Index
OF
Garden
Plants

ROYAL HORTICULTURAL SOCIETY

THE NEW DICTIONARY

Index
OF
Garden
Plants

MARK GRIFFITHS

TIMBER PRESS
Portland, Oregon

Derived from
The New Royal Horticultural Society Dictionary of Gardening
Editor in Chief Anthony Huxley
Editor Mark Griffiths, Managing Editor Margot Levy
in four volumes, 1992

First edition published 1994 by
THE MACMILLAN PRESS LTD,
London and Basingstoke

Associated companies in Auckland, Delhi, Dublin, Gaborone,
Hamburg, Harare, Hong Kong, Johannesburg, Kuala Lumpur,
Lagos, Manzini, Melbourne, Mexico City, Nairobi, New York,
Singapore, Tokyo.

A catalogue record for this book is available from
The British Library.

ISBN 0-333-59149-6

First published in North America in 1994 by
Timber Press, Inc.
9999 S. W. Wilshire, Suite 124
Portland, Oregon 97225, USA

ISBN 0-88192-246-3

Printed in Great Britain

CONTENTS

INTRODUCTION

At first sight, an index to a dictionary may seem superfluous, but the byways of botany are full of free-standing indexes. It is as if, once the Society of Gardeners had published its *Catalogus Plantarum* in 1730, the list became the plantperson's genre of choice. We have *Index Kewensis* (all the botanical names for flowering plants), *Index Londinensis* (illustrations), *Index Filicum* (ferns), the multi-volume garden nomenclator *Index Hortensis*, and a tangled undergrowth of other works to show what is known, grown or sold. Most botanical gardens produce an *index viventium* – a catalogue of their living rather than their pressed or pickled accessions. Through the combined expertise of hundreds of plant-lovers world-wide, the present volume is an *index viventium* for the global garden.

It has three aims: to list currently accepted botanical names, synonyms and popular names for some 60,000 plants in cultivation; to furnish each plant with a brief description; and to demystify the ways in which such names arise and sometimes change.

Gardeners are on intimate terms with a wider range of plants than even some botanists would expect to know. The force of that intimacy gives us in gardens a rich and vital sampling of the world's flora. We are accordingly among the main clients of taxonomy, the science of naming and classifying living things. We need to be able to identify and name with confidence and precision. Botanical understanding not only provides us with a vocabulary for the plants we grow, it may also help us to realize their full horticultural potential. The getting of this understanding is often seen as a process of diffusion from the botanist to the gardener – with unwelcome results: name changes (apparently wilful), the lumping or splitting of seemingly distinct or coherent species, and the pedantic rigmarole of nomenclature. All of which elicits a sigh from the gardener, who might agree with Pope that those responsible '... just like fools, at war about a name/Have full as oft no meaning, or the same'.

Resistance to taxonomic change is perfectly natural, unless, of course, we see such change as an index of the very awareness of biodiversity we would all wish to cultivate. Scanning the tens of thousands of botanical names in this volume, I am aware of a still more basic resistance – to Latin itself – and am reminded of William Gilpin's quip (a hardy perennial since the 1790s) that to treat plants in such a way 'so that nobody but a botanist can find them out, appears ... something like writing an English grammar in Hebrew. You explain a thing by making it unintelligible.' But plenty of people other than botanists can and do 'find them out', gardeners especially, precisely because the system of botanical nomenclature is intelligent and, with very little effort, intelligible. The alternative is the eclectic roll-call of popular names also to be found in the Index – again, thousands of them, from every conceivable language and culture, no less important than the universal Latin but inevitably less helpful.

The arts of the garden and the enquiries of natural philosophy enjoy an ancient alliance. John Parkinson's *Paradisi* of 1629 catalogues and describes almost a thousand garden plants according to scientific principles and illustrates them in plates whose method would grace any modern monograph. Parkinson the gardener became 'Botanicus Regius Primarius'. The Royal Society's first sponsored publication was John Evelyn's *Sylva* (1664), an account of his lifelong interest in arboriculture. In the 1768 edition of his *Gardener's Dictionary*, Philip Miller took the revolutionary step of adopting Linnaeus's system of botanical nomenclature which, in essence, we use to this day. We think of Linnaeus himself, 'the Father of Taxonomy', as patriarch of the purest of sciences, but his own system was inspired in part by the wealth of exotics he encountered as garden superintendent to the Dutch merchant George Clifford. *Hortus Cliffortianus* (1737) is the log of a *Beagle*-like voyage of discovery embarked upon within the confines of a garden.

Two centuries later, the American horticulturalist Liberty Hyde Bailey blessed the union of taxonomy and horticulture with the 'Hortorium', a place for the systematic study of garden plants. In the British Isles, the botanist's mission remained closely linked to the enrichment of gardens. Alongside Kew and other great clearing houses of our new garden flora, the Royal Horticultural Society strove to propagate and distribute not only the plants themselves but also information about them of the highest quality. This was the spirit in which the society undertook the *Dictionary of Gardening*, published in 1951. Forty years on, the same spirit informs *The New Royal Horticultural Society Dictionary of Gardening*. The necessary originality of this work bears witness to rapid progress in horticulture and plant systematics. These two fields, then, come together with great mutual benefit at times of exciting horticultural expansion. The present is just such a time. If we are to manage the proliferation of plants of wild and cultivated origin in our gardens and give renewed vigour to the oldest branch of botany, theirs is a symbiosis we should encourage.

It used to be said that most people looked to the *RHS Dictionary* of 1951 'for the botany', i.e. names and descriptions, somewhat at the expense of its horticultural content. *The New RHS Dictionary* contains many more species and cultivars than its predecessor. Its chief purpose is to convey a broad view of gardening at all times and levels. The need to turn to something 'for the botany' alone, for a reliable name, a concise description, is clearly a general need and one best answered with a purpose-built and widely available publication.

A botanist was once heard to remark that the label was more important than what grew behind it. It would be too easy to present in this handbook a list of botanical epithets with only the occasional popular name like Love-in-Idleness or Midnight Horror for colour. I have attempted to provide just enough descriptive data for each plant to convey something of its appearance and garden value. For the most part, these descriptions are based on the text of the *New RHS Dictionary*. While they certainly go beyond the information offered by (say) T.W. Sanders in his celebrated *Encyclopaedia* ('saddle-shaped', 'yellow', 'tall'), they are not so very detailed as the *Dictionary* itself. Sometimes to good effect. The extreme economy of the *Index* can result in the selection of just a few strictly comparable characteristics. This leads to easy identification. At other times, particularly within very large or homogeneous genera, it has been possible only to sketch qualities that distinguish and commend a plant. Any arbitrariness in the characters chosen for description throughout the *Index* can usually be explained in terms of their significance to the gardener. It has not been feasible to include the vast array of cultivars of *Rosa* and *Rhododendron*, or those of economic plants, comprehensive treatments of which can be found in the *New RHS Dictionary of Gardening*. Measurements given for plants in the *Index* tend to be 'averages' or a range. At times, however, a maximum measurement may represent an extreme unlikely to occur in cultivation. This is true particularly of trees and of large plants of tropical or subtropical origin. Unless qualified, measurements are of length. The basic method of the descriptions is key-like – features described for the genus as a whole are not usually repeated in the species that follow. Where a feature is described for one or two species among several, it should be assumed that the others do not possess that feature. Infraspecific taxa and cultivars are often described in comparative terms (e.g. 'leaves larger'), the comparison being with the typical plant described under the species name. The single species of monotypic genera are described within the genus and merely named thereafter. Infraspecific taxa of monotypic genera, for example the cultivars of *Ginkgo*, are described after the specific epithet. Author abbreviations follow those in the *New RHS Dictionary*. In descriptions of cacti, the number of spines stated is the number per areole. Climatic zones are given either for a genus as a whole or for individual species where their hardiness differs. These follow the system adopted in the *Dictionary*. The range of average annual minimum temperature for each zone is stated in the table at the end of the List of Abbreviations. The zones are an approximate indication of the coldest climatic band in which the plant will thrive.

The New RHS Dictionary of Gardening was the work of many hands. I can only reaffirm here the gratitude expressed in the Preface to the *Dictionary*, where the authors' names are stated in full. Many of their contributions have been extensively adapted for the *Index* – it is hoped without having strayed too far from the authors' original intentions.

It remains to acknowledge a debt of gratitude to those who participated in the exacting task of preparing the work for publication, notably Margot Levy of Macmillan Publishers, without whom the *Index* would never have been realized. Warmest thanks are also due to the artists, Vana Haggerty, Christine Hart-Davies, Paula Rudall, Fiona Bell-Currie and Camilla Speight, and to Morton Wordprocessing of Scarborough, Yorkshire.

London 1994   Mark Griffiths

THE NAMING OF PLANTS

The naming and classification of plants is known as systematic or taxonomic botany. To distinguish, group and name are three essentially human activities; in this respect, taxonomy has in some form been practised wherever humans have journeyed or settled. Within the context of one very early and rather important garden at least, taxonomy can claim to be the oldest profession. So long-lived an activity will have passed through many phases: the localized 'folk' taxonomy of vernacular names; the first 'pure' taxonomic distinctions of Aristotle; the proto-scientific classifications of the earliest botanists and herbalists such as Dioscorides based on the crudest similarities, and the medicinal or economic value of plants to man; the emergence of a science of botany with concepts such as a taxonomic hierarchy under Bauhin, the genus and species under Ray and Tournefort; Linnaeus's invention of a universal system based on the binomial; the great eras of botanical inquiry and exploration, both during the Enlightenment and later with the building of empires; the factoring in of time to the taxonomic equation by evolutionary taxonomists; the establishment of a code of nomenclature for botanical names; the birth of biosystematics which combines taxonomy with genetics and ecology; the addition of chemical and other micro-studies to the taxonomist's weaponry; the code of nomenclature for cultivated plants; the analytical rigours of cladistics.

These episodes suggest a highly charged discipline evolving far faster than any of the life forms it may ever be called on to classify. Recently, however, systematics has passed through a crisis. The usefulness of whole plant study and classification has been questioned; the 'harder' or 'purer' sciences have won by far the greater part of available funds and practitioners. Taxonomy suffered to the extent that in Britain the House of Lords commissioned an enquiry into its purpose and prospects. In the evidence submitted to that enquiry, a succinct and principled definition is recorded: systematics is described as 'the language of biodiversity'.

The modern study of biodiversity is in many ways comparable to the old-fashioned natural history, only informed by a fusion of many scientific disciplines and methods and given great urgency by the rapid disappearance of flora and fauna. 'The language of biodiversity' is in a very real sense, the language of life itself. While taxonomy may use Latin and sometimes, it seems, be governed by an unaccountable *nomenklatura*, it nonetheless has every characteristic of a living language – the growth of new terms and remodelling of old, adaptations of vocabulary to reflect a ceaseless shift of concepts, themselves arising from continuous discovery. Without systematics which makes a single accessible text of living things, without a lingua franca governed by universal rules, that one 'language' would become many tongues, vernaculars, many argots and slangs: biodiversity would be Babel, and then fall silent.

In 1658, Thomas Browne, meditating on the subject of gardens and gardeners, answered the question why taxonomy should concern us:

..a large field is yet left unto sharper discerners to enlarge upon this order, to search out the figured draughts of nature and moderating the study of names and mere nomenclature of plants, to erect generalities, disclose unobserved proprieties ...; affording delightful Truths confirmable by sense and observation, which seems to me the surest path, to trace the Labyrinth of Truth.

Nomenclature is the scientific naming of living things according to universal principles. Today the naming of plants of wild origin is regulated by the International Code of Botanical Nomenclature, that of plants of cultivated origin by the International Code of Nomenclature for Cultivated Plants.

The first botanist to address the need for a standardized nomenclature was Carl von Linné (Linnaeus) (1707-1778). Prior to Linnaeus, plants *were* named with generic and specific concepts and in Latin forms which largely resemble those we use today. These names, however, were unregulated both in application and style. Different botanists and gardeners were free to apply different names to the same plant. The names tended to be rambling descriptive phrases. Caspar Bauhin, for example, named the Creeping Buttercup *Ranunculus pratensis repens hirsutus*. The coconut was named *Palma indica coccifera angulosa*. Linnaeus determined that the significance of names was not their descriptive content (how, after all, did 'Carl von Linné' describe *him*?) but their uniqueness, their specificity as labels. By 1753, with the publication of *Species Plantarum*, Linnaeus had resolved that the fundamental unit of naming was the **binomial**, a combination of two words, the first a noun representing the lowest class of plants (genus), the second usually an adjective describing the member of that class (species). This breakthrough simply took into the world of science what was already a basic pattern of human thought: we name each other according to a binary system and what are Germander Speedwell, Rock Speedwell, Silver Speedwell, Digger's Speedwell, Common Speedwell, Marsh Speedwell and Thyme-leaved Speedwell if not species of the genus Speedwell? The genius of the binomial, however, lay in the fact that it could be applied to one species and one only, and that it was clearly based on a single specimen or illustration that provided an unambiguous reference point for all other users of the name. This is known as the **type**.

Since 1753, the binomial system has undergone many changes and refinements. Two of the most important of these are the rules of **publication** and **priority**. A taxon (plural taxa) is a unit of naming applied to plants with a distinct set of characters: *Buddleja* and *Quercus*, for example, are taxa at genus level; *Buddleja davidii* and *Quercus robur* taxa at species level. The cultivar *Buddleja davidii* 'Black Knight' is a taxon of cultivated origin. Although taxon means 'name', in botanical parlance it means the thing itself — the entity or group of entities to which we give a name and rank.

To be recognized as valid, a botanical taxon must be furnished with a Latin name and described in Latin in a printed publication widely available to botanists. A type specimen for the new taxon must be deposited in one or more herbaria. For taxa of garden origin, the requirements are not so exacting, but a widely available description and the deposition of a type specimen are nonetheless recommended.

A validly published taxon does not necessarily pass muster. The new taxon will only be judged legitimate if its naming infringes neither the relevant code of nomenclature nor the rule of priority. The rule of priority dictates that the first published of two or more validly published names for the same plant will be judged to be the good name. For botanical taxa, the Anno Domini for this rule is the year in which *Species Plantarum* was published. Names published before 1753 are termed pre-Linnaean, those published since must conform to this first-past-the-post system.

The rule of priority is of interest to gardeners in that it leads inevitably to the thing we fear most, **name changes**. Botanists change scientific names either in order to reflect their changing view of the plants themselves or for procedural reasons. An invalidly published name must be amended or rejected in favour of one that is validly published. No two genera may have the same name (although some come close – *Carpenteria, Carpentaria, Discocactus, Disocactus, Oplopanax, Opopanax*). No two species or infraspecific taxa may have the same combination of names. One species may be judged to be synonymous with another, in which case the older of the two names is maintained and the younger becomes a **taxonomic synonym**. If it is discovered that two or more names have been based on the same type, again, only the oldest remains, the others become **nomenclatural synonyms.** A synonym is one of two or more names given to the same taxon. It is usually rejected in favour of the accepted or correct name. Sometimes when naming a plant a botanist may be unaware that the plant in question has already been named or that his name has already been used for a different plant. When the latter happens, the later name becomes a **homonym**.

A homonym is the same name used repeatedly for different plants. Clearly, only one of these applications (usually the earliest) can be correct. For example, *Phlox amoena* Sims is the valid name for a taxon published in 1810. Later authors and horticultural custom have misapplied this name to a different plant validly published by Lehmann in 1802 as *Phlox* x *procumbens*. This could be stated: *P. amoena* hort. non Sims = *P.*x *procumbens*. 'Hort.' here stands for 'hortorum', of gardens; 'auctt.' (auctorum, of authors), is also used to denote misapplied names. Where the perpetrator of the misapplication is known, his name abbreviation can be used in the same way as 'hort.' above. For example, *Berberis integerrima* Franch. non Bunge represents Franchet's misapplication of a name already published by Bunge for a completely different plant. Rendered as a synonym, this would read: *B. integerrima* Franch. non Bunge = *B. jamesiana*. With his name, Franchet had not intended to name the type already described by Bunge as *B. integerrima*, but a plant ultimately given its 'good' name by George Forrest and William Smith.

Species may be transferred from one genus to another; genera may be split or pushed together. In each of these cases, the previous and now disregarded name becomes a synonym of the 'new' one. Names also change when it is decided that a species is in fact no more than a subspecies or variety of another or, conversely, when a variety or subspecies is judged so distinctive as to merit recognition as a species in its own right. Voss, for example, decided that *Pinus monophylla* Torr. & Frém. was no more than a variety of *Pinus cembroides*. This new combination is written *P. cembroides* var. *monophylla* (Torr. & Frém.) Voss; it has a synonym *P. monophylla* Torr. & Frém. (= *P. cembroides* var. *monophylla*). In the *Index*, however, *P.monophylla* is maintained as a species. Its synonymy is therefore reversed: *P. cembroides* var. *monophylla* (Torr. & Frém.) Voss = *P. monophylla*.

Such differences of opinion bring taxonomy into disrepute. A new name for an old plant is no more welcome than the new names forced upon the ancient counties of England and Wales, unless, that is, we accept that they arise because someone suspects they know something new, or because the old names have been cast aside under the implementation of one of the Codes — which, after all, exist to achieve the Linnaean goal, stability of names.

Despite all differences of opinion, the office of taxonomy remains to make diversity accessible. For this reason, the Plant Kingdom is divided into a series of subordinate ranks (**principal taxonomic ranks**) – Division, Subdivision, Class, Order, Family, Genus, Section and Species.

The **Division** is the highest of these categories. Divisions of interest to us here are the Pteridophyta (ferns), Gymnospermae (cone-bearers, or plants with naked seeds) and Angiospermae or Magnoliophyta (the flowering plants). The **Subdivisions** of Gymnospermae are Cycadophytina (cycads), Gnetophytina (*Gnetum, Ephedra*, etc.), Ginkgophytina (*Ginkgo*), Pinophytina (most conifers) and Taxophytina (yews). Some authors prefer to treat these as **Classes**, viz. Cycadopsida, Gnetopsida, Ginkgopsida, Pinopsida, Taxopsida. The Division of flowering plants, Angiospermae, is divided into two Classes, the Dicotyledonae (dicots) and Monocotyledonae (monocots). Classes break down into **Subclasses**, the names of which end -dae. These in turn are made up of Orders.

The **Order** is the rank immediately above the Family; the names of orders end in -ales. Thus, the Class Dicotyledonae contains within the Subclass Magnoliidae the Order Ranunculales, which includes the families Ranunculaceae, Berberidaceae and Lardizabalaceae. In the Monocotyledonae Subclass Commelinidae, the Order Commelinales embraces the families Rapateaceae, Xyridaceae, Mayacaceae and Commelinaceae – only two of which are horticulturally important.

The **Family** is comprised of genera; its name is formed from the name of the type genus and usually ends in -aceae ('relating to'), thus Ranunculaceae (type genus, *Ranunculus*), the buttercup family, Ericaceae (type genus, *Erica*), the heather family, Primulaceae (type genus, *Primula*), the primula family. Some families were identified as 'natural' groups long before the strict implementation of our present system. These retain their old family names (Compositae, Cruciferae, Gramineae, Guttiferae, Labiatae, Leguminosae, Palmae, Umbelliferae); the names also have modern equivalents (Asteraceae, Brassicaceae, Poaceae, Clusiaceae, Lamiaceae, Fabaceae, Arecaceae and Apiaceae respectively).

The family is a natural grouping, defined and distinguished from others by a broad suite of resemblances, reproductive and chemical characters among them. The idea of family values is, however, no easier to enforce in the Plant Kingdom than in the human realm. The limits of families are often unclear, blurred by link-plants and others of uncertain position. One example of these is the genus *Montezuma*, which shuttles between the families Bombacaceae and Malvaceae. There are many others, each of them presenting an argument for redefining one of the families involved in narrower terms or creating an even larger conglomerate of genera, and always offering fascinating clues as to the development and interrelations, the *phylogeny* of the group as a whole.

There exist some large and long-established families, formed on the basis of scant and superseded evidence and fattened to unfeasible dimensions by a slow admixture of disparate genera over many years – included here are the Dogwood family, Cornaceae, and the 'Lilies', Liliaceae. The modern remedy for these 'traditional' families is dissolution. In the Cornaceae, genera of horticultural interest such as *Aucuba*, *Griselinia* and *Helwingia* have been placed in monogeneric families of their own (Aucubaceae, Griseliniaceae, Helwingiaceae), as has *Davidia* (but not without a sojourn in the Tupelo family, Nyssaceae), while *Corokia* has served time in the Grossulariaceae (Escalloniaceae).

If this type of diaspora is a contemporary trend in systematics, it is not always endorsed by modern systematists. Arthur Cronquist (1919–92) preferred the broad or traditional view of the Dogwoods for the pragmatic reason that there was more to bind them together than there was to attach them to anything else. This eminently reasonable position is usually shared by gardeners, who are not only accustomed to the larger, older families but often show an innate sensitivity to their cohesive similarities and can navigate the mazes of their variation.

There is no better illustration of this than the families Liliaceae and Amaryllidaceae. Those genera with a superior ovary such as *Lilium*, *Ruscus*, *Paris*, *Agapanthus* and *Allium* were traditionally placed in the family Liliaceae. Those with inferior ovary (e.g. *Narcissus*, *Amaryllis*, *Alstroemeria*) were assigned to the Amaryllidaceae. The Kew botanist John Hutchinson (1884–1972) deprecated the separation of these families on the basis of ovary position alone. He left *Lilium* in Liliaceae, moved *Allium* and *Agapanthus* to Amaryllidaceae on account of their spathaceous, umbellate inflorescences, placed *Paris* in Trilliaceae, *Ruscus* in

Ruscaceae and *Alstroemeria* in Alstroemeriaceae. Many botanists hesitated to accept such changes. Cronquist not only upheld the broad 'classical' Liliaceae but added Amaryllidaceae to it. To no avail – the balkanization of the Lilies had begun.

Rolf Dahlgren (1932–1987) proposed numerous smaller families of more uniform content: Trilliaceae, Convallariaceae, Asparagaceae, Ruscaceae, Asphodelaceae, Anthericaceae, Agavaceae, Hyacinthaceae, Alliaceae, Amaryllidaceae, Colchicaceae, Alstroemeriaceae, Liliaceae and Melanthiaceae. Other Liliaceae segregates of various vintages include Aloeaceae, Aphyllanthaceae, Doryanthaceae, Dracaenaceae, Hemerocallidaceae, Hostaceae, Hypoxidaceae, Phormaceae, Smilacaceae, Tecophilaeaceae, Xanthorrhoeaceae. Having been one of the largest families of petaloid monocotyledons, Liliaceae became one of the smallest. The system of Dahlgren, Clifford and Yeo (1985) has not been followed in the *Index*. Instead, the broad groupings of the petaloid monocots familiar to generations of horticulturists as the Liliaceae (distinguished by the superior ovary) and the Amaryllidaceae (with an inferior ovary) are maintained. Agavaceae, a family of heterogeneous origins, has also been retained on the strength of its apparent morphological unity, as have the distinctive Hypoxidaceae and Xanthorrhoeaceae. The families into which Dahlgren *et al.* would place each genus are indicated in parenthesis after the traditional family. e.g. *Colchicum* Liliaceae (Colchicaceae); *Trillium* Liliaceae (Trilliaceae).

The Family, then, is open to varying interpretations, none of them 'wrong'. Readers wishing to take these territorial disputes further are referred to *Vascular Plant Families and Genera* (R.K. Brummitt, Royal Botanic Gardens, Kew, 1992), where the world's vascular plant genera are listed, as are their families, together with a telling analysis of eight major systems of plant classification from Bentham's and Hooker's (1862-83) to that of Cronquist (1988). The *Index* adopts the Kew system for ferns, whose taxonomy was in some flux at the time of completing the *New RHS Dictionary*.

Families vary greatly in size. The Compositae contains some 1200 genera comprising 21,000 species in all. The 800 genera of Orchidaceae account for perhaps 18,000 species. Families of great magnitude or diversity are often divided into **Subfamilies**, the names of which terminate -oideae (resembling). In the Orchidaceae there are three subfamilies. The Apostasioideae is limited to two genera (*Apostasia* and *Neuwiedia*) from Asia and Australasia. These are rather grassy plants with almost asphodel-like spikes of flowers with 2-3 distinct stalked 'anthers', not the sac-enclosed pollinia of most Orchidaceae. On the basis of this and other distinctions, subfamily Apostasioideae is sometimes recognized as Family Apostasiaceae. The Cypripedioideae contains the slipper orchids, *Cypripedium*, *Paphiopedilum*, *Phragmipedium*, *Selenipedium*. Because of their slipper-like labellum and large staminode, these are sometimes separated from Orchidaceae as family Cypripediaceae. The remaining genera (the vast majority) are placed in the Orchidoideae. So unwieldy a grouping requires **Tribes** to establish order.

The names of tribes terminate -eae. In Subfamily Orchidoideae, these are four - Neottieae (largely terrestrial orchids lacking pseudobulbs), e.g. *Epipactis, Neottia, Spiranthes*; Orchideae (again mostly terrestrial and lacking pseudobulbs), e.g. *Disa, Orchis, Pterostylis*; Epidendreae (largely tropical epiphytes with pseudobulbs), e.g. *Cattleya, Masdevallia*; Vandeae (again pseudobulbous tropicals for the most part), e.g. *Cymbidium, Vanda*. It has been suggested that the Vandeae are not *monophyletic*, that is, they are not a unified and exclusive group at the end of a single line of evolutionary development, but represent a number of lines of development derived from the Epidendreae. Certainly the grouping of *Lycaste* with *Phalaenopsis* at anything below family level seems fanciful and arbitrary to those of us who only grow these plants. The subfamilies of the Compositae (Asteroideae and Lactucoideae), their Tribes (Lactuceae, Senecioneae, Heliantheae, Astereae, etc.) and their numerous **Subtribes** are altogether more convincing groupings, making diversity accessible.

For scale and range, few families compete with the daisies and orchids. Some are **monogeneric**, containing only one genus. These can arise as a result of segregation, as has happened with Cornaceae. Others are 'loners' of long standing. The genus *Sparganium*, Bur Reed, contains twelve species, the only members of the family Sparganiaceae. These fall under the Subclass Commelinidae along with the Spiderworts; their order, however, is Typhales, which they share with another monogeneric family of rushes, Typhaceae (single genus, *Typha*, the Reed Mace, 12 spp.). The Bur Reeds and the Reed Maces are otherwise alone, adrift somewhere between the true grasses and the bromeliads and gingers. Some families are smaller still, containing only one genus of one species. The best known of these is probably Ginkgoaceae. *Ginkgo biloba* is the last survivor of a large genus within a family of at least five others, gradually extinguished over 200,000,000 years. Not only is the family Ginkgoaceae **monotypic**, but so, effectively, is the entire class, Ginkgopsida.

In his *History of Astronomy*, (*c*1750), Adam Smith used the hypothesis of a foundling species to illustrate the yearning of botanists to relate everything to something:

> With what curious attention does a naturalist examine a singular plant, or a singular fossil, that is presented to him? He is at no loss to refer it to the general genus of plants or fossils; but this does not satisfy him, and when he considers all the different tribes or species of either with which he has hitherto been acquainted, they all, he thinks, refuse to admit the new object among them. It stands alone in his imagination, and as it were detached from all ... other species... He labours, however, to connect it with some one or other of them. Sometimes he thinks it may be placed in this, and sometimes in that other assortment; nor is he ever satisfied, till he has fallen upon one which, in most of its qualities, it resembles. When he cannot do this, rather than it should stand quite by itself, he will enlarge the precincts ... of some species, in order to make room

for it; or he will create a new species on purpose to receive it, ... or give it some other appellation, under which he arranges all the oddities that he knows not what else to do with.

Because of abundant fossil evidence, we can relate *Ginkgo biloba* with certainty to a larger class, however extinct. Other monotypic families evade such attempts. The small white-flowered shrub *Medusagyne oppositifolia* sits in rather less than splendid isolation in the Seychelles. We could place its family Medusagynaceae in the Order Theales alongside Theaceae (the Tea or Camellia Family) and the Guttiferae (St John's Wort Family) as did Cronquist, or lose it in the Family Guttiferae as did Dalla Torre and Harms (*c*1900), or include it in the Order Scytopetalales (Young in Bedell & Reveal, 1982), or give it an order of its own, Medusagynales (Takhtajan, 1987). The only thing that can be stated with clarity is that its affinities are unclear.

The principal rank in the taxonomic hierarchy between Family and species is the **genus** (pl. genera). The genus represents a single highly distinctive species (a monotypic or monospecific genus) such as *Argyrocytisus, Bignonia, Cercidiphyllum, Ginkgo* or *Ravenala* or, more frequently, a number of species united by a distinctive suite of common characters. As a unit the genus varies greatly in size and distinctiveness: it is, for example, difficult to compare *Cercidiphyllum*, with one species so distinct as to claim for itself a monogeneric family, with the symphonic range of the 2000-strong *Euphorbia*, which includes annual and perennial herbs, succulents, shrubs and trees standing alongside a further 320 genera in the Euphorbiaceae. Other 'giants' include *Astragalus* (2000 species), *Acacia, Bulbophyllum, Carex, Piper* and *Solanum* (with 1000-1500 species each) and *Allium, Dendrobium, Erica, Ficus, Oxalis, Rhododendron, Schefflera, Senecio* and *Silene* (each with 500-1000 species).

Infrageneric ranks (subgenus, section, subsection and series) can be used to divide up any genus of more than one species, but are particularly useful in the larger genera. Within *Rhododendron* (*c*800 species) the Subgenera Azaleastrum, Candidastrum, Hymenanthes, Mumeazalea, Pentanthera, Rhododendron, Therorhodion and Tsutsusi have been recognized. *Rhododendron ponticum* belongs to Subgenus Hymenanthes, Section Ponticum Subsection Ponticum; *R.simsii* (the Indian Azalea) belongs to Subgenus Tsutsusi, Section Tsutsusi.

No binomial is complete without a genus name, or its abbreviation, and a specific, cultivar or hybrid epithet. *Lilium auratum*, *Lilium* 'Stargazer', *Lilium* x *pardaboldtii* are acceptable binominals, as are *L. auratum*, *L.* 'Stargazer', *L.* x *pardaboldtii*. Detached from the generic name, the epithets *auratum*, 'Stargazer' and x *pardaboldtii* are taxonomically meaningless.

To be validly published, a generic name requires a type species – usually the first to be discovered, or the first published taxon within a new segregate. The French botanist de Labillardière based the genus *Anigozanthos*, Kangaroo Paw, on the species *A. rufus*, which he described in 1798. The type specimen, collected on the south coast of Western Australia in1792 and now in the Paris Herbarium, furnishes the *idea* of the genus with its evidential basis. Since 1798, a further twelve species of Kangaroo or Cat's Paw have been added to the genus. Even if , as new species are discovered, and a genus fills out over time, the type should prove to be the least 'typical' member of the genus, so long as it remains a member its status remains sacrosanct: it is a starting point. As with most botanical names, the genus has an **author**, normally abbreviated and cited after the name, e.g. *Lilium* L. (named by Linnaeus), *Anigozanthos* Labill. (named by de Labillardière).

The genus or generic name is italicized, underlined or in bold type, and takes a capital letter. It may be formed in a number of ways, most commonly by relating an important character of one (the type) or all of its members, e.g. *Anigozanthos*, from the Greek *anisos*, unequal, and *anthos*, flower, referring to the unequal perianth lobes; *Indigofera*, from the Latin *indigo* and *fero*, to bear; *Orchis*, from the Greek for testicle, which the tubers of these plants resemble. Generic names may also be commemorative (e.g. *Linnaea*, *Wellingtonia*) or derived from names used in the plants' native places (e.g. *Ananas*, from 'nana', the Tupi Indian word for pineapple; *Ginkgo*, a corruption of the Japanese *gin* (silver), *kyo* (apricot), itself an adaptation of the Chinese 'yin-kuo'; *Tamarindus*, from the Arabic 'tamarhindi'). Genera are sometimes named by mythological allusion (e.g. *Narcissus*, *Daphne*, or, to risk greater complexity, *Heliconia*, named by Linnaeus for Mount Helicon, the home of the Muses, a pun reflecting the propinquity of this genus to *Musa*). Some generic names come down to us unaltered from Classical antiquity (e.g. *Lilium*, *Fraxinus*). Genus names may also be derived from others to demonstrate true affinity, false resemblance or the status of a segregate and be formed by prefixes (e.g. *Chamaecereus*, *Metasequoia*, *Nothofagus*, *Parahebe*, *Pseudomuscari*), by suffixes (e.g. *Cymbidiella*, *Stapeliopsis*), or even by anagramatizing the name of the original genus from which another has been split (e.g. *Muilla* from *Allium*, *Phinaea* from *Niphaea*, *Sedirea* from *Aerides*, *Tellima* from *Mitella*, *Tylecodon* from *Cotyledon*). The names of intergeneric hybrids are equivalent to those of genera; for rules governing their formation, see Plants of Garden Origin below.

In linguistic terms, the genus is a noun treated as a Latin word, irrespective of its etymology. Generic names therefore have gender – masculine, feminine or neuter, and all subordinate botanical names must agree in gender with the genus. Masculine generic names end most frequently in -us, for example *Abelmoschus*, in which the name of one species (Okra) is *esculentus*, not *esculenta* or *esculentum*. Others include *Galanthus*, *Helleborus*, *Mimulus*, *Philadelphus*, *Pleioblastus*, *Ranunculus*, *Zygocactus*. Although they may appear masculine, the names of trees ending -us or -os, notably those coined in Classical times, are feminine, e.g. *Cocos*, *Ficus*, *Fagus*, *Pinus*, *Pyrus*, *Quercus*, *Zizyphus*. The Greek ending -os corresponds to the Latin -us: *Anigozanthos* and *Symphoricarpos* are masculine. Some names terminating in -on are also masculine (viz.

Cotyledon, *Lysichiton*, *Platycodon*), although -on more usually corresponds to the Latin neuter -um (e.g. *Rhododendron*).

Feminine names often end in -a, for example *Artemisia*, *Campanula*, *Daboecia*, *Hosta*, *Onoclea*, *Punica*, *Thunbergia*, *Viola*. Some apparently feminine genera are in fact neuter, having been derived from the neuter Greek words -derma (e.g *Argyroderma*), -loma (*Lysiloma*), -agma (*Tristagma*), -nema (*Aglaeonema*), -paegma (*Anemopaegma*), -phragma (*Schizophragma*), -trema (*Isotrema*), -sperma (*Dictyosperma*), -stemma (*Dichelostemma*), stigma (*Ceratostigma*). *Phyteuma* is neuter; *Glechoma*, however, is feminine. Other feminine endings include -ago (*Plumbago*), -anthe (*Stromanthe*), -es (*Menyanthes*), -is (*Clematis*, *Parrotiopsis*, *Vitis*), -ix (*Tamarix*), -odes (*Omphalodes*) and -oides (*Hyacinthoides*).

Neuter names end -um, or -dendron; e.g. *Arum*, *Dendrobium*, *Glaucidium*, *Hippeastrum*, *Leucadendron*, *Leucanthemum*, *Rehderodendron*, *Symphytum*, *Trillium*, *Trochodendron*, *Zygopetalum*.

With these few pointers, it should be possible to determine the gender of most genera. Botanical Latin is itself a multigeneric hybrid; the etymology and gender of a genus are not always evident. Names that do not fit the scheme outlined above – for example, *Arundo* (a feminine genus simply taken from the Latin for reed) or *Bombax* (neuter, from the Greek *bombyx*, silk) or *Cycas* (feminine, from Greek *koikas*, the Doum Palm) have to be assimilated by slow osmosis. Some, such as *Styrax*, prove almost impossible to sex, as the gender of the ancient tongues at its root conflict with each other and then with the gender employed by its botanical namer, which in turn conflicts with botanical convention, and so on. The *obiter dicta* on all questions to do with botanical names, their forms and derivations are provided by Professor W.T. Stearn, whose *Dictionary of Plant Names for Gardeners* (Cassell, 1992) is indispensable.

We have already remarked on the susceptibility of Families to differing interpretations and boundary changes. As a concept, the genus is even more assailable: genera shrink, grow, are put together or asunder for a variety of of reasons, some to do with actual increase in numbers (there are many more *Rhododendron* species known today than were known to Linnaeus), mostly to do with taxonomic judgements (Linnaeus's *Azalea* is now included in *Rhododendron*). 'What makes a genus?' is perhaps the most vexed question a botanist might face and certainly one with great impact on horticulture. Why should we accept the break-up of *Chrysanthemum* when other large and catholic genera go untouched? Differing standards of difference seem to be at work. Such 'inconsistencies' combined with the apparently fickle nature of taxonomic change give rise to charges of subjectivity and whim on the part of the taxonomist. This rather presumes that systematics has ever pretended to be a truly pure science untainted by human agency, by *interpretation*, or by historical change. The tale of taxonomy, from early natural history which was content to describe and catalogue, to 'objective' biosystematics, modern-day chemotaxonomy and cladistics, does suggest an increasingly scientific rigour and the emergence of an orthodox 'method'. In practice, the methods and results are as diverse as the genera they address. The dissent these results excite should be welcomed as proof that our picture of the living world is not a static tableau, but the changing image of a live interest. Over the next few years, for example, we will witness a push to unite *Mahonia* and *Berberis* in a single monophyletic *Berberis*. The arguments for this union seem incontrovertible and the consequences for name-users dire. Agreed, many *Mahonia* species have been combined in the genus *Berberis* before, providing what amounts to traditional support for a radical position, but more recently the horticultural and botanical worlds have quite naturally accepted a distinction between these two genera based on absence or presence of stem spines, compound/simple leaves and pseudo-terminal/axillary inflorescence. That gardeners deal happily with long-established large and seemingly discordant genera suggests that eventually a leviathan *Berberis* will be accepted and will have arrived by virtue of a reasoned revision, rather than an *ad hoc* accrescence. We sense little hardship in seeing as neighbours London Pride, say, and *Saxifraga* 'Wisley', or Poinsettia and *Euphorbia obesa*, or the Rosebay Willowherb and the California Fuchsia, as if we knew that a 'good' genus somehow makes sense of its parts, however diverse. This type of intuition was perhaps in Linnaeus's thoughts when, in *Philosophia Botanica* (1751) he stated: "Know that the characters do not constitute the genus, but the genus the characters; that the characters flow from the genus; that it is not the characters that make the genus but the genus that makes the characters.'

The **species** (abbreviated sp., plural spp.) is the lowest principal taxonomic rank. It usually describes very closely related, morphologically similar individuals often found within a distinct geographical range. Otherwise put, the species can be viewed as a population or series of populations exhibiting a suite of characters, or several suites of characters, which consistently distinguish it from other populations. The definition of a species does not necessarily take origin into account. Detailed knowledge of distribution set within the broader context of floras obviously provides a sound basis for judging a species' limits, but the origins and relations of some highly distinctive 'species' are poorly understood (notably, exotics brought into cultivation in the 19th century), while others have been distributed and developed by man for so long as to be 'unplaceable' (the Sweet Flag and Taro, for example).

The species is the basic unit of naming, forming a binomial when combined with the generic name. The species itself is signified by a **specific epithet**, or 'trivial name'. The values given to characters used to assess whether or not a plant or set of plants merits species rank are ultimately matters of judgement based on experience, contrast with existing taxa and 'harder' evidence gathered from scientific research. As with higher ranks, differences of opinion exist over the limits of species. Different populations regarded by one botanist as distinct species and named accordingly may be regarded by another as subspecies, varieties or formas of one variable or 'collective' species. The Tree Lucerne (*Chamaecytisus proliferus*), for example, may be recognized in a wide sense (**sensu lato**) with three infraspecific taxa, subspecies *palmensis*, ssp. *proliferus* (the typical state of the species) and ssp. *angustifolius*, or, more narrowly (**sensu stricto**), the first two might be accepted as distinct species, *C.palmensis* and *C. proliferus*. Disputes in the ranks are not confined to the infraspecific level. As a result of a clean sweep made of the brooms some years ago, the highly distinctive Moroccan Broom, *Cytisus battandieri*, was transferred to a genus of its own, becoming *Argyrocytisus battandieri*. The author of the original combination (**basionym**) was Maire, the author of the new genus and, therefore, of the new combination is Reynaud. To show that the plant has been moved to a new genus, a **double citation** is used, with the name of the original author in parentheses, *Argyrocytisus battandieri* (Maire) Reynaud. The same procedure is followed if an infraspecific taxon is promoted to species rank, or when a species is reduced in status. *Paeonia arietina* of Anderson, for example, was judged by Cullen and Heywood to be a subspecies of *Paeonia mascula*. The new name is written *P.mascula* ssp. *arietina* (Anderson) Cullen & Heywood.

The specific epithet is lower case and italic or underlined. Specific epithets, like the names of genera, may be derived from a variety of languages and express a range of features or associations. Some are descriptive, such as *albus*, white; *candidus*, shining white; *praecox*, early; *scandens*, climbing; *phaeus*, dusky; *glaber*, glabrous; *glandulifer*, gland-bearing; *pulchellus*, pretty. These epithets clearly refer to a distinctive character of the species – in naming *Lilium auratum*, Lindley was gilding the Lily. Others refer to places of origin or habitat – *americanus*, from the Americas, *coum*, from Kos, *indicus*, Indian or East Asian, *sinensis*, Chinese, *eboracensis*, from York, England, *noveboracensis*, from New York, *australis*, southern (not necessarily Australian), *littoralis*, of the seashore, *silvicola*, of woods. The names of interspecific hybrids are equivalent to specific epithets; for rules governing their formation, see Plants of Garden Origin below.

Specific epithets are adjectival, participial or substantive. With the last of these types, no gender agreement with the genus name is required. Epithets of the first two groups have agreement and can be divided into three categories: (a) Masculine, feminine and neuter having different endings, -us, -a, -um; e.g. *albus* (masc.), *alba* (fem.), *album* (neut.), *glaber* (masc.), *glabra* (fem.), *glabrum* (neut.). (b) Masculine and feminine having the same ending, -is, -is, -e; e.g. *brevis* (masc.), *brevis* (fem.), *breve* (neut.), *rivalis* (masc.), *rivalis* (fem.), *rivale* (neut.), *spectabilis* (masc.), *spectabilis* (fem.) *spectabile* (neut.). (c) Masculine, feminine and neuter having the same endings; e.g. *concolor* (masc.), *concolor* (fem.), *concolor* (neut.),*cupresoides* (masc.), *cupressoides* (fem.), *cupressoides* (neut.); others in this category include *bicolor*, *hians*, *luxurians*, *lycopodioides*, *praecox*, *pubescens*, *repens* and *simplex*.

A further group of names have no agreement: these are attributive and formed in the genitive. Examples include *fullonum* (of fullers), *officinarum* (of apothecaries' shops), *poetarum* (of poets) and *tuguriorum* (of huts or cottages). Within this group are some habitat names such as *deserti* (of the desert), *desertorum* (of deserts) and *dumetorum* (of hedges).

Place names are usually turned into adjectival epithets with the suffix -ensis; they agree in gender with the genus – thus *Conophytum khamiesbergense* (from the Khamiesberg Mountains) is neuter, *Passiflora costaricensis* is feminine, *Lysichyton camtschatcensis* masculine.

Persons can be commemorated in specific epithets. These names take two forms, the first, the possessive form, is the name of the person celebrated latinized and in the genitive case; thus *sieboldii* (from Sieboldius), of Philipp Franz von Siebold, *willmottiae*, for Miss Willmott, *wilsonii* (from Wilsonius), for E.H. Wilson. These names are latinized simply by adding -ius to their endings in the case of men, -ia for women; in the genitive case, they become -ii and -iae respectively. Exceptions to this rule are names with existing classical or medieval forms, thus *caroli* (from Carolus), *helenae* (from Helena); names ending -er, which are latinized -us or -a for the sake of euphony (thus *farreri*, not farrerii, *hillieri*, not hillierii, *hookerae*, not hookeriae, *rehderi*, not rehderii). Names already terminating in a vowel are also latinized -us or -a (thus *henryi*, not henryii, *greyi*, not greyii, *makinoi*, not makinoii, *louisae*, not louisiae, *fortunei*, not fortuneii), although a terminal -u is latinized 'v', causing Monsieur Bureau to be remembered in plants named *bureavii*. Commemorative names formed in the genitive can also be plural – *baileyorum*, for example, means of the Bailey family, but *baileyi* of one Bailey only. The second form of commemorative name is adjectival; it entails forming an adjective from the person's name and ensuring gender agreement with the genus. Thus while *Arctostaphylos hookeri* is Hooker's Manzanita, *Crinodendron hookeranum* is the Hookerian *Crinodendron*. The adjectival epithet is made by adding -ianus, -iana, -ianum to the person's name; again, the -i- of the suffix is dropped where that name ends in -er or a vowel. Examples of this type of epithet include *Cotoneaster henryanus* (masculine), *Vanda rothschildiana* (feminine) and *Rhododendron bainbridgeanum* (neuter).

'Borrowed names' comprise the last category of specific epithets; all of these are nouns and do not agree with the genus in gender. They are of four kinds. Long-defunct herbal or botanical names formerly used at generic level are sometimes taken up as specific epithets, e.g. *Campanula elatines, Cucumis melo, Nymphaea lotus. Liriodendron tulipifera* and *Sedum rosea* are commonly written *Liriodendron tulipiferum* and *Sedum roseum* by people assuming quite reasonably that the epithets are adjectival ('tulip-bearing', 'rosy') and ought to agree in gender with the genus. In these two cases and a very few others, what appear to be descriptive epithets are in fact the names of long-disused genera. Names of genera currently in use are sometimes taken as specific epithets, for example *Cam-panula saxifraga, Corokia cotoneaster, Diervilla lonicera.* Vernacular names may also be used as specific epithets, e.g. *Albizia lebbeck, Aloe vaombe, Codonopsis tangshen, Musa basjoo, Podocarpus totara, Sabal palmetto, Zamia chigua.*

Finally, vernacular names are sometimes used as specific epithets in Latin translation, e.g. *clava-herculis*, Hercules' club, *crus-galli*, cock'scomb, *crux-andreae*, St Andrew's Cross, *lacryma-jobi*, Job's tears, *unguis-cati*, cat's claw, *vulpis-cauda*, foxtail. Not all compound epithets are hyphenated. Clearly those mentioned above, and others such as *agnus-castus, burle-marxii, coeli-rosa, ferdinandi-coburgi, spina-christi* and *uva-ursi*, must retain their hyphens; others, traditionally hyphenated, are now treated as single words. The hyphen is removed in cases where the component words cannot stand in their own right. For example, pseudo-sieboldianum becomes *pseudosieboldianum*, aureo-marginata, *aureomarginata*, neo-caledonicum *neocaledonicum*, albo-picta, *albopicta*. The distinction can be illustrated from the genus *Euphorbia*: unhyphenated, *E. fructus-pini*, a plant which resembles a pine cone, might easily be taken for a plant with spiny fruit. The hyphen is always retained, however, where the last letter of the first component and the first of the second are both vowels, e.g. *griseo-argentea, sino-ornata*.

Some compound epithets are intended to show similarity with another genus. They are usually formed by combining a genitive form of the name of that genus with an adjectival particle naming the feature in question, for example -florus, -a, -um, folius, -a, -um. Feminine genera terminating in -a are rendered -i (formerly -ae); thus *hederifolius*, from *Hedera*, with ivy-like leaves. Those terminating -ia, or -ea, are rendered -ii or -ei; thus *begoniiflorus*, from *Begonia*, with Begonia-like flowers, *castaneifolius*, from *Castanea*, with chestnut-like leaves. Masculine and neuter genera are treated similarly, e.g. *cistiflorus*, with flowers like *Cistus*; *anethifolius*, with leaves like *Anethum*. Care should be taken with genera with irregular endings – for example, *ilicifolius*, holly-leaved, from *Ilex*; *caryopteridifolius*, from *Caryopteris*; *cycadifolius*, from *Cycas*. Still greater care should be taken with epithets formed in this way but based, despite appearances, not on current generic names but their ancient forbears. One such name, commonly encountered is *asplenifolius*, -a, -um, not aspleniifolium from *Asplenium*, but derived from a common ancestor, the Greek word *asplenon* (asplenum), spleenwort.

It has already been stated that the species can be a loose and variable assemblage, much after the fashion of the genus. Where botanists wish to maintain a broad species concept and demonstrate variation, they name infraspecific taxa. These are in descending order of distinctiveness **subspecies** (abbreviated ssp.; plural sspp.), **variety** or varietas (var.) and **forma** (f.) Like the species epithet, the names of infraspecific taxa take the lower case in italics or are underlined; they follow the same rules of name formation and gender agreement as the species. They must be preceded by an unambiguous statement of rank and, for obvious reasons, are meaningless unless clearly assigned to a species. In full botanical citations, infraspecific taxa should also be followed by the author's name or names. *Lilium pyrenaicum* Gouan now contains the following infraspecific taxa:

ssp. *pyrenaicum*
    f. *pyrenaicum*
    f. *rubrum* Stoker
ssp. *carniolicum* (W.Koch) V. Matthews
    var. *carniolicum*
    var. *albanicum* (Griseb.) V. Matthews
    var. *jankae* (Kern.) V.Matthews
ssp. *ponticum* (C.Koch) V.Matthews
    var. *ponticum*
    var. *artvinense* (Misch.) V.Matthews

The subspecies and varieties here were formerly held to be species in their own right. As more data on these plants and their distributions came to light, it became clear that they were in fact examples of variation of varying degrees of distinctiveness within a broader circumscription of *Lilium pyrenaicum*. In order to name the two new subspecies of *L. pyrenaicum* (sspp. *carniolicum* and *ponticum*), the author has designated a typical subspecies, ssp. *pyrenaicum*. This duplicates the species epithet and carries no author citation. The procedure is repeated when varieties of the new subspecies are named: ssp. *carniolicum* var. *jankae* is balanced by ssp. *carniolicum* var. *carniolicum*, which now applies strictly to the plant described originally by Koch as *L. carniolicum*. This method allows botanists to maintain a broad species concept containing named variants while still indicating the type with precision.

Plants of garden origin. These are subject to a different set of rules, The International Code of Nomenclature for Cultivated Plants. Such plants are of three types, the cultivar, the group and hybrids. The **cultivar** (abbreviated cv., plural cvs), a cultivated variety, is an assemblage of plants arising and/or maintained in cultivation distinguished by one or more characters and which, when reproduced either sexually or asexually, retains its distinguishing character. Cultivars are often called **'selections'**, a reference to the discrimination required by the grower to choose and develop a significant variant. The characters for which growers might value and select a cultivar are many and various – flower colour, double flowers, variegated leaves, low spreading habit, tall fastigiate habit, large fruit, seedless fruit are just a few. A cultivar can be a clone, a line, a number of individuals showing some genetic differences yet distinguishable as a whole from other cultivars, or a uniform assemblage of individuals that is maintained clonally, or by inbreeding or by recurrent first-generation hybridization.

Cultivars, in other words, may be selected in order to come true from seed (these are sometimes called **races**) or propagated vegetatively (these are called **clones**). Clonal cultivars may constitute either a single genetically uniform clone, e.g. *Daphne* x *burkwoodii* 'Carol Mackie', or a group of clones genetically unalike but consistently distinguished by one or more characters, e.g. *Geranium sylvaticum* 'Album'. Cultivars of

the second type are often equivalent to formas or groups.

A cultivar is named with a cultivar (or fancy) epithet, a word or words formed according to the many strictures of the Code in a vernacular language (unless published prior to 1959, or a botanical (i.e. Latin) epithet already established for a taxon now deemed to be a cultivar). Latin names used for cultivars are subject to the same rules of gender agreement as those of botanical ranks. The epithet is printed in roman characters, takes a capital first letter, and is enclosed in quotation marks, e.g. *Hosta kikutii* 'Green Fountain', *Silene uniflora* 'Weisskehlchen', *Phalaris arundinacea* 'Picta'. A cultivar may not be clearly assignable to a single species, in which case the generic name and cultivar epithet only are used in combination, e.g. *Heuchera* 'Palace Purple'. This form is also sometimes used for reasons of economy: *Pieris japonica* 'Bert Chandler' might equally be styled *Pieris* 'Bert Chandler'.

The **group** is a category used to distinguish (1) an assemblage of two or more similar cultivars within a species or hybrid; (2) plants derived from a hybrid of unknown parentage; (3) a range of individuals of a species or hybrid which, although different, share certain characters that give them coherence as a unit. Group names are written in roman script, take a capital inital letter, have no quotation marks and are followed by the word 'group', e.g. *Brassica oleracea* Tronchuda group, *Photinia* Undulata group. When followed by a cultivar, the group name is placed in parentheses, e.g. *Clematis* (Patens group) 'Nellie Moser', *Rhododendron cinnabarinum* (Concatenans group) 'Copper'. These last two examples show group names formed from botanical epithets previously published at other ranks. It is permissible, however, to publish a group name in a modern language provided it conforms to the articles of the International Code of Nomenclature for Cultivated Plants, e.g. *Phaseolus vulgaris* (Dwarf French Bean group) 'Masterpiece', *Lolium perenne* (Early group) 'Deron Eaver'. In some cases, group names may be non-alphabetic and their generic names non-botanical, being those of crops or highly developed ornamentals such as Rose or Lily, e.g. Maize (200-299 maturity group) 'W240'.

The names of many fern cultivars were formed from a Latin tag showing the type of frond variation for which the plant had been selected together with the name of the selector. Since Latin is inadmissable for cultivated plants named after 1959, many fern cultivars were found to have illegitimate names. Growers who had previously used the combined Latin/vernacular names found they no longer had recourse to an informative and precise system of naming. A compromise was struck whereby the Latin name is used as a group epithet and the personal name identifies the cultivar in question. In this way *Athyrium filix-femina* 'Plumosum Jones' (published after 1959) becomes *Athyrium filix-femina* (Plumosum group) 'Jones'.

Conceptually akin to the group is the **grex** (Latin, 'herd'). The grex is a group name for all plants derived from the crossing of the same two or more species. Unlike the group, the grex relates very specifically to an established parentage or lineage. Its use is limited to orchid hybrids. For example, *Paphiopedilum callosum* x *Paphiopedilum lawrenceanum* gives rise to the grex *P.* Maudiae. The grex name is written in roman script, takes a captial initial letter and no quotation marks. As with the group, cultivars can be added to the grex name to denote particular clones, e.g. *Paphiopedilum* Maudiae 'The Queen'.

Hybrids are the offspring of the sexual union of plants belonging to different taxa. A natural hybrid arises in the wild; a spontaneous hybrid arises in cultivation but without human intervention; an artificial hybrid is deliberately made by man. The names of all three types are formed in the same way. They are treated collectively here. A hybrid binomial covers all the progeny of a particular union, e.g. *Mahonia* x *media* (*Mahonia japonica* x *Mahonia lomariifolia*) including selections such as 'Faith', 'Hope', 'Charity', 'Lionel Fortescue', 'Underway', 'Winter Sun'. Hybrids between species of the same genus are termed **interspecific**, or specific. Where one selection of a hybrid is meant, the cultivar name is simply added to the hybrid binomial, thus *Mahonia* x *media* 'Charity'. This can also be written *M.* 'Charity'. Hybrid epithets are formed in the same way as botanical names: x *arendsii*, x *speciosa*, x *kewensis* are examples of commemorative, descriptive and place-type names respectively. Sometimes hybrid epithets are formed from portmanteau combinations of the parents' names, e.g. *Epimedium* x *perralchicum* (*E. perralderianum* x *E. pinnatum* ssp. *colchicum*). All agree in gender with the genus, appear in lower case italics and are preceded by a multiplication sign. Like botanical ranks, the hybrid binomial requires a statement of authority in a full citation; in the case of the example above, *M.* x *media* C.D. Brickell.

Intergeneric hybrids are the offspring of the union of species belonging to two or more genera. The names of intergeneric hybrids are usually portmanteau words, e.g. x *Mahoberberis* (*Mahonia* x *Berberis*), x*Solidaster* (*Solidago* x *Aster*), x*Carmispartium* (*Carmichaelia* x *Notospartium*). These are treated as conventional genus names but must be preceded by a multiplication sign. The offspring of a precisely known cross is treated as if a species and forms a binomial with the intergeneric

hybrid name; thus x *Mahoberberis neubertii* represents the result of the cross between *Mahonia aquifolium* and *Berberis vulgaris*, x*Chionoscilla allenii* covers all offspring produced by *Chionodoxa siehei* crossed with *Scilla bifoliata*.

Multigeneric hybrids are the progeny of crosses made between three or more genera. The names of those involving three genera may be either portmanteau, e.g. x*Sophrolaeliocattleya* (*Cattleya* x *Laelia* x *Sophronitis*) or commemorative and terminate in -ara, e.g. x*Wilsonara* (*Cochlioda* x *Odontoglossum* x *Oncidium*). Names of hybrids between more than three genera are invariably commemorative, e.g. x *Potinara* (*Brassavola* x *Cattleya* x *Laelia* x *Sophronitis*).

The word 'hybrid' occurs in two other contexts.

Hybrid groups are assemblages of cultivars selected from the progeny of a single hybrid or several successive hybrids. These are usually plants that have undergone intensive horticultural development, have been crossed, selected, recrossed, backcrossed, etc. to the point where it is nonsense to assign them to any one specified parentage. In the *Index*, this is best illustrated by *Primula* Pruhonicensis Hybrids.

Graft hybrids (graft chimaeras) are non-sexual hybrids formed by the fusion and mingling of tissues belonging to the stock and scion of a graft. The proliferation of both tissue types causes the production of growth typical of both taxa involved, and in mutated 'hybrid' forms intermediate between them. The graft hybrid name is formed in the same way as an intergeneric hybrid name, but prefixed by an addition sign. +*Laburnocytisus adamii*, for example, is a graft hybrid between *Laburnum anagyroides* and *Chamaecytisus purpureus*. It is a small, *Laburnum*-like tree which produces *Laburnum*-type foliage and flowers, also *Laburnum*-type flowers with purple-pink colouring, also Broom-type flowers in buff or purple-pink, foliage intermediate between Broom and *Laburnum* and sporadic outbreaks of 'true' Broom-like growth. Other intergeneric graft hybrids include + *Crataegomespilus dardarii* (*Crataegus monogyna* + *Mespilus germanica*); this has the cultivars 'Bronvaux' and 'Jules d'Asnières'. *Syringa* + *correlata* is an example of an interspecific graft hybrid, *Syringa* x *chinensis* + *S. vulgaris*.

USING THE INDEX

POPULAR NAME

GENUS

GENUS AUTHOR

POPULAR NAME

FAMILY

DISTRIBUTION
of the genus

Flowering season

CLIMATIC ZONE

SPECIES

forma

AUTHOR CITATION
(in this case a double
citation with the basionym
author in parentheses)

CULTIVAR

DISTRIBUTION
of the species

HYBRID BINOMIAL
(parentage in
parenthesis)

Jasmin *Gardenia augusta.*
Jasmine *Jasminum.*
Jasmine Tobacco *Nicotiana alata.*
Jasmine Tree *Holarrhena pubescens.*

Jasminocereus Britt. & Rose Cactaceae. 1 arborescent cactus to 8m. Br. segmented, green or grey-green; ribs 11–22; areoles 5–25mm apart; central spines usually 2–4, to 7.5cm, radial spines shorter. Fls salverform, 5–9×2–6cm, nocturnal, creamy white. Galapagos Is. Z9.
J. *thouarsii* (Weber) Backeb.

Jasminum L. JASMINE; JESSAMINE. Oleaceae. 200 shrubs and woody climbers. Lvs trifoliolate, imparipinnate or with only one leaflet. Fls in term. or axill. cymes; cor. tubular, 5-lobed. Fr. a 2-valved berry. Trop. and temp. Old World, 1 sp. in Amer.
J. *affine* Carr. = *J. officinale* 'Affine'.
J. *angulare* Vahl. Everg. climbing shrub, lfts 3, rarely 5, ovate to lanceolate. Fls unscented, in threes, to 3cm diam., white. S Africa. Z9.
J. *azoricum* L. Everg. twining shrub. Lfts 3, ovate, undulate. Fls fragrant, in term. pan.; white. Late summer. Azores. Z9.
J. *beesianum* Forr. & Diels. Decid., sprawling to twining shrub. Lvs simple, ovate-lanceolate, slightly downy. Fls in threes, fragrant, pale pink to deep rose, 1cm diam. Fr. black, glossy. Early summer. China. Z7.
J. *blinii* Lév. = *J. polyanthum.*
J. *farreri* Gilmour = *J. humile* f. *farreri.*
J. *floridum* Bunge. Erect to semi-pendent, semi-everg. shrub. Lfts 3–5, oval to ovate, acuminate, glab. Fls in cymes, profuse, yellow. Late summer. China. Z9.
J. *fluminense* hort. = *J. azoricum.*
J. *fruticans* L. Dense everg. or semi-everg. shrub to 1.25m. Lfts 3, tough, narrow-oblong, obtuse, minutely ciliate. Fls to 5 per term. cyme, yellow. Summer. Medit., Asia Minor. Z8.
J. *giraldii* hort. = *J. humile* f. *farreri.*
J. *grandiflorum* L. = *J. officinale* f. *grandiflorum.*
J. *humile* L. ITALIAN YELLOW JASMINE. Everg. or semi-everg. shrub to 6m, erect. Lfts to 7, ovate-lanceolate. Fls in near-umbellate clusters, yellow, poorly scented, 1cm wide. Summer. Middle East, Burm., China. 'Revolutum' Semi-everg. Lfts 3–7. Fls 2.5cm wide, yellow, fragrant. Summer. f. *farreri* (Gilmour) P. Green. Everg. shrub to 1.5m; lfts 3, oval-lanceolate, acuminate. Fls yellow. Summer. Upper Burm. f. *wallichianum* (Lindl.) P. Green. Shoots v. angular. Lfts 7–13, ovate-lanceolate. Fls to 3 per pendent cyme. Nepal. Z8.
J. *humile* var. *glabrum* (DC.) Kob. = *J. humile* f. *wallichianum.*
J. *humile* var. *revolutum* (Sims) Stokes = *J. humile* 'Revolutum'.
J. *mesnyi* Hance. PRIMROSE JASMINE. Everg. rambling shrub to 2m. Lfts 3, subsessile, lanceolate, glossy. Fls 3–5cm wide, usually semi-double, bright yellow. Summer. W China. Z8.
J. *nudiflorum* Lindl. WINTER JASMINE. Decid., slender, pendent shrub, to 3m. Lfts 3, oval-oblong, dark green, glab., ciliate. Fls solitary to 3cm wide, yellow. Winter–early spring. N China. 'Aureum': lvs yellow, liable to revert to green. 'Nanum': dwarf, slow-growing, compact. Z6.
J. *officinale* L. COMMON JASMINE; TRUE JASMINE; JESSAMINE. Decid. scandent to twining shrub to 10m. Lfts 5–9, elliptic, acuminate, margins minutely downy. Fls to 5 per cyme, highly fragrant, white, 2cm wide. Summer–early autumn. Asia Minor, Himal., China. 'Affine': fls larger, exterior pink. 'Aureum': lvs blotched golden yellow. f. *grandiflorum* (L.) Kob. More robust; lfts 5–7. Fls to 4cm diam., white flushed pink at base. Summer. Himal. Z7.
J. *parkeri* Dunn. Everg. dwarf shrub, to 30cm. Lfts 3–5, ovate, acuminate, entire, sessile. Fls solitary or paired, yellow, 1.5cm wide. Summer. NW India. Z7.
J. *polyanthum* Franch. Semi-evergreen climber. Lfts 5–7, lanceolate, narrow-acuminate, coriaceous. Fls in axill. pan., highly fragrant, white, exterior pink. Summer. SW China. Z8.
J. *primulinum* Hemsl. = *J. mesnyi.*
J. *pubigerum* var. *glabrum* DC. = *J. humile* f. *wallichianum.*
J. *reevesii* hort. = *J. humile* 'Revolutum'.
J. *revolutum* Sims. = *J. humile* 'Revolutum'.
J. *rex* S.T. Dunn. Everg. climber. Lft large, 1, broadly ovate. Fls 2–3 per axill. cyme, unscented, white, tube to 2.5cm. Summer. Thail. Z8.
J. *sambac* (L.) Ait. ARABIAN JASMINE. Everg. climber. Lvs shiny broad-ovate. Fls in clusters 3–12, highly fragrant, waxy white, pink with age, tube 12mm. Flowers continuously. Widespread through cult.; may originate in India. 'Grand Duke of Tuscany': fls double. Z9.
J. *sieboldianum* Bl. = *J. nudiflorum.*
J. ×*stephanense* Lemoine. (*J. beesianum* ×*J. officinale.*) Vigorous twiner to 5m. Lvs simple or 3–5-parted, flushed cream on emergence. Fls pale pink, small, in sparse cymes. Mid-summer. Gdn origin, also said to occur wild in W China. Z7.

J. triumphans hort. = *J. humile* 'Revolutum'.
J. wallichianum Lindl. = *J. humile* f. *wallichianum*.

Jata de Guanbacoa *Copernicia macroglossa*.
Jata-uba *Syagrus cocoides*.

Jatropha L. TARTOGO; GOUT PLANT; BARBADOS NUT; PHYSIC NUT; CORAL PLANT; PEREGRINA; JICAMILLA. Euphorbiaceae. 170 tall perenn. herbs and shrubs, or trees with milky or watery sap. Lvs simple or palmately lobed or cut. Fls small, 5-merous in terminal, flat-topped, many-branched cymes, peduncle stout, often coloured. Trop. and warm temp., mainly S Amer. Z10.
J. curcas L. PHYSIC NUT; PURGING NUT; PULZA; BARBADOS NUT. Shrub or small tree, 2.5–6m, decid. Lvs to 15cm diam. ovate to 3–5-palmately lobed. Fls green-yellow to yellow-white. Trop. Amer.
J. hastata Jacq. = *J. integerrima*.
J. integerrima Jacq. PEREGRINA; SPICY JATROPHA. Everg. tree to 6m. Lvs dark green, pandurately 3-lobed, green-brown beneath. Fls bright rose-red. Cuba, W Indies.
J. multifida L. CORAL PLANT; PHYSIC NUT. Shrub or tree, to 7m. Lvs to 30cm diam., palmately 7–11 lobed, lobes finely dissected. Fls scarlet. Trop. Amer.
J. pandurifolia Andrew = *J. integerrima*.
J. podagrica Hook. GOUT PLANT; TARTOGO. St. to 2.5m, gouty, with a central swelling. Lvs orbicular-ovate, to 30cm wide, 3–5-lobed, blue-green. Fls coral red. Guat. and Panama.
J. texana Muell. Arg. = *Cnidoscolus texanus*.
J. urens L. = *Cnidoscolus urens*.
J. urens var. *inermis* Calvino = *Cnidoscolus chayamansa*.

Java Apple *Syzygium samarangense*.
Java Dacryberry *Dacrycarpus imbricatus*.
Java Glory Bean *Clerodendrum* ×*speciosum*.
Javanese Ixora *Ixora javanica*.
Javan Grape *Tetrastigma*.
Java Olives *Sterculia foetida*.
Java Staghorn Fern *Platycerium willinckii*.
Java Tree *Ficus benjamina*.
Java Willow *Ficus virens*.
Jazmin Del Monte *Brunfelsia lactea*.

Jeffersonia Barton. TWIN LEAF. Berberidaceae. 2 perenn. herbs. Lvs round to reniform, radical, 2-lobed, peltate, angled to toothed, long-petioled. Fls solitary, on slender scapes; pet. 5–8, flat, oblong, sta. 8. N Amer., E Asia. Z5.
J. diphylla (L.) Pers. RHEUMATISM ROOT. Lvs to 15cm across, glaucous beneath. Scapes exceeding petioles; fls white, 2.5cm across. Spring. Ont. to Tenn.
J. dubia (Maxim.) Benth. and Hook. f. ex Bak. & Moore. Lvs to 10cm across, glaucous, tinged mauve. Scapes shorter than petioles; fls lavender to pale blue, 3cm. across. Spring–summer. NE Asia.

Jeffrey's Pine *Pinus jeffreyi*.

Jehlia Rose = *Lopezia*.

Jelly Palm *Butia*; *B. yatay*.
Jenneb *Cordia africana*.

Jensenobotrya Herre. Aizoaceae. 1 dwarf shrub. St. woody, with withered lf remains. Lvs to 1.5cm diam., spherical, v. succulent, red-flushed. Fls solitary or paired, 2–2.5cm diam., pale magenta. Nam. Z9.
J. lossowiana Herre.

Jepsonia Small. Saxifragaceae. 3 rhizomatous, perenn. herbs. Rhiz. tuber-like. Lvs basal, orbicular-cordate, palmatifid to serrate; petiole long. Fls small, 5-merous in scapose cymes. S Calif. Z7.
J. parryi (Torr.) Small. Lvs 5cm diam. Scape to 30cm, fls 4; cal. tube to 1cm, olive striped purple; pet. to 1cm, white marked purple. Autumn. *J. heterandra* Eastw. and *J. malvifolia* (Green) Small are closely related sp. sometimes included in *J. parryi*. Both differ from this sp. in having branching rhiz. and ± 10 fls per scape.
→*Saxifraga*.

Jeriva *Syagrus comosa*.
Jersey Elm *Ulmus* 'Sarniensis'.
Jersey Lily *Amaryllis belladonna*.
Jerusalem Artichoke *Helianthus tuberosus*.

JUNCACEAE Juss. 10/325. *Juncus*, *Luzula*.

NUMBER OF SPECIES known to science (approximate)

SYNONYM (cross referring to the accepted name, where the plant is described)

SYNONYM leading to the genus where the plant is described

MONOTYPIC GENUS the single species in this genus is described under the generic name

cross reference to another genus where synonyms for *Jepsonia* can be found

FAMILY followed by Family Author, Total Number of genera/species in the family, and a list of genera described in the Index

GENERAL ABBREVIATIONS

alt.	alternate	fl.	flower	perenn.	perennial
ann.	annual	-fld	-flowered	pubesc.	pubescent
anth.	anther(s)	fls	flowers	rac.	raceme(s)
axill.	axillary	flt(s)	floret(s)	rhiz.	rhizome
bienn.	biennial	fr.	fruit	seg.	segment(s)
br.	branch(es)	gdn	garden	sep.	sepal(s)
cal.	calyx, calyses	glab.	glabrous	sp.	species
cap.	capitulum,	gland.	glandular	spp.	species (pl.)
	capitula	inc.	including	ssp.	subspecies
c	circa	introd.	introduced	sspp.	subspecies (pl.)
cor.	corolla	infl.	inflorescence	st.	stem(s)
cult.	cultivation/	lat.	lateral	sta.	stamens(s)
	cultivated	lf	leaf	temp.	temperate
cv., cvs	cultivar,	lfts	leaflets	tep.	tepal(s)
	cultivars	lvs	leaves	term.	terminal
decid.	deciduous	mts	mountains	trop.	tropical
distrib.	distributed/	nat.	naturalized	v.	very
	distribution	occas.	occasionally	var.	variety
dors.	dorsal	pan.	panicle,	♂	male
epical.	epicalyx		panicles	♀	female
esp.	especially	perenn.	perennial	☿	bisexual
everg.	evergreen	pet.	petal, petals	+/–	more or less
f.	forma	pb., pbs	pseudobulb,	0	[zero] absent
fil.	filament(s)		pseudobulbs		

GEOGRAPHICAL ABBREVIATIONS

Afghan.	Afghanistan	Cauc.	Caucasus	It.	Italy
Afr.	Africa	Circumtrop.	Circumtropic	Jam.	Jamaica
Alab.	Alabama	Colomb.	Colombia	Jap.	Japan
Alask.	Alaska	Conn.	Connecticut	Jord.	Jordan
Alg.	Algeria	Cont.	Continental	Kans.	Kansas
Amaz.	Amazon	Cosmop.	Cosmopolitan	Kent.	Kentucky
Amer.	America	Czech.	Czechoslovakia	Leb.	Lebanon
Antarc.	Antarctica	Dak.	Dakota	Les.	Lesotho
Arc.	Arctic	Denm.	Denmark	Madag.	Madagascar
Arg.	Argentina	Ecuad.	Ecuador	Manch.	Manchuria
Ariz.	Arizona	Eng.	England	Manit.	Manitoba
Ark.	Arkansas	Equat.	Equatorial	Masc.	Mascarene
Aus.	Australia	Ethiop.	Ethiopia	Mass.	Massachusetts
Balk.	Balkans	Eur.	Europe	Maur.	Mauritius
BC	British	Flor.	Florida	Medit.	Mediterranean
	Columbia	Fr.	France	Mex.	Mexico
Boliv.	Bolivia	Germ.	Germany	Mich.	Michigan
Bots.	Botswana	Guat.	Guatemala	Minn.	Minnesota
Braz.	Brazil	Hemis.	Hemisphere	Miss.	Mississippi
Br.	British	Himal.	Himalaya	Mong.	Mongolia
Bulg.	Bulgaria	Hispan.	Hispaniola	Mont.	Montana
Burm.	Burma	Hond.	Honduras	Moroc.	Morocco
Calif.	California	Hung.	Hungary	Moz.	Mozambique
Cantab.	Cantabrian	Ill.	Illinois	NJ	New Jersey
Carib.	Caribbean	Indomal.	Indomalaya	NY	New York
Carol.	Carolina	Indon.	Indonesia	NZ	New Zealand
Carpath.	Carpathians	Isr.	Israel	Nam.	Namibia

Neb.	Nebraska	Queensld	Queensland	Tob.	Tobago
Neotrop.	Neotropics	Rep.	Republic	Transcauc.	Transcaucasia
Nic.	Nicaragua	Rom.	Romania	Trin.	Trinidad
OFS	Orange Free State	Saskatch.	Saskatchewan	Trop.	Tropics
		Scand.	Scandinavia	Turk.	Turkey
Okl.	Oklahoma	Seych.	Seychelles	Tun.	Tunisia
Ont.	Ontario	Sib.	Siberia	Tvl	Transvaal
Oreg.	Oregon	Subcosmop.	Subcosmopolitan	Urug.	Uruguay
OW	Old World	Subtrop.	Subtropics	Venez.	Venezuela
Pak.	Pakistan	Swaz.	Swaziland	Verm.	Vermont
Pantrop.	Pantropical	Switz.	Switzerland	Vict.	Victoria
Parag.	Paraguay	Syr.	Syria	Virg.	Virginia
Penn.	Pennsylvania	Tanz.	Tanzania	Wisc.	Wisconsin
Philipp.	Philippines	Tasm.	Tasmania	Wyom.	Wyoming
Polyn.	Polynesia	Tenn.	Tennesee	Zam.	Zambia
Port.	Portugal	Tex.	Texas	Zimb.	Zimbabwe
Pyren.	Pyrenees	Thail.	Thailand		

TEMPERATURE CONVERSION

$$°C = 5/9(°F - 32) \qquad °F = 9/5°C + 32$$

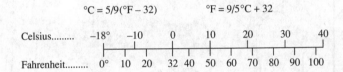

CONVERSIONS OF MEASUREMENTS

Length	1 millimetre	=	0.0394 inch
	1 centimetre	=	0.3937 inch
	1 metre	=	1.0936 yards
	1 kilometre	=	0.6214 miles

RANGE OF AVERAGE ANNUAL MINIMUM TEMPERATURE FOR EACH CLIMATIC ZONE

Zone	°F	°C
1	< −50	< −45.5
2	−50 to −40	−45.5 to −40.1
3	−40 to −30	−40.0 to −34.5
4	−30 to −20	−34.4 to −28.9
5	−20 to −10	−28.8 to −23.4
6	−10 to 0	−23.3 to −17.8
7	0 to +10	−17.7 to −12.3
8	+10 to +20	−12.2 to −6.7
9	+20 to +30	−6.6 to −1.2
10	+30 to +40	−1.1 to +4.4
11	> +40	> +4.4

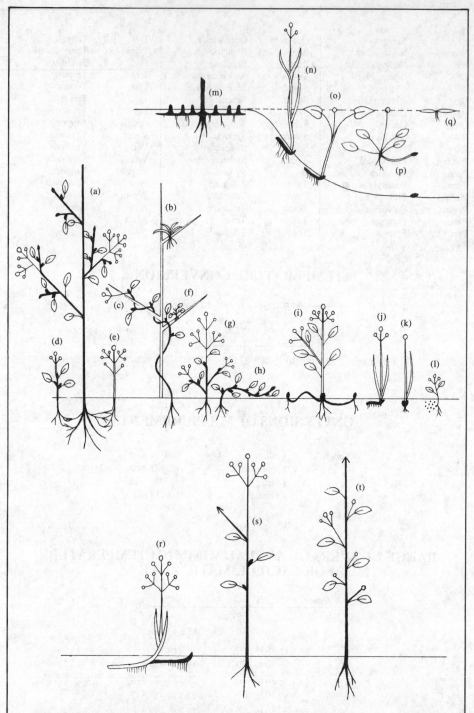

Life forms and growth habits (Open circles indicate flowers. Thick black regions indicate perennial parts, except in (r), where black indicates subsequent season's growth). (a) Phancrophyte. (b) Epiphyte. (c) Climber (liane). (d) Partial parasite. (e) Obligate parasite (f) Epiphytic partial parasite. (g,h) Chamaephytes. (i) Hemicryptophyte. (j) Cryptophyte-geophyte (rhizomatous). (k) Cryptophyte-geophyte (cormous or bulbous). (l) therophyte (annual). (m) Mangrove with pneumatophores. (n) Cryptophyte-helophyte. (o) Cryptophyte-hydrophte. (p) Cryptophyte-hydrophte (submerged). (q) Cryptophyte-hydrophte (surface floating). (r) Cryptophyte with sympodial growth. (s) Phanerophyte with sympodial growth. (t) Phanerophyte with monopodial growth.

GLOSSARY

a-, an- prefix meaning without.

ab- prefix meaning from or away from (i.e. deviant).

abaxial of the surface or part of a lateral organ, turned or facing away from the axis and toward the plant's base; thus the underside of a leaf or perianth segment even when that surface may be uppermost because of the twisting of a stalk, strong incurving of petals or the hanging attitude of a branch or inflorescence; cf. adaxial.

abbreviated shortened.

aberrant unusual or atypical, differing from the normal form.

abortive (of reproductive organs) undeveloped or not perfectly developed, and therefore barren; (of seeds) failing to develop normally.

above (1) pertaining to the adaxial surface of a leaf, petal, sepal or scale; (2) pertaining to the upper portions of a stem, bulb, tuber, branch or inflorescence.

abrupt of a leaf or perianth segment tip, terminating suddenly without tapering, usually when broadly rounded or squared; 'abruptly acute' refers to parts terminating in this way but tipped with a short sharp point; 'abruptly acuminate' is used where a longer point is meant.

abscission, abscissing (abscising) (of leaves, branches etc.) a separating or falling away, caused by disintegration of a layer of plant tissues at the base of the organ (e.g., as the result of environmental conditions or pollination leading to hormonal action), with a subsequent development of scar tissue or periderm at the point of abscission.

acaulescent of a plant whose stem is absent or, more usually, appears to be absent, being very short or subterranean.
inconspicuous.

accepted a name is said to be accepted when a botanist proposes or adopts it as the correct name for a taxon.

accessory fruit a fruit or aggregate fruit in which the conspicuous and, usually, fleshy parts are distinct from the pistil, as in the enlarged torus of the strawberry.

accrescent growing together or becoming larger or longer with age, or after fertilization, as in the calyx of *Physalis*.

accumbent lying against; (of cotyledons) lying face to face, the edges of one side lying against the radicle in the seed.

-aceous suffix denoting resemblance, e.g. foliaceous, 'leaf-like'; or 'belonging or relation to', e.g. asclepiadaceous genera belong to the Asclepiadaceae; papilionaceous flowers are those of Leguminosae subfamily Papilionoideae.

achene a dry, small, indehiscent fruit with a tight thin pericarp, strictly consisting of one free carpel as in Ranunculaceae, but sometimes applied to Compositae with more than one seed.

achenocarp any dry indehiscent fruit.

achlamydeous lacking a perianth.

acicular needle-shaped, and usually rounded rather than flat in cross-section.

aciculate of texture or coloration, marked as if scored with a needle.

acinaceous full of kernels.

acinaciform shaped like a scimitar.

acinose resembling a bunch of grapes, composed of granular bodies tightly packed.

acondylose of stems lacking joints or nodes.

acropetal of organs such as leaves or flowers, produced, developing or opening in succession from base to apex, the opposite of basipetal.

acroscopic directed towards the apex of a frond: the first lateral vein or leaflet on a pinna branching off in an upwards direction.

actinomorphic of regular flowers possessing radial symmetry, capable of division in two or more planes into similar halves.

actinostelic said of a vascular strand with radiating ribs.

aculeate prickly, bearing sharp prickles.

aculeiform prickle-shaped.

acuminate (of leaves and perianth segments) with the tip or, less commonly, the base tapering gradually to a point, usually with somewhat concave sides.

acutangular when stems are sharply angular.

acute (of the tips or bases of leaves or perianth segments) where two almost straight or slightly convex sides converge to terminate in a sharp point, the point shorter and usually broader than in an acuminate leaf tip.

acyclic with parts arranged spirally, not in pairs or whorls.

adaxial turned or facing toward the axis and apex, thus the upper, if not always the uppermost surface of an organ, sometimes used interchangeably with ventral.

adherent of parts usually free or separate (i.e. petals) but clinging or held closely together. Such parts are sometimes loosely described as united or, inaccurately, as fused, which is strictly synonymous with coherent. Some authors use this word to describe the fusion of dissimilar parts.

adnate attached by its whole length or surface to the face of an organ.

adpressed (appressed) (of indumentum, leaves, etc.) used of an organ which lies flat and close to the stem or leaf to which it is attached.

adventitious (adventive) occurring in an unusual location, originating from other than the normal place – applied to non-native plants introduced deliberately or accidentally; to buds developing along a stem rather than at leaf axils; to viviparously produced plantlets and to roots that develop not from the radicle and its subdivisions but from another part such as the stem or leaf axil.

aerenchyma air-conducting tissue in roots and stems composed of thin-walled cells and large intercellular spaces; a feature of some plants of wet places securing aeration and (in genera like *Neptunia* and *Eichhornia*) buoyancy.

aerial used broadly of all plant parts found above ground or (in the case of aquatics) water.

aerial roots roots borne wholly above ground, either adventitiously as in *Hedera* or from the rooting axis as in many epiphytes.

aestivation the arrangement of floral parts before flowering.

affixed fixed upon.

afoliate leafless.

ageotropic (apogeotropic) applied to parts that are negatively geotropic, i.e. growing upwards against the influence of gravity as in the pneumatophores of mangrove species, the knee roots of *Taxodium* and the coralloid roots of many Zamiaceae.

agglomerate crowded together in a head, as in the flowers of *Scabiosa* spp.

agglutinate glued together, as in the pollen masses of Orchidaceae.

aggregate flowers gathered together, usually in a tight

LEAF ARRANGEMENTS 1

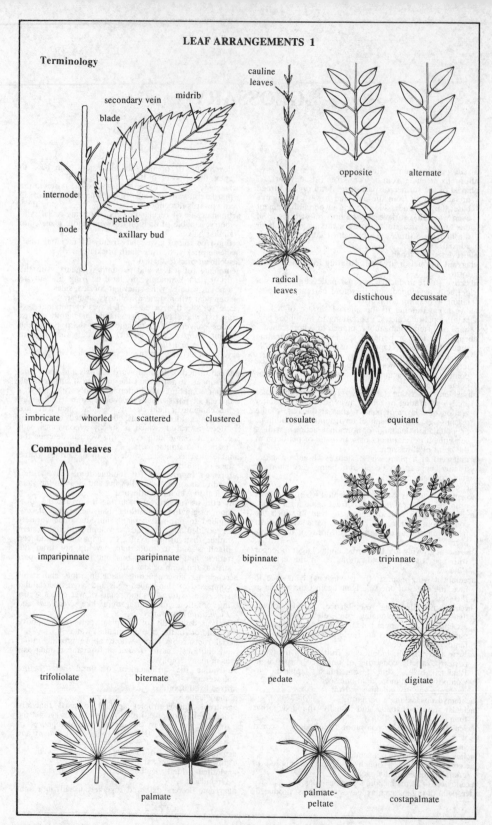

Terminology

cauline leaves

secondary vein

blade

midrib

internode

node

petiole

axillary bud

radical leaves

opposite

alternate

distichous

decussate

imbricate   whorled   scattered   clustered   rosulate   equitant

Compound leaves

imparipinnate   paripinnate   bipinnate   tripinnate

trifoliolate   biternate   pedate   digitate

palmate   palmate-peltate   costapalmate

rounded bunch or head as in Dipsacaceae without being capitulate as in Compositae.

aggregate fruits a collection of separate carpels produced by a single flower and borne on a common receptacle, as in the fleshy 'fruit' of *Rubus*.

alate winged, usually of stems, petioles and fruits where the main body is furnished with marginal membranous bands.

albumen the storage tissue for starchy or oily nutritive material, as food supply for the embryo; see endosperm and perisperm.

aliferous bearing wings.

alternate (1) of leaves, branches, pedicels, etc., arranged in two ranks along the stem, rachis, etc., with the insertions of the two ranks not parallel but alternating, thus the antithesis of paired or opposite; (2) of two types of organ or structure, when one is placed in an alternating sequence with another, thus petals alternate with calyx lobes = petals placed between calyx lobes.

alternation of generations the complete life-cycle of organisms with strongly differentiated sexual and asexual phases (i.e. the succession of gametophytes and sporophytes), as found in Pteridophytes.

alveolate honey-combed.

ament see catkin.

amphicarpic producing two different types of fruit, sometimes used of plants bearing two crops per season.

amphicarpogenous producing buried fruit, as in the peanut.

amphigeal producing two types of flower, one from the rootstock or stem base, the other from the upper stems.

amphimixis sexual reproduction, the union of parental characters.

amplexicaul (of a leaf base or dilated petiole or stipule) enlarged and embracing or clasping the stem.

ampulla an organ shaped like a squat, rounded flask or a bladder.

ampullaceous ampulla-shaped.

anadromous when the first branch of a frond or vein of a primary pinna is produced on the side facing towards the frond apex, cf. catadromous.

anastomosing of veins forming a network, united at their points of contact.

ancipitous with two sharp edges.

androdioecious a species with two forms, one with male flowers only, the other with hermaphrodite flowers.

androecium the male component of a flower, the stamen or stamens as a whole.

androgynophore a stalk-like axis subtended by the perianth and bearing stamens and pistil.

androgynous hermaphrodite or, sometimes, monoecious.

andromonoecious a species with two forms, one with only male flowers, the other with only perfect flowers, but no purely female flowers.

androphore the base (if distinct) of a staminal column, as in Malvaceae, or a stalk supporting an androecium.

anfractuose (anfractuous) closely or tightly sinuous, or spirally twisted.

angiosperms plants with their seeds enclosed in an ovary, i.e. flowering plants as opposed to gymnosperms, non-flowering plants with naked seeds.

angular, angulate with laterally projecting angles, as in longitudinally ridged and angled stems.

anisophyllous of paired leaves differing one from the other in size or shape, a common feature in the trailing-stemmed Gesneriaceae.

annual a plant which completes its entire life-cycle within the space of a year.

annular of organs of parts in a circular arrangement or forming rings.

annulate ring-shaped.

annulus a ring: (1) the corona or rim of the corolla in Asclepiadaceae, (2) in ferns, an elastic ring of cells that partially invests and bursts the sporangium at dehiscence.

antemarginal lying within, or extending just short of, the margin.

anterior of the surface or part of an organ turned away from or furthest from the axis and projecting forward or toward the base or (in the case of a flower) any subtending bract; close to abaxial but broader in definition, meaning not only 'beneath' but also lower (of two, as in the lower lip of a bilabiate flower) or furthest as in the tip of an organ, cf. posterior.

anther the pollen-bearing portion of the stamen, either sessile or attached to a filament.

anther cap in Orchidaceae, the case enclosing the pollinia.

anther sac a sac-shaped unit containing pollen. In many plants, the anther consists of four pollen sacs disposed in two lobes, the tissues separating the members of each pair usually break down prior to anthesis, giving rise to a biloculate (two-celled) anther.

antheridium in cryptogams, the structure producing male gametes; the equivalent of the anther in flowering plants.

antheriferous bearing anthers.

antheroid anther-like.

antherozoid a male gamete or sperm.

anthesis the expansion or opening of a flower, the period in which the anthers and stigmas become functional, enabling fertilization to take place.

anti- prefix meaning against or opposed to.

antipetalous opposite to or superposed on a petal, i.e. not alternate.

antisepalous opposite to or superposed on a sepal, i.e. not alternate.

antrorse turned, curved or bent upward or forward, toward the apex; cf. retrorse.

ap-, apo- prefix meaning not.

apetalous lacking petals.

apex the growing point of a stem or root; the tip of an organ or structure, most commonly used of a leaf tip.

aphyllous lacking leaves.

apical borne at the apex of an organ, farthest from the point of attachment; pertaining to the apex.

apical dominance the dominance of the apical meristem which produces hormones to prevent lateral buds developing while it is active.

apiculate possessing an apicule.

apicule a short sharp but not rigid point terminating a leaf, bract or perianth segment.

apocarpous of a gynoecium with the carpels distinct from one another; the opposite of syncarpous.

apogeotropic see ageotropic.

apomict see clone.

apomictic asexual reproduction, often through viable seeds but without fusion of gametes.

apomixis the process of reproducing without fusion of gametes, ie. asexually; plants in which seeds develop from unfertilized cells are termed apomicts. The offspring of such plants are genetically uniform. The term is sometimes extended to cover other asexual (vegetative) means of increase.

apophysis a swelling or enlargement, noticeable in the cone-scale of some conifers, or in the stalk or seta at the base of the capsule in some mosses.

aposepalous with free sepals.

appendage secondary part or process attached to or developed from any larger organ, e.g. the leafy appendages terminating the lower inflorescence bracts of some *Heliconia* spp. or the whisker-like appendages of a *Tacca* inflorescence.

appendix a long, narrowed development of the spadix in Araceae.

appendiculate furnished with appendages.

applanate flattened.

appressed see adpressed.

approximate drawn very closely together, sometimes confused with *proximate*.

apterous without wings.

apud (Lat. with, among or in) when a name and diagnosis belonging to one author were published by another, this connective was required for the author citation, often with the work in which they were published (e.g. *Ceratozamia latifolia* Miq. apud Tijdschr.

Wis. en Nat. I, 1846). More commonly, the connective 'in' was used for this purpose and today almost without exception.

aquatic a plant growing naturally in water, either entirely or partially submerged.

arachnoid interlaced with a cobweb of fine white hair, as in some tightly growing succulent rosette plants.

araneous arachnoid.

arborescent with the habit or stature of a tree.

archegone a term for the egg cell produced in the archegonium.

archegonium a flask-shaped organ producing female gametes in some cryptogams and gymnosperms.

arching curved gently downwards, usually of branches, stems, large leaves and inflorescences, usually more freely than *arcuate* and less markedly than *pendent*.

arcuate curved downwards, bow-shaped, usually applied to a smaller, more rigid structure than would be described as arching, e.g. the column of an orchid.

areole a small area or space, often between anastomosing veins; also a depression or elevation on a cactus stem, bearing spines.

aril a generally fleshy appendage of the funiculus or hilum, partially or entirely enveloping the seed.

arillate possessing an aril; more loosely, any outgrowth or appendage on the testa.

aristate of a leaf apex abruptly terminated in an acicular continuation of the midrib. Otherwise, awned.

aristulate bearing a small awn.

articulate, articulated jointed; possessing distinct nodes or joints, sometimes swollen at their attachment and breaking easily.

arundinaceous reed-like, resembling a cane or reed.

ascending rising or extending upwards, usually from an oblique or horizontal position, thus differing from erect.

aseptate lacking partitions or divisions.

asexual lacking sexual characteristics or (of reproductive processes) occurring without the fusion of gametes, thus the asexual generation of a fern is the sporophyte and asexual means of increase include apogamy, viviparity and mechanical methods such as grafting, cuttings and division.

asperous rough.

asperulous of a very rough surface, possessing short, hard projections or points.

assurgent rising, extending upwards.

astragaloid dice-shaped.

asymmetric, asymmetrical (1) irregular or unequal in outline or shape, (2) of a flower incapable of being cut in any vertical plane into similar halves.

attenuate (of the apex or base) tapering finely and concavely to a long drawn out point.

auctoris, auctorum [abbrev. auct., auctt.] (Lat. of an author, of authors) used to cite a name applied by authors to the wrong entity and usually with the 'non' formula to contrast it with the true type as embodied by the correct author citation. Thus: *Betula platyphylla* auct. non Sukachev, where some authors call what is in fact *B. mandschurica* by a valid name belonging to a wholly different plant. This formula is sometimes used interchangeably with 'hort.' and 'misapplied'.

auricle an ear-like lobe or outgrowth, often at the base of an organ (i.e. a leaf), or the junction of leaf sheath and blade in some Gramineae.

auricled see auriculate.

auriculate (of the base of a leaf blade or perianth segment) possessing two rounded, ear-shaped lobes that project beyond the general outline of the organ.

author in taxonomy, the first worker validly to publish a new name or combination for a taxon. The author name, usually abbreviated, follows that of the taxon in a citation. For example, *Physalis alkekengi* L., where L. stands for Linnaeus. The author citation can be qualified to denote a msapplied name (e.g. *Physalis alkekengi* hort. non L., to describe a name wrongly used by some growers for a plant more correctly named *P. alkekengi* var. *franchetii*), or used in a double citation to indicate that a name first

described at one rank (here a species) has been relegated to the status of variety within another species, e.g. *Physalis alkekengi* var. *franchetii* (Mast.) Mak. In this case Makino, has reduced Masters's species *P. franchetii* to a variety of *P. alkekengi*. The convention is also used when a name is transferred to a different genus entirely.

autogamous self-fertilizing.

autonym authors naming – say – a new subspecies or variety also designate a typical form of the species at the same rank as the new one, based on the original type of the species and duplicating its epithet. This method enables botanists to maintain broad concepts of species containing many variants, while still defining the type quite precisely.

awl-shaped narrowly wedge-shaped and tapering finely to a point, subulate.

awn a slender sharp point or bristle-like appendage found particularly on the glumes of grasses.

awned see aristate.

axe-shaped dolabriform.

axial relating to the morphological axis.

axil the upper angle between an axis and any off-shoot or lateral organ arising from it, especially a leaf.

axillary situated in, or arising from, or pertaining to an axil.

axis a notional point or line around or along which organs are developed or arranged, whether a stem, stalk or clump; thus the vegetative or growth axis and the floral axis describe the configuration and development of buds and shoots and flowers respectively, and any stem or point of origination on which they are found.

baccate of fruit, berry-like, with a juicy, pulpy rind.

bacciform berry-shaped.

baciliform rod- or club-shaped.

backbulb a dormant pseudobulb having completed its growth cycle and been surpassed by a new pseudobulb or the lead growth.

backcross a cross between a hybrid and one of its parent plants.

baculiform rod-like.

barb a hooked semi-rigid hair.

barbate bearded, with hairs in long weak tufts.

barbed of bristles or awns with short, stiff lateral or terminal hairs which are hooked sharply backward or downward.

barbellae short, stiff hairs, e.g. those of the pappus in Compositae.

barbellate furnished with barbellae.

basal at or arising from the base or point of attachment of a whole plant or organ, thus basal leaves arise from the rootstock or a very short or buried stem and a basal inflorescence arises from the rootstock or the base of a stem or storage organ.

basifixed (of an organ) attached by its base rather than its back, as an anther joined to its filament by its base.

basionym the base name of a taxon that has been transferred by a later author from one rank to another within a species, or to a new species or genus altogether. For example, in 1964 Cullen and Heywood judged that *Paeonia arietina* (published by Anderson 146 years earlier) was in fact a subspecies of *Paeonia mascula*. *P. arietina* Anderson became *P. mascula* ssp. *arietina* (Anderson) Cullen & Heywood. The original name is now the basionym or base name of the new combination and synonymous with it. To make this change clear and to indicate that the type of Cullen and Heywood's *arietina* is one and the same as Anderson's, the basionym author is cited in parentheses.

basipetalous developing from apex to base, as in an inflorescence where the terminal flowers open first, cf. acropetal.

basiscopic directed towards the base of a frond: the first lateral vein or leaflet on a pinna branching off in a downwards direction.

beak a long, pointed, horn-like projection; particularly applied to the terminal points of fruits and pistils.

beaked furnished with a beak.

LEAF ARRANGEMENTS 2

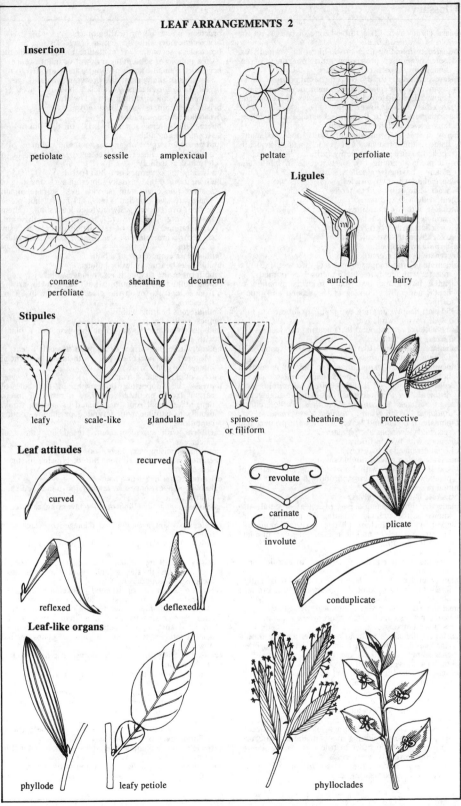

Insertion

petiolate sessile amplexicaul peltate perfoliate

connate-perfoliate sheathing decurrent

Ligules

auricled hairy

Stipules

leafy scale-like glandular spinose or filiform sheathing protective

Leaf attitudes

curved recurved revolute carinate involute plicate

reflexed deflexed conduplicate

Leaf-like organs

phyllode leafy petiole phylloclades

beard (1) an awn; (2) a tuft or zone of hair as on the falls of bearded irises.

bearded terminating in a bristle-like hair (awned); or, more generally, possessing tufts or zones of indumentum on parts of the surface.

below pertaining to the lower, basal portions of an organ or whole plant, thus 'stems devoid of leaves below'. 'Lvs ciliate below' meaning lvs whose margins are ciliate in their lower half.

beneath pertaining to the abaxial surface of an organ, thus 'leaves tomentose beneath'.

berry a baccate, indehiscent fruit, one- to many-seeded; the product of a single pistil. Frequently applied to any pulpy or fleshy fruit.

bi- a prefix denoting two or twice; as in bifoliolate, meaning having two leaflets.

biauriculate with two auricles.

bibracteolate with two bracteoles.

bicalcarate with two spurs.

bicallose with two callosities.

bicarinate with two keels.

bicarpellate with a two-celled fruit.

bicolor distinctly two-coloured.

bicornute two-horned.

bicrenate doubly crenate.

bidentate (1) (of an apex) possessing two teeth; (2) of a margin, with teeth, the teeth themselves toothed.

biennial lasting for two years from germination to death, generally blooming in the second and monocarpic.

bifid cleft deeply, forming two points or lobes.

bifoliate with two leaves.

bifoliolate (of a compound leaf) bearing two leaflets.

bifurcate twice forked.

bilabiate possessing two lips, as in the corolla of Labiatae and Acanthaceae.

binomial a binary name, the basic unit of naming in botany comprising a generic name and a species, cultivar, group or hybrid epithet describing and distinguishing the individual belonging to that genus, e.g. *Buddleja alternifolia*, *Buddleja* 'Petite Indito', *Buddleja* Davidii group, *Buddleja* ×*weyeriana*.

bipinnate of compound leaves where both primary and secondary divisions are pinnate.

biseptate with two partitions.

biserial arranged in two rows.

biserrate with a row of double saw-teeth.

bisexual of flowers with both stamens and pistils; of plants with perfect (hermaphrodite) flowers.

bitten praemorse.

bivalvate having two valves.

blade the thin, expanded part of a leaf or petal, also known as the lamina, excluding the petiole, stipe or claw; (in the strap-shaped leaves of certain monocots, i.e. grasses, orchids and bromeliads) the part of a leaf above the sheath.

blistered see bullate.

bloom the waxy or pruinose covering of certain fruits, leaves and stems.

blunt rounded, as in a leaf or bud tip that is neither finely tapered or pointed nor abruptly cut off. See obtuse, retuse.

boat-shaped see carinate, cymbiform, navicular.

bole the main stem of a tree or arborescent plant.

bossed see umbonate.

bostryx a uniparous helicoid cyme, i.e. a cyme producing one axis with each branching; often used interchangeably with helicoid cyme.

botuliform sausage-shaped.

bract a modified protective leaf associated with the inflorescence (clothing the stalk and subtending the flowers), with buds and with newly emerging shoots and stems. Bracts exhibit varying degrees of reduction, from the leafy inflorescence bracts of *Euphorbia pulcherrima* to the navicular bracts of *Heliconia*, or the thin scale-like stem bracts of many herbaceous species. In the developing shoots of the last category, a progression from bract to true leaf can be seen as the shoot develops.

bract scale in conifers, the scale of a female cone that subtends the seed-bearing scale.

bracteate possessing or bearing bracts.

bracteolate possessing or bearing bracteoles.

bracteole a secondary or miniature bract, often borne on a petiole or subtending a flower or inflorescence.

branchlet a small branch or twig, usually applied to the branches of the current and preceding years.

break (1) to produce new branches, buds or leaves: (2) a sporadic colour variation in a flower.

bristly see echinate, hispid and setose.

brushlike see muscariform.

buccae the lateral sepals (wings) in the flowers of *Aconitum* and allies.

bud an undeveloped organ or shoot; the rudiment of a branch, leaf cluster, inflorescence or flower, be it terminal or axillary.

bud scales the coverings of a bud (perules).

bulb a modified bud, usually subterranean, consisting of a short thickened stem, serving as a storage organ. There are two principal kinds, (1) naked, composed of free, overlapping scaly modified leaves, all of them fleshy, e.g. *Lilium*; (2) tunicated, with thin, membranous, fibrous or reticulated outer and fleshy concentric inner layers, e.g. *Allium*. The 'solid bulb' is a corm.

bulb scale a component of a bulb.

bulbiferous bearing bulbs or bulbils.

bulbiform in the shape of, resembling, a bulb.

bulbil, bulblet a small bulb or bulb-like growth, arising from a leaf axil or in the place of flowers in an inflorescence.

bulbiliferous bearing bulbils.

bulbose bulb-like.

bulbous (of a stem) swollen at the base; (of a plant) with a bulb.

bullate where the surface of an organ (usually a leaf) is 'blistered' or puckered (i.e. with many superficial interveinal convexities).

burr a prickly headed fruit.

buttress the supporting outgrowths of the bole of certain trees, produced either as a result of fused, flange-like aerial roots or a fluted or swollen trunk, usually to contend with saturated or shallow-rooting conditions.

cactiform with succulent stems resembling those of Cactaceae.

caducous abscising very early, soon falling.

caespitose a habit description: tufted, growing in small, dense clumps.

calcarate furnished with a spur.

calceolate slipper-shaped; resembling a round-toed shoe in form.

calcicole a plant dwelling on and favouring calcareous soils.

calcifuge a plant avoiding and damaged by calcareous soils.

callose (1) bearing callosities; (2) hard and thick in texture.

callosity a leathery or hard isolated thickening of an organ, callus in the second sense (i.e. not as a response to wounding).

callus an abnormal or isolated thickening of tissue, either produced in response to wounding or abscission or as a stable surface feature of leaves and perianth segments, thus the callus that forms on the wounded surface of a cutting and the calli (superficial protuberances) on the lips of many orchid flowers.

callused bearing callus, usually in response to wounding or abscission.

calycle, calyculus the epicalyx, an involucre of bracts or bracteoles simulating and subtending the true calyx.

calyptra in flowering plants, a hood or cap-like structure terminating a circumscissile calyx or pyxis.

calyptrate bearing a calyptra.

calyx a collective term for the sepals, whether separate or united, which form the outer whorl of the perianth or floral envelope.

calyx lobe the remaining free, apical portion of sepal in a fused calyx or hypanthium.

calyx tube a tube produced by fusion of the sepals.

cambium a secondary or inner meristem which increases the girth of a plant stem or root by adding vascular tissue.

campanulate (of a corolla) bell-shaped; a broad tube terminating in a flared limb or lobes.

campestral growing in fields.

camptodromous venation where the secondary veins curve toward the margin without forming loops.

canaliculate channelled with a long, concave groove, like a gutter.

candelabriform (of branching patterns and stellate hairs) candelabra-like, with tiered whorls or ranks of radiating or divergent branches.

canescent hoary, or becoming so; densely covered with short, grey-white pubescence.

cano-tomentose indumentum midway between canescent and tomentose.

cap see calyptra.

capillary slender and hair-like; much as filiform, but even more delicate.

capitate (1) arranged in heads, as in the inflorescence of Compositae; (2) terminating in a knob or somewhat spherical tip.

capitellate (1) minutely head-shaped; (2) clustered in a small, compact, capitate group.

capitiform, capitose see capitate.

capitulum a head of densely clustered and sessile or subsessile flowers on a compressed axis.

capsular attached to or resembling a capsule.

capsule a dry, dehiscent seed vessel.

carina keel, (1) the anterior petals of a papilionaceous flower; (2) the keel of the glume in flowers of Gramineae; (3) the midvein of a leaf, petal or sepal, prominent to ridged beneath.

carinate of a leaf, bract or perianth segment, boat-shaped or, more usually, keeled, with a line or ridge along the centre of its dorsal surface.

carnivorous used of plants which derive nutrients directly from animal remains, having entrapped them by specialized means.

carpel a female sporophyll, a simple pistil or one element of a compound pistil bearing an ovule.

carpellate, carpelled bearing or consisting of carpels; when written 2-carpellate, 3-carpellate etc., meaning composed of 2, 3, etc. carpels.

carpophore a slender stalk forming an extension of the receptacle and furnishing an axis for a carpel or carpels.

cartilaginous hard and tough in texture, but flexible.

caruncle a small protuberance near the hilum.

carunculate possessing a caruncle.

caryophyllaceous (1) pertaining to members of the Caryophyllaceae; (2) (of petals) bearing a long basal claw.

caryopsis (of Gramineae) a one-celled, one-seeded, superior fruit in which the pericarp and seed-wall are adherent.

cassideous helmet-shaped.

castaneous deep reddish brown or chestnut coloured.

casual an occasional weed of cultivation, not naturalized.

catadromous when the first branch of a frond or vein of a primary pinna is produced on the side facing towards the base of a frond cf. anadromous.

cataphyll any of the several types of reduced or scarcely developed leaves produced either at the start of a plant's life (i.e. cotyledons) or in the early stages of shoot, leaf or flower development (e.g. the bract-like rhizome scales of some monocots, those subtending and enveloping pseudobulbs, those found in the crowns of cycads alternating with whorls of developed leaves, or the imperfect leaf forms found, progressing up the stem from the most reduced scales, in the basal portions of the stems of many herbs).

catkin (ament) a cylindrical, bracteate spike or spike-like inflorescence composed of single flowers or cymules, the flowers usually apetalous and unisexual.

caudate (of a leaf or perianth segment apex) tapering gradually into a long tail-shaped appendage.

caudex strictly, the basal axis of a plant comprising both stem and root; sometimes applied to the aerial stems of palms and superficially palm-like plants. The term is, however, most often used in connection with plants with stout, swollen or succulent simple stems (sometimes by no means distinct from the root axis), usually crowned with narrower branches, leaves or inflorescences.

caudiciform resembling or possessing a caudex, encountered in the phrase caudiciform succulents, a disparate group of horticultural importance defined only by its members' exhibiting a caudex.

caulescent producing a well-developed stem above ground.

cauliflory the production of flowers directly from older wood, i.e. springing from the trunk or branches as in the Judas tree, *Cercis*, cocoa, *Theobroma*, and *Goethea*. Such plants are termed cauliflorous.

cauline attached to or arising from the stem.

cell (1) the primal operating unit of living matter, consisting of protoplasm in the form of cytoplasm and usually a single nucleus, contained within walls of cellulose; (2) the lobe of an anther or locule of an ovary or pericarp.

centrifugal progressing or extending from the centre towards the margin.

centripetal developing or progressing towards the centre from the margin.

cephalanthium the capitulum or flowerhead of Compositae.

cephalium a woolly growth bearing flowers, terminating the stem of certain Cactaceae.

ceriferous wax-producing.

cernuous nodding, usually applied to flowers with curved or drooping pedicels attached to a straight or erect inflorescence axis; cf. nutant.

cespitose see caespitose.

chaff dry thin membranous bracts or scales.

chaffy see paleaceous.

chalaza the part of an ovule where nucellus, integument and funicle are joined.

channelled (channeled) see canaliculate and sulcate.

chartaceous (of leaf and bract texture) thin and papery.

chimaera, chimera a plant constituted of tissues of differing genetic composition; can be the result of mutation or graft-hybridization.

chlamydia (1) bud scales; (2) perianth envelopes.

choripetalous see polypetalous.

cilia (*sing.* cilium) fine marginal hairs.

ciliate bearing a marginal fringe of fine hairs.

ciliolate bearing a marginal fringe of minute hairs.

cincinnal pertaining to cincinni or other curled inflorescences.

cincinnus a uniparous scorpioid cyme.

cinereous ashy grey.

circinate of an unexpanded leaflet, frond or frond segment, rolled up in a close coil with the tip at its centre, like a crozier.

circumscissile a form of dehiscence in which a pod opens along a line parallel with its circumference, allowing the top to come off like a lid; see calyptra.

cirrhous (cirrose) (of the apex) terminating in a coiled or spiralling continuation of the midrib.

cladophyll (cladode) 'stem-leaf', a stem simulating a leaf, a flattened or acicular branch which takes on the form and function of a leaf, arising from the axil of a minute, bractlike, and usually caducous true leaf, e.g. in *Ruscus, Phyllanthus*.

clambering of a vine climbing or growing over obstacles without the support of twining stems or tendrils.

clasping partially or wholly surrounding an organ, as a leaf-base clasps a stem.

class the principal category of taxa intermediate in rank between Division and Order: e.g. Monocotyledonae.

clathrate latticed, pierced with holes and windows.

clavate shaped like a club or a baseball bat; thickening to the apex from a tapered base.

clavellate a diminutive of clavate; club-shaped, but smaller.

claviculate bearing hooks or tendrils.

claviform club-shaped.

claw the narrowed petiole-like base of some sepals and petals; cf. caryophyllaceous, unguiculate.

clawed possessing a claw.

LEAF SHAPES 1

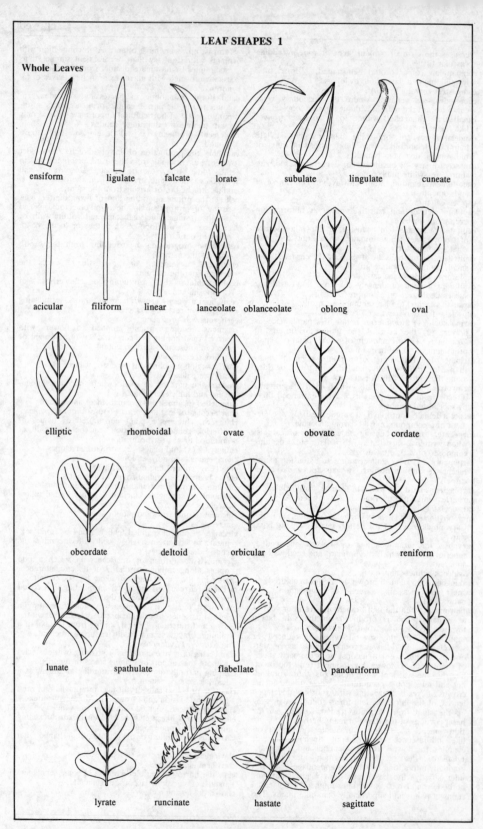

Whole Leaves

ensiform   ligulate   falcate   lorate   subulate   lingulate   cuneate

acicular   filiform   linear   lanceolate   oblanceolate   oblong   oval

elliptic   rhomboidal   ovate   obovate   cordate

obcordate   deltoid   orbicular   reniform

lunate   spathulate   flabellate   panduriform

lyrate   runcinate   hastate   sagittate

cleft of a flat organ (i.e. leaf or perianth segment), cut almost to the middle.

cleistogamous with self-pollination occurring in the closed flower.

climber any plant that climbs or has a tendency to do so, by means of various adaptations of stems, leaves or roots. See aerial root, scrambler, self-clinging, tendril, twiner.

clinandrium in orchids, the part of the column containing the anther.

clone the asexually produced offspring of a single parent to which it is genetically identical.

club-shaped gradually thickened upwards from a slender base, clavate.

clypeate shield-shaped.

coalescent union by growth.

coarctate crowded together.

coccus part of a schizocarp or lobed fruit.

cochlea a tightly coiled legume.

cochlear, cochleariform, spoon-shaped.

cochleate coiled like a snail's shell.

coensorus a extended sorus or a combination of sori united so as to appear as one.

coherent of parts usually free or separate fused together, as in a corolla tube. This term is sometimes used to describe the adhesion of similar parts; cf. adherent.

coleoptile a sheath protecting the plumule of a germinating grass seedling.

coleorhiza a sheath protecting the radicle of a germinating grass seedling.

collateral standing side by side.

columella the central axis of a multi-carpelled fruit.

column (1) a feature of orchids where the style and stamens are fused together in a single structure; (2) the column- or tube-like configuration formed by the fusion of staminal filaments in some Bombacaceae, Malvaceae and Sterculiaceae.

column foot a basal platform found in the column of some Orchidaceae, to which the lip is attached.

coma (1) a tuft of hairs projecting from a seed, as in Asclepiadaceae; (2) a tuft of leaves or bracts terminating an inflorescence or syncarp, i.e. the crown of a pineapple; (3) a leafy head in the crown of a tree or shrub.

comate bearing a coma.

combination the name of a taxon below the rank of the genus, being comprised of the genus name together with the specific and any infraspecific epithets.

commercial synonym an alternative legitimate name for a cultivar, or a shortened form of the original cultivar name used where the original name is not commercially acceptable or at the instigation or with the consent of the originator of the cultivar.

commissure the face by which two parts (often carpels) meet or cohere.

comose bearing a coma.

complanate flattened, compressed.

complete (of flowers) possessing all four whorls (sepals, petals, stamens, carpels).

complex a group of highly similar taxa of uncertain delimitation.

composite cultivar a cultivar composed of several closely related cultivars. See group; grex.

compound divided into two or more subsidiary parts or orders.

compressed flattened, usually applied to bulbs, tubers and fruit and qualified by 'laterally', 'dorsally' and 'ventrally'.

con-, co-, com- prefix meaning 'with'.

concatenate linked as in a chain.

concolorous of a uniform colour.

conduplicate (of leaves) folded once lengthwise, so that the sides are parallel or applied; (of cotyledons) folded in this manner, with one cotyledon enclosed within the other, and enclosing the radicle in its fold.

cone (1) (in gymnosperms) an assemblage or bracts and sporophylls, usually densely crowded and overlapping in an ovoid, spherical or cylindrical structure on a single axis and (in the female cone) persisting to the seed-bearing stage. In some families, i.e. Gnetaceae and Podocarpaceae, the bracts or scales may be very few so that the whole scarcely resembles a cone, but the term is retained here, as is strobilus, to avoid misleading use of 'inflorescence'; (2) (in flowering plants) a compact spike or raceme with conspicuous and congested bracts suggesting a true cone (i.e. def. 1), as is found in Zingiberaceae.

conferted closely packed or crowded.

confluent merging one into the other.

congested crowded.

conglomerate tightly clustered, usually into a ball.

congregate (*adj.*) collected into close proximity.

conic, conical cone-shaped; tapering evenly from base to apex in three dimensions.

conjugate coupled, a linked pair, as in the leaflets of a pinnate leaf.

connate united, usually applied to similar features when fused in a single structure.

connate-perfoliate where opposite sessile leaves are joined by their bases, through which the axis appears to pass.

connective the part in a stamen that connects the lobes of an anther at the point of attachment to the filament.

connivent converging, and even coming into contact, but not fused; (of petals) gradually inclining toward the centre of their flower.

conoid resembling or shaped like a cone.

conservation (of names) an International Botanical Congress may decide to conserve, that is to maintain as valid and accepted, what is strictly an illegitimate name – a measure that retains in parlance many highly familiar names that would otherwise be lost in synonymy.

conspecific 'belonging to the same species', often used of highly similar populations scarcely worthy of recognition as separate species.

conspicuous easily visible to the naked eye, often used to mean enlarged or showy (as in 'conspicuously veined'); cf. prominent.

constipate (*adj.*) crowded or massed together.

constricted abruptly narrowed, contracted.

contiguous in contact, touching but not fused.

continuous an uninterrupted symmetrical arrangement, sometimes used as a synonym of decurrent.

contorted twisted or bent, in aestivation the same as convolute.

contracted narrowed and/or shortened.

contractile applied to roots which contract in length and pull parts of a plant further into the soil.

convergent see connivent.

convolute rolled or twisted together longitudinally, with the margins overlapping, as leaves or petals in the bud.

coralloid resembling coral in structure, applied to certain types of root adapted to house blue-green algae or, in the case of saprophytes, fungi, to the heavily cristate inflorescence of some *Celosia* cultivars and body shapes of some cacti, and to the calli and stigmatic surfaces of some monocots.

cordate heart-shaped, applied to leaves and leafy stipules, usually ovate-acute in outline with a rounded base and a deep basal sinus or notch where the petiole is inserted.

coriaceous leathery or tough but smooth and pliable in texture.

cork a protective tissue, usually elastic and spongy in texture and with air-filled outer cells; it replaces epidermis in the older superficial parts of some plants.

corky composed of cork or of a porous, elastic and cork-like texture.

corm a solid, swollen, subterranean, bulb-like stem or stem-base; it is annual, the next year's corm developing from the terminal bud or, in its absence, one of the lateral buds.

cormel (cormlet) a small corm developing from and around the mother corm.

cormous bearing corms.

corniculate bearing or terminating in a small horn-like protuberance.

corolla the interior perianth whorl; a floral envelope

LEAF SHAPES 2

Leaf tips

 acuminate

 acute

 abruptly acute

 apiculate

 aristate

 caudate

 cirrhose

 cupsidate

 pungent

 mucronate

 mucronulate

 obtuse

 rounded

 truncate

 praemorse

 retuse

 emarginate

cleft

Leaf bases

 acute

 acuminate

 attenuate

 cuneate

 cordate

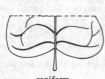 reniform

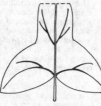 hastate

 sagittate

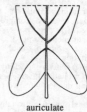 auriculate

 rounded

 obtuse

 truncate

 unequal

 oblique

xxxii

composed of free or fused petals. Where the petals are separate, a corolla is termed choripetalous or polypetalous; where they are fused, the corolla is gamopetalous or sympetalous, in such cases the petals may be discernible only as lobes or teeth on the rim of a corolla tube, cup or disc.

corolliform resembling a corolla.

corona 'crown', a crown- or cup-like appendage or ring of appendages, this may be a development of the perianth (e.g. *Narcissus*), of the staminal circle, as in *Asclepias*, or located between perianth and stamens as in *Passiflora*.

coronal, coronate bearing a corona.

corrugate (*adj.*) crumpled or wrinkled but more loosely so than in rugose. Corrugate aestivation describes the irregular and apparently crumpled folding of a perianth in bud, as in *Papaver*.

cortex the bark or rind, ground tissue between stele and epidermis.

corticate covered with bark, with a hard coating, but softer centre.

corymb an indeterminate flat-topped or convex inflorescence, where the outer flowers open first; cf. umbel.

corymbose, corymbiform resembling or forming a corymb.

costa a single pronounced midvein or midrib; less frequently, the rachis of a pinnately compound leaf.

costapalmate strictly a pinnate leaf where the pinnae are congested in a radial, fan-like order and perhaps to some degree united, the whole therefore appearing palmate; or where the petiole of a palmate leaf continues through the blade as a distinct midrib.

costate with a single, pronounced vein, the midrib.

cotyledon the primary leaf, or seed leaf, either solitary (monocots), paired (dicots) or whorled as in some conifers, it may remain within the seed-coat or emerge and become green during germination.

crateriform shaped like a goblet; a concave hemisphere slightly contracted at the base.

cremocarp a dry, seed-like fruit consisting of two one-seeded carpels with an epigynous calyx; these separate into mericarps on ripening.

crenate scalloped, with shallow, rounded teeth; bicrenate is where the teeth themselves have crenate teeth.

crenulate minutely crenate.

crest an irregular or dentate elevation or ridge, generally applied to an outgrowth of the funiculus in seeds but also found on the summit of some organs and on the lip of some orchids.

cretaceous chalky, as the chalk-glands in porophyllous saxifrages.

crinoid lily-like.

crispate curled and twisted extremely irregularly, used either of a leaf-blade or, more often, of hairs.

crispy-hairy (of hairs) wavy and curved, in dense short ringlets.

cristate crested or, less commonly, 'crest-like', sometimes used to denote the presence of crests (cristae) (e.g. *Coelogyne cristata*), more often used to describe an abnormality of growth showing, for example, closely sculpted brain- or coral-like ridges as in *Celosia*, or ruffled and usually forked tips to fern fronds.

cross a hybrid.

crowded (of leaves) arranged close to each other or gathered toward a stem or branch tip, often in whorled or scattered fashion.

crown (1) a corona; (2) a collective term for the main stem divisions and foliage of a tree or shrub and the branching pattern and overall habit (i.e. domed, spreading, narrowly conical, etc.) that they assume; (3) the basal portions of a herbaceous plant, usually where root or rhizome and aerial stems or resting buds meet; (4) a length of rhizome with a strong terminal bud, used for propagation as, for example, with *Convallaria*; (5) the head of a single-stemmed tree-like plant or shrub bearing a distinct apical whorl, rosette or flush of foliage; (6) the leaves and terminal buds of a low-growing plant when arranged

in a fashion resembling that of the larger plants mentioned under (5), e.g. many ferns.

crownshaft a characteristic of some Palms in which the overlapping leaf bases form a tight cylindrical or vase-shaped shaft distinct from the (usually) bare stem below.

crozier the coiled young frond of a fern.

cruciate, cruciform cross-shaped.

cruciferous belonging to the Cruciferae.

crumpled see corrugate.

crustaceous of a hard, brittle nature.

cryptogams flowerless and seedless plants that nonetheless increase by means of sexual fusion (i.e. neither angiosperms nor gymnosperms, but pteridophytes, bryophytes, etc.).

ctenoid comb-like.

cubiform dice-shaped, cubic.

cucullate furnished with or shaped like a hood.

cucumiform cucumber-like.

culm the stems of Gramineae.

cultigen a plant found only in cultivation or in the wild having escaped from cultivation; included here are many hybrids and cultivars, some exotic ornamentals whose wild origins have become lost or were never recorded, and several ancient and important crops that have undergone development and distribution at man's hands for so long a time that, although they may have 'wild' distributions, their original forms and native places are lost or confused.

cultispec a cultigen deserving recognition at species level, i.e. possessing many distinctive qualities apparently unassignable to any one established species or known only in gardens but almost certainly of obscure wild origins.

cultivar class a taxon within which the use of the same cultivar name for two different cultivars would cause confusion; this is particularly acute in the case of older, latinized cultivar names.

cultivar, cv. 'a cultivated variety', a distinct assemblage of plants arising and/or maintained in cultivation which, when reproduced sexually or asexually, retains its distinguishing character. A cultivar is named with a cultivar (or fancy) epithet, a word or words in a vernacular language (unless published prior to 1959, or a botanical (Latin) epithet already established for a taxon now deemed to be a cultivar). The epithet is printed in roman characters, takes a capital first letter and is either enclosed in single quotation marks or prefixed by the abbreviation cv.

culton a distinct plant originating in or maintained in cultivation. This term has been proposed to reflect the fact that not all such entities can be deemed cultivars.

cultrate, cultriform knife-shaped, resembling the blade of a knife.

cuneate, cuneiform inversely triangular, wedge-shaped.

cupreous with the colour and lustre of copper.

cupressoid with *Cupressus*-like foliage, i.e. narrow branchlets clothed with scale-like leaves.

cupular furnished with a cupule.

cupule a cup-shaped involucre of hardened, coherent bracts, subtending a fruit or group of fruits, as in the acorn. See also Cyathium.

cupuliform resembling a cupule.

cushion (1) a pulvinus, the enlarged area of tissue above, beneath or either side of an insertion or at the axis of two branches or stem and branch; (2) *cushion plants* have a low, tightly branched, packed and rounded habit, as in many high alpines.

cusp a short, stiff, abrupt point.

cusped see cuspidate.

cuspidate (of apices) terminating abruptly in a sharp, inflexible point, or cusp.

cuspidulate minutely cuspidate.

cuticle the outermost skin, multi-layered and waxy tissues composed of the epidermis and containing cutin, fatty acids and cellulose.

cyathiform shaped like a cup; as urceolate but without the marginal contraction.

cyathium an inflorescence-type characteristic of *Euphorbia*, it consists of a cupule (an involucre of small

Margins

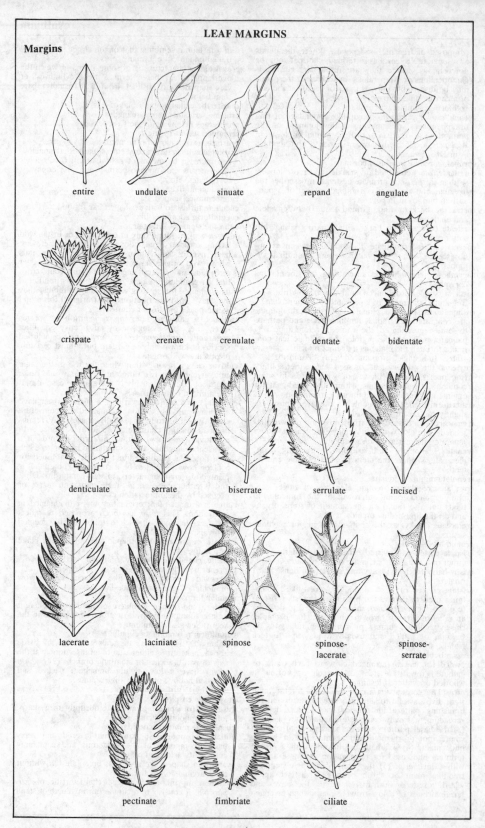

entire undulate sinuate repand angulate

crispate crenate crenulate dentate bidentate

denticulate serrate biserrate serrulate incised

lacerate laciniate spinose spinose-lacerate spinose-serrate

pectinate fimbriate ciliate

bracts sometimes furnished with glands and subtended by petaloid bracts or appendages) enclosing several 'stamens', each equivalent to a single male flower, and a stalked trilocular 'ovary' (a 3-carpelled pistil equivalent to the female flower). In dioecious species the male or female is lacking according to the sex of the individual.

cyclic disposed in whorls or circles.

cylindric, cylindrical elongated and virtually circular in cross-section.

cymbiform boat-shaped, attenuated and upturned at both ends with an external dorsal ridge as in the keel of many papilionaceous flowers.

cyme a more or less flat-topped and determinate inflorescence, the central or terminal flower opening first.

cymose arranged in or resembling a cyme or bearing cymes.

cymule a small and generally few-flowered cyme.

cypsela an achene invested by an adnate calyx as in the fruit of Compositae.

dactyloid, dactylose fingerlike.

dealbate whitened, covered with a white powder.

deciduous (1) falling off when no longer functional, as non-evergreen leaves, or the petals of many flowers; (2) a plant that sheds its leaves annually, or at certain periods, as opposed to evergreen plants.

declinate bent or curved downward or forward.

decompound a compound leaf with two or more orders of division, e.g., bipinnate, tripinnate, triternate, etc.

decrescent gradually reduced in size.

decumbent of a stem, lying horizontally along the ground, but with the apex ascending and almost erect.

decurrent where the base of a leaf blade extends down and is adnate to the petiole (if any) and the stem.

decurved curved downwards.

decussate of leaves, arranged in opposite pairs with adjacent pairs at right angles to each other, thus forming four longitudinal rows.

deflected bent or turned abruptly downwards.

deflexed bent downward and outwards; cf. reflexed.

deflorate past the flowering state.

defoliate with leaves shed.

deformed disfigured or distorted.

dehiscence the mode and process of opening (i.e. by valves, slits, pores or splitting) of a seed capsule or anther to release seed or pollen.

dehiscent, dehiscence of a seed capsule, splitting open along definite lines to release seeds when ripe.

deltoid (deltate) an equilateral triangle attached by the broad end rather than the point; shaped like the Greek letter delta.

demersed of a part constantly submersed under water.

dendritic, dendroid ramifying finely at the apex, in the manner of the head of a tree.

dentate toothed, of the margins of leaf blades and other flattened organs, cut with teeth. Strictly, the teeth are shallow and represent two sides of a roughly equilateral triangle, in contrast to serrate (saw-toothed), where the teeth are sharper and curved forwards, or crenate, where the teeth are blunt and rounded. Less precisely, the term is used to cover any type of toothed margin.

dentation the teeth on the margin of an organ.

denticulate minutely dentate.

dentiform tooth-shaped.

denudate stripped, made bare.

denuded see naked.

depauperate reduced in stature, number or function as if starved and ill-formed. Species with organs described thus are, however, usually perfectly healthy but adapted to cope with some ecological factor.

dependent hanging downward as a result of its weight, as in a flower- or fruit-laden branch.

deplanate flattened or expanded.

depressed sunken or flattened as if pressed from above.

descending tending gradually downwards.

determinate of inflorescences such as cymes that end in a bud where the central or terminal flower opens first, thus ending extension of the main axis.

diadelphous of stamens, borne in two distinct bundles or, with several stamens united and a further solitary stamen apart from them, as in many Leguminosae.

diagnosis a short statement of the principal character or characters that distinguish a new taxon from others.

dialypetalous see polypetalous.

diandrous possessing two perfect stamens.

dichasium a type of determinate inflorescence; the basic structure has three flowers (members), one terminating the primary axis, the other two carried on more or less equal secondary branches arising from beneath the primary member in a false dichotomy. The secondary members may themselves be dichasia. Such a structure is known as a *dichasial cyme* or a *compound dichasial cyme*, although the former term has been applied by some authors to the basic dichasium itself.

dichogamous (of flowers) preventing natural self-pollination by the failure of pollen dehiscence and stigma receptivity to occur simultaneously.

dichotomous branching regularly by forking repeatedly in two; the two branches of each division are basically equal.

dicotyledonous possessing two cotyledons.

dicotyledons (dicots) one of the two major divisions of the angiosperms, characterized by (usually) two cotyledons, the presence of cambium in many species and floral parts most often occurring in fours and fives.

didymous twinned, (in pairs) the two parts similar and attached by a short portion of the inner surface.

didynamous possessing two pairs of stamens, the two pairs being of unequal lengths.

difform dissimilar.

diffuse spreading widely outwards by frequent branching.

digamous having the two sexes in the same flower cluster as in Compositae.

digitate 'fingered', of a compound leaf, palmately arranged with the leaflets arising from the same point at the apex of the petiole.

digonous two-angled, as the stems of some cacti.

digynous with two separated styles or carpels.

dilated, dilating broadened, expanded.

dimidiate said of a pinna or pinnule with the blade much reduced or lacking on the basiscopic side.

dimorphic, dimorphous occurring in two dissimilar forms or shapes, either at the same stage in a plant's life history, as in ferns where dimorphism can be exhibited by fronds (sterile and fertile) or at different stages in a plant's development, as in juvenile and adult foliage.

dioecious with male and female sporophylls or staminate and pistillate flowers on different plants.

diplostemonous bearing the stamens in an outer whorl, alternate with the petals, and an inner whorl, opposite the petals.

disc, disk (1) a fleshy or raised development of the torus within the calyx, or within the corolla and stamens, or composed of coalesced nectaries or staminodes and surrounding the pistil; (2) (in Compositae) the central, or sometimes whole, part of the capitulum bearing short tubular florets as opposed to the peripheral ray florets; (3) the central part of the lip in Orchidaceae, often elevated and callused or crested; (4) a circular flattened organ, e.g. the disc-like tendril tips of some plants climbing by adhesion; (5) the basal plate of a bulb around which scales are arranged.

disc floret (of Compositae) a flower with a tubular corolla, often toothed, found in the centre of a radiate capitulum or occupying the whole of a discoid capitulum. See also ray floret.

disciform, discoid circular and flattened.

discoid (1) of leaves, with a round fleshy blade and thickened margins; (2) (more commonly) pertaining to the capitula of some Compositae, composed entirely of disc florets.

dissected cut in any way, a general term applicable to leaf blades or other flattened organs that are incised, lacerate, laciniate, pinnatisect or palmatisect.

LEAF LOBING AND VEINING

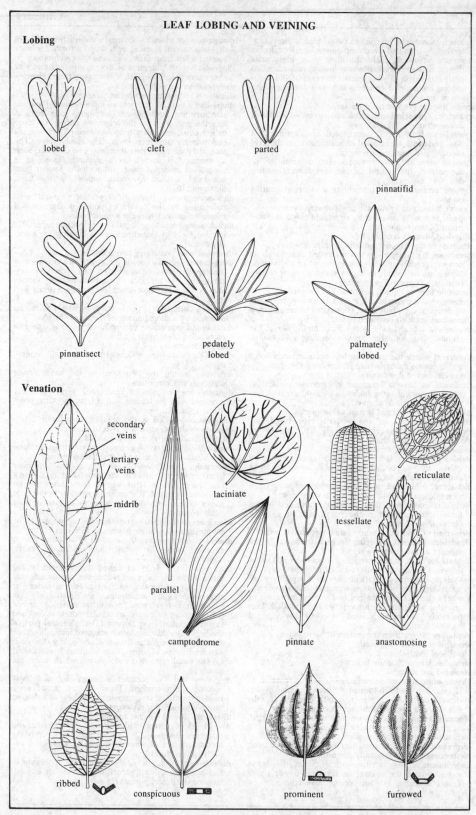

Lobing

lobed

cleft

parted

pinnatifid

pinnatisect

pedately lobed

palmately lobed

Venation

secondary veins

tertiary veins

midrib

laciniate

reticulate

tessellate

parallel

camptodrome

pinnate

anastomosing

ribbed

conspicuous

prominent

furrowed

distal the part furthest from the axis, thus the tip of a leaf is distal; cf. proximal.

distant (of leaves on a stem, stipes on a rhizome or flowers on a floral axis) widely spaced, synonymous with remote and the antithesis of proximate.

distichous (of leaves) distinctly arranged in two opposite ranks along a stem or branch.

distinct separate, not connate or in any way united, with similar parts; more generally meaning evident or obvious, easily distinguishable.

diurnal of activity taking place only during daylight.

divaricate broadly divergent and spreading, a term usually applied to branching patterns where branches spread from 70° to 90° outwards from the main axis.

divergent broadly spreading from the centre.

divided a vague term meaning compound or deeply cut, lobed or cleft.

division the highest rank of the principal categories in the plant kingdom. The names of Divisions end in *-phyta* ('plants'). The widely used late-19th-century classifications of Eichler and Engler and Prantl accepted four: Thallophyta (including the bacteria, slime moulds, algae, fungi, and lichens). Bryophyta (mosses and liverworts), Pteridophyta (ferns and fern-allies), and Spermatophyta (seed plants). Since then many further divisions have been proposed.

dolabriform hatchet-shaped.

doleiform barrel-shaped.

dorsal pertaining to the back of an organ, or to the surface turned away from the axis, thus abaxial. A term confused by some authors with its opposite, ventral.

dorsifixed of an organ attached by its dorsal surface to another.

dorsiventral flattened, and having separate dorsal and ventral surfaces, as most leaves and leaf-blades.

double a flower is said to be double when it has more than the usual complement of petals or petal-like elements (petaloid sepals, staminodes or colourful bracts). In flowers with tubular corollas, a further form of doubling is the hose-in-hose arrangement where additional corollas are held within each other. The capitula of Compositae are said to be double when they consist wholly of ray florets.

double citation an author citation in which the basionym author is shown in brackets and before the author of the later combination. For example, *Gentiana lagodechiana* (Kusnezov) Grossheim ex Möllers, where Kusnezov originally named this plant as a variety of *G. septemfida* (*G. septemfida* var. *lagodechiana* Kusnezov).

downy see pubescent.

drepanium a sickle-shaped cyme.

drip-point, drip-tip a leaf tip, either acuminate, caudate or aristate, from which water readily drips in wet conditions.

drupaceous resembling, or pertaining to a drupe; with a juicy seed coat.

drupe an indehiscent, one- to several-seeded fruit, in which the endocarp is osseous or cartilaginous, and is contained within a soft, fleshy pericarp; as in stone fruits, such as mango, or plums.

drupelet a small drupe, generally a part of an aggregate fruit such as a blackberry (*Rubus*).

e-, ex- (prefix) meaning 'without' or 'deprived of', e.g. estipellate, without stipels.

ear the spike of corn or an auricle.

ebracteate without bracts.

ecallose not callused.

eccentric one-sided, off-centre.

echinate covered with many stiff hairs or bristles, or thick, blunt prickles.

eciliate lacking cilia, not ciliate.

eglandular without glands.

elaiosome oil-secreting appendages or processes (arils, crests, etc.) on the seeds of myrmechorous plants offered to the ants as food bodies.

eligulate not ligulate; not possessing ligules.

ellipsoid elliptic, but 3-dimensional.

elliptic, elliptical ellipse-shaped; midway between oblong and ovate but with equally rounded or narrowed ends, with two planes of symmetry and widest across the middle.

elongate lengthened, as if stretched or extended.

emarginate (of the apex) shallowly notched, the indentation (sinus) being acute.

embracing clasping by the base.

embryo the rudimentary plant within the seed.

embryotega a cap-like or disc-like callosity near the hilum of certain testa, and detached by the radicle during germination.

emersed raised out of and above the water.

endemic confined to a particular region.

endo- (prefix) meaning 'within', 'inner', e.g. endodermis, the inner layer of skin in a periderm.

endocarp the innermost layer or wall or a pericarp, enclosing the seed, and either membranous or bony or cartilaginous.

endosperm the albumen, when it is stored inside the embryo sac.

ensiform sword-shaped, straighter than lorate, and with an acute point.

entire continuous; uninterrupted by divisions or teeth or lobes, thus 'leaves entire' meaning, margins not toothed or lobed.

ephemeral very short-lived plants, or flowers lasting for only one day or less.

epi- (prefix) meaning 'upon', 'uppermost', as epigynous, growing upon or arising from the ovary.

epicalyx an involucre of bracts surrounding a calyx, a false calyx.

epicarp see exocarp.

epichile the terminal part of a tripartite lip, as found in some Orchidaceae, e.g. *Stanhopea*.

epicormic (of branches, buds etc.) developing on or from the trunk of a tree; the growth can be latent or adventitious.

epicotyl the portion of the stem of an embryo or seedling above the cotyledons.

epidermis the outer layer of a periderm.

epilithic growing on rocks.

epipetalous growing on or arising from the petals.

epiphyllic, epiphyllous positioned on or growing from the leaf, as in an epiphyllous flower or inflorescence, e.g. *Helwingia*.

epiphyte a plant which grows on another plant, but is not parasitic and does not depend on it for nourishment.

epiphytic growing on plants without being parasitic.

epithet any word in a binomial which is neither the generic name nor a term denoting rank, the epithet qualifies a generic name or a name of lower rank: e.g. *Primula vulgaris* ssp. *sibthorpii*, where *Primula* is the genus name, *vulgaris* the specific epithet, and *sibthorpii* the subspecific epithet.

epruinose lacking a pruinose coating.

equal, equalling said of parts or categories of plants held in comparison where one is the same as the other in length or, less often, number, e.g. 'corolla equals calyx' means that the corolla is more or less the same length as the calyx and terminates at much the same point but *not* that the corolla is the same as the calyx, or undifferentiated from it 'Petiole equalling blade' means that the petiole, seen as discrete from the leaf blade and midrib, is of the same length as the blade. An equal leaf is one with longitudinal symmetry, a term often used of the base of the leaf blade alone.

equilateral equal-sided.

equitant when conduplicate leaves overlap or stand inside each other in two ranks in a strongly compressed fan, as in many Iridaceae.

erect of habit, organ or arrangement of parts upright, perpendicular to the ground or point of attachment.

erianthous woolly flowered.

ericaceous (1) in broad terms, resembling *Erica* in habit, e.g. *Fabiana*, or certain Epacridaceae; (2) pertaining to members of the family Ericaceae.

erinous prickly, coarsely textured with sharp points.

erose irregularly dentate, as if gnawed or eroded.

erumpent on the point of breaking through, or apparently so.

LEAF SURFACES 1

glabrous

lustrous

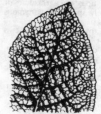

rugose

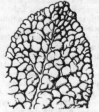

bullate

punctate

pustulate

squarrose

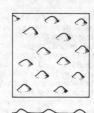

muricate

scabrous

setose

strigose

hispid

hirsute

paleaceous/
chaffy

pilose

bifid
hairs

bifid T-shaped
hairs

stellate hairs (various)

dendritic
hairs

etiolated drawn out and bleached or blanched by exclusion of light.

eu- true (Gk, good).

evergreen (having) foliage that remains green for at least a year, through more than one growing season.

everlasting plants with inflorescences that retain their shape and colour after drying.

evolute unfolded.

ex- [Lat. from, according to] used in citations to connect author names where the second author cited validly published a name proposed but not published by the first: e.g. *Hyacinthoides non-scripta* (L.) Chouard ex Rothmaler, or, less commonly, to connect the names of two authors where the second has published as a synonym a name proposed but again never published by the first.

exarate grooved.

exceed, exceeding said of parts or categories of parts held in comparison where one is longer than the other. Thus 'corolla exceeds calyx' means that the corolla is literally longer than and therefore surpasses the calyx; however, 'petiole exceeding blade' means that the petiole is absolutely longer than the leaf blade but, of course, not that it surpasses it, i.e. goes after or beyond it in the arrangement of parts from the axis outwards; cf. *equal*.

excentric one-sided, out of the centre.

excrescence an outgrowth or abnormal development.

excurrent (1) projecting beyond the margin or apex of its organ, as a midvein terminating in a mucro or an awn; (2) a growth habit where the primary axis remains dominant and recognizable throughout life and the branches secondary to it – as in a strongly single-stemmed tree with a remote, tiered branching pattern.

exfoliating peeling off in thin layers, shreds or plates.

exindusiate without an indusium.

exine, extine the outer wall of a microspore.

exo- prefix meaning outward.

exocarp the outermost wall of a pericarp.

exotic a plant in cultivation outside its native lands.

explanate spread out, flat.

exserted obviously projecting or extending beyond the organs or parts surrounding it, as stamens sticking out from the corolla; cf. *included*.

exstipulate, estipulate without stipules.

extra- (prefix) meaning 'outside', e.g. extrafloral, outside the flower proper.

extrafloral outside the true flower (as bracts, nectaries, etc.).

extrastaminal outside the stamens; mostly used of the disc, a useful character for identification in, say, the genus *Acer*.

extrorse turned or facing outwards, abaxial, often used of the dehiscence of an anther; cf. *introrse*.

eye (1) the centre of a flower, if differing from the rest in colour; (2) a stem-cutting with a single lateral bud; (3) the undeveloped bud on a tuber.

F1 see filial generation.

facies the overall appearance of a plant.

facultative not obligate, able to exist without.

falcate strongly curved sideways, resembling a scythe or sickle.

fall one of the drooping or spreading petals, often bearded, of an *Iris* perianth.

false indusium a covering over the sorus formed by a reflexed leaf margin.

family the principal category of taxa intermediate between Order and genus, e.g. Rosaceae. The names of most families derive from that of the type genus (*Rosa* above) and are plural nouns ending in *-aceae*. Among the exceptions to this rule are Palmae, Gramineae, Leguminosae, Umbelliferae; these too have modern equivalents in Arecaceae, Poaceae, Fabaceae and Apiaceae, respectively.

fancy term used of names published in accordance with the International Code of Nomenclature for Cultivated Plants and applied to cultivars, grexes and hybrids. It is invariably formed in a vernacular language, not Latin, i.e. *Lupinus* 'Loveliness', *Heuchera* 'Palace Purple'.

farina the powdery or mealy coating on the stems, leaves, and sometimes flowers of certain plants, notably primulas.

farinose see farinaceous.

farinose, farinaceous having a mealy, granular texture.

fasciated (of stems or similar axes, 'bundled') where two or more narrow parts grow abnormally together lengthwise in a congested manner; (of one part) flattened and misshapen as if composed of several parts joined in that way.

fascicle a cluster or bundle of flowers, racemes, leaves, stems or roots, almost always independent but appearing to arise from a common point.

fascicled arranged in a fascicle or fascicles.

fasciculate see fascicled.

fastigiate describing the habit of trees and shrubs – often cultivars – with a strongly erect, narrow crown, and branches virtually erect and parallel with the main stem.

father plant the pollen parent of a hybrid.

fauces (*sing.* faux) the throat of a gamopetalous corolla; term used particularly when the throat is in some way distinguished, i.e. by colour, texture or appendages such as faucal scales.

faveolate honey-combed.

favose honey-combed.

feather-veined applied to leaves whose veins all arise pinnately from a single mid-rib.

felted-tomentose tomentose, but more woolly and matted, the hairs curling and closely adpressed to the surface.

fenestrate irregularly perforated by numerous openings or translucent zones.

ferruginous brown-red, rust-coloured.

fertile producing viable seed; said of anthers containing functional pollen, of flowers with active pistils, of fruit bearing seeds and of spore-bearing fern fronds. A fertile shoot is one bearing flowers, as opposed to a sterile shoot.

fertilization the union of male and female gametes to make a new cell.

fibrillate finely striated or fibrous.

fibrillose with thread-like fibres or scales.

fibrous of a thread-like, woody texture.

fiddle-shaped see pandurate.

filament (1) a stalk which bears the anther at its tip, together forming a stamen; (2) a threadlike or filiform organ, hair or appendage.

filamentous composed of or bearing filaments.

filial generation a cross-bred generation, i.e. hybrid offspring, the first denoted by the symbol F1, the second F2, etc.

filiferous bearing filiform appendages.

filiform (of leaves, branches etc.) filament-like, i.e. long and very slender, rounded in cross-section.

filmy fern a fern of shady, wet places with exceptionally thin frond blades; usually of the family *Hymenophyllaceae*.

fimbria a fringe.

fimbriate bordered with a fringe of slender processes, usually derived from the lamina rather than attached as hairs; cf. ciliate.

fissile splitting easily.

fistulose, fistular hollow and cylindrical like a pipe.

flabellate, flabelliform fan-shaped, with a wedge-shaped outline and sometimes conspicuously pleated or nerved.

flaccid weak, limp, floppy, lax etc.

flagellate with whip-like runners, sarmentose.

flagelliform long, tapering, supple; whiplike.

fleshy-rooted used of plants with thick fleshy roots or storage organs.

flexuous (of an axis) zig-zag, bending or curving in alternate and opposite directions.

floccose possessing dense, woolly hairs that fall away easily in tufts.

flocculent, flocculose slightly floccose, woolly.

floret a very small flower, generally part of a congested inflorescence; in grasses, a collective term embracing the lemma, palea, lodicules and enclosed flower.

floricane a biennial stem which fruits and flowers in its

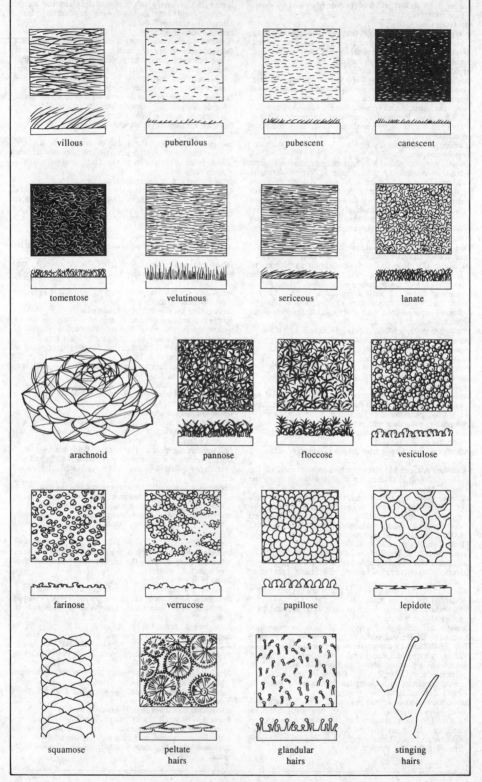

LEAF SURFACES 2

villous

puberulous

pubescent

canescent

tomentose

velutinous

sericeous

lanate

arachnoid

pannose

floccose

vesiculose

farinose

verrucose

papillose

lepidote

squamose

peltate
hairs

glandular
hairs

stinging
hairs

second year, particularly of a bramble (*Rubus*).

floriferous bearing flowers freely.

flower an axis bearing one or more pistils or stamens, or both, usually with some floral envelope; if surrounded by a perianth of calyx and corolla it is termed perfect.

fluted (of a trunk) with long rounded grooves running vertically.

foetid, fetid having an unpleasant odour.

foliaceous resembling a leaf, in appearance or texture.

foliate bearing leaves.

foliolate bearing leaflets.

follicle a dry, dehiscent, one- to many-seeded fruit, derived from a single carpel and dehiscing by a single suture along its ventral side.

form, forma [abbrev. f.] an infraspecific taxon subordinate to subspecies and variety, e.g. *Hosta crispula* f. *viridis*. The lowest rank in the taxonomic hierarchy, the forma is usually distinguished by characters such as flower colour, habit, leaf division – features of importance to gardeners if 'minor' for taxonomists.

formula the designation of parentage or name given to a hybrid or hybrid group and formed by combining the names or parts of the names of its parents. Thus, (*Chilopsis* × *Catalpa*) and × *Chitalpa* are both hybrid formulae.

foveolate with shallow, precise indentations.

fractiflex in intermittent zig-zag lines.

free (strictly of dissimilar parts or organs) separate, not fused or attached to each other. 'Distinct' describes the separateness of similar organs.

fringed see fimbriate.

frond the leaf of a fern; more loosely, a large compound leaf, such as those of palms.

frondose leafy and frond-like.

fructiferous bearing fruit.

fructification fruiting.

fruit the fertilized and ripened ovary of a plant together with any adnate parts.

frutescent shrubby, or becoming so.

fruticose shrub-like, bearing stems or branches, but without a single main trunk.

fugacious falling off or withering rapidly; transitory.

funicle, funiculus the stalk or thread sometimes bearing the ovule or seed and attaching it to the placenta.

funnelform of a corolla tube which widens gradually upward toward and into the spreading limb.

furcate forked, the terminal lobes prong-like.

furfuraceous scurfy, with soft, bran-like scales.

furrowed channelled or grooved lengthwise, a term covering both sulcate and conspicuously striate.

fuscous dusky, blackish.

fused (of parts usually free or separate) joined together to form a continuous surface; cf. coherent.

fusiform spindle-shaped, swollen in the middle and tapering to both ends.

fusoid somewhat fusiform.

galea a helmet-shaped organ, usually a vaulted and enlarged upper petal as in *Aconitum*.

galeate helmet-shaped, hollow and domed.

gall a local tumour, swelling or other congested monstrous growth; a symptom of disease, usually spread by an insect vector.

gamete a fertile reproductive cell of either sex.

gametophyte the stage in the life-cycle of a plant when gametes are produced.

gamopetalous with petals united by their margins, forming a tubular or funnelform corolla, or at least by their bases.

gamophyllous with leaves or leaflike organs united by their margins.

gamosepalous with sepals united by their margins.

geminate paired.

gemma an asexual reproductive body, bud-like and detaching itself from the parent plant.

gemmiparous bearing vegetative buds.

gene a chromosomal unit which carries heritable information.

geniculate bent abruptly, in the form of a flexed knee.

geniculum a knee-like joint or node where an organ or axis is sharply bent.

genus (pl. genera) the principal rank in the taxonomic hierarchy between Family and species. The genus represents a single highly distinctive species (monotypic or monospecific genus) such as *Ginkgo* or, more often, a number of species united by a common suite of distinctive characters. The genus or generic name is italicized and takes a capital letter.

geocarpy subterranean ripening of fruits developed from flowers borne above ground, as in peanuts.

geophyte a plant growing with stem or tuber below ground, usually applied to bulbous or tuberous species from arid lands.

gibbosity a basal or apical swelling.

gibbous swollen on one side or at the base.

glabrate see glabrescent.

glabrescent (1) nearly glabrous, or becoming glabrous with age; (2) minutely and invisibly pubescent.

glabrous smooth, hairless.

gladiate sword-like.

gland any cell or cells secreting a substance or substances, such as oil, calcium or sugar, e.g. nectaries.

glandspine in some Cactaceae, a short spine borne in the upper part of an areole, nectariferous in its first year.

glandular generally, beaing glands; (of hairs) bearing a gland, or gland-like prominence at the tip.

glandular-pubescent either covered with intermixed glands and hairs, or possessing hairs terminated by glands.

glaucescent slightly glaucous.

glaucous coated with a fine bloom, whitish, or blue-green or grey and easily rubbed off.

globose spherical, sometimes used to mean near-spherical.

globular composed of globose forms, as in the aggregate fruits of *Rubus*; sometimes used where globose is meant.

globulose diminutive of globose.

glochid a barbed spine or bristle, often tufted on the areoles of cacti.

glochidate possessing barbed spines or hairs (glochids), often in tufts, as in many Cactaceae.

glomerate aggregated in one or more dense or compact clusters.

glomerule a cluster of capitula or grouped flowers, strictly subtended by a single involucre.

glumaceous resembling glumes in Gramineae, i.e. dry, chaffy.

glume a small, dry, membranous bract found in the inflorescences of Gramineae and Cyperaceae and usually disposed in two ranks.

glutinose, glutinous see viscid.

gourd fleshy, one-loculed, many-seeded fruit, with parietal placentation, as in Cucurbitaceae.

graft chimaera, graft hybrid a non-sexual 'hybrid', a new plant formed by the intimate association and mingling of tissues belonging to the stock and scion of a graft. A graft chimaera is designated by a formula name prefixed by a crucifix-type cross, e.g. + *Laburnocytisus* (*Laburnum* + *Chamaecytisus*).

grain a term applied for cereals, e.g. wheat, barley, oats, etc.

graminaceous grassy, resembling grass in texture or habit.

granular (of a leaf) composed of granules, or minute knobs or knots; (of its surface) grainy, as if covered by small granules.

grex a group name for all plants derived from the crossing of the same two or more species. The grex (herd or hybrid swarm) is close in some senses to the group, but relates far more specifically to an established parentage or lineage. The term has become limited to orchid hybrids. It is printed in roman with a capital initial. The grex may be combined with a cultivar name which is printed within quotation marks, e.g. *Paphiopedilum* Maudiae 'The Queen'.

grooved a more general term for striate or sulcate.

group a category intermediate between species and cultivar used to distinguish (1) an assemblage of two or more similar cultivars and/or individuals within a species or hybrid; (2) plants derived from a hybrid of

Climbers and roots   (a) Rattan (climbing palm) with hooked spines on leaf extension (b) *Clematis* with clasping petioles (c) Virginia creeper with adhesive pads on branched tendrils (d) Rose with hooked thorns (e) Twining tendrils (*Passiflora*) (f) Cirrhous leaves (*Gloriosa*) (g) Adventitious roots (ivy) (h) Prop or stilt roots (mangrove) (i) Buttress roots (j) Aerial roots (epiphytic orchid) (k) Liane (*Monstera*) with main stem and descending aerial roots (l) Strangler fig with anastomosing roots uncertain parentage; (3) a range of individuals of a species or hybrid which, although different, share certain characters that give them coherence as a unit. Group names are written in roman script, take a capital initial letter, no quotation marks and are always linked to the word group, with a lower case initial and never abbreviated.

guard-cells two cells which open or close the stoma (pl. stomata).

gum a viscid secretion usually exuded from stems and hardening in the air.

gymnosperm a plant in which seeds are borne naked on a sporophyll rather than enclosed in an ovary, the ovules developing without the tegumentory pericarp found in angiosperms.

gynandrium a structure in which the stamens are adnate to the pistils.

gynandrous with the stamens adnate to the pistils, as in Orchidaceae.

gynobase an elongated or enlarged receptacle in which the pistil is borne.

gynobasic of a style attached to the gynobase.

gynodioecious bearing perfect or pistillate flowers on separate plants.

gynoecium the female element of a flower comprising the pistil or pistils.

gynomonoecious bearing separate female and bisexual flowers on the same individual.

gynophore the stalk of a pistil which raises it above the receptacle.

gynostegium the staminal crown in Asclepiadaceae.

gynostemium a single structure combining androecium and gynoecium, as in the column of Orchidaceae.

gyrate curving in a circular or spiral fashion.

habit the characteristics of a plant's appearance, concerning shape and growth and plant type (i.e. herb, shrub or tree).

habitat the area or type of locality in which a plant grows naturally.

haft the base of an organ when narrow or constricted, most often applied to the haft of the falls in Iris flowers.

hair an outgrowth of the epidermis, unicellular or comprising a row of cells and conforming to one of several types (i.e. dendritic, stellate, scale-like, peltate, etc.) according to branching, form, grouping and attachment.

halophyte a plant tolerant of or adapted to saline soil.

hamate hooked at the tip.

hapaxanthic with only a single flowering period.

hastate arrow-shaped, triangular, with two equal and approximately triangular basal lobes, pointing laterally outward rather than toward the stalk (see sagittate).

haustorium (pl. haustoria) a sucker attachment in parasitic plants penetrating the host.

head a dense cluster or spike of flowers; a capitulum.

helically spirally, in a spiral arrangement.

helicoid spirally clustered, in the shape of a spring or a snail-shell.

helicoid cyme see bostryx.

helminthoid worm-shaped.

helophyte a plant growing in permanent or seasonal mud.

herb (1) strictly, a plant without persistent stems above ground, often confined to perennials with annual stems or leaves arising from a persistent subterranean stem or rootstock. More generally, any non-woody plant; (2) a plant with culinary or officinal properties.

herbaceous (1) pertaining to herbs, i.e. lacking persistent aerial parts (as in the idea of a herbaceous perennial or the herbaceous border) or lacking woody parts; thus Hosta is strictly herbaceous in the first sense, but Liriope is also an herbaceous perennial; (2) softly leafy, pertaining to leaves; (3) thin, soft and bright green in texture and colour, as in the leaf blades of some grasses and many other herbs.

hermaphroditic bisexual, having both pistils and stamens in the same flower.

hesperidium a berry, pulpy within with a tough rind, e.g. the fruits of Citrus.

heterogamous (1) bearing two types of flower, as in the ray and disc florets of Compositae; (2) with sexual organs abnormally arranged or developed, or with function transferred from flowers of one sex to another.

heteromorphic assuming different forms or shapes at different stages in the life-history of the plant, as opposed to polymorphic, where different forms occur at the same stage of a plant's development.

heterophyllous bearing two or more differnt forms of leaf on the same plant, either contemporaneously or at different times; sometimes used of different leaf forms exhibited by individuals of the same species.

heterosporous producing spores of two sexes, which develop into male and female gametophytes as in Isoetes.

heterostylous of species whose flowers differ in the presence or number of styles, i.e. some unisexual, some hermaphrodite.

hibernaculum the winter-resting body of some plants, usually a bud-like arrangement of reduced leaves.

hilum the scar on a seed at the point at which the funicle was attached.

hip the fleshy, developed floral cup and the enclosed achenes of a rose.

hippocrepiform shaped like a horse-shoe.

hirsute with long hairs, usually rather coarse and distinct.

hirsutullous slightly hirsute.

hirtellous minutely or softly hirsute.

hirtuse see hirsute.

hispid with stiff, bristly hairs, not so distinct or sharp as when setose.

hispidulous minutely hispid.

hoary densely covered with white or grey hairs.

homochlamydeous with an undifferentiated perianth of tepals.

homogamous having hermaphrodite flowers, or flowers of the same sex.

homologous of organs or parts that resemble each other in form or function.

homomorphic having the same shape.

homonym a scientific name bestowed two or more times for plants of the same taxonomic rank but quite distinct from one another. The names are identical, but based on different types.

homosporous (1) producing only one kind of seed; (2) developed from only one kind of spore.

hooded cucullate or, more loosely, referring to inarching parts enclosing others in the resulting concavity.

horn appendage shaped like an animal's horn, see cornute.

horny hard and brittle, but with a fine texture and easily cut.

hort., horti, 'of the garden', **hortorum** 'of gardens', **hortulanorum,** 'of gardeners'; all three are abbreviated hort., never capitalized lest the citation be mistaken for the name of a botanist. The last two of these are used to indicate either the misapplication of a name by gardeners when it is, in fact, a homonym of some other validly published name or to denote the origination and effective publication of a name in horticultural writings of confused authorship or of no standing as vehicles of valid publication. The citation horti (again shortened to hort.) usually precedes a grower's name and indicates a plant name published in a nursery catalogue, e.g. hort. Lemoine, hort. Spaeth.

hose-in-hose a form of double flower, where the corolla or corolla-like calyx – usually tubular – is duplicated with one inserted in the throat of the other.

host a plant that nourishes a parasite.

husk the outer layer of certain fruits (Juglans, Physalis), generally originating from the perianth or involucre.

hyaline transparent, translucent, usually applied to the margins of leaves and bracts.

hybrid a plant produced by the cross-breeding of two or more genetically dissimilar parents; the parents generally belong to distinct taxa. A natural hybrid is one arising in nature, a spontaneous hybrid one aris-

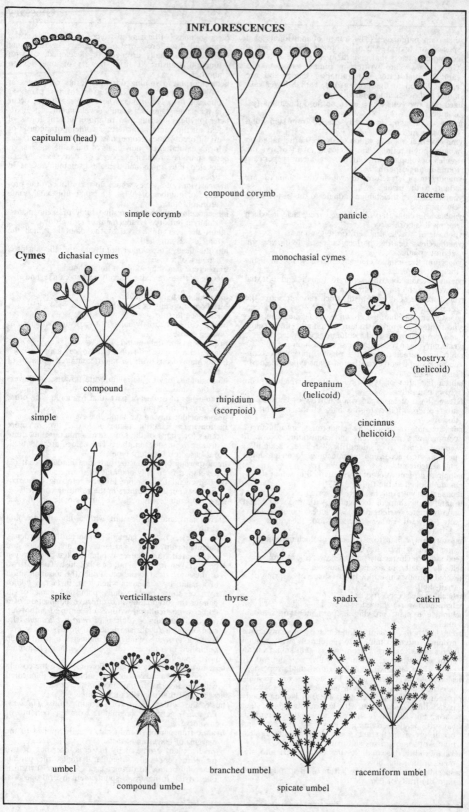

INFLORESCENCES

capitulum (head)

simple corymb

compound corymb

panicle

raceme

Cymes   dichasial cymes   monochasial cymes

simple

compound

rhipidium
(scorpioid)

drepanium
(helicoid)

cincinnus
(helicoid)

bostryx
(helicoid)

spike   verticillasters   thyrse   spadix   catkin

umbel

compound umbel

branched umbel

spicate umbel

racemiform umbel

ing without the direct intervention of man but, usually, in gardens, an artificial hybrid is a cross deliberately made by man. Specific hybrids (interspecific hybrids) are those between species belonging to the same genus, intergeneric hybrids those between taxa belonging to different genera – the number of genera involved is usually denoted by a prefix, e.g. bigeneric, trigeneric, etc.

hydathode a water-secreting gland on the surface or margin of a leaf: usually situated at the end of a vein and often surrounded by a concretion of white salts; similar to a stoma but with functionless guard cells; popularly termed lime-dot.

hydrophyte plants growing partly or wholly in water.

hygroscopic expanding when water is present, contracting in its absence.

hypanthium cup-, ring- or tube-like structure formed by the enlargement and fusion of the basal portions of calyx, corolla and stamens, together with the receptacle and on which these parts are borne, as in Rosaceae. Sometimes termed the floral cup or, inaccurately, the calyx tube.

hypochile the lower or basal part of the complex lip of certain orchids, usually swollen or inflated and distinct in form from the mesochile (central portion) and epichile (apical portion).

hypocotyl the axis of an embryo lying beneath the cotyledons and on germination developing into the radicle.

hypocrateriform see salverform.

hypogynous borne beneath the ovary, generally on the receptacle; said of the calyx, corolla and stamens of a superior ovary.

hysteranthous with the leaves developing after the flowers; cf. precocious and synanthous.

idioblasts specialized epidermal cells producing slime or gum.

illegitimate said of a name published validly but *in contravention* of one or more articles of the Code of Botanical Nomenclature or the Code of Nomenclature for Cultivated Plants.

imbricate (of organs such as leaves or bracts) overlapping; more strictly applied to such organs when closely overlapping in a regular pattern, sometimes encircling the axis.

immersed (1) entirely submerged in water, cf. emersed; (2) of features embedded and sunken below the surface of a leaf blade.

imparipinnate where a pinnately compound leaf terminates in a single leaflet, pinna or tendril (see paripinnate).

imperfect when certain parts usually present are not developed. Imperfect flowers are unisexual.

impressed sunken into the surface.

incised dissected, but cut deeply and irregularly with the segments joined by broad lamina.

included 'enclosed within', as in a grass floret by its glume, or stamens within a corolla; neither projecting nor exserted.

incomplete (of flowers) lacking one or more of the four whorls of the complete flower.

incrassate thickened; especially of skin.

incumbent folded inward and lying on or leaning against another organ; said of cotyledons when the radicle lies on one side instead of along the edge, of an anther when it lies against the inner face of its filament.

incurved bending inwards from without; (of an ovule) curved to the extent that the micropyle almost meets the funicle.

indehiscent not splitting open to release its seeds or spores; the opposite of dehiscent, and generally applied to fruit types such as achenes, berries, drupes and pomes.

indeterminate used of an inflorescence with the lower flowers opening first, thus not arresting the elongation or development of the primary axes, e.g. a panicle, raceme or corymb. An inflorescence not terminated by a single flower.

indigenous native, not exotic.

indumentum a covering of hair, scurf or scales, most often used in the general sense of 'hair'.

induplicate folded inwards.

indurate hardened and toughened.

indusium the epidermal tissue which covers or surrounds a sorus.

inerm, inermous unarmed, without spines, prickles or teeth.

inferior beneath.

inflated bladder-like, blown up and swollen, as in the lip of *Cypripedium*; cf. saccate.

inflected bent or flexed.

inflexed bent inwards towards the main axis.

inflorescence the arrangement of flowers and their accessory parts on an axis.

infra- as a prefix, denotes 'below', as infrastipular, meaning below the stipules.

infrageneric said of any taxon of a rank below that of genus, i.e. subgenus, species, subspecies, variety, forma, cultivar.

infraspecific said of any taxon of a rank below that of species, i.e. subspecies, variety, forma, cultivar.

infructescence fruiting stage of the inflorescence.

infundibular, infundibuliform funnel-shaped.

insectivorous see Carnivorous.

inserted attached to or placed upon, as in 'stamens inserted on corolla'; *not* the antithesis of exserted.

insertion the point or mode of attachment for a body to its support, a leaf insertion is where the leaf joins the stem forming an axil.

integument the layers of tissue covering the ovule, and developing into the seed coat.

inter- as a prefix, denotes 'between' or 'among', as in interstaminal, meaning between the stamens.

intergeneric used of a hybrid produced by crossing members of two or more genera and designated by a multiplication sign before a hybrid generic name, e.g. ×*Sorbopyrus*.

intermediate used of hybrids apparently combining the characters of their parents in equal measure and standing midway between them: cf. *segregate*.

internode the portion of stem between two nodes.

interrupted not continuous; the disturbance of an otherwise symmetrical arrangement by, for instance, the interposition of small or undeveloped leaflets or segments.

interspecific used of hybrids between two different species belonging to the same genus, denoted by a hybrid binomial, that is, for interspecific hybrids, genus name plus multiplication sign plus hybrid epithet, e.g. *Helleborus* ×*nigercors*.

intra- as a prefix, denotes 'within' or 'inside', as intrastaminal, meaning inside the stamens or the circle of stamens.

intricate entangled.

introduction a non-indigenous plant, usually purposefully introduced.

introrse turned or facing inwards, towards the axis, as an anther which opens towards the centre of its flower.

invaginated enclosed in a sheath.

invalid applied to names published without requisite description, diagnosis, type designation, etc., or outside a vehicle of valid publication.

involucel a secondary or diminutive involucre.

involucral forming an involucre.

involucrate possessing an involucre.

involucre a single, highly conspicuous bract, bract pair, whorl or whorls of small bracts or leaves subtending a flower or inflorescence.

involute rolled inward, toward the uppermost side (see revolute).

irregular zygomorphic; asymmetrical.

jointed see articulate.

jugate see paired.

jugum a pair, especially of lobes or leaflets.

juvenile the early, non-adult phases of a plant's life, evidenced by sexual immaturity and/or by different habit and foliage forms.

keel (1) a prominent ridge, like the keel of a boat, running longitudinally down the centre of the undersurface of a leaf, petiole, bracts, petal or sepal; (2) the two lower united petals of a papilionaceous flower.

keeled possessing a keel; see also carinate.

kernel the inner part of a seed or the whole body within the coats.

kidney-shaped reniform.

knees the apogeotropic and exposed spongy roots of *Taxodium* when growing in saturated conditions; these are held to perform the same aerating function as the pneumatophores of mangroves.

knobbed see capitate.

knotted see torulose.

labellum a lip, especially the enlarged or otherwise distinctive third petal of an orchid.

labiate possessing a lip or lips, thus 'corolla bilabiate'.

labium one of the lip-like divisions of a labiate corolla or calyx.

lacecap a flat-topped inflorescence in which the outer flowers are sterile and enlarged, e.g. *Hydrangea* cvs, *Viburnum plicatum* 'Mariesii'.

lacerate irregularly, and more or less broadly and shallowly, cut, as if torn.

laciniate irregularly and finely cut, as if slashed.

lacrimiform, lachrymaeform tear-shaped.

lacticifer, lactifer a latex-producing duct.

lactiferous, lacticiferous containing or producing latex.

lacuna a cavity or depression, especially an air-hole in plant tissue.

lacunose pitted with many deep depressions or holes.

laevigate appearing smoothly polished.

lageniform flask-shaped.

lamellate composed of one or more thin, flat scales or plates.

lamina see blade.

lanate woolly, possessing long, densely matted and curling hairs.

lanceolate lance-shaped, narrowly ovate, but 3–6 times as long as broad and with the broadest point below the middle, tapering to a spear-like apex.

lanose woolly, see lanate.

lanuginose as lanate, but with the hairs shorter; somewhat woolly or cottony.

lanulose as lanate, but with extremely short hairs.

lateral on or to the side of an axis or organ.

latex a milky fluid or sap, usually colourless, white or pale yellow, found in plants such as *Asclepias* and *Euphorbia*.

lax loose, e.g. of flowers in an inflorescence or a loose arrangement of leaves; or hardly coherent, e.g. loose cells in a tissue.

laxpendent hanging loosely.

leaf a lateral member borne on the shoot or stem of a plant, generally differing from the stem in form and structure.

leaflet one of the leaf- or blade-like ultimate units of a compound leaf.

leathery coriaceous.

legimate a name is said to be legitimate when published validly and in accordance with the rules of nomenclature set out in either the Code of Nomenclature of Cultivated Plants or the Code of Botanical Nomenclature.

legume the seed vessel of Leguminosae, one-celled, two-valved and dehiscing along both sutures – typically the pea or bean pod.

lemma the lower and stouter of the two glumes which immediately enclose the floret in most Gramineae; also referred to as the flowering glume.

lenticel an elliptical and raised cellular pore on the surface of bark, or the suberous tissue of fruit, through which gases can penetrate.

lenticellate possessing lenticels.

lenticular, lenticulate lens-shaped; almost flattened and elliptical, but with both sides convex.

lentiginous minutely dotted, as if with dust.

lepidote, leprous covered with tiny, scurfy, peltate scales.

leprous see lepidote.

liana, liane a woody climbing vine.

lianoid resembling a liana.

ligneous, lignose woody in texture.

lignotuber the swollen woody base of some shrubs adapted to withstand fire and drought.

ligulate (1) possessing a ligule; (2) strap-shaped, usually more narrowly so than in lorate.

ligule (1) a strap-shaped body, such as the limb of ray florets in Compositae; (2) the thin, scarious, sometimes hairy projection from the top of the leaf sheath in Gramineae and some other families, e.g. Palmae, Zingiberaceae; (3) any strap-shaped appendage; (4) an envelope sheathing the emerging foliage of Palmae.

limb a broadened, flattened part of an organ, extending from a narrower base, as in the flared upper part of a gamopetalous corolla.

lime-dots see hydathode.

line a term used by plant breeders to describe a more or less uniform assemblage of individuals; equivalent to a cultivar.

linear slender, elongated, the margins parallel or virtually so.

lineate see striated.

lined see striated.

lingulate resembling a tongue.

lip (1) in, for example, Labiatae, one of the two distinct corolla divisions, one, the upper, often hooded, the other, lower, often forming a flattened landing platform for pollinators; (2) a staminode or petal modified or differentiated from the others.

lithophyte a plant that grows on rocks or stony soil, deriving nourishment from the atmosphere rather than the soil.

littoral, litoral growing on the sea-shore.

lobe see lobed.

lobed divided into (usually rounded) segments – lobes – separated from adjacent segments by sinuses which reach halfway or less to the middle of the organ (see cleft).

lobulate possessing or bearing lobules.

lobule diminutive of lobe; a small lobe.

locular, loculate furnished with locules; divided into separate chambers or compartments.

locule a cavity or chamber within an ovary, anther or fruit.

loculicidal (dehiscence); splitting longitudinally and dorsally, directly into a capsule through a capsule wall.

lodicule one of two, or sometimes three minute extrastaminal scales, adpressed to the base of the ovary in most Gramineae; they swell at flowering-time to cause the divergence of the lemma and palea (the two bracts immediately enclosing the floret).

loment a leguminous pod which contracts between the seeds, drying and splitting transversely into one-seeded segments at maturity.

lorate strap-shaped.

lunate crescent-shaped.

lyrate pinnatifid, but with a large, rounded terminal lobe and smaller lateral lobes diminishing in size toward the base of the whole.

macrospore see megaspore.

maculate blotched by wide, irregular patches of colour.

mallee a small tree or shrub producing slender, short-lived stems from a swollen woody base – a bushfire survival adaptation found in *Eucalyptus*.

mamillate, mammillate furnished with nipple-like prominences.

marcescent withered but persisting, as in the leaf margins of some bamboos and palms.

marginal (1) affixed at the edge or margin of an organ; (2) growing at the water's edge.

marginate with a distinct or conspicuous margin or border.

maturation the stage of development in a fruit immediately preceding ripeness.

mealy farinose.

median pertaining to the central transverse area of a leaf, thus 'median width', width through midpoint, 'median leaflet', the leaflet at the midpoint of a pinnate leaf.

medullary consisting of pith, spongy.

megasporangium a sporangium which produces megaspores.

megaspore the larger of the two types of spores produced by heterosporous plants, they develop into female gametophytes.

megasporophyll in non-flowering plants, a sporophyll bearing megaspores; in angiosperms, a carpel.

membranous [membraneous], membranaceous thin-textured, soft and flexible.

mentum a chin-like extension of the flower, formed by the association of the bases of the lateral sepals with the foot of the column in many orchids.

mericarp a one-seeded carpel, one of a pair split apart at maturity from a syncarpous or schizocarpous ovary.

meristem undifferentiated tissue capable of developing into organs or special tissues.

-merous a suffix denoting number and disposition of parts, often combined simply with an arabic number, thus a 3-merous or trimerous flower has parts arranged in threes.

mesocarp the middle layer of a pericarp, often fleshy, occasionally fibrous, rarely membranaceous or spongy.

mesochile the middle part of the distinctly tripartite, complex lip of some orchids, such as *Stanhopea*.

mesophyte a plant halfway between hydrophytic and xerophytic, i.e. the vast majority of plants growing on land and requiring regular water supplies at least when in growth.

mesosperm the middle coat of a seed.

micropylar relating to the micropyle.

micropyle an opening in the wall of an ovule, through which the pollen tube enters.

microsporangium a sporangium which produces microspores; in angiosperms, an anther sac.

microspore the smaller of the two types of spore produced in heterosporous plants, and which develop into male gametophytes.

microsporophyll in non-flowering plants, a sporophyll bearing microsporangia; in angiosperms, a stamen bearing anther sacs.

midrib the primary vein of a leaf or leaflet, usually running down its centre as a continuation of the petiole or petiolule.

midvein see midrib.

mimosiform, mimosoid possessing globose or spiciform flower heads resembling those of the genus *Mimosa* in which cal. and cor. are inconspicuous or reduced and sta. showy.

misapplied when a published name is applied to the wrong plant it is said to be misapplied. Such names are *homonyms* and, of course, synonyms of the taxa to which they truly relate.

monadelphous stamens united by fusion of their filaments into a single group or bundle.

moniliform where a cylindrical or terete organ is regularly constricted, giving the appearance of a string of beads or a knotted rope; cf. torulose.

mono- (prefix) denoting 'one'.

monocarpellary (of a fruit) derived from a single carpel.

monocarpic dying after bearing fruit (i.e. flowering) only once.

monocephalous having one flower head.

monochasial cyme as a dichasial cyme but with the branches missing from one side.

monochlamydeous with only one perianth whorl.

monocolpate (of pollen grains) with one furrow or groove.

monocot a monocotyledonous plant. The monocots are one of the two primarily divisions of the angiosperms, the other being the dicots. They are characterized by the single, not double, cotyledon in the seed, usually the absence of cambium and thus woody tissue and, in many cases, parallel venation. The monocotyledons include Gramineae, Musaceae, Agavaceae, Liliaceae, Amaryllidaceae, Orchidaceae, Araceae, Iridaceae, Bromeliaceae, Palmae, etc.

monocotyledonous containing only one cotyledon in the seed; pertaining to monocots.

monoecious with bisexual flowers or both staminate and pistillate flowers present on the same plant; cf. dioecious.

monoembryonic of ovules or seeds containing only one embryo.

monogeneric of a family or grouping of higher rank containing a single genus.

monopetalous strictly, with one petal; often loosely used for gamopetalous.

monopodial of a stem or rhizome in which growth continues indefinitely from the apical or terminal bud, and which generally exhibits little or no secondary branching.

monospecific see monotypic.

monotypic having only one component, e.g. a genus with one species. The term is misleading for all genera, no matter how large, are based on a single type; equally, a genus with a single species may be termed monotypic yet contain many distinctive named entities (varieties and cultivars) each of which will have its own type. In such cases, the term monospecific is sometimes preferred.

morphology here, the study of plant structure. Morphological terms form the basic vocabulary of botanical description.

mother plant (1) the parent plant from which propagules are derived; (2) the seed parent of a hybrid.

motile (of hairs, appendages and lobes) capable of movement; (of spores, sperms etc.) self-propelling, using cilia etc.

mucilage a viscous substance or solution.

mucilaginous slimy.

mucro an abrupt, sharp, terminal spur, spine or tip.

mucronate (of an apex) terminating suddenly with an abrupt spur or spine developed from the midrib.

mucronulate diminutive of mucronate.

multi- as a prefix, denoting many, e.g. multicarpellate, many-seeded.

multifid as bifid, but cleft more than once, forming many lobes.

multifoliate many-leaved.

multigeneric refers to hybrids with more than two genera involved in their ancestry, e.g. ×*Potinara* (*Brassavola* ×*Cattleya* ×*Laelia* ×*Sophronitis*). Multigeneric hybrid names are formed either by combining the generic names of the parents, as for example in ×*Sophrolaeliocattleya*, or, as in the case above, by creating a commemorative personal name using the suffix -ara.

multiline a term used by plant breeders to describe a horticultural variety (or seed issue) made up of several closely related lines.

multiple fruit a fruit derived from an entire inflorescence, i.e. from the ovaries (and/or other parts) of a number of flowers.

muricate rough-surfaced, furnished with many short, hard, pointed projections.

muriculate slightly muricate.

muscariform in the shape of a broom or brush.

mutant an individual produced as a result of mutation.

mycorrhizal a term describing roots which associate with a fungal mycelium, and can derive a benefit, through symbiosis or digestion, from the latter.

myrmecophyte a plant in symbiosis with ants – such plants are myrmecophilous.

navicular, naviculate shaped like a deeply keeled boat.

nec 'nor': see non.

neck used of the upper part of a bulb, where the leaves and flower stem emerge.

nectar a sweet, liquid secretion often attractive to pollinators.

nectariferous possessing nectaries.

nectary a gland, often in the form of a protuberance or depression, which secretes and sometimes absorbs nectar.

needle a linear stiff leaf as found in conifers.

needle-like see acicular.

nervation see venation.

nerved furnished with ribs or veins.

nervose see nerved.

FLOWERS

BRACTS

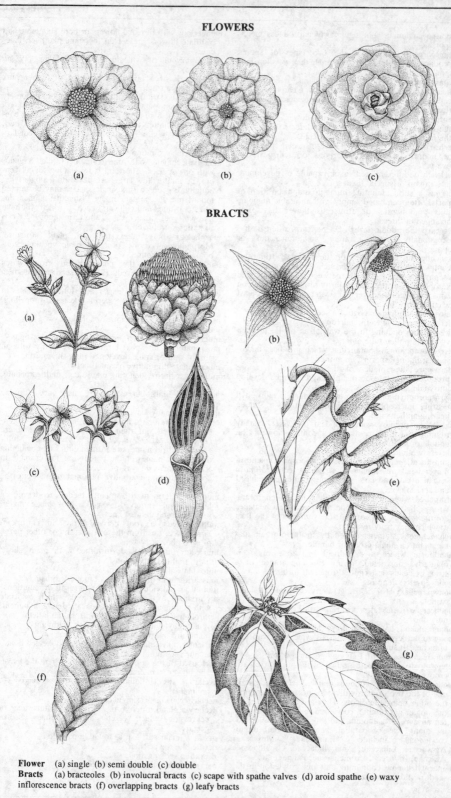

Flower (a) single (b) semi double (c) double
Bracts (a) bracteoles (b) involucral bracts (c) scape with spathe valves (d) aroid spathe (e) waxy inflorescence bracts (f) overlapping bracts (g) leafy bracts

netted reticulate, net-veined.

neuter, neutral sterile, asexual; (of flowers) lacking both pistils and stamens.

nigrescent turning black.

nocturnal opening or active only during the night.

node the point on an axis where one or more leaves, shoots, whorls, branches or flowers are attached.

nodose possessing many closely packed nodes; knobbly.

nodule a small, virtually spherical protuberance.

nomen [Latin 'name', pl. nomina, abbrev. nom.] a term used in one of the following forms:

(a) **nomen confusum (nom. confus.), nomina confusa** a 'confused' name is one based on a type composed of material (specimens, images, etc.) that is later discovered to represent not one but two or more taxa.

(b) **nomen conservandum (nom. cons.), nomina conservanda** a name to be conserved.

(c) **nomen ambiguum (nom. ambig.), nomina ambigua** a name applied different taxa with the result that it has become 'a long-persistent source of error'. It has been suggested that such names be abandoned.

(d) **nomen novum (nom. nov.)** a name proposed as a substitute for an earlier one that has been rejected for a variety of reasons. Such names may be preferred over existing names (these then appear in synonymy) or replace existing names as the basionyms of new combinations.

(e) **nomen illegitimum (nom. illegit.)** an illegitimate name, one that is validly published yet contravenes the Codes of Nomenclature.

(f) **nomen nudum (nom. nud.) nomina nuda** 'a naked name', one published with neither description nor diagnosis and therefore in contravention of the Codes of Nomenclature.

(g) **nomen rejiciendum (nom. rejic.) nomina rejicienda** 'a name to be rejected', a name rejected when another is conserved.

non [Latin 'not'] used in the citations of later homonyms to differentiate between the various applications of the name in question to different entities by different authors, e.g. *Artemisia lanata* Willd. non Lam. represents Willdenow's misapplication in 1823 of a name published by Lamarck in 1783 for a wholly different plant.

non-resupinate (of a leaf or flower) inverted by a twisting of the petiole or pedicels – in the case of some orchids this results in "upside-down' flowers with the lip uppermost.

nonvascular without vascular tissue, as algae, lichens, fungi etc.

nothomorph a taxonomic term for different hybrid forms derived from the same parent species, equivalent in rank to a variety.

novirame a flowering or fruiting shoot arising from a primocane.

nucellar arising from the nucellus.

nucellus the central tissue of an ovule, containing the embryo sac.

nut (1) an indehiscent, one-celled and one-seeded, hard, ligneous or osseous fruit, as the acorn of *Quercus*; (2) more loosely applied to a drupe with a thin exocarp and a large pyrene, or to the pyrene itself.

nutant nodding, usually applied to a whole inflorescence or stem; cf. cernuous.

nutlet a small nut or a small stone of a drupaceous fruit; as an achene, but with a harder and thicker pericarp.

ob- a prefix, meaning inverted; thus oblanceolate, means lanceolate, but with the broadest part furthest from the base.

obconic, obconical as conic, but with the point of attachment at the narrower end.

obcordate as with cordate, but with the sinus at the apex rather than the base.

obcuneate as cuneate, but with the point of attachment at the broad end.

obhastate as hastate, but with the triangular lobes at the apex.

oblanceolate as with lanceolate, but with the broadest part above the middle, and tapering to the base

rather than the apex.

oblate spherical but dorsally and ventrally compressed.

obligate essential, unable to exist without; cf. facultative.

oblique (1) (of the base) with sides of unequal angles and dimensions; (2) (of direction) extending laterally, the margin upwards and the apex pointed horizontally.

oblong essentially linear, about 2–3 times as long as broad, with virtually parallel sides terminating obtusely at both ends.

obovate ovate, but broadest above rather than below the middle, thus narrowest toward the base rather than the apex.

obovoid as ovoid, but broadest below the middle; obovate in cross-section.

obpyramidal inversely pyramidal, tapering from the apex.

obpyriform inversely pear-shaped, thus narrowing toward the base.

obsolescent (of an organ) reduced to the point of being vestigial.

obsolete extinct, or not evident; where an organ is absent, or apparently absent, from its expected location.

obtuse (of apex or base) terminating gradually in a blunt or rounded end.

ocrea, ochrea a tubular or inflated sheath at the base of the petiole formed by a pair of coherent stipules, as in Polygonaceae, or an expansion of the leaf sheath, as in some Palmae.

oleaginous oily, though of a fleshy nature.

oligo- as a prefix, denoting few, as oligopetalous, meaning few-petalled.

oogonium the organ in thallophytes which produces female gametes.

opercular, operculate possessing a lid or cap.

operculum the lid or cap of a capsule with circumscissile dehiscence.

opposite two organs at the same level, or at the same or parallel nodes, on opposite sides of the axis.

orbicular perfectly circular, or nearly so.

ordo, order the principal category of taxa intermediate in rank between Class and Family, e.g. Commelinales, the order containing the families Rapateaceae, Xyridaceae, Mayacaceae and Commelinaceae. Until the present century, botanists used *ordo* to denote the rank of family and *cohors* for the modern order.

osseous bony and brittle, but difficult to cut.

ovary the basal part of a pistil, containing the ovules; a simple ovary is derived from a single carpel, a compound ovary from two or more; a superior ovary is borne above the point of attachment of perianth and stamens, an inferior ovary is borne beneath, and a subinferior, semi-inferior or half-inferior ovary is intermediate between these two positions. See also epigynous and hypogynous.

ovate egg-shaped in outline, rounded at both ends but broadest below the middle, and 1.5–2 times as long as it is broad (see elliptic).

oviform egg-shaped.

oviparous producing female gametes.

ovoid egg-shaped, ovate but 3-dimensional.

ovule the body in the ovary which bears the megasporangium, developing into a seed after pollination.

pachycarpous with a thick pericarp.

pachycaul thick-stemmed, sometimes applied to tree-like herbs or shrubs with strong, simple, erect stems, e.g. high altitude giant lobelias or simple-stemmed trees *Carica* spp.

paired usually applied to flowers or leaflets in opposite pairs; bi-, tri-, and multijugate describe compound leaves with two, three or many such pairs or leaflets.

palaceous with the stalk attached to the margin.

palate the lower lip of a personate corolla, apparently closing its throat.

palea specifically the upper and generally slimmer of the two glumes enclosing the floret in most Gramineae; more generally a small, dry bract or scale.

paleaceous bearing small, chaffy bracts or scales (paleae); more generally, chaffy in texture.

palmate with three or more free lobes or similar segments originating in a palm-like manner from the same basal point. (Of venation) three or more veins arising from the point of attachment of the petiole.

palmatifid palmately cleft rather than lobed.

palmatisect palmately cut rather than cleft or lobed into segments almost to the base of the leaf.

pandurate fiddle-shaped; rounded at both ends, one end being enlarged, and markedly constricted or indented on both sides in or around the middle.

panduriform see pandurate.

panicle an indeterminate branched inflorescence, the branches generally racemose or corymbose.

paniculate resembling, or in the form of a panicle.

pannose felt-like in texture, being densely covered in woolly hairs.

papilionaceous of the pea-type corolla characteristic of papilionoid legumes, having five petals: a large standard, two lateral wings, paired and clawed, and the two lower petals united along their lower margin to form a carinate structure (keel) enclosing the stamens and pistil.

papillae small, soft, pimple-like excrescences or protuberances of various sizes.

papillate, papillose covered with small, soft pimple-like excrescences or protuberances of varying sizes.

pappus a whorl or tuft of delicate bristles or scales in the place of the calyx, found in some flowers of Compositae.

papule a relatively large pustule or papilla.

papyraceous papery.

paraclade an inflorescence on a lateral axis which repeats the symmetry of the primary axis.

parallel where the veins are more or less parallel to the margins, running lengthwise.

parallel-ribbed, penniparallel where the veins extend laterally at or almost at right angles to the midrib.

paraphysis, paraphyses a sterile filament or hair borne among sporangia; may be simple or branched, pointed or clubbed.

parasite an organism that lives at the expense of another (the host).

paripinnate where a pinnately compound leaf is not terminated by a single leaflet pinna or tendril.

parted divided almost to the base into a determinate number of segments; a more general term for, e.g. pinnate, palmate, etc.

parthenocarpic fruiting without fertilization having taken place.

parthenogenesis the development of a seed without fertilization having taken place.

partite see parted.

patellate see patelliform.

patelliform orbicular and thick, having a convex lower surface and a concave upper surface.

patent spreading.

pea-like see papilionaceous.

pectinate pinnately divided, the segments being many, slender and long, and close together, like the teeth of a comb.

pedate palmate, but for the basal/lowest lobes on each side, which are themselves lobed.

pedicel the stalk supporting an individual flower or fruit.

pedicelled, pedicellate growing on a pedicel.

peduncle the stalk of an inflorescence.

peduncled, peduncular, pedunculate borne on or possessing a peduncle.

pellicle a thin, generally non-cellular coat or skin.

pellucid virtually transparent.

peltate of a leaf whose stalk is attached inside its margin rather than at the edge, usually at the centre beneath.

pendent hanging downwards, more markedly than arching or nodding but not as a result of the weight of the part in question or the weakness of its attachment or support (pendulous).

pendulous dependent, but as a result of the weakness of the support, as in a slender-stalked heavy fruit or a densely flowered weeping raceme.

penicillate brush-shaped, or like a tuft of hairs.

penninerved, penniveined, penniribbed with closely arranged veins extending from the midrib in a feather-like manner.

pentamerous with parts in groups of five, or multiples of five; often written 5-merous.

pentangular five-angled.

pepo a multicarpellate fruit with fleshy pulp but a hard exocarp derived from the receptacle.

perennate to survive from year to year; to overwinter.

perennial a plant lasting longer than two years.

perfect a bisexual flower or an organ with all its constituent members.

perfoliate of a sessile leaf where the basal lobes are united surrounding the stem which passes through the blade. cf. connate-perfoliate.

perianth the collective term for the floral envelopes, the corolla and calyx, especially when the two are not clearly differentiated.

pericarp the wall of a ripened ovary or fruit, sometimes differentiated into exocarp, mesocarp and endocarp.

periderm a three-layered tissue of skin.

perigone the perianth, especially when undifferentiated, or anything surrounding a reproductive structure.

perigynous of flowers in which the perianth and stamens are apparently basally united and borne on the margins of a cup-shaped rim, itself borne on the receptacle of a superior ovary, and are thus neither above nor below the ovary.

persistent of an organ, neither falling off nor withering.

personate a sympetalous corolla with an undifferentiated limb, the upper lip arching and the lower lip prominent and addressed to it.

perulate (of buds) covered in scales.

perule a bud scale.

petal one of the modified leaves of the corolla, generally brightly coloured and often providing a place on which pollinators may alight.

petaloid petal-like in colour, shape and texture; e.g. a petaloid staminode in a double *Camellia*.

petiolate, petioled furnished with a petiole.

petiole the leaf stalk.

petiolulate possessing a petiolule.

petiolule the stalk of a leaflet.

phanerogam a spermatophyte, a plant reproducing by means of seeds not spores, unlike a cryptogam.

phenotypic adaptation in direct response to environmental conditions, thus neither stable nor heritable (genotypic). Such changes are often found in horticulture where species are grown in a wide range of conditions.

phyllary one of the bracts which subtends a flower or inflorescence, composing an involucre.

phylloclad, phylloclade a stem or branch, flattened and functioning as a leaf, as in *Phyllocladus*, *Opuntia*, etc.

phyllocladous (of stems or branches) functioning as a leaf.

phyllode an expanded petiole, taking on the function of a leaf-blade, as in *Acacia*.

phyllopodium an outgrowth of the rhizome of some ferns to which the frond is joined.

pilose covered with diffuse, soft, slender hairs.

pilosulous slightly pilose.

pinna (*pl*. pinnae) the primary division of a pinnately compound leaf. See pinnate.

pinnate (of a compound leaf) feather-like; an arrangement of leaflets (pinnae) in two rows along the rachis; bipinnate refers to a leaf in which the pinnae are themselves divided into rachiae and petiolules bearing leaflets (pinnules). Also applied to veins in a feather-like arrangement.

pinnately veined see penninerved.

pinnatifid pinnately cleft nearly to the midrib in broad divisions, but without separating into distinct leaflets or pinnae.

pinnatipartite see pinnatifid.

pinnatisect deeply and pinnately cut to, or near to, the midrib; the divisions, narrower than when pinnatifid, are themselves not truly distinct segments.

pinnule the ultimate division of a (generally pinnate) compound leaf; for example, a segment of a pinnately divided pinna.

pistil one of the female reproductive organs of a flower, together making up the gynostemium, and usually composed of ovary, style and stigma. A simple pistil consists of one carpel, a compound pistil of two or more.

pistillate a unisexual, female flower bearing a pistil or pistils but no functional stamens.

pistillode a sterile, vestigial pistil remaining in a staminate flower.

pitch resinous exudate.

pitcher a tubular or cup-like vessel, usually a modified leaf. In several carnivorous genera, these are trapping adaptations.

pitcher-shaped campanulate but with a distinct narrowing toward the orifice.

pitted see lacunose.

placenta the tissue containing or bearing the ovules in an ovary.

placentation the arrangement of the ovules in the placenta. Several types are found: apical, where one or few ovules develop at the top of a simple or compound ovary; axile, where ovules are borne at or around the centre of a compound ovary on an axis formed from joined portions (septa); basal, where one or few ovules develop at the base of a simple or compound ovary; free central, where ovules develop on a central column in a compound ovary lacking septa or with septa at base only; lamellate, with ovules on thin extensions of the placentae into a compound ovary; marginal or ventral, with ovules borne on the wall along the ventral suture of a simple ovary; parietal, where ovules develop on the wall or on the slight outgrowths of the wall forming broken partitions within a compound ovary.

plane flat; a flat surface.

plantlet a small or secondary plant, developing on a larger plant.

plate flattened structure.

pleated see plicate.

plicate folded lengthwise, pleated, as a closed fan.

plumed see plumose.

plumose feather-like; with long, fine hairs, which themselves have fine secondary hairs.

plumule the axis (stem) of an embryo or seedling.

plur-, pluri- a prefix denoting many, as plurilocular, many-celled.

pneumatophore an air-filled apogeotropic root, taking the function of a respiratory organ, found in plants of wet places.

pod a general term for any dry, dehiscent fruit.

pollen the microspores, spores or grains producing male gametes and borne by an anther in a flowering plant.

pollination the mechanical or physical transfer of pollen from an anther to a receptive stigma.

pollinator the agent by which pollination is effected.

pollinium a regular mass of more or less coherent pollen grains.

polycarpellary (of a fruit) derived from two or more fused carpels.

polyembryonic containing several embryos.

polygamodioecious (1) a plant that is functionally dioecious but contains some perfect flowers in its inflorescence; (2) a species which has perfect and imperfect flowers on separate individuals.

polygamous bearing both unisexual and bisexual flowers on the same or different plants within the same species.

polymorphic occurring in more than two distinct forms, possessing variety in some morphological feature.

polypetalous with a corolla composed of separated or distinct petals.

polyploid with more than the regular two sets of chromosomes.

polysepalous with a calyx composed of separate sepals.

polystichous arranged in many rows.

polytrichous having many hairs.

pome a multiloculate fruit, formed by the fusion of an inferior ovary and the hypanthium, from which the flesh, which is tough but not woody or bony, is derived; typical examples include the apple and pear.

pore an aperture, small and approximately circular, as covered by the operculum of a circumscissile capsule.

poricidal a form of dehiscence in which the pollen is released through pores at the apex of the anther.

porrect extending or stretching outward and forward.

posterior at or towards the back and adaxial surface.

praemorse raggedly or irregularly truncated, as if gnawed or bitten.

precocious appearing or developing early. Precocious flowers appear before the leaves; cf. hysteranthous.

prickle a small, weak thorn-like outgrowth from the bark or outer layers, generally irregularly arranged.

primocane as floricane, but in its first year of growth, prior to flowering.

primordium a tissue or organ in its earliest state, having undergone differentiation and just prior to emergence.

priority the nomenclatural rule whereby the first published of two or more validly published names for the same entity is judged to be the accepted name. The rule may be waived where names are *conserved*. For vascular plants at family, genus, species and lower ranks, the starting point for priority begins with Linnaeus, *Species Plantarum* Ed. I. (1753). Names published before 1 May 1753 are termed 'pre-Linnaean'.

proboscis see beak.

procumbent trailing loosely or lying flat along the surface of the ground, without rooting.

pro hybrida (pro hybr.) 'as a hybrid', used in citations to denote that a taxon now deemed to be a species was originally published as a hybrid.

projecting of stamens and styles and stigmas, clearly thrust outwards beyond the apical margins or (where a flared and flattened limb is present) throat of a corolla, as in *Hibiscus*.

proliferating producing buds or off-shoots, especially from unusual organs, e.g. plants or plantlets from stolons or runners.

proliferous see proliferating.

prominent (usually applied to veins and surface features) clearly visible or palpable, standing out from the surface.

pro parte (p.p.) 'in part', used in citations to show that a taxon in the sense of one author represents only part of the elements on which it was based by its original author.

prop root a root that arises adventitiously from the stem of a plant, roots in the ground and supports the stem.

prophyll (1) the bracteole subtending a single flower or pedicel; (2) the conspicuous first bract borne on the peduncle and, sometimes, inflorescence branches of some monocots.

pro specie (pro sp.) 'as a species', used in citations to denote that a taxon originally thought to be a species is now judged to be and designated a hybrid.

prostrate lying flat on the ground.

protandrous describes a flower in which pollen is released from the mature anthers before the stigma of the same flower becomes receptive; in incomplete protandry the shedding of pollen continues after the stigma becomes receptive, enabling self-pollination to take place.

prothallus the gametophyte generation of ferns and other cryptogams, a delicate liverwort-like structure bearing the antheridia and archegonia on its lower surface and providing a site for the fusion of gametes and development of the sporophyte generation.

protogynous of a flower in which the stigma becomes receptive before pollen is shed from the anthers of the flower.

protologue all of the appurtenances of botanical publication, i.e. diagnosis, description, synonymy, citation of specimens, illustrations, etc.

protruding exserted, e.g. with stamens or style longer than or passing clearly beyond the perianth segments.

proximal the part nearest to the axis, thus the base of a leaf is proximal; cf. distal.

proximate close together; see distant.

pruinose thickly frosted with white, rather than blue-grey bloom, usually on a dark ground colour, e.g. garnet or black.

pseud-, pseudo- as a prefix, meaning 'apparently, but not actually'.

pseudanthium (*pl.* pseudanthia) an inflorescence which simulates a simple flower, but is composed of more than a single axis with subsidiary flowers.

pseudobulb the water-storing thickened 'bulb-like' stems found in many sympodial orchids – predominantly aerial and in epiphytic or lithophytic species but also in some terrestrials (e.g. *Eulophia, Calanthe*), where they may be buried. Pseudobulbs arise from a rhizome, sometimes so short as to give them the appearance of being clumped. They vary in shape and size from species to species and usually grow actively for only one season, persisting thereafter as backbulbs.

pseudobulbous resembling or pertaining to the pseudobulb.

pseudocarp see accessory fruit.

pseudostem an erect aerial 'stem' apparently furnished with leaves but in fact composed of the packed or overlapping sheaths and stalks of essentially basal leaves – a common feature of Musaceae, Zingiberaceae, Heliconiaceae, Strelitziaceae and Cannaceae.

pseudoterminal (of buds) a lateral or axillary bud which takes the place of an abscised or damaged terminal bud; (of an inflorescence or solitary flower) situated at a stem apex but in fact axillary.

pteridophyte the general name for ferns and fern allies.

puberulent, puberulous minutely pubescent; covered with minute, soft hairs.

puberulose, puberulous see puberulent.

pubescent generally hairy; more specifically, covered with short, fine, soft hairs.

pulp the juicy or fleshy tissue of a fruit.

pulverulent powdery, covered in a fine bloom.

pulvinate possessing a pulvinus; also sometimes used of cushion-like plants.

pulvinus a cushion of enlarged tissue on a stem at the insertion of a petiole, or on a rachis at the base of a petiolule; generally articulated, and sometimes responsive to environmental conditions, such as heat, light or movement.

punctate dotted with minute, translucent impressions, pits or dark spots.

puncticulate minutely punctate.

pungent ending in a rigid and sharp long point.

pustular, pustulate of a surface covered with pustules.

pustule a pimple-like or blister-like eruption.

pustuliform blister-like.

pyramidal conical, but with more angular sides.

pyrene the nutlet of a drupe or drupelet; a seed and the bony endocarp which surrounds it.

pyriform pear-shaped.

pyxis a capsule exhibiting circumscissile dehiscence.

quadrangular four-angled, as in the stems of some *Passiflora* and succulent *Euphorbia* spp.

quadrate more or less square.

quadrilateral four-sided.

quadripinnate pinnately divided into four pinnae, or groups of four pinnae.

quinate possessing five leaflets emanating from the same point of attachment.

raceme an indeterminate, unbranched and, usually, elongate inflorescence composed of pedicelled flowers.

racemiform of an inflorescence that appears to be a raceme, i.e. slender, simple and with apparently stalked flowers.

racemose of flowers borne in a raceme; of an inflorescence that is a raceme.

rachilla the secondary axis of a decompound leaf or inflorescence.

rachis (rachises, rachides) the axis of a compound leaf or a compound inflorescence, as an extension of the petiole or peduncle, respectively.

radiate (1) spreading outward from a common centre; (2) possessing ray florets, as in the typically daisy-like capitula of many Compositae.

radical arising directly from the root, rootstock or root-like stems, usually applied to leaves that are basal rather than cauline.

radicle the rudimentary root of the embryo.

radius (*pl.* radii) the outermost florets when distinct from discoid ones in Compositae.

ramentaceous (on stems or leaves) possessing small, loose, brownish scales.

ramet (1) an individual member of a clone; (2) an underground tree system giving rise to large sucker-ing colonies.

ramiflorous bearing flowers directly on large branches and leafless twigs, but not the trunk.

ramiform branched, branch-like.

ramose bearing or divided into many branches.

rank (1) a vertical row or column, e.g. of leaves; (2) in taxonomy, the position of a taxon in the hierarchy.

raphe the generally ridged portion of a funicle which is in contact with the integument.

raphide an elongated, needle-like crystal of calcium oxalate, sometimes in a bundle and found in the vegetative parts of many plants.

ray (1) the primary division of an umbel or umbelli-form inflorescence; (2) a ray flower, or a circle of ray flowers, or the corolla of a ray flower.

ray flower, ray floret a small flower with a tubular corolla and the limb expanded and flattened in a strap-like blade (ligule), these usually occupy the peripheral rings of a radiate Compositae capitulum; cf. disc floret.

receptacle the enlarged or elongated, and either flat, concave or convex, end of the stem from which the floral parts or the perigynous zone derive.

receptacular borne on a receptacle, pertaining to the receptacle.

reclinate see reclining.

reclining tending gradually backwards from the vertical.

reflexed abruptly deflexed at more than a 90° angle.

regular see actinomorphic.

remontant of a plant that flowers twice or more in a season, in distinct phases.

remote see distant.

reniform kidney-shaped; lunate, but with the concave centre of the shape attached to the base, and the ends obtuse.

repand sinuate, with less pronounced undulations.

replum the frame-like placenta which remains after the valves of a silique fall away.

resiniferous see resinous.

resinous containing or exuding resin.

resupinate, resupine (of a leaf or flower) inverted by a twisting of 180° of the petiole or stalk; cf. non-resupinate.

reticulate netted, i.e. with a close or open network of anastomosing veins, ribs or colouring. A reticulate tunic in cormous plants is composed of a lattice of fibres.

reticulation a network of reticulate veins, ribs, colour-ing or fibres.

retrorse (usually of a minor organ attached to a larger part, e.g. a prickle on a stem, a barb on a leaf or a callus on a lip) turned, curved or bent downwards or backwards, away from the apex; cf. introrse.

retuse (of apices) emarginate, but with a small, rounded sinus, and the adjacent lobes blunt.

revolute of margins, rolled under, i.e. toward the dorsal surface, the antithesis of involute.

rhizoid a structure resembling a root in appearance and function, but differing anatomically.

rhizomatous producing or possessing rhizomes; rhizome-like.

rhizome a specialized stem, slender or swollen, branch-ing or simple, subterranean or lying close to the soil surface (except in epiphytes), that produces roots and aerial parts (stems, leaves, inflorescences) along its length and at its apex, common to many perennial herbs.

rhomboid (of leaves, tepals etc.) diamond-shaped, angularly oval, the base and apex forming acute

FLOWER FORMS AND ARRANGEMENTS

Parts of the flower

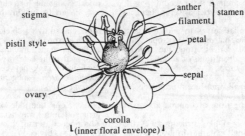

stigma

pistil style

ovary

anther
filament] stamen

petal

sepal

corolla
(inner floral envelope)
calyx (outer floral envelope)

polypetalous flower

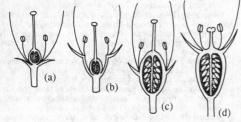

(a)

(b)

(c)

(d)

Position of ovary
(a) ovary superior, perianth and stamens hypogynous
(b) ovary superior, petals and stamens perigynous
(c) ovary partly inferior, petals and stamens epigynous
(d) ovary inferior, petals and stamens epigynous

gamopetalous
flower

unisexual flowers
(salix)

anther

connective

filament

basifixed
stamen

dorsifixed
stamen

sessile
stigma

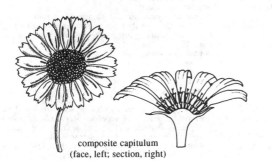

composite capitulum
(face, left; section, right)

ray floret

disc floret

angles, and both sides forming obtuse angles.

ribbed possessing one or more prominent veins or nerves.

rind the outer bark of a tree outside the cambium.

ripening (1) the maturescence of a fruit as developmental changes occur to prepare it for seed dispersal; (2) the hardening of wood, particularly the lignification of soft stems.

root the axis of a plant that serves to anchor it and absorb nutrients from the soil, usually geotropic, subterranean, endose and derived from the radicle; roots may, however, be adventitious or aerial.

rootlet a small or secondary root.

rootstock see rhizome.

roridulous covered with small, translucent prominences, giving the appearance of dewdrops.

rosette (of leaves) radiating from a common crown or . centre.

rostellum (1) any small beak-like structure; (2) the beak-like tissue separating the anther from the stigma in Orchidaceae.

rostrate see beaked.

rosulate of leaves arranged in a basal rosette or rosettes.

rotate wheel-shaped; of a corolla with a short tube and spreading circular limb or segments.

rotund rounded, curved like the arc of a circle.

ruderal growing in waste places.

rudimentary fragmentary, imperfectly developed.

rufescent, rufous reddish-brown.

rugose wrinkled by irregular lines and veins.

rugulose finely rugose.

ruminate appearing as if chewed.

runcinate of a leaf, petal or petal-like structure, usually oblanceolate in outline and with sharp, prominent teeth or broad, incised lobes pointing backwards towards the base, away from a generally acute apex.

runner see stolon.

sac see locule.

saccate bag- or pouch-like, shaped like a round shoe.

sagittate arrow- or spear-shaped, where the equal and approximately triangular basal lobes point downward or toward the stalk; see hastate.

salverform of a corolla with a long, slim tube and an abruptly expanded, flattened limb.

samara a one-seeded, indehiscent, alate fruit, as in maple or ash.

samaroid resembling a samara, an indehiscent fruit of which part of the wall is alate.

saprophyte a plant deriving nutrition from dead or decayed organic matter and usually lacking chlorophyll.

saprophytic deriving its nutrition from dissolved or decayed organic matter.

sarmentose producing long, slender stolons.

saxicolous growing in or near rocky places, or on rocks.

scaberulous finely or minutely scabrous.

scabrid a little scabrous, or rough.

scabridulous minutely scabrid.

scabrous rough, harsh to the touch because of minute projections, scales, tiny teeth or bristles.

scale leaves specialized, scale-like leaves, including those covering buds or forming bulbs.

scaly possessing minute scales, attached at one end.

scandent climbing.

scape an erect, leafless stalk bearing a terminal inflorescence or flower.

scapose producing scapes or borne on a scape.

scarabaeiform beetle-shaped.

scariose see scarious.

scarious thin, dry and shrivelled; consisting of more or less translucent tissue.

scarred bearing scars where bodies have fallen off, e.g. leaf scars on stems.

schizocarp a dry, usually dehiscent syncarpous ovary which splits into separate, one-seeded halves, or mericarps, at maturity.

sclerophyll tissue abounding in schlerenchyma, composed of cells with thick, ligneous walls retaining water; a common adaptation of plants at risk from true or physiological drought and evidenced by hard,

leathery or glassy leaf surfaces.

scorpioid cyme (cincinnus) a coiled, determinate inflorescence with flowers or branches alternating in two opposite ranks.

scrambler a plant with long stems, often equipped with prickles enabling it to climb through shrubs and trees.

scurfy covered with tiny bran-like scales, or scale-like particles.

scutate shaped like a shield or buckler; with a concrete centre surrounded by an elevated margin.

scutelliform shaped like a small shield.

sectio, section the category of supplementary taxa intermediate in rank between subgenus and series, e.g. *Rhododendron* subgenus *Rhododendron* section *Pogonanthum*.

secund (of flowers, leaves) where all the parts are borne along one side of the axis, or appear to be arranged in this way because of twists in their stalks.

seed a ripened, fertilized ovule; an embryonic plant.

seed leaf see cotyledon.

seedling a young plant which develops from a seed.

segment a discrete portion of an organ or appendage which is deeply divided but not compound; thus the segments of a pinnatifid leaf, or the segments (free apical portions) of a fused calyx or corolla.

segregate (1) a genus split from another for taxonomic reasons, e.g. *Dracula* from *Masdevallia*; (2) a hybrid in which the characters of one of the parents are more evident than those of the other(s); cf. *intermediate*.

selection a distinct form of a plant, sexual or asexual in origin, selected and propagated for its ornamental or economic virtues and named as a cultivar.

self-clinging used of plants that climb without the support of others, as by aerial roots or adhesive tendrils.

semi- prefix meaning half or partly.

semiterete a semi-cylindrical form, terete on one side, but flattened on the other, as some petioles.

senescent undergoing the processes following maturity and resulting in the death of tissue.

sensu 'in the sense of', often used before the first author cited in citation of a homonym where two or more authors are contrasted by 'non' and 'nec'; e.g. *Mimulus luteus* sensu Greene non L., where Linnaeus's taxon is the one to which the name should correctly be applied.

sensu lato 'in the broad sense', used of a taxon when it is cited in such a way as to signify its broadest interpretation, i.e. embracing variants.

sensu stricto 'in the narrow sense', used of a taxon when it is cited in such a way as to signify only its type.

sepal one of the members of the outer floral envelope, enclosing and protecting the inner floral parts prior to anthesis, the segments composing the calyx, sometimes leafy, sometimes bract- or scale-like, sometimes petaloid. Sepals when described as such are usually free; they may, however, be wholly or partially fused in a calyx tube, a sepaline cup or a synsepalum.

sepaline pertaining to the sepals.

sepaloid sepal-like.

sept a small depression or cavity, e.g. between carpels on the exterior of an ovary.

septate see locular.

septicidal when, in dehiscence, a capsule splits or breaks through its lines of junction, splitting into its interior septa (partitions) and not into the locule itself.

septifragal when, in dehiscence, the valves break away from their partitions.

septum a partition or wall, particularly in an ovary.

seriate in a row or whorl; generally prefixed by a number, e.g. monoseriate, in one row, multiseriate, in many rows.

sericeous, silky covered with fine, soft, adpressed hairs.

series the category of supplementary taxa intermediate in rank between section and species, e.g. *Saxifraga* section *Porphyrion*, series *Juniperifoliae*.

serrate essentially dentate, but with apically directed teeth resembling those of a saw; biserrate is when the teeth are themselves serrate. (See dentate.)

FLOWER FORMS AND ARRANGEMENTS

Perianth forms

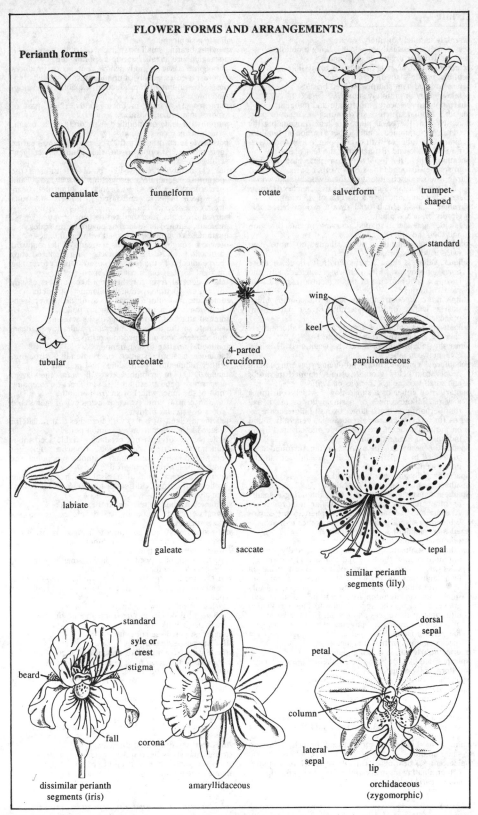

campanulate

funnelform

rotate

salverform

trumpet-shaped

tubular

urceolate

4-parted (cruciform)

standard

wing

keel

papilionaceous

labiate

galeate

saccate

tepal

similar perianth segments (lily)

standard

syle or crest

stigma

beard

fall

dissimilar perianth segments (iris)

corona

amaryllidaceous

dorsal sepal

petal

column

lateral sepal

lip

orchidaceous (zygomorphic)

serrulate minutely or finely serrate.

sessile stalkless, usually of a leaf lacking a petiole.

seta a bristle, or bristle-shaped organ.

setaceous either bearing bristles, or bristle-like.

setiform bristle-shaped.

setose covered with sharply pointed bristles.

setulose finely or minutely setose.

sharp-pointed see acute, mucronate and pungent.

sheath a tubular structure surrounding an organ or part; most often, the basal part of a leaf surrounding the stem in Gramineae and other monocot families, either as a tube, or with overlapping edges and therefore tube-like and distinct from the leaf blade.

sheathing where the tubular or convolute base of a leaf or spathe surrounds the stem or other parts.

shrub a loose descriptive term for a woody plant which produces multiple stems, shoots or branches from its base, but does not have a distinct single trunk.

shrublet a small shrub or a dwarf, woody-based and closely branched plant.

sigmoid, sigmoidal S-shaped, curving in one direction and then the other.

silicle, silicula, silicule a short silique, no more than twice as long as broad.

siliqua, silique a thin, 2-carpelled fruit, three or more times as long as wide, dehiscing longitudinally and leaving a central frame of tissue (septum); peculiar to the Cruciferae.

simple not compound; not divided into secondary units, such as leaflets or branches, thus in one part or un-branched.

sinuate (of the outline of a margin) wavy, alternatively concave and convex. (See undulate.)

sinus the indentation or space between two divisions, e.g. between lobes.

soboliferous clump-forming, producing suckering lateral shoots from below ground, usually applied to shrubs and small trees, e.g. *Aesculus parviflora*.

solitary used either of a single flower which constitutes a whole inflorescence, or a single flower in an axil (but perhaps in a much larger overall inflorescence).

sorus (in ferns) a cluster of sporangia, generally found on the underside of the leaf blade and covered by an indusium or false indusium.

spadix the fleshy axis of a spike, often surrounded or subtended by a spathe. Typically the club- or tail-like inflorescence of Araceae.

spartoid rigidly and sharply rush-like.

spathaceous furnished with a spathe.

spathe a conspicuous leaf or bract subtending a spadix or other inflorescence, of particular importance in Araceae and Palmae, but also applied to the valves subtending scapose flowers in many other monocots.

spatheole a small or secondary spathe.

spathiform spathe-shaped.

spathulate, spatulate spatula-shaped, essentially oblong, but attenuated at the base and rounded at the apex.

species the category of taxa of the lowest principal taxonomic rank, occurring below genus level and usually containing closely related, morphologically similar individuals often found within a distinct geographical range. The species may further be divided into subspecies, variety and forma. It is the basic unit of naming, forming a binomial in combination with the generic name. The species itself is signified by a specific epithet, or trivial name.

spermatophyte a seed-bearing plant.

spicate spike-like, or borne in a spikelike inflorescence.

spiciform spike-shaped.

spiculate furnished with fine, fleshy points.

spike an indeterminate inflorescence bearing sessile flowers on an unbranched axis.

spikelet a small spike, forming one spicate part of a compound inflorescence, especially the flower head of Gramineae, composed of flowers and their bracts or glumes.

spine a modified stem or reduced branch, stiff and sharp pointed.

spinescent (1) bearing or capable of developing spines; (2) terminating in, or modified to, a spine-like tip.

spinose bearing spines.

spinule a small spine.

spinulose bearing small or sparsely distributed spines.

sporangiophore a stalk bearing a sporangium.

sporangium a sac or body which contains or produces spores, used especially of cryptogams.

spore a basic unit of reproduction, capable of developing into a gametophyte.

sporocarp (1) a spore-producing body; (2) a mass of spores in a sac or capsule.

sporophyll a leaf, or modified leaf, or leaf-like organ, which bears spores.

sporophyte in cryptogams, the vegetative, spore-bearing generation, as opposed to the gametophyte generation.

spur (1) a tubular or sac-like basal extension of the perianth, generally projecting backwards and nectariferous; (2) a short branch or branchlet, bearing whorls of leaves and fascicled flowers and fruits from closely spaced nodes.

spurred calcarate, furnished with a spur or spurs.

squamate, squamose, squamous covered with scales.

squamulose covered or furnished with small scales.

squarrose rough or hostile as a result of the outward projection of scales or bracts with reflexed tips perpendicular to the axis; also used of parts spreading at right angles from a common axis.

stalk a general term for the stem-like support of any organ, e.g. petiole, peduncle, filament, stipe etc.

stamen the male floral organ, bearing an anther, generally on a filament, and producing pollen.

staminal attached to or relating to the stamen.

staminate of the male, a unisexual, male flower, bearing stamens and no functional pistils.

staminodal relating to a staminode.

staminode a sterile stamen or stamen-like structure, either rudimentary or modified and petal-like.

standard (1) in papilionaceous flowers, the large, uppermost petal (vexillum); (2) an erect or ascending unit of the inner whorl of an *Iris* perianth.

stele the central core (vascular cylinder) of stems and roots of vascular plants.

stellate star-like, (of hairs) with branches that radiate in a star-like manner from a common point.

sterile (of sex organs) not producing viable seed, non-functional, barren; (of shoots, branches etc.) not bearing flowers; (of plants) without functional sex organs, or not producing fruit.

stigma the apical unit of a pistil which receives the pollen and normally differs in texture from the rest of the style.

stigmatic attached or relating to the stigma.

stigmatose having especially well-developed or conspicuous stigmas.

stilt-roots the oblique adventitious support roots of the mangrove, screw pine and other woody plants of warm coastal and flooded places.

stipe the stalk of a pistil or a similar small organ; also, the petiole of a fern or palm frond.

stipel (stipella, stipellae) the secondary stipule of a compound leaf, i.e. at the base of a leaflet or petiolule.

stipellate furnished with stipels.

stipitate provided with, or borne on a stipe or small stalk or stalk-like base.

stipular, stipuled see stipulate.

stipulate possessing stipules.

stipule a leafy or bractlike appendage at the base of a petiole, usually occurring in pairs and soon shed.

stolon a prostrate or trailing stem, taking root and giving rise to plantlets at its apex and sometimes at nodes.

stoloniferous producing stolons.

stoloniform resembling a stolon.

stoma (*pl.* stomata) an aperture or pore in the epidermis of a leaf or stem, allowing gaseous exchange.

stone fruit see drupe and drupelet.

stramineous straw-like, in colour, texture or shape.

straw the jointed hollow culm of grasses.

striate striped with fine longitudinal lines, grooves or ridges.

FRUITS 1

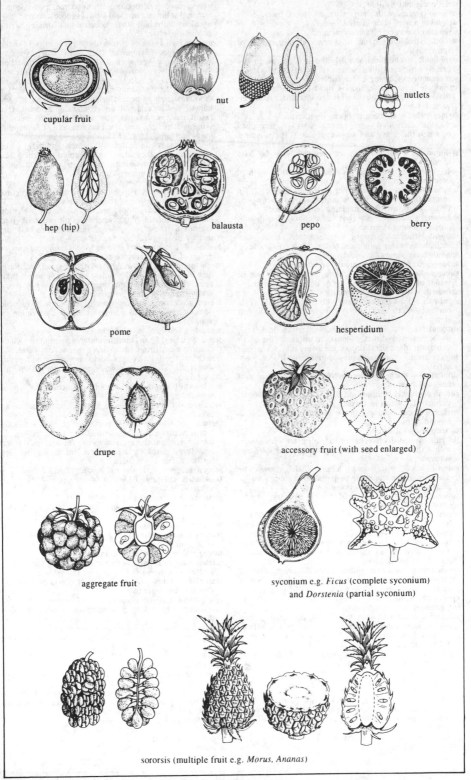

cupular fruit

nut

nutlets

hep (hip)

balausta

pepo

berry

pome

hesperidium

drupe

accessory fruit (with seed enlarged)

aggregate fruit

syconium e.g. *Ficus* (complete syconium)
and *Dorstenia* (partial syconium)

sororsis (multiple fruit e.g. *Morus, Ananas*)

strict erect and straight.

strigose covered with sharp, stiff, adpressed hairs.

strigulose minutely or finely strigose.

striolated gently or obscurely striated.

strobile, strobilus a cone, or dense cone-like cluster of sporophylls.

strobiloid, strobiliform shaped like a cone, as in the closely bracteate inflorescence of some Acanthaceae.

strophiolate possessing a strophiole.

strophiole a small swelling on the ridge caused by the fusion of the funiculus with the nucellus of an inverted ovary.

stylar, styled possessing or borne on a style.

style the elongated and narrow part of the pistil between the ovary and stigma; absent if the stigma is sessile.

stylopodium a disciform enlargement at the stylar base in some Umbelliferae.

sub- a prefix meaning (1) (in conjunction with a descriptive term) slightly, somewhat, nearly, as in subacute, meaning somewhat or slightly acute; (2) (in conjunction with an anatomical term) below or under, as in subapical, meaning below the apex.

suberous, suberose corky (not to be confused with suberose, 'somewhat erose').

subgenus the category of supplementary taxa intermediate between genus and order: see sectio above.

subimbricate somewhat overlapping.

submerged, submersed beneath the water.

subopposite more or less opposite, but with one leaf or leaflet of a pair slightly above or below its partner.

subsessile with a partial or minute stalk.

subshrub (1) a very small but truly woody shrub; (2) a perennial herb with a woody base and partially soft stems.

subtend (verb) of a bract, bracteole, spathe, leaf, etc., to be inserted directly below a different organ or structure, often sheathing or enclosing it.

subterranean, subterraneous underground, i.e. not aerial.

subulate awl-shaped, tapering from a narrow base to a fine, sharp point.

succulent thickly cellular and fleshy, a plant with roots, stems or lvs with this quality.

sucker a shoot arising from a plant's roots or underground stem.

suffrutex see subshrub.

suffruticose, suffrutescent of a subshrub, perennial, with a shrubby, woody, persistent base, and soft stem summits.

sulcate lined with deep longitudinal grooves or channels, often confined to parts possessing a single deep gulley, i.e. some petioles.

super-, supra- (in combined form) meaning above, greater than, superior to.

superior above, uppermost; a superior ovary is one borne above the insertion of the floral envelope and stamens, or of a hypanthium from which it is distinct.

suture a seam or groove marking the junction between organs such as the valves of a seed capsule, and/or the line of dehiscence.

syconium a fruit-like inflorescence characteristic of *Ficus* where the interior of the globose, fleshy, hollow receptacle is lined with flowers.

symmetric, symmetrical actinomorphic.

sympetalous see gamopetalous.

sympodial a form of growth in which the terminal bud dies or terminates in an inflorescence, and growth is continued by successive secondary axes growing from lateral buds; cf. monopodial.

synandrium an androecium composed of fused or connate anthers.

synangium a mass or cluster of connate sporangia.

synanthous (of leaves) appearing alongside the flowers; cf. hysteranthous.

syncarp an aggregate or multiple fruit produced from the connate or coherent pistils of one or more flowers, and composed of massed and more or less coalescent fruits.

syncarpous with two or more carpels fused or united in a compound pistil.

synflorescence a compound inflorescence, possessing a terminal inflorescence and lateral inflorescences.

syngenious with the anthers connate and forming a ring around the style.

synonym (syn.) one of two or more names used for the same taxon. Synonyms fall into two types – *nomenclatural* synonyms are different names based on the same type; *taxonomic* synonyms are different names based on different types that are later judged to belong to the same taxon. Of whichever sort, a synonym tends to be a later name for a taxon already named and is rejected on grounds of priority. If a taxon is recombined, its older names become synonyms of the new combination, e.g. *Chrysanthemum indicum*, a syn. of *Dendranthema indicum*.

'Synonymy' indicates all names applied to the same taxon other than its accepted or proposed name. Homonyms join the synonymy of the taxon to which they were misapplied.

synsepalous see gamosepalous.

synsepalum a calyx cup or tube; a discrete structure formed by the fusion of two or more sepals.

taproot the primary root, serving to convey nutrition and to anchor the plant; where a plant is described as taprooted, these long, deep, scarcely branched and usually fusiform roots persist in adult life.

taxon (*pl.* taxa) a general term for a taxonomic unit or group of any category or rank.

teeth marginal lobes, usually relatively small, regularly disposed and with the sides tapering toward their apex, thus differing from broad lobes or very narrow divisions; see dentate, serrate.

tendril a slender modified branch, leaf or axis, capable of attaching itself to a support either by twining or adhesion.

tentacle a sensitive glandular hair.

tepal a unit of an undifferentiated perianth, which cannot be distinguished as a sepal or petal. In orchids, the term is applied to the sepals and petals minus the labellum and was originally coined for this purpose.

terete cylindrical, and smoothly circular in cross-section.

terminal at the tip or apex of a stem, the summit of an axis.

ternate (of leaves, sepals, petals) in threes; a ternate leaf is a compound leaf divided into three leaflets; in a biternate leaf these divisions are themselves divided into three parts; in a triternate leaf these parts are further divided into three.

terrestrial growing in the soil; a land plant.

tessellated chequered, marked with a grid of small squares.

testa the outer coating of a seed.

tetra- prefix denoting four, e.g. tetrandrous, having four stamens.

tetrad a group of four.

tetradynamous having four long stamens and two short as in Cruciferae.

tetragonal, tetragonous four-angled.

tetramerous with parts in fours, or groups of four; often written as 4-merous.

tetraploid having four basic sets of chromosomes, instead of the usual two.

tetrapterous four-winged.

thallophyte a cryptogam consisting principally of a thallus.

thallus an undifferentiated vegetative growth.

theca a case; specifically, the pollen-sac in flowering plants or the capsule in bryophytes.

thorn a sharp hard outgrowth from the stem wood.

threadlike see filiform.

throat the orifice of the tubular part of a corolla, calyx or perianth, between the tube and the limb.

thyrse, thyrsus an indeterminate, paniculate or racemose primary axis, with determinate cymose or dichasially compound lateral axes.

thyrsiform, thyrsoid thyrse-like.

tomentose with densely woolly, short, rigid hairs, perceptible to the touch.

tomentulose slightly tomentose.

tomentum a tomentose pubescence.

toothed possessing teeth, usually used of margins, often interchangeably with dentate or, qualified, as saw-toothed or bluntly toothed.

tortuous irregularly bent and turned in many directions.

torulose of a cylindrical, ellipsoid or terete body, swollen and constricted at intervals but less markedly and regularly so than moniliform.

torus a receptacle, the region in which floral parts are inserted. An elongated torus is a gynophore.

trailing (of stems) prostrate but not rooting.

trapeziform asymmetrical and four-sided, as a trapezium.

tree a woody, perennial plant with a single main stem, generally branching at some distance from the ground and possessing a more or less distinct, elevated crown.

tri- prefix denoting three.

triadelphous stamens connate by their filaments in three groups or fascicles.

tribe a category of taxa intermediate between subfamily and genus.

trichome a unbranched, hair-like outgrowth of the epidermis, often glandular-tipped.

trichotomous branching regularly by dividing regularly into three.

tricolpate (of pollen grains) with three colpi (grooves).

tridentate when the teeth of a margin have teeth which are themselves toothed.

tridenticulate finely or minutely tridentate.

tridynamous when three stamens out of six are longer than the rest.

trifid as bifid, but twice cleft into three lobe-like divisions.

trifoliate three-leaved.

trifoliolate having three leaflets (a ternate leaf is trifoliolate).

trifurcate with three branches or forked in three.

trigonal three-angled.

trigonous a solid body which is triangular but obtusely angled in cross-section.

trilobed having three lobes.

trilocular having three locules.

trimerous 3-merous, with parts in threes.

trimorphic as polymorphic, or dimorphic, but occurring in three distinct forms.

trinervate three-nerved.

tripartite divided almost to the base in three segments.

tripinnate when the ultimate divisions of a bipinnate leaf are themselves pinnate.

tripinnatifid when the leaflets of a pinnatifid leaf have pinnatifid divisions which are themselves divided in a pinnatifid manner.

tripinnatisect when the leaflets of a pinnatisect leaf are divided into pinnatisect divisions which are themselves divided in a pinnatisect manner.

triplinerved (of venation) in which a midrib produces two lateral veins from a little above its base.

triploid having three basic sets of chromosomes.

tripterous three-winged.

triquetrous triangular in cross-section.

tristylous in which the styles of the flowers of a plant have three different relative lengths.

trisulcate with three grooves or furrows.

trullate, trulliform trowel-shaped.

truncate where the organ is abruptly terminated as if cut cleanly straight across, perpendicular to the mid-rib.

trunk the main stem of a tree, or the hard, thickened stem of certain primulas and cyclamens, and of tree ferns.

tryma drupaceous nut with dehiscent exocarp, as the walnut.

tuber a swollen, generally subterranean stem, branch or root used for storage.

tubercle a small, warty, conical to spherical excrescence.

tubercular, tuberculose see tuberculate.

tuberculate, tubercled covered with small, blunt, warty excrescences.

tuberiferous bearing tubers.

tuberous bearing tubers, or resembling a tuber.

tumid see turgid.

tunic a loose, dry, papery, membranous, fibrous or reticulate skin covering a bulb or corm.

tunicate (1) enclosed in a tunic; (2) having concentrically layered coats, the outermost being a tunic, like an onion.

turbinate top-shaped; inversely conical, but contracted near the apex.

turgid more or less swollen or inflated, sometimes by fluid contents.

turion a detached winter-bud, often thick and fleshy, by which aquatic plants perennate; also an adventitious shoot or sucker.

twig a small branch of a woody plant.

twiner a climbing plant that twines around a support.

type one of several categories of specimen or, less commonly, image or description, used by a taxonomist as the evidential basis of a taxon.

More loosely, the 'type of a species' describes material close or identical to the author's original idea in naming a new taxon or redefined as 'typical' as the result of later taxonomic work. In works such as the *Index*, named variants are often described by means of contrast with the 'type' or typical state of a species, e.g. 'lvs woollier than type', 'fls larger'.

umbel a flat-topped inflorescence like a corymb, but with all the flowered pedicels (rays) arising from the same point at the apex of the main axis; in a compound umbel, all the peduncles supporting each secondary umbel (umbellule) arise from a common point on their primary ray.

umbellate borne in or furnished with an umbel; resembling an umbel.

umbelliform in the form of or resembling an umbel.

umbellule the umbel which terminates a compound umbel.

umbilicate with a more or less central depression, like a navel.

umbo a rough, conical projection, arising from the centre of a surface, as the raised part of the scale in a pine-cone.

umbonate bossed; orbicular, with a point projecting from the centre.

umbraculiferous shaped like a parasol.

unarmed devoid of spines, prickles or other sharp points.

uncinate (of hairs) hooked, where the tips are acutely deflexed, or where the sides are denticulate, or bear minute, retrorse barbs.

undershrub a low shrub.

undifferentiated of parts or tissues with no apparent characters to distinguish them – e.g. the units of an undifferentiated perianth, where sepals and petals resemble each other so closely as to be indistinguishable; cf. tepal.

undulate wavy, but of the margin's surface rather than outline (see sinuate).

unguiculate of petals and sepals, bearing a basal claw.

uni- prefix denoting one.

unicarpellate possessing a single carpel.

unifoliate a simple leaf, sometimes applied to essentially compound leaves with only a single leaflet.

unifoliolate a compound leaf of which only a single leaflet remains; can be distinguished from a simple leaf by the vestigial point of articulation between the leaflet and the petiole.

uniform of one type only (by contrast with dimorphous or polymorphic).

unijugate see paired.

unilateral one-sided; borne or arranged on one side only.

unilocular, uniloculate having a single locule or cavity.

uniovular, uniovulate having a single ovule.

unisexual either staminate or pistillate; with flowers of one sex only.

united of parts usually free or separate held closely or clinging together so as to be scarcely distinguishable (e.g. stamens in tight bundles) or wholly fused forming a single whole (e.g. perianth lobes united in a tube). The term covers both adherent and coherent.

unitegmic with only one covering to the ovule.

FRUITS 2

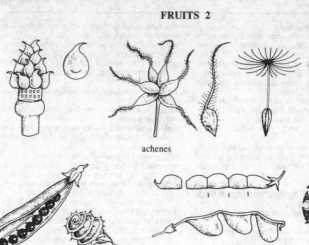

achenes

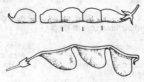

caryopsis

legume

loment

follicle

 silique silicle

Capsules (showing different modes of dehiscence)

loculicidal

septicidal

septifragal

poricidal

valvate

circumscissile
(pyxis)

utricle

schizocarp

samara

strobilus (conifer)

strobilus (angiosperm
e.g. *Humulus*)

urceolate (of a corolla) urn-shaped; globose to sub-cylindrical but with a considerable constriction at or below the mouth.

utricle a round, inflated sheath or appendage, also a bladder-like, one- to two-seeded, indehiscent fruit with a loose, thin pericarp.

vaginate possessing or enclosed by a sheath.

valid a name is valid when it is published in accordance with the Codes of Nomenclature.

valvate (1) describing parts with touching but not over-lapping margins; (2) opening by or pertaining to valves.

valve one of the parts into which a dehiscent fruit or capsule splits at maturity.

variegated marked irregularly with various colours.

varietal relating to a variety.

variety, varietas (var.) the category of taxa intermediate between subspecies and forma.

vascular possessing or pertaining to tissues or vessels which conduct water, minerals, sugar and other organic substances. Vascular plants include ferns, gymnosperms and angiosperms.

vein an externally visible strand of vascular tissues.

velamen corky epidermis of aerial roots in some epiphytes, through which atmospheric moisture is absorbed.

velutinous coated with fine soft hairs, more densely so than in tomentose and giving the appearance and texture of velvet.

velvety see velutinous.

venation the arrangement or disposition of veins on the surface of an organ.

venose possessing veins.

ventral attached or relating to the inner or adaxial sur-face or part of an organ; sometimes wrongly applied to the undersurface.

ventricose unequally swollen; inflated on one side in a more pronounced manner than if gibbous.

vermiculate worm-shaped, with a pattern of impressed, close, wavy lines.

vernal appearing in spring.

vernation the arrangement of leaves in the bud, some-times an important character for identification, as in the case of *Galanthus* where the emerging lvs have convolute (rolled), reduplicate (folded back) or flat margins if viewed in cross-section while in the sheath.

verrucose warty

verruculose finely verrucose.

versatile of an attached or supported body capable of free movement, e.g. an anther, attached to a filament by its middle and able to be rotated.

verticil a ring or whorl of three or more parts at one node.

verticillaster a false whorl where opposite cymes, being almost sessile, appear to surround the stem in a whorl.

verticillate forming or appearing to form a whorl.

vesicle a small, bladder-like sac or cavity, filled with fluid or air.

vesicular of, possessing, or composed of vesicles.

vestigial of a part or organ which was functional and fully developed in ancestral forms, but is now reduced and obsolete.

vestiture, vesture see indumentum.

vexillum the standard of a papilionaceous flower.

viable of seed, capable of germination.

villous with shaggy pubescence.

virescence the appearance of green pigmentation in plant tissues not ordinarily green.

virgate long, slim and straight, like a rod or wand.

viscid covered in a sticky or gelatinous exudation.

vitta, vittae an aromatic oil tube found in the pericarp of Umbelliferae, a similar oily gland with a dot or dash-like appearance, for example on the ovary of *Hypericum* spp.

viviparous with seeds which germinate, or buds or bulbs which become plantlets while still attached to the parent plant.

volubile twining.

whorl when three or more organs are arranged in a circle at one node or, loosely, around the same axis.

wing (1) a thin, flat, often membranous extension or appendage or an organ; (2) a lateral petal of a papilionaceous flower.

wood the lignified portion of plants.

woody ligneous, approaching the nature of wood.

woolly see lanate, lanuginose and tomentose.

xerophyte a plant adapted to survival in an arid habitat.

xerophytic adapted to withstand drought.

zygomorphic bilaterally symmetrical, having only one plane of symmetry by which it can be divided into two equal halves.

A

Aaron's Beard *Hypericum calycinum.*
Aaron's Rod *Verbascum thapsus.*
Abaca *Musa textilis.*
Abata Cola *Cola acuminata.*
Abbéville Iris *Iris* × *nelsonii.*
Abele *Populus alba.*

Abelia R. Br. Caprifoliaceae. 15 small to medium-sized shrubs, everg. to decid. Lvs opp. or in 3s, entire or toothed. Fls 1–8 in lat. cymes or term. pan.; sep. 2–5, persistent; cor. tubular, 5-lobed. China, Jap., Himal., Mex.
A. buddleoides W.W. Sm. Close to *A. triflora*; lvs smaller; sep. to 0.5×length cor. tube. SW China. Z8.
A. chinensis R. Br. non hort. Spreading decid., to 1.5m. Br. initially lanuginose. Fls fragrant, paired, in term. pan.; sep. to 0.6cm, 5, rose-tinted; cor. 1.25cm, white, downy. China. Z7.
A. chinensis hort. non R. Br. = *A.* × *grandiflora.*
A. 'Edward Goucher'. (*A.* × *grandiflora* × *A. schumannii.*) Semi-everg. Lvs close to *A.* × *grandiflora*, but fls larger, lilac-pink with orange-yellow throat. Z5.
A. engleriana (Gräbn.) Rehd. Decid. to 1.8m. Bark glossy at first, then peeling. Lvs 2–4cm, ovate-elliptic, acute, ± serrate, glab. above, ciliate. Fls paired; sep. 2; cor. to 1.6cm, rose, curved. W China. Z6.
A. floribunda Decne. Everg. to 3m. Br. arching; bark papery. Lvs to 4.5cm, ovate, acute, ± toothed, dark glossy green. Fls in nodding clusters; sep. to 0.8cm, 5, narrow, green; cor. to 5cm, pale rose to cherry pink, narrow-tubular. Mex. Z7.
A. graebneriana Rehd. Decid. to 3m. Lvs 4–5cm, ovate-acuminate, serrate, ciliolate. Fls clustered at br. tips; sep. 2, narrow; cor. 2.5cm, apricot to pink, throat yellow. C China. 'Vedrariensis': lvs larger; fls tubular, throat yellow blotched. Z5.
A. × **grandiflora** (André) Rehd. (*A. chinensis* × *A. uniflora.*) Semi-everg. to 1.8m. Branchlets downy. Lvs 1.5–6.5cm, ovate-acute, ± serrate, bronze-pink at first, hardening dark green, purple-bronze in fall. Fls clustered; sep. to 2cm, 2–5, tinted bronze-pink; cor. 2cm, white tinted pink. Origin unknown. 'Aurea': to 1.2m, spreading; lvs dark amber at first. 'Compacta': low-growing; lvs deep green, glossy; fls small, white, clustered. 'Francis Mason' ('Variegata'): to 1.5m, densely branched; lvs flushed orange-bronze at first, later green edged gold with a dark green central patch, eventually fading; fls white, profuse. 'Gold Strike': lvs variegated bright gold. 'Goldsport': to 1.5m; lvs variegated yellow; fls tubular, pink and white. 'Prostrata': to 50cm, habit spreading; lvs shiny, tinted red when young; fls small, white. Z5.
A. integrifolia Koidz. Decid. to 2m. Br. rufous then grey, fissured. Lvs 3.5–5cm, obovate-elliptic, entire. Fls usually paired; sep. to 1.8cm; cor. 2cm, white. Jap. Z6.
A. ionandra Hayata. Decid. to 1m. Bark brown-grey. Lvs 1.5cm, ovate. Infl. cymose; fls 1–2 per axil; sep. to 0.6cm, 5; cor. to 1.3cm. Taiwan. Z8.
A. longituba Rehd. = *A. schumannii.*
A. rupestris Lindl. = *A. chinensis.*
A. rupestris hort. non Lindl. = *A.* × *grandiflora.*
A. rupestris var. *grandiflora* André. = *A.* × *grandiflora.*
A. schumannii (Gräbn.) Rehd. Semi-everg., to 2m. Br. initially purple-tinted, downy. Lvs 1.5–3cm, ovate, entire or ± toothed. Fls 1 per axil; sep. 0.7cm, rounded; cor. 2.5cm, rose-pink, funnelform, gibbous, downy. C China. Z6.
A. serrata Sieb. & Zucc. Decid. to 2m. Br. rufous. Lvs 2–8cm, ovate, serrulate. Fls 1–7 per cluster; sep. to 1cm, 2–3(–4); cor. white, tinted rose or madder, downy, lobes spreading. Jap. var. *buchwaldii* (Gräbn.) Nak. Lvs and fls larger. Z6.
A. spathulata Sieb. & Zucc. Decid. to 1.2m. Br. thinly pubesc. Lvs to 5cm, oval-lanceolate to rhomboid, serrate, tinted red at first. Fls paired; sep. 5, downy, spathulate, equalling cor. to 2.5cm, broad, white marked yellow or apricot in throat. Jap. f. *colorata* (Hara & Kurosawa) H. Hara. Fl. buds dark red; fls rosy red. Jap.
A. triflora R. Br. ex Wallich. Decid. or semi-everg. to 3.5m, erect. Bark grey, riven; br. initially bristly. Lvs 3.5–7.5cm, ovate-lanceolate to linear-lanceolate. Fls 3 per cluster, fragrant; sep. to 1.6cm, 5, slender, red, feathery; cor. 2cm+, pink fading to white. NW Himal. Z6.
A. umbellata (Gräbn. & Buchw.) Rehd. Decid. to 3m. Br. pubesc. Lvs 4–7.7cm, elliptic-lanceolate, entire or toothed, edged red, glossy. Fls fragrant, 4–7 per cluster; sep. 4, obovate-lanceolate; cor. to 1.5cm, white, pale rose in bud. W China. Z7.
A. uniflora R. Br. Everg. to 1.8m. Lvs 2–5cm, ovate-acuminate, ± serrate. Fls 2–3 per axil; sep. (2–3)–4; cor. to 2.5cm, foxglove-like, opal-white, marked orange in throat. China. Z7.
A. zanderi (Gräbn.) Rehd. Decid., to 3m. Branchlets bristly at base. Lvs 7cm, ovate-lanceolate, entire or ± toothed. Fls paired; sep. 4, small, slender; cor. white tinted rose, tube to 1cm, lobes spreading. China. 'Sherwoodii': seldom exceeds 75cm. Z6.
→*Zabelia.*

Abeliophyllum Nak. WHITE FORSYTHIA. Oleaceae. 1 decid. sprawling shrub to 2m. Br. 4-angled, warty, at first tinted maroon. Lvs to 5cm, ovate-acuminate. Fls nodding, fragrant; cal. maroon-tinted; pet. 4, to 1.5cm, narrowly oblong, bright white flushed rose at base. Late winter–early spring. Korea. Z5.
A. distichum Nak. 'Roseum': fls flushed pink.

Abelmoschus Medik. Malvaceae. 15 ann. or perenn. herbs, usually pubesc. St. erect. Lvs large, usually palmately lobed. Fls solitary, axill. or in term. rac.; epical. 4–16-lobed; cal. lobes thin, toothed; pet. 5. Fr. a 5-celled capsule. OW Trop. Z9 unless treated as an ann.
A. esculentus (L.) Moench. OKRA; GUMBO; LADY'S-FINGER. Ann. to 2m, glabrate to hispid. Lvs to 20cm, lobes 5–7, toothed. Fls solitary in upper axils; pet. 4–8cm, white to yellow blotched red or purple at base. Fr. 5–20cm, 5-angled, fleshy, pod-like, green or red-skinned. OW Trop., widely nat.
A. manihot (L.) Medik. AIBIKA. Perenn. to 2m, hispid. Lvs to 45cm, lobes 3–7. Fls solitary or in rac.; pet. white to yellow, maroon at base. Fr. to 8cm, ovate-ellipsoid, deeply 5-angled. SE Asia.
A. moschatus Medik. MUSK MALLOW. Differs from *A. manihot* in linear not ovate epical. seg. and cylindrical or obscurely angled fr. on longer stalks (to 12cm). Trop. Asia. 'Mischief': compact and bushy; fls bright red with white centres. 'Pacific Light Pink': bushy, to 40cm high; fls to 10cm diam., dark pink edges blending into pale pink centre; heat and sun-tolerant. 'Pacific Orange Scarlet' ('Oriental Red'): as 'Pacific Light Pink' but fls vivid scarlet, with white centre.
→*Hibiscus.*

Abies Mill. FIR; SILVER FIR. Pinaceae. 50 everg. coniferous trees. Bark and winter buds often resinous. Lvs single, linear-acicular, flattened, keeled beneath, spirally or pectinately arranged, margins revolute; stomata ± conspicuous in 2 pale or silvery-white lines beneath, sometimes sparsely above. ♂ cones pendulous, ♀ erect, described below – the colour given is that of the unhardened cone. N Temp., C Amer.
A. alba Mill. SILVER FIR; EUROPEAN SILVER FIR; CHRISTMAS TREE. 60m. Crown regular; bark grey; br. whorled. Lvs to 3.5cm, 2-ranked, dark shiny green above, silvery beneath. Cones to 18×3.5cm, cylindric, bronze-green at first. Many cvs are available, varying in habit from the dwarf 'Microphylla' to the narrow erect 'Fastigiata', densely conical 'Pyramidalis', or the weeping 'Pendula' or 'Pendula Gracilis'. Br. may be short and upturned as in 'Columnaris', twisted as in 'Tortuosa', or few and slender, like those of 'Virgata'. Foliage varies from the dark green of 'Compacta' to the bright green of 'Tortuosa'. 'Aurea' and 'Aureovariegata' are variegated golden-coloured selections. Z4.
A. alba var. *acutifolia* Turrill. = *A. borisiiregis.*
A. amabilis Douglas ex Forbes. PACIFIC SILVER FIR; RED SILVER FIR; CHRISTMAS TREE. To 35m. Crown conic; bark smooth to soft and thick, silvery when young; br. tiered. Lvs to 3.5×0.25cm, crowded, orange-scented when crushed, truncate, dark glossy green, grooved above, white beneath. Cones to 17×7cm, conic-ovoid, deep purple. S Alask. to W Oreg. 'Compacta': broadly ovoid, dense, v. slow-growing. 'Spreading Star': low-growing, spreading; br. horizontal. Z5.
A. arizonica Merriam. = *A. lasiocarpa* ssp. *arizonica.*
A. × **arnoldiana** Nitz. (*A. koreana* × *A. veitchii.*) Hybrid resembling *A. koreana* in producing cones when young and *A. veitchii* in its luxuriant growth. 'Graciosa': cones green ripening yellow-brown. 'Violet': cones violet-purple. Z5.

A. balsamea (L.) Mill. BALM OF GILEAD; BALSAM FIR. 25m. Crown conic; bark grey; br. ascending. Lvs to 2.5cm, glossy dark green above, balsam-scented when crushed, 2-ranked, apex rounded with a glaucous patch. Cones to 8×2.5cm, oblong-cylindric, gummy, purple ripening brown-grey. N Amer. Cvs vary in habit from the low, spreading, compact 'Andover' and the dwarf rounded 'Nana' to the erect 'Columnaris'. Foliage colour varies: 'Coerulea' is green above, silver beneath, 'Coerulescens' is silver-blue, 'Lutescens' is straw-yellow, becoming bronze, and 'Nana' is dark green above, pale yellow beneath with white stomatal bands. 'Denudata' and 'Nudicaulis' form a single unbranched st. f. *hudsonia* (Jacques) Fern. & Weatherby. Habit dwarf, broad. Lvs short, broad, blue-green beneath. var. *phanerolepis* Fern. Cone bracts exserted, reflexed. Z2.

A. beissneriana Rehd. & Wils. = *A. recurvata* var. *ernestii*.

A. bifida Sieb. & Zucc. = *A. firma*.

A. borisiiregis Mattf. (*A. alba* ×*A. cephalonica*?) To 45m. Lvs to 3cm, dark green above with 2 glaucous bands beneath, crowded, acute or emarginate, ridged above. Cones to 18×3.5cm, cylindric to conic; bracts exserted, reflexed. Balk. Z6.

A. bornmuelleriana Mattf. = *A. nordmanniana* ssp. *equitrojani*.

A. brachyphylla Maxim. = *A. homolepis*.

A. bracteata (D. Don) D. Don ex Poit. BRISTLECONE FIR; SANTA LUCIA FIR. To 40m. Crown dense becoming open and conical; bark red-brown, smooth. Buds long, narrow. Lvs to 6×0.4cm, 2-ranked, spine-tipped, dark, rigid, glossy, obscurely grooved. Cones to 8×0.5cm, ovoid, golden-green; bracts long, spine-tipped, exserted. SW Calif. Z7.

A. cephalonica Loud. GREEK FIR; GRECIAN FIR. To 40m. Crown conic; br. low, spreading; bark grey. Lvs to 3×0.3cm, radially arranged, rigid, acuminate. Cones to 18×2.5cm, cylindric, tapering, brown. Greece. 'Meyer's Dwarf': broad, low habit; branchlets rigid; lvs short. Other variants have been described but are uncommon in cult. var. *graeca* (Fraas) Liu. Lvs emarginate. Cone bracts long, exserted, reflexed. N & E Greece. Z5.

A. chengii Rushforth. (*A. forrestii* ×*A. chensiensis*?) To 25m. Bark grey, smooth. Lvs to 6×0.3cm, adpressed or spreading, 2-ranked, dark glossy green above with pale bands beneath, apex cleft. Cones to 9cm, cylindric-ovoid, pale purple. SW China. Z7.

A. chensiensis Tieghem. SHENSI FIR. To 55m. Crown columnar; bark grey to dark brown. Lvs to 4×0.3cm, ascending, 2-ranked, apex acute, obtuse or incised. Cones to 10×3cm, ovoid-oblong to cylindric, green. N China. ssp. *salouenensis* (Borderes & Gauss.) Rushforth. Lvs to 7.5cm. SW Yunnan to Assam. ssp. *yulongxueshanensis* Rushforth. Cones to 14×4cm. NW Yunnan. Z6.

A. cilicica (Antoine & Kotschy) Carr. CILICIAN FIR. To 35m. Crown narrowly conic; bark grey; br. whorled, decurved to ascending. Lvs to 4×0.2cm, loosely pectinate, apex rounded or emarginate. Cones to 24×4cm, cylindric, red-brown. S Turk., NW Syr., Leb. Z5.

A. coahuilensis Johnst. = *A. durangensis* var. *coahuilensis*.

A. colimensis Rushforth & Narave. To 30m. Bark smooth, silver-grey to brown; lower br. horizontal, upper ascending. Lvs to 4×0.2cm, curved, adpressed, glaucous, acute. Cones to 14×8cm, ovoid-conic, purple. SW Mex. Z8.

A. concolor (Gordon & Glend.) Lindl. ex Hildebr. WHITE FIR; COLORADO FIR. To 50m. Crown conic to columnar; bark pale grey, rough; br. whorled, spreading. Lvs to 6×0.25cm, scattered, falcate, apex acute to rounded, blue-green. Cones 12×4cm, cylindric, tapering, green to green-purple. US. Cvs range in habit and form from the dwarf 'Globosa' and 'Compacta' to the erect 'Fastigiata' and the weeping 'Pendula' and 'Gables Weeping'. Foliage is variable: 'Violacea' is a v. bright glaucous blue-green tree; 'Albospica' has white lvs that become grey-green; those of 'Archer's Dwarf' are powder blue, 'Candicans' has lvs silver-white; 'Husky Pup' is dark green, 'Aurea' is gold, becoming silver-grey, and lvs of 'Wintergold' become deep yellow in winter. ssp. *lowiana* (Gordon) E. Murray. SIERRA WHITE FIR; PACIFIC WHITE FIR; LOW'S FIR. To 70m. Crown narrow-conic, regular. Upper lvs to 6×0.2cm in 2 ranks. Cones to 9×3cm, green at first. Z4.

A. delavayi Franch. DELAVAY'S FIR. To 25m. Crown candelabriform; br. ascending. Lvs to 4×0.2cm, radially arranged, flexible, sometimes curved, midrib prominent beneath, margins revolute, bright green above, stomatal bands silver beneath. Cones to 12×4cm, narrow-cylindric, dark blue to violet, ripening black. China to NE India and N Burm. 'Major Neishe' ('Nana'): dwarf, to 2m; buds orange-brown. Z7.

A. delavayi var. *fabri* (Mast.) Hunt = *A. fabri*.

A. delavayi var. *faxoniana* (Rehd. & Wils.) A.B. Jackson = *A. fargesii*.

A. delavayi var. *forestii* (C. Coltm.) A.B. Jackson = *A. forrestii*.

A. delavayi var. *smithii* (Vig. & Gauss.) Liu = *A. forrestii*.

A. densa Griff. SIKKIM FIR. To 25m. Bark smooth, riven at base. Lvs to 4.5×0.25cm, radially arranged, margins revolute. Cones to 10×4.5cm, cylindric. Sometimes misnamed *A. spectabilis*. E Nepal, Sikkim, Bhutan, NW Assam. Z8.

A. durangensis Martinez. To 35m. Crown narrowly conic; bark dark brown, tinged red or grey, riven. Lvs to 3.5×0.2cm, pale green, grooved above, obtuse. Cones to 10×3cm, oblong-cylindric, fawn to violet. NW Mex. var. *coahuilensis* (Johnst.) Martinez. Shoots greener and more pubesc. Z8.

A. ernestii Rehd. = *A. recurvata* var. *ernestii*.

A. excelsior Franco = *A. grandis*.

A. fabri (Mast.) Craib. FABER'S FIR. To 25m. Bark grey, furrowed. Lvs to 3×0.25cm, 2-ranked, dark green above, bright white beneath, apex emarginate, revolute. Cones to 9×5cm, blue-black. W China. ssp. *minensis* (Borderes & Gauss.) Rushforth. Winter buds strongly purple (not green tinged purple), lvs flatter, longer pectinately arranged. Z7.

A. fargesii Franch. To 30m. Crown conic, becoming flat. Lvs to 3×0.25cm in 2 or more ranks, dark green, grooved above, with 2 glaucous bands beneath, acute or cleft. Cones to 8×4cm, violet. C & NW China. Z6.

A. fargesii hort. non Franch. = *A. chengii*.

A. faxoniana Rehd. & Wils. = *A. fargesii*.

A. firma Sieb. & Zucc. JAPANESE FIR; MOMI FIR. To 35m+. Crown broadly conic; bark grey, tinged yellow or pink, becoming corky; br. spreading to ascending. Lvs to 3.5×0.25cm, pectinately arranged, rigid, cleft or blunt, pale green, furrowed above, contracted at base. Cones to 15×5cm, usually smaller, green tinged yellow. Jap. 'Bedgebury': low-growing; lvs dense, pale green. Z6.

A. flinckii Rushforth. To 35m. Bark smooth, grey, becoming scaly; br. outspread to decurved. Lvs 3.5–7×0.2cm, in 2–3 rows, mid-green, cleft or blunt. Cones to 16×5cm, long-conic to cylindric, green-brown or purple. SW Mex. Z9.

A. forrestii C. Coltm. To 30m. Crown conic; bark grey, smooth, becoming cracked, plated and riven. Lvs to 4×0.25cm, dark green above, silvery beneath, pectinately arranged, ridged above, blunt or cleft. Cones to 11×5cm, ovoid or cylindric, blue-black to purple. W China. var. *smithii* Vig. & Gauss. Shoots densely hairy. Z7.

A. fraseri (Pursh) Poir. To 20m. Crown conic; bark smooth, becoming cracked. Lvs to 2×0.25cm, blunt or notched, dark green, grooved above, silvery beneath. Cones to 7×2.5cm, ovoid to oblong-cylindric, purple or green tinged yellow, bracts long-exserted. E US. 'Coerulea': low-growing, vigorous, spreading. 'Prostrata': low-growing; br. horizontal, branchlets pale with red-tinged down; lvs pale above, white beneath. Z4.

A. gamblei Hickel. To 30m. Crown conic to columnar; bark grey. Young shoots pale red-brown. Lvs to 4cm, radially arranged, grooved above, glossy green, acute or notched. Cones to 14×5cm, conic, purple-blue. NW India. Z7.

A. georgei Orr. = *A. forrestii* var. *smithii*.

A. gracilis Komar. = *A. sachalinensis* var. *gracilis*.

A. grandis (Douglas ex D. Don) Lindl. GIANT FIR; GRAND FIR. Fast-growing, to 75m. Crown conic to broken columnar; bark blistered, brown, becoming grey-brown, ridged; br. arching to ascending. Lvs to 4.5×0.2cm, pectinately arranged, grooved above, bright green above with 2 glaucous bands beneath, cleft, aromatic. Cones to 10×3.5cm, cylindric, tapering, green. NW Amer. 'Aurea': young growth golden-yellow. 'Compacta': dwarf; lvs 1–1.5cm. 'Crassa': compact. 'Pendula': br. weeping. var. *idahoensis* Silba. To 55m. Lvs to 5cm, less regularly arranged. Cones shorter and broader. Z6.

A. guatemalensis Rehd. To 50m. Bark smooth, grey, scaly; br. level to decurved. Lvs 1.5–5×0.13cm, 2-ranked, bright green, apex cleft. Cones to 10×4cm, ovoid-cylindric, green-brown or purple. Guat., Hond., El Salvador. var. *tacanensis* (Lundell) Martinez. Lvs shorter and denser. Cone bracts longer (exserted to 2mm). S Mex. Z9.

A. hickelii Flous & Gauss. To 30m. Crown conic; br. level; bark smooth, grey, becoming fissured, plated. Lvs to 3.5×0.15cm, pectinately arranged, green above, apex rounded or notched. Cones to 8×3.5cm, green-purple, bracts exserted. SE Mex. var. *oaxacana* (Martinez) Farjon & Silba. Cones to 12×5cm; bracts shorter. Z8.

A. hirtella (HBK) Lindl. = *A. religiosa*.

A. holophylla Maxim. MANCHURIAN FIR. To 25m. Bark yellow-brown to grey, ridged, exfoliating in scales. Lvs to 4.5×0.2cm, crowded, leathery, shiny green, acuminate. Cones to 14×4cm, green, gummy. Korea, Manch. Z5.

A. homolepis Sieb. & Zucc. NIKKO FIR. To 40m. Crown broadly conic; br. slightly ascending; bark yellow to pink-grey, flaking. Lvs to 3×0.2cm, densely pectinately arranged, dark green above with 2 chalky bands beneath, blunt or cleft. Cones to 11×3cm, cylindric, smooth, gummy, green tinged purple. C & S

Jap. 'Prostrata': low-spreading; lvs profuse, glossy dark green. 'Scottiae': dwarf. 'Shelter Island': semi-prostrate, growth irregular; foliage golden-yellow. 'Tomomi': slender, br. sparse. var. **umbellata** (Mayr) Wils. Cone apices dimpled. Possibly *A. homolepis* × *A. firma*. Z4.

A. hudsonia Jacques = *A. balsamea* f. *hudsonia*.

A. ×*insignis* Carr. ex Bailly. (*A. pinsapo* × *A. nordmanniana*.) Fr. 'Andreana': lvs lax, spreading, central lvs erect. 'Beissneriana': lvs distichous, unequal, central lvs erect. 'Kentiana': lvs regular, upturned, dense, silvery. 'Mastersiana': lat. lvs spreading, central lvs ascending, forward-pointing. 'Pendula': br. weeping, close to the trunk. 'Speciosa': lvs radially arranged. Z6.

A. kawakamii (Hayata) Itô. FORMOSAN FIR; TAIWAN FIR. To 35m. Crown open, conic; bark corky, grey-tan. Lvs to 2.5×0.2cm, glaucous at first then green with 2 pale lines beneath, apex rounded, shallowly cleft. Cones to 11×4cm, ovoid-cylindric, apex rounded, purple. Taiwan. Z6.

A. koreana Wils. To 15m. Crown broadly conic; bark rough. Lvs to 2cm, crowded, radially arranged, apex acute or notched, dark glossy green above, white beneath. Cones to 8×2.5cm, cylindric, purple or green at first, apex tapering. S Korea. Cvs vary in habit from the dwarf spherical 'Silberkugel' or prostrate 'Piccolo' and 'Prostrate Beauty' to forms v. similar to the sp. Foliage colour is from blue-green ('Blauer Pfiff'), dense dark green ('Horstmann') or dull green tinged yellow ('Nisbet'). 'Silberlocke' is slow-growing with lvs twisted upwards, silver beneath. 'Blue Standard' and 'Brevifolia' produce violet cones, while 'Compact Dwarf' and 'Piccolo' have brown buds. Z5.

A. lasiocarpa (Hook.) Nutt. SUBALPINE FIR; ALPINE FIR. To 25m. Crown narrowly conic to columnar; bark thin, smooth, silver grey or grey-brown. Lvs to 4×0.15cm, pale grey-green, ridged, apex rounded or notched, in a loose, brush-like arrangement. Cones to 13×3cm, cylindric-conic, dark purple; scales orange-pubesc. N Amer. 'Compacta': dense, conic dwarf; lvs silver-blue. 'Green Globe': globose, dwarf, densely branched. 'Nana': dwarf, slow-growing. 'Roger Watson': broad, conical, dwarf; foliage grey-green. ssp. *arizonica* (Merriam) E. Murray. CORKBARK FIR. Bark creamy, corky. Lvs densely arranged, steel-blue. 'Argentea' ('Glauca'): lvs silver-white. Z5.

A. lowiana (Gordon) A. Murray = *A. concolor* ssp. *lowiana*.

A. magnifica A. Murray RED FIR; CALIFORNIAN RED FIR. To 60m. Crown narrow-conic; bark smooth, grey to red-brown, fissured. Lvs to 4×0.1cm, grey-green or blue-green, carinate, sparse, obtuse. Cones to 25×9cm, broadly-cylindric, golden-green or purple. S Oreg. to Calif. 'Glauca': lvs deep glaucous green. 'Nana': dwarf, low, spreading. 'Prostrata': br. prostrate, spreading; lvs glaucous. var. *shastensis* Lemmon. Cones to 16×7cm with bracts exserted, not included as above. Z5.

A. mariesii Mast. To 30m. Lower br. downswept, upper ascending; bark pale grey, smooth, becoming dark grey. Young shoots red-brown, downy. Lvs to 2.5×0.2cm, densely arranged, glossy dark green above with silvery bands beneath, apex rounded, cleft. Cones to 11×4.5cm, ellipsoid-conic, purple. Jap. Z6.

A. mariesii var. *kawakamii* Hayata = *A. kawakamii*.

A. marocana Trabut. = *A. pinsapo* var. *marocana*.

A. mexicana Martinez. To 30m. Crown conic; br. level; bark grey-brown cracked in square plates. Lvs to 2.5×0.2cm, pectinately arranged, olive-green. Cones to 10×4cm, yellow-green. NE Mex. Z8.

A. momi Sieb. = *A. firma*.

A. nebrodensis (Lojac.) Mattei. SICILIAN FIR. To 25m. Crown conic, broad then spreading, flat. Lvs to 2×0.2cm, densely, spreading, acute or bluntly cleft. Cones to 18×3.5cm, cylindric-ellipsoid. N Sicily. Z7.

A. nephrolepis (Trautv. ex Maxim.) Maxim. MANCHURIAN FIR; KHINGAN FIR. To 35m. Bark grey-brown, smooth then fissured. Lvs to 2.5×0.2cm, outspread, crowded, yellow-green, grooved above, blunt. Cones to 7×2.5cm, cylindric to ovoid-oblong, purple or green tinged red. Manch., Korea, N China. 'Elegans': compact: lvs bright green. Z3.

A. nobilis (Douglas & Lamb.) Lindl. = *A. procera*.

A. nordmanniana (Steven) Spach. CAUCASIAN FIR; CHRISTMAS TREE. To 55m. Crown conic becoming columnar; br. whorled and downswept. Lvs to 3×0.2cm, glossy, dark green above, silvery beneath, ridged above apex notched (often persisting for many years). Cones to 18×4.5cm, red tinged green. Cauc., NE Turk. Cvs vary in habit from the upright 'Erecta' and pendent 'Jansen', 'Pendula' (semi-prostrate, spreading, tips pendulous), to dwarf forms which may be prostrate ('Horizontalis') or conic ('Refracta'). Foliage colour is from pale green ('Nana Compacta') to blue-green ('Glauca') and yellow ('Aurea'). 'Golden Spreader' ('Aurea Nana') is dwarf with spreading br. and pale yellow lvs. 'Tortifolia': lvs twisted, falcate, irregular. ssp. *equitrojani* (Asch. & Sint. ex Boiss.) Coode & Cullen. Lvs to 4.5×0.2cm, some stomata present above near apex. Z4.

A. nordmanniana ssp. *bornmuelleriana* (Mattf.) Coode & Cullen. = *A. nordmanniana* ssp. *equitrojani*.

A. numidica Delannoy ex Carr. ALGERIAN FIR. To 35m. Crown conic, dense. Lvs to 2×0.3cm, crowded, ascending, brush-like, grey-blue with broad stomatal bands beneath and apical zone above. Cones to 18×4cm, cylindric, erect, green bloomed violet. NE Alg. 'Glauca': lvs short, broad, radially set, blue to dark blue, stomatal lines white. 'Lawrenceville': dwarf; lvs pale green. 'Nana': dwarf; lvs blue-green. 'Pendula': br. weeping. Z6.

A. oaxacana Martinez = *A. hickelii* var. *oaxacana*.

A. pectinata DC. = *A. alba*.

A. pectinata var. *nebrodensis* Lojac. = *A. nebrodensis*.

A. pectinata var. *equitrojani* Asch. & Sint. ex Boiss. = *A. nordmanniana* ssp. *equitrojani*.

A. pichta Forbes = *A. sibirica*.

A. pindrow Royle. WEST HIMALAYAN FIR. To 40m. Crown narrow-conic to columnar; bark smooth, grey tinged yellow to grey-brown, fissured. Lvs to 8×0.2cm, slender, drooping or short, semi-erect, dark green above with grey-green bands beneath, apex cleft. Cones to 16×4.5cm, often smaller, strong purple-blue. W Himal. var. *intermedia* Henry. Lvs to 5.5cm, convex beneath, pectinately arranged. (*A. pindrow* × *A. spectabilis*?). Z8.

A. pindrow var. *brevifolia* Dallim. & A.B. Jackson = *A. gamblei*.

A. pinsapo Boiss. SPANISH FIR; HEDGEHOG FIR. To 35m. Crown broadly conic; br. crowded, whorled; bark smooth, rusty brown, becoming rough. Lvs to 1.8×0.3cm, radially arranged, rigid, dark green with blue-white bands. Cones to 16×3.4cm, green bloomed pink or violet. S Spain. Z8. 'Argentea': lvs silver to tinged blue-grey. 'Aurea': slow-growing; young lvs light gold. 'Clarke': dwarf, v. slow-growing (1m in 20 years). 'Fastigiata': dense and columnar; br. short. 'Glauca': dwarf, becoming arboreal with age; lvs glaucous. 'Hamondii': dwarf, spreading, st. short. 'Horstmann': br. short, twiggy; foliage silver-blue. 'Kelleris' ('Keller'); hardy dwarf; lvs thick and waxy, sea-blue. 'Nana': dwarf, v. slow-growing (1m in 20 years). 'Pygmaea': dense, conic dwarf. 'San Diego Creeper': procumbent; lvs glossy green. var. *marocana* (Trabut) Ceballos & Bolaños. MOROCCAN FIR. Lvs more pectinately arranged with fewer stomata above. N Moroc. var. *tazaotana* (Cozar ex Huguet) Pourtet. Taller with resinous buds and cones larger, green bloomed white. N Moroc. Z6.

A. procera Rehd. NOBLE FIR; CHRISTMAS TREE. To 70m. Crown conic, slender or broad, irregular; bark smooth, silver-grey, blistered, later brown, fissured. Lvs to 3.5cm, arranged to sides and along upper surface of shoots, upper lvs longest, blue-green with glaucous stomatal bands. Cones to 23×7cm, oblong-cylindric, purple; bracts long-exserted, reflexed. NW US. 'Aurea': lvs bright golden-yellow. 'Blaue Hexe': broad, flat, globose; br. short and dense. 'Glauca' ('Argentea'): lvs silver-blue; profusely cone-bearing. 'Glauca Prostrata': low, flat, spreading; lvs silver-blue. 'Jeddeloh': dwarf, flat, globose; lvs green-blue. 'Noble': dwarf, broad, br. becoming erect; lvs blue, dense, smaller at the br. base and apex. 'Prostrata': dwarf; habit irregular, flat, bushy. 'Sherwoodii': lvs golden-yellow. Z5.

A. recurvata Mast. MIN FIR. To 25m (taller in wild). Crown conic, then flat, spreading; bark rough, flaking, brown or grey-brown sometimes tinted orange. Lvs to 2.5×0.2cm, thick, rigid, glossy green, acute. Cones to 8×3.5cm, ovoid to oblong, purple. China. var. *ernestii* (Rehd.) Kuan. Cones to 3.5cm, bloomed grey above. Z6.

A. religiosa (HBK) Schldl. & Cham. SACRED FIR. To 60m. Crown conic; bark smooth brown-grey, later scaly, rough. Lvs to 4×0.2cm, above and to either side of shoot, dark green above with pale bands beneath, curved and tapered, acute. Cones to 16×5cm, cylindric-conic, tapering to apex, purple-blue. C & S Mex., Guat. Z8.

A. sachalinensis (Schmidt) Mast. SAKHALIN FIR. To 30m. Bark pale-grey, fissured. Shoots not densely white-pubesc. (cf. *A. sibirica*). Lvs to 3×0.1cm, with dull or green-white stomatal bands, apex round or notched. Cones to 7×2.3cm, cylindric, green tinged yellow or violet; bracts exserted or slightly reflexed. N Jap. var. *gracilis* (Komar.) Farjon. Lvs flatter. Kamchatka. var. *mayriana* Miyabe & Kudô. Bark smooth. Cone bracts longer, reflexed. Z5.

A. salouenensis Borderes & Gauss. = *A. chensiensis* ssp. *salouenensis*.

A. semenovii B. Fedtsch. = *A. sibirica* ssp. *semenovii*.

A. sibirica Ledeb. To 35m. Crown narrow-conic; bark smooth, grey, with resin blisters, shoots densely white-pubesc. Lvs to 3×0.1cm, radially arranged on upper surface of shoot, aromatic, apex acute or emarginate. Cones to 7.5×3cm, cylindric, tinged blue. Cvs, valued in Canada and US for cold-tolerance, range in habit from the conic, dwarf 'Compacta Glauca' to the large, shortly branched 'Monstrosa' and the erect, vertically branched

'Candelabrum'. Foliage colour is from dark green to glaucous; 'Alba' is pale green above, white beneath, while 'Variegata' has some yellow-white lvs. ssp. *semenovii* (B. Fedtsch.) Farjon. To 40m. Shoots yellow brown, not silver-grey or beige, as in type, buds only slighty resinous. Tienshan Mts. Z1.

A. *sibirica* var. *nephrolepis* Trautv. = A. *nephrolepis*.

A. *sikokiana* Nak. = A. *veitchii* var. *sikokiana*.

A. *spectabilis* (D. Don) Spach HIMALAYAN FIR. To 30m. Crown conic, broad; br. spreading then ascending; bark scaly, rough. Buds large, globose, sticky. Lvs to 5×0.3cm, linear, tough, 4-ranked, dark green above, silvery beneath, apex bifid. Cones to 15×5cm, cylindric to oblong-ovoid, pale blue-grey. Himal. 'Affinis': lvs blue-green beneath. 'Obovata': lvs white beneath. Z7.

A. *spectabilis* hort. non (D. Don) Spach. = A. *densa*.

A. *squamata* Mast. FLAKY FIR. To 15m in cult., 40m in wild. Crown columnar; bark red-brown, peeling and shaggy. Lvs to 2.5×0.2cm, crowded, spreading below shoot, grey-green, apex acute or cleft. Cones to 6×3.5cm, ovoid, violet. SW China. Z6.

A. *subalpina* Engelm. = A. *lasiocarpa*.

A. *sutchuenensis* (Franch.) Rehd. & Wils. = A. *fargesii*.

A. *tazaotana* Cozar ex Huguet. = A. *pinsapo* var. *tazaotana*.

A. ×*vasconcellosiana* Franco. (A. *pindrow* ×A. *pinsapo*.) Close to A. *pindrow* in habit; lvs 1–3cm, ± curved, glossy dark green above with 2 silvery bands beneath. Gdn origin. 'Amaral Franco': crown conic, dense.

A. *veitchii* Lindl. CHRISTMAS TREE. To 35m. Crown narrow-conic; br. short, spreading; bark grey, smooth, paler towards crown, fluted below. Lvs to 3×0.18cm, ranked along upper surface of br. and forward-pointing, pliable, apex truncate, cleft, glossy dark green above, silver beneath. Cones to 7×2.5cm, cylindric, blue-purple or green. S & C Jap. var. *sikokiana* (Nak.) Kusaka. Lvs to 2.5cm. Midway in appearance between type and A. *koreana*. Z3.

A. *veitchii* var. *sachalinensis* Schmidt. = A. *sachalinensis*.

A. *vejarii* Martinez. To 40m. Crown conic; br. level; bark smooth, grey, then scaly, fissured. Lvs to 2×0.1cm, forward-pointing and upcurved, grey-green to glaucous blue. Cones to 15×5cm, ovoid-cylindric, stout, blue-grey with orange down at base of scales. NE Mex. Z7.

A. *vejarii* var. *mexicana* (Martinez) Liu. = A. *mexicana*.

A. *venusta* (Douglas) K. Koch. = A. *bracteata*.

A. ×*vilmorinii* Mast. (A. *cephalonica* ×A. *pinsapo*.) Crown broadly conic. Lvs to 3×0.2cm, close to A. *pinsapo*, dark green above, silvery beneath. Cones to 16×3cm, tapering. Z6.

A. *webbiana* Lindl. = A. *spectabilis*.

Abromeitiella Mez. Bromeliaceae. 2 low-growing everg. perenn. Lvs triangular, fleshy, rigid, spiny, scurfy, in small rosettes forming a broad cushion. Infl. term., long-stalked, branched; fls in 3s; pet. & sep. twisted, yellow-green. S Boliv., NW Arg. Z9.

A. *brevifolia* (Griseb.) Cast. Lvs to 2cm, spiny only at base. Sep. to 13mm; pet. bright green, basal scale not fringed. S Boliv.

A. *chlorantha* (Speg.) Mez. = A. *brevifolia*.

A. *lorentziana* (Mez) Cast. Lvs to 3cm, spiny throughout. Sep. to 16mm; pet. green, basal scale fringed. NW Arg.

A. *pulvinata* Mez. = A. *brevifolia*.

→*Dyckia*.

Abronia Juss. SAND VERBENA. Nyctaginaceae. c35 trailing or decumbent, ann. or perenn. herbs, often viscid. Lvs fleshy. Fls fragrant, in a head subtended by conspicuous bracts; perianth tubular to salverform, limb small, 4–5-lobed. Summer. W N Amer. Z8.

A. *alba* var. *platyphylla* (Standl.) Jeps. = A. *umbellata*.

A. *arenaria* Menz. = A. *latifolia*.

A. *californica* Rausch. = A. *umbellata*.

A. *crux-maltae* Kellogg. Erect or procumbent, much-branched, villous-viscid ann. Lvs 2–6cm, broadly ovate to elliptic-oblong. Fls 2–2.5cm, rose, throat green. SW Calif.

A. *cycloptera* A. Gray. Erect or decumbent perenn., sparsely gland. or glab. Lvs to 7.5cm. Fls to 3.5cm, bright pink. Tex., Mex.

A. *fragrans* Nutt. Tufted, branching, semi-erect perenn., viscid-villous. Lvs ovate to elliptic. Fls to 2.5cm, white, sweetly scented. S Dak., Idaho, Ariz.

A. *latifolia* Eschsch. YELLOW SAND VERBENA. St. to 1m, viscid. Lvs 1–6cm, ovate to orbicular. Fls to 1.8cm, tube yellow-green, limb broad, yellow. Coastal Calif. to BC.

A. *maritima* Nutt. ex S. Wats. Perenn. St. to 1m, much-branched, somewhat succulent, prostrate, glandular-villous. Lvs to 6cm, ovate to ovate-lanceolate. Fls to 1.4cm, dark crimson to red-purple. Coastal Calif., Baja Calif.

A. *pinetorum* Abrams. = A. *villosa* var. *aurita*.

A. *platyphylla* Standl. = A. *umbellata*.

A. *pogonantha* Heimerl. MOJAVE SAND VERBENA. Trailing perenn., glandular-villous. Lvs 1–4cm, oblong-ovate to suborbicular. Fls 1.2–1.8cm, white to rose-pink tube v. slender, limb 0.8cm wide. Mojave and Colorado deserts to Ariz., Calif.

A. *rosea* Hartw. ex Loud. = A. *umbellata*.

A. *rotundifolia* Gaertn. f. = A. *umbellata*.

A. *umbellata* Lam. PINK SAND VERBENA; BEACH SAND VERBENA. Prostrate ann. or perenn., glab. to viscid-pubesc. Lvs ovate-linear, acute. Fls rose-pink, in dense term. clusters, lightly fragrant; bracts pink or white. Coastal Calif. to BC. 'Grandiflora': lvs and fls larger. 'Rosea': fls paler pink. ssp. *platyphylla* St. viscid-villous. Lvs 1.5–3cm, suborbicular to broadly elliptic. (Standl.) Munz.

A. *villosa* S. Wats. Much-branched ann., procumbent to ascending, st. viscid. Lvs oblong-ovate to suborbicular. Fls 1.2–1.6cm, purple-rose, limb 1cm wide, white tinged pink. Nevada, Ariz., S Calif., Baja Calif. var. *aurita* (Abrams) Jeps.

Abrotanella Cass. Compositae. c16 dwarf cushion-forming perenn. herbs. Lvs closely imbricate. Cap. discoid, term., small; flts tubular, usually purple-brown. Aus., NZ, New Guinea, temp. S Amer. Z7.

A. *emarginata* (Cass. ex Gaudich.) Cass. Forming small, mossy cushions or mats. Lvs 2–5mm, oblong, truncate and forked at apex. Cap. sessile. Spring–summer. Southern S Amer.

A. *forsterioides* (Hook. f.) Benth. Forming green velvety cushions in large patches. Lvs 4–6mm, oblong, acuminate. Cap. stalked. Tasm.

A. *marginata* hort. = A. *emarginata*.

Absinthe *Artemisia absinthium*.

Abutilon Mill. FLOWERING MAPLE; PARLOUR MAPLE; INDIAN MALLOW. Malvaceae. 150 glab. or pubesc. perenn. or ann. herbs, shrubs, trees. Lvs cordate-ovate to elliptic, simple to palmately lobed, entire or toothed. Fls solitary or grouped in axils, sometimes arranged in rac. or pans.; epical. 0; cal. shallowly tubular, lobes 5; pet. obovate, ± erect, 5; sta. many fused in a tubular column. Early spring–autumn. Trop. and subtrop.

A. *avicennae* Gaertn. = A. *theophrasti*.

A. *bedfordianum* St.-Hil. Small tree. St. glab. Lvs to 20cm, ovate-acuminate, serrate, glab. Fls 1–2 per axil; pet. to 3.5cm, yellow veined red, equalling staminal column. Braz. Z9.

A. *darwinii* Hook. f. Velutinous shrub to 2m. Lvs to 15cm, cordate, lobes (0–)3–7, minutely toothed. Fls 1–3 per axil, drooping; pet. to 4cm, orange-red veined blood red; staminal column dark red. Braz. Z8.

A. *esculentum* St.-Hil. = A. *purpurascens*.

A. *globosum* hort. = A. ×*hybridum*.

A. *grandiflorum* hort. non G. Don. = A. ×*hybridum*.

A. *graveolens* (Roxb. ex Hornem.) Wight & Arn. = A. *hirtum*.

A. *hirtum* (Lam.) Sweet. Viscid-pubesc. perenn. herb to 2.5m. Lvs to 7cm, rounded to cordate-acuminate, downy, toothed. Fls in a term. pseudopanicle; pet. to 2cm, orange-yellow, dark red at centre. Trop. Afr., Asia and Aus.; nat. C & S Amer. Z9.

A. ×*hybridum* hort. CHINESE LANTERN. Shrub to 2–5m, glabrate. Lvs 0–5-lobed, often variegated. Fls 1 per axil, long-stalked, drooping; pet. to 5cm, white, red, yellow or orange. 'Album': lvs dark green; fls soft white. 'Amsterdam': habit compact; fls v. open, red tinted orange. 'Apricot' ('Apricot Belle'): lvs pubesc.; fls salmon, veins darker. 'Ashford Red': lvs large, light green; fls vibrant soft red. 'Boule de Neige': v. vigorous; fls white. 'Canary Bird': fls lemon. 'Cannington Carol': dwarf; lvs variegated gold; fls flaming orange. 'Cerise Queen': fls pinky red. 'Clementine Variegated': compact; lvs marbled white; fls scarlet. 'Crimson Belle': fls royal red. 'Cynthia Pike': fls red and apricot. 'Golden Fleece': lvs crenate, downy, obscurely lobed; fls rich yellow. 'Kentish Belle': fls flaming orange. 'Louise Marignac': fls pale pink. 'Luteum': fls chrome yellow. 'Master Michael': fls wavy, vermilion. 'Moonchimes': dwarf; fls large, intense yellow. 'Nabob': lvs dark green; fls large, burgundy tinted plum. 'Old Rose Belle': fls large, deep rose. 'Patrick Synge': fls flame red. 'Roseum': fls pale pink with darker veins. 'Satin Pink Belle': fls large, bright pink with darker veins. 'Savitzii': dwarf, bushy; lvs lobed and toothed as in tinted grey, heavily marbled soft white. 'Silver Belle': fls pure white, sta. brilliant yellow. 'Souvenir de Bonn': erect to 3.5m; lvs maple-shaped, tinted grey, edged and sometimes marbled creamy white; fls large, salmon orange, veins darker. 'Tangerine' ('Tangerine Belle'): fls large, golden orange, veins bright pink. 'Vesuvius Red': fls vivid flame red. 'Violetta': fls deepest plum. 'Yellow Belle': fls large, clear butter yellow. Z8.

A. *indicum* (L.) Sweet. Grey-pubesc. perenn. herb or subshrub to 2.5m. Lvs to 10cm, broadly ovate-cordate, lobes 0–3, toothed, downy. Fls 1 per axil; pet. to 1.6cm, yellow. OW tropics. Z10.

A. insigne Planch. Rusty-pubesc. shrub to 1.2m. Lvs to 15cm, cordate-ovate, toothed, lobes 0–3. Fls 3–7 per axil, drooping; pet. to 5cm, white to rose veined and edged dark crimson. Colomb. and Venez. Z9.

A. integerrimum (Hook.) Triana & Planch. = *Bakeridesia integerrima*.

A. 'Margherita Manns' = *A. ochsenii*.

A. megapotamicum (Spreng.) St.-Hil. & Naudin. TRAILING ABUTILON. Glab., slender-branched, spreading shrub to 2.5m. Lvs to 8cm, cordate-lanceolate, rarely lobed, toothed. Fls 1 per axil, drooping; cal. to 2.5cm, tubular, red; pet. to 4cm, yellow. Braz. 'Variegatum': lvs mottled yellow. 'Wisley Red': fls rich red. Z8.

A. × milleri hort. (*A. megapotamicum × A. pictum*?) Lvs broader, longer than in *A. megapotamicum*. Fls sometimes paired; cal. green tinted rose; pet. yellow veined crimson; staminal column carmine. Gdn origin. 'Variegatum': lvs mottled yellow. Z8.

A. mollissimum (Cav.) Sweet. Shrub or small tree to 3m; branchlets pilose. Lvs to 15cm, cordate-acuminate, lobes 0–3. Fls 1–5 in a long-stalked umbel; pet. to 1.8cm, sulphur-yellow. S Amer. Z9.

A. ochsenii (Philippi) Philippi. Shrub to 4cm, similar to *A. vitifolium*, but less downy. Lvs to 8cm, lobes 3, toothed. Fls 1–3 per axil; pet. to 2.8cm, lavender to violet, spotted within. Chile. Z8.

A. pictum (Gillies ex Hook. & Arn.) Walp. Shrub or small tree to 5m, glab. Lvs to 15cm, lobes 3–5–7. Fls 1, long-stalked, drooping; pet. 2–4cm, yellow-orange veined crimson. Braz., nat. elsewhere in C & S Amer. 'Aureomaculatum': lvs green heavily spattered yellow; fls coral red with darker veins. 'Gold Dust': lvs light green, heavily mottled gold; fls orange. 'Goldprince': habit dwarf and bushy; lvs small, variegated cream. 'Thompsonii': habit upright, compact; lvs deeply lobed, mottled yellow; fls salmon flushed orange. 'Pleniflorum': lvs sometimes variegated; fls double. Z9.

A. purpurascens (Link) Schum. Shrub to 2m. Lvs to 12cm, cordate-acuminate, serrate, downy beneath. Fls 1–3 per axil, long-stalked, drooping; pet. to 2cm, purple. Braz. Z9.

A. striatum G. Dickson ex Lindl. = *A. pictum*.

A. × suntense C. Brickell. (*A. ochsenii × A. vitifolium*.) Intermediate between parents. 'Gorer's White': fls white. 'Jermyns': fls deep purple. 'Violetta': fls violet to indigo. 'White Charm': fls to 5cm diam., white.

A. theophrasti Medik. VELVET LEAF; BUTTER-PRINT; CHINA JUTE. Ann. herb to 1m. Lvs to 25cm diam., cordate-acuminate, crenate. Fls in small cymes; pet. to 1.2cm, yellow. Trop. Asia, nat. SE Eur., Medit. and US. Z4.

A. venosum Walp. Shrub or small tree to 5m. Lvs to 20cm, lobes 5–7, toothed, acuminate. Fls 1 per axil, long-stalked; pet. to 5.5cm, golden yellow to orange, net-veined brown. Braz. Z9.

A. vexillarium E. Morr. = *A. megapotamicum*.

A. vitifolium (Cav.) Presl. Softly downy shrub or small tree to 8m. Lvs to 15cm, 3–5–7-lobed, toothed. Fls 1 per axil or in cymes; pet. to 4cm, white or pale lilac. Chile. 'Album': fls snow white. 'Tennant's White': lvs grey-felted; fls v. large, white. 'Veronica Tennant': lvs grey-felted; fls large, lavender, profuse. Z8.

→*Corynabutilon* and *Sida*.

Abyssinian Banana *Ensete ventricosum*.
Abyssinian Cabbage *Brassica carinata*.

Acacallis Lindl. Orchidaceae. 1 epiphytic orchid. Pb. to 5cm, ovoid, compressed with 1–2 tough oblong-lanceolate lvs at apex. Infl. basal, erect or arching; fls few, to 6cm diam.; tep. fleshy, blue-mauve tinted pink; lip gold-bronze. Braz., Venez., Colomb. Z10.

A. cyanea Lindl.
→*Aganisia*.

Acacia Mill. WATTLE; MIMOSA. Leguminosae (Mimosoideae). 700–1200 shrubs trees and lianes. Br. often spiny-stipulate. Lvs bipinnate, particularly in juveniles, but often replaced by simple phyllodes – the adult condition is given below. Fls small, crowded in 'fluffy' ball-like heads, sometimes arranged in a spike or raceme, usually yellow; cal. a 4–5-lobed tube; pet. united; sta. numerous. Spring. C & S Amer., Afr., Aus., Polyn. Z9 unless specified.

A. accola Maid. & Betche. = *A. adunca*.

A. acinacea Lindl. GOLD-DUST WATTLE. Shrub to 2×4m, occas. prostrate. Phyllodes 2.5×1.5cm, thin, orbicular to narrow-oblong. Infl. globose, 12–20-fld. E Aus. 'Ruby Tips': br. tips vivid red.

A. aculeatissima Macbr. THIN-LEAF WATTLE; CREEPING WATTLE. Spreading to prostate shrub to 0.5×3m. Phyllodes to 2×0.1cm, rigid, prickly. Stipules stiff, persistent. Infl. globose, to 20-fld.

SE Aus.

A. adansonii Guillem. & Perrott. = *A. nilotica* ssp. *adansonii*.

A. adunca Cunn. ex G. Don. WALLANGARRA WATTLE. Tall shrub or small tree. Phyllodes 11×0.3cm. Infl. showy, profuse, globose, bright orange-yellow. E Aus.

A. alata R. Br. WINGED WATTLE. Shrub to 2.5m. St. flexuous, broad-winged. Phyllodes spiny. Stipules spiny. Infl. globose, orange-yellow. W Aus. Z8.

A. aneura F. Muell. ex Benth. MULGA. Shrub-tree to 15m. St. angular. Phyllodes 2–25×1cm, blunt. Infl. cylindric, bright golden-yellow. Aus.

A. angustissima (Mill.) Kuntze. TIMBE. Shrub to 4m. Br. furrowed. Lvs bipinnate; lfts numerous, acute. Infl. globose, white tinged pink or mauve. US, Mex. to Costa Rica.

A. arabica (Lam.) Willd. = *A. nilotica* ssp. *tomentosa*.

A. armata R. Br. = *A. paradoxa*.

A. aspera Lindl. ROUGH WATTLE. Shrub to 3×3m. Br. grooved. Phyllodes 3×0.5cm. Infl. globose, 30–50-fld pale or bright yellow. SE Aus.

A. auriculiformis Cunn. ex Benth. BLACK WATTLE. Tree to 30m, crown spreading, dense. Phyllodes 20×3cm. Infl. spicate, paired, dull yellow.

A. baileyana F. Muell. COOTAMUNDRA WATTLE; GOLDEN MIMOSA. Shrub or small tree to 8m. Br. arching. Lvs to 5cm, glaucous, grey-green, finely bipinnate. Infl. globose in dense rac., golden yellow. SE Aus. 'Purpurea': lvs tinted purple when young. Z8.

A. bidentata Benth. Shrub to 1×1.5m. Branchlets often sharply pointed. Phyllodes 1×0.5cm. Stipules spiny. Fls cream to pale yellow. W Aus.

A. binervata DC. TWO-VEINED HICKORY WATTLE. Shrub or tree to 6m. Phyllodes to 10cm, 2-veined, oblong-lanceolate. Infl. globose in rac., yellow. E Aus.

A. binervia (H.L. Wendl.) Macbr. COASTAL MYALL; SALLY WATTLE. Tree to 20m. Phyllodes 15×2cm, 3-veined, lanceolate. Infl. in dense axill. spikes, bright yellow. E Aus.

A. botrycephala (Vent.) Desford. = *A. terminalis*.

A. brachybotrya Benth. GREY MULGA. Shrub to 4m across. Phyllodes 3.5×1.5cm obovate to ovate. Infl. globose, 20–30-fld in rac., yellow. Aus.

A. brunioides G. Don. Shrub to 2m. Phyllodes to 1cm, oblong, terete, sharply pointed. Infl. 10–25-fld, globose, yellow. Aus.

A. buxifolia Cunn. BOX LEAF WATTLE. Shrub to 3m. Br. angled. Phyllodes 3.5×1cm, elliptic, obtuse or acute, grey-green. Infl. 6–20-fld, deep golden yellow. SE Aus.

A. bynoeana hort. = *A. sclerophyllodes*.

A. caffra (Thunb.) Willd. Tree to 12m. Bark gnarled. Lvs to 23cm, bipinnate, lfts mucronate. Infl. spicate, cream, fragrant. Trop. Afr. to S Afr.

A. calamifolia Sweet ex Lindl. BROOM WATTLE; WALLOWA. Shrub to 4m. Phyllodes 12×0.5cm, flexible, linear, mucronate. Infl. globose, 30–40-fld, bright yellow. SE Aus.

A. cardiophylloides Cunn. ex Benth. WYALONG WATTLE. Shrub or small tree to 5m. Lvs bipinnate, pubesc., lfts to 2mm in 6–12 pairs. Infl. 20–30-fld in branched or simple rac., golden yellow. SE Aus. 'Gold Lace': habit prostrate.

A. catechu Benth. CATECHU; WADALEE-GUM TREE; KHAIR; CUTCH. Tree to 25m. Spines hooked. Lvs to 15cm, bipinnate; lfts 0.5mm, gland. Infl. cylindrical, pale to dark yellow. W Pak. to Burm.

A. cavenia (Molina) Molina. Small tree to 6m. Trunk twisted. Lvs bipinnate; lfts in 12–20 pairs. Stipules spinescent. Infl. yellow, globose. Temp. S Amer.

A. centrinervia Maid. & Blakely. Pyramidal shrub. Phyllodes 3×0.5cm, linear-lanceolate. Infl. globose, 20-fld, yellow. Aus.

A. choriophyllodes Benth. Tree to 9m, unarmed. Stipules minute. Lvs to 20cm; lfts 1.5×3cm. Infl. globose. Bahamas.

A. cognata Domin. NARROW-LEAVED BOWER WATTLE. Shrub or small tree to 8m. Br. weeping. Phyllodes 10×0.3cm, linear-oblong, dark green. Infl. globose, lemon yellow. Aus.

A. colletioides Benth. WAIT-A-WHILE; SPINE BUSH; NORKA. Shrub to 4×4m, rarely small tree. Phyllodes 4×0.2cm, narrowly cylindric, pungent. Infl. globose, 12–15-fld, deep golden yellow. Aus.

A. cornigera (L.) Willd. BULL HORN ACACIA. Large shrub or small tree with swollen, ant-inhabited spines. Lvs bipinnate, lfts to 0.6cm. Infl. in dense spike, yellow. C & S Amer., nat. in Carib. and SE US.

A. cultriformis Cunn. ex G. Don. KNIFE-LEAF WATTLE. Shrub to 4m. Phyllodes to 3.5×1.5cm, fleshy, ovate to deltoid. Infl. 8–20-fld, yellow. NSW. Z8.

A. cuneata Benth. = *A. truncata*.

A. cyanophylloides Lindl. = *A. saligna*.

A. cyclops Cunn. COASTAL WATTLE; WESTERN COASTAL WATTLE; ROOIKRANS. Shrub to 4m, dense, rounded. Phyllodes 9×1.2cm, leathery, narrowly oblong, rigidly mucronate. Infl. globose, 0.5cm diam. W Aus.

A. dealbata Link. SILVER WATTLE; MIMOSA. Everg. tree to 30m. Lvs to 12cm, bipinnate, silver-green, lfts 4×1mm, 20–40 pairs. Infl. globose, highly fragrant. Tasm., Aus. 'Pendula': habit weeping. Z8.

A. deanei (R. Bak.) Welch. DEANE'S WATTLE. Similar to *A. decurrens* but lfts in 10–25 pairs, coarsely hairy. NSW. Z7.

A. decipiens R. Br. = *A. truncata.*

A. decora Rchb. WESTERN SILVER WATTLE; SHOWY WATTLE; GRACE-FUL WATTLE. Rounded shrub to 2m or tree to 5m. Phyllodes 2–6×1cm, lanceolate, mucronate. Infl. 15–30-fld, bright gold, fragrant. E Aus.

A. decurrens (Wendl.) Willd. EARLY BLACK WATTLE; GREEN WATTLE. Tree to 12m. Br. grooved. Lvs to 7cm, bipinnate; pinnae 5–12, lfts 0.5–1.5cm, crowded, acicular. Infl. 20–30-fld in axillary rac. NSW. Z7.

A. decurrens var. *mollis* Lindl. = *A. mearnsii.*

A. denudata Lehm. = *A. pulchella.*

A. diffusa Lindl. = *A. genistifolia.*

A. discolor (Andrews) Willd. = *A. terminalis.*

A. dodonaeifolia (Pers.) Willd. STICKY WATTLE. Tall shrub or small tree to 6m. Br. angular, ridged. Phyllodes 10×0.1cm, narrowly lanceolate, rigid, gland. Infl. globose, solitary or in pairs. S Aus.

A. doratoxylon Cunn. SPEARWOOD; LANCEWOOD; CURRAWANG. Tall shrub or small open tree to 8m. Phyllodes 20×1cm, narrowly lanceolate, subfalcate, olive green. Infl. cylindric in axill. rac. NSW to Queensld.

A. drummondii Lindl. DRUMMOND'S WATTLE. Shrub to 2m, br. flimsy. Lvs bipinnate; pinnae in 1–3 pairs, lfts to 0.5cm, few. Infl. solitary, cylindric. W Aus.

A. dunnii (Maid.) Turrill. ELEPHANT EAR WATTLE. Shrub or small tree to 4m. Phyllodes 30×13cm, broadly falcate, blue-grey. Infl. globose in axill. rac. N Aus.

A. elata A. Cunn. ex Benth. CEDAR WATTLE. Tree to 20m. Lvs to 40cm, bipinnate; pinnae in 6–8 pairs, lfts to 6cm, in 10–20 pairs. Infl. globose, in rac. or pan. NSW.

A. elongata Sieber ex DC. SWAMP WATTLE; SLENDER WATTLE. Shrub to 3m. Branchlets white silky hairy. Phyllodes to 13×0.5cm, linear, rigid hooked at apex. SE Aus.

A. erioloba E. Mey. CAMEL THORN. Tree to 15m. Br. spreading, tips pendulous. Lvs bipinnate; pinnae in 2–5 pairs, blue-green. Infl. axill., solitary. Trop. Afr.

A. euthycarpa J.M. Black. = *A. calamifolia.*

A. 'Exeter Hybrid' (*A. longifolia×A. riceana*). Medium to large shrub; br. arching; phyllodes narrow; infl. rich yellow, fragrant. Gdn origin. Z9.

A. extensa Lindl. WIRY WATTLE. Erect shrub to 3m. Phyllodes 20×0.2cm, linear, scabrous, hooked. Infl. globose, solitary. W Aus.

A. falcata Willd. Shrub or small tree to 6m. Phyllodes 15×4cm, lanceolate, falcate. Infl. globose in short axill. rac. SE Aus.

A. farinosa Lindl. MEALY WATTLE. Similar to *A. sclerophyllodes* except branchlets, flowerheads and peduncles hoary or white-mealy. SE Aus.

A. farnesiana (L.) Willd. MIMOSA BUSH; SWEET WATTLE; SWEET ACACIA; SCENTED WATTLE. Shrub or small tree to 7m. Lvs bipinnate; pinnae 2–6 pairs, lfts to 1cm, linear, 10–20 pairs. Infl. globose, bright orange-yellow. Trop. Amer. (uncertain). Z8.

A. fimbriata Cunn. ex G. Don. FRINGED WATTLE. Bushy shrub or small tree to 5m. Phyllodes to 5×0.6cm, narrowly lanceolate, grey-green. Infl. golden yellow in rac. exceeding phyllodes. Aus.

A. flexifolia Cunn. ex Benth. BENT-LEAF WATTLE. Erect shrub to 1.5m. Phyllodes 5×0.2cm, narrow-linear, erect or bent near base. Infl. lemon yellow, fragrant, solitary or paired. NSW.

A. floribunda (Vent.) Willd. WHITE SALLOW; SALLY WATTLE; GOSSAMER WATTLE. Bushy shrub or small tree to 8m. Phyllodes 17×1cm linear to lanceolate. Infl. oblong, to 8cm, lemon yellow, solitary or paired. E Aus.

A. genistifolia Link. SPREADING WATTLE. Everg. shrub to 3×2m, erect or spreading. Phyllodes to 5cm, linear, rigid. Infl. axill., globose, pale or bright yellow. Aus., Tasm.

A. giraffae Burchell. = *A. erioloba.*

A. gladiiformis Cunn. ex Benth. SWORD-LEAF WATTLE. Erect shrub to 3m. Phyllodes 15×1.2cm lanceolate, obtuse, apex hooked. Infl. 40–50-fld, globose, bright yellow. NSW.

A. glandulicarpa Reader. HAIRY-POD WATTLE. Dense spreading shrub to 2m. Phyllodes to 1.5×0.6cm, ovate-acute, sinuate, erect. Infl. deep golden yellow, fragrant, globose. S Aus.

A. glaucescens Willd. = *A. binervia.*

A. glaucocarpa Maid. & Blakely. Shrub or tall tree. Lvs bipinnate; pinnae 4–5 pairs, lfts 8–20 pairs, elliptic-oblong. Infl. globose, yellow, in rac. Aus.

A. glaucoptera Benth. CLAY WATTLE; FLAT WATTLE. Shrub 2.5×2m, much branched. Young shoots bright orange-red. Phyllodes deltoid, acute, hooked, 2-ranked, blue-green. Infl.

bright yellow, globose, inserted on phyllodesde midribs. W Aus.

A. graminea Lehm. = *A. extensa.*

A. grandis Henfr. = *A. pulchella.*

A. hakeoides Cunn. ex Benth. HAKEA-LEAF WATTLE; WESTERN BLACK WATTLE. Spreading shrub to 4×5m, occas. small tree to 10m. Phyllodes 14×1.5cm, linear-oblong, thick. Infl. globose, bright yellow, in rac. of 6–12. E Aus.

A. hanburyana Winter ex Berger. Shrub to small tree. Lower part of lvs phyllodesdinous, upper part with 3–4 pairs of pinnae. Infl. globose in axill. rac. (*A. dealbata ×A. podalyriifolia?*).

A. harveyi Benth. Shrub. Branchlets winged. Phyllodes oblong to linear-oblanceolate. Infl. globose, in rac. Aus.

A. hastulata Sm. Shrub to 1m, much branched. St. red-tinged. Phyllodes to 0.5cm, ovate-triangular, pungent, thick. Infl. globose, few-fld, solitary. W Aus.

A. hemiteles Benth. TAN WATTLE. Shrub, erect or spreading. Phyllodes 7.5×0.7cm, leathery, oblong-linear. Infl. globose, in rac. Aus.

A. hispidissima DC. = *A. pulchella.*

A. holosericea Cunn. ex G. Don. Shrub or small tree to 6m. Phyllodes to 25×9.6cm, erect, ovate-oblong, blue-green, seric-eous. Infl. oblong, solitary or paired, bright yellow. NE Aus. Z7.

A. horrida hort. non Willd. = *A. karroo.*

A. howittii F. Muell. = *A. verniciflua.*

A. implexa Benth. LIGHTWOOD WATTLE; HICKORY WATTLE. Tree to 15m. Phyllodes 18×2.5cm, lanceolate-falcate; bipinnate lvs may persist. Infl. globose, cream to pale yellow. Aus.

A. iteaphyllodes F. Muell. ex Benth. WINTER WATTLE. Shrub to 3×4m. Br. ascending or pendulous. Phyllodes 14×1cm, narrow-lanceolate, blue green with silver sheen. Infl. lemon yellow, fragrant in rac. S Aus. 'Parson's Cascade': prostrate.

A. jonesii F. Muell. Shrub to 2m. Lvs bipinnate, deep green; pinnae in 5–6 pairs, lfts to 0.6cm, linear. Infl. globose in rac. SE Aus.

A. julibrissin (Durazz.) Willd. = *Albizia julibrissin.*

A. juniperina Willd. = *A. ulicifolia.*

A. karroo Hayne. Tree to 15m, occas. spreading shrub; pinnae in 2–6 pairs, lfts obovate-oblong. Stipules spinescent, often in-flated. Lvs bipinnate. Infl. globose, bright yellow, fragrant, clustered. S Afr. Z8.

A. kettlewelliae Maid. BUFFALO WATTLE. Shrub or small tree to 9m. Phyllodes 10×1cm, lanceolate, mucronate. Infl. globose, in dense clusters, bright yellow. SE Aus.

A. koa A. Gray. KOA. Tree to 20m. Phyllodes to 12.5×1cm, lanceolate-falcate. Infl. 50–60-fld, globose, yellow. Hawaii.

A. latifolia hort. = *A. longifolia.*

A. lebbek Willd. = *Albizia lebbek.*

A. leioderma Maslin. Shrub to 3m. Lvs bipinnate; pinnae 1–3, lfts to 1cm, oblong. Infl. globose, pale yellow. W Aus.

A. leprosa Sieber ex DC. CINNAMON WATTLE. Shrub or small tree to 8m. Br. arching. Phyllodes 12×1cm, linear-lanceolate, curved, mealy. Infl. globose in axill. rac., primrose yellow. SE Aus. Z8.

A. leptoclada Cunn. ex Benth. Small shrub. Lvs bipinnate, leathery; pinnae 3–5 pairs, lfts to 0.3cm, oblong. Infl. globose, bright yellow in crowded rac. E Aus.

A. ligulata Cunn. ex Benth. Bushy shrub or small tree to 5m. Phyllodes 10×0.5cm, oblanceolate to linear-oblong. Infl. globose, bright yellow, solitary or in rac. of up to 5. Aus.

A. linearis Sims non (H.L. Wendl.) Macbr.= *A. longissima.*

A. linearis (H.L. Wendl.) Macbr. non Sims. = *A. linifolia.*

A. lineata Cunn. ex G. Don. STREAKED WATTLE. Shrub to 2×2.5m, dense, rounded. Phyllodes 2×1cm, linear, rigid, acute. Infl. solitary or paired, golden yellow. Aus.

A. linifolia (Vent.) Willd. FLAX WATTLE. Shrub to 4m. Shoots arching-pendulous. Phyllodes 5×0.3cm, linear. Infl. in short rac., fragrant, yellow. Aus.

A. linophylloides Fitzg. = *A. ramulosa.*

A. longifolia (Andrews) Willd. SYDNEY GOLDEN WATTLE; SALLOW WATTLE. As for *A. floribunda* but less bushy. Phyllodes to 15cm, oblong-lanceolate, dark green. Infl. deep yellow. E Aus. 'Lisette': fls pale yellow, fragrant. Similar to *A. sophorae.* Z8.

A. longifolia var. *sophorae* (Labill.) F. Muell. = *A. sophorae.*

A. longissima H.L. Wendl. FLAX WATTLE; NARROW-LEAVED WATTLE. Shrub to 3m. Branchlets drooping. Phyllodes 20×0.5cm, linear, often curved, dark green. Infl. globose in cylindric rac., cream to pale yellow. SE Aus., Tasm.

A. lophantha Willd. = *Albizia lophantha.*

A. lutea Leavenw. = *Neptunia lutea.*

A. macracantha Humb. & Bonpl. ex Willd. STEEL ACACIA. Multi-stemmed tree to 10m, spiny. Lvs bipinnate; pinnae in 15–20 pairs, lfts crowded, linear-oblong. Infl. globose, fascicled, yellow, fragrant. W Indies, Venez.

A. macracanthoides Bertero ex DC. = *A. macracantha.*

A. macradenia Benth. ZIG-ZAG WATTLE. Shrub or small tree to

5×4m. Br. flexuous. Young shoots red. Phyllodes 25×2.5cm, linear-lanceolate, spreading or reflexed. Infl. in rac., bright yellow, fragrant. Queensld.

A. maidenii F. Muell. MAIDEN'S WATTLE. Bushy shrub or tree to 15m. Phyllodes 18×2cm, thin, lanceolate, curved. Infl. spicate, paired. Aus.

A. marginata R. Br. non Steud. = *A. myrtifolia*.

A. mearnsii De Wildeman. BLACK WATTLE. As for *A. decurrens* but branchlets not ribbed. Lvs bipinnate; pinnae in 9–20 pairs, lfts to 0.5cm, broader, downy, pale yellow. Tasm., Aus.

A. meissneri Lehm. Dense shrub to 3×4m. Branchlets laterally compressed. Phyllodes 2.5×1cm, oblong-ovate, acute. Infl. globose, solitary or to 30 in branching rac. W Aus.

A. melanoxylon R. Br. BLACKWOOD. Tree to 30m. Phyllodes 14×2.5cm, oblanceolate, acute. Infl. globose in branched rac. Aus. Z8.

A. microbotrya Benth. MANNA WATTLE. Shrub or small tree to 6×5m. Phyllodes 13×1.5cm, lanceolate, acute, grey-green. Infl. globose, 3–5 per rac., peduncles yellow-orange-pubesc. W Aus.

A. montana Benth. MALLEE WATTLE. Shrub to 2m, spreading. Bark red-brown. Phyllodes to 4×0.6cm, linear-oblong, obtuse. Infl. globose, solitary or paired. E Aus.

A. mucronata Willd. VARIABLE SALLOW WATTLE. As for *A. longifolia* except infl. lax. Aus. Z8.

A. myrtifolia (Sm.) Willd. MYRTLE WATTLE; RED STEM WATTLE. Shrub to 3m, stiff, erect. Phyllodes 2.5–14×0.5–3cm, leathery, tinged red, oblanceolate to linear. Infl. cream to lemon yellow. Aus., Tasm.

A. nigricans R. Br. Shrub to 3m. St. ribbed. Lvs bipinnate, pinnae in 1–3 pairs; lfts to 0.5cm, linear-oblong. Infl. globose, axill., solitary. W Aus.

A. nilotica (L.) Willd. ex Delile. GUM ARABIC TREE; SUNTWOOD; BABUL. Tree to 10m. Lvs bipinnate; pinnae in 5–11 pairs, lfts to 0.5cm, linear-oblong; stipules to 7.5cm, spinescent. Infl. axillary, solitary or clustered 2–6. Trop. Afr. ssp. *adansonii* (Guillem & Perrott.) Brenan. Fr. glab. to sparsely hairy. ssp. *tomentosa* (Benth.) Brenan. GUM ARABIC TREE; EGYPTIAN MIMOSA; EGYPTIAN THORN. Fr. grey-white-tomentose.

A. notabilis F. Muell. Shrub to 3×6m. Bark smooth. Phyllodes to 15×2.5cm, leathery, oblanceolate, obtuse. Infl. globose, bright yellow, 4–15 per rac. Aus.

A. obliqua Cunn. ex Benth. = *A. rotundifolia*.

A. obliqua auct. non Cunn. ex Benth. = *A. acinacea*.

A. obtusata Sieber ex DC. BLUNT-LEAVED WATTLE. Shrub to 3m. Phyllodes to 11×1.6cm, oblanceolate to linear, truncate. Infl. in dense axill. rac. NSW.

A. omalophyllodes Cunn. ex Benth. GIDGEE MYALL; FRAGRANT MYALL; MYALLWOOD; YARRAN; VIOLETWOOD. Tree to 10m. Phyllodes to 10×0.8cm, grey, linear-lanceolate. Infl. 2–5 per short rac. Aus.

A. ornithophora Sweet. = *A. paradoxa*.

A. oxycedrus Sieber ex DC. SPIKE WATTLE. Dense shrub to spreading tree to 9m. Phyllodes 3×0.5cm, linear-lanceolate, acuminate, grey-green. Rac. to 3cm, dense, cylindric. SE Aus.

A. paradoxa DC. KANGAROO THORN; HEDGE WATTLE. Shrub to 5m. Phyllodes 1–3×1cm, oblong to lanceolate, dark green, undulate; stipules to 1cm, paired, spinescent. Infl. globose, axill., solitary. NSW. 'Pendula': habit straggling. var. *angustifolia* Benth. Phyllodes narrowly oblong. Z8.

A. pendula Cunn. WEEPING MYALL; BOREE. Tree to 10m. Br. pendulous. Phyllodes 10×1cm, blue-green, narrowly lanceolate. Infl. in short, cylindrical pan. lemon yellow. E Aus.

A. penninervis Sieber ex DC. HICKORY WATTLE; MOUNTAIN HICKORY. Shrub or small tree to 12m. Phyllodes 15×5cm, oblong to broadly lanceolate, mucronate. Infl. in loose term. rac., cream or pale yellow. E Aus.

A. platyptera Lindl. = *A. alata*.

A. podalyriifolia G. Don. MT. MORGAN WATTLE; QUEENSLAND SILVER WATTLE. Shrub or small tree to 5m. Phyllodes 5×2cm, ovate to elliptic, acute, often undulate white-tomentose. Infl. in branched rac., bright yellow. NE Aus. Z8.

A. polyacantha Willd. Tree. Lvs bipinnate; pinnae in 11–27 pairs, lfts to 0.5cm. Infl. in loose axill. spikes. India, Sri Lanka.

A. polybotrya hort. = *A. glaucocarpa*.

A. pravissima F. Muell. OVEN'S WATTLE. Bushy shrub or small tree to 8m. Br. pendulous or arching. Phyllodes 2×1.5cm, deltoid to cuneate, 2-veined, glaucous with an apical spine beneath. Infl. in loose rac., bright yellow. SE Aus. Z8.

A. prominens Cunn. ex D. Don. GOSFORD WATTLE; GOLDEN RAIN WATTLE; GREY SALLY. Shrub or small tree to 9m, rarely 25m. Phyllodes 6×1cm, crowded, lanceolate-falcate, mucronate, with basal gland. Infl. in dense, drooping rac. SE Aus.

A. pruinosa Cunn. ex Benth. FROSTY WATTLE. Small tree to 6m. Foliage bronze at first. Lvs bipinnate; pinnae in 3–5 pairs, lfts to 2cm. Infl. in pan. or rac. SE Aus.

A. pubescens (Vent.) R. Br. DOWNY WATTLE. Shrub or small tree

to 6×3m. Lvs bipinnate; pinnae in 6–12 pairs, lfts to 0.5cm. Infl. in arching rac., fragrant. Aus.

A. pulchella R. Br. PRICKLY MOSES. Shrub to 3m. Br. occas. spiny. Lvs bipinnate; pinnae in 1 pair, lfts to 0.5cm. Infl. in clusters of 2–3, bright yellow. W Aus. Z8.

A. pulverulenta Cunn. ex Benth. = *A. calamifolia*.

A. pycnantha Benth. GOLDEN WATTLE. Small tree to 8m. Phyllodes to 20×5cm, leathery, broadly lanceolate, obtuse, lustrous green. Infl. globose, in axill. rac., golden yellow. SE Aus. Z8.

A. ramulosa Fitzg. Spreading shrub, to 2m. Phyllodes to 15cm acicular, pungent. Infl. in dense subsessile spikes. Aus.

A. redolens Maslin. Dense shrub, 3–8m. Phyllodes 2.5–7×0.5–1.5cm, straight to falcate, glaucous grey-green, sweet scented. W Aus. 'Prostrata': habit dense and low; phyllodes strong golden green.

A. restiacea Benth. Shrub, rush-like in appearance. St. green, ribbed. Phyllodes needle-like. Infl. in rac.; buds with overlapping bracts. Aus.

A. retinodes Schldl. WIRILDA; MIMOSE DE QUATRE SAISONS. Shrub, or small tree to 6m. Phyllodes 18×1.5cm, linear-lanceolate, acute, grey-green. Infl. in rac. or pan., pale yellow, highly fragrant. S Aus., Tasm. Z8.

A. riceana Hensl. RICE'S WATTLE. Dense shrub or small tree 2–10m, occas. prostrate. Young shoots red-brown. Phyllodes to 5.5×0.5cm, linear, acute. Infl. in dense rac., bright yellow. Differs from *A. verticillata* in its phyllodes – clustered, not whorled. S Tasm. Z8.

A. rigens Cunn. NEALIE; NEEDLE-BUSH WATTLE. Shrub to 3m. Br. yellow-ribbed. Phyllodes to 12.5cm, cylindric, flexible. Infl. in axill. clusters. SE Aus.

A. roemeriana Scheele. Shrub or tree to 5m. Lvs bipinnate; pinnae in 10–20 pairs, lfts to 1.5cm. Infl. axill., solitary, globose. Tex., N Mex.

A. rostellifera Benth. Spreading shrub or small tree to 5m. Br. drooping; branchlets yellow-ribbed, flexuous. Phyllodes to 12.5cm, linear-lanceolate with apical hook. Infl. in loose axill. rac. W. Aus.

A. rotundifolia Hook. Shrub. Br. pendent. Phyllodes to 1×1cm, ovate-orbicular, cleft. Infl. axill., solitary or paired, globose. Calif., Ariz.

A. rubida Cunn. RED-STEMMED WATTLE. Bushy shrub or small tree 1.5–12m. Branchlets compressed, tinted red. Phyllodes 18.5×2.5cm, lanceolate, often tinged red. Infl. in loose, red-stalked rac. E Aus.

A. salicina Lindl. BROUGHTON WILLOW; NATIVE WILLOW; WILLOW WATTLE; COOBA. Shrub or tree to 15m, often suckering. Phyllodes to 17.5×3cm, oblong-linear, acute, pendent, pale to blue green. Infl. 2–8 per rac., pale yellow. Aus.

A. saligna (Labill.) H. Wendl. BLUE-LEAVED WATTLE; GOLDEN WREATH WATTLE. Shrub or small tree to 6m, spreading and suckering. Phyllodes 15–30×1–3cm, linear-oblong to lanceolate. Infl. globose in rac. to 7.5cm. W Aus.

A. schinoides Benth. FROSTY WATTLE. Tree to 8m. Br. glaucous. Lvs bipinnate, pinnae in 2–4 pairs, lfts to 2cm. Infl. cream in loosely branched rac. SE Aus.

A. sclerophyllodes Lindl. HARD-LEAF WATTLE. Shrub to 2×5m, dense, spreading. Phyllodes to 4×0.5cm, oblong in oblanceolate, mucronate. Infl. solitary or grouped in axils, bright yellow, fragrant. S Aus.

A. scorpioides (L.) W. Wight = *A. nilotica*.

A. senegal (L.) Willd. GUM ARABIC TREE; SUDAN GUM ARABIC. Shrub or small tree to 4m. Bark exfoliating. Lvs bipinnate; pinnae 3–8 pairs, lfts grey-green; stipules spinescent. Infl. axillary, white to cream, fragrant. Senegal to Nigeria.

A. seyal Delile. GUM ARABIC TREE; WHISTLING TREE; THIRTY THORN. Tree to 10m, thorny. Bark powdery, orange red; young growth white with red glands. Lvs bipinnate; pinnae 2–8 pairs, lfts to 5mm. Infl. fragrant. Egypt to Kenya.

A. sieberiana DC. Tree 5–8m. Stipules straight, 12.5cm. Lvs to 10cm, bipinnate; pinnae 6–23, lfts to 6.5mm. Fls white to cream. Trop. Afr. 'Woodsii': habit spreading, to 8m tall; bark corky, exfoliating; lvs finely pinnate; infl. off-white.

A. sophorae (Labill.) R. Br. COASTAL WATTLE. Shrub. Branchlets angular, becoming terete. Phyllodes to 10×3.5cm, elliptic to oblong-elliptic. Infl. to 3cm, axill., dense. E Aus.

A. spadicigera Schldl. & Cham. = *A. cornigera*.

A. spectabilis Cunn. ex Benth. MUDGEE; GLORY WATTLE. Shrub or small tree 2–6m, spreading. Lvs bipinnate, to 10cm; pinnae 2–7 pairs, lfts to 1.5cm. Infl. in pan., bright yellow, fragrant. E Aus.

A. spilleriana J.E. Br. = *A. brachybotrya*.

A. spinescens Benth. SPINY WATTLE. Shrub to 1m. Branchlets grooved, spiny. Lvs bipinnate. Phyllodes sometimes present, narrowly ovate. Infl. solitary, axill., golden-yellow. S & E Aus.

A. stenophyllodes Cunn. ex Benth. DALBY MYALL; EUMONG. Tree to 10m. Br. drooping, spreading. Phyllodes to 40×1cm, linear, coriaceous. Infl. in rac. or solitary, pale yellow. Aus.

A. suaveolens (Sm.) Willd. SWEET-SCENTED WATTLE. SWEET WATTLE. Shrub 1–3m. Phyllodes to 15×1cm, blue green, linear, acute, fleshy. Infl. in dense, short, axill. rac., pale yellow. E Aus. 'Boddy's Variegatum': phyllodes yellow and pale green with paler splashes.

A. subporosa F. Muell. Resembles *A. cognata* but much larger with broader phyllodes. Aus. 'Emerald Cascade': habit creeping; phyllodes narrow, bright green, drooping; fls yellow, in paired puffs.

A. subulata Bonpl. AWL-LEAF WATTLE. Slender shrub to 3m. Young shoots hairy, weeping. Phyllodes 15×0.2cm linear, acute. Infl. in flimsy rac., cream to pale yellow. SE Aus. Z8.

A. suma (Roxb.) Kurz. = *A. polyacantha*.

A. sutherlandii (F. Muell.) F. Muell. CORKWOOD WATTLE. Medium shrub or tree to 12m. Br. arching. Lvs bipinnate, to 30cm; pinnae 15–20 pairs, lfts to 3mm. Infl. to 5cm, cylindric, pale yellow. NE Aus.

A. tenuifolia F. Muell. non L. = *A. aculeatissima*.

A. terminalis (Salisb.) Macbr. SUNSHINE WATTLE. Shrub or small tree to 3m. Lvs bipinnate; pinnae 4–5 pairs, lfts elliptic. Infl. in terminal rac., few-fld, globose. SE Aus.

A. torulosa Benth. Shrub or small tree to 7m. Crown dense. Phyllodes to 20×1cm, linear-lanceolate. Infl. to 6cm, in groups of 1–3, cylindric, bright yellow. NE Aus.

A. trineura F. Muell. THREE-VEINED WATTLE. Shrub to 5m. Phyllodes to 6×0.5cm, cuneate-oblong. Infl. 3–8 per axill. rac. Aus.

A. truncata Hoffsgg. Shrub 1–3m. Br. ascending. Phyllodes to 2×1cm, obliquely cuneate. Infl. bright yellow. W Aus.

A. ulicifolia (Salisb.) Court. JUNIPER WATTLE. Shrub to 3.5m. Phyllodes to 2cm, acicular, spreading. Infl. solitary, globose, cream to pale yellow. SE Aus. 'Brownii': to 60cm, compact; infl. large, rich yellow.

A. undulata Lindl. Shrub to 3m. Branchlets arching. Phyllodes 0.5–2.5cm, cuneate-deltoid, undulate, soft pubesc. Infl. solitary or paired, lemon-yellow. E Aus.

A. undulifolia C. Fraser ex Lodd. = *A. undulata*.

A. 'Veitchiana' = *A.* 'Exeter Hybrid'.

A. verniciflua Cunn. VARNISH WATTLE. Shrub or small tree to 5m. Shoots sticky. Phyllodes to 12×1.5cm, subulate-oblong to linear. Infl. axill., 50–60-fld, solitary or paired. Aus., Tasm.

A. verticillata (L'Hérit.) Willd. PRICKLY MOSES. Low shrub or small open tree to 9m. Base and roots offensively scented. Phyllodes 2×0.2cm, linear-subulate, in whorls of 6. Infl. cylindric, bright yellow. SE Aus., Tasm. Z8.

A. vestita Ker-Gawl. HAIRY WATTLE; WEEPING BOREE. Spreading, multistemmed shrub, to 4×3m. Br. pendulous. Phyllodes to 2×1cm, elliptic, undulate, tip hooked. Infl. in terminal rac., bright yellow. SE Aus.

A. victoriae Benth. BRAMBLE ACACIA; BRAMBLE WATTLE; GUN-DABLUE WATTLE. Shrub or small tree to 7m. Phyllodes to 8×1cm, lanceolate to oblanceolate, mucronate. Stipules to 1cm, in pairs, spinescent. Infl. in pairs or term. rac., creamy to pale yellow. E Aus.

A. viscidula Benth. Shrub to 3×2m. Phyllodes to 8×0.3cm, oblong to linear, fleshy, pitted, sticky, hairy. Infl. axill., globose. Aus.

A. xanthophloea Benth. Tree to 25m. Branchlets purple-brown. Lvs bipinnate, glab.; pinnae 3–8 pairs, lfts to 0.5cm. Infl. axill., white to purple tinged or yellow to golden. Afr.

Acaena Mutis ex L. NEW ZEALAND BUR; BIDI-BIDI; SHEEP'S BURRS. Rosaceae. *c*100 perenn. herbs or subshrubs. St. creeping. Lvs imparipinnate; lfts dentate. Fls v. small in crowded, 'prickly' burr-like cap. or spikes. Summer. S hemis. to Calif. and Hawaii, notably NZ, S Amer. Z6.

A. adenocarpa Bitter. = *A. splendens*.

A. adscendens Vahl. Creeping to 20cm. Br. pink, rooting. Lvs to 12cm; lfts to 13, vividly glaucous. Infl. globose, long-stalked, dark purple. S Amer., NZ.

A. affinis Hook. f. = *A. adscendens*.

A. anserinifolia (Forst. & Forst. f.) Druce. Stoloniferous or scandent perenn. Lvs to 7.5cm; lfts 9–13, dull green, pubesc. Infl. globose, rose or white. NZ. 'Blue Haze' ('Pewter'): lvs pale blue; infl. red; late summer. 'Bronze': lvs bronze; infl. brown; late summer.

A. anserinifolia hort. non (Forst. & Forst. f.) Druce. = *A. novae-zelandiae*.

A. argentea Ruiz & Pav. St. prostrate to 60cm. Lvs to 14cm; lfts 9–15, grey blue above, silvery pubesc. beneath. Infl. globose, purple. Peru, Chile.

A. buchananii Hook. f. Rhizomatous. Lvs to 9cm; lfts 11–17, grey or milky green. Infl. globose, sessile, pale. NZ.

A. caesiiglauca (Bitter) Bergmans. Stoloniferous to 14cm. Lvs to 10cm; lfts 7–11, grey-green tinged red. Infl. obconic, red-brown. NZ.

A. coerulea hort. = *A. caesiiglauca*.

A. cuneata Hook. & Arn. = *A. sericea*.

A. fissistipula Bitter. Stoloniferous to 11cm. Lvs to 17cm; lfts 2–6, green-glaucous. Infl. globose, purple-red. NZ.

A. fuegina Philippi. = *A. sericea*.

A. glabra Buch. Creeping, shrubby, to 10cm. Lvs to 7cm; lfts 9–13, glossy above, glaucescent beneath, teeth red. Infl. globose, pale or red. NZ.

A. glauca hort. = *A. caesiiglauca*.

A. glaucophylla Bitter. = *A. magellanica*.

A. inermis Hook. f. Rhizomatous to 6cm. Lvs to 7cm; lfts 11–15, purple brown or pale olive. Infl. globose, pale with red spines. NZ, nat. GB.

A. integerrima Gillies ex Hook. & Arn. = *A. splendens*.

A. laevigata Ait. Decumbent. Lvs 5cm; lfts 13–15, green, glab. Infl. ellipsoid, long-stalked. Falkland Is.

A. lucida (Lam.) Vahl. St. procumbent or ascending. Lvs to 4cm; lfts 11–21, pilose or sericeous. Infl. term., globose, purple. W Arg., E Chile, Falkland Is.

A. magellanica (Lam.) M. Vahl. Stoloniferous to 15cm. Lvs to 15cm; lfts 11–17, grey green above, pilose beneath. Infl. globose, dark red. S S Amer., Subantarctic Is.

A. microphylla Hook. f. Rhizomatous, to 4cm. Lvs to 3cm; lfts 9–15, grey-green tinted bronze and glossy above. Infl. globose, crimson. NZ. 'Copper Carpet' ('Kupferteppich', 'Purple Carpet'): lvs bronze; Infl. red; late summer. 'Pulchella': lvs deep blue-green; infl. red; late summer.

A. microphylla 'Glauca' = *A. caesiiglauca*.

A. microphylla var. *inermis* (Hook. f.) T. Kirk. = *A. inermis*.

A. multifida Hook. f. = *A. pinnatifida*.

A. myriophylla Lindl. Prostrate to 70cm. Lvs to 12cm; lfts 15–31, deeply divided. Infl. a spike, purple. Chile, Arg.

A. novae-zelandiae T. Kirk. PIRRI-PIRRI BUR; BIDGEE-WIDGEE; BIDDY BIDDY. Shrubby, creeping to 15cm. Lvs to 11cm; lfts 9–15, rachis often flushed red. Infl. globose, green-white, spines red. SE Aus., New Guinea, NZ, nat. GB.

A. ovalifolia Ruiz & Pav. St. to 80cm, prostrate or ascending. Lvs to 6cm; lfts 5–9. Infl. globose, anth. purple. S Amer., Falkland Is., nat. GB.

A. ovina Cunn. To 60cm. Lvs to 20cm; lfts 11–29, dense pilose beneath. Infl. an interrupted spike. Aus.

A. pallida (T. Kirk) Allan. Stoloniferous to 15cm. Lvs to 12cm; lfts 9–15, glossy green, paler, pubesc. beneath. Infl. globose, spines red-brown. SE Aus., NZ.

A. parvifolia Philippi. = *A. lucida*.

A. philippi Dusén. = *A. sericea*.

A. pinnatifida Ruiz & Pav. St. to 15cm. Lvs to 8cm; lfts 9–27, divided, downy beneath. Infl. a long cylindric-globose spike, purple-black. Arg., Chile.

A. platyacantha Speg. Resembles *A. pinnatifida* but infl. more rounded. Arg.

A. pumila Vahl. Prostrate, to 5cm. Lvs to 6cm; lfts 15–25, stipules purple. Infl. a few-fld short-stalked spike. Arg., Chile, Falkland Is.

A. saccaticupula Bitter. Stoloniferous herb to 25cm. Lvs to 13cm; lfts 9–15, glaucous. Infl. globose to obconic, red-spined. NZ.

A. sanguisorbae (L. f.) Vahl. = *A. anserinifolia*.

A. sericea Jacq. f. St. to 50cm. Lvs to 8cm; lfts 7–15, oblong, silky beneath; petiole to 7cm. Infl. globose, purple. Arg., Chile.

A. splendens Hook. & Arn. Resembles *A. sericea* but lfts obovate and infl. globose to cylindric. Arg.

A. trifida Ruiz & Pav. Base woody. Lvs mainly basal, to 9cm; lfts 9–17, deeply toothed, pubesc. Infl. globose. Chile.

Acajou Mill. = *Anacardium*.

Acalypha L. Euphorbiaceae. 430 herbs, shrubs or trees. Lvs simple, ovate, toothed. Fls small in catkin-like rac. or spikes. Trop. Z10.

A. godseffiana hort. Sander ex Mast. Dwarf, bushy shrub. Lvs ovate-lanceolate, deeply cut, variegated ivory or pale yellow. Infl. green-yellow. New Guinea. 'Heterophylla': br. pendulous; lvs ragged, narrow, edges yellow, wavy.

A. hispida Burm. f. RED HOT CAT'S TAIL. Shrub to 4m. Lvs to 14cm, broadly ovate, acute, bright green, thinly hairy, toothed. Catkins 50cm, bright red. New Guinea, Malaya. 'Alba': infl. off-white, tinged pink.

A. sanderi N.E. Br. = *A. hispida*.

A. sanderiana Schum. = *A. hispida*.

A. tricolor Seem. = *A. wilkesiana*.

A. wilkesiana Muell. Arg. JACOB'S COAT; COPPERLEAF; BEEFSTEAK PLANT. Shrub to 4.5m. Lvs to 20cm, elliptic to ovate-acuminate, toothed, copper-green splashed pink and red.

Catkins to 20cm, red. Pacific Is. 'Ceylon': lvs copper-maroon, round, twisted, margins bordered white to pink. 'Hoffmannia': lvs twisted, narrow, fringed with ivory lobes. 'Macafeeana': lvs red with bronze and crimson markings. 'Macrophylla': lvs large, red-brown. 'Marginata': lvs usually edged crimson. 'Miltoniana': lvs oblong, drooping, margins white, irregular. 'Mooreana': lvs broad, black tinged copper, waxy, margins twisted, crenate, small, green shaded red. 'Musaica': lvs green marked orange and red. 'Obovata': lvs green tinged bronze, margined pink.

Acampe Lindl. Orchidaceae. 13 epiphytic or lithophytic mono-podial orchids. St. robust. Lvs 2-ranked, fleshy, strap-shaped, tough. Infl. axill., cylindric or subcapitate; fls waxy, fragrant, to 1.8cm diam. Indo-Malaya, Afr. Z10.
A. dentata Lindl. = *A. ochracea.*
A. multiflora (Lindl.) Lindl. = *A. rigida.*
A. ochracea (Lindl.) Hochr. To 60cm. Tep. yellow-white blotched brown, lip white streaked purple. India.
A. papillosa (Lindl.) Lindl. To 90cm. Lvs to 15cm. Tep. yellow blotched brown, lip white, papillose. Himal. to Burm.
A. rigida (Buch.-Ham. ex Sm.) P. Hunt. To 40cm. Lvs to 45cm. Tep. rounded, yellow spotted red-brown or crimson, lip white. Asia, E Afr.

ACANTHACEAE Juss. 346/4300. *Acanthopsis, Acanthus, Anisacanthus, Aphelandra, Asystasia, Barleria, Chameranthemum, Crossandra, Dicliptera, Dyschoriste, Eranthemum, Fittonia, Graptophyllum, Hemigraphis, Hygrophila, Hypoestes, Justicia, Lankesteria, Mackaya, Megaskepasma, Odontonema, Pachystachys, Peristrophe, Phlogacanthus, Pseuderanthemum, Ruellia, Ruspolia, Ruttya, Sanchezia, Schaueria, Sciaphyllum, Stenandrium, Strobilanthes, Thunbergia, Whitfieldia, Xantheranthemum.*

Acanthephippium Bl. Orchidaceae. 15 terrestrial orchids. Pb. ovoid-subconical with 3 large, plicate, elliptic-lanceolate lvs at apex. Infl. a lat. rac.; fls to 5cm, few, fleshy, fragrant; sep. connate enclosing pet. free, spathulate; lip 3-lobed, lat. lobes erect; sometimes spurred. Asia to Fiji. Z10.
A. bicolor Lindl. Pbs 5cm. Lvs to 30×10cm. Fls fragrant, pale yellow streaked red-brown. Indochina.
A. javanicum Bl. Pbs to 25cm. Lvs to 60×20cm. Fls fragrant, dull yellow streaked or spotted pink, lip yellow and white, tipped purple. Malaysia.
A. matinianum Lindl. & Cogn. Pbs to 5cm, dark purple. Lvs to 30×13cm, fleshy, purple-tinted. Fls yellow striped dull red, lip yellow to gold. Philipp.
A. striatum Lindl. Pbs to 20cm. Lvs. Fls white to ivory tinged dull red; lip with maroon calli. N India.
A. sylhetense Lindl. Close to *A. bicolor,* but larger in all respects with fls cream to dull yellow, spotted and streaked maroon. Himal.

Acanthocalycium Backeb.
A. aurantiacum Rausch = *Echinopsis thionantha.*
A. chionanthum (Speg.) Backeb. = *Echinopsis thionantha.*
A. glaucum Ritter = *Echinopsis thionantha.*
A. hyalacanthum (Speg.) Backeb. = *Echinopsis huascha.*
A. klimpelianum (Weidlich & Werderm.) Backeb. = *Echinopsis spiniflora.*
A. peitscherianum Backeb. = *Echinopsis spiniflora.*
A. spiniflorum (Schum.) Backeb. = *Echinopsis spiniflora.*
A. thionanthum (Speg.) Backeb. = *Echinopsis thionantha.*
A. variiflorum Backeb. = *Echinopsis thionantha.*
A. violaceum (Werderm.) Backeb. = *Echinopsis spiniflora.*

Acanthocereus (Berger) Britt. & Rose. Cactaceae. 6+ cacti, shrubs or weakly scandent; st. segmented or not, ribbed. Fls funnelform, nocturnal, white; tube elongate; perianth broad. Trop. Amer., Carib. Z9.
A. acutangulus (Pfeiff.) Backeb. & F. Knuth = *A. tetragonus.*
A. baxaniensis (Karw.) Britt. & Rose = *A. tetragonus.*
A. colombianus Britt. & Rose. Similar to *A. tetragonus.* Shrubby, erect, 2–3m, branching below, st. 9cm broad, red-brown at first; ribs 3, wing-like; central spines 1–3, 4–5.5cm, v. stout. Fls 25cm, tube 23.5cm. Colomb.
A. guatemalensis hort. = *A. colombianus.*
A. horridus Britt. & Rose. Stout shrub; st. 8–10cm diam., grey-green; ribs 3, or 5–6 on young growth, deeply crenate; central spines 1(–2), to 8cm, stout. Fls 18–20cm, tube 12cm. Guat. and perhaps Mex.
A. occidentalis Britt. & Rose. Shrubby, forming thickets; st. weak and slender, 4–5cm diam., often bronzed; ribs 3–5, slightly sinuate; spines to 7cm, tinged yellow. Fls 14–18cm. W Mex.

A. pentagonus (L.) Britt. & Rose = *A. tetragonus.*
A. pitajaya (Jacq.) Dugand ex Croizat. = *A. colombianus.*
A. subinermis Britt. & Rose. Low shrub, to 1m; st. seg. 5–7cm broad, shining green; ribs 3–4; spines to 1.5cm. Fls 15–22cm; outer tep. tinged red. S Mex.
A. tetragonus (L.) Hummelinck. Gaunt shrub; st. to 3m+, arching, sometimes rooting at tips; ribs 3–5, wing-like; spines 5–8, to 4cm, stout. Fls 17–25cm; tube to 15cm. Summer. S US, W. Indies, Central Amer.
→*Cereus.*

Acantholimon Boiss. Plumbaginaceae. 120 perenn. everg. sub-shrubs and herbs, tufted or cushion-forming. Sometimes heterophyllous: spring lvs short, broad, fleshy; summer lvs linear to subcylindric, ending in a spine. Infl. simple or branched, short or long-stalked; fls small in bracteate spikelets; cal. funnelform, 5–10-lobed; pet. 5. E Medit. to C Asia. Z3.
A. acerosum (Willd.) Boiss. Densely tufted, woody-based. Lvs 1–7cm, 3-angled, mucronate, with lime dots and coarse margins. Infl. simple; spikelets 5–15; cal. white-pink; cor. white-pink. Asia Minor.
A. alberti Reg. Loosely tufted, woody-based. Lvs to 3cm, linear-subulate, short-pubesc. Infl. to 15cm, branched, downy; spike-lets 4–8; cal. white to pink; cor. bright pink. C Asia.
A. androsaceum (Jaub. & Spach) Boiss. = *A. ulicinum.*
A. androsaceum ssp. *lycaonicum* (Boiss. & Heldr.) Bokh. = *A. ulicinum* ssp. *lycaonicum.*
A. androsaceum var. *creticum* Boiss. = *A. ulicinum* var. *creticum.*
A. androsaceum var. *purpurascens* Bokh. = *A. ulicinum* var. *purpurascens.*
A. araxanum Bunge. Loosely tufted, woody-based, domed. Lvs to 5cm, narrow, glaucous, ciliate. Infl. to 20cm, glab., branched at apex; spikelets 1-fld; cal. 1.5cm; cor. bright pink. S Russia, Armenia to Kurdistan. f. *microcalyx* Lincz. Cal. to 1cm.
A. armenum Boiss. & Huet. Cushion-forming subshrub. Lvs to 4cm, linear-lanceolate, rigid, ± 3-angled. Infl. flexuous; spikelets 1-fld; cal. white-brown veined mauve; cor. pink. Asia Minor.
A. assyriacum Boiss. = *A. venustrum* var. *assyriacum.*
A. assyriacum var. *micracme* Nab. & Bornm. = *A. acerosum.*
A. avenaceum Bunge. Loosely cushion-forming subshrub. Lvs to 3cm, linear-subulate, pale green, ciliate. Infl. to 30cm, branched; spikelets 1-fld; cal. purple-white with darker veins; cor. bright pink. C Asia.
A. bracteatum (Girard) Boiss. Compact subshrub. Lvs 3–6cm, 3-angled or flat, rigid, ciliate. Infl. to 18cm, simple; spikes capitate; spikelets 3–5-fld; cal. pink-purple; cor. bright pink. Cauc. and Iran.
A. caryophyllaceum Boiss. Subshrub to 30cm, loosely tufted. Lvs 2–5cm, linear, 3-angled, pubesc. Infl. flexuous; spikes distichous; cal. white veined purple; cor. bright pink. Cauc., Armenia, Kurdistan.
A. caryophyllaceum var. *brachystachyum* Boiss. = *A. libanoticum.*
A. confertiflorum Bokh. Glaucous, cushion-forming subshrub. Lvs 3–5cm, linear-subulate, exceeding infl. Spikes to 3cm; spike-lets 8–12, to 1.5cm; cal. limb puple; cor. pink. Iran to Turk.
A. creticum (Boiss.) Rech. f. = *A. ulicinum.*
A. echinus Boiss. = *A. ulicinum.*
A. glumaceum (Jaub. & Spach) Boiss. Woody-based, cushion-forming herb. Lvs to 3cm, linear-lanceolate, 3-angled, downy beneath. Infl. to 15cm, pubesc.; spikelets 6–8, 1-fld; cal. to 2cm, white, downy; cor. rose. Cauc., Armenia, Kurdistan, Asia Minor.
A. hohenackeri (Jaub. & Spach) Boiss. Cushion-forming, woody-based herb. Lvs to 2cm, linear-subulate, rigid. Infl. to 10cm, finely pubesc.; spikes distichous; spikelets 1-fld. Cauc., Iran.
A. iskanderi Lipsky = *A. tataricum.*
A. kotschyi (Jaub. & Spach) Boiss. Glaucous cushion-forming subshrub. Lvs 1.5–4cm, 3-angled to flattened, scabrous. Infl. flexuous; spikelets 10–20 per spike; cal. white veined purple above; cor. bright pink. S Turk.
A. laxiflorum Boiss. ex Bunge = *A. venustum* var. *laxiflorum.*
A. libanoticum Boiss. Glaucous, cushion-forming shrublet. Lvs to 2cm, 3-angled, scabrid, equalling infl. Spikelets 1cm, 10–12 per spike; cal. red, tipped white; cor. bright pink. E Medit.
A. litvinovii Lincz. Cushion-forming. Lvs narrow, tinged blue. Infl. short-stalked; spikelets 5–8 per spike; cor. pale pink. C Asia.
A. olivieri Boiss. Lvs flat, sea-green. Infl. 1–2 rows spikelets; cor. bright deep pink. Asia Minor, Cilician Taurus.
A. pulchellum Korov. Loosely cushion-forming subshrub. Lvs 2–2.5cm, linear-subulate, ciliate. Infl. to 15cm, sometimes

branched; spikes to 2cm with 6–8, 1-fld spikelets; cal. white; cor. bright pink. C Asia.

A. raddeanum Czerniak. Loosely cushion-forming. Lvs turning bronze in winter. Fls pink. C Asia.

A. splendidum Bunge = *A. bracteatum*.

A. tataricum Boiss. Compact, cushion-forming subshrub. Lvs 1.5–2.5cm, linear-lanceolate, glaucous, rigid. Infl. to 15cm, usually simple; spikelets 5–10, 2–4-fld; cal. white veined purple; cor. bright pink. C Asia.

A. tournefortii (Jaub. & Spach) Boiss. = *A. ulicinum*.

A. trautvetteri Kusn. = *A. araxanum*.

A. ulicinum (Willd. ex Schult.) Boiss. Cushion-forming subshrub. Lvs 0.5–2cm, linear, 3-angled, glaucous. Infl. short; spikes 1–2, spikelets 3–7; cal. white or purple; cor. large; pink. E Medit. and Balk. to Asia Minor. var. *creticum* (Boiss.) Bokh. & Edmonds. Lvs to 0.8cm. Spikelets 2–3-fld; cal. white. Crete. var. *purpurascens* (Bokh.) Bokh. & Edmonds. Cal. purple. E Medit. ssp. *lycaonicum* (Boiss. & Heldr.) Bokh. & Edmonds. Lvs ± glaucous. Infl. with 2 spikes; bracts purple-tinted. Asia Minor.

A. venustum Boiss. Loosely cushion-forming shrublet. Lvs 1.5–4cm, linear-lanceolate, rigid, revolute, silver-green. Infl. exceeding lvs with 12–20, 1-fld spikelets; cal. dull yellow veined purple; cor. pink. Asia Minor. var. *venustum*. Infl. bracts glab., outermost triangular. W Syr. to W Iran. var. *assyriacum* (Boiss.) Boiss. Infl. bracts pubesc. Turk. var. *laxiflorum* (Boiss. ex Bunge) Bokh. Infl. bracts glab., outermost lanceolate, not triangular. W Syr., N Iran.

→*Statice*.

Acanthopanax (Miq.) Decne. & Planch.

A. aculeatus (Ait.) Witte = *Eleutherococcus trifoliatus*.

A. divaricatus (Sieb. & Zucc.) Seem. = *Eleutherococcus divaricatus*.

A. evodiifolius Franch. = *Gamblea evodiifolia*.

A. giraldii Harms = *Eleutherococcus giraldii*.

A. gracilistylus W.W. Sm. = *Eleutherococcus gracilistylus*.

A. henryi (Oliv.) Harms = *Eleutherococcus henryi*.

A. innovans (Sieb. & Zucc.) Seem. = *Gamblea innovans*.

A. lasiogyne Harms = *Eleutherococcus lasiogyne*.

A. leucorrhizus (Oliv.) Harms = *Eleutherococcus leucorrhizus*.

A. pentaphyllus (Sieb. & Zucc.) Marchal. = *Eleutherococcus sieboldianus*.

A. rehderianus Harms = *Eleutherococcus rehderianus*.

A. ricinifolius (Sieb. & Zucc.) Seem. = *Kalopanax septemlobus*.

A. senticosus (Rupr. & Maxim.) Harms = *Eleutherococcus senticosus*.

A. sessiliflorus (Rupr. & Maxim.) Seem. = *Eleutherococcus sessiliflorus*.

A. setchuensis Harms ex Diels. = *Eleutherococcus setchuensis*.

A. sieboldianus Mak. = *Eleutherococcus sieboldianus*.

A. sieboldianus f. *variegatus* (Nichols.) Rehd. = *Eleutherococcus sieboldianus* 'Variegatus'.

A. simonii Schneid. = *Eleutherococcus simonii*.

A. spinosus auctt., non (L. f.) Miq. = *Eleutherococcus gracilistylus* or *Eleutherococcus*

A. spinosus auct., non (L. f.) Miq. = *Eleutherococcus sieboldianus*.

A. spinosus (L. f.) Miq. = *Eleutherococcus spinosus*.

A. ternatus Rehd. = *Eleutherococcus lasiogyne*.

A. trichodon Franch. & Savat. = *Eleutherococcus trichodon*.

A. trifoliatus (L.) Voss = *Eleutherococcus trifoliatus*.

A. wardii W.W. Sm. = *Eleutherococcus lasiogyne*.

Acanthophoenix H.A. Wendl. Palmae. BARBEL PALM. 1 palm to 18m. St. solitary, closely ringed, swollen at base; crownshaft prominent. Lvs pinnate; sheaths to 1.5m, prickly; pinnae numerous, spreading, slender, closely set, apically cleft, conspicuously veined. Mascarene Is. Z10.

A. crinita (Bory) H.A. Wendl. = *A. rubra*.

A. rubra (Bory) H.A. Wendl.

Acanthophyllum C.A. Mey. Caryophyllaceae. 50 suffruticose perenn. Lvs spine-like. Fls sessile; cal. tubular, 5-toothed; pet. 5, white to pink. Z6.

A. glandulosum Bunge ex Boiss. Shrublet to 30cm, densely gland. hairy. Lvs to 3.5cm. Fls white in condensed infl. Mts of NE Iran to the Altai.

A. grandiflorum Stocks. Dense cushion plant, grey hairy. Lvs to 1cm. Fls solitary, purple. Pak. (Baluchistan).

A. pungens (Bunge) Boiss. To 30cm. Lvs to 5cm. Fls pink in heads. Widespread and variable, from Armenia and Iran to Mong.

A. spinosum C.A. Mey. = *A. pungens*.

Acanthopsis Harv. Acanthaceae. 7 perenn. herbs, differing from *Acanthus* in seeds with hygroscopic hairs. S Afr. Z9.

A. carduifolia (L.f.) Schinz. Coarsely hairy short-stemmed, woody-based herb. Lvs to 7.5cm, pinnatifid, spiny, biserrate. Spike to 7cm with broad, spiny bracts and blue fls to 2.25cm. S Afr.

→*Acanthus* and *Blepharis*.

Acanthosicyos Welw. ex Hook. f. Cucurbitaceae. 2 xerophytic perenn. Lvs reduced to scales. ♂ fls solitary or clustered, ♀ fls solitary, pet. coriaceous. Kalahari. Z10.

A. horridus Welw. ex Hook. f. NARA; NARRAS. Bush to 1m. Roots to 12m deep. Pet. yellow. Fr. orange-yellow to 7cm.

Acanthostachys Klotzsch. Bromeliaceae. 1 perenn. epiphyte with short, sprawling rhiz. Lvs to 1m, linear, loosely bundled, arching, scaly, tightly involute, remotely toothed. Infl. 3–7cm, long-stalked, an ovoid, pineapple-like head with sterile apical bracts, pet. yellow. E Braz., Parag., NE Arg. Z10.

A. strobilacea (Schult. f.) Klotzsch.

Acanthus L. BEAR'S BREECHES. Acanthaceae. 30 perenn. herbs and shrubs. Lvs basal in those listed (except *A. montanus*), oblanceolate, pinnately lobed, toothed, spiny. Infl. a conspicuously bracteate, long-stalked spike; cal. 4; cor. hooded-tubular, lower lip 3-lobed. Trop. and temp. OW, largely Medit., Asia Minor.

A. balcanicus Heyw. & Richardson. Lvs pinnatisect, lobes ovate, toothed, not spiny. Infl. to 1.5m; bracts ovate-acuminate, spiny, red-purple; cor. pale-pink flushed mauve. Balk., Rom., Greece. Z8.

A. boissieri Freyn non Hausskn. = *A. dioscoridis*.

A. carduifolius L. f. = *Acanthopsis carduifolia*.

A. caroli-alexandri Hausskn. Possibly a hybrid between *A. spinosus* and *A. hirsutus*.

A. dioscoridis L. ed. Willd. Stoloniferous. Lvs to 4cm across, entire, laciniate or lobed, silver-green, seldom spiny. Infl. to 40cm; bracts incised, 7-veined; fls to 5cm, purple-pink. Turk., Iraq, Iran. var. *brevicaulis* (Freyn) E. Hoss. Seldom exceeding 15cm: (*A. dioscoridis* × *A. hirsutus*?). var. *laciniatus* Freyn. Lvs cut to half-way. var. *perringii* (Siehe) E. Hoss. Lvs pinnatisect with toothed and spiny lobes. Z8.

A. hirsutus Boiss. Lvs pinnatifid, lobes acute, ragged, spiny, with cobwebby hairs. Infl. to 45cm, few-fld; bracts broadly ovate, woolly, toothed; cor. cream to yellow. W Turk. Z8.

A. hispanicus hort. = *A. mollis* 'Niger'.

A. hungaricus Baenitz = *A. balcanicus*.

A. latifolius hort. ex Goeze = *A. mollis* Latifolius group.

A. longifolius Host non Poir. = *A. balcanicus*.

A. lusitanicus hort. = *A. mollis*.

A. mollis L. Lvs to 100×20cm, pinnatifid, lobes oblong, toothed, softy spiny, glossy dark green. Infl. to 2m; bracts ovate, sharply toothed, flushed mauve; cor. white. S Eur., NW Afr. Latifolius group – large plants with v. broad, glossy lvs, sometimes barely dissected, includes: 'Niger': lvs v. dark, glossy green; fls suffused mauve. 'Oak Leaf': lvs large, deep green, oak lf-shaped. Z6.

A. montanus (Nees) Anderson. MOUNTAIN THISTLE. Sparse shrub to 2m. Lvs to 3cm, oblong, sinuate to shallowly pinnatifid, coarsely spiny, semi-rigid, dark green with silvering. Infl. term., stout, to 25cm; cor. white or rose tinted mauve. W Trop. Afr. Z10.

A. niger hort. = *A. mollis* 'Niger'.

A. perringii Siehe. = *A. dioscoridis* var. *perringii*.

A. schotii hort. = *A. balcanicus*.

A. spinosissimus Desf. = *A. spinosus* Spinosissimus group.

A. spinosus L. Lvs to 30cm across, to 3×pinnatifid, semi-rigid, lobes narrow, strongly spiny and revolute, dark green with silvery weak hairs above. Infl. to 1m, slender; bracts ovate-acuminate, spiny-toothed; cor. white. Medit. Z6. Spinosissimus group: hybrids between *A. spinosus* and *A. mollis* with broad, sharply spiny, deeply cut lvs.

A. spinosus hort. = *A. spinosus* Spinosissimus group.

A. syriacus Boiss. Lvs lanceolate, lacerate, spiny, thinly pubesc., midrib silvery. Infl. to 60cm; bracts purple-tinted, recurved, spiny; cor. green-white tinted purple. W Syr., E Medit., Greece. Z8.

Acca O. Berg. Myrtaceae. 2 everg. shrubs. Fls solitary, axill.; cal. lobes and pet. 4; sta. many, long-exserted. Fr. an oblong berry. S Braz.

A. sellowiana (O. Berg.) Burrett. PINEAPPLE GUAVA. To 6m. Lvs to 7.5cm, elliptic-oblong, dull sea green above, silvery or grey-downy beneath. Fls to 4cm diam.; pet. fleshy, tinted purple; sta. dark red. Fr. 5–7cm, green tinged red. S Braz. to N Arg. Z8.

→*Feijoa*.

Acer L. MAPLE. Aceraceae. 150 decid. or everg. trees and shrubs. Lvs simple, entire to deeply lobed or with 3–7 lfts. Fls 4–5-merous in axill. or terminal pan. or rac. Fr. 2 1-seeded samaras, fused at ovaries. N & C Amer., Eur., N Afr., Asia.

A. acuminatum Wallich ex D. Don To 6m. Young twigs purple-brown, glab. Lvs 6–11cm, dark green above, pale green beneath, flushed red when young, pubesc. beneath, lobes 3–5, triangular, biserrate, acuminate. W Himal. Z6.

A. albopurpurascens Hayata. Tree to 15m, everg. Br. pubesc., then glab. Lvs 6–13×2.5–5cm, coriaceous, oblong-lanceolate, acuminate, entire, base cuneate, pale green glab. above, red-white to blue beneath, v. pubesc. when young; petiole to 3cm tinged blue. China, Taiwan. Z7.

A. ambiguum Dipp. non Heer = *A. mono* f. *ambiguum*.

A. amplum Rehd. = *A. longipes* ssp. *amplum*.

A. angustilobum Hu = *A. wilsonii*.

A. argutum Maxim. POINTED-LEAF MAPLE. To 8m, usually shorter, shrubby. Twigs pubesc. Lvs broadly elliptic to oval, dark green above, paler beneath, turning yellow in autumn, lobes 5–7 narrow-acuminate, serrate; petiole to 6cm. Jap. Z5.

A. barbatum Booth non Michx. = *A.* ×*rotundilobum*.

A. barbinerve Maxim. Distinguished from *A. argutum* by larger fr. and more coarsely biserrate lvs. Manch., Korea. Z6.

A. bodinieri Lév. = *A. mono* var. *tricuspis*.

A. ×*bornmuelleri* Borb. (*A. campestre* ×*A. monspessulanum.*) Small tree, similar to *A. campestre*. Young br. smooth. Lvs 5–6cm, base cordate, 3–5 lobed, glab., shiny above, subglabrous beneath. SE Eur., Balk., reported in Greece. Z6.

A. buergerianum Miq. THREE-TOOTHED MAPLE. Small tree. Br. glab. Lvs to 8×10cm, dark green above, paler or glaucescent beneath, pubesc., at first, broadly cuneate, lobes 3–5, acute-triangular, entire to crenulate; petiole to 7cm. E China, Jap. 'Maruba Tokaede': lvs firmer, lobes blunt, sometimes 0. var. *formosanum* (Hayata) Sas. Lvs 3-lobed, obtuse, base cordate. var. *ningpoense* (Hance) Rehd. Lvs with lobes pointing sideways, blue-green. China. var. *trinerve* (Siesmeyr) Rehd. Shrubby, to 3–6m. Lvs with 3 deep, narrow lobes, lobes dentate to biserrate. China. Z6.

A. caesium Wallich ex Brandis. To 25m; bark grey. Lvs to 14×20cm, narrow cordate, pubesc., blue-green beneath, glab. at tip, lobes 5, caudate, biserrate. China, Himal. Z6.

A. caesium ssp. *giraldii* (Pax) E. Murray = *A. giraldii*.

A. campbellii ssp. *flabellatum* (Rehd.) Murray = *A. flabellatum*.

A. campbellii ssp. *wilsonii* (Rehd.) De Jong = *A. wilsonii*.

A. campbellii Hook. f. & Thoms. ex Hiern. To 30m. Young br. red-brown, glab. Lvs to 12×15cm, narrow, glab. beneath at tip, pubesc. when young, lobes 5–7 ovate-caudate, deeply dentate, base rounded, entire. Nepal to Burm. ssp. *sinense* (Pax) De Jong. To 10m; bark grey, rough. Lvs glossy green above, blue-green beneath, lobes 5, acuminate-cordate; petiole red, pubesc. China. Z7.

A. campbellii var. *yunnanense* Rehd. = *A. flabellatum* var. *yunnanense*.

A. campestre L. HEDGE MAPLE; FIELD MAPLE. Shrub or tree to 12m, crown rounded. Young growth pubesc. often becoming corky. Lvs to 8×10cm, dull green above, pubesc. beneath, lobes 3–5, obtuse, entire to denticulate; petiole containing milky sap. Eur., W Asia. 'Albomaculatum': lvs tinged white. 'Albo-variegatum': lvs blotched white; fr. downy. 'Eastleigh Weeping': habit pendulous. 'Elsrijk': habit broadly conical, v. dense; lvs small, 4–6cm, deep green. 'Fastigiatum': upright; br. v. corky; lvs 5-lobed, pubesc. beneath. 'Laetum': upright; lvs light green. 'Nanum' ('Compactum'): shrubby, dense, rounded. 'Pendulum': br. pendulous. 'Postelense': small tree, shrubby or mop-headed; lvs golden-yellow becoming yellow-green, petioles red. 'Pulverulentum': lvs dusted white, blotched green. 'Schwerinii': lvs opening blood-red, later becoming purple. 'Zorgvlied': crown slender-ovoid. var. *austriacum* (Tratt.) DC. Lvs subcoriaceous, lobes 5 entire to undulate, glab. beneath. N Medit. var. *leiocarpon* Wallr. Fr. glab., not pubesc. as in type. SE Eur. var. *tauricum* (Kirchn.) Pax. Less robust. Lobes 3–5, bluntly acute, pubesc. beneath. Z4.

A. campestre var. *hebecarpum* DC. = *A. campestre*.

A. capillipes Maxim. To 13m. Bark green-brown striped white; twiglets coral-red at first. Lvs to 11cm, ovate-acute in outline, 3-lobed, serrate, dark green, glab.; petiole red. Jap. Z5.

A. cappadocicum Gled. CAUCASIAN MAPLE. To 20m, suckering. Young growth pruinose then lustrous green. Lvs to 14cm wide, reticulate beneath, golden yellow in autumn, lobes 5–7, triangular, acuminate, entire; petiole to 18cm, containing milky sap. Cauc., Asia Minor to N India. 'Aureum': lvs bright green, turning golden yellow in spring and autumn. 'Rubrum': lvs blood-red when young, green with age; young twigs red. 'Tricolor': lvs pink when young, later white powdered on green; young twigs pink-red. var. *indicum* (Pax) Rehd. Small tree, 6–8m; young growth red-brown, lenticillate. Lvs finely pubesc.

along midrib. var. *tricaudatum* (Rehd.) Rehd. To 9m; bark dark grey. Young br. grey, glab. Lvs smaller, 3-lobed. ssp. *lobelii* (Ten.) De Jong. To 18m, columnar with age. Young growth pruinose. Lvs larger, usually with 5 entire to undulate lobes. It. ssp. *sinicum* (Rehd.) Hand.-Mazz. Young shoots red-brown, deeply punctate. Lvs to 10cm wide, deeply punctate. Himal. to China (Yunnan). Z6.

A. carpinifolium Sieb. & Zucc. HORNBEAM MAPLE. To 10m; young br. glab., brown. Lvs to 11×4cm, simple, obovate, acute, biserrate, chartaceous, penninerved; petiole to 3cm. Jap. 'Esveld Select': habit fastigiate. Z5.

A. catalpifolium Rehd. = *A. longipes* ssp. *catalpifolium*.

A. caudatifolium Hayata. To 20m; shoots glab. Lvs to 10×7cm, ovate-oblong, narrow-acuminate, biserrate, glab. beneath, mid-lobe ovate, acuminate longer than lat. lobes; petiole to 7cm. China, Taiwan. Z8.

A. caudatum Nichols. non Wallich ex Rehd. = *A. acuminatum*.

A. caudatum Wallich ex Rehd. = *A. ukurunduense* ssp. *caudatum*.

A. caudatum var. *ukurunduense* (Trautv. & Mey.) Rehd. = *A. ukurunduense*.

A. chienii Hu & Cheng = *A. pectinatum* ssp. *taronense*.

A. chloranthum Merrill = *A. pectinatum* ssp. *taronense*.

A. chunii Fang = *A. longipes* ssp. *catalpifolium*.

A. circinatum Pursh. VINE MAPLE. To 12m; young growth glab., green brown. Lvs to 12cm wide, almost circular, pale green above, pubesc. beneath, lobes 7–9, acute, acute, biserrate. N Am. BC to Calif. 'Little Gem': a selection of witches' broom. 'Monroe': lvs deeply dissected, lobes themselves deeply dissected. Z5.

A. circumlobatum var. *pseudo-sieboldianum* Pax = *A. pseudo-sieboldianum*.

A. cissifolium (Sieb. & Zucc.) K. Koch. To 12m; bark grey, smooth. Young growth pubesc. Lfts 3, to 8cm, ovate, acute, coarsely serrate, dark green above, paler beneath, orange-red in autumn; petiole red, glab. Jap. ssp. *henryi* (Pax) E. Murray. To 10m. Lfts 3, to 10cm, elliptic, acuminate, cuneate, entire to denticulate, crimson in autumn. C China. Z6.

A. colchicum Booth ex Gordon = *A. cappadocicum*.

A. cordatum Pax. To 3–9m, shrubby; bark grey, glab. Br. grey, smooth, pruinose. Lvs 6×3.5cm, ovate, acute, unribbed, base cordate, serrulate, glossy green above, tinged with blue beneath, pubesc. at base. China. Z6.

A. coriaceifolium Lév. Tree; young growth tomentose. Lvs 8–15×2.5–5cm, everg., oblong, grey to yellow-tomentose; petiole red. C China. Z8.

A. ×*coriaceum* Bosc ex Tausch. (*A. monspessulanum* ×*A. pseudoplatanus*.) Shrub, compact, rounded; twigs glab. Lvs to 8cm wide, glossy green above, tinged blue beneath, lobes usually 3, triangular or rounded, unevenly serrate. Origin unknown. Z6.

A. crataegifolium Sieb. & Zucc. HAWTHORN MAPLE. To 10m; bark striped white. Br. glab., purple-red with white stripes. Lvs to 8cm, ovate, unevenly serrate, blue green above, paler beneath, shallowly 3–5 lobed. Jap. 'Veitchii': marbled lime, cream and white, flushed pink at base when emerging. Z6.

A. creticum L., non F. Schmidt = *A. sempervirens*.

A. creticum F. Schmidt, non L. = *A.* ×*coriaceum*.

A. cultratum Wallich = *A. cappadocicum* var. *indicum*.

A. dasycarpum Ehrh. = *A. saccharinum*.

A. davidii Franch. SNAKEBARK MAPLE. To 15m, often multi-stemmed; bark green or purple when young. Young growth glab., striped white. Lvs to 15cm, ovate to oblong, simple or shallowly 3-lobed, dark, glossy, green above, deeply serrate; petioles. China. 'Ernest Wilson': crown round, compact; lvs to 11.5×7cm, internodes to 6cm, light green. 'George Forrest': crown open, loose; lvs to 18×13cm, deep green; petioles red. 'Madeleine Spitta': habit erect, columnar; lvs orange in fall. 'Serpentine': lvs smaller; young wood brown. ssp. *grosseri* (Pax) De Jong. To 9m; bark grey-green, striped white. Lvs to 7cm, ovate-cordate, light brown pubesc. beneath, biserrate. N China. Z6.

A. decandrum Merrill = *A. garrettii*.

A. diabolicum Bl. ex Koch. HORNED MAPLE. To 10m, round-headed. Twigs pilose, glab. at tip. Lvs to 16cm wide, densely pilose when young, then glab., lobes 5, broad-ovate, sparsely serrate. Fr. tinted red, bristly. Jap. f. *purpurascens* (Franch. & Savat.) Rehd. Lvs purple-red when young. Jap. Z5.

A. ×*dieckii* Pax. (*A. platanoides* ×*A. cappadocicum* ssp. *lobelii*.) Tree, 15–18m. Lvs 10–12cm, lobes 3–5, deltoid, entire, dark green above, paler beneath, turning red-brown or golden yellow in autumn. Gdn origin. Z5.

A. distylum Sieb. & Zucc. LINDEN-LEAVED MAPLE. To 15m. Br. pubesc. Lvs to 15cm, simple, ovate, deeply cordate, serrate, green, lustrous beneath. Jap. Z7.

A. divergens Pax. Large shrub or small tree, similar to *A. campestre*. Lvs 5- or sometimes 3-lobed. Transcauc.

A. douglasii Hook. = *A. glabrum* ssp. *douglasii*.

A. drummondii Hook. & Arn. = *A. rubrum* var. *drummondii*.

A. × durettii Pax. (*A. pseudoplatanus* × *A. monspessulanum* or *A. opalus.*) Tree, to 12m. Br. glab. Lvs to 12×9cm, light green and glab. above, lobes 3–5, triangular, serrate. Origin unknown, in cult. since 1892. Z6.

A. erianthum Schwerin. Small tree. Young shoots green, glab. Lvs to 12cm, dark green above, glab., paler beneath, lobes 3–7, acuminate, coarsely dentate. China. Z6.

A. eriocarpum Michx. = *A. saccharinum*.

A. fabri Hance. To 18m; bark smooth, grey. Br. glab., pink when young. Lvs to 10×3cm, simple, coriaceous, narrow obovate, entire, lustrous green above, paler beneath, tinged pink on emergence. C & E China. f. *rubrocarpum* (Metcalf) Rehd. Fr. purple. Z8.

A. fargesii (Veitch) Rehd. = *A. fabri*.

A. flabellatum Rehd. Tree, 6–9m. Twigs grey, thinly striate. Lvs with 7 lobes ovate, serrate, dark green above, paler beneath, glossy. China. var. *yunnanense* (Rehd.) Fang. Slender tree. Lvs deeply 5-lobed; petioles red. Z5.

A. formosanum Koidz. = *A. oliverianum* ssp. *formosanum*.

A. forrestii Diels = *A. pectinatum* ssp. *forrestii*.

A. franchetii Pax = *A. sterculiaceum* ssp. *franchetii*.

A. fulvescens Rehd. = *A. longipes*.

A. garrettii Craib. Small tree, usually everg. Twigs red-blue. Lvs to 15×7.5cm simple, entire, oblong, coriaceous, blue green beneath. S China. Z8.

A. ginnala Maxim. = *A. tataricum* ssp. *ginnala*.

A. ginnala var. *aidzuense* Franch. = *A. tataricum* ssp. *aidzuense*.

A. giraldii Pax. To 18m. Young br. flushed red, striped white, closely spotted and scarred, glab. Lvs to 11×13cm, shiny dark green above, blue-green beneath, coriaceous, lobes 3, acuminate, entire to crenate. China. Z6.

A. glabrum Torr. ROCKY MOUNTAIN MAPLE; ROCK MAPLE. To 10m. Br. red-brown, subglabrous. Lvs to 12cm wide, glab., narrow, lustrous green above, paler blue-green beneath, lobes 3–5, coarsely biserrate, acute, subcordate to cuneate. N US, Canada. var. *tripartitum* (Nutt.) Pax. Lower lvs lobed almost to centre. Colorado, New Mex. ssp. *douglasii* (Hook.) Wesm. To 6m. Shoots tinged red, upright. Lvs to 10cm wide, dull green above, paler beneath, shallowly 3-lobed, lobes acuminate. Alask. to NW US. Z5.

A. grandidentatum Nutt. ex Torr. & A. Gray = *A. saccharum* ssp. *grandidentatum*.

A. griseum (Franch.) Pax. PAPERBARK MAPLE. To 12m; bark red-brown, smooth and glossy at first, peeling in thin flakes after one season. Br. pubesc. to glab. Lfts 3, 3–5cm, elliptic to obovate, 3–5 pairs of coarse teeth, dark green above, blue-green beneath, glaucous, red-purple in autumn. C China. Z5.

A. grosseri Pax = *A. davidii* ssp. *grosseri*.

A. grosseri var. *hersii* (Rehd.) Rehd. = *A. davidii* ssp. *grosseri*.

A. heldreichii Orph. ex Boiss. GREEK MAPLE. To 16m. Br. dark red-brown, glab. Lvs to 13cm wide, chartaceous, glossy dark green above, paler and glaucous beneath, deeply 5-lobed, lobes oblong-lanceolate, coarsely dentate. SE Eur. ssp. *trautvetteri* (Medv.) Murray. RED BUD MAPLE. To 16m. Brs. glab., dark red-brown. Cauc., N Turk. ssp. *visianii* Maly. Lvs larger. Balkans. Z6.

A. henryi Pax = *A. cissifolium* ssp. *henryi*.

A. hersii Rehd. = *A. davidii* ssp. *grosseri*.

A. heterophyllum Willd. = *A. sempervirens*.

A. × hillieri Lancaster. (*A. cappadocicum* × *A. miyabei*.) Small tree. Lvs 5-lobed, turning butter yellow in autumn. 'Summer Gold': lvs tinged yellow in summer. 'Westhill': the typical state. Z5.

A. hispanicum Pourr. = *A. opalus* ssp. *hispanicum*.

A. hookeri Miq. = *A. sikkimense* ssp. *hookeri*.

A. × hybridum Bosc. (*A. opalus* × *A. pseudoplatanus*.) To 15m, crown rounded. Shoots glab., covered with lenticels. Lvs cordate, lobes 3, forward-pointing, serrate, dull green above, pubesc. beneath. Z6.

A. hyrcanum Fisch. & Mey. BALKAN MAPLE. Tree, to 10m, compact. Br. glab., grey-brown. Lvs to 9cm wide, chartaceous, 5-lobed, angular acute, dark green glab. above, glaucous beneath; petiole crimson. Crimea, Cauc., Balk. ssp. *keckianum* (Pax) Yaltirik. Shrub to 3.5m. Lvs smaller, densely pubesc. beneath. Turk. ssp. *reginae-amaliae* (Orph. & Boiss.) De Jong. Lvs smaller. Found on drier soils. Greece, W Turk. ssp. *stevenii* (Pojark.) E. Murray. Lvs glaucous and dark blue-green above, paler beneath, pubesc., lobes acuminate. Crimea. ssp. *tauricolum* (Boiss. & Bal.) Yaltirik. Tree or shrub. Br. dark brown. Lvs dark green above, veined red beneath. Asia Minor. Z5.

A. ibericum Bieb. = *A. monspessulanum* var. *ibericum*.

A. italicum var. *hyrcanum* Pax = *A. hyrcanum*.

A. italum Lauth. = *A. opalus*.

A. japonicum Thunb. FULL MOON MAPLE; JAPANESE MAPLE. To 10m. Shoots glab. Lvs to 14cm wide, suborbicular in outline, lobes 7–11, ovate to lanceolate, unevenly biserrate, bright green, silky white-haired beneath, becoming glab., crimson in autumn. Fls red. Jap. 'Aconitifolium': to 3m, rounded; lvs finely 9–11-lobed, lobes deeply incised, each lobe further divided, sharply dentate, autumn colour crimson. 'Green Cascade': habit pendulous; lvs deeply divided. 'Microphyllum': lvs smaller. 'Vitifolium': lvs fan-shaped, broad, 10–12-lobed. Z5.

A. japonicum var. *aureum* Schwerin = *A. shirasawanum* 'Aureum'.

A. japonicum var. *microphyllum* hort. (Veitch) = *A. shirasawanum*.

A. japonicum var. *sieboldianum* Franch. & Savat. = *A. sieboldianum*.

A. kawakamii Koidz. = *A. caudatifolium*.

A. laetum C.A. Mey. non Schwerin = *A. cappadocicum*.

A. laetum var. *cultratum* (Wallich) Pax = *A. cappadocicum* var. *indicum*.

A. laevigatum Wallich non Pax. To 12m; semi-everg.; bark dark grey. Br. olive green. Lvs to 13×5cm, simple, oblong-lanceolate, entire to remotely serrate, coriaceous, red becoming bright green. Himal., C & E China. var. *salweenense* (W.W. Sm.) Cowan ex Fang. To 9m; young growth pale grey, densely pubesc. Tibet, Yunnan. Z8.

A. laevigatum var. *fargesii* hort. Veitch = *A. fabri*.

A. lasiocarpum Lév. & Vaniot = *A. ukurunduense*.

A. laxiflorum Pax = *A. pectinatum* ssp. *laxiflorum*.

A. laxiflorum var. *ningpoense* Pax = *A. davidii*.

A. laxifolium var. *longilobum* Rehd. = *A. pectinatum* ssp. *taronense*.

A. leucoderme Small = *A. saccharum* ssp. *leucoderme*.

A. lipskyi Rehd. = *A. platanoides* ssp. *turkestanicum*.

A. lobelii Ten. = *A. cappadocicum* ssp. *lobelii*.

A. lobelii var. *indicum* Pax = *A. cappadocicum* var. *indicum*.

A. longipes Franch. ex Rehd. To 10m; bark smooth. Twigs glab., green when young. Lvs to 15cm wide, light green beneath, pilose, tinged red-purple on emergence, lobes 0–3, acuminate, entire; petiole containing milky sap. W China. ssp. *amplum* (Rehd.) De Jong. Brs. green, glab., punctate. Lvs glossy dark green above, paler beneath, 3–5 lobed, obovate, subcoriaceous. C China. ssp. *catalpifolium* (Rehd.) De Jong. To 20m; bark grey, inner bark red-brown. Twigs punctate. Lvs to 20cm, simple, ovate, oblong. W China. Z6.

A. macrophyllum Pursh. OREGON MAPLE; BIG LEAF MAPLE. To 30m, trunk to 1m diam. Br. stout, glab. Lvs to 28cm wide, dark lustrous green above, paler and pubesc. beneath, orange in autumn. W N tmer. 'Seattle Sentinel': habit fastigiate. 'Tricolor': lvs variegated pink and white. Z6.

A. mandschuricum Maxim. MANCHURIAN MAPLE. To 10m. Br. glab. Lfts 3 to 10×3.5cm, oblong to lanceolate, acuminate, dark green above, glaucous beneath, midrib pubesc.; petiole to 10cm, red. Manch., Korea. Z4.

A. × martinii Jordan. (*A. monspessulanum* × *A. opalus*.) Small tree. Young growth brown, smooth. Lvs with 3 lobes, deltoid, coarsely serrate, glab. and rugose, blue-green beneath, tomentose at bud break. NE Spain, S Fr., It., Switz., Balk. Z6.

A. maximowiczianum Miq. NIKKO MAPLE. To 15m, round-headed. Twigs pilose in first year. Lfts 3, to 12×6cm, ovate to oblong, dull green above, grey-green, shaggy beneath, vividly flame-coloured in fall, entire to dentate, petiole pubesc. Jap., C China. var. *megalocarpum* Rehd. Lfts to 10×5cm, oblong, pale white-green beneath, pubesc. Z5.

A. maximowiczii Pax = *A. pectinatum* ssp. *maximowiczii*.

A. mayrii Schwerin = *A. mono* var. *mayrii*.

A. mexicanum (DC.) Pax = *A. negundo* ssp. *mexicanum*.

A. micranthum Sieb. & Zucc. Small tree. Br. russet. Lvs to 8×8cm, base cordate, glab., lobes 5–7, ovate, acuminate, biserrate, red to yellow in autumn; petiole pubesc. Jap. Z6.

A. mirabile Hand.-Mazz. = *A. wardii*.

A. miyabei Maxim. To 12m, round-headed; bark corky. Young growth pubesc. Lvs to 13cm wide, deep olive green, puberulent above, blue-green pubesc. beneath, yellow in autumn, lobes 3–5, acuminate, bluntly dentate; petiole containing milky sap. Jap. Z5.

A. mono Maxim. To 15m. Brs. glab., turning yellow-grey in second year. Lvs to 15cm wide, subcordate, bright green, usually glab., lobes 5–7, ovate-deltoid, entire, apiculate; petiole with milky sap. China, Manch., Korea. 'Marmoratum': habit shrublike; lvs finely punctate and pulverulent, marked white to white-green. f. *ambiguum* (Pax) Rehd. Twigs rough, covered with lenticels. Lvs pilose beneath, midlobe larger. Jap. f. *connivens* (Nichols.) Rehd. Fr. wings upright. f. *dissectum* Wesm. Lvs deeply incised, glab. beneath, narrowly acuminate. var. *mayrii* (Schwerin) Nak. To 25m; bark smooth. Twigs blue-pruinose, glab. at tip. Lf lobes 3–5, broad-ovate, glab. beneath.

Jap. var. *savatieri* (Pax) Nak. Lvs deeply cordate, usually 7-lobed. var. *tricuspis* (Rehd.) Rehd. To 7m. Lvs to 6×6cm, lobes 0–3, glossy green above. C China. ssp. *okamotoanum* (Nak.) De Jong. Bark russet, becoming grey, smooth. Lvs to 9-lobed. Korea. Z6.

A. monspessulanum L. MONTPELLIER MAPLE. To 12m, sometimes shrubby, crown rounded. Differs from *A. campestre* in lvs lacking hair, glaucous beneath; petioles lacking milky sap. Lvs to 8cm wide, lobes 3, deltoid-ovate, lustrous green above, paler beneath, pubesc. SE Eur. to W Asia. var. *boissieri* Schwerin. Lvs to 2cm, plubesc. Iran. var. *paxii* Schwerin. Lvs to 1.5×2cm, glab. S Iran. var. *ibericum* (Bieb.) Willd. Lvs larger, midlobe with secondary lobes. W Asia. ssp. *turcomanicum* (Pojark.) E. Murray. Lvs russet, pubesc. beneath, lobes rounded. Asia Minor. f. *commutatum* Presl. Lf lobes more deeply incised. Balk. f. *hispanicum* Schwerin. Lvs, twiglets and petioles pubesc. beneath when mature. Spain. f. *illyricum* (Jacq. f.) Spach. Lvs with 3 deltoid, cuspidate lobes. Balk., Asia Minor. f. *liburnicum* Pax. Lvs smaller with short distinct basal lobes. Balk., Asia Minor. f. *maroccanum* Schwerin. Lvs with 3 cuneate lobes. var. *microphyllum* Boiss. Lvs small. ssp. *cinerascens* (Boiss.) Yaltirik. Shrub; bark olive green blotched black. Lvs sometimes with 2 additional small lobes to 6cm. Asia Minor. Z5.

A. montanum Ait. = *A. spicatum*.

A. morrisonense Hayata. = *A. caudatifolium*.

A. neapolitanum Ten. = *A. opalus* ssp. *obtusatum*.

A. neglectum Láng non Hoffsgg. = *A. × zoeschense*.

A. negundo L. ASH-LEAVED MAPLE; BOX ELDER. Tree to 20m, crown spreading. Br. glab. Lvs to 22cm, pinnate, lfts (3–)5(–7) lanceolate to oblong, to 10cm, term. lft further 3-lobed, serrate, bright green above, paler beneath, slightly pubesc.; petiole 5–8cm. C & N Amer. 'Auratum': lvs golden. 'Elegans': lvs edged bright yellow. 'Flamingo': mature lvs resembling those of 'Variegatum' but flushed rose when young, as are branchlets. 'Variegatum': lvs marbled light green and cream; tends to revert. ssp. *californicum* (Torr. & A. Gray) Wesm. Twigs tomentose. Lfts 3, rarely 5, pubesc. above, tomentose beneath when young. ♂ fls tinted pink, showy. Calif. var. *texanum* Pax. Br. pale-tomentose. Lfts 3. Tex. var. *violaceum* (Kirchn.) Jaeg. Young shoots purple-black, glaucous; fls in pink-tinted tassels. ssp. *mexicanum* (DC.) Wesm. Young twigs densely pubesc. Lfts 3, 6–8×2.5–3cm, elliptic, cuneate, serrate, tomentose; petiole white-pubesc. Mex., Guat. Z2.

A. negundo Sieb. & Zucc. non L. = *A. cissifolium*.

A. nigrum Michx. f. = *A. saccharum* ssp. *nigrum*.

A. nikoense (Maxim.) Miq. = *A. maximowiczianum*.

A. nikoense var. *griseum* Franch. = *A. griseum*.

A. nipponicum Hara. Small tree. Young br. brown-pubesc., later glab. Lvs to 15×15cm, cordate, biserrate, light green, rusty-pubesc. beneath when young, shallowly 3–5 lobed, lobes ovate. Jap.

A. nudicarpum Nak. = *A. pseudo-sieboldianum*.

A. oblongum Wallich ex DC. Tree to 10m, semi-decid. Bark grey, peeling. Br. glab. Lvs 5–12cm, 0–3-lobed, obovate, glab., subcoriaceous, entire, glaucous beneath, red on emergence; petiole 1.5 to 4cm. Himal., C & W China. var. *concolor* Pax. Lvs glaucous above, pale green beneath, glossy. var. *latialatum* Pax. Fr. wings to 3×1.5cm. Z7.

A. obtusatum Willd. = *A. opalus* ssp. *obtusatum*.

A. obtusifolium Sibth. & Sm. To 9m, everg. Lvs to 5cm wide, 0–3-lobed, coriaceous, dark green above, olive beneath, glab. E Medit. Z7.

A. okamotoanum Nak. = *A. mono* ssp. *okamotoanum*.

A. okamotoi Nak. = *A. pseudo-sieboldianum*.

A. oliverianum Pax. To 10m. Lvs to 10cm wide, truncate, dark lustrous green above, bright green beneath, glab., lobes 5, ovate, caudate, finely serrate. C China. Z6. ssp. *formosanum* (Koidz.) Murray. To 20m. Twigs tinged red. Lvs to 10×7cm, oval, base cordate, palmate, 5-lobed, lobes biserrate. China, Taiwan. Z7.

A. opalus Mill. ITALIAN MAPLE. To 15m. Lvs to 10cm wide, cordate to truncate, glossy dark green above, paler and pubesc. beneath, lobes 5, short, broad, petiole to 9cm. Fls yellow, precocious in crowded corymbs. SE Eur., It. ssp. *hispanicum* (Pourr.) E. Murray. Lvs to 7.5cm wide, 5-lobed, pubesc. Spain, SW Fr. var. *microphyllum* Kirchn. Dwarf, bark almost black. Br. short, russet. Lvs to 3cm wide, rotund, lobe tips tridentate. var. *tomentosum* (Tausch) Rehd. Lvs to 16cm wide, pale tomentose beneath, cordate, lobes shallow, rounded. It. ssp. *obtusatum* (Willd.) Gams. Lvs to 12cm wide, grey-green-pubesc. beneath, lobes 5–7, irregularly dentate. S Eur. Z5.

A. opalus var. *hyrcanum* (Fisch. & Mey.) Rehd. = *A. hyrcanum*.

A. opulifolium Vill. = *A. opalus*.

A. orientale auct. non L. = *A. sempervirens*.

A. osmastonii Gamble. Small tree. Lvs to 14cm, 0–3 lobed,

serrate, base rounded to cuneate. Himal. Z6.

A. ovatifolium Koidz. = *A. caudatifolium*.

A. palmatum Thunb. JAPANESE MAPLE. To 8m, crown rounded. Lvs to 10cm wide, suborbicular, bright green, glab., above, paler beneath, palmately 5–7 lobed, lobes deeply divided, lanceolate to oblong, biserrate, cuspidate; petioles to 4cm. Korea, Jap. Z5. There is a vast number of cvs of Japanese and European origin: a group classification has been adopted.

(a) PALMATUM GROUP. Cvs with palmately 5–7 lobed lvs; included are those cvs hitherto placed under var. *heptalobum* (Septemlobum group) excepting those intermediate between var. *heptalobum* and the Dissectum group. Ranging in habit from upright ('Okagami') to compact and bushy ('Lutescens'); young twigs may be brilliant red ('Senaki'); lvs 5-lobed ('Aureum') to 9-lobed ('Ki Hachijo'), lobes deep ('Umegal') to shallow ('Hogyoku'), scarcely toothed ('Oshu Beni') to deeply cut ('Koreanum'), broadly lanceolate ('Kiyohima') to slenderly tapering ('Koreanum'), foliage wine red ('Atropurpureum') to red-tinted ('Rubrum') to gold ('Aureum') to purple-edged ('Tsuma Beni'), summer foliage wine-red ('Bloodgood') to green ('Lutescens') to yellow-mottled ('Ukon'), autumn foliage flushed with rose ('Ki Hachijo') to scarlet ('Okagami') to gold ('Aureum').

(b) ELEGANS GROUP. Lvs mostly 7-lobed, divided to the base or near it, lobes narrowly lanceolate, toothed or slightly incised, broader and less finely cut than the Dissectum group. 'Beni kagami': shrub-like to 6.5m, young lvs dark red, autumn foliage red. 'Elegans': lf lobes widely spreading, autumn colour orange. 'Katsura': 1.25m, young lvs pale orange-yellow. 'Hessei': lvs bronze in fall. 'Omurayama': young lvs dark red turning green. 'Kinran': pendulous.

(c) DISSECTUM GROUP. Lvs 5–9-lobed, incised nearly to the base, lobes pinnatisect and deeply serrate. To 3m ('Crimson Queen'), usually vigorous in habit; lobes finely cut ('Ornatum') to deeply cut ('Garnet'), young foliage edged with red ('Dissectum Roseomarginatum') to bronze-red ('Ornatum'), summer foliage splashed with white and pink ('Dissectum Variegatum') to green ('Ornatum'), autumn foliage gold ('Filigree') to red ('Ornatum').

(d) LINEARILOBUM GROUP. Lvs divided almost to the base into 5–7 narrow lobes which are denticulate but not incised. 'Linearilobum Atropurpureum': erect, shrub-like; lvs brown-red at first, bronze in fall.

(e) VARIEGATED CULTIVARS. 'Butterfly': habit dense; lvs light green, shaped almost as in the Elegans group, irregularly edged with cream. 'Higasayama': lvs divided into 7 deeply and coarsely dentate, slenderly lanceolate lobes, margins white interrupted by green bands along veins. 'Kagero': lvs with 7 oblanceolate to obovate-acuminate lobes, the basal pair backward-pointing, irregularly variegated with yellow. 'Kagiri Nishiki': upright open habit; lvs 5-lobed, lobes distorted, irregularly denticulate, sea-green with a pink flushed margin of varying width which turns cream-white later. 'Orido Nishiki': lvs with 5–7 long-tapered, doubly dentate, narrow lobes, shiny dark green with a v. irregular white variegation which can cover the whole lf; young foliage predominantly pink. 'Shigitatsu Sawa': lvs mostly 7-lobed, not deeply divided, yellow-green, veined green. 'Ukigumo': lvs deeply lobed with blended variegation of white and green. 'Versicolor': lvs mostly 7-lobed, splashed with white, pink-tinged markings of various sizes; inclined to revert.

var. *palmatum*. Lobes coarsely serrate. var. *heptalobum* Rehd. Lvs large, mostly 7-lobed, lobes obovate, finely biserrate. ssp. *amoenum* (Carr.) Hara. Lvs to 12cm wide, lobes 7, serrate. Jap. ssp. *matsumurae* Koidz. Lvs to 11cm wide, lobes 5–9, ovate to lanceolate, deeply biserrate. ssp. *pubescens* (Li) Murray. Br. white-pubesc. Lvs to 5cm, pubesc.; petiole pubesc. Taiwan.

A. palmifolium Borkh. = *A. saccharum*.

A. papilio King. = *A. ukurunduense* ssp. *caudatum*.

A. parsonii hort. (Veitch). = *A. japonicum* 'Aconitifolium'.

A. parviflorum Franch. & Savat. non Tausch. = *A. nipponicum*.

A. parvifolium Tausch non Franch. & Savat. = *A. × coriaceum*.

A. paxii Franch. To 10m, everg. Br. purple to grey-brown. Lvs to 7×4cm, persistent, coriaceous, obovate, lustrous light green above, blue-green, glaucous beneath, 0–3-lobed, lobes abruptly acuminate; petiole to 4cm. C China. Z8.

A. pectinatum Wallich. To 15m. Br. purple to brown-grey, striped chalk white. Lvs to 14×7cm, lobes 3–5, triangular to ovate, caudate, finely serrate, or biserrate with awn-tipped teeth. Himal. ssp. *forrestii* (Diels) Murray. To 12m. Lvs to 8.5–6.5cm, dark green, glab. above, paler beneath, lobes 3, biserrate, lacking awn-tipped teeth. China. ssp. *laxiflorum* (Pax) Murray. To 12m. Young br. tinged red. Lvs usually 3-lobed, serrate, subcoriaceous. W China, Tibet. ssp. *maximowiczii* (Pax) Murray. Small tree; bark grey. Lvs to 8×10cm, ovate-oblong, dark green above, white-green beneath, glaucous, 3–5 lobed, midlobe elongated. C China. ssp. *taronense* (Hand.-Mazz.) Murray. Small, spreading tree. Br. grey-brown, pruinose, becoming red-brown, glab. Lvs to 10×10cm, ovate, lobes 5, deltoid, biserrate. Himal., NE Burm., China. Z6.

A. pensylvanicum L. MOOSEWOOD; STRIPED MAPLE; SNAKE BARK MAPLE; GOOSE FOOT. To 12m. Br. green, red-brown later, smooth, becoming white-striped. Lvs 12–18cm, obovate, subcordate, lobes 3, acuminate, serrulate, bright green, rusty beneath when young; petiole pubesc. NE US to E Canada. 'Erythocladum': br. bright red in winter. 'Silver Vein': habit spreading; bark with conspicuous silver striations, persisting even on the lower trunk. Z3.

A. pentaphyllum Diels. To 10m, spreading; bark ash-grey. Lvs palmate, lfts 5–7, to 7×1.5cm, oblanceolate, light green above, tinged blue and glab. beneath, lower lfts almost sessile; petiole red-brown. SW China. Z6.

A. pentapotamicum Stewart ex Brandis. To 9m; bark grey, smooth. Lvs to 10×15cm, grey-green, lobes 3, deeply incised, caudate, serrate; petiole to 8cm. NW Himal. Z6.

A. pictum Thunb. ex Murray. = *A. mono*.

A. pictum var. *ambiguum* Pax. = *A. mono* f. *ambiguum*.

A. pictum var. *angustilobum* Mak. = *A. mono* f. *dissectum*.

A. pictum var. *mono* Maxim. = *A. mono*.

A. pictum var. *paxii* Schwerin. = *A. mono* f. *ambiguum*.

A. pictum f. *tricuspis* Rehd. = *A. mono* var. *tricuspis*.

A. platanoides L. NORWAY MAPLE. To 30m, crown dense; bark dark grey. Br. glab. Lvs to 18cm wide, lobes 5, acuminate, sparsely dentate, dark green, lustrous beneath, yellow in autumn; petiole with milky sap. N Eur. to Cauc., nat. N Amer. A great range of cvs encompasses forms ranging in habit from narrowly columnar ('Columnare') to globose ('Charles F. Irish') to dwarf ('Pygmaeum'); lvs symmetrical ('Dissectum') to v. irregular ('Dilaceratum'), 3-lobed ('Stollii') to 5-lobed ('Plicatum'), lobes shallow ('Walderseei') to deeply dentate ('Palmatifidum'), bullate ('Roseobullatum') to glossy ('Faassen's Black') to wrinkled ('Goldsworth Purple'), margin entire ('Plicatum') to revolute ('Schwedleri') to crispate ('Undulatum'), base rounded ('Cucullatum') to cuneate ('Argutum'), venation red ('Buntzalii') to black-red ('Reitenbachii'), young foliage cream-white ('Albescens') to dark green ('Superform Miller') to dark red-brown ('Crimson King'), summer foliage light green ('Laehm'), rich crimson-purple ('Crimson king') to black-red ('Reitenbachii'), autumn foliage orange-red ('Meyering') to yellow-brown ('Palmatifolium'), variegation ranging in from large yellow-gold specks ('Aureovariegatum') to white-zoned ('Pueckleri'), deeply white-edged ('Drummondii') to pink-brown striped and white-punctate ('Walderseei'); infl. purple-red ('Faassen's Black') to green ('Rubrum'). ssp. *turkestanicum* (Pax) De Jong. Twigs red. Lvs to 20cm, lobes 5–7, entire; petiole to 12cm. NE Afghan., Turkestan. Z3.

A. polymorphum Sieb. & Zucc. = *A. palmatum*.

A. pseudolaetum Radde-Fom. = *A. platanoides* ssp. *turkestanicum*.

A. pseudoplatanus L. SYCAMORE; GREAT MAPLE; SCOTTISH MAPLE. To 40m, crown broad; bark pale grey, flaky. Br. glab. Lvs to 16cm wide, cordate, lobes 5, ovate, crenate-serrate, dark green glab. above, grey-green, glaucous beneath, yellow in autumn. NW to C Eur., It., W Asia. Cvs range in habit from broadly pyramidal ('Negenia') to narrowly upright ('Erectum') to shrub-like ('Prinz Handjery'); lvs 3-lobed ('Trilobatum') to 5-lobed ('Erectum'), lobes long-acuminate ('Argutum') to broadly ovate ('Alberti'), glossy ('Metallicum') to bullate ('Rugosum'), margin serrate ('Heterophyllum') to crenate ('Opizii') to dentate ('Wordleei'), symmetrical ('Rotterdam') to asymmetrical ('Heterophyllum'), base broadly cordate ('Latifolium') to truncate ('Trilobatum'), venation yellow ('Crispum') to green ('Nervosum'), young foliage pink changing to yellow then green ('Brilliantissimum'), yellow-pink ('Discolor') to dark orange ('Wordleei') to blood-red ('Rafinesquianum'), mature foliage green ('Cruciatum') to light yellow, beneath dark purple ('Purpureum') to white-green ('Opalifolium') to grey ('Euchlorum'), variegation from densely red and orange-speckled ('Nizetii'), grey-white punctate ('Pulverulentum') to zonally yellow ('Aureovariegatum'); petiole red ('Opalifolium') to yellow ('Euchlorum'); fr. wings light violet ('Purpurascens') to green ('Purpureum') to red ('Erythrocarpum'). Z5.

A. pseudosieboldianum (Pax) Komar. KOREAN MAPLE. Small tree. Young growth white-pruinose. Lvs suborbicular, cordate, lobes 9–11, oblanceolate, bisserrate lustrous green above, pubesc. beneath. Manch. to Korea. Z5.

A. purpurascens Franch. & Savat. = *A. diabolicum* f. *purpurascens*.

A. pycnanthum K. Koch. Like a smaller *A. rubrum*. Twigs tinged blue. Lvs to 8×7cm, shallowly 3-lobed, lobes deltoid, biserrate, dark green glab. above, tinged with blue, glaucous beneath. Jap., Korea. Z6.

A. regelii Pax = *A. pentapotamicum*.

A. reginae-amaliae Orph. & Boiss. = *A. hyrcanum* ssp. *reginae-amaliae*.

A. ×rotundilobum Schwerin. (*A. opalus* ssp. *obtusatum* ×*A. monspessulanum*.) To 20m. Twigs tinged red with grey lenticels. Lvs to 9cm, orbicular, glab., coriaceous, dark green above, paler beneath, red when young. Z6.

A. rubrocarpum Metcalf = *A. fabri* f. *rubrocarpum*.

A. rubrum L. RED MAPLE; SCARLET MAPLE; SWAMP MAPLE. To 40m; bark grey. Br. glab., red when young. Lvs to 10cm, subcordate, lobes 5–7, deltoid, abruptly acuminate, crenate-serrate, lustrous dark green, glab. above, glaucous beneath, scarlet and yellow in autumn. E & C N Amer. 'Albovariegatum': lvs spotted white. 'Columnare': to 20cm, habit broadly columnar. 'Gerling': broadly conical. 'Globosum': dwarf form, habit dense, rounded; lvs deep red. 'October Glory': lvs shiny green becoming crimson in autumn. 'Red Sunset': habit dense, growth upright; distinct red lvs in autumn. 'Sanguineum': shrubby; twigs pink-red; lvs smaller, deep green above, intense blue-green beneath, pubesc., base deeply cordate, deep red in autumn; fls carmine. 'Scanlon': habit conical. 'Schlesingeri': lvs to 12cm, base almost truncate, scarlet, normal autumn foliage; petiole red. 'Tilford': habit globose. 'Wagneri': twigs pendulous; lvs large, deeply 5-lobed; fls red. var. *drummondii* (Hook. & Arn. ex Nutt.) Sarg. DRUMMOND MAPLE. Br. red, densely tomentose. Lvs to 14cm wide, pale green veined red above, white-tomentose beneath. SE US. var. *pallidiflorum* K. Koch. Lvs turning yellow in autumn. var. *tomentosum* (Desf.) Koch. Br. deep red-brown. Lvs smaller, coarsely serrate, deep green above, tomentose beneath; petiole red. var. *trilobum* Torr. & A. Gray ex Koch. Lvs ovate, 3-lobed, deeply serrate, blue-green, pubesc. beneath. Z3.

A. rubrum var. *pycnanthum* (Koch) Mak. = *A. pycnanthum*.

A. rufinerve Sieb. & Zucc. To 12m. Bark striped white. Young brs. glaucous blue-white. Lvs to 12cm, rounded at base, 3-lobed, spreading, unevenly biserrate, dark green, glab. above, paler veined red beneath. Jap. 'Albolimbatum': lvs dotted white at margins (1869). Z6.

A. saccharinum L. SILVER MAPLE. To 40m, habit loose. Bark grey. Br. glab., pendulous. Lvs to 14cm, lobes 5, deep, acuminate, bidentate, light green, glab. above, silver pubesc. beneath, midlobe often with secondary lobules. N Amer. f. *tripartitum* (Schwerin) Pax. Twigs with large white lenticels. Lvs deeply 3-lobed. f. *lutescens* (Späth) Pax. Lvs yellow, bronze when young. f. *pendulum* (Nichols.) Pax. Br. pendulous. Lvs deeply incised. f. *pyramidale* (Späth) Pax. Br. upright forming a narrow pyramidal crown. f. *laciniatum* (Carr.) Rehd. SKINNER MAPLE. Lvs deeply cleft, lobes dissected, narrow. 'Wieri' (WIER MAPLE): br. pendulous; lvs deeply cut. Z3.

A. saccharinum Waugh non L. = *A. saccharum*.

A. saccharophorum Koch = *A. saccharum*.

A. saccharum Marshall. SUGAR MAPLE; ROCK MAPLE. To 40m, resembling *A. platanoides*, crown rounded; bark furrowed, grey. Br. glab., brown-grey. Lvs to 14cm wide, cordate, dull green above, pale grey-green beneath, lobes 3–5, acuminate, serrate, chartaceous, colouring brilliantly in fall. Alask. and Canada to SE US. 'Newton Sentry': narrowly columnar, no distinct trunk, with few, short, ascending side-branches; lvs deep green, coarse, tough, margin wavy as with *A. saccharum* ssp. *nigrum*. 'Slavin's Upright': narrow, upright form. 'Temple's Upright': habit broadly columnar, no main st., branched densely; lvs thin, pale green, margin flat. f. *glaucum* (Schmidt) Pax. Lvs sea-green beneath. var. *rugelii* (Pax) Rehd. Lvs thin-textured, lobes 3, deltoid. var. *sinuosum* (Rehd.) Sarg. Lvs obtusely 5-lobed, margins nervose. ssp. *floridanum* (Chapm.) Desmarais. Small tree; bark chalky grey. Lvs glaucous and pubesc. beneath. ssp. *grandidentatum* (Nutt. ex Torr. & A. Gray) Desmarais . To 12m; bark deep brown. Br. russet, glab. Lvs to 8cm wide lustrous green above, pubesc. beneath. W N Amer. ssp. *leucoderme* (Small) Desmarais. To 8m; bark pale grey to brown. Br. glab. Lvs to 8cm wide, dark green above, yellow-green and white-pilose beneath. SE US. ssp. *nigrum* (Michx. f.) Desmarais. BLACK MAPLE. To 40m; bark black, deeply fissured. Lvs to 14cm, deep dull green above, grey-green and pilose beneath, usually 3-lobed. E & C N Amer. Z3.

A. salweenense W.W. Sm. = *A. laevigatum* var. *salweenense*.

A. savatieri Pax = *A. mono* var. *savatieri*.

A. semenovii Reg. & Herd. = *A. tataricum* ssp. *semenovii*.

A. sempervirens L. CRETAN MAPLE. To 5m. Br. usually glab. Lvs ovate and entire to 3-lobed, coriaceous, glab., bright green, persisting into winter. E Medit. Z7.

A. ×sericeum Schwerin. (*A. pseudoplatanus* ×?) Small tree. Lvs to 9×11cm, 5-lobed, membranous to coriaceous, cordate, shiny yellow-green above, white-tomentose beneath. Z5.

A. serrulatum Hayata = *A. oliverianum* ssp. *formosanum*.

A. shibatai Nak. = *A. miyabei*.

A. shirasawanum Koidz. Small tree. Lvs to 6×6cm, suborbicular,

11–13-lobed, biserrate, red in autumn. Jap. 'Aureum': shrub; lvs pale yellow. var. *tenuifolium* Koidz. Lvs membranous, downy beneath when young. Z6.

A. sieboldianum Miq. Small tree, resembling *A. japonicum*. Shoots densely pubesc. Lvs to 8cm, cordate, 7–9 lobed, obovate, serrate, red in autumn, petioles densely downy. Jap. var. *microphyllum* Maxim. Lvs smaller, to 6cm wide. Z6.

A. sikkimense Miq. Small tree. Lvs 10–18×8–9cm, elliptic-oblong, glab., coriaceous, base cordate; petiole 3–4cm. E Himal., Sikkim, China. ssp. *hookeri* (Miq.) Wesm. Twiglets red, glab., buds red. Lvs broad-lanceolate, unlobed, membraneous, serrate; petiole 2–4cm. Z7.

A. 'Silver Vein'. (*A. laxiflorum* × *A. pensylvanicum* 'Erythrocladum'.) Strong-growing, br. arching, streaked green and white. Lvs 3-lobed above middle, acuminate, deep green above, yellow in autumn; petiole red.

A. spicatum Lam. MOUNTAIN MAPLE. To 10m. Br. russet, grey pubesc. when young. Lvs to 12cm, cordate, yellow-green above, grey pubesc. beneath, scarlet in autumn, lobes 3–5, acuminate, serrate. E N Amer. Z2.

A. stachyophyllum Hiern. Slender tree to 10m. Br. Lvs to 7cm, simple, occas. lobed, ovate to oblong, dentate, truncate, bright green above, paler beneath, pubesc. at first; petiole to 5cm. Himal. to C China. ssp. *betulifolium* (Maxim.) De Jong. Habit suckering; lvs birch-like. Z6.

A. sterculiaceum Wallich. Tree; bark grey. Twigs brown, tomentose. Lvs to 20cm wide, 3–5 lobed, cordate, chartaceous, tomentose above when young, deep green, tomentose and grey-green beneath, serrate. Himal. ssp. *franchetii* (Pax) E. Murray. To 6m. Lvs 3-lobed, smaller. SW China. Z8.

A. stevenii Pojark. = *A. hyrcanum* ssp. *stevenii*.

A. striatum Duroi = *A. pensylvanicum*.

A. syriacum Boiss. & Gaill. = *A. obtusifolium*.

A. taronense Hand.-Mazz. = *A. pectinatum* ssp. *taronense*.

A. tataricum L. TATARIAN MAPLE. To 10m. Br. glab., pale green at first, later striped chalk-white. Lvs to 10cm, simple, broadly ovate, unevenly biserrate, bright green, glab. above, pubesc. beneath, yellow in autumn. SE Asia to Asia Minor. var. *slendzinskii* Racib. Lvs usually unlobed. var. *torminaloides* Pax. Lvs 3-lobed. ssp. *aidzuense* (Franch.) De Jong. Lvs deep green, membranous. ssp. *ginnala* (Maxim.) Wesm. AMUR MAPLE. To 6m, vigorous, spreading. Br. slender. Lvs 4–8×3–6cm, 3-lobed, midlobe markedly longer, shiny deep green above, paler beneath, orange to crimson in autumn. NE Asia, NW US. 'Albovariegatum': lvs irregular, spattered with white. 'Durand Dwarf': 50–60cm, densely branched, twiglets crimson; lvs distinctly smaller. 'Pulverulentum': lvs speckled and zoned white. ssp. *semenovii* (Reg. & Herd.) Pax. Sparse, open shrub. Lvs duller and smaller than in ssp. *ginnala*, more deeply 3–5-lobed. Turkestan. Z4.

A. tauricolum Boiss. & Bal. = *A. hyrcanum* ssp. *tauricolum*.

A. tegmentosum Maxim. To 10m. Br. glab., pale green at first, later striped chalk-white. Lvs to 16cm, cordate, glab., dull green above, paler beneath, lobes 3–5, acuminate, spreading, biserrate; petiole to 8cm. Manch., Korea. Z5.

A. tenellum Pax. To 9m; shoots glab. Lvs deltoid, truncate or cordate, 3-lobed, lateral lobes short, bright green glab. above, tufted beneath; petiole with milky sap. China. Z6.

A. tenellum auct. non Pax = *A. mono* var. *tricuspis*.

A. tenuifolium (Koidz.) Koidz. = *A. shirasawanum* var. *tenuifolium*.

A. tetramerum Pax = *A. stachyophyllum*.

A. tibetense Fang. Young brs. brown to purple. Lvs 5–10cm wide, lobes 5, ovate, yellow-grey tomentose beneath; petiole 5–7cm. SE Tibet. Z6.

A. tomentosum Desf. = *A. rubrum* var. *tomentosum*.

A. tonkinense Lecompte. Twiglets olive to purple or grey-brown. Lvs 9–15cm wide, coriaceous, 3-toothed to 3-lobed, lobes acute; petiole thick, to 2.5cm. SW China, N Vietnam. Z9.

A. trautvetteri Medv. = *A. heldreichii* ssp. *trautvetteri*.

A. trifidum Hook. ex Arn. non Thunb. = *A. buergerianum*.

A. triflorum Komar. THREE-FLOWERED MAPLE. To 12m; bark eventually peeling. Shoots warty. Lvs to 8cm, trifoliate, lfts ovate to oblanceolate, pilose above, glab. and glaucous beneath; petiole pilose. Manch., Korea. Z6.

A. truncatum Bunge. SHANTUNG MAPLE. To 8m. Brs. glab., tinged purple when young. Lvs to 10cm, truncate, bright green, glab. above, paler, pubesc. beneath, lobes 5, deeply divided, deltoid; petiole to 8cm, with milky sap. N China, Manch., Korea. 'Akikaze Nishiki': lvs deep green, marked with white, some wholly white, some merely striped white. Z6.

A. tschonoskii Maxim. To 6m. Shoots glab. Lvs orbicular-ovate, to 10cm wide, bright green and glab. above, russet pubesc. beneath, yellow in autumn, lobes 5–7, ovate, biserrate; petiole to 4cm. Jap. Z5.

A. turcomanicum Pojark. = *A. monspessulanum* ssp. *turcomani-*

cum.

A. turkestanicum Pax = *A. platanoides* ssp. *turkestanicum*.

A. ukurunduense Trautv. & Mey. Small tree. Shoots pubesc. Lvs to 14cm wide, cordate, lobes 5–7, narrow ovate, serrate, densely yellow-grey pubesc. beneath; petiole pubesc., to 10cm. Jap., Korea, Manch. ssp. *caudatum* (Wallich) De Jong. Young br. ash grey, glab. Lvs to 12×12cm, yellow-brown pubesc. beneath, lobes 5, deltoid. E Himal. Z6.

A. urophyllum Maxim. = *A. pectinatum* ssp. *maximowiczii*.

A. velutinum Boiss. Tall tree. Lvs to 15cm wide, subcordate, lobes 5, broad-lanceolate, serrate, bright green above, tinged with blue and densely pubesc. beneath. Cauc., N Persia. f. *glabrescens* (Boiss. & Buhse) Rehd. Young growth brown-pink. var. *vanvolxemii* (Mast.) Rehd. Lvs to 30cm wide, veins pubesc. E Cauc. f. *wolfii* (Schwerin) Rehd. Lvs to 25×23cm, glab., maroon beneath. Z5.

A. villosum Wallich = *A. sterculiaceum*.

A. wardii W.W. Sm. To 10m. Br. stiffly pubesc. Lvs to 9cm wide, lustrous green-yellow above, rufous-pilose beneath, serrate, lobes 3, rounded. SW China, E Tibet. Z5.

A. wilsonii Rehd. To 13m. Shoots glab. Lvs to 9×10cm, lobes 3, deeply incised, lanceolate, forward pointing, glaucous blue-green beneath. China. Z7.

A. yuii Fang. Small tree. Twigs tinged red to grey-brown. Lvs 5×7.5cm wide, 3-lobed to deltoid, deep green above, yellow-green beneath with yellow pubesc.; petiole 2.5–5cm, flushed red. W China. Z5.

A. ×*zoeschense* Pax. (*A. campestre* × *A. cappadocicum* ssp. *lobelii*.) To 16m. Shoots finely downy. Lvs to 11cm wide, cordate, dark green above, later glab. and lustrous beneath, lobes 5, acuminate; petiole with milky sap. 'Annae': lvs deep red at bud break, later turning olive-green. 'Elongatum': lvs 3-lobed, lobes long and narrow-acuminate, outside lobes slightly further lobed, margin wavy, venation scarlet; petioles red. 'Frederici': young growth white-yellow; lvs later golden veined red. Z5.

ACERACEAE Juss. 2/113. *Acer, Dipteronia*.

Aceras R. Br. Orchidaceae. 1 tuberous terrestrial orchid, 10–60cm. Lvs to 12cm, oblong-lanceolate, basal or reduced on st. Spike term; fls to 3cm, olive green tinted red; tep. hooded; lip slender, 3-lobed, midlobe elongate, cleft. Summer. W & C Eur. Z5.

A. anthropophorum (L.) Ait. f. MAN ORCHID.

Aceriphyllum Engelm.

A. rossii (Oliv.) Engelm. = *Mukdenia rossii*.

Acerola *Malpighia*.

Achillea L. YARROW; MILFOIL. Compositae. 85 perenn., often aromatic herbs. Lvs entire or pinnately divided and ferny. Cap. radiate, small, term., solitary or in dense umbel-like clusters. N temp. regions. Z6 unless specified.

A. abrotanifolia L. = *Tanacetum abrotanifolium*.

A. abrotanoides (Vis.) Vis. To 40cm, glabrescent. Lvs to 3cm, 1–2-pinnatifid, lobes lanceolate to linear, entire, pubesc. Cap. in corymbs of 12–30; involucre 5–7mm diam.; ray flts *c*4mm, white. W Balk.

A. aegyptiaca L. 20–50cm; grey-tomentose, lvs to 10cm, pinnately dissected with crenate or serrate lobes. Cap. in corymbs of 15 to many; involucre to 4mm diam.; ray flts to 1mm, yellow. S Greece, S Aegean. Z5.

A. ageratifolia (Sibth. & Sm.) Boiss. To 30cm. Lvs grey-tomentose, to 4cm, spathulate, entire or crenulate, occas. pinnately divided at base. Involucre 5–15mm diam.; ray flts 7–9mm, white. C Balk. Z3.

A. ageratum L. SWEET NANCY. To 80cm, hairy. Lvs to 5cm, sometimes hairy, pinnately divided to simple, serrate. Cap. in corymbs of 15 to many; involucre *c*3mm diam.; ray flts to 1mm, yellow. W Medit., Port. 'Flowers of Sulphur': flts sulphur yellow, ageing pale cream. 'Hartington White': fls bright white. 'Moonshine': fls pale yellow. 'Moonwalker': fls bright yellow, sweetly scented even when dried. 'Salmon Beauty': fls salmon red ageing to pale creamy yellow, flowering successively. 'Weserandstein': fls salmon red ageing creamy yellow. 'W.G. Childs': ray flts white, disc dark. Z7.

A. aizoon (Griseb.) Hal. = *A. ageratifolia*.

A. alpina L. = *A. sibirica*.

A. ambigua Poll. = *A. millefolium*.

A. argentea hort. non Lam. = *A. umbellatum*.

A. argentea Lam. non hort. = *Tanacetum argenteum*.

A. atrata L. To 30cm, brown-green. Lvs 1–4cm, twice pinnatifid, ± hairy, seg. with to 3 lanceolate lobes. Cap. 2–10, in corymbs; involucre 8–12mm diam.; ray flts *c*6mm, white. Alps.

A. aurea hort. = *A. tomentosa*.

A. barbeyana Heldr. & Heimerl. To 15cm, silky. Lvs 1cm, elliptic to lanceolate dissected, lobes lanceolate. Cap. in corymbs of 5–20; involucre 4mm diam.; ray flts 3mm, white. SC Greece.

A. barrelieri (Ten.) Schultz-Bip. To 15cm, silky tomentose. Lvs elliptic to lanceolate, twice pinnatifid, basal lvs 2–7cm, petiolate, st. lvs to 2×0.4cm, sessile. Involucre 10mm diam.; ray flts 7–9mm, white. C to S Apennines.

A. biebersteinii Afan. Differs from *A. micrantha* in st. unbranched; ray flts 1.5mm. SW & SC Asia, S Bulg.

A. brachyphylla Boiss. & Hausskn. To 20cm. Lvs to 1.2cm, woolly, pinnatisect, lobes toothed. Cap. 1–3; involucre to 8×10mm; ray flts 4–5mm white. Turk.

A. buglossis Friv. = *A. lingulata*.

A. cartilaginea Ledeb. ex Rchb. Resembles *A. ptarmica* but lvs slightly pubesc. with gland. spots on both surfaces; involucre 4–8mm diam.; ray flts 3mm. Russia to Germ.; SW Rom.

A. chrysocoma Friv. Resembles *A. tomentosa* but involucre 3.5–5mm diam.; ray flts c3mm. Albania, Macedonia. 'Grandiflora': heads large.

A. clavennae L. To 40cm, silky-silvery. Lvs to 8cm, pinnatifid, with few lobes. Cap. in corymbs of 6–25; involucre 4–8mm diam.; ray flts 4–6mm, white. E Alps, W Balk. Z3.

A. clusiana Tausch. Resembles *A. atrata* but strongly aromatic; st. white-pubesc.; lf seg. 10-lobed; involucre 5–7mm diam. E Alps, mts of Bulg. and S Balk.

A. clypeolata Sm. To 70cm, short-tomentose. Lvs to 18cm pinnately dissected, weakly glandular-spotted, lobes ovate, serrate to pinnatifid toothed. Cap. 50–150 in corymbs; involucre to 4×3mm; ray flts 2–4mm, yellow. Spring–summer. Balk., SE Rom. Crossed with *A. filipendulina* to produce 'Coronation Gold' (to 1m, vigorous; fls deep yellow in flat heads, drying well), and with *A.* 'Taygetea', producing 'Moonshine' (lvs tomentose, v. silver; fls bright yellow).

A. coarctata Poir. 15–70cm, silky-woolly. Lvs to 30cm, pinnatisect, lobes divided once or twice to 1-pinnatifid. Cap. 20–150 or more; involucre 3–4mm diam.; ray flts c1cm, 5–6, yellow. Spring–summer. Balk., Rom., Ukraine.

A. compacta Willd. = *A. coarctata*.

A. decolorans Schräd. = *A. ageratum*.

A. depressa Janka. To 30cm, hairy. Lvs to 3cm, lanceolate to linear, pectinate or pinnatifid. Cap. 15 to many, in corymbs; involucre 2–3mm diam.; ray flts 1–1.5mm, pale yellow. EC Eur. and Balk.

A. distans Waldst. & Kit. ex Willd. To 120cm. Lvs to 8cm, lanceolate, deeply divided, seg. 1–2cm, ovate to lanceolate, 1–2-serrate or divided. Involucre to 7×4mm; ray flts 1–4mm, white or pink. SW Alps to E Carpath. and Bulg.

A. erba-rotta All. ± glab. Lvs simple or divided, ovate to spathulate, rarely lanceolate. Cap. in corymbs of 3–15; involucre 5–6mm diam.; ray flts 2–3mm, white. Alps, Apennines, EC Greece. ssp. *ambigua* (Heimerl) I.B.K. Richardson. Lvs divided. W Alps, Apennines. ssp. *moschata* (Wulf.) I.B.K. Richardson. To 10cm; infl. aromatic. C Alps.

A. eupatorium Bieb. = *A. filipendulina*.

A. filipendulina Lam. 60–100cm, loosely hairy. Lvs densely hairy, with gland. spots, to 20cm, oblong, pinnatisect divided with oblong to lanceolate, lobed or toothed seg. Cap. numerous in corymbs 4–10cm diam.; involucre to 5×3.5mm; ray flts c1mm, 2–4, gold. Summer. Cauc., Iran, Afghan., C Asia. 'Altgold': to 80cm; fls dark gold. 'Cloth of Gold': fls gold, in flat heads. 'Gold Plate': st. tall and stiff; fls small, white in a flat head; dries well. 'Neugold': to 60cm; fls profuse, gold. 'Parker's Variety': fls yellow. 'Sonnengold': fls light gold. Also crossed with *A. ptarmica* producing *A.* 'Schwefelblüte' ('Flowers of Sulphur') with bright sulphur to cream flowerheads, and 'Schwellenburg', to 40cm, with lemon yellow fls. Z3.

A. grandifolia Friv. 30–100cm, pubesc. Lvs to 13cm, deeply divided or dissected, ovate, with lobed or dentate lanceolate seg. Cap. in corymbs 6–11cm diam.; involucre to 4×3mm; ray flts to 2.5mm, white. Spring–summer. S & C Balk.

A. herba-rotta hort. = *A. erba-rotta*.

A. holosericea Sibth. & Sm. 15–60cm, pubesc. Lvs 1-pinnatifid, silky, 3–30cm, lobes serrate to entire. Cap. 10 to many; involucre 5mm diam.; ray flts to 2.5mm, round, yellow. S & SW Balk.

A. impatiens L. 45–100cm, slightly pubesc. above. Lvs to 8cm, lanceolate, 2-pinnatifid (upper st. lvs 1-pinnatifid), lobes serrulate. Cap. in corymbs of 3–10; involucre 6–8mm diam.; ray flts 4–5mm, white. C Rom., Sib.

A. ×jaborneggii Hal. (*A. clavennae* ×*A. erba-rotta* ssp. *moschata*.) Intermediate between parents, lacking silvery sheen of *A. clavennae*. Flowerheads white, in short-stalked, loose corymbs. Z3.

A. ×kellereri Sunderm. (*A. clypeolata* ×*A. ageratifolia*.) To 25cm. Lvs ferny, grey-green. Cap. large, daisy-like, to 8 per br. of lax, erect corymb; ray flts white to cream, disc flts pale yellow. Gdn origin.

A. ×kolbiana Sunderm. (*A. clavennae* ×*A. umbellata*.) Cushion-forming. Lvs pinnate. Flowerheads white. Midsummer. Z6.

A. lanulosa Nutt. = *A. millefolium*.

A. leptophylla Bieb. To 25cm, woolly. Lvs to 5cm, pinnatisect, lobes 3-fid, or simple. Cap. in corymbs of 3–15; involucre 4–5mm diam.; ray flts 1.5mm, yellow. SE Eur.

A. ×lewisii Ingwersen. (*A. clavennae* ×*A. clypeolata*.) 'King Edward': semi-evergreen, compact, woody-based perenn. to 10cm. Lvs feathery, soft silver-grey. Cap. minute in compact corymbs; flts buff-yellow. Gdn origin. Z5.

A. ligustica All. 30–100cm. Lvs to 3cm, ovate, 2-pinnatifid to -pinnatisect, pubesc., seg. lanceolate, divided. Involucre to 4×2mm; ray flts 1.5mm. Medit.

A. lingulata Waldst. & Kit. 10–40cm, brown-pubesc. above. Lvs 2–5cm, simple, spathulate, serrulate, with gland. spots. Cap. in corymbs of 10–30; involucre 5–8mm diam.; ray flts 3mm, white. E & S Carpath., mts of Balk. from C Balk. to N Greece.

A. micrantha Willd. To 50cm, tomentose. Lvs to 12cm pinnatisect, lobes divided, mucronate, lanceolate to linear. Cap. in corymbs of 15 to many; involucre 2mm diam.; ray flts 0.5–1mm, yellow. S Russia.

A. millefolium L. 10–100cm. Lvs to 20cm, pubesc., linear to lanceolate, 2–3-pinnatisect. Cap. 50 to numerous in corymbs 4–15cm diam.; involucre to 5.5×4mm; ray flts 4–6, to 2.5mm, white or pink. Summer–autumn. Eur. to W Asia, widely nat. in temp. regions. 'Apfelblüte' (*A. millefolium* ×*A.* 'Taygetea'): to 60cm; fls dark rose. 'Burgundy': to 1m, vigorous; fls deep burgundy. 'Cerise Queen': to 1.5m, vigorous; lvs tomentose; fls vivid pink. 'Fanal' ('The Beacon') (*A. millefolium* ×*A.* 'Taygetea'): fls 'double', snow-white, in profuse, rosette-like cap. 'Fawcett Beauty': to 80cm; fls dark lavender. 'Fire King': fls bright pink. 'Hoffnung' ('Great Expectations') (*A. millefolium* ×*A.* 'Taygetea'): to 75cm, robust; fls profuse, maize-yellow. 'Kelwayi': fls magenta-red. 'Lachsschönheit': fls salmon-pink. 'Landsdörferglut': fls delicate pink. 'Lilac Beauty': st. leafy; fls lavender. 'Paprika': to 60cm; fls sunset red, some yellow. 'Purpurea': fls pink tinged with purple. 'Red Beauty': st. to 45cm; lvs silver-grey; fls in flat heads, rich rose-red. 'Rosea': fls pink. 'Rubra': fls dark pink. 'Sammetriese': large; fls red. 'White Beauty': fls snow-white. Z2.

A. mongolica Fisch. ex Spreng. = *A. sibirica*.

A. monocephala Boiss. & Bal. 20–40cm. Lvs to 2cm with short, adpressed hairs, narrowly filiform, dissected, seg. undivided or 3-lobed. Cap. 1–8; involucre to 6×8mm; ray flts 1–2.5mm, sulphur-yellow. Turk.

A. moschata Wulf. = *A. erba-rotta* ssp. *moschata*.

A. multifida (DC.) Boiss. 10–30cm. Lvs hairy, to 4cm, oblong-lanceolate, 2–3-pinnatifid or pinnatisect. Cap. 4–20 in corymbs 2–6cm across; involucre 4×6mm; ray flts to 5mm, 6–9, white. Turk. Z5.

A. nana L. To 15cm, tomentose, strongly aromatic. Lvs to 4.5cm, oblong-lanceolate to spathulate, 1–2-pinnatifid, lobes entire. Cap. in corymbs of 4–8; involucre 5–7mm diam.; ray flts 2–3.5mm, white. Alps, Apennines.

A. nobilis L. To 60cm. Lvs to 3cm, ovate, pinnatisect, seg. to 8mm, elliptic, dissected. Involucre 2.5×1.5mm; ray flts to 1.5mm, 3–5, pale ochre above, white below. Summer. S & C Eur., S Russia.

A. odorata L. To 30cm. Lvs to 1cm, elliptic to ovate, 1–2-pinnatisect, pubesc.; seg. to 4mm, serrate to pinnatifid. Involucre to 3×2mm; ray flts 1mm, white or pale yellow. SW Eur.

A. olympica Heimerl Hal. = *A. erba-rotta* ssp. *olympica*.

A. oxyloba (DC.) Schultz-Bip. To 20cm. Lvs oblong-elliptic, 1–2-pinnatifid, 3–5cm. Cap. in corymbs of 1–3; involucre 10mm diam., ray flts 6–10mm, white. SE Alps, Apennines, E & S Carpath.

A. pseudopectinaria Janka ex Boiss. = *A. depressa*.

A. ptarmica L. SNEEZEWORT. To 150cm; somewhat pubesc. above. Lvs to 9cm, lanceolate, undivided, ± serrate, sessile, glab. Cap. in corymbs of 1–15; involucre to 12mm diam.; ray flts c5mm, white. Eur. N of Medit. 'Angel's Breath': fls double, white. 'Ballerina': small to 40cm; fls white, double. 'Boule de Neige' ('Schneeball' 'The Pearl'): st. strong; flts double, in branched heads, snow white. 'Nana Compacta': flts in flat heads, white, centres grey-green. 'Perry's White': loose heads of button-shaped white cap. Z5.

A. ptarmicifolia (Willd.) Rupr. ex Heimerl. 15–60cm. Lvs linear, basal lvs to 7×0.4cm, 2-pinnatisect, withering at flowering, st. lvs to 10×0.5cm, 1-pinnatifid. Ray flts, to 9mm, white. Cauc.

A. pubescens auct. non L. = *A. biebersteinii*.

A. pyrenaica Sibth. ex Godron. 20–60cm, slightly pubesc. above. Lvs to 5cm, lanceolate, undivided, serrate, sessile. Cap. 2–6; involucre 12mm diam.; ray flts 5mm, white. Pyren., SC Fr.

A. rupestris Porta. = *A. erba-rotta* ssp. *rupestris*.

A. serbica Nyman. = *A. ageratifolia*.

A. sericea Janka. = *A. coarctata*.

A. serrata hort. = *A. ageratum*.

A. sibirica Ledeb. 30–75cm, pilose. Lvs to 9cm, sessile, linear to lanceolate, pinnatifid or pinnatisect, lobes linear, pinnatifid. Cap. in corymbs; ray flts to 3mm, white. E Sib., E Russia.

A. sudetica Opiz. = *A. millefolium* ssp. *sudetica*.

A. 'Summer Pastels'. Fls in range of pastel shades of pink, rose, salmon to orange, purple to grey.

A. tanacetifolia All. = *A. distans*.

A. 'Taygetea'. To 60cm. Lvs feathery, grey. Corymbs of flat cap.; ray flts lemon yellow. Close to *A.* 'Moonshine' but with paler cap. in more openly branched corymbs.

A. taygetea Boiss. & Heldr. non *A.* 'Taygetea' hort. = *A. aegyptiaca*.

A. tomentosa L. To 40cm, silky. Lvs to 8cm, 2-pinnatisect, lobes linear, ± terete. Cap. 15 or more in corymbs; involucre 3mm diam.; ray flts to 2mm, bright yellow. SW Eur. to C It. 'Aurea': dwarf, to 15cm. Compact, mat-forming with v. woolly lvs and deep yellow fls. 'Maynard's Gold': fls bright yellow. Z3.

A. tournefortii DC. = *A. aegyptiaca*.

A. umbellata Sibth. & Sm. To 15cm, white-tomentose. Lvs 1–2cm, ovate, pinnatisect, lobes entire, spathulate. Cap. umbellate to 8, in corymbs; involucre 4–6mm diam.; ray flts 3–5mm, white. S Greece. 'Alba': fls white. 'Weston': lvs silver, mat-forming; fls snow-white.

A. vermicularis Trin. 20–60cm. Lvs densely hairy, linear, to 2.5cm, pinnatisect, seg. with 3 finely toothed lobes. Cap. 2–30 or more in corymbs 2–10cm diam.; involucre to 6×8mm; ray flts gold, 1–2.4mm. Transcauc., Iran, N Iraq.

A. ×wilczekii Sunderm. (*A. ageratifolia* ×*A. lingulata*.) Mat-forming. Lvs in rosettes, silver-grey. Fl. stalks 15–20cm; slightly nodding, fls white.

→*Pyrethrum*.

×Achimenantha H.E. Moore. Gesneriaceae. Gdn origin.

×A. naegelioides (Van Houtte) H.E. Moore. (*Achimenes glabrata* ×*Smithiantha zebrina*.) Closer to *Achimenes* parent. Fls pink to white, sometimes flushed yellow, spotted pink, maroon or purple. 'Cerulean Mink': lvs woolly; fls lavender-pink. 'Dutch Treat': resembles a smaller 'Inferno'. 'Ginger Peachy': habit compact; fls deep peach-pink, numerous. 'Inferno': fls vivid red, with a large, yellow centre, veined with red. 'Rose Bouquet': lvs v. small; fls double, magenta red, numerous. 'Royal': fls azure, with a white throat.

Achimenes P. Browne. HOT WATER PLANT. Gesneriaceae. 25 perenn. herbs. Rhiz. scaly, fleshy. St. simple or branched. Lvs simple, toothed, ± fleshy, usually pubesc. Fls 1 to several per axil or in cymes; cal. 5-parted; cor. tubular to salverform, lower lip 3-lobed, upper lip 2-lobed. W Indies, Mex. to C Amer. Z10.

A. andrieuxii DC. = *Eucodonia andrieuxii*.

A. antirrhina (DC.) Morton. To 30cm, downy. Lvs to 10cm, ovate, red beneath. Fls 1 per axil, ivory to yellow, exterior striped maroon to purple, interior yellow marked red. W Mex., Guat. 'Red Cap': upright, to 75cm; lvs light green; fl. tube yellow, with red spots inside, limb deep rust red.

A. atrosanguinea Lindl. = *A. antirrhina*.

A. bella C. Morton. To 30cm, downy. Lvs to 12.5cm, elliptic-ovate, crenate. Fls 1 per axil, to 3cm, violet with 3 yellow stripes within lower lobes. W Mex.

A. candida Lindl. To 50cm, glabrate. Lvs to 8cm, elliptic, serrate. Fls 2–3 per axil, white marked maroon outside, throat blotched yellow, lined red. Guat.

A. candida hort. non Lindl. = *A. longiflora* 'Alba'.

A. cettoana H.E. Moore. To 30cm, densely hairy. Lvs linear-lanceolate, toothed. Fls 1 per axil, to 2.5cm, bright purple, somewhat flattened. S Mex.

A. coccinea (Scop.) Pers. = *A. erecta*.

A. dulcis Morton. To 60cm, densely hairy. Lvs to 11.5cm, ovate-lanceolate, toothed, pubesc. above. Fls 1 per axil, to 5cm, white, throat yellow. W Mex.

A. ehrenbergii (Hanst.) H.E. Moore. To 45cm. Lvs to 15cm, ovate, crenate, tomentose beneath. Fls 1–2 per axil, to 4cm, pale mauve, throat orange spotted and lined yellow. S Mex.

A. erecta (Lam.) H.P. Fuchs. To 45cm. Lvs to 6cm, acuminate, toothed. Fls bright red, lobes to 1cm. Jam., Mex. to Panama. 'Mexican Dwarf': dense and bushy, to 22cm high; fls tiny, pink.

A. flava C. Morton. To 60cm, sparsely hirsute. Lvs to 8cm, ovate, serrate. Fls 1 or more per axil, to 2.5cm, yellow spotted white. W Mex.

A. foliosa Morr. = *A. antirrhina*.

A. grandiflora Schiede. To 45cm. Lvs to 15cm, ovate, toothed, thinly hirsute, red beneath. Fls 1 to several per axil, to 4.5cm, maroon with pale, purple-spotted zone in throat. Mex. to Hond. 'Atropurpurea': dwarf; foliage purple-flushed; fls darker.

A. gymnostoma (Griseb.) Fritsch. = *Gloxinia gymnostoma*.

A. jauregia Hanst. = *A. longiflora* 'Alba'.

A. lanata (Planch. & Lindl. ex Lem.) Hanst. = *A. ehrenbergii*.

A. longiflora DC. To 60cm, hirsute. Lvs to 8cm, ovate-oblong to lanceolate, serrate, usually red beneath. Fls 1 per axil, to 6cm, violet, maroon or white, variously marked. Mex. to Panama. 'Alba': cor. white with a large yellow spot, lobes marked with purple lines. 'Ambroise Verschaffelt': as for 'Alba' but throat marked heavily with purple lines and spots. 'Margarita': as for 'Alba' but cor. pure white, throat yellow. 'Andersonii': st. slender; lvs small, ovate; fls nodding, salverform, mauve with a white blotch below. 'Dentoniana': fls to 3cm, pale purple, throat white blotched yellow, spotted red. 'Galatea': fls violet, stained purple on throat, white below. 'Major': lvs metallic green; fls to 7.5cm diam., lavender to pale-purple, throat golden; tube yellow. 'Paul Arnold': lvs burgundy beneath; fls dark purple, throat white, tinged yellow, with red dots.

A. longiflora var. *alba* F.A. Haage, Jr. = *A. longiflora* 'Alba'.

A. margaritae hort. = *A. longiflora* 'Margarita'.

A. maxima hort. = *A. longiflora* 'Alba'.

A. mexicana Seem. To 60cm, hirsute. Lvs to 12.5cm, ovate, dentate. Fls 1 per axil, 5cm, purple or blue, throat pale mauve. Name sometimes misapplied to *A. longiflora* cvs. W Mex.

A. misera Lindl. To 20cm, downy. Lvs to 6cm, ovate, dentate. Fls 1–2 per axil, to 1cm, white with 3 crests marked mauve within. Guat.

A. patens Benth. To 30cm, downy. Lvs to 7.5cm, elliptic to ovate, marked purple-red beneath. Fls 1 per axil, maroon-violet marked yellow, throat spotted purple within. W Mex. 'Major': fls with purple-pink throat.

A. pedunculata Benth. To 85cm, puberulous. Lvs to 15cm, broadly elliptic, acuminate, dentate. Fls 1–3 on a common stalk, to 3cm, scarlet, throat spotted darker red. Mex. to Hond.

A. pulchella L'Hérit. = *A. erecta*.

A. robusta nom. nud. = *A. grandiflora*.

A. rosea Lindl. = *A. erecta*.

A. scheeri Glend. = *A. mexicana*.

A. skinneri Lindl. To 90cm, pubesc. Lvs to 8cm, ovate, serrate. Fls 1–2 per axil, long-stalked, to 3cm, pink, throat yellow marked red. Guat.

A. tubiflora (Hook.) Britton. = *Sinningia tubiflora*.

A. verschaffeltii hort. = *A. longiflora* 'Ambroise Verschaffelt'.

A. violacea hort. = *A.* 'Violacea Semiplena'.

A. warscewicziana (Reg.) H.E. Moore. To 30cm, viscid pubesc. Lvs to 11.5cm, elliptic-ovate, dentate. Fls 1–2 per axil, to 1cm, white spotted rust or maroon. S Mex. to El Salvador.

A. cvs. Habit prostrate to erect – 'Pendent Purple': habit v. vigorously trailing; 'Dazzler': habit bushy; 'Jubilee Gem': habit robust, vigorous, upright; 'Burnt Orange': habit erect to spreading. 'National Velvet U.S.A.': lvs unusually dark glossy green; 'Jennifer Goode': lvs numerous, strikingly shiny. 'Brilliant': fls scarlet. 'Ruby': fls small, deep ruby-crimson; 'Little Beauty': fls deep pink with yellow eye; 'Mauve Queen': fls showy, purple; 'Charm': fls coral-pink with a crimson-velvet sheen; 'Pearly Queen': fls tinged pink and lilac with a cream centre, giving the appearance of mother-of pearl; 'Peach Blossom': trailing; fls peach pink. 'Show Off': fls extremely numerous, pink-lilac; 'Glacier': fls snow-white, tinged ice-blue.

Achiote *Bixa orellana*.

Achira *Canna indica*.

Achyranthes L.

A. bettzichiana (Reg.) Standl. = *Alternanthera bettzichiana*.

A. herbstii hort. = *Iresine herbstii*.

A. philoxeroides (Mart.) Standl. = *Alternanthera philoxeroides*.

Acianthus R. Br. Orchidaceae. 20 tuberous, terrestrial herbs. Lf solitary, ovate, usually entire, subtended by basal sheath. Infl. a scapose rac.; fls insect-like; dors. sep. incurved, tapering, other tep. slender; lip entire, callose or tuberculate. Aus., NZ, Solomon Is., New Caledonia. Z8.

A. brunonis F. Muell. = *A. fornicatus*.

A. caudatus R. Br. MAYFLY ORCHID. Lf to 4cm. Infl. to 22cm; fls violet- to maroon-black, dors. sep. to 3.5cm; lip dark rose to violet, tip gland. C & SE Aus.

A. exsertus R. Br. MOSQUITO ORCHID. Lf to 4.5cm. Infl. to 21cm; fls green tinted red or mauve, dors. sep. to 0.8cm, lip with gland. tip. Temp. Aus.

A. fornicatus R. Br. PIXIE CAPS. Lf 2.5–5cm, sometimes sinuate or lobed. Infl. to 30cm; fls green spotted and flushed purple, dors. sep. to 1.2cm, lip green with mauve calli and maroon papillae. E Aus.

A. reniformis (R. Br.) Schltr. = *Cyrtostylis reniformis*.

Acidanthera Hochst.

A. bicolor Hochst. = *Gladiolus callianthus*.

Acineta Lindl. Orchidaceae. 15 epiphytic perenn. herbs. Pbs clustered, ovoid, with basal sheaths and 2–4 oblanceolate, stalked ribbed lvs at apex. Infl. to 70cm, a basal pendulous rac.; fls clustered, fleshy, waxy, fragrant; tep. ± equal, lanceolate, cupped. Trop. Amer. Z10.

A. barkeri (Batem.) Lindl. Fls to 4.5cm diam., spicily scented, strongly cupped, ochre to golden yellow, flecked or spotted blood-red within, lip marbled maroon. Mex.

A. chrysantha (Morr.) Lindl. & Paxt. Fls to 6cm diam., vanilla-scented, yellow, flecked red on pet., lip mottled maroon. Guat., Costa Rica, Panama.

A. densa Lindl. & Paxt. = *A. chrysantha*.

A. erythroxantha Rchb. f. Fls to 6cm diam., golden yellow spotted dark maroon at base within, lip ivory flushed maroon, spotted blood red. Venez., Colomb.

A. superba (HBK) Rchb. f. Fls to 8cm diam., muskily fragrant, golden-yellow to ochre, spotted maroon or bronze, mottled oxblood to chocolate. Panama to Peru.

A. warscewiczii Klotzsch. = *A. chrysantha*.

→*Peristeria*.

Acinos Mill. CALAMINTHA; SATUREJA. Labiatae. 10 annuals and woody everg. perennials, small, tufted, bushy or spreading. Lvs small, simple, opposite. Fls whorled in spikes; cor. tubular, markedly 2-lipped. Eurasia.

A. alpinus (L.) Moench. ALPINE CALAMINT. Pubesc. perenn. to 45cm. Lvs 6–20mm, elliptic to suborbicular, entire or denticulate. Fls 10–20mm, violet with white marks on lower lip. Mts of C & S Eur. ssp. *meridionalis* (Nyman) P.W. Ball. Fls 10–14mm; cal. with crispate hairs. Z5.

A. arvensis (Lam.) Dandy. BASIL THYME; MOTHER OF THYME. Ann. or short-lived perenn., faintly aromatic, 20cm+. Lvs 8–15mm, ovate to elliptic, obscurely toothed, pubesc. Fls 7–10mm, violet marked white on lower lip. Summer–autumn. Eurasia, Medit., N Eur. Z4.

A. corsicus (Pers.) Getliffe. Procumbent, pubesc. perenn. to 10cm. Lvs 4–10mm, obovate-spathulate to suborbicular, obtuse, entire. Fls 12–16mm, violet. Corsica. Z6.

A. graveolens (Bieb.) Link. = *A. rotundifolius*.

A. rotundifolius Pers. Pubesc. ann. to 40cm. Lvs 8–15mm, obovate-orbicular to orbicular, obtuse or acuminate, entire or denticulate. Fls 7–10mm, violet with white marks on lower lip. SE Eur. Z4.

A. thymoides Moench. = *A. arvensis*.

→*Calamintha*, *Micromeria* and *Satureja*.

Aciphylla Forst. & Forst. f. Umbelliferae. 40 small or giant perenn. herbs, yucca- or palm-like in overall appearance. Lvs basal, usually rigid, linear and simple or compound with linear lfts. Infl. a large, terminal, candelabriform pan. composed of compound umbels; fls cream or white. Summer. NZ, Aus.

A. aurea W. Oliv. Lvs to 70cm, 1–2-pinnate; lfts to 3×1cm in 2–4 pairs, pungent. Infl. to 80cm. NZ. Z5.

A. colensoi Hook. f. COLENSO'S SPANIARD; WILD SPANIARD. Lvs to 50cm, ensiform or pinnate, glaucous; lfts to 20×1.2cm, pungent, midrib red, margins serrulate. Infl. to 3m. NZ. Z5.

A. congesta Cheesem. Lvs pinnate, soft; lfts to 6cm, finely pungent. NZ.

A. crenulata J.B. Armstr. Lvs to 15cm, pinnate, soft; lfts to 15cm, in 2–3 pairs, midrib red, margins serrulate. Infl. to 60cm. NZ.

A. dobsonii Hook. f. Lvs to 15cm in compact, cushioned rosettes; lfts 3, tough, pungent. NZ.

A. ferox W. Oliv. Lvs to 40cm, pinnate; lfts to 15cm, in 2–4 pairs, striate, serrulate, pungent. Infl. to 1m. NZ.

A. glaucescens W. Oliv. Lvs to 1.5m, glaucous, 3-pinnate; lfts to 20cm (term. lfts longer), serrulate. Infl. to 2m. NZ.

A. gracilis W. Oliv. = *A. montana* var. *gracilis*.

A. hectori Buch. Lfts 3 per lf, 3–6cm, rigid, serrulate. Infl. to 15cm. NZ.

A. horrida W. Oliv. Lvs to 80cm, pinnate, tough; lfts 5–7, to 40cm, curved, striate, pungent, serrulate. NZ.

A. latifolia Ckn. = *Anisotome latifolia*.

A. lecomtei Dawson. Lvs to 25cm, pinnate; lfts to 10cm, in 4 pairs, sharply pungent. NZ.

A. lyallii Hook. f. Lvs to 30cm, trifoliolate or pinnate; lfts to 10cm, 3–5, pungent, margins smooth. NZ.

A. monroi Hook. f. Lvs to 10cm, pinnate; lfts to 4.5cm, in 4–6 pairs. Umbels to 2.5cm diam. NZ.

A. montana Armstr. Lvs to 30cm, pinnate; lfts to 13cm, in 2–4 pairs, tough, yellow-green, pungent. NZ. var. *gracilis* (W. Oliv.) Dawson. Lvs to 23cm; lfts in 2 pairs. Infl. to 40cm. C S Is.

A. pinnatifida Petrie. Lvs to 20cm, pinnatifid, midrib yellow; seg. to 10cm, pungent. NZ.

A. procumbens F. Muell. ex Benth. Densely tufted, spreading. Lvs to 5cm, 2-pinnate; lfts crowded, bristle-tipped. Tasm.

A. scott-thomsonii Ckn. & Allan. GIANT SPANIARD. Lvs to 1.5m, 1–2-pinnate; lfts to 45cm, glaucous, midrib tinted red, margins v. finely serrulate. cf. *A. colensoi*. NZ.

A. similis Cheesem. Lvs to 23cm, pinnate; lfts to 6.5cm, leathery, yellow-green, pungent. NZ.

A. simplex Petrie. Cushion-forming. Lvs 3–10cm, simple, mucronulate, prominently veined. Infl. a globose pan. NZ.

A. simplicifolia (F. Muell.) Benth. Tufted. Lvs to 25cm, simple, linear, blunt, ribbed. Aus. (Vict.).

A. spedenii Cheesem. Similar to *A. congesta* but with shorter, sub-flabellate lvs; lfts to 8cm. NZ.

A. squarrosa Forst. & Forst. f. SPEARGRASS; BAYONET PLANT. Lvs 2–3-pinnate; seg. to 25cm, crenate-serrulate, pungent. Infl. to 1m. NZ. Z5.

A. subflabellata W. Oliv. Lvs to 50cm, 2-pinnate, subflabellate; lfts to 23cm, in 3–4 pairs, tips acicular, margins serrulate. NZ.

Ackama A. Cunn.

A. paniculata Endl. = *Caldcluvia paniculosa*.

Acmadenia Bartling & Wendl. Rutaceae. 33 small everg. shrubs. Lvs linear to orbicular. Fls often solitary, usually term.; bracts sometimes leaflike; cal. 5-lobed; pet. 5, pink or white sometimes bearded. Spring–summer. S Afr. (Cape Prov.). Z9.

A. tetragona (L. f.) Bartling & Wendl. PAGODA FLOWER. To 60cm, spreading. Lvs to 5cm, orbicular, gland-dotted, ciliate. Infl. to 2.5cm diam.; cal. tinted purple; pet. to 1.3cm, white or pink, midrib red.

→*Diosma*.

Acmella Rich. ex Pers. Compositae. *c*30 ann. or perenn. herbs. Lvs mostly basal, opposite, glab. to tomentose; petioles occas. winged. Cap. radiate, sometimes appearing discoid, scapose, solitary or few. Trop. and subtrop., esp. US. Z9.

A. oppositifolia (Lam.) R.K. Jansen. Short perenn., often decumbent. Lvs to 10cm, broadly ovate to lanceolate, glab. or hairy, dentate. Involucre to 5mm diam.; flts orange-yellow, to 1cm. Late summer. S US.

→*Spilanthes*.

Acmena DC. Myrtaceae. 7 small or large trees. Lvs opp., entire, oil-dotted. Fls small, in axill. rac. or pan. Fr. a berry. Aus. to New Guinea. Z10.

A. australis (C. Moore) L. Johnson. RED APPLE; COBUN-BUN. Small spreading tree. Lvs elliptic, glossy, undulate. Fls to 0.5cm diam., cream, in pan. Fr. to 4cm diam., red. Aus. (Queensld, NSW).

A. brachyandra Merrill & Perry. = *A. australis*.

A. smithii (Poir.) Merrill & Perry LILLY PILLY. Small tree. Bark brown. Lvs 2–10cm, lanceolate-ovate, glossy, tip attenuate. Fls small, green, crowded in pan. Fr. to 1.5cm diam., white, pink or purple. Aus. (Queensld, NSW, Vict., N Territ.). var. *minor* Maid. Low-growing with smaller lvs and fr.

Acmopyle Pilger. Podocarpaceae. 2 everg. conifers to 20m; habit as for *Podocarpus*. Lvs 2-ranked, dimorphic, linear on weak shoots, scale-like on strong shoots. ♀ and ♂ cones separate. New Caledonia, Fiji. Z10.

A. alba Buchholz. = *A. pancheri*.

A. pancheri (Brongn. & Griseb.) Pilger. To 20m. Bark smooth at first. Lvs to 2.5×0.3cm. ♀ cones to 22mm, long-stalked. New Caledonia.

A. sahniana Buchholz & N. Gray. Similar to *A. pancheri* except to 10m. ♀ cones to 5mm, short-stalked. Fiji.

Acoelorraphe H.A. Wendl. PAUROTIS PALM; SAW CABBAGE PALM; SILVER SAW PALM; EVERGLADES PALM. Palmae. 1 palm. St. numerous, clustered. Crown compact. Lvs costapalmate, to 2×1m, orbicular; petioles to 1.2m, spiny; lamina silvery beneath. W Indies, S Flor., Mex., C Amer. Z10.

A. wrightii (Griseb. & H.A. Wendl.) H.A. Wendl. ex Becc.

→*Serenoa*.

Acokanthera G. Don. BUSHMAN'S-POISON; POISON BUSH; POISON TREE. Apocynaceae. 5 highly toxic everg. trees and shrubs. Lvs entire, leathery. Fls in pan., white or red, fragrant; cor. tubular-salverform, lobes 5. Fr a berry. Arabia to E & S Afr. Z10.

A. longiflora Stapf. = *A. oppositifolia*.

A. oblongifolia (Hochst.) Codd. WINTERSWEET; POISON ARROW PLANT. To 6m. Lvs 6–12.25cm, elliptic. Cor. white, tube 1.4–2cm, lobes 0.3–0.7cm. Moz., S Afr.

A. oppositifolia (Lam.) Codd. To 6m. Lvs 4–13.5cm, obovate, more strongly veined than in *A. oblongifolia*. Cor. tube

0.6–2cm, pink, lobes 0.25cm, white. E trop. & S Afr.
A. spectabilis (Sonder) Hook. f. = *A. oblongifolia*.
A. venenata auctt. non G. Don. = *A. oppositifolia*.
A. venenata var. *scabra* (Sonder) Markgr. = *A. oppositifolia*.
→*Carissa*.

Aconitum L. MONK'S-HOOD. Ranunculaceae. c100 ann., bienn. or perenn. herbs, often tuberous. St. erect to scrambling. Lvs basal and rosulate or cauline and alt., palmately lobed, often again divided. Infl. a rac. or racemose pan.; fls showy, bilaterally symmetric; sep. 5, petal-like, uppermost hemispheric to cylindric, large, erect, forming a helmet; pet. 2–10, small, concealed within sep., uppermost pair with long, nectar-secreting spurs projecting into the helmet. Temp. regions of the N Hemis.
A. ×*acutum* Rchb. = *A.* ×*cammarum*.
A. ambiguum Rchb. = *A. napellus*.
A. ampliflorum Rchb. = *A. napellus*.
A. anglicum Stapf. = *A. napellus* ssp. *napellus*.
A. angustifolium Bernh. in Rchb. St. to 60cm. Lvs deeply 5–7-lobed, long-petiolate, lobes cuneate, to narrowly linear. Infl. paniculate, broad, lax; fls violet-blue; helmet 2cm. Balk. Z6.
A. anthora L. St. erect. Lvs orbicular, seg. numerous linear, glab. to sparsely lanate. Infl. racemose; fls numerous, yellow, spurs straight. Summer. S Eur., W & C Asia. var. *caeruleum* Hoelzl. Lvs strongly adpressed-hairy; fls smaller, blue-violet. Galicia. Z6.
A. ×*arendsii* hort. = *A. carmichaelii* Arendsii group.
A. autumnale Lindl. = *A. napellus* ssp. *neomontanum*.
A. bakeri Greene. St. 40–60cm. Lvs sparsely minutely pubesc., lobes 3–5, rhombic-cuneate, twice cleft, broadly lanceolate. Infl. subspicate; fls v. dark blue; helmet 18–20mm. Summer. Rocky Mts. Z5.
A. barbatum Pers. = *A. lycoctonum* ssp. *lycoctonum*.
A. bicolor Schult. = *A.* ×*cammarum*.
A. biflorum Fisch. St. 15–40cm, erect, pubesc. above. Lvs 3–5cm, orbicular, glab., lobes 3, dissected, seg. linear, 5–20mm. Infl. racemose; fls azure; helmet 10–15mm, low, boat-shaped, spurless. Late summer. C Asia. Z2.
A. brachypodum Diels. St. to 60cm. Lvs pale green beneath, glab. above, lobes 5–7, linear to narrowly deltoid. Infl. racemose; fls to 4cm, bright blue, paler toward base; helmet beaked; spurs small. Early autumn. W China.
A. bulbiferum T.J. Howell. = *A. howellii*.
A. bullatifolium A. Lév. 30–50cm. St. silky. Lvs ± coriaceous, bullate, lobes 5, acutely dissected. Fls in a narrow spike, blue, pubesc.; helmet acutely beaked. Yunnan. Z6.
A. ×*cammarum* L. Apparently *A. variegatum* ×*A. napellus*. St. 90cm. Lvs 5–10cm wide, lobes 5–7, often with 3 lanceolate lobules. Infl. somewhat branched, pyramidal; fls 4cm, mostly white, sometimes red or purple or variegated; helmet short-beaked, purple-margined. Summer. Eur. 'Bicolor': tall, wide-branching; fls blue and white, hood nodding, infl. loose. 'Caeruleum': upright, wide; fls deep blue, infl. loose. 'Doppelgänger': tall, vigorous; fls large, dark blue. 'France Marc': upright, wide, vigorous; fls large, deep blue. 'Grandiflorum Album': fls large, white. 'Nachthimmel': tall; fls large, dark violet, hood bulbous. Z3.
A. carmichaelii Debeaux. St. erect to 2m. Lvs ovate, lobes 3–5, dark green above, pale green beneath, coriaceous, sparsely dentate or lobed. Infl. densely paniculate, br. upright; fls deep purple within, paler mauve or almost white without; helmet sparsely crisped-hairy. Summer. C & W China, N Amer. Arendsii group; 85–120cm tall, with stout flowerstalks, branching infl. and large, deep blue fls; valued for late flowering and cutting. 'Arendsii': fls azure blue. 'Latecrop': fls blue, autumn flowering. Z3.
A. chinense Sieb. & Zucc. St. erect, branched, 80–120cm, tinged purple. Lvs 3-parted, rather thick, lobes 10–15cm, cuneate, deeply incised and dentate. Infl. erect, branched; fls large, 3–4cm, deep bright blue to indigo; spurs short. Summer. China. Z6.
A. ×*cordatum* Royle. (*A. heterophyllum* ×*A. kashmiricum*.) St. erect, to 120cm. Lvs broadly ovate-cordate, 5-lobed to entire, 5–10cm wide. Infl. finely villous; fls bright blue or somewhat green with purple veining; hemlet 2cm high. Late summer. Kashmir.
A. coriophyllum Hand.-Mazz. St. 50–100cm, densely pubesc. Lvs rounded-cordate, 10–20cm wide, 3-fid to middle, subcoriaceous, dentate. Infl. racemose, somewhat branched at base, elongate; fls 4cm, yellow tinged green. Autumn. Yunnan. Z6.
A. delavayi Franch. St. to 30cm, slender, flexuous, villous above. Lf lobes 5, deeply cut, somewhat pilose. Infl. a short rac.; fls 3–5, violet-blue; helmet conic, pubesc. Summer–autumn. Yunnan. Z6.
A. delphinense Gáyer. Glandular-pubesc. St. 1–1.5m. Lvs divided to base, into almost linear lobes. Infl. simple or branched; fls

violet to blue; helmet 7–14mm. Summer. SE Fr. Z6.
A. delphiniifolium DC. = *A. napellus* ssp. *vulgare*.
A. dielsianum Airy Shaw. St. to 75cm, velvety above. Lvs 8.5–12.5cm, lobes 3, dentate, lateral lobes deeply 2-fid, midlobe 3-fid. Infl. to 30cm, occas. branched at base; fls 3cm, deep blue; helmet narrow; spurs 0. Autumn. W China. Z6.
A. duclouxii A. Lév. St. erect, 30–50cm, hairy. Lvs palmatisect; lobes cuneate, deeply cut. Fls blue; helmet longer than wide; spur circinate. W China. Z6.
A. elatum Salisb. = *A. pyramidale*.
A. eminens Koch ex Rchb. = *A. napellus* ssp. *neomontanum*.
A. ×*exaltatum* Bernh. (*A. firmum* ×*A. gracile*.) St., 2m. Lvs 5–8cm, lobes 5–7, rhombic, often 3-lobed. Infl. elongate, racemose; fls pale lilac; helmet tall, pointed at top. Summer. Czech. Z6.
A. excelsum Rchb. St. 70–200cm, erect. Lvs to 15cm, orbicular-cordate, lobes 3–9, subrhombic, apically 3-cleft. Infl. racemose, lax; fls dull violet to grey-violet; helmet 15–25mm, cylindric-conic; spurs circinate. Summer. N Eurasia. Z2.
A. ferox Wallich. St. 90–180cm. Lvs 7–15cm, ovate or suborbicular, lobes 5, cuneate-ovate, incised. Infl. 15–30cm, racemose, dense; fls large, pale dingy blue; helmet rounded, with short sharp beak. Late summer. Himal. Z6.
A. firmum Rchb. = *A. napellus*.
A. fischeri Forbes and Hemsl. non Rchb. = *A. carmichaelii*.
A. formosanum Rchb. = *A. napellus* ssp. *hians*.
A. forrestii Stapf. St. 90–150cm, erect. Lvs 9cm, ovate-orbicular, lobes 3, to 6cm, rhomboid to lanceolate, dentate. Infl. laxly paniculate; fls blue; helmet 18–20mm high. Yunnan. Z6.
A. funiculare Stapf. St. 45cm, slender. Lvs to 3cm, reniform, fleshy, lobes 5, seg. broadly linear to linear-lanceolate. Infl. laxly racemose; fls 4–6, lilac; helmet 18–20mm, erect, flattened at apex. Summer. Bhutan. Z6.
A. gigas Lév. & Van't. St. stout; 30–100cm. Lvs 10–20cm wide, orbicular-reniform, 7–9-parted, lobes 3-cleft or incised, dentate, vivid green, thinly pilose beneath. Infl. to 30cm, racemose, branched; fls 2.5cm, numerous, pale yellow. Jap. Z6.
A. gmelinii Rchb. St. to 60cm, erect. Lvs 10–16cm wide, orbicular to reniform, dissected, seg. narrow, hairy beneath, glossy above. Rac. 8–25cm, v. lax; fls cream to sulphur-yellow; helmet cylindric-conic. Summer. Sib. Z6.
A. gracile (Rchb.) Rchb. ex Gáyer. = *A. variegatum*.
A. gymnandrum Maxim. Ann., 15–90cm. Lvs 3–6cm, reniform to broadly ovate, bipinnatisect, pubesc. above, white-villous beneath, seg. linear-oblong, dentate. Infl. a dense rac.; fls violet or deep blue; helmet 15–20mm, boat-shaped. Summer. Bhutan, Tibet, W China. Z6.
A. halleri Rchb. = *A. napellus* ssp. *neomontanum*.
A. handelianum Comber. St. to 60cm, flexuous, hairy. Lvs 5cm, broadly cordate to reniform, hairy, lobes 5, 2–3-pinnatifid, seg. ligulate. Infl. usually simple, about 20-fld, hairy; fls rich blue-purple; helmet 2cm. Autumn. Yunnan. Z6.
A. hemsleyanum Pritz. St. scrambling to twining. Lvs ovate, dark green above, paler beneath, glab. or sparsely lanate, lobes 3–5, broadly dentate. Rac. widely spreading; fls dark purple-blue to indigo; helmet hemispheric-cylindric, downy. Summer. C & W China. Z4.
A. henryi Pritz. St. erect below, twining or scrambling above. Lvs ovate, lobes 3(–5), narrow, dentate or lobed. Infl. racemose; fls few, indigo; helmet hemispheric. Summer. C & W China. 'Spark' ('Spark's Variety'): tall, wide-branched; fls deep violet blue. Z4.
A. heterophyllum Wallich ex Royle. St. 30–90cm, erect. Lvs 40–100cm, broadly ovate-cordate or orbicular-ovate, lobes 5, crenate. Infl. racemose, or paniculate, many-fld; fls 2.5–3cm, bright blue or blue-green with purple veins; helmet rounded, broader than long. Late summer. W Himal. (Pak. to W Nepal). Z6.
A. hookeri Stapf. St. slender, to 10cm. Lvs rounded-cordate to reniform, 1–1.5cm across, rather fleshy, lobes 3–5, cut into narrow seg. Fls 2.5–3cm, 1 or few, deeply blue or purple; helmet strongly curved, projecting forward. Late summer. SW China to Nepal and Sikkim. Z6.
A. hosteanum Schur. = *A. lycoctonum* ssp. *moldavicum*.
A. howellii A. Nels. & Macbr. St. 80–150cm, ascending or reclining, slender, weak, bulbiliferous. Lvs 4–7cm, lobes 4–7, cuneate, deeply cleft and dentate. Infl. lax, with slender br.; helmet 1.5–2cm, deeply saccate. Summer. W USA. Z5.
A. ×*illitinum* Rchb. Close to *A. gracile*; sterile.
A. japonicum Thunb. St. 50–100cm, erect to slightly scandent. Lvs 5–10cm across, lobes 3, obovate-rhombic, dentate. Infl. laxly corymbose; fls 3cm, few, blue-purple or somewhat tinged red; helmet conic, abruptly mucronate. Summer. Jap. Z6.
A. jucundum Diels. St. 60–90cm. Lvs to 13cm, ± 5-angled, thin, lobes 5, cuneate-obovate, sharply dentate. Infl. slender, sometimes branched at base; fls rosy purple; helmet 18–20mm,

slender with curved beak. Summer. W China. Z6.

A. judenbergense (Rchb.) Gáyer. St. erect, tall. Lf lobes short, broadly lanceolate, sometimes hairy. Infl. branched, racemose; fls purple or white; helmet 2.5cm+ high, arched, broadly rounded above. E Alps, Bulg. Z6.

A. kashmiricum Stapf ex Coventry. St. 10–30cm. Lvs 1–3.5cm across, rounded-cordate, lobes 3–5, broad, dentate. Fls 2–2.5cm, solitary, paired or in few-fld rac., deep blue; helmet with small crest near apex. Late summer. Kashmir. Z6.

A. kusnetzowii Rchb. St. 180–240cm, erect, slender. Lf lobes 3, cuneate-lanceolate, middle lobe 3-lobed, lat. lobes bifid, pinnately dentate. Infl. racemose, branched at base, dense; fls large, pale blue; helmet hemispheric-conic with a broad beak. Kamchatka. Z6.

A. lamarckii Rchb. = *A. lycoctonum* ssp. *neapolitanum*.

A. latemarense Degen & Gáyer. Slender st. 30–60cm. Lf lobes 5, rhomboid, deeply cut with dentate divisions. Infl. densely racemose; fls bright violet; helmet hemispheric or depressed, gaping. Summer. Austria (Tyrol). Z6.

A. leucanthum Stapf or Rchb. = *A. lycoctonum* ssp. *lycoctonum*.

A. linnaeanum Gáyer. St. to 60cm, erect. Lvs glossy above, lobes 5, lanceolate, dentate. Rac. short, rather dense; fls purple, maroon or white, softly hairy; helmet 18–20mm, rounded above with a short point, open. Summer. Eur. Alps. Z6.

A. lutescens Nels. St. 40–80cm. Lvs 5–10cm wide, glab., lobes 3–5, rhombic, cut into lanceolate seg. Fls white tinged yellow; helmet 1.5cm. Summer. N Amer. (Rocky Mts). Z5.

A. lycoctonum L. ssp. *lycoctonum*. WOLFSBANE; BADGER'S BANE. St. tall, erect. Lvs orbicular, glab. or hairy above, hairy along veins beneath, lobes 5–7, dentate or lobulate. Infl. paniculate, lax to dense; fls few to many, purple-lilac or white or yellow; helmet cylindric or saccate, usually hairy. Summer. Eur., N Afr. ssp. *moldavicum* (Hacq.) Jalas. Lf lobes 3-fid. Infl. branched, glandular-pubesc.; fls few, blue to purple. Summer. E Eur. (Carpath., Rom.). ssp. *neapolitanum* (Ten.) Nyman. Lf lobes deeply divided. Infl. branched; fls numerous, tinged yellow. Summer. S Eur. (mts), Moroc. ssp. *vulparia* (Rchb.) Schinz & Keller. Lf lobes deep, incised-serrate to v. deeply laciniate-dentate. Infl. simple or branched, lax to dense; fls few, pale yellow. Summer. C & S Eur. Z3.

A. mairei Lév. St. to 30cm, branched below, slender, flexuous, pubesc. Lf lobes 5, deeply cut into short, linear lobes. Rac. short; fls rather crowded, violet-blue marked with white and yellow; helmet 18–20mm, conic, straight, mouth gaping. Summer–autumn. Yunnan. Z6.

A. maximum Pall. = *A. carmichaelii*.

A. meloctonum Rchb. = *A. lycoctonum* ssp. *lycoctonum*.

A. moldavicum Hacq. ex Rchb. = *A. lycoctonum* ssp. *moldavicum*.

A. × molle Rchb. (*A. compactum* × *A. paniculatum*.) St. 1m. Lvs large, lobes 5–7, cuneate, 3-fid, deeply cut and dentate. Infl. broadly pyramidal; fls large, violet-purple; helmet 25–30mm, cuneate, closed. Summer. Switz. Z6.

A. multifidum Koch. = *A. napellus* ssp. *vulgare*.

A. napellus L. HELMET FLOWER; FRIAR'S-CAP; SOLDIER'S-CAP; TURK'S-CAP; BEAR'S-FOOT; GARDEN WOLFSBANE; GARDEN MONKSHOOD. St. erect. Lvs ± orbicular, lobes 5–7, glab. or sparsely hairy, lobed or dentate. Infl. racemose, dense; fls blue or tinged purple; helmet hemispheric. Summer. Eur., Asia, Amer. ssp. *napellus*. To 1m. Lf lobes narrowly cuneate. Infl. racemose, usually dense; fls blue-lilac. Late spring–summer. Engl. ssp. *hians* (Rchb.) Gáyer. St. 30–60cm. Lf lobes 5, rhomboid, deeply cut with dentate divisions. Infl. laxly racemose; fls violet; helmet hairy. Summer. C Eur. ssp. *neomontanum* (Wulf.) Gáyer. St. erect, 1m. Lf lobes 5, lanceolate, dentate. Infl. with 2–4 short lat. br.; fls purple, maroon or white, softly hairy; helmet 18–20mm. Summer. Eur. Alps. ssp. *tauricum* (Wulf.) Gáyer Close to *A. napellus* but infl. glab., nearly always simple; fls violet to blue; helmet 7–14mm. Summer. E Alps, Rom. ssp. *vulgare* (Rchb.) Rouy & Foucaud. St. 90cm. Lf lobes narrowly linear. Infl. simple or branched, crisped-hairy; fls violet to blue; helmet 7–14mm, softly hairy. Summer. W Alps and Pyren. 'Album' ('Albidum'): fls white. Z6.

A. naviculare (Brühl) Stapf. St. 10 to 30cm, erect. Lvs in a loose rosette, rounded-cordate, 1–3.5cm wide, pubesc., lobes 3–5, 2–3-lobed, somewhat crenate. Fls 1–4, solitary or in a short rac., white and violet, flushed blue-purple, with darker veins, hairy; helmet 20–25mm, boat-shaped. Summer. Himal. Z6.

A. neomontanum Wulf. = *A. napellus* ssp. *neomontanum*.

A. novoluridum Munz. St. 60–90cm, erect. Lvs 7–15cm, rounded-cordate to reniform, pubesc., lobes 5, ovate-cuneate, 2–5-fid, crenate. Infl. 15–30cm, simple, racemose, yellow-pubesc.; fls dull red to maroon; helmet dome-like, with long beak, brown-tomentose. Summer. E Himal. Z6.

A. orientale Mill. St. to 120–180cm, erect. Lvs ± orbicular, large,

glab. or hairy above, veins hairy beneath, lobes 5–7, broad, 3-fid, seg. narrowly lanceolate, dentate. Infl. to 60cm+, racemose, compact; fls few, tinged dark blue, or white flushed yellow; helmet tall, cylindric or saccate, shortly beaked. Summer. Turk. and Cauc. to Iran. Z6.

A. orochryseum Stapf. St. 40–50cm, slender, ± flexuous, golden-hairy. Lvs 3.5–5cm, cordate to reniform, seg. 5, oblong to lanceolate, 2–3cm wide, dentate. Infl. racemose, lax, yellow-pubesc.; fls 2–10, white tinged golden-yellow and blue, pubesc.; helmet 2.5cm, beaked; pet. tinged black at apex, lobes deep violet. Summer. Himal. (Mt Everest, Bhutan). Z6.

A. ottonianum Rchb. = *A. × cammarum*.

A. ouvrardiaum Hand.-Mazz. St. 25–90cm, erect. Lvs 6–9cm diam., broadly orbicular, lobes 5, broadly rhombic, cut, bright green, membranous. Infl. racemose, dense; fls 2cm, numerous, intense blue or violet or white tinged blue; helmet, 1cm high, boat-shaped, with a short broad beak. China. Z6.

A. paniculatum Lam. St. erect, 60–150cm, branched. Lvs ± orbicular, lobes 5–7, dentate or lobed. Infl. openly paniculate, glandular-pubesc.; fls blue or blue-violet; helmet hemispheric, often pilose. Summer. SC Eur. 'Nanum': dwarf. Rom., Balk. Z6.

A. pulchellum Hand.-Mazz. St. 8–50cm, slender, flexuous. Lvs 2–5cm diam., orbicular-cordate, glab. or v. sparsely pilose above, lobes 3, rhombic-cuneate. Fls 2.5–3.5cm, solitary or paired or in lax rac., 2.5–3.5cm, deep blue; helmet boat-shaped, scarcely beaked, slightly hairy. Summer. China. Z6.

A. pyrenaicum L. = *A. lycoctonum* ssp. *neapolitanum*.

A. ranunculifolium Rchb. = *A. lycoctonum* ssp. *neapolitanum*.

A. reclinatum Gray. TRAILING WOLF'S-BANE. St. to 3m, slender, erect, reclining or scandent. Lf lobes 5, cuneate-obovate, coarsely incised. Infl. elongate, usually compound; fls white; helmet elevated into slender subcylindric projection. Summer. E US. Z6.

A. rostratum Bernh. St. to 60cm, slender. Lf lobes dissected, rather short, seg. sublinear. Infl. branched, few-fld; fls small to medium-sized, red to purple or white; helmet 25mm, hemispheric to cuneate, high, arched. Summer. Switz. Z6.

A. rotundifolium Karel. & Kir. St. 12–60cm, erect, simple. Lvs 2–4cm, orbicular-cordate, lobes 5–7, 2–3-lobed, apically dentate. Infl. term., racemose, lax; fls 15–20mm, pale lilac, veins dark, prominent; helmet boat-shaped. Summer. C Asia.

A. senanense Nak. St. 60–90cm, ± arching. Lf lobes 3, laterals 2-fid, seg. deeply cut. Pan. few-fld, corymbiform; fls pale blue or variegated with white; helmet conic, hairy. Jap. Z6.

A. septentrionale Koelle. = *A. lycoctonum* ssp. *lycoctonum*.

A. souliei Finet & Gagnep. St. 25–60cm, erect, 4-angled. Lvs 5cm, velvety above, lobes obcuneate-rhombic, obtusely 3-lobed at apex. Infl. paniculate, sprawling; fls 6mm, pale yellow; helmet broadly hemispheric, with short straight beak. Summer. SW China. Z6.

A. × stoerkianum Rchb. (*A. neomontanum* × *A. variegatum*.) St. to 1m. Lvs orbicular-cordate, pale lustrous green, lobes 7, rhombic, coarsely dentate. Infl. racemose, term., lax, branched below; fls large, violet, or white, with violet border, silky; helmet vaulted. Summer. Austria, Switz. Z6.

A. tatsienense Finet & Gagnep. St. 25–75cm, erect. Lvs 5.5–8cm, lobes obcuneate-rhombic, dentate, upper 3-lobed. Infl. racemose or paniculate, densely downy; fls 12mm, v. pale blue; helmet hemispheric, beak obtusely conic. W China. Z6.

A. tenue Rydb. St. to 30cm, slender. Lvs few, thin, shining, lobes 5–7, rhombic, 3-cleft then divided again. Infl. racemose, 2–6-fld; fls blue; helmet 15–18mm. Summer. US (Mont.). Z4.

A. thyraicum Blocki. = *A. lycoctonum* ssp. *vulparia*.

A. uncinatum L. St. 60–120cm, twining or scrambling, thin. Lvs ovate, dark green above, paler beneath, glab., lobes 3–5, trapezoid, broad, sparsely dentate. Rac. ± umbellate, lax; fls deep blue; helmet obtusely conical. Summer. E US. Z6.

A. variegatum L. St. erect, frequently branched. Lvs ± orbicular, lobes 5–7, dentate or lobed. Infl. openly paniculate; fls blue or blue-violet and white, helmet campanulate, often pilose. Summer. C & S Eur., Turk. Z6.

A. venatorium Diels. St. to 90cm. Lvs 10–12.5cm, glab., lobes 3, 3-5-fid, deeply dentate. Infl. 35–40cm, racemose, narrow; fls deep violet; helmet 2.5cm, shortly beaked. Autumn. Upper Burm., W China. Z6.

A. vilmorinianum Komar. St. 2m, erect below, twining or scrambling above. Lvs broadly ovate, lobes 3(–5), pale green, lanceolate to ovate, dentate or lobed. Infl. racemose, flexuous; fls few, indigo; helmet taller than wide, rounded at apex. Autumn. W & C China. Z6.

A. violaceum Jacq. ex Stapf. St. 10–60cm. Lvs 2–10cm, sub-orbicular to cordate or reniform, lobes finely dissected into seg. 1–3mm across. Infl. spike-like, dense, or fls solitary or few; fls 2–2.5cm, dark to pale blue, marked white. Summer–autumn. Himal. (Pak. to C Nepal). Z6.

A. volubile Pall. St. twining or scrambling, to 4m. Lvs 3–9cm, suborbicular, ternately lobed, hairy. Infl. 12–20cm, racemose; fls 2–3cm, purple and green or tinged blue and green; helmet hemispheric-conic. Summer–autumn. E Asia. Z2.

A. vulparia Rchb. = *A. lycoctonum* ssp. *vulparia*.

A. willdenowii Rchb. ex Gáyer. = *A. napellus* ssp. *vulgare*.

A. wilsonii Stapf ex Mollet. = *A. carmichaelii*.

A. yezoense Nak. St. erect, slightly flexuous above. Lf lobes 3, narrowly lobed, 7–10cm, lat. lobes bipartite, seg. lanceolate. Infl. term. and axill., dense; fls 3cm, blue-purple. Summer. Jap. Z6.

A. cvs. 'Bergfürst': tall; fls deep blue, long-lasting, early, infl. compact. 'Blue Sceptre': fls violet blue and white. 'Bressingham Spire': tall; fls violet blue, infl. tapering. 'Carneum': fls murky salmon pink. 'Gletschereis': fls white, long-lasting, early 'Newry Blue': fls deep blue, infl. upright, compact. 'Rubellum' ('Roseum'): fls light pink.

ACORACEAE Martinov. See *Acorus*.

Acorn Banksia *Banksia prionotes*.

Acorus L. Araceae (Acoraceae). 2 perenn. herbs. Rhiz. horizontal, aromatic. Lvs equitant, sheathing, grass- or iris-like. Spathe and stalk fused in a lf-like blade; spadix club-shaped, carried at 45° toward summit of blade. OW, N Amer.

A. calamus L. SWEET FLAG; SWEET CALAMUS; MYRTLE FLAG; CALAMUS; FLAGROOT. Lvs to 1.5m, resembling a flag iris, bright green. Infl. blade 2–3-ridged; spadix to 10×1.2cm, yellow-green. Asia, SE US, widely nat. N hemis. 'Variegatus': lvs striped cream and yellow. var. *angustifolius* (Schott) Engl. Lvs to 1.5cm wide, grass-like, thin-textured. SE Asia. Z3.

A. gramineus Ait. Lvs 8–50cm, glossy, sedge-like, finely tapering, arranged in a fan. Spadix 4.5–8cm. E Asia. 'Albovariegatus' ('Argenteostriatus'): dwarf, lvs striped white. 'Pusillus': dwarf and compact, lvs seldom exceeding 8cm. 'Oborozuki': lvs vibrant yellow. 'Ogon' ('Wogon'): lvs variegated chartreuse and cream. 'Variegatus' ('Aureovariegatus'): lvs striped cream and yellow. 'Yodonoyuki': lvs variegated pale green. Z5.
→*Carex*.

Acourtia D. Don. Compositae. *c*40 perenn. herbs or subshrubs. Lvs leathery, with a spined or toothed margin. Cap. radiate, cymose. N Amer. Z8.

A. microcephala DC. Erect, to 1.4m. Lvs 10–20cm, oblong, base broad, clasping, minutely toothed, rough and hairy. Cap. to 12mm, in a broad pan. with leafy bracts; flts rose, lavender-pink or white. Summer. Calif.
→*Perezia*.

Acradenia Kipp. Rutaceae. 2 closely branched shrubs and trees. Lvs trifoliolate, glandular-punctate, leathery, aromatic. Fls small, paniculate; sep. 5–6; pet. 5–6. E Aus. Z8.

A. frankliniae Kipp. WHITEY WOOD. To 7m. Br. angled, gland. Lfts to 6cm, oblong-lanceolate. Infl. to 5cm, few-fld; fls to 7mm, white. Tasm.

Acridocarpus Guillem., Perrott. & A. Rich. Malpighiaceae. 30 trees and shrubs, sometimes climbers. Lvs often gland. beneath. Infl. term. or axill., rac. or corymb; sep. 5; pet. 5, spreading, clawed. Fr. a samara. Trop. Afr., Madag., New Caledonia. Z10.

A. natalitius A. Juss. Climber. Lvs 7.5–12.5cm, oblong-obovate, glossy. Infl. to 15cm; pet. to 1cm, pale yellow, toothed. S Afr.

Acriopsis Reinw. ex Bl. Orchidaceae. 5 small epiphytes. Pbs crowded, ovoid, sheathed, with 2–4 linear lvs at apex. Infl. a lat. rac. or pan.; fls twisted, dors. sep. incurved, lat. sep. fused behind lip, lip ± tubular. SE Asia to Solomon Is. Z10.

A. densiflora Lindl. Tep. dark purple, lip edged white. Borneo, Sumatra.

A. javanica Reinw. ex Bl. Sep. pale yellow ± striped purple; pet. white to cream blotched or striped purple; lip crimson-purple edged white. Sumatra to New Guinea.

A. picta Lindl. = *A. javanica*.
→*Spathoglottis*.

Acrocarpus Wight ex Arn. Leguminosae (Caesalpinioideae). 2 trees to 60m. Lvs bipinnate. Infl. a simple or branched rac.; cal. seg. 5, unequal; pet. 5, unequal; sta. 5, exserted. Indomal. Z10.

A. fraxinifolius Arn. SHINGLE TREE; PINK CEDAR; RED CEDAR. Lvs coral-tinted, downy, then glab.; pinnae to 30cm, in 3–5 pairs; lfts to 14cm, ovate-oblong. Infl. spike-like; fls scarlet, downy. Z10.

Acroclinium A. Gray. EVERLASTING FLOWER; STRAWFLOWER. Compositae. *c*90 ann. to perenn. herbs, subshrubs or shrubs. Lvs entire. Cap. discoid, solitary or in corymbose infl.; phyllaries numerous, pet.-like, persistent. Aus., S Afr.

A. roseum Hook. PINK AND WHITE EVERLASTING; ROSY SUNRAY; PINK PAPER-DAISY. Ann. erect to 60cm. Lvs to 3.5cm, linear, glab. Cap. to 5cm diam., solitary, phyllaries bright pink. SW Aus.
→*Helipterum*.

Acrocomia Mart. Palmae. 1 palm. St. subterranean or erect to 15m×40cm, sometimes swollen above, with persistent lf bases or caducous spines, becoming smooth, ringed. Lvs to 3m, pinnate; petiole with spines and bristles; sheath green, blue-grey, or tinged red, disintegrating into tangled fibres; pinnae crowded, linear, acute or shallowly divided, usually grouped and held in differing planes along rachis, coriaceous, glab. above, glaucous or pubesc. beneath. Central S Amer. Z10.

A. aculeata (Jacq.) Lodd. ex Mart. MACAMBA; GRU GRU; MBOCAYA TOTA; MUCAJA.

Acrodon N.E. Br. Aizoaceae. 4 mat-forming succulents. Lvs triangular, toothed, in a rosette. S Afr. Z9.

A. bellidiflorum (L.) N.E. Br. Lvs 3–5cm, grey-green with white, horny, toothed edges. Fls 2.5–4cm diam., white edged pink to red. W Cape.

Acronychia Forst. & Forst. f. Rutaceae. 44 trees and shrubs. Lvs simple or trifoliolate, entire, gland-dotted. Fls small, 4-merous, in cymes or pan., white to yellow. Fr. a drupe. Aus., Trop. Asia, Pacific Is. Z10.

A. baueri Schott. Tree. Lvs to 15cm, simple, ovate-elliptic. Fls downy; ovary pubesc. Aus.

A. laevis Forst. & Forst. f. Shrub or small tree. Lvs to 9.5cm, simple, elliptic to obovate. Fls glab.; ovary glab. Aus., New Caledonia.

Acropera Lindl.

A. armeniaca Lindl. & Paxt. = *Gongora armeniaca*.

A. cornuta Klotzsch. = *Gongora armeniaca*.

A. loddigesii Lindl. = *Gongora galatea*.

Acropogon Schltr. Sterculiaceae. 26 trees and shrubs. Infl. cauliflorous; fls campanulate; sep. 5. Follicles woody, dehiscent. New Caledonia. Z10.

A. austro-caledonicus (Hook. f.) Morat. Tree. Lvs 12–60cm, palmately lobed; petiole 30–60cm. Fls red-yellow. New Caledonia.
→*Sterculia*.

Acrostichum L. Pteridaceae. 3 massive ferns of wet, warm places. Rhiz. stout. Fronds pinnate, clustered, erect; pinnae leathery, entire, topmost fertile. Pantrop. Z10.

A. alpinum Bolton = *Woodsia alpina*.

A. apiifolium (J. Sm.) Hook. = *Psomiocarpa apiifolia*.

A. aureum L. LEATHER FERN. Fronds to 3m; fertile pinnae to 40cm, broadly ligulate-oblong. Pantrop.

A. cervinum (L.) Sw. = *Olfersia cervina*.

A. chrysophyllum Sw. = *Pityrogramma chrysophylla*.

A. danaeifolium Langsd. & Fisch. GIANT LEATHER FERN. Fertile fronds to 3.5m, taller, more erect than sterile fronds, with pinnae closer than in *A. aureum*. Flor., C & S Amer., W Indies.

A. drynarioides Hook. = *Merinthosorus drynarioides*.

A. ebeneum L. = *Pityrogramma tartarea*.

A. excelsum Maxon. = *A. danaeifolium*.

A. harlandii Hook. = *Hemigramma decurrens*.

A. ilvense L. = *Woodsia ilvensis*.

A. latifolium (Meyen) Hook. = *Hemigramma latifolia*.

A. osmundaceum (Willd.) Hook. = *Polybotrya osmundacea*.

A. peltatum (Sw.) Sw. = *Peltapteris peltata*.

A. platyneuron L. = *Asplenium platyneuron*.

A. punctatum L. = *Microsorium punctatum*.

A. repandum Bl. = *Bolbitis quoyana*.

A. ruta-muraria (L.) Lam. = *Asplenium ruta-muraria*.

A. scandens L. = *Stenochlaena palustris*.

A. septentrionale L. = *Asplenium septentrionale*.

A. sinuatum Lagasca ex Sw. = *Cheilanthes sinuata*.

A. sorbifolium L. = *Stenochlaena sorbifolia*.

A. speciosum Willd. MANGROVE FERN. Fronds to 1.5cm; sterile pinnae narrowly acuminate. Trop. Asia & Aus.

A. tartareum Cav. = *Pityrogramma tartarea*.

A. variabile Hook. = *Leptochilus decurrens*.

Acrotriche R. Br. Epacridaceae. *c*14 erect to prostrate everg. shrubs. Lvs small, rigid. Fls small; pet. 5, fused below. Aus. Z9.

A. cordata (Labill.) R. Br. COAST GROUND-BERRY. Dense, erect or spreading shrub, to 1m. Lvs to 1cm, pungent. Fls white to pale green, v. small. S & W Aus., Tasm.

A. divaricata R. Br. TALL GROUND-BERRY. Spreading shrub to 2.4m. Lvs to 1cm, pungent. Fls to 2cm, pale green. SW Aus.

A. ovalifolia R. Br. = *A. cordata*.
→*Styphelia*.

Actaea L. Ranunculaceae. BANEBERRY. 8 rhizomatous perenn. herbs. Lvs 2–3-ternate, basal lvs long-stalked. Fls small, white in term. rac.; sep. 3, 4 or 5, petaloid; pet. 0–4, nectariferous; sta. numerous. Fr. a glossy berry, toxic. Early summer. N temp. regions.

A. acuminata Wallich = *A. spicata* var. *acuminata*.

A. alba (L.) Mill. non Mackenzie & Rydb. WHITE BANEBERRY; DOLL'S EYES. 40–80cm. Resembles *A. rubra*. Rac. 4×3cm, to 22cm in fr.; fls to 1cm. Fr. to 8mm, white or pale red. E N Amer. f. *rubrocarpa* (Killip) Fern. Fr. bright red. Z3.

A. alba Mackenzie & Rydb. non (L.) Mill. = *A. rubra* f. *neglecta*.

A. arguta Nutt. = *A. rubra* ssp. *arguta*.

A. asiatica Hara. To 70cm. Lfts acuminate. Fr. to 6mm, black. China, Korea, Jap. Z6.

A. cimicifuga L. = *Cimicifuga foetida*.

A. eburnea Rydb. = *A. rubra* f. *neglecta*.

A. erythrocarpa Fisch. To 70cm. Resembles *A. spicata*. Rac. oval in outline. Fr. red. NE Eur. to Sib., Jap. var. *leucocarpa* hort. Fr. white. Z2.

A. japonica Thunb. = *Cimicifuga japonica*.

A. neglecta Gilman = *A. rubra* f. *neglecta*.

A. nigra (L.) Gaertn., Mey. & Scherb. = *A. spicata*.

A. pachypoda Elliott = *A. alba*.

A. rubra (Ait.) Willd. RED BANEBERRY; SNAKEBERRY. To 80cm. Lvs to 45cm. Fls c8mm diam., white or tinged purple. Fr. scarlet. N Amer. f. *neglecta* (Gilman) Robinson. Taller. Fr. white, slender-stalked. ssp. *arguta* (Nutt.) Hult. Lvs smaller, more deeply cut. W N Amer. Z3.

A. spicata L. 60–80cm. Lvs to 60cm, sometimes pinnate. Rac. loosely conical. Fr. purple-black. Eur. to W Asia. var. *acuminata* (Wallich) Hara. Lfts lanceolate-acuminate. Afghan. to China. Z5.

A. spicata 'Nigra' = *A. asiatica*.

A. spicata ssp. *erythrocarpa* (Fisch.) Hult. = *A. erythrocarpa*.

A. spicata var. *rubra* Ait. = *A. rubra*.

Actinella Pers.

A. acaulis Nutt. = *Tetraneuris acaulis*.

A. grandiflora Torr. & A. Gray = *Tetraneuris grandiflora*.

A. lanata Pursh = *Eriophyllum lanatum*.

A. scaposa Nutt. = *Tetraneuris scaposa*.

Actinidia Lindl. Actinidiaceae. 40 climbing decid. or everg. shrubs. St. twining. Lvs simple. Fls unisexual, 5-merous, solitary or in axill. cymes. Fr. a large many-seeded berry, sometimes edible. E Asia.

A. arguta (Sieb. & Zucc.) Planch. ex Miq. TARA VINE; YANG-TAO. Lvs to 15cm, broadly ovate, glab., serrate. Fls white; anth. purple. Fr. to 2.5cm diam., oblong, yellow-green, edible. Temp. E Asia. 'Ananasnaya': v. hardy, vigorous; fls attractive, fragrant; fr. small in large clusters. 'Issai': self-fertile. 'Meader Female': ♀ clone, to be pollinated by 'Male' or 'Meader Male'. var.*cordifolia* Dunn. Lvs cordate. Z4.

A. callosa Lindl. Lvs to 13cm, ovate-oblong, glab., finely toothed. Fls white; anth. yellow. Fr. to 2.5cm diam., ovoid, green spotted red. E Asia. Z7.

A. chinensis hort. non Planch. = *A. deliciosa*.

A. coriacea (Finet & Gagnep.) Dunn. Lvs to 15cm, oblonglanceolate, glab., dentate. Fls red; anth. yellow. Fr. to 2cm, ovoid, brown. China. Z6.

A. deliciosa C.S. Liang & A.R. Fergusson KIWI FRUIT; CHINESE GOOSEBERRY; YANGTAO. Lvs to 20cm, cordate-acuminate, bristly-downy. Fr. to 6.5cm, oblong-ellipsoid, brown-bristly, flesh green, edible. China. 'Aureovariegata': lvs marked cream and yellow. 'Blake': ♀, fast-cropping and self-fertile; recommended for smaller gardens. 'Tomuri': ♂ st. red, hairy; lvs oval, dark green; fls less abundant, large, cream, late flowering. Commercially, ♀ cvs like 'Bruno' (fr. elongated) and 'Hayward' (fr. large) are used, with ♂ pollinators such as 'Male', 'Matua' and 'Tomuri'. Z7.

A. giraldii Diels. Close to *A. arguta*, vigorous, lvs ovate-elliptic, fls white. Summer. C. China.

A. kolomikta (Rupr. & Maxim.) Maxim. Lvs to 15cm, cordateovate, glab., zoned pale green, bronze, pink and white toward slender tip. Temp. E Asia. 'Arctic Beauty': v. hardy; lvs to 12cm, opening purple, mature to combination of pink, white and green; fls small, white, fragrant. 'Krupnoplodnaya': hardy; lvs red in summer. Z4.

A. lanceolata Dunn. Lvs to 6.5cm, ovate-lanceolate, puberulent above, hoary beneath. Fls green; anth. yellow. Fr. to 1cm. China. Z6.

A. melanandra Franch. Lvs to 9cm, ovate-oblong, sparsely rusty-pubesc. beneath. Fls white; anth. mauve. Fr. to 3cm, glab., red-brown. Jap., China. Z6.

A. polygama (Sieb. & Zucc.) Maxim. SILVER VINE. Lvs to 15cm, ovate to oblong, ± silvery or golden above. Fls white; anth. yellow. Fr. to 2.5cm diam., yellow, edible. Temp. E Asia. Z4.

A. purpurea Rehd. Cf. *A. arguta*, but lvs longer, narrower, fr. flushed purple, sweet-tasting. China. Z6.

A. volubilis (Sieb. & Zucc.) Miq. = *A. polygama*.

ACTINIDIACEAE Hutch. 3/355. *Actinidia*, *Clematoclethra*.

ACTINIOPTERIDACEAE Pic. Serm. See *Actiniopteris*.

Actiniopteris Link. Actiniopteridaceae. 5 terrestrial ferns. Rhiz. scaly, slender, creeping. Fronds clustered, fan-shaped, palmately compound. Trop. Asia & Afr., Madag., Masc. Z10.

A. radiata (Sw.) Link. Frond blade to 4cm, deeply cleft, 5–6× dichotomously divided; seg. linear, wider toward tip; stipe 3–5x blade length. Distrib. as for the genus, inc. Arabia.

A. semiflabellata Pichi-Serm. Frond blade to 20cm, not cleft, 4–5× dichotomously divided; seg. narrowly ensiform, narrower toward tip; stipe 1.5–2x blade length. Afr., Madag., Maur., N India.

Actinodium Schauer. Myrtaceae. 2 small aromatic shrubs. Fls small, in daisy-like arrangement, outermost enlarged, sterile. SW Aus. Z9.

A. cunninghamii Schauer. SWAMP DAISY; ALBANY DAISY. Dwarf. Br. erect. Lvs to 5mm, linear, erect, overlapping. Infl. to 4cm across, white and red.

Actinomeris Nutt.

A. alternifolia (L.) DC. = *Verbesina alternifolia*.

A. procera Steud. = *Verbesina alternifolia*.

A. squarrosa (L.) DC. = *Verbesina alternifolia*.

Actinophloeus (Becc.) Becc.

A. macarthurii (H.A. Wendl.) Becc. = *Ptychosperma macarthurii*.

A. sanderianus (Ridl.) Burret. = *Ptychosperma sanderianum*.

Actinorhytis H.A. Wendl. & Drude.

A. calapparia Vidal = *Veitchia merrillii*.

Actinostemma Griff. Cucurbitaceae. 1 scandent herb. Lvs round to reniform. Fls small, green-yellow, ♂ fls in pan. or rac.; ♀ fls solitary. Fr. soft-spiny, 1cm across.

A. lobatum (Maxim.) Maxim. = *A. tenerum*.

A. tenerum Griff. GOKIZURU.

Actinostrobus Miq. Cupressaceae. 3 evergr. conifers to 5m. Crown conical. Br. erect. Lvs decussate, in whorls of 3: juveniles acicular, adult scale-like. ♀ cones with sterile thin scales in whorls, increasing in size, forming a ray-like base, and thick, woody fertile scales. W Aus. Z10.

A. acuminatus Parl. To 2m. Adult lvs 1–2mm. Cones to 15mm, ovoid-acuminate, fertile scales spreading after opening.

A. arenarius Gdn. Close to *A. pyramidalis* but taller, with longer, more unspread lvs and cones ovoid-acute with scales straight after opening.

A. pyramidalis Miq. To 3m. Adult lvs to 3mm, spreading. Cones to 15mm, ovoid-globose, blunt, scales incurved after opening.

A. pyramidalis var. *arenarius* (Gdn) Silba = *A. arenarius*.

Actinotus Labill. FLANNEL FLOWER. Umbelliferae. 17 ann. to perenn. herbs. Lvs pinnately lobed or 2-ternate. Fls minute in dense umbels subtended by conspicuous bracts. Aus., NZ.

A. helianthi Labill. Woolly, erect perenn. to 60cm. Lvs 2–3× pinnatifid, seg. narrow. Infl. white, short-stemmed, bracts to 5cm, 10–18, petal-like, woolly. Summer. Aus.

Action Plant *Mimosa pudica*.

Acumo *Syagrus flexuosa*.

Acumo Rasteiro *Syagrus petraea*.

Ada Lindl. Orchidaceae. 2 epiphytic orchids. Pbs ovoid, compressed, clothed with leafy bracts. Lvs 1–2 per pb., flexible, strap-shaped. Rac. lat., arching; fls numerous; tep. narrow, equal. Colombian Andes, New Grenada. Z9.

A. aurantiaca Lindl. Pbs to 10cm. Lvs to 30cm. Tep. to 2.5cm, dark orange to cinnabar red, forward-pointing, overlapping, tips

recurved.
A. lehmannii Rolfe = *A. aurantiaca*.

Adam's Apple *Tabernaemontana divaricata*.
Adam's Needle *Yucca filamentosa, Y. smalliana*.

Adansonia L. BAOBAB; MONKEY-BREAD TREE. Bombacaceae. 9 decid. trees with massive swollen trunks and short br. Fls pendulous, large, usually white, opening at night; sta. in a dense, stalked boss. Fr. cylindrical, large, woody. Afr., Madag., NW Aus. Z10.
A. digitata L. BAOBAB. To 20m. Trunk to 10m diam. Lvs simple to 7-digitate. Pet. to 12cm, white, obovate-spathulate, crisped. Subsaharan Afr.

Adder's Fern *Polypodium vulgare*.
Adder's Tongue *Erythronium*.
Adder's Tongue Fern *Ophioglossum vulgatum*.

Adelocaryum Brand.
A. coelestinum (Lindl.) Brand. = *Cynoglossum coelestinum*.

Adelonenga Becc.
A. microspadix Becc. = *Hydriastele microspadix*.

Adenandra Willd. Labiatae. 18 much-branched everg. shrubs. Lvs simple. Fls white suffused red below. S Afr. (Cape Prov.). Z9.
A. amoena (Lodd.) Link = *A. fragrans*.
A. coriacea Lichtenst. ex Roem. & Schult. To 45cm. Lvs 0.4–1.2cm, ovate-elliptic, entire to crenulate, ± glab. Infl. few-fld; cor. white inside, suffused pink to brick red outside.
A. cuspidata E. Mey. ex Bartling & Wendl. = *A. villosa*.
A. fragrans (Sims) Roem. & Schult. To 1m. Lvs to 2cm, oblong-oblanceolate, gland., crenate. Infl. 4–18-fld; cor. white outside, pink inside, red-veined.
A. uniflora (L.) Willd. To 40cm, sparsely branched. Lvs 0.4–1.4cm, oblong to elliptic glab. Fls usually solitary, white to pink.
A. villosa (P. Bergius) Lichtenst. ex Roem. & Schult. To 1m, ascending to erect. Lvs 0.4–1cm, glabrescent, glandular-punctate. Fls solitary or in few-fld umbels, white inside, often suffused red outside.

Adenanthera L. Leguminosae (Mimosoideae). 4 decid. trees to 30m. Lvs bipinnate. Fls in spiciform rac.; pet. small, yellow-white; sta. 10, showy, white to yellow. Fr. linear, straight or spiraling; seeds brilliant red. Trop. Asia and Pacific. Z10.
A. pavonina L. CORALWOOD; REDWOOD; RED SANDALWOOD TREE; PEACOCK FLOWER FENCE; BARBADOS PRIDE; CORAL PEA. To 18m. Lvs to 40cm; lfts to 4.5cm, ovate, on 3–5 pairs pinnae. Rac. to 30cm. Fr. to 22cm, coiling in dehiscence. SE Asia.

Adenanthos Labill. Proteaceae. 33 shrubs and small trees. Lvs variable, entire or lobed. Fls pink red or yellow, solitary or clustered; tep. 4, fused; nectary scales 4, basal. S & W Aus. Z9.
A. barbigerus Lindl. HAIRY JUGFLOWER. Shrub to 1m. Lvs elliptic-lanceolate. Fls red, produced on upper third of st.; tep. silky hairy. W Aus.
A. cuneatus Labill. COASTAL JUGFLOWER. Shrub to 2m, rarely prostrate. Lvs lobed or toothed, bronze red when young, turning silver. Fls red, ± term. W Aus.
A. cygnorum Diels. COMMON WOOLLYBUSH. To 4m. Lvs finely divided, grey-green, with term. extrafloral nectary. W Aus. ssp. *chamaephyton* Nels. Smaller in all parts.
A. detmoldii F. Muell. SCOTT RIVER JUGFLOWER. Erect shrub to 3m. Lvs narrow. Fls yellow and orange in lf axils. W Aus.
A. obovatus Labill. BASKET FLOWER. Low shrub to 1m. Lvs obovate, glab. Fls orange to red to 25cm. Yellow-fld forms available. W Aus.
A. ×pamela hort. (*A. detmoldii* × *A. obovatus*.) Intermediate between parents.
A. sericeus Labill. WOOLLYBUSH. Shrub to 5m. Lvs finely divided, silver-grey, silky hairy. Fls red, inconspicuous.
A. teges A.S. George = *A. cygnorum*.

Adenia Forssk. Passifloraceae. 90 decid. shrubs. St. climbing, sprawling or bushy, with thorns or tendrils, arising from a massive caudex. Lvs simple or digitately lobed. Fls 5-merous, green, cream or yellow, borne in cymes, pet. of ♀ smaller than ♂. Afr. to Asia.
A. digitata (Harv.) Engl. Climber to 3m. Lvs 3–5-lobed, lfts to 15cm, linear to obovate, sometimes divided. Fls tubular, ♂ fls 5–10 per cyme, ♀ 1–10; ♂ pet. to 12mm. Afr.
A. fruticosa Davy. Shrub to 6m. Lvs simple or 3–5-lobed, lfts to

6cm, ovate to orbicular, entire. Fls campanulate, ♂ fls 2–5 per cyme, ♀ 1–3; ♂ pet. to 8mm. S Afr.
A. pechuelii (Engl.) Harms. Thorny shrub to 1.5m. Lvs to 6cm, sparse, tough, ovate to lanceolate, entire or 3-lobed. Fls campanulate, 1–3 per cyme; ♂ pet. to 5mm. S Afr.
A. spinosa Davy. Thorny shrub to 1.5m. Lvs to 3.5cm, ovate to elliptic, simple. Fls tubular-campanulate, ♂ fls 2–6 per cyme, ♀ 1–3; ♂ pet. to 10mm. S Afr.

Adenium Roem. & Schult. MOCK AZALEA; DESERT ROSE; IMPALA LILY; KUDU LILY; SABI STAR. Apocynaceae. 1 pachycaul, succulent shrub or tree. Caudex conical-globose, often ± subterranean; br. thick. Lvs to 15cm, lanceolate-obovate, coriaceous. Fls in term. corymbs; cor. 2–5cm, tubular, lobes 5, spreading, red with a white eye, pink or white. Trop. and S Afr., Arabia, Socotra. Z9.
A. arabicum Balf. f. = *A. obesum*.
A. boehmianum Schinz. = *A. obesum* ssp. *boehmianum*.
A. coetaneum Stapf = *A. obesum*.
A. honghel A. DC. = *A. obesum*.
A. lugardii N.E. Br. = *A. obesum* ssp. *boehmianum*.
A. multiflorum Klotzsch = *A. obesum*.
A. obesum (Forssk.) Roem. & Schult. ssp. **boehmianum** (Schinz) G. Rowley. Fls pink-purple with dark throat. Nam., S Angola. ssp. **oleifolium** (Stapf) G. Rowley. Caudex mainly subterranean. SE Nam., N Cape, S Bots. ssp. **socotranum** (Vierh.) Lavranos. Trunk massive. Fls bright pink. Socotra. ssp. **somalense** (Balf. f.) G. Rowley. Small tree. E Afr. ssp. **swazicum** (Stapf) G. Rowley. Caudex partly subterranean. Lvs large. Transvaal, Swaz., S Natal.
A. oleifolium Stapf = *A. obesum* ssp. *oleifolium*.
A. socotranum Vierh. = *A. obesum* ssp. *socotranum*.
A. somalense Balf. f. = *A. obesum* ssp. *somalense*.
A. swazicum Stapf = *A. obesum* ssp. *swazicum*.

Adenocalymma Mart. ex Meissn. Bignoniaceae. 34 lianes. St. 4-ribbed. Lvs usually trifoliolate, term. leaflet often replaced by tendril. Rac. axill. or term.; cal. cupular; cor. yellow, tubular-funnelform to tubular-campanulate, slightly pubesc. outside. Mex. to Arg., mostly in Braz. Z10.
A. alboviolaceum Loes. = *Mansoa hymenaea*.
A. apurense (HBK) Sandw. Lfts 3, oblong-elliptic, shortly mucronate, short-pilose beneath. Fls to 6cm, 3cm diam., densely pubesc. Braz.
A. calderonii (Standl.) Seib. = *A. inundatum*.
A. ciliolatum Blake. = *Mansoa hymenaea*.
A. comosum (Cham.) A. DC. Lfts ovate to lanceolate, shorter and wider than *A. longeracemosum*, gland. Rac. densely bracteate; fls 5cm diam. at mouth. Braz.
A. dusenii Kränzl. CIPO-CRUZ-AMARELO. Lfts 15cm, ovate or oblong-elliptic, mucronate, base rounded to subcordate, leathery. Infl. 12cm diam., densely pubesc.; fls 4.5–6cm, cream to yellow, pubesc. to 3.5cm diam. Braz.
A. floribundum DC. = *Cuspidaria floribunda*.
A. friesianum Kränzl. = *Arrabidaea corallina*.
A. grenadense Urban = *A. inundatum*.
A. hintonii Sandw. = *A. inundatum*.
A. hosmeca Pittier = *Mansoa hymenaea*.
A. inundatum Mart. ex DC. Lfts 4.5–17cm, 2–3, ovate to ovate-elliptic, membranous to papery, grey, shining. Fls 2.5–6.9cm, to 2cm diam. at mouth. Mex. to N Venez., Braz., Grenada.
A. laevigatum Mart. ex DC. non Bur. & Schum. = *A. marginatum*.
A. laevigatum Bur. & Schum. non Mart. ex DC. = *Mansoa hymenaea*.
A. longeracemosum Mart. ex DC. Lfts to 25cm, oblong-lanceolate. Rac. long, puberulent-velutinous; cor. golden. Braz.
A. macrocarpum Donn = *Mansoa hymenaea*.
A. marginatum (Cham.) DC. Lfts 2–13cm, elliptic to ovate-elliptic, emarginate, leathery or rigid-papery. Infl. densely pubesc.; cor. 3–5.5cm, densely pubesc., limb to 5cm diam. Braz., to Parag., Urug., N Arg. var. *apterospermum* Sandw. Lfts usually 8cm, rounded or emarginate at apex. Braz.
A. obovatum Urban = *Mansoa hymenaea*.
A. portoricense Stahl. = *Arrabidaea chica*.
A. splendens Bur. & Schum. = *Mansoa difficilis*.
→*Bignonia* and *Tabebuia*.

Adenocarpus DC. Leguminosae (Papilionoideae). 20 shrubs or small trees. Lvs trifoliolate, in crowded whorls. Fls pea-like, showy, golden-yellow, in arching rac. Summer unless specified. Medit., Asia Minor, N & W Afr.
A. anagyrifolius Coss. & Bal. Decid. shrub, erect to 2m. Lfts to 3.5cm, ovate to elliptic, mucronate, thinly downy beneath. Rac. to 20cm; standard to 1.5cm, yellow. Atlas Mts. Z8.
A. anagyrus L'Hérit. non Spreng. = *A. hispanicus*.

A. anagyrus Spreng. non L'Hérit. = *A. viscosus*.

A. commutatus Guss. = *A. complicatus*.

A. complicatus (L.) Gay. Decid. shrub to 1m. Lfts to 2cm, oblanceolate to ovate, thinly to thickly pubesc. beneath. Rac. v. crowded; standard often tinted red. S Eur. Z9.

A. decorticans Boiss. Decid. shrub to 3m. Bark ash-grey. Lfts to 2cm, narrow-elliptic, adpressed-pubesc. throughout. Rac. to 6cm, dense; standard 1–5cm. Spain. Z8.

A. foliolosus (Ait.) DC. Semi-everg. shrub to 1m. Lfts to 0.5cm, obovate-lanceolate, pubesc. beneath. Standard to 1cm, broadly ovate, hairy. Canary Is. Z8.

A. grandiflorus Boiss. = *A. telonensis*.

A. hispanicus (Lam.) DC. Decid. shrub to 4m. Lfts to 3cm, oblanceolate, downy. Standard to 2.5cm, broadly ovate. Spain. Port. Z8.

A. intermedius DC. = *A. complicatus*.

A. parvifolius (Lam.) DC. = *A. complicatus*.

A. telonensis (Lois.) DC. Semi-everg. shrub to 1m. Lfts to 1cm, obovate, thinly hairy beneath. Rac. sometimes capitate; standard to 2cm, broadly ovate. Port., Spain, S Fr., Moroc. Z8.

A. viscosus (Willd.) Webb & Berth. Semi-everg. to 2m. Lfts to 1cm, narrowly elliptic, grey-green. Standard to 1cm, broadly ovate, tip hairy. Spring. Tenerife. Z8.

Adenophora Fisch. LADYBELLS; GLAND BELLFLOWER. Campanulaceae. *c*40 perenn. herbs, close to *Campanula*. Roots fleshy. Fls pendulous, 5-merous; cor. campanulate, blue or white. Eurasia, Jap.

A. bulleyana Diels. To 100cm. Lvs serrate. Fls oft. in 3s, pale blue. W China. Z3.

A. chinensis hort. = *A. sinensis*.

A. coelestis Diels. To 45cm. Fls few, in term. rac., broad, bright blue. W China. Z6.

A. communis Fisch. = *A. liliifolia*.

A. confusa Nannf. To 90cm. Lvs numerous, bluntly dentate, sessile. Fls in term. pan., dark blue. W China. Z3.

A. coronata A. DC. = *A. intermedia*.

A. coronifolia Fisch. = *A. nikoensis*.

A. denticulata Fisch. To 45cm. Lvs dentate. Fls many, small, blue, in term. rac. Dahuria. Z7.

A. diplodonta Diels. To 90cm. Lvs biserrate. Fls in long rac., white to blue. W China. Z3.

A. farreri hort. = *A. confusa*.

A. gmelinii Fisch. To 60cm. Upper lvs narrow linear. Fls blue, in secund, elongate rac. Dahuria. Z7.

A. hakusanensis Nak. = *A. triphylla* var. *hakusanensis*.

A. intermedia Sweet. To 90cm. Lower lvs cordate. Infl. racemose; fls pale blue. Sib. Z2.

A. koreana Kitam. To 90cm. Lower lvs whorled. Fls in term. rac., broad campanulate, blue. Korea. Z7.

A. lamarckii Fisch. To 60cm. Lvs serrate. Infl. a dense pan.; fls blue. E Eur. Z6.

A. latifolia hort. = *A. pereskiifolia*.

A. liliiflora Schur. = *A. liliifolia*.

A. liliifolia (L.) Ledeb. ex A. DC. To 50cm. Fls fragrant, in a spreading pan., pale blue to white. C Eur. to Sib. Z2.

A. marsupiiflora (Roem. & Schult.) Fisch. = *A. stenanthina*.

A. maximowicziana Mak. To 60cm, oft. decumbent. Infl. corymbose, to 10-fld; fls blue. Jap. Z6.

A. megalantha Diels. To 45cm. Lvs attenuate to base. Fls large, dark blue in rac. W China. Z6.

A. morrisonensis Hayata. Similar to *A. nikoensis*, lvs narrower. Fls violet. Taiwan. Z7.

A. nikoensis Franch. & Savat. To 40cm. Lvs usually sessile. Fls in lax rac., tinged blue. Jap. var. *stenophylla* (Kitam.) Ohwi. Lvs and cal. lobes narrower. Z6.

A. nipponica Kitam. = *A. nikoensis* var. *stenophylla*.

A. ornata Diels. To 1m. Lvs serrate, subsessile. Fls in loose pan., blue. W China. Z6.

A. palustris Komar. To 60cm. St. tinged purple. Fls in narrow rac., 1.5cm, lavender blue. China, Jap. Z6.

A. pereskiifolia G. Don. To 45cm. Lvs whorled, incised. Fls numerous, blue. Dahuria. Z7.

A. periplocifolia A. DC. To 10cm. St. ascending. Fls term., occas. solitary, pale blue. Sib. Z2.

A. polyantha Nak. To 90cm. Lvs in remote whorls. Fls numerous, sometimes constricted above, azure. Korea, Manch. Z7.

A. polymorpha Ledeb. = *A. nikoensis*.

A. potaninii Korsh. To 90cm. St. weak. Fls in rac.; cal. lobes serrate; cor. violet. W China. 'Alba': fls white. Z3.

A. remotiflora (Sieb. & Zucc.) Miq. To 1m. Lvs to 20cm. Fls in large lax pan., blue. Jap., Korea, Manch. Z6.

A. scabridula Nannf. = *A. polyantha*.

A. sinensis A. DC. To 75cm. Lvs to 8cm, biserrate. Fls in pan., indigo. China. Z6.

A. stenanthina (Ledeb.) Kitag. To 90cm, slender. Fls in rac., tinged blue. Russia, Manch. Z6.

A. stricta Miq. To 1m, sparsely white spreading pilose. Fls in dense pan., violet. China, Jap. Z7.

A. stylosa (Lam.) Fisch. = *A. liliifolia*.

A. takedae Mak. To 70cm, slender. Lvs involute, membranous. Fls in open rac., violet to blue. Jap. var. *howozara* (Tak.) Sugimoto. Compact, lvs rounded. Z7.

A. tashiroi (Mak. & Nak.) Mak. & Nak. To 30cm, decumbent. Fls few in a rac., violet. Jap. Z7.

A. thunbergiana Kudô = *A. triphylla* var. *japonica*.

A. tricuspidata A. DC. = *A. denticulata*.

A. triphylla (Thunb.) A. DC. To 90cm. Lvs to 10cm, usually in whorls of 4. Fls pale blue to violet. Jap., Taiwan, China. var. *hakusanensis* (Nak.) Kitam. To 50cm. Fls in dense clusters. var. *japonica* (Reg.) Hara. Cor. more openly campanulate. Z7.

A. verticillata (Pall.) Fisch. = *A. triphylla*.

A. verticillata var. *angustifolia* Miq. = *A. triphylla*.

A. wawreana Zahlbr. Similar to *A. polyantha* except cal. lobes lanceolate. N China. Z6.

Adenostoma Hook. & Arn. Rosaceae. 2 everg. shrubs and small trees to 6m with peeling red bark, resinous, heath-like foliage and small, white, scented fls in term. paniculate rac. W US.

A. brevifolium Nutt. = *A. fasciculatum* var. *obtusifolium*.

A. fasciculatum Hook. & Arn. CHAMISE; GREASEWOOD. Lvs 0.5–1cm, linear, glab., clustered. Infl. 5–10cm, dense. Calif. var. *obtusifolium* Wats. Lvs smaller, blunter. Z8.

A. fasciculatum var. *densiflorum* Eastw. = *A. fasciculatum*.

A. sparsifolium Torr. RIBBONWOOD; REDSHANKS. Lvs 0.6–1.5cm, filiform, gland., alt. Infl. 2–6cm, loose; fls sometimes pink. S Calif. Z8.

Adenostyles Cass.

A. albifrons (L. f.) Rchb. = *Cacalia alliariae*.

A. alliariae (Gouan) Kerner = *Cacalia alliariae*.

A. alpina hort. = *Cacalia glabra*.

A. glabra (Mill.) DC. = *Cacalia glabra*.

A. leucophylla (Willd.) Rchb. = *Cacalia leucophylla*.

Adhatoda Medik.

A. vasica (L.) Nees = *Justicia adhatoda*.

ADIANTACEAE (C. Presl.) Ching. 34. *Adiantopsis, Adiantum, Anogramma, Bommeria, Cheilanthes, Coniogramme, Cryptogramma, Doryopteris, Gymnopteris, Hemionitis, Jamesonia, Llavea, Onychium, Paraceterach, Pellaea, Pityrogramma*.

Adiantopsis Fée. Adiantaceae. 7 small terrestrial ferns. Rhiz. short, creeping, scaly. Fronds erect, blade 1–4-pinnate. Trop. Amer.

A. radiata (L.) Fée. Fronds to 50cm, 2-pinnate, pinnae 7–9, radiating from top of stipe, pinnules to 1.4cm, oblong. Trop. Amer. Z10.

Adiantum L. MAIDENHAIR; MAIDENHAIR FERN. Adiantaceae. 200 ferns. Rhiz. short, suberect to long, creeping. Fronds 1–5-pinnate, pale green, often emerging bronze or pink; pinnules usually flabellate or cuneate, thin-textured; stipes slender, dark. Cosmop. Z10 unless specified.

A. achilleifolium Lam. = *Asplenium rutifolium*.

A. aemulum T. Moore = *A. raddianum* var. *majus*.

A. aethiopicum L. COMMON MAIDENHAIR FERN; BUSH MAIDENHAIR FERN. Fronds to 80cm; blade triangular 2–3-pinnate; pinnules broadly cuneate. Aus., NZ, S Afr. (SW Cape). Z9.

A. affine Willd. = *A. cunninghamii*.

A. amoenum Wallich ex Hook. & Grev. = *A. flabellulatum*.

A. anceps Maxon & Morton. Fronds to 130cm, arching; stipe black, scaly; blade narrowly triangular, bronze-pink at first, 2–3-pinnate; pinnules ovate-cuneate, acuminate. Ecuad., Peru.

A. asarifolium Willd. = *A. reniforme*.

A. bellum T. Moore. BERMUDA MAIDENHAIR FERN. Frond blade to 15cm, ovate-lanceolate, 2-pinnate; pinnules to 2cm, erose, cuneate, stalked, shallowly lobed. Bermuda. Z9.

A. birkenheadii T. Moore = *A. diaphanum*.

A. capillus-junonis Rupr. Frond blade to 20cm, oblong-lanceolate, 1-pinnate; pinnae orbicular, crenate and finely lobed. Manch., Jap. Z8.

A. capillus-veneris L. COMMON MAIDENHAIR; SOUTHERN MAIDENHAIR; VENUS MAIDENHAIR. Fronds to 70cm, arching; blade narrowly triangular, bronze-pink at first, 2–3-pinnate; pinnules to 2cm, broadly cuneate to flabellate, sometimes lobed; stipe to 20cm, dark. Eur., Afr., India, Sri Lanka, China, Jap., Polyn., Americas, Aus. 'Fimbriatum': pinnules deeply and irregularly cut with serrate margins, irregular in size, some failing to develop, lobes twisted, variously disposed. 'Imbricatum':

pinnules flabellate, overlapping, deeply and irregularly incised or lobed. Z8.

A. *cardiochlaenum* Kunze. = A. *polyphyllum*.

A. *caudatum* L. TRAILING MAIDENHAIR; WALKING MAIDENHAIR FERN. Fronds to 60cm, rooting at apex, trailing, 1-pinnate; pinnae to 2cm, cuneate, sometimes lobed or cut; stipes shaggy. China, India, Sri Lanka, Malaysia, Taiwan, Philipp., New Guinea.

A. *chilense* Kaulf. Frond blade to 30cm, ovate-triangular, 3-pinnate; pinnules subrhombic-reniform, lobed; stipe glossy black. Chile, Peru, Juan Fernandez Is. Z8.

A. *chusanum* L. = *Sphenomeris chinensis*.

A. *clavatum* L. = *Sphenomeris clavata*.

A. *collisii* T. Moore. Frond blade to 60cm across, triangular, 6-pinnate; pinnules rhombic-truncate, sometimes lobed; stipe to 45cm. Origin obscure.

A. *concinnum* Humb. & Bonpl. ex Willd. BRITTLE MAIDENHAIR. Fronds to 80cm; blade narrowly triangular, 2–3-pinnate; pinnules to 1.5cm, subrhombic to flabellate, deeply cut. Mex., Peru, Venez., Braz., W Indies. Z9.

A. *cristatum* L. Fronds to 100cm; blade to 3-pinnate, term. pinnae pronounced, laterals remote, shorter; pinnules to 1.5cm, rhombic-oblong, finely toothed, apex subfalcate or obtuse. Greater & Lesser Antilles, Venez.

A. *cuneatum* Langsd. & Fisch. = A. *raddianum*.

A. *cunninghamii* Hook. Fronds to 100cm; blade broadly triangular, 2-pinnate, dark mauve hardening blue-green; pinnules to 2.5cm, oblong-rhombic. Australasia (Queensld, New Guinea, NZ, Kermadec Is.). Z9.

A. *curvatum* Kaulf. Fronds pedate, 2–3-pinnate, to 100cm; pinnules to 2cm, narrow-trapeziform, shallowly lobed. Braz.

A. *deflectens* C. Mart. Fronds to 40cm; blade lanceolate, 1-pinnate, rooting at tip; pinnae narrowly cuneate to flabellate, toothed or cleft, fragile. C & S Amer.

A. *diaphanum* Bl. FILMY MAIDENHAIR. Fronds semi-transparent; blade to 30cm, arching 1–2-pinnate; pinnules to 0.5cm, rhombic, many held close together. Trop. Asia, Malaysia, Jap., Aus., NZ. Z9.

A. *dolabriforme* Hook. Fronds rooting at tip; blade oblong, pinnate; pinnules thin-textured, obliquely subrotund, deeply lobed. Braz., Panama.

A. *edgeworthii* Hook. Fronds rooting at tip; blade to 12cm, lanceolate, pinnate; pinnae to 1.5cm, 5–20 pairs, obliquely flabellate, subentire, membranous. India, China, Jap. Z9.

A. *emarginatum* Hook. = A. *jordanii*.

A. *excisum* Kunze. CHILEAN MAIDENHAIR. Fronds densely tufted; blade to 40cm, triangular, 2–3-pinnate; pinnules many, short; stipes wiry. Chile, Panama, Mex., Boliv.

A. *farleyense* T. Moore = A. *tenerum* 'Farleyense'.

A. *feei* T. Moore ex Fée. Frond blade to 60cm, 3-pinnate; ultimate pinnae with to 7 suborbicular-cuneate pinnules. Mex., Guat.

A. *fergusonii* T. Moore = A. *tenerum* 'Fergusonii'.

A. *flabellulatum* L. Frond blade to 55cm, pedate, 2-pinnate; pinnules 5–18 pairs, upper margin rounded, sometimes notched. India, China, Jap., Taiwan, Philipp., Malaysia.

A. *formosum* R. Br. GIANT MAIDENHAIR FERN; PLUMED MAIDENHAIR; AUSTRALIAN MAIDENHAIR FERN. Fronds to 100cm, held erect; blade broadly triangular, 2–4-pinnate; pinnules 2cm, triangular, deeply cut. Aus., NZ. Z9.

A. *fovearum* Raddi = A. *latifolium*.

A. *fructosum* Poepp. ex Spreng. Fronds erect; blade to 100cm, ovate-triangular, 2-pinnate; pinnules transversely oblong, dark green, some serrate. Mex., W Indies, Venez., Peru, Braz.

A. *fulvum* Raoul. Frond blade to 40cm, ovate-triangular, 3-pinnate; pinnules ± lax, cuneate to subrhombic; stipes to 30cm, red-brown with tawny scales. Polyn., Aus., NZ.

A. *ghiesbreghtii* hort. = A. *tenerum* 'Scutum Roseum'.

A. *hendersonii* Lind. = A. *fructosum*.

A. *henslovianum* Hook. Fronds to 90cm; blade ovate-triangular, 2–3-pinnate; pinnules broadly cuneate to subflabellate, lobed, with fine pale hairs beneath; stipes to 40cm, glabrate. Venez., Galapagos Is., Ecuad., Peru.

A. *hispidulum* Sw. ROUGH MAIDENHAIR FERN; ROSY MAIDENHAIR FERN. Fronds to 50cm, pink-bronze when young; blade pedate or 2–3-pinnate, hispidulous; pinnules to 2cm, rhombic, overlapping. Afr., S India, Malaysia, Polyn., Aus., NZ, US (nat., Hawaii).

A. *incisum* Forssk. Fronds to 35cm, rooting at tip; blade narrow, 1-pinnate; pinnae small, oblong-cuneate, rusty-pubesc. Trop. Afr., subtrop. Afr., Yemen, India, Cape Verde Is.

A. *jordanii* K. Muell. CALIFORNIA MAIDENHAIR FERN. Fronds to 60cm; blade narrowly triangular, 2–3-pinnate; pinnules crescent-shaped, finely toothed or deeply notched. US (Oreg., Calif.). Z8.

A. *kaulfussii* Kunze = A. *petiolatum*.

A. *latifolium* Lam. GLAUCOUS MAIDENHAIR FERN. Fronds to 70cm; blade 1–2-pinnate; pinnules oblong, bluntly tapered, glaucous beneath; stipes with curly scales. Trop. Amer.

A. *lucidum* (Cav.) Sw. Frond blade to 60cm, lanceolate-oblong, 1-pinnate; pinnae to 10cm, acuminate, sometimes serrate; stipe to 30cm, black. Trop. S Amer., W Indies.

A. *lunulatum* Burm. f. = A. *philippense*.

A. *macrophyllum* Sw. Frond blade to 70cm, 1-pinnate; pinnae to 8cm, in 3–8 pairs, ovate-triangular, sometime incised emerging pink-bronze; stipe black, glab. W Indies, C Amer., Braz., Boliv., Galapagos Is.

A. × *mairisii* T. Moore. (Possibly A. *capillus-veneris* × A. *raddianum*.) Frond blade to 50cm, broadly triangular, 3–4-pinnate; pinnules broadly cuneate to subrhombic, lobed, serrulate. Gdn origin.

A. *monochlamys* D.C. Eaton. Frond blade to 25cm, narrowly triangular, 3–4-pinnate; pinnules obtriangular, subcoriaceous; stipe to 20cm, chestnut. S Korea, Taiwan, China, Jap. Z9.

A. *obliquum* Willd. Frond blade semi-rigid, to 30cm, lanceolate, pinnate; pinnae oblong-triangular, sometimes hastate or pinnatifid. W Indies, C Amer., S to Braz. and Boliv.

A. *paradiseae* Bak. = A. *capillus-veneris*.

A. *patens* Willd. Frond blade to 65cm, pedate; pinnules subrhombic to crescent-shaped, some crenate; stipe to 40cm, pale rust. Trop. Amer.

A. *pedatum* L. FIVE-FINGERED MAIDENHAIR FERN; AMERICAN MAIDENHAIR FERN. Frond blade pedate, 2-pinnate; pinnae to 30cm, linear-lanceolate; pinnules obliquely triangular to oblong, pale green, glaucescent beneath; stipes to 50cm. N Amer., E Asia. Several forms have been named. 'Japonicum' (EARLY RED MAIDENHAIR): Fronds to 30cm, purple-pink on emergence. 'Laceratum': to 20cm, pinnules deeply cut; 'Miss Sharples': 30–40cm, a golden green form. var. *aleuticum* Rupr. ALEUTIAN MAIDENHAIR. To 40cm. Pinnules obliquely triangular. Alask., Aleutian Is., Canada. ssp. *subpumilum* Wagner ('Minus', 'Minor'). To 15cm, habit dwarf, congested. Z5.

A. *pentadactylon* Langsd. & Fisch. Similar to A. *trapeziforme*; pinnules trapeziform, deeply lobed; stipe black, glabrescent, the colour suffusing pinnules. Braz. 'Sanctae Catherinae': fronds erect; pinnules oblong-trapeziform to rhombic-ovate, with lobes 5mm deep, strongly scented.

A. *peruvianum* Klotzsch. SILVER DOLLAR MAIDENHAIR FERN. To 1m. Frond blade triangular, 1–3-pinnate, dark green; pinnules 7cm, rhombic-trapeziform, silver-rose on emergence. cf. A. *anceps*. Ecuad., Peru, Boliv.

A. *petiolatum* Desv. Frond to 60cm; blade oblong to triangular, 1-pinnate; pinnae lanceolate-triangular, serrulate to pinnatisect; stipes to 40cm, black. W Indies, Trop. Amer.

A. *philippense* L. WALKING MAIDENHAIR FERN; WILD TEA LEAVES. Fronds rooting at apex; blade to 30cm, 1-pinnate; pinnae to 2cm, crescent-shaped, lobed, glossy, term. pinna large, subflabellate. Trop.

A. *platyphyllum* Sw. Fronds to 70cm; blade broadly triangular to ovate, 2-pinnate; pinnules 5–10cm, ovate-lanceolate, long-acuminate, glaucous beneath; stipe chalky black. Peru, Ecuad., Boliv., Braz.

A. *poiretii* Wikstr. Fronds to 50cm, arching; blade ovate-triangular, 3–4-pinnate; pinnules to 1.5cm, suborbicular to flabellate, suffused with dark colouring of stipe and rachis. Trop. var. *sulphureum* (Kaulf.) Tryon. Pinnules coated with yellow gland-hair secretion beneath. Peru, Arg., Chile. Z9.

A. *polyphyllum* Willd. Fronds to 150cm, emerging pale pink; blade 2–3-pinnate; pinnules to 2.5cm, suboblong, lobed; stipe to 40cm. Colomb., Venez., Boliv., Trin.

A. *princeps* T. Moore. Differs from A. *tenerum* in longer fronds and larger pinnules. Colomb.

A. *pubescens* Schkuhr. Differs from A. *hispidulum* in blade always pedate and pinnules thinly and stiffly pubesc. beneath. India, Ceylon, Australasia, Pacific Is.

A. *pulverulentum* L. Fronds to 100cm; blade oblong to ovate, 2-pinnate; pinnules falcate, glabrate to scaly beneath; stipe to 60cm. W Indies, C Amer., trop. S Amer.

A. *pyramidale* (L.) Willd. = A. *cristatum*.

A. *raddianum* C. Presl. DELTA MAIDENHAIR FERN. Fronds to 60cm; blade narrowly triangular, 3-pinnate; pinnules 1cm, cuneate to rhombic, lobed on outer margins; stipe to 10cm, black. Trop. Amer., W Indies. 'Fritz-Luthii': fronds bright green; 'Grandiceps': fronds elegantly tasselled. var. *majus* Hoshizaki. Frond blade narrower, larger; pinnules more deeply divided. Urug., Braz., Parag.

A. *reniforme* L. Fronds to 20cm; blade simple, reniform, tough; stipe to 15cm, hairy. Kenya, Tenerife, Madeira, Canary Is. Z9.

A. *rubellum* T. Moore = A. *raddianum*.

A. *sanctae-catherinae* hort. = A. *pentadactylon* 'Sanctae Catherinae'.

A. *seemannii* Hook. Fronds to 60cm; blade broadly triangular,

1–2-pinnate; pinnules 6–10cm, broadly ovate, sharply serrate, glaucous beneath; stipes to 20cm. Mex., Hond., Nic., Costa Rica, Panama, Colomb.

A. setulosum J. Sm. = *A. diaphanum*.

A. silvaticum Tind. Fronds to 80cm; blade 2–3-pinnate, thin; pinnae branching away from rachis; pinnules bright green, cuneate to attenuate. Aus. (Queensld, NSW).

A. tenerum Sw. BRITTLE MAIDENHAIR FERN; MAIDENHAIR FERN. Fronds to 110cm; blade broadly triangular, 3–5-pinnate; pinnules 1–2cm, trapeziform to rhombic to flabellate, sometimes cleft and toothed; stipes to 30cm, glossy maroon-black. S US, W Indies, C Amer., N S Amer. 'Farleyense' (FARLEY MAIDENHAIR FERN; BARBADOS MAIDENHAIR FERN; GLORY FERN): Fronds to 90cm, arching, 4–5-pinnate; pinnules 6–10cm, broadly flabellate, incised and crisped. 'Fergusonii': fronds to 60cm, narrowly triangular, 3-pinnate, terminal pinnules fused to each other and the rachis. 'Glory of Moordrecht': fronds erect, hardy. 'Scutum Roseum': fronds erect, to 50cm, 3-pinnate, pinnules broad, crowded, rose-pink when young. Z9.

A. tetraphyllum Humb. & Bonpl. ex Willd. Fronds to 100cm; blade ovate to triangular, 2-pinnate; pinnules long-rectangular, cuspidate. Trop. Amer., W Indies.

A. ×*tracyi* C.C. Hall. (*A. jordanii* ×*A. pedatum*.) TRACY'S MAIDENHAIR. Fronds to 75cm; blade pedately 3-pinnate; pinnules intermediate in shape between those of parents. W US. Z8.

A. trapeziforme L. GIANT MAIDENHAIR; DIAMOND MAIDENHAIR. Fronds to 200cm; blade broadly triangular, 2–3-pinnate; pinnules 4–7cm, oblong-rhombic to trapeziform, shallowly lobed; stipe to 50cm with dark brown basal scales. cf. *A. pentadactylon*. Trop. Amer., W Indies, Cuba.

A. venustum D. Don. EVERGREEN MAIDENHAIR. Fronds to 80cm; blade broadly triangular, 3–4-pinnate; pinnules to 1cm, ovate-cuneate, outer margins serrate, glaucous beneath; stipe to 24cm. Afghan., Himal. Z8.

A. villosum L. Fronds to 100cm, ascending; blade ovate to triangular, 2-pinnate; pinnules subrectangular, acute or caudate, some biserrate; stipe to 60cm, brown-black. C & S Amer., W Indies.

A. waltonii T. Moore = *A. excisum*.

Adlumia Raf. ex DC. Fumariaceae. 1 herbaceous, bienn. vine, to 5m +. Lvs fern-like, to 25cm. Fls pale pink or white, similar to *Dicentra*. Summer. NE Amer., Korea. Z6.

A. fungosa (Ait.) Greene ex BSP. CLIMBING FUMITORY; MOUNTAIN FRINGE; ALLEGHENY VINE.
→*Fumaria*.

Adobe-lily *Fritillaria pluriflora*.

Adonidia Becc.
A. merrillii (Becc.) Becc. = *Veitchia merrillii*.

Adonis L. Ranunculaceae. *c*20 ann. or perenn. rhizomatous herbs. St. simple or branched, leafy. Lvs bi- and tri-pinnate, lobes narrow. Fls terminal, solitary, large; sep. 5–8, petaloid; pet. 3–30, spreading to cupped not nectariferous; sta. numerous, anth. yellow in perenn. sp., black-purple in annuals. Eur., Asia.

A. aestivalis L. Differs from *A. annua* in sep. closely adpressed to spreading pet. Summer. Eur. var. *citrina* Hoffm. Fls yellow. Spring. Z6.

A. aleppica Boiss. Ann., st. branched to 40cm. Lf lobes linear. Fls to 5cm diam.; sep. purple; pet. cuneate-obovate, crimson, not marked. Spring–summer. W Asia. Z7.

A. amurensis Reg. & Radde. Perenn. 5–15cm, occas. branched above. Cauline lvs deltoid-ovate, to 10cm, pinnatisect, lobes lanceolate, dentate; petioles long. Fls 3–4cm diam., sometimes double; sep. pale lilac; pet. 20–30, yellow, bronze outside, oblong-elliptic. Winter–spring. Manch., Jap., Korea. 'Benten': fls near white, fringed. 'Fukujukai': fls semi-double, large, bright yellow, sterile. 'Fukurokuju': fls double, v. large, brilliant yellow. 'Hino moto': fls green, bronze and orange-red. 'Pleniflora' ('Plena'): fls double, yellow to green. 'Ramosa': fls double, red to brown. Z3.

A. annua L. PHEASANT'S EYE. Ann., erect, branched to 40cm. Lvs tripinnate, lobes linear. Fls to 2.5cm diam.; sep. green or dull purple; pet. 5–8, narrowly obovate, crimson with black base. Summer. S Eur. to SW Asia, nat. N Eur. Z3.

A. autumnalis L. = *A. annua*.

A. chrysocyathus Hook. f. & Thoms. Perenn. St. to 40cm, unbranched, with lvs above. Upper cauline lvs sessile, tripinnatifid, triangular in outline, to 16cm, lobes to 1cm, oval-rhombic to sublanceolate. Fls to 5cm diam.; sep. brown to lilac; pet. 16–24, oblanceolate, golden yellow. Summer. W Himal.

(Pak. to W Nepal), Tibet. Z7.

A. davurica hort. = *A. amurensis*.

A. flammea Jacq. Close to *A. annua*, but larger. Fls to 3cm diam.; pet. linear-oblong, deep scarlet or yellow. Summer. S & C Eur., NW Afr. to Cauc. and W Iran.

A. pyrenaica DC. Perenn. to 40cm, erect. Lower lvs long-petiolate, tripinnatifid, lobes linear. Fls to 6cm diam.; pet. 12–20, golden yellow. Spring–summer. Pyren., Maritime Alps. Z6.

A. vernalis L. Perenn, 20cm. Cauline lvs sessile, oval in outline, palmately, lobed, lobes 2cm, linear, entire. Fls to 8cm, diam.; sep. dull green; pet. 12–20, oblong-elliptic, yellow. Spring. Eur. 'Alba': fls white. Z3.

A. volgensis Steven in DC. Perenn. to 30cm, branched from middle. Lf lobes broader than in *A. vernalis*, dentate. Fls to 4.5cm diam.; sep. lilac; pet. narrowly lanceolate, to 22×7mm, more numerous than in *A. vernalis*, pale yellow. Spring. E. Eur.

ADOXACEAE Trautv. See *Adoxa*.

Adoxa L. Adoxaceae. 1 delicate spreading, perenn. herb to 20cm. Lvs radical, ternately decompound, with long petioles, seg. 3-partite. Infl. a single long-stalked head, to 2mm diam.; fls green-yellow, one facing upwards, others facing outwards.

A. moschatellina L. MUSKROOT; MOSCHATEL; TOWNHALL CLOCK.

Adriatic Bellflower *Campanula elatines*.

Adromischus Lem. Crassulaceae. 26 succulent herbs and subshrubs. Br. usually prostrate, slightly fleshy. Lvs fleshy, clustered. Infl. a spike-like complex cyme; sep. 5, fused at base, pointed; pet. 5, fused to form a cylindrical floral tube, free portions spreading. Summer. S Afr. Z9.

A. alstonii (Schönl. and Bak. f.) C.A. Sm. To 35cm. St. prostrate, to 15cm. Lvs 3–11cm, oblong-lanceolate, blunt, bristle-tipped, grey-green spotted purple. Infl. purple-green, 35cm; pet. 10–15mm, brown-green, lobes pink to white, tipped red.

A. alveolatus P.C. Hutchison = *A. marianae* var. *immaculatus*.

A. antidorcadum Poelln. = *A. marianae* var. *immaculatus*.

A. bolusii (Schönl.) A. Berger = *A. caryophyllaceus*.

A. caryophyllaceus (Burm. f.) Lem. To 60cm. St. prostrate or erect. Lvs 8–45mm, oblanceolate-linear, obtuse, grey or brown-green. Infl. to 40cm; pet. 22–27mm, grey-green, lobes pointed, rough, white-pink, sometimes striped purple.

A. cooperi (Bak.) A. Berger. St. much-branched. Lvs 40–70mm, oblong to obtriangular, tapering abruptly to petiole, compressed or terete, grey-green, sometimes with dark spots. Infl. to 40cm; cor. 12–16mm, light pink, dusted grey, lobes pointed, darker pink at margins.

A. cristatus (Haw.) Lem. CRINKLE-LEAF PLANT. St. erect, 20–80mm, with red-brown, aerial roots. Lvs 20–50mm, triangular to oblanceolate, grey-green spotted purple, terete or slightly compressed, puberulent, margin callused, crispate. Infl. to 20cm, cor. 12–16mm, grey-green, lobes white edged pink. ssp. *clavifolius* (Haw.) Toelken. Lvs triangular, margin horny, v. wide. Infl. glandular-hairy.

A. cuneatus (Thunb.) Lem. = *Cotyledon cuneata*.

A. festivus C.A. Sm. = *A. cooperi*.

A. filicaulis (Ecklon & Zeyh.) C.A. Sm. To 35cm, prostrate to ascending, branching. Lvs 20–80mm, oblong-lanceolate, green to grey-green, sometimes with dark purple spots, terete, or compressed. Infl. to 35cm; cor. 11–15mm, yellow-green, lobes bristle-tipped, tinged mauve. ssp. *marlothii* (Schönl.) Toelken. Roots 2–3mm thick, stiff, stilt-like. Lvs lanceolate, acute, rarely spotted purple.

A. grandiflorus Uitew. = *A. caryophyllaceus*.

A. hemisphaericus (L.) Lem. To 50cm, prostrate to ascending. Lvs 10–45mm, tightly packed, grey-green, waxy, rarely spotted purple, ovate-oblanceolate, blunt, margin horny. Infl. to 25cm; cor. 11–16mm, green-brown, lobes white, suffused pink.

A. kleinioides C.A. Sm. = *A. filicaulis*.

A. maculatus (Salm-Dyck) Lem. St. prostate, sparsely branching. Lvs 30–100mm, oblanceolate, grey-green to grey-brown, spotted purple, entire, margin horny. Infl. grey-green; cor. 10–16mm, pale yellow-green, lobes pale pink to cream, edged purple.

A. mammillaris (L. f.) Lem. St. prostrate, sparsely branching. Lvs 20–50mm, linear-lanceolate, pointed, ± terete, grey-green, margin horny. Infl. 35cm, grey-green; cor. 15–18mm, grey-green, lobes white suffused pink, edged mauve.

A. marianae (Marloth) A. Berger. St. erect or prostrate. Lvs 30–70mm, linear-obovate, acute or obtuse, terete, grooved above, grey-green or brown, occas. spotted dark purple, margin horny. Infl. to 35cm; cor. 12–15mm, white to light pink, thickly dusted, lobes edged purple. var. *immaculatus* Uitew. Lvs unspotted, margin white, not horny.

A. poellnitzianus Werderm. = *A. cristatus* ssp. *clavifolius.*

A. roaneanus Uitew. Differs from *A. hemisphericus* in st. slender, wavy; lvs lax; pet. light green, tips pink.

A. rotundifolius (Haw.) C.A. Sm. = *A. umbracticola.*

A. saxicola C.A. Sm. = *A. umbracticola.*

A. schaeferianus (Dinter) A. Berger. = *Tylecodon schaeferianus.*

A. schuldtianus (Poelln.) Poelln. Differs from *A. trigynus* in lvs oblanceolate, tapering to base, grey-green, spotted, margin horny above.

A. sphenophyllus C.A. Sm. St. sparsely branched. Lvs 25–70mm, gradually tapering to base, blunt, glaucous, flecked lime to emerald, margin horny. Infl. to 45cm; cor. 11–16mm, light green, suffused red, lobes white-pink, edged dark purple.

A. tricolor C.A. Sm. = *A. filicaulis* ssp. *marlothii.*

A. triebneri Poelln. = *A. alstonii.*

A. triflorus (L. f.) A. Berger. Differs from *A. mammillaris* in lvs oblanceolate to triangular, 30–60mm, spotted purple-red, margin horny above.

A. trigynus (Burchell) Poelln. To 50cm. Base tuberous, branching. St. erect. Lvs 15–40mm, round to obovate, apex round, sometimes bristle-tipped, grey-green, dark-spotted, margin horny. Infl. to 35cm; cor. 11–16mm, yellow-green, lobes white, pink at base.

A. umbracticola C.A. Sm. Differs from *A. trigynus* in lvs to 50mm, oblanceolate, rarely dark-spotted, margin horny or smooth. Cor. tube tinged pink. S Afr.

→*Cotyledon.*

Adzuki Bean, Aduki Bean *Vigna angularis.*

Aechmea Ruiz & Pav. Bromeliaceae. 170 perenn. herbs. Lvs strap-shaped, rigid or pliable, often with spiny margins, in a basal bundle or rosette forming a funnel or 'tank'. Infl. term., scapose, simple or branched; bracts primary and floral (treated below as 'bracts'; the second colour, where different, refers to the floral bracts); fls small. C & S Amer.

A. amazonica Ule. = *A. chantinii.*

A. aquilegia (Salisb.) Griseb. To 1m. Lvs serrate, brown-scaly. Infl. branched; bracts bright red; pet. yellow. Costa Rica, Venez., Guyana, NE Braz., Trin. & Tob. Z10.

A. aureorosea (Antoine) Bak. = *A. nudicaulis* var. *aureorosea.*

A. barleei Bak. = *A. bracteata.*

A. benrathii Mez. = *A. recurvata* var. *benrathii.*

A. 'Bert'. (*A. orlandiana* ×*A. fosteriana.*) To 70cm. Lvs short, banded brown-purple with dark spines. Infl. nodding; bracts red; pet. pale.

A. blumenavii Reitz. To 70cm. Lvs banded white beneath, flushed purple above, toothed. Infl. simple; scape violet; bracts tinted pink; pet. yellow. Braz. Z10.

A. bracteata (Sw.) Griseb. 50–170cm. Lvs pale green, white-scaly, wavy-toothed. Infl. branched; bracts bright red; pet. yellow. E Mex. to Colomb. and Venez. Z9.

A. brasiliensis Reg. = *A. distichantha.*

A. bromeliifolia (Rudge) Bak. To 90cm. Lvs white-scaly with retrorse spines. Infl. spiciform, tomentose; bracts leathery; pet. green-yellow. C Amer. to Arg. Z9.

A. calyculata (E. Morr.) Bak. To 60cm. Lvs pale-scaly, serrulate. Infl. simple, globose, floccose; bracts yellow to red; pet. lemon-yellow. S Braz., NE Arg. Z9.

A. caudata Lindm. To 90cm. Lvs minutely spiny, brown at base. Infl. paniculate, deflexed; bracts red; pet. yellow. Braz. var. *variegata* M.B. Fost. Lvs striped cream. Z9.

A. chantinii (Carr.) Bak. To 1m. Lvs banded white beneath. Infl. branched, floccose, deflexed; bracts bright red; pet. white or pale blue. Colomb., Peru, Amazonian Venez. and Braz. Z10.

A. coelestis (K. Koch) E. Morr. 40–100cm. Lvs spiny, banded dark green beneath, ± blue at base. Infl. pyramidal; bracts red to pink; pet. pale blue. Braz. var. *albomarginata* M.B. Fost. Lvs edged white. Z10.

A. coerulescens hort. = *A. luddemanniana.*

A. conspicuarmata Bak. = *A. bromeliifolia.*

A. cornui Carr. = *A. nudicaulis* var. *aureorosea.*

A. dichlamydea Bak. To 1m. Lvs pale-scaly, spiny. Infl. loosely compound; bracts bright red or blue marked purple; pet. yellow. Trin. & Tob., N Venez. Z10.

A. distichantha Lem. 30–100cm. Lvs with dark spines. Infl. decompound, long-stemmed; bracts thick, pink overlapping in short, horizontal br.; fls in close ranks; sep. rose pink; pet. purple or blue. S Braz., Parag., Urug., NE Arg. var. *glaziovii* (Bak.) L.B. Sm. To 30cm. Infl. compact; fls bright blue. S Braz. Z9.

A. fasciata (Lindl.) Bak. To 100cm. Lvs broad, grey-green with silver scales, these thinner or falling to make darker green bands; spines short. Infl. pyramidal; bracts rose pink; pet. blue, purple or red.

A. filicaulis (Griseb.) Mez. To 60cm. Lvs linear, glabrate, spiny at base. Infl. lax, pendulous; bracts bright red; fls white on whorled br. N. Venez. Z9.

A. fosteriana L.B. Sm. To 90cm. Lvs mottled and banded brown-purple, toothed. Infl. paniculate; scape purple, glab.; bracts red; sep. green; pet. yellow-orange. Braz. Z10.

A. 'Foster's Favorite'. Lvs burgundy, glossy. Infl. pendulous; sep. bright red; pet. dark blue.

A. 'Foster's Favorite Favorite'. Sport of 'Foster's Favorite' – lvs copper edged cream.

A. fulgens Brongn. CORAL BERRY. To 50cm. Lvs scaly, spiny. Infl. loosely pyramidal; scape red; bracts pink; sep. dark purple pet. blue or purple turning red. Fr. scarlet. Braz. var. *discolor* (Morr.) Brongn. ex Bak. Lvs glossy purple. Braz. Z9.

A. gamosepala Wittm. To 70cm. Lvs subentire, pale-scaly. Infl. slender, simple; bracts thin, decid. or red-purple; sep. pink; pet. blue or purple. Braz. Z10.

A. germinyana (Carr.) Bak. To 1m. Lvs papery, scaly, serrate. Infl. simple, comose; bracts scarlet; pet. white to pink. Colomb., Panama. Z9.

A. gracile Lindm. To 50cm. Lvs subentire, sometimes banded beneath and purple below. Infl. simple or branched at base; bracts red; pet. pale blue. Braz. Z10.

A. hystrix E. Morr. = *A. ornatum.*

A. lasseri L.B. Sm. To 1.5m. Lvs pale-scaly, serrate, sometimes flushed red. Infl. pendent, branched; bracts papery, pink; pet. white-green. Fr. blue. Venez. Z9.

A. legrelliana (Bak.) Bak. = *A. recurvata.*

A. lindenii (E. Morr.) Bak. To 1m. Lvs white-scaly, spiny, closely bundled. Infl. simple; bracts brown or red; sep. red; pet. yellow. Braz. 'Makoyana': lvs with broad, longitudinal yellow or ivory-white stripes. Gdn origin. Z9.

A. lineata hort. = *A. lindenii* 'Makoyana'.

A. luddemanniana (K. Koch) Mez. To 70cm. Lvs pale-scaly, spiny, sometimes flushed rose. Infl. paniculate; scape mealy; bracts papery; pet. indigo then carmine. S Mex., Guat., Hond. Z10.

A. macracantha Brongn. ex André = *A. bracteata.*

A. ×maginalii Nally. (*A. miniata* var. *discolor* ×*A. fulgens* var. *discolor.*) Lvs narrow below. Bracts pink; fls blue. Z9.

A. makoyana hort. = *A. lindenii* 'Makoyana'.

A. marmorata (Lem.) Mez. = *Quesnelia marmorata.*

A. mertensii (Mey.) Schult. f. Lvs white-scaly with dark spines and purple bases. Infl. decompound, woolly, coral-pink; bracts pink; pet. yellow then red. Trin., Venez., Guiana, Surinam to Colomb. and Peru. Z9.

A. mexicana Bak. To 1m. Lvs pale-scaly in dense rosette. Infl. paniculate, pyramidal, scurfy; bracts straw yellow; pet. red or lilac. S Mex. to Ecuad. Z9.

A. miniata (Beer) hort. ex Bak. To 40cm. Lvs channelled, spiny. Infl. compound, red; bracts short-lived; pet. blue. Braz. var. *discolor* (Beer) Beer ex Bak. Lvs maroon or rose below. Z9.

A. mucroniflora Hook. = *A. mertensii.*

A. mulfordii L.B. Sm. To 1m. Lvs scaly, spiny, faintly banded. Infl. tripinnate; scape red; bracts red or yellow; pet. yellow. Braz. Z10.

A. myriophylla E. Morr. ex Bak. = *A. distichantha.*

A. nudicaulis (L.) Griseb. Lvs to 1m, scaly, with dark teeth and dark inflated bases. Infl. simple, sometimes arching; bracts red; pet. yellow. Mex. and W Indies to Ecuad. and Peru. var. *aureorosea* (Antoine) L.B. Sm. Sep. red; pet. red tipped yellow. CE Braz. Z10.

A. orlandiana L.B. Sm. FINGER OF GOD. To 40cm. Lvs with dark spines and banding or mottling beneath. Infl. bipinnate; scape red; bracts scarlet; pet. pale yellow edged white. Braz. Z10.

A. ornata (Gaud.-Beaup.) Bak. To 80cm. Lvs grey-scaly, spiny in a flat rosette. Infl. cylindric; bracts leafy; pet. pale red or pink, spine-tipped. Braz. Z10.

A. ortgiesii Bak. = *A. recurvata* var. *ortgiesii.*

A. polystachya (Vell.) Mez = *A. distichantha.*

A. purpurea Bak. = *Nidularium billbergioides.*

A. purpureorosea (Hook.) Wawra. To 80cm. Lvs few, glossy with dark spines. Infl. paniculate; scape slender, red; bracts pink; sep. pink; pet. purple or blue. Braz. Z9.

A. racinae L.B. Sm. CHRISTMAS JEWELS. To 50cm. Lvs glossy, midgreen to red-brown, serrulate, in a tubular rosette. Infl. simple, pendulous; bracts narrow, red-brown; sep. red; pet. yellow. Fr. bright red. Braz.

A. recurvata (Klotzsch) L.B. Sm. To 20cm. Lvs thick, grooved, scaly beneath, ± spiny, dilated and blue-tinted at base. Infl. simple, short, torch-like; bracts red; pet. purple or pink. S Braz., Parag., Urug., NE Arg. var. *benrathii* (Mez) Reitz. Smaller in all parts. Infl. deeply sunken in rosette; bracts maroon. Braz. var. *ortgiesii* (Bak.) Reitz. Lvs strongly toothed, yellow-green, the bases enclosing infl. S Braz. Z9.

A. **'Red Wing'**. (*A. penduliflora* ×*A. mutica.*) Lvs large, copper-purple. Scape claret; fls yellow. Fr. pink-purple.

A. *regularis* Bak. = *A. bracteata*.

A. *rosea* (E. Morr.) Bak. non hort. = *Canistrum lindenii* var. *roseum*.

A. *rosea* hort. = *A. purpureorosea*.

A. **'Royal Wine'**. (*A. miniata* var. *discolor* ×*A. victoriana* var. *discolor.*) Lvs bright green, cerise at base. Infl. branched, nodding; pet. azure. Fr. orange.

A. *schiedeana* Schldl. = *A. bracteata*.

A. *serrata* (L.) Mez. To 80cm. Lvs with brown teeth and white scales in lines. Infl. decompound, shorter than lvs; bracts pink, scaly, inrolled; pet. dark purple. Lesser Antilles. Z10.

A. *skinneri* Bak. = *Androlepis skinneri*.

A. *tessmannii* Harms. To 1m. Lvs narrow, white-scaly, toothed. Infl. decompound; bracts bright red or green tipped orange; pet. orange. Colomb., Ecuad., Peru. Z10.

A. *tinctoria* (Mart.) Mez. = *A. bromeliifolia*.

A. *victoriana* L.B. Sm. Lvs pale green, minutely spiny. Infl. lax. simple; pet. purple edged white. Braz. var. *discolor* Fost. Lvs flushed red beneath.

A. *viridis* (E. Morr.) Bak. = *Canistrum lindenii* var. *viride*.

A. *zebrina* L.B. Sm. To 80cm. Lvs silver-banded, faintly above, strongly beneath. Infl. decompound; bracts tend to pink-orange; pet. yellow. Colomb., Ecuad. Z10.

→*Portea* and *Wittmackia*.

Aegilops L. GOAT GRASS. Gramineae. 21 ann. grasses. St. slender. Lvs linear, flat. Infl. rigid, spicate, lanceolate to ovoid; spikelets cylindric to ovoid, glumes oblong to ovoid. Summer. Medit., Asia Minor, N Afr. Z9.

A. *kotschyi* Boiss. GOAT GRASS. To 25cm. Lvs glab. or downy beneath. Spikelets to 3cm, narrow-lanceolate. Afghan., Egypt, N Afr.

A. *ovata* L. To 30cm, decumbent. Lvs pubesc. Infl. ovoid; spikelets in fascicles, glumes awned.

A. *triuncalis* L. To 45cm. Lvs pubesc. Infl. narrow-lanceolate, constricted between to 7 spikelets, glumes awned.

A. *ventricosa* Tausch. To 45cm. Lvs puberulous. Infl. constricted between to 10 spikelets, glumes awnless.

Aeginetia L. Orobanchaceae. 3 chlorophyll-free, leafless, largely subterranean, parasitic perenn. herbs. Fls large, solitary, scapose, cal. spathe-like; cor. tubular. E Asia. Z10.

A. *indica* L. INDIAN BROOMRAPE. Parasitic on sugar cane and other large grasses. Flg st. pale bronze to yellow, streaked or mottled pink, to 15cm. Cor. white, flushed mauve. India to Jap.

Aegopodium L. Umbelliferae. 5 perenn. herbs. Rhiz. creeping. Lvs 1–2-ternate. Umbels compound; involucre usually 0. Eur., W Asia.

A. *podagraria* L. BISHOP'S WEED; GOUTWEED; GROUND ELDER; HERB GERARD; ASH WEED; GROUND ASH. Rhiz. aromatic. Lf seg. 3(–9), to 8cm, ovate-acuminate, toothed, stalked. Umbels 2–6cm diam.; fls white-cream. Early summer. Eur., nat. N Amer. 'Variegatum': lvs edged and splashed ivory.

Aeonium (L.) Webb & Berth. Crassulaceae. 31 succulent shrubs and herbs, mostly perenn. Br. often candelabriform, thick. Lvs mostly in apical rosettes, succulent, base usually cuneate, apex usually mucronate, often ciliate. Infl. mostly cymose, term., usually 3-branched, obconic. With many small fls. Canary Is., Madeira, S Moroc., E Afr. and Yemen; all described below are from the Atlantic Is. Z9.

A. *arboreum* (L.) Webb & Berth. St. erect, to 2m, br. often grouped. Lvs to 15×4.5×0.7mm, obovate to oblanceolate, glossy, ciliate. Gran Canaria, naturalized California, Mexico, northern S America, Mediterranean. 'Atropurpureum': all parts strongly flushed dark red-purple to maroon. 'Schwarzkopf': lvs narrow, dark glossy purple-black, emerald green at base. 'Variegatum': lvs zoned or splashed cream and/or white. var. *holochrysum* H.-Y. Liu. Pedicels glabrate. Las Palmas, Tenerife. var. *rubrolineatum* (Svent.) H.-Y. Liu. Fls veined red. Summer, lvs usually drop when flowering. Gomera.

A. *balsamiferum* Webb & Berth. Perenn. subshrub with strong balsamic odour. St. to 1.5m, br. frequently in groups. Lvs to 7×3.5cm, obtrullate, recurved, glab., grey green, occas. striped brown near margin, mottled beneath with numerous cream lines, ciliate. Spring–summer. Lanzarote, Cape Verde Is.

A. *bentejui* Webb ex Christ = *A. spathulatum*.

A. *berthelotianum* Bolle = *A. tabuliforme*.

A. *bethencourtianum* (Webb) Webb = *Aichryson bethencourtianum*.

A. *caespitosum* (C. Sm. ex Otto) Webb & Berth. = *A. simsii*.

A. *canariense*. CANARY ISLAND AEONIUM; VELVET ROSE; GIANT VELVET ROSE. Perenn. herb. St. to 35cm, erect, usually un-

branched. Lvs to 20×8×0.8cm, obovate to oblanceolate, flattened to undulate, apex rounded to mucronate, pubesc. Canary Is., Tenerife. var. *palmense* (Webb ex Christ) H.-Y. Liu. Lvs in cup-shaped rosettes, glandular-hairy, viscid. Spring–summer. A parent of natural hybrids. Las Palmas, Hierro. var. *subplanum* (Praeger) H.-Y. Liu. Lvs in flattened to planar rosettes, loosely imbricate, sparsely pubesc. Spring–summer. Hybridizes frequently. Gomera. var. *virgineum* (Webb ex Christ) H.-Y. Liu. Smaller and more branching than other ssp. Lvs more rigid. in cup-shaped rosettes to 25cm, occas. tinged red or yellow, pubesc., occas. undulate. Spring. Gran Canaria.

A. *castello-paivae* Bolle. Perenn. subshrub. St. to 70cm, minutely pubesc. Lvs to 3.5×2cm, glabrate, glaucous, pale green occas. variegated, ciliate, flushed red. Spring–summer. Gomera.

A. *ciliatum* Webb & Berth. Perenn. subshrub, to 1m; br. few. Lvs to 12×5×0.8cm, obovate to spathulate, apex acute, glabrate, glaucous, deep green, ciliate. Spring–summer. Tenerife.

A. *cruentum* Webb & Berth. = *A. spathulatum*.

A. *cuneatum* Webb & Berth. Perenn. herb. St. v. short, erect, frequently stoloniferous. Lvs to 25×8×0.9cm, cupped, obovate to oblanceolate, glabrate, ciliate, occas. undulate. Spring–summer. Tenerife.

A. *decorum* Webb ex Bolle. Perenn. subshrub to 60cm, br. numerous. Lvs to 5×1.5cm, oblanceolate, minutely pubesc., glossy, dark green to yellow tinged, ciliate, glaucous. Spring–summer. Gomera.

A. *domesticum* (Praeger) A. Berger = *Aichryson* ×*domesticum*.

A. *floribundum* A. Berger = *A.* ×*hybridum*.

A. *giganteum* Webb ex Christ = *A. canariense*.

A. *glandulosum* (Ait.) Webb & Berth. Bienn. or perenn. herb with strong balsamic odour. St. short, erect, unbranched. Lvs to 12×6cm, obovate to oblanceolate, minutely pubesc. Spring–summer. Madeira archipel.

A. *glutinosum* (Ait.) Webb & Berth. Perenn. viscid subshrub to 1.5m. Lvs to 12×6cm in cup-shaped rosettes, obovate-spathulate, slightly folded, glabrate, dull pale green to fresh green, midrib usually with brown stripes, viscid when young, ciliate. Spring–summer. Madeira archipel.

A. *gomerense* (Praeger) Praeger. Perenn. subshrub to 2m, br. few, lax. Lvs to 14×4×0.7cm obovate to oblanceolate, glaucous, glabrate, ciliate, flushed red. Spring–summer. Gomera.

A. *goochiae* Webb & Berth. Perenn. subshrub to 40cm, young br. pubesc. green viscid. Lvs to 1.5×0.25×0.3cm, upper part elliptic, pubesc., pale to yellow green, base attenuate, margin involute. Winter–spring. Las Palmas.

A. *haworthii* Salm-Dyck ex Webb & Berth. PINWHEEL. Perenn. v. similar to *A. ciliatum* and *A. urbicum*, which also lose their lvs while flowering. St. to 60cm, with adventitious roots. Lvs to 5.5×3cm, obovate, glaucous, margin ciliate, tinged red. Spring–summer. Tenerife.

A. *hierrense* (R.P. Murray) Pitard & Proust. Perenn. subshrub to 1.2m, usually unbranched. Lvs to 30×8×0.7cm, obovate to oblanceolate, apex caudate, glaucous, dark green, ciliate, tinged red or purple. Spring. Hierro and Las Palmas.

A. *holochrysum* auct. non Webb & Berth. = *A. arboreum* var. *holochrysum*.

A. ×*hybridum* (Haw.) G. Rowley. (*A. simsii* ×*A. spathulatum*.) Perenn. to 15cm, branched horizontally. Lvs 25–40×6–7mm, green above, paler beneath with raised green or sunken brown, oblong glands, margin irregularly beaded. Widespread in cult., not known in the wild.

A. *lancerottense* (Praeger) Praeger. Perenn. subshrub to 60cm, adventitious roots abundant. Lvs to 9×4×0.6cm, obovate to oblanceolate, apex caudate, often folded, glaucous, tinged red beneath, slightly denticulate, ciliate. Spring–summer. Lanzarote.

A. *lindleyi* Webb & Berth. Perenn. dense subshrub with balsamic odour, to 50cm. Lvs to 4.5×1.5×0.7cm, obovate to oblanceolate, base attenuate, apex obtuse to acute, pubesc., viscid, margin tinged brown or yellow. Tenerife. var. *viscatum* (Bolle) H.-Y. Liu. St. to 40cm. Lvs to 4mm thick, strongly viscid, not variegated, appearing glab., margin entire. Spring. Gomera.

A. *longithrysum* (Burchard) Svent. = *A. canariense* var. *palmense*.

A. *macrolepum* Webb ex Christ = *A. tabuliforme*.

A. *manriqueorum* C. Bolle = *A. arboreum* var. *arboreum*.

A. *meyerheimii* Bolle = *A. glandulosum*.

A. *nobile* (Praeger) Praeger. Perenn. subshrub, malodorous, to 60cm, usually unbranched, erect. Lvs to 30×20×0.1cm, obovate, viscid when young, acute margin ciliate, tinged brown. Spring. Las Palmas.

A. *palmense* Webb ex Christ = *A. canariense* var. *palmense*.

A. *percarneum* (R.P. Murray) Pitard & Proust. Perenn. subshrub to 1.5m, branched. Lvs to 10×4×0.6cm, obovate to oblanceolate, caudate, glaucous, dark green, tinged purple or red, margin subentire to denticulate, tinged red. Spring–summer. Gran Canaria.

A. pseudotabuliforme hort. = *A. undulatum*.

A. saundersii Bolle. Perenn. subshrub with a balsamic odour, to 25cm. Lvs to 3.5×1.3cm, overlapping and incurved during dry spells, elliptic to obovate, concave, apex retuse or rounded, pubesc., variegated above. Spring. Gomera.

A. sedifolium (Webb ex Bolle) Pitard & Proust. Dense, dwarf perenn. subshrub to 40cm. Lvs to 1.5×1×0.5cm, incurved in dry season, ovate to obovate, apex rounded, green, variegated with brown and red, glossy minutely pubesc., viscid. Spring––summer. Tenerife, Las Palmas.

A. simsii (Sweet) Stearn. Tufted perenn. herb to 15cm, stoloniferous. Lvs to 6×2cm, lanceolate, lorate, apex acuminate, minutely pubesc., with prominent longitudinal stripes, ciliate. Spring–summer. Tenerife.

A. smithii (Sims) Webb & Berth. Perenn. herb to 60cm, erect, br. hispid. Lvs to 7×3×0.1cm, obtrullate, apex acuminate, ciliate, usually undulate, minutely pubesc., glossy above with distinct stripes. Spring–autumn. Tenerife.

A. spathulatum (Hornem.) Praeger. Perenn. subshrub to 60cm, suberect, br. slender. Lvs to 2.5×1cm, obovate to spathulate, 1mm thick, apex obtuse, minutely pubesc., with conspicious stripes beneath, ciliate. Spring. Macaronesia.

A. spathulatum var. *cruentum* (Webb & Berth.) Praeger = *A. spathulatum*.

A. strepsicladum Webb & Berth. = *A. spathulatum*.

A. subplanum Praeger. = *A. canariense* var. *subplanum*.

A. tabuliforme (Haw.) Webb & Berth. Bienn. or perenn. herb to 25cm, unbranched, occas. caespitose. Lvs to 20×4×0.6cm, many in flat, stemless rosettes to 40cm, closely imbricate, obovate to oblanceolate, apex rounded to mucronulate, minutely pubesc. when young, pale to grass green, ciliate. Spring–summer. Tenerife.

A. undulatum Webb & Berth. SAUCER PLANT. Perenn. subshrub to 25cm, clump-forming. Lvs to 18×5×0.3cm, flattened, spathulate, apex acute, glossy, dark green, variegated with brown lines, ciliate, often tinged brown. Spring. Gran Canaria.

A. urbicum (C. Sm. ex Hornem.) Webb & Berth. Perenn. sub-shrub, unbranched to 2m. Lvs 18×4.5×0.7cm, oblanceolate, glaucous, apiculate, ciliate. Spring–autumn. Tenerife, Gomera.

A. valverdense (Praeger) Praeger. Perenn. subshrub to 1m. Lvs to 12×6×0.8cm obovate, caudate, minutely pubesc., glaucous, tinged yellow, brown and/or pink, ciliate. Spring. Hierro.

A. vestitum Svent. = *A. arboreum* var. *holochrysum*.

A. virgineum Webb ex Christ = *A. canariense* var. *virgineum*.

A. viscatum Bolle = *A. lindleyi* var. *viscatum*.

A. youngianum Webb & Berth. = *A. undulatum*.

→*Aichryson, Sedum* and *Sempervivum*.

Aerangis Rchb. f. Orchidaceae. 50 epiphytic monopodial orchids with short or long st. clothed with strap-shaped or broad fleshy or leathery lvs in 2 ranks and fls in axillary rac., white, ivory or green, spur sometimes tinged pink. Mainland Afr., Madag. and Masc. Is.; 1 sp. Sri Lanka. Z10.

A. apiculatum Hook. = *A. biloba*.

A. appendiculata (De Wildeman) Schltr. St. short. Lvs to 8cm, obovate. Rac. to 15cm; fls white, long-spurred; tep. to 8mm, elliptic-obovate. Zam., Malawi, Zimb., Moz.

A. arachnopus (Rchb. f.) Schltr. St. to 12cm. Lvs to 20cm, oblanceolate. Rac. to 60cm, pendent; fls white; tep. to 18mm, linear-lanceolate, spur long, pink. W Afr. to Zaire.

A. articulata (Rchb. f.) Schltr. St. to 30cm. Lvs to 15cm, v. dark green. Rac. to 25cm, pendent; fls white, fragrant, long-spurred; tep. to 20mm, elliptic. Madag.

A. biloba (Lindl.) Schltr. St. to 20cm. Lvs to 18cm, obovate, reticulated. Rac. to 40cm, pendent; fls white; tep. to 25mm, lanceolate, spur long, pink. W Afr.

A. brachycarpa (A. Rich.) Dur. & Schinz. St. to 20cm. Lvs to 25cm, obovate, ± dotted black. Rac. to 40cm, arching; fls white; tep. to 45mm, narrow-lanceolate, spur v. long, pink. E Afr., Zam., Angola.

A. calantha (Schltr.) Schltr. St. to 3cm. Lvs to 8cm, linear. Rac. to 11cm, arching; fls white; tep. to 12mm, oblong-lanceolate, spur pink, curved forward. Trop. Afr.

A. calligera (Rchb. f.) Garay = *A. ellisii*.

A. citrata (Thouars) Schltr. St. to 6cm. Lvs to 12cm, elliptic. Rac. to 25cm; fls to 1.8cm diam., yellow-cream, held in one plane, spur swollen at tip. Madag.

A. clavigera H. Perrier = *A. macrocentra*.

A. confusa Joyce Stewart. St. to 10cm. Lvs 5–24cm, obovate. Rac. to 20cm; fls white; tep. to 25mm, lanceolate, spur long, pink. Kenya, Tanz.

A. coriacea Summerh. St. to 10cm. Lvs to 22cm, obovate-ligulate, reticulated. Rac. to 40cm, arching; fls white, tep. to 20mm, oblanceolate-elliptic, spur v. long pink or green. Kenya, Tanz.

A. cryptodon (Rchb. f.) Schltr. St. short. Lvs to 15cm, oblong. Rac. to 40cm, arching; fls white; tep. to 18mm, lanceolate, spur long, pink. Madag.

A. curnowiana (Rchb. f.) Schltr. St. v. short. Lvs to 4cm, obovate, grey-green. Rac. to 8cm; fls 1–2, white; tep. to 20mm, lanceolate, spur long curved, tinted pink. Madag.

A. decaryana H. Perrier. St. v. short. Lvs to 10cm, oblanceolate, undulate, grey-green tinted pink-brown. Rac. to 40cm, pendent; fls white, fragrant, spur long, tinted brown. Madag.

A. distincta Joyce Stewart & I.F. la Croix. St. to 15cm. Lvs to 16cm, narrowly triangular, spotted black. Rac. to 27cm, pendent; fls white sometimes tinted salmon pink; tep. to 60mm, narrow-lanceolate, spur long, straight. Malawi.

A. ellisii (Rchb. f.) Schltr. St. to 80cm, branched. Lvs to 15cm, fleshy, remote. Rac. to 40cm; fls white, fragrant, long-spurred; tep. to 22mm, ovate. Madag. var. *grandiflora* Joyce Stewart. Fls larger.

A. fastuosa (Rchb. f.) Schltr. St. v. short. Lvs to 8cm, oblong. Rac. to 6cm; fls sparkling white, spur tipped green, ± coiled; tep. to 30mm, oblong. Madag.

A. fuscata (Rchb. f.) Schltr. St. short. Lvs to 8cm, elliptic-obovate, glossy. Rac. few-fld; fls white sometimes tinted pink or green, long-spurred; tep. to 30mm, lanceolate. Madag.

A. gracillima (Kränzl.) J.C. Arends & Joyce Stewart. St. to 8cm. Lvs to 24cm, falcate-obovate. Rac. to 75cm, pendent; fls white sometimes tinted-rusty red with a long, spoon-shaped spur; tep. to 30mm, narrowly elliptic. Cameroun, Gabon.

A. hyaloides (Rchb. f.) Schltr. St. v. short. Lvs to 7cm, elliptic. Rac. to 7cm, erect; fls sparkling white, v. short-spurred; tep. to 8mm, somewhat cupped. Madag.

A. kirkii (Rchb. f.) Schltr. St. short. Lvs to 15cm, oblanceolate, deep grey-green. Rac. to 17cm, pendent; fls white, spur long, tinted pink; tep. to 20mm, oblanceolate. Kenya, Tanz., Moz.

A. kotschyana (Rchb. f.) Schltr. St. to 20cm, thick. Lvs to 30cm, obovate. Rac. to 45cm, arching; fls white flushed salmon pink, spur long, spiralling, tip dilated. Widespread in trop. Afr.

A. luteoalba (Kränzl.) Schltr. St. v. short. Lvs to 15cm, linear-oblong. Rac. to 35cm, arching; fls in 1 plane, white to ivory, spur to 4cm, incurved; tep. oblanceolate-rhomboid, to 20mm. Zaire, Uganda. var. *rhodosticta* (Kränzl.) Joyce Stewart. Column bright orange-red. Central African Rep., Cameroun, Zaire, Ethiop., Uganda, Kenya, Tanz.

A. macrocentra (Schltr.) Schltr. St. short. Lvs to 20cm, lanceolate-falcate, blue-green. Rac. to 30cm, pendent; 2-ranked; fls white sometimes tinted-pink, nodding short-spurred; tep. to 10mm, oblong. Madag.

A. modesta (Hook.) Schltr. St. to 15cm. Lvs to 12.5cm, obovate. Rac. to 30cm, pendent; fls remote, white, slender-spurred, term. fl. largest and first to open, none opening fully; tep. to 12mm, lanceolate. Madag.

A. mooreana (Rolfe ex Sander) Cribb & Joyce Stewart. Short-stemmed. Lvs to 12cm, oblong. Rac. to 18cm, pendent; fls white sometimes tinted-pink, long-spurred; tep. to 10mm, lanceolate-obovate. Madag.

A. mystacidii (Rchb. f.) Schltr. St. short. Lvs to 23cm, oblanceolate. Rac. to 20cm, arching; fls white sometimes tinted-pink; tep. to 1.4mm, oblong (to 1/8 length of spur). Tanz., Malawi, Moz., Zam., Zimb., Swaz., S Afr.

A. pallidiflora H. Perrier. St. v. short. Lvs to 7×2cm, forming a fan. Rac. to 20cm; fls to 1.5cm diam., yellow-green, star-shaped, short-spurred. Madag.

A. punctata Joyce Stewart. Dwarf. St. v. short. Lvs to 3.5cm, elliptic-oblong, grey-green dotted silver. Fls to 4cm diam., solitary, long-spurred, white sometimes tinted-green or brown. Madag.

A. seegeri Sengh. = *A. pallidiflora*.

A. somalensis (Schltr.) Schltr. St. short. Lvs to 11cm, oblong-obovate, sometimes reticulated and red-tinted. Rac. to 20cm; fls white sometimes tinted-salmon pink, long-spurred; tep. to 12mm, ovate. Ethiop., Tanz., Malawi, S Afr.

A. stylosa (Rolfe) Schltr. St. short. Lvs to 17cm, grey-green edged red. Rac. to 60cm, arching; fls white sometimes tinted-pink or brown, long-spurred; tep. to 20mm, oblanceolate. Madag.

A. thomsonii (Rolfe) Schltr. St. 10–100cm, woody. Lvs to 28cm, strap-shaped. Rac. to 30cm, arching; fls white in 2 rows with long, flexuous spurs; tep. to 20mm, lanceolate-elliptic. E Afr.

A. ugandensis Summerh. St. to 20cm. Lvs to 15cm, oblanceolate, dotted black. Rac. to 15cm, pendent; fls white sometimes tinted-green; tep. to 12mm, oblong-lanceolate, to 0.5× length spur. EC Afr.

A. umbonata Schltr. = *A. fuscata*.

A. verdickii (De Wildeman) Schltr. St. to 6cm. Lvs to 20cm, oblong-ligulate, grey-green tinted purple, undulate. Rac. to 40cm; fls white, fragrant; tep. to 22mm, ovate-oblong, 0.2–0.1× length spur. C Afr.

→*Angraecum*.

Aeranthes Lindl. Orchidaceae. 40 epiphytic monopodial orchids. Lvs strap-shaped, fleshy or leathery, few in 2 loose ranks clothing short st. Infl. simple or branched, racemose; pedicel usually wiry, drooping; fls large, translucent green to white. Madag., Masc. Is., Comoros Is., with 2 sp. on mainland Afr. Z10.

A. arachnites Lindl. Lvs to 30cm. Rac. to 40cm; fls few, pale green; tep. to 2cm, tapering abruptly and finely. Réunion.

A. caudata Rolfe Lvs to 15cm. Rac. to 60cm; fls pale green; tep. to 12cm, long-caudate. Madag.

A. grandiflora Lindl. Lvs to 30cm. Rac. to 100cm, pendent, sheathed; fls yellow-green; tep to 6cm, long-caudate. Madag.

A. henrici Schltr. Lvs to 8cm. Rac. to 40cm, pendent; fls white; tep. to 10cm, lanceolate tapering finely; lip fringed. Madag.

A. peyrotii Bosser. Lvs to 40cm, linear. Infl. to 50cm, a remontant pan.; fls bright green 1 opening at a time; tep. to 4cm, lanceolate. Madag.

A. ramosa Rolfe. Lvs to 28cm. Infl. to 30cm, pendent; fls dark green, spur white; tep. to 4cm, ovate-lanceolate, long-acuminate. Madag.

Aerides Lour. Orchidaceae. 40 epiphytic monopodial orchids. St. erect, simple, clothed with strap-shaped lvs in 2 ranks. Fls fragrant in axill. rac.; tep. broad, spreading; lip entire or 3-lobed at apex; spur usually short, ± saccate, forward-pointing. Trop. & E Asia, W Malaysia. Z10.

A. affinis Wallich = *A. multiflora*.

A. arachnites Sw. = *Arachnis flos-aeris*.

A. calceolaris Buch.-Ham. ex Sm. = *Gastrochilus calceolaris*.

A. crassifolia Parish & Burb. Lvs to 20cm, rigid, thick. Fls to 50 per rac.; tep. magenta to violet, white at base, lip midlobe dark mauve, ovate, cleft. Burm., Laos, Thail.

A. crispa Lindl. Lvs to 22cm, tough. Fls white suffused rose-purple, crowded in pendulous rac., lip midlobe ovate, fringed. India.

A. expansa Rchb. f. = *A. falcata*.

A. falcata Lindl. Lvs to 20cm, glaucescent above, maroon-streaked beneath, leathery. Fls white blotched violet in lax rac., lip midlobe violet, obovate, dentate. SE Asia.

A. falcata var. *houlletiana* (Rchb. f.) Veitch = *A. houlletiana*.

A. fieldingii Williams. Lvs to 35cm, strongly keeled. Fls white spotted or suffused amethyst in dense rac. to 60cm, lip midlobe amethyst, sagittate. India.

A. flabellata Rolfe. Lvs to 10cm, keeled, curved. Tep. maroon; lip white blotched purple, midlobe flabelliform, fringed. Burm., China, Thail.

A. houlletiana Rchb. f. Lvs strap-shaped. Tep. fleshy, yellow-brown marked purple, lip cream blotched magenta or rusty red at centre, midlobe subrhombic, fringed. Thail., Vietnam, Cambodia.

A. japonica Lind. & Rchb. f. = *Sedirea japonica*.

A. jarckiana Schltr. = *A. quinquevulnera*.

A. kraibiensis Seidenf. St. small. Lvs conduplicate, tapering rigidly. Fls few on short rac.; tep. white or purple edged violet or wholly purple, lip paler, lobes shallow, rounded. Thail.

A. lawrenceae Rchb. f. Lvs to 30cm. Fls in dense rac., to 30cm; tep. white blotched violet-rose, lip midlobe ligulate, violet streaked red. Philipp.

A. lindleyana Wight = *A. crispa*.

A. lobbii hort. ex Lem. = *A. multiflora*.

A. maculosa Lindl. St. short. Lvs to 20cm. Fls crowded in branched infl. to 40cm; tep. white suffused rose, spotted purple, tipped violet, lip amethyst, midlobe ovate-oblong, undulate. India.

A. mitrata Rchb. f. = *Seidenfadenia mitrata*.

A. multiflora Roxb. Lvs to 35cm, strongly keeled. Fls crowded in rac. to 30cm, fragrant; tep. rose-purple or white, lip pale amethyst, midlobe cordate-hastate. Himal., India to Thail., Indochina.

A. odorata Lour. Lvs to 30cm, oblong-ligulate. Fls to 30 per pendent rac., fragrant, white to mauve, often spotted or tipped purple; lip midlobe oblong-lanceolate, incurved. India, SE Asia, Java to Philipp.

A. paniculata Ker-Gawl. = *Cleisostoma paniculatum*.

A. quinquevulnera Lindl. Lvs to 35cm. Fls crowded, fragrant, waxy in rac. to 40cm, white spotted purple-red; lip midlobe oblong-linear, strongly incurved, pale purple. Philipp.

A. racemifera Lindl. = *Cleisostoma racemiferum*.

A. vandarum Rchb. f. = *Papilionanthe vandarum*.

A. williamsii Warner = *A. fieldingii*.

Aeschynanthus Jack. Gesneriaceae. BASKET PLANT; BLUSH WORT *c*100 epiphytic or climbing perenn. herbs and subshrubs. St. shrubby and sprawling or ± unbranched, cascading. Lvs opposite in subequal pairs or whorled, somewhat fleshy. Fls in

axils or in term. clusters; cal., tubular, shortly 5-dentate or 5-partite; cor., tubular, hooded, decurved, limb bilabiate, upper lip bilobed; lower lip trilobed. Indomal. Z10.

A. acuminatus Wallich ex A. DC. St. trailing. Lvs to 8cm, elliptic, acuminate, slightly glaucous. Fls in term. clusters; cal. divided almost to base, glab.; cor. to 1.5cm, yellow-green, upper lip yellow, lower lip often red at margin. Himal., Sikkim to Assam.

A. albidus Steud. Lvs 5–13.5cm, oblong-lanceolate, acuminate, shallowly dentate, pale green and purple-blotched beneath. Fls 1–2 per axil, or 2–8 in a term. cluster; cal. divided to base; cor. to 2cm, outside green, inside brown with red streaks and spots, lobes pubesc. Java.

A. bracteatus Wallich ex A. DC. Scrambling. Lvs to 10cm, elliptic to ovate, acuminate. Fls in a terminal cluster on red peduncles; floral bracts red; cal. divided nearly to base, red; cor. to 3cm, bright red, lower lobes often maroon-spotted. E Himal.

A. ceylanicus Gardn. St. branching. Lvs to 8.5cm, narrowly lanceolate. Fls 2 per axil; sep. linear; cor. to 2.5cm, orange-red, pubesc. or subglabrous. Sri Lanka.

A. cordifolius Hook. Br. pendent. Lvs to 6cm, cordate to ovate, fleshy, short-acuminate. Fls in axill. fascicles; cal. turbinate, obscurely 5 angled, slightly tomentose; cor. to 5cm, deep red, glandular-villous, lower lobes yellow at base. Borneo.

A. ellipticus Laut. & Schum. St. red-pilose. Lvs elliptic, lustrous dark green. Fls in axill. and term. clusters; cal. incised to base, puberulent; cor. to 6cm, bright pink, pale maroon-hairy, flesh-coloured inside. New Guinea.

A. evrardii Pelleg. St. branching. Lvs to 11cm, lanceolate. Fls in clusters toward br. tips; cal. incised to about middle, glab.; cor. to 8cm, orange-red with yellow-orange throat, upper lobes glandular-pilose, red-striped, lower lobes yellow. Malaysia.

A. fecundus P. Woods. St. spreading. Lvs 4–8.5cm, lanceolate to elliptic-lanceolate, dark green with pale veins above, pale green beneath, margin with purple glands. Fls 1–3, often cleistogamous; cal. yellow-green, sep. free; cor. to 1.8cm, yellow becoming red at apex, lobes glandular-ciliate, hairy at base. Malaysia.

A. fulgens Wallich. Epiphyte with stout br. Lvs to 12.5cm, narrowly lanceolate. Fls in a term. fascicle; cal. narrowly tubular, 5-toothed, subglabrous; cor. scarlet, pubesc., limb orange with purple markings. Malaysia.

A. gracilis Parish. Br. slender, elongate, rooting at nodes, red-tinged. Lvs to 1.2cm, broadly lanceolate, base cuneate or rounded, pubesc. Fls 1(–2) per axil; cal. deeply lobed, villous; cor. to 2.5cm scarlet, villous, mouth orange with purple-black markings. E Himal.

A. grandiflorus (D. Don) Spreng. = *A. parasiticus*.

A. hartleyi P. Woods. Lvs to 10cm, elliptic or lanceolate, acuminate. Fls 1–3 per axil; cal. glabrescent, seg. subulate; cor. pale orange, to 2cm, glandular-puberulent. New Guinea.

A. hians A. DC. St. elongate, pendent. Lvs to 10cm, ovate, acuminate, base rhombic, coriaceous. Fls solitary to several; cal. broadly obconic, villous; cor. to 2.5cm, bright red, villous, lobes spotted black. Borneo.

A. 'Hillbrandii' = *A. hildebrandii*.

A. hildebrandii Hemsl. Dwarf creeping subshrub. Lvs to 2.5cm, crowded, ovate, subacute, minutely hairy, margins flushed red, ciliate. Fls 1–3 per axil; cal. 4-partite, seg. ovate-lanceolate, glandular-hairy; cor. to 2.5cm, orange-red. Burm.

A. horsfieldii R. Br. Epiphyte to 1.5m. Lvs to 9.5cm, ovate-oblong-lanceolate, acuminate. Fls 2+ per axil; cal. flushed red, divided to base; cor. to 3cm, bright red with slightly inflated green base, glab. to densely pubesc., seg. blotched dark red. Malaysia.

A. hosseusianus Kränzl. Lvs to 3cm, oblanceolate, obtuse, dark green and pilose above, white-tomentose beneath. Fls in term. pairs; cal. seg. linear; cor. to 3cm, inflated at middle, narrowing to throat, purple, sparsely pilose. Thail.

A. javanicus hort. = *A. radicans*.

A. lamponga Miq. To 30cm. Lvs ovate, obtuse, fleshy. Fls in axill. clusters; cal. tubular, not deeply incised, purple-brown; cor. 4–5cm, orange-red. Java.

A. lanceolatus Ridl. St. creeping, slender. Lvs to 1.8cm, coriaceous, linear-lanceolate; apex acuminate. Fls solitary, term.; cal. tubular-cylindric, sparsely pubesc., lobes short, ovate, cor. to 5.8cm, red, sparsely pubesc. Malay Penins.

A. lobbianus Hook. LIPSTICK PLANT. St. deep purple. Lvs fleshy, elliptic, grey-green, apex acute, margin purple, entire to remotely toothed. Fls in a term. corymb; floral bracts cordate, dark purple; cal. cylindric, lustrous black-purple, black-tomentose, 5-partite; cor. deep red, downy, limb marked with maroon lines and spots. Java.

A. longicaulis R. Br. St. branching. Lvs to 8cm, lanceolate, obscurely falcate, fleshy. Fls in axill. and term. cymes, sep. narrowly linear-lanceolate cor. to 2.2cm, orange-red, glab. Malaysia.

A. ***longiflorus*** (Bl.) DC. Robust epiphyte to 80cm. Lvs to 16cm, ovate-oblong, acuminate, lustrous dark green above, paler beneath. Fls 2–7 per cluster; cal. to 2cm, divided to base, dark red; cor. to 11cm, dark red, short-hairy; lobes with an orange-red, black-margined blotch. Malaysia.

A. ***maculatus*** Lindl. Lvs to 10cm, lanceolate. Fls in axill. clusters; cal. deeply divided; cor. to 12cm, red, lobes orange marked with black-purple. India.

A. ***marmoratus*** T. Moore. St. to 1m, slender, shrubby. Lvs to 10cm, elliptic-lanceolate, semirigid, glossy, purple beneath, pale green marbled or striped purple above. Fls solitary; cal. lobes slender, downy; cor. to 3.5cm, olive green, flecked maroon on lobes. Burm., Thail., Malaysia.

A. ***micranthus*** C.B. Clarke. Br. elongate, often rooting. Lvs to 6cm, elliptic or oblong, shortly acuminate, coriaceous. Fls 1–5 per cluster; cal. deeply divided, sparsely villous; cor. to 2cm, narrow, bright red, mouth orange, lobes purple-spotted. Subtrop. Himal.

A. ***motleyi*** C.B. Clarke = *A. albidus*.

A. ***musaensis*** P. Woods. St. elongate, creeping or pendent; to 1m, red-brown. Lvs to 9.3cm, fleshy, broadly elliptic to oblong, apex acuminate. Fls axillary, 1 or 2; floral bracts pale green, red-brown at margins; cal. glab., tubular, pale green, purple at margin; cor. to 7cm, maroon-purple, lobes marked with dark lines, glandular-pubesc. Malaysia.

A. ***myrmecophilus*** P. Woods. St. creeping or pendulous. Lvs to 3.5cm, ovate or orbicular, succulent, dentate. Fls solitary; sep. glandular-pubesc. linear-lanceolate, pale green; cor. to 2.3cm, cream-yellow, glandular-pubesc., lobes flushed to spotted with red. Malaysia.

A. ***nummularius*** (Burkill & S. Moore) Schum. St. creeping, rooting, brown-tomentose. Lvs to 1.3cm, rounded. Fls on narrow stalks; cal. puberulent; cor. to 5cm. New Guinea.

A. ***obconicus*** C.B. Clarke St. slender, pendent to ascending, glab. Lvs to 8cm, ovate-orbicular to elliptic-oblong, fleshy. Fls in axill. pairs; cal. broadly obconic, slightly 5-toothed; cor. to 2cm, maroon marked yellow, villous. Summer. Malay Penins.

A. ***parasiticus*** (Roxb.) Wallich. St. elongate. Lvs to 10cm, lanceolate. Fls in term. clusters; cal. incised to base; cor. to 3cm, inflated at middle, narrowed to throat, pilose, orange-red with red lines, lobes edged orange, marked red. India.

A. ***parviflorus*** Ridl., non (D. Don) Spreng. = *A. fecundus*.

A. ***parviflorus*** (D. Don) Spreng., non Ridl. = *A. parasiticus*.

A. ***pulcher*** (Bl.) G. Don. LIPSTICK PLANT; RED BUGLE VINE; ROYAL RED BUGLER; SCARLET BASKET VINE. Br. slender. Lvs broadly ovate, fleshy, obscurely toothed. Fls in a term. corymb; floral bracts cordate; cal. cylindric-urceolate, glab., yellow-green, flushed red above, incised to one quarter length; cor. to 6cm, deep red, glab. except for lips, seg. ovate bright yellow in throat. Java.

A. ***radicans*** Jack. LIPSTICK PLANT. Epiphyte or creeper, to 1.5m. Lvs to 7.5cm, orbicular to broadly ovate, entire or dentate-lobate, somewhat fleshy. Fls in axill. pairs; cal. green to maroon, divided to above middle; cor. to 7.5cm, bright red, pubesc., blotched yellow in throat. Malaysia.

A. ***ramosissimus*** Wallich = *A. parasiticus*.

A. ***sanguineus*** Schltr. St. scandent, branching; br. filiform, flexuous. Lvs to 8.5cm, elliptic or obovate-oblong, apex acuminate, glab., flushed red. Fls in pairs; floral bracts linear; sep. linear, puberulent; cor. to 5cm, blood-red, papillose. New Guinea.

A. ***sikkimensis*** Stapf. Br. pendulous. Lvs to 15cm, oblong-lanceolate, apex acuminate, entire or remotely toothed, fleshy-coriaceous. Fls 6–9 per cyme; floral bracts linear to subulate, to 5mm; cal. teeth, linear-lanceolate; cor. to 3cm, scarlet with short glandular-pubescence outside, yellow and almost glab. inside, lobes streaked black. India.

A. ***speciosus*** Hook. Robust, shrubby. Lvs 6.5–11cm, in pseudo-whorls, ovate-lanceolate, apex acuminate, glab. Fls in term. fascicles; cal. divided almost to base, yellow-green, marked red at apex; cor. to 11cm, short-hairy, orange-yellow in lower part to orange-red at apex, lobes blotched dark red, throat marked yellow. Malaysia.

A. ***splendens*** = *A. speciosus*.

A. ×***splendidus*** T. Moore. (*A. parasiticus* × *A. speciosus*.) Differs from *A. speciosus* in cal. tube equalling lobes; cor. lobes with large marginal blotches of black-maroon, not marked orange at base. Gdn origin.

A. ***tricolor*** Hook. Br. climbing or pendent, rooting, slightly tomentose. Lvs to 2.5cm, ovate, acuminate, slightly downy, entire. Fls in clusters of 3–5; pedicels curved upwards; cal. cupulate, red, 5-partite, villous; cor. to 5cm, scarlet, streaked with bright yellow and black, glandular-hirsute, seg. yellow at base and margins. Borneo.

A. ***vinaceus*** P. Woods. St. to 1m, pendent or creeping, purple-brown. Lvs 6–11cm, lanceolate or ovate-lanceolate, apex

acuminate. Fls axill.; cal. flushed purple, 2-lipped; cor. to 3.2cm, maroon-purple, margins ciliate. Malaysia.

A. ***zebrinus*** Van Houtte = *A. marmoratus*.

A. **cvs.** 'Big Apple': habit compact, erect; fls deep red, tubular. 'Black Pagoda': lvs mottled, green above, purple beneath; fls green at base, deep orange at tips. 'Topaz': similar to *A. hildebrandii*, differing in its yellow fls.

Aesculus L. Hippocastanaceae. 15 decid. trees and shrubs. Twigs lenticellate; buds viscous. Lvs palmately lobed; petioles long. Fls in erect, term. pyramidal pan. or rac.; cal. campanulate-tubular, 5-lobed; pet. 4–5, usually unequal, lobed or crested; sta. exserted. Fr. a capsule, smooth, rugose or prickly; seeds 1–6 with woody coating and pale hilum. Summer. N Amer., SE Eur., E Asia.

A. ***arguta*** Buckley = *A. glabra* var. *arguta*.

A. ×***arnoldiana*** Sarg. ((*A. glabra* × *A. flava*) × *A. pavia*.) To 25m. Lfts 5, elliptic, glab., serrate. Fls yellow tinged red. Fr. subglobose, scaly, spines short. Gdn origin. Z5.

A. ***assamica*** Griff. To 25m. Lfts 5–7, lanceolate-oblong, lustrous, serrulate. Fls white, pale rose at centre. Fr. ovoid, unarmed. Bhutan, Sikkim, N Vietnam. Z8.

A. ×***bushii*** Schneid. (*A. glabra* × *A. pavia*.) To 7m, low, spreading. Lfts denticulate. Fls yellow, pink or red on same infl. Fr. warty. N Amer. Z5.

A. ***californica*** (Spach) Nutt. CALIFORNIA BUCKEYE. To 12m, small. Multi-stemmed tree or spreading shrub. Lfts 5–7, narrow-oblong, acute, glossy, dark green, serrate. Fls white (-pink); fil. mauve. Fr. pyriform, rough. Calif. Z7.

A. ×***carnea*** Hayne. (*A. hippocastanum* × *A. pavia*.) RED HORSE CHESTNUT. To 25m. Lfts 5–7, obovate, puckered and somewhat misshapen, dark green, bicrenate. Fls rose to scarlet blotched yellow. Fr. spherical, spiny. 'Briotii': infl. large; pet. pale blood-red, fr. laxly spined. 'Plantierensis': lfts usually 7, sessile, ribbed, uneven; fls delicate pink, fr. prickly but undeveloped, triploid. Z4.

A. ***chinensis*** Bunge. CHINESE HORSE CHESTNUT. To 30m. Lfts 5–7, oblong-obovate, serrate. Fls white; sta. shortly exserted. Fr. depressed-globose, scabrous. N China. Z6.

A. **+** ***dallimorei*** Sealy. (*A. hippocastanum* + *A. flava*.) Lfts 5, broadly elliptic, dark green above, hoary beneath. Fls usually staminate, white blotched maroon or cream blotched ochre. Z5.

A. ***discolor*** Pursh = *A. pavia*.

A. ***flava*** Sol. SWEET BUCKEYE; YELLOW BUCKEYE. To 28m. Lfts 5–7, obovate to ovate, veins downy. Fls yellow. Fr. subspherical. N Amer. Z5.

A. ***georgiana*** Sarg. = *A. sylvatica*.

A. ***glabra*** Willd. OHIO BUCKEYE. Shrub or tree to 30m. Lfts 5–7, obovate to elliptic, acuminate, glab. or tomentose beneath. Fls yellow-green; anth. orange. Fr. ovoid, prickly or smooth. SE and C US. var. ***arguta*** (Buckley) Robinson. Small tree or shrub to 6m. Br. arching; twigs hairy. Lfts 7–9, lanceolate, subcaudate. Fls cream. S US. Z5.

A. ***glaucescens*** Sarg. Shrub or tree 3–9m. Lfts 5, midrib hairy above, glaucous beneath. Fls yellow-green. Fr. subglobose. SE US. Z5.

A. ***hippocastanum*** L. HORSE CHESTNUT. To 25m. Lfts 5–7, obovate-acuminate, dark green above, paler, ± pubesc. beneath. Fls white blotched rose or yellow, speckled red, fringed. Fr. globose, softly spiny. NW Greece, C & S Albania, Bulg. 'Baumannii': fls double, sterile, longer-lasting. 'Henkellii': lfts smaller, more deeply toothed. 'Laciniata': lfts linear-laciniate. 'Pumila': dwarf form, lfts deeply incised. 'Pyramidalis': br. ascending, habit pyramidal. Z3.

A. ×***hybrida*** DC. (*A. flava* × *A. pavia*.) To 18m. Lfts 5, obovate, downy beneath. Fls red, yellow or yellow tinged red. Fr. spherical. US (Allegheny Mts). Z5.

A. ***indica*** (Wallich ex Cambess.) Hook. INDIAN HORSE CHESTNUT. To 30m. Lfts 5–9, obovate-lanceolate, ± glab., serrulate, emerging bronze-pink, then dark green, glaucous beneath. Fls similar to *A. hippocastanum*, pet. narrower, sta. more incurved, infl. slender, remote. NE Himal. 'Sydney Pearce': strongly vigorous, lvs dark olive green, petioles red; fls in large, erect pan., white flushed pink, marked yellow. Z7.

A. ×***marylandica*** Booth. (*A. glabra* × *A. flava*.) To 10m. Lfts 3–7, lanceolate-ovate, lustrous above, rusty-pubesc. on veins beneath. Fls yellow. Cult. hybrid. Z5.

A. ×***mississippiensis*** Sarg. = *A. ×bushii*.

A. ×***mutabilis*** (Spach) Schelle. (*A. pavia* × *A. sylvatica*.) To 5m. Lfts 5–7, oval to oblong, downy beneath. Fls yellow and red. Cult. hybrid. 'Harbisonii': lvs smoother, somewhat glaucous beneath; fls bright red. 'Induta': lvs smoother beneath; fls yellow, flushed pink. Z5.

A. ×***neglecta*** Lindl. (*A. flava* × *A. sylvatica*.) To 20m. Lfts 5, obovate, entire or serrate, emerging pink, then pale green, veins downy beneath. Fls yellow suffused red at centre. SE US.

'Erythroblastos': new growth red, fls peach to pink. Z5.
A. octandra Marshall = *A. flava*.
A. ohioensis DC. = *A. glabra*.
A. parviflora Walter. Tree-like shrub to 5m, suckering. Lfts 5–7, oval-obovate, smooth, dark green, paler, downy beneath. Fls white in slender pan.; anth. far-exserted. S US. f. *serotina* Rehd. Lvs ± glaucous. Infl. longer. SE US. Z5.
A. pavia L. RED BUCKEYE. Shrub or small tree to 4m. Lfts 5–7, obovate to oblong-lanceolate ± tomentose beneath, serrate. Fls carmine or yellow or red marked yellow. Fr. ovoid, unarmed. N Amer. 'Atrosanguinea': fls dark red. 'Humilis': trailing or prostrate shrub. Z5.
A. ×*plantierensis* André = *A.* ×*carnea* 'Plantierensis'.
A. rubicunda Loisel. = *A.* ×*carnea*.
A. splendens Sarg. = *A. pavia*.
A. sylvatica Bartr. Shrub to 2m. Lfts 5, oval to obovate, puberulent. Fls yellow then red, downy. Fr. obovoid. SE US. Z5.
A. turbinata Bl. JAPANESE HORSE CHESTNUT. Tree to 30m. Lfts 3–7, cuneate-obovate, large, glaucous beneath, serrate. Fls cream spotted red. Fr. pyriform, scabrous, bumpy. Jap. Z6.
A. wilsonii Rehd. Tree to 25m. Lfts 5–7, oval to oblanceolate, acuminate, glabrescent, serrulate. Fls white, spotted yellow in upper half. Fr. ovoid, spiny. China. Z6.
A. ×*woerlitzensis* Koehne. (*A.* ×*hybrida* ×*A. sylvatica.*) To 20m. Lfts 5–7, obovate-oblong, yellow-green. Fls red. Gdn. origin. Z6.

Aetheopappus Cass.
A. pulcherrimus (Willd.) Cass. = *Centaurea pulcherrima*.

Aethionema R. Br. STONE CRESS. Cruciferae. *c*40 ann. or perenn. herbs. Lvs fleshy, entire, usually sessile. Fls in term., crowded rac., 4-merous, red-purple or white. All below are perenn. unless stated otherwise. Eur., Medit., SW Asia. Z7.
A. arabicum (L.) Andrz. Ann. to 15cm. Fls crowded, white-pink or purple. Greece to SW Asia.
A. armenum Boiss. Densely tufted, to 20cm. Lvs glaucous. Fls in close rac.; pet. 3–6mm, pink-white. Armenia, Cauc. 'Warley Rose': lvs blue-grey, tinted red dense; fls dark pink, striped; sterile. 'Warley Ruber': fls deep maroon.
A. buxbaumii (Fisch. ex Hornem.) DC. = *A. arabicum*.
A. cardiophyllum Boiss. & Heldr. = *A. cordatum*.
A. cordatum (Desf.) Boiss. Shrubby, 15–20cm. Lvs 8mm, blunt. Fls sulphur yellow; pet. 7mm. Greece to SW Asia.
A. coridifolium DC. Similar to *A. grandiflorum* except to 20cm, pet. to 5mm. Leb.
A. diastrophis Bunge. To 25cm. St. numerous. Rac. elongate in fr.; pet. 3–4mm, white pink. Armenia.
A. gracile DC. = *A. saxatile*.
A. grandiflorum Boiss. & Hohen. Loosely branching, to 45cm. Pet. to 11mm, rose pink, distinctly clawed. Iran, Iraq, Cauc.
A. iberideum (Boiss.) Boiss. To 15cm; st. branching from base. Fls white, fragrant; pet. to 8mm. E Medit. to Cauc.
A. kotschyi hort. = *A. grandiflorum*.
A. oppositifolium (Pers.) Hedge. Tufted, woody based, to 5cm. Sep. purple; pet. to 8mm, pink-lilac. Leb., Cauc.
A. pulchellum Boiss. & Huet = *A. grandiflorum*.
A. saxatile (L.) R. Br. Ann. or perenn. to 30cm. Fls small, in loose rac., purple-white. S & SC Eur.
A. schistosum (Boiss. & Kotschy) Kotschy. 6–10cm, much branched. Rac. not elongating; fls pink. Turk.
A. speciosum Boiss. & Huet. 15–25cm; base woody. Flg st. simple; fls pink. E Turk. to N Iraq.
A. spicatum Post. To 15cm. Rhiz. woody. Rac. dense, not elongating; pet. 5–8mm, pink. Syr.
A. stylosum DC. Shrubby, 7–20cm. Rac. compact; fls large, rose pink to white. Leb. to W Syr.
→*Eunomia, Iberis* and *Lepidium*.

Aframomum Schum. Zingiberaceae. *c*50 perenn. rhizomatous herbs. Lvs alt. in 2 ranks on erect st. Infl. congested. Fls subtended by 2 bracts; posterior pet. erect, laterals slender; lip oblong to suborbicular. Fr. a fleshy berry. Trop. Afr., Madag. Z10.
A. daniellii Schum. To 75cm. Lvs 20–30cm. Fls several, red; lip rose, yellow at base, margin white. W Afr.
A. melegueta (Roscoe) Schum. GRAINS OF PARADISE; GUINEA GRAINS; MELAGUETA PEPPER. To 2m. Lvs to 20cm. Fls solitary, white to rose; lip pale violet, yellow at base. W Afr.
A. zambesiacum (Bak.) Schum. To 2m. Lvs 20–45cm. Fls 25–50, white to cream or pink; lip crimson at base. W Afr.
→*Amomum*.

African Bowstring Hemp *Sansevieria hyacinthoides*.
African Boxwood *Myrsine africana*.
African Cabbage *Brassica carinata*.

African Cherry Orange *Citropsis*.
African Cypress *Widdringtonia*.
African Daisy *Arctotis*; *Lonas*.
African Fern Pine *Afrocarpus gracilior*.
African Fountain Grass *Pennisetum setaceum*.
African Hairbell *Dierama*.
African Hemp *Sparmannia africana*.
African Holly *Solanum giganteum*.
African Honeysuckle *Halleria lucida*.
African Horned Cucumber *Cucumis metuliferus*.
African Juniper *Juniperus procera*.
African Lily *Agapanthus africanus*.
African Love Grass *Eragrostis curvula*.
African Marigold *Tagetes erecta*.
African Milk Barrel *Euphorbia horrida*.
African Millett *Eleusine coracana*.
African Moringo *Moringa ovalifolia*.
African Oil Palm *Elaeis guineensis*.
African Poison Oak *Smodingium argutum*.
African Sage *Salvia aethiopis*.
African Sandalwood *Baphia nitida*.
African Tulip *Spathodea campanulata*.
African Valerian *Fedia cornucopiae*.
African Violet *Saintpaulia*; (*S. ionantha*).
African Walnut *Schotia brachypetala*.
African Yellowwood *Podocarpus elongatus*.

Afrocarpus (Buchholz & Gray) Page. YELLOWWOOD. Podocarpaceae. 6 everg. coniferous trees or shrubs, resembling *Podocarpus*. Crown columnar; twigs rhombic in section. Lvs narrow lanceolate-elliptic, distichous, bilaterally flattened, coriaceous, midrib prominent. Cones drupe-like, usually solitary, subglobose to ovoid, thinly fleshy, to 2cm diam.; bracts fleshy, pruinose; receptacle not swollen. Equat. to S & SE Afr. Z10.
A. falcatus (Thunb.) Page. OTENIQUA YELLOWWOOD; COMMON YELLOWWOOD; BASTARD YELLOWWOOD. To 30m+. Lvs opposite to spirally arranged; juvenile lvs to 12cm×8mm, becoming densely arranged, to 2.5cm×2–3mm when mature, acute or obtuse. S Afr. (Cape Prov., Natal) to Angola.
A. gracilior (Pilger) Page. AFRICAN FERN PINE. To 20m. Lvs loosely arranged, to 10cm×6mm on young trees, on mature trees, densely arranged, linear, 2–6cm×13–5mm, yellow-green, apex acuminate, midrib projecting beneath. Subtrop. Afr. (mts of Uganda, Ethiop., Kenya).
A. mannii (Hook. f.) Page. To 15m+. Lvs sessile, linear or slightly curved, to 16cm×11mm on young trees, to 7cm×5mm on mature trees, coriaceous, apex long-acuminate. W Afr. (Sao Tomé Is.).
A. usambarensis (Pilger) Page. To 5mm+. Lvs 7cm×5mm, to 10cm on young trees and only 5cm on old trees; linear to falcate, long acuminate. C Africa.
→*Decussocarpus* and *Podocarpus*.

Afzelia Sm. Leguminosae (Caesalpinioideae). 8 everg. or decid. trees. Lvs pinnate. Fls spirally arranged in erect rac. or pan.; cor. reduced to 1 showy pet. Fr. a large woody legume. Malesia, Trop. Afr. Z10.
A. quanzensis Welw. MAKOLA. To 35m. Lvs to 30cm, lfts ovate-elliptic. Fls to 5cm, scarlet, fragrant. Fr. to 28cm; seeds black with red aril. Trop. Afr. Z9.

Agalinis Raf. Scrophulariaceae. *c*40 semi-parasitic ann. and perenn. herbs. Lvs simple, opposite. Fls in rac. or solitary; cal. 5-lobed; cor. tube campanulate, 5-lobed, 2 upper lobes arched, lower lobes spreading. Summer. US and W Indies. Z8.
A. pedicularia (L.) S.F. Blake = *Aureolaria pedicularia*.
A. purpurea (L.) Penn. Ann. to 1.2m. Lvs linear, 38×2mm. Cor. tube to 2.5cm, damask pink, throat with 2 yellow stripes and red to maroon spots.
A. tenuifolia Raf. Perenn. to 60cm. Lvs linear, 31×2mm. Cor. tube to 1.2cm, violet.
A. virginica (L.) S.F. Blake = *Aureolaria virginica*.
→*Gerardia*.

Agalmyla Bl. Gesneriaceae. 6 creeping perenn. herbs, often epiphytic. Lvs opposte, in unequal pairs. Fls in dense axill. cymes; cal. seg. 5, broadly lanceolate-obovate; cor. tubular, widening toward apex, limb 5-lobed, bilabiate. Malaysia, New Guinea. Z10.
A. parasitica (Lam.) Kuntze. SCARLET ROOT BLOSSOM. Larger lf of each pair elliptic to ovate-oblong, 15–30cm, villous beneath, glab. or pubesc. above. Cal. red villous, to 1.5cm; cor. bright red, tube yellow-pink within, lobes obtuse, 3 anterior lobes blotched purple. Malaysia.

Aganisia Lindl. Orchidaceae. 3 small epiphytic orchids related to *Zygopetalum*. Spring–summer.
A. brachystalix (Rchb. f.) Rolfe = *Otostylis brachystalix*.
A. coerulea Rchb. f. = *Acacallis cyanea*.
A. ionoptera (Lind. & Rchb. f.) Nichols. = *Koellensteinia ionoptera*.
A. kellneriana (Rchb. f.) Benth. = *Koellensteinia kellneriana*.
A. lepida Lind. & Rchb. f. = *Otostylis lepida*.
A. pulchella Lindl. Pbs remote, ovoid, terminating in single oblong-lanceolate lf to 12cm. Rac. to 12cm, basal; fls to 4cm, white, lip spotted red with yellow disc. Guyana, N Braz. Z10.
A. tricolor (Lindl.) Bois. = *Warrea warreana*.

Agapanthus L'Hérit. Liliaceae (Alliaceae). 10 perenn. herbs. Roots fleshy. St. thickened, short. Lvs basal, strap-shaped, 2-ranked, glossy, thinly fleshy. Fls tubular to campanulate in scapose term. umbels. S Afr.
A. africanus (L.) Hoffm. AFRICAN LILY; BLUE AFRICAN LILY; LILY OF THE NILE. Lvs to 35cm, ± persistent. Scape 25–60cm; per. 2.5–5cm, tubular, deep violet-blue, exceeding sta. 'Albus': fls white. 'Albus Nanus': small; fls white. 'Sapphire': fls dark blue. Z9.
A. campanulatus F.M. Leighton. Lvs to 40cm, decid. Scape 40–100cm; per. 2–3.5cm, campanulate, blue to white, exceeding sta. 'Albus': fls white. 'Iris': large heads of clear lavender-blue fls. 'Isis': to 75cm; fls deep blue, in dense heads. 'Profusion': to 90cm; fls abundant, pet. light and dark blue striped. 'Royal Blue': fls intense rich blue. 'Variegatus': lvs striped cream, fading later. ssp. *patens* (F.M. Leighton) F.M. Leighton. Smaller in all parts. Per. widely spreading. Z7.
A. caulescens Sprenger. Lvs to 60cm, forming pseudostem to 25cm. Scape to 130cm; per. to 5cm, dark or bright blue; sta. exserted. Z7.
A. inapertus Beauv. Lvs to 70cm, glaucous, decid., from short pseudostem. Scape to 180cm; per. to 5cm, bright blue to violet, tubular, equalling sta. 'Albus': fls creamy white. Z7.
A. minor Lodd. = *A. africanus*.
A. nutans F.M. Leighton. Lvs to 50cm, glaucous, decid. Scape to 90cm; fls usually nodding; per. 3.5–6cm, pale blue, not opening fully, exceeding sta. Z7.
A. orientalis F.M. Leighton = *A. praecox* ssp. *orientalis*.
A. patens F.M. Leighton = *A. campanulatus* ssp. *patens*.
A. pendulus L. Bol. Differs from *A. nutans* in indigo fls to 3.75cm, always drooping. Z7.
A. praecox Willd. Lvs to 70cm, persistent, fleshy. Scape to 100cm; per. to 7cm, bright to pale blue (-white); sta. usually exserted. 'Aureovittatus': lvs striped yellow. 'Plenus': fls double. ssp. *minimus* (Lindl.) F.M. Leighton. Lvs to 2.5cm across; per. to 5cm. ssp. *orientalis* (F.M. Leighton) F.M. Leighton. Small, forming dense clumps. Scape stout; per. to 5cm. 'Albus' ('Albidus'): fls white. 'Nanus': habit dwarf. 'Variegatus': lvs striped silvery white. Z9.
A. cvs. 'Albatross': similar to 'Maximus Albus'; fls large, white. 'Ardernei': to 90cm; fls white, pedicels and buds flushed purple. 'Blue Giant': to 1m; fls rich blue. 'Blue Moon': fls pale blue, in dense heads. 'Blue Triumphator': fls clear blue. 'Bressingham White': lvs broad; fls pure white. 'Castle of Mey': tall; fls deep blue. Giant Hybrids: to 90cm; fls in shades of blue. 'Golden Rule': lvs edged gold; fls pale blue. Headbourne Hybrids (Palmer Hybrids): to 90cm, vigorous and hardy; fls in a range of bright colours. 'Kingston Blue': st. strongly erect; fls brilliant blue. 'Liliput': dwarf, to 45cm; fls dark blue. 'Loch Hope': to 1.2m; umbels large, abundant, fls dark blue; late-flowering. 'Maximus Albus': fls large, white. 'Midnight Blue': to 40cm; fls deepest blue. 'Peter Pan': to 30cm; fls mid blue. 'Torbay': fls mid blue, profuse. 'Zella Thomas': to 75cm; fls rich blue. Z7.
A. umbellatus L'Hérit., non Redouté = *A. africanus*.
A. umbellatus Redouté non L'Hérit. = *A. praecox* ssp. *orientalis*.
A. umbellatus var. *maximus* Edwards = *A. praecox* ssp. *orientalis*.
A. weilloghii hort. = *A. inapertus*.

Agapetes D. Don ex G. Don f. Ericaceae. 95 everg. scandent shrubs. Br. slender, arching, ± lenticellate. Lvs leathery, large and sparse or small and clothing st., v. short-stalked. Fls solitary or in short cymes, axill., pendent, tubular-urceolate, pentagonal, waxy, lobes 5, short. E Asia to N Aus. Z9.
A. affinis (Griff.) Airy Shaw. Lvs to 20cm, oblong-lanceolate, whorled. Fls to 1.5cm, green, white or brick-red, cymose. Himal. to Assam.
A. buxifolia Nutt. Lvs to 3cm, ovate-oblong. Fls to 2.5cm, bright red. Bhutan.
A. glabra (Griff.) C.B. Clarke = *A. affinis*.
A. 'Ludgvan Cross' (*A. rugosum* × *A. serpens.*) Lvs to 3.5cm, ovate. Fls pink with red V-marking; cal. crimson. Gdn origin.

A. macrantha Benth. & Hook. f. Lvs to 12cm, laurel-like. Fls to 4.5cm, white-rose with red V-markings, lobes tipped green. NE India.
A. mannii Hemsl. Lvs to 2cm, elliptic. Fls to 1cm, pale green to off-white, throat darker green.
A. moorei Hemsl. Lvs to 7cm, elliptic. Fls to 2.5cm, orange-red tipped green at first. Burm.
A. obovata (Wight) Hook. f. Lvs to 1.8cm, obovate-spathulate. Fls to 0.6cm, green flushed dull red. Assam.
A. rugosa (Hook.) Sleumer. Lvs to 2cm, ovate-lanceolate, rugose. Fls to 2cm, white marbled or banded purple-red. Khasi Hills. Z8.
A. serpens (Wight) Sleumer. Lvs to 2cm, lanceolate-ovate. Fls to 2cm, orange-red to scarlet with crimson V-markings. Nepal, Bhutan, N Assam. 'Nepal Cream': fls ivory.
A. setigera (Wallich) D. Don ex G. Don. Lvs to 15cm, lanceolate. Fls to 2.5cm, red. India.
A. speciosa Hemsl. Lvs to 11cm, lanceolate-oblong. Fls to 4cm, crimson with darker V-markings, lobes green-yellow. Probably Burm.
A. variegata (Roxb.) G. Don. Lvs to 20cm, broadly lanceolate. Fls to 2.5cm, pale red to yellow-green with dark red banding. Assam.
A. variegata var. *macrantha* (Hook. f.) Airy Shaw = *A. macrantha*.
→*Pentapterygium*.

Agarista G. Don. Ericaceae. 20 small everg. shrubs. Lvs leathery, entire. Fls in drooping racemose pan.; cor. urceolate, 5-lobed. S Amer., Maur. Z9.
A. neriifolia G. Don. To 60cm. Lvs to 8cm, lanceolate. Fls to 0.8cm, scarlet, limb pale pink. Braz.
A. pulchra G. Don. To 60cm. Lvs c2.5cm, ovate-cordate. Fls scarlet or pale green. Braz.
→*Andromeda*.

Agastache Clayton ex Gronov. MEXICAN HYSSOP; GIANT HYSSOP. Labiatae. c20 aromatic upright or procumbent perennials. Inflorescence spicate or narrowly paniculate, fls in dense verticils, bracts often conspicuous; cal. turbinate or tubular, with 5 teeth; cor. tubular, 2-lipped; sta. 4, paired, usually exserted beyond upper lip. N Amer., China & Jap.
A. anethiodora Britt. = *A. foeniculum*.
A. anisata hort. = *A. foeniculum*.
A. barberi Epling. St. to 60cm unbranched. Lvs 3–5cm, deltoid to deltoid-ovate, coarsely crenate-serrate. Verticils 15–30cm, in a loose, showy, red-purple spike; cal. red-purple, cor. rose, to 30mm. Ariz. to N Mex. 'Firebird': fls orange tinted copper. 'Tutti-frutti': lvs strongly scented; fls raspberry purple.
A. barberi hort. = *A. pallidiflora*.
A. cana (Hook.) Wooton & Standl. St. 50–60cm, much-branched. Lower lvs 1–3cm, deltoid to deltoid-ovate, crenate-serrate or entire. Minutely puberulent, gland-dotted. Infl. paniculate or interrupted spikes to 30cm; cal. off-white or tinged rose; cor. rose, 16–25mm. S US. Z9.
A. foeniculum (Pursh) Kuntze. ANISE HYSSOP. St. 50–80cm, little-branched. Lvs 5–8cm, anise-scented, ovate or deltoid-ovate, serrate, densely puberulent beneath, white or glaucous. Spikes 4–8cm, pubesc., compact; bracts ovate, often violet; cal. violet (white in albino plants); cor. blue or white, 6–8mm. N Amer. 'Alabaster' ('Alba'): fls white. 'Fragrant Delight': fls blue, yellow, red, pink and white, each coloured spike with individual fragrance from peppermint to aniseed. Z8.
A. mexicana (Kunth) Link & Epling. St. 50–60cm. Lvs 4–6cm, lanceolate or ovate-lanceolate, apex acute, hirtellous or glab., serrate. Verticils 12-fld in a spike to 30cm, cal. green or rose-tinged; cor. rose or crimson, 20–27mm. Mex. Z9.
A. nepetoides (L.) Kuntze. YELLOW GIANT HYSSOP. St. 150–180cm, stout. Lvs 5–15cm, ovate, apex acute, crenate. Verticils to 12.5cm; cor. yellow-green. S Canada to SE US.
A. pallidiflora Rydb. St. 40–100cm. Lvs 2.5–4cm, deltoid-ovate, apex obtuse, crenate-serrate hirtellous to pubesc. Spikes cylindrical cal. green, rose or deep purple; cor. white or rose, 9–18mm. N Amer. Z8.
A. rugosa (Fisch. & Mey.) Kuntze. St. to 120cm, branching above. Lvs 6–8cm, ovate, apex acute to acuminate, serrate, glab. to hirtellous. Spikes cylindrical 5–10cm; bracts inconspicuous; cal. rose or violet with white teeth; cor. violet to rose, 7–10mm. China, Jap. Z8.
A. urticifolia (Benth.) Kuntze. St. to 2m. Lvs 3.5–8cm, ovate to deltoid-ovate, often acuminate, coarsely serrate, glab. to pubesc. Infl. 4–15cm, tapering, compact; bracts ovate to lanceolate, acuminate; cal. green or rose; cor. violet to rose, tube 8–13mm. W US. Z8.
→*Cedronella*.

Agastachys R. Br. Proteaceae. 1 suckering shrub to 3m. Lvs 2.5–8cm, narrow-oblong. Fls white to cream, to 0.8cm, clustered in term. 'spikes' to 12cm. Summer. Tasm.
A. odorata R. Br. WHITE WARATAH.

Agathis Salisb. DAMMAR PINE; KAURI PINE. Araucariaceae. 20 everg. conifers. Bark resinous. Br. whorled and tiered. Lvs flat, ovate to lanceolate, spiralling on br., alt. on branchlets, bronze at first, then olive green. ♂ cones subsessile, cylindric, axillary; ♀ cones stalked, globose, subterminal. Sumatra and Philippine Is. to NZ. Mostly Z9.
A. alba (Bl.) Foxw. = A. dammara.
A. atropurpurea B. Hyland. BLUE KAURI; To 50m. Bark purple-black. Lvs to 4.5cm, oval-elliptic, glaucous. Aus. (N Queensld).
A. australis (D. Don) Salisb. KAURI; KAURI PINE. To 50m. Bark purple-grey. Lvs to 6cm, ovate-lanceolate (larger and broader on young plants), glaucescent mid-green. NZ. Z9.
A. beccarii Warb. = A. borneensis.
A. borneensis Warb. To 50m+. Bark dark grey. Lvs to 9cm, ovate-elliptic, revolute, pale lustrous green. Malaysia, Sumatra, Borneo.
A. dammara (Lamb.) Rich. AMBOINA PINE. To 50m. Bark red-grey. Lvs to 12cm, oblong-lanceolate, obtuse, revolute. Malaysia.
A. dammara (Lamb.) Rich. in part = A. philippinensis.
A. lanceolata Lindl. ex Warb. KOGHIS KAURI. To 40m. Bark rusty, scaly. Lvs to 8cm, lanceolate-elliptic, acute, revolute (juv. lvs larger). New Caledonia.
A. latifolia Meijden = A. borneensis.
A. loranthifolia Salisb. = A. dammara.
A. macrophylla (Lindl.) Mast. To 30m+. Bark white, scaly. Lvs to 18cm, ovate-lanceolate, acuminate, revolute, leathery. Solomon Is., New Hebrides, Fiji.
A. microstachya J.F. Bail. & C.T. White. ATHERTON KAURI; BULL KAURI. To 50m. Bark brown-grey. Lvs to 7cm, lanceolate-elliptic, obtuse. Aus. (N Queensld).
A. moorei (Lindl.) Mast. KAURI BLANC. To 30m. Bark ivory to ash-grey. Lvs to 7cm (juvs to 20cm, stalked), lanceolate to elliptic, acute, dark above, pale beneath. New Caledonia.
A. obtusa (Lindl.) Mast. = A. macrophylla.
A. orientalis (D. Don) Hook. = A. dammara.
A. ovata Warb. SCRUB KAURI. Shrub to 1m or tree to 8m+. Bark rough, grey. Lvs to 11cm, ovate-elliptic, tapered and curved, deep green above, blue-green beneath. New Caledonia.
A. palmerstonii (F. Muell.) Bail. = A. robusta.
A. philippinensis Warb. To 60m. Bark red-grey. Lvs to 5cm, narrow-lanceolate, blunt, dark green (juv. to 7cm, oval, acute). Melanesia, Philipp.
A. rhomboidalis Warb. = A. borneensis.
A. robusta (C. Moore ex F. Muell.) Bail. SMOOTH BARK KAURI; QUEENSLAND KAURI. To 50m. Bark grey-brown, exfoliating. Lvs to 12cm, lanceolate to elliptic-ovate, revolute, dark green tinged red at first. Aus. (S Queensld).
A. vitiensis (Seem.) Benth. & Hook. f. = A. macrophylla.

Agathosma Willd. Rutaceae. 135 aromatic heath-like shrubs and subshrubs. St. erect or decumbent. Lvs crowded. Fls 5-merous, 1 to few in axils or term. clusters. S Afr. Z9.
A. apiculata G. Mey. Lvs to 8mm, ovate to oblong-lanceolate, glab. Fls in term. umbels; pet. to 4mm, white.
A. betulina (Bergius) Pill. Lvs to 20mm, obovate, serrate, glab. Fls solitary, terminating branchlets; pet. to 10mm, pink.
A. ciliata (L.) Link. Lvs to 12mm, ovate-lanceolate, ± ciliate. Fls in term. clusters; pet. to 5mm, white.
A. corymbosa (Montin) G. Don. Lvs to 6mm, ovate-lanceolate, imbricate, pubesc. beneath. Fls in terminal umbels; pet. to 6mm, white, lilac or purple.
A. crenulata (L.) Pill. BUCHU. Lvs to 35mm, ovate to oblong-lanceolate, serrate, glab. Fls solitary terminating branchlets; pet. to 9mm, white.
A. hirta (Lam.) Bartling & Wendl. Lvs to 15mm, ovate-lanceolate, concave, glab. above, pilose beneath. Fls in term. clusters and axils; pet. to 5mm, white or red.
A. imbricata (L.) Willd. Lvs to 5mm, linear-lanceolate to ovate, glab., concave above, sometimes pubesc. beneath. Fls in term. clusters; pet. to 7.5mm, pale purple.
A. ovata (Thunb.) Pill. Lvs to 15mm, oblong-orbicular, glab. or puberulent. Fls in axillary clusters; pet. to 4.5mm, white.
A. pulchella (L.) Link. Lvs to 6mm, ovate to ovate-lanceolate, glab. Fls 1–2 in axils; pet. to 3mm, white to pale mauve.
A. rugosa Link. Lvs to 8mm, lanceolate to oblong-lanceolate, imbricate, rugulose, puberulous. Fls in term. umbels; pet. to 6.5mm, white tinged mauve.
A. ventenatiana (Roem. & Schult.) Bartling & Wendl. = A. corymbosa.

A. villosa (Willd.) Willd. = A. corymbosa.
→Barosma and Diosma.

AGAVACEAE Endl. (including Dracaenaceae and Nolinaceae). 18/580. Agave, Beschorneria, Cordyline, Dasylirion, Doryanthes, Dracaena, Furcraea, Hesperaloe, Manfreda, Nolina, Phormium, Polianthes, Sansevieria, Yucca.

Agave L. CENTURY PLANT; MAGUEY. Agavaceae. c300 succulent perennials. Some st. short, stout. Lvs large in rosettes, often rigid, with a sharp term. spine and marginal teeth, sometimes filiferous. Infl. a scapose, term. spike, rac. or pan.; fls in umbellate clusters; perianth tubular or infundibular, tep. 6, erect to curved; sta. 6, exserted. N Amer., N S Amer. Z9 unless specified.
A. albicans Jacobi = A. celsii var. albicans.
A. albomarginata Gent. Lvs to 125×4cm, narrowly linear-lanceolate, ascending, convex beneath, grey-green, margin white, horny; teeth to 4mm, remote, white, recurved, term.; spine to 1.5cm, grey. Infl. to 6m, a slender spike, loosely fld; fls to 4cm, yellow-green. Mex.
A. americana L. Lvs to 200×25cm, curved or reflexed, lanceolate, acuminate, light green to grey, undulate to crenate; teeth to 10mm, brown to grey, term. spine to 5cm, brown to grey. Infl. to 9m, with 15–35 spreading, umbellate br., fls to 10cm, pale yellow. E Mex. 'Marginata': lvs widely edged yellow. 'Mediopicta': lvs with wide central pale yellow stripe. 'Striata': lvs striped yellow to white. 'Variegata': lvs edged white. var. expansa (Jacobi) Gent. Lvs to 150×25cm, erect or ascending, glaucous grey, margin straight or crenate; teeth to 8mm, at 4cm intervals, brown to grey, terminal spine to 3cm. Infl. to 9m, a pan. with 20 to 30 lat. br.; fls to 8.5cm, pale yellow. W Mex. var. oaxacensis Gent. Lvs to 200×24cm, fleshy, spreading, linear, convex near base, glaucous-white, undulate or repand; teeth to 5mm, at 3cm intervals, dark brown, sometimes flexuous, term. spine to 3cm. Infl. to 10m, a pan., with some 30 umbels; fls to 10cm, yellow-green. Mex. var. picta (Salm-Dyck) A. Terracc. Lvs larger, green, sometimes with yellow margins, furrowed and straight or curved.
A. 'Andromeda' Lvs to 1m in a compact, rounded rosette, almost totally white.
A. angustifolia Haw. Lvs to 120×10cm, fleshy, firm, ascending to horizontal, lanceolate to linear, base attenuate, entire to undulate, pale green to glaucous grey, sometimes concave above, convex beneath, teeth to 5mm, dark brown, term. spine to 3.5cm, dark brown. Infl. to 5m, with 10 to 18 small umbels; fls to 6.5cm, yellow to green, short-lived. Trop. Amer. 'Marginata': lvs deeply edged white.
A. applanata Koch ex Jacobi. Lvs to 140×10cm, glaucous-grey, rigid-fleshy, linear-lanceolate, strongly fibrous; teeth to 15mm, sharp, remote, dark brown, term. spine to 7cm, dark red-brown becoming grey. Infl. to 8m, a pan.; fls yellow. N & E Mex.
A. asperrima Jacobi = A. scabra.
A. atrovirens Karw. ex Salm-Dyck. Lvs to 200×40cm, succulent, lanceolate, green to glaucous, smooth, concave above, convex beneath; teeth to 7mm, brown or brown-grey, remote, term. spine to 5cm. Infl. to 12m, a pan., with 18 to 30 lat. br. above; fls to 10cm, red to purple at first, becoming yellow, fleshy. Mex.
A. attenuata Salm-Dyck. Lvs to 70×16cm, succulent, ovate-oblong, acuminate, pale yellow-green to glaucous grey, entire to serrulate, plane to concave, term. spine 0. Infl. to 3.5m, a rac., densely fld; fls to 5cm, yellow-green. Mex.
A. aurea Brandg. Lvs to 110×12cm, arching, narrowly lanceolate to linear, fleshy, base rounded, glaucous to green, sometimes undulate; teeth to 0.7cm, at 2cm intervals, light brown to dark brown, term. spine to 3.5cm, dark brown or grey-brown. Infl. to 5m, a diffuse pan., with 15 to 25 umbels above; peduncle red; fls to 7cm, yellow or yellow-orange, red in bud. Baja Calif.
A. bourgaei Trel. Lvs to 150×15cm, grey, repand; teeth triangular, at 1cm intervals; spine to 3cm, grey. Infl. to 3m, a pan.; fls to 7.5cm. C Mex.
A. bovicornuta Gent. Lvs to 80×17cm, spathulate to lanceolate, green or yellow-green, crenate, teeth to 12mm, dark brown to grey-brown. Infl. to 7m, a pan., with 20–30 lat. br. above; fls to 6.5cm, yellow-green. Mex.
A. bracteosa S. Wats. ex Engelm. Lvs to 70×5cm, narrowly lanceolate, green-yellow, succulent, arching, minutely serrulate, convex beneath, term. spine 0. Infl. 170cm, a spicate rac., erect to ascending, densely fld; fls to 2.6cm, white to pale yellow. NE Mex.
A. brevispina Trel. Lvs to 100×10cm, broadly lanceolate, dull dark green; teeth straight or recurved, furrowed. Infl. to 4m, a pan.; fls to 4cm, yellow. Haiti.
A. candalabrum Tod. = A. cantala.
A. cantala Roxb. Lvs to 200×9cm, elongate, narrowly linear, long-acuminate, fleshy, strongly fibrous, light to dark green;

teeth to 4mm, brown, at 3cm intervals, term. spine to 15mm. Infl. to 8m, a diffuse pan., with some 20 umbels above; fls to 8.5cm, green tinged red or purple. Trop. Amer.

A. carchariodonta Pamp. = *A. xylonacantha*.

A. celsii Hook. Lvs to 70×13cm, ascending, spathulate or oblong to ovate, short-acuminate, concave above, convex beneath, green to glaucous grey, sometimes undulate, teeth to 3mm, closely set, white to red-brown, term. spine to 2cm, green-brown or brown. Infl. to 2.5cm, spicate, densely fld; fls to 6cm, fleshy, exterior green, interior yellow to red-purple or lavender. E Mex. var. *albicans* (Jacobi) Gent. Lvs pale glaucous. Tep. larger, to 2.7cm. E Mex.

A. chrysantha Peebles. Lvs to 75×10cm, yellow to grey-green, lanceolate to linear-lanceolate, grooved, rigid, teeth to 1cm, at 3cm intervals, erect or flexed, term. spine to 4.5cm, brown or grey-brown. Infl. to 7m, a pan., with 8–18 clustered umbels above; fls to 5.5cm, yellow. Ariz.

A. cochlearis Jacobi = *A. salmiana*.

A. colimana Gent. Lvs to 70×2.5cm, linear, green with brown margin, glab., terminal spine to 8mm, dark brown to grey-brown. Infl. to 3m, spicate, erect, slender; fls to 5cm, pale yellow or lavender. W Mex.

A. colorata Gent. Lvs to 60×18cm, few, lanceolate to ovate, short-acuminate, firm, sometimes concave above, convex beneath, glaucous, sometimes tinged red, crenate; teeth to 1cm, at 3cm intervals, grey to brown, term. spine to 5cm, grey to brown. Infl. to 3m, a pan., densely-fld, with 15–20 umbels above; fls to 7cm, yellow, red in bud. Mex.

A. cubensis Haw. = *Furcraea hexapetala*.

A. cupreata Trel. & Berger. Lvs to 80×20cm, bright green, ovate to broadly lanceolate, plane to somewhat concave above, strongly crenate, teeth to 15mm, copper-coloured, on prominent teats, at intervals of 6cm, erect or curved, term. spine to 5cm, light brown to grey. Infl. to 7m, a pan., with diffuse umbels of fls; fls to 6cm, orange-yellow. W Mex.

A. decipiens Bak. To 3m, arborescent. Lvs to 100×10cm, fleshy, narrowly lanceolate, acuminate, concave, with enlarged, thick-ened bases, teeth to 3mm, at 2cm intervals, dark brown, term. spine to 2cm, dark brown Infl. to 5m, a pan., with some 12 umbellate br. above; fls to 8cm, green-yellow. Flor.

A. deserti Engelm. Lvs to 40×8cm, thick, rigid, linear to linear-lanceolate, acuminate, concave above, convex beneath, glaucous grey, teeth to 0.8cm, at 3cm intervals, grey, term. spine to 4cm, light brown to grey. Infl. to 4cm, a pan., with 6–15 short umbellate br. above; fls to 6cm, yellow. Calif., Ariz., Baja Calif.

A. desmettiana Jacobi. Lvs to 80×12cm, arching, brittle, narrowly lanceolate, base attenuate, finely fibrous, sometimes armed, teeth to 2mm, chestnut brown, term. spine to 3cm, dark brown. Infl. to 3m, a pan., with 20–25 lat. umbellate br. above; fls to 6cm, pale yellow. E Mex.

A. difformis Berger. Lvs to 80×6cm, ascending, yellow-green or green, margin light grey, concave above, convex beneath, some-times undulate, teeth to 1cm, at 3cm intervals, grey to dark brown, term. spine to 3cm, grey to dark brown. Infl. a spike to 5m, slender; fls to 4cm, light green to yellow and pink. Mex.

A. eborispina Hester = *A. utahensis* var. *eborispina*.

A. ellemeetiana Jacobi. Lvs to 70×20cm, few, succulent, oblong to ovate, acuminate, slightly recurved, smooth, bright green, finely serrulate, term. spine 0. Infl. to 4.5m, a rac., erect, densely-fld; fls to 4cm, pale yellow-green. Mex.

A. expansa Jacobi = *A. americana* var. *expansa*.

A. fenzliana Jacobi. Lvs to 150×20cm, lanceolate, dull light green or yellow-green, teeth small, unequal, dark brown, curved, raised on prominences, terminal spine to 6cm, brown. Infl. to 10m, a pan.; fls to 8cm, yellow. Mex.

A. ferdinandi-regis A. Berger = *A. victoriae-reginae*.

A. ferox Koch. Lvs to 1.25m×3.25cm, spreading to prostrate, tip recurved, keeled beneath, lustrous dark green, teeth to 2.5cm, dark brown to black, hooked; term. spine 8cm. Infl. to 10m, a pan.; fls to 8cm, yellow. Mex. Sometimes treated as a var. of *A. salmiana*.

Á. filifera Salm-Dyck. Lvs to 30×4cm, lanceolate, acuminate, convex above and beneath, finely filiferous, term. spine to 2cm, grey. Infl. a spike to 2.5m, densely-fld above; fls to 3.5cm, red. E Mex. 'Compacta': small; lvs to 10cm, striped white, spines black.

A. foetida L. = *Furcraea foetida*.

A. fourcroydes Lem. Lvs to 180×12cm, rigid, linear, acuminate, teeth to 6mm, dark brown, slender, term. spine to 3cm, dark brown. Infl. to 6m, a pan., with 10 to 18 umbels above; fls to 7cm, yellow-green. Mex. Z8.

A. franzosinii Bak. Lvs to 220×35cm, narrowly lanceolate, reflexed or recurved, white-grey or blue-grey, teeth to 10mm, remote, triangular, dark brown, term. spine to 6cm, dark brown. Infl. to 11.5m, a large pan.; fls to 7.5cm, yellow. Mex.

A. funifera Lem. = *Hesperaloe funifera*.

A. funkiana Koch & Bouché. Lvs to 80×5.5cm, rigid, dark to yellow-green, concave above, clasping at base, often with a pale central stripe; teeth to 5mm, at intervals of 2.5cm, grey to brown, slender, term. spine to 3cm, white to brown. Infl. a slender spike to 4.5m; fls to 4.5cm, pale glaucous green. E Mex.

A. ghiesbreghtii Lem. ex Jacobi. Lvs to 40×10cm, few, ovate or broadly lanceolate to deltoid or linear, straight or curved, light green to dark green, teeth to 8mm, grey to brown, term. spine to 4cm, grey to brown, subulate, shallowly furrowed above. Infl. a spike to 4m, densely-fld; fls to 5cm, purple to brown-green. Mex.

A. gracilispina Engelm. ex Trel. = *A. americana*.

A. guadalajarana Trel. Lvs to 30×12cm, rigid, oblong to obovate, obtuse, overlapping, glaucous to dull grey, basal teeth to 4mm, at 10mm intervals, red-brown to grey, apical teeth larger, remote, term. spine to 2.5cm, grey. Infl. to 5m, a pan. of 15–20 small umbels; fls to 6cm, red to purple. Mex.

A. guiengola Gent. Lvs to 50×25cm, white glaucous-grey, ascending, ovate to ovate-lanceolate, short-acuminate, densely papillate, dentate-serrate, terminal spine to 3cm, dark brown. Infl. to 2m, an erect spike; fls to 3.5cm, pale yellow or white-yellow. Mex.

A. horrida Lem. ex Jacobi. Lvs to 35×7.5cm, rigid-fleshy, ovate or obovate to elliptic-lanceolate, short-acuminate, lustrous dark green to yellow-green, convex beneath, teeth to 1.5cm, light grey, term. spine to 4cm, red-brown to grey. Infl. to 2.5m, a slender spike; fls to 4cm, variously coloured. Mex.

A. kaibabensis McKelv. = *A. utahensis* ssp. *kaibabensis*.

A. karwinskii Zucc. St. to 3m, arborescent. Lvs to 40×3cm, spreading to ascending, narrowly oblong to linear-lanceolate, acuminate, furrowed or concave above, convex beneath, teeth to 5mm, dark brown, triangular, at 4cm intervals, term. spine to 4cm, grey to black. Infl. to 3.5m, a diffuse pan., branched above; fls to 6cm, pale yellow to green. C Mex.

A. kewensis Jacobi. Lvs to 180×15cm, arching, succulent, narrowly lanceolate, yellow-green, furrowed, teeth to 4mm, at 3cm intervals, term. spine to 4.5cm. Infl. to 5m, a pan. of 12–20 umbels; fls to 7.5cm, yellow. Mex.

A. latissima Jacobi = *A. atrovirens*.

A. lechuguilla Torr. Lvs to 50×4cm, erect to ascending or falcately spreading, linear-lanceolate, convex beneath, concave above, yellow-green to light green, often pale-striped above, teeth to 0.5cm, light brown to grey, term. spine to 4cm, grey. Infl. to 3.5m, a spike; fls to 4.5cm, yellow or red to purple. Tex., N Mex.

A. lophantha Schiede. Lvs to 70×5cm, thin, pliant, pale green or yellow-green, lanceolate to linear, spreading sometimes concave above, sinuous to crenate, horny, teeth to 8mm on low broad teats, term. spine to 2cm, grey to red-brown. Infl. to 4.5cm, a slender spike; fls to 4.7cm, pale grey-green to yellow. E Mex.

A. lurida Ait. Lvs to 150×18cm, ascending or spreading, ensi-form, glaucous-grey to dull green, teeth to 6mm, regular, at 2cm intervals, term. spine to 45mm, grey-brown. Infl. to 7m, a pan. of some 20 umbellate br., diffusely spreading; fls to 6.5cm, yellow-green. Mex.

A. macroacantha Zucc. Lvs to 35×3cm, rigid, spreading, elongate-lanceolate to linear-lanceolate, blue-grey, convex be-neath, sometimes undulate, teeth to 4mm, at 3cm intervals, dark brown, term. spine to 3.5cm, grey to dark brown. Infl. to 2m, a slender pan. with 10–14 spreading br. above; fls to 6cm, pruinose-green, tinged purple. Mex.

A. maculosa Rose = *Manfreda maculosa*.

A. marmorata Roezl. Lvs to 135×30cm, spreading, lanceolate to oblanceolate, spathulate, light grey to light green or white, roughly scabrous, often undulate, sinuate, teeth to 12mm, at 5cm intervals, term. spine to 3cm. Infl. to 6.5m, a pan. of 20–25 diffuse umbels; fls to 5cm, bright yellow or golden yellow. C Mex.

A. micracantha Salm-Dyck = *A. celsii*.

A. mirandorensis Jacobi = *A. desmettiana*.

A. missionum Trel. Lvs to 250×20cm, broadly lanceolate, grey-green to dark grey, teeth small, triangular, straight or slightly curved, term. spine to 2.5cm, grey to brown. Infl. to 7m, a pan.; fls to 6.5cm, yellow. Virgin Is.

A. mitis Mart. ex Salm-Dyck = *A. celsii*.

A. mitriformis Jacobi = *A. salmiana*.

A. multifilifera Gent. Lvs to 80×3.5cm, erect-ascending to recurved, narrowly linear-lanceolate, filiferous, pale green, teeth 0, term. spine to 1.5cm. Infl. to 5m, a densely fld spike, erect; fls to 4.3cm, pale green tinged pink, waxy. Mex.

A. murpheyi F. Gibson. Lvs to 65×8cm, firm, linear, short-acuminate light blue-green to yellow-green, undulate, teeth to 4mm, at 2cm intervals, term. spine to 2cm, dark brown to grey. Infl. to 4m, a bulbiliferous pan.; fls to 7.5cm, pale green, apices purple to brown. Ariz., Mex. (Sonora).

A. neomexicana Wooton & Standl. Lvs to 45×12cm, rigid, oblong to ovate-lanceolate, short-acuminate, blue-green, concave above, rounded beneath, teeth to 7mm, term. spine to 4cm. Infl. to 4m, a pan., with 10–17 umbellate br. above; fls to 6.5cm, red to orange in bud, becoming yellow. New Mex.

A. nevadensis (Engelm.) Hester = *A. utahensis* var. *nevadensis*.

A. nizandensis Cutak. Lvs to 30×2.5cm, linear to lanceolate, flat above, dark green with light green central stripe, convex beneath, serrulate but without marginal spines, term. spine to 8mm, dark red. Infl. to 2m, a rac. or a pan.; fls to 4cm, pale green or yellow-green. Mex.

A. ocahui Gent. Lvs to 50×2.5cm, erect to ascending, usually rigid, linear-lanceolate, flat above, margin red-brown, teeth 0, terminal spine to 2cm, grey-brown. Infl. to 3m, a slender spike, densely-fld; fls to 3.8cm, yellow. Mex.

A. odorata Pers. = *Furcraea hexapetala*.

A. pachyacantha Trel. = *A. shawii*.

A. palmeri Engelm. Lvs to 75×10cm, rigid, lanceolate, acuminate, glaucous-green or pale green, sometimes tinged red, convex beneath, teeth small, terminal spine to 6cm, fine, brown to grey. Infl. to 5m, a pan., br. horizontal; fls to 5.5cm, red in bud becoming pale yellow-green to white. New Mex. and Ariz. to Mex.

A. parrasana Berger. Lvs to 30×12cm, rigid, overlapping, ovate or obovate, acute to acuminate, dull green with a light blue-grey bloom, flat to concave above, teeth to 1.5cm, grey-brown, curved, term. spine to 4cm, grey to dark brown. Infl. to 4m, a pan.; fls to 6cm, yellow, flushed red or purple. NC Mex.

A. parryi Engelm. Lvs to 40×12cm, in rounded rosettes, overlapping, rigid, broadly oblong to obovate, flat to concave above, rounded beneath, glaucous grey to light green, teeth to 7mm, grey to dark brown, term. spine to 3cm, dark brown becoming grey. Infl. to 6m, a stout pan.; fls to 7.5cm, red to pink in bud, becoming yellow. SW US to Mex. Z8.

A. parviflora Torr. Lvs to 20×1.8cm, linear-lanceolate, rigid in a dense rosette, dark green with broad white tracery left by contact with other lvs, margins with curling white fibres. Infl. spicate, to 1.5m; fls to 2cm, green-yellow. Ariz. to N. Mex.

A. peacockii Crouch. Lvs to 145×16cm, rigid, erect to spreading or horizontal, ensiform to obovate-lanceolate, dark green, flat to concave above, convex beneath, fibrous, teeth to 2.5cm, hooked, term. spine to 9cm, acicular to subulate, grey to dark brown. Infl. to 5m, a spike or a rac.; fls to 5.5cm, green to yellow, marked red. C Mex.

A. pedunculifera Trel. Lvs to 80×15cm, succulent, ascending-horizontal, lanceolate or ovate, acuminate, flat to concave above, base convex, pale green to green-white, denticulate, term. spine to 1cm. Infl. to 3m, a densely-fld spike, erect or recurved; fls to 5.2cm, yellow. Mex.

A. pendula Schnittsp. Lvs to 75×11cm, ascending to arching, narrowly lanceolate, flat to concave above, light green or yellow-green with a pale central stripe, teeth small, brown, term. spine to 8mm, brown. Infl. to 180cm, a slender spike, pendent, loosely-fld above; fls to 4.5cm, green, sometimes tinged lavender, interior white. Mex.

A. picta Salm-Dyck = *A. americana* var. *picta*.

A. polyacantha Haw. Lvs to 65×10cm, ascending to arching, fleshy, oblong to lanceolate, acuminate, dark green or yellow-green, usually plane, teeth to 3mm, closely spaced, dark brown to red, term. spine to 2.5cm, dark brown. Infl. a spike to 3m; fls to 5cm, red. E Mex.

A. potatorum Zucc. Lvs to 40×18cm, fleshy-rigid, obovate to lanceolate, glaucous white to green, undulate to crenate, teeth to 1cm, rust-brown to grey-brown, term. spines to 4.5cm, brown. Infl. to 6m, a rac. or a pan.; fls to 8cm, light green to yellow, tinged red-purple in bud. Mex.

A. potatorum var. *verschaffeltii* (Lem.) Berger. = *A. potatorum*.

A. pumila De Smet ex Bak. Dwarf, persisting in juvenile form for several years. Young lvs to 4×4cm, succulent grey-green, striped dark green beneath, ovate-rotund, concave above, margin white, with a few small teeth, terminal spine small, conical; mature lvs 38×4.5cm, rigid, deltoid-lanceolate, grey-green without stripes, margin white-horny; teeth to 2mm; spine to 1.5cm. Infl. not seen. Mex.

A. salmiana Otto ex Salm-Dyck. Lvs to 200×35cm, fleshy, erect-spreading, linear-lanceolate, acuminate, repand, teeth to 10mm, term. spine to 10cm, dark brown. Infl. to 8m, a broad pan., with 15–20 umbels above; fls to 11cm, fleshy, yellow or green-yellow. C Mex.

A. sartorii Koch = *A. pendula*.

A. scabra Salm-Dyck. Lvs to 110×16cm, rigid, lanceolate, acuminate, plane above, convex beneath, glaucous grey to light green, scabrous teeth to 15mm, often deflected, term. spine to 6cm. Infl. to 6m, a pan. with 8–12 br. above; fls to 8cm, yellow. Tex., N Mex.

A. schidigera Lem. Lvs to 50×4cm, thin, pliant, spreading, line-

ar, acuminate, light green, convex beneath, white-filiferous, term. spine to 2cm, grey to brown. Infl. to 3.5m, a slender spike, loosely-fld; fls to 4.5cm, yellow to green or red-purple. Mex.

A. schottii Engelm. Lvs to 50×1cm, pliant, incurved, linear, green to yellow-green, convex beneath, sparsely filiferous, term. spine to 12mm, grey. Infl. to 2.5m, a slender spike; fls to 4cm, yellow. Ariz. to Mex. (Sonora).

A. seemanniana Jacobi. Lvs to 50×20cm, succulent, ovate to oblong-spathulate, glaucous to light green, usually plane, undulate to crenate, teeth to 1cm, dark brown or grey-brown, term. spine to 4cm, dark brown to grey. Infl. to 4m, a pan. with 18–30 umbels above; fls to 7cm, yellow. C Amer.

A. shawii Engelm. Lvs to 50×20cm, fleshy-rigid, ovate to elongate-spathulate, acuminate, lustrous light to dark green, teeth to 2cm, red to dark brown, hooked, term. spine to 4cm, acicular, dark red-brown. Infl. to 4m, a pan., many-fld; fls to 10cm, green-yellow, red or purple in bud. S Calif. to Mex. (Sonora).

A. sisalana Perring. SISAL. Lvs to 130×12cm, spreading, fleshy, narrowly lanceolate or ensiform, bright green, smooth, fibrous, sometimes denticulate, terminal spine to 2.5cm, dark brown. Infl. to 6m, a diffuse pan., often bulbiferous; fls to 6.5cm, yellow-green, foul-scented. E Mex. 'Minima': habit small; lvs tinted blue.

A. sobria Brandg. Lvs to 80×10cm, lanceolate to linear, acuminate, flat to concave above, grey-green, undulate, teeth to 1cm, remote, red-brown, term. spine to 6cm. Infl. to 4m, a slender pan., sometimes arcuate, with 12–20 short br.; fls to 5.5cm, light yellow. Baja Calif.

A. striata Zucc. Lvs to 60×1cm, spreading, rigid, linear, convex above, grey-green striped dark green, term. spine to 5cm, red-brown to dark grey. Infl. to 2.5m, an erect spike, loosely-fld; fls to 4cm, yellow-green to red or purple. Mex. 'Nana': dwarf; lvs small, tinted grey.

A. stricta Salm-Dyck. Lvs to 50×1cm, rigid, erect-spreading or incurved, linear-lanceolate, green, scabrous, serrulate, term. spine to 2cm, grey. Infl. to 2.5m, a spike; fls to 3cm, red to purple. Mex. 'Dwarf': habit small and dense.

A. toumeyana Trel. Lvs to 30×2cm, rigid, linear to subulate, dark green, filiferous, term. spine to 2cm, grey to brown. Infl. to 2.5m, a rac.; fls to 2.5cm, green and white or pale yellow. Ariz.

A. triangularis Jacobi. Lvs to 60×7cm, rigid, spreading, triangular-lanceolate, long-acuminate, dul grey-green or yellow-green, margin grey-horny, sometimes toothed, term. spine to 4cm, grey. Infl. unknown. Mex.

A. univittata Haw. = *A. lophantha*.

A. utahensis Engelm. Lvs to 30×3cm, linear-lanceolate, convex beneath, grey-green, teeth to 4mm, triangular, light grey, term. spine to 4cm, light grey. Infl. to 4m, a spike, a rac. or a pan.; fls to 3cm, yellow. SW US. ssp. *kaibabensis* (McKelv.) Gent. Lvs to 50×5cm, numerous, rigid, lanceolate, acuminate, light green; teeth to 5mm, white to grey; spine to 4cm, white to grey. Infl. to 5m, a pan., stout; lat. br. numerous, to 10cm. SW US. var. *eborispina* (Hester) Breitung. Term. spine to 20cm, stout, ivory-white. var. *nevadensis* Engelm. Resembles *A. utahensis* except smaller, to 25cm. Lvs blue-grey, usually undulate, term. spine to 15cm, brown to white.

A. utahensis var. *kaibabensis* (McKelv.) Breitung = *A. utahensis* ssp. *kaibabensis*.

A. variegata Jacobi = *Manfreda variegata*.

A. verschaffeltii Lem. = *A. potatorum*.

A. victoriae-reginae T. Moore. Lvs to 25×6cm, rigid, overlapping, packed, tongue-shaped, flat to concave above, rounded beneath, dark green with white lines (traced impressions of surrounding lvs), margins white-horny, teeth 0, term. spine to 3cm, black. Infl. to 5m, a spike, erect, densely-fld above; fls to 4.5cm, usually green. Sometimes tinged red or purple. Mex.

A. vilmoriniana Berger. Lvs to 180×10cm, erect to recurved, linear-lanceolate, acuminate, deeply furrowed, concave above, teeth 0, term. spine to 2cm, brown to grey-brown. Infl. to 5m, a spike, densely-fld, sometimes bulbiferous; fls to 4cm, yellow. NW Mex.

A. virginica L. = *Manfreda virginica*.

A. warelliana Bak. Lvs to 75×14cm, fleshy, erect to spreading, linear-lanceolate, light green, slightly serrulate, term. spine to 2cm, brown. Infl. to 5m, a spike; fls to 9.5cm, light green, spotted violet-brown. Mex.

A. weberi Cels ex Poiss. Lvs to 160×18cm, fleshy, becoming recurved, oblong-lanceolate, teeth 0 or minute, term. spine to 4.5cm, grey to brown. Infl. to 8m, a diffuse pan., sometimes bulbiliferous; fls to 8cm, bright yellow. Mex.

A. wercklei Weber ex Berger. Lvs to 150cm, fleshy, lanceolate or ovate, acuminate, apex involute, margins straight to undulate, term. teeth to 4mm, black, terminal spine to 3cm, black or dark brown. Infl. to 8m, a much-branched pan., bulbiferous; br.

umbellate, short, spreading, densely-fld; fls to 6cm, golden-yellow. C Amer.

A. wislizenii Engelm. = *A. parrasana*.

A. xylonacantha Salm-Dyck. Lvs to 90×10cm, fleshy-rigid, lanceolate-ensiform, acuminate, flat to concave above, rounded beneath, grey-green or yellow-green, sometimes with a pale median stripe, teeth to 15mm, light grey, teerminal spine to 5cm, light grey-brown. Infl. to 6m, an erect spike; fls to 5cm, pale yellow to green. C Mex.

A. yuccifolia DC. Lvs to 65×3.5cm, slightly succulent, becoming recurved, linear, green with a pale central stripe, sometimes spotted red or purple, concave above, convex beneath, slightly serrulate, term. spine to 8mm, brown. Infl. to 3m, a slender rac., arcuate; fls to 4cm, yellow-green, foul-scented. Mex.

Agdestis Moc. & Sessé ex DC. Phytolaccaceae. 1 vine with red st. to 15m arising from a massive grey tuber. Lvs to 10cm, cordate-oblong, foetid. Fls white, starry, fragrant in pan. to 15cm. Mex., Guat. Z9.

A. clematidea Moc. & Sessé ex DC.

Ageratina Spach. Compositae. *c*230 ann. to perenn. herbs or shrubs. Lvs usually opposite, petiolate. Cap. small, discoid, in corymbs; receptacle slightly convex; flts tubular or funnelform. E US, C and W S Amer.

A. adenophora (Spreng.) R. King & H. Robinson. Subshrub, to 1.5m. Lvs 3–10cm, ovate to deltoid, acute to acuminate, glab. above, pubesc. beneath, dentate to serrate, glandular-pubesc. Cap. clustered in rounded corymbs; flts white. Spring–early summer. Mex., nat. elsewhere. Z10.

A. altissima (L.) R. King & H. Robinson. Perenn. to 2m, grey-green, pubesc. Lvs 4–10cm, lanceolate to elliptic-oblong, apex, acuminate, serrate. Cap. clustered in corymbs; flts white. Late summer. E N Amer. 'Braunlaub': lvs tinted brown. Z6.

A. aromatica (L.) Spach. Perenn., to 1.5m. Lvs 3–10cm, ovate, crenate to serrate. Cap. numerous, in a loose corymb; flts white. Late summer. N & E US, S Canada. Z4.

A. glechonophylla (Less.) R. King & H. Robinson. Subshrub or perenn. herb, to 2m. Lvs to 6cm, triangular-ovate, acute, slightly pubesc., coarsely dentate. Cap. in loose corymbs; flts white or tinged pink. Autumn–winter. Chile. Z9.

A. grandifolia (Reg.) R. King & H. Robinson. Subshrub, to 1.5m. Lvs to 12cm, triangular-ovate, acute or acuminate, serrate. Cap. in loose clusters, usually exceeded by lvs; flts white. Mex. Z10.

A. herbacea (A. Gray) R. King & H. Robinson. Perenn. woody-based herb, to 60cm. Lvs to 5cm, deltoid to ovoid-deltoid, acute, grey-green, pubesc., crenate to serrate. Cap. in dense corymbs; flts white. Autumn. SW to SC US. Z5.

A. hidalgensis (Robinson) R. King & H. Robinson. Shrub to 2m; br. dark purple. Lvs 1.5–3cm, rhombic-oblong, glab. above, subentire. Cap. in dense term. corymbs; flts white. Mex. Z10.

A. ligustrina (DC.) R. King & H. Robinson. Shrub, to over 5m, densely branched. Lvs 5–10cm, elliptic to elliptic-lanceolate, acuminate, glandular-punctate beneath, sparsely dentate. Cap. in clusters of corymbs to 20cm wide; flts cream-white or rose-tinged, fragrant. Autumn. Mex. to Costa Rica. Z10.

A. modesta (Kunth) R. King & H. Robinson. Shrub, to 3m, viscid. Lvs 2.5–6cm, ovate to rhombic-oblong, serrulate to entire. Cap. in term. pan.; flts pale pink. W Indies, S Amer. Z10.

A. occidentalis (Hook.) R. King & H. Robinson. Perenn. to 70cm. Lvs to 4cm, deltoid to deltoid-ovate, glandular-punctate beneath, entire or dentate. Cap. in term. corymbs clusters; flts white tinted purple. Late summer. W US. Z6.

A. petiolaris (Moc. & Sessé ex DC.) R. King & H. Robinson. Shrub, to 5m. St. white-pubesc. Lvs 3.5–10cm, ovate to ovate-cordate, pubesc. beneath, resin-dotted, crenate-dentate. Cap. in large, dense, term. corymbs; flts white. Winter. Mex. Z10.

A. proba (N.E. Br.) R. King & H. Robinson. Like *A. adenophora*, but perenn. herb to 1m; lvs to 4cm; cap. few in flat-topped corymbs. Winter. Peru. Z10.

A. purpusii (Brandg.) R. King & H. Robinson. Perenn. herb to 1.5m. Lvs 5–15cm, ovate-orbicular, base cordate, narrowed to apex, coarsely dentate. Cap. few to many, in corymbs; flts white, becoming pink-lilac. Early spring. NW Mex. Z9.

A. riparia (Reg.) R. King & H. Robinson. Woody-based perenn. herb, to 60cm. St. flexuous, finely pubesc. Lvs 5–10cm, lanceolate, attenuate, slightly pubesc. on veins, serrate. Cap. clustered in a corymbose pan.; flts white. Early spring. Mex. Z10.

A. vernalis (Vatke & Kurtz) R. King & H. Robinson. Shrub or perenn. herb, to 1m. Lvs to 10cm oblong-ovate, acuminate, base cordate, grey-white-pubesc. beneath, coarsely dentate. Cap. in loose, subpyramidal corymbs; flts white. Winter. Mex. to Guat. Z10.

→*Ageratum* and *Eupatorium*.

Ageratum L. Compositae. 43 ann. or perenn. herbs and shrubs. Cap. discoid, solitary or in a pan. forming a round-topped cluster; flts tubular, with 5 lobes, giving the flower-head a tassel-like appearance. Trop. Amer. Z10.

A. altissimum L. = *Ageratina altissima*.

A. caeruleum hort. = *A. houstonianum*.

A. conyzoides L. Ann. or perenn. herb to 1m. St. erect, branching, red. Lvs ovate to oblong, rounded at base, hairy, to 10cm. Cap. 4–18 in terminal, cymose clusters, mauve, blue or white. S & C Amer. Z9.

A. corymbosum Zucc. ex Pers. Shrub, to 2m. Lvs to 10cm, ovate to lanceolate, subentire or toothed, dull green above, canescent beneath. Cap. numerous, in dense clusters, blue, lavender or white. C Amer. Z9.

A. houstonianum Mill. Ann., to 70cm. St. sometimes branched, red or green. Lvs to 9cm, ovate to deltoid, sometimes downy, apex usually rounded, base heart-shaped, crenate. Cap. 5–15 in term., usually loose clusters, blue, lilac or lavender. C Amer., W Indies. Many seed strains and hybrids: taller blues include 'Blue Horizon' and 'Blue Bouquet'; 'Blue Danube' and 'Blue Blazer' are low and hummock-forming. Other colours include white, lavender, pink (e.g. 'Pinkie') and bicolours. Z8.

A. lasseauxii Carr. = *Barrosoa candolleana*.

A. mexicanum Sims = *A. houstonianum*.

A. petiolatum (Hook. & Arn.) Hemsl. Ann. or perenn., to 70cm. Lvs to 7cm, ovate to triangular, shiny, green and hairy above, pale green beneath, crenate or serrate. Cap. 3–9 in term. clusters, lavender. Nic. to Panama. Z8.

A. scabriusculum (Benth.) Hemsl. = *A. petiolatum*.

A. wendlandii hort. ex P.L. Vilm. = *A. houstonianum*.

Aglaomorpha Schott. Polypodiaceae. 10 epiphytic ferns. Fronds dimorphic, arising from creeping, fleshy, rusty-scaly rhiz., blade entire to lobed at base, pinnatifid to pinnate at apex, more so in fertile fronds where circular sori occupy narrow term. seg. Trop. Asia. Z10.

A. brooksii Copel. Fronds to 120cm, short-stalked, base to 35cm across, apex to 25cm across, fertile pinnae to 2×1cm. Philipp.

A. coronans (Wallich ex Mett.) Copel. = *Pseudodrynaria coronans*.

A. heraclea (Kunze) Copel. = *Drynariopsis heraclea*.

A. meyeniana Schott. BEAR'S PAW FERN. Fronds to 80cm, sessile, cordate, lobed at base, median seg. to 15cm, linear-oblong, fertile pinnae to 20cm, linear, constricted. Taiwan, Philipp. 'Roberts': of uncertain parentage, perhaps related to *A. meyeniana*; fronds uniform, entirely sterile, to 1.5m.

A. pilosa (J. Sm.) Copel. Fronds to 90cm, short-stalked, narrow at base, median seg. to 25cm, oblong, fertile pinnae scattered. Philipp.

A. splendens (J. Sm.) Copel. Fronds to 90cm, sessile, shallowly lobed at base, median seg. to 20cm, oblong-lanceolate, acute, fertile pinnae to 25×2cm. Malaysia to Philipp.

→*Polypodium*.

Aglaonema Schott. Araceae. 21 perenn. herbs. St. erect or creeping and rooting. Lvs usually oblong-lanceolate, variegated. Spathe stalked, ovate, green-yellow; spadix cylindrical to club-shaped. Fr. ripening red or white. Trop. Asia. Z10.

A. acutispathum N.E. Br. = *A. modestum*.

A. angustifolium N.E. Br. = *A. simplex*.

A. brevispathum (Engl.) Engl. Creeping. Lvs to 20cm, lanceolate-elliptic, plain green or with central white stripe or spots. SE Asia. f. *brevispathum* (Engl.) Nicols. Lvs unspotted. f. *hospitum* (Williams) Nicols. Lvs spotted.

A. clarkei Hook. f. = *A. hookerianum*.

A. commutatum Schott. Erect, 20–150cm, becoming decumbent. Lvs 13–30cm, banded yellow-white along primary veins, or spotted. Philipp. and NE Celebes. 'Albovariegatum': petiole, st., spathe white. 'Fransher' (*A. commutatum* 'Treubii' ×*A.c.* 'Tricolor'): slender; lvs lanceolate, fleshy, milky green with cream variegation, petioles white. 'Malay Beauty': as 'Pseudobracteatum', but larger, lvs to 30cm, less variegation. 'Pseudobracteatum': st. white with green marking; lvs spattered grey-green, spotted white, areas round primary veins white. 'Treubii': lvs narrow, spathe long. 'Tricolor': petiole mottled white to pink; If variegation hazy to streaked. 'White Rajah': massive white variegation throughout lvs. var. *elegans* (Engl.) Nicols. Lvs larger, more markedly variegated. var. *maculatum* (Hook. f.) Nicols. Lvs striped pale green along primary veins. var. *robustum* (Alderw.) Nicols. Lvs to 45cm long.

A. costatum N.E. Br. Creeping. Lvs to 20cm, ovate-lanceolate, with scattered spots throughout and/or white midrib. SE Asia. f. *immaculatum* (Ridl.) Nicols. Lvs unmarked except for white midrib.

A. crispum (Pitcher & Manda) Nicols. PAINTED DROP TONGUE. Erect, to 120cm. Lvs 14–32cm, elliptic to narrow-elliptic, largely

variegated silver-grey above. Philipp.
A. elegans Engl. = *A. commutatum* var. *elegans*.
A. gracile Schott. = *A. pictum*.
A. hookerianum Schott. Erect, to 50cm. Lvs to 27cm, ovate to elliptic-lanceolate, plain green. NE India, Bangladesh, coastal W Burma.
A. integrifolium (Link) Schott. = *A. nitidum*.
A. marantifolium var. *tricolor* Graf. = *A. commutatum* 'Tricolor'.
A. modestum Schott ex Engl. St. dark green. To 50cm. Lvs to 24cm, ovate-lanceolate, unmarked. S China, N Laos, N Thail. 'Maria': lvs small, rounded, dark green. 'Variegatum': lvs lanceolate, to 25cm, deep green boldly variegated cream.
A. nebulosum N.E. Br. Erect, 10–60cm. Lvs to 18cm, elliptic-oblong, dull green usually blotched silver-grey. Spathe inflated. Malaya, Borneo, islands E of Sumatra. f. *nanum* (Hook. f.) Nicols. Habit compact; lvs unmarked.
A. nitidum (Jack) Kunth. Erect, to 1m. Lvs to 45cm, unmarked or barred or blotched cream. Spathe ageing white. S Burm., Malaysia, Sumatra, Borneo. 'Curtisii': lvs striped silver along primary veins. 'Parrot Jungle' (*A. nitidum* 'Curtisii' ✕?): lvs lanceolate, somewhat leathery, matt dark green with silvery markings above; spathes ivory. 'Silver King' (*A. nitidum* 'Curtisii' ✕ *A. pictum* 'Tricolor'): lvs to 30cm, heavily streaked silverwhite. 'Silver Queen': as 'Silver King', but freely branched, lvs narrower, silvery white marbling.
A. oblongifolium Schott non (Roxb.) Kunth. = *A. nitidum*.
A. pictum (Roxb.) Kunth. Erect, 30–50cm. Lvs to 16cm, narrowelliptic, lustrous, aquamarine to dark green, blotched silver, midrib grey-green. Spathe inflated. Sumatra and Nias Is. 'Tricolor': lvs deep green, smooth surface, spattered silver and green tinted yellow.
A. roebelinii Pitcher & Manda. = *A. crispum*.
A. rotundum N.E. Br. Decumbent with age. Lvs to 14cm, broadovate, dark, glossy green, veined white-pink, violet-red beneath. N Sumatra.
A. simplex Bl. Erect, to 120cm. Lvs to 25cm, unmarked. Infl. with decumbent spadix. S Burm. to W Moluccas. 'Angustifolium': lvs narrower than sp., shiny dark green, waxy. 'Shingii': compact, freely branched; lvs ovate-pointed, thick, to 25cm, apple green, edged in dark green.
A. treubii hort. non Engl. = *A. commutatum* 'Treubii'.
A. versicolor hort. Bull. = *A. pictum*.

Agonis (DC.) Sweet. Myrtaceae. 11 shrubs and small trees. Bark fibrous. Lvs entire. Fls small, clustered; pet. 5, orbicular, spreading. W Aus.
A. flexuosa (Willd.) Sweet WILLOW MYRTLE; WILLOW PEPPERMINT. Small tree. Br. weeping. Lvs to 15cm, linear-elliptic, silky at first. Fls to 1cm diam., white; clusters axill. Selected forms are available, some with v. fine, pendulous foliage. 'Variegata': lvs variegated.
A. juniperina Schauer. JUNIPER MYRTLE. Medium shrub. Br. erect. Lvs to 1cm, linear, rigidly pungent, silky at first. Fls white, brown at centre; clusters term.
A. linearifolia (DC.) Sweet. Medium to tall shrub. Br. erect. Lvs to 2.5cm, linear-lanceolate, softly pungent. Fls white; clusters axill.
A. marginata (Labill.) Sweet. Medium shrub. Br. erect to spreading. Lvs to 3cm, oval-lanceolate, ciliate. Fls white; clusters axill. and term.
A. perviceps Schauer. Similar to *A. junipera*, but smaller, fls pure white.

Agoseris Raf. MOUNTAIN DANDELION. Compositae. 10 ann. or perenn. dandelion-like herbs with milky latex. Lvs mostly in a basal rosette. Cap. ligulate, stalked, to 6cm diam., solitary. W N Amer., temp. S Amer.
A. aurantiaca (Hook.) Greene. To 50cm. Lvs 5–25cm, linear to broadly oblanceolate, subentire to laciniate, glab. or villous; petioles purple. Flts orange mostly turning purple to pink. Summer. W US.
A. cuspidata (Pursh) Raf. To 35cm. Lvs to 20cm, linearlanceolate, white-pubesc. Flts yellow. Summer. C US.
A. glauca (Pursh) Raf. To 50cm. Lvs linear to narrowly lanceolate, obscurely toothed, sparsely hairy. Flts yellow. W N Amer. var. *dasycephala* (Torr. & A. Gray) Jeps. To 20cm. Lvs pubesc., usually entire.
→*Troximon*.

Agrimonia L. AGRIMONY; COCKLEBUR; HARVEST-LICE. Rosaceae. 15 rhizomatous perenn. herbs. St. erect, hairy and gland. Lvs irregularly pinnate. Fls small in dense term., spike-like rac.; pet. c6mm, yellow, 5. Summer. Chiefly N Temp.
A. asiatica Juz. = *A. eupatoria*.
A. dahurica Willd. ex Ser. = *A. pilosa*.

A. eupatoria L. AGRIMONY. To 1.2m. Lfts 4–14 pairs, small and large pairs alternating, hoary beneath. Rac. to 35cm, loose. Eur., N & S Afr., N Asia.
A. odorata auct., non Mill. = *A. procera*.
A. odorata Mill. non auct. = *A. repens*.
A. parviflora Ait. To 2m. Lfts 5–7, lanceolate-acuminate, glandular-punctate beneath. US.
A. pilosa Ledeb. To 1.5m. Lfts glandular-pubesc., toothed. E Eur. to Jap.
A. procera Wallr. FRAGRANT AGRIMONY. To 120cm. Lfts elliptic deeply incised, glutinous-pubesc. beneath. Eur.
A. repens L. To 1m. Lfts to 6.5cm, elliptic, overlapping, coriaceous, dark green above, grey-green beneath. Turk., Iraq.
A. suaveolens Pursh = *A. parviflora*.

Agrimony *Agrimonia* (*A. eupatoria*).

Agropyron Gaertn. WHEATGRASS; DOG GRASS. Gramineae. 40 perenn. grasses. Rhiz. creeping; aerial st. erect. Infl. spicate; spikelets sessile, alt. Temp. and cool regions.
A. cristatum (L.) Gaertn. CRESTED WHEATGRASS; FAIRWAY CRESTED WHEATGRASS. Spikes to 6cm, ovate-oblong; spikelets crowded, divergent from rachis. Eurasia; introd. N Amer.
A. elongatum (Host) Scribn. & J.G. Sm.) Rydb. = *Elymus elongatus*.
A. inerme (Scribn. & J.G. Sm.) Rydb. = *Elymus spicatus*.
A. intermedium (Host) P. Beauv. = *Elymus hispidus*.
A. littorale Nash = *Schizachyrium scoparium* var. *litorrale*.
A. pauciflorum (Schweinf.) A. Hitchc. = *Elymus trachycaulos*.
A. pectiniforme Roem. & Schult. = *A. cristatum*.
A. pseudoagropyron (Griseb.) Franch. = *Leymus chinensis*.
A. sibiricum (L.) Beauv. = *Elymus sibiricus*.
A. spicatum (Pursh) Scribn. & J.G. Sm. = *Elymus spicatus*.
A. tenerum Vasey = *Elymus trachycaulos*.

Agrostemma L. CORN-COCKLE. Caryophyllaceae. 2–4 ann. herbs erect, to 1m. Lvs opp., linear. Fls large, magenta to white, usually solitary; sep. 5, fused; pet. 5, large, clawed; sta. 10. Medit.
A. coeli-rosa L. = *Silene coeli-rosa*.
A. coronaria L. = *Lychnis coronaria*.
A. flos-jovis L. = *Lychnis flos-jovis*.
A. githago L. As above. 'Milas': fls to 5cm diam., plum pink. 'Milas Cerise': fls to 6cm diam., deep red. 'Milas Rosea': fls to 5cm diam., pale lilac-pink.
A. milas hort. = *A. githago* 'Milas'.
A. tomentosum hort. = *Lychnis coronaria*.

Agrostis L. BENT GRASS. Gramineae. 120 ann. and perenn. grasses, stoloniferous or tufted. Lvs linear, flat to filiform, revolute. Spikelets numerous, whorled, single-fld in pan. Summer. Cosmop. (esp. N Hemis.).
A. alba L. = *Poa nemoralis*.
A. algeriensis hort. = *Aira elegantissima*.
A. arundinacea L. = *Calamagrostis arundinacea*.
A. canina L. VELVET BENT; VELVET BENT GRASS; BROWN BENT; RHODE ISLAND BENT. Perenn. to 60cm, tufted. Lvs to 8cm, flat, scabrous. Infl. to 11✕5cm, br. spreading; glumes, purple, awn exserted. Eur. 'Silver Needles': lvs v. small and fine, edged silver-white; sometimes offered as *Festuca rubra* 'Silver Needles'.
A. capillaris hort. non L. = *A. nebulosa*.
A. elegans Thore = *A. nebulosa*.
A. nebulosa Boiss. & Reut. CLOUD GRASS. Ann. to 35cm, tufted. Lvs flat. Infl. to 15cm; spikelets lacking awns. Moroc., Iberia. Z7.
A. pulchella (R. Br.) Roth. = *Sporobolus pulchellus*.
A. setacea Curtis. BRISTLE-LEAVED BENT GRASS. Perenn., closely tufted, glaucous. Infl. purple, dense, rough-stalked; outer glume long-awned. Eur.
A. spica-venti L. = *Apera spica-venti*.
A. tenerrima Trin. Ann. to 30cm, tufted. Lvs to 10cm. Infl. to 15cm; spikelets lacking awns. W Medit. Z6.

Agrostocrinum F. Muell. BLUEGRASS LILY; FALSE BLIND-GRASS. Liliaceae (Asphodelaceae). 1 tufted perenn. to 45cm. Lvs grasslike. Fls to 3cm diam., star-shaped, blue, in a loose, longstalked pseudoumbel. W Aus.
A. scabrum (R. Br.) Bail.

Aguacate *Persea americana*.
Ague Root *Aletris farinosa*.
Ague Weed *Gentianella quinquefolia*.
Agui *Ormosia coccinea*.
Aibika *Abelmoschus manihot*.

Aichryson Webb & Berth. Crassulaceae. *c*15 ann. to short-lived perenn. herbs or subshrubs, many monocarpic. St. erect, br. often forking, shrubby. Lvs scattered or in loose rosettes, thin to slightly fleshy. Infl. a pan.; fls; cal. fleshy; pet. yellow. Atlantic Is., Moroc., Port. Z9.

A. bethencourtianum Bolle. Perenn. herb, 20–30cm, br. hairy. Lvs 20–30mm, broadly spathulate to suborbicular, fleshy, covered with soft hairs; petiole to 1.5cm. Pet.8–9. Late summer. Canary Is.

A. bollei Webb ex Bolle. Ann. or bienn. monocarpic herb, 30–35cm; st. slender, unbranched, with white hairs. Lvs 4.5cm, spathulate, hairy, slightly grooved surface covered with adpressed hairs, entire, toothed or sinuate, with black glands. Pet. 8. Late summer. Canary Is.

A. dicotomum (DC.) Webb & Berth. = *A. laxum*.

A. divaricatum (Ait.) Praeger. Ann. herb to 15cm; st. erect, glab., purple, branching above. lvs 2cm, broad ovate, blunt. Pet. 6–7. Madeira.

A. ×domesticum Praeger. (*A. tortuosum* ×*A. punctatum* Berth.) YOUTH-AND-OLD-AGE. Perenn. subshrub to 30cm; br. forking, sparsely hairy. Lvs 1×2cm, narrowing gradually to petiole, clustered at ends of br., dark green to white. Pet. 7–8. Early summer. Canary Is. 'Variegatum': shoots occas. white; lvs with broad white edges.

A. laxum (Haw.) Bramw. Ann. or bienn., erect herb to 30cm with upright forked br. Lvs to 3cm, broad-ovate, widest near the base, somewhat fleshy, pale to bright green, sometimes with purple markings. Pet. 9–12. Canary Is.

A. palmense Webb ex Bolle. Resembles *A. laxum*, but to 15cm, monocarpic; st. much branched with short brown hairs. Lvs broadly ovate to spathulate-rounded, v. fleshy, petiole v. hairy. Pet. 8–9. Canary Is.

A. porphyrogennetos Bolle. Resembles *A. laxum* but with widely spreading br.; st. purple-red, with short white hairs; br. bright red. Lvs red-purple. Canary Is.

A. pulchellum C.A. Mey. = *Aeonium spathulatum*.

A. pygmaeum C.A. Sm. = *A. tortuosum*.

A. sedifolium Webb ex Bolle = *Aeonium sedifolium*.

A. tortuosum (Ait.) Praeger. Perenn. subshrub to 10cm, downy. Lvs 12mm, crowded, fleshy, obovate-spathulate to cuneate, sometimes tinged red, hairy. Pet 8. Late spring. Canary Is.

A. villosum (Ait.) Webb & Berth. Ann. to 20cm. Erect st. sticky white-hairy. Pet. 6–9, golden yellow. Late spring. Azores, Madeira.

→*Aeonium, Sedum* and *Sempervivum*.

Ailanthus Desf. Simaroubaceae. 5 decid. spreading trees and shrubs. Lvs imparipinnate. Fls small, in long term. pan.; pet. 5–6, oblong; sta. 10. Fr. 1–6 oblong samaras. E & SE Asia to Aus.

A. altissima (Mill.) Swingle. TREE OF HEAVEN. Tree to 30m; bark grey, fissured; young branchlets minutely pubesc., red to bronze. Lvs 45–60cm, lfts to 15cm, 15–30, lanceolate-ovate, finely ciliate with 2–4 coarse teeth near base. Pan. term. to 20cm, white-green, malodorous. Fr. 4cm, green-pink to red-brown. Summer. N China; widespread urban weed. var. *sutchuenensis* (Dode) Rehd. & E.H. Wils. Young shoots glab., red-brown, lustrous. Lfts not ciliate, strongly cuneate at base; petioles purple. W China.

A. giraldii Dode. Similar to *A. altissima*. Young shoots puberulous, brown. Lvs to 90cm; lfts 7.5–15cm, 33–41, lanceolate, long-acuminate, dark green above, light green and loosely pubesc. beneath; petiole purple. Pan. to 30cm. Fr. 6.5cm. W China. var. *duclouxii* Dode. Branchlets light orange. Lfts sparingly pilose beneath, more densely so on veins; petiole green.

A. glandulosa Desf. = *A. altissima*.

A. malabarica DC. Large tree; bark thick, rough, often with bright red grains of resin. Lfts in 5–10 pairs, lanceolate, glab. Fr. 7.5–13cm, oblong, red-brown. Spring. India, Sri Lanka, Malay Penins., China.

A. sutchuenensis Dode = *A. altissima* var. *sutchuenensis*.

A. vilmoriniana Dode. Tree to 18m; branchlets softly spiny. Lvs to 90cm; lfts to 15cm, 17–35, lanceolate-oblong, acuminate, with 2–4 teeth near base, glab. or pubesc. above, glaucescent, pubesc. beneath; petiole often red and prickly. W China.

Ainsliaea DC. Compositae. 40 perenn. herbs. Lvs mostly basal, cordate, entire to dentate. Cap. discoid, small, in a spike or narrow pan. E Asia to W Malesia.

A. aptera DC. To 1m. Lvs to 10cm, glab. to pubesc., entire to sinuate. Cap. in long scapose spikes, pendent; flts pink or white. Pak. to Bhutan. Z10.

A. walkerae Hook. To 30cm. Lvs to 10cm, narrow, recurved, dark green, mucronate, dentate near apex. Cap. in an erect, spike-like pan., arching near apex; flts white; anth. pale red-purple. Spring. Hong Kong. Z10.

Aiphanes Willd. RUFFLE PALM. Palmae. *c*38 palms. St. usually solitary, ringed with long black needle-like spines. Lvs pinnate or entire and emarginate; sheaths disintegrate into woven fibres, spiny and tomentose; petiole spiny; pinnae linear-lanceolate to rhombic, regularly spaced or clustered. NW, C & S Amer., W Indies. Z10.

A. acanthophylla (Mart.) Burret. To 4.5m, trunk with aerial prop roots, ringed with 5cm black spines. Lvs to 3.6m; pinnae to 45cm, near-opposite, sparsely black spiny. Fr. 1.25cm, glossy red, endocarp white, edible, oily, coconut-like fr. Puerto Rico, Haiti, San Domingo.

A. aculeata Willd. Trunk to 3.6m×15cm. Lvs to 1.5m; pinnae in 4 opposite pairs, white-canescent beneath. Venez.

A. caryotifolia (HBK) H.A. Wendl. RUFFLE PALM; SPINE PALM. Slender, 7.5–12m. Trunk, petioles and rachis spiny. Pinnae in clusters of 4–10, 15–30cm, apices cuneate, dentate, veins prickly. N S Amer., Columbia.

A. corallina (Mart.) H.A. Wendl. Trunk to 7m×10cm, densely spiny. Lvs to 2m; pinnae 40–75cm, crowded, to 40 per side, alt. to near-opposite, apex truncate, fimbriate to denticulate. Martinique.

A. erosa (Lind.) Burret. MACAW PALM. Trunk to 6m, tapered to apex, spines to 6cm. Lvs to 2m; rachis armed; pinnae 15–25cm, regularly or irregularly spaced along rachis, linear, apex praemorse. W Indies.

A. lindeniana (H.A. Wendl.) H.A. Wendl. To 5m. Pinnae clustered, subopposite, apex truncate, tattered, narrow cuneate; petiole and rachis densely black-spiny. Colomb.

A. minima (Gaertn.) Burret = *A. erosa*.

A. truncata (Brongn. ex Mart.) H. Wendl. To 4m. Lvs 1.2–1.5m; pinnae 20–25cm, in groups of 4–6, subopposite, apex truncate and denticulate. Boliv.

→*Bactris, Curima* and *Euterpe*.

Aira L. HAIR GRASS. Gramineae. 9 ann. grasses. St. narrow, flimsy. Lvs filiform or narrow-linear, often inrolled, grooved; ligules membranous. Pan. lax, finely branched; spikelets small, laterally compressed, each with 2 fls, usually awned, shiny. Medit., Asia, Afr., Maur. Z6.

A. capillaris Host = *A. elegantissima*.

A. caryophyllea L. SILVER HAIR GRASS. To 30cm. St. tufted. Lvs to 50×1mm, grooved, scaberulous; sheath rough; ligule to 5mm. Pan. loose, spreading, to 10cm; spikelets 2.5–3mm, tinged grey or purple. Summer. Eur., N & W Asia, N Afr., Trop. Afr. (mts).

A. cespitosa L. = *Deschampsia cespitosa*.

A. elegans auct. = *A. elegantissima*.

A. elegantissima Schur. To 30cm. St. loosely tufted. Lvs to 50×1mm; ligule to 5mm. Pan. loose, 2.5–10cm; br. spreading, diffusely divided; spikelets long-stalked, 2.5–3mm. Spring–summer. Medit.

A. praecox L. EARLY HAIR GRASS. To 20cm. St. solitary or tufted. Lvs to 50×0.5mm, sheaths somewhat inflated, smooth; ligule to 3mm. Pan. spike-like, narrow-obovate, to 5cm; spikelets to 3mm. Late spring–early summmer. N, C & W Eur.

A. provincialis Jordan. Similar to *A. caryophyllea*. To 40cm. St. solitary or tufted. Lvs grooved. Pan. v. diffuse; br. spreading; spikelets to 3mm. Summer. S Fr.

A. pulchella Link = *A. tenorei*.

A. tenorei Guss. 10–40cm. St. solitary or tufted. Pan. diffuse; br. spreading; spikelets to 1mm, lacking awns. Spring. S Eur.

→*Agrostis*.

Airplane Plant *Crassula perfoliata* var. *falcata*.

Airplane Propellers *Crassula cultrata; C. perfoliata* var. *falcata*.

Air Plant *Tillandsia*.

Air Potato *Dioscorea bulbifera*.

AIZOACEAE Rud. 114/2400. *Acrodon, Aloinopsis, Aptenia, Argyroderma,* ×*Argyrops, Aridaria, Astridia, Bergeranthus, Bijlia, Braunsia, Carpobrotus, Carruanthus, Cephalophyllum, Cerochlamys, Chasmatophyllum, Cheiridopsis, Conicosia, Conophytum, Cylindrophyllum, Dactylopsis, Delosperma, Didymaotus, Dinteranthus, Diplosoma, Disphyma, Dorotheanthus, Dracophilus, Drosanthemum, Ebracteola, Erepsia, Faucaria, Fenestraria, Frithia, Gibbaeum, Glottiphyllum, Hereroa, Herrea, Herreanthus, Jacobsenia, Jensenobotrya, Jordaaniella, Juttadinteria, Kensitia, Lampranthus, Lapidaria, Leipoldtia, Lithops, Machairophyllum, Malephora, Mesembryanthemum, Mestoklema, Meyerophytum, Mitrophyllum, Monilaria, Muiria, Namibia, Nananthus, Neohenricia, Odontophorus, Oophytum, Pleiospilos, Psammophora, Psilocaulon, Rabiea, Rhinephyllum, Rhombophyllum, Ruschia, Ruschianthus, Sceletium, Schwantesia, Scopelogena, Semnanthe, Sphalmanthus, Stomatium, Tanquana, Titanopsis, Trichodiadema, Vanheerdia.*

Ajania Polj. Compositae. 30 perenn. herbs or shrubs. Cap. radiate, in corymbose or racemose clusters. C & E Asia.

A. **adenantha** (Diels) Muld. Aromatic, tufted perenn. herb, 15–30cm. Lvs 1–1.5cm, pinnatifid, lobes entire or divided, white-tomentose beneath. Cap. to 5mm diam., in loose corymbs; flts orange-yellow. W China.
→*Tanacetum*.

Ajuga L. BUGLE. Labiatae. 40 spreading ann. or perenn. everg. herbs, generally rhizomatous. St. tetragonal. Lvs entire, generally whorled, becoming bracts on erect flowering st.; cal. 10– or more veined; cor. tubular, lower lip larger than upper. Spring–early summer. Temp. Eurasia, nat. Aus. and S Afr. Z6.

A. **alpina** L. = *A. genevensis*.

A. **argyrea** Stapf = *A. bombycina*.

A. **australis** R. Br. Aromatic perenn. St. to 30cm, downy. Lvs narrow-oblong, thick, pubesc. Whorls *c*6-fld; bracts exceeding cor.; cor. to 15mm, blue or purple. Aus.

A. **bombycina** Boiss. Prostrate perenn. 3–15cm. Basal lvs obovate to oblong, crenate-dentate. Whorls covered in silvery hairs, 2-fld; cor. 12–16mm, yellow. S & C Turk.

A. **chamaepitys** (L.) Schreb. YELLOW BUGLE; GROUND PINE. Low-growing ann. or perenn., faintly aromatic. Lvs with 3 narrow lobes. Fls 1–2 per node; bracts lf-like; cor. yellow dotted red. Eur., Br. Isles, N Afr. Z6.

A. **genevensis** L. BLUE BUGLE; UPRIGHT BUGLE. Perenn., not stoloniferous. St. to 40cm. Basal lvs to 12×5cm, obovate, long-petioled. Spike leafy; whorls to 6-fld; bracts obovate, tinged violet-blue; cor. to 18mm, bright blue. S Eur. 'Alba': fls creamy. 'Robusta': larger in all aspects. 'Rosea': fls rose pink. 'Tottenham': fls lilac-pink in dense spikes. 'Variegata': lvs mottled creamy white.

A. **metallica** hort. = *A. pyramidalis*.

A. **orientalis** L. Woolly perenn. St. to 40cm. Lower lvs to 9×4cm, ovate, dentate. Whorls to 6-fld; bracts tinged blue; cor. to 16mm, upper lip lobed. S Eur.

A. **piskoi** Deg. & Bald. St. 30–50cm, angles hispid. Lower lvs 6–8.5cm, ovate, serrate. Bracts exceeding fls, fls 2 at each node; cor. 25–35mm, pink veined purple. Albania.

A. **pyramidalis** L. PYRAMID BUGLE. Everg. creeping perenn., not stoloniferous. Basal lvs to 11×4.5cm, dark green, pubesc., obovate, slightly toothed. Whorls 2–4-fld in a compact leafy pyramid; bracts tinged red-violet; cor. to 18mm, blue. Eur. 'Metallica Crispa': to 10cm; lvs purple tinted brown, iridescent, crinkled edges.

A. **repens** N. Tayl. = *A. reptans*.

A. **reptans** L. Stoloniferous, carpeting. Lvs to 9×4cm, oblong to spathulate, glab., ± toothed. Spikes to 12cm, leafy; whorls to 6-fld; bracts tinged purple-blue; cor. to 17mm, azure; sta. protruding. Eur., Iran, Cauc., Transcauc. 'Alba': lvs dark green; fls off-white. 'Atropurpurea': lvs dark purple tinted bronze. 'Braunherz' lvs darkest purple, shiny. 'Bronze Beauty': lvs brilliant bronze. 'Burgundy Glow': lvs silvery green variegated deep red. 'Catlin's Giant': lvs large, bronze. 'Jungle Beauty': lvs large, dark green, st. tall, fls indigo. 'Jungle Bronze': tall; lvs bronze, crinkled. 'Multicolor' ('Tricolor'): lvs dark bronze with red pink and gold splashes. 'Pink Elf': (smaller than 'Rosea', fls pink). 'Rosea': fls pink. 'Silver Carpet': mat-forming; lvs silver. 'Variegata': habit dense; lvs grey-green edged pale cream.

A. **rugosa** Host = *A. genevensis*.

A. **tenorii** C. Presl. Rhizomatous perenn., stemless or with a short st. to 5cm. Lvs 1.8–5×12cm, oblong-obovate to spathulate, crenate-denate. Bracts lanceolate; cor. 16–25mm, bright blue; sta. exserted. Mts of It. and Sicily.

Akebia Decne. CHOCOLATE VINE. Lardizabalaceae. 4 everg. or decid. slender twining vines. Lvs digitately lobed. Fls unisexual in nodding rac.: ♂ small, several, ± sessile, at tip of infl.; ♀ larger, few, stalked, at base of infl.; pet. 0; sep. 3–4, maroon to chocolate, petaloid, rounded. Fr. fleshy, ovoid-oblong, purple. Spring. Jap., China, Korea.

A. **lobata** Decne. = *A. trifoliata*.

A. ×**pentaphylla** Mak. (*A. quinata* × *A. trifoliata*.) Lfts 4–5 (6–7), oval to ovate, crenate or entire. Fls slightly fragrant. Jap. Z5.

A. **quinata** Houtt. Lfts 5, 3–5cm, oblong or ovate, entire. Fls strongly vanilla-scented: ♂ 0.5–1cm diam.; ♀ 2–3cm diam. China, Korea, Jap. Z5.

A. **trifoliata** (Thunb.) Koidz. Lfts 3, 3–6cm, ovate to broadly elliptic, shallow-lobed or entire, apex notched. Fls unscented; ♂ to 0.5cm diam; ♀ to 2cm diam. China, Jap. Z5.
→*Rajania*.

Akee *Blighia*.
Akikaze-giboshi *Hosta cathayana*.
Alabaster Plant *Dudleya virens*.

Alangiaceae Lam. See *Alangium*.

Alangium Lam. Alangiaceae. 17 trees, shrubs and climbers. Lvs simple or sometimes lobed. Fls axill. cymes; cal. 4–10-toothed; pet. equalling cal. teeth in number, ligulate; sta. numerous, alternating with pet. Fr. a drupe. Trop. Afr., China to E Aus. Z9.

A. **chinense** (Lour.) Harms. Everg. shrub or tree to 17m. Lvs to 30cm, oblong-ovate to rounded, slender-toothed or 3–5-pinnatifid. Pet. to 2cm, 5–9, white, ivory or orange- or red-flushed. Fr to 1.25cm, purple-red. Widespread throughout genus range except Aus.

A. **lamarckii** Thwaites = *A. salviifolium*.

A. **platanifolium** (Sieb. & Zucc.) Harms. Differs from *A. chinense* in lvs decid., pet. to 2.5cm. var. *macrophyllum* Lvs larger, broader. Jap., Korea.

A. **salviifolium** (L. f.) Wangerin. Scrambling shrub or small tree to 12m, oft. spiny. Lvs to 25cm, lanceolate to obovate, entire. Pet. 2.5cm, 5–10, green-white or ivory. Fr. to 2.2cm, dark red. Trop. Asia, Comoros Is.

Alaskan Holly Fern *Polystichum setigerum*.
Alaska Violet *Viola langsdorfii*.
Albany Bottlebrush *Callistemon speciosus*.
Albany Cat's-paw *Anigozanthos preissii*.
Albany Daisy *Actinodium cunninghamii*.

Albizia Durazz. Leguminosae (Mimosoideae). *c*150 decid. trees, shrubs or lianes, occas. armed. Lvs bipinnate. Infl. simple, fascicled or compound, mimosa-like, composed of umbellate heads or spikes; cal. campanulate or tubular, dentate; cor. lobed to centre, tubular below; sta. numerous, showy. Trop.

A. **adianthifolia** (Schumacher) Wight. Tree to 30m. Crown flattened. Pinnae in 5–8 pairs; lfts to 2×1cm, in 9–17 pairs, rhombic to oblong, mucronate, sparsely pubesc. above, densely so beneath. Fl. heads in compound rac., red to light-green marked-pink. Summer. Trop. Afr. Z9.

A. **basaltica** Benth. Shrub to 6×2m. Pinnae 1–2 pairs; lfts to 0.5cm, in 5–10 pairs, oblong or ovate, obtuse, rigid. Fl. heads solitary or in axillary pairs, globose. Spring. Aus. (Queensld). Z9.

A. **distachya** (Vent.) Macbr. = *A. lophantha*.

A. **fastigiata** (E. Mey.) Oliv. = *A. adianthifolia*.

A. **julibrissin** Durazz. SILK TREE. Tree to 6m. Crown domed to flat-topped. Pinnae in 5–18 pairs; lfts to 1.5cm, in 20–30 pairs, oblong-falcate, mucronate. Fl. heads to 3.5cm diam., lime green to ivory to pink, in corymbose rac. Summer. Iran to Jap., nat. US. 'Alba': fls white. var. *mollis* (Wallich) Benth. Densely pubesc. throughout. var. *rosea* Mouill. Tree smaller, fls candy-pink. 'Ernest Wilson': crown broad, fls white and pink, profuse, long-lasting. Cvs with some resistance to vascular wilt disease include 'Charlotte' and 'Tryon'. Z7.

A. **lebbeck** (L.) Benth. SIRIS TREE. Tree to 15m. Crown spreading. Pinnae in 2–4 pairs; lfts to 5×2.5cm, in 4–9 pairs, obovate. Fl. heads to 3cm diam., axillary, umbellate, fragrant, cream to pale yellow. OW Trop. Z9.

A. **lophantha** Benth. PLUME ALBIZIA. Shrub or small tree to 5m. Pinnae in 4–12 pairs; lfts to 1×2.5cm in 20–30 pairs, oblong, acute. Fl. heads pale green to golden, in spikes to 6cm. Spring. Aus. Z9.

A. **procera** (Roxb.) Benth. Tree to 8m. Crown spreading. Pinnae in 2–3 pairs; lfts to 3×1cm, in 6–9 pairs, oblong, obtuse, minutely hairy, shiny above. Fl. heads globose, yellow-green to cream, clustered in loose pan. Summer. Temp. Asia to Aus. Z9.

A. **saman** F. Muell. RAIN TREE; SAMAN; MONKEY POD; ZAMANG. Tree to 30m. Crown widespread. Pinnae in 3–6 pairs; lfts to 4×2cm, in 4–8 pairs, elliptic, puberulent. Fl. heads to 6m diam., umbellate, clustered in lf axils. Summer. C Amer. to Braz. Z9.
→*Acacia, Pithecellobium* and *Samanea*.

Albuca L. Liliaceae (Hyacinthaceae). 30 perenn. bulbous herbs. Lvs linear or lanceolate, basal, terete to flat. Fls racemose; tep. 6. Arabia, Afr., chiefly S Afr.

A. **altissima** Dryand. Lvs 70–90cm, lanceolate, glab. Racs loose, 30–45cm; tep. 1.5–2cm, white with broad green median stripe. S Afr.

A. **aurea** Jacq. Lvs 45–60cm, linear-lanceolate, flat. Fls erect, rac. to 30cm; tep. 2–3cm, pale yellow with green to red-brown stripe. S Afr.

A. **canadensis** (L.) F.M. Leighton. Lvs 7.5–15cm, lanceolate, grooved above, keeled. Fls to 7, nodding; tep. 1.5–2cm, pale green-yellow with wide green stripe. S Afr.

A. **cooperi** Bak. Lvs 15–30cm, linear. Fls 10–12; tep. 1.5–2cm with broad green to red-brown stripe. S Afr.

A. fragrans Jacq. Close to *A. aurea*. Fls ± pendulous, highly fragrant; tep. 1.5–2cm, yellow with green stripe. S Afr.

A. humilis Bak. Lvs 7.5–15cm, linear. Fls 1–3; tep. 1.5cm, white, outer with green stripe, inner unstriped, oft. with yellow tip. S Afr.

A. major L. Close to *A. canadensis* but more robust. Lvs 20–60cm. Fls 6–12; tep. with green or brown stripe. S Afr.

A. minor L. = *A. canadensis*.

A. namaquensis Bak. Lvs 10–15cm, v. narrow, pubesc. Fls 6–10 per rac., 10–20cm; tep. 1.5–2cm, inner with yellow tips. S Afr.

A. nelsonii N.E. Br. Lvs 90–120cm, lanceolate-acuminate. Rac. to 30cm; tep. 3–4cm, white with green or dull red stripe. S Afr.

A. wakefieldii Bak. Lvs 30–45cm, linear. Rac. 15–23cm; tep. to 2.5cm, outer green, inner white striped green. E Afr.

Alcea L. HOLLYHOCK. Malvaceae. 60 hairy bienn. or short-lived perenn. herbs, rarely shrubs. St. usually erect, simple or few-branched. Lvs unlobed or palmately divided. Fls in erect, term. elongate racemose infl.; epical. lobed; cal. lobes 5; pet. 5; staminal column tubular, 5-angled; anth. yellow. SW to C Asia.

A. ficifolia L. ANTWERP HOLLYHOCK. Perenn. or bienn. to 2.25m. Lvs to 18cm diam., lobes 7, oblong-obtuse, toothed. Fls yellow or orange, single or double. Sib. Z3.

A. heldreichii (Boiss.) Boiss. Perenn. herb. Upper lvs rhomboid-ovate, undivided or obscurely lobed. Epical. 1/2 as long as cal.; cal. conspicuously veined; pet. 3–4.5cm, white or pink. Bulg., Greece, Balk., Turk., S Ukraine.

A. lavateriflora (DC.) Boiss. Perenn. herb to 1.8m. Lvs yellow-tomentose, palmatifid or with 3–7 obovate, serrate lobes. Epical. seg. 2/3–4/5 length of cal.; cal. striate; pet. 3.5–4cm, violet with yellow base. Turk. in Eur. and in Asia.

A. pallida (Willd.) Waldst. & Kit. Bienn. to 2m. Lvs ± thick, cordate-orbicular to rhombic-deltate, undivided or 3–5-lobed, grey-tomentose beneath. Epical. equalling or slightly shorter than cal.; pet. 3–4.5cm, rose or lilac, not overlapping. SE & C Eur., Turk.

A. rosea L. HOLLYHOCK. Bienn. or perenn. to 3m. Lvs orbicular, 3-, 5- or 7-lobed. Epical. slightly over 1/2 length of cal.; pet. 3–5cm, white, pink or purple, sometimes pale yellow, usu. overlapping. Origin probably Turk. or Asia. Many cvs and seed races, ranging in height from 1–3m; fls single to double, 8–12cm across, white to dark red, including Chater's Double Hybrids (fls peony-shaped, double, a range of colours), 'Indian Spring' (to 2.5m; fls single, white, yellow, rose, pink); Majorette Mixed (to 90cm; fls semi-double, lacy, pastel colours), Pinafore Mixed (to 1.2m; to 6 st. per plant; fls semi-double, ruffled and lacy, compact, many colours); Powder Puffs Mixed (to 2m; fls fully double, white, yellow, rose, red); 'Nigra' (to 2m; fls deepest maroon).

A. rugosa Alef. Similar to *A. rosea*, but st. with longer white hairs. Lf lobes 5, oblong, obtuse, irregularly crenate. Epical. seg. half as long as cal.; pet. 3.5×5.5cm, pale or clear yellow or orange-yellow. Ukraine, S Russia.

A. striata (DC.) Alef. Perenn. to 1.5m. Lvs cordate-orbicular, grey-tomentose sides, upper lvs ± unlobed. Epical. in fl. less than half as long as cal.; sep. striate pet. 2.5–3.5cm, pink, crimson, purple, white or yellow. ssp. *striata*. Lvs unlobed or v. shallowly lobed. Aegean Is., Asian Turk., Isr., Jord., Sinai. ssp. *rufescens* (Boiss.) Cullen. Lvs distinctly 3-, or 5-lobed.

A. sulphurea (Boiss. & Hohen.) Alef. Low perenn. herb. Lvs rounded, 0–3-lobed, floccose beneath. Epical. as long as cal.; pet. pale yellow. Iraq and Iran.

→*Althaea*.

Alchemilla L. Rosaceae. LADY'S MANTLE. 300 perenn. herbs. Basal lvs palmately lobed, sometimes compound; st. lvs with fewer lobes and large stipules. Infl. cymose, much-branched, fls numerous, small; perianth green, epical. seg. 4, sep. 4, pet. 0. Fr. an achene. Summer. Widespread in Eur. and Asia sp. in the mts of Eur. and NZ may be introductions.

A. abyssinica Fres. St. villous, creeping, rooting; br. short, few-fld. Lvs to 4cm, reniform, lobes 7, shortly cuneate, with 3–5 long, curved teeth, sparsely hairy. E African mts.

A. acutangula Buser = *A. acutiloba*.

A. acutiloba Opiz. Robust, to 65cm; summer lvs to 10cm across, lobes 9–13 almost triangular, teeth unequal; hairy, except infl. and upper lf surface. Most of Eur.

A. alpestris misapplied = *A. glabra*.

A. alpina L. ALPINE LADY'S MANTLE. Rootstock creeping, woody; flg st. to 15cm, densely hairy. Lfts 5–7, lanceolate-obovate, apex toothed, dark green and glab. above, silvery-hairy beneath. Eur.

A. alpina hort. non L. = *A. plicatula* and *A. conjuncta*.

A. asterophylla Buser = *A. plicatula*.

A. caucasica Buser = *A. erythropoda*.

A. conjuncta Bab. Fl. st. to 30cm, silky-hairy. Lvs ± thick, glab. above, silky-hairy beneath, circular, seg. 7–9, lanceolate to elliptic, teeth almost hidden by silky hair. Jura and SW Alps; nat. Scotland; commonly cult. and often sold as 'A. alpina'.

A. elisabethae Juz. Dwarf, blue-green; fl. st. to 15cm, with ascending hairs. Lf seg. 7, flattened, incised, teeth 3 or 4, broad and blunt. Cauc.

A. ellenbeckii Engl. Small, prostrate, sparsely hairy, rooting at nodes. Lvs to 2cm across, lobes 5, wedge-shaped, with few small blunt teeth. E African mts.

A. epipsila Juz. Differs from *A. mollis* in lf lobes deeper, glab. above. Balk. Penins. (mts).

A. erythropoda Juz. Like *A. glaucescens* but grey or blue-green, with incisions, up to about two-fifths, between truncate lf-lobes. Balk. Penins. mts, W Carpath., Cauc.

A. erythropodoides Pawl. = *A. erythropoda*.

A. faeroensis (Lange) Buser. Differs from *A. conjuncta* in lvs reniform, usually 7-lobed, with deep incisions; teeth large, acute, in upper half of lobes. E Iceland, Faeroe Is. var. *pumila* (Rostrup) Simmons. V. dwarf, to 5cm.

A. fulgens Buser. Differs from *A. conjuncta* in lf lobes broader and shorter, with acute teeth, and separated by toothless, V-shaped incisions to less than half depth of blade. Pyren.

A. glabra Neygenfind. Flowering st. to 60cm, almost glab. Lvs ± reniform, lobes 9–11, triangular-ovate, teeth 7–9, rather wide acute, unequal. N & C Eur.

A. glaucescens Wallr. Small plant, spreading hairy, flg st. to 20cm. Lvs circular; lobes 7–9, shallow, rounded with 4–6 teeth, basal lobes overlapping. Ireland and C Fr. to Russia.

A. grandiflora hort. = *A. mollis*.

A. hoppeana misapplied = *A. plicatula*.

A. hybrida misapplied = *A. glaucescens*.

A. hybrida (L.) L. nom. ambig. = *A. lapeyrousii*.

A. indivisa Rothm. = *A. epipsila*.

A. lapeyrousii Buser. Medium-sized, flg st. to 25cm. Lvs ascending-hairy, reniform, lobes 7–9, ± triangular, fairly shallow, teeth on lobes 5 or 6. Pyren.

A. minor misapplied = *A. glaucescens*.

A. mollis (Buser) Rothm. LADY'S MANTLE. Large, flg st. to 80cm, spreading-hairy. Lvs to 15cm, circular; lobes 9–11, v. shallow, semicircular, with 7–9 wide, ovate, unequal teeth. Infl. showy, yellow. E Carpath., Cauc. 'Variegata': lvs variably marked yellow. 'Robusta': indistinguishable from *A. mollis*. 'Mr Poland's Variety' is *A. venosa*.

A. monticola Opiz. Medium-sized, flowering st. to 50cm, densely spreading-hairy. Lvs to 8cm across, ± circular, lobes 9–11, rounded, separated by short incisions, teeth 7–9, regular. Eur.

A. multiflora Rothm. = *A. tytthantha*.

A. pastoralis Buser = *A. monticola*.

A. pedata A. Rich. = *A. abyssinica*.

A. pentaphylla L. Dwarf, often prostrate, subglab., fl. shoots rooting at the nodes. Lvs to 2cm, lfts 5, deeply cut into narrowing seg. Fls few. Alps.

A. plicatula Gand. Like *A. alpina* but more robust, with st. to 20cm; lvs circular with 7 (rarely 9) seg., the middle one free to the base, the others joined near the base. Eur. mts (Pyren. to Balk. Penins.), Turk.

A. pratensis nom. ambig. = *A. xanthochlora*.

A. pubescens misapplied = *A. glaucescens*.

A. rigida Buser. Like *A. sericata* but indumentum less closely adpressed, lvs deeper green, reniform, basal lobes not or scarcely overlapping, teeth broader, 4–5 per lobe. Mts of Turk. and Cauc.

A. sericata Rchb. Small, slender, flg st. to 20cm, silky-hairy. Lvs circular, lobes 7, semicircular; teeth 5 or 6, acute, light green above, pale green silky beneath, st. and stalks red in sun. Cauc.

A. sericea Willd. Like *A. alpina* but with more conspicuous, irregular teeth in the upper half of the lfts, and thin adpressed hairs on the upper surface of lvs. Turk., Cauc.

A. speciosa Buser. Differs from *A. mollis* in deeply lobed lvs (to two-fifths) with narrower, acute teeth, and in its ascending hairiness. Pedicels hairy, not subglab. as in *A. mollis*. Cauc.

A. splendens misapplied = *A. fulgens*.

A. tytthantha Juz. Medium-sized, flg st. to 50cm; lvs almost circular, spreading hairy, lobes 9–11, shallow, teeth 6–8. Crimea.

A. venosa Juz. Medium-sized flowering st. to 40cm, with ± adpressed hairs. Lvs thin, circular, with lobes 9–11, semicircular, incised to one-third; lf-teeth 6–8, upper lf surface hairless. Cauc.

A. vetteri Buser. Small, flg st. to 20cm, with ± adpressed hairs. Lvs ± glab. along the folds above, silky-hairy beneath, circular, lobes 7–9 truncate with 5 or 6 teeth. Mts of SW Eur.

A. vulgaris hort. non L. = Cf. *A. mollis*.

A. xanthochlora Rothm. Flg st. to 50cm; lvs ± reniform, hairless above, spreading-hairy beneath, yellow-green; lf lobes 9–11, rounded, with 7–9 wide, acute, almost equal teeth. Eur.

Alcock's Spruce *Picea alcoquiana.*
Alder *Alnus.*
Alder Buckthorn *Rhamnus frangula.*
Alder-leaved Service Berry *Amelanchier alnifolia.*

Aldrovanda L. WATERWHEEL PLANT. Droseraceae. 1 floating, aquatic, carnivorous perenn. St. slender, branching, to 15cm. Lvs in whorls of 6–9, terminating in 4–6 bristly seg. and a folded, round lobe, closing to trap prey. Fls emergent, solitary, green-white. C & S Eur., Afr., Asia to Aus.
A. vesiculosa L.

Alecost *Tanacetum balsamita.*

Alectorurus Mak. Liliaceae (Asphodelaceae). 1 rhizomatous perenn. herb. Lvs 10–50cm, narrowly ligulate, distichous, everg. Scape 15–40cm, obscurely winged; fls white tinged lilac or pink, campanulate, in an arching pan. Summer. Jap.
A. yedoensis (Franch. & Savat.) Mak.

Alectryon Gaertn. Sapindaceae. 17 everg. trees. Lvs pinnate. Infl. paniculate, axill. or term., many-fld; fls usually unisexual; cal. pubesc. within, unequally 4–5 lobed, pet. 0; sta. 5–8, v. short. Fr. a woody, subglobose, 1–4 lobed, crested capsule; seeds with a red fleshy aril. Malesia, W Pacific to NZ.
A. excelsus Gaertn. TITOKI. Young growth silky-red-pubesc. Lvs to 40cm, lfts 8–12, to 10cm, oval to lanceolate, undulate, coarsely crenate to entire. Infl. to 30cm. NZ. Z8.
A. subcinereus (A. Gray) Radlk. SMOOTH RAMBUTAN. Lvs to 20cm, lfts 2–8, 7–13cm, oblong-elliptic to elliptic-ovate, Infl. to 20cm. E Aus. Z10.
A. tomentosus (F. Muell.) Radlk. Lfts 4–8 to 15cm, ovate to elliptic-oblong. Infl. to 15cm. W Aus. Z10.
→*Cupania.*

Alehoof *Glechoma hederacea.*
Aleppo Grass *Sorghum halapense.*
Aleppo Pine *Pinus halepensis.*
Alerce *Tetraclinis articulata.*

Aletris L. STAR GRASS; COLIC ROOT. Liliaceae (Melanthiaceae). 10 fibrous-rooted perennials. Lvs grassy in a basal rosette. Rac. spike-like, scapose, tep. 6, united into a tube, exterior wrinkled and 6-ridged, appearing mealy. Summer. E N Amer., E Asia.
A. aurea Walter. To 70cm. Fls campanulate, tep. to 0.6cm, ovate, yellow. SE US.
A. farinosa L. UNICORN ROOT; CROW CORN; AGUE ROOT; COLIC ROOT. To 1m. Fls tubular; tep. to 1.2cm, ovate, white; anth. orange-red, exserted. SE US.

Aleurites Forst. & Forst. f. Euphorbiaceae. 6 everg. trees with milky latex. Lvs entire or lobed; petioles long, with extrafloral nectaries. Fls small, in term. paniculate cymes, sep. 2–5; pet. 5. Fr. a drupe. Indomalesia, W Pacific. Z10.
A. cordata (Thunb.) R. Br. To 6m. Lvs ovate, cordate, apex acute to trilobate, glossy above, paper-thin. Fls white. Fr. to 2cm diam. SW Asia.
A. fordii Hemsl. To 7m. Lvs to 25×25cm. Fls red-tinged. Fr. to 7cm diam. Asia.
A. moluccana (L.) Willd. CANDLENUT TREE. To 20m. Lvs to 20cm, ovate, sometimes 3–5-lobed, stellate-pubesc. Fls white in infl. to 25cm. Fr. to 6cm diam., yielding oil. SE Asia, widely cult in Tropics.

Aleuritopteris Fée.
A. candida (Mart. & Gal.) Fée = *Cheilanthes candida.*

Aleutian Maidenhair *Adiantum pedatum* var. *aleuticum.*

✕**Alexanderara.** (*Brassia* ✕*Cochlioda* ✕*Odontoglossum* ✕*Oncidium.*) Orchidaceae. Gdn hybrids with large, branching spikes of small to medium-sized fls, usually yellow with brown spots. Z10.

Alexander Palm *Ptychosperma elegans.*
Alexanders *Angelica atropurpurea*; *Smyrnium olusatrum.*
Alexandra Palm *Archontophoenix alexandrae.*
Alexandrian Laurel *Danaë racemosa.*
Alexandrian Senna *Senna alexandrina.*
Alfalfa *Medicago sativa.*

Alfredia Cass. Compositae. 3 perenn. herbs. Lvs spinulose. Cap. discoid, large, terminal; receptacle bristly; phyllaries apppendaged; flts yellow, narrowly tubular. C Asia, Sib.

A. cernua (L.) Cass. St. to 3m, strongly branched above, thick, hollow. Lvs to 50cm, ovate-cordate or oblong, erose-dentate, spinulose, green, almost glab. and rough above, grey or white beneath. Cap. numerous; phyllaries black-hairy with golden-yellow appendage.

Algarobia Benth.
A. glandulosa (Torr.) R. Cooper = *Prosopis glandulosa.*

Algarroba Bean *Ceratonia.*
Algerian Black Pine *Pinus nigra* var. *mauretanica.*
Algerian Fir *Abies numidica.*
Algerian Ivy *Hedera algeriensis.*
Algerian Oak *Quercus canariensis.*
Algerian Winter Iris *Iris unguicularis.*

Alibertia A. Rich. Rubiaceae. 20 shrubs or everg. trees. Lvs opposite, often leathery. Fls unisexual, ♀ solitary, ♂ in term. clusters; hypanthium hemispheric or globose; cal. short or tubular, cor. tubular, leathery, lobes 4–8; sta. 4–8, inserted. Fr. a fleshy berry. Trop. Amer. Z10.
A. edulis (Rich.) A. Rich. WILD GUAVA. To 5m. Lvs to 20cm, oblong to ovate, acute, lustrous above. ♂ fls 6–8, sessile, with cor. to 2.5cm, white or cream, lobes 4–5, ovate or lanceolate, half as long as tube or more. ♀ fls with cor. to 3cm, lobes lanceolate to ovate. Fr. 2.5cm in diam., fleshy, yellow to green. Summer. C Amer.

✕**Aliceara.** (*Brassia* ✕*Miltonia* ✕*Oncidium.*) Orchidaceae. Gdn hybrids with long sprays of yellow-brown, cream, green or chestnut fls with narrow tep. and large lip. Z10.

Alice Holt Cypress ✕ *Cupressocyparis notabilis.*

Alisma L. Alismataceae. 9 aquatic, perenn. herbs. Lvs basal, stalked, submerged or emergent, linear, cordate or ovate. Scape erect; fls small, in umbellate, whorled pan., rac. or umbels; pet. 3, green-white, often tinted brown or pink. Summer. N temp. regions, Aus. Z6.
A. canaliculatum A. Braun & Bouché. Lvs grey to dark green, oblanceolate to lanceolate. Infl. to 80cm; pet. to 4mm, white, entire, obtuse. S China, S Jap.
A. gramineum Lej. Submerged lvs, narrow-linear, aerial lvs to 10×4.5cm, dark green, narrow-elliptic to lanceolate, apex acute to obtuse. Pet. 2.5–3.5mm, white or purple-white. Eur., Asia, central N Amer., N Afr.
A. lanceolatum With. Aerial lvs to 27×7.5cm, dark green, lanceolate to elliptic, apex acute or acuminate. Pet. to 7mm purple-pink, emarginate. Eur., C & SW Asia, Afr.
A. loiselii Gorski = *A. gramineum.*
A. natans L. = *Luronium natans.*
A. parviflorum Pursh = *A. plantago-aquatica* var. *parviflorum.*
A. plantago auct. = *A. plantago-aquatica.*
A. plantago-aquatica L. WATER PLANTAIN. Lvs to 30×12cm, usually smaller, largely aerial, in rosettes, grey to deep green, elliptic or ovate to lanceolate, apex acuminate (linear if submerged). Pet. 3.5–6.5mm, white or purple-white. Eur., E Asia, N & S Afr., N US. var. *americanum* Schult. & Schult. f. Pet. white; fruiting heads larger. var. *parviflorum* (Pursh) Torr. Fls 3–3.5mm diam.
A. plantago-aquatica ssp. *graminifolium* (Ehrh. ex Steud.) Hegi. = *A. gramineum.*
A. ranunculoides L. = *Baldellia ranunculoides.*
A. subcordatum Raf. = *A. plantago-aquatica* var. *parviflorum.*
A. triviale Pursh = *A. plantago-aquatica* var. *americanum.*
A. wahlenbergii (Holmb.) Juz. Lvs usually submerged, to 45×0.3cm, narrow-linear, sometimes narrowly elliptic-oblong. Infl. short; fls usually submerged, pet. slightly longer, white or faintly purple-white. Scand., W Russia.

ALISMATACEAE Vent. 11/95. *Alisma, Baldellia, Damasonium, Echinodorus, Luronium, Ranalisma, Sagittaria.*

Aliso *Platanus racemosa.*
Alkali Blue Curls *Trichostema ovatum.*
Alkali Grass *Zigadenus elegans.*

Alkanna Tausch. Boraginaceae. c30 ann. or perenn. herbs. Lvs basal, entire, hairy, often gland. Fls in term., branching cymes; cor. infundibular or salverform, with downy ring in throat. S Eur. to Iran.
A. incana Boiss. 10–25cm, white-tomentose. Lvs to 15cm, linear-lanceolate to lanceolate, acuminate. Fls 1.1cm, sky blue. S & SW Anatolia. Z8.
A. lehmannii (Tineo) A. DC. = *A. tinctoria.*

A. orientalis (L.) Boiss. To 30cm, setose-pubesc. Lvs to 8cm, green or white-green, linear to oblong-lanceolate or narrowly obovate, acute or obtuse. Fls to 1.2cm, white or yellow, scented. S Eur., SW Asia.

A. tinctoria (L.) Tausch. To 30cm, bristly. Lvs to 8cm, linear to obovate. Fls to 1.2cm, bright blue. S Eur.

A. tuberculata (Forssk.) Meikle = *A. tinctoria*.

→*Anchusa* and *Lithospermum*.

Allagoptera Nees. Palmae. 5 unarmed, small palms. St. usually buried. Lvs pinnate, pinnae folded. Braz., Parag.

A. arenaria (Gomes) Kuntze. St. subterranean. Lvs to 1m, pinnae *c*100 in groups of 2–5, held in differing planes along rachis, silvery beneath.

Allamanda L. Apocynaceae. 12 ± everg., erect or scandent shrubs. Lvs glossy, lanceolate to oblong-obovate, whorled. Fls showy, trumpet-shaped, in term. cymes, yellow to purple-red, limb 5-lobed, flared. Trop. Amer.

A. blanchetii A. DC. PURPLE ALLAMANDA. Usually ± erect. Fls rose-purple, darker in throat. S Amer.

A. cathartica L. COMMON ALLAMANDA; GOLDEN-TRUMPET. Climbing to 6m. Fls golden yellow marked white in throat, longtubular, 3.25cm diam. S Amer. 'Grandiflora': fls freely produced, exceptionally large. 'Hendersonii': fls orange-yellow with white spots in throat, tinged bronze, lobes thick and waxy. 'Nobilis': lvs large and strongly whorled; fls v. large, pure gold.

A. neriifolia Hook. f. = *A. schottii*.

A. purpurea hort. = *A. violacea*.

A. schottii Pohl. BUSH ALLAMANDA. More bushy than *A. cathartica*. Fls deep golden-yellow streaked orange-red within, short-tubular. S Amer.

A. violacea Gardn. & Fielding = *A. blanchetii*.

Allardia Decne. Compositae. Tufted perenn. herbs. Lvs entire, toothed or 2–3-pinnatisect. Cap. radiate, large, term.; ray flts white to lilac; disc flts yellow. Himal., C Asia.

A. tomentosa Decne. Densely white-tomentose perenn. to 20cm. Lvs to 8cm, 1–2-pinnatisect, oblong to linear-oblong. Cap. to 10cm diam.; ray flts to 2.5cm, linear, pink or white. W Himal.
→*Waldheimia*.

Allegheny Blackberry *Rubus allegheniensis*.
Allegheny Chinkapin *Castanea pumila*.
Allegheny Monkey Flower *Mimulus ringens*.
Allegheny Moss *Robinia kelseyi*.
Allegheny Plum *Prunus alleghaniensis*.
Allegheny Sand Myrtle *Leiophyllum buxifolium* var. *prostratum*.
Allegheny Serviceberry *Amelanchier laevis*.
Allegheny Vine *Adlumia fungosa*.
Alleluia *Oxalis acetosella*.
Allgood *Chenopodium bonus-henricus*.
Alligator Juniper *Juniperus deppeana*.
Alligator Lily *Hymenocallis palmeri*.
Alligator Pear *Persea americana*.
Alligator Weed *Alternanthera philoxeroides*.

Alliona L.

A. linearis Pursh = *Mirabilis linearis*.

A. nyctaginea Michx. = *Mirabilis nyctaginea*.

Allium L. Liliaceae (Alliaceae). *c*700 perenn. and bienn. bulbous herbs, many pungently aromatic. Lvs basal or sheathing st., linear to elliptic, flat, grooved or terete. Fls in a scapose spathaceous umbel; tep. 6. Summer unless otherwise indicated. N hemis.

A. acuminatum Hook. 10–30cm. Lvs 2–4, channelled, linear, shorter than st. Fls 10–30, in a loose umbel 4–6cm wide; tep. 8–15mm, white to deep rose-pink. Pacific NW Amer. Z6.

A. acuminatum var. *bidwelliae* Jeps. = *A. campanulatum*.

A. acutangulum Schräd. = *A. angulosum*.

A. affine Boiss. & Heldr. = *A. vineale*.

A. aflatunense B. Fedtsch. 80–150cm. Lvs 6–8, slightly glaucous, 2–10cm diam., much shorter than st. Fls numerous; infl. spherical; tep. 7–8mm, violet with dark central veins. C Asia. 'Purple Sensation': to 1m; fls intense deep violet. Z8.

A. akaka S. Gmel. ex Roem. & Schult. f. 5–15cm. Lvs 1–3, to 20×6cm, oblong-elliptic. Fls numerous in a short-stalked spherical umbel 3–10cm wide; spathes 1, lobed; tep. 6.5–8.5mm, white to lilac-pink. Turk., Cauc., Iran. Z8.

A. albidum Fisch. ex Bieb. = *A. denudatum*.

A. albidum ssp. *caucasicum* (Reg.) Stearn. = *A. denudatum*.

A. albopilosum C.H. Wright = *A. christophii*.

A. album Santi = *A. neapolitanum*.

A. album var. *purpurascens* Maire & Weiller = *A. subvillosum*.

A. alleghaniense Small = *A. cernuum*.

A. alpinum Hegetschw. non Reg. = *A. schoenoprasum*.

A. alpinum Reg. non Hegetschw. = *A. narcissiflorum*.

A. altaicum Pall. 12–70cm. St. hollow, swollen in mid-region. Lvs 2–6, 6–30cm, hollow, terete. Fls bell-shaped in a dense spherical umbel; tep. 6–8mm, glossy yellow. Sib., Mong. Z5.

A. altissimum Reg. 65–150cm. Lvs 4–6, 15–35mm wide, linearlanceolate. Umbels dense; tep. 6–8mm, violet with dark central vein. C Asia. Z6.

A. amabile Stapf. 10–20cm. Lvs 2–4, grassy. Fls 2–5, funnelshaped, often pendent; tep. to 1.5cm, deep pink to magenta with darker spotting. SW China. Z6.

A. ambiguum Sm. = *A. roseum* var. *carneum*.

A. amblyanthum Zahar. = *A. pallens*.

A. amethystinum Tausch. 30–120cm. Often tinged red above. Lvs 3–7, to 50×0.8cm, linear, hollow. Fls numerous; umbel 3–5cm wide, spherical; tep. purple. Balk., It., Sicily, Crete. Z9.

A. ammophilum Heuff. = *A. denudatum*.

A. amoenum G. Don = *A. roseum* var. *carneum*.

A. ampeloprasum L. WILD LEEK; LEVANT GARLIC; KURRAT. 45–180cm. Lvs 4–10, to 50×4cm, flat, margins rough. Fls cupshaped, to 500; umbel 5–10cm wide, spherical; tep. 4–5.5mm, pink or dark red. S Eur., Cauc., Iran, Turk., N Afr. var. *babingtonii* (Borrer) Syme. Numerous bulbils and few fls. SW Engl., Channel Is., Ireland. Z6.

A. ampeloprasum var. *bulbiferum* Syme = *A. ampeloprasum* var. *babingtonii*.

A. ampeloprasum var. *bulbiliferum* Lloyd = *A. ampeloprasum* var. *babingtonii*.

A. ampeloprasum var. *porrum* (L.) Reg. = *A. porrum*.

A. amplectens Torr. St. 20–50cm. Lvs 2–4, narrow, flat, twisting with age. Fls numerous; umbel spherical; tep. 6–7mm, white to pink. NW US. Z7.

A. anceps var. *lemmonii* (Jeps.) Jeps. = *A. lemmonii*.

A. angulosum L. MOUSE GARLIC. 20–45cm. Lvs 10–25×1.5–6mm, 4–6, channelled. Fls cup-shaped; umbel 2.5–4.5cm wide, hemispherical; tep. 4–6mm, white to pale purple. Eur., Sib. Z5.

A. angulosum ssp. *ammophilum* K. Richt. = *A. denudatum*.

A. angulosum var. *caucasicum* Reg. = *A. denudatum*.

A. angulosum var. *flavescens* Reg. = *A. denudatum*.

A. angustipetalum Wendelbo = *A. rosenbachianum*.

A. antonii-bolosii Palau Ferrer = *A. cupanii*.

A. arvense Guss. = *A. sphaerocephalon* ssp. *arvense*.

A. ascalonicum auct. non L. = *A. cepa*.

A. assimile Hal. = *A. vineale*.

A. atropurpureum Waldst. & Kit. 40–100cm. Lvs 15–35cm, 3–7, linear. Fls numerous; umbel 3–7cm wide; tep. 7–9×1mm, dark purple. S Eur. Z8.

A. atrosanguineum Schrenk = *A. monadelphum*.

A. atroviolaceum Boiss. 50–120cm. Lvs 3–6, 0.4–1.2cm, flat, denticulate. Fls many, cup-shaped, in globose umbel 3–6cm diam.; tep. to 5×2.5mm, dark purple, sometimes tinged green. SE & E Eur.

A. attenuifolium Kellogg = *A. amplectens*.

A. attenuifolium var. *monospermum* Jeps. = *A. amplectens*.

A. aureum Lam. = *A. moly*.

A. austinae Jones = *A. campanulatum*.

A. azureum Ledeb. = *A. caeruleum*.

A. babingtonii Borrer = *A. ampeloprasum* var. *babingtonii*.

A. bakeri Reg. = *A. chinense*.

A. bauerianum Bak. = *A. nigrum*.

A. beesianum W.W. Sm. 15–20cm. Lvs 15–20×0.4–1cm, 2–4. Fls 6–12, pendent, bell-shaped or tubular; tep. 1–1.5cm, blue; sta. blue. W China. f. *album*. Fls white. Z8.

A. bidwelliae S. Wats. = *A. campanulatum*.

A. bisceptrum S. Wats. 10–30cm. Bulbs producing numerous bulblets. Lvs 3–10mm wide, 2–3, flat. Fls 15–40, umbel globose; tep. 6–10mm, rose-purple. W US. Z8.

A. boissieri Reg. = *A. borszczowii*.

A. bolanderi S. Wats. 10–25cm. Lvs 2, 1–2.5mm wide. Fls 6–25; tep. 8–15mm, white to rose-purple, toothed. S Oreg., N Calif. var. *stenanthum* (Drew) Jeps. Taller. Fls white or pale pink. Z7.

A. borszczowii Reg. 10–30cm. St. flexuous. Lvs 10–30cm, linear, hollow. Fls many, campanulate; umbel loose rounded; tep. 5–7mm, white or pink with purple median vein. Iran, Afghan.

A. boryanum Kunth = *A. callimischon*.

A. brahuicum Boiss. = *A. caspium*.

A. breweri S. Wats. St. to 8cm, flat. Lvs longer than st., 3–8mm wide, curved. Fls numerous, in an umbel; tep. 7–10mm, deep purple. US (C Calif.). Z8.

A. bucharicum Reg. St. 10–30cm. Lvs 10–30×0.7–2cm, 3–6, margin scabrid. Fls many in loose hemispheric umbel, starshaped; tep. 8–10mm, white with dull purple-green vein. Afghan.

A. buhseanum Reg. = *A. schoenoprasum*.

A. bulgaricum (Janka) Prodan. = *Nectaroscordum siculum* ssp.

bulgaricum.

A. caeruleum Pall. St. 20–80cm, 3-angled. Lvs 7cm, 2–4, linear, 3-angled. Fls numerous; umbel 3–4cm diam., spherical; tep. 3.5–4.5×1–1.5mm, blue with darker central vein. Sib., Turkestan. var. *bulbiliferum* Schrenk. Umbels with bulbils. Z7.

A. caesium Schrenk. 25–65cm. Lvs 1–3mm wide, 2–4, hollow, sheathing st. Fls numerous; umbel 1.5–2cm wide; tep. 4–5×2mm, violet-blue with green central vein, occas. white. Infl. sometimes bulbiliferous. Sib. to C Asia, Pamir and Tien Shan Mts. Z7.

A. callimischon Link. 9–38cm. Lvs to 30×0.1cm, 3–5. Fls 8–25, cup-shaped, in clusters; umbel fastigiate, 2–3cm wide; tep. 5–7×1.5mm, white to pink with brown or red central veins. Autumn. Greece, W Turk. ssp. *haemostictum* Stearn. Tep. spotted red. Crete, Peloponnese. Z9.

A. campanulatum S. Wats. 10–30cm. Lvs to 30×0.3–0.5cm, 2–3. Fls 15–40, cup-shaped in an umbel; tep. 5–8mm, white to pale pink. US (Calif., Nevada). Z8.

A. canadense L. CANADA GARLIC; MEADOW LEEK; ROSE LEEK. To 30cm. Lvs to 5mm wide; 3, channelled, shorter than st. Fls bell-shaped; umbel bulbiliferous; tep. 4–7mm, white to pink. N Amer. var. *fraseri* F.M. Ownb. Tep. white. var. *mobilense* (Reg.) F.M. Ownb. Tep. pink, no bulbils in infl. Z4.

A. candissimum Cav. = *A. neapolitanum.*

A. capillare Cav. = *A. moschatum.*

A. carinatum L. KEELED GARLIC. 30–60cm. Lvs 20×0.1–0.25cm, 2–4 glab. Fls cup-shaped, to 30 in an umbel 2–5cm wide, usually with bulbils; tep. 4–6×1.5–2mm, purple. C & S Eur., Russia, Turk. ssp. *pulchellum* (G. Don) Bonnier & Layens. St. purple. Infl. bulbils 0. S Eur. f. *album.* Fls white. Z7.

A. carneum Bertol. = *A. roseum* var. *carneum.*

A. caspium Bieb. 10–20cm. Lvs to 25×3.5cm, 3–6, linear. Fls numerous, bell-shaped; umbel loose, 5–20cm diam.; tep. 5–11×2–3mm, lilac tinged green. Cauc., C Asia. Z8.

A. caucasicum Bieb. = *A. paniculatum.*

A. cepa L. ONION; SHALLOT; TREE ONION. Bienn. St. to 100cm, hollow. Lvs to 40×2cm, to 10, hollow, flattened. Fls star-shaped, in umbel 4–9cm diam., with or without bulbils; tep. 3–4.5mm, white with green central vein. Not known in wild. Cepa group: bulbs solitary; bulbils lacking from infl. (includes onions). Aggregatum group: bulbs clustered; bulbils lacking from infl. (includes shallots, multiplier onions and potato onions). Proliferum group: bulbils in infl. (includes Egyptian onions and tree onions). Not known in wild. Z5.

A. cernuum Roth. LADY'S LEEK; NODDING ONION; WILD ONION. St. 30–70cm, terete or angled. Lvs 10–20×0.5–0.7cm, 4–6, flat. Fls cup-shaped, 30–40, nodding; umbel 3–5cm diam.; tep. 4–6mm, white, deep pink or maroon. Canada to Mex. Z6.

A. chamaemoly L. Lvs 3–27cm, 2–5, linear, ciliate, rosulate. Fls 2–20, star-shaped, in umbel 2cm diam.; tep. white with green or purple central veins. Winter–spring. S Eur., N Afr. Z9.

A. chinense G. Don. RAKKYO; CH'IAO T'OU. 28–30cm. Lvs to 30×0.1–0.3cm, 3, hollow, 3- or 5-angled. Fls cup-shaped, to 18 in a hemispherical umbel; tep. 5mm, pale violet. Autumn. China. Z7.

A. christophii Trautv. STAR OF PERSIA. St. 15–50cm, ribbed. Lvs 15–40×1–4cm, 2–7, glaucous, hairy beneath. Fls 2–3cm diam., numerous, star-shaped; umbel loose, 10–20cm diam.; tep. 1–2cm, purple-violet with metallic sheen. Iran, Turk., C Asia. 'Gladiator': to 1.2m, fls large, lilac-mauve; 'Globus' (*A. christophii* ×*A. giganteum*): st. to 35cm, fls blue, in large heads; 'Lucy Ball': to 1.2m, fls dark lilac in compact head; 'Rien Poortvliet': to 1.2m, fls lilac. Z9.

A. chrysonemum Stearn. 30–60cm. Lvs to 15×0.2cm, 3–4, hairy. Fls numerous, cup-shaped, umbel to 4cm diam.; tep. 4.5–5mm, pale yellow with green central vein. Fr. 4mm. Spain. Z7.

A. ciliatum Cirillo = *A. subhirsutum.*

A. cirrhosum Vand. = *A. carinatum* ssp. *pulchellum.*

A. coerulescens G. Don = *A. caeruleum.*

A. coloratum Spreng. = *A. carinatum* ssp. *pulchellum.*

A. compactum Thuill. = *A. vineale.*

A. complanatum Boreau = *A. oleraceum.*

A. continuum Small = *A. canadense.*

A. contortum Stokes = *A. sativum* var. *ophioscordum.*

A. controversum Schräd. ex Willd. = *A. sativum* var. *ophioscordum.*

A. coppoleri Tineo = *A. pallens.*

A. coryi M.E. Jones. To 30cm. Lvs 2–3, shorter than st. Fls 10–25, bell-shaped; tep. 6–9mm, chrome-yellow, occas. tinged red. US (W Tex.). Z8.

A. cowanii Lindl. = *A. neapolitanum.*

A. crenulatum Wiegand. St. 5–8cm, 2-angled, edges dentate. Lvs 3–10×0.3–0.6cm, 1–2, margins dentate. Fls few, umbel hemispherical; tep. 6–12mm, white, pink or purple. W N Amer. Z7.

A. crispum Greene = *A. peninsulare* var. *crispum.*

A. cupanii Raf. 10–25cm. Lvs to 10×0.05cm, 3–5. Fls bell-shaped, to 15; umbel fastigiate, 2–4cm diam.; tep. 5.5–9mm, white to pink with dark central vein, rarely white. Medit. Z8.

A. cusickii S. Wats. = *A. tolmiei.*

A. cuspidatum Fern. = *A. acuminatum.*

A. cuthbertii Small. STRIPED GARLIC. To 50cm. Lvs to 5mm wide, shorter than st. Fls numerous in umbels; spathes conspicuously veined; tep. to 6mm, white. SE US. Z8.

A. cyaneum Reg. 10–45cm. Lvs 15cm, 1–3, semi-cylindric. Fls 5–18, bell-shaped, pendent; tep. violet-blue to purple with dark blue or green central vein. China. Z9.

A. cyaneum var. *brachystemon* Reg. = *A. sikkimense.*

A. cyathophorum Bur. & Franch. var. *farreri* (Stearn) Stearn. St. 19–42cm, 3-angled. Lvs 18–24.5×0.1–0.5cm, 3–6. Fls bell-shaped, 6–30 in loose umbel; tep. 6–8×1.5–2mm, maroon. China. Z9.

A. cyrilli Ten. 50–60cm. Lvs 15–35cm, 3–7, linear. Fls numerous, cup-shaped; umbel 4–7cm diam.; tep. 6–7mm, white with green central vein. S Eur. Z8.

A. darwasicum Reg. St. 10–50cm, ribbed. Lvs shorter than st. 1–2, linear, margins rough. Fls numerous, bell-shaped; tep. white with green central vein. C Asia. Z5.

A. denudatum (Delaroche f.) Redouté. 10–30cm. Lvs to 14×0.25cm, 5–9, flat. Fls numerous, star-shaped; umbel 1.5–2.5cm diam.; tep. 3.5–1–1.5mm, white to pale yellow. W Russia, Bulg., Rom. Z9.

A. descendens L. = *A. sphaerocephalon.*

A. descendens auct., non L. = *A. amethystinum.*

A. deserticola(M.E. Jones) Wooton & Standl. = *A. macropetalum.*

A. dichlamydeum E. Greene. 10–30cm. Lvs 1–2mm wide, as long as st. flat, 1–3. Fls bell-shaped, umbel close; tep. 9–11mm, rose-purple. Calif. Z8.

A. dictyotum E. Greene = *A. geyeri.*

A. dioscoridis Sibth. & Small = *Nectaroscordum siculum* ssp. *bulgaricum.*

A. douglasii Hook. To 25cm. Lvs 6–8mm wide, shorter than st., 2. Fls numerous; tep. to 8mm, white to pink. NW US. Z6.

A. drummondii Reg. 10–20cm. Lvs 10–15×0.1–0.4cm, 3 or more, channelled. Fls 10–25, bell-shaped; tep. 4–7mm, white, pink or red. Spring. SW N Amer. Z7.

A. elatum Reg. = *A. macleanii.*

A. euboicum Rchb. f. = *A. paniculatum.*

A. falcifolium Hook. & Arn. St. 5–12cm, with 2 wings. Lvs 25×0.9cm, 1–2, falcate, grey-green. Fls 10–30, bell-shaped; umbel 4–5cm diam., compact; tep. 8–15mm, deep pink to purple or green-white tinged with pink. S Oreg. to N Calif. Z8.

A. fallax Schult. & Schult. f. = *A. senescens* ssp. *montanum.*

A. farreri Stearn = *A. cyathophorum* var. *farreri.*

A. fedtschenkoanum Reg. = *A. monadelphum.*

A. fibrillum M.E. Jones. To 10cm. Lvs 3–5mm wide, as long as or longer than st. Fls numerous; tep. 8–12mm, white to pale pink. US (Idaho). Z5.

A. fibrosum Rydb. = *A. rubrum.*

A. fimbriatum S. Wats. 3–10cm. Lvs twice as long as st. Fls 8–10, in umbel; spathes with apical bristles; tep. 7–15mm, pink to purple with darker central vein. Calif. Z7.

A. fimbriatum var. *purdyi* Eastw. = *A. purdyi.*

A. fistulosum L. WELSH ONION; JAPANESE BUNCHING ONION; JAPANESE LEEK. St. 12–70cm, hollow. Lvs 6–30cm, 2–6, hollow, terete. Fls bell-shaped, sometimes replaced by bulbils in loose umbel, 1.5–5cm diam.; spathes 1–2; tep. 6–9mm, yellow-white. Not known in the wild. Z5.

A. flavescens Besser = *A. denudatum.*

A. flavescens var. *ammophilum* (Heuff.) Zahar. = *A. denudatum.*

A. flavum L. SMALL YELLOW ONION. 8–30cm. Lvs 20cm, cylindric, glaucous. Fls 9–60, scented, bell-shaped; umbel hemispherical, 1.5–3cm diam.; tep. 4.5–5mm, lemon-yellow. C Eur. to W Asia. 'Blue Leaf' ('Glaucum'): strong-growing; lvs blue; fls yellow. 'Minus': smaller, fls with purple fil. Z7.

A. flavum var. *pulchellum* (G. Don) Reg. = *A. carinatum* ssp. *pulchellum.*

A. flavum var. *purpurascens* Mert. & Koch = *A. carinatum* ssp. *pulchellum.*

A. flexum Waldst. & Kit. = *A. carinatum.*

A. flexum var. *capsuliferum* Koch = *A. carinatum* ssp. *pulchellum.*

A. fragrans Vent. = *Nothoscordum gracile.*

A. fraseri (F.M. Ownb.) Shinn = *A. canadense* var. *fraseri.*

A. frigidum Boiss. & Heldr. To 25cm. Lvs 5cm, 2–3, thread-like. Fls 3–16; umbel fastigiate, 1.5–4cm diam.; tep. 5–6mm, yellow tinged with red. Greece (Peloponnese). Z8.

A. funiculosum Nels. = *A. geyeri.*

A. fuscum Waldst. & Kit. = *A. paniculatum.*

A. gaditanum Pérez Lara ex Willk. = *A. guttatum* ssp. *sardoum.*

A. galanthum Karel. & Kir. To 50cm. Lvs 25–35×1cm, 2–3,

cylindric, fistular. Fls numerous; tep. 5mm, white; sta. joined to tep. forming a basal ring. Sib. Z5.

A. geyeri S. Wats. 15–50cm. Lvs 10–20×0.2–0.4cm, channelled. Fls 10–25, pedicels long; tep. 4–10mm, white to pink, slightly toothed. Spring. W US. Z7.

A. giganteum Reg. 80–200cm. Lvs 30–100×5–10cm, basal, grey-green. Fls star-shaped; umbel dense, spherical, 10–15cm diam.; tep. 5–7mm, purple or white, elliptic. Spring. C Asia. Z8.

A. glandulosum Link & Otto. St. 20–55cm, laterally compressed. Lvs to 30×0.6cm, 2–5, nearly basal, strongly veined. Fls star-shaped; umbel compressed, 4–9cm diam.; tep. 6–9mm, maroon, lanceolate, spreading. Autumn. US (Tex., Ariz.), Mex. Z7.

A. glaucum Schräd. = *A. senescens* var. *glaucum*.

A. globosum DC. in Redouté. To 60cm. Lvs 5–6, thread-like. Fls numerous; spathe 2 or 3× as long as umbel; tep. 5mm, deep pink with dark midrib. Cauc. Z6.

A. gmelinianum Misch. = *A. globosum*.

A. gracile Dryand. in Ait. = *Nothoscordum gracile*.

A. grandiflorum Lam. = *A. narcissiflorum*.

A. grandisceptrum Davidson = *A. unifolium*.

A. gredense Rivas Mart. = *A. schoenoprasum*.

A. grossii Font Quer. 30–40cm. Lvs linear. Fls numerous, bell-shaped; umbel 5.5cm diam.; tep. purple with dark midrib. Balearic Is. Z9.

A. guttatum Steven. 10–90cm. Lvs 30×0.3cm, 2–5, hollow. Fls numerous, bell-shaped to tubular; umbel dense spherical, 1.5–5cm diam.; tep. 2.5–4.5×1–1.5mm, white with green or pink veins and purple blotch. SE Eur. ssp. *guttatum*. Tep. white with purple blotch. Aegean to Ukr. ssp. *sardoum* (Moris) Stearn. Tep. white with green or pink stripe. S Port. to Turk. Z6.

A. haematochiton S. Wats. RED-SKINNED ONION. Bulb tunics white to deep red. St. 10–40cm, slightly flattened. Lvs 10–20×0.1–0.4cm, several, flat, bases broad, sheathing. Fls 10–30; tep. 6–8mm, white to pink with darker central vein. Spring. Calif. Z6.

A. halleri S. Don = *A. ampeloprasum*.

A. heldreichii Boiss. 20–60cm. Lvs 5–30×0.1–0.3cm, 2–4, hollow, cylindric. Fls bell-shaped, numerous; umbel 2.5–4.5cm diam., globose; tep. 10×2.5–3mm, pink, acute. N Greece. Z8.

A. helleri Small = *A. drummondii*.

A. hirtovaginatum Kunth = *A. cupanii*.

A. hyalinum var. *praecox* (Brandg.) Jeps. = *A. praecox*.

A. hymenorrhizum Ledeb. 30–90cm. Lvs 30×0.6cm, 4–6. Fls numerous, bell-shaped; umbel spherical or hemispherical, 2–3.5cm diam.; tep. 4–6×1.5–2mm, deep pink. C Asia, W Sib., Iran, Afghan. Z7.

A. illyricum Jacq. = *A. roseum*.

A. incarnatum Hornem. = *A. roseum* var. *carneum*.

A. insubricum Boiss. & Reut. St. 2-edged, 16–30cm. Lvs 12–20×0.2–0.5cm, 3–4, flat glaucous. Fls 3–5, bell-shaped, pendent; umbel fastigiate; tep. to 18mm, purple. N It. cf. *A. narcissiflorum*. Z8.

A. intermedium DC. = *A. paniculatum*.

A. jacquemontii Reg. non Kunth. = *A. przewalskianum*.

A. jajlae Vved. = *A. scorodoprasum* ssp. *jajlae*.

A. japonicum Reg. = *A. thunbergii*.

A. kansuense Reg. = *A. sikkimense*.

A. karataviense Reg. 10–25cm. Lvs 15–23cm, 2–3, broadly elliptic, grey flushed with purple. Fls numerous, star-shaped; umbel to 20cm diam.; tep. 5–8mm, white to pale purple-pink with darker midrib. Spring. C Asia. Z8.

A. kaufmannii Reg. = *A. monadelphum*.

A. kharputense Freyn & Sint. 10–30cm. Lvs 2–3, 2–4cm wide, broad-lanceolate, twisted. Umbel dense, rounded, 3.5–8.5cm diam.; pedicels long; tep. 5–6mm, linear, white or cream. Turk. to Iran.

A. kochii Lange. 30–120cm. Lvs 15–60×0.15–0.4cm, 2–4, hollow. Fls bell-shaped, numerous; umbel to 3cm diam.; tep. 2–4.5mm, dark red. Baltic region, N Afr., W Asia. Z6.

A. kunthii G. Don. To 40cm. Lvs to 10cm, 3mm wide, 2–4, triangular in section, channelled. Fls numerous; tep. to 6mm, white to pink, midrib dark red. New Mex. to Mex. Z7.

A. lacteum Sm. = *A. neapolitanum*.

A. lacunosum S. Wats. 10–20cm. Lvs 1–2, terete. Fls 8–25; tep. 5–7mm, white to white with green or red midribs. Spring. C & S Calif. Z8.

A. latifolium Jaub. & Spach = *A. akaka*.

A. lavendulare var. *fraseri* Shinn = *A. canadense* var. *fraseri*.

A. ledebourianum Roem. & Schult. f. 40–80cm. Lvs to 1cm wide, 1–2, fistular. Fls bell-shaped, in a dense umbel; tep. 7–12mm, glossy violet-pink with dark midrib. Sib. Z5.

A. lemmonii S. Wats. St. 10–20cm, 2-edged. Lvs 2–5mm wide, 2, flat. Fls numerous; tep. 6–8mm, white to pale rose. Spring–summer. Calif. Z8.

A. libani Boiss. St. to 8cm. Lvs narrow, exceeding st., 2–3. Fls

numerous; tep. 6mm, white with red midrib. Asia Minor. Z9.

A. lineare L. 30–60cm, ribbed. Lvs 18cm, 2–4, linear, flat, denticulate. Fls bell-shaped; umbel dense, to 3cm diam.; tep. 4–5mm, rose-pink. Fr. to 4mm. Sib. Z6.

A. lineare var. *strictum* (Schrad.) Krylov = *A. strictum*.

A. longispathum Delaroche = *A. paniculatum*.

A. lusitanicum Lam. = *A. senescens* ssp. *montanum*.

A. macleanii Bak. St. 60–100cm, deeply ridged. Lvs to 30×2–8cm, 2–5, basal. Fls star-shaped; umbel dense, spherical 7–10cm diam.; tep. 6–8mm, deep violet. Spring–summer. C Asia. Z8.

A. macnabianum hort. ex Reg. To 30cm. Lvs 25×0.6cm, linear, channelled. Fls numerous; tep. deep magenta. N Amer. Z8.

A. macranthum Bak. St. 20–30cm, 3-angled. Lvs 15–45×0.3cm, many, channelled. Fls pendulous, bell-shaped; umbel loose, spherical, 7–10cm diam.; tep. 8–12×4mm, deep purple. W China, Sikkim. Z8.

A. macropetalum Rydb. 5–20cm. Lvs 1–3mm wide, longer than st., 2. Fls 10–20, bell-shaped; tep. 8–12mm, pink with deep pink or red midrib. NW Amer. Z5.

A. macrorrhizum Boiss. = *A. hymenorrhizum*.

A. mairei Lév. St. 10–40cm, 2-angled. Lvs to 25×1cm. Fls 2–6, bell-shaped, erect; tep. 8–12mm, white to pink with red spotting. Autumn. SW China. Z9.

A. mairei var. *amabile* Stapf = *A. amabile*.

A. margaritaceum Sm. non Moench = *A. guttatum* ssp. *sardoum*.

A. margaritaceum var. *guttatum* (Steven) Steven = *A. guttatum* ssp. *guttatum*.

A. maritimum Benth. = *Muilla maritima*.

A. marvinii Davidson = *A. haematochiton*.

A. meliophilum Juz. = *Nectaroscordum siculum* ssp. *bulgaricum*.

A. mobilense Reg. = *A. canadense* var. *mobilense*.

A. modocense Jeps. = *A. parvum*.

A. moly L. YELLOW ONION; LILY LEEK. 12–35cm. Lvs 20–30cm, 1–3, lanceolate, glaucous. Fls star-shaped; umbel 4–7cm diam.; tep. 9–12mm, golden-yellow above, keeled beneath. S & SW Eur. 'Jeannine': often 2 fig st.; fls bright yellow, in large umbels. Z7.

A. moly var. *xericense* Pérez Lara = *A. scorzonerifolium* var. *xericense*.

A. monadelphum Turcz. ex Kunth. 10–60cm. Lvs to 60cm, 1–3, cylindric, fistular. Fls few, bell-shaped; tep. 7–14mm, bright yellow becoming red or dark purple. C Asia, Sib. Z8.

A. monospermum Jeps. = *A. amplectens*.

A. monspessulanum Gouan = *A. nigrum*.

A. montanum Schrank = *A. senescens* ssp. *montanum*.

A. montigenum Davidson = *A. peninsulare*.

A. moschatum L. 10–35cm. Lvs 14×0.05cm, 3–6, margins rough beneath. Fls 3–12, bell-shaped; umbel fastigiate, 1–3cm diam.; tep. 5–7mm, white to pink with darker midrib. S Eur. Z8.

A. multibulbosum Jacq. = *A. nigrum*.

A. murrayanum Reg. = *A. acuminatum*.

A. murrayanum misapplied = *A. unifolium*.

A. mutabile Michx. = *A. canadense*.

A. narcissiflorum Vill. St. 15–35cm, 2-edged. Lvs 9–18×0.2–0.6cm, 3–5, flat, grey-green. Fls 5–8, bell-shaped; umbel fastigiate; tep. 10–15mm, bright pink to purple. N It., Port. Z8.

A. narcissiflorum var. *insubricum* (Boiss. & Reut.) Fiori = *A. insubricum*.

A. neapolitanum Cirillo. DAFFODIL GARLIC; FLOWERING ONION; NAPLES GARLIC. St. 20–50cm, 3-angled. Lvs 8–35cm, 2, basal, linear-lanceolate. Fls numerous, cup-shaped or stellate; umbel loose, fastigiate or hemispherical, 5–11cm diam.; tep. 7–12mm, glistening white. Spring. Medit., S Eur., Asia Minor, N Afr. 'Grandiflorum': fls white with a dark eye, umb. large and loose. Z8.

A. neriniflorum (Herb.) Bak. = *Caloscordum neriniflorum*.

A. nevii S. Wats. To 25cm. Lvs shorter than st., narrow, 2. Fls several; tep. to 6mm, light rose-pink. NW US. Z5.

A. nigrum L. 40–90cm. Lvs to 50cm, 3–6, basal, lanceolate. Fls 1–1.5cm diam., numerous, star-shaped; umbel 6–9cm diam.; tep. 6–9mm, white, pink or purple with green midribs. Spring. S Eur., N Afr., Asia Minor, Cyprus. Z8.

A. nigrum var. *atropurpureum* (Waldst. & Kit.) Vis. = *A. atropurpureum*.

A. nitens Sauzé & Maillard = *A. vineale*.

A. nutans L. St. 30–60cm, 2-angled. Lvs to 30×1.5cm, 6–8, glaucous. Fls numerous, cup-shaped; umbel spherical, to 6cm diam.; tep. 4–6mm, rose-pink or lilac. Sib. Z5.

A. nuttallii S. Wats. = *A. drumondii*.

A. obliquum L. 60–100cm. Lvs to 35×2cm, 4–10, broadly linear. Fls cup-chaped to spherical; umbel 3–4cm diam., dense; tep. 4–5mm, pale sulphur-green. Rom., Sib., C Asia. Z7.

A. occidentale A. Gray = *A. amplectens*.

A. ochroleucum Waldst. & Kit. 15–30cm. Lvs 3–4, linear, flat, margins rough. Fls cup-shaped; umbels dense, globose, 1.5–2cm diam.; tep. white to yellow, with red midrib. It. Z8.

A. odorum L. = *A. ramosum.*

A. oleraceum L. FIELD GARLIC. St. 25–100cm, slightly ridged. Lvs to 25cm, 2–4, linear, channelled. Fls numerous, cup-shaped, outer pendulous; umbel 2–4cm diam., bulbils replacing some fls; tep. 5–7mm, white tinged green, pink or brown. Eur. Z5.

A. oliganthum Karel. & Kir. = *A. schoenoprasum.*

A. olympicum Boiss. 30–50cm. Lvs 2–3, narrow-linear, flat. Fls campanulate; umbel 1–4cm diam., dense, rounded; tep. 3–4mm, ovate, obtuse, violet-red or lilac-pink. Turk.

A. ophioscorodon Link = *A. sativum* var. *ophioscorodon.*

A. oreophilum C.A. Mey. 5–20cm. Lvs longer than st., linear. Fls numerous, bell-shaped; umbels loose, spherical; tep. 8–11mm, pink to purple with darker midrib. Spring–summer. Turkestan, Cauc., C Asia. 'Zwanenburg': fls deep carmine. Z8.

A. orientale Boiss. 10–40cm. Lvs to 40cm, 3–4, narrow, lanceolate, rosulate. Fls stellate; umbels to 5cm diam., hemispherical; tep. 5–9mm, narrow, white with green midrib. Spring. E Medit. Z8.

A. ostrowskianum Reg. = *A. oreophilum.*

A. oviflorum Reg. = *A. macranthum.*

A. oxyphilum Wherry = *A. cernuum.*

A. pallens L. 10–30cm. Lvs to 30×0.5cm, 3–4. Fls cup-shaped; umbel 1.5–3cm diam., compact; tep. 3.5–5mm, white or pink. S Eur. Z8.

A. paniculatum L. 30–70cm. Lvs 25cm, 3–5, ribbed beneath. Fls bell-shaped; umbel loose, 3.5–7cm diam.; tep. 4.5–7mm, white, pink or yellow-brown. Eur. Z5.

A. paniculatum var. *pallens* (L.) Gren. & Godron = *A. pallens.*

A. paradoxum (Bieb.) G. Don. FEW-FLOWERED LEEK. St. 15–30cm, triangular. Lvs to 30×2.5cm, 1, keeled. Umbels ± bulbiliferous; fls 1–10, bell-shaped; tep. 8–12mm, white with pale green midrib. Spring. Cauc., Iran. var. *paradoxum.* Umbel with 1 or no fls, many bulbils. var. *normale* Stearn. Umbels with to 10 fls and no bulbils. Z8.

A. parciflorum Viv. 9–30cm. Lvs to 10cm, 3–4. Fls 2–10, bell-shaped; umbel fastigiate; tep. 5mm, pink. Corsica, Sardinia. Z9.

A. parishii S. Wats. 10–20cm. Lf much longer than st., 1, terete. Fls 10 or more in an umbel; tep. 15mm, pale pink, spreading. Spring. Calif., W Nevada. Z6.

A. parvum Kellogg. 3–5cm. Lvs to 10×0.4cm, 2, curved. Fls 8–100 in an umbel; tep. 7–10mm, pink to purple with darker midrib. Spring–summer. Calif., Oreg., Idaho, Utah, Nevada. Z5.

A. pedemontanum Willd. = *A. narcissiflorum.*

A. pendulinum Ten. St. 6–25cm, triangular. Lvs to 25×0.7cm, 2, keeled. Fls 5–9, erect becoming pendent, stellate; tep. 3–5mm, white with green midrib. Spring. S It., Corsica, Sardinia, Sicily. Z8.

A. peninsulare Lemmon ex Greene. 20–40cm. Lvs equal st., 1–6mm wide, 2–4. Fls 6–25; tep. 10–13mm, deep pink to purple, outer tep. spreading. Spring–summer. Calif. var. *crispum* (Greene) Jeps. Inner tep. with wavy margins. Z8.

A. perdulce S. Fraser. 10–20cm. Lvs as least as long as st., to 2mm wide, 3 or more, channelled. Fls urceolate, fragrant, 5–25 per umbel; tep. 10mm, erect, deep rose to purple. Spring. US (Dak., Iowa, Tex., New Mex.). Z5.

A. pikeanum Rydb. = *A. geyeri.*

A. pilosum Sibth. & Sm. 2.5–15cm. Lvs 9cm, thread-like, hairy. Fls cup-shaped; umbel 1.5–4cm diam.; tep. 3–4mm, lilac. Greece. Z9.

A. platycaule S. Wats. St. 4–12cm, flat. Lvs longer than st., 8–15mm wide, 2, sickle-shaped. Fls numerous; tep. 12mm, deep pink with paler tips. Spring. US (Calif., Nevada, Oreg.). Z6.

A. platystemon Karel. & Kir. = *A. oreophilum.*

A. plummerae S. Wats. 30–50cm. Lvs to 27cm, to 10, channelled, sometimes denticulate. Fls stellate, 10–25 in an erect umbel; tep. 5–10mm, white to pink. SW US, N Mex. Z8.

A. polyanthum Schult. & Schult. f. 40–80cm. Lvs 10–25cm, 3–6, flat. Fls many; umbel 4–8cm diam.; tep. to 5mm, elliptic, pink, midvein rough. SW Eur.

A. porphyroprasum Heldr. = *A. scordoprasum* ssp. *rotundum.*

A. porrum L. LEEK. Bienn. grown as an ann. Pseudostem continuous with fleshy, elongated, solitary bulb. Lvs linear-lanceolate. Fls white to pink, in a large spherical umbel. N temp. zones. Z6.

A. porrum ssp. *euampeloprasum* Breistr. = *A. ampeloprasum.*

A. porrum var. *ampeloprasum* Mirb. = *A. ampeloprasum.*

A. praecox Brandg. 20–50cm. Lvs 20–50×0.1–0.5cm, 2–4, flat. Fls 6–30 in a loose umbel; tep. 9–12mm, white with pink to purple midrib. Spring. Calif. Z9.

A. przewalskianum Reg. 15–30cm. Lvs to 35cm, 3–4. Fls numerous, stellate; umbel hemispherical, 1.5–2.5cm diam.; tep. 4–5mm, mauve. Himal., W China. Z8.

A. pseudoflavum Vved. = *A. stamineum.*

A. pulchellum G. Don = *A. carinatum* ssp. *pulchellum.*

A. pulchrum Clarke = *A. subhirsutum.*

A. purdomii W.W. Sm. = *A. cyaneum.*

A. purdyi Eastw. 10–30cm. Lf 1, exceeding st. Fls numerous, in an umbel; tep. to 10mm, pale pink with darker midrib. Spring. Calif. Z8.

A. purpurascens Losa. = *A. schoenoprasum.*

A. pyrenaicum Costa & Vayr. 55–100cm. Lvs to 45cm, 5–6, linear, keeled, toothed. Fls campanulate; umbel 4–7cm diam.; tep. 7–9mm, white with green midrib. E Pyren. Z7.

A. raddeanum Reg. = *A. schoenoprasum.*

A. ramosum L. FRAGRANT-FLOWERED GARLIC. 24–50cm. Lvs to 35cm, 4–9, hollow. Fls bell-shaped; umbel fastigiate, 3–5cm wide; tep. 8–18mm, white with dark red midrib. C Asia. Z7.

A. ramosum Jacq. = *A. obliquum.*

A. recurvatum Rydb. = *A. cernuum.*

A. regelii Trautv. To 100cm. Lvs to 5cm wide, 2–4, margins often rough. Fls bell-shaped, erect, in whorls of 6, lowest 8–10cm diam.; tep. 9–13mm, pale pink to purple with darker central vein. C Asia. Z9.

A. reticulatum G. Don non Presl & C. Presl = *A. textile.*

A. reticulatum var. *deserticola* M.E. Jones = *A. macropetalum.*

A. reticulatum var. *nuttallii* (S. Wats.) M.E. Jones = *A. drummondii.*

A. rhodopeum Velen. = *A. paniculatum.*

A. rilaense Panov. = *A. vineale.*

A. rollii Terracc. = *A. amethystinum.*

A. rosenbachianum Reg. St. to 100cm, ribbed. Lvs 1–5cm wide, much shorter than st., 2–4. Fls stellate; umbel to 10cm diam., spherical; tep. 6–10mm, deep purple or white. Spring. C Asia. 'Album': to 75cm; fls white, slightly tinted green. 'Purple King': st. tall; fls dark violet, sta. white, in loose, round umbel. Z8.

A. roseum L. ROSY GARLIC. 10–65cm. Lvs 12–35×1–1.5cm, 2–7. Fls 5–30, cup-shaped; umbels 2–8cm diam., fastigiate or hemispherical, ± bulbiliferous; tep. 7–12mm, white to bright pink. Spring–summer. S Eur., N Afr., Turk. var. *roseum.* Infl. without bulbils. var. *bulbiliferum* DC. Infl. with bulbils. var. *carneum* (Bertol.) Rchb. Infl. with bulbils, tep. pale pink. Z8.

A. roseum var. *bulbiferum* DC. = *A. roseum* var. *carneum.*

A. rotundum L. = *A. scordoprasum* ssp. *rotundum.*

A. rubens Schräd. ex Willd. St. 10–25cm, ridged. Lvs 5–20cm, 5–6, channelled. Fls bell-shaped; umbel lax, 2–3cm diam.; tep. 4–5mm, purple. N & C Asia, Russia. Z4.

A. rubrum Osterh. To 25cm. Lvs to 6mm wide. Fls few; umbels bulbiliferous; tep. 6mm, white to pink. New Mex. to BC. Z3.

A. rydbergii Macbr. = *A. rubrum.*

A. sardoum Moris. = *A. guttatum* ssp. *sardoum.*

A. sativum L. GARLIC. Pungently aromatic, 25–100cm. Bulbs composed of bulblets. Lvs 60cm, linear, flat above. Fls few; umbels 2.5–5cm diam., containing bulbils; tep. 3–5mm, white to pink, tinged green or purple. Not known in the wild. var. *ophioscorodon* (Link) Döll. ROCAMBOLE; SERPENT GARLIC. St. coiled at first. Z8.

A. sativum var. *subrotundum* Gren. & Godron. = *A. sativum* var. *ophioscorodon.*

A. scaposum Benth. = *A. kunthii.*

A. schmitzii var. *duriminium* Cout. = *A. schoenoprasum.*

A. schoenoprasum L. CHIVES; CIVE; SCHNITTLAUGH. 10–60cm. Lvs to 35×0.6cm, 1–2, cylindric, hollow. Fls bell-shaped; umbel dense, 1.5–5cm diam.; tep. 7–15mm, white or purple, with darker midrib. Eur., Asia, N Amer. 'Forescate': vigorous, to 50cm; fls rose-pink, edible. 'Fruhlau': to 25cm; early and plentiful; F1 hybrid. 'Shepherds Crook': to 5cm; lvs contorted. 'Schnittlauch': dwarf, to 20cm. var. *sibiricum* (L.) Hartm. St. to 40cm. Tep. deep rose becoming violet. Balk., Sib., Asia Minor. Z5.

A. schrenkii Reg. = *A. strictum.*

A. schubertii Zucc. St. 30–60mm, hollow. Lvs 20–45cm, broadly linear, wavy, glaucous. Fls stellate, umbel 2–4cm diam., some fls on v. much longer pedicels; tep. 6–10mm, white, pink or violet, with purple midribs. Spring. E Medit. to C Asia. Z8.

A. scorodoprasum L. SAND LEEK; GIANT GARLIC; SPANISH GARLIC. 25–90cm. Lvs to 27cm, 2–5, linear. Fls ovoid, many replaced by purple bulbils; tep. 4–7mm, lilac to dark purple. E Eur., Cauc., Turk., N Iran. *jajlae* (Vved.) Stearn. Bulbils 0; fls rose-violet. Crimea, Cauc. ssp. *rotundum* (L.) Stearn. Umbel rounded, without bulbils; tep. purple, inner paler with white margins and dark purple midrib. S Eur., W Russia, W Asia, Iran. Z7.

A. scorodoprasum ssp. *babingtonii* (Borrer) K. Richt. = *A. ampeloprasum* var. *babingtonii.*

A. scorodoprasum var. *babingtonii* (Borrer) Reg. = *A. ampeloprasum* var. *babingtonii.*

A. scorzonerifolium Desf. ex DC. in Redouté. St. 14–30cm, angular. Lvs 18–40cm, 1–3, linear, glaucous. Fls to 15, stellate; umbel 4–5cm diam., fastigiate; tep. 7–10mm, yellow. Spain, Port. var. *scorzonerifolium.* Umbel with many bulbils. var.

xericense Fernandes. Umbel lacking bulbils. Z8.

A. segetum Schult. & Schult. f. = *A. amethystinum*.

A. semenowii Reg. St. 10–40cm. Lvs 5–15mm wide, linear, channelled. Fls bell-shaped, few; tep. 10–15mm, yellow becoming red. C Asia. Z6.

A. senescens L. GERMAN GARLIC. St. 7–60cm, flattened. Lvs 4–30cm, 4–9, basal, flat. Fls numerous, cup-shaped; umbel 2–5cm diam.; tep. 3.5–8mm, lilac. Summer–autumn. Eur., N Asia. 'Roseum': fls pink. ssp. *senescens*. St. to 60cm. Lvs to 1cm wide. N Asia. ssp. *montanum* (Schrank) Holub. St. to 45cm. Lvs to 6mm wide. Eur. var. *calcareum* (Wallr.) Hylander. St. to 45cm. Lvs 1–6mm wide, grey, curled on surface of soil. var. *glaucum* (Schrad.) Reg. Lvs glaucous, swirling; fls lilac. Z5.

A. serbicum Vis. & Pančič. = *A. pallens*.

A. serotinum Lapeyr. = *A. senescens* ssp. *montanum*.

A. serratum S. Wats. 20–35cm. Lvs to 3mm wide; 2–4. Umbels dense; tep. 7–9mm, pink to purple, papery. Spring. Calif. Z8.

A. serratum var. *dichlamydeum* Jones. = *A. dichlamydeum*.

A. setaceum Waldst. & Kit. = *A. moschatum*.

A. sibiricum L. = *A. schoenoprasum* var. *sibiricum*.

A. siculum Ucria = *Nectaroscordum siculum*.

A. sieberianum Schult. & Schult. f. = *A. neapolitanum*.

A. sikkimense Bak. 10–40cm. Lvs to 30cm, 2–5, linear, flat. Fls bell-shaped, pendent; tep. 6–10mm, deep blue or purple. Himal., Tibet, China. Z8.

A. speciosum Cirillo = *A. nigrum*.

A. sphaerocephalon ssp. *rollii* (Terracc.) K. Richt. = *A. amethystinum*.

A. sphaerocephalum L. ROUND-HEADED LEEK. St. to 90cm, terete, hollow. Lvs 7–35cm, 2–6, hollow. Fls cylindric, numerous; umbel 2–3cm diam., many contain bulbils; tep. pink to dark red-brown. Eur., N Afr., W Asia. ssp. *sphaerocephalon*. Fls red. ssp. *arvense* (Guss.) Arcang. Tep. white, midrib green; pedicels smooth. ssp. *trachypus* (Boiss.) Richter Tep. white, midrib green; pedicels rough. Z5.

A. splendens Willd. 25–50cm. Lvs to 4mm wide, 3–4, linear, flat, margins rough. Fls bell-shaped; umbel hemispherical, dense; tep. to 4mm, bright pink with purple midrib. Sib., Mong., Jap., China. Z5.

A. stamineum Boiss. 10–35cm. Lvs to 15×0.1cm, 3–4. Fls cup-shaped; umbel to 7cm diam., lax; tep. 5mm, pale purple, sometimes yellow. Summer. N Greece, Turk., Asia Minor, Cauc. Z7.

A. stellatum Ker-Gawl. PRAIRIE ONION. 30–70cm. Lvs 1–2mm wide, 3–6, thick, keeled. Fls numerous, cup-shaped; tep. 4–7mm, pink, ovate. Summer. N Amer. 'Album': fls white. Z6.

A. stellerianum Willd. St. 10–30cm, ridged. Lvs to 21×0.15cm, 4–6, margins rough. Fls cup-shaped, few; umbel 2–3cm diam.; tep. 4–5mm, white to yellow. Sib., Mong., C Ural Mts. Z4.

A. stenanthum Drew = *A. bolanderi* var. *stenanthum*.

A. stevenii Ledeb. = *A. globosum*.

A. stipitatum Reg. St. to 150cm, ribbed. Lvs 2–4cm wide, pubesc., glaucous. Fls star-shaped, fragrant; umbel 8–12cm diam.; tep. 8–9mm, pale lilac or white, thin. E Afghan., Pak., Pamir and Tien-Shan Mts. Z8.

A. stojanovii Kovachev = *A. amethystinum*.

A. stramineum Boiss. & Reut. = *A. scorzonerifolium* var. *xericense*.

A. striatum Jacq. = *Nothoscordum bivalve*.

A. strictum Schräd. St. 40–60cm, mild. Lvs to 5mm wide, flat, rigid, margins rough. Fls bell-shaped; umbel dense; tep. 4–5mm, pink with purple midrib. C Eur., W Asia. Z4.

A. subangulatum Reg. To 25cm. Lvs thread-like, dentate. Fls numerous; tep. to 6mm, purple. China.

A. subhirsutum L. 7–30cm. Lvs 8–50×0.1–2cm, 2–3, basal, flat, margins pubesc. Fls stellate; umbel 2–8cm diam., loose; tep. 7–9mm, white. Spring. Medit. Z9.

A. subvillosum Schult. & Schult. f. 10–60cm. Lvs 6–40×0.2–2cm, margins ciliate. Fls cup-shaped; umbel 2.5–4.5cm diam.; tep. 5–9mm, white. Spring. W Medit., Canary Is., N Afr. Z9.

A. sulcatum DC. = *A. neapolitanum*.

A. suworowii Reg. 30–100cm. Lvs to 3cm wide, 2–6, margins rough, glaucous. Fls numerous, stellate; tep. 4–5.5mm, purple, linear. C Asia. Z8.

A. tanguticum Reg. LAVENDER GLOBE LILY. To 40cm. Lvs to 3mm wide, shorter than st., flat, linear. Fls numerous; tep. 3mm, purple, with darker midribs. W China. Z7.

A. tataricum L. f. = *A. ramosum*.

A. tauricum Rchb. = *A. flavum*.

A. tenellum Davidson = *A. campanulatum*.

A. tenorii Spreng. = *A. roseum* var. *carneum*.

A. tenuiflorum Ten. = *A. pallens*.

A. textile Nels. & Macbr. 5–30cm. Lvs to 30×0.5cm, 1–3, channelled, denticulate. Fls 15–30, bell-shaped; tep. 5–7mm, white or pink with red or brown midribs. N Amer. Z6.

A. thunbergii G. Don To 60cm. Lvs 2–3, linear. Fls numerous; tep. to 5mm, purple. Jap. 'Ozawas': low, to 30cm high; fls violet tinted red. Z8.

A. tibeticum Rendle = *A. sikkimense*.

A. tolmiei Bak. St. 5–12cm, flattened. Lvs 2–8mm wide, 2, sickle-shaped. Fls 15–30; tep. 7–10mm, white with broad pink midrib. Spring–summer. Calif. to Utah. Z5.

A. trachypus Boiss. = *A. sphaerocephalon* ssp. *trachypus*.

A. tribracteatum var. *andersonii* S. Wats. = *A. parvum*.

A. tribracteatum var. *parvum* Jeps. = *A. parvum*.

A. tricoccum Ait. WILD LEEK; RAMP. 10–40cm. Lvs 10–30×2.5–5cm, 2–3, petiolate. Fls numerous, stellate, umbel loose; tep. 4–6mm, white, obtuse. Quebec to Virg. to Iowa. Z6.

A. triquetrum L. TRIQUETROUS LEEK; THREE-CORNERED LEEK. St. to 30cm, 3-angled. Lvs to 50cm, 2–5, triangular in section. Fls pendent; umbel 4–7cm diam., loose, secund; tep. 1–2cm, white with green midrib. Spring. S Eur. Z8.

A. triquetrum ssp. *pendulinum* K. Richt. = *A. pendulinum*.

A. triquetrum var. *pendulinum* Reg. = *A. pendulinum*.

A. tuberosum Rottl. ex Spreng. CHINESE CHIVES; GARLIC CHIVES; ORIENTAL GARLIC. St. to 50cm, angled. Lvs 35–0.8cm, 4–9, solid, keeled. Fls fragrant, stellate; umbel 3–5cm diam.; tep. 4–7mm, white with green or brown stripe. Summer–autumn. SE Asia. Z7.

A. ucrainicum Bordz. = *A. ursinum*.

A. uliginosum Ledeb. non G. Don = *A. ledebourianum*.

A. uliginosum G. Don. non Ledeb. = *A. tuberosum*.

A. unifolium Kellogg. To 60cm. Lvs 7mm wide, shorter than st., flat, channelled, 1 from each bulblet. Fls 5–20, bell-shaped; umbel 5cm diam.; tep. 1–1.5cm, deep pink. Spring–summer. US (Oreg., Calif.). Z8.

A. urceolatum Reg. = *A. caesium*.

A. ursinum L. RAMSONS; WILD GARLIC; WOOD GARLIC. St. 10–50cm, angular. Lvs 6–20×1–8cm, 2–3, dark green, petiolate. Fls 6–20, stellate; umbel 2.5–6cm diam.; tep. 7–12mm, white, acute. Spring. Eur., Russia. Z5.

A. validum S. Wats. SWAMP ONION. St. to 50–100cm, flattened, angled. Lvs 5–12mm wide, nearly as long as st., 3–6. Fls numerous; tep. 6–10mm, white to pink, with basal pouches. Calif. Z8.

A. vancouverense Macoun. = *A. crenulatum*.

A. vernale Tineo = *A. subvillosum*.

A. victorialis L. ALPINE LEEK. 30–60cm. Lvs 8–25cm, 2–3, lanceolate, narrow. Fls stellate; umbel 3–5cm diam.; tep. 4–5mm, white to yellow. Eur., Asia, Aleutian Is. Z7.

A. vineale L. CROW GARLIC; FALSE GARLIC; STAG'S GARLIC. 30–120cm. Lvs 15–60cm, 2–4, hollow. Fls bell-shaped; umbel 2–5cm diam., sometimes bulbiliferous; tep. 2–4.5mm, white or pink, tinged green. Eur., N Afr., W Asia. Z5.

A. vineale var. *kochii* H.P.G. Koch = *A. kochii*.

A. violaceum Willd. = *A. carinatum*.

A. virens Lam. = *A. oleraceum*.

A. virescens DC. = *A. oleraceum*.

A. viviparum Karw. & Kir. = *A. caeruleum* var. *bulbiliferum*.

A. volhynicum Besser = *A. strictum*.

A. wallichianum Steud. = *A. wallichii*.

A. wallichii Kunth. St. 30–75cm, triangular. Lvs 60–90×0.8–2cm, flat, keeled. Fls stellate; umbel 5–7.5cm diam., loose; tep. 7–11mm, magenta to purple, papery. Nepal to W China. Z8.

A. yatei Aitch. & Bak. = *A. regelii*.

A. yunnanense Diels = *A. mairei*.

A. zebdanense Boiss. & Noë. 25–40cm. Lvs 3–6mm wide, shorter than st., 2. Fls 3–10, bell-shaped; umbel 3–5cm diam.; tep. 9–13mm, white with red midrib. Spring. Leb. Z9.

A. zenobiae Cory. Resembles *A. canadense* var. *mobilense*; umbels bulbiliferous, to 6.5cm diam.; tep. to 6mm, lavender. S Tex. Z8.

Alloplectus Mart. Gesneriaceae. 65 shrubs and perenn. herbs. St. scandent, rooting. Lvs opposite in unequal pairs. Fls axill., solitary or clustered; cal. 5-fid, often red and hairy; cor. gibbous at base, tube cylindric or ventricose, often contracted at the mouth, lobes 5 rounded. Trop. Amer. Z10.

A. ambiguus Urban = *Trichantha ambigua*.

A. calochlamys J.D. Sm. Terrestrial or epiphytic subshrub to 60cm, pilose. Lvs oblong-lanceolate, 6–20cm, sericeous, serrate. Fls to 2.5cm, red, densely sericeous appearing white except at tips. C Amer.

A. dichrous DC. = *Nematanthus hirtellus*.

A. domingensis Urban = *Trichantha domingensis*.

A. forgetii Sprague = *Nautilocalyx forgetii*.

A. hirtellus (Schott) Preston ex Hoehne = *Nematanthus hirtellus*.

A. microsepalus Morton = *Pentadenia microsepala*.

A. nummularia (Hanst.) Wiehl = *Nematanthus gregarius*.

A. savannarum Morton. Epiphytic vine to 5m, yellow-tomentose. Lvs oblong-elliptic, to 16cm. Fls to 3cm, glab. below, yellow-

sericeous at apex. Guyana.
A. sparsifolius Mart. = *Nematanthus hirtellus*.

Allspice *Calycanthus*.

Alluaudia Drake. Didiereaceae. 6 succulent shrubs or trees; br. ascending or spreading, densely thorny. Lvs below thorns, rounded to elliptic, sessile, ± fleshy, falling in dry season. Madag. Z10.
A. ascendens (Drake) Drake. Tree, 5–12m; st. thick, grey-brown with few erect br.; thorns 1.5–2cm, conical, gre-white. Lvs 13.5–25mm, circular to oblique-obcordate, swollen at tips, fleshy, dark green.
A. comosa Drake. Shrub or tree, 1–10m, dividing into 4–5 erect br. with many twigs; thorns, thin, 1.5–3.5cm. Lvs 10–22mm, obovate to circular, often with slight indentation at tips.
A. dumosa Drake. Shrub to 2m or tree to 8m; br. erect, succulent, dividing; thorns to 2cm. Lvs short-cylindric.
A. humbertii Choux. Tree to 6–7m; forking; br. thin, twisted; thorns 0.5–2cm, slender. Lvs 5–16mm, ovate-obcordate.
A. montagnacii Rauh. Tree to 8m, with no or few br.; st. columnar, with annular constrictions, apex curving strongly; thorns to 2.5cm, silver-grey, tips black. Lvs to 17mm, broadly obovate to oblong-oval, tip deeply indented, base subterete.
A. procera (Drake) Drake. Tree to 20m; br. ascending, curved slightly outwards; thorns spirally arranged, 2–2.5cm. Lvs 7–25mm, obovate to obovate-oblong, fleshy.
→*Didierea*.

Alluaudiopsis Humb. & Choux. Didiereaceae. 2 shrubs resembling *Alluaudia*. Madagascar.
A. fiherensis Humb. & Choux. Shrub to 3m; br. long, slender; thorns to 1.5cm, solitary. Lvs fleshy, 9–40mm, oblong-linear. Fls white-yellow. SW Madag.
A. marnieriana Rauh. Shrub, 1–2m; br. spreading; thorns paired 1–1.5cm. Lvs fleshy, 10–15mm, oblong-oval. Fls crimson. Madag.

Allysum *Alyssum; Berteroa incana; Lobularia*.
Almond *Prunus dulcis*.
Almond Geranium *Pelargonium quercifolium*.
Almond-leaved Willow *Salix triandra*.
Almond Tree *Prunus dulcis*.

Alniphyllum Matsum. Styracaceae. 3 decid. shrubs or trees. Fls racemose, clustered or solitary; cal. cup-shaped, 5-lobed, golden stellate-tomentose; cor. gamopetalous, lobes 5, oblong, golden stellate-tomentose; sta. 10. E Asia.
A. fortunei (Hemsl.) Perkins. Shrub or tree, 3–10m. Bark white; young shoots yellow-tomentose. Lvs sparsely stellate-pilose, 8–16cm, obovate to broadly ovate, base rounded, apex acuminate to rounded. Infl. to 15cm; fls 2.5cm, white. W China.
A. pterospermum Matsum. Shrub or tree to 10.5m; young shoots tawny-stellate pubesc. Lvs tawny-pilose, oblong-lanceolate, 11–14cm, base cuneate to rounded-cuneate, apex acute. Infl. to 8cm; fls 1.5cm, white to pink. Taiwan, China.
→*Halesia*.

Alnus Ehrh. ALDER. Betulaceae. 35 decid. trees or shrubs. Lvs alt., toothed. Fls unisexual in separate catkins; ♂ catkins cylindric, slender, pendulous, formed in autumn, flowering in early spring; ♀ catkins (described below) in clusters, term. on short side-branches, oblong to oval, short, erect; scales numerous, woody. N hemis. from subarc. S to the Himal. and Andes, where S to Peru.
A. ×aschersoniana Callier. (*A. serrulata* ×*A. rugosa*.) Small tree, shoots sometimes downy. Lvs 5–9cm, broadly oval or elliptic, apex obtuse, base cuneate, sharply toothed, blue-green or grey beneath, felted yellow. Catkins short-stalked or sessile, in clusters of 6–8. Occurring with the parents.
A. barbata C.A. Mey. = *A. glutinosa* var. *barbata*.
A. californica hort. = *A. rhombifolia*.
A. cordata Desf. ITALIAN ALDER. Tree to 30m, crown ovoid-conic; shoots angled, soon glab., sticky, red-brown. Lvs 5–12cm, broadly ovate to rounded, apex pointed, base cordate, sticky at first, coriaceous, finely toothed, deep lustrous green above, paler beneath with vein axils yellow-brown tufted-hirsute; vein pairs 6–10. Catkins 2–3cm, erect, ovoid in clusters of 1–5. It., Corsica. Z6. 'Purpurea': lvs emerging purple-brown.
A. cordifolia Ten. = *A. cordata*.
A. cremastogyne Burkill. Tree to 25cm, crown slender, bark grey, smooth; shoots angled, soon glab. Lvs 7–11cm, obovate to oval, pointed, base cuneate, sharply toothed, lustrous green above, paler beneath, brown-downy, vein pairs 8–11. Catkins 2×0.5cm, solitary, on pedicels 5–8cm. W China. Z8.
A. crispa (Ait.) Pursh = *A. viridis* ssp. *crispa*.

A. ×elliptica Reg. (*A. cordata* ×*A. glutinosa*.) Tree to 20m+. Lvs 3.5–7cm, slender, oval or rounded, apex blunt, base rounded, finely serrate, lustrous green above, almost glab. beneath. Catkins 2×1cm, in clusters of 3–5. Corsica. 'Itolanda': more vigorous; lvs elliptic.
A. fauriei Lév. Large shrub or small tree; young shoots glab. Lvs to 10cm, base rounded to cuneate, apex truncate, emarginate, glab. above, with tufts of brown hairs in vein axils beneath. N & C Jap.
A. fiekii Callier = *A. ×silesiaca*.
A. firma Sieb. & Zucc. Tree or shrub to 15m; br. long, slender; shoots glab., sticky, becoming grey-brown. Lvs 5–12cm, ovate-oblong to oblong-lanceolate, apex tapered, base rounded-cuneate, finely toothed, adpressed-hairy, vein pairs 12–15, pubesc. Catkins 2cm, solitary, oval or subglobose, stalk glandular-hirsute. Spring. Jap. Z7. var. *hirtella* Franch. & Savat. Shoots downy. Lvs 5–12cm, oval-oblong to oval-lanceolate, vein pairs 10–16. Jap. Z6. var. *multinervis* Reg. Tree 5–10m; shoots soon glab., brown. Lvs 5–12cm, oblong-lanceolate, apex tapered, base rounded-cuneate, vein pairs 18–26. Jap. Z6.
A. firma var. *yasha* (Matsum.) Winkl. = *A. firma* var. *hirtella*.
A. fruticosa Rupr. Tree or shrub to 10m; shoots red-brown at first, becoming grey. Lvs 3–5cm, broadly ovate, apex tapered, slightly lobed, vein pairs 7(–10). Catkins 1cm. Sib., Manch. Z2.
A. glutinosa (L.) Gaertn. COMMON ALDER; EUROPEAN ALDER. Tree to 20m, rarely 30m, crown narrow-pyramidal, open; bark brown-black; shoots glab., with glutinous glands. Lvs 4–10cm, broad obovate to orbicular, apex rounded, base acuminate, margins irregularly rounded or bidentate, dark green, glab. except for axial tufts beneath, vein pairs 5–6. Catkins 1–2cm, ovoid, long-stalked, in groups of 3–8. Spring. Eur. to Cauc. and Sib., N Afr. Z3. 'Aurea': lvs yellow ageing yellow-green. 'Imperialis': lvs deeply cut into narrow lobes. 'Incisa': lvs rounded, small, deeply serrate to almost pinnate. 'Laciniata': similar to 'Imperialis' but strong-growing, lobes wider. 'Maculata': lvs dotted white. 'Pyramidalis': habit stiff, erect; lvs rounded. var. *barbata* (C.A. Mey.) Ledeb. Lvs oval-oblong, finely toothed, acute, downy beneath. Cauc., N Iran. Z5. var. *denticulata* (C.A. Mey.) Ledeb. Lvs 5–10cm, broad-elliptic to obovate, apex blunt, base tapered, biserrate, rarely lobulate, vein pairs 7–9. Asia Minor, Cauc. f. *graeca* Callier. Lvs 2.5–3.5cm, coriaceous, thick. Greece (Naxos, Euboea). f. *lacera* (Mela) Mela. Shrub or small tree; lvs 4–7cm, oblong-oval, with 5–6 oblong dentate, lobes in apical half. N Eur. f. *parvifolia* (Kuntze) Callier. Lvs 3–5cm, rounded. Eur.
A. glutinosa f. *fastigiata* Beissn. = *A. glutinosa* 'Pyramidalis'.
A. glutinosa f. *pyramidalis* Späth. = *A. glutinosa* 'Pyramidalis'.
A. hirsuta (Spach) Rupr. MANCHURIAN ALDER. Tree to 20m, crown broadly pyramidal; bark black-brown; shoots thickly downy at first, red-brown, older shoots grey-bloomy, smooth. Lvs 6–13cm, broadly ovate, apex shortly pointed, base cuneate, biserrate to lobed, dull green, lightly pubesc. above, red-brown downy beneath, vein pairs 9–12. Catkins 2×1cm in rac. of 2–6. Jap., China (Manch.). Z3. var. *mandschurica* Callier Lvs to 10×8cm, broadly elliptic, apex obtuse, short, base rounded, margins with shallow lobes, slightly downy above, pale green or blue-green beneath, veins thickly downy beneath, 8–10 pairs. Manch. Z3. var. *sibirica* (Spach) Schneid. Shoots glab. Lvs glab., downy only on midrib and veins beneath. Jap., NE Asia. Z3.
A. hybrida A. Br. = *A. ×pubescens*.
A. incana (L.) Moench. GREY ALDER. Tree to 30m, bark smooth, pale grey; shoots grey-downy. Lvs 4–10cm, broadly ovate or oval, base rounded or cuneate, dull, rugose above, pubesc. at first, white-grey downy beneath, vein pairs 9–14. Catkins 1.5cm, ovoid, in bunches of 4–12. Eur., Cauc. Z2. 'Aurea': br. yellow, ageing orange-red; lvs yellow, felted beneath; catkins orange at first. 'Bolleana': lvs spotted yellow. 'Laciniata': lvs with narrow lobes. 'Monstrosa': low, wide spreading shrub; br. fasciate. 'Oxyacanthoides': lvs with triangular teeth. 'Pendula': br. weeping; lvs grey-green. 'Ramulis Coccineis': winter shoots and buds red; catkins orange. 'Variegata': lvs splashed white. f. *blyttiana* Callier. Lvs 2.5–3cm, ovate to broadly elliptic, apex blunt, shallowly bluntly lobed, green or blue-green, slightly downy, vein pairs 7–8. Finland, Norway. var. *hypochlora* Callier. Lvs elliptic to broadly ovate, apex abruptly tapered, margins rounded-lobed, glab. or lightly downy, vein pairs 8–10. Finland to It. f. *parvifolia* Reg. Lvs 1–1.5cm, rounded, grey-green beneath, vein pairs 5–7. Finland.
A. incana ssp. *rugosa* Duroi = *A. rugosa*.
A. incana ssp. *tenuifolia* (Nutt.) Breitung = *A. tenuifolia*.
A. incana var. *acuminata* Reg. = *A. incana* 'Laciniata'.
A. incana var. *americana* Reg. = *A. rugosa*.
A. incana var. *glauca* Loud. = *A. ×pubescens* var. *americana*.
A. incana var. *hirsuta* Spach = *A. hirsuta*.
A. incana var. *incisa* Bean = *A. incana* 'Laciniata'.

A. incana var. *pinnatifida* Dipp. = *A. incana* 'Laciniata'.

A. incana f. *acuminata* (Reg.) Callier = *A. incana* 'Laciniata'.

A. incana f. *acutiloba* (K. Koch) Hallier = *A. incana* 'Laciniata'.

A. jackii Hu = *A. trabeculosa.*

A. japonica (Thunb.) Steud. JAPANESE ALDER. Tree to 25m, densely leafy, crown conical; shoots glab. or downy near base. Lvs 6–10cm, ovate or oval, apex and base acuminate, finely dentate, glab. dark green and glossy above, paler and tufted in vein axils beneath. Catkins 1.5–2.5cm, oval, stalked, in clusters of 2–6. Jap., Korea, China (Manch.). Z4. var. *koreana* Callier. Lvs 3–5.5cm, broadly ovate, obtuse, with large blunt teeth, dull green above, densely downy beneath, vein pairs 7–8. Korea. var. *minor* Miq. Lvs 4–6.5cm, elliptic, tapered, with short acute teeth, short flocked-downy beneath, vein pairs 7–8(–10). Jap.

A. jorullensis HBK. Tree to 25m; bark with distinct rings. Lvs 6–9cm, oblong-elliptic, abruptly short-tapered, irregularly toothed, base entire, glab. above, yellow-pubesc. beneath, vein pairs. Mex. Z8. ssp. *lutea* Furlow. Lvs with yellow glands beneath. Z9.

A. ×koehnei Callier. (*A. incana* ×*A. subcordata.*) Shoots stout, bristly. Lvs 6–9cm, elliptic, base rounded, toothed, glab., or with scattered down above, densely bristly beneath. Origin unknown.

A. lanata Duthie. Tree 15–18m; bark smooth, yellow-grey; shoots brown, bristly, gland. Lvs 8–14cm, obovate, apex short, base rounded-cuneate, unevenly toothed in apical half, dull green felted above, densely brown-tomentose beneath. Catkins solitary. W China. Z8.

A. mandschurica (Callier) Hand.-Mazz. = *A. hirsuta* var. *mandschurica.*

A. maritima (Marsh) Muhlenb. SEASIDE ALDER. Shrub or small tree to 10m, usually shrubby; shoots soon glab., orange-brown. Lvs 6–10cm, obovate, oval or ovate, apex usually pointed, base cuneate, finely glandular-dentate, dark lustrous green above, dull green and glab. beneath except for tufts in vein axils, vein pairs 8–10. Catkins to 2cm, ovoid. Autumn. US. Z7.

A. matsumurae Callier. Tree; shoots yellow-brown, glab., with orange lenticels. Lvs 7cm, rounded-obovate to orbicular, base concave, slightly lobed, biserrate, apex truncate or notched, dull green above, sparsely grey-green and downy to glab. beneath, vein pairs 8–9. Catkins obovoid to elliptic. Jap. Z5.

A. maximowiczii Callier. Shrub or small tree to 10m. Shoots angled, pale brown, later grey. Lvs 5–10cm, broadly ovate, apex acute, base rounded or slightly cordate, teeth fine, slender, dark green glab. above, paler beneath, axial tufts of down, and midrib speckled, vein pairs 8–11. Catkins 1.5–2cm, ovoid or cylindrical, in groups of 4–5. Jap. (Sakhalin). Z4.

A. ×mayrii Callier. (*A. japonica* ×*A. hirsuta.*) As *A. japonica* but lvs broader, apex acute, not acuminate.

A. mitchelliana M.A. Curtis. = *A. viridis* ssp. *crispa.*

A. mollis Fern. = *A. viridis* ssp. *crispa* var. *mollis.*

A. multinervis (Reg.) Callier. = *A. firma* var. *multinervis.*

A. nepalensis D. Don. NEPAL ALDER. Tree to 25m, bark dark silver-grey; shoots grey-brown, white-glandular, glab. or slightly downy. Lvs 8–22cm, ovate or narrowly oval, apex acute, base usually tapered, shallow-toothed, dark green and glab. above, paler beneath, loosely downy on veins, vein pairs 10–18. Catkins 1.5–2.5cm, ovoid or cylindrical, 10–12, in a short pan. Autumn. Himal., SW Yunnan. Z9.

A. nitida (Spach) Endl. Tree to 30m; bark black, eventually forming square scales; shoots soon glab., yellow-brown. Lvs 8–14cm, ovate to oval, v. slender, apex tapered, base broadly cuneate, coarsely dentate to subentire, dark lustrous green above, paler beneath with axial tufts, vein pairs 9–12. Catkins 2–3cm, erect, 3–5 in a cluster, oblong. Autumn. Himal. Z8.

A. oblongata Mill. = *A. maritima.*

A. oblongifolia Torr. ARIZONA ALDER. Tree to 18m; shoots glab., red-brown. Lvs 5.5–7cm, oblong-ovate to lanceolate, apex and base broadly tapered, sharply biserrate, dark green and glossy above, glab. or slightly downy beneath. US (Ariz. to Calif.). Z8.

A. occidentalis Dipp. = *A. tenuifolia* var. *occidentalis.*

A. oregona Nutt. = *A. rubra.*

A. orientalis Decne. Tree to 15m, shoots angled, red-brown, lenticels orange. Lvs 4–12cm, ovate or oval, unevenly toothed, dark lustrous green above, paler beneath, glab. except for axial tufts beneath, vein pairs 8–10. Catkins 2.5–1.5–2cm, ovoid-rounded, solitary, paired or in clusters of 3. Syr., Cyprus, S Turk. Z7.

A. pendula Matsum. = *A. cremastogyne* var. *multinervis.*

A. ×pubescens Tausch (*A. glutinosa* ×*A. incana.*) Shoots downy at first. Lvs 3–6cm, obovate to ovate, apex slightly tapered, margins lobed, undulating, dark green above, blue-green, downy or slightly felted beneath, vein pairs 7–8. Eur.

A. ×purpusii Callier. (*A. rugosa* ×*A. tenuifolia.*) Tree; buds densely downy. Lvs 3–6cm, ovate, densely covered with rust-coloured felted down, shallowly obtusely lobed, vein pairs 8. WN America.

A. rhombifolia Nutt. WHITE ALDER. Tree to 20m, crown thin, spreading, rounded; br. slender, nodding; shoots soon glab. Lvs 6–10cm, ovate, oval or rounded, apex acute, base tapered, finely biserrate, densely downy at first, becoming dark shiny green above, paler yellow-green beneath and remaining downy. Catkins 1.5cm. W US. Z7.

A. rubra Bong. RED ALDER; OREGON ALDER. Tree to 40m, crown slender, pyramidal; br. ± pendent; shoots angled, glab., sticky, dark red at first. Lvs 8–17cm, ovate or oval, apex acute, base broadly cuneate, shallowly lobed or large-toothed, teeth bicrenate, dark green above, grey or blue-grey beneath, red-brown pubesc. when young, vein pairs 12–15, red. Catkins to 3cm, barrel-shaped, in clusters of 3–6 on orange-red pedicels. Alask. to Calif. Z6.

A. rugosa (Duroi) Spreng. SPECKLED ALDER. Tree or shrub to 6m; shoots glab. or scattered with rust-coloured down, occas. sticky. Lvs 5–12cm, ovate or oval, apex rounded or pointed, base rounded or tapering, shallowly lobed, finely biserrate, glab. above, paler, grey-hairy to glab. beneath, venation brown-downy. Catkins erect, 1–1.5cm, in clusters of 4–10. Canada, NE US. Z2. f. *emersoniana* Fern. Lvs 3–5cm, rounded to suborbicular, grey-felted beneath, v. shallowly lobed or entire, finely serrate, vein pairs 7–9. E US.

A. serrulata (Ait.) Willd. HAZEL ALDER; SMOOTH ALDER. Shrub 2–4m, or small tree to 6m; shoots soon glab.; buds sticky. Lvs 5–9cm, obovate, apex short, blunt, base cuneate, finely sharp-toothed, deep lustrous green above, glab. beneath except for axial tufts, vein pairs 8–9. Catkins in clusters of 3–4. E US.

A. sibirica Fisch. = *A. hirsuta* var. *sibirica.*

A. sieboldiana Matsum. = *A. firma.*

A. ×silesiaca Fiek. (*A. serrulata* ×*A. glutinosa.*) Lvs 6–8cm, rounded-elliptic, apex blunt, base rounded to cordate, indistinctly lobed, finely sharp-toothed, vein pairs 10–12, rusty-downy beneath. Catkins in clusters of 4–8. Gdn origin.

A. sinuata (Reg.) Rydb. SITKA ALDER. Shrub or small tree to 10m, crown slender; br. almost horizontal, short; shoots soon glab., densely gland. Lvs 6–9cm, ovate, apex rounded-cuneate, slightly lobed, biserrate, light green above, paler and shiny beneath, vein pairs 5–10, downy. Catkins ellipsoid, 3–6 in a term. rac. Alask. to Calif. Z2.

A. sitchensis Sarg. = *A. sinuata.*

A. ×spaethii Callier. (*A. japonica* ×*A. subcordata.*) Tree 15–20m, shoots with scattered soft down, sparsely gland. Lvs 6–16cm, lanceolate-ovate, apex short, coriaceous, coarsely serrate, dark lustrous green above, glab. beneath, violet-purple when young, retaining a dark central band, vein pairs 8–11. Gdn origin.

A. ×spectabilis Callier. (*A. incana* ×*A. japonica.*) Close to *A. japonica.* Lvs 5–7(–10)cm, oval or obovate, apex blunt, rounded or acute, base tapered, crenate or serrate, dull and dark green above, pale green, glab. beneath, vein pairs 8–9, downy beneath. Only known in cult.

A. spuria Callier. = *A. ×pubescens.*

A. subcordata C.A. Mey. CAUCASIAN ALDER. Tree to 15m, shoots angled, downy. Lvs 5–16cm, emerging red-brown, ovate to oval, apex abruptly acute, base rounded or slightly cordate, finely biserrate, dark green, glab. above, paler beneath, vein pairs 8–10, downy beneath. Catkins nodding, solitary or to 5 in clusters. Mid winter–early spring. Cauc. (Iran). Z5.

A. tenuifolia Nutt. THINLEAF ALDER; MOUNTAIN ALDER. Tree 7–10m, crown globose; shoots soon glab. veins. Lvs 5–10cm, oval or ovate, apex acute, base rounded or shallowly cordate, slightly lobed, crenate, dark green above, veins downy, paler, pubesc. beneath, vein pairs 10. Catkins 1.5cm, ovoid, in clusters of 3–5. BC to Calif. Z2. var. *occidentalis* (Dipp.) Callier. Lvs 8–15cm apex strongly pointed, lobes pointed, slightly glaucous beneath, vein pairs 10–12. Z5. var. *virescens* (Wats.) Callier. Lvs 8–15cm apex blunt, lobes short, blunt, pale green-yellow beneath, vein pairs 8.

A. tiliacea hort. ex Rehd. = *A. cordata.*

A. tinctoria Sarg. = *A. hirsuta.*

A. trabeculosa Hand.-Mazz. Small tree to 7m, bark smooth, flaking or fissured; shoots grey at first. Lvs 5.5–7.5cm, obovate, apex abruptly pointed, base cuneate, coriaceous, sharply toothed, dark green and glab., veins slightly downy. SE China. Z5.

A. viridis (Chaix) DC. GREEN ALDER. Multistemmed shrub to 2.5m, shoots sticky. Lvs 3–6cm, ovate or rounded-oval, apex abruptly acute, base rounded or slightly cuneate, sticky at first, serrate, matt green above, more yellow and glossy beneath, glab., vein pairs 5–10, downy beneath. Catkins 0.7–1.5cm, oval, in rac. of 2–15, yellow-brown. Eur. Z4. 'Grandifolia': lvs 6–11×5–9cm, vein pairs 6–10. 'Laciniata': lvs deeply cut. 'Microphylla': lvs rounded, small. var. *pumila* Cesati. To 0.5m.

Lvs 1–1.5cm, glab., vein pairs 6–10. Z3. ssp. *crispa* (Ait.) Turrill. Shrub, prostrate or to 3m. Lvs 3–8cm, ovate-broadly elliptic, base rounded or shallowly cordate, finely serrate, slightly sticky at first, aromatic, bright green, vein pairs 5–10. Canada, NE US. Z2. var. *mollis* (Fern.) Fern. Shoots downy; lvs larger, downy beneath. Canada, NE US. Z3. var. *repens* (Wormsk.) Callier. Prostrate shrub. Lvs 3–7cm, vein pairs 5–7(–9), glab. beneath.

A. *viridis* var. *parviflora* Dipp. = A. *viridis* var. *pumila*.

A. *viridis* var. *brembana* (Rota) Callier = A. *viridis* var. *pumila*.

A. *viridis* var. *sibirica* Reg. pro parte = A. *fruticosa*.

A. *yasha* Matsum. = A. *firma* var. *hirtella*.

Alocasia (Schott) G. Don f. ELEPHANT'S-EAR PLANT. Araceae. c70 large rhizomatous or tuberous herbs. St. erect, short, stout. Lvs glab., usually peltate, erect or deflexed, cordate to sagittate, petiole long. Peduncle shorter than petioles; spathe margins overlapping below, forming cylindric or ovoid tube, limb ovate, cymbiform, yellow to green; spadix shorter than spathe, terminated by conic appendage. Trop. S & SE Asia. Z10.

A. ×*amazonica* André. (A. *lowii* ×A. *sanderiana*.) Lvs to 60×30cm, shallowly sinuous or undulate, dark green, purple beneath, veins silver. Gdn origin. 'Green Velvet' (A. ×*amazonica* ×A. *micholitziana*): lvs as A. ×*amazonica*, emerald green, satiny, veins white.

A. ×*argyraea* hort. Sander (A. *korthalsii* ×A. *putzeysii*.) Lvs 60×25cm, ovate, sagittate, acuminate, coriaceous, dark metallic silver-green above, glossy red-brown beneath. Gdn origin.

A. *cucullata* (Lour.) G. Don f. CHINESE TARO. To 1.5m. Lvs 15–40×10–28cm, broad-ovate-cordate, quilted, basal lobes united for less than half length, glossy green, veins prominent; petiole to 1m. Sri Lanka to N India, Burm.

A. *cuprea* (Koch & Bouché) Koch. To 1m. Lvs 20–30×10–18cm, oblong-ovate to elliptic, cordate, basal lobes almost wholly united, obtuse, green with purple or coppery iridescent sheen between black-green zones around sunken veins and midrib above, red-violet beneath; petiole to 60cm. Malaysia, Borneo.

A. *eminens* N.E. Br. = A. *longiloba*.

A. *indica* (Lour.) Spach misapplied = A. *macrorrhiza*.

A. *indica* var. *metallica* Schott ex Engl. misapplied = A. *plumbea*.

A. *indica* var. *violacea* Engl. = A. *macrorrhiza* 'Violacea'.

A. *jenningsii* Veitch = Colocasia affinis.

A. *johnstonii* Bull. = Cyrtosperma johnstonii.

A. *korthalsii* Schott. To 50cm. St. short. Lvs to 35×18cm, ovate, sagittate, basal lobes obtuse, united for half length, dark olive-green with metallic sheen above, margins and veins zoned grey, purple beneath. Borneo.

A. *lindenii* Rodigas = Homalomena lindenii.

A. *longiloba* Miq. To 1m. Lvs 30–70×15–27cm, narrow-triangular to sagittate, basal lobes nearly half length main lobe, united at base, acute, deep glossy green, or blue-green, margin and veins grey, purple beneath. Malaysia, Borneo, Java.

A. *lowii* Hook. To 60cm+. Rhiz. long; st. short. Lvs to 50×18cm, cordate-sagittate, basal lobes to half length main lobe, united for quarter length, obtuse, olive green, veins broad, white, deep purple beneath. Borneo. 'Lowica' (A. *lowii* ×A. ×*amazonica*): lvs metallic green, ribs ivory, margins wavy, purple.

A. *lowii* var. *grandis* hort. ex Nichols. = A. *korthalsii*.

A. *lowii* var. *veitchii* (Lindl.) Engl. = A. *veitchii*.

A. *macrorrhiza* (L.) G. Don. GIANT TARO. To 4m+. St. stout. 1–2m. Lvs 125×75cm, ovate, sagittate, glossy green above, veins green-white; petiole to 1.5m. Sri Lanka, India to Malaysia; cult. widely in tropics for edible rhiz. and shoots, frequently nat. 'Variegata': lvs blotched cream-white, grey-green or dark-green; petioles green and white-striped. 'Violacea': lvs tinged violet.

A. *macrorrhiza* var. *rubra* (Hassk.) Furt. = A. *plumbea*.

A. *macrorrhiza* var. *variegata* (K. Koch & Bouché) Furt. = A. *macrorrhiza* 'Variegata'.

A. *micholitziana* Sander. To 1m. St. to 35cm. Lvs to 25cm, narrow-sagittate, sometimes peltate, basal lobes shortly united, undulate, rick dark green above, soft-textured, pale green beneath, veins white to cream; petiole to 35cm, marbled purple. Philipp. 'Maxkowskii' ('African Mask', 'Green Velvet', 'Green Goddess'): lvs cordate, margins less undulate, dark green, veins v. white; petiole not marbled.

A. ×*mortefontanensis* André. (A. *lowii* ×A. *sanderiana*.) To 1.5m. St. erect, to 50cm. Lvs to 60cm, oblong-sagittate, acute, deeply lobed, green, margin and veins white, violet beneath; petiole to 60cm, olive green with opaque bands. Gdn origin.

A. *odora* (Lodd.) Spach. Close to A. *macrorrhiza*. St. to 60cm. Lvs to 100cm, sagittate-ovate, peltate, erect or spreading, basal lobes rounded. Trop. Asia.

A. *picta* hort. = A. *veitchii*.

A. *plumbea* (K. Koch) Van Houtte. Differs from A. *macrorrhiza* in foliage coloured or tinged purple. Lvs 75×50cm+, weakly sinuate, glossy dark olive-green or purple, silvery-purple beneath, veins purple; petiole purple or marbled. Java. 'Metallica': lvs with purple sheen. 'Nigra': lvs dark green to black. 'Rubra': lvs tinted red.

A. *portei* Schott. To 2m+. St. to 60cm. Mature lvs to 2m, ovate-sagittate, pinnatisect, seg. c8 per side, linear-lanceolate, obtuse, undulate, dark metallic green; juvenile lvs oblong-triangular, shallowly 5–7-lobed; petiole to 2m, green marbled red-purple. Philipp.

A. *putzeysii* N.E. Br. To 1m. Lvs 30–40cm, ovate-sagittate, median lobe triangular, basal lobes one-third length median, dark green above, margin and veins white, metallic violet when young, purple-violet beneath; petiole to 60cm, pale red-purple, spotted brown. Java.

A. *regnieri* Lind. & Rodigas = A. *portei*.

A. *sanderiana* Bull. KRIS PLANT. To 2m. Lvs 30–40×12–20cm, sagittate, margin deeply lobed or sinuous, basal lobes triangular, shortly united, metallic dark black-green above, edged silver, green or purple beneath, lat. veins widely spreading, white; petiole to 40cm, brown-green. Philipp. 'Gandavensis': lvs purple-tinged above when young, purple beneath, veins tinged vermilion, becoming green beneath. 'Van Houtte': dwarf; lvs broad, ribs coloured grey-white.

A. *scabriuscula* N.E. Br. To 2m. St. short, erect. Lvs 40–90×30–45cm, sagittate, erect, glossy dark green above, pale green beneath; petiole to 1m. Borneo.

A. ×*sedenii* hort. ex Mast. & T. Moore. (A. *cuprea* ×A. *veitchii*.) To 1m. Lvs to 40cm, ovate-elliptic, basal lobes obtuse, united for three-quarters length, dark green above, midrib grey-green, red-purple to dark purple beneath; petiole red-purple, green above. Gdn origin.

A. *thibautiana* Mast. = A. *korthalsii*.

A. *veitchii* (Lindl.) Schott. St. to 75cm. Lvs to 90×45cm, narrow-triangular-sagittate, basal lobes half length main lobe, shortly united, dark green above, veined and edged grey, red-purple beneath; petiole to 1.3m, green to purple, dark-banded. Borneo.

A. *watsoniana* Mast. To 1.5m. Lvs 90×45cm, elliptic-ovate, sagittate, bullate, basal lobes half length main lobe, united to half length, blue-green above, edged and veined silver-grey, red-purple beneath; petiole pink or green. Malaysia, Indon.

A. *zebrina* K. Koch ex Veitch. To 1m+. St. short. Lvs to 35×20cm, triangular, cordate-sagittate or sagittate, obtuse, green; petiole to 60cm, banded pale green and black. Philipp.

A. cvs. 'Hilo Beauty': small; stalks black, glaucous; lvs thin, marked pale lime yellow, grey beneath. 'Spotted Papua': vigorous; stalks marked brown; lvs hastate, thick, tinted copper and spotted yellow above, tinted purple beneath.

→Schizocasia.

Aloe L. Liliaceae (Aloeaceae). 325 perenn. herbs, shrubs or trees. Lvs in basal or term. rosettes or an open spiral, succulent, margins horny, toothed or spiny (width given below is that of the clasping base). Infl. lat. or term., racemose, scapose, sometimes branched, capitate to cylindric (heights below include scape); perianth usually tubular, tep. 6. S Afr., Madag., Cape Verde Is. Some spp. widely nat. elsewhere.

A. *aculeata* Pole-Evans. RED HOT POKER ALOE. St. procumbent. Lvs in a compact rosette, to 60cm, lanceolate-attenuate, dull green to glaucous, teeth red-brown, scattered, v. spiny below. Infl. 2–4-branched near base, to 1m; fls to 4cm, orange in bud, opening lemon-yellow. Early winter. S Afr., Zimb. Z9.

A. *africana* Mill. St. usually unbranched, to 4m. Lvs in a dense rosette, dull green to glaucous, to 65×12cm, spines red-tinged sometimes scattered below. Infl. 2–4-branched, to 80cm; fls to 5.5cm, dull red in bud, opening yellow to orange-yellow, upper half upcurved. Summer. S Afr. (Cape Prov.). Z9.

A. *albida* (Stapf) G. Reynolds. Stemless, solitary. Lvs suberect, 15×0.5cm, narrow-linear, dull green, marginal teeth minute white. Infl. unbranched, to 18cm; rac. capitate, fls 8–16, creamy white, green at the tip. Autumn. S Afr. Z9.

A. *albiflora* Guillaum. Stemless, forming small groups. Lvs spiralling or rosulate, to 15×0.5cm, linear-attenuate, grey-green, muricate, with dull white spots, margins dull white, teeth crowded. Infl. unbranched, to 60cm, buds striped grey-brown; fls 1cm, white, campanulate. Winter. Madag. Z9.

A. *albocincta* Haw. = A. *striata*.

A. *alooides* (Bol.) Van Druten. St. stout, erect usually unbranched, to 2m. Lvs in dense rosettes, to 130×18cm, ensiform, recurved, green, margins and teeth red. Infl. unbranched, to 1.3m; fls to 1cm, lemon yellow, campanulate. Winter. S Afr. Z10.

A. *andringitrensis* H. Perrier. Stemless. Lvs ascending, to 50×7cm, rough, grey-green, marginal teeth small, pink-tinged.

Infl. 6–8-branched to 150cm; fls to 2cm, orange-red in bud, opening dull orange to yellow. Winter. Madag. Z10.

A. **arborescens** Mill. CANDELABRA ALOE; OCTOPUS PLANT; TORCH PLANT. Much-branched candelabriform shrub to 3m. Lvs to 60cm, grey-green above, dull-green beneath, marginal teeth forward-curving. Infl. usually unbranched, to 80cm; fls 4cm, scarlet tipped green-white. Summer. S Afr., Zimb., Moz., Malawi. 'Spineless': lvs tinted blue, margins smooth. Variegata': lvs blue-green, striped cream. Z9.

A. **arenicola** G. Reynolds. St. to 1m, slender simple or branched, procumbent, to suberect. Lvs to 18×5.5cm, lanceolate-attenuate, green tinged blue, with white spots, margins white, serrulate. Infl. to 50cm, br. 0–2; fls to 4cm, peach-red, paler at the mouth. Winter–summer. S Afr. (Cape Prov.). Z9.

A. **aristata** Haw. TORCH PLANT; LACE ALOE. Stemless, forming clusters of dense rosettes. Lvs incurved, lanceolate, tapering to a tufted bristle, to 10×1.5cm, green with scattered white spots in bands with sparse white spines, teeth soft, white. Infl. (0)–6-branched, to 50cm; fls to 4cm, red. Early summer. S Afr., Les. 'Variegata': lvs striped white. Z9.

A. **audhalica** Lavranos & Hardy. Rosettes solitary. Lvs to 45×15cm, triangular-acute, ascending, glaucous if grown in shade, otherwise brown, tinged pink, rough, teeth strong, brown. Infl. 1–4-branched to 1m; fls scarlet. S Yemen. Z10.

A. **ausana** Dinter = A. variegata.

A. **bainesii** Dyer. Tree to 18m, trunk stout; br. forking. Lvs 60–90cm, sword-shaped, green, marginal teeth scattered, horny, white, tipped brown. Infl. usually 3-branched, to 60cm; fls to 4cm, rose tipped green. Winter. S Afr., Swaz., Moz. Z9.

A. **bakeri** Scott-Elliot. St. to 20cm, slender, sprawling, offsetting. Lvs c7cm, tapering, chocolate to green-brown banded brick-red or dull pink, with scattered green spots, margins white-toothed. Infl. unbranched, to 30cm; fls scarlet, tinged apricot below, orange towards apex, yellow at green-tipped mouth. Winter. Madag. Z10.

A. **barbadensis** Mill. = A. vera.

A. **barbertoniae** Pole-Evans. St. 0 or v. short. Lvs lanceolate, spreading, to 50cm including dry, twisted apex, tinged red-brown above, with white spots ± forming bands; margins wavy, brown, sharp-toothed. Infl. 5–8-branched, to 1m; fls dull pink tinged red. Summer. S Afr. Z9.

A. **bayfieldii** Salm-Dyck = × Gasterhaworthia bayfieldii.

A. **beguinii** Radl. = × Gasteraloe beguinii.

A. **bellatula** G. Reynolds. Stemless, suckering, tufted. Lvs to 13×1×0.3cm, linear, ascending, dark green, with pale green spots, verrucose, softly toothed. Infl. 0–1-branched, to 60cm; fls to 1.3cm, pale coral-red, campanulate. Summer. Madag. Z10.

A. **branddraaiensis** Groenew. Stemless. Lvs in rosette, or 2-ranked, to 35×10cm, lanceolate, tapering, brown-tinged toward dried, twisted apex, with pale striations and scattered pale blotches, margins wavy, teeth hard, brown. Infl. much-branched, to 1.5m; fls dull scarlet, paler at mouth. Summer. S Afr. Z9.

A. **brevifolia** Mill. Stemless, forming groups of compact rosettes. Lvs 6×2cm, triangular-lanceolate, glaucous, sparsely and softly spiny beneath, toothed. Infl. unbranched, to 40cm; fls light scarlet, mouth green. Early summer. S Afr. (Cape Prov.). Z9.

A. **broomii** Schönl. BERG ALWYN. St. procumbent, to 1m, unbranched or forked above. Lvs to 30×10cm, ovate-lanceolate, pungent, teeth, pale-tipped, margins wavy, red-brown. Infl. unbranched, to 1.5m; fls pale lemon, to 2.5cm, concealed by white-yellow bracteoles. Spring. S Afr. Z9.

A. **buettneri** A. Berger. Stemless, solitary, base bulbous. Lvs leathery, decid., to 45×10cm, narrowing to an acute apex, green, white- to pink-toothed. Infl. 3–5-branched, to 90cm; fls to 4cm, green, tinged yellow, to pink, tinged brown or scarlet. W & C Afr. S to Nam. Z10.

A. **bulbilifera** H. Perrier. Usually stemless. Lvs to 60×10cm, triangular, margins wavy, toothed. Infl. many-branched, sprawling, to 2.5m; fls scarlet, oft. replaced by plantlets. Madag. Z10.

A. **cameronii** Hemsl. St. branched below, to 1m, shrubby. Lvs 40–50×5–7cm, green, bronze-red in winter, teeth pale brown. Infl. dichotomously 2–3-branched, 60–90cm; fls to 4.5cm, bright scarlet. Winter. Zam., Malawi, Zimb., Moz. Z10.

A. **camperi** Schweinf. St. 0.5–1m, branched below, erect to decumbent. Lvs to 60×12cm, tapering dark green, with elongated white spots, margins red-tinged, teeth brown-red. Infl. 6–8-branched, 70–100cm; fls 2cm, orange to yellow. Early winter. Ethiop. Z10. 'Maculata': lvs smaller, glaucous, heavily spotted cream, spines pale, prominent.

A. **candelabrum** Berger. St. 2–4m, unbranched. Lvs to 100×15cm, dull or glaucous green, channelled above, ± spiny beneath, margins red, teeth small red-brown. Infl. with 6–12 br., 50–80cm; fls 3cm, scarlet, rose-pink or orange, tips white. Winter. S Afr. (Natal). Z9.

A. **capitata** Bak. St. 0 or short. Lvs ascending, apex slightly twisted, rounded, to 50×6cm, green, tinged red, margins brown-red, teeth red. Infl. 3–4-branched, to 80cm, capitate to subglobose; fls to 2.5cm, orange-yellow, campanulate. Madag. Z10.

A. **castanea** Schönl. Arborescent, to 4m, trunk often much branched below. Lvs to 1m×10cm, dull green, margins and teeth pale red-brown. Infl. unbranched; fls to 2cm, chestnut brown, campanulate, nectariferous. Winter. S Afr. Z9.

A. **chabaudii** Schönl. St. short or 0, forming groups. Lvs to 50×10cm, ovate-lanceolate, grey- to blue-green, with a few irregular spots, margins grey-tinged, teeth small, hooked. Infl. much-branched, to 1m; fls to 4cm, usually pale brick-red. Autumn–winter. S Afr., Moz., to Zaire. Z9.

A. **ciliaris** Haw. CLIMBING ALOE. St. slender, climbing to 5m. Lvs distant, to 10–15×1.5cm, linear-lanceolate, white-toothed. Infl. lat., usually unbranched, to 30cm; fls 3cm scarlet, green tinged with yellow at the mouth. S Afr. (Cape Prov.). Z9.

A. **comosa** Marloth & A. Berger. St. unbranched, to 2m. Lvs in a dense term. rosette, to 65×12cm, lanceolate-ensiform, glaucous, sometimes tinged brown and pink, teeth small. Infl. usually unbranched, to 2.5m; fls pink in bud, opening to 2.5cm, rose-cream to ivory tinged pink. Summer. S Afr. (Cape Prov.). Z9.

A. **cooperi** Bak. St. 0 or v. short, offsetting. Lvs usually 2-ranked, to 80×6cm, green, with white spots beneath, white-toothed. Infl. unbranched, to 1m; fls salmon-pink, tipped green. Summer. S Afr., Swaz. Z9.

A. **cremnophila** G. Reynolds & Bally. St. to 20cm, narrow, procumbent, much-branched. Lvs about 10cm, 2cm wide at base, grey-green, teeth pale brown. Infl. unbranched, pendent then ascending to 30cm; fls scarlet, tipped yellow-green. Early summer. Somalia. Z9.

A. **cryptopoda** Bak. Rosettes several, ± stemless. Lvs to 90×15cm, ensiform, erect to bow-shaped, dark green, tinged red or blue, teeth small, red-brown. Infl. 5–8-branched, to 1.75m; fls to 4cm, scarlet, green-tipped. Winter. S Afr., Moz., Malawi, Zam., Bots. Z9.

A. **davyana** Schönl. Stemless. Lvs to 20×10cm, triangular-lanceolate, tip dry, twisted, oblong, with banded or scattered white spots above, margins wavy, brown-toothed. Infl. 3–5-branched to 1m; fls to 3.5cm, flesh-pink to dull brick-red. Winter. S Afr. Z9.

A. **descoingsii** G. Reynolds. St. 0 or v. short, suckering. Lvs to 3×1.5cm, ovate-acuminate, dull green, with dull white tubercles, teeth firm, white. Infl. unbranched, to 15cm; fls to 1cm, scarlet tipped orange. Madag. Z10.

A. **dichotoma** Masson. Flat-topped tree to 9m. Trunk thick; branching dichotomous. Lvs to 35×5cm, linear-lanceolate, glaucous, margins brown-yellow, teeth to 1mm. Infl. 3–5-branched to 30cm; fls bright yellow. Winter. S Afr. (Cape Prov.), Nam. Z9.

A. **dinteri** A. Berger ex Dinter. Stemless. Lvs to 30×8cm narrowly lanceolate, chocolate to green tinged brown, with white spots in interrupted bands, margins white, toothed. Infl. 3–8-branched to 85cm; fls to 3cm, pale rose-pink, tipped white, glaucous. Winter. Nam. Z9.

A. **distans** Haw. JEWELLED ALOE. St. decumbent, rooting, to 3m. Lvs to 15×7cm, lanceolate, glaucous with pale subtuberculate spots and an apical spine, teeth golden yellow. Infl. branched, to 60cm; fls dull scarlet or lemon yellow with an orange keel. Summer. S Afr. (Cape Prov.). Z9.

A. **divaricata** A. Berger. Shrub 3m+, usually branched. Lvs to 65×7cm, ensiform, dull grey-green tinged red, teeth sharp, red-brown. Infl. much branched and re-branched to 1m; fls to 3cm, scarlet. Winter. Madag. Z10.

A. **doei** Lavranos. Usually solitary. Lvs 35×10cm, dull green and flat, with scattered white spots above. Infl. 2–3-branched, to 70cm; fls to 2.5cm, yellow. Summer. S Yemen. Z10.

A. **dorotheae** A. Berger. St. 0 or short, suckering. Lvs to 25×5cm, tapering, green, becoming brown-red, with elongated spots denser on paler lower surface, margins wavy, toothed. Infl. usually unbranched, to 60cm; fls to 3.5cm, yellow or red, tipped green. Winter. Tanz. Z10.

A. **echinata** Willd. = A. humilis var. echinata.

A. **ecklonis** Salm-Dyck. St. short or 0, grouped 7. Lvs many-ranked, to 40×9cm, unspotted above, dull green sometimes with white spots beneath, margins and teeth white. Infl. unbranched, to 50cm; fls to 2.5cm, yellow to orange, purple to red. S Afr., Les., Swaz. Z9.

A. **erinacea** Hardy. St. sometimes decumbent, to 60cm, solitary or in groups. Lvs lanceolate-triangular, 8–16×4cm, grey-green, with black spines near apex, 5–8 black teeth on keel beneath, toothed. Infl. unbranched, to 1m, buds crimson tipped grey; fls red and white, tinged yellow and tipped green. Nam. Z9.

A. **eru** A. Berger = A. camperi.

A. **esculenta** Leach. St. 0 or to 40cm, decumbent, branched. Lvs

40–50×8cm, grey-green to pink tinged brown, with white spots in irregular bands, more densely spotted beneath, with dark-tipped white, tuberculate teeth, margins wavy, brown-toothed. Infl. 3–5-branched, ±1.5m; fls to 3cm, dark pink, striped cream or yellow, becoming yellow. Angola, Zam., Nam., Bots. Z9.

A. *excelsa* A. Berger. Tree to 9m, unbranched. Lvs to 80×15cm, spiny when young, usually tuberculate beneath, marginal teeth red-brown. Infl. much-branched; fls to 3cm, orange to deep red. Winter. Zimb., Zam., Malawi, Moz., S Afr. (Transvaal). Z9.

A. *ferox* Mill. CAPE ALOE.   St. to 3m. Lvs to 1m×15cm, lanceolate-ensiform, fleshy, sometimes tinged red, smooth to spiny throughout, margins sinuate, with stout red-brown teeth. Infl. branched; fls to 3.5cm, scarlet, sometimes orange. Winter–spring. S Afr. (Cape Prov.). Z9.

A. *fosteri* Pill.   Usually stemless. Lvs to 50×8cm, lanceolate-attenuate, tip dry and twisted, dark green or blue-grey, with pale green spots in bands, margins sinuate, teeth pale brown. Infl. compound to 1.5m, lower fls to 3.5cm, orange-red, upper fls golden-yellow. Early winter. S Afr. Z9.

A. *gariepensis* Pill. St. 0 or to 1m, branched or simple, erect or sprawling. Lvs to 40×8cm, narrowly lanceolate, dull green to red-brown, spotted or unspotted, teeth red-brown. Infl. simple to 120cm; buds sometimes red, fls to 3cm, yellow. Winter. S Afr., Nam. Z9.

A. *glauca* Mill.   St. usually short. Lvs to 15×4cm, lanceolate, glaucous, somewhat spiny below, teeth red-brown. Infl. simple to 80cm; fls pale red, faintly green-tipped. Spring. S Afr. (Cape Prov.). Z9.

A. *globuligemma* Pole Evans.   St. many, slender, procumbent. Lvs to 50×9cm, lanceolate, glaucous, margins dull white, teeth brown-tipped. Infl. much-branched to 1m, buds tinged red; fls to 2.5cm, sulphur yellow to ivory, tinged red at base. Winter. S Afr., Zimb., Bots. Z9.

A. *grandidentata* Salm-Dyck. Suckering. St. short or 0. Lvs to 20×7cm dried twisted, lanceolate, green, tinged brown, spots white, oblong, in broken bands, margins undulate, teeth red-brown. Infl. branched to 90cm; fls dull red, rarely pale pink, edged white to 3cm. Winter–spring. S Afr. Z9.

A. *greenii* Bak. Stemless, stoloniferous. Lvs to 45×8cm, broadly linear-lanceolate, bright green, with paler spots in irregular bands, margins undulate with light brown to pink teeth. Infl. 5–7-branched to 1.3m; fls pale to dark flesh pink. S Afr. (Natal). Z9.

A. *hanburiana* Naudin = A. *striata*.

A. *harlana* G. Reynolds. St. 0 or short, sometimes dividing. Lvs to 15×15cm, lanceolate, tapered, olive green, sometimes with a few pale green blotches. Infl. 6–8-branched to 90cm; scape with broken green lines; fls to 3cm, dark red, sometimes yellow. Summer. Ethiop. Z9.

A. *haworthioides* Bak.   Stemless, sometimes suckering. Lvs to 4cm, narrow, mucronate, margins ciliate, teeth white. Infl. un-branched, to 30cm; fls to 1cm, white to light pink. Madag. Z9.

A. *hereroensis* Engl. St. 0, or short, procumbent. Lvs to 30×6cm, lanceolate-deltoid, arched, v. glaucous with scattered spots beneath, margins undulate, teeth short, red-brown. Infl. branched, 1m, fls to 3cm, yellow, orange or scarlet to dull red. Winter. Nam., S Afr. Z9.

A. *humilis* (L.) Mill. SPIDER ALOE; HEDGEHOG ALOE; CROCODILE JAWS.   Stemless, forming clumps. Lvs to 10×1.8cm, ovate-lanceolate, acuminate, glaucous, tuberculate, teeth white. Infl. simple, to 35cm; fls scarlet, sometimes orange, 4cm. Spring. Cape Prov. Z9. var. *echinata* (Willd.) Bak.   'Globosa': lvs tinged blue.

A. *inermis* Forssk. St. to 50cm, decumbent to erect, suckering. Lvs to 30×7cm, lanceolate or ensiform, entire grey-green or olive green, sometimes with white, elongated spots toward base. Infl. 6–9-branched, to 70cm; fls to 3cm, dull scarlet or yellow. Yemen, S Yemen, Somalia. Z10.

A. *jacksonii* G. Reynolds. St. to 20cm, simple or branched below, erect or sprawling. Lvs subulate, to 15×1.5cm, obtusely mucronate with pale green spots, sometimes in interrupted bands, marginal teeth red-brown, tipped white. Infl. un-branched, to 30cm; fls to 3cm, scarlet. Ethiop. Z10.

A. *jucunda* G. Reynolds. St. 0 or short, clumped. Lvs 4×2.5cm, ovate-acuminate, dark green, brown-tinged in upper half with pale spots, teeth red-brown. Infl. unbranched, to 33cm; fls to 2cm, pale rose pink, mouth white. Somalia. Z10.

A. *juttae* Dinter = A. *microstigma*.

A. *juvenna* Brandham & S. Carter.   St. to 45cm, erect or decumbent, suckering. Lvs to 4×2cm, triangular, bright green, blotched and spotted, margins toothed. Infl. simple or with 1 br., to 25cm; fls bright pink, green-tipped in bud, mouth yellow, to 3cm. Known only in cult. Z9.

A. *karasbergensis* Pill. St. 0 or to 30cm, unbranched or forming groups. Lvs to 50×20cm, ovate-lanceolate, acuminate, glaucous, green-veined, margins dull white, entire. Infl. much-

branched, to 60cm; fls to 3cm, pink to pale coral, tipped green. S Afr. (Cape Prov.), Nam. Z9.

A. *krapohliana* Marloth.   St. 0, or to 20cm. Lvs to 20×4cm, narrowly lanceolate, acuminate, glaucous, banded beneath, teeth small, white. Infl. 0–2-branched to 40cm; fls to 3.5cm, scarlet tipped green. Winter. S Afr. (Cape Prov.). Z9.

A. *latifolia* Haw. = A. *saponaria*.

A. *littoralis* Bak. St. unbranched, to 4m. Lvs to 60×13cm, grey-green, usually unmarked, margins undulate, brown-toothed, sparse superficial teeth sometimes also present. Infl. 8–10-branched, to 1.5m; fls to 3.5cm, pink to bright red, paler and tinged yellow toward mouth, pruinose. Autumn. Angola, Nam., Zam., Moz., Bots., S Afr. Z9.

A. *longistyla* Bak.   Stemless, usually solitary. Lvs to 15×3cm, spine-tipped, grey-green with white spines and tubercles, margins white-toothed. Infl. simple, to 20cm, fls to 5cm, pale salmon pink to rose-red, tipped green. Winter. S Afr. (Cape Prov.). Z9.

A. *lutescens* Groenew. St. short or to 80cm, forming dense clumps. Lvs 60×9cm, lanceolate, attenuate, glossy yellow-green, becoming yellow, teeth pink-brown. Infl. 3-branched, to 1.5m; buds scarlet; fls to 3.5cm, yellow. Winter. S Afr., Zimb. Z9.

A. *macracantha* Bak. = A. *saponaria*.

A. *macroclada* Bak.   Stemless. Lvs to 75×15cm, ensiform-attenuate, ascending, margins wavy, horny, teeth tipped orange-brown. Infl. usually simple, to 1.75m; fls pale red, tinged green in mouth, campanulate. Madag. Z10.

A. *marlothii* A. Berger.   St. unbranched, 2–4m. Lvs to 1.5m×25cm, lanceolate, grey-green with red-brown spines esp. below, marginal teeth red-brown. Infl. much branched, to 80cm; fls to 3.5cm, orange to yellow-orange, ± tipped mauve. Winter. S Afr., Bots., Swaz. Z9.

A. *melanacantha* A. Berger.   St. short, or procumbent to 50cm. Lvs to 20×4cm, lanceolate, dull dark green to brown-green, leathery, keel and margins black-spiny-toothed. Infl. usually simple, to 1m, fls to 4.5cm, scarlet turning yellow, tipped-green. Winter. (Cape Prov., Nam. Z9.

A. *microstigma* Salm-Dyck. St. short, procumbent, to 50cm. Lvs to 30×6.5cm, lanceolate, acuminate, green, occas. tinged red, often with scattered spots, margins undulate, teeth red-brown. Infl. simple, to 80cm; buds dull red, fls orange, turning green tinged yellow, sometimes dull red. Winter. Cape Prov. Z9.

A. *millotii* G. Reynolds.   St. much branched, decumbent or ascending to 25cm. Lvs 2-ranked rosulate, to 10×0.9cm, grey-green, often red-tinged, spots few above, many beneath, marginal teeth white. Infl. simple, to 15cm; fls to 2.5cm scarlet, paler at the mouth. Madag. Z9.

A. *mitriformis* Mill. St. procumbent, to 2m, branched below. Lvs to 20×5cm, ovate-lanceolate, glaucous to green, often sparingly spotted, teeth golden yellow. Infl. 2–5-branched, to 60cm; fls to 4.5cm, dull scarlet. Summer. S Afr. (Cape Prov.). Z9.

A. *myriacantha* (Haw.) Roem. & Schult. GRASS ALOE.   Stemless. Lvs to 30×0.8cm, linear, dull green, with white spots, marginal teeth minute, white. Infl. 1–2, simple; fls to 2cm, dull pink, tinged red. Summer. Cape Prov. to Kenya. Z9.

A. *niebuhriana* Lavranos.   Stemless, suckering. Lvs to 45×10cm, grey-green tinged purple, apex mucronate, marginal teeth dark brown. Infl. 0–(2)-branched, to 1m; fls to 3cm, scarlet becoming yellow, tinged green at apices. S Yemen. Z10.

A. *ortholopha* Christian & Milne-Redh.   Stemless. Lvs to 50×14cm, lanceolate, grey-green tinged pink, margins brown, tinged pink or red, teeth brown. Infl. usually 2–3 branched, to 90cm; fls to 4cm, orange-scarlet. Winter. Zimb. Z9.

A. *pachygaster* Dinter.   Stemless, forming dense groups. Lvs 25×5cm, grey-green, convex on both sides, teeth yellow becoming black. Infl. simple, to 90cm; fls to 4cm, brown-red, paler at mouth. Nam. Z9.

A. *parvibracteata* Schönl.   St. 0 or v. short, grouped. Lvs to 40×8cm, narrow, lanceolate, green to green tinged brown, with white spots in interrupted, wavy bands or scattered, margins wavy, brown-toothed. Infl. branched; fls to 3cm, dull to glossy red. Winter. S Afr., Swaz., Moz. Z9.

A. *parvula* A. Berger.   Stemless, solitary or grouped. Lvs to 10×1.2cm, pale blue-grey, unspotted, muricate, marginal teeth white. Infl. simple, to 35cm; fls to 2.5cm, pale coral red, edged white. Early summer. Madag. Z10.

A. *pearsonii* Schönl.   St. much branched, erect, 1–2m. Lvs deflexed, to 9×4cm, ovate-acute to ovate-lanceolate, becoming dull red during drought, teeth white to red. Infl. 2–3-branched, to 40cm; fls to 2.5cm, yellow or brick-red. Summer. S Afr. (Cape Prov.), Nam. Z9.

A. *peglerae* Schönl.   St. 0 or v. short, procumbent. Lvs to 25×7cm, lanceolate-acuminate, dull green, tip spiny, red-tinged, with sparse tuberculate spines beneath, teeth tipped red-brown. Infl. to 40cm sometimes forked; fls to 3cm, cream tinged green and red, dull red in bud. Winter. S Afr. Z9.

A. perfoliata L. = *A. vera*.

A. perryi Bak. SOCOTRINE ALOE. St. unbranched, to 30cm. Lvs to 35×7.5cm, lanceolate-acuminate, grey-green, tinged red, teeth light brown. Infl. 2–3-branched, to 60cm; fls to 2.5cm, red, green-tipped. S Yemen (Socotra). Z10.

A. petricola Pole Evans. St. 0, or v. short. Lvs to 60×10cm, lanceolate, glaucous, with sparse spines throughout. Infl. 3–6-branched, to 1m; fls to 3cm, cream, green-white or orange. Winter. S Afr. Z9.

A. picta Thunb. = *A. saponaria*.

A. pienaarii Pole Evans = *A. cryptopoda*.

A. pillansii L. Guthrie. Tree to 10m, bole thick, br. simple to dichotomously branched. Lvs to 60×1.5cm, lanceolate, tapered, grey-green to green, tinged brown, teeth white. Infl. densely branched to 50cm; fls lemon yellow. Spring. S Afr. (Cape Prov.), Nam. Z9.

A. plicatilis (L.) Mill. FAN ALOE. Shrub or small tree, to 5m, much branched. Lvs to 30×4cm in 2 ranks, flat, broadly linear, obtuse, dull green to glaucous. Infl. simple to 50cm; fls to 5cm, scarlet tipped green. Winter. S Afr. (Cape Prov.). Z9.

A. pluridens Haw. St. to 6m, simple or branched. Lvs to 70×6cm, long-acuminate, pale green to yellow-green, margins undulate, white, teeth incurved. Infl. branched, to 1m; fls to 4.5cm, bright pink. Winter. S Afr. Z9.

A. polyphylla Schönl. ex Pill. St. 0 or v. short. Lvs to 30×10cm, spirally arranged, ovate-acuminate, grey-green, apex tinged purple, margins with pale triangular teeth. Infl. 3–8-branched, to 60cm; fls to 5cm, pale red to salmon-pink, rarely yellow. Spring. Les. Z7.

A. pratensis Bak. Stemless, usually in groups. Lvs to 15×5cm, lanceolate or ovate-lanceolate, glaucous, usually with a few brown spines beneath, margins sharp-toothed. Infl. unbranched, to 60cm; fls to 4cm, red. Spring. E S Afr. Z9.

A. pretoriensis Pole Evans. St. single, to 1m. Lvs to 60×15cm, lanceolate, pale green to grey-green tip, tinged red, teeth red-tinged, yellow or brown-yellow. Infl. much-branched 1.5m ±; fls to 4.5cm rose to peach. Winter. S Afr., Swaz., Zimb. Z9.

A. purpurascens Haw. = *A. succotrina*.

A. ramosissima Pill. Shrub to 2–3m. St. repeatedly branched from below. Lvs to 20×0.7cm, linear-lanceolate, margin pale yellow, teeth pale brown. Infl. to 20cm; 2-branched, fls canary yellow, sometimes tinged green, to 3.5cm. Winter. S Afr. (Cape Prov.), Nam. Z9.

A. rauhii G. Reynolds. St. 0 or v. short, clumped. Lvs to 10×2cm, lanceolate-triangular, grey-green, with scattered spots, margins white, minutely toothed. Infl. 0–(1)-branched, to 30cm; fls 2.5cm, pink-red. Early summer. Madag. Z10.

A. recurvifolia Groenew. = *A. alooides*.

A. reitzii G. Reynolds. St. 0 or to 60cm, procumbent. Lvs to 65×12cm, ensiform, sometimes with spines in mid-line near apex beneath, teeth brown to red-brown. Infl. 2–6-branched, to 1.3m; fls to 5cm, bright red above, lemon below. Late summer. S Afr. Z10.

A. rigens G. Reynolds & Bally. St. 0 or v. short. Lvs to 80×15cm, grey-green, sometimes tinged red, teeth tinged brown. Infl. 3–4-branched, to 1.75m. Summer. Somalia. Z10.

A. rubriflora (L. Bol.) G. Rowley = *Poellnitzia rubrifolia*.

A. rubrolutea Schinz. = *A. littoralis*.

A. rubroviolacea Schweinf. St. unbranched, to 1m. Lvs to 60×11cm, lanceolate-ensiform, violet, tinged red or purple near base, with a violet bloom, margins red-tinged, teeth hooked. Infl. unbranched or forked, to 1m; fls to 4cm, bright red. Spring. Yemen. Z10.

A. saponaria (Ait. f.) Haw. SOAP ALOE. St. 0, clumped, suckering or to 50cm, unbranched. Lvs to 30×8–12cm, lanceolate, pale to dark green with dull white markings in broken bands above, margins wavy, teeth brown. Infl. forked 50–100cm; fls to 4cm, yellow, salmon-pink, orange-scarlet to scarlet. S Afr., Zimb., Bots. Z9.

A. secundiflora Engl. St. 0, or v. short. Lvs to 45×14cm, ovate-lanceolate, dull green, margins wavy with sharp brown teeth. Infl. 10–12-branched, to 1.5m; fls to 3.5cm, rose to dull red, speckled white. Spring. Tanz., Kenya, Sudan, Ethiop. Z10.

A. simii Pole Evans. St. 0. Lvs to 60×12cm, dull milky green, usually unspotted, U-shaped in cross-section, margins wavy, teeth pale brown. Infl. to 1.5m, br. 5–9, bowed, compound; fls 4cm, strawberry pink. Late summer. S Afr. Z9.

A. sinkatana G. Reynolds. Stemless. Lvs to 60×8cm, dull grey-green, apex rounded, toothed, unspotted above, with dull white spots beneath, marginal teeth red. Infl. 5–6-branched, to 90cm; fls 2cm, yellow, orange or scarlet. Sudan. Z10.

A. sladeniana Pole-Evans. Stemless, suckering. Lvs 3-ranked, 4–8×3–4cm, with white markings scattered or in broken bands, keel and margins minutely white-toothed. Infl. to 50cm, 0–2-branched; fls to 3cm, dull pink, tinged green at the mouth.

Summer. Nam. Z9.

A. somaliensis C.H. Wright. St. 0 or v. short. Lvs to 20×7cm, usually lanceolate, tinged brown with many light green spots, margins wavy, teeth red-brown. Infl. 5–8-branched, to 80cm; fls 3cm, pink, tinged scarlet, minutely speckled. Somalia. Z10.

A. speciosa Bak. Shrubby to tree-like, st. often unbranched, sometimes to 6m. Lvs to 80×8cm, ensiform, glaucous blue or red, margins dark pink to pale red, teeth red. Infl. unbranched, to 50cm; fls to 3.5cm, green-white, buds red. Winter. S Afr. (Cape Prov.). Z9.

A. squarrosa Bak. St. 0, or low, branching. Lvs to 8×2cm, triangular to lanceolate, rough, green with bands of white spots, margins toothed. Infl. unbranched, to 15cm; fls 2cm, scarlet. S Yemen (Socotra). Z10.

A. steudneri Schweinf. St. short, branching from base. Lvs to 60×15cm, teeth small. Infl. 0–5-branched to 90cm; fls to 4.5cm, dark red. Spring. Ethiop. (Tigre, Eritrea). Z10.

A. striata Haw. CORAL ALOE. St. decumbent, to 1m, unbranched. Lvs to 50×20cm, ovate-lanceolate, entire, unspotted, striate, margins pale pink to red. Infl. 1m; fls to 2.5cm, peach-red to coral-red. Winter. S Afr. (Cape Prov.). Z9. 'Picta' (*A. striata* ×*A. saponaria*): lvs dark green striped cream, banded green-yellow.

A. striatula Haw. Shrub to 1.75m. Lvs to 25×2.5cm, linear-lanceolate, glossy, sheaths, striped green, teeth minute, white. Infl. unbranched, to 40cm; fls to 4.5cm, orange to red-orange. Summer. S Afr. (Cape Prov.), Les. Z9.

A. succotrina Lam. St. short, unbranched, or to 1–2m, branched. Lvs to 50×10cm, arching, dull green to grey-green, sometimes white-spotted teeth white. Infl. unbranched, to 1m; fls to 4cm, red tipped green. S Afr. (Cape Prov.). Z9.

A. suprafoliata Pole-Evans. St. 0 or to 60cm. Lvs to 40×7cm, lanceolate, blue-grey, red-brown near dry and twisted apex, teeth red-brown. Infl. unbranched, to 1m; buds red with blue-grey tips; fls 4cm, rose-pink to scarlet, tipped green. Early winter. Swaz., S Afr. Z9.

A. suzannae Decary. St. usually unbranched, 3–4m. Lvs to 1m×9cm, leathery, dull green, teeth light brown. Infl. unbranched, to 3m; fls 3cm, cream tinged pale pink. Madag. Z10.

A. swynnertonii Rendle. St. 0. Lvs to 40cm, apex dried and twisted, lanceolate, dark green with spots in wavy bands above, margins wavy, teeth red-brown. Infl. 8–12-branched, to 1.75m; fls 3cm, dull pink to red with a bloom, margins white. Winter. Zimb., Moz., Malawi. Z9.

A. tenuior Haw. St. to 3m, scrambling or arching, from swollen rootstock. Lvs to 15×1.5cm, linear-lanceolate, glaucous, teeth minute, white. Infl. to c30cm, br. 0–2; fls to 1.5cm, yellow. Summer. S Afr. Z9.

A. thorncroftii Pole-Evans. St. 0 or v. short. Lvs to 40×10–14cm, broadly lanceolate, dull grey-green becoming red-tinged, tip dried, margins wavy, teeth red-brown. Infl. to 1m, unbranched; fls 5cm, dull rose-red to scarlet with a pale grey bloom. Winter. S Afr. Z9.

A. thraskii Bak. St., unbranched, 1–4m. Lvs to 1.5m×22cm, dull green to glaucous, few, curved, with median spines beneath, teeth small red. Infl. 3–6-branched; fls 2.5cm, lemon yellow to pale orange, tipped green. Winter. S Afr. (Natal). Z9.

A. turkanensis Christian. St. procumbent, forming groups. Lvs to 55×10cm, lanceolate, blue-green, rough, with dull white, scattered spots, margins white, teeth brown-tipped. Infl. to 12-branched; fls 2.5cm, dull red, tinged pink. Kenya. Z10.

A. vaombe Decorse & Poiss. St. unbranched usually 2–3m. Lvs to 1m×20cm, dull green, margins wavy, toothed. Infl. to about 90cm, to 12-branched; fls 3cm, bright red. Madag. Z10.

A. vaotsanda Decary. St. unbranched, to 4m. Lvs to 1m×15cm, tinged red, margins toothed. Infl. branched, to 50cm; fls 2cm, orange-yellow. Winter. Madag. Z10.

A. variegata L. PARTRIDGE BREAST ALOE; KANNIEDOOD ALOE; TIGER ALOE. St. 0 or short, forming dense clumps. Lvs 10–15×6cm, triangular, fleshy, dark green with oblong white blotches in irregular bands, keel and margins horny, white, minutely notched. Infl. 0–2-branched, to 30cm; fls to 4cm, flesh pink to dull scarlet. Winter. S Afr. Nam. Z9.

A. vera (L.) Burm. f. St. 0 or short, suckering. Lvs grey-green tinged red, sometimes spotted; margins slightly pink with pale teeth. Infl. 0–2-branched to 90cm; fls 3cm, yellow. Cape Verde Is., Canary Is., Medit. region, Barbados, Jam., Mex., Venez., Peru, Boliv. Z8.

A. 'Walmsley's Blue'. Lvs soft, tapering, in small rosettes, blue-green tinged bronze at base, with inconspicuous cream teeth.

A. wickensii Pole Evans. St. 0 or short, forming small groups. Lvs to 80×12cm, ensiform, incurved, dull grey-green, marginal teeth dark. Infl. 3–4-branched to 1.5m; buds dark red; fls to 3.5cm, chrome yellow. Winter. S Afr. Z9.

A. wildii G. Reynolds. Stemless, sometimes forming groups. Lvs 10–20×5–10cm, 2-ranked, linear dull green tinged brown with scattered spots, margins white-toothed. Infl. unbranched, to 30cm; fls to 4cm, bright orange-red, tipped green. Spring. Zimb., Moz. Z9.

A. yuccifolia Gray = *Hesperaloe parviflora*.

A. zebrina Bak. ZEBRA LEAF ALOE. St. 0 or to 30cm, suckering. Lvs to 30×7cm, linear, dark green, powdery, with white blotches in irregular bands, margins wavy, teeth brown-tipped. Infl. much-branched to 1.6m; fls 3cm, dull red. Late summer. Nam. to Malawi, Moz. Z9.

ALOEACEAE Batsch. See LILIACEAE.

Aloinopsis Schwantes. Aizoaceae. 15 fleshy-rooted dwarf, tufted, succulent perennials. Lvs usually rosulate on creeping st., velvety pubesc. or glab. and tuberculate, broadly spathulate, subclavate. Fls stalked, opening in the late afternoon to evening. S Afr. (Cape Prov.).

A. albinota (Haw.) Schwantes = *Rabiea albinota*.

A. albipuncta (Haw.) Schwantes = *Rabiea albipuncta*.

A. aloides (Haw.) Schwantes = *Nananthus aloides*.

A. crassipes (Marloth) L. Bol. = *A. spathulata*.

A. dyeri (L. Bol.) L. Bol. = *A. rubrolineata*.

A. hilmarii (L. Bol.) L. Bol. Lvs 2–2.5cm, abruptly tapered, flat and somewhat widened above, rounded beneath, grey, often flushed red, velvety. Fls 3cm diam., yellow.

A. jamesii L. Bol. Lvs to 1.8cm, triangular to long-tapered, carinate at tip, grey-green, rough-tuberculate. Fls 0.6cm diam., golden-yellow striped red.

A. lodewykii L. Bol. Lvs reniform to semicylindrical above, 10–15mm across, compressed and widened at tip, blue-green to red-brown, tuberculate, tip area with white tubercles. Fls 1.5cm diam., pale pink.

A. luckhoffii (L. Bol.) L. Bol. Lvs 1.8cm, triangular, with a chin-like keel, blue-tinged to grass-green, with grey-green tubercles. Fls 2.5cm diam., pale yellow.

A. malherbei (L. Bol.) L. Bol. Lvs broadly spathulate to fan-shaped and truncate, blue-green, tuberculate below, margins with white tubercles above. Fls 2.5cm diam., pale brown to flesh-coloured.

A. orpenii (N.E. Br.) L. Bol. Lvs to 2cm, ovate-lanceolate, lower surface keeled towards tip, blue-green, glab. or puberulous, prominently spotted. Fls 3.5cm diam., yellow, tipped red.

A. peersii (L. Bol.) L. Bol. Lvs 2–2.2cm, obtusely triangular to tapered, tip carinate beneath, smooth blue-green to grey-green, spotted, minutely puberulous. Fls 2.5cm diam., yellow.

A. rosulata (Kensit) Schwantes. Lvs 2.5–3cm long, broadly spathulate, margins blunt, dark glossy green, tip rounded, covered with pale tubercles. Fls 3–3.5cm diam., yellow.

A. rubrolineata (N.E. Br.) Schwantes. Lvs ovate-acute, 2.5cm long, tapering to a broad, rounded tip, grey-green, rough above with flat white tubercles, angles rough-tuberculate. Fls yellow-white lined red.

A. schooneesii L. Bol. Shoots forming dense clusters. Lvs v. small, broadly spathulate, tip rounded-triangular, blue-green. Fls 1–1.5cm diam., yellow-red, silky.

A. setifera (L. Bol.) L. Bol. Lvs 4cm, tip slightly widened and obliquely rounded-triangular, rough-tuberculate beneath, blue-green to deep crimson, angles and tip with bristly teeth. Fls 2–5cm diam., golden-yellow to salmon-pink.

A. spathulata (Thunb.) L. Bol. Lvs hatchet-shaped, tapered toward base, apiculate, grey-green with a tuberculate tip, margins reddened. Fls 3cm diam., deep red.

A. transvaalensis (Rolfe) Schwantes = *Nananthus transvaalensis*.

A. villetii (L. Bol.) L. Bol. Lvs 2cm, broadly spathulate, rounded above, blue-green with dense white tubercles. Fls 2cm diam., pale yellow, tipped copper-red.

A. vittata (N.E. Br.) Schwantes = *Nananthus vittatus*.

A. wilmaniae L. Bol. = *Nananthus wilmaniae*.

→*Acaulon, Cheiridopsis, Mesembryanthemum, Nananthus, Prepodesma* and *Titanopsis*.

Alonsoa Ruiz & Pav. MASK FLOWER. Scrophulariaceae. 12 shrubs or branched herbs; br. often 4-angled. Infl. usually term., racemose, glandular-pubescent; fls long-stalked; cal. 5-parted; cor. zygomorphic, rotate, tube short, cleft at base. W Trop. Amer. (Mex. to Peru). Z10.

A. acutifolia Ruiz & Pav. Small shrub. 50–90cm. Lvs 2–3cm, lanceolate, rigidly serrate, acute, ± pubesc. Fls 2–2.5cm diam., orange to cinnabar-red. Peruvian and Boliv. Andes. var. *candida* Voss. Fls white.

A. albiflora hort. = *A. acutifolia* var. *candida*.

A. caulialata Ruiz & Pav. = *A. meridionalis*.

A. grandiflora hort. = *A. warscewiczii*.

A. incisifolia Ruiz & Pav. Erect subshrub, 30–90cm. Lvs to 6cm, ovate to ovate-lanceolate, deeply incised. Fls 1.5cm diam.,

rather hooded, deep scarlet with purple-black throat, rarely white. Late spring–autumn. Peru to Chile.

A. ×*intermedia* Lodd. (*A. incisifolia* ×*A. linearis.*) Shrubby plant. Lvs 2cm, entire to weakly serrate. Fls red.

A. linearis (Jacq.) Ruiz & Pav. Shrub to 1m. Lvs 3–4cm, linear to narrowly ovate-lanceolate, entire to minutely serrate. Fls 8–10mm, brick red. Late spring–autumn. Peru. var. *gracilis* hort. More slender in all parts.

A. linifolia Roezl. = *A. linearis*.

A. mathewsii Benth. in DC. Perenn. herb to 30cm. Lvs to 3.5cm, mostly in whorls of 3, ovate to oblong-ovate, serrate. Fls red, sparsely pubesc. Summer. Amazonian Peru.

A. meridionalis (L. f.) Kuntze. Herb, subshrub or shrub. Lvs 3–3.5cm, ovate to lanceolate, serrate to dentate. Fls orange to dark red. Peru.

A. miniata hort. = *A.* ×*intermedia*.

A. myrtifolia Roezl. = *A. acutifolia*.

A. warscewiczii Reg. MASK FLOWER. Perenn. herb or shrub, often treated as gdn ann., 45–60cm. Lvs broadly ovate to lanceolate-cordate to cordate, bidentate to crenate-serrate. Fls 1.5–2cm diam., scarlet to light cinnabar-red, occas. white. Summer–autumn. Peru.

Alopecurus L. FOXTAIL GRASS. Gramineae. 25 ann. or perenn. grasses. St. erect, tufted. Lvs flat; ligules usually obtuse. Infl. a spicate, cylindric, soft pan.; spikelets in a dense spiral, 1-fld, laterally compressed; awn 2–3× length of spikelet. N temp. regions. Z5.

A. alpinus Sm. Low-growing perenn. Lf sheaths somewhat dilated; lower lvs narrow, upper lvs broader. Pan. ovoid or short-cylindric, to 2cm×9mm, pubesc., grey; spikelets ovoid, to 4.5mm, dark purple; awn straight, to 1.5mm. Summer. Scotland, Arc. Eur.

A. armenus K. Koch = *A. arundinaceus*.

A. arundinaceus Poir. Perenn. to 1m. Lf sheaths inflated, glab. to pubesc.; lvs linear, to 4.5cm, scabrid above and on margins. Pan. broad-cylindric, to 7×1.5cm, green to green-purple; spikelets urceolate, to 7mm; awn to 7.5mm, usually curved. Temp. Eurasia.

A. arundinaceus ssp. *armenus* (K. Koch) Tzvelev. = *A. arundinaceus*.

A. lanatus Sibth. & Sm. Perenn. to 30cm. Lf sheaths tomentose, inflated; lvs mostly basal, linear, usually convolute, to 5.5cm, white-tomentose. Pan. ovoid-globose, to 1.5×1.3cm; spikelets to 6mm; awn to 11mm, geniculate, tortuous in lower half. E Medit.

A. nigricans Hornem. = *A. arundinaceus*.

A. phaleioides K. Koch = *A. lanatus*.

A. pratensis L. MEADOW FOXTAIL. Perenn. to 1.2m. Lvs flat, scabrous, to 8mm across; sheath somewhat inflated, smooth. Pan. cylindric, dense, to 10×1cm, pale green, often tinged purple; spikelets to 7mm; awn exserted. Summer. Eurasia, NE Afr. 'Aureomarginatus' ('Aureovariegatus'): lvs striped and edged gold. 'Aureus': lvs gold.

A. ventricosus Pers. non Huds. = *A. arundinaceus*.

Alophia Herb. Iridaceae. 4 cormous perenn. herbs. Lvs radical or few on st. in 2 ranks, plicate, linear-lanceolate. Rac. few-fld, term., subtended by 2 spathes; flowering st. sometimes branching. Tep. 6, outer 3 exceeding inner, ovate with a median band of hairs; style br. 3, cleft. S US to C & S Amer. Z9.

A. amoena (Griseb.) Kuntze = *Herbertia amoena*.

A. caerulea Herb. = *A. drummondii*.

A. drummondiana Herb. = *A. drummondii*.

A. drummondii (Graham) Fost. Lvs 15–30cm. Flowering st. 12–38cm; outer perianth seg. to 2.5cm, inner 1.5cm, violet to indigo, fading to white spotted brown at centre and on claws, margins inrolled. Early summer. S US, Mex., Guinas.

A. lahue (Molina) Espin. = *Herbertia lahue*.

→*Eustylis, Gelasine, Herbertia* and *Trifurcia*.

Aloysia Ortega & Palau ex L'Hérit. Verbenaceae. 37 aromatic shrubs. Lvs opposite or whorled, simple. Fls small in slender spikes or rac.; cal. tubular-campanulate, 4-lobed; cor. hypocrateriform. Americas. Z8.

A. triphylla (L'Hérit.) Britt. LEMON VERBENA; CIDRON; LIMONETTO. To 3m. Lvs to 10cm, membranous, lanceolate, acuminate, entire or dentate, glandular-dotted beneath, strongly lemon-scented. Fls white, sometimes tinted purple, whorled, in axill. spikes or term. pan. Arg., Chile.

A. wrightii (A. Gray) Heller. Lvs to 1.5cm, suborbicular to ovate, rounded, crenate to serrate, grey or yellow-tomentose. Fls white, crowded in pubesc. spikes. SE US, N Mex.

→*Lippia* and *Verbena*.

Alpine Anemone *Pulsatilla alpina*.

Alpine Ash *Eucalyptus delegatensis.*
Alpine Avens *Geum montanum.*
Alpine Azalea *Loiseleuria procumbens.*
Alpine Baeckea *Baeckea gunniana.*
Alpine Balsam *Erinus alpinus.*
Alpine Bartsia *Bartsia alpina.*
Alpine Bearberry *Arctostaphylos alpina.*
Alpine Bistort *Polygonum viviparum.*
Alpine Bottlebrush *Callistemon sieberi.*
Alpine Buttercup *Ranunculus alpestris.*
Alpine Calamint *Acinos alpinus.*
Alpine Catchfly Tree *Lychnis alpina.*
Alpine Celery Pine *Phyllocladus alpinus.*
Alpine Cider Gum *Eucalyptus archeri.*
Alpine Cinquefoil *Potentilla crantzii.*
Alpine Clover *Trifolium alpinum.*
Alpine Collomia *Collomia debilis.*
Alpine Coltsfoot *Homogyne alpina.*
Alpine Columbine *Aquilegia alpina.*
Alpine Currant *Ribes alpinum.*
Alpine Everlasting *Helichrysum acuminatum.*
Alpine Filmy Fern *Hymenophyllum peltatum.*
Alpine Fir *Abies lasiocarpa.*
Alpine Fleabane *Erigeron borealis.*
Alpine Forget-me-not *Eritrichium.*
Alpine Geranium *Erodium reichardii.*
Alpine Golden Chain *Laburnum alpinum.*
Alpine Grey Willow *Salix glaucosericea.*
Alpine Heath *Epacris paludosa; Erica carnea.*
Alpine Knotweed *Polygonum alpinum.*
Alpine Lady Fern *Athyrium distentifolium.*
Alpine Lady's Mantle *Alchemilla alpina; A. conjuncta.*
Alpine Leek *Allium victorialis.*
Alpine Lovage *Ligusticum; (L. mutellina).*
Alpine Marsh Violet *Viola palustris.*
Alpine Meadow Grass *Poa alpina.*
Alpine Milk Vetch *Astragalus alpinus.*
Alpine Mouse-ear *Cerastium alpinum.*
Alpine Orites *Orites lancifolia.*
Alpine Pasque Flower *Pulsatilla alpina.*
Alpine Penny-cress *Thlaspi alpestre.*
Alpine Penstemon *Penstemon tolmiei.*
Alpine Pink *Dianthus alpinus.*
Alpine Poppy *Papaver alpinum.*
Alpine Rock Butterweed *Packera werneriifolia.*
Alpine Scurvy Grass *Rhizobotrya alpina.*
Alpine Snowbell *Soldanella alpina.*
Alpine Strawberry *Fragaria vesca.*
Alpine Thistle *Carlina acaulis.*
Alpine Toadflax *Linaria alpina.*
Alpine Totara *Podocarpus nivalis.*
Alpine Violet *Cyclamen.*
Alpine Wintergreen *Gaultheria humifusa.*

Alpinia Roxb. GINGER LILY. Zingiberaceae. *c*200 perenn. herbs with aromatic rhiz. Lvs lanceolate, acuminate, in 2 ranks on reed-like st. Infl. sometimes bracteate, term. on leafy shoot, racemose or paniculate; cal. 3-lobed, tubular; pet. 3, waxy, posterior pet. largest; lip 2-lobed, larger than pet.; lat. staminodes small or 0. Asia, Australasia. Z10.
A. albolineata = *A. vittata.*
A. allughas Roscoe = *A. nigra.*
A. antillarum Roem. & Schult. = *Renealmia jamaicensis.*
A. calcarata (Haw.) Roscoe. INDIAN GINGER. To 1m. Lvs to 30cm, sparsely ciliate. Infl. 10cm, erect to horizontal; fls green-white; lip to 3cm, yellow, veined red or maroon. Autumn. China, India.
A. cernua Sims = *A. calcarata.*
A. coerulea Benth. To 1.5m. Lvs to 40cm. Infl. paniculate; fls white to rose; lip 1.2cm wide; staminode purple. Spring. Aus. (Queensld).
A. elatior Jack = *Etlingera elatior.*
A. formosana Schum. To 4m. Resembles *A. zerumbet* but with lvs to 70cm. Infl. erect, 15cm; axis glab. S Jap., Taiwan.
A. galanga (L.) Willd. SIAMESE GINGER; GALANGAL. To 2m. Lvs 50cm, margins downy. Infl. to 25cm, usually branched, erect; fls short-lived; pale green; lip 2.5cm, white with pink line. SE Asia.
A. jamaicensis Gaertn. = *Renealmia jamaicensis.*
A. japonica (Thunb.) Miq. To 60cm. Lvs to 40cm. Infl. spicate, to 15cm; fls to 2.5cm, white veined red. China, C Jap., S Jap., Taiwan.
A. kumatake Mak. = *A. formosana.*
A. magnifica Roscoe = *Etlingera elatior.*
A. malaccensis (Burm.) Roscoe. To 3m. Lvs 90cm, pubesc. beneath. Infl. erect; fls large; pet. 2.5cm, silky, white; lip 2cm, ovate, striped yellow and red. Spring. India.

A. mutica Roxb. SMALL SHELL GINGER; ORCHID GINGER. Resembles *A. zerumbet.* To 2m. Lvs to 50cm. Infl. erect; pet. white, to 2.5cm; lip 3–3.5cm, yellow-orange with red lines and spots, crispate. India, Malaysia.
A. nigra B.L. Burtt. To 2m. Lvs 40cm. Fls numerous, in long-branched pan.; cor. pale green; lip pink, 3cm. Winter–early spring. India.
A. nutans hort. non Roscoe = *A. zerumbet.*
A. oceanica hort. = *A. vittata* 'Oceanica'.
A. officinarum Hance. LESSER GALANGAL. To 1.5m. Lvs to 30cm. Infl. 10cm, simple, erect; fls white; lip 2cm, white veined red. China.
A. pauciflora (Griseb. ex Petersen) Kuntze = *Renealmia jamaicensis.*
A. purpurata (Vieill.) Schum. RED GINGER. 3–4m. Lvs to 80cm. Infl. 50cm, erect to nodding, cylindrical, with densely overlapping purple-red bracts concealing small white fls. SE Pacific. 'Eileen McDonald': bracts candy pink. 'Pink Princess': bracts rose. 'Tahitian Ginger': infl. v. large, deep scarlet.
A. rafflesiana Wallich ex Bak. To 1.5m. Lvs to 60cm, short-pubesc. Infl. 8cm, horizontal, each bract subtending 1–5 small white fls. Malaysia.
A. sanderae hort. Sander = *A. vittata.*
A. speciosa (Wendl.) Schum. = *A. zerumbet.*
A. tricolor hort. Sander = *A. vittata.*
A. ventricosa (Griseb.) Kuntze = *Renealmia jamaicensis.*
A. vittata Bull. VARIEGATED GINGER. To 1.5m. Lvs 15cm, with white or cream stripes. Infl. to nodding; bracts green, tinged pink; fls pale green. Solomon Is. 'Oceanica': a smaller plant (to 60cm), st. slender, somewhat inclined; lvs narrow, dark green with broken flashes of white and cream.
A. zerumbet (Pers.) B.L. Burtt & Rosemary M. Sm. SHELL GINGER; PINK PORCELAIN LILY. To 3m. Lvs to 60cm, oblong-lanceolate. Infl. 40cm, pendent; axis red-brown; fls fragrant, white, tinged purple-pink; lip 4cm, crinkled, yellow, with red and brown stripes. Spring–summer. E Asia. 'Variegata': lvs dark green with pale yellow stripes or bands.
A. zingiberina Hook. = *A. galanga.*
→*Catimbium, Globba, Languas* and *Zerumbet.*

Alseuosmia A. Cunn. Alseuosmiaceae. 5 everg. shrubs. Lvs simple, alt., petiolate. Fls axill., solitary or in small cymose fascicles, strongly scented; sep. 4 or 5; cor. tubular or funnel-shaped, 4- or 5-lobed; sta. 4 or 5, anth. exserted. Fr. a crimson berry. N Zealand. Z9.
A. macrophylla A. Cunn. To 2m. Branchlets red-brown, slender. Lvs to 15cm, coriaceous, narrowly ovate to oblanceolate, serrate to entire. Fls to 4cm, dull red or crimson to cream-white; cor. lobes fimbriate. NZ.

ALSEUOSMIACEAE Airy Shaw. 3/8. *Alseuosmia.*

Alsine L. Caryophyllaceae.
A. aretioides (Sommerauer); Mert. & Koch = *Minuartia cherlerioides.*
A. graminifolia Vitm. = *Minuartia graminifolia.*
A. laricifolia (L.) Crantz = *Minuartia laricifolia.*
A. octandra (Sieber) Kerner = *Minuartia cherlerioides.*
A. recurva (All.) Wahlenb. = *Minuartia recurva.*
A. sedoides (L.) Kittel. = *Minuartia sedoides.*
A. verna (L.) Wahlenb. = *Minuartia verna.*

Alsinopsis Small.
A. obtusiloba Rydb. = *Minuartia obtusiloba.*

Alsobia Hanst. Gesneriaceae. 2 perenn. herbs related to *Episcia.* Trop. Amer.
A. dianthiflora (H.E. Moore & R.G. Wils.) Wiehler. LACE-FLOWER VINE. St. creeping, stoloniferous. Lvs to 4cm, elliptic to ovate, obtuse, toothed, thinly fleshy, dark green, glandular-hispidulous, often veined purple-red. Fls solitary; cor. pearly white, tube broad, to 3cm, purple-spotted at base, lobes 1cm, rounded, spreading, fringed. Costa Rica, Mex.
→*Episcia.*

Alsomitra (Bl.) M. Roem. Cucurbitaceae. 2 woody climbers. St. slender. Tendrils bifid. Lvs entire to 3-lobed, broadly ovate to rounded, base rounded to cordate. Fls white; cor. rotate, lobes fleshy: ♂ in pan., ♀ in rac. Fr. large, semi-globose. Indomal. Z10.
A. macrocarpa (Bl.) M. Roem. Lvs 12–17cm. Fr. *c*25cm diam., brown, smooth.

Alsophila R. Br.
A. aculeata (Raddi) J. Sm. = *Cyathea microdonta.*
A. australis R. Br. = *Cyathea australis.*

A. baileyana Domin. = *Cyathea baileyana.*
A. colensoi Hook. f. = *Cyathea colensoi.*
A. cooperi F. Muell. = *Cyathea cooperi.*
A. cunninghamii (Hook. f.) Tryon = *Cyathea cunninghamii.*
A. dregei (Kunze) Tryon = *Cyathea dregei.*
A. leichhardtiana F. Muell. = *Cyathea leichhardtiana.*
A. microdonta (Desv.) Desv. = *Cyathea microdonta.*
A. polypodioides Hook. = *Macrothelypteris polypodioides.*
A. rebeccae F. Muell. = *Cyathea rebeccae.*
A. robertsiana F. Muell. = *Cyathea robertsiana.*
A. smithii (Hook. f.) Hook. = *Cyathea smithii.*
A. subglandulosa Hance = *Ctenitis subglandulosa.*
A. tricolor (Colenso) Tryon = *Cyathea dealbata.*
A. walkerae (Hook.) J. Sm. = *Cyathea walkerae.*
A. woollsiana F. Muell. = *Cyathea woollsiana.*

Alstonia R. Br. Apocynaceae. 45 tall, everg. shrubs or trees with milky sap. Lvs whorled or opposite, entire. Fls small, white, in term. corymbose cymes; cal. 5-lobed; cor. salverform, tube hairy below, limb 5-lobed. Follicles paired, pod-like, elongate. Afr., C Amer., SE Asia to W Pacific Is. Z10.
A. scholaris (L.) R. Br. DEVIL TREE; PALI-MARI; DITA BARK. Tree to 20m. Lvs whorled, to 20cm, oblanceolate, leathery. Cymes compact; cor. to 1.25cm diam., green-white, pubesc. Fr. to 60×0.3cm, pendent. Aus., Malaysia, India and Afr.

Alstroemeria L. LILY OF THE INCAS; PERUVIAN LILY. Liliaceae (Alstroemeriaceae). 50 fleshy rooted herbaceous perennials. St. erect. Lvs usually lanceolate, alt. or scattered, narrowing to a twisted petiole. Fls zygomorphic, in a term. umbel; tep. 6, clawed, 3 inner narrower and longer than outer; sta. 6, declinate. S Amer. Z9 unless specified.
A. aurantiaca D. Don = *A. aurea.*
A. aurea Graham. To 1m+. Lvs 7–10cm. Umbels 3–7-rayed with 1–3 fls per ray; tep. 4–5cm, bright orange or yellow, outer tep. tipped green, inner tep. flecked red above. Summer. Chile. 'Dover Orange': tall; fls deep orange. 'Lutea': fls yellow marked carmine. 'Moerheim Orange': to 1m; fls deep orange and yellow, veined darkly. 'Orange King': to 90cm; fls large in shades of orange. Z7.
A. brasiliensis Spreng. To 120cm. Lvs 5–10cm, linear. Umbels usually 5-rayed, fls 1–3 per ray; tep. *c*4cm, red-yellow, inner tep. flecked brown. Summer–early autumn. C Braz.
A. chilensis hort. To 75cm. Lvs scattered, narrowly obovate. Umbels 5–6-rayed, fls 2 per ray; tep. pale pink to blood red, upper inner tep., yellow striped red-purple. Origin obscure.
A. haemantha Ruiz & Pav. To 90cm. Lvs 7–15cm. Umbel 3–15-rayed; fls 1–4 per ray; tep. 4–5cm, orange to deep vermilion, outer tep. tipped green, upper inner tep. yellow-orange striped purple, lowermost tep. orange to orange-red, striped dark red. Chile. 'Rosea': fls rose.
A. hookeri Lodd. Resembles *A. pelegrina* but shorter (10–15cm), tep. pink, upper inner tep. blotched yellow and flecked red-purple. Peru.
A. ligtu L. ST MARTIN'S FLOWER. To 60cm. Lvs 5–8cm. Umbels 3–8-rayed; fls 2–3 per ray; tep. white to pale lilac to pink-red, upper inner tep. usually yellow, spotted and streaked white or purple or yellow and red. Summer. Chile, Arg. 'Angustifolia': lvs narrow. Fls pale pink. 'Pulchra': fls larger; tep. acute, spotted purple in upper half. Z8.
A. pelegrina L. 30–60cm. Lvs 5–8cm. Fls solitary or in 2–3-rayed umbels; tep. *c*5cm, off-white flushed mauve or pink with a darker central zone, inner tep. yellow at base, flecked brown or maroon. Summer–autumn. Peru. 'Alba': fls white, flushed green, inner upper tep. spotted green and often blotched yellow, 'Rosea': fls deep rose.
A. psittacina Lehm. To 90cm. Lvs to 7.5cm. Umbels 4–6-rayed; tep. 4–4.5cm, green overlaid with dark wine red, spotted and streaked red or maroon. Summer. N Braz. Z8.
A. pulchella L. f. Scarcely distinct from *A. psittacina*. Plants labelled *A. pulchella* are usually *A. psittacina* or *A. ligtu*. Z8.
A. pygmaea Herb. Close to *A. aurea*, but st. ± subterranean, producing a group of lvs to 2.5cm, grey-green; tep. to 5cm, yellow, inner spotted red. Arg.
A. versicolor Ruiz & Pav. Resembles *A. psittacina* but smaller, umbels 2–4-rayed; tep. 2.5cm, yellow orange, flecked purple. Summer–autumn. Chile.
A. violacea Philippi. 50–100cm. Lvs 6–9cm, ovate-oblong, scattered. Umbels 3–6-rayed, fls 3–5 per ray; tep. 3.5–5.5cm, bright violet, inner tep. white at base, spotted purple, sometimes flushed orange. Summer. N Chile.
A. hybrids and cvs. *A. aurea* is the parent of several hybrids, largely confined to the cut-flower trade. More frequently encountered in gardens are the Ligtu Hybrids (*A. ligtu* ×*A. haemantha*), varying in height and habit with fls in a range of colours from soft pink to orange and yellow, and Dr Salter's

Hybrids with fls in carmine, orange, yellow and pink, whiskered, veined or mottled dark red to purple black. Named selections include: 'Afterglow': fls deep flame orange; 'Ballerina': fls light pink; 'Parigo Charm': fls in salmon-pink, primrose-yellow and deep pink; 'Sonata': fls deep pink, often tinged green or brown with splashes with yellow and dark markings; 'Margaret': to 1m; fls deep red and 'Walter Fleming' ('Orchid'): to 1m; fls deep yellow tinged purple spotted red-purple.

ALSTROEMERIACEAE Dumort. See LILIACEAE.

Altai Mountain Thorn *Crataegus altaica.*

Altamiranoa Rose.
A. batesii (Hemsl.) Rose = *Villadia batesii.*
A. cucullata (Rose) Walth. = *Villadia cucullata.*
A. elongata Rose = *Villadia elongata.*
A. grandyi (Hamet) Berger = *Villadia grandyi.*
A. guatemalensis (Rose) Walth. = *Villadia guatemalensis.*
A. imbricata (Rose) Walth. = *Villadia imbricata.*
A. jurgensenii (Hemsl.) Rose = *Villadia jurgensenii.*

Alternanthera Forssk. JOSEPH'S COAT; CHAFF-FLOWER; JOYWEED; BROAD PATH; COPPERLEAF. Amaranthaceae. 200 ann. or perenn. herbs. St. procumbent to erect or floating. Lvs entire or obscurely toothed, opposite, often brightly coloured. Fls small, apetalous, in bracteolate spikes. Trop. and subtrop. Amer. Z8.
A. amoena (Lem.) Voss = *A. ficoidea* var. *amoena.*
A. axillaris Hornem. ex Willd. Erect or ascending to 1m, branched. Lvs to 6×2cm, oblong to oblong-ovate, acute. Cuba.
A. bettzichiana (Reg.) Nichols. CALICO PLANT. Ann. or short-lived perenn. erect to 1m. Lvs narrow-spathulate, olive green to yellow, mottled and stained red to purple. Braz. Probably not truly distinct from *A. ficoidea.* 'Aurea Nana': dwarf; lvs yellow-green. 'Brilliantissima': lvs bright red.
A. dentata (Moench) Scheygr. Erect to 45cm. Lvs 10×5cm, ovate to linear-lanceolate, dark green, often coloured red or purple, pale beneath, rounded or sharply cuneate at base. W Indies. 'Rubiginosa' (INDOOR CLOVER): lvs red to purple.
A. ficoidea (L.) R. Br. Erect or procumbent ann., 30×50cm. St. striate, creeping. Lvs to 2.6×2cm, elliptic to ovate or obovate, pubesc. to glab., acuminate to acute, mucronate, green blotched red and purple or yellow and green or red and orange, often with carmine veins; petioles ± winged. Mex., S Amer. 'Snowball': lvs minute, chalk-white and jade green. 'Versicolor': lvs copper or blood-red to maroon, spathulate. var. *amoena* (Lem.) L.B. Sm. & Downs. PARROT LEAF; SHOOFLY; JOYWEED. Mat-forming. Lvs lanceolate to elliptic, mottled and veined brown, red, orange, yellow and purple. Braz. 'Rosea Nana': lvs rose to carmine. 'Sessilis': lvs ± sessile, green to purple.
A. philoxeroides (Mart.) Griseb. ALLIGATOR WEED. Aquatic perenn. St. to 1.2m, rooting, glab., decumbent to ascending, often swollen. Lvs to 8×2.5cm, glab., lanceolate to obovate, acute, cuneate at base. Colomb. to Braz., Arg.
A. polygonoides (L.) R. Br. Procumbent to mat-forming perenn. to 80cm. Br. soon glab., striate, yellow or red. Lvs to 4.3×1.2cm, villous to glab. above, thinly pilose beneath, acute to mucronate, cuneate to attenuate at base; petioles often winged. Fls white in globose-cylindric spikes to 1cm. Mex. to Arg.
A. ramosissima hort. = *A. dentata.*
A. ramosissima 'Versicolor' = *A. dentata* 'Rubiginosa'.
A. spinosa Hornem. = *A. axillaris.*
→*Achyranthes* and *Telanthera.*

Althaea L. Malvaceae. 12 ann. or perenn. herbs. Lvs shallowly to deeply lobed or parted. Fls to 3.5cm diam., in rac. or pan.; epical. seg. 6–9, united at base; pet. 5, obovate; sta. united in a cylindrical column; anth. purple-red. W Eur. to C Asia.
A. armeniaca Ten. Perenn. herb to 1.2m, sparsely pubesc. Lvs palmately 3- or 5-parted, seg. linear-lanceolate to obovate, coarsely dentate. Fls pink, several, on axill. peduncles, as long as or exceeding subtending lf. SE Russia, C & SW Asia. Z6.
A. cannabina L. Perenn. to 1.8m, stellate-pubesc. pink. Lvs palmately lobed, often to base, lobes 3–5, lanceolate or linear, irregularly dentate, sometimes segmented. Fls pink, solitary or in clusters on long often branched axill. peduncles, exceeding subtending lvs, sometimes forming term. rac. S & E to C Eur. Z4.
A. frutex hort. ex Mill. = *Hibiscus syriacus.*
A. heldreichii Boiss. = *Alcea heldreichii.*
A. kragujevacensis Pančić. = *A. officinalis.*
A. lavateriflora DC. = *Alcea lavateriflora.*
A. narbonensis Pourr. ex Cav. = *A. cannabina.*

A. officinalis L. MARSH MALLOW; WHITE MALLOW. Perenn. to 2m, grey stellate-hairy. Lvs triangular-ovate or broadly ovate, undivided or shallowly, palmately 3- or 5-lobed, acute, crenate-serrate. Fls pale lilac-pink to pink, solitary or in axill. and term. clusters, shorter than subtending lf. Eur., nat. E US. Z3.

A. pallida Willd. = *Alcea pallida*.

A. rosea (L.) Cav. = *Alcea rosea*.

A. striata DC. = *Alcea striata*.

A. sulphurea Boiss. & Hohen. = *Alcea sulphurea*.

A. syriaca hort. = *Hibiscus syriacus*.

A. taurinensis C.A. Mey., non DC. = *A. armeniaca*.

A. taurinensis DC., non C.A. Mey. = *A. officinalis*.

Aluminium Plant *Pilea cadierei*.

Alum Root *Heuchera*.

×**Alworthia** G. Rowley. (*Aloe* ×*Haworthia*.) Liliaceae (Aloeaceae). 2 small, perenn. succulents. Lvs soft, sessile, linear-lanceolate, acute, in compact or lax rosettes.

×**A. 'Black Gem'** (*Haworthia cymbiformis* ×*Aloe* sp.) Rosettes small, offsetting to produce a carpet. Lvs to 10×2.5cm, deep black-purple, soft and thick, channelled above, rounded beneath, with a few tiny white marginal teeth near apex. Z9.

Alyogyne Alef. Malvaceae. 4 shrubs. Lvs petiolate, unlobed to deeply palmately lobed. Fls axillary, solitary, on long articulate pedicels; epical. seg. 4–12, forming a toothed cup; cal. 5-lobed, exceeding epical.; pet. 5, obovate, stellate-hairy outside; staminal column with numerous whorled fil. S & W Aus. Z10.

A. hakeifolia (Giord.) Alef. Shrub to 3m, glab. Lvs 5–10cm, linear, almost terete, bipinnate or divided into 2–3 linear seg. Epical. seg. 4–7; pet. 5–7.5cm, pale lilac to lilac-purple, with dark purple spot at base.

A. huegelii (Endl.) Fryx. LILAC HIBISCUS. Shrub to 2.5m, stellate-hairy. Lvs 3–8cm, broadly ovate or obovate, palmately 5-lobed, rarely bipinnatifid, lobes crenate or dentate. Epical. seg. 7–12; pet. to 10cm, lilac or purple-red, dark spotted at base.

Alyssoides Mill. Cruciferae. 3 mat-forming perenn. herbs, to 40cm. Foliage and habit v. similar to *Alyssum*. Fls small, yellow. Silicle inflated. Eur. to Asia.

A. cretica (L.) Medik. = *Lutzia cretica*.

A. sinuata (L.) Medik. = *Aurinia sinuata*.

A. utriculata (L.) Medik. Stock woody, much-branched. Lvs densely crowded, oblong-spathulate to lanceolate, stellate-hairy. Pet. 2mm. Fr. 10–12mm, ovoid to globose, style 7–10mm. Spring–summer. Alps, Balk. *A. graeca* (Reut.) Jav. differs in having simple and stellate hairs on the rosette lvs. Z7.

Alyssum L. MADWORT. Cruciferae. 168 ann. or perenn. herbs or subshrubs, often stellate-pubescent. Lvs simple. Infl. a rac., sometimes corymbose. Fls small, 4-merous; pet. obovate-spathulate, clawed. C & S Eur., SW & C Asia, N Afr.

A. alpestre L. To 15cm, usually procumbent, suffruticose. Lvs 4–7mm, obovate-oblong, white-pubesc. Rac. short, simple; pet. to 3.5mm, pale yellow, rounded, entire. Summer. S Eur. Z6.

A. alyssoides (L.) L. Erect ann. or bienn., to 30cm, grey-pubesc. Lvs to 2.5cm, oblanceolate-obovate to spathulate. Infl. a term. rac.; pet. 2mm, notched, yellow-white. C & S Eur. Z6.

A. argenteum All. Dense erect long-stemmed perenn., to 45cm. Lvs oblong-spathulate, silvery, flowering st. lvs larger than basal lvs. Corymb flat, wide, loose; pet. deep golden yellow, to 4mm, entire. Summer. S Alps. Z6.

A. armenum Boiss. To 15cm. Base woody. St. lvs obovate-oblanceolate, acute, larger above. Rac. simple, compact, 2–5cm; pet. 4–5mm, entire, golden yellow. Armenia, Kurdistan, Turk. Z6.

A. atlanticum Desf. Similar to *A. cuneifolium* except basal lvs sessile, st. lvs oblanceolate. SE Spain. Z9.

A. bertolonii Desv. Erect, to 60cm. Lvs 12mm, spathulate, hoary; flowering st. lvs oblanceolate, 25mm. Pet. entire, to 3.5mm. SW Eur. Z7.

A. bornmuelleri Hausskn. ex Deg. To 5cm. Lvs spathulate-obovate; flowering st. lvs lanceolate, hoary. Rac. 10–15-fld; pet. 5–7mm, bilobed. Turk. Z7.

A. borzaeanum Nyár. To 30cm. Base woody. St. erect. Basal lvs 6–7mm, spathulate-obovate; st. lvs oblanceolate, larger above, hoary. Pet. to 2.5mm. Bulg. and Rom. Z6.

A. calycinum L. = *A. alyssoides*.

A. clypeatum L. = *Fibigia clypeata*.

A. condensatum Boiss. & Hausskn. To 20cm. Base woody. Lvs 0.5–2cm, obovate-spathulate, silver-pubesc. Rac. large and corymbose; pet. 2.5–3.5mm, lemon yellow, obovate, notched. Summer. Syr., Leb., Turk., Iran. Z7.

A. corsicum Duby. 30–60cm. St. branching, woody. Lvs in sterile rosettes, 15mm, spathulate-round; flowering st. lvs 25–35mm, oblong-spathulate. Corymb broad; pet. to 3mm, golden yellow, obovate. W Turk., Cauc., Crete. Z8.

A. corymbosum (Griseb.) Boiss. = *Aurinia corymbosa*.

A. creticum L. = *Lutzia cretica*.

A. cuneifolium Ten. Tufted, 5–15cm, stellate-pubesc. Lvs in rossetes, obovate-oblong, tapering to petiole or narrow, obtuse on flexuous flowering st. Rac. short, dense; pet. yellow, 5–8mm, notched. S Eur. Z6.

A. desertorum Stapf. Ann., to 15cm. St. slender, ascending. Lvs 5–15mm, oblong-grey-green, linear-lanceolate above. Pet. 2–3mm, pale yellow, entire to notched. Spring and autumn. Eur. to Asia, nat. W US. Z6.

A. diffusum Ten. Differs from *A. montanum* in flowering st. long, straight, prostrate. Pet. to 7mm. S Eur. Z6.

A. edentulum Waldst. & Kit. = *Aurinia petraea*.

A. floribundum Boiss. & Bal. To 1m, shrubby. Lvs 5–20mm, linear-oblong, grey-hairy, reduced above. Rac. corymbose, compact; pet. 2–2.5mm, lemon-yellow, obovate. Turk. Z7.

A. gemonense L. = *Aurinia petraea*.

A. grandiflorum (Hook.) Kuntze = *Lesquerella grandiflora*.

A. grayanum Kuntze = *Lesquerella montana*.

A. idaeum Boiss. & Heldr. Diffuse; to 5cm. St. slender, prostrate. Lvs round-oblong to narrow-ovate, pointed, ciliate, silver-green. Rac. simple; pet. 4–6mm, soft yellow, oblong to cuneate, entire. Greece, Crete. Z7.

A. incanum L. = *Berteroa incana*.

A. janchenii Nyár = *A. bertolonii*.

A. lapeyrousianum Jordan. Tufted subshrub to 30cm. Lvs oblong-lanceolate, obtuse, basally acuminate, silver-pubesc. Pet. obovate, white. Pyren. Z7.

A. longicaule Boiss. Laxly tufted, to 60cm. Base woody. St. brittle. Basal lvs spathulate-obovate, tapering to petiole; flowering st. lvs linear-lanceolate. Pet. white. Spain. Z7.

A. ludovicianum Nutt. = *Lesquerella ludoviciana*.

A. maritimum (L.) Lam. = *Lobularia maritima*.

A. markgrafii O. Schulz. To 50cm. St. erect, stellate-pubesc. Lvs 1.5cm, linear-spathulate; flowering st. lvs 2.2cm, oblanceolate, grey beneath. Pan. dense; pet. 2–2.5mm, entire, bright yellow. Balk. Z7.

A. minimum Willd. non L. = *A. desertorum*.

A. moellendorfianum Asch. ex G. Beck. Tufted, 5–15cm. St. ascending. Lvs spathulate-oblong to obovate-round, silver scaly in dense rosettes on short st. Rac. long; pet. to 6mm, notched, yellow. Summer. Balk. Z6.

A. montanum L. Tufted 5–25cm. St. prostrate to erect, dense. Lvs obovate to oblong in rosettes on sterile st., becoming more spathulate above, grey-pubesc. Rac. many-fld; fls fragrant; pet. 3.5–6mm, bright yellow, notched. Summer. Eur. 'Berggold' ('Mountain Gold'): low-growing, spreading to 15cm; fls golden yellow. Z6.

A. murale Waldst. & Kit. YELLOW TUFT. Tufted to 60cm. Lvs spathulate-obovate, grey-green; flowering st. lvs 10–20mm, oblanceolate or lanceolate, larger than basal lvs, grey-green. Corymb term., many-fld; pet. 2–3.5mm, entire, yellow. SE Eur. Z7.

A. orientale Ard. = *Aurinia saxatilis*.

A. ovirense Kerner. Prostrate, to 12cm; stellate-pubesc. Lvs of sterile st. in rosettes, round to ovate; flowering st. lvs oblong-lanceolate, blunt. Pet. 6–8mm, pale yellow, entire or notched, hairy. SE Alps. Z6.

A. persicum Boiss. Perenn. subshrub, 15–30cm. St. divaricate, woody at base. Lvs 1–2.5cm, oblong-lanceolate, blunt. Pet. straw-yellow, obovate, entire. Iran. Z7.

A. petraeum Ard. = *Aurinia petraea*.

A. pulvinare Velen. Cushion-forming, to 15cm. Lvs to 10mm, oblong-spathulate, stellate-pubesc., in rosettes, upper lvs long-petioled. Pet. to 6mm, lemon yellow, obovate. Bulg. Z6.

A. purpureum Lagasca & Rodr. Densely tufted, 2–5cm. Lvs to 5mm, linear to spathulate, scurfy. Pet. rose-red to purple. Spain. Z7.

A. pyrenaicum Lapeyr. Tufted, to 50cm. Stock woody. Lvs silver-pubesc., lanceolate-obovate, tapering to base. Infl. a dense corymb; pet. white, near-round. E Pyren. Z6.

A. repens Baumg. Diffuse to erect, to 60cm. Lvs on sterile st., spathulate-obovate, acute; flowering st. lvs linear-lanceolate, smaller. Rac. to 30cm; pet. 4–7mm, golden-yellow, notched. S & C Eur., SW Asia. Z7.

A. rostratum Steven. Ann. or bienn., 20–60cm. Lvs spathulate-obovate to lanceolate. Rac. lax; pet. 4.5–6mm, yellow, notched, hairy beneath. SE Eur. Z8.

A. rupestre Ten. = *Aurinia rupestris*.

A. saxatile L. = *Aurinia saxatilis*.

A. serpyllifolium Desf. Similar to *A. alpestre* except to 30cm, basal lvs to 18mm, st. lvs broad-spathulate. SW Eur. Z8.

A. sibiricum Willd. Erect or prostrate, 5–20cm. Base woody, stout. Basal lvs 7mm, spathulate, grey-green to white; st. lvs rounded to oblanceolate, grey-green, larger. Pet. to 2.5mm. SE Eur. Z7.

A. sinuatum L. = *Aurinia sinuata*.

A. speciosum Pomel. = *A. atlanticum*.

A. spinosum L. Small shrub, to 60cm. St. much-branched, becoming spiny. Lvs spathulate-obovate to linear-lanceolate, silver-scaly. Pet. white, sometimes tinged purple. S Fr., SE Spain. 'Roseum': fls deep rose. Z8.

A. stribrnyi Velen. Diffuse, 6–25cm. Base woody. Sterile st. long. Lvs obovate or spathulate, silvery; flowering st. lvs oblanceolate, densely pubesc. Pet. 5.5–6.5mm, orange-yellow, notched. E Balk. to W Turk. Z7.

A. tortuosum Willd. Prostrate or erect, around 30cm, shrubby below. Br. tortuous. Basal lvs lanceolate-spathulate, coarsely hairy, to 25mm; st. lvs larger. Rac. corymbose; pet. 2.5mm, yellow. SE Eur. Z7.

A. troodii Boiss. Subshrub, 10–25cm. Base woody. St. erect, ridged, much-branched; sterile shoots with dense lf clusters. Lvs 5–10mm, obovate-spathulate. Rac. corymbose, dense; pet. 3mm, golden-yellow, blunt. Cyprus. Z8.

A. vesicaria L. = *Coluteocarpus vesicaria*.

A. wierzbickii Heuff. Ann. or short lived perenn., 30–75cm. St. erect, rigid, sparsely branched. Lvs oval-oblong, stellate-pubesc. Infl. a dense corymb, 4cm diam.; pet. 5–7mm, deep yellow. Summer. Bulg., Serbia, Rom. Z6.

A. wulfenianum Bernh. Erect or prostrate, to 20cm, white stellate-pubesc. Lvs on sterile st. in rosettes, oblong-obovate, blunt; flowering st. lvs oblanceolate. Infl. corymbose; pet. 5.5–6.5mm, bilobed, pale yellow. Summer. Asia Minor. Z7.

→*Hormathophylla* and *Ptilotrichum*.

Amana Honda.

A. edulis (Miq.) Honda = *Tulipa edulis*.

A. latifolia (Mak.) Honda = *Tulipa edulis* var. *latifolia*.

Amaracus Gled.

A. tournefortii (Ait.) Benth. = *Origanum tournefortii*.

AMARANTHACEAE Juss. 71/800. *Alternanthera, Amaranthus, Celosia, Froelichia, Gomphrena, Iresine, Ptilotus.*

Amaranthus L. Amaranthaceae. c60 ann., herbs, erect, spreading or prostrate, often red-tinted and glandular-pubescent. Lvs alt., entire or sinuate; petioles usually long. Fls small, unisexual, bright red or green packed in term. or soft catkin-like spikes. Cosmop. as weeds of wasteland and tilled land; native to temp. and trop. regions. Z5.

A. blitum L. = *A. lividus*.

A. caudatus L. LOVE-LIES-BLEEDING; VELVET FLOWER; TASSEL FLOWER. Erect to 1.5m. St. striate, red to purple, sparingly branched, glab. or pilose. Lvs 2.5–15cm, ovate to ovate-oblong, pilose on margin and beneath. Infl. long, drooping, tassel-like, to 30×1.5cm, crimson to blood red. Summer. Peru, Afr., India. 'Viridis' ('Green Thumb'): spikes long-lasting, vivid green.

A. cruentus L. PURPLE AMARANTH; RED AMARANTH; PRINCE'S FEATHER. Erect, pubesc. to 2m. Lvs 3–15cm, ovate to lanceolate, glab. above, pubesc. beneath, entire to minutely crenulate. Infl. to 60cm, drooping, cylindric, 5–15mm across, green tinged red. Americas. 'Golden Giant': infl. large, golden. 'Reselected': stalks, lvs, and infl. red.

A. gangeticus L. = *A. tricolor*.

A. hybridus ssp. *cruentus* Thell. = *A. cruentus*.

A. hybridus ssp. *hypochondriacus* (L.) Thell. = *A. hypochondriacus*.

A. hypochondriacus L. PRINCE'S FEATHER. Erect to 1.5m, pubesc above. Lvs 2–15cm, oblong-lanceolate, entire to crenulate, green to purple. Spikes dense, blunt, erect, 6–12mm across, crimson. Summer. S US, Mex., India, China. 'Erythrostachys': to 1.5m; lvs stained purple; pan. dense, erect to 20cm, blood red. 'Pygmy Torch': spikes erect, deepest maroon.

A. lividus Willd. Erect or prostrate to 90cm. Lvs 1–8cm, sub-ovate, green tinged red, retuse. Infl. to 11×2cm, green to pale purple. Trop. Amer., S Eur. ssp. *polygonoides* (Moq.) Probst. Small, prostrate to decumbent. Lvs to 4cm, acute, ovate, midrib tinged red.

A. mangostanus L. = *A. tricolor*.

A. melancholicus L. = *A. tricolor*.

A. oleraceus L. = *A. lividus*.

A. paniculatus L. = *A. cruentus*.

A. patulus Bertol. = *A. cruentus*.

A. polygamus L. = *A. lividus*.

A. salicifolius hort. Veitch. = *A. tricolor* var. *salicifolius*.

A. speciosus Sims. = *A. cruentes*.

A. spinosus L. Erect, glab. or pilose, to 1.5m; st. yellow or red-green, with 2 spines per lf axil. Lvs 3–10cm, narrowly ovate to rhomboid-ovate, glab. or pilose, veins pale yellow beneath; petioles green or pink, to 9cm. Infl. to 15×1cm, green to red and purple. Autumn-winter. Trop. C Asia, Afr.

A. tricolor L. TAMPALA; CHINESE SPINACH. Erect to 1.3m; pubesc above. Lvs to 22cm, elliptic or ovate, green or purple; petioles to 8cm. Infl. 4–25mm diam., pale green or red with green mid-rib. Afr., Indochina. 'Splendens': lvs deep red, uppermost brilliant light red. 'Molten Fire': lvs brown-red to maroon, with a scarlet growing centre. 'Joseph's Coat': upper lvs light crimson-scarlet and gold; lower lvs chocolate, yellow and green. 'Illumination': upper lvs bright rose-red topped with gold, lower lvs green and chocolate. 'Flaming Fountain': lvs carmine, crimson and bronze, willow-like. var. *salicifolius* (hort. Veitch) Allen. Habit pyramidal. Lvs long, narrow, drooping.

A. tristis L. = *A. tricolor*.

×**Amarcrinum** Coutts. Amaryllidaceae. (*Amaryllis* ×*Crinum*.) Habit similar to *Crinum*, bulb long-necked, lvs to 60×5cm, everg., 2-ranked. Fls similar to *Amaryllis*, shell-pink, fragrant with perianth tube narrow and curved. Autumn. Gdn origin. Z8.

×*A. howardii* Coutts = ×*A. memoria-corsii*.

×*A. memoria-corsii* (Ragion.) H.E. Moore. (*Amaryllis belladonna* ×*Crinum moorei*.)

→×*Crinodonna*.

Amarelle Cherry *Prunus cerasus* var. *caproniana*.

×**Amarygia** Cif. & Giac. (*Amaryllis* ×*Brunsvigia*.) Amaryllidaceae. Intergeneric hybrids close to *Brunsvigia*. Z9.

×*A. bidwillii* (Worsley) H.E. Moore. (*Amaryllis belladonna* ×*Brunsvigia orientalis*.) Similar to ×A. parkeri, but fls shorter and tep. broader.

×*A. parkeri* (Will. Wats.) H.E. Moore. (*Amaryllis belladonna* ×*Brunsvigia josephinae*.) NAKED LADY LILY. Fls clear deep rose suffused carmine, varying in self-crosses and back-crosses. 'Alba': fls pure white, fragrant.

→*Amaryllis*, × *Brunsdonna* and *Brunsvigia*.

AMARYLLIDACEAE J. St.-Hil. 70/1390. ×*Amarcrinum*, ×*Amarygia*, *Amaryllis*, *Ammocharis*, *Apodolirion*, *Bomarea*, *Boophone*, *Brunsvigia*, *Calostemma*, *Carpolyza*, *Chlidanthus*, *Clivia*, *Crinum*, *Cyanella*, *Cybistetes*, *Cyrtanthus*, *Eucharis*, *Eucrosia*, *Eustephia*, *Galanthus*, *Gethyllis*, *Griffinia*, *Habranthus*, *Haemanthus*, *Hippeastrum*, *Hymenocallis*, *Ixiolirion*, *Lapiedra*, *Lepidochiton*, *Leucojum*, *Lycoris*, *Narcissus*, *Nerine*, *Pamianthe*, *Pancratium*, *Paramongaia*, *Phaedranassa*, *Phycella*, *Plagiolirion*, *Proiphys*, *Pyrolirion*, *Rhodophiala*, *Scadoxus*, *Sprekelia*, *Stenomesson*, *Sternbergia*, *Strumaria*, *Ungernia*, *Urceolina*, *Vagaria*, *Worsleya*, *Zephyranthes*.

Amaryllis *Hippeastrum*.

Amaryllis L. Amaryllidaceae. 1 bulbous perenn. herb. Lvs to 50cm, in 2 ranks, strap-shaped, glossy, mid green. Scape to 60cm, before lvs, stout, flushed red-purple; fls sweetly scented, short-stalked, 6 or more in an umbel, perianth 6–10cm, purple-pink to pink, often white below, funnelform, lobes 6, spreading, oblanceolate, acute; style and sta. declinate. Late summer–autumn. S Afr. Z8.

A. advena Ker-Gawl. = *Rhodophiala advena*.

A. aglaiae Cast. = *Hippeastrum aglaiae*.

A. ambigua (Herb.) Sweet ex Steud. = *Hippeastrum ambiguum*.

A. andersonii (Herb.) Griseb. = *Habranthus tubispathus*.

A. andreana (Bak.) Traub & Uphof = *Hippeastrum andreanum*.

A. araucana (Philippi) Traub & Uphof = *Rhodophiala araucana*.

A. argentina (Pax) Ravenna = *Hippeastrum argentinum*.

A. atamasca L. = *Zephyranthes atamasca*.

A. aulica Ker-Gawl. = *Hippeastrum aulicum*.

A. aurea Ruiz & Pav. = *Pyrolirion aureum*.

A. bagnoldii (Herb.) Dietr. = *Rhodophiala bagnoldii*.

A. barlowii Traub & Mold. = *Rhodophiala rosea*.

A. belladonna L. JERSEY LILY; BELLADONNA LILY. 'Barberton': fls dark rose pink. 'Capetown': fls deep rose. 'Hathor': fls white. 'Jagersfontein': fls deep pink. 'Johannesburg': fls pale pink, centre lighter; free-flowering. 'Kewensis': fls deep pink. 'Kimberley': fls deep carmine pink, centre white. 'Major': st. dark pink; fls dark pink, scented. 'Pallida': robust; fls large, rose pink, abundant. 'Purpurea': fls purple. 'Rosea': fls rose, segs. striped white, pointed, late. 'Spectabilis': fls rose, interior white, umbels large.

A. bifida (Herb.) Spreng. = *Rhodophiala bifida*.

A. blossfeldiae Traub & Doran. = *Hippeastrum blossfeldiae*.

A. blumenavia (K. Koch) & Bouché ex Carr.) Traub. =

Hippeastrum blumenavium.
A. bukasovii Vargas = *Hippeastrum bukasovii.*
A. calyptrata Ker-Gawl. = *Hippeastrum calyptratum.*
A. candida (Stapf) Traub & Uphof = *Hippeastrum candidum.*
A. caspia Willd. = *Allium caspium.*
A. chilensis L'Hérit. = *Rhodophiala chilensis.*
A. coranica Ker-Gawl. = *Ammocharis coranica.*
A. cybister (Herb.) Traub & Uphof = *Hippeastrum cybister.*
A. doraniae Traub. = *Hippeastrum doraniae.*
A. dryades Vell. = *Griffinia dryades.*
A. elegans Spreng. = *Hippeastrum elegans.*
A. elegans var. *ambigua* (Herb.) Traub & Mold. = *Hippeastrum ambiguum.*
A. elwesii (C.W. Wright) Traub & Uphof = *Rhodophiala elwesii.*
A. equestris Ait. = *Hippeastrum puniceum.*
A. evansiae Traub & Nels. = *Hippeastrum evansiae.*
A. formosissima L. = *Sprekelia formosissima.*
A. gigantea Van Marum = *Brunsvigia josephinae.*
A. hyacinthina Ker-Gawl. = *Griffinia hyacinthina.*
A. immaculata Traub & Mold. = *Hippeastrum candidum.*
A. josephinae Redouté = *Brunsvigia josephinae.*
A. lapacensis Cárdenas = *Hippeastrum lapacense.*
A. leopoldii (Dombrain) H.E. Moore = *Hippeastrum leopoldii.*
A. longifolia L. = *Cybistetes longifolia.*
A. machupijchensis Vargas = *Hippeastrum machupijchense.*
A. maracasa Traub. = *Hippeastrum organense.*
A. maranensis Ker-Gawl. = *Hippeastrum stylosum.*
A. oconequensis Traub. = *Hippeastrum oconequense.*
A. organensis Bury = *Hippeastrum organensis.*
A. orientalis L. = *Brunsvigia orientalis.*
A. papilio (Ravenna) = *Hippeastrum papilio.*
A. pardina Hook. f. = *Hippeastrum pardinum.*
A. ×*parkeri* Will. Wats. = ×*Amarygia parkeri.*
A. phycelloides (Herb.) Traub & Uphof = *Phycella phycelloides.*
A. pratensis Poepp. = *Rhodophiala pratensis.*
A. procera Duchartre = *Worsleya rayneri.*
A. psittacina Ker-Gawl. = *Hippeastrum psittacinum.*
A. puniceum Lam. = *Hippeastrum puniceum.*
A. purpurea Ait. = *Cyrtanthus elatus.*
A. rayneri Hook. = *Worsleya rayneri.*
A. reginae L. = *Hippeastrum reginae.*
A. reticulata L'Hérit. = *Hippeastrum reticulatum.*
A. rosea Lam. = *A. belladonna.*
A. rosea (Sweet) Traub & Uphof non Lam. = *Rhodophiala rosea.*
A. rutila Ker-Gawl. = *Hippeastrum striatum.*
A. striata Lam. = *Hippeastrum striatum.*
A. traubii (Mold.) = *Hippeastrum traubii.*
A. tubispatha L'Hérit. = *Habranthus tubispathus.*
A. variabilis Jacq. = *Crinum variabile.*
A. vittata L'Hérit. = *Hippeastrum vittatum.*
A. vivipara Lam. = *Crinum defixum.*
→*Brunsvigia* and *Coburgia.*

Amasonia L. f. Verbenaceae. 8 herbs or decid. subshrubs. Lvs simple, mostly clustered beneath infl. Infl. paniculate or racemiform, erect, cymes short-stalked subtended by large, coloured bracts. Fls solitary or in 3-fld cymules; cal. campanulate, lobes 5; cor. yellow or white, limb 5-lobed, slightly 2-lipped. Drupe black, glossy. C & S Amer. Z10.
A. calycina Hook. f. Tall shrub or subshrub, with red viscid hairs. Lvs to 17cm, thin-textured, broadly lanceolate or elliptic, minutely puberulent or glabrate. Infl. to 20cm, nodding, with purple-red hairs; bracts to 19cm, brilliant red, lanceolate, apiculate-dentate; cal. to 1.9cm, red, densely gland.; cor. to 3cm, lobes strongly recurved. N S Amer.
A. campestris (Aubl.) Mold. Herb or subshrub to 2m, brown-pubesc. Lvs to 28cm, chartaceous, elliptic, narrowly obovate to oblanceolate, minutely dentate or serrate, pubesc. to glabrate. Infl. to 30cm; bracts to 5cm, elliptic or lanceolate, flushed red, often yellow or green; cal. to 1.2cm, red or yellow-green flushed red; cor. to 3cm, lobes broadly ovate. Venez. to NE Braz.
A. punicea hort. ex Hook. f. = *A. calycina.*
A. spruceana Mold. = *A. campestris.*

Amatungulu *Carissa macrocarpa.*

Amauropelta Kunze. Thelypteridaceae. *c*200 epiphytic or terrestrial ferns. Rhiz. erect or decumbent. Frond blades 1-pinnate or pinnatifid. Trop. Amer., Afr., Polyn. Z10.
A. resinifera (Desv.) Pichi-Serm. Rhiz. ultimately trunk-like to 80×25cm. Fronds erect to spreading like a shuttlecock, lanceolate or elliptic, gland. to resinous beneath, pinnae to 3×2cm, 30–40 pairs, falcate, linear to lanceolate or deltoid, seg. linear to oblong; stipes to 15cm, straw-coloured to red-brown. W Indies.
→*Dryopteris, Polypodium* and *Thelypteris.*

Amazon Lily *Eucharis* ×*grandiflora.*
Amazon Sword Plant *Echinodorus paniculatus.*
Amazon Water Lily *Victoria amazonica.*
Ambarella *Spondias dulcis.*
Amberbell *Erythronium americanum.*

Amberboa (Pers.) Less. Compositae. 6 ann. or bienn. herbs. Lvs undivided to pinnatifid. Cap. radiate, solitary; sometimes long-stalked; involucre ovoid; phyllaries in many series, imbricate; flts tubular, the outer elongated, spreading. Medit. to C Asia. Z8.
A. moschata (L.) DC. SWEET SULTAN. St. to 70cm. Basal lvs undivided, toothed or lyrate, petiolate; st. lvs lobed or pinnatifid, minutely toothed, sessile. Cap. fragrant, long-stalked; involucre to 20×16mm; flts pink, laciniate. Spring–summer. SW Asia. 'The Bride': cap. pure white. Imperialis Series: white to yellow, pink, carmine or purple.
A. muricata (L.) DC. = *Cyanopsis muricata.*
→*Centaurea.*

Ambiguous Knight's Star Lily *Hippeastrum ambiguum.*

Amblostoma Scheidw. Orchidaceae. 3 epiphytic or lithophytic orchids. Pbs clustered, narrow-ellipsoid or cylindric. Lvs thin, linear-lanceolate. Infl. term., erect, dense; fls small, delicate; lip midlobe smaller than lat. lobes. Summer. Brazilian Andes. Z10.
A. tridactyle (Lindl.) Rchb. f. Pbs slender, to 20cm. Lvs to 25cm. Infl. to 15cm; fls to 1.25cm diam., green to ivory. Braz.

Amboina Pine *Agathis dammara.*

Amelanchier Medik. SERVICEBERRY; JUNEBERRY; SHADBUSH; SARVICEBERRY; SHAD; SUGARPLUM. Rosaceae. 25 decid. shrubs or small trees. Lvs often emerging pink-bronze, simple, entire or sharp-serrate, colouring well in fall. Fls white, in term. rac., often produced before or with lvs; cal. tube campanulate; pet. 5, obovate to lanceolate; sta. 10–20. Fr. a small globose or pyriform pome, purple to maroon. N Amer., Eur., Asia.
A. alnifolia (Nutt.) Nutt. ALDER-LEAVED SERVICE BERRY. Stoloniferous shrub or small tree to 4m. Branchlets soft-tomentose at first. Lvs to 5cm, oval to rounded, tomentose beneath when young, coarse-dentate, vein pairs 8–13. Fls cream-white, small, fragrant, in 5–15-fld, erect rac. to 4cm. Fr. 1.5cm diam., purple-black, pruinose. Spring. NW N Amer. 'Alta Glow': columnar, to 6m; lvs yellow, burgundy and brown in autumn; fr. cream. 'Regent': lvs dark green, bright yellow to red in fall. var. *cusickii* (Fern.) C. Hitchc. Shrub to 3m. Young br. red and glossy. Lvs to 5.5cm, oval, apex acute or rounded, base round to cordate, glab., sharp-toothed, vein pairs 7–10. Fls large, 3–8-fascicled in rac. to 5cm. Fr. 1cm diam., red, later blue-black. NW US. var. *semiintegrifolia* (Hook.) C. Hitchc. Shrub or small tree to 12m. Young branchlets rufous and tomentose. Lvs to 4cm, oval to oblong, rounded, base acute to cordate, tomentose, later glab. and fresh green, teeth triangular, pointed outward, vein pairs 8–12. Fls to 3cm diam., fragrant, in upright, 5–15-fld rac. to 8cm. Fr. to 13mm diam., pruinose, purple-black. Spring. NW US. Z2.
A. amabilis Wiegand. = *A. sanguinea.*
A. arborea (Michx. f.) Fern. Shrub or tree to 20m. Branchlets pubesc. Lvs to 10cm, ovate to oval, apex short-acuminate, base cordate or round, dark green above, paler beneath, finely sharp-toothed, vein pairs 11–17. Fls pure white, fragrant, in 4–10-fld, pendulous rac. to 7.5cm. Fr. to 1cm diam., red-purple. Spring–summer. E N Amer. Z4.
A. asiatica (Sieb. & Zucc.) Walp. Graceful shrub or tree to 12m. Branchlets thin, grey-brown. Lvs to 7cm, ovate, apex acute, base subcordate to round, finely-serrate, white- or yellow-tomentose beneath at first, glab., dark green above, red-orange in autumn. Fls in lanate rac. to 6cm. Fr. blue-black. Spring. Jap., China, Korea. var. *sinica* C. Schneid. Lvs to 5cm, serrate only above, somewhat tomentose when young, later glab. Rac. usually glab. Fr. smaller, blue-black. China. Z5.
A. bartramiana (Tausch) M. Roem. Open shrub to 3m. Branchlets glab. Lvs to 6cm, oval to elliptic or obovate, acute, glab., dark green, paler beneath, finely toothed, vein pairs 10–16. Fls to 2.5cm diam., pure white, solitary or 3-fasciculate. Fr. to 1.5cm diam., pruinose, black. Spring. E N Amer. Z5.
A. basalticola Piper. Shrub, 1–3m; branchlets glab. Lvs appearing before fls, 1.5–3cm, obovate-orbicular, blue-green, glab., sharply toothed, vein pairs 10–13. Fls white, in 4–8-fld, glab. pan. Fr. 9–12mm diam., dark purple. NW US. Z5.
A. botryapium (L. f.) Borkh. non DC. = *A. canadensis.*
A. botryapium DC. non (L. f.) Borkh. = *A. lamarckii.*
A. botryapium var. *lanceolata* hort. Simon-Louis = *A.* × *grandiflora.*
A. canadensis K. Koch non (L.) Medik. = *A. lamarckii.*

A. canadensis (L.) Medik. Stoloniferous shrub to 8m. Branchlets grey, glab. Lvs to 5cm, elliptic, apex acute or rounded, base usually rounded, with shallow, sharp teeth, ± glab., vein pairs 9–13. Fls white, in erect rac. to 6cm, initially white-pubesc. Fr. 1cm diam., purple-black, blue-pruinose. Spring. E N Amer. 'Micropetala': tall and upright; lvs richly coloured in fall; fls small. 'Prince William': low, to 3.5m, multistemmed; fr. purple, edible, abundant. 'Springtyme': oval, upright, compact, to 3.5m; lvs yellow-orange in fall. 'Tradition': oval, upright, well branched, to 7.5m; fls early.

A. canadensis Sieb & Zucc. non L. = *A. arborea*.

A. canadensis var. *botryapium* (DC.) Koehne = *A. lamarckii*.

A. canadensis var. *japonica* Miq. = *A. asiatica*.

A. canadensis grandiflora Zab. = *A.* ✕ *grandiflora*.

A. confusa N. Hylander. Shrub to 2–3m. Lvs 3–5.5cm, elliptic to broad-ovate, apex acute, base rounded to subcordate, serrate above, pale green above, light blue-green beneath, sericeous at first. Fls 2.5–3.5cm diam., 6–8 in a long 3–8cm rac. Fr. 7–9mm diam., black. Late spring–early summer. Origin unknown, nat. S Sweden. Z5.

A. confusa Schmeil & Fitschen non N. Hylander = *A. lamarckii*.

A. crenata Greene = *A. utahensis*.

A. cusickii Fern. = *A. alnifolia* var. *cusickii*.

A. florida Lindl. = *A. alnifolia* var. *semiintegrifolia*.

A. ✕ *grandiflora* Rehd. (*A. arborea* ✕ *A. laevis*.) Differs from *A. arborea* in larger fls, longer slender, less pubesc. rac., and densely floccose-tomentose, purple young lvs; from *A. laevis* in tomentose young lvs, villous rac., more numerous fls, and larger fr. Gdn origin. 'Autumn Brilliance': br. moderately spreading, thick; bark light grey; lvs brilliant red in fall. 'Ballerina': vigorous; fls pure white, in large heads; fr. blue-black, edible. 'Cole's Select': vigorous; vivid autumn colours. 'Cumulus': upright, vigorous; lvs leathery, orange-red in fall; fls abundant; fr. red later purple. 'Princess Diana': small tree, gracefully spreading; lvs bright red in fall; fr. purple. 'Robin Hill': narrowly upright, branching open; fls pale pink fading to white, nodding; fr. small, red, juicy. 'Rubescens': fls blush pink, purple tinted pink in bud. 'Strata': branching horizontal. Z4.

A. ✕ *grandiflora* Franco non Rehd. = *A. lamarckii*.

A. humilis Wiegand. Differs from *A. stolonifera*, in lvs more coarsely toothed, v. densely white-tomentose beneath. Z4.

A. intermedia Spach. = *A. canadensis*.

A. laevis Wiegand. ALLEGHENY SERVICEBERRY. Shrub or tree to 13m. Branchlets glab. Lvs to 6cm, tough, ovate to oval, apex short-acuminate, base rounded to cordate, glab., ± blue-green, serrate, vein pairs 12–17. Fls glab., numerous, in pendulous rac. to 12cm. Fr. to 18mm diam., pruinose, purple to nearly black. Spring. 'Prince Charles': habit somewhat rounded, vigorous; fls abundant; lvs orange and red in fall; fr. blue, edible. Z4.

A. laevis Clapham, Tutin & Warb. = *A. lamarckii*.

A. laevis f. *villosa* Pelkwijk = *A. lamarckii*.

A. lamarckii F.-G. Schröd. Shrub or tree to 10m, of graceful, wide-branching habit. Branchlets sericeous. Lvs to 8.5cm, elliptic, oblong-elliptic, or oblong-obovate, obtuse to subacute or bluntly short-acuminate, rounded to cordate at base, sericeous at first, finely serrate. Fls white, in lax, 6–10-fld rac. to 7.5cm, initially pubesc. Fr. 9.5mm diam., purple-black. Spring. E Canada. 'Rubescens': buds purple-pink, soft pale pink in full bloom. Z4.

A. mormonica Schneid. = *A. utahensis*.

A. oblongifolia Roem. = *A. canadensis*.

A. oligocarpa M. Roem. = *A. bartramiana*.

A. oreophila A. Nels. = *A. utahensis*.

A. ovalis Medik. Stoloniferous shrub or small tree. Young growth lanate. Lvs to 4.5cm, ovate to oval, base and apex rounded, white-lanate at first, later glab., serrate or entire. Fls often 4cm diam., in white-tomentose, 3–8-fld, erect rac. Fr. pruinose, dark blue, almost black. Spring. C & S Eur. (esp. mts). ssp. *embergeri* Favarger & Stearn. Pet. longer, to 1.9cm, not 1.5cm. Z5.

A. ovalis Borkh. non Medik. = *A. spicata*.

A. oxyodon Koehne = *A. alnifolia* var. *semiintegrifolia*.

A. prunifolia Greene = *A. utahensis*.

A. purpusii Koehne = *A. utahensis*.

A. racemosa Lindl. = *Exochorda racemosa*.

A. rotundifolia Roem. non (Lam.) Dum.-Cours. = *A. sanguinea*.

A. rotundifolia (Lam.) Dum-Cours. non Roem. = *A. ovalis*.

A. sanguinea (Pursh) DC. Shrub to 3m. Young branchlets red or grey. Lvs to 7cm, oval to rounded, acute or obtuse, rounded to slightly cordate at base, white- to yellow-tomentose beneath, later glab., teeth sharp, vein pairs 11–13. Fls white to light pink in 4–10-fld, ascending to pendulous rac. to 8cm. Fr. pruinose, purple-black. Spring. NE Amer. Z4.

A. sinica (Schneid.) Chun. = *A. asiatica* var. *sinica*.

A. spicata (Lam.) K. Koch. Shrub to 2m. Young shoots lanuginose. Lvs to 5cm, oval, broad-ovate or rounded, acute, base rounded to cordate, white-tomentose beneath, later glab., teeth fine, vein pairs 7–9. Fls white to pale pink in dense, erect, lanate, 4–10-fld rac. to 4cm. Fr. to 8mm diam., pruinose, purple-black. Spring. NE Amer. Z4.

A. spicata auct. non (Lam.) K. Koch = *A. stolonifera*.

A. stolonifera Wiegand. Stoloniferous shrub to 2m. Lvs to 5cm, oval, oblong or suborbicular, rounded and mucronate, fine-dentate, white-lanuginose beneath, soon glab., vein pairs 7–10. Fls white, in short, dense, erect rac. Fr. blue-black, juicy. Spring. NE Amer. Z4.

A. utahensis Koehne. Shrub or small tree to 5m. Lvs to 3cm, rounded to oval, apex rounded to emarginate, grey-green, fine-tomentose, large-toothed, vein pairs 11–13. Fls in 3–6-fld, erect or ascending rac. to 3cm. Fr. to 1cm diam., purple-black. W N Amer. Z3.

A. vulgaris Moench. = *A. ovalis*.

→*Aronia, Pyrus* and *Mespilus*.

✕ **Amelasorbus** Rehd. Rosaceae. (*Amelanchier* ✕ *Sorbus*.) NW US. Z3.

✕ *A. jackii* Rehd. (*Amelanchier alnifolia* var. *semiintegrifolia* ✕ *Sorbus scopulina*.) Decid. shrub to 2m. Lvs ovate to elliptic, to 10cm, coarsely toothed often slightly sinuate, irregularly lobed or entire, soon glab. Pan. to 5cm; pet. white, oblong, 2cm diam. Fr. small, subglobose, dark red, pruinose. Idaho, Oregon, Nat. hybrid.

Amellus L. Compositae. 12 ann. and perenn. herbs, usually hairy. Lvs linear to lanceolate or spathulate, entire or with 1–3 teeth per side. Cap. radiate, solitary, pedunculate; ray flts generally in a single series, disc flts numerous. S Afr. Z8.

A. alternifolius Roth. ann. or perenn., to 50cm. Lvs to 5×0.5cm, linear, pale green, with erect bristles. Peduncles long; involucre to 19mm diam. ray flts to 22, to 18×3.2mm, blue-violet, seldom white.

A. annuus hort. non Willd. = *A. strigosus*.

A. annuus Willd. = *A. alternifolius*.

A. asteroides (L.) Druce. Perenn. subshrub, to 50cm. Lvs to 3×1cm, broadly oblanceolate to spathulate, entire or minutely toothed, hairy. Peduncle to 6cm; involucre 16mm diam.; ray flts 20–30, to 13×1.5mm, blue-violet, rarely white.

A. diffusus Forst. f. = *Chiliotrichum diffusum*.

A. fruticosus L. ex Jackson = *A. asteroides*.

A. lychnitis L. = *A. asteroides*.

A. pallidus Salisb. = *A. asteroides*.

A. strigosus (Thunb.) Less. Ann. or bienn. herb to 40cm. Lvs to 4×0.5cm, linear or oblanceolate, olive green, bristly. Peduncle to 5cm; involucre to 15mm diam.; ray flts 11–14, to 9.5×3.0mm, blue-violet.

→*Kaulfussia*.

Amentotaxus Pilger. CATKIN YEW. Cephalotaxaceae. 4 everg. conifers similar to *Cephalotaxus*. Br. long, thin. Lvs in two ranks, flat or upswept, ± opposite, flattened, thick and fleshy, lanceolate, matt or shiny green above, becoming glossy with time; stomata in two broad bands beneath. Fr. fleshy, drupe-like, ovoid, green-red or yellow, seed 1, stony, projecting from apex. SE Asia.

A. argotaenia (Hance) Pilger CATKIN YEW. Shrub or small tree to 4m. Lvs 4–7cm×6mm, glossy to dull green above, with two white stomatal bands beneath. Fr. 2–2.5cm. S China. var. *brevifolia* Li. Lvs shorter, 2–3.7cm. Z9.

A. assamica Ferg. Tree to 20m. Lvs falcate or S-shaped, 7–15cm, two white or silvery stomatal bands beneath. Fr. unknown. Assam. Z9.

A. cathayensis Li = *A. argotaenia*.

A. formosana Li. Small tree to 10m or shrub. Lvs falcate, 5–8cm×6–10mm, two broad bright silver stomatal bands beneath. Fr. 2–2.5cm. Taiwan. Z9.

A. yunnanensis Li. Small tree to 15m or shrub. Lvs falcate, 4–9cm×10mm, two off-white stomatal bands beneath. Fr. 2–3cm. China. var. *poilanei* De Ferré & Rouane. Lvs narrower, thick and ribbed. Vietnam. Z9.

A. yunnanensis var. *assamica* (Ferg.) Silba = *A. assamica*.

A. yunnanensis var. *formosana* (Li) Silba = *A. formosana*.

American Alpine Speedwell *Veronica wormskjoldii*.
American Angelica Tree *Aralia spinosa*.
American Arbor-vitae *Thuja occidentalis*.
American Arrowhead *Sagittaria latifolia*.
American Aspen *Populus tremuloides*.
American Basswood *Tilia americana*.
American Beech *Fagus grandifolia*.
American Bittersweet *Celastrus scandens*.
American Blueberry *Vaccinium corymbosum*.
American Blue Vervain *Verbena hastata*.

American Brooklime *Veronica americana*.
American Bugbane *Cimicifuga americana*.
American Chestnut *Castanea dentata*.
American Cowslip *Dodecatheon* (*D. meadia*).
American Cranberry *Vaccinium macrocarpon*.
American Cranberry Bush *Viburnum trilobum*.
American Cress *Barbarea verna*.
American Dewberry *Rubus canadensis; R. flagellaris*.
American Dog Violet *Viola conspersa*.
American Dogwood *Cornus stolonifera*.
American Dwarf Birch *Betula pumila*.
American Elder *Sambucus canadensis*.
American Elm *Ulmus americana*.
American Featherfoil *Hottonia inflata*.
American Feverfew *Parthenium integrifolium*.
American Frogbit *Limnobium spongia*.
American Germander *Teucrium canadense*.
American Ginseng *Panax quinquefolius*.
American Hazel *Corylus americana*.
American Holly *Ilex opaca*.
American Hop Hornbeam *Ostrya virginiana*.
American Hornbeam *Carpinus caroliniana*.
American Ipecacuanha *Gillenia stipulata*.
American Larch *Larix laricina*.
American Lime *Tilia americana*.
American Lotus *Nelumbo lutea*.
American Maidenhair Fern *Adiantum pedatum*.
American Mistletoe *Phoradendron serotinum*.
American Mountain Ash *Sorbus americana*.
American Mountain Gooseberry *Ribes oxyacanthoides*.
American Mountain Mint *Pycnanthemum*.
American Oil Palm *Elaeis oleifera*.
American Parsley Fern *Cryptogramma acrostichoides*.
American Persimmon *Diospyros virginiana*.
American Pistachio *Pistacia texana*.
American Plane *Platanus occidentalis*.
American Raspberry *Rubus idaeus* var. *strigosus*.
American Red Birch *Betula fontinalis*.
American Red Elder *Sambucus pubens*.
American Red Plum *Prunus americana*.
American Rock-brake *Cryptogramma acrostichoides*.
American Rubber Plant *Peperomia obtusifolia*.
American Smokewood *Cotinus obovatus*.
American Spatterdock *Nuphar advena*.
American Spikenard *Aralia racemosa*.
American Sweet Chestnut *Castanea dentata*.
American Sweet Gum *Liquidambar styraciflua*.
American Sycamore *Platanus occidentalis*.
American Turkey Oak *Quercus laevis*.
American Wall Fern *Polypodium virginianum*.
American White Elm *Ulmus americana*.
American White Oak *Quercus alba*.
American Wisteria *Wisteria frutescens*.
American Wonder Lemon *Citrus ponderosa*.
American Wormseed *Chenopodium ambrosioides*.

Amesiella Garay. Orchidaceae. 1 monopodial, epiphytic orchid. St. 3–6cm. Lvs 2.5–5cm, elliptic-oblong, obtuse, fleshy, 2-ranked. Rac. axill., few-fld; peduncle winged; fls white; dors. sep. to 2.2cm, elliptic, lat. sep. similar; pet. spathulate; lip lateral lobes oblong, midlobe rounded, spur slender. Philipp. Z10.
A. philippinensis (Ames) Garay.
→*Angraecum*.

Amesium Newman.
A. ruta-muraria (L.) Newman = *Asplenium ruta-muraria*.
A. sasaki Hayata = *Asplenium septentrionale*.

Amethysteya L. Labiatae. 1 erect glab. ann. St. erect, branched, to 80cm. Lvs 3–6cm, ovate to ovate-lanceolate, 3–5-parted, seg. lanceolate, incised. Fls whorled in narrow term. pan.; cor. blue, tubular; bilabiate. Temp. Asia, Turk. to Jap. Z7.
A. caerulea L.

Amianthum A. Gray. Liliaceae (Melanthiaceae). 1 highly toxic bulbous perenn. herb to 120cm. Lvs to 60cm, linear, largely basal. Rac. term., bracteate to 12.5cm; tep. free, spreading, white. Summer. E N Amer. Z4.
A. muscitoxicum (Walter) A. Gray. FLY POISON.
→*Zigadenus*.

Amicia Kunth. Leguminosae (Papilionoideae). 7 herbs or shrubs. Lvs long-petiolate, bijugate; lfts entire, cuneate, obcordate or emarginate, with pellucid glands; bracts and stipules leaflike. Rac. axill.; fls pea-like. Andes, Mex.

A. zygomeris DC. Perenn. herb to 1.5m. Lfts to 7×5.5cm, elongate-obcordate; petioles to 10cm, downy. Rac. to 12cm, 3–10-fld; pet. yellow splashed or veined purple, standard to 3cm across, yellow. Summer–autumn. E Mex. Z9.

Amitostigma Schltr. Orchidaceae. 15 small terrestrial orchids. St. erect. Lvs linear to lanceolate. Rac., many-fld; sep. oblong to ovate; pet. similar, forming a hood; lip trilobed, spur short. India, E Asia. Z8.
A. keiskei (Maxim.) Schltr. St. 5–15cm. Lvs 3–7cm, oblong, basally sheathing. Fls pale rose-purple; dors. sep. elliptic; pet. ovate, incurved, margins speckled red; lip with 2 broken purple lines at base, midlobe cleft. Summer. Jap.

Ammi L. Umbelliferae. 6 ann. or perenn. herbs. Roots fusiform. Lvs pinnatisect, finely cut. Fls white in compound umbels; involucral bracts leafy or pinnatifid. Macaronesia, Eur., W Asia.
A. majus L. FALSE BISHOP'S WEED. Ann. 40–60cm, glaucous. Lvs 1–2-pinnatisect, seg. linear, deeply toothed, tipped white. Umbel many-rayed, spreading; bracts cut into filiform seg. Summer. Eur., Asia. Z6.

Ammobium R. Br. WINGED EVERLASTING. Compositae. 3 erect, branched or unbranched perenn. herbs. St. winged. Lvs in a basal rosette, lanceolate, white-tomentose, st. lvs smaller, decurrent. Cap. term., discoid; involucre hemispherical; receptacle scaly; phyllaries petal-like or scarious; flts numerous, orange-yellow. E Aus. Z9.
A. alatum R. Br. 50–100cm, with a stout rootstock. Lvs to 18cm, apex acute. Cap. in a loose pan.; involucre *c*2cm diam.; phyllaries silvery white, broadly ovate. NSW, Queensld.
A. grandiflorum hort. = *A. alatum*.

Ammocharis Herb. Amaryllidaceae. 5 bulbous, herbaceous perennials. Lvs prostrate, or semi-erect, distichous, in a fan, ligulate or linear, margins coarse, incised to lacerate. Umbel term., scapose; perianth funnelform, tube cylindrical, tep. equal, flat or recurved, narrowly oblanceolate; sta. strongly exserted, straight. Afr. Z9.
A. coranica (Ker-Gawl.) Herb. Bulb v. large. Scape to 35cm; fls fragrant; pedicels to 6cm; perianth tube to 2.5cm, pink to copper or crimson, veined white; seg. 2.8–5.5cm, apex recurved; fil. and style carmine. Summer–autumn. S Afr.
A. falcata (Jacq.) Herb. = *Cybistetes longifolia*.
→*Amaryllis*.

Ammophila Host. MARRAM GRASS; BEACH GRASS; MEL GRASS. Gramineae. 2 coarse, perenn. grasses to 1.3m. Rhiz. long, hard, scaly. Lvs to 60×0.5cm, tough, sharp, grey-green, rolled in dry weather. Pan. dense, spike-like, pale yellow to straw-coloured; spikelets single-fld, somewhat flattened. Eur., N Afr., N Amer. Z5.
A. arenaria (L.) Link. Ligule to 3cm, bifid, flimsy. Pan. to 25cm; spikelets ascending. Summer. Eur., N Afr.
A. breviligulata Fern. Ligule to 0.3cm, rigid. Pan. to 30cm, narrower than *A. arenaria*. NE Amer.

Amoebophyllum N.E. Br.
A. guerichianum (Pasc.) N.E. Br. = *Mesembryanthemum guerichianum*.

Amole *Chlorogalum*.

Amomum Roxb. Zingiberaceae. 90 perenn. herbs. Rhiz. aromatic. Lvs lanceolate on reed-like erect shoots. Infl. pyramidal, bracteate, scapose; cor. 3-lobed; lip showy; lat. staminodes small or 0. Capsule 3-valved. E Asia to Australasia. Z10.
A. cardamomum auct. = *A. compactum*.
A. cardamomum L. non auct. = *Elettaria cardamomum*.
A. compactum Sol. ex Maton. ROUND CARDAMOM. To 1m. Lvs 25cm, glab. Scape 5–10cm; cor. yellow, pet. 1cm, obtuse, lip elliptic, 1.5cm, yellow with purple or purple-edged stripe. Fr. aromatic; seeds with white aril. Summer. Java.
A. kepulaga Sprague & Burkill = *A. compactum*.
A. melegueta Roscoe = *Aframomum melegueta*.
A. zambesiacum Bak. = *Aframomum zambesiacum*.
A. zerumbet L. = *Zingiber zerumbet* (not *Alpinia zerumbet*).

Amomyrtus (Burret) Legrand & Kausel. Myrtaceae. 2 everg. aromatic shrubs or trees. Bark smooth or scaly. Lvs opp., leathery. Fls solitary, 5-merous. Fr. a berry. S Amer. Z9.
A. luma (Molina) Legrand & Kausel. LUMA; PALO MADRONO; CAUCHAO. To 20m. Lvs to 3cm, ovate, elliptic or lanceolate, copper later dark glossy green, petioles red-tinted. Fls fragrant; pet. to 0.3cm, white, rounded. Fr. to 1cm, black, edible. Chile,

Arg.
→*Eugenia, Myrcia* and *Myrtus*.

Amorpha L. Leguminosae (Papilionoideae). 15 often aromatic shrubs. Lvs imparipinnate; lfts glandular-punctate. Rac. to 30cm, erect, crowded, paniculate or spike-like; pet. 1 (others aborted), erect, clawed, obovate to obcordate, bilobed at apex; sta. 10, forming a tube, exserted. N Amer.

A. angustifolia (Pursh) F.E. Boynt. = *A. fruticosa*.

A. brachycarpa Palmer = *A. canescens*.

A. californica Nutt. To 4m. Young shoots hairy with pointed, orange-red resin glands. Lvs to 20cm; rachis gland.; lfts 11–25, to 4cm, oblong to elliptic, obtuse, usually emarginate, sparsely hairy. Pet. to 1cm, red to indigo, broadly obovate, tapering to a claw, emarginate to truncate, enveloping sta. tube. Summer. Calif. Z7.

A. canescens Pursh. LEAD PLANT. To 1m. Lvs 6–15cm; lfts to 2.5cm, 11–47, overlapping, ovate-oblong to elliptic, mucronate, leathery, grey-white tomentose. Pet. to 0.5cm, broadly obcordate, arched and involute, emarginate, violet, margins ragged. Summer. S Canada to New Mex. Z2.

A. croceolanata Wats. = *A. fruticosa*.

A. fragrans Sweet = *A. fruticosa*.

A. fruticosa L. BASTARD INDIGO. To 4m. Young shoots glab. or pilose. Lvs to 30cm; lfts to 5cm, 9–30, oblong to elliptic, acute, rarely emarginate, gland. Pet. to 0.5cm, broadly obovate, clawed, entire or emarginate, dark purple, rarely pale blue or white. Summer. US. 'Albiflora': fls white. 'Coerulea': fls pale blue. 'Crispa': lfts crinkled at edges. 'Lewisii': fls large. 'Pendula': br. prostrate to pendulous. Z4.

A. glabra Desf. ex Poir. To 2m. Young shoots light to dark purple-brown, glab. Lvs to 30cm; lfts to 7.5cm, 7–21, glab., elliptic to ovate, rarely suborbicular, obtuse. Pet. to 1cm, broadly obcordate, blue to maroon. Summer. Appalachians. Z6.

A. microphylla Pursh = *A. nana*.

A. montana F.E. Boynt. = *A. glabra*.

A. nana Nutt. non Sims. To 60cm. Young shoots red-brown, hairy at first. Lvs to 10cm; petioles to 1cm, red-brown; lfts to 2cm, 7–31, narrowly to broadly oblong, cuneate at base, mucronate. Pet. to 0.5cm, broadly obcordate, arched and involute, purple. Summer. Minn. to Rocky Mts. Z4.

A. nitens F.E. Boynt. To 3m. Young shoots brown, sparsely hairy. Lvs to 20cm; lfts to 7cm, 7–19, oblong or ovate, obtuse, often emarginate, glossy dark green above. Pet. broadly obovate, clawed, maroon to mauve. Summer. S US. Z7.

A. occidentalis Abrams. = *A. fruticosa*.

A. tenessensis Shuttlew. ex Kunze = *A. fruticosa*.

A. virgata Small = *A. fruticosa*.

Amorphophallus Bl. ex Decne. DEVIL'S TONGUE; SNAKE PALM. Araceae. 90 cormous perenn. herbs. Corm large, sometimes edible. Lf usually solitary, after fl., with 3 usually bipinnatifid seg.; petiole erect, stout. Infl. large; peduncle stout; spathe campanulate to funnel-shaped, ventricose, margins overlapping below to form tube, limb spreading, undulate; spadix with large, foetid appendix. OW Trop. and subtrop. Z10.

A. bulbifer (Curtis) Bl. Corm to 7cm diam. subglobose. Lvs to 60cm across, main seg. dissected to base, lobes to 20cm, obovate or lanceolate, bearing cormlets; petiole to 1m, marbled or spotted, dull brown to pink or dull white. Spathe 15–20cm, limb dull green, mottled pink externally, dull green or white, tinged pink within; spadix 7×2.5cm, appendix ovoid, pink. Spring. Burm.

A. campanulatus (Roxb.) Bl. ex Decne. = *A. paeoniifolius*.

A. konjac K. Koch = *A. rivieri* 'Konjac'.

A. paeoniifolius (Dennst.) Nicols. ELEPHANT YAM; TELINGO POTATO. Corm to 25cm thick, flattened, edible. Lvs 60–90×60cm, occas. 2, trifid, lat. lobes pinnate; petiole to 75cm, dark green with pale spots, sometimes verrucose. Spathe to 20cm, externally green, spotted white, tube deep purple, verrucose within, limb ovate, green to purple, undulate; spadix to 30cm, appendix globose-conic, deep purple. India to New Guinea.

A. rivieri Durieu. DEVIL'S TONGUE; SNAKE PALM; UMBRELLA ARUM. Corm to 25cm diam., depressed-globose. Lf to 1.3m diam. seg. 1–2× dichotomous, then bipinnate, lobes oblong-elliptic, cuspidate; petiole to 1m, brown green, mottled white. Spathe to 40cm, tube green, spotted green-white, limb broadly round-cordate, undulate, green externally, dark purple within; spadix exceeding spathe, appendix to 55cm, narrowly conic, dark red-brown. Spring. SE Asia. 'Konjac': infl. large, limb oblong; widely cult. for edible corms. Indon. to Jap.

A. titanum Becc. TITAN ARUM. Corm to 50cm diam. Lf to 4m+ across, trifid, lobes to 40cm, ovate or oblong, abruptly acuminate; petiole to 4m, pale green, spotted white. Spathe campanulate, to 150cm, 3m in circumference, margin recurved, v. irregular, green, spotted white externally, rich dark crimson within, green-yellow at base; spadix appendix to 2m, tapering upwards, obtuse, furrowed, dirty dull yellow, v. malodorous. Sumatra.

Ampelodesmos Link. DISS GRASS; MAURITANIA VINE REED. Gramineae. 1 robust, perenn. grass forming large clumps. St. to 3m, glab., pale green. Lf sheaths striate; ligule to 1.5cm, ciliate; blades to 1m×8mm, wiry, curved, scabrous. Pan. to 50cm, br. slender, pendulous, apparently one-sided, scabrous; spikelets crowded, green-yellow, suffused purple, pilose. Medit. Z8.

A. mauritanicus (Poir.) T. Dur. & Schinz.

→*Arundo*.

Ampelopsis Michx. Vitaceae. 25 decid. shrubs or woody vines climbing by tendrils lacking adhesive disks. Lvs simple or compound. Fls in forked cymes, small, 4-merous, yellow tinged green. Fr. a thin-fleshed berry, produced in early autumn. N Amer., Asia.

A. aconitifolia Bunge. Vine; st. slender, young shoots glab. Lvs palmate, 5–12cm diam., deep glossy green above, paler beneath; lfts 3–5, 2.5–7.5cm, lanceolate to rhombic, coarsely dentate to 3–5-lobed; petiole 1–5cm. Fr. 5–6mm, rounded-obovate, blue turning yellow to brown. N China, Mong. var. *glaba* Diels. Lvs generally 3-parted, seg. lobed or dentate. Z4.

A. aegeriophylla (Bunge) Boiss. = *A. vitifolia*.

A. arborea (L.) Koehne. PEPPER VINE. Vine, high-climbing; shoots flexuous, rather angular, tinged purple, glab.; tendrils slender, forked, or lacking. Lvs 10–20cm, broadly deltoid, 2–3× pinnate, dark green and glab. above, downy on veins beneath at first; lfts 1.2–4.5cm, ovate to rhombic, acute at apex, cuneate at base, deeply dentate. Fr. 8mm diam., dark purple. E US. Z7.

A. bipinnata Michx. = *A. arborea*.

A. bodinieri (Lév. & Vaniot) Rehd. Vine to 6.5m; shoots sometimes tinged purple, glab. Lvs 6–12cm, rounded to triangular-ovate, shallowly cordate to truncate at base, acute at apex, triangular-dentate, 3-lobed glittering green above, pale or glaucous beneath, glab.; petiole 4–7.5cm, tinged purple. Fr. 4–5mm diam., flattened-globose, dark blue. C China. Z5.

A. brevipedunculata (Maxim.) Trautv. Vine, climbing vigorously; young shoots roughly hairy. Lvs 5–15cm, 3(–5)-lobed, lobes spreading, cordate at base, mucronate-crenate, dark green and v. sparsely pubesc. above at first, setose beneath; petiole hairy, particularly at first. Fr. 6–8mm diam., amethyst purple to bright blue. China, Jap., Korea. var. *maximowiczii* (Reg.) Rehd. Young shoots ± glab.; lvs variable – broadly cordate and unlobed to deeply 3–5-lobed, glab. or slightly downy beneath. Fr. porcelain blue. China, Jap., Korea. Z4. 'Citrulloides': lf lobes 5, narrow, some lobed again. 'Elegans': smaller; shoots tinged pink; lvs variegated, flushed pink, white, green or yellow. Z9.

A. brevipedunculata var. *citrulloides* (Lebas.) Bail. = *A. brevipedunculata* var. *maximowiczii* 'Citrulloides'.

A. brevipedunculata var. *elegans* Bail. = *A. brevipedunculata* var. *maximowiczii* 'Elegans'.

A. cantoniensis (Hook. & Arn.) Planch. Vine, climbing high. Lvs pinnate to bipinnate with lowest pinna bearing 3–5 lfts and upper ones entire; lfts ovate to ovate-oblong, serrate, term. leaflet 3–7cm, subcoriaceous, glab., glaucous beneath, stalked. Fr. ovoid-globose, black tinged blue. S China to Malaysia. Z9.

A. chaffanjonii (Lév.) Rehd. Vine, glab. throughout. Lvs to 30cm, pinnate, lustrous green above, claret purple beneath, brilliantly coloured in autumn; lfts 3.5–11cm, 5–7, ovate to oblong, long-acuminate at apex, sparsely dentate. Fr. pea-sized, red turning black. China. Z5.

A. citrulloides Lebas. = *A. brevipedunculata* var. *maximowiczii* 'Citrulloides'.

A. cordata Michx. Vine, climbing high; bark warted, ± glab.; tendrils forked. Lvs 6–12cm, ovate-deltoid, serrate, broadly truncate to subcordate at base, acuminate at apex, ± glab.; petiole long, downy. Fr. 7–10mm diam., blue or blue-green. E & C US. Z4.

A. delavayana Planch. Vine; st. swollen at nodes, tinged pink and hairy when young. Lvs pinnate, lfts 3.5–10cm, 3–5, narrowly ovate, tapered to both ends, coarsely dentate, rough above, pubesc. beneath when young; term. lft stalked; laterals sometimes lobed; petiole tinged pink. Fr. small, dark blue. W China. Z5.

A. engelmannii hort. ex Rehd. in Bail. = *Parthenocissus quinquefolia* var. *engelmannii*.

A. hederacea (Ehrh.) DC. = *Parthenocissus quinquefolia*.

A. henryana (Hemsl.) Rehd. in L.H. Bail. = *Parthenocissus henryana*.

A. heterophylla (Thunb.) Sieb. & Zucc. non Bl. = *A. brevipedunculata* var. *maximowiczii*.

A. heterophylla var. *amurensis* Planch. = *A. brevipedunculata*.

A. himalayana Royle = *Parthenocissus himalayana*.

A. hoggii Nichols. = *Parthenocissus tricuspidata*.

A. humulifolia Bunge. Vine to 6.5m; shoots often tinged purple, glab. Lvs 6–12cm, rounded to triangular-ovate, shallowly cordate to truncate at base, triangular-dentate, 3–5-lobed with rounded sinuses, or unlobed, lustrous bright green above, white tinged blue beneath, thick glab.; petiole tinged purple. Fr. flattened-globose, 4–5mm diam., pale yellow becoming pale blue. N China. Z5.

A. japonica (Thunb.) Mak. Vine, creeping; shoots slender, glab.; roots tuberous. Lvs pinnate, 5–12cm, dark green above, pale glossy green beneath, glab.; lfts 2.5–7.5cm, 3–5, lanceolate, dentate, lowest pair sometimes pinnately divided; rachis winged. Fr. 6mm, pale violet-blue with darker spots. Summer. China, Jap., Korea. Z7.

A. leeoides (Maxim.) Planch. Woody vine, decid.; br. glab., with lenticels; tendrils bifid. Lvs 12–30cm, ternately 2–3-pinnate, ± glab.; lowest lfts ternately parted or lobed, others ovate to oblong, acuminate at apex, adpressed-dentate, stalked. Fr. globose, red. Jap., Ryukyu Is., Taiwan. Z7.

A. lowii Cook = *Parthenocissus tricuspidata* 'Lowii'.

A. megalophylla (Veitch) Diels & Gilg. Vine, climbing vigorously, 10–12m, glab.; shoots ± glaucous. Lvs 45–60cm, pinnate, pinnae 7–9 on larger lvs, lower pairs again pinnate, seg. 5–15cm, ovate to ovate-oblong, mucronate-dentate, deep green above, glaucous beneath. Fr. top-shaped, 6mm diam., dark purple to black. W China. Z5.

A. micans Rehd. = *A. bodinieri*.

A. orientalis (Lam.) Planch. Bushy shrub, sometimes climbing; shoots slightly ribbed, glab.; tendrils few. Lvs 1–2× pinnate or biternate; lfts 2.5–7.5cm, usually 9, ovate, rhombic or obovate, tapered to base, apex coarsely dentate, dull dark green above, paler grey-green beneath, glab. Fr. rounded top-shaped, 6mm diam., red. Asia Minor, Syr.

A. quinquefolia (L.) Michx. = *Parthenocissus quinquefolia*.

A. saint-paulii hort. ex Rehd. = *Parthenocissus quinquefolia* var. *saint-paulii*.

A. sempervirens hort. ex Veitch = *Cissus striata*.

A. serjaniifolia Bunge = *A. japonica*.

A. tricuspidata Sieb. & Zucc. = *Parthenocissus tricuspidata*.

A. variegata hort. = *A. brevipedunculata* var. *maximowiczii* 'Elegans'.

A. veitchii hort. = *Parthenocissus tricuspidata* 'Veitchii'.

A. vitifolia (Boiss.) Planch. Shrub, glab., slightly glaucous; tendrils 0; shoots erect, weakly striate. Lvs 4–7cm across, apex coarsely dentate, dull dark green above, paler grey-green beneath, glab. Fr. rounded top-shaped, 6mm diam., red. Iran, Turkestan to NW Himal. Z6.

A. watsoniana Wils. = *A. chaffanjonii*.

→*Cissus* and *Vitis*.

Ampelopteris Kunze. Thelypteridaceae. 1 terrestrial fern. Rhiz. to 4mm diam., creeping. Stipes 30–60cm; frond-blades to 100cm+, pinnate, term. pinna petiolate, lat. pinnae sessile, apex acuminate, base cordate to truncate, to 20×2cm, herbaceous, plantlets produced at nodes of rachis. OW Trop. and subtrop. Z10.

A. prolifera (Retz.) Copel.

→*Hemionitis*.

Amphicarpaea Elliott ex Nutt. HOG PEANUT. Leguminosae (Papilionoideae). 3 fleshy-rooted twining ann. or perenn. herbs. Lvs trifoliolate. Fls dimorphic: pea-like, racemose toward summit of plant, apetalous, clustered lower on plant. Upper fr. a linear-oblong, 3–4-seeded legume; lower fr. often subterranean, 1-seeded. Afr., Asia, N Amer.

A. bracteata (L.) Rickett & Stafleu. Ann. to 1.5m. Petioles to 10cm; lfts to 8.25cm, ovate to deltoid, acute, dark green above, lighter beneath, adpressed-hairy. Upper fls in axill. rac. to 15cm; purple-maroon, standard to 1.5×0.5cm. Summer–early autumn. E US, SE Canada. Z7.

Amphicome G. Don.

A. arguta Royle = *Incarvillea arguta*.

A. diffusa (Royle) Sprague = *Incarvillea arguta*.

A. emodi Lindl. = *Incarvillea emodi*.

Amphilophium Kunth. Bignoniaceae. 7 cane-like climbers. Br. hexagonal. Lvs 2–3-pinnate, term. pinnae often replaced by tendril. Infl. a pan.; cal. campanulate; cor. tubular, 2-lipped, upper lip 2-lobed, lower 3-lobed. Fr. a woody capsule. Americas. Z10.

A. macrophyllum HBK = *A. paniculatum* var. *molle*.

A. molle Schldl. & Cham. = *A. paniculatum* var. *molle*.

A. mutisii HBK = *A. paniculatum*.

A. paniculatum (L.) HBK. St. 10cm diam. Lvs 2-pinnate, membranous. Fls to 4cm, fragrant, white-yellow becoming purple. Mex. to N Arg. var. *molle* (Schldl. & Cham.) Standl. Densely soft pubesc. throughout. Mex. to Peru.

A. paraguariense Hassl. ex O. Schulz. = *A. paniculatum*.

A. purpureum Brandg. = *A. paniculatum*.

A. vauthieri DC. = *A. paniculatum*.

A. xerophilum Pittier = *A. paniculatum*.

→*Endoloma*.

Amphineuron Holtt. Thelypteridaceae. 12 epiphytic or lithophytic ferns. Fronds uniform or dimorphic; pinnae lobed, pubesc. and gland.; stipes setose-pubescent, scaly at base. SE Asia to Polyn., Afr. Z10.

A. opulentum (Kaulf.) Holtt. Rhiz. short-creeping, brown-scaly. Lamina to 90×50cm, (if sterile, wider and less erect), ovate to oblong, apex narrowly acute, base lobed; pinnae 25, to 30×3cm, alt., narrowly acute at apex, lobes to 5mm distant, spreading, subfalcate, linear to oblong; stipes to 70cm, pubesc. and gland., purple to brown.

→*Aspidium* and *Thelypteris*.

Amphitecna Miers. Bignoniaceae. 18 small trees. Fls solitary or in clusters; cal. bilabiate, irregularly split; cor. white to green, tubular-campanulate. Fr. a calabash or pepo, spherical to ellipsoid, shell woody, thin, pulpy within. W Indies and Mex., to Venez., Ecuad. Z10.

A. latifolia (Mill.) A. Gentry BLACK CALABASH; SAVANA CALABASH; WILD CALABASH; RIVER CALABASH; CALABASH TREE. To 10m. Lvs 7–19×3.3–10.6cm, obovate, rigid and brittle to leathery, glab. beneath. Cor. tube 2–4cm, lobes 0.8–1.5cm. Fr. 6–9cm, spherical. Ecuad. to Costa Rica.

A. macrophylla (Seem.) Miers ex Baill. 2–7m. Lvs 28–53×5–13cm, oblanceolate, leathery, glab. Cor. 3.7–5×1–1.5cm wide at apex of tube, undulate. Fr. narrowly ellipsoid, to 1.6cm diam. Mex.

A. nigripes (Lind.) Baill. = *A. macrophylla*.

A. obovata (Benth.) L.O. Williams = *A. latifolia*.

A. regalis (Lind.) A. Gentry. 4–12m. Lvs 69–100×18–35cm, oblanceolate, leathery, glab. Cor. 2.5–3.3cm diam. at apex, undulate. Fr. unknown. Mex.

A. regia hort. ex Seem. = *A. macrophylla*.

→*Crescentia, Enallagma* and *Ferdinandia*.

Amsinckia Lehm. FIDDLENECK. Boraginaceae. *c*50 ann. herbs, hispid. Lvs ovate to linear. Spike terminal, elongate, scorpioid; cal. accrescent, deeply 5-lobed; cor. salverform to infundibular. Americas, Eur. Z7.

A. calycina (Morris) Chater. St. to 5cm. Lvs to 15cm, linear-lanceolate, erect-patent pubesc. Cor. to 8mm, yellow. N & W Eur., S Amer., S N Amer.

A. intermedia Fisch. & C.A. Mey. COMMON AMSINCKIA. St. to 70cm. Lvs to 4cm, lanceolate to broadly linear. Cor. to 12mm, yellow-orange. W US.

A. lycopsoides (Lehm.) Lehm. BUGLOSS AMSINCKIA. St. to 1m. Basal lvs to 15cm, linear to linear-oblanceolate, erect patent-pubesc., cauline lvs narrowly ovate or lanceolate. Cor. to 10mm, rich yellow, interior pubesc. W US, Eur.

→*Lithospermum*.

Amsonia Walter. BLUE STAR. Apocynaceae. 20 perenn. herbs and subshrubs with milky sap. Lvs entire. Fls in term. pan.; cal. 5-lobed; cor. funnelform, tube narrow, limb flared, with 5 spreading lobes. S Eur., Asia Minor, Jap., N Amer.

A. angustifolia (Ait.) Michx. = *A. ciliata*.

A. ciliata Walter. 30–90cm, pubesc. when young. Lvs 2.5–5cm, crowded, linear-lanceolate, revolute. Cor. periwinkle blue, lobes ovate-oblong to linear-oblong. SE US. Z7.

A. illustris Woodson. To 1m, often clump-forming. Lvs ovate to lanceolate or elliptic, thick textured, leathery. C US. Z5.

A. orientalis Decne. Subshrub to 1m. Lvs 2.5–5cm, narrowly ovate to oval, apex acuminate, ciliate. Cor. 1.5cm, bright blue to dark violet. Early summer. Greece to Turk. Z8.

A. rigida Shuttlew. To 1.5m. Lvs 6cm, elliptic, glaucous beneath. Fls in loose cymes; cor. blue tinged purple, tube to 1cm. N Amer. Z8.

A. salicifolia Pursh = *A. tabernaemontana* var. *salicifolia*.

A. tabernaemontana Walter. To 1m, often clump-forming. Lvs ovate to lanceolate or elliptic, matt green. Cor. tube to 0.6cm; lobes, slate blue, lanceolate, exterior pubesc. Spring–summer. SE US. var. *salicifolia* (Pursh) Woodson. Lvs narrowly linear-lanceolate, acuminate. Summer. SE US. Z8.

→*Rhazya*.

Amur Cherry *Prunus maackii*.

Amur Cork Tree *Phellodendron amurense*.

Amur Grape *Vitis amurensis.*
Amur Maple *Acer tataricum.*
Amur Silver Grass *Miscanthus sacchariflorus.*

Amyris P. Browne.
A. polygama Cav. = *Schinus polygamus.*

Anaba *Ficus palmeri.*

Anabasis L.
A. ammodendron C.A. Mey. = *Haloxylon ammodendron.*

Anacampseros L. Portulacaceae. 56 small, low-growing, succulent perennials. Lvs fleshy, rosulate or spirally arranged on thick st., or small, adpressed; stipules sometimes reduced to bristle-hairs. Fls solitary or cymose, with 2 sep. and 5 pet., short-lived. S Afr., Nam., C & E Afr., S Aus. Z10.
A. affinis Pearson & Stephenson. St. short. Lvs 8–12mm, obovate to conic, pointed to tapering, lower surface slightly convex, bristles numerous, 3cm, white, glossy. Fls 1–4, 3cm diam., red. SW Cape Prov.
A. albissima Marloth. St. numerous, branching, to 4cm. Lvs v. small, spirally arranged, hidden by adpressed, rounded, papery stipules. Fls 1–3, white. SW Cape Prov. var. *caespitosa* Poelln. St. subterranean, branching at tips above ground, erect to creeping. Nam. var. *laciniata* Poelln. Stipules lanceolate and laciniate. Nam.
A. alstonii Schönl. Caudex napiform, flat-topped, 6cm+ diam. St. simple, numerous, to 3cm. Lvs v concealed by stipules, in 5 rows along st.; stipules silvery, adpressed, triangular, 2mm. Fls 1, 3cm diam., white. Nam., SW Cape.
A. arachnoides (Haw.) Sims. St. to 5cm, densely leafy. Lvs 20mm, broadly ovate, tapering, thick, tip tuberculate, covered with a few v° te threads, bristles few, shorter than lvs, white. Fls several, 3cm diam., white-pink. S Africa. var. *hispidula* (A. Berger) Poelln. Lvs always felty white; fls white. Cape Province.
A. arachnoides hort. non (Haw.) Sims = *A. rufescens.*
A. arachnoides var. *grandiflora* Sonder = *A. rufescens.*
A. asperula A. Berger = *A. arachnoides* var. *hispidula.*
A. avasmontana Dinter = *A. albissima.*
A. baeseckeri Dinter. St. branching to 5cm, densely leafy. Lvs 3–4mm, rounded above, ± tuberculate beneath, white-felted, bristle hairs, 3–4mm. Fls several, 6mm diam., carmine edged white. Cape Province.
A. bremekampii (Poelln. St. to 1cm, simple, numerous from a short root-stock 1cm diam. Lvs spirally arranged, small, half covered by 2mm papery, broadly ovate, silvery stipules. Fls 6mm diam., 1, pink. SW Cape Prov.
A. buderiana Poelln. St. 1.5cm, simple, erect, forming circular mounds. Lvs spirally arranged, v. small, hidden by adpressed silvery-white stipules, basal hairs often present. Fls 5mm diam., 1, white. SW Cape Prov.
A. comptonii Pill. Caudex 1–1.5×1–2cm, st. short. Lvs 2–4, 3–5mm, semi-ovate to rounded with short tapering tip, flat or somewhat grooved, olive to bronze, bristle hairs 4–5mm. Fls 5–6mm diam., 1, purple, pink or white, long-stalked. SW Cape Prov., Nam.
A. crinita Dinter. St. forming a dense carpet. Lvs 4mm, crowded, ovate-orbicular, light green, young lvs white-felted, bristle hairs 15mm, wavy, off-white to red-brown. Fls 2–6, 2cm diam., pale purple or purple-red edged white. Namibia; SW Cape Province.
A. dielsiana Dinter. Rosette-forming, 2–2.5cm diam., stemless. Lvs 12–15mm, subterete, clavate, floccose when young; whole rosette covered in grey wool. Fls 2–3, 1.5cm diam., pink. Namibia.
A. dinteri Schinz. St. numerous, creeping, to 10cm. Lvs spirally arranged, covered by adpressed pointed silvery stipules 3–5mm. Fls 1, red. Nam.
A. filamentosa (Haw.) Sims. Roots tuberous. St. 5cm, densely leafy. Lvs 6–10mm, ovate to spherical, tip truncate, rough, covered with fine threads, bristles long, curly, off-white. Fls 3–5.3cm diam., pink. SW Cape Prov.
A. filamentosa De Wildeman non (Haw.) Sims. = *A. rufescens.*
A. fissa Poelln. Caudex 2×4cm. St. numerous, erect, simple. Lvs spirally arranged, half covered by 2mm silvery stipules with basal hairs, long-oval to truncate, tip divided. Fls 1. Transvaal.
A. gracilis Poelln. St. 5–7cm, branching, erect. Lvs 8mm, ovate-lanceolate, apiculate, red-green, flat above, covex beneath, young lvs felted, bristle-hairs bushy, white. Fls 2.5cm diam., white striped red. S Africa.
A. hispidula A. Berger = *A. arachnoides* var. *hispidula.*
A. intermedia Nichols. = *A. filamentosa.*
A. intermedia Haw. = *A. telephiastrum.*
A. karasmontana Dinter. Lvs 10–12mm, crowded, cuneate, flat to convex above, convex beneath, green to green-red, covered

with white felt, bristle hairs numerous, glossy, curly, 2cm. Fls 2cm diam., pink. Nam.
A. lanceolata (Haw.) Sweet. St. short. Lvs 35mm, numerous, narrow-lanceolate to lanceolate, abruptly pointed with a spiny tip, rounded beneath, bristle hairs numerous, 5mm, white, curly. Fls 1–4, 3cm diam., red or white. S Afr.
A. lanigera Burchell. St. 2cm thick. Lvs 4mm, crowded, rounded to obovate, white-felted, tip tuberculate, bristle hairs 4mm, curly, white. Fls 2cm diam., pink. S Afr.
A. margaretae Dinter = *A. tomentosa* var. *margaretae.*
A. meyeri Poelln. St. tuberous, short, br. numerous, erect, 7cm. Lvs spirally arranged, small, hidden by adpressed, off-white stipules with a yellow-white nerve. Fls 1cm diam., off-white. S Afr.
A. papyracea E. Mey. Roots tuberous. St. short, 5–6cm, many-branched, prostrate. Lvs spirally arranged, small, hidden by adpressed, broad-ovate, blunt, white stipules. Fls 10–12mm diam., green-white. S Afr.
A. populifolia (Pall.) Haw. = *Hylotelephium populifolium.*
A. quinaria E. Mey. Caudex to 2.5cm, fleshy; st. to 1.5cm, br. numerous. Lvs spirally arranged, hemispheric, covered by stipules, stipules ovate to triangular, silvery, spotted brown. Fls to 1.5cm diam., 1, purple. Great Namaqualand, SW Cape.
A. recurvata Schönl. Roots tuberous. Br. 2.5cm, simple. Lvs to 2mm, spirally arranged, hemispheric, stipules 3mm lanceolate, curved outwards with a light green median nerve. Little Namaqualand.
A. retusa Poelln. Caudex thick grey, br. 4cm. Lvs crowded, slightly hairy at first, somewhat carinate, tip rough, truncate and grooved, bristle hairs numerous, 15mm, white to yellow-white. Fls 2.5cm diam., pink. SW Cape Prov.
A. rhodesiaca N.E. Br. Br. 1cm, numerous. Lvs spirally arranged, stipules rounded-ovate, silvery, short-pointed, 2.5mm, curving outwards. Fls 0.6cm diam., 1, white to pale flesh-coloured. Zimb.
A. rotundifolia Sweet = *A. telephiastrum.*
A. rubens hort. = *A. rufescens.*
A. rufescens (Haw.) Schwantes. Caudex thick; st. 5–8cm, forming dense mats. Lvs 20mm in a dense spiral, dark green to red-brown, obovate-lanceolate, tapering, bristle hairs long, sometimes wavy. Fls 3–4cm diam., 2–4, pink to purple-red. S Afr.
A. sempervirens Haw. = *Hylotelephium anacampseros.*
A. spectabilis (Boreau) Jordan & Fourr. = *Hylotelephium spectabile.*
A. telephiastrum DC. Mat-forming; st. to 5cm. Lvs 18mm, compressed, rosulate, ovate to rounded, short-pointed, glab., bristles short and sparse. Fls 1–4, 3–3.5cm diam., pink-carmine. S Afr.
A. telephioides (Michx.) Haw. = *Hylotelephium telephioides.*
A. tomentosa A. Berger. Clump-forming; st. to 5cm. Lvs 10mm, overlapping, obovate, truncate, tuberculate, flattened above, brown-green, white-felted, bristle hairs few, 10mm, curved. Fls several, 3cm diam., pink. Nam. var. *margaretae* (Dinter) Poelln. Lvs smaller, red-brown, bristle hairs longer, more numerous; fls darker pink.
A. ustulata E. Mey. Lvs spirally arranged, short-reniform, stipules 1.5–2×1–1.25mm, adpressed, broad-ovate, apiculate. Fls 1, pink. S Afr., Botswana.
A. varians Sweet = *A. telephiastrum.*
→*Portulaca* and *Rulingia.*

Anacamptis Rich. Orchidaceae. 1 tuberous, terrest. orchid to 40cm. Lvs lanceolate, diminishing to bracts on fl. st. Spike crowded, pyramidal; fls to 1.6cm, across, rose pink to pale mauve, narrowly spurred. Eur., N Afr. Z6.
A. pyramidalis (L.) Rich. PYRAMID ORCHID.

ANACARDIACEAE Lindl. 73/850. *Anacardium, Cotinus, Harpephyllum, Lithrea, Malosma, Mangifera, Pistacia, Pleiogynium, Poupartia, Rhodosphaera, Rhus, Schinus, Sclerocarya, Semecarpus, Smodingium, Spondias, Toxicodendron.*

Anacardium L. Anacardiaceae. 8 trees and shrubs. Lvs entire. Infl. term. or axill., paniculate or corymbose; cal. 5-lobed; pet. 5, puberulous; sta. 7–10. Fr. a drupe; receptacle or peduncle enlarged and fleshy. Trop. Amer. Z10.
A. occidentale L. CASHEW; MARANON; ACAJOU. Tree to 12m. Trunk rarely straight; bark smooth, brown. Lvs 4–22cm, obovate to broadly elliptic, coriaceous, glab. Infl. to 26cm, pubesc.; pet. 0.7–1cm, linear, pale green to red. Fr. to 3×2cm, reniform, grey-brown. Trop. Amer., nat. Malaysia.
→*Acajou* and *Cassuvium.*

Anacyclus L. Compositae. 9 ann. or perenn. herbs. St. erect or creeping. Lvs 2–3-pinnatifid or pinnatisect, in basal rosettes and cauline. Cap. usually radiate, long-stalked, solitary or paired, term.; receptacle flat to conic, scaly; disc flts yellow. Medit. Z6.
A. atlanticus Litard. & Maire = *Heliocauta atlantica*.

A. clavatus (Desf.) Pers. Ann., to 30cm. St. procumbent to erect, branching. Lvs to 13×4cm, oblanceolate, 2–3-pinnatisect, lobes in 3–12 pairs. Cap. to 40, in a loose cyme; peduncle clavate, ray flts 16.5×7mm, cream, trifid, obtuse. Medit.
A. clavatus ssp. *maroccanus* Ball = *A. maroccanus*.
A. depressus Ball = *A. pyrethrum* var. *depressus*.

A. maroccanus (Ball) Ball. Low ann. Lvs 3-pinnatisect, lobes in 7–12 pairs. Cap. 2–12 in a compact cyme; involucre to 1cm diam.; ray flts to 25×5mm, white with a red stripe. Moroc.

A. pyrethrum (L.) Link. Low, rosette-forming perenn. St. with persistent lf bases. Lvs grey green, mostly in a basal rosette, to 14×3cm, 3-pinnatisect, lobes in 4–9 pairs. Involucre to 2.5cm diam., ray flts to 15×5mm, white with a red stripe beneath. Spain, Alg., Moroc. var. *depressus* (Ball) Maire. Lf bases not persistent. Involucre to 1.2cm diam.

A. radiatus Lois. YELLOW ANACYCLUS. Ann. or bienn. St. erect, simple, to 12cm, often tinged red. Lvs in a basal rosette, to 16×5cm, 3-pinnatisect, lobes in 6–14 pairs. Peduncle clavate; involucre to 2cm diam.; ray flts to 17×7mm, yellow, cream or white, often striped maroon beneath. W & C Medit.
A. valentina var. *maroccanus* Ball ex Pitard. = *A. maroccanus*.
→*Anthemis*.

Anadenanthera Speg. Leguminosae (Mimosoideae). 2 trees or shrubs. Bark grey to black. Lvs bipinnate; rachis red, grooved; petioles with a black or white gland near base; lfts v. small, entire. Infl. axill., globose-capitate, 30–50-fld; flts 5-merous; cal. campanulate; cor. tubular, puberulent; sta. to 1cm, showy, far-exserted. Trop. Amer. Z10.

A. colubrina (Vell.) Brenan. Shrub or tree to 30m. Lvs to 20cm; pinnae to 7cm, in 7–35 pairs; lfts in 20–80 pairs, oblong to lanceolate. Infl. to 2cm diam., 5–7 together, white to pale yellow-orange. Braz., Arg.
→*Piptadenia*.

Anagallis L. PIMPERNEL. Primulaceae. 20 glab. herbs, st. erect or creeping, rooting. Lvs entire, short-petiolate. Fls 5-merous, solitary and axill., or in rac.; cor. rotate or infundibuliform. Summer. Cosmop. Z7.

A. arvensis L. SHEPHERD'S CLOCK; POOR MAN'S WEATHERGLASS; COMMON PIMPERNEL; SCARLET PIMPERNEL. Diminutive ann., bienn. or short-lived perenn.; st. to 50cm, quadrangular, slender, diffuse, creeping to ascending. Lvs to 1.8cm, opposite, sessile, gland., margins scarious, ovate to lanceolate. Fls solitary, closing in dark or cold conditions; pedicels to 3.5cm, cor. to 1cm diam., scarlet or white, lobes ovate to elliptic. Eur. var. *caerulea* (L.) Govan. Fls sky blue. var. *latifolia* (L.) Lange. Lvs broader. Many other variants occur; these range in fl. size and colour from white through pink (e.g. 'Sunrise') to dark scarlet, blues and yellows.
A. caerulea (Schreb.) Baumg. = *A. arvensis* var. *caerulea*.
A. collina Schousb. = *A. monellii* ssp. *linifolia*.
A. fruticosa Vent. = *A. monellii* ssp. *linifolia*.
A. grandiflora Andrews = *A. monellii* ssp. *linifolia*.

A. monellii L. BLUE PIMPERNEL. Perenn., erect or ascending; st. to 50cm, terete. Lvs to 2.5cm, oblong-ovate to elliptic, opposite or verticillate. Fls solitary, pedicels to 5cm; cor. to 1cm diam., typically blue above and tinted red below, sometimes blue or red only, rarely other paler shades, lobes obovate to elliptic. Medit. 'Phillipii': to 25cm; fls royal blue. ssp. *linifolia* (L.) Maire. Lvs linear-lanceolate.

A. tenella (L.) L. BOG PIMPERNEL. Procumbent perenn., freely rooting. St. to 15cm. Lvs to 1cm, usually opposite, suborbicular to broad-elliptic, entire. Fls solitary; pedicels to 3.5cm, thread-like; cor. to 1cm diam., rose pink, rarely white, infundibuliform, lobes lanceolate, cleft. W Eur. 'Studland': fls deep pink, sweetly scented.

Anagyris L. Leguminosae (Papilionoideae). 2 shrubs to 3m. Lvs trifoliolate. Fls pea-like in short axillary rac. Medit., Aegean, Balk., Canary Is.
A. foetida L. STINKING BEAN TREFOIL. Lfts to 4cm, elliptic, sage-green foetid when crushed. Rac. to 7.5cm; fls to 20 per rac., yellow, standard marked black. Summer. Medit. Z8.

Ananas Mill. PINEAPPLE. Bromeliaceae. 8 terrestrial perenn. herbs. Lvs linear-triangular, rigid, erect, scurfy, in a basal rosette, margins spiny. Infl. term., scapose, bracteate, comose, the whole becoming a fleshy syncarp. S Amer. Z10.
A. ananas Voss = *A. comosus*.

A. ananassoides (Bak.) L.B. Sm. To 1m. Infl. to 15cm; fls red-purple. Fr. to 20cm, inedible. Braz.
A. ananassoides var. *nanus* L.B. Sm. = *A. nanus*.
A. bracamorensis Lindm. = *A. lucidus*.

A. bracteatus (Lindl.) Schult. f. RED PINEAPPLE; WILD PINEAPPLE. To 1m. Infl. to 15cm; bracts tinted red; fls red to lilac. Fr. green-brown, edible. var. *tricolor* (Bertoni) L.B. Sm. Lvs striped cream, flushed and edged red-pink. Fr. pink.

A. comosus (L.) Merr. PINEAPPLE. Infl. to 30cm; bracts yellow-red. Fr. orange-brown, edible, seedless. Braz. (cultigen). 'Porteanus': lvs with central yellow stripe. 'Variegatus': lvs striped yellow, sometimes marked red.
A. comosus var. *variegatus* (Lowe) Mold. = *A. comosus* 'Variegatus'.
A. comosus f. *lucidus* (Mill.) Mez. = *A. lucidus*.
A. glaber Mill. = *A. lucidus*.

A. lucidus Mill. To 1m. Lvs scarcely armed. Infl. to 20cm; fls white or lilac. Fr. inedible. Venez., Peru, Braz.

A. nanus (L.B. Sm.) L.B. Sm. To 60cm. Infl. to 10cm; fls lilac-red. Fr. to 15cm, usually seedless. Braz., Surinam.
A. porteanus K. Koch = *A. comosus*.
A. sativus Schult. = *A. comosus*.
A. sativus var. *bracteatus* (Lindl.) Mez. = *A. bracteatus*.
A. sativus var. *lucidus* (Mill.) Bak. = *A. lucidus*.
A. semiserratus (Willd.) Schult. f. = *A. lucidus*.
A. striatifolius hort. = *A. comosus* 'Variegatus'.

Anapalina N.E. Br.
A. burchellii (N.E. Br.) N.E. Br. = *Tritoniopsis burchellii*.
A. caffra (Bak.) Lewis = *Tritoniopsis caffra*.
A. intermedia (Bak.) Lewis = *Tritoniopsis intermedia*.
A. nervosa (Thunb.) Lewis = *Tritoniopsis nervosa*.
A. pulchra (Bak.) N.E. Br. = *Tritoniopsis pulchra*.

Anaphalis DC. PEARLY EVERLASTING. Compositae. c100 white-tomentose, perenn. herbs. Lvs cauline, linear, entire, entire. Cap. discoid, small, crowded in clusters or in loose corymbs; phyllaries imbricate, white, papery, woolly below; flts yellow. N temp., trop. mts.

A. alpicola Mak. To 20cm, grey white-tomentose. Lvs to 10cm, oblanceolate, acute. Cap. in a ± dense corymb; phyllaries ovate, obtuse, white to brown-red. Jap. Z7.
A. cinnamomea DC. = *A. margaritacea* var. *cinnamomea*.
A. cuneifolia Hook. f. = *A. nepalensis* var. *nepalensis*.

A. margaritacea (L.) Benth. & Hook. f. PEARLY EVERLASTING. To 1m. Lvs to 15cm, linear to narrowly lanceolate, green above, thinly white-tomentose beneath, revolute. Cap. crowded in a terminal corymb to 15cm diam.; phyllaries oblong, rounded, pearly white, papery. Summer. N N Amer., N & C Eur., NE Asia. var. *angustior* (Miq.) Nak. Lvs to 10cm, lanceolate to narrowly oblong, woolly above at first, grey-brown villous beneath. Outer phyllaries tinged brown, scarious, inner phyllaries, white at tip. Late summer–early autumn. China. var. *cinnamomea* (DC.) Herd. ex Maxim. Lvs 2.5–10cm, densely grey white- or cinnamon-woolly. India. var. *yedoensis* (Franch. & Savat.) Ohwi. Lvs to 6cm, linear, 1-nerved, tomentose. Phyllaries yellow-brown near base. Jap. Z3.

A. nepalensis (Spreng.) Hand.-Mazz. To 8cm. Lvs to 1.5cm; spathulate, tomentose. Cap. solitary or few in a globose corymb to 1×2cm; phyllaries ovate. Himal., W China. var. *nepalensis*. To 30cm. Lvs often to 2cm wide, lanceolate. Cap. few, in a dense term. cluster to 1cm across. Summer, early autumn. var. *monocephala* (DC.) Hand.-Mazz. Low tufted herb to 10cm. Lvs 1–1.5cm, oblanceolate to linear-lanceolate, white-tomentose. Cap. few or solitary, 1–1.5cm across; phyllaries white. Summer. Himal. Z6.
A. nubigena DC. = *A. nepalensis* var. *monocephala*.

A. royleana DC. To 15cm. Lvs to 3.5cm, linear to linear-oblong, 1-nerved, tomentose, sometimes revolute. Cap. to 1cm diam., in corymbs; phyllaries ovate, white. Autumn. Himal. Z6.

A. sinica Hance. To 50cm, grey-tomentose. Lvs to 6cm, oblanceolate, mucronate, often viscid, sparsely grey-tomentose above. Cap. in a globose corymb; phyllaries in 5 or more series, brown, pubesc., apex white. Late summer–early autumn. Jap. ssp. *morii* (Nak.) Kitam. 5–20cm. Lvs 2cm. Cap. few, rarely solitary. Jap., Korea, China. Z7.

A. trinervis (Forst. f.) F. Muell. To 60cm, cobwebby. Lvs to 12cm, oblanceolate, acute or apiculate, glab. above, white-woolly beneath. Cap. 3–5, in corymbs to 1.5cm diam.; phyllaries white, radiating. NZ. Z7.

A. triplinervis (Sims) C.B. Clarke. To 90cm, tomentose. Lvs to 10cm, spathulate or obovate to elliptic-oblong, 3–5-nerved. Cap. to 1cm diam., many, in dense, domed clusters; phyllaries ovate-lanceolate to lanceolate, lustrous white-papery, spreading. Summer–autumn. Afghan. to SW China. Z5.

A. triplinervis var. *intermedia* (DC.) Airy Shaw = *A. nepalensis*

var. *nepalensis*.
A. triplinervis var. *monocephala* (DC.) Airy Shaw =
A. nepalensis var. *monocephala*.
A. yedoensis (Franch. & Savat.) Maxim. = *A. margaritacea* var.
yedoensis.
→*Antennaria, Gnaphalium* and *Helichrysum*.

Anarrhinum Desf. Scrophulariaceae. 8 bienn. or perenn. herbs
or subshrubs, allied to *Antirrhinum* but lacking the palate in the
cor. throat. Basal lvs entire to palmately lobed. Summer. S Eur.
Z8.
A. bellidifolium (L.) Willd. Bienn. or perenn., erect, to 80cm.
Basal lvs 2–8cm, obovate to spathulate to lanceolate, irregularly
toothed or entire, st. lvs with seg. linear to lanceolate. Infl.
densely branched; cor. tube pale lilac to blue, 4–5cm. SW Eur.
A. durminium (Brot.) Pers. Bienn. or perenn. erect to 20cm,
glandular-pubesc. Basal lvs obovate to spathulate, crenate to
bi-serrate, st. lvs lanceolate to suborbicular. Infl. dense, many-
branched; cor. pale yellow to white, basal spur slender. SW
Eur.
A. fruticosum Desf. Glab., erect, subshrub to 70cm. Lvs simple,
entire, rarely serrate. Infl. simple or branched, dense; cor.
white. Medit.
A. hirsutum Hoffsgg. & Link. = *A. durminium*.
A. laxiflorum Boiss. As *A. bellidifolium* but basal lvs broad-ovate
to spathulate, trilobed, st. lvs narrow, entire. Infl. sparsely
branching; cor. white to pale mauve or sky blue. S Spain.
→*Simbuleta*.

Anarthropteris Copel. Polypodiaceae. 5 epiphytic and lithophytic ferns. Rhiz. creeping. Fronds simple, lanceolate to oblong,
leathery, glab.; stipes tufted. NZ. Z10.
A. lanceolata (Hook. f.) Pichi-Serm. Rhiz. short- to long-
creeping, covered with pubesc. roots and brown scales. Fronds
to 25×2cm, lanceolate, attenuate at apex and base, entire to
somewhat lobed, leathery to fleshy, midrib prominent; stipes to
7cm, winged. NZ.

Anastatica L. ROSE OF JERICHO; RESURRECTION PLANT. Cruciferae. 1 ann. herb to 15cm. St. much-branched radiating in a
basal rosette, dying and curling inwards to form a tight skeletal
ball in drought – this rolls freely until made wet when it reopens
and releases seed. Lvs small, obovate-spathulate, stellate-
pubesc. Fls small, 4-merous, white, in spikes along br. Summer.
Moroc. to S Iran. Z9.
A. hierochuntica L.

Anceps Bamboo *Yushania anceps*.
Anchovy Pear *Grias cauliflora*.

Anchusa L. Boraginaceae. 35 ann., bienn. or perenn. herbs,
pubesc. Fls in terminal and axill. cymes; cal. 5-lobed; cor. 5-
lobed, infundibular to hypocrateriform, faucal scales ovate or
oblong, papillose or pubesc.; sta. 5, included or slightly
exserted. Eur., Afr., W Asia.
A. angustifolia L. = *A. officinalis*.
A. angustissima K. Koch = *A. leptophylla* ssp. *incana*.
A. azurea Mill. Perenn., to 150cm, erect, hispid-tuberculate. Lvs
to 35cm, linear-elliptic to lanceolate, entire, hispid. Cor. deep
blue to violet, tube to 10mm, limb to 10mm diam. Eur., N Afr.,
W Asia. 'Dropmore': to 1.8m; fls deep blue tinted purple,
profuse. 'Feltham Pride': to 90cm; fls blue. 'Little John': dwarf,
to 45cm; lvs coarse; fls deep blue, long-lasting. 'Loddon Royal-
ist': to 1m, bushy; fls large, royal blue. 'Morning Glory': to
1.2m; pure gentian blue. 'Opal': to 1m; lvs dark green tinted
grey; fls sky blue. 'Royal Blue': to 1.2m; fls vivid gentian blue.
Z3.
A. azurea Mill. = *A. italica*.
A. barrelieri (All.) Vitm. Perenn., to 80cm, erect, hispid-
tuberculate. Lvs to 7cm, elliptic or lanceolate to oblong-
spathulate, subentire to undulate. Cor. blue or blue-violet, tube
to 1.5mm, limb to 10mm diam. Eur., Asia Minor. Z3.
A. caespitosa Lam. Perenn., to 10cm, tufted, hispid-tuberculate.
Lvs to 5cm, narrowly linear. Cor. deep blue, tube to 7mm,
white, limb to 12mm diam. Crete. Z5.
A. caespitosa hort. non Lam. = *A. leptophylla* ssp. *incana*.
A. capensis Thunb. Bienn., to 60cm, erect, hirsute. Lvs to
12.5cm, linear to narrowly lanceolate, tuberculate-hirsute. Cor.
blue, throat white. S Afr. 'Blue Angel': dwarf and compact, to
20cm; fls vivid ultramarine, profuse. 'Blue Bird': to 45cm; fls
vivid indigo, in sprays. 'Pink Bird': fls pink. Z9.
A. leptophylla Roem. & Schult. ssp. *incana* (Ledeb.) Chamberl.
To 40cm. Lvs narrow-lanceolate, dark green, in loose rosettes.
Fls bright azure.
A. myosotidifolia Lehm. = *Brunnera macrophylla*.

A. ochroleuca Bieb. Perenn. or bienn., to 80cm, erect, densely
adpressed-pubesc. Lvs to 10cm. Cor. pale yellow, tube to
10mm, limb to 10mm diam. Eur. Z5.
A. officinalis L. Perenn. or bienn., to 1m, erect, hispid. Lvs to
12cm, linear to linear-oblanceolate. Cor. dark blue, violet or
red, sometimes white or yellow, tube to 7mm, limb to 15mm
diam. Eur., Asia Minor. 'Angustifolia': lvs narrow. 'Incarnata':
fls flesh pink. Z5.
A. orientalis L. = *Alkanna orientalis*.
A. osmanica Velen. = *A. officinalis*.
A. riparia DC. Bienn. or perenn. to 80cm, erect, setose. Lvs to
15cm, narrowly lanceolate or oblanceolate, hispid or setose.
Cor. blue to red-purple. S Afr. Z9.
A. sempervirens L. = *Pentaglottis sempervirens*.
A. tinctoria (L.) L. = *Alkanna tinctoria*.
A. zeylanica Vahl. = *Cynoglossum zeylanicum*.
→*Buglossum*.

Ancient Pine *Pinus longaeva*.

Ancistrocactus Britt. & Rose.
A. brevihamatus (Engelm.) Britt. & Rose = *Sclerocactus breviha-
matus*.
A. crassihamatus (F.A.C. Weber) L. Bens. = *Sclerocactus unci-
natus*.
A. megarhizus (Rose) Britt. & Rose = *Sclerocactus scheeri*.
A. scheeri (Salm-Dyck) Britt. & Rose = *Sclerocactus scheeri*.
A. uncinatus (Gal. ex Pfeiff. & Otto) L. Bens. = *Sclerocactus
uncinatus*.

Ancistrochilus Rolfe. Orchidaceae. 2 epiphytic orchids. Pbs
clustered, globose-pyriform, with 1–2 plicate, lanceolate lvs.
Rac. basal; fls large, few; tep. narrow, reflexed; lip 3-lobed,
midlobe tapering, recurved. W Afr. to Uganda. Z10.
A. rothschildianus O'Brien. Rac. 2–5-fld; tep. to 3cm, elliptic-
lanceolate, rose to mauve; lip to 1.7cm, pink or purple. Distrib.
as for the genus.
A. thomsonianus (Rchb. f.) Rolfe. Rac. 2–3-fld; tep. to 4.5cm,
oblong-lanceolate, white; lip green marked brown, midlobe
purple, proboscis-like. Nigeria, Cameroun.

Ancistrorhynchus Finet. Orchidaceae. 13 epiphytic orchids. St.
usually short lvs; strap-shaped 2-ranked. Fls many, small, white,
green or ivory, spurred, in axillary rac. Trop. Afr. Z10.
A. capitatus (Lindl.) Summerh. Lvs 17–44cm. Rac. short, dense;
fls 0.6–1.2cm across, white to pale rose, lip marked yellow. W
Afr., Zaire, Uganda.
A. cephalotes (Rchb. f.) Summerh. Lvs 7–35cm. Rac. short,
dense; fls 0.8–1.4cm across, fragrant, white blotched green or
yellow on lip. W Afr.
A. clandestinus (Lindl.) Schltr. Lvs to 180cm. Rac. to 4cm; fls
0.7–1cm across, white marked green on lip. W Afr. to Zaire.
A. ovatus Summerh. Lvs 7–20cm. Rac. to 2cm, dense; fls 0.6–1cm
across, white. Zaire, Uganda.
A. refractus (Kränzl.) Summerh. Lvs 5–11cm in a pendulous fan.
Rac. 2–fld; fls to 2.6cm across, lustrous white. Tanz.
A. serratus Summerh. St. elongated, branched. Lvs 5–11cm. Rac.
± capitate, v. short; fls c0.6cm across, white to ivory. Nigeria,
Cameroun.

Ancylostemon Craib. Gesneriaceae. 5 perenn., stemless herbs.
Lvs rosulate, hairy, crenulate to lobed. Fls solitary or few in a
cymose or umbellate infl.; cal. lobes 5, lanceolate, denticulate;
cor. tubular, slightly inflated, glandular-hairy, lobes 5. W China.
Z8.
A. aureus (Franch.) B.L. Burtt. Lvs to 10×6cm, ovate or
oblong-ovate, truncate to cordate at base, sparsely brown-
pilose, dentate-lobulate. Cor. tube to 2cm, bright orange, lobes
oblong or ovate, emarginate. Yunnan.

Andelmin *Andira*.

Andersonia R. Br. Epacridaceae. 22 heath-like everg. shrubs.
Lvs arranged spirally, overlapping, rigid, concave, bases sheathing st. Fls subtended by bracteoles, in term. infl.; cor. tube usually shorter than sep., lobes recurved or deflexed, hairy within.
SW Aus. Z9.
A. coerulea R. Br. To 75cm. Lvs to 1.5cm, ovate-lanceolate,
sharply pointed, usually spirally twisted and sinuate. Fls in a
dense term. spike or short cluster; sep. to 1cm, linear-
lanceolate, lilac, pale blue or white; cor. shorter than the cal.,
blue, densely bearded. Summer.
A. depressa R. Br. To 70cm. Lvs to 1cm, closely set, subulate,
often twisted. Fls in a term. spikelet; cal. to 1cm white-green;
cor. blue. Summer.

A. *homatostoma* Benth. To 45cm. Lvs to 1.5cm, narrowly ovate-oblong, curved or twisted, apex acuminate. Fls in crowded term. spikes; sep. to 0.5cm suffused red; cor. dark blue, longer than cal. Summer.

A. *sprengelioides* R. Br. To 50cm. Lvs to 1cm, ovate tapering to a fine point, sometimes incised. Fls in term. clusters; cal. pink to lilac; cor. tube to 1cm, shorter than cal., mauve to blue. Summer.

Andira Juss. ANGELIM; ANDELMIN. Leguminosae (Papilionoideae). 21 everg. trees. Leavs imparipinnate. Pan. term.; fls pea-like. Trop. Amer., W Afr.

A. *inermis* (Wright) HBK ex DC. CABBAGE TREE. Tree to 30m, base buttressed. Crown spreading. Bark cabbage-scented, grey to dark brown, exfoliating. Lvs to 40cm; lfts 9–15, ovate-lanceolate to elliptic-oblong. Infl. to 60cm, hairy; fls to 1.5cm, fragrant, pink to violet-red. Summer. Z9.

Andrachne L. Euphorbiaceae. 12 shrubs, subshrubs or perenn. herbs. Lvs alt., simple, usually entire. Fls small, axill., 5- to 6-merous, on long pedicels; ♂ fls clustered, with pet. smaller than sep., ♀ fls solitary, ± apetalous. N Amer., Afr., Asia, S Amer. Z6.

A. *colchica* Fisch. & C.A. Mey. To 60cm; habit dense, erect. Br. numerous, ascending. Lvs 1.5–2.5cm, ovate, obtuse, thin, margins thickened. Fls to 1cm diam., yellow-green. Asia Minor.

A. *phyllanthoides* (Nutt.) Muell. Arg. To 30cm, with slender br. Lvs 1.5–2cm, oval to obovate, obtuse, glab. or slightly pubesc. beneath. Fls to 0.5cm diam., yellow green. C US.

Androcymbium Willd. Liliaceae (Colchicaceae). 12 perenn. cormous herbs. Lvs basal, rosulate, 2–4, linear to lanceolate, usually lying flat on ground. Scape barely emerging above ground; spike umbellate, subtended and partly enclosed by large cupped bracts; fls small, tep. 6, free, green, green-white or cream, with yellow glands at base. Medit. to S Afr. Z9.

A. *capense* (L.) Krause. Lvs 10–24cm, lanceolate, undulate, pale green. Bracts to 8cm, pale green; fls 2–8. S Afr. (Cape Penins.).

A. *ciliolatum* Schltr. & Krause. Lvs to 15cm, broadly lanceolate, minutely fringed. Bracts to 15cm, pale green, almost white; fls many. Spring. S Afr.

A. *eucomioides* (Jacq.) Willd. Lvs 6–15cm, lanceolate to ovate, undulate, slightly keeled, dark green. Bracts pale, shorter and broader than lvs; fls 2–5. Winter. S Afr.

A. *fenestratum* Schltr. & Krause = A. *ciliolatum*.

A. *leucanthum* hort. = A. *eucomioides*.

A. *melanthoides* Willd. BABOON'S SHOES; PYJAMA FLOWER. Lvs narrow-linear, narrowing to a tail 20cm long. Bracts to 7.5cm, white veined green, flushed pink; fls 6–8. S Afr.

Androlepis Brongn. ex Houll. Bromeliaceae. 1 mealy perenn. herb to 2m in fl. Lvs rosulate, ligulate-acuminate, spiny-serrate, red in full sun. Infl. pyramidal-cylindric, compound, scapose; bracts papery, straw-yellow, overlapping; fls spicate, yellow. Guat. to Costa Rica. Z9.

A. *skinneri* Brongn. ex Houll.
→*Aechmea*.

Andromeda L. Ericaceae. 2 spreading, low, everg. shrubs. Lvs 0.8–5cm, linear-lanceolate to narrowly oblong, revolute, dark green to grey, coriaceous. Fls in term., nodding umbels; cal. glab., lobes 5; cor. urceolate, teeth 5, short, reflexed. Arc., Temp. N hemis.

A. *acuminata* Ait. = *Leucothoe populifolia*.

A. *arborea* L. = *Oxydendrum arboreum*.

A. *bryantha* L. = *Bryanthus gmelinii*.

A. *cassinifolia* Vent. = *Zenobia pulverulenta*.

A. *catesbaei* Walter = *Leucothoe catesbaei*.

A. *glaucophylla* Link. BOG ROSEMARY. Wiry shrub, 10–70cm. St. glaucous, scandent. Lvs linear to narrowly oblong, tomentellous beneath. Fls packed in pendulous umbels; cal. off-white; cor. 4–7mm, white or pink. Late spring–early summer. Arc., Canada, NE US. Z2.

A. *mariana* L. = *Lyonia mariana*.

A. *nana* Maxim. = *Arcterica nana*.

A. *neriifolia* Cham. & Schldl. = *Agarista neriifolia*.

A. *polifolia* L. MARSH ANDROMEDA; COMMON BOG ROSEMARY. Erect to decumbent shrub, 10–40cm. St. wiry. Lvs linear-oblong, sharp-tipped, glaucous beneath. Fls 2–8 in terminal umbels; cal. tinged red; cor. 5–7mm, white to pale pink. Late spring–summer. N Eur., S Alps, SC Russia, E Carpath. 'Alba': fls white. 'Compacta': to 30cm, compact, dense; lvs tinged grey; fls pink. 'Compacta Alba': habit compact; fls near white. 'Grandiflora': habit dwarf, compact; lvs blue-grey; fls large, cream tinged pink. 'Grandiflora Compacta': habit compact; lvs tinged blue; fls pale pink. 'Kiri-Kaming': dwarf, upright; lvs

narrow, dark tinged red; fls pendent, pink. 'Macrophylla': low-growing; fls pink. 'Major': tail; lvs broad, mostly grey. 'Minima': to 8cm, prostrate; lvs needle-like, tinged blue beneath; fls pale pink. 'Montana': compact; lvs dark. 'Nana': vigorous; fls in clusters, pink, globe-shaped. 'Nana Alba': lvs silver-blue; fls white. 'Nikko': habit compact. 'Red Winter': habit tall; good autumn leaf-colour. 'Shibutsu': compact; fls pink.

A. *racemosa* L. = *Leucothoe racemosa*.

A. *recurva* Buckl. = *Leucothoe recurva*.

A. *rosmarinifolia* Gilib. = A. *polifolia*.

A. *speciosa* Michx. = *Zenobia pulverulenta*.

Andropogon L. Gramineae. *c*100 ann. or perenn. grasses. Rhiz. creeping. St. clumped, occas. branched toward summit. Lvs flat. Infl. compound, rac. paired or palmately arranged, flimsy, on a jointed pubesc. rachis, usually sheathed; spikelets paired, one sessile, the other stalked, with a fine apical hair. Warm temp. and trop. regions.

A. *annulatus* Forssk. = *Dichanthium annulatum*.

A. *argenteus* Sw. = *Bothriochloa saccharoides*.

A. *capillipes* Nash. To 80cm. St. erect, branching above, glaucous. Lf sheaths distichous, chalk white, yellow-green or somewhat purple; basal lvs elongate, to 5mm diam. Infl. of 2+ rac., subtended by purple-bronze inflated spathes. SE US. Z8.

A. *caricosus* L. = *Dichanthium caricosum*.

A. *caucasicus* Trin. = *Bothriochloa caucasica*.

A. *citratus* DC. ex Nees = *Cymbopogon citratus*.

A. *elliottii* Chapm. To 1m. St. tufted, upper node strongly bearded. Lf sheaths pilose. Lvs flat, elongate, later curled or tortuous. Rac. silky, primary rac. long-exserted from sheath, secondary rac. paired, rarely exserted. Autumn. E US. Z5.

A. *furcatus* Muhlenb. = A. *gerardii*.

A. *gerardii* Vitm. Perenn. to 2m, forming large clumps. Rhiz. short, basal sheaths and lvs blue-green turning purple-bronze; blades flat, to 1cm wide, margin rough. Infl. of 3–6 purple-tinged rac. to 10cm, terminal on far-exserted stalk. Summer. Canada to Mex. Z4.

A. *glomeratus* (Walter) BSP. Perenn. St. erect, forming tussocks. St. laterally flattened. Lf sheaths crowded at st. base, keeled. Infl. a dense, feathery, club-shaped pan. Summer. C Amer., W Indies. Z6.

A. *halapensis* (L.) Brot. = *Sorghum halapense*.

A. *hallii* Hackel. As for A. *gerardii*, except rhiz. spreading. Lvs pale green or glaucous grey-green. Rac. shorter, with straw-coloured hairs. Summer. N Amer. Z5.

A. *intermedius* Retz = *Bothriochloa bladhii*.

A. *ischaemum* L. = *Bothriochloa ischaemum*.

A. *littoralis* Nash = *Schizachyrium scoparium* var. *littorale*.

A. *longiberbis* Hackel. To 80cm. St. wiry, branching above. Lf sheaths grey-villous; lvs narrow, arching. Pan. elongate, with paired, distant rac.; spathes to 6cm, narrow; pedicels pilose. Autumn. SE US. Z6.

A. *macrourus* Michx. = A. *glomeratus*.

A. *muricatus* Retz. = *Vetiveria zizanoides*.

A. *nardus* L. = *Cymbopogon nardus*.

A. *nodosus* (Willem.) Nash. = *Dichanthium aristatum*.

A. *schoenanthus* L. = *Cymbopogon schoenanthus*.

A. *scoparius* Michx. = *Schizachyrium scoparium*.

A. *sibiricus* (Trin.) Steud. = *Spodiopogon sibiricus*.

A. *sorghum* (L.) Brot. = *Sorghum bicolor*.

A. *ternarius* Michx. SPLITBEARD BLUESTEM. Perenn. to 120cm. St. tufted, erect, branching above. Lvs purple-glaucous, glab. or lax-villous beneath. Infl. lax, elongate; rac. to 6cm, to 12-jointed, silver-cream, or grey-plumose, usually on long-exserted peduncles from slender spathes. Spring–autumn. SE US. Z6.

A. *virginicus* L. BROOM SEDGE. To 120cm. St. tufted, branching above, lvs slender, pubesc. above, green, glaucous or somewhat purple. Infl. simple, paniculate or corymbiform; spathes to 6cm, rac. later exserted; rachis slender, flexuous, silky. Autumn. SE US. Z6.

A. *zizanoides* (L.) Urban = *Vetiveria zizanoides*.

Androsace L. ROCK JASMINE. Primulaceae. 100 ann., bienn. or perenn. often cushion-forming herbs. Lvs usually sessile, basal, rosulate. Fls solitary or in scapose umbels; cal. campanulate or subglobose, lobes triangular; cor. salverform or funnelform, tube short, limb spreading, lobes 5. Summer. N temp. Z5.

A. *adenocephala* Hand-Mazz. Similar to A. *sarmentosa* but smaller and with v. short runners. Fls pink. Nepal. Z6.

A. *albana* Steven. Pubesc. ann. Lvs to 2cm, in a dense rosette, spathulate to ovate, 2- or 3-toothed, apex obtuse, usually ciliate. Infl. far exceeding lvs, many-fld; pedicels v. short; cor. white or pink, to 1cm diam., lobes ovate-spathulate. Spring. Cauc. Z6.

A. *alpina* (L.) Lam. Loosely tufted perenn., forming flat loose cushions. Lvs to 1cm, loosely imbricate, oblong or oblanceolate, pubesc. Fls solitary; pedicels to 1cm; cor. to 1cm diam., white or pink with yellow throat. Early summer. Switz. Z5.

A. aretioides Heer ex Duby = *A. imbricata*.

A. argentea Lapeyr. = *A. imbricata*.

A. brevis (Hegetschw.) Cesati. Close to *A. alpina*, but more densely tufted, forming smaller cushions; lvs to 0.5cm, spathulate, more closely overlapping. E Alps. Z7.

A. brigantiaca Jordan & Fourr. = *A. carnea* ssp. *brigantiaca*.

A. carnea L. Loosely tufted perenn. Lvs to 2cm, linear, sometimes fleshy, ciliate. Scape to 6cm, 2- to many-fld; cor. to 5mm, white or pink. A hybrid between this sp. and *A. pyrenaica* is grown. W Eur. (mts). ssp. *brigantiaca* (Jordan & Fourr.) I.K. Ferg. Robust. Lvs to 3cm, flat, puberulent, sometimes dentate. Cor. to 5mm diam., white. ssp. *laggeri* (Huet) Nyman. Smaller, usually densely tufted. Lvs to 0.5cm, canaliculate, ± fleshy, glab., shortly ciliate. Cor. usually pink. ssp. *rosea* (Jordan & Fourr.) Rouy. Rosettes fewer, larger. Lvs to 2.5cm, entire, flat, glab. or slightly puberulent apex above, shortly ciliate. Cor. pink. Z5.

A. chaixii Gren. & Godron. Similar to *A. septentrionalis* but infl. lax, 5–8-fld; cor. to 5mm. SE Fr. Z6.

A. chamaejasme Wulf. in Jacq. Loosely tufted perenn., shortly stoloniferous. Lvs to 1.5cm, oblong-lanceolate, in flattened rosettes, entire, ciliate. Scape to 7cm, 3–7-fld; cor. to 5mm diam., white or pink. Early summer. N Hemis. Z5.

A. charpentieri Heering = *A. brevis*.

A. ciliata DC. in Lam. & DC. Differs from *A. pubescens* in lvs to 1.5cm, ovate-spathulate or oblong-ovate, ciliate, ± pubesc. Pedicels to 1.5cm; cor. to 1cm diam., pink or violet with orange or yellow throat. Early summer. Pyren. Z6.

A. cylindrica DC. in Lam. & DC. Densely tufted perenn., forming cushions. Lvs to 1cm, oblong-lanceolate, pubesc., densely imbricate, dead lvs persistent, forming columnar shoots. Fls solitary; pedicels to 2cm; cor. to 1cm diam., pink with yellow throat, lobes obovate. Early summer. Pyren. A hybrid between this sp. and *A. hirtella* is grown. Z6.

A. delavayi Franch. Tufted. St. repeatedly forked, erect, with persistent dead lvs. Lvs to 0.5cm, densely crowded, broadly obovate, downy, apex rounded. Fls solitary; pedicels to 5mm; cor. white or pale pink, to 1cm diam., lobes broad-obovate, emarginate. Spring. Himal. to SW China. Z6.

A. elongata L. Ann. Lvs to 1.5cm, lanceolate or oblanceolate, entire or dentate, ciliate. Scape to 10cm; infl. many-fld, loose; cor. to 5mm diam., white, lobes ovate-lanceolate, entire. Early summer. Mid-Eur., temp. Asia. Z6.

A. × escheri Bruegg. (*A. chamaejasme* × *A. obtusifolia*.) Closer to *A. chamaejasme*; fls white.

A. filiformis Retz. Ann. Lvs to 4cm, ovate to elliptic, dentate; petiole distinct. Scape to 15cm; infl. many-fld, loose; pedicels to 5cm, glandular-pubesc.; cor. to 3mm diam., white. Sib., W US. Z2.

A. foliosa Duby. Stoloniferous perenn. Lvs to 10cm, basal but not forming rosette, elliptic-oblong or obovate, to lanceolate-ovate, entire, pubesc., ciliate, apex acute, base attenuate. Scape stout, to 35cm, many-fld; pedicels pilose; cor. to 1cm diam., pale pink becoming white, throat yellow, lobes obovate, rounded. Summer. W Himal. Z6.

A. geraniifolia Watt. Loosely hairy, stoloniferous perenn. Lvs 4cm diam., ± cordate, 7-lobed, 3-partite, obtuse; petiole to 8cm. Scape to 16cm, 6–14-fld; pedicels to 3cm, pilose; cor. pink, to 5mm diam., lobes oblong-ovate, emarginate. Himal., Tibet, W China. Z6.

A. globifera Duby. Tufted, br. forking, slender. Lvs to 5mm diam., densely overlapping in small globes, spathulate to ovate-lanceolate, downy, obtuse. Scape short, 1- or 2-fld; cor. to 5mm diam., pink, lobes obovate. WC Himal. Z4.

A. hausmannii Leyb. Tufted perenn., rosettes few, not forming cushions. Lvs to 1cm, linear-lanceolate, densely pubesc. Fls solitary; pedicels to 1cm, pubesc.; cor. to 5mm diam., pink with yellow throat, lobes rounded-obovate. Austria. Z6.

A. hedraeantha Griseb. Differs from *A. obtusifolia* in infl. sub-capitate, 5–10-fld; bracts glab., not puberulent. Balk. Z6.

A. × heeri Koch. (*A. helvetica* × *A. alpina*.) To 3cm, br. crowded, hairy. Lvs v. small, lanceolate, obtuse. Fls ± unstalked; cor. pink, to 5mm diam., lobes rounded-obovate. Switz. Z6.

A. helvetica (L.) All. Densely tufted perenn., forming deep, dense, hemispherical cushions. Lvs to 0.6×0.2cm, lanceolate, oblong or spathulate, pubesc., closely overlapping, persistent and forming columnar shoots. Fls solitary, ± unstalked; cor. to 5mm diam., white with yellow throat, lobes rounded-obovate. Switz., Austria. Z6.

A. hirtella Dufour. Densely tufted, white-hairy, br. leafy. Lvs to 1cm, densely overlapping in rosettes, linear, obtuse, green becoming darker and stained black. Fls solitary, v. short-stalked; cor. white, to 5mm diam., lobes obovate. Pyren. Z6.

A. hookeriana Klatt. Slender, stoloniferous, loosely tufted

perenn. to 8cm. Lvs to 2cm in rosettes, lower lvs obovate, sessile, upper lvs ovate-lanceolate, with winged petiole. Scape to 10cm; cor. to 1cm diam., pink, lobes round-obovate, emarginate. Himal., S Tibet. Z5.

A. × hybrida Kerner. (*A. helvetica* × *A. pubescens*.) Intermediate between parents. Alps.

A. imbricata Lam. Differs from *A. helvetica* in lvs linear-lanceolate, densely white-tomentose; fls on stalks to 1cm. Alps, Pyren. Z6.

A. jacquemontii Duby = *A. villosa* var. *jacquemontii*.

A. lactea L. Perenn., loosely tufted or rosettes solitary, shortly stoloniferous. Lvs to 2cm, linear, glab. or sparsely hairy. Infl. 1–4-fld, arising from axils of lower lvs; cor. to 1cm diam., white with yellow throat, lobes obcordate. Alps. Z6.

A. lactiflora Pall. Glab. ann. to 25cm. Lvs to 4cm in rosettes, linear-lanceolate or linear-spathulate, apex toothed; petiole winged. Infl. scapose, many-fld; pedicels 2–6cm, pendent; cor. to 1cm diam., white, lobes cuneate-ovate, emarginate. Sib., Mong. Z4.

A. laevigata (A. Gray) Wendelbo = *Douglasia laevigata*.

A. laggeri Huet = *A. carnea* ssp. *laggeri*.

A. lanuginosa Wallich. Prostrate white-lanuginose perenn. Lvs to 1.5cm, lanceolate-ovate, apex acute, base tapering. Scape to 4cm, many-fld; pedicels to 1cm; cor. to 1cm diam., pink, lobes round-obovate, emarginate. Summer–early autumn. Himal. 'Leichtlinii': fls deeper pink. Z6.

A. lehmannii Duby. Tufted. Br. closely packed. Lvs to 0.5cm, overlapping in loose globes, linear, acute, soon glab., persistent. Infl. many-fld; cor. pink, lobes obovate, obtuse. Himal. Z3.

A. mathildae Lév. Tufted perenn. Lvs to 1.5cm, linear, glab., imbricate. Fls solitary on short downy stalks; cor. to 5mm diam., white or pink, lobes ovate. C Apennines. Z6.

A. maxima L. Ann. Lvs to 3cm, ovate, obovate, or oblong-lanceolate, sessile or short-stalked, dentate, glab. or sparsely hairy. Scapes to 15cm, many-fld; cor. to 5mm diam., white or pink, lobes lanceolate, obtuse. Eur., E Russia. Z5.

A. montana (A. Gray) Wendelbo. = *Douglasia montana*.

A. mucronifolia G. Watt. Loosely tufted, stoloniferous, perenn. Lvs to 0.5cm, overlapping in rosettes, obovate, ciliate, mucronate. Scape short, 3–6-fld; cor. pink to lilac. Himal., Tibet. Z5.

A. muscoidea Duby. Resembling *A. villosa* var. *arachnoidea*. Fls 9mm diam., 1–3 per umbel, white with green-yellow eye. Himal. Z5. f. *longiscapa* (Knuth) Hand.-Mazz. Taller. Fls lilac-pink.

A. nivalis (Lindl.) Wendelbo = *Douglasia nivalis*.

A. obtusifolia All. Perenn. growths loosely tufted or in solitary rosettes. Lvs to 2cm, lanceolate or oblong-lanceolate, base tapered, scarcely petiolate, sparsely hairy or ciliate. Scape to 12cm, tomentose, 1–7-fld; pedicels to 2.5cm, densely hairy; cor. to 1cm diam., white or pink, lobes round-ovate. Spring. C Eur. Z4.

A. × pedemontana Rchb. (*A. carnea* × *A. obtusifolia*.) Tufted perenn. lvs ligulate, wavy-toothed. Fls white with orange eye, slender-stalked. N It. Z6.

A. primuloides Duby. Stolons to 10cm, diffuse, hairy at first. Lvs to 1.5cm in rosettes, lanceolate to linear, obtuse, white-hairy. Scape to 7cm, axillary, hairy; cor. pink, to 1cm diam., lobes round-ovate. NW Himal. Z6.

A. pubescens DC. in Lam. & DC. Tufted perenn., forming loose cushions. Lvs to 1cm, spathulate or oblong-lanceolate, hairy, overlapping in term. rosettes. Fls solitary, short-stalked; cor. to 5mm diam., white or pink with yellow throat. C & SW Alps, Pyren. Z5.

A. pyrenaica Lam. Perenn. forming, dense cushions. Lvs to 1cm, linear-oblong, pubesc., ciliate, overlapping, persistent, forming columnar shoots. Fls solitary, short-stalked; cor. to 5mm diam., white with yellow eye. Summer. Pyren. Z6.

A. rigida Hand.-Mazz. Lvs to 1cm, oblong, spathulate or round, fleshy, hairy, sessile. Scape to 4cm, 1–7-fld; pedicels to 5mm; cor. to 10mm diam., pink, lobes suborbicular or obovate. SW China. Z6.

A. rosea Jordan & Fourr. = *A. carnea* ssp. *rosea*.

A. rotundifolia Hardw. Hairy perenn. Lvs to 3cm, orbicular to reniform, usually 7-lobed, lobes 3-fid; petiole to 8cm. Scape to 15cm, many-fld; cor. pale pink, lobes ovate, sometimes emarginate, subacute. N India. Z4.

A. salicifolia hort. = *A. lactiflora*.

A. sarmentosa Wallich. Stolons to 10cm. Lvs to 3cm rosulate, lanceolate to ovate-lanceolate, silvery-hairy at first. Scape to 10cm, many-fld; pedicels to 2cm; cor. deep pink, to 5mm diam., lobes rounded, obovate. Himal. 'Brilliant': fls carmine-pink. var. *chumbyi* hort. Densely tufted. Lvs in congested rosettes, densely hairy. Pedicels v. short. var. *watkinsii* Hook. f. Lvs congested, smaller. var. *yunnanensis* Knuth. Lvs smaller. Z3.

A. sempervivoides Jacquem. ex Duby. Lvs to 0.5cm, in rosettes on stolons, ovate to spathulate, closely overlapping, ciliate. Scapes to 10cm, gland.; cor. to 5mm diam., pink, lobes obovate, emarginate. Kashmir, Tibet. Z5.

A. septentrionalis L. Ann. Lvs to 35cm, oblong-lanceolate or elliptic, dentate, ± sessile, glab. or sparsely hairy. Scapes to 30cm, 5–30-fld; cor. to 5mm diam., white or pink, lobes obovate. N Hemis. Z4.

A. spinulifera (Franch.) Knuth. Hairy perenn. to 30cm. Lvs to 5×1cm, overlapping in globose rosettes, scale-like, then linear or obovate, acute with a rigid spiny hair at tip. Scape to 20cm, many-fld; pedicels to 1.5cm; cor. to 1cm diam., deep purple. C China, Yunnan. Z6.

A. strigillosa Franch. Tufted perenn. to 30cm, covered with stiff hairs. Lvs to 6cm, oblong to obovate, usually hairy, apex obtuse to subacute, hard, base attenuate. Infl. 5–10-fld; pedicels to 2.5cm; cor. to 5mm diam., purple to violet, lobes obovate, emarginate. Himal. Z7.

A. tapete Maxim. Densely tufted. Lvs overlapping in dense globes, outer lvs scarious, obovate, obtuse, margins white, inner lvs oblong or oblong-spathulate, glaucous, hairy. Fls ± un-stalked; cor. to 5mm diam., white, lobes orbiculate. Himal., W China. Z6.

A. taurica Orcz. = *A. villosa* var. *taurica*.

A. vandellii (Turra) Chiov. = *A. imbricata*.

A. villosa L. Similar to *A. chamaejasme*, but usually more densely tufted with numerous cushion-forming rosettes; lvs in hemi-spherical rosettes, villous. Eur., Asia (mts). var. *jacquemontii* (Duby) Pax & Knuth. Rosettes 1cm wide; fls pink. var. *taurica* (Orcz.) R. Knuth. More pubesc., less vigorous. Fls larger, age-ing bright pink. Z4.

A. vitaliana (L.) Lapeyr. = *Vitaliana primuliflora*.

A. wulfeniana Sieber ex Koch. Similar to *A. alpina* but cushions usually denser; lvs to 0.5cm, lanceolate, acute, somewhat fleshy and keeled, sparsely pubesc.; cor. to 1cm diam., deep pink with yellow throat. E Alps. Z5.

A. zambalensis Hand.-Mazz. Lvs spathulate or linear-spathulate, to obovate. Infl. 3–7-fld, short-stalked; cor. white. Himal., S Tibet. Z5.

Androstephium Torr. Liliaceae (Alliaceae). 2 perenn. cormous herbs. Lvs basal, linear, channelled. Scape erect; umbel term. subtended by scarious bracts; perianth funnelform, seg. 6, narrow-oblong, united below; sta. 6, fil. partly united into petaloid corona. SW US. Z8.

A. caeruleum (Scheele) Greene. BLUE FUNNEL LILY; BLUE BETHLEHEM. Lvs v. narrow. Scape 10–12cm, stout; fls 3–6, to 3.75cm diam., pale blue to lilac or mauve. Spring. CE US.

A. violaceum Torr. = *A. caeruleum*.

Andryala L. Compositae. 25 ann. to perenn., latex-producing, densely hairy herbs. St. usually solitary. Lvs entire to pinnatisect. Cap. ligulate, few to numerous, in loose paniculate infl.; receptacle pitted, flat; flts yellow, the outer row sometimes with a red stripe beneath. Medit. Z7.

A. aghardii Haensl. ex DC. Perenn. with woody stock, clothed in persistent petiole bases. St. to 15cm, glandular-hairy. Lvs with silky-white hairs; basal lvs to 4cm, spathulate to oblanceolate, entire; petiole long, winged; st. lvs few, linear. Cap. solitary; in-volucre to 1.2×1.4cm. S Spain.

A. integrifolia L. Ann. to perenn. St. to 80cm, sometimes with gland. hairs. Lvs to 8cm, densely hairy, linear, lanceolate or ovate, entire to pinnatisect, mostly cauline, upper lvs broader. Cap. few to many; involucre to 1×1cm. Medit.

A. lanata L. = *Hieracium lanatum*.

A. mogadorensis Coss. ex Hook. f. Subshrub. St. to 60cm, strag-gling, white-tomentose, black-hairy above. Lvs to 15cm, obovate-spathulate, petiole, upper lvs auricled, sessile, ovate to oblong, entire to dentate. Cap. to 3cm diam., in corymbs of 6–10. Summer. Moroc.

A. sinuata L. = *A. integrifolia*.

Aneilema R. Br. Commelinaceae. 60 ann. and perenn. herbs. Fls zygomorphic in single cincinni or thyrses of cincinni; sep. 3; pet. 3, often unequal and differing in colour, upper pair clawed, lower usually much reduced. Trop. and subtrop., predominantly Afr. Z10.

A. biflorum R. Br. Creeping perenn. Lvs lanceolate, petiolate. Infl. of 1–4 2-fld cincinni on short lat. shoots; fls to 1cm, blue. Summer. Aus.

A. sinicum Ker-Gawl. = *Murdannia simplex*.

A. zebrinum Chiov. Creeping perenn. Lvs to 4cm, shiny, grey-green, striped paler and sometimes with maroon lines. Infl. usu-ally a single cincinnus, 4–6-fld; fls to 1cm, pale lilac. Summer–winter. Ethiop.

Anemarrhena Bunge. Liliaceae (Asphodelaceae). 1 rhizomatous perenn. herb. Lvs 15–30cm, basal, linear, grass-like, persistent. Flowering st. erect, with a few-bract-like lvs above; spike dense, interrupted, 15–22cm; fls nocturnally fragrant; perianth funnel-shaped, white, keels sometimes brown or green, lobes 6, 0.5cm, linear; anth. yellow. Summer. N China, Jap.

A. asphodeloides Bunge.

Anemia Sw. FLOWERING FERN. Schizaeaceae. *c*90 terrestrial or lithophytic ferns. Rhiz. creeping or ascending, generally short, hairy. Stipe long. Fronds pinnatifid to pinnately compound; basal pinnae erect, fertile, greatly exceeding others; sterile pinnae leafy, pinnate to decompound. Sori numerous, small, forming a pan., distinct from sterile part of frond and similar to a fl. spike. Trop. Amer., Trop. & S Afr. Z10.

A. adiantifolia (L.) Sw. PINE FERN. Stipes 30–45cm. Sterile pinnae to 30×15cm, deltoid-ovate, 2–3-pinnate, pinnules oblong-obovate, erose-denticulate. S Flor., W Indies, C Amer.

A. dregeana anon. Stipes 20–30cm. Sterile pinnae 2.5–4×1–2cm, ovate-deltoid, upper side subcordate, incised-crenate. S Afr.

A. mandioccana Maddi. Stipes 15–30cm. Fronds 30×5–10cm, pinnae with apex tapered, acute, minutely serrate, coriaceous, finely pilose. Braz.

A. mexicana Klotzsch. Stipes to 25cm. Sterile part of frond to 22×15cm, deltoid-ovate, pinnae 5–9, elliptic-lanceolate, minutely serrate. S US, Mex. to Colomb.

A. phyllitidis (L.) Sw. Stipes to 60cm. Fronds 10–30cm, sterile portion ovate-oblong, pinnae in 4–12 pairs, 13–18cm, ovate-lanceolate, acuminate, base rounded or cuneate, entire. Mex. to Arg., W Indies.

A. rotundifolia Schräd. Stipes 15–18cm. Fronds 20–30×2.5–5cm, apex often elongate and rooting, pinnae 2.5×2cm, rhombic to flabellate, obtuse, minutely serrate, pubesc. Braz.

A. tomentosa (Savigny) Sw. Stipes 15–30cm. Fronds 6–35×3–20cm, sterile portion ovate-deltoid, bipinnatifid or bipinnate, pinnae 6–13 pairs, pinnules ovate, pilose. Trop. Amer.

A. underwoodiana Maxon. Fronds anise-scented when crushed. Stipes 8–23cm. Fertile fronds 15–40cm, pinnae stiffly erect, sterile fronds 8–18×8–14cm, linear-lanceolate, pinnate, pinnae in 3–7 pairs, attenuate at apex, cuneate at base, minutely undulate-crenate, pale green, v. thin. W Indies.

Anemone L. Ranunculaceae. WINDFLOWER. *c*120 perenn. herbs. Roots rhizomatous, tuberous or fibrous. Basal lvs usually lobed, dissected, st. lvs often whorled below infl., sessile or short-petiolate. Fls solitary or in cymes; shallowly dish-shaped; tep. petaloid; sta. numerous (petaloid staminodes in double forms). N & S temp. regions.

A. acutiloba (DC.) Laws. = *Hepatica acutiloba*.

A. albana Steven = *Pulsatilla albana*.

A. albana ssp. *armena* (Boiss.) Smirnov. = *Pulsatilla armena*.

A. alpina L. = *Pulsatilla alpina*.

A. altaica Mey. To 20cm. Rhiz. cylindrical, creeping. Basal lf solitary, petiolate, seg. toothed above, often cut; st. lvs tripartite, in whorls of 3, divided and toothed. Fls solitary, 2–4cm diam., white veined violet inside; tep. 8–9, rarely to 12. Spring. Arc. Russia, Jap. Z2.

A. angulosa auct. non Lam. = *Hepatica transsylvanica*.

A. apennina L. To 15cm. Rhiz. stout, creeping. Basal lvs divided into 3 seg., each lobed and cut; st. lvs with 3 seg., lobed or divided, petiole distinct. Fls solitary, 2.5–3cm diam., pedicel 2–3cm; tep. 8–23, oblong, blunt, blue rarely flushed pink or white. Early spring. S Eur. 'Petrovac': vigorous, fls multi-petalled, rich blue. 'Purpurea': fls soft purple-rose. var. *albiflora* Strobl. Fls white. Z6.

A. armena Boiss. = *Pulsatilla armena*.

A. baicalensis Turcz. & Ledeb. 15–35cm. Rhiz. cylindrical. St. lvs often v. reduced. Fls solitary or in pairs; tep. 6, broad to rounded ovate, white. Spring. E Asia. Z5.

A. baldensis L. To 20cm. Rootstock fibrous. Basal lvs petiolate, 3-parted, lfts deeply 3-lobed; st. lvs petiolate, multifid. Fls solitary, 2.5–4cm, slightly nodding, tep. (5–)8–10, oblong-oval, white, sometimes flushed pink or purple. Summer. CS Eur. Z6.

A. biarmiensis Juz. Differs from *A. narcissiflora* in lvs with 3, stalked, primary divisions. NE Russia. Z3.

A. biflora DC. To 20cm. Rhiz. tuberous. Basal lvs petiolate, 3-parted, seg. lobed and cut; lvs flattened at base to form a lobed wing-like structure. Fls nodding, 2–3 together, 2–5cm diam.; 5, hairy outside, crimson, orange or yellow. Spring. Iran, Afghan., Pak., Kashmir. Z6.

A. blanda Schott & Kotschy. To 18cm. Rhiz. thick, tuberous. Basal lf 0 or solitary, broadly triangular, petiolate, 3-parted, seg. unevenly lobed; st. lvs 2–3, lobed or divided into 3 seg. covered with flattened hairs. Fls solitary, 2–4cm diam. pedicel 2–5cm; tep. 9–15, narrow, blue, mauve, white or pink, glab.

Spring. SE Eur., Cyprus, W Turk., Cauc. 'Atrocaerulea' ('Ingramii'): fls deep blue. 'Blue Shades': lvs v. finely divided; fls pale to deep blue. 'Blue Star': fls pale blue. 'Bridesmaid': fls large, pure white. 'Bright Star': fls bright pink. 'Charmer': fls deep pink. 'Fairy': fls snow white. 'Pink Star': fls large, pale pink. 'Radar': fls magenta, centre white. 'Rosea': fls pale pink. 'Violet Star': fls large, amethyst, white outside. 'White Splendour': tall; fls large, white, exterior pink. var. *scythinica* Jenk. Fls white, exterior blue. N Turkestan. Z5.

A. blanda var. *parvula* DC. = *A. caucasica.*

A. borealis Richards = *A. parviflora.*

A. bucharica (Reg.) Finet & Gagnep. To 20cm. Rhiz. tuberous. Basal lvs petiolate, 3-parted, seg. lobed and cut; st. lvs with basal part flattened forming a 3-parted wing-like structure. Fls usually paired, 3–4cm diam., erect; tep. 5, red or violet-red, hairy. Spring. C Asia. Z5.

A. canadensis L. Differs from *A. virginica* in sessile involucral lvs. Summer. N Amer. Z3.

A. capensis Lam. 8–60cm. Rootstock ± woody. Basal lvs 2–3-parted, seg. deeply cut; involucral lvs often poorly developed. Fls solitary or few; tep. numerous, narrow, white suffused pale pink. S Afr.

A. caroliniana Walter. To 25cm. Rhiz. tuberous. Lvs slender-petiolate, 3-parted, seg. 3-fid, dentate; st. lvs 3-lobed, seg. cut. Fls erect, 2–4cm diam.; tep. 6–20, oblong-linear, purple or white-purple, pubesc. E US. Z4.

A. caucasica Rupr. Resembles a smaller, more delicate *A. blanda.* St. 6–13cm. St. lvs short-stalked, eventually glab. Tep. 8–11, blue or white. Cauc., N Iran. Z5.

A. coerulea DC. 10–25cm. Rootstock long, thin. Lvs deeply divided, seg. narrow-linear. Tep. 5, ovate or elliptic, blue or white, hairy outside. Altai Mts. var. *uralensis* Korsh. Fls pink to white. Ural Mts. Z5.

A. coronaria L. To 60cm. Rhiz. tuberous. Basal lvs tripartite, seg. finely dissected; st. lvs sessile, deeply cleft. Fls solitary, 3–8cm, diam.; tep. 5–8, oval, scarlet, blue, pink, white or bicoloured, exterior pubesc. Spring. S Eur., Medit. Over 20 cvs or groups: fls 6–10cm diam., single to semi-double, wide range of bright and pastel colours, also bicolours. De Caen group (fls single, poppy-shaped, large, white, bright pink, red or purple, with black anth.; collective name for single-fld cvs), 'His Excellency' (fls large, single, scarlet with white eye, similar to *A. ×fulgens*), 'Mr Fokker' (fls single, blue), 'The Bride' (fls single, white). Mona Lisa group (F1 hybrids; to 60cm tall; fls single, to 10cm diam., v. abundant, full colour range), 'Sylphide' (fls single, mauve) and St Brigid group (fls semi-double, many bright, pastel and bicolours; collective name for semi-double cvs), 'Lord Lieutenant' (fls semi-double, blue), 'Mt Everest' (fls white, semi-double form of 'The Bride'), 'The Admiral' (fls semi-double, deep pink). var. *coronaria.* Fls scarlet. var. *alba* (Goaty & Pons) Burnat. Fls white. var. *cyanea* (Risso) Ard. Fls blue. var. *rosea* (Henry) Rouy & Foucaud. Fls pink. Z8.

A. cylindrica Gray. 20–60cm, silky; root-stock, fibrous. Basal lvs 5-parted, lfts narrow, deeply divided, incised; st. lvs smaller. Fls 0.5–2cm, in clusters of 2–6 on erect stalks 10–28cm long; tep. 5–6, white, often tinged green. Summer. W US. Z5.

A. deltoidea Hook. 15–30cm, slender. Rhiz. slender, horizontal. Basal lvs 3-lobed, seg. ovate, dentate; st. lvs sessile, entire. Fls solitary; tep. 15–25mm, white. Summer. US, Rocky Mts. Z5.

A. demissa Hook. f. & Thoms. Differs from *A. tetrasepala* in st. 15–40cm, basal lvs smaller, rounded, divided into wedge-shaped seg.; st. lvs smaller, 3-fid. Fls 3–6 in spreading umbels, white, blue or purple. W Himal. to SW China. Z5.

A. dichotoma L. 20–80cm. Rhiz. thin, black-brown. St. frequently branched. Basal lvs on long petioles, deeply cut and dentate, seg. broad, 5–7; st. lvs sessile with 2–3 deep lobes. Fls solitary, 2–3cm, on long pedicels; tep. 5, white. Early summer. Sib., Jap., Manch., Korea, US. Z4.

A. ×elegans Decne. = *A. ×hybrida.*

A. elongata D. Don. 30–60cm. St. erect, stout, hairy. Lvs resembling those of *A. sylvestris*, hairy. Fls 1–3, to 2.5cm diam.; tep. 4–6, dull white. Early summer. Himal. Z6.

A. eranthoides Reg. To 12cm. Rhiz. tuberous. Basal lvs petiolate, 3–5-parted, each leaflet with 3 seg., toothed; st. lvs sessile, narrowly obovate, divided into 3 seg. Fls paired, 1–2.5cm diam., golden yellow inside, yellow-green outside; tep. to 8, adpressed-hairy outside. Spring. C Asia. Z5.

A. fanninii Harv. 60–150cm. Lvs petiolate, suborbicular, indented with 5–7 toothed lobes, coriaceous, softly pubesc. above, hirsute beneath. Fls 6–9cm diam., scented; tep. 12–30, linear-lanceolate, white; pedicels 18–25cm. Early summer. S Afr. Z8.

A. fasciculata L. = *A. narcissiflora.*

A. flaccida Schmidt. 5–20cm. Rhiz. thick, black. St. erect, unbranched. Lvs thick, in mounds, bronze at first, later dark green with white markings at base; petioles long, lobes 3, lat. lobes

dissected, central lobe 3-cleft. Fls 1–3, 1.5–3cm diam.; tep. 5(–7), cream-white sometimes flushed pink. Late spring. E Russia, China, Jap. Z6.

A. fragifera Wulf. = *A. baldensis.*

A. ×fulgens Gay. (*A. pavonina* × *A. hortensis.*) Less robust than *A. pavonina.* Fls solitary; tep. 15, scarlet, narrower than in *A. pavonina.* C Medit. 'Annulata Grandiflora': to 30cm; fls scarlet, centre yellow-cream. 'Multipetala': fls semi-double, tep. 20+, pointed, selection of 'Annulata Grandiflora'. Z8.

A. glaucifolia Franch. To 90cm; rootstock thick. Basal lvs to 20cm, oblanceolate, pinnately lobed, sparsely long white-hirsute; st. lvs 3, linear-oblong, dentate. Fls 3.5–10cm diam., erect, solitary or in sparse umbels, mauve, silky externally; tep. obovate. Summer. SW China. Z7.

A. glaucophylla hort. = *A. glaucifolia.*

A. globosa Pritz. = *A. multifida.*

A. gortschakowii Karel. & Kir. To 15cm. Rhiz. tuberous. Basal lvs petiolate, 3-parted, seg. bifid or 3-fid and lobed; basal portion of st. lvs wing-like, 3-parted. Fls usually in pairs, 1–2cm diam.; tep. 5, pale yellow occas. flushed red, exterior thickly hairy. Spring. C Asia. Z4.

A. heldreichiana (Boiss.) Gand. Resembles *A. hortensis*, but tep. blue-grey outside, white inside. Spring. Crete. Z8.

A. hepatica auct. non L. = *Hepatica americana.*

A. hepatica L. = *Hepatica nobilis.*

A. hirsutissima Britt. = *Pulsatilla hirsutissima.*

A. hortensis L. To 30cm. Rhiz. tuberous. Basal lvs petiolate, seg. 3, unevenly lobed and finely dissected; st. lvs sessile, unlobed, toothed. Fls solitary, 2–4cm diam.; tep. 12–20, pink-mauve. Spring. C Medit. Z8.

A. hudsoniana Richardson = *A. multifida.*

A. hupehensis Lem. To 60cm. Roots fibrous. St. branching. Basal lvs 3-parted, sometimes entire at first, sharply toothed, lightly pubesc. beneath; st. lvs 3–4, resembling reduced basal lvs. Fls in umbels; tep. 5–6, rounded, exterior hairy, white, often tinged mauve or pink. Late summer–autumn. C China. 'Bowles' Pink' ('E.A. Bowles'): to 90cm; fls large, deep pink-purple. 'Elegans': to 75cm; fls pale rose. 'Hadspen Abundance': perianth seg. bitoned pink-purple, the smallest ones darkest. 'Rosenschale': vigorous; perianth seg. rounded at base, pale outside. 'September Charm' ('September Glow'): fls often drooping, silvery-pink, darker exterior; probably a hybrid; prolific. var. *japonica* (Thunb.) Bowles & Stearn. Sturdy, tep. 20+ deep pink-purple. Jap., S China. 'Bodnant Burgundy': tall, to 1m. 'Bressingham Glow': similar to 'Prinz Heinrich' but to 90cm, compact; fls semi-double; tep. fluted, deep pink. 'Praecox': early, fls dark pink, deeper outside. 'Prinz Heinrich' ('Prince Henry'): st. thinner; lvs less acute; fls darker, tep. longer, more numerous, flatter. Z6.

A. ×hybrida Paxt. Robust, to 1.5m, closely resembles *A. hupehensis* but taller and generally lacks fertile pollen; tep. 6–11, occas. to 15. Late summer–autumn. Gdn origin. Over 30 cvs: height 0.8–1.5m; st. robust to wiry; fls single to fully double, white through cream to deep pink and mauve; perianth seg. to 45, sometimes overlapping or waved. 'Alice': strong-grower; fls with a double row of tep., rose pink with a silvery edge. 'Coupe d'Argent': fls cream, fading white; perianth seg. 34–45, wavy. 'Elegantissima': to 1.5m; fls with a double row of tep., satin pink. 'Géante des Blanches' ('White Giant', 'White Queen'): large, to 1m; fls white with 15–20 tep., quilled at base. 'Honorine Jobert': lvs dark green; fls pure white. 'Königin Charlotte' ('Reine Charlotte', 'Queen Charlotte'): vigorous; fls semi-double, with 10–15 tep., pale purple, tips ragged. 'Kriemhilde': fls semi-double with 10–15 tep., pale purple-pink, darker on outside. 'Lady Gilmour': large; fls semi-double, pure pink. 'Margarette': fls semi-double, deep pink. 'Max Vogel': st. wiry; fls pink-mauve. 'Prince Heinrich': fls to 80cm; fls purple-red, semi-double. 'Rosenschale' ('Pink Shell'): fls v. large, single, deep pink. 'Whirlwind' ('Wirbelwind'): fls semi-double, with 20–30 narrow twisted tep., white. Z6.

A. ×intermedia Winkl. = *A. ×lipsiensis.*

A. japonica (Thunb.) Sieb. & Zucc. non Hoult. = *A. hupehensis* var. *japonica.*

A. keiskeana Itô ex Maxim. To 15cm. Rhiz. thin, creeping; st. erect, unbranched. Basal lvs with 3 stalked triangular-ovate lfts; st. lvs sessile, narrowly ovate to slender-oblong, pinnately incised. Fls solitary, 1.5–3.5cm diam.; tep. 12–15, mauve, occas. white within. Early spring. Jap. Z6.

A. lancifolia Pursh. To 8cm, closely resembling *A. quinquefolia* but larger. Rootstock fleshy. Basal lvs 3-parted, lfts petiolate, lanceolate, crenate; involucral lf 3-parted. Fls solitary; tep. 5, 1–2cm, white, ovate, acute. Early summer. E US. Z4.

A. ×lesseri Wehrh. (*A. multifida* × *A. sylvestris.*) Closely resembling *A. multifida*, basal lvs large, long-stalked, rounded, palmately lobed; fls larger, 2–4cm diam.; tep. 5–8, wide-spreading, purple, yellow, white or pink, pubesc. outside, shining within. Early summer. Gdn origin. Z3.

A. leveillei Ulbr. To 60cm. Rootstock fibrous. Basal lvs 12–20cm, reniform, lobes 3, deeply divided, toothed, hairy; st. lvs 3, ovate, deeply incised. Fls to 4cm diam.; tep. 8, narrowly elliptic, white, exterior pink and hairy. C China. Z6.

A. ×*lipsiensis* Beck. (*A. ranunculoides* ×*A. nemorosa.*) Fls 1.5–2cm, pale sulphur yellow. Nat. hybrid. Z4.

A. lithophila Rydb. 10–20cm, sparsely silky-pubesc. Basal lvs with 3–5 dissected seg. to 3cm. Tep. 1.5cm wide, elliptic, cream-white tinged blue, silky. US.

A. ludoviciana DC. = *Pulsatilla patens*.

A. magellanica hort. ex Wehrh. Close to *A. multifida*. To 20cm. Basal lvs with 3–5 lobes divided into many narrow seg., hairy. Fls solitary, 1.5–2.5cm diam., cream-yellow. S Chile, S Arg.

A. mexicana HBK. 22–30cm, st. simple. Basal lvs 3-parted, lfts rhomboid, 3-fid, serrate, teeth rounded; st. lvs 2–3. Fls erect, 2.5–4cm diam., tep. 5, ovate, white, pink or pink-purple, exterior tomentose. Mex. Z8.

A. montana Hoppe = *Pulsatilla montana*.

A. multifida Poir. 10–60cm, silky. Rootstock sturdy, erect. Basal lvs petiolate, lfts 3–5, incised in 2–3 linear lobes; st. lvs 2–3 sessile, or 0. Fls 2–3, 0.5–2cm diam., tep. 5–9, elliptic, obtuse, white, yellow-cream or red. Spring–autumn. N Amer. 'Major': to 20cm, robust; fls cream-yellow. Z2.

A. narcissiflora L. To 40cm; rootstock ± woody. Basal lvs numerous, petiolate, lfts 5, cut into linear-lanceolate acute lobes; st. lvs sessile, 3–5-fid. Fls 3–8 in umbels, 2–4cm diam.; tep. 5–6, ovate or oval, acute or obtuse, white, occas. stained pink or blue outside. Summer. C & S Eur., Turk., Russia, Jap., US. var. *villosa* Royle. All parts hairy. Z3.

A. nemorosa L. WINDFLOWER; WOOD ANEMONE. To 30cm. Rhiz. slender, creeping. Basal lvs petiolate, trisect, lateral seg. 3-fid, toothed to divided; st. lvs similar, on short, stout petioles. Fls 2–3cm diam., solitary, held 2–3cm above the involucre; tep. 6–8, rarely 5–12, white, occas. flushed purple or pink, rarely blue. Early spring. Eur., widespread except in Medit. 'Alba Plena': closely resembling 'Vestal' and much confused with it, but fls smaller, petaloid sta. more irregular, tep. 6. 'Allenii': petioles maroon; pedicel brown; fls rich lilac or pale blue outside, lavender inside. 'Blue Beauty': lvs tinted bronze; fls large, pale blue, pearly beneath. 'Blue Bonnet': late flowering; fls large, blue. 'Bracteata': fls large, loose double, narrow, white, outer seg. wholly or partly green. 'Grandiflora': fls large, white. 'Green Fingers': tep. white, tinged green; fl. red. 'Leeds Variety': fls to 6cm diam., white, faintly flushed pink as they age, early. 'Lychette': fls large, white. 'Monstrosa': tep. serrate, outer few green. 'Plena': fls double. 'Robinsoniana': pedicel maroon; fls clear grey outside, lavender within. 'Rosea': fls pink in bud, tep. white at first, ageing deep pink especially on exterior. 'Royal Blue': fls blue. 'Vestal': late, fl. centre a button of petaloid seg. 'Vindobonensis': fls cream. 'Virescens': fls replaced by a pyramid of small leaflike bracts. 'Wilk's Giant': fls large, white, single. Z5.

A. nigricans (Stork) Fritsch. = *Pulsatilla pratensis* ssp. *nigricans*.

A. nikoensis Maxim. Differs from *A. nemorosa*, in more sharply toothed and divided lvs; fls solitary, large, often to 5cm diam., white. Jap. Z6.

A. nipponica Merrill. = *A. hupehensis* var. *japonica*.

A. nuttalliana DC. = *Pulsatilla hirsutissima*.

A. obtusiloba D. Don. To 30cm, closely resembling *A. tetrasepala*. St. spreading. Basal lvs rounded, seg. rounded, crenate. Fls in umbels; tep. 4–6, white, red or purple-blue, rarely yellow. Late spring–summer. Pak. to Bhutan. 'Alba': to 15cm; fls yellow white. Z5.

A. occidentalis Wats. = *Pulsatilla occidentalis*.

A. oregana A. Gray = *A. quinquefolia* var. *oregana*.

A. palmata L. To 15cm. Rhiz. tuberous. Basal lvs petiolate, orbicular with 3–5 shallow, toothed lobes; st. lvs with 3–5 linear-lanceolate seg. Fls solitary or paired, 2.5–3.5cm diam.; tep. 10–15, oblong, obtuse, yellow often red flushed outside. Spring. SW Eur. 'Alba': lvs violet beneath; fls white. 'Flore Pleno': fls double. 'Lutea': fls yellow. Z8.

A. parviflora Michx. 10–30cm. Rhiz. thin. Basal lvs petiolate, cordate, seg. 3, wedge-shaped with 3 lobes, crenate; st. lvs ± sessile. Fls solitary to 3cm diam.; tep. 5–6, oval, blunt, white sometimes flushed pale blue. N US, N Asia. Z4.

A. patens 'Nuttalliana'. = *Pulsatilla hirsutissima*.

A. patens L. = *Pulsatilla patens*.

A. pavonina Lam. To 30cm, hairy. Rhiz. tuberous. Basal lvs petiolate, seg. 3, deeply lobed and divided; st. lvs simple, sparsely toothed. Fls solitary, 3–10cm diam.; tep. 7–9, broad, scarlet, violet, purple or pink, rarely white or yellow, base white. Spring. Medit. 'Barr Salmon': fls deep salmon, fading somewhat. St Bavo Group: to 30cm, strong-growing; fls rose, lavender to violet. var. *ocellata* (Moggr.) Bowles & Stearn. Fls scarlet, centre white. var. *purpureoviolacea* (Boiss.) Hal. Fls

violet or pink-violet, centre white. Z8.

A. pennsylvanica Ledeb., non L. = *A. canadensis*.

A. petiolulosa Juz. To 18cm. Rhiz. tuberous. Basal lvs petiolate, seg. 3, 3-parted, deeply lobed and cut; basal part of st. lvs flattened, 3-lobed, toothed. Fls 2–4.5cm diam., slightly pendulous, usually in clusters of 2–4; tep. 5, yellow, exterior flushed red, covered with adpressed hairs. Spring. C Asia. Z5.

A. polyanthes D. Don. To 50cm, closely resembling *A. tetrasepala*; basal lvs rounded, shallowly lobed, seg. rounded; fls numerous, in umbels; tep. 4–6, white, red or purple-blue. Late spring. Pak. to Bhutan. Z6.

A. pratensis L. = *Pulsatilla pratensis*.

A. pulsatilla L. = *Pulsatilla vulgaris*.

A. quinquefolia L. Resembles *A. nemorosa*. Rhiz. stout. St. to 30cm. Basal lf solitary, 3-parted, rhomboidal, strongly dentate, less lobed than in *A. nemorosa*. Fls solitary; tep. usually 5, occas. 4–9, variable, 0.5–2.5cm, white, often flushed pink. US. var. *oregana* (A. Gray) Robinson. Tep. 1–2cm, blue or pink. US. Z7.

A. raddeana Reg. To 15cm. Rhiz. short. Basal lf 0 or solitary with 3 long-petiolate, broadly ovate, seg. often further lobed, clothed in long hairs; st. lvs in whorls of 3, 3-parted. Fls solitary, 2–4cm diam.; tep. 10–15, white, exterior flushed purple. Spring. Manch., Sakhalin, Jap., Korea. Z6.

A. ranunculoides L. To 15cm. Rhiz. slender. Basal lf 0 or solitary, seg. 3, deeply divided and lobed; st. lvs similar, short-stalked. Fls 1.5–2cm diam., solitary, held 2–3cm above involucre; tep. 5–6, elliptic, deep yellow, pubesc. outside. Early spring. Eur., widespread except in Medit. 'Flore Pleno': fls semi-double; yellow; tep. 12+. 'Grandiflora': fls large to 2.5cm diam. 'Superba': lvs bronzed green; fls bright yellow. Z4.

A. reflexa Stephan. To 25cm, closely resembling *A. nemorosa*; rhiz. thin; tep. 5–6, strongly recurved, white-green. NE Asia. Z6.

A. riparia Fern. THIMBLEWEED. Resembles *A. cylindrica*. St. 1–4, villous. Basal lvs with 3–5 deeply cut lfts; st. lvs 3-lobed. Fls 1–10, each with a whorl of bracts, except central fl.; tep. 4–6, 1–2cm, white or red. US. Z4.

A. rivularis DC. To 90cm; rootstock swollen, woody. Basal lvs petiolate, 8–15cm wide, seg. 3, obovate, 3-fid, lobes cut, dentate; st. lvs sessile, apex pinnately cut. Fls in umbels, each with 2–5 fls, 1.5–3cm diam.; tep. 5–8, oval, white, exterior stained blue. Late spring–summer. N India, SW China. Z7.

A. rupicola Cambess. To 15cm; rootstock long, woody, fibrous. Basal lvs petiolate, seg. 3, strongly lobed and toothed; st. lvs 2, sessile, less divided. Fl. 4–8cm diam., solitary; tep. 5(–6), 2–3cm, broadly elliptic, white, exterior stained pink or blue and silky-hairy. Summer. Afghan. to SW China. Z6.

A. ×*seemannii* Camus = *A.* ×*lipsiensis*.

A. sibirica L. Basal lvs somewhat orbicular, lfts 3, palmately incised, stalked, petioles hirsute; st. lvs 3, divided, seg. lanceolate. Fls solitary, yellow. Sib. Z2.

A. stellata Risso, non Lam. = *A.* ×*fulgens*.

A. stellata Lam., non Risso = *A. hortensis*.

A. stellata var. *heldreichii* Boiss. = *A. heldreichiana*.

A. sylvestris L. SNOWDROP WINDFLOWER. 15–30cm; rhiz. woody, branching. Basal lvs petiolate, palmately lobed, seg. obovate, lobed, pubesc. beneath; st. lvs smaller, toothed. Fls solitary or paired, 2.5–8cm diam., slightly drooping, fragrant; tep. 5+, elliptic, white. Early summer. C & E Eur., Cauc. 'Grandiflora': fls large, held well up from plant, nodding, fragrant, white; sta. yellow. 'Elisa Fellmann' ('Plena'): fls semi-double. 'Macrantha': v. vigorous, fls large, white, fragrant, nodding. 'Wienerwald': fls large. Z4.

A. tetrasepala Royle. To 75cm; rootstock woody, sturdy. Basal lvs petiolate, coriaceous, dentate and lobed; st. lvs 4, sessile, smaller, lobes narrower. Fls in umbels, each br. with 3–5 stalked fls; tep. 4(–5–7), white. Summer. W Himal. Z6.

A. thalictroides L. = *Anemonella thalictroides*.

A. tomentosa (Maxim.) P'ei. To 1m+; st. branching, tomentose woody. Basal lvs 3-parted, or entire, strongly toothed, tomentose beneath; st. lvs smaller. Fls 5–8cm diam. in term. clusters; tep. 5–6, pale pink. Late summer–early autumn. N China. 'Robustissima': lvs large, grey-green beneath; fls soft pink, numerous. 'Superba': habit smaller; fls large. Z3.

A. transsylvanica (Fuss.) Heuft. = *Hepatica transsylvanica*.

A. trifolia L. To 15cm, occas. to 20cm. Rhiz. thin, creeping, brown. Basal lvs absent or 3-parted, on long petioles, toothed; st. lvs stalked, in whorls of 3, lfts 3, ovate-lanceolate, toothed. Fls solitary, 2cm diam., on long pedicels above the last whorl, erect; tep. 5–8(–12), elliptic, blunt, white, rarely flushed pink. Spring. S Eur. ssp. *albida* (Mariz.) Tutin. Anth. white, not blue. NW Spain and Port. Z6.

A. trifolia L. in part = *A. lancifolia*.

A. trullifolia Hook. & Thomps. Differs from *A. obtusiloba*, differs in narrower, long-cuneate basal lvs, with 3, 3-lobed apical lobes; fls blue or white. Summer. E Himal. to SW China. Z5.

A. tschernjaewii Reg. To 30cm. Rhiz. tuberous. Basal lvs petiolate, seg. 3, sessile, shallowly divided into 3 further seg.; st. lvs smaller. Fls 2–3 together, 2–4.5cm diam.; tep. 5, white, base flushed purple-pink. Spring. C Asia. Z5.

A. tuberosa Rydb. To 30cm. Rhiz. tuberous. Basal lvs petiolate, solitary, 3-parted, lfts 2.5–5cm, ovate, 3-parted, seg. lobed and toothed; st. lvs 3, to 8cm, similarly lobed or toothed. Fls solitary; tep. to 1.5cm, linear oblong, white or pink. US. Z5.

A. vernalis L. = *Pulsatilla vernalis*.

A. villosissima (DC.) Juz. Differs from *A. narcissiflora* in covering of long, white or cream hairs; pedicels v. short; fls in a tight head. NW US, Altai Mts. Z5.

A. virginiana L. 30–60cm; rootstock woody, thick. Basal lvs with 3–5 seg. diamond-shaped to ovate in outline, incised toward apex, petiolate; st. lvs reduced. Fls arising from each st. axil in groups of 2–3, to 2.5cm diam.; tep. 5–6, white often tinged green. Summer. C & E US. Z4.

A. vitifolia DC. To 90cm. Rootstock woody, thick. Basal lvs petiolate, large, 5-lobed, crenately toothed, white-tomentose beneath; st. lvs similar but smaller. Fls 3.5–5cm in lax term. umbels; tep. 5–6, white. Late summer to early autumn. Afghan. to W China and Burm. Z5.

A. vitifolia misapplied = *A. tomentosa*.

A. zephyra Nels. Differs from *A. narcissiflora* in lvs less divided; fls solitary, pale yellow. W US (Rocky Mts). Z5.

Anemonella Spach. Ranunculaceae. 1 perenn. herb to 25cm, glab., roots tuberous. Lvs basal, 2–3-ternate. Fls white, 2–5, on slender pedicels; sep. 5–10, petaloid, spreading; cor. 0; sta. numerous. E N Amer. Z4.

A. thalictroides (L.) Spach. RUE-ANEMONE. 'Flore Pleno': fls double. 'Rosea': fls pale pink. 'Rosea Plena' ('Schoaff's Double Pink'): fls double, pale pink, long-lasting.

→*Anemone* and *Thalictrum*.

Anemonopsis Sieb. & Zucc. Ranunculaceae. 1 rhizomatous, perenn. herb to 80cm. Lvs basal or cauline, 2–3-ternate, dark glossy green; lfts rhombic-ovate to oblong, to 8cm, 3-lobed, dentate; petioles dilated below. Fls 10+, nodding, slender-stalked in loose racemose pan., lavender, waxy; sep. 7–10, to 2cm, petaloid, oblong; 10, obovate, to 1.2cm; sta. many, exceeding sep. Jap. Z4.

A. macrophylla Sieb. & Zucc.

Anemopaegma Mart. ex Meissn. Bignoniaceae. 43 lianes. Lvs pinnate, 1–3-jugate, often with a tendril. Fls racemose; cal. cupular, truncate, margin gland.; cor. tubular-campanulate. Mex. to Braz. and Arg. Z10.

A. belizeanum Blake = *A. chrysoleucum*.

A. carrerense Armitage. Lfts 6–7cm, ovate. Fls to 6cm, pale to deep yellow. Trin.

A. chamberlaynii (Sims) Bur. and Schum. Lfts 5–14cm, oblong-ovate to lanceolate. Fls to 5cm, pale yellow. Braz.

A. chrysoleucum (HBK) Sandw. Lfts 5.5–15cm, narrowly elliptic. Fls fragrant, 6–10cm, cream inside, yellow outside, glandular-lepidote, tube yellow, striped orange. Mex. to N Braz.

A. grandiflorum Sprague = *A. paraense*.

A. lehmannii Sandw. = *A. puberulum*.

A. macrocarpum Standl. = *A. chrysoleucum*.

A. pachypus Schum. = *Mansoa hymenaea*.

A. paraense Bur. & Schum. Lfts ovate to oblong-ovate, cuspidate or pointed. Fls yellow or cream, densely scaly inside. Trin., Guyana, Peru, Braz.

A. puberulum (Siebert) Miranda. Lfts 8–13cm, ovate-elliptic. Fls 5cm, yellow. Spring–summer. Mex. to E Ecuad.

A. punctulatum Pittier & Standl. = *A. chrysoleucum*.

A. rugosum (Schldl.) Sprague. Lfts 5–7.5cm, broadly ovate, rugose. Fls 6.25cm, yellow. Venez.

A. scandens Méllo ex Schum. = *A. chamberlaynii*.

A. tonduzianum Kränzl. = *Cydista aequinoctialis* var. *hirtella*.

→*Bignonia* and *Chondranthus*.

Anemopsis Hook. & Arn. Saururaceae. 1 aromatic perenn. herb of marshy places. Basal lvs to 14cm, elliptic-oblong, apex blunt or rounded, base truncate to cordate, glandular-punctate, ± ciliate; petioles exceeding blades. Scapes to 5cm, erect; spike packed, subpyramidal to 4cm; fls small, green-white, subtended by white, sometimes rust-spotted bracts to 2.5cm, the whole resembling an *Anemone* fl. SW US to Mex. Z8.

A. californica (Nutt.) Hook. & Arn. YERBA MANSA.

Anethum L. Umbelliferae. 2 ann. or bienn. herbs scented of anise. Lvs finely 3–4-pinnate; seg. filiform. Fls yellow, small, in compound umbels. OW. Z8.

A. graveolens L. DILL. Ann. to 60cm. Lvs to 35×20cm, v. finely divided. Umbel rays 2–9cm, 15–30. SW Asia.

A. sowa hort. non Roxb. ex Flem. = *A. graveolens*.

→*Peucedanum*.

Angelica *Polyscias filicifolia*.

Angelica L. Umbelliferae. 50 bienn., monocarpic or perenn. herbs. Lvs ternate to 3-pinnate; seg. broad, toothed or lobed. Umbels compound, many-rayed; fls white, green or pink-tinged. N Hemis.

A. acutiloba (Sieb. & Zucc.) Kitag. To 1m. Lf blades to 25cm, 1–2-pinnate; lfts to 10cm, lanceolate, toothed. Fls white. Jap. Z7.

A. archangelica L. GARDEN ANGELICA; ARCHANGEL; WILD PARSNIP. Monocarpic. To 2m. Lf blades to 60cm, 2–3-pinnate; seg. 3-parted, upper lvs with inflated petiole base. Fls green-white to cream. N & E Eur. to C Asia, Greenland. Z4.

A. atropurpurea L. ALEXANDERS; MASTERWORT. Perenn. to 2m. St. purple. Lf blades to 25cm, 2-pinnate to 3-ternate; lfts ovate, serrate. Fls white. C US. Z4.

A. curtisii Buckley = *A. triquinata*.

A. florentii Franch. & Savat. ex Maxim. Perenn. to 50cm. Lf blades to 15cm, 2–3-pinnate or ternate; seg. linear-lanceolate, entire or 3-parted. Fls white. Jap. Z7.

A. hirsuta (Torr. & A. Gray) Chapm. = *A. venenosa*.

A. maximowiczii (F. Schmidt) Benth. = *A. florentii*.

A. montana Brot. = *A. sylvestris*.

A. officinalis Moench = *A. archangelica*.

A. pancicii Vandas = *A. sylvestris*.

A. polyclada Franch. = *A. pubescens*.

A. pubescens Maxim. Perenn. to 2m. Lvs 3- to ternately pinnate; seg. to 10cm, ovate-elliptic, serrate. Fls white. Jap. Z7.

A. sylvestris L. WILD ANGELICA. Bienn. to 2m. St. tinged purple. Lf blades to 60cm, 2–3-pinnate; seg. 1.5–8cm, oblong-ovate, hispid, serrate. Fls white to pink. Eur. Z7.

A. triquinata Michx. Perenn. to 1.5m. Lf blades to 30cm, biternate or ternately pinnate; seg. 4–6cm, ovate to lanceolate, serrate. Fls white. Canada. Z3.

A. venenosa (Greenway) Fern. Perenn. to 2m. Lf blades to 25cm, ternately pinnate; seg. to 2.5cm, ovate-lanceolate, toothed. Fls white. E US. Z4.

→*Ligusticum* and *Oestericum*.

Angelica Tree *Aralia elata*.

Angelim *Andira*.

Angelonia Humb. & Bonpl. Scrophulariaceae. 30 subshrubs or perenn. herbs, related to *Alonsoa*. Fls solitary in lf axils or in term. rac.; cor. lacking spur, tube reduced or 0, upper lip 2-lobed, lower lip 3-lobed. C & S Amer. Z9.

A. angustifolia Benth. Perenn. St. glab., 30–45cm. Lvs lanceolate, serrulate. Fls deep mauve to violet. Summer. Mex., W Indies. 'Alba': fls white. 'Blue Pacific': floriferous; fls indigo blue and white.

A. gardneri Hook. Glandular-pubesc. perenn. St. angular, erect; to 1m. Lvs lanceolate, serrate. Fls purple, centre white, spotted red. Summer. Braz.

A. integerrima Spreng. Perenn. Lvs lanceolate, entire. Fls sky blue, spotted purple. Summer. S Braz., Parag.

A. salicariifolia Humb. & Bonpl. Perenn. to 70cm, viscid, glandular-pubesc. Lvs broadly lanceolate, sparsely serrulate. Fls opaline-mauve. C Amer., W Indies. 'Grandiflora': fls white, large.

Angels' Eyes *Veronica chamaedrys*.

Angel's Fishing Rod *Angelica archangelica*; *Dierama pulcherrimum*.

Angel's Hair *Artemisia schmidtiana*.

Angel's Tears *Narcissus triandrus*; *Soleirolia soleirolii*.

Angel's Trumpet *Brugmansia arborea*; *Datura innoxia*.

Angel's Wings *Caladium bicolor*.

Angel-wing Begonia *Begonia* × *argenteoguttata*; *B. coccinea*.

Angel Wings *Caladium*.

Angiopteris Hoffm. TURNIP FERN; GIANT FERN; KING FERN. Marattiaceae. 1 giant fern. Rhiz. massive, erect, woody, supported by thick roots; stipes erect, green, smooth, base swollen, enclosed by dilated, brown-scurfy stipules. Fronds to 5m+, deltoid, 3-pinnate; pinnae spreading, 30–90cm, lowest longest, swollen at base; pinnules 10–30cm, linear-oblong, acuminate, entire or finely dentate, leathery, pale to mid green. Pacific Trop. Z10.

A. evecta (Forst.) Hoffm.

Angled Loofah *Luffa acutangula*.

Angled Solomon's Seal *Polygonatum odoratum.*
Angleton Bluestem, Angleton Grass *Dichanthium aristatum.*

Angophora Cav. Myrtaceae. 8 shrubs or trees. Lvs leathery. Fls in dense term. clusters, 5-merous, white-cream, buds not operculate. cf. *Eucalyptus.* Fr. a ribbed woody capsule *c*1cm diam. E Aus. Z9.

A. bakeri C. Hall. NARROW-LEAVED APPLE. Bark rough. Lvs to 7.5cm, lanceolate-acuminate. Fls to 1.5cm diam.

A. cordifolia Cav. SMOOTH-BARK APPLE. Bark smooth, falling in flakes, orange-brown to pink. Fls to 2cm diam., stalks ± hairy.

A. costata (Gaertn.) Britten) = *A. cordifolia.*

A. floribunda (Sm.) Sweet. ROUGH-BARKED APPLE. Bark furrowed-fibrous. Lvs to 15cm, oblong-acuminate. Fls to 2cm diam., v. profuse, stalks ± hispid.

A. hispida (Sm.) Blaxell. DWARF APPLE. Bark flaky; branchlets red-hairy. Lvs to 10cm, oval to oblong-cordate. Fls to 2cm diam., stalks red-hairy.

A. hispida (Sm.) Blaxell = *A. cordifolia.*

A. intermedia DC. BROAD-LEAVED APPLE. Bark rough; branchlets thinly red-hairy. Lvs to 12cm, cordate-lanceolate. Fls to 1.5cm diam., stalks red-hairy.

A. lanceolata Cav. = *A. cordifolia.*

A. subvelutina F. Muell. = *A. intermedia.*

Angraecopsis Kränzl. Orchidaceae. 16 epiphytic monopodial orchids. Lvs 2-ranked, often curved, in one plane. Fls small, white, green or ivory in pendent axill. rac. Trop. Afr., Madag., Masc. Is., Comoros Is. Z10.

A. amaniensis Summerh. Dwarf, ± stemless. Lvs to 4cm, elliptic. Rac. to 7cm; fls many, to 1.4cm across, ivory or green-white, fragrant. Kenya to Zimb.

A. boutonii (Rchb. f.) H. Perrier = *Microterangis boutonii.*

A. gracillima (Rolfe) Summerh. St. to 7cm, pendent. Lvs linear-falcate. Rac. to 16cm; fls few, to 2cm across, white tinged orange. Kenya to Zam.

A. parviflora (Thouars) Schltr. St. short. Lvs to 25cm, ligulate-falcate. Rac. to 10cm; fls many, to 0.8cm across, green-white to ivory. W Afr., Tanz. to Zimb., Moz., Madag., Masc. Is.

A. tenerrima Kränzl. St. short, pendent. Lvs to 20cm, linear-oblanceolate-falcate. Rac. to 20cm; fls few, to 2.2cm across, white, spur tinged green. Tanz.

Angraecum Bory. Orchidaceae. 100–150 epiphytic monopodial orchids. St. long or short, clothed with 2-ranked lvs. Fls in axill. rac., white green or ivory; tep. spreading, similar; lip shell- or boat-shaped, spurred. Trop. and S Afr., Indian Ocean Is. Z9.

A. arachnites Schltr. To 30cm. Lvs to 2cm, oblong. Fls solitary, pale green with white, lip shell-shaped tapering to 3cm, long-spurred. Madag.

A. arachnopus Rchb. f. = *Aerangis arachnopus.*

A. arcuatum Lindl. = *Cyrtorchis arcuata.*

A. articulatum Rchb. f. = *Aerangis articulata.*

A. bicallosum H. Perrier. To 15cm. Lvs *c*20cm, elliptic. Fls solitary, tawny, lip white, broadly ovate to 3cm, long-spurred. Madag.

A. bidens Sw. = *Diaphananthe bidens.*

A. bilobum Lindl. = *Aerangis biloba.*

A. birrimense Rolfe. Long-stemmed. Lvs to 14cm, ligulate. Fls 2–3 per rac., pale green, lip to 3.5cm, rounded, apiculate, white blotched green, spur short. W Afr.

A. boutonii Rchb. f. = *Microterangis boutonii.*

A. brongniartianum Rchb. f. = *A. eburneum* ssp. *superbum.*

A. buyssonii Godef.-Leb. = *Aerangis ellisii.*

A. calceolus Thouars. Short-stemmed. Lvs 3–10cm, lanceolate-ligulate. Infl. ± paniculate; fls pale green, lip to 1cm, ovate-acuminate, spur short. Indian Ocean Is.

A. calligerum Rchb. f. = *Aerangis ellisii.*

A. capense (L. f.) Lindl. = *Mystacidium capense.*

A. caudatum Lindl. = *Plectrelminthus caudatus.*

A. chailluanum Hook. f. = *Cyrtorchis chailluana.*

A. christyanum Rchb. f. = *Calyptrochilum christyanum.*

A. citratum Thouars. = *Aerangis citrata.*

A. comorense Kränzl. = *A. eburneum.*

A. compactum Schltr. St. short. Lvs to 10cm, thick, leathery. Fls solitary, white, lip to 2.5cm, boat-shaped, shortly apiculate, spur to 12cm. Madag.

A. conchiferum Lindl. St. to 30cm. Lvs to 5cm, linear-ligulate. Fls solitary or paired, white, lip to 1.3cm, shell-shaped, apiculate. Kenya to S Afr.

A. cryptodon Rchb. f. = *Aerangis cryptodon.*

A. cultriforme Summerh. St. to 20cm. Lvs falcate. Fls solitary straw-coloured to orange, lip to 1.5cm, boat-shaped, spur short. Kenya to S Afr.

A. dasycarpum Schltr. St. to 10cm. Lvs to 1cm, oblong. Fls solitary, white, lip to 0.6cm, oblong-ligulate, spur short. Madag.

A. dendrobiopsis Schltr. St. to 60cm, pendent. Lvs 5–12cm, linear-lanceolate. Fls 1–4 per rac., white, fleshy, lip to 2cm, rhomboid, apiculate, spur short. Madag.

A. descendens Rchb. f. = *Aerangis articulata.*

A. didieri Baill. ex Finet. St. to 15cm. Lvs to 5cm, ligulate. Fls solitary, white, lip to 3cm, ovate, concave. Madag.

A. distichum Lindl. St. to 25cm. Lvs to 1.1cm, elliptic-oblong, strongly 2-ranked. Fls solitary, white, lip to 0.3cm, ovate-oblong, ± 3-lobed. W Afr., Zaire, Uganda, Angola.

A. eburneum Bory. St. to 1m. Lvs to 40cm, ligulate. Fls many, sep. green, pet. and lip white, lip to 3.5cm, uppermost, ovate, concave, acuminate, spur to 7cm. Indian Ocean Is. ssp. *giryamae* (Rendle) Cribb & Sengh. Lip broader, spur shorter. E Afr. ssp. *superbum* (Thouars) H. Perrier. Fls larger, whiter. Madag. var. *longicalcar* Bosser. Fls larger, spur v. long. Madag. ssp. *xerophilum* H. Perrier. Fls smaller except spur to 8cm. Madag.

A. eichlerianum Kränzl. St. elongated. Lvs to 12cm, elliptic-ligulate. Fls 2–3 per rac., green with a white-edged lip to 3.5cm. Nigeria to Angola.

A. elephantinum Schltr. St. to 15cm. Lvs to 12cm, ligulate. Fls white, sometimes tinted rose, solitary; lip to 4cm, ovate, concave, spur v. long, slender. Madag.

A. emarginatum Sw. = *Calyptrochilum emarginatum.*

A. equitans Schltr. St. to 10cm. Lvs to 6cm, fleshy, spreading, curved. Fls 1–3 per rac., white, lip to 2cm, elliptic, spur long, slender. Madag.

A. fastuosum Rchb. f. = *Aerangis fastuosa.*

A. florulentum Rchb. f. St. to 30cm. Lvs to 7cm, narrowly lanceolate, strongly 2-ranked. Fls white, 2–4 per rac., lip to 2.3cm, v. concave, spur long, slender. Comoros Is.

A. fragrans Thouars = *Jumellea fragrans.*

A. fuscatum Rchb. f. = *Aerangis fuscata.*

A. germinyanum Hook. f. St. to 1m, branched. Lvs to 4cm, oblong. Fls solitary, white (tep. sometimes pale amber), lip to 2.5cm, shell-shaped, long-acuminate, short-spurred. Madag.

A. hamatum Rolfe = *Cyrtorchis hamata.*

A. hildebrandtii Rchb. f. = *Microterangis hildebrandtii.*

A. humbertii H. Perrier. St. to 20cm. Lvs to 12cm, linear-ligulate. Fls 4–8 per rac., green-white, lip to 5cm, v. concave, green, v. long-spurred. Madag.

A. humblotii Rchb. f. = *A. leonis.*

A. hyaloides Rchb. f. = *Aerangis hyaloides.*

A. imbricatum Lindl. = *Calyptrochilum emarginatum.*

A. infundibulare Lindl. St. 1–2m robust. Lvs to 11cm, broadly ligulate. Fls solitary, green-white to ivory, lip to 8cm, oblong, concave, v. long-spurred. Nigeria to Zaire, Uganda, Kenya.

A. kirkii Rchb. f. = *Aerangis kirkii.*

A. kotschyanum Rchb. f. = *Aerangis kotschyana.*

A. leonis (Rchb. f.) Veitch. St. v. short. Lvs to 20cm, fleshy, falcate, usually 4, ± decussate. Fls 2–4 per rac., white, fleshy, lip to 5cm, carinate, long-spurred. Madag., Comoros Is.

A. magdalenae Schltr. St. short. Lvs to 30cm, oblong-ligulate. Fls 1–2 per rac., white, fleshy, lip to 5cm obovate, spur long, sigmoid. Madag.

A. mauritianum (Poir.) Frappier. St. to 40cm, pendent, branched. Lvs to 6cm, oblong-lanceolate. Fls solitary, white, lip to 1.5cm, lanceolate-acute, spur 8cm. Masc. Is.

A. maxillarioides Ridl. = *Jumellea maxillarioides.*

A. mirabile Schltr. St. to 15cm. Lvs to 5cm, narrow-linear, margins inrolled. Fls solitary, white, yellow-tinged, lip to 3cm, shell-shaped, long-acuminate, long-spurred. Madag.

A. modestum Hook. f. = *Aerangis modesta.*

A. mooreanum Rolfe ex Sander = *Aerangis mooreana.*

A. mystacidium Rchb. f. = *Aerangis mystacidii.*

A. ochraceum (Ridl.) Schltr. St. short. Lvs to 10cm, narrowly linear-lanceolate. Fls small, solitary, ochre-yellow, lip carinate, acute. Madag.

A. pellucidum Lindl. = *Diaphananthe pellucida.*

A. pertusum Lindl. = *Listrostachys pertusa.*

A. philippinense Ames = *Amesiella philippinensis.*

A. reygaertii De Wildeman. St. elongated. Lvs to 15cm, oblong. Fls solitary white except for lip green at base, to 2.5cm, oblong-lanceolate, spur to 5cm. Cameroun, Zaire, Uganda.

A. rhodostictum Kränzl. = *Aerangis luteoalba* var. *rhodosticta.*

A. rothschildianum O'Brien = *Eurychone rothschildiana.*

A. rutenbergianum Kränzl. St. to 12cm. Lvs to 6cm, linear. Fls solitary, white, spur green, lip to 3.5cm, rhomboid-elliptic, apiculate, v. long-spurred. Madag.

A. sanderianum Rchb. f. = *Aerangis modesta.*

A. scottianum Rchb. f. St. to 30cm, slender. Lvs few, to 10cm, terete, grooved. Fls 1–4 per rac., white, lip to 3cm, transversely oblong, apiculate, spur to 15cm. Comoros Is.

A. sesquipedale Thouars. COMET ORCHID. St. to 1.2m, robust. Lvs to 40cm, ligulate. Fls 1–4 per rac. white to ivory, fleshy, v. large, lip to 9cm, pandurate-acuminate, spur to 35cm. Madag.

A. somalense Schltr. = *Aerangis somalensis.*

A. sororium Schltr. St. to 1m. Lvs to 30cm, ligulate. Fls 1–4 per rac., white, lip to 6cm, broadly ovate, tip conical, narrow, spur to 32cm. Madag.

A. striatum Thouars. St. 5–7cm. Lvs to 24cm, ligulate. Fls 5–7 per rac., white except green spur and column, lip to 1.2cm, ovate, spur 0.4cm. Masc. Is.

A. stylosum Rolfe = *Aerangis stylosa.*

A. superbum Thouars. = *A. eburneum* ssp. *superbum.*

A. teretifolium Ridl. St. to 40cm, pendent, often branched. Lvs to 11cm, terete, grooved. Fls solitary, green-white to white tinged brown, lip to 3cm, carinate-apiculate, long-spurred. Madag.

A. tridactylites Rolfe = *Tridactyle tridactylites.*

A. triquetrum Thouars. St. v. short, branched at base. Lvs to 9cm, ligulate, forming a fan. Fls solitary, white, lip to 2cm suborbicular, apiculate, spur 7cm. Réunion.

A. Veitchii (*A. sesquipedale* × *A. eburneum*). To 1.5m. Lvs to 30cm, strap-shaped. Fls 9–12cm diam.; tep. to 7cm, white tinged green; lip to 7cm, carinate, acuminate; spur to 15cm.

A. vigueri Schltr. St. short. Lvs to 14cm, linear-ligulate. Fls solitary, white or tinged brown, pink or yellow, lip to 7cm, shell-shaped, long-acuminate, long-spurred. Madag.

A. wakefieldii Rolfe = *Solenangis wakefieldii.*

Anguloa Ruiz & Pav. CRADLE ORCHID; TULIP ORCHID. Orchidaceae. 10 terrestrial and epiphytic species. Pbs large, cylindric to ovoid, clustered with leafy sheaths and 2–3 broadly lanceolate, plicate lvs at apex. Fls fragrant, large, waxy, solitary, basal; tep. ovate-lanceolate, strongly cupped enclosing 3-lobed, hinged lip. Colomb. to Peru. Z10.

A. brevilabris Rolfe. Differs from *A. ruckeri* in smaller fls, duller yellow within. Colomb.

A. cliftonii Rolfe. Fls to 9cm, pale yellow to ochre, flecked maroon within. Colomb.

A. clowesii Lindl. CRADLE ORCHID. Fls to 8cm, lemon or golden yellow. Colomb., Venez.

A. eburnea Williams = *A. uniflora.*

A. ruckeri Lindl. Fls to 9cm, ext. olive green to pale bronze, int. ochre spotted blood red or solid maroon or ivory. Colomb.

A. uniflora Ruiz & Pav. Fls to 10.5cm, ivory tinted rose within, spotted red at base; lip ivory mottled chocolate. Throughout genus range.

A. virginalis Lindl. = *A. uniflora.*

✗ Angulocaste. (*Anguloa* × *Lycaste*.) Orchidaceae. Gdn hybrids intermediate in habit between the parents with large, cupped waxy fls in shades of white, rose to red, orange or yellow, sometimes stained gold or marked red.

Anibak *Arrabidaea floribunda.*

Anigozanthos Labill. KANGAROO PAW; CAT'S PAW; AUSTRALIAN SWORD LILY. Haemodoraceae. 11 perenn. herbs. Lvs basal, clumped to equitant, linear-lanceolate to lorate, conduplicate to subterete, grass or iris-like. Scape subterminal, erect, slender, simple or branched; fls 2-ranked, racemose; perianth zygomorphic, saccate at base then tubular, curving, dilating and hooded above with 6 unequal lobes, splitting beneath to form a deep ventral cleavage, exterior felty. W Aus. Z9.

A. bicolor Endl. LITTLE KANGAROO PAW. Lvs 30–40×1–1.25cm, flat, strap-shaped, glab. or puberulous, usually bristly ciliate, mid-green to grey-blue green. Scape 10–60cm, simple; perianth 4–6cm, exterior olive green, with bright red indumentum at base, interior olive to blue-green. Spring–summer. ssp. *minor* (Benth.) Hopper. Lvs 5–10cm. Scape 5–20cm. Perianth 3–4.5cm.

A. bicolor var. *minor* hort. non Benth. = *A. gabrielae.*

A. coccineus Lindl. ex Paxt. = *A. flavidus.*

A. flavidus DC. TALL KANGAROO PAW; EVERGREEN KANGAROO PAW. Lvs 35–100×2–4cm, glab., olive to mid-green. Scape 1–3m, downy, branched; perianth 3.5–5.5cm, sulphur-yellow to lime green, sometimes red, orange or pink or multicoloured, with yellow-green, red or brown indumentum, lobes forward-pointing; sta. orange. Early summer–summer. Hybrids include 'Mini Red': dwarf, compact, with bright red perianth indumentum; 'Pink Joey': seldom exceeding 50cm; fls smoky-pink and 'Werit-Woorata': to 50cm; fls dark red to burgundy and green.

A. gabrielae Domin DWARF KANGAROO PAW. Lvs 3–12×0.1–0.3cm, glab., green to blue-green. Scape 5–20cm, unbranched; perianth 2.5–4cm, constricted above middle, not curved as in *A. bicolor* and rather broad, lobes strongly recurved, green with a red or yellow base.

A. grandiflorus Salisb. = *A. flavidus.*

A. humilis Lindl. COMMON CAT'S PAW. Lvs 15–20×1–1.5cm, not usually persisting, flat, falcate, usually ciliate. Scape 10–50cm,

rarely forked, flocculose; perianth to 5cm, yellow-green with yellow, orange-red or pink indumentum, lobes slightly recurved or with central lobes horizontal, forward-pointing and lat. lobes reflexed. ssp. *chrysanthus* Hopper. Fls pure sulphur yellow.

A. humilis hort. non Lindl. = *A. onycis.*

A. kalbarriensis Hopper. Lvs 12–20×0.3–1cm, flat, falcate, blue-green. Scape 10–20cm, unbranched; perianth 3–6cm, ± falcate, margins decurved, lobes strongly recurved, yellow-green with red-green indumentum, usually red below. Spring.

A. manglesii D. Don. Lvs 10–40×0.5–1.2cm, straight, glab. grey-green. Scape 30–110cm, red-floccose above, simple or few-branched; perianth 7–12cm, curved, lobes reflexed, yellow-green, with lime green indumentum, often red below and on ovary. Spring–early summer. ssp. *quadrans* Hopper. Perianth indumentum orange-red throughout.

A. onycis A.S. George. BRANCHED CAT'S PAW. Lvs 5–15×0.2–1.5cm, broadly keeled, conduplicate, glab., not usually persisting. Scape 15–30cm, floccose, branched; perianth 5–7cm, straight, yellow green, with cream to green or dull red indumentum, lobes spreading. Spring.

A. preissii Endl. ALBANY CAT'S PAW. Lvs 10–25×0.1–0.5cm, subterete, tapering finely, seldom persisting. Scape 20–70cm, red-pubesc., simple or forked; perianth 6.4–8.2cm, curved, cream or yellow-green with lime to orange indumentum deepening to red at base, lobes deeply cut, slender, those in centre forward-pointing, others spreading. Spring–early summer.

A. pulcherrimus Hook. YELLOW KANGAROO PAW. Differs from *A. rufus* in lvs 5–15mm wide, tomentose or glab., and fls with yellow, never red or dark purple, indumentum. Summer.

A. rufus Labill. Lvs 20–40×0.2–0.6cm, flattened, conduplicate, margins bristly or scabrous. Scape 5–150cm, strongly branched red-flocculose above; perianth 3.5–5cm, straight or slightly curved, olive green with deep red, dark purple, or, rarely, yellow indumentum, lobes spreading to reflexed; sta. green. Spring–summer.

A. tyrianthinus Hook. = *A. rufus.*

A. viridis Endl. GREEN KANGAROO PAW. Lvs 5–50×0.1–0.5cm, flat to subterete, glab., dark or grey-green, seldom persisting. Scapes to 0.8m, ± arched, floccose, usually simple; perianth 5–8.5cm, curved, yellow-green with uniform sulphur yellow or lime green indumentum, lobes strongly recurved. Spring–early summer.

A. viridis var. *major* (Benth.) Geer. = *A. bicolor.*

The Black Kangaroo Paw from SW Aus., *Macropidia fuliginosa* is sometimes grown and quite often seen as a cut flower. It has robust, broadly branching pan. of large, sulphur yellow to lime green fls thickly felted in black. The monotypic genus *Macropidia* J.L. Drumm. ex Harvey has been included in *Anigozanthos*, from which it differs chiefly in its deeply cut perianth and large seeds.

Anikab *Macfadyena unguis-cati.*

Animated Oat *Avena sterilis.*

Anisacanthus Nees. Acanthaceae. 8. Subshrubs and shrubs. Lvs opp., entire. Fls in spikes or rac.; bracts short-lived; cor. funnel-form, 4-lobed. SW US, Mex. Z9.

A. wrightii (Torr.) A. Gray. To 1.5m. Lvs to 5cm, oblong to lanceolate. Fls to 3.5cm, vermilion to red-purple in paniculate spikes. Tex., N Mex.

Anise, Aniseed *Pimpinella anisum.*

Aniseed Tree *Backhousia anisata.*

Anise Hyssop *Agastache foeniculum.*

Anise Magnolia *Magnolia salicifolia.*

Anise Root *Osmorhiza longistylis.*

Anise Tree *Illicium.*

Anisodontea Presl. Malvaceae. 19 shrubby perenn. herbs or everg. shrubs, decumbent or ascending. Fls axill., solitary or few in cymose, corymbose or racemose infl.; epical. seg. 3; cal. campanulate; pet. usually 5, spreading, exceeding cal., often with a darker basal spot; sta. united in columns. S Afr. Z9.

A. capensis (L.) Bates. Perenn. woody-based herb to 1m, stellate-hairy. Lvs to 2.5cm, shallowly to deeply 3- or 5-lobed, lobes 1–3-pinnate-lobed, serrate or crenate-dentate. Infl. racemose; pet. 0.8–1.4cm, pale to deep magenta with darker veins and basal spot; staminal column 0.5–0.7cm. Cape Prov.

A. elegans (Cav.) Bates. Shrub to 1.5m, white-, grey- or yellow-pubesc. Lvs to 8cm, dark green to yellow-green, deeply 3- or 5-lobed or trifoliate, dentate-serrate. Infl. racemose; pet. 1.8–3.8cm, pale rose-magenta to magenta, with darker veins towards base, notched; staminal column 0.6–1.1cm. Cape Prov.

A. ×hypomandarum (Sprague) Bates. (Parentage unknown.) Shrub to 3m, br. slender, hairy. Lvs to 3.5cm, lobes 3, spathulate or obovate to obovate-oblong, dentate, stellate-hairy beneath, with simple hairs above. Fls solitary or in groups of 2–3; pet. to 1.5cm, white or flushed pink, with deep purple veins fused at base; staminal column to 0.6cm. Gdn orig.

A. scabrosa (L.) Bates. Shrub to 2m, pubesc., often viscid and aromatic, br. soft-woody. Lvs 2–7cm, linear to orbicular, 3- 5-lobed, crenate to serrate. Fls solitary or 4–5 in axill. cymes, sometimes campanulate; pet. 1.2–2cm, flushed rose-purple or deep rose magenta, rarely white, more intensely coloured toward base, with a diffuse-margined spot. Cape Prov.

→*Malvastrum* and *Sphaeralcea*.

Anisotome Hook. f. Umbelliferae. 13 perenn. herbs. Lvs rigid, pinnate or delicate, fern-like, basal. Infl. robust; umbels large, compound, involucrate; fls white to purple-red. NZ, Subantarctic Is. Z8.

A. aromatica Hook. f. To 50cm. Lf blades to 40cm, pinnate; lfts 6–12 pairs, cuneate-orbicular, tough, toothed to pinnatifid, seg. linear. NZ.

A. aromatica var. *dissecta* Allan = *A. flexuosa*.

A. capillifolia (Cheesem.) Ckn. To 25cm. Lf blades to 20cm, 3–4-pinnate; pinnae 8–12 pairs, ovate, seg. linear. NZ.

A. flexuosa Dawson. To 3m. Lf blades to 15cm, 2-pinnate; pinnae 7–12 pairs, ovate, seg. linear. NZ.

A. haastii (F. Muell. ex Hook. f.) Ckn. & Laing. To 60cm. Lf blades to 55cm, 3–4-pinnate; pinnae 8–12 pairs, ovate-lanceolate, seg. linear. NZ.

A. imbricata (Hook. f.) Ckn. Compact, cushion-forming. Lf blade 1–4cm, pinnate; pinnae overlapping, linear-ovate, finely pinnatifid. NZ.

A. latifolia Hook. f. To 2m. Lf blades to 60cm, 2–3-pinnate, leathery; pinnae 5–10 pairs, ovate-lanceolate, seg. toothed. Auckland, Campbell Is.

A. pilifera (Hook. f.) Ckn. & Laing. To 45cm. Lf blades to 30cm, pinnate; pinnae 4–10 pairs, overlapping, ovate, tough, serrately incised to pinnatifid. NZ.

→*Aciphylla* and *Ligusticum*.

Anisum Hill.

A. vulgare Gaertn. = *Pimpinella anisum*.

Annatto *Bixa orellana*.

Annona L. Annonaceae. 100 trees and shrubs, everg. or semideciduous. Lvs entire, petiolate, aromatic. Fls solitary or in clusters, ♂ ; sep. 3; pet. 6, fleshy inner whorl reduced; sta. and pistils numerous. Fr. a syncarp, usually green and leathery, checkered with outlines of fleshy carpels. Trop. Amer. and Afr. Z9.

A. cherimola Mill. CHERIMOYA; CHIRIMOYA; CUSTARD APPLE; CHERIMALLA. To 7m. Lvs to 15cm, ovate to lanceolate, acuminate, velutinous beneath. Fls to 2.5cm, fragrant, exterior pale yellow- to brown-pubesc., interior spotted purple at base. Fr. to 20cm, conical to subglobose, pale green, smooth or obscurely tubercled; pulp white. Peru and Ecuad., widely nat.

A. diversifolia Safford. ILAMA; ANONA BLANCA. To 8m. Lvs to 14cm, elliptic to oblanceolate; petioles with leafy bracts. Fls to 2.5cm, maroon. Fr. to 16cm, ellipsoid to subglobose, pale green, often flushing pink, strongly tubercled, rarely smooth. Mex., C Amer. 'Imery': large, pink-fleshed.

A. glabra L. POND APPLE. To 10m. Lvs to 15cm, ovate to oblong, acute or briefly acuminate. Fls to 3cm, fragrant, yellow-white, interior marked red at base. Fr. to 15cm, globose to ovoid, ripening yellow; pulp peach to orange, highly fragrant. Trop. Amer., W Afr.

A. muricata L. SOURSOP; GUANABANA; PRICKLY CUSTARD APPLE. To 7m. Lvs 10–25cm, obovate to elliptic. Fls solitary to 3cm, nodding, yellow-green. Fr. to 20cm, irregularly ovoid, dark green with longitudinally arranged, curved prickles; pulp white. C Amer., W Indies. Cvs with smooth, melting flesh include 'Cuban Fiberless' and 'Whitman Fiberless'.

A. reticulata L. BULLOCK'S HEART; CUSTARD APPLE. To 10m. Lvs to 15cm, oblong-lanceolate to lanceolate, glabrescent beneath. Fls to 3cm, clustered, yellow-white to yellow-green, outer pet. with purple blotch at base. Fr. to 12cm diam., often globose, ripening red-green, fairly smooth and marked with outlines of obscure carpels; pulp yellow, granular. Subtrop. and trop. Amer.

A. squamosa L. SUGAR APPLE; CUSTARD APPLE; SWEETSOP. To 8m. Lvs to 12cm, oblong-lanceolate to narrow-elliptic, somewhat glaucous. Fls to 2.5cm, clustered, yellow-green, interior of outer pet. spotted purple near base. Fr. to 10cm diam., roughly globose, olive green, glaucous, coarsely tubercled and bulging and splitting along the outline of the carpels; pulp white. Trop. Amer. 'Seedless': seedless. 'Ubol': hard skin prevents fr. splitting.

A. cvs. The Atemoya, a hybrid between *A. cherimola* and *A. squamosa* combines the best qualities of both parents, succeeding in warmer regions than *A. cherimola*. A widespread cv., 'African Pride', is dwarf and fruits twice a year; other cvs include 'Bradley', 'Geffner', 'Page', 'Pink's Mammoth' (v. large) and 'Priestly'.

ANNONACEAE Juss. 128/2050. *Annona, Artabotrys, Asimina, Cananga, Monodora, Xylopia*.

Annual Beard Grass *Polypogon monspeliensis*.
Annual Fern *Anogramma leptophylla*.
Annual Phlox *Phlox drummondii*.
Annual Wild Rice *Zizania aquatica*.

Anoda Cav. Malvaceae. 10 ann. or perenn. herbs or subshrubs. Lvs variable even on the same plant, petiolate, unlobed or palmately lobed. Fls solitary or paired in erect rac. or pan.; epical. 0; sep. 5; pet. 5, spreading, obovate; sta. united into a tubular column. Trop. Amer. Z9.

A. cristata (L.) Schldl. Ann. or short-lived herbaceous perenn. to 1.5m, glab. or sparsely hairy. Lvs unlobed or 3-, 5- or 7-lobed, entire or serrate-dentate. Fls axill., solitary or paired, pet. 8–20mm, white, lavender or purple-blue. SW US, Mex., W Indies to S Amer., nat. Trop. 'Opal Cup': to 1m; lvs marked purple; fls pale lilac with iridescent sheen and darker veins. 'Silver Cup' and 'Snowdrop': fls white.

A. dilleniana Cav. = *A. cristata*.
A. hastata Cav. = *A. cristata*.
A. lavateroides Medik. = *A. cristata*.
A. thurberi A. Gray. Perenn., glab. to puberulent. Lvs cordate-ovate, dentate, upper lvs often lanceolate, hastate. Fls numerous, in densely branched leafy pan.; pet. blue or purple, 4–6mm. New Mex., S Ariz., Mex.
A. triangularis (Willd.) DC. = *A. cristata*.
A. wrightii A. Gray. Ann. herb, upper lvs smaller, deltoid-ovate to lanceolate or hastate, roughly villous, obtuse, lower lvs to 4cm, often cordate. Fls long-stalked; pet. 8–12mm, yellow or yellow-orange, often purple at base. New Mex., S Ariz., Mex.

Anoectochilus Bl. JEWEL ORCHID. Orchidaceae. 25 small orchids. Rhiz. creeping, fleshy. St. ascending. Lvs to 6cm, ovate-cordate to elliptic, alt. or in loose rosette, velvety-papillose, conspicuously veined. Fls small, white, cream or green in slender term. spikes. Asia to W Pacific. Z10.

A. regalis Bl. Lvs dark green netted gold above, purple beneath. S India, Sri Lanka.
A. reinwardtii Bl. Lvs black-red netted gold above. Sumatra, Java.
A. roxburghii Wallich (Lindl.). Lvs black-green netted copper with central broad stripe of gold on lime. N India.
A. sanderianus hort. = *Macodes sanderiana*.
A. sikkimensis King & Pantl. Lvs black-maroon netted pale gold above, dull red-green beneath. Sikkim.

Anogra Spach.
A. albicaulis (Pursh) Britt. = *Oenothera albicaulis*.
A. californica Small = *Oenothera californica*.
A. pallida (Lindl.) Britt. = *Oenothera pallida*.

Anogramma Link. Adiantaceae. 7 small, short-lived, delicate ferns, with ephemeral sporophytes and tuberous perennating prothalli. Rhiz. rudimentary. Stipe slender, fronds 1–4× pinnate, pinnules decurrent. Temp. regions. Z9.

A. chaerophylla (Desv.) Link. Stipe 2.5–10cm; fronds 5–10cm, 2-pinnate; pinnules flabellate, lobes deltoid. C & S Amer., W Indies.

A. leptophylla (L.) Link. ANNUAL FERN; JERSEY FERN. Stipe tinted red, 2.5–10cm; fronds to 7.5cm, 2–4-pinnate; pinnules flabellate, lobes oblong. Fronds die back to tuberous gametophyte. Cosmop.

A. schizophylla (Bak. ex Jenman) Diels. = *Pityrogramma schizophylla*.

Anoiganthus Bak.
A. breviflorus Harv. = *Cyrtanthus breviflorus*.

Anomalesia N.E. Br.
A. cunonia (L.) N.E. Br. = *Gladiolus cunonius*.
A. saccata (Klatt) N.E. Br. = *Gladiolus saccatus*.
A. splendens (Sweet) N.E. Br. = *Gladiolus splendens*.

Anomatheca Ker-Gawl. Iridaceae. 6 cormous perenn. herbs. Lvs basal and cauline, lanceolate-ensiform. Flowering st. simple or branched; bracts 2, unequal; perianth zygomorphic, seg. arranged in two groups of three, tube straight or curved, slightly expanded towards apex; anth. and style exserted. S & C Afr.

A. cruenta Lindl. = *A. laxa*.

A. laxa (Thunb.) Goldbl. To 30cm. Fls 2–5, to 2cm across, red, white or pale blue, with red or purple marking at base of lower 3 seg.; perianth tube straight, pale green, striped red. S Afr., Moz.

A. viridis (Ait.) Goldbl. To 35cm. Fls 2–10, green, sometimes fragrant; perianth tube 2–3cm, curved; seg. 1–2cm, reflexed. S Afr. (Cape Prov.).

→*Lapeirousia*.

Anona Blanca *Annona diversifolia.*

Anopteris Prantl. ex Diels. Pteridaceae. 1 small terrestrial fern. Rhiz. short, erect, with dark scales. Stipes 8–25cm; frond-blade 10–30cm, deltate or ovate-deltate, fertile fronds slightly narrower and more stiffly erect than sterile, 2–4-pinnate, dark green, glab. and firm. Bermuda, Hispan., Jam. Z10.

A. hexagona (L.) C. Chr.

→*Pteris*.

Anopterus Labill. Grossulariaceae. 2 everg. shrubs to trees. Fls usually 6-merous, waxy, white, sometimes tinted rose, campanulate, in short, erect term. rac. Aus., Tasm. Z8.

A. glandulosus Labill. TASMANIAN LAUREL. Shrub or small tree to 10m. Lvs 6–18cm, obovate to lanceolate-elliptic, tapered to stout stalks, coarsely glandular-toothed, leathery, dark shining green. Infl. 5–15cm; fls 2cm diam. Spring. Tasm.

A. macleayanus F. Muell. Resembles *A. glandulosus*, but to 15m; lvs to 30cm, less leathery. Queensld, NSW.

Anredera Juss. Basellaceae. 10 tuberous lianes or twining herbs. Lvs ovate, cordate or elliptic, fleshy. Fls small in axill. spikes or rac.; perianth seg. 5, basally united. S Amer., nat. S Eur. Z9.

A. cordifolia (Ten.) Steenis. MADEIRA VINE; MIGNONETTE VINE. Tuber oblong.Stems twining to 6m. lvs 2.5–10cm, ovate-lanceolate, base cordate; petioles often bearing tubers in axils. Rac. to 30cm; fls white, fragrant. Braz. to N Arg. Most plants grown as *A. baselloides* are *A. cordifolia*. *A. baselloides* (H.B.K.) Ten. has a simple, not trifid style.

→*Boussingaultia*.

Ansellia Lindl. Orchidaceae. 1 variable epiphytic orchid. Pbs to 60cm, narrowly cylindric or cane-like. Lvs 15–50cm, lanceolate-oblong, ribbed, alt. on pbs. Pan. lax, term.; tep. elliptic-oblanceolate, to 3.5cm, spreading, yellow variably spotted or blotched brown to black. Trop. & S Afr. Z9.

A. africana Lindl. LEOPARD ORCHID.

A. gigantea Rchb. f. = *A. africana*.

A. nilotica (Bak.) N.E. Br. = *A. africana*.

Antarctic Beech *Nothofagus antarctica.*
Antelope Bush *Purshia.*
Antelope Ears *Platycerium.*

Antennaria Gaertn. CAT'S EARS; EVERLASTING; PUSSY-TOES; LADIES' TOBACCO. Compositae. *c*45 small woolly, perenn. herbs. Lvs in basal rosettes and smaller, narrower on st. Cap. discoid, small, solitary or in dense corymbs; phyllaries imbricate, apex white or coloured, scarious; flts usually white. N temp. regions, Asia and S Amer.

A. alpina (L.) Gaertn. Mat-forming, to 15cm. Lvs to 1.5cm, apiculate, grey-tomentose, linear-oblong to oblong. Cap. 1–5, sessile; phyllaries dark green-brown towards apex; flts cream. Midsummer. N Amer., N Eur. to N Russia. Z2.

A. anaphaloides Rydb. Tufted or stoloniferous, to 50cm. Lvs to 15cm, lanceolate to linear, acute, tomentose. Cap. several in a lax corymb; phyllaries tipped white to pale pink. Early summer. Canada to C US. Z3.

A. aprica Greene = *A. parvifolia*.

A. campestris Rydb. = *A. neglecta*.

A. candida E. Greene = *A. dioica*.

A. carpatica (Wahlenb.) Bluff & Fingerh. Sometimes tufted, to 15cm. Lvs 10cm, oblanceolate, to linear, sparsely tomentose. Cap. 2–6; phyllaries with dark centre, brown above; flts cream, sometimes purple-tinged. Summer. Eur. mts, Arc. Z2.

A. chilensis Rémy. = *A. rosea*.

A. dioica (L.) Gaertn. Mat-forming, densely tomentose, stoloniferous. Lvs to 4cm, spathulate, obtuse or apiculate, grey above, white-tomentose beneath. Cap. in groups of 2–15; phyllaries pink-white. Midsummer. Eur., N Amer., N Asia. var. **hyperborea** (D. Don) DC. Lvs wider, densely tomentose, throughout. 'Nyewood': compact; infl. deep rose-pink. 'Rosea': infl. rose-pink. 'Rubra': infl. dark red. Z5.

A. dioica var. *tomentosa* hort. = *A. dioica*.

A. dioica var. *rosea* (E. Greene) D.C. Eaton = *A. rosea*.

A. fallax E. Greene = *A. parlinii* ssp. *fallax*.

A. gaspensis Fern. = *A. rosea* ssp. *pulvinata*.

A. geyeri A. Gray. St. several, erect to 15cm. Lvs to 3cm, oblanceolate, tomentose. Involucre lanate; phyllaries usually with pink, scarious tips. W N Amer. Z5.

A. hyperborea D. Don = *A. dioica* var. *hyperborea*.

A. imbricata E.E. Nels. = *A. rosea* ssp. *rosea*.

A. lanata (Hook.) Greene. Perenn. compactly branched, tomentose, to 20cm. Lvs 3–10cm, tufted. Cap. several in a compact cyme; phyllaries dark brown or green-black below, paler toward apex. W N Amer. Z5.

A. macrophylla hort. = *A. microphylla*.

A. magellanica Schultz-Bip. = *A. rosea*.

A. margaritacea R. Br. = *Anaphalis margaritacea*.

A. media E. Greene = *A. alpina*.

A. microphylla Rydb. Slender, to 40cm, finely pubesc., usually stoloniferous. Lvs to 1cm, spathulate to linear-oblong. Cap. in an open corymb, phyllaries green-yellow tinged, margins white, scarious. Summer. C & SW US. Z4.

A. monocephala DC. = *A. alpina*.

A. neglecta Greene. 7–30cm, stolons slender. Lvs to 6cm, oblanceolate, glab. above. St. lvs linear. Phyllaries green to red, tipped white. S Canada to Calif. var. **attenuata** (Fern.) Cronq. Stolons short, lvs somewhat petiolate. var. **gaspensis** Fern. Stolons short, lvs smaller than those of var. *attenuata*.

A. neodioica Greene. St. to 40cm. Lvs 10–40×5–15mm, rosetted, obovate-spathulate to spathulate. Cap. corymbose; phyllaries brown below. SC Canada. Z2.

A. obovata E.E. Nels. = *A. plantaginifolia*.

A. oxyphylla E. Greene = *A. rosea* ssp. *rosea*.

A. parlinii Fern. Mat-forming, stoloniferous, to 40cm. Lvs to 6cm, obovate to spathulate, glab. above, hairy beneath. Cap. 4–8; phyllaries occas. tipped white. SE US. ssp. *fallax* (Greene) Bayer & Stebb. Basal lvs tomentose above. Z3.

A. parvifolia Nutt. Mat-forming, to 25cm, stoloniferous. Lvs to 3cm, spathulate to oblanceolate, white-grey tomentose. Cap. scapose in a small corymbose cyme; phyllaries white or pink-rose. Late spring–summer. W US and SW Canada. Z3.

A. plantaginifolia (L.) Richardson. LADIES' TOBACCO. Stoloniferous, to 40cm. Lvs to 10cm, ovate-elliptic to obovate, 3–5-nerved, tomentose to glabrate. Cap. scapose, in a cyme-like cluster; phyllaries white above, tinged pink below. Spring–summer. N Amer. Z3.

A. rosea Greene. Mat-forming, tufted, to 50cm. Lvs to 4cm, oblanceolate to spathulate, acute, grey-tomentose. Cap. small, several in a corymbose cluster; phyllaries cream to rose. Late spring–summer. Mts of W N Amer. ssp. *rosea*. 10–40cm; lvs 1–4cm; sep. ssp. *pulvinata* (Greene) R. Bayer. 4–17cm; lvs 1–1.8cm. Z4.

A. speciosa E.E. Nels. = *A. rosea*.

A. steetziana Turcz. = *Leontopodium leontopodioides*.

A. tomentosa hort. = *A. dioica*.

A. triplinervis Sims = *Anaphalis triplinervis*.

Anthemis L. DOG FENNEL. Compositae. 100 hairy aromatic herbs or dwarf shrubs. St. usually branched. Lvs usually 1–3-pinnatisect. Cap. solitary, term., pedunculate; involucre hemispherical; ray flts with spreading 2–3-toothed ligules, white or yellow, rarely purple; disc flts, tubular, 5-toothed, yellow, rarely purple. Medit. to Iran.

A. altissima L. Erect, subglabrous ann., to 120cm. Lvs 3–7cm, ovate, 2–3-pinnatisect, lobes to 4×1mm. Cap. 2.5–5cm diam.; peduncle to 7.5cm; ligules to 2cm. S Eur., Crimea, Cauc., C Asia. Z6.

A. arabica L. = *Cladanthus arabicus*.

A. carpatica Willd. = *A. cretica* ssp. *carpatica*.

A. cinerea Pančić. Resembles *A. cretica* ssp. *carpatica* but with white-silky down. SE Eur., E Pyren. Z6.

A. cota L. = *A. altissima*.

A. cotula L. MAYWEED; STINKING CHAMOMILE. Aromatic, glab. or sparsely pubesc. ann. to 70cm. Lvs to 6.5×3cm, ovate or ovate-oblong, 2–3-pinnatisect with narrow linear lobes, sometimes fleshy. Cap. 1.2–3cm diam.; peduncle to 15cm; ligules 0.5–1.4cm. Summer. Eur. to N Afr., Syr. and Iran. Z5.

A. cretica L. Perenn., cushion-forming, sometimes with grey or white down. St. to 30cm, usually simple. Lvs to 5cm, pinnatisect, often folded along rachis, petiolate. Involucre to 1.5cm diam.; ray flts white, ligules to 1.25cm, disc flts yellow. Spring–summer. S Eur. (mts) to Turk. ssp. *cretica*. St. erect, to 30cm. Lvs to 8cm, glandular-spotted. Cap. to 4.5cm diam.; ligules to 1.7cm. ssp. *carpatica* (Willd.) Grierson. Usually glab. St. to 15cm. Lf seg. 1mm across, entire or 3-fid, involucre to 1.3cm diam.; phyllaries edged dark brown or black. ssp. *pontica* (Willd.) Grierson St. to 20cm. Lvs 3–4cm, simple or 3-fid above, seg. 7–8mm, involucre to 1cm diam.; phyllaries edged white or pale brown. Z6.

A. cupaniana Tod. ex Nyman = *A. punctata* ssp. *cupaniana*.

A. frutescens hort. & Siebert & Voss = *Argyranthemum frutescens*.

A. haussknechtii Boiss. & Reut. Sparsely pubesc., decumbent ann., 8–20cm. Lvs to 4.5cm, 3-pinnatisect, ovate, lobes to 3mm; involucre to 1.25cm diam.; ligules to 7.5mm, disc flts 3mm, turning purple. Spring. Syr., Iran, Turk. Z7.

A. macedonica Boiss. & Orph. Ann. or bienn. to 32cm. Lvs to 2cm, 1–2-pinnatisect, with gland. spots, lobes linear, mucronate. Cap. to 2.5cm diam.; peduncles long and thin; ligules c9mm. C & S Bulg., NE Greece. Z7.

A. marschalliana Willd. Grey or yellow-silky perenn., to 30cm. Lvs to 7cm, 2-pinnatisect, obovate or obovate. Involucre to 1.3cm diam.; phyllaries brown- or black-margined; ligules to 6mm, yellow. Summer. NE Anatolia, S Cauc. Z7.

A. mixta L. = *Chamaemelum mixta*.

A. montana L. = *A. cretica* ssp. *cretica*.

A. nobilis L. = *Chamaemelum nobile*.

A. pedunculata Bory & Chaub. = *Anacyclus clavatus*.

A. punctata Vahl. Perenn., glab. to white-silky, woody at base. St. to 60cm, usually branched. Lvs to 12×5.5cm, 1–2-pinnatisect, glandular-punctate, lobes to 7mm wide. Cap. to 6cm diam.; peduncle to 2.5cm; ligules to 24mm, white. Eur., NW Afr. ssp. *cupaniana* (Tod. ex Nyman) R. Fernandes. Lvs silver-grey. Sicily. Z7.

A. purpurascens Nyman = *Anacyclus radiatus*.

A. rigescens hort. = *A. triumfettii*.

A. rosea Sm. Erect or decumbent pubesc. ann. St. to 20cm. Lvs 2–3-pinnatisect, to 2cm, ovate-oblong, lobes v. narrow. Involucre to 1cm diam.; ligules to 1cm, pink-mauve. Spring–summer. E Medit. Z6.

A. sancti-johannis Turrill. Tufted, sparsely woolly perenn. to 90cm. Lvs pinnatisect, oblong, tipped white; rachis toothed. Cap. 4–5cm diam.; peduncle long; ligules to 1.5cm, orange-yellow. SW Bulg. Z6.

A. styriaca Vest. Differs from *A. cretica* ssp. *carpatica* in st. to only 16cm, lf lobes wider, cap. larger, ligules broader. Austria. Z6.

A. tinctoria L. DYERS' CHAMOMILE; YELLOW CHAMOMILE. Sparsely hairy to white-woolly perenn. to 60cm. Lvs 2–3-bipinnatisect, 1–5cm, oblanceolate or obovate with oblong to linear seg. and involute lobes. Cap. 3cm diam.; involucre to 2cm diam.; ligules yellow to pale cream, to 1cm. Spring–autumn. Eur., Cauc., Iran. 'Alba': forming a low-spreading mound 45–60cm high; lvs dark green, finely divided; rays yellow, disc white. 'Beauty of Grallagh': to 90cm; st. erect; lvs dark green, finely divided; fls bright gold. 'E.C. Buxton': to 60cm, bushy; lvs dark green, fern-like; fls pale yellow. 'Grallagh Gold': 60–90cm; fls golden-orange. 'Sauce Hollandaise': to 60cm; lvs dark green, finely divided; fls v. pale yellow changing to creamy white. 'Wargrave': st. to 90cm; lvs dark green; similar to 'E.C. Buxton' but fls slightly deeper yellow. Z6.

A. tinctoria var. *triumfettii* L. = *A. triumfettii*.

A. triumfettii (L.) All. Resembles *A. tinctoria* but to 60cm, br. fastigiate above; lvs 3–4cm with flat seg.; involucre to 1.8cm diam.; ligules white, to 18mm. Summer–early autumn. N Medit. to Cauc. Z7.

A. tuberculata Boiss. Woolly perenn., sometimes short-lived, to 45cm. Lvs to 5cm, 1–2-pinnatifid, glandular-punctate. Cap. to 4.5cm diam.; peduncle to 1.6cm. C & S Spain. Z7.

→*Santolina*.

Anthericum L. Liliaceae (Asphodelaceae). 50 perenn. fleshy-rooted herbs. St. simple. Lvs radical, grasslike. Rac. or pan. scapose; bracts usually small, scarious; perianth rotate, white; tep. oblong-elliptic, connate or free, with 3 green-tinted veins. Late spring–early summer. S Eur., Turk., Afr. Z7.

A. algeriense Boiss. & Reut. = *A. liliago*.

A. bulbosum R. Br. = *Bulbinopsis bulbosa*.

A. incurvum Thunb. = *Bulbine frutescens* var. *incurva*.

A. latifolium L. f. = *Bulbine latifolia*.

A. liliago L. ST. BERNARD'S LILY. To 90cm. Lvs to 40cm. Fls to 2cm across in slender rac., star-like; style curved upwards, ovary green. S Eur. 'Major': st. 90cm; fls pure white, large, opening flat.

A. liliastrum L. = *Paradisea liliastrum*.

A. plumosum Ruiz & Pav. = *Trichopetalum plumosum*.

A. ramosum L. To 60cm. Ls to 40cm. Fls to 1.5cm across in pan.; style straight, ovary yellow. S Eur.

A. rostratum Jacq. = *Bulbine frutescens* var. *rostrata*.

A. semibarbatum R. Br. = *Bulbinopsis semibarbata*.

→*Phalangium*.

Antheropeas Rydb. DWARF DAISY. Compositae. 5 small ann. herbs. Cap. radiate. N Amer.

A. wallacei (A. Gray) Rydb. 1–15cm, diffusely branched or tufted. Lvs 7–15mm, obovate-spathulate, entire or lobed above. Cap. scattered, short-stalked; ray flts 3–4mm, 5–10, golden or yellow, disc flts yellow. Spring–early summer. SW US, N Mex. var. *rubellum* (A. Gray) A. Gray. Ray flts rose or purple, rarely white.

→*Eriophyllum*.

Anthocercis Labill. Solanaceae. 9 everg. shrubs. Fls axill., solitary, or in cymes or pan., somewhat zygomorphic, subtended by bracts; cal. campanulate to cupular, 5-lobed; cor. tubular to campanulate, lobes 5, spreading. Aus., Tasm. Z9.

A. albicans Cunn. = *Cyphanthera albicans*.

A. ilicifolia Hook. Erect glab. shrub, to 2.5m+. Br. few, tinged purple. Lvs to 8cm, spathulate-ovate, dentate. Fls paniculate; cor. to yellow, lobes to 1.8cm. Summer. W Aus.

A. littorea Labill. Erect shrub, to 3m, densely branched. Lvs to 6cm, obovate. Fls solitary to clustered; cor. to 3.2cm, yellow, streaked purple to purple brown, lobes to 2.5cm. Summer. W Aus.

A. viscosa R. Br. STICKY TAIL FLOWER. Erect to spreading shrub, to 2.5m+, viscid-pubesc. Lvs to 6cm, ovate to obovate, denticulate to entire. Fls cymose; cor. cream, streaked green to purple to 5cm. Summer. W Aus.

A. zambesiaca Bak. = *Cyphanthera albicans*.

Anthocleista Afzel. ex R. Br. Loganiaceae. 14 trees, shrubs and climbers. Infl. a 1–5-branched cyme, terminal, upright; lower bracts leaflike, others v. small; fls large, regular, sweetly fragrant; sep. 4, free or connate at base, ± circular; cor. funnel-form, fleshy, lobes 8–16, bent backwards; sta. alt. to cor. lobes, protruding; fil. v. short, usually united into a tube. Trop. Afr., Comoros, Madag. Z10.

A. grandiflora Gilg. CABBAGE TREE. Tree, to 35m. Bole straight; br. short, high up; bark grey-brown. Lvs to 135cm, narrow-obovate, papery to leathery, veins conspicuous. Cor. to 7cm, creamy white, lobes 11–13, narrow-elliptic, spreading or reflexed.

A. zambesiaca Bak. = *A. grandiflora*.

Antholyza L.

A. abbreviata (Andrews) Pers. = *Gladiolus abbreviatus*.

A. aethiopica L. = *Chasmanthe aethiopica*.

A. bicolor Gasp. = *Chasmanthe bicolor*.

A. burchellii N.E. Br. = *Tritoniopsis burchellii*.

A. caffra Ker-Gawl. ex Bak. = *Tritoniopsis caffra*.

A. cunonia L. = *Gladiolus cunonius*.

A. floribunda Salisb. = *Chasmanthe floribunda*.

A. intermedia Bak. = *Tritoniopsis intermedia*.

A. nervosa Thunb. = *Tritoniopsis nervosa*.

A. paniculata Klatt. = *Crocosmia paniculata*.

A. plicata L. f. = *Babiana thunbergii*.

A. priorii N.E. Br. = *Gladiolus priorii*.

A. pulchra Bak. = *Tritoniopsis pulchra*.

A. quadrangularis Burm. f. = *Gladiolus quadrangularis*.

A. revoluta (Pers.) Bak. = *Gladiolus watsonius* or *G. priorii*.

A. ringens L. = *Babiana ringens*.

A. saccata (Klatt) Bak. = *Gladiolus saccatus*.

A. schweinfurthii Bak. = *Gladiolus schweinfurthii*.

A. splendens (Sweet) Steud. = *Gladiolus splendens*.

A. vittigera Salisb. = *Chasmanthe aethiopica*.

A. watsonioides (Bak.) Bak. = *Gladiolus watsonioides*.

Anthospermum L. Rubiaceae. c40 small shrubs or herbs. Fls sessile, axill. and solitary or term. and paniculate; floral bracts to 3; cal. tube obovoid or ellipsoid, 2–4-lobed or 4–5-toothed, 1 or 2 lobes sometimes forming a leaf-like appendage; cor. bell- or funnel-shaped, lobes 4–5, spreading; sta. 3–5, exserted. Trop. Afr., Madag. Z9.

A. aethiopicum L. Heath-like, everg. shrub to 1m. Br. erect, clustered, downy. Lvs to 12mm, opposite or 3-whorled, linear-lanceolate to filiform, revolute. Fls clustered in leafy spikes to 5cm; cor. 4-lobed, white or pale yellow. Summer. S Afr.

Anthoxanthum L. VERNAL GRASS. Gramineae. 15 ann. or perenn. grasses. Lvs flat, aromatic when crushed. Pan. dense, spikelets somewhat laterally compressed; flts 3 per spikelet, 2 sterile. Eurasia, E Afr., N & S Amer. Zone 7.

A. gracile Biv. Ann. To 30cm, forming loose tussocks. Lf blades arching, downy above. Pan. ovate, silver-grey pan.; spikelets to 1.2cm. Spring. Medit.

A. odoratum Lagasca. SWEET VERNAL GRASS. Perenn. to 60cm, most parts sweetly scented. St. clustered. Lvs glab., to 1cm wide, becoming straw-coloured. Pan. to 8cm; spikelets to 1cm. Spring. Eurasia.

Anthriscus Pers. Umbelliferae. 12 ann., bienn. or perenn. herbs. Lvs 2–3-pinnate to ternate. Fls small, white in compound umbels. Eur., N Afr., Asia. Z7.

A. cerefolium (L.) Hoffm. CHERVIL.   Ann. to 60cm. St. furrowed, hairy at nodes. Lvs 2–3-pinnate; seg. to 1cm, ovate, toothed to pinnatifid, hairy beneath. Umbels 2–6-rayed. Eur., W Asia.

A. sylvestris (L.) Hoffm. COW PARSLEY; KECK.   Bienn. or perenn. to 150cm. St. furrowed, glab. above. Lvs ferny, 3-pinnate; seg. to 3cm, ovate, pinnatifid. Umbels 6–12-rayed. Eur., W Asia, N Afr. 'Moonlit Night': to 1m; lvs bronze-green turning deep purple. 'Ravenswing': lvs brown-purple.
→*Chaerophyllum*.

Anthurium Schott. FLAMINGO FLOWER; TAILFLOWER. Araceae. *c*900 often epiphytic everg. perennials. Roots adventitious. St. usually short, erect, sometimes elongate, climbing. Lvs entire or palmately lobed, ± coriaceous; petiole pulvinate at apex. Scape long; spathe persistent, flat to hooded, erect, spreading or reflexed, margins not overlapping at base; spadix cylindric, often tapering, sometimes twisted. Berries globose. Trop. Amer. Z10.

A. acaule misapplied = *A. crenatum*.

A. aemulum Schott = *A. pentaphyllum* var. *bombacifolium*.

A. amnicola Dressler. Lvs lanceolate-elliptic to oblong-elliptic, acute, sparsely gland. above; petiole to 9cm. Scape to 40cm; spathe narrow- to broad-ovate, violet-purple; spadix to 2cm, dark violet-purple, fragrant. Fr. white. Panama.

A. andraeanum André. FLAMINGO FLOWER.   Lvs 17–50×11–22cm, ovate, sagittate, coriaceous, dark green; petiole to 60cm. Scape to 1m+; spathe 6–15cm, broad-ovate to rounded, cordate, bright red, bullate, veins prominent; spadix to 9cm, white to yellow. Fr. red. Colomb., Ecuad. 'Anitas' (*A. andraeanum* ×*A. antrophyoides*): 'Aztec': spathe red, spadix golden yellow. 'Brazilian Surprize': spathe orange to red, spadix white later gold. 'Flamingo': spathe large, bright pink, spadix white later ivory. 'Nova': spathe white turning dark pink, spadix lemon.

A. bakeri Hook. f. Lvs 19–55×3–9cm, narrow-lanceolate-elliptic to narrow-oblanceolate, coriaceous, dark green; petiole to 17cm. Scape to 30cm; spathe 5cm, oblong-lanceolate, reflexed, yellow-green; spadix to 20cm, cream. Fr. scarlet. Summer. Guat. to Colomb.

A. berriozabalense Matuda.   Lvs to 25×20cm, reflexed, triangular, subhastate, basal lobes widely spaced; petioles to 40cm. Spathe to 5cm, narrow, green; spadix nearly equalling spathe. S Mex.

A. bogotense Schott. Lvs to 45×30cm, sagittate-lanceolate, basal lobes v. expanded, olive-green; petioles to 60cm. Scape to 15cm; spathe to 7.5cm, ovate-lanceolate, dull white; spadix short. N S Amer.

A. ×*carneum* Reg. = *A.* ×*ferrierense*.

A. ×*chelsiense* N.E. Br. (*A. andraeanum* ×*A. veitchii*.)   Lvs ovate. Spathe 13cm, broadly cordate, cuspidate, deep crimson, glossy; spadix 8cm, white below, yellow above. Gdn origin.

A. clarinervium Matuda. Lvs 12.5×10cm, ovate, deeply-cordate, velvety, dark green above, veins pale green; petioles to 16cm. Scape to 38cm, erect; spathe to 6.5cm, lanceolate, pale green; spadix green, suffused violet. Fr. orange. S Mex.

A. clavigerum Poepp. & Endl.   Climber to 4m. Lvs 80–200cm across, palmate, lfts 7–13, sinuous or pinnate with 3–4 lobes per side, bright green; petiole to 1m. Scape pendent, to 90cm; spathe 30–65cm, lanceolate, violet-purple; spadix to 75cm, pale purple. Fr. purple. N S Amer.

A. cordatum K. Koch & Sello = *A. leuconeurum*.

A. corrugatum Sodiro.   Climber. Lvs to 60×40cm, deflexed, broad-ovate to elliptic, sagittate-cordate, bullate; petiole to 90cm. Scape equalling petiole; spathe to 20cm, lanceolate, reflexed, green; spadix 15–20cm, pale green. Colomb., Ecuad.

A. crassinervium (Jacq.) Schott. Lvs 45–110×9–35cm, rosulate, oblanceolate to obovate, acuminate; petiole to 20cm, almost quadrangular. Scape to 60cm; spathe to 15cm, oblong-lanceolate, spreading, green; spadix to 20cm, dull red-violet. Fr. red. Venez.

A. crassinervium misapplied = *A. schlechtendalii*.

A. crenatum Kunth.   Lvs 40–100×6–30cm, rosulate, oblong-lanceolate to oblanceolate; petiole 5–25cm. Scape to 1m; spathe 6–15cm, linear-lanceolate, red-brown, soon withering; spadix 10–35cm, green-brown, fragrant. Fr. obovoid, red. Carib.

A. crystallinum Lind. & André.   Lvs 30–45×25–30cm, ovate to narrow-ovate, cordate, acute to acuminate, deflexed, silky emerald green above, veins crystalline white, suffused pink-bronze when young; petiole to 20cm. Scape to 60cm; spathe to 13.5cm, oblong-lanceolate, reflexed, red-purple; spadix to 19cm, yellow-green. Fr. white, tinged red-purple. Panama to

Peru.

A. ×*cultorum* Birdsey = *A.* ×*ferrierense*.

A. digitatum (Jacq.) G. Don f.   Climber, similar to *A. pentaphyllum*. Lvs palmate, lfts 10–22×4–10cm, 7–13, oblong-oblanceolate, dark green; petioles to 60cm. Scape to 20cm; spathe to 7cm, ovate-lanceolate, green to red-purple, decid.; spadix to 15cm, purple. Fr. red to purple. Venez.

A. dussii Engl. Lvs to 35×9cm, rosulate, elongate-elliptic, obtuse at base, bright green; petioles to 6.5cm. Scape to 30cm; spathe 12cm, lanceolate to linear; spadix equalling spathe, dark purple. Guadeloupe.

A. elegans Engl. = *A. pedatum*.

A. ellipticum Koch & Bouché = *A. crassinervium*.

A. enneaphyllum (Vell. Conc.) Stellf. = *A. pentaphyllum*.

A. ×*ferrierense* Mast. & T. Moore. (*A. andraeanum* ×*A. nymphaeifolium*.)   Scape exceeding petioles; spathe to 9cm, cordate, smooth or bullate, usually glossy, white, pink, salmon, orange to dark red; spadix curved downwards or straight, sometimes yellow and white. 'Album': spathe round cordate, quilted, white, thick; spadix white tinted mauve, tip yellow; lvs glossy. 'Atrosanguineum': spathes blood red. 'Giganteum': spathes large, salmon red. 'Guatemala': dense habit; spathe wide, thick, bright red; spadix yellow. 'Reidii': spathes large, deep pink. 'Rhodochlorum': spathes v. large, to 30cm, pink. 'Roseum': spathe large, quilted, deep red; spadix white, tip yellow. 'Salmoneum': spathe salmon tinted yellow.

A. fissum Reg. = *A. palmatum*.

A. flavidum N.E. Br.   Climber. Lvs to 40cm, triangular-ovate, deflexed, coriaceous, bright green; petiole to 45cm. Spathe 12.5cm, oblong, abruptly acuminate, spreading, yellow-green; spadix 5cm, pale violet. Colomb.

A. forgetii N.E. Br.   Lvs 20–30×15–22cm, ovate, peltate, acuminate, rounded or with shallow sinus, olive-green, soft-textured, with veins outlined in pale green; petiole to 25cm. Scape to 60cm, spathe 8–15cm, linear-lanceolate, green; spadix to 15cm, yellow. Fr. white, tinged purple. Colomb.

A. fortunatum Bunting = *A. pedatum*.

A. fraternum misapplied = *A. huixtlense*.

A. gracile (Rudge) Lindl.   Lvs 15–40cm, linear to linear-lanceolate, acute to acuminate, cuneate at base, coriaceous, dark green above, paler beneath, glandular-punctate; petiole to 10cm. Scape equalling or shorter than lvs; spathe to 4cm, linear-lanceolate, red; spadix to 8cm. Fr. orange-red. C Amer. to N S Amer.

A. grandifolium (Jacq.) Kunth. JUNCTION ROOT; WILD COCO.   Lvs 75×60cm+, clustered, ovate to deltate, cordate, acute to obtuse; petiole 90cm. Scape to 60cm; spathe recurved, green; spadix to 25cm+, far exceeding spathe, dark purple-brown. Fr. dark red-purple. Venez., Carib.

A. holtonianum Schott = *A. clavigerum*.

A. hookeri Kunth. Lvs 35–140×10–45cm, rosulate, obovate, or elliptic to ovate, short-acuminate, black-punctate, glaucous; petiole to 14cm, angular. Scape to 90cm; spathe 9–23cm, oblong, reflexed, green, dull purple beneath; spadix to 30cm, pale violet-purple. Fr. white, red to purple at apex. Lesser Antilles to Surinam.

A. ×*hortulanum* Birdsey. (*A. scherzerianum* ×?).   St. short. Lvs oblong-elliptic to oblong-lanceolate, acuminate, 15–48×-3.5–9cm, dark green; petioles to 25cm. Scape green to red; spathe broadly ovate, short-cuspidate, 5–14cm, subcoriaceous, white to yellow, pink to blood red or purple, sometimes freckled or streaked, spadix twisted or curved, white or yellow to orange and scarlet, to 13cm. Fr. scarlet. Gdn origin.

A. huegelii Schott = *A. hookeri*.

A. huixtlense Matuda.   Lvs 17–70×10–36cm, ovate to broad-ovate, sagittate, coriaceous; petiole to 70cm. Scape to 40cm; spathe to 15cm, oblong-lanceolate, pale green-white; spadix to 14cm, dark pink to pale purple. Fr. orange. Mex. to Nic.

A. kalbreyeri N.E. Br. = *A. clavigerum*.

A. latihastatum Engl. ex K. Krause. St. long, ascending. Lvs to 30×38cm, 3-lobed, hastate, median leaflet elongate-triangular, 8.5cm across at base, lat. lfts to 20×6cm, oblong, curved; petiole to 30cm. Scape 20cm; spathe to 12.5cm, linear-lanceolate; spadix to 10cm. Costa Rica.

A. leuconeurum Lemoine. (Possibly wild hybrid *A. clarinervium* ×*A. berriozabalense*.)   Lvs 10–15×10–15cm, round-cordate, sinus broad, coriaceous, dark green above, glaucous beneath. Scape 40–50cm; spathe to 8.5cm, broad-lanceolate, glaucous green; spadix to 15cm, grey-green. Mex.

A. lilacinum Dressler non Bunting = *A. amnicola*.

A. lindenianum K. Koch & Augustin = *A. nymphaeifolium*.

A. magnificum Lind. Lvs 30–40×20–25cm, ovate, deeply cordate, basal lobes large, rounded, velvety, olive-green, veins white; petiole to 40cm, quadrangular, grooved. Scape to 60cm, winged above; spathe 15–20cm, lanceolate, long-acuminate, recurved, green, sometimes tinged red; spadix to 25cm, dull purple.

Colomb.

A. **microphyllum** (Hook.) G. Don f. Lvs to 15×7.5cm, elliptic-lanceolate or elliptic-ovate, truncate at base, glossy dark green; petiole to 20cm. Scape to 40cm; spathe 3cm, ovate-lanceolate, reflexed, yellow-green; spadix to 12cm, purple. Braz., Venez.

A. **nymphaeifolium** K. Koch & Bouché. Lvs 30–70×20–40cm, broad-ovate, rounded, deeply cordate, lobes close to overlapping, veins impressed, subcoriaceous; petiole 50–90cm. Scape 35–95cm; spathe 10–20cm, oblong-elliptic to narrow-obovate, white, tinged green, pink with age, or red; spadix to 14cm, white to pink, red or purple. Berries red. Venez., Colomb. 'Album': fls white.

A. **ornatum** Schott = A. nymphaeifolium.

A. **palmatum** (L.) G. Don f. Climber. Lvs reflexed, orbicular in outline, palmate, lfts 25–40×4–6cm, 5–11, oblanceolate; petiole to 1m. Scape to 85cm; spathe 6–18cm, lanceolate, green; spadix to 16cm, violet. Fr. red. Lesser Antilles.

A. **panduratum** Mart. = A. clavigerum.

A. **papilionense** = A. corrugatum.

A. **papillosum** Markgr. = A. corrugatum.

A. **pedatoradiatum** Schott. Lvs to 60cm diam., orbicular in outline, pedate, seg. to 32.5×7.5cm, 11–13, united below, narrow-lanceolate to oblong; petiole to 1m. Scape to 60cm; spathe to 15cm, narrow-lanceolate, reflexed; spadix purple. Fr. orange. S Mex. ssp. **helleborifolium** (Schott) Croat. Lvs smaller, seg. 7–11, median seg. deeply divided. Spadix green, becoming brown.

A. **pedatum** HBK Lvs cordate-ovate in outline, palmate, lfts 20–45×5–8cm, 9–13, median leaflet linear-lanceolate, laterals to 30cm, undulate, coriaceous, glossy, midrib purple; petiole 30–75cm. Scape 15–60cm, spathe 6–10cm, lanceolate, spreading, yellow-green, spadix to 12cm, pendent, green or purple. Fr. deep purple. Colomb.

A. **pentaphyllum** (Aubl.) G. Don f. Creeping or climbing. Lvs palmate, deflexed, seg. to 30cm, 5–9, oblanceolate to narrow-elliptic or ovate; petiole to 45cm. Scape 1–13cm; spathe 15cm, lanceolate to ovate, pale green or purple, persistent; spadix to 10cm, pale violet. Fr. red to dark-red-violet. Trin., coastal S Amer. to Braz. var. **bombacifolium** (Schott) Madison. Spathe soon falling. Mex. to Panama.

A. **pictamayo** invalid = A. polyschistum.

A. **podophyllum** (Cham. & Schldl.) Kunth. Lvs to 90cm across, palmatisect to palmate, seg. 5–11, to 2cm, pinnatisect with 5–12 lobes, or merely undulate, pale green; petioles 40–80cm. Scape to 1m; spathe 5–8cm, lanceolate, green; spadix to 15cm, green or purple. Fr. red. Mex.

A. **polyschistum** Schult. & Idrobo. Climbing or creeping. Lvs palmate, lfts 8–15cm, 11–15, linear-lanceolate, thin, bright green, crispate; petioles to 23cm. Scape to 28cm; spathe 6–10cm, narrow-lanceolate, reflexed, green; spadix to 14cm, pale green. Fr. violet-purple to red-violet. Colomb., Ecuad., N Peru.

A. **polytomum** Schott = A. podophyllum.

A. **putumayo** invalid = A. polyschistum.

A. **radicans** K. Koch. Creeper. Lvs 10–16cm, ovate, cordate, arched along midrib, coriaceous, bullate, veins impressed; petiole to 10cm. Scape to 8cm; spathe to 5cm, ovate, cordate, dull red; spadix to 4cm, red-green to brown. Braz.

A. **regale** Lind. Lvs 30–55cm, ovate to oblong, cordate, coriaceous, bright green above, with pale green or white veins; petiole to 40cm. Scape to 70cm; spathe 7–19cm, lanceolate, long-acuminate, reflexed, green; spadix to 25cm, green-white. Peru. 'Robustum': lvs large, shiny, dark matt green, veins paler; spathe thin, green.

A. ×**roseum** Closon. = A. ×ferrierense.

A. ×**rothschildianum** Bergman & Veitch = A. scherzerianum 'Rothschildianum'.

A. **rugosum** Schott = A. crassinervium.

A. **salviniae** Hemsl. Lvs 60–180cm, rosulate, oblanceolate or elliptic-oblong; petiole short. Scape pendent, exceeding lvs; spathe 15cm, lanceolate, brown-purple to purple-green; spadix to 40cm, lavender. Mex. to Colomb.

A. **scandens** (Aubl.) Engl. Climber. Lvs 4–16cm, elliptic to ovate-lanceolate, black-punctate beneath; petioles 1–6cm. Scape 2–8cm, slender; spathe lanceolate to oblong-lanceolate, reflexed, green to purple; spadix to 3cm, green, or becoming pale purple. Fr. white, becoming pale mauve. Carib., Mex. to Peru and Guyana.

A. **scherzerianum** Schott. Lvs to 26cm, linear to elliptic or lanceolate, acuminate, coriaceous; petioles to 20cm. Scape to 50cm, red or green; spathe to 12cm, elliptic to ovate, glossy bright red to orange-red; spadix 2–8cm, spirally contorted, orange to red. Fr. orange to red. Costa Rica. 'Atrosanguineum': spathe deep red. 'Rothschildianum': spathe red, spotted white, spadix yellow. 'Wardii': st. red, spathe large, dark burgundy, spadix long, red. Cvs of hybrid origin are referable to A. ×hortulanum.

A. **scherzerianum** hort. non Schott = A. ×hortulanum.

A. **schlechtendalii** Kunth. Lvs 30–110cm, oblong to obovate-elliptic or obovate-lanceolate, coriaceous, glaucous green above; petioles 12–23cm, angled. Scape to 35cm; spathe 15–28cm, linear-lanceolate to lanceolate, reflexed, green to violet; spadix to 34cm, green, sometimes tinged violet. Fr. red. Mex. to Nic.

A. **scolopendrinum** (Hamilt.) Kunth = A. gracile.

A. **spectabile** Schott. Lvs 65–135cm, oblong-lanceolate to oblong or oblong-triangular, weakly lobed, subcoriaceous; petiole to 60cm, quadrangular. Scape to 28cm; spathe to 32cm, narrow-ovate, base rounded or subcordate, green or violet-purple within, green externally; spadix to 38cm, yellow-green. Fr. orange. Costa Rica.

A. **tetragonum** (Hook.) Schott = A. schlechtendalii.

A. **undatum** Kunth = A. pentaphyllum.

A. **veitchii** Mast. KING ANTHURIUM. Lvs 25–100cm, pendent, oblong-ovate, cordate, sinus narrow, coriaceous, deep green, veins impressed; petiole to 70cm. Scape to 30cm; spathe 7–13cm, ovate to ovate-lanceolate, spreading, ivory-white; spadix 5–9cm, cream or rose-white; pollen purple. Fr. red. Colomb.

A. **violaceum** (Sw.) Schott = A. scandens.

A. **warocqueanum** J.W. Moore. Climbing or creeping, to 100cm. Lvs 50–90cm, pendent, narrow-ovate to oblong-ovate, thinly fleshy, deep velvety green above, veins pale; petiole 15–60cm. Scape 6–30cm; spathe to 10cm, narrow-ovate-lanceolate, reflexed, green; spadix to 30cm, yellow-green. Fr. red. Colomb. 'Robustum': vigorous.

A. **watermaliense** Bail. Lvs 30–60cm, ovate-triangular, sagittate, basal lobes longer than broad, undulate, dark green; petioles 10–90cm. Scape 12–65cm; spathe 15–21cm, lanceolate-triangular, green to dark violet or coppery-black; spadix to 10cm, white to green, yellow or purple. Fr. yellow to orange. Costa Rica to Colomb.

A. **wendlingeri** Barroso. St. pendent, to 20cm. Lvs 32–80cm, ligulate, obtuse or rounded at base, coriaceous, dark-punctate; petiole to 30cm. Scape to 42cm, spreading to pendent; spathe to 7.5cm, oblong, green, sometimes tinged purple, soon decid.; spadix to 80cm, spiralling, pale green, purple to brown. Fr. orange. Costa Rica.

A. **cvs.** 'Evans' Huegellii': tall; lvs thick, midrib prominent, lat. veins indented. 'Negrito': lvs sagittate, large basal lobes; spathe deep bronze. 'Splendidum Hybrid': lvs thick, corrugated, metallic green, pale beneath; spathe pale green, spadix plum.

Anthyllis L. Leguminosae (Papilionoideae). c25 ann. or perenn. herbs or shrubs. Lvs imparipinnate, or with lat. lfts rudimentary, giving appearance of 1 leaflet only. Rac. capitate, umbellate, densely flowered, subtended by a palmate bract; fls pea-like. Medit.

A. **barba-jovis** L. JUPITER'S BEARD. Everg. shrub to 4m, grey-pubesc. Petioles to 5cm; lfts to 2.5cm, 11–18, elliptic-oblong. Infl. umbellate, 10–20-fld; cor. to 1cm, white or cream. Spring. Spain. Z8.

A. **erinacea** L. = Erinacea anthyllis.

A. **hermanniae** L. Shrub to 1m. Br. diffuse, ± spiny, grey-white-pubesc. Lvs apparently simple or trifoliolate; lfts to 1cm, oblong to oblanceolate, revolute, mucronate. Infl. 2–8-fld; cor. to 0.5cm, yellow, standard marked orange. Spring. Medit. 'Minor' ('Compacta'): habit domed, dense, to 20cm high; lvs tiny, grey-green; fls gold, abundant. Z8.

A. **montana** L. Perenn. herb to 30cm, forming low clumps. Young shoots clothed in lf bases. Lfts to 1cm, ovate to elliptic-oblong silky, to 8–15 pairs. Infl. capitate; cor. to 1cm, purple, red, white or rose. Spring. Medit. Alps. 'Atropurpurea': fls darkest purple. 'Rubra': lvs grey; fls crimson. Z7.

A. **tetraphylla** L. Ann. herb, procumbent, villous. Lfts to 2.5cm, 1–5, obovate, lateral lfts reduced. Fls in axill. clusters of 1–6; cal., silky, much inflated and tinted yellow or red in fr.; cor. yellow-cream, occas. marked red. Summer. Medit. Z8.

A. **vulneraria** L. KIDNEY VETCH. Ann. or short-lived perenn., to 50cm. St. forming a basal rosette, pubesc. Lvs with term. lfts to 5cm, and lat. lfts reduced, obovate to lanceolate. Infl. umbellate, many-fld, to 1.5cm; cor. yellow, cream, often tinged or tipped maroon sometimes deep red. Summer. N Afr., Eur., W Asia. Z7.

Antiaris Leschen. Moraceae. 4 highly toxic decid. trees and shrubs. Fls small, unisexual; ♂ fls in heads; ♀ fls solitary. Drupe fleshy ellipsoid. Trop. Afr., Madag., Trop. Asia to Philipp. and Fiji Is. Z10.

A. **africana** Engl. Tree to 40m. Lvs to 16cm, broad oblong obovate to oblong, base cordate to rounded, tips rounded to acute, rough, rough-pubesc. beneath. Fr. to 1.5cm, tomentose, orange or red. Trop. Afr.

A. toxicaria (Rumphius ex Pers.) Leschen. UPAS TREE. To 45m. Lvs to 20cm, oblong-elliptic, sometimes few-toothed, smooth. Fr. to 4.5cm, red or purple. Distrib. as for genus.

Anticlea Kunth.
A. elegans (Pursh) Rydb. = *Zigadenus elegans*.

Antidesma L. Euphorbiaceae. *c*70 trop., unisexual trees and shrubs. Lvs alt., simple. Fls small, apetalous in rac. or spikes. Berry small, fleshy, currant-like. Afr., Asia, Aus., Pacific. Z10.
A. bunius (L.) Spreng. Tree to 13.5m. Lvs 7.5–17.5cm, elliptic to oblong, dark glossy green. Fr. edible, red 20–40 per cluster. India, Malaya.
A. dallachyanum Baill. Small tree. Lvs 5–10cm, ovate or lanceolate-elliptic, thin. Aus.

Antigonon Endl. Polygonaceae. 3 fast-growing perenn. climbers. St. slender, jointed, flexuous. Rac. branching, terminating in tendrils; sep. 5 papery, red-pink or green-white. Achene within enlarged perianth, bluntly 3-angled. Mex., C Amer. Z10.
A. guatemalense Meissn. Differs from *A. leptopus* in lvs broadly cordate, 3–9cm, pubesc.; sep. orbicular, 1cm, tomentose pink; fr. obscurely 3-angled. Mex., Guat., Costa Rica, W Indies.
A. leptopus Hook. & Arn. CORAL VINE; CONFEDERATE VINE; MEXICAN CREEPER; CHAIN OF LOVE; ROSA DE MONTANA. To 12m, roots tuberous. Lvs deltoid or cordate, 3–14cm usually glab. Sep. cordate, 0.8–2.5cm, coral-pink to -red, minutely pubesc. Fr. about 1cm, strongly angled. Summer–early autumn. Mex. 'Album': fls white.
A. macrocarpum Britt. & Small = *A. guatemalense*.

Antimima N.E. Br.
A. dualis (N.E. Br.) N.E. Br. = *Ruschia dualis*.

Antirrhinum L. Scrophulariaceae. *c*40 annuals, herbaceous perennials and subshrubs. St. intricately branched. Lvs linear-lanceolate to ovate. Fls solitary in lf axils or term. rac.; cor. tube closed at mouth, saccate at base, lobes erect to reflexed on upper lip, spreading on lower lip, midlobe with large bearded palate. Spring–summer. Temp. Old and New World. Z7.
A. asarina L. = *Asarina procumbens*.
A. bipartitum Vent. = *Linaria bipartita*.
A. braun-blanquetii Rothm. Perenn., glab. except for glandular-pubesc. infl. St. to 120cm, erect, branched. Lvs 2.5–6cm, linear-oblong to elliptic, acute. Fls 3–4cm, yellow. NW Spain, NE Port. Z8.
A. calcycinum Lam. Glab. ann., to 45cm. Lvs 5cm, narrowly elliptic, entire. Fls to 2cm, purple. Port., It.
A. coulterianum Benth. Erect or scandent ann., to 1m; br. tendril-like. Lvs to 3cm, ovate-elliptic, to lanceolate-elliptic, entire. Fls 1–1.5cm, white with pale yellow palate. Calif.
A. dalmaticum L. = *Linaria genistifolia* ssp. *dalmatica*.
A. filipes A. Gray = *Asarina filipes*.
A. glandulosum Lindl. = *A. multiflorum*.
A. glutinosum Boiss. & Reut., non Brot. = *A. hispanicum* ssp. *hispanicum*.
A. hispanicum Chav. Much-branched dwarf shrub, villous to glandular-pubesc. procumbent to ascending, 20–60cm. Lvs 0.5–3cm, lanceolate to orbicular. Fls to 2.5cm, white or pink, palate often yellow. W & SE Spain. 'Album': fls white. 'Roseum': fls pink.
A. latifolium Mill. Perenn., erect to 1m, usually glandular-pubesc. throughout. Lvs 2–7cm, ovate, obtuse, basally truncate. Fls pale yellow, 3–5cm. SC Eur.
A. majus L. SNAPDRAGON. Perenn., erect or straggling, to 2m. Lvs 1–7cm, linear to ovate, acute to obtuse, cuneate at base. Fls 3–4.5cm, usually purple or pink, exterior pubesc. SW Eur., Medit. Many cvs and seed races ranging in habit from dwarf (e.g. 'Tom Thumb', 'Magic Carpet', 'Floral Carpet') to intermediates (Monarch Series, 'Pixie') to tall (e.g. Rocket and Penstemon-fld types); the fls range in colour from white to yellow, orange, peach, rose, red and purple. ssp. *tortuosum* (Vent.) Rouy. Lvs 1–7.5cm, narrow-oblong to linear. Fls purple-pink; palate yellow or white.
A. minus L. = *Linaria viscida*.
A. molle L. Dwarf pubesc. shrub to 40cm, procumbent to ascending. Lvs 0.8–2cm, broadly ovate to elliptic, sometimes suborbicular. Fls 2.5–3cm, pale pink or white; palate yellow, exterior pubesc. NE Spain, Port.
A. multiflorum Pennell. Herbaceous perenn. to 1.5m, erect, pubesc., viscid, often soapy-scented. Lvs 2.5–3.8cm, lanceolate to linear. Fls 1.5–2cm, pale pink to carmine; palate white, withering and becoming brown to tan as fl. opens. SW US.
A. multipunctatum Brot. = *Linaria amethystea* ssp. *multipunctata*.
A. nevinianum A. Gray = *A. coulterianum*.

A. nuttallianum Benth. Ann. to 2m, erect, pubesc. Branchlets tendril-like. Lvs 6cm, ovate-elliptic, acute. Fls lavender to blue-purple, tube and palate white, veined violet. SW US.
A. orcuttianum A. Gray = *A. coulterianum*.
A. orontium L. = *Misopates orontium*.
A. ovatum Eastw. Ann. to 60cm, many-branched, spreading to erect. Lvs lanceolate, oblanceolate or ovate. Fls to 2cm, cream, flushed pink on upper lip and tube. SW US.
A. pulverulentum Laz.-Ibiza. Close to *A. sempervirens*, differing in longer hair and upper lvs alt. (all opposite in *A. sempervirens*); fls pale yellow. E Spain. Z8.
A. sempervirens Lapeyr. Dwarf decumbent shrub to 40cm, pubesc. to villous. Lvs 0.5–3cm, oblong to broadly elliptic. Fls 2–2.5cm, cream or white, venation often purple, violet patch on upper lip, palate yellow or white. Pyren., EC Spain.
A. siculum Mill. Perenn. herb to 50cm, glab., erect. Lvs linear or linear-elliptic. Fls 1.7–2.5cm, pale yellow, sometimes with red veins, palate darker. Medit.
A. speciosum (Nutt.) A. Gray = *Galvezia speciosa*.
→*Howellia* and *Neogaerrhinum*.

Ant Orchid *Chiloglottis formicifera*.
Ant-plants *Myrmecodia*.
Ant Tree *Triplaris* (*T. americana*).
Antwerp Hollyhock *Alcea ficifolia*.

Anubias Schott. Araceae. 7 everg., semi-aquatic, everg. rhizomatous perenn. herbs. Lvs entire or lobed, lanceolate, rounded or hastate, tough; petiole long, apex pulvinate; base sheathing. Peduncle ± equalling petioles; spathe open or with margins overlapping at base; spadix exceeding spathe. Trop. C & W Afr.
A. afzelii Schott. Lvs 15–55×3–17cm, lanceolate to oblong-elliptic, mucronate, dark green; petiole to 40cm, sheathing to half length. Spathe to 6.5cm, green, margins overlapping at base. W Afr.
A. barteri Schott. Lvs 15–25×5–10cm, rounded, apex rounded to acuminate, base truncate to cordate; petiole sheathing only below. Spathe 4–5cm, green. W Afr.
A. lanceolata misapplied = *A. afzelii*.

Apache Pine *Pinus engelmannii*.
Apache Plume *Fallugia*.

Apera Adans. SILKY BENT. Gramineae. 3 ann. grasses. Lvs flat or revolute, narrowly linear, somewhat scabrous, glab.; sheaths tinged purple; ligules papery. Pan. often tinged purple; spikelets laterally flattened, 1-fld. Summer. Eur., N Asia. Z6.
A. interrupta (L.) P. Beauv. DENSE SILKY BENT; WIND GRASS. To 0.7m. Lvs to 0.4cm wide; sheaths smooth; ligules acute. Pan. narrow-ovate, to 25cm, tinged purple, br. distant, interrupted, spreading.
A. spica-venti (L.) P. Beauv. LOOSE SILKY BENT. To 1m. Lvs 0.5–1cm wide; sheaths scabrous; ligules obtuse. Pan. ovate to oblong, to 25cm, densely branched, tinged purple.
→*Agrostis*.

Aphanamixis Bl. Meliaceae. 23 everg., medium-sized trees. Lvs imparipinnate. Fls in axillary spikes or pan.; sep. 5; pet. 3; anth. 3–6, fil. united in a tube. Capsule leathery; seeds arillate. SE Asia. Z10.
A. polystachya (Wallich) Parker. To 20m. Lvs to 90cm; lfts 7–23cm, 9–15, oblong to elliptic-oblong, ♂ pan. 30cm, ♀ spikes 35–45cm. Seeds with scarlet aril. Sri Lanka, Sumatra.

Aphananthe Planch. Ulmaceae. 5 trees or shrubs. Lvs simple, serrate, alt. in 2 rows, stipulate, petiolate. Fls small, apetalous; ♂ in dense corymbs, sta. 5; ♀ solitary in term. lf axils. Drupe small, ovoid or subglobose, somewhat flattened. Madag., E Asia to Aus., Mex.
A. aspera (Bl.) Planch. To 20m, decid.; crown dense, rounded; bark grey-brown, scaly; twigs finely pubesc., lenticulate. Lvs to 9cm, obliquely ovate-oblong, acute to acuminate, coriaceous, serrate, dark green above, lighter beneath. Fr. 6–8mm, black, pubesc. Jap., Korea, E China. Z7.

Aphania Bl.
A. rubra (Roxb.) Radlk. = *Lepisanthes senegalensis*.

Aphanostephus DC. LAZY DAISY. Compositae. 6 ann. to perenn. herbs, sometimes woody-based. Lvs entire to pinnatisect. Cap. radiate, solitary, term.; phyllaries in 3–6 series; ray flts lanceolate to elliptic-oblong; disc flts yellow. SW US, N & C Mex. Z8.
A. arkansanus (DC.) A. Gray = *A. skirrhobasis*.

A. ramosissimus DC. Many-stemmed, downy ann., to 45cm. Lvs to 6×2cm, toothed to pinnatisect. Involucre to 1cm diam.; ray flts to 1cm, white, often pink or purple below. SW US, N Mex.

A. skirrhobasis (DC.) Trel. Single-stemmed or branched, grey-downy ann., to 50cm. Lvs to 6×2cm, oblanceolate to oblong. Involucre to 1.3cm diam.; ray flts to 1.5cm, white above, cherry-red or rose-purple below. N SW US, Mex.
→*Keerlia*.

Aphelandra R. Br. Acanthaceae. 170 everg. shrubs and sub-shrubs. Lvs opp., simple. Infl. term., a 4-sided spike with showy, overlapping bracts enclosing tubular 2-lipped fls. Trop. Amer. Z10.

A. aurantiaca (Scheidw.) Lindl. Lvs to 10cm, ovate-elliptic, dark to silver green, puckered. Infl. to 18cm, fls scarlet to vermilion. Mex., Colomb. 'Roezlii' (FIERY SPIKE): lvs strongly puckered or twisted, leaden, distinctly silvered on veins above sometimes flushed purple beneath and on young st.; fls brilliant scarlet.

A. chamissoniana Nees. YELLOW PAGODA. Lvs to 10cm, narrow-elliptic, dark green broadly veined silver-white. Infl. bracts yellow, tipped green, spiny; fls yellow. Braz.

A. fascinator Lind. & André = *A. aurantiaca* 'Roezlii'.

A. nitens Hook. f. = *A. aurantiaca*.

A. squarrosa Nees. ZEBRA PLANT; SAFFRON SPIKE. Lvs to 30cm, glossy, tough, ovate-elliptic, dark green, veins sunken, broadly edged and zoned silver or yellow above. Infl. to 20cm; bracts yellow ± tinted maroon, waxy; fls yellow. Braz. 'Citrina': fls citron yellow. 'Dania': compact, to 1m; lvs to 30cm, veined white; spikes to 15cm, bracts yellow. 'Leopoldii': lvs v. dark green, midrib and veins pure white; infl. bracts oxblood; fls pale yellow. 'Louisae': midrib and veins v. clearly outlined in silver-white on an emerald background; fls golden. 'Fritz Prinsler': lvs narrow, veins outlined in white or golden yellow; infl. bracts deep yellow, stained green; fls bright yellow. 'Saffron Spike Zebra': lvs waxy, dark green, ovate, veins silver-white; fls pale yellow; bracts orange. 'Snow Queen': lvs with white vein color-ation covering most of blade; fls pale lemon.

A. tetragona (Vahl) Nees. Lvs to 24cm, broadly ovate. Infl. strongly tetragonal; bracts to 1.25cm; fls to 8cm, scarlet. W In-dies, N S Amer.

Aphyllanthes L. Liliaceae (Aphyllanthaceae). 1 fibrous-rooted perenn. herb. St. 15–40cm, numerous, v. slender, terete, wiry, striate, chalky. Lvs reduced to membranous sheaths. Fls 2cm diameter, term., solitary or in groups of 2–3; tep. 6, spreading, pale lilac to deep blue. Early summer. SW Eur. and Moroc. Z8.

A. monspeliensis L.

APIACEAE Lindl. See Umbelliferae.

Apicra Willd. non Haw.

A. aspera Haw. non Willd. = *Astroloba muricata*.

A. rubriflora L. Bol. = *Poellnitzia rubrifolia*.

Apios Fabr. Leguminosae (Papilionoideae). 10 twining perenn. herbs. Roots tuberous. Lvs imparipinnate. Rac. short axill.; fls pea-like. Legume linear, laterally compressed. N Amer., Asia.

A. americana Medik. WILD BEAN; POTATO BEAN; INDIAN POTATO. Roots bearing chains of white tubers. Vine to 3m+. Lvs to 15cm; lfts 5–7, lanceolate or ovate. Fls fragrant, red-brown or dull purple. Summer–autumn. N Amer. Z3.

A. tuberosa Moench = *A. americana*.

Apium L. Umbelliferae. 20 glab. herbs. Lvs pinnate to ternate above. Fls white in compound short-stalked or sessile umbels. Eur., Temp. Asia.

A. dulce Mill. = *A. graveolens* var. *dulce*.

A. graveolens L. WILD CELERY. Strongly aromatic perenn. to 1m. Lf seg. 1–5cm, rhombic-lanceolate, toothed or lobed; petiole thick, long, grooved. Eur. 'Tricolor': lvs glossy green, tinted bronze at first, later edged cream with a central silver stripe. var. *dulce* (Mill.) Pers. CELERY. Lvs erect; petioles enlarged, closely overlapping, thick, ribbed. var. *rapaceum* (Mill.) Gaudich. CELERIAC; TURNIP-ROOTED CELERY. Taproot grossly swollen. Lvs short.

A. rapaceum Mill. = *A. graveolens* var. *rapaceum*.

Aplopappus Cass. = *Haplopappus*.

APOCYNACEAE Juss. 215/2100. *Acokanthera, Adenium, Alla-manda, Alstonia, Amsonia, Apocynum, Beaumontia, Carissa, Catharanthus, Cerbera, Forsteronia, Holarrhena, Kopsia, Macrosiphonia, Mandevilla, Nerium, Ochrosia, Odontadenia, Pachypodium, Parsonsia, Plumeria, Prestonia, Rauvolfia, Stem-madenia, Strophanthus, Tabernaemontana, Thevetia, Trach-elospermum, Vallaris, Vallesia, Vinca, Wrightia*.

Apocynum L. DOGBANE. Apocynaceae. 9 often poisonous perenn. herbs with milky sap. Lvs thin, entire. Fls in small cymose infl.; cal. 5-parted; cor. tubular to campanulate. Temp. N Amer., E Eur. and Asia. Z4.

A. androsaemifolium L. COMMON DOGBANE; SPREADING DOGBANE. 30–60cm. Lvs 2.5–10cm, ovate to lanceolate, mucronate, glab. to pubesc. and pale beneath. Fls to 0.9cm, campanulate, pale red. N Amer.

A. cannabinum L. To 120cm. Lvs to 15cm, ovate to ovate-lanceolate. Fls 0.3cm, tubular, white tinged green. NE US, Canada.

A. pumilum (A. Gray) Greene. ROCKY MOUNTAIN DOGBANE. Differs from *A. androsaemifolium* in lvs always glab.; fls 0.6cm, tubular to urceolate. N Amer.

A. venetum L. To 150cm. Lvs 1.8cm, elliptic-lanceolate, to ovate-oblong. Fls campanulate, purple-red or pink. E Eur. to China.
→*Trachomitum*.

Apodanthera Arn. Cucurbitaceae. 15 climbing or prostrate perennials. Lvs reniform to rounded, entire to lobed. Fls yellow; cal. funnel-shaped to cylindrical, lobes 5; cor. lobes 5, oblong-obovate; ♂ racemose; ♀ fls solitary. Fr. ovoid, fleshy. N Amer. Z9.

A. undulata A. Gray. MELON-LOCO. Br. to 3m, prostrate spread-ing, from thick root. Lvs to 15cm diam., reniform, dentate to shallow-lobed, undulate, strigose. Fr. longitudinally ridged, 6–10cm. Summer. W Tex., S Ariz. to Mex.

Apodolirion Bak. Amaryllidaceae. 6 bulbous perenn. herbs, differing from *Gethyllis* in sta. in 2 ranks near throat. Lvs to 22cm, grass-like. Scape subterranean; fls solitary; perianth narrowly funnelform, seg. ovate-lanceolate. S Afr.

A. buchananii Bak. Fls white tinged red. Summer.

A. ettae Bak. = *A. buchananii*.

A. lanceolatum Benth. & Hook. f. Fls white. Summer.

Aponogeton L. f. Aponogetonaceae. 44 perenn., aquatic herbs to 1m. Rhiz. tuberous. Lvs in a basal rosette generally oblong, long-stalked usually floating, some submerged, rarely emergent, veins tessellated. Fls waxy small, arranged in 2 opposite or spiral ranks, on an emergent long-stalked pan. of spike-like rac.; peri-anth seg. 1–6; sta. 6+ in 2 or more whorls. OW tropics and sub-trop.

A. abyssinicus Hochst. ex A. Rich. Lvs 4–16×2–5cm, oval, oblong, ovate or linear, cuneate to truncate at base, cuneate to narrowly obtuse at apex. Fls purple unscented, in a forked, dense rac., each br. to 5cm. Afr., India. Z10.

A. angustifolius Ait. Lvs 3–11×0.5–1.5cm, linear, lanceolate or narrowly oblong, cuneate at base, acute to obtuse at apex. Fls white tinged pink unscented, in a forked rac., 4–8 per br.; br. distichous, to 2cm. S Afr. Z9.

A. bernerianus (Decne.) Hook. Lvs 11–50×1.5–10cm, cuneate, rounded or cordate at base, cuneate, with an acute or obtuse point at apex, puckered, undulate, dark green or red-brown. Infl. of 3–10 pale pink, densely-fld rac. to 8cm. Madag. Z9.

A. boivinianus Baill. ex Jum. Lvs 6–30×1.5–8cm, rounded at base, narrowly cuneate, apex, strongly puckered, stiff, midrib wide; petiole to 13cm. Infl. of 2–3, rac. to 20cm, unscented, white or pink; anth. cream. Madag. Z10.

A. crispus Thunb. Lvs to 30×6cm, cordate to narrow ovate, base truncate to rounded, or linear with narrowly cuneate base, apex cuneate or rounded, rigid, light green to purple-green, undulate to crisped; petiole to 45cm. Fls white to pink, unscented, in a simple, spike-like, loose rac. to 18cm. Sri Lanka. Z10.

A. desertorum Zeyh. ex Spreng. Lvs to 30×7.5cm, lanceolate, oval or ovate, cuneate to cordate at base, obtuse, acute or cordate at apex. Fls fragrant, white or yellow in a dense, forked rac., each br. to 9cm. Madag. Z9.

A. dinteri Engl. & Krause = *A. desertorum*.

A. distachyos L. f. CAPE PONDWEED; WATER HAWTHORN. Lvs to 15cm, oblong-lanceolate, entire, bright green. Fls strongly scented, in a forked rac., each br. to 10cm, white; anth. purple-brown. S Afr. 'Giganteus': larger. 'Grandiflorus': perianth seg. larger. 'Lagrangei': lvs mauve beneath; fls mauve. Z9.

A. echinatus Roxb. = *A. crispus*.

A. elongatus F. Muell. ex Benth. Lvs 15–55cm, oblong to oblong-lanceolate, cuneate or rounded at base and apex, un-dulate or flat, bright green; petiole to 50cm. Fls fragrant, yellow in a simple, sparsely-fld spike-like rac. to 20cm. N & E Aus. Z10.

A. fenestralis (Pers.) Hook. f. = *A. madagascariensis*.

A. henckelianus Baum. = *A. madagascariensis*.

A. junceus Lehm. Lvs rarely floating, 4–43cm, linear-subulate, rush-like, triangular in section, obtuse. Fls unscented, arranged dorsally in a loose-fld, forked rac.; each br. to 7.5cm, white or pink. Afr. Z10.

A. kraussianus Hochst. ex Krauss = *A. desertorum*.

A. leptostachyus Mey. = *A. desertorum*.

A. madagascariensis (Mirb.) H. Bruggen. LACE LEAF; LATTICE LEAF. Lvs submerged, to 55×16cm, ovate obovate or lanceolate, lamina reduced to a network of dark or emerald veins; petiole to 35cm. Fls in a pan. of 2–6, densely fld spikes to 20cm, white or mauve. Madag. Z10.

A. natalensis Peter = *A. nudiflorus*.

A. natans (L.) Engl. & K. Krause. Lvs to 15×3cm, oblong or lanceolate, cordate to truncate basally, light green; petioles to 30cm. Fls in a simple, dense, spike-like rac. to 10cm, white, pink or mauve. Sri Lanka, India. Z10.

A. nudiflorus Peter. Lvs floating, to 10.5×3cm, linear, oblong or ovate, truncate at base, obtuse to cuneate at apex. ♂ fls in loose-fld, forked infl. to 6cm; perianth seg., white; sta. green. ♀ fls in densely fld, forked infl. to 5cm; perianth seg. and sta. 0. Afr. Z9.

A. quadrangularis Bak. = *A. bernerianus*.

A. stachyosporus De Wit = *A. undulatus*.

A. ulvaceus Bak. Lvs submerged, to 35×8cm, linear-oblong, cuneate to rounded at base, obtuse to acute at apex, flat, undulate or twisted, membranous, bright green; petiole to 25cm. Fls fragrant, in a dense, forked spike-like rac.; br. to 15cm, white yellow or mauve. Madag. Z10.

A. undulatus Roxb. Lvs submerged, to 25×4cm, ovate-oblong to lanceolate, cuneate or obtuse at base and apex, undulate, with transparent patches; petiole to 35cm. Fls in a simple, loose, spike-like rac. to 10cm, white, sometimes tinged pink. India to Malay Archipel. Z10.

APONOGETONACEAE L. f. See *Aponogeton*.

Aporocactus Lem. Cactaceae. 2 epiphytic or lithophytic cacti; st. ascending at first, soon decumbent then pendent, slender, cylindric; ribs low, sometimes producing aerial roots; spines bristly, tinged yellow. Fls narrowly tubular funnelform, ± zygomorphic. Mex. Z6.

A. conzattii Britt. & Rose = *A. martianus*.

A. flagelliformis (L.) Lem. RAT'S-TAIL CACTUS. St. to 1m+, ×c1cm; ribs 7–12; spines 9–14; 4–5mm. Fls 5–8×2.5–4cm, purple-pink; tube sharply curved. Spring.

A. flagriformis (Zucc. ex Pfeiff.) Lem. ex Britt. & Rose = *A. flagelliformis*.

A. leptophis (DC.) Britt. & Rose. = *A. flagelliformis*.

A. martianus (Zucc.) Britt. & Rose. St. 2–5m×1.2–2.5cm; ribs 8–10; spines 8–20, 5–12mm. Fls 6–9×5–6cm, scarlet; tube almost straight. Summer.

Apothecaries' Rose *Rosa gallica*.
Apple *Malus*.
Appleblossom Cassia *Cassia grandis*.
Apple Box *Eucalyptus bridgesiana*.
Apple Geranium *Pelargonium odoratissimum*.
Apple Guava *Psidium guajava*.
Apple Gum *Eucalyptus clavigera*.
Applemint *Mentha suaveolens*.
Apple of Peru *Nicandra physaloides*.
Apple of Sodom *Solanum linnaeanum*.
Apricot *Prunus armeniaca*.
Apricot Vine *Passiflora incarnata*.

Aptenia N.E. Br. Aizoaceae. 2 dwarf, succulent, freely branching prostrate subshrubs; br. green, papillose, terete. Lvs opposite, cordate or lanceolate, ± fleshy, minutely papillose. Fls c1.5cm diam., solitary or 3 together. S Afr. Z4.

A. cordifolia (L. f.) Schwantes. Lvs to 25×25mm, cordate-ovate. Fls purple-red. E Cape. 'Variegata': lvs smaller, bordered cream.

A. lancifolia L. Bol. Lvs 32×6mm, lanceolate to narrow-lanceolate, grooved above, bluntly keeled beneath. Fls pink. NE Transvaal.

→*Lithocarpus*.

AQUIFOLIACEAE Bartling. 4/420. *Ilex, Nemopanthus*.

Aquilegia L. COLUMBINE; GRANNY'S BONNET. Ranunculaceae. c70 perenn. herbs. Rootstock woody; roots fibrous. St. erect, branched. Basal lvs long-petiolate, 1–3-ternate; cauline lvs gradually reduced. Fls term., pendent to erect; sep. 5, petaloid, regular; pet. 5, with forward-pointing lamina and long hollow nectar-secreting spur projecting backwards. Circumpolar N temp.

A. adoxoides (DC.) Ohwi = *Semiaquilegia adoxoides*.

A. akitensis Huth = *A. flabellata*.

A. akitensis auct. non Huth = *A. flabellata* var. *pumila*.

A. alpina L. 15–80cm. Basal lvs 2-ternate, lfts 2–3-fid, seg. linear, subglabrous. Fls 2–3 per st., nodding, bright blue or blue and white; sep. to 4.5cm; pet. to 1.7cm, oblong, spur straight or curved, to 2.5cm. Spring. Alps. 'Alba': fls white. 'Atroviolacea': fls dark violet; probably hybrid. 'Blue Spurs': tall; fls large, spurred, deep blue. 'Caerulea': fls blue. 'Hensol Harebell': dwarf; lvs fine, purple; fls soft blue. 'Superba': large, vigorous. Z5.

A. amaliae Heldr. ex Boiss. 20–30cm. Basal lvs 2-ternate, lfts 2–3-fid, hairy beneath. Fls nodding, bicoloured; sep. 1.8cm, pale blue-violet; pet. 1.4cm, white, rounded, spur 1.4cm, pale violet, hooked. Spring–summer. Balk. Z5.

A. arctica Loud. = *A. formosa*.

A. atrata Koch. To 80cm. Basal lvs 2-ternate, lfts 2–3-fid, glab. Fls nodding, rich deep purple-violet or chocolate; sep. to 2.4–0.9cm; pet. to 1.2cm, spur to 1.5cm, hooked. Summer. Alps, Apennines. Z5.

A. atropurpurea Miq. non Willd. = *A. buergeriana*.

A. atropurpurea Willd. non Miq. = *A. viridiflora*.

A. bernardii Gren. & Godron. To 80cm. Basal lvs 2-ternate, lfts 2–3-fid, crenulate, glab. Fls 3–7 per st., nodding, pale blue; sep. to 3.5cm; pet. to 2cm, spur to 1.7cm, straight or slightly curved. Summer. Corsica, Sardinia. Z8.

A. bertolonii Schott. 10–30cm. Basal lvs 2-ternate, lfts 2–3-fid, dark green, glaucous. Fls 2–4 per st., nodding, blue-violet; sep. to 3.3cm, rounded; pet. to 1.4cm, almost truncate, spur to 1.4cm, straight or curved, inflated at apex. Spring–summer. S Fr., It. 'Blue Berry': to 15cm; fls dark blue. Z5.

A. bicolor Ehrh. = *A. sibirica*.

A. brevistyla Hook. 40–100cm. Basal lvs 2-ternate, lfts 3-fid, coarsely crenate. Fls small, nodding, bicoloured; sep. to 1.5cm, blue, lanceolate; pet. yellow-white, spur to 0.8cm, hooked. Summer. NW Amer. Z2.

A. brevistyla Coult. non Hook. = *A. saximontana*.

A. buergeriana Sieb. & Zucc. 30–60cm. Basal lvs 2-ternate, lfts sessile, 2–3-fid, glaucescent. Fls nodding; sep. to 2.5cm, narrow-ovate, brown-purple to dull yellow; pet. to 1.5cm, yellow, spur to 2cm, dull purple, straight. Summer. Jap. Z7.

A. buergeriana var. *oxysepala* (Trautv. & Mey.) Kitam. = *A. oxysepala*.

A. caerulea James. 20–60cm. Basal lvs 2-ternate, lfts deeply 2–3-fid, lobes rounded, glab. Fls erect, bicoloured; sep. blue, pink or white, 2–4cm, ovate-lanceolate; pet. to 2.5cm, white or cream, spur to 5cm, straight or curving. Summer. Colorado, New Mexico to Idaho, California. 'Candidissima': fls large, snow white. 'Citrina': fls lemon yellow. 'Crimson Star': fls red and white or cream; hybrid. 'Cuprea': fls red flushed copper. 'Heavenly Blue': fls long-spurred, deep blue, pet. white. 'Helenae' (*A. caerulea* ×*A. flabellata*): fls vivid blue. 'Koralle' ('Coral'): fls pale flesh pink; hybrid. 'Maxistar': fls bright yellow, long-spurred. 'Olympia': fls red and yellow. 'Rotstern' ('Red Star'): fls carmine and off-white. var. *daileyae* Eastw. Sep. blue, spurless. Colorado. var. *ochroleuca* Hook. Sep. somewhat white. Rocky Mts. Z3.

A. caerulea var. *calcarea* M.E. Jones = *A. scopulorum* var. *calcarea*.

A. californica Hartweg ex Lindl. = *A. formosa* var. *truncata*.

A. canadensis L. MEETING HOUSES; HONEYSUCKLE. 30–60cm. Basal lvs 2-ternate, 2–3-fid. Fls several per st., nodding, glandular-pubesc.; sep. red, ovate, 1.5cm, not reflexed; pet. to 1cm, yellow, truncate, spur to 2.5cm, red, straight. Spring–summer. E N Amer. 'Nana': to 30cm. 'Corbett': to 60cm; fls bright yellow, long-spurred. var. *latiuscula* (Greene) Munz. Basal lvs 2-ternate, lfts deeply cleft. Z3.

A. canadensis var. *flavescens* P.H. Davis = *A. flavescens*.

A. caucasica Ledeb. ex Rupr. = *A. olympica*.

A. cazorlensis Heyw. 15–25cm. Basal lvs 2-ternate, lobed. Fls nodding, bright blue; sep. 1.5cm; pet. 1cm, spur 0.7cm, slightly curved. Spring–summer. S Spain. Z7.

A. chrysantha A. Gray. 30–100cm. Basal lvs 3-ternate, lfts 3-fid. Fls several, horizontal; sep. to 3cm, yellow, sometimes tinged pink, lanceolate; pet. yellow, to 2cm, rounded, spur 3–7.5cm, curving outward. Spring–summer. S US. 'Alba': fls off-white. 'Alba Plena': fls double, white. 'Flore Pleno': fls double, yellow. 'Grandiflora Sulphurea': fls creamy yellow, sep. large, dark cream. 'Nana': habit dwarf; fls gold. 'Silver Queen': fls pure white, long-lasting. 'Yellow Queen': st. to 120cm; fls bright yellow, long-spurred, profuse. Z3.

A. dichroa Freyn. 20–75cm. Lvs 2-ternate, lfts 2–3-fid, crenate. Fls nodding; sep. to 2cm, blue, ovate-lanceolate; pet. to 0.8cm, blue tipped white, spur 1.2cm, blue, hooked. Spring–summer. Port., NW Spain. Z7.

A. discolor Levier & Leresche. 10–15cm. Lvs ternate, glab. Fls ± erect when open; sep. 1cm, deep blue; pet. to 0.6cm, white, spur to 1cm, straight, blue. Spring–summer. N Spain. Z8.

A. ecalcarata Maxim. = *Semiaquilegia ecalcarata*.

A. einseleana F.W. Schultz. 10–45cm. Basal lvs 2-ternate, lfts 2–3-fid. Fls nodding, blue-violet; sep. to 2cm; pet. to 1cm, spur to 1cm, straight. Spring–summer. Alps. Z5.

A. elegantula Greene = *A. canadensis*.

A. eximia Van Houtte ex Planch. = *A. formosa* var. *truncata*.

A. fauriei Lév. & Van't non Lév. = *A. flabellata* var. *pumila*.

A. flabellata Sieb. & Zucc. 20–50cm. Basal lvs few, 1–2-ternate, lfts 3-fid, glaucous beneath. Fls 1–2 per st., nodding, on glandular-pubesc. pedicels; sep. 2.5cm, blue-purple to lilac or white; pet. 1.5cm, lilac tipped pale yellow or entirely white, spur to 2cm, lilac or white, curved. Spring–summer. Jap., E Asia. 'Alba': fls white. var. *pumila* (Huth) Kudô. To 15cm. Lvs less glaucous. Fls 1–3, bicoloured or white, slighty smaller. Japan. 'Alba' ('Pumila Alba', 'Nana Alba', var. *alba*): fls white. 'Kurilensis': to 10cm. 'Ministar': sep. bright blue, pet. white; vigorous. Z3.

A. flavescens S. Wats. 20–70cm. Basal lvs 2–3-ternate, lfts 2–3-fid, glab. to pubesc., glaucous beneath. Fls nodding; sep. 2cm, yellow; pet. to 1cm, cream-coloured, spur to 2cm, yellow, hooked at apex. Spring–summer. Rocky Mts. Z4.

A. formosa Fisch. 50–100cm. Basal lvs 2-ternate, lfts 2–3-fid; glab. to pubesc., glaucous beneath. Fls many, nodding; sep. to 2.5cm, spreading, ovate-lanceolate, red; pet. to 2cm, rounded to truncate or emarginate, yellow, spur red, straight. Spring–summer. W N Amer. 'Nana': habit dwarf; fls pale pink. 'Nana Alba': habit dwarf; fls white. 'Rubra Plena': fls double, red. 'Western Red': to 90cm; fls red and yellow. var. *truncata* (Fisch. & C.A. Mey.) Bak. Pet. much reduced. Calif., S Oreg., W Nevada. Z3.

A. fragrans Benth. 40–80cm. Basal lvs 2-ternate, lfts 3-fid, lobes toothed, glaucous above. Fls horizontal to nodding, white or cream-coloured, sweetly fragrant; sep. to 3cm; pet. to 2cm, cuneate-oblong, spur to 2cm, straight or hooked. Summer. W Himal. Z7.

A. glandulosa Fisch. ex Link. 12–35cm. Basal lvs 2-ternate, lfts 3-fid, dentate. Fls nodding, solitary or 2–3; sep. to 5cm; blue; pet. to 2.5cm, violet-blue, rounded, spur to 1.5cm, strongly hooked. Spring–summer. C Asia to Sib. var. *jucunda* (Fisch. & Avé-Lall.) Bak. Smaller; pet. white, broader. Sib. Z3.

A. glauca Lindl. = *A. fragrans*.

A. grata F. Maly ex Zimm. 15–45cm. Basal lvs 2-ternate, lfts 3-fid, glandular-pubesc. Fls nodding, bright blue; sep. to 3cm; pet. to 1cm, spur to 2cm, straight. Spring. Balk. Z6.

A. helenae hort. ex Bergmans = *A. caerulea*.

A. japonica Nak. & Hara = *A. flabellata* var. *pumila*.

A. jonesii Parry. To 10cm. Basal lvs 2-ternate, lfts 3–5-fid, pubesc. Fls solitary, erect; sep. to 1.5cm, blue or purple; pet. to 0.8cm, blue, broad, rounded, spur to 1cm, incurved. Summer. Rocky Mts. Z3.

A. jucunda Fisch. & Avé-Lall. = *A. glandulosa* var. *jucunda*.

A. kitaibelii Schott. 15–30cm. Basal lvs 2-ternate, lfts pubesc. Fls 1–3 per st., suberect, red-violet to blue-violet; sep. to 2cm; pet. to 1.5cm, spur to 1cm, straight or slightly curved. Spring–summer. It., Balk. Z6.

A. lactiflora Karel. & Kir. 40–80cm. Basal lvs 2-ternate or imparipinnate, lfts deeply lobed, glaucous or tomentose beneath. Fls nodding, densely pubesc., milk-white, pink or lilac; sep. to 2.5cm, lanceolate; pet. 1cm, spathulate, sometimes yellow, spur to 2cm, straight or slightly curved. Spring–summer. C Asia. Z5.

A. laramiensis A. Nels. 20–30cm. Basal lvs 2-ternate, lfts 2–3-fid, lobes rounded, sparsely pubesc. Fls small, barely surpassing foliage; sep. white; pet. cream, spur to 0.8cm, straight. Summer. Wyom. Z3.

A. latiuscula Greene = *A. canadensis* var. *latiuscula*.

A. leptocera Nutt. = *A. caerulea*.

A. leptoceras Fisch. & Mey. 20–30cm. Basal lvs 2-ternate, lfts lobed. Fls nodding, lilac-blue; sep. to 2.5cm, elliptic or oblong; pet. 1cm, edged cream, spur to 2cm, slightly curved. Spring–summer. E Sib. Z3.

A. longissima A. Gray. To 1m. Basal lvs 3-ternate, lfts 2–3-fid, glaucous. Fls erect, yellow, slighty glandular-pubesc.; sep. 2.5cm, sometimes tinged red; pet. to 2.5cm, spur to 1.5cm, slender, straight. Summer. W Tex., N Mex. Z8.

A. macrantha Hook. & Arn. = *A. caerulea*.

A. mexicana Hook. = *A. skinneri*.

A. micrantha Eastw. 40–50cm. Basal lvs 2-ternate, lfts broadly cuneate. Fls erect; sep. 1cm, oval, white or pale blue, sometimes tinged red; pet. 0.8cm, truncate, white or tinged red, spur 1.5cm, straight or curving outward. Summer. Utah, Colorado, Arizona. Z4.

A. montana Sternb. = *A. alpina*.

A. moorcroftiana Wallich ex Royle. 20–40cm. Basal lvs 2-ternate, lfts 2–3-fid, glaucous, glab. above, pubesc. beneath. Fls several or solitary, nodding, purple; sep. to 2cm, lanceolate-ovate; pet. 1.3cm, tipped white, obovate, spur 1.7cm, straight or slightly

curved. Summer. Afghan. to SE Tibet. Z7.

A. nigricans Baumg. Differs from *A. atrata* in st. glandular-hairy, lvs smaller; fls few to numerous, purple or bright blue, larger, spur strongly hooked. Summer. C & SE Eur. Z4.

A. nivalis Falc. ex Jackson. 10–20cm. Basal lvs 2-ternate, lfts reniform, deeply 3-fid, glandular-pubesc. above, glab. beneath. Fls usually solitary, nodding; sep. large, purple-blue; pet. limb black-purple, spur 0.3–1cm, purple-blue, strongly hooked. Summer. W Himal. Z7.

A. olympica Boiss. 30–60cm. Basal lvs 2-ternate, lfts 2–3-fid, ± glaucous beneath. Fls nodding, blue or pink; sep. to 4.5cm, ovate; pet. to 1.5cm, white, spur to 2cm, curved, with gland. hairs at apex. Spring–summer. Cauc., W Asia. Z5.

A. ottonis Orph. & Boiss. Differs from *A. amaliae* in pet. 1.6–2cm, truncate, sta. exserted. Greece, It. Z7.

A. oxysepala Trautv. & Mey. Close to *A. buergeriana*, but slightly taller. Fls nodding or horizontal; sep. 2.5cm, claret to violet; pet. 1.5cm; yellow-white, spur to 2cm, claret to violet, strongly hooked. Spring–summer. Jap., Manch., E Sib. Z3.

A. pubescens Cov. 20–45cm. Basal lvs ternate to 2-ternate, lfts deeply 2–3-fid, glab. to pubesc., sometimes glaucous beneath. Fls erect, glandular-pubesc.; sep. to 2cm, cream to yellow or pink; pet. paler, to 1.2cm, spur to 4cm, straight or slightly spreading. Spring–summer. US (Sierra Nevada). Z5.

A. pyrenaica DC. 10–30cm. Basal lvs 2-ternate, lfts 2–3-fid, subglabrous; cauline lvs simple, linear. Fls nodding, bright blue; sep. ovate, 2–3.5cm; pet. to 1.5cm, oblong-obovate, spur to 16mm, straight or slightly curved. Spring–summer. Pyren., N Spain. Z5.

A. reuteri Boiss. = *A. bertolonii*.

A. rubicunda Tidestr. = *A. micrantha*.

A. saximontana Rydb. 10–20cm. Basal lvs 2-ternate, lfts obovate, 2–3-fid. Fls nodding; sep. 1.5cm, blue; pet. 0.8cm, pale yellow, spur 0.5–0.7cm, blue, hooked. Spring–summer. US (Colorado, Utah). Z4.

A. scopulorum Tidestr. 10–20cm. Basal lvs 2-ternate, lfts crowded, sessile, 3-fid, glaucous. Fls erect; sep. to 2cm, ovate-oblong, blue to white, sometimes red; pet. 1.5cm, white to pale yellow, oblong, rounded, spur 3–5cm, straight, blue to red. Spring–summer. W US. var. *calcarea* (M.E. Jones) Munz. Petioles glandular-pubesc. Z3.

A. shockleyi Eastw. 20–30cm. Lvs 2–3-ternate, thin, blue-green. Fls pendulous, glandular-pubesc., spurs red; nectariferous glands yellow. Calif. Z7.

A. sibirica Lam. 25–70cm. Basal lvs ternate, lfts large, ± glaucous beneath. Fls nodding; sep. 2–7cm, lilac-blue; pet. 1.5cm, blue or white, spur 2cm, blue, hooked or strongly incurved. Spring–summer. Sib. 'Flore Pleno': fls double. Z2.

A. skinneri Hook. 60–100cm. Basal lvs 3-ternate, lfts deeply 3-fid, glaucous. Fls many, nodding; sep. to 2.5cm, green, lanceolate, not spreading; pet. to 1.5cm, green-orange, spur to 5cm, bright red. Summer. New Mex. 'Flore Pleno': fls double. Z8.

A. stellata hort. ex Steud. = *A. vulgaris*.

A. ×stuartii Balf. f. (*A. glandulosa* ×*A. olympica.*) 15–25cm. Fls nodding, deep violet-blue; sep. 3.5cm; pet. tipped white. Spring–summer. Gdn origin. Z4.

A. thalictrifolia Schott & Kotschy. Close to *A. einseleana*. St. to 60cm, glandular-pubesc. as are lvs and petioles. Fls nodding to suberect, lilac-blue; sep. to 2cm; pet. 1.3cm, spur to 1.1cm, straight or slightly curved. Spring–summer. N It. Z7.

A. transsilvanica Schur. = *A. glandulosa*.

A. truncata Fisch. & C.A. Mey. = *A. formosa* var. *truncata*.

A. viridiflora Pall. 15–30cm. Basal lvs 2-ternate, lfts 3-fid, glaucous. Fls nodding; sep. 2cm, green, ovate; pet. 1.5cm, chocolate to purple-brown or yellow-green, truncate, spur to 1.7cm, brown, straight or slightly curved. Spring–summer. E Sib., W China. Z3.

A. vulgaris L. COLUMBINE; GRANNY'S BONNETS. 30–70cm. Basal lvs 2-ternate, lfts 2–3-fid, glab. above, pubesc. beneath. Fls nodding, blue to purple, red or white, sometimes double or lacking spurs; sep. to 2.5cm, ovate to ovate-lanceolate; pet. to 1.3cm, spur to 2.2cm, strongly hooked. Spring–summer. W, C & S Eur., nat. N Amer. Many cvs and hybrids. Fls single or double ('Plena'), colours range from white through yellow, red to blue, sometimes with coloured edges or markings, occas. fragrant ('Scented Form'). 'Nivea' ('Alba', 'Munstead'): vigorous; fls pure white. 'Clematiflora Alba' ('White Spurless'): fls spurless, pure white, also in other colour forms. 'Nora Barlow': fls double, pom-pom form, pink and lime green fading to white. 'Gisela Powell': fls yellow-orange. 'Tom Fairhurst': fls pale pink and red. 'Red Star': fls red with white cor. 'Double Red': low; fls double, dark red. 'Adelaide Addison': fls blue, centres double white with blue edge. Lvs marbled yellow in Vervaeneana group. Z4.

A. vulgaris ssp. *atroviolacea* Avé-Lall. = *A. atrata*.

A. cvs and seed races. Biedermeier Mixed: compact and dwarf; fls mixed delicate colours. Blackmore and Langdon: fls large, long-spurred, wide colour range. Blue Shades: to 65cm; fls large, long-spurred, mix of blues. 'Celestial Blue': to 60cm; fls vivid blue. Dragonfly Hybrids: to 45cm; fls mixed colours. Dynasty Series: compact, to 20cm; fls long-spurred, heavy texture, range of colours; F1 hybrids. colours; F1 hybrids. Harbutt's Hybrids: fls long-spurred, range of colours, v. profuse. Harlequin Mixed: to 90cm; fls long-spurred, bright colours and bicolors, early-flowering. early-flowering. 'Kristall': to 60cm; fls long-spurred, white. Langdon's Rainbow Hybrids: to 90cm; fls v. long-spurred, mix of bright colours. Lowdham Strain: to 90cm; fls long-spurred, burnished colours. McKenna Hybrids: vigorous; fls large, long and flared spurs, abundant, mixed colours. colours. Mrs Scott Elliot's Var.: to 90cm; fls v. long-spurred, pale colours. Music Hybrids: compact, to 45cm; fls large, long-spurred, brightly coloured; F1 hybrid. hybrid. 'Rose Queen': to 75cm; fls rose, cor. white. 'Schneekonigin' ('Snow Queen'): fls spurred, pure white. 'Spring Song Mixed': vigorous, fls large, gracefully spurred, bold coloured; F1 hybrid.

Arabian Coffee *Coffea arabica.*
Arabian Jasmine *Jasminum sambac.*
Arabian Tea *Catha edulis.*

Arabis L. ROCKCRESS. Cruciferae. c120 ann. to perenn. herbs. St. oft. woody, much branched. Lvs simple. Fls 4-merous; pet. white to deep purple. Temp. N Amer., Eur., Asia.
A. albida Steven ex Bieb. = *A. caucasica.*
A. allionii DC. Perenn. to 45cm, pet. 6–7mm, white. C Eur. (mts). Z6.
A. alpina L. Perenn. 5–40cm. Rac. hairy; fls white, rarely pink. Cvs include, 'Alba', 'Coccinea', 'Compacta', 'Grandiflora', 'Nana', 'Rosea', 'Superba' and 'Variegata'. Eur. (mts). Z5.
A. androsacea Fenzl. Dense tufted perenn., 2–5cm. Lvs silver-hairy. Fls white. Turk. Z6.
A. ×*arendsii* Wehrh. (*A. aubrietoides* ×*A. caucasica.*) Similar to *A. aubrietioides* except st. creeping to ascending, pet. rose-red. Gdn origin. 'Atrorosea': fls persistently deep magenta. 'Coccinea': fls scarlet. 'Compinkie': spreading; lvs silver-tinted; fls vivid pink. 'Hedi': compact, fls deep pink. 'La Fraîcheur': fls deep rose red. 'Monte Rosa': fls bright maroon. 'Rosabella': fls rose pink. 'Rosenquarz': fls lilac. 'Rubin': fls claret. Z5.
A. arenosa (L.) Scop. = *Cardaminopsis arenosa.*
A. aubrietoides Boiss. Dwarf, dense tufted perenn., 7–15cm. Pet. rose-purple. Turk. Z6.
A. bellidifolia Jacq. = *A. soyeri* ssp.*jacquinii.*
A. billardieri DC. = *A. caucasica.*
A. blepharophylla Hook. & Arn. Perenn., 7–10cm. Fls rose-purple. Calif. 'Alba': fls white. 'Frühlingszauber' ('Spring Charm'): habit compact, to 10cm; lvs in rosettes; fls rich carmine. Z7.
A. brassiciformis Wallr. = *Fourraea alpina.*
A. breweri S. Wats. Tufted perenn. to 20cm. Pet. red-purple to pink, narrow-clawed. Calif., Oreg. Z7.
A. bryoides Boiss. Dense tufted perenn., 2–6cm. Lvs silky white-hairy, minute. Fls white. Greece, Balk. Penins. Z7.
A. caerulea (All.) Haenke. Tufted perenn. Rac. nodding; fls pale or grey-blue. Alps. Z6.
A. carduchorum Boiss. Densely tufted perenn. Flg st. naked. Fls large, white. Armenia. Z6.
A. caucasica Schldl. Similar to *A. alpina.* Lvs grey-green. S Eur. 'Gillian Sharman': lvs green, gold-edged and occas. striped; fls white. 'Variegata': lvs green and white edged; fls profuse, white. Those selected for fls include 'Bakkely': compact, fls white. 'Compacta Schneeball': to 15cm, fls white. 'Flore Plena': habit spreading, fls double, white. 'Grandiflora': fls large, white. 'Pink Pearl': habit mat-forming, fls deep pink. 'Plena': habit tall, fls double, white. 'Rosabella': to 15cm; spreading; fls single, deep pink. 'Snowcap': habit low-spreading, fls white. 'Sulphurea': fls sulphur yellow. Z4.
A. constricta Griseb. = *A. allionii.*
A. corymbiflora Vest. Bienn. or perenn., 6–30cm. Fls small, white. C Eur. (mts). Z6.
A. drummondii A. Gray. Bienn. or perenn., 30–90cm. Fls pink or white. N Amer. Z2.
A. ferdinandi-coburgi Kellerer & Sünderm. Similar to *A. procurrens* but lvs narrower, hairy. Bulg. 'Limedrop': to 10cm, mat-forming; lvs deep green with lime centre. 'Old Gold': to 10cm, mat-forming; lvs shiny, green and gold variegated; fls white. 'Reversed': to 10cm, mat-forming; lvs white, edged and heavily splashed with green. 'Variegata': to 10cm, mat-forming; lvs green, edged and heavily splashed with ivory, often tinted purple in winter; fls white. Z7.
A. furcata S. Wats. Perenn. to 40cm. Pet. to 8mm, white. Oreg., Washington. Z5.
A. glabra (L.) Bernh. = *Turritis glabra.*

A. holboellii Hornem. Bienn. or perenn. 10–90cm. Lvs densely hairy. Fls purple pink to white. W N Amer. Z3.
A. japonica A. Gray = *A. stelleri.*
A. ×*kellereri* Sünderm. (*A. bryoides* ×*A. ferdinandi-coburgi.*) Resembles *A. bryoides* but densely cushion-forming. Gdn origin. Z6.
A. muralis Bertol. Perenn., 10–30cm. Fls large, rose-purple or white. SE & C Eur. Z6.
A. nivalis Guss. = *A. serpillifolia.*
A. oregana Rollins. Perenn., 30–50cm. Fls purple. N Calif. Z7.
A. perfoliata Lam. = *Turritis glabra.*
A. petraea Lam. = *Cardaminopsis petraea.*
A. procurrens Waldst. & Kit. Stoloniferous perenn., 10–30cm. Fls large, white. Carpath., Balk. 'Schneeteppich': to 15cm; fls pure white. 'Neuschnee': lvs dark; profuse, long-lasting. 'Variegata': to 25cm; lvs green mottled white; fls white. Z5.
A. pumila Jacq. = *A. bellidifolia.*
A. purpurascens Howell ex Greene non C. Presl = *A. oregana.*
A. scabra All. = *A. stricta.*
A. scopoliana Boiss. Perenn. to 10cm. Pet. white. Alps, Balk. Z6.
A. serpillifolia Vill. Loosely tufted bienn. or perenn. to 25cm. Fls white, rarely pink. C & S Eur. (mts). Z6.
A. serrata Franch. & Savat. Somewhat tufted perenn., 10–30cm. Fls white. Jap. Z7.
A. soyeri Reut. & Huet. Perenn., 15–50cm. Lvs dark, glossy green. Fls white. Pyren., Alps, W Carpath. ssp. *jacquinii* (G. Beck) B.M.G. Jones. Lvs fleshy. Z6.
A. stelleri DC. Perenn., 15–70cm. Rac. many-fld; fls straw yellow or white. Jap. Z7.
A. stelleri DC. = *A. japonica.*
A. stricta Huds. Perenn. 5–25cm. Lvs leathery, dark, glossy green. Fls yellow. Pyren., Alps, SW GB. Z6.
A. sudetica Tausch = *A. allionii.*
A. ×*sundermannii* Kellerer ex Sünderm. (*A. ferdinandi-coburgi* ×*A. procurrens.*) Similar to *A. procurrens* but lvs long-stalked. Gdn origin. Z6.
A. thaliana L. = *Arabidopsis thaliana.*
A. turrita L. Bienn. or perenn. to 75cm. Rac. dense; pet. pale yellow. C & S Eur. Z6.
A. verna (L.) R. Br. Ann. 5–40cm. Fls small; pet. pale purple, claw white-yellow. E Medit. Z7.
A. vochinensis Spreng. Similar to *A. procurrens* but smaller. SE Alps. Z6.
A. ×*wilczekii* Sünderm. (*A. bryoides* ×*A. carduchorum.*) Similar to *A. caduchorum* but lvs hispid throughout. Gdn origin. Z6.

Arab's Turban *Crassula haemisphaerica.*

ARACEAE Juss. 106/2950. *Acorus, Aglaonema, Alocasia, Amorphophallus, Anthurium, Anubias, Arisaema, Arisarum, Arum, Biarum, Caladium, Calla, Colocasia, Cryptocoryne, Cyrtosperma, Dieffenbachia, Dracontium, Dracunculus, Eminium, Epipremnum, Homalomena, Lagenandra, Lysichiton, Monstera, Nephthytis, Orontium, Peltandra, Philodendron, Pinellia, Pistia, Remusatia, Rhaphidophora, Rhektophyllum, Sauromatum, Schismatoglottis, Scindapsus, Spathicarpa, Spathiphyllum, Stenospermation, Symplocarpus, Syngonium, Taccarum, Typhonium, Xanthosoma, Zamioculcas, Zantedeschia.*

Arachis L. Leguminosae (Papilionoideae). 22 ann. or perenn. herbs. Lvs pinnate; stipules persistent. Fls pea-like in short, dense axill. spikes; usually procumbent. Fr. developing below ground, on elongated gynophores ('pegs'), oblong or swollen cylindric, weakly torulose, ± curved, woody-fibrous, strongly reticulate. S Amer.
A. hypogaea L. PEANUT; GROUNDNUT; MONKEY NUT. Ann. erect or procumbent to 30cm. Lfts 4, 1–7cm, obovate or elliptic, glab. or sparsely pilose beneath. Fls yellow veined red. Fr. to 6×1.5cm; seeds to 2cm, 1–3, irregularly ovoid. Summer. Origins obscure, widely nat. and cult. Z8.

Arachniodes Bl. Dryopteridaceae. c40 terrestrial ferns. Rhiz. mostly long-creeping, scaly. Fronds deltoid or ovate, broadened at base, bipinnate or more profusely divided, pinnules rhomboid, awned or spinose. E Asia, Malaysia, NZ.
A. amabilis (Bl.) Tind. Rhiz. short-creeping. Fronds 25–45×15–25cm, ovate to broad-ovate, simply pinnate or more often with a pinnate br. on the lower side in the lowest pairs; pinnae 12–20cm, petiolate, lanceolate; pinnules 1.5–3cm; short-petiolate, deltoid-ovate to oblong-ovate, spine-tipped and -toothed, subcoriaceous; stipes to 40cm. E Asia. Z10.
A. aristata (Forst.) Tind. Fronds 20–40×12–25cm, bipinnate to tripinnate, with 1 to few pinnate br. on the lowest pinnae, ovate to broad-ovate, caudate; pinnules to 2cm, oblong-ovate, spine-tipped, spine-toothed, coriaceous; stipes to 60cm. E Asia, Poly-

nesia. 'Variegata': fronds 20–50cm, deep glossy green, yellow near midrib. Z10.

A. hasseltii (Bl.) Ching. Fronds to 30cm, almost 4-pinnate, triangular-ovate, acuminate, coriaceous; pinnae to 15cm, triangular-ovate, pinnules ovate, to 4cm, seg. to 7.5cm, ovate-oblong, obtuse, deeply pinnatifid at base, confluent above with a v. narrow wing, base cuneate, seg. obliquely truncate, oblong to rhombic-ovate, obtuse, crenate or entire. Java. Z10.

A. maximowiczii (Bak.) Ohwi. Rhiz. short-creeping. Fronds 15–25×15–25cm, tripinnate to tripinnatsect, pinnae to 18cm, petiolate, narrowly deltoid-ovate, short-attenuate; pinnules oblong-ovate, obtuse, minutely dentate; stipe to 35cm. Jap., Korea. Z9.

A. mutica (Franch. & Savat.) Ohwi. Rhiz. erect to ascending, stout. Fronds 25–50×13–25cm, tripinnate, ovate, short-acuminate; pinnae narrowly ovate, acuminate, to 10cm; pinnules to 2.5cm, narrowly ovate, mucronate- to obtuse-toothed, pinnately divided to parted, lustrous above, paler and scaly beneath; stipes to 35cm. Jap. Z9.

A. nipponica (Rosenstock) Ohwi. Fronds 4–60×25–35cm, narrowly ovate, long-acuminate, vivid green above, subcoriaceous; pinnae 6–8 pairs, to 30cm, petiolate, pinnate or partially bipinnate, long-acuminate; pinnules to 3cm, pinnately lobed or parted, ovate or oblong, acute; stipes to 45cm. Jap., China. Z9.

A. simplicior (Mak.) Ohwi. Rhiz. short-creepping, knotty. Fronds pinnate, 25–40×15–25cm, broadly ovate; pinnae 2–5 pairs, gradually acuminate, lowest with elongate pinnate br.; term. pinna, linear-lanceolate, acuminate, dark green and lustrous above; pinnules to 2.5cm, oblong-ovate, obscurely auricled on anterior side, obtuse, spine-tipped and -toothed, sometimes lobulate; stipes to 60cm. Jap., China. var. *major* (Tag.) Ohwi. Term. pinna lanceolate-deltoid, broadened at base, gradually merging into the upper lat. pinnae. Jap. Z9.

A. standishii (Moore) Ohwi. Rhiz. short-creeping. Fronds 40–60×20–30cm, 4-pinnatisect to 4-pinnate, oblong-ovate, short-acuminate, vivid green, thinly herbaceous; pinnae 12–15 pairs; pinnules 0.5–1cm, oblong-ovate, acute to obtuse, sometimes lobed or parted, acutely dentate, vivid green above; stipes to 50cm. Jap., Korea. Z9.

A. webbiana (A. Br.) Schelpe. Fronds to 60cm, 3- to 4-pinnate, broad subtriangular-ovate, glossy, membranous, coriaceous; primary and secondary pinnae ovate-lanceolate, narrowly acuminate; pinnules oblong-obovate, acute, bristly-sessile, subdecurrent, serrate; stipes to 60cm. Madeira. Z9.

→*Dryopteris, Lastrea, Polystichopsis* and *Polystichum.*

Arachnis Bl. SCORPION ORCHID. Orchidaceae. 7 monopodial epiphytic orchids. St. to 2m, narrow, clothed with 2-ranked, leathery, strap-shaped lvs to 20cm. Infl. an axill. rac., often branched; fls large, fleshy; tep. narrowly oblanceolate, obtuse, spreading; lip small. SE Asia, W Malaysia. Z10.

A. flos-aeris (L.) Rchb. f. Fls dark green to yellow-red banded or blotched maroon or chestnut, lip pale, with orange ridges. Malaysia to Philipp.

A. hookeriana (Rchb. f.) Rchb. f. Fls cream dotted purple, lip purple or purple-striped. Malaysia.

A. lowii (Lindl.) Rchb. f. = *Dimorphorchis lowii.*

→*Aerides.*

Araiostegia Copel. Davalliaceae. 12 epiphytic or terrestrial ferns. Rhiz. creeping, fleshy. Fronds stipitate, finely pinnate or pinnatifid, thin-textured; stipes approximate, jointed to rhiz., glab. or scaly. Trop. Asia. Z10.

A. hymenophylloides (Bl.) Copel. Rhiz. scales attenuate to narrowly acute, brown. Fronds 50×30cm, 4-pinnate to 5-pinnatifid, deltoid, lacy, decid., membranous, pinnae ovate-lanceolate or deltoid, to 15×5cm, pinnules ovate to oblong, 4–5-lobed, ovate, lower lobes incised, rhomboid to oblong; stipes to 40cm. India to Malaysia and Philipp.

A. pulchra (D. Don) Copel. Rhiz. scales obtuse, grey-brown or chalky white. Fronds to 35×20cm, 3–4-pinnate or -pinnatifid, ovate or lanceolate to deltoid, membranous, sometimes decid., pinnae ovate to lanceolate, narrowly acute, to 15×5cm, pinnules 5-lobed, lanceolate, lobes incised, stipes to 15cm. India, China.

Aralia L. Araliaceae. c40 everg. or decid., trees, shrubs, lianes and rhizomatous herbs. Lvs pinnately compound or simple. Infl. terminal or pseudo-axillary, mostly paniculate; fls small, green-tinged, yellow or white, in umbels, heads or racemes. Fr. drupaceous, small, usually black. S & E Asia, Malesia, Americas.

A. amboinensis Versch. ex Sowerby = *Schefflera littorea.*

A. arborea L. = *Dendropanax arboreus.*

A. balfouriana Sander ex André = *Polyscias scutellaria* 'Balfourii'.

A. cachemirica Decne. Unarmed erect shrub to 3m. Lvs large, 1–3× compound; lfts on each primary or secondary pinna 5–9, stalked or sessile, to 15×7.5cm, toothed or lobed, paler beneath, somewhat hispid. Infl. compound, paniculate; primary br. to 30cm+. Himal. Z7.

A. californica S. Wats. ELK CLOVER; SPIKENARD. Unarmed, branching, woody-based herbaceous perenn. to 3m. Lvs 2–3× compound, uppermost ternate; lfts stalked, to 30×19cm, usually smaller, shallowly toothed, base cordate to truncate. Infl. term. or axill., paniculate, to 40cm, primary br. shorter. Oreg., Calif. Z8.

A. capitata Jacq. = *Oreopanax capitatus.*

A. chinensis auct., non L. = *A. elata* and *A. stipulata.*

A. chinensis var. *mandshurica* (Rupr. & Maxim.) Rehd. = *A. elata.*

A. chinensis var. *nuda* Nak. = *A. elata.*

A. chinensis var. *nuda* auct., non Nak. = *A. stipulata.*

A. continentalis Kitag. MANCHURIAN SPIKENARD. Differs from *A. cordata* in infl. more compact, up to 3× compound; umbels of ♂ fls smaller. Summer. W & N China, E Russia, Korea. Z8.

A. cordata Thunb. UDO; JAPANESE SPIKENARD. Unarmed herbaceous perenn. to 2.7m. Lvs 2–3× compound, uppermost trifoliolate or simple; lfts ovate, to 15×10cm, finely toothed. Infl. term., paniculate, 1–2× compound, to 45cm. Summer. EC & S China, Jap. Z8.

A. cordata Thunb. pro parte = *A. continentalis.*

A. dactylifolia hort. = *Oreopanax dactylifolius.*

A. deleauana Lind. = *Polyscias* 'Deleauana'.

A. digitata Roxb. ex Carey = *Schefflera roxburghii.*

A. edulis Sieb. & Zucc. = *A. cordata.*

A. elata (Miq.) Seem. ANGELICA TREE; JAPANESE ANGELICA TREE. Clump-forming, decid. shrub or tree to 14m, with pithy, spiny st. arising from underground br. Lvs large, 2× compound, in terminal rosettes; petiole and rachis often prickly; lfts 5–9 per pinna, ovate to elliptic, to 12cm, toothed, downy- to rough-pubesc. beneath. Infl. term., paniculate, 3–4× compound, primary br. to 60cm. Summer. China, USSR. The less hairy form (*A. chinensis* var. *nuda*) is more commonly cultivated. 'Albovariegata': lfts white-bordered. 'Aureomarginata': lfts yellow-bordered. 'Aureovariegata': lfts wide, yellow-variegated. 'Pyramidalis': br. narrowly upright, lvs smaller. 'Variegata': lfts white-bordered. Z4.

A. elegantissima Veitch = *Schefflera elegantissima.*

A. excelsa Lind. = *Polyscias* 'Excelsa'.

A. filicifolia C. Moore ex E. Fourn. = *Polyscias filicifolia.*

A. guilfoylei Bull = *Polyscias guilfoylei.*

A. hispida Vent. BRISTLY SARSAPARILLA; DWARF-ELDER. Woody-based rhizomatous herb to 1m, shoots slender; st. leafy, densely bristly. Lvs 2× compound; nerves spiny beneath, petioles to 15cm; lfts oblong to ovate, 3.5–7.5cm, serrate, veins bristly beneath. Infl. term., compound, cyme-like. Late spring–early summer. Z3.

A. japonica Thunb. = *Fatsia japonica.*

A. kerchoveiana Veitch ex W. Richards. = *Schefflera kerchoveiana.*

A. longifolia hort., non Reinw. = *Schefflera longifolia.*

A. macrophylla Lindl. = *A. cachemirica.*

A. mandshurica Rupr. & Maxim. = *A. elata.*

A. maximowiczii Van Houtte = *Kalopanax septemlobus* var. *maximowiczii.*

A. mitsde Sieb. = *Dendropanax trifidus.*

A. monstrosa Williams = *Polyscias guilfoylei* 'Monstrosa'.

A. moorei Muell. = *Schefflera pubigera.*

A. moseri hort. = *Fatsia japonica* 'Moseri'.

A. nudicaulis L. WILD SARSAPARILLA. Rhizomatous, perenn. herb; br. forming erect, woody stocks, producing a single lf to 40cm and scapes to 20cm. Lvs glab., 2–3× compound, petiole to 15cm; primary division ternate, seg. pinnate; lfts 3–5, elliptic-ovate, to 18×11cm, finely serrate. Infl. terminal, once compound, with 2–7 (usually 3) umbels radiating in a single whorl. N Amer. Z4.

A. nymphaeifolia Lind. ex Hibb. = *Oreopanax nymphaeifolius.*

A. papyrifera Hook. = *Tetrapanax papyrifer.*

A. pentaphylla Sieb. & Zucc., non Thunb. = *Eleutherococcus sieboldianus.*

A. pentaphylla Thunb. = *Eleutherococcus spinosus.*

A. pulchra hort. = *Schefflera pueckleri.*

A. racemosa L. AMERICAN SPIKENARD; PETTY MOREL; LIFE-OF-MAN. Unarmed, widely branched, rhizomatous herbaceous perenn. to 3m. Lvs 2–3× compound, to 75cm, lfts stalked, to 23×16cm, usually smaller, ovate, bidentate, base cordate, pubesc. beneath. Infl. racemose or paniculate, simple or 1–3× compound, shorter than or equalling lvs, primary br. many. Late spring. N Amer. Populations in southwest N America have been named as *A. arizonica* Eastwood. Z4.

A. racemosa var. *sachalinensis.* = *A. schmidtii.*

A. reticulata hort., non Willd. ex Roem. = *Meryta denhamii*.
A. schmidtii Pojark. SAKHALIN SPIKENARD. Differs from *A. racemosa* in umbels 3.5–4cm diam. Sakhalin, Jap. Z5.
A. sieboldii hort. ex de Vriese = *Fatsia japonica*.
A. sieboldii var. *variegata* Veitch ex T. Moore = *Fatsia japonica* 'Variegata'.
A. spectabilis Lind. & André non Bull = *Delarbrea paradoxa*.
A. spectabilis Auct., non Lind. & André = *Polyscias filicifolia*.
A. spinosa L. AMERICAN ANGELICA TREE; DEVIL'S-WALKING-STICK; HERCULES'-CLUB. Clump-forming decid. shrub or small tree to 12m; st. spiny. Lvs to 70cm, 2–3× compound, in term. rosettes; petiole prickly; lfts 7–13 per pinna, ± sessile, to 18×12cm, ovate, toothed, base obtuse, main veins sometimes spinose, glab. and white-tinged beneath, often softly hairy. Infl. terminal, off-white, paniculate, 3–4× compound, often longer than lvs, main axis elongate, primary br. spreading. Summer. E US. Z5.
A. spinosa auctt., non L. = *A. elata* and *A. stipulata*.
A. spinulosa Williams = *Polyscias* 'Spinulosa'.
A. stipulata Franch. CHINESE ANGELICA TREE. Similar to *A. spinosa*; shrub or small tree to 9m; st. sometimes prickly. Lvs 60–120cm, long, conspicuous; petiole ± unarmed; lfts to 15cm, tinged white beneath, glab. Infl. conical, main axis to 30cm+, primary br. several to many, 25–30cm. Summer. W China. Z5.
A. tomentella Franch. Decid. shrub or tree to 9.5m. Lvs pinnate, to 40cm; lfts 3–5, ± sessile, to 17.5×10cm, ovate, shallowly serrate. Infl. term., paniculate, twice-compound, densely rusty-pubesc., to 30×17.5cm. Late summer. W China. Z5.
A. veitchii Veitch ex Carr. = *Schefflera veitchii*.
A. veitchii var. *gracillima* Fourn. = *Schefflera veitchii* 'Gracillima'.
A. warmingiana (Marchal) Marchal. CAROBA-GUAZU; SABUGUERO. Unarmed, glab., decid. tree to 20×0.8m; bark grey. Lvs 2× compound, to 70cm+; lfts to 8×3.5cm, ovate or oblong, stalked. Infl. term., paniculate, compound, axes to 22cm; fls purple. Autumn. Arg., Braz. Z9.
→*Dimorphanthus, Megalopanax* and *Pentapanax*.

ARALIACEAE Juss. 57/800. *Aralia, Cussonia, Delarbrea, Dendropanax, Eleutherococcus, ×Fatshedera, Fatsia, Gamblea, Gastonia, Hedera, Kalopanax, Meryta, Metapanax, Oplopanax, Oreopanax, Osmoxylon, Panax, Polyscias, Pseudopanax, Schefflera, Tetrapanax, Tetraplasandra, Trevesia*.

Aral Wild Rye *Leymus multicaulie*.

×Aranda. (*Arachnis ×Vanda.*) Orchidaceae. Gdn hybrids intermediate in habit between parents with tall upright spikes of fls in shades of pink, lilac, violet and yellow, often with darker spots and tessellations and a differently coloured lip.

Arar *Tetraclinis articulata*.

Araucaria Juss. Araucariaceae. 20 large everg. coniferous trees. Br. spreading, whorled; branchlets pendent then upturned, clothed with overlapping lvs, ± needle-like in juveniles, adults (described below) scale-like, spiralling or decussate. Old trees often bare of br. except at summit. Bark hard, dark grey-brown, ridged horizontally, resinous. Cones, to 25cm wide, large, woody, ovoid to globose. SW Pacific, S Amer.
A. angustifolia (Bertol.) Kuntze. PARANA PINE; CANDELABRA TREE; BRAZILIAN PINE. To 35m. Br. somewhat descending, raised at ends, spreading horizontally in whorls of 4–8; lower br. lost early; branchlets long and pendent. Lvs leathery, loosely overlapping, oblong-lanceolate, 3–6×0.6cm, pungent, shorter on fertile shoots, glaucous. S Braz., N Arg. 'Elegans': lvs narrow, dense, less stiffly pointed. 'Ridolfiana': vigorous, lvs long and broad. 'Saviana': lvs narrower and more glaucous. Z9.
A. araucana (Molina) K. Koch. MONKEY PUZZLE; CHILE PINE. To 30m. Crown ovoid-conic becoming domed atop a bare trunk. Branching generally in fives, horizontal at first with uppermost br. ascending, lower pendulous; branchlets paired, curving upwards when young, to 2m. Lvs stiff, leathery, triangular-ovate to lanceolate, pungent, spirally arranged, 3–5×2–2.5cm on main st., concave, bright green. C Chile, N Patagonia. 'Adenzwerg': slow-growing dwarf; lvs short. 'Angustifolia': br. longer, more slender; lvs thinner and narrower. 'Aurea': foliage golden. 'Aureovariegata': similar to 'Aurea'; lvs variegated yellow. 'Densa': br. sparse and irregular; lvs short and dense. 'Denudata': br. v. sparse; lvs smaller. 'Distans': vigorous, br. whorled, sparse; lvs short, dense. 'Platifolia' ('Platyfolia'): lvs short and v. broad. 'Striata': bark, branchlets and lvs green with yellow stripes. 'Variegata': some br. entirely green; lvs straw-yellow, some green. Z8.
A. balansae Brongn. & Gris. To 18m. Br. 5 per tier; pendent; branchlets distichous, narrow, deflexed with age. Lvs subulate,

to 3mm, dark olive green, imbricate, stiff. New Caledonia. Z10.
A. beccarii Warb. = *A. cunninghamii* var. *papuana*.
A. bidwillii Hook. f. BUNYA BUNYA. To 45m, narrow, becoming broadly domed with age; br. horizontal; branchlets long, pendent. Lvs 2–3cm, overlapping, twisted, ovate, glossy, pungent, rigid and woody. NE Aus. Z9.
A. brasiliensis Lindl. = *A. angustifolia*.
A. columnaris (Forst. f.) Hook. NEW CALEDONIA PINE. Slender columnar tree to 60m, lower br. shed and replaced by tufts of young shoots from dormant buds, columnar spreading to a short crown. Lvs 0.6–1.5cm, densely imbricate, short-ovate, obtuse, midrib prominent. New Caledonia, New Hebrides. 'Aurea': foliage golden yellow. 'Rigida': lvs silvery. Z10.
A. cookii R. Br. ex Endl. = *A. columnaris*.
A. cunninghamii D. Don HOOP PINE; MORETON BAY PINE. Tree 45–60m, tall with tufted twig clusters at ends of naked br.; upper br. ascending, lower horizontal. Lvs 0.8–2cm, usually shorter, scale-like, triangular-lanceolate, crowded, imbricate. E Aus. 'Glauca': needles glaucous with silver tint. 'Longifolia': vigorous; lvs longer and straighter. 'Pendula': br. arching. 'Taxifolia': needles v. dense, almost distichous. var. *papuana* Laut. Br. less ascending. New Guinea. Z10.
A. excelsa (Lamb.) R. Br. = *A. columnaris*.
A. excelsa hort. non (Lamb.) R. Br. = *A. heterophylla*.
A. heterophylla (Salisb.) Franco. NORFOLK ISLAND PINE; HOUSE PINE. To 60m. Juvenile lvs to 1cm, subulate, curved inwards, laterally flattened and decurrent, light green, soft; adult lvs to 0.6cm, imbricate, scale-like, ovate-triangular. Norfolk Is. 'Albospica': needles and br. variegated silver. 'Aureovariegata': slender; lvs striped pale yellow. 'Compacta': densely compact. 'Glauca': lvs blue-green. 'Gracilis': habit compact and ornamental. 'Leopoldii': compact, needles blue-green. 'Monstrosa': br. in clusters, some tipped white. 'Muelleri': v. vigorous. 'Robusta': vigorous; needles dark green. 'Speciosissima': similar to *A. cunninghamii*, coarser and tighter, needles curved, to 4cm. 'Virgata': br. whiplike. Z9.
A. hunsteinii Schum. To 45m. Juvenile lvs, similar in shape to *A. columnaris* to 10cm; adult lvs broad, overlapping, similar to *A. bidwillii*. NE New Guinea. Z10.
A. imbricata Pav. = *A. araucana*.
A. klinkii Laut. ex Engl. = *A. hunsteinii*.
A. rulei F. Muell. ex Lindl. To 15m. Branchlets pendulous, to 3cm wide, densely covering st. on all sides. Juvenile lvs dark green, obscurely 4-angled, subulate; adult lvs to 2cm, oval to elliptic, imbricate, concave, obtuse with a prominent dors. nerve, silvery grey above, glossy green beneath. New Caledonia. 'Elegans': br. in tight whorls, branchlets slender; lvs smaller. 'Goldieana': lvs narrower and br. more erect. 'Intermedia': lf form intermediate between *A. columnaris* and *A. rulei*. 'Polymorpha': young shoots usually pendulous; lvs compressed, 4-angled. Z10.

ARAUCARIACEAE Henkel & Hochst. 2/32. *Agathis, Araucaria*.

Araujia Brot. Asclepiadaceae. 4 everg. twining shrubs. Fls fragrant, waxy, in axill. umbels or cymes; cor. salverform or campanulate, inflated at base, lobes 5; pollen sticky, entrapping proboscides of moths overnight to ensure pollination. S Amer.
A. albens G. Don = *A. sericofera*.
A. angustifolia Steud. To 6m. Lvs narrow-lanceolate, hastate, acuminate. Fls rotate-campanulate, green-white to purple. Autumn. Urug. Z10.
A. graveolens Mast. Yellow-hairy climber; malodorous when bruised. Lvs obovate, to 11.5cm, slender, narrowing to cordate base. Fls white, funnel-shaped, 5–6cm diam. Autumn. Braz. Z9.
A. sericofera Brot. CRUEL PLANT. To 10m, covered with pale down when young, emitting latex when bruised. Lvs oval-oblong, acute, 5–10cm, pale green. Fls to 3cm diam., white, salverform. Summer–autumn. S Amer., nat. Queensld. Z9.
→*Physianthus* and *Schubertia*.

Arbutus (Tourn.) L. MANZANIIA; MANZANITA; MADROÑA; STRAWBERRY TREE. Ericaceae. 14 large everg. shrubs or trees; bark smooth red or silver-grey, flaking. Lvs alt., simple, leathery. Fls in term. pan., often scented, cor. urceolate, to 1.5cm, lobes. 5 spreading. Fr. a pendent berry, globose, smooth or densely bumpy. W N & C Amer., S & W Eur., Asia Minor.
A. andrachne L. Tree to 12m, bark peeling, red-brown. Lvs to 10cm, oval to oblong, obtuse, dark green above, paler beneath, glab., leathery, usually entire. Pan. leafy, compact, erect, glandular-downy, 10cm; fls dull white. Fr. orange, granular, 1.5cm diam. Late spring. SE Eur., Asia Minor. Most plants in cult. under this name are *A. ×andrachnoides*. 'Serratula': lf tips serrate. Z8.

A. ×andrachnoides Link. (*A. unedo* ×*A. andrachne*.) Large shrub or small tree to 10m, bark deep red. oval, oblong, elliptic or lanceolate, acute, dark green above, lighter and pubesc. beneath, finely serrate. Pan. leafy-bracteate, pendent; fls ivory to white. Fr. 1cm wide, smoother than in *A. unedo*, rarely seen. Late autumn or spring. SE Eur., Asia Minor. 'Milleri': bark rough, shedding. Z8.

A. arizonica (A. Gray) Sarg. To 15m, bark grey to white. Lvs to 8cm, oblong to lanceolate, dark green above, pale beneath, glab., entire. Pan. spreading, erect 5–7cm; fls white. Fr. deep orange-red. Spring. SW US. Z6.

A. canariensis Duh. Shrub or small tree to 10m. Lvs to 15cm, oblong to lanceolate, serrate, glaucous beneath. Pan. loose, erect, gland.; fls green-white tinted pink. Fr. bright orange, granular, warty. Early summer. Canary Is. Z8.

A. densiflora Benth. = *A. xalapensis*.

A. hybrida Ker-Gawl. = *A. ×andrachnoides*.

A. integrifolia Lam. = *A. andrachne*.

A. laurifolia Lindl. = *A. xalapensis*.

A. lucida hort. ex Steudner = *A. andrachne*.

A. menziesii Pursh. MADRONE. Tree to 30m; bark rusty red. Lvs to 15cm, elliptic-ovate, obtuse, entire, sometimes serrate on young plants, dark shining green pubesc. above, glaucous beneath. Pan. term., subpyramidal to 15cm. Fr. orange-red, to 1.5cm wide. Late spring. NW US. Z7.

A. milleri Sweet = *A. ×andrachnoides* 'Milleri'.

A. mollis HBK = *A. xalapensis*.

A. procera Sol. = *A. canariensis*.

A. procera Douglas non Sol. = *A. menziesii*.

A. serratifolia Lodd. = *A. ×andrachnoides*.

A. serratula Pursh = *A. andrachne* 'Serratula'.

A. texana Buckley = *A. xalapensis*.

A. unedo L. STRAWBERRY TREE. Tall shrub or small tree to 10m, bark red coarse and flaking, young twigs gland. pubesc. Lvs 5–7cm, elliptic to obovate, glab., subcoriaceous, serrate, acute, shining above. Pan. crowded, term., pendent to 5cm; fls white or pink-tinged. Fr. scarlet, globose, rough, edible but bland. Late autumn. S Eur., SW Ireland, Asia Minor. 'Compacta': dwarf shrub. 'Microphylla': lvs smaller. f. *integerrima* (Sims) Hegi. Lvs entire. f. *rubra* (Ait.) Rehd. Fls rich pink to red. Z7.

A. xalapensis HBK. Shrub or small tree to 12m. Lvs to 10cm, oblong to lanceolate or ovate, acute or obtuse, entire to serrate, leathery, pubesc. or glaucous beneath, pale brown when young. Pan. loose; fls white or pink. Fr. dark red. Summer. Guat., Mex., S US. Z8.

A. xalapensis var. *arizonica* A. Gray = *A. arizonica*.

Arceuthos Antoine & Kotschy.

A. drupacea (Labill.) Antoine & Kotschy = *Juniperus drupacea*.

Archangel *Angelica archangelica*.

Archangelica Hoffm. = *Angelica*.

Archontophoenix H.A. Wendl. & Drude. KING PALM; BANGALOW PALM. Palmae. 2 graceful, unarmed palms. St. simple, slender, grey-green, ringed, swollen at base. Crownshaft prominent. Lvs 2–3.5m, pinnate; pinnae lanceolate, single-fold, acute, silvery-scurfy beneath or throughout. E Aus. Z10.

A. alexandrae (F.J. Muell.) H.A. Wendl. & Drude. ALEXANDRA PALM; NORTHERN BANGALOW PALM. Trunk to 25m×20cm, swollen at base, prominently ringed.

A. cunninghamiana H.A. Wendl. & Drude. PICCABBEN PALM. Trunk to 22m×20cm, straight. var. *beatrice* (F.J. Muell.) T.C. White. Bole basally swollen with deep rings, giving the trunk a stepped appearance.

→*Ptychosperma* and *Seaforthia*.

Arctanthemum Tzvelev. Compositae. 5 herbaceous, perenn., halophytes, often woody-based. Lvs entire or pinnatifid. Cap. radiate, in loose corymbs or solitary; ray flts white or purple; disc flts tubular. Arc. & subarc.

A. arcticum (L.) Tzvelev. To 50cm, erect, or decumbent. Basal lvs to 16×5cm, obovate or ovate, glaucous, toothed or lobed, petiole to 8cm. Cap. to 3cm diam.; ray flts white, often tinged pink. Late summer–autumn. Arc. Russia, Alask. Z1.

→*Chrysanthemum* and *Dendranthema*.

Arcterica Cov. Ericaceae. 1 cushion-forming everg. shrublet, 0.5–10cm. Lvs 0.5–1cm, in whorls of 3 or paired, oblong to ovate-elliptic, mucronate, base rounded, revolute, dark, glossy above, paler beneath, tinted red-bronze in winter, leathery. Fls fragrant, pendent, 3–8 in short, term. clusters or rac.; cal. lobes 5, green-pink, ciliate; cor. to 0.5cm, white, spherical-urceolate, lobes 5, short. Spring–autumn. NE Asia, Bering Straits, Jap. Z1.

A. nana (Maxim.) Mak. KOMEBA-TSUGAZAKURA.

→*Andromeda* and *Pieris*.

Arctic Birch *Betula nana*.

Arctic Bramble *Rubus arcticus*.

Arctic Creeping Willow *Salix reptans*.

Arctic Grey Willow *Salix glauca*.

Arctic Poppy *Papaver nudicaule*.

Arctic Willow *Salix arctica*.

Arctium L. BURDOCK. Compositae. 10 erect taprooted biennials. Lvs alt., tomentose, entire or obscurely toothed. Cap. discoid, solitary or in clusters; involucre ovoid-conical to spherical, with many spiny bracts; receptacle flat; phyllaries numerous, imbricate, with hooked apices; flts hermaphrodite, tubular, purple or white. Temp. Eurasia. Z3.

A. lappa L. GREAT BURDOCK. To c150cm. Basal lvs to 50cm, ovate, cordate; petioles solid. Infl. corymbose; involucre to 25×42mm, hemispherical; phyllaries shiny, golden-green; flts equalling phyllaries. Eur., Asia Minor.

A. minus Bernh. COMMON BURDOCK; LESSER BURDOCK. To 150cm. Basal lvs to 50cm, ovate, cordate; petioles hollow. Infl. racemose; involucre to 18×25mm, spherical; phyllaries green or purple stained, often hairy at first; flts exceeding phyllaries. Eur., N Afr.

Arctomecon Torr. & Frém. Papaveraceae. 3 taprooted perenn. herbs. Lvs mostly basal, cuneate-oblanceolate, emarginate, densely hairy; st. lvs alt., lanceolate, entire to 5-lobed. Fls to 7cm diam., long-stalked; sep. 2–3, glab. to hairy; pet. 4–6, obovate; sta. many. Summer. SW US. Z9.

A. californica Torr. & Frém. To 60cm. Lvs to 6cm, oblanceolate to cuneate. Fls 6–20, clustered in a subumbellate rac.; pet. 4, yellow.

A. merriamii Cov. DESERT POPPY. To 35cm. Lvs to 3cm, cuneate-oblanceolate, 3-toothed at apex, glaucous, with shaggy white hairs. Fls solitary; pet. 6, white.

Arctostaphylos Adans. BEARBERRY; MANZANITA. Ericaceae. c50 shrubs, mostly prostrate, or small trees, everg. (except *A. alpina*). Bark flaking, red-brown. Lvs simple, generally entire, obtuse, short-stalked. Pan. or rac. term.; fls small, pendulous; cal. 5-parted; cor. urceolate to campanulate, 4–5-lobed. Drupe berry-like, globose, smooth or warted. NW to C Amer.

A. alpina (L.) Spreng. ALPINE BEARBERRY; BLACK BEARBERRY. Dwarf shrub, creeping, 10–15cm high. Lvs 2–3cm, oblanceolate (larger, subspathulate in var. *japonica* (Nak.) Hult.), finely serrate and ciliate, fresh green in summer, bright red in autumn. Cor. 3–4mm, white flushed pink, tips ciliate. Fr. 6mm, red becoming blue-black. Spring–early summer. Circumpolar. Z1.

A. andersonii A. Gray. HEARTLEAF MANZANITA. Shrub, erect, 1–4m, young twigs thick, shortly pubesc., sometimes gland. Lvs 3–7cm, oblong to ovate-oblong, lobed at base, acute, entire or finely serrate, bright green. Pan. glandular-pubesc.; cor. 6–7mm, white to pink; ovaries densely gland. Winter–early spring. W US. var. *pallida* (Eastw.) J.E. Adams ex McMinn. Lvs pale green, glab.; fls white; fr. clear red. Z8.

A. andersonii var. *auriculata* (Eastw.) Jeps. = *A. auriculata*.

A. auriculata Eastw. Differs from *A. andersonii* in lvs densely white-tomentose; ovaries pubesc., eglandular. Late winter–early spring. Calif. Z8.

A. bakeri Eastw. = *A. stanfordiana* ssp. *bakeri*.

A. bicolor (Nutt.) A. Gray. MISSION MANZANITA. Shrub, densely branched, 1–2m. Lvs 2–6cm, ovate to elliptic-oblong, revolute, dark green above, white-tomentose beneath, coriaceous. Infl. paniculate, dense, few-fld, minutely tomentose; cor. white or flushed pink; ovaries pubesc. Fr. 6–9mm, maroon, dry. S Calif. & Baja Calif. Z8.

A. bracteosa (DC.) Abrams = *A. tomentosa* var. *trichoclada*.

A. canescens Eastw. HOARY MANZANITA. Shrub, erect, to 2m, often much smaller, densely branched, gnarled; twigs white-tomentose when young. Lvs 2–4cm, ovate to oblong or rounded, densely white-tomentose when young. Infl. paniculate, short, dense, white-tomentose; pet. 8–9mm, pink; ovaries white-pubesc. eglandular. Fr. 8mm, brown. Winter–spring. S Oreg. to Calif. Z7.

A. columbiana Piper. HAIRY MANZANITA. Shrub, erect, 1–3m, twigs white-tomentose when young. Lvs 2–7cm, ovate to oblong, acute at apex, base rounded, tomentose when young. Infl. paniculate, dense, tomentose-setose; cor. 6mm, white; ovaries often glandular-, pubesc. Fr. 8mm, light red, viscid white-pubesc. Spring. NW America. Z7. 'Oregon Hybrid': low-growing, compact, bark red; lvs grey-green; fls white; fr. flushed red.

A. crustacea Eastw. BRITTLELEAF MANZANITA. Shrub, erect, 1–2m; young twigs white-tomentose. Lvs 2–4cm, ovate-oblong, obtuse to subcordate at base, entire or minutely serrate, bright green, brittle, ± glab. Infl. paniculate, pubesc.; cor. white or rosy pink; ovary hairy or glab., eglandular. Fr. 6mm, red-brown, sparsely pubesc. or glabrate. Late winter–spring. Calif. Z8.

A. cushingiana Eastw. = *A. glandulosa* f. *cushingiana*.

A. densiflora M.S. Bak. SONOMA MANZANITA. Procumbent shrub; br. slender, sinuous, rooting. Lvs 1–3cm, elliptic, glossy green. Infl. a congested short pan.; fls white or pink. Spring. Calif. 'Emerald Carpet': mound-forming, 23–35cm, dense, lustrous green carpet. 'Harmony': close to 'Howard McMinn' but taller, broader, with pale pink fls. 'Howard McMinn': to 1.5–1.8×2m, mound-forming; fls white-pink. 'Sentinel': erect, to 1.8×2.4m; lvs pale green, downy. Z8.

A. diversifolia Parry. SUMMER-HOLLY. Shrub, erect, 2–5m; twigs canescent-tomentose. Lvs 3–8cm, oblong to elliptic, rounded to acute, entire to minutely serrate, revolute, glossy above, minutely tomentose beneath. Infl. racemose, 3–6cm, tomentose; cor. 6mm, white, minutely pubesc.; ovary pubesc. Fr. 5–6mm, red, granular-rugose. Late spring–early summer. Calif. & Baja Calif. var. *planifolia* . Lvs broader, margins plane. Z8.

A. drupacea (Parry) Macbr.= *A. pringlei* var. *drupacea*.

A. edmundsii J.T. Howell. LITTLE SUR MANZANITA. St. rooting, ± prostrate. Lvs to 3cm, elliptic to broadly ovate, truncate to cordate. Fls pink, with leafy bracts; ovary glab. Fr. brown. Calif. 'Carmel Sur': mound-growing groundcover; new growth bronze. 'Danville': to 60cm, spreading; lvs to 2.5cm, rounded, light green, petioles red; fls pink. 'Little Sur': dense, prostrate, new growth bronze-red; fls pink.

A. glandulosa Eastw. EASTWOOD MANZANITA. Shrub, erect and spreading, to 2m, viscid glandular-pubesc. Lvs to 5cm, ovate to ovate-lanceolate, cuneate to obtuse at base, often minutely scabrous, sometimes glaucescent. Cor. white; ovaries glandular-pubesc. Fr. red-brown. Winter–early spring. Oreg. to S Calif. f. *cushingiana* (Eastw.) Wells. Plant eglandular; lvs elliptic to ovate, glabrescent to canescent, bright green to grey-green or subglaucous. ssp. *zacaensis* f. *howellii* (Eastw.) Wells. Branchlets, lvs and petioles minutely pubesc., not gland. or hispid; infl. glandular-hispid; lvs rounded, truncate to sub-cordate at base, often dentate, glaucous. Z8.

A. glauca Lindl. BIG BERRY MANZANITA. Erect, tree-like shrub to 6m. Lvs to 3.25cm, oblong, elliptic to ovate, glaucous. Fls white or pink; ovary gland. Fr. brown. Calif. to Baja Calif.

A. hookeri G. Don. MONTEREY MANZANITA. Low carpeting shrub, 15cm–1m; branchlets ashy-pubesc., rooting. Lvs 1.5–2.5cm, ovate to elliptic, acute, lustrous, thin-textured. Fls in small congested clusters; cor. to 0.4cm, white or pink; ovaries glab. Fr. to 6mm diam., pale red, glossy. Spring. C Calif. 'Monterey Carpet': compact, to 0.3×3.5m. 'Wayside': to 1.2×2.4m, dense. Z8.

A. manzanita Parry. MANZANITA; PARRY MANZANITA. Shrub, erect, 2–4.5m, or tree to 6m; twigs somewhat sinuous, densely pubesc. when young. Lvs 2.5–5cm, broadly ovate, obtuse, mucronate, light to grey-green, coriaceous. Infl. paniculate, pendulous, to 3cm; cor. 1cm, white to pink. Fr. white then red-brown. Late winter–spring. Calif. Z8. 'Dr Hurd': treelike to 5m; bark mahogany; lvs dark green; fls white.

A. ×media Greene. (*A. columbiana* ×*A. uva-ursi*.) Shrub, procumbent with erect or ascending br. to 25cm.Lvs 2.5cm, obovate, apex obtuse to acute, base tapered, softly pubesc. beneath. Infl. racemose, compact; cor. 6mm, white to pale pink. Fr. 6mm. Spring. NW US. 'Grandiflora': fls larger. Z7.

A. myrtifolia Parry. IONE MANZANITA. Low shrub, 0.5–1m; br. procumbent and rooting, sinuous, glaucous and glandular-setose when young scaly. Lvs 0.5–1.5cm, elliptic to narrowly ovate, apex acute, base obtuse to acute, glossy light green above. Infl. small, pubesc.; cor. 4mm, white to pink; ovaries pubesc. Fr. 4mm, green. Winter. Calif. Z8.

A. nevadensis A. Gray. PINE-MAT MANZANITA. Mat-forming shrub, 15–40cm; br. erect, rooting, young twigs grey-pubesc., becoming viscid. Lvs 2–3cm, narrowly lanceolate to broadly obovate, with short, distinct tip, light green, glab. to sparsely pubesc. Infl. erect, compact, pubesc.; cor. 5mm, white to pink. Fr. globose, dark brown. Spring–early summer. Oreg. and Calif. Z6.

A. nummularia A. Gray. FORT BRAGG MANZANITA. Mat-forming or rounded shrub; br. erect to 1m, creeping then ascending, densely leafy; white-downy. Lvs 1–1.5cm, elliptic to ovate, lustrous, entire to ciliate, base ± cordate. Infl. small; cor. to 5mm, white; ovaries puberulous. Fr. 3–4mm, green. Calif. Z6.

A. pallida Eastw. = *A. andersonii* var. *pallida*.

A. patula Greene. GREEN MANZANITA. Shrub, erect, 1–2m; st. many, crown regular, twigs minutely glandular-pubesc. Lvs 3–5cm, broadly oval to oblong, obtuse, rounded at base, thick,

Infl. paniculate, lax, broad, gland.; cor. 5–8mm, pink; ovaries glab. Fr. 8–10mm, dark brown. Spring. Calif. Z6.

A. pringlei Parry. PINK-BRACTED MANZANITA. Shrub, erect, 1–2.5m, br. spreading; branchlets glandular-pubesc. Lvs 2.5–5cm, ovate to suborbicular, rounded to subcordate at base, grey-green, minutely glandular-pubesc. Infl. racemose, glandular-pilose; bracts slender, pink; cor. white to rosy pink. Fr. 6–12mm, ovoid to dark red, glandular-pubesc. Spring. Ariz. & Baja Calif. var. *drupacea* Parry. Nutlets united into single solid stones, not divisible. Late winter–early spring. Z8.

A. pumila Nutt. DUNE MANZANITA. Shrub, mat-forming, procumbent; twigs ascending, 15–30cm, pubesc. when young. Lvs 1.5–2cm, obovate, subacute, dull or glossy, glab. above, ± white-tomentose beneath. Rac. short, dense, pubesc.; cor. 3–4mm, white or tinged pink; ovary glab. Fr. globose to oblong, 5mm, red-brown. Late winter–early spring. Calif. Z8.

A. regismontana Eastw. = *A. andersonii*.

A. stanfordiana Parry. Shrub, erect, 1.5–2.5m; twigs slender, dark red, glab. or finely pubesc. Lvs 3–6cm, erect, oblanceolate to narrowly ovate, glossy. Pan. elongate, axis red, finely pubesc.; cor. 4–5mm, pink to white flushed pale pink; ovaries glab. Fr. 5–7mm, light red. Late winter–early spring. Calif. Z6. 'Louis Edmunds': everg., upright; fls pink. ssp. *bakeri* (Eastw.) J.E. Adams. Branchlets with longer hairs; fls larger.

A. tomentosa (Pursh) Lindl. DOWNY MANZANITA; WOOLLY MANZANITA. Shrub, erect, openly branched usually with a single st., 1–2.5m; bark peeling in long strips, twigs white-tomentose. Lvs 2.5–4.5cm, oblong to ovate, glab. and glossy above, densely white-tomentose beneath. Infl. paniculate, short, broad, tomentose; cor. 5–6mm, white; ovaries white-pubesc., eglandular. Fr. 8–10mm, finely pubesc. Winter–early spring. Z8. var. *trichoclada* (DC.) Munz. Branchlets, lvs, infl. gland.

A. uva-ursi (L.) A. Gray. COMMON BEARBERRY; MEALBERRY; HOG CRANBERRY; KINNIKINICK; SANDBERRY; MOUNTAIN BOX; BEAR'S GRAPE; CREASHAK. Mat-forming shrub; br. procumbent, rooting. Lvs 1–3cm, obovate, coriaceous, dark green, pale beneath. Fls to 0.6cm, white tinted pink in short, nodding rac. Fr. scarlet. N Amer., N Eurasia. Z4. 'Anchor Bay': dense groundcover; lvs oblong, deep-green, glossy. 'Massachusetts': vigorous, mat-forming; lvs deep-green, glossy. 'Point Reyes': groundcover; lvs rounded, bright. 'Radiant': lvs paler green; fr. large, bright red, abundant. 'Vancouver Jade': everg.; lvs glossy; fls pink, small. 'Vulcan's Peak': dense groundcover; fls abundant; fr. red.

A. cvs. 'Clyde Robins': slow-growing; fls white. 'Emerald Carpet': dense carpet to 40cm; lvs to 1.8cm, bright green; fls small, pink. 'Tilden Park': low-growing; lvs dark, rounded. 'Sunset': (*A. hookeri* ×*A. pajaroensis*) new growth coppery red; fls pink-white. 'Wood's Red': dwarf; young growth tinged red; fls pink; fr. large, red.

→*Arctous* and *Comarostaphylis*.

Arctotheca Wendl. Compositae. 5 white-tomentose, perenn. herbs. St. 0 or decumbent. Lvs basal and rosulate or alt. on st., usually lyrate-pinnatifid. Cap. radiate, scapose; receptacle flat; involucre campanulate or hemispheric; phyllaries oblong to oblong-linear; ray flts in 1 row, mostly yellow; disc flts tubular, 5-lobed. Summer–autumn. S Afr., nat. Eur. and elsewhere. Z9.

A. calendula (L.) Levyns. Perenn. herb to 50cm, scapose or decumbent. Lvs to 15×5cm, lyrate-pinnatifid or entire, white-tomentose beneath. Cap. to 5cm diam.; ray flts to 20mm, pale yellow above, tinged purple below.

A. forbesiana (DC.) Lewin. Stemless perenn. herb. Lvs basal, to 20×5cm, with linear-lanceolate lobes, white-tomentose beneath, revolute. Cap. to 4cm diam.; ray flts yellow-brown, to 25mm.

A. nivea (L. f.) Lewin = *A. populifolia*.

A. populifolia (A. Berger) Norl. Perenn. herb to 30cm, white-tomentose, decumbent to erect, branched. Lvs to 7×7cm, elliptic to ovate, rarely lyrate-pinnatifid, obtuse or rounded. Cap. 1.5–2cm diam.; ray flts yellow.

→*Arctotis*, *Cryptostemma* and *Venidium*.

Arctotis L. AFRICAN DAISY. Compositae. *c*50 ann. to perenn. herbs, rarely subshrubs. Lvs in basal rosettes and cauline. Cap. to 10cm diam., radiate, solitary on long stout scapes. S Afr. to Angola. Z9.

A. acaulis L. Stemless perenn. Lvs to *c*25cm, lobed or lyrate, to 20cm, green above, white-woolly beneath, undulate. Ray flts yellow orange-yellow to red, copper-red below; disc flts purple-black. Summer. S Afr.

A. angustifolia L. Herbaceous perenn. Lvs to 6cm, lanceolate to oblong or elliptic-oblong, scabrous to hispid above, white-woolly beneath, entire to remotely toothed. S Afr.

A. anthemoides L. = *Ursinia anthemoides*.

A. aspera L. Subshrub to 1m. St. hispid. Lvs pinnatifid, lobed or deeply incised, tomentose beneath, hispid above. Ray flts yellow. S Afr.

A. breviscapa Thunb. Stemless ann. to 15cm. Lvs to 15cm, oblong-lanceolate, pinnately lobed or lyrate, serrate or dentate, tomentose beneath. Ray flts orange-yellow, coppery beneath, often brown-blue at base; disc flts dark brown. Summer–early autumn. S Afr.

A. calendula L. = *Arctotheca calendula.*

A. calendulacea Thunb. = *Arctotheca calendula.*

A. candida Thunb. Herbaceous, short-stemmed perenn. Lvs to 12cm, pinnatisect, lobes narrow, white-woolly beneath, pilose above, ray flts cream-yellow above, tinged purple below. S Afr.

A. crithmoides P. Bergius. = *Ursinia crithmoides.*

A. decurrens Jacq. = *Arctotheca calendula.*

A. dentata L. = *Ursinia dentata.*

A. grandis hort. = *A. venusta.*

A. fastuosa Jacq. CAPE DAISY. Hoary ann. To 80cm. Lvs to 15cm, oblanceolate, lyrate-lobed. Ray flts orange with purple-brown base; disc flts maroon to black. Summer. S Afr. Z8.

A. ×hybrida hort. (*A. venusta* ×*A. fastuosa.*) Robust hyrids to 40cm, intermediate between the parents, sometimes persisting as subshrubby perennials but usually treated as annuals. Lvs thinly felty, dull to silver-grey, sinuately toothed. Fls in a range of colours from pale grey-blue to peach, or vivid orange. Harlequin Hybrids: 'Apricot', 'Flame', 'Pink', 'Rosita', 'Wine', selections named and cloned for the predominant fl. colour. There are also Harlequin New Hybrids, with fls ranging in colour from white and cream to apricot, carmine and red, some with dark centres.

A. pilifera A. Berger = *Ursinia pilifera.*

A. revoluta Jacq. Subshrub to 40cm. St. tomentose. Lvs pinnatisect, lobes linear to lanceolate, white-tomentose, dentate. Ray flts yellow, tinged brown below. S Afr.

A. roodae Hutch. Subshrub to 20cm. St. pubesc. Lvs to 15cm, oblanceolate-spathulate, lobed, denticulate. Ray flts orange-red to red-purple, with black mark at base; disc flts black. S Afr.

A. scapigera Thunb. = *A. acaulis.*

A. sericea Thunb. = *Ursinia sericea.*

A. speciosa Jacq. = *A. breviscapa.*

A. stoechadifolia hort. = *A. venusta.*

A. venusta Norl. BLUE-EYED AFRICAN DAISY. Ann. to 60cm, st. ribbed. Lvs elliptic-obovate, obtuse, grey-white pubesc., sinuate-dentate to pinnatisect. Ray flts purple-red; disc flts blue-red. Summer–autumn. S Afr. 'Circus-Circus': to 30–45cm; lvs silver-green; flowerheads to 10–12cm diam., white, yellow, pink, orange, bronze and lavender.

→ × *Venidioarctotis* and *Venidium.*

Arctous (A. Gray) Niedenzu.

A. alpinus (L.) Niedenzu = *Arctostaphylos alpina.*

Ardisia Sw. Myrsinaceae. *c*250 everg., small trees, shrubs or sub-shrubs, some scandent. Lvs in spirals or whorls, petiolate, often leathery, entire or toothed. Fls small, 5-merous, racemose in long-stalked corymbs among or below lvs, or in dense term. pan; cal. lobes ± free or fused, cor. fleshy, star-shaped. Drupe globose, 1-seeded. Trop. and warm-temperate Asia, Australasia and the Americas.

A. acuminata Willd. = *A. guianensis.*

A. crenata Sims. CORALBERRY; SPICEBERRY. Glab. shrub to 2m. Lvs to 20cm, oblanceolate to elliptic-lanceolate, crenate-undulate. Fls white or pink. Fr. coral-red to scarlet. Jap. to N India. 'Alba': fls white. Z7.

A. crenulata Lodd. = *A. crenata.*

A. crispa (Thunb.) DC. Shrub, 60–120cm; twigs hairy when young. Lvs 6–14cm, elliptic-lanceolate, leathery dark green. Fls pink with darker spots. Fr. red. Indon. and the Philipp. to In-dia, S China and Jap. 'Alba': fr. white. 'Variegata': lvs irregularly edged white, pink-red when young. Z7.

A. escallonioides Cham. & Schldl. MARLBERRY; DOG-BERRY. Shrub or small tree to 7.5m, bark white, scaly, twigs stout. Lvs 6–16cm, oblanceolate to elliptic, leathery, yellow-green or dark green. Infl. term. pan.; fls white with purple dots and lines. Fr. glossy black. US and Mex. to Guat. and N W Indies. Z9.

A. guianensis (Aubl.) Mez. Small tree to 6m. Lvs to 15cm, oblong-elliptic, membranous, crenate. Infl. a term. pan., fls gland-dotted white. Fr. red to purple-black, gland-dotted. N S Amer., Trin. Z9.

A. japonica (Thunb.) Bl. MARLBERRY. Procumbent shrub, 25–40cm, br. erect, twigs red-brown, hairy. Lvs 5–7cm, oval-ovate, glossy dark green, toothed. Rac. pendulous, fls white to pale pink. Fr. pink. Summer. China, Jap. 'Hakuokan': lvs white and silver-green. 'Hinotsukasa': slow-growing; lvs irregular, toothed, largely coloured cream. 'Ito Fukurin': lvs variegated green and white. 'Matsu-Shima': st. pink; lvs waxy, dark green,

variegated with cream centre, margins frilled and deeply toothed. 'Nishiki' ('Hokan Nishiki'): lvs variegated gold and pink. Z8.

A. paniculata (Nutt.) Sarg. = *A. escallonioides.*

A. pickeringia Torr. & A. Gray = *A. escallonioides.*

A. pusilla A. DC. Stoloniferous, decumbent shrub to 30cm, twigs rusty-brown hairy. Lvs 2–5cm, elliptic-ovate, coarsely toothed, rusty-brown hairy, pink when young. Fls white or pink-white, *c*12 per rac. Fr. red. S China, Jap. Z6.

A. solanacea Roxb. Low shrub or small tree to 3–4m. Lvs to 17cm, oblong-ovate or elliptic, glab., fleshy, leathery, gland-dotted. Fr. black, juice purple, flesh white. Summer. India, China, SE Asia. Z9.

Ardisiandra Hook. f. Primulaceae. 3 creeping, perenn. herbs. St. to 35cm. Lvs 3–4cm, ovate or round, apex rounded, base cordate, dentate or with denticulate lobes; petiole equalling or exceeding lamina. Fls clustered or solitary, axillary, pedicellate; cal. cylindrical, lobes 5; cor. white, campanulate, lobes oblong, ciliate, rounded. Summer. Trop. Afr. (mts). Z10.

A. sibthorpioides Hook. f. Fls to 0.5cm diam., 3–4 per cluster.

Areca L. Palmae. 50–60 palms. St. usually erect, conspicuously scarred. Crownshaft smooth. Lvs arching or *c*2m, undivided and pinnately ribbed or pinnate; term. pinnae fused into a fish-tail shape. Indomal. to trop. Aus. and Solomon Is. Z10.

A. alba Bory = *Dictyosperma album.*

A. aurea hort. ex Balf. f. = *Dictyosperma album.*

A. baueri (Seem.) Hook. f. = *Rhopalostylis baueri.*

A. catechu L. BETEL PALM; BETEL-NUT PALM; ARECA NUT PALM; CATECHU; PINANG. St. solitary, to 20m×20cm. Crownshaft grey-green. Lvs to 2m; pinnae crowded, several-ribbed, apices truncate, toothed. Fr. yellow to orange or scarlet, to 5cm. Origin unknown.

A. langloisiana Potztal. = *A. vestiaria.*

A. lutescens Bory = *Chrysalidocarpus lutescens.*

A. madagascariensis hort. = *Chrysalidocarpus madagascariensis.*

A. oleracea Jacq. = *Roystonea oleracea.*

A. purpurea hort. ex André = *Hyophorbe lagenicaulis.*

A. speciosa hort. ex Versch. = *Hyophorbe lagenicaulis.*

A. triandra Roxb. St. clustered, to 7m×5cm, sometimes with stilt roots. Crownshaft green. Lvs to 2m; petioles to 30cm; pinnae truncate, apex toothed. E India to Philipp.

A. verschaffeltii hort. = *Hyophorbe verschaffeltii.*

A. vestiaria Giseke. St. clustered to 10m×10cm, with stilt roots. Crownshaft orange-red. Lvs to 2m; pinnae obliquely truncate, praemorse. Sulawesi, Moluccas.

ARECACEAE C.H. Schultz. See Palmae.

Areca Nut Palm *Areca catechu.*

Areca Palm *Chrysalidocarpus lutescens.*

Arecastrum (Drude) Becc.

A. romanzoffianum (Cham.) Becc. = *Syagrus romanzoffianus.*

A. romanzoffianum var. *botryphorum* (Mart.) Becc. = *Syagrus botryphorus.*

Arenaria L. SANDWORT. Caryophyllaceae. *c*160 low-growing, largely perenn., woody-based herbs. Lvs in opposite pairs, line-ar or circular. Fls small, in cymes or solitary, slender-stalked; sep. 5, ovate-lanceolate free; pet. ovate-oblanceolate, usually 5 and white. Widespread, esp. in N hemis.

A. aggregata (L.) Lois. Dense cushion-plant with small, 4-ranked, lanceolate, lvs. Fls solitary; sep. 4–6mm; pet. slightly longer than sep. Summer. Mts of SW Eur. Z6.

A. balearica L. Mat-forming, with slender, prostrate, rooting st. Lvs 2–4mm, broadly ovate to almost circular, pubesc., shiny. Fls solitary; sep. 3mm; pet. about 5mm. Summer. Is. of W Medit. Z7.

A. caespitosa auct. = *Sagina subulata.*

A. capillaris Poir. Loosely mat-forming, with narrowly linear lvs. Infl. a few-fld cyme; sep. 3–5mm, obtuse; pet. at least 1.5× length sep. Summer. Sib.; Alask. to Nevada. *A. kingii* (S. Wats.) M.E. Jones, differs in acute sep. and eglandular st., occurs in W America from Oregon to California. Plants in cult. in North American gardens are mostly *A. kingii.* Z2.

A. capitata Lam. = *A. aggregata.*

A. ciliata L. Loosely tufted, with small, broadly ovate, ± glab. lvs. Flowering shoots to 7cm, with 1–6 fls; sep. about 3mm; pet. 4–5mm. Summer. N Eur. and mts of C Eur. Z1.

A. erinacea Boiss. = *A. aggregata.*

A. formosa Fisch. ex DC. = *A. capillaris.*

A. graminifolia Schräd. non Ard. = *A. procera.*

A. graminifolia Ard. non Schräd. = *Minuartia graminifolia.*

A. hookeri Nutt. Cushion-plant with linear, rigid, pungent lvs, and glandular-hairy flowering st. to 15cm. Infl. a dense cyme; sep. 6–8mm; pet. slightly longer than sep. Summer. NW Amer., Rocky Mts to Tex. *A. franklinii* Douglas ex Hook., with looser habit, glab. flowering st. and smaller pet., occurs from Washington State to Nevada. Z6.

A. laricifolia L. = *Minuartia laricifolia.*

A. laricifolia auctt. non L. = *Minuartia obtusiloba.*

A. ledebouriana Fenzl. Tufted, somewhat spiny, glab. plant with closely packed, rigid, subulate lvs, and branched flowering st. to 15cm. Cyme loose; sep. 3–4mm; pet. about 8mm. Summer. Turk. Z6.

A. montana L. Broadly resembling *Cerastium* spp., from which it may be distinguished by its entire pet. Robust, grey-green, hairy plant with prostrate shoots and ascending flowering st. Lvs to 4cm, oblong-lanceolate to linear. Fls solitary or in few-fld cymes; sep. 6–8mm; pet. 1.5–2cm. Summer. SW Eur. Z4.

A. norvegica Gunn. = *A. ciliata.*

A. obtusa Torr. = *Minuartia obtusiloba.*

A. procera Spreng. Tufted, from a branched woody stock, with grass-like basal lvs and flowering st. to 40cm. Pan. few-fld; sep. 2–5mm; pet. 4–10mm, slightly indented. Summer. Temp. Asia & E Eur. Z3.

A. purpurascens DC. Loosely tufted, st. ascending to 10cm, branching and leafy above. Fls (1–)2–4 together; sep. 5mm; pet. 7–10mm, pale purple, rarely white. Summer. Pyren. and mts of N Spain. 'Elliot's Variety': fls pink, v. abundant. Z6.

A. recurva All. = *Minuartia recurva.*

A. sajanensis auct. amer. non Schltr. = *Minuartia obtusiloba.*

A. sedoides (L.) F.J. Hanb. = *Minuartia sedoides.*

A. tetraquetra L. Differs from *A. aggregata*, in 4, not 5 pet. Summer. Pyren., N Spain. Z6.

A. tmolea Boiss. Mat-forming, densely glandular-hairy, with ovate-elliptic, acute lvs. Flowering st. to 8cm; infl. 1–6-fld; sep. 3–5mm; pet. about twice cal. Summer. Turk. Z6.

A. verna L. = *Minuartia verna.*

Arenga Labill. Palmae. 17 usually monocarpic palms. Trunk simple or multiple, clothed with persistent lf bases. Lvs pinnate or entire. SE Asia. Z10.

A. ambong Becc. = *A. undulatifolia.*

A. brevipes Becc. To 2m, densely clustered. Lvs to 6m; pinnae linear to cuneate, proximal pinnae clustered. Sumatra, Borneo.

A. caudata (Lour.) H.E. Moore. To 2.75m. St. ringed. Pinnae cuneate, apex terminating in a long, toothed tail. Thail., Burm., Indochina.

A. engleri Becc. To 1.8m. St. clothed with dark grey fibres. Lvs to 1.4m; pinnae to 43cm, dark green above, grey beneath. Taiwan, Ryukyu Is.

A. hastata (Becc.) Whitm. To 1m. St. slender, clustered. Pinnae 3–4, to 13×5cm. Malay Penins.

A. hookeri (Becc.) Whitm. To 45cm. St. slender, clustered. Lvs to 40cm, simple or imparipinnate, oblong. Malaya.

A. microcarpa Becc. To 8m. St. clustering. Lvs to 3m; pinnae to 75cm, linear, base rounded. New Guinea, Moluccas.

A. obtusifolia Mart. To 10m. Trunk dark grey, clothed with fibres. Lvs to 5m; pinnae to 90×5cm, linear-lanceolate, glaucous beneath, apex obtuse. W Java, Sumatra, Malay Penins.

A. pinnata Merrill. SUGAR PALM. To 20m. Trunk clothed with persistent black lf sheaths and bases. Lvs to 12×3m; pinnae to 70×5cm, in 1–6 rows, oblong, apex drooping, margins dentate. Malay Archipel.

A. porphyrocarpa (Bl.) H.E. Moore. To 3m. St. cane-like, densely clustered. Lvs to 5m; pinnae to 45×15cm, alt., white beneath, long-cuneate-flabellate, apex tattered. W Java.

A. tremula (Blanco) Becc. DUMA YAKA. To 4m. St. clustered. Lvs to 6m; pinnae to 35×2cm, narrow-linear, apex dentate. Philipp.

A. undulatifolia Becc. To 7m. St. clustered. Lvs to 6m; pinnae to 100×15cm, margins sometimes undulate. Borneo, Celebes.

A. westerhoutii Griff. LANGKAP. St. short, solitary, ringed. Lvs to 10×2m, ascending; pinnae to 70×5cm, oblong, apex fishtail-shaped, margin dentate. Malaya, Penins. Thail.

→*Blancoa, Caryota, Didymosperma* and, Wallichia.

Arequipa Britt. & Rose.

A. leucotricha sensu Britt. & Rose = *Oreocereus hempelianus.*

Arethusa L. Orchidaceae. 2 terrestrial cormous orchids. Lvs slender, solitary. Fls solitary on slender stalks; tep. ± linear-oblong to lanceolate, forming hood; lip reflexed, erose, crested. N Amer., Jap. Z3.

A. bulbosa L. SWAMP PINK; DRAGON'S MOUTH; BOG ROSE. Lf to 23cm, grass-like. Fls to 5cm, pale to dark rose-purple, fragrant, lip paler with yellow crest and purple apex. Canada, US.

A. divaricata L. = *Cleistes divaricata.*

A. ophioglossoides L. = *Pogonia ophioglossoides.*

Argemone L. PRICKLY POPPY; ARGEMONY. Papaveraceae. 28 ann. or perenn. herbs and 1 shrub, with pale yellow to orange latex. St. erect or ascending, glaucous, smooth to prickly. Lvs entire to deeply lobed, prickly to smooth, glaucous blue, spiny-dentate, becoming narrower and more shallowly lobed on st. Sep. 3–6, smooth to prickly, terminating in a spine; pet. usually in 2 whorls of 3, sta. numerous, pale yellow. Capsules elliptic to oblong, smooth to densely spiny. SE & S US, W Indies, C & S Amer., Hawaii.

A. alba James = *A. polyanthemos.*

A. albiflora Hornem. Ann. or bienn. to 1.5m, much-branched, sparsely prickly. Lvs glaucous grey-green, prickly on main veins beneath, oblanceolate, deeply to shallowly lobed, lobes oblong. Fls to 10cm diam.; sep. smooth, spiny to 1cm; pet. white or mauve, suborbicular to obovate; sta. 150+, anth. yellow. Spring–summer. S US. Z7.

A. grandiflora Sweet. Ann. or short-lived perenn. to 1.5m, much-branched, smooth to densely prickly. Lvs prickly on veins beneath with prickle-tipped teeth, deeply lobed, upper lvs more shallowly lobed. Fls to 10cm diam.; sep. spine to 1.5cm; pet. white or yellow, suborbicular to cuneate; sta. 150+. Summer. Mex. Z8.

A. hispida A. Gray. Perenn. to 60cm; branched above, densely prickly, hispid. Lvs blue-green, prickly on veins above, deeply lobed. Fls to 10cm diam.; sep. densely prickly; pet. white; sta. 150+. Fr. ovoid, with straight to incurved prickles. Summer. Rocky Mts. Z5.

A. intermedia Eastw. = *A. polyanthemos.*

A. mexicana L. DEVIL'S FIG; MEXICAN POPPY. Ann. to 1m, branching below, sparsely prickly. Lvs glaucous, with striking grey-white markings over veins, smooth, oblanceolate to ovate deeply lobed, marginal teeth mucronate. Fls to 7cm diam.; sep. spiny, horn to 1cm; pet. bright to pale yellow, outer pet. obovate, inner obcuneate; sta. 30–50. Summer. S US, W Indies, C Amer. var. *ochroleuca* Lindl. Pet. cream-yellow. 'Alba': fls white. 'Yellow Lustre': to 50cm; lvs blue-green veined silver; fls pale lemon-tangerine. Z8.

A. munita Dur. & Hilg. Ann. or perenn. to 160cm, sparsely to densely branched, sparsely prickly, sometimes marked purple. Lower lvs oblanceolate, deeply lobed, margins and veins prickly, upper lvs elliptic, shallowly lobed. Fls to 13cm diam.; sep. smooth to prickly, spine to 1cm; pet. obcuneate to obovate; sta. 150–250+. Summer. Calif. to New Mex. Z7.

A. platyceras Link & Otto. Ann. to 75cm, branched above, with sparse weak spines. Lvs glaucous blue, sharply spiny to dentate, veins sparsely prickly to smooth, oblanceolate, deeply lobed, to elliptic to ovate, shallowly lobed. Fls to 15cm diam.; sep. spine to 1cm, soft; pet. white to yellow, obcuneate; sta. about 75, anth. yellow to mauve. Summer. Mex. Z8.

A. polyanthemos (Fedde) Ownb. Ann. or bienn. to 120cm, branched above apex, sparsely prickly. Lvs glaucous, succulent, sparsely prickly on veins above, oblanceolate, deeply lobed to elliptic-ovate, shallowly lobed. Fls to 10cm diam.; sep. smooth, spines to 1cm; pet. white or pale mauve, inner pet. broadly obovate, erose; sta. to 150+. Summer. W US. Z6.

A. sanguinea Greene. Ann., bienn. or short-lived perenn. to 120cm. Lvs glaucous, veins light blue-green, lower lvs deeply loved, upper lvs shallowly lobed, spiny-serrate. Fls to 9cm diam.; sep. slightly prickly, spines to 1cm; pet. obovate to suborbicular, white to mauve, erose; sta. to 150+, fil. yellow to red, anth. yellow to mauve. Summer. S Tex. to NE Mex. Z7.

Argemony *Argemone.*

Argentine Trumpet Vine *Clytostoma callistigioides.*

Argyle Apple *Eucalyptus cinerea.*

Argylia D. Don. Bignoniaceae. 10 caudiciform perenn. herbs. St. erect, branched, viscid, pubesc. Lvs peltate-digitate, 2–3-pinnatifid, petiolate, seg. linear-rhombic, fleshy. Fls axill. or in term. corymb; cal. lobes 5, narrow; cor. tube dilated to 5-lobed, indistinctly bilabiate limb. Peru, Chile. Z9.

A. canescens D. Don. Caudex 19cm diam. St. fleshy, terete. Lvs 5–8.75cm; petiole 10–20cm. Fls intense yellow, 2.5–3.75cm, streaked red in throat. Summer. Chile.

Argyranthemum Webb ex Schultz-Bip. MARGUERITE. Compositae. 22 perenn. subshrubs, to 2m. St. branched, procumbent or ascending. Lvs entire to finely dissected. Cap. radiate, 2 to many in loose corymbs; involucre cup-shaped. Macronesia. Z9.

A. broussonetii (Pers.) Humphries. St. to 1.5cm. Lvs to 16×8cm, ovate to oblong, bipinnatisect, with 2–18 primary seg. Involucre to c20mm diam.; ray flts to 40×8mm, white; disc flts 4mm, yellow. Canary Is.

A. callichrysum Habit compact; foliage finely divided; ray flts cream to golden yellow. Gomera. Cv. Prado is selection.

A.foeniculaceum (Willd.) Webb ex Schultz-Bip. St. to 1m. Lvs to 10×6.5cm, blue grey, 2–3-pinnatisect with 2–8 obovate primary seg. Involucre to c20mm diam.; ray flts to 20×5mm, white; disc flts to c3.5mm, yellow. Tenerife.

A.frutescens (L.) Schultz-Bip. St. to 1m. Lvs to 10×6cm, 1–2-pinnatisect, blue grey, primary seg. 2–10, leathery, thinly succulent, narrowly obovate, involucre to over 20mm diam.; ray flts to 15×5mm, white; disc flts to 4mm yellow. Canary Is. ssp. *frutescens*. St. to 70cm. Lvs to 5×3cm, with 2–6 primary seg. lobes, dentate. Involucre to 12mm diam.; ray flts to 15×4mm. ssp. *canariae* (Christ) Humphries. St. to 50cm. Lvs to 8×4cm, with 2–8, 1–4 lobed primary seg. Ray flts to 30×5mm.

A.gracile Schultz-Bip. St. to 1.5m. Lvs 2–10cm, finely pinnatisect, primary seg. 2–6. Involucre to 12mm diam.; ray flts to 14×4mm white, disc flts 3mm, yellow. Tenerife.

A.haemotomma Ray flts white to rose; disc flts purple-red. Bugio, Deserta Grande.

A.maderense (D. Don) Humphries. St. to 1m. Lvs to 10×3cm, obovate, dark green, lobes 2–6. Involucre to 15mm diam.; ray flts to 25×5mm, pale yellow, disc flts to 3.5mm, yellow. Lanzarote.

A. cvs. Fls pink 'Mary Cheek': 20–40cm; lvs fine; infl. double, rounded, mid pink. 'Mary Woolton': to 90cm; lvs coarse; infl. double; disc flts peach to pink, pompom-like, ray flts spreading, shell-pink. 'Petite Pink': 20–40cm, compact; lvs fine slightly fleshy; infl. single, disc flts golden, ray flts pale pink. 'Powder Puff': miniature; lvs fine; infl. double, slightly ragged, mid to pale pink. 'Rollason's Red': 20–40cm; lvs coarse; infl. single, ray flts crimson to scarlet, gold at base forming ring around dark disc. 'Vancouver': erect to 90cm; lvs coarse; infl double, candy pink, ray flts spreading, disc dense, pompom-like. *Fls yellow* 'Cornish Gold': resembling a superior 'Jamaica Primrose'. 'Double Yellow': sprawling, coarse-lvd; infl. double, golden yellow. 'Jamaica Primrose': bushy, to 1m; lvs grey-green, broad-ly lobed; flts large single, pale to bright gold. 'Levada Cream': lvs more finely divided than 'Jamaica Primrose', flts single, primrose to cream, long-stalked. 'Peach Cheeks': low, spreading habit; infl. single to double or anemone – centred, peach-apricot to white with a yellow centre. *Fls white* (in singles, ray flts white, disc golden yellow) 'Chelsea Girl': 40–70cm; lvs v. fine; infl. single. 'Margaret Lynch': a selection of *A. frutescens* ssp. *succulentum*, lvs v. succulent, slender, infl. single. 'Royal Haze': to 90cm, lvs finely cut, blue-grey; infl. single. 'Snow-storm': compact, rounded, to 40cm; lvs blue-green; infl. single. 'Snowflake': compact; lvs blue-grey; infl. double, small, pompom-like, pure white. 'Edelweiss': compact; lvs fine blue-grey; infl. double, spreading, disc stained gold. 'Qinta White': large plant with ivory-white, double chrysanthemum-like infl.

→*Anthemis, Chrysanthemum* and *Pyrethrum*.

Argyreia Lour. Convolvulaceae. c90 mainly woody climbers. Lvs petiolate, entire, usually orbicular. Infl. 1- to many-fld, axill.; sep. 5; cor. funnel-shaped, tubular or campanulate, entire to lobed, usually with hairy bands on seg. Trop. Asia to Aus. Z9.

A. capitata (Vahl) Choisy. Woody climber to 15m. Lvs 7.5–18cm, ovate to orbicular or oblong-lanceolate, apex acuminate, base cordate, brown or yellow-hairy. Infl. long-stalked, capitate, dense, patent-hairy; flts subsessile; cor. 4.5–5.5cm, funnel-shaped, maroon, pale violet or pink, sometimes white. Indon. and Malaysia to Vietnam and Bangladesh.

A. nervosa (Burm. f.) Bojer. WOOLLY MORNING GLORY. Woody climber to 10m. Lvs 18–27cm, ovate to orbicular, apex obtuse, acute or with a short cusp, base cordate, densely white, grey or yellow-hairy beneath. Infl. stalked, subcapitate, white-tomentose; cor. 6–6.5cm, tubular to funnel-shaped, lavender, base of tube darker, tube densely woolly outside. N India; pantropically nat.

A. tiliifolia Wight. = *Stictocardia campanulata*.

Argyrocytisus (Maire) Reyn. Leguminosae (Papilionoideae). 1 decid. shrub to 4m. Br. dark green, becoming grey-brown and weakly woody; young shoots dark green, densely silver-pilose. Lvs trifoliolate; petiole to 5cm; lfts to 11cm, obovate or ovate-oblong, mucronate, dark green, silky-pubescent. Fls to 2cm, pea-like, golden-yellow, pineapple-scented, in dense term. rac. to 11cm. Summer. Moroc. Z7.

A. battandieri (Maire) Reyn. MOROCCAN BROOM; PINEAPPLE BROOM. 'Yellow Tail': fls striking yellow, in long spikes.

→*Cytisus*.

Argyrodendron F. Muell.
A. trifoliolatum F. Muell. = *Heritiera trifoliolata*.

Argyroderma N.E. Br. Aizoaceae. 10 v. succulent perennials. Lvs cylindrical to semi-ovoid, above ground or level with the

soil, the stemless spp. resembling a round, fleshy body with a gaping fissure, 2 borne per season, opposite, base connate, upper surface plane, lower surface forming a chin, occas. keeled, covered with silvery wax, older lvs sometimes persistent, forming a column. Fls with a distinct cal. tube; sta. pendulous. S Afr. Z9.

A. angustipetalum L. Bol. = *A. congregatum*.
A. australe L. Bol. = *A. delaetii*.
A. blandum L. Bol. = *A. delaetii*.
A. braunsii (Schwantes) Schwantes = *A. fissum*.
A. brevipes (Schltr.) L. Bol. = *A. fissum*.
A. citrinum L. Bol. = *A. delaetii*.
A. congregatum L. Bol. Forming clusters with age. Lvs hood-shaped. Fls yellow or purple.
A. crateriforme (L. Bol.) N.E. Br. Largely subterranean. Lvs hood-shaped. Fls yellow, occas. purple or white.
A. delaetii Maass. Largely subterranean. Lvs semi-ovoid. Fls white, or in shades of purple or yellow.
A. duale (N.E. Br.) N.E. Br. = *Ruschia dualis*.
A. fissum (Haw.) L. Bol. Forms patches with age. Lvs finger-shaped, 5–12cm long, green to yellow. Fls with outer pet. purple or yellow, inner pet. white.
A. formosum L. Bol. = *A. delaetii*.
A. framesii L. Bol. Forming clumps with age. Lvs hood-shaped, keeled, lf-pair not longer than 11mm across the top, fissure to 5mm wide. Fls purple or purple and white. ssp. *hallii* (L. Bol.) H. Hartm. Lf-pair 15–20mm across the top, fissure wider than 5mm. Fls purple and white, rarely yellow.
A. ×kleijnhansii L. Bol. Naturally occurring hybrids involving and resembling *A. fissum*.
A. lesliei L. Bol. = *A. delaetii*.
A. margaretae (Schwantes) N.E. Br. = *Lapidaria margaretae*.
A. nortieri L. Bol. = *A. congregatum*.
A. orientale L. Bol. = *A. fissum*.
A. patens L. Bol. Forming clusters with age. Lvs hood-shaped, keeled. Fls in shades of purple to white, rarely lemon.
A. pearsonii (N.E. Br.) Schwantes. Sometimes clustered, above the ground. Lvs semi-globose, fissure narrow. Fls mostly purple and white, outer pet. occas. orange, inner pet. yellow, rarely white.
A. reniforme L. Bol. = *A. delaetii*.
A. ringens L. Bol. Plants with one or a few bodies. Lvs hood-shaped, ascending, fissure as wide as lvs. Outer pet. purple, in-ner pet. white.
A. roseatum N.E. Br. = *Lapidaria margaretae*.
A. roseum Schwantes = *A. delaetii*.
A. schlechteri Schwantes = *A. pearsonii*.
A. schuldtii Schwantes = *A. delaetii*.
A. subalbum (N.E. Br.) N.E. Br. Forming clumps with age. Lvs semi-globose, upper surfaces closely pressed together, leaving no fissure. Outer pet. purple, inner pet. white.
A. subrotundum L. Bol. = *A. crateriforme*.
A. testiculare (Ait.) N.E. Br. Usually unbranched, growing above the ground. Lvs semi-ovoid, keeled, fissure narrow. Fls purple, rarely white.
A. villetii L. Bol. = *A. subalbum*.

→*Roodia*.

×**Argyrops** Kimnach. (*Argyroderma* × *Lithops*.) Aizoaceae. Lf pairs several, each fushed below; free part of lvs green-white, smooth, 1.5cm thick toward apex, upper surface flat, lower surface rounded, apex obtuse, obscurely carinate, marked with olive-green, dentritic streaks. Fls 2cm diam., yellow. Gdn origin. Z9.

×*A.* 'Moonstones'.

Argyropsis Roem.
A. candida (Lindl.) Roem. = *Zephyranthes candida*.

Argyroxiphium DC. SILVERSWORD. Compositae. 4 erect or spreading, rosette-forming shrubs. Lvs ligulate to lanceolate, helical or in whorls, glab. to silver-hairy. Cap. usually radiate, few to numerous, in large elongated rac. or pan. Hawaii, Maui. Z10.

A. sandwicense DC. Trunk short, simple, stout. Lvs to 40×1.5cm, helical, ± linear, rigid, succulent, silvery hairy. Infl. to 2.5×1m; ray flts to 2×0.6cm, pink to red, 2–4-lobed; central disc flts yellow, peripheral disc flts pink or red.

Aridaria N.E. Br. Aizoaceae. 35 shrubby taprooted perennials; st. woody. Lvs opposite, papillose, usually cylindrical. Fls several or solitary, pedicellate usually noctural and fragrant. S Afr., Nam. Z9.

A. canaliculata (Haw.) Friedr. = *Sphalmanthus canaliculatus*.
A. noctiflora (L.) Schwantes. Erect or prostrate shrub to 90cm. Lvs 5–40×3–10mm, semi-cylindrical, green to blue-green. Fls

solitary, opening at night, 0.5–4.5cm diam., white or pale pink inside, darker outside.

A. resurgens (Kensit) L. Bol. = *Sphalmanthus resurgens*.

A. splendens (L.) Schwantes = *Sphalmanthus splendens*.

Ariocarpus Scheidw. LIVING ROCK. Cactaceae. 6 slow-growing cacti; rootstock stout; st. usually unbranched; tubercles spiralled or rosulate, ± triangular; spines usually 0. Fls short-funnelform; tube naked; perianth-limb spreading. N & E Mex., S Tex. Z9.

A. agavoides (Castañeda) E.F. Anderson. St. (including tubercles) 5–8cm diam., occas. branching; tubercles to 40mm, dark green to green-brown, tip dying when old, bearing a large woolly areole above with a few short spines. Fls 4–5×4–5cm, magenta; stigma lobes 5–6. Autumn–winter. Z7.

A. elongatus (Salm-Dyck) M.H. Lee = *A. trigonus* or *A. retusus*.

A. fissuratus (Engelm.) Schum. St. 5–10cm diam. (to 15cm in var. *lloydii* (Rose) W.T. Marshall); tubercles 10–20mm, grey-green to grey-brown, deeply fissured and wrinkled (less so in var. *lloydii*), with a woolly groove above. Fls 1.5–3.5×2.5–4.5cm, pale to deep magenta, stigma lobes 5–10. Autumn. Z7.

A. furfuraceus (S. Wats.) C. Thomps. = *A. retusus*.

A. intermedius (Backeb. & Kilian) Voldan = *A. fissuratus*.

A. kotschoubeyanus (Lem.) Schum. St. 2–7cm diam., occas. branched; tubercles 5–13mm, dark green to brown-tinged, only slightly roughened, with a woolly groove above. Fls 1.8–2.5×1.5–2.5cm, magenta or white; stigma lobes 4–6. Autumn–winter. Z6.

A. lloydii Rose = *A. fissuratus*.

A. macdowellii W.T. Marshall, invalid name = *A. kotschoubeyanus*.

A. retusus Scheidw. St. 10–25cm diam.; tubercles 15–40mm, spreading, light grey-, yellow- or blue-green, surface smooth or slightly undulating, with or without an areole near the tip, not grooved above. Fls 2–4.2×4–5cm, white or pale pink; stigma lobes 7–16. Autumn. Z7.

A. scaphirostris Boed. St. 4–9cm diam.; tubercles to 50mm, ascending to incurved like the prow of a ship, v. dark green to brown, finely roughened, lacking an areole, not grooved. Fls to 4×4cm, magneta; stigma lobes 3–5. Autumn. Z9.

A. strobiliformis Werderm. = *Pelecyphora strobiliformis*.

A. sulcatus (Salm-Dyck) Schum. = *A. kotschoubeyanus*.

A. trigonus (F.A. Weber) Schum. St. 7–30cm diam.; tubercles 35–80mm, erect or curving upwards or inwards, yellow-green or bronzed grey-green, smooth, lacking an areole, not grooved above, sharply pointed. Fls 2.5–4×3–5cm, pale yellow; stigma-lobes 6–10. Autumn. Z9.

→*Neogomesia* and *Roseocactus*.

Ariry *Syagrus petraea*.

Arisaema Mart. Araceae. *c*150 tuberous or rhizomatous herbaceous perennials. Lvs compound, trifoliate, pedate or radiate, petioles long, sheathed at base, forming a pseudostem, often spotted or mottled. Infl. solitary, terminating pseudostem; spathe usually borne below foliage, base and convolute forming a tube, limb flat or concave, apex hooded or erect; spadix with conspicuous appendix, cylindric, clavate, fimbriate or v. long and slender, erect or drooping. E & C Afr., temp. and trop. Asia, E N Amer.

A. abbreviatum Schott = *A. flavum*.

A. amurense Maxim. To 45cm. Lf 1(–2), lfts 5, entire, radiate; pseudostem dull purple. Spathe white, striped dark purple to green; spadix appendix cylindric, truncate at base. Spring. N Asia. Z5.

A. atrorubens (Ait.) Bl. = *A. triphyllum*.

A. candidissimum W.W. Sm. To 40cm. Lf 1, lfts 10–20cm, 3, suborbicular to ovate; petiole 25–35cm, sheathed by mottled pink-brown basal bracts. Spathe 8–15cm, tube green striped white, limb ovate, long-acuminate, slightly hooded, white striped pink; spadix appendix 5–6cm, subcylindric, tapering above, green. Early summer. W China. Z6.

A. concinnum Schott. To 50cm. Lf 1, lfts 15–30cm, 7–11, radiate, oblanceolate, acuminate. Spathe tube 5cm, cylindric, limb 5cm, ovate-lanceolate, green, striped white, apex 2–7cm, long-acuminate, green or dark purple; spadix slender, apex thickened and roughened. Early summer. E Himal. to Burm. Z8.

A. consanguineum Schott. To 1m. Lf 1, lfts to 40cm, 11–20, radiate, lanceolate to linear-lanceolate, apex filiform. Spathe to 12cm, tube glaucous green, deep purple within, limb oblong-ovate, curved, green, sometimes tinged brown, narrowly striped white, apex 5–15cm, long-acuminate; spadix appendix 3cm, cylindric, sparsely bristly at base, green. Early summer. E Himal. to N Thail. and C China. Z7.

A. costatum (Wallich) Mart. ex Schott & Endl. To 50cm+. Lf 1, lfts to 40cm, 3, elliptic to ovate, edged red. Spathe to 15cm, dark red-purple striped white, limb 1–4cm, oblong-lanceolate,

incurved, apex long-acuminate; spadix appendix to 45cm, narrowing to twisted filiform tail, reaching to ground. Early summer. C & E Nepal. Z7.

A. curvatum (Roxb.) Kunth = *A. tortuosum*.

A. dracontium (L.) Schott. To 80cm. Lf 1, pedate, seg. 10–15cm, 7–15, oblong-elliptic to lanceolate, acuminate; petiole mottled. Spathe poorly differentiated into tube and limb, base 5–7cm, narrow, apical portion to 5cm, oblong-ovate, short-acuminate; spadix appendix to 15cm, white at base, tip green, filiform. Spring. E N Amer. Z4.

A. elephas Buchet. To 30cm. Lf 1, lfts 3, to 15cm, ovate, undulate, brown-purple. Spathe tube 3.5cm, limb to 12cm, obovate-oblong, dark liver-purple, striped white toward base; spadix appendix 25–30cm, curved, apex filiform, reaching ground, dark black-purple. Early summer. W China. Z5.

A. erubescens (Wallich) Schott. To 45cm. Lf 1, lfts to 17cm, 7–14, radiate, narrow-lanceolate, acuminate, undulate; petiole dull pink, mottled red-brown. Spathe to 15cm, tube cylindric, limb ovate, long-acuminate, incurved, red-brown or dull green, pink and white, striped white within; spadix appendix stout, subcylindric, scarcely exserted from tube. Early summer. E Himal. Z4.

A. fimbriatum Mast. To 45cm. Lvs 1–2, lfts to 15cm, 3, ovate, acute. Spathe tube to 6.5cm, funnel-shaped, striped green and white, limb to 11cm, erect or incurved, ovate-lanceolate, striped purple and white; spadix appendix to 10cm, red-purple, pendulous, slender, with numerous filiform rudimentary sterile fls. Malaysia. Z10.

A. flavum (Forssk.) Schott. To 45cm. Lvs 2, pedate, lfts 2.5–12cm, 5–11, oblong-lanceolate, acute; petioles streaked pink-brown. Spathe 2–4cm, tube ovoid to subglobose, green, marked yellow, limb sharply incurved, slender-acuminate, yellow-green to yellow, purple within; spadix included, appendix short, clavate. Early summer. Yemen to W China. Z7.

A. griffithii Schott. To 70cm. Lvs 2, lfts 10–70cm, 3, rhombic-ovate; petiole stout, spotted or blotched green or purple. Spathe tube to 8cm, purple ribbed white, limb 10–20×10–16cm, v. broadly ovate, folded over and downwards, dull purple conspicuously netted green beneath (i.e. on the facing surface), interior purple to grey or green-white with purple blotches, veins and stripes, tip to 10cm, acuminate, purple; spadix appendix to 1m, purple, narrowing to a twisted tail. Early summer. E Himal. Z8.

A. helleborifolium Schott = *A. tortuosum*.

A. hookerianum Schott = *A. griffithii*.

A. jacquemontii Bl. 10–70cm. Lvs 1–2, digitate, lfts 5–15cm, 3–9, narrow-elliptic to ovate, acuminate. Spathe to 15cm, green, sometimes narrowly white-striped, limb to 7.5cm, slightly incurved, apex long-acuminate, upcurved, sometimes purple; spadix appendix, cylindric, slender, upcurved, dark purple above. Early summer. Afghan. to SE Tibet. Z6.

A. japonicum Bl. = *A. serratum*.

A. kiushianum Mak. To 40cm. Lf 1, radiate, lfts 10–20cm, 7–13, lanceolate, long-acuminate. Spathe dark purple, limb broad-ovate, strongly incurved, cuspidate, interior marked white; spadix appendix to 18cm, slender, long-exserted. Early summer. Jap. Z7.

A. nepenthoides (Wallich) Mart. ex Schott. COBRA PLANT. To 50cm. Lvs 2, digitate, lfts 6–12cm, 5, narrow-elliptic, acuminate; petiole dull yellow, spotted red-brown. Peduncle mottled dull purple; spathe tube to 7.5cm, cylindric, limb to 15cm, mottled green-brown to red-brown, striped white, triangular-ovate, incurved forming reflexed auricles at junction with tube, dull green-brown, edged brown; spadix appendix subcylindric, erect, shortly exceeding tube, green. Early summer: Himal. to SW China, Burm. Z8.

A. praecox Koch = *A. ringens*.

A. propinquum Schott. To 70cm. Lvs 2, lfts 8–20cm, 3, rhombic-ovate; petiole spotted brown or dark green. Spathe 10–15cm, tube green-purple to purple, striped white, limb oblong, incurved, apex to 4cm, acuminate, purple, netted white toward margins; spadix appendix 8–20cm, apex filiform, long exserted. Early summer. Kashmir to SE Tibet. Z5.

A. ringens (Thunb.) Schott. To 30cm. Lvs 2, lfts 15–20cm, 3, broad-ovate, long-acuminate, apex filiform, glossy green; petiole sometimes tinged purple. Spathe tube to 3.5cm, obconic, green to purple, striped white or pale green, limb sharply incurved, helmet-shaped, purple or green, sometimes striped, with dark auricles at junction with tube; spadix enclosed in spathe, erect or curved, cylindric, white to pale yellow. Early spring. Jap., Korea, China. Z7.

A. robustum (Engl.) Nak. To 60cm. Lf 1, palmate, lfts 10–15cm, 5, obovate to ovate, short-acuminate. Spathe green, striped white, or dark purple, limb 5–6cm, ovate, long-acuminate; spadix appendix cylindric. Early summer. Jap. Z7.

A. sazensoo misapplied = *A. sikokianum*.

A. serratum (Thunb.) Schott. To 1m. Lvs 2, pedate, lfts to

12.5cm, 7–20, obovate to lanceolate, entire or dentate; pseudostem pale green, densely mottled purple. Spathe 8–12cm, tube 5–7cm, cylindric, limb incurved, ovate, short-acuminate, pale green to dark purple, or purple-spotted, sometimes striped white; spadix appendix 4–5cm, cylindric to clavate, yellow-green, erect. Spring. NE Asia. Z5.

A. **sikokianum** Franch. & Savat. To 50cm. Lvs 2, pedate, lfts to 15cm, oblong-elliptic to broad-ovate, short-acuminate, toothed. Spathe 15–20cm, tube funnel-shaped, interior yellow-white, dull purple at base, exterior deep purple or brown-purple, limb erect or slightly incurved, narrow-ovate, long-acuminate, green to purple-green striped green-white within; spadix appendix erect, white, apex thickened, rounded, club-like. Early summer. Jap. Z5.

A. **speciosum** (Wallich) Mart. ex Schott. To 60cm. Lf 1, lfts 20–45cm, 3, triangular-ovate to lanceolate, margins flushed red; petiole marbled dark purple. Spathe to 20cm, dark black-purple, striped white, tube ribbed, white within, limb ovate-lanceolate, long-acuminate, incurved; spadix appendix to 80cm, ovoid at base, apex long-filiform, purple. Early summer. C Nepal to SW China. Z8.

A. **thunbergii** Bl. To 60cm. Lf 1, radiate, lfts 10–25cm, 9–17, lanceolate, acuminate. Spathe red-purple to dark purple, limb ovate, strongly incurved, apex long-caudate-acuminate; spadix appendix 30–50cm, filliform, erect, wrinkled and thickened at base, tip pendulous. Spring. Jap. ssp. *urashima* (Hara) Mak. To 50cm. Lfts to 18cm, 11–15, oblanceolate to broad-lanceolate, acuminate. Spadix appendix to 60cm, smooth at base. Spring. Jap. Z7.

A. **tortuosum** (Wallich) Schott. To 150cm. Lvs 2–3, pedate, lfts 5–17, ovate to linear-lanceolate; petiole mottled. Spathe to 18cm, green or purple, ± glaucous, tube cylindric, limb ovate, acute, incurved or erect; spadix appendix long-exserted, 'S'-curved, erect toward apex, tapering, green to dark purple. Early summer. Himal. Z7.

A. **triphyllum** (L.) Torr. JACK-IN-THE-PULPIT; INDIAN TURNIP. To 60cm. Lvs (1–)2(–3), lfts 8–15cm, 3, ovate to oblong-ovate, acute; petiole sometimes spotted purple. Spathe to 15cm, green to purple, striped green or white, margins reflexed, limb acute-acuminate, incurved; spadix appendix to 7cm, erect, exserted from tube, clavate to cylindric, green to purple, or purple-flecked. Summer. S Canada to Louisiana and Kans. Z4.

A. **utile** Hook. f. ex Schott. To 50cm. Close to A. *griffithii*; lfts to 25cm, rhombic-ovate or obovate, margins flushed red; petiole spotted. Spathe to 15cm, dark purple, striped or netted white, tube campanulate, limb 7.5×10cm, obovate, incurved, apex to 3cm; spadix appendix 15cm, filiform. Early summer. Himal. Z5.

A. **wallichianum** Hook. f. = A. *propinquum*.

A. **yamatense** (Nak.) Nak. To 40cm. Lvs 2, pedate, lfts 7–12cm, 7–11, broad-oblanceolate, long-acuminate. Spathe green, tube margins recurved above, limb 4–7cm, ovate to broad-ovate, short-acuminate, papillose, yellow within; spadix appendix erect, narrow-cylindric, abruptly capitellate. Spring. Jap. Z7.

Arisarum Targ.-Tozz. Araceae. 3 tuberous or rhizomatous perenn. herbs. Lvs radical, long-petiolate, sagittate-hastate, forming dense cover ± concealing infl. Spathe tubular, below expanded, limb hooded and forward-pointing; spadix shorter than or barely equalling spathe, long-appendaged. Medit., Atlantic Is. Z7.

A. **proboscideum** (L.) Savi. MOUSE PLANT. Rhiz. slender. Lvs 6–15cm, petiole 7–25cm. Spathe 6–18cm, white, bulbous below, upper two-thirds forming a slender, upturned tail-like tip projecting from strongly hooded blade, chocolate brown to maroon-black; spadix tipped white, enclosed within spathe. It., Spain.

A. **vulgare** Targ.-Tozz. FRIAR'S COWL. Tuber irregularly shaped. Lf 5–12cm; petiole 12–30cm. Spathe 4–6cm, tubular, green to silver-white striped dark purple-brown below, then strongly decurved and expanded to form a dark metallic maroon or violet-black hood; spadix fleshy green to purple, protruding from spathe. Medit., Canaries, Azores.

Aristea Sol. ex Ait. Iridaceae. 50 perenn. rhizomatous herbs, usually everg. Basal lvs erect or equitant; st. lvs sheathing. Fls in term. or lateral clusters, short-lived, opening in the morning; perianth seg. 6, joined at base, subequal, spreading; style lobed, not branched. Trop. & S Afr., Madag. Z9.

A. **africana** (L.) Hoffsgg. St. 10–25cm, slender, slightly flattened, often much branched. Lvs narrowly linear, 4–15cm. Fl. clusters single at end of each br.; fls bright blue, rarely white; tep. 10–12mm, oblong, blue. Late winter–summer. S Afr.

A. **biflora** Weimarck. St. 20–40cm, flattened, fls large, blue or lilac, marked with dark green or black. Spring. S Afr.

A. **capitata** Ker-Gawl. = A. *major*.

A. **corymbosa** (Benth. & Hook. f.) Bak. = *Nivenia corymbosa*.

A. **cyanea** Sol. ex Ait. = A. *africana*.

A. **ecklonii** Bak. 40–90cm, st. winged. Lvs to 60cm, arching. Infl. paniculate; fls blue, in lax clusters; outer tep. 8–11mm, inner 9–15mm. Spring–summer. E S Afr., Swaz.

A. **fruticosa** L. f. = *Nivenia fruticosa*.

A. **lugens** (L. f.) Steud. 30–50cm, st. ± flattened. Lvs linear, in basal rosette. Fls c2cm diam.; outer tep. dark blue, inner smaller, pale blue or violet. Spring–summer. S Afr.

A. **macrocarpa** G. Lewis. 1–1.5m, st. terete. Lvs equitant, lanceolate. Infl. lax; fls pale blue, c3cm diam. Summer. S Afr.

A. **major** Andrews. St. 1–1.5m, with short, erect br. Lvs 100–120cm, linear, ± glaucous. Infl. with many fl. clusters; fls pale blue; tep. 16–20mm, inner slightly larger than outer. Summer. S Afr. (Cape Penins.).

A. **platycaulis** Bak. 20–30cm, st. flattened. Lvs 20–30cm, lanceolate. Infl. a pan. or rac.; fls blue. Summer. S Afr.

A. **pusilla** (Thunb.) Ker-Gawl. Slender plants 5–40cm tall, forming tufts; st. angular, lvs 4–23cm, linear. Infl. 1–2-fld; fls blue; tep. 13–24mm, inner wider than outer. Spring–summer. S Afr.

A. **spiralis** (L. f.) Ker-Gawl. St. 20–60cm tall, flattened, unbranched. Lvs 20–55cm, linear. Infl. lax, with 2–4 lat. fl. clusters; fls white or pale blue, marked purple at base; tep. to 30mm, outer with green-brown median line. Late winter–spring. S Afr. (Cape Penins.).

A. **thyrsiflora** (Delaroche) N.E. Br. = A. *major*.

Aristida L.

A. **pennata** Trin. = *Stipagrostis pennata*.

Aristolochia L. BIRTHWORT; DUTCHMAN'S PIPE. Aristolochiaceae. c300 lianes, shrubs or perenn. herbs. Lvs entire or 2–7-lobed, often cordate or subhastate at base. Fls malodorous, usually zygomorphic, often strangely coloured and shaped; perianth straight, curved or S-shaped, usually inflated at base, contracted above into cylindric or funnel-shaped tube graduating into limb, limb entire or lobed. Cosmop.

A. **altissima** Desf. = A. *sempervirens*.

A. **brasiliensis** Mart. & Zucc. = A. *labiata*.

A. **californica** Torr. Climber to 5m. Lvs broadly cordate, acute to obtuse at apex, strigose above, tomentose beneath, 4–12×3–10cm. Fls solitary, geniculate, dull purple; U-shaped, unevenly inflated, to 3cm, abruptly narrowed at limb; limb 3-lobed, smooth, 2×2cm, lobes concave, divergent. Summer. Calif. Z8.

A. **chrysops** (Stapf) Hemsl. To 6m; br. hairy. Lvs to 13cm, ovate, downy, auricled. Fls to 4cm, tubular, sigmoid on pendulous stalks, grey-green, mouth flared, purple-brown, throat yellow. Late spring. China.

A. **clematitis** L. BIRTHWORT. Glab. perenn. herb. St. ± unbranched, erect, to 1m. Lvs broadly cordate, obtuse at apex, base deeply cordate, 6–15×6cm. Fls in congested axill. fascicles, dull green-yellow, base spherical, 0.5cm; tube 1cm, slightly curved, limb 1-lobed, triangular, gradually expanding. Summer. Eur., E to Cauc. Z6.

A. **clypeata** Lind. & André = A. *gigantea*.

A. **cymbifera** Mart. & Zucc. Climber to 7m+. Lvs to 15×8cm reniform, grey-green. Fls ivory to white, mottled and heavily veined chocolate to maroon; base strongly inflated, to 8cm; tube to 4cm, slightly recurved; upper lip to 18cm across, suborbicular, drooping and often folded, minutely and closely veined, lower lip lanceolate, replicate, beak-like, ciliate, green-white marked brown. Summer. Braz. Z10.

A. **durior** Hill = A. *macrophylla*.

A. **elegans** Mast. = A. *littoralis*.

A. **fimbriata** Cham. Climber to 2m+. Lvs suborbicular, cordate to reniform, to 9cm across. Fls with strongly curved green tube; limb erect, 2.5cm across, ciliate with long hairs, exterior green-brown, interior purple-brown veined yellow. Autumn. Braz. Z10.

A. **galeata** Mart. & Zucc. = A. *labiata*.

A. **gigantea** Mart. & Zucc. Vigorous climber. Lvs broadly triangular, acuminate, basally subtruncate, 12–16×10–15cm, deep green above, white-tomentose beneath. Fls purple and yellow-orange; base swollen, obpyriform, 10cm; tube not sharply differentiated, U-shaped, 4cm; limb 1-lobed, abruptly spreading from tube, broadly cordate, 16×14cm, exterior white netted purple, interior maroon broken with white or ivory. Panama. Z10.

A. **gigas** Lindl. = A. *grandiflora*.

A. **grandiflora** Sw. PELICAN FLOWER. Lvs triangular cordate, acute to acuminate, base cordate, 10–20×8–15cm, deep green. Fls solitary, axill., twice geniculate, blotched with purple, white, yellow, red and green; base obpyriform, gibbous, 6–17cm, tube bent at middle, 7–15cm; limb abruptly spreading, 1-lobed,

20–50×50–300cm (width including long tape-like appendage hanging from lower lip of limb). Summer. C Amer., Carib. Z10.

A. indica L.   Climber, 3m+. Lvs elliptic, obtuse, emarginate, slightly cordate at base. Fls purple, erect, many on peduncles. Summer. India. Z10.

A. ×kewensis Will. Wats. (*A. labiata* ×*A. trilobata.*) Vigorous climber, intermediate between parents. Lvs triangular-cordate, almost as large as *A. labiata*, veins tinged red. Fls dull yellow, netted red-brown; tail-like lip crimson. Summer. Gdn origin. Z10.

A. labiata Willd. ROOSTER FLOWER.   Climber. Lvs broadly cordate, apex obtuse, 7–12×7–15cm. Fls solitary, geniculate, mottled red, yellow, green and purple; base subglobose, 7cm, tube straight, emerging at sharp angle from base, 4cm; limb with 2 superposed lobes, upper lobe suborbicular, clawed, ruffled, pendent, 13–15×14–18cm, lower lobe stiffly erect, narrowly lanceolate, 10–15cm. Summer. S Amer. Z10.

A. labiosa Ker-Gawl. = *A. labiata.*

A. littoralis L. Parodi. CALICO FLOWER.   Graceful climber. Lvs cordate to reniform, apex obtuse, base cordate, 7–9×6–10cm, ± glaucous. Fls solitary, axill., geniculate, green-yellow to white, limb veined and marbled purple to maroon, with a darker zone in the throat and yellow in tube; base subcylindric, 3.5cm; tube bent, 3cm; limb 1-lobed, orbicular, abruptly spreading from tube, 10×10cm, often smaller. S Amer., nat. C Amer. and S US. Z9.

A. macrophylla Lam. DUTCHMAN'S PIPE.   Climber to 9m. Lvs broadly cordate, apex obtuse to acute, basally cordate, 7–50×7–45cm, ± glab. Fls solitary, geniculate, green spotted purple, brown and yellow, limb bordered purple-brown, base cylindric, 5mm; tube curved upward, narrowing to limb, 2.5cm; limb 2×2cm, lobes 3, concave, divergent, unappendaged. Summer. E US (Appalachians). Z6.

A. macroura Gomes = *A. trilobata.*

A. manshuriensis Komar. Differs from *A. macrophylla* in young shoots and lf undersides downy. Fls yellow, flushed purple; limb 3cm across, with abruptly acuminate points. Manch., Korea. Z7.

A. moupinensis Franch. Decid. climber. Lvs 10–12cm, reniform, pointed, downy. Fls to 5cm, pale green, tube bent, limb 3-lobed, yellow with purple spots. W China. Z9.

A. pistolochia L.   Pubesc. tuberous perenn. herb, erect, to 80cm. Lvs ovate-triangular, 5×3cm, margin and veins beneath with cartilaginous teeth or papillae. Fls brown, 2–5cm; limb, dark purple, ovate-lanceolate, shorter than tube. Spring. Sardinia to Port. Z8.

A. ringens Vahl non Link & Otto. Glaucous climber, 7m+. Lvs broadly cordate, apex obtuse, 7–12×7–15cm. Fls solitary, geniculate, mottled red, yellow, green and purple; base subglobose, woolly within, 7cm; tube straight, emerging at sharp angle, 4cm; limb with 2 superposed lobes, upper lobe obovate-spathulate, not deflexed, 8×5cm, lower lobe stiffly erect, narrowly lanceolate, 16–20cm. Summer. C Amer., Carib., Flor. Z9.

A. ringens Link & Otto non Vahl = *A. labiata.*

A. rotunda L. Perenn. herb to 20cm. Lvs to 7cm, oval-reniform with a deep basal sinus. Fls solitary 3–5cm, yellow, hairy, limb dark brown. S Eur. Z9.

A. sempervirens L.   Everg. climber, occas. procumbent, to 5m. Lvs triangular-ovate, cordate, leathery, basal sinus shallow, 10×6cm. Fls 2–5cm, yellow striped purple, tube strongly curved; limb purple or dull brown-purple. Spring. S It. to Crete. Z8.

A. serpentaria L. VIRGINIA SNAKEROOT.   Glab. to pubesc. herb. Lvs narrowly lanceolate to broadly ovate, apex acute to acuminate, bse truncate, sagittate or hastate-cordate, 5–15×1–5cm, smooth. Fls borne at base of st. in racemose clusters, geniculate, dull purple; base subglobose; limb indistinctly 3-lobed, smooth, 5×5mm, slightly convex. Summer. SE US. Z8.

A. sipho L'Hérit. = *A. macrophylla.*

A. sturtevantii hort. = *A. grandiflora.*

A. tomentosa Sims.   Climber to 10m. Lvs broadly cordate, apex acute to obtuse, base cordate, 9–20×8–15cm, tomentose beneath. Fls solitary, geniculate, purple, yellow and green; base cylindric, 7mm; tube constricted, sharply bent, 1.5cm, throat ring prominent, purple, rugose; limb smooth, 3-lobed, lobes convex, unequal, strongly revolute, 2×2cm. Summer. SE–SC US. Z8.

A. trilobata L.   Vigorous climber. Lvs obscurely 3-lobed, 10–15×3–15cm. Fls solitary, green mottled brown, term. lobe and tail deep brown, geniculate; base ellipsoid, 4–5cm; tube bent, 5–7cm; limb 1-lobed, narrowly triangular, 15–20×2–5cm, including length of tail-like apical appendage; limb and tube resembling *Sarracenia* pitcher. Summer. E C Amer., Carib. Z9.

ARISTOLOCHIACEAE Juss. 7/410. *Aristolochia, Asarum.*

Aristotelia L'Hérit. Elaeocarpaceae. 5 everg. or decid. shrubs or small trees. Lvs simple or rarely pinnatifid (*A. peduncularis*), entire or toothed. Fls in axill. clusters or term. corymbs; cal. 4–5-parted; pet. 4–5, 3-lobed, toothed or subentire; sta. distinct, downy. Fr. a small berry. Aus., NZ, Chile to Peru. Z8.

A. chilensis (Molina) Stuntz. Everg. shrub or small tree to 5m. Lvs 5–10cm, ovate, toothed, glossy dark green above, paler beneath. Fls to 0.6cm diam., white-green, in 3-fld clusters. Fr. purple, ripening black. Chile. 'Variegata': lvs variegated white.

A. fruticosa Hook. f. MOUNTAIN WINEBERRY.   Intricately branched everg. shrub resembling *Corokia*. Lvs linear to oblong-obovate, leathery. Fls v. small. Fr. red to purple-black. NZ.

A. macqui L'Hérit. = *A. chilensis.*

A. peduncularis (Labill.) Hook. f. Everg. rangy shrub to 3m. Lvs 2.5–7.5cm, lanceolate to ovate-lanceolate, serrate, rarely pinnatifid. Fls to 2.5cm diam., white spotted orange, 1–3 per axil on nodding stalks to 2cm. Fr. pink to red, ripening black. Tasm.

A. racemosa Hook. f. = *A. serrata.*

A. serrata (Forst. & Forst. f.) Oliv. NEW ZEALAND WINE BERRY. Decid. shrub or tree to 8m. New growth downy. Lvs 5–10cm, ovate to ovate-cordate, deeply serrate. Fls to 0.6cm diam., pale pink, crowded in axill. pan. to 10cm. Fr. dark red, ripening black. NZ.

Arizona Alder *Alnus oblongifolia.*
Arizona Ash *Fraxinus velutina.*
Arizona Bugbane *Cimicifuga arizonica.*
Arizona Cypress *Cupressus arizonica.*
Arizona Douglas Fir *Pseudotsuga menziesii* var. *flahaultii.*
Arizona Pine *Pinus arizonica.*
Arizona Single-leaf Pinyon *Pinus californiarum.*
Arizona Sycamore *Platanus wrightii.*
Arizona White Oak *Quercus arizonica.*
Arizona Wild Cotton *Gossypium thurberi.*

Armand Pine *Pinus armandii.*

Armatocereus Backeb. Cactaceae. c10 shrubby or tree-like cacti; st. stout, erect or ascending, cylindric, segmented. Fls nocturnal, tubular. Colomb., Ecuad., Peru.

A. cartwrightianus (Britt. & Rose) Backeb. To 12m; trunk to 2m×30cm; seg. 15–60×7–10cm, dark green; ribs 6–9; central spines 1–4, 2–10cm (to 20cm on the trunk); radial spines c20, 0.5–2.5cm. Fls narrowly funnelform, 7–9×4–5cm; outer tep. red-brown outside; inner tep. white. Ecuad. Z9.

A. godingianus (Britt. & Rose) Backeb. To 10m, trunk to 1.5m×50cm; seg. 15–60×7–10cm, dark green; ribs 7–11; spines 15–25, 1–3(–5)cm. Fls narrowly funnelform, 7–9×5–7cm; outer tep. red-green; inner tep. white. Ecuad. Z9.

A. laetus (Kunth) Backeb. To 6m; trunk short; br. erect, grey- or blue-green; seg. cylindric, 20–80× to 15cm; ribs 6–9; central spines 2–5, 7–30mm; radial spines 7–10, 5–10mm. Fls narrowly funnelform, to 10×6cm; tep. brown-green, pubesc.; inner tep. white, red-tipped. N Peru, S Ecuad. Z9.

A. matucanensis Backeb. Differs from *A. laetus* in more shrubby habit, spines more numerous; central spines 3–8, 2–11cm; radial spines 10–18, 0.5–1.5cm. Peru. Z9.
→*Lemaireocereus.*

Armenian Oak *Quercus pontica.*

Armeria (DC.) Willd. THRIFT; SEA PINK. Plumbaginaceae. c80 herbaceous or shrubby perennials, low-growing, tufted, sometimes cushion-forming. Lvs radical, rosulate, usually linear. Cap. dense, scapose, subtended by scarious bracts; fls small, packed; cal. 5-lobed or -parted, often awned, 5–10-ribbed; cor. 5-parted. Eur., Asia Minor, N Afr., Pacific coast of Americas.

A. alliacea (Cav.) Hoffsgg. & Link. Lvs 5–15×0.5–1.5cm, linear-lanceolate to oblong-lanceolate. Scape to 50cm; cap. about 1–2cm diam.; fls white (f. *leucantha*) to pale purple. Port. to S Germ. Formosa Hybrids: cushion-forming; fls deep pink to white. Z7.

A. alliacea auct. non (Cav.) Hoffsgg. & Link = *A. arenaria.*

A. allioides Boiss. = *A. alliacea.*

A. alpina Willd. Lvs 3–8×0.2–0.5cm, linear-lanceolate. Scape to 30cm often shorter; cap. to 3cm diam.; fls deep rose to white. Mts of S & C Eur. Z4.

A. arctica (Cham.) Wallr. Lvs 2–8×0.1cm, linear, occas. conduplicate. Scape 5–20cm; cap. 1–2cm diam., globose. Fls violet. Summer. Alask. Z1.

A. arenaria (Pers.) Schultz. Lvs 5–18×0.1–1cm, linear-lanceolate. Scape 20–60cm; cap. 1.5–2cm, globose; fls violet, pink or white. C & S Eur. Z4.

A. argyrocephala Wallr. = *A. undulata*.

A. atrosanguinea hort. = *A. pseudarmeria*.

A. berlengensis Daveau. Dwarf shrublet. Lvs 5–6×0.5–1cm, lanceolate to obovate-lanceolate. Cap. about 2.5cm diam.; fls pink to white. Port. Z7.

A. bottendorfensis Wein = *A. maritima*.

A. caespitosa (Cav.) Boiss. Shrublet to 15cm, densely branching. Lvs 0.4–1.5×0.1cm, linear, ciliate, pungent. Scape to 3cm, cap. 1–1.5cm diam.; fls purple to pink. Spain. 'Alba': densely tufted; fls white. 'Beechwood': cushion-forming, compact; fls deep pink. 'Bevan's Variety': small dense mounds, to 5cm; lvs dark; fls pink, st. v. short. Z8.

A. canescens (Host) Boiss. Woody-based herb. Outer lvs about 3mm wide, shorter than inner, linear to linear-spathulate, inner 1–1.5mm wide, linear-lanceolate. Scape to 70cm; cap. about 2cm diam. Fls pink to purple. SC Eur. ssp. *nebrodensis* (Guss.) P. Silva. Outer lvs wide, margins scarious, veins ciliate. Scape to 20cm. Z6.

A. cantabrica Boiss. & Reut. ex Willk. Tufted herb or shrublet. Lvs to 8×0.5cm, linear to linear-lanceolate. Scape to 30cm, cap. 2–3cm diam; fls deep pink, purple, or white. Medit., N Spain to Balk. Z6.

A. cephalotes (Ait.) Hoffsgg. & Link. = *A. pseudoarmeria*.

A. cinerea Boiss. & Welw. Differs from *A. welwitschii* in lvs and fls clothed in short dense down. N & C Port. Z8.

A. corsica hort. = *A. leucocephala* 'Corsica'.

A. dalmatica G. Beck = *A. canescens*.

A. elongata (Hoffm.) Koch = *A. maritima* ssp. *elongata*.

A. fasciculata (Vent.) Willd. = *A. pungens*.

A. filicaulis (Boiss.) Boiss. Herb, br. slender, long. Lvs heterophyllous, mucronate, outer lvs 1–3×0.1–0.2cm, linear-lanceolate, inner lvs 1.5–6×0.1cm, linear to filiform. Scape 20–30cm; cap. about 1cm diam.; fls pink or white. SE Fr., S Spain. Z7.

A. formosa (hort.) Vilm.-Andr. = *A. pseudarmeria*.

A. gaditana Boiss. Herb, glab. Lvs 10–25×1–4cm, lanceolate to ± spathulate, acute. Scape to 90cm, usually shorter; cap. about 3cm diam.; fls deep rose. S Iberia. Z8.

A. girardii (Bernis) Litard. Herb, to 22cm, tufted, outer lvs about 1.5×0.1cm, linear to linear-triangular, muticous, sometimes glaucous, inner lvs 1.5–4×0.1cm. Scape to 15cm; cap. 1–1.5cm diam.; fls pink. S Fr. 'Alba': fls white. Z8.

A. grandifolia Boiss. = *A. pseudarmeria*.

A. gussonei Boiss. = *A. morisii*.

A. halleri Wallr. = *A. maritima* ssp. *halleri*.

A. juncea Girard non Wallr. = *A. girardii*.

A. juniperifolia (Vahl) Hoffsgg. = *A. caespitosa*.

A. juniperina Willd. ex Hoffsgg. & Link. = *A. caespitosa*.

A. labradorica Wallr. Lvs 3.5×0.1cm, densely tufted, linear. Cap. to 2cm diam., hemispheric; fls lilac. Labrador, Greenland. Z2.

A. latifolia Willd. = *A. pseudoarmeria*.

A. laucheana hort. = *A. maritima* 'Laucheana'.

A. leucocephala Salzm. ex Koch. Short-branched dwarf shrublet. Lvs 3–6×0.1–0.9cm, linear, mucronate, usually revolute, sometimes pubesc. Scape 15–25cm, sometimes tuberculate; cap. about 2cm diam.; fls rose to white. Corsica, Sardinia. 'Corsica': short tussocks; fls small, brick red. Z8.

A. macrophylla Boiss. & Reut. Differs from *A. pinifolia* in lvs longer, to 25cm, filiform to linear. Scape sometimes pubesc. below. SW Iberia. Z8.

A. macrophylla Boiss. & Reut. = *A. pinifolia*.

A. majellensis Boiss. Woody-based, tufted, glab. herb to 30cm. Outer lvs short-lanceolate, sometimes undulate, channelled, margins cartilaginous, inner lvs straight, long. Cap. 2cm diam., hemispherical; fls purple-pink. Summer. N Medit. and Asia Minor. Z8.

A. maritima (Mill.) Willd. Tufted herb or dwarf subshrub to 30cm. Lvs to 10cm linear to linear-spathulate, obtuse, muticous. Scape to 30cm; cap. 1–3cm; fls red to pink or white. Eur., Asia Minor, N Afr., N Amer. Z4. 'Alba' (fls small, white); 'Bee's Ruby' (fls shocking pink); 'Bloodstone' (to 20cm; fls large, intense blood red); 'Düsseldorfer Stolz' (fls rich crimson); 'Glory of Holland' (to 25cm; st. strong; fls large, pink); 'Laucheana' (lvs dark, spiky; fls bright pink); 'Minor' (v. dwarf, fls white); 'Ruby Glow' (to 15cm; fls brilliant red); 'Splendens' (fls carmine, ball-shaped); 'Vindictive' (to 15cm; fls rich rose pink). ssp. *elongata* (Hoffm.) Bonnier. Lvs to 15cm, linear, ciliate, to 30cm+; fls pale pink. N & C Eur. ssp. *halleri* (Wallr.) Rothm. Lvs 3–10×0.1–0.2cm, linear, ciliate. Scape to 30cm; fls pink to red. C Eur.

A. maritima ssp. *alpina* (Willd.) P. Silva = *A. alpina*.

A. maritima var. *sibirica* auct. = *A. sibirica*.

A. mauritanica Wallr. Shrub to 60cm, tufted, glab., glaucous. Lvs to 15cm, oblong-lanceolate to spathulate, margins white-scarious. Cap. to 5cm diam.; fls pink. Spain, N Afr. Z8.

A. morisii Boiss. Herb. Lvs 2–5×0.5–1cm, lanceolate to lanceolate-spathulate, muticous, subcoriaceous. Scape to 40cm; cap. about 2cm diam.; fls rose. Sardinia, Sicily. Z8.

A. muelleri Huet. Tufted. Lvs narrow linear; fls rose to violet. W Eur. (Netherlands to Pyren.). Z7.

A. pinifolia (Brot.) Hoffsgg. & Link. Herb to 70cm. Lvs 6–25×0.1cm, narrowly lanceolate to linear. Scape to 50cm; cap. about 2cm diam.; fls pink or white. SW Port.

A. plataginea (All.) Willd. = *A. arenaria*.

A. pseudarmeria (Murray) Mansf. Dwarf shrublet, compact. Lvs about 2.5×0.2cm, lanceolate, muticous. Scape 25–50cm; cap. 3–4cm diam., fls white to dark rose. WC Port. 'Rubra': fls brilliant red. Z8.

A. pubinervis Boiss. = *A. alpina* and *A. cantabrica*.

A. pungens (Link) Hoffsgg. & Link. PRICKLY THRIFT; SPINY THRIFT. Tufted woody-based perenn. to 50cm. Lvs about 10×0.7cm, linear, pungent, glaucous. Scape to 35cm; cap. 3cm diam.; fls rose, large. SW Iberia, Corsica, Sardinia. var. *velutina* Cout. Lvs pubesc., narrower; scapes longer. SW Port. Z8.

A. rouyana Daveau.   To 30cm, mat-forming. Lvs 9–16× 0.1–0.3cm, filiform to linear, convolute. Fls rose. SW Port. Z8.

A. rumelica Boiss. Short-branched, tufted herb, outer lvs 2–3mm wide, linear, inner lvs 1–2mm wide, narrowly linear, mucronulate. Fls purple-pink. S Balk. Z7.

A. ruscinononesis (Kuntze) Girard. Dwarf subshrub or herb; stock stout. Lvs 3.5–10×0.2–0.5cm, linear-lanceolate, sometimes somewhat spathulate, coriaceous. Scape to 4cm; cap. about 2cm diam., fls white to rose. S Fr., N Spain. Z8.

A. setacea Delile ex Godron = *A. girardii*.

A. sibirica Turcz. ex Boiss. Tufted perenn. herb. Lvs linear, obtuse. Cap. about 1.5cm diam., fls white. Sib., Mong. Z2.

A. soleirolii Duby. Dwarf subshrub. Outer lvs to 5×0.5cm, linear-spathulate, pubesc., inner lvs to 8×0.3cm, linear-lanceolate, glab. or puberulent. Scape to 40cm, sometimes pubesc.; cap. to 2cm diam.; fls white to pale rose. Corsica, Sardinia. Z8.

A. splendens (Lagasca & Rodr.) Webb. Densely tufted, glab. subshrub. Lvs linear, obtuse. Scape 2–8cm; fls deep rose to purple. Summer. Spain. Z7.

A. undulata (Bory & Chaub.) Boiss. Woody-based perenn. Lower lvs short-lanceolate to linear lanceolate, serrulate, upper lvs linear-setaceous, mucronate. Early summer. Greece. Z8.

A. vulgaris var. *arctica* (Cham.) Ledeb. ex B. Fedtsch. & Flerov. = *A. arctica*.

A. welwitschii Boiss. Dwarf subshrub to 30cm, compact, somewhat glaucous. Lvs 5–10×0.2–1cm, linear to linear-spathulate, sometimes convolute. Scape 15–25cm; fls white to bright pink. W Port. Z8.

→*Statice*.

Armoracia P. Gaertn., Mey. & Scherb. Cruciferae. 3 perenn. herbs. Taproots deep, woody or fleshy. Lvs variable, small or to 1m, st. lvs generally reduced, sessile to clasping. Infl. a rac. or pan. greatly elongating in fr.; fls small, white, 4-merous. SE Eur. to Sib.

A. rusticana P. Gaertn., Mey. & Scherb. HORSE RADISH; RED COLE. To 1m. Roots fleshy, pungently scented. Lvs 30–50cm, oblong bullate, serrate-crenate. Infl. paniculate. SE Eur., nat. throughout Eur. and N Amer. Z5. 'Variegata': lvs splashed cream or white.

→*Cochlearia, Nasturtium, Radicula* and *Rorippa*.

Arnebia Forssk. Boraginaceae. 25 hispid ann. to perenn. herbs. St. simple or branched, erect to decumbent. Cymes scorpioid, usually term., simple or branched; cal. lobes accrescent, linear to lanceolate; cor. infundibular or hypocrateriform, lobes 5, spreading, rounded. N Afr. to C Asia and Himal. Z7.

A. benthamii (Wallich ex G. Don) Johnst. Perenn. St. to 90cm, solitary, simple, white-setaceous. Lvs to 3cm, lanceolate, silvery-setose. Infl. to 35cm; cor. pink or purple to maroon, to 2.5cm. S Asia.

A. cephalotes DC. = *A. densiflora*.

A. cornuta (Ledeb.) Fisch. = *A. decumbens*.

A. decumbens (Vent.) Coss. & Král. Ann. St. to 30cm, usually numerous, branched, densely white-setose. Lvs to 3cm, ovate-oblong, setaceous. Infl. to 9cm; cor. to 1.2cm, yellow, exterior densely pubesc. Eur. and N Afr. to W China.

A. densiflora (Ledeb. ex Nordm.) Ledeb. Perenn. St. to 40cm, simple, velutinous, hispid. Lvs to 15cm, linear-elliptic to linear-lanceolate, setose, velutinous. Infl. dense; cor. to 4.5cm, yellow, exterior slightly pubesc. Greece, Turk.

A. echioides (L.) DC. = *A. pulchra*.

A. griffithii Boiss. Ann. St. to 30cm, erect, pale brown, branched, white-setose, lvs to 7cm, obovate-oblong to linear. Infl. to 10cm; cor. to 2.5cm, orange or yellow, limb spotted purple. Afghan., Pak.

A. linearifolia A. DC. Ann. St. to 15cm, ± erect, usually numerous, branched, glab. to densely white-setose, lvs to 5cm, oblong, densely setose above, subglabrous. Infl. to 12cm; cor. to 1.5cm, yellow, exterior densely pubesc. Egypt and SW Asia to Pak.

A. macrothyrsa Stapf = A. densiflora.

A. pulchra (Willd. ex Roem. & Schult.) Edmondson. PROPHET FLOWER. Perenn. St. to 42cm, simple, densely branched. Lvs to 15cm, oblong to lanceolate, pilose to hispid. Infl. compact, term.; cor. to 2.5cm, yellow, tube puberulent, limb spotted maroon or black. Asia Minor, Iran, Cauc.
→Echium, Echioides, Lithospermum and Lycopsis.

Arnica L. Compositae. 32 rhizomatous, usually perenn. herbs. Lvs opposite, mostly toward st. base. Cap. radiate, solitary or many in a cymose infl. Flts yellow. N temp. and Arc. regions.
A. alpina (L.) Olin = A. angustifolia.
A. amplexicaulis Nutt. To 1m. Lvs to 12cm, ovate to lanceolate, toothed, sessile, amplexicaul, sparsely pubesc. Cap. 5–9; ray flts to 16×6mm, 8–14. Alask. to Calif. and Mont. Z2.
A. angustifolia Vahl. To 50cm. Lvs lanceolate, entire or toothed, ciliate. Cap. 1–7; ray flts often strigose below. N Amer., Arc., N Eurasia. ssp. **alpina** (L.) I.K. Ferguson. 10–30cm. Stalk eglandular-hairy. Z2.
A. betonicifolia Greene = A. latifolia.
A. chamissonis Less. To 1m+. Lvs sessile, lanceolate. Cap. 5–15; ray flts to 20mm. Alask. to New Mex. Z2.
A. cordifolia Hook. f. To 50cm. Lvs c11cm, ovate to lanceolate. Cap. 1–5; ray flts 9–13, c10×5mm. Alask. to New Mex. Z2.
A. crenata Thunb. = Mairia crenata.
A. foliosa Nutt. = A. chamissonis.
A. fulgens Pursh. To 60cm. Lvs to 20cm, oblanceolate, entire. Cap. 1–4; ray flts to 25×10mm, 12–20, dark yellow or orange. W N Amer.
A. latifolia Bong. To 60cm. Lvs to 12cm, sessile, pubesc., ovate to lanceolate. Cap. 1–5; ray flts to 22×6mm, 8–12. Alask. to Calif. and Colorado. Z2.
A. lessingii Greene. To 30cm. Lvs to 10cm, lanceolate, entire or toothed. Cap. 1, often nodding; phyllaries deep red; ray flts to 20×10mm, 8–13, sometimes orange; anth. purple. NW N Amer., NE Asia. Z4.
A. longifolia D.C. Eaton. To 60cm. Lvs to 12cm, lanceolate, entire or minutely toothed. Cap. 7–20; ray flts to 20×6mm, 8–11, pale to deep yellow. W US. Z4.
A. mollis Hook. St. to 50cm, unbranched. Lvs lanceolate to ovate or obovate, subentire to deeply serrate. Cap. 1–3; ray flts to 2.5×1cm, 14–18. W N Amer. Z4.
A. montana L. St. to 75cm, usually simple. Lvs to 20cm, ovate to lanceolate, sheathing below. Cap. 1–5; ray flts to 25×10mm, 11–15. Most of Eur., W Asia. Z6.
A. montana var. alpina L. = A. angustifolia ssp. alpina.
A. oporina Forst. f. = Olearia oporina.
A. pedunculata Rydb. = A. fulgens.
A. sachalinensis (Reg.) A. Gray. To 1m. Lvs to 15cm, lanceolate, sheathing below, serrate. Cap. 1–15; ray flts 10–16, to 25×8mm. Sakhalin Is., NE Sib. Z2.
A. scorpioides sensu Jacq. = Doronicum grandiflorum.
A. unalasohensis Less. To 12cm, ovate or obovate to oblanceolate. Cap. 1; ray flts 12–19, 17×7mm. Admiralty Is., Aleutians, Commander Is., Japanese Archipel. Z5.

Aroeira Schinus terebinthifolius.
Aroeira Blanca Schinus chichita.
Aroeira Branca Lithrea molleoides.
Aroeira Brava Lithrea molleoides.
Aroeira Mansa Schinus terebinthifolius var. acutifolius.
Arolla Pine Pinus cembra.

Aronia Medik. CHOKEBERRY. Rosaceae. 2 decid. shrubs. Lvs simple, crenate, black-glandular on midrib above. Fls small, in small corymbs; pet. 5, concave; sta. many, anth. purple. Fr. a small, red, purple or black, berry-like pome. N Amer. Z4.
A. alnifolia Nutt. = Amelanchier alnifolia.
A. arbutifolia (L.) Pers. Shrub to 2m. Young twigs downy. Lvs to 8cm, elliptic to oblong-obovate, dull green, scarlet in fall, grey-tomentose beneath. Fls white or pink, 1cm diam., in grey-tomentose corymbs. Fr. 6.5mm diam., bright red, late-ripening, persisting into winter. Summer. E N Amer. 'Brilliant' ('Brilliantissima'): to 2.5m; lvs brilliant red in fall; fr. vivid red, long-lasting. 'Erecta': habit fastigiate; lvs oblanceolate to oblong, bright crimson in fall. f. **macrophylla** (Hook.) Rehd. To 6m. Lvs to 10.5cm. S US. var. **pumila** (Schmidt) Rehd. Shorter. Lvs smaller. Fr. deep red.
A. asiatica Sieb. & Zucc. = Amelanchier asiatica.
A. atropurpurea Britt. = A. ×prunifolia.
A. densiflora Spach = × Sorbaronia alpina.

A. dippelii Zab. = × Sorbaronia dippelii.
A. floribunda Spach = A. ×prunifolia.
A. heterophylla Zab. = × Sorbaronia fallax.
A. melanocarpa (Michx.) Elliott. BLACK CHOKEBERRY. Shrub to 1m, stoloniferous. Young twigs glabrescent. Lvs to 6cm, elliptic to oblong-oblanceolate, shiny, deep green above, brown-red in autumn, glab. beneath. Fls white, 1.5cm diam., in glab. corymbs. Fr. to 8.5mm diam., shiny, black or black-purple, ripening in autumn, falling early. Summer. E N Amer. var. **elata** Rehd. To 3m. Lvs, fls and fr. larger. var. **grandifolia** (Lindl.) Schneid. To 2.5m. Lvs obovate to broad-obovate. Fls and fr. larger.
A. nigra Dipp. = A. melanocarpa.
A. ×prunifolia (Schneid.) Gräbn. (A. arbutifolia ×A. melanocarpa.) PURPLE-FRUITED CHOKEBERRY. To 4m. Favours A. arbutifolia with tomentose young twigs but infl. lax, cal. downy, tips usually lacking glands. Fr. purple or purple-black, 8mm diam. E N Amer.
A. prunifolia (Marshall) Rehd. = A. ×prunifolia.
→Pyrus and Sorbus.

Aronicum Neck.
A. clusii (All.) Koch = Doronicum clusii.
A. corsicum (Lois.) DC. = Doronicum corsicum.

Arpophyllum La Ll. & Lex. BOTTLEBRUSH ORCHID. Orchidaceae. 3 epiphytic orchids. Pbs long, narrowly cylindric, compressed, terminating in a long, rigid, linear to ligulate, ± conduplicate lf. Infl. a term. spike, crowded, cylindrical. Mex. to Venez., W Indies. Z10.
A. alpinum Lindl. Pbs to 30cm. Lvs to 60cm, ligulate. Infl. to 15cm; fls to 1.75cm diam., magenta, lip white to pale pink or lilac. Mex., Guat., Hond.
A. cardinale Lind. ex Rchb. f. = A. giganteum.
A. giganteum Hartw. ex Lindl. Pbs to 20cm. Lvs to 55cm, ligulate. Infl. to 25cm; fls to 2cm diam., deep rose pink to magenta. Throughout genus range.
A. medium Rchb. f. = A. alpinum.
A. spicatum La Ll. & Lex. Taller than above (to 1.2m) with bright rose fls to 1.5cm diam. Throughout genus range.

Arrabidaea DC. Bignoniaceae. c50 lianes, small trees or shrubs. Lvs usually trifoliate, term. lft often replaced by tendril. Fls in crowded pan.; cal. cupular, truncate or bilabiate, 5-denticulate, pubesc.; cor. campanulate to salverform, lobes pubesc. outside. Mex., W Indies to Arg.
A. acuminata (Johnst.) Urban = A. corallina.
A. acutifolia DC. = A. chica.
A. barquisimetensis Pittier = A. corallina.
A. chica (Humb. & Bonpl.) Verl. Young br. tinged red. Lfts 3, 3–12 ovate. Infl. puberulent; cor. 1.6–3×0.5–1.4cm at mouth of tube, tube 1.1–2.1cm. Spring–autumn. Mex. to Arg.
A. corallina (Jacq.) Sandw. Lfts 3, 1–18cm, ovate. Infl. puberulent; cor. tube campanulate, 2.7–4.6×2.1–2.8×0.8–1.2cm, lilac to purple-red, white inside. Mex. to Arg.
A. corymbifera Bur. ex Schum. = A. selloi.
A. dichotoma (Vell.) Bur. = A. selloi.
A. floribunda (HBK) Loes. ANIBAK. Lfts to 6.25cm, oblong-elliptic. Fls 1.7cm, purple, funnelform. Mex.
A. guaricensis Pittier = A. corallina.
A. guatamalensis Schum. & Loes. = Cydista aequinoctialis var. hirtella.
A. isthmica Standl. = Cydista aequinoctialis.
A. larensis Pittier = A. chica.
A. littoralis (HBK) Wendl. Lfts to 13cm, 2–3, ovate. Fls red, funnelform. Spring–summer. Mex.
A. magnifica Sprague ex Steenis = Saritaea magnifica.
A. mollis Bur. ex Schum. Lfts to 12.5cm, 3, ovate, downy. Fls small, downy-pubesc. Fr. Guyana.
A. mollissima (HBK) Bur. ex Schum. Lfts 3–10cm, 2–3, ovate to suborbicular. Fls fragrant, dark purple or white, tube 2–5×0.8–1.6cm. Venez.
A. obliqua var. hirsuta (DC.) Dugand. = A. corallina.
A. ovalifolia Pittier = A. corallina.
A. praecox Hassl. = A. corallina.
A. pseudochica Kränzl. = Cydista aequinoctialis.
A. rhodantha Bur. & Schum. = A. corallina.
A. rhodantha var. oxyphylla Sprague ex Sandw. = A. corallina.
A. rosea DC. = A. chica.
A. rotundata (DC.) Bur. ex Schum. = A. corallina.
A. selloi (Spreng.) Sandw. Lfts to 10cm, 2–3, ovate to elliptic. Cor. pink to violet, tube 2–3cm, exterior pubesc., limb 2–2.5cm diam., interior pubesc. N Braz. to N Arg.
A. spraguei Pittier = A. corallina.
→Adenocalymma, Bignonia, Cremastus, Panterpa, Paramansoa, Pentelesia, Petastoma, Piriadacus and Scobinaria.

Artemisia

Arrayán *Luma apiculata.*
Arrayán Blanco *Luma chequen.*

Arrhenatherum P. Beauv. OAT GRASS. Gramineae. 6 perenn. grasses. Culms erect or spreading; basal nodes occas. swollen into bulbous or pear-shaped structures. Lvs flat; sheaths usually glab. Pan. narrow; spikelets 2-fld, somewhat flattened laterally. Eur., N Afr., N & W Asia. Z6.
A. avenaceum P. Beauv. = *A. elatius.*
A. bulbosum (Willd.) C. Presl. = *A. elatius* ssp. *bulbosum.*
A. elatius (L.) Presl & C. Presl. FALSE OAT; FRENCH RYE. To 1.5m. Culms forming tussocks, usually glab. Lvs scabrous, to 40×1cm. Rac. lanceolate to oblong, often purple-tinged, lustrous, to 30cm; spikelets to 1cm. Summer. Eur. 'Variegatum': lvs erect, narrow, boldly striped and edged pure white. ssp. *bulbosum* (Willd.) Schübl. & Martens. Basal internodes swollen into a chain of bulbous organs to 1cm diam. Eur.
A. tuberosum (Gilib.) F.W. Schultz. = *A. elatium* ssp. *bulbosum.*
→*Avena.*

Arrojadoa Britt. & Rose. Cactaceae. 3 low, shrubby cacti; st. cylindric, sometimes segmented; spines small or bristly. Flowering areoles tufted with bristles and forming ring-like subterminal cephalia through which growth continues after flowering leaving a collar of bristles. Fls small, often numerous, tubular, diurnal. E Braz. Z10.
A. penicillata (Gürke) Britt. & Rose. St. ascending or sprawling, 1–2m×1–1.5cm; ribs 10–12; central spines 1–2, 1–3cm; radial spines 8–12. Fls c3cm, pale to deep pink, limb spreading. Summer. E Braz. Z9.
A. polyantha (Werderm.) D. Hunt = *Micranthocereus polyanthus.*
A. rhodantha (Gürke) Britt. & Rose. St. erect at first, later sprawling or clambering, 1–2m×1–5cm; ribs 10–13; central spines 5–6, to 3cm; radial spines c20. Fls 3–4cm, deep pink, limb erect. E Braz. Z9.

Arrow Arum *Peltandra.*
Arrow Bamboo *Pseudosasa japonica.*
Arrow Grass *Triglochin.*
Arrowhead *Sagittaria.*
Arrow-leaf Violet *Viola sagittata.*
Arrowroot *Canna indica.*
Arrowroot *Maranta arundinacea.*
Arrow Wood *Viburnum dentatum, V. recognitum.*
Arroyo Willow *Salix lasiolepis.*

Arrudaria Macedo.
A. cerifera (Mart.) Macedo = *Copernicia prunifera.*

Artabotrys R. Br. TAIL GRAPE. Annonaceae. 100 shrubs climbing by means of hook-like, modified peduncles. Lvs glossy. Fls solitary, paired or in clusters on long woody peduncles, fragrant; pet. 6, in 2 whorls, valvate, swollen at base, concealing crowded sta. OW Trop. Z10.
A. hexapetalus (L. f.) Bhand. CLIMBING ILANG-ILANG. Shrub, climbing to 4m. Lvs 10–20cm, oblong-lanceolate. Fls highly fragrant; pet. to 2.5cm, yellow-white to ivory. S India, Sri Lanka, introd. throughout OW Trop.
A. odoratissimus R. Br. = *A. hexapetalus.*
A. uncinatus (Lam.) Merrill = *A. hexapetalus.*

Artanthe Miq.
A. magnifica Lindl. = *Piper magnificum.*

Artedia L. Umbelliferae. 1 ann. herb to 50cm. Lvs 3-pinnate; seg. fine. Umbels compound; outer flts white, radiating, inner sterile, purple, bristle-like. E Medit. Z8.
A. squamata L.

Artemisia L. WORMWOOD; SAGE BRUSH; MUGWORT. Compositae. c300 ann., bienn. or perenn. herbs or shrubs, mostly aromatic. Lvs usually pinnately divided or finely dissected, often white-silky-hairy. Cap. small, discoid, often grey, hairy in a paniculate, racemose or corymbose infl. N temp., W S Amer., S Afr.
A. abrotanum L. SOUTHERNWOOD. Strongly aromatic herb to 1m. Lvs to 6cm, 1–3-pinnatisect, lobes linear or filiform, glab. above, grey-pubesc. beneath. Cap. globose, in dense pan. Summer. Origin uncertain; nat. E, S & SC Eur. Z4.
A. absinthium L. ABSINTHE; COMMON WORMWOOD; OLD MAN; LAD'S LOVE. Aromatic, silky perenn. erect to 1m. Lvs to 10cm, 2- or 3-pinnatisect, lobes to 20×6mm, oblong. Cap. hemispherical, nodding, in leafy pan. Summer–autumn. Temp. Eurasia, N Afr. 'Lambrook Silver' and 'Lambrook Giant': to 75cm; lvs silver, much-divided. Z4.

A. alba Turra. Aromatic subshrub to 1m, glab. to white-tomentose, branched below, lvs 1–2–3-pinnatisect, lobes linear to filiform, to 10×1mm, simple above. Cap. hemispherical, nodding, in a long racemose pan. S Eur., N Afr. Z6.
A. albula Wooton = *A. ludoviciana* var. *albula.*
A. annua L. SWEET WORMWOOD. Erect, glab. ann. to 1.5m; st. often red. Lvs (1–)2–3-pinnatisect, lobes to 5×1mm, linear-lanceolate, entire or toothed. Cap. hemispheric, in a loose spreading pan. Summer–autumn. SE Eur. to Iran. Z8.
A. arborea hort. = *A. arborescens.*
A. arborescens L. Glab. aromatic perenn. to 1m; base woody. Lvs 1- or 2-pinnatisect, lobes to 25×2mm. Cap. hemispheric, nodding or erect, in large pan. Summer–autumn. Medit. 'Faith Raven': to 1m, hardy; lvs silver. 'Powis Castle', a fine shrubby plant with silvery filigree lvs, is sometimes assigned here: it is probably a hybrid between *A. arborescens* and *A. absinthium.* Z8.
A. arbuscula Nutt. SAGE BRUSH. Compact shrub to 30cm. Lvs small cuneate, lobes 3, often pinnately divided. Cap. erect, in a simple spike-like pan. NW US. Z3.
A. argentea hort. = *A. arborescens.*
A. armeniaca Lam. Erect perenn. 0.3–1m; st. simple, grey-hairy. Basal lvs 2- or 3-pinnatisect, densely grey-silky-hairy, lobes curling, filigree-like, to 10×4mm, sparsely hairy above, woolly beneath, serrate. Cap. hemispheric, nodding, in a narrow pan. Late summer. C & S Russia, Cauc., N Iran. Z5.
A. assoana Willk. = *A. caucasica.*
A. baumgartenii Besser = *A. eriantha.*
A. borealis Pall. = *A. campestris* ssp. *borealis.*
A. caerulescens L. = *Seriphidium caerulescens.*
A. californica Less. CALIFORNIA SAGEBRUSH. Shrub to 2m, densely branched. Lvs grey-pubesc., to 5cm, palmately 1- or 2-pinnatisect, seg. linear-filiform, upper lvs sometimes entire. Cap. numerous, in long racemose pan. Summer–late autumn. Calif. Z3.
A. campestris L. Perenn. herb to 1.5m, scarcely aromatic; st. erect, glab., red-brown, base woody. Lvs silky at first, 2- or 3-pinnatisect, to entire. Cap. oblong, erect in a widely spreading pan. Summer–autumn. Eur., NW Afr. ssp. *borealis* (Pall.) H.M. Hall & Clements. St. to 25cm. Pan. br. with 1–3 cap. Alps, Arc. Russia. Z2.
A. camphorata Vill. = *A. alba.*
A. cana Pursh = *Seriphidium canum.*
A. canadensis Michx. = *A. campestris* ssp. *borealis.*
A. canariensis (Besser) Less. Shrub to 1m. Lvs to 10cm, clustered, ovate, 2-pinnate, lobes, linear, hairy. Cap. in loose pan. Canary Is. Z9.
A. canescens hort. = *A. armeniaca.*
A. caucasica Willd. Tufted white-woolly perenn. to 30cm. Lvs palmatifid to pinnatifid, lobes linear. Cap. to 6mm diam., hemispheric, nodding in maturity in a simple or branched rac. with pinnatifid bracts. C Spain to S Ukraine. Z5.
A. chamaemelifolia Vill. Aromatic, ± perenn. to 60cm. Lvs 2- or 3-pinnatisect, lobes filiform. Cap. hemispheric, in a narrow, many-fld, leafy pan. Summer–autumn. SW Alps, Pyren., Bulg., Cauc., N Iran, Sib. Z3.
A. chinensis L. = *Crossostephium chinense.*
A. discolor Douglas ex Besser = *A. michauxiana.*
A. douglasiana Besser. Perenn. to 3m; st. herbaceous. Lvs to 15cm, elliptic to lanceolate and entire, or oblanceolate to obovate and lobed near apex or coarsely dentate, grey-tomentose beneath, green above. Cap. in an open or dense elongated pan. W US. Z3.
A. dracunculus L. TARRAGON; ESTRAGON. Aromatic, glab. much-branched perenn., 1–2m. Lvs to 10cm, blue-green, linear to lanceolate, entire or slightly toothed. Cap. recurved, globose, pedunculate, in a spreading pan. SE Russia. Z3.
A. eriantha Ten. Tufted, silky-tomentose perenn. to 25cm. Basal lvs usually 2-ternate, lobes linear-lanceolate, upper st. lvs digitate to pinnatifid, rarely entire. Cap. hemispheric, ultimately nodding in a dense, simple rac. Pyren., SW Alps, Apennines, Balk., Carpath. Z5.
A. filifolia Torr. SILVERY WORMWOOD; SAND SAGE. Silvery-haired shrub, to 1m; br. erect. Lvs to 5cm, trifid, seg. filiform. Cap. in compact leafy pan. C & S US, Mex. Z3.
A. frigida Willd. Tufted, woody-based silky perenn., to 50cm. Lvs 1- or 2-pinnatisect, lobes to 5×1mm, linear, uppermost lvs palmately divided. Cap. hemispheric, nodding, in a v. narrow pan. SE & E Russia. Z4.
A. genipi Weber. Resembling *A. eriantha* but less hairy, lvs pinnately lobed or deeply toothed. Alps. Z4.
A. glacialis Willd. Densely tufted perenn., to 18cm, silky-hairy. Lvs divided into 5seg., seg. 3-lobed, lobes, narrowly linear. Cap. in a compact terminal corymb. SW Alps. Z5.
A. gmelinii Weber ex Stechm. Ann. or bienn. subshrub, to 1.5m, grey-pubesc. Lvs to 7cm, ovate, bipinnate, lobes linear to

linear-lanceolate. Cap. in leafy terminal pan. to 40cm. S Russia
to Sib. and NE Asia. 'Viridis': to 3m, vigorous; lvs light green,
much-divided. Z3.

A. gnaphalodes Nutt. = *A. ludoviciana.*

A. gracilis hort. = *A. scoparia.*

A. granatensis Boiss. Resembling *A. glacialis*, but cap. often
solitary and larger with more numerous flts, phyllaries often red
at centre; flts purple, not yellow. S Spain. Z8.

A. haussknechtii Boiss. Resembling *A. splendens* but not tufted
or hummock-forming, basal lvs 0 at anthesis, lower lvs with
blunt, elliptic seg. Autumn. Turk. to N Iraq, Iran. Z8.

A. indica Willd. Ann. or perenn. to 120cm. Lvs to 12×10cm,
oblong to elliptic, pinnatifid, seg. in 2–3 pairs, green above,
white-woolly beneath, uppermost lvs entire. Cap. many, in
narrow pan. Jap., China, to India. Z7.

A. japonica Thunb. Herb to 1.4m. Lvs in an apical tuft, to 8cm,
spathulate, pinnately lobed, dentate, silky; lvs on flowering st. thick, to 8cm, cuneate-spathulate, dentate or divided,
lobes divided. Cap. shiny yellow-green, in leafy pan. Late
summer–autumn. China to Jap. and Philipp. Z8.

A. lactiflora Wallich. WHITE MUGWORT. Perenn. herb erect to 2m;
st. glab. Lvs to 25cm, pinnatisect to pinnate, seg. toothed or
lobed, to 8cm. Cap. in loose pan. China. 'Variegata': lvs
variegated green and grey. Z4.

A. lanata Willd. non Lam. = *A. caucasica.*

A. laxa Fritsch = *A. umbelliformis.*

A. longifolia Nutt. Perenn. herb to 1m; st. simple, herbaceous.
Lvs to 12cm, entire, linear to lanceolate, white-hairy beneath.
Cap. erect, clustered in a rac. N Amer. Z3.

A. ludoviciana Nutt. WESTERN MUGWORT; WHITE SAGE; CUDWEED.
Perenn. herb to 1m; st. white-tomentose. Lvs to 11cm, linear or
lanceolate, white-hairy beneath, lower lvs toothed or divided,
upper lvs entire. Cap. often in glomerules, in dense elongate
pan. Summer–autumn. W US, Mex. 'Silver Frost': lvs finely cut,
silver. 'Silver King': to 1m, lvs silver, frosty and aromatic, finely
cut. 'Silver Queen': to 75cm, lvs jagged, silver; fls in plumes,
yellow-grey. 'Valerie Finnis': to 60cm; lvs grey-silver, jagged.
var. *albula* (Wooton) Shinn. SILVER KING. Lvs to 2cm,
lanceolate, and entire or obovate to elliptic and toothed or
lobed, white-hairy. Calif. var. *latiloba* To 80cm; lvs grey-white,
jagged. Z5.

A. maritima L. = *Seriphidium maritimum.*

A. michauxiana Besser. Perenn. herb to 45cm, woody at base.
Lvs to c3cm, 1- or 2-pinnatisect, seg. linear to lanceolate, green
above, white-hairy beneath. Cap. in narrow pan. W US, SW
Canada. Z3.

A. mutellina Vill. non S.G. Gmel. = *A. umbelliformis.*

A. nana Gaudin = *A. campestris* ssp. *borealis.*

A. nitida Bertol. Resembling *A. umbelliformis* but to 40cm, cap.
more numerous, nodding when mature. SE Alps. Z5.

A. nutans Willd. = *Seriphidium nutans.*

A. palmeri A. Gray = *Seriphidium palmeri.*

A. palmeri hort. = *A. ludoviciana.*

A. paniculata Lam. = *A. abrotanum.*

A. pedemontana Balb. = *A. caucasica.*

A. petrosa Fritsch = *A. eriantha.*

A. pontica L. ROMAN WORMWOOD. Aromatic perenn. to 80cm,
grey-tomentose. Lvs to 4cm, 1- or 2-pinnatifid, densely pubesc.,
lbes to 0.5mm wide, linear-lanceolate. Cap. ovoid, nodding, in a
long, narrow, racemose pan. with pinnatifid bracts. C & E Eur.
'Old Warrior': to 50cm; lvs finely-cut, pewter-grey, fragrant, fls
yellow-grey. Z4.

A. 'Powis Castle'. See *A. arborescens.*

A. procera Willd. = *A. abrotanum.*

A. purshiana Besser = *A. ludoviciana.*

A. pycnocephala (Less.) DC. Subshrub to 70cm, erect to ascending. Lvs to 2.5cm, clustered, 1–3-pinnate, lobes linear, densely
silky-tomentose. Cap. erect, in dense, leafy, narrow pan.
Summer. Calif., Oreg. Z3.

A. redowskii Ledeb. = *A. dracunculus.*

A. rothrockii A. Gray = *Seriphidium rothrockii.*

A. roxburghiana Besser. Erect perenn. herb; st. becoming
purple. Lvs small, bipinnatifid or bipinnatisect, seg. linear, glab.
above, downy beneath. Cap. ovoid, in a narrow pan. Z7.

A. rupestris L. Shrub to 45cm; procumbent to ascending. Lvs 1 or
2-pinnatisect, lobes to 6×1mm, acute. Cap. nodding, clustered
in a rac. or pan. Baltic, NW Russia to C Asia. Z3.

A. sacrorum Ledeb. = *A. gmelinii.*

A. schmidtiana Maxim. Rhizomatous tufted perenn. to 60cm. Lvs
to 4.5cm, palmately 2-pinnatisect, seg. linear, silver-hairy. Cap.
to 5mm diam., in pyramidal pan. Jap. 'Nana': dwarf, to 8cm; lvs
in rounded cushions of silver filigree. 'Silver Mound': lvs silver,
finely cut; hardy. Z4.

A. scoparia Waldst. & Kit. Bienn. to 60cm; st. solitary, usually
red, often slightly hairy. Lvs 1–2-pinnatisect, seg. filiform, lower
lvs withered at anthesis. Cap. oblong-globose, nodding, in a

broad pan. Summer–autumn. C & E Eur., SW Asia, Sib. Z3.

A. sericea Weber. Perenn. to 70cm, with creeping rhiz. Lvs silky-
downy, 1–2-pinnatisect, primary seg. in 1–2 pairs, upper lvs 1-
pinnatisect or simple, lobes to 17×2mm, entire. Cap. hemispheric, nodding, in a narrow, sometimes lax, pan. S, C & E
Russia. Z3.

A. spicata Wulf. = *A. genipi.*

A. spinescens D.C. Eaton. BUD SAGEBRUSH. Spiny shrub, to
50cm, strongly aromatic, branching at base; branchlets white-
tomentose. Lvs to 2×1.5cm, pedately 5–7-parted, seg. 3-lobed,
linear or spathulate, grey-hairy. Cap. few, clustered in spikes
persisting as spines the following year. Spring. W US. Z3.

A. splendens Willd. Tufted or hummock-forming perenn. erect,
to 30cm, with silky hairs. Lvs to 2cm, 2-pinnatisect, seg. oblong
to narrowly elliptic, silky-hairy. Cap. globose, erect or nodding,
in a rac. or narrow pan. Summer–autumn. Cauc., N Iran, N
Iraq. Z5.

A. stelleriana Besser. BEACH WORMWOOD; OLD WOMAN; DUSTY
MILLER. Perenn. to 60cm, densely white-tomentose. Lower lvs
lobed or deeply toothed, cuneate, upper lvs sometimes entire.
Cap. campanulate, erect or nodding, clustered in a racemose
pan. with leaf-like bracts. NE Asia, E US. 'Mori' ('Boughton
Silver'): to 15cm, habit compact, semi-prostrate; lvs white. Z3.

A. tridentata Nutt. = *Seriphidium tridentatum.*

A. tripartita Rydb. = *Seriphidium tripartitum.*

A. umbelliformis Lam. Tufted, aromatic perenn. to 25cm, white-
silky. Lvs palmately divided, seg. of lower lvs 3-fid, lobes linear,
seg. of upper lvs entire. Cap. ovoid, erect, in a loose rac. Alps,
N Apennines. Z4.

A. vallesiaca All. = *Seriphidium vallesiacum.*

A. villarsii Gren. & Godron = *A. eriantha.*

A. vulgaris L. MUGWORT. Tufted aromatic perenn. to 2.5m; st.
red or purple, sparsely hairy. Lvs 1-pinnatisect, glab. and dark
green above, white and downy beneath, seg. entire, pinnatifid
or coarsely dentate. Cap. numerous, erect, in a broad, bracteate
pan. Summer–autumn. Eur. to Iran and Sib., N Afr.
'Variegata': lvs variegated with white flecks. Z3.

A. vulgaris var. *heterophylla* (Nutt.) Jeps. = *A. douglasiana.*

Arthrocereus (A. Berger) Backeb. & Knuth Cactaceae. 5
shrubby cacti, branching basally; st. cylindric; ribs low and
narrow; spines numerous, thin. Fls tubular-salverform,
nocturnal; pericarpel and tube elongate; usually with wool and
hair-spines. Braz.

A. campos-portoi (Werderm.) Backeb. = *A. glaziovii.*

A. glaziovii (Schum.) N. Tayl. & Zappi. St. prostrate or ascending, simple or clustering; seg. cylindric, 10–60×2.5–4cm; ribs
10–14; central spines to 6, to 4cm, brown, radial spines 25–35,
white. Fls 10–15×6.5–10cm, white, tube almost naked. E Braz.
Z9.

A. itabiriticola P. Braun = *A. glaziovii.*

A. melanurus (Schumann) Diers et al. Shrub to 1m+, branching
below; st. to 2–2.5cm diam.; ribs 10–17; spines glassy yellow or
yellow-brown; central spines 5–7, 3–5cm; radial spines to c30,
4–8mm. Fl. 5–10×5–8cm; tube with small scales and yellow to
black-brown hairs; outer tep. green, tinged brown; inner tep.
white. E Braz. Z9.

A. mello-barretoi Backeb. & Voll. = *A. glaziovii.*

A. microsphaericus sensu A. Berger, not *Cereus microsphaericus*
Schum. = *A. glaziovii.*

A. mirabilis (Speg.) W.T. Marshall = *Echinopsis mirabilis.*

A. rondonianus Backeb. & Voll ex Backeb. St. slender, ascending, to 75×2.5cm; ribs 14–18; spines 40–50, green- to golden
yellow, central 2–7cm, radials 0.5cm. Fls c11cm, fragrant; tep.
pale lilac-pink, tube with bristly hairy spines. E Braz. Z9.

→*Cereus* and *Leocereus.*

Arthrochilus F. Muell. Orchidaceae. 4 tuberous terrestrial
orchids. Lvs 0 at flg. Fls racemose; tep. slender, spreading; lip
uppermost, jointed, callus insect-like. SE Aus. Z9.

A. irritabilis F. Muell. Lvs 3–10cm, ovate-lanceolate. Fls few to
many, golden green ± flushed or spotted red; tep. slender; lip to
1.2cm, mauve-maroon, swollen, glossy, gland.

→*Drakaea* and *Spiculaea.*

Arthromeris (T. Moore) J. Sm. Polypodiaceae. 8 epiphytic or
terrestrial ferns. Rhiz. long-creeping, stout. Fronds stipitate,
uniform, pinnate, pinnae ± lanceolate, entire and cartilaginous,
leathery or membranous. N India to China, Taiwan. Z7.

A. wallichiana (Spreng.) Ching. Rhiz. rusty-scaly. Fronds to
60×30cm; lat. pinnae to 15×5cm, to 21 pairs, oblong to
lanceolate, apex acute, base rounded, margin swollen and undulate, leathery to membranous; stipes to 30cm+, brown. N India, Himal., China. Z7.

→*Polypodium.*

Arthrophyllum Bl.
A. ceylanicum Miq. = *Oroxylum indicum*.
A. reticulatum Bl. ex Miq. = *Oroxylum indicum*.

Arthrophytum Schrenk.
A. acutifolium Minkw. = *Haloxylon persicum*.
A. ammodendron var. *acutifolium* Minkw. = *Haloxylon persicum*.
A. ammodendron Litv. = *Haloxylon ammodendron*.
A. arborescens Litv. = *Haloxylon persicum*.

Arthropodium R. Br. Liliaceae (Asphodelaceae). 12 everg. or decid. rhizomatous tufted perennials. Lvs radical, linear or lanceolate, basally sheathing. Rac. or pan. terminal; fls solitary or 2–3 in axils of scarious bracts; pedicels jointed; tep. 6, spreading; sta. 6, the anth. bearing hairy appendages; attached to the fil. Aus., NZ, New Guinea, New Caledonia, Madag. Z8.
A. candidum Raoul. Lvs 10–30×0.3–1cm, grass-like, decid. Scape to 30cm; pan. few-branched; fls 1cm diam., white; anth. tails white, wholly joined to fil. NZ. 'Maculatum': lvs dull flesh pink mottled and spotted bronze; fls white.
A. cirrhatum (Forst. f.) R. Br. RIENGA LILY; ROCK LILY. Lvs 30–60×3–10cm, everg., lanceolate, white-green or glaucous beneath. Scape to 1m, stout; pan. to 30cm diam., br. many, short, spreading; fls 2–4cm diam., white; anth. tails purple at base, white midway, shading to yellow at free, recurved tips. NZ.
A. milleflorum (DC.) Macbr. Lvs 30×1–3cm, narrow-lanceolate, decid. Scape 1m, pan. br. few to many, erect or ascending; fls to 1.5cm diam., buds mauve, opening white or mauve; anth. tails yellow, sometimes free and recurved. E Aus.
A. minus R. Br. Lvs to 20×0.2–0.4cm, decid. Scape to 30cm; pan. br. few, erect; fls fragrant, to 1cm diam., deep purple; anth. tails deep purple, attached to fil. for all of their length. Aus.
A. paniculatum R. Br. = *A. milleflorum*.
A. pendulum invalid. = *A. milleflorum*.
A. reflexum Colenso. = *A. candidum*.

Arthropteris J. Sm. Oleandraceae. 20 epiphytic or lithophytic ferns. Rhiz. scandent or long-creeping. Fronds uniform, pinnate, pinnae jointed to rachis, oblique; stipes remote, 2-ranked, joined to rhiz. on short phyllopodia. Trop. and subtrop. OW. Z10.
A. articulata (Brackenr.) C. Chr. Fronds to 35×6cm, lanceolate in outline, apex caudate middle and upper pinnae to 4×0.8cm, lobed, auriculate at base, lower pinnae curved and smaller; rachis and costa pubesc.; stipes to 12cm. Polyn.
A. tenella (Forst. f.) J. Sm. Fronds to 50×15cm, elliptic or lanceolate to obovate in outline, glab., pinnae erect to spreading, alt., entire or notched, middle and upper pinnae to 10×1cm, falcate, linear to elliptic or lanceolate, lower pinnae smaller; stipes to 8cm. Aus., NZ.
→*Aspidium* and *Lastrea*.

Arthrostylidium Rupr.
A. longifolium (Fourn.) Camus. = *Otatea acuminata*.

Artillery Plant *Pilea microphylla*.

Artocarpus Forst. & Forst. f. Moraceae. *c*50 everg. or decid., latex-bearing trees. Lvs large, pinnately lobed or entire; stipules large, conical. Fls small: ♂ in catkins, ♀ in dense heads. Fr. a massive, spherical syncarp composed of swollen and compacted receptacles and perianths, exterior usually leathery, green, with interlocking outlines of individual fr., interior white, fleshy, starchy. Trop. Z10.
A. altilis (Parkinson) Fosb. BREADFRUIT. Tree to 18m+, everg.; crown spreading. Lvs to 60cm, ovate, deeply pinnately 3-lobed, dark green, lustrous, coriaceous. Fr. to 20×20cm, subglobose, yellow-green, usually with 0 seeds. Probably originating in Malayan Archipel. The BREADNUT is a race of *A. altilis* with chestnut-like seeds.
A. blumei Trécul. = *A. elasticus*.
A. cannonii Bull ex Van Houtte = *Ficus aspera* 'Cannonii'.
A. communis Forst. & Forst. f. = *A. altilis*.
A. elasticus Reinw. ex Bl. Tree to 45(–65)m, everg., strongly buttressed; twigs pachycaul, short-hispid, annulate. Lvs 10–60cm, ovate-elliptic, bi- or tri-pinnatifid in juveniles, later entire or shallowly crenate, dark green above, paler beneath. Fr. on stalk, 6.5–12cm; pericarp thin, horny, testa fleshy. Malesia.
A. heterophyllus Lam. JACKFRUIT. Tree 10–15m, everg., scarcely buttressed, twigs glab., annulate. Lvs 5–25cm, elliptic to obovate-elliptic, with 1–2 pairs of lat. lobes in juveniles. Fr. massive (to 30kg), borne directly on br. and trunks on stalks to

10cm; endocarps separated, horny, enclosed by gelatinous exocarp. India to Malay Penins.
A. hirsutus Lam. Tree to *c*24m. Lvs 15–22.5cm, subentire, rough beneath. Fr. erect, 5–7.5cm, spiny; seeds to *c*1.9cm, ovoid, hirsute. S India
A. hypargyraeus Hance ex Benth. Tree with rusty-pubesc. br. Lvs 7.5–12.5cm, oblong, entire to sinuately toothed, narrow-acuminate, shiny above, white-tomentose beneath. Fr. obovoid, on tomentose stalks. S China, Hong Kong.
A. incisa L. = *A. altilis*.
A. integer (Thunb.) Merrill. Tree to 20m, everg., scarcely buttressed; twigs pilose, ± annulate. Lvs 5–25cm, obovate-elliptic, acuminate, entire, juveniles with 1–2 pairs lat. lobes. Fr. yellow, brown when dry, with a strong, odour carried on br. and trunks on stalks to 9cm. Malaysia.
A. integrifolius auct., non L. f. = *A. heterophyllus*.
A. kunstleri King = *A. elasticus*.
A. lakoocha Roxb. ex Buch.-Ham. MONKEY JACK. Tree to 18m, decid.; br. villous-tomentose. Lvs 15–30cm, elliptic or oblong, entire, pubesc. beneath. Fr. to 7.5cm diam., wrinkled or smooth, yellow, on v. short peduncle. India to Burm.
A. odoratissimus Blanco. Tree. Lvs 7–9-lobed, villous beneath, pilose along veins above, lobes lanceolate. Fr. globose, small, many-seeded. Philipp.
A. pubescens auct. non Willd. = *A. elasticus*.

Arum L. Araceae. 26 tuberous perenn. herbs. Lvs radical, entire, hastate to sagittate; petioles long, sheathing at base. Peduncle shorter than or equalling petioles; spathe with margins overlapping below to form tube, contracted at throat, limb expanded above; spadix elongate, usually shorter than spathe, with conic to cylindric appendix. Berries orange to red. Eur., esp. Medit., Asia to W Himal.
A. albispathum Steven = *A. italicum* ssp. *albispathum*.
A. alpinum Schott & Kotschy. Lvs 9–13×3–7.5cm, sagittate to sagittate-hastate, acute to obtuse, mid-green; petiole 12–18cm, green. Peduncle to 18cm; spathe to 14cm, tube oblong-cylindric, to 3cm, pale green externally, purple with white at base within, limb erect, elliptic-lanceolate, pale green; spadix to 8cm, appendix slender, ± clavate, pale chocolate-brown to dull purple, to 5cm. Fr. bright orange-red. Early summer. S Spain to NW Turk., Sweden to Crete. Z7.
A. concinnatum Schott. Lvs 15–55×10–32cm, sagittate-hastate to oblong-sagittate, dark green, blotched silver-grey; petiole to 45cm. Peduncle to 14cm; spathe to 29cm, tube oblong-cylindric, to 5cm, pale green externally, margin purple, interior white below, purple above, limb erect, lanceolate-elliptic to elliptic, apex acuminate, exterior pale green with purple margins, green-white with translucent patches and purple margins within; spadix shorter than or just exceeding spathe, appendix conic-cylindric to clavate-cylindric, dull yellow, pale cream-purple or purple. S Greece to SW Turk. Z7.
A. conophalloides Kotschy ex Schott = *A. rupicola*.
A. conophalloides var. *virescens* Bornm. & Gauba = *A. rupicola* var. *virescens*.
A. creticum Boiss. & Heldr. Lvs 8–26×4–18cm, hastate-sagittate, glossy dark green; petiole 10–35cm. Peduncle to 45cm; spathe 15–25cm, bright yellow to yellow-green or green-white, tube much inflated and scarcely constricted, limb recurved and twisted; spadix equalling or exceeding spathe, appendix yellow or purple. Crete, Karpathos. Z7.
A. detruncatum C.A. Mey. ex Schott = *A. rupicola*.
A. dioscoridis Sm. Lvs 13–45×9–27cm, oblong-hastate to narrow-sagittate-hastate, acute, mid-green, veins often paler; petiole 13–50cm. Peduncle usually shorter than petioles, 3.5–10cm; spathe 11–40cm, tube to 8cm, green suffused with purple above and on margin, green-white within, limb erect, lanceolate to lanceolate-elliptic, acute to acuminate, green externally, sometimes stained purple, pale green within, usually blotched and spotted purple-maroon to black purple, or unspotted (var. *syriacum* (Bl.) Engl.) or uniformly purple (var. *philistaeum* (Kotschy ex Schott) Boiss.); spadix malodorous, 12–28cm, appendix stout, cylindric, dark purple, rarely dull yellow. Fr. orange. Late spring. Cyprus to Iraq. var. *dioscoridis*. Spathe limb 16–37cm, blotches confluent, with basal two-thirds stained purple with darker spots, apical portion green, unspotted. SW & SC Turk., Cyprus. var. *cyprium* (Schott) Engl. Spathe limb pale green, not stained purple, with large discrete spots. E Aegean Is., Syr., Leb., Isr. var. *syriacum* (Bl.) Engl. Spathe limb pale green, not stained purple, blotches 0 or small and scattered. SC Turk., N Syr. var. *philistaeum* (Kotschy ex Schott) Boiss. Spathe limb to 14cm, uniformly purple. NW Syr. Possibly a hybrid with *A. palaestinum*. Z8.
A. dioscoridis f. *atropurpureum* Hruby = *A. dioscoridis* var. *philistaeum*.
A. dracunculus L. = *Dracunculus vulgaris*.

A. gratum Schott. Lvs 9–18×7–12, emerging in early winter, hastate-sagittate to oblong-hastate, deep green; petiole 17.5–30cm. Peduncle often remaining below grown, to 2.5cm; spathe to 18.5cm, tube often partly subterranean, oblong-ventricose, to 3.5cm, exterior pale green below, purple-stained above, interior green-white below, purple above, limb cucullate, elliptic-ovate, externally green flushed purple, olive-green stained purple within; spadix to 6.5m, appendix clavate, red- to green-purple, fragrant. Spring–early summer. Syr., Leb., W Turk. Z8.

A. hygrophilum Boiss. Lvs 8–45×5–14cm, lanceolate-hastate, acute, bright to dark green; petiole 9–75cm. Peduncle shorter than lvs, to 45cm; spathe to 14cm, tube ellipsoid, to 3.8cm, green or purple externally, deep purple within, limb erect to cucullate, oblong- to elliptic-lanceolate, acuminate, pale-green externally, green-white within, edged purple; spadix to 9cm, appendix slender, deep purple. Spring. Moroc., Cyprus, Levant. Z8.

A. idaeum Coust. & Gand. Lvs oblong-sagittate, acute, 10–22.5×8–17cm; petiole to 21cm, stained purple. Peduncle 5–17cm; spathe to 11cm, tube oblong-cylindric, to 4cm, pale lime-green externally, faintly marked purple at base, margin and interior white-green, limb erect to cucullate, narrow-elliptic to lanceolate, acute, white tinged green externally, white with translucent patches within, margin purple; spadix to 9.5cm, appendix laterally marbled purple, pale purple, or yellow marbled purple. Crete. Close to *A. creticum*, sometimes known as 'white creticum'. Z7.

A. italicum Mill. Lvs 15–35cm, emerging in autumn or early winter, sagittate to hastate, glossy dark green with various markings; petiole 15–40cm. Peduncle to half length of, or subequal to petioles; spathe 15–40cm, tube oblong-cylindric, 5cm, white within, limb erect, becoming cucullate, green-yellow or white, margins purple; spadix one-third to half length spathe, appendix stout, yellow. Fr. orange-red. Late spring–early summer. S & W Eur. ssp. *italicum*. Lf veins often marked with creamy-white or yellow-green, or lvs sometimes mottled grey-green. Spathe pale green-yellow. The plants cultivated as *A. italicum* 'Pictum' and 'Marmoratum' belong here. Throughout sp. range, except N. 'Chamaeleon': lvs broad, marbled grey-green and yellow-green. 'Tiny': dwarf; lvs small, marbled cream. 'White Winter': to 20cm; lvs slender with bold white marbling. ssp. *neglectum* (C. Towns.) Prime. Lvs uniform green, or with dark spots, not marked cream or grey-green as ssp. *italicum*. Peduncle shorter than petioles, spathe pale green-yellow. W Eur. ssp. *albispathum* (Steven) Prime. Close to ssp. *neglectum*, but spathe pure white within, green externally. Crimea, SW Asia. ssp. *byzantinum* (Bl.) Nyman. Close to ssp. *neglectum* but peduncle subequal to petioles; spathe pale green, tinged purple at margin. Crete, E Balk. Z6.

A. korolkowii Reg. Lvs 8–16×5–13cm, emerging in early winter, sagittate-hastate to oblong-sagittate; petiole to 35cm, striped brown-green. Peduncle to 46cm; spathe 14–20cm, tube oblong-cylindric, to 3.7cm, green externally, white within, limb erect, narrow-lanceolate, acuminate, green externally, paler green with pale purple tinge within; spadix to 14cm, appendix dull cream, marbled red-brown, purple-brown below. N Iran, Afghan., C Asia. Z6.

A. maculatum L. LORDS-AND-LADIES; CUCKOO-PINT; JACK-IN-THE-PULPIT. Lvs 7–20cm, emerging in early spring, hastate to sagittate, obtuse, glossy green, often with dark spots; petiole 15–25cm. Peduncle two-thirds length of, to equalling petioles; spathe 15–25cm, tube oblong, limb erect, becoming cucullate, pale green, often spotted purple-black, sometimes flushed dull purple, margin purple; spadix to 12cm, appendix purple or yellow. Fr. orange-red. Spring. Eur., E to Ukraine. 'Immaculatum': lvs unspotted; fls spathe tube white interior at base, splashed purple above, blade green, sometimes purple edged interior. 'Pleddel': lvs blotched cream. Z6.

A. marmoratum Schott. non hort. = *A. concinnatum*.

A. neglectum (C. Towns.) Ridl. = *A. italicum* ssp. *neglectum*.

A. nickelii Schott = *A. concinnatum*.

A. nigrum Schott. Lvs 10–20cm, emerging in autumn, hastate to hastate-sagittate, dull green; petiole 20–30cm. peduncle to 5cm; spathe 15–20cm, tube green externally, white to green or dull purple within, limb ovate- to elliptic-oblong, purple-black within; spadix less than half length spathe, appendix stout, dark purple-grey. Spring. W Balk., N Greece. Z6.

A. orientale Bieb. = *A. nigrum*.

A. palaestinum Boiss. Lvs to 20cm, emerging in spring, hastate to broadly hastate-sagittate, median lobe 12.5×10cm, ovate-oblong; petioles 20–30cm. Peduncle shorter than lvs; spathe 15–20cm, tube campanulate, scarcely constricted at apex, 4cm, green-white externally, deep purple within, limb spreading, oblong-lanceolate, twisted at apex, dark red-purple within; spadix shorter than spathe, appendix cylindric, black-purple.

Spring. Isr. Z9.

A. petteri misapplied = *A. nigrum*.

A. pictum L. f. Lvs 15–30cm, emerging in autumn, cordate-sagittate, glossy dark green, finely white-veined, margin red; petiole 20–25cm. Peduncle 5–10cm, mostly subterranean; spathe 15–25cm, tube oblong, 3.5cm, green, marked white externally, limb erect, acuminate, dark red-purple; spadix much shorter than spathe, appendix dark red-purple. Autumn. Is., W Medit. Z8.

A. purpureospathum Boyce. Lvs 20–30×15–20cm, emerging in autumn, hastate, dark green; petioles 20–25cm. Peduncle 6–8cm; spathe dark purple throughout, limb erect, becoming cucullate; spadix to half length spathe, appendix dark purple. Fr. orange-red. Crete. Z8.

A. rupicola Boiss. Lvs 8–25×4–18.5cm, emerging in early winter, oblong-sagittate to -hastate, mid-green; petioles 10–55cm. Peduncle 10–65cm; spathe to 40cm, tube oblong-cylindric, to 7cm, green or brown edged purple, white within, limb soon reflexed or cucullate, apex twisted, exterior usually green with purple margin, occas. purple or brown, green-white stained maroon to brown within; spadix to 33cm, appendix cylindric to conic-cylindric, purple to grey-lilac, or brown to yellow. var. *rupicola*. Spathe limb deep purple or maroon within; spadix appendix purple, occas. brown to yellow. Spring–early summer. W Asia, E Medit. var. *virescens* (Stapf) Boyce. Spathe limb green-white within, narrowly bordered purple. Spadix appendix grey-lilac. Spring–early summer. Z8.

A. stevensii Boyce nom. nud. = *A. gratum*.

A. virescens Stapf = *A. rupicola* var. *virescens*.

Arum Lily *Zantedeschia*.

Aruncus L. GOAT'S BEARD. Rosaceae. 3 tall, rhizomatous perenn. herbs. Lvs basal and on st., 2- or 3-pinnate; lfts toothed; petioles long. Fls small, white or cream, in feathery elongate, term. pan.; pet. 5, spathulate; sta. 20–30. N Temp. & subarc. regions.

A. aethusifolius (Lév.) Nak. 20–40cm, compact. Lvs to 25cm, 3–4-pinnate, seg. 1–2cm, ovate, deeply incised; petiole 7–10cm. Fls 2mm diam., in an open pan. Summer. Korea.

A. astilboides Maxim. = *A. dioicus* var. *astilboides*.

A. dioicus (Walter) Fern. GOAT'S BEARD. To 2m. Lvs large, 2-pinnate; seg. to 10cm, ovate, biserrate; petiole to 20cm. Fls 5mm diam., malodorous, in frothy pyramidal pan. to 50cm. Summer. W & C Eur., S Russia, Cauc. Z4. 'Kneiffii': vigorous, to 1m; lvs finely divided into thread-like seg.; fls cream. var. *astilboides* (Maxim.) Hara. Somewhat smaller. Jap. Z7.

A. parvulus Kom. 'Dagalet': to 30cm; lvs ferny, forming a close mat, bronze in autumn; fls cream in ± erect pan.

A. sinensis hort. Differs from *A. dioicus* in more coarsely toothed brown-tinted growth, tighter habit and later flowering time. Usually represented by 'Zweiweltenkind' ('Child of Two Worlds').

A. sylvester Kostel. = *A. dioicus*.

A. sylvester var. *astilboides* (Maxim.) Mak. = *A. dioicus* var. *astilboides*.

A. vulgaris Raf. = *A. dioicus*.

A. vulgaris var. *astilboides* (Maxim.) Nemoto = *A. dioicus* var. *astilboides*.

→*Spiraea*.

Arundina Bl. Orchidaceae. 5 terrestrial orchids. St. clumped, reed-like, sheathed with narrow, grassy lvs. Fls term., solitary or several; tep. lanceolate, spreading (pet. broader than sep.); lip ± funnel-shaped. Himal. to Pacific. Z10.

A. bambusifolia (Roxb.) Lindl. = *A. graminifolia*.

A. chinensis Bl. Smaller than *A. graminifolia*; tep. pale lavender; lip midlobe distinct, blotched crimson. Java, Hong Kong, China.

A. densa Lindl. = *A. graminifolia*.

A. graminifolia (D. Don) Hochr. To 2.5m. Lvs to 30cm. Fls to 8cm across, scented, short-lived, white, mauve, rose-lilac or pale pink, lip obscurely 3-lobed, purple with white disc. Indochina, Thail., Malaya.

A. speciosa Bl. = *A. graminifolia*.

Arundinaria Michx. Gramineae. 1 bamboo; rhiz. running. Culms 2–10m×2–7cm, stout, terete, erect; sheaths glabrescent, usually with coarse dark bristles and auricles; br. many, erect, produced from upper part of culm in its second year. Lvs 10–30×2.5–4cm, tessellate, margins scabrous. SE US. Z6.

A. amabilis McClure = *Pseudosasa amabilis*.

A. anceps Mitford = *Yushania anceps*.

A. argenteostriata (Reg.) Vilm. = *Pleioblastus argenteostriatus*.

A. aristata Gamble = *Thamnocalamus aristatus*.

A. atropurpurea Nak. = *Sasaella masumuneana*.

A. auricoma Mitford = *Pleioblastus auricoma*.
A. borealis (Hackel) Mak. = *Sasamorpha borealis*.
A. chino Franch. & Savat. = *Pleioblastus chino*.
A. chino var. *argenteostriata* f. *elegantissima* Mak. = *Pleioblastus chino* f. *gracilis*.
A. disticha (Mitford) Pfitz. = *Pleioblastus pygmaeus* var. *distichus*.
A. falcata Nees = *Drepanostachyum falcatum*.
A. falconeri (Hook. ex Munro) Benth & Hook. f. = *Drepanostachyum falconeri*.
A. fastuosa (Marliac ex Mitford) Houz. = *Semiarundinaria fastuosa*.
A. fortunei (Van Houtte) Nak. = *Pleioblastus variegatus*.
A. gauntlettii auct. = *Pleioblastus humilis* var. *pumilus*.
A. gigantea (Walter) Muhlenb. GIANT REED; CANE REED; SWITCH CANE.
A. graminea (Bean) Mak. = *Pleioblastus gramineus*.
A. hookeriana Munro = *Drepanostachyum hookerianum*.
A. humilis Mitford = *Pleioblastus humilis*.
A. japonica Sieb. & Zucc. ex Steud. = *Pseudosasa japonica*.
A. jaunsarensis Gamble = *Yushania anceps*.
A. latifolia Keng. = *Indocalamus latifolius*.
A. linearis Hackel = *Pleioblastus linearis*.
A. macrosperma Michx. = *A. gigantea*.
A. maling Gamble = *Yushania maling*.
A. marmorea (Mitford) Mak. = *Chimonobambusa marmorea*.
A. murielae Gamble = *Thamnocalamus spathaceus*.
A. narihira Mak. = *Semiarundinaria fastuosa*.
A. niitikayamensis Lawson, non Hayata = *Yushania anceps* 'Pitt White'.
A. nitida Mitford = *Sinarundinaria nitida*.
A. pumila Mitford = *Pleioblastus humilis* var. *pumilus*.
A. pygmaea (Miq.) Mitford = *Pleioblastus pygmaeus*.
A. quadrangularis (Fenzi) Mak. = *Chimonobambusa quadrangularis*.
A. racemosa auct. non Munro = *Yushania maling*.
A. ragamowskii (Nichols.) Pfitz. = *Indocalamus tessellatus*.
A. simonii (Carr.) A. & C. Riv. = *Pleioblastus simonii*.
A. simonii var. *albostriata* Bean = *Pleioblastus simonii* f. *variegatus*.
A. simonii var. *striata* Mitford = *Pleioblastus simonii* f. *variegatus*.
A. spathacea (Franch.) D. McClintock = *Thamnocalamus spathaceus*.
A. spathiflora Trin. = *Thamnocalamus spathiflorus*.
A. tecta (Walter) Muhlenb. = *A. gigantea*.
A. tessellata (Nees) Munro = *Thamnocalamus tessellatus*.
A. vagans Gamble = *Sasaella ramosa*.
A. variegata (Sieb. ex Miq.) Mak. = *Pleioblastus variegatus*.
A. variegata var. *akebono* Mak. = *Pleioblastus akebono*.
A. viridistriata (Reg.) Mak. ex Nak. = *Pleioblastus auricoma*.

Arundinella Raddi. Gramineae. 47 ann. or perenn. grasses, culms erect. Lvs linear, flat or rolled, rarely flaccid and lanceolate; ligule short, scarious, ciliate. Infl. an oblong pan.; spikelets in pairs, yellow-green or purple-tinged. Pantrop. Z7.
A. ecklonii Nees = *A. nepalensis*.
A. nepalensis Trin. Tufted perenn. to 180cm. Lvs linear or convolute, to 30×1cm, glab. to hirsute. Pan. oblong or contracted, to 40cm, br. densely spiculate, spikelets lanceolate, to 6mm. Trop.

Arundo L. GIANT REED. Gramineae. 3 giant rhizomatous, perenn. grasses. Lvs alt., 2-ranked on thick, reed-like st., deflexed, broad-linear, flat, slightly scabrous, bases sheathing. Pan. large, term., dense, feathery. Trop. and subtrop. OW. Z7.
A. ampelodesmos Cyr. = *Ampelodesmos mauritanicus*.
A. bicolor Desf., non Poir. = *Ampelodesmos mauritanicus*.
A. conspicua Forst. f. = *Chionochloa conspicua*.
A. donax L.   St. to 6m, clumped. Lvs to 60×6cm, slightly scabrous, grey-green. Pan. to 60cm, tinged red at first, then silvery grey. Autumn. Medit. 'Macrophylla': st. sometimes tinted mauve; lvs larger, to 100×9cm, glaucous, grey-green to blue-green. var. *versicolor* (Mill.) Stokes. Lf blades striped white. 'Variegata': to 3m; lvs striped and edged off-white. 'Variegata Superba': lvs to 30×6.5cm, striped and edged off-white, closer together on culms.
A. festucoides Desf. = *Ampelodesmos mauritanicus*.
A. madagascariensis Kunth = *Neyraudia arundinacea*.
A. mauritanica Poir. = *Ampelodesmos mauritanicus*.
A. phragmites L. = *Phragmites australis*.
A. plinii Turra. Resembles *A. donax*, but smaller, less hardy, with smooth pan. br. Medit.
A. richardii Endl. = *Cortaderia richardii*.
A. selloana Schult. = *Cortaderia selloana*.
A. tenax Vahl. = *Ampelodesmos mauritanicus*.

Asafoetida *Ferula assa-foetida*.
Asarabacca *Asarum* (*A. europaeum*).

Asarina Mill. TWINING SNAPDRAGON. Scrophulariaceae. 16 diffuse or twining perenn. herbs. Fls slender-stalked, solitary, axill.; sep. 5; cor. tubular, bilabiate, with ventral basal pouch and prominent ventral ridges sometimes united into a palate. Mex. & SW US, S Eur. Z9 unless specified.
A. **antirrhinifolia** (Humb. & Bonpl.) Pennell. VIOLET TWINING SNAPDRAGON. Glab.; st. diffuse, twining. Lvs 1.5–2.5cm, ovate-hastate, apex acuminate, base narrowly cordate; petioles twining. Cor. 2–2.5cm, tube pale and dull, lobes purple to violet, palate closing throat white tinged yellow, marked with dark lines. Spring–summer. Calif. to Tex. to S Mex.
A. **barclaiana** (Lindl.) Penn. Vine, to 3m+, woody at base. Lvs 2cm, cordate to broadly hastate, long-acute, angular, entire, glab.; petioles twining. Cor. funneliform, without palate, lobes 3–7cm, spreading, rounded, white to pink darkening to deep purple, purple downy without, tube tinged green. Summer. Mex.
A. **erubescens** (D. Don) Penn. CREEPING GLOXINIA. Vine, softly glandular-pubesc., grey-green, woody at base. Lvs 4–7.5cm, deltoid, dentate, petioles twining. Cor. 7cm, glandular-pubesc., lobes obtuse or notched, rose-pink, tube ventricose, white, marbled within. Summer. Mex. 'Alba': fls white.
A. **filipes** (A. Gray) Pennell. YELLOW TWINING SNAPDRAGON. Glab., slightly glaucous; st. diffuse, twining. Lvs 3–5cm, ovate-lanceolate, entire; petioles twining. Cor. 1–1.2cm, yellow, palate raised, golden yellow with black spots. Spring. SW US.
A. **lophospermum** (L.H. Bail.) Penn. Similar to *A. erubescens*, except slightly pubesc. to glabrate; cor. rose-purple, somewhat spotted, tube not ventricose, white. Summer. Mex.
A. **procumbens** Mill. Glandular-pubesc. procumbent. Lvs to 6cm, ovate-cordate to reniform, crenate-dentate, rarely ± palmatifid. Cor. 3–3.5cm, tube white with faint purple veins, lobes pale yellow or sometimes pale pink, palate deep yellow. S Fr., NE Spain. Z7.
A. **purpusii** (Brandg.) Penn. Tuberous; glab. or glandular-pubesc.; st. 30–45cm, prostrate, slender. Lvs triangular-ovate to deltoid, sometimes dentate, long-petiolate. Cor. 4cm, purple-carmine, lacking palate. Mex.
A. **scandens** (Cav.) Penn. Similar to *A. barclaiana* except cal. glab., not glandular-pilose; cor. funneliform with spreading lobes 4–5cm, pale violet to lavender or pink, tube paler. Mex.
→*Antirrhinum, Lophospermum* and *Maurandya*.

Asarum L. WILD GINGER; ASARABACCA. Aristolochiaceae. *c*70 low-growing everg. perenn. herbs. Rhiz. aromatic. Lvs long-petiolate, 1 or 2 per shoot, reniform to cordate or sagittate, usually glab. and leathery. Fls solitary, short-stalked, at basal axils or between paired lvs with 3 narrow lobes, (sep.) spreading from the annular rim of a fleshy, cup-like receptacle, usually dull green to purple-brown, aromatic. Temp. E Asia, N Amer.
A. albivenium Reg. = *A. blumei*.
A. **arifolium** Michx. Lvs triangular-sagittate to subrotund, obtuse, 16–20×5–25cm, marked light green to silver between principal veins. Perianth pyriform with prominent spreading lobes or ovoid with short erect lobes, tube 1–3cm long, 6–12mm wide. Spring. SE US. Z7.
A. **asaroides** (Morr. & Decne.) Mak. Lvs broadly ovate to deltoid-ovate, 8–12×5–10cm, obtuse, pubesc. on veins above, spotted. Perianth tube pyriform 2–2.5cm, prominently constricted at apex, purple-green, finely net-veined inside, lobes orbicular-cordate or deltoid-orbicular, spreading, undulate, 1–1.5cm. Spring. Jap. Z7.
A. **blumei** Duchartre. Lvs broadly hastate-ovate to broadly ovate, 6–10×4–8cm, acute to obtuse, dark green with white veins, short-pubesc. Perianth tube 1×1cm, bluntly 4-angled; yellow spotted red, lobes net-veined inside, spreading, ovate-orbicular, incurved at apex. Spring. Jap. Z7.
A. **canadense** L. WILD GINGER. Lvs decid., broadly reniform, dark green, short-acuminate, finely pubesc., 6–10×10–17cm. Perianth 2.5cm across, purple-brown, tube ovoid, lobes spreading, ovate-lanceolate, acute or long-acuminate, sometimes caudate to 2cm. Spring. Manit. to N Carol. Z4.
A. **caudatum** Lindl. Lvs cordate-reniform, obtuse-rounded to subacute 2–10cm long, pubesc. beneath and on veins above. Perianth red-brown, tube rounded, lobes attenuate-caudate, twisted, 2.5–8.5cm. Spring. W N Amer. Z7.
A. **europaeum** L. ASARABACCA. Lvs reniform, 2.5–10cm, broader than long, deeply cordate at base, apex v. obtuse, dark glossy green, pubesc. on veins above. Perianth dull brown, 1.5cm, pubesc. outside, lobes deltoid, acuminate, half as long as tube. Spring. W Eur. Z5.
A. **grandiflorum** Klotzsch = *A. arifolium*.

A. hartwegii S. Wats. Lvs to 10cm diam., cordate to ovate, acute, dark green to bronze, mottled silver, pubesc. beneath. Perianth hairy, lobes 2.5–6.5cm. Spring. Calif., Oreg. Z7.

A. leucodictyon Miq. = *A. blumei*.

A. lewisii Fern. Lvs reniform, dark green with red and silver spots. Fls 2.5–5cm. N Am. Z7.

A. maximum Hemsl. Lvs cordate, 20cm across, dark green mottled grey. Perianth 6cm across, maroon, pyriform, strongly constricted at orifice, inner walls ridged, annulus white or yellow, eye-like, lobes papillose. Spring. China. Z7.

A. shuttleworthii Britten & Bak. f. Lvs 5–10×4–7.5cm, cordate to orbicular-cordate, mid-green, usually marked silver. Perianth campanulate to urceolate, pale brown spotted brown to blood red, tube to 1.5–4×2cm, tessellated with ridges inside, lobes large, spreading, 1×2cm at base. Spring. SE US. Z7.

A. thunbergii A. Braun = *A. asaroides*.

A. virginicum L. Lvs cordate, rounded, to orbicular-cordate or retuse, dark green with purple and silver mottling. Perianth tube brown cylindric with slight flare below constriction, thick-walled, 1–1.5×1cm, ridged within, lobes tessellated, 3.5×7.5mm, erect to spreading. Spring. SE US. Z7.

→*Hexastylis*.

ASCLEPIADACEAE R. Br. 347/2850. *Araujia, Asclepias, Brachystelma, Caralluma, Ceropegia, Cionura, Cryptostegia, Cynanchum, Dischidia, Dregea, Duvalia, Duvaliandra, Echidnopsis, Edithcolea, Fockea, Folotsia, Frerea, Hoodia, Hoodiopsis, Hoya, Huernia, Huerniopsis, Karimbolea, Kinepetalum, Notechidnopsis, Orbea, Orbeanthus, Orbeopsis, Pachycymbium, Pectinaria, Periploca, Piaranthus, Pseudolithos, Quaqua, Raphionacme, Rhytidocaulon, Sarcostemma, Stapelia, Stapelianthus, Stapeliopsis, Stephanotis, Stultitia, Tavaresia, Trichocaulon, Tridentea, Tromotriche, Tweedia, Vincetoxicum, Whitesloanea*.

Asclepias L. SILKWEED; MILKWEED. Asclepiadaceae. 108 annuals, perenn. herbs, subshrubs and shrubs; st. simple or divaricate, erect or exuding milky sap. Fls small, starry, numerous, in flat-topped cymes; sep. 5; cor. rotate, lobes 5; corona usually conspicuous, composed of 5 'hood lobes', composed of the hood and (usually) the horn (an incurved, slender appendage within the hood); sta. 5, fused to form staminal column. Pods or follicles globose to fusiform, paired, smooth or spiny; seeds with silky apical tuft. Americas, S Afr., nat. Eur.

A. aphylla Thunb. = *Cynanchum aphyllum*.

A. asperula (Decne.) Woodson. Multi-stemmed; sprawling, perenn. herb. Lvs 7–20cm, narrow-lanceolate, alt. Fls 15–20 per head; cor. lobes to 1.25cm, chartreuse green; hoods deep purple, almost black. SW US. Z7.

A. cornuttii Decne. = *A. syriaca*.

A. curassavica L. BLOOD FLOWER; SWALLOW WORT; MATAL; INDIAN ROOT; BASTARD PECACUANHA. Ann. or short-lived everg. subshrub to 1.5m. Lvs to 15cm, elliptic-lanceolate, acuminate, opposite. Fls in axill. or subterminal cymes; cor. 1cm across, cinnabar red, sometimes white or yellow; hoods yellow-orange. Summer–later autumn. S Amer.; pantrop. weed. Z9.

A. fruticosa L. Slender-stemmed, perenn. subshrub to 1m. Lvs to 12.5cm, lanceolate to oblanceolate, opposite. Infl. axill.; cor. lobes to 1.2cm, cream to white. Fr. to 7.5cm, ovoid, silver-green, strongly inflated, softly spiny. Afr., nat. C & S Amer. Z8.

A. hallii A. Gray. Erect perenn. to 1m, allied to *A. purpurascens* but with narrower, alt. lvs and smaller fls. Lvs to 13cm, lanceolate to narrow-ovate, acuminate. Fls deep pink. W US. Z3.

A. incarnata L. SWAMP MILKWEED. Densely branching, thick-stemmed perenn. to 1.75m. Lvs 5–15cm, linear-elliptic to narrowly ovate, opposite. Infl. axill., toward ends of st.; cor. lobes to 0.5cm, white to pink. NE & SE US. Z3.

A. lanceolata Walter. Perenn. to 1.5m, slender, erect then arching. Lvs to 25cm, narrow-lanceolate, opposite. Infl. sparse, term.; cor. lobes to 0.75cm, brick- to sealing-wax red, often orange and yellow. Neb. to SW US. Z4.

A. mexicana Cav. Slender-stemmed perenn. to 75cm. Lvs to 12cm, elliptic to lanceolate, whorled. Infl. toward ends of br.; cor. white tinged purple, lobes to 1.2cm. Mex. Z6.

A. ovalifolia Decne. Differs from *A. syriaca* in its slender st. and green-white, sometimes purple-tinted fls in lax fascicles. W N Amer. Z6.

A. physocarpa (E. Mey.) Schltr. SWAN PLANT. Downy, somewhat viscid, slender, shrub, erect to 2m. Lvs to 10cm, narrow-lanceolate. Fls cream to green-white; cor. lobes to 0.5cm. Fr. to 6cm diam., subglobose, strongly inflated, translucent pale green, softly spiny; pedicel sigmoid. S Afr. Z9.

A. pumila (A. Gray) Vail. Low, tufted perenn. to 35cm. Lvs to 4.5cm, linear-lanceolate to filiform, loosely whorled to alt. Fls borne terminally and in upper axils, white, sometimes flushed rose or lime green; cor. lobes to 0.4cm. W N Amer. Z6.

A. purpurascens L. PURPLE SILKWEED. Perenn. to 1m. Lvs to 20cm, opposite, ovate to broadly lanceolate, dark glossy green above, downy beneath. Fls borne terminally; cor. deep rose to purple, lobes to 0.8cm. E N Amer. Z5.

A. quadrifolia Jacq. Slender-stemmed perenn., 20–50cm. Lvs to 15cm, usually far shorter, ovate, paired in 4-lvd pseudowhorls. Fls borne terminally, pale pink to ivory; cor. lobes to 1cm. E N Amer. Z5.

A. rubra L. Differs from *A. lanceolata* in its broader lvs and red, mauve or lavender fls. E N Amer. Z5.

A. speciosa Torr. Differs from *A. purpurascens* in its hoary growth, axill. infl., cor. green tinted purple-red, lobes to 1.2cm. Fr. sometimes spiny. W N Amer. Z2.

A. subulata Decne. Gaunt broom-like shrub to 2m. Lvs narrow-subulate, caducous. Fls to 2.5cm diam., off-white, in axill. infl. SW US, Mex. Z6.

A. syriaca L. Perenn. herb 1–2m. Lvs 7.25cm, ovate-oblong. Fls solitary, axillary, or in nodding cymes toward br. ends, pink to mauve or white, to 2.3cm diam. E N Amer., nat. Eur. Z3.

A. tuberosa L. BUTTERFLY WEED; CHIEGER FLOWER; PLEURISY ROOT; TUBER ROOT; INDIAN PAINTBRUSH. Erect, hispidulous tuberous-rooted and woody-based perenn., to 1m. Lvs to 11.5cm, narrow-lanceolate, loosely spiralling. Cymes axill.; cor. lobes to 0.8cm, yellow, orange or vermilion. E & S US. Gay Butterflies Mixed: to 60cm high; fls red, pink, orange, gold and bicolors, abundant; seed race. 'Orange Flame': to 60cm high; fls vibrant orange, scented. 'Vermilion': to 100cm; fls vermilion. Z3.

A. viridiflora Raf. Perenn. to 1m; st. simple. Lvs to 13cm, linear to rounded, opposite to alt. Infl. subterminal; cor. pale green, lobes to 5mm. E US to Ariz. and Mex.

→*Gomphocarpus*.

X**Ascocenda**. (*Ascocentrum* ×*Vanda*.) Orchidaceae. Gdn hybrids intermediate between parents in habit with erect sprays of large spreading fls in shades of yellow, orange, red, rose and cream, sometimes with darker or differently coloured spotting or tessellation.

Ascocentrum Schltr. ex J.J. Sm. Orchidaceae. 5 small epiphytic orchids. St. narrow. Lvs rigid, strap-shaped, 2-ranked. Fls to 2cm diam. in dense, erect, ± cylindric rac.; tep. flat, rounded; lip small, 3-lobed; spur short. Himal. to Borneo. Z10.

A. ampullaceum (Roxb.) Schltr. Lvs to 14cm. Fls sparkling rose red. Himal., Burm.

A. curvifolium (Lindl.) Schltr. Lvs decurved. Fls scarlet with golden-yellow lip, column and spur orange to red. Himal.

A. hendersonianum Rchb. f. = *Dyakia hendersoniana*.

A. miniatum (Lindl.) Schltr. Lvs to 8.5cm. Fls golden to orange. Himal., Malaysia.

→*Saccolabium*.

X**Ascofinetia**. (*Ascocentrum* ×*Neofinetia*.) Orchidaceae. Gdn hybrids with slender, offsetting growth and sprays of small pink fls.

Ascoglossum Schltr. Orchidaceae. 2 epiphytic orchids. Lvs linear-ligulate, 2-ranked. Infl. a branched axill. rac.; fls many, spurred. New Guinea, Solomon Is. Z10.

A. calopterum (Rchb. f.) Schltr. To 30cm. Lvs to 18.5cm. Fls to 2.2cm diam., pale purple to magenta. New Guinea.

→*Saccolabium*.

X**Asconopsis**. (*Ascocentrum* ×*Phalaenopsis*.) Orchidaceae. Gdn hybrids with broad 2-ranked lvs and erect branching spikes of dainty, rounded fls in shades of pink, orange and apricot.

Ash *Fraxinus*.
Ashanti Pepper *Piper guineense*.
Ashby's Banksia *Banksia ashbyi*.
Ashe Chinkapin *Castanea pumila* var. *ashei*.
Ashe Juniper *Juniperus ashei*.
Ash Gourd *Benincasa hispida*.
Ash-leaved Maple *Acer negundo*.
Ash Plant *Leucophyllum frutescens*.
Ash Weed *Aegopodium podagraria*.
Ashy Sunflower *Helianthus mollis*.
Asian Black Birch *Betula davurica*.
Asian Sword Fern *Nephrolepis multiflora*.
Asiatic Poppy *Meconopsis*.
Asiatic Sweetleaf *Symplocos paniculata*.

Asimina Adans. Annonaceae. 8 everg. or decid. subshrubs or small trees. Lvs entire. Fls nodding, subcampanulate, axill., solitary or in small clusters; sep. 3; pet. 6, in 2 whorls; sta. numerous. Fr. a berry, ellipsoid to oblong. E N Amer. Z5.

A. triloba (L.) Dunal PAPAW; PAWPAW. Decid. tree or shrub to 10m. Buds red-hairy. Lvs 10–25cm, obovate-oblong. Fls solitary, precocious; outer pet. to 2.5cm, broadly ovate, thick, veined, purple to maroon, inner pet. reduced, banded yellow. Fr. to 16cm, ovoid, green ripening yellow-brown, edible, aromatic. SE US.

Aspalathus L. emend R. Dahlgr. Leguminosae (Papilionoideae). *c*270 shrubs or small trees. Br. often armed. Lvs (1–)3-foliolate or unifoliolate, lf base occas. developed into a spine; lfts plane to tightly inrolled. Fls pea-like in bracteate clusters or umbels. S Afr. Z9.

A. capensis (Walp.) R. Dahlgr. Erect, shrub to 3m+. Young shoots pale green, downy. Lfts 3, linear, terete, mucronate, light green. Infl. 1–3-fld; cor. bright yellow, standard to 2cm. Summer. Cape Penins.

A. carnosa Berger. YELLOW GORSE. Rigidly erect shrub to 3.5m; young br. short-tomentose. Lfts 3, linear, ± terete, often pungent. Infl. 1–7-fld; cor. bright yellow, standard to 1.4cm, acute, flushed red. Summer. SW Cape.

A. linearis (Burm. f.) R. Dahlgr. ROOIBOS. Erect or decumbent shrub to 2m. Young br. white-tomentose. Lfts 1, linear, subterete, silvery. Infl. 1–10-fld; cor. yellow, standard to 6.5cm. Summer. S & SW Cape. Plants grown as *A. contaminata* may well belong here.

A. sarcodes Vogel ex Benth. = *A. capensis*.
→*Psoralea*.

Asparagus L. Liliaceae (Asparagaceae). *c*300 perenn., rhizomatous herbs, 'shrubs' or climbers, usually tuberous. St. of 1–3 years duration, erect, spreading, or climbing. True lvs small, scale-like, often spiny; cladophylls green, needle or leaf-like. Fls inconspicuous, green, white or yellow. Fr. a spherical berry. OW.

A. acutifolius L. St. to 2m, wiry, erect, somewhat woody, white or grey, with faint ridges; br. rigid, 17.5–15cm. Cladophylls 2–10×0.5mm, awl-shaped, rigid, spreading, glaucous, terete, spine-tipped, in clusters of 10–30. Fls in axill. clusters. Fr. black. Medit. Z8.

A. aethiopicus L. Close to *A. falcatus*. St. to 7m, climbing. Cladophylls 1–4cm×1–2mm, flat, rigid, ascending, mucronate, in clusters of 3–6. C & S Afr. Z9.

A. africanus Lam. St. to 3m, glab., climbing, woody, much-branched. Cladophylls 5–10mm, terete, thread-like, rigid, in clusters of 8 to 20. Fls in axill. umbels. Fr. red. S Afr. Z9.

A. albus L. St. to 1m, erect, woody, with faint ridges. Cladophylls 5–25×0.5–1.5mm, ridged, with 3 angles, in clusters of 10–20. Fr. black. W Medit. Z8.

A. asparagoides (L. Druce. St. to 1.5m, bright green, twining, glab. or slightly ridged. Cladophylls 1.5–3.5cm×0.8–2cm, ovate, alt., leathery, round or cordate at base. Fls solitary or paired in lf axils. Fr. red. S Afr. 'Myrtifolius': habit small, elegant; lvs to 2cm. Z10.

A. cooperi Bak. = *A. africanus*.

A. crispus Lam. St. to 1m, green, herbaceous, flexuous, climbing or drooping, much-branched. Cladophylls 0.3–1×0.1cm, 3-angled, reflexed, linear, in clusters of 2 or 3. Fls solitary, fragrant. Fr. pale black. S Afr. Z9.

A. densiflorus (Kunth) Jessop. EMERALD FERN. St. to 1m, somewhat woody, erect or trailing, finely ridged, somewhat spiny, green or brown. Cladophylls 0.5–1.5×0.1–0.2cm, usually flat, linear, narrowly falcate, 1-nerved, in clusters of 1–3. Fls in axill. rac. Fr. bright red. S Afr. 'Compactus' ('Nanus'): compact; br. short. 'Deflexus': cladophylls wider, with metallic tint. 'Myersii' (FOXTAIL FERN): lat. br. ± the same length; cladophylls needle-like, dark green, creating soft ferny cylinders. The forms of *A. densiflorus* usually seen belong to the Sprengeri group, with whorls of 3 cladophylls and gracefully arching st. Z9.

A. drepanophyllus Welw. St. to 10m, terete, woody, climbing, with faint ridges. Cladophylls with papillose margins, flat, in a single, horizontal plane on each shoot, 2–7cm. Fls in erect rac. on older shoots. Fr. bright scarlet. W & C Afr. Z9.

A. falcatus L. St. to 12m or more, climbing, terete, woody, grey-brown. Cladophylls 5–9×0.5–0.7cm, bright green, linear-oblong, falcate, with a conspicuous midrib, in clusters of 1–3. Fls fragrant in axill. rac. Fr. brown. S Afr., E Afr., Ceylon. Z10.

A. filicinus D. Don. FERN ASPARAGUS. St. to 2m, erect, herbaceous, with branchlets and cladophylls in horizontal plane. Cladophylls 0.6–2×0.1–0.2cm, lanceolate, strongly falcate, flat in clusters of 3–5. Fls solitary or paired at each node. Fr. black. India, China. Z8.

A. laricinus Burchell. St. to 2m, erect, woody, white, grooved, much-branched; br. ascending, flexuous. Cladophylls 0.8–3cm, bright green, awl-shaped, terete, rigid, ascending, clusters of 15 to 60. Fls in axill. or terminal clusters. Fr. dull red. S Afr. Z9.

A. lucidus Lindl. St. to 3m, woody, slender, flexuous, branching freely. Cladophylls 2.5–5×0.1–0.2cm, bright green, flat, narrow, falcate, in clusters of 2 to 6. Fls in axill. clusters. Fr. brown. China, Korea, Jap., Taiwan. Z7.

A. madagascariensis Bak. St. to 60cm+, erect, green, angled, much-branched with hooked prickles. Cladophylls 1–2×0.5–0.7cm, lanceolate, acute, glab., dark olive-green, in clusters of 3 in a single plane on each twig. Fls in term. umbels. Fr. red, somewhat 3-lobed. Madag. Z9.

A. medeoloides (L.) Thunb. = *A. asparagoides*.

A. meyeri = *A. densiflorus* 'Myersii'.

A. officinalis L. ASPARAGUS. St. to 1m, herbaceous, usually erect, feathery, much-branched. Cladophylls 1–2.5cm, terete, filiform, in clusters of 4–25, dark green. Fls axillary, drooping, solitary or clustered. Fr. bright red. Eur., Asia, N Afr. Z4.

A. officinalis var. *pseudoscaber* Asch. & Gräbn. = *A. pseudo-scaber*.

A. plumosus Bak. = *A. setaceus*.

A. pseudoscaber (Asch. & Gräbn.) Grecescu. Close to *A. officinalis*. St. grooved with papillose ridges. Cladophylls 0.5–2×0.05cm, weakly 4-angled. E Eur., W Russia. 'Spitzen-schleier': foliage exceptionally graceful. Z4.

A. racemosus Willd. St. to 7m+, climbing, grey to brown, branched above. Cladophylls 1–2×0.1cm, often falcate, with grey-green, ridge-like angles, in clusters of 3 to 8. Fls fragrant, racemose. Fr. black or red. S Afr., E Afr., Asia. Z9.

A. retrofractus L. Close to *A. laricinus*. St. scrambling or weakly cascading, brown with age; br. flexuous. Fls in axill. umbels. Fr. orange. S Afr. Z9.

A. scandens Thunb. St. to 2.5m, scrambling or climbing, terete, herbaceous, weak, much-branched above. Cladophylls 0.5–1.5×0.1–0.2cm, linear-lanceolate, flat, glab., light green, in lax whorls of 2 or 3. Fls nodding, axill., solitary or in clusters. Fr. scarlet. S Afr. Z9.

A. setaceus (Kunth) Jessop. St. climbing or scrambling, woody or wiry, green, glab. Cladophylls to 1cm, bright or dark green, finely-pointed, in clusters of 8–20, in a single plane, forming a flat leaf-like spray, triangular in outline. Fls solitary, term. Fr. red. S & E Afr. 'Cupressoides': compact, narrowly pyramidal. 'Nanus': habit more compact, upright; cladophylls crowded, shorter. 'Pyramidalis': loose pyramidal habit. 'Robustus': strong-growing. Z9.

A. sprengeri Reg. = *A. densiflorus* Sprengeri group.

A. tenuifolius Lam. St. to 1m, herbaceous, erect, wiry, green. Cladophylls 1–3×0.05cm, linear, thread-like, grey-green or dark-green, soft, 2–4-angled, in whorls of 15–40. Fls axill., in clusters. Fr. bright red. Medit. Z7.

A. ternifolius Hook. f. = *A. aethiopicus*.

A. tetragonus Bresl. = *A. racemosus*.

A. trichophyllus Bunge. St. 2m, erect, flexuous, much-branched above; br. green with curved prickles. Cladophylls 1.2–2.5cm, setose, stiff, awl-shaped, 2–4-angled, in whorls of 20–30. Fls usually solitary, or in axillary clusters of 1–3. Sib., N China. Z6.

A. umbellatus Link. St. to 5m, slender, wiry, grooved, much branched above. Cladophylls 1–3×0.1cm, stiff, almost spine-like, with 3 or 4 papillose angles, in clusters of 10 to 30. Fls in term. umbels of 1 to 4. Fr. yellow orange. Canary Is. Z9.

A. verticillatus L. St. to 2.5m, 1.5cm thick, climbing, woody, much-branched, with short prickles. Cladophylls 1–6×0.05–0.15cm, with 3 strong, papillose angles, filiform, in whorls of 10 to 20. Fls in whorls. Fr. black. SE Eur. to Russia. 'Floribundus': fls and berries produced freely. Z6.

A. virgatus Bak. St. to 1m erect, much-branched above, woody, with grooves and ridges; br. long, straight or drooping. Cladophylls to 2.5cm, rigid, dark green, in whorls of 3–7. Fls in axill. clusters of 3–7. Fr. dull red. S Afr. Z9.

→*Medeola* and *Myrsiphyllum*.

Asparagus *Asparagus officinalis*.
Asparagus Bean *Vigna unguiculata*.
Asparagus Pea *Lotus tetragonolobus*; *Psophocarpus tetragono-lobus*.

Aspasia Lindl. Orchidaceae. 5 epiphytic orchids. Pbs to 12cm, oblong-ellipsoid. Lvs to 30cm, lanceolate-ligulate, 2 at pb. apex, 2 basal, sheathing. Fls 1–9 in erect basal rac.; tep. narrow, spreading; lip ± crenately callused. Trop. Amer. Z10.

A. epidendroides Lindl. Fls to 3.5cm diam., fragrant; sep. yellow-green banded brown; pet. mauve-bronze; lip white, yellow and purple at centre. Guat. to Colomb.

A. fragrans Klotzsch = *A. epidendroides*.

A. lunata Lindl. Fls to 3.5cm diam.; tep. green banded and spotted brown; lip white, purple at centre. Braz.

A. principissa Rchb. f. Fls to 6cm diam.; tep. green striped brown or ochre; lip ivory, disc yellow. Costa Rica, Panama.

A. variegata Lindl. Fls to 5cm diam., fragrant; tep. green banded maroon-chocolate at base; lip white spotted purple. Costa Rica, Panama.

Aspen *Populus tremula.*

Asperula L. WOODRUFF. Rubiaceae. *c*100 ann. or perenn. herbs, or dwarf shrubs. St. 4-angled. Lvs ± sessile, opposite or in whorls. Fls in branched, often involucrate, term. and/or axill. pan. or cymose cap.; cal. tube 0, limb swollen or minutely 4–5-toothed; cor. bell-, funnel-, cup-shaped, tubular, or hypocrateriform, lobes usually 4. Eur., Asia, Aus.

A. arcadiensis Sims. Perenn. St. tufted, woody at base, to 18cm, grey-woolly pubesc. Lvs to 1.2cm, 6–8-whorled, linear to lanceolate, somewhat revolute, grey-woolly. Cap. to 8-fld term.; cor. rose-pink to pale purple, funnel-shaped, tube to 12mm, lobes lanceolate to ovate, to 3mm. Greece. Z8.

A. aristata L. f. Perenn. St. tufted, ascending, to 70cm, glab. to pubesc., rough and papillose. Lvs to 4cm, 4-whorled, linear to lanceolate, tip hyaline, revolute. Cymes loose, many-fld, term., paniculate; cor. funnel-shaped to hypocrateriform, smooth to papillose, tube to 5mm, lobes to 2mm, abruptly acute. S Eur. Z8.

A. athoa Boiss. = *A. suberosa.*

A. caespitosa Boiss. = *A. lilaciflora.*

A. calabrica L. f. = *Putoria calabrica.*

A. cynanchica L. SQUINANCY WORT. Perenn. St. tufted, erect to sprawling, woody or herbaceous, glab. to rough. Lvs to 4cm, 4–6-whorled, obovate to narrowly linear. Corymbs or cymes short-stalked in lax, few-fld, much-branched; cor. white to pink or pale purple, funnel-shaped, exterior rough, tube to 6mm, lobes 3–4, spreading, appendaged. Summer–autumn. Eur., W Asia. Z6.

A. cynanchica ssp. *aristata* (L. f.) Bég. = *A. aristata.*

A. gussonii Boiss. Perenn. St. to 9cm, densely tufted, compact, woody at base, glab., frosted and glaucous. Lvs to 1cm, glaucescent, 4-whorled, overlapping, incurved, ovate-oblong to linear. Cap. dense, to 15-fld, term.; cor. buff to dark red, funnel-shaped to hypocrateriform, exterior smooth, tube to 5mm, lobes ovate, indistinctly appendaged, to 2mm. Sicily. Z7.

A. hirta Ramond. Perenn. St. to 15cm, tufted and mat-forming, erect, glab. or pubesc. Lvs to 1.5cm, 4–7-whorled, linear to lanceolate, acute or cuspidate, revolute, pubesc. Cap. pedunculate, term.; cor. white turning pink, funnel-shaped, glab., tube to 5mm, lobes to 3mm. Summer–autumn. Pyren. Z6.

A. humifusa (Bieb.) Bieb. = *Galium humifusum.*

A. lilaciflora Boiss. Perenn. St. tufted, to 30cm. Lvs to 2cm, 4-whorled, linear, acute. Fls in term. clusters, pink to pink-lilac. W to C Asia. Z5.

A. longifolia Sibth. & Sm. = *Galium longifolium.*

A. nitida Sibth. & Sm. Perenn. St. to 25cm, tufted, cushion-forming, erect or ascending. Lvs to 1.5cm, 4-whorled, linear to lanceolate, apex acute and hyaline, ± revolute and ciliate. Fls few in term. clusters; cor. pale pink to purple, funnel-shaped to hypocrateriform, glab., tube to 6mm, lobes distinctly appendaged, to 2mm. Summer. Greece. Z7.

A. odorata L. = *Galium odoratum.*

A. suberosa Sibth. & Sm. St. to 10cm, tufted, short-pubesc., frosted. Lvs to 1cm, 4-whorled, narrowly linear, revolute. Fl. clusters elongate-spike-forming; cor. pink, hypocrateriform, tube to 6mm, lobes to 2mm. Summer. Bulg., Greece. Z7.

A. suberosa Guss., non Sibth. & Sm. = *A. gussonii.*

A. taurina L. PINK WOODRUFF. Perenn. St. to 60cm, erect or ascending, spreading via creeping, orange-red stolons, usually glab. Lvs to 6cm, 4-whorled, lanceolate to ovate, acute, short-pubesc. to ciliate. Corymbs term. and axill. capitulate; cor. white to yellow or pink, funnel-shaped to tubular, tube to 1cm, lobes 4, strap-shaped, to 4mm. Spring–summer. S to E Eur. ssp. *leucanthera* (G. Beck) Hayek in Hegi. Anth. white or light yellow. Balk. Z4.

A. tinctoria L. DYER'S WOODRUFF. Perenn. St. to 80cm, erect to prostrate, with stolons as for *A. taurina*. Lvs to 5cm, 6-whorled, opposite, ovate, linear to lanceolate, revolute and ± scabrous on margin, glab. or short-pubesc. Cymes loose, 3-branched; cor. white (red in bud), funnel-shaped to tubular, tube to 3mm, lobes 3, to 3mm, glab. or pubesc. Summer. Eur. Z4.

→*Galium.*

Asphodel *Asphodelus aestivus.*

Asphodeline Rchb. JACOB'S ROD. Liliaceae (Asphodelaceae). 20 rhizomatous perenn. or bienn. herbs to 130cm. St. unbranched, erect, straight or flexuous. Lvs numerous, linear to subulate, bases wide, membranous, grey-green, margins often scarious, basal or on st. Rac. term., cylindrical, erect, bracts papery; tep. 6, to 3cm, joined near base, each with 3 central veins. Medit. to Cauc.

A. balansae Bak. = *A. damascena.*

A. brevicaulis (Bertol.) Bak. Similar to *A. liburnica* but st. to 50cm, often flexuous; lower lvs to 15cm, narrow, subulate. Infl. usually branched; tep. pale yellow veined green, to 2cm. Asia Minor. Z8.

A. damascena (Boiss.) Bak. Related to *A. taurica*. Bienn. St. to 60cm, leafy below. Lvs linear, rosulate, to 22cm. Infl. usually unbranched, 15–30cm; tep. white to light pink, to 2.5cm. Summer. Asia Minor. Z9.

A. isthmocarpa Bak. = *A. damascena.*

A. liburnica (Scop.) Rchb. Perenn., to 60cm. St. leafy below. Lvs to 10cm. Infl. usually unbranched, to 22cm; tep. to 3cm, yellow striped green. Summer. Greece, Austria, It., Balk. Z7.

A. lutea (L.) Rchb. KING'S SPEAR; YELLOW ASPHODEL. Perenn. to 130cm. St. leafy throughout. Lvs linear-subulate, to 30cm, furrowed, silver to dark green with paler veins, margins smooth, or rough. Infl. scented, unbranched to 20cm, tep. to 3cm, yellow. Late spring–summer. Medit. 'Florepleno': fls double, long-lasting. 'Yellow Candle' is a selected form. Z7.

A. taurica (Pall.) Endl. Perenn. to 60cm, st. leafy except infl. Lvs to 22.5cm, narrow-subulate. Infl. unbranched, dense, to 30cm; tep. to 1.7cm, white with buff midvein. Summer. Greece, Asia Minor, to Cauc. Z7.

A. tenuior (Fisch.) Ledeb. Related to *A. taurica*. To 40cm, leafy below, margins of sheathing lvs ciliate. Infl. sometimes branched, to 10cm; tep. to 2cm, white tinged pink. Summer. Turk., Iran, Cauc. Z8.

→*Asphodelus.*

Asphodelus L. Liliaceae (Asphodelaceae). 12 rhizomatous annuals or perennials. Flowering st. erect or 0. Lvs radical, linear, with membranous sheathing base. Fls in dense racs or pan. with thin bracts; tep. 6 in 2 whorls, free or joined at base, 1-veined. Medit. to Himal.

A. acaulis Desf. Perenn. St. 0 or v. short. Lvs flat, to 30cm. Bracts white; tep. to 4cm across, white or pale pink with pale green midvein. Spring. N Afr. Z9.

A. aestivus Brot. Perenn. St. to 2m, solid with short br. Bracts grey-green to green-white; tep. to 4cm, white with tan midvein. Spring–early summer. Canary Is., S Eur., N Afr., Turk. Z8.

A. albus Mill. Perenn. st. to 1m, solid, sometimes branched. Lvs flat, to 60cm. Bracts white or dark brown; tep. to 2cm, white or rose-pink with deeper midvein. Late spring–summer. C & S Eur. Z6

A. cerasiferus Gay = *A. ramosus.*

A. delphinensis Gren. & Godron = *A. albus.*

A. fistulosus L. Ann. or short-lived perenn. St. hollow, to 70cm, branched or unbranched. Lvs to 35cm, cylindric, hollow. Bracts white; tep. to 1.2cm, white or rose-pink with tan midvein. Summer. SW Eur., Medit., SW Asia; widely nat. elsewhere. Z8.

A. liburnicus Scop. = *Asphodeline liburnica.*

A. luteus L. = *Asphodeline lutea.*

A. microcarpus Salzm. & Viv. = *A. aestivus.*

A. ramosus L. Perenn. St. to 150cm, solid, with many long br. Lvs to 40cm, flat, with shallow keel. Bracts white to pale green; tep. to 2cm, white with rust midvein. Summer. S Eur., N Afr. Z7.

A. tenuifolius Cav. = *A. fistulosus.*

Aspidistra Ker-Gawl. Liliaceae (Convallariaceae). 8 everg., perenn. herbs. Rhiz. thick, creeping. Lvs basal, solitary or in groups along rhiz., lanceolate to elliptic, dark green, glossy, coriaceous, base narrowing to a long petiole. Fls solitary, ± stemless on rhiz. at ground level; perianth fleshy, campanulate to urceolate, shallowly 6–8-lobed. Himal. to Jap.

A. elatior Bl. CAST-IRON PLANT; BAR-ROOM PLANT. Lvs 50–60cm, ovate to lanceolate, arising singly, 16–20-veined. Fls 2–3cm diam., 8-lobed, cream, spotted purple, interior claret. Spring. China. 'Green Leaf': lvs large, shiny, mid-green. 'Milky Way' ('Minor'): lvs speckled white. 'Variegata': lvs longer, variegated cream. 'Variegata Ashei': lvs irregularly streaked white, centre pales with age. 'Variegata Exotica': lvs v. boldly streaked white. Z7.

A. lurida Ker-Gawl. Lvs 15–20cm, lanceolate, 2–3 per node, 5–9-veined. Fls 8-lobed, deep red-purple. Spring. China. Plants offered under this name are usually *A. elatior*. Z8.

A. typica Baill. Lvs 20–40cm, elliptic to lanceolate, 5–9-veined.

Fls 2cm diam., 6-lobed, green, exterior spotted red-purple, interior stained purple. Spring. China. Z8.

Aspidium Sw.
A. albopunctatum Luerssen, non Bory ex Willd. = *Arthropteris articulata.*
A. alatum Brackenr. non Wallich = *Tectaria decurrens.*
A. alpestre Hoppe = *Athyrium distentifolium.*
A. amabile Bl. = *Arachniodes amabilis.*
A. argutum Kaulf. = *Dryopteris arguta.*
A. aristatum var. *simplicius* Mak. = *Arachniodes simplicior.*
A. atratum Wallich ex Kunze = *Dryopteris atrata.*
A. biserratum Sw. = *Nephrolepis biserrata.*
A. braunii Spenn. = *Polystichum braunii.*
A. caducum (Humb. & Bonpl. ex Willd.) Kunth. = *Cyclopeltis semicordata.*
A. californicum D.C. Eaton = *Polystichum californicum.*
A. caryotideum Wallich = *Cyrtomium caryotideum.*
A. championii Benth. = *Dryopteris championii.*
A. cicutarium (L.) Sw. = *Tectaria cicutaria.*
A. cicutarium Sim non (L.) Sw. = *Tectaria gemmifera.*
A. coadnatum var. *gemmiferum* (Fée) Mett. = *Tectaria gemmifera.*
A. coadnatum Hook. & Grev. = *Tectaria macrodonta.*
A. commutatum Franch. & Savat. = *Arachniodes maximowiczii.*
A. craspedosorum Maxim. = *Polystichum craspedosorum.*
A. cunninghamianum Colenso = *Rumohra adiantiformis.*
A. cystolepidotum Miq. = *Dryopteris cystolepidota.*
A. cystostegia Hook. = *Polystichum cystostegia.*
A. davallioides Sw. = *Nephrolepis davallioides.*
A. decompositum var. *marginans* F. Muell. = *Lastreopsis marginans.*
A. decompositum var. *quinquangulare* (Kunze) Mett. = *Lastreopsis microsora.*
A. decompositum (R. Br.) Spreng. = *Lastreopsis decomposita.*
A. decurrens Presl = *Tectaria decurrens.*
A. dickinsii Franch. & Savat. = *Dryopteris dickinsii.*
A. erythrosorum Eaton = *Dryopteris erythrosora.*
A. exile Hance = *Arachniodes aristata.*
A. filix-mas (L.) = *Dryopteris filix-mas.*
A. fragrans L. = *Dryopteris fragrans.*
A. frondosum Lowe = *Arachniodes webbiana.*
A. gemmiferum (Fée) Ching = *Tectaria gemmifera.*
A. glanduligerum Kunze = *Parathelypteris glanduligera.*
A. heracleifolium Willd. = *Tectaria heracleifolia.*
A. hispidum Sw. = *Lastreopsis hispida.*
A. hokutoense Hayata = *Tectaria subtriphylla.*
A. lachenense Hook. = *Polystichum lachenense.*
A. latifolium Presl = *Tectaria mexicana.*
A. lepidocaulon Hook. = *Polystichum lepidocaulon.*
A. lobatum (Huds.) Sw. = *Polystichum aculeatum.*
A. lonchitis (L.) Sw. = *Polystichum lonchitis.*
A. longifolium Desv. = *Tectaria incisa.*
A. macleayi Bak. = *Polystichum macleayi.*
A. macrophyllum Rudolphi = *Tectaria incisa.*
A. martinicense Spreng. = *Tectaria incisa.*
A. meniscioides Willd. = *Cyclodium meniscioides.*
A. munitum Kaulf. = *Polystichum munitum.*
A. muticum Franch. & Savat. = *Arachniodes mutica.*
A. noveboracense Sw. = *Parathelypteris novae-boracensis.*
A. obtusum (Spreng.) Willd. = *Woodsia obtusa.*
A. opulentum Kaulf. = *Amphineuron opulentum.*
A. pachyphyllum (Moore) Kunze = *Tectaria crenata.*
A. parallelogramma Kunze = *Dryopteris wallichiana.*
A. patens Sw. = *Christella patens.*
A. pectinatum Willd. = *Nephrolepis pectinata.*
A. plumieri Presl = *Tectaria trifoliata.*
A. polyblepharum Roem. ex Kunze = *Polystichum polyblepharum.*
A. prescottianum Wallich. = *Polystichum prescottianum.*
A. proliferum Hook. & Grev. = *Fadyenia hookeri.*
A. purdiaei Jenman = *Tectaria trifoliata.*
A. quinquangulare Kunze = *Lastreopsis microsora.*
A. repandum Willd. = *Tectaria crenata.*
A. rufescens Bl. = *Lastreopsis rufescens.*
A. sabae Franch. & Savat. = *Tectaria sabae.*
A. scandicinum Willd. = *Athyrium scandicinum.*
A. semicordatum (Sw.) Sw. = *Cyclopeltis semicordata.*
A. simulatum Davenp. = *Parathelypteris simulata.*
A. speluncae (L.) Willd. = *Microlepia speluncae.*
A. spinulosum ssp. *genuinum* var. *amurense* Milde = *Dryopteris amurensis.*
A. thelypteris (L.) Sw. = *Thelypteris palustris.*
A. trifoliatum (L.) Sw. = *Tectaria trifoliata.*
A. trifoliatum Hook. & Bauer, non (L.) Sw. = *Tectaria heracleifolia.*

A. tripteron Kunze = *Polystichum tripteron.*
A. truncatulum Sw. = *Didymochlaena truncatula.*
A. tsussimense Hook. = *Polystichum tsussimense.*
A. velutinum A. Rich. = *Lastreopsis velutina.*
A. wallichianum Spreng. = *Dryopteris wallichiana.*
A. webbianum A. Br. = *Arachniodes webbiana.*

Aspidotis (Nutt. ex Hook.) Copel.
A. densa (Brackenr.) Lellinger = *Cheilanthes siliquosa.*

ASPLENIACEAE Mett. ex A. B. Frank. 9 genera. *Asplenium, Pleurosorus, Schaffneria.*

Asplenium L. SPLEENWORT. Aspleniaceae. *c*700 terrestrial, rupestral, or epiphytic ferns. Rhiz. short and erect to creeping, covered with massed roots, hairs and scales. Fronds stipitate, usually uniform, 1–4-pinnate to -pinnatifid, apex occas. proliferous. Trop. and subtrop.
A. achilleifolium Ogata, non Liebm. = *A. prolongatum.*
A. achilleifolium (Lam.) Christ, non Liebm. = *A. rutifolium.*
A. acrostichoides Sw. = *Deparia acrostichoides.*
A. acutum Willd. = *A. onopteris.*
A. adiantoides Raoul, non Raddi = *A. hookerianum.*
A. adiantoides (L.) Christ = *A. polyodon.*
A. adiantoides var. *richardii* Hook. f. = *A. richardii.*
A. adiantum-nigrum L. BLACK SPLEENWORT. Fronds to 35×10cm, to 3-pinnate to -pinnatifid, ovate to deltoid, narrowly acute, leathery and glab., pinnae to 8×5cm, ovate to lanceolate, pinnules ovate to spathulate, lobed, seg. toothed, rachis winged; stipes to 15cm, base scaly, chestnut or brown to black, scales black. Eur., Afr., Asia. Z6.
A. adulterinum Milde. Fronds to 12×1cm, pinnate, linear to lanceolate, attenuate to obtuse, sparsely glandular-pubesc. beneath, pinnae to 8×5mm, ovate or rhomboid to suborbicular, apex obtuse, toothed to notched; stipes to 10cm, green to red-brown or black, wiry, base scaly. Scand., C Eur., Balk. Z4.
A. aethiopicum (Burm. f.) Bech. Fronds to 60×20cm, 2–3-pinnate, linear or oblong to lanceolate, apex acute to caudate, thinly leathery, sparsely pubesc., pinnae to 12×4cm, lanceolate to deltoid, apex acute to caudate, seg. rolled in drought, ovate or elliptic to oblong, apex attenuate, toothed to notched, rachis scaly, brown; stipes to 28cm, initially scaly, brown to black. Afr. Z9.
A. africanum Desv. Fronds to 45×8cm, simple, lanceolate, attenuate to acute, base attenuate, margin undulate, leathery; stipes to 15cm, grooved, lustrous, black. Trop. W Afr. Z10.
A. angustifolium Michx., non Jacq. = *Athyrium pycnocarpon.*
A. antiquum Mak. Fronds to 80×10cm, simple, linear to oblanceolate, apex attenuate to acute, base attenuate and decurrent, entire or subentire, leathery, lustrous, costa grooved above, brown; stipes short or 0, winged above, base scaly. Taiwan, Jap. Z9.
A. apicidens Moore = *A. vieillardii.*
A. aspidiiforme Fée = *Diplazium franconis.*
A. atkinsonii (Bedd.) C.B. Clarke = *Athyrium atkinsonii.*
A. attenuatum R. Br. Fronds to 35×1cm, simple, stiff, rosulate, linear or oblong to lanceolate, apex attenuate to acute, proliferous, entire to lobed, leathery to papery; stipes to 10cm, scaly. Aus. Z10.
A. aureum Cav. Fronds to 30×8cm, pinnate to pinnatifid, lanceolate, apex and base attenuate, densely scaly beneath; pinnae alt., oblong, obtuse, notched; stipes scaly. Canary Is., Madeira. Z9.
A. auritum Sw. Fronds to 30×12cm, 1–2-pinnate to -pinnatifid, erect or ascending to spreading, deltoid or lanceolate to oblong, apex narrowly acute, base truncate, papery to leathery, glab., pinnae to 75×15mm, 10–20 pairs, linear or oblong to deltoid, apex acute or obtuse, cuneate and auriculate, subentire to notched, lobed, or incised, initially sparsely scaly; stipes to 15cm, grooved, initially scaly, green to purple. W Indies, Mex. to Boliv. Z10.
A. australasicum (J. Sm.) Hook. BIRD'S NEST FERN; CROW'S NEST FERN. Fronds to 1.5m×20cm, short-stipitate, simple, erect or ascending to spreading, nest-forming and rosulate, lanceolate, apex attenuate to narrowly acute, base attenuate, entire to undulate, leathery to papery, lustrous, costa sharply keeled below, initially scaly, black; stipes often obsolete. Aus. to Polyn. Z10.
A. australe (R. Br.) Brackenr., non Sw. = *Diplazium australe.*
A. baptistii Moore = *A. vieillardii.*
A. beddomei Mett. = *A. crinicaule.*
A. belangeri (Bory) Kunze = *A. thunbergii.*
A. billotii F.W. Schultz. LANCEOLATE SPLEENWORT. Fronds to 25×10cm, 2-pinnate to -pinnatifid, ovate or lanceolate to elliptic, apex caudate, membranous, sparsely scaly, pinnae to 4×1cm, to 9 pairs, falcate, lanceolate, apex obtuse, base cuneate to truncate, pinnules 6–9 pairs, ovate or rhomboid to

oblong, base attenuate to cuneate, toothed, rachis often glandular-pubesc., green to brown; stipes to 10cm, ± glab., lustrous, chestnut. W Eur. Z7.

A. bipinnatifidum Bak. Fronds to 20×5cm, 2-pinnatifid to pinnate at apex, occas. scaly, eesp. on veins, pinnae to 25×20mm, 9–12 pairs, deltoid, seg. to 1mm wide, 3–5, linear, apex obtuse, base cuneate, rachis minutely scaly; stipes to 12cm, green, scales fimbriate to hair-tipped, red-brown. Polyn. Z10.

A. bipinnatum Brackenr., non Rosb. = *A. bipinnatifidum.*

A. brachycarpum (Mett.) Kuhn. Fronds to 45×20cm, 4-pinnate to -pinnatifid, erect, deltoid to lanceolate, pinnules to 8×3cm, lanceolate to deltoid, seg. linear, entire to bifid; stipes to 30cm, glab. New Hebrides. Z8.

A. brachypteron Kunze ex Houlst. & Moore. = *A. dregeanum.*

A. bradleyi D.C. Eaton. Fronds to 20×5cm, 1–2-pinnate to -pinnatifid, lanceolate to oblong, apex acute, base truncate, pinnae to 25×12mm, 8–12 pairs, alt., ovate or lanceolate to oblong, apex obtuse, base auriculate, toothed or notched to lobed, seg. ovate or obovate, toothed; stipes to 8cm, grooved, ± glab., lustrous, chestnut to black. E to S US. Z6.

A. bulbiferum Forst. f. HEN & CHICKENS FERN; MOTHER SPLEEN-WORT. Fronds to 1.2m×30cm, 2–3-pinnate, freely producing plantlets, erect or ascending to arched, ovate, deltoid, or lanceolate to oblong, thin-textured and flaccid, membranous to leathery, pinnae to 20×5cm, ovate to lanceolate, pinnules to 40×15mm, ovate, deltoid or lanceolate to oblong, apex obtuse, toothed to lobed, seg. to 15mm, oblong, subentire to notched, rachis winged, scaly, green; stipes to 30cm, flattened, grooved, base scaly, green to brown. Aus., NZ. Z10.

A. camptosorum Mett. ex Kuhn = *A. serra.*

A. caudatum Forst. f. Fronds to 60×15cm, pinnate, pinnatifid at apex, lanceolate, apex narrowly acute, papery, sparsely scaly on veins, pinnae to 15×2cm, subfalcate, lanceolate, apex attenuate to acute or caudate, base cuneate to truncate, notched to lobed, seg. oblique, apex obtuse, toothed; stipes to 50cm, scaly, purple to brown, scales spreading, occas. fimbriate. Malaysia to Polyn. Z10.

A. celtibericum Rivas Mart. = *A. seelosii.*

A. centripetale Bak. = *Diplazium celtidifolium.*

A. ceterach L. RUSTY BACK FERN. Fronds to 20×5cm, pinnate, spreading, lanceolate to linear, oblong, or spathulate, apex and base attenuate, leathery, scaly, pinnae to 10×6mm, 6–15 pairs, alt., oblong to suborbicular, apex obtuse, base truncate, notched; stipes to 5cm, scaly. W Medit. Z8.

A. cheilosorum Kunze ex Mett. Rhiz. to 3mm wide, short-creeping. Fronds to 40×5cm, pinnate, pinnatifid at apex, linear to lanceolate, apex narrowly acute, base attenuate, membranous, pinnae to 25×10mm, lowest reduced, to 40 pairs, ovate, apex obtuse, base cuneate to truncate, lower margin entire, upper margin toothed or notched to lobed, seg. ovate, apex obtuse, toothed, rachis lustrous, purple; stipes to 20cm, base scaly, lustrous, purple to brown, scales brown to black. Trop. Asia. Z10.

A. chihuahense Bak. = *A. adiantum-nigrum.*

A. cicutarium Sw. = *A. cristatum.*

A. comorense Christ = *A. sandersonii.*

A. crinicaule Hance. Fronds to 25×4cm, pinnate, erect, leathery, pinnae 15 pairs, horizontal, apex obtuse, base obliquely truncate and auriculate; stipes to 10cm, sparsely brown-pubesc. China. Z8.

A. cristatum Lam. Fronds to 40×15cm, 3-pinnate to -pinnatifid, suberect, lanceolate or deltoid to oblong, apex narrowly acute, base attenuate to truncate, membranous, pinnae to 9×3cm, 15–20 pairs, lanceolate to oblong, apex acute to narrowly acute, pinnules to 12×6mm, ovate, rhomboid, or deltoid to oblong, apex obtuse, base truncate and auriculate, toothed to lobed, seg. to 2mm wide, simple or bifid, elliptic to oblong, apex acute, rachis and costa winged above; stipes to 25cm, grey or green to brown. Trop. Amer. Z10.

A. cuneatum var. *laserpitiifolium* (Lam.) Luerssen = *A. laserpitiifolium.*

A. cuneatum var. *splendens* (Kunze) Sim. = *A. splendens.*

A. cuneifolium Viv. Fronds to 30×10cm, 2–3-pinnate to -pinnatifid, ovate to lanceolate, apex acute, leathery and glab., pinnae to 7×4cm, distant, ovate or deltoid to lanceolate, apex obtuse, pinnules toothed to lobed, seg. obovate, to flabellate, apex truncate, base cuneate, toothed; stipes to 20cm, red-brown. GB, C to S Eur. Z5.

A. cymbifolium Christ. Fronds to 100×50cm, simple, ovate to lanceolate, apex attenuate to acute or obtuse, base cordate and dilated, entire, leathery and glab., rachis scaly. Trop. Asia to Polyn. Z10.

A. dalhousiae Hook. Fronds to 15×5cm, deeply pinnatifid, oblanceolate, apex acute or obtuse, base attenuate to acute, thick-textured, seg. deltoid to oblong, apex obtuse, rachis somewhat scaly; stipes to 1cm, scaly, straw-coloured to brown. US

(Ariz.). Z6.

A. dareoides Desv. Fronds to 10×2cm, 1–2-pinnate, ovate or deltoid to lanceolate, membranous, glab., pinnae to 5×1cm, ovate to cuneate, apex and base attenuate to acute, pinnules ovate to rhomboid, notched to lobed, seg. falcate, ovate, toothed; stipes to 12cm, lustrous, brown. S Amer. Z9.

A. daucifolium Lam. MAURITIUS SPLEENWORT. Fronds to 60×20cm, 1–4-pinnate, ovate to lanceolate, apex proliferous, leathery to membranous, somewhat scaly, pinnae to 15×5cm, lanceolate, apex narrowly acute, seg. to 10×1mm, linear, filiform, or subulate; stipes to 20cm. Maur., Réunion Is. Z10.

A. debile Mett. ex Kuhn, non Fée. = *A. sandersonii.*

A. difforme R. Br. Fronds to 30×10cm, pinnate to pinnatifid, erect to arched or pendent, ovate to deltoid, margin cartilaginous, thin-textured or leathery to fleshy, sparsely scaly, pinnae to 6×2cm, ovate to oblong, apex obtuse, notched to lobed, seg. oblong to suborbicular, undulate, rachis and costa winged; stipes to 15cm, base scaly, grey to brown.

A. dimorphum Kunze. THREE-IN-ONE FERN. Fronds to 90×35cm, 2–3-pinnate to -pinnatifid, ovate to deltoid, lower and sterile pinnae to 20×5cm, ovate to deltoid, upper and fertile pinnae to 20×5cm, sterile seg. to 25×12mm, ovate, toothed, fertile seg. to 25×12mm, linear, lobed; stipes to 30cm, glab. to scaly. Norfolk Is. Z9.

A. distans Fée = *Diplazium franconis.*

A. divaricatum Kunze. Fronds to 25×10cm, 2–3-pinnate, lanceolate to elliptic, apex narrowly acute to caudate, base attenuate, thin-textured, membranous to papery, pinnae 10–20 pairs, oblong, apex obtuse, pinnules, obovate or elliptic to trapeziform, seg. ovate to linear or oblong, apex obtuse, base cuneate; stipes to 8cm, grooved, glab., grey or green to brown. Mex., C to S Amer. Z10.

A. diversifolium Wallich, non Bl. = *A. dimorphum.*

A. dregeanum Kunze. Fronds to 40×6cm, 2-pinnate to -pinnatifid, arched, linear or oblong to lanceolate or elliptic, apex acute to caudate and proliferous, glab. to minutely scaly on veins, pinnae to 35×11mm, 12–32 pairs, petiolate, horizontal, oblong, apex acute, base cuneate and acroscopically auriculate, seg. to 6×2mm, simple or bifid, linear to oblong, apex obtuse; stipes to 17cm, winged, scaly, grey or green to brown. Trop. Afr. Z10.

A. dubiosum Davenp. = *A. adiantum-nigrum.*

A. ebeneum Ait. = *A. platyneuron.*

A. ebenoides Scott. Fronds to 20×8cm, pinnate at base to pinnatifid, lanceolate, apex attenuate to acute or caudate and, occas., proliferous, base truncate, thin-textured, sparsely pubesc. below, pinnae short-petiolate, alt., ascending, ovate or deltoid to linear, apex acute to caudate, base acute or cordate, margin notched to undulate, veins forked, rachis and costa green to brown; stipes to 10cm, ± glab., lustrous, red or purple to brown. E & S US. Z6.

A. elegantulum Hook. = *A. incisum.*

A. erectum var. *lunulatum* Sw. = *A. lunulatum.*

A. falcatum Lam. = *A. polyodon.*

A. fauriei Christ = *A. oligophlebium.*

A. fissum Kit. ex Willd. Fronds to 13×5cm, 3–4-pinnate to -pinnatifid, lanceolate or deltoid to oblong, glab., pinnae petiolate, alt., spreading, distant, ovate or lanceolate to suborbicular, apex acute, pinnules spreading, flabellate to cuneate, margin lobed, seg. to 1mm wide, bifid, linear, base cuneate, rachis and costa compressed; stipes to 15cm, lustrous, green to brown or black. S Eur. Z6.

A. flabellifolium Cav. Fronds to 40×3cm, pinnate, spreading to arched or sprawling, linear to lanceolate, apex attenuate to caudate and proliferous, flaccid, membranous, pinnae to 25×20mm, upper reduced, 5–18 pairs, sessile to short-petiolate, subopposite, distant, rhomboid or flabellate to cuneate, margin toothed to notched, veins flabellate, stipes to 10cm, scaly, green. Aus., Tasm., NZ. Z9.

A. flaccidum Forst. f. WEEPING SPLEENWORT. Fronds to 90×30cm, pinnate to pinnatifid, erect to pendent, variably shaped but ± ovate or lanceolate to oblong, apex acute to narrowly acute, pinnae to 20×1cm, alt., spreading to pendent, falcate, stiff to flaccid, distant, lanceolate or deltoid to linear or oblong, seg. to 2cm, erect to spreading, oblique, subfalcate, distant, linear, apex acute, veins indistinct, rachis and costa winged, sparsely scaly; stipes to 20cm, base scaly. S Afr., Aus. and NZ. Z9.

A. flaccidum var. *aucklandicum* Hook. f. = *A. scleroprium.*

A. flaccidum var. *shuttleworthianum* Hook. f. = *A. shuttleworthianum.*

A. fontanum (L.) Bernh. SMOOTH ROCK SPLEENWORT. Fronds to 15×4cm, 1–2-pinnate to -pinnatifid, spreading to arched, elliptic or lanceolate to oblong, apex and base attenuate, soft-textured, pinnae to 15mm, lowest reduced and deflexed, horizontal, ovate to oblong, apex attenuate, pinnules to 3mm, 3–8 pairs, petiolate, oblong, base cuneate, margin undulate to lobed, margin of seg. toothed, rachis and costa occas. glandular-pubesc.; stipes to 10cm, green to chestnut. C to S Eur., to C Asia. Z6.

A. foresiacum (Le Grand) Christ = *A. forisiense*.

A. foreziense Hérib. = *A. forisiense*.

A. forisiense Le Grand. Fronds to 20cm, 2-pinnate to -pinnatifid, linear to lanceolate, apex acute to narrowly acute, base attenuate to cuneate, thick-textured, leathery to membranous, pinnae to 12mm, sessile, spreading, lowest deflexed, falcate, approximate, ovate, apex attenuate to obtuse, pinnules 1–3 pairs, obovate, base attenuate to obtuse, margin entire to toothed; stipes to 10cm, green to red or brown. Medit. Z7.

A. formosum Willd. Fronds to 30×4cm, pinnate, ascending and rosulate, linear to oblanceolate, apex acute to narrowly acute, base attenuate, glab. to minutely pubesc., pinnae to 18×6mm, lowest reduced, 20–50 pairs, sessile to subsessile, subopposite to alt., horizontal and spreading, approximate to distant, deltoid to linear or oblong, apex acute, base obliquely cuneate to truncate, margin entire to toothed or notched, veins 4–6 pairs per pinna, simple or forked, oblique, rachis grooved above, glab.; stipes to 5cm, wiry, grooved, glab., purple. Trop. Amer., Afr., Asia. Z10.

A. furcatum Thunb. = *A. aethiopicum*.

A. furcatum Brackenr. non Thunb. = *A. bipinnatifidum*.

A. furcatum Jenman, non Thunb. = *A. praemorsum*.

A. gemmiferum Schräd. Fronds to 70×25cm, pinnate, arched, lanceolate to oblong, leathery or fleshy to papery, glab. above, scaly below, pinnae to 15×4cm, to 12 pairs, petiolate, oblique, ovate or lanceolate to oblong, apex narrowly acute, base cuneate and (term. pinna) gemmiferous, margin entire to minutely notched, rachis winged, initially scaly; stipes to 30cm, initially scaly, grey to green. Trop. E & S Afr. Z10.

A. gracile Peter, non D. Don = *A. dregeanum*.

A. guineense Schum. = *A. africanum*.

A. hemionitis L. Fronds to 15×15cm, palmately lobed, ascending to spreading, papery, lat. lobes to 3cm, 1–2 pairs, imbricate, cordate to orbicular, apex acute, base auriculate, term. lobe solitary, deltoid, apex acute, veins forked, approximate; stipes to 20cm, base scaly, purple to brown. SW Eur., N Afr., Atlantic Is. Z9.

A. heterocarpum Wallich (nom. nud.) Hook. = *A. cheilosorum*.

A. hookerianum Col. Fronds to 25×10cm, 1–2-pinnate, suberect, ovate or lanceolate to oblong, apex acute to narrowly acute, membranous, pinnae to 8×2cm, to 11 pairs, subsessile to petiolate, erect to spreading, stiff, ovate to oblong, pinnules 1×1cm, 3–10, subsessile to petiolate, spreading, obovate or rhomboid to oblong, base obliquely cuneate, margin notched, veins forked, rachis and costa flattened, glab. to scaly; stipes to 15cm, base scaly. NZ. Z9.

A. hybridum (Milde) Bange. Fronds to 20×5cm, pinnatifid, ovate or lanceolate to linear or oblong, apex and base attenuate to obtuse; seg. suborbicular to deltoid or oblong, apex attenuate to subacute; stipes to 10cm, scaly. Medit. Z8.

A. incisum Thunb. Fronds somewhat dimorphous, linear to lanceolate or oblanceolate, apex narrowly acute, glab., sterile to 15×5cm, pinnate to 2-pinnatifid, fertile to 35×7cm, 2–3-pinnatifid, pinnae sessile to short-petiolate, spreading, distant sterile to 1×1cm, orbicular to kidney-shaped, apex obtuse, base cordate, margin toothed, fertile to 35×15mm, lanceolate to deltoid, apex acute, margin lobed, seg. ovate to rhomboid, apex obtuse, base truncate, margin notched, rachis green above, chestnut to brown below; stipes to 2cm (sterile) or 5cm (fertile), scaly, green to purple, scales lanceolate, apex attenuate, black. E Asia. Z8.

A. insigne Liebm. = *A. serra*.

A. japonicum Thunb. = *Deparia petersenii*.

A. laciniatum D. Don. Fronds to 15×4cm, 1–2-pinnate to -pinnatifid, ovate or lanceolate to oblong, apex narrowly acute or obtuse, membranous, pinnae to 30×6mm, lowest reduced, 3–8 pairs, petiolate, spreading, oblique, ovate or rhomboid to orbicular, apex obtuse, base cuneate, pinnules to 5×4mm, ovate or obovate to rhomboid or flabellate, base cuneate, margin toothed to lobed, veins forked, rachis and costa indistinct; stipes to 10cm, initially somewhat scaly, grey to green. Trop. Asia. Z10.

A. lanceolatum Huds., non Forssk. = *A. billotii*.

A. lanceum Thunb. = *Diplazium lanceum*.

A. laserpitiifolium Lam. JOHNSTON RIVER FERN. Fronds 120×45cm, 3–4-pinnate to -pinnatifid, arched to pendent, ovate or deltoid to lanceolate, apex narrowly acute, membranous, glab., pinnae to 15×7cm, petiolate, pinnules to 8×3cm, apex caudate and toothed, seg. 6–8, free or decurrent, margin lobed, lobes linear or oblong to rhomboid or trapeziform, margin toothed, veins forked to flabellate, parallel; stipes to 40cm, scaly, purple to brown or black. Trop. Asia to Aus., Polyn.

Z10.

A. lepidum Presl. Fronds to 10×4cm, 2-pinnate, lanceolate to deltoid, apex attenuate to acute, base cuneate, thin-textured, gland., pinnae petiolate, alt., spreading, distant, deltoid, apex acute, apex of pinnules acute, base cuneate, margin notched, rachis and costa grooved above; stipes persistent, wiry. Eur. (Alps). Z6.

A. longissimum Bl. Fronds to 100×15cm or more, pinnate, lanceolate, apex and base attenuate of indefinite growth at apex until bud forms proliferation, initially scaly on veins, pinnae to 85×15mm, lowest reduced, 50–70 pairs, sessile, spreading, apex narrowly acute, base truncate to cuneate and acroscopically auriculate, margin toothed to lobed, seg. oblique, margin subentire to toothed, veins forked, distinct, rachis and costa grooved above; stipes to 30cm, scaly, black, scales adpressed, scattered, apex occas. hair-tipped, brown. Malaysia. Z10.

A. lucidum Forst. f., non Salisb., et non Burm. f. = *A. lyallii*.

A. lucidum var. *lyallii* Hook. f. = *A. lyallii*.

A. lucidum var. *obliquum* (Forst. f.) Moore = *A. obliquum*.

A. lucidum var. *scleroprium* Moore = *A. scleroprium*.

A. lunulatum Sw. Fronds to 30×5cm, pinnate, to pinnatifid at apex, erect, lanceolate to linear or oblong, apex narrowly acute and proliferous, membranous, glab., pinnae to 25×5mm, lowest reduced and deflexed, 15–20 pairs, opposite, horizontal, falcate, approximate to distant, rhomboid to oblong, apex obtuse, base truncate and acroscopically auriculate, margin notched to lobed, veins forked to pinnate, rachis ± terete, stiff; stipes to 12cm, glab., green to brown. Trop. Afr. Z10.

A. lyallii (Hook. f.) Moore. Fronds to 45×25cm, 1–2-pinnate, ovate to elliptic, leathery, scaly, pinnae to 15×5cm, 30–50 pairs, ovate to deltoid to lanceolate, apex and base attenuate, middle margin notched, pinnules petiolate, oblique, ovate to linear or oblong, apex obtuse, base cuneate, margin toothed; stipes to 45cm, scaly, grey to brown. NZ. Z9.

A. macraei Hook. non Grev. & Hook. = *A. cristatum*.

A. macrolobium Peter = *A. gemmiferum*.

A. magellanicum Kaulf. = *A. dareoides*.

A. majoricum Litard. Fronds to 8cm, 2-pinnate to -pinnatifid, oblanceolate, glab. to gland., pinnae to 12mm, 8–11 pairs, subsessile, approximate, ovate or oblong to suborbicular, seg. 5–6, apex obtuse, margin toothed to notched, rachis and costa grooved; stipes to 3cm, wiry, lustrous, green to purple or black. Majorca. Z9.

A. marinum L. SEA SPLEENWORT. Fronds to 40×10cm, pinnate, to pinnatifid at apex, ascending to spreading, linear or oblong to deltoid or lanceolate, thick-textured and stiff, leathery to fleshy, pinnae to 35×15mm, subsessile to short-petiolate, alt., ovate or deltoid to oblong, apex acute or obtuse, base cuneate to truncate, acroscopically auriculate, margin toothed or notched to lobed, veins forked; stipes to 15cm, purple to brown. W Eur., Atlantic Is. Z10.

A. maximum D. Don = *Diplazium dilatatum*.

A. michauxii Spreng. = *Athyrium filix-femina* ssp. *angustum*.

A. monodon Liebm. = *A. auritum*.

A. montanum Willd. MOUNTAIN SPLEENWORT. Fronds to 11×8cm, 1–2-pinnate to -pinnatifid, ovate or deltoid to lanceolate, apex acute to narrowly acute, base truncate or obtuse, pubesc. and sparsely scaly below, pinnae to 30×25mm, lowest reduced, short-petiolate, alt., ovate or deltoid to lanceolate or oblong, margin toothed or notched to lobed, pinnules to 12×6mm, petiolate, ovate or elliptic to oblong, base cuneate, margin lobed, seg. obovate to oblong, margin toothed, veins forked; stipes to 9cm, terete to flattened, grooved, base scaly, green to brown. E & S US. Z6.

A. multifidum Brackenr. = *A. shuttleworthianum*.

A. musifolium Mett. Fronds to 120×30cm, simple, ascending to arched, nest-forming and rosulate, ovate to lanceolate, apex attenuate to mucronate or obtuse, base attenuate, margin entire, leathery, glab., veins occas. marginally connivent, simple or forked, parallel, rachis and costa prominent above, initially scaly; stipes to 30cm, scaly, black. Trop. Asia. Z10.

A. nanum Willd. = *A. formosum*.

A. nidus L. BIRD'S NEST FERN. Fronds to 150×20cm, sessile to short-stipitate, simple, erect and stiff, nest-forming and rosulate, ovate to lanceolate, apex and base attenuate to acute, margin entire, leathery and glab., veins occas. marginally connivent, simple or forked, parallel, to 1cm distant, rachis prominent above, initially scaly; stipes to 5cm, scaly, black, apex of scales hair-tipped. Trop. OW. Z10.

A. nidus var. *musifolium* = *A. musifolium*.

A. nigricans Kunze. = *A. praemorsum*.

A. nigripes (Fée) Hook. = *Schaffneria nigripes*.

A. nipponicum Mett. = *Athyrium nipponicum*.

A. normale D. Don. Fronds to 50×4cm, pinnate, erect to arched, linear to lanceolate, apex narrowly acute and, occas., proliferous, membranous, pinnae to 15×7mm, upper reduced, to 45 pairs, sessile to short-petiolate, spreading, lowest deflexed, oblique, approximate to imbricate, ovate to oblong, apex truncate to obtuse, base truncate to cuneate and acroscopically auriculate, margin entire to toothed or notched, veins forked, oblique, distinct, rachis and costa grooved above; stipes to 15cm, terete, base initially scaly, lustrous, purple to brown, scales sparse, adpressed, ciliate. Trop. OW. Z10.

A. obliquum Forst. f. Fronds to 30×15cm, pinnate, erect to arched to pendent, linear to oblong, cartilaginous, pinnae to 10×3cm, petiolate, subopposite to alt., markedly oblique, oblong to lanceolate, apex attenuate to acute, base cuneate, margin notched, veins simple or forked; stipes to 50cm, base scaly. NZ. Z9.

A. oblongifolium Col. SHINING SPLEENWORT. Fronds to 60×45cm, pinnate, ovate to elliptic, apex attenuate to acute, membranous, scaly, pinnae to 25×5cm, 15–20 pairs, opposite, spreading to ascending, approximate to distant, ovate to oblong, apex attenuate to narrowly acute, base truncate to cordate, margin shallowly toothed; stipes to 50cm, scaly, green to brown. NZ. Z9.

A. obovatum Viv. Fronds to 30×10cm, 2-pinnate to -pinnatifid, ovate to lanceolate, apex caudate, base attenuate, stiff, pinnae to 4×1cm, 18–20 pairs, short-petiolate, subopposite to alt., approximate to distant, ovate or deltoid to lanceolate, pinnules short-petiolate, oblique, approximate to imbricate, ovate to suborbicular, base cuneate and acroscopically auriculate, margin toothed, veins forked, rachis and costa sparsely scaly; stipes to 10cm, base scaly, red to purple or brown. W Eur., Atlantic Is. Z8.

A. obtusatum Forst. f. Fronds to 30×10cm, pinnate, erect to arched or pendent, ovate to deltoid to oblong, leathery to fleshy, sparsely scaly, pinnae to 6×2cm, 4–15 pairs, short-petiolate, subopposite to alt., ovate to oblong, apex obtuse, base truncate to cuneate and acroscopically auriculate, margin notched to somewhat lobed and cartilaginous, veins simple or forked, approximate, rachis and costa winged; stipes to 15cm, base scaly, grey to brown. S Amer., Aus., Tasm., NZ, Polyn. Z9.

A. obtusatum var. *difforme* (R. Br.) Benth. = *A. difforme*.
A. obtusatum var. *obliquum* (Forst. f.) Hook. f. = *A. obliquum*.
A. obtusilobium Hook., non Desv. = *A. bipinnatifidum*.
A. oceanicum Christ = *A. bipinnatifidum*.

A. oligophlebium Bak. Fronds to 15×4cm, pinnate, lanceolate, thin-textured, glab., pinnae to 15×5mm, sessile, subdeltoid to lanceolate, apex obtuse, base obliquely cuneate, margin entire to toothed, veins simple or forked; stipes to 8cm, glab., lustrous, purple to brown. Jap. Z8.

A. onopteris L. Rupestral. Rhiz. short and ascending to creeping; scales filiform, apex attenuate, brown. Fronds to 40cm, 2–4-pinnate to -pinnatifid, deltoid to lanceolate, apex narrowly acute to caudate, lustrous and leathery, pinnae to 7cm, 10–25 pairs, falcate, ovate to linear, apex attenuate to caudate, pinnules falcate, lanceolate, apex attenuate to caudate, seg. lanceolate to linear, apex acute, base attenuate, margin toothed; stipes to 10cm, base distended and scaly, lustrous, green to purple or brown. C to S Eur. Z6.

A. opacum Kunze = *A. normale*.
A. otophorum Miq. = *Athyrium otophorum*.

A. paleaceum R. Br. CHAFFY SPLEENWORT. Fronds to 25×5cm, pinnate, ascending to arched or pendent, apex proliferous, leathery, pubesc. below, pinnae to 25×12mm, 12–20 pairs, sub-sessile to petiolate, spreading, oblique, approximate, ovate or rhomboid to flabellate, apex obtuse, base truncate and acroscopically auriculate, margin toothed to notched, veins forked to flabellate, approximate, rachis and costa pubesc. and scaly, green above; stipes to 8cm, pubesc. and scaly, scales persistent, spreading. Aus., New Guinea. Z10.

A. palmatum Lam. = *A. hemionitis*.
A. parvulum Mart. & Gal., non Hook. = *A. resiliens*.
A. petersenii Kunze = *Deparia petersenii*.

A. petrarchae (Guérin) DC. Fronds to 10×1cm, 2-pinnate to -pinnatifid, linear or oblong to lanceolate or elliptic, membranous, glandular-pubesc., pinnae to 6×5mm, 6–10 pairs, petiolate, horizontal and spreading, ovate to oblong, apex obtuse, base truncate or cordate, margin notched to lobed; stipes to 5cm, persistently glandular-pubesc., green or brown or black. Medit. Z8.

A. phyllitidis Christ, non D. Don = *A. australisicum*.

A. pinnatifidum Nutt. LOBED SPLEENWORT. Fronds to 15×4cm, simple and pinnatifid at base, linear to lanceolate or deltoid, apex attenuate to acute or caudate and, occas., proliferous, base truncate or subcordate, thick-textured, leathery, glandular-pubesc., lobes to 12×10mm, opposite or alt., approximate, ovate, deltoid, or oblong to suborbicular, apex obtuse, margin erose and undulate, veins forked; stipes to 10cm, terete to

flattened, grooved, green to brown or black. E & S US. Z6.
A. planicaule Wallich ex Hook. Fronds to 30×5cm, pinnate, to pinnatifid at apex, lanceolate to oblong, apex narrowly acute, leathery, pinnae to 35×10mm, lowest occas. reduced, 12–20 pairs, petiolate, horizontal, rhomboid, apex acute, base obliquely truncate to cuneate and acroscopically auriculate, margin entire to deeply notched and somewhat lobed, veins forked, approximate, rachis and costa compressed, sparsely scaly, indistinct; stipes to 15cm, glab. or scaly, brown, scales lanceolate, apex attenuate, margin subentire. Trop. Asia. Z10.

A. plantagineum L. = *Diplazium plantaginifolium*.
A. plantaginifolium L. = *Diplazium plantaginifolium*.

A. platyneuron (L.) Oakes. EBONY SPLEENWORT. Fronds to 40×8cm, pinnate, linear to lanceolate, membranous, glab. above, minutely scaly below, pinnae to 25×3mm, lowest re-duced, 20–50 pairs, sessile to subsessile, oblique, linear or oblong to lanceolate, apex acute or obtuse, base cordate and acroscopically auriculate, margin notched, veins indistinct; stipes to 5cm, initially scaly, chestnut to purple. Trop. Afr., US, W Indies. Z5.

A. polyodon Forst. f. SICKLE SPLEENWORT. Fronds to 45×20cm, pinnate, to pinnatifid at apex, pendent, elliptic, apex attenuate to acute, base truncate, pinnae to 12×3cm, 6–20 pairs, sessile to short-petiolate, opposite, horizontal, distant, lanceolate, apex attenuate to narrowly acute, base obliquely truncate to cuneate, margin toothed to lobed, veins forked, oblique, indistinct above, rachis and costa scaly; stipes to 20cm, base initially scaly, brown. Madag., Trop. Asia to Aus., Polyn. Z10.

A. praemorsum Sw. Fronds to 35×10cm, 1–2-pinnate to -pinnatifid, erect to ascending and stiff, ovate or deltoid to lanceolate or oblong, apex attenuate, leathery, scaly below, ipnnae to 8×3cm, 7–15 pairs, short-petiolate, opposite or alt., lanceolate or deltoid to quadrangular, base unequal, pinnules to 35×25mm, 3–5, obovate, deltoid, or flabellate to linear or oblong, base cuneate, margin entire to lobed, seg. to 4mm wide, 2–4, unequal, oblong, veins forked, parallel, approximate, rachis scaly; stipes to 15cm, grooved above, scaly, brown to black, scales to 5mm, dense, spreading, apex attenuate. W In-dies, Mex. to Arg. Z10.

A. progrediens Fée = *A. serra*.
A. proliferum Lam. = *Diplazium proliferum*.
A. proliferum Sw. = *Fadyenia hookeri*.

A. prolongatum Hook. Fronds to 30×8cm, 2–3-pinnate to -pinnatifid, spreading and rosulate, linear to lanceolate, apex proliferous, pinnae to 40×12mm, 10–20 pairs, petiolate, ascend-ing, oblique, ovate or deltoid to oblong, apex obtuse, pinnules to 10×2mm, to 5 pairs, sessile, erect or ascending to spreading, distant, linear, apex obtuse and occas., bifid, margin entire to lobed, seg. erect to spreading, linear; stipes to 25cm, flattened, base scaly, green, scales to 1mm, sparse, spreading. Trop. Asia. Z8.

A. pteridoides Bak. Fronds to 25cm, to 3-pinnate to -pinnatifid, deltoid to oblong, flaccid, pinnae to 5cm wide, petiolate, approximate, lanceolate to deltoid, pinnules sessile, erect to spreading, rhomboid, margin lobed, rachis grooved; stipes to 10cm, grooved, glab. Lord Howe Is. Z9.

A. pycnocarpon Spreng. = *Athyrium pycnocarpon*.
A. raoulii var. *richardii* (Hook. f.) Mett. = *A. richardii*.
A. resectum Sm. = *A. unilaterale*.

A. resiliens Kunze. LITTLE EBONY SPLEENWORT; BLACK-STEM SPLEENWORT. Fronds to 20×3cm, pinnate, erect, linear or oblong to oblanceolate or elliptic, apex narrowly acute or sub-obtuse, base attenuate, leathery, sparsely gland. below, glands adpressed, clavate, pinnae to 15×8mm, lowest reduced and deflexed, 20–40 pairs, subopposite to alt., horizontal or deflexed, approximate and imbricate to distant, linear or oblong to deltoid, apex obtuse, base cordate and acroscopically auriculate, margin entire to somewhat notched, veins indistinct, rachis winged above; stipes to 7cm, terete, winged, glab. to sparsely scaly, lustrous, purple to black. Trop. Amer. Z6.

A. rhizophyllum L. WALKING FERN. Fronds to 30×5cm, simple to pinnatifid at base, deltoid or lanceolate to linear, apex attenuate and proliferous, base cordate, margin entire and plane, glab., apex of lobes usually obtuse, veins occas. anastomosing; stipes to 15cm, base scaly, green to red-brown. N Amer. Z6.

A. richardii Hook. f. Fronds to 25×15cm, 2–3-pinnate, erect to ascending, ovate to lanceolate, apex narrowly acute, leathery, pinnae to 10×4cm, to 14 pairs, petiolate, ovate to lanceolate, apex acute to narrowly acute, pinnules to 2×2cm, approximate to imbricate, ovate to oblong, seg. to 5mm, linear to lanceolate, apex acute or subacute to apiculate, rachis glab. to scaly; stipes to 15cm, stiff, initially scaly, green. NZ. Z9.

A. ruprechtii Kurata. Fronds dimorphous, simple, leathery, sterile to 25×10mm, ovate, apex acute, fertile to 15cm×0.6cm, apex caudate and proliferous, base attenuate; stipes to 8cm, glab., brown. Sib. to China, Jap. Z3.

A. rutaefolium Mak., non Kunze. = *A. prolongatum*.

A. ruta-muraria L. WALL RUE. Fronds to 40×25mm, 2-pinnate to -pinnatifid, ascending to spreading, ovate or deltoid to lanceolate, leathery, pinnae to 3 pairs, petiolate, alt., distant, pinnules to 6×5mm, 1 term. and 1–2 pairs lateral, obovate, rhomboid, or flabellate to orbicular, apex obtuse, base cuneate, margin entire to minutely toothed or notched, veins forked to flabellate, parallel, indistinct, rachis grooved above; stipes to 6cm, scaly, green to brown, scales linear to subulate, margin gland., black, glands decid., capitate. N Amer., Eur., Trop. Asia. Z6.

A. rutifolium (Bergins) Kunze. Fronds to 15×8cm, 1–3-pinnate to -pinnatifid, erect to arched, elliptic to oblong, apex acute, leathery, glab. to sparsely scaly below, pinnae to 50×12mm, to 19 pairs, petiolate, deltoid to lanceolate or oblong-apex attenuate to obtuse, base cuneate and acroscopically auriculate, pinnules to 1mm wide, linear to oblong, apex obtuse, seg. obovate or oblanceolate to oblong, apex acute, rachis sparsely scaly; stipes to 16cm, glab. to sparsely scaly, green to brown, scales scattered, ovate, apex narrowly acute. Trop. E Afr., Madag. Z10.

A. sagittatum (DC.) Bange. MULE'S FERN. Fronds to 15cm, simple to pinnatifid, ovate or lanceolate, to oblong, apex obtuse, base sagittate to hastate or cordate and acroscopically auriculate, margin entire to lobed, lobes deltoid to suborbicular, apex attenuate to subacute; stipes to 15cm, somewhat fibrillose. Medit. Z8.

A. sandersonii Hook. Fronds to 20×3cm, pinnate to pinnatifid, arched, linear, apex caudate and proliferous, leathery to fleshy, sparsely stellate-pubesc. to scaly below, pinnae to 13×7mm, lowest reduced, to 32 pairs, petiolate, horizontal, rhomboid or lunate to cuneate, base attenuate, margin (lower) entire and plane, (upper) notched to lobed, seg. to 9, apex obtuse, margin entire, rachis winged, sparsely pubesc. and scaly; stipes to 7cm, grooved, sparsely scaly, straw-coloured, scales to 2mm, sub-ulate, margin minutely notched. Trop. Afr., Madag. Z10.

A. schimperi (Moug. ex Fée) A. Braun = *Athyrium schimperi*.

A. scizodon Moore = *A. vieillardii*.

A. scleroprium Hombron & Jacq. Fronds to 100×30cm, pinnate to pinnatifid, lanceolate, apex narrowly acute, thick-textured and fleshy, pinnae to 12×2cm, 8–15 pairs, petiolate, sub-opposite to alt., lanceolate, apex narrowly acute, base obliquely cuneate, margin deeply toothed to lobed; seg. linear, margin en-tire to toothed, veins simple or forked, distinct, rachis winged, scaly; stipes to 40cm, base scaly. NZ. Z9.

A. scolopendrium L. HART'S TONGUE FERN. Fronds to 40×6cm, simple, lanceolate to strap-shaped, apex acute, base cordate and basioscopically auriculate, margin entire to undulate and some-what hyaline, leathery, flaccid, initially minutely scaly below, veins forked, costa initially scaly; stipes to 20cm, scaly, scales as those on rhiz. N Amer., Eur. (incl. GB), Asia. 'Crispum': frond entire, deeply pleated or goffered along each margin with the undulations so deep and close in the best forms as to resemble an Elizabethan ruff. Many forms were grown in past; some selected forms offered occas. are 'Crispum Bolton's Nobile' (a fine broad form, 20–30cm, up to 10cm broad; sterile); 'Crispum Golden Queen' (suffused with yellow, 20–30cm; sterile); 'Crispum Moly' (frond tapers quickly to sharp point, 20–30cm; sometimes fertile); 'Fimbriatum' (30cm, margins fimbriate; fertile; 'Speciosum' (tall, 30–50cm, deeply folded, slightly variegated; sterile). 'Cristatum': 30cm; frond apex crested, real-ly a capitatum. 'Laceratum Kaye': 20cm; the best of the known laceratums, frond broad and margin torn into narrow irregular lobes. 'Marginatum': 35cm; fleshy ridges along frond surfaces. 'Muricatum': 35cm; frond surface rough and leathery. 'Ramo-cristatum': 20–35cm; frond branched, terminals crested. 'Un-dulatum': 20–30cm; frond margins wavy, approaching 'Crispum'; usually fertile. 'Sagittatum': 15–30cm; lobes produced at base of frond, forming an arrowhead shape: these lobes can be greatly enlarged giving a brachiate frond; often associated with crested and crisped characters, hence. 'Sagittato-cristatum' and 'Sagittato-crispum'. Z5.

A. seelosii Leyb. Fronds to 7×3cm, palmately lobed, rhomboid or cuneate to oblong, leathery, glab. to glandular-pubesc., seg. to 2mm wide, 3, subequal, rhomboid, base decurrent, margin toothed to notched, veins forked, parallel, sunken; stipes to 10cm, wiry, grooved, glab., green to brown. W to C Eur. (Pyren., Alps). Z6.

A. septentrionale (L.) Hoffm. GRASS FERN. Fronds to 8×1cm, simple to pinnatifid, erect, seg. to 35×1mm, 2–3, linear, margin entire to toothed; stipes to 8cm, scaly, green to black; scales lanceolate, black. N Amer., Eur., Indochina, Taiwan. Z3.

A. serpentini Tausch = *A. cuneifolium*.

A. serra Langsd. & Fisch. Fronds to 125×40cm, pinnate, erect to spreading or arched, oblong, apex narrowly acute, leathery to papery, pinnae to 20×3cm, 15–20 pairs, short-petiolate, sub-

opposite to alt., horizontal and spreading, oblique, distant, line-ar to lanceolate, apex attenuate to caudate, base unequal and obtuse or cuneate, margin notched, veins forked, oblique, rachis and costa glab. to scaly; stipes to 25cm, 4-angled, scaly, purple to brown. Trop. Amer., Trop. Afr. Z10.

A. serratum L. BIRD'S NEST FERN; WILD BIRD'S NEST FERN. Fronds to 100×15cm, subsessile to short-petiolate, simple, nest-forming and rosulate, linear to oblanceolate, apex acute to narrowly acute, base attenuate to cuneate, margin subentire to irregularly toothed or notched, undulate and cartilaginous, papery, glab., veins forked, parallel, oblique, rachis prominent; stipes to 5cm, 3-angled, scaly, green to purple. Trop. Amer. Z10.

A. shepherdii Spreng. = *Diplazium shepherdii*.

A. shuttleworthianum Kunze. Fronds to 75×45cm, 3–4-pinnate, erect to pendent, ovate or elliptic to oblong, apex attenuate to acute, leathery to fleshy, ± glab., pinnae to 15×5cm, to 10 pairs, petiolate, subopposite to alt., ovate, to lanceolate, apex ± acute, pinnules to 3×1cm, petiolate, lobes to 1cm, seg. to 2mm wide, linear or oblong to spathulate, apex ± acute and un-dulate, rachis and costa glab. to scaly; stipes to 15cm, scaly, green to brown. NZ, Polyn. Z9.

A. simplicifrons F. Muell. Fronds to 60×3cm, subsessile, simple, erect to spreading, nest-forming and rosulate, spathulate to strap-shaped, apex attenuate to acute, membranous; stipes ± obsolete. Aus. Z9.

A. sinuatum P. Beauv., non Salisb. = *A. africanum*.

A. spinulosum (Maxim.) Bak. = *Athyrium spinulosum*.

A. splendens Kunze. Fronds to 37×18cm, 2–3-pinnate, ovate to deltoid, thin-textured, leathery, glab. above, scaly below, pinnae to 5cm wide, 9–16 pairs, petiolate, deltoid, pinnules to 12mm wide, to 16, cuneate to trapeziform or flabellate, apex obtuse, margin of seg. toothed to notched; stipes to 25cm, to 2cm distant, scaly, brown, scales to 5mm, fimbriate. S Afr. Z9.

A. subalatum Hook. & Arn. = *A. formosum*.

A. subsinuatum Wallich, ex Hook. & Grev. = *Diplazium lanceum*.

A. suntense Bl. = *A. vittiforme*.

A. tenerum Forst. f. Fronds to 40×10cm, pinnate to pinnatifid at apex, erect to spreading and rosulate, linear or oblong to lanceolate, apex narrowly acute to caudate and proliferous, base truncate, pinnae to 4×1cm, 10–20 pairs, sessile to short-petiolate, horizontal and spreading, lowest deflexed, approx-imate, lanceolate to oblong, apex acute or obtuse, base cuneate to truncate and acroscopically auriculate, margin toothed to notched, veins simple or forked to pinnate, distinct, rachis and costa fragile, winged, scaly below; stipes to 20cm, grooved, initi-ally scaly, grey to green, scales ovate, brown. Trop. Asia to Polyn. Z10.

A. tenerum var. *belangeri* Bory = *A. thunbergii*.

A. terrestre Brownsey. Fronds to 45×22cm, 2–30-pinnate, erect and stiff, elliptic, apex acute, leathery to fleshy, pinnae to 15×4cm, petiolate, alt., approximate, elliptic or lanceolate to deltoid, apex attenuate to acute, base acute, pinnules ovate or elliptic to linear, apex acute or obtuse, margin subentire to lobed, rachis and costa scaly; stipes to 20cm, scaly, green to brown. Aus., NZ. Z9.

A. thelypteroides Michx. = *Deparia acrostichoides*.

A. thunbergii Mett. Fronds to 35×10cm, 2-pinnate, linear to lanceolate, apex attenuate to acute and proliferous, membranous, pinnae to 4×1cm, sessile, horizontal and spread-ing, oblong, apex obtuse, base cuneate to truncate, pinnules to 6×1mm, erect to spreading, linear or oblong to spathulate, apex obtuse, base cuneate, margin entire, veins simple to forked or pinnate, rachis and costa compressed, sparsely scaly; stipes to 10cm, straw-coloured. Malaysia. Z10.

A. trichomanes L. MAIDENHAIR SPLEENWORT. Fronds to 30×2cm, pinnate, erect or ascending to spreading or arched, linear, apex attenuate to obtuse, base attenuate, leathery, pinnae to 12×6mm, 15–30 pairs, sessile or subsessile, opposite or sub-opposite, horizontal and spreading, distant, ovate or obovate to elliptic or oblong, apex obtuse, base obliquely cuneate to truncate and, occas., acroscopically auriculate, margin subentire to toothed or notched, veins forked to pinnate, indistinct, rachis and costa stiff winged above; stipes to 10cm, wiry, stiff, base scaly, lustrous, brown to purple or black. N temp., trop. mts. 'Cristatum': 10cm; tip of frond crested, strictly a capitate var. as the pinnae are not crested; in some forms the frond may br. near the mid-point, hence 'Ramo-cristatum'. 'Incisum': 15cm; pinnules deltate and deeply incised, the best forms completely sterile, e.g. 'Greenfield' (Incisum group). 'Incisum Moule' ('Moulei'): 10cm; pinnules linear and shallowly incised, texture hard, fertile form comes true from spore. 'Trogyense': 10cm; pinnae deltate and incised, fertile; a form of *A. trichomanes* spp. *pachyrachis*. Z2.

A. trichomanoides Houtt. = *A. trichomanes*.

A. unilaterale Lam. Fronds to 25×8cm but variable, pinnate, to pinnatifid at apex, erect, linear or oblong to lanceolate, apex attenuate to acute, thin-textured and membranous, glab., pinnae to 35×10mm, lowest somewhat reduced and deflexed, 10–30 pairs, short-petiolate, horizontal and spreading, approximate, lanceolate to rhomboid, apex truncate or attenuate to mucronate, base cuneate to truncate, margin entire to toothed or notched, plane or falcate, veins forked, distinct, rachis and costa grooved above, initially scaly; stipes to 20cm, to 4cm distant, base scaly, lustrous, brown to purple or black. Trop. Afr., Asia, Polyn. Z10.

A. vagans Bak. = *A. sandersoni.*

A. varians Hook. & Grev. = *A. laciniatum.*

A. veitchianum Moore = *A. thunbergii.*

A. venosum Hook. = *A. africanum.*

A. vidalii Franch. & Savat. = *Athyrium vidalii.*

A. *vieillardii* Mett. Fronds to 23×20cm, pinnate, obovate, apex caudate, scaly below, pinnae to 10×2cm, 3–4 pairs, sessile to petiolate, alt., erect to spreading, linear to lanceolate, apex narrowly acute, base cuneate to truncate and acroscopically auriculate, margin toothed to notched, rachis and costa scaly; stipes to 35cm, scaly, scales to 3mm, lanceolate, ciliate. Polyn. Z10.

A. virgilii Bory = *A. onopteris.*

A. *viride* Huds. GREEN SPLEENWORT. Fronds to 12×1cm, pinnate, suberect to spreading or arched, linear to lanceolate, apex obtuse, glab., pinnae to 6×5mm, 10–20 pairs, sessile to short-petiolate, ovate or rhomboid to suborbicular or flabellate, apex obtuse, base obliquely cuneate to truncate, margin toothed to notched, veins forked, indistinct, rachis and costa grooved above; stipes to 10cm, grooved above, lustrous, green to purple or brown. N Amer., Eur., Asia (Sib., Indochina to Taiwan, Jap.). Z5.

A. vitiense Bak. = *Diplazium esculentum.*

A. *vittiforme* Cav. Fronds to 45×10cm, simple, erect, lanceolate to oblong, apex attenuate to acute, base attenuate, margin somewhat toothed to notched, membranous, pubesc. below, veins approximate; stipes to 8cm, glab. Malaysia to Polyn. Z10.

A. viviparum (L. f.) Presl, non Bl. = *A. daucifolium.*

A. woodwardioideum Gardn. = *A. serra.*

A. yokoscense Franch. & Savat. = *Athyrium yokoscense.*

A. yoshinagae Mak. = *A. planicaule.*

→*Acrostichum, Adiantum, Amesium, Camptosorus, Ceterach, Loxoscaphe, Neottopteris, Phyllitis, Scolopendrium* and *Thamnopteris.*

Assai Palm *Euterpe; E. edulis; E. oleracea.*
Assam Rubber *Ficus elastica.*
Assyrian Plum *Cordia myxa.*

Astelia R. Br. Liliaceae (Asteliaceae). 25 everg., perenn. herbs. Rhiz. short, thick. Lvs linear, crowded at base of st., covered with chaffy or silky hairs or scales particularly beneath. Fls inconspicuous, in pan., on long scapes or short-stalked and held in lf rosette; tep. 6. Fr. a berry. Australasia, Polyn., Réunion, Maur., Falkland Is. Z9.

A. *banksii* Cunn. Lvs 100–250×3–4.5cm, closely packed, linear, apex slender-acuminate, base narrowed then broadly sheathing, sericeous, upper surface covered in fused scales, undersurface densely white-felty, margins recurved, veins 3+. Infl. to 50cm, much-branched; fls pale green tinted ivory. Fr. white, ripening purple-black. NZ.

A. cockaynei Cheesem. = *A. nervosa.*

A. cunninghamii Hook. f. = *A. solandri.*

A. montana (Cheesem.) Ckn. = *A. nervosa.*

A. *nervosa* Hook. f. Lvs 50–200×2–6cm, linear, rigid, narrowed and conduplicate just above sheath, then arching outwards, covered above with fused scales, with white-brown scales beneath, over a layer of hairs, veins 1–2, subsidiary and parallel to midrib. Infl. to 40cm, much-branched; fls fragrant, green-purple to bronze or dark red. Fr. orange to red. NZ.

A. *petriei* Ckn. Similar to *A. nervosa.* Lvs 25–100×2.5–6cm, not narrowing above sheath, green above, glab. when mature, white-scaly beneath, veins 10. Fr. orange to red. NZ.

A. *solandri* Cunn. Lvs 100–200×2–3.5cm, linear-ensiform, spreading, recurved, narrowing to green-black sheathing base, glab. above, with white scales beneath, 3-veined. Pan. few-branched, on stalks 30–100cm; fls lemon-yellow. Fr. bright red. NZ.

Aster L. Compositae. *c*250 mainly herbaceous perennials, some annuals and biennials. Lvs usually stalked below, narrower and ± sessile higher on st. (those below often withering before flowering). Cap. discoid or radiate, solitary or clustered in corymbs or rac. S Amer., Eurasia, Afr., Asia. Z7. The China Aster is *Callistephus chinensis.*

A. abatus Blake = *Machaeranthera tortifolia.*

A. acris L. = *A. sedifolius.*

A. *acuminatus* Michx. Rhizomatous perenn. herb to 80cm. Lvs to 15cm, elliptic to obovate, acuminate, dentate, glab. Cap. in a corymbose pan.; ray flts white, or tinged purple; disc flts yellow. NE N Amer. Z4.

A. aestivus Dryand. = *A. longifolius.*

A. aethiopicus Burm. f. = *Felicia aethiopica.*

A. ageratoides Turcz. = *A. trinervius* ssp. *ageratoides* var. *microcephalus.*

A. *albescens* (DC.) Hand.-Mazz. Diffuse shrub to 2m. Lvs to 12cm, lanceolate, ± entire. Cap. in cymes; ray flts lilac; disc flts yellow. Late summer–autumn. Kashmir, SW Tibet. Z6.

A. ×*alpellus* hort. (*A. alpinus* ×*A. amellus.*) Compact perenn. herb 20–30cm. Ray flts blue; disc flts orange. Summer. Gdn origin. 'Triumph': fls white with orange discs, fragrant. Z3.

A. *alpigenus* (Torr. & A. Gray) A. Gray. Taprooted, decumbent perenn. herb to 20cm. Lvs to 15cm, tufted, linear-spathulate or oblanceolate. Cap. to 4cm diam.; ray flts deep violet to purple. Summer–early autumn. W US. ssp. *andersonii* (A. Gray) Ouno. Low, mat-forming, tomentose above. Lvs to 35cm, linear to linear-elliptic. Cap. 2–3.5cm diam., ray flts purple. Summer. SW US. Z7.

A. *alpinus* L. Perenn. herb to 25cm, ascending or erect. Lvs mainly basal, entire, pubesc., oblong-spathulate to lanceolate. Cap. to 4cm diam., solitary; ray flts violet to blue-violet, disc flts yellow. Summer. Alps, Pyren. 'Abendschein': to 25cm; fls brilliant pink. 'Albus': to 25cm; fls white. 'Beechwood': fls clear blue. 'Blue': fls blue. 'Coeruleus': st. to 25cm; fls blue, ligulate. 'Dunkel Schöne' ('Dark Beauty'): to 25cm, fls purple in Summer. 'Happy End': to 25cm; fls pink. 'Roseus': st. to 15cm, fls pale rose, ligulate. 'Rubra': fls purple rose, ligulate. 'Superbus': fl. heads large, fls purple, ligulate. Trimix: to 20cm; fls tricolour mix of pink, blue and white. 'Violet Blue': fls violet. 'Wargrave Variety' ('Wargrave Park'): fls pale pink tinged with purple. 'White Beauty': fls white. Z3.

A. alpinus var. *himalaicus* Turcz. = *A. himalaicus.*

A. altaicus Willd. = *Heteropappus altaicus.*

A. amellius hort. = *A. amellus.*

A. amelloides hort. = *Felicia amelloides.*

A. *amellus* L. Perenn. herb; st. pubesc., ascending to 70cm. Lvs hirsute, lanceolate to obovate. Cap. clustered, to 5cm diam.; ray flts purple, rarely white, disc flts yellow. Autumn. Eur., W Asia. Over 30 cvs; the wild form is relatively rare and most closely approximates to 'Ultramarine' and 'Violet Queen' ('Veilchenkönigin'); others range from the soft lavender of 'Lac de Génève', the lilac 'Nocturne' and the deep violets of 'King George', 'Blue King' and 'Rudolf van Goethe', to pink cvs, such as the rose-pink 'Sonia', the bright pink 'Brilliant' and the deeper pink of 'Mrs Ralph Woods' and 'Lady Hindlip'. ssp. *ibericus* (Steven) Avetisyan. Ray flts dark blue. Asia Minor and Cauc. Z5.

A. amellus hort. pro parte = *A. indamellus.*

A. amellus var. *frikartii* hort. = *A. ×frikartii.*

A. ×*amethystinus* Nutt. (*A. ericoides* ×*A. novae-angliae.*) Resembling *A. ericoides* but ray flts blue or purple. SC Canada. Z3.

A. amygdalinus Lam. = *A. umbellatus.*

A. andersonii A. Gray = *A. alpigenus* ssp. *andersonii.*

A. argenteus Michx. = *A. sericeus.*

A. argophyllus Labill. = *Olearia argophylla.*

A. asper Nees = *A. bakerianus.*

A. *asteroides* (DC.) Kuntze. Glandular-pubesc., perenn. erect to 15cm; with swollen rhiz. Lvs to 4cm, ovate to lanceolate, toothed or entire. Cap. solitary, c5cm diam.; ray flts blue-purple to mauve. Early summer. Tibet, Bhutan, W China. Z6.

A. azureus Lindl. ex Hook. = *A. oolentangiensis.*

A. *bakerianus* Davy ex C.A. Sm. To 30cm; roots ruberous; st. erect, scabrous. Lvs 5–12cm, ovate-oblong to oblong-lanceolate, entire or remotely dentate, scabrous-pubesc. Cap. solitary, to 5cm diam.; ray flts distant, narrow, light to dark blue or white; disc flts yellow. S Afr. Z9.

A. barrowianus hort. = *A. albescens.*

A. *bellidiastrum* (L.) Scop. DAISY-STAR ASTER. Perenn. herb erect to 40cm. Lvs basal, spathulate or suborbicular to elliptic, entire or crenate, ± hirsute. Cap. solitary; ray flts white or pink; disc flts yellow. S & E Eur. Z6.

A. bigelovii A. Gray = *Machaeranthera bigelovii.*

A. blandus Pursh = *A. puniceus.*

A. *brachytrichis* Franch. Rhizomatous, hirsute, perenn. herb to 30cm. Lvs to 6cm, obovate-spathulate to obovate, entire. Cap. solitary, 5cm diam.; ray flts violet; disc flts yellow. China. Z6.

A. caespitosus hort. = *A. novi-belgii.*

A. canescens Pursh = *Machaeranthera canescens.*

A. canus Waldst. & Kit. = *A. sedifolius* ssp. *canus.*

A. capensis Less. = *Felicia amelloides.*

A. carolinianus Walter. Straggling shrub to 4m, softly grey-tomentose. Lvs 5–10cm, oblong-lanceolate to elliptic. Cap. term. on br.; ray flts pale pink or purple; disc flts yellow. Autumn. US (Flor. to N Carol.) Z8.

A. cassiarabicus Maund. = *A. amellus* ssp. *ibericus*.

A. caucasicus Willd. Erect, rhizomatous, perenn. herb to 75cm. Lvs to 15cm, ovate to oblanceolate, scabrid, serrate. Cap. 1 to 6 in a corymb, 5cm diam.; ray flts purple. Summer. Cauc. Z6.

A. chapmanii Torr. & A. Gray. To 1m; st. slender. Lvs to 18cm, linear-spathulate to filiform. Cap. to 1.5cm diam., solitary; flts violet. Autumn. US (Flor.) Z8.

A. chilensis Nees. Perenn. herb to 1m, erect or ascending. Lvs to 12cm, oblanceolate, serrulate, margins scabrous; petioles winged. Cap. numerous in a pan.; ray flts violet to pale purple, disc flts yellow. Summer–autumn. Calif. Z8.

A. chinensis L. = *Callistephus chinensis*.

A. ciliolatus Lindl. Stout, erect perenn. herb to 80cm. Lvs to 10cm, ovate to cordate, dentate, petioles long-winged. Cap. few in a pan.; ray flts blue. BC. Z2.

A. coelestis Cass. = *Felicia amelloides*.

A. ×*commixtus* (Nees) Kunth. Slender, branched, 60–90cm, somewhat scabrid. Lvs 5–15cm, ovate, remotely dentate, scabrid above, somewhat pubesc. on main veins. Cap. 2.5–4cm diam.; ray flts violet. Late summer–autumn. E US. Z6.

A. commutatus (Torr. & A. Gray) A. Gray. = *A. falcatus*.

A. concolor L. Perenn. herb to 80cm. Lvs to 6cm, elliptic-oblong to lanceolate, silky becoming glab. Cap. to 2.5cm diam., in a spicate rac.; ray flts blue, violet or pink; disc flts yellow. US (Mass. to Kent.) Z4.

A. conspicuus Lindl. Gland., perenn. herb erect to 1m. Lvs ovate to obovate, dentate, scabrid above, hirsute beneath. Cap. 4cm diam., in a corymb; ray flts violet. US (BC, Washington, Oreg., S Dak.) Z4.

A. cordifolius L. Perenn. herb to 1.5m. Lvs to 12cm, narrowly to broadly cordate; petioles scarcely winged. Cap. 2cm diam., in a loose pan.; ray flts pale blue; disc flts yellow. E N Amer. 'Aldeboran': tall; fls profuse, pale blue with darker centres. 'Elegans': fls in sprays, small, white. 'Esther': compact, bushy; fls small, pink. 'Ideal': to 120cm; fls tinted violet. 'Little Carlow': to 90cm; fls profuse, single, violet-blue. 'Little Dorrit': to 1m, habit shapely and upright; fls mauve-pink. 'Photograph': fls in arching sprays, tinted lilac. 'Silver Queen': fls pale in silvered, frothy infl. 'Silver Spray': to 1m; lvs feathery; fls light violet-blue. 'Sweet Lavender': fls lavender, in arching sprays. ssp. *sagittifolius* (Wedem. ex Willd.) A.G. Jones. Lvs to 15cm, cordate or sagittate, sharply dentate, thick. Cap. to 2cm diam., crowded; ray flts pale blue, lilac or white. Late summer–autumn. N Amer. Z3.

A. coriaceus Forst. f. = *Celmisia coriacea*.

A. corymbosus Ait. = *A. divaricatus*.

A. crenatus Less. = *Mairia crenata*.

A. curtisii Torr. & A. Gray = *A. retroflexus*.

A. dahuricus (DC.) Benth. ex Bak. Perenn. to 1m. Lvs oblong-linear, entire, acute, glandular-punctate. Cap. large; ray flts white. Summer. Sib. Z2.

A. delavayi Franch. = *A. diplostephioides*.

A. diffusus DC. = *A. lateriflorus*.

A. diplostephioides (DC.) C.B. Clarke. Perenn. herb to 50cm. Lvs to 8cm, oblanceolate to linear-lanceolate, entire. Cap. solitary, to 7cm diam.; ray flts narrow, reflexed; disc flts brown-rust to orange. Pappus silky, tinged red. Late summer–autumn. Kashmir, China. Z5.

A. divaricatus L. Perenn. herb to 60cm; st. dark purple. Lvs to 6cm wide, cordate-ovate to triangular. Cap. clustered in a cyme; ray flts white; disc flts yellow. E US. Z4.

A. dracunculoides Lam. = *A. sedifolius* ssp. *dracunculoides*.

A. drummondii Lindl. Perenn. herb to 1.3m. Lvs to 15cm, cordate, shallow-dentate, scabrid above, pubesc. beneath; petioles winged. Cap. 1.5cm diam., in a dense pan.; ray flts bright blue; disc flts yellow. CE to CS US. Z5.

A. dumosus L. Perenn. herb to 1m. Lvs to 12cm, linear-lanceolate or narrow-elliptic, entire, scabrous above, glab. beneath. Cap. c1.2cm diam., in a loose pan.; ray flts lavender, blue or white; disc flts yellow. SE US. Many cvs, known as the dwarf asters; all are bushy and free-flowering, suited to the fronts of borders or to small gardens. See *A. novi-belgii*. Z3.

A. elongatus Thunb. = *Felicia elongata*.

A. eminens Willd. = *A. praealtus*.

A. englemannii var. *ledophyllus* A. Gray = *A. ledophyllus*.

A. ensifolius Scop. = *Inula ensifolia*.

A. ericoides L. Perenn. herb to 1m; st. slender, much-branched above. Lvs to 6cm, numerous, linear to linear-lanceolate. Cap. to 12mm diam., somewhat secund on divergent br.; ray flts white, occas. blue or pink; disc flts yellow. C & E US. 'Blue Star': compact; fls pale blue. 'Blue Wonder': fls rich blue. 'Brimstone': fls cream with yellow centres. 'Cinderella': fls

white. 'Delight': fls white. 'Enchantress': fls mauve. 'Erlkönig': to 120cm; fls light lilac. 'Esther': to 70cm; fls profuse; lilac-rose. 'Golden Spray': to 1m; fls single, white with gold disc. 'Herbstmyrte': small; fls violet. 'Hon. Edith Gibbs': to 90cm; fls lavender. 'Hon. Vicary Gibbs': to 90cm; fls lilac. 'Ideal': to 1.2m; fls soft mauve. 'Lovely': to 80cm; fls light pink. 'Maidenhood': to 1.5m, elegant and tall; fls in white sprays. 'Monte Cassino': to 140cm; fls snow-white. 'Perfection': fls white. 'Pink Cloud': to 90cm, feathery and bushy; fls in light pink sprays. 'Ringdove': to 90cm, upright; fls in pale rose-mauve sprays. 'Rosy Veil': fls light pink; feathery. 'Schneegitter': fls white. 'Schneetanne': to 120cm; fls snow-white. 'Vimmer's Delight': habit compact; fls white. 'White Heather': to 90cm, upright; fls in snow-white compact sprays. Z3.

A. falcatus Lindl. WHITE PRAIRIE ASTER. Perenn. herb to 80cm, much-branched, scabrid-hirsute. Lvs to 4cm, linear to linear-lanceolate. Cap. few, 2.5cm diam.; ray flts white; disc flts yellow. W N Amer. Z4.

A. falconeri (C.B. Clarke) Hutch. Perenn. herb to 40cm. Lvs to 15cm, basal, oblanceolate, distantly dentate. Cap. c8cm diam., solitary; ray flts pale purple with white base. Late summer. Himal. of Pak., Nepal. Z6.

A. farreri W.W. Sm. & Jeffrey. Tufted perenn. herb to 60cm. Lvs to 12cm, lanceolate, hirsute. Cap. to 3cm diam., solitary; ray flts narrow, violet; disc flts gold to orange. Summer. Tibet. Z4.

A. fastigiatus Ledeb. = *A. hauptii*.

A. fendleri A. Gray. Tufted perenn. herb erect to 40cm. Lvs to 4.5cm, linear, ciliate, finely serrate. Cap. to 4cm diam. in a short rac.; ray flts pale blue; disc flts yellow. SC US. Z5.

A. filaginifolius Hook. & Arn. = *Corethrogyne filaginifolia*.

A. flaccidus Bunge. Hirsute perenn. herb to 15cm. Lvs mainly in a basal cluster, oblanceolate, undulate. Cap. solitary, 4cm diam.; ray flts mauve. Midsummer. Afghan., Pamirs, Altai, China. Z6.

A. floribundus Willd. = *A. novi-belgii*.

A. foliaceus Lindl. ex DC. Perenn. herb to 1m. Lvs to 12cm, oblanceolate to obovate. Cap. to 6cm diam. in a cymose pan.; ray flts rose-purple or blue or violet; disc flts yellow. Late summer–autumn. W N Amer. Z2.

A. foliosus Pers. = *A. lateriflorus*.

A. forestii Stapf = *A. souliei*.

A. fragilis Willd. To 1.2m; st. slender. Lvs to 10cm, linear-lanceolate, mucronate, minutely serrulate or entire. Cap. numerous, in loose pan., often second. Late summer–autumn. E US. Z5.

A. ×*frikartii* hort. (*A. amellus* ×*A. thomsonii*.) Perenn. herb to 70cm. Lvs oblong, dark green, scabrid. Cap. to 5cm diam., solitary on many br.; ray flts light violet-blue; disc flts orange. Autumn. Gdn origin. 'Flora's Delight': dense and bushy; fls light lilac with yellow discs. 'Jungfrau': to 70cm; fls deep clear blue. 'Monch': to 40cm, upright and free-flowering; fls profuse, clear light blue, long-blooming. 'Wonder of Staffa' ('Wunder von Stäfa'): to 70cm; upright; fls radiant lavender-blue, long-blooming, early summer to early autumn. Z4.

A. frostii F. Muell. = *Olearia frostii*.

A. fruticosus L. = *Felicia fruticosa*.

A. furcatus Burgess. Perenn. to 80cm. Lvs 15cm, ovate-acuminate, serrate to minutely mucronate-dentate, base cordate, thick, scabrous above, pubesc. beneath; petiole often laciniate-winged. Cap. in a rounded or flat-topped corymb; ray flts usually white, occas. becoming lilac or rose with age. Summer. CE US. Z4.

A. furfuraceus A. Rich. = *Olearia furfuracea*.

A. fuscescens Bur. & Franch. Rhizomatous perenn. herb erect to 60cm. Lvs to 13cm, ovate, cordate, hirsute, long-stalked. Cap. to 3.5cm diam., clustered in a corymb; ray flts blue to purple; disc flts yellow or orange. Summer. China, Tibet, Burm. Z6.

A. geyeri (A. Gray) T.J. Howell = *A. laevis* var. *geyeri*.

A. glandulosus Labill. = *Olearia glandulosa*.

A. glaucoes S.F. Blake. To 60cm, erect, branched. Lvs 3–3cm, linear-oblong, acute, glaucous. Cap. in dense corymbs; ray flts purple or white flushed rose. C US. Z4.

A. glaucus auct. = *A. glaucodes*.

A. glehnii F. Schmidt. To 1.5m, branched above, minutely powdery-pubesc. Lvs crowded, oblong to linear, remotely dentate, chartaceous, minutely pubesc, glandular-punctate beneath. Cap. to 1.5cm diam., in dense corymbs; ray flts to 2cm, white. Late summer–autumn. Jap. Z7.

A. glehnii auctt. = *A. trinervius* ssp. *ageratoides* var. *microcephalus*.

A. glutinosus Cav. = *Grindelia glutinosa*.

A. gracilis Nutt. Cauciciform perenn. to 60cm. Basal lvs to 6.5cm, elliptic, entire, petiole longer than blade; st. lvs to 9cm, narrow. Cap. to 2cm diam. in a corymb; ray flts blue-violet to purple. CE US. Z5.

A. graminifolius Pursh = *Erigeron aureus*.

A. grandiflorus L. Perenn. herb to 2m, branched, gland. Lvs to 7.5cm, oblong or lanceolate-oblong, entire, firm, scabrid. Cap. to 4; ray flts to 2cm, blue or purple, occas. rose. Late autumn. US (Virg. to Flor.) Z7.

A. greatai Parish. Perenn. herb to 1.2m, sparsely pubesc. above. Lvs mostly basal, oblanceolate to lanceolate-elliptic, stalked to amplexicaul, to 15cm. Cap. in a cymose pan.; ray flts to 12mm, pale purple; disc flts yellow. Autumn. US (Calif.) Z8.

A. gymnocephalus (DC.) A. Gray = *Machaeranthera blephariphylla.*

A. hauptii Ledeb. To 60cm, erect. Lvs linear-oblong or linear, margins scabrid. Cap. to 5cm diam.; ray flts purple. Autumn. Sib. Z2.

A. haydenii Porter = *A. alpigenus.*

A. ×*herveyi* A. Gray = *A.* ×*commixtus.*

A. heterochaeta Benth. & C.B. Clarke = *A. asteroides.*

A. heterochaeta auctt., non Benth. ex C.B. Clarke = *A. flaccidus.*

A. himalaicus C.B. Clarke. Perenn. herb to 15cm. Lvs to 8cm, obovate-spathulate to narrow-elliptic. Cap. solitary, 3.5cm diam.; ray flts lilac; disc flts brown-yellow. Autumn. Nepal to China. Z6.

A. hispidus Thunb. = *Heteropappus hispidus.*

A. holosericeus Forst. f. = *Celmisia holosericea.*

A. hybridus var. *luteus* hort. = × *Solidaster luteus.*

A. hybridus var. *nanus* hort. = × *Solidaster luteus.*

A. incisus Fisch. = *Kalimeris incisa.*

A. indamellus Grierson. Perenn. herb; st. many, branching above. Lvs to 5cm, oblong, entire or dentate. Cap. 4cm diam., in a lax cyme. Autumn. Kashmir, Nepal. Z6.

A. integrifolius Nutt. Perenn. herb to 70cm, villous to glandular-pubesc. Lvs to 20cm, oblanceolate to elliptic, entire, thick, glab. to white-pilose. Cap. in a cyme; ray flts to 1.5cm; purple or violet; disc flts yellow. Late summer–autumn. US (Calif.) Z7.

A. japonicus (Miq.) Matsum. = *A. maackiana.*

A. junciformis Rydb. Slender perenn. herb to 80cm above. Lvs to 8cm, linear to lanceolate- or oblong-linear, ampelixicaul. Cap. to 2cm diam., in an open pan.; ray flts white to pale blue or lavender. Late summer–autumn. Alask. to WC US. Z2.

A. kumleinii Fries ex A. Gray = *A. oblongifolius.*

A. laevigatus hort. = *A.* ×*versicolor.*

A. laevis L. Perenn. to 1m, often glaucous; st. stout, maroon. Lvs to 12.5cm, ovate-lanceolate to lanceolate, auriculate, entire to slightly dentate, basal lvs with winged petiole. Cap. to 2.5cm diam., in a pan.; ray flts violet to blue; disc flts yellow. Autumn. N Amer. 'Albus': fls white. 'Blauschleier': to 1.5m; fls light blue. var. *geyeri* A. Gray. To 60cm. Involucral bracts longer, narrower. NW US. Z4.

A. lanceolatus Willd. Perenn. herb to 2m; st. tinged purple. Lvs oblong-lanceolate to linear-lanceolate, entire or slightly dentate. Cap. to 2cm diam., in a narrow pan.; ray flts white, sometimes violet-blue; disc flts yellow. Autumn. N Amer., nat. Eur. 'Edwin Beckett': fls off-white. ssp. *lanceolatus.* Lvs to 15cm, linear. S Canada to C US. ssp. *simplex* (Willd.) A.G. Jones. To 1.5m. Lvs to 20cm, oblong-lanceolate to oblanceolate, somewhat serrate. E to central N Amer. Z4.

A. lateriflorus (L.) Britt. Perenn. herb to 1m. Lvs to 15cm, broad-linear to linear-lanceolate. Cap. 1.5cm diam., in branched corymbs; ray flts white, apex often purple. N Amer., nat. Eur. 'Coombe Fishacre': fls with tinted pink rays, darker centres. 'Delight': lvs grey; fls white. 'Lovely': fls pink. var. *hirsuticaulis* (Lindl.) Porter. Lvs 15cm, serrate, minutely pubesc. on midrib beneath. Ray flts white. var. *horizontalis* (Desf.) D.E. Greene. St. widely spreading; ray flts cream, disc chocolate. Z3.

A. ledifolius Cunn. ex DC. = *Olearia ledifolia.*

A. ledophyllus (A. Gray) A. Gray. Perenn. herb ascending to 60cm. Lvs to 6cm, narrow-lanceolate to elliptic-oblanceolate, sessile, tomentose beneath. Cap. corymbose or solitary on glandular-tomentose peduncle; ray flts c1.5cm, lavender-purple. Late summer–autumn. US (Calif.) Z6.

A. lepidophyllus Pers. = *Olearia lepidophylla.*

A. leucopsis Greene = *A. chilensis.*

A. likiangensis Franch. = *A. asteroides.*

A. limitataneus = *A. souliei.*

A. linariifolius L. Perenn. herb to 60cm; st. bristly. Lvs to 4cm, numerous, linear, scabrous. Cap. in a corymb or solitary; ray flts to 12mm, broad, violet or white. Summer–autumn. N Amer. (Quebec to Flor. and Tex.) 'Albus': fls white. 'Purpureus': fls purple. 'Roseus': fls pink. Z4.

A. lindleyanus Torr. & A. Gray = *A. ciliolatus.*

A. linearifolius hort. = *A. linariifolius.*

A. linosyris (L.) Bernh. GOLDILOCKS. Perenn. herb to 70cm, decumbent to erect, densely leafy. Lvs narrow-lanceolate, often gland. above. Cap. discoid, small, many, in a dense corymb; ray flts 0; disc flts gold. Autumn. S & SE Eur. 'Gold Dust': earlier flowering. Z4.

A. lipskii Komar. Perenn. herb to 45cm erect, slender, hirsute. Lvs basal, lanceolate, irregularly toothed, long-petiolate. Cap. to 6.5cm diam., solitary; ray flts deep violet; disc flts yellow. Early summer. Tibet. Z6.

A. liratus Sims = *Olearia liratii.*

A. longifolius Lam. Perenn. to 90cm, branched, leafy. Lvs to 20cm, lanceolate to linear-lanceolate, ± entire. Cap. numerous, to 2.5cm diam.; ray flts violet or pale purple. Summer. N N Amer. Z3.

A. lowrieanus Porter = *A. cordifolius.*

A. luteus hort. = × *Solidaster luteus.*

A. maackii Reg. Rhizomatous perenn. herb to 1m, hirsute. Lvs to 10cm, lanceolate, sessile, upper lvs to 2cm, oblong. Cap. to 4cm diam., clustered; ray flts blue; disc flts yellow. Jap., Korea, Manch. Z7.

A. macrophyllus L. Perenn. herb to 1m; st. glandular-pubesc., twisted. Lvs coarsely dentate, to 14cm, broad, petiolate, ovate-cordate. Cap. in a corymb; ray flts pale violet, fading to white; disc flts yellow. N Amer., nat. Eur. 'Albus': fls white. Z3.

A. menziesii Lindl. ex Hook. = *A. chilensis.*

A. miqueliana Hara. Perenn. herb to 90cm; st. slender. Lvs to 9cm, ovate-cordate, acute to acuminate, incised-serrate, pilose, long-petiolate to sessile. Cap. to 2.5cm diam., on slender pedicels; ray flts 15×2mm. Fr. 4mm. Late summer–autumn. Jap. Z7.

A. modestus Lindl. Perenn. to 1m, glandular-pubesc. above. Lvs to 13cm, lanceolate, entire to serrulate, auriculate-amplexicaul, glab. to pubesc. beneath. Cap. several or numerous in a short infl.; ray flts 1–1.5cm, dark purple. Summer. N Amer. Z3.

A. mohavensis Cov. non Kuntze. = *Machaeranthera tortifolia.*

A. mongolicus = *Kalimeris mongolicus.*

A. multiflorus Ait. = *A. ericoides.*

A. myrsinoides Labill. = *Olearia myrsinoides.*

A. natalensis (Schultz-Bip.) Harv. = *Felicia rosulata.*

A. nebraskensis Rydb. = *A. praealtus* var. *nebraskensis.*

A. nemoralis Sol. Slender perenn. to 60cm. Lvs 5cm, linear to oblong, ± entire, often revolute, firm, scabrous above, minutely pubesc. beneath. Cap. solitary or several in corymb, slender-stalked; ray flts to 1.5cm, broad, pink to lilac-purple. Summer. E N Amer. Z2.

A. nernstii F. Muell. = *Olearia nernstii.*

A. novae-angliae L. NEW ENGLAND ASTER. Perenn. herb to 1.5m; st. stiffly hirsute. Lvs to 12cm, lanceolate to oblanceolate, entire, base cordate or auriculate. Cap. 4cm diam., in a crowded pan., ray flts deep purple; disc flts yellow. Autumn. E N Amer. 'Albus': fls white. 'Andenken an Alma Potschke' ('Alma Potschke'): to 1.2m, compact; fls fiery salmon-red. 'Andenken an Paul Gerber': fls deep claret. 'Barr's Blue': fls blue. 'Barr's Pink': fls pink. 'Barr's Violet': fls pale violet-blue. 'Dr Eckener': fls red washed purple. 'Guinton Menzies': fls red. 'Harrington's Pink': to 1.2m; fls crystal clear pink. 'Lye End Beauty': to 1.75m; fls pale plum. 'Lye End Companion': to 1.75m; fls purple. 'Mrs S.T. Wright': to 1.2m; fls pink-violet. 'Purple Cloud': fls purple. 'Red Cloud': to 1.4m; fls red. 'Rosa Sieger': to 1.3m; fls large, light pink. 'Roseus': fls pink. 'Röter Stern': fls pale pink. 'Rubinschatz': fls ruby red. 'Rudelsburg': to 1.2m; fls deep pink. 'September Ruby' ('September Rubin'): to 120cm, v. vigorous; fls rose-pink. 'Treasure': to 1.6m; fls light purple. 'Violetta': to 1.6m; fls rich purple. Z2.

A. novi-belgii L. MICHAELMAS DAISY. Perenn. herb to 120cm. Lvs oval-lanceolate to linear-lanceolate, base auriculate, remotely dentate. Cap. to 5cm diam., in a corymbose pan.; ray flts violet-blue; disc flts yellow. N Amer., widely nat. in Eur. Nearly 400 cvs in Europe and the US, differentiated by height and colour. The dwarfs, derived in part from *A. dumosus,* range from 15–50cm and from pink to light blue; they include the pink 'Heinz Richard', 'Pink Lace', 'Rosenwitchel' and 'Little Pink Beauty', the blue 'Audrey' and 'Remembrance', the popular purple 'Jenny' and the white 'Snow Cushion'; colours in the large type (mostly around 1m) range from white ('Mount Everest', 'Snowsprite'), pink ('Hilda Ballard', 'Lady Frances'), crimson ('Crimson Brocade') to powder and lavender blues ('Marie Ballard', 'Cloudy Blue', 'Blue Eyes') and purples ('Sailor Boy', 'Tovarich', 'Chequers'); 'Starlight' is bright red; others, such as 'Royal Velvet' are notable for their resistance to mildew or for the vigour of their growth ('Climax', 'Fellowship'). ssp. *tardiflorus* (L.) A.G. Jones. Lvs long-acuminate, serrate to subentire, semi-amplexicaul at base. Late summer–autumn. NE US, Canada. Z2.

A. oblongifolius Nutt. Perenn. to 1m; rhiz. creeping; st. brittle, gland., often scabrous. Lvs to 8cm, oblong or lanceolate-oblong, entire, ± auriculate-amplexicaul, scabrous. Cap. several to numerous; ray flts to 1.5cm, blue, purple or rose. Late summer–autumn. E to NC US. 'Roseus': rose pink. Z9.

A. occidentalis (Nutt.) Torr. & A. Gray Perenn. herb to 50cm with creeping rootstock; st. slender, tinged red. Lvs to 10cm, linear-oblanceolate, entire, lower lvs with winged, ciliate petioles. Cap. solitary or cymose; ray flts lavender or violet, to 10mm; disc flts yellow. Late summer–autumn. N Amer. (Alask. to Calif.) Z3.

A. *oolentangiensis* Riddell Perenn. to 1.5m. Lvs to 13cm, lanceolate or ovate, cordate or subcordate, entire to serrate, thick and firm, hispid above, pubesc. beneath. Cap. long-stalked in an open pan.; ray flts to 12mm, blue or pink. Summer–autumn. E N Amer. Z5.

A. *oreophilus* Franch. Perenn. herb to 50cm; st. tinged purple. Lvs to 12.5cm, oblanceolate to spathulate, entire to shallowly serrate, petiole narrowly winged, roughly pubesc. Cap. to 5cm diam., solitary or paired; ray flts pale lilac to blue-mauve. Early summer. W China. Z6.

A. *paniculatus* Lam. = A. *novi-belgii*.

A. *paniculatus* hort. non Lam. = A. *lanceolatus* ssp. *lanceolatus*.

A. *pappei* Harv. = Felicia amoena.

A. *patens* Ait. Perenn. to 1.5m with short caudex; st. slender, brittle, pubesc. Lvs to 15cm, broadly ovate to oblong, entire, base cordate and semi-amplexicaul, hairy or scabrous. Cap. few to numerous, in a spreading pan.; ray flts to 1.5cm, blue, occas. pink. Late summer–autumn. SE US. Z4.

A. *paternus* Cronq. Perenn. to 60cm with branched caudex; st. several. Lvs to 10cm, broadly oblanceolate to elliptic or sub-rotund, dentate, sometimes hairy. Cap. in small glomerules forming corymbs; ray flts to 8mm, white or pink. Summer. E US. Z5.

A. *pattersonii* A. Gray = Machaeranthera bigelovii.

A. *patulus* Lam. Perenn. to 1.2m. Lvs to 15cm, oval to oblong-lanceolate, entire, membranous, petioles winged. Cap. numerous, to 2.5cm diam., in pan.; flts violet-purple or white. Autumn. N Amer. Z5.

A. *paucicapitatus* Robinson. To 40cm, erect or ascending, gland. and thinly pilose. Lvs to 3.5cm, elliptic or elliptic-oblong, entire, narrowed to base, ± sessile. Cap. 2.5–4cm diam., 1–4 per st.; ray flts white turning pink. Late summer. NW US. Z6.

A. *pendulus* Ait. = A. *lateriflorus*.

A. *peregrinus* Pursh. Perenn. herb to 70cm. Lvs linear-oblanceolate to spathulate, tapered to petiole. Cap. solitary or few; ray flts to 2.5cm, white to purple. Summer. N Canada. Z3.

A. *petiolaris* Kuntze = Felicia petiolata.

A. *phlogopappa* Labill. = Olearia phlogopappa.

A. *piccolii* Hook. f. Perenn. herb to 1m, suberect. Lvs to 10cm, oblong, coarsely dentate. Cap. 3.5–5cm diam., in loose corymbs; ray flts lilac; disc flts yellow. China. Z6.

A. *pilosus* Willd. Perenn. herb to 1m. Lvs linear to linear-lanceolate, entire, slightly hirsute. Cap. many, in a wide pan. on long stalks with linear lvs; ray flts white becoming purple. N Amer., nat. Eur. var. *demotus* Blake. Lvs narrow-linear. E US. Z5.

A. *polyphyllus* Moench = A. *macrophyllus*.

A. *porteri* A. Gray. To 30cm, unbranched or branched above, glab. Lvs to 10cm, linear or linear-spathulate. Cap. numerous, broad, in a thyrse or corymb; ray flts 8mm, bright white, occas. becoming rosy-purple. C US. Z4.

A. *praealtus* Poir. Perenn. to 2m with a creeping rhiz.; st. stout, scaberulous. Lvs to 13cm, linear, ± entire; sessile or tapered to subpetiolate base, thick, firm, hairy, ± glab. Cap. in densely leafy infl.; ray flts to 1.5cm, indigo or white. Autumn. SE to C & SW US. var. *nebraskensis* (Britt.) Wiegand. St. and lower lvs minutely pubesc. Z4.

A. *prenanthoides* Muhlenb. Perenn. to 1m from long, creeping rhiz.; st. often flexuous. Lvs to 20cm, ovate to lanceolate, serrate, acuminate, petiole long, winged, auriculate-amplexicaul. Cap. several or numerous in open infl.; ray flts to 1.5cm, blue-mauve or white. Late summer–autumn. E & NC US. Z4.

A. *pseudamellus* Hook. = A. *indamellus*.

A. *ptarmicoides* (Nees) Torr. & A. Gray. Perenn. to 70cm with branched caudex; st. clad in persistent lf remains. Lvs 20cm, linear-oblanceolate, firm, glab. or scabrous. Cap. in an open corymb; ray flts to 9mm, white or pale yellow; disc flts white. Summer. Central N Amer. 'Major': to 40cm; white. Z3.

A. *punctatus* Walst. & Kit. = A. *sedifolius* ssp. *sedifolius*.

A. *puniceus* L. Perenn. to 1.3m; st. stout, maroon, hipsid. Lvs to 16cm, ovate-lanceolate to lanceolate, serrate, auriculate, scabrid. Cap. in a divaricately branched pan.; ray flts to 1.6cm, violet-blue, rose or white. Autumn. E N Amer., widely nat. Eur. Z4.

A. *purdomii* Hutch. = A. *flaccidus*.

A. *pyrenaeus* Desf. ex DC. Perenn. to 90cm; st. erect, stout. Lvs oblong-lanceolate, dentate, auriculate, setulose. Cap. solitary, few, or laxly corymbose; ray flts blue tinged lilac. Eur. (Pyren.) 'Lutetia': to 60cm; fls dark blue. Z6.

A. *radula* Ait. Perenn. to 1.2m; st. striate-angled. Lvs to 10cm, elliptic to oblong or lanceolate-oblong, ± serrate, scabrous

above, pubesc. beneath. Cap. in a short, broad corymb or solitary; ray flts to 1.5cm, violet. Summer. Vancouver to Labrador. Z5.

A. *ramosus* G. Don = A. *sedifolius*.

A. *reflexus* L. = Polyarrhena reflexa.

A. *retroflexus* Lindl. St. with short br. Lvs linear-lanceolate, entire, subglabrous to reduced, distant, linear-subulate, recurved. Cap. solitary, term.; involucral bracts squarrose, ray flts blue; disc flts white. N Amer. Z5.

A. *rotundifolius* Thunb. = Felicia amelloides.

A. *sagittifolius* Wedem. ex Willd. = A. *cordifolius* ssp. *sagittifolius*.

A. *salicifolius* Ait. = A. *praealtus*.

A. ×*salignus* Willd. (A. *lanceolatus* ×A. *novi-belgii*.) Perenn. to 1.2m. Lvs ovate-lanceolate to linear-lanceolate, remotely dentate. Cap. in a symmetric pan.; ray flts light violet-blue. Gdn origin, widely nat. Z2.

A. *salsuginosus* Less. = A. *sibiricus*.

A. *saundersii* Burgess = A. *ciliolatus*.

A. *savatieri* Mak. Erect perenn. herb. Lvs to 10cm, lanceolate, sharply dentate, petiolate to sessile. Cap. 3.5–5cm diam.; ray flts 15–18, broadly oblanceolate. Jap. Z7.

A. *scaber* Thunb. To 1.5m, stout, branched above. Lvs to 24cm, cordate to ovate-deltoid, shortly acuminate, 1–2-dentate, deep green above, chartaceous, scabrous, with narrowly winged petioles. Cap. to 2.5cm diam., in loose corymbs; ray flts white. Late summer–autumn. NE Asia Z7.

A. *scopulorum* A. Gray. To 12cm with compact, branched caudex; st. numerous, tufted, ascending, simple, densely leafy, hairy. Lvs to 1.4cm, elliptic to oblong or linear, sessile, callous-cusped, pale green, rigid, minutely hispid, with white margins. Cap. solitary, 1.5–2.5cm diam.; ray flts to 12mm, violet or purple. Summer. W US. Z7.

A. *sedifolius* L. Perenn., or ann., to 1.2m, erect, scabrid. Lvs narrowly linear to broadly lanceolate or elliptic, entire, sessile. Cap. corymbse, paniculate or solitary; ray flts sometimes few or 0, blue to lilac-pink. S, E & C Eur. 'Nanus': dwarf, to 45cm; fls profuse, with narrow clear blue ray flts, long-flowering, mid-summer–early autumn. 'Roseus': pink. ssp. *sedifolius*. Lvs glandular-punctate, scabrid. ssp. *canus* (Waldst. & Kit.) Merxm. Lvs grey, arachnoid, ± floccose. EC & SE Eur. ssp. *dracunculoides* (Lam.) Merxm. Lvs glandular-punctate to eglandular, scabrid to nearly smooth. S Russia to SE Rom. Z6.

A. *sericeus* Vent. Perenn. to 70cm from short, branched caudex; st. several, brittle, wiry. Lvs to 4cm, oblanceolate to lanceolate to oblong or elliptic, entire, stalked to sessile, thinly sericeous. Cap. in a widely branched corymb or pan., often in term. clusters; ray flts to 1.5cm, deep violet to rosy purple, or white. Late summer–autumn. C & E US. Z4.

A. *shortii* Lindl. Perenn. to 1.2m from short, branched caudex. Lvs to 15cm, lanceolate to narrowly ovate, entire or few-toothed, subcordate at base, petiolate, glab. or minutely scabrous above, hirtellous beneath. Cap. in an open pan.; ray flts to 1.5cm, blue, occas. rose or white. Late summer–autumn. SE US. Z4.

A. *sibiricus* L. Perenn., to 40cm, ascending, often tinged purple. Lvs ovate-lanceolate to oblong, serrate-dentate, lower often panduriform or tapered to petiole, upper semi-amplexicaul. Cap. solitary or in v. loose corymbs; ray flts violet. Arc. Asia. Z3.

A. *sikkimensis* Hook. f. & Thoms. To 1.2m, erect, much-branched, leafy, br. flexuous. Lvs to 17cm, lanceolate, entire or subserrate, membranous; petiole broad, short, clasping. Cap. to 2cm diam., numerous, stalked, corymbose; ray flts blue. Himal. Z6.

A. *simplex* Willd. = A. *lanceolatus* ssp. *simplex*.

A. *simplex* var. *ramossisimus* (Torr. & A. Gray) Cronq. = A. *lanceolatus* ssp. *lanceolatus*.

A. *sinensis* hort. = Callistephus chinensis.

A. *souliei* Franch. Erect perenn. to 30cm. Lvs to 11cm, rosulate or tufted, spathulate, oblanceolate or obovate, entire to obscurely crenate, pubesc. to glab. above, pilose beneath on veins. Cap. solitary, to 7.5cm diam.; ray flts blue or mauve; disc flts orange. Early summer. SW China. Z5.

A. *stenomeres* A. Gray. To 30cm; rootstock woody; st. numerous, tufted, simple, rigid, densely leafy. Lvs to 3cm, spathulate to linear, entire, sessile, callous-pinted, pale green, rigid, minutely hispid. Cap. solitary, 3–5cm diam., long-stalked; ray flts 1–2cm, violet. Summer. NW N Amer. Z4.

A. *stracheyi* Hook. f. Dwarf perenn., pubesc. or villous; st. creeping, often with leafy runners to 20cm. Lvs to 5cm, obovate-spathulate, remotely dentate. Cap. 1.5–4cm diam., solitary, scapose; ray flts slender, often recurved. Summer. Himal. Z6.

A. *subcoeruleus* S. Moore = A. *tongolensis*.

A. *subspicatus* Nees. To 1m; st. slender, br. ascending. Lvs to 13cm, lanceolate, serrate above, subglabrous, often slightly amplexicaul, lowest lvs narrowed to winged base. Cap. to 3cm diam., in a cymose pan.; ray flts violet. Summer. US (Alask. to Calif.) Z2.

A. tanacetifolius Kunth = *Machaeranthera tanacetifolia*.

A. tardiflorus L. = *A. novi-belgii* ssp. *tardiflorus*.

A. tataricus L. f.   Perenn. to 2m from stout caudex, coarse, rough-hairy. Lvs to 40cm, narrowly to broadly elliptic, strongly dentate, long-petiolate. Cap. in a flat-topped corymb; ray flts 1–2cm, purple or blue. Summer–autumn. Sib. Z3.

A. tenellus Thunb. = *Felicia tenella*.

A. tenuifolius hort. = *A. pilosus* var. *de motus*.

A. thomsonii C.B. Clarke.   To 90cm; st. erect, villous; br. slender, flexuous. Lvs to 10cm, ovate to elliptic, coarsely dentate, tapered to semi-amplexicaul base. Cap. 3.5–5cm diam., solitary, term.; ray flts purple. Summer. Pak. to Uttar Pradesh. Z7.

A. tibeticus Hook. f. = *A. flaccidus*.

A. tomentosus Wendl. = *Olearia tomentosa*.

A. tongolensis Franch.   Stoloniferous perenn. to 30cm. Lvs to 9cm, oblong or oblong-lanceolate, ± entire, sessile, often pub-esc. Cap. to 5cm diam., solitary; ray flts pale blue. Early summer. W China to India. 'Berggarten': fls lavender-blue with vivid orange discs. 'Lavender Star': to 30cm; fls lavender-blue. 'Leuchtenburg' ('Shining Mountain'): fls amethyst-violet with bright orange discs. 'Napsbury': to 25cm; fls dark blue with bright orange disc. 'Sternschnuppe': to 40cm; fls lilac. 'Summer Greeting': to 45cm, fls single, lilac-blue; long-flowering. 'Wartburgstern' ('Wartburg Star'): mound-forming to 100cm; fls deep violet-blue. Z8.

A. tortifolius A. Gray non Michx. = *Machaeranthera tortifolia*.

A. tortifolius var. *funereus* Jones. = *Machaeranthera tortifolia*.

A. tradescantii L. = *A. lateriflorus*.

A. tradescantii pro parte. hort. non L. = *A. lanceolatus*.

A. tricephalus Clarke.   Minutely pubesc.; st. erect, leafy. Basal lvs obovate-spathulate, petiolate; st. lvs oblong, semi-amplexicaul. Cap. 1–3; ray flts v. narrow. Himal. (Sikkim). Z7.

A. trinervis (Pers.) Nees = *A. sedifolius*.

A. trinervius Roxb. ex D. Don.   Erect herbaceous perenn. to 1m; st. slender, leafy. Lvs to 10cm, lanceolate to elliptic, irregularly dentate. Cap. to 2cm diam., in a lax, much-branched corymb; ray flts to 1cm, white. Summer. W Nepal to SW China. ssp. *ageratoides* var. *microcephalus* (Miq.) Mak. To 40cm; st. tufted. Lvs to 6cm, linear, mucronate, thinly setulose above. Ray flts pale blue. Autumn. Jap. Z7.

A. tripolinum L. = *A. tripolium*.

A. tripolium L.   Ann. or short-lived perenn., to 60cm; st. erect or ascending, often red. Lvs lanceolate to linear, ± succulent and terete. Cap. in corymbs or pan.; ray flts bright blue to lilac. Eur. Z6.

A. turbinellus Lindl.   Perenn. to 1.2m from short, branched caudex; st. several. Lvs to 10cm, firm, broadly linear to oblong or lanceolate-elliptic, scabrous-ciliate. Cap. long-stalked; ray flts to 12mm, violet. Autumn. EC US. 'Roseus': pink. Z5.

A. umbellatus Mill.   Perenn. to 2m. Lvs 16cm, elliptic to elliptic-ovate, acute or acuminate, entire, scabrous above, glab. to minutely pubesc. beneath. Cap. long-stalked in a dense corymb; ray flts to 1cm, white, disc flts yellow. Summer. E N Amer. Z3.

A. undulatus L.   Perenn. to 1.2m from branched caudex; st. densely pubesc. Lvs to 14cm, lanceolate-ovate to ovate, entire to dentate, scabrous to glab. above, sessile or with clasping petiole base. Cap. in an open pan.; ray flts to 1cm, blue or lilac. Late summer–autumn. E US. Z5.

A. vahlii (Gaudich.) Hook. & Arn.   Rhizomatous perenn. to 35cm. Lvs to 8cm, oblanceolate to elliptic-lanceolate, or linear, ciliate; petiole to 5cm, ciliate. Cap. 3.5–4cm diam., usually solitary or 2–3 together; ray flts pale purple, or white. Falkland Is., Tierra del Fuego. Z6.

A. ×versicolor Willd. (*A. laevis* ×*A. novi-belgii*.)   Perenn. to 2m; st. erect, often tinged purple. Lvs ovate, remotely dentate, sub-glaucous beneath. Cap. stalked; ray flts violet-blue. Gdn origin, widely nat. Z2.

A. vimineus auctt. non Lam. = *A. fragilis*.

A. vimineus Lam. = *A. lateriflorus*.

A. viscosus Labill. = *Olearia viscosa*.

A. yunnanensis Franch.   Perenn. to 60cm; st. darkly gland., base with fibrous lf remains. Lvs to 16cm, lanceolate or oblanceolate to ovate, entire to minutely dentate, base cordate sessile, pilose, gland. Cap. 6.5cm diam., usually 2–6, ray flts broad, blue-mauve. Early summer. W China to SE Tibet. Z5.

→*Boltonia* and *Chrysocoma*.

ASTERACEAE Dumort. See Compositae.

✗ **Asterago** Everett. = ✗ *Solidaster*.

Asteranthera Klotzsch & Hanst. Gesneriaceae. 1 everg., woody scrambler, to 4.5m. Lvs to 3cm in unequal pairs, ovate-orbicular

to ovate-elliptic, pilose, dentate. Fls axill., solitary or paired, on bracteate stalks to 5cm; cal. 5-lobed; cor. to 6cm, bright red, tube narrow, widening to 2-lipped limb, to 3cm across, upper lip 2-lobed, lower lip 3-lobed, marked yellow; sta. 4, exserted. Chile. Z9.

A. ovata Hanst.

Asteriscus Mill. Compositae. 4 ann. to perenn. herbs. St. leafy. Lvs entire or rarely dentate. Cap. radiate, term. on br.; ray flts cuneate, in 2 rows, apex 3-toothed, yellow; disc flts numerous, yellow. Medit., Cape Verde Is., Canary Is. Z7.

A. maritimus (L.) Less.   Hispid, perenn. to 25cm. St. woody, much-branched, ascending. Lvs oblanceolate to spathulate, hirsute. Cap. solitary; ray flts 30, to c1cm, orange-yellow. W Medit., S Port., Canary Is., Greece.

A. sericeus (L. f.) DC. = *Nauplius sericeus*.

→*Buphthalmum* and *Odontospermum*.

Asteromyrtus Schauer. Myrtaceae. 7 shrubs to trees close to *Melaleuca*. Infl. a several- to many-fld head, globose to oblong; fls sessile, subtended by a bract; sep. 5; pet. 5; sta. numerous, showy, fil. basally connate and aggregated into five groups or bundles, alternating with sep. New Guinea to N Aus. Z9.

A. magnifica (Specht) Craven.   Shrub to 3.5m. Bark flaky. Lvs 4–8cm, narrowly elliptical or narrowly ovate, acute, appressed pubesc. Infl. a many-fld dense globose term. head to 6cm diam.; pet. cream, 6.5–9mm; sta. cream to yellow, fil. 6–17mm. Aus. (N Territ.)

A. symphyocarpa (F. Muell.) Craven.   Shrub or small tree to 12m. Bark hard, fissured. Lvs 3–9cm, narrowly obovate to elliptical, obtuse, glab. Infl. a dense, globose 5–15-fld head; pet. yellow-orange, 2.7–3mm; sta. orange to yellow, sometimes turning red, fil. 10–15mm. New Guinea, N Aus.

→*Melaleuca* and *Sinoga*.

Asterotrichion Klotzsch. CURRAJONG. Malvaceae. 1 shrub or small tree; young growth covered with white or brown hairs. Lvs 5–15cm, lanceolate to ovate-lanceolate, acute, serrate. Fls in short rac. or pan.; epical. 0. ♂ with cal. 3–4mm, campanulate, stellate-pubescent; pet. 6–8mm, spreading, cream-white, ovate; sta. 15–20; ♀ with cal. 4mm, tubular, pet. slighty longer; sta. small and abortive. Tasm. Z9.

A. discolor (Hook.) Melville. CURRAJONG.

→*Plagianthus* and *Sida*.

Astilbe Buch.-Ham. ex D. Don. SPIRAEA (commercial name still occas. used). Saxifragaceae. 12 rhizomatous herbaceous perennials. Lvs 2–3 ternately compound stipulate, rachis swollen and conspicuously jointed at base and junction of petiolules; petiole glossy red-green. Fls small, numerous, in broadly pyramidal, branching erect pan.; pet. 0 or 5; sta. to 10. E Asia, N Amer.

A. ×arendsii Arends.   Hybrids involving *A. chinensis* var. *davidii*, *A. astilboides* ×*A. chinensis* var. *davidii*; fls in loose pan., sta. and pet. longer than sep. *A. chinensis* var. *davidii* ×*A. ×rosea*; fls purple-pink to rose or white. *A. chinensis* var. *davidii* ×*A. thunbergii*; erect to 1.75m; pan. large, nodding. 'Amethyst': to 1m; fls lilac tinted pink. 'Anita Pfeifer': to 80cm; fls salmon pink. 'Bergkristall': to 1m, white, midseason. 'Braut-schleier' ('Bridal Veil'): to 70cm; fls snow white, nodding, early. 'Bressingham Beauty': 1.2m, bright pink, midseason. 'Cattleya': to 1.2m, vigorous; fls lilac pink, late. 'Ceres': to 90cm; fls lilac. 'Diamant' ('Diamond'): to 90cm, white, early. 'Else Schluck': to 80cm, carmine, midseason. 'Fanal': to 80cm; lvs dark; fls crimson, early. 'Federsee': fls deep salmon pink. 'Feuer' ('Fire'): to 80cm; fls salmon, late. 'Gloria': to 70cm, deep pink, early flowering. 'Glut' ('Glow'): to 80cm; fls bright red, late. 'Granat': to 80cm; fls crimson. 'Grete Pungel': to 100cm; fls light pink, early. 'Hyazinth' ('Hyacinth'): to 1m; fls dark lilac-pink. 'Irrlicht': to 40cm, white, early flowering. 'Lilli Goos': to 80cm; lvs tinted brown or purple. 'Obergärtner Jürgens': to 60cm, fls carmine, early flowering. 'Rosa Pearl' ('Pink Pearl'): to 70cm; fls coral pink. 'Rotlicht': to 80cm, lvs darkly tinted, fls bright red, midseason. 'Salland': to 1.8m, carmine, midseason. 'Spartan': to 60cm, fls deep red, midseason. 'Spinell': to 90cm; fls salmon red. 'Venus': to 90cm; fls shell pink. 'Weisse Gloria': to 1m, white, late-flowering. Z6.

A. astilboides (Maxim.) E. Lemoine.   Plants offered under this name are usually a selection in *A. japonica* with large pan. (to 1.25m) of small, densely packed white fls. Summer. Jap. Z6.

A. biternata Vent. & Britt. FALSE GOATSBEARD.   To 1m. Lvs to 75cm wide; lfts to 12cm, ovate-cordate, serrate. Fls in spike-like rac., v. profuse, creamy-white to yellow; pet. ± 0. Early summer. N Amer. Z6.

A. chinensis (Maxim.) Franch.   To 7cm. Lfts elliptic-ovate, biserrate. Fls in short-stemmed pan. arising from tomentose axis, white, flushed rose or magenta, densely clustered. Summer. China, Jap. 'Finale': to 40cm; fls bright pink, held low. 'Intermezzo': to 60cm; fls salmon pink. 'Pumila': dwarf, to 25cm; lvs short-stemmed, tufted in appearance, red-green to maroon, pubesc.; fls pink-burgundy, borne densely on broad pan. appearing disproportionately large for plant. 'Serenade': to 40cm; fls pink-red, feathery. 'Spatsommer': to 40cm; fls pink. 'Veronica Klose': to 40cm; fls dark pink. var. *davidii* French. To 2m; lvs emerging bronze. Fls purple-pink packed in slender, tapering pan.; pet. narrow-acute, longer than sta.; fil. 10, purple, anth. blue-pink. Summer. China. var. *taguetii* (Lév.) Vilm. To 1m; fls purple tinted pink. 'Purpurkerze': to 1m; fls purple tinted pink. 'Purpurlanze' ('Purple Lance'): to 1m; st. tall, erect; fls rose to purple. 'Superba': to 1m; fls purple tinted pink. Z5.

A. ×*crispa* (Arends) Bergmans. 'Dagalet': a synonym of *Aruncus parvulus* 'Dagalet'. 'Liliput': low; fls salmon pink. 'Perkeo': lvs finely divided, bronze when young; fls dark pink. 'Peter Pan': fls deep pink. Z6.

A. davidii (Franch.) Henry = *A. chinensis* var. *davidii*.

A. decandra D. Don = *A. biternata*.

A. *glaberrima* Nak. 'Saxatilis': dwarf; st. to 8cm; lvs deep green, tinted red beneath, edges recurved; fls mauve, tipped white. Z6.

A. *grandis* Stapf ex Wils. To 2m. Lvs ternate; lfts ovate, to 6cm, biserrate, coarsely pubesc. on veins; petiole pilose. Fls in pyramidal pan. to 1.25m, white; pet. three times longer than sep.; sta. exceeding pet. Summer. China. Z6.

A. ×*hybrida* hort. ex Ievinya & Lusinya. Over 20 cvs and hybrids; height ranges from 60–180cm; lvs dark green; fls white to pink to purple. Over 20 cvs and hybrids: height ranges from 60–180cm; lvs dark green; fls white to pink to purple. 'Betsy Cuperus': large, to 1.1m; fls pale pink in arching sprays. 'Bressingham Beauty': to 120cm; fls bright pink. 'Drayton Glory': to 70cm; fls pale pink. 'Jo Ophurst': to 90cm; fls dark pink to red, in dense upright spikes. 'Salland': to 1.8m; st. dark; lvs dark green; fls rich purple. 'Snowdrift': to 60cm; fls white. Z6.

A. *japonica* Morr. & Decne. SPIRAEA. To 1m. Lfts narrow, ovate-lanceolate, basally cuneate, rigidly dentate. Fls white, small in erect pan.; pet. slender, obtuse, exceeding sta. Summer. Jap. 'Bremen': to 60cm; fls dark pink. 'Bonn': to 70cm; fls carmine. 'Deutschland': to 50cm; fls white. 'Emden': to 50cm; fls purple-pink. 'Europa': to 60cm; fls pale pink, in dense spikes. 'Koblenz': to 60cm; fls carmine. 'Köln': to 50cm; fls deep pink. 'Mainz': to 60cm; fls lilac. 'Montgomery': to 70cm, fls dark red. 'Möve': to 60cm, fls salmon pink. 'Red Sentinel': to 90cm; fls deep red, in loose spikes. 'Washington': to 60cm; fls white. Z5.

A. *koreana* Nak. To 60cm. Lvs pinnate or bipinnate; lfts lanceolate, tapering, finely dissected, fern-like. Fls rose-pink in bud, off-white when open, borne densely in lax, arching pan. Summer. Z7.

A. ×*lemoinei* E. Lemoine. A race of hybrids, mostly to 60cm. Fls in loose pan. to 50cm, white to rose-pink. Summer. Gdn origin. Z6.

A. *rivularis* Buch.-Ham. ex D. Don. To 1.5m. Lvs to 7cm, biternate; lfts ovate, dentate, woolly beneath. Fls yellow-white or dull red in large pan. with broad, well-defined br.; pet. 0. Late summer. Nepal. Z7.

A. ×*rosea* Van Waveren & Kruyff. (*A. chinensis* ×*A. japonica*.) Resembling *A. japonica* but with pink fls. Summer. Gdn origin. 'Peach Blossom': fls pale pink. 'Queen Alexandra': fls rose pink. Z6.

A. ×*rubella* hort. (Lemoine). (*A. chinensis* var. *davidii* ×*A.* ×*lemoinei*.) Resembles *A.* ×*lemoinei* but with fls rose in compact pan. Summer. Gdn origin. Z6.

A. sikokumontana Koidz. = *A. thunbergii* var. *sikokumontana*.

A. *simplicifolia* Mak. To 40cm. Lvs to 7cm, simple, ovate, lobed or sharply dissected, glossy, glab. Fls white, star-like, in narrow pan. Summer. Jap. The parent of many hybrids including 'Alba': fls white. 'Aphrodite': to 40cm; fls carmine. 'Atrorosea': to 50cm; fls dark salmon pink, in arching sprays. 'Bronce Elegans' ('Bronze Elegance'): to 30cm; fls clear pink tinted bronze, late-flowering. 'Carnea': to 30cm; fls flesh pink. 'Dunkellanchs': to 30cm; lvs tinted copper; fls flesh pink. 'Gnome': to 15cm; lvs deeply cut, red-green; fls pink in dense rac. 'Inshriach Pink': to 35cm; fls pink. 'Peter Barrow': fls white. 'Praecox': to 40cm; fls pink, early-flowering. 'Praecox Alba': to 30cm; fls white, early-flowering. 'Rosea': to 35cm; fls rose. 'Sprite': to 50cm; fls soft pink. 'Willy Buchanan': dwarf, to 20cm; fls pink. Z7.

A. taquetii (Lév.) Koidz. = *A. chinensis* var. *taquetii*.

A. *thunbergii* (Sieb. & Zucc.) Miq. To 50cm high. Lvs irregularly pinnate or bipinnate; lfts broadly ovate, olive green, sharply dentate, downy. Fls small, white turning pink, crowded in pyramidal pan.; peduncles red-green, puberulent. Early

summer. Jap. 'Moerheimii': to 90cm; fls white. 'Professor Van der Wielen': to 45cm; fls white. 'Straussenfeder' ('Ostrich Plume'): fls rich coral pink, in open plumes. var. *fujisanensis* (Nak.) Ohwi. Lvs smaller rigid; lfts biserrate. Pet equalling sta., short. var. *sikokumontana* (Koidz.) Morata. Lfts narrow-lanceolate, biserrate. Z7.

Astilboides (Hemsl.) Engl. Saxifragaceae. 1 perenn. herb to 1.5m. Lf blades shield-shaped, v. large, broadly lobed, dentate; petiole long. Flowering st. lower than topmost lvs; infl. resembling that of *Astilbe*; fls numerous, small, white. Z7.

A. tabularis (Hemsl.) Engl.

→*Rodgersia*.

Astragalus L. MILK VETCH. Leguminosae (Papilionoideae). *c*2000 ann. or perenn. herbs or shrubs. Lvs pinnate, rarely 1–3-foliolate, term. leaflet occas. reduced to a filiform appendage. Fls pea-like in spikes or rac. or in upper lf axils forming a compound infl., rarely solitary. Fr. a legume. N Temp. zone.

A. *adsurgens* Pall. Perenn. herb to 30cm, pubesc. Lvs to 17cm; lfts to 30cm, oblong to elliptic. Fls crowded in ascending, cylindrical, spike-like rac. to 13cm, maroon to dull grey-blue, rarely cream, standard to 4cm, erect, recurved. E Asia, W N Amer. Z6.

A. *agrestis* Douglas ex G. Don. Perenn. to 30cm. St. tufted. Lvs to 10cm; lfts to 2cm, 13–23, lanceolate to ovate. Fls crowded in short ovoid to subglobose heads, maroon, pale lilac or cream, standard to 2cm, recurved, emarginate, wings tipped white. Summer. US. Z7.

A. *alopecuroides* L. Perenn. herb to 75cm. St. erect, hairy. Lvs to 20cm; lfts in 12–15 pairs, ovate-oblong. Fls in globose heads; pale yellow, standard to 3cm, broadly ovate. Summer. Spain, S Fr. Z6.

A. *alpinus* L. ALPINE MILK VETCH. Perenn. herb to 30cm. St. tufted, often decumbent. Lvs to 14cm; lfts to 2.5cm, in to 27 pairs, ovate to suborbicular, obtuse. Infl. dense, stalk erect to 17cm; fls pendent; standard to 1.5cm, ovate-cuneate, emarginate, light mauve, tipped purple, keel tip spotted maroon, wings pale purple. Summer. Mts of N Eur., Asia, N Amer. Z5.

A. *angustifolius* Lam. Cushion-forming shrub to 50cm; st. armed. Lvs to 6cm; lfts in 5–12 pairs, elliptic to ovate, obtuse, sparsely hairy. Rac. to 14-fld, crowded; fls light purple to cream-yellow or dull-white, standard to 2cm; emarginate. Summer. Greece, Asia Minor. Z8.

A. *aristatus* L'Hérit. Subshrub to 15cm, woody, white-lanate. Lvs to 6cm, clustered; lfts in 6–10 pairs, oblong to linear-oblong, grey-green, mucronate, white-lanate. Fls in capitate rac., white to pale pink or pale purple. S Eur.

A. *barrii* Barneby. Cushion-forming shrub to 50cm across, with lustrous, silver-grey hairs. Lvs to 5cm; lfts to 1cm, linear-lanceolate to elliptic-ovate. Rac. to 22cm; fls 2–4, purple, with a darker stripe in standard fold, standard to 2cm, obovate. Summer. US (S Dak.). Z8.

A. *bisulcatus* (Hook.) A. Gray. Perenn. herb. St. to 70cm, often prostrate. Lvs to 12cm; lfts 7–35, ovate, obtuse, to 3cm. Rac. to 80-fld, ovoid, to 25cm, pendulous; cal. red to purple, hairy, becoming papery; cor. white, cream, dull yellow, purple-marked or bright violet, standard to 2cm, oblanceolate to oval-obovate. Summer. US. Z8.

A. *boeticus* L. Ann. herb erect to 60cm. Lvs to 20cm; lfts in 15 pairs, narrowly oblong to ovate, truncate or emarginate, sparsely hairy beneath. Rac. densely 5–15-fld; fls yellow, standard to 1.5cm. Summer. Eur. Z8.

A. campestris L. = *Oxytropis campestris*.

A. *canadensis* L. Perenn. herb to 1m, mostly erect. Lvs to 35cm; lfts to 0.5cm, 7–35, broadly lanceolate to elliptic. Fls crowded in a cylindric spike to 16cm, pale green, cream or green tinged with mauve, standard to 2cm, oblanceolate, emarginate. Summer. US. Z8.

A. caryocarus Ker.-Gawl. = *A. crassicarpus*.

A. *centralpinus* Braun-Blanquet. Perenn. herb to 1m. St. erect, hairy. Lvs to 30cm; lfts in 20–30 pairs, elliptic to ovate-lanceolate, sparsely hairy beneath. Fls in sessile, ovoid rac., golden-yellow, standard to 2cm. Summer. Alps, S Bulg. Z6.

A. *coccineus* Brandg. Tufted perenn., densely tomentose. Lvs to 10cm, radical; lfts obovate-cuneate to elliptic; stipules persistent, forming a crown. Rac. to 2.5cm, loosely 5–10-fld; fls scarlet, standard to 4cm, recurved, broadly oblanceolate. Summer S US. Z8.

A. *crassicarpus* Nutt. GROUND PLUM. Perenn. herb to 40cm, upbesc. St. ± prostrate. Lvs to 15cm; lfts to 2.5cm, 15–33, broadly ovate to linear-elliptic. Rac. to 7.5cm, densely 20–35-fld; fls purple, lilac, cream or pale green, standard to 3cm, obovate-cuneate, keel tipped pink or purple. Fr. to 4cm, globose to obovoid, brown-red. US Rocky Mts. Z7.

A. danicus Retz. PURPLE MILK VETCH. Perenn. herb to 30cm. St. erect. Lvs to 10cm; lfts 12–26, obovate, obtuse or emarginate, sparsely hairy. Rac. densely fld, globose to ovoid; fls purple or violet, standard to 2cm. Spring–summer. S & W Eur. Z5.

A. depressus L. Perenn. herb. Stemless or with st. to 10cm, prostrate, pubesc. Lvs to 30cm; lfts to 30, obovate to obcordate, hairy beneath. Rac. oblong to 14-fld; fls cream or blue-violet, standard to 1cm, emarginate. Spring. S Eur. (mts). Z6.

A. echinus DC. Perenn. herb to 50cm, spiny, spines black with age. Lfts in 5–7 pairs, oblanceolate, adpressed hairy, mucronate. Fls creamy-yellow, standard panduriform. Summer. Syr.

A. eriocarpus Bieb. Perenn. herb erect to 30cm. Lvs to 20cm; lfts to 2cm, 20–36, elliptic, sparsely sericeous. Rac. densely 20–35-fld, cylindric; fls pale green to pale violet, standard to 2cm, ovate. Summer. Iran. Z9.

A. exscapus L. Perenn. herb. St. v. short. Lvs to 30cm, erect; lfts to 3cm, 20–60, elliptic to ovate, hairy. Rac. capitate, densely 3–10-fld; fls yellow, standard to 3cm. Summer. C Eur. Z5.

A. foetidus Vill. = *Oxytropis foetida*.

A. frigidus (L.) A. Gray. Perenn. sparsely branched herb to 30cm. Lvs to 10cm; lfts to 3.5cm, to 7–13 pairs, ovate-oblong, ciliate. Rac. to 8cm, loosely 5–11-fld erect; fls cream, standard 2cm, spathulate. Summer. N Amer. Z5.

A. galegiformis L. Sparsely hairy, erect perenn. herb, 0.5–1m. Lvs 10cm; lfts in 8–15 pairs, elliptic to linear-oblong, mucronate, grey beneath. Fls drooping, in loose 12–20-fld rac. Asia Minor, Cauc.

A. gerardianus Graham = *Caragana gerardiana*.

A. gilviflorus E. Sheldon. Tufted erenn. herb to 10cm, densely silver-hairy. Lvs to 10cm; lfts 0.5–4cm, 3, obovate-cuneate to rhombic-ovate. Fls 1–3, white, rarely maroon, standard to 3cm, oblanceolate, emarginate. N Amer. Z6.

A. glareosus Douglas ex Hook. = *A. purshii*.

A. glycyphyllos L. WILD LIQUORICE. Perenn. herb; st. to 1.5m, procumbent. Lvs to 20cm; lfts 8–16, elliptic, obtuse, minutely hairy beneath. Fls pale yellow, standard to 1.5cm, emarginate. Summer. Eur. Z3.

A. goniatus Nutt. = *A. agrestis*.

A. lapponicus (Wahlenb.) Burnat = *Oxytropis lapponica*.

A. leontinus Wulf. Perenn. herb to 20cm, sometime stemless. Lvs to 12cm; lfts to 1.5cm, 5–10 pairs, ovate, obtuse or truncate, hairy. Rac. ovoid, densely to 20-fld; fls purple to pale mauve, standard to 2cm. Alps, Nw Balk. Z5.

A. lusitanicus Lam. Perenn. herb to 60cm. St. erect, minutely white-hiary. Lvs to 20cm; lfts to 3.5cm, to 20, oblong-lanceolate, mucronate, adpressed hairy beneath. Rac. densely to 20-fld, oblong; fls white, standard to 3cm. Summer. Port., SW Spain, S Greece, Turk. Z9.

A. massiliensis (Mill.) Lam. Tufted woody-based perenn. to 30cm. Lvs to 7cm, spiny at apex; lfts to 2.5cm, 12–24, oblong or elliptic, obtuse or truncate, mucronate, densely pubesc. Rac. densely 3–8-fld, globose, hairy; fls white, standard to 2cm. Summer. SW Eur. Z6.

A. mexicanus DC. = *A. crassicarpus var. berlandieri*.

A. missouriensis Nutt. Tufted perenn. to 1.5m. St. often prostrate, strigose. Lvs to 14cm; lfts to 2cm, 5–21, elliptic to narrowly obovate. Rac. to 4cm, somewhat umbellate, to 15-fld; fls pink-purple, rarely white, standard to 2.5cm, rhombic-ovate to obovate-cuneate. Spring–summer. N Amer. Z7.

A. monspessulanus L. Stemless grey-hairy, woody-based, perenn. herb. Lvs to 20cm, in basal rosettes, persisting when dead; lfts to 1cm, 14–40, suborbicular to oblong, obtuse, hairy beneath. Rac. ovoid or oblong, to 30-fld; fls purple or red, rarely white, standard to 3cm. Summer. S Eur. Z6.

A. montanus L. = *Oxytropis jacquinii*.

A. narbonensis Gouan = *A. alopecuroides*.

A. nuttallii (Torr. & A. Gray) Howell. Robust perenn. herb to 1m, white-villous to sparsely hairy. St. ascending or prostrate, forming mats. Lvs to 17cm; lfts to 3cm, 21–45, obovate to broadly oblanceolate, mucronate. Rac. densely 15–125-fld, erect; fls pale green to white, occas. tiped and marked lilac, standard to 1.5cm, rhombic-spathulate, emarginate. Summer. Calif. Z9.

A. onobrychis L. Perenn. woody-based herb to 60cm, procumbent and ascending. Lvs to 10cm; lfts to 2cm, 16–30, narrowly elliptic, adpressed-hairy. Rac. 20-fld, oblong; fls pale or dark purple, cream or pale yellow, standard to 3cm. Summer. Eur. Z5.

A. penduliflorus Lam. Perenn. herb to 50cm; st. erect, pubesc. below. Lvs to 10cm; lfts to 0.5cm, in 7–15 pairs, elliptic to oblong-lanceolate, sparsely hairy. Rac. to 4cm, densely to 20-fld; fls yellow; standard to 1cm, obtuse, recurved. N Eur. (mts). Z5.

A. pilosus L. = *Oxytropis pilosa*.

A. purshii Douglas ex Hook. Mat-forming perenn. herb, villous,

with interspersed silky hairs. Lvs to 15cm; lfts to 2cm, 5–21, suborbicular to narrowly elliptic. Rac. composed of umbellate clusters of 2–11 fls; peduncle to 20cm; fls white, cream, pale pink or purple, standard to 2.5cm, recurved, emarginate, keel spotted purple at apex. Summer. Rocky Mts. Z4.

A. sempervirens Lam. Perenn. herb to 40cm. St. procumbent or ascending. Lvs to 7cm; lfts in 4–10 pairs, linear to obovate. Rac. 3–8-fld; fls white to mauve, rarely yellow. S Eur. (mts). Z5.

A. sempervirens Lam. = *A. aristatus*.

A. sericeus Lam. = *Oxytropis halleri*.

A. shinanensis Ohwi. Perenn. herb to 30cm. St. simple, erect. Lvs to 8cm; lfts in 6–9 pairs, obovate, obtuse, ± glab. Rac. densely 5–10-fld; fls cream-white. Jap. Z7.

A. shiroumaensis Mak. Perenn. herb to 30cm. St. erect, black-hairy. Lvs to 9cm; lfts to 2cm, 5–8, narrowly oblong to lanceolate, emarginate. Rac. axillary, densely 7–15-fld; fls white, occas. mauve toward apex, standard to 1.5cm, obovate-elliptic. Jap. Z8.

A. sirinicus Ten. Differs from *A. massiliensis* in lfts subacute; fls to 15 per rac., yellow, marked with mauve. C Medit., SW Balk. Z9.

A. spatulatus E. Sheldon. Mat-forming perenn. herb to 1.5cm. Lvs much reduced, oblanceolate to spathulate, mucronate, occas. bearing 1–2 pairs of oblanceolate, involute. Rac. capitate, loosely 1–11-fld; fls bright magenta, rarely cream, standard to 1cm, obovate, emarginate, clawed. US. Z7.

A. succulentus Richardson = *A. crassicarpus*.

A. tragacantha L. pro parte = *A. massiliensis*.

A. trichopodus (Nutt.) A. Gray. Perenn. herb to 1m, finely hairy. Lvs to 16cm; lfts to 2.5cm, to 40, ovate to lanceolate; obtuse, mucronate or emarginate. Rac. densely to 50-fld; fls cream, pale green, rarely cream or white marked with purple, standard to 2cm, oblanceolate, emarginate, clawed. US. Z9.

A. tridactylicus A. Gray. ± stemless, mat-forming, perenn. herb to 1.5cm. Lvs to 6cm; lfts to 2cm, obovate to oblanceolate. Rac. loosely 2–10-fld; silver-pilose; recurved, pink-purple, standard to 1cm, obovate-cunate. US Rocky Mts. Z7.

A. velutinus Sieber ex Steud. = *Oxytropis halleri* ssp. *velutina*.

Astranthium Nutt. Compositae. 10 ann., bienn. or perenn. herbs. St. striate, strigose. Cap. radiate, secondary heads much smaller, nodding, in lf axils, long-pedunculate. S US and Mex. Z7.

A. integrifolium (Michx.) Nutt. Ann., to 45cm. St. erect, densely pubesc. below. Basal lvs 1.8–8cm, spathulate, obtuse or mucronate, base long-attenuate, ciliate, st. lvs smaller, spathulate to linear-lanceolate. Cap. 1 to many; peduncles to 20cm; ray flts white, or lavender beneath and pale above. Early spring–early summer. C US.

→*Bellis*.

Astrantia L. MASTERWORT. Umbelliferae. 10 perenn. herbs. Lvs palmately partite or lobed, glab. Fls long-stalked (sterile) or subsessile (fertile) in simple umbels subtended by showy, papery bracts, usually toothed and netted. Eur. to Asia. Z6.

A. bavarica F.W. Schultz. To 60cm. Lvs 5-lobed; seg. lanceolate-cuneate, toothed. Infl. bracts lanceolate, entire, green tinged white or purple, exceeding umbel rays. E Alps

A. biebersteinii Trautv. = *A. major*.

A. carinthiaca Hoppe ex Mart. & Koch = *A. major*.

A. carniolica Wulf. Differs from *A. bavarica* in lf seg. ovate and involucre not exceeding umbel rays. SE Alps. 'Rubra': infl. silver tinted pink.

A. carniolica hort. non Wulf. = *A. major*.

A. gracilis Bartling = *A. carniolica*.

A. helleborifolia Salisb. = *A. maxima*.

A. heterophylla Willd. = *A. maxima*.

A. major L. GREATER MASTERWORT. To 80cm. Lvs 3–7-partite; seg. oblanceolate to obovate, toothed. Infl. bracts lanceolate, fused, toothed, white netted green or rose, equalling or exceeding umbel rays. C & E Eur. 'Alba': infl. white. 'Barrister': habit compact; lvs veined white. 'Sunningdale Variegated' ('Variegata'): to 75cm; lvs large, pointed, marked with cream and yellow; involucre white flushed pale pink. ssp. *involucrata* Koch. Involucre large, dissected. 'Margery Fish' ('Shaggy'): to 75cm; involucre large, shaggy, pink-white. 'Rosea': to 75cm; infl. pink to rose. 'Rosensymphonie': infl. silver-rose. 'Rubra': to 50cm; infl. tinted claret.

A. maxima Pall. To 90cm. Lvs 3–5-partite, seg. elliptic-ovate, serrulate to crenulate. Infl. bracts elliptic to ovate, fused, ciliate-serrate, shell pink, equalling or exceeding umbel rays. S Eur., Cauc. 'Alba': bracts large, white. 'Hadspen Blood': a hybrid with *A. major*; infl. large, dark pink.

A. minor L. To 40cm. Lvs 7-partite; seg. lanceolate to obovate, serrate. Infl. bracts lanceolate, white sometimes tinged red, exceeding umbel rays. Pyren., SW Alps, Apennines.

A. *pauciflora* Bertol. Differs from *A. minor* in lvs 5–7-partite; seg. linear-lanceolate, toothed. Umbels larger, clustered, bracts white. It.

A. *trifida* Hoffm. = *A. major*.

Astridia Dinter & Schwantes. Aizoaceae. 10 succulent shrubs. Lvs erect or spreading, long-persistent, subfalcate, narrowing toward obtuse or rounded tip. Fls mostly solitary; pedicel short with 2 bracts. S Afr., Nam. Z9.

A. *hallii* L. Bol. Shrubby, to 30cm; lvs and young st. grey-green, velvety. Lvs 50–80×2–3×2–3mm, lanceolate, acute to tapered, acutely carinate, widest at midpoint. Fls to 7.5cm diam., glassy white. Nam.

A. *herrei* L. Bol. Robust, to 30cm. Lvs 75×10×14mm, thumb-shaped or 57×7–9×16mm, falcate, tip rounded, lower surface rounded, rough grey tinged purple, margins and keel line lined red when young. Fls 3–5cm diam., red, paler on the outside. W Cape.

A. *longifolia* (L. Bol.) L. Bol. Erect subshrub to 24cm. Lvs 90×7–10×16mm, falcate, keel and margins indistinct, somewhat compressed laterally, blue-green, velvety. Fls 5.3cm diam., scarlet, white-centred. W Cape.

A. *velutina* (Dinter) Dinter & Schwantes. To 30cm. Lvs lunate, margins rounded, mucronate with a rounded keel, minutely white-papillose, appearing velvety, 2.5–3.5cm×1.5cm× 11–21mm. Fls 4cm diam., pure white or violet-pink. W Cape, Nam.

→*Ruschia*.

Astroloba Uitew. Liliaceae (Aloeaceae). 4 small everg. succulents similar to *Haworthia*. Lvs clothing st. in 5 spiralling rows. S Afr. (Cape Prov.). Z9.

A. *aspera* Uitew. = *A. muricata*.

A. *bicarinata* Uitew. = *A. bullulata*.

A. *bullulata* (Jacq.) Uitew. St. 15–30cm, erect to prostrate. Lvs 2.5–4×1.5–2.5cm, triangular-lanceolate, grey-green to olive green, covered in green tubercles often forming crossbands, tip brown; fls 9–12mm, cream to light green, midveins darker, tipped yellow to cream.

A. *congesta* Uitew. = *A. spiralis* ssp. *foliolosa*.

A. *deltoidea* (Haw.) Uitew. = *A. spiralis* ssp. *foliolosa*.

A. *dodsoniana* Uitew. = *A. herrei* 'Dodsonia'.

A. *egregia* Uitew. = *A. bullulata*.

A. *foliolosa* Uitew. = *A. spiralis* ssp. *foliolosa*.

A. *hallii* hort. = *A. bullulata*.

A. *herrei* Uitew. St. to 20cm, erect to ascending. Lvs in 2–2.5×1–1.5cm, ovate to orbicular-ovate, deep green to lighter blue-green, glossy, dark-striate beneath, crenulate, pungent. Fls 7–10mm, hexagonal, white, midveins green, angles inflated, undulating, tipped yellow. 'Dodsonia': more vigorous, to 25cm; lvs pale green-green to glaucous white, inconspicuously veined.

A. *muricata* Groenew. St. 10–20cm, erect to sprawling. Lvs 12–25×12–15cm, stiff, pale green to red-green, tubercles numerous, to 0.5mm diam., tip often recurved. Fls 7–12mm, cream to pale green, midveins darker tipped cream to white.

A. *pentagona* Uitew. = *A. spiralis* ssp. *foliolosa* 'Pentagona'.

A. *skinneri* Uitew. = ×*Astroworthia skinneri*.

A. *spiralis* (L.) Uitew. St. 10–20cm, erect. Lvs 2–3×1–1.5cm, ovate to triangular-lanceolate, grey-green to blue-green, tubercles 0, crenulate, pungent. Fls 7–13mm, hexagonal to cylindrical, white, midveins pale green, angles swollen, tipped yellow. ssp. *foliolosa* (Haw.) Groenew. Perianth tube yellow, not inflated or roughened; tep. tips white. 'Pentagona': lvs in almost straight rows, not spiralling, occas. with scattered paler spots; perianth tube yellow.

A. *turgida* Jacobs. = *A. spiralis* ssp. *foliolosa*.

→*Apicra*.

Astroloma R. Br. Epacridaceae. 18 low, erect or prostrate, much-branched everg. shrubs of heath-like habit. Lvs crowded. Fls solitary, bracts grading into sep.; cor. tube elongate, lobes valvate, usually bearded. Fr. a drupe. Aus., Tasm. Z8.

A. *denticulatum* R. Br. = *A. humifusum*.

A. *humifusum* (Cav.) R. Br. CRANBERRY HEATH; NATIVE CRANBERRY. Small, intricately branched, prostrate or ascending shrub, to 30cm. Lvs 0.6–1.8cm, linear-elliptic, pungent. Fls to 1cm scarlet. S & W Aus., Tasm.

A. *humifusum* var. *denticulatum* (R. Br.) J.M. Black = *A. humifusum*.

A. *longiflorum* Sonder. Small, prostrate or spreading shrub. Lvs to 1.3m, narrow-lanceolate, cuspidate. Fls to 2cm, blood red. Aus.

A. *pinifolium* (R. Br.) Benth. PINE HEATH. Much branched dwarf shrub, to 90cm. Lvs to 3cm, linear, pungent, revolute. Fls to 2cm, red or lime, base yellow, lobes green. SW Aus., Tasm.

→*Stenanthera*, *Styphelia* and *Ventenatia*.

Astrophytum Lem. Cactaceae. BISHOP'S HAT. 4 hemispheric, globose or shortly columnar cacti; st. simple, usually covered with minute, chalky scales; ribs 4–10; areoles large; spines present or 0. Fls apical, shortly funnelform. E Mex., S Tex. Z9.

A. *asterias* (Karw. ex Zucc.) Lem. SEA URCHIN; SILVER DOLLAR CACTUS. St. ± flat or hemispheric, 4–15cm diam.; ribs 6–10, broad and low; spines 0. Fls $c3×4–6.5$cm; yellow with orange or red throat, or tinged red. Summer. NE Mex., Tex. Z9.

A. *capricorne* (A. Dietr.) Britt. & Rose. St. globose to columnar, to 25×15cm; ribs 7–9, acute; spines 1–20, to 7cm or more, flattened, curved and twisted. Fls $c7×6–10$cm, yellow with red throat. Summer. N Mex. Z7.

A. *coahuilense* (H. Möller) Kayser = *A. myriostigma*.

A. *myriostigma* Lem. St. globose or shortly columnar, to 30×10–20cm; scales usually dense, rarely 0 (cv Nudum); ribs (3–)4–5 or more (5–10 in var. *tulense* (Kayser) Borg), acute to rounded; spines 0, except in seedlings. Fls $c4–6$cm in diameter, yellow 9with red to orange throat in var. *coahuilense* (Kayser) Borg). Summer. NE Mex. Z7.

A. *ornatum* (DC.) Britt. & Rose. St. globose to columnar, eventually 1m×20–30cm; scales forming stripes on ribs in young plants; ribs 6–8; spines 5–11, to 3cm, straight. Fls $c7×7–10$cm, pale to deep yellow. Summer. CE Mex. Z7.

A. *senile* Frič. = *A. capricorne*.

→*Echinocactus*.

×**Astroworthia** G. Rowley. (*Astroloba* ×*Haworthia*.) Liliaceae (Aloeaceae). 2 naturally occurring hybrids. Compact, everg. succulents with the habit of *Haworthia*, but with fls lacking strongly bilabiate perianth. S Afr. Z9.

×*A.* *skinneri* (A. Berger) Pilb. (*A. muricata* ×*Haworthia margaritifera*.) St. 15–30cm, erect to prostrate. Lvs 3–5×1.5–2.5cm, ovate-lanceolate, acute, firm, dark green, with a double keel, with conspicuous, warty tubercles and white spots, margins thickened and rough. Fls tubular, cream to pale green with darker midveins. Cape Prov.

→*Astroloba*.

Asyneuma Griseb. & Schenk. Campanulaceae. *c*50 perenn. or bienn. herbs, close to *Phyteuma*. Lvs simple. Infl. simple or branched, a lax spike or pan.; cal. lacking interlobal appendages; cor. divided nearly to base, lilac to indigo. S Eur. to E Asia. Z5.

A. *campanuloides* (Bieb.) Bornm. To 60cm. Infl. spicate; fls dark violet to blue. Cauc.

A. *canescens* (Waldst. & Kit.) Griseb. & Schenk. To 80cm. Infl. paniculate; fls pale lilac. S Eur., Balk. to Greece.

A. *limoniifolium* (L.) Janch. To 1m. Infl. paniculate or spicate; fls violet. S Eur., Balk. to Turk.

A. *lobelioides* (Willd.) Hand.-Mazz. To 60cm. Short-pubesc. Infl. a lax spike or pan.; fls lilac to pale blue. Asia Minor.

A. *michauxioides* (Boiss.) Damboldt. To 1m. Short-pubesc. to dense hispid. Fls pendulous, pale to azure blue. Turk.

→*Phyteuma*.

Asystasia Bl. Acanthaceae. 70 perenn. herbs and shrubs. Lvs opp., simple. Fls in axil. and terminal bracteate rac. or spikes; cor. tubular-campanulate, 5-lobed. Trop. of the E hemis.

A. *bella* hort. = *Mackaya bella*.

A. *coromandeliana* Nees = *A. gangetica*.

A. *gangetica* (L.) Anderson. Downy perenn. St. to 130cm, procumbent. Lvs ovate. Fls to 3cm, lavender-pink in secund rac. to 10cm.

A. *violacea* Dalz. = *A. gangetica*.

Ataenidia Gagnep. Marantaceae. 1 rhizomatous herb, erect and branching. Lf blades 40×20cm, elliptic, acuminate, green above, red-violet beneath; petiole to 10cm+. Infl. branching, v. dense, lat.; bracts imbricate; cor. to 20mm, white to rose; outer staminodes 2, petaloid, inner staminode hooded. Trop. Afr. to Angola. Z10.

A. *conferta* (Benth.) Milne-Redh.

A. *gabonensis* Gagnep. = *A. conferta*.

→*Calathea* and *Phrynium*.

Atalantia Corr. Serr.

A. *buxifolia* (Poir.) Oliv. = *Severinia buxifolia*.

A. *hindsii* (Champ.) Oliv. ex Benth. = *Fortunella hindsii*.

Atamasco Lily *Zephyranthes atamasca*.

Ateje De Costa *Bourreria succulenta*.

Athamanta L. Umbelliferae. 15 downy perenn. herbs. Lvs 2–5-pinnate, seg. narrow. Fls white or yellow in involucrate umbels. Medit., Eurasia. Z6.

A. cretensis L. CANDY CARROT. To 60cm. Lvs 3–5-pinnate; seg. to 0.7cm, grey-green, filiform. Umbels 6–15-rayed; fls white or red-tinged. SE Spain and E Fr., to C Balk.

A. haynaldii Borb. & Üchtr. = *A. turbith* ssp. *haynaldii*.

A. mathioli Wulf. = *A. turbith*.

A. turbith (L.) Brot. To 50cm. Lvs 2–4-pinnate; seg. bright green, to 3.5cm, linear. Umbels c25-rayed; fls white. S Carpath., Balk. Penins. to NE It. ssp. *haynaldii* (Borb. & Üchtr.) Tutin. Lf seg. to 2cm, shallow-linear. Umbels 15–25-rayed. W Balk., Albania.

Athanasia L. Compositae. 35 often aromatic shrubs and sub-shrubs. Lvs crowded on st., simple or pinnate, entire or dentate. Cap. discoid, often numerous, in corymbs; involucre cylindrical to subspherical; phyllaries in many imbricate series; flts tubular, yellow, lobes often spreading. Trop. & S Afr. Z9.

A. capitata (L.) L. Subshrub, to 80cm. St. diffusely branched, villous. Lvs to 3cm, oblong to obovate, entire or slightly dentate, often villous. Cap. campanulate, phyllaries villous. Cape Prov.

A. crithmifolia L. Shrub to 1m. St. densely branched, silky at first. Lvs to 6cm, 3–5-lobed, lobes linear, mucronate. Cap. ovoid; phyllaries glab. Cape Prov.

A. parviflora L. = *Hymenolepis parviflora*.

A. pubescens (L.) = *Hymenolepis parviflora*.

Atherosperma Labill. Monimiaceae. 1 large everg. tree. Lvs 5–10cm, lanceolate, toothed or entire, glaucous, downy-white beneath. Fls solitary, to 2.5cm diam.; pedicels recurved to 1.25cm, subtended by 2 bracts; tep. cream, 8–10, in 2 ranks; sta. 10–18, fil. with 2 long appendages; ♀ fls densely silky with staminodes. Aus. (Vict., NSW, Tasm.). Z9.

A. moschatum Labill.

A. novae-zealandiae Hook. f. = *Laurelia novae-zealandiae*.

Atherton Kauri *Agathis microstachya*.
Atherton Palm *Laccospadix*.
Athl *Tamarix aphylla*.

Athrixia Ker-Gawl. Compositae. 14 low ann. or perenn. herbs and subshrubs. Lvs usually narrow, entire, hairy. Cap. radiate, usually solitary. Trop. & S Afr., Madag. Z9.

A. capensis Ker-Gawl. Subshrub to 50cm. Lvs to 2cm, narrow-linear, acute, often revolute, shiny, glandular-hairy above, tomentose beneath. Flts white, pink or purple. Early summer. S Afr.

Athrotaxis D. Don. Cupressaceae. 3 coniferous everg. trees to 30m. Bark red- to grey-brown, fissured, flaking in long shreds. Lvs spirally arranged, subulate or scale-like, adpressed to shoot or spreading, glossy deep green, margins often translucent. Cones globose or ovoid, 1–3cm across, green, becoming orange or brown; cone scales united to bract scales; thinly woody, mucronate. Tasm. Z8.

A. cupressoides D. Don. SMOOTH TASMANIAN CEDAR. To 16m; crown ovoid. Lvs to 0.4cm, adpressed, scale-like, oblong, obtuse, keeled, dark green; margins translucent, minutely dentate. Cones 7–10mm diam.; scales abruptly acute.

A. ×laxifolia Hook. (*A. cupressoides* × *A. selaginoides*.) SUMMIT CEDAR. To 20m; crown broadly conical, domed. Lvs 0.5cm, ovate-lanceolate, loosely adpressed, slightly spreading, apices incurved, glossy yellow-green becoming dark green, margin translucent. Cone scales with reflexed apical spine.

A. selaginoides D. Don. KING WILLIAM PINE. To 30m; crown conical. Lvs 1–1.5cm, subulate, lanceolate-ovate, convex, spreading, outer surface bright green, inner with 2 blue-white stomatal bands. Cones 20–30mm diam.; scales with recurved spine at apex.

Athyrium Roth. Woodsiaceae. c100 terrestrial or rupestral ferns. Rhiz. short and erect and, occas., arborescent, to creeping; scales entire to toothed, brown to black. Fronds stipitate, uniform, 1–3-pinnate to -pinnatifid, or, rarely, simple, herbaceous, leathery to membranous, usually glab.; rachis and costa grooved above; stipes tufted, occas. papillose to spinulose from bases of decid. scales. Temp. and trop. regions.

A. accidens (Bl.) Milde. = *Diplazium proliferum*.

A. acrostichoides (Sw.) Diels = *Deparia acrostichoides*.

A. alpestre (Hoppe) Ryl. = *A. distentifolium*.

A. angustifolium (Michx.) Milde = *A. pycnocarpon*.

A. angustum (Willd.) Presl = *A. filix-femina* ssp. *angustum*.

A. asplenioides (Michx.) D.C. Eaton = *A. filix-femina* ssp. *asple-nioides*.

A. atkinsonii Bedd. Terrestrial Fronds to 1m., 3-pinnate to -pinnatifid, ovate to deltoid, thin-textured, herbaceous, glab. above, glandular-pubesc. below, pinnae to 40×20cm, petiolate, ovate, apex narrowly acute, pinnules petiolate, seg. to

25×15mm, short-petiolate, oblong, apex obtuse, base cuneate, margin toothed; stipes to 40cm, base scaly, red-brown. Himal. to China, Taiwan, Jap. Z7.

A. australe (R. Br.) Presl = *Diplazium australe*.

A. bantamense (Bl.) Milde = *Diplazium bantamense*.

A. bourgaei Fourn. = *A. filix-femina*.

A. commixtum Koidz. = *A. vidalii*.

A. crenatum (Sommerf.) Rupr. = *Diplazium sibiricum*.

A. decurrenti-alatum (Hook.) Copel. Terrestrial. Rhiz. creeping; scales ovate, entire, brown. Fronds to 45×30cm, 2-pinnate to -pinnatifid, ovate or deltoid to oblong, glab., pinnae to 15×5cm, 6–9 pairs, sessile or subsessile, subopposite to opposite, spreading, lowest falcate, lanceolate, apex narrowly acute, pinnules to 35×10mm, ovate to oblong, apex subacute or obtuse, base decurrent, margin entire to toothed or somewhat notched; stipes to 40cm, somewhat scaly, straw-coloured or green to purple, brown. China, Taiwan, Korea, Jap. Z7.

A. deltoidofrons Mak. Terrestrial. Fronds to 70×50cm, 3-pinnate, ovate to deltoid, apex narrowly acute, herbaceous, glab., pinnae to 30×7cm, 9–12 pairs, short-petiolate, spreading, apex narrowly acute, pinnules to 40×12mm, subsessile to short-petiolate, ovate or lanceolate to deltoid, apex acute to narrowly acute, seg. to 7mm, ovate to oblong, apex subuacute or obtuse, margin toothed; stipes to 60cm, base scaly, straw-coloured. Jap. Z7.

A. dilatatum (Bl.) Milde = *Diplazium dilatatum*.

A. distentifolium Tausch & Opiz. ALPINE LADY FERN. Terrestrial Rhiz. short and erect or ascending to creeping. Fronds to 40×20cm, 2–3-pinnate, erect to arched, ovate or lanceolate to linear or oblong, apex and base attenuate, herbaceous, initially sparsely scaly, pinnae to 10×3cm, 8–10 pairs, sessile, sub-opposite, ascending to spreading, oblong to lanceolate, apex narrowly acute, pinnules to 20×8mm, sessile ovate to oblong, apex acute, base cuneate, seg. elliptic, apex obtuse, margin toothed; rachis and costa initially scaly below; stipes to 30cm, scaly, green to red. N Amer., Eur. to Asia. Z5.

A. dubium (D. Don) Ohwi = *Diplazium lanceum*.

A. dubium var. *crenatum* (Mak.) Ohwi = *Diplazium tomitaroa-num*.

A. esculentum (Retz.) Copel. = *Diplazium esculentum*.

A. filix-femina (L.) Roth. LADY FERN. Terrestrial. Rhiz. to 7mm wide, short and suberect or ascending to creeping; scales lanceolate, brown. Fronds to 1m×35cm, 2–3-pinnate to -pinnatifid, suberect or ascending to spreading or arched, ovate, lanceolate or elliptic to linear, apex and base attenuate to acute, thin-textured and leathery, glab., pinnae to 15×4cm, lowest re-duced and deflexed, short-petiolate, ascending to spreading, horizontal to falcate, elliptic to lanceolate, apex attenuate to narrowly acute, pinnules to 2cm, sessile to short-petiolate, to 6mm distant, lanceolate to oblong, apex acute or obtuse, base decurrent, margin of seg. toothed to notched; stipes to 30cm, glab. to sparsely scaly at base, green or straw-coloured to purple. N temp.

'Angustato-cruciatum': 70–80cm; pinnae short, hence narrow cruciate form, tip of frond crested. 'Capitatum' ('Coronatum'): 70–100cm; frond apex alone crested, pinnae not crested. 'Clarissi-mum': two v. similar forms known (Jones and Bolton): the archetypal graceful uncrested fern, to 100cm; pinnules narrow and long giving the frond an airy appearance; v. rare. 'Clarissimum Cristatum Garnett' ('Fimbriatum Cristatum Garnett'): 80cm; resembling a crested form of 'Clarissimum'; v. rare. 'Congestu-mum': 30–40cm; congested, character often combined with crest-ing. 'Cristatum': 70–100cm; frond and pinnae crested. 'Cruciatum': 30–50cm; pinnae forked at point of attachment to midrib, resembling series of crosses along midrib, usually crested. 'Corymbiferum': 70–100cm; frond apex divided in several planes. 'Fieldii': 80–100cm; a cruciate var. with pinnae of normal length. 'Frizelliae' (TATTING FERN): 10–20cm; pinnae reduced to balls almong midrib; crested and branched forms are in cult. – beware of cruciate forms being offered under this name. 'Gemmatum': 50cm; frond and pinnae carrying dense corymbose crests; rare. 'Grandiceps': 30–70cm; term. crest wider than frond. 'Kalothrix': 20–30cm; a delicate pale green uncrested var., each pinna seg. ending in a hairlike point; long thought extinct but recently re-raised; v. beautiful, v. rare. 'Minutissimum': 10–30cm, a dwarf form. 'Multifidum': 50–70cm; divisions of crests long and slender. 'Nudicaule Cristatum': 20–30cm; large 3-dimensional crests carried on rachis with all, or most, pinnae missing. 'Percristatum': 40–80cm; frond apex, pinnae and pinnules crested. 'Plumosum': a section including some of the best forms of lady fern (see also 'Kalothrix' above); several new forms raised in the 1980s but not in general cult. 'Plumosum Axminster': 60–80cm; one of the original plumosums, a finely cut form, uncrested. 'Plumosum Penny': 60–70cm; a newish form named in the 1950s, a large un-crested plumosum.

C.T. Druery, a prominent fern collector and writer at the turn of the century, raised several named varieties of great gdn value, three of which are still known in cult.: 'Plumosum Druery': 50cm, the finest most feathery form, raised from 'Plumosum Superbum Druery', uncrested, rare; 'Plumosum Superbum Druery': 40cm, flat crested, plumose, percristate form raised from the now extinct 'Plumosum Elegans Parsons', rare; 'Plumosum Superbum Dissectum Druery': 50cm, a dissected uncrested form, often bulbiferous on underside, raised from 'Plumosum Superbum Druery', rare. 'Setigerum': 30–60cm; pinnule seg. narrow with pointed teeth or bristles – crested forms are common. 'Uncoglomeratum': 10–20cm; progeny of 'Acrocladon' with finer ultimate divisions; described by Druery as 'resembling a green coral', v. attractive and v. rare. 'Victoriae': percruciate (i.e. pinnae and pinnules br. at base to form crosses); the original clone found in 1861 still exists in cult. but is v. rare; spore progeny is common, smaller and usually only cruciate, not percruciate. 'Victoriae': of nursery catalogues is usually 'Cruciatum'.

ssp. *angustum* Willd. NORTHERN LADY FERN. Rhiz. to 35mm wide, erect to ascending; scales to 15mm, persistent, rough. Fronds to 75×30cm, rhomboid, apex acute, base attenuate to acute or obtuse; stipes to 35cm. NE N Amer. ssp. *asplenioides* (Michx.) Farw. SOUTHERN LADY FERN. Rhiz. to 3cm wide, ascending to creeping; scales decid. Fronds to 50×25cm, lanceolate, apex acute, base truncate; stipes to 50cm. S & E N Amer. Z2.

A. filix-femina var. *deltoideum* Mak. = *A. deltoidofrons*.

A. filix-femina var. *michauxii* (Spreng.) Farw. = *A. filix-femina* ssp. *angustum*.

A. flaccidum C. Chr. = *A. yokoscense*.

A. frangulum Tag. Terrestrial. Rhiz. short and erect. Fronds to 40×25cm, 2-pinnate, ovate to oblong, apex narrowly acute, thin-textured, pinnae to 25×10mm, sessile to short-petiolate, ovate or lanceolate to oblong, apex acute or obtuse, base obliquely cuneate, margin of seg. toothed; costa sparsely bristly above; stipes to 35cm, base somewhat scaly, purple. Jap. Z7.

A. goeringianum (Kunze) T.V. Moore. = *A. nipponicum*.

A. iseanum var. *fragile* Tag. = *A. frangulum*.

A. japonicum (Thunb.) Copel. = *Deparia petersenii*.

A. lanceum (Thunb.) Milde, non Moore = *Diplazium lanceum*.

A. laxum Pappe & Rawson = *A. scandicinum*.

A. matsumurae C. Chr. = *A. nipponicum*.

A. maximum (D. Don) Copel. = *Diplazium dilatatum*.

A. microsorum Mak. = *A. atkinsonii*.

A. monticola Rosenst. = *A. atkinsonii*.

A. multifidum Rosenst. = *A. deltoidofrons*.

A. nipponicum (Mett.) Hance. Terrestrial. Rhiz. to 3mm wide, short and ascending to creeping; scales lanceolate, apex hairtipped, red-brown. Fronds to 35×25cm or more, 2–3-pinnate to -pinnatifid at apex, ascending to arched, ovate to lanceolate, apex narrowly acute to caudate, pinnae to 9×3cm, 6–10 pairs, petiolate, opposite to alt., ascending, oblique, distant, lanceolate to oblong, apex narrowly acute, pinnules to 30×12mm, sessile to short-petiolate, ovate or lanceolate to oblong, apex acute to narrowly acute or obtuse, base decurrent, margin subentire to notched or lobed; rachis minutely pubesc. above, purple; stipes to 40cm, sparsely scaly, lustrous, straw-coloured. E Asia. 'Pictum': PAINTED LADY FERN. 20–30cm; a form with purple-red rachis suffusing into a silver grey and aquamarine green lamina; crested forms are known. Z4.

A. otophorum (Miq.) Koidz. Terrestrial. Rhiz. short and erect. Fronds to 45×30cm, 2-pinnate, ovate to oblong, apex narrowly acute to caudate, glab., pinnae to 7×4cm, 8–10 pairs, sessile or subsessile, spreading, lanceolate, apex narrowly acute, pinnules to 25×12mm, sessile, ovate, apex acute or obtuse, base cuneate and acroscopically auriculate, margin toothed to somewhat lobed; stipes to 30cm, base scaly, straw-coloured to purple. E Asia. Z7.

A. paucifrons C. Chr. = *A. filix-femina*.

A. pycnocarpon (Spreng.) Tidestr. GLADE FERN; SILVERY SPLEENWORT; NARROW-LEAVED SPLEENWORT. Terrestrial. Rhiz. to 5mm wide, short-creeping; scales lanceolate, brown. Fronds to 75×20cm, pinnate, lanceolate to oblong, apex acute to narrowly acute, base acute, pinnae to 13×3cm, lowest reduced, 20–30 pairs, subsessile, opposite or alt., lanceolate to linear or oblong, apex narrowly acute, base truncate, margin subentire to somewhat notched; rachis ± glab., green; stipes to 30cm, base scaly, straw-coloured to chestnut. N Amer. Z7.

A. rigescens Mak. = *A. otophorum*.

A. scandicinum (Willd.) Presl. Terrestrial. Rhiz. to 5mm wide, short and erect; scales to 7mm, lanceolate to oblong, margin entire, brown. Fronds to 60×35cm, 3-pinnate-pinnatifid, arched, ovate to deltoid, apex narrowly acute to caudate, glab., pinnae to 20×6cm, lowest somewhat reduced, lanceolate to deltoid, apex narrowly acute to caudate, pinnules unequal, lanceolate, seg. to 4mm wide, ovate to oblong, margin toothed to notched; rachis winged above, glab. to minutely pubesc., brown; stipes to 55cm, glab. to sparsely scaly, green to brown. Trop. E Afr. Z10.

A. schimperi Moug. ex Fée. Terrestrial or rupestral. Rhiz. to 6mm wide, short-creeping; scales to 7mm, lanceolate, apex narrowly acute, red-brown. Fronds to 70×28cm, 3-pinnate to -pinnatifid, erect, lanceolate or deltoid to oblong, apex acute to narrowly acute, membranous, glab., pinnae to 16×5cm, petiolate, lowest somewhat reduced and distant, approximate, ovate to lanceolate, apex attenuate, pinnules approximate, seg. approximate, oblong, margin toothed to notched; rachis winged above, glab. to minutely pubesc., brown; stipes to 45cm, base scaly, brown. Trop. E Afr. Z10.

A. solutum Rosenst., non C. Chr. = *A. deltoidofrons*.

A. spinulosum (Maxim.) Milde. Terrestrial. Rhiz. short-creeping. Fronds to 30×35cm, 3-pinnate, deltoid, apex narrowly acute, glab., pinnae to 25×12cm, upper reduced, 5–6 pairs, short-petiolate, ovate to lanceolate, apex narrowly acute, pinnules to 10×5mm, sessile, ovate to oblong, apex obtuse, seg. to 4×2mm, 6–9, rhomboid to oblong, apex mucronate, margin toothed; rachis minutely pubesc. above; stipes to 50cm, distant, somewhat scaly, straw-coloured. C Asia to China, Korea, Jap. Z7.

A. thelypteroides (Michx.) Desv. = *Deparia acrostichoides*.

A. uropteron (Miq.) C. Chr. = *A. nipponicum*.

A. vidalii (Franch. & Savat.) Nak. Terrestrial. Rhiz. short and erect to ascending; scales persistent, lanceolate, apex attenuate, brown. Fronds to 35×25cm, 2-pinnate, ovate to deltoid, apex narrowly acute, pinnae to 15×5cm, lowest reduced, subsessile to short-petiolate, ascending, lanceolate, apex narrowly acute, pinnules to 30×13mm, sessile, oblique, ovate or deltoid to lanceolate, apex acute to narrowly acute, base truncate to cuneate and adnate, seg. elliptic to oblong, apex obtuse, margin toothed to somewhat notched; rachis and costa grooved above and spinulose; stipes to 25cm, base scaly, straw-coloured. E Asia. Z7.

A. yokoscense (Franch. & Savat.) C. Chr. Terrestrial fern. Rhiz. short and erect. Fronds to 40×20cm, 2-pinnate, ovate to oblong, apex narrowly acute, base attenuate, glab., pinnae to 50×25mm, 10–15 pairs, lanceolate, apex narrowly acute, pinnules to 12×5mm, ovate to oblong, apex acute or obtuse, base adnate, margin toothed to somewhat lobed; stipes to 25cm, base scaly, straw-coloured. E Asia. Z7.

→*Aspidium*, *Asplenium*, *Cystopteris*, *Diplazium* and *Gymnogramma*.

Atlantic Ivy *Hedera hibernica*.
Atlas Cedar *Cedrus libani*.
Atlas Fescue *Festuca mairei*.

Atragene L.
A. alpina L. = *Clematis alpina*.
A. americana Sims = *Clematis verticillaris*.
A. columbiana Nutt. = *Clematis columbiana*.
A. sibirica L. = *Clematis alpina* var. *sibirica*.
A. zeylanica L. = *Naravelia zeylanica*.

Atraphaxis L. Polygonaceae. 18 decid., often spiny shrubs or subshrubs. Lvs alt., with a pair of pale, membranous, sheathing stipules. Fls in term. rac.; sep. 4 or 5, petal-like, small, inner 2 or 3 sep. persistent, maintaining their colour and enlarging to surround fr. Fr. a 2- or 3-angled achene. SE Eur., N Afr., W & C Asia.

A. billardieri Jaub. & Spach. Spiny shrub, 30–75cm, semi-prostrate. Lvs 0.3×0.8cm, narrowly oval to lanceolate, acute, green, glab., entire. Fls in rounded clusters, inner sep. ovate or cordate, to 5mm, rose-pink. Fr. 3-angled. Summer. SE Eur. to W Asia. Z6.

A. buxifolia (Bieb.) Jaub. & Spach = *A. caucasica*.

A. caucasica (Hoffm.) Pavlov. Shrub 30–80cm, with slender, spreading br., occas. spiny, bark red-grey. Lvs 1.5–1.7cm, broad obovate or elliptic, obtuse or short-acuminate, dull green, glab., undulate-crispate. Fls in rac. to 4cm, inner sep. pink-red, 5–6mm. Fr. 3-angled. Early summer. Cauc. Z6.

A. frutescens (L.) K. Koch. Erect shrub to 70cm, mostly spineless, br. slender, bark white-grey. Lvs lanceolate to oblong-ovate, mucronate, 1–2.5cm, grey-green, wavy or bluntly toothed. Fls in loose term. rac., 2.5–8.5cm, inner sep. 4–5mm, rose-pink. Fr. 3-angled. Late summer. S Eur. to C Asia and S Russia. Z6.

A. lanceolata (Bieb.) Meissn. = *A. frutescens*.

A. muschketowii Krasn. Loose straggling shrub, to 2.4m, spineless, bark deeply furrowed, red-brown. Lvs oblong to elliptic, 3–6cm, light green, glab., crispate. Fls to 7mm diam., in 3–6cm rac., white or pale pink. Fr. 3-angled. Late spring–early summer. C Asia. Z5.

A. spinosa L. Low sprawling shrub to 60cm, resembles *A. frutescens* but br. slender and often spiny. Lvs ovate or elliptic, 0.7–1cm. Fls 8mm diam., in axill. rac.; sep. pink with white margins. Fr. 2-angled. Summer. SE Eur., W & C Asia to S Russia. Z6.

A. tournefortii Jaub. & Spach. Shrub, 30–80cm, br. spreading, unarmed, bark yellow-grey. Lvs 1.2–2.5cm, oblong-elliptic, green, undulate-crispate. Fls in rounded, term. rac., white or tinged pink; inner sep. 5–6mm. Fr. 3-angled. Late spring–early summer. Near East. Z9.

Atriplex L. ORACH; SALTBUSH. Chenopodiaceae. *c*100 shrubs or ann. herbs, usually grey or white in appearance, farinose. St. often striped. Lvs flat, toothed or lobed. Fls small; ♂ with 5 perianth seg. and 5 sta., ♀ perianth, usually replaced by 2 large persistent bracteoles. Temp. and subtrop. regions.

A. californica Moq. Taprooted, prostrate perenn. St. divaricate, 20–50cm, white-farinose, glabrescent. Lvs 0.5–1.8cm, lanceolate to oblanceolate, acute, grey-farinose. Fls ♂ and ♀ in axill. clusters or ♂ in term. spike. Summer. Coastal Calif. & Baja Calif. Z8.

A. canescens (Pursh) Nutt. Erect, divaricate shrub to 2m. Br. grey-farinose. Lvs 1.5–5cm, linear-spathulate to narrow-oblong, hoary, revolute. ♂ fls in terminal pan. of dense spikes, ♀ fls in dense, leafy, bracteate spikes and pan. Summer. W N Amer. Z7.

A. confertifolia (Torr. & Frém.) S. Wats. Erect, rounded, spiny shrub to 1m. Br. rigid; branchlest farinose. Lvs farinose, round-ovate or obovate to elliptic, obtuse, entire, 1–2cm. ♂ fls in upper axils, almost spicate, ♀ fls 1 to few in upper axils. Summer. W US, Mex. Z7.

A. halimus L. TREE PURSLANE. Erect, loosely spreading, white-farinose shrub to 2.5m. Lvs to 6cm, ovate-rhombic or deltate, leathery, entire or dentate, silvery-white. Cymes remote in paniculate infl. Summer. S Eur. (saltmarshes). Z8.

A. hortensis L. ORACH; MOUNTAIN SPINACH. Erect ann. to 2.5m. Lvs cordate- or hastate-triangular, shallow-dentate to entire, 10cm+, slightly farinose, green or often purple-brown. Infl. term., spicate. Summer. Asia, nat. C & S Eur. and N Amer. var. *rubra* L. Lvs purple-red or crimson. 'Cupreatorosea': st. and lvs red with coppery lustre. 'Rosea': lvs paler red, veins and petioles dark red. Z6.

A. hortensis var. *atrosanguinea* hort. ex L.H. Bail. = *A. hortensis* var. *rubra*.

A. hymenelytra (Torr.) S. Wats. DESERT HOLLY. Low, compact shrub, white-farinose, 20–100cm. Lvs 1.5–3.5cm, rounded to rhombic, obtuse at apex, rounded to subcordate at base, dentate, silvery. ♂ fls in short leafy pan., ♀ fls in short dense spikes. Spring. W US. Z8.

A. lentiformis (Torr.) S. Wats. QUAIL BUSH; WHITE THISTLE. Erect, spreading shrub, 1–3m. Lvs 1.5–4cm, silvery-farinose, oblong to ovate-deltoid, entire. Fls in term. pan. Summer. SW US, N Mex. ssp. *breweri* (S. Wats.) A.W. Hill & Clements. Lvs longer and broader. Fruiting bracteoles longer (4–7mm) convex, entire or undulate, not crenulate. Calif. Z8.

A. mexicana hort. = *Chenopodium botrys*.

A. nummularia Lindl. Erect shrub, grey-farinose, to 3.5m. Twigs striate. Lvs 3–6.5cm, rounded to obtuse, slightly entire to serrate. ♂ fls in short spikes forming large pan., ♀ fls in dense pan. Spring–summer. Aus., nat. Calif. Z8.

A. nuttallii S. Wats. Much-branched subshrub to 1m. St. stout, erect or decumbent. Lvs linear- to oblong-spathulate, entire, 2–4cm, farinose. Fls in axillary clusters or interrupted paniculate spikes. Summer. W US. Z6.

Atropa L. Solanaceae. 4 highly toxic perenn. herbs, to 2m. St. erect, branching. Fls axill., solitary; cal. campanulate, lobes 5, spreading; cor. tubular-campanulate to funnel-shaped, 5-lobed. Fr. a 2-chambered berry. W Eur. to Himal. Z7.

A. belladonna L. DEADLY NIGHTSHADE; BELLADONNA. To 1.5m+. St. sap red. Lvs ovate to elliptic, to 15cm. Fls pendent; cor. to 3cm, lobes tinged purple brown to green. Fr. to 2cm diam., glossy purple-black. Summer–autumn. Eurasia, Medit. 'Lutea': fls yellow green.

Atropanthe Pascher. Solanaceae. 1 glab., erect herb to 1m. Lvs to 15cm, ovate to elliptic, acuminate, dark green, short-stalked. Fls solitary, axill., to 5cm, nodding; cal. globose, to 0.5cm, teeth triangular; cor. funnel-shaped, lobes 5 subequal recurved, yellow-green, netted green within, shiny. China. Z6.

A. sinensis (Hemsl.) Pascher.
→*Scopolia*.

Atsuba-giboshi *Hosta crassifolia*.

Attalea Kunth. Palmae. 22 palms. St. underground or erect, becoming bare and scarred. Lvs pinnate, marcescent, sheath thick, fibrous; pinnae crowded, linear-lanceolate, single-fold,

regularly spaced or in groups, apices notched, margins covered with scales, midrib prominent. Panama to Braz. and Peru. Z10.

A. amygdalina HBK. Lvs to 5.4m; petiole rusty-scaly; pinnae to 90×3cm, to 100 each side. Braz.

A. funifera Mart. ex Spreng. PISSABA PALM; BAHIA PIASSAVA; BAHIA COQUILLA. St. to 10m×30cm. Lvs equalling st., deep green; petiole with long, pendent black fibres; pinnae to 60×5cm, in clusters of 3–5. Braz.

Aubergine *Solanum melongena*.
Aubretia *Aubrieta*.

Aubrieta Adans. Cruciferae. AUBRETIA. 12 cushion or mat-forming everg. herbs. Lvs obovate-oblong, usually hairy, small, entire to angular-toothed. Rac. lax, term.; sep. 4, pouched at base; pet. 4, clawed. Eur. to C Asia.

A. canescens (Boiss.) Bornm. Lvs grey at first, usually round-obovate, entire or with small teeth; pet. 11–19mm, lilac-violet. Asia Minor. ssp. *cilicica* (Boiss.) Cullen. 10–25cm. Turk. Z5.

A. cilicica Boiss. = *A. canescens* ssp. *cilicica*.

A. columnae Guss. Lvs small, spathulate, entire. Pet. 11–18mm, lilac-red to purple. N Medit., It. to Rom. ssp. *croatica* (Schott, Nyman & Kotschy) Mattf. Tufted. Lvs broad-ovate. Albania, Balk., Rom. ssp. *italica* (Boiss.) Mattf. Creeping. Lvs broad-ovate. It., Sicily. Z6.

A. croatica Schott, Nyman & Kotschy. = *A. columnae* ssp. *croatica*.

A. ×cultorum Bergmans. Complex gdn hybrids, often of obscure parentage, probably involving *A. deltoidea*; habit mat-forming, from 8–15cm tall, to 60cm diam.; fls single to double, 1–3cm diam., white through pink to deep purple. 'Barker's Double': fls double, large, purple tinted rose, long lasting. 'Berach's White': fls ivory. 'Blue Emperor': fls deep violet blue, early. 'Bressingham Pink': fls double, large, pink, in groups of to 6. 'Dr Mules': fls rich violet blue. 'Godstone' and 'Gurgedyke': fls large, bright purple. 'Lavender Queen': fls large, pale purple. 'Leichtlinii': fls pink, profuse. 'Mrs Lloyd Edwards': fls lilac. 'Neuling': fls light indigo, early. 'Purple Cascade': fls brilliant purple. 'Red Cascade' and 'Magician': fls deep magenta. 'Riverslea': fls large, pink tinted mauve. 'Royal Cascade': habit trailing, fls rose. 'Schloss Eckeberg': densely cushion-forming, fls blue-indigo. 'Red Carpet': fls strong red. 'Rosengarten': fls purple-pink. 'Rotkäppehen': fls carmine. There are over 10 seed races, notable are Giant Superbissima Mixed (fls purple, rose and red), Monarch (habit trailing; fls large, wide colour range).

A. deltoidea (L.) DC. Lvs rhomboid-ovoid, entire or with 1–3 pairs of large teeth. Pet. 12–28mm, lilac to red-purple. Aegean, nat. SW Eur. Large numbers of cvs have been raised, including double-fld forms and forms differing in fl. colour and habit. 'Argenteovariegata': lvs edged silver; fls purple. 'Aureovariegata': lvs edged gold; fls mauve. 'Tauricola': fls deep purple flushed blue. var. *microphylla* Boiss. Densely cushion-forming, lvs v. small. Z7.

A. deltoidea var. *cilicica* Boiss. = *A. canescens* ssp. *cilicica*.

A. erubescens Griseb. Lvs oblong-spathulate, sparsely hairy, entire or with one pair of small teeth. Pet. 8–11mm, white becoming lilac-pink. N Greece. Z6.

A. glabrescens Turrill. Lvs elliptic-lanceolate, glab., entire or with 1 pair of teeth. Pet. 13–15.5m, violet. Summer. Greece. Z7.

A. gracilis Sprun. ex Boiss. Lvs linear-lanceolate or oblong-ovate, stellate and simple-pubesc. entire to sparsely toothed. Pet. 10–20mm, purple. Summer. Balk. Penins. Z7.

A. italica Boiss. = *A. columnae* ssp. *italica*.

A. kotschyi Boiss. & Hohen. = *A. parviflora*.

A. libanotica Boiss. Lvs obovate-spathulate to long-spathulate, grey-hairy, rarely glab., entire to toothed. Pet. purple. Summer. Leb. Z8.

A. olympica Boiss. Lvs spathulate or obovate-oblong, entire, occas. toothed. Pet. violet, 11–19mm. Turk. Z8.

A. parviflora Boiss. Lvs 1–3.5cm, triangular-spathulate, 2–6-toothed. Pet. to 8mm, white to pale lilac. Syr., Turk., Iran. Z8.

A. pinardii Boiss. Lvs linear-oblong or linear-spathulate, entire. Pet. 18–19mm, purple. Turk. Z8.

Aucuba Thunb. Cornaceae (Aucubaceae). 3 everg. shrubs and small trees. St. green. Lvs coriaceous, glossy. Fls unisexual, small, 4-merous in cymose pan., star-shaped, maroon to green. Fr. an ovoid berry. E Asia. Z7.

A. chinensis Benth. Shrub to 3m. Lvs to 20cm, broad-lanceolate to oval; irregularly and rather bluntly toothed to entire, veins impressed, matt green above, blue-green beneath. Fr. red. SW China. Z8.

A. himalaica Hook. Tree to 10m. Lvs 45cm, lanceolate, coriaceous, finely serrate in basal half; petiole to 4cm, suffused purple. Fr. orange. E Himal., Sikkim. Z6.

A. japonica Thunb. SPOTTED LAUREL. Shrub to 4m. Lvs to 20cm, elliptic to narrow-ovate, ± serrate. Fls purple-maroon, ♂ with cream anth. Fr. scarlet, rarely yellow (f. *luteocarpa*), or white (f. *leucocarpa*). Late spring. China, Taiwan, S Jap. 'Bicolor': lvs green, central spot yellow, marginal teeth large. 'Crotonoides': ♀; lvs mottled gold. 'Crotonifolia': ♀ lvs dense, finely speckled and blotched gold. 'Dentata': lvs undulate, teeth at apex 1–2. 'Fructu-albo': lvs sparsely blotched and spotted pale green and old; fr. yellow-white. 'Gold Dust': lvs speckled gold; fr. red. 'Hillieri': lvs large, deep green; fr. carmine. 'Lance Leaf': ♀; lvs lanceolate, bright green. 'Nana': dwarf. 'Nana Rotundifolia': dwarf; st. sea-green; lvs deep green, broad, rarely spotted; free-fruiting. 'Picturata': lvs centrally blotched gold. 'Salicifolia': lvs dark green, narrow. Fr. red. 'Sulphurea': st. sea-green; lf margins pale yellow. 'Variegata': ♀; lvs spotted and blotched yellow. 'Viridis' ('Concolor'): lvs dark green, unspotted. Z7.

AUCUBACEAE J. Agardh. See *Aucuba*.

Audibertia Benth.
A. clevelandii A. Gray = *Salvia clevelandii*.
A. dorrii Kellogg = *Salvia dorrii*.
A. grandiflora Benth. = *Salvia spathacea*.
A. humilis Benth. = *Salvia sonomensis*.
A. polystachya Benth. = *Salvia apiana*.
A. stachyoides var. *revoluta* Brandg. = *Salvia brandegei*.
A. vaseyi Porter = *Salvia vaseyi*.

August Lily *Hosta plantaginea*.
August Plum *Prunus americana*.

Aureolaria Raf. FALSE FOXGLOVE. Scrophulariaceae. 11 herbs, semi-parasite on *Quercus* and Ericaceae. St. erect, branched. Lvs entire or lobed. Fls in erect leafy rac., pan. or solitary; cor. narrow, campanulate, lobes 5, spreading. Summer. N Amer. Z7.
A. flava (L.) Farw. Perenn., to 180cm. Lvs oblong-lanceolate, to 12cm; lower lvs lobed or pinnatisect. Cor. yellow to ochre, to 5cm, exterior glab.
A. glauca (Eddy) Raf. = *A. flava*.
A. pectinata (Nutt.) Penn. Ann., to 55cm. Lvs to 4cm, bipinnatifid, glandular-pubesc. Cor. yellow stained bronze, to 4.5cm, exterior glandular-pubesc. Summer–autumn.
A. pedicularia (L.) Raf. Ann. 60–120cm. Lvs slightly pubesc., lanceolate, bluntly dentate, bi-pinnatifid. Cor. yellow with brown hue, to 4cm.
A. virginica (L.) Penn. Perenn., to 90cm. Lvs elliptic, entire to obscurely cut. Cor. bright yellow, to 5cm. Spring–autumn.
→*Agalinis* and *Gerardia*.

Auricula *Primula* section *Auricula*.

Aurinia Desv. Cruciferae. 7 bienn. or perenn. herbs similar to *Alyssum*. Petiole base long, swollen. Fls yellow to white. Fr. a silicle, compressed or inflated. C & S Eur., E to Ukraine and Turk.
A. corymbosa Griseb. Perenn. Infl. a corymb; pet. bilobed. Balk. Penins. Z7.
A. petraea (Ard.) Schur. Perenn. Infl. racemose; pet. yellow, bilobed. C & SE Eur., nat. NW Amer. Z7.
A. rupestris (Ten.) Cullen & Dudley. Rootstock thick. Lvs grey stellate-hairy. Fls white. SE Eur., Turk. Z7.
A. saxatilis (L.) Desv. Perenn. Lvs grey stellate-hairy. Infl. paniculate; fls pale yellow. C & SE Eur. 'Argentea': lvs v. silvered; fls bright. 'Citrina': fls profuse, bright lemon; late spring. 'Compacta': to 20cm; fls gold. 'Dudley Neville': to 20cm; fls rich cream tinted apricot. 'Dudley Neville Variegated' (also unnamed reversed form): to 20cm; lvs grey variegated white; fls rich cream tinted apricot. 'Gold Dust': to 30cm; fls gold. 'Golden Queen': low-growing; lvs tinted grey; fls profuse, light yellow; spring. 'Goldkugel' ('Gold Ball'): to 15cm, compact; fls gold. 'Plena': to 20cm; fls double, dark golden yellow; sterile. 'Silver Queen': to 25cm; fls lemon. 'Sulphurea': to 20cm; fls striking yellow. 'Tom Thumb': to 10cm; lvs small; fls small. 'Variegata': lvs yellow variegated white; weak-growing. Z3.
A. sinuata (L.) Griseb. Perenn. St. only woody at v. base. Lvs grey-pubesc. Pet. notched. Spain, It., Balk. Z7.
→*Alyssum* and *Vesicaria*.

Australia Chestnut *Castanospermum*.
Australia Flame Pea *Chorizema cordata*.
Australian Banyan *Ficus macrophylla*.
Australian Beech *Nothofagus moorei*.
Australian Bluebell *Sollya heterophylla*.
Australian Bracken *Pteris tremula*.

Australian Brush Cherry *Syzygium paniculatum*.
Australian Cabbage Palm *Livistonia australis*.
Australian Daffodil *Calostemma luteum*.
Australian Desert Lime *Eremocitrus*.
Australian Fan Palm *Livistonia australis*.
Australian Firewheel Tree *Stenocarpus sinuatis*.
Australian Flame Tree *Brachychiton acerifolium*.
Australian Fuschia *Correa*.
Australian Hare's Foot *Davallia pyxidata*.
Australian Heath *Epacris*.
Australian Ivy-palm *Schefflera actinophylla*.
Australian Maidenhair Fern *Adiantum formosum*.
Australian Mint Bush *Prostanthera*.
Australian Nut Palm *Cycas media*.
Australian Palm *Livistonia australis*.
Australian Pea *Dipogon lignosus*.
Australian Pine *Casuarina*.
Australian Pitcher Plant *Cephalotus*.
Australian Round Lime *Microcitrus australis*.
Australian Sarsparilla *Hardenbergia violacea*.
Australian Sassafras *Atherosperma moschatum*.
Australian Sword Lily *Anigozanthos*.
Australian Tea Tree *Leptospermum laevigatum*.
Australian Tree Fern *Cyathea australis; Dicksonia antarctica*.
Australian Violet *Viola hederacea*.
Australian Water Lily *Nymphaea gigantea*.
Australian Weeping Grass *Chloris ventricosa*.
Australian Willow *Geijera*.
Austral Lady Fern *Diplazium australe*.
Austrian Copper Briar *Rosa foetida*.
Austrian Pea *Lathyrus hirsutus*.
Austrian Pine *Pinus nigra*.
Austrian Yellow Rose *Rosa foetida*.

Austrocactus Britt. & Rose. Cactaceae. 5 low shrubby cacti; st. simple or branched below; ribs ± tuberculate; central spines hooked or straight. Fls subapical (lat. in *A. spinoflorus*), urceolate or campanulate; floral areoles with woolly hairs and usually bristles; sta. in two series, the lower encircling style; stigmas usually purple-red. S Arg., S Chile.
A. hibernus Ritter. Low shrub; st. prostrate or decumbent, 10–40×1cm, green; ribs 7–8, low; areoles at first with scale-like lf rudiment; central spines 1–4, 1–3cm; radial spines 5–8, 1.5–2cm. Fls 4–5cm; tep. yellow- or red-brown. Chile. Z6.
A. patagonicus (Weber ex Speg.) Backeb. Caespitose shrub; st. to 50×5–8cm; ribs 9–12, prominent; central spines 1–4, 1.5–4cm, with bulbous base; radial spines 6–10, 1–1.5cm. Fls 4×5cm, fragrant; outer tep. pink; inner white or pink with violet mid-stripe, or yellow. S Arg., S Chile. Z6.
A. spiniflorus (Philippi) Ritter. Low caespitose and stoloniferous shrub; st. 6–8×2–3cm, dark green or bronze; ribs 6–8; central spines 1–3, 1.5–2.5cm; radial spines 5–8, 0.5–1cm. Fls 6.5–7.5cm; outer tep. tinged red, inner pale yellow; style off-white. Chile. Z6.
→*Corryocactus* and *Erdisia*.

Austrocedrus Florin & Boutelje. Cupressaceae. 1 everg. conifer allied to *Calocedrus*. Crown broad ovoid to narrow conic; bole flutted; bark dark brown to orange-grey, exfoliating in narrow stringy plates; twigs crowded in 2 ranks, pinnate. Lvs marked white, imbricate, in 4 ranks; lat. lvs acute, keeled, exceeding and obscuring facial lvs, grooved; facial lvs smaller, obtuse, obscurely gland. Chile & W Arg. Z8.
A. chilensis (D. Don) Pichi-Serm. & Bizzarri. CHILEAN CEDAR.
→*Libocedrus*.

Austrocephalocereus Backeb.
A. dybowskii (Roland-Goss.) Backeb. = *Espostoopsis dybowskii*.

Austrocylindropuntia Backeb.
Austrocylindropuntia cylindrica (Lam.) Backeb. = *Opuntia cylindrica*.
Austrocylindropuntia salmiana (Pfeiff.) Backeb. = *Opuntia salmiana*.

Austrotaxus Compton. NEW CALEDONIAN YEW. Taxaceae. 1 everg. conifer to 25m, resembling *Podocarpus*. Crown dense; bark brown tinged red, flaky. Lvs spirally arranged, 8–12cm, narrow lanceolate, coriaceous, acuminate, revolute, midrib sunken above. Fr. similar in structure to *Taxus* but larger, 2.5–3cm. C & NE New Caledonia. Z10.
A. spicata Compton.

Autograph Tree *Clusia major*.
Autumn Crocus *Colchicum autumnale*.
Autumn Daffodil *Sternbergia*.

Autumn Damask Rose *Rosa* ×*damascena* var. *semperflorens*.
Autumn Phlox *Phlox paniculata*.
Autumn Pumpkin *Cucurbita pepo*.
Autumn Sage *Salvia greggii*.
Autumn Snowdrop *Galanthus reginae-olgae*.
Autumn Snowflake *Leucojum autumnale*.
Autumn Squash *Cucurbita maxima*; *C. pepo*.
Avalanche Lily *Erythronium grandiflorum*; *E. montanum*.
Avaram *Senna auriculata*.

Avena L. OATS. Gramineae. c15 ann. grasses. St. solitary or tufted. Lvs flat, linear; sheaths slightly hairy to smooth; ligule obtuse, papery. Flts few, in v. loose pan., spikelets 1–7-fld, scattered, pendulous, slender-stalked, flattened. Eurasia, N Afr. Z5.
A. barbata Pott ex Link. SLENDER WILD OATS. To 170cm. Lvs to 25×2cm, pilose to glab. Pan. to 36×15cm; spikelets to 2.5cm, 2–3-fld; awn to 4cm, tortuous below. Spring–summer. Medit., Cauc., Asia.
A. elatior L. = *Arrhenatherum elatius*.
A. sempervirens Vill. = *Helictotrichon sempervirens*.
A. sterilis L. ANIMATED OAT. To 1m. Lvs to 30×1cm, rough. Pan. to 30×20cm; spikelets to 4cm, 3–5-fld; awns to 7.5cm. Summer. Atlantic Is., Medit., C Asia.

Avens *Geum*.

Averrhoa L. Oxalidaceae. 2 everg. shrubs or trees. Lvs spirally arranged to terminally clustered, imparipinnate. Infl. loosely cymose, axill. or cauliflorous; sep. fused below to form a short tube; pet. creamy to dark red, marked white; sta. 10. Fr. fleshy. Indigenous to Malesia, now cult. and nat. in many trop. and subtrop. regions. Z10.
A. bilimbi L. BLIMBI; CUCUMBER TREE. Shrub or tree to 15m, br. erect. Pinnae to 12×4cm, green beneath. Infl. caulifloral, fasciculate and pendulous; pedicels to 17mm; sep. to 8mm, purple to yellow-red; pet. to 20×4mm, lanceolate-spathulate. Fr. to 10×5cm, green-yellow, ellipsoid to obovate, round to obscurely 5-angular in cross-section, base tapering.
A. carambola L. CARAMBOLA; STARFRUIT. Tree to 14m, br. pendent. Pinnae to 10×4cm, glaucous beneath. Infl. axill.; pedicels to 6mm; sep. to 4×2mm, dull glossy red; pet. to 8×2mm, obovate to lanceolate. Fr. to 12.5×6cm, yellow, ovoid to ellipsoid, v. strongly (3–)5-ribbed, star-shaped in cross-section. Range as for the genus.

Avignon Berry *Rhamnus saxatilis*.
Avocado Pear *Persea americana*.
Awl-leaf Wattle *Acacia subulata*.
Awl Tree *Morinda citrifolia*.
Awlwort *Subularia*.

Ayapana Spach. Compositae. c15 ann. to perenn. herbs. Lvs narrowly ovate to lanceolate, sessile, base sometimes winged. Cap. discoid, in a lax corymb or pan.; flts tubular or funnel-shaped, white or pink. Trop. Amer.
A. triplinervis (Vahl) R. King & H. Robinson. Somewhat shrubby perenn. to 1.5m. Lvs to 15cm, lanceolate to oblong- or elliptic-lanceolate, usually entire, subglabrous. Cap. few, in lax corymbs; peduncles slender, 1–2cm. N & S Amer., W Indies. →*Eupatorium*.

Aylostera Speg. = *Rebutia*.

Ayo *Tetrastigma harmandii*.

Azara Ruiz & Pav. Flacourtiaceae. 10 everg. shrubs or small trees, to 8m. Lvs alt. or paired, entire or toothed, tough, base often with 1–2 small, accessory lvs. Fls small, green or yellow, often fragrant, in axill. spikes or corymbs; cal. 4- or 5-lobed; pet. 0; sta. numerous. Fr. a round, fleshy berry. Chile, NW Arg., Boliv., Urug. Z8.
A. bergii F. Philippi = *A. serrata*.
A. berteroniana Steud. = *A. integrifolia*.
A. borealis F. Philippi in Philippi = *A. microphylla*.
A. brasiliensis Lign. & Beyer = *A. uruguayensis*.
A. browneae F. Philippi = *A. integrifolia* var. *browneae*.
A. brumalis Gand. = *A. lanceolata*.
A. celastrina D. Don. Shrub or small tree, to 3m. Lvs to 4×2.5cm, elliptic or sublanceolate, entire or regularly toothed, grey-green; accessory lvs single or 0, abscising, oblong, to 6mm. Fr. black, 6mm diam. Chile.
A. celastrina var. *tomentosa* (Steud.) Reiche = *A. dentata*.
A. chiloensis Hook. f. = *A. lanceolata*.
A. crassifolia hort. Booth = *A. petiolaris*.

A. dentata Ruiz & Pav. Small tree, 1–2m. Lvs 3.5×2cm, elliptic, pale green, toothed, veins in 4 pairs; accessory lvs similar but one-third smaller. Fr. yellow, 4–6mm diam. Chile.
A. dubia Steud. = *A. serrata*.
A. emiliae Harms. = *A. uruguayensis*.
A. gilliesii Hook. & Arn. = *A. petiolaris*.
A. hirtella Miq. = *A. integrifolia*.
A. integrifolia Ruiz & Pav. Shrub, to 4m. Lvs to 4×3cm, entire; accessory lvs 1–2, 0.8×1.2cm. Fr. black, pruinose, 5–6mm diam. Chile. var. *browneae* (Philippi) Bean. Lvs to 6×3cm, to 4 teeth per side near apex. Chile. 'Variegata': lvs smaller, edged pale pink or white.
A. intermedia Gay = *A. integrifolia*.
A. lanceolata Hook. f. Shrub or small tree, to 6m. Lvs to 7×1.5cm, lanceolate, subacute, shiny and glab. above, serrate; accessory lvs to 1.5cm, persistent. Fr. dark violet, 7–10mm diam. Chile, Arg.
A. lechleriana Steud. = *A. integrifolia*.
A. lilen Bertero = *A. celastrina*.
A. microphylla Hook. f. Small tree, to 8m. Lvs to 1.5×0.8cm, obovate or round, often emarginate, entire or obscurely toothed; accessory lvs single, to 0.8cm, persistent. Fr. blood-red, 3mm diam. Chile, Arg. 'Variegata': lvs edged pale yellow.
A. petiolaris (D. Don) I.M. Johnst. Tree, to 5m. Lvs to 4×3.5cm, ovate-elliptic, obtuse, shiny above, sharp-serrate; accessory lvs 1–2, 8–10mm diam. Fr. nearly black pruinose, 8mm diam. Chile.
A. pycnophylla Philippi = *A. integrifolia*.
A. serrata Ruiz & Pav. Shrub, to 4m. Lvs to 6×3cm, oblong or elliptic, deep green and shiny above, often glab., sharply serrate; accessory lvs single, to 2cm. Fr. black, 7mm diam. Chile.
A. serrata var. *chiloensis* (Hook. f.) Reiche = *A. lanceolata*.
A. sparsiflora Steud. = *A. celastrina*.
A. subandina Philippi = *A. serrata*.
A. tomentosa Bertero ex Steud. = *A. dentata*.
A. umbellata Philippi = *A. serrata*.
A. uruguayensis (Speg.) Sleumer. Shrub or small tree, to 6m. Lvs to 8.5×4.5cm, deep green, glab., entire or regularly toothed; lat. lvs to 2.2cm, entire or slightly toothed. Fr. rose to blue, pruinose, to 8mm diam. Urug.
A. valdiviae Lechl. ex Steud. = *A. microphylla*.

Azarole *Crataegus azarolus*.

Azolla Lam. MOSQUITO FERN; WATER FERN; FAIRY MOSS. Azollaceae. 8 small, free-floating, aquatic ferns, usually perenn. and surviving by means of submerged fragments. Rhiz. pinnately or dichotomously branched, densely covered with overlapping scale-like 2-ranked lvs above, rooting below, velvety pea green, turning dark red or purple toward end of season. Cosmop.
A. caroliniana Willd. MOSQUITO FERN. Plant body 0.5–1.5cm broad and long, suborbicular; alternately branched, br. pseudo-dichotomous. Lvs to 1mm, oval, green, pink or bronze-red, minutely papillose-puberulous, lower lobes pale green. E US, Carib. and trop. Amer., nat. W & S Eur. Z7.
A. filiculoides Lam. Plant body to 10cm, elliptic, pinnately branched, br. mostly 2-pinnate, often separating. Lvs 2.5mm, obtuse, green turning dark red to purple. N & S Amer., nat. Eur. Z7.
A. mexicana Presl. Scarcely discernible from *A. filiculoides*. SW US to Boliv. Z8.
A. pinnata R. Br. Plant body to 2.5cm, broadly ovate, more slender and feathered than *A. caroliniana*; rhiz. 1- or 2-pinnate. Lvs ovate, obtuse, concave, loosely imbricate. S Afr., SE Asia. Z9.
A. portoricensis Spreng. = *A. caroliniana*.

AZOLLACEAE Wettst. See *Azolla*.

Azorella Lam. Umbelliferae. 70 caespitose or cushion-forming perennials. Lvs everg., entire, toothed or cut; petioles basally sheathing. Umbels subsessile, simple; involucral bracts conspicuous; fls v. small, yellow-white to golden brown. S Amer., Antarc. Is., NZ.
A. glebaria (Comm. ex Gaudich.) A. Gray = *Bolax gummifera*.
A. peduncularis (Spreng.) Mathias & Constance = *A. pedunculata*.
A. pedunculata (Spreng.) Mathias & Constance. Growths tufted, forming cushions. Lvs 5–10×2–7mm, overlapping and crowded, spathulate, leathery, with 4 or more apical teeth. Umbel 10–20-fld; involucral bracts 8–10. Ecuad. Z8.
A. trifurcata (Gaertn.) Pers. St. diffusely branched, forming compact mats or cushions. Lvs 6–12×2–5mm, grey-green, crowded, deeply 3-parted, lobes triangular, acute, leathery. Umbel 6–9-fld; involucral bracts 4–8. Summer. Chile, Arg.

'Nana': doubtfully distinct.
A. umbellata hort. = *A. trifurcata*.
A. utriculata Griseb. = *A. trifurcata*.

Azores Laurel Cherry *Prunus lusitanica*.

Azorina Feer.
A. vidalii (H. Wats.) Feer = *Campanula vidalii*.

Aztec Lily *Sprekelia formosissima*.
Aztec Marigold *Tagetes erecta*.

Aztekium Boed. Cactaceae. 1 cactus; st. to 5×5cm, simple or clustering, grey-green; ribs 8–11, rugose, with longitudinal rib-like ridges; areoles woolly, with 1–3 upward-curved and adpressed, flattened, yellow to grey spines to c4mm. Fls apical, funnel-form, c12×14mm; outer tep. red-purple, purple outside, inner tep. white. NE Mex. Z7.
A. ritteri (Boed.) Boed.

Azuma-zasa *Sasaella ramosa*.
Azure Ceanothus *Ceanothus coeruleus*.

Azureocereus Akers & Johnson.
A. hertlingianus (Backeb.) Backeb. = *Browningia hertlingiana*.
A. nobilis Akers = *Browningia hertlingiana*.
A. viridis Rauh & Backeb. = *Browningia viridis*.

B

Babaco *Carica pentagonia.*
Babao *Syagrus comosa.*
Babassu *Orbignya phalerata.*

Babiana Ker-Gawl. BABOON FLOWER. Iridaceae. 50–60 cormous, perenn. herbs. Lvs linear to oblong-lanceolate, plicate, hairy. Spike simple or branched, fls regular or irregular, scented; perianth tubular, seg. 6. Winter–spring. S Afr. Z9.
B. ambigua (Roem. & Schult.) Lewis. St. 1–5cm. Spike short, densely 4–5-fld; fls 2-lipped, scented, blue or mauve-blue, lower side lobes usually white or pale yellow in centre with purple W-shaped mark. SW Cape.
B. disticha Ker-Gawl. = *B. plicata.*
B. gawleri N.E. Br. = *B. sambucina.*
B. hypogaea Burchell. Spikes clustered at base of plant, densely 2–8-fld; fls scented, funnel-shaped, somewhat 2-lipped, blue-mauve, lower tep. sometimes with yellow streaks and irregular purple bands. S Afr.
B. macrantha MacOwan = *B. pygmaea.*
B. nana (Andrews) Spreng. Spike densely 2–6-fld, distichous; fls scented, irregular, widely bell-shaped, blue, mauve or pink, the lower side lobes marked with yellow or white and purple. SW Cape.
B. plicata Ker-Gawl. St. 7–20cm, sometimes with 1–3 short br. Spike 4–10-fld; fls scented, irregular, pale blue, violet or white, the lower side lobes usually with a yellow blotch and 2 purple dots toward base. W Cape.
B. purpurea (Jacq.) Ker-Gawl. St. 10–15cm, simple or 1–3-branched. Spike distichous, 4–10-fld; fls scented, usually regular, purple-mauve, tube purple, outside of lobes with purple median line. W Cape.
B. pygmaea (Burm. f.) N.E. Br. St. 2–6(–15)cm, usually unbranched; spike 2–5-fld. Fls regular, yellow, purple-maroon in centre, sometimes tinged with purple outside. W Cape.
B. ringens (L.) Ker-Gawl. Spike branched, many-fld; fls red or maroon, laterally compressed. Cape Penins.
B. rubrocyanea (Jacq.) Ker-Gawl. St. 5–20cm. Spike 5–10-fld; fls spirally arranged, regular, the basal third of lobes scarlet, curving up, the apical two-thirds blue, spreading. W Cape.
B. sambucina (Jacq.) Ker-Gawl. St. 1–2cm. Spike short, 2–6-fld; fls scented, irregular, purple, violet or pale blue-mauve, lower side lobes with white mark near centre. Cape Prov.
B. stricta (Ait.) Ker-Gawl. Spike, short, 4–8-fld; fls spirally arranged, ± regular, sometimes scented, purple, mauve or blue, the 2 lower or 3 inner lobes paler, sometimes yellow. SW Cape. var. *sulphurea* (Jacq.) Bak. Fls sulphur-yellow, tube purple or blue, lobes sometimes flushed with purple outside; anth. purple-black.
B. thunbergii Ker-Gawl. Spike branched, many-fld on upper side; fls bright red or pink-red with green patches on lip. W & NW Cape.
B. tubata (Jacq.) Sweet = *B. tubulosa.*
B. tubiflora var. *filifolia* Pappe ex Bak. = *B. tubulosa* var. *tubiflora.*
B. tubulosa (Burm. f.) Ker-Gawl. St. short, 1–3-branched. Spike 8–12-fld; fls bilabiate, cream with red arrow-shaped or triangular marks on 3 lower lobes, tube flushed with purple or red-purple, outer lobes usually lined red line on outside. W Cape. var. *tubiflora* (L. f.) Lewis. Spike 2- to many-fld; floral tube 65–80mm, slender, only slightly wider towards throat.
B. villosa Ker-Gawl. St. 12–20cm, sometimes with 1 br. Spike 4–8-fld, distichous, fls ± regular, deep red or red-purple; anth. large, purple-black. SW Cape.
B. villosula (Gmel.) Ker-Gawl. ex Steud. St. 1–5cm, erect, usually simple; spike distichous, 2–4-(–8)fld; fls regular, pale blue or mauve, white in centre. W Cape.
B. cvs. Mostly derived from *B. stricta* and producing fls in a range of colours from pearly white with a dark eye through to yellow, rose, red, mauve and indigo.
→*Antholyza.*

Baboon Flower *Babiana.*
Baboon's Shoes *Androcymbium melanthoides.*
Babul *Acacia nilotica.*
Baby-blue-eyes *Nemophila menziesii.*
Babylon Weeping Willow *Salix babylonica.*
Baby Pepper *Rivina humilis.*

Baby Primrose *Primula malacoides.*
Baby Rose *Rosa multiflora.*
Baby Rubber Plant *Peperomia obtusifolia.*
Baby's Breath *Gypsophila paniculata.*
Baby Snapdragon *Linaria maroccana.*
Baby's Tears *Soleirolia soleirolii.*
Baby's Toes *Fenestraria rhopalophylla.*

Baccharis L. Compositae. *c*350 dioecious shrubs. St. often flattened, acting as lvs. Cap. discoid, clustered in pan. or corymbs. Fr. with dense downy pappus. Americas.
B. angustifolia auct. = *B. neglecta.*
B. brasiliana L. = *Vernonia brasiliana.*
B. glomeruliflora Pers. 1–3m, glab.; br. angled, sometimes scurfy. Lvs to 5cm, obovate to spathulate, coarsely dentate above or entire, obtuse, light green, coriaceous. Cap. in axils of upper lvs, sessile. Pappus brilliant white. Autumn. SE US. Z8.
B. glutinosa Pers. = *B. salicifolia.*
B. halimifolia L. GROUNDSEL-TREE; COTTON-SEED TREE. 1–3m, glab.; br. angled, sometimes scurfy. Lvs 3–7cm, obovate to deltoid or oblanceolate, coarsely dentate or entire, obtuse. Cap. solitary or to 5 in clusters, pedunculate. Pappus brilliant white. E & SC US, W Indies. Z5.
B. magellanica (Lam.) Pers. St. to 30cm, prostrate to erect, minutely scabrous, striate, viscid. Lvs 5–9cm, spathulate, remotely crenate or entire, glab. or minutely scabrid on margins, viscid when young. Cap. solitary, terminal on short lat. br., sessile or shortly pedunculate; flts yellow. Summer. S Chile, S Arg., Falkland Is. Z8.
B. neglecta Britt. To 1.5m, glab. or slightly glutinous; br. ascending, slender. Lvs 3–7cm, linear to linear-lanceolate, entire or remotely and minutely dentate. Cap. in clusters, shortly pedunculate. Pappus dull white. Late summer. Neb. to Tex. and N Mex. 4.
B. neriifolia L. = *Brachylaena neriifolia.*
B. patagonica Hook. & Arn. To 1.5m. St. erect, glab., occas. gland. Lvs 1cm, elliptic to oblong or elliptic-oblong, obtuse, serrate, punctate, gland. above. Cap. sessile at tips of short lat. br., forming a spike; flts yellow. Papus white or v. pale. Summer. S Chile, S Arg. Z8.
B. pilularis DC. DWARF CHAPARRAL-BROOM. To 50cm, matted, widely spreading. St. ± prostrate, glab., resinous-granular, brown, striate. Lvs 1–4cm, obovate to ovate, obtuse, subentire or serrate above, 1-nerved, thick. Cap. numerous, in axill. glomerules or spikes clustered at br. apices, tinged white. Summer. Calif. 'Twin Peaks': ♂, growth rate moderate, lvs small, dark green. 'Pigeon Point': to 1×4m, fast-growing with larger, lighter lvs. Z8.
B. rosmarinifolia Hook. & Arn. To 2.5m, branched, pulverulent-glandular. Lvs 1–3cm, linear, obtuse or mucronate, revolute, entire to 1–3-dentate, coriaceous. Cap. in corymbs of 3–12, forming a rac. Pappus white. Chile. Z9.
B. salicifolia (Ruiz & Pav.) Pers. 1–2m, branched, gland., densely leafy. Lvs 4–9cm, lanceolate to linear, acute, serrate above, 3-nerved, glutinous. Cap. clustered in dense corymbs. Pappus white. S Amer. Z9.
B. salicina Torr. & A. Gray. 1–2m, br. ascending, glab. and glutinous. Lvs 2.5–4cm, oblong-lanceolate to oblanceolate, obtuse, 3-nerved, remotely dentate to entire, firm. Cap. pedunculate, to 7 in clusters. Pappus nearly white. Summer. SC US. Z4.
B. trimera (Less.) DC. 40–50cm, glab., glutinous. St. 3-winged. Lvs reduced to inconspicuous bracts. Cap. inconspicuous, clustered in truncated spikes at br. apices. Pappus white. S Braz., NE Arg. Z9.
B. viminea DC. MULE FAT. To 4m, gland., densely leafy. Lvs 4–9cm, lanceolate, acute, entire or minutely dentate, 3-nerved. Cap. clustered in small cymes or pan., term. on st. and main br., usually flushed purple. Pappus white. Spring–summer. Calif., Baja Calif. Z8.

Bachelor's Buttons *Craspedia* (*C. glauca; C. uniflora*); *Gomphrena globosa.*

Backebergia Bravo.
B. militaris (Audot) Sanchez-Mej. = *Pachycereus militaris.*

Backhousia Hook. & Harv. Myrtaceae. 7 shrubs or trees. Lvs entire, aromatic. Fls small, white, in cymes, umbels or pan.; pet. 4; sta. showy, spreading. Z9.

B. anisata Vick. ANISEED TREE. Large tree. Lvs 5–10cm, lanceolate, shiny green, anise-scented. Fls creamy-white, 0.5–0.8cm diam., in term. umbels.

B. bancroftii Bail. JOHNSTONE RIVER HARDWOOD. Medium to tall tree. Lvs 7–12cm, elliptic, bright green, shiny. Fls c0.8cm diam., creamy white, in term. clusters.

B. citrodora F. Muell. LEMON IRONWOOD; LEMON SCENTED MYRTLE. Medium shrub to tree. Lvs 5–10cm, ovate, lanceolate, pale green, tinted red when young, slightly toothed, strongly lemon-scented. Fls creamy white, 0.5–0.7cm diam., numerous in umbel-like clusters.

B. hughesii C.T. White. STONE WOOD; LIME WOOD. Tall spreading tree. Lvs 3–6cm, ovate or lanceolate, dark green, shiny. Fls c0.5cm diam., white, in conspicuous clusters.

B. myrtifolia Hook. & Harv. Tall shrub or small bushy tree. Lvs 2.5–7cm, ovate or lanceolate, dark green, shiny. Fls 1.5–2cm diam., white, in axill. cymes or term. pan.

B. sciadophora F. Muell. SHATTERWOOD; IRONWOOD. Small to medium tree. Lvs 2.5–8cm, broadly ovate, dark green, shiny, obtuse, aromatic. Fls c0.4cm, white, in dense cymes or umbels in the upper lf axils.

Bacon-and-eggs *Daviesia*.

Bacopa Aubl. WATER HYSSOP. Scrophulariaceae. 56 aquatic or semi-aquatic perennials creeping to erect, often succulent. Lvs entire, dentate or finely dissected. Fls small, axill.; cal. 5-lobed; cor. campanulate, lobes spreading. Summer. Asia, Afr., Aus., Amer. Z8.

B. amplexicaulis (Michx.) Wettst. = *B. caroliniana*.

B. caroliniana (Walter) Robinson. St. creeping to ascending, pubesc., simple. Lvs to 2.5cm, ovate, entire, lemon-scented. Fls blue. N Amer.

B. monnieri (L.) Pennell. Glab., succulent, st. mat-forming. Lvs to 1.9cm, spathulate to cuneate-obovate, entire or apex dentate. Fls white to pale blue. Pantrop.

→*Herpestis*.

Bactris Jacq. ex Scop. SPINY-CLUB PALM. Palmae. 239 solitary or clustered palms. St. short, erect, from underground rhiz. or tall with conspicuous and scaly lf scars. Lvs pinnately divided or simple and cleft, petiole unarmed or spiny; pinnae 1- to many-fold, regularly spaced or clustered and in differing planes along rachis, margins often bristly. Fr. to 6cm, ellipsoid to subglobose.

B. acanthophylla Mart. = *Aiphanes acanthophylla*.

B. balanoidea (Ørst.) H.A. Wendl. = *B. major*.

B. erosa Mart. = *Aiphanes acanthophylla*.

B. gasipaes HBK. PEACH PALM; PEJIBEYE; PEJIVALLE; PUPUNHA; CHONTA. St. solitary or clustered, 20m×15cm, ringed with sharp spines. Lvs to 3m; petioles to 1m, spiny; pinnae bright green, crowded in different planes along rachis; rachis spiny. Fr. orange-red. Widely cult. C Amer., origin unknown.

B. guineensis (L.) H.E. Moore. TOBAGO CANE; PRICKLY-POLE. St. several, to 3.6m, pale green. Petiole spiny. Pinnae 20–30 per side, regularly spaced along rachis, short and narrow. Fr. black. C Amer.

B. horrida Ørst. = *B. guineensis*.

B. major Jacq. PRICKLY PALM; BLACK ROSEAU. St. clustered to 7.5m×5cm, prickly then smooth. Lvs to 2.4m, dull green, glab.; petiole densely prickly; pinnae c30 per side, regularly spaced along rachis. Fr. purple. C Amer.

B. minor Jacq. = *B. guineensis*.

→*Guilelma*.

Badger's Bane *Aconitum lycoctonum*.

Baeckea L. Myrtaceae. 70 prostrate undershrubs to tall shrubs. Lvs small, entire or lobulate. Fls small, solitary or in clusters, white to pink; pet. 5, spreading, orbicular; sta. c20. Aus., Pacific Is., Asia. Z9.

B. astarteoides Benth. Dwarf to small shrub. Branchlets arching. Lvs c5mm, narrow, fleshy. Fls c5mm diam., pink. Aus.

B. behrii (Schldl.) F. Muell. BROOM BAECKEA; BROOMBRUSH. Slender small shrub. St. erect, thin. Lvs 3–8mm, terete, tips recurved. Fls 6–8mm diam., white or pink. Aus.

B. camphorata R. Br. CAMPHOR BUSH. Sparse spreading small to medium shrub. Lvs 4–6mm, oblong, flat, bright green. Fls 4–6mm diam., white. Aus.

B. camphorosmae Endl. CAMPHOR MYRTLE. Dwarf shrub, compact or spreading. Lvs to c5mm, narrow, heath-like, in clusters. Fls 1–1.5cm diam., white to pink. Aus.

B. crassifolia Lindl. DESERT BAECKEA. Slender dwarf shrub. Lvs 1–3mm, oblong, blunt, thick. Fls 4–8mm diam., white, pink to pale violet. Aus.

B. dimorphandra F. Muell. ex Benth. Dwarf shrub. Br. slender, erect, twiggy. Lvs to 5mm, narrow, blunt. Fls c1cm diam., pink. Aus.

B. frutescens L. Medium to tall slender shrub. Br. thin, weeping, often bronze. Lvs 1–2cm, linear, acute, spreading. Fls 3–5mm diam., white. Aus.

B. gunniana Schauer. ALPINE BAECKEA; MOUNTAIN HEATH MYRTLE. Small wiry shrub. Young br. tinged red. Lvs 2–5mm, concave or terete, bright green, fleshy. Fls 5–8mm diam., white. Aus.

B. imbricata (Gaertn.) Druce. Compact or spindly dwarf shrub. Br. arising from near ground level. Lvs 2–4mm, obovate, yellow-green, concave. Fls 2–4mm diam., white. Aus.

B. linifolia Rudge. WEEPING BAECKEA. Slender small to medium shrub. Br. thin, drooping, often bronze or red. Lvs 5–15mm, linear, terete, pointed. Fls 3–5mm diam., white. Aus.

B. ramosissima A. Cunn. ROSY BAECKEA. Dwarf erect or decumbent shrub. St. thin, much-branched. Lvs 4–10mm, linear, flat, often thickened. Fls 6–12mm diam., white through shades of pink to red. Aus.

B. thymoides S. Moore. Dwarf to small shrub. Lvs c2–3mm, ovate to oblong, flat, sessile, decussate. Fls c8mm diam., white to pale pink. Name sometimes misapplied to *Scholtzia teretifolia* Benth., a low, spreading sp. with pale pink fls and ± terete lvs. Aus.

B. virgata (Forst. & Forst. f.) Andrews. TALL BAECKEA; TWIGGY BAECKEA. Shrub to small tree. Br. loose, erect, spreading, sometimes weeping. Lvs 1–2.5cm, linear-lanceolate or oblong, sessile, dark green. Fls 5–6mm diam., white. Aus. 'Howie's Feathertips': dense weeping shrub with fine foliage. 'Howie's Sweet Midget': compact, dwarf shrub.

Baeometra Salisb. Liliaceae (Colchicaceae). 1 cormous perenn. herb. St. 15–30cm. Lower lvs 15–20cm, 2-ranked, linear, upper lvs reduced. Rac. 1–7-fld; tep. to 1.25cm, 6, erect, yellow inside with a purple spot at base, red outside. Spring. S Afr. (Cape Penins.). Z9.

B. columellaris Salisb. = *B. uniflora*.

B. uniflora (Jacq.) G. Lewis

Baeria Fisch. & C.A. Mey.

B. chrysostoma Fisch. & C.A. Mey. = *Lasthenia chrysostoma*.

B. coronaria (Nutt.) A. Gray = *Lasthenia coronaria*.

B. gracilis (DC.) A. Gray = *Lasthenia chrysostoma* ssp. *gracilis*.

Ba'gambil *Cordia africana*.
Bag Flower *Clerodendrum thomsoniae*.
Bagras *Eucalyptus deglupta*.
Bahama Grass *Cynodon dactylon*.
Bahamas Phymosia *Phymosia abutiloides*.
Bahamas Pine *Pinus caribaea* var. *bahamensis*.

Bahia Lagasca. Compositae. c12 pubesc. ann. to perenn. herbs. Lvs alt. or opposite, entire to deeply dissected. Cap. radiate, term.; ray flts ♀, yellow; disc flts many, yellow. Fr. 4-angled, pappus of scales or 0. SW US, Mex., Chile. Z9.

B. confertiflorum DC. = *Eriophyllum confertiflorum*.

B. dissecta (A. Gray) Nutt. Bienn. or short lived perenn. 30–80cm. St. branched, red. Lvs 2–7cm, ternately divided, lobes narrow. Ray flts to 0.6cm. SW US, Mex.

B. lanata (Pursh) DC. = *Eriophyllum lanatum*.

→*Villanova*.

Bahia Coquilla *Attalea funifera*.
Bahia Grass *Paspalum notatum*.
Bahia Piassava *Attalea funifera*.
Bake Apple, Baked-apple, Baked Berry *Rubus chamaemorus*.

Baileya A. Gray. Compositae. 3 densely hairy ann. or perenn. herbs. Lvs alt. Cap. radiate, solitary, long-stalked. WN Amer. Z7.

B. multiradiata Harv. & A. Gray ex Torr. DESERT MARIGOLD. Ann. to 35cm. Lvs pinnatifid to entire, grey. Cap. to 5cm diam., ray flts 20–50, yellow, disc flts yellow. Spring–autumn. W US.

Bakeridesia Hochr. Malvaceae. 13 shrubs or small trees, hairy at first. Lvs entire, ± ovate. Fls axill., solitary or in cymes; epical. 0; cal. campanulate, lobes 5; cor. campanulate to rotate, pet. 5. S Amer. Z10.

B. integerrima (Hook.) Bates. Shrub or small tree to 6m. Lvs to 21×18cm, entire or slightly sinuate. Lvs solitary or in leafy cymes; pet. 2.5–4cm, pale to deep yellow, usually deep red towards the centre; staminal column to 1cm. Mex., Hond.,

Colomb., Venez.
→*Abutilon*.

Balata *Manilkara bidentata*; *M. zapota*.
Bald Cypress *Taxodium distichum*.

Baldellia Parl. Alismataceae. 2 aquatic perenn. herbs, sometimes stoloniferous. Lvs basal and rosulate or cauline and clasping, elliptic to linear-lanceolate. Fls whorled, in umbels or rac. Eur., N Afr. Z7.
B. ranunculoides (L.) Parl. To 30cm. Lvs 10×1.5cm+, submerged lvs linear; petioles to 25cm. Fls to 1.5cm diam.; pet. white or pale pink with a yellow blotch at base. Summer.
→*Alisma* and *Echinodorus*.

Baldmoney *Meum athamanticum*.
Balearic Boxwood *Buxus balearica*.
Balfour Aralia *Polyscias scutellaria*.
Balisier *Heliconia bihai*; *H. caribaea*.
Balkan Blue Grass *Sesleria hempleriana*.
Balkan Maple *Acer hyrcanum*.
Balkan Pine *Pinus peuce*.
Ball Fern *Davallia mariesii*; *D. trichomanoides*.
Ball Moss *Tillandsia recurvata*.
Ball Nightshade *Solanum carolinense*.
Balloon Flower *Platycodon*.
Balloon Pea *Sutherlandia frutescens*.
Balloon Vine *Cardiospermum halicacabum*.

Ballota L. Labiatae. 35 perenn. herbs or subshrubs. Lvs dentate to crenate. Bracteoles linear to spathulate; fls in verticillasters; cal. tubular to funnel-shaped, limb spreading, dish-like, toothed; cor. tubular, 2-lipped, shorter than or equalling cal. Medit., N & C Eur., W Asia. Z8.
B. acetabulosa Benth. Shrub to 1m, thickly tomentose, woody at base. Lvs to 5cm, broadly cordate, obtuse, crenate, grey-woolly, spreading. Verticillasters 6–12-fld; cal. limb 12–20mm diam., lobes rounded; cor. 15–18mm, white with purple markings. Greece, E Medit.
B. 'All Hallow's Green'. Habit low. Lvs soft, lime green. Fls light green.
B. frutescens J. Woods. Woolly subshrub to 60cm. Lvs to 2.5cm, ovate, obtuse, entire, denticulate. Verticillasters 2–6-fld; cal. limb 12–15mm diam., irregularly dentate, lobes awned; cor. 12–15mm, lilac or white. SW Alps.
B. nigra L. BLACK HOREHOUND. Perenn. herb erect to 130cm. Lvs 2.5–7cm, ovate, acute, crenate. Verticillasters 12-fld; cal. limb dentate, lobes 5 subequal; cor. 9–15mm, white, lilac or pink. Eurasia, N Afr., nat. NE US. 'Archer's Variety' ('Variegata'): to 45cm; lvs spotted and streaked white. 'Zanzibar': to 90cm; lvs spotted and streaked pale green in winter.
B. pseudodictamnus Benth. Differs from *B. acetabulosa* in st. 30–50cm; lvs shorter, ovate, less markedly cordate and crenate, cal. limb 7–8mm diam., cor. 14–15mm. S Aegean.

Balm Mint Bush *Prostanthera melissifolia*.
Balm of Gilead *Populus ×jackii*.
Balsa *Ochroma*.
Balsam *Impatiens*.
Balsam Apple *Clusia rosea*; *Momordica balsamina*.
Balsam Fir *Abies balsamea*.
Balsam Groundsel *Packera paupercula*.

BALSAMINACEAE A. Rich. 2/850. *Impatiens*.

Balsamita Desf.
B. major Desf. = *Tanacetum balsamita*.
B. vulgaris Willd. = *Tanacetum balsamita*.

Balsam of Peru *Myroxylon balsamum* var. *pereirae*.

Balsamorhiza Hook. ex Nutt. BALSAM ROOT. Compositae. 5 perenn. herbs. St. erect or ascending, scapose, sparingly leafy, from a branched base. Lvs mostly in basal rosettes, opposite, lanceolate to sagittate. Cap. radiate, large, usually solitary; ray flts yellow, 2–3-toothed; disc flts usually yellow. W N Amer.
B. deltoidea Nutt. 20–90cm. Lvs to 50cm, elongate-triangular to ovate-deltoid, cordate or sagittate with blunt lobes, gland., minutely hispid, entire or coarsely toothed; petiole longer than lamina. Ray flts 2–5cm, 12–20. Spring-early summer.
B. hookeri (Hook.) Nutt. 10–30cm. Lvs 10–30cm, lanceolate, pinnatifid, divisions cleft into spreading lobes, thinly silky to woolly; petioles much shorter than lamina, often pilose. Ray flts 1.5–2.5cm, 10–16. Spring-early summer.

B. incana Nutt. 20–90cm. Lvs 10–45cm, pinnatifid, lanceolate to oblong, lobes lanceolate, oblong to ovate, dentate or deeply incised, lanate; petioles much shorter than lamina. Ray flts 3–5cm, 13+.
B. sagittata (Pursh) Nutt. 20–60cm. Lvs 15–30cm, deltoid to deltoid-ovate, cordate-sagittate or cordate-hastate at base, entire, with grey-white fine hairs or soft wool, glandular-punctate, greener and less hairy above when mature; petioles equalling lamina. Ray flts to 4cm, 13–21. Summer.
B. serrata Nels. & Macbr. To 30cm. Lvs 7–25cm, lanceolate to ovate-oblong, base subtruncate or cuneate, coriaceous, scabrous, serrate to pinnatifid. Ray flts 2–4cm, mostly 10–16. Late spring-early summer.

Balsam Pear *Momordica charantia*.
Balsam Poplar *Populus balsamifera*.
Balsam Root *Balsamorhiza*.
Balsam Willow *Salix pyrifolia*.
Baltic Rush *Juncus balticus*.
Bamboo. See *Arundinaria*, *Bambusa*, *Chimonobambusa*, *Chusquea*, *Dendrocalamus*, *Drepanostachyum*, *Hibanobambusa*, *Indocalamus*, *Otatea*, *Phyllostachys*, *Pleioblastus*, *Pseudosasa*, *Sasa*, *Sasaella*, *Sasamorpha*, *Semiarundinaria*, *Shibataea*, *Sinarundinaria*, *Sinobambusa*, *Thamnocalamus*.
Bamboo Fern *Coniogramme japonica*.
Bamboo-leaved Oak *Quercus bambusifolia*.
Bamboo Lily *Lilium japonicum*.
Bamboo Palm *Chamaedorea erumpens*; *Rhapis excelsa*.

Bambusa Schreb. Gramineae. 120 clumping bamboos. Culms mostly hollow, glab., terete, sometimes distorted; sheaths ± thick, blade broad; br. many, compound. Lvs small or medium-sized, rarely tessellated. Trop. & subtrop. Asia.
B. argentea hort. = *B. multiplex*.
B. glaucescens (Willd.) Sieb. ex Munro = *B. multiplex*.
B. multiplex (Lour.) Rausch. HEDGE BAMBOO. Culms 3–15m×1–4.5cm, slender, arching, glabrescent; sheaths usually glab. and lacking auricles and bristles; nodes prominent. Lvs 2.5–15×0.5–1.5cm, in 2 rows, somewhat silvery beneath; lf sheaths almost glab., lacking auricles and bristles. S China. 'Alphonse Karr': culms and br. striped orange-yellow and green, tinged pink when young, sheaths similarly striped. 'Fernleaf' ('Wang Tsai'): smaller, culms narrower with numerous small lvs. 'Golden Goddess': small; culms golden; lvs larger. 'Riviereorum' (CHINESE GODDESS BAMBOO): culms delicate, somewhat sinuous; lvs 1.6–3×0.3–0.8cm. 'Silver Stripe': the largest variant: culms, sheaths and lvs striped white or yellow. Z9.
B. nana Roxb. = *B. multiplex*.
B. oldhamii Munro. OLDHAM BAMBOO. Culms 6–15m×3–13cm, erect, glab., with white powder below nodes; sheaths glabrescent with few or small auricles and bristles; nodes not prominent. Lvs 15–30×3–6cm, tough and broad, denticulate; sheaths usually lacking auricles and bristles. China, Taiwan. Z9.
B. ventricosa McClure. BUDDHA'S BELLY BAMBOO. Culms 8–20m×3–5.5cm, glab., often shorter and swollen between nodes; sheaths glab., usually with auricles and bristles; nodes not prominent. Lvs 10–20×1.5–3cm, sheaths with small auricles and bristles. S China. Z9.
B. vulgaris Schräd. ex Wendl. COMMON BAMBOO. Culms 5–25m×5–25cm, glabrescent; sheaths dark brown-pubesc., esp. above, with auricles and bristles; nodes prominent. Lvs 10–25×1.8–4cm, near-glabrous; sheaths with auricles and bristles. Native distribution obscured by cult. 'Vittata': culms, sheaths and, often, lvs striped green and yellow. Z10.
→*Dendrocalamopsis*, *Leleba* and *Sinocalamus*.

Banana *Musa*.
Banana Passion Fruit *Passiflora antioquiensis*; *P. mollissima*.
Banana Plant *Nymphoides aquatica*.
Banana Shrub *Michelia figo*.
Banana Yucca *Yucca baccata*.
Banded Violet *Viola missouriensis*.
Baneberry *Actaea*.
Bangalay *Eucalyptus botryoides*.
Bangalow Palm *Archontophoenix*.
Banjo Fig *Ficus lyrata*.

Banksia L. f. Proteaceae. 50 trees and shrubs, sometimes with lignotubers. Lvs alt. or whorled, coriaceous, entire to dentate or lobed. Infl. spicate, dense, terminal, globose to cylindric; perianth tube short, slender, seg. concave; style slender, exserted. Fr. a compressed woody capsule in 'cones', with hardened bracts. Aus. Z9.
B. aculeata A.S. George. Robust, erect shrub, to 2m; new growth velvety. Lvs 4cm, broadly linear to narrowly cuneate,

sometimes canaliculate and prickly toothed. Infl. 4cm, pendent, cylindrical, green opening pink. W Aus.

B. aemula R. Br. WALLUM BANKSIA. Shrub or tree to 8m, bark corky. Lvs 12–15cm, obovate, serrate, red with coarse hairs. Fls yellow green in cylindrical heads. E Aus.

B. ashbyi Bak. f. ASHBY'S BANKSIA. Spreading tall shrub or tree to 8×3m. Lvs 10–30cm, linear, deeply wavy-serrate. Fls bright orange in 15–20cm spikes. W Aus.

B. attenuata R. Br. SLENDER BANKSIA. Shrub to tree, 2–10×2–10m. Lvs 8–14cm, broadly linear to linear-lanceolate, serrate, hairy beneath. Infl. cylindrical, to 26cm, green-yellow opening yellow. W Aus.

B. baueri R. Br. WOOLLY BANKSIA. Compact low shrub to 2m. Lvs 4–13cm, oblong-cuneate, serrate, brown-green at first. Infl. 20×13cm, woolly, orange-brown to grey. W Aus.

B. baxteri R. Br. BAXTER'S BANKSIA. Spreading shrub to 4×4m. Lvs 7–17cm, rusty brown then bright green, divided into triangular lobes. Flowering spikes globose, 5–8cm diam., green; young buds red-brown. W Aus.

B. benthamiana C. Gardn. Shrub to 4×3m. Lvs 10–25cm, erect, narrow-linear, broadly serrate, rusty red at first. Infl. yellow or orange, cylindrical-ovoid, 6cm wide. W Aus.

B. blechnifolia F. Muell. Prostrate. Lvs 25–45cm, erect, long-stalked, divided almost to midrib, lobes 8–22, margins slightly recurved. Infl. term., produced at ground level, cylindrical, to 16cm, red-pink. W Aus.

B. brownii Baxter ex R. Br. FEATHER-LEAVED BANKSIA. Tall shrub to 4×2m. Lvs 11cm, feather-like, soft, in whorls, white beneath, seg. linear-falcate. Infl. 15–20cm, oblong-cylindrical, fls cream at the base, grey-brown above. W Aus.

B. burdettii Bak. f. BURDETT'S BANKSIA. Compact shrub to 4×3m. Lvs 12–15cm, olive green, cuneate-oblong, shortly dentate. Infl. term., 7–8cm wide, fls pale orange with grey-white hairs, in bud. W Aus.

B. caleyi R. Br. CALEY'S BANKSIA. Bushy shrub to 2×2m. Lvs 7–14cm, narrow-cuneate, green, grey beneath, prickly-toothed. Infl. cylindrical to barrel-shaped, pendulous or decurved, pink to red. W Aus.

B. candolleana Meissn. PROPELLER BANKSIA. Many-stemmed spreading shrub to 13×2m. Lvs 30–40cm, linear, with many small triangular lobes. Infl. globose to ovoid, 5–6cm diam., golden-yellow. W Aus.

B. canei J.H. Willis. MOUNTAIN BANKSIA. Rounded spreading shrub to 3m. Lvs to 5cm, entire, broad-linear to obovate, dark green above, silver beneath. Infl. 15cm, cylindrical, pink to mauve in bud, opening yellow. Vict. 'Celia Rosser': low, spreading; lvs 6cm, deeply lobed; infl. 2–4cm.

B. coccinea R. Br. SCARLET BANKSIA. Shrub to small tree 2–5m×1–1.5m. Lvs to 9cm, oblong, dentate, velvety pink-brown at first, then deep green above, silver beneath. Infl. erect, globose, grey; styles scarlet. W Aus.

B. cuneata A.S. George MATCH-STICK BANKSIA. Erect, 1-stemmed, ± dense shrub to small tree. Lvs 5cm, obovate-cuneate, flat, sharp-toothed. Infl. globose; fls pink at base, then cream to lime green. W Aus.

B. dentata L. f. TROPICAL BANKSIA. Small tree to 7m. Lvs to 2.2cm, narrow-obovate, toothed. Infl. 5–15cm, cylindrical, cream opening yellow. N Aus.

B. dryandroides Baxter ex Sweet. DRYANDRA-LEAVED BANKSIA. Dense spreading shrub to 1×1.5m. Lvs 17cm, broadly linear, seg. triangular. Infl. pale brown to dull orange, spherical, 3cm diam. W Aus.

B. elderiana F. Muell. & Tate. SWORDFISH BANKSIA. Tangled bushy plant to 2–3m. Lvs 3–4cm, erect, rigid, linear, serrate, rusty brown, ageing to dark brown. Infl. broadly cylindrical, pendent, 5–7.5cm diam., yellow. W Aus.

B. ericifolia L. f. HEATH-LEAVED BANKSIA. Compact shrub to 5m high. Lvs 2cm, narrow-linear. Infl. to 25cm, cylindrical, erect, orange-red to russet. E Aus. var. *macrantha* A.S. George. Lvs more crowded, fls larger and often deeper in colour. A form with a grey perianth tube and orange style has been recorded.

B. gardneri A.S. George. Dwarf, prostrate; st. densely tomentose. Young lvs and fl. buds rusty brown. Lvs 14–40cm, erect, deeply divided. Infl. 10cm, cylindrical, dark red-brown. W Aus.

B. 'Giant Candles'. (*B. ericifolia* ×*B. spinulosa*.) Lvs to 4.5cm, linear, toothed, slightly revolute. Infl. to 40cm, deep orange.

B. goodii R. Br. GOOD'S BANKSIA. Low to prostrate shrub to 45cm. Lvs 45cm, few, obovate, irregularly toothed, deep red-purple at first. Infl. rusty brown. W Aus.

B. grandis Willd. BULL BANKSIA. Tall robust tree to 10m. Lvs 45cm, deeply lobed, pink-brown at first, then bright green. Infl. to 40cm, yellow, cylindrical. W Aus.

B. grossa A.S. George. Small open shrub to 1m. Lvs 12cm, linear, revolute, velvety brown ageing dark green or blue-green. Fls yellow to red-brown in cylindrical spikes. W Aus.

B. hookeriana Meissn. HOOKER'S BANKSIA. Many-stemmed, bushy shrub to 1.2m. Lvs 20cm, narrow-linear, finely toothed; young lvs rusty brown. Infl. 15cm, cylindrical, woolly white, opening orange. W Aus. A natural hybrid, *B. hookeriana* ×*B. menziesii*, has been recorded: fls lemon yellow.

B. ilicifolia R. Br. HOLLY-LEAVED BANKSIA. Erect, stout tree to 10m. Lvs to 10cm, obovate to elliptic, shiny, entire or prickly toothed. Buds pink tipped bright green. Fls in sessile, term. heads, cream ageing to pink or red. W Aus.

B. integrifolia L. f. COAST BANKSIA. Low shrub to large robust tree, to 25m. Lvs to 10cm, green, white in whorls of 3–5(8), narrow-obovate. Infl. cylindrical, 10–12cm, pale yellow. E Aus.

B. laevigata Meissn. TENNIS BALL BANKSIA. Open to bushy shrub to 3.5m. Lvs 10–14cm, broadly linear or narrow obovate, rusty-brown toothed. Fls yellow and brown in tightly spherical heads. W Aus.

B. laricina C. Gardn. ROSE BANKSIA. Rounded shrub to 1.2m. Lvs 1–1.5cm, narrow-linear. Fls yellow to red-brown in spherical heads. Fruiting cones brown-green with duckbill-like follicles.

B. lemanniana Meissn. Bushy shrub, 1–4m. Lvs 5–9cm, obovate, toothed, young growth bronze-brown. Infl. pendulous, lemon-yellow, cylindrical, to 11cm. W Aus.

B. littoralis R. Br. SWAMP BANKSIA. Stout, often gnarled tree to 10m. Lvs 15–20cm, linear, silver beneath. Infl. 1–2cm, cylindrical, numerous, lemon-yellow. W Aus.

B. marginata Cav. SILVER BANKSIA. Low shrub or tree, to 12m tree. Lvs 1.5–6cm, linear to wedge-shaped, entire or serrate. Infl. cylindrical, 5–10cm, lemon yellow. E Aus.

B. media R. Br. SOUTHERN PLAINS BANKSIA. Dense shrub, 2–5(10)m. Lvs 5–12cm, pale brown when young, wedge-shaped, toothed. Infl. cylindrical, 10–15cm, forming a bright yellow dome.

B. meissneri Lehm. MEISSNER'S BANKSIA. Medium spreading shrub, 1.5×2m. Lvs 7cm, linear to narrow elliptic, deflexed. Infl. spherical, brown, apex delicate pink. W Aus.

B. menziesii R. Br. FIREWOOD BANKSIA. Low shrub to medium tree, to 10m; bark with spherical projections. Lvs 10–25cm, oblong, with small teeth. Infl. ± cylindrical, 12cm, pink, red, yellow to bronze or chocolate. W Aus.

B. nutans R. Br. NODDING BANKSIA. Compact rounded shrub to 1m. Lvs 1.5–2cm, linear, blue-green, revolute. Infl. cylindrical, nodding; young fl. buds green ageing to pink purple, opening rusty brown with an onion-like smell. Spring–summer. W Aus.

B. oblongifolia Cav. Low spreading shrub to 1m. Lvs 8–11cm, oblong, usually serrate. Infl. 10cm, cylindrical, green-yellow. E Aus.

B. occidentalis R. Br. RED SWAMP BANKSIA. Erect bushy shrub, 3×2–3m. Lvs 10–13cm, linear, whorled, silver beneath. Infl. red, cylindrical, to 14cm. W Aus.

B. oreophila A.S. George. WESTERN MOUNTAIN BANKSIA. Spreading shrub to 3m high. Lvs 1cm, narrowly obovate, blue-green, pungent. Infl. to 9cm, grey-mauve. W Aus.

B. ornata F. Muell. ex Meissn. DESERT BANKSIA. Shrub to 2.5m. Lvs 10cm, narrowly obovate, serrate. Infl. to 10cm, cylindrical, grey-green opening yellow-green, then brown. E Aus.

B. paludosa R. Br. SWAMP BANKSIA. Compact shrub to 1m high, 1.5m wide. Lvs 8–10cm, sometimes whorled, narrow-obovate, toothed or entire. Infl. cylindrical, to 13cm, yellow-brown. E Aus.

B. petiolaris F. Muell. Prostrate shrub, to 50cm. Lvs 40cm, toothed, oblong, silver-grey beneath, long-stalked. Infl. to 16cm, cylindrical, cream, borne at ground level. W Aus.

B. pilostylis C. Gardn. Dense, diffuse shrub to 2m. Lvs 15cm, wedge-shaped, toothed, silver-grey beneath, new growth brown. Infl. 10cm, cylindrical, cream. W Aus.

B. praemorsa Andrews. CUT-LEAF BANKSIA. Compact, dense shrub 3–4×3–4m. Lvs 2–6cm, obovate, toothed, apex abrupt. Infl. robust, 20–25×8cm, creamy-brown. Summer. W Aus.

B. prionotes Lindl. ACORN BANKSIA. Shrub or tree to 10m. Lvs 15–30cm, broad-linear, grey-green, toothed. Infl. cylindrical, to 15cm, densely woolly in bud, opening orange. W Aus.

B. pulchella R. Br. TEASEL BANKSIA. Small, spreading shrub to 1m. Lvs 1–1.3cm, linear. Infl. cylindrical, 2.5cm, orange-brown. W Aus.

B. quercifolia R. Br. OAK-LEAVED BANKSIA. Erect, bushy shrub, 3×2m. Lvs 3–15cm, cuneate, serrate. Infl. red and green opening rusty-brown, narrow, cylindrical, 10cm. Autumn-winter. W Aus.

B. repens Labill. CREEPING BANKSIA. Prostrate. Lvs erect, to 30cm, irregularly lobed, young lvs rusty brown. Infl. cylindrical, 10cm, pink-brown. Spring. W Aus.

B. robur Cav. SWAMP BANKSIA. Open shrub to 2m. Lvs 30cm, leathery, midvein prominent, yellow or brown. Infl. cylindrical, 17cm, yellow-green. E Aus.

B. seminuda (A.S. George) Rye. SWAMP BANKSIA. Robust shrub or tree to 25m. Lvs 10cm, broad-linear, silver beneath. Infl. cylindrical, 15cm, yellow or red. W Aus.

B. serrata L. SAW BANKSIA. Small tree, 2–15m. Lvs 15cm, narrowly obovate, serrate. Infl. cylindrical, 15cm, green-yellow. E Aus.

B. solandri R. Br. SOLANDER'S BANKSIA. Spreading, open shrub to 4m. Lvs 25cm, obovate, apex truncate, dark green, broadly toothed. Infl. cylindrical, 16cm, fawn. W Aus.

B. speciosa R. Br. SHOWY BANKSIA. Large shrub or tree to 6m. Lvs to 40cm, linear, grey-green, silver beneath, deeply incised. Infl. 12cm, squat, rounded, white opening yellow-green. W Aus.

B. sphaerocarpa R. Br. ROUND-FRUITED BANKSIA. Open, rounded shrub to 2m. Lvs 10cm, linear, revolute. Infl. spherical, 8cm across, brown. Summer–winter. W Aus.

B. spinulosa Sm. HAIRPIN BANKSIA. Dense rounded shrub to 2m. Lvs 8–12cm, linear, revolute. Infl. cylindrical, 18cm; styles yellow to red. Autumn–winter. E Aus.

B. tricuspis Meissn. Shrub to 4m. Lvs 10cm, linear, revolute, apex tricuspidate. Infl. cylindrical, 10–15cm, lemon-yellow. W Aus.

B. verticillata R. Br. GRANITE BANKSIA. Spreading shrub to small tree to 4m. Lvs 9cm, oblong, dark green, silver beneath. Infl. yellow, cylindrical, 20cm. W Aus.

B. victoriae Meissn. WOOLLY ORANGE BANKSIA. Tall, rounded shrub to 5m. Lvs 20–30cm, broad linear, with deep pungent lobes. Infl. cylindrical, 10–12cm, white and hairy in bud, opening orange. W Aus.

B. violacea C. Gardn. VIOLET BANKSIA. Low shrub to 1.5m. Lvs 2cm, linear. Infl. spherical, 6cm diam., purple. W Aus.

Banksian Rose *Rosa banksiae*.
Banyan *Ficus benghalensis*.
Baobab *Adansonia digitata*.

Baphia Afzel. ex Lodd. Leguminosae (Papilionoideae). 60 erect or scrambling shrubs or trees. Lvs simple, entire. Fls fragrant, pea-like; sta. 10, free. Trop. Afr., Madag. Z9.

B. massaiensis Taub. Shrub or small tree. Lvs to 12×8cm, elliptic to obovate, glab. or hairy. Fls in axill. clusters; standard to 2.5×2cm, white, cream or pale mauve. C Tanz. ssp. *obovata* (Schinz) Brummitt. Lvs to 10×6cm, hairy. Fls occas. in axill. cymes; standard to 2×2cm.

B. nitida Lodd. AFRICAN SANDALWOOD; CAMWOOD. Shrub or small tree. Lvs to 21×9cm, ovate to oblong-elliptic or lanceolate, glab. Fls in axill. clusters of 2–5 or solitary; standard to 2×2cm, white. Afr.

B. obovata Schinz = *B. massaiensis* ssp. *obovata*.

B. racemosa (Hochst.) Bak. f. CAMWOOD; VIOLET PEA. Shrub or small tree. Lvs to 11×5.5cm, ovate to lanceolate, occas. elliptic, hairy. Fls in axill. rac., violet-scented, standard to 1.5×1.5cm, white veined purple. Spring. S Afr.

Baptisia Vent. FALSE INDIGO; WILD INDIGO. Leguminosae (Papilionoideae). 17 perenn. herbs. Lvs usually trifoliolate. US.

B. alba (L.) Vent. Bushy herb to 2m, glab., often glaucous. Lvs to 5cm; lfts obovate to narrowly elliptic-lanceolate. Rac. erect, to 20-fld; cream-white, occas. streaked with darker patches, standard often marked with purple near base. Virg. to Florid. 'Pendula': habit nodding.

B. australis (L.) R. Br. BLUE FALSE INDIGO. Upright or spreading herb to 1.5m, glab., often glaucous. Lvs to 8cm; lfts to 4cm, ovate to oblanceolate. Fls in 5 to many-fld rac.; cor. light mauve streaked purple or deep indigo, keel white or cream. Summer. E US.

B. ×bicolor Greenm. & Larisey. (*B. australis* ×*B. bracteata*.) Spreading herb, pubesc. Lfts to 5cm, oblanceolate. Fls in arching, many-fld rac.; standard mauve, keel and wings cream. Summer. Oklah., Kansas, Missouri.

B. bracteata Muhlenb. ex Elliott. Spreading or ascending herb to 70cm, pubesc. Lfts to 10cm, oblanceolate to cuneate-obovate. Fls in ascending or horizontal, 5–20-fld rac.; cor. white to bright yellow. Spring. E US.

B. caerulea Michx. = *B. australis*.

B. cinerea (Raf.) Fern. & Schubert. Erect or low-spreading herb. St. to 80cm. Lfts to 7.5cm, obovate, oblanceolate or narrowly elliptic, leathery, glab. above. Fls in erect or arching rac.; cor. bright yellow. Spring–summer. N & S Carolina.

B. confusa Sweet ex G. Don = *B. australis*.

B. exaltata Sweet = *B. australis*.

B. lactea (Raf.) Thieret. WHITE FALSE INDIGO. Erect or spreading herb to 2m, glab. Lfts to 8cm, elliptic-obovate to oblanceolate. Fls in term., many-fld rac.; cor. cream-white, standard occas. marked purple. Spring. E US.

B. leucantha Torr. & A. Gray = *B. lactea*.

B. leucophaea Nutt. = *B. bracteata*.

B. minor Lehm. = *B. australis*.

B. nepalensis Hook. = *Piptanthus nepalensis*.

B. perfoliata (L.) R. Br. Erect herb to 30cm, glab., glaucous. Lvs to 8cm, simple, perfoliate. Fls axill., solitary, bright yellow. Summer. SE US.

B. tinctoria (L.) Vent. HORSEFLY WEED; RATTLE WEED; WILD INDIGO. Much-branched, erect herb to 1m, glab., often glaucous. Lfts to 4cm, obovate-cuneate to spathulate. Fls in numerous, 4–20-fld, arching rac.; cor. yellow, margins often ruffled. Summer. E US.

B. versicolor Lodd. = *B. australis*.

B. villosa auctt. = *B. bracteata* or *B. cinerea*.

Baracaro *Ormosia coarctata*.

Barbacenia Vand.
B. gracile Brongn. = *Dasylirion acrotrichum*.
B. squamata Herb. = *Vellozia squamata*.

Barba de Boi Grande *Syagrus macrocarpa*.
Barbados Cherry *Malpighia emarginata*; *M. glabra*.
Barbados Flower Fence *Caesalpinia pulcherrima*.
Barbados Gooseberry *Pereskia aculeata*.
Barbados Lily *Hippeastrum puniceum*.
Barbados Maidenhair Fern *Adiantum tenerum*.
Barbados Nut *Jatropha curcas*.
Barbados Pride *Adenanthera pavonina*; *Caesalpinia pulcherrima*.

Barbarea R. Br. ST. BARBARA'S HERB. Cruciferae. 12 bienn. or perenn. herbs. St. erect. Lvs mostly radical, pinnately cut or entire. Fls small, 4-merous, racemose. N temp. regions. Z6.

B. praecox (Sm.) R. Br. = *B. verna*.

B. verna (Mill.) Asch. LAND CRESS; AMERICAN CRESS; BELLE ISLE CRESS; EARLY WINTER CRESS. Bienn. or perenn. grown as ann., to 75cm. Lvs with 6–10 pairs of lateral lobes, pinnatisect on upper part of st. Pet. 5–7mm, yellow. SW Eur.

B. vulgaris R. Br. YELLOW ROCKET; ROCKCRESS; BITTERCRESS. To 1m. Lvs with 2–5 pairs lat. lobes, becoming simple up st. Pet. 5–7mm, yellow. Eur. 'Flore Pleno' (DOUBLE YELLOW ROCKET): fls double. 'Variegata': lvs splashed yellow. Z6.

→*Erysium* and *Sisymbrium*.

Barbary Fig *Opuntia ficus-indica*.
Barbasco *Jacquinia barbasco*.
Barbed Wire Plant *Tylecodon reticulatus*.
Barbel Palm *Acanthophoenix*.
Barberry *Berberis*.
Barberton Cycad *Encephalartos paucidentatus*.
Barberton Daisy *Gerbera jamesonii*.

Barbosella Schltr. Orchidaceae. 20 diminutive epiphytic orchids. St. tufted, bearing 1 linear to lanceolate lf. Fls solitary, long-stalked, from lf insertion; dors. sep. semi-erect, concave above, lat. sep. fused in synsepalum; pet. free, often fringed; lip shorter than tep., trilobed, hinged. Venez., Colomb., Ecuad., Peru. Z10.

B. cucullata (Lindl.) Schltr. Lvs to 5×0.75cm. Fls 4cm across, golden-green, on stalk to 8cm.

B. miersii (Lindl.) Schltr. = *Barbrodria miersii*.

→*Pleurothallis* and *Restrepia*.

Barbrodria Luer. Orchidaceae. 1 epiphytic orchid. Rhiz. creeping. St. short bearing 1 fleshy elliptic lf. Infl. filiform, exceeding lvs, 1-fld; lateral sep. connate at base, pet. serrulate; lip hinged.

B. miersii (Lindl.) Luer.

→*Barbosella, Pleurothallis* and *Restrepia*.

Baria *Cordia gerascanthus*.

Barkeria Knowles & Westc. Orchidaceae. ± 10 epiphytic or lithophytic orchids. Roots thick, silver-grey. Pbs clustered, cane-like. Lvs alt., lanceolate to ovate, sheathing, slightly fleshy. Rac. long-stalked, term.; tep. ± narrow, reflexed; lip ovate-rhombic, spreading; callus carinate, marked yellow or white. Z10.

B. cyclotella Rchb. f. Close to *B. lindleyana*; smaller with narrower, purple or red-tinted lvs; fls vivid magenta to crimson. Mex.

B. lindleyana Batem. ex Lindl. Pbs to 15cm. Lvs to 15×4cm, linear-lanceolate to oblong-lanceolate, sometimes flushed rosy-purple. Fls to 7.5cm diam., white or lilac to deep purple, lip to 35×25mm often lined red-purple. Mex. to Costa Rica.

B. skinneri (Batem. ex Lindl.) Paxt. Pbs to 14cm. Lvs to 15×2cm, fleshy, elliptic to elliptic-lanceolate, pale green. Fls to 4cm diam., lilac-purple or rose-purple to red-magenta; lip 15–18×1–15mm. Guat.

B. spectabilis Batem. ex Lindl. Pbs to 15cm. Lvs to 15×4cm, ovate to linear-lanceolate. Fls usually pale lilac; lip spotted red-purple, 28–35×20–25mm. S Mex., Guat., El Salvador. →*Epidendrum*.

Barleria L. Acanthaceae. 250 everg. herbs and shrubs, usually spiny. Lvs entire. Fls in spikes, with spinose bracts; sep. 4; cor. tubular, expanded at mouth, lobes 5, broad, spreading. OW tropics and subtrop. Z10.
B. cristata L. PHILIPPINE VIOLET. Bristly shrublet. Lvs 2.5–10cm, oblong-elliptic. Fls 3–5cm, in dense axill. spikes, pale blue-violet, sometimes pink or white; sep. spiny. Summer. India, Burm.
B. lupulina Lindl. HOP-HEADED BARLERIA. Spiny shrublet. Lvs 10cm, narrowly lanceolate, green, midvein pink to red. Fls 2.5cm, in term. hop-like spikes, yellow, bracts overlapping. Summer. Maur.
B. obtusa Nees. Unarmed shrublet. Lvs to 7.5cm, usually smaller, elliptic. Fls 3cm, purple in loose axill. infl. Winter–spring. S Afr.

Barley *Hordeum*.

Barlia Parl. Orchidaceae. 1 terrestrial tuberous orchid, 25–60cm. Lvs oblong to ovate, reduced on st. Fls fragrant in a dense spike to 23cm; tep. olive to violet spotted purple, lip to 2cm, rose spotted purple, lobes 3, green, laterals undulate, midlobe longer, straight, cleft. Medit. Z6.
B. robertiana (Lois.) Greuter. GIANT ORCHID.
→*Himantoglossum*.

Barnedesia L. f. Compositae. 22 shrubs or small trees, often spiny. Lvs entire. Cap. radiate, receptacle flat; phyllaries multiseriate; ray flts bilabiate, pink or purple; disc flts few. Colomb. to NE Arg. Z9.
B. caryophylla (Vell.) S.F. Blake. Shrub to 60cm. Lvs ovate, acute. Cap. solitary; flts rose-pink. S Amer.
B. rosea Lindl. = *B. caryophylla*.

Barnyard Grass, Barnyard Millet *Echinochloa crus-galli*.
Barometer Bush *Leucophyllum frutescens*.

Barosma Willd.
B. betulina (Bergius) Bartling & H.L. Wendl. = *Agathosma betulina*.
B. crenulata (L.) Hook. = *Agathosma crenulata*.
B. ovata (Thunb.) Bartling & Wendl. = *Agathosma ovata*.
B. pulchella (L.) Bartling & Wendl. = *Agathosma pulchella*.

Barrel Cactus *Ferocactus*.
Barrens Claw-flower *Calothamnus validus*.
Barren Strawberry *Waldsteinia fragarioides*.
Barrenwort *Epimedium alpinum*.

Barringtonia Forst. & Forst. f. Lecythidaceae. 39 everg. trees or shrubs. Lvs simple, entire or crenate-serrate. Fls in rac. or spikes, usually pendulous; cal. splitting into 5 lobes or circumscissile; pet. 3–5; sta. numerous, protruding. E Afr. Z10.
B. acutangula (L.) Gaertn. INDIAN OAK. Shrub or small tree, to 13m. Lvs in 16×6cm, oblanceolate to obovate, finely toothed. Fls in pendulous rac.; pet. 4, red; sta. to 2cm, in 3 whorls. Afghan. to N Aus.
B. asiatica (L.) Kurz. Tree, to 20m. Lvs in 38×8cm, obovate, entire, glossy. Fls in erect rac.; pet. 4, to 8.5cm, white; sta. to 12cm, in 6 whorls, purple. Madag. to Pacific.
B. racemosa (L.) Spreng. Shrub or small tree, to 20m. Lvs to 13×13cm, obovate, crenate to serrate. Fls in pendulous rac. or spikes; pet. to 2.5cm, white or red. E & S Afr., SE Asia, N Aus., S Pacific.
B. samoensis A. Gray. Shrub or small tree, to 12m. Lvs to 100×24cm, obovate, crenate to serrate. Fls in term. or ramiflorous, pendulous rac.; pet. 4, to 3.5cm, white or red. SE Celebes to Micronesia, New Guinea, Polyn.
B. speciosa Forst. & Forst. f. = *B. asiatica*.

Bar-room Plant *Aspidistra elatior*.

Barrosoa R. King & H. Robinson. Compositae. 9 perenn. herbs. St. erect, densely pubesc. Lvs lanceolate to broad ovate, toothed. Cap. discoid, in a dense corymb; receptacle conic; phyllaries 15–24; flts funnelform. Trop. S Amer. Z10.
B. candolleana (Hook. & Arn.) R. King & H. Robinson. 40–100cm. Lvs 3–8cm, ovate to lanceolate, serrate. Cap. 4–5mm; flts dull pink to purple. Trop. S Amer.
→*Ageratum* and *Eupatorium*.

Bartholina R. Br. Orchidaceae. 2 dwarf tuberous terrestrial orchids. Lf solitary, to 2cm diam., orbicular, fleshy, lying on soil surface. Fl. solitary on a slender, hairy stalk erect to 8cm; tep. small, lanceolate, connivent; lip to 6cm diam., flabellate, deeply and finely cut, beard-like. S Afr. Z10.
B. burmanniana (L.) Ker-Gawl. Fls pale lilac.

Bartlettina R. King & H. Robinson. Compositae. 23 erect shrubs or small trees. St. branched. Lvs lanceolate to broadly ovate. Cap. discoid, shortly pedunculate, usually in corymbose pan.; phyllaries in 3–5 series; flts few to numerous. Trop. Amer. Z10.
B. sordida (Less.) R. King & H. Robinson. Shrub to 3m. St. densely red tomentose at first. Lvs to 10cm, broadly ovate, dentate. Cap. to 1.2cm diam., corymbose; flts fragrant, violet. Mex.
→*Eupatorium*.

Bartonia Pursh ex Sims.
B. aurea Lindl. = *Mentzelia lindleyi*.

Bartram's Oak *Quercus ×heterophylla*.

Bartschella Britt. & Rose.
B. schumannii (Hildm.) Britt. & Rose = *Mammillaria schumannii*.

Bartsia L. Scrophulariaceae. *c*60 root parasites often found on grasses. Lvs opposite. Rac. bracteate; cal. seg. 4; cor. 2-lipped, upper lip 2-lobed, lower lip 3-lobed. Eur., Andes. Z6.
B. alpina L. VELVET BELLS; ALPINE BARTSIA. Pubesc. ann. to 20cm. Lvs ovate, crenate-serrate. Bracts dull purple lip; cor. 15–20mm, dark purple. Summer. Eur.
B. coccinea L. = *Castilleja coccinea*.
B. odontites (L.) Huds. = *Odontites verna*.
B. pallida L. = *Castilleja pallida*.

Basella L. MALABAR NIGHTSHADE. Basellaceae. 5 glab., twining herbs. Lvs oblong or rounded, fleshy. Fls small in axill. spikes; perianth swelling to enclose fr. Trop. Afr. and Asia. Z10.
B. alba L. INDIAN SPINACH; MALABAR SPINACH; CEYLON SPINACH. 1–9m. Lvs 5–15×4–12cm, oblong to broadly ovate, base shallow-cordate, glossy pale green. Infl. to 15cm; fls white, rose, red or purple. Fr. 6mm, black, dark red or white, glossy. Afr., SE Asia, now pantrop. 'Rubra': st., petioles and fls flushed red-pink.
B. tuberosa (Caldas) Humb. = *Ullucus tuberosus*.

BASELLACEAE Moq. 4/15. *Anredera, Basella, Ullucus*.

Basil *Ocimum*.

Basilicum Moench.
B. myriostachyum (Benth.) Kuntze = *Tetradenia riparia*.

Basil Thyme *Acinos arvensis*.
Basket Fern *Drynaria rigidula*; *Nephrolepis pectinata*.
Basket Flower *Adenanthos obovatus*; *Hymenocallis narcissiflora*.
Basket Grass *Oplismenus hirtellus*.
Basket Oak *Quercus prinus*.
Basket-of-gold *Aurinia*.
Basket Plant *Aeschynanthus*.
Basket Spike Moss *Selaginella apoda*.
Basket Willow *Salix purpurea*.

Bassia All. Chenopodiaceae. 26 ann. or perenn. herbs. Lvs usually narrow, entire, sometimes downy. Infl. spicate; fls inconspicuous. Cosmop. Z6.
B. scoparia (L.) A.J. Scott. SUMMER CYPRESS; BURNING BUSH; BELVEDERE. Erect, densely-branched, cypress-shaped ann., 20–150cm. Lvs narrow-lanceolate or oblong, 5cm, thin. Asia; widely nat. Eur. & N Amer. f. *trichophylla* (Schmeiss) Schinz & Thell. Form usually cultivated; lvs narrow, turning deep to brilliant purple-red in late summer (hence 'burning bush').
→*Kochia*.

Basswood *Tilia americana*.
Bastard Balm *Melittis*.
Bastard Cabbage Tree *Geoffroea*; *Schefflera umbellifera*.
Bastard Cinnamon *Cinnamomum aromaticum*.
Bastard Indigo *Amorpha fruticosa*.
Bastard Olive *Buddleja saligna*.
Bastard Pecacuanha *Asclepias curassavica*.
Bastard Rocket *Reseda odorata*.
Bastard Sandalwood *Myoporum sandwicense*.
Bastard Toadflax *Comandra*.
Bastard Vervain *Stachytarpheta*.

Bastard Yellowwood *Afrocarpus falcatus.*

Batemannia Lindl. Orchidaceae. 2 epiphytic orchids. Pbs clustered, oblong-ovoid, tetragonal. Lvs apical, paired, elliptic-lanceolate. Fls to 5, in a basal rac., dors. sep. elliptic-oblong, lat. sep. narrow; pet. oblong-ovoid; lip trilobed, fleshy. Braz. to Boliv. Z10.
B. colleyi Lindl. Pbs to 6cm. Lvs to 20cm. Fls 7.5cm diam., lustrous rusty red to maroon tipped or edged pale green, lip white stained garnet at base of midlobe.
B. grandiflora (A. Rich.) Rchb. f. = *Mendoncella grandiflora.*
B. meleagris (Lindl.) Rchb. f. = *Huntleya meleagris.*

Bat Flower *Tacca chantrieri*; *T. integrifolia.*
Bath Asparagus *Ornithogalum pyrenaicum.*
Bat-leaf Passion Flower *Passiflora coriacea.*
Batoko Plum *Flacourtia indica.*

Batschia J.F. Gmel.
B. canescens Michx. = *Lithospermum canescens.*
B. disticha G. Don = *Lithospermum distichum.*

Bat Tree *Ficus amplissima.*

Bauera Banks ex Andrews. Cunoniaceae. 3 everg. shrubs. Br. slender. Lvs in whorls appearing to consist of 6 lfts. Fls solitary, axill., often clustered toward ends of br.; cal. 4–10-lobed; pet. 4–10; sta. 4–10. E Aus., Tasm. Z9.
B. capitata Ser. ex DC. Dwarf shrub to 40cm, erect or spreading. Lfts to 0.6cm, narrow, with a conspicuous lobe on each side, glab. Fls to 1cm diam., white, subsessile. E Aus.
B. rubioides Andrews. Shrub to 2m, prostrate to bushy, spreading. Lfts to 1.2cm, ovate or obovate to oblong-lanceolate, oft. serrate, glab. or pubesc. Fls to 2cm diam., white or pink; pedicel to 1.5cm. E Aus., Tasm.
B. sessiliflora F. Muell. Shrub to 2m, densely branched. Lfts to 2.5cm, oblong, dark to bright green, entire, pubesc. Fls to 1.5cm diam., rose-purple or magenta, sessile. Vict.

Bauhinia L. MOUNTAIN EBONY; ORCHID TREE. Leguminosae (Caesalpinioideae). 250–300 thorny trees, shrubs or lianes. Lvs reniform to bilobed, rarely entire or bifoliolate. Fls in corymbose rac.; cal. spathe-like; pet. 5, spreading, showy; sta. to 10, long, declinate. Trop. and subtrop. Z9.
B. aculeata L. Tree or shrub. Lvs to 10cm, bilobed, suborbicular-cordate to ovate-oblong, leathery, glab. Thorns paired, curved. Infl. 2–4-fld; pet. to 6cm, white, oblanceolate to obovate, clawed. Summer. C Amer.
B. acuminata L. Shrub to 3m. Lvs to 10cm, suborbicular to ovate, bilobed, finely downy. Rac., few-fld; pet. to 4.5cm, obovate, white to cream. Summer–early autumn. SE Asia.
B. alba hort. = *B. variegata.*
B. aurita Ait. = *B. variegata.*
B. binata Blanco. Shrub. Br. climbing, often with tendrils. Lvs bifoliolate; lfts to 4cm, ovate. Corymbs dense; pet. to 2.5cm, obovate or spathulate, hairy, white; sta. red. Spring. SE Asia (Is.).
B. ×*blakeana* Dunn. (*B. purpurea* ×*B. variegata?*) Everg. shrub or tree to 12m. Lvs bilobed, to 20cm, lobes obtuse. Rac. to 15cm across, tawny-hairy; pet. narrowly obovate, to 8cm, mauve to bright red. Winter. China.
B. candicans Benth. = *B. forficata.*
B. candida Roxb. = *B. variegata* 'Candida'.
B. carronii Muell. QUEENSLAND EBONY. Differs from *B. cunninghamii* in pet. obovate, white. Queensld.
B. championii Benth. Liane, with tendrils. Lvs bilobed to half the length, lobes obtuse, hairy beneath. Fls minute, in rac. to 10cm; pet. white. Hong Kong.
B. corymbosa Roxb. ex DC. PHANERA. Liane, with tendrils. Lvs to 4cm, pale green beneath, suborbicular-cordate, bilobed. Rac. dense; pet. to 1.5cm, white to pink or white streaked with pink. S China.
B. cunninghamii (Benth.) Benth. Tree to 6m. Br. pendulous. Lvs bifoliolate; lfts to 3cm, ovate, leathery. Fls 2–3 per cluster; pet. to 2cm, ovate, cream-white or magenta, hairy. Summer. N Aus.
B. cupulata Benth. Shrub or tree. Lvs to 12cm, bilobed, ovate to subcordate, stiff, lobes obtuse. Fls in short rac.; pet. to 9cm, linear-filiform, white. Winter. Braz., Venez.
B. divaricata L. Shrub or small tree, sparsely hairy. Lvs to 12cm, bilobed ovate to almost square, to 12cm, hairy above, lobes divaricate. Rac. many-fld; pet. to 2cm, unequal, long-clawed, white to pale mauve. Summer–autumn. Antilles, Mex., C Amer.
B. faberi Oliv. Climbing shrub, glab. to sparsely hairy. Lvs to 5.5cm, bilobed, lobes obtuse. Rac. dense; pet. to 1cm, obovate

to spathulate, usually spreading. Summer. SE Asia. var. *microphylla* Oliv. Lvs to 1.5cm.
B. fassoglensis Kotschy ex Schweinf. Vine, climbing via tendrils. Lvs to 12cm, emarginate or bilobed, obcordate to reniform, lobes obtuse. Rac. loose; pet. to 3cm, obovate, yellow. Summer–early autumn. Afr.
B. forficata Link. Spiny shrub or tree to 15m. Lvs to 12cm, bilobed, ovate, slightly downy beneath, lobes acute. Infl. axill., to 4-fld; pet. 5–10cm, linear to lanceolate, white, clawed. Summer. S Amer.
B. galpinii N.E. Br. Spreading or climbing shrub to 3m. Lvs to 5cm, emarginate or bilobed, lobes obtuse. Rac. short, pet. to 4cm, broadly obovate, clawed, orange or red, ruffled. Spring–autumn. S Afr.
B. glabra Jacq. St. and tendrils often compressed. Lvs lustrous, bilobed or bifoliolate, lobes or lfts acute. Pet. to 2cm, clawed, white with purple streaks. Summer–winter. Trop. Amer.
B. glauca hort. = *B. hupehana.*
B. grandiflora hort. = *B. forficata.*
B. hookeri hort. = *B. binata* or *B. tomentosa.*
B. hupehana Craib. Climbing shrub, often with tendrils, hairy becoming glab. Lvs to 8cm, bilobed, ovate, lobes obtuse. Fls many, malodorous; pet. to 1.5cm, obovate, clawed, white or pink. Spring–early summer. China.
B. kappleri Sagot = *B. monandra.*
B. kurzii hort. = *B. purpurea.*
B. malabarica Roxb. Tree to 15m. Lvs to 12cm, bilobed, cordate to reniform, glaucous beneath, lobes acute. Fls many, clustered; pet. to 2cm, white to pink, pubesc. Winter. SE Asia.
B. megalandra Griseb. = *B. multinervia.*
B. mollicella Blake = *B. aculeata.*
B. monandra Kurz. As for *B. variegata* except tree to 6m; fls pale pink, central pet. magenta-streaked. Winter. Burm.
B. multinervia (HBK) DC. Shrub or tree to 4.5m; young parts tomentose. Lvs to 14cm, bilobed, ovate to subcordate, hairy on veins beneath. Fls solitary or 2–3; pet. to 6cm, linear, white. Winter. W Indies, Trin., Venez.
B. pauletia Pers. RAILWAY FENCE BAUHINIA. Spiny shrub or small tree to 7m, occas. climbing. Lvs to 6cm, bilobed, suborbicular to cordate. Infl. few- to many-fld; pet. to 10cm, filiform, pale green. Winter. N S Amer., Antilles, Mex.
B. petersiana Bolle. Spreading shrub or liane. Young shoots short-hairy. Lvs to 6cm, bilobed, cordate to truncate, lobes spreading, obtuse. Infl. few-fld; pet. to 8cm, oblanceolate, clawed, white, ruffled. Summer. Afr.
B. petiolata hort. = *B. acuminata.*
B. picta hort. = *B. tomentosa.*
B. piliostigma hort. = *B. fassoglensis.*
B. polycarpa Wallich ex Benth. = *B. viridescens.*
B. porosa Boiv. ex Baill. Shrub, br. climbing, glabrate. Lvs to 10cm entire or bilobed, orbicular to ovate. Infl. lax; pet. cream to pale yellow, clawed. Summer–early autumn. Madag.
B. punctata Bolle = *B. galpinii.*
B. purpurea L. non hort. Differs from *B. variegata* in pet. not overlapping, oblanceolate. Autumn. India to Malay Penins.
B. purpurea hort. non L. = *B. variegata.*
B. racemosa Lam. Shrub or small tree. Br. straggling or drooping. Lvs to 6cm, bilobed, suborbicular-cordate, occas. pubesc. beneath, lobes obtuse. Fls. clustered; pet. spreading, white to cream. Summer–autumn. SE Asia.
B. reticulata DC. = *B. fassoglensis.*
B. retusa Roxb. Tree. Lvs to 13cm, emarginate, suborbicular to cordate, coriaceous. Infl. compound, corymbose; pet. to 1cm, yellow spotted purple. Autumn–winter. SE Asia.
B. rufescens Lam. Differs from *B. racemosa* in br. spreading; lvs to 2.5cm across; fls fragrant. Throughout the year. Afr.
B. saigonensis Pierre ex Gagnep. = *B. yunnanensis.*
B. taitensis hort. = *B. racemosa* and *B. tomentosa.*
B. tomentosa L. ST. THOMAS TREE; YELLOW BAUHINIA; BELL BAUHINIA. Everg. shrub to 5m. Lvs to 8cm, bilobed, suborbicular, pubesc. to glab. beneath, lobes obtuse. Fls solitary or paired, pendent; pet. to 6cm, overlapping, broadly obovate, yellow to cream, becoming dull pink. Throughout the year. OW Trop.
B. triandra hort. = *B. purpurea.*
B. vahlii Wight & Arn. MALU CREEPER. Liane to 35m climbing by tendrils. Lvs to 30cm, bilobed, suborbicular-cordate, woolly beneath, lobes obtuse. Infl. simple or compound, many-fld; pet. to 2.5cm, obovate, clawed, white to cream, becoming glab., margins ruffled. Summer. India.
B. variegata L. ORCHID TREE; MOUNTAIN EBONY. Tree to 12m, glabrate. Br. spreading. Lvs to 20cm, bilobed, suborbicular to cordate, lobes obtuse. Rac. few-fld; pet. 4–6cm, overlapping, obovate, pale magenta to indigo, often streaked or spotted. Winter–summer. E Asia. 'Candida': fls large, white, often with green markings.

B. violacea hort. = *B. purpurea.*
B. viridescens Desv. Shrub or tree, glabrate. Lvs 6–11cm, bilobed, suborbicular to ovate-cordate, lobes obtuse to acute. Infl. pendent; pet. to 0.5cm, erect, ovate, cream to white. Late autumn. SE Asia.
B. yunnanensis Franch. Everg. shrub or liane climbing by tendrils. Lvs bifoliolate; lfts to 3.5cm, ovate. Infl. many-fld; pet. to 1.5cm, clawed, pink to light mauve. SE Asia.
→*Piliostigma.*

Baxter's Banksia *Banksia baxteri.*
Bay *Laurus*
Bayberry *Myrica pensylvanica.*
Bay Laurel, Bay Tree *Laurus nobilis.*
Bay-leaved Caper *Capparis flexuosa.*
Bayonet Plant *Aciphylla squarrosa.*
Bay Star Vine *Schisandra coccinea.*
Bayur *Pterospermum.*
Bay Willow *Salix pentandra.*
Beach Aster *Erigeron glaucus.*
Beach Berry *Scaevola taccada.*
Beach Grass *Ammophila.*
Beach Heather *Hudsonia* (*H. tomentosa*).
Beach Morning Glory *Ipomoea pes-caprae.*
Beach Pea *Lathyrus japonicus.*
Beach Pine *Pinus contorta.*
Beach Plum *Prunus maritima.*
Beach Sand Verbena *Abronia umbellata.*
Beach Strawberry *Fragaria chiloensis.*
Beach Wormwood *Artemisia stelleriana.*
Bead Fern *Onoclea sensibilis.*
Bead Plant *Nertera granadensis.*
Bead Tree *Melia azedarach*; *Ormosia.*
Bead Tree of India *Elaeocarpus sphaericus.*
Beaked Hazel *Corylus cornuta.*
Bean *Phaseolus*; *Psophocarpus*; *Vicia*; *Vigna.*
Bean Tree *Catalpa bignonioides*; *Laburnum.*
Bearberry *Arctostaphylos.*
Bearberry Willow *Salix uva-ursi.*
Bearded Begonia *Begonia hirtella.*
Bearded Bellflower *Campanula barbata.*
Beard Grass *Polypogon monspeliensis.*
Bear Grass *Dasylirion*; *Nolina microcarpa*; *Xerophyllum tenax*; *Yucca smalliana.*
Bear Oak *Quercus ilicifolia.*
Bear's Breeches *Acanthus.*
Bear's Ears *Primula auricula and cvs.*
Bear's Foot *Aconitum napellus*; *Helleborus foetidus.*
Bear's-foot Fern *Humata tyermannii.*
Bear's Grape *Arctostaphylos uva-ursi.*
Bear's-paw Fern *Aglaomorpha meyeniana.*

Beaucarnea Lem.
B. gracilis Lem. = *Nolina gracilis.*
B. recurvata Lem. = *Nolina recurvata.*
B. stricta Lem. = *Nolina stricta.*

Beaufortia R. Br. Myrtaceae. 17–18 shrubs. Lvs small, usually decussate. Fls many, small, with prominent sta., in globose heads or dense brush-like spikes. Capsules bead-like, woody, usually fused around st. W Aus. Z9.
B. decussata R. Br. Erect medium shrub. Lvs *c*1cm, oval, opposite, concave. Flowerheads oblong to 10×4cm, deep red.
B. incana (Benth.) A.S. George. Medium shrub. Lvs *c*1cm, opposite, canescent. Flowerheads *c*2.5×2.5cm, term. on short branchlets; sta. yellow-green at base, tips deep red.
B. purpurea Lindl. Much-branched dwarf to small shrub. Lvs to 1cm, narrow, grey-green. Flowerheads globose, *c*2cm diam., term., purple-red.
B. sparsa R. Br. SWAMP BOTTLEBRUSH; GRAVEL BOTTLEBRUSH. Upright to spreading medium shrub. Lvs *c*1cm, scattered. Flowerheads *c*5–7×6–7cm, bright red-orange, rarely white.
B. squarrosa Schauer. SAND BOTTLEBRUSH. Small to medium shrub. Lvs *c*0.5cm, oval, dense, bright green, young growth sometimes hairy. Flowerheads *c*3×3cm, term., bright red, orange or yellow.

Beaumontia Wallich. Apocynaceae. 9 everg. vines. Lvs entire, with glands in vein axils. Fls fragrant, in crowded corymbs; cal. 5-parted; cor. funnelform or campanulate, lobes 5, twisted. China, Indomal. Z10.
B. grandiflora Wallich. NEPAL TRUMPET FLOWER; HERALD'S TRUMPET; EASTER LILY VINE. Woody twiner to 5m+. Lvs 10–28cm, broadly oblong-ovate, glossy glab. above, downy beneath, bronze, rusty-pubesc. at first. Fls 7.5–13cm, funnelform-

campanulate, white, exterior tinted green at base, interior deeper in colour. India to Vietnam.

Beauty Bush *Kolkwitzia amabilis.*
Bedding Begonia *Begonia schulziana* Semperflorens Hybrids.
Bedding Conehead *Strobilanthes isophyllus.*
Bedding Geranium *Pelargonium* ×*hortorum.*
Bedding Pansy *Viola cornuta.*

Bedfordia DC. Compositae. 2 shrubs or small trees, ± stellate-tomentose. Cap. *c*1cm discoid; phyllaries *c*8; flts tubular, yellow. SE Aus. Z9.
B. linearis DC. To 3m. Young br. white-tomentose. Lvs 1.5–9cm, linear, obtuse, tough, revolute, silvery beneath. Cap. 1–5, larger than in *B. salicina*, crowded toward br. tips. Tasm.
B. salicina DC. To 5m. Young br. white or rusty-tomentose. Lvs 1.5–15cm, lanceolate-elliptic, tomentose beneath, veins sunken above. Cap. in cylindrical clusters. Vict., NSW, Tasm.

Bedstraw *Galium.*
Bee Balm *Melissa officinalis*; *Monarda didyma.*
Beech *Fagus.*
Beech Fern *Phegopteris connectilis.*
Beef Plant *Iresine herbstii.*
Beefsteak Begonia *Begonia* ×*erythrophylla.*
Beefsteak Geranium *Begonia rex.*
Beefsteak Heliconia *Heliconia mariae.*
Beefsteak Plant *Iresine herbstii.*
Beefwood *Casuarina.*
Bee Orchid *Ophrys apifera.*
Bee Sage *Salvia apiana.*
Beet *Beta.*
Beetleweed *Galax.*
Beetroot *Beta vulgaris.*

Befaria Mutis ex L. = *Bejaria.*

Beggar's Lice *Hackelia.*
Beggar's Ticks *Bidens.*
Beggarweed *Desmodium.*

Begonia L. Begoniaceae. *c*900 herbs, shrubs or climbers. Roots fibrous, rhizomatous or tuberous. St. succulent to 'woody', conspicuously jointed. Lvs alt., simple, lobed or compound, highly varied in colour and texture; stipules 2, often large. Fls unisexual, in cymes or rac., tep. 2+2 in ♂ fls, 2–6 in ♀, waxy, crystalline; sta. numerous, massed or connate. Capsule winged. Trop. and subtrop., esp. Americas. Z10 unless specified.
B. acetosa Vell. Roots fibrous. St. erect. Lvs obliquely cordate, to 30cm across, deep coppery olive-green with white hairs above, wine-red beneath; petioles to 30cm. Peduncles to 45cm; fls white. Spring–early summer. Braz.
B. acida Vell. Rhizomatous. Lvs basal, suborbicular, to 23cm across not lobed, finely toothed, hispid, rugose, bright green, underside and petioles with thick white to pink hairs. Peduncles tall; fls to 1.5cm across, white to pale pink. Winter–spring. Braz.
B. aconitifolia A. DC. Roots fibrous. St. erect, 90–120cm. Lvs ovate, 12.5–18cm, palmately 4–6-lobed, finely dentate, glossy green, spotted white above, red beneath. Fls pendulous, to 5cm across, white or pale pink. Autumn. Braz. 'Metallica' ('Hildegard Schneider'): lvs bronzed, faintly marked white.
B. acuminata Dryand. = *B. acutifolia.*
B. acutangula hort. = *B. stipulacea.*
B. acutangularis hort. = *B. stipulacea.*
B. acutifolia Jacq. HOLLY-LEAF BEGONIA. Roots fibrous. St. 40–100cm, much-branched, red to brown-green. Lvs oblong-oblanceolate, to 10cm, acuminate, dentate, glossy above, hairy beneath on veins. Fls 3–5, white and red, to 2.5cm across. Year-round. Jam., Cuba.
B. albaperfecta hort. = *B. undulata.*
B. albopicta hort. Bull. GUINEA-WING BEGONIA. Roots fibrous. St. erect, 60–100cm, slender, woody, much-branched. Lvs obliquely ovate-lanceolate, 8–9cm, acuminate, sparsely toothed, undulate, coriaceous, glossy, spotted silver-white above. Fls many, pendent, green-white, to 2cm diam. Summer. Braz. 'Rosea' fls rose-pink.
B. ampla Hook. f. Trailing, scandent, to 60cm. Lvs downy then glab., 20–25cm, obliquely round to broad-ovate, base cordate, scaly beneath, toothed toward tip; petiole stout, 13–20cm. Fls similar to those of *B. poculifera.* Summer. Guinea.
B. angularis Raddi St. erect, to 2.5m+, br. many, spreading or pendulous. Lvs large ovate, acuminate, undulate, dentate, glossy dark green above with veins white, tinged red beneath. Fls many in pendent cymes, white, to 1.5cm across. Braz.
B. angularis Raddi. = *B. stipulacea.*

B. annulata K. Koch. Lvs large, obliquely-cordate, short-acuminate, ± sinuate, olive green with broad zones of grey and purple above, suffused purple-red beneath. Peduncle hairy; fls 5–8, white tinged pink. Winter–spring. Assam.

B. arborescens Raddi var. *confertiflora* (Gardn. in Hook.) A. DC. St. woody, 90–120cm. Lvs oblong, to 23×8.5cm, acuminate, finely dentate, glossy dark green above, veins conspicuous; petiole short. Fls small, white or pink, numerous in branched clusters to 12.5cm across. Peru, Braz.

B. argentea Lind. Close to *B. xanthina* and *B. rex*: possibly of hybrid origin. Lvs suffused white, with scattered small green spots; veins yellow. Fls yellow. Assam.

B. × argenteoguttata Lemoine. (*B. albopicta* × *B. olbia*.) TROUT BEGONIA; TROUT-LEAF BEGONIA; ANGEL-WING BEGONIA. Shrubby, erect, to 120cm, st. thick. Lvs 10–15cm, ovate, acuminate, shallowly lobed, dentate, glossy green densely white-spotted above. Fls many, white or tinged pink; ovary pink. Spring–autumn.

B. argyrostigma Fisch. ex Link & Otto = *B. maculata*.

B. aridicaulis Ziesenh. Rhiz. woody, appearing shrivelled. Lvs ovate to broad-lanceolate, to 6.5cm, acute, base deeply cordate, light green with veins silver above, veins red-brown-hairy beneath. Fls few, large, white. Late winter. Mex.

B. barkeri Knowles & Westc. Roots fibrous. St. woody-based, erect, to 60cm, v. hairy. Lvs broad-ovate, 12–18cm, acuminate, lobed and dentate, basal lobes overlapping, bright green, margins suffused red, veins yellow-green. Peduncles erect, red, to 30cm; fls many, large, pink. Spring. Mex.

B. bartonea hort. = *B.* 'Winter Jewel'.

B. × bertinii hort. ex Legros = *B. × intermedia* 'Bertinii'.

B. bhotanensis hort. = *B. deliciosa*.

B. bicolor Wats. = *B. gracilis*.

B. biserrata Lindl. Tuberous. St. erect, tall. Lvs orbicular, to 20cm, palmately-lobed, lobes triangular, acute, or cleft, toothed, ciliate, green, hairy above. Fls in dense axill. cymes, white; tep. serrate. S Mex., Guat.

B. bogneri Ziesenh. Tuberous. St. slender. Lvs 12–15cm, crowded, linear, glossy, sparsely toothed. Fls white-pink. Autumn–winter. Madag.

B. boisiana Gagnep. Shrubby. St. erect, to 50cm, swollen at nodes. Lvs narrow-ovate or lanceolate, 8–10cm, obliquely acuminate, base rounded to cordate, dentate, glossy green above, veins purple beneath. Peduncle to 10cm; fls many, to 2.5cm across, pink and white. Early winter–autumn. Indochina.

B. boliviensis DC. Tuberous. St. erect to 90cm somewhat succulent, drooping with age. Lvs 6–13cm, lanceolate-ovate, pointed, toothed. Fls to 5cm scarlet, in drooping pan. Summer. Boliv.

B. bowerae Ziesenh. EYELASH BEGONIA. Close to *B. strigillosa*. Lvs 2.5–5cm, ovate, acuminate, light green with irregular dark marginal markings, undulate, conspicuously ciliate. Peduncles erect; fls several, small, pink. Winter–early spring. Mex. 'Major': large; lf blotching faint. 'Nigromarga': lvs mint-green, blotched brown, with white cilia.

B. bowringiana hort. non Champ. ex Benth. = *B. cathayana*.

B. bowringiana Champ. ex Benth. = *B. palmata* var. *bowringiana*.

B. bracteosa DC. Shrub-like, 30–250cm. Lvs 7–13cm, obliquely broad-ovate, acuminate, base cordate, wavy, serrate, ciliate. Cymes many-fld; fls rose pink to 2cm diam. Peru.

B. bradei Irmsch. Roots fibrous. St. erect or creeping, hairy. Lvs oblong, 8.5–11cm, base cordate, bronze-green above, red beneath. Fls large, white with crimson hairs. Summer. Braz. 'Pubescens' (*B.* 'Alto da Serra'): lvs rich green edged red, red beneath.

B. brasiliensis hort. non Klotzsch = *B. acida*.

B. breviramosa Irmsch. Shrubby. St. rust-red-pilose above. Lvs ovate or suboval, large, apex shortly acuminate, base obliquely cordate, dentate, ciliate, bullate, glossy dark green, marked white or grey. Fls many, pink. New Guinea.

B. caffra Meissn. = *B. homonyma*.

B. × camelliiflora hort. = *B.* Tuberhybrida Hybrids, Camellia group.

B. cantareira hort. = *B. acetosa*.

B. capensis hort. = *B. sutherlandii*.

B. caraguatatubensis Brade Roots fibrous. St. erect, 30–60cm, brown. Lvs obliquely broad-ovate, 12.5–19cm, acuminate, base cordate, glab., pale glossy green above; petioles with leafy growths at apex. Fls to 6mm across, white in dense cymes. Braz.

B. carolineifolia Reg. St. erect, thick, succulent. Lvs palmate, lfts 6–8, radial, lanceolate to obovate, to 15cm, undulate, dentate, veins deeply impressed. Fls in dichotomous cymes, small, pale pink with darker spots. Winter. Mex., Guat.

B. cathayana Hemsl. Roots fibrous. St. erect, 60–90cm, few-branched, with crimson hairs. Lvs deflexed, obliquely ovate, 15–20cm, apex acuminate, base cordate, dentate, olive green,

veined crimson above, mottled crimson beneath. Fls downy, orange-vermilion or white, to 4.5cm across. Autumn or spring. China.

B. × cheimantha Everett ex C. Weber. (*B. dregei* × *socotrana*.) CHRISTMAS BEGONIA; BLOOMING-FOOL BEGONIA; LORRAINE BEGONIA. Roots fibrous. St. ann., branching. Lvs suborbicular, base cordate, toothed, green. Cyme loose exceeding lvs; peduncle pink; fls large, pink. Winter. Gdn origin.

B. chimborazo hort. = *B. conchifolia*.

B. chlorosticta Sands. St. to 60cm, brown-red, swollen at nodes. Lvs obliquely ovate-oblong, 18–21cm, at first dull maroon above, then dark green with light patches, maroon beneath, margin light green, toothed; petiole to 11cm. Infl. to 27cm; fls crimson at tip, green-white below; ovary scarlet, 3-winged. Malaysia, Sarawak.

B. cinnabarina Hook. Tuberous. St. to 60cm, erect, few-branched. Lvs 10–20cm diam., obliquely ovate, hairy, lobed, serrate; petiole 8–17cm. Infl. 2–6-fld; fls fragrant, orange-red to 4cm. Summer–autumn. Peru, Boliv.

B. coccinea Hook. ANGEL-WING BEGONIA. Roots fibrous. St. 90–120cm, erect, succulent. Lvs obliquely oblong to ovate, to 15cm, serrate, coriaceous, somewhat glaucous above, margin red, dull red beneath. Fls. coral in red-stalked pendent rac.; ovary long, red. Spring. Braz.

B. conchifolia A. Dietr. Rhiz. creeping, succulent, hairy. Lvs ovate, to 6.5cm, acuminate, base cordate, peltate, succulent, glossy green above. Peduncle erect, to 23cm, hairy; fls many, to 1.5cm across, pale pink, fragrant. Spring. Hond. to Panama.

B. confertiflora Gardn. in Hook. = *B. arborescens* var. *confertiflora*.

B. cooperi DC. Roots fibrous. St. erect, to 1m, red-brown-hairy. Lvs elongate-ovate, to 10cm, sharply dentate, glossy green, hairy on veins beneath; petiole short. Peduncles short, hairy; fls many, white. Winter. Costa Rica.

B. corallina Carr. St. to 3m, glab., brown with age. Lvs to 20cm, lanceolate, glossy green with white spots above, red beneath. Fls many, pendent, large, coral red. Spring. Braz. 'Fragrans': fls white, scented. 'Odorata': fls light pink, scented.

B. × crispa hort. = *B.* Tuberhybrida Hybrids, Crispa group.

B. crispamarginata hort. = *B.* Tuberhybrida Hybrids, Marginata group.

B. crispula Brade. Rhizomatous. Lvs prostrate, orbicular, to 15cm across, base cordate, bullate, crispate, dark glossy green; petiole short. Peduncles to 15cm, red-hairy; fls few, to 1.5cm across, white, tinted pink. Braz.

B. × cristata hort. non Koord. = *B.* Tuberhybrida Hybrids, Cristata group.

B. cubensis Hassk. CUBAN HOLLY; HOLLY-LEAF BEGONIA. Roots fibrous. St. erect, branched, brown-hairy. Lvs obliquely ovate, to 5cm, acuminate, dentate, veins hairy. Peduncles short; fls white, to 6mm across. Winter. Cuba.

B. cucullata Willd. Perenn. succulent herb to 1m. Lvs to 10cm, slightly asymmetric, broadly ovate, incurved at base, palmately veined, crenate-serrate, ciliate; petiole to 5cm. Cyme few-fld; fls white. Intermittent flowering. Braz. to Arg. var. *hookeri* (A. DC.) L.B. Sm. & Schubert. Lvs not incurved at base. ♂ fls larger (tep. to 2cm). SE Braz., NE Arg.

B. cuspidata DC. = *B. multinervia*.

B. daedalea E. Lemoine = *B. strigillosa*.

B. davisii hort. Veitch ex Hook. f. DAVIS BEGONIA. Tuberous, acaulescent. Lvs spreading, obliquely ovate, to 10cm, base cordate, membranous, crenate, glossy dark green above, crimson beneath. Fls bright red in red-stalked umbels. Summer. Peru.

B. decora Stapf. HAIRY BEGONIA. Rhiz. short, succulent, red-green, with dark hairy stipules. Lvs ovate, 8–10cm, acuminate, base cordate, dentate, purple-brown with yellow-green veins, becoming dark metallic green, rugose, hispid above, red and soft-hairy beneath. Peduncle to 12.5cm; fls few, large, pink. Spring. Malaysia, Indochina.

B. deliciosa Böhme. Rhizomatous. St. erect, to 60cm, succulent. Lvs deeply cordate, 15–25cm, deeply palmately-lobed, lobes 6–8, sparsely hairy, dentate, dark olive-green spotted-grey above, red beneath. Infl. long-stalked; fls in dense clusters, to 2cm across, pink, fragrant. Late summer–winter. Borneo.

B. diadema Lind. Rhizomatous. St. erect, 30–50cm, succulent, marked with white lines. Lvs palmately lobed, lobes lanceolate, acuminate, crenate to dentate, glab., light green with white spots and tinted red above. Infl. short; fls few, v. small, pink. Spring. Borneo.

B. dichotoma Jacq. KIDNEY BEGONIA. Roots fibrous. St. erect, 75–150cm+, woody with lenticels. Lvs ovate-cordate, to 30×25cm, acuminate, somewhat angular, dentate, ciliate, glossy green above; petiole to 22cm. Peduncle erect; fls many, small, white in dichotomous cymes. Late winter. Venez.

B. dichroa Sprague. Roots fibrous. St. spreading, woody, to

35cm, branched. Lvs obliquely ovate-oblong, 20–30cm, acuminate, base ± cordate, glab., slightly undulate, bright green with silver spots. Fls in dichotomous umbels, pendent, salmon-pink; ovary white. Summer. Braz.

B. dipetala Graham. St. erect, to 60cm, seldom branched. Lvs v. obliquely ovate, acuminate, finely toothed, sparsely hairy, red beneath. Fls few in axillary cymes, pendent, light pink. Year-round. India.

B. diversifolia Graham = B. gracilis.

B. domingensis A. DC. PEANUT-BRITTLE BEGONIA. Roots fibrous. St. erect, to 30cm, pilose. Lvs ovate, 2.5cm, acuminate, base cordate, coriaceous, rugose, glossy, veins and petioles brown-pilose. Fls in dense cymes, small, white or pink. Late winter–early spring. Hispan.

B. dregei Otto & A. Dietr. GRAPE-LEAF BEGONIA; MAPLE-LEAF BEGONIA. tuberous, glab. St. ann. to 1m, succulent. Lvs ovate or rhombic, to 7.5cm, membranous, shallowly lobed and dentate, pale green with grey spots and purple veins above, dull red beneath. Fls few, white, 1.5cm across. Summer. S Afr. 'Macbethii': lvs small, v. notched to lobed, veins green. 'Macbethii Obtusa': as 'Macbethii', but more compact; lvs lacking green veins.

B. echinosepala Reg. Roots fibrous. St. erect, 50–70cm, slender, branched, nodes v. swollen. Lvs ovate-elliptic, 7cm, acute, finely dentate, glossy light green above, paler beneath; petiole short, hairy. Peduncle short; fls few, white, 2cm across; ♂ fls with tep. white-hairy. Summer. Braz.

B. edmundoi Brade. Roots fibrous. St. erect, to 1m, subshrubby. Lvs lanceolate, 10–12cm, long-acuminate; petiole short. Peduncles axill.; fls few in clusters, white, to 5cm across. Spring–autumn. Braz.

B. egregia N.E. Br. Roots fibrous. Lvs oblong-lanceolate, 15–28cm, brittle, bullate, grey-green. Fls many in axill. cymes, white. Winter. Braz.

B. ×elatior hort. = B. ×hiemalis.

B. eminii Warb. Roots fibrous. St. scrambling, rooting. Lvs obliquely ovate to oblong-ovate, 8–14cm, base obliquely cordate, margin red, dentate, veins brown-hairy. Fls 7 per short-stalked cluster, pink, to 3.5cm across; ovary curved, cylindric. Capsule scarlet or white. Trop. Afr.

B. engleri Gilg. Roots fibrous. St. 1–1.5m, usually solitary, purple-spotted. Lvs ovate-oblong, 7.5–12.5cm across, coarsely dentate, shortly hairy, veins purple. Peduncles long, arching; fls in flat pan., clear pink; ovary red hairy. Spring. Trop. E Afr.

B. epipsila Brade. Roots fibrous. St. erect, 40–55cm, woody, red-hairy. Lvs obliquely ovate, 5–8cm, acuminate, base cordate, glossy dark olive-green above, red- lanuginose beneath. Peduncles short, red-hairy; fls many, white, small. Spring. Braz.

B. ×erythrophylla J. Neumann. (B. hydrocotylifolia × B. manicata.) BEEFSTEAK BEGONIA; KIDNEY BEGONIA. Rhiz. stout, creeping. Lvs suborbicular, 14cm, short-acuminate, base cordate appearing almost peltate, coriaceous, white-ciliate, olive-green above, purple beneath, veins pale green; petioles to 15cm, hairy. Peduncle erect, to 30cm; fls many, paniculate, pink, small. Winter–spring. Origin unknown. 'Bunchii' (LETTUCE-LEAF BEGONIA): lvs bright green, thickly crested. 'Helix' (WHIRLPOOL BEGONIA, POND-LILY BEGONIA): lvs with basal lobes spiralled.

B. evansiana Andrews = B. grandis ssp. evansiana.

B. exotica hort. = B. brevirimosa.

B. fagifolia Fisch. = B. glabra.

B. faureana Lind. ex Garn. = B. aconitifolia.

B. ×feastii hort. ex L.H. Bail. = B. ×erythrophylla.

B. fernandoi-costae Irmsch. Roots fibrous. St. erect. Lvs broad-ovate, 11–17.5cm, acuminate, base cordate, entire or shallowly dentate, hairy, bright green above, rose-pink beneath. Peduncle erect, exceeding lvs; fls cymose, white. Summer–autumn. Braz.

B. ficicola Irmsch. Rhizomatous epiphyte. Lvs obliquely ovate-elliptic, 8–11cm, acuminate, bullate; petiole 4–11cm. Peduncle scarcely exceeding lvs; fls few, small, bright yellow; one tep. orange-red. W Afr.

B. ×fimbriata hort. non B. fimbriata Liebm. = B. Tuberhybrida Hybrids, Fimbriata group.

B. floccifera Bedd. Rhizomatous. Lvs suborbicular, 3.5–7.5cm, base cordate, coriaceous, denticulate or subentire, white- or yellow-tomentose, glabrescent above. Peduncle to 45cm; fls many cymose, white, small. India.

B. ×floribunda hort. = B. Tuberhybrida Hybrids, Multiflora group.

B. foliosa HBK. FERN BEGONIA; FERN-LEAVED BEGONIA. Shrubby to 1m+, br. many, slender, succulent. Lvs many, in 2 dense ranks, ovate-oblong, to 3.5cm, slightly toothed, glossy dark green. Peduncles slender; fls 1–2, white, to 1.5cm across. Summer or autumn–winter. Colomb., Venez.

B. foliosa var. **miniata** (Planch.) L.B. Sm. & Schubert = B. fuchsioides.

B. froebelii A. DC. Lvs orbicular, 15–30cm, acuminate, base cordate, shallowly toothed, bright green above, red beneath, with fleshy purple hairs. Peduncles erect, red; fls in pendent cymes, crimson or scarlet, to 5cm across. Late summer–winter. Ecuad.

B. fruticosa A. DC. Roots fibrous. St. erect to scrambling, to 60cm+, much-branched, red-green. Lvs obliquely oblong-ovate, 7.5cm, acuminate, serrate, ciliate, glossy green, veins red beneath. Fls in loose cymes, white, white, to 1.5cm across. Braz.

B. fuchsioides Hook. FUCHSIA BEGONIA; CORAZON-DE-JESUS. Roots fibroui. St. erect, to 1m+, slender, succulent. Lvs in 2 ranks, numerous, oblong-ovate to falcate, 2–5cm, dentate, flushed red when young. Peduncles stout, pendulous; fls red or rose-pink, to 3cm across. Venez.

B. fusca Liebm. Rhiz. succulent. Lvs obliquely broad-ovate, 15–28, acuminate, base cordate, lobed, pubesc.; petioles long, hairy. Fls white or pink; tep. hairy. Summer. S Mex., Guat.

B. ×gigantea hort. non B. gigantea Wallich = B. Tuberhybrida Hybrids, Single group.

B. glabra Aubl. Roots fibrous. St. trailing, 3–10m+, rooting. Lvs broad-ovate, to 14cm, acuminate, base rounded, denticulate, glossy green. Fls in large pendent cyme, white, to 1cm across. Summer. Mex. to Peru and Boliv., W Indies. 'Cordifolia': lvs large, cordate, light green. 'Coralipetiolis': lvs heart-shaped, petiole red-pink.

B. glaucophylla Gower = B. radicans.

B. glaucophylla var. scandens hort. = B. radicans.

B. goegoensis N.E. Br. FIRE-KING BEGONIA. Rhiz. stout, green-red. Lvs ovate-orbicular, 15–23, peltate, cupped, bullate, green with dark bronze blotches above, red beneath; petioles quadrangular, to 10cm. Peduncles to 15cm; fls few, small, rose-pink. Summer–autumn. Is. of Goego, Sumatra.

B. gracilis HBK. HOLLYHOCK BEGONIA. Tuberous. St. erect, 60–100cm, succulent, usually simple. Lvs orbicular to lanceolate, small, succulent, crenate, pale green; bulbils in axils. Peduncles short, axill.; fls pink, to 3cm across; tep. ± serrate. Summer. var. martiana A. DC. St. 30–45cm. Lvs obliquely cordate, to 15cm, entire. Fls to 5cm across, fragrant; tep. entire. Mex., Guat.

B. grandis Dryand. ssp. evansiana (Andrews) Irmsch. HARDY BEGONIA Tuberous. St. erect, 60–100cm, ann., red. Lvs obliquely ovate, large, acuminate, base cordate, v. shallowly lobed, red-hairy, copper to green above with veins red, red beneath. Fls in dichotomous pendent cymes, fragrant, pink or white, to 3cm across. Summer. Malaysia to China and Jap. 'Alba': fls white. 'Claret Jug': lvs flushed red beneath; fls pink. 'Simsii': fls large. Z8.

B. griffithii Hook. = B. annulata.

B. guaduensis HBK. Shrub-like, erect to 2m. Lvs 5–9cm, elliptic to lanceolate, unequal at base, acute at apex, double-toothed; petiole 2–8mm. Fls pink-white to 1.5cm in branched cymes. Panama to Venez.

B. haageana hort. ex Will. Wats. = B. scharffii.

B. handroi Brade. Roots fibrous. St. arching, to 30cm, somewhat hairy. Lvs obliquely ovate, to 11cm, acuminate, base cordate, succulent, denticulate, hairy, glossy above, red beneath. Peduncles short; fls few, white, to 3.5cm across. Braz.

B. hatacoa Buch.-Ham. Rhiz. thick. Lvs narrowly elliptic to lanceolate, to 15cm, acuminate, base weakly cordate, entire or angular to undulate, dark glossy green, brown-tomentose on veins; petiole 5cm. Peduncle to 15cm; fls few, to 2.5cm across green-white sometimes veined red. Spring. Himal.

B. hemsleyana Hook. f. Tuberous. St. erect, to 45cm, br. few, succulent, sparsely hairy, rose-pink. Lvs orbicular, 10–12.5cm across, palmately lobed, lobes 7–9, lanceolate, serrate, margin red when young; petiole to 10cm. Fls light pink, cymose, to 4cm. Summer. Hunan.

B. hepatica maculata hort. = B. stigmosa.

B. heracleifolia Cham. & Schldl. STAR BEGONIA; STAR-LEAF BEGONIA. Rhiz. succulent, creeping, brown. Lvs to 30cm+ across, orbicular in outline, base cordate, deeply palmately lobed, lobes 7–9, lanceolate, sinuate, denticulate and ciliate, bronze-green above, red beneath with green zones along veins, with tufts of hairs; petiole to 35cm, with red blotches, hairy. Peduncle erect, 40–60cm, hairy; fls 15–30, pink. Spring–autumn. S Mex. to Belize. 'Sonderbruchii': lvs deeply cut, streaked bronze; fls pale pink, abundant. var. nigricans Hook. Lvs green, edged black-green; petiole, peduncle and pedicels red. Tep. white; ovary pink. Mex. var. punctata (Link & Otto) Nichols. Lvs less deeply lobed, black-green above with metallic tints, with black blotches. Tep. and ovary pink marked red. var. longipila A. DC. Lvs dark red-brown-green above, pale green along veins, rust-red beneath, veins pink; petiole and peduncle with raised white, green or crimson lines, long-hairy. Mex.

B. herbacea Vell. Rhiz. coarsely hairy. Lvs obovate-lanceolate, to 15cm, serrate, with silver-white spots, petiole v. short. Fls white or pink, 1.5cm across, subtended by large fimbriate bracts. Year-round. Braz.

B. hidalgensis Sm. & Schubert. Rhizomatous. St. short, 1cm thick. Lvs transverse-elliptic, 7–12cm, dark, hairy beneath, usually entire; petiole slender, to 17cm. Cyme irregular, many-fld; fls green-white, small. Spring. Mex.

B. ×hiemalis Fotsch (*B. socotrana* ×*B. ×tuberhybrida*.) WINTER-FLOWERING BEGONIAS. Roots fibrous. Lvs asymmetric, green to bronze. Fls single or double, white to pink, yellow, orange or red. Winter or year-round. Gdn origin.

B. hirtella Link. BEARDED BEGONIA. 20–90cm, simple to branched, hairy. Lvs 3–11cm, obliquely ovate, apex acute, base shallow-cordate, sometimes shallowly lobed, toothed, ciliate; petiole 2–7cm. Fls pink. Summer. W Indies, Braz., Colomb. and Peru.

B. hispida Schott ex A. DC. var. *cucullifera* Irmsch. St. thick, to 1.5m, branched. Lvs obliquely ovate, to 8.5cm, acuminate, base cordate, lobed to deeply toothed, pubesc., with adventitious lfts along veins above; petioles red. Fls white. Braz.

B. holtonis DC. Shrub-like, 120–150cm. Lvs 4–6cm, asymmetric, elliptic, apex acute, crenate-serrate; petiole short. Cymes dichotomously branched, many-fld, 7–30cm; fls white, to 0.8cm. Late winter–summer. Columbia.

B. homonyma Steud. St. to 1m, fleshy, branched. Lvs obliquely reniform-cordate, 5–6.5×7.5–10cm, acute or acuminate, angular, serrate, red-veined beneath; petiole to 7.5cm. Fls 4 in dichotomous cymes, white. S Afr.

B. humilis Ait. St. to 60cm, branched at base. Lvs 5–11cm, transversely ovate, cordate at base, shallowly lobed, serrate, ciliate; petiole 1–4cm. Cymes 2–5-fld, lax; fls white, 3–4mm. Autumn. Trop. S Amer.

B. hydrocotylifolia Otto ex Hook. PENNYWORT BEGONIA. Rhizomatous. Lvs orbicular to cordate, 3.5–6.5cm, peltate, glossy olive-green above, red beneath; petioles short. Peduncles to 45cm, pink; fls rose-pink. Spring–summer. Mex.

B. hypolipara Sandw. Rhiz. thick, hairy, with persistent stipules. Lvs reniform, basal, 7–13×9–15.5cm, apex obtuse, base deeply cordate, somewhat angular, pilose above; petiole to 19cm. Peduncle to 25cm; fls cymose, white or pink, to 3cm across. Winter–spring. Hond.

B. imperialis Lem. Hairy. Rhiz. stout, short. Lvs obliquely cordate, 10–15cm across, acuminate, weakly sinuate, dark red-brown with bright green marking along veins above, red with reticulate green veins beneath; petiole to 15cm. Fls few, to 1.5cm across, white. Year-round. Mex. 'Gruss an Erfurt': small; lvs pointed, bullate, silvery green marked brown along margin. 'Hildegard Epple' (*B. imperialis* ×*B. lindleyana*): vigorous; lvs cordate, silver edged deep green. 'Marbachtaler' (*B. imperialis* ×*B. lindleyana*): strong-growing, rhizomatous; lvs silver webbed dark green. 'Otto Forster': lvs brown marked pale green around veins. var. *smaragdina* Lem. ex A. DC. Lvs wholly emerald green.

B. incana Lindl. = *B. peltata*.

B. incarnata Link & Otto. Roots fibrous. St. erect, to 1m, succulent, red, spotted grey-white. Lvs oblique ovate, ovate-oblong, 10–12cm, acuminate, sinuate-denticulate, ciliate, sometimes white-spotted, sparsely grey-hairy above. Peduncles arching, to 16cm; fls many, to 3.5cm across, pink. Winter–spring. Mex.

B. ×intermedia hort. Veitch ex Van Houtte (*B. boliviensis* ×*B. veitchii*.) Close to *B. boliviensis*, differing in fls larger, light scarlet, more erect. 'Bertinii': (*B. boliviensis* ×*B. ×intermedia*.) To 30cm. Lvs obliquely ovate-lanceolate, to 12.5cm, dentate, hairy. Fls many, in pairs on long pendulous peduncles, to 3cm, vermilion. Bertinii Hybrids derived from this are placed in Tuberhybrida Hybrids, Multiflora group. Summer.

B. involucrata Liebm. Rhizomatous. St. 90–135cm, much-branched, red-brown-pubesc. Lvs obliquely broad-ovate, to 23×18cm, shallowly palmately lobed, lobes 3–5, acute, dentate, white-downy. Peduncles long; fls in loose cymes, white or pink, to 2cm across. Spring. Guat. to Panama.

B. isoptera Dryand. Roots fibrous. St. erect, to 60cm, br. spreading. Lvs obliquely ovate-oblong, to 8.5cm, base somewhat cordate, undulate, dentate, edged red. Fls small, green-white, edged pink. Summer. Java.

B. josephi A. DC. Tuberous, stemless. Lvs peltate, ovate-acuminate, to 15cm, or 3-lobed, or orbicular with many acute lobes, serrate to entire, usually glab. Peduncle to 30cm, much-branched; fls numerous, to 1.5cm across, pink. C Nepal to Bhutan.

B. kellermannii DC. St. 30–60cm, succulent, white-hairy. Lvs peltate, ovate, deeply cupped, 10–23cm, acuminate, entire, green or tinged pink with red margins above, white-tomentose beneath. Peduncles long, erect; fls pink, fragrant, to 2.5cm across. Late winter–early spring. Guat.

B. kenworthyae Ziesenh. Rhiz. erect, to 15cm, simple succulent, green. Lvs 5-lobed, cordate at base, to 30cm, lobes acute, succulent, serrate, red-ciliate, slate-grey with veins green. Fls in dense axill. cymes, white, to 1.5cm across. Winter. Mex.

B. kraussiantha Irmsch. = *B. pringlei*.

B. kunthiana Walp. Root fibrous. St. to 45cm, slender with swollen nodes, purple-brown. Lvs to 7.5cm lanceolate, serrate, glab., dark green above, crimson beneath. Peduncles short; fls in 2 clusters of 3, white to 3.5cm across. Summer. Venez.

B. laciniata Roxb. = *B. palmata*.

B. laeteviridis hort. = *B. bradei*.

B. lepidota Liebm. = *B. manicata*.

B. leptotricha DC. = *B. subvillosa* var. *leptotricha*.

B. liebmannii A. DC. = *B. ludicra*.

B. liminghii K. Koch = *B. radicans*.

B. limmingheiana Morr. = *B. radicans*.

B. lindleyana Walp. Rhiz. erect, to 30cm, red-hairy. Lvs obliquely broad-ovate, 7.5–20cm, acuminate, base cordate, dentate lobed or entire, glabrescent above, red-hairy beneath. Peduncles exceeding lvs, red-hairy; fls white or pink, to 2cm across. Spring–summer. S Mex. to Colomb.

B. listada L.B. Sm. & Wassh. Roots fibrous. St. erect, to 30cm, branched. Lvs ovate, small, acuminate, base cordate, with one lobe much enlarged, denticulate, soft-hairy, dark green with bright emerald green zone along midrib and margins above, red-hairy beneath. Peduncles short; fls few, white, red-hairy, to 5cm across. Autumn–winter. Braz.

B. listida hort. = *B. listada*.

B. ×lloydii hort. = *B.* Tuberhybrida Hybrids, Pendula group.

B. longibarbata Brade. Roots fibrous. St. erect, branched. Lvs obliquely broad-ovate, 18–25cm, acuminate, base cordate, undulate, dentate, ciliate, green above, sinus red, dull purple beneath. Fls few, white to pink, fragrant. Braz.

B. longipes Hook. = *B. reniformis*.

B. loranthoides Hook. f. St. erect, v. stout, woody. Lvs obliquely elliptic-lanceolate, 7.5–8cm, acute, entire, thickly fleshy; petiole short. Peduncle short; fls several, white tinged pink, to 3cm across. Trop. W Afr.

B. lubbersii E. Morr. Rhiz. short, ascending. St. erect, 60–90cm, stout. Lvs peltate, obliquely lanceolate, 15cm, slightly undulate dark green with silver-white spot above, crimson beneath; petiole to 12.5cm. Fls 6 per cyme, white, to 3.5cm across. Year-round. Braz.

B. lucida Haw. = *B. humilis*.

B. ludicra A. DC. Rhiz. erect or procumbent, slender. Lvs obliquely ovate to subpalmate with lobes acute, entire or dentate, green with silver-white spots above, suffused purple beneath. Peduncles short, fls few, green-white, to 3.5cm across. Spring. S Mex. to Panama.

B. ludwigii Irmsch. Roots fibrous. St. to 1m, v. thick, swollen at base. Lvs suborbicular, to 35cm across, shallowly palmately divided, lobes *c*7, acuminate, biserrate, white-hispid, green with veins red at sinus; petiole with collar of hairs. Peduncles 45–90cm, streaked white; fls many, cream-white with green and pink marks, to 2.5cm across. Spring–summer. Ecuad.

B. luxurians Scheidw. PALM-LEAF BEGONIA. Roots fibrous. St. to 1.5m, fleshy, red, soft-hairy. Lvs palmate, lfts 7–17, 7.5–15cm, lanceolate, serrate, hairy, green or bronze above, green beneath; petiole short. Peduncles erect; fls cream-white, 6mm across. Summer. Braz.

B. macrocarpa hort. non Warb. = *B. bradei*.

B. maculata Raddi. Roots fibrous. St. erect, to 1m, branched, becoming woody. Lvs lanceolate, to 16.5cm, base cordate, thick, waxy, undulate, with white spots above, red at margin and beneath. Peduncles pendulous; fls many, pale pink or white to 1.5cm across. Summer. Braz. 'Wightii': st. to 2.5m; lvs larger, v. heavily white-spotted; fls to 2.5cm across, white.

B. malabarica Lam. Roots fibrous. St. subshrubby, 40–60cm, glab. Lvs oblong-ovate, 10–12cm, acuminate, base subcordate, lobed and denticulate, pilose to glab., dark green. Peduncles short; fls 10–12, white or v. pale pink, large. Winter–summer. S India, Sri Lanka.

B. malabarica Roxb. = *B. roxburghii*.

B. malabarica var. *dipetala* C.B. Clarke = *B. dipetala*.

B. manicata Brongn. ex Cels. Rhizomatous. St. erect, or decumbent, to 60cm. Lvs obliquely ovate-cordate, to 16cm, acuminate, dentate and ciliate, glossy light green, glab. above, somewhat red and pilose on veins beneath; petiole to 20cm with collar of hairs. Peduncle erect, to 60cm; fls many, pale pink, v. small; tep. 2. Winter. Mex. 'Aureomaculata' (LEOPARD BEGONIA): Lvs pale green blotched white or flushed red. 'Aureomaculata Crispa' ('Aurea Crispa', 'Aurea Cristata'): lvs pale green, marbled yellow, edge ruffled, becoming pink in sun. 'Crispa': lvs pale green, edge ruffled.

B. mannii Hook. f. St. climbing, to 2m, slender, rusty-tomentose. Lvs oblong-ovate to lanceolate, 10–18cm, acuminate, base cordate, shallowly lobed and toothed, glossy above, rusty-tomentose beneath. Peduncles short; fls numerous, rose-red, to 2cm across. Spring. Trop. W Afr.

B. ×*marginata* hort. = *B.* Tuberhybrida Hybrids, Marginata group.

B. ×*marmorata* hort. = *B.* Tuberhybrida Hybrids, Marmorata group.

B. martiana Link & Otto = *B. gracilis* var. *martiana*.

B. masoniana Irmsch. IRON-CROSS BEGONIA. Rhizomatous. Lvs obliquely broad-cordate, to 20cm, acuminate, toothed, ciliate, rugose, red papillate-bristly, green with large cross-like central chocolate-brown marking radiating along main vein and broadening toward margin. Peduncles erect; fls numerous, green-white, small. Spring-summer. New Guinea.

B. maxima hort. ex Klotzsch = *B. fusca*.

B. ×*maxima* hort. = *B.* Tuberhybrida Hybrids, Multiflora group.

B. mazae Ziesenh. Roots fibrous. St. to 45cm, br. few. Lvs small, obliquely orbicular to broad-ovate, 12.5cm, acuminate, base cordate, remotely dentate, shiny green with green and red spots above, pink at sinus, yellow-green at margin, blood-red beneath. Fls many, fragrant, white spotted red to 1.5cm across. Winter-spring. Mex. 'Nigricans': lvs dark, burnished. var. *viridis* 'Stitchleaf': lvs cordate, pale green with dark purple 'stitches' along edges.

B. megaphylla A. DC. = *B. barkeri*.

B. megaptera A. DC. Rhiz. ascending, stout, green with white stripes. Lvs obliquely broad-ovate, to 17.5cm, acuminate, base cordate, angular, glossy with silver markings above, dark red-purple beneath to 10cm. Peduncle to 20cm; fls few to many, pink, to 5cm across. Himal.

B. metallica W.G. Sm. METALLIC-LEAF BEGONIA. Roots fibrous. St. erect, to 1.2m, much-branched, hairy. Lvs obliquely ovate, to 15cm, apex acuminate, base cordate, angled or lobed, sinuate, serrate, veins metallic purple above. Fls many, pale pink to rose, to 3.5cm across. Summer-autumn. Braz.

B. meyeniana Walp. = *B. humilis*.

B. meyeri-johannis Engl. Roots fibrous. St. scrambling to 7m, woody. Lvs obliquely, ovate, 11cm, acuminate, base cordate, glab., dark green above, red beneath; petiole red. Peduncles short, pendulous; fls few, white or pink, 3–4cm across. year-round. Afr.

B. micranthera Griseb. Tuberous. St. erect, to 50cm. Lvs obliquely ovate, to 30cm, acuminate, base cordate, shallowly lobed, hairy, serrate, ciliate. Peduncles erect; fls 2–3, white or pale pink, to 2.5cm across. Arg., S Boliv.

B. miniata Planch. = *B. fuchsioides*.

B. minor Jacq. Roots fibrous. St. erect, to 2m. Lvs obliquely ovate to reniform, 10–15cm, base cordate, undulate, crenate, glossy dark green above, crystalline pale green beneath; petioles red. Peduncles long; fls many, white or pink, to 5cm across. year-round. Jam. 'Rosea': fls deep pink, scented.

B. mollicaulis Irmsch. St. erect, 30–50cm, woody, short-glandular-pilose; stipules persistent. Lvs obliquely broad-ovate, 11.5cm, acute to short-acuminate, base broadly cordate, dentate, chartaceous, pale green, short-hairy above, hairy on veins beneath. Peduncles to 10cm; cymes to 13cm; fls many, white, to 3cm across. Braz.

B. 'Mrs. W.S. Kimball' = *B. dipetala*.

B. ×*multiflora* hort. = *B.* Tuberhybrida Hybrids, Multiflora group.

B. multinervia Liebm. Rhiz. stout, erect. St. to 3m, woody. Lvs obliquely cordate, to 23cm, undulate, coarsely dentate, glossy green veined red above, pale green, spoted red beneath; petioles short, hairy. Fls white, large in dense cymes. Winter. Costa Rica, Panama.

B. ×*narcissiflora* hort. = *B.* Tuberhybrida Hybrids, Narcissiflora group.

B. nelumbiifolia Cham. & Schldl. LILY-PAD BEGONIA. Rhiz. stout, short, ascending. Lvs peltate, suborbicular, to 45×30cm, short-acuminate, serrulate, ciliate, green; petioles long, hairy. Peduncles, to 60cm; fls cymose, white or pale pink, to 1.5cm across. Winter-spring. S Mex. to Colomb. 'Glabra': small; lvs glab., narrow.

B. nitida Ait. = *B. minor*.

B. octopetala L'Hérit. Tuberous. Lvs basal, cordate, to 20cm, lobed, toothed; petioles 30–45cm, fleshy. Fls ivory-white, in 6–20-fld corymbs; peduncles 2.5–5cm; tep. 6–10, 5–7.5cm wide. Autumn-winter. Peru.

B. odeteiantha Handro. St. erect to 60cm, branched, purple-brown. Lvs in 2 ranks, lanceolate or sublanceolate, 10–15cm, obliquely cordate, glab.; petiole short; stipules large. Peduncle to 8cm; fls many, white, to 3cm across. Late winter-autumn. Braz.

B. odorata Paxt. Close to *B. minor*. St. to 1.2m, slender, hairy. Lvs obliquely ovate, 10–17.5cm, acute, glossy green, veins impressed. Peduncles long; fls many in loose cymes, white or

pale pink, fragrant; to 1.5cm across. Year-round. C Amer. 'Alba': fls white.

B. olbia Kerch. St. erect, 30–70cm, sparsely branched, thick. Lvs ovate, 25–28cm, acuminate, base cordate, irregularly lobed, dentate, bronze-green with white spots and red hairs above, purple-red and glab. beneath. Peduncle v. short; fls pendent, few, green-white, to 5cm across. Spring. Braz.

B. olsoniae L.B. Sm. & Schubert. Roots fibrous. St. ascending, to 14cm. Lvs obliquely broad-ovate to suborbicular, 12.5–20cm, base cordate, pilose, bronze-green, veins pale green, white or pink. Peduncles erect; red; fls few, white to rose-pink. Winter. Braz.

B. oxyloba Welw. To 60cm. St. succulent, stout. Lvs obliquely reniform, 5–18cm diam. palmately 5-lobed, cordate at base, lobes triangular, bristly-toothed; petiole 10–18cm; stipules toothed. Fls cymose, rose red. Guinea.

B. oxysperma A. DC. St. trailing or climbing, hairy. Lvs ovate-acuminate, subcordate, dentate, glab. above, hairy on veins beneath. Peduncle exceeding lvs; fls red. Capsule with solitary large wing. Philipp.

B. palmaris A. DC. = *B. biserrata*.

B. palmata D. Don Rhiz. to 60cm, decumbent. Lvs broad-ovate, 12.5–20cm, acuminate, base cordate, angled to sharply-lobed to laciniate, purple-black with broad green band above, red beneath. Fls several, yellow with red hairs, white within, to 2.5cm across. Summer. India, Burm., to S China. var. *bowringiana* (Champ. ex Benth.) J. Golding & C. Karegeannes. Lvs strongly obliquely cordate, 15–25cm, elongate, irregularly lobed, dark green, hairy above, yellow-green veins, margin red beneath. Fls white edged pink. Hong Kong.

B. palmifolia hort. = *B. vitifolia*.

B. paranaensis Brade. St. thick. Lvs obliquely broad-ovate, 22–25cm, shallowly 7–8-lobed, base deeply cordate, serrate, ciliate, sparsely hairy above, glab. beneath, veins pale; petiole to 16cm with collar of hairs at apex. Peduncle exceeding lvs; fls many in large cymes, white, to 3.5cm across. Spring. Braz.

B. partita Irmsch. Small, shrubby with swollen base. Lvs to 5cm, maple-like, acuminately lobed, pewter-grey. Fls small, white. S. Afr.

B. parva Sprague, non Merrill = *B. mannii*.

B. parvifolia Graham, non Schott nec Klotzsch = *B. dregei*.

B. paulensis A. DC. Rhiz. ascending, to 7.5cm, fleshy, soft-hairy. Lvs peltate, oblong, to 20cm, acuminate, dentate, glossy above with net of white veins, white-hairy, veins and hairs red beneath; petiole with red hairs at apex. Peduncles tall; fls many, white with red hairs, 3.5–5cm across. Braz.

B. pavoniana DC. = *B. humilis*.

B. pavonina Ridl. Rhiz. short, red. Lvs ovate-cordate, 12.5cm, acuminate or acute, basal lobes unequal, entire, deep green with blue iridescence above, red beneath; petioles to 17.5cm, red. Peduncle to 15cm; fls few, pink, to 2.5cm across. Winter-early spring. Malaysia.

B. peltata Otto & A. Dietr. LILY-PAD BEGONIA. Roots fibrous. St. erect, to 60cm, succulent, hairy. Lvs peltate, ovate, to 23cm, acuminate, succulent, white-tomentose. Peduncles long; fls pendent, white, to 2.5cm across. Winter. Mex., Guat.

B. ×*pendula* hort., not *B. pendula* Ridl. = *B.* Tuberhybrida Hybrids, Pendula group.

B. philodendroides Ziesenh. Rhiz. prostrate, succulent. Lvs palmately lobed, 20–25cm across, base cordate, lobes *c*7, acuminate, serrate, glossy green with sparse red hairs above, veins prominent beneath; petioles long. Peduncles marked blood-red; fls few, white, to 2.5cm across. Autumn. Mex.

B. **'Phyllomaniaca'** (*B. incarnata* ×*B. manicata*.) CRAZY-LEAF BEGONIA. St. erect, to 60cm, branched, villous, with many buds and leafy outgrowths. Lvs obliquely cordate, to 20cm, slightly lobed, dentate, ciliate, glossy, with many leafy growths on the upper surface. Peduncles erect; fls pink, to 2.5cm across. Winter. Braz., origin obscure.

B. phyllomaniaca Mart. = *B.* 'Phyllomaniaca'.

B. picta Sm. St. to 38cm. Lvs ovate, 7.5–12.5cm, acuminate, base cordate, biserrate, pilose, dark green mottled white and purple-bronze above; petiole long. Peduncle short; fls pink, 2–3cm across, fragrant. Summer or year-round. Pak. to Bhutan.

B. picta hort. Henderson ex A. DC., non Sm. = *B. annulata*.

B. picta var. *alba* hort. = *B. undulata*.

B. pilifera (Klotzsch) A. DC. = *B. lindleyana*.

B. pinetorum A. DC. Rhizomatous. Lvs obliquely ovate, acuminate, base cordate, undulate, glab. or white-hairy above, red-brown-tomentose beneath. Peduncles tall; fls many, pink, small. Winter. Mex.

B. plagioneura Milne-Redh. Shrubby, erect to 1m. Lvs v. obliquely sublanceolate, 3.5–7cm, acuminate, base subcordate, ± fleshy, glab. except veins beneath, undulate, dentate; petioles to 2.5cm, hairy. Fls cymose, white, to 3cm across. Origin unknown.

B. platanifolia Schott in Spreng. Shrubby erect, to 2m. Lvs reniform in outline, 20–25cm across, 5-lobed to middle, dentate, ciliate, green with silver marking, hispid. Fls many, pendulous, white, tinged pink, large. Winter–spring. Braz.

B. plebeja Liebm. Rhiz. stout, ascending, branched. Lvs obliquely broad-ovate, 7.5–20cm, apex acute, base cordate, dentate, ciliate, glab., green or red above, white-spotted and pilose beneath; petiole long. Peduncle long; fls many, white. Autumn–winter. S Mex. to Panama. 'Brooks': lvs marbled brown, veins pale green.

B. poculifera Hook. f. To 5m, robust. Lvs 12–18cm, obliquely ovate, base rounded, veins and margin red, entire; petiole 15–25mm. Pedicels short; fls cupped by 2 rose-coloured bracts. Guinea.

B. polyantha Ridl. St. short, woody. Lvs orbicular-ovate, 19–20cm, base deeply cordate, denticulate, glab. above except veins, densely red-brown-hairy on veins beneath; petiole to 45cm. Peduncles to 60cm, hairy, brown-red; fls many, white tinged pink or red. Sumatra.

B. polygonoides Hook. f. To 1m; st. slender, shiny. Lvs to 8cm, obliquely elliptic-lanceolate, entire; petiole v. short. Infl. few-fld; tep. white; ovary slender, orange. Year-round. Guinea.

B. popenoei Standl. Rhiz. v. stout, ascending; stolons present. Lvs orbicular, to 23cm, acute, dentate, ciliate, sparsely hairy, bright green, red toward margin. Peduncles tall; fls many, white or pale pink, to 2.5cm across. Spring–summer. Hond.

B. pringlei S. Wats. Rhiz. covered in brown stipules. Lvs obliquely rhombic-ovate, 5–7.5cm, acute, base cordate, dentate, sparsely pubesc. above, tomentose, papillose beneath; petioles to 10cm. Peduncle to 20cm, red, ± pubesc.; fls to 1.5cm across. Mex.

B. prismatocarpa Hook. St. creeping, rooting. Lvs 2.5–5cm, v. obliquely ovate or near round, base cordate-rounded, 2(–3)-lobed, sparsely hairy, wavy-toothed; petiole 2.5–7cm, hairy. Fls yellow. Year-round. Guinea. 'Variegation': lvs marked pale green; fls abundant.

B. pruinata A. DC. Rhizomatous. St. erect, to 30cm, br. few. Lvs ovate, to 7.5cm, acuminate, base cordate, entire, shiny green above, hairy along veins, glaucous pale green beneath. Peduncles to 30cm; fls many, white. Winter. C Amer.

B. pruinosa hort. = *B. pruinata*.

B. pseudolubbersii Brade. Roots fibrous. St. erect, to 75cm, woody. Lvs obliquely oblong-lanceolate, 7.5–12.5cm, spotted silver-white, base cordate, shallowly dentate. Fls few, white with pink margins, to 5cm across. Intermittent throughout year. Braz.

B. pustulata Liebm. Rhizomatous. Lvs basal, obliquely broad-ovate, to 15cm, acuminate, base cordate, bullate, dentate, ciliate, green with silver veins above, red or pink beneath; petioles long, red-hairy. Fls few, rose-pink, small. Summer. Mex., Guat. 'Argentea': lvs variegated with silver patches along veins; fls green-white.

B. quadrialata Warb. Rhizomatous. St. short. Lvs ovate to suborbicular, to 14cm, apex acuminate or rounded, pale green, margin red or pink; petiole pink. Peduncles pink; fls orange-red to yellow streaked orange-red; ovary 4-winged. Spring–autumn. Trop. W Afr.

B. quadrilocularis Brade = *B. egregia*.

B. radicans Vell. SHRIMP BEGONIA. Rhiz. short. St. pendulous, scrambling to 2.5m, green with white spots. Lvs obliquely ovate to oblong-lanceolate, 7.5cm, undulate, glaucous with white spots above, purple beneath, red when young; petiole short. Peduncles short; fls in dense cymes, coral-pink to brick-red, to 2.5cm across. Winter. Braz. 'Purpurea': lvs flushed bronze.

B. radicans hort., non Vell. = *B. glabra*.

B. rajah Ridl. To 15cm. Lvs radical, ± circular, cordate, 8–10×8–15cm, green, blotched red, veins bristly beneath, ciliate; petiole bristly. Infl. hairy; fls rose-pink, 2cm across. Spring. Malaya.

B. reniformis Dryand. Roots fibrous. St. erect, to 1m+, branched, thick, ridged, red-hairy or -glandular. Lvs obliquely obovate, to 14cm, base cordate, serrate, sparsely hairy, glossy yellow-green above, hairy or gland. beneath; petiole long. Peduncles arching, to 20cm; fls many, white, small. Winter. Braz., Colomb.

B. rex Putzeys KING BEGONIA; PAINTED-LEAF BEGONIA. Rhiz. fleshy, creeping, usually buried. Lvs obliquely ovate, 20–30cm, acute, base cordate, undulate, ciliate-denticulate, puckered and sparsely hairy above, pubesc. on veins beneath, rich metallic green with broad zone of silver-white above, dull red beneath; petioles red, hairy. Peduncles erect; fls few, pink, to 5cm across. Winter. Assam. Plants in cult. usually belong to the Rex Cultorum Hybrids.

B. Rex Cultorum Hybrids. REX BEGONIA; BEEFSTEAK GERANIUM. Group of hundreds of named cvs derived from hybrids primarily between *B. rex* and related Asian spp. Chiefly rhizomatous. Lvs

obliquely ovate to lanceolate-ovate, base ± cordate, sometimes with one basal lobe overlapping and forming a spiral, entire to sinuate or sharply lobed, usually dentate, often ciliate, dark green to wine-red or bronze patterned or zoned silver, grey or purple.

B. ×rex-cultorum L.H. Bail. = *B.* Rex Cultorum Hybrids.

B. ×ricinifolia A. Dietr. (*B. heracleifolia* ×*B. peponifolia*.) CASTOR-BEAN BEGONIA; STAR BEGONIA; BRONZE-LEAF BEGONIA. Resembling *B. heracleifolia* but lvs orbicular in outline, to 30×20cm, lobes 5–7, dark bronze-green above, purple-red beneath; petiole to 50cm. Peduncles to 125cm; fls many, white to rose-pink, small.

B. rosiflora Hook. f. = *B. veitchii*.

B. ×rosiflora hort., not *B. rosiflora* Hook. f. = *B.* Tuberhybrida Hybrids, Rosiflora group.

B. rotundifolia Lam. Rhiz. short, slender, creeping. Lvs suborbicular, to 7.5cm across, crenately lobed, basal lobes overlapping, glossy yellow-green; petioles long, red. Peduncles to 23cm; fls few, white or pink, to 3cm across. Year-round. Haiti.

B. roxburghii DC. Rhizomatous. St. 30–100cm, many, erect, thick. Lvs 15–30cm, obliquely ovate, glab., occas. hairy on veins, toothed; petiole 7–23cm. Infl. few-fld; fls white to v. pale pink. Capsule pyramidal. Spring–summer. India.

B. rubra hort. non Bl. = *B. coccinea*.

B. rubrovenia Planch. = *B. hatacoa*.

B. rufosericea Tol. Shrubby. St. erect, 50–100cm, glabrescent or red-brown-hairy. Lvs lanceolate, to 20cm, acuminate, base obtuse, undulate, crispate and biserrate, with red-brown hairs above. Peduncle to 4cm; fls many, white with red hairs, to 2.5cm across. Braz.

B. sanguinea Raddi. Roots fibrous. St. erect, to 45cm, woody at base, glossy, red. Lvs obliquely cordate, ± peltate, 10–15cm, acute, succulent, denticulate, bright green above, crimson beneath. Peduncles to 30cm; fls white, to 2cm across. Spring. Braz.

B. scabrida A. DC. Roots fibrous. St. erect, to 1.5m, thick, rough-hairy. Lvs obliquely broad-ovate, 15–30cm across, base cordate, dentate, rough-hairy, bright green. Peduncles erect; fls white, to 2cm diam., many in cymes to 30cm across. Winter–spring. Venez.

B. scandens Sw. = *B. glabra*.

B. scapigera Hook. f. To 35cm. Lvs radical, 10–20cm, peltate, rounded at base, wavy-toothed or entire; petiole 13–25cm, stout. Scape to 30cm, forked, stout; fls to 4cm diam., erect, solitary or in small, subumbellate clusters. Cameroun.

B. scharffiana Reg. Roots fibrous. St. to 1m, thick, white-hairy. Lvs broad-ovate, to 20cm, acuminate, olive-green above, bright red beneath. Peduncles long; fls few, waxy-textured, white with red marks and hairs. Summer–autumn. Braz.

B. scharffii Hook. f. Roots fibrous. St. erect, to 1.2m, woody, red-hairy. Lvs obliquely ovate, to 25cm, acute, base cordate, shallowly lobed, bronze-green with red veins above, red beneath. Fls pendent in large clusters, pale pink, hairy, to 5cm across. Year-round. Braz.

B. schmidtiana Reg. Roots fibrous. St. ann., to 30cm, hairy. Lvs obliquely ovate, 7.5cm, acuminate, lobed and dentate, hairy, green above, red beneath. Peduncles short; fls many, white or v. pale pink, to 1.5cm across. Winter. Braz.

B. schmidtii hort. Haage & Schmidt = *B. schmidtiana*.

B. schulziana Urban & Ekman. Rhiz. slender, spreading. Lvs broad-ovate in outline, to 7.5cm, deeply 5–7-lobed, white-scaly. Peduncles erect; fls few, white tinted peach. Late winter–early spring. Haiti.

B. Semperflorens-Cultorum Hybrids. BEDDING BEGONIA; WAX BEGONIA. Derived originally from *B. cucullata* var. *hookeri* and *B. schmidtiana*, but now sometimes involving *B. fuchsioides*, *B. gracilis*, *B. minor* and *B. roezlii*. Roots fibrous. St. clumped erect, 15–45cm, branched, fleshy, glab. Lvs ovate to broad-ovate, 5–10cm, obtuse, denticulate, ciliate, green to bronze or black-red, green-lvd cvs often red-tinged in sun, occas. variegated (Calla-lily begonias). Fls in small axill. clusters, single or double, white, pink or red, to 3.5cm across. Summer or year-round.

B. semperflorens Link & Otto = *B. cucullata* var. *hookeri*.

B. ×semperflorens-cultorum hort. = *B.* Semperflorens-Cultorum Hybrids.

B. serratipetala Irmsch. Roots fibrous. St. arching, to 60cm. Lvs obliquely ovate, small, acuminate, sharply lobed, crispate, biserrate, dark olive-green to metallic bronze-green with raised pink spots. Peduncles short; fls few, rose to claret; tep. sometimes serrate. Intermittent throughout year. New Guinea.

B. sikkimensis A. DC. Tuberous. St. erect, to 45cm. Lvs round in outline, 10–15cm across, weakly cordate, 5–7-lobed, lobes further incised, denticulate-ciliate, glab.; petiole to 10cm. Peduncles to 23cm; pedicels, bracts and fls bright red; fls few, to 2.5cm across. Sikkim. 'Gigantea': habit large. 'Variegata'

('Maculata'): lvs blotched.

B. socotrana Hook. f. St. ann., to 30cm, slender, succulent, bulb-like buds at base. Lvs peltate, orbicular, 10–25cm across, depressed in centre, crenate, dark green. Peduncles slender; fls few, rose-pink, 3.5–5cm across. Winter. Socotra.

B. solananthera A. DC. St. trailing or climbing. Lvs to 8cm, broad-ovate, acuminate, shallowly angled, glossy dark green above, pale beneath. Peduncles short, pendent; fls profuse, fragrant, white stained red; ovary white, broadly winged. Winter–spring. Braz.

B. sonderiana Irmsch. St. erect, 30–100cm, often branched. Lvs v. obliquely-ovate, 4–18cm, with 3 triangular lobes, biserrate. Peduncles 8–12; fls many in large cymes, pink or white, to 3cm across. S Afr.

B. spraguei C. Weber = *B. mannii*.

B. squamulosa Hook. f. Rhiz. woody, creeping, scaly-hairy. Lvs oblong-elliptic, 16–23cm, acuminate, base rounded or acute, green and glab. above, red with scattered scaly hairs beneath; petiole 4–25cm; stipules v. large. Peduncle stout; fls clustered, rose-red, to 1.5cm across. Intermittent throughout year. Trop. W Afr.

B. squarrosa Seem., non Liebm. = *B. stigmosa*.

B. staudtii Gilg var. *dispersipilosa* Irmsch. Rhizomatous. St. erect, short, hairy. Lvs peltate, obliquely broad-ovate to suborbicular, 10–11cm, bullate; petiole 6–15cm, long-hairy. Peduncles short; fls bright yellow, large. Spring–autumn. Nigeria.

B. stigmosa Lindl. Rhizomatous. Lvs orbicular, small, thick-coriaceous, weakly angled, light green with liver-coloured markings above, scaly-hairy on principle veins; petioles long, hairy. Peduncles long; fls white to pale pink, small. Winter. S Mex. to Colomb.

B. stipulacea Willd. Roots fibrous. St. spreading or pendulous, to 2.5m. Lvs obliquely ovate, 10–15cm, long-acuminate, glossy, veins grey-white above, dull red beneath. Peduncles erect; fls many, white or pink, to 1.5cm across. Winter. Braz.

B. strigillosa A. Dietr. Rhizomatous. St. bushy. Lvs obliquely ovate, 7.5–15cm, acuminate, base cordate, dentate, ciliate, olive-green above netted with brown veins. Fls few, white to pink edged red to 25cm across. Guat., Costa Rica.

B. subnummarifolia Merrill. Rhiz. slender, creeping. Lvs suborbicular, 2.5–5cm across, apex rounded, base weakly cordate, entre, ciliate, dark green; petioles long. Peduncles exceeding lvs; fls pink, to 6mm across. Intermittent throughout year. Banguey Is.

B. subvillosa Klotzsch. Roots fibrous. St. erect, to 60cm, rust-red-villous or tomentose. Lvs obliquely ovate, 3.5–12.5cm, acute, base cordate, biserrate. Fls pendulous, white, white- to red-hairy, to 2.5cm across. Summer. Braz. var. *leptotricha* (C. DC.) L.B. Sm. & Wassh. MANDA'S WOOLLY BEAR BEGONIA; WOOLLY BEAR BEGONIA. St. to 30cm; lvs to 7.5cm, crenate, matted white-hairy above. Year-round. Parag.

B. sudjanae Jansson. Rhiz. short, stout. Lvs peltate, orbicular to ovate, to 15cm+, acute, ± bullate, densely hairy, light green; petiole hairy. Fls small, white or pale pink. Intermittent throughout year. Sumatra.

B. suffruticosa Meissn. Small, compact. Lvs finely lobed and toothed, bright green with a red spot in each sinus. Fls white to pale pink. S Afr.

B. sutherlandii Hook. f. St. ann., 10–80cm, trailing, red. Lvs lanceolate, 10–15cm, deeply serrate, green with margin and veins red; petioles red. Peduncles pendulous; fls cymose, 2–2.5cm across, orange to orange-red. Summer. Natal to Tanz. Z9.

B. teuscheri Lind. ex André. Roots fibrous. St. erect, to 2m, swollen at base, pilose. Lvs ovate-lanceolate, large, acute, shallowly lobed, serrate, fleshy, dull green with grey markings above, margin red, red beneath. Peduncles short; fls deep pink to bright red. Summer–autumn. Indon.

B. thelmae L.B. Sm. & Wassh. St. trailing or climbing. Lvs in 2 ranks, oblong-elliptic, medium-sized, apex rounded, margin dentate, veins marked white. Fls white. São Tomé.

B. tomentosa Schott. Roots fibrous. St. erect, unbranched, woody, white-hairy. Lvs ovate, 10–15cm, acuminate, base cordate, entire to dentate, white-hairy, margin red. Fls many, pink edged white, red-hairy, to 2.5cm across. Spring. Braz.

B. ×*tuberhybrida* Voss = *B.* Tuberhybrida Hybrids.

B. ×*tuberosa* hort. (non *B. tuberosa* Lam.). = *B.* Tuberhybrida Hybrids.

B. Tuberhybrida Hybrids. HYBRID TUBEROUS BEGONIAS. Many cvs derived from hybrids between the Andean spp. *B. boliviensis*, *B. clarkei*, *B. davisii*, *B. pearcei*, *B. veitchii* and possibly also *B. froebelii* and *B. gracilis*. Tubers large, often concave above. St. 0 or to 60cm, fleshy, usually hairy. Fls in axillary clusters, to 15cm across, single or double, females smaller, single. Summer. Divided into 13 groups. (1) Single group: fls

large, tep. 4, usually flat. (2) Crispa or Frilled group: fls large, single tep. frilled and ruffled. (3) Cristata or Crested group: large, single, with frilled outgrowth in centre of tep. (4) Narcissiflorra or Daffodil-fld group: fls large, double, central tep. spreading-erect resembling corona of *Narcissus*. (5) Camellia or Camelliiflora group: fls large, double tep. regular, resembling a *Camellia* fl.; self-coloured, or ruffled or fimbriate. (6) Ruffled Camellia group: as (5) but fls with tep. ruffled. (7) Rosiflora or Rosebud group: fls large, with centre resembling rose-bud. (8) Fimbriata Plena or Carnation group: fls large, double, tep. fimbriate. (9) Picotee group: fls large, usually double, camellia-shaped, with tep. edged with different shade or colour, or merging with main colour. (10) Marginata group: fls as in (9), precisely edged with distinct colour. (11) Marmorata group: fls as in (5), pink, marbled with white. (12) Pendula or Hanging-basket group: st. trailing or pendulous; fls many, small to large, single or double. (13) Multiflora group: plant low, bushy, compact; fls many, small, single to double.

B. ulmifolia Willd. ELM-LEAF BEGONIA. Roots fibrous. St. erect, to 2m, 4-angled, grooved, pale green. Lvs ovate-oblong, 7.5–12.5cm, rugose, biserrate, sparsely rough-hairy. Fls many, white, to 1.5cm across. Spring. Colomb., Venez.

B. undulata Schott. Roots fibrous. St. erect, 1–2m, much-branched. succulent. Lvs in 2 ranks, oblong-lanceolate. 7.5–12.5cm, acuminate, undulate, glossy. Fls many, pendulous, white, to 2.5cm across. Summer–autumn. Braz.

B. undulata hort., non Schott = *B. radicans*.

B. urophylla Hook. Rhizomatous. Lvs basal, broadly cordate, large, long-acuminate, deeply-toothed. Fls in large pan., white, flushed pink. Origin unknown.

B. valdensium A. DC. PHILODENDRON-LEAF BEGONIA. Roots fibrous. St. erect. Lvs obliquely broad-ovate, to 30cm, acuminate, base cordate, shallowly lobed, flat to undulate, dentate, veins ivory-white above; petiole with hair collar at apex. Fls white edged pink. Summer. Braz.

B. veitchii Hook. Tuberous. St. 30–75cm, short. Lvs 5–10cm, broadly ovate-cordate or reniform, dark green, above, glaucous, hairy beneath, lobed, serrate; petiole stout; stipules red. Infl. 2–4-fld; fls bright scarlet, fragrant, to 6cm diam. Summer. Peru.

B. vellozoana Brade = *B. olsoniae*.

B. venosa Skan ex Hook. f. Roots fibrous. St. erect, thick, with persistent stipules. Lvs reniform with centre depressed, not peltate, large, succulent, crystalline in appearance. Peduncles long, arching, white-hairy; fls few, white or pink, fragrant, small. Late summer–spring. Braz.

B. versicolor Irmsch. FAIRY-CARPET BEGONIA. Rhiz. short, red-pilose. Lvs obliquely broad-ovate or oblong, 7.5–12.5cm across, short-acuminate, denticulate, ciliate, emerald- to apple-green with silver-white markings and red veins above, red beneath. Peduncles hairy; fls cymose, salmon-pink or red, hairy. Intermittent throughout year. China.

B. vitifolia Schott. Roots fibrous. St. erect, to 1.2m, fleshy, glab. Lvs ovate to orbicular, large, base cordate, lobed, finely serrate, hairy. Peduncles erect; fls white, small. Winter–spring. Braz.

B. vitifolia Lindl. non Schott = *B. lindleyana*.

B. wallichiana A. DC. Roots fibrous. St. to 30cm, bushy, glandular-hairy. Lvs obliquely broad-ovate, 5–7.5cm, base cordate, serrate, viscid-pubesc. Peduncle to 5cm; fls few, white or pink-tinged, hairy, to 1.5cm across. Autumn. Origin obscure.

B. ×**weltoniensis** hort. ex André. (*B. dregei* ×*B. sutherlandii*.) MAPLE-LEAF BEGONIA; GRAPEVINE BEGONIA. Tuberous or semituberous. St. to 1m, swollen at base, branched, red. Lvs ovate, to 7.5cm across, acuminate, shallowly-lobed, dentate, dark glossy green veined purple above. Peduncles short; fls many, white or pink. Gdn origin. 'Alba': fls white.

B. 'Winter Jewel'. Roots fibrous. St. many, to 45cm, sparsely hairy. Lvs obliquely ovate, acute, dentate, dark green edged glossy red above, rust-brown beneath. Peduncles short; fls many, pink. Year-round. Origin obscure.

B. wollnyi Herzog. Semituberous. St. erect, to 30cm+, thick. Lvs large, deeply palmately lobed, biserrate, dark green with white markings between veins. Fls green-white. Winter. Boliv.

B. xanthina Hook. Rhiz. stout, short, scaly-hairy. Lvs obliquely ovate-cordate, 15–22cm, short-acuminate, denticulate, ciliate, glossy dark green above, purple-red with veins prominent, hairy beneath petioles to 30cm, purple-red, hairy. Peduncle red-purple, hairy; fls 12–20, pendent, yellow to orange-yellow, tinted red, to 3.5cm across. Spring. Bhutan.

B. zebrina hort. = *B. stipulacea*.

Cv. classification. I CANE-LIKE (1) *Superba*-type 'Esther Albertine' (lvs large, feathery, apple green splashed white; fls pale pink), 'Nokomis' (lvs heavily marked white; fls dusty pink), 'Sophie Cecile' (lvs deeply cut, rich green splashed silver, deep red beneath; fls rose pink). (2) *Mallet*-type 'Aya' (lvs silver, pale pink beneath and venation), 'Margaritaceae' (compact; lvs metallic purple), 'Tingly Mallet' (lvs bronze-red dotted silver, hairs red; fls large). (3) *All others* low (to 60cm): 'Anna Christine' (lvs ruffled, deep bronze; fls coral, everblooming, abundant), 'Flo' Belle Moseley' (lvs dark green speckled white; fls deep pink), 'Martha Floro' (lvs veined red; fls salmon, everblooming, scented, abundant), 'Orange Rubra' (lvs pale green; fls orange, everblooming, abundant); intermediate (to 120cm): 'Di-Anna' (lvs heavily spotted silver; fls salmon-orange), 'Florence Rita' (lvs pointed, soft green; fls pink), 'Looking Glass' (lvs silver-green, veins marked olive, cranberry beneath), 'Tom Ment' (lvs salmon spotted silver; fls coral); tall (over 120cm): 'Di-Erna' (lvs moss green; fls dark coral, everblooming, abundant), 'Interlaken' (vigorous; lvs large, green; fls cherry), 'Pickobeth' (compact; lvs apple green spotted white; fls full, frosted red).

II SHRUB-LIKE (1) *Bare-leaved* large-leaved (over 15cm): 'Paulbee' (lvs slim, puckered; fls cream with burgundy beard) and 'Rosea Gigantea' (fls large, bright red); medium-leaved (10–15cm): 'Dancing Girl' (lvs variously shaped and streaked or spotted silver), 'Druryi' (fls white with red hairs), 'Gloire de Sceaux' (lvs rounded, v. dark bronze; fls pale pink, everblooming, scented, abundant), 'Tea Rose' (bushy; lvs deep green; fls pale pink, everblooming, scented, abundant); small-leaved (under 10cm): 'Decker's Select' (lvs glossy; fls deep rose red), 'Medora' (lvs olive spotted silver; fls pale pink, profuse) and 'Swan Song' (lvs dark green; fls white); small-leaved everblooming (under 10cm): 'Sachsen' (lvs sunset-hued; fls peach, abundant) and 'Tiny Gem' (lvs v. small, crinkle-edged, deep green; fls candy pink). (2) *Hairy-leaved* wide-leaved (over 7cm across): 'Alleryi' (lvs soft green, veins dark; fls pale pink, bearded) and 'Jack Golding' (lvs deep matt green, red beneath; fls white), 'Lorene Brown' (lvs matt pea green; fls pale pink); narrow-leaved (under 7cm across): 'Withlacoochee' (lvs grey and cream; fls pearly white and whitehaired) and the felted 'San Miguel' (lvs v. furry; st. with fine bracts; fls white). (3) *Distinctive foliage* unusual surface and/or colouring: 'Shawne Worley' (compact; lvs small, spotted silver; fls candy pink); listada type: 'Caravan' ('Serlis'; lvs large, matt green splashed cream along veins; fls white) and 'Raymond George Nelson' (compact; lvs dark green with creamy sinus; fls white with red plastics); compact type: 'Midnight Sun' (outer lvs moss green, inner lvs glowing pink with green veins and red beneath; fls white).

III THICK-STEMMED (1) *Bare-leaved* large-leaved (over 15cm): 'Paul Bruant' (lvs deeply cut, glossy; fls pink); medium-leaved (10–15cm): 'Bessie Buxton' (lvs rounded; fls soft pink) and 'Perle de Lorraine' (lvs deep matt green; fls white). (2) *Hairy-leaved* large-leaved (over 15cm): 'Tim O'Reilly' (fls white flushed pink); medium-leaved (10–15cm): 'Tamo' (lvs rounded, brown, oatmeal felted; fls white, scented). (3) *Trunk-like, non-ramified* 'Snow White' (lvs light green, heavily flecked white; fls blush pink). (4) *Thickset* 'Toe' (Cookole 'Toe'; fls pink).

IV SEMPERFLORENS (1) *Single-fld* : including the green-leaved 'Derby' (fls light coral, everblooming, abundant), Frilly Dilly Mixed (lvs bright green; fls range of colours, pet. undulating), Organdy Mixed (fls range of colours, everblooming, abundant) and 'Viva' (lvs vivid deep green; fls pure white); and the bronze-leaved Cocktail Series, for example 'Gin' (lvs metallic green-black; fls deep pink), 'Vodka' (lvs v. dark; fls deep red) and 'Whiskey' (lvs pale bronze; fls white); others are Coco Series (low-growing; lvs pure bronze; fls red or salmon, everblooming, abundant) and Dancia Series (vigorous, dense, bushy; lvs bronze, shiny; fls rose or scarlet, everblooming, abundant). (2) *Double-fld* : over 80 cvs including the green-leaved 'Dainty Maid' (fls fully round, white edged salmon pink, everblooming, abundant), 'Gustav Lind' (fls semi-double/double, pink, everblooming), 'Pink Wonder' (fls v. large, fully round, pink, everblooming), 'Snow White' (fls white, everblooming); and the bronze-leaved 'Curly Locks' (robust; lvs dark bronze; fls sulphur yellow, upper tep. candy pink), Mother Goose Series including 'Bo Peep' (lvs deep bronze; fls extra-double, dark pink) and 'Lucy Locket' (lvs pale bronze; fls pink); others are 'Ernest K.' (lvs v. deep bronze; fls coral red, crested, abundant) and 'Old Lace' (fls fully double, rosy red, lacy). (3) *Variegated lvs*: over 20 cvs including 'Calla Lily' (robust; lvs splashed white; fls single, red), 'Charm' (lvs vivid green, blotched gold and cream; fls single, light pink, everblooming) and 'Ruby Jewel' (dwarf; fls double, frilled, ruby).

V RHIZOMATOUS (1) *Small-leaved* (to 7cm) 'Bethlehem Star' (compact; lvs black with fine cream central star; fls cream dotted pink), 'China Doll' (compact; lvs ice green with irregular red-brown mottling; fls light pink, abundant), 'Libby Lee' (lvs light green, spiky edged; fls white, abundant) and 'Robert Shatzer' (lvs deep green striped and blotched rich brown, some cordate; fls peach, abundant); lobed: 'Baby Perfection' (lvs linden green, edges undulate and marked black; fls candy pink, abundant) and 'Royal Lustre' (lvs silver and lime green, shiny; fls blush pink, red flecked, sparse); cleft: 'Dr. Spelios' (lvs light green, darker edged; fls pale pink) and 'Tondelayo' (lvs with central cream star; fls

pink); parted: 'Cathy Lou' (fls delicate pink); crested-margined: 'Cathedral' (lvs puckered with shining pink 'windows' of colour; fls pink) and 'Small Change' (lvs silver, frilly edged); spiral-leaved: 'Curly Zip' (compact; lvs lime green, sinus red, central double corkscrew; fls pink). (2) *Medium-leaved* (7–15cm) 'Merry-Go-Round' (lvs round, brown-felted; fls pale apricot), 'Red Spider' (lvs tear-shaped, bright green with cherry central star; fls pink) and 'Pearlii' (lvs pointed, metallic blue-green; fls white); lobed: 'Aries' (lvs maple-shaped, fresh green marked deep brown toward edge; fls light pink), 'Burgundy Velvet; (lvs spotted maroon, heart red; fls white flecked red) and 'Virbob' (lvs maple-shaped, deep matt green with light green star; fls pale pink); cleft: 'Black Velvet' (fls rich red), 'Emerald Lacewing' (lvs wing-shaped, vivid green; fls pale pink abundant) and 'Universe' (lvs maple-shaped, mottled burgundy; fls palest pink); parted: 'Helen Jaros' (fls deep pink, abundant); crested margin: 'Munchkin' (lvs v. ruffled and crinkled-edged, bronze, edges hairy and coloured pink/white, claret beneath; fls pink); spiral: 'Stallion' (lvs speckled black and green, central double spiral; fls pearly white to pink) and 'Spellbound' (lvs cupped, light green, curled at sinus, velvety; fls white, ruffled). (3) *Large-leaved* (to 30cm) entire/subentire: 'Bess' (lvs shiny bronze, v. textured) and 'Delia Marleau' (lvs moss green, flecked brown at edges; fls light pink, abundant); lobed: 'Brown Lake' (fls pink) and 'Frosty Knight' (lvs v. shiny; fls pale pink, abundant); cleft: 'Cumbre' (lvs bright green; fls light pink, abundant) and 'Texastar' (lvs star-shaped, black, shiny; fls pale pink); parted: 'Palmgarten' (lvs deep green; fls pink, abundant); compound-leaved: 'Carol Mac' (fls white flushed green); crested margined: 'Crestabruchii' ('Curly Lettuce Lf Begonia'; lvs large, margins thickly crested; fls pink to white); spiral-leaved: 'Sweet Majic' (lvs large, satiny, red-brown; fls white flushed pink, scented, everblooming). (4) *Giant-leaved* (over 30cm) entire/subentire: 'Freddie' (lvs thick, glossy deep green; fls pink, abundant); lobed: 'Shenandoah' (lvs green; fls pink, abundant); cleft: 'Peggy Frost' (fls pink); parted: 'Earl-ee-bee' (lvs v. fine, light green; fls white-green, abundant). (5) *Rhiz. erect* entire/subentire: 'Tancho' (lvs large, green with black 'stitches' at margin; fls white); lobed: 'Dark Forest' (lvs dark green; fls white); cleft: 'Kumwha' (lvs deep green, veins lighter; fls pink); parted: 'Pinwheel' (fls light pink); crested-margined: 'Essie Hunt' (lvs light green, curled at sinus, marked red along veins; fls pale pink) and 'Madame Queen' (lvs v. large, roughly crested, olive green, maroon beneath; fls pink); spiral-leaved: 'Spindrift' (lvs snow white, marked green along veins, edged pink; fls pink, abundant). (6) *Rhiz. joined at or below the soil with erect st.*: 'Charles Jaros' ('Lowe's Rubro-venia'; lvs star-shaped, snow white, speckled; fls bluish pink). (7) *Distinctive Foliage* pustular type (imperialis-like): 'Emerald Jewel' (lvs lush green, lightly marked silver and brown; fls white) and 'Silver Jewel' (lvs rich green streaked silver around veins; fls white); unusual surface/colour; small-leaved (under 7cm): 'Buttercup' (lvs green, v. glossy; fls bright yellow to orange, abundant, everblooming); medium-leaved (to 15cm): 'It' (lvs green marked yellow; fls deep coral pink, scented, abundant, everblooming) and 'Wanda' (lvs mottled silver, glossy, hairs red; fls pale pink); large-leaved (over 15cm): 'Mumtaz' (lvs deep bronze, peltate, veins green, lightly puckered; fls pink), and 'Su Go Go' (lvs large, green and brown, veins lighter, puckered; fls pink); unusual shape/habit of growth: 'Bebe' (lvs long, pointed, midrib protruding and marked red, rosette form; fls palest pink, abundant).

VI REX-CULTORUM (1) *Small-leaved* (under 8cm) include the spiralled 'Merlin' (fls pink); the non-spiralled 'Mini Merry' (lvs rose with cream band surrounded by green, edge rose; fls light pink) and 'Wood Nymph' (lvs rounded, rich brown speckled silver). (2) *Medium-leaved* (to 15cm) include the spiralled 'Carlton's Velma' (lvs gold, dappled metallic red), 'Purple Curly Stardust' (lvs ruffled, purple with cream and pink mottling), 'Purple Petticoats' (lvs silver with lilac along edge and veins, edges curling in; fls pink); the non-spiralled 'Elda Haring' (lvs white laced with red; fls large, purple/pink, scented), 'Her Majesty' (lvs wide, irregularly shaped, satiny, deep purple with olive area splashed frosty pink), 'Roi des Roses' (lvs pale pink mottled silver; fls pink), 'Vista' (lvs black/brown, dappled deep coral pink, satiny). (3) *Large-leaved* (over 15cm) include the spiralled 'Comtesse Louise Erddody' (lvs large, light olive, marked silver-pink between veins, hairs pink), 'Green Gold' (lvs v. large, ruffled, green-gold marked silver, heart and edge purple), 'Persian Swirl' (lvs plum with white lacework), 'Snooky' (lvs moss green with dark purple/brown heart and edge, satiny; fls pink, everblooming); the non-spiralled 'Black Knight' 'Midnight'; lvs black/red with row of pink dots; fls coral pink), 'Cardoza Gardens' (lvs rainbow coloured with olive, silver, purple, violet etc), 'Emerald Giant' (lvs deep green marked with brown heart), 'Merry Christmas (lvs shiny, red surrounded by bright green band, deep red heart and edge), 'Queen Mother' (lvs metallic pink with silver band inside edge), 'Tahara' (lvs long, purple splashed silver and green). (4) *Upright-stemmed* include the spiralled 'Curly Fireflush' (lvs soft green with wide burgundy edge; fls pale pink, scented), 'Dewdrop' (lvs small, round, pearly grey, purple veins and underside), 'Hallelujah' (lvs soft purple dusted silver), 'Maid Marion' (lvs round, silver, metallic rose in bright light; fls red), the non-spiralled 'Dido' (lvs silver with bands of bright colours; fls pink), 'Fire Flush' ('Bettina Rothschild'; lvs cordate, metallic olive with many bright red hairs; fls white, scented), 'Fireworks' (lvs large, maroon, marked white blending to purple between veins; fls pink), 'Helen Lewis' (lvs black with silver stripe; fls creamy white flushed pink), 'Scarlett O'Hara' (lvs marked crimson and frosty green leaving a burgundy heart and edge), 'Tambourine' (lvs bright red with fine green veins and silver stripe; fls pale orange).

VII TUBEROUS (1) *Semituberous* 'Richard Robinson' (lvs pleated, marked silver, fls white) and 'Speckled Roundabout' (lvs spiralled, pleated, deep bronze dotted silver; fls soft pink and white). (2) *Sp. and First Generation Hybrids* low-growing: 'Lulandii' (lvs pointed, deeply cut, bright green; fls large, pink, abundant); tall-growing: 'Torsa' (fls pink). (3) *Tuberhydra*, including the large-fld single 'Bonfire' (lvs bronze; fls bright red); crispa marginata 'Thelma' (fls pink, edges darker); large-fld double 'Allan Langdon' (fls deep cardinal red, abundant), 'Bernat Klein' (fls fully double, pure white, pet. slightly waved), 'Buttermilk' (fls large, cream flushed pinky apricot), 'Elaine Tarttelin' (fls deep rose pink, abundant), 'Tahiti' (fls coral orange), 'Roy Hartley' (fls salmon rose, abundant), 'Sweet Dreams' (fls soft pink), 'Falstaff' (fls rich rose pink); picotee 'Bali Hi' (fls pale cream edged raspberry red), 'Fairylight' (fls milky white finely edged coral pink), 'Jean Blair' (fls yellow edged bright red), 'Saturn' (fls salmon-orange with darker edge); ruffled picotee 'Santa Teresa' (fls white edged pink); grandiflora compacta Champion Series (fls abundant, range of colours); maxima 'Switzerland' (fls dark red, abundant); multiflora 'Madame Richard Galle' (fls orange, abundant), 'Kupfergold' (fls copper-gold, abundant), 'Queen Fabiola' (fls rich soft red, abundant); pendula 'Jo Rene' (fls crimson to pink, abundant), 'Orange Cascade' (fls yellow flushed burnt apricot, abundant), 'Trisha' (fls picotee, yellow edged apricot, abundant); fimbriata 'Pink Princess' (fls pale pink), 'Santa Barbara' (fls bright yellow); bertinii 'Bertinii' (fls red, abundant). (4) *Hiemalis and Hiemalis-like*, including Aphrodite Series (fls double, everblooming, abundant, in rose, pink, peach and red), 'Bolero' (fls double, orange, everblooming, abundant), 'Fantasy' (lvs v. dark, finely cut; fls deep vivid pink, everblooming, abundant), 'Man's Favorite' (fls single, white), 'Renaissance' (lvs deeply cut; fls double, frilled, dark coral red, frilled, everblooming, abundant), 'Schwabenland Orange' (bushy; fls metallic green; fls bright apricot, abundant). (5) *Cheimantha and Cheimantha-like*, including 'Love Me' (fls vivid lilac-pink, abundant), 'Marjorie Gibbs' (lvs round, dark matt green; fls pink, v. abundant), 'White Marina' (vigorous; lvs light green; fls large, white edged soft pink).

VIII TRAILING SCANDENT. 'Florence Carrell' (lvs light green, deeply cut; fls salmon, everblooming), 'Ivy Ever' (lvs small, cordate, marked brown; fls large, bright pink, everblooming), 'Orococco' (lvs textured, pale green edged bronze; fls white, lacy), 'Splotches' (lvs lightly splashed soft yellow; fls pink and white).

BEGONIACEAE Agardh. 2/900. *Begonia*.

Behnia Didr. Liliaceae (Luzuriaceae). 1 climbing perenn. herb. Roots swollen. St. slender, flexuous, much-branched. Lvs 5–7.5cm, ovate to acuminate, glossy, coriaceous. Fls in lax cymes; perianth short-tubular, green-white, seg. to 2cm. S Afr. Z9.
B. reticulata Didr.

Bejaria Mutis ex L. Ericaceae. 25 everg. shrubs or trees. Lvs ovate to oblong, entire. Infl. racemose or corymbose; cal. campanulate, 7-parted; cor. seg. 6–7, distinct, spreading; sta. 12–20. S & C Amer., US.
B. aestuans Mutis ex L. f. Shrub or tree to 8m; branchlets glab. to minutely tomentose. Lvs 3–5cm, elliptic-oblong to oblong-lanceolate, glaucous and tomentose beneath. Infl. to 5cm, rusty-pubesc.; fls to 3cm, rose. Colomb. Z10.
B. cinnamonea Lindl. Shrub, 1–1.5m, or small tree; branchlets darkly glandular-hirsute. Lvs 2–3.5cm, elliptic, glandular-pilose above, then glab. Infl. to 4cm, paniculate, rusty-pubesc.; fls to 2.5cm, purple. Peru and Ecuad. Z10.
B. coarctata Humb. & Bonpl. V. similar to *B. glauca* except most parts ± densely ferruginous-tomentose; cor. pale rose-pink with darker streaks. Colomb., Ecuad., Peru, Boliv. Z10.
B. glauca Humb. & Bonpl. Shrub, 1–2m, rarely tree to 8m; branchlets glab. Lvs 3–4cm, oblong to elliptic-oblong, glossy above, glaucous beneath. Infl. to 8cm, racemose; fls to 1.5cm, fleshy pink. Venez. and Colomb. to Boliv. var. *tomentella* Mansf. & Sleumer. Br. grey-pubesc.; lvs tomentose; fls longer. Peru and Boliv. Z10.

B. glauca var. *coarctata* (Humb. & Bonpl.) Mansf. & Sleumer = *B. coarctata*.
B. ledifolia Humb. & Bonpl. Shrub to 1.5m, much branched; branchlets tinged purple, viscid-pubesc. Lvs 1–2cm, oblong to oblong-ovate, mucronate, revolute, glossy and sparsely glandular-hispid above, glaucous beneath. Infl. to 5cm, racemose, glandular-pilose; fls to 2cm, purple. Venez. and Colomb. Z10.
B. mathewsii Fielding & Gardiner = *B. glauca* var. *tomentella*.
B. phillyraeifolia Benth. = *B. aestuans*.
B. racemosa Muell. Shrub, 1–2m; branchlets oft. coarsely-pubesc. Lvs 4–6cm, elliptic-lanceolate, powdery-pubesc. above, paler and glab. beneath. Infl. to 20cm, term. or paniculate, viscid; fls to 3cm, fragrant, white tinted pink, gummy. SE US. Z9.

Bejuco Colorado *Cydista aequinoctialis*.
Bejuco de Ajo *Mansoa alliacea*.
Bejuco de Danta *Cydista aequinoctialis*.
Bejuco Edmurcielago *Macfadyena unguis-cati*.

Belamcanda Adans. Iridaceae. 2 iris-like, short-lived perenn. herbs. Lvs in fans on branching st. Perianth seg. 6, equal (unlike the falls of *Iris*); styles 3. Eurasia. Z8.
B. chinensis (L.) DC. BLACKBERRY LILY; LEOPARD LILY. Rhiz. slender, stoloniferous. Lvs to 20×1.5cm. Infl. to 1m, loosely branched; fls to 4cm diam., yellow to orange-red, spotted maroon or purple. C Asia, India, China, Jap.
→*Pardanthus*.

Belgian Evergreen *Dracaena sanderiana*.
Belladonna *Atropa belladonna*.
Belladonna Lily *Amaryllis belladonna*.
Bella Sombra *Phytolacca dioica*.
Bell Bauhinia *Bauhinia tomentosa*.
Belle Apple *Passiflora laurifolia*.
Belle de Nuit *Ipomoea alba*.
Belle Isle Cress *Barbarea verna*.

Bellendena R. Br. Proteaceae. 1 compact shrub to 65cm. Lvs grey-green, thick, oblanceolate to cuneate. Infl. 6–10cm, erect; perianth reflexed, white to pale pink. Summer. E Aus. Z9.
B. montana R. Br. MOUNTAIN ROCKET.

Bellevalia Lapeyr. Liliaceae (Hyacinthaceae). *c*45 bulbous perenn. herbs. Lvs 2+, basal, linear-lanceolate. Fls 6-merous, nodding or horizontal, funnelform or tubular, in rac. Medit., Black Sea, Turkestan, NE Afghan.
B. atroviolacea Reg. 8–30cm. Lvs 3–6, glaucous, slightly channelled and waxy, ciliate or scabrous. Rac. 3–6cm, densely conical; fls 8–9mm, campanulate, overlapping and nodding when open, tinged black-violet. C Asia. Z7.
B. azurea (Fenzl) Boiss. = *Muscari azureum*.
B. ciliata (Cyr.) Nees. To 30cm. Lvs 3–5, strongly ciliate. Rac. 10–12cm, broadly conical, v. loose; fls 9–11mm, narrow-campanulate, tube brown or lilac, lobes white or green-tinted. NW Afr., S Eur., W Asia Minor. Z7.
B. dubia (Guss.) Rchb. To 40cm. Lvs 2–5, channelled, trailing. Rac. loose, narrow-cylindric; fls 6–8mm, ellipsoid to weakly campanulate, bright violet-blue with green tips in bud, opening maroon brown with yellow-tinted lobes. Port.
B. flexuosa Boiss. To 50cm. Lvs 4 or 5, usually exceeding scape, trailing, wavy, ciliate or scabrous. Rac. cylindric; fls 7–8mm, campanulate or broadly obconical, white in bud with green veins, sometimes tinged lilac.
B. hyacinthoides (Bertero) Persson & Wendelbo. To 15cm. Lvs 4–8, somewhat fleshy, trailing, slightly channelled, glaucous, ciliate. Rac. spike-like ellipsoid, to cylindric; fls 7–12mm, campanulate, horizontal or turned upwards, v. pale blue with deeper blue to purple-blue veins. Greece. Z7.
B. longipes Post. Close to *B. ciliata* but lvs 3–4 with glab. margins.
B. pycnantha (K. Koch) A. Los. To 40cm. Lvs 3, channelled, dark green, glaucous above. Rac. densely conical with overlapping fls, becoming ellipsoid or cylindric and loose; fls to 6mm, urceolate, blue-black, green-yellow on edges and inner surfaces.
B. romana (L.) Rchb. To 30cm. Lvs 3–6, ± erect, fleshy, channelled. Rac. loose, oblong or ovoid in fl., to 4cm wide; fls 8–10mm, widely campanulate or broadly obconical, white becoming tinged green, violet, or brown; anth. blue-black, conspicuous. S Fr. Z7.
B. savizii Woron. To 40cm. Lvs 3–6, oblong-lanceolate, glaucous above, margins ciliate to scabrous. Rac. cylindric-oblong to ovate, to 15cm; fls 7–10mm, campanulate white, becoming grey-brown to pale grey-green. Afghan., E & S Iran, C Asia. Z7.

B. warburgii Feinbrun. To 60cm. Lvs 3–6, to 3.5cm wide, margins shortly ciliate or scabrous. Rac. loose, becoming cylindric; fls 10–15mm, narrow-campanulate, white, veined green in bud, perianth tube becoming purple-brown when open. Isr. Z8.
→*Hyacinthus* and *Muscari*.

Bell-flowered Cherry *Prunus campanulata*.
Bellflower *Campanula*.
Bell-fruited Mallee *Eucalyptus preissiana*.
Bell Heather *Erica cinerea*.

Bellidiastrum Scop. = *Aster*.

Bellinger River Fig *Ficus watkinsiana*.

Bellis L. DAISY. Compositae. 7 ann. or perenn. herbs. Lvs basal or alt., entire to serrate-crenate. Cap. radiate, solitary, pedunculate; disc flts yellow. Eur., Medit.
B. caerulescens (Hook. f.) Cass. ex Ball. Perenn. to 12cm. Lvs to 8cm, orbicular-reniform to broadly oblong-ovate, sinuate-crenate, cordate, truncate or cuneate at base, adpressed-pubesc.; petiole to 18cm, slender. Cap. 2.5–4cm diam., on stout peduncles 1.5–5cm; ray flts 8–17mm, white to pale blue washed pink. Atlas Mts. Z8.
B. integrifolia Michx. = *Astranthium integrifolium*.
B. monstrosa hort. = *B. perennis* 'Monstrosa'.
B. perennis L. Perenn. Lvs to 1–6cm, oblanceolate to broadly obovate-spathulate, narrowed abruptly to petiole, 1-veined, bright green, adpressed-pubesc. Cap. 1.5–3cm diam., on slender 4–5cm peduncles; ray flts 4–11mm, often tinged maroon below, occas. pink. Late spring–summer. S, W & C Eur., W Asia. White selections include the single-fld 'Aucubifolia' with green and gold variegated lvs and 'Shrewly Gold' with single fls and bright gold lvs; double forms include 'Alba Plena', 'Pomponette' (miniature),the Victorian selection 'Parkinson's Double White' and 'Prolifera' (known as 'Hen and Chickens') with white fls speckled pink and a ring of tiny daisies hanging from the mother fl.; pink selections include the dwarf, small-fld 'Dresden China', the double-fld 'Pink Buttons' and the tall (to 12cm) 'Staffordshire Pink'; red selections include the large-fld 'Monstrosa' and the tall (to 12cm) double scarlet 'Rob Roy'. 'Goliath' is large-fld, red, pink or white. Z4.
B. rotundifolia (Desf.) Boiss. & Reut. Perenn. Lvs 2.5–9cm, orbicular-reniform to broadly oblong-ovate, cordate, toothed, truncate or cuneate at base, adpressed-pubesc.; petiole to 18cm. Cap. 2.5–4cm diam., on stout 1.5–5cm peduncles; ray flts 8–17mm, usually tinged maroon. Spring. SW Spain, NW Afr. Z9.
B. rotundifolia var. *caerulescens* hort. = *B. caerulescens*.
B. sylvestris Cyr. Perenn. Lvs 3–18cm, linear-oblong to narrowly obovate, subentire to remotely serrate, narrowed to a short, scarcely distinct petiole, 3-veined, dark green, adpressed-pubesc. Cap. 2–4cm diam., on stout 10–45cm peduncles; ray flts 8–14mm, tinged maroon below and often above. Spring–autumn. S Eur. Z7.
→*Bellium*.

Bellium L. Compositae. 4 small, ann. or perenn. herbs. Lvs basal, alt. or somewhat whorled, entire, petiolate. Cap. radiate, small, solitary, pedunculate; ray flts white, sometimes tinged red beneath; disc flts yellow. Medit. Z8.
B. bellidioides L. Perenn., with trailing, leafless stolons. Lvs to 12mm, basal, elliptical, tapered to petiole. Cap. 9–15mm diam., on slender, 2–14cm peduncles; ray flts 3–4mm, often tinged red beneath. Summer. W Medit. islands.
B. crassifolium Moris. Perenn.; st. sparingly branched, decumbent, somewhat woody. Lvs 9–15mm, alt. or whorled, orbicular to elliptic-spathulate, fleshy, petiole to 4cm. Cap. 1.5–2cm diam., term. on stout, 5–18cm peduncles; ray flts 4–6mm, 20–30. Summer. Sardinia.
B. minutum (L.) L. Ann. Lvs to 8mm, elliptical-obovate, petiole to c1cm. Cap. 6–7mm diam., on slender, numerous, 2–5cm peduncles; ray flts 7–10, scarcely exceeding involucre. Summer. Medit. is.
B. nivale Req. = *B. bellidioides*.
B. rotundifolium (Desf.) DC. = *Bellis rotundifolia*.

Bellota *Sterculia apetala*.
Bell Rue *Clematis occidentalis*.
Bells of Ireland *Molucella laevis*.
Bellwort *Uvularia*.
Belmore Sentry Palm *Howea belmoreana*.

Beloperone Nees.
B. californica Benth. = *Justicia californica*.

B. guttata Brandg. = *Justicia brandegeana*.
B. 'Super Goldy' = *Pachystachys lutea*.
B. plumbaginifolia Nees = *Justicia plumbaginifolia*.

Belosynapsis Hassk.
B. kewensis Hassk. = *Cyanotis kewensis*.

Belvedere *Bassia scoparia*.

Belvisia Mirb. Polypodiaceae. 15 epiphytic and lithophytic ferns. Rhiz. creeping with woolly roots and scales. Fronds simple, elliptic to lanceolate, leathery to fleshy (fertile fronds with narrow apical seg.). Trop. OW. Z10.
B. platyrrhynchos (J. Sm.) Copel. Fronds to 50×5cm, lanceolate, attenuate and constricted at base, leathery, glab., apical seg. to 7×1cm, oblong. Indon. to Philipp.
B. spicata (L. f.) Mirb. Fronds to 30×3cm, linear to elliptic or lanceolate, attenuate at base, undulate, leathery to fleshy, glab., apical seg. to 10×0.4cm, linear. Trop. Afr.

Ben *Moringa oleifera*.

Bencomia Webb & Berth. Rosaceae. 5 sparsely branched shrubs. Lvs in term. rosettes, blue-green, imparipinnate; lfts toothed. Fls in long axill. spikes; sep. 5; epical. sometimes present; pet. 0; sta. many. Canary Is. Z9.
B. caudata (Ait.) Webb & Berth. To 2m. St. lanate. Lvs 7–11-foliolate; lfts to 6.5cm, ovate, pointed, dentate, lanate beneath, lanuginose above. Fr. pear-shaped to subglobose. Spring.
B. moquiniana Webb & Berth. To 2m. St. red glandular-pubesc. Lvs 7–15-foliolate; lfts to 2.5cm, ovate, crenate. Fr. winged.
→*Marcetella* and *Poterium*.

Bengal Clock Vine *Thunbergia grandiflora*.
Bengal Ginger *Zingiber purpureum*.
Bengal Rose *Rosa chinensis*.
Benghal Bean *Mucuna pruriens* var. *utilis*.

Benincasa Savi. WAX GOURD; WHITE GOURD; CHINESE WATER MELON; ASH GOURD; TALLOW GOURD; TUNKA; ZIT-KWA. Cucurbitaceae. 1 ann., downy vine. Tendrils 2–3-fid. Lvs palmate, 5–7-lobed, hairy, 10–25cm. Fls solitary, axill., yellow, 5-merous; sta. 3. Fr. large, fleshy, globose or oblong, hispid, glaucous, becoming waxy, glabr. Indomal. Z10.
B. cerifera Savi = *B. hispida*.
B. hispida (Thunb.) Cogn.
→*Cucurbita*.

Benin Pepper *Piper guineense*.
Benjamin Bush *Lindera benzoin*.
Benjamin Tree *Ficus benjamina*.

Bensonia Abrams & Bacig.
B. oregona Abrams & Bacig. = *Bensoniella oregona*.

Bensoniella Morton. Saxifragaceae. 1 perenn. herb, allied to *Mitella*; to 20cm. Lvs 5–7-lobed, 2.5–4.5cm, dentate; petioles rusty-villous. Infl. racemose; fls green-yellow; sep. 2mm, 5 fused in a campanulate tube; pet. 3mm, 5, filiform. NW Calif. and SW Oreg. Z6.
B. oregona (Abrams & Bacig.) Morton.
→*Bensonia*.

Bent Grass *Agrostis*.

Benthamidia Spach.
B. florida (L.) Spach = *Cornus florida*.
B. fragifera Lindl. = *Cornus capitata*.
B. japonica (Sieb. & Zucc.) Hara = *Cornus kousa*.
B. kousa (Hance) Nak. = *Cornus kousa*.
B. nuttallii (Aud.) Mold. = *Cornus nuttallii*.

Bentham's Cornel *Cornus capitata*.
Bent-leaf Wattle *Acacia flexifolia*.

Benzoin Nees.
B. aestivale Nees = *Lindera benzoin*.
B. grandifolium Rehd. = *Lindera megaphylla*.
B. obtusilobum Kuntze = *Lindera obtusiloba*.
B. odoriferum Nees = *Lindera benzoin*.
B. praecox Sieb. & Zucc. = *Lindera praecox*.
B. touyunense (Lév.) Rehd. = *Lindera megaphylla*.

BERBERIDACEAE Juss. 15/570. *Berberis, Bongardia, Caulophyllum, Diphylleia, Epimedium, Gymnospermium, Jeffersonia,*

Leontice, ×*Mahoberberis, Mahonia, Nandina, Podophyllum, Ranzania, Vancouveria.*

Berberidopsis Hook. f. CORAL PLANT. Flacourtiaceae. 1 glab. everg., climbing shrub. Lvs to 10cm, oblong, acute, toothed, tough, dark green. Fls to 1.75cm diam., fleshy, bowl-shaped, pink to dark red, on long pendulous red stalks in pairs or short rac. Chile. Z8.
B. corallina Hook. f.

Berberis L. BARBERRY. Berberidaceae. 450 everg. and decid. shrubs. St. spiny; wood yellow. Lvs simple, often armed, alt. or whorled, subtended by simple or several-parted spines. Fls yellow to dark orange-red borne singly or in fascicles, rac., umbels or pan., 6-merous. Fr. a berry. Eurasia, N Afr., Trop. Afr., Americas.
B. actinacantha Mart. in Roem. & Schult. Semi-everg. spreading shrub to 1m; sts. yellow, red, pubesc. when young, spines sparse, tripartite, leaf-like, to 12mm. Lvs to 3cm, obovate, dull green, entire to toothed with to 4 spines per side. Fls 5mm diam., clustered 3–6, deep yellow, fragrant. Fr. to 7mm, blue-black, pruinose. Summer. Chile. Z7.
B. acuminata Stapf non Franch. nec. Veitch = *B. gagnepainii*.
B. acuminata Veitch non Stapf. nec. Franch. = *B. veitchii*.
B. aemulans Schneid. Decid. shrub to 1.5m st. angular, warty, maroon, spines to 11mm, tripartite, grooved, red-yellow, slightly flexible. Lvs to 4cm, obovate, obtuse, base decurrent on petiole, serrate, dull green above, glaucous beneath. Fls to 3 per cluster, pale yellow. Fr. to 1.5cm, orange-yellow. Summer. W China. Z5.
B. aetnensis Presl. Decid. shrub, compact, to 70cm; shoots red, hardening yellow; spines tripartite, to 2cm. Lvs to 3cm, oblong-ovate, grey-green, finely dentate with to 15 spines in apical half. Fls bright yellow, to 7mm diam., in short rac. Fr. red, ripening black, slightly pruinose, oblong to 8mm. Early summer. S It., Sardinia, Corsica. Z7.
B. aggregata Schneid. Decid. shrub, densely branching to 2m; st. yellow, spines tripartite, narrow, to 3cm. Lvs to 2.5cm, oblong-ovate, base cuneate, apex obtuse, olive green above, glaucous beneath, dentate. Fls pale yellow, to 6mm diam. in erect, sub-globose pan. to 3cm. Fr. to 7mm, oval, pale red. Late spring. Gansu, W Sichuan. Good autumn colour. Parent of numerous hybrids. 'Crimson Bead': fr. oblong, to 5mm, dark carmine, in pendulous trusses. 'Ruby Watson': berries deep ruby red. 'Sibbertoft Coral': fr. red, bloomed white with blue tint. 'Stone-field Dawn': lvs tinted yellow; fr. globose, dark carmine. Z6.
B. ahrendtii R. Rao & Uniyal = *B. lycioides*.
B. amoena Dunn. Similar to *B. wilsoniae* var. *stapfiana*. Lvs sea-green, semi-decid. Fr. striking coral red. China.
B. amurensis Rupr. Decid. shrub similar to *B. vulgaris*; erect to 3.5m, st. grey; spines tripartite, to 2cm. Lvs to 8cm, ovate-elliptic, abruptly acuminate, serrulate, light green, nearly glaucous. Fls to 25 in pendent rac. Fr. to 1cm, oblong, vivid red, sometimes pruinose. Late spring. NE Asia. 'Flamboyant': lvs to 5cm, tinted blue beneath, bright red in autumn. Z6.
B. angulizans Massias = *B. canadensis*.
B. angulosa Hook. f. & Thoms. Decid. shrub erect to 1m; shoots erect, grooved, pubesc. dark brown, spines 1.5cm, 3–5-partite, fine, slightly downy. Lvs 4cm, obovate, entire, apex obtuse, glossy, bright green above, paler beneath. Fls solitary, yellow. Fr. to 12mm, subglobose, shining red-purple. Summer. Himal. Z6.
B. ×*antoniana* Ahrendt. (*B. buxifolia* ×*B. darwinii*.) Everg. shrub to 1.5m, suckering freely; st. rusty brown, pubesc.; spines to 1cm. Lvs to 1cm, rigid, elliptic, entire, rarely spinose, glossy dark green above, paler, papillose beneath. Fls solitary, to 1.5cm diam., golden yellow. Fr. to 7.5mm, globose, blue-black, pruinose. Early summer. Gdn origin. Z6.
B. approximata Sprague = *B. dictyophylla* var. *approximata*.
B. aristata DC. CHITRA. Decid. shrub to 3m; st. red-brown, spines to 3cm, 1–3-partite thick. Lvs to 6cm, lanceolate to broadly elliptic, entire or serrate with 5 thorns per side, dark glossy green above, whitish beneath. Fls yellow tinged red, in threes, up to 25 in rac. to 6cm. Fr. to 1cm, ovoid, red, glossy or slightly glaucous. Summer. Nepal. Z6.
B. aristata Parker non DC. = *B. glaucocarpa*.
B. aristata var. *coriacea* (Lindl.) Schneid. = *B. coriaria*.
B. aristata var. *floribunda* (G. Don) Hook. f. & Thoms. = *B. floribunda*.
B. asiatica Roxb. non Griff. Everg. shrub erect to 3.5m; st. slightly bristly at first, spines tripartite, to 3cm. Lvs 7cm, coriaceous, rigid, obovate to orbicular, mucronate, shiny dark green above with pale green veins, pruinose beneath, entire or sparsely serrate. Fls yellow, to 25 in crowded umbels. Fr. to 8mm, long-ovoid red ripening black, pruinose. Early summer. Himal. Z8.

B. atrocarpa Schneid. Everg. shrub to 1.5m, br. dense, spotted black; spines slender, tripartite, to 2cm. Lvs to 8cm, oblanceolate, thick, flexible, dark green above, olive green beneath, with to 10 teeth per side. Fls to 1cm diam., bright yellow, clustered to 10. Fr. to 5mm, ovoid, black, glossy. Summer. W China. Z6.
B. australis Moris ex Schneid. = *B. hispanica*.
B. beaniana Schneid. Decid. shrub to 2.5m; st. yellow-grey; spines tripartite, to 2.5cm. Lvs 5cm, narrowly elliptic, acute, dark green above, grey, papillose beneath, with 12 spines per side. Fls to 20 in open pan., deep yellow. Fr. to 10mm, oblong-ovoid, dark red ripening purple, pruinose. Summer. W China. 'Stonefield Mauve': fr. to 8mm, dark red with lilac tint when ripe. Z6.
B. bergmanniae Schneid. Everg. shrub to 2m, densely branching; spines stout or flattened, to 3cm. Lvs 3–10cm, rigid, elliptic, mucronate, ± glossy above, v. glossy beneath, to 8 large teeth per side. Fls yellow, to 15-clustered. Fr. to 10mm, ovoid, black, pruinose. Summer. W China. var. *acanthophylla* Schneid. Lvs large with to 6 large triangular teeth per side, holly-like. Z6.
B. brachybotrys Edgew. non Gay = *B. edgeworthiana*.
B. brachypoda var. *gibbsii* hort. = *B. mitifolia*.
B. ×*bristolensis* Ahrendt. (*B. calliantha* ×*B. verruculosa*.) Small, compact rounded shrub. Lvs small, prickly, white beneath. Gdn origin.
B. buxifolia Lam. Everg. shrub to 3m; spines to 1.5cm, simple or tripartite. Lvs to 2.5cm, obovate, obtuse, mucronate, entire, coriaceous, tufted alongside spines. Fls 1 or 2 per axil, orange-yellow. Fr. to 8mm, globose, dark purple, grey-pruinose. Late spring. S Chile. 'Aureomarginata': lvs edged gold. 'Nana': dwarf form not exceeding 30cm; lvs ovate; fls sparse. 'Pygmaea': st. slender; spines 0; lvs larger, ovate, grey-papillose beneath; fls rarely produced. Z5.
B. cabrerae Job. Differs from *B. montana* in fls in subumbellate clusters to 6cm. Summer. Arg. Z6.
B. calliantha Mullig. Everg. shrub to 70cm; spines tripartite. Lvs to 6cm, oblong-elliptic, glossy green above, white-pruinose beneath, with to 10 remote teeth per side. Fls clustered 2–3, yellow. Fr. 1cm, ovoid, purple-black, glaucous. Late spring. Tibet. Z7.
B. canadensis Mill. Decid. arching, slender shrub to 1.5m; spines tripartite. Lvs to 5cm, oblong-ovate, obtuse, entire or with to 10 weak spines, dark green above, grey beneath, scarlet in autumn. Fls yellow, 5–15 in rac. to 5cm. Fr. to 9mm, ellipsoid, dark red, glossy. Early summer. E N Amer. Z5.
B. candidula Schneid. Everg. erect shrub to 50cm. Lvs to 3cm, elliptic-ovate, sparsely toothed, strongly revolute, shining, dark green above, white beneath. Fls solitary, small, yellow stained red. Fr. to 9mm, ovoid, grey-pruinose. Late spring. China. Z5.
B. capillaris Ahrendt. Decid. shrub to 1m; shoots smooth, dark red. Lvs to 4cm, entire, grey-green above, glaucous beneath. Fls solitary, golden, to 1.5cm across. Fr. to 1.5×8mm, bright red, slightly pruinose. Late spring. Burm., Yunnan. Z8.
B. ×*carminea* Ahrendt. (*B. aggregata* ×*B. wilsoniae*.) Decid. shrub to 1m. Lvs to 3cm, obovate, to 4 teeth per side, glaucous beneath. Fls in pan. to 5cm. Fr. to 8mm, ovoid, pink to scarlet. Early summer. Gdn origin. 'Aurora': lvs narrow; fr. globose-ovoid, vermilion. 'Autumn Cheer': lvs broad; fr. oblong-ovoid, scarlet. 'Barbarossa': twigs red-brown; lvs entire, semi-evergreen; fr. oblong to ovoid, to 7mm, scarlet. 'Bountiful': fls to 10mm wide; fr. globose to oblong, to 8.5mm, crimson. 'Buccaneer': lvs entire, narrow, semi-evergreen; fr. globose to 9mm, clouded white turning shiny red. 'Fireflame': dense and tall; lvs small; fr. orange-vermilion. 'Pirate King': vigorous; br. pendulous; fr. bright orange. 'Sparkler': fr. conic, tinted tangerine. Z6.
B. caroli var. *hoanghensis* Schneid. = *B. vernae*.
B. caroliniana Loud. = *B. canadensis*.
B. centiflora Diels. Differs from *B. pruinosa* in larger outer sep. (to 5.5×4mm) and conspicuously veined, bright yellow-green lvs, to 4cm with upturned teeth. Early summer. SW China. Z6.
B. ×*chenaultii* Ahrendt = *B.* ×*hybrido-gagnepainii*.
B. chillanensis (Schneid.) Sprague. Decid. shrub to 3m; spines 0 or variable, or tripartite. Lvs 1.5cm, papery, entire, obovate, narrow-acuminate. Fls solitary, to 1.5cm wide, orange. Fr. ovoid, dark red to purple, pruinose. Late spring. var. *hirsutipes* Sprague. Large, slender, erect. Lvs small, glossy, crowded. Fls yellow and orange. Chilean & Peruvian Andes. Z7.
B. chinensis Poir. Differs from *B. poiretii* in its broader lvs and dark red berries. Early summer. China. Z6.
B. chitra var. *sikkimensis* Schneid. = *B. sikkimensis*.
B. chitria Lindl. = *B. aristata*.
B. chrysosphaera Mullig. Everg. shrub differs from *B. candidula* in more open habit; shoots hardening red; spines tripartite, to 2cm. Lvs to 4cm, elliptic-ovate, with to 6 teeth per side, revolute, glossy dark green above, grey-papillose beneath. Fls

solitary, yellow, 1.2cm diam. Fr. to 10mm, ovoid, dark mauve; held semi-erect. Late spring. SE Tibet. Z6.

B. circumserrata Schneid. Decid. shrub to 1m, upright; spines thick, to 4cm. Lvs 3cm, obovate, closely serrate, olive green above, grey, glaucous beneath, scarlet in autumn. Fls in clusters 1–3, yellow, to 1cm diam. Fr. 15mm, ellipsoid, orange. Late spring. NW China. Z5.

B. comberi Sprague & Sandw. Everg. to 1m, suckering, erect; spines 0. Lvs coriaceous, 3cm, oblong-elliptic, coarsely toothed, mucronate, olive green above, pruinose beneath. Fls to 1.5cm diam., in clusters 2–3, pale orange, fragrant. Chilean Andes. Z8.

B. 'Concal'. (*B. concinna* × *B. calliantha*.) Compact, semi-decid.; fls deep lemon yellow.

B. concinna Hook. f. Semi-evergreen shrub to 60cm, densely branching; spines tripartite, orange, to 2cm. Lvs 3cm, oblong-ovate, obtuse or abruptly acuminate, with to 5 teeth per side, shining dark green above, white-pruinose beneath, red in autumn. Fls in clusters; pet. 6mm, deep yellow. Fr. 16mm, ovoid, red. Late spring. Sikkim. Z5.

B. congestiflora C. Gay. Large shrub differing from *B. hakeoides* in thinner lvs and short-stalked fls in dense clusters. Chile.

B. 'Coral Gem'. (*B. concinna* × *B. calliantha*.) Compact to 1m. Lvs red in autumn. Fr. bright red.

B. coriaria Royle ex Lindl. Everg. to 2m; spines tripartite, stout, to 3cm. Lvs 5cm, lanceolate-obovate, acute, entire, olive green above, glossy green beneath. Fls to 25 in rac., to 1.5cm across, yellow. Fr. to 1cm, oblong, glossy red. Late spring. W Himal. Z6.

B. coxii Schneid. Everg. to 1.5m. spines flattened. Lvs 6cm, elliptic-ovate, revolute with spiny teeth incurved, glossy above, white, pruinose beneath. Fls to 6 in clusters, pale yellow, to 1cm across. Fr. to 1cm, obovoid, glaucous blue. Late spring. E Himal. Z6.

B. cretica L. Decid. to 1.5m, often procumbent; spines tripartite, yellow. Lvs to 1.5cm, obovate, entire, base contracted, deep green above, paler beneath. Fls to 6 in clusters, bright yellow. Fr. mauve-black, globose, slightly pruinose. Spring. Medit., Middle E. Z8.

B. crispa C. Gay. Small, dense wiry habit. Lvs to 1.5cm, spathulate, green, spiny-toothed, clustered along st. Chile.

B. darwinii Hook. Everg. to 2m; spines to 8mm, 3–7-partite. Lvs to 2cm, coriaceous, obovate, shining dark green above, paler beneath, with 1–3 spiny teeth per side. Fls in pendulous rac. to 10cm, gold sometimes flushed red. Fr. to 7mm, globose, blue-pruinose. Spring. Chile, Patagonia. 'Flame': to 1.5m; fls vivid dark orange. 'Gold': to 1.5m; fls profuse, vivid gold. 'Blenheim': is a hybrid between this sp. and *B. hakeoides*. 'Nana': dwarf; lvs small; fls sparse. 'Pendula': twigs arching; lvs to 1.8cm; fls golden-red, to 1cm wide. 'Prostrata': dwarf to 50cm; lvs dull green; buds tinted red; fls profuse. 'Rubens': buds red; fls vivid yellow, later tinted red. 'Triumph': hardy, dense and upright to 1m; lvs to 3cm, tinted blue beneath. Z7.

B. darwinii var. *macrophylla* hort. ex Sm. = *B. × antoniana*.

B. dasystachya Maxim. Decid. shrub erect to 4m; spines 0 or simple, 1.5cm. Lvs thick, oblong-elliptic to 6cm, apex obtuse, serrulate with to 35 teeth per side, olive green above, yellow-green, glossy beneath. Fls to 6mm diam., to 30 in narrow, upright rac. to 6cm. Fr. globose to 7mm, glossy bright red. Late spring. China. Z5.

B. × declinata Schräd. (*B. canadensis* × *B. vulgaris*.) Decid. shrub erect to 2m; spines, to 15mm, tripartite. Lvs to 4cm, obovate-elliptic, apex obtuse, finely serrulate or entire, glaucous beneath. Fls to 9 in loose umbels to 5cm, yellow. Fr. to 1cm, ovoid, glossy, dark red. Late spring. Gdn origin. Z4.

B. diaphana Maxim. Decid. shrub to 2m; spines tripartite, thick, to 2cm. Lvs to 4cm, obovate, serrulate with to 10 teeth per side, dull grey-green above with prominent veins, glaucous grey beneath, bright red in autumn. Fls in clusters of up to 5, deep yellow, to 1.5cm diam. Fr. to 1cm, ovoid, glossy, pale, translucent red. Late spring. W China. Z5.

B. dictyoneura Schneid. Decid. shrub to 1.75m; spines tripartite, to 2cm. Lvs to 2.5cm, obovate, obtuse at apex, serrulate, to 15 spines per side, grey-green above, yellow-olive and prominently net-veined beneath. Fls to 6 in rac. to 3cm. Fr. to 4mm obovoid, pale red. Early summer. W China. Z6.

B. dictyophylla Franch. Decid. shrub to 2m; spines tripartite, coarse, to 3cm. Lvs 1–3cm, entire, obovate, cuneate at base, pale matt green above, pruinose white beneath, good autumn colour. Fls to 1.5cm across, solitary, pale yellow. Fr. to 1.25cm, red, pruinose ovoid. Late spring. W China. var. *approximata* (Sprague) Rehd. Lvs smaller, with to 6 sharp teeth per side and smaller fls. Late spring. Z6.

B. dielsiana Fedde. Decid. shrub to 3m; spines simple or tripartite, to 3cm. Lvs to 7cm, acute, finely toothed, green beneath. Fls 10–20 in rac. to 6cm. Fr. ovoid, carmine. W China.

'Compacta': to 1.5m, shoots shorter, denser and more rigid; lvs tinged blue. Z5.

B. dulcis Sweet = *B. buxifolia*.

B. dumicola Schneid. Everg. arching shrub to 1.75m, st. slightly warty, arching; spines tripartite, to 3cm. New growth coral red. Lvs to 6cm, in whorls to 5, thick, coriaceous, elliptic, acuminate, with to 40 spines per side, glossy, dark, convex above with sunken veins, paler beneath. Fls to 20, clustered, yellow, flushed red. Fr. to 7mm, narrow-ovoid, pruinose plum-black. Late spring. W China. Z8.

B. edgeworthiana Schneid. Decid. shrub to 1m. Lvs to 3cm, narrow, elliptic, rarely lanceolate, coriaceous, with to 8 long teeth per side, glab., dull green veins strongly reticulate. Fls to 25 in pan. to 4cm, subsessile. Fr. to 1cm, hard, glossy, vermilion, ovoid. Late spring. NW Himal. Z6.

B. empetrifolia Lam. Everg. semi-prostrate shrub to 30cm; spines to 7-partite, often longer than lvs. Lvs 1cm, elliptic, mucronate, revolute, dark green, above, pruinose beneath. Fls paired, deep yellow. Fr. globose to 7mm, glaucous blue-black. Late spring. Chile, Arg. Z7.

B. erythroclada. Ahrendt = *B. concinna*.

B. fendleri A. Gray. Decid. shrub to 1.5m; st. rigid, v. glossy; spines to 7-partite, to 1cm. Lvs to 5cm, lanceolate, entire, bright green above, paler beneath. Fls to 10, corymbose, orange and pale yellow. Fr. to 5mm, globose, red. Late spring. NW Amer., New Mex. Z6.

B. floribunda G. Don. Decid. shrub to 3m, arching. Differing from *B. coriaria* in dark red to purple-black, pruinose fruits. Early summer. Nepal. Z5.

B. formosana Ahrendt = *B. kawakamii*.

B. forrestii Ahrendt. Decid. arching shrub to 1.5m, sparsely armed or unarmed. Lvs to 6cm, oblong-obovate, apex obtuse, entire, pale green above, glaucous beneath. Rac. subumbellate to 12cm. Fr. to 1.2cm, narrow-ovoid, glossy, bright red. Early summer. SW China. Z6.

B. franchetiana Schneid. Usually grown in the form var. *macrobotrys* Ahrendt: large, arching; fls yellow; fr. red. W China.

B. francisci-ferdinandii Schneid. Decid. shrub to 2m; spines tripartite, to 4cm. Lvs to 7cm, ovate-elliptic, acute, with to 25 fine teeth per side, rarely entire, glossy above, paler beneath. Fls pale yellow, 8mm across, in narrow, pendulous rac. to 12cm. Fr. to 12mm, ovoid-ellipsoid, scarlet, glossy. Late spring. W China. Z6.

B. × frikartii Schneid. ex Van de Laar. (*B. candidula* × *B. verruculosa*.) Everg. shrub to 1.5m; spines tripartite, to 2cm. Lvs elliptic, coriaceous, to 3cm, serrate with to 4 teeth per side, revolute, shining dark green above, grey-pruinose beneath. Fls pale yellow in pairs. Fr. ovoid, blue-black, glaucous. Early summer. Gdn origin. Cvs include 'Amstelveen': br. arching, to 1m; lvs close to *B. candidula* but smaller and paler above, glaucous-white beneath; fast-growing. 'Staefa': the type of the cross; v. hardy. 'Telstar': resembling 'Amstelveen', but larger and more spreading. Z6.

B. gagnepainii Schneid. Everg. shrub to 1.5m; st. erect, suckering; spines, tripartite, slender, to 2cm. Lvs to 4cm, lanceolate, narrow-acuminate, undulate, with to 10 teeth per side, matt grey-green above, glossy yellow-green beneath. Fls bright yellow, to 7 per cluster. Fr. to 1cm, ovoid, purple-black, pruinose. Early summer. W China. Sometimes confused with *B. veitchii*, which has red (not yellow) new growth, with *B. triacanthophora*, which has red-brown mature st. and with *B. panlanensis* with oblanceolate lvs. 'Fernspray': compact; lvs pale green, long, narrow, undulate; 'Green Mantle': arching-pendent; lvs grey-green, v. narrow. 'Klugowski': slow-growing, dense, to 1m; lvs narrow, to 5cm, tinted blue beneath. 'Robin Hood': low-growing, rounded, to 1m; old lvs tinted dark red. 'Rusthof': habit open, to 1m; lvs tinted blue beneath. Z5.

B. geraldii Veitch = *B. aggregata*.

B. gilgiana Fedde. Decid. shrub to 2m; spines solitary, to 2cm. Lvs to 4cm, narrowly elliptic, apex acuminate, base cuneate, entire or with to 9 sparse, irregular teeth, olive green, pubesc. Fls pale yellow in pubesc. spike-like rac. to 6cm. Fr. 1cm, ovoid, wine-red, slightly glaucous. Early summer. China. Z5.

B. giraldii Hesse. Decid. shrub to 2m; spines often solitary, to 3cm. Lvs to 8cm, ovate, serrulate, red hardening deep green, downy beneath. Fls to 1cm across in pendent rac. to 10cm. Fr. ellipsoid, mauve. Early summer. China. 'Emperor': spines yellow, to 1.3mm; lvs glaucous beneath; fls in fascicled rac.; fr. tinted red. Z6.

B. glaucocarpa Stapf. Semi-evergreen shrub to 4m, differing from *B. lycioides* in lvs acute, elliptic, to 6cm, with to 8 broad teeth per side and fls in rigid rac.; fr. to 9mm, black, pruinose, oblong-globose. Early summer. Himal., Punjab. Z6.

B. 'Goldilocks' (*B. darwinii* × *B. valdiviana*.) Large vigorous shrub; br. erect, arching. Lvs dark green, glossy, spiny. Fls golden in pendulous, red-stalked clusters.

B. graminea Ahrendt. Decid. shrub, spreading, prostrate; spines tripartite, to 1cm. Lvs to 2cm, narrowly obovate, mucronate, entire or sparsely serrate, glossy above, grey, papillose beneath. Fls paired. Fr. red. Early summer. SW China. Z6.

B. gyalaica Ahrendt. Decid. arching shrub to 3m; spines tripartite, narrow, to 1cm. Lvs to 1.5cm, elliptic, with to 4 teeth per side, glaucous beneath. Fls in dense pan. Fr. to 1cm, oblong-ovoid, black-blue, glaucous. Summer. SE Tibet. Z6.

B. hakeoides (Hook. f.) Schneid. Everg. erect shrub to 2m; spines leaflike. Lvs paired, to 4cm, orbicular-cordate, rigid, glossy dark green above, grey, papillose beneath, with to 7 spiny teeth per side, subsessile or long-'stalked'. Fls golden, to 20 in clusters. Fr. to 5mm across, globose, blue-black, glaucous. Late spring. Chile. Z8.

B. henryana Schneid. Lvs 2–5cm, elliptic, obtuse, entire or thorny-toothed, distinctly stalked. Fr. ellipsoid, deep red, glaucescent. China.

B. heterophylla Juss. Semi-evergreen suckering shrub to 1.5m; spines tripartite, thick, to 1.5cm. Lvs to 2.5cm, obovate, dimorphic: narrow, entire, pale, soft or rigid, dark, with 3 broad teeth. Fls solitary, pale orange. Fr. to 6mm, globose, black, glaucous. Spring. Chile, Tierra del Fuego. Z8.

B. heteropoda Schrenk. Decid. shrub to 2m; spines tripartite, to 1cm. Lvs to 5cm, obovate-elliptic, entire or indistinctly toothed, glab., glossy, pale. Fls to 9, corymbose. Fr. 1cm across, ovoid, black, glaucescent. Early summer. Turkestan. Z6.

B. heteropoda var. *oblonga* Reg. = *B. oblonga*.

B. hispanica Boiss. & Reut. Decid. upright shrub to 1.5m; spines simple or tripartite, yellow-brown, to 2cm. Lvs to 2.5cm, elliptic-obovate, entire, apex acute, base cuneate, glab. Fls to 15 in clusters or short rac., orange-yellow. Fr. to 9mm, ovoid, blue-black, glaucous. Late spring. SE Spain, coastal N Afr. Z6.

B. hookeri Lem. Everg. shrub to 0.5m; spines tripartite, to 25mm, yellow-brown. Lvs in whorls, to 6cm, oblong-elliptic, with to 15 prominent teeth per side, dark, glossy green above, pruinose white beneath. Fls clustered to 6, green or pale yellow, to 1.5cm across. Fr. to 15mm, oblong, mauve-black, glossy or slightly glaucous. Late spring. Himal. var. *viridis* Schneid. Lvs green, beneath. Fr. smaller. Z6.

B. hookeri var. *latifolia* hort. = *B. manipurana*.

B. × hybrido-gagnepainii Sur. (*B. verruculosa* × *B. gagnepainii*.) Everg. spiny shrub. Lvs to 4cm, ovate, revolute, with to 9 spines per side. Fls resembling *B. gagnepainii* var. *lanceifolia*. Fr. to 7mm, grey-pruinose. Early summer. Gdn origin. 'Chenault': to 2.5m; lvs lanceolate to 3cm, shining above, pruinose beneath; fls golden yellow. 'Chenault Compact': lvs smaller than 'Chenault', shoots more pendulous. 'Genty': dense; to 1m, shoots upright; lvs to 5cm, narrow, tinted blue beneath. 'Hilde': to 1.2m, spreading, compact; young shoots tinted red; lvs to 3cm, tinged blue. 'Minikin': dwarf to 50cm; lvs small, white pruinose beneath, to 2cm. 'Park Juweel': low, dense thorny shrub, lvs mostly unarmed, colouring brilliantly in autumn, sometimes persistent. 'Red Jewel': semi-evergreen; lvs tinted dark red, later dark green. 'Select': habit loose, upright, later spreading; lvs narrow, to 4cm, tinted dull blue beneath. 'Terra Nova': semi-prostrate, densely branching, glossy green above, blue-pruinose beneath. 'Tottenham': to 2m, arching; lvs oblong-ovate, green throughout, colouring red in autumn. The following exhibit the influence of *B. candidula*: 'Gracilis': habit tall, rangy, twigs glab., thin; fls to 4 per cluster. 'Haalboom': vigorous, erect, to 1m; lvs elliptic, to 5cm, glossy green above, tinted blue beneath; fls to 4 per cluster. 'Jytte': similar to 'Haalboom', lvs paler beneath. Z5.

B. hypokerina Airy Shaw. Everg. shrub to 1m, upright, or sprawling; spines 0. Lvs to 12cm, oblong-elliptic with to 10 teeth per side, grey-green above, white-pruinose beneath. Fls to 1cm across, to 12 in clusters. Fr. to 7mm, ellipsoid, blue-black, glaucous. Early summer. N Burm. Z8.

B. ilicifolia Forr. Everg. shrub to 2m; st. yellow, spines to 5-partite, thick, to 2cm. Lvs to 5cm, rigid, oblong-elliptic, with to 7 broad teeth, holly-like, shining grey-green above, yellow-green beneath. Fls to 7 in clusters, orange-yellow, to 2cm across. Fr. to 8mm, obovoid, glaucous blue. Late spring. Chile. Name sometimes misapplied to × *Mahoberberis*. Z7.

B. insignis Hook. f. & Thoms. Everg. shrub to 1.5m; spines 0 or reduced. Lvs solitary or in whorls, to 16cm, coriaceous, lanceolate with to 20 small teeth per side, dark green above, yellow green beneath. Fls to 20 in short rac., pale yellow. Fr. to 8mm, ovoid, black, glossy. Early summer. Sikkim. ssp. *incrassata* (Ahrendt) D.F. Chamberl. & C. Hu. Lvs softer, pet. entire, not emarginate, fr. globose, to 5mm. Early summer. N Burm. var. *tongloensis* Schneid. St. grey-yellow; not red-brown. Lvs narrower and more finely serrate. Early summer. Sikkim, Nepal, Bhutan. Z8.

B. integerrima Franch. non Bunge = *B. jamesiana*.

B. × interposita Ahrendt. (*B. hookeri* var. *viridis* × *B. verruculosa*.) Differs from *B. hookeri* var. *viridis* in smaller lvs, to 3×1cm, grey beneath, solitary fls and fr. to 1cm×6mm. Early summer. Gdn origin. 'Wallich's Purple': habit dense, to 1.5m; young growth tinted copper. Z6.

B. irwinii hort. = *B. × stenophylla* 'Irwinii'.

B. jamesiana Forr. & W.W. Sm. Decid. shrub to 2m; spines tripartite, to 3cm. Lvs thick, obovate, entire or slightly toothed toward apex, olive-green above, grey, pruinose beneath. Fls to 40 in rac. to 10cm, pale-orange. Fr. globose, opaque white ripening translucent pink. Early summer. SW China. Z6.

B. julianae Schneid. Everg. dense, erect shrub to 4m, spines tripartite, coarse, to 4cm. Lvs to 10cm, coriaceous, densely serrate, obovate, glab., dark green above, paler beneath. Fls to 15 in clusters, to 1cm across. Fr. to 8mm, oblong, black, glaucous. Early summer. W China. 'Dart's Superb': br. spreading; lvs small. 'Lombart's Red': lvs tinted light claret beneath. 'Nana': dwarf. Z5.

B. kawakamii Hayata. Everg. shrub, erect to 2m, spines to 3cm, usually solitary. Lvs to 6cm, elliptic-obovate with to 7 teeth per side, tough, pale green beneath, veins reticulate often prominent. Fls to 15 per cluster, pale yellow. Fr. to 6mm, blue-purple, ovoid, glaucous or glossy. Early summer. Taiwan. Z6.

B. knightii hort. = *B. manipurana*.

B. koreana Palib. Compact, suckering shrub to 1.5m; st. red-brown; spines 3–7-partite, palmately arranged or flattened, encircling st. Lvs to 6cm, oblong-ovate, serrate, mottled when young. Fls to 20 in pendent rac. to 5cm. Fr. globose, red, glossy, to 8mm. Late spring. Korea. 'Red Tears': to 2m; br. arching; lvs tinted rich purple; fr. in rac. to 10cm, rich red. Z4.

B. liechtensteinii Schneid. Differs from *B. potaninii* in lvs 3–5cm, obovate with 4–7 coarse thorns per side. W China.

B. lempergiana Ahrendt. Differs from *B. julianae* in broader, paler lvs, fls larger. China.

B. leptoclada Diels = *B. amoena*.

B. levis sensu Schneid. = *B. atrocarpa*.

B. libanotica Ehrenb. = *B. cretica*.

B. linearifolia Philippi. Everg. shrub to 1.5m; st. yellow; spines tripartite, to 1.5cm. Lvs to 5cm, obovate-oblanceolate, entire, revolute. Fls to 2cm across, to 6 per cluster, orange. Fr. to 1cm, ellipsoid, black, glaucous. Late spring. Chilean Andes. 'Comber's Apricot': buds orange, tinted apricot when opening. 'Phoenix': buds vivid red, orange-red when open. 'Jewel': lvs narrower; fls dark orange in bud, opening red-yellow. 'Orange King': vigorous; lvs darker, glossier, narrower; fls deeply coloured, large. Z6.

B. × lologensis Sandw. (*B. darwinii* × *B. linearifolia*.) Everg. shrub; st. angular, red-brown; spines 5-partite, to 7mm. Lvs to 3cm, spathulate. Fls to 7 per umbel, orange-yellow. Fr. ovoid, to 7mm, blue, glaucous. Early summer. Arg. 'Apricot Queen': growth erect; fls orange. 'Gertrude Hardijzer': narrow, upright; fls deep orange. 'Highdown': habit low and broad, spines sharply curved; fls vivid yellow. 'Nymans': fls v. profuse. 'Stapehill': fls orange, tinted vivid red. 'Yellow Beauty': young shoots tinted red; fls gold; fr. white tinted blue. Z6.

B. lycioides Stapf. Semi-evergren shrub to 2.5m; st. grey-yellow; spines to 2cm. Lvs to 7cm, oblanceolate, entire, narrow-acuminate, mucronate, dark green above, glaucous beneath. Fls to 20 per loose, sometimes compound pendent rac. Fr. ovoid, to 1cm, mauve-black, glaucous. Early summer. Himal. Z5.

B. lycium Royle. Decid. shrub to 3m; st. slender, erect, yellow-grey; spines tripartite, to 2cm. Lvs to 5cm, oblanceolate, acute, entire or sparsely toothed, grey-green. Fls to 8mm diam., golden, to 20 in loose rac. Fr. to 1cm, elliptic, black, glaucous. Summer. Himal. Z6.

B. × macracantha Schrad. (*B. aristata* × *B. vulgaris*.) To 4m; thorns to 3cm. Fls yellow in long rac. Fr. purple. Gdn orig.

B. macrophylla hort. = *B. floribunda*.

B. manipurana Ahrendt. Everg. shrub to 2m; spines to 3cm. Lvs to 8cm, ovate-elliptic, semi-rigid, subentire to minutely toothed, shining, reticulate above, olive green beneath. Fls to 12 per cluster, to 1.5cm across. Fr. oblong, to 10mm, black, blue-glaucous. Late spring. Assam. Z6.

B. × media hort. = *B. × hybrido-gagnepainii*.

B. × mentorensis L. Ames. (*B. julianae* × *B. thunbergii*.) Decid. erect shrub to 2m. Lvs to 4cm, elliptic, rigid, entire or with 3 teeth per side. Fls solitary or paired, pale yellow. Fr. red-brown, ellipsoid. Early summer. Gdn origin. Z5.

B. microphylla Forst. = *B. buxifolia*.

B. microphylla var. *nana* Dipp. = *B. buxifolia* 'Nana'.

B. mitifolia Stapf. Decid. shrub to 2m; st. grey-yellow, spotted black; spines tripartite, to 3cm. Lvs to 6cm, oblong-ovate, acute, with to 25 teeth, yellow-green above, pubesc. beneath. Fls 30 in rac. to 9cm, pubesc. Fr. oblong, crimson, glossy. Late spring. W China. Z6.

B. montana C. Gay. Decid. shrub to 2m, erect; st. red-brown; spines tripartite, to 1cm. Lvs to 2cm, papery, obovate, entire, papillose beneath. Fls paired or to 3, to 2cm diam. Fr. ellipsoid, mauve, glaucous. Andes, Chile, Arg. Z6.

B. montana var. *chillanensis* Schneid. = *B. chillanensis*.

B. morrisonensis Hayata. Decid. shrub to 0.5m; st. red, armed. Lvs to 3cm, oblanceolate, with to 7 large teeth per side, glossy yellow-green above, slightly pruinose beneath. Fls pale yellow, to 1.2cm diam., to 5 per cluster. Fr. crimson, ovoid, translucent. Early summer. Taiwan. Z6.

B. mucrifolia Ahrendt. Decid. shrub, compact to 50cm; st. yellow, pubesc.; spines tripartite, to 2cm. Lvs to 2cm, elliptic to narrow obovate, entire, mucronate. Fls solitary, to 1cm diam. Fr. globose to oblong-globose, to 7mm, scarlet. Early summer. Nepal. Z6.

B. nummularia var. *sinica* Schneid. = *B. jamesiana*.

B. oblonga (Reg.) Schneid. Resembles *B. heteropoda* but infl. more crowded. Late spring. Turkestan. Z6.

B. ×ottawensis Schneid. (*B. thunbergii* × *B. vulgaris*.) Decid. shrub differing from *B. thunbergii* in its exceptional vigour, erect yellow-brown st. with large spines and spiny stipules and fls to 10 per long-stalked rac. Early summer. Gdn origin. 'Decora': broad, to 1.75m; lvs like 'Superba' but smaller, with blue to violet flush. 'Purpurea': lvs purple. 'Silver Miles': to 1.75m; lvs variegated silver and purple; fls yellow; v. hardy. 'Superba': vigorous, to 3m; twigs red, thorns flattened, tripartite, to 15mm or simple; lvs to 5.5cm, suborbicular to spathulate, purple-green, serrulate; fls umbellate or fascicled, yellow and red; fr. ovoid, pink-red. 'Suzanne': similar to 'Decora', more upright, lvs more acuminate. Z5.

B. pallens Franch. Close to *B. chinensis*. Tall. Lvs colouring well in autumn. Fr. bright red. W China.

B. panlanensis Ahrendt. Everg. shrub to 2m, compact; st. slender, slightly warty; spines tripartite, to 2cm. Lvs to 3cm, narrow-oblong, acuminate, mucronate, with to 8 teeth per side, grey-green above, glossy, olive beneath. Fls solitary or paired, flushed red. Fr. black, shining, ellipsoid, to 6mm. Late spring. W China. Z6.

B. parisepala Ahrendt. Differs from *B. angulosa*, in height, to 3m, acutely emarginate pet. and persistent style, to 1mm. Late spring. N Assam. Z6.

B. poiretii Schneid. Decid. shrub to 1m; st. arching, angular glossy; spines 0 or simple, to 8mm. Lvs to 4cm, narrow-oblanceolate, acuminate. Fls yellow, flushed red, to 15 per pendent rac. Fr. oblong, pale red. Late spring. N China. Z5.

B. polyantha Hemsl. Medium-sized, erect. Autumn colour v. fine. Fls profuse in drooping pan. Fr. red in grape-like clusters. W China.

B. potaninii Maxim. Everg. shrub to 1m; st. red-brown; spines tripartite, to 4cm. Lvs to 3cm, narrow-obovate, mucronate, with 1–2 prominent teeth per side, rigid, pale beneath. Fls in rac. to 2cm. Fr. to 1cm diam., globose, bright red. Early summer. China. Z6.

B. prattii Schneid. Decid. shrub to 3m; st. yellow, minutely warty; spines tripartite, to 1cm. Lvs 4cm, whorled above, obtuse, base cuneate, entire or sparsely serrate, glossy olive-green above, grey-pruinose beneath. Fls in dense, erect pan. to 20cm. Fr. to 6mm, ovoid, coral pink. Summer. W China. Z5.

B. pruinosa Franch. Everg. shrub to 1.5m; st. hardening yellow; spines tripartite, to 4cm. Lvs to 8cm, elliptic-oblong, coriaceous, dull green above, pruinose white beneath, with to 6 prominent teeth per side. Fls to 25, pale yellow in short-stalked clusters; pet. deeply incised. Fr. ovoid, v. pruinose. Late spring. SW China. 'Barresiana' lvs to 6cm, dentate; fls to 6 per cluster; fr. small. 'Viridifolia': lvs large, glossy green; fr. obovoid. Z6.

B. replicata W.W. Sm. Everg. shrub to 1m; st. arching, yellow; spines tripartite, to 1.5cm. Lvs to 3cm, lanceolate, serrulate above, revolute, dull, dark green above, white beneath. Fls to 10 per cluster, pale yellow. Fr. to 1cm, oblong, red ripening purple-black. Late spring. SW China. Z5.

B. revoluta Sm. ex DC. = *B. empetrifolia*.

B. ×rubrostilla Chitt. (*B. aggregata* × *B. wilsoniae?*) To 1.5m; st. erect or arching, brown, angular; spines tripartite, to 2.5cm, yellow-brown. Lvs to 2cm, oblanceolate, with to 6 teeth per side, grey, pruinose beneath. Fls to 4 in subumbellate rac. to 3cm, pale yellow. Fr. to 1.5cm, ovoid, scarlet, glossy. Early summer. Gdn origin. 'Chealii': fr. garnet-coloured. 'Cherry Ripe': st. red-brown, warty; lvs obovate; fr. green-white ripening scarlet. 'Crawleyensis': lvs larger; fls to 6 in umbels; fr. ovoid-globose, scarlet, to 1.5cm. Z6.

B. sanguinea var. *microphylla* hort. = *B. panlanensis*.

B. sargentiana Schneid. Everg. shrub to 2m; st. dark red, terete; spines coarse, tripartite, to 6cm. Lvs to 10cm, thick, elliptic, acute, with to 25 teeth per side, dark, glossy green above with veins impressed, yellow-green beneath. Fls to 6 per cluster, pale yellow. Fr. to 6mm, purple-black, oblong, glossy. Early summer. W China. Z6.

B. sherriffii Ahrendt. Decid. shrub to 2m, differing from

B. gyalaica in glab. st. and entire or v. sparsely armed narrow obovate lvs to 2cm. Fls in slender pan. to 5cm. Fr. oblong, purple-black, glaucous. Early summer. SE Tibet. Z6.

B. sieboldii Miq. Decid. shrub to 1m, compact; st. glossy, somewhat angular. Lvs to 7cm, rhombic-ovate, obtuse, spiny-ciiate, red when young, later bright green above, paler beneath. Fls to 6 in umbellate rac. to 3cm. Fr. globose, glossy dark red. Late spring. Jap. Z5.

B. sikkimensis (Schneid.) Ahrendt. Decid. shrub to 1.5m; st. yellow-grey, pubesc. at first; spines tripartite, to 2cm, yellow. Lvs to 3cm, obovate, coriaceous, acute, mucronate, base cuneate, subsessile, entire or sparsely toothed, slightly revolute, dull dark green above, at first grey, pruinose beneath. Fls to 9 in rac. to 5cm, yellow. Fr. ovoid, often curving, to 1.5cm, dark red, glossy. Late spring. Sikkim. Z6.

B. silva-taroucana Schneid. Decid. shrub to 2m; st. yellow; spines 0 or solitary, to 7mm. Lvs to 5cm, oblong-ovate, entire, apex obtuse, base abruptly contracted, dark green above, pruinose beneath. Fls to 10 per 5cm-long rac. Fr. ovoid-globose, to 1cm, scarlet. Early summer. W China. Z6.

B. sinensis var. *angustifolia* Reg. = *B. poiretii*.

B. soulieana Schneid. Everg. shrub to 1.5m; st. grey; spines tripartite, to 3cm, rigid. Lvs to 8cm, rigid, oblong-elliptic, narrow-lanceolate, serrate, bright green above, paler, papillose beneath. Fls to 10 per cluster. Fr. ovoid, mauve glaucous-blue. Early summer. China. Z6.

B. sphalera Fedde = *B. potaninii*.

B. stapfiana Schneid. = *B. wilsoniae* var. *stapfiana*.

B. ×stenophylla Lindl. (*B. darwinii* × *B. empetrifolia*.) Everg. shrub to 3m. Lvs to 2cm, linear-lanceolate, mucronate, entire, revolute, dark green above, glaucous beneath. Fls golden, clustered. Fr. globose, purple-black, glaucous, to 7mm. Late spring. Gdn origin. 'Autumnalis': small, graceful shrub flowering again in autumn. 'Brilliant': lvs scarlet in autumn. 'Claret Cascade': young lvs purple-tinted. Fls orange tinged red. 'Coccinea': buds bright red, fls orange. 'Compacta': dwarf, to 60cm. 'Corallina': open, loosely branched small shrub; buds coral pink, opening burnt orange to yellow. 'Corallina Compacta': dwarf, to 30cm. 'Crawley Gem': to 60cm; fls orange tipped red. 'Cream Showers': fls cream-white. 'Etna': lvs dark glossy green; free-flowering, fls clustered, dense, brilliant red-orange. 'Gracilis Nana': dwarf, to 30cm. 'Irwinii': compact; fls golden yellow. 'Latifolia': to 3m; lvs broad. 'Nana': v. compact; fls golden. 'Picturata': lvs variegated white. 'Pink Pearl': lvs deep green or splashed and striped ivory and rose; fls ivory, orange, pink or all three on same plant. 'Prostrata': low habit; buds orange, fls golden. 'Semperflorens': late- and long-flowering, buds red-orange, opening tangerine. Z5.

B. stenophylla Hance non Lindl. = *B. soulieana*.

B. subcaulialata Schneid. = *B. wilsoniae* var. *subcaulialata*.

B. sublevis W.W. Sm. Everg. shrub to 1m; st. slightly warty; spines tripartite, to 2cm. Lvs to 8cm, lanceolate, acuminate, entire or with to 15 small teeth per side, olive green above, paler, somewhat glossy beneath. Fls to 20 per cluster, fragrant, orange. Fr. to 7mm, oblong, glossy purple-black, style 0. Late spring. W China. Z6.

B. taliensis Schneid. Everg. shrub to 0.5m; st. thick, yellow-grey; spines tripartite, to 7mm. Lvs to 4cm, elliptic, acute, mucronate, base cuneate, entire or with to 3 teeth per side, glossy dark green above, pruinose beneath. Fls pale yellow in clusters to 5. Fr. oblong to 1cm, black, glaucous. Early summer. SW China. Z6.

B. taylorii Ahrendt. Medium sized. Fls green-yellow. Fr. ovoid, black, pruinose. Tibet.

B. temolaica Ahrendt. Decid. shrub to 1.5m; st. dark brown, arching; spines tripartite, to 1cm. Lvs to 4cm, oblong-ovate, entire on juvenile shoots, with to 5 broad teeth per side in maturity, grey-green above, white-pruinose beneath. Fls pale yellow, solitary. Fr. oblong, red, glaucous, apex bent. Late spring. SE Tibet. Z5.

B. thunbergii DC. Decid. shrub to 1m; st. angular, dark red; spines simple. Lvs to 2cm, ovate, obtuse, entire, olive green above, grey papillose beneath. Fls to 5 in subumbellate rac., yellow, stained red. Fr. ellipsoid, red, glossy, to 8mm. Late spring. Jap. Good autumn colour. Cvs include: (with unbroken green foliage) 'Erecta': fastigiate; 'Green Ornament': dark green; 'Vermilion': bright red autumn colour. (with red or purple foliage) 'Atropurpurea': lvs at st. red-purple; 'Dart's Red Lady': lvs deep purple turning scarlet. 'Golden Ring': lvs purple edged gold; 'Helmond Pillar': narrowly upright; lvs dark purple. 'Red Chief': tall, to 2m, with narrow red-purple lvs. (with pink-variegated foliage) 'Harlequin': compact, lvs small; 'Pink Queen': lvs red-purple flecked grey and white; 'Rose Glow': variegated white-pink. (with white- or green-variegated foliage) 'Kelleriis': more vigorous than 'Silver Beauty'. (dwarf habit) 'Atropurpurea Nana': dwarf form; lvs red-purple;

'Aurea': lvs golden-yellow; 'Bagatelle': not exceeding 30cm, lvs purple; 'Green Carpet': low, widespreading, lvs green, red in fall; 'Kobold': foliage green; 'Minor': densely branched dwarf to 25cm; 'Red Pillar': improved 'Erecta', densely branched, fastigiate dwarf shrub with purple lvs. Z4.

B. thunbergii var. *enuclea* Weston = *B. vulgaris* 'Asperia'.

B. thunbergii var. *pluriflora* Koehne = *B. ottawensis*.

B. triacanthophora Fedde = *B.* ×*wisleyensis*.

B. tricuspidata Sm. ex DC. = *B. heterophylla*.

B. tsangpoensis Ahrendt. Differs from *B. concinna* in dull, yellow-green lvs, pruinose beneath and procumbent habit. Early summer. SE Tibet. Z6.

B. umbellata Wall. Semi-evergreen shrub to 3m; st. red-brown; spines, 3-partite if present, to 1.5cm. Lvs to 5cm ovate, entire, mucronate, sparsely serrate, glossy above, grey-papillose beneath. Fls to 7 in long-stalked umbels, pale yellow. Fr. oblong, dark red-purple, glaucous. Late spring. Nepal. Z7.

B. valdisepala Ahrendt. Differs from *B. yunnanensis* in shorter spines, smaller fls and fr. Yunnan.

B. valdiviana Philippi. Everg. shrub, upright, to 5m; st. spiny, grey-yellow. Lvs rigid, coriaceous, to 5cm, elliptic, entire, glab., dark green above, yellow green, papillose beneath. Fls to 20 in pendulous rac. to 5cm, burnt orange. Fr. to 6mm diam., globose, mauve-black, glaucous. Late spring. Chile. Z8.

B. veitchii Schneid. Everg. shrub, erect to 1.5m; st. red hardening yellow grey; spines tripartite, thick to 3cm. Lvs to 11cm whorled, linear-lanceolate, acuminate, undulate, with to 24 broad teeth per side, grey-green above, yellow-green beneath. Fls to 8 per cluster, v. pale yellow, flushed brown, pink and green. Fr. ellipsoid to 1cm, purple, pruinose. Late spring. W China. Z6.

B. vernae Schneid. Decid. shrub to 1.5m; st. slender, arching, dark red, slightly warty; spines thick, solitary, yellow to 4cm. Lvs to 4cm, oblanceolate, entire, bright green, glab. Fls to 35 in pendent rac. to 4cm. Fr. to 4mm across, globose, coral pink. Late spring. NW China. Z6.

B. verruculosa Hemsl. & Wils. Everg. shrub to 1.5m; st. arching, yellow-brown, pubesc., warty; spines narrow. Lvs to 2cm, obovate-elliptic, acute, ± serrulate, glossy above, grey-pruinose beneath. Fls solitary or paired, golden. Fr. to 1cm, ovoid or pyriform, purple-black, pruinose. Summer. W China. Z5.

B. virescens Hook. f. & Thoms. Decid. shrub to 3m; st. slender, dark red, glossy, spines tripartite, to 1.5cm. Lvs to 3cm, oblong-obovate, obtuse, or abruptly acuminate, entire, olive green above, grey-pruinose beneath. Fls in subumbellate rac. to 3cm, yellow green. Fr. to 1cm, ovoid, glossy, dark pink. Early summer. Himal. Z6.

B. virgetorum Schneid. Decid. shrub to 2m; st. angular, pale yellow, slender; spines solitary, to 2cm. Lvs to 10cm, oblong-rhombic, abruptly acuminate, entire, slightly undulate, olive green. Fls to 10 in corymbs to 3cm. Fr. oblong, glossy, red. Early summer. China. Z6.

B. vulgaris L. COMMON BARBERRY. Decid. shrub to 2m; st. yellow; spines tripartite. Lvs to 6cm, obovate-elliptic serrulate, matt green. Fls to 20 in pendent rac. to 6cm. Fr. to 1cm, oblong, dull red. Spring. Eur., N Amer., Middle E. 'Alba': fr. white. 'Asperma': fr. seedless. 'Atropurpurea': lvs purple-red. 'Dulcis': fr. sweet. 'Lutea': fr. pale yellow. 'Marginata': margins silver. Z3.

B. wallichiana sensu Hook. f. non DC. = *B. hookeri*.

B. wallichiana var. *latifolia* hort. = *B. manipurana*.

B. wallichiana var. *pallida* Boiss. = *B. candidula*.

B. wilsoniae Hemsl. & Wils. Decid. shrub to 1m; st. red-brown; spines tripartite, to 2cm. Lvs to 3cm, obovate to linear-oblong, semi-rigid, entire, grey-green, mucronate, scarlet in fall. Fls to 6 per cluster, pale yellow, small. Fr. globose to 6mm diam., coral pink. Early summer. W China. var. *stapfiana* (Schneid.) Schneid. Lvs somewhat spathulate, grey beneath. Fr. ellipsoid, deep red. W China. var. *subcaulialata* (Schneid.) Schneid. Lvs blue-green, larger, mucronate or spiny-emarginate. Fr. yellow-red. Wisley Hybrids, showing closest affinity with *B. wilsoniae*, are 'Comet' (fr. rounded, scarlet); 'Coral' (fr. oblong, carmine), 'Ferax' (fr. oblong-ovoid, scarlet); 'Fireball' (fr. conic vermilion): 'Firefly' (fr. ovoid-conic, vermilion); 'Stonefield Surprise' (shoots tinted red; fls and fr. small); 'Tom Thumb' (shoots yellow; lvs broad, persisting). Valuable cvs of *B. wilsoniae* include: 'Joke': vigorous growth; fr. pink flushed red, large, profuse, hardy; and 'Orangeade': semi-prostrate, spreading; fr. orange and pink. Z6.

B. wintonensis Ahrendt. (*B. bergmanniae* ×*B. replicata*.) Favours *B. bergmanniae* but with narrow oblong-elliptic lvs to 5×1cm. Fls borne early and in great abundance. Fr. blue-black, pruinose. Gdn orig.

B. ×*wisleyensis* Ahrendt. Everg. shrub to 1.5m; st. yellow; spines tripartite, to 3cm. Lvs to 5cm, linear-lanceolate, with to 5 teeth per side, grey-green above, pruinose beneath. Fls to 6 per

cluster, yellow flushed red. Fr. to 1cm, oblong, black, pruinose. Early summer. Gdn origin. Z5.

B. ×*wokingensis* Ahrendt = *B. hybrido-gagnepainii*.

B. xanthoxylon hort. = *B. manipurana*.

B. yunnanensis Franch. Decid. shrub to 2m; st. slightly warty; spines tripartite, thick, to 2.5cm. Lvs 6cm, obovate, entire or sparsely serrate, minutely papillose beneath. Fls golden, to 8 per cluster. Fr. to 1cm, ellipsoid, glossy, red. Early summer. W China. Z6.

B. zabeliana Schneid. Decid. shrub to 2m; st. angled; spines tripartite, to 0.8cm, or 0. Lvs to 7cm, oblong-elliptic, base cuneate, apex obtuse, with to 30 spines per side, dull green above, initially glaucous beneath. Fls to 20 in lax pendent rac. to 5cm. Fr. to 1cm, obovoid. Early summer. Kashmir. Z6.

Berchemia Necker ex DC. Rhamnaceae. 12 decid., climbing or scandent perennials, rarely trees or shrubs. Lvs entire. Infl. fasiculate, paniculate or a raceme-like thyrse; fls small, 5-merous green-white. Fr. a small elongate drupe. Spring or summer. S Asia, E Afr., S US, Mex., Guat.

B. flavescens Wallich. Climber, 1.5–3m. Lvs 5–15×2.5–6cm, vein pairs 9–16, base attenuate, shiny green above. Infl. 3–10cm, term., pyramidal, paniculate. Himal., Nepal, Tibet, W China. Z5.

B. giraldiana Schneid. Climber 5–6m. Shoots red-brown. Lvs 3–7cm, ovate-oblong, vein pairs 9–11, apex acute or acuminate, base rounded or slightly cordate, dark green above, glaucous, glab. or sparsely downy beneath. Infl. to 20cm, pyramidal, term., paniculate. Fr. to 1cm, oblong, red to black. Summer. Hupeh, Sichuan, Shansi. Z6.

B. lineata DC. Climber to 5m. Lvs 1–3×0.3–1.5cm, vein pairs 4–9, oval-ovate, base and apex rounded, dark green above, pale, grey-green beneath. Infl. axill. or term. Fr. cylindrical or ovoid, blue-black. N India, China, Taiwan. Z8.

B. racemosa Sieb. & Zucc. Climber to at least 4m. Lvs 3–6cm, vein pairs 6–9, ovate, base slightly cordate, dark green above. Infl. to 15cm, paniculate, pyramidal. Fr. red to black. Late summer. Jap., Taiwan. 'Variegata': lvs variegated cream. Z6.

B. scandens (Hill) K. Koch. SUPPLE JACK; VINE RATTANY. Climber to 5m. Lvs 2–8cm, vein pairs 9–12, narrowly ovate-elliptic to elliptic, base rounded or cuneate, apex acute, often mucronate, glab., dark green above, paler beneath, undulate, clear yellow in fall. Infl. 1–3cm, axill. or term., racemose or paniculate. Fr. dark blue to black. Spring. US., Mex., Guat. Z7. 'Variegata': lvs variegated cream to white.

B. volubilis (L. f.) DC. = *B. scandens*.

Berg Alwyn *Aloe broomii*.
Bergamot *Citrus bergamia*; *Monarda didyma*.
Bergamot Orange *Citrus bergamia*.
Bergbamboes *Thamnocalamus tessellatus*.

Bergenia Moench. Saxifragaceae. 8 perenn. rhizomatous herbs. Lvs in an open rosette, leathery, rounded, entire or toothed; petioles sheathing, sometimes ligulate. Cymes scapose; fls 5-merous. E Asia.

B. ciliata (Haw.) Sternb. Lvs 20–35cm, densely pubesc. orbicular to obovate or elliptic, dentate to undulate, tinted red-bronze in cold weather, ciliate. Infl. to 30cm; fls few, sometimes weakly fragrant, to 5cm diam, white flushed rose, colour often deepening with age; sta., 6–12mm, fil. pink to deep red. Spring. W Pak., S Kashmir to SW Nepal. 'Leichtlinii': lvs tinted red, fls rose. 'Rosea': fls deep rose. Z7.

B. cordifolia (Haw.) Sternb. Lvs orbicular, crenate. Scape and infl. flushed red; fls pale rose to dark pink; sta. 5–8mm, fil. lilac. Late winter–spring. Sib., Mong. 'Morning Red': lvs large, tinted bronze; fls plum. 'Perfect': lvs large, tinted pale purple to brown; fls maroon. 'Purpurea': st. tall, red; lvs large, rounded, tinted purple in winter; fls bright blood red. 'Red Start': lvs tinted bronze; fls deep carmine. 'Rotblum': fls bright red. Z3.

B. coreana Nak. = *B. crassifolia*.

B. crassifolia (L.) Fritsch. Lvs 6–20×4–17cm, glab., shallowly dentate. Fls magenta to crimson; sta. equalling style, anth. tinged pink; styles flushed red. Early spring. Sib., Mong. 'Aureomarginata': lvs variegated cream and purple-green. 'Autumn Red': lvs small, spathulate, bright red in autumn; fls soft pink. Z3.

B. delavayi (Franch.) Engl. = *B. purpurascens*.

B. ligulata Engl. = *B. ciliata*.

B. ×*media* (Haw.) Engl. (*B. cordifolia* ×*B. crassifolia*.) Resembles *B. crassifolia* except smaller with lvs broadly ovate, rounded or cordate at base. Infl. crowded, usually taller than lvs. Late winter, spring. Gdn origin. Z3.

B. milesii Bak. = *B. stracheyi*.

B. purpurascens (Hook. f. Thoms.) Engl. Lvs 7–25×5–17cm, elliptic, suffused purple, entire or with sparse bristle-tipped teeth. Infl. 25–40cm, upper part of scape deep red; fls nodding deep maroon or bright pink; sta. 9–14mm, fil. white or rose pink. Late winter, spring. E Himal. Z4.

B. ×schmidtii (Reg.) Silva-Tar. (*B. ciliata ×B. crassifolia.*) Lvs glab., obovate to elliptic, bluntly toothed. Infl. equalling lvs, nodding at first, becoming erect; fls rose pink, darker at base; fil. white becoming maroon. Early spring, sometimes autumn. Gdn origin. Z5.

B. ×smithii Engl. ex Engl. & Irmsch. (*B. cordifolia ×B. purpurascens.*) Lvs broader than in *B. purpurascens*. Infl. red, glandular-pubesc.; fls pale pink, larger than in *B. cordifolia*, sta. mauve. Late spring. Gdn hybrid. 'Distinction': lvs pale green, bullate; fls clear pink. Z3.

B. ×spathulata Nagels. (*B. ciliata ×B. stracheyi.*) Lvs glab., double-serrate, cuneate at base. Fls numerous, erect, except when young, slightly fragrant, white ageing pink, deeper toward base. India. Z6.

B. stracheyi (Hook. f. & Thoms.) Engl. Lvs 6–20×3–10cm, obovate, glab., dark garnet red in winter, ciliate, finely toothed. Several infl. from 1 rosette; fls numerous, fragrant, nodding pink-cream or white ageing pink; fil. becoming red. Late winter--spring. E Afghan., Pak., W Turkestan, Kashmir, Nepal, Tibet. 'Alba': lvs neat; fls pure white in dense heads. Z6.

B. cvs. 'Abendglocken' ('Evening Bells'): to 40cm; lvs large, tinted red; fls dark red. 'Abendglut' ('Evening Glow'): low; lvs broad, edges crinkled, tinted dark red to bronze; fls semi-double, claret. 'Admiral': lvs erect, oval, dark green, tinted bronze and red in autumn; fls cherry red. 'Baby Doll': fls baby pink, dense. 'Ballawley' ('Delbees'): lvs glossy, flushed purple in winter; st. red; fls wide, vivid red. 'Beethoven': fls white, in large, compact clusters, cal. red. 'Bressingham Bountiful': compact; lvs dark, edged dark red in winter; fls clear pink, darker later, heads branching. 'Bressingham White': fls pure white, abundant. 'Eric Smith': lvs large, crinkled, flushed bronze. 'Glockenturm' ('Bell Tower'): fls red to pink, v. profuse. 'Margery Fish': to 45cm; lvs large, bright green, tinted red in autumn; fls deep rose, early-flowering. 'Morgenrote' ('Morning Blush'): lvs small; fls large, cherry pink, fls twice. 'Oschberg': st. tall, to 60cm; fls bright pink, late-flowering. 'Pinneberg': lvs upright, oblong, tinted bright red in autumn; fls carmine red. 'Profusion': lvs rounded, deeply veined; fls pale pink. 'Pugsley's Pink': to 50cm; lvs tinted pink below; fls pink, sep. brown tinted pink. 'Pugsley's Purple': strong-growing; fls magenta, late-flowering. 'Purpurglocken' ('Purple Bells'): to 40cm; lvs large; fls campanulate, maroon, flowering again in autumn. 'Schneekissen' ('Snow Cushion'): v. tall; lvs crispate at margins; st. to 50cm; fls blush pink. 'Schneekonigen' ('Snow Queen'): to 50cm; lvs large, crispate at margins; fls large, pale pink, darker later. 'Silberlicht' ('Silver Light'): lvs large, somewhat dentate; fls white, later tinted pink, cal. dark. 'Sunningdale': lvs rounded, bronze to red in autumn; fls deep lilac pink. 'Sunshade': lvs small, tinted bronze, not rosette-form; fls lilac-pink, in loose pan. 'Walter Kienli': tall, to 50cm, everg.; fls late. Winter Flowering Hybrids: lvs broad, tinted bronze; winter flowering. 'Wintermarchen' ('Winter Fairy Tale'): lvs small, pointed, somewhat twisted, scarlet beneath; fls dark rose.

Bergeranthus Schwantes. Aizoaceae. 11 compact leaf-succulents. Lvs curved inwards, upper surface flat or trough-shaped, lower surface semi-cylindrical, grey-green, sometimes with minute dark spots. Fls stalked, solitary or several, opening during afternoon. E Cape. Z9.

B. albidus (L.) Schwantes = *Macairophyllum albidum*.

B. artus L. Clump-forming. Lvs 6–8 per shoot, crowded, 3–4cm, yellow-green, lower surface acutely carinate. Fls 2.5cm, diam., yellow-red. Cape Prov.

B. caninus (Haw.) Schwantes = *Carruanthus ringens*.

B. carinans (Haw.) Schwantes = *Hereroa carinans*.

B. cookii (L. Bol.) Schwantes = *Macairophyllum cookii*.

B. derenbergianus (Dinter) Schwantes = *Ebracteola derenbergiana*.

B. firmus L. Bol. = *B. multiceps*.

B. glenensis N.E. Br. Mound-forming. Lvs crowded, 2.5–4cm, oblong-lanceolate, lower surface rounded to rounded-carinate, densely spotted dark green. Fls 3cm diam., glossy yellow. OFS.

B. multiceps (Salm-Dyck) Schwantes. Mat-forming. Lvs 6–8 in a rosette, 2.5–3cm, triangular in cross-section, smooth. Fls 3cm diam., yellow, flushed red. E Cape.

B. puttkamerianus (Dinter & A. Berger) Schwantes = *Hereroa puttkameriana*.

B. rehneltianus (A. Berger) Schwantes = *Hereroa rehneltiana*.

B. rhomboideus (Salm-Dyck) Schwantes = *Rhombophyllum rhomboideum*.

B. scapiger (Haw.) Schwantes. Mat-forming. Lvs 7–12cm, gradually tapering, one lf of the pair longer, with the angle of the keel pulled forward, dark green, margins smooth, pale,

cartilaginous. Fls 4–5cm diam., golden-yellow, tinged red. Cape Prov.

B. vespertinus (A. Berger) Schwantes. Mat-forming. Lvs to 6cm, 3-angled, tapered, carinate above, grey-green with darker spots. Fls yellow. E Cape.

Bergerocactus Britt. & Rose. Cactaceae. 1 shrubby cactus; st. erect, to 60×3–6cm, rather woody; ribs 20–25, somewhat tuberculate; spines 1–4cm. Fls 2×2cm, pale yellow. Fr. globose, densely spiny. Calif., NW Baja Calif. Z9.

B. emoryi (Engelm.) Britt. & Rose.
→*Cereus*.

Berkheya Ehrh. Compositae. *c*80 often spiny, perenn. herbs, subshrubs and shrubs. Lvs pinnate, pinnatisect or pinnatifid, usually petiolate, often white-tomentose beneath. Cap. radiate or discoid, usually terminal, few to several, usually in spreading clusters; ray flts yellow, rarely white, purple or brown-tinged, sometimes 0; disc flts yellow, rarely purple to brown. S Afr. Z8.

B. adlamii Hook. f. = *B. radula*.

B. armata (Vahl) Druce. Woody, rhizomatous, perenn. herb, to 40cm. Lvs subrosulate, to 18cm, narrowly lanceolate to oblong-lanceolate or obovate, base attenuate into a petiole, sinuate-dentate, spiny, white-tomentose beneath, st. lvs ovate-lanceolate to narrowly oblong, sessile, toothed or spiny-ciliate. Cap. 6–10cm diam., usually 3–5 in branched, racemose infl., radiate. Cape Prov.

B. barbata (L. f.) Hutch. Few-branched shrub or subshrub, to 80cm. Lvs opposite, often alt. above, to 6cm, lanceolate to elliptic, apex with long brown spine, base attenuate to a short petiole, sinuate-dentate, teeth spiny, glabrescent above, dull white-tomentose beneath. Cap. 6–10cm diam., solitary at br. apices, radiate. Cape Prov.

B. carduoides (Less.) Hutch. Erect perenn. herb, to 90cm. Lvs basally crowded, to 35cm, lower narrowly oblong, pinnatifid-laciniate, lobes in 12–20 pairs, usually regular, semi-orbicular or subrotund, lightly repand-dentate, teeth spiny, subglabrous, st. lvs sessile, base decurrent; uppermost subentire, bract-like. Cap. 1.5–3cm diam., in an apically branched, subpaniculate or subcorymbose infl., discoid. Cape Prov.

B. grandiflora (Thunb.) Willd. = *B. barbata*.

B. pinnata (Thunb.) Less. = *Heterorhachis aculeata*.

B. macrocephala J.M. Wood. Erect perenn. to 1m. Lvs narrow-oblong, deeply irregularly lobed with sinuate spiny teeth. Cap. to 5.5cm diam. on branched st., radiate, ray flts golden-yellow, disc flts orange-yellow. Natal.

B. purpurea (DC.) Mast. Erect perenn. herb, to 80cm. Lvs bas-ally crowded, to 25cm, lower narrowly obovate-oblong, sinuate, dentate-lobate, teeth spiny, puberulous and cobwebby above, white-tomentose beneath, st. lvs narrowly oblong, base decurrent. Cap. 5–8cm diam., usually few in apical, branched, racemose infl., radiate; ray flts purple or lilac, rarely white; disc flts purple to brown, rarely yellow. S Afr.

B. radula (Harv.) Willd. Erect perenn. herb, to 1m. Lvs sub-rosulate, to 40cm, lower obovate to elliptic-oblong, base attenuate, ± sessile, repand- or lobate-sinuate, lobes to 2cm, semiorbicular, densely spiny, white-tomentose beneath, st. lvs oblong to linear, spinose-dentate, base decurrent. Cap. 4–6cm diam., several, solitary at br. apices, radiate. S Zimb. to S Afr.

→*Gorteria, Stephanacoma* and *Stobaea*.

Berlin Poplar *Populus ×berolinensis*.
Bermuda Buttercup *Oxalis pes-caprae*.
Bermuda Grass *Cynodon dactylon*.
Bermuda Juniper *Juniperus bermudiana*.
Bermuda Lily *Lilium longiflorum*.
Bermuda Maidenhair Fern *Adiantum bellum*.
Bermuda Olive-wood Bark *Cassine laneana*.
Bermuda Palmetto *Sabal bermudana*.

Berresfordia L. Bol.
B. khamiesbergensis L. Bol. = *Conophytum khamiesbergense*.

Berry-bearing Catchfly *Cucubalus*.
Berry Bladder Fern *Cystopteris bulbifera*.

Berteroa DC. Cruciferae. 8 low-growing ann. or perenn. herbs. Lvs lanceolate-obovate, usually entire. Fls racemose; pet. 4, 4–6mm, cleft, white or pale cream, sometimes flushed red. N Temp. OW. Z8.

B. incana (L.) DC. ALLYSUM; HOARY ALISON. Lvs lanceolate, en-tire to remotely toothed. Fls white in dense heads. Fr. 4.5–8mm, narrow-ovoid, downy, inflated. Summer. N & C Eur. to E Asia; nat. N Amer.

B. mutabilis (Vent.) DC. Lvs lanceolate or linear-oblong, entire. Fls in lax rac., tinted red with age. Fr. compressed, glab. Arm-

enia, Cauc.
B. stricta Boiss. & Heldr. = *B. incana.*
→*Alyssum* and *Farsetia*.

Bertholletia Humb. & Bonpl. Lecythidaceae. 1 decid. tree to 50m. Lvs to 36×15cm, oblong, apiculate to mucronate, leathery, entire or undulate. Fls in pan.; sep. 2; pet. 6, oblong-ovate, pale yellow or white, to 3cm; sta. fused to form thick flap. Fr. woody, spherical, to 15cm diam., containing 12–24 hard nuts to 5cm, packed like orange seg. Amazonia. Z10.
B. excelsa Humb. & Bonpl. BRAZIL NUT.

Bertolonia Raddi. Melastomataceae. 14 herbs. Lvs simple, ovate-cordate, crenate. Cymes corymbose, secund; fls saucer-shaped, white, rose or purple. Trop. S Amer. Z10.
B. houtteana Van Houtte. V. short-stemmed. Lvs 10–18cm, ovate to elliptic, yellow-green above, striped bright pink along veins. Gdn origin.
B. maculata Mart. ex DC. St. decumbent, rooting. Lvs 5–8cm, ovate, ciliate, velvety-green above, veins bordered purple or magenta. Fls 2cm diam., 6–7 per rac., violet-purple. NE Braz. 'Wentii': veins bordered silver.
B. marmorata Naudin. St. fleshy, about 15cm. Lvs 5–8cm, ovate-oblong, acute, thinly fleshy, velvety, bullate, bright green with irregular streaks of pure white above, rich purple beneath. N Braz. var. *aenea* (Naudin) Cogn. Lvs dark bronze with green few or no spots. Fls purple. var. *genuina.* Lvs banded white along veins above. 'Sanderiana': lvs banded silver-green along primary veins above.
B. primuliflora hort. ex Triana = *Monolena primuliflora.*
B. cvs. *B.* 'Hrubyana': lf veins connected by bars of white above, green beneath. *B.* 'Mirandaei': lvs in upper part of plant spotted white, in lower part spotted red, purple beneath. red, purple beneath. 'Mosaica': habit low; lvs longitudinally banded white, in a range of iridescent colours. *B.* 'Rodeskiana': like *B.* 'Hrubyana' but lvs dark red above.

Berzelia Brongn. Bruniaceae. 12 compact everg. shrubs. Lvs closely set, usually keeled. Fls in heads, white, 5-merous in round heads; sta. exceeding pet. S Afr. Z9.
B. lanuginosa (L.) Brongn. To 2m. Lvs to 6mm, imbricate, linear-liliform to acicular, slightly pilose. Fl. to 1cm diam., heads creamy-white on short br. S Afr.

Beschorneria Kunth. Agavaceae. 10 perennials, allied to *Agave*. Lvs in a basal rosette, fleshy, lanceolate to ensiform, glaucous. Infl. large, term., scapose, usually inclined and branched above. Summer. Mex. Z9.
B. bracteata Jacobi. Lvs 45–60cm, lanceolate, erect, thin, margin scarious, glaucous. Infl. to 150cm, paniculate, red-brown; fls green-brown; bracts large, red-brown.
B. decosteriana Bak. Lvs 60–75cm, spreading, oblanceolate, long-acuminate, narrowed to 2.5cm above an expanded base, rigid, glaucous, smooth above, denticulate. Infl. to 240cm, green, paniculate; fls tinged red, pendulous.
B. toneliana Jacobi. Lvs to 60×5–6cm, v. glaucous, slender pointed, contracted below, minutely toothed. Infl. to 120cm, paniculate, red-purple; fls bright green, red inside; bracts red-purple.
B. tubiflora (Kunth & Bouché) Kunth. Lvs to 60×2.5cm, glaucous, linear, with fine stripes, denticulate. Infl. to 90cm, racemose, green to red-brown; fls nodding, deep buff to green tinged red; bracts tinged purple.
B. wrightii Hook. f. Differs from *B. decosteriana* in lvs to 150×5cm, ensiform, narrowing to a brown stiff apex; fls hairy.
B. yuccoides Hook. f. Lvs to 60×5–7cm, lanceolate, short-acuminate, grey-green, somewhat glaucous when mature, margin rough. Infl. to 180cm, arching, paniculate, dull pink to red; fls nodding, yellow-green amid fleshy red bracts.

Besleria L. Gesneriaceae. 170 herbs and shrubs. St. erect, creeping or climbing. Lvs paired, usually elliptic. Fls in umbels or solitary; cal. urceolate to campanulate; 5-dentate; cor. limb 5-lobed. Trop. Amer. Z10.
B. flavovirens Nees & Mart. Shrub to 2m. Lvs to 32×12cm, oblong-lanceolate, ± serrate. Fls in umbels; cor. tube to 4mm, white, lobes subequal. N S Amer.
B. imrayi Hook. = *B. lutea.*
B. incarnata Aubl. = *Sinningia incarnata.*
B. insolita Morton. Herb to 1.25m. Lvs to 27×11cm, elliptic to oblong-elliptic, strigilose beneath. Fls in axill. fasicles; cor. tube to 2cm, cream or pale yellow, limb erect, lobes minute. N S Amer.
B. lutea L. Shrub or tree to 7m. Lvs to 28×10cm, ovate, elliptic or oblong, acuminate, serrate. Fls in clusters of 1–6; cor. yellow

rarely white, erect, contracted in throat, lobes to 3mm, rounded. W Indies.

Besom Heath *Erica scoparia.*

Bessera Schult. Liliaceae (Alliaceae). 2 cormous perennials. Lvs narrow-linear. Umbel scapose, fls nodding; perianth campanulate to cylindric; tep. 3–4cm, 6, exterior scarlet or purple veined green, interior ivory, margins and midvein scarlet. Mex. Z9.
B. elegans Schult. CORAL DROPS. To 90cm. Lvs 60–80cm. Infl. 2–30fld.

Besseya Rydb. KITTEN-TAILS. Scrophulariaceae. 9 perenn. rhizomatous herbs. Lvs rosulate, ovate-elliptic, entire to crenate. Rac. spike-like; cal. 4-lobed; cor. tubular, bilabiate, hooded. N Amer., particularly NW.
B. alpina (Gray) Rydb. Lvs 3–6×1–4cm, broadly ovate-elliptic, crenate-dentate, ± glab. Fls red to violet. Summer. Wyom. to New Mex. Z3.
B. arizonica Pennell = *B. plantaginea.*
B. cinerea (Raf.) Penn. = *B. wyomingensis.*
B. gooddingii Pennell = *B. plantaginea.*
B. plantaginea (James) Rydb. Lvs to 20×8cm, broadly elliptic-ovate, entire to dentate, minutely lanate-pubesc. becoming glab. Fls white, sometimes pink. Summer. Wyom. to New Mex. & Ariz. Z5.
B. reflexa (Eastw.) Rydb. = *B. ritteriana.*
B. ritteriana (Eastw.) Rydb. Lvs to 25×8cm, elliptic-lanceolate, entire to dentate, shortly villous. Fls light lemon yellow. Summer. Colorado. Z4.
B. rubra (Douglas) Rydb. Lvs to 11×8cm, ovate, red-tinged doubly crenate to entire, truncate or cordate at base, villous to glabrate. Cor. 0; sta. maroon, cream or cream and maroon, fil. to 9mm. Summer. W Mont. to E Oreg. and Washington. Z4.
B. wyomingensis (A. Nels.) Rydb. To 30cm, softly pubesc. Lvs to 10×5cm, ovate-lanceolate, crenate-serrate, lanate. Cor. 0 or vestigial; fil. 5–10mm, white to pink or maroon. Late spring-–summer. Alberta & Saskatch. to S Dak., Mont. and Colorado. Z3.
→*Synthyris, Veronica* and *Wulfenia.*

Beta L. BEET. Chenopodiaceae. 6 perenn. or bienn. glab. herbs, roots often massively swollen. Lvs entire, sometimes undulate, often glossy. Fls small, solitary or in cymes arranged in spicate infl. Medit. Z5.
B. hortensis hort. = *B. vulgaris* ssp. *vulgaris.*
B. rubra hort. = *B. vulgaris* ssp. *vulgaris.*
B. vulgaris L. Variable ann. or perenn., to 2m in fl. Basal lvs forming a rosette, ovate-cordate to rhombic-cuneate, st. lvs rhombic to lanceolate. Infl. dense, usually branched; fls in clusters, subtended by bracts, small, green. Summer. ssp. *vulgaris* BEETROOT; MANGELWURZEL; MANGOLD. St. to 2m, erect. Root swollen, globose. Lvs to 20cm+. Fls in clusters of 2–8. Plant often flushed red-purple or yellow-white, the root petioles and principal veins esp., but lamina and infl. axis usually green. Derived from ancestral ssp. *provulgaris*: includes all forms with swollen roots providing sugarbeet, forage beets, red and yellow gdn beets. var. *flavescens* (Lam.) Lam. SWISS CHARD. Roots not swollen. 'Dracaenifolia': lvs narrow, deep scarlet; cultivated as an ornamental. 'Macgregor's Favourite': lvs brilliant purple. ssp. *cicla* (L.) Koch. SPINACH BEET. Root not swollen. Lf midrib dark orange or scarlet, lamina sometimes puckered. ssp. *maritima* (L.) Arcang.). St. to 80cm, procumbent to erect. Root not swollen. Lvs to 10cm. Fls in clusters of 1–3.

Betel *Piper betle.*
Betel Palm *Areca catechu.*
Betle Pepper *Piper betle.*

Betonica L.
B. alopecuros L. = *Stachys alopecuros.*
B. annua L. = *Stachys annua.*
B. macrantha K. Koch = *Stachys macrantha.*
B. nivea (Labill.) Steven = *Stachys discolor.*
B. officinalis L. = *Stachys officinalis.*

Betony *Stachys officinalis.*
Betoum *Pistacia atlantica.*

Betula L. Betulaceae. BIRCH. 60 decid. trees and shrubs. Trunk frequently white or shades of pink, amber or glossy brown; bark often exfoliating. Lvs generally ovate, serrate or dentate ♂ catkins cylindric, slender, pendulous; ♀ catkins on short side br., shorter and stiffer than ♂. Temp. and Arc. N Hemis.

B. acuminata Wallich non Ehrh. = *B. alnoides*.

B. alba L. = *B. pendula* or *B. pubescens*.

B. albosinensis Burkill. CHINESE RED BIRCH. Tree, 18–25m; bark glaucous then peeling, thin, orange or red-orange; young twigs gland., pubesc. Lvs 4–7cm, narrowly ovate, acuminate, irregularly biserrate. Fr. catkins ovoid-cylindric, 3–4cm, pendulous. Spring. W China (mts). Z7. var. *septentrionalis* Schneid. Bark orange-pink to red, lightly bloomed violet-white, exfoliating in shaggy rolls; lvs to 12×7cm, lanceolate, drooping. NW China. Z7.

B. alleghaniensis Britt. YELLOW BIRCH. Tree, 20–30m; bark crisped or curled, tinged yellow or grey, peeling in translucent sheets, yellow-brown where exposed; twigs pale olive-green, pubesc. Lvs 6–12cm, ovate to ovate-oblong, acute, coarsely biserrate, dull green, yellow in autumn, ciliate, silky beneath. Fr. catkins 2.5–3cm, erect, thick. E N Amer. Z4. var. *fallax* (Fassett) Brayshaw. Bark as in *B. lenta* and easily confused with it. SE Canada. Z3.

B. alnoides Buch.-Ham. ex D. Don. Tree to 40m; bark papery, grey or brown tinged red, peeling in narrow horizontal silvery scrolls; twigs pendulous, maroon, pubesc. when young, gland. Lvs to 10cm, oblong-elliptic, acute or acuminate, irregularly biserrate, veins brown-tomentose beneath, petiole red. Fr. catkins 5–7cm, in clusters of 2–3. China, NE India, temp. Himal. Z8.

B. alnoides var. *cylindrostachya* (Lindl.) Winkl. = *B. cylindrostachya*.

B. alnoides var. *pyrifolia* Burkill = *B. luminifera*.

B. apoiensis Nak. Shrub to 1m; branchlets resinous-glandular, shortly pubesc. Lvs 1.5–4cm, ovate to ovate-orbicular, irregularly acutely dentate, acute, silky-pubesc. beneath when young. Fr. catkins 1–3×0.6–1.2cm, erect, subglobose to shortly cylindric. Jap. Z3.

B. ×aurata Borkh. (*B. pendula* ×*B. pubescens*.) Shrub to small tree. Growth resembling *B. pubescens* but twigs more slender and young growth pubesc. to glandular-pubesc. Lvs 4–5cm, usually rhombic, fine-toothed. Z2.

B. austrosinensis Chun. Tall tree to 20m, bark white; young twigs thin, glab., scented of wintergreen. Lvs triangular-lanceolate, serrate-dentate, glossy, green, ± glab., sometimes bronze when young, attractively coloured in fall. Fr. catkins 3–4cm, erect. China. Z6.

B. bhojpattra Wallich = *B. utilis*.

B. bhojpattra var. *sinensis* Franch. = *B. albosinensis*.

B. borealis Spach. Low shrub or small tree; bark dark; twigs and young br. densely villous-tomentose to pilose. Lvs 2–5×1–4cm, ovate to broadly ovate or subrhombic, deeply biserrate, acute or obtuse, pubesc. when young. Fr. catkins 1–3cm. N Amer. Z2. Z6.

B. brachylepis V.N. Vassiliev = *B. pendula* var. *lapponica*.

B. ×caerulea Blanchard. (*B. populifolia* ×*B. cordifolia*.) BLUE BIRCH. Tree to 15m; bark white; twigs glab., warty with sparse resinous glands. Lvs 6–8cm, triangular-ovate, acuminate, sharply serrate, dull blue-green above, yellow-green beneath, glab. Fr. catkins 2.5–3×0.8–1cm, cylindric, pubesc. N US, Canada. Z4.

B. calcicola (W.W. Sm.) P.C. Li. Shrub-like; bark oft. white; twigs densely white hairy. Lvs ovate, serrate, deep glossy green. Fr. catkins 3–4cm, erect. SW China. Z7.

B. candelae Koidz. = *B. maximowiczii*.

B. carpinifolia Sieb. & Zucc. non Willd. = *B. grossa*.

B. celtiberica Rothm. & Vasc. Tree or shrub, to 20m; bark dark and deeply furrowed on bole, silvery white and smooth elsewhere; twigs gland., pilose when young. Lvs to 7cm, rhombic-ovate, coarsely serrate, green tinged blue, rather thick, shiny above. Fr. catkins pendent. N & C Spain, Port. Z7.

B. chichibuensis Hara. Tree or shrub; twigs ± gland., densely villous when young. Lvs 3–6cm, ovate to oblong-ovate, minutely biserrate, veins densely white-villous beneath. Fr. catkins 15–25×7–10mm, erect, cylindric. Jap. Z5.

B. chinensis Maxim. Shrub or small tree 1.5–4m, or small tree to 10m; bark grey tinged red; twigs thin, silky-pubesc. Lvs 2.5–5cm, ovate, acute, serrate, dull dark green above, paler beneath. Fr. catkins ovoid, 1–2cm. N China, Jap., Korea. Z4.

B. chinensis var. *delavayi* (Franch.) Schneid. = *B. delavayi*.

B. cordifolia Reg. Small tree or shrub; bark v. white, smooth, papery, peeling; twigs persistently pubesc. Lvs ovate to triangular-ovate, biserrate hairy beneath. Fr. catkins pendulous. NE N Amer. Z2.

B. corylifolia Reg. & Maxim. Tree to 20m; bark grey or off-white; young twigs brown tinged red to dark purple-brown, glab. scented of wintergreen. Lvs 4–6cm, elliptic to obovate, coarsely biserrate with large triangular teeth, vivid green above, glaucous beneath. Fr. catkins 3–5cm, erect, ± curved. Honshu. Z5.

B. costata Trautv. Tree to 30m; bark peeling, scaly when old,

papery, light yellow or tinted grey; branchlets brown, pubesc. with round yellow glands, later glab. Lvs 5–8cm, ovate, cuspidate, finely biserrate, light green beneath, glandular-warty, often rather pubesc. Fr. catkins ellipsoid to subglobose, 2cm. Manch., Korea. Z6.

B. cylindrostachya Lindl. Tall tree; bark grey tinged yellow; twigs brown tinged grey when young, densely gland. Lvs to 8cm, obovate, coarsely serrate, tough to subcoriaceous, glab. above, yellow-tomentose beneath. Fr. catkins narrowly oblong, 2–2.5cm. W China to N Burm. and Assam. Z9.

B. dahurica Reg. = *B. davurica*.

B. davurica Pall. ASIAN BLACK BIRCH. Tree to 15(–30m); bark dense peeling in curling flakes, brown tinged grey, or grey with age; twigs v. resinous, dark grey with white glands, pilose when young. Lvs 5–10cm, ovate-rhombic, unevenly serrate, acute, dark green and glab. above, glandular-punctate beneath. Fr. catkins narrowly oblong, 2–2.5cm. NE Asia. Z3.

B. delavayi Franch. Small tree or shrub to 13m, horizontally branching; bark dark grey; young twigs dark grey with numerous white glands. Lvs to 4cm, ovate-elliptic, unevenly biserrate with long teeth, acute fresh green. Fr. catkins 1.5–2×1cm. Kansu, Sichuan, Yunnan. Z4.

B. delavayi var. *calcicola* W.W. Sm. = *B. calcicola*.

B. ermanii Cham. GOLD BIRCH; ERMAN'S BIRCH; RUSSIAN ROCK BIRCH. Tree or large shrub to 25m, widely spreading; bark peeling, tinged yellow, to white or rufescent, orange-brown to purple-brown on young br.; twigs glandular-warty when young, glab. Lvs 5–10cm, deltoid-cordate, coarsely triangular-serrate, apex cuspidate, with scattered glands. Fr. catkins 2–3×1–1.5cm, erect, ovate-ellipsoid. NE Asia. Z3. var. *japonica* (Shirai) Koidz. Lvs with to 14 (not 7–11) pairs of veins; tips of fr. scales acuminate not oblong. Honshu. Z5. var. *lanata* Reg. Young shoots pubesc.; lvs triangular-ovate; fr. scales pubesc. E Sib. Z2.

B. exalata S. Moore = *B. chinensis*.

B. 'Fetisowii'. Graceful, narrow-headed tree; bark chalk-white, peeling. Hybrid originating in C Asia.

B. fontinalis Sarg. WATER BIRCH; AMERICAN RED BIRCH. Shrub to 6m, or tree to 12m; bark lustrous, dark bronze; shoots resinous and warted when young. Lvs 2.5–5cm, rhomboid-ovate, apex acute biserrate, dark dull green above, paler beneath, gland., slightly hairy above, soon glab. beneath. Fr. catkins 2.5–3cm. NW Amer.

B. fruticosa Pall. = *B. humilis*.

B. glandulifera (Reg.) Butler. Shrub to 2m; twigs thin, resinous-glandular, coarsely hairy. Lvs 2–5cm, obovate to rounded, serrate or crenate, acute. Fr. catkins to 2cm, erect, cylindric. N US and S Canada. Z4.

B. glandulosa Michx. Shrub 1–2m; twigs densely resinous-glandular and warty, not pubesc. Lvs 1–2.5cm, rounded to broadly elliptic or subreniform, conspicuously crenate-dentate, glandular-punctate, glab. Fr. catkins 1.5–2cm, erect. N N Amer. and Greenland. Z1.

B. globispica Shirai. Tree to 20m; bark peeling, papery, pale grey to nearly white; young twigs yellow tinged grey, sparsely pilose when young, lenticels thick. Lvs 4–7cm, ovate to suborbicular, coarsely serrate, shortly acuminate slightly lustrous. Fr. catkins 2.5–3.5cm, ellipsoid to subglobose. C Jap. Z5.

B. grossa Sieb. & Zucc. JAPANESE CHERRY BIRCH. Tree to 25m; bark black-grey, grooved; twigs brown tinged yellow then red, with few pale lenticels, pilose at first. Lvs 5–10cm, ovate-oblong, apex acuminate coarsely biserrate, dull green, adpressed-pubesc. above, gland. beneath. Fr. catkins 20–25mm, solitary, subsessile, ovoid. Jap. Z5.

B. humilis Schrenk. Shrub, much-branched, 0.5–2m; bark brown tinged black; young twigs soon glab., with large resinous warts. Lvs 1–3cm, elliptic to elliptic-ovate, obtuse to subacute, coarsely serrate to crenate, rather thick, glab. Fr. catkins erect, 5–15mm. N & C Eurasia. Z1.

B. hupehensis Schneid. = *B. luminifera*.

B. hybrida Bechst. = *B. ×aurata*.

B. incisa Koidz. = *B. ermanii*.

B. insignis Franch. Tree, 9–12m; bark dark grey; branchlets foxred, with copious white glands. Lvs 5–9cm, ovate-lanceolate, acute or acuminate irregularly biserrate, pubesc. on veins beneath, otherwise glab. Fr. catkins 4–6×1.5cm, erect, subcylindric. W China. Z7.

B. jacquemontii Spach = *B. utilis* var. *jacquemontii*.

B. japonica var. *szechuanica* C. Schneid. = *B. szechuanica*.

B. ×koehnei Schneid. (*B. papyrifera* ×*B. pendula*.) Large tree, open-crowned; twigs pendulous; bark white. Lvs to 9cm, triangular-ovate, more finely serrate than in *B. papyrifera*, tough, soon glab., paler beneath. Z2.

B. lenta L. SWEET BIRCH; CHERRY BIRCH. Tree to 25m, narrowly upright; bark polished red-brown to almost black, fissured, not peeling, aromatic, brown tinged purple when young; twigs silky, soon glab. Lvs 6–12cm, ovate-oblong, acutely biserrate, acute to acuminate, glossy green above, paler beneath, golden in fall. Fr. catkins 2–3.5cm, erect, oblong-ovoid, subsessile. E N Amer. Z3.

B. *luminifera* Winkl. Tree to 20m; bark grey tinged yellow, not peeling; branchlets bright red-brown, ± pale brown-pubesc. Lvs 6–13cm, ovate, apex acute, irregularly serrate ciliate, tinged red when young, finely tomentose to almost glab., glossy resinous-glandular. Fr. catkins 4–10×0.5cm, candle-like, solitary, erect. China. Z8.

B. *lutea* Michx. = B. *alleghaniensis*.

B. *lyalliana* Bean = B. *papyrifera* var. *commutata*.

B. *maackii* Rupr. = B. *davurica*.

B. *mandschurica* (Reg.) Nak. MANCHURIAN BIRCH. Tree to 12(–18)m; bark chalky white, dusty; branchlets brown, warty. Lvs 4–7cm. Manch., SE Sib. Z3. var. *japonica* (Miq.) Rehd. JAPANESE WHITE BIRCH. To 25m; bark cream-white. Young twigs dark brown, densely warty. Lvs 5–8cm, deltoid- or rhombic-ovate, biserrate, acuminate, glab. above, hair tufts in veins axils beneath. Fr. catkins 2–3cm×8mm. N Jap., Sakhalin. Z4. var. *kamtschatica* (Reg.) Rehd. Lvs 3–5cm, lvs and shoots more pubesc. Possibly synonymous with Alaskan B. *papyrifera* var. *kendica*. NE Sib., Kamchatka. Z2.

B. *maximowicziana* Reg. MONARCH BIRCH. Tree to 30m, crown open; bark thin, peeling, tinged orange, grey and white; twigs dark red-brown, glab., lustrous. Lvs 8–14cm, broadly ovate, acute to acuminate, dark green, golden yellow in fall often with red veins. Fr. catkins 3–7cm×6–7mm, in clusters of 3–5, pendulous, cylindric. Jap. Z6.

B. *medwediewii* Reg. TRANSCAUCASIAN BIRCH. Broadly spreading shrub or tree, to 12m; bark peeling, brown, similar to *Corylus*; br. thick, stiff, glossy pale brown, lenticels long; winter buds v. large, narrow, viscid. Lvs 6–14cm, broadly elliptic, unevenly biserrate, apex acute deep green above, paler beneath, bright yellow in autumn, glab. or pubesc. Fr. catkins erect, stalked, 2–4cm. Cauc., NW Iran & NE Turk. Z5.

B. *megrelica* Sosn. Small tree, to 15m; bark pale brown or yellow to grey; twigs stiff, tinged grey, hairy. Lvs 3–7.5cm, ovate to broadly elliptic, serrate. Fr. catkins 2–3cm, erect, stalked. Cauc. Z5.

B. *michauxii* Spach. NEWFOUNDLAND DWARF BIRCH. Dwarf shrub, to 0.5m, strongly branched; st. ashy; twigs strongly tomentose when young. Lvs 1cm, fan-shaped to obovate, deeply crenate esp. above. Fr. catkins 10–12mm, erect, ovate-oblong. NE Canada. Z3.

B. *microphylla* Bunge. Tree; bark tinged yellow; young twigs pubesc. with dense resinous glands. Lvs 2.5–3cm, obovate to rhombic-ovate, entire or serrate, glab. and gland. beneath. Fr catkins subsessile, oblong-cylindric. C Asia. Z4.

B. *middendorffii* Trautv. & Mey. Shrub, 1–3m, sparsely branched; twigs resinous and fine-pubesc. or glab. Lvs 2–4cm, ovate-orbicular, coarsely serrate, yellow-green beneath. Fr. catkins 1.5–2cm. E Sib. Z3.

B. *miijimae* Nak. = B. *apoiensis*.

B. *miyoshii* Nak. = B. *apoiensis*.

B. *nana* L. DWARF BIRCH. Shrub, prostrate or ascending, 50cm (–1m), bark dull, brown, pubesc. Lvs 5–15mm, suborbicular to reniform, apex rounded, coarsely crenate except at base, dark green, tinged yellow in autumn, or dark red, viscid when young. Fr. catkins 7–10mm, erect, v. shortly stalked, ovoid. Subarc. Eurasia & Greenland. Z2.

B. *nana* var. *intermedia* Reg. = B. *glandulosa*.

B. *nana* var. *michauxii* (Spach) Reg. = B. *michauxii*.

B. *neoalaskana* (Sarg.) Raup. YUKON WHITE BIRCH. Tree to 15m; bark white to pale brown; young shoots glab., densely warty. Lvs 3–6cm, deltoid- or rhombic-ovate, coarsely biserrate, apex acuminate, glossy dark green above, glab. or thinly pubesc. on veins beneath. Fr. catkins 3cm, cylindric, pendulous. Alask., Yukon. Z1.

B. *nigra* L. BLACK BIRCH; RED BIRCH; RIVER BIRCH. Tree to 20m; bark thick, peeling in shaggy shales, pink-brown on young trees, on older trees v. dark red tinged black; branchlets pubesc., with pale round warts. Lvs 4–9cm, ovate-rhombic, biserrate, glossy green above, somewhat glaucous beneath, yellow in autumn. Fr. catkins 2.5–4cm×12mm, erect, cylindric, pubesc. E US. 'Heritage': vigorous tree; bark peeling, light brown to cream; lvs dark green, glossy. Z4.

B. *occidentalis* Hook. pro parte = B. *fontinalis*.

B. *odorata* Bechst. = B. *pubescens*.

B. *ovalifolia* Rupr. Shrub to 1m, branched; branchlets gland., pubesc. then glab. Lvs 1–3cm, ovate or obovate, serrate, acute gland. and hairy beneath. Fr. catkins 10–15×4–7mm, erect, oblong cylindric. SE Sib., NE China, Korea, Jap. Z5.

B. *papyracea* Ait. = B. *papyrifera*.

B. *papyrifera* Marsh. PAPER BIRCH; WHITE BIRCH; CANOE BIRCH. Tree to 30m, stout-branched, crown open; bark bright white,

dull white or dull grey-brown, smooth, peeling in papery layers; branchlets red-brown, pubesc. later glab., warty. Lvs 4–9cm, broad ovate, acute, coarsely biserrate, ciliate, black glandular-punctate beneath. Fr. catkins 3–4×0.6–0.8cm, pendulous, cylindric. US, Canada, Greenland. Z1. var. *commutata* (Reg.) Fern. Tree to 40m, bark red-brown to orange or off-white, peeling. Lvs 7–10cm, ovate to broad-ovate, biserrate. Catkins 3–4cm. NW US. var. *kenaica* (W.H. Evans) Henry. To 12m; bark fissured at base on old trees. Lvs smaller, 3–5cm, minutely pubesc. above at first. S Alask. Z2. var. *minor* (Tuckerm.) S. Wats. Smaller in all parts.

B. *papyrifera* var. *cordifolia* (Reg.) Fern. = B. *cordifolia*.

B. *papyrifera* var. *humilis* (Reg.) Fern. & Raup = B. *neoalaskana*.

B. *pendula* Roth. SILVER BIRCH; WARTY BIRCH; EUROPEAN WHITE BIRCH; COMMON BIRCH. Tree to 25(–30)m, crown slender, open; bark peeling and silvery white when young, thick, fissured and black with age at base; branchlets pendulous, v. slender, glab. with resinous glands. Lvs 3–7cm, broadly ovate to ovate-deltate or ± rhombic, biserrate, thin, viscid when young, glab., glandular-punctate. Fr. catkins cylindric, 1.5–3.5cm. Eur., Asia Minor. Z2. 'Dalecarlica' SWEDISH BIRCH: tall, slender tree; branchlets drooping; lvs deeply cut. 'Fastigiata': erect, medium-sized tree. 'Golden Cloud': small tree; br. arching; lvs golden. 'Laciniata': similar to 'Dalecarlica' and commonly grown under that name, habit more markedly weeping, lvs not so deeply cut. 'Obelisk': similar to 'Fastigiata', but not becoming so wide. 'Purpurea': slow-growing tree; br. slender, drooping. 'Tristis': crown narrow; br. slender, weeping. 'Youngii': small tree, ultimately dome- or mushroom-headed; br. pendulous. var. *lapponica* (Lindquist) Clarke. Tree to 15m, bark not fissuring at base, white; lvs coriaceous, slightly thicker, coarsely and bluntly toothed. N Scand. to Urals. Z1.

B. *platyphylla* Sukachev. Closely allied to B. *pendula* var. *lapponica*, tree to 20m; crown light and open; bark pure white, not fissuring at base; branchlets thin, dark grey or red tinged, densely white-gland. Lvs 4–6cm, triangular-ovate, apex shortly acuminate, coarsely serrate, glab., brown-glandular-punctate beneath. Fr. catkins 3cm. C & E Sib., Manch., Korea, Jap. Z5. var. *japonica* (Miq.) Hara. Bark white, twigs glandular-warty. Lvs 4–7.5cm, finely pubesc. or glab. beneath. Catkins to 5cm. Jap.

B. *platyphylla* auct. non Sukachev = B. *mandshurica*.

B. *platyphylla* var. *japonica* (Miq.) Hara = B. *mandshurica* var. *japonica*.

B. *platyphylla* var. *szechuanica* (C. Schneid.) Rehd. = B. *szechuanica*.

B. *populifolia* Marshall. GREY BIRCH. Tree 10–20m, often multi-stemmed; bark not peeling, pale grey to white; twigs ± pendulous, bowed, glab., rough and warty. Lvs 5–9cm, triangular to ovate, coarsely biserrate, apex acuminate cuspidate, glossy green, light yellow in fall, gland. above; petiole black-punctate. Fr. catkins 2–3×0.6cm, pendulous, cylindric, pubesc. E N Amer. Z4.

B. *potaninii* Batal. Shrub 2–3m; lower br. often procumbent or prostrate; bark dark, rough; branchlets pale brown-pubesc. then glab. and warty. Lvs 2–5cm, ovate, unevenly biserrate, apex acuminate, glab. above, pilose beneath, particularly on veins. Fr. catkins 2cm, scales with long white gland. apical hairs. W China. Z4.

B. *pubescens* Ehrh. DOWNY BIRCH; WHITE BIRCH. Tree, to 20(–25)m; bark peeling in strips, dull white to pale brown, with dark horizontal lenticels; branchlets ascending, stiff, pubesc., never warty. Lvs 3–6cm, broadly ovate to rhombic, coarsely and unevenly biserrate, apex straight, thin, soft. Fr. catkins 2.5–3cm. C Eur. to W Sib. ssp. *carpatica* (Willd.) Asch. & Graebn. Small tree, forming a densely branched head. ssp. *tortuosa* (Ledeb.) Nyman. Low shrubby tree, trunk contorted, bark brown; lvs small, less downy. Subarc. Eur. Z1.

B. *pumila* L. AMERICAN DWARF BIRCH. Erect shrub to 1(–5)m; twigs densely tomentose or pubesc., not gland. or warty. Lvs 1–3cm, rounded to broadly elliptic or obovate, acute to obtuse coarsely crenate-dentate, tinged white beneath, densely pubesc., to glabrate. Fr. catkins erect, 1.5–2.5cm. NE Amer. Z2.

B. *pumila* var. *borealis* Reg. = B. *borealis*.

B. *pumila* var. *glandulifera* Reg. = B. *glandulifera*.

B. ×*purpusii* Schneid. (B. *alleghaniensis* ×B. *glandulifera*.) Tree or shrub, 3–6m; bark grey-brown, scented of wintergreen; branchlets thinly pubesc., sparsely gland. Lvs 3–6cm, ovate to oblong or elliptic, dull green and glab. above, paler and at first pubesc. beneath, unevenly crenate-serrate. Catkins 1.5–2.8cm. NE US. Z3.

B. *raddeana* Trautv. Small tree or large shrub; bark silvery grey or slightly tinged pink; branchlets pale-warty, densely velvety. Lvs 3–5cm, broadly ovate, coarsely serrate, acute dull green and slightly hairy above. Fr. catkins 2–4cm, erect, ellipsoid. Cauc.

Z5.

B. resinifera (Reg.) Britt., non Royle = *B. neoalaskana*.

B. rockii (Rehd.) Jansson. Small tree; bark white. Closely allied to *B. platyphylla* and *B. szechuanica*. W China.

B. rubra Michx. = *B. nigra*.

B. schmidtii Reg. Tree to 30m, trunk to 2.5m diam.; bark shaggy-scaly, with thick irregular plates, black to dark brown; br. stout, branchlets brown, glandular-pubesc. Lvs 4–8cm, ovate, irregularly serrulate, apex acuminate, rather dull light green. Fr. catkins solitary or paired, erect, stiff, oblong-cylindric, 2.5–3cm. Jap., Korea, Manch. Z5.

B. shikokiana Nak. = *B. ermanii*.

B. solennis Koidz. = *B. grossa*.

B. szechuanica (C. Schneid.) Jansson. Tree to 25m, bark thin, peeling, chalky white and dusty; branchlets dark grey to red-brown with blue-white resinous warts. Lvs to 5–12cm, ovate-cordate to deltoid, serrate, shortly acuminate, tinged blue above, somewhat glaucous beneath, thick, glab., densely gland. beneath. Fr. catkins 3–5cm. W China. Z6.

B. tatewakiana M. Ohki & Watan. = *B. ovalifolia*.

B. terrae-novae Fern. = *B. michauxii*.

B. tortuosa Ledeb. = *B. pubescens* ssp. *tortuosa*.

B. ulmifolia Sieb. & Zucc. = *B. grossa*.

B. utilis D. Don. HIMALAYAN BIRCH. Tree to 20m; bark thin, peeling in horizontal papery flakes, pink to orange brown, bloomed white; twigs red-brown in autumn, gland., pilose. Lvs 5–12cm, ovate, unevenly serrate, apex acuminate, dark green above, paler beneath, golden-yellow in autumn, coriaceous, glab. or sparsely hairy above, hairy on veins beneath. Fr. catkins 2.5–3.5cm, spreading to subpendulous, cylindric. Himal. Z8. var. *jacquemontii* (Spach) Winkl. Bark startling white; shoots and buds resin-free. Kashmir to C Nepal. Z7. var. *prattii* Burkill. Bark glossy red-brown to dark chocolate, not bloomed, peeling in shaggy layers. W China. Z6. var. *occidentalis* (Kitam.) Ashburner & Schilling. Bark white, often duller, tinged grey; shoots, buds and lvs encrusted with white resin. Afghan. to Kashmir. Z7. 'Grayswood Ghost'; 'Jermyns'; 'Inverleith'; 'Sauwala White'; 'Silver Shadow': selected clones with pure unmarked white bark extending from base of bole to smaller br.

B. utilis var. *sinensis* (Franch.) Winkl. = *B. albosinensis*.

B. verrucosa Ehrh. = *B. pendula*.

B. wilsoniana Schneid. = *B. luminifera*.

B. wilsonii Bean = *B. potaninii*.

B. wutaica Mayr = *B. davurica*.

BETULACEAE Gray. 6/150. *Alnus, Betula, Carpinus, Corylus, Ostrya, Ostryopsis*.

Bhutan Cypress *Cupressus himalaica*.
Bhutan Pine *Pinus wallichiana*.

Biarum Schott. Araceae. 15 tuberous perennials. Lvs entire, ovate or elliptic to linear. Peduncle v. short; spathe tubular at base, limb erect or incurved, oblong to oblong-lanceolate; spadix appendix long, foetid above, sweet scented at base. Medit., W Asia. Z8.

B. bovei Bl. Lvs 6–13.5cm, broad-ovate to elliptic. Spathe tube 3–4cm, limb 6–11cm, elongate-lanceolate, brown-green beneath, brown-purple above; spadix to 14cm, appendix slender. Autumn. S Turk., Leb., Isr.

B. carduchorum (Schott) Engl. Lvs 7.5–14cm, ovate to narrow-elliptic. Spathe tube to 6cm, narrow, cylindric, not inflated, exterior brown-purple or dull white, interior purple to deep purple-black, limb to 19cm, lanceolate, green beneath, deep black-purple above; spadix to 20cm, appendix to 17cm, stipitate. Late summer. Turk. to Iran.

B. davisii Turrill. Lvs 4–6.5cm, ovate to obovate-elliptic, obtuse, undulate. Spathe to 8cm, green-white or cream spotted pink-brown or mauve, tube large, squat, limb triangular, acuminate, hooded, strongly incurved; spadix to 7.5cm, appendix to 5cm, dull red-brown. Autumn. Crete, S Turk.

B. eximium (Schott ex Kotschy) Engl. Lvs to 17cm, ovate-oblong to spathulate-elliptic. Spathe tube 3–4cm, exterior green, interior dark purple, limb to 9cm, oblong-ovate, dull purple with small spots beneath, purple-black above; spadix to 12cm, appendix to 8cm. Autumn. S Turk.

B. pyrami (Schott) Engl. Lvs 8–12cm, ovate-elliptic, obtuse. Spathe tube 4–5cm, subspherical, exterior green, interior lilac to dark purple, blotched orange, limb to 20cm, lanceolate, green-purple, blotched or suffused black-purple within; spadix to 25cm, appendix to 21cm. Autumn. S Turk. to Iraq.

B. tenuifolium (L.) Schott. Lvs 5–20cm, linear to oblong or spathulate. Spathe tube to 6cm, cylindric, limb to 30cm, green beneath, black-purple above, lanceolate-acuminate; spadix to 35cm, apppendix to 30cm, purple-black. Autumn or rarely

spring. Port. to Turk. var. *abbreviatum* (Schott) Engl. Spathe limb to 10×5cm, hooded, green; spadix appendix 10cm, emerging nearly horizontally. It., Balk., N Greece.

Biddy Biddy *Acaena novae-zelandiae*.

Bidens L. TICKSEED; BEGGAR'S TICKS; STICK-TIGHT; BUR-MARIGOLD; PITCHFORKS; SPANISH NEEDLES. Compositae. 200 ann. or perenn. herbs or shrubs. St. often branched, terete or 4-angled. Lvs opposite, simple or pinnate, often dentate. Cap. usually radiate, solitary or clustered in a branched, terminal infl.; disc flts usually yellow. Cosmop.

B. atrosanguinea (Hook.) Ortega = *Cosmos atrosanguineus*.

B. aurea (Ait.) Sherff. Perenn. herb to 1m. Lvs to 6cm, simple, linear-lanceolate to elliptic, serrate, or 3–5 partite or 2-pinnate, seg. linear, entire. Cap. to 5cm diam.; ray flts to 3cm, yellow. Autumn. S US to Guat. Z8.

B. bipinnata L. Ann. herb to 1.5cm. Lvs to 5cm, 2–3-pinnate, ovate to lanceolate, dentate, term. seg. deltoid-lanceolate. Cap. to 0.7cm diam.; ray flts pale yellow, inconspicuous. Autumn. E US, E Asia. Z3.

B. connata Muhlenb. Ann. herb to 1.5cm. Lvs to 16cm, connate, 3-partite, seg. lanceolate. Cap. to 2cm diam.; ray flts minute, gold or 0. Autumn. E & N US, Canada. Z3.

B. coronata (L.) Britt. Ann. or bienn. herb to 1.5m. Lvs to 16cm, usually pinnate, lanceolate, incised. Cap. to 6cm diam.; ray flts to 2.5cm, gold. Autumn. US. Z5.

B. dahlioides S. Wats. = *Cosmos diversifolius*.

B. diversifolia hort. ex DC. = *B. serrulata*.

B. ferulifolia (Jacq.) DC. Ann. or perenn. herb to 1m. Lvs to 8cm, finely 1–3-pinnate, glab. or rough, scarious or fleshy. Cap. to 3cm diam.; ray flts to 2cm, gold. Autumn. S US, Mex., Guat. 'Golden Goddess': lvs feathery; cap. to 5cm diam., bright yellow. Z8.

B. formosa E. Greene = *Cosmos bipinnatus*.

B. grandiflora Balb. = *B. serrulata*.

B. humilis HBK = *B. triplinervia* var. *macrantha*.

B. pinnata L. ex Sherff = *B. bipinnata*.

B. procera D. Don = *B. ferulifolia*.

B. serrulata (Poir.) Desf. Ann. herb to 80cm. Lvs to 13cm, 2–3-pinnate or 3–5-partite, seg. ovate-lanceolate, serrate or incised, sparsely ciliate. Cap. to 6cm diam.; ray flts to 3cm, gold. Autumn. Mex. Z8.

B. sulphurea Schultz-Bip. = *Cosmos sulphureus*.

B. tenuifolia Tausch = *B. bipinnata*.

B. trichosperma (Michx.) Britt. = *B. coronata*.

B. tripartita L. Ann. herb to 70cm. Lvs to 10.5cm, lower lanceolate, dentate, upper 3- or 5-partite, seg. ovate or lanceolate. Cap. discoid, to 2cm diam. Temp. Eurasia. Z6.

B. triplinervia Kunth. Perenn. herb to 50cm. Lvs to 7cm, simple, ovate-lanceolate, serrate. Cap. to 2.5cm diam.; ray flts 3cm, yellow. Autumn. Mex. to Ecuad. var. *macrantha* (Wedd.) Sherff. Lvs 5-partite, 2–3-pinnate, term., seg. to 3mm wide, linear. Autumn. Mex. to Arg. Z9.

Bidgee-widgee *Acaena novae-zelandiae*.
Bidi-bidi *Acaena*.

Biebersteinia Stephan. Geraniaceae. 5 gland. perenn. herbs. Lvs pinnatisect. Fls in spikes or pan., regular, 5-merous; sta. 10. Carpels not beaked. Greece to C Asia. Z8.

B. odora Stephan ex Fisch. Aromatic herb to 30cm. Lvs 10×1cm, fern-like, round, lobed, toothed, glandular-hairy. Fls yellow in term. rac. Summer. Pak. to Kashmir.

B. orphanidis Boiss. Rootstock tuberous. Lvs broad, oblong-lanceolate, hairy, 3-pinnatisect, lobes oblong-linear, acute. Fls rose clustered in dense spikes. Early summer. Greece.

Bifrenaria Lindl. Orchidaceae. 16 epiphytic or terrestrial orchids. Pbs ovoid to conical, olive green to yellow, often with a black collar at apex. Lvs solitary, apical, stalked, broad-elliptic, coriaceous. Infl. short, basal, semi-erect; fls waxy, fragrant; tep. spreading, oval; lip trilobed disc, velvety, fleshy, ridged. Spring. S Amer. Z10.

B. atropurpurea (Lodd.) Lindl. Fls to 5 per infl., to 5.5cm diam., damask with a central zone of yellow-cream, lip white or rose. Braz.

B. aurantiaca Lindl. Fls to 4cm diam. to 3 per infl., golden, marked chocolate above, flushed pink-brown below, margins recurved, lip glossy pink-brown with thick, white pubescence. Guyana, Venez., Colomb., Peru, Amaz.

B. harrisoniae (Hook.) Rchb. f. Fls to 7.5cm diam., 1–2 per infl., v. waxy and fragrant, ivory, lip tipped mauve to garnet or blood red, with darker veins and dense pubescence above, disc golden-pubesc. Braz.

B. inodora Lindl. Resembles *B. harrisoniae* except fls sometimes unscented, sep. yellow to lime green, acute, far exceeding pet., lip white, ivory or rose flushed claret. Braz.

B. longicornis Lindl. Fls 2.75cm diam., 1 per infl., light bronze or yellow, marked oxblood, lip ivory edged pale rose; lat. sep. basally fused to form pseudospur to 1cm. Venez., Peru, Amaz.

B. maguirei Schweinf. Fls to 12cm diam., 1–3 on a long-stalked infl. fleshy, ochre, flushed pink beneath, margins becoming revolute, lip white, veined dark purple. Venez.

B. tetragona (Lindl.) Schltr. Fls to 5.5cm diam., 3–4 per infl., green-white to bronze flecked chocolate or maroon, lip suffused violet at base. Braz.

B. tyrianthina (Loud.) Rchb. f. Resembles *B. harrisoniae* except fls to 8.5cm diam., ivory flushed red-mauve towards tips, lip strongly marked amethyst and densely white-pubesc. Braz.

B. wageneri Rchb. f. = *Teuscheria wageneri*.

Bigarade *Citrus aurantium*.
Big Berry Manzanita *Arctostaphylos glauca*.
Big-boy *Lyonia ligustrina*.
Big-bud Hickory *Carya tomentosa*.
Big-cone Douglas Fir *Pseudotsuga macrocarpa*.

Bigelowia DC.
B. douglasii A. Gray = *Chrysothamnus viscidiflorus*.

Big Galleta *Hilaria rigida*.
Big-horned Euphorbia *Euphorbia grandicornis*.
Big-leaf Maple *Acer macrophyllum*.
Big-leaf Podocarp *Podocarpus macrophyllus*.
Big Marigold *Tagetes erecta*.

Bignonia L. Bignoniaceae. 1 everg. vine climbing by 3-fid tendrils. Lfts jugate. Fls 1–5 per cyme; cal. campanulate, lobes 5; cor. to 5cm, funnelform, orange to scarlet, limb bilabiate. N Amer. Z6.
B. aequinoctialis L. = *Cydista aequinoctialis*.
B. apurensis HBK = *Adenocalymma apurense*.
B. australis Ait. = *Pandorea pandorana*.
B. callistigioides Cham. = *Clytostoma callistigioides*.
B. capensis Thunb. = *Tecomaria capensis* ssp. *capensis*.
B. capreolata L. CROSS-VINE; QUARTERVINE; TRUMPET FLOWER. 'Atrosanguinea': lvs narrow, long; fls dark purple, tinted brown.
B. chamberlaynii Sims = *Anemopaegma chamberlaynii*.
B. cherere Lindl. = *Distictis buccinatoria*.
B. chica Humb. & Bonpl. = *Arrabidaea chica*.
B. chinensis Lam. = *Campsis grandiflora*.
B. chrysantha Jacq. = *Tabebuia chrysantha*.
B. chrysoleuca HBK = *Anemopaegma chrysoleucum*.
B. crucigera L. = *B. capreolata*.
B. grandiflora Thunb. = *Campsis grandiflora*.
B. ignea Vell. = *Pyrostegia venusta*.
B. jasminoides hort. non Thunb. = *Pandorea jasminoides*.
B. lactiflora Vahl = *Distictis lactiflora*.
B. linearis Cav. = *Chilopsis linearis*.
B. littoralis HBK = *Arrabidaea littoralis*.
B. magnifica hort. = *Saritaea magnifica*.
B. mollis Vahl = *Arrabidaea mollis*.
B. mollissima HBK = *Arrabidaea mollissima*.
B. muricata HBK = *Pithecoctenium crucigerum*.
B. pallida Lindl. = *Tabebuia pallida*.
B. pandorana Andrews = *Pandorea pandorana*.
B. radicans L. = *Campsis radicans*.
B. rotundata DC. = *Arrabidaea corallina*.
B. rugosa Schdl. = *Anemopaegma rugosum*.
B. spathacea L. = *Dolichandrone spathacea*.
B. speciosa Graham = *Clytostoma callistigioides*.
B. spectabilis Vahl = *Cydista aequinoctialis*.
B. stans L. = *Tecoma stans*.
B. tagliabuana hort. = *Campsis* × *tagliabuana*.
B. tweediana Lindl. = *Macfadyena unguis-cati*.
B. unguis-cati L. = *Macfadyena unguis-cati*.
B. variabilis Jacq. = *Pleonotoma variabilis*.
B. venusta Ker-Gawl. = *Pyrostegia venusta*.
B. violacea hort., non DC. = *Clytostoma callistigioides*.
→*Anostichus, Campsis* and *Doxantha*.

BIGNONIACEAE Juss. 112/725. *Adenocalymma, Amphilophium, Amphitecna, Anemopaegma, Argylia, Arrabidaea, Bignonia, Campsidium, Campsis, Catalpa, Chilopsis,* × *Chitalpa, Clytostoma, Colea, Crescentia, Cuspidaria, Cybistax, Cydista, Delostoma, Deplanchea, Distictis, Dolichandra, Dolichandrone, Eccremocarpus, Fernandoa, Godmania, Incarvillea, Jacaranda, Kigelia, Macfadyena, Mansoa, Markhamia, Millingtonia, Newbouldia, Nyctocalos, Ophiocolea, Oroxylum, Pandorea, Parmentiera, Phryganocydia, Pithecoctenium, Pleonotoma, Po-*

dranea, Pyrostegia, Radermachera, Rhigozum, Saritaea, Sparattosperma, Spathodea, Stereospermum, Stizophyllum, Tabebuia, Tecoma, Tecomanthe, Tecomaria, Tecomella.

Big-pine *Pinus coulteri*.
Bigpod Ceanothus *Ceanothus megacarpus*.
Bigroot *Marah*.
Big Shellbark *Carya laciniosa*.
Big-toothed Aspen *Populus grandidentata*.
Big-toothed Euphorbia *Euphorbia grandidens*.
Big Tree *Sequoiadendron*.
Big-tree Plum *Prunus mexicana*.

Bijlia N.E. Br. Aizoaceae. 1 mat-forming succulent. Lvs in a rosette *c*3cm long, triquetrous, rhombic or cylindric, strongly keeled, tip incurved, grey-green. Fls short-pedicellate, 3.5cm diam., yellow. S Afr. Z10.
B. cana N.E. Br.

Bilberry *Vaccinium membranaceum; V. myrtillus*.

Bilderdykia Dumort.
B. aubertii (L. Henry) Dumort. = *Polygonum aubertii*.
B. baldschuanica (Reg.) Webb = *Polygonum baldschuanicum*.

Billardiera Sm. Pittosporaceae. 8 perenn., everg. vines. Lvs entire, usually lanceolate. Fls solitary, 5-merous, pendulous, yellow or purple. Fr. a berry. Aus. Z8.
B. longiflora Labill. BLUEBERRY. Slender climber to 2m. Lvs 1.5–4.5cm. Fls solitary, 1.5–3.5cm, yellow-green then pink or purple. Fr. to 2.5cm, purple-blue (rarely pink or white, 'Fructualbo'), glossy, oblong-ellipsoid, obscurely lobed. Tasm.

Billbergia Thunb. Bromeliaceae. 54 epiphytic perenn. herbs. Lvs in a tubular or funnel-shaped rosette, serrate, ligulate. Scape term., erect or arching, bracts often conspicuous; axis scurfy; fls tubular. Mex. to N Arg. and Peru. Z9.
B. alfonsi-joannis Reitz. To 60cm. Lvs rigid, spiny-serrate, banded white beneath; lf sheaths scaly, flushed violet. Infl. simple, nodding, white-mealy; bracts pink-red; fls yellow-green. Braz.
B. amabilis Beer = *B. vittata*.
B. amoena (Lodd.) Lindl. To 1m. Lvs sometimes flushed red or mottled white, serrulate. Infl. loosely compound, erect; bracts dark red; fls green. Braz.
B. baraquiniana Lem. = *B. decora*.
B. bicolor Lodd. = *B. pyramidalis*.
B. brasiliensis L.B. Sm. To 1m. Lvs banded white beneath, spiny-toothed. Infl. simple, arching; bracts pink clustered below infl., fls blue or purple, white at base. SE Braz.
B. buchholtzii Mez. Lf rosette funnel-shaped. Infl. simple; bracts bright pink; fls blue. Gdn origin.
B. canterae André = *B. zebrina*.
B. 'Catherine Wilson'. (*B. amoena* var. *viridis* × *B. iridifolia*.) To 45cm. Lvs pale green flushed pink and splashed cream. Bracts rose; fls green and blue.
B. chiapensis Matuda. To 1m. Lvs linear-triangular, densely pale grey-scaly, laxly toothed. Infl. simple, arching, tomentose; bracts leathery; fls papery, conspicuously veined. Mex.
B. chlorosticta hort. Saund. RAINBOW PLANT. To 50cm. Lvs mottled creamy-white, red-brown beneath, toothed. Infl. simple, arching; bracts large, red; fls green-yellow tipped blue. Braz.
B. croyana De Jonghe ex Lem. = *B. pyramidalis*.
B. decora Poepp. & Endl. To 80cm. Lvs banded white beneath, sometimes spotted yellow, laxly toothed, spines stout. Infl. pendent, scurfy; bracts large, bright pink; fls pale green. Peru, Braz., Boliv.
B. distachya (Vell.) Mez. To 40–60cm. Lvs narrowly triangular, ± serrulate, flushed purple, in a cylindric or bulbous-based rosette. Infl. lax, arching, short-branched; bracts pink; fls few, pale green, tipped blue. E Braz. var. *straussiana* (Wittm.) L.B. Sm. Pet. entirely pale green, sep. tipped blue. Braz.
B. elegans Mart. ex Schult. f. To 45cm. Lvs light green, toothed. Infl. simple, arching, densely mealy; bracts large, pink; fls pale green tipped purple or dark blue. Braz.
B. euphemiae E. Morr. To 80cm. Lvs in an upright tubular rosette, grey-green banded silver, toothed. Infl. sparse, nodding; scape pink, scaly; bracts pale pink; fls blue. S Braz. var. *purpurea* M.B. Fost. Lvs red-purple, not banded. var. *saundersoides* L.B. Sm. Lvs longer and narrower, spotted white and pink.
B. 'Fantasia'. (*B. pyramidalis* × *B. saundersii*.) Lvs to 30cm, densely blotched cream. Bracts red; fls violet-red.
B. farinosa Lindl. & Hoffsgg. = *B. zebrina*.

B. fosteriana L.B. Sm. Lvs pale-scaly, banded grey beneath, un-armed. Infl. erect, floccose; bracts pink, fading to yellow; sep. lavender; pet. blue-green at apex. Braz.

B. 'Gerda'. (*B. horrida* × *B. amoena*.) Lvs banded white. Infl. open.

B. 'Henry Teuscher'. (*B. pyramidalis* × *B. venezuelana*.) Lvs thick, silver-grey. Bracts rose.

B. horrida Reg. To 50cm. Lvs dark, broadly banded grey or white, conspicuously spiny-toothed. Infl. simple, crowded, glab.; bracts long, dark brown, becoming green; fls nocturnally fragrant, pale green, apex dark blue. CE Braz. var. *tigrina* hort. ex Bak. Lvs maroon strongly banded white.

B. ianthina hort. ex E. Morr. = *B. braziliensis*.

B. iridifolia (Nees & Mart.) Lindl. To 30cm. Lvs in a tubular ros-ette, silver-scaly, serrulate to subentire. Infl. simple, lax, nodding, axis red, glab.; sep. red tipped dark blue; pet. pale yellow tipped blue. var. *concolor* L.B. Sm. Pet. pale yellow throughout.

B. leptopoda L.B. Sm. To 40cm. Lvs pale-blotched, scaly be-neath, laxly toothed, apex curled back; sheaths pale violet. Infl. lax; bracts pink; fls green, tipped dark blue. Braz.

B. liboniana De Jonghe = *Quesnelia liboniana*.

B. lietzei E. Morr. To 25cm. Lvs elliptic-ligulate, blotched yellow, laxly toothed. Infl. simple, erect; sep. red; pet. chartreuse green, tipped blue. Braz.

B. macrocalyx Hook. To 1m. Lvs spotted or banded silver, scaly beneath, toothed. Infl. erect, mealy; bracts red clustered below fls; pet. pale green edged violet-blue. Braz.

B. macrolepis L.B. Sm. To 1m+. Lvs spotted white or grey be-neath, sparsely toothed. Infl. many-fld, scurfy; scape red, floccose, arching; fls bronze-green. Costa Rica to Venez.

B. meyeri Mez. To 1m+. Lvs in a tubular rosette, banded silver and white, laxly toothed, channelled. Infl. arching, simple, white-mealy; bracts rose-pink clustered below fls; floral bracts large, violet; fls green or green-white, tipped blue. Boliv., Braz.

B. minarum L.B. Sm. To 40cm+. Lvs linear, spotted cream, scurfy beneath, short-toothed. Infl. nodding-pendent, short-branched; bracts red to pink; fls green tipped blue. Braz.

B. morelii Brongn. To 60cm. Lvs densely toothed. Infl. simple, arching, scurfy; scape red; bracts large, brilliant red; sep. pink-red; pet. pale green, tipped lilac to dark blue. E Braz.

B. 'Muriel Waterman'. (*B. horrida* var. *tigrina* × *B. euphemiae* var. *purpurea*.) Lvs plum banded silver. Bracts dull pink; fls metallic blue.

B. nutans H. Wendl. ex Reg. FRIENDSHIP PLANT; QUEEN'S TEARS. To 40cm, suckering. Lvs narrow, scaly beneath, entire to toothed. Infl. simple, arching; bracts slender, rose-pink, over-lapping; fls pale yellow-green, banded or edged violet-blue. var. *nutans* Lvs toothed. Pet. tipped green. S Braz., Parag., Urug., N Arg. var. *schimperiana* (Wittm. ex Bak.) Mez. Lvs entire. Pet. tipped violet-blue. S Braz., Parag.

B. pallescens Bak. = *B. distachya* var. *straussiana*.

B. pallida (Ker-Gawl.) Beer = *B. amoena*.

B. pallidiflora Liebm. To 70cm. Lvs tinged red, banded silver, spiny-toothed. Infl. simple, many-fld, arching; bracts pale pink, densely overlapping; fls green to golden brown. Mex. to Nic.

B. porteana Brongn. ex Beer. To 1m+. Lvs banded beneath, oft. blotched yellow, with dark spiny teeth. Infl. simple, arching to pendent, scurfy; bracts bright pink, papery; fls green or yellow-green. Braz., Parag. Z8.

B. pyramidalis (Sims) Lindl. To 60cm. Lvs oft. flushed purple, banded white beneath, scaly, laxly toothed. Infl. erect pyramidal, corymbose, scurfy; bracts bright rose-pink; fls bright red or orange-pink, sometimes tipped kingfisher blue. E Braz. var. *concolor* L.B. Sm. Fls wholly red. Gdn origin.

B. quintusiana hort. Makoy ex Wittm. = *B. macrocalyx*.

B. reichardtii Wawra. To 80cm. Lvs with broad pale bands be-neath, laxly toothed. Infl. compound, few-fld, arching to pendent, glabrate; bracts red, papery; fls yellow or green tipped dark blue. Braz.

B. rosea hort. ex Beer. To 1m+. Lvs scurfy, spiny-toothed. Infl. simple, many-fld, scurfy; bracts rose-pink; fls lime-green, pet. spirally recurved. Venez., Trin.

B. roseomarginata K. Koch = *Quesnelia quesneliana*.

B. sanderiana E. Morr. To 60cm. Lvs to 40cm, in a slender funnel with sharp, black marginal teeth. Infl. compound, arching to pendent; bracts broad, lavender-pink; sep. green tipped blue; pet. yellow-green tipped violet. Braz.

B. saundersii hort. Bull ex K. Koch = *B. chlorosticta*.

B. seidelii L.B. Sm. & Reitz. To 70cm. Lvs in a tubular rosette, banded white beneath, scaly, laxly toothed. Infl. compound, few-fld, subglabrous; bracts rose-pink, scaly, rolled into a cylinder; fls green tipped indigo. Braz.

B. setosa hort. ex Bak. = *B. pyramidalis*.

B. splendida Lem. = *B. pyramidalis*.

B. thyrsoidea Mart. ex Schult. f. = *B. pyramidalis*.

B. tweedieana Bak. To 2m, in dense clusters. Lvs white-scaly, toothed, caudate. Infl. erect, few-fld, laxly paniculate, floccose; bracts rose-pink, papery; fls pale green tipped pale blue. Braz.

B. venezuelana Mez. To 1m+. Lvs 1m, spotted dark maroon, banded cream or silver, scaly beneath, densely and darkly toothed. Infl. simple, pendent, scurfy; bracts bright pink, scaly; fls chartreuse green tipped violet-blue, pet. spirally recurved. Venez.

B. viridiflora H. Wendl. To 60cm. Lvs scaly, oft. banded white beneath and tinted purple, spiny. Infl. simple, arching, scurfy; bracts large, bright red, papery; fls green. S Mex., Guat., Belize.

B. vittata Brongn. ex Morel. To 90cm. Lvs olive green to maroon, oft. spotted or banded white, serrulate or spiny. Infl. compound, narrowly pyramidal, glab.; bracts bright red, rose-pink or orange; sep. orange-red tipped blue; pet white or pale green tipped dark blue. E Braz.

B. wetherellii Hook. = *B. morelii*.

B. × *windii* hort. Makoy ex E. Morr. (*B. decora* × *B. nutans*.) Lvs obscurely banded grey beneath. Infl. pendent; bracts flamingo pink to dark rose; fls green edged red, tipped blue-green. Gdn origin.

B. zebrina (Herb.) Lindl. To 1m. Lvs banded silver or white, sometimes bronze-purple, scaly, laxly toothed. Infl. simple, dense, arching to pendent, scurfy; bracts pink, papery; fls green becoming yellow. SE Braz., Parag., Urug., NE Arg.
→*Bromelia*.

Billy Buttons *Craspedia* (*C. uniflora*).

× **Biltanthus** hort. = × *Cryptbergia*.

Biltmore Ash *Fraxinus biltmoreana*.
Bimble Box *Eucalyptus populnea*.
Bimli *Hibiscus cannabinus*.
Bindweed *Calystegia* (*C. sepium*); *Convolvulus*.
Bine *Humulus lupulus*.

Binghamia Britt. & Rose.
B. acrantha (Vaupel) Britt. & Rose = *Haageocereus limensis*.
B. melanostele (Vaupel) Britt. & Rose = *Espostoa melanostele*.
B. pseudomelanostele (Werderm. & Backeb.) Backeb. = *Haageo-cereus multangularis*.

Bingliu *Polyscias nodosa*.

Biophytum DC. Oxalidaceae. 50–75 ann. or perenn. herbs or dwarf shrubs. Lvs in term. tufts, pinnate, touch-sensitive; lfts oblong. Fls 5-merous, in stalked, involucrate pseudoumbels, white, pink, yellow or orange. Pantrop. Z10.
B. cumingianum (Turcz.) Edgw. = *B. sensitivum*.
B. dendroides (HBK) DC. Perenn. herb to 35cm, becoming branched, woody. Lvs 2–7cm, lfts in 9–16 pairs, overlapping, hairy, decreasing in size toward base. Fls to 1cm diam., pink to lavender, to 7 per infl. S Amer.
B. sensitivum (L.) DC. Ann. to 35cm; st. smooth, simple. Lvs 3–7cm, lfts in 7–14 pairs, folding when touched, rarely overlap-ping, ± glab., decreasing in size toward base. Fls *c*1cm diam. yellow below, purple veined yellow above, to 10 per infl. SE Asia.
→*Oxalis*.

Biota Endl.
B. orientalis (L. f.) Endl. = *Platycladus orientalis*.

Birch *Betula*.
Birch-bark Tree *Prunus serrula*.
Bird-catcher Tree *Pisonia umbellifera*.
Bird Cherry *Prunus avium*; *P. cornuta*; *P. padus*; *P. pensylvanica*.
Bird-of-paradise *Caesalpinia gilliesii*; *Strelitzia reginae*.
Bird-on-the-wing *Polygala paucifolia*.
Birdseed Grass *Phalaris canariensis*.
Bird's-eye *Veronica chamaedrys*.
Bird's-eye Bush *Ochna serrulata*.
Bird's-eye Primrose *Primula farinosa*.
Bird's-eye Primula *Primula* section *Aleuritia*.
Birds Eyes *Gilia tricolor*.
Bird's-foot Euphorbia *Euphorbia ornithopus*.
Bird's-foot Fern *Pellaea mucronata*.
Bird's-foot Ivy *Hedera helix*.
Bird's-foot Sedge *Carex ornithopoda*.
Bird's-foot Trefoil *Lotus corniculatus*.
Bird's-foot Violet *Viola pedata*.
Birds-nest Bromeliad *Nidularium innocentii*.
Bird's-nest Fern *Asplenium australasicum*; *A. nidus*; *A. serratum*.
Bird Vetch *Vicia cracca*.

Birthroot *Trillium.*
Birthwort *Aristolochia clematitis.*

Bischofia Bl. Euphorbiaceae. 1 everg. or decid. tree to 30m. Lvs trifoliolate; lfts 5–15cm, ovate-acuminate, serrulate, bronze-green. Fls small, apetalous, unisexual, green, racemose. Fr. to 1.5cm diam., berry-like, yellow, bronze, blue-black or red. Trop. Asia. Z10.
B. javanica Blume.

Biscochito *Ruprechtia coriacea.*

Biscutella L. Cruciferae. 40 herbs or small shrubs. Lvs in basal rosettes and on st., oblong, entire, toothed or pinnatifid. Fls 4-merous, yellow, in corymbose rac. Fr. a flattened silicle. C & S Eur., Asia Minor. Z8.
B. frutescens Coss. To 50cm, white-tomentose. Basal lvs 20×6cm, ovate, wavy, toothed; st. lvs sessile. Infl. much branched; pet. 4mm. Fr. 7×3.5mm. SW Spain, Balearic Is.
B. laevigata L. BUCKLER MUSTARD. To 70cm. Basal lvs 1.5–13×0.3–2cm, linear to ovate-lanceolate, glab. to hairy; st. lvs resembling rosette lvs. Pet. 4–8mm. Fr. 8–14×4–8mm. SE Eur.
B. megalocarpa Fisch. ex DC. = *Megacarpaea megalocarpa.*
B. suffrutescens Willk. = *B. frutescens.*

Bishop Pine *Pinus muricata.*
Bishop's Cap *Mitella.*
Bishop's Hat *Astrophytum; Epimedium.*
Bishop's Mitre *Epimedium.*
Bishop's Weed *Aegopodium podagraria.*
Bishop's Wort *Stachys officinalis.*
Bistort *Polygonum bistorta.*

Bistorta (L.) Adans.
B. affinis (D. Don) Greene = *Polygonum affine.*
B. amplexicaulis (D. Don) Greene = *Polygonum amplexicaule.*
B. bistortoides (Pursh) Small = *Polygonum bistortoides.*
B. emodi (Meissn.) Hara = *Polygonum emodi.*
B. griffithii (Hook. f.) Grierson = *Polygonum griffithii.*
B. macrophylla (D. Don) Soják = *Polygonum macrophyllum.*
B. major Gray = *Polygonum bistorta.*
B. milletii Lév. = *Polygonum milletii.*
B. tenuicaulis (Bisset & Moore) Nak. = *Polygonum tenuicaule.*
B. vacciniifolia (Wallich ex Meissn.) Greene = *Polygonum vacciniifolium.*
B. vivipara (L.) Gray = *Polygonum viviparum.*

Biting Stonecrop *Sedum acre.*
Bitter Apple *Citrullus colocynthis.*
Bitter Bark *Pinckneya pubens.*
Bitter Bloom *Sabatia angularis.*
Bitter Cassava *Manihot esculenta.*
Bittercress *Barbarea vulgaris; Cardamine.*
Bitter Cucumber *Momordica charantia.*
Bitter Gourd *Momordica charantia.*
Bitter Melon *Momordica.*
Bitternut *Carya cordiformis.*
Bitter Orange *Citrus aurantium; Poncirus trifoliata.*
Bitter Peas *Daviesia.*
Bitter Pecan *Carya aquatica.*
Bitterroot *Lewisia rediviva.*
Bitter Sneezeweed *Helenium amarum.*
Bittersweet *Celastrus; Solanum dulcamara.*
Bitter Vetch *Vicia orobus.*
Bitterweed *Helenium amarum; Picris.*
Bitterwood *Lonchocarpus; Quassia amara.*

Bixa L. Bixaceae. 1 tree to 7m. Branching intricate. Lvs to 20cm, broadly ovate, long-acuminate, entire. Pan. term., 5-fld; fls to 5cm diam., pet. 5, to 2.5cm, obovate, spreading, pink or white tinged purple. Fr. to 5cm, an ovoid capsule, chestnut to sealing-wax red, strigose. Trop. Amer. Z10.
B. orellana L. ANNATTO; LIPSTICK TREE; ACHIOTE.

BIXACEAE Link. 3/16. *Bixa, Cochlospermum.*

Black Alder *Ilex verticillata.*
Black Apricot *Prunus ×dasycarpa.*
Black Ash *Fraxinus nigra.*
Black Bamboo *Phyllostachys nigra.*
Black Bead *Pithecellobium keyense.*
Black Bean *Kennedia nigricans.*
Blackbean Tree *Castanospermum australe.*
Black Bearberry *Arctostaphylos alpina.*
Blackbeard *Pithecellobium unguis-cati.*

Black Beech *Nothofagus solanderi.*
Blackberry *Rubus.*
Blackberry Lily *Belamcanda chinensis.*
Black Birch *Betula nigra.*
Black Box *Eucalyptus largiflorens.*
Black Boy *Xanthorrhoea preisii.*
Blackbutt *Eucalyptus pilularis.*
Black Calabash *Amphitecna latifolia.*
Black Caladium *Colocasia esculenta.*
Blackcap *Rubus occidentalis.*
Black Caterpillar Fern *Davallia plumosa; Scyphularia pentaphylla.*
Black Cherry *Prunus serotina.*
Black Chokeberry *Aronia melanocarpa.*
Black Cohosh *Cimicifuga racemosa.*
Black Coral Pea *Kennedia nigricans.*
Black Cottonwood *Populus trichocarpa.*
Black Crowberry *Empetrum nigrum.*
Black Cumin *Nigella sativa.*
Black Currant *Ribes nigrum.*
Black Cypress-pine *Callitris endlicheri.*
Black Elder *Sambucus nigra.*
Black-eyed Pea *Vigna unguiculata.*
Black-eyed Sundew *Drosera platystigma.*
Black-eyed Susan *Rudbeckia hirta; Thunbergia alata.*
Black False Hellebore *Veratrum nigrum.*
Blackfoot Daisy *Melampodium.*
Black Fritillary *Fritillaria biflora.*
Black-gold Philodendron *Philodendron melanochrysum.*
Black Gum *Eucalyptus aggregata; Nyssa sylvatica.*
Black Haw *Bumelia lanuginosa; Viburnum prunifolium.*
Black Henbane *Hyoscyamus niger.*
Black Highbush Blueberry *Vaccinium atrococcum.*
Black Horehound *Ballota nigra.*
Black Huckleberry *Gaylussacia baccata; Vaccinium atrococcum.*
Black Ironwood *Olea capensis.*
Black Italian Poplar *Populus ×canadensis.*
Blackjack Oak *Quercus marilandica.*
Black Jessie *Pithecellobium unguis-cati.*
Black Juniper *Juniperus wallichiana.*
Black-leaf Panamica *Pilea repens.*
Black Locust *Robinia pseudoacacia.*
Black Lovage *Smyrnium olusatrum.*
Black Mallee *Eucalyptus stellulata.*
Black Maple *Acer saccharum.*
Black Marlock *Eucalyptus redunca.*
Black Medick *Medicago lupulina.*
Black Mulberry *Morus nigra.*
Black Mustard *Brassica nigra.*
Black Nightshade *Solanum nigrum.*
Black Oak *Quercus velutina.*
Black Palm *Normanbya.*
Black Parsley *Melanoselinum decipiens.*
Black Pea *Lathyrus niger.*
Black Pepper *Piper nigrum.*
Black Pine *Pinus nigra.*
Black Poplar *Populus nigra.*
Black Raspberry *Rubus occidentalis.*
Blackroot *Veronicastrum virginicum.*
Black Roseau *Bactris major.*
Black Rosewood *Dalbergia latifolia.*
Black Sally *Eucalyptus stellulata.*
Black Sarana *Fritillaria camschatcensis.*
Black Snakeroot *Cimicifuga racemosa.*
Black Spleenwort *Asplenium adiantum-nigrum.*
Black Spruce *Picea mariana.*
Black Stem *Blechnum nudum.*
Black-stem Spleenwort *Asplenium resiliens.*
Blackthorn *Crataegus calpodendron; Prunus spinosa.*
Black Titi *Cyrilla racemiflora.*
Black Tree Fern *Cyathea medullaris.*
Black Walnut *Juglans nigra.*
Black Wattle *Acacia auriculiformis; A. mearnsii; Callicoma serratifolia.*
Black Widow *Geranium phaeum.*
Black Willow *Salix nigra.*
Blackwood *Acacia melanoxylon.*
Bladder Cherry *Physalis alkekengi.*
Bladder Fern *Cystopteris.*
Bladder Ketmia *Hibiscus trionum.*
Bladdernut *Staphylea (S. pinnata).*
Bladder Pod *Lesquerella; Physaria.*
Bladder Sage *Salazaria.*
Bladder Senna *Colutea arborescens.*
Bladderwort *Utricularia.*
Blaeberry *Vaccinium myrtillus.*

Blancoa Bl.
B. caudata (Lour.) Kuntze = *Arenga caudata.*

Blandfordia Sm. CHRISTMAS BELLS. Liliaceae (Blandfordiaceae). 4 rhizomatous, perenn. herbs. Lvs grass-like, triquetrous. Rac. term.; pedicels recurved; perianth funnelform to campanulate, seg. 6. E Aus., Tasm. Z9.
B. aurea Hook. f. = *B. grandiflora.*
B. cunninghamii Lindl. To 85cm. Lvs smooth-margined. Fls 5–20 in a dense rac.; perianth +5cm, copper red, stained red at base, lobes 3.5mm, yellow. NSW.
B. flammea Lindl. ex Paxt. = *B. grandiflora.*
B. grandiflora R. Br. To 60cm. Lvs minutely crenulate. Fls 7–10 in a loose rac.; perianth 4–6cm, red with yellow lobes to entirely yellow. Spring–early summer. Queensld, NSW.
B. marginata Herb. = *B. punicea.*
B. nobilis Sm. 40–70cm. Lvs v. finely toothed. Fls 3–15 in a loose rac.; perianth 2–3cm, copper red to orange, often stained yellow, to entirely yellow. Spring–early summer. NSW.
B. princeps W.G. Sm. = *B. grandiflora.*
B. punicea (Labill.) Sweet. TASMANIAN CHRISTMAS BELLS. 80–100cm. Lvs somewhat ligulate, finely toothed. Fls 15–25, in a loose rac.; perianth pink-scarlet, interior yellow, lobes tipped golden yellow. Summer. Tasm.

Blanket Flower *Gaillardia pulchella.*
Blaxland's Stringybark *Eucalyptus blaxlandii.*
Blazing Star *Chamaelirion luteum*; *Liatris*; *Mentzelia livicaulis.*

Blechnaceae (C. Presl) Copel. 9 genera. *Blechnum, Doodia, Sadleria, Stenochlaena* and *Woodwardia.*

Blechnum L. HARD FERN. Blechnaceae. 200 terrestrial or epiphytic ferns. Rhiz. erect, or running. Fronds often emerging red, bronze or pink, mostly 1-pinnate. Cosmop. Z9 unless specified.
B. alpina Mett. = *B. penna-marina.*
B. ambiguum (Presl) Kaulf. ex C. Chr. Rhiz. short-creeping, thick. Sterile fronds 3–15×1–2.5cm; pinnae obliquely truncate and short-stalked at base, entire or serrulate, those of fertile fronds narrower. NSW.
B. atherstonii Pappe & Raws = *B. punctulatum.*
B. attenuatum (Sw.) Mett. CLIMBING BLECHNUM. Rhiz. creeping, often ascending, long. Sterile frond blades 50–100×10–30cm, pinnatisect, pinnate at base, broadly lanceolate, v. attenuate below, pinnae c15–23×1–1.5cm, becoming gradually smaller downwards; fertile fronds 6–10×0.1–1.5cm, with pinnae more remote, sessile, linear, apiculate or acuminate. NSW, NZ, Norfolk Is., Polyn., Chile.
B. auriculatum Cav. Rhiz. stout, short, scaly. Fronds to 70cm, rigid, pinnate, bright green, coriaceous; pinnae of sterile fronds ± sessile, deltoid-lanceolate, acute, auricled at base, fertile pinnae narrower, with large auricles at base. S Braz. to Arg.
B. australe L. Rhiz. creeping, slender, scaly. Fronds 22–50×2–7cm, lanceolate; sterile pinnae 4×1cm, numerous, spreading, linear, hastate-cordate or auricled at base, coriaceous; fertile pinnae narrower. Natal to Réunion, Madag.
B. banksii (Hook. f.) Diels. Rhiz. erect or inclined, stout, short. Sterile fronds 5–45×1–4cm, narrowly elliptic, dark green, pinnatisect, lobes 12×6mm, spreading, oblong, lower pinnae reduced; fertile fronds shorter than sterile, pinnae narrower, straight or curved, shorter, rather far apart; stipes v. short. NZ.
B. blechnoides (Lagasca) Sw. Rhiz. decumbent to erect, stoloniferous, slender. Fronds 60×6cm, erect, linear to narrowly elliptic, deeply pinnatisect; middle seg. narrowly oblong; stipes much shorter than blades. Greater Antilles, Jam., Martinique, Mex. to S Braz.
B. boreale Sw. = *B. spicant.*
B. brasiliense Desv. Trunk erect, stout, to 30cm+. Fronds 90×30cm, oblong-lanceolate, narrowing gradually downwards; pinnae 10–15×1.5cm, close, erecto-patent, linear, narrowed gradually toward point, v. finely dentate, coriaceous, glab. Braz., Peru.
B. camfieldii Tind. LANCE WATER FERN. Rhiz. erect, scaly, forming a short trunk, producing short stolons. Frond blades 60–100cm (2× length of stipe), ovate-lanceolate; sterile pinnae short-stalked, lower ones auricle-like, much reduced, fertile pinnae auriculate at base. Queensld, NSW.
B. capense (L.) Schldl. COMMON KIOKI. Rhiz. short-creeping, scaly. Frond blade elliptic, 20–250×8–60cm (equalling stipes); pinnae 5–35cm, oblong to linear, acuminate, auricle-like toward base of blade. Fertile fronds narrower. NZ.
B. cartilagineum Sw. Rhiz. short-creeping, stoloniferous. Fronds 60–90×15–30cm, ovate-oblong; pinnae 10–15×1.2cm, elongate-triangular to linear, finely dentate, fertile pinnae slightly narrower than sterile. Philipp., Aus.

B. chilense (Kaulf.) Mett. = *B. cordatum.*
B. cognatum Presl = *B. australe.*
B. colensoi (Hook. f.) Wakef. Rhiz. short-creeping, short. Frond blades to 90cm, equalling or far exceeding stipes, pendulous, entire, lobed or pinnatifid, dark green, smooth, shining, v. coriaceous; sterile pinnules 5–13×2.5–5cm, remote, linear-lanceolate, falcate, acuminate, often serrate at tip, decurrent; fertile frond pinnules v. slender. NZ, Java, India, Malay and Pacific Is.
B. corcovadense var. *crispum* Raddi = *B. brasiliense.*
B. cordatum (Desv.) Hieron. Rhiz. long-creeping with numerous dark scales. Frond blades ovate-lanceolate, coriaceous; sterile pinnae alt., oblong, apex acute, base auriculate, serrate; fertile pinnae linear-lanceolate, acuminate, base cordate. Chile, Arg. Z8.
B. cycadoides (Pappe & Raws) Kuhn = *B. tabulare.*
B. dalgairnsiae (Pappe & Raws) Kuhn = *B. tabulare.*
B. discolor (Forst.) Keys. CROWN FERN. Rhiz. ascending to 60cm, stout, producing stolons at base. Frond blades 90×5–15cm, dimorphic, gradually tapering at both ends, stiff; sterile lobes spreading, cut nearly to rachis, fertile lobes narrower and shorter than sterile, free. NZ.
B. durum (Moore) C. Chr. Rhiz. erect, stout, sometimes forming a short trunk. Sterile frond blades pinnatisect, 30–75×3–10cm, v. gradually narrowed to the base, dark green, fleshy to tough, lowest pinnae lobe-like, median pinnae oblong-subfalcate, upper pinnae narrower; fertile fronds shorter and narrower than sterile. NZ. Z6.
B. elongatum Mett. = *B. patersonii.*
B. filiforme (A. Cunn.) Ettingsh. THREAD FERN. Rhiz. branched, stout, long. Sterile fronds ovate-lanceolate, those on lower part of creeping rhiz. 8–15×1–2.5cm, deeply dentate, those above pendulous, 30–75×7.5–15cm, green to dark green, stiff, pinnae linear; fertile fronds ovate, pinnae 7.5–15×0.3cm, linear; stipes distant, to 10cm. NZ, Fiji.
B. fluviatile (R. Br.) Salom. RAY WATER FERN. Rhiz. semi-erect, forming a short stout trunk. Sterile fronds in a low rosette, 30–75×2–4cm, linear, dark green to olive-green, pinnae 12–20×6–10mm, oblong; fertile fronds erect, pinnae strongly ascending, 5–15×3mm, linear-oblong; stipes 2–8cm. Vict., Tasm., NZ.
B. fraseri (A. Cunn.) Luers. Rhiz. erect, elongated into caudex to 75cm, stoloniferous. Fronds 30–45×10–15cm, ovate, acuminate, 2-pinnatifid, dark green, glistening; pinnae linear-lanceolate; pinnules linear-oblong, slightly dentate, bases decurrent on rachis as a pinnatifid wing with triangular lobes; fertile pinnules slightly narrower; stipes 15cm. NZ. Z8.
B. fraxineum Willd. Rhiz. creeping, slender. Fronds 30×20cm, pinnate; pinnae 7.5–10×1cm, 3–8 pairs, strongly curved, narrowed gradually towards apex, coriaceous, glab.; stipes to 30cm. Trop. Amer. Z10.
B. germainii (Hook.) Christ. Rhiz. elongated. Sterile fronds 5–7.5×2–2.5cm, oblong-lanceolate; pinnae overlapping, linear-obtuse, crenate; fertile pinnae, nearly as broad; stipe to 5cm. Chile, Braz.
B. gibbum (Labill.) Mett. MINIATURE TREE FERN. Trunk erect, to 90cm high, narrow, black, rooting. Sterile fronds 90×30cm, oblong-lanceolate, pinnatisect, seg. 10–15×0.5cm, entire, dilated and connected at base; fertile pinnae 10–15×0.3cm, v. numerous, ± erect. Fiji.
B. glandulosum Link. Similar to *B. occidentale* but smaller, pinnae ovate-oblong. Mex., Venez.
B. gregsonii (Watts) Tind. Rhiz. creeping. Pinnae v. shortly and distinctly stalked, or articulated, rounded or slightly auriculate at base, pale green, shiny, fertile pinnae slightly narrower. NSW.
B. hastatum Kaulf. = *B. auriculatum.*
B. indicum Burm. f. Rhiz. short and thick or longer and creeping. Fronds 30–60×15–22cm, oblong-acuminate; pinnae 10–13×1cm, 12–24 pairs, articulate, linear-oblong, obtuse or occas. abruptly acute, narrowed gradually towards base and apex, serrulate, smooth, coriaceous; stipe to 15cm. Amer., Asia, Trop. Aus.
B. longifolium HBK = *B. fraxineum.*
B. magellanicum (Hook.) Mett. Rhiz. trunk-like, to 30cm, dark brown. Sterile fronds to 30cm, erect, ovate-oblong, pinnae linear-oblong, sessile, base truncate, cordate, or auricled, dark green above, rufescent beneath; fertile fronds oblong, obtuse, pinnae v. closely spaced, broad-linear, sessile; stipe to 30cm. Tierra del Fuego, Falkland Is.
B. membranaceum (Colenso) Mett. Rhiz. erect, stout, short. Sterile fronds, 6–25×1–4cm, narrow-oblong, membranous, smooth; pinnae suborbicular-oblong, obtuse, toothed; fertile fronds usually longer than sterile, pinnae distant, narrow. NZ.
B. meridionale Presl = *B. glandulosum.*
B. minus (R. Br.) Ettingsh. Rhiz. short-creeping. Sterile frond

blade equalling stipe, 10–65×4–20cm; sterile pinnae in 5–20 pairs, 2–10×0–6–1.3cm, oblong, much reduced toward base; fertile blade usually larger than sterile blade, erect, pinnae narrower. Aus., NZ.

B. nigrum (Colenso) Mett. Rhiz. erect, stout, short. Sterile fronds 10–15×2.5–4cm spreading, linear-oblong, black-green or lurid-green, lobes 3–12, 0.8–3–5×0.6–2.5cm, round-oblong; fertile fronds few, erect, pinnae distant. NZ.

B. niponicum (Kunze) Mak. Rhiz. erect, stout, short, densely scaly. Sterile fronds, 20–30×5–8cm, oblanceolate to oblong-oblanceolate, apex abruptly contracted to a narrow tail to 2cm, pinnae 3–10×3–7mm, broadly linear, obtuse or subobtuse, entire; fertile pinnae 15–30×2–3mm, distant, linear, obtuse. Jap.

B. norfolkianum (Heward) C. Chr. Rhiz. erect, stout, short, scaly. Sterile fronds 30–90×7.5–15cm, numerous, erect or spreading, forming a large crown, tapering from the middle to both ends, dark green, subcoriaceous, pinnae oblong-lanceolate, straight to subfalcate; fertile fronds to 15cm, widely spaced; stipes to 10cm, black. Norfolk Is.

B. nudum (Labill.) Mett. ex Luerss. FISHBONE WATER FERN; BLACK-STEM. Rhiz. erect, sometimes forming a sturdy trunk. Sterile frond blades dimorphic, 40–100×10–25cm, fertile blades 20–70×5–12cm, lanceolate-ovate, apex attenuate, stiffly erect; stipes short, glossy black. W Aus., Tasm.

B. occidentale L. HAMMOCK FERN. Rhiz. erect or ascending, slender to rather stout, usually stoloniferous. Fronds 23–45×10–20cm, ascending or spreading, pinnate at base, pinnatisect distally, linear-oblong or lanceolate to narrowly deltate, widest at base; pinnae 12–24, linear-oblong or v. narrowly deltate, apex obtuse or acuminate, base subcordate and sometimes dilated. Trop. Amer., W Indies, Chile.

B. occidentale var. *minor* L. = *B. glandulosum*.

B. orientale L. Rhiz. erect, stout, scaly at crown. Fronds 50–100×20–40cm, oblong-acuminate; pinnae numerous, oblong-lanceolate, acuminate, entire, cordate at base, coriaceous, glab.; stipe to 50cm, grooved, rusty. Aus. and Polyn., S China to Himal.

B. parvifolium (Colenso) C. Chr. = *B. penna-marina*.

B. patersonii (R. Br.) Mett. STRAP WATERFERN. Rhiz. creeping, stout, short, scaly, occas. stoloniferous. Sterile fronds 15–90×2.5–30cm ovate-acuminate, simple or forked, shining dark green above, paler beneath, stiff; fertile fronds as long, 1cm broad. India, Malaya, NZ, Pacific Is.

B. penna-marina (Poir.) Kuhn. Rhiz. creeping, slender, stoloniferous. Fronds tufted; sterile fronds 10–20×1–2cm, spreading, linear-lanceolate, dark green, thick and firm, pinnae 12×3mm, linear-oblong, obtuse; fertile fronds erect, longer than sterile, pinnae numerous, brown-green rather distant, shorter and narrower; stipes to 30cm. Temp. & Subantarctic S Amer. & Australasia. Z8.

B. polypodioides (Sw.) Kuhn. Rhiz. scandent, to 10m+, 'woody', densely scaly. Sterile frond blades 30–45×2.5–5cm, linear to lanceolate, tapering at both ends, pinnatisect, seg. 25–75 pairs, narrowly oblong-deltate; stipes to 10cm; fertile fronds lanceolate to ovate with pinnae to 4cm, remote, pod-like. C Amer., S Mex., Greater Antilles. Z10.

B. polypodioides Raddi non (Sw.) Kuhn = *B. blechnoides*.

B. procerum (Forst. f.) Labill. Rhiz. erect or inclined, sometimes prostrate, stout, short. Fronds numerous, v. variable in size, bright green or brown-green, v. stiff and rigid, or membranous; sterile pinnae finely serrate, acuminate, shining, fertile pinnae remote, narrowly linear. Mex., Malaysia, NZ.

B. punctulatum Rhiz. stout, densely scaly at crown. Sterile fronds 30–60×10–15cm, oblong-lanceolate, pinnae 5–7.5×0.5–1cm, numerous, linear, subfalcate, lowest reduced to auricles; fertile fronds with pinnae 5–7.5cm×3mm; stipes erect, strong, to 15cm. S Afr.

B. remotum Presl = *B. auriculatum*.

B. serrulatum Rich. = *B. indicum*.

B. spicant (L.) Roth. DEER FERN; HARD FERN. Rhiz. short-creeping to erect, stout. Sterile fronds 15–22×2.5–4cm, patent, lanceolate-linear; pinnae 15–20×3mm, 20–60 pairs, linear, subobtuse or mucronate, slightly dilated at base, stipes to 7.5cm; fertile fronds often 30×5cm, erect, narrowly linear, pinnae 6–10mm apart, dilated at base, 1–2mm broad; stipes to 22cm. N Amer., Eur., Asia, Jap. 'Cristatum': 10–20cm, tip of frond crested. Serratum group: 10–20cm; pinnae lobed, uncrested. Z5.

B. tabulare (Thunb.) Kuhn. Rhiz. erect, stout, to 60cm, woody. Sterile fronds 30–60×15–20cm, ovate, pinnae 7.5–15×1cm, close, erecto-patent, lanceolate, attenuate; fertile pinnae rather close, narrow, linear. S Afr., Aus., W Indies, Falklands Is. 8.

B. unilaterale Sw. Rhiz. elongate, densely scaly at crown. Fronds 15–30×2–5cm, lanceolate; pinnae 20–25×6–10mm, numerous, spreading, linear, apex mucronate, base dilated, entire, herbaceous; stipes to 10cm, erect. Mex. to W Indies, to Peru and S

Braz. Z10.

B. vulcanicum (Bl.) Kuhn. Rhiz. erect or inclined, stout, short. Sterile fronds 10–35×5–13cm, ovate-lanceolate, dull green, stiff, pinnae spreading, lanceolate, slightly dilated at base, acute or subobtuse; fertile pinnae distant, linear, dilated at base; stipes to 15cm. Aus., Pacific Is., Malaya, Java, NZ. Z10.

B. wurunuran Parris. Rhiz. medium-creeping, wiry, much branched, scaly. Fronds to 60cm, erect, dimorphic, dark green; pinnae shortly petiolate, curved, obtuse, lower pinnae not reduced, fertile pinnae much narrower. Queensld.

→*Lomaria* and *Stenochlaena*.

Bleeding Heart *Dicentra spectabilis.*
Bleeding-heart Tree *Homalanthus populifolius.*
Bleeding-heart Vine *Clerodendrum thomsoniae.*

Blepharanthera Schltr.
B. dinteri Schltr. = *Brachystelma blepharanthera.*
B. edulis Schltr. = *Brachystelma blepharanthera.*

Blepharis Juss.
B. carduifolius (L.f.) Anderson = *Acanthopsis carduifolia.*

Blessed Thistle *Cnicus*; *Silybum marianum.*

Bletia Ruiz & Pav. Orchidaceae. 50 decid., terrestrial orchids. Pbs corm-like. Lvs lanceolate, plicate. Rac. erect, leafless, lat. or term.; tep. free, showy; lip entire or trilobed. Spring–summer. Amer. Subtrop., Trop. Z10.
B. catenulata Ruiz & Pav. Lvs to 60cm. Infl. to 88cm; fls to 9, to 4.5cm diam., rose pink to magenta, lip magenta, margins and keels cream or white. Braz., Peru.
B. florida (Salisb.) R. Br. = *B. purpurea.*
B. gracilis Lodd. Lvs to 30cm, somewhat purple. Infl. to 45cm; fls to 8, to 3.75cm diam., yellow, pale bronze, mauve or magenta, lip green, veined blood-red or violet, flushed pink at base. Mex., Guat.
B. hyacinthina (Sm.) R. Br. = *Bletilla striata.*
B. patula Hook. Lvs to 60cm. Infl. to 90cm; fls to 6, to 6cm diam., seldom opening fully, rose madder or deep magenta, lip keeled white. Cuba, Hispan., Puerto Rico.
B. purpurea (Lam.) DC. Lvs to 90cm. Infl. to 1.5m, sometimes branching; fls to 4.5cm diam., rose, magenta, mauve or white, lip darker with yellow-white keel. Throughout species range.
B. shepherdii Hook. = *B. purpurea.*
B. striata (Thunb.) Druce = *Bletilla striata.*
B. verecunda R. Br. = *B. purpurea.*

Bletilla Rchb. f. Orchidaceae. 10 decid. terrestrial, orchids; pb. corm-like. Lvs linear to obovate-lanceolate, plicate. Rac. term., lax; tep. oblanceolate; lip obovate, lat. lobes erect, disc callused or papillose. E. Asia.
B. hyacinthina (Sm.) Rchb. f. = *B. striata.*
B. striata (Thunb.) Rchb. f. St. to 60cm. Lvs to 45cm, oblong-lanceolate, narrow-acuminate. Infl. erect; fls rose to magenta, rarely white; lip to 3.5cm, throat white to ivory, disc with 5 frilled white or mauve calli. Early summer. Jap., China, Tibet. Z7. 'Variegata': lvs striped white.
→*Bletia.*

Blighia Koenig. AKEE. Sapindaceae. 4 everg. trees and shrubs. Lvs pinnate; pinnae entire. Fls unisexual, 5-merous. Fr. a capsule, fleshy, 3-chambered. W Afr., widely planted W Indies. Z9.
B. sapida Koenig. Tree to 20m. Pinnae 6–10, to 12×6–8cm, oblong or obovate. Fls small, in sessile cymes, white tinged green. Fr. to 7.5cm, straw-coloured to magenta, each chamber opening to expose 3 shiny seeds with fleshy, cream-coloured arils.
→*Cupania.*

Blimbi *Averrhoa bilimbi.*

Blitium L.
B. capitatum L. = *Chenopodium capitatum.*
B. virgatum L. = *Chenopodium foliosum.*

Blonde Lilian *Erythronium albidum.*
Blood Berry *Rivina humilis.*
Blood Flower *Asclepias curassavica*; *Haemathus coccineus.*
Bloodleaf *Iresine.*
Blood Lily *Haemanthus coccineus.*
Blood-red Net-bush *Calothamnus sanguineus.*
Bloodroot *Sanguinaria.*
Blood-twig *Cornus sanguinea.*
Blood Warrior *Castilleja coccinea.*

Bloodwood Tree *Haematoxylum campechianum*; *Pterocarpus angolensis*.
Bloody Cranesbill *Geranium sanguineum*.

Bloomeria Kellogg. Liliaceae (Alliaceae). 3 bulbous perenn. herbs. Infl. a many-fld, long-stemmed spherical umbel, jointed toward top; perianth seg. 6; fil. dilated at base to form a 2-toothed cup. SW US, Mex. Z8.
B. aurea Kellogg = *B. crocea*.
B. crocea (Torr.) Cov. Bulb c1cm diam. Lvs 30×1cm, solitary, linear. Scape to 30cm; fls to 2.5cm diam., golden yellow with darker midstripes, in dense umbels. Spring. S Calif., Baja Calif.
B. maritima Macbr. = *Muilla maritima*.

Blooming-fool Begonia *Begonia* ×*cheimantha*.

Blossfeldia Werderm. Cactaceae. 1 tiny, button-like cactus; st. simple or caespitose, not ribbed; spines 0. Fls 0.6–1.5cm, off-white. Andes of N Arg. and Boliv. Z9.
B. liliputana Werderm.
→*Parodia*.

Blotiella Tryon. Dennstaedtiaceae. 15 terrestrial ferns. Rhiz. ascending, or creeping. Fronds stipitate, uniform, to 3 times pinnate, deltoid, seg. undulate or notched. Afr. and Madag.; Amer. Z10.
B. currori (Hook.) Tryon. Rhiz. russet-hairy. Fronds to 1m, 2-pinnate or -pinnatifid, lanceolate to oblong; term. pinna hastate, lat. pinnae sessile, opposite, distant, oblong, acute at apex, deeply lobed, to 40cm, seg. to 8cm, deltoid to lanceolate, somewhat undulate; stipes to 0.6m, erect, straw-coloured. Trop. Afr.
B. lindeniana (Hook.) Tryon. TOMATO FERN. Rhiz. clump-forming, suberect to ascending, fleshy to woody, hairy. Fronds to 5m, shining deep green, 1–2-pinnate or -pinnatifid, deltoid, hoary; pinnae subsessile, paired, seg. deltoid to oblong, entire to lobed or notched, to 2cm wide; stipes to 2m, pubesc. and spiny or setose. Trop. Amer.
B. natalensis (Hook.) Tryon. Rhiz. erect, brown-hairy. Fronds to 1.5m, 2-pinnate or -pinnatifid, lanceolate; pinnae to 55cm, oblong, acute, deeply lobed, pinnules petiolate, oblong, lobed, seg. notched, puberulent; stipes to 1m, pubesc., straw-coloured. Trop. Afr., Comoros Is.
B. pubescens Willd. ex Kaulf. Rhiz. suberect to creeping, brown-hairy. Fronds to 1.2m, 1–3-pinnatifid; pinnae to 45cm, winged, ± sessile, lanceolate, pinnules deltoid to ovate, deeply lobed, pinnatifid or entire, seg. oblong, undulate; stipes to 90cm, erect, densely pubesc. Trop. Afr. and is.
→*Lonchitis*.

Bloukeur *Psoralea aphylla*.
Blowballs *Taraxacum*.
Blue African Lily *Agapanthus africanus*.
Blue Amaryllis *Worsleya rayneri*.
Blue Ash *Fraxinus quadrangulata*.
Blue Atlas Cedar *Cedrus libani* ssp. *atlantica* 'Glauca'.
Bluebeard *Caryopteris*; *Clintonia borealis*.
Bluebell *Campanula rotundifolia*; *Hyacinthoides non-scripta*.
Bluebell Creeper *Sollya heterophylla*.
Blueberry *Billardiera longiflora*; (Edible) *Vaccinium*.
Blueberry Ash *Elaeocarpus reticulatus*.
Blue Bethlehem *Androstephium caeruleum*.
Blue Birch *Betula* ×*caerulea*.
Blue Bird Vine *Petrea*.
Blueblossom *Ceanothus thyrsiflorus*.
Blue Boronia *Boronia coerulescens*.
Bluebottle *Centaurea cyanus*.
Blue Box *Eucalyptus baueriana*.
Blueboy *Stirlingia latifolia*.
Blue Brush *Ceanothus thyrsiflorus*.
Blue Bugle *Ajuga genevensis*.
Blue Buttons *Knautia arvensis*.
Blue Buttons Devil's Bit Scabious *Succisa pratensis*.
Blue Calico Flower *Downingia elegans*.
Blue Candle *Myrtillocactus geometrizans*.
Blue Cardinal Flower *Lobelia siphilitica*.
Blue Chalksticks *Senecio serpens*.
Blue Cohosh *Caulophyllum thalictrioides*.
Blue Cupidone *Catananche caerulea*.
Blue Curls *Phacelia congesta*; *Trichostema*.
Blue Daisy *Felicia*; (*F. amelloides*).
Blue Dawn Flower *Ipomoea indica*.
Blue Dicks *Dichelostemma pulchellum*.
Blue Douglas Fir *Pseudotsuga menziesii*.
Blue Elder, Blue Elderberry *Sambucus caerulea*.
Blue-eyed African Daisy *Arctotis venusta*.
Blue-eyed Grass *Sisyrinchium angustifolium*; *S. bermudianum*.

Blue-eyed Mary *Collinsia verna*.
Blue False Indigo *Baptisia australis*.
Blue Fan Palm *Brahea armata*.
Blue Fern *Phlebodium aureum* var. *areolatum*.
Blue Fescue *Festuca glauca*.
Blue Flag *Iris versicolor*.
Blue Fleabane *Erigeron acer*.
Blue-flowered Torch *Tillandsia lindenii*.
Blue Funnel Lily *Androstephium caeruleum*.
Blue Gem *Craterostigma plantagineum*.
Blue Ginger *Dichorisandra thyrsiflora*.
Blue Grama *Bouteloua gracilis*.
Blue Grape *Vitis bicolor*.
Blue Grass *Poa* (*P. alpina*).
Bluegrass Lily *Agrostocrinum*.
Blue-green Saxifrage *Saxifraga caesia*.
Blue Gum *Eucalyptus globulus*; *E. leucoxylon*.
Blue Hakea *Hakea lehmanniana*.
Blue Haze *Selago spuria*.
Bluehearts *Buchnera*.
Blue Hesper Palm *Brahea armata*.
Blue Hibiscus *Alyogyne*.
Blue Holly *Ilex* ×*meserveae*.
Blue Huckleberry *Vaccinium membranaceum*.
Bluejack Oak *Quercus incana*.
Blue Jasmine *Clematis crispa*.
Blue Kauri *Agathis atropurpurea*.
Blue Laceflower *Trachymene coerulea*.
Blue Latan *Latania loddigesii*.
Blue-leaved Ironbark *Eucalyptus fibrosa*.
Blue-leaved Stringy Bark *Eucalyptus agglomerata*.
Blue-leaved Wattle *Acacia saligna*.
Blue Lettuce *Lactuca perennis*.
Blue Lilly Pilly *Syzygium oleosum*.
Blue Lotus *Nymphaea caerulea*.
Blue Marguerite *Felicia amelloides*.
Blue Mountain Pine *Microstrobus fitzgeraldii*.
Blue Mountains Mallee *Eucalyptus stricta*.
Blue Oak *Quercus douglasii*.
Blue Oat Grass *Helictotrichon sempervirens*.
Blue Oxalis *Parochetus communis*.
Blue Palmetto *Rhapidophyllum hystrix*; *Sabal palmetto*.
Blue Passion Flower *Passiflora caerulea*.
Blue Pea *Clitoria ternatea*; *Psoralea pinnata*.
Blue Petrea *Petrea arborea*.
Blue Phlox *Phlox divaricata*.
Blue Pimpernel *Anagallis monellii*.
Blue Pincushion *Brunonia australis*.
Blue Pine *Pinus wallichiana*.
Blue Poppy *Meconopsis betonicifolia*.
Blue Potato Bush *Lycianthes rantonnetii*.
Blue Rat's Tail *Stachytarpheta urticifolia*.
Blue Sage *Eranthemum pulchellum*.
Blue Skyflower *Thunbergia grandiflora*.
Blue Snakeweed *Stachytarpheta jamaicensis*.
Blue Spike Moss *Selaginella uncinata*.
Blue Spiraea *Caryopteris incana*.
Blue Spruce *Picea pungens*.
Blue Star *Amsonia*.
Blue Stem *Schizachyrium scoparium*.
Blue-stemmed Penstemon *Penstemon ternatus*.
Blue Tannia, Blue Taro *Xanthosoma violaceum*.
Blue Thimble Flower *Gilia capitata*.
Blue Trumpet Vine *Thunbergia grandiflora*.
Bluets *Houstonia caerulea*.
Blue Vine *Clitoria ternatea*.
Blue Waxweed *Cuphea viscosissima*.
Blue Weed *Helianthus ciliaris*.
Blue Willow *Salix caesia*.
Bluewings *Torenia fournieri*.
Blue Witch *Solanum umbelliferum*.
Blue Yucca *Yucca baccata*.

Blumenbachia Schräd. Loasaceae. 6 ann. or bienn. herbs, covered in vicious, bristle-like, stinging hairs. St. climbing or trailing. Lvs lobed. Fls axill., solitary, bracteate, usually long-stalked; pet. 5, strongly concave; sta. in clusters. Fr. a twisted capsule. S Amer.
B. insignis Schräd. To 70m, tightly twining. Lvs to 7.5cm, 5–7-lobed near base of st., pinnatifid above, segs sharply pinnately lobed. Fls to 2.5cm diam. white, spotted or streaked orange to scarlet at centre, long-stalked. Braz. to Arg.
B. lateritia (Klotzsch) Griseb. = *Caiophora lateritia*.

Blunt Everlasting *Helichrysum obtusifolium*.
Blunt flowered Rush *Juncus subnodulosus*.

Blunt-leaf Heath *Epacris obtusifolia.*
Blunt-leaved Chilean Mallow *Sphaeralcea obtusiloba.*
Blunt-leaved Wattle *Acacia obtusata.*
Blunt-lobed Woodsia *Woodsia obtusa.*
Blushing Bride *Serruria florida.*
Blushing Bromeliad *Neoregelia carolinae.*
Blushing Philodendron *Philodendron erubescens.*
Blushwort *Aeschynanthus.*
Boar Thistle *Cirsium vulgare.*
Boat Lily *Tradescantia spathacea.*

Bobartia L. Iridaceae. About 14 perenn. herbs. Lvs basal in a tight rosette, hard, linear, rigid, scabrous. Cymes few-fld, crowded into a dense head with rigid spathes; fls large, short-lived. S Afr. Z8.
B. gladiata (L. f.) Ker-Gawl. Lvs to 80cm often distichous, 3–4mm wide. Infl. flat, made up of 3–12 alt. cymes; fls 1–3 in axils of upper bracts, yellow, often spotted or tinged red-brown. Spring–summer.
B. indica L. Lvs 100–175cm, spreading, terete. Infl. a dense head of 6–40 cymes; fls usually 1 per axil of upper bracts, lemon yellow. Spring–autumn.
B. spathacea Ker-Gawl. = *B. indica.*

Bocconia L. Papaveraceae. 9 trees, shrubs or perenn. herbs, latex yellow. Lvs pinnately nerved or lobed, often glaucous. Fls apetalous, to 2.5cm diam., in terminal, spreading pan. Trop. & subtrop. Amer. Z9.
B. arborea S. Wats. Tree to 7.5m. Lvs to 45×30cm, pinnatifid, glab. above, glab. to downy beneath, lobes linear-lanceolate, to 15cm, serrate. Rac. to 20; sta. 12. Summer. C Amer.
B. cordata Willd. = *Macleaya cordata.*
B. frutescens L. TREE CELANDINE. Tree to 7.5m. Lvs 15–35×10–20cm, pinnatifid, truncate or broadly obtuse at base, glab. above, grey-green, densely hairy beneath at first, becoming sparsely hairy. Rac. to 20cm; sta. 16. Summer. C Amer.
B. integrifolia Humbl. & Bonpl. Tree or shrub to 5m, much branched. Lvs to 30×10cm, oblong, deltoid in upper part, entire, crenate or serrate, grey-white farinose beneath. Rac. to 35cm; sta. 10. Spring. Colomb., Boliv., Peru.
B. japonica André = *Macleaya cordata.*
B. microcarpa Maxim. = *Macleaya microcarpa.*

Boea Comm. ex Lam. Gesneriaceae. 17 rosulate or caulescent herbs. Lvs hairy. Fls in axill. cymes, sometimes branching; cal. seg. 5; cor. campanulate or with a short tube and flat limb, equally 5-lobed or bilabiate, upper lip 2-lobed, lower lip 3-lobed. SE Asia, Aus. Z10.
B. hygrometrica (Bunge) R. Br. Stemless. Lvs to 7.5cm, orbicular-ovate to obovate, apex crenate. Fls few, inflated, pale blue, throat yellow. S Asia.
B. hygroscopica F. Muell. Lvs to 15cm, crowded on st., ovate, crenate, densely pubesc. Fls many bright purple, throat with a yellow blotch. Queensld.

Boehmeria Jacq. FALSE NETTLE. Urticaceae. 100 small trees, shrubs, subshrubs or herbs allied to *Urtica* but without stinging hairs. Trop. and N temp. regions. Z7.
B. argentea hort. = *Myriocarpa stipitata.*
B. biloba Wedd. 30–70cm; st. rugose, tinged red. Lvs 6–15cm, broadly ovate, apex usually 2-lobed, finely toothed, veins sparsely pubesc. Summer. Jap.
B. japonica var. *platanifolia* (Franch. & Savat.) Maxim. = *B. platanifolia.*
B. nivea (L.) Gaudich. RAMIE; CHINESE SILK PLANT; CHINA GRASS. To 2m; st. densely sericeous to hispid. Lvs 7–15cm, oval, long-acuminate, serrate, densely white-tomentose beneath. Autumn. Jap. to Malaysia. 'Candicans': white-pubesc. var. *tenacissima* (Gaudich.) Miq. RHEA. Lvs green throughout. Malay Penins.
B. platanifolia Franch. & Savat. 1m. Lvs orbicular to elliptic, base rounded, pubesc., irregularly serrate, apex prominently 3–5-lobed, lobes toothed. Autumn. China, Jap., Korea.

Boenninghausenia Rchb. ex. Meissn. Rutaceae. 1 rue-like subshrub to 80cm. Lvs 5–10cm, ternately 2–3-pinnatisect, lfts 1–2.5cm, glaucous, obovate or elliptic, white beneath, glandular-punctate. Fls white on slender pedicels in term. pan., 4-merous; sep. 1mm, pet. 3–4mm, oblong. Assam to Jap. Z8.
B. albiflora (Hook.) Rchb. ex Meissn.

Boerboon *Schotia.*

Boerlagiodendron Harris.
B. eminens (Bull) Merrill = *Osmoxylon eminens.*

Boesenbergia Kuntze. Zingiberaceae. 30 perenn. herbs, apparently tufted. Lvs 1 to several, usually long-stalked. Infl. term. on leafy shoot with lanceolate bracts; cal. tubular, cor. 3-lobed, lip concave, lat. staminodes petaloid. SE Asia. Z10.
B. lancifolia Schltr. = *Scaphochlamys malaccana.*
B. ornata (N.E. Br.) Rosemary M. Sm. Lvs 10–20cm, lanceolate, green feathered silver above, purple beneath. Fls crowded, in stalkless spike; yellow, lip yellow, spotted orange at base. Borneo.
B. pandurata (Roxb.) Schltr. = *B. rotunda.*
B. rotunda (L.) Mansf. Lvs 28cm, ovate-oblong, green, midrib downy beneath. Fls few, on stalked spike; white to pink, lip white, spotted pink. Indon.
B. vittata (N.E. Br.) Loes. To 20cm. Lvs 8–12cm, elliptic, dark green, with silky sheen and silver central stripe above, grey-green beneath. Fls numerous, almost hidden by bracts, white, lip white, yellow at centre. Indon.
→*Kaempferia.*

Bogang *Clerodendrum buchananii.*
Bog Arum *Calla.*
Bog Asphodel *Narthecium* (*N. ossifragum*).
Bog Bean *Menyanthes.*
Bog Bilberry *Vaccinium uliginosum.*
Bog Kalmia *Kalmia polifolia.*
Bog Laurel *Kalmia polifolia.*
Bogmat *Wolffiella gladiata.*
Bog Myrtle *Myrica gale.*
Bog Pimpernel *Anagallis tenella.*
Bog Rhubarb *Petasites hybridus.*
Bog Rose *Arethusa bulbosa.*
Bog Rosemary *Andromeda glaucophylla.*
Bog Sage *Salvia uliginosa.*
Bog Star *Parnassia.*
Bog Whortleberry *Vaccinium uliginosum.*
Bog Wintergreen *Pyrola asarifolia.*
Bois Casava *Cornutia pyramidata.*
Bois Chavanon *Catalpa speciosa.*
Bois-chene *Catalpa longissima.*
Bois d'eponge *Gastonia cutispongia.*

Boisduvalia Spach. Onagraceae. , 6 ann. herbs, erect to decumbent, bark exfoliating. Lvs glab., in spirals above, or opposite, ± connate below, pubesc. Fls in axils of leaflike bracts, in an erect infl.; floral tube conspicuous; sep. 4, erect; pet. 4, deeply notched, purple or pink to white. N & S Amer. Z8.
B. bipartita Greene = *B. densiflora.*
B. densiflora (Lindl.) S. Wats. Villous or strigulose. Lvs 1.2–8.5cm, narrowly lanceolate to linear, ± toothed. Infl. crowded, bracteate; pet. 2–9×1.2–5mm, magenta to white. Summer.
B. sparsiflora A.A. Heller = *B. densiflora.*
→*Oenothera.*

Bois Nan-non *Ormosia krugii.*

Bolandra A. Gray. Saxifragaceae. 2 perenn. rhizomatous herbs, to 30cm. Lvs orbicular to reniform, often stipulate, ribbed beneath, crenate or incised; stalked. Fls small, paniculate, 5-merous; sep. fused in campanulate floral cup, lobes spreading; pet. linear. W & NW US. Z6.
B. californica A. Gray. To 40cm. Basal lvs 5×7cm, divided into 4–6 lobes at least half as deep as lf is long. Fls to 12, green marked purple marking. Summer. Calif.
B. imnahaensis Peck = *B. oregona.*
B. oregona Wats. To 50cm. Basal lvs 5–7cm, divided into 6–15 lobes up to half as deep as lf is long. Fls to 40, green suffused purple. Early summer. Oreg., Washington, N Calif.
→*Hemieva.*

Bolax Comm. ex Juss. Umbelliferae. 2–3 perenn. cushion-forming herbs. Lvs crowded, simple. Umbels simple; fls green-white. S Amer. Z7.
B. glebaria Comm. ex Gaudich. = *B. gummifera.*
B. gummifera (Lam.) Spreng. Lvs 2–6.5mm, 3-lobed or parted, lobes ovate, obtuse, leathery. Umbels with 3–20 fls; involucre of 4 bracts. Summer. W Arg., Chile, Falkland Is.
→*Azorella.*

Bolbitis Schott. Lomariopsidaceae. 44 terrestrial then epiphytic ferns. Rhiz. creeping. Fronds simple and entire to pinnate or 1-pinnate-pinnatifid, glab.; fertile fronds taller and finer than sterile. Trop. Z10.
B. cladorrhizans (Spreng.) Ching in C. Chr. = *B. portoricensis.*

B. heteroclita (Presl.) Ching in C. Chr. Rhiz. woody. Sterile fronds simple or with 1–3 pairs of pinnae, lateral pinnae 7.5–15×2.5–5cm, apex sometimes elongate and rooting; fertile pinnae 5–7.5×1cm; stipes to 30cm. Trop. Asia.

B. nicotianifolia (Sw.) Alston. Rhiz. wide-creeping, sometimes climbing. Sterile fronds to 1m, lat. pinnae 1–4 pairs, 15–20×5–9cm, mostly stalked, oblong to elliptic-oval, abruptly long-acuminate; fertile pinnae to 15×2.5–5cm on longer-stalked fronds. W Indies, Guat. to Panama, Fr. Guiana to Peru.

B. portoricensis (Spreng.) Hennipman. Rhiz. short-creeping, scaly esp. at apex. Sterile fronds 30–60×20–50cm, deltate-oblong and long-acuminate, apex sometimes whip-like and viviparous, the lower part 1-pinnate to pinnatifid, pinnae deeply lobed; stipes to 60cm, near base; fertile fronds shorter than the sterile but with longer stipes. W Indies, Mex. to Venez., Colomb. and Ecuad.

B. quoyana (Gaudich) Ching in C. Chr. Rhiz. short-creeping, somewhat flattened. Sterile fronds to 1.2m; sterile pinnae 15×2.5cm, long-tapered, caudate, grey-green, stipes dull grey, fleshy; fertile fronds pale, pinnae reduced, stalked, to 7.5cm; stipe usually c2/3 length of frond blade.

→*Acrostichum, Gymnopteris* and *Leptochilus.*

Bolboschoenus Asch. ex Palla. Cyperaceae. 8 ann. or perenn. herbs. St. tuberous and swollen at base. Lvs grass-like, thin. Infl. term., usually simple, bracts leaflike, exceeding infl.; fls v. small, spirally arranged. E Asia, NE Amer.

B. maritimus (L.) Palla. Rhiz. creeping, scaly. St. solitary, 3-angled, leafy below. Lvs 10–35cm, rough; spikelets 1–3cm, to 10, pungent; glumes 3–4mm, sparsely hairy, tipped with 3–6 white bristles. Summer. Cosmop. Z6.

→*Scirpus.*

Boldo *Peumus boldus.*

Boldoa Cav. ex Lagasca.
B. fragrans (Pers.) Endl. = *Peumus boldus.*
B. chilensis Molina = *Peumus boldus.*

Bolinas Ridge Ceanothus *Ceanothus masonii.*

Bolivicereus Cárdenas.
B. samaipatanus Cárdenas = *Cleistocactus samaipatanus.*
B. serpens (Kunth) Backeb. = *Cleistocactus serpens.*

Bollea Rchb. f. Orchidaceae. 6 epiphytic orchids. Pbs 0. Lvs strap-shaped, 2-ranked in fans. Fls waxy, solitary, axill.; tep. obovate, spreading, lip rhombic, obovate, callose. Summer. Colomb., Guianas, Venez. Z10.

B. coelestis (Rchb. f.) Rchb. f. Lvs to 30×5cm. Fls to 9cm diam., hyacinth-scented, cream flushed amethyst, opal or sapphiree, lip with an ochre disc. Colomb.

B. hemixantha Rchb. f. Lvs to 30×4cm. Fls to 7.5cm diam., ivory at centre fading to white, then lemon yellow to ochre at tips, lip lemon yellow with a golden callus. Venez., Colomb.

B. lawrenceana (Rchb. f.) Rchb. f. Resembles *B. coelestis* except fls to 8cm diam., white tipped red-mauve, lip lilac, callus violet or claret. Colomb.

B. violacea (Lindl.) Rchb. f. Closely resembles *B. coelestis* except fls deep amethyst edged white, lip dark violet, disc yellow. Guianas.

Bollwyller Pear ✕ *Sorbopyrus auricularis.*

Boltonia L'Hérit. FALSE CHAMOMILE. Compositae. 8 tall, perenn. herbs. Lvs entire or minutely toothed, sessile, often twisted at base, erect. Cap. radiate, in large pan.; ray flts white, pink, purple or violet; disc flts yellow. C & E NE Asia.

B. asteroides (L.) L'Hérit. To 2.5m. Lvs oblanceolate, upper lvs to 12cm, narrow, serrulate. Cap. to 2cm diam.; ray flts white to violet or purple. E US. var. *latisquama* (A. Gray) Cronq. Cap. over 2cm diam.; ray flts mauve to violet. Missouri to Okl. 'Nana': dwarf, to 90cm; white. 'Snowbank': to 2m, vigorous; snow-white.

B. cantoniensis Franch. & Savat. = *Kalimeris pinnatifida.*
B. glastifolia (Hill) L'Hérit. = *B. asteroides.*
B. incisa (Fisch.) Benth. = *B. kalimeris incisa.*
B. indica hort. = *Kalimeris pinnatifida.*
B. japonica Benth. & Hook. f. = *Aster miqueliana.*
B. latisquama A. Gray = *B. asteroides* var. *latisquama.*
→*Matricaria.*

Bolusanthus Harms Leguminosae (Papilionoideae). 1 small tree, 3–6m, bark pale to dark brown. Lvs imparipinnate to 15cm; lfts 4–8cm, ovate-lanceolate or lanceolate, in 3–7 pairs, sericeous. Fls 1.5–1.8cm, pea-like, blue-violet, in many-fld drooping, pub-

esc., terminally clustered rac. 10–25cm long. Spring. S Afr., Zimb., Moz., Angola. Z9.

B. speciosus (Bol.) Harms. WILD WISTERIA; ELEPHANTWOOD; SOUTH AFRICAN WISTERIA.

Bomarea Mirb. Liliaceae (Alstroemeriaceae). 100 tuberous-rooted perenn. herbs. St. slender, twining to 6m. Lvs to 15cm, oblong-lanceolate, apex acuminate. Fls tubular-campanulate, stalked in nodding term. umbels; tep. 6 in 2 whorls. S Amer. Z9.

B. acutifolia (Link & Otto) Herb. Differs from in *B. shuttleworthii* in lvs lanceolate to ovate-lanceolate, pubesc. on the veins beneath, outer tep. red, not spotted.
B. caldasiana Herb. = *B. caldasii.*
B. caldasii (HBK) Asch. & Gräbn. Fls in a simple umbel; outer tep. 2–2.5cm, red-brown, inner 2.5–3.5cm, bright yellow to orange, occas. flecked green, brown or red. N S Amer.
B. cardieri Mast. Fls in compound umbels, tep. 5.5–6.5cm, outer pink, flecked mauve above, with a short, green callus below apex, inner pink or green, spotted mauve. Colomb.
B. conferta Benth. = *B. patacocensis.*
B. edulis (Tussac) Herb. Fls in compound umbels, tep. 2.5–3cm, outer pink, inner bright green or yellow, spotted purple or dark pink. W Indies, C Amer., N S Amer.
B. frondea (Mast.) Differs from *B. patacocensis* in outer tep. yellow and inner tep. bright yellow, spotted dark red.
B. multiflora (L.f.) Mirb. Fls in simple umbels; tep. 2.5cm, outer tinged red, inner red-yellow with brown flecks. N S Amer.
B. oligantha Bak. Similar to *B. multiflora* but fls 6–8 not 20–40 per umbel.
B. patacocensis Herb. Fls in simple umbels; outer tep. to 3.3cm, orange or crimson, inner to 6.5cm, chrome-yellow or crimson, flecked chocolate or violet, with orange tips. Andes of Colomb. and Ecuad.
B. racemosa Killip. Differs from *B. patacocensis* in st. deep red; scarlet outer tep., 5–6.3cm, and scarlet inner tep., spotted brown with yellow base, 6.3–7.5cm. S Amer.
B. salsilla (L.) Herb. Fls in compound umbels; tep. 1–15cm, crimson or purple-red, tinged green at tips. Chile.
B. shuttleworthii Mast. Lvs glab. beneath. Fls in compound umbels, tep. to 5cm, outer orange-red with dark spots towards the tip, inner yellow at the base with green, dark-spotted tips and a red midrib. Colomb.

BOMBACACEAE Kunth. 30/250. *Adansonia, Bombax, Ceiba, Chorisia, Durio, Montezuma, Ochroma, Pseudobombax.*

Bombacopsis Pittier.
B. fendleri (Seem.) Pittier = *Pachira fendleri.*

Bombax L. SILK-COTTON TREE. Bombacaceae. 8 decid. trees; trunks spiny when young, buttressed with age; br. spreading. Lvs palmate, lfts 5–9, oblong-ovate to lanceolate. Fls large, axill., before lvs, clustered; epical. and cal. 5-lobed, cup-shaped, fleshy; pet. 5, oblong to oblong-obovate, tomentose beneath; sta. in whorls, or fascicles, fused at base. Capsule massive, woody; seeds embedded in silky fibre. Trop. Afr., Asia, Aus. Z10.
B. angulicarpum Ulbr. = *B. buonopozense.*
B. buonopozense P. Beauv. GOLD COAST BOMBAX. To 40m; trunk with large conical spines. Lfts to 18cm, 5–9, oblong-ovate. Fls solitary or clustered; pet. to 8.5cm, red; sta. in 2 whorls. Fr. to 18cm oblong, 5-angled. Trop. W Afr.
B. ceiba L. RED SILK-COTTON TREE; SIMUL. To 25m+; trunk spiny when young, becoming buttressed. Lfts to 25cm, 3–7, elliptic-obovate or lanceolate. Fls solitary, appearing clustered; pet. to 8cm, dull to bright red; sta. in 2 whorls. Fr. to 15cm, oblong-ovoid. India to S China, SE Asia.
B. malabaricum DC. = *B. ceiba.*
→*Salmalia.*

Bombay Arrowroot *Curcuma angustifolia.*

Bommeria Fourn. ex Baill. Adiantiaceae. 4 terrestrial or lithophytic ferns. Rhiz. short to creeping. Fronds 1–3✕ pinnatifid, deltoid to pentagonal; rachis winged. Tex. & Calif. to Guat. Z9.

B. hispida (Mett.) Underw. Rhiz. creeping, slender; stipes 7–18cm. Fronds 3–10×3–10cm, pentagonal, rusty-tomentose beneath, lower seg. bipinnatifid, median seg. oblong-elliptic, pinnatifid. W Tex. to Ariz. and Mex.

Bonatea Willd. Orchidaceae. 20 terrestrial orchids. St. leafy. Rac. term; fls green or yellow-green and white; dors. sep. forming hood with pet.; pet. bilobed, lower lobe adnate to stigmatic arms, lip trilobed, spurred at base. Afr. Z9.

B. antennifera Rolfe. To 70cm. Lvs to 9cm, ovate. Fls green and white; lip 40–45mm, joined to stigma for 8mm at base, lobes filiform, midlobe 25–35mm, lat. lobes 20–30mm; spur 30–50mm, slender. Zimb., Moz., S Afr.

B. cassidea Sonder. 25–50cm. Lvs 1–4cm, falcate. Fls green, lower pet. lobes and lat. lobes of lip white; lip 16–20mm, claw 8mm, midlobe linear, lat. lobes 9–15mm, semi-orbicular from a narrow base; spur 11–25mm, slightly swollen in apical half. Zimb., S Afr.

B. pulchella Summerh. 25cm. Lvs 5–10cm, lanceolate to ovate. Fls green and white; lip claw 5mm, midlobe 24–30mm, narrowly linear, lateral lobes 45–55mm, filiform; spur 5.5–7cm. Moz., S Afr.

B. speciosa (L. f.) Willd. 40–50cm. Lvs to 10cm, lanceolate to ovate. Fls green and white with a slightly spicy scent; lip 25–32mm, claw 10mm, all lobes linear, 20–23mm; spur 3.5–4cm. Zimb., S Afr.

B. steudneri (Rchb. f.) T. Dur. & Schinz. To 1m. Lvs 7–12.5cm, ovate, amplexicaul. Fls green and white; lip claw 20mm, lobes 45–50mm, linear, tapering; spur 10–21cm, slender. E trop. Afr.; Yemen.

B. ugandae Summerh. = *B. steudneri*.
→*Habenaria*.

Bonavist *Lablab purpureus*.
Boneset *Eupatorium perfoliatum*.

Bongardia C.A. Mey. Berberidaceae. 1 tuberous perenn. herb, to 60cm. Lvs 10–25cm, radical, pinnate; lfts oval-oblong, 3–5-cleft, glaucous, often purple-red at base. Pan. lax, scapose; sep. 3–6, petaloid, tinged red, nearly round; pet. 6, 8–12mm, golden. S Greece, S Aegean. Z9.
B. chrysogonum (L.) Griseb.
B. rauwolfii C.A. Mey. = *B. chrysogonum*.
→*Leontice*.

Bonifazia Standl. & Steyerm.
B. quezalteca Standl. & Steyerm. = *Disocactus quezaltecus*.

Bonin Isles Juniper *Juniperus procumbens*.

Bonjeanea L.
B. recta (L.) Rchb. = *Dorycnium rectum*.

Bonnet Bellflower *Codonopsis*.

Bontia L. Myoporaceae. 1 everg., shrub or small tree; trunk slender. Lvs 3–11mm, oblong to linear-lanceolate, entire, fleshy, glandular-punctate. Fls solitary; peduncles 1–3cm; cor. 2cm, 2-lipped, central lobes with dense long hairs, tawny yellow with purple blotches. W Indies, N S Amer. Z9.
B. daphnoides L. MANGLE BOBO.

Boobyalla *Myoporum insulare*.
Boojum Tree *Fouquieria columnaris*.
Bookleaf *Daviesia cordata*.

Boophone Herb. Amaryllidaceae. 6 bulbous herbs with a pungent, onion-like odour. Umbel to 30cm diam., dense, globose, scapose; tep. 6, lanceolate, united at base, rose, red or mauve; pedicels straight, ray-like, lengthening greatly in fr. S & E Afr. Z10.
B. disticha (L. f.) Herb. CAPE POISON BULB. Lvs to 45cm, in 2 rows, ligulate, glaucous. Scape to 30cm; pedicels rigid, ultimately to 10cm; fls to 4cm, pink to red. S & E Afr.

Booyong *Heritiera trifoliolata*.
Borage *Borago officinalis*.

BORAGINACEAE Juss. 154/2500. *Alkanna, Amsinckia, Anchusa, Arnebia, Borago, Bourreria, Brunnera, Buglossoides, Caccinia, Carmona, Cerinthe, Cordia, Cryptantha, Cynoglossum, Echium, Ehretia, Eritrichium, Hackelia, Heliotropium, Lindelofia, Lithodora, Lithospermum, Mertensia, Moltkia, Myosotidium, Myosotis, Omphalodes, Onosma, Paracaryum, Pentaglottis, Plagiobothrys, Pulmonaria, Solenanthus, Symphytum, Tournefortia, Trachystemon*.

Borago L. Boraginaceae. 3 ann. or perenn. herbs, erect or decumbent, hispid. Lvs simple. Infl. branched, cymose, drooping; cal., lobes 5, linear-lanceolate; cor. rotate to campanulate, lobes spreading or suberect, scales conspicuous, often darkly coloured. Eur. Z7.
B. crassifolia Vent. = *Caccinia macrantha* var. *crassifolia*.
B. laxifolia Poir. = *B. pygmaea*.

B. officinalis L. TAILWORT; BORAGE. Hispid ann. herb to 60cm, st. erect. Basal lvs to 15cm, lanceolate or ovate, base rounded or subcordate, dull green. Cor. rotate; lobes to 1.5cm, deltoid to truncate-deltoid, sky blue to mid blue. Eur. 'Alba': fls white. 'Variegata': lvs variegated.
B. orientalis L. = *Trachystemon orientalis*.
B. pygmaea (DC.) Chater & Greuter. Hispidulous perenn. herb to 60cm. St. ultimately decumbent. Basal lvs to 20cm, obovate to oblong. Cor. campanulate; lobes to 0.8cm, ovate, acute, light blue. Eur.

Borassus L. Palmae. 7 tall, stout, solitary palms. Trunks dark grey, ringed, smooth or rough. Lvs costapalmate, suborbicular to cuneate; petiole armed; blade rigid, blue-green, divided to half depth into spreading seg. Fr. subglobose, yellow to brown. Afr., Madag., India, Sri Lanka, SE Asia, Malay Archipel. to New Guinea.
B. aethiopium Mart. Trunk to 30m, swollen at base and often near middle, clothed with lf bases becoming bare, ringed. Lf blades 1–2m, seg. 60–80 held in differing planes. Trop. Afr.
B. caudatum Lour. = *Arenga caudata*.
B. flabellifer L. PALMYRA PALM; TODDY PALM; WINE PALM; TALA PALM; DOUB PALM; LONTAR PALM. Trunk to 20m, swollen at base and middle, sometimes clothed with persistent lf bases. Lf blades 2.5–3m, seg. 80. Sri Lanka, India, SE Asia, Malay Archipel. to New Guinea.

Border Pinyon *Pinus discolor*.
Boree *Acacia pendula*.

Bornmuellera Hausskn. Cruciferae. 6 tuft-forming woody-based perenn. herbs. Lvs entire. Fls in rac.; pet. 4, white, entire, short-clawed. Asia Minor. Z7.
B. cappadocica (DC.) Cullen & Dudley. 5–10cm. Base shrubby. Lvs linear-oblanceolate, grey-hairy when young. Pet. 4–6mm. Turk.
→*Iberis* and *Schivereckia*.

Boro Dina *Solanum uporo*.

Boronia Sm. Rutaceae. 95 everg. shrubs. Lvs simple or compound, often aromatic. Fls usually fragrant, small, 4-merous, ± cupped, usually axill. and solitary or in cymes, more rarely in term. umbels or clusters. Aus. Z9.
B. alata Sm. To 130cm, glab. or sparsely puberulent. Lfts to 2cm, 9–15, elliptic or oblong, crenulate towards apex, glab. Fls to 2.5cm diam., white to pink. W Aus.
B. anemonifolia A. Cunn. STICKY BORONIA. To 2m, glab. or pubesc.; br. glandular-tuberculate. Lvs to 1.5cm, simple or trifoliolate; lfts narrowly linear, acute, often dentate, strongly aromatic. Fls to 1.5cm diam., white to pink. Queensld to Tasm.
B. citriodora Gunnerus ex Hook. f. LEMON-SCENTED BORONIA. To 1m; br. short-pubesc. Lfts 3–7, to 1.5cm, coriaceous, bright green, strongly lemon-scented, sometimes slightly pubesc. Fls to 1.5cm diam., white to pink. Vict., Tasm.
B. coerulescens F. Muell. BLUE BORONIA. To 1m, glab. or minutely pubesc.; br. usually gland. Lvs to 1cm, simple, usually erect, linear or linear-cuneate. Fls to 1.5cm diam., white, lilac, rose-purple or blue. S & W Aus.
B. crenulata Sm. To 1m; branchlets glab. or puberulent. Lvs to 2.6cm, narrowly elliptic or obovate to linear, acute or obtuse, entire or dentate, glab., aromatic. Fls to 1.5cm diam., pink or pale red. W Aus.
B. cymosa Endl. GRANITE BORONIA. To 1m; branchlets terete, smooth. Lvs to 3cm, simple, narrowly linear, entire. Fls to 1cm diam., rose-pink to mauve-pink, in terminal cymes. W Aus.
B. deanei Maid. & Betche. DEANE'S BORONIA. To 2m; br. glab., often tinged red. Lvs to 1cm, simple, linear to subterete, strongly aromatic. Fls to 1.5cm diam., white to bright pink, term., solitary or in few-fld cymes. NSW.
B. denticulata Sm. To 2.5m, glab.; br. gland. Lvs to 4cm, simple, strongly aromatic, linear or lanceolate, acute, minutely dentate, somewhat glaucous. Fls to 1cm diam., bright pink, mauve or white, in terminal cymes or corymbs. W Aus.
B. elatior Bartling = *B. molloyae*.
B. fastigiata Bartling. To 1m glab., br. usually erect, sometimes decumbent. Lvs to 2.5cm, simple, obovate to elliptic, margins often tinged red, serrate, sessile. Fls to 1.5cm diam., bright mauve-pink to dark red, in term. or axill. clusters. W Aus.
B. filifolia F. Muell. SLENDER BORONIA. To 50cm glab.; br. numerous, slender. Lvs to 2cm, simple or trifoliate; lfts slender, linear-terete, often tinged purple. Fls to 1cm diam., pink, term. or axill., solitary or in cymes. Vict., S Aus.
B. floribunda Seib. ex Spreng. PALE-PINK BORONIA. To 1.5m, much-branched. Lfts to 2.5cm, 5–9, dark green, sometimes tinged red or bronze, aromatic. Fls to 2cm diam., usually pale

pink, sometimes white or deep pink, strongly fragrant, in axillary, few-fld cymes. NSW.

B. fraseri Hook. FRASER'S BORONIA. To 1m glab., br. numerous, angular or compressed. Lfts to 3cm, 3–5, oblong-lanceolate, obtuse, glab., dark green above, paler beneath. Fls to 1.5cm diam., pink, in term. clusters. NSW.

B. heterophylla F. Muell. RED BORONIA; KALGAN. To 2m glab., much-branched. Lvs simple or 3–5 foliolate; lfts to 3cm, linear, coriaceous, dark green. Fls to 1cm, pink or scarlet, sweetly fragrant, solitary. W Aus.

B. inornata Turcz. DESERT BORONIA. To 1m, usually glab.; br. numerous, gland. Lfts to 1cm, 3–5, narrow, linear-terete, obtuse. Fls to 1.5cm diam., pink or white, term., solitary or 2–3 in short-stalked in cymes. Vict., S Aus., W Aus.

B. ledifolia (Vent.) Gay. LEDUM BORONIA. To 1.5m; br. gland., densely tomentose. Lvs to 4cm, simple or 3–7-foliolate; lfts narrowly elliptic, oblong or linear, densely pubesc. beneath, strongly aromatic. Fls to 2cm diam., bright pink, solitary. Queensld, NSW, Vict.

B. megastigma Nees ex Bartling SCENTED BORONIA; BROWN BORONIA. To 3m glab. Lfts to 1.5cm, 3–5, soft, narrow, linear or acicular. Fls to 1cm diam., exterior dark brown or purple-brown to yellow-green, interior pale yellow or yellow-green, solitary, strongly fragrant. W Aus. 'Brown Meg': fls large, brown, heavily scented, abundant. 'Heaven Scent': compact; fls chocolate, centre yellow, heavily scented. 'Lutea': fls clear yellow, lime-scented.

B. microphylla Sieb. ex Spreng. To 1m glab., br. gland., pendent. Lfts to 0.8cm, 5–11, rigid, linear or oblong to obovate, acute or obtuse, dark green. Fls to 1cm diam., bright pink, in axill. cymes. Queensld, NSW.

B. mollis A. Cunn. SOFT BORONIA. To 2m; br. densely hirsute. Lvs to 4cm; lfts 3–7, oblong or lanceolate, subglabrous above, tomentose or villous beneath. Fls to 2cm diam., bright pink, in term. or axill. umbels. NSW.

B. molloyae Drumm. TALL BORONIA. To 4m; br. densely pubesc. Lvs to 5cm, sparsely pubesc.; lfts to 2cm, 5–13, narrowly oblong or narrowly elliptic, strongly aromatic, entire or crenulate. Fls to 0.5cm, campanulate, red-pink, solitary. W Aus.

B. muelleri (Benth.) Cheel. FOREST BORONIA; PINK BORONIA. To 6m; br. often tuberculate. Lfts to 2.5cm, 7–15, linear to lanceolate, glab., often minutely serrate, sweetly fragrant, green to bronze. Fls to 1.5cm diam., white or pale pink, in terminal clusters. NSW, Vict.

B. pilosa Labill. HAIRY BORONIA. To 1m; br. usually densely pubesc. Lfts to 1cm, 3–7, linear, acute, pubesc. Fls to 1.5cm diam., white to pink, in term. or axill. cymes. Vict., Tasm., S Aus.

B. pinnata Sm. PINNATE BORONIA. To 1.5m; br. usually angular. Lfts to 2.5cm, 5–9, linear to oblong-lanceolate, acute, rigid. Fls to 2cm diam., pink, in loose, axill. or subterminal corymbs. NSW.

B. polygalifolia Sm. MILKWORT BORONIA. To 60cm, glab. Lvs to 2cm, usually simple, linear to lanceolate, acute, lustrous dark green. Fls to 1cm diam., red-pink to white, solitary, axill. Queensld, NSW.

B. serrulata Sm. SYDNEY ROCK ROSE. To 1m glab. Lvs to 2cm, simple, broadly obovate or rhombic, serrulate. Fls to 1.5cm diam., bright pink or white, strongly scented, in dense term. clusters or solitary. NSW.

B. viminea Lindl. To 1m glab. Lvs to 2.5cm, simple, linear-lanceolate or linear-cuneate. Fls to 0.5cm diam., pink, solitary on term. or axillary pedicels. W Aus.

B. cvs. 'Southern Star': compact, strong-growing, to 1m; fls star-shaped, bright rose pink, long-lasting. 'Sunset Serenade': spreading, to 75cm; lvs pinnate, light green; fls star-shaped, creamy to pale pink, later bright pink.

Borzicactus Riccob.

B. acanthurus (Vaup.) Britt. & Rose = Cleistocactus acanthurus.
B. aurantiacus (Vaup.) Kimnach & Hutchison = Matucana aurantiaca.
B. aureispinus (Ritter) P.C. Hutchison & Kimnach = Cleistocactus winteri.
B. celsianus (Cels ex Salm-Dyck) Kimnach = Oreocereus celsianus.
B. decumbens (Vaup.) Britt. & Rose = Haageocereus decumbens.
B. doelzianus (Backeb.) Kimnach = Oreocereus doelzianus.
B. fossulatus Kimnach = Oreocereus pseudofossulatus.
B. haynei (Otto ex Salm-Dyck) Kimnach = Matucana haynei.
B. hendriksenianus (Backeb.) Kimnach = Oreocereus leucotrichus.
B. humboldtii (Kunth) Britt. & Rose = Cleistocactus icosagonus.
B. icosagonus (Kunth) Britt. & Rose = Cleistocactus icosagonus.
B. leucotrichus sensu Kimnach = Oreocereus hempelianus.
B. madisoniorum P.C. Hutchison = Matucana madisoniorum.
B. samaipatanus (Cárdenas) Kimnach = Cleistocactus samaipat-

anus.
B. trollii (Kupper) Kimnach = Oreocereus trollii.

Bosisto's Box Eucalyptus bosistoana.
Bosnian Pine Pinus heldreichii.

Bossiaea Vent. WATER BUSH; SUN BUSH. Leguminosae (Papilionoideae). 40 shrubs, sometimes dwarf. Lvs entire or simple, sometimes 0. Fls pea-like, often opening only in bright sunshine, solitary or 2–3 per cluster. Aus. Z9.

B. aquifolium Benth. WATER BUSH. 1–2m. Lvs to 1.5×2cm, green, emerging brown, cordate, hirsute, coarsely spiny-toothed, pungent. Fls 1.5–2cm, standard yellow, keel brown. W Aus.

B. biloba Benth. HORN-LEAVED BOSSIAEA. 30cm–1m. Lvs 2.5–5×0.5cm, apex broad, lobed, base acuminate, occas. downy beneath, green, revolute. Fls 2cm, standard yellow, keel brown. Spring–autumn. W Aus.

B. linophylla R. Br. 2–3m. Lvs to 2.5cm, linear-lanceolate, green to deep copper, central vein protuberant and sharp-tipped, revolute. Fls to 1cm, standard orange-yellow, keel red. Summer–autumn. W Aus.

B. ornata Benth. 50cm–1m. Lvs 2–5×0.3–2cm, lanceolate, mid-green, widening towards base, central vein prominent, pungent, revolute. Fls c2cm diam., red and yellow. Summer–winter. W Aus.

Boston Fern Nephrolepis exaltata.
Boston Ivy Parthenocissus tricuspidata.
Botany Bay Fig Ficus rubiginosa.
Botany Bay Gum Xanthorrhoea arborea; X. preisii.

Bothriochilus Lem.
B. bellus Lem. = Coelia bella.

Bothriochloa Kuntze. Gramineae. 28 perenn. grasses to 1.5m. Rac. ascending to erect. Summer. Cosmop.

B. bladhii (Retz.) S.T. Blake. Rac. to 7cm; rachis with simple br. or, rarely, divided br. at base; spikelets to 4.5mm. Indochina, Malaysia. Z7.

B. caucasica (Trin.) C. Hubb. PURPLE BEARD GRASS; CAUCASIAN BLUE STEM. As for B. bladhii except rac. loose, open, purple; spikelets to 3mm. C Asia, India. Z5.

B. intermedia (R. Br.) Camus = B. bladhii.

B. ischaemum (L.) Keng. YELLOW BLUE STEM. St. upright, to 1m. Fls in a term., palmate cluster of 3–15 pan. to 7cm; spikelets to 4.5mm, narrow. S Eur. Z5.

B. saccharoides (Sw.) Rydb. SILVER BEARD GRASS. St. to 120cm. Lvs glab., blue-green. Fls in a much-branched, oblong, pan. to 15cm, rac. to 5cm numerous upright, grey-downy; spikelets to 4mm. N Amer. to Braz. Z6.
→Andropogon.

Bo Tree Ficus religiosa.

Botryanthus Kunth.
B. aucheri Boiss. = Muscari aucheri.

Botrychium Sw. GRAPE FERN; MOONWORT. Ophioglossaceae. 40 terrestrial ferns. Rhiz. short; roots fleshy. Sterile fronds 1–3-pinnate or dissected; fertile frond an erect offshoot of the sterile frond with sporangia, clustered like a bunch of grapes. Temp. regions.

B. australe R. Br. PARSLEY FERN. Fronds 5–50cm, usually solitary, 2–5-pinnate or dissected, succulent, broadly deltoid, deeply dissected, resembling parsley. Australasia.

B. dissectum Spreng. Fronds to 45×15cm, ternately compound with divisions 1–3-pinnate, dark green, minutely crenate to serrate. Autumn. SE Canada to SE US.

B. lunaria (L.) Sw. COMMON MOONWORT. Fronds 3–7×1–2.5cm, broadest at base; pinnae in 3–9 pairs, semilunar-cuneate at base, often semicircular, entire or notched, cuneate-flabellate. Amer., Eurasia, Aus.

B. matricariifolium A. Br. ex Koch. DAISY-LEAVED GRAPE FERN. Fronds to 20cm, sessile or shortly petiolate, oblong, ovate or deltate-ovate, 2-pinnate; pinnae in 2–7 pairs, oblong to ovate, bluntly tapered, entire or crenate, glab. N Amer., Eurasia.

B. multifidum (Gmel.) Rupr. LEATHERY GRAPE FERN. Fronds 5–20cm, triangular, broader than long, 2–3-pinnate, sparsely hairy, pinnae imbricate, ovate to round, obtuse, entire to crenate. Summer. Eur. ssp. **silaifolium** (Presl) R.T. Clausen. Blades larger and more coriaceous. N & W US and Canada.

B. silaifolium Presl = B. multifidum ssp. silaifolium.

B. ternatum Sw., non Hook. & Bak. Fronds 8–15×8–15cm, deltoid, 4-pinnatifid, on stipe to 10cm; pinnae ovate-lanceolate, deeply pinnatifid or pinnate; seg. minutely dentate. N Amer.,

Asia, Australasia.
B. ternatum Hook. & Bak. non Sw. = *B. australe.*
B. virginianum (L.) Sw. RATTLESNAKE FERN. Fronds 10–30×10–30cm, deltoid, 4-pinnatifid, sessile, lower pinnae greatly exceeding others; pinnules ovate-oblong, close-set, finely dissected into numerous linear-oblong seg. N & S Amer., Temp. Eurasia.

Botryopanax Miq. = *Polyscias.*

Bottionea Colla.
B. thysanthoides Colla = *Trichopetalum plumosum.*

Bottlebrush *Melaleuca.*
Bottlebrush Buckeye *Aesculus parviflora.*
Bottlebrush Bush *Callistemon.*
Bottlebrush Grass *Hystrix.*
Bottlebrush Orchid *Arpophyllum*; *Dendrobium smilliae.*
Bottle Cactus *Hatiora salicornioides.*
Bottle Gentian *Gentiana andrewsii.*
Bottle Gourd *Lagenaria* (*L. siceraria*).
Bottle Palm *Hyophorbe*; *Nolina recurvata.*
Bottle Plant *Hatiora salicornioides.*
Bottletree *Brachychiton.*

Boucerosia Wight ex Arn.
B. aaronis Hart. = *Caralluma aaronis.*
B. aucheriana Decne. = *Caralluma aucherana.*
B. awdeliana Deflers = *Caralluma awedeliana.*
B. campanulata Wight = *Caralluma umbellata.*
B. crenulata Wight & Arn. = *Caralluma crenulata.*
B. edulis Edgew. = *Caralluma edulis.*
B. europaea Guss. = *Caralluma europaea.*
B. lasiantha Wight = *Caralluma umbellata.*
B. maroccana Hook. f. = *Caralluma europaea* var. *maroccana.*
B. munbyana var. *hispanica* Jiminez & Iban. = *Caralluma europaea* var. *confusa.*
B. pauciflora Wight non Deflers. = *Caralluma pauciflora.*
B. pauciflora Deflers non Wight. = *Caralluma penicillata.*
B. russeliana Corb. = *Caralluma acutangula.*
B. sinaica Decne. = *Caralluma sinaica.*
B. socotrana Balf. f. = *Caralluma socotrana.*
B. stocksiana Boiss. = *Caralluma edulis.*
B. truncato-coronata Sedgwick = *Caralluma truncato-coronata.*
B. umbellata Wight & Arn. = *Caralluma umbellata.*

Bougainvillea Comm. ex Juss. Nyctaginaceae. 14 shrubs, climbing, often thorny. Lvs ovate to broadly elliptic, acute to acuminate. Fls small tubular, white or yellow, 1–3 subtended by persistent, highly coloured leaf-like bracts. Trop. and subtrop. S Amer. Z9.
B. 'Bois de Rose'. (*B. glabra* ×*B. spectabilis*.) Lvs dull green. Bracts not persistent, soft rose madder; perianth tube to 2.5cm or longer. Gdn origin.
B. brasiliensis Rausch = *B. spectabilis.*
B. ×buttiana Holtt. & Standl. (*B. glabra* ×*B. peruviana*.) Lvs to 11.5×8cm, ovate, apex acuminate, glab., midrib pubesc. Bracts 3.5×3.2cm, undulate to crispate, purple to orange, glab., veins pubesc.; perianth tube to 2mm diam. angled, pubesc. Gdn origin. 'Crimson Lake': closely resembles 'Mrs Butt'. 'Golden Glow': bracts pale to golden yellow. 'Louis Wathen': bracts apricot to red. 'Miss Luzon': bracts scarlet to blood red; perianth tube open in fl. 'Miss Manila': bracts red-pink. 'Mrs Butt': bracts purple. 'Mrs Mclean': bracts apricot to amber. 'Pigeon Blood': bracts oxblood. 'Scarlet Queen': bracts purple red.
B. glabra Choisy in DC. PAPER FLOWER. Lvs to 13×6cm, elliptic, glab. to sparsely pubesc., paler beneath with raised pubesc. veins. Bracts white or magenta, fading with age, weakly undulate, sometimes persisting after flowering; perianth tube inflated, pentagonal, short-pubesc., hairs curving upwards. Summer. Braz. 'Cypheri': bracts to 4.5cm, deep flamingo pink, not persistent. 'Formosa': shrubby; bracts magenta. 'Lady Huggins': bracts pale red-purple. 'Mrs Leano': bracts bright red, to 4cm, not persistent. 'Magnifica': bracts vivid purple, not persistent, to 4.5cm or longer. 'Penang': bracts elliptic, abruptly attenuate, dark violet. 'Pink Beauty': bracts to 4cm, damask pink to pale magenta. 'Rainbow': bracts coral red, becoming multicoloured as they fade. 'Sanderiana': bracts persistent, magenta to mauve, rhombic to triangular. 'Snow White': bracts white, persistent. 'Variegata': lvs variegated grey-green and cream.
B. peruviana Humb. & Bonpl. Lvs to 10.5×8cm, broadly ovate. Bracts to 3.5×2cm, pale magenta, wrinkled, glab.; perianth tube slender, to 1mm diam., angles obscure, lobes flared, pubesc. below. Columbia, Ecuad., Peru. 'Ecuador Pink', 'Lady Hudson', 'Princess Margaret Rose' are all v. similar.

B. refulgens Bull. Lvs dark green, pubesc. Fls in long pendent rac.; bracts bright purple. Braz.
B. spectabilis Willd. Lvs to 10×6cm, ovate, tomentose or velutinous. Bracts 5–6cm, purple or pink; perianth tube obscurely angled, long-pubesc. Spring. Braz. 'Lady Wilson': bracts cerise, less than 3.5cm, brick red. 'Lateritia': bracts to 3.5cm, brick red. 'Thomasii': bracts to 6cm, pink.

Boulder Raspberry *Rubus deliciosus.*

Bourreria P. Browne. Boraginaceae. 50 pubesc. shrubs or trees. Lvs elliptic, obovate or suborbicular, entire. Fls abundant, white, in term. cymes; cal. globose or ovoid, 2–5-lobed; cor. lobes broad, spreading. Fr. a drupe, orange to red. Americas, E Afr. Z10.
B. montana C. Wright ex Griseb. = *B. succulenta* var. *revoluta.*
B. ovata Miers. STRONG BACK. Shrub to 3.5m. Lvs 3.6–7.5cm, green to green-yellow, glossy above, paler beneath, apex acute, emarginate or rounded, base cuneate or tapered, midrib yellow. Corymbs 15–20-fld. Cor to 1.2cm diam., glab. W Indies.
B. revoluta HBK = *B. succulenta* var. *revoluta.*
B. succulenta Jacq. ATEJE DE COSTA; ROBLE GUAYO; FRUTA DA CATEY. Shrub or tree to 10m. Lvs 5–12cm, apex obtuse, acute or emarginate, base tapered to obtuse, scabrous above. Corymbs 10–60-fld. Cor. to 1cm diam., glab. W Indies. var. *revoluta* (HBK) O. Schulz. HIERRO DE COSTA; RASPA LENGUA DE HOJA CHIZA. Lvs to 6cm; cor. pilose. Cuba, Bahamas, Hispan., Puerto Rico.
B. tomentosa G. Don = *B. succulenta* var. *revoluta.*
→*Ehretia.*

Bourtree *Sambucus nigra.*

Boussingaultia HBK.
B. cordifolia Ten. = *Anredera cordifolia.*
B. gracilis var. *pseudobasselloides* (Hauman) Bail. = *Anredera cordifolia.*
B. gracilis f. *pseudobasselloides* Hauman = *Anredera cordifolia.*
B. gracilis Miers = *Anredera cordifolia.*

Bouteloua Lagasca. GRAMA GRASS. Gramineae. 39 ann. or perenn. grasses; st. in clusters or clumps, stiff, slender. Lvs mostly basal; blades flat or folded. Fls in a 1- to many-branched pan.; br. spicate; spikelets 'mosquito-like', sessile, in 2 rows on one side of wiry rachis. US, W Indies, C & S Amer.
B. curtipendula (Michx.) Torr. SIDEOATS GRASS. To 80cm. Lf blades to 0.5cm wide, scabrous or slightly hairy. Fls in a 30–80-branched pan.; spikelets 1–12 per br., to 1cm. Summer. Canada to Arg. Z6.
B. gracilis (HBK) Griffiths. BLUE GRAMA; MOSQUITO GRASS. To 60cm. Lf blades to 0.3cm wide, scabrous. Fls in a 1–4-branched, dense, arching pan.; spikelets 40–90 per br., to 0.5cm. Summer. S & W US, Mex. Z8.
B. oligostachya Torr. ex A. Gray = *B. gracilis.*

Bouvardia Salisb. Rubiaceae. 30 perenn. herbs or shrubs. Lvs ovate or lanceolate to oblong, entire to laciniate, stipules sheathing. Fls in term. cymes or corymbs or solitary, white to yellow or pink to red; cal. tube globose to campanulate, lobes 4, linear; cor. tubular to salver-shaped, lobes 4, erect to spreading. N Amer. to N S Amer. Z9.
B. angustifolia HBK = *B. ternifolia.*
B. bicolor Kunze = *B. versicolor.*
B. cavanillesii Schult. = *B. multiflora.*
B. corymbosa Ørst. = *B. leiantha.*
B. flava Decne. = *B. laevis.*
B. hirtella HBK = *B. ternifolia.*
B. humboldtii hort. = *B. longiflora.*
B. jacquinii HBK = *B. triphylla.*
B. laevis Mart. & Gal. St. obscurely tetragonal, glab. to sparsely and minutely pubesc., bark grey. Lvs to 11cm, ovate, apex attenuate to acute, base obtuse or truncate, glab. Fls yellow or red in term., to 7 per cyme, cor. tube to 3cm. Mex.
B. leiantha Benth. Shrub. St. terete, initially pubesc., bark grey to brown. Lvs to 7cm, ovate to oblong, apex attenuate to narrowly acute, base obtuse, pubesc. to tomentose. Fls red in dense, term. cymes or corymbs to 9cm wide; cor. tube to 1.6cm. Summer–autumn. Mex. to Costa Rica.
B. longiflora (Cav.) HBK. Shrub. St. obscurely tetragonal, glab., bark grey to brown. Lvs to 45×17mm, ovate to lanceolate to oblong, apex acute to acuminate, base attenuate to acute or cuneate, laciniate to lobed, glab. Fls white, fragrant, axill. or term. and solitary, or in cymes or corymbs; cor. tube to 9cm. Mex.
B. mollis Lind. = *B. laevis.*

B. multiflora (Cav.) Schult. Shrub. St. terete or tetragonal, initially minutely pubesc., bark grey to brown. Lvs to 5cm, ovate to lanceolate, apex attenuate to acute or obtuse, base narrowly acute or obtuse and decurrent, toothed to laciniate, glab. to minutely pubesc. Fls white to green or red, to 5 per sessile or short-stalked cyme; cor. tube to 1.5cm. Spring. Mex.

B. obovata Benth., non HBK = *B. scabra*.

B. scabra Hook. & Arn. Herb or shrub. St. terete or obscurely tetragonal, densely pubesc. Lvs to 8cm, ovate or elliptic to rhomboid or suborbicular, apex attenuate to acute, thick-textured, pubesc. Fls white or pink to red in dense cymes or corymbs to 14cm wide; cor. tube to 2cm. Winter. Mex.

B. ternifolia (Cav.) Schldl. Herb or shrub, to 1m. Bark white to grey. Lvs to 3cm, ovate or lanceolate to oblong, glab. above, pubesc. beneath. Fls red in cymes or corymbs; cor. tube to 3cm. Ariz., Tex., Mex.

B. triphylla Salisb. Lvs to 7cm, apex attenuate to acute, base acute or obtuse, thin-textured, rough, pubesc. beneath. Fls red in term., few-fld cymes or corymbs; cor. tube to 3cm. Tex., Mex.

B. versicolor Ker-Gawl. Shrub, to 1m. St. terete, initially pubesc., bark grey. Lvs ovate or lanceolate, apex attenuate to acute, base obtuse, veins pubesc. Fls yellow to red, to 5 per term. cyme; cor. tube to 3.5cm. Summer–autumn. Mex.
→*Houstonia*.

Bowenia Hook. ex Hook. f. BYFIELD FERN. Zamiaceae. 2 everg. cone-bearing perennials. St. swollen, buried or short. Lvs to 2m, few, long-stalked and forked above with spreading pinnately compound divisions; pinnules bronze then glossy pale green, to 10cm, rhombic-lanceolate. Queensld. Z10.

B. serrulata (Bull) Chamberl. Pinnules sharply and regularly serrate at tips.

B. spectabilis Hook. ex Hook. f. Pinnules ± entire.

Bower Plant *Pandorea jasminoides*.

Bowiea Harv. & Hook. f. Liliaceae (Hyacinthaceae). 3 perenn. bulbous herbs with ann. twining st. Bulbs large, composed of concentric scales. St. succulent, green, intricately branching. Lvs small, short-lived. Fls small, green-white or yellow. S & Trop. Afr. Z10.

B. kilimandscharica Mildbr. Close to *B. volubilis*; bulb smaller. Fls yellow-hyaline. Fr. to 3cm, pointed. Tanz.

B. volubilis Harv. & Hook. f. CLIMBING-ONION. Bulb light shining green, growing above soil level, to 20cm diam. St. thin, bright green. Fls green-white. Fr. to 1.4cm, obtuse. S Afr.
→*Schizobasopsis*.

Bowkeria Harv. Scrophulariaceae. 5 trees or shrubs. Lvs usually in whorls of 3. Infl. axill. or subterminal; cal. seg. 5; cor. 2-lipped, lower lip bladder-like. Summer. S Afr. Z9.

B. citrina Thode. Lvs to 4cm, narrow-elliptic, in whorls of 3. Fls yellow, lemon-scented.

B. gerrardiana Harv. ex Hiern. Shrub to 3m. Lvs to 15cm, elliptic to lanceolate. Fls white, spotted red within, resembling *Calceolaria*.

Bowman's Root *Gillenia trifoliata*; *Veronicastrum virginicum*.
Bowstring Hemp *Sansevieria*.
Bow Wood *Maclura*.
Box *Buxus*.
Box Elder *Acer negundo*.
Box Holly *Ruscus aculeatus*.
Box Huckleberry *Gaylussacia brachycera*.
Box-leaved Fig *Ficus lingua*.
Box-leaved Holly *Ilex crenata*.
Box-leaf Wattle *Acacia buxifolia*.
Box-orange *Severinia*.
Boxthorn *Lycium*.
Boxwood *Buxus*.

Boykinia Nutt. Saxifragaceae. 9 perenn., glandular-pubesc. herbs; rhiz. scaly. Lvs orbicular to reniform, sometimes succulent, petioles long. Fls crowded in pan., 5-merous. N Amer., Jap.

B. aconitifolia Nutt. Lvs 4–8×5–13cm, 4–8-lobed, toothed ×2–3; petiole 3–18cm, soft-pubesc. to glab. Sep. 1.5–3.5mm; pet. 3–6×1–3mm, white, spathulate. Summer. Appalachians. Z6.

B. elata (Nutt.) Greene = *B. occidentalis*.

B. heucheriformis (Rydb.) C. Rosend. Similar to *B. aconitifolia* except lvs 1–5×1.3–7cm, reniform or orbicular to cordate. Sep 2–6mm; pet. spathulate, violet-purple, close to sep. length. Rocky Mts, Alberta to Wyom. Z5.

B. jamesii (Torr.) Engl. Similar to *B. aconitifolia* except lvs 1–3×1.5–4cm; margin toothed ×1–2. Sep. 2–6mm; pet.

spathulate, crimson suffused purple, 2–3× longer than sep. Colorado. Z5.

B. major A. Gray. Lvs 5–22×7–26cm, pubesc. beneath, glab. above. Sep. 2–4mm; pet. white, orbicular. N & W US. Z5.

B. occidentalis Torr. & Gray. Lvs orbicular, cordate, occas. reniform, 4–10-lobed. Sep. 1–2.5mm; pet. 2–3× longer than sep. Vancouver Is to S Calif. Z8.

B. rotundifolia Parry. Lvs 4–16×4–18cm, orbicular, cordate, occas. reniform, shallowly lobed. Sep. 1.5–2mm; pet. 1.5× longer than sep. S Calif. Z8.

B. tellimoides (Maxim.) Engl. = *Peltoboykinia tellimoides*.
B. watanabei (Yatabe) Mak. = *Peltoboykinia watanabei*.
→*Saxifraga, Telesonix* and *Therofon*.

Boymia A. Juss.
B. glabrifolia Champ. ex Benth. = *Tetradium glabrifolium*.
B. ruticarpa A. Juss. = *Tetradium ruticarpum*.

Boz Pirnal Oak *Quercus aucheri*.
Bracelet *Melaleuca armillaris*.
Bracelet Honey Myrtle *Melaleuca armillaris*.
Bracelet Wood *Jacquinia barbasco*.

Brachiaria (Trin.) Griseb. Gramineae. 90 ann. or perenn. grasses. Lvs linear to lanceolate. Infl. branched, racemose; spikelets solitary or in pairs, ovate to oblong, obtuse to acute. Trop. and subtrop. Z10.

B. eruciformis (Sm.) Griseb. Loosely tufted ann. to 60cm. Lvs to 15×0.6cm. Infl. of 3–14 rac. to 2.5cm on an axis to 8cm; spikelets solitary, to 3mm. Trop. to Subtrop.

B. mutica (Forssk.) Stapf. Sprawling perenn. to 125cm. Lvs to 30×1.5cm. Infl. of 5–20 rac. to 10cm on an axis to 20cm; spikelets usually in pairs, to 4mm. Trop. Afr.

B. ramosa (L.) Stapf. Loosely tufted ann. to 70cm. Lvs 25×1.5cm. Infl. of 3–15 rac. to 8cm on an axis to 10cm; spikelets to 2mm. Trop. Afr., Middle E, Trop. Asia.

B. subquadripara (Trin.) Hitchc. Creeping ann. to 50cm. Lvs to 20×1cm. Infl. of 3–5 rac. to 6cm on an axis to 10cm; spikelets solitary, 3–4mm. Trop. Asia, Australasia.
→*Panicum*.

Brachycereus Britt. & Rose. Cactaceae. 1 shrubby cactus. St. to 60×3–5cm, forming clumps up to 2m across; ribs 16–22; spines 0.5–5cm. Fls narrowly funnelform, 6–11cm; outer tep. green- or red-brown; inner tep. creamy white. Galapagos Is. Z9.

B. nesioticus (Schum. ex Robinson) Backeb. LAVA CACTUS.

Brachychilum (R. Br. ex Wallich) Petersen. Zingiberaceae. 1 rhizomatous perenn. herb. St. to 2m slender. Lvs sheathing, lanceolate. Infl. term. Fls 2 or more per bract, white, perianth tube long, slender, yellow-stained, pet. to 1.8cm, pendent, twisted; staminodes petaloid. Fr. orange within; seeds red. Java. Z10.

B. horsfieldii (R. Br. ex Wallich) Petersen.

Brachychiton Schott & Endl. BOTTLETREE. Sterculiaceae. 31 trees and shrubs, sometimes with swollen trunks. Lvs entire to palmatifid. Fls in panicle-like cymes; cal. petaloid, 5-lobed; pet. 0; sta. fused in a staminal column with numerous anth. in 5 bundles. Aus., Papua New Guinea. Z10.

B. acerifolius Cunn. ex F. Muell. FLAME TREE; FLAME KURRAJONG. Tree to 30m. Lvs 10–25cm, glab., ovate or palmatifid. Fls precocious; cal. 1.5–2cm, bright red, 5–6-lobed, glab. or slightly hairy. Queensld to NSW.

B. australis (Schott & Endl.) A. Terracc. BROAD-LEAVED BOTTLETREE; FLAME TREE. Tree. Trunk bottle-shaped. Lvs 10–25cm, broadly ovate, lobes 5–7 ovate-acuminate to lanceolate. Fls in short pan. or rac.; cal. 2–2.5cm, white, downy. Queensld, N Aus.

B. bidwillii Hook. Shrub to 4m. Lvs 5–25cm, ovate to broadly ovate, slightly stellate-pubesc. above, densely ferruginous-pubesc. beneath, lobes 5, acute to acuminate. Fls precocious in clusters; cal. to 3.5cm, red or crimson, tube sometimes yellow, cream inside hairy. Queensld.

B. discolor F. Muell. SCRUB BOTTLETREE; QUEENSLAND LACE-BARK; HAT TREE. Tree to 30m. Lvs 6–16cm, 3–5(–7)-lobed, deeply lobed in juveniles, shallowly lobed or almost entire in adults, broadly ovate, ± glab. above, hairy beneath. Fls precocious in dense pan.; cal. +4–6cm, red or pink, stellate-pubesc. N Aus., Queensld, NSW.

B. gregorii F. Muell. DESERT KURRAJONG. Tree to 10m. Lvs 9–20cm, glab., lobes 3–5, linear-lanceolate, acuminate. Fls in short pan.; cal. 1–2cm, pale-yellow, stellate-hairy, margins often red. S, C & W Aus.

B. ×hybridus hort. (*B. acerifolius* ×*B. populneus*.) Lvs usually simple. Fls paler than in *B. acerifolius.* Gdn origin.

B. luridus C. Moore ex F. Muell. = *B. discolor.*

B. paradoxus Schott & Endl. Shrub or small tree. Lvs 8–15cm, tomentose, cordate-ovate to suborbicular, obscurely 3–5-lobed to entire. Fls in axill. clusters; cal. 2.5–4cm, red. N Aus., Queensld.

B. populneus (Schott & Endl.) R. Br. KURRAJONG. Tree to 20m. Lvs 4–12cm, ovate to broadly ovate, entire or 3–5-lobed, glab., attenuate or aristate, base cuneate, margin thick, crenulate or irregular. Fls in short pan.; cal. 1–1.5cm, pale green, slightly pubesc. outside. Queensld, NSW.

B. ramiflorus R. Br. = *B. paradoxus.*

B. rupestris (Mitch. ex Lindl.) Schum. QUEENSLAND BOTTLETREE; NARROW-LEAVED BOTTLETREE. Large tree, trunk becoming bottle-shaped. Lvs simple on mature trees, 8–15cm, oblong-linear to lanceolate, on juveniles digitately 3–9-divided. Cal. 6–8mm, campanulate, cream blotched with red inside, stellate-pubesc. Queensld.

→*Sterculia* and *Trichosiphon.*

Brachycome Cass. SWAN RIVER DAISY. Compositae. *c*70 ann. or perenn. herbs. St. simple or branched, glab. or glandular-hairy. Cap. 1 to several, radiate; ray flts usually numerous, white, blue, pink or purple, rarely yellow; disc flts yellow. Aus., NZ, New Guinea, Tasm. Z8.

B. aculeata (Labill.) Less. Erect perenn. to 65cm. Rosulate lvs to 10cm, oblanceolate-spathulate, distally lobed, base attenuate; st. lvs linear or cuneate, distally dentate. Ray flts to 35, to 8×2mm, white, blue or pale purple. Summer–autumn. Aus.

B. angustifolia A.M. Cunn. ex DC. Perenn. to 35cm. Lvs to 6cm, alt., basal and cauline, linear-lanceolate to elliptic, entire or irregularly lobed. Ray flts to 29, 10×3mm, pale pink, blue or purple. Summer. Aus.

B. cardiocarpa var. *alpina* F. Muell. ex Benth. = *B. nivalis* var. *alpina.*

B. diversifolia Fisch. & Mey. Ann. or perenn. to 50cm. St. white-grey hairy. Lvs to 14cm, basal and cauline, apex toothed or lobed, seg. linear to oblong, obcuneate, to 1cm. Ray flts to 15mm, white. Early summer. Aus.

B. iberidifolia Benth. SWAN RIVER DAISY. To 45cm, pubesc. Lvs to 10cm, cauline, usually pinnatisect, seg. to 1.3cm, broadly linear. Ray flts 16×4mm, white, blue or violet. Summer–autumn. S Aus. 'Purple Splendour': flts rich purple.

B. microcarpa F. Muell. To 60cm, pubesc. Lvs to 7cm, cauline, opposite, orbicular, pinnatisect, pinnatifid or crenate, lower lvs petiolate, upper lvs sessile. Ray flts to 5×1mm, white or pale blue. Summer–autumn. E Aus.

B. multifida DC. Glab. ann. to 45cm. Lvs to 7cm, cauline, pinnatisect, seg. *c*10, to 3.5cm, filiform to oblanceolate or cuneate, acute, entire, dentate or lobed. Ray flts to 10×2mm, purple, pink or white. Summer–autumn. SE Aus.

B. nivalis F. Muell. To 30cm. Lvs to 15cm, rosulate, spathulate, entire to pinnatipartite or 2-pinnatisect. Ray flts to 3×1mm. Aus. var. *alpina* F. Muell. ex Benth. Lvs linear to narrowly spathulate, seg. linear, to 5mm.

B. rigida hort. = *B. rigidula.*

B. rigidula (DC.) G.L. Davis. Perenn. to 40cm. Lvs to 3cm, cauline, crowded, pinnatisect, seg. linear, spreading, to 8mm. Ray flts to 40, to 8mm, blue-purple. Summer–autumn. Aus.

B. scapiformis DC. = *B. spathulata.*

B. scapigera Sieb. ex Spreng. Perenn., to 40cm. Lvs to 19cm, rosulate, linear, acute, entire. Ray flts to 9×2mm, white or purple. Summer–autumn. S Aus.

B. segmentosa Morr. & Muell. Perenn. to 34cm. Lvs to 5cm, cauline, pinnatisect, seg. 7, cuneate, to 1cm, lobed or toothed above. Ray flts to 7×1mm, white. Summer–autumn. Aus.

B. spathulata Gaudin. Perenn. to 30cm. Lvs alt., obovate or oblong-cuneate, sometimes toothed above. Ray flts white to pale blue. Autumn. Aus.

B. stolonifera G.L. Davis. Perenn. to 8cm. Lvs 3cm, radical, broadly linear, entire, apex obtuse, base sheathing. Ray flts to 6×2mm, white. Summer–autumn. SE Aus.

B. tenuiscapa Hook. f. Perenn. to 30cm. Lvs oblanceolate to ovate, dentate to crenate, base distally sheathing. Ray flts to 60, to 7×2mm, white or purple. Summer–autumn. SE Aus.

→*Steiroglossa.*

Brachycorythis Lindl. Orchidaceae. 30 terrestrial or epiphytic orchids. Roots swollen. St. leafy. Rac. terminal, many-fld; sep. free; pet. usually adnate at base to side of column; lip spurred or saccate at base. Trop. & S Afr., trop. Asia. Z9.

B. kalbreyeri Rchb. f. Epiphytic, 15–40cm, herbaceous. Lvs 11×2.5cm, lanceolate. Fls pale lilac or mauve or almost white, about 5cm diam. with spicy scent; spur 0. W Afr., Zaire, E Afr.

B. macrantha (Lindl.) Summerh. Terrestrial, to 40cm. Lvs to 13×5cm, broadly lanceolate. Fls green and mauve; spur 7.5–10mm, conical. W Afr.

Brachyglottis Forst. & Forst. f. Compositae. *c*30 trees, shrubs, vines or perenn. herbs. Lvs alt. Cap. radiate or discoid, usually in corymbose pan., rarely solitary, fragrant; ray flts yellow to white; disc flts yellow to cream. NZ, Chatham Is., Tasm.

B. bidwillii (Hook. f.) R. Nordenstam. Shrub to 1m; br. stout, densely white- to buff-tomentose at first. Lvs 2–2.5cm, elliptic-oblong to oblong to obovate-oblong, coriaceous, glab. above, densely tomentose beneath. Cap. to 1.5cm diam., radiate or discoid, campanulate, in corymbose pan. to 5cm diam.; ray flts 3–5; disc flts many. Summer. NZ.

B. buchananii (J.B. Armstr.) R. Nordenstam. Robust shrub to 1.5m; br. grooved, branchlets pale-tomentose. Lvs 2.5–5cm, broadly oblong, obtuse, glab. above, silvery-tomentose beneath. Cap. to 1cm diam., discoid, campanulate to subcylindric, in a short rac.; flts numerous, yellow to cream. Summer. NZ.

B. compacta (T. Kirk) R. Nordenstam. Shrub to 1m; br. stout, branchlets densely white-tomentose. Lvs 2–4cm, obovate to oblong, obtuse, crenulate, undulate, densely tomentose at first. Cap. to 3cm diam,. radiate, solitary or few together in rac.; ray flts 10+, spreading, bright yellow. Summer. NZ.

B. **Dunedin Hybrids.** (*B. compacta* × *B. greyi* × *B. laxifolia*). Shrub to 1.5cm, bushy and somewhat straggling, white-tomentose at first. Lvs 3–7cm, obovate to ovate, obtuse, rounded at base, entire to sinuate, grey to dark green above, white-tomentose beneath. Cap. to 2.5cm diam., radiate, in loose term. pan.; ray flts 11–15, bright yellow. The plant most often seen is 'Sunshine' (*Senecio greyi* of gardens). 'Moira Read' has lvs variegated.

B. elaeagnifolia (Hook. f.) R. Nordenstam. Shrub to 3m; br. grooved, pale-tomentose. Lvs 6–9cm, obovate to lanceolate-oblong, obtuse, markedly veined, glab. above, silvery-tomentose beneath. Cap. to 1cm diam., discoid, in a pyramidal to subracemose pan. to 15cm. Summer. NZ.

B. greyi (Hook. f.) R. Nordenstam. Shrub to 2m; br. spreading, white-tomentose. Lvs 4–8cm, oblong to ovate-oblong, obtuse, rounded to shallowly cordate at base, entire to shallowly sinuate, coriaceous, white-tomentose, becoming glab. above. Cap. to 3cm diam., radiate, in large term. corymbs; ray flts to 1cm, 12–15, bright yellow. Summer. NZ.

B. haastii (Hook. f.) R. Nordenstam. Low, spreading, densely white-tomentose. Lvs 3–15cm, basal, oblong to suborbicular, obtuse, cordate to truncate at base, submembranous. Cap. 2–4cm diam., radiate, 1–3 together on scapes to 35cm; ray flts yellow. Summer. NZ.

B. hectoris (Buch.) R. Nordenstam. Shrub to 4m; br. spreading, stout, brittle, tomentose. Lvs 10–25cm, densely arranged toward br. apices, oblanceolate, pinnatifid to pinnatisect toward base, serrate-dentate, membranous, thinly tomentose beneath at first. Cap. to 5cm diam., radiate, in large, lax term. corymbs; ray flts white. Summer. NZ.

B. huntii (F. Muell.) R. Nordenstam. Shrub or tree to 6m+. Lvs 5–10cm, lanceolate-oblong to elliptic-oblong; sessile, narrowed to base, adpressed, fulvous-tomentose at first, slightly revolute. Cap. to 2cm diam., radiate, in a dense, leafy term. pan., on stout peduncles; ray flts 15–20, broad, recurved, yellow. Summer. NZ.

B. kirkii (Hook. f. ex T. Kirk) C.J. Webb. Shrub to 3m; br. brittle. Lvs 4–10cm, obovate-cuneate to oblong, coarsely, sinuate-dentate to sinuate-entire, rather fleshy. Cap. to 5cm diam., radiate, in corymbs to 30cm diam.; ray flts spreading, 2–3cm, white. Summer. NZ.

B. lagopus (Raoul) R. Nordenstam. Perenn. to 2m; rootstock stout. Lvs 2.5–15cm, ovate-oblong to suborbicular, obtuse, cordate at base, coriaceous, hispid above, densely lanate beneath, to 10cm. Cap. 10cm diam., radiate, on scapes to 35cm; ray flts to 2cm, yellow. Summer. NZ.

B. laxifolia (Buch.) R. Nordenstam. Shrub to 1m, laxly branched; branchlets tomentose at first. Lvs 2–6cm, clustered, elliptic to lanceolate-oblong, acute, entire to remotely crenate-sinuate, subcoriaceous, subglabrous above, densely white-tomentose beneath. Cap. to 2cm diam, radiate, in a loose pan.; ray flts to 10mm, 10–15, spreading, yellow; disc flts dark red to rust-coloured. Summer. NZ.

B. monroi (Hook. f.) R. Nordenstam. Shrub to 1m, much-branched, tomentose. Lvs 2–4cm, densely arranged, narrowly to obovate-oblong, obtuse, coriaceous, green tinged brown and glab. above, adpressed-tomentose beneath, sinuate-crenate. Cap. to 2cm diam., radiate, in a term. corymb; ray flts 10–15, spreading to recurved, broad, yellow. Summer. NZ.

B. perdicioides (Hook. f.) R. Nordenstam. Shrub to 2m; br. slender, striate, pubesc. Lvs 2.5–5cm, oblong to elliptic, finely crenate-serrate, membranous. Cap. to 1cm diam., radiate, in crowded corymbs; ray flts to 8mm, usually 1–3, broad, yellow.

Summer. NZ.

B. rangiora Buch = *B. repanda*.

B. repanda Forst. & Forst. f. Shrub or tree to 6m+; br. spreading, stout, white- to buff-tomentose. Lvs 5–25cm, long-stalked, broadly oblong to ovate-oblong, obtuse to subacute, cordate to truncate at base, remotely dentate-lobed to sinuate. Cap. 5mm diam., discoid, in spreading, branched pan. Spring. NZ. 'Purpurea': lvs purple above, white below. 'Variegata': lvs dark green, irregularly stippled yellow-green, grey-green and cream.

B. rotundifolia Forst. & Forst. f. Shrub or tree to 6m+; br. stout, pale buff- to white-tomentose. Lvs 4–10cm, broadly ovate to suborbicular, coriaceous, adpressed-tomentose beneath. Cap. to 1cm diam., discoid, campanulate, in pan. to 20cm. Summer. NZ.

B. saxifragoides (Hook. f.) R. Nordenstam. Perenn. to 2m; rootstock stout, lanate. Lvs 7–20cm, long-stalked, ovate-oblong to suborbicular, obtuse, cordate at base, coriaceous, pilose above, tomentose beneath. Cap. 2–4cm diam., radiate, on branched scapes to 45cm; ray flts to 3cm, yellow. Summer–autumn. NZ.
→*Senecio*.

Brachylaena R. Br. Compositae. 23 strongly scented or shrubs. Lvs alt., somewhat leathery, ± sessile, often tomentose beneath. Cap. discoid, numerous, in axill. or term. branching rac. or pan. Trop. and S Afr. to Madag. and the Masc. Is. Z10.

B. dentata Less. = *B. glabra*.

B. glabra (L. f.) Druce. Like *B. neriifolia* but lvs 7.5–10cm, oblong or lanceolate-oblong, somewhat acute, entire, or sinuate-toothed near apex, sometimes revolute, cap. in a branched term. racemose infl. S Afr.

B. huillensis O. Hoffm. Everg. tree or shrub, to 30m. Trunk fluted, br. grooved, grey-white downy at first. Lvs 4–13cm, oblanceolate, obovate- or elliptic-oblong, acute, mucronate, often sinuate toward apex, shiny above, white-tomentose beneath. Cap. in erect, axill. pan.; flts cream-white. Trop. & S Afr.

B. hutchinsii Hutch. = *B. huillensis*.

B. neriifolia (L.) R. Br. Large leafy shrub or small tree, to 6m. Lvs 6–12cm, lanceolate, linear-lanceolate or oblanceolate, acute or acuminate, entire or with 1 to few teeth near apex, rusty beneath at first. Cap. numerous, in erect, term., pyramidal pan.; flts yellow. Late summer–late autumn. S Afr.
→*Baccharis*.

Brachyloma Sonder. Epacridaceae. 7 heath-like shrubs. Lvs small, entire, rigid. Fls small, solitary; cor. tube with clustered of hairs or scales at the base of each lobe. S & W Aus., Tasm. Z9.

B. ciliatum (R. Br.) Benth. Slender dwarf shrub 20–45cm; sometimes procumbent; branchlets ascending. Lvs to 1cm, subsessile, oblong-lanceolate. Cor. tube white, 3.5mm, campanulate, with 5 tufts of long hairs in throat, lobes ovate-deltoid, globose. Autumn. S Aus., Tasm.

B. daphnoides (Sm.) Benth. DAPHNE HEATH. Small, upright shrub to 80cm. Lvs to 1.3cm, oblong-ovate to elliptic. Fls sweetly fragrant; cor. cream, tube to 4.5mm, long-urceolate with a few hairs at the throat, lobes acuminate. Autumn. S Aus., Tasm.

B. ericoides (Schldl.) Sonder. BRUSH HEATH. Dense dwarf shrub to 1m. Lvs 0.4–1.8cm, linear to broadly elliptic; cor. pink to orange, tube to 4.5mm, campanulate to urceolate, with 5 fringed scales in tube. Summer. S & W Aus.
→*Leucopogon* and *Styphelia*.

Brachypodium P. Beauv. Gramineae. 17 ann. or perenn. grasses. St. upright, somewhat flimsy, forming tussocks. Lvs flat or revolute. Flts in spike-like rac.; spikelets short-pedicellate, compressed, 5–25-fld. Summer. Temp. N hemis. Z5.

B. pinnatum (L.) P. Beauv. TOR GRASS. Perenn. to 1.2m. St. stiff, forming tussocks. Lvs to 45×0.5cm, stiff, linear, glab., scabrous, yellow-green to light green. Rac. to 25cm, erect; spikelets to 25-fld, to 4cm. N hemis.

B. sylvaticum (Huds.) P. Beauv. SLENDER FALSE BROME; WOOD FALSE BROME. Perenn. to 90cm. St. upright, forming tussocks. Lvs 35×1cm, linear-lanceolate to scabrous, pubesc., green to yellow-green, sheaths hairy. Rac. to 20cm, erect to arching; spikelets, 8–16-fld, to 4.5cm. Eur., temp. Asia, N Afr.

Brachysema R. Br. SWAN RIVER PEA. Leguminosae (Papilionoideae). 15 shrubs. St. foliose or phyllocladous. Lvs simple, occas. aborted. Fls pea-like, solitary or in clusters; cal. tubular or campanulate, lobes 5, upper 2 or 3 often united; pet. united in part, standard recurved. Aus. Z9.

B. acuminatum hort. ex Jacques = *B. celsianum*.

B. celsianum Lem. Spreading or prostrate, everg. shrub to 2m. Lvs to 6.5cm, lanceolate, acute, coriaceous, dark green above,

silver-grey beneath. Fls in clusters of 2–3 scarlet, often yellow near base. Throughout the year. W Aus. Z9.

B. lanceolatum Meissn. = *B. celsianum*.

Brachystegia Benth. Leguminosae (Caesalpinioideae). 30 medium to tall trees; bark fibrous. Lvs pinnate; young foliage colourful. Fls olive-coloured, small, in pan. or rac., generally term. Fr. flat, valves spiralling to expel seeds. Zimb. to Kenya, Moz., Angola. Z10.

B. spiciformis Benth. MSASA. Large shrub or tree to 25m; crown diffuse or rounded. Trunk to 1m diam. Bark pale grey and smooth, rough and splitting with age. Lvs emerging scarlet to crimson, turning bronze then lustrous green; lfts 2–8cm, in 2–6, generally 4 pairs, ± circular to narrow-ovate. Fls small, fragrant, green, in crowded term. rac. Zimb., Zam., Malawi.

Brachystelma R. Br. Asclepiadaceae. 100 perenn. herbs. Roots tuberous-caudiciform or fusiform; st. simple or branching, leafy. Fls solitary at nodes or in an umbel; cor. round, disc-like or short-tubed, lobes 5, free or united at tips. Trop. Afr., Ethiop., S Afr., Nam.

B. arnottii Bak. Caudex flattened. Lvs 1–2cm, lanceolate to ovate-lanceolate, densely grey-hispid beneath, wavy. Fls 2–4; cor. small, lobes spreading, with margin folded back, puberulous below, glab. above, dark purple-brown with green warty thickening at lip. E Cape, Nam.

B. barberiae Harv. ex Hook. f. Caudex flattened; st. v. short. Lvs 7–20cm, linear-oblong. Infl. 10–12cm diam., spherical, capitate, fls malodorous, dirty purple, yellow in centre, spotted; cor. lobes 2.5cm, 3-angled, tails thin, fused at tips. Transvaal, E Cape.

B. barbertonensis hort. = *B. barberiae*.

B. bingeri A. Chev. Caudex subspheric or oblong; st. branching. Lvs 2.5–6cm, broadly elliptic to oblanceolate. Fls 1–4; cor. 1.2cm across, red-white, puberulous, tube 2–3mm, lobes 7mm, triangular-ovate. Sudan.

B. blepharanthera H. Huber. Caudex flattened; st. branching. Lvs oblong-spathulate, blunt, margins slightly wavy. Fls 1–2; cor. 9mm. Nam.

B. brevipedicillatum Turrill = *B. dinteri*.

B. buchananii N.E. Br. Caudex large, fleshy. Lvs 4–12cm, elliptic-ovate, blunt, rounded, puberulous. Fls 20–30 in an umbel; cor. 2–2.5cm diam., plate-shaped, black-purple, lobes triangular. Malawi, Tanz., Zimb., Zaire.

B. caffrum (Schltr.) N.E. Br. Caudex compressed-spheric with a long neck; st. numerous, prostrate. Lvs ovate or lanceolate, fairly thick, with minute rigid cilia. Fls 1–2; cor. 10–13mm diam., lobes fleshy, pale yellow, 2–4×1–2mm, ovate, ciliate. Cape Prov.

B. campanulatum N.E. Br. Caudex flattened or napiform; br. prostrate. Lvs 2–4×0.6–1cm, elliptic, ovate to obovate, wavy, puberulous. Cor. campanulate, densely woolly, exterior green, interior green-yellow, upper part with purple-brown spots and longitudinal veins, stiffly hairy, lobes 3–5mm. Cape Prov.

B. cathcartense R.A. Dyer. Caudex flattened; st. 5cm, with few br. Lvs 1–2.5cm, linear-lanceolate, thinly hispid. Fls 1–2 in lf axils, malodorous; cor. 2–2.2cm, 10-ribbed, tube almost campanulate, to 9.5mm, lobes 11–13mm, triangular, ciliate, exterior of tube and lobe bases spotted brown, lower half of tube spotted yellow and striped brown, tips curved inwards, green, hairy. Cape Prov.

B. caudatum (Thunb.) N.E. Br. Caudex flattened; st. several, 10–15cm. Lvs 1.2–2cm, linear-lanceolate to obovate-spathulate, undulate. Fls 2–8; cor. green outside, puberulous, tube and base of lobes spotted purple-brown, interior and base of lobes glab., yellow or off-white with purple-brown tuberculate spots, lobes 2–3cm, ovate-attenuate. Cape Prov.

B. cinereum (Schltr.) N.E. Br. = *B. circinatum*.

B. circinatum E. Mey. Caudex flattened; st. 1 or several, branching. Lvs 0.5–2cm, linear or elliptic-lanceolate. Fls in clusters, or solitary; cor. lobes united at tip, conical, spherical to almost cylindric, exterior glab., interior puberulous, interior and exterior cream in multi-fld forms, interior pink, exterior green in solitary-fld forms, lobes to 12mm. Cape Prov. to Nam.

B. coddii R.A. Dyer. Br. prostrate, 5–15cm. Lvs short-petiolate, 2.5cm, ovate to broad-ovate. Fls solitary, 17–20mm across; lobes 6–7mm long, almost black with purple, red and white blotches. E Transvaal.

B. comptum N.E. Br. Caudex long, thick, fleshy, narrowly fusiform; st. simple or branching, puberulous. Lvs 0.7–1.2cm, oblong or rounded-ovate. Fls solitary; tube flat, 1mm deep, glab., lobes free, 7–8×2mm, margins slightly incurving, with a tuft of long, purple, clavate hairs. Cape Prov.

B. constrictum J.B. Hall. Caudex disc-like, br. prostrate. Lvs to 6cm, narrow-linear. Fls 1–2 in axils; cor. purple, exterior warty, interior white-hairy, tube 4.5mm long, 5mm diam., lobes

9–12mm, caudate, interior with leathery longitudinal band. Ghana.

B. crispum Graham = *B. caudatum*.

B. cupulatum R.A. Dyer.   Caudex flattened; st. simple or branched. Lvs 3–8cm, ovate-lanceolate, elliptic or linear. Fls several together; cor. 1cm across, green-yellow to dark brown or velvety black, interior glab., lobes oblong, narrowing at tip, margins slightly recurved; outer corona cup-shaped. Nam.

B. dinteri Schltr.   Caudex 3–5cm diam., flat on top; st. seldom branching. Lvs 4cm, lanceolate, pointed, velvety. Fls 9–12 in a spherical umbel; cor. flat, 10mm across, green spotted brown. Nam.

B. distinctum N.E. Br. = *B. elongatum*.

B. duplicatum (R.A. Dyer) R.A. Dyer.   Lvs to 1cm, oblong-lanceolate, with papillose hairs, blue-green. Fls 2–3; cor. 22–24mm across, tube campanulate, 2–3mm deep, interior with several stiff hairs, lobes 1–1.2cm, margins recurved, pale green, 3 mauve veins at base. OFS.

B. elongatum (Schltr.) N.E. Br.   Caudex flattened. Lvs 2–4cm, linear to linear-lanceolate. Fls solitary or 2–6; cor. tube 3mm, campanulate, spotted white-purple, exterior glab., with clavate white hairs down to base of lobes, lobes 12–20mm, united at tips. Cape Prov.

B. exile Bullock.   Caudex disc-like. Lvs 7cm, lanceolate. Fls solitary; tube cup-shaped, 2mm, lobes 2.5–4cm, subulate-linear, with 4mm purple hairs. Nigeria, Cameroun.

B. filiformis Harv. = *B. circinatum*.

B. floribundum R.A. Dyer = *B. duplicatum*.

B. foetidum Schltr.   Caudex flattened; br. velvety-hairy, densely leafy. Lvs 1–2.5cm, ovate to ovate-spathulate, velvety, wavy. Fls 1–2; cor. exterior hairy, interior dark purple-brown, lobes 1.3cm, united. Transvaal.

B. galpinii (Schltr.) N.E. Br. = *B. circinatum*.

B. grossartii Dinter = *B. arnotii*.

B. hirsuta E. Mey. = *Raphionacme hirsuta*.

B. johnstonii N.E. Br.   Lvs 1.25–2.5cm, linear, pointed, plicate, undulate, puberulous beneath. Fls 4–5; cor. glab., exterior purple or green-brown, tube purple-brown ringed off-white or yellow at mouth, lobes 7.5×5mm, with thread-like extension, interior white-hairy. Uganda, Kenya.

B. lanceolatum Turrill = *B. johnstonii*.

B. lineare A. Rich.   St. 7.5–10cm, branching. Lvs 3–4cm, linear. Fls 1–2, malodorous; tube campanulate, lobes 1–1.5cm, tapering, linear, base yellow with coalescing brown spots. Sudan, Ethiop., Kenya.

B. linearifolium Turrill = *B. lineare*.

B. magicum N.E. Br. = *B. buchananii*.

B. micranthum E. Mey.   Caudex flattened; st. several, branching. Lvs 1cm, linear-lanceolate to elliptic. Fls 1–2, minute, lobes ovate-lanceolate, spreading. Cape Prov.

B. modestum R.A. Dyer.   St. simple or branching 2–3cm. Lvs 1–1.5cm, oblong-elliptic, glab., finely hairy above. Fls 1–2; tube 5×10mm, campanulate, interior white striped dark red, lobes triangular, winged, dark red. Natal.

B. montanum R.A. Dyer.   Caudex hemispheric to 2.3cm. St. subterranean and aerial. Lvs to 2.3cm, oblong to linear-oblong. Fls 2; cor. to 1.5cm, tube to 4.5×4.5mm, campanulate, lobes to 1cm, linear, base broad, hairy. Cape Prov.

B. natalense (Schltr.) N.E. Br.   Caudex thick, fleshy, fusiform; st. 15–30cm. Lvs 2.5–6cm, ovate to round-ovate, hairy. Fls 2–4; cor. nodding, 3–4mm across, upper two-thirds lobed, flat cup-shaped below, lobes 2×1.5mm, ovate-lanceolate, dull green. Natal.

B. nauseosum Willd. = *B. buchananii*.

B. occidentale Schltr.   Caudex almost spherical. Lvs 0.3–1.2cm, linear, somewhat fleshy, ciliate. Fls usually 2 together; cor. tube 2mm, cup-shaped, lobes free, 2mm, oblong-lanceolate, campanulate, spreading, margins incurved midway, tips thickened, incurved to hooked, yellow-white, interior spotted white-red. Cape Prov.

B. oianthum Schltr.   Lvs 1.5–5cm, linear-lanceolate, blunt to pointed, hairy, somewhat wavy. Cor. 2.2×1.7cm, ovoid, constricted, interior hairy, dark purple-brown or yellow densely spotted dark purple-brown, lobes ovate-triangular, tapering, ciliate, tips free. Transvaal.

B. omissum Bullock.   Caudex disc-like, fleshy; st. stout, to 30cm. Lvs to 6cm, oblong-lanceolate, hispid. Fls in an umbel; cor. densely tomentose within, purple, tube short, to 2cm across, lobes v. short, deltoid. Cameroun.

B. ovatum Oliv. = *B. circinatum*.

B. pachypodium R.A. Dyer.   Caudex irregularly shaped; st. stump-like. Lvs 2.5–5cm, broad-ovate or broadly elliptic-ovate. Fls 1–2; cor. 20–23mm, tube white within, lobes linear-lanceolate, 17mm, interior green-yellow, margins curved back, tips united. Transvaal.

B. pallida (Schltr.) N.E. Br. = *B. circinatum*.

B. phyteumoides Schum. = *B. lineare*.

B. pilosum R.A. Dyer.   St. 4–5mm diam., branching from soil level, 25cm. Lvs 1–1.5cm, oblong, margins folded upwards, slightly wavy. Fls usually paired; cor. 16–18mm, base saucer-shaped, 1–1.5mm, lobes lanceolate, united above, underside hairy. Transvaal.

B. plocamoides Oliv.   Caudex large, fleshy, napiform; st. 20–25cm, repeatedly branching. Lvs 0.5–0.8cm, linear, hooked. Fl. solitary; cor. stellate, lobed almost to base, 15mm long, 2–4mm wide at base, pointed, dark purple. Tanz., Zam., Zimb.

B. pulchellum (Harv.) Schltr.   Caudex spherical to conical; trunk-small; st. creeping, branched, purple-red, with curly hairs. Lvs 1–1.5cm, broad-ovate, fleshy, dark purple-green above, margins with minute curly hairs. Fls solitary; cor. purple to chestnut brown, 11–15mm across, exterior minutely spotted, lobes 4–6mm. Natal.

B. pygmaeum (Schltr.) N.E. Br.   Caudex napiform; st. simple or branching. Lvs to 1cm, linear-spathulate. Fls 1–3; cor. tube flat, cup-shaped, exterior glab., interior puberulous, yellow or tinged green, lobes 4–5mm, linear, from a triangular base, attached at tips, olive green or purple-brown. Transvaal. ssp. *flavidum* (Schltr.) R.A. Dyer. Fls with lobes free, tinged yellow. Natal.

B. ramosissimum (Schltr.) N.E. Br.   Roots fusiform, bunched; st. to 15cm, br. angular. Lvs 1.3–2cm, linear-oblong to lanceolate, ciliate. Fls 2–4 in clusters; cor. 6mm diam., pale yellow or white, united part flat, lobes free, 3–4mm, margins involute, sparsely hairy. Transvaal.

B. rehmannii Schltr. = *B. foetidum*.

B. ringens E.A. Bruce = *B. dinteri*.

B. sandersonii (Oliv.) N.E. Br.   Roots clustered, long, fleshy, cylindric or narrow-fusiform; st. 20–45cm, simple or branching. Lvs 1.2–3cm, linear-oblong to elliptic-oblong, rough-ciliate. Fls in clusters of 2–6; tube 1–2mm deep, cup-shaped, lobes free, 3–5×2mm, edges folded back, ciliate, white, striped pink or pale purple. Natal, Zululand.

B. schinzii (Schum.) N.E. Br.   Caudex conical-ovate; st. single; br. creeping. Lvs 2–5cm, linear or terete, margins recurved, ± hairy. Fls usually in pairs; cor. round, almost 1cm across, purple-brown with white centre, lobes 3×3mm, pointed, covered with purple hairs. Nam.

B. schizoglossoides (Schltr.) N.E. Br.   Roots clustered, narrow-fusiform; st. solitary, fluted. Lvs 1–4cm, linear, pointed. Fls 1–3 in a cluster; tube cup-shaped, lobes free, 1.5–2×1.5–2mm, tips incurved, pale cream-yellow, ciliate. Cape Prov.

B. shirense Schltr. = *B. buchananii*.

B. spathulatum Lindl. = *B. caudatum*.

B. stellatum E.A. Bruce & R.A. Dyer.   Caudex flat-spherical; st. 1–4. Lvs 1cm, ovate to round, rather fleshy, ciliate. Fls 1–2, 9–10mm across; tube 2–2.5mm deep, cream marked purple, covered with purple hairs, lobes projecting, 2mm long, white at base, upper two-thirds yellow-green, covered with long white hairs. Transvaal.

B. stenophyllum (Schltr.) R.A. Dyer.   Caudex flat, disc-like; st. 1–3. Lvs 7–9cm, narrowly linear-lanceolate or spathulate. Fls 2–4 in an umbel-like infl.; cor. 15mm, campanulate, lobes long, united at tips, green to brown-green, interior pale yellow-green. Nam.

B. tavalla Schum.   Caudex spherical; st. mostly simple, somewhat woolly above. Lvs 1.25–3cm, woolly. Fls solitary or in pairs; cor. round, interior violet-green with dense purple wool, exterior puberulous near base, tube 3mm, lobes 12mm, linear. Tanz.

B. tenue R.A. Dyer.   Caudex slightly compressed; st. branching. Lvs 1–2cm, ovate to oblong-elliptic, sparsely hairy. Fls 1–2 at nodes; cor. yellow-brown, around 15mm, exterior sparsely hairy, tube cup-shaped, 1mm deep, lobes linear, united at tips. Natal.

B. togoense Schltr.   Caudex disc-shaped; st. stout. Lvs to 11cm, oblong-lanceolate, pubesc. Fls in a term. umbel; cor. glab. or pubesc. within, yellow, green or purple, broadly funnel-shaped, to 17–18mm across, lobes 11mm long, triangular. Ghana, Togo, Benin, Nigeria, Zam.

B. tuberosum R. Br.   Caudex 3.5cm diam.; st. 1 or several. Lvs 2–4cm, linear-lanceolate to obovate, plicate, ciliate. Fls 2–4; cor. 2cm across, exterior green spotted purple-brown, tube campanulate, interior yellow with purple-brown bands, lobes 6mm, dark purple-brown, free, margins recurved and long-hairy. Cape Prov.

B. undulatum (Schltr.) N.E. Br. = *B. circinatum*.

B. vahrmeijeri R.A. Dyer.   Caudex slightly compressed, red; st. several. Lvs to 3cm, elliptic-lanceolate. Fls 2–3; cor. yellow-green or cream, rarely white or brown, 4mm wide at mouth, lobes 5mm ovate-triangular, spreading, fleshy. Natal.

B. viridiflorum Turrill = *Raphionacme burkei*.

B. zeyheri (Schltr.) N.E. Br. = *B. circinatum*.

→*Blepharanthera, Brachystelmaria, Craterostemma, Dichaelia, Lasiostelma, Siphonostelma, Sisyranthus, Stapelia* and

Tapeinostelma.

Brachystelmaria Schltr.
B. natalensis Schltr. = *Brachystelma sandersonii.*
B. occidentale Schltr. = *Brachystelma occidentale.*
B. ramosissima Schltr. = *Brachystelma ramosissimum.*

Bracken *Pteridium aquilinum.*

Brahea Mart. SOYA; ROCK PALM; HESPER PALM. Palmae. 12
palms. St. usually solitary, erect, clothed with fibrous lf sheaths,
becoming bare and ringed. Lvs costapalmate, induplicate; blade
orbicular; seg. glab., waxy or floccose, apex divided, acuminate
midribs prominent. Mex., Guat. Z10.
B. aculeata (Brandg.) H.E. Moore. SINDALOA HESPER PALM.
Trunk to 6m×20cm, ringed. Petiole to 60cm with 2mm spines;
blade divided to half way or more; pinnae 30–40, apices divided.
Mex.
B. armata S. Wats. BLUE HESPER PALM; SHORT BLUE HESPER; GREY
GODDESS; BLUE FAN PALM; MEXICAN BLUE FAN PALM. Trunk to
15m×45cm. Petioles to 1.5m, with decurved marginal spines; lf
blades blue-green, waxy, divided to half depth. Mex., Baja
Calif.
B. brandegeei (C.A. Purpus) H.E. Moore. SAN JOSE HESPER PALM.
To 12m. Lvs marcescent; petiole to 1m, with 7mm spines; seg.
50–60, almost free. Baja Calif.
B. calcarata hort. = *B. calcarea.*
B. calcarea Liebm. Trunk 5–10m. Lvs neatly abscising; petiole
unarmed; blade green above, glaucous waxy or tomentose beneath; seg. 50–70, apex shallowly emarginate. Mex., Guat.
B. dulcis (HBK) Mart. Trunk to 6m×20cm. Petiole with short
recurved spines; blade orbicular, green; seg. 36–50, linear-
acuminate, semi-rigid. S Mex.
B. edulis Wendl. ex S. Wats. GUADALUPE PALM. Trunk to
12m×40cm, irregularly ringed. Petiole to 1.5m, with rounded
teeth; blade to 2m, often waxy, divided to half depth into erect
seg., apices divided. Mex.
B. elegans (Fenzi ex Becc.) H.E. Moore. FRANCESCHI PALM.
Trunk *c*1m, clothed with dead lvs. Petiole to 65cm, with single
or double spines; seg. 50, divided to half length. Mex.
B. nitida André = *B. calcarea.*
B. pimo Becc. To 4.5m, trunk with fibrous sheaths at apex.
Petiole densely hairy becoming glab., with short spiny teeth;
blade green, with minute scales beneath; seg. 50, shallowly
divided at apex. Mex.
B. roezlii Lind. = *B. armata.*
B. salvadorensis H.A. Wendl. ex Becc. To 6m. Trunk clothed
with fibrous sheaths above. Lvs neatly abscising; petiole hairy
when young, with acute spinose teeth; blade green with minute
scales beneath; seg. 70, shallowly divided. Guat., El Salvador,
Hond.
→*Corypha, Erythea* and *Glaucothea.*

Brahman Grass *Dichanthium annulatum.*
Brain Plant *Calathea makoyana.*
Brake *Pteridium aquilinum; Pteris.*
Bramble *Rubus ulmifolius.*
Bramble Acacia *Acacia victoriae.*
Bramble Fern *Odontosoria.*
Bramble Wattle *Acacia victoriae.*
Branched Burr Reed *Sparganium erectum.*
Branched Cat's Paw *Anigozanthos onycis.*
Branch Thorn *Erinacea anthyllis.*
Brandegee's Fig *Ficus brandegeei.*
Brandy Bottle *Nuphar lutea.*

Brasenia Schreb. Cabombaceae. 1 aquatic herb. St. to 2m,
slender, long-branching. Lvs to 12×8cm, red-brown, coriaceous, floating, ovate, entire, long-petiolate. Fls solitary in lf
axils, small, red-purple. N Amer., Trop. Amer.
B. schreberi J.F. Gmel.

Brasilettia Britt. & Rose.
B. violacea (Mill.) Britt. & Rose = *Caesalpinia violacea.*
B. platyloba (Wats.) Britt. & Rose = *Caesalpinia platyloba.*

Brasilicereus Backeb. Cactaceae. Shrubby cacti; st. cylindric, ±
woody, ribbed, areoles small, close-set; spines acicular. Fls
nocturnal, short tubular-campanulate; tube short, stout; scales
fleshy; tep. spreading; staminal throat circle present. Braz.
B. phaeacanthus (Gürke) Backeb. St. to 4m×4–9cm, erect or
ascending, branching below; ribs *c*13; areoles 5mm apart; spines
numerous, 1–1.5cm, yellow-brown. Fls 7×5.5cm; outer tep.
green-brown, inner white. Braz. Z9.

Brasiliopuntia (Schum.) A. Berger = *Opuntia.*

Brassaia Endl.
B. actinophylla Endl. = *Schefflera actinophylla.*
B. littorea Seem. = *Schefflera littorea.*

Brassavola R. Br. Orchidaceae. 15 epiphytic or lithophytic
orchids. Lvs narrowly cylindrical, solitary, slender, tough. Fls
solitary or to 7 per rac., borne terminally or from rhiz.
(*B. acaulis*), often pendulous, white, ivory or green, nocturnally
fragrant. Summer or continuously. C & S Amer. Z10.
B. acaulis Lindl. & Paxt. Pbs to 15cm. Lvs to 60cm, usually shorter, strongly pendulous, terete. Infl. borne on rhiz.; fls 1–5,
waxy, v. fragrant, to 8cm diam.; tep. slender, nodding to
hooded, green, white tinted green, or deep ivory; lip bright
white. Guat., Costa Rica, Panama.
B. appendiculata A. Rich. = *B. cucullata.*
B. cebolleta Rchb. f. Differs from *B. tuberculata* in fls fewer, to
5cm diam., tep. ivory to yellow-green, lip pure white. Braz.
B. cordata Lindl. Pbs to 16cm, terete. Lvs to 45cm, slender,
terete, ascending or pendulous. Fls solitary or in sparse rac.; to
4.5cm diam., vanilla-scented; tep. lime green to ivory, lip white.
W Indies, Braz.
B. cucullata (L.) R. Br. Pbs to 12cm, v. slender. Lvs to 25cm,
pendulous, semi-terete, sulcate. Fls solitary, fragrant,
pendulous; tep. drooping, linear-lanceolate, to 7cm, ivory
tipped green; lip white tinted green at apex, tip narrowly
pointed, base fringed and often stained red. Mex., Guat., El
Salvador, Hond., Venez., W Indies.
B. digbyana Lindl. = *Rhyncholaelia digbyana.*
B. flagellaris Barb. Rodr. Pbs v. slender, to 30cm. Lvs to 45cm,
terete. Infl. 2–9-fld; fls to 6.5cm diam.; tep. linear, outspread,
ivory; lip white or cream stained lime green in throat. Braz.
B. glauca Lindl. = *Rhyncholaelia glauca.*
B. lineata Hook. = *B. acaulis.*
B. martiana Lindl. Resembles *B. cucullata* except smaller, fls to 6
on stalks to 8cm; tep. linear, to 5cm, pale green, slightly
revolute; lip to 3×2cm, white flushed pale yellow at throat, basally fringed. N Braz., Guianas, Venez., Amaz.
B. nodosa (L.) Lindl. LADY OF THE NIGHT. Pbs 0 or reduced to a
slender st. to 15cm. Lvs to 18×3cm (usually less), erect or
pendent, linear to horn-like, fleshy, sulcate. Infl. bearing 3–5 fls
to 7.5cm diam., scented at night; tep. narrow, pale green, ivory
or white; lip green to pure white at apex, throat sparsely spotted
maroon. Throughout genus range.
B. perrinii Lindl. = *B. tuberculata.*
B. subulifolia Lindl. = *B. cordata.*
B. tuberculata Hook. Pbs v. slender, to 14cm. Lvs to 25cm,
terete, strongly sulcate. Infl. a short rac.; fls 3–6, to 7cm diam.,
strongly fragrant at night, not opening fully; tep. linear, yellow-
ivory or lime green sometimes with blood red spots (*B. perrinii*);
lip elliptic, white often flushed bright green in throat. Braz.

Brass Buttons *Cotula coronopifolia.*

Brassia R. Br. Orchidaceae. 25 epiphytic or terrestrial orchids.
Pbs usually distant, ovoid-subglobose to cylindrical, bases with
leafy sheaths. Lvs coriaceous, ligulate to oblong-lanceolate.
Rac. lateral; fls usually large, held horizontally in 2 opposite
ranks; sep. v. long and slender, in 1 vertical plane, or spreading,
starry, lat. sep. larger than dors.; pet. shorter; lip shorter than
sep., simple or obscurely trilobed, callus bilamellate, bicarinate
or heavily warted. Trop. Amer. Z10.
B. angusta Lindl. = *B. lawrenceana.*
B. bidens Lindl. Tep. erect, yellow-green marked chocolate-
brown, to 8cm, linear-lanceolate, acuminate; lip to 4cm,
yellow-green marked chocolate-brown, oblong-rhombic, interior slightly verrucose, yellow at base. Venez., Peru, Braz.,
Guyana.
B. brachiata Lindl. = *B. verrucosa.*
B. caudata (L.) Lindl. Tep. light yellow-green to yellow-orange,
often marked red-brown, linear-lanceolate, lat. sep. to 18cm,
oblique; pet. shorter; lip to 4cm, light yellow to green, base
spotted red-brown, oblong-lanceolate to elliptic-obovate,
acuminate. Mex. to Panama, Flor., W Indies.
B. cochleata Knowles & Westc. = *B. lawrenceana.*
B. elegantula (Rchb. f.) Rchb. f. Tep. green barred brown to
1.2cm, lanceolate or oblong-lanceolate; lip white, lightly spotted
purple, oblong to ovate-oblong, acute. Peru.
B. forgetiana hort. ex Gdn. Fls fragrant; tep. light yellow-green
or green-white, barred brown, lateral sep. to 7cm, linear-
lanceolate, long-acuminate; lip cream-yellow, basally spotted
dark brown, to 4.5cm, oblong-pandurate, rounded, callus white
marked bright yellow. Peru, Venez.
B. gireoudiana Rchb. f. & Warsc. Tep. yellow-green marked
brown at base, lat. sep. to 15cm; lip to 4.5cm, yellow, finely
spotted brown in centre, rhombic. Costa Rica, Panama.
B. guttata Lindl. = *B. maculata.*

B. lanceana Lindl. Tep. yellow to yellow-green or yellow-brown, marked dark brown-maroon, lateral sep. to 6.5cm; lip to 3.5cm, cream slightly spotted brown, elliptic-oblong, long-acuminate, callus white, tipped bright yellow. Panama, Colomb., Braz., Venez., Tob., Guyana, Surinam.

B. lawrenceana Lindl. SPIDER ORCHID. Tep. pale green or yellow, spotted red-purple at base the margins often inrolled; lat. sep. to 7cm; lip to 4.5cm, white to pale green or pale yellow, obovate-pandurate, acute to long-acuminate, callus yellow. Braz., Surinam, Venez., Guyana.

B. maculata R. Br. Tep. yellow-green marked or spotted purple; lat. sep. to 8cm, oblique, linear-lanceolate, strongly upturned; lip to 4cm, yellow-spotted purple, callus yellow to orange. W Indies, Guat., Hond., Belize.

B. pumila Lindl. = *B. lanceana*.

B. Rex. Large hybrid with v. showy fls similar to *B. verrucosa*.

B. verrucosa Lindl. SPIDER ORCHID. Fls muskily fragrant; tep. sulphur yellow to lime green, base marked or finely spotted red-brown to black, v. slender, sep. to 12cm, linear-lanceolate, acuminate; lip to 5cm, white spotted brown at base, sub-pandurate, with green warts, callus frilly. Mex., Guat., Venez., Hond.

B. wrayae Skinner = *B. maculata*.

Brassica L. Cruciferae. 30 ann. or bienn. herbs, occas. perenn. St. erect, branched. Lvs simple, toothed, pinnately cut or lobed or lyrate. Rac. term.; fls 4-merous; pet. yellow to yellow-white, clawed. Fr. a silique, oblong or linear. Medit. to temp. Asia, widely nat.

B. acephala auctt. = *B. oleracea* Acephala group.

B. alba (L.) Rabenh., non Gilib. = *Sinapis alba*.

B. alboglabra L.H. Bail. = *B. oleracea* Alboglabra group.

B. alpina L. = *Fourraea alpina*.

B. arvensis (L.) Rabenh., non L. = *Sinapis arvensis*.

B. botrytis (L.) Mill. = *B. oleracea*, Botrytis group.

B. campestris L. Ann., lvs 10–20cm, pinnately lobed or cut. Pet. 6–8mm, spathulate. Fr. to 7cm, not torulose. Spring. Eur. Z7.

B. campestris L. = *B. rapa*.

B. carinata A. Braun. ETHIOPIAN CABBAGE; ABYSSINIAN CABBAGE; AFRICAN CABBAGE. Ann., st. tinged purple. Lower lvs lobed, lobes oval, 7.5–12cm, shallowly lobed. Ethiop. 'TexSel': short-stemmed, lvs in a rosette, light green, glaucous.

B. chinensis L. = *B. rapa* Chinensis group.

B. fimbriata Mill. = *B. napus* Pabularia group.

B. hirta Moench. WHITE MUSTARD. Somewhat hairy ann. Lvs 10–20cm, lyrate to pinnately cut. Pet. 8–11mm. Fr. to 3cm, torulose. Medit. to W Asia. Z8.

B. juncea (L.) Czerniak. CHINESE MUSTARD; MUSTARD CABBAGE; INDIAN MUSTARD; SWATOW MUSTARD; GAI CHOI; KAI TSOI; KARASHINA. Ann. Lvs with 2–3 lobes on either side, term. lobe large, ovate, toothed. Pet. 6–9mm. Fr. to 6cm, torulose. Russia to C Asia. Z7. 'Crispifolia': lf margins crisped.

B. kaber (DC.) Wheeler. CHARLOCK; CALIFORNIA RAPE. Ann. Lvs 5–15cm, oblong-ovate to obovate, lyrate. Pet. 8mm. Fr. to 2.5cm, torulose. Eur. and Asia, N Amer. Z7.

B. moricandioides Boiss. = *Moricandia moricandioides*.

B. napobrassica Mill. = *B. napus* Napobrassica group.

B. napus L. RAPE; COLZA. Similar to *B. campestris* except more glab., term. lobe of lf v. large. Pet 9–14mm. Fr. 5–9cm. Spring. Eur. Z7.

B. nigra (L.) Koch. BLACK MUSTARD. Ann. Lvs pinnately cut or lyrate, hairy. Pet. 7–9mm. Fr. tapering to a long sterile beak to 2cm. Eur. Z7.

B. oleracea L. WILD CABBAGE. Ann. or perenn, herb. Base woody. Lvs c45cm, closely packed, fleshy, glaucous, lyrate or pinnately divided, undulate, 5-lobed. Pet. 12–20mm. Fr. 5–10cm, terete. Summer. W Eur. Z8.

Acephala group (KALE, COLEWORT, COLLARD, DECORATIVE KALE, FLOWERING KALE, FLOWERING CABBAGE, SCOTCH KALE). St. usually unbranched; lvs in loose rosettes, not solid heads, thick, glaucous; in ornamental cvs tinted white, pink or purple, margins sometimes fringed.

Alboglabra group (CHINESE BROCCOLI, CHINESE KALE, GAI-LOHN, FAT-SHAN). Ann. to 90cm, glab. and glaucous; lvs thick, lower lvs elliptic, to 25cm, sinuate, upper st. lvs oblong, stalked.

Botrytis group (CAULIFLOWER, PERENNIAL BROCCOLI). St. short and stout; infl. a dense term. head exceeded by lvs.

Capitata group (CABBAGE, SAVOY CABBAGE, RED CABBAGE). St. short; lvs in a dense term. head, in Savoy Cabbage blistered and puckered, in Red Cabbage deep purple-red.

Gemmifera group (BRUSSELS SPROUTS). St. to 90cm, simple, erect; buds small, tight.

Gongylodes group (KOHLRABI); Bienn.; tuber enlarged; lvs to 25cm, elliptic, petioles long.

Italica group (ITALIAN BROCCOLI, ASPARAGUS BROCCOLI, SPROUTING BROCCOLI, PRUPLE CAULIFLOWER, CAPE BROCCOLI). St.

shorter and thicker than in Botrytis group, flowerheads not condensed into a solid head.

Tronchuda group (TRONCHUDA KALE; PORTUGUESE CABBAGE, COUVE TRONCHUDA, BRAGANZA, SEAKALE CABBAGE). Low-growing ann. resembling cabbage, lvs spreading, petiole fleshy, midrib broad.

B. oleracea var. *fimbriata* Mill. = *B. napus*, Pabularia group.

B. oleracea var. *gemmifera* Zenk. = *B. oleracea* Gemmifera group.

B. parachinensis L.H. Bail. See *B. rapa* Chinensis group.

B. pekinensis (Lour.) Rupr. = *B. rapa* Pekinensis group.

B. perviridis (L.H. Bail.) L.H. Bail. = *B. rapa*, Perviridis group.

B. rapa L. FIELD MUSTARD; TURNIP; FODDER TURNIP. Ann. or bienn. Lvs to 50cm, lyrate or pinnately cut, hairy. Pet. 6–10mm. Fr. 6cm. Summer. Eur.

Chinensis group (CELERY MUSTARD, CHINESE MUSTARD, CHINESE WHITE CABBAGE, PAK-CHOI). Ann. or bienn.; lvs obovate, slightly succulent, entire or nearly so; fr. to 7cm. *B. parachinensis* L.H. Bail. (FALSE PAK-CHOI) has more rounded lvs, st. lvs narrowed to base, not clasping.

Pekinensis group (CELERY CABBAGE, CHINESE CABBAGE, PE-TSAI). Ann., mostly glab., becoming glaucous; lvs soft, basal lvs broad, undulate or sparsely toothed, petiole with jagged wings; fr. to 7.5cm.

Perviridis group (HENDERGREEN, SPINACH MUSTARD). Ann. to bienn. to 180cm, branching above; root crown thickened and tuberous; lvs oblong-spathulate, subentire, soft, glossy green.

Rapifera group (TURNIP, RAPINI). Stout leafy bienn., v. glaucous; lower lvs deeply lobed. Taproot swollen, spherical in turnip.

Ruvo group (RUVO KALE, TURNIP BROCCOLI, ITALIAN BROCCOLI, BROCCOLI RAAB). Ann. to bienn. to 1m; lvs lyrate-pinnatifid, dark green, often glossy; fr. to 5cm; cf. *B. oleracea*, Italica group.

Sarson group (TORIA; SARSON). Ann. or bienn. to 1.5m. Lvs dark green, glab. to hairy; seeds oliferous.

B. repanda (Willd.) DC. Tufted perenn. Lvs 1–15cm, spathulate or obovate, blunt, usually glab., somewhat fleshy, deeply toothed to entire; petiole long. Pet. 7–30mm. Fr. 1–8cm. Alps and S Spain. Z7.

B. sylvestris (L.) Mill. = *B. oleracea*.

→*Diplotaxis* and *Sinapis*.

BRASSICACEAE Burnett. See Cruciferae.

✕**Brassocattleya**. (*Brassavola* (*Rhyncholaelia*) ✕ *Cattleya*.) Orchidaceae. Gdn hybrids ranging widely in habit and size from dwarf and tufted to tall and rangy with large fleshy lvs. The fls vary from small and neat to exceptionally large and frilly, in shades of white, pink, magenta, purple, red, orange, apricot, yellow and lime-green. Z10.

✕**Brassoepidendrum**. (*Brassavola* (*Rhyncholaelia*) ✕ *Epidendrum*.) Orchidaceae. Compact hybrids with large fls in shades of white, yellow and green.

✕**Brassolaeliocattleya**. (*Brassavola* (*Rhyncholaelia*) ✕ *Cattleya* ✕ *Laelia*.) Orchidaceae. Extensive range of gdn hybrids - habit dwarf, medium or large, squat, robust or reedy. Fls slender and starry to broad and lacy in shades of white, rose, magenta, mauve, red, orange, apricot, yellow, green or cream often flushed, veined or marked a different colour. Z10.

Braunsia Schwantes. Aizoaceae. 4 dwarf, creeping succulents. Lvs 1–2 pairs per br., lunate, triangular, carinate, united below, glab. or velutinous, often spotted. Fls term., ± sessile, pink or white. Cape Prov. Z9.

B. apiculata (Kensit) L. Bol. To 20cm. Lvs to 3cm, velvety, carinate. Fls 2cm diam., pink. Karroo.

B. bina (N.E. Br.) Schwantes = *B. apiculata*.

B. edentula (Haw.) N.E. Br. = *Ruschia edentula*.

B. geminata (Haw.) L. Bol. To 15cm, branching dichotomously. Lvs to 2.5cm, triangular, margins cartilaginous. Fls to 4cm diam., white. Karroo.

→*Echinus*.

Bravoa La Ll. & Lex. = *Polianthes*.

Braxireon Raf.
B. humile (Cav.) Raf. = *Narcissus humilis*.

Braya Sternb. & Hoppe. Cruciferae. 20 tufted, perenn. herbs. Lvs basal, narrow-linear, usually entire. Fls small, 4-merous, in rac. on leafy st. Asia to C Eur., Arc. circumpolar.

B. alpina Sternb. & Hoppe. Lvs loosely tufted, lanceolate. Corymb dense; pet. to 4mm, white to rose-mauve. E Alps. Z5.

Brazil *Oreopanax xalapensis.*
Brazil Cherry *Eugenia brasiliensis.*
Brazilian Arrowroot *Manihot esculenta.*
Brazilian Fire Cracker *Manettia luteorubra.*
Brazilian Flame Bush *Calliandra tweedii.*
Brazilian Ironwood *Caesalpinia ferrea.*
Brazilian Jasmine *Mandevilla sanderi.*
Brazilian Monkey Pot *Lecythis pisonis.*
Brazilian Pepper Tree *Schinus terebinthifolius.*
Brazilian Pine *Araucaria angustifolia.*
Brazilian Plume *Justicia carnea.*
Brazilian Potato Tree *Solanum wrightii.*
Brazilian Red Cloak *Megaskepasma erythrochlamys.*
Brazilian Sky Flower *Duranta stenostachys.*
Brazilian Tea *Stachytarpheta cayennensis.*
Brazil Nut *Bertholletia excelsa.*
Brazilwood *Caesalpinia echinata.*
Breadfruit *Artocarpus altilis.*
Breadnut *Brosimum alicastrum.*
Breath of Heaven *Diosma ericoides.*

Brevoortia Alph. Wood.
B. ida-maia Alph. Wood = *Dichelostemma ida-maia.*

Brewer's Mountain Heather *Phyllodoce breweri.*
Brewer's Spruce *Picea breweriana.*

Breynia Forst. & Forst. f. Euphorbiaceae. 25 shrubs and small trees. Lvs alt., simple, sessile often distichous. Fls small, axill.; ♀ fls solitary, ♂ occas. clustered. Fr. a red berry. Trop. Asia, Pacific Is., Aus.
B. distacha Forst. & Forst. f. = *B. nivosa.*
B. nivosa (W.G. Sm.) Small. SNOW BUSH. Slender shrub. Br. flexuous, coral pink to red. Lvs 1.5–2.5cm, ovate, short-stalked, 2-ranked, mottled white. Pacific Is. 'Atropurpurea': lvs dark purple. 'Roseapicta': lvs mottled pink and red.
B. oblongifolia Muell. Arg. Slender shrub. Lvs 1.5–2.5cm, ovate, obtuse, sessile. Aus.
B. turbinata Cordm. Shrub. Lvs to 4cm, rhomboid-ovate, glaucous, acute, punctate beneath. China.
→*Phyllanthus.*

Briançon Apricot *Prunus brigantina.*

Brickellia Elliott. Compositae. *c*90 ann. or perenn. herbs and shrubs. Lvs alt. or opposite, simple, thin to leathery, mostly resinous-dotted, serrate to crenate. Cap. discoid, solitary or in a bracteate pan.; flts white, cream, or pink-purple. Warm Amer.
B. californica (Torr. & A. Gray) A. Gray. Woody perenn. to 1m. St. many, grey or pale purple-brown. Lvs to 4cm, alt., deltoid-ovate, stalked. Cap. many, small, solitary in lf axils or in a lat. cluster; flts 8–18, cream or purple. Late summer–autumn. W US, N Mex.
B. grandiflora (Hook.) Nutt. Perenn. herb, to 70cm. St. simple. Lvs to 11cm, opposite, lanceolate or deltoid-ovate, serrate or crenate, base truncate or cordate, stalked, apex acute. Cap. 1.4cm diam., slightly nodding, in a term. corymb or lax pan.; flts 20–38, green or pale cream; styles conspicuous. Summer–early autumn. W US.
B. incana A. Gray. Shrub, to 1m, white-tomentose, erect or ascending. Lvs 1–3cm, alt., ovate, sessile, leathery, serrulate to entire. Cap. *c*2cm diam., solitary, at br. apices; flts around 60. Spring–autumn. SW US.

Bridal Bouquet *Porana paniculata.*
Bridal Heath *Erica bauera.*
Bridal Veil *Gibasis pellucida.*
Bridal Wreath *Francoa ramosa*; *Spiraea* ×*arguta*; *Stephanotis floribunda*.
Bridalwreath Spiraea *Spiraea prunifolia.*
Bride's Bonnet *Clintonia uniflora.*
Bridewort *Spiraea salicifolia.*

Bridgesia Bertero ex Cambess.
B. spicata Hook. & Arn. = *Ercilla spicata.*

Briggsia Craib. Gesneriaceae. 23 rhizomatous perenn. herbs. Lvs in a basal rosette or opposite on st., often pubesc. Fls solitary or many in umbellate cymes; cal. lobes 5; cor. cylindric becoming inflated toward apex, upper lip 2-lobed, lower lip 3-lobed. India and S China. Z8.
B. kurzii (C.B. Clarke) W.E. Evans = *Loxostigma kurzii.*
B. muscicola (Diels) Craib. Lvs to 6.5cm, rosulate, elliptic to lanceolate, crenate, white-tomentose. Fls to 1cm, 2–6 per cyme, exterior yellow-green, interior orange-yellow marked purple. Yunnan and Bhutan to SE Tibet.

Brimeura Salisb. Liliaceae (Hyacinthaceae). 2 small perenn. bulbous herbs. Rac. slender-stalked; perianth 1cm, tubular, lobes 6. S Eur. Z5.
B. amethystina (L.) Chouard. Perianth narrowly campanulate, bright blue, sometimes indigo or white, tube cylindric or waisted below throat, lobes to two-thirds length of tube. Late spring–early summer. NW Balk. 'Alba': fls white.
B. fastigiata (Viv.) Chouard. Perianth campanulate appearing star-shaped, lilac, lilac-pink or white, lobes exceeding tube, spreading. Is. of W Medit., Greece.
→*Hyacinthus.*

Brinjal *Solanum melongena.*
Brisbane Box *Tristania conferta.*
Brisbane Lily *Proiphys cunninghamii.*
Bristle Club Rush *Isolepis setacea.*
Bristlecone Fir *Abies bracteata.*
Bristlecone Pine *Pinus aristata.*
Bristle Fern *Trichomanes.*
Bristle-leaved Bent Grass *Agrostis setacea.*
Bristle-pointed Iris *Iris setosa.*
Bristle Scirpus *Isolepis setacea.*
Bristly Black Currant *Ribes lacustre.*
Bristly Fig *Ficus hispida.*
Bristly Locust *Robinia hispida.*
Bristly Ox-tongue *Picris echioides.*
Bristly Sarsparilla *Aralia hispida.*
Bristly Shield Fern *Lastreopsis hispida.*
Bristly Tree Fern *Dicksonia youngiae.*
Brittle Bladder Fern *Cystopteris fragilis.*
Brittle Bush *Encelia farinosa.*
Brittle Fern *Cystopteris fragilis.*
Brittle Gum *Eucalyptus mannifera.*
Brittleleaf Manzanita *Arctostaphylos crustacea.*
Brittle Maidenhair Fern *Adiantum tenerum.*
Brittle Thatch *Thrinax morrisii.*
Brittle Willow *Salix fragilis.*

Briza L. QUAKING GRASS. Gramineae. 12 ann. or perenn. grasses. Lvs flat. Infl. racemose; spikelets on filiform pedicels, ovate, laterally flattened with overlapping, papery glumes like a rattlesnake's tail. Summer. Cosmop. Z5.
B. geniculata Thunb. = *Eragrostis obtusa.*
B. gracilis hort. = *B. minor.*
B. major C. Presl = *B. maxima.*
B. maxima L. GREAT QUAKING GRASS. Ann. to 60cm. St. solitary or tufted. Lvs to 20×1cm. Fls in lax, nodding pan. to 10cm; spikelets to 2.5cm, 7–20-fld, cordate or ovate to oblong, tinged red-brown, light grey or purple. Medit. 'Rubra': lemmas tinted red-pink edged white.
B. media L. COMMON QUAKING GRASS; DIDDER; TOTTER. Perenn. to 1m. St. forming tussocks. Lvs to 15×0.5cm. Fls in erect, deltoid pan. to 18cm; spikelets to 1cm, 4–12-fld, ovate to broadly deltoid, often tinged purple. Eurasia.
B. minima hort. ex Nichols. = *B. minor.*
B. minor L. LESSER QUAKING GRASS. Ann. to 60cm. St. forming loose tussocks. Lvs to 15×1cm. Fls in a lax deltoid pan. to 20cm, br. ascending; spikelets to 5mm, 4–8-fld, rounded to deltoid-ovate, light green to purple-tinged, lustrous. Eurasia.

Broad Bean *Vicia faba.*
Broad Beech Fern *Phegopteris hexagonoptera.*
Broad Buckler Fern *Dryopteris dilatata.*
Broad-leaf Drumsticks *Isopogon anemonifolius.*
Broad-leaf Fig *Ficus platyphylla.*
Broad-leaf Kafferboom *Erythrina latissima.*
Broad-leaved Apple *Angophora intermedia.*
Broad-leaved Bottletree *Brachychiton australis.*
Broad-leaved Cotton Grass *Eriophorum latifolium.*
Broad-leaved Everlasting Pea *Lathyrus latifolius.*
Broad-leaved Geebung *Persoonia cornifolia*; *P. levis.*
Broad-leaved Helleborine *Epipactis atrorubens.*
Broad-leaved Ironbark *Eucalyptus fibrosa.*
Broad-leaved Lime *Tilia platyphyllos.*
Broad-leaved Marsh Orchid *Dactylorhiza majalis.*
Broad-leaved Meadowgrass *Poa chaixii.*
Broad-leaved Paperbark *Melaleuca leucadendra.*
Broad-leaved Penstemon *Penstemon ovatus.*
Broad-leaved Peppermint *Eucalyptus dives.*
Broad-leaved Pondweed *Potamogeton natans.*
Broad-leaved Snow Tussock *Chionochloa flavescens.*
Broad-leaved Teatree *Melaleuca leucadendra.*
Broad-leaved White Mahogany *Eucalyptus umbra.*
Broad Path *Alternanthera.*
Broad Sword Fern *Nephrolepis biserrata.*

Brocchinia Schult. f. Bromeliaceae. 18 usually erect, terrestrial perenn. herbs. Lvs linear-triangular, sword-like, pungent in dense rosettes. Infl. term., erect, much-branched, scapose; fls numerous, small; sep. free; pet. white or green. Autumn. Braz., Guyana, Colomb., Venez. Z9.
B. andreana hort. = *B. micrantha*.
B. cordylinoides Bak. = *B. micrantha*.
B. demerarensis hort. = *B. micrantha*.
B. micrantha (Bak.) Mez. St. short, columnar, woody. Lvs to 1.2m. Infl. to 2.6m, smooth; fls to 5mm, white; bracts lanceolate. E Guyana, Venez.
B. paniculata Schult. f. Differs from *B. micrantha* in scale-covered infl., ovate floral bracts, fls to 15mm. SE Colomb., Venez.
B. reducta Bak. Carnivore. Lvs to 55cm, few, erect, grey-green, scaly, forming a cylinder. Infl. 50–70cm; bracts to 3.5cm, remote; fls 5mm. Guyana, Venez.

Brodiaea Sm. Liliaceae (Alliaceae). 15 cormous herbs. Lvs linear, elongate. Fls campanulate or funnelform, subtended by papery bracts in scapose umbels; tep. 6, outer narrower than inner, widely spreading. W US, W S Amer. Z8.
B. bridgesii Wats. = *Triteleia bridgesii*.
B. californica Lindl. Scape to 70cm. Fls 2–12 per umbel; tep. 3–4.5cm, lilac to violet or pink, recurved, tube membranous erect. Calif.
B. candida Bak. = *Triteleia laxa*.
B. capitata Benth. = *Dichelostemma pulchellum*.
B. coccinea A. Gray = *Dichelostemma ida-maia*.
B. congesta Sm. = *Dichelostemma congestum*.
B. coronaria (Salisb.) Engl. Scape to 30cm. Fls 2–7 per umbel, blue-purple to deep mauve; perianth 2.4–4cm, tube ovoid to narrow-campanulate, thick-textured. Often mistaken for *B. terrestris*. NW US.
B. coronaria var. *macropoda* (Torr.) Hoover = *B. terrestris*.
B. coronaria var. *mundula* Jeps. = *B. elegans*.
B. douglasii Piper = *Triteleia grandiflora*.
B. elegans Hoover. Scape to 50cm. Fls 2–12 per umbel; perianth to 4cm; tep. 2× length of tube, deep mauve, strongly recurved; tube funnelform, thick-textured. Oreg., Calif.
B. grandiflora Sm. = *B. coronaria*.
B. grandiflora Macbr. non Sm. = *Triteleia grandiflora*.
B. grandiflora var. *elatior* Benth. = *B. californica*.
B. grandiflora var. *macropoda* Torr. = *B. terrestris*.
B. grandiflora var. *minor* Benth. = *B. minor*.
B. hendersonii (Greene) Wats. = *Triteleia hendersonii*.
B. howellii Eastw. = *B. coronaria*.
B. hyacintha (Lindl.) Bak. = *Triteleia hyacintha*.
B. ida-maia (Wood) Greene = *Dichelostemma ida-maia*.
B. ixioides Hook. non (Ait.) Wats. = *Leucocoryne ixioides*.
B. ixioides (Ait.) Wats. non Hook. = *Triteleia ixioides*.
B. lactea S. Wats. = *Triteleia hyacintha*.
B. laxa (Benth.) Wats. = *Triteleia laxa*.
B. lutea Lindl. = *Triteleia ixioides*.
B. minor (Benth.) S. Wats. Scape to 30cm. Fls to 2.5cm; tep. 1.7–2.4cm, pink to violet, linear, spreading then recurved, to twice the length of apically constricted tube. Calif.
B. multiflora Benth. = *Dichelostemma multiflorum*.
B. peduncularis (Lindl.) Wats. = *Triteleia peduncularis*.
B. pulchella (Salisb.) Greene = *Dichelostemma pulchellum*.
B. purdyi Eastw. = *B. minor*.
B. terrestris Kellogg. Scape to 7cm. Fls mauve-pink, tep. 2–2.4cm, ascending and recurved; tube ovoid to narrow-campanulate, not usually constricted above ovary, thick. W US.
→*Hookera*.

Brome *Bromus*.

Bromelia L. Bromeliaceae. 47 perenn., usually terrestrial herbs. Rhizomatous or suckering, forming dense col. Lvs in a rosette, long and rigid, with large, hooked marginal spines, colouring red in full sunlight. Infl. term., compound, sessile or scapose, hoary, bracteate; sep. free or fused, pet. joined into a tube by fil. Mex. and W Indies to N Arg., Parag., Boliv. and Peru. Z9.
B. agavifolia Brongn. ex Houll. To 2m in fl. Lvs to 5m in a dense rosette, dark green, innermost scarlet, spinose. Infl. to 10cm diam., densely paniculate, globose, pet. to 30mm, white tipped red. Known only in cult.
B. antiacantha Bertol. To 3m in fl. Lvs to 3m, linear, inner smaller, red, serrate. Infl. 20–100cm, subcylindric; pet. to 30mm, red-violet. SE Braz., Urug.
B. balansae Mez. HEART OF FLAME. To over 1m in fl. Lvs 1m, spreading, inner bright red in fl., linear, laxly spine-toothed. Infl. to 22cm, dense, cylindric; bracts slender, sharp-toothed, spreading, bright red; pet. 25mm, maroon or violet edged white. Braz., Parag., N Arg., Boliv., Colomb.

B. binotii E. Morr. ex Mez. To 1m in fl. Lvs 1.2m, inner bright red in fl., linear, laxly toothed. Infl. loosely pyramidal; pet. 27mm, violet-purple. Braz.
B. carnea Beer = *Ochagavia carnea*.
B. fastuosa Reg. = *B. antiacantha*.
B. humilis Jacq. Stoloniferous. Lvs to 30cm, in a dense rosette, inner lvs flushed red or purple, spiny-serrate. Infl. stemless; pet. 40mm, white tipped purple. N Venez., Trin., Windward Is.
B. karatas L. = *B. plumieri*.
B. laciniosa Mart. ex Schult. f. To 1.5m in fl. Lvs to 1.5m. Infl. 15–70cm; pet. 35mm, purple. NE Braz.
B. legrellae (E. Morr.) Mez. Lvs to 2m in a spreading rosette, inner short, red, with hooked spines. Infl. 7cm, globose, densely paniculate, on a v. short scape; pet. 30mm, blue edged white. Braz.
B. morreniana (Reg.) Mez. Lvs to 50cm, in a bundle-like rosette, red and scaly beneath, spiny-toothed. Infl. sparse, sessile; pet. 40mm, white, brown-scaly. Braz.
B. plumieri (E. Morr.) L.B. Sm. To 3m in fl. Lvs 1.5–3m, linear, coarsely serrate, inner lvs red. Infl. densely corymbose, flat, stemless; pet. to 40mm, rose-pink or purple edged white. Mex. and W Indies to Braz. and Ecuad.
B. scarlatina (hort. ex Henriq.) E. Morr. Lvs to 75cm, lanceolate or ovate, inner lvs bright red, sessile, toothed. Infl. densely capitate, sessile; pet. 27mm, violet-purple, edged white. Braz.
B. sceptrum Fenzl ex Hueg. = *B. antiacantha*.
B. serra Griseb. To 40cm in fl. Lvs to 1.5m, in a dense rosette, turning pink in strong light, linear base bulb-like; spines 5mm long. Infl. 6cm, densely globose, white-pubesc.; scape short, with bright red bracts; pet. 25–35mm, blue-purple edged white. C Braz. and Boliv. to Parag. and N Arg.
B. urbaniana L.B. Sm. Stoloniferous. Lvs 30cm, a loose rosette, linear, red-brown, spines 3–4mm, curved, brown. Infl. 3cm diam., sparse, sessile; pet. 20mm, white to pale rose. Arg.
B. zebrina Herb. = *Billbergia zebrina*.
→*Rhodostachys*.

BROMELIACEAE Juss. 46/2110. *Abromeitiella, Acanthostachys, Aechmea, Ananas, Androlepis, Billbergia, Brocchinia, Bromelia, Canistrum, Catopsis, Cottendorfia, Cryptanthus,* ✗ *Cryptbergia, Deuterocohnia, Dyckia, Encholirium, Fascicularia, Fosterella, Griegia, Guzmania, Hechtia, Hohenbergia, Navia, Neoglazovia, Neoregelia, Nidularium, Ochagavia, Orthophytum, Pitcairnia, Portea, Puya, Quesnelia, Streptocalyx, Tillandsia, Vriesea, Wittrockia.*

Bromheadia Lindl. Orchidaceae. 11 terrestrial or epiphytic orchids. St. slender. Lvs alt. Infl. term.; fls ephemeral; tep. lanceolate, spreading (pet. wider, shorter), lip midlobe recurved, papillose, lat. lobes erect. Malaysia to Aus. Z10.
B. finlaysoniana (Lindl.) Miq. St. to 2m. Lvs lanceolate, fleshy. Infl. branched with jointed axils; fls white, lip midlobe with yellow crest, lat. lobes veined purple. Thail., Malaysia.
B. palustris Lindl. = *B. findlaysoniana*.

Brompton Stock *Matthiola incana*.

Bromus L. BROME; CHESS. Gramineae. *c*100 ann., bienn. or perenn. grasses. Lvs flat or revolute; sheaths tubular, usually pubesc.; ligules translucent, papery. Fls in spreading or contracted pan.; spikelets 1- to many-fld. Summer. Temp. regions. Z5.
B. anomalus Rupr. Perenn. to 1.6m. Pan. to 30cm; spikelets laterally compressed, to 3cm. Mex.
B. arvensis L. FIELD BROME. Ann. to 1m. Pan. to 25cm; spikelets, narrow-lanceolate to oblong, to 2.5cm, on long, flimsy branchlets. Eur., temp. Asia.
B. asper Murray = *B. ramosus*.
B. briziformis Fisch. & Mey. Ann. to 60cm. Pan. to 25cm, loose, broadly pyramidal, sometimes tinged purple; br. somewhat pendent, bearing 1–2 spikelets; spikelets to 2cm, compressed, lanceolate to ovate. Eur., temp. Asia.
B. canadensis Michx. FRINGED BROME. Perenn. to 120cm. Pan. to 25.5cm, lax, br. slender, pendulous; spikelets to 15cm, somewhat compressed, occas. tinged bronze or purple. US, Mex.
B. ciliatus auct. non L. = *B. canadensis*.
B. danthoniae Trin. Ann. to 45cm. Pan. narrow, erect, often purple-tinged; spikelets to 5cm, lanceolate or oblong, pubesc. or glab., shiny; awns tinged purple or maroon. SW & C Asia.
B. erectus Huds. Perenn. to 1.2m. Pan. to 25cm, narrow, erect, br. ascending; spikelets red-purple. Eur., SW Asia, NW Afr.
B. fibrosus Hackel. Perenn. tufted. Lvs long, arching, with soft, semi-glaucous tinge. E Eur.
B. inermis Leysser. Perenn. to 1m. Pan. to 20cm, contracted or diffuse, erect or nodding, lower br. to 10cm; spikelets narrow-oblong, pale green to grey-purple. Eur., temp. Asia.

B. japonicus Thunb. Ann. or bienn. to 80cm. Pan. to 20cm, spreading, broadly pyramidal, nodding; br. pendent; spikelets to 4cm, lanceolate to oblong, often tinged purple. Medit., temp. Asia.

B. lanceolatus Roth = *B. macrostachys.*

B. lanuginosus Poir. = *B. macrostachys* var. *lanuginosus.*

B. macrostachys Desf. Ann. to 60cm. Pan. to 20cm, dense, narrow, contracted, often tinged purple; spikelets to 3cm, sparse. Medit. var. *lanuginosus* (Poir.) Coss. & Dur. Spikelets covered in pale grey hairs.

B. madritensis L. COMPACT BROME. Ann. to 60cm. Pan. to 15cm, upright, obtusely conic, often tinged purple; spikelets to 6cm, oblong, laterally flattened, becoming outspread, cuneate. Medit.

B. ramosus Huds. Perenn. to 1.5m. Pan. to 40cm, v. lax, pendulous; br. rough, mostly paired, patent or pendulous; spikelets to 4cm, linear-oblong, pendent, green or green-purple, short-pubesc. Eur., N Afr., SW Asia.

B. squarrosus L. ROUGH BROME. Ann. or bienn. to 60cm. Pan. near-secund; spikelets to 7cm, laterally flattened, ovate to elliptic. Medit.

B. tectorum L. DROOPING BROME. Ann. to 90cm. Pan. to 18cm, dense, nodding; spikelets to 2cm, cuneate, laterally flattened, tinged purple, glistening. Medit.

Bronvaux Medlar + *Crataegomespilus.*
Bronze-leaf Begonia *Begonia* ×*ricinifolia.*
Bronze Shower *Cassia moschata.*
Brookleaf Mallee *Eucalyptus kruseana.*
Brooklime *Veronica americana*; *V. beccabunga.*
Broom *Cytisus*; *Genista.*
Broom Baeckea *Baeckea behrii.*
Broom Beard Grass *Schizachyrium scoparium.*
Broom Brush *Baeckea behrii.*
Broom Corn Millet *Panicum miliaceum.*
Broom Crowberry *Corema.*
Broom Hickory *Carya glabra.*
Broom Palm *Thrinax parviflora.*
Broomrape *Orobanche.*
Broom Sedge *Andropogon virginicus.*
Broom Wattle *Acacia calamifolia.*
Broomweed *Gutierrezia.*

Brosimum Sw. COW TREE; MILK TREE; BREADNUT. Moraceae. *c*50 trees or shrubs containing abundant latex (drunk in the case of *B. utile*); trunk sometimes buttressed. Lvs usually entire, leathery. Fls 1 ♀, many ♂ in a spherical head. Fr. immersed in a fleshy receptacle. Trop. Amer.

B. alicastrum Sw. BREADNUT. To 30m. Crown broad, spreading. Lvs *c*18cm, entire, sometimes dentate or repand. Lvs used as animal fodder; seeds eaten roasted or boiled.

Broughtonia R. Br. Orchidaceae. 1 epiphytic orchid. Pbs clustered, globose to subcylindric. Lvs to 18cm, paired, narrow-oblong. Infl. term.; fls to 2.25cm diam.; tep. brilliant crimson, rarely white or yellow, lip crispate, yellow to ivory at base with bright magenta veins. Jam. Z10.

B. coccinea Hook. = *B. sanguinea.*

B. domingensis (Lindl.) Rolfe = *Laeliopsis domingensis.*

B. sanguinea (Sw.) R. Br.

Broughton Willow *Acacia salicina.*

Broussonetia L'Hérit. ex Vent. PAPER MULBERRY. Moraceae. 8 decid. trees or shrubs. Lvs to 20cm, large, serrate, entire or lobed. ♂ fls in pendulous catkins. Fr. aggregate in globose heads, orange-red, 1-seeded, in mass of persistent cal. and bracts. E Asia, Polyn.

B. kaempferi Sieb. = *B. kazinoki.*

B. kazinoki Sieb. Shrub to 2m; twigs thin, red-brown, pubesc. at first. Lvs ovate, long-acuminate, finely serrate, occas. 2–3-lobed, rough above, glabrescent beneath. Catkins 1.25cm. Fr. red, pubesc. Korea, Jap. Z7.

B. papyrifera (L.) L'Hérit. PAPER MULBERRY. Tree or shrub to 15m; twigs sometimes grey-red, thick, soft-pubesc. Lvs broad-ovate, short-acuminate or 3-lobed, dentate, rough above, velvety beneath. Catkins 3.75–7.5cm. Fr. orange-red to scarlet. Jap., China. 'Billardii': resembles 'Laciniata' but a stronger grower and more upright. 'Cucullata': lvs large, unlobed, irregular, convex. 'Laciniata': lvs usually consisting only of a tiny remnant of blade at the tip of the midvein. 'Leucocarpa': fr. white. 'Macrophylla': lvs esp. large, normally undivided, base cordate. 'Variegata': lvs white or yellow variegated. Z8.

B. sieboldii Bl. = *B. kazinoki.*

Browallia L. BUSH VIOLET. Solanaceae. 3 ann. or perenn. herbs or shrubs. Fls axill.; cal. cylindric, 5-lobed; cor. salverform, blue or white. Trop. S Amer. Z9.

B. americana L. Ann., viscid-pubesc., to 60cm. Lvs to 7cm, ovate. Fls blue to violet or white; cor. tube to 2cm, lobes to 2.5cm, notched. Summer. 'Caerulea': fls pale blue. 'Compacta': compact habit. 'Grandiflora' and 'Major': fls larger. 'Nana': dwarf form.

B. demissa L. = *B. americana.*

B. elata L. = *B. americana.*

B. gigantea Morner = *B. speciosa.*

B. grandiflora Graham = *B. americana.*

B. jamesonii Benth. = *Streptosolen jamesonii.*

B. lenetta Miers = *B. americana.*

B. speciosa Hook. Shrubby perenn. to 1.5m. Lvs to 9cm ovate or elliptic. Fls blue or deep purple, eye white; cor. tube to 2.5cm. Colomb. 'Blue Bells': fls lavender-blue. 'Blue Bells Improved': fls violet-blue turning lavender-blue. 'Blue Troll': to 25cm; habit neat, rounded, slow-growing; fls clear blue, abundant. 'Dawn Blue': to 45cm; fls pale lilac-blue. 'Heavenly Bells': fls large, pale sky-blue. Jingle Bells Hybrids: fls in shades of blue, white and lavender. 'Major' (SAPPHIRE FLOWER): fls large, blue-purple; 'Marine Bells': fls indigo-blue. 'Powder Blue': fls lilac. 'Silver Bells': habit bushy; fls pure white. 'Sky Bells': fls powder blue. 'Vanja': fls large, open, deep blue with white eye. 'White Bell' ('Weissglocken'): compact, bushy; fls clear white. 'White Troll': to 25cm; neat, slow-growing; fls pure white, abundant.

B. viscosa HBK. Ann., 60cm. Lvs 4cm, ovate, viscid pubesc. Fls violet-blue, eye white; cor. tube to 2.5cm, lobes deeply notched. Summer. S Amer. 'Alba': fls white. 'Compacta': small, dense. 'Sapphire': to 25cm; fls sapphire blue.

Brownanthus Schwantes.

B. ciliatus (Ait.) Schwantes = *Psilocaulon ciliatum.*

B. marlothii (Pasc.) Schwantes = *Psilocaulon marlothii.*

Brown Barrel *Eucalyptus fastigata.*
Brown Beaks *Lyperanthus suaveolens.*
Brown Bells *Dipcadi brevifolium*; *Fritillaria micrantha.*
Brown Bent *Agrostis canina.*
Brown Boronia *Boronia megastigma.*
Brown Dogwood *Cornus glabrata.*

Brownea Jacq. Leguminosae (Caesalpinioideae). 26 shrubs and trees to 20m. Lvs large, coriaceous, pinnate, emerging bright pink or red. Fls in bracteate globose heads; pet. 4–5, clawed; sta. 10–15. Trop. Amer. Z10.

B. ariza Benth. Lfts 8–18, elliptic-subcordate. Fls orange to red. Summer. Colomb.

B. coccinea hort. = *B. latifolia.*

B. grandiceps hort. = *B. ariza.*

B. latifolia Jacq. GUARAMACO. Lfts 2–6, ovate or obovate-cuspidate. Fls red. Venez.

B. princeps Lind. ex Otto = *B. ariza.*

Brown-eyed Susan *Rudbeckia triloba.*
Brownies *Scoliopus bigelowii.*

Browningia Britt. & Rose. Cactaceae. 7 shrubby or tree-like cacti; st. cylindric, ribbed. Fls tubular-funnelform, nocturnal; tube curved, scales conspicuous; tep. spreading, short. Boliv., Peru, N Chile. Z9.

B. candelaris (Meyen) Britt. & Rose. Tree-like, 3–5m; trunk to 30cm diam., br. spreading or drooping, green; ribs 30–34. Fls 4–12×6–8cm; inner tep. white or tinged-pink. S Peru, N Chile.

B. chlorocarpa (Kunth) W.T. Marshall. Shrub 1–3m; st. erect, fastigiate, 5–8cm diam.; ribs 9–12. Fls *c*5; outer tep. green; inner tep. white. N Peru.

B. hertlingiana (Backeb.) F. Buxb. Tree-like, to 8m, main st. and side br. erect, to 30cm diam., vivid blue; ribs to 18 ±, tuberculate. Fls 6.5–7×2cm; tube scales ciliate, dark purple-brown, outer tep. white at base, tipped brown; inner tep. white, sometimes tinged pink. Peru.

B. microsperma (Werderm. & Backeb.) W.T. Marshall. Tree-like, 4–6m; trunk to 30cm diam.; ribs to 20 ±. Fls 6×6cm; tep. white. N Peru.

B. viridis (Rauh & Backeb.) F. Buxb. Differs from *B. hertlingiana* in st. to 10m, dark green, v. tuberculate. Peru.

→*Azureocereus* and *Gymnocereus.*

Brown Mallet *Eucalyptus astringens.*
Brown Oak *Heritiera trifoliolata.*
Brown Peru Bark *Cinchona officinalis.*
Brown Pine *Podocarpus elatus.*
Brown Stringybark *Eucalyptus capitellata.*
Brown Trefoil *Trifolium badium.*

Brown-woolly Fig *Ficus drupacea.*

Bruckenthalia Salisb. Ericaceae. 1 everg. shrublet. St. to 25cm, crowded. Lvs 0.5cm, linear, glandular-mucronulate, revolute. Rac. cylindrical, erect to 3cm; cal. 1.5mm, pink, lobes 4; cor. 3mm, campanulate, magenta to candy-pink, lobes 4 equalling tube. Late spring–summer. SE Eur., Asia Minor. Z5.
B. spiculifolia (Salisb.) Rchb. SPIKE HEATH. 'Balkan Red': lvs dark grey-green; fls heliotrope or rose.

Brugmansia Pers. Solanaceae. 5 shrubs or trees. Lvs simple, entire to dentate. Fls solitary, pendulous; cal. spathiform or 2–5-dentate; cor. funnel-shaped, ribbed, pleated in bud, lobes 5, reflexed, narrow. S Amer. Z9.
B. arborea (L.) Lagerh. ANGEL'S TRUMPET; MAIKOA. To 4m. Lvs elliptic-oblong to ovate, pubesc., entire to coarsely toothed. Fls to 15cm, only slightly pendent, white; cal. spathiform. Summer. Andes of Ecuad. to N Chile.
B. aurea Lagerh. To 10m. Lvs minutely pubesc. to glab., coarsely toothed when young, later entire. Fls to 24cm, nocturnally fragrant, white to golden yellow; cal. 2–5-toothed. Andes of C Colomb. to S Ecuad.
B. bicolor Pers. = *B. sanguinea.*
B. ×*candida* Pers. (*B. aurea* ×*B. versicolor.*) To 5m. Lvs oblong-elliptic, undulate, entire to toothed. Fls to 32cm, fragrant, white rarely pink or yellow; cal. spathiform. Ecuad. 'Double White': fls white, double, abundant. 'Knightii': fls double.
B. ×*insignis* (Barb. Rodr.) Lockw. ((*B. suaveolens* ×*B. versicolor*) ×*B. suaveolens*.) Differs from *B. suaveolens* in pubesc. cal. To 4m. Lvs ovate-oblong, glab. Fls to 38cm, pink to white. E Andes. 'Orange': fls large, rich golden-yellow, abundant. 'Pink': fls to 15cm, salmon-pink.
B. ×*rubella* (Safford) Mold. (*B. arborea* ×*B. sanguinea.*) 3m. Lvs ovate to lanceolate, pubesc. Fls to 14cm, red-tinted. S Amer.
B. sanguinea (Ruiz & Pav.) D. Don. RED ANGELS' TRUMPET. Lvs ovate-oblong, undulate, toothed, or entire. Fls to 25cm, yellow-green at base of tube deepening to golden-yellow then deep orange-red to scarlet in throat and limb (pure golden, orange, yellow-green and red forms occur). NC Colomb. to N Chile.
B. suaveolens (Humb. & Bonpl. ex Willd.) Bercht. & Presl. To 5m. Lvs ovate to narrow-elliptic, glab., entire. Fls nocturnally fragrant, to 30cm, white, sometimes yellow or pink, tube constricted; cal. 2–5 toothed. SE Braz.
B. versicolor Lagerh. To 5m. Lvs oblong-elliptic, entire. Fls to 50cm, trumpet-shaped, white, sometimes becoming orange or peach, tube constricted; cal. spathiform. Ecuad. 'Grand Marnier': fls soft apricot.
B. cvs. 'Charles Grimaldi': fls large, bright salmon-pink, abundant.
→*Datura* and *Methysticodendron.*

Brunfelsia Pers. Solanaceae. 40 largely everg. shrubs or small trees. Lvs simple, elliptic to ovate or spathulate, leathery. Fls large, clustered or solitary; cal. tubular or campanulate, 5-lobed; cor. salver-shaped, limb spreading, lobes 5, rounded. Trop. Amer. Z10.
B. americana L. LADY OF THE NIGHT. Shrub or small tree to 5m. Lvs 5–13cm, elliptic to obovate. Cor. white, flushed purple near centre, fading to yellow, tube to 7cm, limb to 2cm diam., erose. Summer. W Indies.
B. australis Benth. YESTERDAY-TODAY-AND-TOMORROW; MORNING-NOON-AND-NIGHT; PARAGUAYAN JASMINE. Shrub to 3.5m. Lvs 4–13cm, broadly elliptic to obovate. Cor. purple with white ring at mouth, fading to white, tube to 3cm, limb to 4cm diam. S Braz. to Parag. and Arg.
B. calycina Benth. = *B. pauciflora.*
B. eximia (Scheidw.) Bosse = *B. pauciflora* 'Floribunda Compacta'.
B. fallax Duch. ex Griseb. = *B. americana.*
B. floribunda hort. = *B. pauciflora* 'Floribunda'.
B. grandiflora D. Don. Shrub or small tree to 3.5m. Lvs 6–23cm, lanceolate to obovate-oblong, acuminate. Cor. purple with white centre, fading with age; tube to 4cm, limb to 5cm diam. Venez. to Boliv. ssp. *schultesii* Plowman. Cor. to 3cm diam., tube 2.5cm.
B. hopeana Hook. = *B. uniflora.*
B. hopeana var. *australis* (Benth.) J.A. Schmidt = *B. australis.*
B. hydrangeiformis (Pohl) Benth. Shrub to 2m. Lvs 12–30cm, oblanceolate to somewhat spathulate. Cor. purple, limb 2–4cm diam., tube 5–9cm. Spring. Braz.
B. jamaicensis Griseb. Shrub to 1.5m. Lvs 7–15, oblong-lanceolate. Cor. white, ageing primrose-yellow, limb 5–6cm diam., tube 7.5–9cm. Summer. W Indies.

B. lactea Krug & Urban. JAZMIN DEL MONTE. Shrub or small tree to 7.5m. Lvs 5–15cm, elliptic to obovate. Fls v. fragrant; cor. white flushed pale yellow or pink with age, limb to 7.5cm diam., tube 6–9cm. E Puerto Rico.
B. latifolia (Pohl) Benth. Low shrub, 30–90cm. Lvs 15–18cm, elliptic to oblong. Fls ± fragrant; cor. pale violet with white centre, fading to white limb to 3cm diam., tube to 2cm. Winter–early spring. Trop. Amer.
B. lindeniana (Planch.) Nichols. = *B. pauciflora.*
B. macrantha Lem. = *B. pauciflora* 'Macrantha'.
B. macrophylla (Cham. & Schldl.) Benth. = *B. hydrangeiformis.*
B. maritima DC. = *B. grandiflora.*
B. nitida Benth. Shrub to 2m. Lvs 4–10cm, obovate. Cor. white, tube to 10cm, limb to 5cm diam. Cuba.
B. paraguayensis Chodat = *B. australis.*
B. parvifolia A. Rich. = *B. nitida.*
B. pauciflora (Cham. & Schldl.) Benth. Shrub to 3m. Lvs 7–15cm, oblong to oblong-lanceolate. Cor. purple, with white eye ringed with blue, limb 3–7.5cm diam., tube 3–4cm. Braz. 'Floribunda': habit somewhat dwarf, spreading; fls violet with small white centre, abundant. 'Floribunda Compacta' ('Eximia'): habit small, compact; fls v. abundant. 'Macrantha': fls v. large.
B. pilosa Plowman. Shrub, 0.5–2m. Lvs 4–7.5cm, lanceolate to obovate. Cor. deep purple with white ring at mouth, fading to pure white, tube 2.5–4cm, limb 3–4cm diam. S Braz.
B. undulata Sw. RAIN TREE. Shrub to 3m or small tree to 6m. Lvs 5–18cm, oblong-lanceolate. Cor. white or tinged creamy yellow with age tube 9–11cm, limb to 5cm diam., undulate. Jam.
B. uniflora (Pohl) D. Don. MANAC; VEGETABLE MERCURY. Shrub to 0.5m. Lvs to 7.5cm, oblong-elliptic to lanceolate or obovate. Cor. blue-violet, yellow in throat, tube to 2.5cm, limb 2–3cm diam. Braz., Venez.
B. violacea Lodd. = *B. americana.*
→*Franciscea.*

Brunia L. Bruniaceae. 7 shrubs. Lvs linear to lanceolate or ovate, closely set or overlapping. Fls in bracteate heads, pan. or rac., tubular; pet. ovate or spathulate; sta. exserted. S Afr. Z9.
B. albiflora E. Phillips. To 3m. Lvs to 12mm, linear-lanceolate, closely set. Fls in heads to 15mm diam.; pet. white, to 6mm.
B. nodiflora L. To 1m. Lvs to 3mm, lanceolate-subulate, overlapping. Fls in heads to 12mm diam.; pet. cream to 2mm.

BRUNIACEAE DC. 11/69. *Berzelia, Brunia.*

Brunnera Steven. Boraginaceae. 3 rhizomatous perenn. herbs. setose or glandular-pubesc. Infl. a term. pan.; cal. campanulate, lobes 5, linear-lanceolate; cor. purple or blue, small, rotate, lobes ovate-orbicular. E Eur. to W Sib. Z3.
B. macrophylla (Adams) Johnst. To 50cm. Basal lvs to 14×10cm, ovate to cordate, coarsely pubesc.; petiole to 20cm; cauline lvs sessile. E Eur. 'Betsy Baring': fls white. 'Dawson's White' ('Variegata'): to 45cm; lvs heart-shaped, deep green variegated white; fls blue. 'Hadspen Cream': to 50cm; lvs light green, splashed cream; fls blue. 'Langtrees' ('Aluminium Spot'): to 50cm; lvs large, rounded, edges spotted silver; fls blue.
→*Anchusa* and *Myosotis.*

Brunonia Sm. Brunoniaceae. 1 pubesc. perenn. herb. Lvs to 4.5cm, obovate, entire, basal, long-stalked. Fls small, blue, 5-merous in long-stalked, pincushion-like heads to 2.5cm diam. Aus. Z9.
B. australis Sm. BLUE PINCUSHION.

×**Brunsdonna** hort.
×*Brunsdonna bidwillii* Worsley = ×*Amarygia bidwillii.*
×*Brunsdonna parkeri* (Will. Wats.) Worsley = ×*Amarygia parkeri.*

Brunsvigia Heist. Amaryllidaceae. 20 bulbous herbs. Lvs radical, ligulate. Scape solid, umbel many-fld., term.; pedicels lengthen after flowering; perianth declinate, funnel-shaped; tep. 6, linear to oblong; sta. and style declinate. S Afr. Z9.
B. gigantea (Van Marum) Traub = *B. josephinae.*
B. gigantea Heist. ex Schult. non (Van Marum) Traub. = *B. orientalis.*
B. josephinae (Redouté) Ker-Gawl. Bulb above ground. Lvs to 90cm, semi-erect, glab. Scape 45–90cm; pedicels 40cm at maturity; perianth tube 1cm, tep. to 5cm, crimson. Summer.
B. multiflora Ait. = *B. orientalis.*
B. orientalis (L.) Ait. ex Ecklon. Bulb subterranean. Lvs to 45cm, prostrate, short-pubesc., above. Scape to 50cm; pedicels to 20cm at maturity; perianth tube to 0.5cm, tep. to 6.5cm, pink or scarlet. Summer.

B. rosea (Lam.) Hann. = *Amaryllis belladonna.*
→*Amaryllis* and *Haemanthus.*

Brush Box *Lophostemon confertus.*
Brush Cherry *Syzygium paniculatum.*
Brush Heath *Brachyloma ericoides.*

Bryanthus Gmel. Ericaceae. 1 everg. shrub to 8cm. Br. wiry, procumbent. Lvs 3–6mm, crowded, linear. Rac. 2–4cm, term. white-downy; cal. 4-lobed; cor. cupped-rotate, pink, lobes to 3mm, 4, oval-oblong. Jap., Kamchatka. Z6.
B. gmelinii D. Don.
B. musciformis Nak. = *B. gmelinii.*
B. taxifolius A. Gray = *Phyllodoce caerulea.*
→*Andromeda, Erica* and *Menziesia.*

Bryonia L. BRYONY. Cucurbitaceae. 12 climbing perenn. herbs. Roots fleshy or tuberous. Tendrils simple. Lvs 3–5 lobed or -angular. Fls to 2cm diam., white to yellow, ♂ in rac. or clusters, sta. 3–5; ♀ in rac. or corymbs, or solitary, sta. replaced by staminodes. Temp. Eur. to W Asia and N Afr. Z6.
B. alba L. WHITE BRYONY. Lvs 5-lobed, or angled. Fls white to pale green. Fr. black, to 1cm. Eur. to Iran.
B. amplexicaulis Lam. = *Solena amplexicaulis.*
B. dioica Jacq. RED BRYONY; WILD HOP. Lvs 5-lobed. Fls pale green. Fr. red to 0.5cm. Summer. Eur., N Afr., W Asia.
B. grandis L. = *Coccinia grandis.*
B. laciniosa hort. = *Diplocyclos palmatus.*
B. palmata L. = *Diplocyclos palmatus.*

Bryony *Bryonia.*

Bryophyllum Salisb.
B. beauverdii (Hamet) Berger = *Kalanchoe beauverdii.*
B. calycinum Salisb. = *Kalanchoe pinnata.*
B. crenatum Bak. = *Kalanchoe laxiflora.*
B. daigremontianum (Hamet & Perrier) Berger = *Kalanchoe daigremontiana.*
B. delagoense (Ecklon & Zeyh.) Schinz = *Kalanchoe delagoensis.*
B. fedtschenkoi (Hamet & Perrier) Lauzac-Marchal = *Kalanchoe gastonis-bonnieri.*
B. manginii (Hamet & Perrier) Northdurft = *Kalanchoe manginii.*
B. pinnatum (Lam.) Oken = *Kalanchoe pinnata.*
B. porphyrocalyx (Bak.) Berger = *Kalanchoe porphyrocalyx.*
B. proliferum Bowie = *Kalanchoe prolifera.*
B. schizophyllum (Bak.) Berger = *Kalanchoe schizophylla.*
B. tubiflorum Harv. = *Kalanchoe delagoensis.*
B. uniflorum (Stapf.) Berger = *Kalanchoe uniflora.*

Buchloe Engelm. BUFFALO GRASS. Gramineae. 1 stoloniferous, tufted grass. Lvs grey-green, sparsely hairy. ♂ infl. to 20cm, br. racemose, spikelets in 2 rows on one side of rachis; ♀ spikelets in short spikes enclosed by lvs. N Amer. Z4.
B. dactyloides (Nutt.) Engelm.

Buchnera L. BLUEHEARTS. Scrophulariaceae. 100 semi-parasitic, perenn. herbs. Lvs simple. Spike term.; fls blue, mauve or white rarely red; cor. tube slender, limb spreading, 5-lobed. Summer. Trop. Afr. Z9.
B. canadensis L. = *Verbena canadensis.*
B. henriquesii Engl. To 25cm, hairy, woody-based. Lvs to 4.5cm, lanceolate or linear. Cor. to 1.2cm.

Buchu *Agathosma crenulata.*

Bucinellina Wiehler. Gesneriaceae. 2 epiphytic perenn. herbs. Lvs paired, unequal. Fls axill.; cal. 5-lobed; cor. tube inflated, curved, limb strongly oblique. Colomb.
B. nariniana Wiehler. St. scandent to pendent. Lvs 2cm, ovate, serrate, pilose beneath. Cor. tube 22mm, yellow, limb small, upper lobes flushed wine-red. Colomb.
B. paramicola Wiehler. St. scandent or rambling. Lvs 8.5cm, lanceolate, entire, white-pilose beneath. Cor. tube 24mm, white towards base, orange above, limb small, upper lobes red. Colomb.

Buck Bean *Menyanthes.*
Buck Brush *Ceanothus cuneatus.*
Bucket Orchid *Coryanthes.*
Buckeye *Aesculus.*
Buckhorn *Osmunda cinnamonea; Plantago lanceolata.*

Buckinghamia F. Muell. Proteaceae. 2 trees. Fls small, white, in term. rac.; perianth tube slender, limb globose. E Aus. Z10.

B. celsissima F. Muell. IVORY CURL FLOWER. Tree to 30m. Juvenile lvs lobed; adult lvs 10–20cm, entire, elliptic, glossy, silver beneath. Rac. 20cm, semi-pendulous; fls cream-white, scented. E Aus.

Bucklandia R. Br. ex Griff.
B. populnea (R. Br.) R.W. Br. = *Exbucklandia populnea.*

Buckler Fern *Dryopteris.*
Buckler Mustard *Biscutella laevigata.*

Buckleya Torr. Santalaceae. 4 decid. parasitic shrubs. Lvs 2-ranked, entire. Fls 4-merous; ♂ in umbel-like rac.; ♀ solitary with sep.-like bracts. Fr. a drupe. E N Amer., China. Z4.
B. distichophylla (Nutt.) Torr. To 4m. Lvs 2–6cm, ovate to lanceolate, subsessile. Fls green. Fr. to 1.5cm, olive green to red-brown. E US.

Buck's-horn Plantain *Plantago coronopus.*
Buckthorn *Rhamnus.*
Buckwheat *Polygonum fagopyrum.*
Buckwheat Tree *Cliftonia monophylla.*
Buddha's-belly Bamboo *Bambusa ventricosa.*

Buddleja L. Loganiaceae. *c*100 decid. or everg. shrubs, and trees. Bark often fibrous with longitudinal fissures. Young growth, lf. undersides and infl. axis usually pale stellate-pubesc. Lvs opposite (alt. in *B. alternifolia* and its hybrids). Infl. term. or axill. pan. composed of thyrses or globose heads; fls 4-parted; cal. ± bell-shaped; cor. tubular, lobes overlapping or valvate; sta. usually included. Trop. and subtrop. Asia, Amer. and Afr.
B. albiflora Hemsl. Decid. shrub to 3m; st. terete or subangular. Lvs 8–30cm, lanceolate, tip acuminate, base cuneate, toothed, glab. above, stell-hairy beneath. Pan. narrow, nearly cylindric to 25cm; fls fragrant; cor. 5–8mm, lobes nearly rounded, lilac. Summer. China. Z6.
B. alternifolia Maxim. Decid. shrub or small tree, to 9m. Br. slender, arching. Lvs 1–7cm, narrow-lanceolate, dark green, entire. Fls fragrant, in dense clusters to 4.5cm, along previous year's wood; cor. usually lilac-purple, 8–13mm. Summer. China. 'Argentea': willow-like; lvs silvery. Z5.
B. americana L. Lvs 9–30cm, narrow ovate to lanceolate, serulate, covered in pale hairs. Fls fragrant, in clusters, white with yellow eye, cor. lobes acute. Autumn. C Mex. to Boliv. and Peru, Cuba and Jam. Z9.
B. asiatica Lour. Everg. shrub or small tree, 0.8–7m. Shoots cylindrical, downy. Lvs 3–30cm, narrow-lanceolate to ovate, acuminate, entire to toothed, glab. to hairy above, floocose beneath. Thryse term. or axill., spike-like, 25cm; fls fragrant; cor. usually white, 3–6mm, lobes rounded. Winter–spring. E Indies. Z8.
B. auriculata Benth. Everg. sprawling shrub or small tree to 3.5m. Lvs 2–13cm, lanceolate to narrow-ovate, base obcordate-hastate, auriculate or rounded, serrate, dark green above, white-floccose beneath. Pan. many-fld; fls sweetly scented, cor. cream, white with orange centre or pink-red, 7–11mm. Autumn–winter. S Afr. Z8.
B. australis Vell. Shrub to 3.5m. Shoots tetragonal. Lvs connate-perfoliate, 5–20cm, lanceolate-ovate to spathulate, acuminate, serrate, dark green above. Infl. axill., to 30cm; fls in a series of tight clusters; cor. yellow or orange, 7–10mm. Winter. Braz., Boliv., Parag., Arg. Z10.
B. bhutanica Yamaz. Shrub to 2m. Similar to *B. asiatica*. Lvs 6–10cm, connate-perfoliate, narrow-oblong, serrate to sub-entire, glab. Pan. term.; fls white, sweetly scented; cor. 4.5–5.5mm. Summer. Bhutan. Z9.
B. brasiliensis Jacq. = *B. australis.*
B. candida Dunn. Shrub with hairy br. Lvs 7–18cm, soft, velvety, narrow-oblong, acuminate, base usually hastate, buff- to silver-pubesc., ultimately glab. and blistered above. Fls violet, in term. pan. to 20cm; cor. 6mm. Winter. Himal. Z8.
B. caryopteridifolia W.W. Sm. = *B. crispa.*
B. colvilei Hook. f. & Thoms. Shrub or small tree to 6m, red-woolly. Lvs 7–20cm, elliptic-lanceolate, acuminate, finely serate, pubesc. Fls large in drooping pan. to 20cm; cor. rose, purple or crimson-marroon, to 2.5cm diam., campanulate. Summer. Himal. 'Kewensis': fls deep red. Z8.
B. crispa Benth. Decid. shrub, to 3.5m. Br. white-floccose. Lvs 1–15cm, lanceolate to ovate or triangular, sinuate to dentate, grey-green, silvery-pubesc. above, woolly beneath. Fls fragrant, in pan. to 12cm; cor. lilac with white or orange throat, 7–16mm. Summer. Himal. Z8.
B. crotonoides Gray. Lvs 4.5–20cm, densely hairy. Infl. spicate; 6–18cm; cor. white, tinged green to yellow, tube 1.5–2.5mm, lobes 1.5–2.5mm. Autumn–winter. Calif. to Costa Rica. Z9.

B. curviflora Hook. & Arn. Shrub to 1.5m. Branchlets stout. Lvs 3–16cm, ovate to narrow-ovate, acuminate or rounded, base cuneate, rounded or almost truncate, entire, tomentose to glab. Thyrses term. to 25cm; cor. purple, 11–22mm, tube curved. Summer. Jap., Taiwan. Z8.

B. davidii Franch. BUTTERFLY BUSH; SUMMER LILAC; ORANGE EYE. Decid. shrub to 3m. Branchlets subquadrangular. Lvs to 20cm, dark green above, felted beneath, lanceolate, acuminate, finely toothed. Pan. to 30cm, term., cymose, tapering; fls fragrant; cor. pale violet to purple with orange eye, also red-purple, white and blue,7.5–14mm. Summer–autumn. China and Jap. var. *alba* Rehd. & Wils. Fls white. Summer. var. *magnifica* Rehd. & Wils. Fls violet-purple; cor. lobes reflexed. Summer. W China. var. *nanhoensis* Rehd. To 1.5m. Lvs narrow and shorter. Infl. to 8cm; fls blue-mauve. Late summer. C China. var. *superba* De Corte. Similar to var. *magnifica* but infl. larger, fls purple-violet. Summer. W China. var. *veitchiana* (Veitch) Rehd. Strong-growing. Shoots arching. Pan. large; fls deep mauve with orange eye. Early summer. C China. 'Amplissima': pan. v. large, mauve. 'Black Knight': fls deep violet. 'Border Beauty': compact habit; fls dark purple-crimson. 'Charming': lavender-pink. 'Dartmoor': infl. paniculate; fls magenta. 'Dubonnet': pan. v. large, dark purple. 'Empire Blue': fls blue-mauve with orange eye. 'Fascinating': bright lilac pink. 'Fortune': long pan., fls lilac with orange eye. 'Harlequin': lvs variegated cream-white; fls red-purple. 'Ile de France': fls bright violet. 'Nanho Blue': fls light blue. 'Nanho Purple': habit lax and spreading; fls dark red-purple with orange eyes. 'Peace': fls white. 'Petite Indigo': to 1.75m, a slender, neatly branched shrub with narrow silvered lvs and short pan. of lavender fls, throat orange. 'Petite Purple': as for 'Petite Indigo' but with darker mauve fls. 'Pink Delight': fls bright pink in long pan. 'Pink Pearl': fls pale lilac pink. 'Royal Red': fls red-purple. 'Salicifolia': lvs and pan. narrow. 'Variegata': lvs variegated. 'White Bouquet': fls white, yellow-eyed, scented. 'White Cloud': fls pure white. 'White Profusion': infl. dense; fls white. Z5.

B. delavayi Gagnep. Shrub to 2m. Shoots subterete. Lvs 4–16cm, elliptic, acuminate, base sometimes decurrent, wavy-toothed to entire, felty, sometimes glandular-hairy above. Pan. term. lax to 12cm; fls fragrant; cor. lavender or rose, tube 10–13.5mm, lobes rounded, 2.5–4.5. Late summer. China. Z7.

B. fallowiana Balf. f. Decid. shrub to 5m. Shoots white-felted, erect, robust. Lvs 4–13cm, ovate to lanceolate, acuminate, base cuneate, densely white-felted beneath, crenate. Infl. term., thyrsoid, to 15cm; fls v. fragrant, white or lavender with orange throat; cor. lobes crenate, spreading, tube 7–10mm. Summer. Burm., W China. var. *alba* Sabourin. Fls white with orange eye. 'Glasnevin': vigorous; lvs wide; fls deep lilac. 'Lochinch': shrub to 2m; young shoots white-tomentose; pan. 3-branched; fls lilac-blue, fragrant; late summer–autumn. 'West Hill': to 3m; pan. narrow arching, 10–30cm; fls fragrant, pale lilac, with gold, bronze or orange centre; late summer–autumn. These last two cvs are almost certainly *B. davidii* ×*B. fallowiana*. Z8.

B. farreri Balf. f. & W.W. Sm. Large shrub. Lvs v. large, hastate, white-woolly beneath, velvety above. Fls lilac-pink, fragrant. Spring. China. Z9.

B. forrestii Diels. Decid., sometimes herb-like shrub, to 6m. Shoot 4-angled, downy. Lvs 5–35cm, lanceolate, acuminate, toothed to subentire, red-brown-downy beneath. Pan. term., cylindric, made up of short-stalked clusters; fls fragrant, mauve, orange, blue, maroon to almost white; cor. tube 7–11mm, 5mm across limb. Summer. W China, Bhutan, Assam, N Burm. Z7.

B. globosa Hope. ORANGE BALL TREE. Semi-everg. shrub or tree to 6m. Shoots obscurely tetragonal. Lvs to 24cm, lanceolate, acuminate, base cuneate, subentire to bluntly toothed, rugose, glossy-glabrous above, floccose beneath. Infl. terminal, made up of long-stalked, many-fld, globose heads, each 2cm diam.; fls fragrant, bright yellow to orange. Summer. Arg., Chile. Z7. 'Lemon Ball': fls lemon-yellow.

B. ×*hybrida* Farq. (*B. asiatica* ×*B. davidii.*) Similar to *B. davidii.* Fls lavender with orange eye. Z8.

B. indica Lam. Shrub with climbing or trailing shoots, to 4m. Lvs to 15cm, orbicular to narrow-elliptic, sinuate. Infl. a thyrse of glomerulate cymes or few-fld individual cymes; fls light yellow to green-yellow, or white; cor. 7–17mm. Winter. Madag. Is. Z10.

B. japonica Hemsl. Shrub to 1m. Shoots ± quadrangular. Lvs 6–20cm, narrowly ovate or elliptic, acuminate, base cuneate or rounded, repand-dentate to subentire, glab. Infl. term., thyrsoid, erect, 6–15cm; cor. lavender, tube often curved, 10.5–16mm. Jap. Z7.

B. ×*lewisiana* Everett. (*B. asiatica* ×*B. madagascariensis.*) Habit spreading and lax. Fl. buds white, opening yellow or orange. Late summer-winter. 'Margaret Pike': st. white-woolly; infl. term. rac., fls light yellow; winter. Z8.

B. lindleyana Fort. ex Lindl. Slender everg. shrub to 3m. Lvs 2–11cm, ovate or elliptic, acute to acuminate, entire to crenulate, pale green. Infl. term., erect to nodding, 4–20cm; cor. purple-violet, tube 11–17mm, usually curved, dilated above, lobes erect. Summer. China. Z8.

B. madagascariensis Lam. Everg. scandent shrub to 10m. Lvs 4–14cm, lanceolate, acute, base cordate or rounded, ± entire. Infl. a term. thyrse or pan., to 25cm; cor. tube slender, 7–10mm, orange-yellow. Autumn–spring. Madag. Z9.

B. ×*madagasiatica* hort. = *B.* ×*lewisiana.*

B. magnifica Rehd. & Wils. = *B. davidii* var. *magnifica.*

B. microphylla HBK = *B. parviflora.*

B. myriantha Diels. Shrub to 3m. Lvs 5–20cm, narrow-elliptic, acuminate, base sometimes decurrent, serrate, crenate or subentire, stellate- and glandular-hairy above, stellate-tomentose beneath. Infl. slender cylindric thyrses, to 22cm; cor. purple or white, tube 6mm, lobes erect, 5–7mm. Summer. Upper Burm., Tibet, China. Z8.

B. nivea Duthie. Differs from *B. candida* lvs narrow-ovate, serrate or crenate, glab. above, white-tomentose beneath; fls violet or purple in dense term. pan. to 30cm, or tomentose, 6–8mm. Late summer. China. Z7.

B. officinalis Maxim. Everg. or semi-decid. shrub to 2m. St. grey-floccose. Lvs 4–15cm, narrow-lanceolate, acuminate, entire to minutely serrate, grey-yellow-woolly beneath. Pan. term., pyramidal, glomerulate; fls fragrant, lilac-mauve with pale middle or pink, throat sometimes orange; cor. 9.5–13mm. Winter. W China. Z8.

B. paniculata Wallich. Shrub or small tree to 6m. Shoots stellate-tomentose. Lvs 2–25cm, narrow-elliptic or -ovate, acuminate, entire to crenate or serrate, bullate, stellate-tomentose. Pan. term., to 25cm; fls pink, lavender, mauve with white limb, or white, usually with orange throat; cor. 7–12mm, lobes spreading, rounded. Summer. N India, Nepal, Bhutan, Burm., China. Z8.

B. parviflora HBK. Shrub or small tree to 5m. Lvs 3–12.5cm, narrow-lanceolate to ovate, toothed or entire, glab. above, thickly tomentose beneath. Pan. glomerulate; fls small, white; cor. campanulate, tube 1–1.5mm. Summer. Mex. Z9.

B. ×*pikei* Fletcher. (*B. alternifolia* ×*B. crispa.*) Decid. straggly shrub, to 1.5m. Lvs to 15cm, ovate, to lanceolate, crenate to lobed, stellate-hairy beneath. Pan. to 30cm; fls fragrant, mauve-pink with orange throat. Late summer. Gdn origin. 'Hever': similar to *B. alternifolia* but habit more lax. Z7.

B. pterocaulis A.B. Jacks. St. winged. Lvs long, pointed. Infl. broad, spike-like; fls lilac. China, Burma.

B. pulchella N.E. Br. Evergr. sometimes scandent shrub, 1–10m. Shoots white-woolly. Lvs 2–10cm, lanceolate to ovate or sometimes hastate, sometimes 1–3 large lobes near base, undulate. Pan. lax to 20cm; fls fragrant; cor. 7–12mm, dull white with orange-red throat. Winter. S & E Afr. Z8.

B. saligna Willd. OLIVE BUDDLEIA; BASTARD OLIVE. Shrub or tree, to 12m. Lvs 1–1.5cm, lanceolate, entire or obscurely sinuate, often revolute, dull-green above, lighter beneath. Pan. crowded, rounded to 15cm; fls fragrant, white, cream or lilac, with orange throat; cor. 1.8–3mm, tube cup-shaped. Autumn. S Afr. Z9.

B. salviifolia L. SOUTH AFRICAN SAGE WOOD. Shrub or small tree, 1–8m. Lvs 4–17cm, narrow-lanceolate, tip acuminate to acute, base cordate to auriculate, crenate, bullate, and glab. above. Pan. to 17cm, arching; fls fragrant, pale lilac to white with an orange centre; cor. 6–9mm. Autumn–early winter. S & E Afr. Z8.

B. sterniana A.D. Cotton = *B. crispa.*

B. tibetica W.W. Sm. = *B. crispa.*

B. tubiflora Benth. Vigorous shrub. Lvs and infl. rusty-pubesc. Fls in axill. clusters; cor. tube orange or yellow, 15–20mm. Autumn–early winter. S Parag., S Braz., Arg. Z9.

B. variabilis Hemsl. = *B. davidii.*

B. ×*weyeriana* Weyer. (*B. davidii* ×*B. globosa.*) Decid. shrub. Lvs lanceolate. Fls yellow to apricot in globose heads packed in ± conical pan. Summer–autumn. Gdn origin. 'Elstead Hybrid': fls pale apricot with brown throat. 'Golden Glow': vigorous; fls light yellow-orange, suffused lilac. 'Moonlight': fls creamy yellow suffused lilac-pink, throat deep orange. 'Sungold': fls deep orange. Z6.

B. ×*whiteana* R.J. Moore. (*B. alternifolia* ×*B. asiatica.*) Lvs to 12cm, lanceolate, deep green above, paler beneath. Pan. terminal, narrow, fls lilac, lobes paler. Autumn. Gdn origin. Z6.

B. yunnanensis Gagnep. Shrub to 2m. Lvs 2–12cm, elliptic, apex acuminate, base decurrent or acuminate, serrate to entire, stellate-tomentose beneath. Spikes dense, term., to 6cm, bracteate; fls lilac; cor. 10–12mm, lobes oblong, erect. Late summer. Yunnan. Z8.

→*Chilianthus* and *Nicodemia.*

Bud Sagebrush *Artemisia spinescens.*

Buffalo Berry *Shepherdia argentea; S. canadensis.*
Buffalo Bur *Solanum rostratum.*
Buffalo Currant *Ribes aureum; R. odoratum.*
Buffalo Euphorbia *Euphorbia bubalina.*
Buffalo Gourd *Cucurbita foetidissima.*
Buffalo Grass *Buchloe; Stenotaphrum secundatum.*
Buffalo Horn *Burchellia bubalina.*
Buffalo Mallee *Eucalyptus mitchelliana.*
Buffalo Nut *Pyrularia pubera.*
Buffalo Thatch *Thrinax morrisii.*
Buffalo Top *Thrinax morrisii.*
Buffalo Wattle *Acacia kettlewelliae.*
Buffalo Wood *Burchellia bubalina.*
Buffel Grass *Cenchrus ciliaris.*
Bugbane *Cimicifuga.*
Bugle *Ajuga.*
Bugleweed *Lycopus virginicus.*
Bugloss Amsinckia *Amsinckia lycopsoides.*

Buglossoides Moench. Boraginaceae. 16 setulose or hispid ann. or perenn. herbs. Lvs entire. Cymes terminal, simple or branched, bracteate; cal. lobes 5, narrow; cor. usually blue or white, infundibular, 5-lobed, throat with 5 distinct longitudinal bands of hairs or glands. Eur., Asia. Z6.
B. gastonii (Benth.) Johnst. Perenn. herb to 30cm, adpressed-pubesc. Lvs to 6.5cm, lanceolate to ovate-lanceolate. Cor. to 14mm, purple becoming blue, exterior pubesc. W Pyren.
B. purpureocaeruleum (L.) Johnst. Perenn. herb to 70cm, pub-esc. Lvs to 8cm, narrowly elliptic to lanceolate. Cor. to 19mm, red-purple, becoming bright blue. W Eur. to Iran.
B. zollingeri (A. DC.) Johnst. Perenn. herb to 20cm, procumbent, strigose. Lvs to 6cm, oblong or ovate to broadly oblanceolate. Cor. to 18mm, blue, or white, interior glandular-pubesc. E Asia.
→*Lithospermum.*

Buglossum Adans.
B. barrelieri All. = *Anchusa barrelieri.*

Bug Orchid *Orchis coriophora.*

Buiningia F. Buxb.
B. brevicylindrica Buin. = *Coleocephalocereus aureus.*

Buisson Ardent *Pyracantha coccinea.*

Bulbine L. Liliaceae (Asphodelaceae). 30–40 succulent and non-succulent herbs and shrubs, perenn. except for *B. annua.* Lvs radical or cauline, soft, fleshy, usually narrow and persistent. Fls many, small, usually yellow, in slender long-stalked rac. S & E Afr. Z9.
B. alooides Willd. Clump-forming. Lvs 15–22cm, aloe-like, lanceolate; linguiform, v. soft and fleshy, light green. Fls yellow. S Afr.
B. annua Willd. Ann.; roots fibrous. Lvs 20–30cm long, 2–5mm thick, erect, subulate, rac. Fls bright yellow. Cape Prov.
B. bulbosa (R. Br.) Haw. = *Bulbinopsis bulbosa.*
B. caulescens L. = *B. frutescens.*
B. caulescens var. *incurva* (Thunb.) Roem. & Schult. = *B. frutescens* var. *incurva.*
B. caulescens var. *rostrata* (Jacq.) Poelln. = *B. frutescens* var. *rostrata.*
B. diphylla Schltr. ex Poelln. Main st. short, arising from 3–7 conical, fleshy roots. Lvs in single pairs succulent, light green, tinged red, larger lf channelled above, 3–5cm, smaller lf terete, thinner. Fls yellow. Cape Prov.
B. frutescens (L.) Willd. Freely branching shrub to 60cm, roots fibrous. Lvs c16cm. Fls bright yellow, orange or white. E Cape. 'Hallmark': fls orange. 'Virgo': fls white. var. *incurva* (Thunb.) G. Rowley. Lvs 4–5cm, incurved. var. *rostrata* (Jacq.) G. Rowley. St. stouter and shorter; lvs glaucous, fls yellow.
B. haworthioides R. Nordenstam. Cape Prov.
B. incurva (Thunb.) Spreng. = *B. frutescens* var. *incurva.*
B. latifolia (L. f.) Haw. Rootstock stout. Br. few. Lvs 20–35cm, in aloe-like rosettes, oblong-lanceolate, flat, margins curled upwards. Fls yellow. Cape Prov.
B. mesembryanthoides Haw. Caudex subglobose. Lvs 1.6cm, 1–2, lemon-shaped, v. soft and watery, pale green. Cape Prov.
B. rostrata (Jacq.) Willd. = *B. frutescens* var. *rostrata.*
B. semibarbata (R. Br.) Haw. = *Bulbinopsis semibarbata.*
B. succulenta Compton. Caudex 3–4cm thick, tipped with tuft of spiny scales. Lvs 6–7cm, 2–4, radical, erect, v. fleshy, light green tinged red. Fls yellow. S Afr.
B. triebneri Dinter. Caudex short, tuberous. Lvs 15–30cm, 10–20, subterete, nearly flat above, glaucous. Fls white. Nam.
→*Anthericum.*

Bulbinella Kunth. Liliaceae (Asphodelaceae). 20 fleshy-rooted perenn. herbs. Lvs ± succulent, radical. Scape exceeding lvs; rac. many-fld; perianth seg. 6. NZ, Afr. Z8.
B. hookeri (Hook. f.) Cheesem. To 60m. Fls ♂, yellow. Fr. short-stalked.
B. rossii (Hook. f.) Cheesem. To 1.25m. Fls functionally unisexual, yellow. Fr. sessile. NZ.

Bulbinopsis Borzi. Liliaceae (Asphodelaceae). 2 perenn. herbs. Lvs to 30cm, linear-subulate, radical. Fls numerous, yellow, in a lax rac. to 60cm. E Aus.
B. bulbosa (R. Br.) Borzi. Caudex bulbous. Fls with 6 bearded fil.
B. semibarbata (R. Br.) Borzi. Root fibrous. Fls with 6 fil. (3 bearded).
→*Anthericum* and *Bulbine.*

Bulblet Bladder Fern *Cystopteris bulbifera.*

Bulbocodium L. Liliaceae (Colchicaceae). 2 perenn., cormous herbs. Lvs basal, blunt, linear-lanceolate, subterete. Fls emerging from a tubular sheath; tep. 6, oblong-lanceolate, clawed, with basal teeth forming a short tube. Spring. S & E Eur. Z4.
B. trigynum Adam non Jank. = *Merendera trigyna.*
B. vernum L. Lvs to 15×1.5cm. Fls 1(–3), rose to magenta, occas. mauve or white, claw flushed or spotted white. SW Alps to S Russia.
B. versicolor (Ker-Gawl.) Spreng. Differs from *B. vernum* in its smaller fls and narrower lvs. E Eur., W Asia.
→*Colchicum.*

Bulbophyllum Thouars. Orchidaceae. *c*1200 epiphytic orchids, mostly small. Lvs 1(–2), ± fleshy, obovate-spathulate, terminating globose to cylindrical pbs widely spaced on rhiz. Fls 1 to many, in scapose, usually lat. umbels, rac. or spikes; dors. sep. free, lat. sep. often far larger, decurved, fused to the column foot, forming a saccate projection, or longer still, hanging vertically and twisted above; pet. free, smaller, sometimes vestigial; lip entire to trilobed, fleshy. Trop. Z10.
B. ambrosia (Hance) Schltr. Fls fragrant, white to pale green, lined maroon, dors. sep. oblong, lateral sep. oblong to round; pet. triangular, lip midlobe ligulate, broad, reflexed. Hong Kong, China.
B. auricomum Lindl. Rac. to 22cm, drooping; fls many, yellow or white marked yellow, fragrant; dors. sep. lanceolate, elongate, lat. sep. longer; pet. ovate-oblong, ciliate; lip oblong-lanceolate, pubesc. India.
B. barbigerum Lindl. Infl. to 20cm, racemose; fls deep red to burgundy; sep. tinged green, linear-lanceolate; pet. minute, triangular; lip linear-ligulate, tip covered with long motile hairs. W & C Afr.
B. beccarii Rchb. f. Lvs unusually long (to 60cm). Rac. to 20cm, packed, pyramidal, pendent; fls malodorous, to 1cm diam., tep. lanceolate yellow, veined and blotched deep red, lip golden, cordate-oblong. Borneo.
B. biflorum Teijsm. & Binnend. Fls 2 per st.; sep. pale green, streaked red-brown, pet. pale green or white, streaked dark red; lat. sep. v. long, linear, upper half tubular, apex club-shaped; lip triangular-ligulate, yellow, speckled red. Java.
B. binnendijkii J.J. Sm. Infl. to 20cm, umbellate; fls pale green, sep. to 10cm, oblong-lanceolate, twisted, green marked violet, lip speckled dark violet, streaked white. Java.
B. calamarium Lindl. Rac. erect to 30cm; sep. ochre, lanceolate, spreading; pet. minute, lip purple, base saccate, midlobe linear-lanceolate, ciliate with longer, crimson hairs at tip. Afr.
B. careyanum (Hook.) Spreng. Rac. to 23cm, nodding, dense cylindric; sep. small, orange-yellow or green, spotted or tinged purple or red-brown, oblong-ovate; pet. minute; lip to 0.5×0.2cm, violet. Autumn–winter. E Himal., Burm., Thail.
B. cocoinum Batem. ex Lindl. Infl. to 45cm, pendent, fls white, green or cream, often suffused purple or pink; sep. lanceolate; pet. oblanceolate, minutely dentate; lip denticulate or fringed. W Afr.
B. comosum Collett & Hemsl. Rac. to 6.5cm, deflexed, cylindric, dense; fls cream tinged green; sep. subequal, translucent, subulate to lanceolate, densely villous; pet. small, linear-oblong; lip lanceolate. Burm.
B. cumingii Rchb. f. Scape to 22cm; infl. umbellate; fls straw-yellow tinged purple; dors. sep. slender, filamentous, fringed, lat. sep. elliptic, narrow, tips fused; pet. linear-triangular, fringed with yellow hairs; lip fleshy. Philipp.
B. cupreum Lindl. Rac. to 25cm, lax; fls copper-yellow; sep. lanceolate, lat. sep. deflexed, ×2 larger than dors.; pet. small, lip trilobed, oblong-ligulate, spurred, ciliate. India.
B. dayanum Rchb. f. Fls to 3, to 2.5cm diam., sep. ovate, fringed,

spreading, pubesc., yellow-green, spotted dark purple, pet. purple edged green, linear-oblong, fringed; lip minute. Burm.

B. dearei Rchb. f. Fls solitary, dors. sep. ovate-lanceolate, to 4.5cm, tawny-yellow, spotted red, lat. sep. lanceolate, falcate, marked purple, pet. linear-lanceolate, tawny-yellow, veins darker, spotted maroon, lip white mottled purple, mobile. Philipp.

B. falcatum (Lindl.) Rchb. f. Infl. to 35cm; rachis lanceolate-falcate, purple or green, flattened, strongly undulate; fls v. short-stalked, situated along both margins, red, purple or green, sometimes marked purple, pet. tipped yellow. Spring–autumn. C Afr.

B. fascinator (Rolfe) Rolfe. Fls solitary, pale green, marked crimson; dors. sep. to 3cm, ovate, with filamentous appendages and purple-fringed margins, lat. sep. to 20cm, fused, apex free, appendages long; pet. to 2cm, falcate-oblong, fringed; lip ovate-oblong, recurved. Malaysia.

B. fletcherianum Rolfe. Fls fleshy, malodorous, clustered; dors. sep. lanceolate, broad, to 5cm, claret, speckled white, lat. sep. similar, with fewer spots. pet. claret, triangular, erect; lip ligulate, 2-ridged. New Guinea.

B. frostii Summerh. Fls purple, lip base pale yellow, faintly veined; sep. papillose beneath, fringed, dors. sep. ovate to orbicular, shortly acuminate, lateral sep. oblong-lanceolate, to 2cm; pet. oblong, margins jagged, fringed; lip to 0.5cm, fleshy, sagittate. Indo-China.

B. godseffianum Weathers = *B. dearei.*

B. gracillimum (Rolfe) Rolfe. Peduncle purple, to 30cm; fls crimson, lip violet-purple; tep. filamentous at apex, fringed, dors. sep. forming hood; lip to 2mm. New Guinea, Malaysia.

B. graveolens (Bail.) J.J. Sm. Fls umbellate, many, tep. yellow to green streaked or suffused rose; dors. sep. concave, cuspidate, lat. sep. to 5cm, linear-oblong; pet. oblong, cuspidate; lip crimson, ovate-oblong, fleshy. New Guinea.

B. guttulatum Wallich ex Hook. f. Fls umbellate, few, tep. yellow or green, speckled purple; sep. spreading, dors. sep. ovate, lat. sep. to 2cm, ovate-lanceolate; lip pale purple, short. India.

B. lemniscatum Parish. Pbs aggregated. Infl. to 15cm, crowded, pendent; sep. orbicular-ovate, purple with long white-banded appendages and hairs; pet. linear-lanceolate, purple streaked white; lip ovate, dark blue-purple. Burm.

B. leopardinum (Wallich) Lindl. Fls paired, to 3cm diam., globose-campanulate, fleshy, pale yellow-brown or green, densely spotted purple or pink, lip deep purple or crimson, ovate-lanceolate. Spring–summer. E Himal. to Burm., N Thail.

B. leysianum Burb. Dors. sep. ovate-lanceolate, fringed, violet tipped green, lat. sep. falcate, pale green flushed violet; pet. white speckled violet; lip green speckled violet, hairy within. Java, Borneo.

B. lobbii Lindl. Fls solitary, to 10cm diam., red-yellow, ochre or pale yellow, veined red or speckled pink and yellow, lined brown; dors. sep. lanceolate, lateral sep. falcate, concave; pet. narrower, spreading; lip ovate. NE India, SE Asia to Philipp.

B. longiflorum Thouars. Infl. to 20cm, umbellate; tep. cream or yellow, spotted red, lip dark red or yellow, suffused dark red; dors. sep. round to elliptic, apex dentate, lat. sep. linear-lanceolate, basally twisted; lip narrow, triangular. Afr., Indon., Aus., Fiji.

B. longissimum (Ridl.) J.J. Sm. Infl. to 20cm, umbellate, pendent; fls white, streaked rose, dors. sep. with 5 red veins, lat. sep. streaked pink; dors. sep. to 2cm, oblong-lanceolate, fringed, lat. sep. to 30cm, linear, apex filamentous; lip ovate-oblong, recurved, fleshy. Borneo, Malaysia.

B. macranthum Lindl. Fls to 6cm diam., solitary, fleshy, burgundy, fading to dull violet, speckled dark violet; sep. pale green or yellow, lat. sep. ovate-triangular, to 3cm. Burm.

B. macrobulbon Rolfe. Rac. 4–5-fld; fls malodorous, yellow-white, lined and blotched purple, pet. base and lip crimson; sep. to 4.5cm, ovate. New Guinea.

B. mandibulare Rchb. f. Tep. bronze, suffused pale green, pet. striped purple above, lip yellow, marked red-brown, triangular-cordate. Borneo.

B. mastersianum (Rolfe) J.J. Sm. Infl. curved or suberect, to 15cm; fls umbellate, yellow, tinged amber; lat. sep. linear-oblong, fused almost to apex, base narrow; pet. to 0.6cm, oblong, falcate, finely fringed; lip to 4cm, fleshy. Malaysia.

B. maximum (Lindl.) Rchb. f. Infl. to 90cm; tep. yellow or green, usually tipped yellow, marked purple or brown; lip cream or yellow, spotted purple, lip fleshy, ovate-oblong, margins at base irregularly divided. Afr.

B. medusae (Lindl.) Rchb. f. Scape arched; fls crowded, umbellate, white or cream, spotted red or yellow; dors. sep. finely caudate, lat. sep. with v. fine apical fil. to 15cm. Winter.

Malay Penins., Thail., Borneo.

B. obrienianum Rolfe. Fls solitary; tep. to 2.5cm, ovate, obtuse, yellow to brown spotted maroon; lip linear-oblong, fleshy, maroon, yellow below. Himal.

B. odoratissimum Lindl. Fls white, fragrant; sep. lanceolate, apices terete; pet. smaller, ovate; lip fringed. India, Burm., S China.

B. ornatissimum (Rchb. f.) J.J. Sm. Fls 3 per scape, straw-yellow, striped and dotted purple; sep. ovate-lanceolate, red-fringed, to 10cm, tips filamentous; lip short. India.

B. pahudii (De Vries) Rchb. f. Infl. to 15cm; fls 10–12, pale brown-yellow or green, speckled red-brown; tep. linear, apices filamentous. Java.

B. paleaceum (Lindl.) Hook. f. = *Sunipia palacea.*

B. patens King ex Hook. f. Infl. bracts yellow, speckled red, overlapping; fls solitary; sep. linear to ovate-lanceolate, white or pale yellow, pet. narrow, tinted and spotted maroon, lip oblong, purple. Malaysia, Sumatra, Java, Borneo.

B. picturatum (Lodd.) Rchb. f. Infl. erect to 25.5cm, green, speckled purple; sheaths speckled red; fls umbellate; dors. sep. hooded, papillose, dull green spotted crimson, lat. sep. long, narrow, pale green, pet. ovate, similar to dors. sep., lip crimson. India.

B. pulchrum (N.E. Br.) J.J. Sm. Dors. sep. circular, bristly, purple, dotted dark purple, lat. sep. slender, fused, pale yellow, mottled purple, pet. purple, minute; lip to 5cm, purple. New Guinea.

B. purpureorhachis (De Wildeman) Schltr. Fls small, maroon, in a line running lengthwise along the centre of either side of a broad, flattened, spiralling, purple-mottled rachis. Zaire.

B. refractum (Zoll.) Rchb. f. Rac. to 40cm; fls orange-yellow; dors. sep. ovate, sparsely pubesc., lateral sep. linear, fringed; pet. triangular, hairy-tipped; lip sigmoid, pubesc. Himal., Java.

B. retusiusculum Rchb. f. Fls pale green to yellow, sometimes marked purple; dors. sep. oblong, truncate, minutely dentate, to 3mm, tinged brown, spotted white, lip dull purple. India, Nepal to Malaysia.

B. rothschildianum (O'Brien) J.J. Sm. Infl. erect, green, speckled purple; fls crimson-purple blotched yellow; dors. sep. yellow, lined purple, forming a hood, fringed; lip triangular. India.

B. roxburghii (Lindl.) Rchb. Dors. sep. and pet. ovate, awned, fringed, yellow striped red, lateral sep. 3–4× longer (1.75cm), linear, yellow; lip maroon. India.

B. rufinum Rchb. f. Infl. decurved; bracts 2–3; fls erect, green and yellow, veined purple; dors. sep. ovate, broad, lat. sep. oblong; pet. oblong; lip compressed, stalked. Himal., India.

B. suavissimum Rolfe. Fls pendent, fragrant; pet. primrose, sep. linear-oblong; pet. shorter, ovate-lanceolate, jagged; lip golden, linear-oblong. Burm.

B. uniflorum (Bl.) Hassk. Infl. borne on rhiz.; fls 1–2, to 4.5cm diam., tep. tan to rust, yellow beneath; dors. sep. oblong, tapering, lat. sep. falcate, long; pet. smaller; lip cordate, red-brown. Java.

B. vaginatum (Lindl.) Rchb. f. Scape to 10cm; fls pale straw-yellow, fringed; dors. sep. ovate, lateral sep. connivent; pet. elliptic-oblong; lip oblong-triangular. Java.

B. wallichii Rchb. f. Fls many, fragrant, pale green, ageing yellow-brown, dotted purple; sep. lanceolate, fringed, larger; pet. triangular, fringed; lip hairs purple, gland., tufted. Himal. to Burm., Thail., Indo-China.

B. watsonianum Rchb. f. = *B. ambrosia.*

B. wendlandianum (Kränzl.) J.J. Sm. Infl. to 10cm; fls umbellate, to 6, tep. yellow, striped purple; dors. sep. to 1.5cm, boot-shaped, apex broadly red-filamentous, lat. sep. narrow, to 15cm; pet. broad, fringed; lip smooth, purple. Burm.

→*Cirrhopetalum.*

Bulbous Meadow Grass *Poa bulbosa.*
Bulbous Saxifrage *Saxifraga granulata.*
Bullace *Prunus × domestica*; *Vitis rotundifolia.*
Bull Banksia *Banksia grandis.*
Bull Bay *Magnolia grandiflora.*
Bullhorn Acacia *Acacia cornigera.*
Bullich *Eucalyptus macrocarpa.*
Bull Kauri *Agathis microstachya.*
Bull Nettle *Solanum elaeagnifolium.*
Bull Oak *Casuarina.*
Bullock's Heart *Annona reticulata.*
Bullocks Heart Ivy *Hedera colchica.*
Bullrush *Typha* (*T. latifolia*).
Bull Thatch *Sabal jamaicensis.*
Bull Thistle *Cirsium vulgare.*

Bumelia Sw. Sapotaceae. 25 everg. or decid. trees and shrubs with milky latex. Lvs simple, leathery. Infl. axill., fascicled; fls small, white; cor. with lateral appendages; sta. and staminodes 5, leafy, alt. with cor. lobes. Fr. a small black berry. US to S Amer. Z6.

B. lanuginosa (Michx.) Pers. CHITTAMWOOD; SHITTIMWOOD; FALSE BUCKTHORN; BLACK HAW. Decid. to 15m, twigs slender, thorny. Lvs 3–8cm, lanceolate to elliptic, brown-lanate when young, sinuate. Fr. 1–2cm, ovoid. Summer. SE US, Mex.

B. lycioides (L.) Pers. SOUTHERN BUCKTHORN; SHITTIMWOOD; MOCK ORANGE. Decid. to 8m, twigs often thorny. Lvs 5–13cm, oval to obovate or elliptic, with silky hairs when young. Fr. 1cm, ellipsoid. SE US.

Bunchberry Cornus canadensis.
Bunchflower Melanthium virginicum.
Bunch-flowered Daffodil Narcissa tazetta.
Bunchgrass Schizachyrium scoparium.

Bunchosia Rich. ex Kunth. Malpighiaceae. 55 everg. shrubs or small trees. Lvs opposite, simple, often with glands close to base below. Rac. axill.; cal. gland.; pet. 5, yellow, spreading, clawed; sta. 10. Fr. a red or yellow drupe. Mex. and Carib. Is. to Parag. and S Braz. Z10.

B. argentea DC. Shrub to 3m; br. pubesc. Lvs lanceolate, silver-pubesc. beneath. N S Amer.

B. glandulifera (Jacq.) Kunth. Shrub or small tree, 2–8m. Lvs to 18cm, broad-ovate to elliptic, glossy above, sparsely pubesc. beneath, with 4 basal glands. Carib. Is., N S Amer.

B. lanceolata Turcz. Small tree 4–6m. Lvs 6.5–20cm, oblong to elliptic or oblong-lanceolate, glossy bright green. Mex. to Boliv.

B. nitida (Jacq.) DC. Shrub or small tree. Lvs to 15cm, elliptic to oblong or lanceolate, becoming glab. lacking glands. Cuba, Lesser Antilles, Colomb.

Bunga Pinanga.

Bunias L. Cruciferae. 6 ann. or perenn., hairy herbs. St. erect, branching. Infl. racemose; fls yellow, large, long-stalked, 4-merous. Medit. Z7.

B. orientalis L. Perenn. to 80cm. Basal lvs long-oblong, runcinate. Pet. 8×4mm, obovate yellow. Infl. much elongated in fr. Cauc., Armenia, S Russia.

Bunnies' Ears Stachys byzantina.
Bunny Ears Opuntia microdasys.
Bunya Bunya Araucaria bidwillii.

Buphthalmum L. OX EYE. Compositae. 2 perenn. herbs. Lvs alt., simple. Cap. medium to large, radiate, solitary, on long, leafy peduncles; ray flts yellow; disc flts yellow. Summer. Eur., W Asia. Z4.

B. aquaticum L. = Nauplius aquaticus.
B. cordifolium Waldst. & Kit. = Telekia speciosa.
B. grandiflorum L. = B. salicifolium.
B. maritimum L. = Asteriscus maritimus.

B. salicifolium L. Hairy perenn., to 1.5m. St. simple or branched. Lvs to 10cm, obovate-lanceolate to linear-lanceolate, entire or toothed. Cap. to 6.5cm; ray flts to 20×3mm. C Eur. 'Golden Wonder' ('Golden Beauty'): vivid gold. 'Sunwheel': to 75cm; bright yellow.

B. sericeum L. f. = Nauplius sericeus.
B. speciosissimum L. = Telekia speciosissima.
B. speciosum Schreb. = Telekia speciosa.

Bupleurum L. THOROW-WAX. Umbelliferae. c100 ann. or perenn. herbs or shrubs. Lvs simple, entire. Umbels compound often subtended by an involucre of leafy bracts, and involucel of broad bracteoles; fls small, usually yellow, occas. green- or red-tinged. Eurasia, Canary Is., N US, S Afr.

B. americanum Coult. & Rose. Perenn. herb to 40cm, lvs 2–16cm, linear to oblong-lanceolate, usually sessile. Umbel rays 4–14, unequal; bracts to 15mm, ovate to lanceolate; bracteoles to 5mm, 6–8; fls yellow, or tinged purple. Alask. to Wyom. and Mont. Z2.

B. angulosum L. Perenn. herb to 40cm. Lower lvs linear to lanceolate, long-stalked; st. lvs 3–5, broad, base amplexicaul. Umbels rays 3–6; bracts 3–4, ovate-lanceolate; bracteoles, small 5–6 rounded, fls yellow-green. Summer. Pyren., NE Spain. Z6.

B. candollii Wallich ex DC, Perenn. to 1m. Upper lvs oblong to ovate, variable; lower lvs broadly lanceolate, to 15cm. Umbel rays 5–12 to 3.5cm; bracts few, ovate; bracteoles 5, lanceolate to ovate, exceeding yellow fls. Summer. Himal. Z7.

B. falcatum L. SICKLE-LEAVED HARE'S EAR. Perenn. to 1m, with woody stock. Basal lvs obovate, elliptic; st. lvs linear or lanceolate, often falcate, prominently veined. Umbel rays 5–8 to 2cm; bracts unequal, 2–5; bracteoles, 4–5 linear-lanceolate; fls yellow. Summer. S, C & E Eur., Asia. var. *scorzonerifolium*

(Willd.) Ledeb. Basal lvs linear to oblong-lanceolate; st. lvs lanceolate to oblong-spathulate. Jap. and Sib. to Pak., India. Z3.

B. fruticescens L. Everg. subshrub to 1m, br. divaricate, sometimes spinescent in upper reaches. Lvs 2–7.5cm, rigid, linear, midrib prominent. Umbels minute, 2–5-rayed in slender, flexuous pan. Summer. SW Eur. Z6.

B. fruticosum L. SHRUBBY HARE'S EAR. Everg. shrub to 3m. Lvs 5–8cm, oblanceolate to oblong-obovate, mucronulate, blue-green, thick, midrib prominent. Umbel rays to 5cm, 5–15; bracts 5–6, ovate to obovate caducous; bracteoles 5–6 obovate; fls yellow. Summer. S Eur. Z7.

B. gibraltaricum Lam. Everg. subshrub to 2m, sparsely branching. Lvs 7.5–15cm, oblanceolate, mucronate, glaucous. Umbels to 7cm diam.; rays 10–30; bracts 5–7, persistent; bracteoles 5 ovate; fls yellow. Summer. S Spain. Z7.

B. graminifolium Vahl = B. petraeum.

B. longifolium L. Herbaceous or suffruticose perenn. to 1.5m. Lower lvs to 6cm, elliptic-spathulate, petiole winged; st. lvs ovate-cordate. Umbel rays 5–10, 2–5cm; bracteoles to 7mm, 5, ovate, often connate at base; fls minute, yellow. Summer. C Eur. to Sib. Z3.

B. multinerve DC. Perenn. to 50cm. Lower lvs linear-lanceolate, 3–15cm; upper lvs smaller, base cordate-clasping. Umbels 10–20-rayed; bracts 2–7, oblong-ovate, shorter than rays; bracteoles, 5 obovate to orbicular, exceeding; fls yellow. Summer. Eurasia. Z3.

B. nipponicum Kozo-Polj. Perenn. to 40cm; st. little-branched. Lower lvs to 15cm, linear to oblong-lanceolate; upper lvs clasping, base auriculate. Umbels 5–8-rayed; bracts few, ovate; bracteoles 5–6, ovate to obovate-oblong, longer than pedicels; fls yellow or tinged purple. Jap. Z7.

B. petraeum L. ROCK HARE'S EAR. Perenn. to 30cm; base ± woody. Lvs to 20cm, in basal rosettes, linear, thick, glaucescent. Umbels c6cm diam., 5–15-rayed; bracts 3–6; bracteoles 5–10, occas. slightly connate; fls yellow. Summer. S Alps. Z6.

B. ranunculoides L. Herbaceous perenn. to 60cm. Basal lvs linear to oblong-lanceolate, glaucescent; st. lvs ovate, clasping. Umbels 5–7-rayed; bracts 1–5; bracteoles 5–6, green-yellow; fls yellow. Summer. Eur. Z6.

B. rotundifolium L. THOROW-WAX. Glaucescent ann. or short-lived perenn. to 60cm. Lvs 2–5cm, elliptic-ovate to suborbicular, amplexicaul to perfoliate, suffused rose when young and prominently veined above. Umbels to 2.5cm diam.; rays 4–8; bracts 0; bracteoles oblanceolate to ovate, connate at base, yellow-green; fls yellow-green. Summer. Eurasia, US. 'Green Gold': to 45cm; lvs light green; fls yellow. Z6.

B. scorzonerifolium Willd. = B. falcatum var. scorzonerifolium.

B. spinosum Gouan. Perenn. to 30cm; st. sparsely branched, base woody; upper br. persisting, becoming spiny. Basal lvs linear-subulate; st. lvs reduced. Umbels 2–7-rayed; bracts usually 5. Summer. S & E Spain. Z7.

Burbidgea Hook. f. Zingiberaceae. 6 perenn. rhizomatous herbs to 1m. Lvs in 2 ranks on fleshy st. Infl. term.; pet. 3, posterior broader than spreading laterals; lip smaller than pet., narrow, erect, 0. Z10.

B. pubescens Ridl. = B. schizocheila.

B. schizocheila Hackett. To 50cm. Lvs to 15cm, elliptic, red-brown beneath. Pet. to 3.5cm; orange-yellow, lip emarginate. Malaysia, Borneo.

Burchardia R. Br. MILKMAIDS. Liliaceae (Colchicaceae). 1 rhizomatous perenn. herb. St. 15–30cm. Lvs 7.5–15cm, linear, cauline. Fls fragrant, white ± tinged red in a term. umbel subtended by linear bracts. Spring. Temp. Aus. Z9.

B. umbellata R. Br.

Burchellia R. Br. Rubiaceae. 1 everg. shrub to 3m+. St. white or mottled grey. Lvs to 13cm, ovate, oblong or lanceolate, entire, pubesc. beneath. Fls in term. heads; cor. deep scarlet to orange, tubular, 2.5cm, 5-lobed. Fr. a red-brown berry, 1.5cm diam. Spring–summer. S Afr. Z9.

B. bubalina (L. f.) Sims. BUFFALO-WOOD; BUFFALO-HORN; WILD POMEGRANATE.

B. capensis R. Br. = B. bubalina.

Bur Cucumber Sicyos angulatus.
Burdett's Banksia Banksia burdettii.
Burdett's Gum Eucalyptus burdettiana.
Burdock Arctium.
Bur Gherkin Cucumis anguria.

Burgsdorffia Moench = Sideritis.

Burgundy Rose Rosa ×centifolia.

Buri Palm *Polyandrococos.*
Buriti Palm *Trithrinax acanthocoma.*

Burlingtonia Lindl. = *Rodriguezia.*

Burma Reed *Neyraudia reynaudiana.*
Bur-marigold *Bidens.*
Burmese Fishtail Palm *Caryota mitis.*
Burmese Rosewood *Pterocarpus indicus.*
Burmese Spruce *Picea farreri.*
Burnet *Sanguisorba minor.*
Burnet Bloodwort *Sanguisorba officinalis.*
Burnet Rose *Rosa pimpinellifolia.*
Burnet Saxifrage *Pimpinella saxifraga.*
Burning Bush *Bassia scoparia; Combretum microphyllum; Dictamnus; Euonymus atropurpureus.*
Burning Love *Ixora coccinea.*
Burnt Orchid *Orchis ustulata.*
Burracoppin Mallee *Eucalyptus burracoppinensis.*
Burrawong *Macrozamia communis.*
Bur Reed *Sparganium.*
Burro's Tail *Sedum morganianum.*

Burrielia DC.
B. chrysostoma var. *macrantha* A. Gray = *Lasthenia macrantha.*

Burr Oak *Quercus macrocarpa.*
Burro's Tail *Sedum morganianum.*

Bursaria Cav. Pittosporaceae. 3 spiny everg. shrubs and small trees. Lvs alt. Fls small, 5-merous in term. pan. Fr. a dry flattened capsule. Aus. Z8.
B. spinosa Cav. Shrub or small tree to 5m, branchlets spiny. Lvs 2–4cm, obovate. Infl. to 15×10cm; fls c1cm diam., many, white, fragrant. Fr. 8mm diam., pouch-like, leathery, red-brown. Summer. NSW, Tasm.

Bursera Jacq. ex L. TORCHWOOD. Burseraceae. 40 decid. shrubs or trees. Bark peeling, sap aromatic. Lvs pinnate. Fls small, in axill. pan. or clusters; cal. 3–5-lobed; pet. 3–5, free; sta. 8–10. Fr. a 1-seeded drupe. Subtrop. and Trop. Amer. Z10.
B. gummifera L. = *B. simaruba.*
B. microphylla A. Gray. ELEPHANT TREE. Polygamous to 3m, br. cherry red with age. Lfts 13–33, to 0.6cm, linear-oblong. Fls in small clusters, white, 5-merous. Ariz., SE Calif., NW Mex.
B. simaruba (L.) Sarg. Dioecious to 25m, br. lustrous light red to dark red with age. Lfts 7–9, to 10cm, ovate, lanceolate or oblong. Infl. to 10cm; ♂ fls 5-merous, white to green-brown; ♀ fls 3-merous, white. S Flor., W Indies, C Amer.

BURSERACEAE Kunth. 18/540. *Bursera, Garuga.*

Burser's Saxifrage *Saxifraga burseriana.*

Burtonia R. Br. Leguminosae (Papilionoideae). 12 low shrubs. Lvs simple or trifoliolate. Fls pea-like, solitary in upper lf axils or in term. rac. W Aus. 10.
B. conferta DC. Erect shrub to 1m. Lvs to 2cm, simple, linear. Fls in short umbelliform rac.; pet. to 1cm, blue-purple, glab. Spring–summer.
B. hendersonii (Paxt.) Benth. RED BONNETS.   To 1.5m. Lvs trifoliolate; lfts 0.5cm, narrow, occas. hooked. Fls solitary in upper lf axils; pet. to 1cm, orange-red and brown. Spring.
B. pulchella Meissn. = *B. scabra.*
B. scabra (Sm.) R. Br. PAINTED LADY. Heath-like shrub to 3m. Lvs trifoliolate; lfts to 1.5cm, narrow. Fls profuse, solitary; pet. to 1.5cm, mauve. Spring.
B. villosa Meissn.   Upright to spreading shrub, to 2m. Lvs trifoliolate; lfts 1cm, narrow. Fls profuse, solitary; pet. 1.5cm, pink to mauve. Spring–summer.
→*Gompholobium.*

Busbeckea Endl.
B. arborea F. Muell. = *Capparis arborea.*
B. mitchellii Lindl. ex F. Muell. = *Capparis mitchellii.*

Bush Allamanda *Allamanda schottii.*
Bush Basil *Ocimum basilicum.*
Bush Chinkapin *Castanea alnifolia.*
Bush Clock Vine *Thunbergia erecta.*
Bush Clover *Lespedeza.*
Bush Fig *Ficus sur.*
Bush Grape *Vitis acerifolia; V. rupestris.*
Bush Grass *Calamagrostis epigejos.*
Bush Groundsel *Baccharis halimiifolia.*
Bush Hibiscus *Radyera farragei.*

Bush Honeysuckle *Diervilla (D. lonicera; D. sessilifolia).*
Bush Lawyer *Calamus; Rubus cissoides.*
Bush Maidenhair Fern *Adiantum aethiopicum.*
Bushman's-poison *Acokanthera.*
Bush Monkey Flower *Mimulus aurantiacus.*
Bush Palmetto *Sabal minor.*
Bush Pepper *Clethra alnifolia.*
Bush Phlox *Phlox speciosa.*
Bush Poppy *Dendromecon.*
Bush Sour Cherry *Prunus cerasus* var. *frutescens.*
Bush Vetch *Vicia sepium.*
Bush Violet *Browallia.*
Bush Willow *Combretum erythrophyllum.*
Bushy Yate *Eucalyptus lehmannii.*
Busy Lizzie *Impatiens walleriana.*
Butcher's Broom *Ruscus aculeatus.*

Butea Roxb. ex Willd. Leguminosae (Papilionoideae). 4 decid. trees, shrubs or lianes. Lvs large, trifoliolate, sericeous, then glab. Fls pea-like, large, in pan. or axill. clusters or term. rac. Burm., India, Malaysia, Sri Lanka. Z10.
B. frondosa Roxb. ex Willd. = *B. monosperma.*
B. monosperma (Lam.) Taub. FLAME OF THE FOREST; DHAK; PALAS.   Erect tree to 15m. Lfts 10–20cm, leathery, ± glab. above, thickly sericeous beneath. Rac. to 16cm; pet. vividly flame-coloured, silvery-tomentose, standard 2.5cm diam. India, Burm., Sir Lanka.

Butia Becc. YATAY PALM; JELLY PALM. Palmae. 12 palms. St. subterranean or erect and clothed with grey lf bases, becoming scarred. Lvs pinnate, unarmed and petiole hairy near base or with stout spines, diminishing to short teeth; pinnae single-fold, regularly spaced in one plane along rachis, often glaucous, line-ar. Fr. spherical to ovoid, beaked. Braz. to Arg. Z10.
B. capitata (Mart.) Becc. St. to 6m×45cm, often clothed with lf bases. Lvs blue-green; pinnae to 75×2cm, ascending. Fr. to 3.4cm, yellow. Braz., Urug., Arg. var. *nehrlingiana* (G. Abbott ex Nehrl.) L.H. Bail. Fr. smaller, bright red. var. *pulposa* (Barb.-Rodr.) Becc. Fr. yellow, pulpy. var. *odorata* (Barb.-Rodr.) Becc. Lvs glaucous. Fr. 2×2.5cm, compressed-globose. var. *strictior* L.H. Bail. Lvs tinged blue, strongly ascending.
B. eriospatha (Mart. ex Drude) Becc. WOOLLY BUTIA PALM.   To 3m. Pinnae green above, blue-green beneath; petiole matted-hairy beneath. Fr. to 2cm, yellow. Braz.
B. yatay (Mart.) Becc. YATAY PALM; JELLY PALM.   St. to 6m×45cm. Fr. to 3.4cm, dark yellow to orange tinged red. Arg. →*Cocos.*

BUTOMACEAE Rich. See *Butomus.*

Butomus L. FLOWERING RUSH; WATER GLADIOLUS; GRASSY RUSH. Butomaceae. 1 perenn., aquatic, rhizomatous herb to 150cm. Lvs emergent, radical, distichous, linear, to 150×1cm, bronze at first, becoming green. Scape to 1m; umbel many-fld; fls often fragrant; tep. 6 to 1.5cm, rose-pink; sta. 6–9, anth. dark red. Summer. Eurasia. Z5.
B. umbellatus L.

Butter-and-eggs *Linaria vulgaris.*
Butterbur *Petasites (P. hybridus).*
Buttercup *Ranunculus.*
Buttercup Witch-hazel *Corylopsis pauciflora.*
Butter Daisy *Verbesina encelioides.*
Butterfly Bush *Buddleja davidii; Clerodendrum ugandense.*
Butterfly Flower *Schizanthus.*
Butterfly Lily *Hedychium coronarium.*
Butterfly Orchid *Orchis papilionacea; Psychopsis.*
Butterfly Palm *Chrysalidocarpus lutescens.*
Butterfly Pea *Centrosema virginianum; Clitoria ternatea.*
Butterfly Tree *Bauhinia purpurea.*
Butterfly Weed *Asclepias tuberosa.*
Butter Nut *Caryocar nuciferum; Juglans cinerea.*
Butter-print *Abutilon theophrasti.*
Butter Tree *Tylecodon paniculata.*
Butterwort *Pinguicula.*
Buttonbush *Cephalanthus (C. occidentalis).*
Button Everlasting *Helichrysum scorpioides.*
Button Fern *Tectaria cicutaria; T. macrodonta.*
Button Flower *Hibbertia.*
Button Snakeroot *Eryngium yuccifolium; Liatris (L. pycno-stachya; L. spicata).*
Button Willow *Cephalanthus occidentalis.*
Buttonwood *Platanus (P. occidentalis).*

BUXACEAE Dumort. 5/60. *Buxus, Notobuxus, Pachysandra, Sarcococca.*

Buxus L. BOX; BOXWOOD. Buxaceae. 70 everg. shrubs or small trees. Lvs short-petioled or sessile, entire, coriaceous. Fls unisexual, small, yellow, apetalous, in rac., spikes or heads; ♂ sep. 4, sta. 4; ♀ sep. 6, styles 3. Eurasia, Trop. and S Afr., Carib., and C Amer.

B. balearica Lam. BALEARIC BOXWOOD. Shrub or small tree to 10m. Lvs 2–4cm, thick, coriaceous, dark green above, oval-oblong, emarginate; petiole short, downy. Infl. 10mm diam. Spring. Balearics, S Spain, N Afr. Z8.

B. chinensis Link = Simmondsia chinensis.

B. harlandii Hance. Semi-tender shrub to 1m. Lvs 2–4cm, spathulate, occas. narrow-oblong, emarginate, shiny above; petiole short or 0. Infl. densely capitate. S China, Hong Kong. B. harlandii of gardens is a dwarf, compact domed selection of B. microphylla var. sinica with bright green oblanceolate lvs.

B. henryi Mayr. Shrub to 3m. Lvs 4–11cm, lanceolate, oblong-lanceolate or ovate-lanceolate, slightly coriaceous, petiole 1–2mm. Infl. axill., dense. W Hubei, W & E Sichuan, Guizhou. Z6.

B. hyrcana Pojark. Shrub or small tree. Lvs 2.7–3.5cm, oblong-lanceolate to ovate-elliptic, emarginate. Formerly included in B. sempervirens. Z6.

B. japonica Muell.-Arg. = B. microphylla var. japonica (Muell.-Arg.) Rehd. & Wils..

B. microphylla Sieb. & Zucc. Compact, rounded shrub to 1m, occas. prostrate. Lvs 1–1.75cm, thin, obovate or lanceolate, rounded. Infl. axillary. 'Apple Green': dense; lvs bright green. 'Compacta': v. dwarf and dense; lvs to 0.5cm. 'Curly Locks': lvs with second growth of tiny lf clusters at lf axils; sport of 'Compacta'. 'Faulkner': small; st. chestnut; lvs rounded oval, emerald. 'Grace Hendrick Phillips': v. dwarf, cone-shaped; lvs varying in size, curled and cuspidate. 'Green Pillow': dome-forming, similar to 'Compacta'; lvs obovate, dark green. 'John Baldwin': upright, to 1.5m; lvs small, thick, oval, tinted blue. 'Kingsville Dwarf': slow-growing; lvs to tiny, to 5mm. var. *insularis* (Nak.) Hatsusima. Young twigs pubesc. Lvs larger, somewhat leathery. 'Brouwer's Seedling': compact, conical; lvs pointed-elliptic, deep green. 'Green Gem': dwarf, globose; lvs narrow oblanceolate, olive; exceptionally hardy. 'Green Mountain': as 'Green Gem', but taller. 'Green Velvet': mound-forming; lvs dark rich green. 'Pincushion': dwarf, cushion-forming; lvs to 1cm, rounded ovate, dull green. 'Tide Hill': low, wide; lvs lanceolate, shiny. 'Winter Gem': compact; lvs oval, dark green, colour good through winter. var. *japonica* (Muell.-Arg.) Rehd. & Wils. 2–5m. Habit open, spreading. Branchlets thicker, 4-angled. Lvs 1–1.5cm, ovate, ovate-elliptic or obovate-lanceolate, leathery. Japan. var. *koreana* Nak. 20–60cm. Lvs 1–1.8cm, ovate to oblong. 'Sunnyside': lvs green through winter. 'Winter Green': dense, rounded; lvs oval, dark green through winter. var. *sinica* Rehd. & Wils. CHINESE BOXWOOD. Shrub or small tree, 1–6m. Lvs 1.5–3cm, pale yellow-green, coriaceous, upper surface shiny, obovate or oblong, apex acute to narrowly obtuse, frequently retuse, revolute. China, Jap., Taiwan. 'Filigree': procumbent; lvs orbicular, light sea green. 'Green Beauty': compact, upright; lvs dark green. 'Green Jade': dense and wide, mound-forming; lvs obovate, somewhat cupped, light green. 'Morris Dwarf': dwarf, tufted; lvs oblong, to 1cm, leathery, dull green; slow-growing. 'Morris Midget': hummock-forming; lvs oblong, deep sage green. 'National': erect, tall; lvs to 3cm, oval, deep green. 'Rubra': lvs yellow to orange. 'Richard': low, bushy; lvs oblong, thick, edges wavy, bright green. Z6.

B. sempervirens L. COMMON BOX. Shrub, multistemmed to 1m, or arching multistemmed tree to 8m (var. *arborescens*). Lvs 1.5–3×0.5–1.3cm, dark green and glossy above, sometimes concave or convex, pale green beneath, ovate, oval-oblong or elliptic, emarginate or obtuse. S Eur., W Asia and N Afr. Z6. Many cvs – habit from dwarf to spreading, pendulous to tall and erect, dense to loose; lvs obovate to linear-lanceolate, small to large, dark to mid green, blue or variegated white or yellow. 'Myosotidifolia': v. dwarf, dense bush, to 30cm; lvs to 1.2cm, narrow, somewhat tinted yellow. 'Vadar Valley': flattened compact mound; lvs broad ovate, dark green. 'Pendula': tall; br. slender, gracefully weeping. 'Suffruticosa': to 1m, compact; lvs ovate to obovate, to 2cm, shining green. 'Handsworthiensis': bushy, dense, upright; lvs broad v. dark green. 'Glauca': upright; lvs broad, blistered, dark blue-green. 'Marginata' ('Aureomarginata', 'Aureolimbata'): upright; lvs misshapen, olive, irregularly blotched and edged yellow. 'Aureopendula': weeping; lvs ovate, streaked yellow. 'Argenteovariegata' ('Argenteomarginata'; lvs ovate, edged white). Z5.

B. wallichiana Baill. HIMALAYAN BOX. Shrub or small tree to 10m. Lvs 1.5–6cm, narrowly oblong-lanceolate, dark green, glab., obtuse or emarginate; petioles and midrib downy. Infl. rounded. NW Himal., India. Z8.

Byblis Salisb. Byblidaceae. 2 glandular-hairy, carnivorous, ann. or perenn. herbs. Lvs linear with sticky stalked and sessile glands. Fls axill., solitary, slender-stalked; pet. spreading, obovate. W Aus., N Aus., New Guinea. Z10.

B. gigantea Lindl. Perenn. to 60cm. Lvs 10–30cm, filiform to linear, ± terete. Fls to 4cm across, iridescent blue, pink or purple. Summer. W Aus.

B. liniflora Salisb. Ann. to 28cm. Lvs to 10cm+, filiform. Fls to 1cm across, pink or lilac. N Aus., New Guinea.

BYBLIDACEAE Domin. See Byblis.

Byfield Fern Bowenia.

Byrnesia Rose.
B. weinbergii Rose = Graptopetalum paraguayense.

Byzantine Gladiolus Gladiolus communis ssp. byzantinus.

C

Caballera De Palo *Oreopanax capitatus.*
Cabbage *Brassica* (*B. oleracea* Capitata group).
Cabbage Bark *Lonchocarpus.*
Cabbage Fern *Platycerium elephantotis.*
Cabbage Gum *Eucalyptus amplifolia*; *E. clavigera.*
Cabbage Palm *Livistona australis.*
Cabbage Palmetto *Sabal palmetto.*
Cabbage Rose *Rosa* ×*centifolia.*
Cabbage Tree *Andira inermis*; *Anthocleista grandiflora*; *Cordyline* (*C. australis*); *Cussonia*; *Sabal palmetto.*
Cabbage-wood *Schefflera umbellifera.*
Cabecudo *Syagrus coronata.*

Cabomba Aubl. Cabombaceae. 7 aquatic herbs. St. submerged, branching. Submerged lvs divided into many filiform seg., opposite or whorled; floating lvs peltate, bifurcate, ovate to narrow-elliptic. Trop. & subtrop. Amer.
C. aquatica Aubl. Internodes yellow-pubesc. when young. Submerged lvs bright green: floating lvs to 1.5cm wide, broadly elliptic. Guiana to Amaz. Z10.
C. australis Speg. Internodes red-pubesc. when young. Submerged lvs lined red; floating lvs to 1.5cm wide. S Braz. to E Arg. Z10.
C. caroliniana A. Gray. Submerged lvs to 7cm: floating lvs to 2cm, ovate, linear-oblong or oblanceolate, obtuse. C & SE US. Z5.
C. caroliniana var. *pulcherrima* Harper = *C. pulcherrima.*
C. pulcherrima (Harper) Fassett. Internodes red-pubesc. when young. Submerged lvs streaked or flecked red; floating lvs to 3cm wide. N Flor., S S Carol. Z8.

CABOMBACEAE A. Rich. 2/8. *Brasenia, Cabomba.*

Cacalia Kuntze. Compositae. 5 perenn. herbs, branched above. Lvs alt., long-petiolate below, short-petiolate or sessile above. Cap. discoid, small, numerous, clustered in corymbs; receptacle flat, flts red-purple. Eur. and Asia Minor. Z6.
C. alliariae Gouan. To 2m. Lvs 50cm across, triangular-cordate, margin with alternating large and small teeth, glab. above, downy beneath, upper lvs with distinct, mostly toothed lobes, amplexicaul. Eur.
C. angulata Vahl = *Solanecio angulatus.*
C. anteuphorbium L. = *Kleinia anteuphorbium.*
C. appendiculata L. f. = *Pericallis appendiculata.*
C. glabra Mill. To 80cm. St. densely pubesc. above. Lvs to 15cm across, coarse, reniform, not amplexicaul, glab. beneath or with short hairs on nerves, regularly toothed. S Eur.
C. javanica hort. = *Emilia coccinea.*
C. leucophylla Willd. To 2m. Lvs to 10cm across, coarse, triangular-cordate, regularly toothed, grey-haired or subglabrous above, densely white-hairy beneath; petioles of upper lvs sometimes with small, entire auricles. W Alps.
C. lutea Mill. = *Emilia coccinea.*
C. odora Forssk. = *Kleinia odora.*
C. pendula Forssk. = *Kleinia pendula.*
C. sagittata hort. = *Emilia coccinea.*
C. sonchifolia L. = *Emilia sonchifolia.*
→*Adenostyles.*

Cacaliopsis A. Gray. Compositae. 1 woolly perenn. herb to 80cm. Lvs to 20cm, mostly basal, round-cordate, palmate, lobes 7–9, obtusely toothed, sparsely downy; petioles to 20cm. Cap. mostly 5–10, discoid, in loose, racemose, apical clusters; flts many, yellow, 5-lobed, fragrant. W US. Z6.
C. nardosmia (A. Gray) A. Gray. SILVER CROWN.
→*Luina.*

Cacao *Theobroma cacao.*

Caccinia Savi. Boraginaceae. 6 hispid bienn. or perenn. herbs. Lvs glaucous. Rac. or pan. term.; cal. accrescent in fr., subglobose, 5-lobed; cor. salverform, tube narrow, lobes oblong to linear, spreading, scales in throat large; sta. exserted. W & C Asia. Z5.
C. glauca Savi = *C. macrantha* var. *crassifolia.*
C. macranthera var. *crassifolia* (Vent.) Brand. Perenn. to 90cm, simple to branched, erect or ascending, glab. Lvs to 23cm, line-

ar, lanceolate or oblong, thick, glaucous, tuberculate. Infl. a term. pan.; bracts broadly lanceolate; fls violet-blue becoming red; cor. tube to 18mm, lobes to 9mm. SW Asia.
C. strigosa Boiss. Glaucous perenn. to 40cm; st. simple, ascending or decumbent, strigose. Lvs to 17cm, obovate to obovate-oblong, obtuse to rounded. Infl. a terminal pan., ebracteate; fls blue, cor. tube to 12mm, lobes to 3mm. SW Asia to Iran.
→*Borago.*

Caconier *Ormosia monosperma.*

CACTACEAE Juss. 130/1650. *Acanthocereus, Aporocactus, Ariocarpus, Armatocereus, Arrojadoa, Arthrocereus, Astrophytum, Austrocactus, Aztekium, Bergerocactus, Blossfeldia, Brachycereus, Brasilicereus, Browningia, Calymmanthium, Carnegiea, Cephalocereus, Cereus, Cipocereus, Cleistocactus, Coleocephalocereus, Copiapoa, Corryocactus, Coryphantha, Denmoza, Discocactus, Disocactus, Echinocactus, Echinocereus, Echinopsis, Epiphyllum, Epithelantha, Eriosyce, Escobaria, Escontria, Espostoa, Espostoopsis, Eulychnia, Facheiroa, Ferocactus, Frailea, Gymnocalycium, Haageocereus, Harrisia, Hatiora, Heliocereus, Hylocereus, Jasminocereus, Leocereus, Lepismium, Leptocereus, Leuchtenbergia, Lophophora, Maihuenia, Mammillaria, Matucana, Melocactus, Micranthocereus, Mila, Myrtillocactus, Neobuxbaumia, Neolloydia, Neoporteria, Neoraimondia, Neowerdermannia, Nopalxochia, Obregonia, Opuntia, Oreocereus, Oroya, Ortegocactus, Pachycereus, Parodia, Pediocactus, Pelecyphora, Peniocereus, Pereskia, Pereskiopsis, Pilosocereus, Polaskia, Pterocactus, Quiabentia, Rathbunia, Rebutia, Rhipsalis, Samaipaticereus, Schlumbergera, Sclerocactus, Selenicereus, Stenocactus, Stenocereus, Stephanocereus, Stetsonia, Strombocactus, Tacinga, Thelocactus, Uebelmannia, Weberocereus.*

Cactus L.
C. bahiensis Britt. & Rose = *Melocactus bahiensis.*
C. broadwayi Britt. & Rose = *Melocactus broadwayi.*
C. caesius (Wendl.) Britt. & Rose = *Melocactus curvispinus.*
C. intortus Mill. = *Melocactus intortus.*
C. maxonii Rose = *Melocactus curvispinus.*
C. royenii L. = *Pilosocereus royenii.*
C. tetragonus Willd. non L. = *Cereus fernambucensis.*

Cactus Euphorbia *Euphorbia ingens.*
Cactus Geranium *Pelargonium echinatum.*

Cadetia Gaudich. Orchidaceae. 55 epiphytic orchids. Pbs slender, tufted, stem-like. Lvs solitary, term., obovate to oblong-elliptic. Fls small, solitary or clustered at lf base; tep. oblong-obovate; lip trilobed, midlobe decurved, pubesc., lat. lobes erect. Papuasia. Z10.
C. hispida (A. Rich.) Schltr. Lf to 7.5cm. Fls solitary, white, marked purple. Solomon Is., New Guinea.
C. taylori (F. Muell.) Schltr. Lf 1.5–5cm. Fls solitary, white, lip pink and yellow. NE Aus., New Guinea.

Caesalpinia L. Leguminosae (Caesalpinioideae). 70+ shrubs, trees and perenn. herbs. Lvs bipinnate (no. of lft pairs per pinna given below). Fls in term., often branched rac.; cal. tube short, 5-toothed; pet. 5, subequal, clawed, usually spreading; sta. 10, usually far-exserted, fil. declinate. Trop. & subtrop. Z10 unless specified.
C. bicolor C.H. Wright = *C. cassioides.*
C. brasiliensis L. = *C. violacea.*
C. cassioides Willd. Shrub or small tree, sparsely thorny. Pinnae 2–5 pairs; lfts to 2.5cm, 5–7 pairs, broad-ovate or elliptic, emarginate. Cor. 1.5cm. tubular-campanulate, orange, red- and dark-veined; sta. 2cm. Peru.
C. conzattii (Rose) Standl. Small tree. Lfts 4–5 pairs, oblong to ovate. Pet. yellow-red to bright red. Mex.
C. coriaria (Jacq.) Willd. DIVI-DIVI. Small flat-topped thornless tree or shrub to 9m. Pinnae 9–17; lfts to 0.7cm, 15–25 pairs, oblong, glab. Pet. to 6cm, yellow to ochre. Autumn. Antilles, S Mex., N S Amer.
C. decapetala (Roth) Alston MYSORE THORN. Climbing shrub to 3m, thorny. Pinnae 6–10 pairs; lfts to 1.5cm, 7–12 pairs, obovate-elliptic to oblong, rounded. Cor. rotate, pet. pale

yellow, sometimes spotted red, unequal, suborbicular; fil. pink, villous. Trop. Asia. Z8. var. *japonica* (Sieb. & Zucc.) Ohashi. Prickly. Lfts 2.5cm, 4–8 pairs. Pet. bright yellow; fil. scarlet. Jap., China. Z9.

C. echinata Lam. BRAZILWOOD; PEACH WOOD; PERNAMBUCO WOOD. Tree with prickly trunk. Lfts numerous, rhombic-oblong. Fls yellow. Trop. Amer.

C. ferrea Mart. ex Tul. BRAZILIAN IRONWOOD. Unarmed tree to 15m. Bark grey, peeling. Lvs 7–9-pinnate; lfts to 2cm, 5–7 pairs, elliptic to obovate; petiole to 12cm. Fls yellow. Summer. E Braz.

C. gilliesii (Wallich ex Hook.) Benth. POINCIANA; BIRD-OF-PARADISE. Shrub or small tree. Br. slender, erect. Lvs 20cm, 9–11-pinnate; lfts to 0.8cm, many, oblong. Cor. 3.5cm diam., rotate, golden yellow; fil. to 7cm, scarlet-red. Summer. Arg., Urug. Z8.

C. glabra (Mill.) Merrill = *C. platyloba*.

C. japonica Sieb. & Zucc. = *C. decapetala* var. *japonica*.

C. mexicana Gray. Shrub or tree to 10m, thornless. Lvs 5–9-pinnate; lfts to 2.5cm, 3–5 pairs, elliptic or ovate-elliptic. Pet. 1.5cm, golden yellow, obovate to obcordate, clawed, standard orange at base; fil. yellow, slightly exserted. Spring. Mex.

C. pectinata Cav. = *C. spinosa*.

C. platyloba Wats. Small tree, unarmed. Pinnae 1–4 pairs; lfts to 6cm, 4–7 pairs, elliptic, acute, somewhat pubesc. Pet. to 1.4cm yellow, obovate; sta. not exserted. Spring. Mex., C Amer.

C. pulcherrima (L.) Sw. BARBADOS-PRIDE; PARADISE FLOWER; PEACOCK FLOWER; BARBADOS FLOWER FENCE; FLAMBOYANT TREE. Shrub or small tree to 3m, unarmed or slightly prickly. Pinnae 3–10 pairs; lfts to 2.5cm, 6–10 pairs, elliptic to obovate. Pet. to 2cm, spreading, undulate yellow-orange or yellow; sta. red, far-exserted. Spring. Trop. Amer. Z9.

C. punctata Willd. QUEBRAHACHA. To 12m. Lvs to 30cm; lfts to 2cm, in 3–5 pairs, oval or obovate. Fls gold patterned orange. Venez.

C. reticulata Britt. Unarmed shrub. Pinnae 2–4 pairs; lfts to 3cm, 2–6 pairs, obovate-elliptic, rounded, glossy, distinctly veined. Pet. 1.5cm, pale yellow. Spring. W Indies.

C. sappan L. Shrub or tree to 4.5cm, prickly. Pinnae 7–10 pairs; lfts to 2.3cm, 10–20 pairs, rhomboid, puberulent to subglabrous. Pet. to 1.5cm, yellow; fil. tangled-pilose. Summer–autumn. Trop. Asia.

C. sepiaria Roxb. = *C. decapetala*.

C. spinosa (Molina) Kuntze. Scandent shrub or small tree, usually prickly. Pinnae 2–5 pairs; lfts to 4.5cm, 5–7 pairs, elliptic, glab., finely punctate, ± viscid. Pet. to 0.7cm, yellow-red, suborbicular. S Amer.

C. tinctoria (HBK) Benth. ex Reiche = *C. spinosa*.

C. vesicaria L. Shrub or tree, armed or unarmed. Pinnae 2–3 pairs; lfts to 3.5cm, 1–3 pairs, obovate, truncate or emarginate, glossy. Pet. 1cm, yellow, subequal; fil. villous. Autumn–winter. C Amer., Antilles.

C. violacea (Mill.) Standl. Unarmed tree. Pinnae 2–4 pairs; lfts to 6cm, 6–9 pairs, ovate to elliptic-oblong, acute, coriaceous, glossy. Pet. yellow, unequal, spotted, standard to 0.8cm, short and stiff. Spring. C & S Amer., Afr., India.

→*Brasilettia, Cassia, Guilandina, Libidibia, Nicarago, Poinciana, Poincinella* and *Tara*.

Caffre Lime *Citrus hystrix*.
Cafta *Catha edulis*.
Caimito *Chrysophyllum cainito*.

Caiophora Presl. Loasaceae. 65 ann. or short-lived perenn. herbs with bristly, stinging hairs. St. usually twining. Lvs pinnately lobed. Fl. solitary, axillary; pet. deeply concave above; sta. clustered opposite pet. Capsule twisted, valves spiralling. S Amer. Z9.

C. lateritia Benth. Bienn. or short-lived perenn. St. to 3m, slender, twining. Lvs 8–18cm, cordate to ovate-lanceolate, pinnately lobed or toothed, with soft hairs and stinging bristles, dull pale green. Fls nodding, on slender stalks; pet. to 3cm, peach to brick-red. Arg.

→*Blumenbachia* and *Loasa*.

Cajanus DC. Leguminosae (Papilionoideae). 2 erect, densely branched shrubby perennials; young st. grey-white pubesc. Lvs trifoliolate, downy. Pan. term., racemose; fls large, pea-like. Fr. narrowly oblong, hirsute, ± torulose. OW Trop. (Asia, Afr.), nat. in other warm regions. Z10.

C. cajan (L.) Huth. CATJANG PEA; RED GRAM; DAHL; DHAL; PIGEON PEA. To 3m. St. ribbed, sericeous. Lfts 2.5–10cm, green and downy above, grey-white pubesc. beneath, dotted with yellow glands; petiole 1–5.5cm. Infl. downy to 7cm; cal. red downy; standard 1.2–1.7cm, yellow lined mahogany or crimson. Fr. 4.5–10cm yellow, streaked purple-black; seeds 3–7, cream,

fawn, brown or ruddy, compressed-globose. Trop. regions (probably native of Afr.).

C. indicus Spreng. = *C. cajan*.

Cajeput Tree *Melaleuca viridiflora* var. *rubriflora*.

Cakile Mill. Cruciferae. 7 ann. or bienn., succulent herbs. St. branching, often spreading. Lvs simple or pinnatisect. Fls 4-merous, racemose. Medit., Arabia, Aus., N Amer. Z6.

C. maritima Scop. SEA ROCKET. Ann., 15–60cm, diffusely branched. Lower lvs fleshy, grey-green, pinnatisect, upper lvs ± entire. Fls 1cm diam. fragrant, violet or rose, rarely white. Range as for the genus.

Calabash *Crescentia cujete*.
Calabash Gourd *Lagenaria siceraria*.
Calabash Nutmeg *Monodora myristica*.
Calabash Tree *Amphitecna latifolia*.
Calabazilla *Cucurbita foetidissima*.
Calabrian Pine *Pinus brutia*.
Calabura *Muntingia calabura*.

Caladenia R. Br. Orchidaceae. 70 terrestrial, tuberous orchids. Lf solitary, oblong or linear-lanceolate, basal. Fls in a lax pan. or rac.; dors. sep. erect, narrow, incurved, forming a hood, lat. sep. similar, spreading or reflexed; pet. erect, narrow; lip basally erect, entire or trilobed, midlobe with sessile or stalked calli, fringed or dentate. Australasia. Z9.

C. alba R. Br. WHITE CALADENIA. To 30cm. Fls 1–2, to 5cm diam., pink or white, midlobe orange- or yellow-tipped; tep. 12–20mm; lip white, trilobed with white or yellow calli in 2 rows, midlobe fringed, undulate; lat. lobes tinted purple or crimson. Mid spring–mid autumn. E Aus.

C. cairnsiana F. Muell. ZEBRA ORCHID. To 30cm. Fls 1–2 pale yellow marked purple or red; tep. linear-lanceolate, glandular-tipped, reflexed; lip erect, clawed, broadly ovate, calli in 2 rows, deep red or purple, with dark apical calli. Summer–mid autumn. SW W Aus.

C. carnea R. Br. 8–20cm. Fls 1–3; tep. green, glandular-pubesc., pink above, lanceolate, 10–16mm; lip to 8mm, with red horizontal broken lines, calli in 2–4 rows, midlobe lanceolate, fringed or dentate. Summer–mid winter. SE Aus., NZ, New Caledonia.

C. carnea var. *alba* (R. Br.) Benth. = *C. alba*.

C. deformis R. Br. To 17cm. Fl solitary, deep blue, rarely yellow, white or pink; tep. with scattered purple glands, dors. sep. 12–25mm, elliptic-lanceolate, lat. sep. lanceolate, pet. oblong-lanceolate, spreading; lip to 15mm, trilobed, calli linear or club-shaped, 4–6 rows, midlobe triangular, fringed. Summer–mid autumn. SE Aus.

C. dilatata R. Br. GREAT COMB; SPIDER ORCHID. St. 15–45cm. Fls solitary, to 10cm; dors. sep. erect, narrowing to a filamentous or clavate tip, lat. sep. deflexed, spreading; pet. lanceolate, tapering, 3–4cm; lip recurved, trilobed, green, maroon and pale yellow, midlobe lanceolate, recurved, toothed, tip maroon. Summer–winter. SE & SW Aus.

C. discoidea Lindl. DANCING ORCHID. St. to 30cm. Fls 1–3, yellow-green lined red; sep. to 1cm, dors. sep. narrow, concave, lat. sep. lanceolate, pet. narrower and longer, lip broadly ovate, veined dark red, fringed. Summer–mid autumn. SW W Aus.

C. flava R. Br. COWSLIP ORCHID. To 30cm. Fls 2–4, to 4.5cm, yellow; tep. ovate-lanceolate dors. sep. with a scarlet central line or blotches, pet. smaller; lip to 1cm, calli in 2 rows, converging, forming a semicircle, midlobe lanceolate. Mid summer–mid autumn. SW W Aus.

C. gemmata Lindl. Fls 1–2, 4–7cm diam., deep blue or white; tep. erect, dors. sep. with tip recurved, elliptic-oblong; lip ovate, erect and recurved, calli small, club-shaped, in rows covering most of lamina. Mid summer–mid autumn. SW W Aus.

C. hirta Lindl. SUGAR CANDY ORCHID. To 30cm. Fls 1–3, white and pink or pure pink; tep. acuminate; lip half sep. length, oblong or oblong-lanceolate, basally constricted and erect, fringed. Mid summer–mid autumn. SW W Aus.

C. latifolia R. Br. To 30cm. Fls 1–4, white to pink; tep. glandular-pubesc, spreading, dors. sep. erect, acute, shorter than laterals, lat. sep. oblong-lanceolate, obtuse; pet. lanceolate; lip, midlobe blotched pink, lat. lobes oblong, lined pink, calli in 2 semicircular rows. Autumn–mid winter. SE & SW Aus.

C. lobata Fitzg. To 45cm. Fls 1–2, yellow-green or yellow, marked red; dors. sep. clavate, incurved, 6–8cm, lat. sep. basally dilated, sharply upcurved; pet. basally dilated, tapering to fili-form; lip to 3cm, central lobe lanceolate, reflexed, minutely dentate, basally inflated, deep maroon; lateral lobes green, fringed with dark calli. Autumn. SW W Aus.

C. magniclavata Nicholls. To 35cm. Fls 1–2, 7–8cm diam.; tep. yellow to yellow-green, striped purple or crimson, lanceolate, basally dilated, tapering to clavate tip, yellow with dark glands, dors. sep. erect, incurved, 4.5–5cm, lat. sep. spreading, pet. shorter and narrower; lip ovate, yellow, blotched maroon, tipped dark purple, margins fringed. Late summer–early autumn. SW W Aus.

C. menziesii R. Br. To 25cm. Fls 1–3, white and pink, rarely wholly white; dors. sep. spathulate-lanceolate, glandular-pubesc., lat. sep. 11–15mm, crescent-shaped, spreading; pet. clavate, apically gland., maroon; lip, orbicular-ovate, to 10mm, white, marked pink, entire. Summer–autumn. SE Aus.

C. patersonii R. Br. To 40cm. Fls 1–4, white or cream, tipped dark purple, rarely crimson, yellow-green, yellow or brown; dors. sep. erect or incurved, basally dilated, tapering to filiform, lat. sep. and pet. spreading, narrower; lip 1.5–3cm, ovate-lanceolate, erect, tipped purple or scarlet, toothed or serrate. Summer–autumn. SE & SW Aus.

C. sericea Lindl. To 35cm. Fls blue or mauve; tep. oblong-lanceolate, dors. sep. erect, concave; lip to 2cm, trilobed, calli linear, often fused at base, forming plates, midlobe recurved, fringed with calli. Mid summer–mid autumn. SW W Aus.

Caladium Vent. ANGEL WINGS; ELEPHANT'S-EAR. Araceae. 7 tuberous perenn. herbs. Lvs usually peltate-sagittate, base hastate to truncate or rounded, petiole long. Peduncle short; spathe tubular below, limb partly expanded, constricted above tube, green to green-white. Trop. S Amer. Z10.

C. argyrites Lem. = *C. humboldtii*.
C. bicolor (Ait.) Vent. Lvs 18–45×12–25cm, peltate, ovate to elliptic, base cordate to sagittate, lobes often obtuse, green with white, pink or red markings; petiole to 60cm variegated. N S Amer. A variable plant; the two main groups were formerly treated as distinct spp: *C. picturatum*, with narrower lvs and acute basal lobes, and *C. marmoratum*, with lvs blotched grey, green and ivory on green. Plants with pure white lvs veined green are sometimes named *C. ×candidum*. Hybrids and selections of these types were grouped under the name *C. ×hortulanum*. These fall into 'fancy leaf' and 'strap leaf' categories. 'Fancy leaf' cvs include whites such as: 'June Bride': lvs flat, white with green edge; 'Mrs Arno Nehrling': lvs large, white with delicate dark green venation and edge, main ribs shaded red; 'White Queen': lvs white with crimson primary veins, green edge and fine tracings; and pinks such as 'Carolyn Whorton': lvs bright pink with deep green-black marbling towards edge and red ribs; 'Fannie Munson': lvs pale pink with fine green edge and some venation, main ribs deep pink; 'Pink Beauty': lvs green with pink marbling in centre and along the red ribs; 'Rosabud': lvs pink, centre shading to white then green, ribs pink; and reds such as 'Freida Hemple': bushy; lvs bright red, ribs scarlet with wide dark green margin; 'Poecile Anglais': lvs dark, dull green with burgundy ribs and central shading. 'Postman Joyner': bushy; lvs pale red, veins darker, margin green; 'Red Flash': lvs dull green with vibrant red centre and ribs, blotched white. 'Strap leaf' cvs include 'Candidum Junior': lvs white delicately traced with dark green veins and edge; 'Gingerland': lvs grey with white ribs, dark green edge and maroon spots; 'White Wing': lvs white with deep green edge; 'Clarice': lvs pink shaded with darker rib, wide dark green edge and venation, blotched white; 'Miss Muffet': dwarf, lvs sage green with white ribs, soft red heart, dark red spotting; 'Red Frill': lvs deep red shading darker towards the deep green margin. Cvs with almost entirely white lvs include 'Speciosum' with lvs quilted, midrib painted white, lat. veins spreading white, and 'Venosum' with small deep green lvs with midribs, lat. veins and inner edge ivory.
C. ×hortulanum Birdsey = *C. bicolor*.
C. humboldtii Schott. Diminutive, lvs 5–10×2–4.5cm, peltate, ovate to oblong, short-acuminate, base sagittate, dull green, blotched and spotted white; petiole to 24cm. Braz. & Venez.
C. lilliputiense Rodigas = *C. humboldtii*.
C. lindenii (André) Madison. Lvs 16–45×10–20cm, not peltate, hastate, main lobe oblong, acute, lat. lobes unequal, obtuse, dark green with main veins marked white, midrib hairy; petioles to 40cm, green, striped purple. Colomb. 'Albescens': lvs heavily marked white at centre and on margin. 'Magnificum': lvs marked cream to white along veins and in a line inside margins.
C. marmoratum Mathieu = *C. bicolor*.
C. picturatum K. Koch = *C. bicolor*.
C. poecile Schott = *C. bicolor*.
C. schomburgkii Schott. Lvs to 20×15cm, not peltate, triangular, ovate, broad lanceolate to rhombic, base emarginate to truncate or rounded, variegated pink or white, undulate, veins silver to red; petiole to 25cm. Guiana, Braz. 'Changju': petioles white; lvs small, ovate, hanging, light shading to dark green, ribs white.

C. 'Venosum' = *C. bicolor*.
C. venosum N.E. Br. = *C. schomburgkii*.
→*Xanthosoma*.

Calamagrostis Adans. REED GRASS. Gramineae. *c*250 reed-like perenn. grasses. Lvs long, linear, flat or channelled. Infl. paniculate, compressed, dense; spikelets narrow lanceolate, 1-fld. Summer. Temp. N hemis. Z7.
C. ×acutiflora (Schräd.) DC. (*C. arundinacea* ×*C. epigejos*.) FEATHER REED GRASS. Tight, tufted, stiffy erect to 2m. Foliage arching, slightly glossy. Infl. loose, branched, soft and silvery bronze to purple-brown. 'Karl Foerster' ('Stricta'): to 2m; infl. held upright, red-bronze, later buff. 'Oredam': to 1m; lvs arching, striped white.
C. arundinacea (L.) Roth. To 125cm. Lvs to 7mm diam., finely pubesc. above. Infl. contracted, to 25cm, many-fld; br. v. scabrous. Summer. Scand., Eur. to Asia Minor.
C. brachytricha Steud. To 1m. Lvs to 1cm diam. Pan. contracted, to 18cm, many-fld; br. v. scabrous spikelets ± purple. Summer–autumn. C to E Asia.
C. canescens (Weber) Roth. To 1.2m. Lvs 0.6cm diam., scabrous. Infl. lanceolate to oblong, tinged purple, green or yellow. W, N, C Eur. 'Variegata': lvs variegated white.
C. epigejos (L.) Roth. WOOD SMALL-REED; BUSH GRASS. To 1.9m. Lvs to 1cm diam. scabrous. Infl. erect, lanceolate to oblong, to 30×6cm, purple, brown or green. Eurasia.
C. 'Hortorum' = *C. ×acutiflora*.
C. lanceolata Roth = *C. canescens*.
C. 'Stricta' = *C. ×acutiflora* 'Karl Foerster'.
C. sylvatica Maxim. = *C. brachytricha*.
C. varia Turcz. = *C. brachytricha*.

Calamint *Calamintha*.

Calamintha Mill. CALAMINT. Labiatae. 7 aromatic perenn. herbs, sometimes woody-based. Lvs ovate or oblong. Cymes axill.; cal. tubular with 13 nerves, 2-lipped; cor. 2-lipped, upper lip entire, sometimes arched, lower lip 3-lobed, tube straight. W Eur. to C Asia, N Amer.
C. acinos (L.) Scheele = *Acinos arvensis*.
C. alpina (L.) Lam. = *Acinos alpinus*.
C. ascendens Jordan = *C. sylvatica*.
C. chinensis Benth. = *Clinopodium chinense*.
C. clinopodium Benth. = *Clinopodium vulgare*.
C. coccinea (Nutt.) Benth. Small. St. tetragonal. Lvs to 3cm, linear to ovate, glab. or minutely pubesc. Fls solitary; cor. to 5cm, red. Summer–autumn. SE US. Z8.
C. cretica (L.) Lam. Densely grey-pubesc., woody-based, prostrate, 10–30cm. Lvs 0.6–1.5cm, broadly ovate, obtuse, tomentose or villous-tomentose, entire to crenate-serrate. Cymes 1–3(6)-fld; cor. to 10mm, white. Crete.
C. georgiana (Harper) Shinn. = *Clinopodium georgianum*.
C. glabella (Michx.) Benth. = *Clinopodium glabellum*.
C. grandiflora (L.) Moench. LARGE-FLOWERED CALAMINT. Rhiz. thin. much-branched, creeping. St. herbaceous, sparsely pubesc., to 60cm. Lvs to 8cm, ovate, toothed, deep green and pilose above, pale green beneath. Cymes to 5-fld; cor. to 4cm, pink. Summer. S & SE Eur., Anatolia, N Iran. 'Variegata' ('Forncett Form'): habit bushy, to 30cm high; lvs strongly flecked off-white; fls pink. Z5.
C. mimuloides Benth. St. slender, glandular-pubesc., to 150cm. Lvs to 6cm, ovate, coarsely toothed. Fls solitary; cor. to 4cm, orange to red. Summer–autumn. Calif. Z8.
C. nepeta (L.) Savi. LESSER CALAMINT. Strongly aromatic, pubesc., to 80cm. Lvs 2–3.5cm, oblong, subentire or with shallow teeth. Cymes whorled, to 15-fld.; cor. to 1.2cm, mauve. Summer. S Eur. to GB. ssp. *glandulosa* (Req.) P.W. Ball. Lvs smaller; fls fewer. Z6.
C. officinalis Moench = *C. nepeta* ssp. *glandulosa*.
C. repens Benth. = *Clinopodium umbrosum*.
C. sylvatica Bromf. COMMON CALAMINT. Pubesc., mint-scented. St. erect to 60cm. Lvs 4cm, oval, apex blunt, base truncate, slightly toothed, dark green, petiolate. Cymes whorled; cal. often purple; cor. to 1.5cm, pink spotted purple. Summer–early autumn. C & S Eur.
C. thessala Hausskn. = *C. nepeta* ssp. *nepeta*.
C. umbrosum Fisch. & Mey. = *Clinopodium umbrosum*.
→*Clinopodium*, *Melissa* and *Satureja*.

Calamondin, Calamondin Orange ×*Citrofortunella microcarpa*.

Calamus L. RATTAN PALM; WAIT-A-WHILE PALM. Palmae. 370 palms, many with slender, spiny, climbing st. Lvs pinnate, sometimes with a sharply toothed and whiplike apical cirrus. Trop. Afr., Asia, Malay Archipel., New Guinea, NE Aus. to Fiji. Z10.

C. australis Mart. LAWYER CANE. Tall and scrambling. St. many, *c*1.5cm diam. Lf sheaths with long, rust-coloured, needle-like spines, blades to 1m; petioles sparsely armed, cirrus whip-like, with hooked spines. Aus., NE Queensld.

C. caryotoides Cunn. ex Mart. FISHTAIL LAWYER CANE. St. slender, clustered. Lf sheaths with short spines; lvs to 30cm; pinnae 8–10, cuneate, apices truncate, armed with spines, term. pinnae usually fused into fishtail shape. Aus., NE Queensld.

C. ciliaris Bl. Climbing by st. armed with reflexed spines. Lvs to 9m; petiole 10–15cm, sparsely spined, lacking cirrus; pinnae 40–50 each side of rachis, hairy. India.

C. muelleri H.A. Wendl. & Drude. WAIT-A-WHILE. Scrambling. St. many, 0.8–1.2cm diam. Lf sheaths with short, weak, grey spines; lvs to 60cm; pinnae 11–14, lanceolate, margins spiny, apical cirrus slender with small, hooks. E Aus., NE NSW, SE Queensld.

C. rotang L. RATTAN CANE. Lvs to 80cm, lacking cirri; pinnae alt. or subopposite, acuminate, glossy above, papery, to 30cm, ciliate. Sri Lanka, S India.

C. roxburghii Griff. = *C. rotang*.

C. zalacca Gaertn. = *Salacca zalacca*.

Calamus *Acorus calamus*.

Calandrinia HBK. Portulacaceae. *c*150 ann. or perenn., low, spreading or trailing herbs. Lvs fleshy, entire. Fls ephemeral, in rac. or pan.; sep. persistent, 2; pet. 5–7, spreading. Widespread throughout trop. and subtrop. and warm temp. areas.

C. buridgii hort. ex Reg. Lvs linear-lanceolate, glab. Fls copperrose or brick-red, small, many, in leafy clusters. S Amer.

C. caulescens HBK = *C. ciliata*.

C. ciliata (Ruiz & Pav.) DC. REDMAIDS. Ann. to 30cm. Lvs to 4.5cm, linear-spathulate. Fls to 1.5cm diam., solitary, purple, or white fading to purple. Peru, Ecuad. var. *menziesii* (Hook.) Macbr. St. to 60cm, diffuse or erect. Lvs to 10cm, oblanceolate to linear. Fls crimson or rose-red, rarely white, 1.2–1.8cm diam., in leafy rac. SW US: Ariz. to Calif.

C. discolor Lindl. Ann. or perenn. 30–45cm. Lvs obovate to spathulate, purple beneath. Fls bright light purple, 4–5cm diam., in long, nodding rac.; sta. yellow. Chile.

C. elegans hort. ex Vilm. = *C. discolor*.

C. grandiflora Lindl. Perenn. to 1m, grown as an ann. St. tinged red. Lvs to 20cm, elliptic, acute, petioles wide. Fls light purple to magenta, 2.5–5cm diam., in rac. Chile.

C. lindleyana hort. ex Vilm. = *C. discolor*.

C. menziesii (Hook.) Torr. & A. Gray = *C. ciliata* var. *menziesii*.

C. polyandra (Hook.) Benth. Small ann. or perenn. herb. Lvs 2.5cm, oblong, sometimes terete. Fls *c*2cm diam., in ascending rac., purple or white.

C. speciosa Lindl. = *C. ciliata* var. *menziesii*.

C. spectabilis Otto & Dietr. To 60cm. Lvs spathulate. Fls 5cm + wide, bright purple. Chile.

C. umbellata (Ruiz & Pav.) DC. ROCK PURSLANE. Perenn. or ann. to 10–15cm, forming compact tufted masses. Lvs 1.5–2cm, grey-green, linear, hairy. Fls upturned and cup-shaped, corymbose, bright crimson-magenta, to 2cm diam. Peru, Chile. 'Amaranth': fls crimson-purple.

Calanthe R. Br. Orchidaceae. 120 terrestrial, rarely epiphytic orchids. Pbs small, corm-like to large, exposed and angularoblong-ellipsoid. Lvs plicately ribbed, petiolate, decid. or everg. Rac. lat.; sep. obovate-elliptic spreading, pet. similar; lip fused to column foot, broadly trilobed, spur slender. Trop. and temp. Asia, Polyn., Madag.

C. alismifolia Lindl. Pbs cylindric, narrow, to 5cm. Lvs elliptic to elliptic-ovate, acuminate, to 15cm; petioles slender, to 15cm. Infl. to 5cm, minutely pubesc; fls to 2cm diam. white, tipped green. India. Z9.

C. alpina Hook. f. Pbs ovoid, subcylindric, 2–2.5cm. Lvs to 17cm, sessile, oblong-elliptic, acuminate. Infl. exceeding lvs, few-fld; fls to 2cm diam., white, tipped green, lip dull red, base and spur pale yellow. India. Z9.

C. ceciliae Rchb. f. Lvs elliptic-oblong, erect, 33–43cm; petiole 11–13cm. Infl. to 45cm; fls to 3cm diam. violet becoming suffused orange, lip white, becoming yellow, spur deep violet. Malaysia. Z10.

C. curculigoides Wallich = *C. pulchra*.

C. discolor Lindl. Pbs small, sheathed and concealed by lf bases. Lvs 10–25cm, elliptic-lanceolate to obovate-oblong. Infl. erect, lax, 40–50cm, minutely pubesc.; fls 4–5cm diam., maroon, bronze, purple or white, lip pale pink. Jap., Ryuku Is. Z8.

C. Dominyi. Everg. plants; short spikes of muddy lilac fls.

C. herbacea Lindl. Pbs to 3cm, subfusiform, sheathed. Lvs 15–25cm, elliptic to elliptic-lanceolate, acuminate; petiole to 15cm. Infl. stout, to 60cm; fls fragrant, brown-green, lip yellow. Sikkim. Z9.

C. masuca (D. Don) Lindl. Pbs elongate, conic. Lvs oblonglanceolate to lanceolate, acuminate, to 50cm. Infl. 10–15cm, dense; fls to 5cm diam., pale lilac-rose, lip violet. India. Z9.

C. natalensis Rchb. f. = *C. sylvatica*.

C. pulchra Lindl. Pbs v. small, apparently 0. Lvs linear to lanceolate, broad, to 70cm. Infl. to 70cm, dense; fls deep orange-yellow, lip orange-red. India. Z9.

C. regnieri Rchb. f. = *C. vestita*.

C. rosea (Lindl.) Benth. Decid. pbs elliptic to fusiform. Lvs oblong-lanceolate. Infl. erect, precocious; fls pale rose, lip paler, becoming white. Burm. Z10.

C. rubens Ridl. Decid. pbs conic or ovoid, furrowed and angled, 5–15cm, silvery. Lvs elliptic, acuminate, to 40cm; petiole short. Infl. to 50cm, emerging before lvs; fls pink, rarely white, lip central stripe crimson, exterior pubesc. Thail., N Malaysia. Z10.

C. sieboldii Decne. ex Reg. = *C. striata*.

C. striata (Banks) R. Br. Pb. 2.5–15cm, narrow. Lvs ellipticlanceolate, 15–25cm; petiole to 20cm. Infl. to 45cm; fls 3.8–6.5cm diam., yellow to bronze, often streaked brown-red. Jap. Z8.

C. sylvatica (Thouars) Lindl. Pbs sheathed by lf bases, small. Lvs elliptic-lanceolate, acuminate, narrowed to petiole, 20–30cm. Infl. to +70cm, erect; fls 2.5–5cm diam., white to lilac, lip white to dark red-purple, callus yellow-orange or white. Masc. Is. Z10.

C. tricarinata Lindl. Pbs short, ovoid. Lvs elliptic or lanceolateelliptic, acute, 17–30cm. Infl. 30–50cm, lax; fls yellow-green, lip brown-red. India, Jap. Z8.

C. triplicata (Willem.) Ames. To 1m. Pbs ovoid. Lvs ovatelanceolate to elliptic-lanceolate, puberulent beneath, 45–60cm; petiole long. Infl. congested above, minutely pubesc.; fls white, sep. tipped pale green, callus orange or yellow. SE Asia to Aus., Fiji. Z10.

C. Veitchii. Decid. plants; tall spikes of pale pink fls in winter.

C. versicolor Lindl. = *C. masuca*.

C. vestita Wallich ex Lindl. Decid., pbs oblong-conical, obscurely angled, 8–12.5cm, with silvery, onion-skin-like sheath vestiges. Lvs lanceolate, broad, 45–60cm, narrowing to petiole. Infl. precocious, suberect then arching, pubesc.; fls 4–5cm diam.; tep. white to pale rose, lip white to rose or magenta, callus golden yellow to crimson or violet, spur ivory to green. Burm., Indochina to Celebes. Z10.

C. volkensii Rolfe = *C. sylvatica*.

Calathea Mey. Marantaceae. *c*300 perenn., rhizomatous or tuberous herbs. Lvs basal or on erect st., ovate to elliptic; petioles usually sheathing at base, pulvinate at apex. Spikes or rac. dense on leafy or naked shoots; bracts spirally arranged or distichous, often coloured; fls in pairs; cor. tube elongated with 1 petaloid staminode. Mex. to Arg. Z9.

C. aemula Körn. Lvs 25cm, oblong, lanceolate, acute to abruptly acuminate, green with pale midzone above, sometimes pubesc. beneath; petiole pubesc. above; sheath villous. Infl. bracts yellow; fls white. Braz.

C. alberti (Pynaert & Van Geert) L.H. Bail. Lvs to 20cm, ovate, obtuse, undulate, grey-green, striped olive-green between veins above, purple beneath. Infl. bracts hairy; fls white. Braz.

C. albicans Schum. = *C. micans*.

C. allouia (Aubl.) Lindl. Roots tuberous. Lvs to 50cm, lanceolate to oblong, light green above, silver-green beneath; petiole to 70cm, striped. Infl. bracts white; fls white. W Indies.

C. applicata Makoy ex E. Morr. Rhiz. tuberous. Lvs to 9cm, ovate-elliptic, white with dark green spots above, rose beneath; petiole to 3cm. Infl. bracts brown, scarious; fls white. Braz.

C. argyraea Körn. Lvs to 12cm, oblong-lanceolate, glab., dark green with silver-grey bands above, purple beneath; petiole to 0.5cm; sheath glab. Origin unknown.

C. bachemiana Morr. Lvs to 22cm, lanceolate, grey-green above with dark green spots along veins, purple beneath, margins tinged purple; petioles to 25cm. Braz.

C. baraquinii (Lem.) Versch. Lvs to 14cm, oblong, acuminate, bright green with bands of silver above, pale and downy beneath; petiole short, downy. Infl. bracts edged purple; fls white. Braz.

C. bella (Bull) Morr. Lvs to 25cm, ±velvety, elliptic-ovate, greygreen with dark green spots along veins above, pale purple beneath, petioles to 15cm. Braz.

C. burle-marxii H. Kenn. Lvs to 72cm, ovate to obtuse, acuminate, bright green with yellow-green midrib, pubesc. toward apex above, grey-green with yellow-green midrib beneath; petiole green, 2–24cm, pubesc.; sheath tinged purple. Infl. bracts waxy; fls yellow. Braz. 'Ice Blue': Infl. bracts blue; fls purple. 'Snow Cone': Infl. bracts white; fls white or purple.

C. chimboracensis Lind. Lvs 18cm, ovate-oblong, green with a dark green, white-edged line either side of midrib above, green beneath; petiole short. Fls yellow. Ecuad.

C. colorata (Hook.) Benth. Lvs to 40cm, lanceolate, acuminate, green, glossy above; petiole about 25cm. Braz.

C. conferta Benth. = *Ataenidia conferta*.

C. crocata E. Morr. & Joriss. Lvs oblong or ovate-elliptic, dark green with grey feathered pattern above, purple beneath; sheath purple, winged. Infl. bracts orange, lanceolate; sep. red, to 8mm; cor. orange. Braz.

C. crotalifera S. Wats. Lvs 40cm, oblong-elliptic to ovate. Infl. compact, bracts many, bronzy; fls yellow. Mex., Ecuad., Panama.

C. cylindrica (Roscoe) Schum. Lvs 80cm, elliptic or oblong, acuminate, pale green; petiole long. Infl. bracts pale green; fls white or yellow. S Braz.

C. discolor Mey. = *C. lutea*.

C. disticha Buc'hoz = *C. lutea*.

C. ecuadoriana H. Kenn. RED ZEBRINA; TIGRINA. Lvs elliptic, dark green, midrib and minor veins yellow to pale green above, dark red beneath; petiole to 24cm, red to purple. Infl. bracts green; fls pale yellow to orange. Autumn. Ecuad.

C. elliptica (Roscoe) Schum. Lvs oblong to ovate-oblong, to 40cm, light green, striped white between veins above, tinted yellow-green beneath; petiole downy, to 10cm. Infl. bracts bright green; fls bright yellow. Colomb., Braz. 'Vittata': lvs pale green striped white above, lime green beneath; fls yellow.

C. eximia (Mathieu) Körn. About 35cm. Roots tuberous. Lvs 15–30cm, oblong, olive-green above with silver lat. bands, midrib yellow-green, deep red, pubesc. beneath; petiole to 8cm. Infl. bracts red-villous; fls villous. C Amer.

C. fasciata (Lind.) Körn. Tufted. Lvs to 30cm, suborbicular, dark olive with silvery white transverse bars, dull grey-green, sometimes tinged purple beneath. Infl. bracts brown; fls transparent, white. Braz. 'Borrusica': dark-leaved form.

C. flavescens Lind. Lvs 25cm, oblong or oblong-lanceolate, light green above, pale green beneath; petiole to 25cm. Fls yellow. Braz.

C. gandersii Kenn. Stemless, to 45cm. Lvs to 18cm, narrowly elliptic, occas. ovate, undulate, mid green above with dark green subrectangular markings along veins, dark purple beneath; petiole pilose, 0.5–2cm; sheaths purple. Infl. bracts green; fls white. Ecuad.

C. glabra hort. = *Ctenanthe glabra*.

C. glazioui Petersen non Benth. = *C. alberti*.

C. grandiflora (Roscoe) Schum. = *C. flavescens*.

C. grandifolia Lindl. = *C. cylindrica*.

C. insignis Petersen. = *C. crotalifera*.

C. insignis hort. ex Bull non Petersen = *C. lancifolia*.

C. kegeliana hort. = *C. bella*.

C. lancifolia Boom RATTLESNAKE PLANT Lvs to 30cm, erect, oblong-linear to narrowly lanceolate, undulate, pale yellow-green, dark at midrib and margin with alternating large and small, dark green, elliptic blotches along lat. veins above, maroon beneath. Braz.

C. legrelliana (Lind.) Reg. Lvs to 15cm, oblong, dark green with olive-green zone between midrib and margin above, violet beneath; petiole downy, to 9cm. Infl. bracts subvillous, grey-red. Colomb., Ecuad.

C. leonia Sonder. Differs from *C. ecuadoriana* in lvs dark green with gold zones near margins above, purple beneath; fls white tipped purple. Origin unknown.

C. leopardina (Bull) Reg. Lvs to 20cm, ovate-lanceolate, acuminate, pale green with dark spots along midrib above; petiole to 20cm. Infl. bracts transparent, lined green; fls yellow. Braz.

C. leucophaea Poepp. & Endl. = *Ischnosiphon leucophaeus*.

C. leucostachys Hook. Lvs to 20cm, oblong or elliptic, green with downy midrib above, purple beneath; petiole downy, to 1cm. Infl. bracts white with yellow hairs; fls white. Costa Rica.

C. libbyana Kenn. Lvs to 40cm, ovate to ovate-elliptic, glaucous green above, red-purple beneath, markings between raised veins cream to yellow above; petiole 3.5–70cm, olive; sheath dark red-purple. Infl. bracts olive green; fls white and purple. Ecuad.

C. lietzei E. Morr. Clump-forming, to 60cm. Lvs to 20cm, ovate-lanceolate, obtuse, undulate, velvety green with olive stripes above, red-purple beneath. Infl. bracts distichous, green; fls white. Braz. 'Greenstar': lvs deep green, grey-green midrib and feathering.

C. lindeniana Wallis. Lvs to 40cm, elliptic, dark green with olive zone along midrib and margins above, green and purple beneath; petiole to 40cm. Fls pale yellow, tipped black. NW Braz., Peru.

C. lindenii Wallis & André = *C. lindeniana*.

C. louisae Gagnep. Lvs to 35cm, undulate, narrowly elliptic-ovate, dark green, feathered with green-white along midrib above, tinted purple beneath. Fls white. Trop. Amer.

C. lucianii Nichols. Lvs to 35cm, elliptic, corrugated, metallic green with silvery band along midrib above, grey-green beneath; petiole to 70cm. Fls yellow. Trop. Amer.

C. lutea (Aubl.) Mey. Lvs to 1.7m, ovate to obovate, green, leathery, concolorous with waxy bloom beneath; petiole to 15cm. Infl. bracts red-brown; fls yellow. Trop. Amer.

C. magnifica Morton & Skutch. = *C. lutea*.

C. majestica H. Kenn. Lvs to 60cm, erect, ovate-lanceolate to ovate, glossy green above, dull red-purple beneath. Infl. bracts ochre; fls white, violet and yellow. Guyana, Colomb., Ecuad. 'Albolineata': lvs with fine white lines along veins above. 'Princeps': lvs light green with darker central band above, violet beneath. 'Roseolineata': lvs with fine pink lines along veins above.

C. makoyana (E. Morr.) E. Morr. PEACOCK PLANT; CATHEDRAL WINDOWS; BRAIN PLANT. Lvs to 33cm, ovate, pale green feathered cream with dark green oblong blotches along veins and dark green border above, with a purple repeating pattern beneath. Infl. bracts green; fls white, lobes purple. E Braz.

C. marzellii hort. = *C. virginalis*.

C. mediopicta (E. Morr.) Makoy ex E. Morr. Lvs to 20cm, oblong-elliptic, dark green with midrib feathered white above, pale green beneath; petiole 4cm. Infl. bracts cream or pale yellow; fls violet. Braz.

C. metallica (K. Koch) Körn. & Reg. Lvs oblong, glab., to 17cm, green with pale feathered mid-zone above, pale green sometimes edged purple beneath; petiole slender, to 15cm, minutely pubesc. Infl. bracts minutely black- or brown-pubesc.; fls white and rose. Colomb., Braz.

C. micans (Mathieu) Körn. Lvs to 13cm, oblong-lanceolate to elliptic, dark green with silvery feathered midrib above, pale green beneath; petiole to 5cm, minutely pubesc. Fls white and violet. Mex. to Braz.

C. musaica (Bull) L.H. Bail. Dwarf. Lvs to 14cm, ovate, bright yellow-green with dark green veins and small green bars diverging from lat. veins above, green beneath. Braz.

C. nitens Bull. Dwarf. Lvs glab., elliptic, glaucous green with olive-green oblong-acute bars on either side of midrib above, dull green tinted red beneath. Braz.

C. oppenheimiana E. Morr. = *Ctenanthe oppenheimiana*.

C. orbiculata Lodd. = *C. truncata*.

C. orbifolia (Lind.) H. Kenn. Differs from *C. fasciata* in lf surface more pleated, with many more minor veins and thinner texture, entirely green or banded white and green. Braz.

C. ornata (Lind.) Körn. = *C. majestica*.

C. ornata var. *sanderiana* hort. = *C.* 'Sanderiana'.

C. pardina Planch. & Lind. = *C. villosa* var. *pardina*.

C. pavonii Körn. Lvs oblong-acute, 25cm, pale green above with a row of paired, dark green blotches along midrib, green beneath; petiole short, downy. Infl. bracts leathery, green; fls yellow. Peru.

C. picta (Bull) Hook. f. = *C. warscewiczii*.

C. picturata (Lind.) K. Koch & Lind. Lvs 25cm, elliptic, acute, dull green with white stripes along midrib and near margin above, purple beneath. Fls white. NW Braz. 'Argentea': lvs glossy blue-green with silver-white feathered central zone. 'Vandenheckei': juvenile phase.

C. princeps (Lind.) Reg. = *C. majestica* 'Princeps'.

C. propinqua (Poepp. & Endl.) Körn. Tuberous. Lvs c30cm, oblanceolate to obovate, silver with dark green margins and stripes between lat. veins and pubesc. midrib above, brown-pubesc. and pale green beneath. Fls sulphur-yellow. Venez., Guyana, N Braz.

C. pseudoveitchiana H. Kenn. Similar to *C. veitchiana*. Lvs abruptly acuminate, deep green with pale green fishtail pattern along midrib and scalloped light green pattern around margin above, red-purple beneath; petiole deep green. Infl. bracts purple; sep. translucent white and purple. Peru.

C. pulchella (E. Morr.) Reg. Resembles a smaller *C. zebrina*; lvs to 10cm, paler with green bands above, violet beneath. Braz.

C. rodeckiana hort. Similar to *C. pulchella* but lvs banded with alt. large and small spots; petiole downy. Braz.

C. roseapicta (Lind.) Reg. Lvs to 20cm, oval, obtuse, green with pink or cream feathered stripes along midrib and between midrib and margin above, red-purple beneath. Infl. bracts green; fls white and violet. NW Braz.

C. rotundifolia (K. Koch) Körn. non Poepp. & Endl. = *C. orbifolia*.

C. rufibarba Fenzl. Lvs to 25cm, narrow, acuminate, glaucous green with red-haired midrib above, violet beneath; petiole red-hairy, to 16cm. Infl. bracts violet-pubesc.; fls yellow. E Braz.

C. 'Sanderiana'. Differs from *C. majestica* in lvs wider, lustrous, olive-green with similar white and pink markings. Peru.

C. sciuroides Petersen. Similar to *C. rufibara* but taller, about 40cm, tuberous-rooted, lvs elliptic. Braz.

C. smaragdina Lind. = *Monotagma smaragdinum*.

C. splendida (Lem.) Reg. Lvs to 35cm, oblong to oblong-lanceolate, deep green and glaucous with yellow-green, almond-shaped spots above or yellow green edged and broadly dark green on veins, purple beneath. Braz.

C. taeniosa Joriss. Lvs in a rosette, oblong, acuminate, dark green with silvery bands above, pale green to grey-green beneath; petiole to 15cm, purple, downy. Infl. bracts rose pink; fls yellow, white and orange. Braz.

C. truncata (Link) Schum. Lvs 35cm, suborbicular, with longitudinal silver stripes above, red beneath. Fls white. Braz.

C. tubispatha Hook. = *C. pavonii*.

C. undulata Lind. & André. Lvs to 10cm, oblong-elliptic, undulate, with a jagged cream stripe along midrib above, tinged purple beneath, ±sessile. Infl. bracts green, edged and spotted white; fls white. Peru, Braz.

C. varians (K. Koch & Mathieu) Körn. Lvs to 35cm, linear-lanceolate, acuminate, purple beneath; petiole downy, variegated purple. Infl. bracts deep brown spotted green, redhairy; fls yellow. Guyana.

C. variegata (K. Koch) Körn. Lvs 35cm, oblong, acute, green with median band of dark green above, paler with deeper green bands beneath. Fls pale yellow. Origin unknown.

C. veitchiana Hook. Lvs ovate-elliptic, dark green with yellow-green blotches along midrib and pale green scalloped longitudinal band between midrib and margins above, paler with purple markings beneath. Infl. bracts green; fls white, spotted violet. Peru. 'Foxii': dwarf; lvs broader; midrib bright rose, markings darker.

C. villosa (Lodd.) Lindl. Lvs to 28cm, oblong or lanceolate, acuminate, pubesc., green above, grey-green beneath; petiole to 2cm, rusty-pubesc. Infl. bracts green, pubesc.; fls orange. Guyana, Colomb., Braz., Venez. var. *pardina* (Planch. & Lind.) Körn. Lvs spotted black. Braz., Venez.

C. virginalis Lind. Lvs 20cm, suborbicular, downy, green with silvery white band along midrib above, deep violet and pubesc. beneath. Infl. bracts red-brown, pubesc., tip violet; fls white. Braz.

C. vittata (Koch) Körn. = *C. elliptica* 'Vittata'.

C. wallisii (Lind.) Reg. Differs from *C. ecuadoriana* in lvs with bright green band along midrib, deep green blotches between raised veins and deep green around margin above. Fls yellow. Peru. 'Discolor': lvs with central white stripe.

C. warscewiczii (Mathieu) Körn. Lvs 33cm, lanceolate or oblong-lanceolate, undulate, dark green with yellow-green blotches along midrib above, deep purple beneath. Infl. bracts leathery, downy, yellow-brown. Costa Rica.

C. wiotiana Makoy ex E. Morr. = *C. wiotii*.

C. wiotii (E. Morr.) Reg. Dwarf. Lvs to 15cm, ovate-oblong to oblong-lanceolate, undulate, light green with a row of dark green blotches along midrib above, sometimes tinged purple with yellow-green patches beneath; petiole to 8cm. Braz.

C. zebrina (Sims) Lindl. ZEBRA PLANT; Lvs to 70cm, elliptic, velvety green with broad chartreuse stripes along veins above, red-purple beneath, sessile; sheath winged. Infl. bracts violet-brown; fls white and violet. SE Braz. 'Exotica': lvs to 15×20cm, midrib grey. 'Humilior': lf with olive veins above, grey-green beneath. 'Putumayo': lvs oblanceolate, dark green with silver feathering. 'Tuxtla': lvs obliquely ovate, green, striped silver along midrib and near edge. ssp. *binotti* hort. ex L.H. Bail. Lvs narrower, to 1.5m, dark green-brown bands extending from midrib above, grey-green beneath.

→*Maranta, Monostiche* and *Phrynium*.

Calathian Violet *Gentiana pneumonanthe*.

Calceolaria L. SLIPPER FLOWER; SLIPPERWORT; POCKETBOOK FLOWER; POUCH FLOWER. Scrophulariaceae. *c*300 herbs and shrubs. Lvs generally hairy and rugose. Fls mostly cymose, showy, slipper-like, cal. 4-parted; cor. tube v. short, limb distinctly bilabiate, lower lip deflexed, inflated, upper smaller, hooded to saccate. Trop. & S Amer., northwards to Mex. Z9 unless specified.

C. acutifolia Witasek. Creeping perenn. Lvs 3–7cm, ovate-oblong to elongate-lanceolate, acute, less pubesc. Fls solitary; cor. yellow, rear of lower lip red-spotted, lower lip pouched, 1.5–2cm, orifice small. Arg.

C. alba Ruiz & Pav. Shrub, 80–100cm; aromatic. Lvs 3–6cm, linear, acute, dentate. Infl. branched, viscid; cor. white, lower lip subglobose, slightly narrowed to base, pressed against upper. Summer. Chile.

C. amplexicaulis HBK. Woody-based perenn. to 1m, glandular-pilose. Lvs to 8cm, oblong-ovate, acuminate at apex, amplexicaul at base, crenate-serrate, pilose. Infl. subumbellate; cor. yellow, 2×1cm, upper lip transversely oblong, lower much larger. Late spring–summer. Peru.

C. andina Benth. in DC. Shrub; br. glandular-hairy. Lvs to 7.5cm, ovate to ovate-lanceolate, dentate, rugose, hairy. Infl. paniculate-cymose; cor. bright yellow, upper lip 5mm, gland., lower lip 7–8mm. Spring. Chile. var. *nana* Philippi. Dwarf form. Z8.

C. angustifolia Sweet = *C. integrifolia* var. *angustifolia*.

C. arachnoidea Graham. Rhizomatous, tufted herb; st. 30–60cm. Lvs 6cm, attenuate to base, obtuse at apex, silver-downy. Cymes compact, short-stalked; cor. violet-purple, lower lip subglobose, 1cm. Summer–early autumn. Chile. var. *lanata* Walp. Lvs densely lanate. var. *viridis* Benth. in DC. Lvs scarcely lanate.

C. bellidifolia Gillies ex Benth. Tufted perenn.; st. 8–15cm, white-hirsute. Lvs mostly basal, to 3cm, obovate-oblong, obtuse, narrowed to petiole, white-villous. Fls 2–4; cor. deep yellow or orange, 1.5–2cm, upper lip v. short, lower lip rounded-saccate. Chile. Z7.

C. benthamii Philippi = *C. volckmannii*.

C. bicolor Ruiz & Pav. Subshrub, ascending to scandent, 1–2m. Lvs 5–8cm, ovate, rounded at base, acute at apex, doubly serrate, deep green above, white-pubesc. to arachnoid-lanate beneath. Cymes 8–16-fld; cor. light yellow, lower lip sacate, upcurved portion 18×14mm. Summer–late autumn. Peru. Z6.

C. biflora Lam. Perenn. herb, 10–30cm. Lvs basal, rosulate, to 7cm, ovate-lanceolate, obtuse at apex, attenuate to petiole-like base, minutely dentate, hairy. Scape glandular-pubesc.; infl. cymose, 2-few-fld; cor. yellow, 12×18mm, upper lip much shorter than cal., subglobose, lower lip far larger. Summer. Chile & Arg. 'Goldcrest': dwarf; lvs in flat rosette; fls yellow. 'John Innes': stoloniferous; fls to 3×4cm, lip indented, deep yellow with red-brown marking. 'Hall's Spotted' is more distinctly marked. Z6.

C. bipartita Philippi = *C. pratensis*.

C. × burbidgei hort. (*C. deflexa* × *C. pavonii*.) Shrub to 1m; shoots red. Lvs ovate, cordate at base, acute to acuminate at apex, dentate, pilose, gland.; petioles dilated at base, connate. Fls showy; cor. golden-yellow with purple markings, minutely pubesc., lower lip 2.5cm. Autumn and winter.

C. cana Cav. Perenn. herb; st. ascending, 40–60cm, hairy and gland. towards apex. Lvs mostly basal, 2–5cm, spathulate, white-felted. Infl. paniculate; fls fragrant; cor. small, yellow, lower lip distinctly narrowed to base, transversely oblong-ovate, 1cm. Chile.

C. chelidonioides HBK. Ann.; st. to 1m, pilose above. Lvs to 20cm, pinnate to pinnatifid, dentate, long-petiolate, bright green above, paler beneath. Infl. subumbellate; cor. yellow, 1.5–4cm, upper lid bifid, lower lip greatly inflated. Summer. Peru.

C. corymbosa Ruiz & Pav. Herb; st. 30–60cm, hairy. Lvs in large, flat basal rosette, to 7cm, ovate, doubly serrate, hairy; petioles long. Infl. cymose, many-fld slender-stalked, cor. yellow, lower lip narrowed to base. Late spring–autumn. Chile.

C. crenata Lam. Herb, erect or ascending, 0.5–1m, sometimes woody below. Lvs 6–12cm, lanceolate, cordate at base, amplexicaul, crenate, glandular-villous. Cymes 6–34-fld; cor. bright yellow or sulphur-yellow, lower lip 18×12mm. Summer. S Colomb., N Ecuad.

C. crenatiflora Cav. Perenn. herb; st. 40–80cm, hairy. Lvs 10–12cm, ovate, entire or minutely dentate, sessile or attenuate to petiole, obtuse or acuminate at apex, dentate, hairy. Infl. cymose; cor. yellow with red or rusty spots, upper lip small, lower transversely ovate, crenate, to 2.5cm. Summer. Chile. Z8.

C. darwinii Benth. in DC. V. similar to *C. uniflora*, except plant subglabrous; cor. somewhat larger, lower lip obtriangular, yellow-ochre streaked blood red within, inner lower lip with a broad white band, exterior dotted and stained ruby red. Summer. S Patagonia, Tierra del Fuego. 'Walter Shrimpton' (*C. darwinii* × *C. fothergillii*): fls yellow and brown with strong white bar across lower lip. Z7.

C. deflexa Ruiz & Pav. Shrub, erect, rarely scrambling, 0.5–2m. Lvs 5–9cm, lanceolate, acute, entire to serrate, dark green above, pale green beneath. Infl. of 2–3 pairs of 8–16-fld cymes; cor. bright orange-yellow to light yellow, lower lip sometimes white below, upper lip flat, 9–12mm, lower lip upcurved, saccate part 1.5–2cm. Winter–spring. Andes of N & C Peru.

C. diffusa Lindl. = *C. bicolor*.

C. falklandica (S. Moore) Kränzl. St. prostrate, short, sparsely hairy. Lvs basal, 10–12cm oblong or oblong-lanceolate, dentate. Infl. corymbose, few- to many-fld, on scapes to 25cm; cor. pale yellow, purple-spotted in throat, 15×13mm, lower lip obovate, inflated. Summer. Falkland Is. Z7.

C. filicaulis Clos. Herb, slender. Lvs basal, rosulate, ovate, finely serrate, attenuate to base, 3–6cm, white-pubesc. Scapes 2–4, 15–40cm, tinged red, glandular-pubesc., cyme few-fld; cor. bright yellow, minutely pubesc., lower lip larger, globose, 8–9mm, pilose. S Arg., Chile.

C. flexuosa Ruiz & Pav. Subshrub, ascending or scrambling. Lvs 4–7cm ovate, pilose, glandular-punctate beneath. Infl. of 2–4 pairs of 4–12-fld cymes; cor. with upper lip light yellow to sulphur-yellow, lower lip bright to golden yellow, throat white to deep yellow with red spots. Peru. Z7.

C. floribunda Hook. = *C. crenata*.

C. fothergillii Sol. in Ait. Perenn. herb 10–15cm. Lvs in basal rosette, to 4cm, spathulate, entire or obscurely serrate, hairy. Fl. solitary, large, scapose; cor. sulphur-yellow, streaked red towards front, lower lip transversely ovate, 1.5cm. Summer. Falkland Is., Patagonia. Z7.

C. Fruticohybrida group. Derived in part from *C. integrifolia*, a complex group of rather shrubby hybrids with somewhat smaller fls than in *C.* Herbeohybrida group. Glorious Hybrids: large, to 25cm; fls large, brightly coloured, in plain, spotted, and bicolours). 'Kentish Hero': fls bronze to orange. 'Paul's Spotted': fls spotted plum. 'Red Slippers': fls numerous, small, bright red.

C. ×*fruticohybrida* Voss = *C.* Fruticohybrida group.

C. fuchsiifolia hort. = *C. deflexa*.

C. glacialis Wedd. Perenn. herb. Lvs 1–2cm, rosulate, spathulate to oblanceolate, attenuate at base, obtuse. Infl. 2–4cm, 1–2-fld; cor. deep yellow, upper lip 3mm, triangular-rounded, lower lip 13×10mm, suborbicular to obovate, dorsally flattened. Summer. Boliv. to N Arg.

C. gracilis HBK = *C. tripartita*.

C. grandiflora Pennell. Perenn. herb; st. ascending, 0.5–2m, white-villous. Lvs 5–8cm, ovate to triangular-ovate, cordate to truncate at base, lobulate and crenate, blade above, glandular-hispid on veins beneath, lanate; petioles 3–6cm, crenate-winged. Infl. of paired 8–12-fld cymes; cor. sulphur-yellow, upper lip 1cm, subglobose, lower lip projecting, 2.5–3cm, circular, flattened. S Ecuad.

C. henrici Hook. f. Shrub to 1m pubesc. Lvs to 12cm, lanceolate, acuminate, serrate, glab. above, tinged yellow and villous beneath, petioles slightly connate. Infl. corymbose to sub-umbellate; cor. 18×13mm, golden yellow, upper lip transversely oblong, lower lip orbicular, orifice minute. Spring. Peru.

C. Herbeohybrida group. (*C. crenatiflora* ×*C. corymbosa* ×*C. cana*.) A complex group of hybrids, usually with soft, bushy growth and large, strongly inflated fls. 'Grandiflora': lvs thin, fresh green; fls to 8cm diam., with inflated lower lip, shades of yellow or red, often marked orange red to maroon. Anytime Hybrids: various colours, early-flowering. Confetti Hybrids: habit compact; fls in large clusters, from yellow to bronze. 'Goldcrest': to 15cm; long-flowering. 'Gold Fever': fls lemon-yellow. Hunt's Choicest: fls v. large, pouched, variegated brilliant colours. 'Jewel Cluster': fls mix of colours, speckled, early-flowering. 'Multiflora Nana': habit dwarf; lvs thin, ovate, toothed and quilted; fls numerous, to 5cm diam., pouch-like, often orange, yellow or red, usually marked with crimson. Pocket Hybrids: compact; lvs bright green; fls from bronze through red and pink to yellow, in large heads. Tiger Spotted Hybrids: to 45cm; fls large, speckled, range of colours.

C. ×*herbeohybrida* Voss = *C.* Herbeohybrida group.

C. herbertiana Lindl. = *C. andina*.

C. hirta Pennell = *C. pavonii*.

C. hyssopifolia HBK. Subshrub, erect or ascending, 20–100cm. Lvs 3–7cm, narrowly elliptic, cuneate at base, entire to minutely dentate, subsessile, smooth, glutinous. Infl. of 1–3 pairs of 4–12-fld cymes; cor. white towards centre, light lemon-yellow in distal parts, upper lip flat, subcircular, 5×7mm, lower lip upcurved, saccate to 1.5cm. Andes of N Ecuad.

C. integrifolia Murray. Viscid subshrub, 60–120cm; br. hairy or glandular-hairy. Lvs to 5cm, linear-lanceolate to ovate-lanceolate, dentate, green above, grey-green and rusty-hairy beneath, rugose; petioles v. short. Infl. cymose-paniculate short; cor. yellow, lips near equal. Late summer. Chile. var. *angustifolia* (Sweet) Lindl. Lvs lanceolate, acute, infl. long. var. *viscosissima* Hook. Lvs oblong, obtuse, auriculate at base, v. viscid, not rusty-hairy beneath, infl. shorter.

C. ×*kellyana* hort. (Parentage unknown.) Dwarf. Scapes viscid-pubesc., few-fld; cor. orange-yellow with purple spots, 2.5cm, upper lip hooded, acute, lower lip far larger, saccate.

C. lobata Cav. Herb, ascending, 30–90cm; st., glandular-pilose. Lvs 3–8cm, suborbicular to subdeltoid, cordate at base, lobed, dentate, pilose. Infl. of 1 pair of 4–20-fld cymes; cor. yellow, throat red or purple spotted within, upper lip 5mm, lower lip 18×12mm. Peru to Boliv.

C. mathewsii Benth. Dwarf; st. leafy. Lvs 1–2.5cm, oblong or suborbicular to spathulate, rather fleshy, villous above, glab. beneath. Fls solitary long-stalked; cor. yellow, 2.5cm, lower lip obovate-oblong, ±equal to upper lip. Summer. Peru, Chile.

C. mendocina Philippi. Perenn. herb, pubesc. Lvs in basal rosette, 3×2cm, ovate, somewhat fleshy. Scapes 1 or 2, 5–7cm, 1-fld; cor. subglobose, clear yellow, lower lip larger, orbicular or

slightly broader than long, gland. Arg., China.

C. mexicana Benth. Ann. herb, 20–50cm, glandular-pubesc. Lvs 3–7cm, ovate to lanceolate, deeply pinnatifid-lobed, rarely sub-entire, cuneate to truncate at base, often tinged purple beneath. Cor. bright yellow, upper lip 2–3mm, lower lip 10×7mm, saccate, shallowly 3-lobed, with horseshoe-shaped dors. ridge. Summer. Mex. to Boliv.

C. multiflora Cav. Shrub, much-branched, low-growing. Lvs 1×0.5cm, ovate to oblong, acute, serrate, minutely pubesc. Infl. a much-branched pan.; cor. yellow, upper lip 2.5×3mm, lower lip elongate-obovate, 10×4.5mm. Peru.

C. nana Sm. = *C. uniflora*.

C. paralia Hook. = *C. corymbosa*.

C. pavonii Benth. in DC. Scandent woody-based herb, 60–120cm, buff-villous. St. ± tetragonal. Lvs 8–20cm, triangular-ovate, cordate at base, minutely lobed and serrate, olive-green, buff-pilose; petioles broadly winged, connate. Infl. of 1–5 pairs of 4–20-fld cymes; cor. light yellow to sulphur-yellow, sometimes banded purple in throat, upper lip 7mm, lower lip 20×14mm. Ecuad., Peru.

C. pendula Sweet = *C. crenatiflora*.

C. petiolaris Cav. Perenn; st. robust, hollow, 50–80cm, gland. Lvs 10–15cm, ovate, lower abruptly narrowed to petiole, upper cordate at base, sessile, serrate, thin; petioles winged, connate-perfoliate. Infl. many-fld, glandular-pubesc.; cor. pale yellow, upper lip to 8mm, lower to 12mm. Peru, Chile.

C. picta Philippi. Perenn. herb; st. 30–60cm, purple, hairy. Lvs oblong, attenuate to base, shortly petiolate, doubly serrate, to 18cm, hairy. Infl. cymose; cor. violet with darker spots and yellow centre, lower lip subglobose, to 1.5cm. Summer. Chile.

C. pinnata L. Ann. herb, 5–50cm; st. succulent. Lvs 5–15cm, ovate to lanceolate, pinnatisect, lobes serrate to pinnatisect; petioles connate, winged. Cor. light to bright yellow or white, unspotted or with purple blotch in throat, lower lip 1–2cm. Summer. Peru, Boliv., N Chile; nat. elsewhere.

C. pisacomensis Meyen ex Walp. Subshrub or shrub, 30–90cm; st. glandular-hirsute. Lvs 3–4cm, ovate to triangular, cordate at base, acute at apex, serrate to crenate, sessile, olive-green, glandular-hirsute. Infl. of 1–3 pairs of 4–20-fld cymes; cor. upper lip, lemon-yellow, lower lip 15×10mm, lemon-yellow at base, orange within, bright red to red tinged brown elsewhere. S Peru.

C. plantaginea Sm. = *C. biflora*.

C. polifolia Hook. Shrub, woody at base, much-branched. Lvs 1–1.5cm, ovate-orbicular to ovate-lanceolate, entire or minutely dentate, white-tomentose. Infl. subumbellate to paniculate; cor. with upper lip inflated, 5mm, pale yellow, lower subglobose, 6–7mm, brilliant yellow. Summer. Chile.

C. polyrrhiza Cav. Prostrate everg. perenn. herb. Lvs 4–6cm, lanceolate, obscurely crenate. Fls usually solitary, long-stalked; cor. yellow with purple spots, 2.5×1cm, upper lip, rounded, lower lip much longer, obovate. Summer. Chile, Patagonia. Z6.

C. polyrrhiza hort. non Cav. = *C. crenatiflora*.

C. pratensis Philippi. Dwarf herb. Lvs basal, 5–7cm, broadly oblong, crenate, petiolate, densely pilose. Infl. subumbellate, few-fld; scapes 20–40cm; cor. yellow, 12×9mm, upper lip v. short, lower lip broadly oblong with small orifice. Summer. Chile. Z9.

C. punctata Vahl = *Jovellana punctata*.

C. purpurea Graham. Perenn., herbaceous or woody-based, viscid-glandular, 60–80cm, branched. Basal lvs rosulate petiolate, st. lvs amplexicaul, opposite, ovate, serrate, to 12cm, rugose. Infl. many-fld; peduncles 1–1.5cm; cor. purple, upper lip 4mm, lower lip subglobose, 8mm. Summer–early autumn. Chile.

C. ribesifolia Rusby = *C. lobata*.

C. rugosa Ruiz & Pav. = *C. integrifolia*.

C. scabiosifolia Roem. & Schult. = *C. tripartita*.

C. scapiflora (Ruiz & Pav.) Benth. in DC. St. v. short. Lvs basal, rosulate, 3cm, ovate to subrhombic, dentate, petiolate, villous. Fls solitary; scapes 10–15cm, glandular-pilose; cor. yellow with purple blotches and stripes. 16×8mm, upper lip exceeding lower. Peru.

C. stewartii hort. = *C. integrifolia*.

C. tenella Poepp. & Endl. Perenn. herb, 8–10cm; st. numerous, creeping, slightly woody. Lvs 0.7–1cm, ovate, finely serrate, shortly petiolate. Infl. few-fld; cor. bright yellow with orange spots, upper lip erect, inflated. Chile.

C. tenerifolia Philippi = *C. pratensis*.

C. tetraphylla Philippi = *C. corymbosa*.

C. thyrsiflora Graham. Shrub, copiously branched, 60–80cm; br. gland. Lvs 1–2cm, linear or linear-lanceolate, dentate, viscid-glandular. Infl. cylindric; cor. bright yellow, globose, glandular-hairy, upper lip inflated, 3–5×5–6mm, lower lip 6mm, arched. Summer. Chile.

C. tomentosa Ruiz & Pav. Herb to 1m; st. fleshy, glandular-pilose above. Lvs to 10cm, triangular-ovate, cordate at base, bidentate; petioles connate, broadly winged. Infl. corymbose; cor. golden yellow, upper lip transversely oblong, 1cm, lower suborbicular, 4×3cm. Peru.

C. tripartita Ruiz & Pav. Herb, erect or ascending, 20–90cm. Lvs 2–9cm, ovate, dissected to midrib to subentire, pinnae in 1–2 pairs, serrate; petioles 1–4cm, unwinged or v. narrowly winged, cor. unspotted, bright to deep yellow, upper lip 4×5mm, lower lip 18×16mm. Late spring–autumn. Mex. to Peru; nat. elsewhere.

C. umbellata Wedd. Herb, ascending, subrosulate, 5–30cm. Lvs 3–7cm, elliptic to lanceolate, entire or shallowly serrate, obscurely petiolate. Infl. of 1–2 pairs of 4–8-fld cymes; peduncles 4–12cm, villous; cor. bright yellow, upper lip 3mm, triangular-rounded, lower lip 13×10mm, obovate, flattened, truncate. S Boliv. to C Arg.

C. uniflora Lam. Perenn. Lvs in flattened rosettes, to 3cm, spathulate, entire to minutely dentate, sparsely glandular-hairy. Scapes 4–8cm, glandular-pubesc.; fls 1(–2), held vertically; cor. yellow, lower lip far exceeding upper, oblong, swollen in centre, spreading, 2cm, white with coloured streaks. Summer. S Patagonia, Tierra del Fuego. Z6.

C. uniflora var. *darwinii* (Benth.) Witasek = *C. darwinii*.

C. valdiviana Philippi = *C. pratensis*.

C. violacea Cav. = *Jovellana violacea*.

C. volckmannii Philippi. Perenn. herb; st. 20cm. Lvs mostly crowded at base of st., ovate-cuneate, narrowed to petiole, glandular-hairy, glandular-punctate. Cymes few-fld; stalks slender, 1–1.5cm, gland., cor. yellow.
→*Fagelia*.

Caldcluvia D. Don. Cunoniaceae. 11 everg. shrubs or trees. Lvs simple or imparipinnate. Pan. term. or axill.; fls small, white, perfect; cal. lobes 5 triangular or ovate pet. 5; sta. 10. S Amer., Aus., New Guinea, Philipp., NZ. Z10.

C. australiensis (Schltr.) Hoogl. Resembles *C. paniculosa*. Lvs 5-foliate, lfts to 8cm, ovate or elliptic, deep green. NE Queensld.

C. paniculata (Cav.) D. Don. Tree to 8m. Lvs to 14cm, simple, oblong-lanceolate glossy. Fls fragrant;; pet. to 2.5mm. S S Amer.

C. paniculosa (F. Muell.) Hoogl. Tree to 40m. Lvs 3–7-foliate, lfts to 15cm, ovate to elliptic; petiole to 5cm. Pet. 10 1mm. Queensld, NSW.
→*Ackama* and *Weinmannia*.

Caledon Bluebell *Gladiolus bullatus*.

Calendula L. MARIGOLD. Compositae. *c*20 ann. or perenn. herbs, often gland. and aromatic. Cap. radiate, solitary, term., receptacle flat; ray flts yellow or orange; disc flts yellow, orange, brown or violet-purple. Medit., Macaronesia.

C. arvensis L. FIELD MARIGOLD. Ann., to 30cm. Lvs to 10×2cm, oblong or narrowly obovate, pubesc., sometimes toothed. Cap. to 3.5cm diam.; ray flts to 1.8cm, yellow or orange; disc flts yellow, orange, brown or violet-purple. S & SC Eur. Z6.

C. chrysanthemifolia (Vent.) DC. = *Dimorphotheca chrysanthemifolia*.

C. cuneata Thunb. = *Dimorphotheca cuneata*.

C. eckerlinii hort. = *Osteospermum ecklonis*.

C. fruticosa L. = *Osteospermum fruticosum*.

C. maderensis DC. Perenn., to 80cm. Lvs to 14×5cm, oblong-spathulate to spathulate, scabrous, pubesc. to bristly, glandular-viscid, entire. Flts orange. Madeira. Z9.

C. maritima Guss. = *C. suffruticosa* ssp. *maritima*.

C. nudicaulis L. = *Castalis nudicaulis*.

C. officinalis L. RUDDLES; COMMON MARIGOLD; SCOTCH MARIGOLD; POT MARIGOLD. Ann. or perenn., to 70cm. Lvs to 17×6cm, oblanceolate to spathulate, glandular-pubesc. to sparsely woolly, sometimes toothed and wavy. Cap. to 7cm diam.; ray flts to 2cm, yellow or orange; disc flts yellow, orange or brown. Origin unknown. Cvs vary in colour from the bright yellow 'Sun Glow' and 'Lemon' to the vivid orange 'Orange Prince' and 'Bon Bon Orange' and the red-tinted 'Indian Prince'; larger-fld seed races include the rich orange, 45cm Mandarin Fl. Hybrids and the mixed orange, yellow and apricot of Pacific Beauty Mixed, the similarly coloured Art Shades Mixed grows up to 60cm. 'Chrysantha': fls double, bright gold. 'Prolifera': fls proliferous. 'Variegata': lvs variegated green and gold. Z6.

C. pinnata Thunb. = *Osteospermum pinnatum*.

C. pluvialis (L.) Moench. = *Dimorphotheca chrysanthemifolia*.

C. stellata Cav. Ann., to 50cm. Lvs to 14×4cm, oblong-lanceolate to obovate, sparsely hairy, slightly toothed. Cap. to 5cm diam., ray flts golden yellow or orange, apex violet; disc flts violet-purple to black. Sicily and N Afr. Z8.

C. suffruticosa Vahl. Woody-based perenn., to 50cm or taller. Lvs to 12×4cm, linear-lanceolate to oblanceolate, glandular-pubesc., sessile, often toothed. Cap. to 5cm diam. numerous, on long peduncles; ray flts to 2cm, yellow or orange; disc flts yellow or orange. Medit., Port. ssp. *maritima* (Guss.) Meikle. Lvs densely glandular-pubesc., fleshy, entire or minutely toothed. Cap. to 5cm diam.; ray flts yellow, rarely orange. W Sicily. Z8.

C. tragus Ait., non Jacq. = *Castalis tragus*.

Caley Pea *Lathyrus hirsutus*.
Caley's Banksia *Banksia caleyi*.
Calico Bush *Kalmia latifolia*.
Calico Flower *Aristolochia littoralis*.
Calico Plant *Alternanthera bettzichiana*.

Calicotome Link. Leguminosae (Papilionoideae). 2 decid. thorny shrubs to 3m; st. Lvs trifoliolate, growing from short spiny twigs; lfts small, elliptic-obovate. Fls bright yellow, pea-like, solitary, clustered or umbellate. Medit. Z8.

C. infesta (Presl) Guss. = *C. villosa*.

C. spinosa (L.) Link. Lfts 5–12×3–6mm, downy or glab. beneath. Fls solitary or 2–4 per cluster; spring–summer. W Medit. coasts.

C. villosa (Poir.) Link. Lfts 4–10×2–5mm, sericeous beneath. Fls fragrant, solitary or to 5 per cluster, or in short rac. Winter–summer. Medit.

California Bay *Umbellularia californica*.
California Bayberry *Myrica californica*.
California Beauty *Fremontodendron*.
California Black Oak *Quercus kelloggii*.
California Black Sage *Salvia mellifera*.
California Bluebell *Phacelia campanularia*.
California Buckeye *Aesculus californica*.
California Buckwheat *Eriogonum fasciculatum*.
California Fan Palm *Washingtonia filifera*.
California Fern *Conium maculatum*.
California Fuchsia *Epilobium canum*.
California Golden Violet *Viola pedunculata*.
California Juniper *Juniperus californica*.
California Laurel *Umbellularia californica*.
California Lilac *Ceanothus*.
California Live Oak *Quercus agrifolia*.
California Maidenhair Fern *Adiantum jordanii*.
Californian Allspice *Calycanthus occidentalis*.
Californian Blackcurrant *Ribes bracteosum*.
Californian Blue-eyed Grass *Sisyrinchium bellum*.
Californian Gold Fern *Pityrogramma triangularis*.
Californian Huckleberry *Vaccinium ovatum*.
Californian Lace Fern *Cheilanthes californica*.
Californian Nutmeg *Torreya californica*.
Californian Pepper Tree *Schinus molle*.
Californian Poppy *Platystemon*.
Californian Red Fir *Abies magnifica*.
Californian Tree Poppy *Romneya*.
Californian Washingtonia *Washingtonia filifera*.
California Olive *Umbellularia californica*.
California Pitcher Plant *Darlingtonia*.
California Poppy *Eschscholzia californica*.
California Privet *Ligustrum ovalifolium*.
California Rape *Brassica kaber*.
California Redbud *Cercis occidentalis*.
California Redwood *Sequoia*.
California Romero *Trichostema lanatum*.
California Sagebrush *Artemisia californica*.
California Scrub Oak *Quercus dumosa*.
California Single-leaf Pinyon *Pinus californiarum*.
California Sycamore *Platanus racemosa*.
California Walnut *Juglans californica*.
California Wax Myrtle *Myrica californica*.
California White Oak *Quercus lobata*.
California White Sage *Salvia apiana*.

Caliphruria Herb.
C. subedentata Bak. = *Eucharis subedentata*.

Calisaya *Cinchona officinalis*.
Calistoga Ceanothus *Ceanothus divergens*.

Calla L. WATER ARUM; BOG ARUM; WILD CALLA; WATER DRAGON. Araceae. 1 perenn. aquatic and marginal herb. Rhiz. creeping, dark green. Lvs 4.5–8cm across, broadly ovate to reniform, apex abruptly acute, base cordate, glossy dark green; petioles to 20cm. Spathe to 6cm diam., usually smaller, white, spadix green to 3cm. Berries bright red. Temp. regions. Z4.

C. aethiopica L. = *Zantedeschia aethiopica*.

C. palustris L.

Calla Lily *Zantedeschia.*
Callery Pear *Pyrus calleryana.*

Calliandra Benth. POWDER PUFF TREES. Leguminosae (Mimosoideae). *c*200 shrubs, small trees and perenn. herbs. Lvs bipinnate. Fls few-fascicled or many in globose mimosa-like heads; cal. campanulate, lobed; sta. many, fil. long, showy. Trop. & subtrop. Amer., India, Madag., W Afr. Z10.

C. anomala (Kunth) Macbr. Erect shrub, 1–2m. Lvs 9–12cm; pinnae 1–3cm, in 6–22 pairs, lfts 2.5–3.5mm, in 20–35 pairs, narrowly oblong, sharp-tipped. Fl. heads in narrow or pyramidal pan.; fil. 40–70mm, dark red or carmine. Summer–autumn. Mex.

C. brevipes Benth. = *C. selloi.*

C. emarginata (Humb. & Bonpl. ex Willd.) Benth. Low-growing, diffuse shrub to 0.5m (–3m). Lvs 4–8cm; pinnae in 1 pair, lfts 30–60mm, in 1–2 pairs, elliptic or obovate, rounded or sharp-tipped, hairy beneath. Fls in spherical heads; fil. *c*30mm deep cerise to near white. Throughout the year. Hond. to S Mex.

C. eriophylla Benth. MOCK MESQUITE; MESQUITILLA; FAIRY-DUSTER. Shrub 0.2–1m. Lvs to 2.5cm; pinnae 5–20mm in 1–4 pairs, lfts 2–6mm, in 6–10 pairs, elliptic or elliptic-oblong, obtuse or sharp-tipped, sericeous beneath. Fls in axill. heads, on delicate stalks; fil 14–25mm, rosy pink to white. Summer–autumn. S Calif., Ariz. to New Mex. and N Mex.

C. guildingii Benth. = *C. tweedii.*

C. haematocephala Hassk. Shrub or small tree to 6m. Lvs to 45cm; pinnae to 20cm, lfts to 8cm, in 5–10 pairs, lanceolate-falcate to semi-elliptic, mucronulate, lustrous above, paler beneath. Fls in heads, on downy peduncles; fil. *c*30mm, white at base, vivid red toward apex. S Amer.

C. hirsuta (G. Don) Benth. Thickly canescent shrub to 1m. Lvs 6–11cm; pinnae 20–45mm, in 7–11 pairs, lfts 2.5–4.5mm, in 20–40 pairs, linear-oblong, sharp-tipped, leathery, sericeous beneath. Fls, in narrow or hemispherical heads, solitary or fascicled; fil. scarlet, 30–35mm. Early summer. S Amer.

C. houstoniana (Mill.) Standl. Delicate shrub or tree, to 2.5m. Lvs 15–25cm; rachis rusty-hirsute; pinnae 4–12cm, in 8–15 pairs, lfts 4–11mm, in 35–55 pairs, linear, apex curved forwards. Fl. heads 3–7 in narrow pan. 10–30cm; fil. 60–80mm, scarlet or dark red. Summer–autumn. S Mex. to Hond.

C. inaequilatera Rusby = *C. haematocephala.*

C. portoricensis (Jacq.) Benth. Small tree or shrub to 6m. Pinnae 38–76mm, in 2–7 pairs; lfts to 16mm, overlapping, linear-oblong, margins pubesc. Fls in globose, axill. heads; fil. to 19mm, white. Summer. S Mex. to Panama, W Indies.

C. schottii Torr. ex S. Wats. Shrub to 1m. Pinnae in 1–3 pairs; lfts 5–12mm, in 4–7 pairs, ovate to irregularly elliptic, sparsely pubesc., glaucous beneath. Fls in heads, axill. or grouped at st. tips, on delicate stalks; fil. 1.5–3cm yellow-white or rose. Summer. S Ariz., Mex.

C. selloi (Spreng.) Macbr. Shrub to 1.8m. Pinnae paired, each 25–32mm; lfts 3–6mm, numerous, linear-oblong, overlapping. Fls in solitary, in short-stalked globose heads; fil. to 25mm or more, red-tipped. Autumn. Braz.

C. surinamensis Benth. Small tree or diffuse shrub, 3–6m. Pinnae 1–3 pairs, lfts 8–17mm, in 7–12 pairs, oblong-lanceolate, sharp-tipped. Fls in erect, axill. heads; fil. to 40mm, white below, deep red above. N S Amer., widespread in cult.

C. tweedii Benth. CUNURE; MEXICAN FLAMEBUSH. Shrub or small tree, 1.8–2m. Pinnae in 2–7 pairs; lfts 4–6mm, in 15–20 pairs, narrowly oblong, overlapping, sericeous when young. Fls in solitary, axill. heads; fil. to 35mm red. Winter–spring. Braz., nat. S US, W Indies.

Callianthemum C.A. Mey. Ranunculaceae. 10 rhizomatous perenn. herbs. Basal lvs pinnate, seg. 2–3-pinnatifid, petiole long; st. lvs 1–2, small. Fls terminal often solitary or 2–3; sep. 5, ovate, green-white, yellow or pink; pet. 5–20, usually with an orange-yellow nectary; sta. numerous. C Eur., C Asia.

C. anemonoides (Zahlbr.) Endl. ex Heynh. To 20cm. Lvs developing after fls, triangular in outline, pinnate; lfts in 2–3 pairs, pinnatifid. Fls solitary, 2.5–3cm diam; pet. 5–15, white to pink, nectaries orange-red. Spring. Austria. Z5.

C. angustifolium Witasek. Perenn. to 20cm. Lvs slender, developing with fls, elliptic in outline, 2-pinnate, seg. 2–4 pairs; petiole long. Fls 2–4cm diam.; pet. white, ovate or linear, rounded or emarginate. Summer. Sib. Z3.

C. cachemirianum Cambess. Perenn. to 10cm. Lvs in basal tuft, pinnate; lfts 3–6 pairs, deeply cut, glaucous; petiole long. Fls 1 or few, 2.5–3cm diam.; pet. 8–12, oblong-cuneate, notched, white tinged red. Summer. Himal. Z7.

C. coriandrifolium Rchb. St. to 30cm, usually shorter. Lvs 5.5–13cm, long-stalked, dull grey-green, ovate-elliptic, seg. 5–7,

finely divided. Fls 2–3cm diam., solitary, rarely 2–3; pet. white, sometimes suffused yellow at centre, 6–13, obovate to broadly elliptic. Summer. Alps, Carpath., Pyren. Z6.

C. kernerianum Freyn ex Kerner. St. 3–12cm, tinted red. Lvs 2.5–7cm, long-stalked, blue-green, developing after fls, pinnate; lfts 2–3 pairs, lower lfts pinnatisect. Fls solitary, *c*2.5cm diam.; pet. 10–15, oblong to linear, white, often flushed or veined pink or red. Spring–summer. S Alps. Z6.

C. pimpinelloides (D. Don) Hook. & Thoms. = *C. cachemirianum.*

C. rutifolium (L.) C.A. Mey. = *C. anemonoides* or *C. coriandrifolium.*

→*Ranunculus.*

Callicarpa L. Verbenaceae. *c*140 trees or shrubs, usually stellate-tomentose. Br. slender, divaricate. Lvs simple, usually toothed with veins impressed. Cymes small, axill., many-fld; fls small; cal. small, tubular or campanulate, with 4 teeth; cor. infundibular or salverform, limb 4-lobed, sta. 4 exserted. Fr. a small, bead-like drupe. Trop. and subtrop.

C. americana L. Shrub to 3m; br. tetragonal or subterete, glabrescent, initially stellate-pubesc. or tomentose. Lvs to 23cm, membranous, ovate or ovate-oblong to elliptic, acute or acuminate, white-tomentose to glabrescent. Cymes to 3.5cm, many-fld; fls blue, pink or red, sometimes white. Fr. to 6mm diam., rose-pink to red-violet or blue. S US, W Indies. 'Lactea': fr. white. Z6.

C. angustata Rehd. = *C. longifolia.*

C. bodinieri Lév. Shrub to 3m; branchlets, softly scurfy. Lvs to 18cm, elliptic to ovate to lanceolate, acuminate, dentate, pubesc. beneath, gold-purple in fall. Cymes to 3.5cm diam. many-fld; fls lilac. Fr. to 2mm diam., violet. C & W China. var. *giraldii* (Hesse ex Rehd.) Rehd. Superior form with graceful br. and lvs and brilliantly coloured violet berries. 'Profusion': young foliage bronze-purple; fr. violet in packed clusters. Z6.

C. dichotoma (Lour.) K. Koch. Shrub to 120cm, subglabrous. Lvs to 6cm, chartaceous, ovate or obovate to elliptic, shortly acuminate, dentate towards apex, gland. beneath. Cymes axill., few- to many-fld; fls pink. Fr. to 2mm diam., lilac-violet. China, Jap. Z6.

C. giraldiana Hesse ex Rehd. = *C. bodinieri* var. *giraldii.*

C. giraldiana var. *subcanescens* Rehd. = *C. bodinieri* var. *giraldii.*

C. japonica Thunb. Compact shrub close to *C. longifolia*; lvs oval, ± glab. and gland. beneath; fls pale pink; fr. violet. Jap. Z8.

C. koreana hort. = *C. dichotoma.*

C. longifolia Lam. Shrub to 5m. Lvs to 20cm, oblong or oblong-lanceolate, long-acuminate dentate towards apex, pubesc. beneath. Fls clustered, rose or purple. Fr. to 2mm diam., white or dark pink. Himal. and Jap. to Philipp., Malay peninsula, Java, Trop. Aus. 'Leucocarpa': Fr. white. var. *luxurians* Rehd. Lvs and infl. larger. Z9.

C. macrophylla Vahl. Shrub to 2.5m, white-tomentose. Lvs large cuneate, hairy above, white-tomentose beneath. Infl. to 9cm diam., dense; fls red or purple. Fr. to 2mm diam., white. Masc. Is., India to Burm. and Malaysia. Z9.

C. nudiflora Hook. & Arn. Shrub or tree to 10m. Lvs to 22cm, ovate-lanceolate to oblong or elliptic-oblong, acute or acuminate, dentate, sparsely pubesc. above, villous beneath. Cymes to 15cm diam.; fls red or purple. Fr. to 3mm diam., blue, black when dry, gland. China, India, Malay Penins. Z8.

C. pedunculata R. Br. Lvs to 15cm, membranous, broadly elliptic to oblong, acuminate, base rounded, serrulate, puberulent above, sparsely stellate-flocculose beneath. Cymes to 5cm diam., stellate-villous. Fr. to 2mm diam., purple to dark violet or white. India, Trop. Aus. Z10.

C. purpurea Juss. = *C. dichotoma.*

C. rubella Lindl. Shrub to 1m. Lvs to 12.5cm, obovate, yellow-green, acuminate, base cordate, dentate above, tomentose. Cymes villous, many-fld; fls pink. Fr. to 2mm diam., red-purple, pubesc. when young. Indochina, Malay Archipel. Z9.

Callicoma Andrews. Cunoniaceae. 1 tree or shrub to 20m. Young shoots brown-pubescent. Lvs to 13cm, ovate to elliptic, acute or acuminate, serrate, densely pubesc. beneath. Fls creamy, small, term., in dense globular heads; sep. 4 or 5, free; pet. 0; sta. numerous, conspicuous. E Aus. Z9.

C. serratifolia Andrews. BLACK WATTLE.

Calliopsis Rchb.
C. basalis Dietr. = *Coreopsis basalis.*

Callipsyche Herb.
C. aurantiaca Bak. = *Eucrosia aurantiaca.*
C. eucrosioides Herb. = *Eucrosia eucrosioides.*
C. mexicana Roem. = *Eucrosia eucrosioides.*

Callirhoë Nutt. POPPY MALLOW. Malvaceae. 8 ann. and perenn. herbs. St. usually erect. Lvs alt., petiolate, lobed or palmately cleft, basal lvs few, suborbicular, upper lvs smaller, lobed. Fls solitary or few in upper axils; epical. 3-parted or 0; cal. 5-lobed; pet. cuneate, truncate at apex; sta. united in a tubular column. US, Mex.

C. alcaeoides (Michx.) A. Gray. Perenn. to 40cm. Lvs strigose-hirsute, lower lvs triangular-cordate, deeply toothed, upper lvs with 5–7 linear lobes. Epical. 0; pet. white or rose-pink. Ill., Missouri, Okl., Alab., Tex., New Mex. Z4.

C. digitata Nutt. FRINGED POPPY MALLOW. Perenn. to 1.2m. Lvs subpeltate. Lobes 5–7 linear, entire or deeply bifid. Epical. 0; pet. rose-red, purple or rose-purple. C US. Z5.

C. involucrata (Torr. & A. Gray) A. Gray. PURPLE POPPY MALLOW. Perenn. to 30cm, procumbent to ascending,. Lvs orbicular, lobes 3–5, narrowly lanceolate, 3–5-toothed. Epical. of 3 seg.; pet. crimson-purple or cherry red. N Dak., Wyom., Missouri, Okl., Tex., New Mex., Utah. Z4.

C. leiocarpa R. Martin. Ann. to 1m. Lf lobes 3–6 entire or toothed. Pet. pale pink to red-purple. Tex. and Okl. Z6.

C. papaver (Cav.) A. Gray. POPPY MALLOW. Perenn. to 1m. Lvs simple or with lobes 3–5 entire or with 1–2 teeth. Epical. seg. 3, pet. violet-red. Okl., Missouri, Ark., Tex., Georgia, Flor. Z6.

C. pedata A. Gray = *C. leiocarpa.*

C. triangulata (Leavenw.) A. Gray CLUSTERED POPPY MALLOW. Perenn. to 1m. Basal lvs mostly triangular, acute, truncate to almost sagittate at base, upper lvs narrower. Epical. lobes 3; pet. deep rose-puple. Alab., Missouri, N Carol., Ind., Ill., Wisc., Neb. Z4.

→*Malva* and *Sida.*

Callisia L. Commelinaceae. 20 perenn. or short-lived herbs. Lvs succulent. Cincinni typically fused in pairs, without conspicuous bracts; fls usually actinomorphic; sep. 3, rarely 2; pet. 3, rarely 2, free; sta. 3–6. SE US, Mex. and trop. Amer.

C. elegans Alexander ex H.E. Moore. STRIPED INCH PLANT. Decumbent succulent herb. Lvs 3.5–10×1.5–3cm, 2-ranked, dark green above with fine silver-white stripes, often flushed purple beneath, velutinous. Infl. 6–15cm, fls white. Winter. Guat. and Hond. Allegedly originating in Mex. Probably a variant of *C. gentlei* Matuda, which has pink fls and unstriped lvs. Z10.

C. fragrans (Lindl.) Woodson. Robust fleshy herb to 1.5m. Lvs to 30×7cm, bright, light green in a loose rosette, producing slender stolons with 2-ranked lvs from lower nodes. Infl. a crowded term. pan.; fls small, white, fragrant. Winter–spring. Mex. 'Melnickoff': lvs pale-striped. Z10.

C. grandiflora J.D. Sm. = *Tripogandra grandiflora.*

C. martensiana (Kunth) C.B. Clarke = *C. multiflora.*

C. micrantha (Torr.) D. Hunt. Resembling *C. navicularis,* but smaller and lacking overwintering dwarf shoots. Tufted or creeping perenn., sometimes trailing. Lvs ± falcate and canaliculate, 1.5–2.5×0.5–0.6cm, succulent, green lined purple beneath. Fls 1–1.5cm diam., bright purple-pink. Summer–autumn. US (SE Tex.). Z9.

C. multiflora (Martens & Gal.) Standl. St. to 80cm, ascending or procumbent, rooting. Lvs 3–9×1–2.5cm, ovate to elliptic-lanceolate, acute or acuminate, rounded at base, pale green, succulent, minutely hairy. Infl. a slender term. pan. to 30cm; fls 6–8mm diam., white, fragrant. Winter. Mex. to Nic. Z10.

C. navicularis (Ortgies) D. Hunt. St. tufted or trailing, succulent, of two types: bulbil-like, (short shoots with overlapping lvs), and stolons with long internodes. Lvs 2–3×1–2cm, lanceolate to broadly ovate, canaliculate, keeled, acute, v. succulent, green above, purple-striate beneath. Fls bright magenta or mauve. Summer–autumn. E & NE Mex. Z10.

C. nizandensis Matuda = *C. tehuantepecana.*

C. repens L. St. slender, creeping, rooting and forming mats. Lvs 1–4×1–2cm, narrowly to broadly ovate, acute, rounded to sub-cordate at base. Infl. spiciform, ascending; pet. 3–5mm, translucent white. Autumn. Tex. and W Indies to Arg. The form of *C. repens* in cult. is possibly a distinct sp. It has small rounded lvs and inconspicuous axill. fls. Its origin is uncertain. It has been confused with *C. cordifolia.* Z9.

C. rosea (Vent.) D. Hunt. St. tufted, erect or ascending, to 40cm, simple or branched. Lvs 5–25×0.1–1.2cm, linear-lanceolate. Paired cincinni term. or term. and axill.; fls 1.5–2.5cm diam. pink. Summer. E US. Z8.

C. tehuantepecana Matuda. Differs from *C. gentlei* and *C. elegans* in the longer and narrower lvs and laxer habit. St. to 80cm, decumbent or erect. Lvs 7–9×1.5–2cm, lanceolate, acuminate, not striate, white-ciliate. Infl. spiciform; fls 1–1.5cm diam., pink. Autumn–winter. S Mex. Z10.

C. warszewicziana (Kunth & Bouché) D. Hunt. Robust bromeliad-like herb; st. stout. Lvs to 30×6.5cm, spirally arranged and densely overlapping, narrowly oblong, acuminate,

succulent, margin often purple. Infl. to 35cm, branched below and sometimes viviparous; pet. 6×6mm, purple-pink. Spring–autumn. S Mex., Guat. Z10.

→*Cuthbertia, Hadrodemas, Phyodina, Setcreasea, Spironema* and *Tradescantia.*

Callistachys Vent.
C. lanceolata Vent. = *Oxylobium lanceolatum.*

Callistemon R. Br. Myrtaceae. BOTTLE-BRUSH BUSH. *c*25 shrubs and trees. Young shoots tinted pink, silky. Lvs narrow, acute or acuminate, often leathery. Fls axill. in bottlebrush-like pseudoterminal spikes, new growth extending beyond flowering zone; sep. 5, decid.; pet. 5, small; sta. free, numerous, fil. colourful, longer than pet. Capsules woody globose to urn-shaped persisting on br. Summer. Aus. Z9 unless stated.

C. acuminatus Cheel. Medium to tall shrub. Lvs 7–11×1–2cm, broad-lanceolate, with v. prominent veins. Spikes 6–10×5–5.5cm; fil. dark crimson, anth. gold.

C. brachyandrus Lindl. PRICKLY BOTTLEBRUSH. Dense, small to tall shrub. Lvs to 4cm, terete or channelled above, rigid, pungent. Spikes to 4×2cm, fil. orange-red, anth. gold.

C. citrinus (Curtis) Skeels. CRIMSON BOTTLEBRUSH. Medium shrub to small tree. Br. sometimes arched or pendulous. Lvs to 10×2cm, tapering, pointed, lemon-scented if crushed. Spikes to 12×6cm; fil. bright crimson, rarely white, anth. dark. 'Burning Bush': compact; lvs dark green; fls carmine red. 'Hannah Ray': semi-weeping; fls bright orange-red. 'Splendens' (var. *splendens* Stapf): lvs linear-lanceolate; spikes dense, cylindrical; fil. 5cm, carmine red. Z8.

C. comboynensis Cheel. CLIFF BOTTLEBRUSH. Small to medium erect or straggly bush. Lvs 5–9×1–1.5cm, pale green, lanceolate, often twisted or recurved. Spikes 4–6×3–5cm; fil. rich red to crimson-purple or occas. pink.

C. lanceolatus DC. = *C. citrinus.*

C. linearifolius DC. Spreading, open, medium shrub. Lvs to 14×1cm, tapering, concave to flat, pungent, margins wavy and thickened. Spikes 6–12×5–6cm; fil. bright red, anth. yellow.

C. linearis DC. NARROW-LEAVED BOTTLEBRUSH. Dense to open, medium shrub. Lvs to 12×0.5cm, concave or flat, ending in a short point, rigid, sometimes twisted or curved. Spikes to *c*12×6cm; fil. dull red, anth. gold. Z8.

C. lophanthus Sweet. CRESTED CALLISTEMON. Medium to tall shrub. Bark papery. Lvs *c*5×1cm, lanceolate, pungent, pale green sometimes glaucous. Spikes *c*10×5cm; cream to yellow.

C. macropunctatus (Dum.-Cours.) Court. SCARLET BOTTLEBRUSH. Open to dense shrub. Lvs 3–8×0.5cm, tapering at both ends, pungent, rough with prominent oil glands, mid-rib and margins thickened. Spikes to 10×5cm; fil. rose red, anth. gold.

C. pachyphyllus Cheel. WALLUM BOTTLEBRUSH. Small, erect, straggly shrub. Lvs 3–6.5×0.3–1.5cm, oblanceolate, dull-green, held upwards, blunt. Spikes 6–10×4–6cm; fil. bright red.

C. pallidus (Bonpl.) DC. LEMON BOTTLEBRUSH. Dense medium to tall shrub. Br. slender to pendulous. Lvs 5–10×0.5–2cm, tapering, grey-green to green. Spikes to 10×5cm; fil. cream to green-yellow, anth. yellow.

C. paludosus F. Muell. RIVER BOTTLEBRUSH. Medium shrub to small tree. Br. slender, often pendulous. Lvs 3–10×0.6–0.8cm, tapering to both ends, ending in a fine point. Spikes 6–8×2–3cm; pet. 0.3cm, green; sta. cream or pink, anth. yellow.

C. phoeniceus Lindl. LESSER BOTTLEBRUSH. Medium shrub. Br. sometimes pendulous. Lvs 4–10×0.5–1cm, rigid, sometimes twisted, grey-green. Spikes to 12×*c*5cm; fil. bright rich red, anth. usually dark.

C. pinifolius DC. Low and spreading, or upright shrub. Lvs to 10cm, linear, channelled above, often terete, pungent. Spikes to 8×4cm; fil. yellow, green or dull red, anth. yellow. 'Viridis': fls bright green.

C. pityoides F. Muell. = *C. sieberi.*

C. rigidus R. Br. STIFF BOTTLEBRUSH. Small to medium shrub. Lvs to 1.5×0.6cm, linear-lanceolate, dull green, veins forming ridged margins. Spikes 2–5×1–2.5cm; fil. deep red.

C. salignus (Sm.) DC. PINK TIPS; WILLOW BOTTLEBRUSH; WHITE BOTTLEBRUSH. Tall shrub to medium tree. Bark white, papery. Lvs 6–10×0.2–0.4cm, narrow-lanceolate. Spikes 3–5×2–3.5cm, fil. green or white but also pink, red or mauve. Z8.

C. sieberi DC. ALPINE BOTTLEBRUSH. Erect to spreading, dwarf to tall shrub. Lvs 1.5–4×0.2–0.5cm, pungent, dense. Spikes 2–15×2–3cm; fil. cream to yellow. Z7.

C. speciosus (Sims) DC. ALBANY BOTTLEBRUSH. Erect, stiff, medium shrub. Br. upright. Lvs to 15×2cm, narrowed at base, rigid, spreading, pungent, veins prominent. Spikes dense to 15×7.5cm; fil. deep red (rarely white), anth. gold.

C. subulatus Cheel. Arching shrub to 1.5m, similar to *C. linearis.*

Lvs narrowly oblong, pungent, silky then bright green. Spikes dense, fil. crimson. Z8.

C. viminalis (Sol. ex Gaertn.) G. Don ex Loud. WEEPING BOTTLE-BRUSH. Small shrub to a small bushy tree. Br. arching or weeping. Lvs 2–6.5×0.5–1cm, lanceolate. Spikes 5–20×3–6cm, fil. bright red. 'Red Cascade': br. pendulous; fls rose-red.

C. viridiflorus (Sims) Sweet. GREEN BOTTLEBRUSH. Upright to spreading, small to medium shrub. Br. short. Lvs c3×1cm, tapering, pungent, arranged densely. Spikes dense c8×4cm; fil. yellow-green, anth. yellow.

C. cvs. 'Captain Cook': low, spreading; fls large, deep crimson. 'Little John': v. small; fls deep red. 'Mauve Mist': compact; fls mauve. 'Red Cluster': compact; fls deep scarlet.

Callistephus Cass. Compositae. 1 erect, herbaceous ann., to 80cm. Lvs to 8cm, ovate or triangular-ovate, coarsely toothed. Cap. to 12cm diam., radiate, term., solitary; ray flts, white to pale mauve to violet; disc flts yellow, often replaced by ray flts. China.

C. chinensis (L.) Nees. CHINA ASTER. Seed races range from single to double, anemone-centred and quilled in form; each mixture has a wide selection of vivid colours; singles include the 60cm lavender to salmon Single Rainbow Hybrids; doubles include the dwarf Pot'n'Patio mixtures, the tall (to 80cm) Perfection Mixture, the compact Pinnochio Mixed and the large-fld Contraster Mixed; anemone-centred mixtures include the robust, bushy 'Milady Mixed'; and the large-fld Operetta Mixed; quilled or 'ostrich feather' mixtures include Crego Mixture (to 60cm) and the neat-fld Burpee's Pompon Mixed; dwarfs include the Burpee Ribbon Series and Burpee's Dwarf Border Mixed.
→*Aster.*

CALLITRICHACEAE Link. See *Callitriche.*

Callitriche L. WATER STARWORT. Callitrichaceae. 25 feathery aquatic or sometimes terrestrial herbs. St. v. slender. Lvs opposite, often forming floating rosettes, linear or spathulate to suborbicular. Fls solitary, axill., minute; perianth 0. Amer., Eur., Asia.

C. autumnalis L. = C. hermaphroditica.

C. hermaphroditica L. St. to 50cm, submerged. Lvs to 30×1mm, lanceolate to linear, subtruncate, entire, clasping at base. N Amer., Eur. Z6.

C. heterophylla Pursh. St. to 30cm, floating or submerged. Submerged lvs to 10mm, filiform or linear, floating lvs spathulate, retuse or rounded; petioles winged. N & C Amer. Z4.

C. intermedia Hoffm. St. to 80cm. Submerged lvs to 25×1mm, linear, often deeply emarginate, floating lvs to 25×5mm, narrowly spathulate to narrowly elliptic. Eur., Greenland. Z3.

C. stagnalis Scop. St. to 60cm. Submerged lvs elliptic to spathulate, slightly emarginate, floating lvs forming a rosette, elliptic to orbicular, rounded or slightly emarginate. S Eur., N Afr. Z8.

Callitris Vent. CYPRESS-PINE. Cupressaceae. 17 everg. coniferous trees or shrubs. Bark tough, furrowed. Br. spreading or erect, branchlets slender, angular. Juvenile lvs needle-like, in decussate whorls of 4; adult lvs scale-like, in decussate whorls of 3, closely adpressed and decurrent along st. Cones term. on short shoots, solitary or clustered, globose to ovoid-conic, dark brown to grey; scales 6, unequally sized in 2 decussate whorls of 3 (4), thick, woody. Aus., New Caledonia.

C. arenosa Dunn = C. columellaris.

C. baileyi C.T. White. To 10m, crown slender. Lvs 2–5mm, acutely keeled, bright green. Cones solitary, opening and falling soon after maturity, globose, 10–13mm. SE Queensld, NE NSW. Z10.

C. calcarata (A. Cunn. ex Mirb.) Muell. = C. endlicheri.

C. canescens (Parl.) S.F. Blake. To 9m; branchlets slender. Lvs 2–4mm, grey-green, dors. surface rounded. Cones 15–20mm, solitary or grouped, remaining closed after maturity, subglobose, grey-brown. SW W Aus. Z10.

C. columellaris F. Muell. To 25m; br. spreading to fastigiate. Lvs 1–3mm, green, occas. glaucous, dors. surface rounded. Cones solitary, opening and falling soon after maturity, depressed-globose, 15–20mm diam. SE Queensld, NE NSW, coastal. Z10.

C. drummondii (Parl.) Muell. Tree to 15m or shrub. Lvs mostly 3–4mm, green, dors. surface acutely keeled. Cones solitary or grouped, remaining closed after maturity, globose, 12–15mm. S coastal W Aus. Z10.

C. endlicheri (Parl.) Bail. RED CYPRESS-PINE; BLACK CYPRESS-PINE. Tree to 25m, br. spreading. Lvs 2–4mm, bluntly keeled, green or glaucous. Cones solitary or clustered, globose, 15–20mm. SE Queensld to E Vict. Z9.

C. glauca R. Br. ex Bak. & H.G. Sm. = C. glaucophylla.

C. glaucophylla Thomps. & Johnson. WHITE CYPRESS-PINE. Small tree or shrub, spreading to fastigiate. Lvs 1–3mm, glaucous blue- or grey-green, dors. surface rounded. Cones solitary, opening and falling soon after maturity, globose, 15–25mm, glaucous. S Aus., mostly NSW. Hybridizes naturally with C. preissii and C. verrucosa. Z9.

C. hugelii auct. = C. glaucophylla.

C. intratropica Bak. & H.G. Sm. Similar to C. columellaris, but lvs more glaucous. Trop. N Aus. Z10.

C. macleayana (Muell.) Muell. STRINGY-BARK; PORT MACQUARIE CYPRESS-PINE. Tree to 20m, rarely 45m, crown spreading, bark fibrous. Lvs mixed juvenile and adult; juvenile lvs to 12mm, glaucous; adult lvs 2–3mm, green, acutely keeled. Cones solitary, remaining closed after maturity, ovoid to conic, acuminate, often distorted, 20–30mm. NE NSW, extreme SE Queensld. Z10.

C. monticola Gdn. STEELHEAD. Erect spreading shrub to 2.5m. Lvs 2–4mm, bluntly keeled, glaucous grey-green. Cones solitary or grouped remaining closed after maturity, subglobose, 15–25mm diam. NE NSW, SE Queensld. Z10.

C. morrisonii Bak. = C. canescens.

C. muelleri (Parl.) Muell. ILLAWARA CYPRESS-PINE. Tree or shrub to 15m, fastigiate. Juvenile lvs occas. retained; adult lvs 4–10mm, bluntly keeled, grey-green. Cones solitary or grouped, remaining closed after maturity, globose, 25–30mm diam., glossy. NSW. Z10.

C. neocaledonica Dümmer To 8m, crown broad. Lvs 3–4mm, acutely keeled. Cones 10mm. New Caledonia. Z10.

C. oblonga Rich. TASMANIAN CYPRESS-PINE. Tree or shrub to 8m, br. dense, erect. Lvs 4–5mm, bluntly keeled, green. Cones solitary or grouped, remaining closed after maturity, ovoid-conic, 15–25×12–22mm. Tasm. Z9.

C. preissii Miq. ROTTNEST ISLAND CYPRESS-PINE. Tree or shrub to 10m. Lvs 2–4mm, not keeled, green, often glaucous. Cones solitary or grouped, remaining closed after maturity, depressed-globose, 20–30mm diam., glaucous at base. W Aus., scattered. ssp. **murrayensis** Gdn. Cones longer than broad. NSW to S Aus. Z10.

C. preissii ssp. **verrucosa** (A. Cunn. ex Endl.) Garden = C. verrucosa.

C. quadrivalvis Vent. = Tetraclinis articulata.

C. rhomboidea R. Br. ex Rich. OYSTER BAY CYPRESS-PINE. Tree or shrub to 15m, spreading to fastigiate. Lvs 2–3mm, bluntly keeled, glaucous grey-green. Cones solitary or grouped, remaining closed after maturity, angular, depressed-globose, 13–18×18–25mm. SE Queensld to Tasm. & S Aus. Z9.

C. roei (Endl.) Muell. Small tree, br. spreading. Lvs 3–5mm, glaucous grey-green, acutely keeled. Cones solitary or grouped, remaining closed after maturity, depressed-globose, 15–20mm diam. SW W Aus. Z10.

C. sulcata (Parl.) Schltr. Tree. Lvs 4–6mm, acutely keeled. Cones solitary, opening and falling soon after maturity, ovoid to depressed-globose, often distorted, 12–18mm. New Caledonia. Z10.

C. sulcata var. **alpina** Compton = C. neocaledonica.

C. tasmanica (Benth.) Bak. & H.G. Sm. = C. rhomboidea.

C. verrucosa (Cunn. ex Endl.) Muell. MALLEE CYPRESS-PINE. Usually a shrub. Lvs 2–4mm, not keeled, glaucous. Cones solitary or grouped, remaining closed after maturity, depressed-globose, 15–25mm. S W Aus. to NSW. Z10.
→*Frenela.*

Callitropsis Compton = Neocallitropsis.

Callose-leaved Fig Ficus callosa.

Calluna Salisb. LING; SCOTS HEATHER. Ericaceae. 1 everg. shrub to 60cm, differing from Erica in cor. concealed by pink cal. Lvs 1–2mm, scale-like, sessile, tightly adpressed to st. Fls crowded in rac.; cal. pink, to 4mm, 4-lobed; stigma exserted. Late summer-autumn. W N Amer., Azores, N & W Eur. to Sib. Z4.

C. vulgaris (L.) Hull. Over 1000 cvs, mostly erect in habit, some dense and narrow ('Darkness', 'Rigida'), other sparser and more freely growing ('Gold Haze', 'Joan Sparkes', 'October White' and 'Serlei' are distinguished by esp. vigorous growth. Height ranges from the cushion-like 'Foxii' and 'Foxii Nana' (7cm) and the prostrate 'Alba Aurea' (10cm) to strong upright growers to 75cm ('Mair's Variety', 'Hammondii') and to 1m ('Alportii'). Some slow-growers, esp. 'Golden Carpet', others v. fast-growing ('Hammondii', 'Hirsuta Typica'). Some prostrate or dwarf with procumbent br. ('Alba Aurea', 'Hibernica', 'Prostrate Orange') and with creeping horizontal br. ('Mrs Roland Gray'), to the more upright cushion-or hummock-forming ('Elkstone White', 'Foxii') and dwarf conifer-like plants ('Gnome', 'Humpty Dumpty'). Of upright growers with simple fls, lvs range through green, yellow, bronze and white-variegated. Green-lvd cvs with fls lilac ('Hiemalis'), pink/carmine ('Alportii', 'Darkness'), or white ('August Beauty', 'October White'). Foliage sunrise yellow ('Gold Haze') or bronze red ('Sunset', 'Spring Torch'); 'Blazeaway' has excellent bright red foliage in winter; others with lvs variegated white or grey-woolly ('Argentea', 'Wilver Queen'). Double-fld forms include the popular 'H.E. Beale' (long infl. of dense pink fls) and 'Alba Plena' (fls dense, snow-white).

Calocapnos Spach.
C. nobilis Spach = *Corydalis nobilis*.

Calocedrus Kurz. INCENSE CEDAR. Cupressaceae. 3, everg. conifers, usually broadly conical and spreading in habitat, but often columnar-fastigiate in cult. Branchlets in 2 flattened rows. Lvs 4-ranked in false whorls of decussate pairs, adnate to st. except at apex, scale-like, tough. Cones with 6, rarely 8 scales in decussate pairs, normally a minute 1–4mm sterile basal pair, a large fertile pair, as long as the whole cone, and a term. fused pair forming a plate between the fertile pair. W N Amer., E Asia.

C. decurrens (Torr.) Florin. INCENSE CEDAR. To 45m. Bark maroon flecked grey, fissured, flaking in long scales. Lvs 4–10mm, acute, glossy green; facial lvs triangular pointed; lateral lvs incurved. Cones oblong, light brown to red-brown, to 2.5cm; scales 6 rarely 8. W US. Most cult. trees are of columnar/fastigiate habit and could be styled 'Columnaris' ('Fastigiata'). 'Aureovariegata': foliage with scattered large pale yellow blotches. 'Compacta': habit globose to columnar, compact, densely branched. 'Depressa': dense, globose dwarf; lvs bronze in winter. 'Glauca': lvs glaucous with conspicuous blue tint. 'Intricata' ('Nana'): dense, upright, compact dwarf; br. increasingly tortuous, tinted brown in winter. 'Riet': globose dwarf to 75×75cm. Z7.

C. formosana (Florin) Florin. To 20m. Bark maroon to rusty-red, smooth. Lvs similar to *C. macrolepis* but less white beneath. Cones oblong, to 1.5cm; scales 6. Taiwan. Z9.

C. macrolepis Kurz. To 30m. Dark light grey-scaly. Lvs larger and flatter than *C. decurrens*, to 1cm, bright green above, blue-white beneath, lateral lvs often curved, acute, facial lvs inverted deltoid. Cones 8–13mm, orange bloomed violet, ellipsoid; scales 6–8. SW China. Z9.

C. macrolepis var. *formosana* (Florin) Cheng & L.K. Fu = *C. formosana*.
→*Libocedrus*.

Calocephalus R. Br. Compositae. 18 ann. or perenn. herbs or small shrubs, usually white-woolly. Lvs entire. Cap. discoid, numerous, clustered into term., globular, compound infl. Temp. Aus. Z9.

C. brownii (Cass.) F. Muell. Shrub to 40cm. St. much-branched, slender, br. woolly, white, intricate. Lvs to 5cm, linear-subulate, erect, closely adpressed. Cap. in spherical clusters to 12mm diam., white. Coastal temp. Aus.

C. chrysanthus Schldl. = *Craspedia chrysantha*.

C. citreus Less. Tufted perenn. herb, to 60cm. St. wiry and erect. Lvs to 8cm, narrowly linear. Cap. in cylindrical-ovoid clusters, to 14mm diam., yellow. Temp. Aus.

Calochortus Pursh. MARIPOSA LILY; SEGO LILY; GLOBE TULIP; STAR TULIP; BUTTERFLY TULIP; MARIPOSA TULIP; FAIRY LANTERN; CAT'S EAR. Liliaceae (Calochortaceae). 60 bulbous, perenn. herbs. Lvs usually linear, basal and cauline. Fls erect or nodding, showy, in cymes or subumbels; sep. 3, lanceolate; pet. 3, obovate to oblanceolate, often bearded, usually with a somewhat flattened gland or depression near the base. Americas. Z6.

C. albus Benth. Fls nodding, globose to globose-campanulate; pet. 1.5–3cm, white with deep red-brown spot, elliptic-obovate, delicately fringed, sparsely pubesc. above gland; gland traversed by about 5 deeply fringed membranes. W US. var. *rubellus* Greene. Fls tinged rose. S Calif.

C. albus var. *amoenus* (Greene) Purdy & Bail. = *C. amoenus*.

C. amabilis Purdy. Fls nodding, globose or globose-campanulate; pet. 1.5–2cm, deep yellow, triangular in outline, clawed, rounded at apex, densely fringed ± glab. near gland, gland deeply depressed, bounded by a transverse line of hairs. W US.

C. amoenus Greene. Fls nodding to erect, narrow-campanulate to globose-campanulate, deep rose-pink or purple; pet. to 1cm; gland broad, arched, slightly depressed, extending across base of pet. W US.

C. barbatus (HBK) Painter. Fls usually 2, campanulate, drooping; pet. 1–2cm, yellow, or tinged purple, obovate, obtuse, or acuminate, entire or fringed, beared with purple hairs; gland circular, naked, encircled by small hairs. Mex.

C. benthamii Bak. = *C. monophyllus*.

C. citrinus auctt. = *C. luteus*.

C. citrinus Bak. = *C. weedii*.

C. clavatus Wats. Fls campanulate to cup-shaped, subumbellate; pet. 3.5–5cm, broadly obovate, yellow with a red-brown line above gland and club-shaped hairs below; gland circular, depressed, covered with short, branched processes, surrounded by laciniate scales. S Carol.

C. coeruleus (Kellogg) Wats. Differs from *C. tolmiei* in pet. blue tinged, broadly obovate, 8–12mm. W US.

C. coeruleus var. *maweanus* (Bak.) Jeps. = *C. tolmiei*.

C. cyaneus Nels. = *C. macrocarpus*.

C. elegans Pursh. Fls open-campanulate, green-white, tinged purple at base above the depressed gland; gland membrane deeply fringed. W US.

C. elegans Hook. f. non Pursh = *C. tolmiei*.

C. flavus Schult. = *C. barbatus*.

C. gunnisonii Wats. Fls erect, campanulate, subumbellate; pet. 3–4cm, white to purple, tinged green within, with a purple stripe above the gland, obovate, rounded, bearded near gland, with dense, gland., branched hairs; gland transverse, oblong, arched above, covered with branched processes. US (Dak., Mont., S to New Mex.).

C. kennedyi Porter. Fls campanulate, erect, in umbels; pet. vermilion to orange, often with brown-purple spot at base, 2.5–5cm, obovate, usually rounded above; gland circular, densely hairy, surrounded by laciniate scales. W US.

C. lilacinus Kellogg = *C. uniflorus*.

C. lobbii Purdy. Fls broadly campanulate, ± erect; sep. with purple spot; pet. white to pale yellow sometimes tinted lilac, fringed with yellow hairs. W US.

C. luteus Douglas ex Lindl. Fls open-campanulate, erect; pet. dark yellow, striped red-brown, occas. with median brown spot; gland transverse, ± crescent-shaped, covered with short, thick processes. W US.

C. luteus var. *citrinus* Wats. = *C. superbus*.

C. luteus var. *octatus* Purdy & Bail. = *C. superbus*.

C. luteus var. *weedii* (Wood) Bak. = *C. weedii*.

C. macrocarpus Douglas. Fls large, open-campanulate, erect, in an umbel; pet. 3.5–6cm, purple, acuminate, pubesc. above gland, with a green stripe; gland sagittate, bound by a fringed membrane covered with slender processes. W US.

C. maweanus Bak. = *C. tolmiei*.

C. monophyllus (Lindl.) Lem. Fls usually erect, spreading-campanulate; pet. obovate, yellow, pubesc. above gland, sparsely fringed; gland naked, spreading across base of pet., with a deeply fringed papillose membrane below and short cilia above. W US.

C. nudus Wats. Fls 1–6, open-campanulate, erect; pet. 1.5–2cm, white or pale lavender, erose-denticulate, glab. except for v. few hairs near gland; gland naked, transverse, shallowly arched above, bounded below by a fringed membrane. W US.

C. pulchellus Benth. Differs from *C. amabilis* in its sep. which do not usually exceed pet., pet. 2.5–3.5cm, largely pubesc. within and lighter yellow, margin more deeply but less densely fringed. W US.

C. pulchellus var. *amabilis* (Purdy) Jeps. = *C. amabilis*.

C. splendens Benth. Fls 1–4, erect, campanulate, pale pink, in cymes of 1–4; pet. 2.5–5cm, pale pink, rounded with irregular, fine teeth above, sparsely pubesc. from above gland to about the middle; gland small, circular, at base of pet., naked or covered with thick, branched processes. W US.

C. subalpinus Piper = *C. lobbii*.

C. superbus How. Close to *C. venustus* differing in sep. not curled under at tip. Fls campanulate; pet. white, cream, or yellow, steaked purple at base, with median brown or maroon spot surrounded with yellow, rounded to acute, slightly hairy near the gland; gland ± inverted V-shaped. W US.

C. tolmiei Hook. & Arn. Fls open-campanulate, erect or spreading, borne in umbels; pet. white or cream, occas. tinged rose or purple, 1–2.5cm, obovate, pubesc., fringed; gland transverse, arched above, naked, bounded below by a toothed to fringed membrane and above by a band of thick papillose processes. W US.

C. uniflorus Hook. & Arn. Fls open-campanulate, erect, long-stalked in loose umbels; pet. 1.5–3cm, pale lilac, rounded and irregularly toothed above, sparsely pubesc. above gland; gland naked, acute below, truncate above, with a fringed membrane below and band of slender processes above. W US.

C. venustus Benth. Fls campanulate, erect, in an umbel; pet. 2–4.5cm, white to yellow, purple or dark red, obovate, rounded above, sparsely pubesc. below, with a median dark red spot; gland circular to diamond-shaped, covered with hair-like appendages. W US.

C. venustus var. *vestae* (Purdy) Wils. = *C. vestae*.

C. vestae Purdy Close to *C. venustus*. Fls campanulate; pet. white to tinged purple, streaked with red to purple near base, usually with a central brown spot, bordered in pale yellow; gland transverse, doubly crescent-shaped, covered with thick, short processes. Calif.

C. weedii Wood. Fls 2, open-campanulate, erect; pet. 2.5–3cm, deep yellow, with purple dots or often margins, ciliate, broadly obovate, rounded to acute, covered with fine yellow hairs; gland circular, ± naked, encircled by dense hairs, sometimes united below in a continuous membrane. W US, Mex.

Calodendrum Thunb. CAPE CHESTNUT. Rutaceae. 1 everg. tree, 10–15m. Trunk smooth, grey, crown spreading, young br. densely tomentose. Lvs 6–13cm, petiolate, elliptic to elliptic-ovate, apex acute to rounded, becoming glab., shiny. Pan. term. to 15cm; sep. 3–5mm, 5, ovate, pet. 3–4cm, 5, overlapping, white, pink or mauve, narrowly oblanceolate straight or recurved, dotted with purple glands, tomentose within; sta. 5, opposite sep. staminodes 5, opposite pet. Fr. a 5-lobed, rugose capsule 3–4cm diam. Coastal S Afr. Z9.

C. capense (L. f.) Thunb.

Calomeria Vent. Compositae. 14 ann. to perenn. herbs. Lvs simple, entire, mostly amplexicaul. Cap. discoid, numerous, in a diffuse, term., pyramidal pan. Afr., Madag., S Aus. Z9.

C. amaranthoides Vent. INCENSE PLANT; PLUME BUSH. Robust, erect, aromatic bienn. or perenn., to 2m+, glab. to glandular-pubesc. Lvs to 25cm, ovate-lanceolate to oblong. Cap. small, red-brown or pink, v. many in a large, drooping pan. Aus. (Vict., NSW).
→*Humea.*

Calonyction Choisy.
C. aculeatum (L.) House = *Ipomoea alba.*

Calophaca Fisch. ex DC. Leguminosae (Papilionoideae). 5 herbs or small decid. shrubs. Lvs imparipinnate. Fls pea-like solitary or in axill. rac. Sometimes grafted as a weeping standard on stocks of *Laburnum* or *Caragana.* Russia to China. Z6.

C. crassicaulis (Bak.) Komar. Subshrub. Branchlets erect, stout, covered in lf remains. Lfts 0.4–0.6cm, 21–25, linear, pubesc. Fls 2cm, solitary, yellow to red. Himal. to W China.

C. cuneata (Benth.) Komar. = *Chesneya cuneata.*

C. grandiflora Reg. Semi-prostrate shrub. Lfts 2.5cm, 17–25, ovate, glabrescent. Fls 2.5–3cm, yellow, in 10–16-fld, erect, downy rac. to 20cm. Summer. Turkestan.

C. wolgarica (L. f.) Fisch. Prostrate shrub. Branchlets glandular-pubesc. when young. Lfts 0.3–1.5cm, 11–17, ovate to orbicular, pubesc. beneath. Fls 2–2.5cm, vivid yellow, in 4–9-fld rac. to 12.5cm. Summer. S & E Ukraine.

Calophyllum L. Guttiferae. 187 everg. trees or shrubs. Lvs entire, coriaceous with many parallel lat. veins. Fls small in pan. or rac.; cor. and cal. seg. 4–12, in 2–3 whorls, not distinct; sta. many. Fr. a 1-seeded yellow to brown drupe. Trop. Z10.

C. brasiliense Cambess. MARIA; SANTA MARIA. Tree to 30m. Lvs to 12cm, oblong to elliptic, obtuse to emarginate. Rac. axill.; fls white, 1.5cm across, fragrant. Fr. 2.5cm diam. Carib., C Amer., N S Amer.

C. calaba L. Tree to 25–40m. Lvs elliptic to oblong-elliptic, obtuse or emarginate, 4–30cm. Rac. axill.; fls sweetly fragrant, to 1.6cm diam. white. Fr. 2–2.5cm diam. Winter. Carib.

C. inophyllum L. ALEXANDRIAN LAUREL; INDIAN LAUREL; LAURELWOOD. Tree to 25 (35)m. Lvs to 20cm, broadly elliptic-oblong. Rac. axillary, to 20cm; fls white, to 2cm across, v. fragrant. Fr. to 3.5cm diam. Coastal S India to Malaysia.

Calopogon R. Br. Orchidaceae. 4 terrestrial cormous orchids. Lvs usually solitary basal, grass-like. Rac. term., lax; sep. and pet. free, spreading; lip obscurely trilobed, lat. lobes minute, midlobe dilated toward papillose apex centre with beard-like hairs; column broadly winged. N Amer. to W Indies. Z3.

C. barbatum (Walter) Ames. Scape to 45cm; infl. subcapitate; fls to 3.5cm diam., usually rose-pink, sometimes white; dors. sep. linear-oblong to elliptic-oblong, lat. sep. obliquely ovate, pet. short-clawed, base rounded, apex obtuse; lip mid-lobe broadly obovate to suborbicular, rounded, hairs on centre of disc deep rust-red, apical papillae pale lavender. SE US.

C. pulchellum (Salisb.) R. Br. = *C. tuberosum.*

C. tuberosum BSP. Scape to 46cm infl. few to many-fld; to 5cm diam. rose to magenta, sometimes white; dors. sep. oblong to elliptic-oblong, lat. sep. ovate to ovate-lanceolate; pet. short-clawed, oblong-pandurate to oblong-elliptic, obtuse or rounded; lip obreniform to cuneate-flabellate, retuse or rounded, disc bearded. Canada, NE US, Cuba, Bahamas.

Caloscordum Herb. Liliaceae (Alliaceae). 1 bulbous perenn. herb, resembling *Allium* but lacking typical pungent odour

when bruised and with sta. fil. fused to pet. Lvs linear, shorter than scape, pale green, channelled above. Scape 10–25cm; fls 10–20, stellate, in a loose umbel; pedicels long, often upturned; tep. reflexed, 6–8mm, bright pink with darker midrib, basal third united. N China, SE Sib. Z7.

C. neriniflorum Herb.
→*Allium* and *Nothoscordum.*

Calostemma R. Br. Amaryllidaceae. 3 bulbous perenn. herbs, 15–50cm. Lvs 4–8mm wide, basal, linear-lorate. Umbels scapose; fls funnel-shaped, asymmetric; tep. 6, to 2.5cm; sta. erect, fil. dilated and united at base to form a tubular toothed corona. Aus. Z9.

C. luteum Sims. AUSTRALIAN DAFFODIL. Fls bright yellow. Spring. S Aus., Queensld, NSW.

C. purpureum R. Br. GARLAND LILY. Fls purple or pink. S Aus., NSW.

Calothamnus Labill. Myrtaceae. c25 shrubs differing from *Callistemon* in fls and fr. often immersed in bark of branchlet, infl. ± 1-sided with sta. in bundles, not free. W Aus. Z9.

C. asper Turcz. ROUGH NET-BUSH. Much-branched medium shrub. Lvs to 2.5cm, linear, flat, blunt or pointed, rigid. Fls in short dense clusters; staminal bundles 4, to 2.5cm, fil. many, red, anth. gold.

C. gilesii F. Muell. GILES NET-BUSH. Upright-branched, open, medium shrub. Lvs to 20cm, terete, pungent, gland. Fls in clusters, usually 2–3; staminal bundles 5, bright red with golden anth.

C. homalophyllus F. Muell. MURCHISON CLAW-FLOWER. Much-branched medium shrub. Lvs to 5cm, flat, thick, tapering to base, blunt-tipped. Fls in one-sided clusters; staminal bundles 4, 2.5cm+, rich red, anth. gold, rarely white to yellow.

C. lehmannii Schauer. Dwarf, branching shrub. Lvs c2.5cm, terete, pungent, crowded. Fls in one-sided clusters to c3cm; staminal bundles 4, c0.8cm, one with 5–7 fil., one with 3–5, two others as a single fil., dark red.

C. longissimus F. Muell. Dwarf to small spreading shrub. Br. corky. Lvs to 30cm, narrow, terete, curving, rigid, gland. Fls in one-sided clusters to 5cm; staminal bundles 4, unequal, upper two about 3cm, broad, flat with many fil., lower two narrow, undivided dark red.

C. pinifolius F. Muell. DENSE CLAW-FLOWER. Upright small to medium shrub. Br. thick, sometimes hairy or corky. Lvs to c3cm, crowded, terete, rigid, pungent. Spikes one-sided to c10cm; staminal bundles 4, to 3cm+, deep red.

C. quadrifidus R. Br. COMMON NET-BUSH. Upright to spreading medium shrub. Lvs to 3cm, linear, terete, or flattened, pointed or blunt, gland., glab. or hairy. Fls in one-sided spikes or surrounding st. to 20cm; staminal bundles 4, c2.5cm, rich red with golden anth.

C. rupestris Schauer. CLIFF NET-BUSH. Bushy small to medium shrub. Br. thick. Lvs to c5cm, linear, terete, pungent. Clusters or spikes one-sided; staminal bundles 4, to 2.5cm, deep pink to red.

C. sanguineus Labill. BLOOD-RED NET-BUSH. Dwarf to medium shrub. Lvs to 4cm, linear, terete, pungent. Clusters or spikes one-sided; staminal bundles 4, not equal, upper 2 united for most of their length, c2.5cm, lower two not united and shorter, rich red, anth. yellow.

C. validus S. Moore. BARRENS CLAW-FLOWER. Upright to rounded medium shrub. Br. erect, many. Lvs to 4cm, terete, incurved, rigid, slightly pungent. Spikes or clusters one-sided to 5cm; staminal bundles 4, 3–4cm, rich red with gold anth.

C. villosus R. Br. SILKY NET-BUSH; WOOLLY NET-BUSH. Upright to spreading small to medium shrub. Br. hairy. Lvs to c2.5cm, linear, terete, incurved, pungent, covered with scattered hairs. Spikes one-sided to spikes to c10cm; staminal bundles 5, bright red with gold anth.

Calotis R. Br. Compositae. 22 ann. to perenn. herbs. Cap. radiate, term.; ray flts in 1 series; disc flts tubular. S & E Aus., NZ. Z9.

C. cuneifolia R. Br. To 30cm. Lvs cuneate, deeply cut, apex toothed. Flts blue. Mid- to late summer. Aus.

C. scabiosifolia Sonder ex F. Muell. Perenn., to 50cm, erect to ascending, sometimes branched. Basal lvs to 20cm, oblong, pinnatifid, petiolate; st. lvs to 5cm, ovate-lanceolate, entire, sessile. Ray flts white to pale blue; disc flts yellow. E Aus.

Calpurnia E. Mey. Leguminosae (Papilionoideae). 6 small trees or shrubs. Lvs imparipinnate. Fls pea-like in lax or crowded rac. Afr., India. Z9.

C. aurea (Ait.) Benth. EAST AFRICAN LABURNUM; NATAL LABURNUM. 2–10m. Br. spindly. Lvs 6–24cm, initially downy; lfts 2.5–4cm, apex obtuse and fine-tipped, base rounded to cuneate, deep green above, glabrescent beneath. Fls vivid yellow, 8–30 in axill. rac. 7–24cm, with thickly downy or bristly axes; standard 9–20mm. Winter. S India, Afr., introd. warm US. ssp. *sylvatica* (Burchell) Brummitt. Lvs and ovary glab. E Cape.

C. floribunda Harv. Similar to *C. glabrata* but thickly pubesc. in most parts. S Afr.

C. glabrata Brummitt. Shrub or small tree, ± glab. Lvs 6–12cm; lfts 1–3cm, in 7–13 pairs, elliptic-oblong, base cuneate, apex blunt or emarginate. Fls golden yellow in rac. 5–12cm; standard 6–12mm. S Afr.

C. lasiogyne E. Mey. = *C. aurea*.

C. sylvatica (Burchell) E. Mey. = *C. aurea* ssp. *sylvatica*.

C. villosa Harv. Differs from *C. aurea* in twigs, lf stalks and peduncles villous. Lvs 5–7.5cm; lfts 0.7–1.5cm, 7–13, elliptic, ± coriaceous, sericeous beneath. Rac. few-fld, cal. pubesc., not glab. S Afr.

Caltha L. Ranunculaceae. 10 perenn. herbs. Lvs simple, base often cordate; petiolate. Fls in corymbose cymes, white or yellow; cal. of 5 or more petaloid sep.; pet. 0; sta. numerous. Temp. regions.

C. alpestris Schott = *C. palustris*.

C. appendiculata Pers. To 8cm. Lvs 6–9cm, ovate to oblong, entire or 3-fld, base cuneate, margins undulate or crenate; petiole to 2cm. Fls white, short-stalked; sep. 5.5–8×1.5–4mm, 5. Winter. W Arg. to Falkland Is. Z7.

C. asarifolia DC. = *C. palustris*.

C. biflora DC. = *C. leptosepala* ssp. *howellii*.

C. chelidonii Greene = *C. leptosepala*.

C. dioneifolia Hook. f. To 5cm. Lvs 2–4cm, ovate to suborbicular, 2-lobed, lobes oblong, obtuse, ciliate; petiole to 8mm. Fls pale yellow short-stalked; sep. 3.5–6×1.5–2mm, 5–7. Autumn–winter. S Chile, Tierra del Fuego, Arg. Z7.

C. laeta Schott, Nyman & Kotschy = *C. palustris* var. *palustris*.

C. leptosepala DC. To 30cm. Lvs 1–6cm, oblong-ovate, base cordate, with shallow sinus, longer than broad, crenate-dentate; petioles long. Fls often solitary, stalk 3–10cm, white; sep. *c*15×6mm, 6–12. Spring–summer. Alask. to Alberta, S to Oreg., Utah and New Mex. ssp. *howellii* (Huth) Smit. To 20cm, st. erect. Lvs to 8cm, broader; petiole long; st. lvs commonly 1. Fls usually 2; sep 7–20mm, 6–9, oblong-elliptic. Spring–summer. Alask. to Calif. Z3.

C. natans Pall. St. floating, or creeping in mud, rooting. Lvs 3–5cm, cordate-reniform, entire to bluntly dentate; petioles long. Fls white, occas. tinged red or grey-brown at margin; sep. *c*5mm, ovate. Summer. Alask. to Minn. and Wisc., also N Asia. Z2.

C. novae-zelandiae Hook. f. To 15cm. Lvs 1–2.5cm, clustered, ovate-oblong to oblong, subcordate, entire to crenate or sinuate; petiole *c*5cm. Fls solitary, pale yellow, fragrant; sep. *c*11×2mm, 5–8, lanceolate. Summer. NZ. Z7.

C. palustris L. sensu lato. KINGCUP; MARSH MARIGOLD; MEADOW BRIGHT; MAY-BLOB. 10–80cm, st. erect or decumbent, branched above. Lvs 3–25cm, reniform, crenate-dentate to ± entire, long-stalked. Fls *c*4cm diam., pale to golden yellow; sep. 4–9, commonly 5, elliptic to obovate. A highly variable sp. with several distinct forms formerly recognized as spp. – *C. asarifolia* from Alaska south to Oregon with leafy decumbent st., reniform lvs to 3cm diam. and small, bright yellow fls; *C. alpestris*, a small form from C. France with largely solitary fls; *C. alpina* with many-fld st. and sharply toothed lvs; *C. polypetala*, a large, vigorous plant from Caucasus, N Iran, E Balkans with glossy reniform-orbicular lvs to 30cm diam. and large golden yellow fls with 6–10 sep. Spring. N Temp. regions. Z8. 'Flore Pleno' ('Multiplex'): fls double. 'Monstrosa': lvs dark; fls fully double. 'Plurisepala' ('Semi-Plena'): fls pale, semi-double. 'Tydermannii': st. procumbent, dark; fls clear yellow. var. *alba* Hook. f. & Thoms. Compact. Fls white. var. *palustris*. St. decumbent to creeping, leafy, lvs 4–10cm, rounded-reniform, crenate, petiole long. Fls often solitary or 2–3, yellow; sep. to 1.5cm, 5–7. Summer. Alask. to Oreg. var. *radicans* (Forst.) Beck. St. long, creeping, rooting. N Temp. Z3.

C. palustris var. *alpina* Schur = *C. palustris*.

C. parnassifolia Raf. = *C. palustris*.

C. polypetala Hochst. ex Lorentz = *C. palustris*.

C. radicans Forst. = *C. palustris* var. *radicans*.

C. rotundifolia (Huth) Greene = *C. leptosepala*.

C. sagittata Cav. To 30cm; rhiz. thick, trailing to ascending. Lvs 1–3.5cm, ovate to triangular, base cordate, undulate-serrate; petiole 1–1.5cm. Fls solitary, yellow; stalk 5–20mm; sep. 4.5–16×1.5–8mm, 5–8. Winter. W Arg., Chile, Falkland Is. Z7.

C. scaposa Hook. f. & Thoms. To 15cm, flowering st. scapose. Lvs 1.5–4cm, ovate, obtuse, base deeply cordate, entire to minutely crenate or dentate; petiole long. Fls yellow; sep.

12×8mm, 5–9, obovate. Summer. Himal., W China. Z6.

C. uniflora Rydb. = *C. leptosepala*.

Caltrop *Tribulus terestris*.

Calvary Clover *Medicago intertexta*.

CALYCANTHACEAE Lindl. 3/9. *Calycanthus, Chimonanthus.*

Calycanthus L. ALLSPICE; SPICEBUSH. Calycanthaceae. 6 spicily aromatic decid. shrubs to 3m. Lvs entire, upper surface rough. Fls solitary, term. on current year's leafy shoots; sep. and pet. similar, spreading narrow-lanceolate to elliptic, numerous; sta. 10–30. Fr. a hard, fig-shaped capsule. Summer. E China, SW & E US.

C. chinensis Cheng & Chang. Lvs to 15cm, elliptic to obovate, abruptly acuminate, glossy green. Fls to 7cm diam., nodding, outer tep. white sometimes tinted pink, inner tep. smaller, pale yellow to white at base with maroon markings. E China.

C. fertilis Walter. Lvs ovate, acute or acuminate, 5–15cm, glossy dark green, glabrescent beneath. Fls purple or red-brown, slightly fragrant, 3–5cm wide. SE US. 'Nanus': dwarf; lvs elliptic or oblong, 4–8cm, lower surface glaucous. 'Purpureus': lvs tinged purple beneath. var. *laevigatus* (Willd.) Bean. Lvs glossy green beneath. Z6.

C. floridus L. CAROLINA ALLSPICE; STRAWBERRY SHRUB. Lvs 5–12cm, oval or oblong, apex acuminate or obtuse, base cuneate, grey-green, densely pubesc. beneath. Fls dark red-brown, 4–5cm wide, strawberry-scented. SE US. Z5.

C. floridus var. *laevigatus* (Willd.) Torr. & Gray = *C. fertilis* var. *laevigatus*.

C. glaucus Willd. = *C. fertilis*.

C. macrophyllus hort. = *C. occidentalis*.

C. mohrii (Small) Pollard. Differs from *C. floridus* in lvs larger, broader, rounded to cordate at base. Fls purple, 5–6cm wide. Fr. tapering only slightly above. SE US. Z6.

C. occidentalis Hook. & Arn. CALIFORNIAN ALLSPICE. Strongly aromatic shrub differing from *C. fertilis* in summer buds not concealed by petiole bases. Lvs 8–20cm, ovate to oblong-lanceolate, acute, rough above, ± glab. beneath. Fls 5–7cm diam., purple-brown fading to yellow, fragrant. SW US. Z7.

C. sterilis Walter = *C. floridus*.

→*Sinocalycanthus*.

Calycomis D. Don. Cunoniaceae. 1 shrub to 2m. Lvs to 10cm, in whorls or opposite, ovate to ovate-oblong, apex acute, base cordate, sharply serrate. Infl. in a compact series of whorls, alternating with lf whorls, each to 3cm diam., consisting of 3, many flowered pan.; sep. to 3×1mm; pet. to 3.5×1mm, obovate-oblong, membranaceous; sta. 10, long-exserted. Aus. (NSW). Z10.

C. australis (A. Cunn.) Hoogl.

→*Weinmannia*.

Calycophyllum DC.

C. coccineum DC. = *Warszewiczia coccinea*.

Calydorea Herb. Iridaceae. 12 cormous perenn. herbs. Lvs narrowly linear or terete. Fls short-lived; tep. subequal, spreading; sta. arising at base of tep. Warm temp. Americas.

C. speciosa Herb = *C. xiphioides*.

C. xiphioides (Poepp.) Espin. To *c*25cm. Lvs 7–25cm, plicate, narrowly linear, fls in a terminal head; tep. blue, yellow in centre *c*2.5cm, obovate. Chile.

Calylophus Spach. Onagraceae. 6 herbaceous to shrubby perennials. St. prostrate to erect. Fls 4-merous, actinomorphic, in axils of upper lvs; floral tube well developed; sep. green yellow, often with purple or red markings, reflexed; pet. yellow, in some sp. becoming red, orange or purple upon wilting; sta. 8, yellow. N Amer.

C. lavandulifolius (Torr. & A. Gray) Raven. Suffrutescent perenn. St. tufted, moderately branched, spreading-decumbent, 4–30cm, grey-strigulose. Lvs 0.6–5cm, dense, linear to narrowly lanceolate. Floral tube 2.5–6cm; sep. to 2cm, with purple marginal stripes; pet. 1.2–2.8cm fading pink to purple. W US.

C. serrulatus (Nutt.) Raven. SHRUBBY EVENING PRIMROSE. Herbaceous to suffrutescent perenn. St. few to many, 10–60cm. Lvs 1–9cm, well spaced, linear to oblanceolate. Floral tube 0.2–1.6cm, pale yellow green; sep. keeled; pet. 0.5–2cm, suborbicular. Canada and W US.

→*Galpinsia, Oenothera* and *Salpingia*.

Calymmanthium Ritter. Cactaceae. 1 or 2 shrubby or arborescent cacti; st. segmented, 3–4-winged, spiny. Fls nocturnal, narrowly tubular-campanulate, tube enclosing the perianth in bud; perianth-limb narrow, spreading. Peru.

C. substerile Ritter. Shrub or tree to 8m; stem-segments to 1m×4–8cm, wings crenate, light green. Spines pale yellow or whitish, 1–5cm. Fls 9.5–11×3.5cm, white or tinged red-brown. Peru. Z9.

Calypso Salisb. Orchidaceae. 1 terrestrial cormous orchid. Lf single, elliptic-oblong or ovate; petiole short. Fls solitary on scape to 10cm; tep. to 2cm, narrow-lanceolate, widely spreading, often reflexed upwards or twisted, magenta; lip to 2.5cm, slipper-shaped with golden fringe, saccate and horned at base, white to rose pink, marked purple. Early spring–mid-summer. Scand., Russia, N Amer. Z5.

C. bulbosa (L.) Oakes. var. *americana* (R. Br.) Luer. Lip densely yellow-pubesc. N Amer. var. *occidentalis* (Holzing.) Cald. & Tayl. Lip irregularly spotted purple, sparsely white-pubesc. N Amer.

Calyptrochilum Kränzl. Orchidaceae. 2 epiphytic orchids. St. long, leafy. Lvs 6–15cm, oblong, fleshy. Rac. borne along st., dense; fls white; sep. and pet. subsimilar; lip trilobed, spurred. Trop. Afr. Z10.

C. christyanum (Rchb. f.) Summerh. Rac. to 4cm, 6–9-fld; rachis flexuous; fls lemon-scented, white, yellow in throat, spur green; tep. 6–10mm, ovate; lip trilobed, midlobe to 10×8mm, oblong, apiculate; spur 8–10mm, geniculate, globose at tip. Trop. Afr. (widespread).

C. emarginatum (Sw.) Schltr. Rac. to 5cm, densely fld; fls strongly scented, white, lip yellow or yellow-green; tep. 6–10mm, ovate, acute; lip 15–17mm, oblong, concave, obscurely trilobed, lat. lobes rounded, midlobe smaller, acute; spur 8mm, incurved, apex swollen. W Afr., Zaire, Angola.
→*Angraecum.*

Calystegia R. Br. BINDWEED. Convolvulaceae. *c*25, rampant perenn., climbing or scrambling herbs, spreading rapidly via rhiz. St. twining containing white latex. Lvs petiolate, bases often lobed. Fls axill., solitary or in small clusters, with 2 large bracteoles concealing cal.; cor. large, tubular or funnel-shaped. Widely distrib. in temp. and subtrop. zones, often introd. or uninvited and nat.

C. hederacea Wallich. Herbaceous climber. St. to 5m. Lvs narrowly sagittate to lanceolate, to 10cm, hairy. Fls solitary, on winged stalks, to 3.5cm diam., rose-pink. Summer–autumn. E Asia; nat. in E US. 'Flore Pleno': fls 'double', – cor. to 5cm diam. bright rose-pink, divided into many narrow, petal-like lobes. Z5.

C. japonica (Thunb.) Miq. = *C. hederacea.*

C. macrostegia (Greene) Brummitt. Herbaceous climber. St. 1–4. Lvs 4–10cm, deltoid-hastate, somewhat fleshy, sparsely hairy, basal lobes with 2–3 coarse, spreading teeth, apices acute. Fls solitary, on 10–20cm stalks; cor. white at first, later pink, 5–6cm. W US. ssp. *cyclostegia* (House) Brummitt. Lvs 2–5cm, triangular-lanceolate to ovate; cor. 2.5–4.5cm, white with purple stripes on outside, sometimes pink when old. Z8.

C. occidentalis (A. Gray) Brummitt. Tall climber. Lvs 1–4cm, triangular-hastate, basal lobes broad, 2-toothed, apex blunt. Fls 1–3 per stalk; cor. 3–4cm, white, yellow-brown or pink, purple with age. S Calif. Z8.

C. pellita (Ledeb.) G. Don = *C. hederacea.*

C. pubescens Lindl. = *C. hederacea* 'Flore Pleno'.

C. pulchra Brummitt & Heyw. Climber. St. hairy when young. Lvs dull green, sagittate, sinus parallel-sided and oblong. Fl. stalk winged; cor. 5–7.5cm diam., pink. Summer–autumn. NE Asia, or perhaps a hybrid of Eur. gdn origin. Z5.

C. sepium (L.) R. Br. BINDWEED; HEDGE BINDWEED; WILD MORNING-GLORY; RUTLAND-BEAUTY. Glab. climber. Lvs sagittate, sinus acute with divergent sides; cor. 3–7cm diam., white or pink. Widely distrib. in Eur., nat. elsewhere. ssp. *spectabilis* Brummitt. Glab. or with st. and petioles hairy. Lf sinus rounded. Cor. usually 5–6cm diam., pink. Summer–autumn. Sib., or perhaps a nat. gdn hybrid of *C. sepium* and *C. pulchra.* Z4.

C. silvatica (Kit.) Griseb. Glab. climber. Lvs sagittate, with a rounded sinus, sides parallel or divergent. Cor. 5–9cm diam., white, centre band of each lobe sometimes flushed pink on outside. Summer–autumn. S Eur., N Afr., nat. further N. Z7.

C. tuguriorum (Forst. f.) R. Br. ex Hook. Slender climber, glab. to puberulent. Lvs 1–4cm, thin, ovate-cordate or deltoid, apex acute or acuminate, sinus broad and shallow. Fl. stalks sometimes narrowly winged; cor. 2.5–5cm diam., white to pink. Summer–autumn. NZ, S Chile. Z5.
→*Convolvulus.*

Calytrix Labill. STARFLOWER. Myrtaceae. 75 shrubs. Lvs small to minute. Fls solitary, axill., often clustered toward ends of branchlets, subtended by two bracteoles, hypanthium long and narrow, sep. 5, usually ending in a hair-like awn; pet. 5; sta. many. Z8.

C. alpestris (Lindl.) Court. SNOW MYRTLE. To 2.5m. Lvs 1–5mm, linear, narrowly elliptic. ovate or lanceolate. Infl. 1, to many, clustered or scattered; pet. white to pink, elliptic, 4–5.75mm; sta. 14–37, white, 0.7–5.5mm. S Aus. and Vict.

C. angulata Lindl. To 1m. Lvs 2–7mm, linear to ovate. Infl. few to many, scattered; pet. cream, yellow below, lanceolate to narrowly elliptic, 5.5–8mm; sta. 30–40, yellow, 1.25–6mm. W Aus.

C. aurea Lindl. To 1.2m. Lvs 5–12mm, pubesc., elliptic, lanceolate or linear. Infl. few to many, clustered; pet. yellow, ovate to elliptic, 6.5–10mm; sta. 25–55, yellow, 3–7mm. W Aus.

C. brevifolia (Meissn.) Benth. To 2.5m. Lvs 3–14mm, ovate, linear, elliptic, or suborbicular. Infl. 1 to many, scattered; pet. pink to magenta, yellow at base, ovate, lanceolate or broadly elliptic, 8–11.5mm; sta. 40–90, yellow, 2.5–8mm. W Aus.

C. depressa (Turcz.) Benth. To 1m. Lvs 2–17mm, linear to linear-lanceolate. Infl. 1 to many, scattered; pet. mauve to violet, yellow, tinged pink below, or cream tinged yellow below, ovate to lanceolate, 5–11mm; sta. 35–75, yellow becoming red-purple, 1.5–7.5mm. W Aus.

C. flavescens Cunn. To 80cm. Lvs (1.5–)4–9mm, linear to narrowly elliptic. Infl. slightly fragrant, few to many; pet. yellow, ovate to lanceolate, 5.5–10mm, sta. 35–60, yellow, 2–6mm. W Aus.

C. fraseri Cunn. To 2m. Lvs 0.8–5mm, oblong, linear, broadly elliptic or obovate. Infl. one to few, not clustered; pet. pink to cerise or pink-purple, yellow at base, lanceolate to elliptic, 6–14mm; sta. 35–55, pink to pink-purple, yellow below, 2.5–8mm. W Aus.

C. genethylloides F. Muell. = *C. alpestris.*

C. glutinosa Lindl. To 1m. Lvs 3–15mm, linear. Infl. one to many, scattered; pet. pink to mauve, white below, lanceolate to elliptic, 9–12.5mm; sta. 10–20, white, 2.5–8mm. W Aus.

C. muricata F. Muell. = *C. brevifolia.*

C. oldfieldii Benth. To 1m. Lvs 1.5–3.5mm, linear, oblong or ovate. Infl. one to few, scattered; pet. mauve, pink, red, magenta or violet, elliptic to ovate, 7.5–9mm; sta. 50–75, yellow; 1.5mm. W Aus.

C. sapphirina Lindl. To 1m. Lvs 2.5–10mm, linear to elliptic. Infl. few to many, usually tightly clustered; pet. deep pink, mauve, magenta or dark purple, elliptic to ovate, 4.5–8mm; sta. 30–45, deep pink to purple, 1.5–5.5mm. W Aus.

C. scabra DC. = *C. tetragona.*

C. sullivanii (F. Muell.) B.D. Jackson = *C. tetragona.*

C. tenuifolia (Meissn.) Benth. = *C. depressa.*

C. tetragona Labill. To 3m. Lvs 0.75–14mm, linear, oblong, ovate, lanceolate, to narrowly elliptic. Infl. one to many, tightly clustered or scattered; pet. white to pink, elliptic to lanceolate, 3.5–7.5mm; sta. 23–45, white, 1–6.5mm. Aus.

C. violacea (Lindl.) Craven. To 4.5m. Lvs 2–8.5mm, linear, linear-oblanceolate or v. narrowly elliptic. Infl. few to many, tightly clustered or scattered; pet. purple, purple-mauve or violet, white-yellow or yellow below; sta. 50–65, yellow to red-purple, 1–6mm. W Aus.

Camas, Camass *Camassia.*

Camassia Lindl. CAMASH; CAMAS; QUAMASH; CAMOSH. Liliaceae (Hyacinthaceae). 5 bulbous perenn. herbs. Lvs basal, narrow-linear, keeled beneath, sheathing at base. Scape terete; rac. term., dense, cylindrical with slender bracts; tep. 6; spreading; sta. 6, fil. slender, anth. versatile. Late spring–early summer. N & S Amer.

C. cusickii S. Wats. Lvs 40–80×2–4cm, glaucous above, undulate. Scape 60–80cm; rac. to 40cm; tep. 2.5–2.7cm, linear-oblong, pale blue; fil. white, anth. yellow. US (NE Oreg.). 'Zwanenburg': fls large, deep blue. Z5.

C. esculenta Lindl. non (Ker-Gawl.) Cov. = *C. quamash.*

C. esculenta (Ker-Gawl.) Cov. non Lindl. = *C. scilloides.*

C. fraseri Torr. = *C. scilloides.*

C. howellii S. Wats. Lvs 30×0.5–1cm. Scape 30–100cm; rac. 20–25cm; tep. 1–2cm, oblong, pale blue or purple, fil. mauve, anth. yellow. US (SW Oreg.).

C. hyacinthina (Raf.) Palmer & Steyerm. = *C. scilloides.*

C. leichtlinii (Bak.) S. Wats. Lvs 20–60×0.5–2.5cm, bright green. Scape 20–130cm; rac. 10–30cm; tep. 2–5cm, oblong-lanceolate, cream-white or blue to violet, fil. blue-white, anth. yellow. W N Amer. 'Blue Danube': fls dark blue. 'Coerulea': fls vivid deep blue. 'Electra': fls to double size, rich blue. 'Plena': tall; fls double, rosette-form, creamy white to yellow. 'Semiplena': fls semi-double, creamy white to yellow. ssp. *leichtlinii.* Fls cream-white. Oreg. ssp. *suksdorfii* (Greenman) Gould. Fls blue to violet. BC to Calif. 'Albocaerulea': fls deep blue-violet. 'Alba': fls white. Z3.

C. quamash (Pursh) Greene. QUAMASH; CAMOSH. Lvs 20–50×0.5–2cm, sometimes glaucous above. Scape 20–80cm, dark green; rac. 5–30cm; tep. 1–3.5cm, linear-oblong, white to pale blue to deep violet-blue, fil. white or pale blue, anth. yellow or blue. W US to Mont. and Idaho. 'Orion': fls dark steely blue, deep purple in bud, infl. dense. 'Purpureocoerulea': fls violet-blue. Z5.

C. scilloides (Raf.) Cory. EASTERN CAMASS; WILD HYACINTH; MEADOW HYACINTH; INDIGO SQUILL. Lvs 20–60×0.5–2cm, bright green. Scape 20–80cm, rac. 8–10cm; tep. 0.5–1.5cm, narrow-oblong, lue, blue-violet or white, fil. same colour as tep. anth. yellow. C & E N Amer. Z7.

C. teapeae St. John = *C. quamash*.

Cambridge Oak *Quercus warburgii*.
Camden Woollybutt *Eucalyptus macarthurii*.

Camelina Crantz. Cruciferae. 10 ann. or bienn. herbs. Lvs mostly basal, hairy; st. lvs clasping. Fls small, pet. 4, clawed; sta. 6, of 3 different lengths. Medit. to C Asia. Z7.

C. glabrata (DC.) Fritsch = *C. sativa*.
C. pilosa (DC.) Vassilcz. = *C. sativa*.
C. sativa (L.) Crantz. GOLD-OF-PLEASURE. 30–80cm. St. erect, unbranched. Lvs 3–9cm, narrow oblong-lanceolate, entire to remotely toothed. Pet. to 5mm, yellow. Distrib. as for the genus.

Camellia L. Theaceae. *c*250 everg. shrubs or trees. Lvs elliptic or oblong or lanceolate or ovate, coriaceous, usually dark green, glossy. Fls v. short-stalked, term. or axill., single, paired or clustered, in cult. often double or semi-double with petaloid staminodes; sep. 5–6, usually concave, pubesc. or glab.; pet. spreading, whorled 5–12, outermost often transitional to sep. or perules; sta. in whorls often forming a showy golden boss. N India, Himal. to Jap. S to N Indon. Z8 unless specified.

C. assimilis Champ. ex Benth. Shrub. Lvs 4–8cm, elliptic to oblong-elliptic, acuminate to caudate, base cuneate to obtuse, bluntly serrulate in upper half to two thirds, dark green above, pale green beneath. Fls nodding, white; pet. 7, to 1.5cm, orbicular to wide-obovate, grey-velutinous beneath. Hong Kong.

C. axillaris Griff. = *C. caudata*.
C. brevistyla (Hayata) Cohen-Stuart. Slender tree, 5–8m. Lvs 3–4.5cm, elliptic, apex obtuse, base cuneate, crenulate-denticulate, villous beneath, verruculose throughout. Fls white; pet. 5, to 1.6cm, obovate to oblanceolate to obcuneate, retuse to deeply emarginate, pubescent tawny-pubesc. Taiwan.

C. caudata Wallich. Erect shrub to small tree, 2–7m. Lvs 5–10cm, elliptic, oblong-elliptic or oblong, apex caudate, base cuneate, crenulate-serrulate, dark glossy above, paler beneath. Fls white, pet. to 1.4cm, 5, broad-obovate to oval or suborbicular, unequal. NE India, N Burma, Vietnam, Hainan, Taiwan.

C. cavaleriana (Lév.) Nak. = *C. pitardii*.
C. chekiangoleosa Hu. Small tree, 3–7m. Lvs 8–12cm, oblong-rounded to obovate-elliptic, acuminate or caudate-acuminate, base cuneate, serrate in upper half, revolute. Fls red: pet. 7, deeply emarginate. S China.

C. chrysantha (Hu) Tuyama. Small tree, 2–5m. Lvs 11–17cm, narrow-oblong to broad-lanceolate, apex acuminate, base cuneate, coriaceous. Fls pure yellow; pet. to 2–5cm, 9–11, waxy. S China.

C. connata (Craib) Craib. Shrub 3–4m or small tree 5–9m. Lvs 1–9cm, elliptic or oblong- to oblanceolate-elliptic, acute to acuminate, base cuneate to rounded, shallowly crenulate to serrulate, deep green above, paler beneath. Fls white; pet. 5, to 1.5cm, broad-elliptic to obovate, rounded, concave. Thail.

C. crapnelliana Tutcher Small tree, 5–7m, bark brick red. Lvs 9.5–12cm, obovate-elliptic to elliptic, apex cuspidate, base cuneate, denticulate, dark green above, v. pale beneath. Fls white, pet. 6–8, obovate to oblanceolate, to 4.2cm. Hong Kong.

C. cuspidata (Kochs) Wright ex Gard. Chron. Shrub 0.6–3m. Lvs 5–7.5cm, narrow-elliptic to lanceolate-elliptic to broad-elliptic, apex blunt-acuminate to caudate, base cuneate, serrulate, dark glossy above, pale beneath. Fls white, pet. 6–7, outermost 2–3 smaller, to 1.5cm, suborbicular, inner. pet. to 3cm, wideobovate, truncate to emarginate. W China. Z7.

C. drupifera Lour. = *C. oleifera*.
C. euryoides Lindl. Shrub or small tree. Lvs 2–4.2cm, elliptic to ovate or lanceolate-elliptic, apex broadly acuminate, base cuneate to rounded, bluntly serrulate, thinly coriaceous, dark above, pale and villous beneath. Fls white, pet. 5, outer 2 to 1.1cm, inner 3 to 1.5cm, ovate, emarginate to truncate. China.

C. forrestii (Diels) Cohen-Stuart. Shrub or small tree, 1–5m. Lvs 2.2–7cm, elliptic to oblong-ovate, or ovate, apex obtuse to acuminate, base cuneate or rounded, serrulate, teeth blacktipped, dark green above, pale green beneath. Fls fragrant,

white, pet. 5–6, unequal, outer 1–2 to 1.2cm, concave, inner 4 to 1.6cm, rounded or emarginate. China, Vietnam.

C. fraterna Hance. Shrub 1–5m. Lvs 4–8cm, elliptic, broad- or oblong-elliptic, apex blunt-acuminate, base cuneate, serrulate, teeth black-tipped, glossy dark green above, pale beneath. Fls fragrant white or white-lilac, pet. 5–6, outer 2 shorter, pubesc. beneath, inner 3–4 to 2.2cm, rounded or emarginate. China.

C. furfuracea (Merrill) Cohen-Stuart. Shrub to 3m. Lvs 8.5–14cm, elliptic to oblong-elliptic, apex acuminate, base cuneate to obtuse, serrulate or mucronulate-denticulate, dark glossy green above, pale beneath with sparse cork-warts. Fls fragrant white; pet. 8, 2 outermost to 1.5cm, inner to 2cm, obovate to narrow-oval. Vietnam, China.

C. gigantocarpa Hu & Huang = *C. crapnelliana*.
C. granthamiana Sealy. Tree 3m. Lvs 8–10cm, oblong-elliptic to broadly so, bluntly acuminate, base rounded or obtuse, bluntly serrulate, glossy dark green with veins impressed above. Fls fragrant white; pet. 8, wide-spreading, to 7cm, ovate, deeply emarginate. Hong Kong.

C. grijsii Hance. Shrub 1–3m. Lvs 4.5–8.3cm, elliptic or oblanceolate-elliptic to oval or ovate, apex acuminate, base cuneate to rounded, sharply serrulate or crenate-serrulate, teeth black-glandular-tipped, dark green above, paler beneath with dark cork-warts. Fls sometimes fragrant, white; pet. 5–6, to 2.7cm, obcordate to cuneiform, deeply bilobed, or obovate and emarginate. China.

C. ×heterophylla Hu. (*C. japonica* ×*C. reticulata*) Intermediate between parents. Wild and gdn. origin. 'Barbara Hillier': large shrub with bold, glossy lvs and showy pink fls.

C. ×hiemalis Nak. (Possibly *C. japonica* ×*C. sasanqua*.) Small tree. Lvs 6–9cm, serrulate. Fls white or pink; pet. 7, 3.5cm. Jap., imported from China.

C. honkongensis Seem. Tree 11m. Lvs 7–12cm, oblong or oblong-elliptic, apex short-acuminate, base cuneate to obtuse, emerging iridescent blue-bronze, hardening coriaceous, glossy green. Fls crimson; pet. 3cm. 6–7, broad-obovate, emarginate or truncate. Hong Kong.

C. hozanensis (Hayata) Hayata = *C. japonica*.
C. irrawadiensis Barua. Tall shrub to 6.5m. Lvs 8–15cm, elliptic or oblanceolate-elliptic, apex bluntly acuminate, base cuneate, blunt-denticulate, or entire and undulate, glab., brick-red turning deep green above, veins yellow-green, bright green beneath. Fls nodding white; pet. to 2cm, 9–10, orbicular to broadobovate, rounded. Burm.

C. japonica L. Shrub or small tree to 15m. Lvs 5–10.5cm, broadly elliptic to elliptic-oblong, apex shortly and bluntly acuminate, base cuneate, denticulate or crenulate-denticulate, rigidly coriaceous, glossy above, pale beneath with brown cork-warts. Fls red; pet. to 3cm, 5–6, oblong-oval to broad-obovate or suborbicular, rounded and deeply emarginate; outer fil. ½ to ⅔ united. Liu Kiu Is., Jap., Korea, China. ssp. *rusticana* (Honda) Kitam. SNOW CAMELLIA. Smaller; pet. wide-spreading; fil. united only at base. Jap.

Over 2000 cvs with varying fl. form, colour and markings; fl. size 5–15cm diam., single, semi-double, and several types of double, colour ranging from white through shades of pink to red, bicolors including striped and picotee forms.

Single: 'Alba Simplex': fls white, flat; mid-season. 'Alexander Hunter': habit upright; fls bright crimson, sta. pale; mid-season. 'Faustine Lechii': fls striped pink and white; early flowering. 'Juno': growth strong; lvs dark, glossy; fls pale red. 'Kingyo Tsubaki' (FISHTAIL CAMELLIA): lvs divided and twisted at tip; fls pale pink, scented. 'Kin-sekai' (from ssp. *rusticana*): lvs variegated; fls pink. 'Yobuko Dori': fls small, pale pink; midseason.

Semi-double: 'Adolphe Audusson': fls scarlet with conspicuous white fil.; mid-season. 'Ama No Kawa': fls white, pet. incurved, creped; mid-season. 'Ann Sothern': habit bushy, upright; fls pink shading to white at centre; mid to late season. 'Berenice Boddy': habit tall; lvs glossy; fls pale pink, outer pet. shaded; early to midseason. 'Bob Hope': fls large, v. darkly tinged; mid-season. 'Gay Chieftain': habit vigorous, open; fls vivid red and white, pet. upright; mid to late season. 'Virginia Carlyon': fls deep crimson.

Anemone Form: 'Barbara Woodroff': outer pet. pale pink, inner petaloids cream; early to mid-season. 'Bob's Tinsie': habit upright, neat; lvs small; fls miniature, abundant, outer pet. deep crimson, petaloids deep crimson and white; mid-season. 'Daitarin' ('Hatsu Zakura'): vigorous, upright; fls rose-pink, mass of petaloids in centre; early season. 'Elegans' ('Chandler'): habit spreading, growth slow; fls large, rose, centre petaloids often spotted white; early to mid-season. 'Elegans Miniata': growth slow; fls lavender pink to nearly white. 'Frosty Morn': habit open; fls large, white; mid-season. 'Koto-Hajime' (from ssp. *rusticana*): miniature; fls white.

Peony Form: 'Blood of China': fls strong red, semi-double to loose peony-shaped; late flowering; scented. 'Daikagura': fls pale red and white, v. variable in marking; v. early flowering. 'Lady Loch': lvs dark, glossy; fls pink, darker-veined, shading to white edge, outer pet. broad, reflexing; long-flowering. 'The Pilgrim': habit upright; fls large, cream, full peony; mid-season. 'Tomorrow': habit open, vigorous, slightly hanging; fls semi-double, with irregular pet. and large petaloids, to full peony form, bright strawberry red; early to mid-season.

Rose Form Double: 'Auburn White': fls cream-white; late flowering. 'Elizabeth Dowd': habit open, erect, vigorous; fls white flecked pink, large. 'Kao-Majima' (from ssp. *rusticana*): miniature; fls red. 'Margaret Davis Picotee': fls white, edged crimson; late season. 'Shima-Chidori' (from ssp. *rusticana*): miniature; fls red spotted white.

Formal Double: 'Bienville': habit compact, vigorous; fls white with incurved pet.; early to late season. 'Berenice Perfection': habit columnar, vigorous; fls pale pink with darker margin; mid-season. 'Lavinia Maggi ('Contessa Lavinia Maggi')': habit upright to 3.6m; fls white striped pink and carmine, likely to sport red; long-flowering. 'Mathotiana': habit compact, upright; fls crimson occas. tinged purple, large; mid to late season. 'Shiragiku': vigorous, upright; fls white, cream at base, late season. 'Wilamina': miniature, growth narrow, upright; lvs rounded; fls pink edged paler, pet. incurved; mid to late season.

Higo Japonicas. A group of cvs developed over the last four centuries in the city of Higo, now Kumamoto, Japan; fls single, flat, in range of colours, with large bosses of golden-yellow anth. 'Hagoromo': fls 10cm or more wide, dark red, with 5–8 pet.; fil. red. 'Hakaku': fls white. 'Higo Hakama': fls bright red. 'Kiyo': fls 9cm wide, shell-pink with 6 pet. 'Kumagai': fls 13cm wide, dark red, with 5–7 pet.; fil. white. 'Show-no-hikara': fls red, with 6 pet. and numerous white petaloids, or broken-coloured. 'Yamato Nishiki': fls to 11cm, irregular, streaked pink and red, sta. white tipped gold, abundant. Z7.

C. kissii Wallich. Shrub or tree to 13m. Lvs 5.5–9cm, oblong-lanceolate to narrow-elliptic or elliptic, apex acuminate to caudate, base cuneate to rounded, serrulate, coriaceous, bright deep green above, pale or glaucous green beneath. Fls white; pet. 7–8, cuneate to obovate-oblanceolate, emarginate to retuse, to 1.8cm. Himal. to Burm., China and Indochina.

C. latilimba Hu = **C. crapnelliana.**

C. luchuensis Itô. Shrub 2–3m. Lvs 2.2–4cm, elliptic to oblong, apex bluntly acute, base cuneate to rounded, bluntly serrulate, bright green. Fls fragrant, white, pet. 6, white, outer 2–3 to 0.7cm, inner 3–4 obovate, emarginate, 1cm. Liu Kiu Is.

C. × maliflora Lindl. (Parents unknown.) Densely leafy shrub to 2.5×2m. Lvs 3.7–5cm, oblong-elliptic or broad-elliptic, apex bluntly acute to acuminate, base cuneate to rounded, denticulate. Fls double, blush rose; outer pet. almost orbicular, 1.7cm across; sta. petaloid. Gdn origin.

C. miyagii (Koidz.) Mak. & Nemoto. Small tree 3m. Lvs 3.3–5.2cm, narrow- or oblong- or obovate-elliptic to elliptic, apex obtuse, base cuneate, crenulate-serrate in upper half, glossy bright green, veins impressed, verruculose. Fls white, outer pet. 1.5cm, inner pet. 2cm, obovate, deeply emarginate. Jap.

C. nokoensis Hayata. Small tree, 5–8m. Lvs 3–4.7cm, elliptic or lanceolate-elliptic, apex acuminate to caudate, base cuneate, serrulate, deep green above, paler beneath. Fls white, outermost pet. suborbicular, inner pet. obovate-oval to suborbicular, to 1.2cm. Taiwan.

C. octopetala Hu = **C. crapnelliana.**

C. oleifera Abel. Small tree to 7m. Lvs 3.5–9cm, elliptic or oblong-elliptic, apex acute or acuminate, base cuneate or obtuse, serrulate, coriaceous, glossy dark green. Fls fragrant white; pet. 5–7, obovate to oblanceolate or long narrow-cuneate, apex rounded, bilobed, to 3.5cm. China, Indochina. 'Jaune' (FORTUNE'S YELLOW CAMELLIA): pet. white with dense yellow petaloids in centre.

C. oleifolia Wallich = **C. kissii.**

C. parviflora Merrill & Chun ex Sealy. Shrub to 3m. Lvs 5.5–14cm, narrow-elliptic or lanceolate, apex obtuse, base cuneate, remotely denticulate, coriaceous, dark glossy. Fls white, pet. 6, 0.5cm, subquadrate to broad-oval, truncate to rounded. China.

C. parvifolia (Hayata) Cohen-Stuart = **C. transarisanensis.**

C. pitardii Cohen-Stuart. Shrub or tree to 7m. Lvs 6.5–10cm, oblong-elliptic to broad-elliptic, apex abruptly acuminate to caudate, base cuneate, serrulate, dark green. Fls white or rose, pet. 3–6, obovate or oval or suborbicular, to 2.2cm, deeply emarginate. W China. var. *yunnanica* Sealy. Young branchlets and lvs pubesc.; lvs attenuate to base and apex, less prominently serrulate. Hunan, Sichuan.

C. polyodonta How ex Hu. Shrub or small tree. Lvs to 9cm, elliptic, apex acute, sharply serrate, heavily veined. Fls red; pet. 5, deeply emarginate. China.

C. reticulata Lindl. Loose-branched shrub or tree to 15m. Lvs 8–11.5cm, broad-elliptic, or oblong-elliptic, apex acute to short-acuminate, often blunt, base cuneate to rounded, serrulate, coriaceous, dark green above, paler beneath with conspicuous veins. Fls red, pink or white, single or semi-double to double (type was a cultivated semi-double now known as 'Captain Rawes': the wild, single-fld state is differentiated as f.*simplex* Sealy); pet. 5–6, suborbicular to obovate or broad-spathulate, emarginate, 3.2–4.3cm. China. Some 400 cvs and hybrids or *C. reticulata* are recorded. 'Arch of Triumph': habit upright, robust; fls large to 17cm, peony 1–1 form to double, crimson with orange hue, pet. wavy; long-flowering. 'Captain Rawes': fls semi-double, v. large, carmine, pet. irregular. 'Curtain Call': habit open; fls large, semi-double, deep coral-pink, pet. irregular; mid to late season. 'Cresta Blanca' (*C. japonica* × *C. reticulata* 'Crimson Robe'): habit upright, vigorous; fls v. large, semi-double, white; mid to late season. 'Dr Clifford Parks' (*C. reticulata* 'Crimson Robe' × *C. japonica* 'Kramer's Supreme'): habit vigorous; fls semi-double to peony or anemone form, dark orange-red; mid-season. 'Interval': habit upright; fls large, semi-double, pink centred cream, colour darker when grown under glass and pet. notched; mid-season. 'Ken Spragg': habit spreading, upright; fls large, semi-double, pink splashed white, inner pet. notched. 'Lila Naff': habit broad; fls large, semi-double, pink, pet. recurved; mid to late season. 'Nôtre Dame': fls loose peony-form, large, deep pink with silver sheen; mid to late season. 'Royalty': br. pendulous; fls semi-double, red; mid to late season. 'William Hertrich': habit tall; fls semi-double to loose peony-form, cherry red with bold centre of golden sta.; mid-season.

C. reticulata var. *rosea* (Mak.) Mak. = **C. × uraku.**

C. rosiflora Hook. Shrub to 1m. Lvs 4.5–8cm, elliptic, bluntly acuminate, base cuneate, crenulate-serrulate, dark green above, pale beneath. Fls soft pink-rose, pet. 6–9, to 1.8cm, spreading, slightly recurved, obovate to suborbicular, round to retuse. China. 'Cascade': br. pendulous; fls small, pale pink.

C. rusticana Honda = **C. japonica** ssp. *rusticana.*

C. salicifolia Champ. ex Benth. Small tree. Lvs 5–10cm, oblong to elliptic-oblong, tapering to long-acuminate or caudate apex, base narrow-cuneate, serrulate, teeth black-tipped, dark green above, villous beneath. Fls white; pet. 5–6, ovate or obovate, acute or short-acuminate to obtuse or rounded, undulate, to 2cm. Hong Kong, Taiwan, China.

C. saluenensis Stapf ex Bean. Compact shrub, 1–5m. Lvs 3–5.5cm, oblong or elliptic or oblong-elliptic, apex acute to obtuse, base cuneate to rounded, denticulate, coriaceous, glossy dark green above, venation prominent. Fls pale pink or deep rose-pink, occas. white; pet. 6–7, obovate or broad-oval, emarginate, 2–3cm. W China. 'Admiration': fls single, rich red. 'Apple Blossom': fls small, single, pink and white. 'Bow Bells': fls semi-double, funnel-shaped, rose-pink shaded at base and darkly veined; mid to late season. 'First Flush': fls single, pale pink; mid-season. 'Flamenco Dancer': fls semi-double, deep coral fading to pale pink, pet. irregular. 'Rose Bowl': fls single, rose-pink, pet. ruffled. Z7.

C. sasanqua Thunb. Shrub or small tree to 5m. Lvs elliptic or oblong- or broad-elliptic, 3–7.5cm, tip acute or with broad cusp to 2mm, base cuneate, crenulate, bright glossy green above, with veins prominent beneath. Fls white to rose; pet. 5–8, to 3.5cm, oblanceolate- to obovate-cuneate, apex truncate rounded or deeply emarginate, margins often recurved. Jap. Over 300 cvs recorded. 'Bert Jones': lvs dark green, glossy; fls large, semi-double, pink tinged silver, long-flowering period. 'Dazzler': br. spreading; fls semi-double, rose-red. 'Kanjiro': disease-resistant, vigorous, bushy; lvs dark green, glossy; fls rose-form double. 'Misty Moon': fls large, irregular, semi-double, pale mauve-pink. 'Navajo': habit compact; fls deep red centred white around sta., pet. wavy. 'Otome': fls pale pink, double, abundant. 'Rainbow': young growth purple; fls single, white banded red. 'Robyn Dunne': fls large, semi-double, pale mauve edged white, pet. notched. 'Snowflake': growth strong, spreading; fls large, white, single. 'Yae Arare': habit upright, strong; lvs large; fls white tipped pink, pet. reflexed, v. broad. 'Viola Spragg': fls small, peony-form, pink to red. 'Winifred Hills': fls large, anemone-form, purple-red. 'Yuletide': habit compact, upright; fls small, single, orange red. Higo Sasanquas include 'Ake Yukusora': fls double, white; 'Chisato-no-aki': fls white; 'Gingetsu': fls single, pink; 'Hiinko': fls small, double, rose-red; 'Kikenjo': fls single, large, pale pink; 'Sekiyo': fls v. large, semi-double, red; 'Trihinoumi': fls single, large, bright red.

C. sasanqua Sims non Thunb. = **C. × maliflora.**

C. semiserrata Chi. Shrub or small tree. Lvs 9–15cm, oblong or elliptic-oblong, gradually acuminate, denticulate above. Fls red; pet. 6–7, 5cm. China.

C. sinensis (L.) Kuntze. TEA. Shrub or small tree 1–6m. Lvs 5–12.5cm, elliptic, apex obtuse to broad-obtuse, occas. minutely cuspidate, base cuneate, bluntly to sinuate-serrulate, teeth black-tipped, dark glossy green above, light green, villous beneath. Fls nodding, white; pet. 7–8, to 2cm, broad-oval to suborbicular, concave. Widely cult. in Asia and elsewhere; wild origin obscure, possibly W China. var. *assamica* (Mast.) Kitam. WILD TEA. Tall tree to 17m. Lvs 8–14cm, broad-elliptic, apex acuminate, base cuneate, denticulate to widely serrulate, glab. or persistently hairy esp. on midrib beneath. N India, Assam, Burm., Indochina, Thail., China.

C. speciosa hort. = *C. saluenensis*.

C. symplicifolia Griff. = *C. kissii*.

C. taliensis (W.W. Sm.) Melch. Small tree, 2–7m. Lvs 9.5–15cm, elliptic, bluntly acute or short-acuminate, base cuneate, serrulate, coriaceous, bright deep green. Fls white; pet. 11, to 3.4cm, suborbicular to obovate. Autumn–winter. SW China.

C. thea Link = *C. sinensis*.

C. transarisanensis (Hayata) Cohen-Stuart. Shrub or small tree, (1.5–)2.5–9m. Lvs 2.5–4.4cm, elliptic or lanceolate-elliptic or lanceolate-ovate, apex v. blunt, deep green above, pale beneath. Fls white; pet. 5–6, orbicular to obovate–cuneate, truncate, to 1cm. Taiwan.

C. transnokoensis Hayata. Small tree to 6m. Lvs 3–5cm, elliptic or oblong, apex broad, bluntly acuminate, base cuneate, crenulate-serrate, dark green above, light green beneath. Fls white; pet. 5–6. Taiwan.

C. tsaii Hu. Small tree, 1–5m. Lvs 6–9.5cm, oblong, lanceolate-oblong to elliptic, apex acuminate or caudate, base cuneate, serrulate, somewhat undulate, deep glossy green above, midrib impressed, hirtellous, light pale, villous beneath. Fls white; pet. 5, suborbicular to broad-obovate, entire or emarginate to bifid, to 1.4cm. Burm., W China, N Vietnam.

C. × uraku Kitam. (Parentage unknown.) Shrub. Lvs 7–12cm, oblong or oblong-elliptic to oblong-lanceolate, apex abruptly acuminate, glossy deep green above, yellow-green beneath with cork-warts. Fls red; pet. 6–7, to 3.5cm. Not known in the wild.

C. × vernalis (Mak.) Mak. (Possibly *C. japonica* × *C. sasanqua*.) Shrub to 3m. Lvs 3.5–7.5cm, elliptic-oblanceolate, apex bluntly acuminate, crenulate-serrulate, glossy green. Fls semi-double, 6–7cm diam., white, sometimes tinged pink. Gdn origin, Jap. 'Dawn': fls white occas. suffused pink, semi-double. 'Egao': fls large, semi-double, deep rose. 'Kocho-no-mai': fls single, red. 'Ryuko': fls small, single, deep red. Z7.

C. vietnamensis Huang ex Hu. Small tree to 9m. Lvs 5–12cm, elliptic, serrulate. Fls 7–11cm diam.; pet. 5–7, white, wide-spreading, emarginate. Vietnam.

C. × williamsii W.W. Sm. (*C. saluenensis* × *C. japonica*.) Lvs 6.5–9.5cm, elliptic to broad-elliptic, shallow-serrulate, bright lustrous green, often with scattered brown spots. Fls closer to *C. saluenensis*, 5–12.5cm diam., white flushed rose. 'Anticipation': growth slow to 3.6×1m; fls large, peony-form, deep pink, abundant; mid to late season. 'Bridal Gown': habit upright, dense; fls peony-form to formal double, white. 'Brigadoon': exceptionally hardy; fls v. large, semi-double, pink tinged rose. 'Caerhays': fls double, pink tinged purple. 'C.F. Coates': lvs 3-lobed at apex; fls single, deep rose. 'Daintiness': habit open, broad; br. horizontal; fls semi-double, pink, sta. cream. 'Donation': to 2.4m wide; large, semi-double pink fls. 'Edna Raley': habit compact, upright; fls large, semi-double to peony-form, white flushed flesh pink. 'J.C. Williams': habit dense; br. fan-shaped; fls single, pale pink, pet. broad, wavy; long-flowering. 'Jury's Yellow': fls anemone-form to full peony; outer pet. white, petaloids yellow, abundant; long-flowering. 'November Pink': flowering November–May. 'Raspberry Delight': vigorous, upright growth; fls large, semi-double, deep pink tinged red, pet. large, fluted; mid to late season. 'Satan's Robe': hardy, vigorous; br. pendulous; fls large, semi-double, red; mid-season. 'St. Ewe': lvs glossy; fls large, single, bright pink, cup-shaped. 'Wilber Foss': habit dense; lvs glossy; fls full deep peony-form, rich claret, pet. broad, thick; mid to late season.

C. yunnanensis (Pitard ex Diels) Cohen-Stuart. Shrub 1.3–7m. Lvs 3.7–6.5cm, elliptic to ovate-elliptic to broad-ovate, apex acute to blunt-acuminate, base wide-cuneate to rounded, serrulate to serrate, coriaceous, dark above, pale, verruculose beneath, midrib red. Fls white; pet. 8–12, broad-oval, or broad-obovate and suborbicular, rounded, to 3.8cm. SW China.

C. cultivars. Miscellaneous hybrids and cvs include:
Single: 'Autumn Glory' (*C. japonica* 'Spencer's Pink' ×*C. granthamiana*): fls large, white flushed pink near edge. 'Baby Willow' (*C. rosiflora* ×*C. tsaii*): habit dwarf, growth pendulous; fls miniature, white. 'Cornish Snow' (*C. cuspidata* ×*C. saluenensis*): fls small, white. 'Michael' is a clone with larger fls; 'Winton' with soft pink fls. 'Frost Prince' (*C. × hiemalis* 'Shishi-Goshura' ×*C. oleifera*): habit upright; fls deep pink.
Semi-double: 'Exuberance' (*C. saluenensis* seedling): habit compact, upright, growth vigorous; fls large pink. 'Inamorata' (*C. reticulata* × *C. saluenensis*): habit close to *C. reticulata*; fls rose-

pink, resembling *C. saluenensis*. 'Inspiration' has same parentage. 'Nicky Crist' (*C. pitardii* ×*C. japonica*): growth slow, compact; fls large, lavender tinged pink; long-flowering. 'Sharlie Rayner' (*C. pitardii* ×*C. japonica*): habit open, upright, fls pale pink fading to white at centre; mid to late season.
Anemone Form: 'Little Lavender' (*C.* 'Philippa Forwood' ×*C. japonica*): habit compact, upright, vigorous; fls miniature, lavender tinged pink. 'Miss Bess' (*C.* 'Donation' ×*C. japonica* 'J.J. Pringle Smith'): fls pale pink.
Peony Form: 'Dr Zhivago' ('William's Lavender' seedling): habit open, upright; fls large, pale mauve tinged pink; mid to late season. 'Fragrant Pink' (*C. japonica* ssp. *rusticana* ×*C. lutchuensis*): habit spreading; fls miniature, deep pink, fragrant; long-flowering. 'Monterey Sunset' ('Robbie' seedling): growth vigorous, compact; fls large, red, outer pet. flat, inner pet. twisted, interspersed with sta.; mid-season.
Rose Form Double: 'Jubilation' (hybrid involving *C. japonica* 'Betty Sheffield Supreme'): habit upright; fls large, pink occas. flecked dark pink; mid to late season. 'Spring Festival' (*C. cuspidata* seedling): habit narrow, upright; fls miniature, pink fading at centre; mid to late season.
Formal Double: 'First Formal' ('Sylvia Mae' seedling): fls v. pale pink. 'Leonard Messel' (*C. × williamsii* 'Mary Christian' ×*C. reticulata*): hardy; fls deep pink; long-flowering. 'Sun Song' ('Elegant Beauty' seedling): fls large, pale pink; long-flowering.
→*Thea*.

Camel Thorn *Acacia erioloba*.

Camissonia Link. Onagraceae. 62 taprooted ann. or perenn. herbs, rarely subshrubs. Fls opening at dawn, usually 4-merous (v. rarely 3-merous); pet. glossy, yellow, rose-purple or white, reflexed at anthesis; sta. and style yellow, sta. 8, rarely 4, stigma capitate. Mainly W US and Mex., extending to the S part of W Canada. Z8.

C. cheiranthifolia (Hornem. ex Spreng.) Raim. Short-lived perenn., with a circle of prostrate, decumbent, or ascending st. to 1.3m, strigose. Lvs 0.5–5cm, narrowly ovate. Pet. 6–20mm, yellow, often red-dotted near base, fading red. W US.

C. graciliflora (Hook. & Arn.) Raven. Ann., stemless or with short ascending lat. br. to 2.5cm. Lvs 1–10cm, linear to narrowly lanceolate, pilose. Pet. 5–18mm, yellow, unspotted. W US.

C. ovata (Nutt. ex Torr. & A. Gray) Raven. Subsucculent stemless perenn. Lvs 3–15cm, ovate to v. narrowly elliptic, white-ciliate; petiole narrowly winged. Pet. 8–23mm, yellow, unspotted. W US.

C. subacaulis (Pursh) Raven. Subsucculent stemless perenn. Lvs 2–22cm, lanceolate to narrowly elliptic, subentire to sinuate or pinnatifid. Pet. 5–16mm, yellow, unspotted. W US.
→*Oenothera* and *Sphaerostigma*.

Camoensia Welw. ex Benth. Leguminosae (Papilionoideae). 2 shrubs or lianes. Lvs trifoliolate. Fls pea-like, large, in thick-stalked, axill. rac. Trop. W Afr. (Gulf of Guinea). Z10.

C. scandens (Welw.) J.B. Gillett. Large spiny liane. Petioles to 10cm; lfts to 15cm, ovate- or obovate-acuminate, glossy. Fls 2–5, to 20cm, in pendulous, rusty-hairy rac.; fls to 12cm, white, edged yellow or gold, standard to 8cm diam., suborbicular, frilled.

Camosh *Camassia* (*C. quamash*).

Campanula L. BELLFLOWER. Campanulaceae. *c*300 ann., bienn. or perenn. herbs. Lvs usually basal and stalked and shorter, narrower, ± sessile on st. Infl. paniculate, racemose or capitate, or fls solitary; cal. tube deeply 5-lobed; cor. campanulate, rarely infundibuliform or rotate, 5-lobed. Temp. N hemis.

C. abietina Griseb. & Schenk. Short-lived perenn. to 50cm, with slender creeping rootstock and slender st. Lvs narrow-ovate or elliptic, crenate, glab. to ciliate, stalked. Fls few, at tips of st., broadly funnelform, star-shaped, pale violet to blue. Summer. SE Eur. Z7.

C. acutangula Leresche & Levier = *C. arvatica*.

C. adsurgens Levier & Leresche. Like *C. elatines*. Lvs cordate-suborbicular, sinuate. Fls in short term. spikes. Spain. Z6.

C. affinis Roem. & Schult. Erect bienn., robust, pubesc., st. leafy. Lvs to 15cm, linear-oblanceolate, sinutate, ciliate, sessile. Fls axill. or terminal in leafy rac., broadly campanulate, lobes short, pale mauve to pink or white. Summer. Spain. Z5.

C. afra Cav. = *C. dichotoma*.

C. albiflora K. Koch = *C. sarmatica*.

C. alliariifolia Willd. Densely pubesc. perenn.; st. to 70cm, erect, simple or branched. Lower lvs to 8cm, broadly-cordate, densely pubesc., white-tomentose beneath, dentate. Fls pendulous, axill. or in a secund rac., blue, infundibular to campanulate, lobes ovate, bearded. Summer. Cauc., Asia Minor. 'Ivory

Bells': fls cream-white. 'Flore Pleno': fls double. Z3.

C. allionii Vill. = *C. alpestris*.

C. alpestris All. Perenn., slowly forming a mat of tiny lf rosettes. Lvs linear-lanceolate, sinuate, ciliate. Fls large, campanulate, mid blue. Summer. W Alps. 'Alba': fls white. 'Rosea': fls pink. Z5.

C. alpina Jacq. Perenn.; st. tufted, erect, simple or branched. Lvs to 5cm, linear to lanceolate, entire to crenate, glab. to pubesc. Fls long-stalked, erect or pendulous, campanulate, pale to deep blue, lobes short. Alps, Carpath. Z4.

C. alsinoides Hook. f. & Thoms. Many-stemmed. Lvs to 1cm, oblong-obovate, remotely dentate, pubesc. Fls small. NW Himal. Z7.

C. altaica DC. = *C. chamissonis*.

C. amabilis Leichtlin = *C. persicifolia*.

C. americana L. Erect ann. or bienn. to 1.8m; st. usually unbranched. Lower lvs rosulate, ovate-cordate, acuminate, petiolate, crenate, pubesc., upper lvs lanceolate, dentate. Fls racemose, rotate, lobes pubesc., pale blue to white. N Amer. Z4.

C. aparinoides Pursh. MARSH BELLFLOWER. Decumbent to prostrate perenn.; st. to 90cm, slender. Lvs to 4cm, ovate-lanceolate, sessile. Fls long-stalked, campanulate, white suffused with blue. E N Amer. Z5.

C. ardonensis Rupr. Densely tufted perenn., st. slender, spreading. Lower lvs to 5cm, narrow-linear, remotely dentate, upper lvs filiform. Fls solitary, narrowly campanulate, dark blue. Cauc. Z6.

C. argyrotricha Wallich. St. many, to 20cm. Lvs lanceolate to elliptic, remotely dentate, white-pubesc. Fls blue, exterior pubesc. NW Himal. Z7.

C. arvatica Lagasca. Perenn. forming a mat of tufted, short-stalked lvs; st. to 14cm, usually topped with a single fl. Lvs rhomboidal to suborbicular, crenate to serrate. Fls few, campanulate-rotate, white to blue or violet. Summer. N Spain. 'Alba': fls white. Z7.

C. attica Boiss. & Heldr. = *C. ramosissima*.

C. aucheri A. DC. Caespitose, pubesc. perenn.; st. short. Lower lvs to 8cm, in dense rosettes, oblong to ovate-spathulate, crenate. Fls solitary, terminating each sparsely lvd st., obconic-campanulate, deep blue to violet. Summer. E Cauc. Z5.

C. autraniana Albov. Tufted, subglabrous perenn. Lower lvs to 8cm, elliptic-cordate, remotely crenate, petiolate, upper lvs linear-lanceolate. Fls solitary, scapose, campanulate, to 2.5cm, blue suffused with purple. W Cauc. Z6.

C. barbata L. BEARDED BELLFLOWER. Short-lived perenn. or bienn., to 50cm, tufted to erect, pubesc., usually unbranched. Rosette lvs lanceolate, hispid, st. lvs ligulate, pubesc. Fls pendulous, in secund spikes, campanulate, ciliate, lavender blue. Summer. Mts of Norway, Alps. 'Alba': fls white. Z6.

C. barrelieri Presl = *C. fragilis*.

C. baumgartenii J. Becker. Like *C. rotundifolia* in habit but lvs lanceolate; fls ± erect. Germ. Z6.

C. beauverdiana Fomin. Erect perenn., to 60cm, st. slender, ascending. Lower lvs obovate, to 6cm, dentate, attenuate, long-stalked, upper lvs linear. Fls solitary or in small clusters, broadly campanulate, blue. Summer. N Persia. Z8.

C. bellardii All. = *C. cochleariifolia*.

C. bellidifolia Adams. Dwarf, tufted perenn., cushion-forming. Lower lvs ovate to broad-elliptic, crenate, long-stalked, upper lvs oblanceolate-attenuate. Fls many, erect, campanulate, deep violet to blue. Summer. C Cauc. Z5.

C. betonicifolia Bieb. = *C. sarmatica*.

C. betulifolia K. Koch. Glab. or finely pubesc. pubesc. perenn.; st. many, ascending and arching tinted purple. Lower lvs to 6cm, ovate to broadly ovate, thick, almost glab., petiolate, dentate, upper lvs smaller, oblong-lanceolate. Fls erect or nodding, corymbose, deeply campanulate, lobes ovate, white or pale coral pink. Armenia.

C. bolosii Vayr. = *C. affinis*.

C. bononiensis L. Shortly pubesc. perenn.; st. to 90cm, erect. Lower lvs cordate, petiolate, upper lvs ovate, subsessile. Fls pendulous, solitary or 2–3 in a spike, infundibular, pubesc. within, blue violet. Summer. E Eur., W Cauc. Z3.

C. brotheri Somm. & Levier = *C. raddeana*.

C. caespitosa Scop. Densely tufted, glab. perenn.; st. many. Lower lvs ovate to rhomboidal, serrate, short-petiolate, upper lvs smaller, linear-lanceolate. Fls in spikes above lvs, campanulate, narrowed at mouth, gentian blue. Dolomites, E Alps. 'Alba': fls white. Z4.

C. calaminthifolia Lam. Short-lived perenn., grey-pubesc. St. to 20cm, decumbent. Lvs to 12mm, in basal rosettes, rotund to spathulate, dentate, petiolate. Fls numerous, erect to 2.5cm diam., white or blue, rotate-campanulate, downy. Greece. Z8.

C. californica (Kellogg) A.A. Heller. Erect perenn., to 45cm; st. weak, scarcely branched. Lvs to 2.5cm, elliptic to oblanceolate,

crenulate, subsessile. Fls campanulate, clear blue. Calif. Z8.

C. carniolica (Sünderm.) Podl. = *C. thyrsoides* 'Carniolica'.

C. carpatica Jacq. TUSSOCK BELLFLOWER. Glab. perenn. forming a dense clump to 45cm. Lower lvs suborbicular, cordate, crenate, long-stalked, upper lvs ovate-acuminate, subsessile. Fls large, erect, solitary, long-stalked, broadly campanulate, blue or white. Summer. Carpath. Mts. 'Blue Clips': fls light sky-blue. 'Blue Moonlight': fls saucer-shaped, light grey-blue. 'Bressingham White': fls white, cup-shaped. 'Chewton Joy': pet. pale blue, edged deeper blue. 'Queen of Sheba': to 45cm, fls china-blue. 'Riverslea': fls 5cm diam., flat, deep purple-blue. 'White Clips': fls white, true from seed. 'Zwergmoeve': fls silver-white. var. *turbinata* (Schott. Nyman & Kotschy) Nichols. Habit smaller; fls pale lavender. 'Alba': fls white. 'Isabel': fls deep violet, widely spreading. 'Jewel': fls bright blue. 'Karl Foerster': fls large, saucer-shaped, deep blue. 'Wheatley Violet': fls deep violet, pubesc. Z3.

C. cashmeriana Royle. Pubesc. perenn., to 15cm, shoots few slender, procumbent. Lvs to 2.5cm, obovate to elliptic, entire, short-stalked, soft grey-green. Fls pendulous, narrow-campanulate, lilac blue. Afghan., Kashmir. Z4.

C. celsii A. DC. Velutinous bienn., with dense lf rosette. Lower lvs ovate, irregularly lobed, lobes lanceolate, crenate. Fls long-stalked erect, to 2.5cm, tubular to campanulate, pubesc., lilac, sometimes suffused with blue. SE Greece. Z7.

C. celtidifolia Boiss. & Huet = *C. lactiflora*.

C. cenisia L. Caespitose to creeping perenn.; st. many, to 8cm. Lvs oblanceolate to broad-obovate, entire, sessile. Fls solitary, erect funnelform to campanulate, lobes lanceolate, pale lilac-blue. Summer. Alps, It. Z5.

C. cervicaria L. Pubesc., erect bienn., to 75cm; st. simple, hispid. Lvs to 15cm, oblong- to linear-lanceolate, serrate, pilose, petiolate. Fls in spikes or clusters, narrow-campanulate to infundibuliform, pubesc., blue to lilac. C & N Eur. Z6.

C. chamissonis Fed. Perenn., st. to 15cm. Lower lvs to 4cm, rosulate, spathulate to oblong, ciliate, glossy, petiolate. Fls solitary, term., erect, campanulate, blue. Summer. Jap., Sib., Sakhalin, Kuriles, Kamchatka, Aleutians, Alask. 'Oyobeni': to 20cm; fls erect, rounded, trumpet-shaped, striped blue and white. Z2.

C. cochleariifolia Lam. FAIRIES' THIMBLES. Perenn.; creeping, producing tufts of lvs and st. Lvs small, orbicular-cordate, to ovate, serrate. Fls pendulous, solitary, terminal, campanulate, mid-blue to grey-blue or white. Summer. Eur. Mts. 'Alba': fls white. 'Blue Tit': fls bright blue. 'Cambridge Blue': fls light blue. 'Elizabeth Oliver': fls double, v. pale blue. 'Flore Pleno': fls small double, pale blue. 'Miranda': fls v. pale grey-blue. 'Miss Willmot': fls pale blue, edged silver. 'Oakington Blue': fls bright blue. 'Patience Bell': fls 10–15cm, rich blue. 'R.B. Loder': close to 'Elizabeth Oliver', but less robust. 'Silver Chimes': fls silver-blue. 'Tubby': fls rotund, china-blue. Z6.

C. collina Bieb. Perenn.; st. pubesc., erect to 30cm. Lower lvs broadly lanceolate to ovate-oblong, acuminate, crenate, petiolate. Fls usually pendulous, large, solitary or to 5 in clusters or rac., broadly campanulate, dark purple to blue-violet. Summer. Cauc. Z5.

C. colorata Wallich ex Roxb. Ann. or perenn.; st. many, slender, branching, pilose, to 60cm. Lvs narrow-ovate, acuminate, remotely serrate. Fls solitary, long-stalked, tubular to campanulate, velutinous, deep purple to violet. Himal., Sikkim, Tibet. Z7.

C. crenulata Franch. Perenn. to 15cm. Lvs low, tufted, ovate or suborbicular, small, sinuate. Fls pendulous, campanulate, in a spike, deep violet to blue. Summer. W China. Z7.

C. dasyantha Bieb. = *C. chamissonis*.

C. denticulata Boiss. = *C. betulifolia*.

C. dichotoma L. Ann., erect, spreading or ascending, hirsute to 15cm; st. divaricately branched. Lvs to 4cm, oblong to lanceolate, entire to crenate. Fls pendulous, tubular to campanulate, purple suffused with pink to blue, pubesc. within. Summer. Spain, Sicily, Alg. Z8.

C. divaricata Michx. SOUTHERN HAREBELL. Glab. perenn., to 90cm; st. slender, upright. Basal lvs to 15cm, oblong to linear-lanceolate, tapering finely. Fls pendulous, numerous, small, in term. pan., campanulate to urceolate, pale blue. Summer. E US. Z6.

C. drabifolia Sibth. & Sm. = *C. ramosissima*.

C. elatines L. ADRIATIC BELLFLOWER. Compact perenn., subglabrous, tufted; st. to 15cm, ascending to spreading. Lvs suborbicular to cordate, finely serrate, long-stalked. Fls in a lax spike or pan.; campanulate to rotate, lobes deflexed, blue or white. Summer. Adriatic coast. 'Alba': fls white. var. *elatinoides* (Moretti) Fiori. V. densely pubesc. and grey, with thicker lvs. var. *fenestrellata* (Feer) L.H. Bail. St. slightly ascending. Lvs larger, deeply serrate, glossy, bright green. 'Alba': fls white. Z6.

C. elatines var. *garganica* (Ten.) Fiori = *C. garganica*.

C. elatinoides Moretti = *C. elatines* var. *elatinoides*.

C. elegans Roem. & Schult. St. to 30cm, simple, pubesc. Lvs linear to narrow-ovate, entire, short-stalked. Fls in spikes or pan.; blue. Sib. Z2.

C. ephesia (DC.) Boiss. Similar to *C. tomentosa*, but larger, white-pubesc., with br. decumbent. Lower lvs to 20cm, lyrate, lobes oblong, crenate. Fls in secund spikes or rac., broad-campanulate, dark blue, white-pubesc. Summer. Asia Minor. Z7.

C. erinus L. Hispid ann.; st. to 25cm, dichotomously branched from base. Lvs oblanceolate to ovate, remotely dentate, occas. lobed, hispid., Fls 1–3 in term. and axill. clusters, cylindric, pale blue, often suffused pink, to white. Summer. S Eur., Moroc., Tenerife.

C. eriocarpa Bieb. = *C. latifolia* 'Eriocarpa'.

C. excisa Schleich. ex Murith. Creeping perenn. forming an open mat; st. to 15cm, slender. Lower lvs suborbicular to spathulate, serrate, petiolate. Fls in few-fld rac., pendulous; funnelform to campanulate, violet to pale lilac-blue. Summer. Switz. Z5.

C. fenestrellata Feer = *C. elatines* var. *fenestrellata*.

C. ×fergusonii hort. ex André. (*C. carpatica* × *C. pyramidalis*.) To 20cm, erect. Infl. like *C. carpatica*, but fls larger, violet blue. Autumn. Gdn origin. Z5.

C. filicaulis Durieu. Compact, tufted perenn.; st. slender, procumbent. Lvs to 6cm, oblanceolate, attenuate to winged base. Fls solitary slender, rotate, suffused with blue. Moroc., Alg. Z8.

C. finitima Fomin = *C. betulifolia*.

C. flexuosa Michx. = *C. divaricata*.

C. floribunda Viv. = *C. isophylla*.

C. formanekiana Deg. & Dörfl. Bienn., erect to 30cm. Lower lvs rosulate, ovate to deltoid, with winged petioles, dentate, upper lvs oblanceolate, sessile, tough, grey. Fls laterally arranged or term., pendulous, campanulate, white to pale lilac. Summer. Balk., Greece. Z7.

C. fragilis Cyr. Perenn., to 10cm; st. prostrate to ascending. Lower lvs orbicular to cordate, fleshy, serrate, long-petiolate. Fls in corymbs, axill. or term., erect, rotate to campanulate, pale blue to blue suffused purple. Summer. S It. 'Jewell': fls soft-blue and white, growth cascading or spreading. 'Hirsuta': lvs and st. conspicuously pubesc. Z8.

C. garganica Ten. Closely resembles *C. elatines*. Basal lvs mostly ovate, acute, green, minutely pubesc. It. 'Alba': fls white. 'Blue Diamond': lvs grey-green; fls grey-blue with deeper blue centre. 'Dickson's Gold': lvs golden; fls star-shaped, blue. 'Erinus Major': fls dark grey. 'Glandore': fls deep blue, with paler centre. 'Hirsuta': fls pubesc., rather grey. 'W.H. Payne': fls erect, starry, with a clean white centre. Z5.

C. 'G.F. Wilson'. (*C. pulla* × *C. carpatica* var. *turbinata*.) To 10cm; tufts of lvs arise from underground runners. Lvs tinged yellow. Fls semi-pendulous, campanulate, deep violet-blue. Summer. Gdn origin. Z5.

C. glomerata L. CLUSTERED BELLFLOWER. Hispid-setose perenn.; st. to 75cm, erect, simple or slightly branched. Lower lvs oblong or ovate-lanceolate, rarely suborbicular-cordate, crenate-dentate, long-stalked. Fls in dense spikes, usually term., subtended by bracts, cylindric-infundibular, lobes lanceolate, violet-blue to white. Summer. Eur., temp. Asia. 'Alba': fls white. 'Alba Nana': fls small, white, densely clustered. 'Crown of Snow' ('Schneekrone'): fls term., white, densely clustered. 'Joan Elliot': dwarf, violet. 'Purple Pixie': fls small, deep violet-purple. 'Schneehäschen': to 15cm; fls large, pure white. 'Schneekissen': habit low; fls white. 'Superba': 60cm; fls violet-purple. 'White Barn': 30cm; fls violet-purple, in dense, round heads, borne on short spikes. var. *dahurica* Fisch. ex Ker-Gawl. To 75cm, fls deep purple. Z2.

C. grandiflora Jacq. = *Platycodon grandiflorus*.

C. grandis Fisch. & C.A. Mey. = *C. latiloba*.

C. grossekii Hueff. Erect perenn. to 80cm; st. branched, setose. Lower lvs rosulate, cordate, coarse, biserrate, long-stalked. Fls solitary or in small clusters, campanulate, blue to violet. Summer. Hung. Z6.

C. ×hallii hort. (*C. cochleariifolia* × *C. portenschlagiana*.) To 10cm; st. slender. Lvs intermediate between parents, glossy, pale green. Fls solitary, semi-erect, campanulate to rotate, white. Summer. Gdn origin. Z5.

C. ×haylodgensis hort. (*C. carpatica* × *C. cochleariifolia*.) Sprawling, tufted perenn., to 15cm. Lvs suborbicular-ovate to cordate, dentate. Fls few, usually term., long-stalked, campanulate, large, pale blue. Summer. Gdn origin. 'Plena': fls double, numerous, small, blue. 'Warley White': fls double, white. Z5.

C. hemschinica K. Koch. Erect bienn.; st. to 45cm, upright. Lower lvs linear, to oblanceolate, sessile to amplexicaul. Fls few, usually term., narrow-campanulate, blue. E Eur. (mts). Z6.

C. ×hendersonii hort. (*C. alliariifolia* × *C. carpatica*.) To 45cm.

Fls in conical spikes, pale lilac. Gdn origin. Z3.

C. hercegovina Degen & Fiala. Lax perenn. herb; st. slender, branched, pubesc. Lower lvs ovate-cordate, deeply serrate, long-petiolate. Fls in lax spikes, campanulate, blue to violet. Balk. 'Nana': dwarf. Z6.

C. heterophylla L. Subglabrous perenn. St. to 20cm, slender, decumbent. Basal lvs oblong-lanceolate, obtuse, short-petiolate; cauline lvs sub-rotund, subsessile. Fls axill., solitary or few, blue, infundibular, pubesc. Greece. Z8.

C. hohenackeri Fisch. & Mey. = *C. sibirica*.

C. hybrida L. = *Legousia hybrida*.

C. imeretina Rupr. Tough, hispid perenn., to 15cm; st. slender, upright. Lower lvs obovate, attenuate to winged petiole, crenulate. Fls few, term., erect, campanulate, purple-violet. Cauc. Z5.

C. incurva Aucher ex A. DC. Pubesc. bienn.; st. to 30cm, sub-erect, pubesc. Basal lvs to 8cm, rosulate, cordate to ovate-oblong, obtuse, serrate, petiolate, finely pubesc. Fls large, inflated, erect, in lavendar loose term. clusters or pan.; broadly campanulate, lavendar blue. Greece. Z8.

C. isophylla Moretti. ITALIAN BELLFLOWER; STAR OF BETHLEHEM; FALLING STARS. Procumbent perenn.; st. to 15cm, soft, slender. Lvs to 6cm, broadly ovate-suborbicular, base cordate, crenate-serrate, long-petiolate. Fls large, erect, in loose clusters; campanulate to funnelform, violet to grey or white. Summer. N It. 'Alba': fls large, white. 'Balchiniana' ('Variegata'): lvs striped cream; fls blue. 'Caerulea': fls clear-blue. Kristal hybrids: fls blue and white. 'Mayi': lvs grey-pubesc.; fls large blue. Z7.

C. jacobaea C. Sm. ex Hook. Perenn. herb to shrub, to 90cm. Lvs to 7cm, obovate to oblong, base attenuate to cordate. Fls campanulate, solitary dark blue to peppermint. Spring. Cape Verde Is. Z9.

C. ×jenkinsae hort. (*C. carpatica* 'Alba' × *C. rotundifolia*.) St. to 30cm, erect. Fls in lax pan., few, white, broadly campanulate. Z5.

C. kachethica Z. Kantsch. Perenn.; st. to 30cm, upright, hispid. Lower lvs to 5cm, obovate, base subcordate, long-petiolate, upper lvs lanceolate, crenate. Fls in clusters or rac.; campanulate to funnelform, white suffused with pale pink, to pale violet-rose. Cauc. Z6.

C. kantschavelii Zagar. Perenn., st. to 30cm, many, tinged with grey, like *C. kachethica*. Fls in lax pan., narrow campanulate, pale violet-blue. Cauc. Z6.

C. kemulariae Fomin. Clump-forming perenn.; st. to 30cm, much-branched. Basal lvs clustered, ovate-cordate, acuminate, biserrate, long-petiolate, stiff, upper lvs incised. Fls long-stalked, campanulate, blue to pale lilac. Summer. Cauc. Z4.

C. ×kewensis hort. (*C. arvatica* × *C. excisa*.) Intermediate between parents. Gdn origin. Z5.

C. khasiana Hook. f. & Thoms. Perenn., to 1.2m erect to ascending. Lvs to 5cm, narrow-ovate, setose, rigid, dentate. Fls in pan. or corymbs, pendulous, campanulate to funnelform, purple. Summer. Khasia Mts. Z6.

C. kolenatiana C.A. Mey. ex Rupr. Monocarpic or perenn.; st. many, erect to ascending. Lower lvs to 3cm, rosulate, ovate-cordate, crenate, pubesc., long-petiolate. Fls solitary or in a few-fld pan., pendulous, campanulate, blue-violet. Cauc. Z5.

C. komarovii Maleev. Woody-based perenn. Lower lvs rosulate, oblanceolate, remotely crenate, pubesc., winged-petiolate. Fls in loose, term. spikes, campanulate, deep violet. Cauc. Z5.

C. laciniata L. Bienn. or perenn., pubesc.; st. to 60cm, erect, usually branched. Lower lvs rosulate, lanceolate, deeply laciniate, lobes linear-oblong, petiole winged. Fls in a large dense rac., widely campanulate, pubesc., blue. Greece, Crete. Z8.

C. lactiflora Bieb. Sparsely setose perenn.; st. to 1.5m, strong, erect, branched. Lower lvs narrowly ovate to ovate-oblong, thin, serrate, short-petiolate. Fls erect, in broad leafy pan.; broadly campanulate, milky blue, fading to a white centre. Summer. Cauc. 'Alba': fls white. 'Loddon Anna': 90cm; fls lilac-pink. 'Macrantha': fls violet-purple. 'Pouffe': habit dwarf; fls mid-blue. 'Pritchard's Variety': 50cm; fls amethyst-violet. 'Superba': fls large, violet-blue. 'White Pouffe': fls white, otherwise as for 'Pouffe'. Z5.

C. lamiifolia Adams = *C. alliariifolia*.

C. lanata Friv. Wooly bienn. or monocarpic perenn.; st. to 70cm, branched, prostrate. Lower lvs large, cordate-acuminate, serrate-crenate, grey-lanate, oblong. Fls solitary, axill., short-stalked, broadly campanulate, bearded, cream to palest pink. Summer. Bulg., N Greece. Z7.

C. lasiocarpa Cham. Subglabrous, tufted, perenn., to 18cm. Lower lvs spathulate to oblanceolate, base cuneate, apex serrate, long-petiolate. Fls suberect, usually solitary, term., funnelform to campanulate violet tinged blue. Summer. N Amer. 'Alba': fls white. Z4.

C. latifolia L. Perenn.; st. to 1m, upright, unbranched, finely pubesc. Lower lvs ovate-oblong, cordate, strongly serrate, velutinous, long-petiolate. Fls in lf-axils or term. clusters infundibular-campanulate, light blue or pale lavendar. Summer. Eur. to Kashmir. 'Alba': fls white, occas. with basal blue ring. 'Brantwood': fls deep violet-blue. 'Eriocarpa': fls purple. 'Gloaming': fls pale lilac. 'Pallida': fls extremely pale blue. 'White Ladies': fls white. var. *macrantha* Fisch. ex Hornem. Fls large, violet-blue. 'Alba': fls white. Z3.

C. latiloba A. DC. Like *C. persicifolia*, but more robust, to 90cm. Lvs lanceolate, acute, dentate, to 10cm, petioles slightly winged. Fls widely campanulate, deep blue. Summer. Sib. Z3.

C. latiloba A. DC. = *C. persicifolia* ssp. *sessiliflora*.

C. leutweinii Heldr. = *C. incurva*.

C. lingulata Waldst. & Kit. Hispid bienn. or perenn. to 30cm, many, erect-ascending. Lower lvs oblanceolate-spathulate, crenate, narrowed to a short petiole. Infl. capitate, cylindric-infundibular, violet. Balk. Z6.

C. linifolia Scop. Erect, tufted perenn.; st. to 25cm, procumbent to upright. Lower lvs ovate-reniform, undulate, petiolate, upper lvs linear. Fls term., solitary or in pan., funnelform to broad-campanulate, blue to mauve. Summer. C Eur. 'Alba': fls white. 'Valdensis': lvs silver-pubesc.; fls numerous, rich-purple. Z5.

C. loeflingii Brot. = *C. lusitanica*.

C. longistyla Fomin. Erect, subglabrous, bienn. or perenn., to 60cm. Lower lvs rosulate, ovate, undulate, petiolate. Fls nodding in spike-like rac. or pan.; campanulate, waisted, deep violet to blue. Summer. Cauc. Z6.

C. lusitanica L. ex Loefl. Ann. to 30cm; st. many, subglabrous to setose. Lvs to 5cm, lower lvs ovate-reniform, upper lvs narrow-ovate. Fls in loose pan., on slender stalks, campanulate, lobes spreading, white at base, grading to blue suffused with violet. Spain, Port., NW Afr. Z8.

C. lyrata Lam. Scabrid bienn. or perenn. to 70cm, erect. Lower lvs lyrate or ovate-oblong to cordate, serrate, lobulate-petiolate. Fls in loose rac. or pan., cylindric to infundibular, violet-blue. Spring–summer. Asia Minor. Z7.

C. macrantha Fisch. = *C. latifolia* var. *macrantha*.

C. macrophylla Sims = *C. alliariifolia*.

C. macrorrhiza Gay ex A. DC. Tufted perenn.; st. to 30cm, ascending. Lower lvs suborbicular-cordate, serrate, petiolate. Fls term. and axill., broad-campanulate, violet-blue. Summer. S Fr., It. Z7.

C. macrostyla Boiss. & Heldr. Finely hispid ann. with long, rigid hairs; st. to 35cm, erect. Lower lvs ovate-lanceolate, upper lvs narrow-ovate, cordate and auricled at base, revolute, hispid. Fls few, solitary, erect, campanulate, short, dull purple netted pink or violet; style long, exserted. Summer. C Turk. Z7.

C. makaschvilii E. Busch. Like *C. alliariifolia*, but smaller. Cauc. Z6.

C. medium L. CANTERBURY BELLS; CUP AND SAUCER. Pubesc. bienn.; st. erect, much-branched, to 90cm. Lower lvs rosulate, elliptic, hispid, crenate, usually sessile. Fls in term. rac.; cal. lobes sometimes enlarged, fused or appendaged; cor. campanulate-urceolate, in shades of blue, through to mauve, purple or rose, lobes short, forming a recurved rim. Summer. S Eur. 'Alba': fls white. 'Bells of Holland': everg., clump-forming bienn.; lvs lanceolate; fls large blue, white or lilac. 'Caerulea': fls blue. 'Calycanthema': cal. lobes petaloid, either divided or coherent, forming a 'saucer' fls generally larger. Dean Hybrid: fls to 12cm, pale grey-blue to dark blue, pink to carmine. Dwarf Musical Bells: dwarf; fls white, blue, pink. 'Flore Pleno': fls hose-in-hose blue, pink, or white. 'Nana': habit dwarf. 'Rosea': fls pink. 'Wigandii': lvs yellow, fls blue. Z8.

C. michauxioides Boiss. Robust bienn., to 1.2m, leafy below. Lvs elliptic-cordate, serrate, long-petiolate. Fls pale blue, obconic in elongated conical rac. Caria. Z6.

C. mirabilis Albov. Monocarpic; st. to 46cm, many, branched below. Lower lvs rosulate, oblong glab., glossy, crenate, stiffly ciliate, with a long, winged petiole. Pan. pyramidal, crowded; fls campanulate, pubesc., lilac to blue. Summer. Cauc. 'Albiflora': fls pale lilac or white, broadly campanulate. 'Mist Maiden': 15cm; fls v. pale grey-white. Z5.

C. moesiaca Velen. Small, subglabrous bienn. Lvs rosulate, broad-linear to oblong, base abruptly attenuate to winged petiole. Fls in dense spikes or clusters, bracteate, campanulate, mauve to blue. Cauc. Z6.

C. mollis L. Softly grey-pubesc. perenn.; st. to c20cm, procumbent to slightly ascending. Lower lvs rosulate, small, spathulate, undulate, sessile. Fls few, long-stalked funnelform, pale lavender or lilac. Summer. S Spain. 'Gibraltarica': larger. 'Molly Pinsent': 20cm; fls violet-blue. Z8.

C. morettiana Rchb. Small, tufted perenn., pubesc.; st. slender. Lower lvs elliptic-cordate, crenate, subglabrous, long-petiolate. Fls erect, pedicellate, usually solitary, campanulate to funnelform, violet-blue, rarely white. Summer. N It., Tyrol. 'Alba': fls white. Z6.

C. muralis Portenschl. = *C. portenschlagiana*.

C. nitida Sol. in Ait. = *C. persicifolia*.

C. nobilis Lindl. = *C. punctata*.

C. oblongifolia (K. Koch) Charadze. Grey-velutinous perenn., to 90cm. Lower lvs obovate, long-petiolate, denticulate, scabrid. Fls in interrupted pan., few; cal. grey-white pubesc.; cor. cylindric to funnelform, elongated. Cauc. Z6.

C. ochroleuca Kem.-Nat. Perenn., to 75cm, resembling *C. alliariifolia*. Lower lvs rosulate, deltoid-cordate, long-petiolate. Fls in spikes or pan.; narrow-campanulate, cream-white; style exserted. Cauc. Z6.

C. olympica Boiss. Sparsely pilose to glab. bienn. or perenn.; st. to 50cm, procumbent to erect. Lower lvs rosulate, spathulate to obovate-elliptic, crenate. Fls erect in pan. or corymbs; funnel-form, violet-blue. Greece, Mt Olympus. Z8.

C. orbelica Pančic. Tufted, subglabrous perenn., to 12cm. Lower lvs oblanceolate. Fls solitary or in many-fld, secund rac., pendulous, campanulate to urceolate, blue. Summer. Greece (Thrace). Z8.

C. oreadum Boiss. & Heldr. Tufted perenn., grey-hispid. St. to 10cm, slender, flexuous. Basal lvs oblong-spathulate, obtuse, entire, petiolate. Fls solitary or few, long-stalked, narrowly campanulate, blue, with hirsute veins. Greece. Z8.

C. orphanidea Boiss. Pubesc. bienn.; st. to 15cm, procumbent to ascending. Lower lvs rosulate, oblong-obtuse, base rounded, crenulate, hirsute, long-petiolate. Fls solitary or to 9 per rac., narrowly campanulate, deep-violet. S Bulg., NE Greece. Z6.

C. ossetica Bieb. = *Symphyandra pendula*.

C. parryi A. Gray. Subglabrous perenn.; st. to 25cm, upright. Lower lvs to 5cm, rosulate, oblanceolate, subentire. Fls erect, usually solitary, terminal, campanulate to rotate, violet-blue. N Amer. (Rocky Mts). 'Alba': fls white. Z4.

C. patula L. Hispid bienn.; st. slender, erect, to 70cm. Lower lvs to 8cm, oblanceolate to obovate, crenulate, petiolate. Fls erect, in corymbs, infundibular, blue-purple or white. Autumn. Eur., W Sib. Z6.

C. pelviformis Lam. Bienn. closely resembling *C. carpatica*; st. to 30cm, erect to ascending. Lvs lanceolate, setose, crenate-serrate. Fls openly campanulate, blue suffused with lilac, rarely white. Crete. Z8.

C. pentagonia (L.) A. DC. = *Legousia pentagonia*.

C. peregrina L. Hispid bienn.; st. to 70cm, ascending. Lower lvs to 11cm, rosulate, ovate to obovate, crenate, attenuate to winged petiole. Fls solitary or in clusters or spikes, broadly campanulate to funnelform, bright to deep blue. Summer. Medit. Z8.

C. persicifolia L. WILLOW BELL; PEACH-BELLS. Glab. perenn.; st. to 70cm, erect, striate. Lower lvs lanceolate to oblong-obovate, crenate, attenuate to long petiole. Fls nodding in slender term. rac.; broadly campanulate, blue or white. Summer. Eur., N Afr., N and W Asia. Many cvs; fls single or double, white through blue to purple-blue. 'Alba': fls white. 'Alba Coronata': fls semi-double, white. 'Alba Flore-Pleno': fls double, white. 'Boule de Neige': fls large, double, white. 'Coerulea Coronata': fls semi-double, blue. 'Coerulea Flore Pleno': fls double, blue. 'Fleur de Neige': fls double, white. 'Flore Pleno': fls double, lilac-blue. 'Gawen': fls semi-double, white. 'Grandiflora Alba': fls white. 'Hampstead White': fls white. 'Loddon Petal': fls dark blue. 'Moerheimii': fls white, semi-double, slender-stalked. 'Porzellan': fls blue. 'Pride of Exmouth': fls purple-blue. 'Telham Beauty' ('Maxima'): fls single, exceptionally large. ssp. *sessiliflora* (K. Koch) Velen. ex Greuter and Burdet. fls unstalked. 'Alba': fls white. 'Hidcote Amethyst': fls pale amethyst, with deeper coloured tips and median stripe. 'Highcliffe': fls deep violet-blue. 'Percy Piper': habit dwarf; fls rich lavender. Z3.

C. petiolata A. DC. = *C. rotundifolia*.

C. petraea L. Grey-pubesc. perenn. or bienn.; st. to 25cm, erect. Lower lvs narrow ovate, crenate-serrate, petiolate. Fls in a bracteate, compact head, campanulate, tomentose, white, occas. tinged yellow. Summer. S Fr., It. Z8.

C. petrophila Rupr. Tufted, subglabrous or thinly downy perenn.; st. to 12cm, procumbent. Lvs ovate to suborbicular, entire or occas. tridentate at apex, long-petiolate. Infl. 1-many-fld; fls erect, long-stalked cylindric to campanulate, pale blue to blue. Cauc. Z4.

C. phrygia Jaub. & Spach. Finely pubesc. ann.; st. to 15cm, slender, flexuous. Lower lvs obovate to orbicular, crenate, subsessile. Fls erect, solitary, terminal, long-stalked, shortly obconic to campanulate, blue suffused with violet, with darker veins. Summer. SE Eur. Z8.

C. phyctidocalyx Boiss. ex Noë. Glab. perenn. resembling *C. persicifolia* but lower growing with longer, narrower cal. lobes and a smaller, shorter cor.; st. to 38cm. Lower lvs to 4cm, oblanceolate, sinuate to crenate, narrowed into a long petiole, upper lvs lanceolate, sessile. Fls erect, solitary or in rac., long-stalked, open-campanulate, blue. Armenia, Persia. Z8.

C. pilosa Herd. = *C. chamissonis*.

C. piperi T.J. Howell. Tufted perenn., subglabrous; st. to 10cm. Lvs to 2.5cm, oblanceolate, serrate, coriaceous, glossy. Fls solitary or clustered, funnelform to open-campanulate, bright blue. N Amer. 'Alba': fls white. 'Souv019regniana': fls large, white. Z7.

C. portenschlagiana Schult. Finely pubesc. perenn., tufted; st. to 25cm, decumbent to ascending. Lvs cordate to suborbicular, crenate, serrate, petiolate. Fls in a loose pan., funnelform to campanulate, lobes short, deflexed, deep lavender. Summer. S Eur. 'Alba': fls white. 'B. Provis': fls numerous, pale violet. 'Bavarica': scarcely distinct from the typical state. 'Major': fls far larger, purple-blue. 'Resholt Variety': fls deep, vivid blue. Z4.

C. poscharskyana Degen. Pubesc. perenn., similar to *C. portenschlagiana*, but less coarse. Lvs slightly more acuminate, finely dentate, ciliate. Fls in a loose rac. or pan., funnelform-star-shaped, lavender to violet. Summer–autumn. N Balk. 'Blue Gown': fls large, mid blue. 'E.H. Frost': fls star-shaped, milk-white. 'Erich G. Arends': fls blue. 'Lilacina': fls lilac-pink. 'Lisduggan Variety': fls lavender-pink. 'Rosea': fls pink. 'Stella': fls star-shaped, vivid violet-blue. Z3.

C. prenanthoides Dur. Perenn.; st. to 75cm, clustered, upright. Lvs to 5cm, lanceolate to elliptic, irregularly deep-serrate, sub-sessile. Fls few, in loose heads, campanulate to funnelform, lobes narrow, pale blue. Calif. Z8.

C. primulifolia Brot. Hispid perenn.; st. to 90cm, branching below angular, succulent. Lower lvs to 15cm, rosulate, obovate, biserrate, with winged petioles. Fls term. and axill. in clusters of 3–5, wide-campanulate, purple-blue with a paler base. Summer. Spain, Port. Z8.

C. ×*pseudoraineri* hort. (*C. raineri* × *C. carpatica* var. *turbinata*.) Close to *C. carpatica* var. *turbinata* but with somewhat greyer lvs. Z4.

C. pulla L. Glab., tufted perenn.; st. to 13cm. Lower lvs rosulate, round-spathulate, obtusely serrate, glossy. Fls nodding, solitary, terminal, stalked, funnelform-campanulate, dark violet. Summer. E Eur. Z6.

C. ×*pulloides* hort. (*C. carpatica* var. *turbinata* × *C. pulla*.) To 15cm, favours *C. pulla*, but with loose basal rosettes, lvs larger, fewer, generally taller. Summer. Gdn origin. 'G.F. Wilson': fls large, widely campanulate, violet-blue. Z6.

C. punctata Lam. Suberect, hispid perenn.; st. to 35cm, vigorous, branched above. Lvs cordate acuminate, fleshy, crenate-serrate, long-petiolate. Fls pendulous, in few-fld, spike-like, term. rac., broad-cylindric, waxy cream to shell pink, sometimes with crimson specks inside. Summer. Sib., Jap. 'Alba': fls white or off-white. 'Nana Alba': habit dwarf; fls cream-white. 'Rosea' (var. *microdonta*): habit small; fls pale pink. 'Rubriflora': fls narrow, cream, tinged purple, with heavy, bright red flecks inside. Z6.

C. pusilla Haenke = *C. cochleariifolia*.

C. pyramidalis L. CHIMNEY BELLFLOWER. Short-lived perenn. to 150cm; st. glab., stout, usually single, erect. Lower lvs broadly ovate, dentate, long-petiolate. Fls to 4cm diam., fragrant, crowded on the spike-like lat. br. of a massive, slender, pyramidal pan., widely campanulate, pale blue to white. Summer. Eur. 'Alba': fls white. 'Aureovariegata': lvs blotched yellow. 'Caerulea': fls blue. 'Compacta': to 70cm; fls larger. Z8.

C. ×*pyraversi* hort. (*C. pyramidalis* × *C. versicolor*.) Longer-lived than *C. pyramidalis*, which it resembles in form and habit. Fls same size and shape as *C. versicolor*, in a wide range of colours. Gdn origin. Z8.

C. raddeana Trautv. Tufted, glab. perenn.; st. to 30cm, slender. Lower lvs rosulate, deltoid-cordate, serrate, glossy, long-petiolate. Fls large, pendulous, in rac., broad-campanulate, deep violet-purple. Summer. Cauc. Z6.

C. raineri Perpenti. Tufted perenn.; st. to 8cm, upright, usually branched. Lvs obovate, dentate, subsessile, grey. Fls large, erect, solitary, terminal, open-campanulate, pale blue. Summer. Switz., It. Z6.

C. ramosissima Sibth. & Sm. Subglabrous ann.; st. to 40cm, upright, simple or branched. Lvs obovate to spathulate, crenate, sparsely setose. Fls erect, solitary, long-stalked, wide-campanulate to rotate, violet or pale blue to white at centre. Summer. S Eur.

C. rapunculoides L. Glab. to shortly pubesc. perenn. to 90cm; st. to 1m, simple, erect, leafy. Lower lvs cordate-acuminate, crenate-serrate, long-petiolate. Fls nodding in a secund spike-like rac., infundibular-campanulate, blue to violet. Summer. Eur. 'Alba': fls white. Z3.

C. rapunculus L. RAMPION. Glab. or finely pubesc. bienn.; st. to 1m, erect. Lower lvs obovate, acute, ± toothed on long winged petioles, upper lvs linear, sessile. Fls small, solitary, rarely in a spike-like rac. or pan.; infundibular, white to pale blue or lilac. Spring. Eur., N Afr.

C. regina Albov = *C. mirabilis*.

C. reiseri Hal. Finely pubesc. perenn.; st. to 40cm, thick, procumbent to ascending. Lower lvs cordate-lanceolate, serrate, with winged petioles. Fls erect, in short, lax, secund rac., cylindric-campanulate, pale blue to violet; style exserted. Summer. Greece. Z8.

C. reuterana Boiss. & Bal. Differs from *C. strigosa* in cor. to 35mm, cal. lobes lanceolate, not subulate. Asia Minor. Z7.

C. rhomboidalis L. Erect, subglabrous perenn.; st. to 60cm, branched above. Lower lvs ovate-lanceolate to rhomboid, sinuate, long-petiolate. Fls few, pendulous, in a rac.; broadly campanulate, deep purple-blue. Summer. Eur. 'Alba': fls white. Z5.

C. rotundifolia L. BLUEBELL; HAREBELL. Perenn.; st. to 45cm, many, erect. Lower lvs rosulate, cordate to suborbicular, sinuate, long-petiolate. Fls pendulous, few in slender-stalked, term. rac. or short pan., or solitary, campanulate, white to deep blue. Summer. Much of Eur., N Hemis. 'Alba': fls white. 'Flore Pleno' (probably *C.* ×*haylodgensis*): fls double. 'Nana': habit dwarf. 'Olympica': 22cm; lvs dark green, serrate. 'Purple Gem': fls rich purple. 'Soldanelloides': cor. composed of many narrow seg. Z3.

C. rupestris Sibth. & Sm. Bienn.; st. to 45cm, erect to procumbent, finely pubesc., grey-green. Lower lvs to 8cm, elliptic to lyrate, with suborbicular terminal lobe, petiolate, tomentose. Fls many in spikes or pan., campanulate, pubesc., blue-mauve. Greece. Z9.

C. ruthenica Bieb. = *C. bononiensis*.

C. sacajaweana Peck = *C. rotundifolia*.

C. sarmatica Ker-Gawl. Coarse, clump-forming perenn.; st. to 50cm, stout, unbranched, erect. Lower lvs deltoid-acuminate, base cordate, irregularly crenate, long-petiolate. Fls pendulous or erect in secund, long, lax rac., campanulate, lobes flaring, bearded, grey-blue. Summer. Cauc. Z5.

C. sartorii Boiss. & Sprun. Bienn. St. to 25cm, procumbent. Basal lvs to 1.5cm diam., rotund-cordate. Fls solitary, erect, infundibular, white or pink. E Medit., Greece. Z8.

C. saxatilis L. Tufted, subglabrous perenn.; st. to 20cm, erect to ascending, flexuous. Lower lvs to 5cm, rosulate, oblanceolate, thick, entire to dentate, petiolate. Fls pendulous in loose clusters or spikes, cylindric-campanulate, finely pubesc., pale blue or deeper, with darker veins. Summer. Crete, Greece. Z8.

C. saxifraga Bieb. Similar in habit to *C. aucheri*, and *C. tridentata*, but with greener foliage. Lower lvs rosulate, linear-lanceolate, margins grey-pubesc., attenuate to petiolate. Fls many, erect, violet-blue. Late spring. Cauc. Z4.

C. scabrella Engelm. Scabrid or finely hispid, tufted perenn., to 10cm. Lower lvs oblanceolate. Fls erect, solitary or in small clusters, blue. NW US. Z6.

C. scheuchzeri Vill. = *C. linifolia*.

C. scouleri Hook. ex A. DC. Like *C. prenanthoides*, but st. shorter, to 30cm, upper lvs broader, mostly petiolate and fls cylindric-campanulate. N. Amer. Z6.

C. sibirica L. Shortly scabrid to hirsute bienn. or monocarpic; st. to 50cm, many, ascending, branched. Lower lvs rosulate, lanceolate to oblong, crenate, petioles winged. Fls numerous or in branched heads, funnelform-campanulate, lobes flaring, sometimes pubesc. within, blue-lilac. Summer. E Eur., temp. Asia. Z6.

C. spathulata Sibth. & Sm. = *C. spruneriana*.

C. spicata L. Erect ann. or bienn., hispid; st. to 65cm, simple. Lower lvs rosulate, spathulate-obovate, subentire to crenate. Fls small, numerous, in long rac., narrow-funnelform, pubesc. within, blue tinged with violet. Tyrol.

C. spruneriana Hampe. Cushion-forming perenn.; st. to 45cm, slender. Lower lvs oblanceolate-obovate, crenate, long-petiolate. Fls erect, solitary, long-stalked, campanulate to wide funnelform, pale blue to nearly white. Greece, Crete, Balk. Z7.

C. 'Stansfieldii'. (*C. carpatica* var. *turbinata* × *C. waldsteiniana*.) Densely tufted, perenn.; runners creeping; st. to 15cm, ascending. Lvs to 5cm, elongate-cordate, undulate, serrate, velutinous. Fls pendulous, solitary, open campanulate, lilac-blue. Summer. Z5.

C. stevenii Bieb. Caespitose perenn.; st. to 60cm, slender, erect or ascending, leafy below. Lower lvs rosulate, narrow obovate, attenuate, petiolate, subentire to crenate. Fls solitary or corymbose, broad-funnelform to campanulate, blue to lilac. Asia Minor, Cauc. 'Nana': habit dwarf, free-flowering. Z5.

C. stricta L. Perenn.; st. to 60cm, ascending, hispid. Lower lvs to 5cm, obovate, petiolate. Fls in a spike or solitary, cylindric, blue. Late summer–autumn. E Medit. Z8.

C. strigosa Banks & Sol. Hispid ann.; st. erect, flexuous, dichotomously branched below. Lvs to 6cm, oblong to oblanceolate, obtuse, entire, sessile, pubesc. Fls erect, term. or

in forks of br., 25–30mm, campanulate, purple tinged with red
to violet-blue. Asia Minor to Persia. Z8.

C. subpyrenaica Timb.-Lag. = *C. persicifolia.*

C.takesimana Nak. Erect perenn. to 60cm. Lvs large in basal rosettes. Fls large, tubular-campanulate, lilac-white spotted
maroon within on nodding stalks in branched infl. Summer.
Korea. Z7.

C.teucrioides Boiss. Dwarf, tufted, subglabrous perenn.; st. to
5cm, procumbent to ascending. Lower lvs rosulate, ovate-
cuneate, pinnatifid, narrowed to short petioles. Fls erect,
narrow funnelform-campanulate, violet to lilac blue. Asia
Minor. Z7.

C.thessela Maire. Procumbent perenn., grey-tomentose. Lower
lvs obovate, lyrate-lobate. Fls in lax pan., cylindric-funnelform,
pale violet. Greece. Z8.

C.thyrsoides L. Monocarpic or bienn., coarse; st. to 70cm, stout,
erect, setose. Lower lvs rosulate, oblong-runcinate to
lanceolate, upper lvs closely packed, lanceolate, v. hispid. Fls in
a dense cylindric to pyramidal spike, pale yellow. Summer. Eur.
Alps. 'Carniolica': to 70cm; spike v. narrow; fls yellow-white.
Z5.

C.tomentosa Lam. Densely tomentose bienn. or perenn.; st. to
45cm, few, erect. Lower lvs large, to 30cm, lyrate. Fls large, in
rac. or pan., tubular-campanulate or urceolate, hoary-pubesc.,
deep blue. Greece. Z8.

C.tommasiniana K. Koch. Glab., tufted perenn.; st. to 30cm,
slender, pendulous. Lvs lanceolate, acute, serrulate, short-
petiolate. Fls in dense pendulous cymes, cylindric-campanulate,
pale violet to lilac-blue. It. Z6.

C. trachelioides Bieb. = *C. rapunculoides.*

C.trachelium L. NETTLE-LEAVED BELLFLOWER; THROATWORT.
Usually setose, erect perenn.; st. to 1m, angled, tinged red.
Lower lvs ovate-cordate, acuminate, crenate, setose, long-
petiolate. Fls forming dense pan. tubular-campanulate, finely
pubesc., blue-purple to violet. Summer. Eur., N Afr., Sib.
'Alba': fls white. 'Alba Flore-Pleno': lvs light green; fls semi-
double, cup-shaped, white. 'Bernice': habit somewhat rigid; fls
double, blue. Z4.

C.trautvetteri Grossh. ex Fed. Perenn. to 30cm, usually pubesc.
Lower lvs rosulate, obovate, base attenuate, serrulate,
petiolate. Fls in term. pan., bracteate, mauve. E Cauc. Z8.

C.tridentata Schreb. Tufted, subglabrous perenn.; st. erect to
ascending. Lvs spathulate, with 3+ crenate teeth at apex, grey-
green pubesc. Fls solitary, erect, long-stalked, campanulate,
pale to deep blue, darker without, white at base. Spring. Cauc.
Z4.

C. turbinata Schott = *C. carpatica* var. *turbinata.*

C. × tymonsii hort. (*C. carpatica* × *C. pyramidalis.*) Resembling a
smaller, more intensely coloured *C. pyramidalis.* Gdn origin.
Z4.

C.uniflora L. Subglabrous, usually tufted perenn., to 20cm; st.
slender, ascending to upright. Lower lvs spathulate, obtuse,
subentire. Fls solitary, erect, campanulate, deep blue to deep
violet. Arc., Rocky Mts. Z2.

C. urticifolia Schum. = *C. trachelium.*

C. valdensis All. = *C. linifolia* 'Valdensis'.

C. × vanhouttei Carr. (?*C. punctata* × *C. latifolia.*) To 40cm. Fls
few, pendulous, campanulate, dark blue-purple. Z4.

C. velutina Velen. non Desf. = *C. lanata.*

C. velutina Desf. non Velen. = *C. mollis.*

C.versicolor Andrews. Upright perenn. to 60cm resembling
C. pyramidalis in habit; st. leafy. Lower lvs ovate to ovate-
cordate, crenate, olive-green, long-petiolate. Fls in long
compound rac., spicily fragrant, rotate-campanulate, violet and
pale blue, bicoloured. Summer. W Greece, Albania, Balk., SE
It. Z8.

C.vidalii H. Wats. Shrubby perenn. with many robust, scarred st.
branching from single main st. to 50cm. Lvs linear, crenate,
glossy, veins impressed. Fls nodding, in elongated rac.,
campanulate, waxy, dusky pink, with a shining orange disc.
Late summer. Azores. Z9.

C.waldsteiniana Schult. Like *C. tommasiniana*, but to 15cm. Lvs
small, ovate-elliptic. Fls erect, broad cylindric, deeper blue.
Dalmatia, Croatia. Z6.

C. × wockei Sünderm. (probably *C. pulla* × *C. waldsteiniana.*)
Closer to *C. pulla.* To 10cm. Lower lvs rosulate, ovate. Fls
campanulate, pendulous, pale blue to lilac. Summer. 'Puck':
15cm; fls pale blue, pendent. Z5.

C.zoysii Wulf. Caespitose, subglabrous perenn., to 10cm. Lower
lvs rosulate obovate to suborbicular, entire, petiolate. Fls term.
or axill., pendulous, cylindric-urceolate, clear blue to pale
mauve. Summer. It. Alps. Z6.

C.hybrids and cvs. 'Abundance' (*C. carpatica* var. *turbinata*
× *C. raineri*): lvs mid-green, cordate, acute with crinkled edged,
minutely pubesc. beneath; fls open cup-shaped. 'Birch Hybrid'
(*C. portenschlagiana* × *C. poscharskyana*): 15cm; fls light blue.

'Burghaltii' (*C. latifolia* × *C. punctata*): fls on erect st., nodding,
funnel-shaped, amethyst-purple in bud, turning pale grey-
mauve with age. 'Constellation': lvs large, acuminate; fls large.
'E.K. Toogood': lvs glab., cordate; fls star-shaped, bright blue
with paler centre. 'Hallii' (*C. cochleariifolia* 'Alba' × *C. portenschlagiana*): lvs glossy, pale green; fls white. 'Joe Elliot'
(*C. raineri* × *C. morettiana*): fls mid-blue, open. 'Lynchmere'
(*C. elatines* × *C. rotundifolia*): miniature; lvs bright green; fls
pendent, rich violet-blue. 'Norman Grove' (*C. isophylla*
× *C.* 'Stansfieldii'): st. tinged red; lvs pale green; fls funnelform,
semi-pendent, rich lilac-blue.
→*Azorina.*

CAMPANULACEAE Juss. 87/1950. *Adenophora, Asyneuma,
Campanula, Canarina, Centropogon, Codonopsis, Cyananthus,
Downingia, Edraianthus, Hypsela, Jasione, Legousia, Lobelia,
Michauxia, Monopsis, Ostrowskia, Petromarula, Phyteuma,
Platycodon, Pratia, Symphyandra, Trachelium, Wahlenbergia.*

Campeachy *Haematoxylum campechianum.*

Campelia Rich.
C. zanonia (L.) Kunth = *Tradescantia zanonia.*

Campernelle Jonquil *Narcissus × odorus.*
Camphor Bush *Baeckea camphorata.*
Camphor Daisy *Haplopappus phyllocephalus.*
Camphor Myrtle *Baeckea camphorosmae.*
Camphor Tree *Cinnamomum* (*C. camphora*).
Camphor-weed *Heterotheca subaxillaris; Trichostema lanceola-
tum.*
Campion *Silene.*

Campsidium Seem. Bignoniaceae. 1 everg. vine climbing to
15m. Lvs 10–15cm, imparipinnate; lfts 2–4cm, 11–13, oblong-
elliptic, entire or serrate. Fls in loose term. rac.; cor. 3cm,
tubular-ventricose, scarlet-orange, pubesc. within, lobes 5,
equal, rounded, dentate, sta. 4, 2 exserted. C & S Chile. Z10.

C. chilense Reisseck & Seem. = *C. valdivianum.*

C. valdivianum (Philippi) Bull.
→*Tecoma.*

Campsis Lour. TRUMPET CREEPER. Bignoniaceae. 2 decid. vines,
climbing by aerial roots. Lvs imparipinnate; lfts lanceolate-
elliptic, serrate. Fls in a term. cyme or pan.; cal. 5-lobed; cor. to
8cm, tubular-funnelform, tube curved and expanded; sta. 4. E
Asia, N Amer.

C. capreolata hort. = *Bignonia capreolata.*

C. chinensis (Lam.) Voiss. = *C. grandiflora.*

C. dendrophila Seem. = *Tecomanthe dendrophila.*

C.grandiflora (Thunb.) Schum. CHINESE TRUMPET CREEPER;
CHINESE TRUMPET VINE. To 6m; aerial roots few. Lfts to 7cm,
7–9, glab. Infl. a loose pan.; cal. lobes lanceolate, to 2cm; cor.
limb to 6cm diam., orange outside, rich yellow inside.
Summer–autumn. Jap., China. 'Thunbergii': fls orange, cor.
tube short, lobes reflexed, somewhat hardier, late-flowering.
Z7.

C. hybrida Zab. = *C. × tagliabuana.*

C.radicans (L.) Seem. TRUMPET HONEYSUCKLE; TRUMPET VINE.
To 10m; aerial roots abundant. Lfts to 6cm, 9–11, midrib pubesc. beneath. Fls in clusters to 4–12; cal. lobes triangular, short;
cor. pale orange, yellow inside, limb scarlet to 4cm diam.
Summer. SE US. 'Crimson Trumpet': fls large, deep velvety
red. 'Flava' ('Yellow Trumpet'): fls rich yellow. 'Praecox': fls
scarlet. 'Speciosa': habit shrubby, poor climber; lfts elliptic; fls
small, flaming orange. Z4.

C. × tagliabuana (Vis.) Rehd. (*C. grandiflora* × *C. radicans.*) Lfts
to 8cm, 7–11, narrow-ovate, lightly pubesc. above and on veins
beneath, apex acuminate, serrate. Pan. loose; cor. orange outside, scarlet inside, limb to 6.5cm across. 'Coccinea': fls brilliant
red. 'Mme Galen': vigorous; lfts to 15, small, dark green; fls to
8cm wide, rich deep apricot, veins darker. Z4.
→*Tecoma.*

Camptandra Ridl. Zingiberaceae. 6 perenn. herbs with leafy
reed-like st. and thick rhiz. Infl. terminal; bracts concave; cor.
tube slender; pet. 3; lat. staminodes circular, spreading, white
to pale mauve; lip broad, 2-lobed. SE Asia. Z10.

C.parvula (King ex Bak.) Ridl. To 20cm. Lvs 10×3cm, elliptic,
flushed pink when young; sheaths sometimes red. Bracts fleshy,
downy; fls 4 per bract, waxy; cor. tube 1.5cm, white to pale
yellow. Borneo, Sarawak.
→*Kaempferia.*

Camptorrhiza Hutch. Liliaceae. 1 cormous perenn. herb with a
bent root tuber. Basal lvs 1–2, linear, canaliculate. Fls in a lax

cyme; rachis flexuous; perianth seg. 6, free, oblong, concave, margins involute; sta. 6, fil. swollen in the middle; style simple. S Afr. to Nam., Bots., Zimb., Moz. Z9.
C. strumosa (Bak.) Oberm.

Camptosema Hook. & Arn. Leguminosae (Papilionoideae). 12 shrubs or subshrubs, climbing or suberect. Lvs trifoliolate, rarely 1- or pinnately foliolate. Fls pea-like in axill., fasciculate rac. S Amer. (esp. Braz.). Z9.
C. rubicundum Hook. & Arn. Tall climbing shrub. Lfts 3, to 5cm, oblong or narrow-oval, apex rounded, often emarginate. Rac. to 25cm; fls deep ruby red, standard to 2.5cm, somewhat hooded. Summer. Braz., Arg.
→*Kennedya*.

Camptosorus Link.
C. rhizophyllus (L.) Link = *Asplenium rhizophyllum*.
C. sibiricus Rupr. = *Asplenium ruprechtii*.

Campylanthus Roth. Scrophulariaceae. 9 shrubs. Rac. term.; cal. 5-parted; cor. tube curved, 5-lobed. Summer. Atlantic Is., N Afr., SW Asia. Z9.
C. salsoloides Roth. To 1.8m, st. wiry. Lvs linear, swollen, 1–4cm. Rac. to 10cm; cor. pink, tube slender, incurved, glandular-pubesc. Canary Is.

Campylobotrys Lem.
C. discolor Lem. = *Hoffmannia discolor*.
C. ghiesbreghtii Lem. = *Hoffmannia ghiesbreghtii*.
C. regalis Lind. = *Hoffmannia regalis*.

Campyloneurum Presl. Polypodiaceae. 25 epiphytic ferns. Rhiz. creeping, stout, covered with roots and scales. Fronds stipitate, uniform, simple or pinnate, stiff and leathery. Trop. Amer. Z10.
C. augustifolium (Sw.) Fée. NARROW-LEAVED STRAP FERN; CENTRAL AMERICAN STRAP FERN. Fronds to 70×3cm, erect, arching, or pendent, lanceolate to linear or strap-shaped, apex acute, base decurrent, margins entire and cartilaginous, lustrous above, veins sunken and indistinct, stipes 0 or to 4cm. Flor., W Indies, Mex. S to Arg.
C. costatum (Kunze) Presl. Fronds to 85×6cm, oblong to elliptic or lanceolate, base and apex narrowly acute; costa prominent, secondary veins indistinct, stipes to 15cm. W Indies, S Mex., S to Ecuad.
C. phyllitidis (L.) Presl. FLORIDA STRAP FERN; RIBBON FERN; COW-TONGUE FERN. Fronds to 120×10cm, erect, crowded, strap-shaped, oblong or linear to lanceolate, apex acute obtuse or attenuate, base attenuate and long-decurrent, margin entire and cartilaginous to undulate or revolute, leathery to papery, lustrous and pale yellow-green to lime, stipes to 10cm. Flor., W Indies, Mex., S to Urug., Braz.
C. phyllitidis var. *costatum* (Kunze) Farw. = *C. costatum*.
→*Grammitis, Marginaria* and *Pleopeltis*.

Campylotropis Bunge. Leguminosae (Papilionoideae). 65 shrubs or subshrubs. Lvs (1–)3-foliolate. Fls pea-like, in axill. and term. rac. E Asia. Z7.
C. macrocarpa (Bunge) Rehd. To 1m; twigs subterete, sericeous when young. Lfts to 5cm, elliptic to oblong, usually emarginate, sericeous beneath. Fls 1cm, purple, in rac. clustered at br. tips. Summer–autumn. N & C China.
→*Lespedeza*.

Camwood *Baphia nitida*; *B. racemosa*.
Cana *Copernicia hospita*.
Canada Garlic *Allium canadense*.
Canada Hemlock *Tsuga canadensis*.
Canada Moonseed *Menispermum canadense*.
Canada Pea *Vicia cracca*.
Canada Plum *Prunus nigra*.
Canada Pumpkin *Cucurbita moschata*.
Canada Thistle *Cirsium arvense*.
Canada Violet *Viola canadensis*.
Canada Wild Rye *Elymus canadensis*.
Canadian Aspen *Populus grandidentata*.
Canadian Blueberry *Vaccinium myrtilloides*.
Canadian Burnet *Sanguisorba canadensis*.
Canadian Fleabane *Conyza canadensis*.
Canadian Lily *Lilium canadense*.
Canadian Plum *Prunus nigra*.
Canadian Pondweed *Elodea canadensis*.
Canadian Poplar *Populus* ×*canadensis*.
Canadian Wild Rice *Zizania aquatica*.
Canadian Yew *Taxus canadensis*.
Canaigre *Rumex hymenosepalus*.

Cana Jata *Sabal japa*.

Cananga (DC.) Hook. & Thoms. Annonaceae. 2 everg. trees. Lvs entire, oblong-ovate, acuminate. Fls in nodding axill. clusters, showy; pet. 6, 2-whorled; sta. crowded. Trop. Asia, Australasia. Z10.
C. odorata Hook. & Thoms. ILANG-ILANG. Lvs to 20cm. Fls highly fragrant; pet. to 2.5cm, yellow-green, narrow-lanceolate, drooping. India, Indon., Philipp.

Canarina L. Campanulaceae. 3 glaucous herbaceous perennials differing from *Campanula* in 6-numerous fls and edible berry-like fr. Canary Is., trop. E Afr.
C. abyssinica Engl. Differs from *C. eminii*, in lvs smaller, base cordate, cor. shorter, pedicels spiralling half way up, fil. basally dilated. Ethiop., Kenya, Uganda. Z10.
C. campanula L. = *C. canariensis*.
C. canariensis (L.) Kuntze. CANARY ISLAND BELLFLOWER. Climbing or trailing; st. to 1.2m. Lvs narrowly ovate to linear, base hastate to cordate, serrate. Fls pendulous; cor. campanulate, lobes recurved, orange-yellow, striped red-brown to maroon. Canary Is. Z9.
C. eminii Asch. Smaller than *C. canariensis*. Branchlets slender, drooping, fleshy. Lvs to 8cm, elongate-ovate, crenate at base or lobed. Fls term.; cor. tubular below, inflated above, lobes 6, deltoid, sulphur yellow, striped green. Kenya. Z10.

Canary Balm *Cedronella canariensis*.
Canary-bird Bush *Crotalaria agatiflora*.
Canary-bird Flower *Tropaeolum*.
Canary-bird Vine *Tropaeolum*.
Canary Creeper *Tropaeolum peregrinum*.
Canary Date Palm *Phoenix canariensis*.
Canary Grass *Phalaris canariensis*.
Canary Island Aeonium *Aeonium canariense*.
Canary Island Bellflower *Canarina canariensis*.
Canary Island Date *Phoenix canariensis*.
Canary Island Hare's Foot Fern *Davallia canariensis*.
Canary Island Ivy *Hedera canariensis*.
Canary Islands Pine *Pinus canariensis*.
Canary Laurel *Laurus azorica*.
Canary Whitewood *Liriodendron tulipifera*.

Canavalia DC. Leguminosae (Papilionoideae). 51 perenn. herbs or lianes. Lvs trifoliolate. Fls pea-like, large, in axill. rac. Trop. and Subtrop., mainly Americas. Z10.
C. africana Dunn. Perenn., scandent or procumbent, 3–15m. Lfts 6–16.5cm, ovate-obtuse or rounded, downy. Standard to 3cm, oblong, pale purple, veined white, wings and keel pale purple-red, white below. Fr. to 18cm, filiform-oblong; seeds brown sometimes marbled black. E Afr.
C. ensiformis (L.) DC. JACK BEAN; WONDER BEAN; GIANT STOCK BEAN. Ann., suberect, or twining to 2m. Lfts to 20cm. Fls purple-pink, standard to 2.5cm. Fr. to 40cm, linear; seeds white. S Amer.
C. gladiata (Jacq.) DC. Differs from *C. ensiformis* in fr. wider (to 5cm across) and seeds deep red, coral or chocolate-brown. OW Trop.
C. virosa (Roxb.) Wight & Arn. = *C. africana*.

Cancer Weed *Salvia lyrata*.
Candelabra Aloe *Aloe arborescens*.
Candelabra Cactus *Euphorbia lactea*.
Candelabra Primula *Primula* Candelabra Hybrids.
Candelabra Tree *Araucaria angustifolia*.
Candellila *Euphorbia antisyphilitica*; *Pedilanthus bracteatus*.
Candia Tulip *Tulipa saxatilis*.
Candleberry *Myrica pensylvanica*.
Candleberry Myrtle *Myrica faya*.
Candlenut Tree *Aleurites moluccana*.
Candle Plant *Senecio articulatus*.
Candle Tree *Parmentiera cereifera*.
Candlewood *Rothmannia capensis*.

Candollea Labill. Stylidiaceae. c20 everg. shrubs. Lvs often amplexicaul. Fls yellow, ± unstalked, clustered or solitary; sep. and pet. 5; sta. united into 5 bundles. W Aus.
C. cuneiformis Labill. Shrub to 3m; shoots downy. Lvs 2–5cm, obovate, base cuneate, 3–5-toothed above. Fls 1.5cm diam., in term. clusters. Spring. W Aus.
C. hugelii Benth. Low everg. shrub; shoots white-downy, soon glab. Lvs 2–6cm, narrow-lanceolate, acute, sometimes pubesc. when young. Fls 2cm diam., in term. clusters. Spring. W Aus.
C. tetrandra Lindl. Shrub to 2m. Lvs 1.5–5cm, oval-lanceolate to oblanceolate, short-pointed, serrate above. Fls 3.5–5cm diam., solitary. W Aus.

Candy Carrot *Athamanta cretensis*.
Candytuft *Iberis*.
Candyweed *Polygala lutea*.

Canella P. Browne. WILD CINNAMON; WHITE CINNAMON. Canellaceae. 1 everg. shrub or tree to 15m. Bark white, strongly scented of cinnamon and cloves. Lvs to 10cm, entire, obovate, cuneate at base, subcoriaceous, lustrous above, white or glaucous beneath laurel-scented. Fls to 2cm, purple, red or violet, fragrant (aromatic if dried and rehydrated) in a term. pan.; sep. 3; pet. 4–12 or 0. Berry, bright red, pulpy. Flor., W Indies. Z10.

C. winterana (L.) Gaertn.

CANELLACEAE Mart. 5/16. *Canella*.

Cane Palm *Chrysalidocarpus lutescens*.
Cane Reed *Arundinaria gigantea*.
Canistel *Pouteria campechiana*.

Canistrum E. Morr. Bromeliaceae. 7 perenn. herbs, mostly epiphytic. Lvs in a basal funnel-shaped rosette, ligulate, usually soft green with dark mottling, margins spiny. Infl. densely corymbose, compound, stemless or on a short scape, with colourful, overlapping bracts. Braz. Z10.

C. eburneum E. Morr. = *C. lindenii*.
C. lindenii (Reg.) Mez. Lvs in a broadly funnel-shaped rosette to 1.5m diam.; sheaths large, dark brown-scaly; blades ligulate, spines 3mm, broad. Infl. to 60cm, 500-fld, on a stout, rusty tomentose scape, involucral bracts ivory to white, to 15cm, scaly; pet. white or pale green. var. *viride* (E. Morr.) Reitz. Infl. bracts green. var. *roseum* (E. Morr.) L.B. Sm. Infl. bracts pink to bright red.
→*Aechmea* and *Nidularium*.

Canna L. Cannaceae. 9 rhizomatous perenn. herbs. St. erect, ± reed like with 2-ranked lvs, bases sheathing, blades lanceolate. Infl. a terminal rac. or pan., bracteate; fls asymmetric; sep. 3; pet. 3, unequal, united in basal tube; sta. 1, petaloid with solitary marginal anth., united at base to fleshy style and staminodes; staminodes 1–4, innermost ('labellum') small and often recurved, outer staminodes exceeding pet. New World tropics and subtrop., widely nat.

C. discolor Lindl. = *C. indica*.
C. edulis Ker-Gawl. = *C. indica*.
C. flaccida Salisb. To 2m. Lvs 20–45cm, elliptic-lanceolate, apex narrowly acute to acuminate, glaucous. Infl. simple; cor. 8–9cm, yellow, tube 3–4cm, lobes reflexed, narrowly oblong-lanceolate; staminodes 9–10cm, broadly obovate. SE US, Antilles, Panama. Z8.
C. ×*generalis* L.H. Bail. CANNA LILY. A large group of complex hybrids, varying in habit from short, stocky to tall and slender, in lf colour and texture from glaucous grey and leathery to dark chocolate-red and rather thin, in fl. shape and colour from small with narrow seg. to large and ruffled, from pale yellow to orange or scarlet. Gdn origin. Bailey originally distinguished between *C.* ×*generalis*, with fls to 10cm diam., not tubular at base, pet. not reflexed, staminodes and lip erect or spreading, and *C.* ×*orchiodes* (derived in part from *C. flaccida*) with v. large fls, tubular at base, with pet. reflexed, usually splashed or mottled and 3 broad, wavy staminodes exceeded by the lip. The first group included the Crozy or French cannas. With continued breeding, the distinction between the 2 groups has become blurred. 'Ambrosia': dwarf to 60cm; fls large, pink. 'America': lvs dark copper-purple; fls red. 'Black Knight': lvs brown; fls red. 'Bonfire': to 90cm; fls orange-scarlet. 'Cherry Red': lvs dark; fls bright red. 'City of Portland': to 100cm, strong grower, compact; fls rosy-pink. 'Cleopatra': lvs splashed black; combination of red and yellow fls, red and yellow bicolors often on same plant. 'Crimson Beauty': dwarf to 60cm; lvs broad; fls bright crimson. 'Cupid': fls pink in large clusters. 'Dazzler': to 120cm; fls burgundy. 'Di Bartolo': lvs brown tinged purple; fls deep pink. 'Eureka': dwarf; fls cream tinged white. 'Feuerzauber' ('Fire Magic'): lvs dark copper-purple; fls orange-red. 'Grumpy': miniature, compact to 50cm; fls brilliant red. 'Halloween': dwarf to 75cm; fls golden with red throats. 'J.B. Van der Schoot': to 90cm; lvs yellow speckled red. 'King City Gold': fls yellow. 'King Midas': to 120cm; fls gold. 'Liebesglut': lvs dark copper-purple; fls orange-red. 'Lucifer': dwarf to 75cm; fls crimson red, broad yellow borders or edging on all seg. 'Orange Perfection': to 75cm; fls pale orange. 'Orchid': fls deep pink. 'Park Princess': dwarf to 75cm, compact; lvs glossy; fls pale pink, abundant. 'Pfitzer's Chinese Coral': dwarf to 75cm; fls pink. 'Pfitzer's Primrose Yellow': dwarf to 75cm, bushy; fls pale yellow in large clusters. Pfitzer's 'Salmon Pink': to 80cm, compact, vigorous; fls pink. 'Pfitzer's Scarlet Beauty': dwarf to

80cm, bushy; fls bright scarlet. 'Picasso': fls both yellow and red. 'President': to 120cm; lvs glossy; fls rich scarlet. 'Rosamund Cole': to 120cm; fls scarlet edged yellow, reverse golden with red overlay. 'Red King Humbert': to 2.1m; bronze-red lvs; fls brilliant orange-scarlet. 'Richard Wallace': to 120cm, vigorous grower; fls golden-yellow. 'Striped Beauty': short; lvs bright green veined in shades of cream; fls scarlet in large truss. 'Wyoming': lvs bronze; fls orange. 'Yellow King Humbert': to 135cm; fls yellow dotted crimson. Z8.
C. gigantea Desf. ex Delaroche = *C. tuerckheimii*.
C. glauca L. To 2m. Lvs 30–50cm, narrow-ovate to narrow-elliptic, apex acuminate, glaucous. Infl. simple; cor. 7–9cm, pale yellow, tube 2cm, lobes narrow-ovate, labellum strongly reflexed, outer staminodes, narrow-obovate to -elliptic, to 10cm. Neotrop. Z10.
C. indica L. INDIAN SHOT; QUEENSLAND; ARROWROOT; ACHIRA; TOUS LES MOIS. To 2m, often shorter. Lvs 20–50cm, narrow-ovate to -elliptic, apex acute to short-acuminate, sometimes lanuginose beneath and on sheath, green sometimes stained red-purple. Infl. branched or simple; cor. to 6cm, red to pink-red or orange, tube 1–2cm, lobes linear, to 4cm; labellum narrow-oblong-ovate, to 6cm, red, often spotted or edged yellow or pink, out staminodes, narrow-elliptic to -obovate, to 7cm, red, sometimes spotted yellow. Neotrop., widely nat. elsewhere. 'Purpurea': to 2m, upright, vigorous; lvs large, purple-bronze; fls small, red. Thompson & Morgan hybrids: to 90cm; lvs often bronze; fls in shades of yellow, red and cream. Z8.
C. iridiflora Ruiz & Pav. To 3m. Lvs to 120cm, broad-oblong, apex acute, blue-green, lanuginose beneath when young. Infl. simple or sparsely branched; fls pendent, deep pink or orange; sep. to 3cm, lanceolate, acuminate; cor. to 10cm, tube 6.5cm, lobes spathulate-lanceolate, reflexed at apex; staminodes to 12cm, round-obovate. Peru. Z9.
C. jaegeriana Urban. Lvs 50–100cm, narrow-elliptic to -ovate, apex short-acuminate, sometimes lanuginose beneath. Infl. simple or branched; cor. to 6.5cm, orange, tube 2cm, lobes to 4.5cm; staminodes to 6.5cm, obovate-elliptic. Andes. Z9.
C. lanuginosa Roscoe = *C. indica*.
C. latifolia Mill. = *C. tuerckheimii*.
C. liliiflora Warsc. ex Planch. To 3m. Lvs 90–120cm, oblong, acuminate. Infl. simple or occas. branched, horizontally deflexed; cor. 12–14cm, white, lobes oblong-linear, 2cm broad; staminodes to 3cm broad. Panama, Boliv. Z10.
C. lutea Mill. = *C. indica*.
C. musifolia hort. = *C. indica*.
C. ×*orchiodes* L.H. Bail. see *C.* ×*generalis*.
C. patens (Ait.) Roscoe = *C. indica*.
C. sanguinea Warsc. = *C. indica*.
C. tuerckheimii Kränzl. To 3.5m. Lvs 35–100cm, narrow-ovate to -elliptic, apex short-acuminate, sheath lanuginose. Infl. branched below; cor. 4–8cm, orange-red to red, tube to 3cm, lobes narrow, to 5cm; staminodes erect, outer staminodes to 8cm, narrow-obovate to spathulate. C Amer. Z9.
C. warszewiczii hort. ex A. Dietr. = *C. indica* 'Purpurea'.

CANNABIDACEAE Endl. 2/3. *Cannabis, Humulus*.

Cannabis L. HEMP; MARIJUANA; GANJA; POT; GRASS. Cannabidaceae. 1 coarse, scabrous, bushy, ann. herb, 3–4m. Lvs palmate, with 3–9 lanceolate, serrate lfts to 12cm, grey-green. Fls unisexual, small, green, clustered. C Asia, widely nat. in N temp. regions. Z9.
C. sativa L. ssp. *sativa*. As above. ssp. *indica* (Lam.) Small & Cronq. To 5m, lfts narrower, linear-lanceolate, slender-acuminate. Indian subcontinent.

CANNACEAE. Juss. See *Canna*.

Canna Lily *Canna* ×*generalis*.
Cannibal's Tomato *Solanum uporo*.
Cannonball Tree *Couroupita guianensis*.
Cannon's Stringybark *Eucalyptus macrorhyncha*.
Canoe Birch *Betula papyrifera*.

Canscora Lam. Gentianaceae. 30 erect ann. herbs, to 60cm. St. quadrangular. Lvs opposite, sessile or amplexicaul. Cor. funnelform, limb oblique, lobes 4, overlapping; sta. exserted. OW Trop. Z9.
C. parishii Hook. f. St. to 60cm slender, erect, branched. Lvs connate, glaucous. Fls solitary, axill., short-stalked; cor. white, tube inflated below, lobes obovate, with 2 yellow spots at base. Summer. S Burm.

Canteloupe Melon *Cucumis melo* Cantalupensis group.
Canterbury Bells *Campanula medium*; *Gloxinia perennis*.

Canthium Lam. Rubiaceae. *c*50 shrubs, lianes and trees. St. sometimes spiny. Fls in dense, pedunculate, axilliary fascicles, corymbose cymes or pan.; cal. tubular, short-limbed, truncate, or 4–5-toothed; cor. cylindric, bell- or funnel-shaped, interior pubesc., lobes 4–5, spreading. Trop. Afr., Asia, Oceania. Z10.

C. attenuatum R. Br. Everg. shrub. Lvs to 15cm, oblong-elliptic or narrowly lanceolate, apex obtuse or acute, base attenuate, leathery, lustrous, bright green, veins prominent. Fls to 5mm. Aus.

C. glabrifolium Hiern = *Psydrax subcordata.*
C. subcordatum DC. = *Psydrax subcordata.*

Cañafistola Sabanera *Cassia moschata.*
Canton Ginger *Zingiber officinale.*

Cantua Juss. ex Lam. Polemoniaceae. 6 everg. shrubs and trees. Corymb term., usually many-fld; cor. 5-lobed, long-tubular, lobes short, obovate or ovate; sta. and style exserted. N Chile, Peru, Boliv. and Ecuad. (mts). Z9.

C. bicolor Lam. Hispid shrub to 1.6m. Lvs to 4cm, oblong-elliptic, entire. Fls solitary; cor. to 3.5cm, tube yellow, limb scarlet. Bolivia.

C. buxifolia Juss. ex Lam. SACRED FLOWER OF THE INCAS; MAGIC FLOWER OF THE INCAS; MAGIC FLOWER. Pubesc. shrub to 1(–5)m. Lvs 1–5cm, elliptic to lanceolate, deeply lobed or entire. Infl. 4–8-fld, pendent from horizontal br.; cor. 6–7.5cm long, 2.4–4cm diam., tube pink or purple with yellow stripes, lobes spreading, intense red. Spring. Mts of Peru, Boliv., N Chile.

C. dependens Pers. = *C. buxifolia.*
C. pyrifolia Juss. ex Lam. Shrub or tree to 2(–5)m. Lvs 4–7.5cm, elliptic to oblong, entire to dentate above. Infl. dense, erect, racemose; cor. to 2.5cm, tube yellow, lobes white. Early spring. Mts of Ecuad., Peru, Boliv.

Canyon *Quercus chrysolepis.*
Canyon Gooseberry *Ribes menziesii.*
Canyon Grape *Vitis arizonica.*
Caoutchouc Tree *Hevea brasiliensis.*

Capanea Decne. Gesneriaceae. 10 herbs, subshrubs and lianes. Lvs in equal, opposite pairs, often dentate. Fls axill., solitary or in an umbellate cyme; sep. 5; cor. campanulate, lobes 5, spreading. C & N S Amer. Z10.

C. humboldtii (Klotzsch) Ørst. Shrub or liane to 2m, finely brown-pubesc. Lvs to 18×8.5cm, oblanceolate. Fls grouped 1–4 on stalks to 1.5cm; sep. 5-ribbed; cor. to 5cm, brown-pubesc, outside, yellow-green inside, throat spotted purple. C Amer.

C. oerstedii (Klotzsch) Ørst. Differs from *C. humboldtii* in lvs glab., or short hairy above; sep. 3-ribbed. Costa Rica.

Capanemia Barb. Rodr. Orchidaceae. 12 epiphytic orchids. Pbs small. Lvs small, fleshy, narrow. Fls racemose, small or minute, usually white or green; tep. oblong to obovate; lip erect, simple, with 1 or 2 fleshy calli. Braz., Parag., Arg.

C. micromera Barb. Rodr. Pbs minute, ovoid or obovoid. Lvs to 2.5cm, linear, subterete. Infl. to 1.5cm, ascending, 1 to few-fld; fls to 0.5cm diam., white; lip oblong-pandurate, acute, callus 1, yellow, flattened. Braz.

C. superflua (Rchb. f.) Garay. Pbs small, elongate. Lvs to 7cm, terete. Infl. to 7cm, erect to pendent, few to many-fld; fls to 0.8cm diam., white; lip broadly spathulate or obcordate to sub-pandurate, retuse, calli 2, elevated. Braz., Arg.
→*Oncidium* and *Quekettia.*

Capassa *Lonchocarpus domingensis.*
Cape Aloe *Aloe ferox.*
Cape Blue Water Lily *Nymphaea capensis.*
Cape Boxwood *Notobuxus macowanii.*
Cape Cherry *Cassine sphaerophylla.*
Cape Chestnut *Calodendrum.*
Cape Cowslip *Lachenalia.*
Cape Dandelion *Arctotheca calendula.*
Cape Fig *Ficus sur.*
Cape Forget-me-not *Anchusa capensis.*
Cape Fuschia *Phygelius capensis.*
Cape Gooseberry *Physalis peruviana.*
Cape Grape *Rhoicissus capensis.*
Cape Honeysuckle *Tecomaria capensis.*
Cape Jasmine *Gardenia jasminioides.*
Cape Jessamine *Gardenia augusta.*
Cape Kafferboom *Erythrina caffra.*
Cape Laburnum *Crotalaria capensis.*
Cape Leadwort *Plumbago auriculata.*
Cape Lilac *Ehretia hottentotica.*
Cape Marigold *Dimorphotheca.*

Cape Myrtle *Myrsine africana*; *Phylica.*
Cape Phillyrea *Cassine capensis.*
Cape Pittosporum *Pittosporum viridiflorum.*
Cape Poison Bulb *Boophone disticha.*
Cape Pondweed *Aponogeton distachyos.*
Cape Primrose *Streptocarpus.*
Caper *Capparis spinosa.*
Caper Bean *Zygophyllum.*
Caper Spurge *Euphorbia lathyris.*
Cape Stock *Heliophila.*
Caper Tree *Capparis flexuosa.*
Cape Sundew *Drosera capensis.*
Cape Tulip *Haemanthus coccineus.*
Cape Yellowwood *Podocarpus elongatus.*
Cappadocian Maple *Acer cappadocicum.*

CAPPARIDACEAE Juss. 45/675. *Capparis, Cleome, Crateva, Polanisia.*

Capparis L. Capparidaceae. *c*250 everg. shrubs or small trees, often scandent. Lvs simple, short-petiolate. Rac. or pan. term. or axill., fls white to cream or pink or purple, often fragrant (harvested in bud for capers); sep. 4; pet. 4, equal or slightly unequal, imbricate, mostly obovate; sta. long, showy, many, exceeding pet. Fr. an elongate to globose berry. Subtrop., Trop. Z10 unless specified.

C. acuminata Lindl. non Willd. = *C. acutifolia.*
C. acutifolia Sweet. Shrub to 5m, glab. Lvs to 13×4cm, apex acute to obtuse, acute to cuneate to base, herbaceous to subcoriaceous. Fls fragrant, in rows of 2–4; pet. to 12×5mm, obovate, rounded, margins tomentose; sta. 28–35. SE China, Taiwan, Vietnam. ssp. *bodinieri* (Lév.) Jacobs. Shrub or small tree to 7m. Lvs to 11×4cm, ovate, obtuse or acuminate, acute to rounded at base. Pet. to 14×5mm. India, Burm., SW China.

C. amygdalina Lam. = *C. indica.*
C. arborea (F. Muell.) Maid. NATIVE POMEGRANATE. Tree to 10m, new growth, hairy. Lvs to 14×15cm, coriaceous, acute or subacuminate. Fls usually solitary; pet. to 31×15mm, obovate, fimbriate; sta. 90–110. E Aus.

C. bodinieri Lév. = *C. acutifolia* ssp. *bodinieri.*
C. breynia L. = *C. indica.*
C. chinensis G. Don = *C. acutifolia.*
C. cynophallophora auct. non L. = *C. flexuosa* or *C. odoratissima.*
C. cynophallophora L. JAMAICA CAPER TREE; MUSTARD TREE. Shrub or small tree to 6m. Lvs to 20×6cm, obovate-oblong to elliptic, coriaceous, obtuse to acuminate, lepidote beneath. Infl. a pan. or a corymb, few- to several-fld; pet. to 15mm, ovate, acute, puberulent, sta. some 32. Carib., S Flor., C Amer., W Indies.

C. flexuosa (L.) L. BAY-LEAVED CAPER; CAPER TREE. Shrub or small tree to 8m; br. flexuous when young, glab. Lvs to 15×6cm, broadly obovate to linear, acute to rounded, obtuse to rounded at base, subcoriaceous, verrucose on veins. Infl. a pan., shorter than lvs, few-fld; pet. to 1.5cm, obovate or ovate; sta. 100 or more. S Flor., C Amer. to Central S Amer.

C. indica (L.) Druce. WHITE WILLOW. Lvs elliptic, leathery, br. somewhat scaly. Infl. racemose-corymb. Sta. 16. S Mex. to N S Amer., W Indies.

C. jamaicensis Jacq. = *C. cynophallophora.*
C. lasiantha R. Br. ex DC. SPLIT JACK. Shrub or climber to 3m, br. tomentose. Lvs to 6.5×2cm, ovate or elongate, obtuse or rounded, rounded at base, coriaceous, blue-green above, yellow-green beneath. Fls solitary or in rows of 2 or 3; pet. to 16×4mm, obovate. Aus.

C. lucida Banks. Br. densely velvet-hairy. Lvs elliptic, acute, entire, glab. E Malesia, Aus.

C. mitchellii (Lindl. ex F. Muell.) Benth. WILD ORANGE; NATIVE ORANGE; TREE CAPER. Small tree to 7m, young growth white-pubesc., bark black. Lvs to 6.5×3.5cm, acute at base, coriaceous, puberulent above, densely pubesc. beneath. Fls term., solitary or few; pet. to 3×2cm, interior verruculose, sometimes clawed, fimbriate, sta. 120–130. Aus.

C. odoratissima Jacq. OLIVE WOOD; OLIVO; NARANJUELO. Shrub or tree to 15m. Lvs to 11×6cm, ovate to elliptic-obovate, obtuse to rounded, acute or obtuse at base, coriaceous, glab. above, lepidote, beneath. Infl. a dense pan., term. or axillary; pet. to 8mm, elliptic-ovate, interior puberulent-papillose; sta. 28. S Mex. to N S Amer., Trin., S W Indies.

C. rupestris Sibth. & Sm. = *C. spinosa* var. *inermis.*
C. spinosa L. CAPER; COMMON CAPER. Prostrate shrub. Lvs to 6×5.5cm, elliptic or suborbicular, obtuse to rounded, truncate to rounded at base; petiole to 1.5cm; stipular thorns present. Fls solitary, upper pet. to 5.5×4cm, subrhomboid, lower pet. to 3.5×3.5cm; sta. 100–190. S Eur. and Asia to Malesia, and Pacific (*C. mariana* Jacq. & *C. cordifolia* Lam.), Aus. (var.

nummularia (DC.) Bail.). var. *inermis* Turra. Stipular thorns 0. W Medit. to N India. Z8.

C. umbonata Lindl. Tree to 5m, glab. Lvs to 23×3cm, linear, acute to rounded, coriaceous, bright or dark green. Fls 1–6 per axil; pet. to 3×1.5cm, obovate, fimbriate, base pubesc. Aus.
→*Busbeckea*.

Capraria L.
C. lanceolata L. = *Freylinia lanceolata*.
C. lucida Ait. = *Teedia lucida*.
C. undulata L. = *Freylinia undulata*.

CAPRIFOLIACEAE Juss. 16/365. *Abelia, Diervilla, Dipelta, Kolkwitzia, Leycesteria, Linnaea, Lonicera, Sambucus, Symphoricarpos, Triosteum, Viburnum, Weigela*.

Capsella Medik. Cruciferae. 5 ann. or bienn. herbs. Lvs pinnatifid or entire. Inflorescence racemose; fls small; sep. 4, erect; pet. 4; sta. free. Fr. heart-shaped to bilobed, compressed. Temp. regions and subtrop. Z7.

C. bursa-pastoris (L.) Medik. SHEPHERD'S PURSE. 4–5cm. St. erect, branching. Lvs v. variable, oblanceolate, deeply pinnatifid to entire. Pet. 2–4mm diam., white. Fr. triangular with 2 keeled valves. Naturalised worldwide. Distrib. as for the genus.
→*Thlaspi*.

Capsicum L. PEPPER; GREEN PEPPER; CHILLI PEPPER. Solanaceae. 10 shrubby, ann. to perenn., herbs. Fls solitary or in groups to 3; cal. campanulate or tubular, fleshy, enlarging slightly after flowering; cor. rotate, limb 5-lobed, stellate; sta. 5, equal, portruding. Fr. a 2–3-chambered, shiny berry. Trop. Amer. Z9.

C. annuum L. var. *annuum*. CAPSICUM; PAPRIKA; CAYENNE PEPPER; RED PEPPER; SWEET PEPPER. To 1.5m. St. branched, erect or creeping, fleshy or woody at base. Lvs ovate to lanceolate, to 12×8cm, entire. Fls solitary, campanulate; green white or green, to 15mm diam. Fr. to 15cm, red, orange, yellow, to black. Unknown in the wild, thought to have originated in trop. America. Most cultivated peppers belong to one of 5 main groups of cvs, varying in fr. shape, flavour and colour. (1) Cerasiforme group (CHERRY PEPPER): fr. small, hot, globose, tinged yellow red or purple; some cult. ornamentals. 'Birdseye': small, much-branched; lvs narrow, thin, bright green; fls small, white, abundant. (2) Conioides group (CONE PEPPER): fr. conic, erect, to 5cm; some cult. ornamentals. 'Acorn': habit low, flattened top; lvs rich green; fr. oval, green turning purple then crimson. 'Candle Pepper': habit broad; lvs small, narrow; fr. erect, conical, white turning orange-red. 'Celestial': habit bushy, compact; lvs ovate, deep green; fr. conical, green turning purple and finally orange-red. 'Red Chilli': fr. cardinal red, glossy, edible. (3) Fasciculatum group (RED CONE PEPPER): fr. erect, clustered, to 7.5cm, red, pungent; some cult. ornamentals. (4) Grossum group (PIMENTO, BELL PEPPER, SWEET PEPPER): fr. irregularly ovoid-campanulate, with a basal depression, thick-skinned, blunt, sweet, the principal salad peppers. (5) Longum group (CAYENNE PEPPER, CHILLI PEPPER): fr. pendent, often finely tapering to 30cm, base to 5cm diam., v. hot. 'Aurora': dwarf to 10cm; fr. purple through tan to bright red. 'Fiesta': habit compact, bushy; fr. slender, curved, cream turning orange then red. 'Filius Blue': dwarf to 20cm; fr. tinged blue, some turning red. 'Holiday Cheer': fr. small, round, cream turning bright red. 'Holiday Time': fr. small, conical, green turning to red or purple. 'Piccolo': ornamental; lvs variegated cream, pale and deep green; fls small, lavender, star-shaped; fr. globose, black-purple. 'Pylon Red': dwarf; fr. red, early. 'Red Missile': habit compact; fr. large, conical, red. 'Robert Craig': densely branched; fr. short, conical, cream splashed purple turning red. 'Treasure Red': habit broad, neat; lvs v. deep green; fr. erect, white turning red. 'Variegated Purple': lvs purple variegated whie; fr. purple turning red. 'Weatherillii': lvs large, glossy, fls white; fr. large, yellow turning red.

C. annuum var. *cerasiforme* (Mill.) Irish = *C. annuum* Cerasiforme group.

C. annuum var. *grossum* (L.) Sendt. = *C. annuum* Grossum group.

C. annuum var. *longum* (DC.) Sendt. = *C. annuum* Longum group.

C. baccatum L. Spreading, herb or shrub, to 3m. Fls solitary or paired, to 1.5cm diam., white to yellow. Fr. erect, to 13×7mm, red. Trop. Amer.

C. chinense Jacq. Small shrub, to 1.5m. Fls pendent, to 2 or more per node, dull white, sometimes tinged green. Fr. red-brown to cream, pendulous. Trop. Amer.

C. frutescens L. TABASCO PEPPER; HOT PEPPER; SPUR PEPPER. Woody-based perenn. herb, to 1.5m+. Lvs elliptic, to 10×5cm.

Fls solitary or in groups of 2–3, pale green to yellow, to 1cm diam. Fls in clusters, to 3 per node, narrowly tapered to subglobose, to 7.5×1cm, green, becoming red, hot. Trop. Amer. 'Chameleon': plant to 30cm; fr. green through yellow, purple then red. 'Fips': plant to 18cm; fr. green through yellow to red. 'Long Gold Spike': fr. conical, yellow. 'Paradicsomalaká Zöld': fr. subglobose, resembling a miniature bell pepper, red, lobed, v. hot. 'Szentesi cseresnyepaprika': small, round, green, v. hot, used for pickling. 'Westlandje': long, thin, green to red fruits.

C. microcarpum Cav. = *C. baccatum*.

C. minimum Roxb. = *C. frutescens*.

C. pubescens Ruiz & Pav. Herb or climbing shrub, to 3m, often pubesc. Lvs ovate, rugose, sometimes ciliate. Fls solitary, violet or purple, with a white eye. Fr. pendent to erect, cylindric to globose, yellow to red or brown. S Amer. (Andes).

C. sinense Murray = *C. chinense*.

Caragana Fabr. PEA TREE; PEA SHRUB. Leguminosae (Papilionoideae). c80 decid. shrubs or small trees, mostly armed. Lvs paripinnate, often clustered; petioles and stipules often spiny and persisting as sharp axill. tufts. Fls pea-like, mostly yellow, solitary or fascicled. E Eur., C Asia.

C. altagana Poir. = *C. microphylla*.

C. arborescens Lam. SIBERIAN PEA-TREE. Shrub to 6m. Young branchlets pubesc. Lfts to 2.5cm, 8–12, elliptic, light green, bristle-tipped. Fls 1–4-per cluster, pale yellow, to 2.2cm. Spring. Sib., Manch. 'Albescens': new growth white-yellow, becoming green. 'Lorbergii': lfts 10–14, to 3.5×0.5cm, v. finely linear-lanceolate; pet. narrow. 'Nana': dwarf; branchlets short, twisted. 'Pendula': weeping, grafted on standards of the type. 'Sericea': lfts 8, all parts densely sericeous. 'Walker': procumbent; lfts v. narrow; best top-grafted on to the type. Z2.

C. arborescens var. *cuneifolia* (Dipp.) Schneid. = *C.* × *sophorifolia*.

C. aurantiaca Koehne. Shrub to 1m; branchlets long and thin, lfts 4, to 1.5cm, oblanceolate, light green, glab., distinctly veined. Fls solitary, orange-yellow. Spring–summer. C Asia. Z5.

C. boisii Schneid. = *C. arborescens*.

C. brevispina Royle. Shrub to 2m; young br. pubesc. Lvs to 7cm, 10–14-foliolate; rachis prickly. Fls yellow, 2–4 per cluster. NW Himal. Z6.

C. chamlagu Lam. = *C. sinica*.

C. cuneifolia Dipp. = *C.* × *sophorifolia*.

C. decorticans Hemsl. Shrub or small tree to 5.5m. Br. dense, corky. Rachis thorned; lfts 6–12, to 1.5cm, oval-elliptic, spine-tipped adpressed-pubesc. Fls 1–2-clustered. Spring–summer. Afghan. Z6.

C. franchetiana Komar. Spiny shrub to 3m; branchlets light brown, pubesc. when young, lfts 10–16 to 1.2cm, narrow-obovate to lanceolate, dull green, ciliate. Fls 1–2-clustered, yellow stained wine-red. SW China. Z6.

C. frutescens DC. = *C. frutex*.

C. frutex (L.) K. Koch. RUSSIAN PEA SHRUB. Upright shrub to 3m, stoloniferous; branchlets thin, yellow, glab. Rachis somewhat thorny; lfts 4, 2cm, obovate, dark green. Fls yellow, 1–3-clustered, to 2.5cm. S Russia to Turkestan and Sib. 'Biflora': fls in pairs 'Globosa': compact and rounded. 'Latifolia': lfts to 3.5×1.5cm, dark green and glossy above. 'Macrantha': fls to 3cm. Z2.

C. gerardiana Benth. Shrub to 1m, compact, densely branched. Branchlets angular, brown, glossy, lanate when young. Rachis thorny; lfts 8–12, to 2cm, obovate-oblanceolate, grey-green, sericeous. Fls solitary, yellow-white. S Tibet. Z5.

C. gerardiana var. *glabrescens* Franch. = *C. franchetiana*.

C. jubata (Pall.) Poir. SHAG-SPINE; PEA SHRUB. Shrub to 1m, sparsely branched. Branchlets short, covered with lanate, spinose, spent rachises, lfts 4–6, 1cm, oblong-lanceolate. Fls 3cm, solitary, red-white. Spring–summer. GB 1796 (B). 'Columnaris': habit narrowly columnar. Z3.

C. lorbergii hort. = *C. arborescens* 'Lorbergii'.

C. maximowicziana Komar. Shrub to 1.5m, spreading, spiny; branchlets thin, rufous. Rachis spiny; lfts 4–6, to 1cm, oblong-lanceolate, thorn-tipped, light green, lanuginose. Fls 2.5cm, yellow. Spring–summer. China, Tibet. Z2.

C. microphylla Lam. Shrub to 3m; branchlets sericeous. Stipules spiny; lfts 12–18, to 0.8cm, oval to obovate, emarginate, dull grey-green, initially sericeous. Fls yellow, 1–2-clustered. Spring–summer. Sib., N China. 'Megalantha': lfts larger, round-obovate, less pubesc.; fls to 3cm Z3.

C. oreophila W.W. Sm. Shrub to 1m, bushy; branchlets lanate. Rachis initially lanate, spiny; lfts usually 16, to 0.7cm, oblong to obovate, sericeous. Fls solitary, 2.5cm, orange, brown-suffused. W China. Z4.

C. pygmaea (L.) DC. Shrub to 1m, often procumbent; branchlets glab. Lfts 4, to 1.5cm, linear-oblanceolate, spine-tipped. Fls solitary, 2cm, yellow. Spring–summer. NW China, Sib. Z3.

C. sibirica Medik. = *C. arborescens*.

C. sinica (Buc'hoz) Rehd. Shrub to 1m, growth sparse; branchlets angular, yellow-brown. Lvs 4-foliolate, in 2 clearly separate pairs; lfts to 3.5cm, obovate, dark green, glossy. Fls 3cm, solitary, pale yellow flushing red-bronze. Spring–summer. N China. Z6.

C. ×sophorifolia Tausch. (*C. arborescens* ×*C. microphylla.*) Lfts mostly in 6 pairs, to 1.5cm. Resembling a dwarf form of *C. arborescens*. Z3.

C. spinosa (L.) DC. Gaunt shrub to 1.5m; br. long, v. spiny, pub-esc. when young. Lfts 4–8, to 2cm, long-petiolulate, linear-oblancolate, subglabrous. Fls 2cm, solitary, bright yellow, sometimes tinted brown. Sib. Z2.

C. sukiensis Schneid. Resembles *C. gerardiana* but branchlets and fr. less lanate, br. not so spiny; rachis pubesc.; lfts 10–14 to 0.8cm, narrow oblong-oblanceolate, clearly parallel-veined, sericeous beneath. Fls 2.5cm, yellow. NW Himal. Z4.

C. tibetica (Schneid.) Komar. Shrub to 25cm, densely branched. Rachis spiny, persistent, white, glab., lfts 6–12, to 1cm, linear-oblong, sericeous. Fls 2.5cm, light yellow. W China. Z4.

C. tragacanthoides (Pall.) Poir. Shrub to 50cm. Branchlets lanuginose when young, v. spiny with many persistent rachises, lfts 4–10, to 1.5cm, obovate, adpressed-pubesc. Fls to 3cm, yellow, solitary on a lanuginose stalk. NW China to Altai and NW Himal. Z4.

C. triflora Lindl. = *C. brevispina*.

C. turkestanica Komar. Differs from *C. decorticans* in lvs 4cm and lfts larger, with scarcely prominent veins. Turkestan. Z6.

→*Astragalus* and *Robinia*.

Caraguata Lindl.

C. angustifolia Bak. = *Guzmania angustifolia*.

C. melionis E. Morr. = *Guzmania melionis*.

Caralluma

R. Br. Asclepiadaceae. *c*80 succulent, clump-forming, perenn. herbs. St. usually 4-angled with rows of rounded or pointed teeth. Lvs reduced to caducous scales. Infl. solitary or umbellate, subterminal or axill.; fls fleshy, sometimes malodorous, cor. 5-lobed, mostly rotate; corona with 2 whorls, the 5 outer lobes cleft, free or fused into a cup-shape, the 5 inner lobes fused to outer whorl. Burm. and India, trop. Afr. to S Spain, Canary Is. Z10 unless specified.

C. aaronis (Hart) N.E. Br. St. to 15–20cm×10–15mm, angles 4 finely dentate, blunt. Fls 1cm diam., lobes triangular-ovate, acute, with motile hairs, yellow marked red, rugose. Jord. Valley. Z9.

C. acutangula N.E. Br. St. 12–18mm thick, ridges 3(–4), acutely angled, finely toothed. Fls 1.5–2cm diam., pale green spotted maroon, lobes triangular-ovate, acute. NE & C Afr. Z9.

C. acutiloba N.E. Br. = *Quaqua acutiloba*.

C. adscendens (Roxb.) R. Br. St. to 60cm, 4-angled, ridges acute or rounded. Fls ± pendent, green or tawny to chestnut-brown, spotted or striped brown or purple, lobes lanceolate. S India, Burm., Sri Lanka. var. *attenuata* (Wight) Gravely & Mayur. St. v. freely branching, highly attenuate at tips, angles blunt, striped red. Fls 1.5cm diam., marked purple. var. *carinata* Gravely & Mayur. St. 20–60×1.5cm, only slightly attenuate, angles acute. Fls 1.5cm diam., usually campanulate, hairy, tinged purple with recurved margins and motile hairs, base banded yellow. Penins. India. var. *fimbriata* (Wallich) Gravely & Mayur. St. angles rounded. Fls small, pendulous and hairy. var. *geniculata* Gravely & Mayur. St. with secondary st. which are often numerous, angles acute. Fls 1cm diam., rotate, not pendulous, lobes marked chestnut-brown; pedicels geniculate. var. *gracilis* Gravely & Mayur. St. to 10mm thick, branching. Fls 1cm diam., rotate, pubesc., tips plicate with dark chestnut-brown markings, lobe base paler. Z9.

C. affinis De Wildeman. = *C. europaea* var. *affinis*.

C. alata Chiov. = *C. priogonium*.

C. aperta (Masson) N.E. Br. = *Tridentea aperta*.

C. arabica N.E. Br. St. 12–15mm thick, 4-angled, grey-green. Fls 1.5cm diam., in large term. umbels, campanulate, lobes triangular-ovate, dark red. S Arabia.

C. arachnoidea (Bally) M. Gilbert. St. to 30cm, angles acute, blunt or denticulate. Fls in apical clusters, white-yellow, mottled purple, tube small, deeply and narrowly lobed. E Afr. Z9.

C. arenicola N.E. Br. = *Quaqua armata* ssp. *arenicola*.

C. armata N.E. Br. = *Quaqua armata*.

C. atrosanguinea N.E. Br. = *Huerniopsis atrosanguinea*.

C. attenuata Wight = *C. adscendens* var. *attenuata*.

C. aucheriana (Decne.) N.E. Br. St. to 15×2cm with 4 acute, serrate-dentate angles, teeth hard. Fls in clusters near st. tips, 1cm diam., yellow. SE Arabia.

C. aurea Lückh. = *Quaqua incarnata* ssp. *aurea*.

C. awdeliana (Deflers) A. Berger. St. to 30×1–3cm, angles 4, sinuate-dentate, spotted red. Fls 5–15 together 0.8–1.5cm, campanulate, pubesc., green-red, exterior spotted red, interior yellow mottled black-purple, lobes erect, triangular. S Arabia.

C. baldratii A. White & B.L. Sloane = *Pachycymbium baldratii*.

C. bhupinderana Sarkaria. St. to 30×1.5cm, tapering, angles acute, speckled purple. Fls in pairs 1.5cm diam., yellow-green below, tips light brown, margins densely hairy. Penins. India.

C. bredae R.A. Dyer = *Stultitia miscella*.

C. brownii Dinter & A. Berger = *Orbeopsis lutea* ssp. *vaga*.

C. burchardii N.E. Br. St. 15–45cm, angles 4, teeth retrorse. Fls 1.3cm diam., in apical clusters, olive green or red-brown, lobes white-ciliate, outer corona yellow. Canary Is., S Moroc. var. *maura* Maire. Fls smaller, campanulate. S Moroc. var. *sventenii* Lamb. Fls red-brown. Canary Is. Z9.

C. campanulata N.E. Br. = *C. umbellata*.

C. carnosa Stent = *Pachycymbium carnosa*.

C. caudata N.E. Br. = *Orbeopsis caudata*.

C. cincta Lückh. = *Quaqua inversa* var. *cincta*.

C. confusa Font Quer = *C. europaea* var. *confusa*.

C. congestiflora Bally. St. to 28cm, angles 4, dentate, teeth 1–2mm, sides deeply grooved, tips whip-like. Fls rounded, in a dense umbel, yellow with green stripe inside, lobes lanceolate with motile hairs at top. Somalia.

C. corrugata N.E. Br. = *C. socotrana*.

C. crassa N.E. Br. = *Whitesloanea crassa*.

C. crenulata Wallich. St. slender, 7–8mm thick, grey-green, tetra-gonal, teeth recurved. Fls 2.3cm diam., in a term. umbel, campanulate-rotate, lobes triangular-ovate, brown-red with yellow spots and stripes and brown hairs. Burm.

C. dalzielii N.E. Br. St. 15–28cm, narrowing above, 4-angled, toothed. Fls 1cm diam., star-like, pendulous, lobes dark purple, base white spotted purple, lanceolate-subulate, with hairs at apex. NC Afr. Z9.

C. decaisneana (Lem.) N.E. Br. = *Pachycymbium decaisneanum*.

C. deflersiana Lavranos = *Pachycymbium deflersianum*.

C. dependens N.E. Br. = *Quaqua parviflora* ssp. *dependens*.

C. dicapuae (Chiov.) Chiov. St. to 60×0.2–1cm, ash-grey, with 3–4 acute angles, teeth conical. Fls in clusters, rarely solitary, lobes 11–14mm, recurved-pendulous, linear-spathulate, inner surface covered in clavate hairs, purple. Ethiop., N Somalia, Kenya. ssp. *seticorona* Bally. Corona lobes covered with stiff hairs. N Somalia. ssp. *turneri* (E.A. Bruce) Bally. St. blotched purple. Cor. lobes dark chestnut-brown with large green-yellow spots. E Afr. ssp. *ukambensis* Bally. Outer corona lobes 2-cleft, tips recurved and almost pointed, inner lobes linear, curved over staminal column. Kenya.

C. dioscoridis Lavranos = *Duvaliandra dioscoridis*.

C. distincta E.A. Bruce. St. 15–25×5–8mm, prostrate, grey striped brown or purple, teeth in alt. and opposite pairs. Fls 3.5–4cm diam., campanulate, tube cream, with band of hairs, lobes oblong-ovate, crimson to chocolate, rugose. Tanz., Kenya.

C. dodsoniana Lavranos. St. 4–6cm, 4-angled, irregularly tuberculate-tessellate. Fls 0.6cm diam., deep red-brown, lobes broadly triangular, revolute, causing the fl. to appear round. N Somalia.

C. dummeri (N.E. Br.) A. White & B.L. Sloane = *Pachycymbium dummeri*.

C. edithae N.E. Br. St. 2.5cm thick, grey-green, 4-(5-) angled, teeth broadly triangular. Fls 1.2cm diam; malodorous, in dense term. umbels, interior warty, dark red-brown, lobes triangular-ovate, with a few hairs at tip. Somalia.

C. edulis (Edgew.) Benth. St. 15–45cm, terete to 4-angled. Fls 0.8cm diam., interior purple, lobes ovate-lanceolate. W Afr., Sudan, Somalia, Arabian Penins., Indian subcontinent.

C. ericeta Nel = *Quaqua parviflora* ssp. *gracilis*.

C. europaea (Guss.) N.E. Br. St. 10–15cm, bluntly tetragonal, procumbent or ascending, grey-green, spotted red. Infl. 10–13-fld; fls to 1.7cm diam.; lobes ovate or suborbicular, yellow with purple bands, tips purple-brown, hairy within or only on margins. N Afr., S Spain, S It. var. *affinis* (De Wildeman) A. Berger. Fls 16–18mm diam., subglabrous, stripes broader than in type. Moroc. var. *confusa* (Font Quer) Font Quer. Corona lobes deeply 2-cleft. S Spain. var. *maroccana* (Hook. f.) A. Berger. Fls larger, lobes red-brown below with yellow bands. Moroc. Z9.

C. fimbriata Hook. f. non Wallich = *C. adscendens* var. *attenuata*.

C. fimbriata Wallich non Hook. f. = *C. adscendens* var. *fimbriata*.

C. foetida E.A. Bruce. St. 10–15cm, tapering to 9mm at the tip, angles with yellow-cartilaginous teeth. Fls malodorous, in term. umbels, 1.5cm diam., dark purple, broad-campanulate, lobes spreading, ovate-triangular, with motile purple hairs. Uganda.

C. foulcheri-delboscii Lavranos = *C. hexagona*.

C. framesii Pill. = *Quaqua framesii*.

C. frerei Rowl. = *Frerea indica*.

C. furta Bally. St. 7cm, 1cm thick at base tapering to a point tip, grey-green with a purple strip along angles. Fls 6cm diam., deeply divided into folded lobes, erect to spreading, pale green at base to pale purple, lobes white to pale green. N Somalia.

C. gemugofana M. Gilbert = *Pachycymbium gemugofanum.*

C. gersterni Letty. = *Orbeopsis gerstneri.*

C. gossweileri S. Moore = *Orbeopsis gossweileri.*

C. gracilipes Schum. St. 30–40cm, 5–6mm thick at base, narrowing toward tip, with 4 finely dentate angles. Fls to 0.7cm diam., arranged along tapered tip. E Afr.

C. gracilis Lückh. = *Quaqua parviflora* ssp. *gracilis.*

C. hahnii Nel. = *Orbeopsis lutea* ssp. *vaga.*

C. hesperidum Maire. St. green-white, 4-angled, teeth flesh-coloured, spine-like. Fls 2cm diam., lobes ovate, pointed, velvety-papillose, dark brown-purple. Moroc.

C. hexagona Lavranos. St. 1–10×1.2–2cm, angles 4–6, divided into tubercles. Fls in clusters near the apex, 1.2–2.2cm diam., rotate to campanulate, lobes ovate-deltoid, exterior green-white with a few red, brown or purple-brown marks, interior purple-brown to green to cream-white, with red-brown papillae. Saudi Arabia, N & S Yemen, Oman.

C. hexagona var. *septentrionalis* Lavranos & Newton = *C. hexagona.*

C. hottentotorum (N.E. Br.) N.E. Br. = *Quaqua incarnata.*

C. huillensis Hiern. = *Orbeopsis huillensis.*

C. incarnata (L. f.) N.E. Br. = *Quaqua incarnata.*

C. incarnata var. *alba* sensu White & B.L. Sloane, non (G. Don) N.E. Br. = *Quaqua incarnata* var. *tentaculata.*

C. inversa N.E. Br. = *Quaqua inversa.*

C. joannis Maire. St. 6–10×1.3–1.5cm, angles 4 rounded seriate-denate. Fls in clusters, 1.5–2.5cm diam., tube campanulate, olive-yellow, red-spotted, lobes purple, ciliate. SW Moroc. Z9.

C. kalambacheriana Lavranos. St. to 25×2cm, angles 4, rounded sinuate-denate. Fls in a spherical umbel, 2cm diam., exterior yellow with orange-red spots, interior yellow covered with small warty spots, lobes deltoid, curved upwards. S Arabia.

C. keithii R.A. Dyer = *Pachycymbium keithii.*

C. knobelii E. Phillips = *Orbeopsis knobelii.*

C. lasiantha N.E. Br. = *C. umbellata.*

C. lateritia N.E. Br. = *Orbeopsis lutea.*

C. lavranii Rauh & Wertel. Freely branching, coral-like. St. to 40×3cm thick, grey waxy-pruinose, angles 4 crenate. Fls 2–3cm diam., solitary, lobes spreading, interior ochre-yellow with wine-red spots, papillose with a tuft of wine-red motile hairs at tips. SE Arabia.

C. linearis N.E. Br. = *Quaqua linearis.*

C. longidens N.E. Br. = *C. edulis.*

C. longipes N.E. Br. = *Pectinaria longipes.*

C. lugardii N.E. Br. St. 10–15cm, bluntly tetragonal, furrowed, grey-green, striped or spotted dark green or brown. Fls 5–6cm diam., chocolate-brown, base campanulate, lobes long, narrow-linear, tips green-yellow, ciliate; corona dark orange. S Afr., Nam. Z9.

C. lutea N.E. Br. = *Orbeopsis lutea.*

C. maculata N.E. Br. = *Orbea maculata.*

C. maculata var. *brevidens* H. Huber = *Orbea rangeana.*

C. mammillaris (L.) N.E. Br. = *Quaqua mammillaris.*

C. maris-mortuae Zoh. = *C. sinaica.*

C. marlothii N.E. Br. = *Quaqua marlothii.*

C. maroccana (Hook. f.) Seemen & Maire = *C. europaea* var. *maroccana.*

C. maughanii R.A. Dyer = *Pectinaria maughanii.*

C. meintjesiana Lavranos = *Pachycymbium meintjesianum.*

C. melanantha Schltr. = *Orbeopsis melanantha.*

C. mijerteina var. *marchandii* Lavranos = *Echidnopsis mijerteina.*

C. mireillae Lavranos. St. 3–10×0.5–1cm, angles 4, rounded, blue-green with brown spots. Fls 1cm diam., campanulate, tube pale yellow, lobes, pale yellow with dark red marks near base. Somalia.

C. mogadoscensis Chiov. = *C. priogonium.*

C. moniliformis Bally. St. to 14×2cm, tapering above, cylindric to moniliform with 4 blunt, dark purple, dentate angles. Infl. almost racemose with 1–2 groups of 2–3 fls; corona tube 1.3×2mm, cup-shaped, interior dark purple-red, lobes 6mm, narrow-triangular, deep purple-red, purple-ciliate. Somalia.

C. mouretii Chev. = *C. edulis.*

C. munbyana (Decne.) N.E. Br. St. 5–15cm, tetragonal, with erect, sinuate teeth. Fls to 0.8cm diam., foetid, campanulate, brown, glab., lobes linear. SE Spain, N Afr. Z9.

C. nebrownii A. Berger = *Orbeopsis lutea* ssp. *vaga.*

C. ortholoba Lavranos = *Quaqua acutiloba.*

C. parviflora (Masson) N.E. Br. non Schltr. = *Quaqua parviflora.*

C. parviflora Schltr. non (Masson) N.E. Br. = *Quaqua parviflora* ssp. *dependens.*

C. pauciflora (Wight) N.E. Br. St. 10–15×0.5cm, 4-angled with downward-pointing, teeth. Fls 2.5cm diam., broadly

campanulate, lobes ovate-tapering, ciliate, pale yellow with brown stripes, wrinkled and minutely hairy. SE India.

C. peckii Bally. St. to 20cm, bluntly tetragonal, blue-green with brown blotches. Infl. strongly attenuate; fls 0.5cm diam., pale yellow, spotted red, lobes elliptic, acute, with purple, clavate, motile hairs at base. N Kenya. Z9.

C. penicillata (Deflers) N.E. Br. St. 40–100×2–3cm, with 4 winged, cartilaginous angles, teeth directed downwards, deltoid. Fls in dense umbels, to 1.5cm diam., lobes ovate-lanceolate, light brown with pale yellow spots, tips with clavate red hairs. Yemen. var. *robusta* (N.E. Br.) White & B.L. Sloane. St. thicker and blue-green, teeth horizontal; fls tuberculate within. Ethiop., Sudan.

C. peschii Nel. Strongly stoloniferous; st. to 10×0.5cm, with 4 blunt angles and conspicuous rudimentary lvs. Fls in pairs, 1cm diam., lobes, pendent, ovate, pointed, yellow-green hairy. Nam.

C. piaranthoides Oberm. = *Pachycymbium schweinfurthii.*

C. pillansii N.E. Br. = *Quaqua pillansii.*

C. priogonium Schum. St. 20–55cm, with 4 acute angles, flowering portion tapering, teeth sharp. Fls in a loose rac., tube 1–2mm deep, lobes 25×1.5mm, linear, v. pointed, interior purple, exterior with white bands or spots. Somalia, Tanz.

C. procumbens Crevost & Mayur. St. mat-forming, 1.5cm thick, acutely angled, teeth scarcely visible. Fls in small rac., 0.8cm diam., campanulate, lobes broad-deltoid, white with red, exterior often marked red. Penins. India.

C. pruinosa (Masson) N.E. Br. = *Quaqua pruinosa.*

C. pseudobrownii Dinter = *Orbeopsis lutea* ssp. *vaga.*

C. ramosa (Masson) N.E. Br. = *Quaqua ramosa.*

C. rangeana Dinter & A. Berger = *Orbea rangeana.*

C. reflexa Lückh. = *Quaqua parviflora* ssp. *dependens.*

C. retrospiciens N.E. Br. = *C. acutangula.*

C. rivae Chiov. = *C. socotrana.*

C. robusta N.E. Br. = *C. penicillata* var. *robusta.*

C. rogersii (L. Bol.) E.A. Bruce & R.A. Dyer = *Pachycymbium rogersii.*

C. rosengreenii Vierh. = *C. socotrana.*

C. russeliana (Corb. ex Brongn.) Cuf. = *C. acutangula.*

C. sarkariae Lavranos & Frandsen. St. to 30×1.5cm, tapering above, with 4 acute angles, mottled purple. Fls paired, 1cm diam., rotate-campanulate, yellow-green with darker, sometimes purple bands. S India.

C. schweinfurthii A. Berger = *Pachycymbium schweinfurthii.*

C. scutellata Deflers. = *Echidnopsis scutellata.*

C. shadbana Lavranos = *C. hexagona.*

C. simulans N.E. Br. = *Quaqua marlothii.*

C. sinaica (Decne.) Benth. & Hook. St. thin, terete to angular and furrowed, grey-green with purple tubercles. Fls 0.5cm diam., solitary or paired, lobes triangular, yellow to pink with white cilia. Sinai Penins., Isr., Dead Sea plains.

C. socotrana (Balf. f.) N.E. Br. St. to 15×0.8–1cm, thick, 4-angled, grey to red, teeth deltoid, thorny, hard, pointed downwards. Fls 1.6–2cm diam., campanulate, upper part of tube concentrically corrugated, lobes spreading, ovate-deltoid, acuminate, dark red. Socotra, Somalia.

C. solenophora Lavranos. St. to 20×2cm, angles 4, green or brown-green, teeth blunt, direct downwards. Fls to 2.2cm, long-tubular, tube constricted partway, somewhat spherical at base, cream-yellow with purple bands, lobes, pointed, deltoid, tipped purple with motile purple hairs. SW Arabia.

C. somalica N.E. Br. St. with 4 acute, slightly dentate angles. Fls in a dense umbel, 1.2–1.4cm diam., campanulate, velvety, lobes, triangular-ovate, pointed. Somalia.

C. speciosa (N.E. Br.) N.E. Br. St. to 1m+, tetragonal. Fls to 5cm diam. in broad umbels, cup-shaped, lobes dark brown, ovate, acute, tube orange to yellow. E Afr. Z10.

C. sprengeri N.E. Br. = *Pachycymbium sprengeri.*

C. staintonii Hara. St. creeping to pendulous, to 1m, 5–12mm thick with round angles. Fls 2–20 together, to 1cm diam., campanulate, exterior pink, lobes, deltoid, aconding, spreading, purple-red, yellow with purple spots at base. W Nepal.

C. stalagmifera C. Fisch. St. erect, attenuate, 5–8mm thick at base, 4-angled with thin angular br. Fls 1cm diam., campanulate, lobes ovate-oblong, dark red with minute red hairs. Penins. India.

C. subterranea Bruce & Bally. Largely subterranean; aerial st. 5–8cm, dying off annually. Fls in umbels, 1.2–1.8cm diam., lobes dark brown to lemon-yellow, covered with silver hairs. Kenya, Tanz.

C. subulata (Forssk.) Decne. St. 20–30×1cm, tapering toward tip, 4-angled below, teeth small, projecting. Fls 1.5cm diam., lobes oblong, tapered to base, awned above, hairy. Yemen.

C. swanepoelii Lavranos = *Quaqua parviflora* ssp. *swanepoelii.*

C. truncatocoronata (Sedgwick) Gravely & Mayur. St. to 15cm×6mm, 4-angled, tuberculate. Fls in umbels, tube

6×6mm, interior spotted purple above, purple with concentric yellow furrows below, lobes with clavate hairs in sinuses. Penins. India.

C. tsumebensis Oberm. = *Orbeopsis tsumebensis*.

C. tuberculata N.E. Br. St. 5–15cm, tetragonal. Fls in bundles, 8cm diam. dark red with pustuliform tubercles, lobes narrowly lanceolate. India, Afghan. Z9.

C. tubiformis Bruce & Bally. Closely related to *C. distincta*. St. erect, with 4 dentate angles. Fls campanulate, interior dark purple, exterior green with red blotches, lobes and interior with long, white hairs. Penins. India, Afghan.

C. turneri E.A. Bruce. St. to 50cm, tetragonal, tapering and obscurely angled above. Infl. tassel-like, axill. clusters; fls to 2cm diam. dark chestnut-brown blotched yellow-green, lobes pendulous, oblong-lanceolate, revolute, basal hairs vibratile, purple. Kenya. Z9.

C. ubomboensis Verdoorn. St. to 4×1cm, angles 4, teeth conical. Fls 1cm diam., dark purple, lobes ovate. S Afr. (Natal).

C. umbellata Haw. Forming dense mats 30–60cm tall; st. 2–5cm diam., angles compressed, winged, sinuate-dentate. Fls in large umbels, lobes broad-ovate, abruptly tapered, yellow or red-brown with darker bands. S India.

C. umdauensis Nel = *Tridentea umdauensis*.

C. vaga (N.E. Br.) A. White & B.L. Sloane = *Orbeopsis lutea* ssp. *vaga*.

C. valida N.E. Br. = *Orbeopsis valida*.

C. variegata hort. = *Orbea variegata*.

C. venenosa Maire. St. to 12×2cm, 4–6-angled, obtuse, with brown spots, tubercles, thick, long. Fls 2–3cm diam., campanulate, tube minutely papillose, red-brown, lobes ovate, hairy, red-brown. Sahara, Sudan.

C. vibratilis E.A. Bruce & Bally. Habit similar to *C. subterranea*. Fls campanulate purple-red with small yellow-green blotches, lobes with motile, clavate hairs. E Afr.

C. villetii Lückh. = *Quaqua inversa*.

C. virescens Lückh. = *Quaqua parviflora*.

C. vittata N.E. Br. = *C. edulis*.

C. wilfriedii Dinter = *Quaqua acutiloba*.

C. wilsonii Bally. St. 5–6cm, angles 4 dentate, blue-green with brown blotches, teeth 1–2cm long, thin. Fls to 1.5cm diam., lobes triangular, pointed, lemon-yellow with small purple blotches and stiff purple bristles. Uganda.

→*Boucerosia, Desmidorchis, Echidnopsis* and *Stapelia*.

Carambola *Averrhoa carambola*.
Caranda *Copernicia alba*.
Caranday *Copernicia alba*.
Caraway *Carum carvi*.
Caraway Thyme *Thymus herba-barona*.

Cardamine L. BITTERCRESS. Cruciferae. *c*150 mostly perenn. rhizomatous or tuberous herbs. Basal lvs sometimes rosette-forming, palmatifid to pinnate, long-petiolate. Infl. a rac. or pan.; sep. 4; pet. 4, spathulate to ovate, erect or spreading. Cosmop. except Antarc., mainly N Hemis.

C. alpina Willd. = *C. bellidifolia*.

C. asarifolia L. 30–45cm; stoloniferous. Lvs large, cordate to round, sinuate to toothed, st. lvs sometimes divided into 3 lfts. Rac. compact; pet. white, 6–10mm. Late spring–summer. S Fr. and N It. (mts). Z5.

C. bellidifolia L. Tufted, to 11cm. Lvs many, lanceolate or rhomboid-spathulate, entire. Rac. corymbose; pet. white, 3.5–5mm. Summer. Arc. and subarc. Eur., Pyren. to Carpath. Z4.

C. bulbifera (L.) Crantz. CORAL ROOT BITTERCRESS. 25–70cm. Rhiz. with fleshy scale lvs. Flowering st. lvs alt., pinnate, upper ± simple, most with axill. bulbils. Fls in a graceful rac.; pet. purple, 10–17mm. Spring. Eur. Z6.

C. californica Greene. 15–60cm. Rhiz. 4–8mm diam. Lvs divided, lfts 3, broad-ovate, 2–5cm wide, crenate; flowering st. lvs 2–4, lfts 3–5, ovate-lanceolate. Rac. many-fld; pet. 9–14mm, pale pink. Spring. Calif., Oreg. Z6.

C. ×digenea Gremli. (*C. heptaphylla* ×*C. pentaphyllos*.) Similar to *C. heptaphylla* but lvs occas. 3-parted. C & S Eur. Z6.

C. diphylla (Michx.) Alph. Wood. CRINKLE ROOT; PEPPER ROOT; TOOTHWORT. 15–30cm. Rhiz. scaly. Lvs divided, lfts 4–10cm, 3, ovate-rhombic, short-stalked, with blunt, setose teeth; flowering st. lvs similar to basal lvs. Pet. white, 1–1.6cm. Spring. N Amer. Z6.

C. enneaphyllos (L.) Crantz. To 35cm. Rhiz. constricted, scaly. St. lvs in a lax whorl, pinnatifid; lfts ovate-lanceolate, pointed, toothed. Fls nodding; pet. 12–16mm, white. Late spring. W Carpath., E Alps, S It. Z7.

C. fontanum Lam. = *Nasturtium officinale*.

C. glanduligera O. Schwarz. To 30cm. Rhiz. scaly. Flowering st. lvs 3 in a whorl, divided, lfts 3, ovate-lanceolate, acuminate,

toothed. Pet. 12–22mm, purple. Late spring. E & C Eur., Carpath. Z6.

C. glauca Spreng. Ann. or perenn. to 25cm. St. lvs glaucous, fleshy, trilobed or entire, to pinnate; lfts obovate, term. leaflet trilobed. Rac. dense; pet. 5–8mm, white, notched. Late spring. S & E Eur. Z7.

C. heptaphylla (Vill.) O. Schulz. 30–60cm. Rhiz. scaly. Flowering st. lvs remote, 3 to many, pinnate, lfts in 3–5 pairs, 2–3 pairs higher up the st., lanceolate-ovate, dark green, sparsely hairy, serrate. Pet. 14–20mm, white-purple. W & C Eur. Z6.

C. ×killiasii (Brügger) O. Schulz. (*C. kitaibelii* ×*C. pentaphyllos*.) Similar to *C. heptaphylla* but more robust; fls pale yellow to pale purple. Balk., Alps, Apennines. Z6.

C. kitaibelii Bech. Perenn., to 30cm. Rhiz. scaly. Flowering st. lvs 3, in a whorl or alt., petiolate, pinnate, lfts 7–9, lanceolate, acuminate, toothed. Pet. 15–22mm, pale yellow. Alps, Apennines, N Balk. Z6.

C. laciniata Wood. Perenn., to 30cm. Rhiz. torulose. St. lvs 3, whorled, divided, lfts 3, linear, entire or deeply toothed. Fls large, rose to palest pink. Spring. N Amer. Z6.

C. latifolia Vahl non Lej. = *C. raphanifolia*.

C. lunaria L. = *Ricotia lunaria*.

C. lyrata Bunge. Stoloniferous. St. to 50cm. St. lvs sessile, pinnate, lfts 11–13, (5–7 higher up st.) lat. lfts 3–10mm, ovate, term. lfts 10–20mm, orbicular, cordate. Rac. many-fld; pet. 8–10mm, white. Late spring. NE Asia. Z7.

C. macrocarpa Nutt. 10–40cm. Roots tuberous-fibrous. Lvs divided, lfts 3, reniform, lobed, entire; flowering st. lvs solitary, bluntly trilobed. Fls rose or purple. W N Amer. Z6.

C. macrophylla Willd. 30–10cm. Rhiz. creeping. Lvs 10–25cm, pinnate, lfts 3–5, ovate-lanceolate, toothed, narrow, hairy. Pet. 6–11mm, pale pink to purple. Summer. NE Russia, Sib. Z6.

C. ×maxima (Nutt.) Alph. Wood. (*C. diphylla* ×*C. concatenata* (Michx.) Schwarz.) To 30cm. Flowering st. lvs 2–3, alt., divided, short-petiolate, ovate or oblong-ovate, coarsely toothed. Pet. *c*10mm, purple-white. E US. Z7.

C. pentaphyllos (L.) Crantz. Similar to *C. heptaphylla* except lvs digitate, lfts glab. apart from margins, fls pale lilac. W & C Eur. (mts). Z6.

C. pinnata (Lam.) R. Br. = *C. heptaphylla*.

C. polyphylla (Waldst. & Kit.) O. Schulz = *C. kitaibelii*.

C. pratensis L. LADY'S SMOCK; CUCKOO FLOWER; MEADOW CRESS. 30–60cm. Lvs rosette-forming, pinnate, pinnae to 1cm, 3–15, obtuse cordate to reniform, denticulate, grey- to glossy dark green; flowering st. lvs 2–4, pinnae narrower, shallow-toothed or lobed. Infl. graceful; pet. to 12mm, white, veined and flushed lilac or pure lilac. Widespread in Eur. 'Edith': fls double, pink in bud, fading to white. 'Flore Pleno': lvs tinted purple; fls double, purple in bud, fading to lilac. 'Improperly Dressed': fls lacking pet. 'Salzach': fls double. 'William': fls deep lilac. Z4.

C. raphanifolia Pourr. 30–60cm. Rhiz. long. Lvs large, pinnate-lyrate; lfts 3–7, rounded, angular, toothed. Pet. 8–12mm, purple, rarely white. Summer. S Eur. (mts). Z5.

C. rotundifolia Michx. Mat-forming, stoloniferous. St. erect-prostrate. St. lvs simple, petiolate, suborbicular to broad-ovate, base cordate, entire to sinuate; lower lvs often trilobed. Fls small, white. E US. Z6.

C. trifolia L. 20–30cm. Rhiz. nodular, creeping. Lvs trifoliolate, long-petiolate; lfts rhomboid to round, toothed, dark green above, purple-green beneath, sessile; flowering st. lvs simple, sessile. Pet. 9–11mm, pink or white. Spring. C & S Eur. Z7.

→*Dentaria*.

Cardaminopsis (C.A. Mey.) Hayek. Cruciferae. 13 ann. or perenn. herbs. Basal lvs simple or pinnatisect, st. lvs smaller, simple. Fls small, in rac.; sep. 4; pet. 4, white tinged pink or purple. N temp. regions.

C. arenosa (L.) Hayek. Ann. or perenn., 5–80cm. St. erect, hairy, branched. Lvs pinnatifid to deeply toothed. Fls numerous; pet. 6–8mm, white to pink. Eur. Z7.

C. halleri (L.) Hayek. Stoloniferous perenn., 10–50cm. St. erect, hairy to glab. Lvs simple to pinnate, with 1–7 round lfts, long-petioled. Fls numerous; pet. to 6mm, lilac-white. Summer. Eur. (mts). Z6.

C. hispida (L.) Hayek = *C. petraea*.

C. neglecta (Schult.) Hayek. Perenn., 5–20cm. St. glab., sparsely branched. Lvs leathery, glab. to sparsely hairy, pinnatisect to subentire. Fls few; pet. to 6mm, purple. Carpath. Z7.

C. petraea (L.) Hiit. Stoloniferous perenn., 5–30cm. St. sparsely branched, hairy below. Lvs pinnatifid, long-petioled. Fls few; pet. to 7mm, white-purple. N & C Eur. Z7.

→*Arabis*.

Cardamom *Elettaria cardamomum*.
Cardboard Palm *Zamia furfuracea*.
Cardinal Climber *Ipomoea* ×*multifida*.

Cardinal Flower *Lobelia cardinalis*.
Cardinal's Guard *Pachystachys coccinea*.
Cardinal-spear *Erythrina herbacea*.

Cardiocrinum (Endl.) Lindl. Liliaceae (Liliaceae). GIANT LILY.
3 giant lily-like bulbous herbs. Lvs broadly ovate-cordate, glossy, long-stalked. Infl. a rac.; fls funneliform; tep. 6. Summer. Himal. to China, Jap. Z7.
C. cathayanum (Wils.) Stearn. St. to 1.5m, leafless below. Lvs 10–13cm, scattered. Fls 1–5, 10–13cm, irregularly funneliform, tep. cream, tipped and spotted purple. E & C China.
C. cordatum (Thunb.) Mak. St. 1.2–2m, leafless below. Lvs 30×30cm, in a loose whorl on lower half of st. Fls to 15cm, irregularly funneliform, lightly fragrant; tep. cream-white, spotted red-brown and blotched yellow at base. Jap., Sakhalin Is.
C. giganteum (Wallich) Mak. St. 1.5–4m, leafy throughout. Lvs to 45×40cm, basal lvs in a rosette, st. lvs gradually smaller. Fls 15–20cm, regularly funneliform, fragrant; tep. white, striped maroon. Himal., NW Burm., SW China. var. **giganteum**. Fls only tinted green when young, opening from base of rac. var. **yunnanense** (Elwes) Stearn. Fls often tinted green, opening from apex of rac. downwards. W & C China.
→*Lilium*.

Cardiospermum L. Sapindaceae. 14 slender vines or lianes, climbing by tendrils. Lvs biternate, coarsely dentate, lfts pinnatifid. Fls small, white, in axill. corymbs with a pair of opposite tendrils; pet. 4, unequal. Capsule subglobose, membranous, inflated; seeds cordate-globose, black. Trop. Afr., Amer. and India. Z9.
C. caillei A. Chev. = *C. grandiflorum*.
C. grandiflorum Sw. HEARTSEED. Robust vine to 8m. Lvs 15–20cm, lfts toothed, hairy beneath. Fr. 7×4cm, ovoid-triangular, usually glab. Trop. Amer. and Afr. f. **hirsutum** (Willd.) Radlk. St. hirsute to setose.
C. halicacabum L. BALLOON VINE; HEART PEA. Slender, short-lived sprawling vine to 2m. Lvs 8–12cm, lfts deeply toothed, glab. Fr. 2.5cm diam., ovoid, 3-angled, v. inflated, pubesc. Trop. India, Afr., Amer.

Cardoon *Cynara cardunculus*.

Carduncellus Adans. Compositae. c30 usually spiny perenn. herbs, ± woolly. Basal lvs pinnate to lyrate; st. lvs sinuate to dentate, teeth often spiny. Cap. discoid; flts tubular, blue or purple. Medit. Z7.
C. caeruleus (L.) C. Presl. St. usually simple. Lvs lustrous, simple, toothed or lobed, lobes in 6–10 pairs, margins spiny. Cap. to 3.5cm; outer phyllaries leaflike, spiny toothed; flts blue. W Medit., C & S Port.
C. mitissimus (L.) DC. To 20cm. St. usually 0. Lvs pinnate to pinnatifid, pinnae or lobes in 6–9 pairs, lanceolate, entire or setulose-dentate, usually subglabrous. Outer phyllaries adpressed, ovate to lanceolate, setulose dentate; flts blue. S, W & C Fr., NE Spain.
C. monspelliensium All. St. ± woolly, to 20cm or 0. Lvs usually rosulate, pinnate to pinnatifid, pinnae or lobes in 6–9 pairs, linear- to oblong-lanceolate, with spinose teeth or lobes; st. lvs 2–6 or 0. Outer phyllaries spreading, leaflike, spiny-toothed. SW Eur.
C. pinnatus (Desf.) DC. To 20cm. St. leafy or 0. Lvs usually rosulate, pinnate, pinnae in 11–13 pairs, ovate to lanceolate-ovate, glaucous, rachis woolly. Outer phyllaries adpressed, toothed or divided toward apex, margin spiny. C Spain, Sicily, N Afr.
C. rhaponticoides Coss. & Dur. Stemless. Lvs rosulate, pressed flat to ground, lanceolate to ovate-lanceolate, spiny-toothed, glab. Cap. to 7cm diam., globose resembling a large, bristly, stalkless cornflower; phyllaries with a scarious apical appendage; flts mauve-blue. Alg.
→*Carthamus*.

Carduus L. THISTLE. Compositae. c90 ann. to perenn. herbs. St. spiny-winged. Lvs usually ovate-linear, sharply spiny-toothed, ± entire in pinnatisect. Cap. receptacle flat or convex, densely bristly; involucre globose, ovoid or cylindrical; phyllaries leathery, glab. or wispy-hairy, imbricate, spine-tipped. Eurasia, Medit. and E African mts. Z7.
C. afer Jacq. = *Ptilostemon afer*.
C. benedictus L. = *Cnicus benedictus*.
C. cyanoides L. = *Jurinea cyanoides*.
C. glycacanthus Sibth. & Sm. = *Jurinea glycacantha*.
C. marianus L. = *Silybum marianum*.
C. mollis L. = *Jurinea mollis*.

C. nutans L. MUSK THISTLE. Perenn. to bienn., to 1.5m. St. pilose wings to 10mm, apical spine to 8mm. Lvs pinnatifid to pinnatisect, ± hairy beneath, lanceolate or oblanceolate, to 40×20cm, seg. 6–10 pairs, spines to 5mm. Cap. to 7cm diam., solitary or few, erect or nodding, on peduncles to 22cm; involucre ± globose; flts violet or white. Eurasia.

Carex L. SEDGE. Cyperaceae. c1000 grass-like, rhizomatous, perenn. herbs. Fertile shoots long, often triangular in section, solid. Lvs usually basal, in 3 ranks, bases sheathing st., blades linear-lanceolate. Infl. a pan., spikes usually unisexual; fls v. small, lacking a perianth: ♂ with 3 sta.; subtended by a glume, ♀ an ovary encased in a utricle subtended by glume, stigmas 2–3, projecting from utricle. Cosmop., esp. temp. and Arc. regions.
C. acuta L. SLENDER-TUFTED SEDGE.   30–120cm. Lvs 30–140cm×3–7mm, glaucous, tip pendulous, sheaths dark red-brown, margin rough. Bracts long, leaf-like, much exceeding nodding infl. Eur. 'Aureovariegata': lvs striped yellow. 'Variegata': lvs with white central stripe. Z3.
C. acutiformis Ehrh. SWAMP SEDGE. To 1m. Lvs 8mm wide, grey-green. Spike to 5×0.8cm, somewhat drooping. E Eur. Z3.
C. alba Scop. Laxly tufted, decid., stoloniferous, 10–40cm. Lvs filiform, 20cm×0.5–2mm, bright green. C & S Eur. to NE Russia. Z7.
C. arenaria L. SAND SEDGE. Rhiz. creeping great distances. Lvs 60cm×1.5–3.5mm, dark green, blade flat, recurved, or keeled, tapering to a 3-angled tip, lower sheaths dark brown. Infl. dense, to 8cm. N & W Eur. Z7.
C. atrata L. To 60cm; basal sheaths dark purple-brown. Lvs shorter than or equal to st., flat or with outward-rolled margins, pale green. N Eur., C & S Eur. Z3.
C. baccans Nees ex Wight. 60–120cm. Lvs 60cm×5–15mm, deep green, flat, leathery, long-acuminate; sheaths brown-purple. Infl. a pan., bracts exceeding infl. spikes. India, Sri Lanka to S China. Z8.
C. baldensis L. SNOW SEDGE. 10–40cm. Lvs 2–4mm wide, grey-green; lower sheaths rust-brown. Infl. capitate, white with long bracts. E Alps. Z7.
C. bergrenii Petrie. Depressed-tufted, small. St. to 3cm, green or red-brown. Lvs to 5cm, linear, obtuse at tip, entire or serrate above. NZ. Bronze, glaucous and narrow-leaved forms are cultivated. Z7.
C. brunnea Thunb.   30–90cm, tufted. St. slender. Lvs 20–60×0.5cm, yellow to bright green, robust; sheaths brown. Summer. Jap., Aus. Z8.
C. buchananii Berggr. LEATHERLEAF SEDGE.   Densely tufted, 10–75cm. Lvs to 40cm×1mm, semiterete, arching, tapering to a flat-pointed tip, red-brown; sheaths dark red-purple. NZ. Z7. 'Viridis': lvs pale green.
C. caryophyllea Latour. SPRING SEDGE. Laxly tufted, 2–30cm. Rhiz. short, creeping. Lvs 20cm×1.5–2.5mm, upper surface rough, reucrved, tip 3-angled; becoming fibrous. Eur. inc. Scand. Z7.
C. comans Berggr. Densely tufted, 6–40cm. St. terete, glab., drooping in fr. Lvs around 40cm×0.5–1.5mm, bronze and pale green, tip drooping, margin rough; lower sheaths dull purple-brown. NZ. Z7.
C. conica Boott. Tufted, 20–50cm. St. 3-angled, smooth. Lvs 2–4mm wide, dark green, rigid, flat, rough. Bract blades short, sheaths brown-purple, inflated. Summer. Jap., S Korea. 'Variegata' ('Hime-Kan-suge'): lvs variegated white. Z7.
C. curvula All. Densely tufted, 2–40cm. St. smooth, blunt, 3-angled. Lvs 1–2.5mm wide, rough, grooved or planoconvex in section. S & C Eur. Z8.
C. digama Nak. = *C. conica*.
C. digitata L. Clump-forming; rhiz. short, ascending. St. to 40cm, leafless, decumbent to erect, smooth or inconspicuously scabrid above. Lvs 2–5mm wide, shorter than or exceeding st., flat, green to dark green. Spikelets narrow, digitate. Eur. Z7.
C. dipsacea Berggr. Densely tufted. St. 30–60cm, erect, slender, smooth. Lvs 2mm wide, exceeding st., numerous, flat, keeled, striate, with sharply scabrid margins. NZ. Z7.
C. dissita Sol. & Boott. Densely tufted. St. 30–75cm, slender, smooth, leafy. Lvs 6mm wide, flat, grass-like, deeply grooved, dark green. Spikelets narrow, digitate. NZ. Z7.
C. elata All. TUFTED SEDGE. Dense tussock-forming, 25–120cm. Rhiz. short, erect. Lvs 40–100cm×1–6mm, glaucous, folded in section, tip flat; sheaths brown-yellow, becoming fibrous. Eur. inc. Scand. 'Bowles Golden': lvs golden-yellow, with green margins. 'Knightshayes': lvs yellow. 'Aurea': lvs with yellow margins. Z7.
C. excisa Boott. = *C. conica*.
C. firma Host. DWARF PILLOW SEDGE.   Densely tufted, mat-forming, to 20cm. St. obscurely 3-angled. Lvs rigid, tapering to pointed apex, 10cm×4mm, blue-green; lower sheaths yellow-

dark brown. C Eur. (mts). 'Variegata': lvs striped creamy yellow. Z7.

C. flacca Schreb. BLUE GREEN SEDGE. St. 20–50cm. Lvs shorter than st., 3–6mm wide, glaucous beneath, dark green above, apex acute. Eur. Z5.

C. fraseri Andrews. Tufted, to 35cm. Lvs 15–60×2.5cm, stiff, smooth, lacking prominent midrib, everg. Spring. W US. Z7.

C. gaudichaudiana Kunth. Loosely tufted, 30–60cm. Rhiz. creeping great distances. St. 6–23cm, 3-angled, subglabrous. Lvs grass-like, v. numerous, 30–60cm×1–2.5mm, plicate; lower sheaths light brown. NZ, New Guinea. Z9.

C. gracilis Curtis = *C. acuta*.

C. grayi Carey. MACE SEDGE. Clump-forming, 30–100cm. Lvs broad, flat, 6–11mm wide, pale green, margin rough. Infl. like a spiked club. Summer. E N Amer. Z7.

C. humilis Leyss. Low, clump-forming, gradually forming a dense semievergreen mat. Lvs 3–5cm, narrow, involute. Z4.

C. intumescens Rudge. 30–100cm. Lvs 3–8mm wide, dark green, soft, rolling inwards when dry. Summer. E N Amer. Z7.

C. kaloides Petrie. Tussock-forming. St. 30–90cm, slender, smooth, drooping at tips. Lvs 2mm wide, shorter than st., flat or involute, grasslike, margins scabrid above. NZ. Z7.

C. maxima Scop. = *C. pendula*.

C. montana L. MOUNTAIN SEDGE. 10–40cm. Rhiz. thick, creeping. St. slender, flexuous, 3- or 6-angled, sometimes leafless. Lvs 10–35cm×1.5–2mm, flat, tapering, soft, becoming glab.; sheaths persistent, becoming fibrous, red. Eur. to C Russia. Z7.

C. morrowii Boott. Tufted, 20–40cm. Lvs everg., 8mm wide, stiff, thick, tapering to the tipp, deep green, margin rough; lower sheaths dark brown, becoming fibrous. Summer. C & S Jap. 'Variegata': lvs narrowly striped white near margin. Z8.

C. muskingumensis Schweinf. Tufted, 35–100cm. Lvs v. numerous, crowded at tips of arching culms, subcordate at base of blade, 3–7mm wide, pale green; sheaths loose, green. Summer. W N Amer. Z7.

C. nigra (L.) Reichard. Clump- or tussock-forming; rhiz. slender, occas. 0. St. 10–60cm, trigonous, usually scabrid. Lvs shorter than or equal to st., green, 3mm wide. Eur. Z5.

C. ornithopoda Willd. BIRD'S FOOT SEDGE. 5–25cm. St. round to 3-angled. Lvs 50–200×1–3mm, blunt-pointed, keeled, soft, margin rough; sheaths red-brown. Infl. digitate, slender, becoming claw-like. NW Eur. 'Variegata': lvs narrowly striped white. Z7.

C. oshimensis Nak. Everg., tufted, similar to *C. morrowii* but with narrower, softer lvs. Jap. 'Evergold': lvs striped bright golden yellow and white.

C. paniculata L. Tussock-forming, 30–150cm. St. rough above. Lvs 20–120×0.5–1cm, dark green, channelled or plicate, tapering to a 3-angled tip, finely serrate. Eur. (except Medit.), Russia. Z7.

C. pendula Huds. Tuft-forming, 50–180cm. Lvs 20–100cm× 15–20mm, keeled, thin, rigid, yellow-green above, glaucous beneath, margin rough, tips curling; sheaths red-brown. Infl. tall, erect to arching with pendulous catkins. WC & S Eur. Z8.

C. petriei Cheesem. Loosely tufted, 10–35cm. St. round or compressed, glab. Lvs to 40cm×0.5–2mm, tinged red, grooved, margin rough, tips curling; sheaths light brown-red. NZ.

C. plagellifera Colenso. Close to *C. buchananii*, but differing in its coarser habit and longer st. (1m+). Z7.

C. plantaginea Lam. Tufted, 25–55cm. St. covered in bladeless purple sheaths. Lvs on sterile shoots, 40×1–3cm, flat-spreading, broad. Spring. N Amer. Z7.

C. polyrrhiza Wallr. = *C. umbrosa*.

C. praecox Jacq. = *C. caryophyllea*.

C. pseudocyperus L. CYPERUS SEDGE. Tufted, 30–90cm. Rhiz. short. St. 3-angled, rough. Lvs 120×1–2mm, flat, longer than st., yellow-green; lower sheaths pale brown; ligule 10–15mm, blunt. Infl. of drooping clustered spikes with long basal bracts. Summer. Temp. regions, nearly Cosmop. Z7.

C. pulchella Berggr. = *C. comans*.

C. riparia Curtis. GREATER POND SEDGE. To 150cm. Rhiz. long, stout. St. sharply 3-angled. Lvs flat, 15mm wide. Spring. Widespread, N hemis. Z6.

C. scaposa Clarke. Rhiz. stout, short, creeping. St. obscurely 3-angled. Lvs 30–2×2–4cm, lanceolate-elliptic, flat, bright green, margin smooth. S China. Z7.

C. secta Hook. Tussock-forming, to 130cm. St. 3-angled, edges rough. Lvs 30cm×1.5–7mm, drooping, grooved, margin and keel rough. NZ. Z7.

C. siderosticha Hance. To 10cm; new shoots tinged red. Lvs broad, decid., similar in outline to *C. plantaginea* but petioles more erect. 'Variegata': striped white along margin, young growth tinged pink. Z7.

C. stricta Good = *C. elata*.

C. sylvatica Huds. WOOD SEDGE. Tuft-forming, 10–80cm. St. nodding, 3-angled. Lvs plicate or keeled, 5–60cm×3–6mm,

sharp-pointed, yellow-green; sheaths pale brown. Eur. inc. Scand. Z6.

C. tenax Berggr. = *C. buchananii*.

C. testacea Sol. ex Boot. Loosely tufted. St. to 45cm, v. slender or slightly scabrid above, occas. reaching 1.5m in fr. Lvs 2mm wide, flat, striate, margins scabrid. NZ. Z7.

C. trifida Cav. Robust, densely tussock-forming, to 1m. St. stout, erect, smooth. Lvs to 1.5m×1.25cm, rigid, striate with scabrid margins. NZ. Z7.

C. umbrosa Host. Densely tufted, to 45cm. Rhiz. creeping. St. bluntly 3-angled. Lvs 5–45cm×1.5–3.5mm, pale green; lower sheaths fibrous, dark or pale brown. C Eur. to N Spain. Z8.

C. uncifolia Cheesem. Spreading, loosely or densely tufted, to 10cm. St. short, usually sheathed to the top by the lvs. Lvs to 25cm, concave in front, convex on the back, margins finely scabrid above. NZ. Z7.

C. uncinata L. f. = *Uncinia uncinata*.

C. variegata hort. = *Acorus gramineus* 'Variegatus'.

C. verna Chaix = *C. caryophyllea*.

C. vulpina L. 30–100cm. Rhiz. short, thick. St. narrowly winged, smooth below, rough above. Lvs 60×0.5–1cm, dark green, keeled, margin rough. N Eur., Russia. Z7.

Caribbean Pine *Pinus caribaea*.
Carib Wood *Sabinea carinalis*.

Carica L. PAPAYA; PAWPAW; MELON TREE. Caricaceae. 22 pachycaul trees and shrubs, often dioecious. Trunk seldom branched, trick, somewhat succulent, marked with petiole scars. Lvs toward summit of trunk and in a spreading crown, palmately lobed; petioles long. Fls white, yellow or green, in axils of lvs or on exposed trunk; cor. 5-lobed, tubular-salverform. Berry v. large, short-stalked, hanging below lvs. S Amer.

C. candamarcensis hort. = *C. pubescens*.

C. ×heilbornii (*C. pubescens* ×*C. stipulata*.) MOUNTAIN PAPAYA. Fr. produced parthenocarpically, eaten raw or cooked.

C. papaya L. PAPAYA; PAWPAW. Trunk to 10m, stout, scarred, unbranched. Lvs to 70cm diam., deeply palmatifid, lobes 7, oblong-elliptic, deeply incised, soft-textured; petioles to 1m, spreading. Fr. to 45cm, elongate-globose to obpyriform, skin leathery, olive green ripening yellow-orange, pulp apricot to salmon pink; seeds black. S Amer. (lowlands), cult. throughout tropics.

C. pubescens Lenné & K. Koch. MOUNTAIN PAWPAW. Differs from *C. papaya* in its shorter, stouter trunk, 5-lobed lvs to 30cm diam., fr. to 25cm, ellipsoid, 5-ribbed, dark green ripening deep yellow. S Amer. (Highlands).

C. quercifolia Benth. & Hook. f. ex Hieron. To 5m, shrubby, sparsely branched. Lvs to 30cm, 3-lobed, lobes broadly sinuately toothed. S Amer. (Highlands).

CARICACEAE Dumort. 4/31. *Carica*.

Caricature Plant *Graptophyllum pictum*.

Carissa L. Apocynaceae. c20 everg. shrubs and small trees. Br. intricate, often spiny. Lvs glossy, entire, coriaceous. Fls clustered, fragrant; cal. 5-parted; cor. tube cylindrical, limb salverform, lobes 5, overlapping to one side. Fr. a berry, bright red ripening purple-black. OW Tro. and Subtrop. 10.

C. acokanthera Pichon = *Acokanthera oppositifolia*.

C. acuminata (E. Mey.) A. DC. = *C. bispinosa*.

C. arduina Lam. = *C. bispinosa*.

C. bispinosa (L.) Desf. ex Brenan. HEDGE THORN. Shrub to 3m. Spines to 3.25cm, usually forked. Lvs to 8cm, ovate-oblong, mucronulate. Fls to 1.5cm diam., white, tube to 3× length of lobes. Fr. to 1.5cm; seeds 1–2. S Afr.

C. grandiflora (E. Mey.) A. DC. = *C. macrocarpa*.

C. longiflora (Stapf) Lawrence = *Acokanthera oppositifolia*.

C. macrocarpa (Ecklon) A. DC. NATAL PLUM; AMATUNGULU. Shrub to 9m. Spines to 4cm, forked. Lvs 3–6.5cm, ovate. Fls to 5cm diam., white, lobes longer than tube. Fr. to 5cm; seeds 6–16. S Afr. 'Boxwood Beauty': habit compact, semi-upright, mound-forming; lvs deep green. 'Boxwood Variegata': v. compact; lvs edged cream. 'Fancy': upright, medium-sized shrub; lvs deep green, luxuriant; fr. bright orange-red. 'Green Carpet': habit dwarf, dense, spreading. 'Horizontalis' (NATAL CREEPER): dense, trailing; lvs small, emerald green; fr. vivid scarlet. 'Humphreyi Variegata': lvs 2cm, oval, striped and edged ivory. 'Nana': small unarmed shrub; pet. conspicuously spirally overlapping. 'Prostrata': habit low and spreading. 'Tuttlei': tightly compact, spreading habit.

C. oppositifolia (Lam.) Pichon = *Acokanthera oppositifolia*.

Carlina L. CARLINE THISTLE. Compositae. 28 ann. to perenn. herbs. Lvs basal or alt., entire to deeply dissected, spiny-toothed. Cap. discoid, large, sessile or pedunculate, solitary or in cymose infl.; phyllaries usually leaflike, spiny-toothed, inner scarious, shining; flts many. Eur., Asia, Medit. region and Macaronesia.

C. *acanthifolia* All. Lvs to 30cm, ovate- to oblong-elliptical, deeply dissected, densely hairy beneath. Cap. to 7cm, diam.; phyllaries to 5.5cm, yellow; flts lilac. S & EC Eur. Z5.

C. *acaulis* L. STEMLESS CARLINE THISTLE. Stemless perenn. Lvs to 30cm, rosulate, elliptic-oblong, dissected, teeth or lobes spiny, glab. or slightly hairy beneath. Cap. to 5cm diam.; phyllaries to 5cm, linear, shiny white or pale pink above, tinged purple-brown beneath; flts white or purple-brown. S & E Eur. 'Bronze Form': lvs tinted silver-bronze. 'Caulescens': lvs grey, tinted silver. 'Splendens': lvs glossy dark green. Z4.

C. *cynara* Pourr. ex Duby = C. *acanthifolia*.

C. *longifolia* Rchb. = C. *vulgaris*.

C. *sicula* Ten. Perenn., to 70cm. St. simple or shortly branched. Lvs to 7cm, oblong, pinnatisect, spiny. Cap. to 3.5cm diam., phyllaries to 4.5cm, silvery above, white or purple beneath; flts yellow. SE It. and Sicily. Z7.

C. *vulgaris* L. COMMON CARLINE THISTLE. Bienn., to 70cm. Lvs to 15cm, linear-oblong to ovate. Cap. 3cm diam.; phyllaries to 3.5cm, spiny, inner to 2cm, straw-coloured. Eurasia.

Carline Thistle *Carlina*.

Carludovica Ruiz & Pav. Cyclanthaceae. 3 v. short-stemmed, palm-like perennials. Lvs fan-shaped, plicate, usually dividing into broad teeth then lobes with drooping, ragged tips; petioles long. Spadix cylindrical, spathaceous. Trop. Amer.

C. *palmata* Ruiz & Pav. PANAMA HAT PLANT. Lvs to 1m across, pliable, bright green, deeply palmatifid, seg. slender, free tips drooping; petioles to 2.5m. Spadix brilliant red in fr. Trop. Amer.

Carmel Ceanothus *Ceanothus griseus*.
Carmel Creeper *Ceanothus griseus* var. *horizontalis*.
Carmel Daisy *Scabiosa prolifera*.

Carmichaelia R. Br. Leguminosae (Papilionoideae). 40 shrubs or small trees, adults leafless or with short-lived scale-like lvs. St. rigid, compressed, green. Fls small, pea-like in short rac., solitary or clustered at st. notches, often fragrant. NZ, Lord Howe Is. Z8 unless specified.

C. *aligera* Simps. Erect shrub or tree to 10m; branchlets finely grooved, to 7mm diam., glab. Rac. 8–12-fld; cor. white, veined and flushed purple. N Is. Z9.

C. *angustata* T. Kirk. Erect or spreading shrub or small tree to 2m; branchlets 2mm diam., pendent, glab., grooved. Rac. 10–40-fld; fls 4×3mm, standard veined and blotched purple, pale toward apex, keel white or purple-flushed, wings white, pale purple-veined. S Is. var. *pubescens* Simps. Branchlets clearly pubesc. Rac. and cal. densely adpressed-pubesc., not thinly pilose. Z9.

C. *arborea* (Forst. f.) Druce. Shrub or tree to 5m, much-branched; branchlets to 3mm diam., striate, glab. Rac. 3–5-fld; fls to 5×4mm; standard purple at centre and purple-veinded, keel white, wings white, veined purple. S Is.

C. *arenaria* Simps. Shrub to 50cm; branchlets ascending, to 10cm×3mm, glab. Rac. 3–5-fld; fls 5×4mm; standard dark purple, keel white, tipped dull purple, wings white. S Is.

C. *astonii* Simps. Low-growing shrub; branchlets ascending, to 12×8mm, pilose, grooved. Rac. loosely 3–7-fld; fls 10×7mm; standard white, veined purple and basally purple-blotched, wings veined purple, keel purple, dark-veined. S Is.

C. *australis* auctt. = C. *arborea*.

C. *australis* var. *grandiflora* Benth. = C. *grandiflora*.

C. *compacta* Petrie. Erect, fastigiate shrub to 1m, much-branched; branchlets 2mm diam., striate, glab. Rac. 3–10-fld; fls 5×5mm; standard dark purple near base, veined and flushed purple above, keel white, wings white, veined purple. S Is.

C. *cunninghamii* Raoul. Shrub to 3m. Branchlets glab. Rac. 3–7-fld; standard flushed purple, keel white tipped with purple, wings white. NZ.

C. *curta* Petrie. Sprawling shrub to 1m, sparsely branched; branchlets to 2mm diam., subterete, grooved. Rac. congested, 8–10-fld; fls 4×3mm; standard cream-white with fine purple lines and 2 purple stripes; keel tipped purple, wings white tipped purple. S Is.

C. *enysii* T. Kirk. Shrub to 30cm, densely branched; branchlets thin, to 25×2mm, finely striate. Rac. 1–3-fld; fls 5×4mm; standard purple, dark-veined, keel green to purple. Summer. S Is. 'Pringle': habit dome-shaped, to 5cm; fls freely.

C. *enysii* var. *orbiculata* (Colenso) T. Kirk = C. *orbiculata*.

C. *flagelliformis* Colenso ex Hook. f. Shrub to 3m, much-branched; br. slender; branchlets 1mm diam., pendent, striate. Rac. 3–7-fld, subumbellate; fls to 4×3mm; standard flushed and veined purple. Summer. N Is.

C. *glabrata* Simps. Bushy shrub to 2m, with spreading br.; branchlets pendent, to 20×0.3cm, groved. Rac. densely 8–15-fld; fls 5×5mm; standard veined and blotched purple, keel and wings white, wings veined and blotched purple. S Is.

C. *gracilis* J.B. Armstr. = C. *kirkii*.

C. *grandiflora* (Benth.) Hook. f. Spreading shrub to 2m, much-branched; branchlets pendent, to 3mm diam., glab., fine-grooved. Rac. 5–10-fld, subumbellate; fls to 8×5mm; standard veined and blotched purple, keel white, wings white. Summer. S Is. var. *alba* T. Kirk. Fls pure white.

C. *kirkii* Hook. f. Semi-liane or scrambler to 4m; br. to 30cm, branchlets 1mm diam., subterete, deep-striate, sericeous to glab. Rac. open, 2–6-fld, slender; fls to 10×8mm; standard white to cream, veined and blotched purple, keel pale green, wings white, faintly purple-veined. S Is.

C. *monroi* Hook. f. Dwarf robust shrub to 15cm; br. erect, close-set; branchlets to 4mm diam., grooved. Rac. 2–5-fld, lax; fls to 10×6mm; standard white, veined and basally blotched purple, keel and wings white. S Is.

C. *nana* auct. = C. *orbiculata*.

C. *nigrans* Simps. Decumbent slender shrub, much-branched; branchlets 1mm diam. ascending, striate, sparse-pubesc. Rac. 5–10-fld; fls 3×2mm; standard white, veined and basally blotched purple, keel white, purple-veined. S Is.

C. *odorata* Colenso ex Hook. f. Bushy shrub to 2m; br. spreading; branchlets pendent, to 20cm×2mm, pilose. Rac. 5–15-fld; fls 4×3mm, white, veined purple. Summer. N Is. Z9.

C. *orbiculata* Colenso. Depressed shrub to 8cm; br. close-set, glab.; branchlets to 3cm×4mm, striate. Rac. 1–3-fld; fls 5×4mm; standard, lilac, blotched purple, keel pale green. N Is.

C. *ovata* Simps. Erect shrub to 2m; br. spreading; branchlets to 2mm diam., fine-grooved, glab. Rac. 1–5-fld; fls to 5×3mm; standard veined and flushed purple, keel and wings white. S Is.

C. *paludosa* Ckn. = C. *arborea*.

C. *petriei* T. Kirk. Stout, erect shrub to 2m, openly branched. Branchlets terete, 10×0.4cm, yellow-green. Rac. 3–8-fld; fls 6×5mm; purple toward tip, standard veined purple, keel pale green, wings white. S Is. var. *minor* Simps. Smaller and more slender shrub to 1.5m; branchlets to 2mm diam. Fls 4×3mm.

C. *subulata* auctt. A name of confused application.

C. *uniflora* T. Kirk. Dwarf rhizomatous shrub to 6m. Branchlets to 2.5cm×1.5mm, finely striate. Fls 1–2 to 10×16mm, standard purple toward base, white near apex, veined purple, wings white, veined purple, keel purple. S Is.

C. *violacea* T. Kirk. Shrub to 1m; br. spreading, grooved; branchlets to 3mm diam., plano-convex, fine-grooved. Rac. 3–8-fld; fls to 5mm, white, standard veined and basally blotched purple, wings veined purple. S Is.

C. *williamsii* T. Kirk. Erect shrub or small tree to 4m; branchlets to 12mm diam., close-grooved, glab. Rac. 1–5-fld; fls to 3cm, yellow, veined and blotched purple. Spring. N Is.

×**Carmispartium** Hutchins ex M.D. Griffiths. Leguminosae (*Carmichaelia* × *Notospartium*).

×C. *astens* Hutchins ex M.D. Griffiths = ×C. *hutchinsii*.

×C. *hutchinsii* M.D. Griffiths. (*Carmichaelia astonii* ×*Notospartium glabrescens*.) Leafless shrub to 1.5m. Branchlets 7.5–15.5× 0.2–0.45cm, olive-green, compressed, striate, notched, pendulous then upturned. Rac. to 3cm, axill., 9–18-fld; standard to 1cm, ovate to orbicular, pale lilac or rose with a white centre, tinged magenta, wings white flushed rose. Gdn origin. Z8.

Carmona Cav. Boraginaceae. 1 shrub or tree to 10m; br. cinereous at first. Lvs ± sessile, dark green, tough, obovate, 0.8–10cm, apex toothed, rounded or acute, shining and scabrous above, minutely hispid beneath, ± revolute. Cymes or glomerules, 2–5cm diam.; peduncle to 4cm; cor. white, lobes spreading, 2.5–4.5mm, tube to 2mm. Fr. a drupe to 6mm diam., red or yellow.

C. *heterophylla* Cav. = C. *retusa*.

C. *microphylla* (Lam.) G. Don = C. *retusa*.

C. *retusa* (Vahl) Masam.

→*Cordia* and *Ehretia*.

Carnation *Dianthus caryophyllus*.
Carnauba *Copernicia prunifera*.

Carnegiea Britt. & Rose. Cactaceae. 1 cactus; columnar or tree-like, erect to 16m, with a trunk 30–75cm diam., eventually with 1 or more lat., fastigiate br.; ribs 12–30; spines 15–30, the longest to 7cm, deflexed, brown or grey. Fls near stem-apex, funnelform-campanulate, 9–12×5–6cm; inner tep. white; sta. v. numerous. SW US, N Mex. Z9.

C. euphorbioides (Haw.) Backeb. = *Neobuxbaumia euphorbioides.*

C. gigantea (Engelm.) Britt. & Rose. SAGUARO; SAHUARO.

C. polylopha (DC.) D. Hunt = *Neobuxbaumia polylopha.*
→*Cereus.*

Caro *Pittosporum crassifolium.*
Carob *Ceratonia.*
Caroba-guazu *Aralia warmingiana.*
Carolina Allspice *Calycanthus floridus.*
Carolina Basswood *Tilia caroliniana.*
Carolina Buckthorn *Rhamnus carolinianus.*
Carolina Hemlock *Tsuga caroliniana.*
Carolina Holly *Ilex ambigua.*
Carolina Jasmine *Gelsemium.*
Carolina Lily *Lilium michauxii.*
Carolina Lupin *Thermopsis villosa.*
Carolina Moonseed *Cocculus carolinus.*
Carolina Rose *Rosa carolina.*

Carpentaria Becc. Palmae. 1 palm to 20m. St. 12–15cm diam., erect, smooth, ringed. Crownshaft prominent. Lvs to 4m, pinnate, tips pendent; pinnae slightly convex above, apices truncate, jagged-toothed with 2–4 long tips, tomentose above, scaly beneath, midrib prominent, clothed with ramenta. Trop. N Aus.. Z10.

C. acuminata (H.A. Wendl. & Drude) Becc.
→*Kentia.*

Carpenteria Torr. Hydrangeaceae (Philadelphaceae). 1 everg. shrub to 2m. Branchlets initially soft, green, bark exfoliating on older st. Lvs 4.25–10.5cm, elliptic-oblong, entire, subcoriaceous, glossy mid- to dark green above, blue-green, thinly downy beneath. Fls 4.5–7.25cm diam., pure white, fragrant; cor. 5–7-parted, rotate; sta. golden, many in a flattened ring or showy boss. Calif. 'Ladham's': fls larger; 'Bodnant': large-fld, hardy; 'Elizabeth': compact with smaller fls. Z8.

C. californica Torr. TREE ANEMONE.

Carpenter's Square *Scrophularia marilandica.*

Carpinus L. HORNBEAM. Betulaceae (Carpinaceae). 35 decid. trees or shrubs to 32m. Bark often smooth, grey-brown or grey. Shoots slender, buds slender conic to ovoid. Lvs alt., in 2 rows, entire or serrate, veins parallel. ♂ fls in catkins; ♀ fls each with a large persistent bract in nodding catkins. Eur., E Asia, N & C Amer.

C. americana Michx. = *C. caroliniana.*

C. betulus L. COMMON HORNBEAM; EUROPEAN HORNBEAM. Tree to 20m. Crown pyramidal, becoming irregular, bark grey. Lvs ovate to ovate-oblong, rounded or cordate at base, 6–12cm, yellow-orange in fall, irregularly dentate, veins in 12–18 pairs. ♀ catkins to 12cm; bracts 3-lobed, to 5cm, often dentate. Spring. Eur., Asia Minor. 'Asplenifolia': lvs deeply and regularly double-toothed. 'Columnaris': small, dense, compact; conical when young. 'Cucullata': broad, columnar; young lvs pale green in spring. 'Fastigiata': erect, pyramidal. 'Frans Fontaine': fastigiate even when mature. 'Horizontalis': br. subhorizontal, becoming reclinate. 'Incisa': lvs narrow, deeply dentate. 'Pendula': semi-dwarf, mound-shaped; br. spreading, nodding at tips. 'Punctata': lvs spotted white. 'Purpurea': young lvs tinged purple. 'Variegata': some lvs marked cream-white. var. *angustifolia* (Medv.) Radde-Fom. Lvs narrowly oblong, long-acute. Floral bracts acuminate. var. *carpinizza* (Host) Neilr. Lvs to 8cm, cordate at base, veins in 7–9 pairs. Rom. var. *parva* Radde-Fom. Lvs ovate, to 6cm. Z5.

C. caroliniana Walter. AMERICAN HORNBEAM; BLUE BEECH. Tree or large shrub to 13m, bark grey. Lvs ovate, acute, 6–10cm, acute-dentate, glaucous blue-green, red-orange in fall, downy beneath, veins in 10–14 pairs. ♀ catkins to 10cm; bracts irregularly 3-lobed, to 2.5cm, dentate. Spring. E N Amer. 'Ascendens': broad, columnar, multi-stemmed; lvs long-acuminate. 'Pyramidalis': fastigiate, becoming spreading. Z5.

C. caucasia Grossh. = *C. betulus.*

C. cordata Bl. Tree to 15m. Bark scaly, fissured. Lvs 6–12cm, broadly cordate, long-acuminate double-dentate, veins in 15–20 pairs, hairy beneath. ♀ catkins to 12.5cm; bracts closely imbricate, ovate, to 3cm, dentate, folded on one side. Spring. Jap., NE China. var. *chinensis* Franch. Young shoots more hairy; lvs narrower, shorter. Spring. China. Z5.

C. coreana Nak. Differs from *C. turczaninovii* in br. pendulous; young shoots dark maroon-brown. Lvs broadly ovate, to 5cm, lustrous green throughout, veins in 10–12 pairs, hairy beneath, not impressed above. Spring. Korea. Z7.

C. duinensis Scop. = *C. orientalis.*

C. erosa Bl. = *C. cordata.*

C. eximia Nak. KOREAN HORNBEAM. Tree to 9m; bark grey. Lvs ovate to oblong, truncate at base, long-acuminate, to 10cm, double-dentate, downy above, veins in 14–16 pairs, downy beneath. ♀ catkins to 7.5cm; bracts semi-ovate, to 3×1cm. Spring. Korea. Z6.

C. faginea Lindl. Young shoots white-grey hairy. Lvs short-acuminate, sparsely hairy beneath, regularly serrate, veins in 12–16 pairs. Fr. bracts with a small, entire lobe on one side. Spring. Himal. Z8.

C. fangiana Hu. Tree to 18m. Bark smooth, grey. Lvs oblong to oblanceolate, cordate at base, long-acuminate, to 30cm, double-serrate, veins in 24–34 pairs. ♀ catkins to 50cm, forming long clusters in fr.; bracts with projecting teeth folded in over fr. Spring. China. Z8.

C. fargesiana H. Winkl. non Franch. Tree to 6m. Trunk grey. Lvs ovate-lanceolate to elliptic or oblong, short-acuminate, rounded at base, to 7cm, glab. above, double-serrate. ♀ catkins to 8cm; bracts semi-ovate, dentate, folded slightly, to 2.5cm. Spring. W China. Z7.

C. fargesii Franch. = *C. laxiflora* var. *macrostachya.*

C. henryana (H. Winkl.) H. Winkl. Tree to 15m. Lvs narrowly lanceolate to ovate, rounded to cordate at base, long-acuminate at apex, to 6cm, glab. above, entire or serrate, veins in 12–16 pairs, silky-hairy beneath. ♀ catkins to 5cm; bracts obliquely ovate, to 2cm, deeply serrate. Spring. C China. Z6.

C. japonica Bl. JAPANESE HORNBEAM. Tree to 15m; br. wide, spreading. Bark fissured, scaly, grey. Lvs ovate-oblong, long-acuminate, rounded to cuneate at base, 5–10cm, downy initially, tinged red, irregularly serrate, corrugated, veins in 20–24 pairs. ♀ catkins to 6cm; bracts closely imbricate, ovate, folded on one side, to 2cm, roughly toothed. Spring. Jap. Z8.

C. kawakamii Hayata. Lvs oblong-lanceolate, acuminate, rounded at base, to 5cm, veins in 14–15 pairs, irregularly serrate; petioles to 1.5cm. ♀ catkins to 6cm; bracts semi-ovate, to 2cm, dentate on one side. Spring. Taiwan. Z7.

C. laxiflora (Sieb. & Zucc.) Bl. Tree to 15m. Lvs ovate to ovate-elliptic, 4–7cm, acuminate, base rounded or subcordate, doubly serrate, pubescence persisting in vein axils; petiole crimson. ♀ catkins to 15cm, bracts usually trilobed. Jap., Korea. var. *macrostachya* Oliv. Lvs larger, to 10×5cm; ♀ catkins to 12cm, with trilobed bracts to 3cm. Korea, N & W China. Z5.

C. mollicoma Hu. Tree to 15m; everg. Lvs 3–6cm, ovate-lanceolate, coarse-serrate, green above, copper beneath; veins reticulate above, white pubesc. beneath; petiole purple, 1cm. SW China. Zone 8.

C. orientalis Mill. ORIENTAL HORNBEAM. Tree or shrub, to 16m, densely branched. Lvs ovate to elliptic, 2–6cm, acute or acuminate, doubly dentate, base rounded, glossy dark green above, midrib and petiole pubesc. ♀ catkins to 6cm; bracts semi-ovate, toothed. SE Eur., Asia Minor. 'Calcarea': lvs coriaceous, subsessile. 'Grandifolia': lvs elliptic; fr. densely clustered. Z5.

C. pubescens Burkill. Tree to 14m. Lvs 4–9cm, oblong to oblong-ovate, bluntly double-serrate; veins pubesc. beneath, in 12–14 pairs. ♀ catkins 5–7cm; bracts asymmetric; broad outer side serrate, narrow inner side entire. SW China. Z8.

C. ×schuschaensis H. Winkl. (*C. betulus* ×*C. orientalis.*) Differs from *C. betulus* in lvs smaller, regularly double-dentate. Catkin bracts smaller; lobes always toothed. N Iran, Cauc. Z6.

C. stipulata H. Winkl. = *C. turczaninovii.*

C. tschonoskii Maxim. Tree to 15m; shoots downy. Lvs 4–9cm, ovate-acuminate, base rounded, sharply double serrate, veins 10–15 pairs, pubesc. beneath. ♀ catkins 5–7cm, bracts ovate, similar to *C. pubescens.* Jap., NE China, Korea. Z5. var. *falcatibracteata* (Hu) P.C. Li. Shoots glab.; lvs to 12cm, 14–16 pairs of veins; ♀ catkins longer with curved bracts. SW China. Z7.

C. turczaninovii Hance. Shrub or small tree to 12m. Young growth emerging red. Lvs broadly ovate, to 5cm, doubly serrate, pubesc. beneath, veins to 12, paired; stipules persisting into winter. Catkin bracts ovate, deeply serrate on one side. N China, Korea, Jap. var. *ovalifolia* Winkl. Lvs to 6cm, markedly serrate. W China. Z7.

C. wilsoniana Hu = *C. fangiana.*

C. yedoensis Maxim. = *C. tschonoskii.*

Carpobrotus N.E. Br. Aizoaceae. 30 closely branching sprawling perennials. Lvs v. succulent, opposite, sessile, shortly united, acute-triquetrous. Fls solitary, term., diurnal, sessile to stalked. Fr. turbinate, juicy. S Afr., Aus., Chile, Mex., Calif.; nat. S Eur., GB and elsewhere.

C. abbreviatus (Haw.) Schwantes. = *C. virescens.*

C. acinaciformis (L.) L. Bol. Lvs to 9×2cm, sabre-shaped, compressed, slightly grey-green, keel much-widened, angles cartilaginous, often slightly undulate and rough. Fls to 12cm diam., crimson-purple. S Afr. (Cape Prov., Natal). Z9.

C. aequilaterus (Haw.) N.E. Br. Lvs 3–9×0.5–1.2cm, dull green, long-tapered, keel minutely crenate abelow tip. Fls 3.5–8cm diam., light purple, paler at base. Aus. (Queensld, NSW, Vict., Tasm.), Mex. (Baja Calif.), US (Calif.). Z8.

C. chilensis (Molina) N.E. Br. Lvs triquetrous, amplexicaul, fleshy. Fls large, violet. Chile, Baja Calif., Calif. Z8.

C. deliciosus (L. Bol.) L. Bol. Lvs 8–10×1.5cm, acute-triquetrous, tapered, dark grey-green, keel horny, crenate. Fls 7–8cm diam., pink-purple. Fr. spherical, edible. S Afr. Z8.

C. edulis (L.) L. Bol. HOTTENTOT FIG; KAFFIR FIG. Lvs 4–8×0.8–1.7cm, curved slightly inwards, tapered above midway, dull green. Fls 7–8.5cm diam., yellow becoming pink. Fr. turbinate, edible. S Afr. nat. Aus., S Eur., Calif. Z8.

C. glaucescens (Haw.) Schwantes. Lvs 3.5–10×0.9–1.5cm, glaucescent, triquetrous, angles thin. Fls 4–6cm diam., light purple, paler to white in centre. Aus. (Queensld, NSW), Norfolk Is. Z9.

C. modestus S.T. Blake. Lvs 3.5–7×0.4–0.7cm, blue-pruinose or tinged red-brown, often curved, keel crenate and rough toward tip. Fls 3cm diam., light purple, centre white. W & S Aus. Z9.

C. muirii (L. Bol.) L. Bol. Lvs 5–7×0.6cm. Fls 6.5–9cm diam., pink-purple. S Afr. Z9.

C. quadrifidus L. Bol. Lvs to 14×1.8cm, broader at midlobe, tapering abruptly at tip, margins horny, tinged blue. Fls to 13cm diam., white to pale pink. S Africa. Z9.

C. quadrifidus f. *roseus* (L. Bol.) G. Rowley = *C. sauerae.*

C. rossii (Haw.) Schwantes. Lvs 3.5–10×0.6–1cm, glaucous, curved inwards, tapered, keel crenate toward tip. Fls 3.5–5.5cm diam., light purple, centre white. W & S Aus. Z9.

C. sauerae Schwantes. Lvs 12×2cm, stiff, lower surface sabre-shaped to sharply carinate, grey to blue-grey, angles often tinged red. Fls to 13cm diam., magenta, base of pet. white. S Afr. (Cape Prov.). Z9.

C. virescens (Haw.) Schwantes. Lvs 3.5–5×0.7–1.7cm, green, slightly glaucous, curved inwards or straight, tapered, upper surface somewhat convex, keel crenate toward tip. Fls 4–6cm diam., purple to light purple, white at base. W Aus. Z9.

→*Mesembryanthemum.*

Carpodetus Forst. & Forst. f. Grossulariaceae. 10 shrubs or small trees. Fls small in sparse pan.; sep., pet. and sta. 5–6. NZ, New Guinea. Z9.

C. serratus Forst. & Forst. f. PUTAPUTAWHETA. Everg. shrub or small tree, 5–10m. Juvenile lvs to 3cm, elliptic to orbicular, sometimes lobed, membranous; adult lvs to 6cm, ovate-elliptic, leathery, hirsute, sometimes mottled, coarsely serrate. Fls white, to 3cm in broad pan. Summer. NZ.

Carpolyza Salisb. Amaryllidaceae. 1 bulbous herb. Lvs 2–5cm, 4–6, subulate, slender. Scape to 10cm, slender, twisted below; umbel 1–4-fld; fls starry; perianth seg. 12mm, 6, white tinted pink, basally fused into a short tube; sta. slightly exserted. Early spring. S Afr. Z9.

C. spiralis (L'Hérit.) Salisb.

C. tenella (L. f.) Leighton = *C. spiralis.*

Carregnoa Boiss.

C. humilis (Cav.) Gray = *Narcissus humilis.*

Carrierea Franch. Flacourtiaceae. 3 decid. trees. Lvs alt., long-petioled, toothed. Fls in rac. or pan.; sep. 5; pet. 0; sta. crowded. E Asia. Z8.

C. calycina Franch. To 18m. Crown broadly spreading. Lvs 5–18cm, ovate-acuminate to elliptic, glossy dark green with wavy, gland-tipped teeth. Fls 1–8, fragrant, in candelabriform rac.; sep. to 2cm, broadly ovate, ivory suffused green, in a cupular arrangement; sta. 80–100. Summer. W China.

Carrion Flower *Stapelia.*
Carrizo *Phragmites australis.*
Carrot *Daucus carota.*
Carrot Fern *Onychium japonicum.*
Carrot Tree *Monizia edulis.*

Carruanthus (Schwantes) Schwantes ex N.E. Br. Aizoaceae. 2 short-stemmed, mat-forming leaf-succulents. Lvs opposite and decussate, oblanceolate to clavate, flat above, carinate beneath, keel pulled forward over tip. Fls solitary. S Afr. Z9.

C. albidus (L.) Schwantes = *Macairophyllum albidum.*

C. caninus (Haw.) Schwantes = *C. ringens.*

C. cookii (L. Bol.) Schwantes = *Macairophyllum cookii.*

C. peersii L. Bol. Lvs to 5×1.5cm, expanded above, narrowed toward apex, usually entire. Fls 4cm diam. yellow tipped pink.

C. ringens (L.) Boom. Lvs to 5×1.8cm, narrower at base, oblanceolate to clavate, triquetrous, margins ± dentate at tip, grey-green. Fls 4–5cm diam., yellow stained red below.

→*Bergeranthus, Mesembryanthemum* and *Tischleria.*

Cartagena Bark *Cinchona cordifolia.*

Carthamus L. Compositae. 14 ± ann. or, rarely, perenn. herbs with gland. and ± woolly hairs. Lvs pinnatifid to pinnatisect, margins spiny. Cap. discoid, term., solitary or in corymbs; phyllaries spiny; flts yellow or pink-purple to violet. Medit., Asia.

C. arborescens L. Perenn., to 2.5m, much-branched and densely gland., woody at base. Lvs to 8.5cm, ovate to lanceolate-ovate, pinnatifid, lobes in 5–6 pairs, spiny-toothed. Cap. to 4cm diam.; flts yellow. S & SE Spain.

C. caeruleus L. = *Carduncellus caeruleus.*

C. flavescens hort. non Willd. = *C. persicus.*

C. flavescens Willd. = *C. oxyacanthus.*

C. lanatus L. DISTAFF THISTLE. Woolly, gland. ann. Lvs to 9cm, pinnatifid or pinnatisect, spiny-toothed, lobes in 3–8 pairs. Cap. *c*2.5cm diam.; flts yellow. S Eur., N Afr. to C Asia.

C. leucocaulos Sibth. & Sm. Subglabrous ann., sometimes woolly and gland. St. white to purple. Basal and lower st. lvs pinnatisect to pinnate, glossy, seg. in 2–3 pairs. Cap. to 1.3cm diam.; flts pale violet. S Greece, Aegean Is.

C. oxyacanthus Bieb. Much-branched ann. to 30cm, with scattered or dense hairs. St. and br. white. Lvs to 15cm, oblong to lanceolate, basal lvs lyrate, lobes in 4–6 pairs, weakly toothed or entire, lower st. lvs sinuate-toothed, upper lvs light green, spines lemon yellow to 1cm. Cap. to 4cm diam.; flts yellow or orange-yellow. Spring–summer. SC Asia.

C. persicus Willd. Subglabrous ann. to 90cm. St. shining white, branched above. Lower st. lvs sinuate-toothed, glandular-hairy beneath, upper lvs to 5cm, light yellow-green, ovate-acuminate, with 3–6 pairs of teeth bearing yellow-white spines. Flts golden yellow, rarely tinged red. Summer–autumn. Turk., N Iraq, S Syr.

C. tinctorius L. SAFFLOWER; FALSE SAFFRON. Subglabrous ann., to 1m. Lower st. lvs ovate, simple or rarely sinuate or pinnate, entire or spiny-toothed. Cap. to 3.5cm diam.; flts yellow, red or orange. W Asia. 'Lasting White': fls creamy white. 'Orange Ball': fls bright orange.

Cart-track-plant *Plantago major.*
Cartwheel Flower *Heracleum mantegazzianum.*

Carum L. Umbelliferae. *c*30 glab. biennials and perennials. Lvs 2–4-pinnate, seg. narrow. Umbels compound; bracts and bracteoles few or 0; pet. obovate, emarginate. Fr. ovoid or oblong, compressed, ridged. Temp. to subtrop.

C. carvi L. CARAWAY. Aromatic glab. bienn. to 60cm; st. slender, striate. Lvs 2–3-pinnate, seg. to 2.5cm, linear-lanceolate to linear, often pinnatifid. Umbels to 4cm diam.; rays 5–16; flts white, occas. pink. Fr. 3–6mm, liquorice-flavoured. Summer. Eur., W Asia, nat. N US. Z3.

C. petroselini (L.) Benth. & Hook. = *Petroselinum crispum.*

Carya Nutt. HICKORY; PECAN. Juglandaceae. *c*25 large decid. trees. Br. smooth, becoming scaly. Lvs imparipinnate. ♂ infl. a pendulous, 3-branched catkin; ♀ infl. a term. spike, 2–20-fld. Fr. globose to ovoid, husk thick, green, separating into 4 valves; nut smooth or angled. E US, C & SE China.

C. alba Nutt. non K. Koch = *C. ovata.*

C. alba K. Koch non Nutt. = *C. tomentosa.*

C. amara Nutt. = *C. cordiformis.*

C. aquatica (Michx. f.) Nutt. BITTER PECAN; WATER HICKORY. To 20m. Bark light brown, peeling. Lfts to 11cm, 7–13, lanceolate, acuminate, yellow-tomentose when young. Fr. ovoid, to 4cm; nut obovoid, compressed, 4-angled, rust-brown, astringent. SE US. Z6.

C. arkansas Sarg. = *C. texana.*

C. austrina Small = *C. glabra* var. *megacarpa.*

C. cathayensis Sarg. CHINESE HICKORY. To 20m. Young br. with orange-yellow scales. Lfts to 14cm, ovate to ovate-lanceolate, green above, yellow-green below, midrib pubesc. Fr. 4-winged, to 25cm; nut ovoid, slightly angled. C & S China. Z6.

C. cordiformis (Wangenh.) K. Koch. BITTERNUT; SWAMP HICKORY. To 28m. Bark rarely scaly, young br. rust-red, puberulent. Lfts 7–13cm, 5–9, ovate-lanceolate, acuminate, light green, ultimately later glab. with veins pubesc. beneath. Fr. suborbicular, to 3cm, 4-winged; nut grey, smooth, thin-shelled, acuminate. NE US. Z4.

C. glabra (Mill.) Sweet. PIGNUT; SMALL-FRUITED HICKORY; BROOM HICKORY. To 30m. Bark grey, narrowly furrowed. Lvs 18–27cm; lfts to 15cm, 3–7, term. lft obovate, lower pairs ovate-lanceolate. Fr. obovate-globose, about 2cm, splitting to middle; fr brown, astringent. E US. var. *megacarpa* (Sarg.) Sarg. COAST PIGNUT HICKORY. Fr. 3–5cm, obovoid, slightly compressed. Z4.

C. illinoensis = *C. illinoinensis*.

C. illinoinensis (Wangenh.) K. Koch. PECAN. To 50m. Lfts 11–17, oblong-lanceolate, acuminate, 9–15cm, usually glab. Fr. in term. spikes, 3–8cm; nut oblong, brown, thin-shelled, acuminate. Iowa and Indiana S to Tex. and Mex. Z5.

C. laciniosa (Michx. f.) Loud. BIG SHELLBARK; KINGNUT. To 40m. Bark peeling in plates, young shoots orange-pubesc. Lvs 25–45cm; lfts 10–20cm, 7–9, oblong-lanceolate, acuminate, pubesc. beneath, term. leaflet larger, obovate. Fr. oval, to 5cm; nut 4- or 6-angled. E US. Z6.

C. × laneyi Sarg. (*C. cordiformis* × *C. ovata*.) Similar to *C. ovata* but bark dark grey, smooth; lfts lanceolate to oblanceolate. Fr. ovate; nut obovoid compressed, thin-shelled. W NY State. Z5.

C. megacarpa Sarg. = *C. glabra* var. *megacarpa*.

C. microcarpa Nutt. = *C. ovalis*.

C. minima Britt. = *C. cordiformis*.

C. myristiciformis (Michx. f.) Nutt. NUTMEG HICKORY. To 30m. Bark dark brown; shoots with yellow, glossy scales. Lvs 15–30cm; lfts 5–11, silvery beneath, term. leaflet obovate, 7–11cm, lower pairs narrower, smaller. Fr. ovoid to obovoid, wings 4, about 4cm; nut ovoid, rust-brown with hard, furrowed shell. S US, Mex. Z9.

C. olivaeformis Nutt. = *C. illinoinensis*.

C. ovalis (Wangenh.) Sarg. SWEET PIGNUT; RED HICKORY. To 30m. Young shoots pubesc. Lfts 5–7, lanceolate to obovate, finely pubesc., term. leaflet to 13cm, others about 8cm. Fr. ovoid, splitting to base. E US. Z6.

C. ovata (Mill.) K. Koch. SHAGBARK HICKORY; LITTLE SHELLBARK HICKORY. To 30m, sometimes more. Bark grey, shaggy; young shoots scaly, pubesc. Lvs to 30cm, pubesc. beneath when young; lfts 11–15cm, 5, obovate, acuminate, lower pair shorter. Fr. to 5cm, splitting to base; nut white, ellipsoid, 4-angled. E US. Z4.

C. pallida (Ashe) Engl. & Gräbn. SAND HICKORY; PALE HICKORY. To 30m. Bark coarsely furrowed to smooth. Lfts to 11cm, 7–9, oblong-lanceolate, light green above, silver-grey scales and hairy beneath when young. Nut subglobose to ovoid, to 3cm, thin-shelled, splitting to base. E US. Z6.

C. pecan Engl. & Gräbn. = *C. illinoinensis*.

C. porcina (Michx. f.) Nutt. = *C. glabra*.

C. sulcata Pursh = *C. laciniosa*.

C. texana Buckley non DC. To 15m. Bark dark, furrowed; young shoots red-brown pubesc. Lfts to 15cm, 7, lanceolate, veins pubesc. beneath. Fr. globose, about 3.5cm, shell splitting to base; nuts acuminate, red-brown. C US. Z6.

C. tomentosa Nutt. MOCKERNUT; BIG BUD HICKORY; WHITE HEART HICKORY. To 30m. Bark furrowed with flattened ridges; shoots initially tomentose. Lfts 7–15cm, 7–9, oblong to oblong-lanceolate, acuminate, 7–15cm. Fr. round to obovoid, to 4.5cm; nut suborbicular to ellipsoid, angled, light brown, thick-shelled. US. Z4.

C. villosa (Sarg.) Schneid. = *C. texana*.

→*Hicoria* and *Juglans*.

Caryocar L. Caryocaraceae. 10 trees or shrubs. Lvs digitately 3–(5–)foliate, coriaceous. Infl. a term. rac.; cal. lobes 5–6, rotund, strongly imbricate; cor. lobes 5–6, imbricate; sta. numerous. Drupe ellipsoid-globose; seeds large, red-brown with an oily pale kernel. Trop. Amer. Z10.

C. amygdaliferum Mutis. Tree to 55m. Lfts to 12cm, 3, oblong to elliptic, coarsely serrate; petiole to 11cm. Fls yellow-green; sta. white. Fr. to 5.5cm; seeds ovoid. Panama, Colomb.

C. glabrum (Aubl.) Pers. Tree to 25m. Lfts to 15cm, 3, elliptic or oblong-elliptic; petioles to 9cm. Fr. to 6×8cm; seeds subreniform. W Indies, Trop. S Amer.

C. nuciferum L. SOUARI NUT; BUTTER NUT. Tree to 45m. Lfts to 34cm, 3, elliptic-lanceolate, obscurely serrate; petioles to 20cm. Fls large, purple or deep red; sta. white. Fr. to 18cm diam.; seeds reniform. Guyana, W Indies.

CARYOCARACEAE Szyszyl. 2/24. *Caryocar*.

CARYOPHYLLACEAE Juss. 89/2070. *Acanthophyllum, Agrostemma, Alsine, Arenaria, Cerastium, Colobanthus, Cucubalus, Dianthus, Drypis, Gypsophila, Herniaria, Illecebrum, Lychnis, Minuartia, Moehringia, Paronychia, Petrocoptis, Petrorhagia, Sagina, Saponaria, Scleranthus, Silene, Spergula, Spergularia, Stellaria, Telephium, Vaccaria*.

Caryopteris Bunge BLUEBEARD. Verbenaceae. 6 herbs sub-shrubs or shrubs, decid., erect or scrambling. Lvs simple, aromatic. Fls white, blue or lavender, in axill. or terminal, pan. or cymes; cal. 5-lobed; cor. 5-lobed, lower lobes concave, entire, fimbriate or dentate, tube short, limb spreading; sta. 4, exserted. E Asia.

C. × clandonensis A. Simmonds ex Rehd. (*C. incana × C. mongholica.*) Shrub to 1.5m. Lvs to 10cm, lanceolate to elliptic-lanceolate or ovate-lanceolate, grey-green above, grey-white beneath, subentire to slightly dentate. Cymes axill. and term., many-fld; cor. to 10mm, bright blue. Gdn origin. 'Arthur Simmonds': fls blue, spikes compact. 'Azurit': fls blue. 'Blue Mist': habit compact; fls blue. 'Dark Knight': habit low; lvs silvery; fls deep blue. 'Ferndown': fls dark blue-violet. 'Heavenly Blue': fls deepest blue. 'Kew Blue': lvs v. silvery; fls strong Cambridge to lavender blue. 'Longwood Blue': to 60cm; lvs silvery; fls sky-blue. 'Worcester Gold': lvs gold; fls blue. Z7.

C. glutinosa Rehd. St. to 2m, erect. Lvs to 2.5cm, lanceolate, obtuse, base attenuate, revolute, glutinous and shiny above, white with dark veins beneath. Cymes axill., many-fld; cor. to 6mm, blue-purple, lower lobe shortly fimbriate. China. Z8.

C. incana (Thunb.) Miq. Shrub or herb to 1.5m, pubesc. Lvs to 7.5cm, ovate to ovate-oblong, obtuse, base truncate, coarsely serrate, pubesc. Cymes axill., pubesc, densely-fld; cor. to 8mm, white-blue to purple, pubesc., lower lobes fimbriate. China, Jap. 'Candida': fls white. 'Nana': habit dwarf. Z6.

C. mastacantha Schauer = *C. incana*.

C. mongholica Bunge. Shrub to 1m. Lvs to 5cm, linear or linear-oblong to linear-lanceolate, acute to obtuse, entire or slightly dentate. Cymes axill., loosely few-fld; cor. to 12mm, blue, lower lobe strongly fimbriate. N China, Mong. Z8.

C. odorata (Hamilt.) Robinson. Shrub to 4m, spreading, densely pubesc. Lvs to 11cm, ovate-elliptic, acute or acuminate, subglabrous above, gland. and pubesc. beneath, coarsely serrate. Cymes term., densely pubesc.; cor. to 10mm, blue-violet, exterior densely pubesc. and gland. India, Himal. Z8.

C. tangutica Maxim. = *C. incana*.

C. wallichiana Schauer = *C. odorata*.

→*Nepeta* and *Volkameria*.

Caryota L. FISHTAIL PALM. Palmae. 12 palms. St. solitary or clustered, clothed with fibrous lf bases and sheaths, becoming bare and ringed. Lvs arching, bipinnate, sheath felted and scaly, disintegrating into black fibres; petiole scurfy or felted; pinnules large, stalked, cuneate-deltoid, apex retuse to emarginate, praemorse, plicately ribbed. SE Asia to N Aus. and the Solomon Is. Z10.

C. aequatoralis (Becc.) Ridl. = *C. maxima*.

C. alberti F. Muell. ex Wendl. & Drude = *C. rumphiana*.

C. cumingii Lodd. ex Mart. St. to 7.5m×20cm. Pinnules erect to spreading, rhombic. Philipp.

C. furfuracea Bl. = *C. mitis*.

C. griffithii Becc. = *C. mitis*.

C. maxima Bl. St. solitary to 30m×30cm. Lvs to 5.4m, pinnules pendent, to 30×6cm. Malay Penins.

C. mitis Lour. BURMESE FISHTAIL PALM; CLUSTERED FISHTAIL PALM; TUFTED FISHTAIL PALM. St. clustered, 3–12m×10cm. Lvs 2–4m; pinnules asymmetrical, deltoid. Burm. to Malay Penins., Java and Philipp.

C. ochlandra Hance. St. solitary, to 1.2m. Pinnules rhombic. S China.

C. rumphiana Mart. St. solitary, to 22.5m×30cm. Solomon Is. to Aus., India, Philipp.

C. sobolifera Wallich ex Mart. = *C. mitis*.

C. tremula Blanco = *Arenga tremula*.

C. urens L. WINE PALM; JAGGERY PALM; SAGO PALM; TODDY PALM; KITUL TREE. St. solitary, to 12m. Crown dense. Lvs to 4m, arching; pinnules to 30cm, pendent. India, Sri Lanka, Malay Penins.

Cascade Penstemon *Penstemon serrulatus*.

Cascara Sagrada *Rhamnus purshianus*.

Cashew *Anacardium occidentale*.

Casimiroa La Ll. Rutaceae. 6 everg. trees or shrubs. Lvs 3–7-foliolate, glandular-dotted. Fls small in a pan. or a corymb; sep. and pet. 5; sta. usually 5. Fr. a drupe. C Amer., Mex. Z9.

C. edulis La Ll. WHITE SAPOTE; MEXICAN APPLE. Tree to 16m, young shoots villous. Lvs digitately 3–5-foliolate; lfts to 12.5cm, ovate to oblanceolate, obtuse, glab. with age. Infl. axill.; fls fragrant, green or green-white. Fr. to 10cm, edible, yellow-green, ± peach-flavoured, pulp cream. Mex., C Amer.

C. tetrameria Millsp. MATASANO. Differs from *C. edulis* in lvs 5-foliolate; lfts to 15cm, elliptic to ovate-oblong, densely pubesc. beneath; fls white or cream; fr. sometimes bitter. C Amer.

Caspian Locust *Gleditsia caspica*.

Cassabanana *Sicana odorifera*.

Cassandra *Chamaedaphne*.

Cassandra D. Don.
C. calyculata (L.) D. Don = *Chamaedaphne calyculata*.

Cassava *Manihot*.

Cassia L. Leguminosae (Caesalpinioideae). SHOWER TREE. 535 trees, shrubs or ann. or perenn. herbs. Lvs pinnate. Fls solitary or in simple or compound rac.; pet. 5, usually yellow, overlapping, obovate or elliptic, sometimes clawed; sta. generally 10. Trop. Z10.
C. abbreviata hort. = *C. afrofistula*.
C. aciphylla Benth. Diffuse, dense shrub to 1.5m. St. prostrate, glab. or pale-pubesc. Lfts 1.5–3cm, in 5–12 pairs, linear, revolute, pungent. Fls 2–4 in umbellate rac.; pet. orbicular or oblong-orbicular. Aus. (NSW, Vict., Queensld).
C. aculeata Pohl ex Benth. = *Senna aculeata*.
C. acutifolia Delile = *Senna alexandrina*.
C. aeschinomene Colladon = *Chamaecrista nictitans*.
C. afrofistula Brenan. Small tree or shrub, 1.2–6m tall. Young branchlets downy. Lfts 2–10cm, in 4–9 pairs, ovate-lanceolate or ovate-elliptic, apex rounded to sharp-tipped, glab. beneath. Fls in pyramidal term. pan.; pet. 1.5–3cm, vivid yellow. E Afr.
C. alata L. = *Senna alata*.
C. angulata Vogel = *Senna angulata*.
C. angustifolia Vahl = *Senna alexandrina*.
C. antillana (Britt. and Rose) Liog. = *Senna nitida*.
C. armata S. Wats. = *Senna armata*.
C. artemisioides DC. = *Senna artemisioides*.
C. auriculata L. = *Senna auriculata*.
C. australis Vell. = *Senna australis*.
C. australis Sims non Vell. = *Senna odorata*.
C. bearana hort. = *C. afrofistula*.
C. bicapsularis L. = *Senna bicapsularis*.
C. biflora L. = *Senna pallida*.
C. brewsteri (F. Muell.) Benth. Tree or shrub 2–12m. Lfts 2.5–6cm, in 2–6 pairs, narrow-ovate to oblong-elliptic, obtuse or retuse, thinly downy when young. Fls in drooping rac. to 20cm; pet. 1–1.2cm, ovate, yellow to orange, to red-brown. Summer. Aus. (Queensld).
C. candolleana Vogel = *Senna candolleana*.
C. carnaval Speg. = *Senna spectabilis*.
C. chamaecrista L. = *Chamaecrista fasciculata*.
C. coluteoides Colladon = *Senna pendula* var. *glabrata*.
C. coquimbensis Vogel = *Senna cumingii* var. *coquimbensis*.
C. corymbosa Lam. = *Senna corymbosa*.
C. covesii A. Gray = *Senna covesii*.
C. didymobotrya Fres. = *Senna didymobotrya*.
C. excelsa HBK = *C. fistula*.
C. fasciculata Michx. = *Chamaecrista fasciculata*.
C. fastuosa Willd. ex Benth. Differs from *C. ferruginea* in long-clawed pet., large median anth. Lower Amazonia, Fr. Guyana.
C. ferruginea (Schräd.) Schräd. ex DC. Tree, 6–20m tall. Branchlets dark chestnut or blue-black. Lfts 2–5cm, 7–23 pairs, oblong. Fls scented, 20–65, in rac. 6–365cm; pet. 9–28mm, yellow, sometimes brick-red later, base cuneate or clawed. E Braz.
C. fistula L. GOLDEN SHOWER TREE; PURGING CASSIA; INDIAN LABURNUM; PUDDING PIPE TREE. Decid. or semi-evergreen tree to 20m, usually far shorter; bark grey, smooth; branchlets with corky spots. Lfts 7–21cm, in 3–8 pairs, ovate to lanceolate, acuminate, papery, vivid green above, pale beneath. Fls scented, 15–75 in drooping, downy rac. 20–40cm; pet. pale to vivid yellow, ovate-elliptic, longest pet. 18–32mm. Summer. SE Asia, C & S Amer., N Aus., Pacific Is.
C. floribunda Cav. = *Senna floribunda*.
C. florida Vahl = *Senna siamea*.
C. fruticosa Mill. = *Senna fruticosa*.
C. gigantea Bertero ex DC. = *Senna siamea*.
C. glandulosa L. = *Chamaecrista glandulosa*.
C. goldmannii Rose = *Senna polyantha*.
C. goratensis Fres. = *Senna singueana*.
C. grandis L. f. PINK SHOWER; HORSE CASSIA; LIQUORICE TREE; APPLEBLOSSOM CASSIA. Semi-evergreen tree to 30m; trunk sometimes armed. Lfts 3.5–8.3cm in 7–21 pairs, oblong-elliptic, hirsute, glossy and yellow-brown above, paler and glabrescent beneath. Fls 15–50 in erect rac. 3–25cm; pet. pink fading to orange-pink, peach or light yellow, white to cream, or white with pink standard to 11mm, oblong-elliptic. C & S Amer.
C. hebecarpa Fern. = *Senna hebecarpa*.
C. helmsii Symon = *Senna helmsii*.
C. hirsuta L. = *Senna hirsuta*.
C. hookeriana Hook. = *Senna birostris* var. *hookeriana*.
C. hybrida Ten. = *Senna × floribunda*.
C. javanica L. PINK SHOWER; RAINBOW SHOWER. Decid. tree to 25m. Young growth thickly downy. Lfts 3–8cm, in 8–17 pairs, elliptic to oblong-elliptic, apex rounded or acute. Fls 10 to many

in subsessile, rigid rac. 5–10cm; pet. to 35mm, crimson or pale pink to buff, downy beneath, broadly rounded to sharp-tipped. SE Asia.
C. laevigata Willd. = *Senna septemtrionalis*.
C. latopetiolata Vogel = *Senna versicolor*.
C. leptocarpa Benth. = *Senna hirsuta* var. *leptocarpa*.
C. leptocarpa var. *hirsuta* Benth. = *Senna hirsuta* var. *hirta*.
C. leptophylla Vogel. Tree to 18m. Branchlets soft-hirsute, lfts 3–7cm, in 9–14 pairs, elliptic-lanceolate, lustrous above, sparsely downy. Fls c30–50 packed in term. rac. to 25cm; pet. yellow, long-clawed. SE Braz.
C. liebmannii Benth. = *Senna racemosa* var. *liebmannii*.
C. ligustrina L. = *Senna ligustrina*.
C. lindheimeriana Scheele = *Senna lindheimeriana*.
C. macranthera DC. ex Colladon = *Senna macranthera*.
C. mannii Oliv. Tree, 15–25m, branchllets downy to glab. Lfts 3.5–8cm, in 5–12 pairs, elliptic to oblong, blunt to sharp tipped, sometimes retuse, subglabrous. Fls in rac. 3–12cm; pet. 15–25mm, rose-purple to white, elliptic. Trop. Afr.
C. marginata Roxb. non Willd. = *C. roxburghii*.
C. marginata Willd. non Roxb. = *Senna polyphylla*.
C. marilandica L. = *Senna marilandica*.
C. medsgeri Shafer = *Senna marilandica*.
C. micans Nees = *Senna macranthera* var. *micans*.
C. moschata HBK. BRONZE SHOWER; CAÑAFISTOLA SABANERA. Tree to 20m. Lfts 2.6–6cm, downy, 10–16 pairs, oblong or oblong-lanceolate or ovate-lanceolate, apex emarginate, blunt or sharp-tipped, base subcordate or rounded. Fls packed in rac. 9–32cm, pet. to 1.5cm, bronze- or golden-yellow, often veined red, elliptic-obovate. C & S Amer., Cuba.
C. multiglandulosa Jacq. = *Senna multiglandulosa*.
C. multijuga Rich. = *Senna multijuga*.
C. nairobensis L.H. Bail. = *Senna didymobotrya*.
C. nicaraguensis Benth. = *Senna nicaraguensis*.
C. nictitans L. = *Chamaecrista nictitans*.
C. nodosa Roxb. = *C. javanica*.
C. obtusifolia L. = *Senna obtusifolia*.
C. occidentalis L. = *Senna occidentalis*.
C. oligophylla F. Muell. = *Senna oligophylla*.
C. pendula Humb. & Bonpl. ex Willd. = *Senna pendula*.
C. phyllodinea R. Br. = *Senna phyllodinea*.
C. polyantha Colladon = *Senna polyantha*.
C. polyphylla Jacq. = *Senna polyphylla*.
C. racemosa Mill. = *Senna racemosa*.
C. renigera hort. = *C. javanica* and *C. grandis*.
C. reticulata Willd. = *Senna reticulata*.
C. robusta (Pollini) Pollini = *Chamaecrista robusta*.
C. roemeriana Scheele = *Senna roemeriana*.
C. roxburghii DC. Tree. Lfts 2–4.5cm, in 12–20 pairs, elliptic-oblong, apex blunt to notched and mucronate, glab. above, soft-hirsute beneath. Fls in axill., often branched rac.; pet. c10–14mm, pink, rose or orange. Summer–autumn. Sri Lanka, S India.
C. roxburghii Willd. non Roxb. = *Senna versicolor*.
C. senna L. = *Senna alexandrina*.
C. septemtrionalis Viv. = *Senna septemtrionalis*.
C. serpens L. = *Chamaecrista serpens*.
C. siamea Lam. = *Senna siamea*.
C. sieberiana hort. = *C. afrofistula*.
C. singueana Delile = *Senna singueana*.
C. sophera L. = *Senna sophera*.
C. speciosa Schräd. non Kunth. See *Senna macranthera* var. *micans*.
C. speciosa Kunth non Schräd. = *Senna spectabilis*.
C. spectabilis DC. = *Senna spectabilis*.
C. splendida Vogel = *Senna splendida*.
C. sturtii R. Br. = *Senna sturtii*.
C. surattensis hort. = *Caesalpinia mexicana*.
C. tomentosa L. = *Senna multiglandulosa*.
C. tora sensu Benth. = *Senna obtusifolia*.
C. versicolor Meyen ex Vogel = *Senna versicolor*.

Cassia *Cinnamomum aromaticum*.
Cassia-bark Tree *Cinnamomum aromaticum*.

Cassine L. Celastraceae. c80 everg. shrubs or trees; twigs 4-angled. Lvs entire or serrate, coriaceous. Fls small, white to yellow-green in simple or compound axill., dichasial cymes; perianth 3–5-merous; sta. as many as pet. Fr. oblong-globose, c2cm. Trop. and subtrop. Z10.
C. australis (Vent.) Kuntze. Shrub or tree to 8m. Lvs to 10cm, ovate to oblong-lanceolate, apex acute to obtuse, base cuneate, entire or crenate. Fr. to 1cm, orange-red. Aus. (C Queensld to S NSW).

C. capensis L. CAPE PHILLYREA. Shrub or tree to 10m. Lvs to 5cm, lanceolate-elliptic, v. obtuse, emarginate, entire at base, spiny-serrate toward apex, somewhat revolute, glossy dark green above, often red-tomentose beneath. Fr. ovoid yellow to purple. S Afr.

C. glauca (Pers.) Kuntze. CEYLON TEA. Shrub or tree to 15m. Lvs 4–15cm, elliptic or ovate, acute or acuminate, crenate or sub-entire, membranous or subcoriaceous. Fr. to 1cm, yellow-green. India.

C. laneana (A.H. Moore) J. Ingram. BERMUDA OLIVE-WOOD BARK. Shrub or tree to 15m. Lvs to 10cm, oblanceolate, shallowly dentate, somewhat lustrous above. Fr. to 2.5cm, white tinged yellow, glossy. Bermuda.

C. laurifolia (Harv.) Davison. Shrub or small tree. Lvs 6–13cm, oblong to elliptic. Fls yellow tinged green. S Afr.

C. orientalis (Jacq.) Kuntze. FALSE OLIVE. Shrub or small tree to 10m. Lvs to 7.5cm, lanceolate to oblong or obovate, crenate, coriaceous, apex slender, base cuneate, midrib dark red when young. Fr. to 1.25cm diam. olive-like. Maur., Madag.

C. papillosa (Hochst.) Kuntze. Shrub to 6m; br. rough. Lvs to 7cm, lanceolate-elliptic, remotely serrate, revolute, dark green above, paler and often rufescent beneath. Fr. to 2cm, yellow. S Afr.

C. sphaerophylla (Ecklon & Zeyh.) Kuntze. CAPE CHERRY; KOOBOO BERRY. Shrub or small tree to 15m. Lvs to 4cm, elliptic, obtuse or slightly emarginate, finely dentate, sometimes velutinous beneath. Fr. to 0.6cm diam. S Afr.

→Elaeodendron and Portenschlagia.

Cassinia R. Br. Compositae. 20 everg. *Erica*-like shrubs or herbs. Lvs entire. Cap. discoid, small, numerous in term. corymbose pan.; receptacle usually with scarious, white-tipped scales, imbricate, scarious or coloured, inner phyllaries often spreading; flts few, pale brown-green, tubular and 5-toothed or filiform. Aus., NZ, S Afr. Z8 unless specified.

C. aculeata R. Br. DOLLY BUSH. Shrub to 4m. St. much-branched, tomentose. Lvs to 3cm, linear, mucronate, revolute, rough above, tomentose beneath. Involucre to 4mm; phyllaries white, rarely pale brown or pink. S & SE Aus.

C. fulvida Hook. f. GOLDEN COTTONWOOD; GOLDEN HEATHER. Shrub to 2m. Br. slender, tomentose, sticky. Lvs to 0.8cm, crowded, sticky, linear to linear-spathulate, green above, yellow beneath, slightly revolute. Cap. clustered in dense corymbs; phyllaries pubesc. or outer glab., inner with white radiating tips. NZ. Z9.

C. leptophylla (Forst. f.) R. Br. Shrub to 2m. Br. slender, erect, tomentose. Lvs to 0.5cm, linear to linear-spathulate, leathery, dark green above, yellow- or white-downy beneath. Cap. numerous; outer phyllaries glab. to pubesc., inner with white radiating tips. NZ.

C. quinquefaria R. Br. Shrub to 2m. Br. tomentose. Lvs to 4cm, linear, revolute. Cap. in large, loose, pyramidal pan.; phyllaries narrow, pale straw-coloured. NSW.

C. retorta .Cunn. ex DC. Shrub to 5m. Br. tomentose. Lvs to 0.5cm, crowded, linear-obovate to oblong, spreading, revolute, leathery, glab. or downy above, white-tomentose beneath. Cap. clustered in small corymbs; phyllaries tomentose, inner with short white tips. NZ.

C. vauvilliersii (Hombron & Jacquinot) Hook. f. MOUNTAIN COTTONWOOD. Shrub to 3m. Br. stout, furrowed, yellow-tomentose, sticky. Lvs to 1.2cm, linear-obovate, leathery, dark green, glab. above, yellow-tomentose beneath. Cap. clustered in rounded corymbs to 5cm diam.; outer phyllaries downy on back, inner with white radiating tips. NZ. var. *albida* T. Kirk. SILVER HEATHER. Br. white-tomentose. Lvs linear-spathulate, white-tomentose beneath.

→Ozothamnus.

Cassiope D. Don. Ericaceae. 12 everg., dwarf shrubs. St. procumbent to ascending; br. heath- or whipcord-like, usually obscured by lvs. Lvs closely overlapping in 4 rows, small, sessile, scale-like. Fls solitary, on slender stalks, often tinted red; cal. lobes 4–6; cor. campanulate-urceolate to hemispherical, lobes usually 4, sometimes 5 or 6, erect or reflexed. N Asia, N Eur., Himal.

C. ericoides (Pall.) D. Don. Br. to 15cm, erect, dense. Lvs small, oblong, margin not membranous, v. finely ciliate, furrowed beneath. Fls small, white. Sib. Z2.

C. fastigiata (Wallich) D. Don. St. 15–25cm, erect. Lvs 2–4mm, lanceolate, dors. surface striate, dark green, margins silver and ciliate, sessile. Fls pendulous; pedicels 6–8mm, decurved; cor. bell-shaped, white, 8–9mm diam., lobes reflexed. Spring. Himal. 'Bearsden' (*C. fastigiata* ×*C. lycopodioides*): low-growing to 15cm, dense; fls white, abundant. 'Edinburgh' (*C. fastigiata* ×*C. tetragona* var. *saximontana*): vigorous to 30cm, lvs deep green; fl. stalks short, fls white in dense groups.

'Medusa' (*C. fastigiata* ×*C. lycopodioides*): vigorous; lf margins finely fringed; fls large, stalks and cal. tinged red. 'Randle Cooke' (*C. fastigiata* ×*C. lycopodioides*): to 15cm, broad; lvs furrowed, fringed; fls large, short-stalked.

C. hypnoides (L.) D. Don. St. to 15cm, branched, prostrate then ascending, mat-forming. Lvs 2–4mm, linear to subulate, sharp-tipped, dark green, glab., ciliate. Fls somewhat pendulous; pedicel 7–10mm; cor. 4–8mm, campanulate, white, lobes 5, rounded. Spring. Arc. N hemis. Z2.

C. lycopodioides (Pall.) D. Don. IWA-HIGE. St. to 8cm sprawling to ascending. Lvs 1.5–2mm. Lvs 1.5–2mm, ovate, entire, blunt, margins transparent, deep green, dors. surface carinate, ventral surface concave and glaucous. Fls pendulous; pedicels 15–30mm; cor. 8mm, tubular-campanulate, pink or white, lobes 4–6. Spring–summer. Jap., NE Asia, Alask. 'Beatrice Lilley': habit compact; fls white, abundant. 'Major': large, to 8cm high; fls in more distinctive bell-shape. 'Rigida': large; cor. cylindrical, lobes longer, narrow. 'Badenoch' (*C. lycopodioides* ×*C. fastigiata*): habit loose; branchlets thin. 'Kathleen Dryden' (*C. lycopodioides* ×*C. fastigiata*): vigorous; branchlets spreading; fls abundant, pendulous. Z3.

C. mertensiana (Bong.) D. Don. WHITE HEATHER. St. 15–30cm, diffuse or erect. Lvs 5mm, ovate to lanceolate, glab., bluntly acuminate, dors. surface carinate, ventral surface concave. Fls pendulous; pedicels to 12mm; cor. bell-shaped, white, sometimes pink tinged, lobes 5, reflexed, to maroon. Spring. Mts of W US. 'Gracilis': mound-forming; br. light green; fls white on red st. Z5.

C. saximontana Small = C. tetragona var. *saximontana*.

C. selaginoides Hook. f. & Thoms. St., 5–25cm. Lvs 2–3mm, lanceolate to oblong-lanceolate, furrowed on dors. surface, sparsely bristly at apex, downy on margins and in groove. Fls pendulous; pedicels to 12–25mm; cor. 6–10mm, bell shaped, white or tinged red, lobes 5, deltoid, recurved. Spring. W China, Himal. 'Nana': to 3cm high; fls rounded. Z4.

C. stelleriana (Pall.) DC. St. to 10cm, diffuse, mat-forming. Lvs c3mm, oblong or narrow-oblong, apex blunt. Fls pendulous; pedicels short; cor. 6–9mm diam., campanulate, white or cream, often tinged pink, conspicuously cleft, lobes 4. Spring. NW Amer., NE Asia. Z4.

C. tetragona (L.) D. Don. St. 10–30cm, decumbent to sprawling, much branched. Lvs 3–5mm, oblong-lanceolate, 3-sided, coriaceous, apex blunt, somewhat downy, dors. surface furrowed, ventral surface concave. Fls pendulous; pedicels c10mm; cor. 6–8mm, bell-shaped, white, occas. pink-tinged; lobes 4–5. Spring. Arc. Eur. var. *saximontana* (Small) Hitchc. Fls smaller. Z3.

C. wardii Marq. St. c20cm, procumbent. Lvs c5mm, lanceolate, dors. surface grooved. Fls pendulous; pedicels short; cor. c8mm, urceolate, white flushed red inside at base, lobes 5, broadly deltoid, apex recurved. Spring. Tibet. 'George Taylor' (*C. wardii* ×*C. fastigiata*): open-growing; lvs fimbriate-ciliate. 'Muirhead' (*C. wardii* ×*C. fastigiata*): low-growing, broad; lvs small, margins fringed; fls abundant.

Cassumar Ginger *Zingiber purpureum*.

Castalis Cass. Compositae. 3 glandular-pilose or glab. perenn. herbs with thick woody rootstock. St. erect or ascending, often branched. Lvs to 7cm. Cap. radiate, solitary and term. at ends of br., c6–7cm diam., pedunculate; receptacle flat or slightly convex; ray flts yellow-orange or lilac-purple on both surfaces, or white above and purple-violet or of mixed colouring beneath. S Afr. Z9.

C. nudicaulis (L.) Norl. 10–30cm. Lvs rigid, membranous, hairy-hispid, narrowly obovate, oblanceolate, oblong- or linear-lanceolate, attenuate below, acute, obtuse or rounded, remotely and coarsely sinuate-dentate, rarely pinnatifid or entire; st. lvs entire or remotely dentate. Peduncles long, scape-like, rigid, densely glandular-hairy to pubesc.; ray flts white above, purple to violet or in places coppery beneath; disc flts yellow beneath, yellow or dark violet above. Cape Prov.

C. spectabilis (Schltr.) Norl. 20–40cm. Lvs erect, rigid, membranous to leathery, lanceolate to narrowly elliptic or linear-lanceolate, apex acute or obtuse, base sessile or semi-amplexicaul, glandular-hairy and rough, or smooth, margin scabrous, entire or dentate, veins white, prominent. Peduncles 5–15cm, rough, glandular-hairy, somewhat rigid; ray flts lilac to purple; disc flts pale yellow beneath, lilac above. Transvaal.

C. tragus (Ait.) Norl. 20–30cm. Lvs membranous, linear, linear-oblong to narrowly spathulate, rounded or obtuse, rarely acute, base decurrent, green or glaucous, glab., entire or finely sinuate-dentate, rough, ciliate. Peduncles 2–6cm, rough, glandular-hairy or glab.; ray flts orange to deep yellow; disc flts pale yellow beneath, dark brown above. Cape Prov.

→Calendula and Dimorphotheca.

Castanea Mill. CHESTNUT; CHINKAPIN; CHINQUAPIN. Fagaceae. 12 decid. trees and shrubs. Bark grey to black, furowed. Lvs usually conspicuously toothed, oblong-lanceolate or narrow-oval, numerous parallel veins angled outwards from midrib. Fls unisexual, small, muskily scented, in axill. catkins. Fr. in clusters; casing a globose involucre or 'burr', covered with branched spines, splitting in 4 sections; nuts 1–7, ovoid-acute, glossy brown with a pale basal scar. Warm temp. regions of E N Amer. and S Eur. E to China and Jap.

C. alnifolia Nutt. BUSH CHINKAPIN; TRAILING CHINQUAPIN. Suckering shrub to 1m. Lvs 5–15cm, oblong to elliptic, toothed, shiny dark green above, initially tawny tomentose beneath, teeth shallow, bristle-tipped. Burr globose with short, stout spines; nut solitary. SE US. Z7. var. *floridana* Sarg. FLORIDA CHINKAPIN. Larger; lvs 8–11cm, less densely tomentose, silky becoming glab. Flor. Z8.

C. americana Raf. = *C. dentata*.

C. arkansana Sarg. = *C. ozarkensis*.

C. ashei (Sudw.) Sudw. ex Ashe = *C. pumila* var. *ashei*.

C. bungeana Bl. = *C. mollissima*.

C. chrysophylla Hook. = *Chrysolepis chrysophylla*.

C. crenata Sieb. & Zucc. JAPANESE CHESTNUT. Spreading, short-trunked tree to 20m. Young shoots scaly to densely downy. Lvs 7–18cm, oblong glab. above, grey downy beneath, apex short-pointed, crenate to serrate, teeth small, aristate. Burr globose with dense slender spines, 4–8cm diam., nuts 1–4, 2–4cm. Jap. Z4.

C. dentata (Marshall) Borkh. AMERICAN SWEET CHESTNUT. Tree to 45m with trunk to 4m diam. or a coppice to 5–10m having survived chestnut blight. Young shoots glab. or slightly scurfy. Lvs 14–22cm, dull green, glab., oblong-lanceolate, apex acuminate, teeth large, gland. Burr globose 5–7cm diam., with dense slender spines; nuts 2–3.5cm, 2–3. E US. Z4.

C. duclouxii Dode = *C. mollissima*.

C. henryi (Skan) Rehd. & Wils. Tree to 25m. Young shoots almost glab. Lvs 10–20cm, glab. above, veins sparsely hairy beneath, oblong-lanceolate, apex acuminate, teeth aristate. Burr prickly 3cm, nut solitary. W & C China. Z6.

C. hupehensis Dode = *C. mollissima*.

C. japonica Bl. = *C. crenata*.

C. mollissima Bl. CHINESE CHESTNUT. Broad-crowned, stout-trunked tree to 20m. Young shoots thinly or velvety hairy. Lvs 12–22cm, glab. above, tomentose on veins beneath, broadly oblong-lanceolate to elliptic, apex acuminate, teeth triangular or aristate. Burr yellow-green 5–8cm with dense slender spines, nuts 1–4, 2–4.5cm. Wild or nat. in Korea and China from Beijing to Yunnan. Z4.

C. nana Muhlenb. = *C. alnifolia*.

C. × neglecta Dode. (*C. dentata × C. pumila*.) Lvs less downy beneath than in *C. pumila*; fr. larger. US (N Carol.).

C. ozarkensis Ashe. OZARK CHINKAPIN. Tree to 20m or shrub, closely related to *C. pumila* but with shoots glab. Lvs larger, 12–23cm, coarsely serrate, tomentose beneath. Burr with dense slender spines; nut solitary. Midwest US. Z6.

C. pubinervis C. Schneid. = *C. crenata*.

C. pumila (L.) Mill. ALLEGHENY CHINKAPIN. Suckering shrub to 4m, or a small tree to 13m. Young shoots tomentose. Lvs 7–15cm, glab. above, pale tomentose beneath, oblong to ovate, acute, teeth short, rigid. Burr 4cm with dense, slender spines; nut 1, 2cm. SE US. Z5. var. *ashei* Sudw. ASHE CHINKAPIN; COASTAL CHINKAPIN. Shrub or small tree to 5m. Lvs 5–8cm, similar to *C. alnifolia*, densely tomentose beneath. Burr globose with scattered short, stout spines. SE US. Z7.

C. sativa Mill. SWEET CHESTNUT; SPANISH CHESTNUT. Tree to 40m. Young shoots pubesc. Lvs 12–25cm, minutely gland. above at first, soon glab., thinly pubesc. beneath, oblong-lanceolate, teeth remote, aristate. Burr 4–7cm, with dense, slender spines; nuts 1–5(–7) in each burr, mostly 2–3cm. Wild or nat. throughout S Eur., NW Afr. and SW Asia from Iberia and Moroc. to Pak. In addition to fr. crop cvs, selections have been made for lf form ('Asplenifolia', Laciniata'), colour ('Albomarginata', 'Aureomarginata', 'Purpurea') mutability ('Heterophylla') and crown form ('Holtii'; narrowly conic). Z5.

C. seguinii Dode. Tree to 10m or shrub. Lvs 6–14cm, glab. above, pubesc. on veins beneath, elliptic-oblong to oblong-lanceolate, apex acuminate, coarsely dentate. Burr globose spiny with 3–5(–7) nuts 1.5cm across. E & C China. Z6.

C. sempervirens Kellogg = *Chrysolepis sempervirens*.

C. vesca Gaertn. = *C. sativa*.

C. vulgaris Lam. = *C. sativa*.

Castanopsis (D. Don) Spach. Fagaceae. *c*110 everg. trees and shrubs; bark scaly. Lvs entire or serrate, leathery. Fls in unisexual erect catkins. Fr. a nut, usually 3 in a prickly 2–4-valved cupule. Warm temp. to subtrop. S & E Asia.

C. chinensis Hance. Tree, to 20m+; bark grey, grooved, twigs dark grey, covered with white lenticels. Lvs 8cm, elliptic, long-acuminate, sparsely serrate above, thick, leathery, glossy above, tinged blue beneath. China. Z7.

C. chrysophylla (Hook. A. DC. = *Chrysolepis chrysophylla*.

C. concolor Rehd. & Wils. = *C. orthacantha*.

C. cuspidata (Thunb.) Schottky. Tree to 25m, br. wide, pendent; bark dark grey, smooth or grooved. Lvs 5–9cm, ovate to oblong, apex cuspidate, base rounded to cuneate, emerging metallic brown nearly white beneath, thick, tough, entire. S Jap., SE China. 'Variegata': lvs with broad pale yellow margin. Z7.

C. delavayi Franch. Tree to 20m+; bark dark grey, twigs grey stellate-tomentose at first. Lvs 7–14cm, elliptic to obovate, margins wavy and irregularly dentate, silver-grey or white beneath. S China. Z8.

C. orthacantha Franch. Tree to 20m+; bark dark grey, finely grooved, twigs glab., rough with white lenticels. Lvs 6–12cm, oblanceolate to oval-elliptic, tough leathery, long-acuminate, irregularly serrate above, glab. blue-green. SW China. Z8.

C. sempervirens (Kellogg) W. Dudley = *Chrysolepis sempervirens*.

Castanospermum Cunn. MORETON BAY CHESTNUT; BLACK BEAN TREE; AUSTRALIA CHESTNUT. Leguminosae (Papilionoideae). 1 tree with heavy twigs and rough bark. Lvs to 15cm, imparipinnate; lfts 11–15, elliptic-oblong, coriaceous. Fls to 4cm, in crowded, puberulent rac., pea-like, yellow, later orange and red. Legume to 30cm, oblong, often curved, turgid, valves ligneous and spongy inside; seeds 1–5, 1.5cm, black. Summer. NE Aus., New Caledonia. Z9.

C. australe Cunn. & Fraser.

Castaño *Oreopanax echinops*.

Castellanoa Traub = *Chlidanthus*.

Castellanosia Cardenas = *Browningia*.

Castilla Sessé. MEXICAN RUBBER; PANAMA RUBBER. Moraceae. 10 lactiferous buttressed trees. Lvs chartaceous, stipules connate, ampexicaull. Principal ♂ infl. pedunculate, fan-shaped, bivalvate, secondary infl. infundibuliform to cyathiform, entire to 2-lobed; sta. solitary or paired along radiating and branching ridges of recpetacle; ♀ infl. solitary, sessile, discoid to subglobose, many- to several-fld. Trop. Amer.

C. elastica Sessé. PANAMA RUBBER TREE; CASTILLA RUBBER TREE. Tree to 40m, with low buttresses; latex white. Lvs 15–40cm, broad, nodding, elliptic to oblong, sometimes pandurate, chartaceous, sometimes with lobes at base, denticulate or dentate, scabrous above, subhispid to strigose beneath; petioles to 10cm; stipules 2–11.5cm, yellow-strigose. Fruiting head red, orange or salmon-pink; fr. 8–10mm, ellipsoid, brown. Flowering throughout the year. S Mex. to N S Amer.

Castilla Rubber Tree *Castilla elastica*.

Castilleja Mutis ex L. f. PAINTED CUPS; INDIAN PAINTBRUSH; PRAIRIE-FIRE. Scrophulariaceae. *c*200 ann. or perenn. herbs, often semi-parasitic on roots of grasses. Fls in term. bracteate spikes; bracts usually conspicuous and brightly coloured; cal. often coloured like bracts; cor. strongly bilabiate, tube narrow, upper lip cleft, arched, galeate, lower lip v. short, 3-toothed. W N Amer., Eurasia, C Amer., Andes.

C. chromosa A. Nels. Perenn. to 40cm, villous. Lvs 8cm, lanceolate-linear, entire to narrowly pinnatifid above. Spike dense, elongate bracts pinnatifid, linear-lanceolate, tipped scarlet; cal. green with scarlet lobes; cor. 2–3cm, green, gland., pubesc., margins red. Spring–summer. W US.

C. coccinea Spreng. BLOODY WARRIOR; WICKAAWEE; ELECTION POSIES. Ann. or bienn. to 30cm, villous. Lvs to 6cm, oblong, obovate or linear tufted, entire or deeply 3–5 cleft. Spike 4–6cm; bracts 3-lobed, scarlet, rarely yellow; cal. scarlet; cor. green-yellow. Spring–summer. W US.

C. collina A. Nels. = *C. chromosa*.

C. crista-galli Rydb. = *C. miniata*.

C. miniata Douglas ex Hook. Perenn., to 24cm, often retrorsely pubesc. Lvs 3cm, entire or cleft, linear-lanceolate, hirsute to scabrous. Spike short, dense, glandular-villous; bracts slender, entire or 2-lobed, gland. pubesc., bright red, purple-red or orange-red; cal. tube yellow, lobes bright red; cor. green tipped red. Spring–summer. N Amer.

C. pallida Spreng. Perenn. to 20cm, glab. or minutely pubesc. Lvs to 7cm, linear, entire, to ovate-lanceolate, dentate. Bracts yellow or white. Spring–summer. Sib., Alask.

→*Bartsia*.

Cast-iron Plant *Aspidistra elatior.*
Castor-bean Begonia *Begonia* ×*ricinifolia.*
Castor-bean Plant, Castor-oil Plant *Ricinus communis.*

Casuarina Adans. BEEFWOOD; BULL OAK; WHISTLING PINE; AUSTRALIAN PINE; SHE OAK. Casuarinaceae. *c*70 everg. trees and shrubs, br. slender, grey, striate, usually weeping; branchlets whip-like, jointed, ridged, resembling *Equisetum* or *Ephedra.* Lvs minute, scale-like. ♂ fls in catkin-like spikes, perianth seg. 1–2, scale-like, sta. 1, ♀ fls in condensed heads, becoming cone-like and woody at maturity. Aus., Pacific. Z9.

C. cunninghamiana Miq. To 35m. Branchlets 7–25cm×0.4–0.7mm, glab., ridges 6–9. Lvs 0.2–0.5mm, usually 8 per whorl, banded brown-green, withering at apex. Cone to 1.4×1cm, cylindric to subglobose, dull grey. Aus. (Queensld, NSW).

C. equisetifolia Forst. & Forst. f. HORSETAIL TREE; SOUTHSEA IRONWOOD; MILE TREE. To 35m. Branchlets 7–20cm×0.5–1mm, pubesc., ridges 6–8. Lvs 0.3–1mm, 6–7 per whorl, not withering (cf. *C. cunninghamiana*). Cone to 2.4×1.8cm, cylindric to subglobose, grey-brown. SE Asia to NE Aus. and Polyn.

C. glauca Spreng. To 20m, often suckering. Branchlets 1–3.5cm×0.9–1.5mm, glab., ridges 12–17. Lvs 0.5–0.9mm, 14–16 per whorl. Cone to 18×13mm, subglobose. Aus. (Queensld, NSW).

C. littoralis Salisb. To 20m. Branchlets to 20cm×0.8mm, usually erect, ridges 6–9. Lvs 0.4–0.9mm, 6–7 per whorl. Cone 1–3×1–2cm, globose, mahogany to black. E Aus., Tasm.

C. nana Sieb. DWARF SHE OAK. Small, closely branched shrub; br. slender, rush-like. W Aus.

C. stricta Ait. = *C. verticillata.*

C. suberosa Otto & Dietr. = *C. littoralis.*

C. torulosa Ait. To 20m, usually less. Bark corky. Branchlets to 10cm×1.5mm, puberulent, ridges 9–13. Lvs 0.7–1.2mm, 9–12 per whorl. Cone 2–4×2–3cm, ovoid, globose, glossy dark brown or black. Aus. (Queensld, NSW).

C. verticillata Lam. To 10m, usually smaller. Bark furrowed. Branchlets to 10cm×1.5mm, puberulent, ridges 9–13. Lvs 0.7–1.2mm, 9–12 per whorl. Cone 2–4×2–3cm, ovoid, globose, glossy dark brown or black. SE Aus.

CASUARINACEAE R. Br. 4/70. *Casuarina.*

Cat *Parmentiera aculeata.*
Catalina Cherry *Prunus lyonii.*
Catalina Ironwood *Lyonothamnus.*
Catalina Mountain Lilac *Ceanothus arboreus.*
Catalina Nightshade *Solanum wallacei.*

Catalpa Scop. Bignoniaceae. 11 decid. trees. Lvs large, entire or shallowly 3-lobed. Infl. an erect term. pan. or rac.; cor. campanulate-funnelform, 2-lipped, upper lip divided once, lower lip 3-lobed, limb crispate-undulate. Fr. a slender, pendulous bean-like capsule. N Amer., Cuba, SW China, Tibet.

C. bignonioides Walter. COMMON CATALPA; EASTERN CATALPA; CATAWBA; INDIAN BEAN; BEAN TREE; SMOKING BEAN; INDIAN CIGAR. To 15m. Lvs 10–20cm, cordate to ovate, apex acuminate, dark green above, entire, rarely with 1–2 lobes, short pubesc. beneath. Infl. paniculate, much branched; cor. white, 3–5cm, with purple spots and yellow stripes in the throat. Capsule to 35cm. Summer. 'Aurea': lvs large, soft golden yellow. 'Koehnei': lvs edged in yellow. 'Nana': habit bushy, densely branched, to 1.8m; lvs small; fls none; usually top grafted onto standard. 'Rehderi': lvs almost triangular, to 15cm, with lat. lobes. 'Variegata': lvs creamy yellow, central splash of yellow-green. Z5.

C. bungei C.A. Mey. Smaller than *C. bignonioides.* Lvs to 15cm, ovate-triangular to trapeziform, glab., apex acuminate, base cordate. Infl. a 3–12-fld corymb; cor. to 3.2cm, rose-pink to white with brown-purple and yellow marks inside. Capsule 30–50cm. Summer. N China. var. *heterophylla* C.A. Mey. Lvs deltoid, caudate-acuminate, glab., base truncate, usually lobed or dentate. Fls fewer, in smaller clusters. Z6.

C. catalpa (L.) Karst. = *C. bignonioides.*

C. cordifolia St.-Hil. = *C. speciosa.*

C. duclouxii Dode = *C. fargesii* f. *duclouxii.*

C. ×*erubescens* Carr. (*C. ovata* ×*C. bignonioides.*) Lvs cordate to deltoid, apex acuminate, base cordate to truncate, often with 1–2 lat. lobes. Infl. a many-fld pan.; cor. *c*3cm, pure white, lined and spotted yellow and purple. Capsule to 40cm. 'Adina': fls "double" – petaloid staminodes surround sta. 'Japonica' (probably *C. bignonioides* ×*C. ovata* 'Flavescens'): lvs large, triangular to cordate, less markedly lobed or downy than in *C. ovata,* glossy; fls in compact infl., pure white, inside spotted purple. 'J.C. Teas' ('Hybrida'): vigorous, to 18m; lvs to 30cm,

broad-ovate, somewhat 3-lobed, cordate, downy beneath, purple when young; fls small, white, stained yellow with purple spots. 'Purpurea': lvs to 8cm, lvs and shoots purple, later dark green; fls to 3cm, white. Z5.

C. fargesii Bur. To 20m. Lvs 8–14cm, elliptic-ovate to deltoid-cordate, apex acuminate, base subcordate to truncate or cuneate, entire or with 1–2 lat. lobes, densely yellow pubesc. beneath and sparsely so above. Infl. a corymb; cor. 3.2cm, rose-pink with yellow and purple-brown marks. Capsule to 55cm. Summer. W China. f. *duclouxii* (Dode) Gilmour. Lvs ovate-acute, 3-lobed; cor. 3.5cm, purple. Capsule to 80cm. W China. Z6.

C. ×*galleana* Dode. (*C. ovata* ×*C. speciosa.*) Lvs 8–10cm, elliptic-ovate becoming cordate, short-acuminate, base truncate, sometimes with 1–2 lat. lobes. Fls similar to *C. speciosa.* C Eur. Z5.

C. henryi Dode = *C. ovata.*

C. ×*hybrida* Späth = *C.* ×*erubescens.*

C. kaempferi Sieb. & Zucc. = *C. ovata.*

C. longissima (Jacq.) Dum.-Cours. BOIS-CHENE; CHENE; CHENE NOIR; CHENE D'AMERIQUE; ST. DOMINGO OAK; SPANISH OAK; JAMAICAN OAK; MAST WOOD; YOKE WOOD. To 25m. Lvs 5–11cm, leathery, lanceolate-elliptic to obovate-elliptic, apex attenuate, entire to undulate. Infl. a lax pan.; cor. 2.5–3cm, lobes white, tinted pink, with purple lines and yellow stripes inside. Capsule 35–67cm. W Indies. Z9.

C. ovata G. Don. To 10m. Lvs 10–25cm, deltoid to cordate, apex acuminate, base cordate, entire, or with 1–5 lat. lobes, glabrescent, with gland. brown markings. Infl. paniculate; cor. 2.2–3cm, white, yellow within with purple and yellow markings, limb crispate. Capsule 32cm. China. 'Flavescens': lvs small, pale; fls to 2cm wide and long, flushed yellow. Z5.

C. punctata Griseb. ROBLE DE OLOR; ROBLILLO. To 20m. Lvs leathery to papery, broadly elliptic, apex and base obtuse, apex emarginate, entire, minute scaly above, glabrescent, scaly beneath. Infl. a few-fld corymb; cor. 1.5–2cm, yellow with brown purple stripes and yellow markings. Capsule to 68cm. Cuba. Z9.

C. speciosa (Warder ex Barney) Engelm. SHAWNEE WOOD; BOIS CHAVANON; HARDY CATALPA; WESTERN CATALPA; NORTHERN CATALPA; EARLY FLOWERING CATALPA; INDIAN CIGAR. To 30m. Lvs 15–30cm, cordate to subcordate, acuminate, entire or with 1–2 lobes, pubesc. beneath, glab. above. Infl. paniculate; cor. 4.5cm, pure white with purple spots and yellow stripes in the throat. Capsules to 55cm. US. 'Albovariegata': lvs spattered off-white. 'Pulverulenta': densely white spotted. Z5.

C. sutchuensis Dode = *C. fargesii* f. *duclouxii.*

C. syringifolia Sims = *C. bignonioides.*

C. teasii Dode = *C.* ×*erubescens.*

C. tibetica Forr. Shrub. Resembling a smaller *C. ovata.* Tibet. Z5.

Catananche L. BLUE CUPIDONE; CUPID'S DART. Compositae. 5 ann. or perenn. latex producing herbs. St. 1 or few, often with adpressed hairs. Lvs linear to linear-oblanceolate, entire or toothed, mostly basal. Cap. 1–5, ligulate, long-stalked; receptacle scaly; phyllaries in several series, scarious, darkly veined; ligules papery, blue, white or yellow. Medit. Z7.

C. bicolor hort. = *C. caerulea.*

C. caerulea L. Perenn., to 90cm. Lvs to 30cm. Cap. to 5cm diam.; peduncle to 30cm; ligules blue. SW Eur. 'Alba': fls white. 'Bicolor': fls white with dark blue centre. 'Blue Giant': lvs tinted silver; fls cornflower-blue, summer. 'Major': fls deep lavender. 'Perry's White': fls white.

C. lutea L. Ann., to 40cm. Lvs to 15cm. Cap. on peduncle to 20cm; ligules yellow. Medit.

Catasetum Rich. ex Kunth. Orchidaceae. 70 epiphytic, lithophytic or terrestrial orchids. Pbs ovoid to fusiform, covered with numerous large sheaths. Lvs alt. in 2 ranks, lanceolate, plicately ribbed. Rac. lat., erect or pendent; fls unisexual, males and females usually on separate infl., rarely perfect; sep. lanceolate-obovate, spreading or reflexed, fleshy or thin; pet. similar to sep., ♂ with lip fleshy, spreading, saccate or galeate, entire, dentate, crenulate or fimbriate; column erect, with 2 antennae. ♀ fewer with lip fleshy, saccate or galeate, entire; column short, stout, lacking antennae. Summer. C Amer., S Amer., W Indies. Z10.

C. barbatum (Lindl.) Lindl. ♂ fls large, membranous; tep. deep green, flecked maroon or violet, margins toothed; sep. to 32×9mm; pet. to 31×7mm; lip pale green marked rose to red, to 20×4mm, oblong, saccate, sac conical, margin lacerate or fimbriate. ♀ fls smaller, fleshy; lip to 2×1.2cm, deeply saccate, sac subrotud, margins undulate. Peru, Braz., Guyana, Colomb., Venez., Ecuad.

C. buccinator (Lindl.) Lindl. ex Stein = *Mormodes buccinator.*

C. bungerothii N.E. Br. = *C. pileatum.*

C. christyanum Rchb. = *C. saccatum*.
C. dilectum Rchb. f. = *Dressleria dilecta*.
C. discolor (Lindl.) Lindl. ♂ fls often inverted, to 4cm; sep. to 15×5.5mm, pale yellow-green, tinted pink-red or pale pink-cream; lip saccate, flattened, exterior and marginal fringe shiny green, tinged red, interior pubesc., green tinted red-pink. ♀ fls similar to males, generally larger. Braz., Venez., Colomb., Surinam, Guyana.
C. eburneum Rolfe = *Dressleria eburnea*.
C. fimbriatum (Morr.) Lindl. ♂ fls to 5cm diam., fragrant, inverted; tep. to 3.8×1.4cm yellow to olive green flushed rose, spotted or streaked maroon, dors. sep. and pet. erect, lat. sep. descending; lip to 3×4cm, yellow-green, margins tinged pink at base, saccate, erose-fimbriate. ♀ fls sometimes on same infl. as ♂ fls, inverted, yellow-green; tep. strongly recurved; lip apiculate, slightly recurved, entire. Trop. S Amer.
C. floribundum Hook. = *C. macrocarpum*.
C. gnomus Lind. & Rchb. f. ♂ fls fleshy, to 7cm diam., green, flecked maroon-purple; sep. to 5×1.8cm, fleshy, spreading; pet. to 4.5×1.2cm; lip to 2cm, white, flecked purple, green at base, deeply saccate, undulate-dentate. ♀ fls tep. similar to ♂; lip pale green, pale yellow marginally, deeply saccate, dentate. Braz.
C. integerrimum Hook. Resembles *C. maculatum* except fls bear few maroon markings and a more broadly conical lip. Guat.
C. macrocarpum Rich. ex Kunth. JUMPING ORCHID. ♂ fls yellow-green, flecked maroon-purple, fleshy, fragrant; sep. to 4.5×1.4cm, incurved, concave; pet. to 4×2.4cm, concave; lip green-yellow, lat. lobes white, interior deep maroon-purple, fleshy, deeply saccate, apex tridentate, midlobe tongue-shaped. ♀ fls on same infl. as ♂ fls; sep. yellow-green flecked maroon-purple; lip exterior green, interior yellow, to 3×2.5cm, galeate. Trop. S Amer., Trin.
C. maculatum Kunth. Fls green to green-brown, tinted or flecked maroon-purple or red-brown, lip green to yellow, tinged maroon-purple or red-brown, column pale green-cream, flecked maroon. ♂ fls with sep. to 4.5×1.8cm, concave; pet. to 4×1.7cm, incurving over column, ciliate; lip to 3.5×2.2cm, fleshy, obconic, fimbriate. ♀ fls fleshy; tep. reflexed, to 2×1cm; lip to 3×1.8cm, saccate, fimbriate. Colomb., Venez., Ecuad., Nic., Costa Rica.
C. maculatum Batem. non Kunth = *C. integerrimum*.
C. microglossum Rolfe. ♂ fls purple or purple-maroon; pet. and dors. sep. erect, to 2.5×0.6cm; lat. sep. broader, parallel; lip yellow, saccate, with many toothlike calluses; column with incurved antennae. ♀ fls lacking antennae, galeate. Peru.
C. oerstedii Rchb. f. = *C. maculatum*.
C. pileatum Rchb. f. ♂ fls to 11cm diam., opening flat, fragrant, usually ivory, variously tinged yellow-green or yellow-cream, sometimes flecked purple; sep. to 7×1.7cm, incurved; pet. to 7×2.5cm, thin; lip to 5×7cm, oblong to rounded, short-saccate, orange-red. ♀ fls cream, lip deep yellow to pale yellow, saccate, margins slightly recurved. Venez., Colomb., Ecuad., Trin., Braz.
C. roseoalbum Hook. = *C. discolor*.
C. roseum (Lindl.) Rchb. f. = *Clowesia rosea*.
C. russellianum Hook. = *Clowesia russelliana*.
C. saccatum Lindl. ♂ fls to 10cm diam., dull green, tinged and dotted purple-brown or olive-brown; sep. to 65×9mm, concave; pet. to 58×8mm, erect, connivent with dors. sep.; lip purple-brown, to 3cm, deeply saccate, trilobed, margins fimbriate. ♀ fls yellow-green dotted red-brown; sep. to 29×7.5mm; pet. to 2.9×1.2cm; lip to 2.9cm, laterally compressed, deeply saccate, margins decurved, fimbriate. Guyana, Braz., Peru.
C. suave Ames & Schweinf. = *Dressleria suavis*.
C. thylaciochilum Lem. = *Clowesia thylaciochila*.
C. tridentatum Hook. = *C. macrocarpum*.
C. warczewitzii Lindl. = *Clowesia warczewitzii*.

Catawba *Catalpa bignonioides*.
Catberry *Ribes grossularioides*.
Catchfly *Lychnis*; *Silene*.
Catechu *Acacia catechu*; *Areca catechu*.
Catelina Perfume *Ribes viburnifolium*.
Caterpillar Fern *Polypodium formosanum*.

Catesbaea L. Rubiaceae. *c*16 spiny everg. shrubs or small trees. Fls usually solitary, axill.; hypanthium oblong or bell-shaped, rounded or 4-sided; cal. with 4 (rarely 5–6) lobes; cor. funnel- or bell-shaped, membranous, lobes 4. Fr. a white berry, crowned by persistent cal. limb. W Indies, Flor. Z9.
C. latifolia Lindl. = *C. spinosa*.
C. macrantha A. Rich. = *C. spinosa*.
C. spinosa L. LILY THORN; SPANISH GUAVA. Shrub, to 3m, with spines to 3cm. Lvs to 2.5cm, sessile, ovate or obovate, acute to rounded at apex, leathery, glab., lustrous above, duller be-

neath. Fls pale yellow, cor. lobes ovate or ovate-deltoid, 2.5cm. Fr. to 5cm diam., edible. Spring. Bahamas, Cuba.

Cat Grape *Vitis palmata*.
Catgut *Tephrosia virginiana*.

Catha Forssk. ex Scop. Celastraceae. 1 everg. shrub or tree, to 7m+. Br. arching. Lvs 5–10cm, narrowly ovate-oblanceolate or elliptic, serrate, coriaceous. Fls white, 5-merous, in short axill. cymes to 8cm. Trop. E Afr. Widely cultivated in Ethiopia, Somalia and Yemen; lvs and tender shoots are chewed fresh or used in an infusion; contains the stimulant cathin. Z10.
C. edulis (Vahl) Forssk. ex Endl. KHAT; CAFTA; QAT; ARABIAN TEA.
C. forsskalii Rich. = *C. edulis*.
→*Celastrus*.

Catharanthus G. Don. PERIWINKLE. Apocynaceae. 8 ann. or perenn. herbs. Habit bushy. Fls solitary or in axill. cymes, sub-sessile; cor. salverform, limb flared, contracted, sericeous at throat; anth. lacking the large apical appendage characteristic of *Vinca*. Madag. Z10.
C. roseus (L.) G. Don. MADAGASCAR PERIWINKLE; OLD MAID; CAYENNE JASMINE; ROSE PERIWINKLE. Erect, perenn. to 60cm. Lvs 2.5–5cm, oblong-spathulate, glab. and glossy with a pale midrib. Fls to 3.75cm across, tube 2.3–3cm, rosy-pink to red, throat mauve. Madag., widely nat. 'Albus': fls white. Ocellatus group (includes Bright Eyes series): fls white or rose, with rose-pink or red eye.
→*Vinca*.

Cathartolinum Rchb. = *Linum*.

Cathaya Chun & Kuang. Pinaceae. 1 coniferous tree to 20m. Bark grey, furrowed. Br. horizontal. Lvs densely spiralled on long shoots, whorled on short shoots, acicular, linear and straight, or cuspidate, 4–5cm×2–3mm, dark green above, with 2 blue-white stomatal bands either side of midrib beneath, apex obtuse, margins slightly revolute. Cones oblong-ovate, 3–5×1–2cm, scales 12–16, in spirals, imbricate, obtuse, 1.5–2.5cm, brown, winged. China. Z8.
C. argyrophylla Chun & Kuang.

Cathedral Windows *Calathea makoyana*.
Catherine's Pincushion *Leucospermum catherinae*.
Catherine-wheel Leucospermum *Leucospermum catherinae*.

Catimbium Lestib. = *Alpinia*.

Catjang *Vigna unguiculata*.
Catjang Pea *Cajanus cajan*.
Catkin Yew *Amentotaxus* (*A. argotaenia*).
Catmint *Nepeta cataria*.
Catnip *Nepeta cataria*.
Catole *Syagrus comosa*.

Catopsis Griseb. Bromeliaceae. 19 stemless, epiphytic, perenn. herbs. Lvs strap-shaped to narrowly triangular with large basal sheaths, in an urn-like rosette, often chalky, entire. Infl. term., scapose, bracteate, simple or with spreading br.; fls small, usually white. S US, Mex. and W Indies to Braz., Peru, Ecuad. Z10.
C. berteroniana (Schult.) Mez. Carnivore. To 90cm in fl. Lvs to 40cm, erect, white-scaly, light green above. S Flor., Greater Antilles, C Amer., Trin. to Braz.
C. hahnii Bak. To 50cm forming dense rosette. Lvs 20–40cm, with powdery coating. S Mex., Guat., Hond. to Nic.
C. nitida (Hook.) Griseb. Rosette elongated, cylindrical to 30cm. Lvs sparse, green, barely undulate, powdery beneath. Hond., Costa Rica, Panama, Guiana.
C. nutans (Sw.) Griseb. To 40cm in fl. Lvs to 24cm, erect or outward-curving, white-scaly. Fls bright yellow. S US, C & S Amer.
C. nutans var. *erecta* Wittm. = *C. sessiliflora*.
C. oerstediana Mez = *C. hahnii*.
C. sessiliflora (Ruiz Pav.) Mez. 10–30cm in fl. Lvs forming upright to spreading slender rosette, tongue shaped, obtuse-mucronate green, ± mealy. S Mex. to S Braz. and Columbia.
C. werckleana Mez. To 54cm in fl. Lvs to 23cm, in a cup-shaped rosette; sheaths brown-scaly; blades short, broad. Costa Rica.
→*Tillandsia*.

Cat's Breeches *Hydrophyllum capitatum*.
Cat's Claw *Pithecellobium unguis-cati*.
Cat's Ear *Calochortus*; *Hypochoeris*.
Cat's Ears *Antennaria*.

Cat's Paws *Anigozanthos*; *Ptilotus spathulatus*.
Cat's Tail *Phleum pratense*; *Typha latifolia*.
Cat's Tail Grass *Rostraria cristata*.
Cat's Valerian *Valeriana officinalis*.
Cat's Whiskers *Tacca chantrieri*.
Cat Thyme *Teucrium marum*.

Cattleya Lindl. Orchidaceae. *c*45 epiphytic or lithophytic orchids. Rhiz. stout, ring-scarred. Pbs erect, stalked, oblong to clavate-cylindric. Lvs oblong to broadly obovate, usually coriaceous, borne 1–2 (–3) at apex of pb. Rac. term., emerging from a thick sheath; fls usually large, showy; sep. subequal, free; pet. usually wider than sep.; lip simple to deeply trilobed, lat. lobes erect, inrolled, midlobe spreading, often broad, with a fringed or ruffled margin. Trop. C & S Amer. Z10.

C. aclandiae Lindl. Infl. 1 or 2-fld; fls fragrant, waxy; sep. 3–5cm, lime green or sulphur yellow to buff, blotched chocolate or spotted maroon, elliptic-oblong, obtuse, undulate; pet. 2.7–4.5cm; lip 3.5–5cm, lateral lobes rose-purple, suberect, rounded, undulate, midlobe bright rose-purple veined deep purple, yellow at base, oblong to reniform, emarginate, undulate. N Braz.

C. alexandrae Lind. & Rolfe = *C. elongata*.
C. amabilis hort. = *C. intermedia*.
C. amethystina Morr. = *C. intermedia*.
C. amethystoglossa Lind. & Rchb. f. ex Warner. Differs from *C. guttata* in tep. white or pale rose spotted dark rose or mauve; lip with white lat. lobes and a magenta midlobe tinted mauve. Braz.

C. aurantiaca (Batem. ex Lindl.) P.N. Don. Infl. 6–10cm, few- to many-fld; fls not always opening fully, orange-yellow to bright vermilion or cinnabar; sep. 0.6–2.5cm, lanceolate to linear-elliptic; pet. smaller, elliptic-lanceolate; lip 1.5–2.5cm, ovate to elliptic-oblong, acute, inrolled-tubular, simple, spotted or streaked red. Guat., Hond., Mex., El Salvador, Nic.

C. bicolor Lindl. Infl. to 20cm, 1- to several-fld; fls strongly fragrant, long-lived; sep. 3–5cm, pale green flushed yellow-brown or copper-brown, oblong-lanceolate, lat. sep. falcate; pet. 3–4.5cm, oblong or obovate, undulate; lip to 3.5cm, crimson-purple, simple, oblong-cuneate, apex bilobed, crisped. Braz.

C. bowringiana O'Brien. Infl. 9–25cm, few- to many-fld; fls rather short-lived, borne v. freely; sep. to 2–5cm, rose to magenta with darker veins, narrowly elliptic to oblong; pet. to 5cm, ovate-oblong, obtuse, undulate; lip 2.25–4cm, pale rose-purple at base, edged dark purple or garnet, throat blotched white, oblong-oblong, tubular, undulate. Guat., Belize.

C. bulbosa Lindl. = *C. walkeriana*.
C. citrina (La Ll. & Lex.) Lindl. = *Encyclia citrina*.
C. deckeri Klotzsch. Infl. 6–15cm, few-fld; sep. 1.5–2.5cm, pale rose-purple, elliptic-lanceolate; pet. slightly broader than sep., undulate; lip deep purple, 1.75–2.5cm, obscurely 3-lobed, obovate-elliptic, midlobe acute. Mex., C Amer., N S Amer., W Indies.

C. dolosa (Rchb. f.) Rchb. f. Infl. 1- to few-fld; fls fragrant; sep. 3.5–5cm, light to dark rose or lavender, elliptic, pet. to 4.5cm, oblanceolate, undulate; lip to 4cm, light rose, base and margins dark rose, undulate, obscurely 3-lobed, disc yellow. Braz.

C. dowiana Batem. & Rchb. f. Infl. short; fls highly fragrant; tep. golden-yellow to pale bronze, pet. sometimes veined purple, sep. 5.5–8.7cm, oblong-lanceolate, pet. 6.5–8cm, elliptic or elliptic-oblong, undulate-crisped; lip 8–10cm, rich velvety crimson-purple with golden-yellow veins, obscurely 3-lobed, midlobe undulate and crispate.

C. elatior Lindl. = *C. guttata*.
C. eldorado Lind. Infl. short; tep. pale rose-pink, sep. 5–7cm, narrowly elliptic-oblong, pet. 5–6.5cm, elliptic; lip to 7cm, cream-white, throat orange-yellow, margins white, midlobe blotched purple in front, emarginate, spreading, erose. Braz.

C. elongata Barb. Rodr. Infl. 20–60cm, 2- to several-fld; fls slightly fragrant; tep. copper-brown to purple-brown, sometimes spotted deep purple-brown, sep. 4–6cm, narrowly oblanceolate to linear-oblong, undulate, pet. similar to sep.; lip to 5cm, light to dark magenta or lavender, 3-lobed, midlobe edged pale lavender, broadly reniform, retuse or emarginate. Braz.

C. flavida Klotzsch = *C. luteola*.
C. forbesii Lindl. Infl. 4.5–12cm, 1- to few-fld; fls fragrant; sep. 2.7–5cm, olive-green, pale bronze or buff, often tinged purple-brown, oblong-ligulate to oblanceolate, spreading; pet. falcate; lip to 4.5cm, tubular, throat yellow-ochre faintly veined red, lat. lobes rounded, white flushed or veined rose, midlobe spreading, crisped-undulate, dull red or buff edged white. Braz.

C. gaskelliana Sander Infl. few-fld; fls fragrant; tep. white to pale amethyst, sometimes darker with a white band, sep. 6–9cm, oblanceolate, pet. ovate to elliptic; lip to 8cm, crisped, 3-lobed, lat. lobes pale purple, midlobe elliptic-oblong, rose-mauve,

throat orange or yellow, with a large white spot on each side, blotched purple toward apex. Venez. var. *alba* Williams ex Warner & Williams. Fls white with yellow blotch on lip.

C. gigas Lind. & André = *C. warscewiczii*.
C. granulosa Lindl. Infl. short, few- to several-fld; fls strongly fragrant, long-lived; tep. green to olive-green, spotted maroon-brown, sep. 5.75–8.5cm, undulate, dors. sep. elliptic-oblong, lat. sep. falcate, elliptic-lanceolate; pet. obovate-oblong, undulate, lip yellow-orange spotted orange to crimson, sides and apex white, lat. lobes triangular-ovate, midlobe flabellate, crisped-undulate, disc granular-papillose. Braz., Guat. var. *buyssoniana* O'Brien. Tep. pure white, lip rose-pink.

C. granulosa f. *schofieldiana* (Rchb. f.) A.D. Hawkes = *C. schofieldiana*.
C. guatemalensis S. Moore = *C. deckeri*.
C. guttata Lindl. Infl. to 25cm, several- to many-fld; fls fragrant, waxy; tep. yellow-green to olive or lime green, spotted to banded maroon, sep. 2.5–3.8cm, oblong to oblong-lanceolate, obtuse, lat. sep. falcate, pet. 2.5–3.5cm, oblong to oblong-elliptic, obtuse, undulate; lip to 2.8cm, lat. lobes white or rose, midlobe rose-purple or bright magenta, obcordate, often undulate. Braz.

C. guttata var. *leopoldii* (Versch. ex Lem.) Rolfe = *C. leopoldii*.
C. guttata f. *prinzii* (Rchb. f.) A.D. Hawkes = *C. amethystoglossa*.
C. harrisoniana Batem. ex Lindl. Infl. to 10cm, few-fld; tep. dark rose to lavender, sep. 4–6.5cm, oblanceolate, lat. sep. falcate, pet. oblong, undulate; lip pale lavender with darker lavender margins, 3-lobed, midlobe subquadrate, crisped, disc yellow or orange-yellow, carinate. Braz. Differs from *C. loddigesii* in its unscented darker fls. var. *alba* Berr. Fls pure white; lip with a yellow, basal blotch.

C. intermedia Graham ex Hook. Infl. to 25cm, few- to several-fld; fls strongly fragrant; tep. white to pale purple, sometimes spotted purple, sep. 4–6.5cm, reflexed, oblong to oblong-lanceolate, lat. sep. falcate, pet. 3.75–5.5cm, oblong to narrowly lanceolate, undulate; lip to 5cm, ovate-oblong, lateral lobes white to pale purple, oblong, rounded, midlobe rich purple, orbicular, crisped-undulate. Braz., Parag., Urug. var. *punctatissima* Sander. Tep. finely spotted red.

C. iricolor Rchb. f. Infl. to 15cm, few-fld; tep. white to cream-white, sep. 3.5–5cm, narrowly elliptic-lanceolate, lat. sep. subfalcate, pet. 3–4cm; lip to 3.5cm, white, central portion orange, striped and suffused purple, midlobe acute, reflexed. Ecuad.

C. jenmanii Rolfe Infl. short, few-fld; tep. lavender, sep. 5.5–8cm, oblong-lanceolate, pet. ovate; lip to 8cm, throat yellow to orange or maroon-orange, grading into white or pale lavender, margins lavender, apex lavender veined and flushed purple. Braz.

C. labiata Lindl. Infl. short, few-fld; fls of sparkling texture and loose, ruffled posture; tep. white-rose to bright rose or mauve, sep. 6–8cm, narrowly oblong to lanceolate, pet. to 7.5cm, ovate or elliptic, spreading, strongly crisped-undulate; lip v. large, ± funnelform, lat. lobes rose, midlobe deep purple-magenta, margins rose-lilac, with a pale yellow blotch lined red-purple, deeply emarginate, crisped-undulate. Braz. var. *alba* Lind. & Rodigas. Fls white, throat sometimes yellow. var. *coerulea* hort. Fls deep lilac to icy opaline blue.

C. labiata var. *dowiana* (Batem. & Rchb. f.) Veitch = *C. dowiana*.
C. labiata var. *lueddemanniana* (Rchb. f.) Rchb. f. = *C. lueddemanniana*.
C. labiata var. *mendelii* (hort.) Rchb. f. = *C. mendelii*.
C. labiata var. *mossiae* (Hook.) Lindl. = *C. mossiae*.
C. labiata var. *percivaliana* Rchb. f. = *C. percivaliana*.
C. labiata var. *warneri* (S. Moore) Veitch = *C. warneri*.
C. labiata var. *warscewiczii* (Rchb. f.) Rchb. f. = *C. warscewiczii*.
C. lawrenceana Rchb. f. Infl. to 15cm, few- to several fld; sep. 4–7cm, white-rose to rose-purple, oblong to narrowly elliptic, lat. sep. subfalcate, pet. 4–7cm, oblong to elliptic or sub-rhombic, undulate; lip to 6cm, light rose-purple, white at centre veined purple, apex dark violet, simple, oblong to elliptic, deeply bilobed, revolute. Venez., Guyana, N Braz.

C. lemoiniana Lindl. = *C. labiata*.
C. leopoldii Versch. ex Lem. Infl. to 30cm, few-fld; sep. 4–6.5cm, pale rose-lilac, oblong-elliptic, lat. sep. falcate, deflexed; pet. to 6cm, undulate; lip light rose-lilac at base, suborbicular, lat. lobes oblong, dentate, midlobe pale amethyst, spreading, crisped, disc white grading to yellow below. S Braz.

C. loddigesii Lindl. Infl. to 30cm, few-fld; fls fragrant, waxy; sep. 4–6.5cm, white tinted pink to pale, sparkling rose-lilac, oblong to oblong-elliptic, lateral sep. subfalcate; pet. broader, obliquely oblong to oblong-elliptic, undulate; lip suborbicular, lat. lobes erect, white to pale rose-lilac, midlobe pale to rich lilac-rose, subquadrate, margin ivory, crisped, like the lip of a shell. Braz., Parag.

C. loddigesii var. *harrisoniana* (Batem. ex Lindl.) Veitch = *C. harrisoniana*.

C. lueddemanniana Rchb. f. Infl. few-fld; fls strongly fragrant; sep. narrowly oblong, undulate, light to dark lavender, suffused white, dors. sep. 6–10cm, laterals to 9cm; pet. to 9.5cm, elliptic, undulate; lip to 9.5cm, lavender, midlobe suborbicular, crisped, emarginate, with 2 yellow blotches near margins, spotted dark lavender. Venez. var. *alba* hort. ex Godef.-Leb. Fls pure white; throat yellow.

C. luteola Lindl. Infl. shorter than lvs, few- to several-fld; fls waxy; sep. to 4.5cm, yellow to yellow-green, oblong or narrowly elliptic-oblong; pet. slightly falcate; lip to 2.8cm, yellow or yellow-green, often spotted or streaked crimson, suborbicular, midlobe crenulate. Braz., Peru, Ecuad., Boliv.

C. maxima Lindl. Infl. to 20cm, few- to many-fld; fls fragrant, long-lived; sep. 6–8.5cm, pale lustrous rose to lilac, narrowly elliptic-lanceolate; pet. wider, ovate-oblong or elliptic-oblong, undulate; lip to 7cm, pale pink veined purple, banded yellow across centre, ovate-subquadrate, lat. lobes shallow, angular, midlobe rounded, undulate. Ecuad., Colomb., Peru. var. *alba* Veitch. Fls white, lip veined purple.

C. mcmorlandii Nichols. = *C. eldorado*.

C. mendelii hort. Infl. few-fld; fls fragrant, long-lived; sep. to 9.5cm, white, often tinged rose, narrowly elliptic-lanceolate; pet. to 9cm, ovate to elliptic, minutely denticulate, undulate; lip to 8.5cm, oblong, lateral lobes white to lilac, midlobe rich purple-crimson, suborbicular, crisped, disc bright to dull yellow, often streaked purple. Colomb.

C. mossiae Hook. Infl. to 30cm, few-fld; fls v. showy, fragrant, long-lived; sep. to 8.5cm, white to rose, pink, pale magenta or lilac, narrowly lanceolate, acute; pet. to 8.5cm, ovate-elliptic, strongly undulate, broadly spreading, appearing lacy and flaccid, erose; lip to 7cm, ± funnelform, white to rose-lilac, throat with a central yellow-orange band lined deep purple to magenta, apex purple, midlobe spreading, undulate-crisped. Venez. var. *coerulea* hort. Fls a cool orchid 'blue', i.e. lilac to washed-out indigo. var. *wageneri* O'Brien. Tep. pure white; lip similar colour to type.

C. nobilior Rchb. f. Infl. to 8cm, slender, 1- to few-fld; fls slightly fragrant; sep. 5.5–7.5cm, rose-lavender, reflexed; pet. far wider than sep., broadly elliptic, undulate; lip to 7cm, rose-lavender, darker toward apex, pandurate, midlobe with a yellow-cream spot, reflexed, undulate. Braz.

C. percivaliana (Rchb. f.) O'Brien. Infl. to 25cm, few-fld; fls with a musty fragrance, short-lived; sep. 4.5–7.5cm, lilac-rose, often tinged purple, elliptic or elliptic-oblanceolate, lat. sep. decurved; pet. 4.5–7.5cm, ovate to subrhombic, undulate, erose; lip maroon veined yellow at base, centre golden-yellow veined maroon, apex deep magenta, broadly elliptic to oblong, truncate. Venez. var. *alba* Sander. Fls pure white, throat yellow.

C. porphyroglossa Lind. & Rchb. f. Infl. to 10cm, several-fld; fls fragrant, long-lived; sep. 3.75–5cm, yellow-brown to green, sometimes suffused faint red, oblong-elliptic to elliptic-lanceolate; pet. 3.5–4.5cm, spathulate to oblanceolate, rounded, undulate; lip to 3.5cm, cream-white suffused magenta, veined purple, lat. lobes triangular, midlobe dentate, disc yellow. Braz.

C. rex O'Brien. Infl. to 20cm, loosely few- to several-fld; sep. 6–8cm, white or cream-white, usually flushed yellow, narrowly elliptic-lanceolate; pet. elliptic-rhomboid, undulate; lip to 8cm, deep yellow, throat marked red-rose or red-brown, obovate to ovate-oblong, entire or obscurely 3-lobed, undulate-crisped. Peru, Colomb.

C. schilleriana Rchb. f. Infl. 1- or 2-fld, short; fls waxy, fragrant; sep. 4.5–6cm, brown or dark olive-brown to dark green, densely spotted or broken-banded dark maroon, lanceolate-oblong, slightly undulate, lat. sep. subfalcate; pet. 4.5–5.5cm, ligulate, obtuse, undulate; lip to 5.5cm, white with purple veins or light red-purple with deep magenta veins, central portion yellow, 3-lobed, apex flabellate, fimbriate. Braz.

C. schofieldiana Rchb. f. Differs from *C. granulosa* in fls larger; tep. tawny yellow, suffused purple or green, densely spotted purple-crimson, lat. sep. abruptly incurved, pet. broad, rounded; lip large, lat. lobes white tinged rose, midlobe magenta, with hair-like excrescences. Braz.

C. schroederae hort. Differs from *C. trianae* in fls larger, strongly fragrant, white to rose-pink or light purple, pet. strongly crisped, broader, lip with larger midlobe, strongly crisped, disc large, orange. Colomb. var. *alba* Sander. Fls white; lip pure white, throat yellow.

C. skinneri Batem. Infl. to 13cm, usually erect; fls slightly fragrant; sep. 4.75–6.5cm, rose to bright purple, elliptic-lanceolate or linear-lanceolate; pet. to 6.7cm, broadly ovate, undulate; lip to 5cm, throat often white or cream, entire to obscurely 3-lobed, obtuse or emarginate. Guat., Hond., Mex., Costa Rica, Venez.,

Belize.

C. skinneri var. *parviflora* Hook. = *C. deckeri*.
C. superba Schomb. ex Lindl. = *C. violacea*.

C. trianae Lind. & Rchb. f. Infl. to 30cm, few-fld; tep. pure white or rose-white to bronze suffused red or deep purple, sep. 6–8.5cm, oblanceolate, pet. 6–8.5cm, ovate-elliptic, obtuse, usually crisped; lip to 8cm, ovate-oblong to elliptic, midlobe usually rich magenta-crimson, sometimes paler or flecked crimson to magenta, disc usually yellow-orange, sometimes streaked pale purple or white. Colomb.

C. velutina Rchb. f. Differs from *C. bicolor* and *C. aclandiae* in fls larger; tep. light orange or yellow-orange, spotted deep purple or brown-purple, oblong, crisped; lip white streaked magenta, midlobe broadly cordate, disc golden-yellow. Braz.

C. vestalis Hoffsgg. = *C. forbesii*.

C. violacea (HBK) Rolfe. Infl. to 30cm, erect or suberect, few- to several-fld; fls fragrant, long-lived; tep. rose-purple, sometimes suffused white, dors. sep. 5.5–7cm, narrowly linear-lanceolate, lat. sep. slightly broader, pet. 4–6.5cm, lanceolate-subrhombic, slightly undulate; lip to 5.5cm, deep violet, marked yellow, basally white, midlobe transversely elliptic-oblong, truncate or emarginate, erose. Venez., Guyana, Braz., Colomb., Peru. var. *alba* (Rolfe) Fowlie. Fls pure white or faint rose-purple. var. *splendens* (Lem.) Fowlie. Fls larger, darker.

C. virginalis Lind. & André = *C. eldorado*.

C. walkeriana Gardn. Infl. to 20cm, 1- to few-fld; fls fragrant; sep. 3–5cm, pale pink-lilac to bright rose-purple, lanceolate or oblong-lanceolate; pet. at least twice width of sep., ovate or elliptic, undulate; lip to 4cm, pandurate, midlobe often bright magenta-purple, spreading, reniform to suborbicular, emarginate, disc white or pale yellow streaked purple. Braz.

C. warneri S. Moore. Differs from *C. labiata* in fls larger, strongly fragrant, tep. pale rose tinged dark amethyst-rose, lip densely veined purple, margins pale amethyst-rose, disc tawny yellow or orange-yellow, streaked pale lilac or white. Braz.

C. warscewiczii Rchb. f. Infl. to 45cm, few- to several-fld; fls fragrant; tep. rose, sep. 6.5–10cm, narrowly oblanceolate, lat. sep. falcate, pet. 8–9.5cm, ovate-elliptic, undulate; lip to 8cm, carmine, throat blotched yellow, oblong-pandurate, midlobe undulate-crisped, reflexed, disc golden-yellow, often lined red-purple. Colomb.

C. grexes and cvs. There are hundreds of *Cattleya* grexes and cvs in addition to intergeneric hybrids with *Brassavola* (*Rhyncholaelia*), *Laelia*, *Sophronitis*, *Broughtonia* etc. The fls range in form from the small, fine and clustered to the large and frilly, in colour from lavender blue to magenta, purple and pink to white, yellow, orange and tan.

Cattley Guava *Psidium littorale* var. *longipes*.

Cattleyopsis Lem. Orchidaceae. 2 small epiphytic orchids. Pbs globose to elongate-ovoid. Lvs paired, rigid, leathery. Rac. or pan. term.; fls small, vivid pink. Winter. Bahamas, Cuba. Z10.

C. lindenii (Lindl.) Cogn. Infl. to 70cm, slender, erect to arching, sometimes branching; fls to 5cm diam., tep. fragile and crystal-line in texture, rose, lip showy, rose to crimson or magenta, lined white with a yellow throat.

C. ortgiesiana (Rchb. f.) Cogn. Infl. to 100cm, fls more spreading than in *C. lindenii*, tep. rose to rose madder or magenta, lip rounded, deep magenta lined a deeper shade again, with white or golden throat.

✕**Cattleytonia** (*Cattleya* ✕ *Broughtonia*.) Orchidaceae. Gdn hybrids with compact growth and small fls in shades of magenta, rose, orange and yellow on tall spikes.

Catunaregam Wolf. Rubiaceae. 6 spiny shrubs or small trees. Lvs clustered on short lat. branchlets, or opposite, simple. Fls 1–3 per cyme; cal. lobes 5; cor. rotate, pubesc., lobes 5. Fr. a leathery, subglobose berry. Afr., Asia. Z10.

C. nilotica (Stapf) Tirv. To 5m, spines alt. Lvs to 7×3cm, obovate to oblanceolate, glab. to pubesc. Cal. glab. or minutely pubesc.; cor. to 1.5cm, white to yellow. Fr. 2cm, ribbed, brown to yellow. Afr. (Nigeria to Kenya).

C. spinosa (Thunb.) Tirv. To 7m, spines opposite or alt. Lvs to 10×5cm, oval or obovate, entire, dark green or glaucous, glab. to densely pubesc. Cal. velutinous; cor. 1.5cm, white to yellow. Fr. to 3cm, yellow-green to green-brown, rugose or velutinous. Zimb., Moz., S Afr., India, China.

→*Gardenia, Lachnosiphonium, Randia* and *Xeromphis*.

Caucasian Alder *Alnus subcordata*.
Caucasian Blue Stem *Bothriochloa caucasica*.
Caucasian Elm *Zelkova carpinifolia*.
Caucasian Fir *Abies nordmanniana*.
Caucasian Lily *Lilium monadelphum*.

Caucasian Lime *Tilia* 'Euchlora'.
Caucasian Maple *Acer cappadocicum.*
Caucasian Oak *Quercus macranthera.*
Caucasian Spruce *Picea orientalis.*
Caucasian Walnut *Pterocarya fraxinifolia.*
Caucasian Whortleberry *Vaccinium arctostaphylos.*
Caucasian Wing Nut *Pterocarya fraxinifolia.*
Cauchao *Amomyrtus luma.*

Caudoleucaena Britt. & Rose.
C. retusa (Benth.) Britt. & Rose = *Leucaena retusa.*

Caularthron Raf. Orchidaceae. 2 epiphytic orchids. Pbs to 25cm, fusiform, elongate-ovoid or cylindric, bases hollow and colonized by ants. Lvs lanceolate to ligulate, to 20cm, glossy green, semi-rigid, fleshy, keeled beneath. Rac. to 30cm, term., erect; tep. elliptic, acuminate, spreading; lip midlobe triangular to lanceolate, disc with 2 erect calli, lat. lobes erect with tooth like projections. Winter–spring. C & S Amer., W Indies. Z10.
C. bicornutum (Hook.) Raf. Fls white, flushed or delicately veined pink; sep. to 30mm; pet. broader than sep.; lip to 28×12mm, white, calli tan, spotted purple. Throughout genus range.
C. bilamellatum (Rchb. f.) R.E. Schult. Fls white, fragrant, often cleistogamous; sep. to 22mm; pet. narrower than sep., flushed pink beneath; lip to 20×8mm, white, calli tinted lime green. Guat. to Panama, Trin., Venez., Colomb.
→*Diacrium* and *Epidendrum.*

Cauliflower Hakea *Hakea corymbosa.*

Caulophyllum Michx. Berberidaceae. 2 perenn., rhizomatous herbs. Rootstock matted. Lf solitary, ternately divided, subtending infl. Fls small, yellow-green, clustered in a rac. or pan.; sep. 6, ovate, petaloid; pet. 6, scale, gland. Berries 2, drupe-like, spherical, blue. N Amer., E Asia. Z8.
C. thalictrioides (L.) Michx. BLUE COHOSH; PAPOOSE ROOT; SQUAW ROOT. 30–75cm. Lf 3-lobed; lobes trifid, seg. ovate-obovate. Fls 12mm across, appearing before lf is fully developed. Fr. to 1.2cm diam., deep rich blue. Spring. E N Amer. Z7.

Cauqui *Chamaedorea oblongata.*

Cautleya (Benth.) Royle ex. Hook. f. Zingiberaceae. 6 perenn. rhizomatous herbs. St. reed-like. Lvs lanceolate to oblong, in 2 ranks, bases sheathing st. Fls yellow, in a loose terminal spike; cal. tubular; cor. funnelform; pet. 3; lat. staminodes petaloid, forming hood together with posterior pet.; lip deeply 2-lobed. Himal. Z8.
C. gracilis (Sm.) Dandy. To 40cm. Lvs 20×2cm, striped purple to brown beneath. Infl. axis dark red; bracts green; cal. red-maroon, longer than bracts. Summer.
C. lutea (Royle) Hook. f. = *C. gracilis.*
C. robusta Bak. = *C. spicata.*
C. spicata (J.M. Sm.) Bak. To 1m. Lvs 35×10cm, green. Infl. bracts red; cal. shorter than bracts.

Cavendishia Lindl. Ericaceae. *c*100 everg. shrubs or small trees. Lvs simple, coriaceous. Fls in axill. rac. or clusters with leathery overlapping bracts; cal. campanulate or hemispherical, limb short, 5-dentate; cor. tubular, lobes 5. Fr. a juicy, black drupe. Trop. S Amer.
C. acuminata (Hook.) Benth. Shrub to 1m; br. pendulous; new growth pink. Lvs 5–7.5cm, ovate to lanceolate or oblong, apex acuminate, base rounded. Racs short; bracts large, scarlet; cor. *c*2cm scarlet to crimson, lobes green. Autumn. Andes of Colomb. and Ecuad.

Cayaponia A. Silva Manso.
C. excisa (Griseb.) Cogn. = *Cionosicyos excisus.*

Cayenne Jasmine *Catharanthus roseus.*
Cayenne Pepper *Capsicum annuum* var. *annuum.*
Cayman Islands Spider-lily *Hymenocallis latifolia.*

Cayratia Juss. Vitaceae. 45 herbs, shrubs or vines. Tendrils forked, sometimes terminating in adhesive pads. Lvs compound, digitate or pedate. Cymes long-stalked, corymbose or umbellate, axill.; fls small, 4-merous; pet. free, green. Fr. a berry, oblong to depressed-globose. OW Trop. Z10.
C. acuminata (A. Gray) A.C. Sm. Vine, subglabrous. Lvs pedately 5-foliolate; lfts 4–6cm, ovate to ovate-oblong or rhombic, long-acuminate, mucronate-serrate. Fiji.
C. japonica (Thunb.) Gagnep. Vine. Lvs pedately 5-foliolate; lfts 3–8cm, ovate to ovate-orbicular, acute or acuminate at apex,

aristate-serrate, glab. or finely pubesc. beneath. Fr. white or blue-black. Summer. E Asia, Malaysia, New Caledonia, Aus.
C. oligocarpa (Lév. & Vaniot) Gagnep. Climbing shrub, cinereous-pubesc. Lvs pedately compound; lfts lanceolate-ovate, narrow-acuminate at apex, glabrescent, central leaflet 6–11cm, laterals 3–5cm. Fr. yellow then black. China, Vietnam.
C. thomsonii (Lawson) Süsseng = *Parthenocissus thomsonii.*
→*Cissus* and *Vitis.*

Ceanothus L. CALIFORNIA LILAC. Rhamnaceae. *c*50 decid. or everg. shrubs or small trees. Twigs sometimes spiny. Lvs pubesc. or glab., soft and pale to glossy coriaceous dark green, short-petiolate, usually serrate. Fls small in umbel-like cymes, rac. or pan.; sep. 5, petaloid, fused to an ureceolate receptacle; pet. 5, hooded and clawed. N Amer., SW Canada, N Mex.
C. 'Albus Plenus'. = *C.* ×*pallidus* 'Plenus'.
C. americanus L. NEW JERSEY TEA; WILD SNOWBALL; MOUNTAIN-SWEET. Decid. shrub, 0.5–1m. Lvs 2–10cm, broadly ovate to ovate-oblong, base rounded, densely hairy beneath, less so above. Infl. cymose, an elongate thyrse to 10cm; fls white. S Canada, E, C & SE US. Z4.
C. arboreus Greene. FELTLEAF CEANOTHUS; CATALINA MOUNTAIN LILAC. Everg. shrub or tree, 3–7m. Lvs 3–8cm, broadly ovate to elliptic, base rounded, apex acute to obtuse, densely white-tomentose beneath. Infl. 5–12cm, pyramidal; fls pale blue, fragrant. Summer. W US. 'Trewithen Blue': spreading everg. shrub, 6–8m; lvs dark green, broadly oval to rounded; infl. to 12cm, fls deep blue. Spring–early summer. Z8.
C. arnouldii Carr. = *C.* ×*delilianus.*
C. 'A.T. Johnson'. (*C. thyrsiflorus* ×?.) Everg. shrub to 2m. Lvs to 3cm, ovate, dentate. Fls rich blue, profuse. Gdn origin. Z8.
C. austromontanus Abrams = *C. foliosus.*
C. 'Autumnal Blue'. (*C. thyrsiflorus* ×?.) Everg. shrub to 1.5m. Lvs elliptic, large, glossy bright green. Fls in large, lax pan., pale to mid china blue. Later summer–autumn. Gdn origin. Z6.
C. 'Blue Jeans'. To 2.5m. Lvs dark green, leathery. Fls pale powder blue in profuse clusters.
C. 'Brilliant'. = *C.* ×*veitchianus.*
C. 'Burkwoodii'. (*C. dentatus* 'Floribundus' ×*C.* ×*delilianus* 'Indigo'.) Dense, everg., spreading shrub to 1.5m. Lvs 1.5–3cm, elliptic, rounded at base and apex, toothed, dark green and glossy above, grey-hairy beneath. Infl. 3–6cm, fls bright blue, sta. and style darker blue. Summer–autumn. Gdn origin. Z8.
C. 'Burtonensis'. (*C. impressus* ×*C. thyrsiflorus?*) Spreading everg. shrub to 2m. Lvs small, circular, dark green and glossy, appearing crinkled. Infl. 2cm across, dense, rounded; fls dark blue, sta. darker. Late spring–early summer. A naturally occurring hybrid. Z8.
C. ×*burtonensis* hort. = *C.* 'Burtonensis'.
C. coeruleus Lagasca. AZURE CEANOTHUS. Medium-sized everg. shrub. Lvs ovate, dark green. Fls sky blue, in long pan. Summer–autumn. Mex. to Guat.
C. 'Concha'. Everg. shrub to 2m tall, dense, spreading to 3m+ across. Lvs to 2.5cm. Fls dark blue, red-hued in bud. Early summer. Gdn origin. Z8.
C. confusus J.T. Howell = *C. divergens* ssp. *confusus.*
C. cordulatus Kellogg. SNOW BUSH. Everg. shrub, 1–2m, much-branched, spreading into flattened clumps, bark white grey; whole plant appearing grey. Lvs 1–2cm, ovate to elliptic, with v. few teeth, glaucous above, greyer beneath. Fls in dense 1.5–3cm clusters, white. US (Calif., Oreg., Nevada), Baja Calif. Z7.
C. crassifolius Torr. HOARY LEAF CEANOTHUS. Everg. shrub, 2–3.5m, openly branching. Lvs *c*1.5cm, broadly elliptic to elliptic-ovate, leathery, revolute, olive green and glab. above, white-hairy beneath, entire to coarsely toothed. Infl. rounded, umbel-like; fls white. S Calif., Baja Calif. Z8.
C. cuneatus (Hook.) Nutt. BUCK BRUSH. Everg. shrub, 1.5–3m, rigidly erect. Lvs 0.5–1.5cm, on spur-like branchlets, spathulate to cuneate-obovate, obtuse at apex, grey-green and glab. above, fine-hairy beneath. Infl. dense, rounded; fls white, lavender or blue. Oreg., Calif., Baja Calif. Z7.
C. cyaneus Eastw. SAN DIEGO CEANOTHUS. Everg. tree-like shrub, 1–5m. Lvs 2–4.5cm, ovate-elliptic, with small teeth, sometimes gland., green and glab. above, slightly hairy beneath. Infl. 5–18cm, compound, term., columnar; fls bright blue, on blue pedicel. Late spring. S Calif. Z8.
C. 'Delight'. (*C. papillosus* ×*C. rigidus.*) Everg. shrub to 5m. Lvs glossy pale green. Infl. a long pan.; fls deep blue. Gdn origin. Z8.
C. ×*delilianus* Spach. FRENCH HYBRID CEANOTHUS. (*C. coeruleus* ×*C. americanus.*) Everg. shrub to 5m. Lvs 4–8cm, elliptic to ovate-oblong, apex acuminate, dark green above, hairy to downy beneath. Pan. large; fls blue. Summer–early autumn. Gdn origin. 'Charles Detriche': fls rich dark blue. 'Gloire de Versailles': large, floriferous form with scented, powder-blue fls; habit rangy, tall; lvs semi-deciduous, to 8cm, dark green,

often paler with age. 'Gloire de Plantières': a low-growing, dwarf form with v. dark blue fls. 'Henri Desfosse': to about 3m; fls dark or violet blue. 'Indigo': fls indigo-blue. Z7.

C. dentatus Torr. & A. Gray. CROPLEAF CEANOTHUS. Everg. shrub, 0.5–1.5m, habit dense. Lvs 0.5–2cm, elliptic to narrowly oblong or linear, apex truncate to retuse, dark green and short-hairy above, grey-hairy beneath, margins revolute and glandular-papillate. Pan. to 3cm, subglobose or cylindrical; fls dark blue. Spring. Calif. 'Floribundus': lvs over 1cm wide, with almost eglandular margins, only partially revolute; infl. dense, v. floriferous. 'Microphyllus': close to *C. papillosus*; lvs less than 6mm wide, margins lacking teeth or glands. Z8.

C. '**Dignity**'. Everg. shrub to 4m. Lvs glossy green. Infl. large; fls clear deep blue. Late spring–early autumn. Gdn origin. Z8.

C. divergens Parry. CALISTOGA CEANOTHUS; MOUNT ST HELENA CEANOTHUS. Everg. shrub, 0.2–1.5m, scrambling to erect, br. arching to divergent, sparse. Lvs 1.2–2.5cm, oblong to obovate, revolute, often undulate with 5–8 spined teeth, bright green above, shortly grey-hairy beneath. Rac. small umbel like; fls dark blue. Spring. US (C Calif.). ssp. *confusus* (J.T. Howell) Abrams. Decumbent, br. tips upward-curving. Lvs 0.6–2cm, denticulate to spinose. Z8.

C. diversifolius Kellogg. PINE MAT. Everg. shrub, 10–30cm, low and clump-forming, br. long and flexible. Lvs 0.5–2.5cm, ovate, orbicular, or elliptic to oblong, pale-glaucous and villous above, paler and hairy beneath, with few small gland. teeth. Infl. about 1cm, simple; fls few blue to near-white. Spring–early summer. Calif. Z8.

C. '**Edinburgh**' ('**Edinensis**'). (*C. griseus* × *C. papillosus?*.) Dense everg. shrub, 2–3m, erect, twigs long. Lvs olive green, to about 7cm. Fls rich blue. Spring–early summer. Gdn origin. Z8.

C. fendleri A. Gray. Everg. shrub, 0.2–2.4m, usually prostrate, densely branched, twigs slender, spiny. Lvs 2.5cm, narrowly elliptic, rarely with few, short, apical, gland. teeth, hairy, or glab. above, grey-hairy beneath. Infl. racemose; fls in umbel-like clusters, white or tinged lilac. Early summer. US (S Dak., Wyom. and Utah) to Mex. Z5.

C. foliosus Parry. WAVY LEAF CEANOTHUS. Everg. shrub, erect to 1m, twigs, flexuous. Lvs 0.5–1.5cm, oblong-elliptic to broadly elliptic, apex obtuse, with small gland. teeth, glossy dark green and strigose above, hairy on veins only beneath. Infl. 0.5–2.5cm, simple, subglobose or sub-cylindrical, sometimes compound and longer; fls dark blue, fil. paler. Spring. Calif. var. *vineatus* McMinn. Prostrate or low and spreading. Lvs 1.3–1.9cm, obovate to broadly elliptic. Spring. N Calif. Z8.

C. fresnensis Dudley ex Abrams. Everg. shrub to 30cm, spreading to form low clumps to 6m across. Lvs 0.6–1.2cm, elliptic or oblanceolate to obovate, slightly toothed at apex, leathery, grey-green above, paler and short-hairy beneath. Umbel ± sessile, few-fld; fls blue. Late spring–early summer. US (C Calif.). Z8.

C. '**Frosty Blue**'. To 2.5×3m. Lvs to 1.25cm, dark green, dense. Fls deep blue frosted white in spiciform clusters to 5cm.

C. '**Gentian Plume**'. To 6×7m. Lvs to 5cm, dark green. Fls dark blue, in spike-like clusters to 20cm.

C. glorious J.T. Howell. POINT REYES CREEPER; POINT REYES CEANOTHUS. Everg. shrub, prostrate to decumbent, forming clumps 2–3m across, br. stout, red-brown. Lvs 2–5cm, broadly oblong to rounded, apex rounded to retuse, thick and leathery, toothed, dark green and glab. above, grey-hairy beneath. Infl., many-fld, umbel-like; fls dark blue to violet or purple. Spring. US (Coastal N Calif.). 'Anchor Bay': to 0.5×2m; foliage v. dense; fls strong Cambridge blue. 'Emily Brown': to 1×4m. Lvs to 2.5cm, dark green, holly-like. Fls dark indigo in clusters to 2.5cm long. var. *exaltatus* J.T. Howell. NAVARRO CEANOTHUS. 1–2m, erect in habit. Lvs 0.5–4cm. var. *porrectus* J.T. Howell. MOUNT VISION CEANOTHUS. 30–50cm, sprawling. Lvs 1–2cm. Z8.

C. greggii A. Gray. Everg. shrub, 0.6–1.8m, erect, br. dense, rigid. Lvs 0.5–1.6cm, elliptic or elliptic-oblong, grey-hairy margins entire or with 1–3 small teeth near base. Infl. a small, umbel-like; fls white. Spring. US (Tex., New Mex., Ariz.), N Mex. var. *perplexans* (Trel.) Jeps. CUP LEAF CEANOTHUS. Lvs 1–2cm, broadly obovate, broadly elliptic or rounded, yellow-green and glab. above, with clusters of fine white hairs in axils beneath, toothed. Spring. S Calif., Baja Calif. Z7.

C. griseus (Trel.) McMinn. CARMEL CEANOTHUS. Large everg. shrub, erect to at least 3m. Lvs 1–5cm, broadly ovate to rounded-ovate, apex blunt, revolute, sinuate between teeth, dark green, glab. above, densely grey-hairy beneath. Infl. 2–5cm, dense, paniculate; fls violet-blue. Spring. Closely related to *C. thyrsiflorus*. Coastal C Calif. var. *horizontalis* McMinn. CARMEL CREEPER. Prostrate to low and spreading. Spring. Coastal C Calif. 'Hurricane Point': fast-growing, forming v. large, low clumps; fls pale blue, sparse. 'Louis Edmunds': 1.3–1.6m tall, clumps to 4m across. 'Santa Ana': to 1.75×5m;

lvs to 1.5cm, dark, lustrous green; fls midnight blue in clusters to 2.5cm long. 'Yankee Point': to 60cm tall, clumps to only 3m across; fls more abundant, bright blue. Z8.

C. '**Hearstiorum**'. To 0.3×2m. Lvs to 3cm, blistered. Fls mid-blue, in clusters to 2.5cm long.

C. herbaceus Raf. = *C. ovatus*.

C. horizontalis hort. = *C. griseus* var. *horizontalis*.

C. impressus Trel. SANTA BARBARA CEANOTHUS. Low everg. shrub, forming clumps to 1.5×1.5m, twigs flexuous. Lvs 0.6–1.2cm, dark glossy green, elliptic to suborbicular, slightly hairy, veins sunken above, margins appearing crenate. Infl. 1–2.5cm, simple, narrow; fls dark blue. Spring. US (Coastal C Calif.). var. *nipomensis* McMinn. NIPOMO CEANOTHUS. To 3m. Lvs 1–2.5cm, pale green, veins scarcely, margins almost flat. Spring. US (Coastal C Calif.). Z7.

C. incanus Torr. & A. Gray. COAST WHITETHORN. Erect everg. shrub, 2–4m, twigs throny, with a white bloom. Lvs 2–6cm, broadly ovate to elliptic, obtuse, subglabrous to hairy, grey-green above, paler beneath, teeth few or 0. Infl. 3–7cm, compound, dense; fls white. Spring. N Calif. Z8.

C. insularis Eastw. Erect everg. shrub, 1–3m, twigs arching. Lvs 1.2–3.5cm, elliptic to cuneate-obovate, apex truncate to retuse, green and glab. above, pale grey beneath. Infl. umbel-like, axill.; fls white, centres sometimes pale blue. Early spring. US (S Calif. Is.). Z8.

C. integerrimus Hook. & Arn. DEER BRUSH. Decid. shrub, 1–4m, br. lax. Lvs 2.5–7cm, broadly elliptical to subovate or oblong, apex acute to obtuse with a few teeth, pale green and somewhat hairy above, paler and more hairy beneath. Infl. 4–15cm, paniculate; fls white to pink or dark blue. Late spring–early summer. W US. Z7.

C. integerrimus var. *parvifolius* S. Wats. = *C. parvifolius*.

C. '**Italian Skies**'. (*C. foliosus* ×?.) Everg. shrub to 1.5m tall, spreading, densely branched, twigs long. Lvs to 1.5cm, oval to oblong-elliptic, obtuse, glossy dark green, with small gland. teeth. Infl. 5–7cm, compound, conical; fls intense blue. Late spring. Gdn origin. Z8.

C. jepsonii Greene. MUSK BUSH. Small spreading shrub close to *C. purpureus*. Lvs dark green, holly-like, strongly coriaceous. Fls rich blue. E US.

C. jepsonii var. *purpureus* (Jeps.) Jeps. = *C. purpureus*.

C. '**John Phelps**'. To 2×4m. Lvs to 2.5cm, mid-green. Fls deep indigo in clusters to 2.5cm long.

C. '**Joyce Coulter**'. To 1.75×4m. Lvs to 2.5cm, mid-green. Fls mid-blue in spicate clusters to 12cm long.

C. leucodermis Greene. CHAPARRAL WHITETHORN. Everg. shrub, 2–4m, br. rigid, spreading widely twigs spinose. Lvs 1–2.5cm, ellipic-oblong to ovate, entire or with small teeth, apex acute or obtuse, glaucous, glab. to pbuesc. Infl. 3–8cm, simple; fls pale blue or white. Spring–early summer. Calif., Baja Calif. Z8.

C. × *lobbianus* (Hook.) McMinn. (*C. dentatus* × *C. griseus*.) Erect everg. shrub to 1m, br. dense. Lvs 2–2.5cm, elliptic, leathery, apex blunt, margins ± revolute, with gland. teeth, dark green and slightly hairy above, paler and more hairy beneath. Infl. axill., rounded; fls strong bright blue, dense, on blue-hairy peduncles. A naturally occurring hybrid. Late spring–early summer. S Calif. 'Russelianus': vigorous, floriferous, with small, glossy lvs. Z8.

C. macrocarpus Nutt. = *C. megacarpus*.

C. maritimus Hoover. MARITIME CEANOTHUS. Prostrate shrub; st. to 1m. Lvs 0.8–2cm, oblong or obovate, apex truncate to emarginate or obcordate, mucronate, revolute, with 1–3 teeth per side, dark green and glossy above, white-hairy beneath; fls pale to dark blue. Spring. S Calif. Z8.

C. masonii McMinn. BOLINAS RIDGE CEANOTHUS. Everg. shrub, 0.6–2m, br. stiff, widely spreading. Lvs 0.6–1.8cm, almost rounded to broadly elliptic, apex obtuse to emarginate, short-toothed, dark green and glab. above, pale grey, puberulous beneath. Infl. umbel-like, many-fld; fls purple to dark blue. Spring. US (C Calif.). Z8.

C. megacarpus Nutt. BIGPOD CEANOTHUS. Everg. shrub, 1–4m, of compact habit, twigs slender. Lvs 1–2cm, spathulate to obovate, base cuneate, apex truncate or emarginate, somewhat revolute, dark green and glab. above, grey-hairy beneath. Infl. to 1.5cm diam., umbel-like, few-fld fls white. Spring. S Calif. Z7.

C. × *mendocinensis* McMinn. MENDOCINO CEANOTHUS. (*C. thyrsiflorus* × *C. velutinus* var. *laevigatus*.) Small to medium-sized shrub. Shoots long, arching. Lvs broadly ovate, dark glossy green, somewhat viscid. Fls pale blue in rac. Spring.

C. '**Mountain Haze**'. (*C. cyaneus* ×?.) Evergeen shrub to 2m. Lvs 2–5cm, ovate-elliptic with gland-tipped teeth, glossy green above, dull beneath, subglabrous. Infl. to 12cm, compound, columnar; fls v. bright blue. Early spring. Gdn origin. Z8.

C. oliganthus Nutt. Everg. shrub or small tree, 1–3m, younger br. tinged red, hairy. Lvs 1.5–4cm, elliptic to ovate or ovate-oblong, with gland. teeth, dark green and slightly hairy above, paler and more hairy beneath. Infl. to 1.5–5cm, simple, lax; fls dark blue or purple. Spring. S Calif. var. *orcuttii* (Parry) Jeps. Fls pale blue. Spring. S Calif. Z8.

C. orcuttii Parry = *C. oliganthus* var. *orcuttii.*

C. ovatus Desf. Erect compact decid. shrub to 1.1m, bark brown or purple-hued. Lvs 2.5–6.5cm, oval-lanceolate to elliptic-lanceolate or oblong-elliptic, margins gland., with small crenate teeth, glossy green above, paler beneath. Infl. a subcorymbose cluster, with lf-like bracts below white fls. Early summer. E & C US, Canada (Manit.). Z5.

C. 'Owlswood Blue'. To 3×4m. Lvs to 6cm, oval, dark green. Fls dark blue, in spicate clusters to 15cm.

C. ×pallidus Lindl. (*C. ×delilianus* × *C. ovatus.*) 'Marie Simon': decid. shrub to 1.5m tall, much-branched; lvs broadly oval; infl. term., conical, dense, fls soft pink. Summer–early autumn. 'Ceres': fls lilac pink. 'Perle Rose': decid. shrub to 1.5m, spreading to 1.5m; lvs broadly oval to elliptic; infl. dense, term., conical to subglobose; fls soft carmine pink to strawberry pink. 'Plenus': fls white, double, pink in bud. Soil type can affect fl. colour. Summer–early autumn.

C. palmeri Trel. Everg. shrub, 1–3.5m. Lvs 1.5–3.5cm, oblong to oblong-ovate, entire, leathery, pale green and glab. above, paler and hairy on midrib beneath. Infl. 7–12cm, compound; fls white. Late spring–early summer. S Calif., Baja Calif. Z8.

C. papillosus Torr. & A. Gray. WART LEAF CEANOTHUS. Everg. shrub, 1–5m, laxly branching. Lvs 1.5–5cm, oblong-elliptic to elliptic, revolute, with gland. teeth, dark green, villous, papillose above, paler and hairy beneth, apex rounded to truncate. Infl. 2–5cm, simple, dense, narrow; fls pale to dark blue or purple-blue. Spring. Calif. var. *roweanus* (Hart.) McMinn. MOUNT TRANQUILLON CEANOTHUS; ROWE CEANOTHUS. Lvs less than 1cm across, linear to oblong, pustular-papillose, apex retuse to truncate. Spring. Calif. 'Supressus': prostrate form. Z8.

C. papillosus var. *regius* Jeps. = *C. ×regius.*

C. parryi Trel. Everg. shrub, 1–5m; twigs angled. Lvs 1.5–4.5cm, oblong or subelliptic, with gland. teeth to subentire, slightly revolute, dark green above, paler and cobwebby beneath. Infl. 5–15cm, compound, downy, fls dark blue. Spring–early summer. N Calif. Z8.

C. parvifolius (S. Wats.) Trel. Decid. to partially everg. shrub, 0.6–1.2m. Lvs 0.6–2.0cm, sometimes slightly toothed near apex, glab., paler green beneath. Infl. 3–7cm, paniculate; fls pale to dark blue. late spring–early summer. US (C Calif.). Z6.

C. 'Percy Picton'. (*?C. impressus* × *C. papillosus.*) Dense everg. shrub to 3m. Lvs small, dense, ovate-oblong. Fls dark blue in small, dense umbels. Early summer. Gdn origin. Z8.

C. perplexans Trel. = *C. greggii* var. *perplexans.*

C. 'Pinguet Guindon'. Fls lavender, suffused pink. Summer.

C. prostratus Benth. SQUAW CARPET; MAHALA MATS. V. low prostrate everg. shrub, forming clumps to over 2.5m across. Lvs 0.8–2.5cm, cuneate-lanceolate to obovate, thick and leathery, sometimes undulate with 3 sharp apical teeth, pale green and glossy above with grey hairs beneath. Infl. term., umbellate; fls pale lavender-blue to dark blue, sometimes white. Spring. NW US. var. *occidentalis* McMinn. Lvs cuneate-spathulate, undulate. Spring. Coastal N Calif. Z7.

C. 'Puget Blue'. (*C. impressus* ×*?C. papillosus.*) Everg. shrub to 3m, dense. Lvs to 2cm, elliptic-oblong, closely glandular-toothed. Infl. 2–5cm, narrowly elongate; fls many, pale to dark blue. Free-flowering. Early summer. Gdn origin. Z7.

C. pumilus Greene. SISKIYOU-MAT. Prostrate or decumbent everg. shrub to 20cm tall, spreading to form clumps 2m across. Lvs 0.4–1.5cm, cuneate-oblong, oblong-obovate or oblanceolate, apex usually with 3 teeth, truncate, leathery, glab. above, white-hairy beneath. Infl. umbel-like, few-fld; fls white or blue. Spring. N Calif.: SW Oreg. Z7.

C. purpureus Jeps. HOLLYLEAF CEANOTHUS. Everg. shrub, 1–2m, erect or spreading, with sparse, red-brown br. Lvs 1.2–2.5cm, holly-like, margins undulate, spinose, glossy dark green above, with short grey hairs beneath. Infl. umbellate, dense, racemose, fls lavender to purple, large. Spring. US (Calif.). Z8.

C. ramulosus (Greene) McMinn. COAST CEANOTHUS. Everg. shrub, 0.6–3m, br. slender, spreading or arching. Lvs 0.6–2cm, obovate or elliptic to suborbicular, apex toothed, blunt or truncate, glab. above, pale grey beneath. Infl. umbel-like; fls pale blue to white. Spring. Calif. var. *fasicularis* McMinn. Lvs clustered, narrowly oblanceolate. Spring. S Calif. Z8.

C. 'Ray Hartman'. (*?C. arboreus* ×*C. griseus.*) Shrub or small tree to 6m, everg., forming clumps to over 6m across. Infl. sub-cylindrical; fls deep blue. Early summer. Gdn origin. Z7.

C. ×regius (Jeps.) McMinn. (Probably *C. papillosus* ×*C. thyrsiflorus.*) Everg. shrub to 3m. Lvs 2–5cm, oblong-ovate to elliptic, dark green and subglabrous above, paler and hairy beneath, slightly revolute gland-toothed. Fls pale to dark blue.

US (Coastal C Calif.). Z8.

C. rigidus Nutt. MONTEREY CEANOTHUS. Everg. shrub, 1–2m tall, much-branched, low and spreading, twigs stiff, slender. Lvs 0.6–1.5cm, cuneate to rounded-obovate, leathery, sometimes with apical teeth, glossy dark green above, paler and hairy between veins beneath. Infl. umbel-like, axill., few-fld; fls bright lilac-blue to dark blue, fragrant. Spring–early summer. US (C Calif.). 'Albus' (WHITE MONTEREY CEANOTHUS): fls white. 'Pallens': lvs coarser, more dentate and glossy; fls in longer clusters. 'Snowball': fls white. 'Snow Flurries': fls white. Z8.

C. rigidus var. *pallens* Sprague = *C. rigidus* 'Pallens'.

C. roweanus Hart = *C. papillosus* var. *roweanus.*

C. sanguineus Pursh. WILD LILAC; OREGON TEA. Decid. shrub, 1.5–3m, erect, twigs red or purple, flexible. Lvs 0.3–1cm, obovate or ovate to broadly elliptic, with gland. teeth, dark green above, paler and downy beneath. Infl. 5–10cm, paniculate; fls white. Late spring–early summer. Calif., to BC. Z5.

C. sorediatus Hook. & Arn. JIM BRUSH. Everg. shrub, 1–5m, br. erect, dense twigs stiff, spinose. Lvs 1–4cm, elliptic to ovate, usually acute, with fine gland. teeth, dark glossy green and glab. above, strigose beneath. Infl. 1–4cm, simple; dense; fls pale to dark blue. Spring (sometimes again in autumn). Calif. Z8.

C. 'Southmead'. (*C. ×lobbianus* ×?.) Everg. shrub to 1.5m tall, dense and bushy, forming clumps to 1.5m across. Lvs oblong, glossy dark green, small. Infl. rounded; fls v. dark, rich blue. Late spring–early summer. Gdn origin. Z8.

C. spinosus Nutt. RED-HEART; GREEN BARK CEANOTHUS. Large shrub or small tree, everg., 2–6m, twigs stiff, ascending, spinose. Lvs 1.2–3cm, elliptic to oblong, apex blunt to emarginate, sometimes with a few teeth, subglabrous, bright green above, paler beneath. Infl. 4–15cm, compound; fls white to pale blue. Spring. S Calif. and Baja Calif. Z8.

C. 'Theodore Payne'. (*C. arboreus* ×*C. spinosus.*) Everg. bush to 4×4m. Fls deep blue. Early summer. Gdn origin. Z8.

C. thyrsiflorus Eschw. BLUEBLOSSOM; BLUE BRUSH. Large shrub or small tree, everg., 1–6m, typically erect, twigs green, angled. Lvs 1–5cm, oblong-ovate to broadly elliptic, glandular-toothed, dark green and glab. above, paler and hairy on veins beneath. Infl. 3–8cm, compound, rounded, axill.; fls pale to dark blue, occas. white. Spring. US (Calif., S Oreg.). 'Cascade': to 8m, habit open, with broadly arching br.; lvs narrow, bright glossy green; pan. lax, cylindrical to 8cm; fls pale blue. 'Skylark': to 2×1.5m; lvs to 5cm, lustrous mid-green; fls dark blue, borne profusely over a long period. var. *repens* McMinn. CREEPING BLUE BLOSSOM. Habit prostrate. Spring–early summer. US (N coastal Calif.). 'Blue Mound': dense, everg. shrub, to 1.5m, spreading to form clumps at least 2m in diam; lvs glossy, dark green, oblong; infl. rounded, fls dark blue. Late spring. Z8.

C. thyrsiflorus var. *griseus* Trel. = *C. griseus.*

C. tomentosus Parry. WOOLLY LEAF CEANOTHUS. Everg. shrub, 1–3m, br. slender, twigs rusty-tomentose. Lvs 1–2.5cm, ovate or elliptic, with gland. teeth, dark green, with fine hairs above, white- or pale-brown wooly beneath. Infl. 2–5cm, compound; fls pale to dark blue. Spring. US (C Calif.). var. *olivaceus* Jeps. Lvs grey-green beneath, denticulate. Spring. S Calif., Baja Calif. Z8.

C. 'Topaz'. (*C. ×delilianus* ×?.) Decid. shrub to 3m. Fls pale indigo blue. Summer. Gdn origin. Z8.

C. ×veitchianus Hook. (*C. griseus* ×*C. rigidus.*) Robust everg. shrub, to 3m. Lvs 1–2cm, obovate to ovate, base cuneate, apex rounded, teeth gland., glossy green above, grey-green hairy beneath. Infl. 2.5–5cm, dense, oblong or capitate; fls intense dark blue, naturally occurring hybrid. Spring. US (Calif.). Z8.

C. velutinus Douglas TOBACCO BRUSH. Everg. aromatic shrub, 1–2cm, spreading, round-topped. Lvs 2.5–8cm, ovate-elliptic, base rounded-subcordate, with dense, fine gland. teeth, glossy dark green above, paler with fine grey hairs beneath. Infl. 5–10cm, compound fls white. Early summer. Calif., Colorado to BC. var. *laevigatus* Torr. & A. Gray. Habit spreading. Lvs large, glossy, somewhat, viscid, often thinly, velutinous beneath. Pan. dense; fls grey-blue-white. Z5.

C. verrucosus Nutt. WARTY-STEM CEANOTHUS. Everg. shrub, 1–3m, br. stiff, twigs woolly, roughened. Lvs 0.5–1.4cm, dense, round to deltoid-obovate, dark green and glab. above, with few fine grey hairs beneath. Infl. 1–2cm, dense, axill.; fls white, centres darker. Spring. S Calif., N Baja Calif. Z8.

Cecropia Loefl. Cecropiaceae. *c*25 lacticiferous trees. Trunk and br. hollow. Lvs palmately lobed, peltate; petioles long, often with basal food bodies. Infl. dense, spicate, spathaceous; fls v. small. W Indies, Mex., Braz. Z9.

C. palmata Willd. SNAKEWOOD TREE. To 15m. Lvs large, scabrous to glabrescent above, white-pubesc. beneath, lobes 7–11, oblong-obovate, blunt. W Indies to Braz.

C. peltata L. TRUMPET TREE; SNAKE WOOD; POP-A-GUN. To 15m. Lvs about 30cm diam., silvery white-tomentose beneath, lobes 7–9, about 10cm, radiating, elliptic, cuspidate. Jam.

CECROPIACEAE C. Berg. 6/200. *Cecropia.*

Cedar *Cedrus.*
Cedar Elm *Ulmus crassifolia.*
Cedar Fig *Ficus superba* var. *henneana.*
Cedar of Goa *Cupressus lusitanica.*
Cedar of Lebanon *Cedrus libani.*
Cedar Wattle *Acacia elata.*
Cedrat *Citrus medica.*

Cedrela P. Browne.
C. sinensis A. Juss. = *Toona sinensis.*

Cedronella Moench. Labiatae. 1 woody-based perenn. herb to 1.5m. Lvs trifoliate, sweetly scented of cedar; lfts lanceolate, glab. above, pubesc. beneath, serrate. Infl. of term. whorls with bracts, simple; cal. tubular to campanulate, 13–15-veined, teeth 5; cor. funnel-shaped, upper lip 2-lobed, lower lip 3-lobed, middle lobe longest, to 20mm, pink, lilac or white, weakly pubesc. Canary Is. Z9.
C. canariensis (L.) Webb & Berth. CANARY BALM.
C. mexicana (Kunth.) Benth. = *Agastache mexicana.*

Cedrus Trew. CEDAR. Pinaceae. 2 everg., coniferous trees. Bark dull grey, smooth, becoming fissured into grey-brown plates. Br. large, spreading, bearing long and short shoots. Lvs linear-acicular, set on persistent pulvini; spirally and radially arranged on long shoots, in pseudowhorls on short shoots, white-blue stomatal lines on all faces. Cones term., utimately erect, ovoid to oblong or cylindric; scales closely imbricate, broad, leathery to woody. E Medit., N Afr., W Himal.
C. atlantica (Endl.) Carr. = *C. libani* ssp. *atlantica.*
C. brevifolia (Hook. f.) Henry = *C. libani* ssp. *brevifolia.*
C. deodara (D. Don) G. Don. DEODAR; HIMALAYAN CEDAR. To 60m in wild, 35m in cult. Bark dark brown, deeply fissured. Crown broadly conic; leader nodding; br. spreading in tiers, tips nodding. Lvs somewhat 4-sided, rich green to grey-green, acuminate, 3–6cm, slender and green on short often thicker more glaucous on long shoots. Cones broadly cylindric, apex round, glaucous blue-grey, becoming brown, 8–14×5.5–7cm; scales ridged at apex. W Himal. (Afghan. to W Nepal). Over 40 cvs described; most selection to find cold-tolerant cvs for E US, Scandinavia and Germany, best are several from seed collected in Paktia Province, Afghanistan, such as 'Eisregen', 'Karl Fuchs', 'Polar Winter' and 'Shalimar'; 'Kashmir', from Kashmir, is also hardy. Many of these have lvs of a bright blue-green. Other cvs selected for v. pale new lvs, to almost white in 'Nivea', or yellow, in 'Aurea'; for fastigiate growth, as in 'Fastigiata'; and dwarf form, as in 'Blue Dwarf' and 'Pygmy'. 'Robusta' has v. with v. long stout, grey-green lvs and heavy branching. Zone 8, clones selected for hardiness to Z5.
C. libani A. Rich. CEDAR OF LEBANON. To 45m. Bark dark brown to dark grey, becoming fissured. Crown conic, becoming flat topped and irregular with age. Main br. tiered, horizontal or slightly ascending. Lvs quadrangular, slightly flattened, acute, mid green, often blue-tinted, 1–3cm. Cones 8–12×5–6.5cm, dull green becoming brown, erect, broadly ovoid, tapering towards apex; scales not ridged at apex. Leb., NW Syr., SC Turk. Cvs are available with golden lvs, dwarf form, erect-branching, etc. 'Aurea': slow-growing to 15m; foliage golden yellow. 'Aurea-Prostrata': dwarf; foliage yellow. 'Golden Dwarf': low and slow-growing; lvs gold. 'Gold Tip': irregular in growth; lvs bright gold at first, later green tinged gold. 'Nana': slow-growing, conical. 'Pendula': weeping; lvs green. 'Purdue Hardy': erect and regular in growth, hardy to −30°C; may belong to ssp. *stenocoma.* 'Sargentii': dwarf, shrubby; br. dense, pendent; foliage blue-green. 'Stricta': narrow, conical; br. ascending; foliage grey-green to silver-grey, glossy.
ssp. *atlantica* (Endl.) Battand. & Trabut. ATLAS CEDAR. To 50m, ovoid-conic when young, eventually becoming flat topped, br. ascending to horizontal. Bark ultimately fissured and dark grey tinged red-brown. Lvs 1.5–3cm, acute, roughly 4-sided, dark green, blue-green to bright pale blue-grey. Cones light green, 6–10×4–5cm, brown bloomed grey, apex depressed to rounded acute ripening; scales not ridged at apex. N Afr. (Atlas Mts). 'Albospica': young shoots snow-white. 'Glauca': foliage silver-blue; numerous clones from seed-raised plants sold under this name. 'Fastigiata': narrowly conic in growth, br. erect, dense and profuse; needles tinged blue. 'Mount Saint Catherine': slow-growing, needles dense and glaucous: witches' broom. 'Pendula': gracefully weeping, needles blue-green; must be

grafted on type. 'Pyramidalis': conic in growth; br. lat. and irregular. 'Rustic': lvs vivid blue.
ssp. *brevifolia* (Hook. f.) Meikle. CYPRUS CEDAR. Tree to 25m. Crown ovoid-conic, growth irregular, flat, umbrella-like; leader arching. Lvs to 2cm, mostly 1–1.2cm, curved, acute, grey-green. Cones 7–11×4–5cm, often with an apical, mucronate depression. Cyprus (mts). 'Hillier Compact': dwarf to 30×65cm after 20 years; needles glaucous, crowded. 'Horizon': dwarf and prostrate in growth. ssp. *stenocoma* (Schwarz) P.H. Davis. To 45–50m. Crown slender ovoid-conic, becoming flat-topped. Br. horizontal to slightly ascending. Lvs 1–2.5cm, light blue-grey. Cones narrower, 7–12×4–6cm, apex depressed to acute. S Turk. Z6.

Ceiba Mill. KAPOK; SILK-COTTON TREE. Bombacaceae. 4 spiny large decid. trees; trunks buttressed, usually spiny. Lvs palmate. Fls axill., solitary or clustered; cal. cup-shaped, truncate or 3–5-lobed; pet. 5, oblong; sta. 5, long. united to form tube. Fr. a leathery or woody capsule; seeds embedded in flossy fibres. Trop. Amer., Afr.; now widely cult. and nat. elsewhere in tropics. Z10.
C. aesculifolia (HBK) Britt. & Bak. f. Medium to large tree, trunk and br. spiny. Lfts 5–8, to 15cm, elliptic to oblanceolate, usually serrulate. Fls before lvs; pet. to 15cm, narrow, yellow or white, exterior brown-tomentose. Fr. to 18cm, ellipsoid. C Amer.
C. casearia Medik. = *C. pentandra.*
C. grandiflora Rose = *C. aesculifolia.*
C. pentandra (L.) Gaertn. KAPOK; WHITE SILK-COTTON TREE. Strongly buttressed, spreading to 70m; trunk spiny. Lfts 5–8, oblong-lanceolate, to 20cm, entire. Fls before lvs; pet. to 3cm, oblong-obovate, yellow, pink or white, exterior tomentose. Fr. to 15cm, ellipsoid to fusiform. S Amer., Afr., widely cult. and nat. elsewhere in tropics.
→*Eriodendron.*

Celandine *Chelidonium.*
Celandine Crocus *Crocus korolkowii.*
Celandine Poppy *Stylophorum diphyllum.*

CELASTRACEAE R. Br. 94/1300. *Cassine, Catha, Celastrus, Euonymus, Maytenus, Paxistima, Putterlickia, Tripterygium.*

Celastrus L. BITTERSWEET; SHRUBBY BITTERSWEET. Celastraceae. c30 mostly dioecious shrubs, usually decid. and scandent or twining. Fls v. small in term. pan. or axill. cymes, white, pale green or cream. Fr. a capsule, small, 3-valved, thinly woody; seeds 1–2 per valve, with a fleshy aril, usually persisting into winter. Afr., Amer., Aus., E & S Asia, Pacific.
C. angulatus Maxim. Shrub, climbing to 7.25m; branchlets angular. Lvs 10–18cm, broadly elliptic-ovate, crenate, glab. Infl. term. Fr. to 9mm diam., interior yellow, seeds orange, aril red. Summer. NW & C China. Z5.
C. articulatus Thunb. = *C. orbiculatus.*
C. australis Harv. & F. Muell. Scandent shrub to 7m. Lvs to 10cm, ovate-lanceolate to oblong-elliptic, entire or minutely dentate. Fr. to 6mm thick; seeds orange-yellow. Aus. (Vict.). Z9.
C. cassinioides L'Hérit. Everg. shrub to 4m, erect, glab. Lvs ovate, dentate, glossy, coriaceous. Fr. globose, pale green to light brown; seed oval, chestnut-brown; aril white, fluffy. Canary Is. Z9.
C. dependens Wallich. Twining shrub, resembling *C. scandens.* Lvs 7.5–10cm, oblong, acuminate, finely crenate, shining deep green above. Fr. close to *C. scandens.* Himal. to SW China. Z8.
C. dispermus F. Muell. Small tree to 8m, glab. Lvs to 8cm, elliptic, obovate-oblong to broadly lanceolate, entire, subcoriaceous. Fr. to 8mm; seeds 1–2, black; aril yellow, thick and fleshy. Aus. (Queensld). Z9.
C. edulis Vahl = *Catha edulis.*
C. flagellaris Rupr. Twining shrub to 8m. Lvs to 5cm, broadly ovate, serrulate, pale green, scaberulous above. Infl. axill. Fr. yellow-green to 6mm diam.; aril orange-red. Summer. China, Jap., S Korea. Z4.
C. gemmatus Loes. Twining shrub to 12m, resembles *C. orbiculatus* but buds long, pointed; lvs to 11cm, glossy, elliptic, tapering finely. C & W China. Z7.
C. glaucophyllus Rehd. & Wils. Scandent shrub to 10m. Lvs to 10cm, elliptic-obovate, acuminate, sparsely crenate, blue-green. Fr. to 1cm, yellow. W China. Z8.
C. heterophyllus Ecklon & Zeyh. Small shrub to 1.5m, much-branched, glab., spiny. Lvs to 4cm, polymorphic, elliptic to obovate-cuneate, obtuse or acute, spiny-dentate. Fr. to 6mm wide, 3-angled, tinged red; aril yellow. S Afr. Z9.
C. hookeri Prain. Vining to 6m; young twigs rusty-pubesc. Lvs elliptic to ovate, apex narrow, rounded or cuneate at base,

coarsely toothed. Fr. to 6mm, orange; aril red. Himal., China. Z6.

C. hypoglaucus Hemsl. = *C. hypoleucus*.

C. hypoleucus (Oliv.) Loes. Twining to 5m; twigs glaucescent. Lvs to 14cm, oblong-elliptic, briefly acuminate, remotely serrulate, dark green above, glaucous blue-green beneath. Fr. to 8mm diam., yellow; aril red. Summer. China. Z8.

C. latifolius Hemsl. = *C. angulatus*.

C. loeseneri Rehd. & Wils. Twining to 6m; twigs smooth, red-brown, obscurely punctate. Lvs 5–11cm, oval to broad ovate to elliptic-lanceolate, acuminate, crenate, deep green above, paler beneath, thick. Fr. 8mm diam., yellow; aril red. C China. Z6.

C. orbiculatus Thunb. ORIENTAL BITTERSWEET; STAFF VINE. Densely twining shrub to 12m; twigs tangled, light brown. Lvs 5 to 10cm, broadly elliptic, to suborbicular, abruptly tapered, finely crenate to serrate, pale green. Infl. axill. Fr. globose, interior yellow; aril coral pink to red. NE Asia, nat. N Amer. Z4. 'Diana': ♀ form. var. *punctatus* (Thunb.) Rehd. Less vigorous; lvs smaller, elliptic-oblong.

C. paniculatus Willd. = *C. dependens*.

C. punctatus Thunb. = *C. orbiculatus* var. *punctatus*.

C. pyracanthus L. = *Putterlickia pyracantha*.

C. rosthornianus Loes. Twining to 5m; twigs v. slender. Lvs to 8cm, narrow-elliptic to elliptic-lanceolate, acuminate, denticulate, pale, lustrous, rather thick. Fr. 6mm diam., ochre to apricot; aril red. C & W China. Z5.

C. rugosus Rehd. & Wils. Twining to 6m; twigs glab., densely punctate. Lvs to 13cm, ovate to oblong, short-acuminate, rugulose above. Fr. abundant, orange-yellow, aril bright red. China. Z6.

C. scandens L. WAXWORK; AMERICAN BITTERSWEET; STAFF TREE; STAFF VINE. Twining to 7m; twigs tough, glab. Lvs to 10cm, ovate-oblong, tapering toward apex, serrate. Infl. term. Fr. globose, 8mm diam., interior yellow; aril carmine-red. N Amer. 'Indian Brave': ♂ form. 'Indian Maiden': ♀ form. Z2.

C. spiciformis Rehd. & Wils. var. *laevis* (Rehd. & Wils.) Rehd. Scandent shrub to 3m. glab. Lvs to 10cm, oval or ovate, sometimes ovate-lanceolate, acuminate, shallow dentate, pale, glaucescent beneath. Fr. to 6mm, orange-yellow; aril shining dark brown. China. Z6.

C. vaniotii (Lév.) Rehd. = *C. spiciformis*.

C. verrucosus E. Mey. = *Putterlickia verrucosa*.

→*Gymnospora*.

Celebes Pepper *Piper ornatum*.
Celeriac *Apium graveolens* var. *rapaceum*.
Celery *Apium graveolens* var. *dulce*.
Celery Pine *Phyllocladus*.
Celery-top Pine *Phyllocladus asplenifolius*.
Celery Wood *Polyscias elegans*.

Celmisia Cass. Compositae. *c*60 perenn. herbs and subshrubs. Lvs in dense tufts or imbricate along br., often silvery above, usually tomentose, at least beneath, bases often forming persistent sheaths. Cap. radiate, solitary, on bracteate, occas. branched scapes; involucre broadly hemispherical; phyllaries imbricate, pubesc.; ray flts white, rarely flushed white or pale mauve to pale yellow; disc flts yellow, rarely purple. Summer. NZ and SE Aus. Z7.

C. angustifolia Ckn. Small subshrub. Br. clothed in old lf remains. Lvs to 5cm, in rosettes at br. tips, linear to linear-spathulate, leathery, viscid, tomentose beneath. Cap. to 4cm diam., solitary, scapose; ray flts to 1.5cm. NZ.

C. argentea T. Kirk Cushion-forming subshrub to 20cm. St. clothed in lf remains. Lvs to 1.2cm, linear-subulate densely imbricate, tomentose. Cap. to 1.2cm diam., ± sessile; ray flts to 1cm. NZ.

C. armstrongii Petrie. Perenn. tuft-forming herb. Lf sheaths densely imbricate around st. Lvs to 40cm, narrowly linear-lanceolate, yellow-green, with a broad yellow band, tomentose beneath, ribbed above. Cap. to 5cm diam., scape *c*25cm, white-tomentose; ray flts to 1.6cm. NZ.

C. bellidioides Hook. f. Creeping, mat-forming perenn. herb. Lvs to 1.5cm, in apical rosettes, obovate-oblong to spathulate, spreading, obtuse, dark green, glossy above, paler beneath, narrowing to a floccose sheathing petiole. Cap. 2cm diam., solitary, on slender pubesc. scape to 5cm; ray flts 1cm above. NZ.

C. coriacea (Forst. f.) Hook. f. Tufted stoloniferous perenn. herb. Lf sheaths forming a pseudostem to 10cm. Lvs to 60cm, lanceolate to lanceolate-oblong, acute to acuminate, leathery, sulcate, lustrous above, tomentose beneath. Cap. on a stout, tomentose scape to 40cm; ray flts to 4cm. NZ.

C. dallii Buch. Viscid, tufted perenn. herb, to 6cm. Lvs to 20cm, obovate-oblong to obovate-lanceolate, leathery, glab. above, tomentose beneath, minutely toothed. Cap. 4cm diam. on a stout, sulcate scape; ray flts to 1.5cm, toothed. NZ.

C. densiflora Hook. f. Subshrubby perenn. herb. Lvs to 12cm, narrowly obovate-oblong, glab. above, tomentose beneath, crenate to sinuate, petioles tapered to a strongly sulcate sheath. Cap. 4cm diam., on a glab., viscid scape to 25cm; ray flts to 2cm. NZ.

C. durietzii Ckn. & Allan ex W. Martin. Subshrub, br. clothed in dead lvs. Lvs to 6cm, in apical rosettes, obovate to spathulate, tomentose beneath, petiole narrow, tapered to a sheath. Cap. 4cm diam., on a scape to 20cm; ray flts to 1.5cm, filiform. NZ.

C. gracilenta Hook. f. Tufted perenn. herb, with pseudostems to 5cm. Lvs to 15cm, linear, rather flaccid, tomentose beneath, sheaths membranous. Cap. to *c*2cm diam. on a slender scape to 40cm; ray flts to 2.5cm, with slender tube. NZ.

C. haastii Hook. f. Low-growing, much-branched subshrub; branchlets clothed in dead lvs. Lvs 8cm, in dense rosettes, elliptic-oblong to obovate-spathulate, glab. above, tomentose beneath, petiole winged. Cap. 4cm diam., on a scape to 15cm; ray flts to 2cm. NZ.

C. hectori hort. = *C. hectoris*.

C. hectoris Hook. f. Ramose subshrub, spreading to 1m, br. clothed in dead lvs. Lvs to 2cm, in rosettes, linear to spathulate-oblong or linear-obovate, entire, leathery, tomentose. Cap. to 2.5cm diam., on a stout floccose scape; ray flts 1.5cm. NZ.

C. hieracifolia Hook. f. Tufted perenn. herb. Lvs to 20cm, oblong-obovate to elliptic-oblong, leathery, crenate, glab. above, yellow-tomentose beneath; petiole short. Cap. to 4cm diam., on a stout viscid scape to 25cm; ray flts 1.2cm. NZ.

C. holosericea (Forst. f.) Hook. f. Perenn. herb, st. covered with umbricate lf sheaths. Lvs to 20cm, radical, oblong to elliptic-lanceolate, denticulate, leathery, glab. above, tomentose beneath; petiole short, tapered to sheath. Cap. to 7cm diam., on a bracteate scape to 30cm; ray flts to 2.5cm, narrow. NZ.

C. hookeri Ckn. Tufted perenn. herb, with st. covered with imbricate lf sheaths. Lvs to 30cm, oblong to broadly lanceolate, glab. above, tomentose beneath, entire, attenuate to short petiole or subsessile, sheath floccose. Cap. to 10cm diam., on a stout, pubesc. scape to 30cm; ray flts 2.5cm. NZ.

C. incana Hook. f. Subshrub, with stout br. clad in reflexed, dead lvs. Lvs to 4cm, in dense rosettes, obovate-oblong, leathery, tomentose, petiole short. Cap. to 3.5cm diam., on a slender scape to 10cm; ray flts to 1.2cm, narrow. NZ.

C. insignis W. Martin. Tufted perenn. herb, with pseudostem to *c*6cm. Lvs to 30cm, linear to linear-oblong, entire, dark green above, tomentose beneath, sheath floccose. Cap. to 4cm diam., on a floccose scape to 30cm; ray flts to 1.6cm, slender. NZ.

C. lanceolata Ckn. Large tufted perenn. herb, with imbricate lf sheaths. Lvs to 30cm, oblong to narrow-lanceolate, entire, tomentose beneath, tapered to short petiole or sessile. Cap. to 7cm diam., on a stout scape to 35cm; ray flts 1.5cm. NZ.

C. lindsayi Hook. f. Robust, low-growing subshrub forming patches, st. creeping or ascending, with persistent dead lvs. Lvs to 18cm, in rosettes, narrow-oblong to elliptic, leathery, viscid, tomentose beneath, sinuate, petiole narrow. Cap. to 4cm diam., on a slender, flexuous scape to 10cm; ray flts 1.5cm. NZ.

C. lyallii Hook. f. Tufted perenn. herb, with pseudostems to 6cm. Lvs to 15cm, linear, entire, glab. above, grooved, tomentose or glab. beneath, narrowed to a tomentose sheath. Cap. to 5cm diam., on a slender, somewhat floccose scape; ray flts to 1.2cm. NZ.

C. lyallii var. *pseudolyallii* Cheesem. = *C.* ×*pseudolyallii*.

C. mackanii Raoul. Tufted perenn. herb, producing offsets from short rhiz. Lvs to 50cm, lanceolate, glab., blue-green above, pale beneath, entire, petiole widening to sheath. Cap. to 5cm diam., on a stout scape to 60cm, with amplexicaul bracts; ray flts sometimes flushed pink. NZ.

C. major Cheesem. Perenn. herb, with pseudostem to 6cm. Lvs to 40cm, tufted, linear, leathery, tomentose beneath, revolute. Cap. to 4cm diam., on a stout scape to 20cm; ray flts to 2cm, slender. NZ.

C. monroi Hook. f. Tufted perenn. herb with pseudostem to 15cm. Lvs to 15cm, lanceolate- to oblong-elliptic, leathery, sulcate, tomentose beneath; petiole tapered to floccose sheath. Cap. to 4cm diam., on a stout floccose scape to 25cm; ray flts to 2cm, slender. NZ.

C. petriei Cheesem. Stout, tufted perenn. herb, with st. clothed in imbricate sheaths. Lvs to 50cm, linear-lanceolatte, leathery, rigid, ribbed above, tomentose beneath. Cap. to 4cmm diam., on a stout floccose scape to 50cm; ray flts to 2cm, narrowly oblong. NZ.

C. prorepens Petrie. Perenn. herb, with st. base clothed in dead lvs and creeping rooting br. Lvs to 8cm, in apical rosettes, elliptic, leathery, strongly wrinkled, petiolate. Cap. to 4cm diam., on stout, angled, viscid scapes to 20cm; ray flts to 2cm. NZ.

C. ×*pseudolyallii* (Cheesem.) Ckn. (*C. lyalii* ×*C. spectabilis* ?) Like *C. lyallii* but lvs to 20–30cm, usually erect, less rigid, thickly tomentose beneath; cap. somewhat floccose. NZ.

C. ramulosa Hook. f. Small shrub or subshrub with stout, procumbent or ascending, branched st., to 20cm. Lvs to 1cm, linear-oblong, leathery, imbricate, glab. above, tomentose beneath, revolute. Cap. to 2.5cm diam., on a slender, glandular-pubesc. scape to 4cm; ray flts narrow. NZ.

C. rigida (T. Kirk) Ckn. = *C. verbascifolia* ssp. *rigida*.

C. sinclairii Hook. f. Small subshrub, br. numerous, ascending to spreading, clothed in dead lvs. Lvs 7cm, in apical rosettes, obovate to elliptic-spathulate, bright green, glab., petiole tapered to sheath. Cap. to 4cm diam., on a slender scape to 15cm; ray flts to 1.2cm, narrow. NZ.

C. spectabilis Hook. f. Rhizomatous perenn. herb, producing large patches, with imbricate lf sheaths forming pseudostems. Lvs to 25cm, ovate to narrowly oblong, leathery, tomentose beneath, entire, petiole tapered to sheath. Cap. to 5cm diam., on a stout, floccose scape to 25cm; ray flts to 2cm, narrow-obovate. NZ.

C. traversii Hook. f. Tuft-forming, perenn. herb, st. clothed in imbricate lf sheaths. Lvs to 40cm, oblong to sublanceolate, glab. above, tomentose, with prominent purple midrib beneath; petiole purple, sheath floccose. Cap. to 5cm diam., on a stout, tomentose scape to 50cm; ray flts to 2cm. NZ.

C. verbascifolia Hook. f. Large, tufted perenn. herb, with st. clothed in imbricate lf sheaths. Lvs to 25cm, oblong-lanceolate to elliptic-ovate, tomentose beneath, margins inrolled; petiole tapered to tomentose sheath. Cap. to 5cm diam., on a stout, sulcate, floccose scape to 40cm; ray flts to 2cm. NZ. ssp. *rigida* (T. Kirk) Given. Lvs to 15cm, scape to 20cm.

C. vernicosa Hook. f. Mat-forming, stoloniferous perenn. herb. Lvs to 10cm, imbricate, in dense rosette 5 to 10cm diam., leathery, glossy green, hard, stiff, glab., revolute. Cap. to 4cm diam., on rigid, sulcate scapes to 25cm; ray flts 1.5cm. NZ.

C. viscosa Hook. f. Stout subshrub, br. numerous, forming patches. Lvs to 15cm, in apical rosettes, linear to narrow-oblong, bright green above, tomentose beneath, toothed. Cap. to 4cm diam., on a stout, glandular-pubesc. scape to 30cm; ray flts to 2cm. NZ.

C. walkeri T. Kirk. Sprawling shrub, with st. to 2m, lf sheaths persistent. Lvs to 5cm, narrow-oblong, leathery, glab. above, tomentose beneath, slightly toothed, tapered to sheath. Cap. to 4cm diam., on a long, slender scape to 20cm; ray flts to 0.6cm. NZ.

→*Aster*.

Celosia L. COCKSCOMB; WOOLFLOWER. Amaranthaceae. 50 ann. or perenn. herbs. Fls v. small, silky in plumose or cristate crowded cymes; perianth seg. 5, scarious. Trop. and subtrop. Asia, Afr., Amer. Z9.

C. argentea L. RED FOX. Ann., erect to 2m. Lvs 2–15cm, linear-lanceolate to lanceolate-ovate. Fls silver-white in spicate cymes. Trop. var. *cristata* (L.) Kuntze. COMMON COCKSCOMB. St. glab., to 20cm. Br. terminated by large, red or yellow, fasciated, cristate or plumose inflorescences. A tetraploid cultigen giving rise to numerous cvs classified in groups. Since dwarf forms occur in each of these the name 'Nana' has not been retained as a collective label. **Childsii group**: bearing globose term. bosses of fls. **Cristata group** (infl. term., broad, flattened and cristate): Big Chef Mixed: to 1m; infl. large, to 15cm diam., cauliflower-shaped; Jewel Box Mixed: infl. crested, 12.5cm diam., deep red, gold, yellow, pink, salmon; 'Jewel Box Red Dark Leaf': lvs deep bronze; infl. 10cm diam., dark red; 'Jewel Box Improved': dwarf; infl. 13cm diam., velvety orange, rose or red. 'Dwarf Fairy Fountain': habit compact, branching; infl. red, pink, and yellow, long-lasting; 'Toreador': infl. to 30cm, red. **Plumosa group** (infl. erect, tapering, plumose): 'Apricot Brandy': habit dwarf, compact; spikes 17.5cm, apricot-orange; Century Series: infl. extra large, to 30cm, red, yellow, rose, cream; Fairy Fountains Mix: habit freely branching; spikes 10–12.5cm, red, orange; 'Forest Fire': lvs maroon; spikes 15cm, bright scarlet; Geisha Series: habit v. dwarf; spikes heavy, dwarf, orange, salmon, yellow, red; Kewpie Series: habit bushy, extremely dwarf; infl. yellow, orange, rose, red; 'New Look': lvs deep bronze; infl. feathery, intense scarlet; 'Pink Castle': fls striking rose-pink. **Spicata group**: infl. metallic pink or yellow in slender heads.

C. cristata L. = *C. argentea* var. *cristata*.

C. debilis S. Moore = *C. argentea*.

C. floribunda A. Gray. Much-branched glab. shrub to 4m, green or glaucous. Lvs to 20cm, triangular, glab. Spikes tight, 2–15×0.4cm, aggregating in dense pan. 7–25cm long. S Calif.

C. huttonii Mart. Bushy ann., to 1.5m. Lvs lanceolate. Spikes cylindrical, oblong, red, to 3cm. Java.

C. splendens Schum. & Thonn. = *C. argentea*.

Celsia L.

C. atroviolacea Somm. & Lév. = *Verbascum phoeniceum*.

C. rechingeri Murb. = *Verbascum phoeniceum*.

Celtis L. NETTLE TREE; HACKBERRY. Ulmaceae. 70+ trees or shrubs, mostly decid. Lvs alt., entire or serrate. Fls unisexual, inconspicuous, usually green; cal. 5-lobed, cor. 0. Fr. drupaceous, 1(–3), somewhat fleshy, c1cm diam., ovoid-globose, on a slender stalk. Trop., SE Eur., N Amer.

C. australis L. MEDITERRANEAN HACKBERRY; EUROPEAN NETTLE TREE; LOTE TREE. To 20m, bark grey, smooth, young twigs pubesc. Lvs 5–15cm, lanceolate to ovate-lanceolate, acuminate, serrate, hirsute, rough, dark green above, green-green, downy beneath. Fr. red becoming brown. Medit., Middle E, widely introd. Z6.

C. berlandieri Klotzsch = *C. laevigata*.

C. biondii Pamp. Tree to shrub to 15m; new growth downy; bark smooth, grey. Lvs 3–10cm, ovate to ovate-oblong, acuminate, entire or serrate above, yellow-green. Fr. orange. C China. var. *cavalieriei* (Lév.) Schneid. New growth rusty pubesc. Lvs coriaceous, ovate-oblong, silky. W China. var. *heterophylla* (Lév.) Schneid. Lvs obovate then truncate with a distinct caudate point, v. coriaceous, smaller toward br. tip. Korea. Z5.

C. bungeana Bl. To 15m, crown rounded; bark smooth, dark grey. Lvs 5–8cm, ovate to ovate-lanceolate, acuminate, dark glossy green above, glabrescent beneath. Fr. black. C & N Asia. Z5.

C. bungeana var. *heterophylla* Lév. = *C. biondii* var. *heterophylla*.

C. canina Raf. = *C. occidentalis* var. *canina*.

C. caucasica Willd. CAUCASIAN NETTLE TREE. Tree to 25mm; bark grey; young twigs downy. Lvs 5–9cm, obovate to ovate-lanceolte, dentate, acuminate, becoming glab. except for tufts in vein axils beneath. Fr. yellow to rust. Cauc., Asia Minor to Afghan. Z6.

C. cavalieriei Lév. = *C. biondii* var. *cavalieriei*.

C. crassifolia (Lam.) A. Gray = *C. occidentalis* var. *cordata*.

C. davidiana Carr. = *C. bungeana*.

C. glabrata Planch. Small tree or shrub; crown rounded; young twigs minutely downy. Lvs 2–5cm, ovate, basally asymmetric, acuminate, coarsely serrate, dark green, scabrous and warted above, paler and smoother beneath. Fr. rust brown. Cauc., Asia Minor. Z6.

C. integrifolia Lam. Tree, everg.; br. somewhat pubesc., crooked. Lvs 5–6cm, ovate to ovate-cordate, entire, short-pubesc. Senegal. Z9.

C. japonica Planch. = *C. sinensis*.

C. koraiensis Nak. Tree to bush to 12m, bark dark grey; shoots glab. Lvs 5–15cm, obovate to oval, denticulate, dark grey-green and glab. above, pubesc. on veins beneath; midrib often extended to form a lobe. Fr. dull orange. Korea, N China, Manch. Z5.

C. labilis Schneid. Tree to 17m; bark pale grey, smooth; young twigs tinged yellow, downy. Lvs to 10cm, ovate to ovate-lanceolate, coarsely serrate ± coriaceous, slenderly acuminate, dark glossy green above, paler and downy veins beneath. Fr. orange. C China. Z6.

C. laevigata Willd. SUGARBERRY. Tree to 30m; crown broad; bark light grey, warty; young shoots downy. Lvs 5–10cm, ovate to ovate-lanceolate, 5–10cm entire or sparsely serrate, acuminate, dark green above, lighter and sparsely pubesc. on veins beneath. Fr. orange-red ripening to black. S US. var. *smallii* (Beadle) Sarg. Lvs sharply serrate. SE US. var. *texana* (Scheele) Sarg. Young shoots pubesc. Lvs to 7cm, coriaceous. S US. Z5.

C. mississippiensis Bosc = *C. laevigata*.

C. occidentalis L. HACKBERRY. Tree to 25m; crown broad; bark grey, rough to warty. Lvs to 12cm, ovate-lanceolate to broadly ovate, acuminate, round to cordate at base, sharply serrate, glossy green above, smooth and slightly pubesc. on veins beneath. Fr. tinged yellow or red ripening to deep purple. N Amer. var. *canina* (Raf.) Sarg. Lvs narrower, oblong-ovate, light green beneath. var. *cordata* (Pers.) Willd. Lvs larger, cordate thick. S US. var. *pumila* (Muhlenb.) Pursh. Lvs smaller, ovate-oblong, downy becoming glab. Z2.

C. pumila Pursh. = *C. occidentalis* var. *pumila*.

C. reticulata Torr. Tree or shrub, to 12m; young twigs downy. Lvs to 10cm, oblique-ovate, rounded or cordate at base, acute, serrate above, or entire, coriaceous, rough and bright green above, darker with downy veins beneath. Fr. red-orange. SW US. Z6.

C. sinensis Pers. JAPANESE HACKBERRY. To 15m; young shoots punctate, pubesc. Lvs to 8cm, oblong to ovate, acuminate, serrate, coriaceous, glab., dark green above, duller beneath. Fr. dark orange. E Asia. Z9.

C. smallii Beadle = *C. laevigata* var. *smallii*.

C. texana Scheele = *C. laevigata* var. *texana*.

C. tournefortii Lam. Small decid. tree or shrub to 8m. Lvs 3–6cm, ovate-acuminate, coarse blunt-serrate, grey-green above, pubesc. beneath. Sicily, Balk., Turk., Crimea. Z7.

C. trinervia Lam. Tree; young br. grey, slightly pubesc. Lvs 5–6cm, ovate to ovate-oblong, acuminate, serrate, glab. except veins beneath, with 3 nerves from base. St Domingo.

C. willdenowiana Schult. = *C. sinensis*.

Cenchrus L. Gramineae. 22 ann. or perenn. grasses. St. slender. Lvs narrow, scabrous; sheath loose, keeled; ligules ciliate. Spikes cylindric; rachis angled; spikelets solitary or clustered, lanceolate to ovate, to 8 per cluster, enclosed by spines or soft bristles. Afr., N Amer., India. Z9.

C. ciliaris L. BUFFEL GRASS. Perenn. to 90cm. Lvs to 30×0.4cm. Infl. dense, to 15×1.6cm, pale green or tinged purple; spikelets surrounded by bristles, inner bristles densely ciliate. Afr. to India.

→*Pennisetum*.

Centaurea L. KNAPWEED; STAR THISTLE. Compositae. *c*450 ann. to perenn. herbs or subshrubs. Cap. discoid, solitary or clustered at br. apices; involucre cylindrical to globose; phyllaries often with a fimbriate or spiny apical appendage; flts tubular, usually deeply lobed, outer sometimes enlarged and radiate. Mostly Medit., also Near E, N Eurasia, N Amer. and Aus.

C. aggregata Fisch. & Mey. ex DC. Perenn., erect to 80cm. Lvs lyrate, lat. seg. in 2–5 opposite pairs, narrowly lanceolate, term. seg. large, lanceolate, lower lvs occas. simple. Cap. in small clusters of 3–5; involucre to 13×5mm, subcylindric, flts purple. Summer. Transcauc., N Iran and N Iraq. Z6.

C. alpestris Hegetschw. Perenn., to 50cm. Lvs pinnatifid, rarely undivided, seg. narrowly elliptic to ovate, obtuse, crenate-dentate. Involucre to 4cm diam., ovoid-globose; flts purple. Mts of C & S Eur. Z6.

C. alpina L. Perenn. erect to 80cm. Lvs pinnate, lower to 35cm, seg. oblong- to linear-lanceolate, often deeply bifid, often serrate near apex. Involucre to 2cm diam., ovoid; flts pale yellow. Summer. S Alps, SE Spain and C Balk. Z6.

C. americana Nutt. Ann., to 1m. Lvs to 10cm, lanceolate to lanceolate-oblong, entire or sparsely dentate, sessile, scabrous or somewhat glandular-punctate. Involucre to 4cm high; flts purple. Summer. SC to SE US. Z4.

C. argentea L. Perenn., erect to 50cm, white-tomentose. Lvs pinnatisect, lower lvs lyrate, seg. oblong, silvery-pubesc. Involucre to 10×7mm, ovoid; flts pale yellow. Summer. Crete. Z8.

C. aspera L. Subshrub, to 50cm. Lvs entire to sinuate-dentate, mucronate, base sometimes auriculate, green, scabrid. Involucre to 2.2cm diam., ovoid to globose; phyllaries tinged pink; flts purple. SW to SC Eur. ssp. *stenophylla* (Dufour) Nyman. Lvs green- to grey-tomentose, lower pinnatifid to deeply dentate. Involucre to 1.5cm diam., ovoid. E Spain, S Port. Z8.

C. atrata Willd. = *C. triumfettii*.

C. atropurpurea Waldst. & Kit. Perenn., to 2m. Lvs pinnatisect, seg. to 3mm wide, rarely wider. Involucre to 3m diam., globose; flts dark purple, rarely yellow. Summer. C Balk., Rom. Z6.

C. austriaca Rchb. = *C. phrygia*.

C. babylonica (L.) L. Bienn. to 3m, erect, grey-tomentose. Lvs lanceolate, repand-dentate to entire, decurrent in broad wings, basal lvs lyrate. Cap. numerous, clustered in an elongate spike; involucre to 2.3×1.5cm; flts yellow. Summer. NE Turk. to Leb. Z6.

C. behen L. Perenn., to 1.5m. Lower lvs to 18cm wide, lyrate to pinnately lobed, petiolate, seg. lanceolate, firm, apparently glab. Cap. numerous; involucre to 2.5×2cm; flts yellow. Summer. Turk. to Leb., Transcauc. and Iran. Z6.

C. bella Trautv. Perenn., to 40cm, forming broad, low cushions. St. arachnoid. Lvs to 12cm, lyrate-pinnatifid, white-tomentose beneath. Cap. to 4.5cm diam.; flts lavender pink to pale purple, outer enlarged. Cauc. Z6.

C. cana hort. = *C. triumfettii*.

C. candidissima hort. = *C. cineraria*.

C. chilensis Hook. & Arn. = *Plectocephalus chilensis*.

C. cineraria L. Perenn., to 90cm, sometimes procumbent. Lvs lyrate to bipinnatisect, seg. elliptic to lanceolate, somewhat tomentose. Cap. fairy small, solitary; flts purple. W & S It. Z4.

C. clementei Boiss. ex DC. Perenn., to 50cm, lanate. Lvs pinnatisect, broadly ovate, dentate, irregularly lobed, petiolate, white-tomentose. Involucre to 2.5cm diam., globose; flts yellow. Summer. Mts of SW Spain. Z6.

C. conifera L. = *Leuzea conifera*.

C. crupina L. = *Crupina vulgaris*.

C. cyanus L. CORNFLOWER; BLUE-BOTTLE. Ann. to bienn., to 90cm. Lvs lanceolate, entire, remotely dentate or lyrate-pinnatisect, acute, petiolate, floccose beneath at first. Involucre to 13mm diam., ovoid-globose; flts violet-blue, outer dark blue, white or purple. Summer. N temp. regions.

C. cynaroides Link. = *Leuzea centauroides*.

C. dealbata Willd. Perenn. to 1m. St. erect, branched. Lvs pinnatisect, long-petiolate, grey-tomentose beneath. Cap. nestled among upper lvs; involucre to 4cm diam.; flts bright pink. Summer. Cauc. Z3.

C. debeauxii Gren. & Godron. Perenn., to 90cm. Lvs ovate to narrowly lanceolate, entire to pinnatifid, scabrid to pale grey arachnoid-pubesc. Cap. usually solitary; involucre to 1.5×1.5cm, ovoid cylindric to globose; flts orange, tinged pink. W Eur. ssp. *nemoralis* (Jordan) Dostál. Lvs bright green. Z7.

C. depressa Bieb. Ann. to bienn. to 60cm. Lvs oblong, entire, occas. lyrate-pinnatisect, obtuse, shortly petiolate, grey-tomentose. Involucre to 12mm diam., ovoid; inner flts violet, outer dark blue. Summer. SW & C Asia. Z7.

C. diffusa Lam. Ann. or bienn., to 50cm. Lvs bipinnatisect, green, somewhat arachnoid. Cap. solitary; involucre to 1×0.5cm, ovoid-cylindric; flts pink. Summer. Medit.

C. fritschii Hayek = *C. grinensis* ssp. *fritschii*.

C. glastifolia L. Perenn., to 90cm. Lvs lanceolate, entire, petiolate, scabrous, sometimes arachnoid, st. lvs narrower. Involucre to 3cm diam., subglobose; flts yellow. Summer. Transcauc., Turk. Z6.

C. grinensis Reut. Perenn., to 1m. St. simple or branched, glab. to floccose. Lvs pinnatifid or entire, floccose, becoming glab., scabrid on lower veins. Involucre ovoid; flts purple. SC Eur., W Balk. ssp. *fritschii* (Hayek) Dostál. To 2m. St. corymbosely branched. Lf seg. oblong-lanceolate. Involucre to 18mm diam.; phyllary appendages with 5–7, not 3–5, fimbriae each side. Czech. to Bulg. and Albania. Z6.

C. gymnocarpa Morris = *C. cineraria*.

C. hypoleuca DC. Perenn., to 50cm. Lvs variable, basal lvs rosulate, elliptic-lanceolate, lyrate, term. seg. ovate-lanceolate, lat. seg. few, small, or pinnatipartite with seg. in to 9 pairs, irregularly dentate to entire, green and sparsely arachnoid above, grey- to white-tomentose beneath. Involucre to 2×2cm, subglobose; flts pink. Late spring–summer. W Transcauc., Turk., N Iran. Z5.

C. iberica Trev. ex Spreng. Bienn., to 1m. Lvs runcinate- to lyrate-pinnatisect, lobes ovate to linear-lanceolate, minutely dentate and setulose, minutely hispid, upper lvs lanceolate. Cap. subsessile, among upper lvs; involucre to 1.5cm diam., ovoid; flts deep purple. Summer. Balk. to SW & C Asia. Z6.

C. imperialis Hausskn. ex Bornm. Perenn. or bienn., to 50cm. Basal lvs large, oblong, entire, obtuse, tapered to petiole, often arachnoid-lanate, st. lvs oblong-lanceolate, entire, sessile. Cap. to 3.5cm diam.; flts rose-pink. Summer. Mts of Iran & Iraq. Z7.

C. imperialis hort. = *Amberboa moschata*.

C. jacea L. Perenn., to 1.5cm. Lvs ovate to broadly lanceolate, entire, dentate or pinnately lobed, usually decurrent, green, scabrid on margins and beneath, hairy. Cap. in corymbose clusters; involucre to 18×12mm, ovoid; flts purple, rarely white. Summer. Eur., W Russia. Z6.

C. kopetaghensis Iljin. Perenn., to 50cm. Lvs oblong, ± entire. Cap. to 1.5cm diam., solitary; involucre ovoid to oblong-ovoid; flts yellow. S Russia. Z6.

C. kotschyana Heuff. ex Koch. Perenn., to 1m. Lvs lyrate-pinnatisect, seg. oblong to linear-lanceolate, dentate or lobed, crispate-hairy. Involucre to 3cm diam., ovoid to globose; flts dark purple. Balk. Z5.

C. leucophylla Bieb. Perenn., to 30cm. Lvs pinnatisect, seg. obtuse, st. lvs lyrate, green tinged with white above, grey-tomentose beneath. Involucre to 1.5cm diam.; flts pink to purple. Summer. Cauc. Z6.

C. macrocephala Pushk. ex Willd. Perenn., to 1m. Lvs to 6cm wide, broadly lanceolate, sessile, shortly decurrent, minutely pubesc., lower lvs petiolate. Cap. enveloped by upper lvs; involucre to 5.5cm diam., hemispheric; flts orange-yellow. Summer. Cauc. Z3.

C. maculosa Lam. Bienn., to 60cm. Lvs bipinnatisect, seg. lanceolate, arachnoid tomentose to glab. Cap. solitary; involucre to 1.5×1.5cm; flts pink. E Eur. Z6.

C. margaritae hort. = *Amberboa moschata*.

C. maritima Dufour = *C. seridis* ssp. *maritima*.

C. marschalliana Spreng. Perenn., to 20cm. Basal lvs pinnatisect, petiolate, seg. oblong, to 12cm, lower lvs entire, middle lvs lyrate, upper lvs entire. Involucre to 1.5cm diam., ovoid; flts purple, tinged pink. NE Bulg. to E Ukraine. Z5.

C. montana L. PERENNIAL CORNFLOWER. Perenn., to 80cm. Lvs ovate to broadly lanceolate, entire, lower lvs sometimes remotely dentate to lobed, soft, patent, floccose-tomentose beneath at first. Involucre to 1.5cm diam., ovoid-cylindric; inner flts violet, outer blue, spreading. Early summer. Mts of Eur. Z3.

C. moschata L. = *Amberboa moschata*.

C. muricata L. = *Cyanopsis muricata*.

C. nervosa Willd. = *C. uniflora* ssp. *nervosa*.

C. nigra L. LESSER KNAPWEED. Perenn., to 1m. Lvs ovate to lanceolate, entire, dentate or lobed, upper lvs lanceolate, entire, green- to grey-arachnoid-pubesc. Cap. solitary or clustered at br. apices; involucre to 18×20mm, globose; flts purple. Summer. NW to C Eur. Z5.

C. orientalis L. Perenn., to 1.2m. Lvs mostly pinnatisect, seg. narrowly oblong to linear, entire or lobed, scabrid at first, becoming glab., lower lvs entire. Involucre to 2.5cm diam., globose; flts cream. Summer. SE Eur. to W Asia. Z7.

C. phrygia L. Perenn., to 1.2m. Lvs lanceolate to ovate, entire or dentate, acute or acuminate, middle lvs acute, base rounded at base or amplexicaul, green to sparsely grey-arachnoid-tomentose. Cap. usually solitary; involucre to 2×2cm, ovoid to globose; flts pink to purple, outer usually longer. Summer. Eur. Z6.

C. pindicola Griseb. Perenn., to 20cm, with short rhiz. Lvs to 5cm, lyrate-pinnatisect, petiolate, lat. lobes in 2–3, opposite pairs, entire or weakly dentate. Cap. to 2cm diam., solitary; involucre ovoid; flts cream. Mts of SW Balk. Z6.

C. polypodiifolia Boiss. Bienn. or perenn., 80cm. Basal lvs pinnatifid, seg. in 6–8 pairs, linear-lanceolate, acute, prominently veined, crisped-hairy, lower lvs pinnatilobate, middle lvs ovate-oblong, broadly decurrent, glab., upper lvs ovate to lanceolate. Cap. clustered in a corymb; involucre to 22×17mm; flts yellow. Summer. Transcauc., N Iran, Iraq. var. *szovitsiana* (Boiss.) Wagenitz. Lf margins scabrous, upper lvs narrowly lanceolate. Involucre to 28×20mm; flts pale yellow. Turk. to Armenia. Z7.

C. pulcherrima Willd. Perenn., to 40cm. Basal lvs rosulate, narrowly lanceolate and dentate to lyrate with large term. lobe, lat. seg. in 1–2 pairs, or pinnatipartite, slightly tomentose to glabrescent above, adpressed grey-tomentose beneath, middle and upper lvs few, sessile, small, often entire. Involucre to 2.5×2.5cm, subglobose; flts rose-purple. Summer. Transcauc. Z6.

C. pulchra DC. = *C. depressa*.

C. putiola hort. = *C. rutifolia*.

C. ragusina L. Perenn., to 60cm, white-tomentose. Lvs pinnatisect, petiolate, seg. ovate to oblong, obtuse, entire or sinuate-dentate or lobed. Involucre to 2.5cm diam., globose; flts yellow. Summer. W Balk. Z7.

C. rhapontica L. = *Leuzea rhapontica*.

C. rothrockii Greenman. Ann., to 1m, usually glab. Lvs to 12cm, lanceolate to oblong-lanceolate, sessile, often semi-amplexicaul. Cap. to 1.5cm diam., solitary; inner flts yellow, outer purple to pink, longer. N Mex., SC & SW US. Z6.

C. ruthenica Lam. Perenn., to 1.5m. Lvs ovate-oblong, pinnate, broadly decurrent, serrate, seg. linear-lanceolate, to 25cm, deep green, glab., lower lvs pinnatipartite. Involucre to 2cm diam., cylindric-ovoid; flts pale yellow. S Russia, to C Rom. Z3.

C. rutifolia Sibth. & Sm. Perenn., to 90cm. Lvs 1–2-pinnatisect, white-tomentose. Cap. solitary; involucre to 13×7mm, ovoid; flts pink. Summer. SE Eur. Z7.

C. scabiosa L. GREATER KNAPWEED. Perenn., to 1.5m. Lvs pinnatisect, or entire to dentate, seg. oblong to linear, entire to dentate or lobed, scabrid, petiolate, upper lvs pinnatisect, sessile. Involucre to 2.5cm diam., ovoid-globose; flts purple. Summer. Eur. Z4.

C. seridis L. Perenn., to 80cm. St. winged. Lvs entire to pinnatisect, petiolate, minutely hispid, lower sinuately lobed, upper lvs pinnately lobed, usually decurrent. Cap. solitary, among upper lvs; involucre to 2.5cm diam., ovoid to sub-globose; flts purple. S & SE Spain. ssp. *maritima* (Dufour) Dostál. Lvs dentate, mucronate, lower lyrate-pinnatifid, upper lvs auriculate-semi-amplexicaul. S & SE Spain. Z8.

C. simplicicaulis Boiss. & Huet. Perenn., to 40cm. Basal lvs to 1.5cm wide, pinnatisect to lyrate, seg. elliptic to orbicular, green, sparsely tomentose above, densely adpressed grey-tomentose beneath, st. lvs pinnatipartite, seg. linear-lanceolate. Involucre to 19×14mm; flts rose. Late spring–summer. Transcauc. Z4.

C. stenolepis A. Kerner. Perenn., to 1m. Lvs entire, ovate to lanceolate, cuneate, base rounded or cordate, or semi-amplexicaul, tomentose, lower lvs petiolate, denticulate and acuminate. Cap. solitary, or in clusters at br. apices; involucre oblong or cylindric-ovoid; flts orange, tinged pink. Summer. C Eur., Balk., Turk. and S Russia. Z5.

C. stenophylla Dufour = *C. aspera* ssp. *stenophylla*.

C. stricta Waldst. & Kit. = *C. triumfettii* ssp. *stricta*.

C. suaveolens Willd. = *Amberboa moschata*.

C. szovitsiana Boiss. = *C. polypodiifolia* var. *szovitsiana*.

C. triumfettii All. Perenn., to 70cm. Lvs oblong to lanceolate,

lower petiolate, usually tomentose or lanate at first. Involucre to 2.5cm diam., ovoid to ovoid-globose or cylindric; inner flts violet, outer blue. Early summer. S & C Eur. to W Asia. ssp. *stricta* (Waldst. & Kit.) Dostál. Lvs narrowly lanceolate, entire or occas. 1–2-dentate, grey-tomentose. Involucre ovoid. EC Eur., N Balk. Z5.

C. uliginosa Brot. = *Cheirolophus uliginosus*.

C. uniflora Turra. Perenn., to 20cm. Lvs entire, green- to grey-lanate, lower lvs oblong-lanceolate, ovate or elliptic, long-attenuate to petiole; middle lvs entire to dentate, truncate, base auriculate or narrowed, upper lvs linear-lanceolate, entire, acuminate. Involucre to 2.5cm diam., ovoid-cylindric to sub-globose; flts violet, occas. white. Summer. Mts of C & SE Eur. ssp. *nervosa* (Willd.) Bonnier & Layens. Upper lvs narrowly elliptic, base truncate, hastate or auriculate-amplexicaul, dentate to sinuate-dentate, green, minutely pubesc. Involucre to 2cm diam.; flts deep purple. Summer. Z4.

→*Chartolepis* and *Serratula*.

Centaurium Hill. CENTAURY. Gentianaceae. *c*30 slender, ann., bienn. or perenn. herbs. St. solitary or several, erect, simple or branched. Lvs usually basal and rosulate and opposite on st., ovate-elliptic to oblong-lanceolate. Infl. flat-topped, cymose; cal. 4–5-lobed; cor. 4–5-lobed. Most N hemis., 1 sp. Chile, 1 sp. Aus. Z8.

C. beyrichii (Torr. & A. Gray) Robinson. To 20cm. Fls deep pink, to 2.5cm. US (Ark. to Tex.).

C. chloodes (Brot.) Gren. & Godron = *C. confertum*.

C. confertum (Pers.) Druce. To 10cm. Fls rose-pink to 1cm. S Eur.

C. floribundum (Benth.) Robinson. To 50cm. Fls pink 1.2cm. Calif.

C. massonii hort. = *C. scilloides*.

C. portense Brot. ex Butch. = *C. scilloides*.

C. scilloides (L. f.) Samp. Tufted perenn. with decumbent non-flowering shoots, to 7.5cm+, erect or semi-prostrate. Fls bright pink, or deep rose-pink to white. W Eur., Azores.

C. venustum (A. Gray) Robinson. Ann. 15–50cm. Fls to 2.5cm diam., pink usually with red spots on white throat. Calif.

→*Erythraea*.

Centaury *Centaurium*.

Centipede Grass *Eremochloa ophiuroides*.

Centipede Plant *Homalocladium*.

Centradenia G. Don. Melastomataceae. 4 everg. herbs or sub-shrubs. Lvs opposite in unequal pairs, entire, 3-veined. Fls in term. or axill. pan. or rac. C Amer. Z9.

C. floribunda Planch. Small shrub; st. obscurely angled, wiry, pubesc., red. Lvs 2.5–5cm, lanceolate, tinted red beneath. Pan. term., 4–10cm; fls lilac-pink beneath, white above. Spring. Guat., Mex.

C. grandifolia (Schldl.) Endl. Shrub to 60cm; br. 4-winged. Lvs 7.5–15cm, oblong-lanceolate, curved, minutely ciliate, bright red beneath, apex long-acuminate. Cyme many-fld, shorter than lvs; fls light rose. Autumn. Mex.

C. inaequilateralis G. Don. To 30cm. Lvs ovate-lanceolate, oblique, ciliate, tinged red beneath. Rac. term. subcorymbose; fls pink. Winter. Mex.

C. ovata Klotzsch. To 1m. St. erect. Lvs ovate, glab., pale and glossy beneath. Cyme many-fld, term., trichotomous; fls pink. C Amer.

C. rosea (Lindl.). = *C. inaequilateralis*.

C. 'Starsprite'. Dwarf; lvs v. small, sickle-shaped; fls light pink, abundant.

Central American Banyan *Ficus pertusa*.

Central American Strap Fern *Campyloneurum augustifolium*.

Central Australian Fan Palm *Livistona mariae*.

Centranthus Necker ex DC. Valerianaceae. 12 ann. or perenn. herbs or subshrubs. Flowering st. erect. Lvs opposite. Infl. cymose, dense, term.; fls small; cor. funnel-form, base spurred, lobes 5 unequal. Eur., Medit.

C. ruber (L.) DC. RED VALERIAN; JUPITER'S BEARD; FOX'S BRUSH. To 80cm. Lvs to 8cm, ovate or lanceolate, slightly toothed to entire, amplexicaul, glaucous. Fls *c*1.25cm, fragrant, crimson to pale red. Eur. and N Afr. to Asia Minor. 'Albus': fls white. 'Atrococcineus': fls deep red. 'Roseus': fls rose.

→*Kentranthus* and *Valeriana*.

Centratherum Cass. Compositae. *c*20 ann. to perenn. herbs and subshrubs. Cap. discoid, solitary or few in clusters; outermost phyllaries leafy; flts red-purple. Pantrop. Z10.

C. intermedium Less. = *C. punctatum*.

C. punctatum Cass. Sprawling to erect, perenn. herb or subshrub. Lvs to 8cm, oval to elliptic, spathulate or rhombic, serrate or lobed, ciliate, glandular-punctate. Cap. solitary. Trop. S & C Amer., W Indies.

Centropogon C. Presl. Campanulaceae. *c*230 herbs and shrubs. Lvs toothed. Fls solitary or paniculate; cor. tube bilabiate, elongate; anth. tube exserted entire. Trop. Amer., W Indies. Z10.

C. austin-smithii Standl. = *C. solanifolius*.

C. coccineus Reg. Glab. shrub to 90cm. Lvs ovate, lobed, biserrulate. Fls pendulous, crimson. Braz.

C. cordifolius Decne. To 60cm. Lvs cordate. Fls pale pink. Autumn. Guat.

C. fastuosus Scheidw. To 6cm. Lvs ovate-acuminate, shallowly dentate. Fls pale pink. Autumn. Mex.

C. ×lucyanus Houll. (*C. fastuosus × Siphocampylus betulifolius?*) Trailing. Lvs linear-lanceolate. Fls rose to claret, tubular, with lat. spurs. Winter.

C. solanifolius Benth. Herb or shrub to 1.5m. Lvs to 12cm, ovate to elliptic. Fls scarlet with yellow tinged lobes. Costa Rica, Venez., S to Ecuad.

C. surinamensis Presl. To 60cm. Lvs to 7cm, narrowly ovate, dentate. Fls pastel pink. Autumn. Surinam.

C. tovarensis Planch. & Lind. Lvs narrow ovate-acuminate. Fls bright pink. Winter. Venez.

Centrosema (DC.) Benth. Leguminosae (Papilionoideae). *c*45 perenn. herbs or shrubs. Lvs 3(–5)-. Fls pea-like turned upwards in axill. rac. Americas.

C. grandiflorum hort. non Benth. = *C. virginianum*.

C. virginianum (L.) Benth. BUTTERFLY PEA; CONCHITA. Perenn. St. sprawling or twining. Lfts to 5cm, oblong-ovate, coarse pubesc. Fls 2.5cm, violet to off-white, 1–4 in clusters. Summer. Trop. Amer., SE US, Afr. Z6.

Century Plant *Agave*.

Cephaelis Sw.

C. ipecacuanha (Brot.) A. Rich. = *Psychotria ipecacuanha*.

C. peduncularis Salisb. = *Psychotria peduncularis*.

Cephalanthera Rich. Orchidaceae. 12 rhizomatous terrestrial herbaceous orchids. St. erect, leafy. Fls few on lax spike; tep. hooded; lip constricted midway, basal portion incurved, sheathing base of column, apical portion spreading with longitudinal ridges or callus. Late spring–early summer. Temp. Eur., Asia, N Afr.

C. damasonium (Mill.) Druce WHITE HELLEBORINE. To 60cm. Lvs 4–10cm, ovate-lanceolate. Fls white or cream, narrowly campanulate; lip golden yellow at base, apex with to 5 golden ridges. N & C Eur., N Afr., Russia. Z6.

C. falcata (Thunb.) Bl. 30–80cm. Lvs 8–15cm, broad-lanceolate. Fls yellow. Jap., Korea, China. Z8.

C. floribunda Woron. = *C. kurdica*.

C. grandiflora Gray = *C. damasonium*.

C. kurdica Bornm. To 70cm. Lvs broad-lanceolate to elliptic. Fls rose-pink; sep. spreading; lip pale rose at base, midlobe white. Eur., Medit., Asia. Z8.

C. longifolia (L.) Fritsch. SWORD-LEAVED HELLEBORINE; WHITE LADY. To 60cm. Lvs linear-lanceolate. Fls white; lip pubesc., golden at base, callus orange, 5–7-ridged. Eur., Medit., Asia. Z7.

C. rubra (L.) Rich. RED HELLEBORINE. 10–60cm. Lvs oblong-lanceolate to linear-lanceolate. Fls bright rose-pink or lilac; lip white edged pink, callus yellow, 7–9-ridged. Eur., Medit., Asia. Z6.

→*Epipactis*.

Cephalanthus L. BUTTONBUSH. Rubiaceae. 10+ shrubs or small trees, decid. and everg. Fls in dense, globose heads; hypanthium turbinate; cal. short-tubular, 4–5-lobed; cor. tubular-funneliform, lobes 4–5. Fr. turbinate. Temp. and trop. N & C Amer., Afr., Asia.

C. natalensis Oliv. Shrub or small tree. Lvs to 4cm, ovate, acute, revolute, lustrous green above, midrib and veins red beneath with gland. hairs in axils. Infl. capitate, to 3cm diam.; cor. rose-red or white, tipped green. Fr. pink, red or white. Spring–summer. S Afr. (Transvaal, Natal, Swaz., Les.). Z9.

C. occidentalis L. BUTTONBUSH; BUTTON-WILLOW; HONEY BELLS. Decid., or everg. shrub or tree, to 7m. Lvs to 18cm, oval to elliptic-lanceolate, rounded to slightly attenuate at apex. Infl. capitate, to 2.5cm, diam., subtended by slender, bracteoles; cor. 7mm, white or cream, interior pilose, lobes with black gland at each sinus. Summer–autumn. Canada to Mex., Calif. to Flor. and Cuba. 'Angustifolius': lvs narrower, usually in whorls of 3.

var. *pubescens* Raf. HAIRY BUTTONBUSH. To 2m. Lvs to 15cm, oblong to ovate-lanceolate, undulate, pubesc. Infl. capitate, to 5cm diam., hairy. US (Indiana to Tex.). Z6.

C. orientalis L. = *Nauclea orientalis*.

Cephalaria Schräd. ex Roem. & Schult. Dipsacaceae. 65 ann. or perenn. herbs related to *Scabiosa*. Lvs toothed or pinnatifid. Fls in globose, term. long-stalked heads with a collar of involucral bracts; cal. cup- or saucer-shaped, toothed, enclosed in epical.; cor. tubular, 4-lobed. Eur. to C Asia, Medit., N & S Afr.

C. alpina (L.) Roem. & Schult. Perenn. to 1.5m. Lvs pinnatisect, coarsely pubesc., seg. 9–15, oval-lanceolate, acute, toothed, st. lvs sometimes simple or with few slender seg. Fls pale yellow in heads to 3cm diam. Eur. Alps.

C. corniculata (Waldst. & Kit.) Roem. & Schult. = *C. uralensis*.

C. flava (Sibth. & Sm.) Z. Szabó. Perenn. to 0.85m. Lvs pinnatisect, seg. usually oblong, toothed or deeply cut. Fls yellow, in heads to 4cm diam. Greece, Balk.

C. gigantea (Ledeb.) Bobrov. GIANT SCABIOUS; YELLOW SCABIOUS. To 2m; st. robust, ridged, pubesc. Lvs pinnatifid, seg. oblong to broadly lanceolate, decurrent, coarsely toothed. Fls ivory to yellow, in heads to 5cm diam. Cauc., Sib.

C. graeca Roem. & Schult. = *C. flava*.

C. radiata Griseb. & Schenk. Differs from *C. tchihatchewii* in height (to 1.25m), and obtuse involucral bracts. Hung.

C. scabra (L. f.) Roem. & Schult. Perenn. to 1m, coarsely pubesc. Lvs pinnately or bipinnately divided, seg. slender, toothed and inrolled. Fls white. S Afr.

C. tatarica hort. non (L.) Roem. & Schult. = *C. gigantea*.

C. tchihatchewii Boiss. Perenn. to 1m, hispid. Lvs lyrate and pinnately cut, seg. 6–10, oblong-lanceolate, toothed to 3–5-lobed. Fls yellow in small heads. Armenia.

C. uralensis (Murr) Roem. & Schult. Perenn. to 1.25m. Lvs pinnatisect, seg. lanceolate-ovate to oblong, entire. Fls primrose-yellow. SE Eur. to S Sib. Double-fld forms are grown. →*Scabiosa*.

Cephalipterum A. Gray. SILVER-FLOWERED EVERLASTING. Compositae. 1 slender, erect ann., to 50cm. Lvs to 5cm, sub-spathulate to linear-lanceolate, sparsely hirsute. Cap. radiate, solitary, glomerate; phyllaries in many series, ovate; flts white, yellow, yellow-green or pink; ray flts recurved. W & S Aus.

C. drummondii A. Gray.

Cephalocereus Pfeiff. Cactaceae. 3 columnar cacti; st. un-branched or few-branched at base, erect, ribbed. Floral areoles distinct usually with hair-like bristles; fls nocturnal, tubular-campanulate, shiny. Mex.

C. alensis (F.A.C. Weber) Britt. & Rose = *Pilosocereus alensis*.

C. apicicephalium Dawson. Columnar or shrubby, to 3m, un-branched or with a few fastigiate basal br.; st. dark blue-green, 6.5–10cm diam.; ribs 22–27; central spines 2–6, 2–4cm, 1 longer; radial spines 9–12, 1cm. Cephalia forming a woolly cap, dis-placed each year by new growth and persisting as woolly rings; fls narrowly campanulate, 5–6×3cm, pink, tinged yellow. S Mex. Z9.

C. arrabidae (Lem.) Britt. & Rose = *Pilosocereus arrabidae*.

C. catingicola (Gürke) Britt. & Rose = *Pilosocereus catingicola*.

C. chrysacanthus (F.A.C. Weber) Britt. & Rose = *Pilosocereus chrysacanthus*.

C. collinsii Britton & Rose = *Pilosocereus collinsii*.

C. colombianus Rose = *Pilosocereus lanuginosus*.

C. columna-trajani (Karw. ex Pfeiff.) Schum. Columnar; st. un-branched 6–10m×4cm, grey-green; ribs 16–26, somewhat tuberculate; central spines 5–8, directed downwards, to 8cm; radial spines 12–18, 1cm. Cephalium densely woolly with hair-spines 4–6cm long, forming a persistent unilateral fleece; fls *c*7×7cm, v. pale yellow. Mex. Z9.

C. dybowskii (Roland-Goss.) Britt. & Rose = *Espostoopsis dybowskii*.

C. euphorbioides (Haw.) Britt. & Rose = *Neobuxbaumia euphorbioides*.

C. gounlei (F.A.C. Weber) Britt. & Rose = *Pilosocereus gounellei*.

C. hoppenstedtii (F.A. Weber) Schum. = *C. columna-trajani*.

C. lanuginosus (L.) Britt. & Rose = *Pilosocereus lanuginosus*.

C. leucocephalus (Poselger) Britt. & Rose = *Pilosocereus leucoce-phalus*.

C. leucostele (Gürke) Britt. & Rose = *Stephanocereus leucostele*.

C. macrocephalus F.A. Weber ex Schum. = *Neobuxbaumia macrocephala*.

C. maxonii Rose = *Pilosocereus leucocephalus*.

C. melanostele Vaupel = *Espostoa melanostele*.

C. mezcalaensis Bravo = *Neobuxbaumia mezcalaensis*.

C. militaris (Audot) H.E. Moore = *Pachycereus militaris*.

C. moritzianus (Otto ex Pfeiff.) Britt. & Rose = *Pilosocereus moritzianus.*

C. nobilis (Haw.) Britt. & Rose = *Pilosocereus royenii.*

C. palmeri Rose = *Pilosocereus leucocephalus.*

C. pentaedrophorus (Labouret) Britt. & Rose = *Pilosocereus pentaedrophorus.*

C. purpusii Britt. & Rose = *Pilosocereus purpusii.*

C. royenii (L.) Britt. & Rose = *Pilosocereus royenii.*

C. senilis (Haw.) Schum. OLD MAN CACTUS. Columnar; st. simple or few-branched below, to 12m×40cm, grey-green; ribs 12+ in young plants, later 25–30; spines 1–5, 1–2cm, slender, tinged yellow, bristle-spines 20–30, 6–12cm, hair-like, white, covering st., decid. Cephalium forming a dense fleece at apex and down one side of st. with abundant wool and bristles; fls 5–9×6cm; tep. off-white and pink midrib. C Mex. Z9.

C. smithianus Britt. & Rose = *Cereus smithianus.*

C. tetetzo (F.A. Weber ex Schum.) Vaupel = *Neobuxbaumia tetetzo.*

→*Neodawsonia* and *Pachycereus.*

Cephalocleistocactus F. Ritter.

C. ritteri (Backeb.) Backeb. = *Cleistocactus ritteri.*

Cephalopentandra Chiov. Cucurbitaceae. 1 tuberous, dioecious climber. St. glab., woody below. Tendrils simple. Lvs elliptic to elliptic-cordate, pinnately lobed or costapalmately lobed, 3–9cm, seg. rounded to dissected. Fls solitary or paired, cream to yellow veined green; cor. lobes 5, 12–28mm. Fr. to 8×4cm, red below. Ethiop., Uganda, Kenya. Z10.

C. ecirrhosa (Cogn.) C. Jeffrey.

C. obbiadensis Chiov. = *C. ecirrhosa.*

→*Coccinia.*

Cephalophora Cav.

C. scaposa DC. = *Tetraneuris scaposa.*

Cephalophyllum (Haw.) N.E. Br. Aizoaceae. 30 prostrate, clump-forming leaf-succulents. Lvs elongated or cylindrical to triangular. Fls usually 1–3 together. Nam., W & SW Cape. Z9.

C. acutum (Haw.) N.E. Br. = *C. subulatoides.*

C. albertinense (L. Bol.) Schwantes = *Jordaaniella dubia.*

C. alstonii Marloth. Lvs to 7cm, cylindric, short-tapered, grey-green with many spots. Fls 5–8cm diam., dark red; sta. violet. W Cape.

C. anemoniflorum (L. Bol.) N.E. Br. = *Jordaaniella dubia.*

C. caespitosum Hartm. & Dehnh. Lvs to 3.5cm, triquetrous, truncate above, angles serrulate. Fls 3.5–4cm diam., copper-red, yellow toward centre. W Cape.

C. calvinianum L. Bol. = *C. roseum.*

C. clavifolium (L. Bol.) L. Bol. ex N.E. Br. = *Jordaaniella clavifolia.*

C. cupreum L. Bol. = *Jordaaniella cuprea.*

C. diversifolium (Haw.) L. Bol. = *C. diversiphyllum.*

C. diversiphyllum (Haw.) N.E. Br. Lvs to 10cm, rosulate, semicylindric, compressed-triquestrous below, tapered, with minute rough spots. Fls glossy yellow, tinted red below. W Cape.

C. dubium (Haw.) L. Bol. = *Jordaaniella dubia.*

C. frutescens L. Bol. = *Leipoldtia frutescens.*

C. loreum (L.) L. Bol. = *C. diversiphyllum.*

C. luxurium Dinter = *Jordaaniella dubia.*

C. maritimum (L. Bol.) Schwantes = *Jordaaniella dubia.*

C. pillansii L. Bol. Lvs 2.5–20cm, cylindric, acute, dark green, spotted. Fls 4–7cm diam., yellow, centre red. W Cape.

C. pittenii L. Bol. = *Jordaaniella dubia.*

C. procumbens (Haw.) Schwantes = *Jordaaniella dubia.*

C. saturatum L. Bol. nom. nud. = *C. pillansii.*

C. subulatoides (Haw.) N.E. Br. Lvs 5–7cm, semicylindric, short-tapered, margins carinate, cartilaginous, grey-green with numerous dots. Fls 4cm diam., purple-red. SW Cape.

C. tricolorum (Haw.) N.E. Br. Lvs 4–8cm, cylindric, long-tapered, light or grey-green, minutely spotted. Fls 4–5cm diam.; pet. yellow, purple at base, tips tinted red below; fil. red. W Cape.

C. uniflorum L. Bol. = *Jordaaniella uniflora.*

C. vanputtenii L. Bol. = *Jordaaniella dubia.*

C. watermeyeri L. Bol. = *Jordaaniella dubia.*

→*Cheiridopsis* and *Mesembryanthemum.*

Cephalorrhynchus Boiss. Compositae. 6 erect, perenn. herbs. Cap. ligulate, clustered in a pan.; involucre *c*2×1cm, cylindrical. SE Eur., SW Asia.

C. macrorhizus (Royle) Tuisl. To 50cm. Lvs to 14cm, petiole to 8cm, linear to oblanceolate or narrowly obovate, pinnatisect, seg. lanceolate to orbicular. Flts blue or pink. Pak. to Iran. Z6.

→*Lactuca* and *Mulgedium.*

CEPHALOTACEAE Labill. See *Cephalotus.*

CEPHALOTAXACEAE Neger. See *Cephalotaxus.*

Cephalotaxus Sieb. & Zucc. COW'S TAIL PINE; PLUM YEW. Cephalotaxaceae. *c*9 everg. coniferous shrubs and small trees. Bark flaking and stripping. Lvs twisted at the base to appear opposite in 2 ranks on lat. br., leathery, linear, midrib prominent with 2 stomatal bands beneath. Fr. an olive-like drupe. Jap., Taiwan, China, NE India.

C. drupacea Sieb. & Zucc. = *C. harringtonia* var. *drupacea.*

C. fortunei Hook. CHINESE PLUM YEW; FORTUNE'S PLUM YEW. Shrub or small tree, to 8m, rarely to 20m. Lvs 2-ranked linear, 5–9(–13)cm×4–5mm, falcate, acuminate, dark to yellow-green above, 2 silver bands of stomata beneath. Fr. ovoid, 2.5–3.5cmmm, olive-green ripening purple-brown. E & C China. 'Grandis': lvs to 13cm; ♀. 'Longifolia: long-lvd, ♂. 'Prostrata' ('Prostrate Spreader'): procumbent ground-covering plant. Z7.

C. griffithii Hook. f. Similar to *C. mannii*; to 15m. Lvs falcate, 4–5cm, green above, white beneath, apex abruptly acute. N Assam. Z9.

C. hainanensis Li. To 20m; closely related to *C. sinensis* but tree-sized; lvs thinner, less fleshy, 2.5–4cm. Subtrop. SW China. Z9.

C. harringtonia (Forbes) Koch. COW'S TAIL PINE; JAPANESE PLUM YEW. Shrub or small tree, to 5m. Lvs in 2 rows raised to give a 'V'-shaped spray, linear to subfalcate, 3–6cm×3–4mm, abruptly acute, shining dark green above, 2 grey bands of stomata beneath. Fr. ovoid or obovoid, 2–3cm, mucronate, purple-brown when ripe. Jap. 'Fastigiata': erect with radially arranged lvs 3–8cm. 'Prostrata': procumbent with no erect leader. var. *drupacea* (Sieb. & Zucc.) Koidz. Large shrubby or bushy tree forming a mound of drooping br. with 2–5cm lvs in a strong v-shaped arrangement and 2–3cm, olive green fr. Jap., C China. var. *koreana* (Nak.) Rehd. Dense shrub to 1.5m. Shoots flatter, lvs less raised, falcate to linear. Fr. dull mauve. Korea, NE China. var. *nana* (Nak.) Rehd. Low-spreading shrub, 0.5–2m high; br. ascending to prostrate; suckering and layering. Fr. 2cm, red. N Jap. Z7.

C. harringtonia var. *sinensis* (Rehd. & Wils.) Rehd. = *C. sinensis.*

C. lanceolata Feng. YUNNAN PLUM YEW. Tree to 8m, rarely 20m, allied to *C. fortunei* but lvs lanceolate, long-acuminate, 5–10cm×4–7mm; fr. 30–45×15–20mm, obovoid. NW Yunnan. Z8.

C. mannii Hook. f. Shrub to 8m, differs from *C. fortunei* in smaller, narrower lvs, 3–5cm×3–4mm, green beneath. Fr. 3–4 on a single pedicel, obovoid to pyriform. NE India, N Burm., SW Yunnan. Z9.

C. nana Nak. = *C. harringtonia* var. *nana.*

C. oliveri Mast. Small shrub, 2–3m. Br. flattened, rigid. Lvs closely linear, 1.5–2(–3)cm×3–4mm; dark green above, 2 glaucous bands beneath. Fr. ellipsoid, 2.5–3cm. W China. Z8.

C. pedunculata Sieb. & Zucc. = *C. harringtonia.*

C. sinensis (Rehd. & Wils.) Li. CHINESE PLUM YEW. Shrub, 2–5m. Resembles *C. harringtonia* but lvs narrower, lanceolate, acuminate, pungent. Fr. obovoid, 2.5×1.7cm, glaucous, mucronate. C & W China. Z7.

C. wilsoniana Hayata. Tree to 10m. Differs from *C. fortunei* in pendulous br. and laxer, small lvs, 3–6cm×2.5–5mm, with margins revolute. Taiwan. Z8.

→*Taxus.*

Cephalotus Labill. AUSTRALIAN PITCHER PLANT. Cephalotaceae. 1 carnivorous perenn. herb. Lvs 2–7cm, ovate in a basal rosette or stalked and modified into squat pitcher-like traps to 5×2.5cm, green marked red-brown with a broad lid, 3 longitudinal ciliate wings and a heavily ribbed, red pitcher rim. W Aus. Z10.

C. follicularis Labill.

Ceradia Lindl.

C. furcata Lindl. = *Othonna furcata.*

Ceraria Pearson & Stephens. Portulacaceae. 6 succulent shrubs. Trunk short, swollen; br. short, spreading. Lvs small, clustered on cushions, oval-cuneate, succulent, green to grey-green. Fls 2–6, pedicellate small; pet. 5, pink or white. S Afr., Nam. Z9.

C. fruticulosa Pearson & Stephens. Highly branched shrub, 30–60cm; br. dichotomous or monopodial, slender, wrinkled, red-brown, lf cushions in 4 ranks. Lvs flattened, obovate to oblong-obovate, minutely apiculate, 4–6mm. S Afr.

C. namaquensis (Sonder) Pearson & Stephens. Highly branched shrub to 2m; br. ascending or horizontal, grey-white, thick, lf cushions in 4–16 rows. Lvs 7–8mm, grey-green, short-subcylindric. Nam., S Afr. (NW Cape).

C. pygmaea (Pill.) Pill. Dwarf shrub with dichotomous br. arising from a rough caudex to 20cm. Lvs 10–14mm, ovate-cuneate, tips rounded and apiculate, rough with rounded papillae, blue-green to yellow-green. S Afr.
→*Portulacaria*.

Cerastium L. MOUSE-EAR CHICKWEED. Caryophyllaceae. 60–100 perenn. or ann. herbs, usually hairy, often tufted or mat-forming. Fls in cymes or solitary; sep. usually 5, free; pet. usually 5, white, bifid or deeply indented; sta. usually 10. Widespread, mostly in N temp. and arctic regions.
C. alpinum L. ALPINE MOUSE EAR. Mat-forming, glandular-hairy perenn. Lvs obovate to elliptic, densely covered with wavy, grey-white hairs. Infl. few or 1-fld.; pet. 1.2–1.8cm, obovate, shallowly bifid. Arc.; Eur. (Mts.) Z3.
C. arvense L. Mat-forming, glandular-hairy perenn. Lvs linear to narrowly elliptical. Infl. few-fld; pet. 1–1.5cm, obovate, bifid. Temp. N Hemis. 'Compactum': low and dense. Z4.
C. biebersteinii DC. = *C. tomentosum*.
C. lanatum Lam. = *C. alpinum*.
C. tomentosum L. SNOW-IN-SUMMER. Differs from *C. arvense* in long, thick, wavy, grey-white hairs. Variable mat-forming perenn., white- to grey-green pubesc. throughout. Flowering sp. to 15cm. Lvs spathulate to linear-lanceolate. Fls to 2.5cm diam.; pet. cleft in apical third. Mts of Eur. and W Asia. 'Silberteppich' ('Silver Carpet'): to 20cm; lvs silver-grey. 'Yo Yo': low, to 15cm; lvs silver-grey. Z4.

Ceratonia L. LOCUST; CAROB; ST JOHN'S BREAD; ALGARROBA BEAN. Leguminosae (Caesalpinioideae). 2 everg. shrubs or trees to 10m. Lvs 10–20cm, paripinnate; lfts 4–6cm, obovate to elliptic, 3–4 pairs, coriaceous, shiny and deep green above, light green beneath, slightly undulate. Fls minute, apetalous, green tinted red, in ascending rac. 2–6cm. Fr. 10–30cm, distended, oblong, black-brown, soft, swollen, leathery. Autumn. Medit., Arabia, Somalia; nat. warm US. Z8. This description applies to *C. siliqua*, the Carob. From Somalia is *C. oreolthauma* Hillc., J. Lewis & Verdc., its putative ancestor.
C. siliqua L.

Ceratopetalum Sm. Cunoniaceae. 5 trees or shrubs. Lvs simple or trifoliate. Pan. or corymb terminal or axill.; cal. 4- or 5-lobed; pet. small, membranaceous, laciniate, sometimes 0; sta. 10. Aus., New Guinea. Z10.
C. apetalum D. Don. Tree to 25m. Lvs to 12cm, simple, oblong to ovate or lanceolate, glab., dentate to serrate. Infl. to 20cm; sep. to 10mm, red, broadly ovate, pubesc.; pet. 0. NSW, Queensld.
C. gummiferum Sm. Tree or shrub to 12m. Lvs trifoliate, lfts to 7cm, narrowly oblong, dentate to serrate, dark green above, pale green beneath. Infl. to 10cm; sep. to 10mm, deep red, sometimes white, broadly ovate, glab.; pet. to 4mm, trifurcate, glab. NSW.
C. succirubrum C.T. White. Tree to 35m. Lvs trifoliate, lfts to 12cm, oblong or obovate-oblong to lanceolate, entire to serrate, glab. Infl. to 20cm; sep. to 12mm, ovate, acute, slightly strigose, interior pubesc. to hirsute; pet. 0. NE Aus., New Guinea.

CERATOPHYLLACEAE Gray. See *Ceratophyllum*.

Ceratophyllum L. Ceratophyllaceae. *c*30 submerged, aquatic herbs, generally free-floating and rootless. St. slender, branched. Lvs 1–4cm in whorls, filiform, often spiny-dentate, rigid and brittle, forked. Eur., Asia, N & Trop. Afr., S & E US. Z8.
C. demersum L. St. 20cm–1.5m, fragile, glab. Lvs dark green, stiff, 5–12 per whorl, forked once or twice, seg. flattened, narrow, teeth short, numerous. Summer. Trop. Afr., Medit., EC Eur.
C. echinatum A. Gray. St. elongated, branching freely. Lvs 9–12 per whorl, forked ×2–4, seg. entire, thread-like. S & E US, N Mex.
C. muricatum Cham. Lvs bright green, soft, forked ×3–4, seg. thread-like, sparsely fine-toothed. Trop. Afr.; Asia.
C. submersum L. St. 20cm–1m. Lvs pale green, 6–8 per whorl, forked ×3–4; seg. narrow, marginal teeth few, tiny, inconspicuous. Eur., N Afr., Asia.

Ceratopteris Brongn. WATER FERN; FLOATING FERN; FLOATING STAG'S-HORN FERN. Parkeriaceae. 4 variable aquatic or semi-aquatic ferns, floating or rooting into marginal substrate. Fronds in rosettes, smooth, sometimes rather succulent, stipes aerenchymatous, sterile fronds simple to irregularly pinnatifid or 3-pinnate, floating or partially submerged, fertile fronds larger, semi-erect, 4–5-pinnate. Trop. Z10.

C. cornuta (P. Beauv.) Lepr. Sterile fronds 10–15cm, lanceolate, pinnate to bipinnate, pinnules irregularly spaced, variously lobed, to 4cm; fertile fronds 20–30cm, bipinnate, pinnules linear. Trop. Afr. and Madag., W Asia to Burm., Indon. and N Aus.
C. pteridioides (Hook.) Hieron. FLOATING FERN. Sterile fronds on short, simple and palmately 3-lobed, or pinnate and 5-lobed, undulate, pale green; fertile fronds to 40cm, erect, 1–4-pinnate. Trop. Amer.
C. thalictroides (L.) Brongn. WATER FERN. Sterile fronds oblong, simple or slightly divided when young, 2–3-pinnate when mature, pinnules narrowly linear to deltoid; fertile fronds 2–3-pinnate, term. pinnules swollen, pod-like; stipes inflated. Pantrop.

Ceratosanthes Burm. ex Adans. Cucurbitaceae. 5 dioecious, tuberous, climbing or trailing perenn. herbs. Tendrils simple. Lvs palmately lobed. Fls white, opening at night; cor. 5-lobed, lobes bifid. Fr. a red berry. S Amer., Trin., Lesser Antilles. Z10.
C. palmata (L.) Urban. St. to 5m. Lvs 1–9cm, broadly ovate, pentagonal or reniform, base cordate, palmately 3–5-lobed, scabrid-punctate. ♂ fls 4–40 per rac.; ♀ fls 1–4 per cluster; cor. lobes to 2×0.4cm. Fr. ovoid or ellipsoid, 1.5–3cm. N S Amer.
→*Trichosanthes*.

Ceratostigma Bunge. Plumbaginaceae. 8 woody-based perenn. herbs or small shrubs producing numerous short-lived st. Lvs alt., simple, ciliate, usually bristly. Fls in dense, bracteate term. heads or clusters; cal. tubular, 5-ribbed, 5-lobed; cor. tubular, slender, lobes 5, spreading. Himal., C China, SE Asia, NE Trop. Afr.
C. abyssinicum (Hochst.) Schwein. & Asch. Ascending shrubby herb to 70cm; st. ridged, tinged red. Lvs 1.5–6cm, coriaceous, narrowly obovate to elliptic, acute, mucronate, adpressed-setose, flushed purple-red in winter. Fls 2–3cm, bright blue. Horn of Afr., Kenya, Sudan. Z9.
C. griffithii C.B. Clarke. Everg., ±procumbent, much-branched shrub, shoots thick, ribbed, with red bristles. Lvs 1–3cm, broadly obovate, crowded, rather thick-textured, dull green with purple tinged margins, ciliate, closely bristly. Fls 1–2cm diam., bright blue. Himal. Z7.
C. minus Stapf ex Prain. Decid. shrub to 1m; st. sometimes weakly ribbed. Lvs 2–6cm, obovate to spathulate rounded at apex, cuneate at base, ciliate, glab. above, bristly beneath. Fls about 2cm, base red-purple, lobes blue. W China. Z7.
C. plumbaginoides Bunge. Herb or subshrub to 50cm; st. slender, ascending, base woody, soft above. Lvs about 9cm, obovate, undulate, thin-textured, bright green, glab. to hispidulous, ciliate. Fls to 2cm, dark blue. W China. Z5.
C. willmottianum Stapf. CHINESE PLUMBAGO. Ascending shrub, 50–100cm, decid.; shoots angled, rather slender, tinged purple, bristly. Lvs 2–5cm, lanceolate to obovate, acuminate, pale-bristly, tinted red in autumn. Fls about 2.5cm, tube red-purple, lobes pale blue. W China to Tibet. Z7.
→*Plumbago* and *Valoradia*.

Ceratotheca Endl. Pedaliaceae. 5 ann. herbs. Fls axill. in tall spikes, cal. 5-partite, glandular-pilose; cor. glandular-pilose, tube curved at base, campanulate above, constricted, limb oblique, lobes 5, ovate, lower 3 longer. Afr. Z10.
C. triloba (Bernh.) Hook. f. Erect ann. or bienn. to 2m, sparsely hairy. Lvs 5–20cm, ovate-cordate to broadly triangular, ± 3-lobed, crenate. Fls turned to one side; cor. 6–8cm, blue-violet or mauve tinged pink to white, glandular-pubesc. S Afr.

Ceratozamia Brongn. Zamiaceae. 9 large, superficially palm-like perennials. Caudex stout, globose-cylindric, scarred. Lvs pinnate, erect to arching, in whorls, rigid; rachis often armed. ♀ cones cylindric dull green, terminating in single spine; sporophylls larger than in ♂, shield-shaped, horned. ♂ cone narrower, slightly felty; sporophylls hexagonal, arranged spirally, 2-horned. Mex., Belize. Z10.
C. hildae Landry & M. Wils. To 1.5m. Caudex small, ovoid. Lvs erect; pinnae to 20×3cm, falcate, lanceolate, papery, in alternating clusters of 3 along rachis. Mex.
C. kuesteriana (Reg.) Moretti, Sabato & Torrez. To 1.5m. Caudex small, subglobose, dull orange. Lvs erect; rachis unarmed, downy at first, later glab., red-brown; pinnae 25×0.8cm, crowded, near-opposite, semi-falcate, linear-lanceolate tapering v. finely, dark green, rigid, upper surface concave. Mex.
C. latifolia Miq. = *C. mexicana* var. *latifolia*.
C. mexicana Brongn. To 2m. Caudex large, subcolumnar. Lvs arching; pinnae to 30×5cm, to 150, narrow to broad-lanceolate, acuminate; rachis heavily armed. Mex. var. *latifolia* (Miq.) Schust. Lvs to 1.5m; pinnae emerge pale green, bloom-

covered, later sap-green, somewhat flaccid, obovate-lanceolate, to 5cm wide, widely spaced. Mex.

C. mexicana var. *robusta* (Miq.) Dyer = *C. robusta*.

C. microstrobilia Vovides. To 1m. Caudex small, ovoid, dull orange. Lvs sparse, bronze at first; rachis orange-brown ± unarmed; pinnae 14×4cm, to 40 pairs, near opposite, obliquely broadly lanceolate, falcate, leathery, olive-green. Mex.

C. robusta Miq. To 3m. Caudex large, columnar. Lvs erect, rachis heavily armed; pinnae to 30×5cm, light green, soft, lanceolate-falcate. S Mex., Belize.

Cerbera L. Apocynaceae. 4 toxic everg. shrubs or trees with milky sap. Lvs entire. Infl. term.; cal. 5-lobed; cor. salverform, tube swollen and hairy at the top with 5 scales in mouth, limb 5-lobed. Trop. Asia, Madag., Seych., Aus., W Pacific Is. Z10.

C. manghas L. Shrub or small tree to 6m. Lvs 15–30cm, narrowly obovate, apiculate, leathery, shining. Pan. large, corymbose; fls 3–8cm across, white with a pink or yellow centre or entirely white, fragrant, lobes ovate, tips incurved. Seych. E to Pacific Is.

C. odollam Gaertn. = *C. manghas*.

Cercidiphyllum Sieb. & Zucc. Cercidiphyllaceae. 1 decid. tree to 30m, single- or multi-stemmed. Shoots red-brown, glossy, slender; spurs adpressed with claw-like buds. Lvs 5–10×3–7.5cm, broadly ovate, base cordate, finely crenate, dark blue-green above, glaucescent beneath, bright yellow to scarlet in fall, when candy-scented. Fls red, inconspicuous. W China and Jap.

C. japonicum Sieb. & Zucc. KATSURA TREE. var. *magnificum* Nak. (Nak.). Smaller tree; lvs 7.5–11cm, more rounded, with large, sometimes overlapping basal lobes. var. *sinense* Rehd. & Wils. Taller, trunk single; lf with pubesc. vein axils beneath. China. f. *pendulum* (Miyoshi) Ohwi. Br. pendulous. Z5.

Cercidium Tul.
C. floridum Benth. ex A. Gray = *Parkinsonia florida*.

Cercis L. Leguminosae (Papilionoideae). 6 decid. shrubs and trees. Lvs broadly cordate to reniform or bilobed. Fls pea-like, in sessile clusters or short rac., often borne directly on old wood and before lvs. Legume oblong-falcate, compressed, red-green becoming leathery to woody, persistent. E Asia, S Eur., US.

C. canadensis L. EASTERN REDBUD; REDBUD. Tree to 14m. Crown domed; br. spreading. Lvs 3.5–12cm, suborbicular-cordate, acute or retuse, shiny above, puberulent beneath. Fls 1cm, crimson or lilac (rarely white), in clusters of 2–8. Spring. N & C Amer. 'Alba': fls snow white. 'Double Flame' ('Flame Plena'): fls double, magenta. 'Flame': habit upright; fls larger, double. 'Forest Pansy': young st. and lvs deep wine red to dark purple. 'Plena': fls double. 'Royal White': compact; fls snow white, larger and earlier than in 'Alba'. 'Ruby Atkinson': fls shell pink, v. abundant. 'Silver Cloud': lvs bordered and mottled silver-white. 'Wither's Pink Charm': fls candy pink. var. *texensis* (S. Wats.) E. Murray. TEXAS RED BUD. Multistemmed shrub or small tree, to 2m. Lvs to 7cm diam., reniform, glossy dark green above, paler, sometimes puberulent beneath. Tex., Colorado. Z4.

C. chinensis Bunge. CHINESE REDBUD. Large upright shrub. Lvs 5–12cm, rounded, shining, subcoriaceous with pale, textured margins, apex abruptly acute, base deeply cordate. Fls 1.5–2cm, lavender to crimson, in clusters of 5–8. Spring. C China. 'Alba': fls white. 'Avondale': to 3m, much-branched; lvs cordate, rich green; fls deep cerise, abundant. 'Nana': habit dwarf and compact; lvs large, cupped. Z6.

C. griffithii Boiss. Spreading shrub or small tree with flattened crown. Differs from *C. siliquastrum* in smaller fr. with a broad wing along the upper suture and fewer seeds. Fls lilac-mauve, sometimes darker. Iran, Afghan., C Asia. Z7.

C. japonica Planch. = *C. chinensis*.

C. nitida Greene = *C. canadensis* var. *texensis*.

C. occidentalis Torr. & A. Gray. WESTERN REDBUD; CALIFORNIA REDBUD. Shrub or small tree to 5m, usually multistemmed. Lvs 2.5–7cm across, reniform, apex rounded, cleft, base deeply cordate, blue-green. Fls 1.2–1.4cm, pink or crimson, 5–6 per cluster. Spring. W US. Z7.

C. racemosa Oliv. Shrub or small tree, to 9m. Lvs 6–10cm, broadly ovate, apex acute, base cordate, pea green above, pubesc. beneath, ultimately sage green, tough. Fls pale pink, to 32 in nodding racs 5–11cm long. Spring. C China. Z7.

C. reniformis Engelm. Tree to 12m, broadly resembling *C. occidentalis*. Lvs 5–7cm across, ovate to reniform, subcoriaceous, downy beneath. Rac. pendent, to 10cm; fls pale pink, to 30. New Mex., Tex. 'Oklahoma': lvs crowded, coriaceous, shining; fls mauve-magenta, carried profusely. Z8.

C. siliquastrum L. JUDAS TREE; LOVE TREE. Tree or shrub to 10m; young shoots maroon. Lvs 6–10×12cm, reniform to broadly and bluntly obcordate, matt grey-green, glab. Fls 1.4–1.8cm, pale rose to magenta, 3–6 per cluster. Spring. E Medit. 'Alba': lvs pale sea green; fls white. 'Bodnant': fls deep magenta. 'Variegated': lvs zoned green and ivory. Z6.

Cercocarpus Kunth. MOUNTAIN MAHOGANY. Rosaceae. 6 everg. or semi-everg. shrubs or small trees. Fls axill. or term. on spur-like branchlets, solitary or clustered; cal. cup-shaped, 5-lobed; pet. 0; sta. numerous. Fr. a small, silky nutlet with a long, persistent, plumose style. W N Amer.

C. alnifolius Rydb. = *C. montanus* var. *blancheae*.

C. argenteus Rydb. = *C. montanus* var. *argenteus*.

C. betulifolius Nutt. = *C. montanus* var. *glaber*.

C. betulifolius var. *blancheae* C. Schneid. = *C. montanus* var. *blancheae*.

C. betuloides Nutt. = *C. montanus* var. *glaber*.

C. betuloides var. *alnifolius* (Rydb.) Dunkle = *C. montanus* var. *blancheae*.

C. breviflorus A. Gray = *C. montanus* var. *paucidentatus*.

C. fothergilloides Kunth. Shrub or small tree to 5m. Lvs to 3.5cm, subelliptic, coriaceous, serrate, dark green and sub-glabrous above, lighter and tomentulose beneath. Cal. tube to 1cm, adpressed-sericeous, limb to 5mm diam.; sta. 20–30. Mex. Z9.

C. hypoleucus Rydb. = *C. ledifolius*.

C. intricatus S. Wats. = *C. ledifolius* var. *intricatus*.

C. ledifolius Nutt. Shrub or tree to 8m, occas. to 12m. Br. tortuous. Lvs to 4cm, lanceolate to linear, entire, coriaceous, resinous, glossy green above, grey- or brown-tomentose beneath, revolute. Cal. tube to 1cm, white-lanate, limb to 6mm diam.; sta. 10–25. Spring–summer. W US. var. *intricatus* (S. Wats.) M.E. Jones. Shrub to 3m, intricately branched. Lvs to 1.5cm, linear, revolute, grey-tomentose beneath. Cal. tube to 5mm, limb to 2mm diam.; sta. 10–15. Z6.

C. minutiflorus Abrams = *C. montanus* var. *minutiflorus*.

C. montanus Raf. Shrub to 4m. Lvs to 3cm, obovate to flabelliform, acute or obtuse, cuneate at base, villous, sericeous or sub-glabrous, 3–6-lateral-veined. Cal. tube to 12mm, sericeous or villous, limb to 5mm diam.; sta. 22–44. Spring–summer. W US. var. *argenteus* (Rydb.) F.L. Martin. Shrub to 5m. Lvs to 4cm, oblanceolate to narrow-elliptic, white-sericeous to subglabrous, 5–6-lateral-veined. Cal. tube to 10mm, sericeous, rarely villous, limb to 5mm diam. Summer. New Mex., Tex. Z5. var. *blancheae* (C. Schneid.) F.L. Martin. Shrub or tree to 10m. Lvs to 6cm, ovate to broad-elliptic, subglabrous to strigose, 6–10-lateral-veined. Cal. tube to 14mm, sericeous to slightly lanate, limb to 7mm diam. Spring–summer. Calif. Z8. var. *glaber* (S. Wats.) F.L. Martin. Shrub or small tree to 8m. Lvs to 3cm, narrow-obovate to almost circular, subglabrous to strigose, 4–6-lateral-veined. Cal. tube to 14mm, limb to 6mm diam. Spring–summer. S Oreg., Calif., Ariz., Baja Calif. Z6. var. *minutiflorus* (Abrams) F.L. Martin. Shrub to 5m. Lvs to 2.5cm, broad-obovate to suborbicular, glossy, light green above, olive green beneath, 3–5-lateral-veined. Cal. tube to 11mm, glab. or sparsely adpressed-sericeous, limb to 4mm diam. Spring–summer. Calif., Baja Calif. Z8. var. *paucidentatus* (S. Wats.) F.L. Martin. Shrub to 5m, often spiny. Lvs lanceolate, oblanceolate or narrow-obovate, entire to short-dentate, short-villous, 3–6-lateral-veined. Cal. tube to 8mm, adpressed-sericeous or patent-villous, limb to 5mm diam. Spring–autumn. Ariz., New Mex., Tex., Mex. Z7. var. *traskiae* (Eastw.) F.L. Martin. Tree to 8m. Lvs to 6cm, broad-obovate to sub-orbicular, coriaceous, revolute, subglabrous above, white-tomentose beneath, 6–8-lateral-veined. Cal. tube to 11mm, white-lanate, limb to 7mm diam. Spring. Calif. Z9.

C. parvifolius Nutt. pro parte. = *C. montanus*.

C. traskiae Eastw. = *C. montanus* var. *traskiae*.

Cerdana Ruiz & Pav.
C. alliodora Ruiz & Pav. = *Cordia alliodora*.
C. gerascanthus (L.) Mold. = *Cordia gerascanthus*.

Cereus Mill. Cactaceae. c40 tree-like or shrubby cacti, usually much branched; st. erect or ascending, strongly ribbed, sometimes segmented; spines numerous. Fls funnelform, nocturnal, usually white; pericarpel and tube elongate, thick, perianth-limb broad or moderately so. W Indies, S Amer.

C. aethiops Haw. Shrub to 2m; st. blue-green; seg. 30cm+, 3–4cm diam.; ribs 7–8, tuberculate; central spine 1.2cm+; radial spines 9–12, black at tip and base. Fls 22×12cm; outer tep. pink, inner white. Arg. Z9.

C. alacriportanus Pfeiff. Shrub to 4(–6)m, young growth blue-green; ribs (4–)5–8, compressed; spines 6–9, to 2.5cm, golden yellow at first. Fls 21–22×10cm; inner tep. white, tinged red. S

Braz., Urug., Parag. Z9.

C. anisitsii Schum. = *C. spegazzinii.*

C. argentinensis Britt. & Rose. Tree-like, 8–12m, br. fastigiate; st. 10–15cm diam.; ribs 4–5; central spines 1–2, 2–5cm; radial spines 3(-5), 10mm. Fls 17–22cm; outer tep. green or tinged red at tips; inner tep. white. Arg. Z9.

C. articulatus Pfeiff. = *Opuntia articulata.*

C. azureus Pfeiff. Shrubby, 2–3m; st. slender, 3–3.5cm diam., blue-pruinose; ribs 6–7, gibbous-crenate; central spines 1–3, to 15mm, dark brown or nearly black; radial spines 8–12, 5–10mm, off-white. Fls 10–30cm; tube pale green; outer tep. tinged brown, inner white. N Arg. Z9.

C. bridgesii Salm-Dyck [not *Echinopsis bridgesii* Salm-Dyck] = *Echinopsis lageniformis.*

C. caesius Salm-Dyck ex Pfeiff. A name used by different authors for a var. of plants.

C. caesius Salm-Dyck (1850) non Salm-Dyck ex Pfeiff. (1837) = *C. pseudocaesius.*

C. campinensis (Backeb. & Voll) P. Braun. Large shrub to 5m; st. erect, to 6cm diam.; ribs 7–9; spines 7–11, 5–15mm, black-tipped. Fls campanulate-funnelform, to 10×6cm; inner tep. white, tinged green. SE Braz. Z9.

C. candelabrum Schum. = *Pachycereus weberi.*

C. catingicola Gürke = *Pilosocereus catingicola.*

C. chalybaeus Otto ex C.F. Först. Shrub to 3m; br. few, ascending, 6–10cm diam., young growth glaucous or tinged purple; ribs 5–6, shallowly crenate; central spines 1–3, 2–3cm; radial spines 7–8, 4–12mm, red at first. Fls c20cm; tube red to dark purple; inner tep. white. N Arg., Urug. Z9.

C. chrysostele Vaup. = *Pilosocereus chrysostele.*

C. coerulescens Salm-Dyck = *C. aethiops.*

C. dayami Speg. Tree, 10–25m, trunk 25–50cm diam.; br. arching-erect, 8–12cm diam., pale green; ribs usually 6, triangular in section; spines 3(-5), 4–12mm, conic. Fls 23–25cm; tube green; tep. white. Parag. Z9.

C. diffusus (Britt. & Rose) Werderm. ex Backeb. Shrub, 1–6m, often forming thickets; st. erect, arching or sprawling, 3–10cm diam., green or grey-green; ribs 4–9, somewhat crenate; central spines 0–4, 2–7.5cm; radial spines 7–13, 5–15cm. Fls 6–9.5×3–4cm; outer tep. green with red midrib; inner tep. white. Ecuad., N Peru. Z9.

C. emoryi Engelm. = *Bergerocactus emoryi.*

C. engelmannii Parry ex Engelm. = *Echinocereus engelmannii.*

C. euphorbioides Haw. = *Neobuxbaumia euphorbioides.*

C. fendleri Engelm. = *Echinocereus fendleri.*

C. fernambucensis Lem. Shrubby, branching below, forming low clumps to 1×4–5m; st. decumbent, sprawling, 5–7cm diam., pale green; ribs 3–6; spines 4–10, yellow-brown or bright yellow, to 5cm. Fls 16cm, white. Braz. Z9.

C. forbesii Otto ex Salm-Dyck see *C. validus.*

C. formosus C.F. Först. = *C. fernambucensis.*

C. geometrizans Mart. ex Pfeiff. = *Myrtillocactus geometrizans.*

C. giganteus Engelm. = *Carnegiea gigantea.*

C. glaucus Salm-Dyck. Large shrub or tree 5–6m+; trunk to c40cm diam.; st. 8–18cm diam., pale blue or blue-green; ribs 6–8 deep; spines 5–15(-20), longest 2–3cm (10cm on trunk). Fls c28cm; outer tep. pale green, inner white. Origin unknown. Z9.

C. grandiflorus (L.) Mill. = *Selenicereus grandiflorus.*

C. greggii Engelm. = *Peniocereus greggii.*

C. haageana (Backeb.) N.P. Tayl. Erect or clambering, to 3m+; st. 2–3cm diam., glaucous; ribs 5, weakly tuberculate; spines 5–8, 2–4mm, thin, black-brown. Fls to 12cm; outer tep. glaucescent, inner white or green-white. Parag. Z9.

C. hexagonus (L.) Mill. Columnar or tree-like, to 8(-15)m, eventually branching below; st. erect, c12cm diam., constricted at intervals; ribs (3-)4–7(-11); spines almost lacking in form usually cultivated, to 14, 7–35mm, in wild plants. Fls 20–29×15–20cm; outer tep. green or green-brown to purple-red, inner tep. white. E Colomb. to Surinam and N Braz. Z9.

C. hildmannianus Schum. Resembling *C. jamacaru*, but nearly spineless. Shrub or tree to 5m, much branched; st. 10–15cm diam.; ribs 5–6; spines 0 or central spine 0–1, to 2cm; radial spines 6–12, 2–8mm, brown-black. Fls 20–23×10–12cm, white. E Braz. (Cult.) Z9.

C. huntingtonianus Weing. Large shrub, to 3×4m, branching; st. segmented, to 25cm diam.; younger seg. cylindric, 6–16×10cm, grey-blue; ribs 6–8; central spine 0–1, to 3(-10)cm; radial spines 1–4, 0.3–8cm. Fls 18×c11cm; outer tep. dark red or pink, sometimes with green midstripe, inner tep. pale pink. Origin unknown. Z9.

C. insularis Hemsl. Much-branched shrub, forming thickets; st. creeping, 2.5–3cm diam.; ribs 6–8; spines 12–15, unequal, yellow. Fls 12.5cm, yellow-white; tube slender. Braz. Z9.

C. jamacaru DC. Tree to 10m; trunk short, to 60cm diam.; st. to 15cm diam., glaucous at first; ribs 4–6(-8); spines of young growth 9–11, yellow, to 2cm, longer and darker on mature

growth. Fls 25–30×18–20cm; outer tep. pale green, inner tep. white. NE Braz. Z9.

C. kunthianus Otto ex Salm-Dyck = *Selenicereus grandiflorus.*

C. lamprochlorus Lem. = *Echinopsis lamprochlorus.*

C. lepidotus Salm-Dyck = *C. hexagonus.*

C. leucostele Gürke = *Stephanocereus leucostele.*

C. lividus Pfeiff. = *C. glaucus.*

C. macdonaldiae Hook. = *Selenicereus macdonaldiae.*

C. marginatus DC. = *Pachycereus marginatus.*

C. maritima Britt. & Rose = *C. diffusus.*

C. melanurus Schum. = *Arthrocereus melanurus.*

C. mojavensis Engelm. & Bigelow = *Echinocereus triglochidiatus* var. *mojavensis.*

C. multiplex Pfeiff. = *Echinopsis oxygona.*

C. neotetragonus Backeb. = *C. fernambucensis.*

?C. obtusus Haw. = *C. fernambucensis.*

C. pachyrrhizus Schum. Thick-rooted shrub to 3m; st. to 10cm diam.; ribs 6, thin; spines 10–13, to 3cm. Fls not described. Parag. Z9.

C. paxtonianus Hook. non Monville. = *C. saxicola.*

C. pentagonus (L. = *Acanthocereus tetragonus.*

C. pernambucensis auct. = *C. fernambucensis.*

C. peruvianus misapplied. = *C. uruguayanus.*

C. piauhyensis Gürke = *Pilosocereus piauhyensis.*

?C. pitajaya (Jacq.) DC. = *Acanthocereus colombianus.*

C. platygonus Speg. non Otto = *C. argentinensis.*

C. pseudocaesius Werderm. Large shrub; st. segmented, 6–30cm diam., pale blue, pruinose; ribs 6–8; spines 16–20, to 1.5(-5)cm. Fls 26–27cm, pure white. Origin unknown. Z9.

C. repandus (L.) Mill. Tree to 12m; trunk 1–3m×25–70cm diam.; br. to 11cm diam., green or grey-green; ribs 7–9; central spines 1+, to 7.5(-17)cm; radial spines 7–15, to 2cm. Fls 6–11×4.5–5cm; white or tinged pink or green. Venez., Antilles. Z9.

C. saxicola Morong. Shrub, branching below; st. suberect or clambering, 1–3m×2–3cm, dark green; ribs 7–10; central spines 1–4, to 2cm, dark brown or black; radial spines 6–10, 5–10mm, bristly, brown. Fls 10–13×6–10cm, outer tep. tinged pink or green; inner tep. white. Spring–autumn. S Braz., Parag. and N Arg. Z9.

C. scheeri Salm-Dyck = *Echinocereus scheeri.*

C. silvestrii Speg. = *Echinopsis chamaecereus.*

C. smithianus (Britt. & Rose) Werderm. Shrub, sometimes with short trunk to 15cm diam.; st. erect or arching and sprawling, to 5m×4–8cm diam., green; ribs 8–11; spines c13, central 3–4cm, red to black at first, radials c1cm, white. Fls 6–8×4cm; scales red-tipped; inner tep. short, rounded and apiculate, white. Venez. Z9.

C. spegazzinii F.A. Weber. Shrub to 2m; st. ascending and arching or prostrate, ± 1.5cm diam., at first blue-green, marbled white; ribs 3–5, sharply tuberculate; spines 2–3 on young growth, short, nearly black, later to 6, to 1.5cm. Fls 10–13×7–9cm; outer tep. tinged purple; inner tep. white. Summer. NE Arg., Parag. Z9.

C. stenogonus Schum. Tree-like, to 6–8m, much branched; trunk 1–2m×55cm, v. spiny; st. 8–10cm diam., blue-grey; ribs 4(-5); spines 2–3, upper 2–5mm, lower 6–7mm, conic. Fls 20–22cm, red. Parag., N Arg. Z9.

C. striatus Brandg. = *Peniocereus striatus.*

C. thurberi Engelm. = *Stenocereus thurberi.*

C. trigonodendron Schum. ex Vaup. Tree to 15m, trunk 5m×30cm, crown much-branched, ribs 3–6, 2–3cm high; areoles woolly; spines 4–7, 2–5.5cm, brown. Fls 10–15cm. E Peru, E Boliv. Z9.

C. uruguayanus Kiesling. Tree to 6m; trunk to 1m×30cm; st. 8–12cm diam., glaucous; ribs usually 8, rounded; spines 5–10, subequal, 1–1.5(-2)cm, radiating, red-brown to black, sometimes yellow when young. Fls 15–18×15cm; outer tep. green, tipped red; inner tep. white. SE Braz. to N Arg. Several monstrose cvs traditionally referred to *C. jamacaru* and *C.* 'Peruvianus' are grown as *C.* 'Monstrosus' or *C.* 'Monstruosus'. *C.* 'Milesimus' (*C. milesimus* Rost.) is a similar plant. Z9.

C. validus Haw. Tree-like, 4–6m; st. to 12cm diam., pale blue-green at first, later grey-green; ribs 4–7, high and thin; central spine 1, to 4.5cm, brown; radial spines 5, lowest pair longest, 1–2cm. Fls 25×20cm; outer tep. pink-red; inner tep. white. Arg. The original identity of both *C. forbesii* and *C. validus* is uncertain; the two names are currently applied to a distinctive and quite widespread Argentinian sp. Z9.

?C. variabilis Pfeiff. = *C. fernambucensis.*

C. viperinus F.A.C. Weber = *Peniocereus viperinus.*

C. xanthocarpus Schum. Shrub or tree to 7m; young st. pale blue-green; ribs 4–6, high, thin; central spines 0–1, 1cm; radial spines 3–5, 5mm, dark brown. Fls 17–20cm; tube 12.5cm; tep. white. Parag. Z9.

→*Cactus*, *Cephalocereus* and *Monvillea*.

Ceriman *Monstera deliciosa*.

Cerinthe L. Boraginaceae. 10 ann., bienn. or perenn. herbs. Lvs often glaucous, sometimes tuberculate, basal and stalked or cauline, shorter, ± sessile. Infl. a term. bracteate cyme, branched, pendent; cal. deeply and unequally lobed; cor. cylindrical, 5-lobed. Eur. Z5.

C. alpina Kit. = *C. glabra*.

C. aspera Roth = *C. glabra*.

C. glabra Mill. Perenn. or bienn. to 50cm, erect to ascending. Basal lvs to 12cm, oblong to narrowly elliptic; petiole to 6cm. Infl. bracts cordate; cor. to 13×4mm, yellow, throat with purple band; lobes erect to strongly recurved, broadly ovate or elliptic. C & S Eur.

C. gymnandra Gasp. = *C. major*.

C. maculata All. = *C. minor*.

C. major L. Ann. to 60cm, erect. Basal lvs to 5cm, obovate-spathulate or obovate, tuberculate, ciliate, short-petiolate. Infl. bracts tinged purple, ovate, base subcordate; cor. to 30×8mm, yellow, tube purple to dark red, lobes short, ovate, acuminate, strongly recurved. S Eur.

C. minor L. Ann., bienn. or perenn., to 70cm, erect. Basal lvs glabrescent, ovate-oblong or oblanceolate to spathulate, obtuse, petiolate. Infl. with cordate bracts; cor. to 12×5mm, yellow, spotted or tinged violet or purple, lobes lanceolate, acute or acuminate. C & S Eur.

C. retorta Sm. & Sibth. Ann. to 50cm. Erect to ascending. Basal lvs to 12cm, broadly spathulate to ovate, tuberculate, obtuse to retuse, short-petiolate. Infl. bracts ovate, base cordate, suffused violet; cor. to 15×5mm, pale yellow, distally tinged violet, curved above. S Eur.

Cerochlamys N.E. Br. Aizoaceae. 1 stemless succulent. Lvs to 6cm, clump-forming, decussate, basally united, 8–10mm wide at base, 16mm wide in upper two-thirds, upper surface flat, lower surface rounded, carinate, pulled forward over briefly tapered tip, brown-green, waxy. Fls purple-red. S Afr.

C. pachyphylla (L. Bol.) L. Bol. var. *albiflora* Jacobsen. Fls white.

→*Mesembryanthemum*.

Ceropegia L. Asclepiadaceae. *c*200 perennials, climbing or erect, often caudiciform or tuberous; many succulent. Fls cymose or solitary, axill.; cal. 5-lobed, pet. 5 united to form a tube, swollen at base, cylindrical or funnel-shaped above, free tips often united creating a lantern-like structure. Canary Is., Trop. & SE Afr., SE Asia, NE Aus. Z10.

C. africana R. Br. St. slender, trailing or erect from small tubers, proliferous. Lvs ovate, elliptic or lanceolate, fleshy. Cor. tube 1–2.5cm, exterior tinged green, brown-violet-striate toward the mouth, lobes linear, 6–12mm, joined at the tip, with dark purple hairs inside. S Afr.

C. albertina S. Moore = *C. aristolochioides* ssp. *albertina*.

C. albisepta var. *viridis* (Choux) H. Huber = *C. viridis*.

C. ampliata E. Mey. St. thick and succulent, grey-green. Lvs 0 or scale-like. Cor. tube 2.5–5cm, broadly cylindric with a swollen base, exterior pale green, interior with a purple band, lobes to 9mm, oblong-lanceolate, dark green, joined at tips. S Afr.

C. arabica H. Huber. St., twining, usually leafless. Cor. tube 2.5–3.5cm, exterior marked purple, interior with hairs in funnel-shaped mouth, lobes triangular or narrow-linear, 1.5–2.5cm, white-pubesc. within, tips joined. Arabia.

C. aristolochioides Decne. St. slender, slightly succulent. Lvs ovate-cordate. Cor. dark purple outside, tube 12–15mm, interior hairy, mouth widened, funnel-shaped, lobes 4–8mm, broad-ovate. Senegal to Ethiop. ssp. *albertina* (S. Moore) H. Huber. Cor. lobes 7–16mm, oblong-linear, narrower at mouth.

C. armandii Rauh. St. v. succulent, erect or prostrate, spotted black; flowering st. elongated, twining. Lvs ovate-lanceolate, decid. Cor. tube urn-shaped, 5×5mm, grey-green, lobes 10–12mm, linear, lime green with a red-brown basal blotch. SW Madag.

C. assimilis N.E. Br. = *C. cancellata*.

C. ballyana Bullock. St. robust, twining. Lvs ovate or elliptic, fleshy. Cor. green-white spotted red-brown, tube 3.5–5cm, lobes 6–7cm, linear, apices twisted together. Kenya.

C. barbertonensis N.E. Br. = *C. linearis* ssp. *woodii*.

C. barklyi Hook. f. Differs from *C. africana* in cor. lobes hirsute inside, equalling or exceeding tube, often twisted together. S Afr.

C. bosseri Rauh & Buchloh. St. v. succulent, prostrate, flattened, finely tuberculate. Lvs rounded-elliptic; flowering st. slender, twining, with scale-like lvs. Cor. tube to 3cm, inflated-obovate below, narrow-tubular above, funnelform at mouth, lobes

13–15mm, linear-subulate, united at tips, margins with white and violet hairs. C Madag.

C. boussingaultiifolia Dinter = *C. nilotica*.

C. brownii Ledger = *C. denticulata* ssp. *brownii*.

C. cancellata Rchb. St. slender, twining, from small tuber. Lvs ovate-oblong to linear, fleshy. Cor. tube 12–20mm, green, interior hairy in central part, lobes 6–12mm, linear, purple-brown, glab., united at tips. S Afr. (Cape Prov.).

C. carnosa E. Mey. St. slender, twining. Lvs, fleshy, ovate to triangular. Cor., cream spotted and striped red-brown, tube 12–19mm, interior hirsute, lobes 4–6mm, ovate, interior sparsely white-hairy, united at tips. S Afr. (Natal, E Cape).

C. ceratophora Svent. St. erect, 1–1.5m tall, succulent. Lvs ephemeral. Infl. flowering persistently over several seasons, 10–20-fld; cor. pale yellow, tube 2cm, scarcely bent, lobes 1cm, united at tips. Canary Is.

C. chrysantha Svent. St. erect, 0.5–1m, succulent. Lvs ephemeral, linear. Infl. persisting, 5–10-fld; cor. 2–2.5cm, tube yellow-white, slightly bent, lobes yellow, 1cm, united at tips. Canary Is.

C. cimiciodora Oberm. St. prostrate or erect, to 1.5m, v. succulent; flowering st. thinner, twining ± leafless. Cor. tube mouth extending to 5 spreading star-shaped, lobes broadly triangular, red-brown. S Afr. (Cape Prov.).

C. connivens Dyer = *C. fimbriata* ssp. *connivens*.

C. constricta N.E. Br. = *C. nilotica*.

C. crassifolia Schltr. Tuberous; st. twining to 3m, with large, circular-ovate or linear lvs. Cor. green-white, speckled red-brown or purple, tube 1.5–3cm, lobes 5–12mm, broad-ovate, sparsely hirsute, veined red-brown. Nam. to Natal.

C. crispata N.E. Br. = *C. crassifolia*.

C. decidua E.A. Bruce. St. short to 15cm, thin, twining, from a small round tuber. Lvs ovate to lanceolate. Cor. tube papillose inside swollen base, lobes to 6mm, linear widening to spathulate at tip, tips united, sometimes with a small canopy, interior purple-ciliate, tube ridged. Kenya to Cape Prov. ssp. *pretoriensis* R.A. Dyer. Cor. tube ridged only in basal two-thirds. Transvaal.

C. denticulata Schum. St. succulent, twining, often 4-angled. Lvs ovate or rhombic, denticulate. Cor. tube 2–4cm, green- or yellow-white, base much swollen, lobes triangular forming a linear beak 1–2cm long, sometimes widened at tips, purple-ciliate. E Afr. ssp. *brownii* (Ledger) Bally. Differs in obliquely constricted, swollen base of cor. Widespread in trop. Afr.

C. devecchii Chiov. St. climbing, succulent. Lvs reduced to scales. Rac. subterminal, few-fld; cor. large, green-white, tube spotted pale purple, lobes and processes with dark purple spots, white within with dark purple band near tip, yellow-green above band, processes pure white within, 12–15×7–8mm, tube 8–10mm, cylindric, funnel-like at apex, processes spreading-deflexed, minutely ciliate. Somalia, Ethiop., Yemen. var. *adelaidae* Bally. St. grey-green mottled red. Lvs claw-shaped, black, spiny. Cor. tube 31mm, exterior white-green spotted red, lobes 4.5×4.5cm, erect, broadly triangular, apiculate, green at base, brown toward apex. Kenya, N Tanz.

C. dichotoma Haw. St. erect or ascending, 33–100cm. Lvs linear. Infl. of 1–9 fls; cor. tube pale yellow, slightly curved, 2–3cm, lobes 1–1.5cm, bright yellow, separating as the fl. dies. Canary Is.

C. dimorpha H. Humb. St. *Stapelia*-like, to 15cm tall, erect; flowering st. segmented, terete, slender, erect. Lvs linear-lanceolate. Cor. tube urn-shaped, 1cm, lobes 1cm, linear, tips united. SW Madag.

C. distincta N.E. Br. St. stout, slightly succulent, twining. Lvs ovate or elliptic. Cor. tube 1.5–3cm, hirsute inside, lobes 1cm, ovate at base extending to a broad-spathulate tip, white-ciliate. Zanzibar.

C. distincta ssp. *lugardae* (N.E. Br.) H. Huber = *C. lugardae*.

C. estelleana R.A. Dyer = *C. fimbriata*.

C. filiformis (Burchell) Schltr. St. twining. Lvs linear to thread-like. Infl. on a short pedicel; cor. tube 12–24mm, exterior off-white to pale green with purple bands and blotches, swollen, lobes filiform, 12–20mm, dark purple, united at tips. S Afr.

C. fimbriata E. Mey. St. v. succulent, twining. Lvs 0 or reduced to scales. Fls foul-smelling; cor. tube 3–5cm, inflated then abruptly narrowing and gradually widening to the funnel-shaped mouth *c*9mm wide, lobes widening above, united to form an umbrella-shaped canopy 1–2cm across, with purple hairs. S Afr. ssp. *connivens* (Dyer) P.V. Bruyns. Cor. tube less constricted above swollen base, clavate hairs borne only below broadened apex of lobes. Karroo. ssp. *geniculata* (Dyer) P.V. Bruyns. Cor. tube only widening to a narrow funnel, lobes sometimes equalling tube, with a conspicuous 'knee' one-quarter of the way up, hairs found only in area of knee. S Cape.

C. fusca Bolle. St. erect or trailing, 2m tall, 2cm thick. Lvs caducous, linear. cor. dark red-brown, tube 14–22mm, lobes narrow-linear, separating as fl. withers. Canary Is.

C. galeata H. Huber. St. v. succulent, twining. Lvs scale-like. Cor. 4cm, yellow-green or light ochre-yellow blotched brown or olive green, inflated below, abruptly constricted to tube above and widening again to funnel-shaped upper part, lobes with a triangular, plicate base, obovate above, united for upper third to form a canopy 2–2.5cm across, purple-ciliate. Kenya.

C. galpinii Schltr. = *C. rendallii*.

C. geniculata Dyer = *C. fimbriata* ssp. *geniculata*.

C. hastata N.E. Br. = *C. linearis* ssp. *woodii*.

C. haygarthii Schltr. St. stout, slight succulent, twining. Lvs ovate or elliptic. Cor. tube 1.5–3cm, with a broad, funnel-sharped neck, lobes with a rounded base, twisted together and narrowing to a filiform stalk 5–14mm long then widening into an ovate tip. S Afr.

C. hians Svent. St. 50–75cm, succulent, stiffly erect, branching. Lvs linear. Infl. perenn., many-fld; cor. tube yellow-white, slightly bent, 2–5.5cm, lobes yellow, separating, 1–1.5cm. Canary Is.

C. infundibuliformis E. Mey. = *C. filiformis*.

C. krainzii Svent. St. stiffly erect, simple or sparsely branched. Lvs caducous, linear. Infl. perenn.; cor. tube yellow-white, slightly curved, 2cm, lobes yellow, separating slightly, 13mm. Canary Is.

C. leroyi Rauh & Marn.-Lap. St. *Stapelia*-like, prostrate, finely tuberculate; twining. St. twining, to 50cm. Lvs linear-lanceolate. Cor. tube broad below, slender and terete above, 2.5–3cm, lobes linear, 6–12mm, tips united. SW Madag.

C. linearis E. Mey. St. thin, twining or cascading, proliferous, from globose tubers. Lvs triangular-ovate, lanceolate or linear, fleshy. Cor. tube 12–15mm, light green with purple stripes, interior dark-hirsute, lobes united above, dark purple-brown, purple-ciliate. S Afr. ssp. *tenuis* (N.E. Br.) P.V. Bruyns. Lvs narrow. Cape. ssp. *woodii* (Schltr.) H. Huber. HEARTS ENTANGLED; SWEETHEART VINE; HEARTS ON A STRING. St. slender, twining, pendent or creeping. Lvs to 1.25cm diam., fleshy, rounded-reniform, cordate, dull purple beneath, sea green above, often with purple and grey-green markings. Cor. tube 1–2cm, dull pink or light green, lobes 5–7mm, purple-brown, purple-ciliate. Zimb. to E Cape.

C. lugardae N.E. Br. St. stout, slightly succulent, twining. Lvs ovate or elliptic. Cor. sometimes downy, lobes triangular-ovate at base, extending to a linear or spathulate tip, 1.5–2cm. Angola, N Nam., Bots., Trop. E Afr. S of Equator.

C. monteiroi Hook. f. = *C. sandersonii*.

C. mozambicensis Schltr. = *C. nilotica*.

C. multiflora Bak. Tuberous; st. to 90cm, slender, twining, glab. Lvs fleshy, round-ovate, elliptic, lanceolate or linear. Infl. many-fld; cor. green-white, tube 12–26mm, interior hirsute, lobes 5–15mm, filiform from a triangular base, lower half projecting obliquely outward, upper half directed almost horizontally inward, tips united. S Afr. ssp. *tentaculata* (N.E. Br.) H. Huber. Cor. lobes usually separating. Angola, Nam., Zimb.

C. nilotica Kotschy. St. somewhat succulent, twining, 4-angled. Lvs ovate or rhombic, finely dentate. Infl. cymose; cor. tube 2–4cm, green- or yellow-white, blotched red-brown, constricted above base, hirsute below, lobes broadly oblong-ovate or triangular, 6–12mm, with a large yellow or white blotch, middle with a purple-brown band, green or red-brown above, interior with fine, purple hairs. Kenya, Sudan, Trop. Afr. S of Equator.

C. nilotica var. *simplex* H. Huber = *C. denticultata*.

C. pachystelma Schltr. Tuber to 10cm diam.; st. slender, twining, downy. Lvs almost cordate, pilose, fleshy. Cor. bronze or yellow-green to off-white, downy, tube 12–24mm, lobes narrow-linear, 5–12mm, light brown below, red above. Moz., Natal, Transvaal, Nam. ssp. *undulata* (N.E. Br.) H. Huber. Cor. lobes 8–12mm, widening to spathulate tip.

C. patersoniae N.E. Br. = *C. zeyheri*.

C. phalangium Dinter = *Kinepetalum schultzei*.

C. plicata E.A. Bruce = *C. nilotica*.

C. racemosa N.E. Br. St. slender, twining, not succulent, short-hairy. Lvs broad-ovate to linear. Infl. elongated; cor. red-brown, tube 1–2cm, lobes long-ovate, 5–12mm, interior sparsely white-hairy. Trop. Afr.

C. radicans Schltr. St. creeping, rooting. Lvs ovate, elliptic or oblong, succulent. Fls often solitary; cor. tube 3.5–5cm, green-white blotched purple, interior hirsute at base, lobes 1.5–3cm, narrow-linear, from a triangular base, with a broad chocolate band then a white stripe surmounted by a dark purple-red band, tip green with long, purple hairs. S Afr. ssp. *smithii* (M.R. Henderson) H. Huber. Lvs smaller, slightly wavy. Cor. lobes 1.5cm, spathulate, obovate to cordate. E Cape.

C. rendallii N.E. Br. Tuber large; st. 8–15cm, slender, twining and proliferous, or erect and dwarf. Lvs fleshy, ovate or linear. Cor. tube 12–20mm, lobes narrow-linear widening above to

spathulate, united to form an umbrella-shaped canopy, margins obscurely 10-lobed, sparsely purple-ciliate. S Afr.

C. robynsiana Werderm. Resembles *C. ballyana*. St. robust, twining. Lvs ovate or elliptic, fleshy. Cor. tube 2.5–3cm, lobes 2cm. Congo.

C. rupicola Deflers. St. terete, to 1m, erect, tips sometimes twining. Lvs broadly ovate, slightly fleshy, decid. Infl. to 15-fld; produced near tips of st.; peduncle 1cm; cor. red-brown, to 5cm, tube narrow slightly widened and curved at base, lobes strongly replicate and joined at tip to form a solid-looking cage, white-ciliate. N Yemen. var. *strictantha* N.P. Tayl. Cor. cream blotched red-brown. Yemen.

C. sandersonii Hook. f. PARACHUTE PLANT; UMBRELLA PLANT. St. robust, v. succulent, twining. Lvs cordate. Cor. green, tube 3.5–5cm, interior of swollen portion hairy, lobes united to form an umbrella-shaped canopy to 2.5cm diam., margin shortly 10-lobed, blotched dark green, covered with white motile hairs. Moz., S Afr.

C. schoenlandii N.E. Br. = *C. linearis* ssp. *woodii*.

C. senegalensis H. Huber. St. slender, twining. Lvs linear, ciliolate. Cor. tube 12–24mm, interior hirsute, lobes narrow-linear, 8–15mm, interior hirsute. Senegal.

C. serpentina E.A. Bruce = *C. sepeliiformis* var. *serpentina*.

C. seticorona E.A. Bruce. St. v. succulent, sparsely downy. Lvs ovate-cordate or lanceolate. Fls many; cor. interior shortly downy, tube 2–2.5cm, base slightly inflated, extremely hairy in central section, lobes spathulate, from a broadly triangular base, 8–10mm. Kenya, N Tanz. var. *dilatiloba* Bally. Cor. tube dilated at base and mouth, lobes ovate, margins sometimes ciliate. E Afr.

C. smithii M.R. Henderson = *C. radicans* ssp. *smithii*.

C. somaliensis Chiov. St. slender, twining, slightly fleshy. Lvs ovate. Cor. downy, tube 1–2cm, hairy inside base and funnel-shaped mouth, lobes narrowing from ovate base to a thread-like stalk, spathulate above, ± equalling tube, interior white-hairy. Somalia, Kenya.

C. squamulata Decne. = *Echidnopsis squamulata*.

C. stapeliiformis Haw. St. to 1.5m tall, shrubby, v. succulent, mottled grey-brown; flowering st. elongated, twining, others appearing fasciated. Lvs scale-like. Infl. several-fld; cor. tube 2–4cm, off-white, or green-white blotched black-purple, lobes linear, from a triangular base, 2.5cm, free, spreading, white, tipped and edged yellow-green, black-purple or dark brown. S Afr. var. *serpentina* (E.A. Bruce) H. Huber. St. longer, more slender. Cor. longer, lobes slimmer, joined for part of length. Transvaal.

C. stentiae E.A. Bruce. Tuber small; st. erect, to 10cm, upper part downy. Lvs fleshy, narrow-linear. Fls 1 or few together; cor. tube 2–3cm, middle section hairy, lobes narrow-linear, as long as tube or longer, hairy toward base, tips united. S Afr.

C. superba D.V. Field & I.S. Collenette. Tubers long-fusiform; st. semi-succulent, twining. Lvs minute, linear-lanceolate. Cor. 6–8cm, base abruptly narrowed to a cylindric portion 2.5–3mm diam., widening at mouth, glab. except at mouth, lobes 23–31mm, base deltoid then replicate and narrow-linear, united at tip, tube and base of lobes dull white with pale purple spots in lines, replicate portion of lobes bright green inside, base with purple band. Saudi Arabia, S Yemen.

C. tabulifera Deflers = *C. variegata*.

C. tentaculata N.E. Br. = *C. multiflora* ssp. *tentaculata*.

C. tenuis N.E. Br. = *C. linearis* ssp. *tenuis*.

C. thorncroftii N.E. Br. = *C. crassifolia*.

C. tuberculata Dinter = *C. crassifolia*.

C. turricula E.A. Bruce. Tuber to 8cm diam.; st. 15–30cm, simple, slender, erect. Lvs few, non-succulent, narrow-linear. Fls few, to 4 per plant, v. large for size of plant; cor. tube 3.6cm base rounded, narrow above, expanding to a wide funnel, lobes to 2.3cm, replicate, tips united, with long purple hairs, bases of tube and lobes dull white spotted light red-brown, lobes white with moss green centre, edged black, tips olive. S Afr.

C. undulata N.E. Br. = *C. pachystelma* ssp. *undulata*.

C. variegata (Forssk.) Decne. St. v. succulent, twining or creeping, ± leafless, mottled green-grey-brown. Cor. tinged pale green or pink, spotted dark red-brown, tube 3.5–4.5cm, base inflated, lobes 1–1.5cm, base triangular-ovate with filiform projections twisted together to form a tip 5mm long. Arabia.

C. variegata var. *cornigera* H. Huber = *C. devecchii*.

C. viridis Choux. St. trailing, robust, succulent. Lvs lanceolate. Cor. green, yellow or off-white, sometimes marked purple, tube mouth widening to 1–1.5cm, lobes triangular, extending to a broad to linear, blunt beak. S Madag. var. *truncata* H. Huber. Lobes much shortened, 3–5mm, beak 0.

C. volubilis var. *crassicaulis* H. Huber = *C. seticorona*.

C. wightii Graham & Wight = *C. africana*.

C. woodii Schltr. = *C. linearis* ssp. *woodii*.

C. zeyheri Schltr. St. twining. Lvs 0, or small, ovate or lanceolate.

Cor. tube 2–5cm, pale green-white; lobes bright green-hairy, deltoid, with long, narrow straight struts terminating in fused ovate-lanceolate tips. S Afr.

Ceroxylon Bonpl. ex DC. WAX PALMS. Palmae. 15–20 palms. St. solitary, ringed, smooth, waxy, often swollen at midpoint. Lvs pinnate; sheaths coriaceous, splitting opposite petiole; petiole channelled above, convex beneath; pinnae linear, acute, single-fold, regularly spaced or grouped along rachis, glossy above, scurfy or waxy beneath. Venez. to Colomb., Ecuad., Peru and Boliv. Z9.

C. alpinum Bonpl. ex DC. Trunk to 30m, pale grey, waxy. Pinnae with yellow midrib, glossy above, silver-grey tomentose beneath. Colomb.

C. andicola Humb. & Bonpl. = *C. alpinum*.

C. ferrugineum André = *C. alpinum*.

C. quindiuense (Karst.) H.A. Wendl. Trunk to 60m, rarely swollen, gleaming white, waxy. Pinnae scaly above, yellow- to white-tomentose beneath, midribs rusty brown. Colomb.

→*Iriartea* and *Klopstockia*.

Cerro Potosi Pinyon *Pinus culminicola*.

Cestrum L. Solanaceae. c175 everg. or decid. shrubs. Lvs simple. Infl. axill. or term., leafy; fls actinomorphic; cal. tubular to campanulate, 5-lobed; cor. tubular to funnel-shaped, limb 5-lobed. Trop. & subtrop. S Amer. Z9.

C. album Ferrero ex Dunal = *C. diurnum*.

C. angustifolium Lodd. = *C. laurifolium*.

C. aurantiacum Lindl. Arborescent or climbing glab. shrub, to 2m. Lvs to 11cm, ovate to lanceolate entire. Infl. term. or axill., paniculate, to 10cm across; cor. bright orange, tube to 18mm, the limb to 13mm diam. Summer. Guat. 'Album': fls white.

C. corymbosum Schldl. To 2m. Lvs to 10cm, elliptic to oblanceolate, coriaceous. Infl. corymbose, to 5cm; cor. red, funnelform, to 2cm; lobes toothed, ovate-acuminate. Braz.

C. × cultum Francey. (*C. elegans × C. parqui*.) To 3m. Lvs 8.5cm, ovate to lanceolate, apex long-acute. Infl. terminal, paniculate, sub-corymbose; cor. violet, tube cylindric, neck funnel-shaped, glab. Gdn origin.

C. diurnum L. non Weston. DAY JESSAMINE. Everg., glab. shrub, to 3m. St. slender, erect. Lvs to 10cm, oblong to oblong-elliptic, glossy, entire. Infl. axill. spicate, 10cm; fls fragrant by day; cor. funnel-shaped, 2cm, white occas. tinged green, lobes reflexed. W Indies.

C. diurnum Weston non L. = *C. laurifolium*.

C. elegans (Brongn.) Schldl. Everg., tree-like shrub, to 3.5m. Br. pendent, soft-pubesc. Lvs to 10cm, ovate-oblong to lanceolate, downy, entire, apex acuminate, base cordate. Pan. corymbose, pendent; cor. tubular, red to purple, to 2.5cm, lobes inflexed, acute. Summer–autumn. Mex. var. *longiflorum* Francey. Fls to 2.5cm and over. var. *smithii* Bail. Fls pink.

C. endlicheri Miers. Shrub, to 180cm, glab., erect. Lvs to 15cm, ovate-lanceolate, apex acuminate. Infl. paniculate, to 15cm; cor. scarlet, funnel-shaped, to 2.5cm, lobes to 2cm, triangular, acuminate. Summer. S Amer.

C. fasciculatum (Schldl.) Miers. Everg. shrub, to 2m. St. slender. Lvs to 7cm, ovate to lanceolate, undulate, apex acute to short-acuminate. Infl. term., clustered, to 8cm wide; cor. to 18mm, pubesc., carmine to red-purple. Spring. Mex. 'Newellii': fls crimson, glab.; possibly *C. elegans × C. fasciculatum*.

C. laurifolium L'Hérit. To 4m. Lvs 7–26cm, usually oblong-elliptic to ovate, coriaceous, slightly revolute, apex usually obtuse to rounded. Infl. paniculate, axill., to 6-fld; cor. funneliform, green to yellow-green. Antilles, Cuba.

C. newellii hort. = *C. fasciculatum* 'Newellii'.

C. nocturnum L. LADY OF THE NIGHT; NIGHT JESSAMINE. Everg. shrub, to 4m, scandent to spreading. Lvs to 13cm, narrow-lanceolate, acuminate. Infl. axill., slender, paniculate to racemose, to 13cm; fls nocturnally fragrant; cor. slender, to 2.5cm, pale green to ivory, limb to 13mm diam. Summer–autumn. W Indies.

C. paniculatum Schldl. = *C. elegans*.

C. parqui L'Hérit. WILLOW-LEAVED JESSAMINE. Decid., glab. shrub, to 3m. Lvs to 14cm, linear-lanceolate to elliptic, apex acute. Infl. cymose, axill. or term., to 13cm; cor. to 2.5cm, yellow-green to yellow, lobes ovoid to 6mm. Summer. Chile. 'Cretian Blue': fls violet-purple.

C. psittacinum Stapf. Scandent everg. shrub, softly pubesc. Lvs to 10cm, elliptic to oblong, apex acute to obtuse. Infl. axill. to term., racemose; cor. vivid orange to 14mm, funnel-shaped, lobes ciliate, rounded to ovoid. Autumn. C Amer.

C. purpureum (Lindl.) Standl. = *C. elegans*.

C. roseum HBK. Everg. shrub, to 180cm. Shoots soft-pubesc. Lvs to 10cm, undulate, oblong to ovate, soft-pubesc. Infl. axill. or term., corymbose; cor. to 3cm, rose to purple; limb to 13mm,

lobes spreading, acute. Mex. 'Illnacullin': fls rose-pink.

C. tinum St.-Lager = *C. corymbosum*.

C. venetatum Lam. = *C. laurifolium*.

Ceterach Willd.

C. aureum (Cav.) Buch. = *Asplenium aureum*.

C. dalhousiae (Hook.) Christ = *Asplenium dalhousiae*.

C. officinarum DC. = *Asplenium ceterach*.

C. rutifolia (R. Br.) Mett. = *Pleurosorus rutifolius*.

C. vulgare Samp. = *Asplenium ceterach*.

Cevennes Black Pine *Pinus nigra*.

Ceylon Bowstring Hemp *Sansevieria zeylanica*.

Ceylon Cardamom *Elettaria cardamomum*.

Ceylon Cinnamon *Cinnamomum zeylanicum*.

Ceylon Gooseberry *Dovyalis hebecarpa*.

Ceylon Oak *Schleichera oleosa*.

Ceylon Spinach *Basella alba*.

Ceylon Tea *Cassine glauca*.

Chaco *Sechium*.

Chaenactis DC. Compositae. c25 ann. to low-growing perenn. herbs. Cap. disciform, solitary or in corymbs, pedunculate; involucre hemispherical to campanulate; phyllaries usually floccose when young. W US. Z7.

C. alpina (A. Gray) M.E. Jones. Perenn., to 10cm. Lvs in term. rosettes, to 6cm, oblong to elliptic, 1–2-pinnate, seg. rounded-crenate. Cap. solitary, peduncle to 5cm, gland., grey-tomentose to glab.; flts white. Oreg. to Mont. and Colorado.

C. douglasii (Hook.) Hook. & Arn. Bienn. to short-lived perenn., to 40cm, floccose at first. Lvs in basal rosettes, to 10cm, 2–3-pinnatifid, tomentose at first. Involucre densely glandular-hairy; flts white or pink. Summer. BC to Ariz.

C. douglasii var. *alpina* A. Gray = *C. alpina*.

C. fremontii A. Gray. Ann., to 40cm, ± tomentose at first. Lvs to 10cm, entire to pinnatifid. Cap. several; flts white or flushed pink, outer flts with palmate limb. Winter. Utah, Ariz., Calif.

C. glabriuscula DC. Ann., to 40cm, thinly floccose at first. Lvs to 3cm, 1–2-pinnatifid or entire. Cap. solitary, peduncle to 10cm; flts yellow, outer flts with palmate limb. Spring. Calif. var. *lanosa* (DC.) Hall. Floccose. Lvs in a basal rosette. var. *tenuifolia* (Nutt.) Hall. Branchlets slender, tough, wiry. Lvs shorter.

C. lanosa DC. = *C. glabriuscula* var. *lanosa*.

C. orcuttiana (Greene) Parish. Like *C. glabriuscula* but stouter and more succulent. Peduncle and involucre coarsely hairy; flts deep yellow. Spring. Calif.

C. tenuifolia Nutt. = *C. glabriuscula* var. *tenuifolia*.

→*Hymenopappus*.

Chaenomeles Lindl. JAPANESE QUINCE; FLOWERING QUINCE; JAPONICA. Rosaceae. 3 decid. shrubs or small trees, sometimes spiny. Lvs ± serrate; stipules broad, leafy. Fls usually precocious, solitary or in clusters; sep. dentate; pet. usually 5, rounded-obovate, large; sta. 40–60, usually golden. Fr. apple-like. E Asia.

C. × californica Weber. (*C. × superba × C. cathayensis*.) Erect spiny shrub to 2m. Lvs lanceolate. Fls to 5cm diam., pink or rose red. Fr. to 6×6cm. Gdn origin. 'Enchantress': fls deep pink.

C. cathayensis (Hemsl.) Schneid. Decid. shrub or small tree to 6m. Br. tortuous, with spiny spurs. Lvs to 13cm, lanceolate or linear-lanceolate, red-lanuginose beneath. Fls 4cm diam., white, occas. flushed pink. Fr. to 15×9cm. Spring. China.

C. japonica (Thunb.) Spach. MAULE'S QUINCE. Spreading, decid., thorny shrub to 1m. Branchlets lanuginose when young. Lvs to 5cm, obovate or oval to suborbicular, glossy-glabrous. Fls 4cm diam., orange-red, scarlet or crimson. Fr. 4cm diam., yellow, red-stained, aromatic. Spring–summer. Jap. f. *alba* (Nak.) Ohwi. Fls white. var. *alpina* Maxim. Dwarf; st. spreading, br. ascending. Fls bright orange-red. Fr. small. Z5.

C. lagenaria (Lois.) Koidz. = *C. speciosa*.

C. lagenaria var. *cathayensis* (Hemsl.) Rehd. = *C. cathayensis*.

C. lagenaria var. *wilsonii* Rehd. = *C. cathayensis*.

C. maulei (T. Moore) Schneid. = *C. japonica*.

C. sinensis (Dum.-Cours.) Schneid. = *Pseudocydonia sinensis*.

C. speciosa (Sweet) Nak. Decid. spreading shrub to 3m. Branchlets spiny, glab. or lanuginose. Lvs to 9cm, oval, dark glossy green above, paler beneath, glab. Fls to 4.5cm diam., scarlet to crimson. Fr. apple- or pear-shaped, to 6.5×6.5cm, green-yellow, speckled, aromatic. Winter–summer. China. 'Apple Blossom': fls white tinted pink and cream. 'Cardinalis': fls crimson-scarlet, 4cm diam. not to be confused with 'Cardinal', a cv. of *C. × californica*. 'Falconnet Charlet' ('Rosea Plena'): fls double, salmon-pink. 'Moerloosii': fls large, white overlaid with pink and carmine, sometimes known erroneously as 'Apple

Blossom'. 'Nivalis': fls pure white. 'Phyllis Moore': fls double, salmon-rose. 'Rubra Grandiflora': habit low and spreading; fls v. large, crimson. 'Simonii': low-growing; fls semi-double, deep red. 'Umbilicata': fls deep pink. Z5.

C. ×*superba* (Frahm) Rehd. (*C. speciosa* ×*C. japonica.*) Shrub to 1.5m. Br. erect-spreading with slender spines. Lvs usually closer to *C. japonica*. Fls white, pink, crimson to orange and orange-scarlet. Spring–summer. Gdn origin. Z5. 'Boule de Feu': fls orange-red. 'Crimson and Gold': pet. crimson; anth. gold. 'Etna' (*C. speciosa* 'Simonii' ×*C.* ×*superba*): small; fls deep orange-red – from the same cross is 'Fire Dance' with glowing bright red fls. 'Hever Castle': fls pink. 'Knap Hill Scarlet': fls bright orange scarlet. 'Rowallane': fls large, deep crimson.

C. *vedrariensis* hort. = *C.* ×*vilmoriana*.

C. ×*vilmoriana* Weber. (*C. speciosa* ×*C. cathayensis.*) Heavily armed shrub to 2.5m. Lvs long. Fls white, pink-flushed. Gdn origin. Z6.

→*Cydonia* and *Pyrus*.

Chaenorrhinum (DC.) Rchb. DWARF SNAPDRAGON. Scrophulariaceae. *c*20 ann. or perenn. herbs. Fls in bracteate term. rac. or solitary in lf axils; cal. 5-lobed; cor. tube sub-cylindrical, elongated at base to a straight spur, upper lip 2-lobed, lower lip 3-lobed. Summer. Medit., Asia Minor. Z8.

C. *glareosum* (Boiss.) Willk. Perenn. to 30cm. St. villous, ascending, flowering st. stoloniferous with scale lvs. Lvs to 12mm, ovate to orbicular. Cor. tube 17–24mm, violet with pink or stained yellow, lips violet to lilac, palate yellow, spur yellow. S Spain.

C. *minus* (L.) Lange in Willk. & Lange. Ann. to 40cm, erect to ascending, pubesc. Lvs linear to oblong-lanceolate, 5–35mm. Cor. pale yellow to purple. Eur., SW Asia, nat. temp. zones.

C. *origanifolium* (L.) Kostel. Perenn. to 50cm, erect, many-stemmed. Lvs lanceolate to suborbicular. Cor. violet to white, palate pale yellow, 9–20mm. SW & SC Eur.

C. *villosum* (L.) Lange in Willk. & Lange Perenn., viscid, pubesc. St. pendent or ascending. Lvs 3–27mm, suborbicular to obovate or rhombic. Cor. tube 10–19mm, lilac to pale yellow, veined violet, palate yellow. S Spain, SW Fr.

→*Linaria*.

Chaerophyllum L. Umbelliferae. 35 annuals, biennials and perennials, taprooted or tuberous. Lvs finely cut, 1–3-pinnate or ternate; petioles sheathing. Umbels compound; involucre commonly 0; involucel of numerous bracteoles; fls small; pet. emarginate. N Temp. Z6.

C. *aureum* L. GOLDEN CHERVIL. Perenn. to 1.5m; st. glab. to puberulent, occas. spotted purple. Lvs 3-pinnate, seg. 1–4cm, lanceolate, golden to lime green, hairy to nearly glab., toothed or lobed. Fls white. Summer. C & S Eur., SW Asia.

C. *bulbosum* L. TURNIP-ROOTED CHERVIL; PARSNIP CHERVIL. Erect bienn. to 2m; roots tuberous; st. hairy at base, often tinged purple-brown. Lvs 2–3-pinnate, seg. linear to lanceolate, to 2mm wide. Fls white. E & C Eur., nat. US.

C. *hirsutum* L. Perenn.; st. to 120cm, hairy. Lvs 2–3-pinnate, seg. slightly overlapping, ovate to cordate, hairy to nearly glab., toothed. Fls white or pink-tinged; pet. ciliate. Summer. Eur. 'Roseum' (Rubrifolium'): lvs and st. strongly flushed purple; fls pink.

C. *sativum* Lam. = *Anthriscus cerefolium*.

Chaetanthera Ruiz & Pav. Compositae. *c*40 ann. to perenn. herbs and dwarf shrubs. Cap. usually radiate, solitary, sessile; inner phyllaries sometimes with a coloured apical appendage. S Peru to Chile. Z9.

C. *ciliata* Ruiz & Pav. Ann. herb to 20cm, spreading or erect. Basal lvs rosulate, to 30mm, spathulate to oblong-spathulate to lanceolate, serrate-mucronate, sericeous-lanate. Innermost phyllaries dark at apex; flts yellow. Summer. Chile.

C. *serrata* Ruiz & Pav. Perenn. herb, creeping, rhizomatous. Lvs to 1.5cm, rosulate, mostly linear, mucronate, cuneate at base, serrate, ± silky. Phyllaries black; ray flts golden-yellow, purple beneath; disc flts yellow. Chile.

Chaetochloa Scrib.

C. *italica* (L.) Scrib. = *Setaria italica*.

C. *palmifolia* A. Hitchc. & Chase = *Setaria palmifolia*.

Chaff-flower *Alternanthera*.

Chaffy Spleenwort *Asplenium paleaceum*.

Chain Cactus *Rhipsalis paradoxa*.

Chain Fern *Woodwardia*.

Chain of Love *Antigonon leptopus*.

Chalice Vine *Solandra*.

Chalk Lettuce *Dudleya pulverulenta*.

Chamaeangis Schltr. Orchidaceae. 7 monopodial epiphytic orchids. Lvs leathery or fleshy. Rac. many-fld, erect or pendulous, fls small; sep. and pet. free; lip entire, spurred. Trop. Afr., Madag., Masc. Is., Comoros Is. Z10.

C. *boutonii* (Rchb. f.) Garay = *Microterangis boutonii*.

C. *hariotiana* (Kränzl.) Schltr. = *Microterangis hariotiana*.

C. *hildebrandtii* (Rchb. f.) Garay = *Microterangis hildebrandtii*.

C. *odoratissima* (Rchb. f.) Schltr. St. to 30cm, pendent. Lvs to 20×2.5cm. Rac. to 15cm, pendent; fls 0.5cm diam., creamy-yellow, turning more yellow with age, scented, arranged in whorls of 4; sep. suborbicular; spur 12mm. W to E Afr., S to Malawi.

C. *orientalis* Summerh. St. to 12cm, woody below. Lvs 8–25×0.7–1.2cm. Rac. to 30cm, erect or pendent; fls 1cm diam., scented, yellow-brown, ochre or salmon, in pairs or whorls of 4; sep. elliptic-ovate; spur 15–20mm. Zaire, E Afr.

C. *vesicata* (Lindl.) Schltr. St. v. short. Lvs 15–40×1–3cm. Rac. to 30cm, pendent, many-fld; fls to 0.7cm diam. fleshy, green or yellow-green in opposite pairs or in threes; sep. ovate, apiculate; spur 4.5–10mm. W to E Afr.

Chamaeanthus Ule non Schltr. = *Geogenanthus*.

Chamaebatia Benth. MOUNTAIN MISERY. Rosaceae. 2 everg., upright shrubs 1(–2)m. Lvs 2–3 pinnate, lfts finely divided and fern-like, gland. pubesc., aromatic. Fls white in small corymbose term. pan.; pet. and sep. 5, sta. many. W US. Z8.

C. *australis* Abrams. Differs from *C. foliolosa* in lvs 2–3-pinnate, less hairy; fls smaller with fewer sta. Summer. S Calif.

C. *foliolosa* Benth. Lvs 2.5–10cm, obovate to ovate, 3–4-pinnate, seg. fine and feathery, glandular-pubesc. and viscid, balsam-scented. Fls 4–8 in term. corymbs; pet. obovate, to 0.5cm; sta. many, anth. yellow. Summer. S Calif.

Chamaebatiaria (Porter) Maxim. Rosaceae. 1 decid. subshrub to 1.5m. Br. erect, glandular-lanuginose, balsam-scented. Lvs ferny, grey-green, bipinnate, to 9cm, lanuginose. Fls in erect, leafy, glandular-tomentose pan. to 12cm; pet. white, 5, rounded, 5mm; sta. many, yellow. Summer. W N Amer. Z5.

C. *millefolium* (Torr.) Maxim.

→*Spiraea*.

Chamaecereus Britt. & Rose.

C. *silvestrii* (Speg.) Britt. & Rose = *Echinopsis chamaecereus*.

Chamaecrista Moench. Leguminosae (Caesalpinioideae). 265 shrubs, small trees or herbs. Lvs paripinnate. Rac. usually axillary; pet. 5, yellow, unequal, obovate, fertile sta. 5–10. Trop. Amer.

C. *fasciculata* (Michx.) Greene. Perenn. herb 10–100cm. St. scandent or procumbent, downy. Lvs 2.5–9cm, lfts in 8–21 pairs, narrow-oblong, rounded with a short sharp tip, glab. or somewhat ciliate or hirsute. Summer–autumn. E, C & SE US. Z5.

C. *glandulosa* (L.) Greene. Perenn., becoming shrubby and tree-like. Low and shrubby. Lvs 4.5–9cm; lfts in 8–24 pairs, oblong to lanceolate oblong-elliptic, soft-pubesc. beneath. Mex. to Boliv., W Indies. Z10.

C. *nictitans* (L.) Moench. ssp. *brachypoda* (Benth.) Irwin & Barneby. Downy somewhat rough, perenn. herb, 40cm–2m. St. usually simple. Lvs 4–10cm; lfts in 6–14 pairs, oblong or ovate-oblong, apiculate or mucronulate. Braz. Z10.

C. *serpens* (L.) Greene. Delicate, procumbent herb, 10–40cm tall, usually soft-hirsute. Lfts 3–14mm, 3–12, narrow-oblong to oblong-oblanceolate, apex triangular and sharp-tipped to blunt, base auricled, glab., occas. stiff-hairy. Z10.

→*Cassia*.

Chamaecyparis Spach. CYPRESS; FALSE CYPRESS. Cupressaceae. 8 everg. coniferous trees. Lvs aromatic, small, paired, opposite, imbricate, clothing flattened, frond-like branchlets: adult lvs scale-like; juvenile lvs larger, awl-shaped to linear. Cones small, globose, composed of woody, peltate scales. E Asia, N Amer.

C. *formosensis* Matsum. TAIWAN CEDAR; TAIWAN CYPRESS. To 60m, slow-growing, broad conic, then columnar. Lvs to 2mm, matt green, often bronze-tinted above, paler beneath. Cones ellipsoid, 5–8mm, brown, scales 10–12 with a quadrangular boss. Taiwan. Z8.

C. *funebris* (Endl.) Franco = *Cupressus funebris*.

C. *henryae* Li = *C. thyoides* ssp. *henryae*.

C. *lawsoniana* (Murray) Parl. LAWSON'S CYPRESS; OREGON CEDAR; PORT ORFORD CEDAR. To 60m in wild, slender conic when young, then columnar. Br. level, branchlets pendulous. Lvs keeled, to 2mm, bright green or tinted blue-grey, with pale lines beneath. Cones globose, 6–13mm, glaucous to rusty-brown, scales 6–10 drying with a sunken centre. W US. Z6. Many cvs are available, ranging in habit from dwarf rounded shrubs to columnar trees in tones of green, blue-green, grey, blue, lime and yellow. Yellow and white-variegated forms are also grown (e.g. 'Albospica', 'Ellwood's White') as are selections with filiform and feathered growth.

C. nootkatensis (D. Don) Spach. NOOTKA CYPRESS; YELLOW CYPRESS. To 40m; slender or broad conic, domed with age. Br. strongly upswept to erect, branchlets pendulous. Lvs to 3mm+; deep green, apices free, acute. Cones globose, 6–12mm, scales 4(–6) with a central soft spike, glaucous ripening purple to brown. W N Amer. 'Aurea': shorter; lvs dull yellow, becoming moss-green. 'Compacta': dwarf, densely bushy; branchlets erect, lvs blue-green. 'Glauca': grey-green. 'Nidifera': dwarf; branchlets few; lvs lax, green. 'Pendula': to 20m, pendulous, green. Z5.

C. obtusa (Sieb. & Zucc.) Endl. HINOKI CYPRESS. To 40m, slow-growing, broad conic, becoming columnar. Foliage dark, in layered fans; keeled lvs to 2mm or longer, facial lvs 1mm, blunt, deep green above, striped bright silver-white beneath. Cones globose, 8–13mm, green then orange-brown, scales 8–12. Jap. Cvs vary from small ('Nana'), dense, compact, globose or flat-topped bushes to medium or large trees; lvs cream-white to dark or blue-green, golden yellow or red-brown. 'Lycopodioides': slow-growing, congested lvs arranged spirally, not opposite as in type. Z6.

C. obtusa var. **formosana** Hayata Rehd. = C. taiwanensis.

C. pisifera (Sieb. & Zucc.) Endl. SAWARA CYPRESS. To 40m, broad conic to irregularly columnar. Bark rusty-brown, peeling. Lvs tapered and pointed, 2–3mm, mossy green above, marked white beneath. Cones globose, 4–7mm across, green then deep brown; scales 6–8 with hardened wavy deeply sunken centre. Jap. Cvs range from dwarf, slow-growing, flattened or globose bushes to medium-sized trees; lvs dense to lax, silver-white to bright yellow-green or steel-blue, sometimes variegated cream. 'Squarrosa' and related cvs (e.g. the silver-blue 'Boulevard') have fully juvenile foliage. 'Plumosa' and related cvs have intermediate foliage, as shown on slightly older normal seedlings. Z6.

C. sphaeroidea Spach = C. thyoides.

C. taiwanensis Masamune & Suzuki. Related to C. obtusa but distinct in lvs acute not white beneath and smaller cones; shoots flatter than in C. obtusa. Distinguished from C. formosensis by globose, few-scaled cone. Taiwan. Z8.

C. thyoides (L.) BSP. WHITE CYPRESS; COAST WHITE CEDAR; WHITE CEDAR. To 30m slow-growing, narrowly conic to irregular ovoid. Lvs to 3mm, in fan-shaped sprays, dark grey-green or gllaucous. Cones glaucous then purple-black to red-brown, ovoid or globose, often irregular; scales 6–10, broadly sunken in centre when dry. E US. 'Andelyensis': bluntly conic shrub to 3m; branchlets fan-like; lvs linear or in whorls of 3, blue-green. 'Andelyensis Nana': smaller, broad-topped bush. 'Aurea': slow-growing, gold to bronze. 'Ericoides': compact, conical, to 1.5m; lvs blue-green, turning bronze to maroon in winter, needle-like, stomatal bands 2. 'Rubicon': lvs bronze-green, burgundy in winter. ssp. **henryae** (Li) E. Murray. Shoots less flattened, lvs bright green, not glaucous; cones larger, to 9mm, not glaucous. SE US. Z5.

→Cupressus and Retinispora.

Chamaecytisus Link. Leguminosae. c30 small trees, shrubs, or subshrubs related to Cytisus. Lvs trifoliolate, petiolate. Fls pea-like. Eur., Canary Is.

C. albus (Hacq.) Rothm. PORTUGUESE BROOM. 30–80cm, ascending or erect. Lfts 1–3cm, oblong-obovate, hirsute throughout, or beneath only. Fls white or pale yellow, in 5–10-fld term. clusters; standard 1.6–2cm. Summer–autumn. SE & C Eur., northwards to S Poland. Z6.

C. albus (Lam.) Link non Hacq. = Cytisus multiflorus.

C. austriacus (L.) Link. 15–100cm, erect or prostrate. Lfts 8–25cm, oblanceolate or obovate, subglabrous to thickly hirsute above, white-sericeous beneath. Fls vivid yellow, in 4–8 fld term. clusters; standard 1.4–2.2cm. Summer. C & SE Eur. Z6.

C. ciliatus (Wahlenb.) Rothm. Closely resembles C. hirsutus but fr. only hairy on margins, not throughout. SE Eur. Z6.

C. glaber (L. f.) Rothm. To 1.5m. Lfts 2–2.5cm, oblong or obovate, glabrescent above. Fls yellow, 2–5 per axil; standard rust-colour dappled. SE & C Eur. Z6.

C. heuffelii (Würzb.) Rothm. Closely resembles C. austriacus but more slender, lfts smaller and fr. more silky. Balk., Rom., Hung. Z6.

C. hirsutus (L.) Link. 20cm–1m, ascending or prostrate. Lfts 0.5–2cm, obovate to elliptic, thinly hirsute or glab. above, sericeous to hirsute beneath. Fls large, rich yellow, 2–4 per axil; standard 18–30mm, occas. brown-speckled. Late spring–summer. C, S & SE Eur. Z6.

C. palmensis (Christ) Bisby & K. Nicholls. TAGASASTE. Lfts 2–3.5cm, oblanceolate or thinly elliptic, glab. above, fine pub-

esc. beneath, bristle-tipped. Fls to 2cm, white, 2–4 per axil. Late winter–spring. Canary Is. Z9.

C. proliferus (L. f.) Link. ESCABON. 3–5m. St. long, delicate. Lfts to 4.5cm, linear, somewhat pubesc. above, sericeous beneath. Fls 2.5cm, white, 4–7 per cluster. Early spring–summer. Tenerife, Gomera. var. **perezii** (Hutch.) Hunkel. Lfts 3.2cm, obovate, sericeous. Similar to C. palmensis. Canaries. Z9.

C. purpureus (Scop.) Link. To 60cm, densely bushy and low-growing. Lfts 0.6–2.4cm, obovate, glab., sharp tipped, dark green. Fls pale pink, lilac flushed ruby or crimson, large, 1–3 per axil; standard 1.5–2.5cm, with a dark central stain. Late spring–summer. SE Eur., S Alpine region, N Balk., N Albania. 'Albocarneus': fls light. 'Albus': fls white. 'Amsaticus': fls red tinted blue. 'Atropurpureus': fls deep burgundy. 'Erectus': habit upright. 'Roseus': fls pale pink. Z6.

C. pygmaeus (Willd.) Rothm. 5–15cm, prostrate to ascending. Lfts 0.5–1.2cm, linear, elliptic or obovate, sericeous. Fls yellow, in 1–4-fld heads; standard 0.7–2cm. Balk. Z6.

C. ratisbonensis (Schaeff.) Rothm. 30–45cm, ascending or prostrate. Lfts 1–1.5cm, obovate, glab. above, sericeous beneath, ultimately glab. Fls vivid yellow, 1–4 in clusters; standard 1.25cm diam., usually spotted peach. Late spring–summer. C Eur. to Cauc. and Sib. Z4.

C. rochelii (Wierzb.) Rothm. 50cm–1m, erect. Lfts 2–2.5cm, oblong-lanceolate, adpressed-hirsute. Fls light yellow, 12–18 in term. heads; standard 1.8–2cm. Summer. E Balk. and Bulg. to W Ukraine. Z6.

C. supinus (L.) Link. 0.15–1m, ascending or prostrate. Lfts 1.5–3.5cm, obovate, elliptic or oblong, glab. or thinly pubesc. above, hirsute beneath. Fls yellow, in term., 2–8-fld heads rarely racemose; standard 2–2.5cm, usually speckled brown at base. Summer. S & C Eur., to C Fr., Bavaria, W Ukraine. Z7.

C. tommasinii (Vis.) Rothm. Differs from C. austriacus in lfts to 2cm, elliptic-lanceolate, glab. above. N Albania, W Balk. Z7.

C. ×versicolor (Kirchn.) Rothm. (C. purpureus × C. hirsutus.) To 50cm, erect or diffuse, br. slender, long. Lfts c2.5cm, obovate, glab. above, pubesc. beneath. Fls 1–3 per axil; standard pale, wing yellow, keel pink-violet. Late spring–early summer. Gdn origin. 'Hillieri': habit low; br. arching; fls large, yellow, later tinted bronze, becoming pink. Z6.

→Cytisus.

Chamaedaphne Moench. LEATHERLEAF; CASSANDRA. Ericaceae. 1 low everg. shrub to 1.5m. Lvs to 5cm, oval, obovate, oblong or lanceolate, entire, undulate or bluntly and irregularly toothed, rusty-scaly beneath. Rac. secund, leafy, term. to 12cm; cor. to 0.6cm, white, urceolate, with 5 small, slightly recurved lobes. N temp. regions. Z7.

C. calyculata (L.) Moench. 'Angustifolia': lvs narrow, undulate-crenate. 'Nana': compact, to 30cm; lvs smaller.

→Cassandra.

Chamaedorea Willd. Palmae. c100 palms. St. solitary or clustered, usually slender and cane-like. Lvs pinnate or entire and emarginate, reduplicate. Infl. interfoliar, branched bracts, papery, overlapping; fls usually yellow-orange. C & S Amer. Z9.

C. adscendens (Dammer) Burret. St. solitary, to 2.5m×1cm. Lvs dull green; petiole 7cm; pinnae to 16×2.5cm, 1–6 per side, dull green, velvety, term. pair often wider, sometimes with one side of lf entire. Belize, Guat.

C. alternans H.A. Wendl. St. to 3m, solitary. Pinnae 8–12 per side, median pinnae to 37.5×6cm, veins 5, prominent; petiole and midrib pale beneath. Mex.

C. arenbergiana H.A. Wendl. St. to 4.5m×2–3cm. Lvs to 2.5m, pinnae, 8–10 each side, shining beneath, oblong-lanceolate, often falcate, apex pendent, largest 60×10cm; petioles to 45cm. Guat. to Panama.

C. atrovirens Mart. St. to 2.7m, simple. Lvs to 75cm, bright green, spreading. Mex.

C. brachypoda Standl. & Steyerm. St. to 1m×1cm, forming colonies. Lvs 25×25cm, entire, base cuneate, apex deeply emarginate, lobes 10×16cm, acute to acuminate; rachis 12cm. Guat.

C. cataractarum Mart. St. to 60cm, tufted, branching, procumbent. Lvs to 27.5×2.5cm, erect, pinnae alt., 13–16 each side, linear-lanceolate, with one conspicuous vein, midrib and petiole pale beneath. S Mex.

C. concolor Mart. Pinnae oblong-rhombic, with slender curved tips. Mex.

C. costaricana Ørst. St. to 3m, tufted. Pinnae c40, linear-lanceolate. Costa Rica.

C. desmoncoides Wendl. = C. elatior.

C. elatior Mart. St. to 4m×2cm, cane-like, weakly climbing, clump forming. Lvs to 3m, entire with apex deeply emarginate, becoming pinnate, pinnae 35×3cm, linear-lanceolate, sometimes curved. Mex., Guat.

C. elegans Mart. PARLOUR PALM. St. to 2m×2cm, erect to decumbent. Lvs few, spreading; pinnae 12–20×1–2cm, 11–20 per side; petiole 12–27cm. S Mex., Guat. 'Bella': habit v. compact with a conspicuous, short crownshaft; lvs to 12cm; infl. golden-yellow. One of the palms most frequently grown as a houseplant.

C. ernesti-augusti H.A. Wendl. St. to 2m×1.5cm, cane-like, usually solitary. Lvs entire, cuneate-obovate, apex deeply emarginate, dull green, to 25×25cm, 13–16-nerved each side, margins dentate; petiole 8–20cm. Mex. to Hond.

C. erumpens H.E. Moore. BAMBOO PALM. St. to 3m, slender, cane-like, clumped. Pinnae 5–15 each side, green, term. pair sometimes larger, largest 27.5×1.6–3cm, lanceolate; petiole 4.5–8cm, rachis 18–47.5cm. Guat., Hond.

C. falcifera H.E. Moore. St. 1–6m×5–7cm, solitary. Petiole 6.5–33cm, pale yellow; rachis 10.5–23cm, pale yellow; pinnae membranous, glossy green above, paler and dull beneath, keeled above, lower pinnae 7.5–21×1–4.5cm, smaller towards st., alt., with prominent nerves. Guat.

C. fragrans (Ruiz & Pav.) Mart. St. tufted, to 1.5m. Lvs entire, deeply emarginate. Infl. intensely fragrant. Peru.

C. fusca Standl. & Steyerm. = *Chamaedorea oblongata*.

C. geonomiformis H.A. Wendl. St. to 1.7m×1cm, solitary. Lvs erect, entire, oblanceolate, apex furcate; petiole 5–15cm; blade 6.5–13cm, margins subscarious, toothed beneath, veins prominent beneath. Belize, Hond., Guat.

C. glaucifolia H.A. Wendl. St. to 4.5m, solitary. Pinnae to 35×1cm, 46–80 each side, clustered in group of 2–4, held in differing planes along rachis, linear. S Mex.

C. graminifolia H.A. Wendl. XIAT. St. solitary. Pinnae 25–30×1cm, 36–42 per side, linear. Guat., Mex.

C. karwinskyana H.A. Wendl. St. to 50cm, stoloniferous. Petiole and midrib pale beneath; pinnae 27–33 each side, 30×3–3.7cm, lanceolate. Mex.

C. klotzschiana H.A. Wendl. St. to 2.4m, solitary. Lvs to 30×3.7cm, pinnae 15–18 each side, slightly curved, in clusters of 2–4 along rachis. Mex.

C. lepidota H.A. Wendl. St. to 45×2cm, solitary. Lvs to 106cm, with minute, pale scales; petiole and rachis green; pinnae to 22.5×4.5cm, 13 per side, lanceolate. Mex.

C. linderiana H.A. Wendl. = *C. concolor*.

C. lunata Liebm. = *Chamaedorea oblongata*.

C. martiniana H.A. Wendl. = *C. cataractarum*.

C. metallica Cook ex H.E. Moore. Resembles *C. ernesti-augusti*, but lvs puckered, broader, borne on shorter st., metallic sea green, 8–9-ribbed each side. Mex.

C. microspadix Burret. St. to 3m×1cm, tufted. Lf blade 55cm, oblong, glaucous; pinnae 9 per side, alt., lanceolate, median pinnae 22×2.8cm, velvety above, blue-green beneath. E Mex.

C. nana N.E. Br. Resembles *C. tenella*. St. to 60cm. Lvs ovate-elliptic, larger than in *C. tenella*, apex divided to middle of blade, dentate, each lobe 11-nerved. Costa Rica.

C. neurochlamys Burret. PACAYA; PACAYO; CHILAC. St. 4–5m×2.5cm, solitary, petiole 15–29cm; pinnae 6–8 each side, rhombic-sigmoid, regularly spaced, apex acuminate, to 30×6cm. S Mex. to Hond.

C. oblongata Mart. CAUQUI. St. 1.5–3m×1.2–5cm, solitary, erect. Petiole 25–31cm; pinnae 6–9 per side, leathery, regularly spaced, rhombic-lanceolate, glossy green, above, paler beneath, median pinnae 17×3.5–10cm, long-acuminate, term. pinnae smaller. E Mex. to Nic.

C. oreophila Mart. St. to 1.2m×10cm, usually solitary. Lvs c75cm; rachis pale below; pinnae 11–18 each side, to 30×3.3cm, alt., lanceolate, straight. Mex.

C. pacaya Ørst. St. to 1.8m, solitary. Petiole and midrib pale beneath, pinnae to 17.5×1.5cm, 5–8 each side of rachis. Costa Rica, Panama.

C. pochutlensis Mart. St. to 3.5m, tufted. Lvs to 1.2m, midrib to 80cm, pinnae 20–28cm, 20–24 per side, regularly spaced, linear-lanceolate, acuminate; petiole to 30cm. W Mex.

C. pulchella Lind. = *C. elegans*.

C. radicalis Mart. St. solitary, suckering, decumbent, sometimes erect. Lvs arched, deep green; pinnae 18 each side, to 32.5×1.6cm, straight, narrow, midrib conspicuous beneath. NE Mex.

C. resinifera Wendl. = *C. elatior*.

C. sartorii Liebm. St. 2.5–4m×2cm, solitary. Lvs to 1m; petiole to 40cm; rachis and petiole pale beneath; pinnae 30×4–5.5cm, 6–8 per side, curved-lanceolate or falcate. Mex. to Hond.

C. scandens Liebm. = *C. elatior*.

C. schiedeana Mart. St. to 3m×2.5cm, solitary. Petiole and rachis green; pinnae to 30×4cm, lanceolate, falcate-cuspidate, 13–14 per side. E Mex.

C. schippii Burret. Multi-stemmed, to 2.7m. Pinnae to 30×2cm,

to 30 per side, linear, straight. Hond.

C. seifrizii Burret. St. scandent. Lf to 40cm; pinnae to 15×2cm, 14 per side, base decurrent; petiole 5cm. Yucatan.

C. stolonifera H.A. Wendl. St. to 90×0.6cm, many, rachis pale below, to 10cm; blade entire, apex deeply emarginate, to 16cm on upper margin. Mex.

C. tenella H.A. Wendl. St. to 60cm, solitary. Lvs entire, apex deeply emarginate, blade to 7.5cm, lat. margin dentate, ribs 11–12 per side. Mex.

C. tepejilote Liebm. PACAYA. St. to 6m, usually solitary, with prop roots. Pinnae to 70×7.5cm, 12–25 per side, linear-lanceolate, apex falcate. Mex. to Colomb.

C. wendlandiana (Ørst.) Hemsl. = *C. tepejilote*.

→*Eleutheropetalum* and *Neanthe*.

Chamaelirion Willd. DEVIL'S BIT. Liliaceae (Melanthiaceae). 1 tuberous, perenn. herb. Basal lvs 5–20cm in a loose rosette, obovate to spathulate, stalked; st. lvs smaller, narrower, sessile. Infl. a dense cylindric rac., often nodding at tip, usually taller (to 1m) and looser in ♀ plants; tep. 3mm, 6, linear-spathulate, white, becoming yellow with age; sta. 6 (staminodes in females). Summer. E N Amer. Z4.

C. luteum (L.) A. Gray. BLAZING STAR; FAIRY WAND; RATTLESNAKE ROOT.

Chamaemelum Mill. CHAMOMILE. Compositae. 4 aromatic ann. or perenn. herbs. Lvs 1–3-pinnatisect. Cap. radiate or discoid, pedunculate; ray flts white; disc flts yellow. Eur., Medit.

C. caucasicum (Willd.) Boiss. = *Tripleurospermum caucasicum*.

C. mixtum (L.) All. Ann., to 60cm, ± pubesc., often much-branched. Lvs oblong pinnatisect to serrate, lobes linear-lanceolate, entire or serrate, mucronate. Involucre 3–5mm; ray flts to 1cm. Medit. and SW Eur. to C Fr.

C. nobile (L.) All. CHAMOMILE. Strongly aromatic decumbent perenn., to 30cm, ± pubesc. Lvs oblong, 2–3-pinnatisect, lobes linear, mucronate. Involucre 4–6mm; ray flts to 1cm, sometimes 0. Summer. W Eur. 'Flore Pleno': to 15cm; infl. 'double'. 'Treneague': to 30cm, non-flowering. Z4.

C. tchihatchewii Boiss. = *Tripleurospermum oreades* var. *tchihatchewii*.

→*Anthemis*.

Chamaenerion Ség.

C. angustifolium (L.) Scop. = *Epilobium angustifolium*.

C. angustissimum (Weber) Sosn. = *Epilobium dodonaei*.

C. dodonaei (Vill.) Schur = *Epilobium dodonaei*.

C. latifolium (L.) T.C.E. Fries & Lange = *Epilobium latifolium*.

C. palustre auct. non (L.) Scop. = *Epilobium dodonaei*.

C. rosmarinifolium Coste pro parte, non (Haenke) Moench = *Epilobium fleischeri*.

Chamaepericlymenum J. Hill.

C. canadense J. Hill = *Cornus canadensis*.

C. suecicum Asch. & Graebn. = *Cornus suecica*.

Chamaerhodiola Nak.

C. dumulosa (Franch.) Nak. = *Rhodiola dumulosa*.

Chamaerops L. Palmae. 1 palm. St. 2–6m, sometimes 0, often clustered, clothed with persistent lf bases, bare and ringed below. Lvs to c80cm, petioles armed; sheaths disintegrating into woven fibres; blades deeply palmately divided; seg. linear-lanceolate, sometimes toothed to tattered at apex, blue-green to grey-green, coarse, scurfy. Medit., eastwards from W Port. and Moroc. Z9.

C. excelsus Mart. = *Trachycarpus fortunei*.

C. fortunei Hook. = *Trachycarpus fortunei*.

C. griffithii Verl. = *Trachycarpus martianus*.

C. humilis L. var. *arborescens* (Pers.) Steud. Trunk tall, simple. 'Nana': scrubby, low, compact, freely suckering, becoming bushy.

C. humilis var. *elatior* hort. = *C. humilis* var. *arborescens*.

C. martianus Wallich = *Trachycarpus martianus*.

Chamaespartium L.

C. sagittale (L.) P. Gibbs = *Genista sagittalis*.

Chambeyronia Vieill. Palmae. 2 palms to 20m. St. solitary, erect, ringed, basally swollen. Crownshaft prominent. Lvs pinnate, emerging purple-red and scurfy; pinnae broadly linear, acute to acuminate, midrib and marginal veins prominent. New Caledonia. Z10.

C. macrocarpa (Brongn.) Vieill. ex Becc. To 18m. Lvs to 2.5m; pinnae to 100×10cm.

→*Kentiopsis*.

Chamelaucium Desf. Myrtaceae. 21 everg. shrubs. Lvs narrow, sessile, usually glab., strongly aromatic. Fls sessile or short-stalked, in upper axils or term. clusters; pet. 5, orbicular, spreading; sta. 10. SW Aus.

C. axillare (F. Muell.) ex Benth. ESPERANCE WAX. Small shrub. Lvs 1–2.5cm, terete to 3-sided, acute. Fls to 2cm diam., white.

C. ciliatum Desf. Dwarf shrub. Lvs to 1cm, linear-lanceolate, acute, ciliate. Fls c1cm diam., white ageing to red.

C. megalopetalum (F. Muell.) ex Benth. Upright, rigid, small shrub. Lvs to 1cm, oblong, flat or concave above, convex beneath, thick, erect, acute or blunt. Fls c1.5cm diam., white or cream ageing to red, centre tinted green.

C. uncinatum Schauer. GERALDTON WAX. Medium to tall shrub, open to dense, foliage lemon-scented. Lvs to 4cm, linear, sub-terete, apex hooked. Fls 1.25–2.5cm diam., faintly scented of sandalwood, dull red, purple, mauve or pink to white. Many cvs in colours ranging from white to cream to pale rose to deep carmine or magenta.

Chameranthemum Nees Acanthaceae. 4 perenn. herbs. Lvs large, thin-textured, often coloured. Fls usually in slender erect spikes or pan.; bracts small; cor. long-tubular, lobes 5, spreading. Trop. Amer. Z10.

C. alatum hort. = *Pseuderanthemum alatum*.

C. gaudichaudii Nees. St. prostrate. Lvs 6–8.5cm, ovate, cordate, dark green overlaid with silver, flushed purple beneath. Spikes single or in threes; bracts purple-flushed; fls to 1.2cm, white tinged rose-purple within. Braz.

C. igneum (Lind.) Reg. = *Xantheranthemum igneum*.

Chamerion (Raf.) Raf. = *Epilobium*.

Chamise *Adenostoma fasciculatum*.

Chamois Cress *Pritzelago alpina*.

Chamomile *Chamaemelum* (*C. nobile*).

Chamomilla Gray.

C. recutita (L.) Rausch. = *Matricaria recutita*.

Champaca *Michelia champaca*.

Chanal, Chanar *Geoffroea*.

Channelled Heath *Erica canaliculata*.

Chaparral Beard-tongue *Penstemon antirrhinoides*.

Chaparral Currant *Ribes malvaceum*.

Chaparral Honeysuckle *Lonicera interrupta*.

Chaparral Lily *Lilium rubescens*.

Chaparral Mallow *Malacothamnus*.

Chaparral Pea *Pickeringia*.

Chaparral Sage *Salvia leucophylla*.

Chaparral Whitethorn *Ceanothus leucodermis*.

Chaplet Flower *Stephanotis floribunda*.

CHARACEAE Agardh. 6/215. *Nitella*.

Charieis Cass.

C. heterophylla Cass. = *Felicia heterophylla*.

C. neesii Cass. = *Felicia heterophylla*.

Charity *Polemonium caeruleum*.

Charlock *Brassica kaber*; *Sinapis arvensis*.

Chartolepis Cass.

C. glastifolia (L.) Cass. = *Centaurea glastifolia*.

Chasmanthe N.E. Br. Iridaceae. 3 cormous perenn. herbs. Lvs distichous, imbricate. Spikes secund or distichous, sometimes branched; fls irregular; perianth tube curved, widening abruptly from a short, tubular base, with 1–3 nectar pouches where the tube expands, seg. 6, the topmost at least twice as long as others. S Afr. (Cape Prov.). Z9.

C. aethiopica (L.) N.E. Br. 40–70cm. Lvs 40–60cm, linear or lanceolate. Spike 15–18cm, unbranched, 7–15-fld, secund; fls to 8cm, red, maroon in throat, tube with yellow stripes. Autumn–winter. SW to SE Cape, coastal areas.

C. bicolor (Gasp. ex Ten.) N.E. Br. 70–130cm. Lvs 50–80cm, sword-shaped, lustrous. Spike 25–30cm, sometimes with 1–2 basal br., 12–28-fld, secund; fls to 8cm, vermilion red and yellow-green, the lobes vermilion, dark red or pink and green. Winter–spring. SW Cape.

C. floribunda (Salisb.) N.E. Br. 50–150cm. Lvs 30–50cm, lanceolate, forming a fan. Spike about 30cm, often branched at base, distichous, many-fld; fls to 8.5cm, orange-red or yellow. Winter–spring. SW Cape. var. *floribunda*. Fls orange-red, tube often with yellow stripes; anth. purple. var. *duckittii* G. Lewis ex L. Bol. Fls primrose yellow; anth. yellow-brown.

C. intermedia (Bak.) N.E. Br. = *Tritoniopsis intermedia*.

C. praealta Rehd. = *C. floribunda*.

C. vittigera (Salisb.) N.E. Br. = *C. aethiopica*.

→*Antholyza*.

Chasmanthium Link. Gramineae. 6 perenn. grasses. Lf blades linear to narrow-lanceolate. Infl. a pan. E US, E Mex. Z4.

C. latifolium (Michx.) Yates. NORTH AMERICA WILD OATS; SPANGLE GRASS; SEA OATS. Loosely tufted, to 1m. Pan. delicately branched; spikelets, oblong-lanceolate to broadly ovate, flattened with overlapping lemmas, like a large flat angular *Briza maxima*. E US, N Mex.

→*Uniola*.

Chasmatophyllum (Schwantes) Dinter & Schwantes. Aizoaceae. 6 shrubby succulents, eventually mat-forming. Lvs decussate, spathulate, lower surface semi-terete or bluntly keeled, sometimes with 1–2 obtuse teeth toward tip, white-tuberculate. Fls solitary, term. Late summer–early autumn. S Afr. Z9.

C. masculinum (Haw.) Dinter & Schwantes. Lvs 1.5–2×0.4–0.6cm, trigonous to semi-terete, bluntly carinate, often 2–4-toothed. Fls 15mm diam., yellow, tipped red. S Afr., Nam.

→*Mesembryanthemum* and *Stomatium*.

Chaste Tree *Vitex agnus-castus*.

Chatham Island Forget-me-not *Myosotidium hortensia*.

Chaubardia Rchb. f. Orchidaceae. 3 epiphytic orchids allied to *Huntleya* and *Chondrorhyncha*. Summer. S Amer. Z10.

C. tigrina Garay & Dunsterv. Pbs 0. Lvs to 20×3cm bases overlapping in a loose fan, pale green, soft, strap-shaped. Fls solitary, to 4.5cm diam. on nodding axillary stalks; tep. sub-equal, broadly lanceolate, acute, olive green to bronze, banded maroon, tipped lime green, lip to 1.5×1.2cm, fleshy, basally saccate, callus 10-ridged, yellow-ochre, spotted purple. Venez.

Chay *Oldenlandia umbellata*.

Chayote *Sechium* (*S. edule*).

Checkerberry *Gaultheria procumbens*.

Checkerbloom *Sidalcea malviflora*.

Checker Mallow *Sidalcea*.

Cheddar Pink *Dianthus gratianopolitanus*.

Chee Grass *Stipa splendens*.

Cheese Berry *Cyathodes glauca*.

Cheeses *Malva sylvestris*.

Cheesewood *Pittosporum undulatum*.

Cheilanthes Sw. LIP FERN. Adiantiaceae. 180 small everg. ferns. Rhiz. short to widely creeping; stipes wiry, stramineous or brown to black. Fronds rigidly spreading, pinnate to bipinnate-pinnatifid, with numerous fine divisions, generally tomentose, coriaceous, glandular-pubescent, farinose or scaly, some resurrection plants, 'shrivelling' in drought, expanding when rehydrated. Cosmop.

C. alabamensis (Buckl.) Kunze. Stipes slender, 8–18cm, black, glab. or villous above; blades to 35×8cm, bipinnate to bipinnatifid, elliptic to narrowly lanceolate, glab. or with sparse white hairs beneath, pinnae numerous, ovate to lanceolate, pinnules triangular-oblong, subobtuse to acute. N Amer. Z6.

C. ambigua A. Rich. = *Hypolepis tenuifolia*.

C. anthriscifolia Schldl. non Willd. = *Hypolepis sparsisora*.

C. arborescens Sw. = *Hypolepis tenuifolia*.

C. argentea (Gmel.) Fée. Stipes 10–25cm, fragile, lustrous, sparsely scaly below; blades 2–8×2–10cm, ternately parted, glab. and glaucous above, white- to cream-farinose beneath, pinnae pinnatipartite, obtuse. E Asia. Z4.

C. aspera Kaulf. = *Hypolepis sparsisora*.

C. bergiana Schldl. Stipes 10–30cm, ferruginous, pubesc., scaly below; blades 10–45×10–45cm, tripinnate to quadripinnatifid, deltoid, herbaceous, pubesc., pinnae deltoid, lowest the largest, pinnules ovate, seg. oblong, obtuse, entire or lobed. S Afr. Z9.

C. bonariensis (Willd.) Proctor. Stipes to 4–25cm, initially pubesc., chestnut to black; blades 10–45×1–3cm, pinnate to pinnatifid, linear to elliptic, apex attenuate to obtuse, base attenuate, pubesc. above, tomentose beneath; pinnae blades lanceolate or deltoid to oblong, lobed, seg. linear to oblong, entire, falcate. W Indies, SW US, Mex. to Chile and Arg. Z10.

C. californica Mett. CALIFORNIAN LACE FERN. Stipes 5–25cm, dark glossy brown, nearly naked; blades usually quadripinnate, deltoid, ultimate seg. 2–3mm, linear to elliptic, bright green, glab. Calif., Baja Calif. Z9.

C. candida Mart. & Gal. Stipes to 15cm, base scaly, black; blades to 15×12cm, pinnate to pinnatifid, ovate or lanceolate to pentagonal, apex attenuate, glab. above with white wax on underside; pinnae 5–10 pairs, linear to oblong, subacute, bluntly

C. canescens (Kunze) Mett. non Kunze = *C. lasiophylla*.

C. clevelandii D.C. Eaton. Stipes stout, pale brown, scaly. Fronds 10–40cm including stipe, oblong to lanceolate, 3–4-pinnate, seg. close-set, suborbicular, revolute, bead-like, green and glab. above, with pale brown scales beneath. Calif., Baja Calif. Z9.

C. colvillei Maxon. Stipes brown or tinged purple, with paler scales; blades 5–30cm, oblong to deltoid, tripinnate, glab. above, densely scaly beneath, seg. oval or suborbicular, bead-like, margins crenate, revolute. Calif. to Nevada, Ariz., Baja Calif. Z8.

C. commutata Kunze = *Hypolepis sparsisora*.

C. concolor Langsd. & Fisch. = *Doryopteris concolor*.

C. dalhousiae Hook. Stipes 8–15cm, densely tufted, dark chestnut brown, ultimately polished, scaly when young; blades 15–30×7–10cm, broadly ovate-lanceolate, tripinnatifid, pinnae, numerous, pinnules linear-oblong, obtuse, sinuate-pinnatifid, glab. N India. Z9.

C. densa (Brackenr.) St. John = *C. siliquosa*.

C. distans (R. Br.) Mett. Stipes 2–7cm, dark brown, scaly; blades 5–15×1–3cm, pinnate to bipinnate, narrow- to ovate-oblong, dull green and ± scaly above, densely brown-scaly beneath, pinnae distant, pinnatifid to pinnatisect, roughly ovate. Australasia. Z10.

C. eatonii Bak. Stipes brown to ferruginous, with scales and hairs; blades to 6cm wide, longer than stipes, tripinnate or tripinnate-pinnatifid, oblong- to narrow-lanceolate, white- to grey- or brown-tomentose above, densely rusty-tomentose beneath, pinnae distant, to 1.5cm wide, ovate-oblong to narrowly triangular-lanceolate, pinnules narrowly triangular-elliptic, divided into 7–9 seg., seg. suborbicular-obovate to broadly elliptic. N Amer. Z4.

C. farinosa (Forssk.) Kaulf. Stipes to length of blade, dark red-brown, sparingly scaly and farinose; blades bipinnate-pinnatifid to pinnate-pinnatifid, ovate-lanceolate to narrowly deltoid, bright green above, white-farinose beneath, pinnae distant, lanceolate, acute, often upturned at apex. pinnules oblong to oblong-lanceolate, obtuse. C & S America, Asia, Afr., Fiji. Z10.

C. feei Moore. Stipes to 12cm, v. slender, maroon to rusty, palely pilose; blades 5–13×1.5–4cm, tripinnate, ovate or deltoid-ovate to linear-oblong, acuminate, delicately herbaceous, glaucous, pinnae spreading, 7–15, deltoid to ovate-oblong, thinly white villous above, densely tawny-tomentose beneath, pinnules in 3–8 pairs, seg. beadlike, suborbicular, crenate. N Amer. Z3.

C. fendleri Hook. Stipes to 18cm×1mm, arched at base, somewhat flexuous above, polished brown, scaly; blades to 15×4.5cm, tripinnate, narrowly ovate-lanceolate to oblong-lanceolate, acuminate, bright glistening green, rigidly herbaceous, glab. above, with overlapping scales beneath, pinnae narrowly oblong to triangular-ovate, alt., oblique, pinnules with 2–4 pairs of seg., seg. broadly rounded to cuneiform. N Amer. Z4.

C. fragrans (L. f.) Sw. = *C. pteridioides*.

C. glauca (Cav.) Mett. Stipes 10–20cm, strong, dark-chestnut brown; blades 7–10×7–10cm, deltoid, 4-pinnatifid, tomentose beneath, pinnules lanceolate-deltoid, seg. cut to rachis, ultimate seg. to 3mm, linear-oblong, crenate. Chile, Mex. Z9.

C. gracillima D.C. Eaton. Stipes dark brown, subglabrous; blades to 24cm including stipe, linear to oblong-lanceolate, bipinnate, pinnae lanceolate-oblong, pinnately divided to linear above, seg. oval to oblong, dull green above, densely cinnamon-tomentose beneath, revolute. NW Amer. Z6.

C. hirta Sw. Stipes 7–15cm, dark brown, white glandular-pilose, rusty with age; blades 15–45×2.5–10cm, tripinnatifid, lanceolate, revolute, minutely crenate, pinnae 2.5–5×1–2cm, ovate or ovate-lanceolate, shortly stalked, pinnules broadly ovate, rounded, cut into 3 pairs of rounded or slightly lobed seg, veins hairy. S Afr., Masc. Is. Z10.

C. hispanica Mett. Stipe 2–3× length of blade, shiny-castaneous, sparsely scaly; blades 6–15×4–8cm, including stipe, bipinnate, deltate, glandular-pubesc. beneath, lower pinnules pinnatifid, ultimate seg. 2–6mm, pinnatifid. Spain and Port. Z8.

C. intertexta Maxon. Stipes purple tinged brown, sparsely scaly at least when young. Fronds to 28cm including stipe, numerous, ovate-deltoid to oblong, tripinnate, dark green with a few pale scales above, underside densely clad with bright castaneous scales, seg. small, revolute, beadlike. S Oreg. to N Calif. and W Nevada. Z7.

C. kuhnii Milde. Fronds bipinnatifid, oblong-lanceolate, membranous, with stalked glands; pinnae subsessile, pinnules 5–6 each side, pinnately parted, narrowly decurrent on winged rachis. SW US. Z8.

C. lanosa (Michx.) D.C. Eaton. Stipes 5–10cm, slightly tomentose; blades 10–20×4–5cm, broadly ovate-lanceolate,

tripinnatifid, pinnae opposite, lowermost distant, cut to rachis, 1–1.5cm; pinnules oblong. N Amer. Z6.

C. lendigera (Cav.) Sw. Stipes 10–25cm, purple-brown, lustrous, pubesc. when young; blades 4–20×2–7cm, tripinnate to quadripinnate, triangular-lanceolate to elliptic-lanceolate, acuminate, bright green above, cobwebby beneath, pinnae narrowly triangular-lanceolate, pinnules narrowly triangular-lanceolate, seg. to 11, often divided again, ultimate seg. minute, orbicular to cuneate-obovate, revolute, pocket-like. S US to Venez. and Ecuad. Z9.

C. marantae (L.) Domin. Stipes to length of blade, dark brown, dull, sparsely scaly. Fronds 10–35×2–5cm, including stipes, linear-lanceolate, pinnae pinnatisect or occas. stipes, linear-lanceolate, pinnules pinnatisect or occas. bipinnate, glab. above, densely clad with pale brown or colourless scales beneath. S Eur., northwards to C Fr. and Austria. Z6.

C. microphylla (Sw.) Sw. Stipes black or dark purple, ± pubesc.; blades bipinnate-bipinnatifid to tripinnate below, elliptic-lanceolate, slightly longer than stipes, pinnae distant, usually alt., ovate-lanceolate, seg. oblong, obtuse to subacute, to 3.5mm broad, crenate, sparsely pubesc.; rachis black. Flor. to C Amer. and W Indies. Z10.

C. multifida Sw. Stipes 10–20cm, glossy black, glabrate, channelled; blades 12–20×7–8cm, occas. longer, oblong-deltoid, 3–4-pinnatifid, dark green above, paler beneath, glossy and glab. throughout, firmly herbaceous, pinnae spreading, deltoid, pinnules cut almost to centre, fertile, revolute, bead-like, sterile, pinnules flat; seg. obliquely ovate, 3–5-lobed, lobes revolute. Trop. & subtrop. S Afr. Z10.

C. myriophylla Desv. Stipes to 18cm, brown, tinged with purple when mature, adpressed-scaly; blades to 20cm, narrowly lanceolate, 3–4-pinnate, pinnae alt., rather distant, ovate to deltoid-lanceolate, pinnules alt., to 12 each side, bipinnate, seg. orbicular to narrowly obovate, bead-like, subglabrous. N Mex. to Chile and Arg. Z9.

C. mysurensis Wallich. Stipes 1.5–5cm, with a pair of raised lat. wings, forming a central groove, dark brown, scaly near base, glabrescent; blades 3–25cm, oblong-ovate to linear-lanceolate, bipinnate, herbaceous, glab., pinnules adnate and decurrent, crenate, rounded at apex. China, India, Taiwan, Sri Lanka, Philipp. Z10.

C. newberryi Domin. COTTON FERN. Stipes tinged purple. Fronds 8–22cm including stipe, oblong-lanceolate, tripinnate, white-tomentose beneath, tawny with age, pinnae in about 10 pairs, lowest longest, pinnules crowded, to 1mm, rounded-ovate. Calif. Z9.

C. olivacea Fée = *C. hirta*.

C. parryi (D.C. Eaton) Domin. PARRY'S LIP-FERN. Stipes to 10cm, glandular-pubesc., base sparsely scaly, purple to black; blades to 12×4cm, 2-pinnate to -pinnatifid, lanceolate, apex acute, base obtuse, white-tomentose throughout; pinnae 5–12 pairs, opposite or alt., distant, pinnules short petiolate, seg. flat, suborbicular.

C. pteridioides (Reichard) C. Chr. Stipe to length of blade, shiny castaneous, sparsely scaly; fronds 3–15×1–3cm, including stipe, bipinnate, subtriangular to linear-lanceolate, with coumarin scent, gland. above, glab. and eglandular beneath, occas. with scattered scales, particularly when young, lower pinnules pinnatifid, seg. 1–3mm, oblong or suborbicular, crenate. S Eur. Z8.

C. pulchella Bory. Stipes 7–22cm, darkly glossy-castaneous; blades 8–30×5–10cm, ovate-lanceolate to deltoid, tripinnate, pinnae 5–7.5cm, few, elongate-oblong, green, coriaceous, pinnules cut to rachis, seg. oblong. Canary Is., Madeira. Z9.

C. repens (L.) Kaulf. = *Hypolepis repens*.

C. rufa D. Don. Stipes 2.5–5cm, densely tomentose; blades 15–22×5–8cm, broadly ovate-lanceolate, bipinnatifid, pinnae opposite, oblong, lowermost distant, pinnules 6–12mm, linear-oblong, farinaceous beneath. N India. Z9.

C. sieberi Kunze. Stipes 10–15cm, slender, v. dark brown, lustrous, glab. except base; blades 5–20×1.5–2.5cm, narrowly oblong, dull green, glab., pinnae to 25mm, ascending, roughly ovate, pinnules 5mm, narrowly oblong, crenate. Aus., NZ, New Caledonia. Z10.

C. siliquosa Maxon. Stipes stout, glossy, darkly castaneous, glab. Fronds to 30cm including stipe, broadly ovate, deltoid-oblong or somewhat pentagonal, tripinnate, mostly fertile, glab., pinnae few, close-set, oblique, basal broadly triangular, lowest longest, seg. narrowly linear, mucroonate, revolute, serrate on sterile fronds. NW Amer. Z9.

C. sinuata (Lagasca ex Sw.) Domin. WAVY CLOAK FERN. Stipes to 10cm, tomentose and scaly, castaneous; blades to 70×5cm, pinnate to pinnatifid, lanceolate to linear or oblong, apex acute or obtuse, base attenuate, scales sparse above, dense beneath, white or brown; pinnae to 2cm, 12–35 pairs, short-petiolate, alt., horizontal, ovate to elliptic, subacute to obtuse, entire to undulate or lobed, seg. 4–6 pairs, irregular, oblique, deltoid to oblong, obtuse, entire. S US and Mex., C Amer. to Arg. Z9.

C. sparsisora Schräd. = *Hypolepis sparsisora*.

C. tenuifolia (Burm.) Sw. Stipes 15cm, dark lustrous brown, scaly at base; blades 10–20×2–5cm, ovate-deltoid, bipinnate to tripinnate, bright to dull green, submembranous, ± glab., pinnae to 6×2cm, ovate-oblong to deltoid, pinnate, pinnules to 1cm; ovate-oblong, pinnatifid to pinnatisect, seg. oblong, crenate to subentire. India and China S to Australasia. Z10.

C. tomentosa Link. Stipes 10–25cm, rather stout, densely beige-tomentose; blades 15–45×3–9cm, oblong- to linear-lanceolate, bipinnate-pinnatifid to tripinnate, acuminate, densely tawny-tomentose, pinnae 5–12mm wide, ovate-oblong to oblong-lanceolate, pinnules to 10×2mm, ovate-oblong to oblong-lanceolate, seg. 0.5–2mm, obovate to broadly elliptic. US; Mexico. Z6.

C. trichomanoides (L.) Mett. Stipes to 10cm, with black-brown scales; blades to 30×3cm, pinnate to pinnatifid, linear, initially stellate-scaly; pinnae petiolate, alt., distant, oblong to deltoid or orbicular, subentire to lobed. Greater Antilles. Z10.

C. vellea F. Muell. Stipes to one-third length of blade; blades 8–25×2–4cm, bipinnate to bipinnate-pinnatifid, linear-lanceolate to oblong-lanceolate, scabrous, coriaceous, dark green and hirsute above, tomentose, frequently tinged brown beneath, pinnae pinnatisect or scalloped. Eur., SW Asia to Afghan. Z6.

→*Acrostichum, Aleuritopteris, Aspidotis, Gymnogramma* and *Notholaena*.

Cheiranthus L.

C. africanus L. = *Heliophila africana*.

C. ×*allionii* (DC.) Kuntze = *Erysimum* ×*allionii*.

C. asperus (Nutt.) DC. = *Erysimum asperum*.

C. cheiri L. = *Erysimum cheiri*.

C. chius L. = *Malcolmia chia*.

C. fruticulosus L. = *Matthiola fruticulosa*.

C. ×*kewensis* hort. = *Erysimum* ×*kewense*.

C. linifolius Pers. = *Erysimum linifolium*.

C. longipetalus Vent. = *Matthiola longipetala*.

C. maritimus L. = *Malcolmia maritima*.

Cheiridopsis N.E. Br. Aizoaceae. 80 v. succulent, clump-forming perennials. Lvs opposite, each pair differing from the previous pair: one shortly united below, the next pair largely united forming a papery sheath. Fls solitary, term., stalked. S Afr. (Cape Prov.), Nam. Z9.

C. acuminata L. Bol. Lvs 5–7cm long, 15mm median width, minutely papillose, with a sheath 1cm long. Fls to 6cm diam., pale yellow. W Cape.

C. aspera L. Bol. Lvs 6cm×5–6mm×5–6mm, united below to form a round sheath, obtuse, apiculate, semicylindric below, light green to grey, rough with cartilaginous, white dots. Fls not known. W Cape.

C. bibracteata (Haw.) N.E. Br. = *C. rostrata*.

C. bifida (Haw.) N.E. Br. = *C. rostrata*.

C. braunsii Schwantes = *Argyroderma fissum*.

C. brevis L. Bol. non Schwantes = *C. cigarettifera*.

C. brevis Schwantes non L. Bol. = *C. verrucosa*.

C. candidissima (Haw.) N.E. Br. = *C. denticulata*.

C. caroli-schmidtii (Dinter & A. Berger) N.E. Br. Lvs united for one-third of their length to form a body 2–4cm long, paired lvs 2–2.5cm across, 12–15mm thick, lower surface semicylindric or bluntly keeled, tip rounded, apiculate, light grey and spotted. Fls golden yellow. Nam.: Great Namaqualand.

C. cigarettifera (A. Berger) N.E. Br. Lf pairs strongly dimorphic, longer pair 2–6cm, united for one-third of their length, the other shorter, rounded on the underside, acutely carinate toward apex, grey-green, waxy-pruinose, rough with translucent spots. Fls 1.2–4.5cm diam., yellow to golden yellow. W Cape.

C. comptonii Jacobsen = *C. speciosa*.

C. crassa L. Bol. = *C. pillansii*.

C. cuprea (L. Bol.) L. Bol. = *Cephalophyllum caespitosum*.

C. denticulata (Haw.) N.E. Br. Lvs rather hard, erect, 8–10cm, subulate, triquetrous, underside semicylindric to carinate, often with a reddened tip, surface smooth, white-grey or tinged blue. Fls yellow to straw-coloured, 7–8cm diam. W Cape.

C. derenbergiana Schwantes. Lvs 30×5–6×5–6mm, acutely carinate, densely haired, grey-green. Fls to 5.5cm diam., lemon yellow.

C. duplessii L. Bol. = *C. cigarettifera*.

C. gibbosa Schick & Tisch. = *C. pillansii*.

C. herrei L. Bol. Lvs 1.5–2cm, compressed and truncate at the tip, rounded-carinate, 9–12mm wide and thick midway with a large basal blister, blue-green to dirty green, papillose. Fls to 6cm diam., yellow. W Cape.

C. hilmarii L. Bol. = *Aloinopsis hilmarii*.

C. lecta (N.E. Br.) N.E. Br. = *C. robusta*.

C. longipes L. Bol. = *C. cigarettifera*.

C. luckhoffii L. Bol. = *C. cigarettifera*.

C. marlothii N.E. Br. = *C. cigarettifera*.

C. mirabilis Schwantes = *C. verrucosa*.

C. noctiflora L. Bol. = *Aloinopsis peersii*.

C. pachyphylla Schwantes = *C. verrucosa*.

C. peculiaris N.E. Br. Largest lf pair flat, resting on the soil, 4–5cm×4–5cm×9–10mm, shortly acute, upper surface flat, lower surface slightly convex, carinate toward tip, grey-green with scattered spots; shorter lf pair completely united, becoming papery. Fls 3.5cm diam., yellow. W Cape.

C. peersii (L. Bol.) L. Bol. = *Aloinopsis peersii*.

C. pillansii L. Bol. Lvs largely united, forming a body 3–4.5×3.5–4.5×1.8–2.5cm, lower surface rounded and chin-like, grey-green to grey-white or blue-green with darker spots. Fls 6–8cm, light yellow to straw-coloured. W Cape.

C. purpurata hort. see *C. purpurea*.

C. purpurea (Salm-Dyck) N.E. Br. Lvs 6cm, obtusely triquetrous with keel pulled over the tip, grey to blue-grey, becoming red, spotted; sheath red and inflated. Fls 4–4.5cm, yellow to deep yellow. W Cape. *C. purpurea* L. Bol. describes a rose-magenta-fld collection – the name is much confused in horticulture.

C. quadrifida (Haw.) Schwantes = *C. rostrata*.

C. robusta (Haw.) N.E. Br. Lvs 4 per st., unequal, 40–45×17×15mm with a basal blister, sheath 9mm, underside rounded-carinate, minutely velvety. Fls 4.2–5.8cm diam., yellow within, orange outside. W Cape.

C. rostrata (L.) N.E. Br. Lvs 4–12cm×5–10mm×5–15mm, sheathed and united to form a cylindrical body, free part narrowed toward the obtuse, spotted, apiculate, grey-green, lower surface rounded-carinate, keel and margins cartilaginous, sometimes spotted. Fls 6.5cm diam., yellow. W Cape.

C. rostratoides (Haw.) N.E. Br. = *C. rostrata*.

C. scabra L. Bol. = *C. cigarettifera*.

C. speciosa L. Bol. Lvs minutely papillose, lowest pair 33mm long with a blister below and a sheath 11mm long, narrow-linear, tip expanded, truncate, 11m thick. Fls 5–6cm diam., coral red. W Cape.

C. tuberculata (Mill.) N.E. Br. = *C. rostrata*.

C. turbinata L. Bol. Lvs semicylindric, blue-green, velvety, to 10cm×17mm×12mm, carinate below the tip, truncate. Fls 7cm diam., lemon yellow. W Cape.

C. vanzylii L. Bol. Lvs 25×14×4mm, upper surface flat, lower surface carinate toward tip, laterally convex, truncate above, finely velutinous, spotted. Fls 6cm diam., yellow. W Cape.

C. velutina L. Bol. = *C. rostrata*.

C. verrucosa L. Bol. Lvs united for half to two-thirds of their length forming spherical bodies 16–20mm, semicylindric below. Fls 2–2.5cm diam., yellow. W Cape.

→*Mesembryanthemum*.

Cheirolophus Cass. Compositae. 3 perenn. herbs. Cap. discoid, solitary on long peduncles, swollen below cap.; involucre ovoid to subglobose; phyllaries imbricate, tips with fimbriate appendages. S Eur.

C. uliginosus (Brot.) Dostál. To 1.5m, pubesc. to subglabrous. Lower lvs lanceolate, dentate, acute, long-petiolate, upper linear-lanceolate to linear, subentire. Involucre 15–20mm; flts blue. Summer. Port. Z8.

→*Centaurea*.

Chelan Penstemon *Penstemon pruinosus*.

Chelidonium L. Papaveraceae. 1 variable bienn. and perenn. herb with orange sap. St. to 1.2m, branching below, erect, leafy. Lvs deeply pinnatifid, crenate to toothed. Fls 2–2.5cm diam., sparsely borne in bracteate umbels; sep. 2, yellow-green, often hairy; pet. 4, orange to yellow; sta. 16–24. Summer. Eur., W Asia, nat. in E US. Z6.

C. majus L. GREATER CELANDINE; SWALLOW WORT. var. *laciniatum* (Mill.) Syme. Lvs deeply incised; pet. cut. 'Flore Pleno': fls double.

Chelone L. SHELLFLOWER. Scrophulariaceae. 6 herbaceous perennials. St. erect, simple or sparsely branched, glab. Lvs glab., dentate. Fls in term. spikes; cor. tube decurved, upper lip arched, 2-lobed, lower lip 3-lobed, interior bearded; staminode present. Summer. N Amer. Z9.

C. barbata Cav. = *Penstemon barbatus*.

C. cuthbertii Small. To 1.8m. Lvs lanceolate to linear-oblong, base rounded. Cor. to 3cm, violet-purple, white or cream; staminode purple. E US. Z3.

C. glabra L. TURTLEHEAD; SNAKEHEAD. To 60cm. Lvs ovate to lanceolate. Cor. to 2.5cm, rose-white, sometimes marked with pale green, pink or purple, beard white. US. 'Montana': cor. lip and throat purple or rose-coloured. var. *elatior* Raf. Cor. flushed rose or purple at throat and apex. Z3.

C. lyonii Pursh. To 120cm. Lvs 5–15cm, ovate to elliptic, serrate, base rounded or truncate. Cor. to 2.5cm, rose-purple, beard yellow. SE US.

C. montana Wherry & Pennell = *C. glabra* var. *elatior*.

C. nemorosa Douglas ex Lindl. To 60cm. Lvs to 5cm, ovate to lanceolate, acute, dentate. Cor. mauve to violet, staminode pubesc. at tip. W N Amer.

C. nemorosa Douglas ex Lindl. = *Penstemon nemorosus*.

C. obliqua L. 60cm. Lvs broadly lanceolate to lanceolate-elliptic, glab., serrate or incised. Cor. to 2cm, deep rose pink to purple, beard sparse, yellow. US. 'Praecox Nana': to 30cm; fls lilac-red, drooping. Z6.

C. penstemon L. = *Penstemon laevigatus*.

Chène *Quercus*; *Catalpa*.
Chène d'Amerique *Catalpa longissima*.
Chène Noir *Catalpa longissima*.
Chenille Plant *Echeveria pulvinata*.

CHENOPODIACEAE Vent. 120/1300. *Atriplex, Bassia, Beta, Chenopodium, Haloxylon, Sarcobatus* and *Spinacia*.

Chenopodium L. GOOSEFOOT; PIGWEED. Chenopodiaceae. 150 herbs or subshrubs, usually mealy or with gland. hairs. St. often striped white or red. Fls minute, usually green in spikes or pan. Fr. 1-seeded, often enclosed in persistent perianth seg., sometimes red and fleshy. Global. Z5.

C. amaranticolor Coste & Reyn. = *C. giganteum*.

C. ambrosioides L. AMERICAN WORMSEED; MEXICAN TEA; SPANISH TEA; WORMSEED. Ann. herb or short-lived perenn. to 120cm. Lvs oblong-lanceolate, crenate, to 12cm. Fls in dense leafy pan. Summer. Trop. Amer., nat. elsewhere.

C. atriplicis L. f. = *C. purpurascens*.

C. bonus-henricus L. GOOD KING HENRY; ALLGOOD; FAT-HEN; GOOSEFOOT; WILD SPINACH; MERCURY. Erect perenn. herb, mealy when young, to 75cm. Lvs triangular to hastate, spinach-like, sinuate. Fls in leafless compound spikes. Summer. C & S Eur., nat. N Eur. and N Amer. Z5.

C. botrys L. FEATHER GERANIUM; JERUSALEM OAK. Differs from *C. ambrosioides* in more erect habit, leafless pan., and smaller, pinnatifid to deeply lobed lvs. Erect ann. herb to 80cm, covered with sticky hairs, aromatic. Fls fragrant, in slender pan. Summer. S Eur. to C Asia, nat. N Amer.

C. capitatum (L.) Asch. STRAWBERRY BLITE; INDIAN PAINT. Erect ann. herb to 60cm, glab. Lvs fleshy, sparsely toothed, triangular-hastate to lanceolate. Fls in clusters forming an interrupted spike. Fr. fleshy, forming a bright red berry-like cluster to 12mm diam. Summer. Eur., nat. N Amer.

C. foliosum Asch. Differs from *C. capitatum* in lvs with dense and coarse teeth, small and more numerous fl. clusters. Asia, S Eur., NW Afr.

C. giganteum D. Don. Erect ann. herb, to 3m. St. glab., much branched, red-green striped white. New growth red-purple. Lvs mealy, triangular-rhombic, irregularly toothed, to 15cm. Fls in large, loose cymes. Fr. dry; seed shiny black. Summer–early autumn. N India.

C. purpurascens Jacq. PURPLE GOOSEFOOT. To 4cm. Lvs flushed garnet, triangular-rhombic, long-stalked. Fls purple pyramidal clusters. Summer–early autumn. China.
→*Atriplex*.

Chequén *Luma chequen*.
Chequered Lily *Fritillaria meleagris*.
Cherimalla *Annona cherimola*.
Cherimoya *Annona cherimola*.

Cherleria L.
C. sedoides L. = *Minuartia sedoides*.

Cherokee Bean *Erythrina herbacea*.
Cherokee Rose *Rosa laevigata*.
Cherry *Prunus*.
Cherry-bark Elm *Ulmus villosa*.
Cherry-bark Red Oak *Quercus falcata* var. *pagodifolia*.
Cherry Bean *Vigna unguiculata*.
Cherry Birch *Betula lenta*.
Cherry Laurel *Prunus caroliniana*; *P. laurocerasus*.
Cherry of the Rio Grande *Eugenia aggregata*.
Cherry Pie *Heliotropium arborescens*.
Cherry Plum *Prunus cerasifera*.
Cherry Tomato *Lycopersicon esculentum* var. *cerasiforme*.
Chervil *Anthriscus cereifolium*.
Cheshire Rose *Rosa* ×*alba*.

Chesneya Lindl. ex Endl. Leguminosae (Papilionoideae). 20 woody-based herbs. Lvs imparipinnate. Fls pea-like, axill., solitary, or in clusters. SW & C Asia to Mong.

C. cuneata (Benth.) Ali. Tufted perenn. to 15cm. Lvs 2–5cm; lfts 0.5–1.5cm, oblong to obovate, apex rounded or emarginate, velutinous. Fls carmine, in clusters of 1–4; standard 2–3cm, hairy. Himal.
→*Calophaca*.

Chess *Bromus*.
Chestnut *Castanea*.
Chestnut Oak *Quercus prinus*.
Chestnut Rose *Rosa roxburghii*.
Chestnut Rush *Juncus castaneus*.
Chestnut Vine *Tetrastigma voinierianum*.
Chiang Mao *Schefflera heptaphylla*.
Ch'iao T'ou *Allium chinense*.

Chiapasia Britt. & Rose.
C. nelsonii Britt. & Rose = *Disocactus nelsonii*.

Chiapas White Pine *Pinus chiapensis*.

Chiastophyllum Stapf ex A. Berger. Crassulaceae. 1 trailing perenn. herb, 15–30cm. Lvs 4–12cm, ovate-orbicular, fleshy, tapering abruptly to petiole, undulate to crenate. Pan. erect, long-stalked, br. pendulous, racemose; cor. to 0.5cm, campanulate, golden-yellow, lobes 5, triangular-lanceolate. Spring. Cauc. Z7.

C. oppositifolium (Ledeb.) A. Berger. 'Frosted Jade': lvs marked white to cream, tinted pink in winter. 'Tropfichen': to 16cm; lvs smooth; fls pale yellow.

Chicasa Plum *Prunus angustifolia*.
Chichester Elm *Ulmus* 'Vegetata'.
Chickasaw Plum *Prunus angustifolia*.
Chicken Gizzard *Iresine herbstii*; *Polyscias scutellaria*.
Chicken Grape *Vitis cordifolia*; *V. vulpina*.
Chick Pea *Cicer arietinum*.
Chickweed *Stellaria* (*S. media*); *Trientalis*.
Chickweed Monkey-flower *Mimulus alsinoides*.
Chicle *Manilkara zapota*.
Chicory *Cichorium* (*C. intybus*).
Chicory Grape *Coccoloba* (*C. venosa*).
Chicot *Gymnocladus dioica*.
Chieger Flower *Asclepias tuberosa*.
Chigaya *Imperata cylindrica*.
Chigo-zasa *Pleioblastus variegatus*.
Chikara-shiba *Pennisetum alopecuroides* var. *purpurascens*.
Chilac *Chamaedorea neurochlamys*.

Childsia J.L. Childs.
C. wercklei J.L. Childs = *Hidalgoa wercklei*.

Chilean Bamboo *Chusquea culeou*.
Chilean Bellflower *Lapageria*.
Chilean Blue Crocus *Tecophilaea cyanocrocus*.
Chilean Cedar *Austrocedrus chilensis*.
Chilean Firebush *Embothrium coccineum*.
Chilean Flameflower *Embothrium coccineum*.
Chilean Gloryflower *Eccremocarpus scaber*.
Chilean Guava *Ugni*.
Chilean Hazelnut *Gevuina*.
Chilean Incense Cedar *Austrocedrus chilensis*.
Chilean Jasmine *Mandevilla laxa*.
Chilean Laurel *Laurelia sempervirens*.
Chilean Maidenhair *Adiantum excisum*.
Chilean Podocarp *Podocarpus nubigenus*.
Chilean Rimu *Lepidothamnus fonkii*.
Chilean Wine Palm *Jubaea*.
Chile Bells *Lapageria*.
Chile Lantern Tree *Crinodendron hookerianum*.
Chile Nut *Gevuina*.
Chile Pine *Araucaria araucana*.
Chile Tarweed *Madia sativa*.
Chilgoza Pine *Pinus gerardiana*.

Chilianthus Burchell.
C. arboreus (L.f.) A.DC. = *Buddleja saligna*.

Chilicothe *Marah macrocarpus*.

Chiliotrichum Cass. Compositae. 2 erect, everg. shrubs. Cap. radiate, solitary, term. Temp. S Amer.
C. amelloides DC. = *C. diffusum*.

C. diffusum (Forst. f.) Kuntze. To 1m. St. ascending to erect, much-branched, bark flaking, grey-brown when mature, twigs white-tomentose. Lvs to 3cm, oblong-lanceolate to subelliptic, revolute, dark glossy green, leathery above, white-tomentose beneath. Cap. to 3cm diam., phyllaries brown tinged purple, ± tomentose; ray flts white. Late spring–summer. S Chile, SW Arg., Falkland Is. Z8.
→*Amellus*.

Chilli Pepper *Capsicum*.

Chiloglottis R. Br. Orchidaceae. 15 tuberous terrestrial orchids. Lvs basal, 2. Scape single-fld; dors. sep. erect, concave, incurved, basally constricted; lat. sep. terete or narrow-linear; pet. lanceolate, falcate; lip oblong-ovate or obovate, entire, callose. Aus., NZ. Z9.
C. formicifera Fitzg. ANT ORCHID. To 12cm. Lvs to 5cm, ovate-lanceolate. Fl. green, marked purple or brown; pet. transparent; calli densely massed, pink to black. Early–mid autumn. SE Aus.
C. gunnii Lindl. To 4cm. Lvs to 10cm, ovate to ovate-lanceolate. Fl. green, violet or maroon; lip purple, with a prominent slender gland near base; calli dark red or black. Autumm–mid winter. SE Aus.
C. truncata D. Jones & M. Clements. To 10cm. Lvs to 6cm, narrow, elliptic, undulate. Fl. green; calli black, glossy. Summer–early autumn. C E Aus.

Chilopsis D. Don. DESERT WILLOW. Bignoniaceae. 1 erect everg. shrub or tree, 2–8m. Lvs 8–14cm, linear. Rac. to 6cm; cor. c3cm, tubular-funnelform, white streaked or tinted lilac or purple-red, sometimes spotted with yellow, limb bilabiate, lobes 5, crenate. SW N Amer., to Mex. Z8.
C. glutinosa Engelm. = *C. linearis* var. *glutinosa*.
C. linearis (Cav.) Sweet var. *linearis*. Branchlets not viscous, usually lanate. Lvs to 30cm, straight. SW US to Mex. 'Alba': fls white. 'Barranca': habit upright; fls deep lavender. var. *arcuata* Fosb. WESTERN DESERT WILLOW. Branchlets not viscous, glab. Lvs 8–14cm, arched. N Baja Calif. and SE Mex. var. *glutinosa* (Engelm.) Fosb. Branchlets and young lvs viscous, glab. Lvs straight, erect.
C. saligna D. Don = *C. linearis* var. *linearis*.
→*Bignonia*.

Chimaphila Pursh. PRINCE'S PINE; PIPISSEWA. Pyrolaceae. 6 shrubby, everg. herbs. Rootstock creeping. St. slender. Lvs often whorled, coriaceous, serrate; petioles short. Fls few, nodding, radial, in a flat-topped or raceme-like, scapose cluster; sep. 5, orbicular; pet. 5, orbicular, concave; sta. 10. Summer. N Amer., Eur., E Asia.
C. astyla Maxim. = *C. japonica*.
C. corymbosa Pursh = *C. umbellata*.
C. japonica Miq. To 10cm. Lvs broadly lanceolate, to 3.5cm, acute, sparsely toothed, deep green with pale white midrib above. Fls 1–2; pet. 7–8mm, white. E Asia. Z6.
C. maculata (L.) Pursh. To 25cm. Lvs ovate to lanceolate, to 7cm, base rounded or cuneate, midrib white, veins bordered white. Fls 2–5; pet. 1cm, white to pale pink. E N Amer. Z6.
C. menziesii (R. Br. ex D. Don) Spreng. LITTLE PRINCE'S PINE. To 15cm. Lvs lanceolate to elliptic, 1–2.5cm, acute, entire to toothed, veins faintly bordered white. Fls 1–3; pet. to 1cm, white turning pink. W N Amer. Z5.
C. occidentalis Rydb. = *C. umbellata*.
C. umbellata (L.) Barton. WESTERN PRINCE'S PINE. To 35cm. Lvs 3–7cm, oblanceolate, obtuse or subacute, toothed, veins not bordered white. Infl. glandular-pubesc.; fls 3–10; pet. to 0.6cm, white to pink to red. E N Amer., N & C Eur., N Asia, Jap. Z4.
→*Pyrola*.

Chimney Bellflower *Campanula pyramidalis*.

Chimonanthus Lindl. WINTERSWEET. Calycanthaceae. 6 decid. or everg. shrubs. Lvs entire. Fls short-stalked, axillary, produced before lvs; pet. and sep. ovate-elliptic, erect to spreading, similar, fleshy, numerous, yellow or white; sta. 5–6. China. Z7.
C. fragrans Lindl. = *C. praecox*.
C. praecox (L.) Link. Decid. to 4m. Lvs ovate-lanceolate, 7–20cm, upper surface rough, glossy green. Fls v. fragrant, 2.5cm wide; sep. and outer pet. sulphur-yellow, inner pet. brown or purple. Winter. China. 'Concolor': fls pale yellow, highly fragrant. 'Grandiflorus': fls less fragrant, 2–3cm wide; sep. and outer pet. pale yellow, inner pet. striped maroon. 'Luteo grandiflorus': fls to 3cm diam., waxy, yellow. 'Luteus': fls clear waxy yellow. 'Parviflorus': fls small, pale yellow-white, inner sep. striped red, inner, pet. edged and spotted purple.

'Patens': fls yellow-white, inner sep. striped purple, inner pet. edged purple. Z7.
C. yunnanensis W.W. Sm. To 6m. Lvs elliptic to elliptic-ovate, base rounded. Fls dull yellow. China.

Chimonobambusa Mak. Gramineae. c20 small to medium-sized bamboos with running rhiz. S & E Asia. Z6.
C. falcata (Nees) Nak. = *Drepanostachyum falcatum*.
C. hookeriana (Munro) Nak. = *Drepanostachyum hookerianum*.
C. jaunsarensis (Gamble) Bahadur & Naithani = *Yushania anceps*.
C. marmorea (Mitford) Mak. KAN-CHIKU. Culms 2–3m×1–2cm, rounded, smooth, often purple-lined; sheaths persistent, mottled purple or pink-brown with white spots when fresh, short-bristly below. Lvs 7.5–16×0.5–1.5cm. Long grown in Jap., origin uncertain.
C. quadrangularis (Fenzi) Mak. SHIKAKUDAKE; SHIHO-CHIKU; SQUARE BAMBOO. Culms 2–10m×1–3cm, often spinulose, with 4 rounded corners; nodes v. prominent, somewhat purple below, the lowest with thorny aborted rootlets; sheaths hairless, soon falling. Lvs 10–29×2.7cm. SE China, Taiwan; long nat. Jap.
→*Arundinaria*.

China Aster *Callistephus chinensis*.
Chinaberry *Melia azedarach*.
China Fir *Cunninghamia*.
China Fleece Vine *Polygonum aubertii*.
China Grass *Boehmeria nivea*.
China Jute *Abutilon theophrasti*.
China Rose *Hibiscus rosa-sinensis*; *Rosa chinensis*.
Chincherinchee *Ornithogalum pruinosum*; *O. thyrsoides*.
Chinese Angelica Tree *Aralia stipulata*.
Chinese Anisatum *Illicium anisatum*.
Chinese Anise *Illicium verum*.
Chinese Arbor-vitae *Thuja orientalis*.
Chinese Artichoke *Stachys affinis*.
Chinese Banyan *Ficus microcarpa*.
Chinese Beech *Fagus engleriana*.
Chinese Bellflower *Platycodon*.
Chinese Bottletree *Firmiana simplex*.
Chinese Box *Murraya paniculata*.
Chinese Box-orange *Severinia buxifolia*.
Chinese Boxthorn *Lycium barbarum*.
Chinese Boxwood *Buxus microphylla* var. *sinica*.
Chinese Butternut *Juglans cathayensis*.
Chinese Chestnut *Castanea mollissima*.
Chinese Chives *Allium tuberosum*.
Chinese Cinnamon *Cinnamomum aromaticum*.
Chinese Cork Oak *Quercus variabilis*.
Chinese Date *Ziziphus jujuba*.
Chinese Deciduous Cypress *Glyptostrobus*.
Chinese Douglas Fir *Pseudotsuga sinensis*.
Chinese Dwarf Lemon *Citrus meyeri*.
Chinese Elm *Ulmus parvifolia*.
Chinese Evergreen *Aglaonema*.
Chinese Fan Palm *Livistona chinensis*.
Chinese Fir *Cunninghamia lanceolata*.
Chinese Flame Tree *Koelreuteria bipinnata*.
Chinese Forget-me-not *Cynoglossum amabile*.
Chinese Fountain Grass *Pennisetum alopecuroides*.
Chinese Fountain Palm *Livistona chinensis*.
Chinese Fringe Tree *Chionanthus retusus*.
Chinese Gall *Rhus chinensis*.
Chinese Glycosmis *Glycosmis parviflora*.
Chinese Gooseberry *Actinidia deliciosa*.
Chinese Ground Orchid *Bletilla*.
Chinese Hat Plant *Holmskioldia sanguinea*.
Chinese Hazel *Corylus chinensis*.
Chinese Hemlock *Tsuga chinensis*.
Chinese Hibiscus *Hibiscus rosa-sinensis*.
Chinese Hickory *Carya cathayensis*.
Chinese Holly *Ilex cornuta*; *Osmanthus heterophyllus*.
Chinese Horse Chestnut *Aesculus chinensis*.
Chinese Houses *Collinsia bicolor*.
Chinese Jujube *Ziziphus jujuba*.
Chinese Juniper *Juniperus chinensis*.
Chinese Lacquer Tree *Toxicodendron verniciIluum*.
Chinese Lantern *Abutilon* ×*hybridum*; *Physalis alkekengi*.
Chinese Lantern Heath *Erica blenna*.
Chinese Lantern Lily *Sandersonia aurantiaca*.
Chinese Lantern Plant *Physalis alkekengi*.
Chinese Larch *Larix potaninii*.
Chinese Lilac *Syringa* ×*chinensis*.
Chinese Magnolia *Magnolia sieboldii*; *M.* ×*soulangiana*.
Chinese Matrimony Vine *Lycium chinense*.

Chinese Mustard *Brassica juncea.*
Chinese Necklace Poplar *Populus lasiocarpa.*
Chinese Nutmeg-yew *Torreya grandis.*
Chinese Parasol Tree *Firmiana simplex.*
Chinese Parsley *Coriandrum sativum.*
Chinese Pennisetum *Pennisetum alopecuroides.*
Chinese Persimmon *Diospyros kaki.*
Chinese Plumbago *Ceratostigma willmottianum.*
Chinese Plum Yew *Cephalotaxus sinensis.*
Chinese Primrose *Primula sinensis.*
Chinese Privet *Ligustrum lucidum.*
Chinese Rain Tree *Koelreuteria* (*K. elegans*).
Chinese Raisin Tree *Hovenia dulcis.*
Chinese Red Birch *Betula albosinensis.*
Chinese Redbud *Cercis chinensis.*
Chinese Red Pine *Pinus tabulaeformis.*
Chinese Rice-paper Plant *Tetrapanax.*
Chinese Scarlet Egg-plant *Solanum integrifolium.*
Chinese Scholar Tree *Sophora japonica.*
Chinese Silk Plant *Boehmeria nivea.*
Chinese Soapberry *Sapindus mukorossi.*
Chinese Spinach *Amaranthus tricolor.*
Chinese Spring Cherry *Prunus changyangensis.*
Chinese Swamp Cypress *Glyptostrobus.*
Chinese Sweet Gum *Liquidambar formosana.*
Chinese Tallow-tree *Sapium sebiferum.*
Chinese Taro *Alocasia cucullata.*
Chinese Thuja *Thuja orientalis.*
Chinese Tree *Tamarix chinensis.*
Chinese Trumpet Creeper *Campsis grandiflora.*
Chinese Trumpet Vine *Campsis grandiflora.*
Chinese Tulip Tree *Liriodendron chinense.*
Chinese Tupelo *Nyssa sinensis.*
Chinese Walnut *Juglans cathayensis.*
Chinese Water Chestnut *Eleocharis dulcis.*
Chinese Water Melon *Benincasa hispida.*
Chinese Weeping Cypress *Cupressus funebris.*
Chinese White Pine *Pinus armandii.*
Chinese White Poplar *Populus* ×*tomentosa.*
Chinese Windmill Palm *Trachycarpus.*
Chinese Wingnut *Pterocarya stenoptera.*
Chinese Wisteria *Wisteria sinensis.*
Chinese Witch-hazel *Hamamelis mollis.*
Chinese Woolflower *Celosia.*
Chinese Yam *Dioscorea batatas.*
Chinese Yew *Taxus chinensis.*
Chinese Zelkova *Zelkova schneiderana.*
Chinkapin *Castanea.*
Chinkapin Oak *Quercus muehlenbergii.*
Chinquapin Rose *Rosa roxburghii.*

Chiococca P. Browne. Rubiaceae. 8 shrubs or trees, erect to climbing. Fls in pan. or rac., fragrant; cal. tube ovoid to turbinate, constricted, lobes 5; cor. campanulate to funnelform, lobes 5, spreading or reflexed. Fr. a berry. Trop. and subtrop. New World. Z10.
C. alba (L.) Hitchc. WEST INDIAN SNOW BERRY. Everg., climbing to 6m. Lvs to 10cm, ovate, lanceolate, or elliptic, apex acute, base attenuate to decurrent, lustrous and leathery. Fls white ageing ivory to pale yellow, ultimately strongly fragrant; cor. tube to 6mm, lobes to 3mm, deltoid. Fr. to 8×6mm, white. Flor. and W Indies, C to S Amer.
C. anguifuga DC. = *C. alba.*
C. racemosa L. = *C. alba.*

Chiogenes Salisb. ex Torr.
C. hispidula (L.) Torr. & A. Gray = *Gaultheria hispidula.*
C. serpyllifolia (Pursh) Salisb. = *Gaultheria hispidula.*

Chionanthus L. FRINGE TREE. Oleaceae. 100 decid. trees or shrubs. Fls white in lax term. pan.; cal. 4-lobed; pet. 4, oblong, slender, fused at base; sta. 2, short. Fr. a purple-blue, single-seeded drupe. E Asia, Korea, Jap., E US.
C. retusus Lindl. CHINESE FRINGE TREE. To 3m. Lvs to 10cm, elliptic to ovate, light green above, downy and white beneath, entire or serrulate on juvenile plants. Fls in erect pan. Summer. Taiwan. Z6.
C. virginicus L. To 5m. Lvs to 20cm, obovate, glossy, dark green above with downy veins beneath, turning pale gold in fall. Fls slightly fragrant, in pendent pan., to 20cm. Summer. E US. 'Angustifolius': lvs narrower, lanceolate. 'Latifolius': lvs to 15cm, broad, ovate. var. *maritimus* Pursh. Lvs broadly elliptic, dull green, slightly downy above, more so beneath; fls in v. loose pan. Z4.

Chionochloa Zotov. Gramineae. SNOW GRASS. 19 coarse perenn. grasses. St. erect, tufted. Lvs narrow-linear, deeply ridged; ligule a line of hairs. Infl. loose or contracted; spikelets several-fld. NZ, 1 sp. SE Aus. Z7.
C. conspicua (Forst. f.) Zotov. HUANGAMOHO GRASS; PLUMED TUSSOCK GRASS. St. densely tufted, to 1.5m. Lvs to 120cm, rigid, flat to concave. Infl. graceful, erect to pendent, compact or loose, to 45cm. Summer. NZ.
C. flavescens (Hook. f.) Zotov. BROAD LEAVED SNOW TUSSOCK. Densely tufted, 60cm–2m. Lvs brown-green. NZ.
C. rigida (Raoul) Zotov. SNOW TUSSOCK. Erect and spreading, to 1.5 tall. Pan. branched, loose, pale straw-coloured. NZ.
C. rubra Zotov. RED TUSSOCK GRASS. Dense, tussock-forming, to 1.5m. Lvs fine, tinged red. NZ.
→*Arundo, Cortaderia* and *Danthonia.*

Chionodoxa Boiss. GLORY OF THE SNOW. Liliaceae (Hyacinthaceae). 6 bulbous perenn. herbs. Lvs basal, linear, usually 2. Fls in a loose rac.; perianth tube short, subspherical, lobes 6, spreading; sta. 6, at apex of perianth tube. W Turk., Crete, Cyprus. Z4.
C. albescens Speta. Like *C. nana* but fls to 1cm, v. pale pink to lavender.
C. cretica Boiss. = *C. nana.*
C. forbesii Bak. Lvs 7–28cm, erect to spreading. Scapes 8–30cm; fls 4–12, slightly drooping, deep blue with white centre, tube 3–5mm, lobes 10–15×4–5mm. W Turk. 'Alba': fls snow white. 'Naburn Blue': fls dark blue, centre white. 'Pink Giant': fls pink with white centre. 'Tmoli': dwarf, to 10cm; fls bright blue.
C. gigantea Whittall = *C. luciliae.*
C. lochiae Meikle. Lvs 7–18cm, erect. Scapes to 18cm; fls 2–4, horizontal or drooping; light blue, tube 5–7mm, lobes 12–13×4–6mm. Cyprus.
C. luciliae Boiss. Lvs 7–20cm, often recurved. Scapes to 14cm; fls 1–2, erect, soft violet-blue with small white central zone, tube 2.5–4mm, lobes 12–20×3–8mm. W Turk. 'Alba': fls white. 'Rosea': fls pink.
C. luciliae auct. non Boiss. = *C. forbesii.*
C. nana (Schult. & Schult.) Boiss. Lvs 8–18cm, spreading. Scapes to 20cm; fls 1–3, erect, blue with white central zone, tube 3–5mm, lobes 6–11×3mm. Crete.
C. sardensis Whittall. Lvs erect or spreading, channelled. Scapes to 40cm; fls 4–12, slightly drooping, deep blue, tube 3–5mm, lobes 8–10×2–4mm. W Turk.
C. siehei Stapf = *C. forbesii.*
C. tmolusi Whittall = *C. forbesii.*

Chionographis Maxim. Liliaceae (Melanthiaceae). 7 rhizomatous, perenn. herbs. Basal lvs long-petioled, st. lvs smaller, sessile. Fls numerous in a delicate term. spike, white; tep. 3–6, the upper 3–4 linear to thread-like, the lower 2–3 small or 0. Spring–early summer. China, Jap., S Korea. Z7.
C. japonica Maxim. 15–45cm. Basal lvs to 8cm, narrowly ovate to oblong, entire, undulate or irregularly toothed; st. lvs to 4cm, linear-lanceolate. Infl. 5–20cm, fls to 1.8cm diam. Jap., Korea.
C. koidzumiana Ohwi. To 20cm. Basal lvs to 3cm, oblong-ovate to ovate, undulate; st. lvs to 2cm, lanceolate. Infl. 3.5cm; fls small. Jap.

×**Chionoscilla** J. Allen ex Nichols. (*Chionodoxa* ×*Scilla.*) Liliaceae (Hyacinthaceae). Natural hybrid, intermediate between the parents, v. variable.
×*C. allenii* Nichols. (*Chinodoxa forbesii* ×*Scilla bifolia.*) Lvs exceeding scape, oblanceolate, acute. Fls starry, perianth seg. fused at base, blue or lilac-pink, with paler central zone; fil. pale blue. Spring. Gdn origin.

Chios Mastic *Pistacia lentiscus.*
Chirimoya *Annona cherimola.*

Chirita Buch.-Ham. ex D. Don. Gesneriaceae. *c*100 downy ann. or perenn. herbs. St. ± erect, somewhat succulent. Fls axill., solitary to clustered, sometimes distinctly stalked; sep. 5; cor. tubular or funnel-shaped, sometimes inflated, upper lip 2-lobed, lower lip 3-lobed. Trop. Asia. Z10.
C. anachoretia Hance. Perenn. to 30cm. Lvs to 18cm, elliptic-ovate, dentate. Fls few in short clusters; cor. to 5cm, bright yellow. China.
C. asperifolia (Bl.) B.L. Burtt. Perenn. to 1m. Lvs to 20cm, elliptic to ovate-elliptic, dentate. Fls in cymose clusters; cor. to 4.5cm, mauve or white, limb white, throat pale purple, rarely pale yellow. Java.
C. barbata Sprague. Bienn. to 60cm. Lvs to 15cm, ovate-oblong. Fls 4–8; cor. to 2.5cm, inflated at throat, indigo-mauve, throat with yellow stripe; anth. hairy. Fr. to 5cm. E Indies.
C. blumei C.B. Clarke = *C. asperifolia.*

C. elphinstonia Craib. Ann. to 1m. Lvs to 15cm, elliptic to oblong. Fls yellow spotted purple, cor. tube to 2cm. Thail.

C. hamosa R. Br. To 30cm. Lvs to 15cm, ovate or elliptic, slightly crenate. Fls ± sessile; cor. to 1.8cm, pale blue to pink. Burm.

C. horsfieldii = *C. lavandulacea.*

C. kurzii (C.B. Clarke) C.B. Clarke = *Loxostigma kurzii.*

C. lavandulacea Stapf. Ann. to 1m. Lvs to 20cm, elliptic-oblong. Fls few to many; pedicels gland.; cor. to 3cm, white, limb mauve-blue. Asia.

C. macrophylla Wallich. To 50cm. Lvs to 15cm, ovate or elliptic. Fls several; cor. to 5.6cm, yellow. Himal.

C. micromusa B.L. Burtt. Ann. to 30cm. Lvs to 25cm, cordate at base. Fls 7–20; cor. to 1.4cm, pale yellow and densely pubesc. outside, limb orange-yellow, throat orange-rust. Thail.

C. pumila D. Don. St. to 50cm. Lvs to 14cm, elliptic, dentate. Fls 1–5; cor. to 3cm, white streaked with indigo-mauve, throat marked with yellow. Himal.

C. sinensis Lindl. Lvs crowded at base, to 20cm, elliptic or ovate-lanceolate, dark green or variegated silver-grey. Fls 1–4, on red-hairy scapes to 15cm; cor. to 2.4cm, white marked yellow, limb pink-purple. Himal.

C. trailliana Forr. & W.W. Sm. St. creeping. Lvs to 20cm, basal, broadly ovate, obtusely dentate, purple at margin. Fls few in clusters on stalks 12.5cm; cor. to 5cm, pale violet outside, pale yellow inside. China.

C. urticifolia Buch.-Ham. ex D. Don. St. to 45cm. Lvs to 12.5cm, elliptic, dentate. Fls 1–4; cor. to 4.3cm, purple, marked yellow inside, pubesc. Himal.

C. zeylanica Hook. Perenn. to 30cm. Lvs ovate, acute, silky brown-pubesc. Fls 3 per stalk; cor. indigo-blue, to 5cm. Sri Lanka.

Chironia L. CHRISTMAS BERRY. Gentianaceae. Some 15 soft or shrubby perenn. herbs. Lvs sessile, opposite, decussate. Fls in loose term. cymes or solitary; cal. seg. pointed; cor. salverform, 5-lobed, tube narrow, limb wide. Fr. a berry-like capsule. S Afr., Madag. Z9.

C. baccifera L. CHRISTMAS BERRY. Shrubby perenn. to 50cm; br. somewhat 4-angled. Lvs to 2cm+, linear-lanceolate, somewhat revolute. Fls to 1cm, dark pink, solitary or clustered at ends of br. Fr. orange-red. S Afr.

C. frutescens L. = *Orphium frutescens.*

C. ixifera hort. = *C. linoides.*

C. linoides L. Herb to 1m, often decumbent and woody at base; br. terete. Lvs to 5cm, linear to linear-lanceolate, erect, fleshy. Fls to 2cm, red, long-stalked, in loose cymes. S Afr.

C. palustris Burchell. Herb to 45cm; st. stout. Basal lvs 9–20cm, oblong-cuneate, persistent, st. lvs linear-lanceolate. Fls to 3cm, white to pink, 2–3 per cyme in term., open pan. S. Afr. ssp. *transvaalensis* (Gilg) Verdoorn. St. to 70cm, forming leafy clumps. Basal lvs to 8cm, not persistent. Fls to 2.5cm. Transvaal, Swaz.

C. transvaalensis Gilg = *C. palustris* ssp. *transvaalensis.*

C. trinervia L. = *Exacum trinervium.*

Chir Pine *Pinus roxburghii.*

✕**Chitalpa**   Elias & Wisura. Bignoniaceae. (*Catalpa* ✕ *Chilopsis.*)

✕*C. tashkentensis* Elias & Wisura. (*Catalpa bignonioides* ✕ *Chilopsis linearis.*) Decid. small to medium-sized tree. Lvs to 17×4.5cm, dull green, glab. above, pilose beneath. Rac. term., erect; fls 2.5cm, pink to white. Gdn origin. 'Pink Dawn': spreading; fls pale pink. 'Morning Cloud': erect; fls v. pale pink to white.

Chitra *Berberis aristata.*

Chittamwood *Bumelia lanuginosa*; *Cotinus obovatus.*

Chives *Allium schoenoprasum.*

Chlamysporum Salisb.
C. dichotomum (Labill.) Kuntze = *Thysanotus dichotomus.*

Chlidanthus Herb. Amaryllidaceae. 1 perenn. bulbous herb. Lvs 15–40cm, linear, channelled, grey-green, margins rough. Scape to 30cm; infl. umbellate; fls fragrant; pedicels to 1.2cm; perianth trumpet-shaped, usually yellow, sometimes red, cinnabar or green striped pink, tube to 7.5cm, lobes 6, lanceolate, shorter than tube. Spring. Peru. Z9.

C. fragrans Herb.
→*Castellanoa.*

CHLORANTHACEAE R. Br. ex Lindl. 4/58. *Sarcandra.*

Chloranthus Sw.
C. brachystachys Bl. = *Sarcandra glabra.*

Chloris Sw. FINGER GRASS; WINDMILL GRASS. Gramineae. 55 tufted or stoloniferous, perenn. or ann. grasses. St. slender. Lvs linear, flat or folded, scabrous. Infl. terminal, spicate, digitate, spikelets laterally flattened, in 2 rows on one side of spike axis. Trop., Subtrop. Z9.

C. barbata Sw. Ann., to 45cm. Lvs linear, flat, to 25×0.6cm. Spikes to 15, to 7.5cm, tinged purple or brown, white-pubesc. Autumn. Trop.

C. berroi Arech. GIANT FINGER GRASS; URUGUAY GRASS. Perenn., to 70cm. Spikes to 5, to 7cm. Urug.

C. crinita Lagasca = *Trichloris crinita.*

C. elegans HBK = *C. virgata.*

C. inflata Link = *C. barbata.*

C. radiata (L.) Sw. Ann., to 45cm. Lvs flat or folded, to 0.6cm wide. Spikes to 10, slender, to 7.5cm, green, occas. tinged purple. Summer–autumn. Trop. Amer.

C. truncata R. Br. STAR GRASS; CREEPING WINDMILL GRASS. Stoloniferous perenn., to 30cm. St. erect, slender. Lvs flat or folded, 0.2–0.3cm diam., spikes to 10, to 8cm, horizontal or reflexed. Autumn. Aus.

C. ventricosa R. Br. AUSTRALIAN WEEPING GRASS. Perenn. to 90cm. St. procumbent to erect, spikes to 6, to 10cm. Aus.

C. virgata Sw. Ann. to 60cm. Lvs flat, to 0.6cm diam.; lf sheaths inflated. Spikes to 12, to 7.5cm, soft-pubesc. to feathery, green to purple-tinged. Summer–autumn. Trop.

Chlorogalum (Lindl.) Kunth. SOAP PLANT; AMOLE. Liliaceae (Hyacinthaceae). 5 bulbous perennials. Lvs linear, mostly basal, undulate. Fls in terminal pan., funnelform-campanulate; tep. 6, free, usually narrow-oblong. Summer. S Oreg. to N Baja Calif. Z8.

C. angustifolium Kellogg. To 45cm. Lvs 30×6cm, grass-like. Tep. 0.8–1.2cm, white with a green-yellow central stripe; sta. equalling tep. N & C Calif.

C. pomeridianum (DC.) Kunth. SOAP PLANT; WILD POTATO. 60–150cm. Lvs to 75×2.5cm, flaccid, glaucous, undulate. Tep. 1–2.5cm, white with a purple or green central stripe; sta. shorter than tep. S Oreg. to N Calif.

Chlorophora Gaudich. FUSTIC. Moraceae. 2 trees with milky latex. ♂ fls in cylindrical spikes, ♀ fls in globose or oblong heads. Trop. Amer., Trop. Afr. Z10.

C. excelsa (Welw.) Benth. & Hook. f. = *Milicia excelsa.*

C. tinctoria (L.) Gaudich. ex Benth. & Hook. f. FUSTIC-TREE. To *c*18m; crown spreading; br. often spiny. Lvs 5–15cm, ovate or ovate-elliptic, rarely lobed. ♂ spikes 3cm; ♀ heads to 0.8cm diam. Trop. Amer. A source of yellow and green dyes.
→*Maclura.*

Chlorophytum Ker-Gawl. Liliaceae (Anthericaceae). 215 everg. perenn. herbs. Rhiz. short with fibrous or thickly fleshy translucent roots. Lvs radial, sessile and linear or petiolate and lanceolate to ovate-acute. Infl. a rac. or pan., sometimes bearing plantlets with or instead of fls; fls small, tep. 6, usually white, spreading free. Trop. & subtrop. Afr., India, SE Asia, Aus., Tasm., Peru, Braz.

C. amaniense Engl. Lvs lanceolate, 12–30×5–8cm, glossy, green, 20–26-nerved, orange-buff and tapered at base; petiole short, channelled. Infl. stout, densely fld, to 17cm. E Afr.

C. arundinaceum Bak. Lvs oblanceolate, 15–45×3.5–5cm, 20–30-nerved; petiole channelled, 5–10cm. Infl. densely fld, 23–50cm, simple or occas. 1-branched. E Himal.

C. bichetii (Karrer) Backer. Lvs linear-lanceolate, 10–20cm× 0.8–1.6cm, striped yellow-white, especially at margins, petiolate. Infl. slender, laxly fld, 10–15cm, usually unbranched. Gabon.

C. capense (L.) Voss. Lvs lanceolate or lorate, 25–60×2–4cm, glaucous, 20–30-veined, apetiolate. Infl. laxly fld, to 120cm, much-branched. S Afr.

C. comosum (Thunb.) Jacques. SPIDER PLANT; SPIDER IVY; RIBBON PLANT. Lvs linear to linear-lanceolate, 20–40×6–20cm, green often striped white, 12–15-nerved, apetiolate. Infl. erect to pendulous, laxly fld, to 60cm, simple or branched, plantlets borne at nodes. S Afr. 'Mandaianum': lvs to 15cm, with a yellow central stripe. 'Milky Way': lvs cream, edged lush green. 'Picturatum': lvs to 30cm, with a yellow central stripe. 'Variegatum': lvs white or cream at margins. 'Vittatum': lvs recurved, with a white central stripe.

C. heynei Bak. Lvs oblanceolate, 30–40×2.5–3.5cm, green, 20–26-nerved, petiole broadly channelled, to 10cm. Infl. densely fld, to 10cm. India, Sri Lanka.

C. hoffmannii Engl. Lvs linear-lanceolate to ovate-lanceolate, green, 8–20×2–3cm, petiolate. Infl. laxly fld, shorter than lvs. Tanz.

C. inornatum Ker-Gawl. Lvs oblong-lanceolate, 15–20×2.5–4cm, green, 12–16-nerved, tapering gradually to petiole. Infl. laxly

fld, to 50cm, simple or once-forked near the base, minutely
scabrid-pubesc. W Afr.

C. macrophyllum (A. Rich.) Asch. ex Bak. Lvs lanceolate,
25–75×2.5–8cm, 30–40-nerved, narrowing at the base. Infl.
densely fld, to 75cm, simple or 1–3-branched at base. Trop. Afr.

C. nepalense (Lindl.) Bak. Lvs linear-lanceolate,
15–50cm×0.6–1cm, pale green above, glaucous beneath, many-
nerved, narrowing at the base. Infl. laxly fld, 30–100cm,
branched. Nepal & Sikkim.

C. orchidastrum Lindl. Lvs oblong to ovate-lanceolate, glossy,
20–25×5–8cm, often undulate, 14–24-nerved; petiole long,
channelled. Infl. laxly fld, br. 25–40cm; peduncle 30–40cm.
Sierra Leone.

C. sternbergianum (Schult. & Schult. f.) Steud. = *C. comosum*.

Chocho *Sechium* (*S. edule*).
Chocolate Cosmos *Cosmos atrosanguineus*.
Chocolate Nut Tree *Theobroma cacao*.
Chocolate Plant *Pseuderanthemum alatum*.
Chocolate Root *Geum rivale*.
Chocolate Vine *Akebia*.

Choisya HBK. Rutaceae. 9 everg. aromatic, gland. shrubs. Lvs
subcoriaceous, glossy, digitately compound. Fls in axillary,
corymb-like cymes near ends of br.; sep. 4 or 5, membranous;
pet. 4 or 5, obovate, spreading; sta. 8 or 10. Mex., Tex., Ariz.,
New Mex. Z7.

C. arizonica Standl. To 1m. Lvs 0.5–1.5cm, petiolate, lfts 3 or 5
(rarely 6 or 7) linear, minutely pubesc., slightly revolute,
shallowly crenulate. Pet. 1cm, white. Ariz. Differing from
C. dumosa in number of lfts and v. short petioles.

C. dumosa (Torr.) A. Gray. 1–2m. Lvs 1.5–2.5cm, shortly
petiolate, lfts 1–4cm, linear-oblong 8–13 rarely 6 or 7, glab. or
sparsely pubesc., slightly revolute, remotely crenulate; pet. to
0.8cm, white. SW US, Mex.

C. grandiflora Reg. = *C. ternata*.

C. ternata HBK. MEXICAN ORANGE; MEXICAN ORANGE BLOSSOM.
1–3m. Lvs petiolate, lfts 3, oblong to obovate, 2–8cm, rounded
at apex, cuneate at base, entire. Pet. 1–1.4cm, white. Mex.
'Aztec Pearl' (*C. ternata* × *C. arizonica*): lvs slenderly divided; fls
scented, tinted pink in bud, opening white. 'Sundance': lvs gold
to lime green.

Chokeberry *Aronia*; *Prunus virginiana*.

Chomelia Jacq. non L. Rubiaceae. 20 shrubs or small trees. Br.
often spiny in axils. Fls white in axill., stalked, cymose clusters;
cal. tube top-shaped or oblong, lobes 4; cor. salver-shaped, tube
narrowly elongate, lobes 4. Trop. Amer. Z10.

C. fasciculata Jacq. Shrub to 1.5m. Lvs ovate, acute, glab. Fls to
2cm, long-pedicelled, usually 3 per axil. Grenada.

C. spinosa Jacq. Spiny shrub or tree to 9m, usually less. Lvs to
8cm, ovate to elliptic or oblong, narrowly acute, membranous.
Fls 3cm, sessile, in pedunculate, cymose clusters, nocturnally
fragrant. C to S Amer.

Chondrorhyncha Lindl. Orchidaceae. 10 epiphytic orchids allied
to *Huntleya*. Pbs 0. Lvs to 40×4cm, 2-ranked, in a loose fan,
overlapping, strap-shaped. Fls solitary, stalked, axill.; tep.
lanceolate-elliptic; lip rolled-tubular. Summer. Mex. to Braz.
Z10.

C. aromatica (Rchb. f.) P. Allen = *Zygopetalum wendlandii*.

C. chestertonii Rchb. f. Fls to 7cm diam., fleshy, highly scented,
ivory to pale green, lip lime green to yellow, fimbriate. Colomb.

C. costaricensis (Schltr.) P. Allen = *Kefersteinia costaricensis*.

C. discolor (Lindl.) P. Allen = *Cochleanthes discolor*.

C. fimbriata (Lind. & Rchb. f.) Rchb. f. Differs from
C. chestertonii in fringed, sulphur-yellow pet. and crispate or
fimbriate ochre lip, streaked or flushed maroon. Colomb.

C. flaveola (Lind. & Rchb. f.) Garay. Fls to 7.5cm diam.; tep.
lemon yellow to golden, pet. fimbriate; lip lemon yellow,
banded chocolate near base. Venez., Colomb., Ecuad., Peru.

C. lactea (Rchb. f.) L.O. Williams = *Kefersteinia lactea*.

C. lendyana Rchb. f. Fls to 5.25cm diam., lemon yellow to ivory
tinted yellow; lip wavy to crispate. Mex., Guat., Costa Rica,
Panama.

C. lipscombiae Rolfe = *Cochleanthes marginata*.

C. lojae (Schltr.) Schweinf. = *Kefersteinia lojae*.

C. rosea Lindl. Fls to 8.5cm diam., tep. pale green fading to ivory
at tips, lip sap green fading to white at tip beneath, lemon
yellow above, basally spotted magenta, golden yellow in centre,
pink to white at apex, callus white spotted pink. Venez.

Chonta *Bactris gasipaes*.

Chordospartium Cheesem. WEEPING TREE BROOM. Leguminosae
(Papilionoideae). 2 shrubs or small trees. St. erect, fissured,
slender; br. often weeping, leafless, slender, grooved. Rac. to
7cm, crowded, axillary, erect or pendulous; fls small, pea-like.
Spring–summer. NZ. Z8.

C. muritai A. Purdie. To 6m. Br. dense, not weeping. Rac. erect,
to 6cm; fls white veined violet.

C. stevensonii Cheesem. To 8m. Br. weeping. Rac. arching, to
7cm; fls pale lilac, lined purple.

Chorisia Kunth. Bombacaceae. 5 decid. trees; trunk sometimes
swollen, usually with stout spines; br. horizontal. Lvs palmate,
lfts 5–7; petiole long. Fls large, solitary or clustered, appearing
before lvs; cal. cup-shaped, irregularly 2–5-lobed; pet. 5,
oblong-obovate; sta. united to form tube with whorl of
staminodes above base and 5 pairs of sessile anth. at apex. Fr. a
large capsule; seeds embedded in silky fibres. Trop. Amer. Z10.

C. insignis Kunth. To 15m; trunk swollen, bottle-shaped, to 2m
diam., spines 0. Lfts to 12.5cm, oblong-obovate, serrate. Pet. to
7.5cm, white to yellow, grey-pubesc. externally, entire or undulate. Peru, Arg.

C. speciosa A. St.-Hil. SILK FLOSS TREE. To 15m+; trunk swollen
at base, covered with stout spines. Lfts to 12.5cm, lanceolate,
serrate. Pet. to 10cm, white or cream at base, white to yellow or
pink, red or violet above, often spotted, densely pubesc. externally. Braz., Arg.

Chorispora R. Br. ex DC. Cruciferae. 10 ann. or perenn. herbs.
Lvs entire to pinnatifid, hairy. Fls small, in rac.; pet. 4, long-
clawed, blade round; sta. 6, free. Summer. E Medit., C Asia.

C. greigii Reg. Perenn., 15–25cm. Lvs long, narrow-oblong,
pinnatifid. Pet. to 18mm, blue-pink. C Asia. Z7.

C. tenella (Pall.) DC. Ann., 8–35cm. Lvs 2.5–12cm, upper
lanceolate, toothed, lower elliptic-oblong, deeply pinnatifid.
Pet. to 10mm, purple. SE Eur. to China, nat. N Amer. Z8.
→*Raphanus*.

Chorizema Labill. Leguminosae (Papilionoideae). 18 twiners or
small shrubs. Lvs simple, entire, or sharply lobed or dentate. Fls
pea-like in rac. Aus., nat. Calif. Z9.

C. cordata Lindl. HEART-LEAVED FLAME PEA; AUSTRALIA FLAME
PEA; FLOWERING OAK. Semi-scandent or dense upright shrub to
3m. Lvs to 5cm, ovate, apex, acuminate, base cordate, sometimes minutely spiny-dentate or lobed. Fls to 1.5cm, in rac. to
15cm; standard red, orange and yellow, keel magenta or mauve.
Summer–early winter. W Aus.

C. dicksonii R.A. Graham. YELLOW-EYED FLAME PEA. Small
many-branched shrub to 1.5m. Lvs to 2cm, linear, pungent,
conspicuously veined, curved. Fls 2cm diam., in lax rac.;
standard orange-red with a lurid central yellow flash, keel
orange-red. Late summer–early winter. W Aus.

C. elegans hort. = *C. ilicifolia*.

C. ilicifolia Labill. HOLLY FLAME PEA. Scrambling herb or shrub
to 1m. Lvs 2–8cm, ovate-acuminate or narrow-oblong, holly-
like, sinuous or notched, glossy, leathery. Rac. to 15cm, 5- to
many-fld; standard orange-red and yellow, strongly reflexed,
sometimes incised, keel rose-mauve. Spring–summer. W Aus.

C. varia Benth. = *C. ilicifolia*.

Chorogi *Stachys affinis*.
Chosen-ki-hagi *Lespedeza maximowiczii*.
Chotito *Polyscias filicifolia*.
Chow Chow *Sechium edule*.
Choyote *Sechium edule*.

Christella Lév. Thelypteridaceae. 50 terrestrial ferns. Rhiz. erect
or creeping. Fronds erect, bipinnatifid; pinnae spreading,
pinnately lobed, linear-elliptic, base auriculate, apex tapered.
OW tropics and subtrop. to Americas. Z10.

C. acuminata (Houtt.) Lév. Rhiz. long-creeping, to 50cm. Fronds
to 60cm, bipinnatifid, deep green above, paler beneath; pinnae
to 2cm wide, linear to lanceolate, acuminate, pinnules obtuse,
mucronate. Temp. Asia.

C. dentata (Forssk.) Brownsey & Jermy. Rhiz. short-creeping,
scaly. Fronds to 100cm, bipinnatifid, softly textured, pubesc.,
pale yellow-green, narrowing towards base into short pinnae,
pinnae in 2–25 pairs. Pantrop.

C. parasitica (L.) Lév. Rhiz. long-creeping, scaly. Fronds to
70cm, chartaceous, orange glands beneath; pinnae 18–24 pairs,
to 1.5cm wide, broadly linear to linear-lanceolate, long-
acuminate, pubesc. Trop. & subtrop.

C. patens (Sw.) Pichi-Serm. Rhiz. stout, erect. Fronds to 100cm,
clustered, bipinnatifid; pinnae to 20cm, linear-oblong,
acuminate. Trop. Amer.

C. serra (Sw.) Pichi-Serm. Rhiz. wide-creeping. Fronds to
100×25cm, broadly lanceolate; pinnae to 25cm, spreading,

coriaceous, pale green, lobes acute. Cuba, Mex.
→*Cyclosorus, Dryopteris* and *Thelypteris*.

Christensenia Maxon. Marattiaceae. 2 terrestrial ferns. SE Asia.
C. aesculifolia (Bl.) Maxon. Rhiz. creeping, succulent; stipes to 70cm, auriculate at base, succulent. Fronds 15–30×7–10cm, palmately parted into 3–5 lobes, resembling horse-chestnut lvs, central division largest, elliptic to oblong-spathulate.
→*Kaulfussia.*

Christia Moench. Leguminosae. 12 sp. from SE Asia, of which only *C. vespertilionis* is in cult.
C. lunata Moench = *C. vespertilionis.*
C. vespertilionis (L. f.) Backh. Everg., semi-scandent shrub. Lvs to 15cm across at tips, with 2 long, spreading lobes, green with silver-grey ribs. Fls small, white in loose term. spikes. SE Asia.

✕**Christieara.** (*Aerides* ✕*Ascocentrum* ✕*Vanda.*) Orchidaceae. Intergeneric hybrids with narrowly channelled, 2-ranked lvs and erect spikes of flat fls in bright colours.

Christmas Begonia *Begonia* ✕*cheimantha.*
Christmas Bells *Blandfordia; Sandersonia aurantiaca.*
Christmas Berry *Chironia* (*C. baccifera*); *Heteromeles; Lycium carolinianum; Photinia.*
Christmas Berry Tree *Schinus terebinthifolius.*
Christmas Box *Sarcococca.*
Christmas Cactus *Schlumbergera* ✕*buckleyi.*
Christmas Candle *Senna alata.*
Christmas Fern *Polystichum acrostichoides.*
Christmas Flower *Euphorbia pulcherrima.*
Christmas Jewels *Aechmea racinae.*
Christmas Palm *Veitchia* (*V. merrillii*).
Christmas Pride *Ruellia macrantha.*
Christmas Rose *Helleborus niger.*
Christmas Star *Euphorbia pulcherrima.*
Christmas Tree *Abies alba; A. amabilis; A. nordmanniana; A. procera; A. veitchii; Metrosideros excelsus; Nuytsia.*
Christmas Tree Kalanchoe *Kalanchoe laciniata.*
Christophine *Sechium edule.*
Christ Plant *Euphorbia milii.*
Christ's Thorn *Paliurus spina-christi; Euphorbia milii.*
Christ Vine *Porana paniculata.*

Chromolaena DC. Compositae. *c*150 perenn. herbs or shrubs. Cap. discoid, few to many in a corymbosely branched thyrse, rarely solitary; phyllaries often with expanded herbaceous or coloured tips. Trop. and warm Amer. Z10.
C. hirsuta (Hook. & Arn.) R. King & H. Robinson. Perenn. herb to 60cm. Lvs to 4cm, triangular-ovate to ovate, coarsely dentate, scabrous. Flts few, mauve tinged blue.
C. odorata (L.) R. King & H. Robinson. Shrub to 2m. Lvs to 10cm, ovate to lanceolate, dentate, base subhastate, membranous, covered with yellow to red glands beneath. Flts 15–30, blue or pale lilac to white.
→*Eupatorium* and *Osmia.*

Chronanthus K. Koch.
C. biflorus (Desf.) Frodin & Heyw. = *Cytisus fontanesii.*

Chrysalidocarpus H.A. Wendl. Palmae. *c*20 palms. St. erect, solitary or clustered, smooth, ringed. Lvs pinnate, arching; sheaths and petioles scaly, or waxy; pinnae single-fold, crowded, linear to lanceolate, glab. above, waxy beneath. Madag., Comoros Is., Pemba Is. Z10.
C. cabadae H.E. Moore. St. clustered, to 9m×12.5cm. Lvs ascending; sheaths blue-green; pinnae 24–60 per side, held in one plane. known only in cult.
C. lucubensis Becc. = *C. madagascariensis* var. *lucubensis.*
C. lutescens (Bory) H.A. Wendl. YELLOW PALM; ARECA PALM; BUTTERFLY PALM; YELLOW BUTTERFLY PALM; CANE PALM; GOLDEN YELLOW PALM. St. clustered, to 9m×12cm. Lvs to 2m, ascending then arching, sheaths and petioles yellow-green, waxy; pinnae to 60 on each side of rachis, held in one plane.
C. madagascariensis Becc. St. clustered, to 10m×15cm. Lvs to 3m; pinnae 100 per side, arranged in groups in several planes. Madag. var. *lucubensis* (Becc.) Jumelle & Perrier. St. solitary.
→*Areca.*

Chrysanthemoides Fabr. Compositae. 3 shrubs. Cap. radiate; flts yellow. S Afr.
C. monilifera (L.) Norl. Erect, 1–3m, densely branched. Laxly arachnoid-woolly, bark later becoming brown-grey and cracked. Lvs to 7cm, obovate to elliptic-oblanceolate, coarsely serrate-dentate to denticulate, teeth often mucronate, cobwebby then glabrescent. Cap. few, in a corymb.
→*Osteospermum.*

Chrysanthemopsis (Maire) Wilcox, Bremer & Humphries. Compositae. 10 somewhat tufted perenn. herbs or subshrubs. Sterile st. usually short and rosulate, fertile st. leafy, taller. Lvs small, usually 3-partite, often becoming entire above. Cap. radiate, solitary and term., on long subscapose peduncles. NW Afr. Z9.
C. atlantica (Ball) Wilcox, Bremer & Humphries. Rhizomatous herb, *c*7–10cm. Lvs to 4cm, radical, unequally 3-partite, middle lobe ternate,, lat. lobes enlarged, laciniate, seg. ovate to broadly oblong, pilose above, glab. beneath. Cap. to 3cm diam., ray flts white tinged red, flushed pink at first beneath; disc flts pale yellow. Morocco.
C. catananche (Ball) Wilcox, Bremer & Humphries. Rhizomatous herb, to 15cm. Lvs to 6.5cm, radical, irregularly 3-partite, dentate, silver-grey. Cap. to 5cm diam.; ray flts yellow, red toward base, disc flts yellow. Morocco.
C. depressa (Ball) Wilcox, Bremer & Humphries. Woody-based herb to 20cm. Lvs to 4cm, crowded, pinnately partite, basal lvs obovate, 3-partite, seg. 2–3-divided, linear, uppermost lvs much smaller, entire or 2-fid, linear, pubesc., sometimes silky-villous. Cap. 1.5–2cm diam.; ray flts white to ± purple tinged or white tinged pink above, red-tinged beneath; disc flts yellow-gold, rarely purple-tinged at apex. Morocc. and Alg.
C. gayana (Coss. & Dur.) Wilcox, Bremer & Humphries. Subshrub to 45cm. Lvs *c*2.5cm, scattered, triangular to oblong, pinnatifid, lobes 3 or more, slender, uppermost lvs linear, entire, soft laxly woolly. Cap. *c*2.5–4cm diam.; ray flts white, rose beneath, disc flts brown. Morocc. and Alg.
C. hosmariensis (Ball) Wilcox, Bremer & Humphries. Like *C. maresii* but more bushy, lvs sessile, cap. to 4cm diam., ray flts white, disc flts yellow. Morocc.
C. maresii (Coss.) Wilcox, Bremer & Humphries. Woody-based herb, to 10–30cm. Lvs crowded, 3-partite, seg. linear, v. short or elongate, divergent, upper lvs often undivided, linear, silvery grey, pubesc. Ray flts yelllow, becoming purple tinged, then black-purple, disc flts yellow, becoming purple at apex. Alg.
→*Chrysanthemum, Leucanthemopsis, Leucanthemum, Pyrethrum.*

Chrysanthemum (of florists and gardens) *Dendranthema* ✕*grandiflorum.*

Chrysanthemum L. Compositae. 5 ann. herbs. Cap. radiate, pedunculate, solitary or 2–5. Eur., N Afr.
C. alpinum L. = *Leucanthemopsis alpina.*
C. anethifolium Brouss. ex Willd. = *Argyranthemum foeniculaceum.*
C. anserinifolium (Hausskn. & Bornm. ex Hausskn.) J. Ingram & Dress = *Tanacetum poteriifolium.*
C. arcticum L. = *Arctanthemum arcticum.*
C. atkinsonii C.B. Clarke = *Tanacetum atkinsonii.*
C. atratum Jacq. = *Leucanthemum atratum.*
C. atrococcineum Hart = *C. carinatum.*
C. aucherianum hort. = *Tanacetum praeteritum.*
C. balsamita L. = *Tanacetum balsamita.*
C. boreale (Mak.) Mak. = *Dendranthema boreale.*
C. broussonetii Pers. = *Argyranthemum broussonetii.*
C. carinatum Schousb. To 1m. Lvs somewhat succulent, stiff, bright green, pinnatifid to pinnatisect with linear lobes. Cap. to 10cm diam., solitary, pedunculate; ray flts white or yellow, occas. tinged red with dark or white basal zone; disc flts purple. Summer–early autumn. Probably originally Moroc. but now widely dispersed. 'Burridgeanum': ray flts with red basal stripe. Court Jester's Mixed: flts vivid red, pink, orange, yellow, maroon and white, zoned red or orange. Dunnetti Choice Mixed: infl. vividly coloured, single and 'double', yellow, bronze and crimson. 'Northern Star': white, yellow-zoned.
C. coccineum Willd. = *Tanacetum coccineum.*
C. coreanum Nak. = *Dendranthema coreanum.*
C. coronarium L. CROWN DAISY. To 80cm, glab. or slightly hairy. Lvs pale green, obovate to oblong, usually 2-pinnatisect, toothed, lanceolate or oblong. Cap. solitary, to 5cm diam.; flts yellow. Late summer. Medit., Port. 'Flore Plenum': fls double. 'Golden Gem': fls deep yellow.
C. corymbosum L. = *Tanacetum corymbosum.*
C. densum (Labill.) Steud. = *Tanacetum densum.*
C. erubescens hort. non Steud. = *Dendranthema zawadskii.*

C. erubescens Steud. = *Dendranthema naktongense*.
C. ferulaceum (Webb) Sunding = *Tanacetum ferulaceum*.
C. flosculosum L. = *Plagius flosculosus*.
C. foeniculaceum (Willd.) Desf. = *Argyranthemum foenicula-
ceum*.
C. frutescens L. = *Argyranthemum frutescens*.
C. grande Hook. f. = *Tanacetum balsamita*.
C. grandiflorum hort. = *Argyranthemum frutescens*.
C. hortorum hort. = *Dendranthema* ×*grandiflorum*.
C. indicum L. = *Dendranthema indicum*.
C. indicum var. *boreale* Mak. = *Dendranthema boreale*.
C. japonicum Mak. = *Dendranthema japonicum*.
C. ×*koreanum* hort. = *Dendranthema* ×*grandiflorum*.
C. lacustre Brot. = *Leucanthemum lacustre*.
C. leucanthemum L. = *Leucanthemum vulgare*.
C. macrophyllum Waldst. & Kit. = *Tanacetum macrophyllum*.
C. makinoi Matsum. & Nak. = *Dendranthema japonicum*.
C. marginatum hort. = *Dendranthema ornatum*.
C. maximum Ramond non hort. = *Leucanthemum maximum*.
C. maximum hort. non Ramond = *Leucanthemum* ×*superbum*.
C. montanum Asch. = *Leucanthemum graminifolium*.
C. ×*morifolium* Ramat. = *Dendranthema* ×*grandiflorum*.
C. naktongense Nak. = *Dendranthema naktongense*.
C. nipponicum (Franch. ex Maxim.) Matsum. = *Nipponan-
themum nipponicum*.
C. ornatum Hemsl. = *Dendranthema ornatum*.
C. pallens Gay = *Leucanthemum pallens*.
C. pallidum Mill. = *Leucanthemopsis pallida*.
C. paludosum Poir. = *Leucanthemum paludosum*.
C. ptarmiciflorum (Webb) Brenan = *Tanacetum ptarmiciflorum*.
C. radicans Pers. = *Leucanthemopsis radicans*.
C. rotundifolium Waldst. & Kit. = *Leucanthemum waldsteinii*.
C. rubellum Sab. = *Dendranthema zawadskii*.
C. segetum L. CORN MARIGOLD. To 80cm, glab., glaucous, some-
what fleshy. Lvs oblong to oblong-obovate, upper lvs entire,
lower and middle lvs deeply cut. Cap. solitary, to 6.5cm diam.;
flts yellow. W Medit. and W Afr., nat. throughout Eur. 'Eastern
Star': primrose with brown disc. 'Evening Star': golden.
C. serotinum L. = *Leucanthemella serotina*.
C. sibiricum Turcz. = *Dendranthema zawadskii*.
C. superbum Bergmans ex J. Ingram = *Leucanthemum*
×*superbum*.
C. tchihatchewii (Boiss.). = *Tripleurospermum oreades* var. *tchi-
hatchewii*.
C. tomentosum Lois. = *Leucanthemopsis alpina* ssp. *tomentosa*.
C. tricolor Andrews = *C. carinatum*.
C. vulgare (L.) Bernh. = *Tanacetum vulgare*.
C. yezoense Mack. = *Dendranthema yezoense*.
C. zawadskii Herbich = *Dendranthema zawadskii*.

CHRYSOBALANACEAE R.Br. 17/460. *Chrysobalanus, Licania*.

Chrysobalanus L. COCO PLUM. Chrysobalanaceae. 2 shrubs or
small trees. Lvs simple, with two glands near junction with
petiole. Infl. a few-fld rac. or cyme; fls small, actinomorphic,
formed of cupuliform receptacle tube, sep. (5) and pet. (5); sta.
12–26, arranged in circle. Fr. a ridged drupe. Trop. Amer., Afr.
C. icaco L. Shrub or small tree to 5m. Lvs 2–8cm, orbicular to
ovate-elliptic, obtuse, glab. Infl. short; receptacle tube and sep.
grey-tomentellous; pet. white. Fr. ovoid 2–5cm, fleshy within,
edible. Trop. Amer., W Afr., nat. E Afr., Vietnam, Fiji.
C. oblongifolius Michx. = *Licania michauxii*.

Chrysocoma L. Compositae. *c*20 small, ann. to perenn. herbs
and shrubs. Lvs linear, lobed. Cap. discoid, term., solitary, or
rarely few in corymbs, shortly pedunculate; flts, yellow. S Afr.
C. coma-aurea L. Shrub, to 50cm. Lvs spreading, recurved. Infl.
button-like, scented. Autumn. S Afr.
C. linosyris L. = *Aster linosyris*.

Chrysocoptis Nutt.
C. occidentalis Nutt. = *Coptis occidentalis*.

Chrysogonum L. GOLDEN KNEE. Compositae. 1 rhizomatous,
perenn. herb to 40cm. Lvs opposite, to 10×7cm, entire to
dentate, base attenuate to subcordate, pubesc. Cap. radiate, to
3cm diam., solitary; ray flts yellow; disc flts yellow. E US.
C. peruvianum L. = *Zinnia peruviana*.
C. virginianum L.

Chrysolarix H.E. Moore.
C. amabilis (J. Nels.) H.E. Moore = *Pseudolarix amabilis*.

Chrysolepis Hjelmqv. GOLDEN CHINKAPIN; GOLDEN CHESTNUT.
Fagaceae. 2 everg. trees and shrubs. Bark red-brown. Shoots
golden-tomentose at first, later scurfy. Lvs simple, entire, oblong-
lanceolate or narrow oval, glossy dark yellow-green above,
densely golden tomentose beneath. Fls in long slender catkins.
Nuts edible, chestnut-like encased in a 2–4cm 7-sectioned burr
covered with branched spines. NW US.
C. chrysophylla (Hook.) Hjelmqv. GOLDEN CHINKAPIN. Tree to
25m; bark furrowed. Lvs 4–15cm. Dist. as for genus. Z7.
'Obovata' ('Obtusata'): small, hardy, free-fruiting tree with
obtuse lvs to 5cm. var. *minor* (Benth.) Hjelmqv. Shrub or small
tree to 10m, lvs, 3–8cm. Calif. coast. Z8.
C. sempervirens (Kellogg) Hjelmqv. DWARF GOLDEN CHINKAPIN.
Shrub to 3m, rarely 5m; bark smooth. Lvs 2–6cm. Calif. Z6.
→*Castanea* and *Castanopsis*.

Chrysolite Lily *Hymenocallis latifolia*.

Chrysophyllum L. Sapotaceae. *c*80 everg. trees or shrubs. Lvs
entire, sometimes coppery or golden-pubescent beneath. Fls
small, white-purple in axill. or cauliflorous clusters, sep.
(4–)5(–6), cor. globose, campanulate or cylindrical, (4–)5(–8)-
lobed, sta. (4–)5(–8). Fr. a berry, often large and fleshy.
Pantrop., esp. Americas. Z10.
C. cainito L. STAR APPLE; CAIMITO. Tree to 18m. Lvs 4.5–15.5cm,
broadly elliptic to oblong-elliptic, glossy green above, with soft,
red-gold or gold pubescence beneath, vein pairs 14–26. Fr.
4–7cm, broadly ellipsoid to globose, smooth, pale green or
purple, pulp white, edible, sweet, translucent; seeds 3–10, star-
shaped in section. C Amer., W Indies.
C. monopyrenum Sw. = *C. cainito*.
C. oliviforme L. SATIN LEAF; DAMSON PLUM. Shrub or small tree
to 10m. Lvs 3–12cm, leathery, elliptic, glab. above, with dense,
red-gold or pale brown tomentum beneath, vein pairs 15–20. Fr.
1.4–3cm, narrowly ellipsoid to ovoid, smooth, purple; seed 1. W
Indies, US (S Flor.).

Chrysopsis (Nutt.) Elliott. GOLDEN ASTER. Compositae. 10 ann.
to perenn. herbs or subshrubs. Cap. radiate, in cymes,
peduncles bracteate; involucre campanulate; flts yellow. SE US.
C. amplifolia Rydb. = *Heterotheca villosa*.
C. camporum Greene = *Heterotheca camporum*.
C. falcata (Pursh) Elliott = *Pityopsis falcata*.
C. gossypina (Michx.) Elliott. Bienn. to perenn., white-
tomentose. St. erect to decumbent, to 1m. Basal lvs to 9cm,
oblanceolate to elliptic; st. lvs smaller, sometimes ciliate or
woolly. Cap. to 4cm diam., few in a loose corymb or cyme,
peduncles and involucre sometimes woolly. SE US. f. *tricophylla*
(Nutt.) Semple. St. erect. Lvs pilose to glabrate, sometimes
ciliate. Peduncles glab.; involucre glab. Carol. to Flor. Z8.
C. mariana (L.) Elliott. Perenn., long-pubesc. St. erect or
ascending, to 90cm, tinted purple. Basal lvs to 25cm, spathulate
to oblanceolate, sparsely dentate, wispy-pubesc., st. lvs to 3cm,
lanceolate to elliptic-oblong, entire. Cap. to 4.5cm diam., in
umbels or cymes, peduncles densely gland. SE US. Z4.
C. microcephala Small = *Pityopsis graminifolia* var. *tenuifolia*.
C. nervosa Willd. = *Pityopsis graminifolia* var. *latifolia*.
C. pinifolia Elliott = *Pityopsis pinifolia*.
C. rutteri (Rothr.) Greene = *Heterotheca rutteri*.
C. trichophylla (Nutt.) Elliott = *C. gossypina* f. *tricophylla*.
C. villosa (Pursh) Nutt. = *Heterotheca villosa*.
C. villosa var. *rutteri* Rothr. = *Heterotheca rutteri*.

Chrysopteris Link.
C. areolata (Humb. & Bonpl. ex Willd.) Fée = *Phlebodium au-
reum* var. *areolatum*.
C. aureum (L.) Link = *Phlebodium aureum*.
C. decumana (Willd.) Fée = *Phlebodium decumanum*.

Chrysosplenium L. GOLDEN SAXIFRAGE. Saxifragaceae. 55
perenn. herbs, occas. stoloniferous. Lvs rounded to reniform,
dentate-lobed, petiole long. Infl. term. cymose, with large leafy
bracts; fls small, occas. solitary; cal. fused at base to form a cup,
4–5-lobed above; pet. 0; sta. 8–10 or 4, on rim of cup. Eur., NE
Asia, NW Amer., S Amer., N Afr.
C. alpinum Schur. = *C. oppositifolium* var. *alpinum*.
C. alternifolium L. To 22cm. Stolons thin. Basal lvs 1–2.5cm, 4–8
lobed, sparsely hispid above; petiole 1.5–5cm. Flowering st.
5–22cm bearing 1–3 small alt. lvs, bracts reniform-round,
yellow-green; fls 4.5–6mm diam., green-yellow. Spring–early
summer. Widespread Br. Isles, Eur., Sib. Z4.
C. americanum Schwein. ex Hook. WATER MAT; WATER CARPET.
To 20cm. Basal lvs 0.5–1.5cm, short-stalked. Flowering st.
5–20cm, with 4–6 paired lvs, bracts ovate, fls 3–4mm diam.,
yellow-green, often purple within. Spring. C & W N Amer. Z3.
C. auriculatum Crantz = *C. oppositifolium*.
C. geoides Fisch. ex Ledeb. = *C. alternifolium*.
C. nivale Schur = *C. alternifolium*.
C. octandrum Caqué ex Steud. = *C. oppositifolium*.

C. oppositifolium L. Differs from *C. alternifolium* in st. lvs opposite and fls and bracts slightly darker in colour. Spring. Br. Isles, Eur. var. *alpinum* (Schur.) Schur. Lvs smaller, glab. Fls deep yellow. Z5.

C. repens Link = *C. oppositifolium*.

C. rotundifolium Schldl. ex Ledeb. = *C. alternifolium*.

→*Saxifraga*.

Chrysothamnus Nutt. RABBIT BRUSH. Compositae. 13 shrubs or subshrubs. Cap. discoid, densely arranged in rac., cymes or pan.; receptacle ± flat; ray flts usually 0, or inconspicuous; disc flts yellow or white, 5-lobed. W N Amer.

C. viscidiflorus (Hook.) Nutt. Rounded, white-barked shrub to 1m. St. glab. to pubesc. Lvs 5cm, linear, lanceolate or elliptic, viscid, glab. or pubesc. Cap. in broad cymes. Summer–early autumn. W US. Z3.

→*Bigelowia*.

Chrysothemis Decne. Gesneriaceae. 7 perenn. herbs. Lvs in equal, opposite pairs, mostly dentate. Fls in axill. cymes; cal. tubular, with 5 short, acute lobes, sometimes 5-angled; cor. tube cylindric, limb recurved, lobes 5, rounded. Trop. Amer. Z10.

C. friedrichsthaliana (Hanst.) H.E. Moore St. to 30cm, erect, sparsely pubesc., succulent. Lvs to 30cm, oblong to oblanceolate, dentate, pale pilose. Fls 3–5 per cluster; cal. 5-angled, inflated at base, green or yellow, often flushed red at apex; cor. to 3cm, orange or orange-yellow, lobes with orange-red stripes. C Amer., W to Colomb.

C. pulchella (Donn ex Sims) Decne. Differs from *C. friedrichsthaliana* in cal. broader, not inflated, bright red; cor. to 6cm. W Indies, Panama, NE S Amer. to Amazonia.

→*Tussaca*.

Chufa *Cyperus esculentus*.

Chulta *Dillenia indica*.

Chuparosa Honeysuckle *Justicia californica*.

Chusan Palm *Trachycarpus*.

Chusquea Kunth. Gramineae. *c*120 bamboos. Culms clumped, terete, pith-filled; sheaths persistent with auricles and bristles; br. basically 3, these soon branching densely near to the base giving the appearance of many primary divisions.

C. breviglumis hort. = *C. culeou* 'Tenuis'.

C. coronalis Söderstr. & Cald. Delicate, clump-forming, with thin culms; br. completely encircling culms. Lvs 2.3–7.0×0.3–0.8cm, not tessellate. C Amer. Z7.

C. culeou E. Desv. Culms yellow-green to olive, erect, stout, 4–6m×1.5–3cm; sheaths persistent, long-tapering, papery white; nodes prominent with white wax below at first; br. 10–80cm, from alt. sides of culm, appearing densely tufted. Lvs 6–13×0.5–1.5cm, tessellate. Chile. Z7. 'Tenuis': culms thinner, shorter, to 2m×0.5cm, growing out at an angle of 45°.

C. culeou var. *tenuis* D. McClintock = *C. culeou* 'Tenuis'.

Chysis Lindl. Orchidaceae. 3 epiphytic orchids. Pbs clavate or fusiform, clothed with papery sheaths. Lvs alt. along upper half of pbs, broad-lanceolate, arching, plicate or ribbed. Rac. lat., arching; fls waxy, fragrant; dors. sep. elliptic, lat. sep. basally fused, forming a conspicuous chin or mentum; pet. resembling sep., but smaller; lip fleshy, united to base of column, inrolled to tubular, midlobe undulate, cleft, broad, disc 3–5-ridged. Summer. Mex. to Peru. Z10.

C. aurea Lindl. Fls to 7.25cm diam., waxy, heavily perfumed, ivory to lemon yellow, lip ivory or white, marked oxblood, disc with to 5 velvety, golden ridges. Throughout genus range.

C. bractescens Lindl. Differs from *C. aurea* chiefly in more conspicuous floral bracts, to 2.75cm. Mex., Belize, Guat.

C. laevis Lindl. Fls to 6.75cm diam., ochre or golden at base, peach or orange in apical half, lip pale yellow to peach, fading at centre to ivory, spotted red, disc 3-ridged. Mex. to Costa Rica.

C. tricostata Schltr. = *C. laevis*.

Cibotium Kaulf. TREE FERN. Dicksoniaceae. 15 tree ferns. Rhiz. decumbent or erect, arborescent, crown and stipes hairy. Fronds oblong-deltoid in outline, bipinnate; pinnules bipinnatifid. Trop. and subtrop. regions (Hawaii, Mex., India, Malaysia, Philippine Is., China). Z9.

C. barometz (L.) J. Sm. SCYTHIAN LAMB. Caudex prostrate, v. short, covered with glossy brown hairs. Fronds to 2m, shining and glab. above, glaucous beneath; pinnae ovate-lanceolate; pinnules linear-acuminate; seg. linear-oblong, acute. Assam, S China, Malaysia.

C. chamissoi Kaulf. HAWAIIAN TREE FERN; HAPUU-II. Caudex to 8m, erect, covered with yellow-brown hairs. Fronds to 4m, sub-coriaceous, glaucous, glab. or covered beneath with arachnoid hairs; pinnae lanceolate, pinnules linear-acuminate; seg. ovate,

obtuse, bluntly serrate; stipes tubercled with yellow-brown hairs at base, and with stiff, black hairs above. Hawaii.

C. glaucum (Sm.) Hook. & Arn. Caudex to 5m, erect, covered with yellow-brown, lustrous hairs. Fronds 30–45cm, ovate-lanceolate, v. glaucous beneath, coriaceous, glab.; pinnae linear-oblong with a long, narrow, serrate tip; pinnules oblong, falcate, crenate-serrate, auricled below; seg. linear oblong. Hawaii.

C. menziesii Hook. Caudex to 8m, erect. Fronds not glaucous beneath, subcoriaceous, glab. throughout; pinnae 30–45cm; pinnules linear-acuminate, cut half way to rachis; seg. rounded. Hawaii.

C. pruinatum Mett. = *C. menziesii*.

C. regale Versch. & Lem. Caudex to 10m, hairy, erect. Fronds to 4m, oblong-deltoid, with conspicuous white bloom beneath; pinnae 45–60cm, oblong-lanceolate; pinnules, to 3cm wide; seg. lanceolate-falcate, incised to pinnatifid; stipes hairy below. Mex.

C. schiedei Schldl. & Cham. MEXICAN TREE FERN. Caudex to 5m, erect, covered with yellow-brown, silky hairs. Fronds to 2m, pale green, glaucous beneath, membranous; pinnae oblong-lanceolate; pinnules linear-lanceolate, finely acuminate; seg. ovate, acute, serrate. Mex.

C. splendens (Gaudich.) Kraj. ex Skottsb. HAPUU; MAN TREE FERN; MAN FERN. Caudex to 3m, erect, similar to *C. glaucum* but fronds slightly glaucous or green and covered with pale cobwebby hairs beneath; pinnules not auricled. Hawaii.

Cicer L. Leguminosae (Papilionoideae). 40 ann. or perenn. herbs, procumbent or erect, glandular-hirsute. Lvs pinnate or trifoliate, tendrils sometimes present. Fls small, pea-like, solitary or in few-fld axill. rac. Legume distended, seeds large, 1–4, with small hilum. W & C Asia, Ethiop., Greece, Moroc. Z8.

C. arietinum L. CHICK PEA; EGYPTIAN PEA; GARBANZO. Ann. herb, 20–100cm. St. procumbent or erect, downy. Lvs paripinnate, lfts 7–19mm, in 5–17 pairs, ovate or elliptic, apex awned or mucronulate. Fls solitary; white or violet, standard 10–22mm. Fr. 20–35mm, ovate-oblong, beaked, glandular-hirsute; seeds 4–14mm, 1–2, smooth, white or tan. S Eur., SW Asia, N Afr.

Cicerbita Wallr. Compositae. *c*18 erect, perenn. herbs with milky sap. Lvs elliptic to obovate-runcinate or deeply lyrate-pinnatisect with a large term. lobe. Cap. numerous, ligulate; ligules blue, lilac or violet, rarely yellow. N temp., esp. mts.

C. alpina (L.) Wallr. MOUNTAIN SOW THISTLE. 50–250cm, red-glandular above. Lvs 8–25cm, glab., glaucous beneath, lowest lyrate or runcinate-pinnatifid, term. lobe triangular, acuminate, base cordate, clasping; petiole winged. Cap. in an elongated pan.; phyllaries purple-green; ligules pale blue. Arc. & Alpine Eur. Z4.

C. bourgaei (Boiss.) Beauv. 1.5–3m. Lvs 9–26cm, oblong to elliptic, lyrate, lobes 2–5, sinuate-toothed, crispate. Cap. in large pan.; phyllaries tinted pink; ligules lavender or lilac-blue. Asia Minor. Z5.

C. macrantha (C.B. Clarke) Beauv. St. smooth, stout, to 70cm. Lvs to 23cm, oblong, pinnately lobed, acute. Cap. pendent, few, in corymbs; phyllaries ciliate; ligules blue. C Nepal to Bhutan. Z6.

C. macrophylla (Willd.) Wallr. Similar to *C. alpina* but lvs setose, lower lvs with cordate term. lobe, lat. lobes 2, pan. wider and corymbose, cap. few in a corymb. C & E Russia, widely nat. ssp. *macrophylla*. Ligules dark violet. ssp. *uralensis* (Rouy) Sell. Ligules lilac. Z4.

C. plumieri (L.) Kirschl. To 1.3m, glab. Lvs 5–60cm, lyrate-pinnatifid, glaucous beneath, term. lobe triangular, lat. lobes several pairs, ovate, undulate, smaller, petioles winged. Cap. in a corymbose pan.; ligules blue. Pyren. to SW Bulg. Z5.

C. racemosa (Willd.) Beauv. To 85cm. glab. or sparsely bristly. Lvs to 20cm, oblanceolate to obovate, usually lyrate-runcinate, petiole winged, toothed. Cap. few to many, in a corymb-like infl.; phyllaries often tinged purple; ligules pale blue, lavender or mauve. Summer–autumn. Cauc., NW Iran. Z6.

→*Lactuca, Mulgedium* and *Sonchus*.

Cichorium L. CHICORY. Compositae. 8 ann. to perenn. herbs, with milky latex. St. usually solitary, diffusely branched. Lvs toothed or pinnatifid. Cap. ligulate, numerous, term. or axill.; receptacle flat; ligules bright blue, rarely pink or white. Eur., Medit., temp. Asia, Ethiop.

C. divaricatum Schousb. = *C. endivia* ssp. *divaricatum*.

C. endivia L. ENDIVE. Like *C. intybus* but usually ann. or bienn., peduncles of terminal cap. markedly swollen. Asia, Eur., widely cult. ssp. *endivia* St. 60–120cm. Lvs dentate to deeply pinnatifid, subglabrous. ssp. *divaricatum* (Schousb.) Sell. St. 5–50cm. Lvs runcinate-dentate, basal lvs pubesc.

C. glandulosum Boiss. & Huet. Ann. to 60cm. St. flexuous, branched. Lvs sparsely pubesc., basal lvs obovate, dentate, shortly petiolate, st. lvs lanceolate, dentate to entire, auriculate, sessile. Cap. few, clustered; peduncle somewhat thickened, glandular-hairy. Summer. Turk., N Syr. Z8.

C. intybus L. CHICORY; SUCCORY; WITLOOF. Perenn., 30–120cm, with a long, thick taproot. St. rigid, grooved, glab. Basal lvs 7–30cm, oblanceolate, runcinate-pinnatifid to toothed, shortly petiolate, sparsely hairy beneath, st. lvs sessile, amplexicaul, sparsely dentate to entire. Cap. with peduncles 0 or slightly swollen. Late spring–autumn. Eur., W Asia, N Afr. Z3.

C. pumilum Jacq. = *C. endivia* ssp. *divaricatum*.

C. spinosum L. Dwarf perenn. St. to 18cm, br. spreading from woody base, the upper terminating in spines. Lvs 2–9cm, oblanceolate, pinnatisect to dentate, glab. Cap. axill. or in term., subsessile clusters. Summer. Medit. Z7.

Cider Gum *Eucalyptus gunnii.*
Cidra *Cucurbita ficifolia.*
Cidron *Aloysia triphylla.*

Cienfuegosia Cav.
C. hakeifolius (Giord.) Hochr. = *Alogyne hakeifolius.*

Cigar Flower *Cuphea ignea.*
Cilantro *Coriandrum.*
Cilician Fir *Abies cilicica.*

Cimicifuga L. BUGBANE; COHOSH; RATTLETOP. Ranunculaceae. 15 erect perenn. herbs. Lvs alt., 1–3-ternate, seg. lobed and toothed; petioles long. Fls small in long, slender, compound rac. or pan., white to cream or tinged pink; sep. 2–5, petaloid; pet. 1–8, commonly 4–5, sometimes 0, small, often 2-lobed, clawed. N temp. regions.

C. acerina (Sieb. & Zucc.) Tan. = *C. japonica* var. *acerina.*

C. americana Michx. AMERICAN BUGBANE; SUMMER COHOSH. To 2m. Lvs 2–3-ternate; lfts 2.5–7cm, almost round, cordate at base, 3 to 5-lobed, lobes toothed, acute. Rac. 30–60cm slender, erect. Summer. E US. Z5.

C. arizonica Wats. ARIZONA BUGBANE. To 1.5m. Lvs biternate, rarely ternate; lfts 9–45cm, ovate or oblong-ovate, serrate to dentate-serrate, often acuminate, base subcordate. Infl. a pan. of virgate to lax rac. Summer. SW US. Z6.

C. biternata (Sieb. & Zucc.) Miq. INUSHOMA. 50–100cm. Lvs ternate or biternate, lfts 3–9, palmately lobed, sharply dentate to serrate and incised. Infl. a spike or spicate rac., 5–30cm, hispid. Summer–autumn. Jap. Z5.

C. cordifolia Pursh = *C. racemosa* var. *cordifolia.*

C. dahurica (Turcz.) Torr. & A. Gray ex Maxim. To 1.5m. Lvs 2–3-ternate; lfts ovate, acuminate, serrate, pinnatifid or lobed at base, term. leaflet cordate. Rac. simple or compound. Summer–autumn. E Sib., Mong., China to Jap. Z5.

C. elata Nutt. 1–2.5m; st. branched and glandular-puberulent above. Lvs 2-ternate, lfts 5–15mm, cordate-ovate, often 3-lobed, lobes shallowly lobed and serrate-dentate. Fls in long rac., or pan. Summer. (Washington to NW Oreg.) Z7.

C. foetida L. FOETID BUGBANE. 1–2m, st. simple or branched above, glandular-hairy. Lvs 2-ternate; lfts ovate-oblong, seg. deeply serrate, term. leaflet usually 3-lobed. Rac. tall, cream, drooping, remotely branched. Summer. Sib., E Asia. Z3.

C. heracleifolia Komar. KOMAROV'S BUGBANE. 50–140cm. Lvs biternate to triternate; lfts 9–25, broadly ovate, 3-lobed, apex acuminate, base rounded to subcordate, serrate-incised. Rac. compound, glandular-hairy. Summer–autumn. N China, E Russia. Z3.

C. japonica (Thunb.) Spreng. 60–80cm. Lvs all basal, 1–2-ternate, lfts 5–10cm, broad-ovate to orbicular, 3–5-lobed, acute or obtuse, base cordate, hairy, long-stalked, toothed. Rac. to 35cm, sometimes branched at base, pubesc. Summer–autumn. Jap. var. *acerina* (Sieb. & Zucc.) Huth. Lvs with long-pointed lobes. Summer–autumn. Jap. Z5.

C. laciniata S. Wats. To 1.5m; st. puberulent and slightly gland. above. Lvs 2–3-ternate; lfts 8–12cm, ovate, acute, base shallowly cordate, lobed to laciniate, coarsely serrate-dentate. Summer. NW US. Z7.

C. racemosa (L.) Nutt. BLACK COHOSH; BLACK SNAKEROOT. To 2.5m, usually shorter. Lvs 2–3-ternate, or ternate then pinnate; lfts ovate or oblong, acute, base cuneate nearly glab., sharply serrate and lobed. Rac. to 90cm, erect, slender, branched; fls fragrant. Summer. N Amer. 'Purpurea': lvs deep purple. var. *cordifolia* (Pursh) Gray. Lfts c20cm, few (i.e. 9–11 per lf), base cordate. Z4.

C. ramosa Nak. To 2m+. Lvs ternate; lfts oblong-oval, biserrate, veins reticulate, impressed. Rac. to 40cm, erect to nodding.

Autumn. Kamchatka. Atropurpurea group: forms with dark purple-red foliage including 'Brunette' (lvs maroon). Z9.

C. rubifolia Kearney. 60–120cm. Lvs 2-ternate, lat. divisions 2-foliate; lfts 12–20cm, ovate to suborbicular, irregularly lobed, lobes acute to acuminate, toothed. Fls in pan. of 2–4, slender, cylindrical rac. to 30cm. Autumn. SE US. Z6.

C. simplex Wormsk. ex DC. 60–120cm. Lvs 2-ternate, lat. divisions, 2-foliate; lfts 12–20cm, ovate to suborbicular, irregularly lobed, lobes acute to acuminate, toothed. Fls in pan. of 2–4, slender rac. to 30cm. Autumn. Mong., E Russia (Kamchatka) Jap. 'Braunlaub': lvs exceptionally dark. 'Elstead' ('Elstead Variety'): buds tinged purple, fls white in feathery rac. 'White Pearl' ('Armleuchter'): lvs v. pale, fls pure white. Z5.

→*Actaea.*

Cinchona L. QUININE; SACRED BARK; JESUIT'S BARK. Rubiaceae. c40 shrubs or trees with bitter bark. Fls in term. pan. or cymes, fragrant; cal. tube pubesc., limb 5-toothed or lobed; cor. tubular, lobes 5, ciliate. S Amer. Z9.

C. calisaya Wedd. = *C. officinalis.*

C. condaminea Humb. ex Bonpl. = *C. officinalis.*

C. cordifolia Mutis ex Humb. CARTAGENA BARK. Shrub to 5m, or tree to 15m. Lvs to 40cm, ovate to orbicular, apex acute, base cordate. Fls in loose, spreading pan., white to green and pink-flushed; cor. to 2cm. Spring–autumn. Peru, Columbia.

C. gratissima Wallich = *Luculia gratissima.*

C. ledgeriana Moens ex Trimen = *C. officinalis* 'Ledgeriana'.

C. micrantha Ruiz & Pav. HUANNCO. Shrub or tree to 8m. Lvs to 17cm, obovate to elliptic, apex acute. Fls in pan., white to yellow, fragrant; cor. to 8mm, tube gibbous at base. Boliv., Peru, Ecuad.

C. officinalis L. CROWN BARK; PERUVIAN BARK; CALISAYA; BROWN PERU BARK. Shrub to 3m, or tree to 8m. Lvs to 18cm, ovate or lanceolate to oblong, apex acute to narrowly acute, base obtuse, lustrous. Fls in axillary or term., corymbose cymes, yellow to green or red, fragrant; cor. to 18mm, tube somewhat 5-angled, sericeous. Peru. 'Ledgeriana' (LEDGER BARK): tree, to 10m; lvs to 12cm, lanceolate or elliptic to oblong, apex acute; fls in term., pendent pan., white to yellow.

C. pubescens Vahl. Tree to 9m. Lvs to 40cm, ovate or elliptic to suborbicular, apex acute or obtuse, base acute or cordate, glossy, sometimes pubesc. beneath. Fls in crowded pan., pink, fragrant; cor. tube to 13mm, pubesc., lobes to 5×2mm, lanceolate to oblong, obtuse. Peru. 'Succirubra' (RED BARK): tree to 12m, with spreading br.; lvs to 25cm, elliptic, pubesc.; fls in dense, term., cymose pan., rose-pink to -red, fragrant. Ecuad., Peru.

C. succirubra Pav. ex Klotzsch = *C. pubescens* 'Succirubra'.

Cinco Hojas *Oreopanax echinops.*

Cineraria (of florists and gardens) *Pericallis* ×*hybrida.*

Cineraria L. Compositae. c50 glab. or hairy herbs or subshrubs. Lvs alt. or radical, usually toothed, lobed or pinnately cut. Cap. small, radiate, in lax corymbs; ray flts yellow, strap-shaped; disc flts yellow, tubular, 5-lobed, lobes conspicuously lined. Mostly S Afr. Z9.

C. albida N.E. Br. Straggling perenn. herb or small shrub, to 1m, white-cobwebby. Lvs to 7.5cm, mostly reniform or coarsely toothed, cobwebby above, glabrescent to white-felted beneath, petioles white-felted. Cap. few to many. S Afr.

C. cruenta hort. = *Pericallis* ×*hybrida.*

C. ×grandiflora hort. = *Pericallis* ×*hybrida.*

C. ×hybrida Willd. = *Pericallis* ×*hybrida.*

C. lobata L'Hérit. Much-branched subshrub, to 1m, glab. Lvs to 7.5cm, rounded-reniform, rarely lyrate, many-lobed, lobes short, 3–5-toothed, teeth callous, petioles slender. Cap. few to many, corymb v. loosely branched. S Afr.

C. macrophylla Ledeb. = *Ligularia macrophylla.*

C. maritima L. = *Senecio cineraria.*

C. multiflora L'Hérit. = *Pericallis multiflora.*

C. petasitis Sims = *Roldana petasitis.*

C. praecox Cav. = *Pittocaulon praecox.*

C. saxifraga DC. Spreading or trailing subshrub, to 1m, glab. Lvs to 4cm, round-reniform, coarsely 5–9-toothed at apex, petioles slender. Cap. few to many, in a simple or branched, leafless corymb. S Afr.

C. sibirica L. = *Ligularia sibirica.*

Cinnamomum Schaeff. CAMPHOR TREE. Lauraceae. c250 everg. trees and shrubs. Wood and bark aromatic. Lvs aromatic, coriaceous, veins usually 3, conspicuous, young lvs often red. Fls inconspicuous, paniculate. E & SE Asia to Aus. Z9.

C. aromaticum Nees. CASSIA-BARK TREE; CASSIA; CHINESE CINNAMON; BASTARD CINNAMON. Tree to 13m. Lvs 15cm, narrowly oblong to lanceolate, apex narrowly acuminate. Burm.

C. camphora (L.) Sieb. CAMPHOR TREE. Tree to 30m. Branchlets yellow-brown to black, hairy. Lvs 7.5–10cm, ovate-lanceolate, narrowly acuminate, glab. and shining above, whitened beneath. Spring–summer. Jap., Taiwan, Malaysia, Trop. Asia. 'Majestic Beauty': erect; lvs large, rich green.

C. cassia (Nees) Nees and Eberm. ex Bl. = *C. aromaticum*.

C. daphnoides Sieb. & Zucc. Large shrub or small tree. Lvs to 3cm, leathery, obovate, obtuse, 3-veined, silvery-hairy beneath. S Jap.

C. glanduliferum (Wallich) Meissn. Tree 20–25m. Bark smooth. Branchlets slender, green-brown, glab. Lvs to 9cm, lanceolate-elliptic, apex abruptly acuminate, green and shining above, paler, blue-green beneath, coriaceous. China.

C. japonicum Sieb. ex Nees. Tree, generally smaller than *C. glanduliferum*. Br. slender, glab. Lvs 6–7cm, oblong-ovate, apex acute, base obtuse, glab. Summer. Korea, Jap., Taiwan.

C. kotoense Kanehira & Sasaki = *C. myrianthum*.

C. micranthum Hayata. Tree to 30m. Br. black-brown, glab. Lvs 9.5–10.5cm, obovate-elliptic, apex acute, coriaceous, shining above, with tufts of hair in vein axils beneath. Taiwan.

C. myrianthum Merrill. Tree. Lvs 15cm, ovate-elliptic, apex acute, base rounded, glab., shining above, glab. and smooth beneath. Philipp., Taiwan.

C. pedunculatum Nees = *C. japonicum*.

C. pseudoloureirii Hayata = *C. japonicum*.

C. zeylanicum Bl. CINNAMON; CEYLON CINNAMON. Tree 10–13m. Bark light rusty brown (cinnamon), papery. Lvs 7–18cm, ovate to ovate-elliptic, apex acute to obtuse, dark glossy green, leathery, glab. S India and Sri Lanka. Z10.
→*Laurus*.

Cinnamon *Cinnamomum zeylanicum*.
Cinnamon Fern *Osmunda cinnamonea*.
Cinnamon Rose *Rosa majalis*.
Cinnamon Vine *Dioscorea batatas*.
Cinnamon Wattle *Acacia leprosa*.
Cinquefoil *Potentilla*.
Cinquefoil Tansy *Tanacetum potentilloides*.

Cionosicyos Griseb. Cucurbitaceae. 3 perenn., herbaceous or partially woody climbers. Tendrils bifid or simple. Lvs palmate or simple. Fls solitary, or in rac., axillary, white to pale green, 1–4cm across; cor. campanulate, lobes 5, ovate to oblong, to 2cm. Fr. globose, smooth; pericarp thick. C Amer., Carib. Z10.

C. excisus (Griseb.) C. Jeffrey. St. glab. Lvs broad, angular-ovate or cordate-ovate, glab. above, sparsely pubesc. on veins beneath, 3–7-lobulate or angulate. Fr. green, sometimes becoming red, 3–5cm. C Amer., Cuba.
→*Cayaponia*.

Cionura Griseb. Asclepiadaceae. 1 decid. shrub to 3.5m. Br. lax, sometimes scandent. Lvs 3–6cm, cordate-ovate, acute, grey-green marbled pewter. Fls fragrant in umbellate axill. cymes; cor. white, seg. 5, spreading. E Medit.

C. erecta (L.) Griseb.
→*Marsdenia*.

Cipocereus Ritter. Cactaceae. 5 shrubby cacti; st. cylindric, rather woody, ribbed; spines 0 to numerous. Fls tubular; pericarpel and tube ribbed or nearly terete, blue-waxy with small scales, wool and sometimes fine spines; tep. short. Braz.

C. pleurocarpus Ritter. St. 2–3cm diam., ascending, branching below; ribs 10–16, ± crenate; central spines 4–6, 8–25mm, yellow; radial spines 8–1, 5–10mm, yellow. Fls c5cm; pericarpel shiny red, tinged yellow, ribbed; outer tep. green with yellow tinge, inner tep. yellow, tinged green. E Braz. Z9.

Cipo-cruz *Cuspidaria pterocarpa*.
Cipo-cruz Amarelo *Adenocalymma dusenii*.

Cipura Aubl. Iridaceae. 5 perenn. bulbous herbs. Lvs plicate, one to several forming a basal fan and one set subtending infl. Infl. of several fl. clusters enclosed in spathes; fls short-lived; tep. 6, outer broadly clawed, inner erect; style with 3 thick br. S Mex. to Boliv., S Braz. and Parag., W Indies. Z10.

C. paludosa Aubl. Basal lvs 1–3, 16–27cm, linear-lanceolate. Fl. clusters several, ± sessile; fls pale blue to violet, outer tep. 25–28mm, oblanceolate, white at base, sometimes wholly white, inner tep. 15mm, obovate. with yellow nectar guide sometimes edged violet. Boliv. and Parag. to S Mex. & W Indies.

Circaea L. Onagraceae. ENCHANTER'S NIGHTSHADE. 7 erect, perenn., rhizomatous herbs. Infl. racemose, branched or simple; fls small, opening at dawn, floral tube minute, to 2mm; sep. 2; pet. 2, notched; sta. 2. N hemis. Z5.

C. alpestris Wallr. = *C. ×intermedia*.

C. alpina L. Erect or decumbent, to 50cm. St. pubesc. Lvs pale to dark green, sometimes variegated red, 1–11cm. Rac. to 17cm; pet. 0.6–2×0.6–1.8mm, white, obtriangular to obovate, scarcely notched. Spring–autumn. N hemis. ssp. *pacifica* (Asch. & Magnus) Raven. St. pubesc. Lvs thin, pale green, translucent; pet. conspicuously notched.

C. alpina var. *intermedia* (Ehrh.) DC. = *C. ×intermedia*.

C. alpina var. *major* Schräd. = *C. ×intermedia*.

C. alpina var. *pacifica* Asch. & Magnus) M.E. Jones = *C. alpina* ssp. *pacifica*.

C. alpina var. *sterilis* Doell = *C. ×intermedia*.

C. alpino-lutetiana G. Mey. = *C. ×intermedia*.

C. canadensis (L.) Hill = *C. ×intermedia*.

C. ×canadensis var. *rishiriensis* Hara = *C. ×intermedia*.

C. ericetorum Martrin-Donos = *C. ×intermedia*.

C. ×intermedia Ehrh. (*C. alpina* ×*C. lutetiana*.) Erect or decumbent, to 70cm. St. rarely pubesc. Lvs 2–11cm, pale to dark green, often blotched, ovate. Rac. to 18cm, pet. 1–3.6×0.6–3.6mm, white or pink. Summer. C & W Eur., Scand., to N US and to E Asia.

C. lutetiana L. Erect to decumbent, to 90cm. Lvs 3–16cm, elliptic to triangular-ovate, glab. or pubesc., ciliate, denticulate. Rac. to 40cm, pubesc.; pet. 1–3.7×1.4–4mm, white or pink, triangular to obovate, deeply notched.

C. lutetiana ssp. *intermedia* (Ehrh.) Rouy & Camus = *C. ×intermedia*.

C. lutetiana var. *intermedia* (Ehrh.) Lév. = *C. ×intermedia*.

C. pacifica Asch. & Magnus = *C. alpina* ssp. *pacifica*.

Circumpolar Pea *Lathyrus japonicus*.

Cirrhaea Lindl. Orchidaceae. 7 epiphytic orchids allied to *Gongora*. Braz. Z10.

C. dependens (Lodd.) Rchb. f. Rac. to 45cm, pendulous; pedicels abruptly decurved; fls to 25, to 5cm diam., scented; tep. oblanceolate, green, ochre or sienna, mottled or banded blood-red or terracotta; lip trilobed, clawed, similar in colour to sep. or wholly maroon; column white. Summer.

Cirrhopetalum Lindl.

C. putridum Teijsm. & Binnend. = *Bulbophyllum fascinator*.

C. gracillimum Rolfe. = *Bulbophyllum gracillimum*.

C. longissimum Ridl. = *Bulbophyllum longissimum*.

C. mastersianum Ridl. = *Bulbophyllum mastersianum*.

C. medusae Lindl. = *Bulbophyllum medusae*.

C. ornatissimum Rchb. = *Bulbophyllum ornatissimum*.

C. picturatum Lodd. = *Bulbophyllum picturatum*.

C. umbellatum (Forster) Hook. & Arn. = *Bulbophyllum wendlandianum*.

Cirsium Mill. PLUME THISTLE. Compositae. *c*200 bienn. to perenn. herbs. Lvs spiny. Cap. usually large, discoid; phyllaries imbricate, spiny. N temp. regions.

C. acaule Scop. Stemless perenn., to 40cm. Lvs oblong-lanceolate, pinnatisect, seg. 2–5, ovate to orbicular, dentate, spines to 12mm. Cap. to 4cm diam.; phyllaries erect, usually compact or slightly loose, spiny; flts purple. Summer. Eur. to C Asia.

C. acaulescens Schum. = *C. foliosum*.

C. arizonicum (A. Gray) Petrak. Perenn., to 12m. Lvs linear, pinnatifid, floccose above, tomentose beneath, margins yellow-spined. Cap. to 4cm diam., phyllaries erect, not reflexed, inner tapered, apices scarlet; flts scarlet. Late spring–autumn. Ariz., Utah (mts).

C. arvense (L.) Scop. CANADA THISTLE; CREEPING THISTLE. Perenn., to 1.5m. Lvs lanceolate to oblong, entire to pinnatifid, apical spines to 10mm, seg. triangular, entire or lobed, glab. or lightly hairy above, tomentose beneath. Cap. to 3cm diam.; phyllaries dense, apex spiny; flts lilac or pink. Summer. Eur., NE US.

C. conspicuum (D. Don) Schultz-Bip. Bienn., to 2m. Lvs pinnatifid, seg. incised, undulate, spines short, brown-purple. Cap. to 3cm diam.; flts scarlet. Mex.

C. coulteri A. Gray. Perenn., to 1.3m. St. spiny-winged. Lvs 1-pinnate, seg. spiny, tomentose beneath, lightly wispy-hairy above. Cap. to 4cm diam., phyllaries weakly spined, outer reflexed; flts crimson. Early summer. W & S US. Z7.

C. dissectum (L.) Hill. Perenn or bienn., to 1m. Lvs entire, rarely pinnatifid, lightly pubesc. above, tomentose beneath, seg. triangular, dentate to lobed. Cap. to 6cm diam.; flts purple. Summer. W Eur. Z7.

C. edule Nutt. Perenn., to 2m. St. robust, branched. Lvs lanceolate to oblong, margins spiny. Cap. to 4cm diam.; phyllaries lanate, purple tinged, tips reflexed; flts rose-pink to purple. Summer. NW US. Z7.

C. eriocephalum A. Gray = *C. scopulorum*.

C. eriophorum (L.) Scop. Bienn., to 1–5m. Lvs pinnatifid, lobes lanceolate, apical spine to 2.5cm. Cap. to 8cm diam.; phyllaries spiny toward apex; flts purple. Summer. W & C Eur., Balk. Penins. Z6.

C. falconeri (Hook. f.) Petrak. Perenn. to 2m, white silvery spiny. Lvs lanceolate to oblong, lobed, upper surface covered by small spines. Cap. 7–9cm diam., nodding; phyllaries densely lanate, spines to 2.5cm; flts cream. Himal. Z6.

C. foliosum (Hook.) DC. Perenn., to 60cm. Lvs lanceolate, dentate, lobed or pinnate, spines weak, yellow. Cap. to 4cm diam.; phyllaries herbaceous, exceeding cap., glab., inner fringed; flts white to pale pink. Summer. N Sierra Nevada. Z6.

C. helenioides (L.) Hill. Perenn., to 1.5m. Lvs lanceolate to oblong, entire to pinnatifid, glab. above, tomentose beneath, seg. triangular to oblong-lanceolate, entire or dentate. Cap. to 5cm diam., flts purple. N Eur. to W Russia. Z5.

C. heterophyllum (L.) Hill = C. helenioides.

C. japonicum DC. NO-AZAMI. Bienn. or perenn., to 2m. Lvs oblong-obovate, mucronate, dentate to 1-pinnate, lobes oblong, lightly pubesc. above, veins pubesc. beneath. Cap. to 5cm diam.; phyllaries loosely hairy, stickly below, spiny above; flts rose-pink to lilac. Summer–autumn. Jap. 'Pink Beauty': to 80cm; soft pink. 'Rose Beauty': deep carmine. Z6.

C. lanceolatum (L.) Scop. = C. vulgare.

C. occidentale (Nutt.) Jeps. Like C. coulteri but rarely to 1m, phyllaries white woolly, flts red-purple. Spring–summer. S Calif. Z9.

C. palustre (L.) Scop. Bienn., to 2.5m. St. spiny-winged above. Lvs lanceolate to lanceolate-linear, undulate, pinnatifid, pubesc. above, woolly beneath, apical spines to 13mm. Cap. to 3cm diam.; flts purple. Summer. N & C Eur., NE US. Z4.

C. pastoris Howell. Bienn., to 1.5m. Lvs oblong to oblanceolate, pinnate, seg. often 2–5-lobed, floccose to woolly beneath. Cap. to 7cm diam.; phyllaries densely woolly, reflexed, spiny; flts bright pink to red. Summer. W US. Z7.

C. rivulare (Jacq.) All. Perenn., to 1.5m. Lvs elliptic to oblong-lanceolate, entire to pinnatifid, seg. oblong or triangular, dentate to lobed, spines to 4mm. Cap. to 3.5cm diam.; phyllaries semi-erect, outer spinulose; flts purple. Summer. C & SW Eur. Z5. 'Atropurpureum': flts deep crimson.

C. scopulorum (Greene) Cockerell. Perenn., to 60cm. Lvs lanceolate to oblanceolate, pinnatifid, lobes triangular to ovate, glab. above, tomentose beneath. Cap. to 3.5cm diam.; phyllaries spiny; flts cream to white. NC US. Z5.

C. spinosissimum (L.) Scop. Perenn., to 1.2m. Lvs oblong to lanceolate or elliptic, pinnatifid, lobes suborbicular, spines to 15mm. Cap. to 3.5cm diam.; phyllaries with apical spine to 1cm; flts pale yellow. Alps, Apennines. Z5.

C. vulgare (Savi) Ten. BULL THISTLE; BOAR THISTLE. Bienn., to 3m. St. winged. Lvs pinnatifid, lobes lanceolate or triangular to elliptic, lightly tomentose, apical spine to 15mm. Cap. to 5cm diam.; phyllaries with apical spine to 3.5mm; flts scented, purple. Summer. Eur., SW Asia, N Afr., Sib., N & C Amer. Z2.

→*Cnicus.*

Cissus L. GRAPE IVY; TREEBINE; IVY. Vitaceae. *c*350 herbs, shrubs or vines, mostly climbing by tendrils. Lvs simple or lobed. Fls small, usually green-white, umbellate in term. or leaf-opposed compound cymes. Fr. a dry berry, usually purple-black. Trop. & Subtrop.

C. acida Chapm., Jacq. or L. = C. trifoliata.

C. acuminata A. Gray = Cayratia acuminata.

C. albonitens hort. ex Nichols. = C. sicyoides 'Albonitens'.

C. amazonica Lind. Woody vine. Lvs simple, ovate to 15cm on mature plants, linear to 5cm on young specimens, glaucous green above, light maroon to red beneath, glab., veins silvery-white above, red beneath. Reputedly Amaz., but known only in cult. Z10.

C. ampelopsis Gray = Ampelopsis cordata.

C. antarctica Vent. KANGAROO VINE. Woody vine; tendrils present. Lvs 7–10cm, ovate to oblong, long acuminate at apex, somewhat cordate at base, entire to sinuate or irregularly dentate, glossy above, glab., coriaceous. Summer. Australasia. 'Minima': dwarf, slow-growing form; br. mostly horizontal. Z10.

C. arborea Gray = Ampelopsis arborea.

C. bainesii Hook. f. = Cyphostemma bainesii.

C. baudiniana Brouss. = C. antarctica.

C. brevipedunculata Maxim. = Ampelopsis brevipedunculata.

C. cactiformis Gilg Succulent vine. St. acutely 4–5-angled, 3–4cm diam., v. fleshy, strongly constricted at nodes, wings undulating, to 2cm broad; tendrils simple. Lvs orbicular, 3-lobed to un-lobed, small, ephemeral. Trop. & S Afr. 10.

C. capensis Willd. = Rhoicissus capensis.

C. capriolata (D. Don) Royle = Tetrastigma serrulatum.

C. chontalensis (Seem.) Planch. Vine. Branchlets angular. Lvs 3-foliolate, bright green; central leaflet elliptic, laterals obliquely ovate, dentate. Fls scarlet. Winter. Nic. Z9.

C. cirrhosa (Thunb.) Willd. = Cyphostemma cirrhosa.

C. cramerana Schinz = Cyphostemma currori.

C. cucumerifolia Planch. Lvs orbicular to broadly ovate, deeply cordate at base, simple to somewhat lobed, densely pilose to tomentose beneath. Malawi. Z10.

C. currori Hook. f. = Cyphostemma currori.

C. davidiana Carr. = Ampelopsis humulifolia.

C. dinteri Schinz = C. nymphaeifolia.

C. discolor Bl. REX BEGONIA VINE. Vine. St. 5–6-angled, flushed red; tendrils bifid. Lvs 6–25cm, ovate-oblong to lanceolate, cordate or truncate at base, acuminate at apex, quilted dark velvety green above with double row of grey-green, silvery-white or pale pink blotches between veins, dark red beneath. Infl. tinted red. SE Asia to Aus. 'Mollis': lvs minutely hirsute; fls carmine-red, cymes large, stalks tall. Z10.

C. endresii Veitch. Vine, climbing vigorously. Shoots tinged crimson; tendrils flushed crimson. Lvs 18–20cm, obovate, cordate at base, acuminate at apex, flushed crimson when young, later bright velvety green above, darker near veins, veins beneath prominent, tinged red. Costa Rica. Z10.

C. erosa Rich. St. quadrangular, grooved or narrowly winged; tendrils numerous. Lvs trifoliolate, glab., subcoriaceous; lfts 5–15cm, lanceolate to ovate, serrate with mucronate teeth. Fls scarlet. Trop. Amer. Z10.

C. glandulosa Poir. = C. antarctica.

C. gongylodes (Burchell ex Bak.) Planch. Vine, villous. St. strongly winged, rather succulent developing specialised, swollen pendulous sections at tips, these eventually dropping and proliferating. Lvs 3-foliolate, 5–18cm; lfts rhombic-obovate, lat. obliquely ovate, acute to acuminate, serrate, undulate-rugose; stipules large, purple tinged brown. Autumn. Braz., Parag. & Peru. Z9.

C. henryana hort. = Parthenocissus henryana.

C. hereroensis Schinz = Cyphostemma hereroensis.

C. himalayana Walp. = Parthenocissus himalayana.

C. hypoglauca A. Gray. Vine. Shoots ferruginous-tomentose when young; tendrils 0. Lvs digitately 5-foliolate; lfts ovate to lanceolate, acuminate at apex, obtuse at base, minutely dentate, light green above, glaucous beneath, coriaceous, glab. Fls yellow. Aus. (NSW, Vict.). Z10.

C. hypoleuca Harv. Vine. St. weak, striate, minutely pubesc. or gland. Lvs pedately 5-foliolate, long-petiolate; lfts broadly lanceolate, shallowly broadly mucronate-dentate, green and glab. above, white-tomentose beneath. S Afr. Z9.

C. incisa (Nutt. in Torr. & A. Gray) Dur. = C. trifoliata.

C. javalensis (Seem.) Planch. Lvs simple, cordate at base, acuminate at apex, mucronate-dentate, green and velvety-pubesc. above, tinged purple and glab. beneath, veins tinged purple. Fls scarlet. Nic. Z9.

C. javana DC. = C. discolor.

C. juttae Dinter & Gilg = Cyphostemma juttae.

C. lindenii André. Vine, woody below, glab. throughout. Adventitious roots descending from base of petiole. Br. some-what warty; tendrils present. Lvs 15–20cm, ovate, cordate at base, long acuminate at apex, laxly serrate, bright deep green above with silvery blotches between veins, paler with veins prominent beneath, tinged pink near base. Colomb. Z9.

C. mexicana Mattei. Vine. Br. angled, velvety; tendrils few. Lvs trifoliolate, lfts acute at apex, mucronate-serrate, velvety, white villous on veins beneath, central leaflet largest, rhombic to ovate-subrhombic, laterals obliquely ovate, semicordate on out-er side at base. Fls scarlet. Mex. Z9.

C. mexicana DC. = Parthenocissus quinquefolia.

C. neilgherrensis Wight = Parthenocissus himalayana.

C. nymphaeifolia (Welw. ex Bak.) Planch. Herb. Lvs simple, suborbicular to ovate, entire, dentate or shallowly lobed, cordate at base, to 15cm diam., ferruginous-tomentose when young, later glabrescent above. Nam., Angola. Z10.

C. oblonga (Benth.) Planch. Vine, decid. St. terete, grey-pubesc.; tendrils simple, pubesc. Lvs 7.5cm, simple, oblong-ovate, truncate to shallowly cordate at base, acute to obtuse at apex, entire or serrate towards apex, glab. when mature. Aus. (Queensld). Z10.

C. obtectum Wallich = Tetrastigma obtectum.

C. olearacea Bol. Rhiz. subterranean, simple, 5–7.5cm diam., woody, with several tubers. St. several, laxly procumbent, simple, sinuous, to 60cm, succulent. Lvs to 19cm, simple, broadly ovate, acutely dentate, glaucous, thick and fleshy. S Afr. Z9.

C. oligocarpa (Lév. & Vant.) L.H. Bail. = Cayratia oligocarpa.

C. orientalis Lam. = Ampelopsis orientalis.

C. pterophora (Bak.) Nichols. = C. gongylodes.

C. quadrangula Salisb. or L. = C. quadrangularis.

C. quadrangularis L. Herb or vine, much-branched, succulent. St. acutely quadrangular, narrowly winged, thick, green, constricted at nodes; tendrils entire. Lvs 3–8cm, on apical part of st. only, ovate to deltoid, entire to 3–5-lobed, obtuse at apex, cordate or truncate at base, green, succulent. Fls green tinged yellow or pink. Afr., S Asia, Malaysia. Z10.

C. quinata (Ait.) Planch. Scandent plant with tendrils. St. slender. Lvs 3–5-foliolate, fleshy; lfts coarsely serrate, glab. or sparsely pilose on veins beneath. S Afr. Z9.

C. rhombifolia Vahl VENEZUELA TREEBINE. Vine. St. yellow, villous when young; tendrils forked. Lvs pedately 3-foliolate, glabrescent; lfts 2.5–10cm, rhombic-ovate, cuneate at base, acute at apex, remotely sharply dentate, glossy dark green above, red-pubesc. on veins beneath; petioles rusty-villous. Trop. Amer. 'Ellen Danica': vigorous growth, bushy; lvs large, deeply lobed, incised, rich, glossy green. 'Mandaiana': st. erect, becoming scandent when older; tendrils 0 when young; lvs glab. above, more coriaceous. Z10.

C. rhomboidea E. Mey. = C. rhombifolia.

C. rocheana Planch. = C. trifoliata.

C. rotundifolia (Forssk.) Vahl. Climbing shrub, much-branched. St. 4–5-angled, woody, thin, pubesc.; tendrils present. Lvs large, broadly ovate to orbicular or reniform, deeply cordate at base, subentire to undulate-dentate, folded and often splitting along main vein, green tinged blue, thick and fleshy. E Afr. to S Arabia. Z10.

C. serrulata Roxb. = Tetrastigma serrulatum.

C. sicyoides L. PRINCESS VINE. Vine, scrambling to some height. Lvs 4–15cm, simple, ovate, obtuse to subcordate at base, acute to acuminate at apex, remotely finely serrate, deep green above, paler beneath, glab. to minutely pubesc., with transparent dots. Trop. Afr. & Amer., N to N Mex.; Galápagos. 'Albonitens': lvs with silvery-white metallic lustre. Z10.

C. striata Ruiz & Pav. IVY OF PARAGUAY; MINIATURE GRAPE IVY. Small vine. St. slender, angled, hairy; tendrils v. slender, threadlike. Lvs palmately 5-foliolate, 4–7.5cm across, somewhat coriaceous; lfts 12–36mm, obovate to oblanceolate, apex coarsely dentate, base tapered, dark green and glab., with a short gland terminating each tooth. Chile & S Braz. Z10.

C. thomsonii (Lawson) Planch. = Parthenocissus thomsonii.

C. trifoliata (L.) L. MARINE IVY; MARINE VINE; POSSUM GRAPE. Vine to 10m. St. slender, striate, initially succulent; tendrils long, stout. Lvs 3-foliolate to 3-partite, rigid and succulent; lfts broadly ovate to obovate, with 1–2 shallow lobes or deeply serrate. Summer. S US, N Mex. Z8.

C. tuberosa Moc. & Sessé ex DC. Vigorous vine; caudex swollen, shapeless. St. somewhat grooved, with internodes fattened, term. sections often becoming detached from parent and proliferating; tendrils long, with adhesive term. discs; aerial roots produced. Lvs 4–9cm, obovate, coarsely serrate to palmate, with incised lobes, sparsely pubesc. or glab. Mex. Z10.

C. uter Exell & Mend. = Cyphostemma uter.

C. velutina Lind. ex Hook. = C. discolor.

C. vitifolia Boiss. = Ampelopsis vitifolia.

C. voinieriana (Pierre ex Nichols. & Mottet) Viala = Tetrastigma voinierianum.

→Ampelopsis, Saelanthus and Vitis.

CISTACEAE Juss. 7/175. *Cistus, Fumana, ✕ Halimiocistus, Halimium, Helianthemum, Hudsonia, Tuberaria.*

Cistus L. ROCK ROSE; SUN ROSE. Cistaceae. c20 small to medium-sized, often low-growing everg. shrubs; st. and lvs occas. viscid, often downy. Lvs ovate to opposite, simple. Fls short-lived solitary or cymose, term., or axill. at br. tips; sep. 3–5; pet. 4–5, rounded, silky, spreading, with or without basal spot; sta. bright yellow, numerous. Flowering recurrent, early to late summer. S Eur., N Afr. Z8.

C. acutifolius hort. = C. psilosepalus, C. pulverulentus.

C. acutifolius Sweet non hort. = C. ✕corbariensis.

C. ✕aguilarii Pau. (C. ladanifer ✕ C. populifolius.) Lvs 10cm, lanceolate, bright green above, paler beneath, undulate. Fls to 3.5cm diam., white. SW Eur., N Afr. 'Maculatus': pet. spotted at base. 8.

C. albidus L. WHITE-LEAVED ROCK ROSE. Compact shrub to 2m, densely white-pubesc. Lvs to 5cm, oblong-ovate. Fls to 4cm diam., rosy-pink to lilac, basal spots yellow. SW Eur. f. *albus* (Warb.) Dansereau. Fls pure white. Z7.

C. algarvensis Sims = Halimium ocymoides.

C. alyssoides Lam. = Halimium alyssoides.

C. atchleyi Warb. Dwarf compact domed shrub. Lvs green, reticulate. Fls white, racemose. N Greece.

C. atriplicifolius Lam. = Halimium atriplicifolium.

C. borgeanus Coss. = C. libanotis.

C. ✕canescens Sweet. (C. albidus ✕ C. incanus.) As for C. albidus

except lvs deeper green, lanceolate, less densely pubesc.; fls pink to dark purple. N Afr. 'Albus': lvs grey; fls white. Z8.

C. clusii Dunal. To 40cm; br. slender, downy. Lvs to 2.5cm, linear, downy, revolute. Fls to 2.5cm diam., white stained yellow at base. SW Eur. Z8.

C. complicatus Lam. = C. parviflorus.

C. ✕corbariensis Pourr. (C. populifolius ✕ C. salviifolius.) Dense, spreading shrub to 1m. Lvs to 5cm, ovate acute, stellate-pubesc., dark green above, paler beneath, undulate, finely ciliate-toothed. Fl. buds red; fls to 3.5cm diam., white, basal spots yellow. S Eur. 'Snow White': fls pure white. Z7.

C. corsicus Lois. = C. incanus ssp. corsicus.

C. creticus L. = C. incanus ssp. creticus.

C. crispus L. Rounded shrub to 60cm. Br. canescent. Lvs 1–4cm, oblong-elliptic, acute, undulate, grey-green with stellate and simple hairs, veins sunken, rugose. Fls 4–6cm diam., purple-red. S Eur. 'Anne Palmer' (C. crispus ✕ C. ladanifer f. latifolius): fls rose-pink. Z8.

C. crispus hort. non L. = C. ✕purpureus.

C. ✕cyprius Lam. (C. ladanifer ✕ C. laurifolius.) To 2m; br. viscid. Lvs 3–10cm, viscid, aromatic, oblong-lanceolate, undulate, acuminate, dark grey-green glab. above, grey-pubesc. beneath. Fls to 7cm diam., white, basal spots carmine. SW Eur. 'Albiflorus': basal spot 0. 'Elma': lvs deep green, glossy, glaucous beneath; fls large, white, abundant. Z7.

C. ✕dansereaui Pinto da Silva. = C. ✕lusitanicus.

C. ✕florentinus Lam. (C. monspeliensis ✕ C. salviifolius.) To 1m, intricately branching. Young st. stellate-pubesc. Lvs 2.5–3cm, elliptic-lanceolate, acute, undulate, initially ashy-tomentose, ultimately dull green, rugulose. Fls 3.5cm diam., white, basal spots yellow. S Eur., N Afr. Z8.

C. formosus Curtis = Halimium lasianthum ssp. formosum.

C. ✕glaucus Pourr. (C. laurifolius ✕ C. monspeliensis.) To 1.75m. Br. slender, white-pubesc. Lvs 2.5–5cm, lanceolate to linear-oblong, clammy above, downy, grey beneath. Fls 4–5cm diam., white. S Eur. Z8.

C. globulariifolius Lam. = Tuberaria globulariifolia.

C. grandiflorus Tausch = C. ✕cyprius.

C. halimiifolius L. = Halimium halimiifolium.

C. heterophyllus Desf. To 1m, erect. Lvs 0.5–2cm, elliptic, dark green, stellate-pubesc., paler, tomentose beneath. Fls 5–6cm diam., purple-pink, basal spots yellow. SE Eur., NW Afr. Z8.

C. hirsutus Lam. To 80cm. Br. covered with long and short hairs. Lvs 3–5cm, ovate-oblong to elliptic-lanceolate, base rounded, white-downy above, stellate-pubesc. beneath. Fls to 3cm diam., white, basal spots yellow. SW Eur. Z8.

C. hirsutus Lam., 1786 not 1778. = C. psilosepalus.

C. ✕hybridus Pourr. = C. ✕corbariensis.

C. incanus L. To 1m. Lvs 1.5–7cm, ovate to elliptic, sometimes undulate, green or silver-pubesc., veins sunken above. Fls 4–6cm diam., pink-purple. S Eur. ssp. corsicus (Lois.) Heyw. Lvs flat, st. densely white-pubesc. ssp. creticus (L.) Heyw. Lvs undulate-crispate. Fls 5–6cm diam., rose pink to purple, basal spots yellow. Z8.

C. ladanifer L. COMMON GUM CISTUS; LADANUM. To 2.5m. St. and lvs viscid, aromatic. Lvs 4–10cm, linear-lanceolate, dark leaden green, glab. above, grey pubesc. beneath. Fls 7–10cm diam., pet. white, usually with a maroon basal spot (f. maculatus (Dunal) Dansereau). SW Eur., N Afr. 'Albiflorus' ('Immaculatus'): fls white. f. latifolius Duveau ST VINCENT CISTUS. 50–10cm bushy. Lvs 2–6cm, oblanceolate to spathulate, conspicuously veined. Fls white, usually unspotted. 'Blanche': lvs elliptic-lanceolate, viscid, aromatic, pubesc. olive-green above, blue grey beneath; fls to 10cm diam., white. 'Paladin': lvs oblong-lanceolate, bright green, viscid above, pale green pubesc. beneath; fls to 12cm diam., solitary, white, basal spots maroon. 'Pat': lvs oblong-lanceolate, bright green viscid above, pubesc. beneath; fls to 13cm diam., white, basal spot maroon. Z7.

C. laevipes L. = Fumana laevipes.

C. laurifolius L. To 1.5cm; st. erect. Young st. pubesc., viscid. Lvs 3–9cm, ovate to ovate-lanceolate, undulate, viscid beneath, dark green glab. above, white-pubesc. Fls 5–6cm diam., white, basal spots yellow. SW Eur. Z7.

C. ✕laxus Ait. f. (C. hirsutus ✕ C. populifolius.) To 1m. Br. initially pilose, viscid. Lvs 5–10cm, ovate-lanceolate, pubesc., viscid. Fls to 5cm diam., white, basal spots yellow. S Eur. Z8.

C. ledon Lam. = C. ✕glaucus.

C. libanotis L. Differs from C. clusii in its slightly larger lvs, clammy, subglabrous infl. and red-hued sep. SW Eur. Z8.

C. ✕loretii Rouy & Foucaud. (C. ladanifer ✕ C. monspeliensis.) To 1m. Lvs linear-lanceolate, viscid, dark green above, grey-pubesc. beneath. Fls to 2.5cm diam., white, basal spots crimson. S Eur., N Afr. Z8.

C. loretii hort. non Rouy & Foucaud = C. ✕lusitanicus 'Decumbens'.

C. ✕lusitanicus Maund non Mill. (C. ladanifer ✕ C. hirsutus.)

Shrub 30–60cm. Br. clammy. Lvs 2.75–6.25cm, oblong-lanceolate, dull, subglabrous, green above, thinly stellate-pubesc. beneath. Fls to 7cm diam., white with crimson basal spots. SW Eur. 'Decumbens': habit low, spreading. Z8.

C. merinoi Pau = *C.* ×*laxus*.

C. monspeliensis L. MONTPELIER ROCK ROSE. To 1.5m, compact, erect; young growth viscid. Lvs 1.5–5cm, linear-lanceolate, dark green, rugulose and thinly pubesc. above, grey pubesc. beneath. Fls to 2.5cm diam., white. SW Eur. Z8.

C. nudifolius Lam. = *Fumana procumbens*.

C. ×*obtusifolius* Sweet. (*C. hirsutus* ×*C. salviifolius.*) To 60cm. Br. slender, ashy-pubesc. Lvs ovate-oblong, grey-pubesc., revolute. Fls to 3cm diam., white, basal spots yellow. SW Eur. Z8.

C. ochreatus see *C. symphytifolius*.

C. ocymoides Lam. = *Halimium ocymoides*.

C. osbekiifolius Christ. Differs from *C. symphytifolius* in lvs, petiole, pubesc. Canary Is. Z9.

C. palhinhae J. Ingram = *C. ladanifer* f. *latifolius*.

C. parviflorus Lam. St. to 1m, spreading, pubesc. Lvs 1–3cm, ovate, acute, grey-tomentose; petiole winged. Fls 2–3cm diam., pink. Aegean, SE It. Z8.

C. 'Peggy Sammons'. (*C. albidus* ×*C. laurifolius.*) To 1m. Lvs oval, grey-green; fls pink. Z8.

C. ×*platysepalus* Sweet. (*C. hirsutus* ×*C. monspeliensis.*) 50–70cm tall. St. white-pubesc. Lvs to 5cm, ovate-lanceolate, glab. except for finely pubesc. veins beneath. Fls white, basal spots yellow. Z8.

C. polymorphus Willk. = *C. incanus*.

C. populifolius L. To 2m. St. initially pubesc., viscid. Lvs 5–9cm, ovate-cordate, glab. green. Fls to 5cm diam., white, basal spots yellow. SW Eur. var. *lasiocalyx* Willk. Lvs broader, undulate; fls to 7.5cm diam. W Medit. ssp. *major* (Pourr. ex Dunal) Heyw. Lvs to 1.5× long as wide, undulate; fls pure white. W Eur. Z8.

C. psilosepalus Sweet. St. to 1m, spreading. Lvs 2–6cm, elliptic-lanceolate, with mixed simple and stellate hairs. Fls 3–4cm diam., white. SW Eur. Z8.

C. ×*pulverulentus* Pourr. (*C. albidus* ×*C. crispus.*) Dense low shrub to 70cm. Lvs 3–5cm, oblong, undulate, grey-pubesc. Fls to 5cm diam., purple-pink to rose. SW Eur. 'Sunset': fls rose pink. 'Warley Rose': fls cerise. Z8.

C. ×*purpureus* Lam. (*C. ladanifer* ×*C. incanus* ssp. *creticus.*) To 1m; st. initially sticky-pubesc. Lvs 3–5cm, oblong-lanceolate, grey-pubesc. beneath. Fls 5–7cm diam., pink, basal spots dark red. S Eur. 'Alan Fradd': pet. white, basal spot dark red. 'Betty Taudevin': pet. crimson, basal spots maroon. 'Brilliancy': fls dark pink spotted rich brown. 'Doris Hibberson': fls pale pink, abundant. Z7.

C. ×*recognitus* Rouy & Foucaud = *C. glaucus*.

C. ×*recognitus* hort., non Rouy & Foucaud = *C.* ×*lusitanicus*.

C. revolii Coste & Soulié = × *Halimiocistus revolii*.

C. rosmarinifolius Pourr. pro parte. = *C. clusii*.

C. sahucii Coste & Soulié = × *Halimiocistus sahucii*.

C. salviifolius L. To 60cm; br. spreading, young growth pubesc. Lvs 1.5–4cm, ovate-oblong, grey-green rugulose above, paler beneath, stellate-pubesc. Fls 3.5–4.5mm diam., white, basal spots yellow. S Eur. 'Prostratus': low, spreading to 35cm; lvs small. Z8.

C. 'Silver Pink'. To 50cm, low, spreading, bushy; st. downy. Lvs 3–7cm, ovate-lanceolate, pale sage green above, pale grey beneath, downy. Fls to 7cm diam., pale silvery pink, possibly *C. incanus* ssp. *creticus* ×*C. laurifolius*. Z8.

C. ×*skanbergii* Lojac. (*C. monspeliensis* ×*C. parviflorus.*) To 1m; st. white-pubesc. Lvs 2.5–5cm, oblong-lanceolate, downy beneath with stellate hairs. Fls pale pink. Greece. Z8.

C. stenophyllus Link = *C.* ×*loretii*.

C. symphytifolius Lam. St. lax, to 1.8m, pilose. Lvs 4–10cm, oblong-elliptic, dark green, sparsely pilose above, densely pubesc. beneath, undulate. Fls to 5cm diam., purple-pink. Canary Is. *C. ochreatus* differs chiefly in its low habit and densely silver-sericeous lvs. Z8.

C. tauricus Presl = *C. incanus*.

C. undulatus Dunal = *C. incanus* ssp. *creticus*.

C. vaginatus Ait. = *C. symphytifolius*.

C. ×*verguinii* Coste and Soulié. (*C. ladanifer* ×*C. salviifolius.*) Erect to 80cm, rather viscid. Lvs to 7cm, oblong-lanceolate, subglabrous or pubesc. beneath. Fls 4–5cm diam., white, basal spots maroon. S Fr. Z8.

C. villosus L. = *C. incanus*.

→*Rhodocistus*.

Citharexylum L. FIDDLEWOOD; ZITHERWOOD. Verbenaceae. 70 trees or shrubs, some armed. Br. tetragonal, lf scars enlarged, corky. Infl. racemiform or spicate, axill. and terminal, simple or sparsely branched, elongate, multi-fld; fls small, fragrant; cal., tubular, thin, apex entire or 5-lobed and toothed; cor.

hypocrateriform, 5-lobed, throat generally pubesc.; sta. 4–6, staminode present. Fr. a drupe, red to black. Z9.

C. berlandieri Robinson. Shrub or small tree to 9m. Br. grey, striate, branchlets pubesc. Lvs to 7cm, membranous, obovate, ovate or rhombic, rarely minutely dentate, pubesc. beneath, puberulent above. Infl. to 10cm, spike-like, nodding; cor. to 3mm, white, lobes rounded, puberulent. Mex.

C. cinereum L. = *C. fruticosum*.

C. cyanocarpum Hook. & Arn. = *Rhaphithamnus spinosus*.

C. fruticosum L. FLORIDA FIDDLEWOOD. Shrub or small tree to 15m. Br. thick, grey, striate, glab. Lvs to 21cm, chartaceous, stiff, bright or yellow-green, shiny, oblong or elliptic, glab., gland.; petioles orange or pink-tinted. Infl. to 27cm, nodding or pendent; cor. to 6mm, white or green-white, lobes rounded. Flor. through the Carib. to N S Amer.

C. quadrangulare Jacq. = *C. spinosum*.

C. spicatum Rusby. Everg. shrub. St. tinted purple. Lvs lanceolate, leathery, dark green. Infl. spike-like, drooping; fls v. small, fragrant, lilac. Bolivia.

C. spinosum L. Shrub or tree to 16m. Br. and branchlets slender, grey, glab. Lvs to 30cm, chartaceous to membranous, dull deep green above, paler beneath, narrowly elliptic to elliptic or oblong, entire, glab.; petioles tinted orange. Infl. to 20cm, nodding; cor. to 8mm, lobes rounded, white or cream, densely villous in mouth. Widely distrib. in W Indies, Trin., Venez. and Guianas; nat. in some areas where it is cult.

C. subserratum Sw. = *C. fruticosum*.

C. villosum Griseb. = *C. fruticosum*.

Citrange × *Citroncirus webberi*.

× **Citrofortunella** J. Ingram & H.E. Moore. (*Citrus* ×*Fortunella*.) Rutaceae. Z9.

×*C. floridana* J. Ingram & H.E. Moore. LIMEQUAT. Everg. tree. Lvs unifoliolate, 5–7.5cm, dark green above, paler beneath. Fls white or slightly streaked with pink. Fr. ovoid or sub-globose, 3–5cm diam., seg. 6–9, pulp light yellow, peel light yellow. Gdn origin. 'Eustis': fls pure white; fr. yellow, to ×3.5cm. 'Lakeland': fls white, striped pink; fr. yellow to orange, to ×4.5cm.

×*C. microcarpa* (Bunge) D.O. Wijnands. CALAMONDIN; CALAMONDIN ORANGE; PANAMA ORANGE. (*Citrus reticulata* ×*Fortunella margarita?*) Small tree, everg., crown v. dense. Lvs 1-foliolate, 5–10cm, elliptic to broadly ovate; petiole narrowly winged. Fls white, highly fragrant. Fr. 2.5–3.5cm, globose or flattened-globose, bright orange, peel loose, pulp sour. Philipp. 'Tiger': lvs edged and streaked white. 'Variegata': compact; lvs mottled white and grey; fr. variegated, later bright orange.

×*C. mitis* (Blanco) J. Ingram & H.E. Moore. = × *C. microcarpa*.

×*C. swinglei* J. Ingram & H.E. Moore. (*Citrus aurantiifolia* ×*Fortunella margarita*.) LIMEQUAT. Everg. tree. Lvs 1-foliolate. Fls pink in bud. Fr. obovoid to ovoid or flattened-globose, 3–5cm diam., peel light yellow, seg. 7–8, pulp pale yellow. Gdn origin.

→*Citrus*.

Citron *Citrullus lanatus* var. *citroides*; *Citrus medica*.

× **Citroncirus** J. Ingram & H.E. Moore (*Citrus* ×*Poncirus*.) Rutaceae. Tree or shrub, everg. or semi-deciduous, spreading, armed with long spines. Lvs generally trifoliolate, large; petiole narrowly winged. Fls to 6cm diam., white, fragrant. Fr. 5–7cm, globose, orange or yellow, pulp acid, bitter.

×*C. webberi* J. Ingram & H.E. Moore. CITRANGE. (*Citrus sinensis* ×*Poncirus trifoliata*.) Gdn origin. Z8.

Citronella D. Don. Icacinaceae. 20 everg. trees and shrubs. Trop.

C. mucronata (Ruiz & Pav.) D. Don. Large everg. shrub. Lvs ovate, leathery, glossy green, with spiny teeth. Fls small, fragrant, cream-white, in dense pan. Fr. to 7.5cm, black, ovoid. C Chile. Z9.

Citronella *Cymbopogon nardus*.

Citropsis (Engl.) Swingle & Kellerm. AFRICAN CHERRY ORANGE. Rutaceae. 8 shrubs or small trees with 1–2 spines per axil. Lvs pinnate, or (1–)3-foliolate; rachis and petiole winged. Infl. axillary, dense, clustered or racemose; fls white, fragrant, 4–5-merous; sta. twice as many as pet. Fr. globose, small, pulpy. Trop. Afr. Z10.

C. gabuensis (Engl.) Swingle & Kellerm. Shrub or small tree. Lvs 1–5-foliolate, lfts 7–14cm, oblong or elliptic, acuminate or caudate at apex. Infl. 1.5–2.5cm; fls v. small, generally 4-merous; pet. 6×2.5mm. Fr. 2cm. Congo.

C. schweinfurthii (Engl.) Swingle & Kellerm. Small tree. Lvs 3–5-foliolate, lfts 10–15cm, oblong to lanceolate, subentire to minutely dentate. Infl. 1–2cm; fls many, 4-merous; pet. 12–15×4–5mm. Fr. 2cm diam., lemon yellow when ripe, fragrant, peel v. thin. N Uganda.

Citrullus Schräd. ex Ecklon & C. Zeyh. Cucurbitaceae. 3 ann. or perenn. herbs, trailing or climbing; tendrils simple, branched or 0. Lvs usually deeply lobed. Fls solitary in axils; cal. tube short; cor. 5-lobed, yellow, campanulate. Fr. broad-cylindric to sub-spherical, pericarp firm, mesocarp fleshy; seeds many, ovate, compresssed. Asia, Afr. Z9.

C. colocynthis (L.) Schräd. COLOCYNTH; BITTER APPLE; VINE OF SODOM. Perenn., trailing. Rootstock woody, tuberous. St. shortly pubesc., later scabrous; tendrils simple. Lvs palmate, ovate, scabrid-pubesc. beneath, 1–8cm, lobes 3–5, midlobe lobulate. Fr. to 5cm diam., globose, smooth, striped green. N Afr. to Afghan. and Pak.; widely cult.

C. fistulosus Stocks = *Praecitrullus fistulosus.*

C. lanatus (Thunb.) Matsum. & Nak. WATER MELON. Ann. coarsely villous climber or trailer. Tendrils branching. Lvs pinnately lobed, ovate, denticulate, smooth, with translucent patches above, pubesc. beneath, lobes 3–5, ovate, obtuse. Fr. globose to cylindric, mottled or striped light and dark green, to 1m×40cm, flesh crystalline pink to red. Nam.; widely nat. and cult. var. *citroides* (L.H. Bail.) Mansf. CITRON; PRESERVING MELON. Fr. smaller, with white flesh.

C. vulgaris Schräd. ex Ecklon & Zeyh. = *C. lanatus.*

→*Cucumis, Cucurbita* and *Momordica.*

Citrus L. Rutaceae. 16 aromatic small, everg. trees or shrubs, with spines in lf axils. Lvs simple; petiole, ± winged. Fls axill., solitary or corymbose, waxy, fragrant, usually white; pet. 5, less often 4, linear, thick; sta. usually c4× as many as pet. Fr. a hesperidium; pulp vesicles filled with v. watery tissue, seg. surrounded by white endocarp, outer peel dotted with oil glands, yellow or orange when fully ripe. SE Asia, Pacific Is.

C. aurantiifolia (Christm.) Swingle. LIME. (Possibly a hybrid of *C. medica* and another sp.) Small tree, 3–5m; spines short, stiff, v. sharp. Lvs elliptic-ovate to oblong-ovate, minutely crenate, obtusely pointed at apex, rounded at base, 5–7.5cm; petioles narrowly spathulate-winged. Fr. ovoid, 3–6cm diam., green tinged yellow when ripe, peel prominently glandular-punctate, v. thin, pulp v. sour. Trop. Asia; widely cult., particularly in W Indies. Z9.

C. aurantium L. SEVILLE ORANGE; BITTER ORANGE; SOUR ORANGE; BIGARADE; MARMALADE ORANGE. (Perhaps a backcross of *C. maxima* ×*C. reticulata.*) Tree to 10m with rounded crown; spines single, slender, blunt, short to 8cm. Lvs 7–10cm, ovate, bluntly pointed, cuneate to broadly rounded at base; petioles 2–3cm, wing rapidly tapering to st. Fr. subglobose, depressed at ends, 5–7cm diam., orange tinged red, peel thick and rough, pulp acid. SE Asia. 'Chinotto': compact, conical; lvs fine, dense; fls abundant. Z9.

C. aurantium ssp. *bergamia* (Risso & Poit.) Wight & Arn. = *C. bergamia.*

C. aurantium var. *myrtifolia* Ker-Gawl. = *C. myrtifolia.*

C. bergamia Risso & Poit. BERGAMOT; BERGAMOT ORANGE. Small tree. Lvs ovate-oblong; petioles long, winged. Fls v. fragrant. Fr. globose to pyriform, 7.5–10cm diam., peel thin, smooth, pale to bright yellow, containing green oil, pulp aromatic. S It., Sicily. Z9.

C. bigaradia Risso & Poit. = *C. aurantium.*

C. decumana L. = *C. maxima.*

C. deliciosa Ten. = *C. reticulata.*

C. grandis Osbeck = *C. maxima.*

C. hybrida L. = *C. kotokan.*

C. hystrix DC. MAURITIUS PAPEDA; LEECH LIME; CAFFRE LIME. Differs from *C. ichangensis* in petiole wings triangular; fls smaller, 5–7mm diam.; fr. 5–7cm diam., yellow or tinged green. SE Asia, widely nat., original distrib. uncertain. Z9.

C. ichangensis Swingle. ICHANG LEMON; ICHANT PAPEDA. Shrub or small tree, 1.5–4.5m; twigs angular; spines stout, sharp, 1.5–2.5cm. Lvs 8–12cm, lanceolate, emarginate at apex, rounded or bluntly pointed at base; petioles large, with obovate to oblong-spathulate wing. Fr. 7–10×3.5–5cm, lemon-shaped, pulp vesicles v. few, juice tasty but acid, peel rough, 4mm thick. W & SW China. Z8.

C. jambhiri Lushington. JAMBHIRI ORANGE LIME LOOSEJACKET. Shrub or small tree, generally unarmed. Lvs ovate to elliptic, tapered, crenate-serrate, emarginate at apex, lemon-scented; petiole narrowly margined or wingless. Fr. ovoid to subglobose, 5–7.5cm diam., peel thick, lemon-yellow, slightly lemon-flavoured, pulp pale yellow, v. sour. India. Z10.

C. japonica Thunb. = *Fortunella japonica.*

C. kotokan Hayata. (Possibly a 4-way hybrid, *C. aurantium* ×*C. sinensis* ×*C. nobilis* ×*C. maxima.*) Spreading shrub, 4m; spines to 6mm. Lvs 10cm, oblong, entire to obscurely crenate; petiole 1–2cm, broadly winged, tapering to base. Fr. 7–8×11cm, depressed-globose, not hollow in centre; peel rough, thick. Asia. Z9.

C. limetta Risso. SWEET LEMON; SWEET LIME. Small tree or erect shrub, much-branched, armed. Lvs 8–10cm, ovate, acute at apex, obtusely serrate below; petioles short, scarcely winged. Fr. rounded or lemon-shaped, to 6.5cm diam., yellow tinged green, not aromatic, pulp v. pale watery green, flavour insipid. Origin unknown; found in Medit. gardens. Z9.

C. limettoides Tan. Shrub or small tree. Lvs ovate or elliptic, obtuse and often shortly mucronate, rounded to acute at base; petiole unwinged. Fls white. Fr. subglobose to ellipsoid, sulphur-yellow, rind v. thin, pulp sweet, not aromatic. India. Z10.

C. limon (L.) Burm. f. LEMON. (Perhaps *C. medica* ×*C. aurantiifolia.*) Small tree, 2–7m; spines short, thick, stiff. Lvs elongate-ovate, acute at apex, ± serrate; petiole narrowly winged. Fls tinged purple below. Fr. 7–15×5–7cm, oval pulp v. sour, peel thick, conspicuously glandular-punctate, yellow. 'Sungold': medium-sized, oblong, many-seeded, with tricoloured skin and lvs. 'Variegated Lemon': lvs variegated cream; fr. striped green, later fully yellow. Z9.

C. limon 'Meyer'. = *C. meyeri.*

C. limon 'Ponderosa'. = *C. ponderosa.*

C. ×limonia Osbeck (Probably *C. limon* ×*C. reticulata.*) RANGPUR; RANGPUR LIME; MANDARIN LIME; LEMANDARIN; OTAHEITE ORANGE. Tree, medium-sized; br. spreading and pendulous; spines few, small. Lvs oblong to elliptic, dull green. Fls flushed purple. Fr. globose to broadly obovoid, pulp orange, v. acid, peel thin, orange tinged yellow or flushed red. Included here is *C. otaitense* Risso & Poit. OTAHEITE ORANGE, a small bush, unarmed; fr. depressed-globose to globose, 5cm diam., juice rather sweet and insipid. Often grown as an ornamental potplant; this and ×*Citrofortunella microcarpa* are the florist's miniature potted oranges.

C. limonum Risso = *C. limon.*

C. madurensis Lour. = *Fortunella japonica.*

C. maxima (Burm.) Merrill. PUMMELO; SHADDOCK. Large tree with rounded crown, to 5.5m; branching regular, twigs pubesc. when young; spines blunt, thin, or 0. Lvs large, ovate-elliptic, apex acute, base rounded, glossy above, pubesc. beneath; petioles cordate-winged. Fr. globose or broadly pyriform, 10–15cm diam., rind thick, lemon-yellow, pulp somewhat acid. Polyn. 'Chandler': large; flesh pink. Z9.

C. medica L. CITRON. Shrub or small tree, 4–5m; twigs flushed purple when young; spines solitary, stout, short. Lvs 10–18cm, elliptic-ovate, serrate, apex rounded, base rounded or cuneate; petioles short, scarcely winged. Fls flushed pink. Fr. 15–30×10–15cm, ovoid or oblong, fragrant, lemon-yellow when ripe, rind v. thick and rough, filled with pale green acid or slightly sweet pulp. Cult. in E Indies and Medit.; origin uncertain. 'Etrog'; (ETROG; ESROG; CEDRAT): fr. lemon-sized, elongate, fragrant. Z9.

C. meyeri Tan. (Possibly of hybrid origin, *C. limon* ×*C. sinensis.*) MEYER LEMON; CHINESE DWARF LEMON; DWARF LEMON. V. similar to *C. limon*, except fr. rounded, 7–8cm diam., peel thin and v. smooth. The hardiest and most compact lemon, often growth as a potplant. Z9.

C. microcarpa Bunge = × *Citrofortunella microcarpa.*

C. mitis Blanco = × *Citrofortunella microcarpa.*

C. myrtifolia Raf. Similar to *C. aurantium*, except often unarmed; lvs much smaller; fr. a quarter to half size of those of *C. aurantium.* Known only in cult. Z9.

C. nobilis Lour. TANGOR; FLORIDA ORANGE; KING ORANGE; KING MANDARIN; KING-OF-SIAM. (*C. reticulata* ×*C. sinensis?*) Tree to 4.5m; br. ascending, twigs glab.; spines present on suckers, 0 on flowering br. Lvs 4–8cm, ovate-oblong to ovate-lanceolate, narrowed to obtuse or slightly emarginate apex, cuneate or obtuse at base; petiole v. narrowly winged. Fr. depressed-globose, 5–8cm diam., peel thin, green to orange tinged yellow. Vietnam. Z9.

C. nobilis Andrews non Lour. = *C. reticulata.*

C. otaitense Risso & Poit. see *C. ×limonia.*

C. papeda Miq. = *C. hystrix.*

C. ×paradisi Macfad. in Hook. GRAPEFRUIT; PAMPLEMOUSSE; POMELO. (Origin unknown, perhaps *C. maxima* ×*C. sinensis.*) Tree, large, crown rounded with dense foliage; twigs slender, angled when young. Lvs ovate, blunt at apex, rounded at base; petioles with broad obovate wing. Fr. 10–12cm diam. globose, peel yellow or tinged slightly orange, pulp light yellow or flushed red, v. juicy. W Indies, known in the 18th century, though perhaps imported from China. Z9.

C. ponderosa hort. GIANT LEMON; WONDER LEMON; AMERICAN

WONDER LEMON. Like *C. limon* except fr. rounded, to 12cm diam. and 1kg+, peel thick and rough, yellow tinged orange. Z9.

C. reticulata Blanco. MANDARIN ORANGE; TANGERINE; CLEMENTINE; SATSUMA. Shrub or small tree, armed; twigs slender. Lvs 4cm, lanceolate, petiole narrowly winged. Fr. subglobose to flattened globose, to 8cm diam., yellow-orange to flame-orange when ripe, peel thin, loose, pulp aromatic, v. sweet. SE Asia. Z9.

C. sinensis (L.) Osbeck. ORANGE; SWEET ORANGE. (Perhaps introgressed hybrid of *C. maxima* ×*C. reticulata.*) Tree, 8–13m, crown rounded; twigs angled when young; spines flexible, slender, sometimes 0. Lvs medium-sized, acute at apex, rounded at base; petioles narrowly winged, articulate. Fr. oval to flattened-globose, pulp sweet, peel thin, orange or golden. Origin unknown; probably S China & Vietnam; cult. worldwide. Z9.

C. taitensis Risso = *C. otaitense* (see *C.* ×*limonia*).

C. ×*tangelo* J. Ingram & H.E. Moore. TANGELO; UGLI FRUIT. (*C. paradisi* ×*C. reticulata.*) Lvs unifoliate; petiole narrowly winged. Fr. to 12cm diam. aromatic, yellow-orange to flame-orange, peel thick, pitted, flesh sweeter than *C. paradisi.* Gdn origin. Cvs include 'Orlando' and 'Minneola'. Z9.

C. trifoliata L. = *Poncirus trifoliata.*

C. wilsonii Tan. Tree, 9–11m, glab., armed. Lvs 1–2.5cm, elliptic-oblong, entire or sinuate-dentate, long acuminate or rounded at apex, broadly cuneate at base; petiole wing obcordate. Fr. globose, peel v. thick and rough. China. Z9.

Cive *Allium schoenoprasum.*

Cladanthus Cass. Compositae. 4 ann. herbs with branching st. Lvs 1–2-pinnatisect. Cap. solitary, radiate; ray flts yellow or white; disc flts yellow, 5-lobed. Spain, NW Afr. Z7.

C. arabicus (L.) Cass. Aromatic, puberulent and pungent. Lvs 2–3cm, lobes linear or trifid, upper lvs surrounding cap.; ray flts yellow. S Spain, NW Afr.
→*Anthemis.*

Cladium P. Browne. Cyperaceae. 2 perenn., rhizomatous herbs. St. terete. Lvs grass-like, linear, tip triangular in section. Infl. a term. pan. of clustered spikelets. Cosmop.

C. mariscus (L.) Pohl. ELK SEDGE. 125–250cm. Rhiz. widely creeping. St. hollow, leafy. Lvs 200cm×10–15mm, keeled, finely toothed. Pan. 30–70×5–12cm, glumes, bristle-like, yellow-brown. Summer. N Afr. to Scand. and Sib. Z3.

Cladobium Lindl.
C. violaceum Lindl. = *Scaphyglottis violacea.*

Cladosicyos Hook. f.
C. edulis Hook. f. = *Cucumeropsis mannii.*

Cladothamnus Bong. Ericaceae. 1 decid. shrub, 90cm–3m. St. ferruginous, erect, angled. Lvs 2.5–6cm, oblanceolate or narrowly oval, acute, glab., subsessile. Fls 1.8–2.5cm diam., usually solitary, pendulous; pet. 5, oblong, pink with yellow tips; sta. 10. N Amer. Z5.

C. pyroliflorus Bong.
→*Elliottia.*

Cladrastis Raf. Leguminosae (Papilionoideae). 5 decid. trees. Lvs imparipinnate. Fls pea-like in term. pan. or rac. E Asia, N Amer.

C. amurensis (Rupr. & Maxim.) Koch = *Maackia amurensis.*

C. kentukea (Dum.-Cours.) Rudd = *C. lutea.*

C. lutea (Michx. f.) K. Koch. KENTUCKY YELLOW-WOOD. Round-headed tree, to 15m. Shoots glab. Lfts to 12.5cm, 7–11, ovate or oval. Fls to 3cm, white, fragrant, in drooping pan. to 40cm. US. Z3.

C. platycarpa (Maxim.) Mak. JAPANESE YELLOW-WOOD. Lfts to 10cm, 8–13, ovate-oblong, acute to acuminate, somewhat adpressed-pubesc. beneath. Fls to 1.5cm, white marked yellow, in pan. to 25cm. Summer. Jap., China. Z4.

C. sinensis Hemsl. CHINESE YELLOW-WOOD. To 21m. Lfts 10cm, 9–13, oblong or ovate, pubesc. and tinged grey beneath. Fls 1.75cm, white, often flushed pink, in erect, pyramidal pan. to 40cm. China. Z6.

C. tinctoria Raf. = *C. lutea.*

C. wilsonii Tak. Tree to 10m. Shoots flushed red, brown-pubesc., lenticellate. Lfts 7–9 to 7cm, narrowly ovate, deep green, shining above, grey-blue beneath with pubesc. veins. Infl. 12–18cm; fls white. C China. Z6.
→*Platyosprion* and *Sophora.*

Clammy Cuphea *Cuphea viscosissima.*

Clammy Ground Cherry *Physalis heterophylla.*
Clammy Locust *Robinia viscosa.*
Clamshell Orchid *Encyclia cochleata.*
Clanwilliam Cedar *Widdringtonia cedarbergensis.*
Claret Ash *Fraxinus angustifolia* 'Raywood'.

Clarkia Pursh FAREWELL TO SPRING; GODETIA. Onagraceae. 33 ann. herbs. Fls in leafy spike or rac.; hypanthium obconical, funnelform, campanulate, or slender, usually with a ring of hairs within; sep. 4, reflexed, free, paired or united, often red; pet. 4, oblanceolate to obovate, frequently lobed or clawed, sta. 8 in two series, or reduced to one series of 4. W N Amer., S Amer.

C. amoena (Lehm.) Nels. & Macbr. SATIN FLOWER. Erect or decumbent to 1m. Lvs linear to lanceolate, entire to denticulate, 1–6cm. Infl. erect; pet. 1–6cm, obovate to fan-shaped, pink to lavender, sometimes darker or shading to white at the base, usually blotched bright red. Coastal N Calif. Azalea-fld series: intermediate in height with semi-double pink fls. Elegans Hybrids: to 75cm; fls double in shades of lavender, red, pink and white. Grace Hybrids: habit vigorous, compact, to 50cm high; fls abundant in shades of pink and red. Princess Series: intermediate in height with frilled fls in shades of pink. ssp. *lindleyi* (Douglas) F.H. & M.E. Lewis. Erect to 2m. Lvs 3–4cm, linear-lanceolate. Pet. lavender, often streaked with white near base, dark-red central spot often 0 or represented by a small spot or line. Oreg. and Washington. ssp. *whitneyi* (A. Gray) F.H. & M.E. Lewis. Coarse, often sprawling, to 1m. Lvs 2–5cm, lanceolate. Fls large; pet. lavender, with a bright red spot. Calif.

C. breweri (A. Gray) Greene. FAIRY FANS. Erect or decumbent, to 20cm. Lvs 2–5cm, lanceolate to linear, entire. Infl. ± erect; pet. 1.5–2.6cm, pink, paler or white at the base, scarcely clawed, 3-lobed. Calif.

C. concinna (Fisch. & C.A. Mey.) Greene. RED RIBBONS. Erect, to 40cm. Lvs 2–4.5cm, lanceolate to elliptic or ovate, entire or subentire. Infl. erect; pet. 1–2.5cm, deep bright pink, often streaked white and purple, clawed, 3-lobed. Calif. 'Pink Ribbons': to 30cm, rounded, bushy; fls feathery, deep rose, abundant.

C. elegans Douglas = *C. unguiculata.*

C. grandiflora Lindl. = *C. amoena.*

C. lindleyi (Douglas) Spach = *C. amoena* ssp. *lindleyi.*

C. pulchella Pursh. Erect, to 50cm. Lvs 2–8cm, linear to lanceolate, entire. Infl. erect; pet. 1–3cm, bright pink to lavender, sometimes white or purple-veined, 3-lobed, clawed, with a prominent pair of lat. teeth. Rocky Mts to Pacific Coast.

C. purpurea (Curtis) Nels. & Macbr. Erect or decumbent herb to 1m. Lvs 2–7cm, linear to narrowly oblanceolate, sometimes ovate, entire. Infl. erect; pet. fan-shaped, obovate, pale pink, rarely white, to purple or deep wine red, with or without a red spot. Washington to Ariz., Baja Calif. ssp. *quadrivulnera* (Douglas) F.H. & M.E. Lewis. Lvs linear to narrowly lanceolate. Pet. less than 15mm long. Baja Calif., Ariz. ssp. *viminea* (Douglas) F.H. & M.E. Lewis. Lvs linear to narrowly lanceolate. Pet. 15–25mm. Calif., Oreg.

C. quadrivulnera (Douglas) Spach = *C. purpurea* ssp. *quadrivulnera.*

C. rubicunda (Lindl.) F.H. & M.E. Lewis. Erect to prostrate, to 1.5m. Lvs 1–4cm, lanceolate or elliptic, entire to denticulate. Infl. erect; pet. 1–3cm, obovate to fan-shaped, subentire to erose, sometimes emarginate, scarcely clawed, rosy-pink to lavender with a bright red or red-purple base. Coastal C Calif.

C. speciosa F.H. & M.E. Lewis. Erect to decumbent, to 60cm. Lvs 1–6cm, linear to narrowly lanceolate, ± entire. Infl. erect; pet. 1–2.5cm, fan-shaped, subentire to erose, purple-red with a white or yellow base, to lavender shading to cream at base, or wholly cream, usually with a bright red or purplish-red spot. S coastal ranges, Calif.

C. tenella (Cav.) F.H. & M.E. Lewis. Erect or decumbent, to 50cm. Lvs 1–6cm, linear to oblanceolate or elliptical, entire. Infl. erect; pet. 7–25mm, obovate to fan-shaped, entire or erose, lavender to blue or dark red-purple. Arg.

C. unguiculata Lindl. Erect, to 1m. Lvs 1–6cm, lanceolate to ovate or elliptic, entire to denticulate. Infl. erect; pet. 10–20mm, lavender-pink to salmon or purple to dark red-purple, occas. white, sometimes with a darker spot at the base, clawed. Calif. 'Albatross': to 60cm; fls double, pure white. 'Chieftain': to 60cm; fls double, pale mauve. 'Brilliant': to 60cm; fls double, carmine-pink. 'La France': to 60cm; fls double, salmon-pink. 'Purple King': to 60cm; fls double, deep purple. 'Rosy Morn': to 60cm; fls double, rose-pink. Royal Bouquet Hybrids: fls fully double in range of colours including white, shades of pink, red and purple. 'Vesuvius': to 60cm; fls double, bright scarlet.

C. viminea (Douglas) Spach = *C. purpurea* ssp. *viminea.*
→*Godetia.*

Clary *Salvia sclarea.*

Clausena Burm. f. Rutaceae. 23 trees and shrubs, wood white. Lvs imparipinnate, anise-scented. Fls to 0.5cm diam., white, 4–5 merous in pyramidal cymose pan. to 30cm; cal. cupulate, lobed to middle; pet. free, elliptic; sta. 10, in 2 whorls; gynophore, hour-glass-shaped. Fr. a hesperidium, subglobose or ovoid, small. S Asia, Trop. Afr., Aus. and Pacific Is. Z10.

C. excavata Burm. f. Small tree. Lvs 15–30-foliolate, 15–30cm, lfts ovate to lanceolate, acuminate at apex, crenate, tomentose. Fls 4-merous. Fr. broadly oblong, to 2cm diam. India to Himal. and S China, Indochina, Malaysia, New Guinea, Philipp.

C. lansium (Lour.) Skeels. WAMPI. Shrub or tree, 7.5–12m. Lvs 5-, 7- or 9-foliolate, 20–25cm; lfts ovate to lanceolate, obtuse or almost emarginate at apex, undulate-crenate or minutely serrate, glabrescent. Fls 5-merous. Fr. to 2.5cm diam., ovoid-globose, white or yellow, pubesc., succulent, edible. SE Asia; cult. in S China for popular lime-like fr., which can be sour or sweet depending on var.

C. punctata Wight & Arn. non Rehd. & Wils. = *C. excavata.*
C. punctata Rehd. & Wils. non Wight & Arn. = *C. lansium.*
C. wampi (Blanco) Oliv. = *C. lansium.*

Clavija Ruiz & Pav. Theophrastaceae. 55 pachycaul, cauliflorous, everg. trees. St. unbranched, erect, bearing an apical tuft of lvs. Lvs oblong lanceolate, or ovate, tough, sometimes spiny-serrate. Fls in short, axill. rac. S Amer. Z10.

C. ernestii Hook. f. = *C. nobilis.*
C. longifolia Mez. Lvs 40–50cm, lanceolate, sharply acute and spiny-serrate. Rac. to 12cm, pendent; fls orange. Venez.
C. nobilis Mez. Lvs to 30–45cm, elliptic-oblong to oblanceolate, acute, entire. Rac. to 12cm, pendulous, crowded; fls to 2cm, apricot. Venez.
C. ornata D. Don = *C. longifolia.*
C. schwackeana Mez. Lvs 35–48cm, oblong, apex broad, rounded, base acuminate. Rac. to 14cm, lax; fls pale yellow. Braz.
→*Theophrasta.*

Claw Fern *Onychium.*

Claytonia L. SPRING BEAUTY; PURSLANE. Portulacaceae. 15 small, succulent herbs. Lvs fleshy, basal lvs rosulate, stalked; st. lvs opposite, sessile, sometimes connate. Fls in term. rac., occas. solitary; sep. 2, persistent; pet. 5, spreading; sta. 5. Mostly W N Amer. but also in S Amer. and Aus. and NZ and Asia.

C. australasica Hook. f. WHITE PURSLANE. St. creeping, rooting. Lvs 4–10cm, linear-lanceolate, blunt, base winged at surrounding st. Infl. a loose term. cyme; fls *c*1.5–2cm wide, fragrant, white. NZ and Aus. Z6.
C. caroliniana Michx. Cormous. St. weak, to 30cm. Lvs to 5×2cm, obtuse, stalked. Fls 2–15 per rac., pink to white marked with pink. E N Amer. Z6.
C. flagellaris Bong. = *C. parvifolia* var. *flagellaris.*
C. lanceolata Pursh. Cormous. St. to 25cm. Basal lvs 0, st. lvs elliptic-lanceolate to ovate, sessile. Fls 1–15, per rac., pink to white, marked pink, sometimes blotched with yellow. E Amer. Z5.
C. megarhiza (A. Gray) Parry ex S. Wats. Taproot long. Basal lvs to 15cm, spathulate to obovate, obtuse, stalks winged; st. lvs oblanceolate to linear. Fls in a dense rac., white to light and dark pink. N Amer. var. *nivalis* (English) C. Hitchc. Fls deep rose. Washington. Z4.
C. nivalis English = *C. megarhiza* var. *nivalis.*
C. parvifolia Moc. ex DC. Stoloniferous. St. to 30cm, spreading or decumbent, slender. Basal lvs to 5.5cm, obovate to oblanceolate, st. lvs sometimes bearing bulbils in the axils. Fls 1–8, white to pink. W N AMerica. var. *flagellaris* (Bong.) R.J. Davis. With long whip-like stolons. Fls larger (to 3cm diam.). Coastal Alask. to S Oreg. Z5.
C. rosea Rydb. Differs from *C. lanceolata* in basal lvs present, st. lvs linear to linear-lanceolate, narrower, and pet. rose pink, tips rounded to acute, not emarginate or retuse. Rocky Mts. Z4.
C. virginica L. SPRING BEAUTY. Cormous. St. 1 to many, to 30cm+. Basal lvs to 12.5cm, linear or linear-lanceolate, st. lvs 5–15cm. Fls to 15 per rac., white marked with pink. E N Amer. 'Lutea': fls orange-yellow veined with red. 'Robusta': to 50cm; lvs to 2.5cm wide. Z6.
→*Montia.*

Clay Wattle *Acacia glaucoptera.*
Clearing Nut *Strychnos* (*S. potatorum*).
Cleavers *Galium* (*G. aparine*).
Cleftstone *Pleiospilos nelii.*

Cleisostoma Bl. Orchidaceae. *c*100 epiphytic, monopodial orchids. Lvs narrowly strap-shaped. Infl. pendent or erect, simple or branched; fls usually small, fleshy, spurred; tep. elliptic-oblong, spreading; lip trilobed, fused to column base, callus conspicuous, midlobe triangular, lat. lobes triangular, erect, spur cylindric or conic. Nepal to New Guinea. Z9.

C. micranthum King & Pantl. = *Smitinandia micrantha.*
C. paniculatum (Ker-Gawl.) Garay. Lvs linear. Fls white marked purple; pet. undulate. India.
C. racemiferum (Lindl.) Garay. Lvs ligulate. Fls violet-black, edged yellow, lip white or yellow. India, Nepal, Thail., Burm.
C. siamense Rolfe ex Downie = *Pomatocalpa siamensis.*
C. spathulatum Bl. = *Robiquetia spathulata.*
→*Aerides* and *Sarcanthus.*

Cleistes Rich. Orchidaceae. *c*25 terrestrial orchids. St. erect, unifoliate. Rac. 1 to 3-fld; fls term. large, subtended by a conspicuous bract; pet. usually held forward over lip; lip funnelform, simple to trilobed, disc crested. N & S Amer.

C. divaricata (L.) Ames. SPREADING POGONIA; FUNNEL-CREST ROSEBUD ORCHID. To 75cm. Lvs to 20cm, oblong-elliptic. Tep. magenta-pink to white and brown, sep. to 65×5mm, linear-lanceolate, pet. to 45×14mm, oblanceolate-spathulate, joined to lip forming a tube; lip to 45×20mm, pale pink, broadly oblong, obscurely 3-lobed, midlobe ovate-triangular, revolute, crest marked dark pink, fleshy-papillose. NE US. Z5.
C. rosea Lindl. To 1.5m. Lvs to 12cm, lanceolate. Tep. rose, dors. sep. to 65×8mm, linear-elliptic to elliptic-lanceolate, pet. to 65×16mm, elliptic to ovate-elliptic, lip to 55×30mm, dark rose, narrowly obovate to broadly oblanceolate, apex serrulate. Panama, N S Amer. Z9.
→*Arethusa* and *Pogonia.*

Cleistocactus Lem. Cactaceae. 30–50 shrubby or tree-like cacti; st. erect to procumbent or pendent, cylindric, usually slender; fls narrowly tubular, regular or somewhat zygomorphic; perianth tube straight or kinked and ± S-shaped, limb unexpanded or expanded; tep. not or only slightly spreading, strongly oblique if expanded. S Ecuad. to Boliv. and N Arg., Parag. and Urug.

C. acanthurus (Vaup.) D. Hunt. Low shrub to 30cm; st. spreading, or pendent, 2–5cm diam.; ribs 15–18, rounded, obscurely tuberculate; spines *c*20–25, short, yellow, to 15mm. Fls 4–5×*c*2.5cm, straight or slightly curved, scarlet; limb expanded; anth. yellow. Peru. Z9.
C. aequatorialis Backeb. = *C. sepium.*
C. anguinus (Gürke) Britt. & Rose. Similar to *C. baumannii.* Decumbent; ribs 10–11; central spines 1–2, yellow; radial spines 18–22. Fls 7cm, yellow-orange; limb unexpanded. Parag. Z9.
C. baumannii (Lem.) Lem. St. erect or arching, to 2m, ×2.5–3.5cm, branching below, ribs 12–16; spines 15–20, to 4cm. Fls 5–7×1cm, orange or scarlet, upcurved and narrowly S-shaped; limb unexpanded. NE Arg., Parag., Urug., SW Braz. Z9.
C. brookei Cárdenas. St. to 50×3–4.5cm, usually unbranched; ribs 22–24; spines 25–40, *c*1cm, bristly, pale yellow. Fls *c*5cm×8mm, red or orange; tube sharply upcurved and somewhat inflated, then S-shaped and somewhat flattened; limb unexpanded. S Boliv. Z9.
C. buchtienii Backeb. = *C. tupizensis.*
C. candelilla Cárdenas. Resembling *C. smaragdiflorus.* St. to 1m×3cm, erect or decumbent; ribs 11–12; fls 3–3.5cm; limb unexpanded; outer tep. yellow, inner tep. tinged purple, bordered white. SE Boliv. Z9.
C. colubrinus Otto ex Fost. Lem. = *C. baumannii.*
C. dependens Cárdenas. St. pendent or clambering, 3–3.5cm diam., dull green; ribs 10–12, obtuse; central spines 3–4, 10–15mm, black-tipped; radial spines 8–13, 2–3mm, red-grey. Fls 4–4.5cm×7mm; pericarpel dark purple; tube red; limb unexpanded; outer tep. pink at base, green-yellow above, tipped dark brown; inner tep. green. Spring–summer. Boliv. Z9.
C. eriotrichus Werderm. & Backeb.) Backeb. = *C. acanthurus.*
C. faustianus Backeb. = *C. acanthurus.*
C. fieldianus (Britt. & Rose) D. Hunt. Large shrub, forming thickets 3–6m tall; erect then decumbent; ribs 5–7, stout, constricted between areoles; spines 6–10, to 5cm. Fls 6–7×3–3.5cm, red; limb expanded. Peru. Z9.
C. fossulatus Mottram = *Oreocereus pseudofossulatus.*
C. fusiflorus Cárdenas. Resembling *C. smaragdiflorus.* Ribs 13–14. Fls 3.5cm; tube pale yellow at first, later tinged red; limb unexpanded; outer tep. pink below, brown-green above, inner tep. purple. SE Boliv. Z9.
C. herzogianus Backeb. = *C. parviflorus.*
C. hyalacanthus (Schum.) Roland-Goss. Low shrub, to 1m, branching below; st. 4–6cm diam.; ribs *c*20; spines 20–30, to

3cm+, yellow or brown. Fls 3.5–4cm, pale red outside; inner tep. purple-pink. N Arg., S Boliv. Z9.

C. icosagonus (Kunth) F.A. Weber ex Roland-Goss. St. procumbent and ascending, 20–60×3–5cm; ribs 12–20; spines 25–50, to 1.5cm, bristly, golden yellow, with finer bristles at flowering areoles. Flower-buds with white hairs; fls 7–8cm, orange to scarlet or pink, nearly straight; limb oblique. S Ecuad., N Peru. Z9.

C. jujuyensis (Backeb.) Backeb. = *C. hyalacanthus*.

C. laniceps (Schum.) Roland-Goss. Resembling *C. roezlii*. Shrub or small tree to 4m; st. erect, 5cm diam.; ribs 9, obtuse, tubercled and cross-furrowed; spines few, to 15mm, grey. Fl. tubular-funnelform, 3.5cm, red. Summer. Boliv. Z9.

C. luminosus Johnson ex Backeb. = *C. morawetzianus*.

C. luribayensis Cárdenas. Similar to *C. tupizensis*, but with smaller fls. Shrub, 2–3m, with numerous fastigiate br., tapering, 4–6cm diam.; ribs c19, transversely furrowed; spines 16–22, 5–15mm, white to light brown. Fls 3cm×5mm; outer tep. pink with dark red midstripe, inner tep. salmon pink. Boliv. Z9.

C. morawetzianus Backeb. Shrub to 2m, much branched; st. c5cm diam., grey-green; ribs 12–14; spines to 14, longest 15–50mm, yellow becoming grey. Fls c5.5cm×9mm, white, or tinged pale green or pink; style long-exserted. C Peru. Z9.

C. morleyanus Britt. & Rose = *C. sepium*.

C. parviflorus (Schum.) Roland-Goss. Shrub to 2–3m; st. 3cm diam., segmented; ribs 12, 3–4mm high; central spine 0–1, to 15mm; radial spines 5–7, to 4mm, dark yellow. Fls 2.5–3cm, red. Boliv. Z9.

C. ritteri Backeb. Shrub to 1m+; branching below; st. c3cm diam.; ribs 12–14+; spines 1cm, yellow or white. Flowering areoles with long white, bristly spines; fls c4cm×5mm, lemon-yellow. C Boliv. Z9.

C. roezlii (F. Haage ex Schum.) Backeb. Broad shrub or small tree 1–3m; st. 4.5–6cm diam.; ribs 7–14; central spine 1, 2–4(–6)cm; radial spines 9–14+, to 1cm, pale brown. Fls 6–7×2cm, red, somewhat curved above; limb narrow, scarcely expanded. N Peru. Z9.

C. samaipatanus (Cárdenas) D. Hunt. Erect shrub to 1.5m, branching below; st. 3.5–4cm diam.; ribs 14–16, rounded; spines 13–22, shortest 4mm, others 1–3cm, straw-yellow or brown to white. Fls 3.5×2cm, bright red; tube S-shaped; limb expanded, oblique; sta. and style exserted; fil. and anth. tinged purple; stigmas green-yellow. Boliv. Z9.

C. sepium (Kunth) F.A. Weber ex Roland-Goss. Simple or shrubby, to 2m, branched below; st. erect 0.5–3m×3–10cm; ribs 6–18, somewhat tuberculate; spines 10–30, 0.5–5(–9)cm. Fls 5–8×2–4cm, bright red, straight; tube c1.5cm diam., scales with dark brown hairs; limb expanded, oblique; sta. violet. Ecuad. Z9.

C. sepium (Kunth) Britt. & Rose = *C. sepium*.

C. serpens (Kunth) F.A. Weber ex Roland-Goss. St. prostrate, slender, 2–3m×5–20mm; ribs 8–11; central spines 1(–4), 5–40mm, light yellow to brown; radial spines 10–15, fine, short. Fls 5cm, pink or scarlet; limb expanded, oblique. Peru. Z9.

C. sextonianus (Backeb.) D. Hunt. St. prostrate, to 1.5m×3cm, branching laterally; ribs c13; central spines 1–2, to 3cm; radial spines 20–30, 5mm, v. thin. Fls 5–6cm, red; tube v. slender, woolly; limb expanded, oblique. Peru. Z9.

C. smaragdiflorus (F.A. Weber) Britt. & Rose. Arching or decumbent, to 1m; st. 2–3cm diam.; ribs 12–14; central spines 4–6, 15–35mm, yellow or brown; radial spines 10–14, to 10mm. Fls 4–5cm; tube slightly constricted above pericarpel; scales red; areoles with white hair; limb unexpanded; outer tep. yellow, inner vivid emerald green. N Arg. Z9.

C. strausii (Heese) Backeb. Erect and branching below, 1–3m; st. 4–8cm diam.; ribs 25–30; spines to 2cm, pale yellow and pure white. Fls 8–9cm, dark red; tube with silky hairs; limb unexpanded, style long-exserted. S Boliv. Z9.

C. tenuiserpens Rauh & Backeb. Resembling *Aporocactus*. St. arching-erect or prostrate, v. slender, to 2m×5mm, ribs 9–10, obscure; spines to 3mm, thin. Fls as in *C. serpens*, but larger. Peru. Z9.

C. tominensis (Weing.) Backeb. St. erect, to 2m×5cm; ribs 18–22, low, transversely furrowed; spines 8–9, to 2cm. Fls 2.6cm, narrow, green, yellow or red, or green below and red above; limb unexpanded. Boliv. Z9.

C. tupizensis (Vaup.) Backeb. Shrub, 2–3m; st. 4–5cm diam.; ribs 18–24; spines c22, red-brown to tinged yellow or white, to 4.5cm. Fls 6–8cm, straight or upcurved, purple or wine-red; limb unexpanded. C & S Boliv. Z9.

C. vulpis-cauda Ritter & Cullm. Procumbent, to 1.5m; ribs 18–22. Spines to 50, 10–20mm, white to red-brown. Fls as in *C. brookei*, produced almost throughout year. S Boliv. Z9.

C. websterianus Backeb. = *C. sepium*.

C. wendlandiorum Backeb. = *C. brookei*.

C. winteri D. Hunt. St. procumbent or pendent, to 1.5m×2.5cm,

with 16–17 ribs; spines 5–10mm, golden yellow. Fls 4–6×5cm, orange-red; limb expanded, nearly regular, inner tep. white or pale pink; anth. violet; stigmas green-yellow. Boliv. Z9.

→*Bolivicereus*, *Borzicactus*, *Cephalocleistocactus*, *Hildewintera*, *Loxanthocereus*, *Matucana* and *Seticereus*.

Clematis L. VIRGIN'S BOWER; LEATHER FLOWER; VASE VINE. Ranunculaceae. 200+ decid. or everg., semi-woody to woody climbers or woody-based perennials. Lvs simple to pinnately compound with ternate divisions. Fls urceolate to spreading, solitary, clustered or in pan.; sep. 4–8, petaloid; pet. 0, staminodes sometimes petaloid; sta. numerous. Achenes numerous with long, persistent, often silky-plumose styles. N & S Temp. regions, mts of Trop. Afr.

C. addisonii Britt. Low shrub to 1m. Br. erect, later procumbent. Lvs to 8cm, glaucous, lower lvs simple, broad-ovate, subsessile, sometimes lobed, obtuse, upper lvs simple to 2–4(–6)-foliolate; lfts ovate. Fls urceolate, solitary, pendulous; sep. purple, lanceolate, recurved. Spring–summer. E N Amer. Z6.

C. aethusifolia Turcz. Erect or scandent perenn. to 60cm. St. slender. Lvs to 20.5cm, bright green, pinnatisect, seg. deeply lobed or trifoliate; lfts to 3cm, linear to obovate or oblong, dentate, lanuginose. Fls narrow-campanulate, pendulous, in 1–3-fld cymes; peduncles erect, to 5cm; sep. pale yellow to cream white, to 4cm, narrow-oblong, acute, white-lanuginose at margins. Summer. N China, Korea. Z5. var. *latisecta* Maxim. Lvs larger, seg. broader.

C. afoliata Buch. Semi-scandent, ± leafless shrub to 2m. Br. slender, wire-like, striate, dark green. Juvenile lvs sometimes present, trifoliolate; lfts minute. Fls 2.5cm diam. 1–6 per cymes; peduncles to 5cm; sep. green-white, 4–6, lanceolate, patent, sericeous. Spring–summer. NZ. Z8.

C. akebioides (Maxim.) hort. ex Veitch. Close to *C. orientalis*. Lvs pinnate, lfts 5–7, glaucous, thick-textured, bluntly toothed to obscurely lobed. Fls clustered in axils; sep. yellow, sometimes stained red or purple beneath, to 2.5cm, fairly thickly textured, ovate, erect or spreading. W China. Z5.

C. albicoma Wherry. Close to *C. ochroleuca*. Br. to 60cm, erect. Lvs 4–5cm, ovate, entire, ultimately glab. Fls solitary, nodding, campanulate; sep. purple, tips recurved. Spring. NE US. Z5.

C. alpina (L.) Mill. Decid. climber to 2.5m. Lvs to 15cm, biternate; lfts 9, to 5cm, ovate-lanceolate, coarse-serrate. Fls solitary, pendulous, stellate-campanulate; peduncles to 10cm; sep. 4, to 4cm, blue or mauve, oblong, sericeous; staminodes petaloid, white spoon-shaped. Spring. N Eur. & mts of C & S Eur., N Asia. 'Bluebell': as 'Pamela Jackman', fls blue. 'Burford White': to 4m; fls large, clear white, bell-shaped, tep. pointed. 'Columbine': fls pale lavender, almost campanulate; sep. long and acute. 'Columbine White': to 4m; lvs pale; fls white, on upright st. 'Frances Rivis' ('Blue Giant'): sep. to 5×2cm, ovate, rich sky blue; staminodes to 1.5×0.3cm. 'Grandiflora': fls large. 'Helsingborg': fls deep purple; sta. petaloid, dark purple. 'Inshriach': fls small on slender, swan-necked pedicels; sep. narrow, decurved to spreading, sometimes slightly twisted, dark lilac to pale mauve, staminodes white tipped mauve, in a tight boss. 'Jacqueline du Pré': fls large, warm pink, interior soft pink, staminodes blush pink. 'Pamela Jackman': fls to 8cm diam., dark azure; sep. to 4.5×1.5cm; staminodes tinted blue. 'Pauline': fls Oxford blue flushed violet, centre white. 'Rosy Pagoda': fls pale pink. 'Ruby': fls soft red, staminodes cream. 'Willy': fls pale pink, deep pink at base of sta., early-flowering. var. *ochotensis* (Pall.) S. Wats. Sep. indigo, more acute; staminodes narrow to broadly spathulate, downy. E Sib., Sachalin, Kamchatka, Korea, Jap. var. *sibirica* (L.) Schneid. Lfts more coarsely and irregularly serrate, pale. Sep. yellow-white, rarely flushed blue, elliptic-lanceolate, long-acuminate; staminodes pale cream, spathulate, dense-pubesc. N Norway and Finland to E Sib., C Urals and Manch. 'Gravetye': fls large, milky yellow, v. early-flowering. 'White Moth': fls semi-double, white. Z5.

C. alpina var. *occidentalis* (Hornem.) A. Gray = *C. occidentalis*.

C. alpina var. *thibetica* hort. = *C. alpina* 'Frances Rivis'.

C. aphylla Col. = *C. afoliata*.

C. apiifolia DC. Decid. climber to 4.5m. St. slender. Lvs trifoliolate, occas. pinnately compound with the lower seg. trifoliolate; lfts to 7.5cm, broad-ovate to ovate-lanceolate, deeply incised, often trilobed, pubesc. on veins beneath. Fls 16mm diam., in axill. pan. to 15cm; sep. dull white, patent, lanuginose. Autumn. China, Jap. Z7.

C. aristata R. Br. Climber. St. initially downy. Lvs long-petioled, 1–2× ternate; lfts coriaceous, toothed or entire. Fls axill. forming a pan.; sep. 2–2.5cm, 4–5, white or ivory, oblong or oblong-lanceolate, spreading, glab. or downy, anth. aristate. Summer. Aus. Z7.

C. armandii Franch. Everg. climber to 9m. Lvs coriaceous, trifoliolate; lfts to 15cm, oblong-lanceolate to ovate, apex acute, rounded or cordate at base, emerging bronze then glossy dark green, prominently veined. Fls to 6.5cm diam., in dense clusters; sep. pure white or cream, later rose-tinted, 4–7, narrow-oblong, 2.5cm. Spring. C & W China. 'Apple Blossom': fls cup-shaped, pink in bud, fading to white. 'Snowdrift': fls large, on drooping stalks, white, waxy, v. fragrant.

C. ×*aromatica* Lenné & Koch. (*C. flammula* ×*C. integrifolia.*) Erect subshrub to 2m. St. slender. Lvs simple, trilobed to 5-foliolate; lfts to 3cm, ovate to broad-oval, entire. Fls 4cm diam., in lax cymes; peduncles 5cm; sep. dark violet, 4, oblong, patent, lanuginose at margins; fil. white or yellow. Summer–autumn. Z4.

C. australis T. Kirk. Climber. Lvs trifoliolate; lfts to 4cm, pinnate-pinnatifid. Fls solitary or few in pan.; sep. white or pale yellow, 5–8, 2cm, sericeous. NZ. 'Green Velvet': hybrid with *C. petriei*; lvs dark green, crenately lobed; fls downy, emerald green. Z8.

C. baldwinii Torr. & A. Gray. PINE HYACINTH. Erect herb to 60cm. Lvs to 10cm, simple, sometimes trifoliolate, elliptic to lanceolate or linear. Fls purple or purple-pink, urceolate, 2.5cm, pendulous. S US. Z7.

C. balearica Rich. = *C. cirrhosa* var. *balearica*.

C. barbellata Edgew. Climber to 4m, similar to *C. montana*, readily identified by fl. colour. Lvs trifoliolate; lfts to 8cm, ovate-lanceolate, acute, lobed and irregularly sharp-serrate. Fls campanulate, solitary or several-grouped; sep. 4, oblong-ovate, to 4cm, lanuginose, dull purple to brown-violet; fil. dilated, lanuginose. Spring–summer. W Himal. 'Pruinina': fls plum, lantern-shaped, sta. petaloid, white; late-flowering.

C. bergeronii Lav. = *C.* ×*eriostemon* 'Bergeronii'.

C. brachiata Thunb. Climber. Lvs 5-foliolate, rarley bipinnate; lfts rounded to ovate, serrate. Fls numerous; sep. cream or white, to 2.5cm. S Afr. Z9.

C. brevicaudata DC. Vigorous climber. St. densely tangled. Lvs 5–7-foliolate, lower lobes ternate; lfts to 7cm, ovate-lanceolate, long-acuminate, sinuate-serrate. Fls many in axill. cymes, grouped in term. pan.; sep. white to yellow, to 1.5cm, pubesc. Summer. Jap., China, W Mong. Z5.

C. buchananiana DC. Vigorous climber. Lvs pinnately 5–7-foliolate; lfts to 10cm, broad-ovate, cordate at base, serrate or lobed, pubesc. Fls tubular, in long leafy pan.; sep. 4, to 2.5cm, cream-white to pale yellow, stout, linear-oblong, recurved at apex, lanuginose and ribbed. Summer–autumn. Himal. Z6.

C. buchananiana Finet & Gagnep., non DC. = *C. rehderiana*.

C. caerulea var. *odorata* hort. = *C.* ×*aromatica*.

C. calycina Sol. Everg. climber to 4.5m. Lvs ternate or biternate, to 7.5cm; lfts deep-lobed or coarse-serrate, purple-bronze in winter. Fls yellow-white, spotted red, to 5cm diam., solitary; pedicel to 2.5cm. Autumn–winter. S Eur. Z7.

C. calyciona Ait. = *C. cirrhosa* var. *balearica*.

C. campaniflora Brot. Decid. climber to 6m. St. slender. Lvs with 5–7 pinnate divisions, each ternately divided; lfts to 7.5cm, narrow-lanceolate, ovate or oval, simple or lobed. Fls bowl-shaped, solitary or several-grouped, pendulous; peduncles to 7.5cm; sep. white tinged violet, 4, 2cm, oblong, abruptly acuminate and recurved. Summer. Port. Z6.

C. ×*cartmanii* hort. (*C. marmoraria* ×*C. paniculata.*) Bushy, dwarf with finely dissected green lvs and large pan. of white fls. Gdn origin. 'Joe' (♂ selection): shrub, not climbing; br. glab., purple-tinted; fls to 4cm diam., white, to 30 per pan.

C. catesbyana Pursh. Climber. Lvs biternate; lfts membranous, lobed or entire. Fls 2.5cm diam., in cymose pan.; sep. white, linear to cuneate. SE US. Z8.

C. chinensis Retz. Decid. climber. Lvs pinnately 5-foliolate; lfts to 7.5cm, ovate or cordate, usually cordate at base, midrib lanuginose. Fls to 2cm diam., in many-fld cymose pan.; sep. white, 4, v. narrow, downy. Autumn. C & W China. Z6.

C. chrysocoma Franch. Decid. climber to 2.5m. St. brown-yellow, lanuginose when young. Lvs trifoliolate, brown-yellow villous-lanuginose; lfts 2.5–5cm, broad-ovate or rhomboid to narrow-obovate, trilobed, sometimes only serrate. Fls 4.5cm diam., solitary; peduncles to 7.5cm, dense brown-yellow lanuginose; sep. white tinged pink, 4, broad-oblong, abruptly acuminate, sericeous; sta. forming a cluster 2.5cm diam. Summer–autumn. SW China. 'Rosea': fls soft pink, sep. winged, sta. yellow. Z7.

C. chrysocoma var. *sericea* (Franch.) Schneid. = *C. spooneri*.

C. cirrhosa L. Everg. climber to 4m. Lvs to 5cm, simple, dentate or trilobed, or ternate or biternate with dentate or lobed lfts, glossy. Fls ± pendulous, broad-campanulate, solitary or in axill. fascicles, subtended by a small cuplike pair of bracteoles; pedicels to 5cm; sep. ovate, to 2.5cm, cream, rarely spotted red. Winter–spring. S Eur., Medit. 'Wisley Cream': lvs simple, light green; fls cream. var. *balearica* (Rich.) Willk. & Lange. Sep. pale cream, always spotted and flecked red-maroon within, on slender pedicels. 'Freckles': sep. to 4cm, cream, intensely

flecked and spotted maroon to violet within, on exceptionally long pedicels. Z7.

C. coccinea Engelm. = *C. texensis*.

C. coerulea Lindl. = *C. patens*.

C. colensoi Hook. f. Everg. climber, much-branched. Br. slender. Lvs 7cm, triangular, eventually pinnatisect or pinnately trifoliolate; lfts rounded. Fls 10-grouped; sep. green, 6, narrow-lanceolate, sericeous. Spring–summer. NZ. Z8.

C. columbiana (Nutt.) Torr. & A. Gray. Semi-woody climber. Lvs pinnately trifoliolate; lfts 4cm, thin, ovate, acute, cordate at base, entire or coarse-serrate. Fls solitary; sep. purple or blue, lanceolate, to 5cm. N Amer. Z4.

C. connata DC. Vigorous decid. climber to 8m. Lvs 3- or 5-foliolate, petiole bases connate, forming a large clasping disc at each node; lfts to 12.5cm, ovate, sometimes trilobed, finely acuminate, cordate at base, coarse-serrate, glab. or lanuginose, bright green. Fls campanulate, pendulous, in pan. to 12.5cm; sep. soft yellow, oblong, to 2.5cm, acute and recurved at apex, lanuginose inside. Summer–autumn. Himal., SW China. Z6.

C. **County Park Hybrids.** (*C. petriei* ×*C. marmoraria*.) 'Pixie': everg., trailing subshrub. Lvs to 4cm, trifoliolate; lfts lobed. Fls pale yellow-green in a congested pan. ♂ selection. Spring. 'Fairy': ♀ selection, differs from 'Pixie' in 8–10 staminodes, silky golden styles; fr. with downy achenes. Z6.

C. crispa L. BLUE JASMINE; MARSH CLEMATIS; CURLY CLEMATIS; CURLFLOWER. Climbing decid. shrub to 2.5m. Lvs to 20.5cm, pinnately 3-, 5- or 7-foliolate; lfts to 7.5cm, often ternate or lobed, thin, lanceolate to broad-ovate, cordate at base, entire. Fls campanulate, solitary, term., pendulous; peduncles to 7.5cm; sep. to 5cm, connate below, lavender, pale at margins, thin and sinuate. SE US. 'Distorta': sep. curled. Z5.

C. delavayi Franch. Erect shrub to 1.5m. Lvs to 10cm, pinnate; lfts to 3.5cm, lanceolate to elliptic-ovate, acute, entire, deep green above, silver-white, sericeous beneath. Fls to 3cm diam., 3–6-grouped in terminal cymes; sep. 4–6, white, obovate, pubesc. Summer. China. Z5.

C. dioscoreifolia Alév. & Vaniot = *C. terniflora*.

C. distorta Lav. = *C. crispa* 'Distorta'.

C. ×*divaricata* Jacq. (*C. integrifolia* ×*C. viorna*.) Erect, non-climbing shrub. Lvs pinnate or simple and irregularly lobed; lfts 3–7. Fls to 2.5cm, short-stalked, nodding, campanulate; sep. red-lilac, spreading. Summer. Gdn origin. Z6.

C. douglasii Hook. Herbaceous, non-climbing perenn. to 60cm. Lvs simple below, pinnate above with pinnate or lobed divisions; lfts oblong, lanceolate or ovate, entire, sometimes sparsely serrate, villous. Fls tubular or campanulate, 2.5cm, solitary; peduncles long, erect to nodding; sep. 4, deep mauve to violet, thick, oblong, 2.5cm, reflexed, paler outside. Spring–summer. NW Amer. var. *scottii* (T.C. Porter) Coult. To 1m. Lvs ± glaucous, 1–2-pinnate; lfts narrow-lanceolate, downy beneath. Fls to 4cm, urceolate, nodding; sep. 4, strongly recurved at tips, lavender to pale magenta, downy. BC, Washington E to Mont., Wyom. 'Rosea': fls rose pink. Z6.

C. ×*durandii* Kuntze. (*C.* ×*jackmanii* ×*C. integrifolia*.) Robust erect semi-scandent shrub to 180cm. Lvs to 15cm, simple, ovate, acute, somewhat cordate at base, glossy green, subglabrous, longitudinally 3–5-veined. Fls usually 3-grouped; sep. deep violet-blue, 4, to 6, patent or reflexed, obovate, 4cm diam., slightly undulate; sta. yellow. Summer–autumn. 'Pallida': fls paler, violet-rose. Z5.

C. erecta L. = *C. recta*.

C. ×*eriostemon* Decne. (*C. integrifolia* ×*C. viticella*.) Sprawling semi-woody shrub to 3m. Lvs pinnately 7-foliolate; lfts elliptic, acute, deep green, term. lfts usually slightly lobed. Fls 1–3-grouped, term.; peduncles to 10cm; sep. 4, dark violet to lavender, spathulate, 4cm, abrupt-acuminate and reflexed, 3-veined. Gdn origin. 'Bergeronii': to 3m; lvs thick; lfts large, oval, wide; fls almost campanulate, sep. spathulate-cuneate, to 1.5cm diam., mauve. 'Hendersonii': to 2.5m; fls to 6.5cm diam., solitary, violet; sep. patent, 2cm diam.; summer–autumn. 'Intermedia': as 'Hendersonii', but st. thicker; fls similar to *C. integrifolia*, violet blue. Z4.

C. fargesii Franch. Decid. climber to 6m. Lvs to 23cm, bipinnate, 5–7-foliolate; lfts 2.5–5cm, ovate, deeply irregularly- and coarsely-serrate, sometimes trilobed, sericeous-lanuginose. Fls to 6.5cm diam., axillary, 1–3-grouped; peduncles to 18cm; sep. pure white, 6, obovate, yellow and lanuginose outside; anth. pale yellow. Summer–autumn. China. Z6.

C. fasciculiflora Franch. Everg. climber to 6m. Lvs trifoliolate; lfts oval-oblong, to 10cm. Fls yellow-white, lanate, in dense axill. clusters; peduncles to 2cm. SW China. Z8.

C. finetiana Lév. & Vaniot. Semi-evergreen climber to 4m. Lvs trifoliolate; lfts to 10cm, thin, ± coriaceous, narrow-ovate, acute, rounded at base, entire, bright green. Fls axill., in 3–7-fld infl.; peduncles to 5cm; sep. white, exterior green-white, 4, lanceolate, 1.5cm, acute, patent. Summer. C & W China.

Possibly not distinct from *C. pavoliniana.* Z8.

C.flammula L. Scandent decid., subshrub to 5m. Lvs with 3–5 divisions, sometimes trifoliolate; lfts narrow-lanceolate to rounded, 2–3-lobed, bright green, glab., often coriaceous. Fls v. fragrant, in lax, many-fld, axill. pan. to 30cm; sep. pure white, 4, to 12mm, obtuse. Summer–autumn. S Eur., N Afr., W Syr., Iran, Turk. Z6.

C.flammula var. *rubromarginata* Cripps = *C. terniflora.*

C.flammula var. *robusta* Carr. = *C. maximowicziana.*

C.florida Thunb. Decid. or semi-evergreen climber to 4m. St. wiry. Lvs to 12.5cm, biternate; lfts to 5cm, ovate to lanceolate, entire or coarse-serrate, shiny deep green above, pubesc. beneath. Fls white or cream white, green-striate, to 7.5cm diam., flat, solitary, axill.; peduncles to 10cm; sep. 4–6, ovate, acuminate, patent; staminodes sometimes present, deep violet, to 2.5cm, fil. white, anth. violet. Summer. China, Jap. 'Alba Plena': fls double, staminodes and sep. white flushed green, exterior with central green stripe. 'Sieboldii' ('Bicolor'): fls white with purple staminodes forming anemone centre. Z7.

C.foetida Raoul. Everg. climber. Young shoots grooved, fulvous-tomentose. Lvs to 12cm, glab. or sparse-pubesc., trifoliolate; lfts to 9cm, ovate, obtuse to acute, entire to sinuate, rarely crenate-lobed or serrate, thinly coriaceous. Fls scented, in axill., cymes; pedicels bracteate; bracts 2, connate; sep. yellow, 5–8, imbricate, to 23mm, ovate-oblong, pilose beneath. NZ. Z8.

C. forrestii W.W. Sm. = *C. napaulensis.*

C.forsteri J.F. Gmel. Everg. climber. Lvs to 16cm, glab., trifoliolate; lfts to 7cm, lanceolate to broad-ovate, entire, crenate-dentate, deeply pinnatifid, bi-pinnatisect or pinnate, coriaceous. Fls pure yellow, solitary or 2–6-grouped, pedicels with paired, connate bracts; sep. 5–8, white, overlapping, lanceolate, ovate or narrow-oblong, to 3cm. Summer. NZ. 'Tempo': ♂ selection, v. vigorous; fls to 4cm diam., pale green becoming white. Z8.

C. ×francofurtensis Rinz. (*C.florida* × *C. viticella.*) Close to *C. viticella.* Lvs bipinnate; lfts ovate, acute, downy beneath. Fls large; sep. 6, purple, interior pure white; sta. violet. Summer. Gdn origin. Z6.

C.fremontii Wats. FREMONT'S CROWFOOT. Stout, erect perenn. to 50cm. Lvs to 10cm, simple, tough, ovate-lanceolate to broad-ovate, entire or subentire, sparse villous-tomentose, conspicuously net-veined. Fls 2.5cm, pendulous, solitary; sep. purple, 4, thick, reflexed at apex, tomentose at margins. Summer. NW Amer. Z4.

C.fruticosa Turcz. Similar to *C. recta.* Subshrub to 50cm, closely branched. Lvs lanceolate, entire or toothed, dark green, glab. Fls 1–4 per cluster; sep. to 2cm, 4, yellow, spreading. Summer. C Asia to Mong. and China. Z5.

C.fusca Turcz. Climber to 3m. Young br. angled. Lvs to 20cm, pinnately 5–7-foliolate; lfts to 6cm, ovate, acute, rounded or cordate at base, glab. or lanuginose beneath, term. leaflet often 0. Fls urceolate, nodding, solitary; peduncles to 2.5cm, rufous-pubesc.; sep. violet inside, densely rufous-pubesc. outside, 4–6, oblong-ovate, to 2.5cm, acuminate and reflexed at apex, lanate. Summer. NE Asia. var. *violacea* Maxim. Fls violet. Korea. Z5.

C.fusca hort. non Turcz. = *C. japonica.*

C. gebleriana Bongard. = *C. songarica.*

C. gentianoides DC. Prostrate or creeping to 120cm. Lvs simple or trifoliolate; lfts lanceolate or lanceolate-ovate. Fls solitary or few-clustered; sep. white, 4, oblong. Tasm. Z9.

C. glauca Willd. Scandent shrub to 4m. Lvs pinnate or bipinnate; lfts to 5cm, elliptic to lanceolate, 2–3-lobed, blue-green. Fls solitary or paired, in paniculate infl.; peduncles to 8cm; sep. yellow, to 2cm, ovate-lanceolate, acuminate, broad-patent. Summer–autumn. W China to Sib. Z4.

C. glauca auctt. non Willd. = *C. intricata* or *C. ladakhiana.*

C. glauca var. *akebioides* (Maxim.) Rehd. & Wils. = *C. akebioides.*

C. glycioides DC. Differs from *C.aristata* in lvs always with 3, thinner-textured, broad and sparsely toothed lfts and smaller fls with anth. not aristate. Aus. Z7.

C. gouriana Roxb. Vigorous climber. Lvs 5- or 7-foliolate; lfts to 8cm, ovate-oblong, long-acuminate, subcordate at base, often entire, shiny above, pubesc. when young. Fls white, to 2cm diam., in large pan. Himal., China. Z6.

C. gouriana var. *finetii* Rehd. & Wils. = *C. peterae.*

C. gracilifolia Rehd. & Wils. Decid. climber to 4m. Lvs ternate or pinnately 3-, 5- or 7-foliolate; lfts to 4cm, ovate, coarse-serrate or trlobed, ± lanuginose. Fls to 5cm diam., 2-4-grouped; pedicels slender, to 7.5cm; sep. white, 4, obovate, patent, lanuginose. Summer. W China. Z5.

C. grata Wallich. Vigorous climber to 10m. Lvs pubesc., pinnately 5-foliolate; lfts to 6cm, broad-ovate, coarsely dentate, sometimes lobed, pubesc. beneath. Pan. many-fld; sep. 4, cream white, ovate-oblong, to 1cm, patent, lanate outside. Autumn. Himal. var. *grandidentata* Rehd. & Wils. To 9m. Lvs 15cm+,

tri- or 5-foliolate; lfts to 7.5cm, ovate, acuminate, coarsely and irregularly dentate, grey-lanuginose, term. leaflet often deep-trilobed. Fls 2.5cm diam., 3-grouped in small pan.; sep. 4–5, white, narrow-oblong, tomentose outside. Spring–summer. China. Z5.

C. grata var. *argentilucida* (Lév. & Vaniot) Rehd. = *C. grata* var. *grandidentata.*

C. graveolens Lindl. Climber to 4m. Close to *C. orientalis* but with more finely divided lvs, spreading sep. and a heavy scent. Lvs 1–3-pinnate, glaucous green; lfts irregularly lobed or dentate. Fls 1–3-grouped; sep. 4, yellow, ovate-obovate, emarginate, 3–4cm. Summer. Himal. Z7.

C. grewiiflora DC. Climber. Lvs pinnately 3- or 5-foliolate; lfts to 10cm, broad-ovate, acute, usually 5-lobed, serrate, lanate. Fls broad-campanulate, tomentose, in many-fld pan.; sep. tawny-yellow, 4, ovate, to 3cm. Summer. Himal., Burm. Z8.

C. ×guascoi Lem. (*C. patens* ×*C. viticella.*) Tall climber. Lfts 5, glab. Fls to 8cm diam., solitary; sep. 4–6, obovate, violet-red, downy. Spring. Gdn origin. 'Minor': blue tinted carmine; 'Albert Victor': lavender with paler limb; 'Fair Rosamond': pink-white; 'The Queen': lilac-blue. Z7.

C. henryi Oliv. Climber to 4m. Lvs simple, ovate-oblong, to 12cm, acute or long-acuminate, cordate at base, entire or denticulate. Fls solitary, axillary; sep. 4, light pink, somewhat brown outside, oblong-elliptic, to 3cm, acute, patent. Winter. China, Vietnam, Taiwan. Z6.

C. heracleifolia DC. Woody-based perenn. herb to 1.5m; st. erect. Lvs trifoliolate; lfts to 6.5cm, rounded-ovate, irregularly and shallowly serrate, light-pubesc., term. leaflet to 12.5cm. Fls tubular, gibbous, in dense, axill. clusters; pedicels to 2.5cm, lanuginose; sep. to 2.5cm, 4, deep blue, recurved at apex, lanuginose. Summer–autumn. C & N China. 'Campanile': to 1.5m; fls 2cm, numerous, densely clustered, mid-blue. 'Côte d'Azur': hyacinth blue. 'Jaggards': fls deep blue. var. *davidiana* (Verl.) Hemsl. To 1m. Lvs coriaceous. Fls fragrant, in dense fascicles; sep. spreading, indigo-blue. 'Manchu': fls deep blue. 'Wyevale': lvs broad, much divided; fls small, deep blue, hyacinth-like, fragrant, clustered. var. *ichangensis* Rehd. & Wils. Lfts rounded at base, pubesc., esp. beneath. Fls blue, exterior silver-pubesc., interior dark blue. C & N China. Z3.

C. heracleifolia var. *stans* (Sieb. & Zucc.) Kuntze = *C. stans.*

C. hilarii Spreng. Vigorous climber. Lvs pinnately compound; lfts to 7.5cm, coriaceous, trilobed or tridentate. Fls white, to 2.5cm diam., in few-fld pan. Braz. to Arg. Z9.

C. hirsutissima Pursh. = *C. douglasii.*

C. hookeriana Allan. Differs from *C. paniculata* in lfts deep-lobed, sep. green-yellow to light yellow, staminate fls to 2.5cm diam. NZ. Z8.

C. indivisa Willd. = *C. paniculata.*

C. integrifolia L. Erect perenn. or subshrub to 1m. Lvs to 9cm, coriaceous, ovate-lanceolate, acute, glab. above, pubesc., beneath, prominently veined. Fls stellate-campanulate, flat, usually solitary, nodding; pedicels 4cm; sep. dark violet or blue, rarely white, 4, lanceolate, to 5cm, short-acuminate, patent, sinuate; fil. dilated, yellow. Summer. C Eur., SW Russia, W & C Asia. 'Alba': fls white. 'Olgae': fls scented, clear light blue, sep. long and recurved. 'Pastel Blue': fls delicate powder blue. 'Pastel Pink': fls soft light pink. 'Rosea': fls sugar pink, underside darker, scented. 'Tapestry': fls large, mauve to rich red. Z3.

C. integrifolia var. *pinnata* hort. = *C. ×divaricata.*

C. intricata Bunge. Close to *C. akebioides*, from which it differs in its foliage (closer to *C. orientalis*), sep. outspread, never reflexed, sometimes flushed purple beneath. N China, S Mong. Z5.

C. ×jackmanii T. Moore. (Probably *C. lanuginosa* ×*C. viticella.*) Climber to 4m. Lvs simple to trifoliolate; lfts to 12cm, broad-ovate, acute, cordate at base, deep green and glab. above, paler and light-pubesc. beneath. Fls velvety, violet-purple, in 3-fld cymes; sep. 4–6, to 6cm, broad-obovate, flat-patent, pubesc. outside; fil. green-white. Summer–autumn. Gdn origin. 'Alba': fls palest grey, double. 'Purpurea Superba': fls deep violet. 'Rubra': fls red to plum, double. Z5.

C. japonica Thunb. Scandent downy subshrub. Lvs ternate; lfts 5–8cm, coarsely toothed. Fls to 3cm, 1 to few-clustered, nodding, campanulate; peduncles to 10cm with a pair of small bracts; sep. purple-red to maroon, 4 broadly lanceolate, somewhat fleshy. Summer. Honshu, Jap. Z6.

C. ×jeuneiana Symons-Jeune. (*C. armandii* ×*C. finetiana.*) Vigorous scandent everg., foliage like *C. armandii.* Fls to 2.5cm diam., to 30-fld, axill. cymes; sep. 5–6, white, silver-pink beneath, oval-lanceolate. Summer. Z8.

C. ×jouiniana Schneid. (*C. heracleifolia* var. *davidiana* ×*C. vitalba.*) Vigorous, sprawling, semi-evergreen, woody-based perenn. or semi-scandent shrub to 4m. Lvs 3- or 5-foliolate; lfts to 10cm, ovate, coarse-dentate, weakly pubesc. Fls fragrant, in corymbs to 15cm, forming term. and axill. pan.; sep.

4, white to ivory deepening to opal then lilac or sky blue toward tips, strap-shaped, 2cm, somewhat recurved. Autumn. Gdn origin. 'Mrs Robert Brydon': lvs coarse; fls small, off-white, somewhat tinted blue. 'Oiseau Bleu': to 90cm, open habit; lvs small; fls mauve to pink. 'Praecox': vigorous; fls pale blue flushed silver. Z4.

C. kamtschatica Boug. = *C. fusca.*
C. koreana Komar. Prostrate decid. shrub. Lvs trifoliolate, thin-pubesc.; lfts to 8cm, cordate-ovate, long-acuminate, coarse-dentate, often trilobed or ternate. Fls to 3.5cm, solitary; peduncles to 15cm; sep. dull violet, elliptic-lanceolate, to 3cm, lanuginose on margins. Summer. Korea. Z6.
C. kousabotan Decne. = *C. stans.*
C. ladakhiana Grey-Wilson. Climber to 3m. st. tinged brown-purple. Lvs pinnate to bipinnate, lfts narrow, acuminate. Fls mostly grouped 3–7 in axils, pedicels 1.5–12cm; sep. spreading, narrowly elliptic, yellow to orange-yellow, usually with darker markings. Summer. India, Tibet. Z6.
C. lanuginosa Lindl. Decid. climber to 2m+. Lvs to 10cm, simple, ovate, acuminate, cordate, or trifoliolate with lfts to 12.5cm, thick, ovate to oval-lanceolate, acute, cordate at base, glab. above, soft-grey-lanate beneath. Fls term., solitary or 2–3-grouped in cymes; sep. white to pale lilac, 6–8, ovate or obovate, to 10cm, imbricate, expanded, lanuginose outside. Spring–autumn. China. 'Candida': fls large, sep. white, heavy, broad and round. Z6.
C. lasiandra Maxim. Vigorous decid. climber, to 4m. St. slender, angular, glutinous when young. Lvs to 20cm, 1–2× ternate; lfts to 10cm, ovate to lanceolate, slender-acuminate, coarse-serrate, sparse-lanuginose and deep green above, glab. and lighter beneath. Fls campanulate, usually 3-grouped, sometimes in axill. cymes to 5cm; peduncles to 7cm; sep. white, violet-traced, oblong, reflexed at apex; sta. yellow-white. Autumn. C & W China, Jap. Z6.
C. lasiantha Nutt. Climber to 5m. Lvs trifoliolate; lfts to 5cm, broad-ovate, rounded to subcordate at base, coarse-serrate to trilobed, teeth rounded, strigose beneath. Fls 1-, 3- or 5-grouped; peduncles to 12cm, bracteate; sep. white, broad-oblong, to 2.5cm, sericeous. W US. Z8.
C. × lawsoniana Moore & Jackm. (*C. lanuginosa × C. patens*). = C. Lanuginosa group.
C. leiocarpa Oliv. = *C. uncinata.*
C. ligusticifolia Torr. & A. Gray. Climber to 6m. Lvs pinnately 5–7-foliolate; lfts to 7cm, tough, ovate to lanceolate, long-acuminate, dentate and often trilobed, yellow-green, glab. or slightly setose. Fls in corymbose pan.; sep. white, to 1.5cm, patent, lanuginose. Summer–autumn. W N Amer. var. *californica* S. Wats. Lvs lanuginose or velutinous. Z5.
C. linearifolia Steud. = *C. microphylla.*
C. macropetala Ledeb. Decid. climber, to 1m. Lvs to 15cm, biternate; lfts to 4cm, ovate to lanceolate, acute, rounded or tapered, sometimes cordate at base, serrate to lobed, sub-glabrous. Fls nodding, solitary; pedicels 7.5cm+; sep. blue or violet-blue, 4, oblong-lanceolate, acuminate, to 5cm, pubesc.; staminodes numerous, lanuginose, outer violet-blue, inner blue-white. Spring–summer. N China, E Sib., Mong. 'Ballet Blanc': fls v. double, small, white. 'Blue Bird' (*C. macropetala × C. alpina* var. *sibirica*): 'Jan Lindmark': fls pale purple. 'Maidwell Hall' ('Lagoon'): fls semi-double, to 5cm diam., deep blue. 'Markham's Pink' ('Markhamii'): fls strawberry pink. 'Rosy O'Grady' (*C. macropetala × C. alpina*): fls to 7cm diam., semi-double, deep bright pink. 'White Swan' (*C. macropetala × C. alpina* var. *sibirica*): fls large, pure white. 'Snow Bird': fls white, late-flowering. Z5.
C. mandschurica Rupr. Decumbent or scandent perenn. Lvs 1–2-pinnatisect, upper lvs often ternate; lfts coriaceous, lanceolate-ovate, short-acuminate, cuneate or cordate at base, sparse-pubesc. beneath. Fls in many-fld, terminal and axill. infl.; pedicels bracteate; sep. white, oblong, to 1.5cm, white-pubesc. Summer. Jap., China. Z7.
C. marata J.B. Armstr. Low, slender, everg. climber. Lvs to 7cm, dull green, pubesc., trifoliolate; lfts to 2.5cm, linear, entire or 3+-lobed, lobes spathulate, sometimes pinnatifid, coriaceous. Fls solitary or 2–4-grouped, unisexual; sep. to 1.2cm, green-yellow, 4, sometimes 5, ovate-oblong, pubesc. beneath. NZ. Z8.
C. marmoraria Sneddon. Prostrate, dwarf everg. shrub. Lvs 1–4cm, ferny, trifoliolate; lfts deeply and closely divided, glossy green, rigid. Fls to 2cm diam., solitary or clustered, long-stalked, erect; sep. 5–8, green-white becoming creamy white; fil. green, flattened. NZ. Z8.
C. maximowicziana Franch. & Savat. = *C. terniflora.*
C. meyeniana Walp. Vigorous everg. climber to 5m+. St. wiry, purple-brown. Lvs trifoliolate; lfts broad-ovate to lanceolate, to 12.5cm, apex acuminate, cordate or rounded at base, coriaceous. Fls in large, lax, many-fld pan.; sep. white, 4, narrow-

oblong, 1.2cm, emarginate, lanate at margins, 3-veined; anth. gold-yellow. Spring. SE China. Z8.
C. microphylla DC. Climber. Lvs bi- or tri-ternate; lfts linear or lanceolate-oblong. Fls in short pan.; sep. 4, cream to 2.5cm. Aus. Z9.
C. montana Buch.-Ham. ex DC. V. vigorous, climber to 8m. Lvs trifoliolate; lfts to 10cm, ovate-lanceolate, acute, tapered or rounded at base, serrate, rarely entire, glab. Fls 1–5-grouped, axill.; peduncles to 21cm; sep. white or pink, 4, rarely 5, elliptic, to 4cm, patent, pubesc. on veins outside, lanuginose on margins. Spring–summer. C & W China, Himal. 'Alba': fls off-white. 'Alexander': fls to 10cm diam., creamy white; sta. yellow; scented. 'Peveril': fls to 8cm diam., pure white, sta. long and shimmering. 'Vera': lvs dark green; fls pink, fragrant. f. *grandiflora* Rehd. Exceptionally vigorous, to 12m; fls white, abundant. China. var. *rubens* Kuntze. New growth tinged purple, later bronzed; fls 5–6cm diam., pink-red. China. 'Elizabeth': fls palest pink; sta. yellow; vanilla-scented. 'Freda': lvs bronze; fls cherry pink, sep. edged crimson. 'Lilacina' (*C. montana* f. *grandiflora × C. montana* var. *rubens*): fls pale mauve. 'Marjorie': vigorous; fls semi-double, creamy pink tinted orange, sta. petal-like, salmon. 'Mayleen': lvs tinted bronze; fls large, to 7.5cm diam., pink, sep. gold. 'Odorata': fls palest pink, sweetly scented, abundant. 'Perfecta' (*C. montana* f. *grandiflora × C. montana* var. *rubens*): vigorous; br. deep brown tinted red; fls to 9cm diam., white flushed lilac. 'Picton's': fls small, deep satin pink, anth. gold. 'Pink Perfection': vigorous; fls small, deep pink, sep. round, profuse. 'Superba' (possibly *C. montana* var. *rubens × C.* 'Mrs Geo. Jackman'): vigorous; fls large, white. 'Tetrarose': tetraploid; st. tinted ruby; lvs bronze; fls large, to 10cm diam., rich rose. 'Undulata': strong-grower; fls white, flushed mauve, sep. reflexed, profuse. var. *wilsonii* Sprague. Fls small, white, fragrant, borne in great profusion. China. Z6.
C. montana var. *sericea* Franch. = *C. spooneri.*
C. nannophylla Maxim. Erect decid. shrub 120cm+, of dense habit. Lvs to 6.5cm, trilobed or deeply pinnatisect; lfts narrow, sharp-acuminate, glab. Fls to 3cm diam., solitary to 3-grouped, term.; sep. golden-yellow, brown at centre, 4, ovate or oval. China. Z7.
C. napaulensis DC. Everg. vine to 7m. Lvs 3- or 5-foliolate; lfts to 9cm, slender, oval-lanceolate, acute, entire, sparse-dentate or trilobed, glab. Fls narrow-campanulate, 6–10-grouped; pedicels to 4cm, bracteate; sep. 2.5cm, cream-yellow, 4, ovate, somewhat patent, sericeous; sta. numerous, to 2.5cm, anth. purple. Winter–spring. SW China, N India. Z8.
C. nutans Royle. Woody scrambler to 5m. Lvs pinnately 5–7-foliolate; lfts to 8cm, oblong, ovate, or lanceolate, usually 3–5-lobed, lanuginose. Fls campanulate, nodding, in paniculate infl.; sep. pale yellow, 4, oblong, to 4cm, lanuginose. Summer. Himal. Z8.
C. nutans hort., non Royle = *C. rehderiana.*
C. nutans var. *thyrsoidea* Rehd. & Wils. pro parte. = *C. rehderiana.*
C. occidentalis (Hornem.) DC. BELL RUE. Climbing or trailing shrub to 2.5m. Lvs trifoliolate; lfts 5–7cm, lanceolate-ovate, base cordate, entire to 2–3-lobed, often serrate. Fls solitary, long-stalked, nodding; sep. to 6cm, 4, lanceolate, blue to violet or rosy mauve, spreading, prominently veined; staminodes petaloid, narrow-spathulate. Spring. NE and NW N Amer. var. *dissecta* (C.L. Hitch.) Pringle. Seldom attaining 1m. Lfts deeply cut. Sep. to 3.25cm, rosy mauve to indigo. Washington State (Cascade Mts). var. *grosseserrata* (Rydb.) Pringle. Usually exceeding 3m. Lfts usually entire; sep. to 6cm, indigo, rarely white. Saskatch., Yukon, Colorado. Z6.
C. ochotensis (Pall.) Poir. = *C. alpina* var. *ochotensis.*
C. ochroleuca Ait. CURLY-HEADS. Perenn. or subshrub to 60cm. Lvs to 10cm, ovate, obtuse, entire or lobed, lanate beneath. Fls campanulate, erect, solitary; sep. 4, thick, ovate, 2.5cm+, recurved at apex, lanate, white inside, dull yellow and grey-pubesc. outside, sometimes maroon. Spring–summer. E N Amer. Z6.
C. odorata hort. = *C. × aromatica.*
C. 'Orange Peel' see *C. tibetana* ssp. *vernayi.*
C. oreophila Hance = *C. meyeniana.*
C. orientalis L. Decid. vine or scrambler to 8m. Lvs to 20cm, pinnately (3–)5–7(–9)-foliolate; lfts oblong to broad-elliptic, acute or acuminate, trilobed, entire or dentate, subcoriaceous, grey-green, glab. to coriaceous, glaucous. Fls solitary or in 3- to many-fld, pan.; peduncles to 10cm; sep. yellow or green-yellow, 4, oblong or elliptic, to 1.4cm, acuminate, patent, later recurved, thick, sericeous; sta. dilated above, maroon. Summer–autumn. Aegean, Ukr., SE Russia, Iran, W Himal., W China, Korea. Z6.
C. orientalis hort. non L. = *C. tibetana* ssp. *vernayi.*
C. orientalis var. *acutifolia* Hook. f. & Thomps. = *C. ladakhiana.*

C. orientalis var. *akebioides* Maxim. = *C. akebioides*.

C. orientalis var. *daurica* (Pers.) Kuntze = *C. ladakhiana*.

C. orientalis var. *glauca* Maxim. = *C. intricata*.

C. orientalis var. *serrata* Maxim. = *C. serratifolia*.

C. orientalis var. *tangutica* Maxim. = *C. tangutica*.

C. paniculata Gmel. Everg. climber 9m+. Lvs trifoliolate; lfts to 7.5cm, ovate, obtuse, rounded or cordate at base, entire, crenate or lobed, coriaceous, glossy. Fls unisexual, in lax, many-fld, axill. pan. to 30.5cm; pedicels to 11.5cm, bracteate; sep. white, 6–8, narrow-oblong, to 1.3cm; fil. yellow, anth. rose. Spring–summer. NZ. var. *lobata* Hook. Lvs lobed. Z5.

C. paniculata Thunb., non Gmel. = *C. terniflora*.

C. parviflora Cunn. Everg. woody climber. Lvs to 16cm, tawny pubesc., trifoliolate; lfts to 8cm, thin, ovate, acute to obtuse, entire to serrate, sometimes dissected. Fls unisexual, in axill., dichasial cymes; peduncles bracteate; sep. yellow, 5–8, imbricate, narrow-oblong to elliptic-oblong, to 2.2cm. NZ. Z8.

C. patens Morr. & Decne. Decid. climber to 4m. Lvs pinnately 3–5-foliolate; lfts to 10cm, ovate or oval-lanceolate, acute, slightly pubesc. Fls solitary, term.; pedicels ebracteate, lanuginose; sep. cream white, violet or bright blue, 6–8, overlapping, elliptic-obovate, to 8cm, long-acuminate; anth. purplebrown. Spring–summer. Jap., China. 'Fortunei': fls to 12cm diam., milky white turning pink, double. 'Standishii': fls to 14cm diam., pale lilac lustrous, centre lilac-rose. Z6.

C. pauciflora Nutt. Low-growing climber. Lvs 3- or 5-foliolate; lfts cordate to cuneate-obovate, to 2cm, usually tri-dentate or -lobed, glab. to tomentose. Fls solitary or in few-fld pan.; sep. 1.2cm, lanceolate-oblong. S Calif., N Baja Calif. Z9.

C. pavoliniana Pamp. Everg. climber. 4.5m. Lvs trifoliolate; lfts to 7.5cm, narrow-ovate, acute, rounded or cordate at base, glab. Fls to 4cm diam., 3–7-clustered, axill.; sep. pure white, 4, lanceolate. Summer. China. Z7.

C. peterae Hand.-Mazz. Woody climber. Lvs pinnate; lfts to 7.5cm, ovate or elliptic, acuminate, rounded or cordate at base, entire or 1–4-dentate, pubesc. Fls in many-fld, lax pan.; sep. white or yellow-white, oblong, to 1.2cm. China. Z7.

C. petriei Allan. Sprawling woody vine to 4m. Lvs bi or tripinnate; lfts to 3cm, coriaceous, ovate-oblong, obtuse, entire or bluntly 1–2-dentate. Fls axill., solitary or in few-fld bracteate pan.; sep. yellow-green, 6–8, ovate-oblong, 2cm, lanuginose. Summer–autumn. NZ. 'Limelight': ♂ selection with purple foliage and lime green fls. 'Princess': ♀ selection, similar to 'Limelight' but with smaller fls and showy seed heads. Z8.

C. phlebantha L.H. Williams. Shrub, erect to 60cm, sometimes trailing. Lvs to 7.5cm, pinnate, lanate; lfts 1.5cm, 5–9, coarsely 3–5-lobed, sessile, acute, broad-cuneate at base, green and sericeous above, dense white-lanate beneath. Fls solitary, axill.; pedicels to 8cm, bracts 2, simple or trilobed; sep. white, 5–7, red-veined, elliptic to obovate, to 2cm, cupped to patent, lanate outside; anth. yellow. Spring–summer. W Nepal. Z7.

C. pitcheri Torr. & A. Gray. Decid. climber to 3.5m+. Lvs pinnately 3–7-foliolate; lfts to 7.5cm, ovate, 2–3-lobed, rounded or cordate at base, thick, lanuginose beneath, term. leaflet often reduced to a tendril. Fls urceolate, solitary; pedicels to 10cm; sep. 4, thick, green-yellow inside, violet outside, ovate, to 3cm, acuminate, somewhat reflexed. Spring–autumn. SE US. Z4.

C. platysepala (Trautv. & C.A. Mey.) Hand.-Mazz. = *C. alpina* var. *ochotensis*.

C. potaninii Maxim. Woody-based climber to 3m. Lvs biternate; lfts to 7cm, ovate, acuminate, rounded or tapered at base, lobed or serrate. Fls solitary or paired in axill., bracteolate cymes; sep. white, sometimes yellow-flushed, 6, obovate, to 4cm, mucronate, patent, lanuginose outside, anth. yellow. Summer. SW China. var. *souliei* Finet & Gagnep. Fls larger. Z7.

C. potaninii var. *fargesii* (Franch.) Hand.-Mazz. = *C. fargesii*.

C. pseudoalpina (Kuntze) J. Coult. & A. Nels. Climber. Lvs bi or tri-foliolate; lfts to 4cm, lanceolate to ovate-lanceolate, acuminate, serrate or 2–3-lobed. Fls purple or blue, rarely white; sep. 4, lanceolate, to 5cm; staminodes present, with rudimentary anth. Spring–summer. S US. Z8.

C. pseudoalpina (Kuntze) Coulter & A. Nelson = *C. occidentalis*.

C. ×pseudococcinia Schneid. (*C. ×jackmanii ×C. texensis.*) Similar to *C. texensis* but to 3m with fls campanulate, sep. 4–6. 'Admiration': sep. salmon, interior white. 'Countess of Onslow': pink tinted mauve, sep. with central. red bar. 'Duchess of Albany': deep pink, erect, centre tinted brown, ventral side striped white. 'Duchess of York': pink, midstripe darker. 'Grace Darling': pale carmine pink, profuse. 'Sir Trevor Lawrence': bright crimson edged light violet, sta. cream. Z5.

C. ×pseudococcinia Schneid. (*C. ×jackmanii ×C. texensis*) = C. Texensis group.

C. pseudoflammula Schmalh. ex Lipsky. Erect perenn. to 70cm, resembling a herbaceous *C. flammula*. Lvs to 25cm, bipinnate; lfts to 5cm, oblong-ovate or oblong-linear, usually entire, glab.

or somewhat pubesc. Fls 2cm diam., fragrant, erect; sep. creamy white, narrow-obcuneate. Summer. S Russia, S & E Ukraine. Z5.

C. pubescens Benth. Climber. Lvs trifoliolate; lfts acuminate, subcordate at base, entire or coarse-serrate, sericeous. Fls small, solitary, paired or 3-grouped; sep. white, ovate, downy. Mex. Z9.

C. quinquefoliolata Hutch. Tall, everg. climber. Lvs pinnately 5-foliolate; lfts to 10cm, lanceolate to ovate-lanceolate, obtuse or short-acuminate, rounded or cordate at base, glab. except lanuginose, grooved midrib above. Fls axillary, in 3-, 5- or 7-fld cymes; sep. milk white, 4–6, narrow-oblong, to 0.7cm, lanceolate; sta. many, anth. yellow. Autumn. China. Z8.

C. ranunculoides Franch. Erect perenn. herb to 50cm or climber to 2m. Br. angular. Lvs trifoliolate or pinnately 5-foliolate, or simple and trilobed; lfts rounded-obovate or ovate, to 5cm, coarse-dentate, pubesc. Fls nodding, solitary or few-grouped; peduncles short, slender; sep. purple to pink, 4, oblong, 1.5cm, broad-patent, much reflexed,lanuginose, 3-ribbed. Spring –autumn. China. Z6.

C. recta L. Erect perenn. to 1.5m, much branched. Lvs to 15cm, pinnately 5–7-foliolate; lfts to 9cm, oval-lanceolate, acuminate, glab. and deep blue-green above, paler beneath. Fls 2cm diam., starry, erect, in many-fld, term. pan.; sep. milk white, 4, narrow-ovate or oblong-obcuneate, to 18mm, patent. Summer. S & C Eur. 'Grandiflora': fls large, v. abundant. 'Peveril': st. upright, to 90cm; fls profuse, scented. 'Plena': fls double. 'Purpurea': br. and lvs flushed bronze to red; fls white. Z3.

C. recta var. *mandshurica* Maxim. = *C. mandshurica*.

C. recta f. *fruticosa* (Turcz.) O. Kuntze. = *C. fruticosa*.

C. rehderiana Craib. Vigorous, decid. climber to 7.5m. Lvs to 23cm, pinnately 7- or 9-foliolate; lfts to 7.5cm, broad-ovate, acute, cordate or rounded at base, often trilobed, coarse-serrate, lanuginose. Fls campanulate, nodding, in several-fld, erect pan. to 23cm; sep. soft primrose yellow or pale green, 4, to 2cm, tips reflexed, velutinous outside. Summer–autumn. W China. Z6.

C. reticulata Walter. Woody climber to 3m. Lvs pinnately 3–7-foliolate; lfts to 7cm, broad-ovate to ovate-lanceolate, acute or obtuse and mucronate, coriaceous, slightly pubesc. Fls campanulate or urceolate, nodding, solitary; peduncles bracteate; sep. 2cm, lilac inside, grey-yellow and pubesc. outside, reflexed. Summer. SE US. Z6.

C. scottii T.C. Porter. = *C. douglasii* var. *scottii*.

C. serratifolia Rehd. Decid. scrambler to 3m. Lvs biternate; lfts to 7.5cm, ovate to lanceolate, long-acuminate, serrate, thin, glab. Fls star-shaped, 1–3 in cymes; sep. soft yellow, violet-tinged or -veined, 4, lanceolate or narrow-oblong, 2.5cm, acuminate, villous inside; sta. purple. Summer–autumn. Korea, NE China. Z6.

C. sibirica (L.) Mill. = *C. alpina* var. *sibirica*.

C. simsii Sweet = *C. crispa*.

C. simsii sensu Britt. & A. Br., non Sweet = *C. pitcheri*.

C. songarica Bunge. Erect or semi-scandent woody-based perenn. to 1.5m. Lvs to 10cm, linear to lanceolate, entire to serrate-dentate, thick, blue-green, glaucous. Fls numerous, nodding, paniculate; pedicels slender, to 5cm; sep. yellow-white, oblong-obovate or elliptic, to 2cm, lanuginose. Summer–autumn. Mong., Korea, S Sib., Turkestan. Z6.

C. spooneri Rehd. & Wils. Decid. climber to 6m. Shoots lanuginose. Lvs trifoliolate; lfts to 7cm, oval or ovate, serrate, yellow-sericeous beneath. Fls solitary or paired; pedicels to 18cm; sep. white, 4, rounded-oval or obovate, to 2.5cm, yellow-sericeous, outside. Spring. China. Z6.

C. spooneri 'Rosea' = *C. ×vedrariensis* 'Rosea'.

C. standishii Van Houtte = *C. patens* 'Standishii'.

C. stanleyi Hook. = *Clematopsis stanleyi*.

C. stans Sieb. & Zucc. Herbaceous subshrub or climber to 1.8m. Lvs trifoliolate; lfts to 15cm, broad-ovate, serrate, veins distinct, lanuginose. Fls tubular, clustered and axill., and in term. pan. to 25cm+; sep. 1cm, recurved, blue, white and tomentose outside. Jap. Z4.

C. stenophylla Fraser = *C. microphylla*.

C. stenosepala DC. = *C. glycinoides*.

C. tangutica (Maxim.) Korsh. Climber to 3m. Lvs pinnate or bipinnate; lfts to 8cm, oblong to lanceolate, sometimes 2–3-lobed, dentate, bright green. Fls campanulate to lantern-shaped, to 3.4cm, nodding, usually solitary; peduncles erect, to 15cm; sep. gold-yellow, 4, oval-lanceolate, to 4cm, acuminate, erect (i.e. pointing downwards), to spreading, exterior sericeous. Summer–autumn. Mong., NW China. 'Bill Mackenzie' (possibly *C. tangutica ×C. tibetana* ssp. *vernayi*): vigorous; fls large, yellow, thick-textured. 'Corry' (*C. tangutica* ssp. *obtusiuscula ×C. tibetana*): fls large, v. open, lemon. 'Drake's Form': fls large. 'Lambton Park': fls large, to 7cm diam., yellow, nodding. ssp. **obtusiuscula** (Rehd. & Wils.) Grey-Wilson. Young shoots

lanuginose-pubesc., lfts smaller, less serrate. Fls rich yellow, solitary, opening widely; peduncles to 10cm, lanuginose; sep. to 3cm, obtuse-elliptic or short-acuminate. China. Z5.

C. tenuiloba A. Gray. Procumbent vine. Lvs biternate; lfts to 2.5cm, usually pinnatisect, seg. ovate or lanceolate. Sep. blue or purple, to 4cm, acuminate, patent. W US. Z4.

C. ternata Mak. = *C. japonica*.

C. terniflora DC. Erect perenn. to 5m; st. tangle-forming. Lvs pinnately 3–5-foliolate; lfts to 10cm, cordate or ovate, entire, subglabrous, dark green. Fls 3cm diam. in many-fld. pan. to 10cm; sep. white, 4, linear. Autumn. Jap. Z6.

C. terniflora var. *mandschurica* (Rupr.) Ohwi = *C. mandschurica*.

C. texensis Buckl. Scandent subshrub or herbaceous perenn. to 2m. Lvs glaucous, pinnately 4–8-foliolate; lfts to 8cm, ovate to rounded, sometimes lobed, tough, blue-green, term. leaflet reduced to a tendril. Fls urceolate, much narrowed towards mouth, solitary, nodding; peduncles to 15cm; sep. to 3cm, scarlet-red or carmine, thick, narrow-ovate, tips reflexed. Summer–autumn. SW US. 'Major': fls to 3cm, exterior scarlet, interior pale yellow or white, thick-textured. 'Passiflora': fls to 2cm, scarlet throughout, rather more thinly textured. Z5.

C. thunbergii Steud. Scandent. Lvs pubesc., pinnate or ternate; lfts ovate, serrate or cut. Fls to 5cm diam. in many-fld pan.; sep. lanceolate, acuminate, patent. S Afr. Z9.

C. tibetana Kuntze. Differs from *C. orientalis* in the finely cut, smooth and glaucous foliage and thickly textured pale yellow fls. N India. ssp. *vernayi* (Fisch.) Grey-Wilson. Lvs v. glaucous. Fls to 5cm, solitary or in threes, nodding, narrow-campanulate then outspread; sep. green-yellow to burnt orange, thickly fleshy, somewhat rugulose; sta. dark purple. Nepal, Tibet. The thick sep. of this ssp. have won it the soubriquet ORANGE PEEL CLEMATIS. 'Orange Peel' has also been applied as a cv. name. Z6.

C. ×*triternata* DC. (*C. flammula* × *C. viticella*.) Climber to 4m. Lvs simple or bipinnate; lfts entire. Fls 3cm diam., in term. pan.; sep. lilac, 6. Gdn origin. 'Rubromarginata': fls white, edged wine red, profuse. Z6.

C. troutbeckiana Spring = *C. versicolor*.

C. tubulosa Turcz. Climbing shrub. Lvs trifoliolate, lfts ovate to rhomboidal, serrate. Infl. paniculate-corymbose; fls campanulate; sep. pale blue-lilac, slightly recurved at tips. Late summer. China. Z6.

C. uncinata Benth. Semi-evergreen climber to 4.5m. Lvs 3- or 5-divided, each division trifoliolate; lfts to 10cm, ovate to ovate-lanceolate, acute, blue-green, somewhat glaucous beneath, 3–5-veined. Fls 2.5cm diam., in many-fld, cymes grouped into pan. to 30cm diam.; sep. cream white, narrow-oblong; anth. linear, yellow. Summer. C China. Z6.

C. ×*vedrariensis* Vilm. (*C.* ×*chrysocoma* × *C. montana* var. *rubens*.) Closely resembles *C. montana* var. *rubens*. Vigorous everg. climber, 6m. Lvs trifoliolate; lfts to 6.5cm, ovate, acute, rounded or broad-cuneate at base, often trilobed, coarse-serrate, dull purple-green and pale-pubesc. above, paler and more densely pubesc. beneath. Fls to 6.5cm, solitary, axill.; peduncles slender, to 12.5cm, pubesc.; sep. rose, lilac or pink, 4, occas. 5–6, rounded-oval, patent; sta. yellow. Spring–summer. Gdn origin. 'Hidcote': fls small, deep pink. 'Highdown': fls pink. 'Rosea': fls large, to 10cm diam., pale pink. Z6.

C. veitchiana Craib. Closely resembles *C. rehderiana*. Lvs bipinnate; lfts to 6cm, often 20+, ovate to oval-lanceolate, ternate or 3-lobed, incised sericeous beneath. Fls yellow-white, campanulate, in bracteate pan. Autumn. W China. Z6.

C. venosa (Carr.) K. Koch. = *C.* ×*francofurtensis*.

C. verrieriensis hort. = *C.* ×*vedrariensis*.

C. versicolor Small. LEATHER FLOWER. Climber to 3.5m. Lvs pinnately 8-foliolate; lfts to 6cm, oval-oblong, blunt, cordate at base, often 2–3-lobed, coriaceous, blue-green, glab. above, glaucous beneath. Fls ovoid-campanulate, nodding, solitary; sep. purple or blue, 4, thin, lanceolate, 2cm, tips recurved. Summer. S US. Z6.

C. ×*violacea* hort. = *C.* ×*triternata*.

C. viorna L. LEATHER FLOWER; VASE VINE. Scandent shrub or subshrub to 3m. Lvs 5–7-foliolate; lfts to 7cm, ovate to elliptic-lanceolate, often cordate at base, entire or somewhat lobed, deep green, glab. Fls urceolate, nodding, solitary; peduncles to 7.5cm; sep. violet or dull purple, 4, v. thick, coriaceous, to 3cm, acute, recurved, margins grey-white-pubesc. Spring–summer. E N Amer. Z4.

C. virginiana L. WOODBINE; LEATHER FLOWER; VIRGIN'S BOWER; DEVIL'S-DARNING-NEEDLE. Decid. semi-woody climber to 6m. Lvs 3(–5)-foliolate; lfts to 9cm, broad-ovate, acuminate, rounded or cordate at base, coarsely serrate or lobed, glab. Fls in many-fld, axill. pan. to 15cm; sep. dull white, 4, rarely 5, thin, oblong or spathulate, to 1.5cm, patent, pubesc. outside. Summer–autumn. E N Amer. Z4.

C. vitalba L. TRAVELLER'S JOY; OLD MAN'S BEARD. Decid. semi-woody climber to 30m. Lvs pinnately (3–)5-foliolate; lfts ovate, rarely linear-lanceolate, dentate or subentire, pilose to glab. Fls in axill. pan.; sep. to 1cm, green-white, oblong, obtuse, white-tomentose. Achenes with long, plumose styles. Summer. Eur., Leb., Cauc., N Iran, Afghan. Z4.

C. viticella L. Decid. semi-woody climber to 3.5m. Lvs to 12.5cm, pinnately trifoliolate; lfts to 6.5cm, lanceolate to broad-ovate, often 2–3-lobed, somewhat coriaceous, pubesc. Fls slightly nodding; pedicels to 10cm; sep. blue, purple or rose-purple, 4, obovate, to 4cm, patent, undulate. Summer–autumn. S Eur. 'Coerulea': fls violet. 'Marmorata': fls small, blue-grey. 'Nana': bushy, non-climbing. 'Plena': fls double, violet. 'Purpurea': fls plum. 'Purpurea Plena Elegans': fls to 8cm diam., v. double, deep violet. 'Rubra': fls small, delicate, wine red. 'Rubra Grandiflora': fls large, sep. 6, carmine red. f. *albiflora* (Kuntze) Rehd. Fls white. Z6.

C. wilfordii (Maxim.) Komar. = *C. serratifolia*.

C. cvs.

FLORIDA GROUP. Woody climbers, 2.5–3m, flowering spring to summer on previous year's wood; fls usually semi-double or double, spring–summer but usually single later in the season, 15–22cm diam., white to lilac and deep violet. 'Belle of Woking' (double, mauve flushed silver, rosette form, sta. yellow), 'Duchess of Edinburgh' (double, small, to 15cm diam., rose-shaped, white), 'Haku Ookan' (fls semi-double, rich violet, sta. white), 'Kathleen Dunford' (large, to 22cm diam., semi-double, rosy purple, sta. gold), 'Miss Crawshay' (small, to 15cm diam., semi-double, mauve-pink, sta. gold), 'Proteus' (semi-double, deep coral pink), 'Sylvia Denny' (double, white, sta. pink).

JACKMANII GROUP. Woody climbers, 2–6m, flowering summer to autumn, on new shoots; fls 12–20cm diam., sep. usually 4, wide to narrow and pointed, shell pink, red, blue to purple. 'Comtesse de Bouchard' (strong-growing; fls almost circular, satin pink flushed lilac, abundant, sta. cream), 'Gipsy Queen' (fls to 15cm diam., rich purple with 3 red stripes, abundant), 'Hagley Hybrid' (fls cup-shaped, sep. pointed, shell pink, abundant, sta. brown), 'Madame Baron Veillard' (vigorous; sep. pointed, lilac-pink, profuse, long-lasting, sta. white), 'Madame Edouard André' (low; sep. acuminate, deep claret, sta. cream), 'Madame Grange' (sep. incurving, purple-tinted bronze with brown midstripe, silky pink beneath), 'Mrs Cholmondeley' (vigorous, to 5m; fls to 22cm diam., sep. long and narrow, lavender, profuse, anth. brown; long-flowering), 'Niobe' (sep. pointed, dark velvety ruby, darker in bud, sta. gold), 'Perle d'Azur' (vigorous, to 5m; fls sky blue, sep. slightly corrugated, semi-pendent, profuse, sta. green), 'Rouge Cardinal' (low; fls to 18cm diam., 6 recurving and blunt sep. deep crimson, darker in bud, sta. brown), 'Star of India' (to 6m; fls to 12cm diam., plum with red midstripe, abundant, sta. yellow).

LANUGINOSA GROUP. Woody climbers, 2.5–5m, flowering on short side-shoots on current year's growth; fls v. large, loosely arranged, summer to autumn, appearing consecutively, single or double, 15–22cm diam., white through cream to lavender or deep red. 'Beauty of Worcester' (small, double, deep blue tinted violet, sta. creamy white), 'Bracebridge Star' (fls lavender with crimson midstripe, sta. plum), 'Edith' (clear white, sta. dark red), 'Fair Rosamond' (small, to 15cm diam., white flushed blue with red midstripe, sta. purple; scented), 'General Sikorski' (fls blue, edges crenulate, sta. gold), 'Henryi' (robust; fls large, to 20cm diam., to 8 acuminate sep. creamy white, sta. coffee-coloured; long-flowering), 'Horn of Plenty' (cup-shaped, rosy purple with darker midstripe, sta. plum), 'Lady Caroline Nevill' (semi-double, soft lilac with darker midstripe, sta. beige), 'Marie Boisselet' ('Madame le Coultre'); (vigorous, to 5m; sep. to 6, overlapping, flat, palest pink fading to pure white; anth. pale yellow to pale brown), 'Nelly Moser' (large, to 22cm diam., sep. pointed, palest lilac with carmine midstripe, anth. rusty-red), 'Silver Moon' (palest pearly lilac, sta. yellow), 'William Kennet' (vigorous; sep. to 8, overlapping, edges crimped, lavender blue with darker midstripe, abundant).

PATENS GROUP. Woody climbers, 2–3.5m, flowering in spring on old wood; fls with pointed sep., usually single, 15–25cm diam., sep. wide and overlapping to pointed, flat to wavy edged, white to purple, often with darker midstripe. 'Barbara Dibley' (small; sep. long, deep red to violet, midstripe darker, sta. plum), 'Barbara Jackman' (small, to 16cm diam., 6 broad, acuminate sep., violet with dark pink to red midstripe, anth. cream), 'Bees Jubilee' (pinky mauve, midstripe deep carmine sta. brown), 'Captain Thuilleaux' ('Souvenir de Captain Thuilleaux'); (sep. pointed, cream with broad strawberry midstripe, anth. brown), 'Countess of Lovelace' (double, lilac-blue, rosette-form), 'Daniel Deronda' (semi-double, violet-blue, sta. cream), 'Dawn' (compact, fls large, pearly pink sep. overlapping, sta. carmine), 'Doctor Ruppell' (rose madder with carmine midstripe, sta. gold), 'Elsa Spath' ('Xerxes') (fls large, to 20cm diam., sep. to 6, deep violet with dark purple midstripe, sta. plum), 'Gillian Blades' (fls large, to 22cm diam., pure white, sep. flat with frilled edges), 'H.F. Young' (to 3.5m; sep. pointed and overlapping, Wedgwood blue, sta. cream, early-flowering, abundant), 'Lasurstern' (to 3.5m; to 22cm diam., sep. narrow, wavy-edged, rich blue, anth. white; long-flowering), 'Lincoln Star' (to 2m; sep. pointed, raspberry pink, centre plum, anth. burgundy), 'Lord Nevill' (dark violet blue, crenulate, sta. red), 'Miss Bateman' (fls small, to 15cm diam., stellate, 8 overlapping sep. creamy white, sta. rusty red), 'Mrs George Jackman' (semi-double, sep. overlapping and elliptic, creamy white, abundant, anth. brown), 'Prins Hendrik' (to 25cm diam., sep. pointed and wavy-edged, lavender, sta. purple), 'Richard Pennell' (fls saucer-shaped, sep. overlapping, rosy purple, anth. red and gold), 'The President' (to 18cm diam., saucer-shaped, 8 sep., purple with paler midstripe, stigma and fil. off-white), 'Vyvyan Pennell' (double, large, deep violet, later single and paler, sta. gold), 'Wada's Primrose' ('Moonlight', 'Yellow Queen'); (fls small, to 15cm diam., primrose with yellow anth.), 'Walter Pennell' (double, deep pink flushed mauve, sta. buff).

TEXENSIS GROUP. Non-scandent shrubs or woody-based semi-herbaceous perennials, flowering abundantly on young shoots over a long summer period; fls campanulate. 'Duchess of Albany' (fls tubular, nodding, bright pink to lilac at margins; summer–early autumn. 'Etoile Rex': fls to 5cm, nodding, bell-shaped, cerise to mauve, margin silver-pink; summer–early autumn. 'Gravetye Beauty': fls cerise to scarlet, tubular-campanulate, then outspread. 'Lady Bird Johnson': fls dusky red, later edged purple, sta. creamy yellow. 'The Princess of Wales': fls deep vivid pink, sta. creamy yellow.

VITICELLA GROUP. Woody climbers, 2.5–6m, flowering abundantly, short fl. season, fls appearing consecutively, 15cm diam., single to double, white to red and deep purple with coloured midstripe or veins. 'Alba Luxurians' (creamy white, sep. tipped green, centres dark; vigorous), 'Ascotiensis' (large, to 20cm diam., bright blue, sep. pointed, sta. green), 'Duchess of Suther-land' (small, claret with lighter midstripe, sta. gold), 'Ernst Mark-ham' (to 15cm diam., sep. blunt-tipped, vibrant petunia red, profuse, sta. gold), 'Etoile Violette' (fls deep purple, sep. blunt-tipped, sta. gold), 'Huldine' (vigorous, to 6m; fls to 10cm diam., pearly white with lilac midstripes beneath, profuse), 'Kermesina' (fls wine red, sta. brown), 'Lady Betty Balfour' (to 6m, vigorous; deep violet-blue, sta. yellow. late-flowering), 'Little Nell' (to 5cm diam., white with creamy midstripe shading to lavender at margins, abundant), 'Madame Julia Correvon' (to 8cm diam., ruby red, sep. twisted and recurved), 'Margot Koster' (to 2.5m; fls to 10cm diam., deep lilac-pink, sep. spaced, abundant), 'Mary Rose' (fls small, double, spiky, dusky amethyst, profuse), 'Minuet' (large, cream, sep. edged lavender; st. long and erect), 'Mrs Spencer Castle' (small, double, heliotrope pink, sta. gold), 'Royal Velours' (fls deep velvety purple), 'Venosa Violacea' (sep. boat-shaped, violet with paler centre, veins dark purple), 'Ville de Lyon' (vigorous; sep. wide and rounded, carmine-red edged dark-er, profuse; sta. gold), 'Voluceau' (petunia red, sta. yellow).
→Atragene and Viorna.

Clematoclethra Franch. Actinidiaceae. 10 scandent shrubs, usu-ally dioecious, decid. Lvs simple, usually dentate. Fls c1cm diam., solitary or in axill. cymes, white; sep. 5; pet. 5; sta. 10, fil. white. Fr. a berry, c1cm diam. C & W Asia. Z6.
C. integrifolia Maxim. Shoots to 8m, smooth. Lvs to 6.5cm, ovate to ovate-oblong, dentate, base rounded, smooth and glaucous beneath. Fr. black. W China.
C. lasioclada Maxim. Shoots to 6m, pilose. Lvs to 10cm, ovate, acuminate, dentate, rounded to cordate at base, midrib pubesc. above, sparsely pubesc. and light green beneath. Fr. black. W China.
C. scandens Franch. Shoots to 8m, brown-setose. Lvs to 12.5cm, ovate-lanceolate to oblong, acute, dentate, rounded or narrowed at base, veins setose beneath. Fr. red. W China.

Clematopsis Bojer ex Hutch. Ranunculaceae. 18 Clematis-like shrubs. Trop. and S Afr., Madag. Z10.
C. stanleyi (Hook.) Hutch. Tall shrub, hairy throughout. Lvs to 15cm, 1–3-pinnate; lfts oblong-cuneate, incised to toothed, sericeous. Fls to 6cm diam., pink to pale blue-purple, in droop-ing pan. Summer. S Afr.
→Clematis.

Clementine Citrus reticulata.

Clementsia Rose.
C. rhodantha (Gray) Rose = Rhodiola rhodantha.
C. semenowii Boriss. = Rhodiola semenowii.

Cleome L. SPIDER FLOWER. Capparidaceae. c150 ann. or perenn. herbs. Lvs usually palmatifid. Infl. a rac., term. or lat., 1- to many-fld; sep. free; pet. 4, subequal, usually clawed; sta. usu-ally 6, fil. slender, long-exserted. Pantrop. & subtrop. zones.
C. aculeata L. Ann. herb to 90cm, glandular-pubesc. lfts 3, to 3.5cm, ovate-elliptic to obovate or oblong. Infl. 1- to few-fld; pet. to 6mm, white or pale yellow, elliptic or obovate; fil. green to 5mm. Mex. & S Amer. to WIndies.
C. gigantea L. = C. viridiflora.
C. gynandra L. Ann. herb to 130cm, glandular-pubesc. Lfts 3–7, to 7cm, rhomboid or oblanceolate to elliptic, glab. to glandular-pubesc., dentate to glandular-ciliate. Infl. to 40cm, few- to many-fld, pet. to 20mm, white or pink, sometimes yellow or purple, broadly ovate or suborbicular; fil. to 25mm. Trop. & subtrop.
C. hassleriana Chodat. SPIDER FLOWER; SPIDER PLANT. Ann. herb to 150cm, glandular-pubesc. Lfts 5–7, to 12cm, ovate to lanceolate, acute, entire to minutely denticulate, glandular-pubesc. Infl. dense, term.; pet. to 3cm, white to pink or purple, broadly oblong to suborbicular; fil. exceeding pet. Parag., Arg., S Braz., Urug. 'Helen Campbell': fls white. 'Violet Queen': fls purple.
C. lutea Hook. Ann. herb to 120cm, glab. Lfts 5, to 5cm, oblong or oblong-lanceolate, acute or rounded to obtuse, entire. Fls yellow. W N Amer.
C. monophylla L. Ann. herb to 50cm, erect, branched, glandular-pubesc. Lvs to 7cm, simple, ovate-oblong to linear-lanceolate, entire, pubesc. Infl. terminal; pet. to 9mm, white to pink or pale mauve, with a transverse yellow band, spathulate; fil. to 1cm. Trop. & S Afr., S Asia.
C. pentaphylla L. = C. gynandra.
C. pungens Willd. = C. spinosa.
C. rubella Burchell. Ann. herb to 40cm, erect, branched, glandular-pubesc. Lfts 5–7, to 2cm, linear-spathulate.Infl. term.; pet. to 8mm, rose to mauve-pink, oblanceolate, rounded; fil. to 8mm, rose-pink. S Afr.
C. serrulata Pursh. ROCKY MOUNTAIN BEE PLANT. Ann. herb to 1m, erect, simple or branched, glab. Lfts 3, to 5cm, oblong to elliptic-lanceolate. Fls deep pink, sometimes white. W N Amer.
C. speciosa Raf. Herb to 1.5m, erect, glab. Lfts 7 to 12cm, lanceolate, acuminate. Infl. to 40cm; pet. to 30mm, bright pink or rose-purple to white, lanceolate to oblanceolate-spathulate; fil. to 5cm. Mex. to N S Amer.
C. speciosissima Deppe ex Lindl. = C. speciosa.
C. spinosa hort. non Jacq. = C. hassleriana.
C. spinosa Jacq. Differs from C. hassleriana in pet. to 2cm, dingy white, ± downy, oblong to obovate-spathulate. S Amer., W In-dies.
C. violacea L. Herb to 5cm. St. erect, often branched. Lfts linear or linear-lanceolate. Infl. bracteate; pet. 4, violet, sometimes yellow, unequal, larger to 6mm. SW Eur., NW Afr.
C. viridiflora Schreb. Shrub to 2m, erect, pubesc.; gland. when young. Lfts 7, to 18cm, oblanceolate to lanceolate-oblong. Infl. to 60cm, term.; fls green-yellow; pet. to 5cm, linear; fil. to 7.5cm, green tinged red towards apex. Trop. Amer. Z10.
C. viscosa L. TICKWEED. Ann. herb to 15cm, erect, glandular-pubesc., usually branched, viscid. Lfts 3–5 to 6cm, oblong to elliptic-oblanceolate. Fls few, in axils of reduced lvs; pet. to 14mm, pale to bright yellow, obovate to oblong, rounded, glab.; fil. to 8mm. Pantrop.
→Gynandropsis.

Cleretum N.E. Br.
C. cuneifolium (Jacq.) N.E. Br. = Dorotheanthus bellidiformis.
C. gramineum (Haw.) N.E. Br. = Dorotheanthus gramineus.
C. limpidum (Ait.) N.E. Br. = Dorotheanthus bellidiformis.

Clerodendrum L. Verbenaceae. c400 trees, shrubs or vines. Lvs entire or dentate. Cymes terminal or axill., often in pan. or corymbs; cal. campanulate or tubular, truncate or 5-lobed; cor. salverform, tube cylindrical, straight or curved, limb 5-lobed, spreading or reflexed; sta. 4, long-exserted. Fr. a drupe. Trop. and subtrop. regions, mostly Asia and Afr. Z10 unless specified.
C. aculeatum (L.) Schldl. Vine-like shrub, br. puberulent, spinescent. Lvs to 7.5cm, lanceolate or elliptic-obovate to oblong, glab. or puberulent above, puberulent beneath. Cymes axill., few-fld; cor. white, tube to 18mm, lobes to 8mm, reflexed; fil. purple. W Indies.
C. bakeri Gürke. Shrub to 1.5m, br. erect or ascending, glab. Lvs to 15cm, obovate or elliptic to oblong, cuspidate, base, glab., serrate. Cymes many-fld, long-stalked; cor. white, fragrant, tube to 36mm, lobes to 4mm, obovate. Trop. Afr.
C. blumeanum Schauer = C. buchananii.
C. buchananii (Roxb.) Walp. MATA AJAM; KEMBANG; BOGANG. Shrub to 2m, erect. Lvs to 30cm, ovate, patent-pubesc. Cymes

in a pan. to 20cm; cor. bright red, tube to 3cm, lobes to 1.5cm. Fr. blue-violet. Java.

C. bungei Steud. GLORY FLOWER. Suckering erect shrub to 2m, glab. to pubesc. Lvs to 23cm, ovate or ovate-deltoid, dark purple-green above, serrate, sparsely strigulose, muskily scented. Cymes in rounded term. pan. to 15cm, puberulent; fls sweetly fragrant; cor. rose to red to purple, tube to 2.5cm, limb to 14mm diam. China, N India, nat. Mex., S Amer. Z8.

C. cunninghamii Benth. Erect shrub. Lvs to 25cm, broadly ovate to oblong, base rounded or subcordate, pubesc. beneath. Cymes in a term. corymb, adprsesed-pubesc., to 25cm diam., many-fld; cor. white or yellow-white, tube to 6cm, lobes to 1cm. Fr. black. Aus., Java.

C. fallax Lindl. = *C. speciosissimum*.

C. floribundum R. Br. LOLLY BUSH. Tree or shrub to 6.5m, erect, glab. Lvs to 18cm, ovate to narrowly elliptic, acute, base acute or subcordate. Infl. term. or axill., a corymb or pan.; fls fragrant; cor. white, tube to 35mm, lobes to 7mm, ovate. Fr. purple or black-purple. Aus., New Guinea.

C. foetidum Bunge = *C. bungei*.

C. fragrans (Vent.) R. Br. = *C. philippinum*.

C. glabrum E. Mey. Small tree or shrub to 12m, much-branched. Lvs to 12.5cm, oblong or ovate to ovate-elliptic, glab. or somewhat pubesc. beneath, lustrous dark green above. Cymes term. or axill., to 7.5cm, densely many-fld, in pan.; fls fragrant; cor. white or pale pink, tube to 8mm, exterior glab. puberulent, lobes to 4mm, obovate. Fr. white to yellow. Afr.

C. hastatum (Roxb.) Lindl. Erect shrub to 2m. Lvs to 25cm, deeply 3 or 5-lobed, lobes ovate or ovate-oblong, base cordate or hastate, villous above, pubesc. beneath. Cymes in a pan. to 15cm, villous, many-fld; cal. tinged red-purple; cor. white or yellow-white, tube to 13cm, exterior patent-villous, lobes to 2cm. Fr. blue-black. SE Asia.

C. heterophyllum (Poir.) R. Br. Shrub or small tree, puberulent to adprescent. Lvs to 10cm, elliptic or elliptic-lanceolate, glab. to puberulent, densely punctate, entire or with few teeth. Cymes to 4cm, axill., forming a corymb, few-fld, grey-puberulent; cor. white, tube to 11mm, exterior minutely puberulent, lobes to 6mm. Masc. Is.

C. indicum (L.) Kuntze. Shrub to 2m, erect, slightly branched. Lvs to 23cm, elliptic or oblong to oblanceolate, entire, glab. Cymes in a term. pan. to 45cm, few-fld, glab.; cor. white or yellow-white, tube to 14cm, glab., curved, lobes to 1cm. Fr. dark blue. India, Burm., nat. W Indies, N S Amer.

C. inerme (L.) Gaertn. Shrub erect or straggling, pubesc. Lvs to 14cm, ovate-oblong to elliptic-lanceolate, entire, slightly pubesc. beneath, gland. Cymes usually axill.; cor. pure white, tube to 3.5cm, sometimes pale lilac, glab., lobes to 5mm; sta. and style red. Fr. black. India, China, Malaysia, Aus., Polyn.

C. infortunatum L. Shrub or small tree to 5m, br. adpressed-pubesc. Lvs to 25cm, ovate, short-acuminate, base truncate or subcordate, pubesc. or pilose. Pan. term. to 22cm, adpressed-pubesc.; cor. white, tube to 30mm, exterior ferruginous-villous, limb to 5cm diam. Fr. black or black-violet. Ceylon, Andaman Is.

C. japonicum (Thunb.) Sweet. Shrub to 2.5m. Shoots glab., 4-angled. Lvs to 20cm, cordate, acuminate, glab. above, scaly beneath, dentate. Pan. to 25cm; cor. scarlet, tube to 2cm, lobes 2cm, obovate, rounded. India, China, Jap.

C. kaempferi (Jacq.) Sieb. ex Steud. Shrub to 3m. Lvs to 22cm, broadly ovate, acute or acuminate, base cordate, entire to denticulate, scaly beneath, lustrous deep green above. Pan. term. to 35cm, many-fld; fls fragrant; cor. bright scarlet, sometimes white, tube to 15mm, lobes to 5mm. Fr. red to blue or blue-black. India, China.

C. nutans Wallich ex D. Don = *C. wallichii*.

C. paniculatum L. PAGODA FLOWER. Erect shrub to 130cm. Lvs to 40cm, orbicular to ovate, base cordate, lower lvs lobed, upper entire or crenate-dentate. Pan. term., broad, much-branched, to 30cm; cor. orange-red or scarlet, tube to 17mm, lobes to 5mm, spreading. SE Asia.

C. philippinum Schauer. GLORY BOWER. Shrub to 3m, pubesc. or tomentose, br. angular. Lvs to 25cm, broadly ovate to ovate-triangular, acute or acuminate, base cordate to truncate, densely pubesc. beneath, dentate. Cymes in term. corymbs, many-fld; fls fragrant; cor. to 2.5cm, pink or white, sometimes tinged blue. China, Jap., nat. tropics.

C. phlomidis L. f. Shrub or small tree to 9m, br. pubesc. Lvs to 7cm, ovate to rhomboid or deltoid, puberulent to glabrescent, entire or serrate. Cymes axill. and term., to 9cm, pubesc.; cor. white or yellow-white to red, tube to 25mm, exterior slightly puberulent. Fr. black. S Asia.

C. phlomoides Willd. = *C. phlomidis*.

C. schweinfurthii var. *bakeri* (Gürke) Thomas = *C. bakeri*.

C. speciosissimum Van Geert ex Morr. Erect shrub to 4m, st. tetragonal. Lvs to 30cm, broadly ovate, acute or acuminate,

base cordate, densely pubesc., deep green. Cymes in an erect term. pan. to 45cm; cor. bright scarlet, tube to 3.5cm, lobes to 2.5cm. Fr. dark blue. Java.

C. ×speciosum Dombr. (*C. splendens* ×*C. thomsoniae*.) JAVA GLORY BEAN; PAGODA FLOWER. Resembles *C. thomsoniae* except cal. pale red or pink; cor. deep rose shaded violet.

C. splendens G. Don ex James. Twining shrub to 2m, glab. Lvs to 18cm, broadly ovate to oblong, entire, lustrous dark green above, paler beneath. Cymes in a term. pan., many-fld; cor. bright red to scarlet, tube to 2cm, lobes to 2cm, obovate. Trop. Afr.

C. squamatum Vahl = *C. kaempferi*.

C. thomsoniae Balf. f. BAG FLOWER; BLEEDING HEART VINE. Twining shrub to 4m, glab. Lvs to 17cm, ovate to ovate-oblong, entire. Cymes term. and axill., 8 to 20-fld, pubesc.; cal. white; cor. dark red, tube to 2cm, glandular-pubesc., lobes to 1cm. Fr. dark red to black. Trop. W Afr.

C. tomentosum (Vent.) R. Br. LOLLY BUSH. Everg. shrub or tree to 10m, velvety-tomentose. Lvs to 14cm, lanceolate to ovate-elliptic, tomentose. Fls in term. corymbs; cor. white, tube to 25mm, lobes to 7mm, usually tomentose, anth. yellow. Fr. black. Aus.

C. trichotomum Thunb. Decid. rounded tree or shrub to 7m, shoots downy. Lvs to 20cm, ovate, entire or sparsely dentate, pubesc., foetid. Cymes to 22cm diam., fragrant, drooping on slender stalks in upper lf-axils; cal. red; cor. white, to 3cm diam., lobes narrowly oblong. Fr. bright blue. Jap. Z8. var. *fargesii* (Dode) Rehd. is a hardier plant with glab. growth and freely fruiting.

C. ugandense Prain. BUTTERFLY BUSH. Glab., erect shrub to 3.5m. Lvs to 10cm, narrowly obovate or elliptic, dentate. Pan. term. to 15cm; cal. crimson; cor. to 2.5cm, violet blue, to pale blue; fil. blue-purple, anth. blue. Trop. Afr.

C. viscosum Vent. Erect shrub to 2m, softly pubesc. Lvs to 25cm, ovate, subentire to dentate, adpressed-pubesc. Pan. term. to 25cm; cal. bright red in fr.; cor. tube to 13mm, white, lobes to 15mm; sta. to 3cm, anth. green. Fr. blue-black. India to Malay Penins. and Archipel.

C. wallichii Merrill. Glab., erect shrub to 2m. Lvs to 26cm, oblong-lanceolate to obovate, subentire. Pan. term. to 35cm, pendent; cal., often tinged red; cor. white or yellow-white, tube to 16mm, lobes to 14mm. Fr. purple-black. SE Asia.

→*Siphonanthus* and *Volkameria*.

Clethra L. WHITE ALDER; SUMMER-SWEET. Clethraceae. *c*30 mainly decid. small trees and shrubs. Lvs obovate to lanceolate, usually serrate. Fls white, often fragrant, racemose; rachis and pedicels stellate-pubescent; sep. 5, petaloid; pet. 5, free; sta. 10, in 2 whorls. Summer–autumn. Asia, E N Amer., Madeira Is., Neotrop.

C. acuminata Michx. Shrub or small tree to 4m. Lvs to 18cm, elliptic to oblong, glab. beneath, apex acuminate, serrate. Fls in term. solitary rac. to 15cm; pet. white, to 6mm. Summer. SE US. Z6.

C. alnifolia L. SWEET PEPPER BUSH; SUMMER-SWEET; PINK SPIRE; NANA; BUSH PEPPER. Tree or shrub to 4m. St. pubesc. at first. Lvs to 10cm, obovate to oblong, serrate above. Rac. erect paniculate cylindrical to 15cm; fls 1cm diam., fragrant; pet. white, obovate. Summer or autumn. E N Amer. Z3. 'Paniculata': superior form; pan. term. 'Rosea' and 'Pink Spire' both have pink-tinted fls and glossy lvs.

C. alnifolia var. *pubescens* Ait. = *C. tomentosa*.

C. arborea Ait. LILY OF THE VALLEY TREE; FOLHADO. Everg. shrub or small tree to 8m. St. pubesc., tinged red when young. Lvs to 14cm, elliptic to oblanceolate, acuminate, deep green and glab. above, finely serrate, midrib and petiole pubesc. Fls to 8mm, pure white, cup-shaped, in slender rac. Summer or autumn. Madeira Is. Z9.

C. barbinervis Sieb. & Zucc. Shrub to 10m, bushy; st. minutely pubesc. when young. Lvs to 14cm, obovate-elliptic, apex acuminate, base cuneate and acute, glab. above, serrate, villous beneath. Fls to 8mm, white, in paniculate terminal rac. to 15cm, rachis densely villous; pet. obovate, emarginate and fringed. Summer–autumn. E China to Jap. Z5.

C. canescens Forbes & Hemsl. = *C. barbinervis*.

C. confusa Briq. = *C. lanata*.

C. delavayi Franch. Decid. tree to 13m; st. villous when young, downy later. Lvs to 15cm, elliptic-oblong to lanceolate, apex acuminate or acute, serrate, hispid above, tomentose beneath. Fls nodding, cup-shaped; rac. solitary, term., to 25cm; sep. rose; pet. rounded, pubesc., white to cream, emarginate, ciliate. Summer. W China. Z5.

C. fargesii Franch. Decid. shrub to 4m; st. initially pubesc. Lvs to 14cm, ovate to lanceolate, dark green, near glab., apex acuminate, serrate. Fls fragrant, white, in packed villous term.

paniculate rac. to 17cm. Summer. C China. Z5.

C. guadalajarensis Briq. = *C. lanata*.

C. lanata M. Martens & Gal.. Tree to 12m; branchlets brown-tomentose. Lvs to 15cm, obovate, apex rounded to subacute, thick, entire to sparsely dentate, glab. above. Fls in packed, paniculate rac. to 20cm. C Amer., S Mex. to Panama. Z9.

C. mexicana DC. JABONCILLO. Shrub or small tree to 9m; branchlets tomentose. Lvs to 20cm, obovate to oval, apex and base acute or obtuse, serrate to entire, tomentose beneath. Fls v. fragrant, in packed rac. to 20cm. C Amer. Z9.

C. monostachya Rehd. & Wils. Decid. shrub to 8m. Lvs to 14cm, elliptic-ovate rarely lanceolate, dark glab. green above, pubesc. on midrib and veins, acuminate to apiculate, serrate. Fls pure white in solitary tomentose term. rac. to 20cm. Pet. glab., papillate outside. Summer. C China. Z6.

C. palmeri Britt. = *C. mexicana*.

C. paniculata Ait. = *C. alnifolia* 'Paniculata'.

C. schlechtendalii Briq. = *C. mexicana*.

C. sleumeriana Hao = *C. fargesii*.

C. tomentosa Lam. Shrub to 3m. Lvs to 10cm, obovate, grey-blue villous beneath, apex acute or acuminate, serrate. Rac. erect solitary or few to 15cm, terminal; fls pure white, fragrant. Late summer. SE US. Z8.

CLETHRACEAE Klotzsch. See *Clethra*.

Cleyera Thunb. Theaceae. 17 trees or shrubs, everg. or decid. Fls solitary or in axillary clusters; pedicels short, thickened at apex; sep. 5, connate at base; pet. 5, obovate, pale yellow, cream or white; sta. *c*25. Jap. to Himal., Mex. to Panama.

C. fortunei Hook. f. = *C. japonica* 'Fortunei'.

C. japonica Thunb. SAKAKI. Everg. glab. shrub to 4.5m with green br. Lvs 7–10cm, narrowly oblong or ovate-oblong, obtuse, deep green above, paler beneath, entire. Pet. 1cm, cream, thick. Jap., Korea, China. 'Tricolor': lvs elliptic to linear-lanceolate at first, tinged pink, bordered pale green and yellow, striped grey and cream; fls pale yellow. 'Fortunei': lvs elliptic, slender-pointed, bright green, variegated golden-yellow and rose toward margins. Z8.

C. japonica var. *tricolor* Kob. = *C. japonica* 'Tricolor'.

C. ochnacea DC. Shrub to 1.8m. Lvs oval-oblong, narrowed at both ends, toothed near apex or entire. Fls white-yellow, fragrant. Himal., Jap. Z8.

C. theoides (Sw.) Choisy. Shrub or small tree to 6m; branchlets adpressed-pilose. Lvs 4–8cm, obovate or oblong-obovate, bluntly acuminate, crenate. Pet. 1cm, cream-white. Jam. Z10.

Clianthus Sol. ex Lindl. Leguminosae (Papilionoideae). 2 everg., trailing or climbing shrubs or subshrubs (*C. formosus* short-lived). Lvs imparipinnate. Fls pea-like; in short, pendulous, axill. rac. or on erect peduncles; standard broad, sharply reflexed, wings short, keel long, carinate, v. sharply tapered, curved downwards, like a lobster claw. Aus., NZ.

C. dampieri Cunn. ex Lindl. = *C. formosus*.

C. formosus (G. Don) Ford & Vick. DESERT PEA; GLORY PEA; STURT'S DESERT PEA. Prostrate perenn. subshrub, silky-pubesc. Lvs 12–17cm; lfts 1–3cm, 9–21, oval, grey-green, densely downy beneath. Rac. erect; cor. vivid scarlet, standard 5–6cm, ovate-acuminate, with a glossy protuberant black basal blotch, keel 5–6.5cm. Winter–late summer. Aus. (Queensld, S & W Aus., NSW, N Territ.). Z9.

C. puniceus (G. Don) Sol. ex Lindl. GLORY PEA; PARROT'S BEAK; PARROT'S BILL; LOBSTER CLAW. Everg. shrub erect to 5m; br. divaricate, arching. Lvs 7–15cm; lfts 1–3cm, 13–25, narrow-oblong, glossy dark green above, canescent beneath. Rac. drooping; cor. scarlet, vermilion, coral-pink or white, lustrous, standard 4–5cm, ovate, keel 6.5cm. Summer–late autumn. NZ. 'Albus': fls white tinted green to ivory. 'Flamingo': fls deep rose pink. 'Magnificus': lfts to 3cm; fls small, deep red. 'Red Admiral': fls red, profuse. 'Red Cardinal': lvs soft green; fls red. 'White Heron': fls pure white. Z8.

C. speciosus (G. Don) Asch. & Gräbn. = *C. formosus*.

Clifants River Cycad *Encephalartos lanatus*.
Cliff Bottlebrush *Callistemon comboynensis*.
Cliff-brake *Pellaea*.
Cliffbush *Jamesia*.
Cliff Date *Phoenix rupicola*.
Cliff Green *Paxistima canbyi*.
Cliff Net-bush *Calothamnus rupestris*.
Cliff Rose *Cowania*.

Cliftonia Banks ex Gaertn. f. Cyrillaceae. 1 everg. shrub or small tree to 7.3m, glab. throughout. Shoots slender. Lvs 2.5–5.5cm, narrowly oval to oblanceolate, entire, apex blunt, base wedge-shaped, coriaceous, dark-green, lustrous above,

glaucous beneath. Fls *c*6mm diam., 5-merous, white or pink, fragrant, in axill. or term., cylindric rac. 3–6.2cm long. Spring. SE US.

C. ligustrina (Willd.) Spreng. = *C. monophylla*.

C. monophylla (Lam.) Sarg. BUCKWHEAT TREE; TITI; IRONWOOD.

Climbing Aloe *Aloe ciliaris*.
Climbing Bird's-nest Fern *Microsorium punctatum*.
Climbing Blechnum *Blechnum attenuatum*.
Climbing Butcher's Broom *Semele*.
Climbing Corydalis *Corydalis claviculata*.
Climbing Dahlia *Hidalgoa*.
Climbing Fern *Lygodium*; *Stenochlaena palustris*.
Climbing Fig *Ficus pumila*.
Climbing Fumitory *Adlumia fungosa*.
Climbing Heath *Prionotes cerinthoides*.
Climbing Hemp-vine *Mikania scandens*.
Climbing Hydrangea *Decumaria barbara*.
Climbing Ilang-ilang *Artabotrys hexapetalus*.
Climbing Lily *Gloriosa*.
Climbing Maidenhair Fern *Lygodium microphyllum*.
Climbing Nightshade *Solanum dulcamara*.
Climbing Oleander *Strophanthus gratus*.
Climbing Onion *Bowiea volubilis*.
Climbing Rose *Rosa setigera*.

Clinelymus (Griseb.) Nevski.

C. sibiricus (L.) Nevski = *Elymus sibiricus*.

Clinopodium L. Labiatae. 10 aromatic perenn. herbs. Lvs ovate to lanceolate, petiolate. Infl. composed of dense whorls; cal. tube curved, 13-veined; cor. tubular, bilabiate, upper lip entire, lower lip 3-lobed. Temp. Eur. and E Asia, SE US. Z7.

C. carolinianum hort. non (Michx.) A.A. Heller = *C. georgianum*.

C. chinense (Benth.) Kuntze. To 80cm. St. erect, white-pubesc. Lvs to 4cm, ovate, acute, rounded at base. Fls rose-purple, 12mm. Late summer. E Asia.

C. coccineum (Nutt.) Kuntze = *Calamintha coccinea*.

C. georgianum Harper. Subshrub to 60cm. St. slightly pubesc. Lvs to 2.5cm, elliptic, crenulate. Fls 12mm, pink. SE US.

C. glabellum Kuntze. To 25cm. St. hirsute at nodes. Lvs to 4cm, oblanceolate, dentate. Fls to 30mm, purple. Summer. E US.

C. grandiflorum (L.) Kuntze = *Calamintha grandiflora*.

C. mimuloides Kuntze = *Calamintha mimuloides*.

C. nepeta Kuntze = *Calamintha nepeta*.

C. umbrosum (Bieb.) K. Koch. To 60cm. St. ascending, tetra-gonal, sparsely pubesc. Lvs ovate or cuneate, serrate. Fls to 10mm, pale purple. Summer–early autumn. Anatolia, Afghan., Cauc.

C. vulgare L. WILD BASIL; CUSHION CALAMINT. To 80cm. Lvs to 5cm, ovate, denticulate or entire. Fls to 20mm, rose-purple. Late summer–autumn. Eurasia.

C. vulgaris (L.) Hal. non Clairv. = *C. vulgare*.

→*Calamintha*, *Melissa* and *Satureja*.

Clintonia Raf. Liliaceae (Convallariaceae). 5 perenn. rhizomatous herbs. Lvs largely basal, sheathing at base, entire, glossy. Flowering st. erect, simple; fls in terminal umbels or rac., bell- to star-shaped; tep. 6, free. Fr. a berry. Himal., E Asia, N Amer.

C. alpina Bak. = *C. udensis*.

C. andrewsiana Torr. Lvs 15–25cm, elliptic to broadly ovate, sparsely ciliate. Flowering st. 25–50cm; fls in a large umbel sub-tended by secondary umbels; tep. 1–1.8cm, deep rose-purple. Fr. blue. Summer. Calif. Z8.

C. borealis (Ait.) Raf. CORN LILY; BLUEBEARD. Lvs 10–30cm, oblanceolate to obovate, minutely ciliate. Flowering st. to 30cm; fls 2–8, nodding in a loose umbel and sometimes smaller, secondary umbels; tep. 0.5–1cm, green-yellow. Fr. blue, or white. Spring–early summer. E N Amer. Z3.

C. udensis Trautv. & Mey. Lvs 8–35cm, oblanceolate to obovate or oblong, ciliate. Flowering st. 10–85cm; fls in a loose 2–10-fld rac. often umbellate, erect; tep. 0.7–1.5cm, yellow-green, white or lilac. Fr. dark blue to purple-black. Summer. E Sib., Himal., Jap. Z3.

C. umbellata Torr. = *C. umbellulata*.

C. umbellulata (Michx.) Morong. SPECKLED WOOD LILY. Lvs 8–30cm, oblanceolate to obovate or oblong, minutely ciliate. Flowering st. 15–30cm; fls in a dense, 5–30-fld umbel, erect or nodding; tep. 0.5–1cm, white spotted green and purple. Fr. black. Late spring–summer. E N Amer. Z4.

C. uniflora (Schult.) Kunth BRIDE'S BONNET; QUEEN CUP. Lvs 7–15cm, oblanceolate to obovate, hairy beneath. Flowering st. 10–20cm; fls 1(–2), erect; tep. 1.8–2.5cm, white. Fr. blue. Summer. W N Amer. (mts). Z6.

Clitoria L. Leguminosae (Papilionoideae). 70 herbs or shrubs, some climbing or prostrate. Lvs trifoliolate or imparipinnate. Fls solitary clustered, or in few-fld, axill. rac.; standard orbicular or broadly obovate, larger than other pet., keel small, incurved, sharp-tipped, wings oblong to falcate. Trop. Z10.

C. amazonum Mart. Tall semi-erect climbing shrub. Lfts 3, ovate, tapering to apex. Fls white or pale rose, standard to 7.5cm, with dark lines. N Braz.

C. cajanifolia (Presl) Benth. = C. laurifolia.

C. fairchildiana R. Howard. Tree to 8m+. Lfts 3, lanceolate, long-acuminate. Fls violet with red-purple throat. Braz.

C. heterophylla Lam. Everg. twining herb. Lfts 5, orbicular to oval, lanceolate or linear. Fls similar to those of C. ternatea, but smaller. Trop. Asia.

C. laurifolia Poir. Erect, perenn. shrub, 30–70cm. Lfts oblong to linear-oblong, sharp-tipped or rounded. Fls 5–6cm, white to purple. Late winter–spring. Trop. S Amer., Aus.

C. mariana L. Perenn. climber to 1m. Lfts 3, ovate to lanceolate, sharp-tipped to blunt and emarginate. Fls pale blue or lilac, standard 4–6cm. Summer. SE US, Mex.

C. racemosa Benth. non G. Don = C. fairchildiana.

C. ternatea L. BLUE PEA; BLUE VINE; BUTTERFLY PEA; PIGEON WINGS. Herbaceous vine, trailing or scandent to 3m. Lvs 6–12cm, lfts 5–7, elliptic-ovate, sharp-tipped to rounded. Fls 3–5cm, standard large, clear blue fading to white at centre with yellow stain, sometimes more strongly marked or pure white. Late summer–early autumn. Trop. Asia, nat. throughout tropics and subtrop. 'Blue Sails': habit climbing; fls semi-double, deep blue.

Clivia Lindl. KAFFIR LILY. Amaryllidaceae. 4 perenn., ± stemless everg. herbs. Lvs bright green, strap-shaped; in 2 distinct, opposite ranks, sheathing at base. Infl. scapose, umbellate; perianth funnel-shaped, seg. longer than tube; sta. declinate. Fr. a red berry. S Afr. Z10.

C. caulescens R.A. Dyer. St. distinct. Lvs to 180×2.5–5cm. Fls drooping, salmon pink tipped with green and yellow; perianth narrowly funnel-shaped, seg. 3.5–4cm, sta. as long as perianth. Spring.

C. ×cyrtanthiflora (Van Houtte) Wittm. (C. miniata × C. nobilis.) Fls rich salmon pink or light flame-coloured; perianth tube narrow with inner seg. twice as broad as outer seg.

C. gardenii Hook. f. Lvs to 75×2.5–4cm. Fls to 7.5cm, narrowly funnel-shaped, red, tinged orange or yellow; perianth seg. oblanceolate, 3.5–5cm, margins yellow above, tips spreading, green; sta. equal to or longer than perianth. Winter–spring.

C. grandiflora Hort. = C. miniata.

C. hybrida hort. = C. ×cyrtanthiflora.

C. miniata Reg. Lvs to 60×3–7cm. Fls erect to spreading; perianth tube to 1.3cm, bright scarlet, throat yellow, broadly funnel-shaped, seg. oblanceolate-oblong, to 7cm, inner broader than outer; perianth longer than sta. and style. Spring–summer. 'Aurea': fls golden yellow. 'Grandiflora': fls large. 'Flame': lvs wide, rich green; fls deep orange-red. French Hybrid: fls strong orange. 'Striata': lvs variegated white to cream.

C. nobilis Lindl. GREENTIP KAFFIR LILY. Lvs to 45×5cm. Fls drooping, narrower and shorter than in C. miniata; perianth seg. to 3cm, oblanceolate, red and yellow, tipped green, overlapping; sta. exserted. Spring.

Clock Vine Thunbergia grandiflora.
Clog Plant Nematanthus gregarius.
Closed Gentian Gentiana andrewsii; G. clausa.
Cloth-of-gold Crocus Crocus angustifolius.
Cloudberry Rubus chamaemorus.
Cloud Grass Agrostis nebulosa.
Cloud Podocarp Podocarpus nubigenus.
Clove Syzygium aromaticum.
Clove Cherry Prunus apetala.
Clove Currant Ribes odoratum.
Cloven-lip Toadflax Linaria bipartita.
Clove Pink Dianthus caryophyllus.
Clover Trifolium.
Cloveroot Geum urbanum.

Clowesia Lindl. Orchidaceae. 5 epiphytic orchids. Pbs stout, ovoid to pyriform. Lvs oblong-lanceolate, large, plicate. Rac. lat. pendent; fls ♂; dors. sep. free, concave, lat. sep. erect; pet. similar, often fringed; lip fleshy, 3-lobed, saccate or spurred, lateral lobes erect, midlobe reflexed, apex fimbriate or denticulate. Mex. to Venez. Z10.

C. rosea Lindl. Fls campanulate, deep rose-pink to light pink; dors. sep. to 1.7cm, elliptic, lat. sep. to 2cm, paler than dors. sep., slightly connate; pet. erose-lacerate; lip to 2cm, gibbous at base, obovate, ciliate-fimbriate. Early winter. Mex.

C. russelliana (Hook.) Dodson. Fls sweetly fragrant; tep. clear-green to white-green, veined dark green; dors. sep. to 3.5cm, elliptic-oblong, apiculate, concave, lateral sep. to 4cm, obliquely oblong to elliptic-oblong, pet. minutely erose; lip to 4cm, base green grading to white, saccate below, elliptic-obovate, crisped-dentate. Mex. to Panama and Venez.

C. thylaciochila (Lem.) Dodson. Fls yellow-green, veined brown; tep. to 3.5cm, lanceolate to oblong-linear; lip to 3.5cm, saccate at base, ovate-triangular. Mex.

C. warczewitzii (Lindl.) Dodson. Fls fragrant; tep. clear-green or green-white to white veined pale green; sep. ovate or elliptic-ovate, to 1.8cm, pet. to 1.7cm, ovate-suborbicular, concave, obtuse; lip to 2.5cm, saccate at base, lateral lobes fimbriate, midlobe, fimbriate-lacerate. Costa Rica, Panama, Colomb., Venez., Guyana.

→ *Catasetum*.

Clown Fig Ficus aspera.
Clown Orchid Rossioglossum grande.
Club Gourd Trichosanthes cucumerina var. anguina.
Clubmoss Lycopodium, Selaginella.
Club-rush Scirpus.

Clusia L. Guttiferae. 145 trees and shrubs, sometimes epiphytic or strangling, st. 4-angled. Lvs large, often obovate, coriaceous. Fls few, terminal; sep. 4–6; pet. 4–9 spreading; sta. numerous in ♂ fls. Fr. a leathery capsule. Trop. & subtrop. Amer. Z9.

C. major (Jacq.) L. AUTOGRAPH TREE; BALSAM APPLE; COPEY; FAT PORK TREE; SCOTCH-ATTORNEY. Tree to 20m, epiphytic or lithophytic. Lvs 6–18cm, obovate. Infl. terminal, 3-fld; pet. creamy-white or pink, 6–8, 3–4cm, oblong-obovate. Fr. globose, green-white, 5–8cm diam. Summer. Range as for the genus.

C. rosea Jacq. = C. major.

CLUSIACEAE Lindl. See Guttiferae.

Cluster Bean Cyamopsis tetragonolobus.
Clustered Bellflower Campanula glomerata.
Clustered Everlasting Helichrysum semipapposum.
Clustered Fishtail Palm Caryota mitis.
Clustered Ivy Hedera helix 'Conglomerata'
Clustered Poppy Mallow Callirhoë triangulata.
Cluster Fig Ficus racemosa.
Cluster Rose Rosa pisocarpa.

Clypeola L.
C. maritima L. = Lobularia maritima.

Clytostoma Miers Bignoniaceae. 9 everg. vines. Lvs 2–3-foliolate; rachis extended into tendril. Fls in axill. or term. pairs or pan.; cal. campanulate, lobes 5; cor. funnelform-campanulate, lobes 5. Spring–Summer. Trop. Amer. Z10.

C. binatum (Thunb.) Sandw. Lfts to 8cm, elliptic to oblong-ovate, apex acuminate, green above, paler beneath, entire, sometimes dentate. Cor. pale purple, with white centre, tube 2.5cm, lobes spreading, ovate. Urug.

C. callistigioides Bur. & Schum. ARGENTINE TRUMPET VINE; LOVE-CHARM. Lfts to 8cm, oblong-elliptic, apex acuminate, glossy green above, reticulate beneath, undulate. Cor. 7cm, yellow striped lilac, lobes purple, spreading, ovate, sinuate. S Braz., Arg.

C. purpureum Rehd. = C. binatum.

→ *Bignonia*.

CNEORACEAE Link. See Cneorum.

Cneorum L. Cneoraceae. 2 everg. shrubs and 1 small tree (the Cuban C. trimerum (Urban) Chodat). Lvs leathery, entire. Fls small; sep. 3 or 4; pet. 3 or 4 yellow. Fr. a schizocarp. Early summer. Medit., Canary Is., Cuba. Z9.

C. pulverulentum Vent. To 1.5m, usually smaller. Young growth grey-downy. Lvs 2.5–7cm, linear to oblanceolate, obtuse. Fls pale yellow, solitary. Fr. green-grey. Canary Is.

C. tricoccon L. SPURGE OLIVE. To 60cm. Young shoots slender, glab., grey-green. Lvs 3–5cm, erect on the st., linear-oblong, apex obtuse, tapering to base, glab., glossy dark to grey-green. Fls deep yellow, in small clusters. Fr. bright red, black when ripe. Early summer. W Medit.

Cnicus L. BLESSED THISTLE. Compositae. 1 ann. herb, to 60cm. St. villous. Lvs ± leathery, oblong, minutely spiny toothed, light-green, white-veined beneath, to 30cm, deeply dissected. Cap. to 4×3cm, solitary, discoid; phyllaries imbricate, with spine at apex; flts tubular, yellow. Summer–autumn. Medit. and Port. Z8.

C. acaulis Willd. = *Cirsium acaule*.
C. afer (Jacq.) Willd. = *Ptilostemon afer*.
C. benedictus L.
C. casabonae (L.) Roth = *Ptilostemon casabonae*.
C. centauroides L. = *Leuzea centauroides*.
C. conspicuus Hemsl. = *Cirsium conspicuum*.
C. falconeri Hook. f. = *Cirsium falconeri*.
C. spinosissimus L. = *Cirsium spinosissimum*.
→*Carduus*.

Cnidoscolus Pohl. TREAD-SOFTLY; SPURGE NETTLE. Euphorbia-ceae. 75 perenn. herbs, shrubs or small trees, usually armed with stinging hairs; milky latex in st. and lvs. Fls apetalous, cymose; cal. showy, white; sta. 8–10. Trop. & subtrop. Amer. Z10.
C. chayamansa McVaugh. Succulent, ± glab. shrub to *c*2m, with few stinging hairs. Lvs broader than long, 3-lobed, lat. lobes often divided; petioles short fleshy. Mex. to Braz.
C. texanus (Muell. Arg.) Small. To 60cm, armed with stiff yellow hairs. Lvs to 15cm wide, long-stalked, deeply divided into 3–5 toothed or cut lobes. Ark. to Tex.
C. urens (L.) Arthur. SPURGE NETTLE; TREAD-SOFTLY; DEVIL NETTLE; PICA-PICA. Small shrub or large herb with soft woody st., to 3m tall, all parts densely armed and stinging hairs. Lvs 7–15cm, 3–5-lobed, ovate to suborbicular. C & S Amer.
→*Jatropha*.

Coach-whip *Fouquieria splendens*.
Coamatl *Oreopanax capitatus*.
Coarse-flowered Mallee *Eucalyptus grossa*.
Coastal Brake *Pteris comans*.
Coastal Chinkapin *Castanea pumila* var. *ashei*.
Coastal Gum-plant *Grindelia latifolia*.
Coastal Jugflower *Adenanthos cuneatus*.
Coastal Myall *Acacia binervia*.
Coastal Wall Flower *Erysimum capitatum*.
Coastal Wattle *Acacia cyclops*; *A. sophorae*.
Coast Banksia *Banksia integrifolia*.
Coast Ceanothus *Ceanothus ramulosus*.
Coast Grey Box *Eucalyptus bosistoana*.
Coast Ground-berry *Acrotriche cordata*.
Coast Lily *Lilium maritimum*.
Coast Pignut Hickory *Carya glabra* var. *megacarpa*.
Coast Polypody *Polypodium scouleri*.
Coast Redwood *Sequoia*.
Coast Tarweed *Madia sativa*.
Coast Violet *Viola brittoniana*.
Coast White Cedar *Chamaecyparis thyoides*.
Coast White-thorn *Ceanothus incanus*.

Cobaea Cav. Polemoniaceae. *c*20 herbaceous or shrubby perenn. climbers. Lvs pinnate, with a term. tendril. Fls solitary in axils, usually fragrant; cal. lobes 5, leafy; cor. 5-lobed; sta. 5, exserted, fil. curving upwards, anth. yellow. Mex. to Trop. S Amer. Z9.
C. scandens Cav. CUP AND SAUCER VINE; MEXICAN IVY; MONASTERY BELLS. Rampant glab. climber. Lvs with large leafy stipules, lfts to 10cm, 4–6, oblong or elliptic, tendrils hook-tipped. Cal. saucer-like, subtending the 'cup' of cor.; cor broadly campanulate to 5×4cm, green-cream and musky-scented at first, later violet then deep purple with a honey-like fragrance. Summer–autumn. Mex., but widely nat., esp. in the Neotrop. 'Alba': fls white.

Cobija *Copernicia tectorum*.
Cobnut *Corylus avellana*.
Cobra Lily *Darlingtonia*.
Cobra Plant *Arisaema nepenthoides*.
Cobun-bun *Acmena australis*.

Coburgia Sweet.
C. belladonna (L.) Herb. = *Amaryllis belladonna*.
C. fulva Herb. = *Stenomesson variegatum*.

Cobweb Aloe *Haworthia arachnoidea*.
Cobweb Houseleek *Sempervivum arachnoideum*.

Coccinia Wright & Arn. Cucurbitaceae. *c*30 climbers or trailers. Tendrils usually simple. Lvs simple, palmate, 5-angled or 5-lobed, usually stalked. Fls white or yellow; cal. short, campanulate, 5-lobed; cor. campanulate, acutely 5-lobed, long; ♂ clustered or racemose with sta. 3, fil. connate or coherent; ♀ solitary with 3 staminodes. Fr. a berry, soft, globose to elongate. Trop. Afr. to India and Malesia. Z9.
C. cordifolia hort. = *C. grandis*.
C. ecirrhosa Cogn. = *Cephalopentandra ecirrhosa*.

C. grandis (L.) Voigt. IVY GOURD; SCARLET-FRUITED GOURD. Perenn., rarely prostrate, to 30m. St. terete, glab. or sealy. Lvs broadly ovate, cordate to 5-angled or 3–5-lobed, 5–10cm. Fr. cylindric to fusiform, to 5cm, bright red, beaked. Trop. Afr. and Asia to N Aus., introd. to Trop. Amer.
C. indica Wright & Arn. = *C. grandis*.
C. palmata (Sonder) Cogn. Perenn. climber, to 8m. St. sulcate, glab. Tendrils bifid. Lvs palmate, ovate-oblong, occas. scabrid above, often gland. beneath, 4–12cm, lobes 5, deeply divided, ovate-lanceolate, minutely dentate. Fr. narrow. oblong-fusiform, red, 5–8cm. S & E Afr.
C. sessilifolia (Sonder) Cogn. Perenn. herbaceous climber to 5m. St. smooth. Lvs sessile, palmate, to 12cm, lobes 5, oblong-lanceolate, dentate or lobulate. Fr. red. to 9cm. S Afr.
→*Bryonia*.

Coccoloba P. Browne. SEA GRAPE; CHICORY GRAPE; PIGEON PLUM. Polygonaceae. *c*150 trees, shrubs or lianes, mostly everg. Lvs entire, leathery, often v. large, lvs of juvenile shoots commonly larger and different in shape. Fls in spikes, rac. or pan.; sep. 5, green-white; sta. usually 8. Fr. a dark achene, 3-angled, surrounded by brightly coloured, fleshy perianth. Trop. & subtrop. Americas. Z10.
C. diversifolia Jacq. PIGEON PLUM; SNAIL SEED. Everg., slow-growing tree to 3m. Lvs oblong to ovate, 5–10cm, bright green, leathery, smooth. Fls in short rac., pale yellow-green. Fr. pear-shaped, to 1.5cm, purple. S Flor., Carib.
C. floridana Meissn. = *C. diversifolia*.
C. grandifolia Jacq. = *C. pubescens*.
C. laurifolia Lindau non Jacq. = *C. diversifolia*.
C. pubescens L. Sparsely branched tree to 24m. Lvs orbicular, 2.5–45cm, rarely to 90cm diam., ± undulate, bright green above, veins prominent, rusty-pubesc. beneath. Fls in erect term. rac., to 60cm, white-green. Fr 2cm diam. Spring. W Indies.
C. uvifera (L.) L. SEA GRAPE; JAMAICAN KINO; PLATTER LEAF. Everg. pachycaul shrub or tree to 10m. Lvs orbicular to cordate at base, rounded to emarginate, to 20cm wide, leathery, glossy, bright green, undulate, veins yellow-green to red. Fls fragrant, in erect, dense rac. to 20cm, white. Fr. in grape-like bunches, spherical to pyriform, 1.5–2cm, green ripening purple. Spring–summer. Trop. Amer. on ocean beach margin.
C. venosa L. CHICORY GRAPE. Small decid. tree to 9m, crown spreading. Lvs drooping, in 2 rows, elliptic to obovate, 9–20cm, green and shiny above, prominently veined beneath. Fls in slender, spike-like rac., to 18cm, green-yellow. Fr. ovoid, to 0.5cm, white-pink, fleshy. Summer. W Indies.

Coccothrinax Sarg. BROOM; SILVER PALM; THATCH PALM. Palmae. 49 palms. St. usually solitary, rarely clustered, clothed with long matted fibres or stout spines, becoming bare, ringed. Lvs palmate, marcescent; blade broad, divided into linear-lanceolate tapering and acuminate seg. radiating from a prominent hastula further divided at apex, glab. above, silver-grey punctate, hairy or glab. beneath. W Indies. Z10.
C. acuminata Sarg. ex Becc. = *C. miraguama*.
C. alta (Cook) Becc. St., to 10m, clothed with straw-coloured webbing at first. Lf blade orbicular, to 75cm, green above, silvery and silky beneath; seg. to 4cm wide. Puerto Rico, St. Thomas Is. Group.
C. argentata (Jacq.) L.H. Bail. SILVER PALM; FLORIDA SILVER PALM. St. to 8m, to 15cm diam. Lvs 45–60cm diam., pale yellow-green shining above, silvery white beneath; seg. narrower than *C. argentea*, pendent. Flor., Bahamas.
C. argentea (Lodd. ex Schult.) Sarg. ex Becc. GUANO; LATANIER BALAI. St. to 10m, to 10cm diam., clothed with webbing. Lf blade to 75cm, orbicular, base cordate, divided into 30 or more seg. to 3cm across, dull green above, silvery and pubesc. beneath. Hispan.
C. argentea auct. non Sarg. = *C. argentata*.
C. barbadensis (Lodd. ex Mart.) Becc. = *Coccothrinax dussiana*.
C. crinita Becc. THATCH PALM. St. to 9m, to 20cm diam., clothed above with long fine fibres. Lvs to 2m, blade 60–70cm, divided into some 52 seg. Cuba.
C. dussiana L.H. Bail. To 16m. St. to 18cm diam. Lvs green above, silver and lightly pubesc. beneath; seg. to 5cm diam.; petiole with sharp margins. Guadeloupe.
C. fragrans Burret. SILVER THATCH. St. to 5m, slender, bare, or with loose webbing. Seg. narrow, shiny above, but less so than in *C. argentata* and blue glaucous. Haiti, E Cuba.
C. garberi Sarg. = *C. argentata*.
C. jucunda Sarg. = *C. argentata*.
C. miraguama (HBK) Becc. St. to 4.5m, 10–15cm diam. Lvs 1.5–2m, rigid, sheath fibrous; petiole slender; blade orbicular and silvery beneath, seg. 24–28, to 65cm. Cuba.
C. radiata (Lodd. ex Schult. & Schult. f.) Sarg. ex

Schum. = *Thrinax radiata*.
C. scoparia Becc. = *C. argentea*.
C. spissa L.H. Bail. St. 3–8m, straight or swollen to 30cm diam. at middle or above, lightly ringed, webbed. Lf blades to 75cm, suborbicular, seg. 40 or more semi-rigid or pendent, 3cm across, deeply divided at apex, pale grey beneath. Hispan.
→*Thrinax*.

Cocculus DC. Menispermaceae. 11 decid. or everg. climbers, shrubs and small trees. Fls small unisexual, in axill. pan. or rac.; sep. 6, pubesc.; pet. 6, usually cleft: ♂ with 6–9 sta., ♀ 0 to 6 staminodes. Fr. a small globose drupe; seeds horseshoe-shaped. S & E Asia, Afr., N Amer.
C. carolinus (L.) DC. CAROLINA MOONSEED; RED MOONSEED; CORAL BEADS; SNAILSEED. Decid. twiner to 4m. Lvs 5–10cm ovate to cordate, sometimes obscurely 3–5-lobed, 3–7-veined. Fls green-white, ♂ in short pan., ♀ in rac. Fr. to 0.75cm diam., bright red. SE US.
C. laurifolius (Roxb.) DC. Erect everg. shrub or small tree to 15m. Lvs to 15cm, oblong-lanceolate to narrowly elliptic, 3-veined, glossy dark green. Fls yellow-green, in slender erect pan. to 10cm. Fr. to 0.5cm diam., black. Himal. to Jap.
C. orbiculatus (L.) DC. Resembles *C. carolinus*. Lvs 4–10cm, ovate to broadly ovate, sometimes cordate- hastate or shallowly 3-lobed, 3–5-veined. Fls cream to off-white or yellow-green, in clusters. Fr. to 0.75cm diam., black, pruinose. Temp. & Trop. E Asia.
C. trilobus (Thunb.) DC. = *C. orbiculatus*.

Cochemiea (Brandg.) Walton.
C. halei (Brandg.) Walton = *Mammillaria halei*.
C. maritima Lindsay = *Mammillaria maritima*.
C. pondii (Greene) Walton = *Mammillaria pondii*.
C. poselgeri (Hildm.) Britt. & Rose preserved. = *Mammillaria poselgeri*.
C. setispina (J. Coult.) Walton = *Mammillaria setispina*.

Cochleanthes Raf. Orchidaceae. 14 epiphytic orchids. Pbs 0. Lvs 2-ranked, in a loose fan, basally overlapping, linear-lanceolate, pale green. Fls solitary, axill., on long pedicels; sep. spreading, broadly lanceolate, acuminate; pet. thin, spreading, slender, erect; lip entire or obscurely trilobed, concave to semi-tubular. Summer. C Amer. Z10.
C. discolor (Lindl.) R.E. Schult. & Garay. Tep. to 3.5×1.8cm, sep. pale green, veined and tipped deeper green; pet. green to ivory, veined and flushed rose-violet below; lip to 3.8×4.5cm, fleshy,± funnel-shaped, deep violet veined amethyst, edged paler mauve or white, callus golden. Cuba, Hond., Costa Rica, Panama, Venez.
C. flabelliformis (Sw.) R.E. Schult. & Garay. Tep. to 2.8×1cm, fleshy, ivory to lime green; lip to 4.5×3.5cm, lat. lobes incurved, midlobe flabellate, white suffused mauve, veined violet, callus veined violet. Throughout C Amer.
C. marginata (Rchb. f.) R.E. Schult. & Garay. Tep. to 3.5×1.8cm, sep. semi-rigid, pale green ageing ivory or white; pet. off-white, weaker than sep.; lip to 4×4cm, white suffused and veined violet at centre, edged rose-purple, callus white, sometimes lightly stained mauve. Venez., Colomb., Ecuad.
→*Chondrorhyncha*, *Warscewiczella* and *Zygopetalum*.

Cochlearia L. Cruciferae. 25 ann. and perenn. herbs. Lvs simple, stalked in basal rosettes and ± sessile, lobed and toothed on flowering st. Fls small, 4-merous, racemose. N temp. regions. Z6.
C. armoracia L. = *Armoracia rusticana*.
C. danica L. Tufted ann., to 20cm. Basal lvs to 2.5cm, reniform-rounded, st. lvs palmately 3–7-lobed. Pet. to 3mm, white-purple. Summer. N temp. regions.
C. officinalis L. COMMON SCURVY GRASS. Bienn. or perenn., to 50cm. Basal lvs reniform-cordate, st. lvs sessile, toothed. Pet. 3–7mm, white. Spring. Coastal NW Eur., Alps.
C. saxatilis L. = *Kernera saxatilis*.
C. sibirica Willd. = *Sobolewskia sibirica*.

Cochlioda Lindl. Orchidaceae. 6 compact epiphytic orchids. Pbs ovoid, laterally compressed. Rac. to slender, arching; fls 3–5cm diam.; sep. and pet. spreading, elliptic, tips obtuse, recurved; lip trilobed, lat. lobes rounded, midlobe subcordate, disc 4-ridged. Peru. Z10.
C. Floryi. Fls small bright orange on long sprays.
C. noezliana (Rchb. f.) Rolfe. Infl. to 45cm; fls vivid scarlet; lat. lobes of lip rounded. Summer–autumn.
C. rosea (Lindl.) Benth. Fls deep rose madder to crimson; lat. lobes of lip rhombic, midlobe narrow-oblong, exceeding lat. lobes. Late spring–summer.
C. sanguinea (Rchb. f.) Benth. = *Symphyglossum sanguineum*.

C. vulcanica (Rchb. f.) Benth. Smaller than preceding spp. Fls rose to damask pink, lip with a faded, central region, midlobe cordate to ovate, lat. lobes rounded or square. Late summer–winter.

Cochliostema Lem. Commelinaceae. 2 robust stemless epiphytic perenn. herbs. Lvs in rosettes, large, oblong or lanceolate. Thyrses axill.; fls zygomorphic, v. fragrant; sep. 3; pet. 3, short-clawed, long-ciliate; fertile sta. 3, with fil. basally united, hooded above, enveloping anth. and produced into a tubular horn, anth. coiled staminodes 3. Nic. to Ecuad.
C. odoratissimum Lem. Lvs 40–100×10–15cm, acuminate, leathery, glab. Infl. 30–80cm diam.; fls 3–6cm diam.; sep. violet-blue; pet. pale blue; lateral staminodes 5–10mm, long-ciliate with pale violet hairs. Autumn. Nic. to Ecuad. Z9.

COCHLOSPERMACEAE Planch. See *Cochlospermum*.

Cochlospermum Kunth. Bixaceae (Cochlospermaceae). 15 decid. trees or shrubs. Lvs palmatifid to palmate. Rac. or a pan. term.; fls, showy; sep. 5; pet. 5; sta. numerous. Capsule ellipsoid, velutinous, seeds small, covered in cotton down. Trop. Amer., introd. throughout Trop.
C. gossypium (L.) DC. = *C. religiosum*.
C. religiosum (L.) Alston. SILK COTTON TREE. To 7.5m. Lvs to 22cm, deeply 3 to 5-lobed, lobes acute, entire, downy beneath. Pet. to 7cm, golden, broadly obovate. Fr. to 13cm. Trop. Amer.
C. vitifolium (Willd.) Spreng. To 12m. Lvs to 30cm diam., deeply divided, lobes acute to acuminate, sub-entire to crenulate-serrulate, veins sometimes puberulent. Pet. to 6cm, bright yellow, obovate. Fr. to 8cm. Trop. Amer.

Cockies Tongue *Templetonia retusa*.
Cocklebur *Agrimonia*; *Huernia pillansii*.
Cockle Orchid *Encyclia cochleata*.
Cockroach Berry *Solanum capsicoides*.
Cockscomb *Celosia*.
Cock's Eggs *Salpichroa origanifolia*.
Cocksfoot *Dactylis glomerata*.
Cockspur *Echinochloa crus-galli*.
Cockspur Coral Tree *Erythrina crista-galli*.
Cockspur Thorn *Crataegus crus-galli*.
Cocoa *Theobroma cacao*.
Cococito *Syagrus orinocensis*.
Coco de Macao *Orbignya phalerata*.
Coco de Mer *Lodoicea*.
Coco do Vaquero *Syagrus flexuosa*.
Coconut *Cocos*.
Cocoon Plant *Senecio haworthii*.
Coco Plum *Chrysobalanus*.

Cocos L. COCONUT. Palmae. 1 palm to 30m. Trunk grey, to 30cm diam., often curved and basally swollen. Lvs to 6m, pinnate; sheath of light brown woven fibres; pinnae single-fold, to 90cm, linear, regularly spaced and held in one plane. Fr. 1-seeded, 20–35cm, globose to ellipsoid or ovoid, dull green to bright orange, yellow or white, epicarp smooth, mesocarp fibrous, endocarp (coconut) woody, brown, with 3 large basal pores, endosperm white, solid, oily, with fluid-filled central lacuna. Possibly originated in W Pacific or Indian Ocean Is.; cult. throughout tropics. Z10.
C. acrocomoides Drude = *Syagrus romanzoffianum*.
C. arechavaletana Barb. Rodr. = *Syagrus romanzoffianum*.
C. australis Mart. = *Syagrus romanzoffianum*.
C. botryophora Mart. = *Syagrus botryophora*.
C. campestris Mart. = *Syagrus flexuosa*.
C. capitata Mart. = *Butia capitata*.
C. comosa Mart. = *Syagrus comosa*.
C. coronata Mart. = *Syagrus coronata*.
C. datil Griseb. & Drude = *Syagrus romanzoffianum*.
C. drudei Becc. = *Syagrus cocoides*.
C. eriospatha Mart. ex Drude = *Butia eriospatha*.
C. flexuosa Mart. = *Syagrus flexuosa*.
C. geriba Barb. Rodr. = *Syagrus romanzoffianum*.
C. glazioviana Dammer = *Syagrus petraea*.
C. macrocarpa (Barb. Rodr.) Barb. Rodr. = *Syagrus macrocarpa*.
C. martiana Drude and Glazebr. ex Drude = *Syagrus romanzoffianum*.
C. nehrlingiana G. Abbott ex Nehrl. = *Butia capitata* var. *nehrlingiana*.
C. nucifera L. 'Dwarf Golden Malay': to 8m; fr. small, numerous, yellow, green, or red. 'Dwarf Green': fr. green, with improved resistance to coconut yellows. 'Dwarf Samoan': trunk short, stout; fr. large, rounded; husk green or red. 'Niño': habit compact; lvs graceful, lfts set closely, long, narrow, shiny, green.

C. odorata Barb. Rodr. = *Butia capitata* var. *odorata*.
C. orinocensis Spruce = *Syagrus orinocensis*.
C. petraea Mart. = *Syagrus petraea*.
C. plumosa Hook. = *Syagrus romanzoffianum*.
C. procopiana Glaz. ex Drude = *Syagrus macrocarpa*.
C. quinquefaria Barb. Rodr. = *Syagrus coronata*.
C. romanzoffiana Cham. = *Syagrus romanzoffianum*.
C. syagrus Drude = *Syagrus cocoides*.
C. urbaniana Dammer = *Syagrus flexuosa*.
C. weddellii Drude = *Syagrus cocoides*.
C. yatay Mart. = *Butia yatay*.

Cocoyam *Colocasia* (*C. esculenta*).

Codariocalyx Hassk. Leguminosae (Papilionoideae). 2 erect shrubs. Lvs generally trifoliolate; term. lfts largest, laterals 0 or v. small. Fls pea-like in sparse pan. or rac. Trop. Aus., E Asia. Z10.
C. motorius (Houtt.) Ohashi. SEMAPHORE PLANT; TELEGRAPH PLANT. Slender shrub 20–180cm with sleep movements and lat. lfts. gyrating slowly at high temperatures. Term. lfts 1.5–12×0.5–4cm, ovate or elliptic, downy beneath, lat. lfts 0.8–2.5×0.2–0.5cm, or 0, elliptic or narrowly obovate. Infl. 2-3-fld; cor. lilac, pale mauve or orange, standard 0.7–1cm. Aus.
→*Desmodium*.

Codiaeum A. Juss. Euphorbiaceae. 6 everg. trees and shrubs. Lvs simple, leathery glossy. Fls small in slender, axill. rac. Malaya, Pacific Is. Z10.
C. variegatum (L.) Bl. var. *pictum* (Lodd.) Muell. Arg. CROTON. Shrub to 1.8m. Lvs linear to ovate, entire or lobed, or spirally twisted, occas. crisped, sometimes deeply cut, variegated with white, yellow and or red. Fls white. S India, Sri Lanka, Malaya. 'Andreanum': compact; lvs oval, pointed, green tinged copper with yellow veins turning red-orange, yellow variegation near margins. 'Big Dipper': large, bushy; lvs broad obovate, blueblack, variegated orange and dark green. 'Commotion': lvs lightly lobed, deep blue-green and bright green marked pink, yellow and cream turning crimson. 'Daisy-O': lvs broad-elliptic, metallic brown-black, variegated and shaded orange-red. 'Evening Embers': vigorous, dense; lvs to 25cm, lightly lobed, blueblack splashed red and green, veined deep red. 'Fascination': lvs v. narrow, striped yellow, flushed red. 'Gloriosum Superbum': lvs broad, coarsely undulate, bluntly and irregularly lobed, dark green veined gold, suffused orange and flame red. 'Imperialis': small, compact; lvs elliptic, almost entirely yellow turning orange to red, midrib green. 'Majesticum': pendulous; lvs to 25cm long, narrow, deep green with yellow ribs, later olive ribbed crimson. 'Mrs. Iceton': lvs oval, black-green heavily marked between veins with red and pink, young lvs marked cream. 'Nepenthifolium': lvs narrowly oblong, dark green spotted yellow, midrib projecting as slender stalk terminating in small cup-like lobe. 'Norma': hardy; lvs variegated green, black and purple overlaid with cream, orange and red. 'Reidii': lvs large, broad, black veined deep red, young lvs veined yellow. 'Sunrise': vigorous; lvs narrow-lanceolate, veined and edged orange-red, young growth green and yellow. 'Tortilis': lvs linear, twisted, large, dark green marked orange-red.
→*Croton*.

Codlins and Cream *Epilobium hirsutum*.

Codonanthe (Mart.) Hanst. Gesneriaceae. 13 myrmecophilous epiphytic shrubs with creeping st. Lvs opposite in pairs, usually thick, fleshy, often with red extrafloral nectaries below. Fls axill.; cor. funnel-shaped to subcampanulate, upper lip 2-lobed, lower lip 3-lobed. Trop. Amer. Z10.
C. 'Aurora'. Habit compact; lvs v. small, satiny; fls small, rosepink.
C. caribaea Urban. Lvs to 8×3.5cm, ovate or ovate-lanceolate, glab. Fls 1-2(-4); cor. to 3.5cm, white, yellow at throat, lobes translucent. Trin.
C. carnosa (Gardn.) Hanst. Lvs to 2.5×1.5cm, equal ovate, obovate or broadly elliptic, brown-hairy. Fls 1–2; cor. white, flushed pink at base, exterior hirsute, blotched red-brown at throat, tube to 1.3cm, lobes to 1cm. S Braz.
C. crassifolia (Focke) Morton. Lvs to 8.5×3.9cm equal, elliptic or narrowly oblong to ovate, thick. Fls 1–4; cor. to 3cm, white, often pink on lobes below, yellow on lower inner surface, spur to 4mm, lobes. Mex., Hond., Braz., Peru.
C. devosiana Lem. = *C. carnosa*.
C. dissimulata H.E. Moore. Lvs to 9×3.6cm markedly unequal, elliptic, smaller lf often caducous. Fls 1–2; cor. to 2.5cm, white, flushed yellow below inside, spur to 4mm, lobes spreading, to 4mm. Peru.

C. gracilis (Mart.) Hanst. Lvs in almost equal pairs, narrowly elliptic to ovate, strigose. Fls 1–2; cor. to 2.2cm, white or yellow at base, spotted red or maroon, lobes to 6mm, minutely gland. S Braz.
C. luteola Wiehler. Lvs to 3.5×1.9cm, equal, obovate, obtuse, succulent, beneath. Fls cymose; cor. light yellow, spur spotted red, throat to 4cm, marked with deep pink, limb to 1.7cm diam. Panama.
C. macradenia F.D. Sm. Lvs to 7.5×2.6cm equal, elliptic to orbicular, sometimes shallowly toothed above. Fls 1–2; cor. to 3.5cm, white, sometimes flushed pink, spotted red inside, curved, upper lip erect, to 5mm, lower lobes spreading, to 7mm. S Mex. to N Colomb.
C. triplinervia Britt. = *C. caribaea*.
C. uleana Fritsch. Lvs to 7×3.5cm equal, elliptic to ovate, obovate or oblanceolate, shallow-toothed toward apex, sometimes tinged red. Fls 1–3; cor. to 3.3cm, white flushed with yellow below, lobes flushed pink, to 4mm, spreading. Braz., Boliv., Colomb., Peru.
C. ulei (Mansf.) H.E. Moore. Lvs to 30×9cm, oblanceolate to obovate, markedly unequal, smaller lf aborted. Fls many together, cor. to 1.8cm, pale pink, spotted purple, lobes rounded, to 2mm. Braz., Peru.
C. ventricosa (Vell.) Hoehne = *C. gracilis*.

Codonopsis Wallich. BONNET BELLFLOWER. Campanulaceae. c30 foetid, scandent perenn. herbs. Lvs opposite or alt. Fls nodding, usually solitary and term.; cal. lobes 5, large; cor. broadly campanulate, often with colourful basal nectaries and net veins within, lobes 5 short. Himal. to Jap. and Malesia.
C. affinis Hook. f. & Thoms. Slender, perenn. herb, twining to 2m. Lvs to 16cm, oblong to elliptic, cordate, entire to denticulate, pubesc. Fls to 1.5cm, campanulate, purple or green, lobes purple. C Himal. Z7.
C. bulleyana Forr. & Diels. Tufted perenn. to 50cm; branchlets usually tomentose. Lvs to 1.5cm, lanceolate-cordate, villous. Fls tubular in lower half, waisted in middle, then flared, pale blue with darker net veins within. SW China, Tibet. Z4.
C. cardiophylla Diels ex Komar. Differs from *C. clematidea* in more cordate lvs with thin, white, slightly thickened margin. Fls small. Summer. China to Tibet. Z4.
C. clematidea (Schrenk ex Fisch. & C.A. Mey.) C.B. Clarke. Erect perenn. to 80cm, branched, eventually sprawling. Lvs to 2.5cm, narrowly ovate, scarcely pubesc. Fls pale blue with tangerine and black markings at base within. Summer. C Asia, from S Russia to W Himal. Z4.
C. convolvulacea Kurz. Perenn., twiner to 3m. Lvs to 6cm, lanceolate-ovate, occas. with a cordate base, entire to denticulate, long-petiolate. Fls rotate-campanulate, with distinct lobes, azure to violet-blue. SW China and N Himal. Z5.
C. convolvulacea var. *forrestii* (Diels) Ballard = *C. forrestii*.
C. cordifolia Komar. Slender twiner, st. smooth, branched. Lvs to 7cm, lanceolate, deeply cordate. Fls to 2.5cm campanulate, green flushed yellow, marked with purple. SW China. Z7.
C. forrestii Diels. To 3.5m, usually shorter, scrambling. Lvs to 10cm, broadly oval, base cordate, glaucous beneath, serrate. Fls lavender blue with claret basal spots within. Summer. SW China. Z7.
C. handeliana Nannf. = *C. tubulosa*.
C. japonica Miq. = *C. lanceolata*.
C. lanceolata (Maxim.) Benth. & Hook. f. Glab. perenn. twiner. Lvs to 5cm, elliptic-ovate to oblong, usually entire, occas. undulate, glaucous beneath. Fls campanulate, lobes to 2.5cm, deltoid pale blue suffused mauve, spotted and striped violet within. Autumn. China. Z7.
C. macrocalyx Diels. St. 60–80cm, weakly twining, sparsely branched. Lvs oblong-ovate, crenate. Fls with cal. inflated, cor. tubular campanulate, yellow-green marked purple at base. W China. Z4.
C. meleagris Diels. Tufted, erect perenn. to 30cm. Lvs usually clustered, ovate, undulate, finely pubesc. Fls campanulate, purple with reticulate dark brown markings, sometimes spotted yellow within. Summer. SW China. Z4.
C. mollis Chippd. St. to 1m forming a clump. Lvs to 4.5cm, ovate, tomentose, grey-green. Fls tubular, blue, throat purple, conspicuously veined within. China, Tibet. Z7.
C. ovata Benth. Perenn., ascending to 30cm. Lvs oval-acuminate, mostly basal, finely pubesc. Fls funnelform, lobes longer than wide, pale blue with darker veins within, base nearly black, green-margined. Summer. W Himal. Z4.
C. pilosula (Franch.) Nannf. Twining to 1.7m. Lvs to 2cm, lanceolate to cordate at base, pilose. Fls to 2.5cm, campanulate, green flushed with dull purple. N China. Z6.
C. rotundifolia Benth. Twining to 3m. Lvs ovate to lanceolate, sometimes cordate at base, sinuate, sparsely pubesc. Fls

C. campanulate, yellow-green with purple-black net veins. Himal. Z7.

C. **tangshen** Oliv. Twining to 2m, glab. or scaberulous. Lvs broadly lanceolate, coarsely dentate, pubesc. Fls campanulate yellow to olive green strongly net-veined and spotted purple at base within. Summer. W China. Z4.

C. **thalictrifolia** Wallich. Tufted perenn., to 25cm, usually erect. Lvs to 0.8cm, ovate to elliptic, entire or sprasely dentate, villous. Fls narrow-funnelform, pale blue with claret veins at base within. Nepal, Sikkim, Tibet. Z7.

C. **tibetica** hort. = *C. forrestii*.

C. **tubulosa** Komar. Twining perenn. herb to 1.5m, glab. Lvs ovate-lanceolate. Fls tinged lime to yellow, with faint purple veins within. SW China. Z7.

C. **ussuriensis** (Rupr.) Hemsl. = *C. lanceolata*.

C. **vinciflora** Komar. = *C. convolvulacea*.

C. **viridiflora** Maxim. Semi-climbing, to 1.2m, pubesc. Lvs to 2.5cm, ovate to lanceolate, crenate, tomentose. Fls to 2cm, campanulate, green tinged yellow. C China. Z7.

Coelia Lindl. Orchidaceae. 5 epiphytic or terrestrial orchids. Pbs clustered, glossy, ovoid to ellipsoid. Lvs to 5, petiolate, narrow lanceolate, soft, ribbed or plicate. Rac. bracteate, basal; fls fleshy, fragrant, often not opening fully, thus ± tubular-campanulate. Summer. Mex., C Amer. Z10.

C. **baueriana** Lindl. = *C. triptera*.

C. **bella** (Lem.) Rchb. f. Lvs to 50cm, usually shorter. Infl. to 12cm; fls to 6, to 5.5cm, held upright, sweetly scented, ivory tipped rose or violet, lip midlobe golden to orange. Mex., Guat., Hond.

C. **densiflora** Rolfe. Lvs broader than in *C. bella*. Infl. packed, short; fls to 1.5cm, spirally arranged, v. fragrant, translucent, sparkling white. Guat., Hond.

C. **guatemalensis** Rchb. f. Lvs shorter than in other spp. Infl. to 18cm, with hooded, conspicuous bracts; fls to 7, to 2cm, white tipped rose, lip centrally thickened. Guat.

C. **macrostachya** Lindl. Lvs to 80×5cm. Infl. to 60cm, crowded; fls to 1cm, highly fragrant, white to glistening rose; lip with a bilobed basal sac. Throughout genus range.

C. **triptera** (Sm.) G. Don ex Steud. Lvs to 38×4.5cm. Infl. to 16cm; fls to 1.5cm, never opening fully, fragrant, crystalline white; ovary winged. Mex., Guat., W Indies.

→*Bothriochilus*.

Coeliopsis Rchb. f. Orchidaceae. 1 epiphytic orchid. Pbs elongate-ovoid, to 10cm. Lvs to 60×8cm, lanceolate, plicate, petiolate. Rac. dense basal, capitate, sharply decurved to pendulous, to 8.5cm, stout; fls to 2.25cm diam., seldom opening fully, waxy, fragrant, sep. ovate, cream, lateral sep. fused at base, forming a blunt spur; pet. concave, broadly lanceolate, ivory; lip trilobed, fleshy, white stained gold to orange at base, midlobe truncate-ovate, reflexed, fimbriate, lat. lobes, erect, fimbriate. Summer. Costa Rica, Panama. Z10.

C. **hyacinthosma** Rchb. f.

Coeloglossum Hartm. FROG ORCHID. Orchidaceae. 1 tuberous terrestrial orchid, 6–40cm. Lvs light green, ovate to lanceolate-oblong. Spike 2–15cm, bracteate, cylindric, 5–25-fld; tep. sometimes forming hood, green to yellow-green, suffused purple, with red margins; lip 6–8mm, linear-oblong, central lobe shorter than laterals, yellow or yellow-brown, spur pale green, short. Late spring–summer. Eur., Asia. Z6.

C. **viride** (L.) Hartm.

Coelogyne Lindl. Orchidaceae. *c*200 epiphytic orchids. Pbs cylindric to globose, clustered or remote. Lvs elliptic to lanceolate. Rac. usually terminal, erect or pendent; tep. ovate to linear; lip trilobed, disc keeled. Indomal., Trop. China, W Pacific. Z10.

C. **asperata** Lindl. Infl. to 30cm, arching, crowded; fls cream-white, fragrant; sep. lanceolate; pet. narrower, 3.5×0.5cm; lip midlobe ovate, acute, warty, lat. lobes veined brown; disc brown, 2-keeled. Malaysia to New Guinea.

C. **barbata** Griff. Infl. erect or arched, to 45cm, to 10-fld; fls to 7cm diam., fragrant, white; dors. sep, carinate, lat. sep. subfalcate; pet. linear-lanceolate; lip midlobe triangular, fringed, lat. lobes rounded, disc 3-keeled, brown, fringed. India.

C. **beccarii** Rchb. f. Fls 3, ivory, sep. ligulate, pet. linear; midlobe triangular-hastate, acute, lat. lobes and keels cinnamon. New Guinea.

C. **brachyptera** Rchb. f. Infl. to 18cm, to 7-fld; fls green-yellow; dors. sep. ovate-lanceolate, subacute, 3.2–3.8cm, lat. sep. oblong-lanceolate; pet. similar to lat. sep.; lip to 2.5cm with dark dots midlobe orbicular, undulate, lat. lobes rounded, disc orange with 3, wavy keels, apex warty. Burm.

C. **brunnea** Lindl. = *C. fuscescens* var. *brunnea*.

C. **Burfordiense** (*C. asperata* ×*C. pandurata*.) Rac. dense; fls similar to *C. pandurata*, lime green, lip marked black fading to brown.

C. **corymbosa** Lindl. Infl. erect or pendent, to 20cm, 2–4-fld; fls white; sep. lanceolate, 2.5–4cm; pet. lanceolate, narrow; lip to 3×2cm, midlobe ovate-lanceolate, with 4 yellow blotches edged orange-red, lateral lobes erose disc ridges 3. Himal.

C. **cristata** Lindl. Infl. pendent, 3–10-fld, 15–30cm; fls fragrant, white; sep. elliptic-oblong, undulate, to 5×2cm; pet. similar, to 4.5–2cm; lip to 4×3.5cm, midlobe suborbicular marked yellow, lateral lobes large, rounded, keels golden-yellow, fringed. E Himal. var. *hololeuca* Rchb. f. Fls pure white. India.

C. **cumingii** Lindl. Infl. axill., 3–5-fld; fls white; sep. ovate-lanceolate; pet. linear-lanceolate, lip white or cream stained orange, oblong, broad, midlobe ovate-obovate, obtuse, undulate, crisped, minutely dentate, keels 3 crisped, crested. Singapore, Malaysia.

C. **dayana** (Rchb. f.) Rolfe. Rac. 4–100cm, 20–30-fld; fls cream to pale brown; sep. lanceolate, acute, to 3.5cm; pet. shorter, narrower; lip brown with white streak, lat. lobes streaked yellow, rounded, crenate, broad, disc 2–3-ridged, crispate. Borneo.

C. **Mem. W. Micholitz.** Fls large, white, golden orange at base of lip with chestnut hairs.

C. **fimbriata** Lindl. Infl. to 5cm, 1–3-fld; fls pale yellow; sep. lanceolate; pet. linear-filiform, to 2cm; lip white or pale yellow, marked brown, midlobe oblong to subquadrate, fringed, obtuse or retuse, lat. lobes oblong-elliptic, keels 4, fringed, undulate. India, Vietnam to Hong Kong.

C. **flaccida** Lindl. Infl. to 20cm, pendent, to 9-fld; fls to 3.5cm diam., white; sep. lanceolate; pet. linear, reflexed; lip blotched yellow, midlobe ovate-lanceolate, spotted at base, reflexed, acute, lat. lobes striped yellow-red oblong, rounded, erect, keels 3, undulate. E Himal.

C. **fuliginosa** Hook. Infl. to 4-fld; fls buff to orange-yellow; sep. oblong-lanceolate; pet. filiform; lip to 2×1cm, stained or streaked brown, midlobe ovate, fringed, lat. lobes oblong, inner margins hirsute, fringed. Burm., Java.

C. **fuscescens** Lindl. Infl. suberect; fls 3.5–5cm diam., pale yellow or pale yellow-green, apex flushed brown; sep. oblong-lanceolate; pet. linear; lip white marked brown, central stripe pale yellow-green elliptic-oblong, narrow, 3–4cm, midlobe ovate to cordate, broad, acute, lat. lobes oblong, keels 3, fleshy. India, Nepal. var. *brunnea* (Lindl.) Lindl. Fls darker, lip marked solid brown. Burm., Thail. to Vietnam.

C. **huettneriana** Rchb. f. Infl. arched, to 18cm, 8–10-fld; fls white; sep. ovate-lanceolate, acuminate; pet. linear; lip midlobe ovate, dentate, lateral lobes rounded, keels 3, crisped. Burm.

C. **lactea** Rchb. f. Infl. to 18cm, to 10-fld, horizontal; fls to 4cm diam., cream-white; sep. oblong; pet. linear; lip to 2cm, midlobe ovate, acute, lat. lobes shorter, brown, ovate, upcurved, flanking column, keels 3, undulate. Burm., Thail., Laos, Vietnam.

C. **lawrenceana** Rolfe. Infl. 17–20cm; fl. solitary, green-yellow to yellow; sep. to 7cm, oblong-lanceolate; pet. linear; lip white tipped sulphur yellow, base weakly saccate, midlobe ovate, broad, weakly undulate, obtuse, sometimes notched, lat. lobes oblong, broad, erect, disc mottled pale brown, keels 5, fringed. Vietnam, Malaysia, India.

C. **lentiginosa** Lindl. Infl. erect, 6–16cm, 4–5-fld; fls pale green; tep. lanceolate, narrow, 1.7–2.2cm; lip white marked brown weakly arched, 1–8cm, midlobe blotched orange spreading, base broadly clawed, apex ovate, subacute, lat. lobes along, narrow, rounded, keels 3, undulate. Burm., Thail., Vietnam.

C. **massangeana** Rchb. f. Infl. pendulous, to 30-fld, axis flexuous, wiry, to 45cm; fls to 6cm diam., pale yellow, ivory or tan; sep. oblong-lanceolate; pet. narrower, lip midlobe veined brown and pale yellow, oblong, obtuse, pendent, lat. lobes veined yellow or white, brown-maroon or blue-grey with age, elliptic-oblong, narrow or rounded, erect, disc warty, fringed. Malaysia to Java.

C. **mooreana** hort. ex Rolfe. Fls white; sep. lanceolate, broad, to 5×1.3cm; pet. similar; lip to 4×3cm, midlobe ovate, acute, lat. lobes rounded, broad, enveloping column, disc ochre or orange, fringed. Vietnam.

C. **nitida** (Wallich) Lindl. Infl. to 20cm, erect or pendent, 3–6-fld; fls sweetly scented, to 4cm diam., white; sep. oblong, narrow; lip subovate, 1.9×1.6cm, midlobe round to cordate, lat. lobes marked yellow, oblong to rounded, disc with blotches yellow edged red. India to Burm. and Laos.

C. **occulata** Hook. f. Infl. exceeding lvs, 2–4-fld; fls to 5cm diam., white; sep. oblanceolate; pet. narrower; lip to 3.5cm blotched and streaked yellow, midlobe oblong, acute, decurved, lat. lobes rounded, minutely crenate, keels 3, crenulate. India.

C. **ocellata** Lindl. = *C. nitida*.

C. **ochracea** Lindl. = *C. nitida*.

C. **ovalis** Lindl. Infl. to 8cm, few-fld; fls pale tan; sep. ovate-lanceolate, to 3×1.5cm; pet. linear; lip marked bronze to dark brown, midlobe ovate, shortly fringed, lat. lobes triangular or oblong, fringed, keels 3 undulate. India, Nepal, China to Thail.

C. pandurata Lindl. Infl. 15–30cm; fls few, fragrant, jade to lime green, mottled or netted dark violet to black on midlobe of lip, sometimes overlaying white, operculum sometimes blue-grey; dors. sep. linear-oblong, 3.5–5×1.3cm; pet. clawed, sub-spathulate, to 4.5×1.2cm; lip to 4cm, pandurate, midlobe crispate to undulate, keels 2, warty. Malaysia to Borneo.

C. parishii Hook. f. Infl. pendent or erect, 3–5-fld; fls green to yellow-green, lip blue-green, blotched dark purple; sep. lanceolate, to 2.3×1.6cm; lip to 3cm, pandurate, midlobe un-dulate, keels 4, combed, becoming warty. Burm.

C. rochussenii De Vries. Infl. to 70cm, to 40-fld; fls 3–7cm diam., fragrant, lemon yellow; sep. lanceolate; pet. oblanceolate; lip to 3cm, midlobe lanceolate, acuminate, decurved, lat. lobes rounded, keels rounded, toothed. Malaya, Sumatra to Philipp.

C. rumphii Lindl. Rac. 10–20cm, 4–5-fld; fls pale green; sep. lanceolate, broad, pet. linear; lip white blotched orange elliptic-oblong, midlobe marked brown obcordate, broad, lat. lobes dotted brown-red obtuse, rounded, oblique, erect. Malaysia, New Guinea.

C. schilleriana Rchb. f. Fls tawny yellow; sep. to 4cm lanceolate; pet. linear, pendent; lip forward-pointing, lyrate, midlobe blotched and spotted orange, orbicular, dentate, undulate, apex bifid, lat. lobes oblong, incurved over column, disc orange, ridged. Burm.

C. speciosa (Bl.) Lindl. Infl. erect to nodding, 1–3-fld; fls green-yellow to pale bronze-pink; sep. oblong-lanceolate, to 6×0.9cm; pet. linear, reflexed, acute, to 5×0.3cm; lip to 5cm, dark flesh pink to brown, apex white, midlobe rounded, erose, lat. lobes obtuse, toothed, disc warty with tubular projections. Java, Malaysia to Sumatra. var. *salmonicolor* Rchb. f. Fl. solitary, salmon pink, lip chequered brown.

C. suaveolens Hook. f. Infl. 15–20cm; fls many, white; sep. oblong-lanceolate, 1.2–1.5cm; pet. oblong-ovate; lip midlobe ovate or orbicular, broad, lat. lobes rounded, keels yellow, 4–6, crenate. India.

C. swaniana Rolfe. Infl. pendent, 20–40cm, many-fld; fls to 5cm diam., white; sep. oblong-lanceolate, pet. narrower than sep.; lip pale brown with darker margins entire, midlobe orbicular-ovate, obtuse, lat. lobes short, rounded, keels crested, some fringed. Philipp., Borneo.

C. testacea Lindl. Infl. pendent, to 40cm, 8–10-fld; fls to 4cm diam., pale brown, sep. and pet. similar, oblong-lanceolate, obtuse, apiculate; lip oblong, broad, recurved, midlobe obtuse, weakly undulate, lat. lobes dark brown edged white rounded, short, keels 4, fringed or crested. Malaysia.

C. tomentosa Lindl. Infl. 30–45cm; bracts pubesc., persistent; fls numerous, salmon pink or pale orange; sep. oblong, 2.5–3.5×0.7cm; pet. oblong-lanceolate, streaked brown; lip 2.5×1.7cm, yellow, midlobe ovate, lat. lobes streaked brown, rounded, erect, keels papillose. Malaysia to Borneo.

C. virescens Rolfe = *C. brachyptera*.

C. viscosa Rchb. f. Infl. erect, 10–15cm, 2–4-fld; fls fragrant, to 4cm diam., white to ivory; sep. ovate-lanceolate, to 3×1cm; pet. linear-lanceolate, reflexed; lip midlobe ovate, broad, lat. lobes veined brown rounded, keels 3. India.

Coetocapnia Link & Otto = *Polianthes*.

Coffea L. COFFEE. Rubiaceae. *c*40 shrubs or small trees. Fls 4–8-merous, axill., bracteolate, usually in clusters, white or cream, fragrant; cal. tube turbinate, campanulate, or subcylindric, or oblong; cor. salverform or funnel-shaped, lobes oblong. Fr. a berry, ellipsoid to subglobose, fleshy; pyrenes 2, 1-seeded. Trop. Asia and Africa, and in widespread trop. cult. Z10.

C. arabica L. COFFEE; ARABIAN COFFEE. Shrub to 7m, usually shorter. Lvs to 10×8cm, elliptic to ovate or oblong, leathery, often undulate, lustrous, dark green. Fls several, in axill. clusters, white, fragrant; cor. tube 12mm, lobes 13×6mm, 5. Fr. 15mm, subglobose to ellipsoid or obovoid, ripening red, yellow or purple. Autumn. Ethiopia, Sudan.

C. bengalensis Roxb. = *Psilanthus bengalensis*.

C. canephora Pierre ex Fröhner. ROBUSTA COFFEE; RIO NUNEZ COFFEE. Shrub or tree to 9m. Lvs to 35×12cm, elliptic to obovate or lanceolate, often undulate. Fls in massed axill. clusters; bracteoles with somewhat leaflike; cor. tube 15mm, lobes 5–6, to 20×6mm. Fr. to 17mm ellipsoid to oblong. W Afr. (Congo Basin).

C. dewevrei De Wildeman & T. Dur. = *C. liberica*.

C. laurina Poir. = *Craterispermum laurinum*.

C. liberica Bull ex Hiern. LIBERIAN COFFEE. Tree to 10m. Lvs to 40×20cm, obovate to oblanceolate or elliptic, leathery or papery, lustrous to dull green above, paler beneath. Fls in sub-sessile clusters; cor. tube to 13mm, lobes usually 7, occas. 5–9,

to 15mm. Fr. to 25mm, ellipsoid to oblong, red or yellow flecked red or rust. W Afr.

C. racemosa Lour. WILD COFFEE. Shrub or tree to 6m. Lvs to 9×5cm, elliptic, oval or lanceolate, narrowed at apex and base, undulate. Fls axill., solitary or few in rac., white or pink, fragrant; cor. tube to 16mm, lobes 6–8. Fr. subglobose, to 14mm, red to purple. S Afr., Moz., Zimb.

C. robusta Lind. = *C. canephora*.

C. stenophylla G. Don. SIERRA LEONE COFFEE; NARROW-LEAVED COFFEE. Shrub or tree to 6m. Lvs to 15×3cm, narrowly oblanceolate to oblong or obovate, long-pointed at apex, gland. in vein axils beneath. fls axill., solitary or 2–3; cor. tube to 1cm, lobes 6–9, to 1cm. Fr. ellipsoid, 12mm, purple to black. W Afr. (Sierra Leone, Guinea).

C. zanguebariae Lour. IBO COFFEE; LARGE-LEAVED WILD COFFEE. Shrub or tree to 5m. Lvs to 14×8cm, elliptic, occas. undulate, papery, veins pubese, beneath. Fls axill., solitary or clustered, white; cor. tube to 1cm, lobes 6–8, to 12mm. Fr. to 20mm, ovoid or oblong, minutely pubesc., green and red-striped to deep red or black. Moz.

Coffee *Coffea* (*C. arabica*).
Coffeeberry *Rhamnus californicus*.
Coffee Fern *Pellaea andromedifolia*.
Coffee Rose *Tabernaemontana divaricata*.
Coffee Senna *Senna occidentalis*.
Coffee Tree *Polyscias guilfoylei*.
Coffin Juniper *Juniperus recurva* var. *coxii*.
Coffin Tree *Taiwania cryptomerioides* var. *flousiana*.
Cohosh *Cimicifuga*.
Cohete *Oreopanax sanderianus*.
Cohune Palm *Orbignya cohune*.
Coigüe *Nothofagus dombeyi*.
Coigüe de Chiloe *Nothofagus nitida*.
Coigüe de Magellanes *Nothofagus betuloides*.

Coix L. Gramineae. 6 ann. or perenn. grasses. Lvs flat, sheathing st. Infl. in upper lf axils, compound, racemose, long-stalked; ♀ spikelet protected by a hollow, globose to pyriform utricle, ♂ spikelets tassel-like in fascicles of 2–3, exserted from infl. bracts. Trop. Asia. Z9.

C. lacryma-jobi L. JOB'S TEARS. Ann. to 1.5m. Lvs narrow-lanceolate, to 60×5cm. Infl. arching gracefully; utricles bead-like, ovoid-globose, to 13mm, white to grey tinged blue to brown. Autumn. SE Asia.

Cojomaria *Paramongaia weberbaueri*.
Cola *Cola acuminata*.

Cola Schott & Endl. Sterculiaceae. *c*125 trees. Lvs simple, palmately lobed or digitately divided; petioles often pulvinate. Fls in axill. rac., pan. or clusters; cal. 4–5 (–7)-lobed; pet. 0: ♂ with 5–12 anth. in 1–2 rings on an androphore ♀ with (3)4–5(–10) coherent carpels, styles many free, or united in a single column. Trop. Afr. Z10.

C. acuminata (Pall.) Schott & Endl. COLA; ABATA COLA; GOORA NUT. Everg. tree to 20m. Lvs to 20cm+, leathery, entire, obovate to elliptic, short acuminate. Rac. many-fld axill. corymbose; fls yellow, 1.2cm in diam.; cal. scurfy-tomentose; cal. tube short, campanulate, lobes 5–6 oblong, subacute, spreading. Fr. 8–20cm; seeds 2.5cm.

C. nitida (Vent.) A. Chev. Differs from *C. acuminata* in lvs. oblong-lanceolate, to 30cm; fls to 4cm diam., pale yellow lined purple, stellate-pubesc.; cal. lobes 5.

Colax Lindl.
C. jugosus (Lindl.) Lindl. = *Pabstia jugosa*.

Colchicum L. AUTUMN CROCUS; NAKED LADIES. Liliaceae (Colchicaceae). 45 perenn. cormous herbs. Lvs basal, linear, lorate, lanceolate or elliptic ovate, smooth to plicate, developing with or after fls. Fls solitary or in clusters, v. short-stalked; perianth campanulate, funnelform or star-shaped, lobes 6, in 2± equal whorls; sta. borne near base of perianth lobes, in 1 or 2 series, fil. slender, anth. dorsifixed and versatile or basifixed and rigid; styles 3, free. E Eur., N Afr. to W Asia, through Afghan. to N India and W China.

C. agrippinum Bak. (*C. variegatum* × *C. autumnale* ?) Lvs to 15cm, erect, dull glaucous green, somewhat undulate. Fls numerous, funnel-shaped; tube to 6cm, white; seg. to 5×1.5cm, heavily but indistinctly tesselated purple and white; anth. purple; styles purple. Early autumn. Greece to SW Turk. Z5.

C. alpinum DC. Lvs 8–15cm, strap-shaped to linear-lanceolate, glab. Fls 1 or 2, narrowly campanulate to funnelform; perianth lobes 1.7–3×0.4–1cm, narrowly oblong-elliptic, purple-pink, occas. white; anth. dorsifixed, yellow; styles straight. Late summer–autumn. Fr., Switz., It., Corsica and Sardinia. Z4.

C. ancyrense B.L. Burtt = *C. triphyllum*.

C. andrium Rech. & P.H. Davis see *C. stevenii*.

C. arenarium Waldst. & Kit. Like *C. alpinum* but lvs longer and broader, fls slightly larger. Summer–autumn. EC Eur. Z6.

C. arenarium Waldst. & Kit. = *C. umbrosum*.

C. armenum B. Fedtsch. = *C. szovitsii*.

C. atropurpureum Stearn. Close to *C. turcicum* but fls small, dark magenta-red, white in bud. Balk., SW Turk. Z6.

C. atticum Tomm. = *Merendera attica*.

C. autumnale L. Lvs 14–35cm, coriaceous, linear-lanceolate to broadly lanceolate, erect to spreading. Fls 1–6, campanulate; perianth lobes 4–6×1–1.5cm, narrowly elliptic to oblong-elliptic, purple-pink to white, occas. tessellated; anth. yellow, dorsifixed; styles curved at apex. Late summer–autumn. W & C Eur. 'Alboplenum': fls double, white. 'Album': fls small, dull white. 'Plenum': fls double, lilac-pink. Z5.

C. balansae Planch. Lvs 18–24cm, erect to spreading, elliptic to oblong-elliptic, inner lvs more strap-shaped. Fls 3–11, funnel-form; perianth lobes 4.5–7.5×0.5–1.3cm, narrowly oblong-elliptic, white to purple-pink; anth. dorsifixed, yellow; styles curved at apex. Late summer–autumn. Turk., Greece. Z7.

C. balansae var. *macrophyllum* Siehe = *C. cilicicum*.

C. baytopiorum C. Brickell. Lvs 1–8cm at flowering, 20–32×2.5–4.5cm at maturity, narrowly lanceolate. Fls 1–3 to 5, campanulate or funnelform; perianth lobes 2.2–4.2×0.5–1.1cm, elliptic or oblong-elliptic to oblanceolate, bright purple-pink; anth. yellow; styles straight. Autumn. W Turk. Z8.

C. biebersteinii Rouy = *C. triphyllum*.

C. bifolium (Freyn & Sint.) Bordz. = *C. szovitsii*.

C. bivonae Guss. Lvs 12–30cm, ±erect, strap-shaped or linear-lanceolate. Fls 1–6, campanulate, sometimes broadly so; peri-anth lobes 4–8.5×0.8–3.5cm, elliptic to obovate-elliptic, rosy purple, strongly tessellated, sometimes white at base; anth. dorsifixed, purple-black or purple-brown; styles curved and slightly swollen at apex. Late summer–autumn. S Eur. from Corsica and Sardinia to W Turk. Z6.

C. boissieri Orph. Lvs 11–22cm, erect, linear. Fls 1 or 2, campanulate to narrowly funnelform; perianth lobes 2.5–5×0.5–1.5cm, narrowly elliptic to narrowly elliptic-obovate, rosy lilac; anth. dorsifixed, yellow; style straight or slightly curved at apex. Autumn. S Greece, W Turk. Z8.

C. bornmuelleri Freyn. Lvs 17–25cm, ±erect, v. narrowly elliptic. Fls 1–6, campanulate; perianth lobes 4.5–7×1.1–2.4cm, oblanceolate to narrowly elliptic, rosy purple throat usually white; anth. purple or purple-brown, dorsifixed; styles slightly curved. Late summer–autumn. Turk. Z5.

C. bowlesianum B.L. Burtt = *C. bivonae*.

C. brachyphyllum Boiss. Like *C. szovitsii* but lvs narrowly ovate to lanceolate. Fls to 15. Syr., Leb. Z8.

C. bulbocodioides Bieb. non Brot. = *C. triphyllum*.

C. bulbocodium Ker-Gawl. = *Bulbocodium vernum*.

C. burttii Meikle. Lvs erect to spreading and 1–4cm at flowering, recurved and 10–15cm, narrowly linear to linear-lanceolate, hairy on margins. Fls 1–4, funnelform, becoming star-shaped; perianth lobes 1.5–4×0.3–0.8cm, narrowly oblanceolate, white or pale purple-pink; anth. dorsifixed, dark purple-black or black; styles straight. Early spring. W Turk. Z7.

C. byzantinum Ker-Gawl. Lvs to 30cm, strongly ribbed or pleated, emerging in spring, bright green. Fls numerous, pale lilac-pink; tube to 8cm, white: seg. to 5cm, oval, keeled, apex spotted dark purple; anth. pale brown; styles white, stigma hooked, crimson-purple. Turk., Syr., Leb. 'Album': fls white, tipped purple. Z6.

C. byzantinum auct. non Ker-Gawl. = *C. cilicicum*.

C. byzantinum var. *cilicicum* Boiss. = *C. cilicicum*.

C. candidum Boiss. = *C. balansae*.

C. candidum var. *hirtiflorum* Boiss. = *C. kotschyi*.

C. catacuzenium Stef. = *C. triphyllum*.

C. caucasicum (Bieb.) Spreng. = *Merendera trigyna*.

C. chalcedonicum Aznav. Like *C. lingulatum* but fls deep rosy purple, tessellated. NW Turk. Z6.

C. cilicicum (Boiss.) Dammer. Lvs 30–40cm, ±erect, narrowly elliptic to elliptic-lanceolate. Fls 3–25, funnelform to campanulate; perianth lobes 4–7.5×1.2–2.5cm, oblanceolate to elliptic, pale lilac to deep rose-purple, occas. faintly tessellated; anth. bright yellow; styles straight or slightly curved at apex. Autumn. Turk., Syr., Leb. 'Purpureum': fls deep rosy purple. Z6.

C. corsicum Bak. Like *C. alpinum* but lvs shorter and broader. Summer–autumn. Corsica. Z7.

C. crociflorum Reg. = *C. kesselringii*.

C. crocifolium Boiss. Like *C. falcifolium* but lvs glab. or covered in rough hairs. Fls numerous, star-shaped, white and pink. Syr., Iran, Iraq. Z8.

C. cupanii Guss. Lvs to 10cm at flowering, to 15cm at maturity,

linear to linear-lanceolate. Fls 1–12, funnelform to star-shaped; perianth lobes 1.8–2.5×0.3–0.5cm, narrowly elliptic, pale to deep purple-pink; anth. dorsifixed, purple-black; styles straight. Autumn–early winter. N Afr., Fr., It., Greece, Crete. Z8.

C. decaisnei Boiss. = *C. troodii*.

C. decaisnei misapplied = *C. cilicicum*.

C. doerfleri Hal. = *C. hungaricum*.

C. falcifolium Stapf. Lvs 1–8cm at flowering, 9–20cm at maturity, narrowly linear, channelled, glab. or roughly hairy (*C. hirsutum*). Fls 1–8, star-shaped or narrowly funnelform; perianth lobes 1.3–2.5×0.2–0.6cm, narrowly elliptic or oblanceolate, white to purple-pink; anth. dorsifixed, black, green-black or black-brown; styles straight. Late winter–early spring. S Russia, Turk., Iran, Iraq, W Syr. Z8.

C. fasciculare (L.) R. Br. Like *C. falcifolium* but lvs glab. and broader. Fls numerous, star-shaped, white and pink. Syr. Z8.

C. giganteum Arn. Differs from *C. speciosum* in fls broadly funnel-shaped, not campanulate. Z5.

C. glossophyllum Heldr. = *C. cupanii*.

C. hirsutum Stef. see *C. falcifolium*.

C. hungaricum Janka. Lvs 3–10cm at flowering, to 20cm at maturity, narrowly linear-lanceolate, erect, ciliate, sometimes hirsute above. Fls 1–8, campanulate to funnelform; perianth lobes 2–3×0.6–0.7cm, elliptic-lanceolate or narrowly elliptic, purple-pink to white; anth. dorsifixed, purple-black, styles straight or slightly curved at apex. Late winter–early spring. Hung., Balk., Albania, Bulg., Greece. f. *albiflorum* Maly. Fls white. Z7.

C. illyricum superbum invalid = *C. giganteum*.

C. imperator-frederici Siehe = *C. kotschyi*.

C. kesselringii Reg. Lvs ± erect, 1–2cm at flowering, 7–10cm at maturity, linear-lanceolate. Fls 1–4, narrowly campanulate to funnelform; perianth lobes 1.5–3×0.2–0.7cm, narrowly linear-lanceolate to narrowly elliptic, white with pale to deep red-purple, central stripes; anth. yellow, basifixed; styles straight. Early spring–summer. C Asia, N Afghan. Z6.

C. kotschyi Boiss. Lvs 10–16cm, erect to spreading, elliptic-lanceolate to oblong-elliptic, slightly undulate. Fls 3–12, funnel-form; perianth lobes 2.3–5.5×0.4–1.2cm, narrowly oblanceolate to oblong-elliptic, white to purple-pink; anth. dorsifixed, yellow; styles curved at apex. Late summer–autumn. Turk., Iran, Iraq. Z7.

C. kurdicum (Bornm.) Stef. = *Merendera kurdica*.

C. laetum Steven. Like *C. autumnale* but fls 1–3, smaller. Plants in cult. as *C. laetum* with numerous star-shaped, pale purple-pink fls are close to *C. byzantinum*. Z7.

C. latifolium Sibth. & Sm. = *C. bivonae*.

C. latifolium misapplied = *C. macrophyllum*.

C. latifolium var. *longistylum* Pamp. = *C. macrophyllum*.

C. lingulatum Boiss. Lvs spreading, oblong to strap-shaped, margins cartilaginous and wavy. Fls funnelform to campanulate; perianth lobes 2.5–5×0.2–1.2cm, narrowly oblanceolate to narrowly oblong-elliptic, pale to deep purple-pink sometimes faintly tessellated; anth. dorsifixed, yellow; styles curved at apex. Late summer–autumn. Greece, NW Turk. Z8.

C. longiflorum Cast. Like *C. autumnale* but lvs shorter, linear-lanceolate, and fls slightly smaller. S Eur. Z7.

C. lusitanicum Brot. Like *C. autumnale* but fls lightly tessellated; anth. pale or deep purple-black. SW Eur., N Afr. Z8.

C. luteum Bak. Lvs ±erect, 1–3cm at flowering, 10–30cm at maturity, ±linear-lanceolate. Fls 1–4, funnelform to narrowly campanulate; perianth lobes 1.5–2.5×0.2–0.6cm, narrowly oblong-lanceolate, pale to deep yellow, tube sometimes purple-brown; anth. yellow, basifixed; styles straight. Spring–summer. C Asia, Afghan., N India, SW China. Z7.

C. macrophyllum B.L. Burtt. Lvs 24–42cm, erect to spreading, ovate to elliptic-ovate, plicate. Fls 1–5; perianth lobes 4.5–7×1.5–3cm, elliptic or oblong-elliptic, spreading, lilac-purple to rosy purple, tessellated, often paler or white in throat; anth. purple, dorsifixed; styles shortly curved at apex. Autumn. Greece (Crete, Rhodes), SW Turk. Z8.

C. micranthum Boiss. Lvs 10–20cm, ±erect, linear to narrowly linear-oblanceolate. Fls 1–2, narrowly campanulate or funnel-form; perianth lobes 1.8–4×0.3–1.1cm, narrowly oblanceolate, or narrowly linear-elliptic, white to pale purple-pink; anth. dorsifixed, yellow; styles straight, shortly curved, slightly swollen at apex. Autumn. NW Turk. Z7.

C. montanum hort. = *C. triphyllum*.

C. montanum var. *pusillum* (Sieb.) Fiori = *C. pusillum*.

C. neapolitanum Ten. = *C. longiflorum*.

C. nivale Boiss. & Huet ex Stef. = *C. szovitsii*.

C. parkinsonii Hook. = *C. variegatum*.

C. parlatoris Orph. Lvs 7–10cm, linear, developing after flower-ing. Fls 1 or 2, narrowly campanulate; perianth lobes 8–50×4–12mm, narrowly elliptic, purple-pink; anth. dorsifixed, yellow; styles straight. Late summer–autumn. S Greece. Z8.

C. parnassicum Boiss. Differs from *C. autumnale* in corm tunics membranous, never coriaceous, lvs arched. Greece. Z8.

C. peloponnesiacum Rech. & P.H. Davis see *C. stevenii*.

C. persicum Bak. = *C. kotschyi*.

C. procurrens Bak. = *C. boissieri*.

C. psaridis Hal. Lvs 7–9cm at flowering, 7–15×0.2–1.5cm at maturity, ±erect, narrowly linear to narrowly linear-lanceolate. Fls 1–3, star-shaped to narrowly funnelform; perianth lobes 1.1–2.7×0.2–0.6cm, v. narrowly elliptic or narrowly elliptic-oblong, white to pink-purple; anth. black or purple-black, dorsifixed; styles straight. Autumn. S Greece, W Turk. Z8.

C. pusillum Sieb. Lvs ±erect and 1–4cm at flowering, recurved and 8–11cm at maturity, 3–8, narrowly linear, sometimes hairy. Fls 1–6, funnelform, opening star-shaped; perianth lobes 1–2×1.5–4cm, narrowly oblanceolate to narrowly oblong-oblanceolate, pale rosy lilac to white; anth. dorsifixed, purple-black, brown-black or grey-brown, styles straight. Autumn. Greece, Crete, Cyprus. Z8.

C. regelii Stef. = *C. kesselringii*.

C. serpentinum Misch. = *C. falcifolium*.

C. sibthorpii Bak. = *C. bivonae*.

C. soboliferum (Mey.) Stef. = *Merendera sobolifera*.

C. speciosum Steven. Lvs 18–25cm, ±erect, narrowly elliptic to oblong-lanceolate, glab. Fls 1–3, campanulate; perianth tube green or white flushed purple, lobes 4.5–8×1–2.7cm, oblanceolate to oblong-oblanceolate or elliptic, pale to deep rose-purple, sometimes white or white at throat, anth. dorsifixed, orange-yellow; style curved. Autumn. N Turk., Iran, Russia (Cauc.). 'Album': fls large, white, throat green. 'Atrorubens': fls purple-red. Variants with white-throated fls and yellow anth. are sometimes misnamed *C. bornmuelleri*. Z6.

C. speciosum var. *bornmuelleri* (Freyn) Bergmans = *C. bornmuelleri*.

C. stevenii Kunth. Lvs 1–12cm at flowering, 8–18cm at maturity, erect, recurved, often wavy, glab. or ciliate. Fls 1–10, funnelform; perianth lobes 1.5–3×0.2–0.9cm, oblong-elliptic to oblanceolate, bright purple-pink; anth. yellow; styles straight. Autumn–early winter. Cyprus, Turkey, W. Syria. var.*C. peloponnesiacum* Rech. f. & P.H. Davis and var.*C. andrium* Rech. f. & P.H. Davis are v. similar, closely related spp. from Greece and the Islands. Z8.

C. szovitsii Fisch. & Mey. Lvs 2–12cm at flowering, 12–25cm at maturity, lorate or v. narrowly linear-lanceolate, ±erect, glab. Fls 1–7, ovoid- or narrow-campanulate; perianth lobes 2.1–3.5×0.4–1cm, oblanceolate to v. narrowly elliptic, deep to pale purple-pink or white, strongly suffused purple-pink; anth. dorsifixed, purple-black or green-black; styles straight. Early spring–summer. Turk., Iran, Russia (Cauc.). Z6.

C. szovitsii auct. non Fisch. & Mey. = *C. falcifolium*.

C. szovitsii var. *freynii* Stef. = *C. falcifolium*.

C. tauri Stef. = *C. falcifolium*.

C. tenorii Parl. Differs from *C. autumnale* in fls slightly tessellated, stigma tips tinged purple. It. Z8.

C. triphyllum Kunze. Lvs to 2–9cm at flowering, 11–15cm at maturity, erect to spreading, linear-lanceolate. Fls 1–6, campanulate to funnelform; perianth lobes 1.5–3×0.5–1.2cm, narrowly elliptic to oblanceolate, purple-pink or white flushed purple-pink; anth. dorsifixed, purple-black or purple-green; styles straight. Early–late spring. NW Afr., Spain, Greece, Turk., S Russia. Z8.

C. troodii Kotschy Lvs 10–30cm, erect to spreading, lorate, glab., ciliate or thinly hairy. Fls 2–12, narrowly funnelform to star-shaped; perianth lobes 2.8–4.5×0.4–1.1cm, narrowly oblong-lanceolate, white to pale purple-pink; anth. dorsifixed, yellow; styles erect or slightly curved at apex. Autumn–winter. Cyprus, Turk., W Syr., Isr., Leb. Z8.

C. turcicum Janka. Lvs 9–19cm, erect and often twisted at apex, lorate to narrowly lanceolate, somewhat glaucous, ciliate. Fls 1–8, campanulate to funnelform; perianth lobes 3–5×0.3–1.3cm, elliptic to narrowly obovate, red-purple, occas. paler, sometimes lightly tessellated; anth. yellow, sometimes tinged purple, dorsifixed; styles straight, curved at apex. Late summer–autumn. Balk., NW Turk. Z7.

C. umbrosum Steven. Lvs 8–17cm, ±erect, strap-shaped to narrowly lanceolate. Fls 1–6, funnelform at first, star-shaped when fully open; perianth lobes 1.5–3×0.2–0.6cm, narrowly oblanceolate to linear-elliptic, white to purple-pink; anth. dorsifixed, yellow; styles straight or slightly curved and swollen at apex. Late summer–autumn. Rom., Crimea, N Turk. Z6.

C. varians Freyn & Bornm. = *C. falcifolium*.

C. variegatum L. Lvs 9–15cm, linear-lanceolate or lorate, margins cartilaginous, wavy. Fls 1–2; perianth lobes 2–2.7×0.5–2.5cm, spreading, lanceolate to elliptic or oblanceolate, deep red or violet-purple, occas. paler or white at base, tessellated, apex frequently slightly twisted; anth. dorsifixed, purple-black or purple-brown; styles straight, occas. slightly curved and swollen

at apex. Autumn. Greece, SW Turk. Frequently confused with *C. agrippinum* which has semi-erect rather faintly tessellated perianth lobes. Z8.

C. vernum (L.) Ker-Gawl. = *Bulbocodium vernum*.

C. visianii Parl. = *C. bivonae*.

C. cvs. 'Autumn Queen' ('Prinses Astrid'): fls tessellated, rosy-lilac, tube ray-like; summer. 'Beaconsfield': fls tulip-shaped, lilac-pink, faintly tessellated, tube white. 'The Giant': fls large, lilac-pink with faint tessellation, white in centre, tube white. 'Lilac Wonder': fls pale lilac; seg. to 7cm, narrow, tube long, soon collapsing, white. 'Pink Goblet': fls large, rounded, rosy-pink, tube pink. 'Violet Queen': fls large, blue-lilac, tessellated purple, throat and tube white. 'Waterlily': fls double, deep rose-pink, tube white.

Colchis Ivy *Hedera colchica.*

Colea Bojer. Bignoniaceae. 15 shrubs or small trees, often un-branched. Lvs whorled in a term. crown, imparipinnate. Rac. or pan. cauliflorous; cor. funnelform, 5-lobed. Is. of SW Indian Ocean. Z10.

C. colei Green. Lvs 5–13cm, lfts 5 green-yellow, finely pubesc, and roughened beneath. Fls deep pink. Maur.

C. floribunda Bojer ex Lindl. = *Ophiocolea floribunda*.

C. mauritiana Bojer = *C. colei*.

C. undulata Reg. Shrub. Lvs 60–120cm, lfts 7–17, green above, paler beneath, undulate. Fls pale yellow with rose to lilac lobes. Madag.

Colebrookea Sm. Labiatae. 1 everg., tomentose, low-growing, aromatic subshrub. Lvs to 3×1.5cm, opposite or in whorls of 3, elliptic to ovate, densely white to rusty-tomentose, gland. Fls v. small, off-white, in small lax spikes. W India. Z9.

C. oppositifolia Sm.

C. tenuifolia D. Don = *C. oppositifolia*.

Colenso's Spaniard *Aciphylla colensoi.*

Coleocephalocereus Backeb. Cactaceae. 6 shrubby cacti; st. slender cylindric to columnar; ribs few to many; areoles close-set; spines weak or strong. Flowering areoles confluent, bearded with wool and bristles, forming an apical and lateral cephalium. Fls tubular to campanulate-funnelform, nocturnal. E & SE Braz.

C. aureus Ritter. St. globose to shortly cylindric, to 30(-115)×17cm, pale yellow-to grey-green; ribs up to 18, broad; spines strong, yellow, to 6cm. Cephalium subapical then extending down one side. Fls tubular, 3×1.5cm, light yellow-green limb creet. E Braz. Z9.

C. brevicylindricus (Buining) Ritter = *C. aureus*.

C. fluminensis (Miq.) Backeb. Shrubby; st. ascending and decumbent, to 2m×10cm, dark green; ribs 10–17 acute; spines to 3cm, flexible, tinged yellow. Fls campanulate-funnelform, 5.5–7×4–5cm; limb widely spreading; outer tep. pink-tinged, inner tep. white. SE Braz. Z9.

C. goebelianus (Vaup.) Buining. Columnar, unbranched, to 6m; ribs 12–30+ central spines to 5cm, brown, shorter and hooked in seedlings; radial spines to 1cm, white. E Braz. Z9.

→*Buiningia*.

Coleonema Bartling & H.L. Wendl. Verbenaceae. 8 shrubs. Lvs glab., gland-dotted, petiolate. Fls solitary, term. or axill., sub-tended by several small bracts; sep. 5; pet. 5, spreading; sta. 5. S Afr. Z9.

C. album (Thunb.) Bartling ex H.L. Wendl. Shrub to 1m; br. glab., spreading. Lvs to 1.3cm, linear-oblanceolate, acute, spreading to recurved. Fls white; pet. to 5×2mm, obovate. S Afr.

C. calycinum (Steud.) Williams. Shrub to 2.5m, much-branched, glab. Lvs to 1.9cm, linear, acute, subglabrous. Fls white; pet. to 4.5×2.5mm, obovate spreading. S Afr.

C. juniperinum Sonder. Shrub to 50cm; br. sprawling, glab., red-brown. Lvs to 0.7cm, linear-lanceolate, acute glab. Fls white; pet. to 2×1mm, obovate, obtuse. S Afr.

C. pulchrum Hook. Shrub to 120cm; br. erect, slender. Lvs to 3.5cm, linear, glab., pale green, ciliolate. Fls pink; pet to 8.5×4mm, obovate, apiculate. S Afr.

→*Diosma*.

Coleostephus Cass. Compositae. 2 ann. herbs. Cap. radiate. W Eur. and N Afr.

C. myconis (L.) Rchb. f. To 45cm. Basal lvs to 5cm, obovate to obovate-spathulate, bluntly toothed, petiolate, st. lvs amplexicaul, ovate-oblong. Cap. to 2cm diam.; ray flts to 15mm, yellow, white or 2-toned. S Eur.

→*Chrysanthemum*.

Coleotrype C.B. Clarke. Commelinaceae. 9 perenn. herbs. Lvs lanceolate. Infl. breaking through lf sheaths, ± sessile, cincinni congested and contracted; sep. 3, free; pet. 3, united at base into a slender tube; sta. 6, fertile, fil. bearded. S Afr. and Madag. Z9.

C. natalensis C.B. Clarke. St. decumbent, to 30cm, little-branched. Lvs to 12cm, lanceolate to narrowly elliptic, bright green, striate. Infl. congested, 3–8–fld; cor. tube 15×0.5mm, lobes 10mm, blue or violet. Summer–autumn. S Afr. Z9.

Coleus *Solenostemon scutellarioides*.

Coleus Lour.
C. amboinicus Lour. = *Plectranthus amboinicus*.
C. aromaticus Benth. = *Plectranthus amboinicus*.
C. barbatus = *Plectranthus barbatus*.
C. blumei Benth. = *Solenostemon scutellarioides*.
C. crassifolius Benth. = *Plectranthus amboinicus*.
C. esculentus = *Plectranthus esculentus*.
C. hybridus = *Solenostemon scutellarioides*.
C. madagascariensis (Pers.) A. Chev. = *Plectranthus madagascariensis*.
C. pumilus = *Solenostemon scutellarioides*.
C. rehneltianus = *Solenostemon scutellarioides*.
C. scutellarioides (L.) Benth. = *Solenostemon scutellarioides*.
C. spicatus = *Plectranthus caninus*.
C. thyrsoideus Bak. = *Plectranthus thyrsoideus*.
C. shirensis Gürke = *Solenostemon shirensis*.
C. verschaffeltii = *Solenstemon scutellarioides*.

Colic Root *Aletris* (*A. farinosa*).
Coliseum Ivy *Cymbalaria muralis*.

Colletia Comm. ex Juss. Rhamnaceae. 17 extremely thorny shrubs, densely clothed with decussate spines derived from st. and br., sometimes thick and flattened. Lvs 0, or v. small and short-lived. Fls small, solitary or clustered below thorns. covering br.; cal. campanulate or tubular, 4–6-merous; pet. 0. Spring–autumn. Temp. S Amer. Z8.

C. armata Miers = *C. hystrix*.
C. crenata Clos. = *Discaria crenata*.
C. cruciata Gillies & Hook. = *C. paradoxa*.
C. discolor Hook. = *Discaria chacaye*.
C. hystrix Clos. Dark green, to 2m with dense, terete, rigid, ± downy spines 1–2.5cm long. Fls waxy-white with hawthorn-like fragrance. Late summer–autumn. S Chile. 'Rosea': fls tinted pink.
C. infausta N.E. Br. = *C. spinosissima*.
C. paradoxa (Spreng.) Escal. Chalky, glaucous to 2m, with spines flattened broadly triangular and subterete. Fls yellow-white, almond-scented. Autumn–winter. Urug., S Braz.
C. spinosissima Gmel. Olive green, to 2.5m with dense, slender, glab., terete spines 1–2.5cm long. Fls brown or green-white with a dull red hue. Spring–early summer. S Chile.

Collimamol *Luma apiculata*.

Collinsia Nutt. Scrophulariaceae. 25 ann. herbs. Fls whorled in rac. or solitary; cal. campanulate, 5-cleft, cor. tubular, saccate at base, deeply bilabiate, upper lip erect, 2-lobed, double-ridged at base, lower lip deflexed, median lobe shorter than laterals and folded. Spring–summer. N Amer., Mex. Z9.

C. bicolor Benth. CHINESE-HOUSES; INNOCENCE. St. weak, to 60cm, glab., or glandular-pubesc. Lvs to 8cm, ovate-lanceolate, base cordate, denticulate or entire. Fls in whorls of 2–7 to 3cm, upper lip and cor. tube white, lower lip rose-purple. Summer. Calif. 'Alba': fls white, lower lip green-white. 'Candidissima': fls pure white. 'Multicolor': fls marked white, lilac and rose. 'Marmorata': fls striped and spotted carmine.
C. candidissima hort. = *C. bicolor* 'Candidissima'.
C. grandiflora Dougl. ex Lindl. BLUE LIPS. To 35cm. Lvs to 5cm, oblong to linear, toothed or entire. Fls to 2cm, upper lip pale purple to white, lower lip dark blue, violet or crimson. BC to Calif.
C. heterophylla Buist ex Graham = *C. bicolor*.
C. tinctoria Hartweg. St. to 30cm, glandular-pubesc. Lvs to 8cm, oblong, lanceolate or ovate, entire or serrate. Infl. crowded; fls to 1.5cm tube yellow-white, lobes deep lavender with purple dots and stripes. Summer. Calif. 'Purpurea': fls purple.
C. verna Nutt. BLUE-EYED MARY. St. weak, to 40cm, often decumbent, finely glandular-pubesc. Lvs triangular-ovate or oblong-ovate, base truncate, entire or serrate. Fls in 4–5-fld whorls or solitary to 1.5cm, upper lip white to pale blue, lower lip bright blue, lobes emarginate. Spring. E US.
C. violacea Nutt. To 37.5cm. St. pubesc. Lvs to 5cm, lanceolate

to oblong-lanceolate, entire or toothed. Fls to 1.25cm, lower lip violet, upper lip pale. SC US. Z5.

Collinsonia L. HORSE BALM; STONE ROOT. Labiatae. 5 perenn. aromatic herbs. Pan. term.; cor. tube obliquely campanulate, 5-lobed bilabiate, lower lip 3-lobed with middle lobe larger and incised or fringed. US.

C. canadensis L. St. erect. 30–80cm, branching above. Lvs 2–8cm, oblong elliptic or oval, serrate. Pan. puberulent, cor. 1cm. yellow, lobes rounded-ovate, middle lobe of lower lip to 5mm. E US. Z4.

Collomia Nutt. Polemoniaceae. 15 ann. or perenn. herbs. Fls in a cymose, term. cluster or solitary in axils, with leafy bracts; cal. 5-lobed campanulate to obconic; cor. 5-lobed narrowly funnelform-hypocrateriform, lobes lanceolate to spathulate. Americas.

C. biflora (Ruiz & Pav.) Brandg. Ann. to 60cm, pubesc. Lvs 3–6cm, ovate-lanceolate to linear-lanceolate, entire, toothed or lobed. Infl. axill., at st. apices; cor. 1.5cm scarlet, lobes elliptic, tube buff-hued outside. Arg., Chile, Boliv. Z7.

C. debilis (S. Wats.) Greene. ALPINE COLLOMIA. Erect or decumbent tufted perenn., 2.5–12cm. Lvs 0.3–4cm. obovate to lanceolate, entire to 3–7 toothed or -lobed, glandular-pubesc. Infl. a compact term. cluster; cor. 1.5–3.5cm, lobes 5–7mm, lavender, cream, pink, white or blue. Summer. NW US. Z4.

C. grandiflora Douglas ex Lindl. Erect ann. to 1m, glab., puberulent or gland. Lvs 3–5cm, linear to lanceolate, entire. Infl. a dense, term. cluster; cor. 1.5–3cm, lobes lanceolate, salmon-pink to yellow to almost white. Spring–early summer. W Canada to W. US; introd. W & C Eur. Z6

✕ Colmanara Intergeneric orchid hybrids involving *Miltonia*, *Oncidium* and *Odontoglossum*.

Colobanthus Bartling. Caryophyllaceae. 15–20 densely tufted, glab. perenn. herbs. Lvs somewhat fleshy, narrow, in overlapping pairs joined at base. Fls small, green, solitary, on elongated stalks; sep. 4 or 5; pet. 0. S Hemis., a characteristic cushion plant of the Antarc.; most spp. in NZ. Z8.

C. canaliculatus T. Kirk. Dwarf cushion plant. Lvs 3–4mm, subulate, canaliculate, abruptly acuminate, with small basal sheath. Sep. 5. NZ.

C. muscoides Hook. f. Plant forming large deep cushions. Lvs 4–10mm, linear to subulate, obtuse, with conspicuous, basal sheath. Sep. 4. NZ.

Colocasia Schott. COCOYAM; TARO; DASHEEN. Araceae. 6 perenn. tuberous herbs. Lvs peltate, sagittate or ovate-cordate, large, glab.; petiole long. Peduncle shorter than petioles; spathe constricted, convolute-tubular at base, apical portion forming elongate, hooded or flattened limb; spadix shorter than spathe with appendix. Trop. Asia, some widely nat. in Trop. and warm temp. regions. Z10.

C. affinis Schott. Tuber small, rounded. Lvs 10–15×7–10cm, ovate or orbicular-ovate, base rounded-retuse to cordate, apex acuminate, green with purple markings between veins, glaucous beneath; petiole to 35cm. Spathe tube pale green, limb 7.5–12.5cm, linear-lanceolate, yellow. Trop. E Himal.

C. antiquorum Schott = *C. esculenta* 'Antiquorum'.

C. esculenta (L.) Schott. COCOYAM; TARO; DASHEEN. Tuber massive, edible, rounded-turbinate, brown. Lvs to 60×35cm, deflexed, cordate-sagittate, basal lobes rounded or angular, apex acute, veins conspicuous; petiole to 1m. Spathe tube green, limb 15–35cm, caudate-acuminate, pale yellow. Trop. E Asia, nat. throughout tropics and warm temp. regions. 'Antiquorum' (EDDO): tubers smaller, nutty-flavoured. 'Euchlora': lvs dark green edged violet; petioles violet. 'Fontanesii': petioles and peduncles dark red-purple or violet; lamina dark green, margin and veins violet, colour suffusing lamina; spathe tube dark violet. 'Illustris' (IMPERIAL TARO; BLACK CALADIUM): lvs light green, marked blue-black between primary veins.

C. marshallii Bull = *C. affinis*.

→*Alocasia*.

Colocynth *Citrullus colocynthis*.
Colombia Buttercup *Oncidium cheirophorum*.
Coloradillo *Hamelia patens*.
Colorado Douglas Fir *Pseudotsuga menziesii*.
Colorado Fir *Abies concolor*.
Colorado Spruce *Picea pungens*.

Colquhounia Wallich. Labiatae. 3 everg. shrubs. Fls in axill. whorls or term. rac.; cor. tubular-bilabiate with upper lip entire or emarginate, shorter than lower, tube curving, somewhat inflated. E Himal. to SW China. Z8.

C. coccinea Wallich. Densely white-felted. St. to 3m, tetragonal. Lvs to 15cm, ovate to lanceolate or cordate, crenate-serrate. Fls in axill. whorls; cor. 25mm, scarlet, yellow within. Late summer. var. *vestita* Prain (var. *mollis*). Shorter and more spreading, woolly rather than felty.

Coltsfoot *Galax*; *Tussilago*.
Columbia Synthyris *Synthyris stellata*.
Columbia Tiger Lily *Lilium columbianum*.
Columbine *Aquilegia* (*A. vulgaris*).
Columbo *Frasera*.

Columella Vell.
C. japonica (Thunb.) Alston = *Cayratia japonica*.
C. oligocarpa (Lév. & Vant.) Rehd. = *Cayratia oligocarpa*.

Columnea L. Gesneriaceae. 160 usually epiphytic shrubs. St. often pendulous and sparsely branched, borne in a cascade from a low crown. Lvs in opposite pairs. Fls solitary or in axill. fascicles, cal. 5-partite; cor. gibbous at base, tube gradually expanded toward apex, limb 2-lipped, upper lip with a central hook-like lobe and 2 spreading lat. lobes, lower lip entire, recurved or reflexed. Trop. Amer., W Indies Z9.
C. allenii Morton. Pendulous epiphyte; st. sparsely red-strigose. Lvs to 2cm, oblong-elliptic, succulent, short-acuminate, rounded at base, entire, glab. Fls 1 per axil; cal. to 3cm, tinged red, lobes long-acuminate; cor. to 7.5cm, scarlet, sparsely strigose, hood to 4cm. Panama.
C. ambigua (Urban) Morley = *Trichantha ambigua*.
C. anisophylla DC. = *Trichantha anisophylla*.
C. argentea Griseb. St. stout, white-sericeous. Lvs to 17cm, narrowly elliptic or oblanceolate, grey-sericeous, remotely and shallowly toothed. Fls 1–4 per axil; cal. densely sericeous, seg. to 2.5cm, oblong-linear, entire; cor. to 5cm, pale yellow, sericeous, tube to 2.5cm, upper lip to 2.5cm. Jam.
C. arguta Morton. St. pendent, red-hirsute. Lvs 2cm, lanceolate, long-acuminate, rounded at base, succulent, entire, tinged red beneath, ciliate. Fls 1 per axil; cal. erect, lobes to 1.5cm hirsute; cor. to 6cm. red streaked white, pilose, hood to 2cm. Panama.
C. aurantica Wiehler. St. to 60cm, erect or descending, grey. Lvs 4–5cm, elliptic, acute, obscurely serrulate, blue-green above, spotted or marbled maroon beneath. Fls 1 per axil; cal. lobes to 1.5cm, lanceolate, toothed, pink to pale maroon; cor. to 6.6cm, golden orange-red, hood 1.2cm, pilose, spur cream-white. Panama.
C. ×banksii Lynch. (*C. schiedeana* ×*C. oerstediana*.) St. pendent. Lvs to 4cm, ovate or oblong-ovate, glab. above, thinly strigose beneath. Fls 1 per axil; cal. lobes often flushed maroon; cor. to 7.5cm, hood to 2cm, basally saccate, red marked yellow. Gdn origin.
C. billbergiana Beurling. St. brown, branched, sparsely strigose when young. Lvs 2–3cm, ovate-lanceolate, acute, broadly cuneate at base, glab. above, pale beneath. Fls 1 per axil; cal. to 12mm, red, lobes ovate-lanceolate; cor. to 5cm, red, tube only slightly enlarged toward apex, sparsely gland., hood 2×0.7cm. Panama.
C. brenneri (Wiehler) Morley = *Trichantha brenneri*.
C. brevipila Urban. St. grey, hariy becoming glab. Lvs to 11cm, narrowly oblong-elliptic, short-acuminate, base cuneate, strigilose, remotely toothed. Fls 1–5 per axil; cor. yellow, sericeous. Jam.
C. calotricha J.D. Sm. = *Trichantha calotricha*.
C. canerina Wiehler. St. to 50cm, becoming woody, erect or spreading. Lvs strongly unequal 4–12cm, elliptic or oblanceolate, acuminate, dentate, sparsely strigose above, pale green marked red beneath. Fls 2–4 per axil; cal. lobes to 3.6×0.9cm, lanceolate-elliptic, serrate, yellow; cor. to 6.5cm, spurred, canary yellow, pilose. Panama.
C. cerropirrana Skog = *Trichantha cerropirrana*.
C. chiricana Wiehler. Herb or subshrub pendent, to 2m. Lvs 2–2.8cm, ovate, acuminate or acute, weakly serrate, rounded at base, succulent, strigose, occas. tinted red. Fls 1 per axil; cal. lobes to 1.6×0.5cm, oblanceolate, marked rose; cor. to 8.5cm, spurred, bright pink of carmine, pilose, hood to 2×2.5cm. Panama.
C. costaricensis Kuntze = *Trichantha sanguinolenta*.
C. crassifolia Brongn. St. erect, to 30cm, pilose soon glab. Lvs to 10cm, narrowly elliptic, lustrous dark green above, pale yellow-green with a maroon-brown midrib and sparse hairs beneath. Fls 1 per axil; cal. to 2.5cm, brown-green, lobes lanceolate; cor. to 10cm, bright scarlet, red-pilose, tube curved, hood entire. Guat., Mex. 'Stella Nova': habit rigid; st. thick; lvs to 15cm long; fls dark orange-red.
C. dissimilis Morton = *Trichantha dissimilis*.
C. dodsonii Wiehler. St. pendent, to 1m sparsely pilose, Lvs to 2cm, broadly ovate, acuminate, entire, cordate, sparsely pilose

above, margins rose. Fls 1 per axil; cal. lobes ovate to 1.5cm, long-acuminate; cor. to 3.8cm, orange-red striped yellow, with a basal yellow spur, pilose. Ecuad.
C. domingensis Morley = *Trichantha domingensis*.
C. erythrophaea Decne. St. ascending or trailing. Lvs to 6.5cm, elliptic, long-acuminate. Fls 1–3; cal. lobes marked orange-red and yellow; cor. to 5cm, orange-red marked yellow, hood to 3cm. Mex.
C. erythrophylla Hanst. = *Trichantha erythrophylla*.
C. ×euphora H.E. Moore. (*C. gloriosa* ×*C. lepidocaula*.) St. ascending or trailing, to 1m, red-pilose. Lvs to 5.5cm, ovate, rounded or subcordate at base, dark green with pale erect hairs above, pale-hairy beneath. Fls 1 per axil; cal. lobes to 1cm, ovate, green, hairy; cor. to 6cm, softly hairy, vermilion shading to yellow at base, lobes yellow at base. Gdn origin. 'Ithacan': vigorous, scrambling; lvs small, opposite, matt green; fls 8cm long, tubular, 2-lipped, orange-red. 'Othello': lvs tinged red-purple; sep. tinged purple; tube yellow on lower part.
C. fawcettii (Urban) Morton. St. grey, white-pilose, Lvs unequal, shortly strigillose, 5–10cm, elliptic or narrowly elliptic, short-acuminate, base cuneate, remotely toothed. Fls 1–3; cal. red, hirsute, seg. to 3cm, narrowly lanceolate; cor. to 5cm, red banded yellow, with long white hairs, upper lip to 2.8cm. Jam.
C. fendleri Sprague. St. erect, fleshy, to 60cm. Lvs 2.5–4.5cm, elliptic-oblong, obtuse, hirsute beneath, margins red. Fls 1–3 per axil; cal. lobes to 1.5cm, erect, toothed, sparsely hairy; cor. to 6.5cm, orange-red, hood to 1.5cm, cuneate-rotund. Venez.
C. flaccida Seem. St. to 2m, glabrescent. Lvs 2.5–3cm oblong-lanceolate, long-acuminate, base round, entire, sparsely strigose. Fls 1 per axil; cal. red, lobes to 1.5cm, linear-lanceolate, red-hairy, lacerate; cor. to 6cm, carmine marked yellow, hood to 2.5cm. Costa Rica, Panama.
C. flava Martens & Gal. St. succulent, ascending or spreading. Lvs to 10cm, elliptic-ovate, acute, flushed red beneath. Fls 1–3; cal. lobes marked pink; cor. to 6.5cm, yellow. Mex.
C. gallicauda Wiehler. Shrubby, spreading or ascending to 1m. Lvs strongly unequal, larger to 30cm, lanceolate, sharply acuminate, lustrous dark green above, flushed red beneath, smaller if caducous. Fls 2–4 per axil; cal. lobes to 3.5cm, lanceolate, serrate, flushed maroon; cor. to 8.5cm, erect, spurred at base, glandular-pilose, orange-yellow banded maroon, hood to 1.5cm, maroon. Panama.
C. glabra Ørst. St. erect, sparsely pilose. Lvs to 2.5cm, oblanceolate to elliptic or ovate, succulent, glab. lustrous dark green above. Fls 1 per axil; cal. lobes to 1.2cm, narrowly elliptic; cor. to 5cm, red, pilose, tube to 4cm, lower lobe to 0.9cm. Costa Rica.
C. gloriosa Sprague. GOLDFISH PLANT. St. ascending to spreading, hairy. Lvs to 3cm, ovate or ovate-oblong, obtuse, rounded at base ± revolute, densely hairy. Fls 1 per axil; cal. lobes to 1.2cm, ovate, red-pilose, reflexed; cor. to 7.5cm, scarlet with yellow throat, hood to 5cm, lat. lobes spreading. C Amer. 'Purpurea': lvs tinted purple-red to bronze. Fls deep scarlet.
C. harrisii (Urban) Britt. ex Morton. Subshrub. Lvs tomentose, unequal, 4–14cm, ovate-elliptic, acute, rounded or cuneate at base, remotely denticulate. Fls 1–4 per axil; sep. to 2cm, lanceolate, entire or denticulate, tomentose; cor. to 4.8cm, funnel-shaped, inflated at middle, yellow banded red; limb to 2.5cm, densely red-pilose. Jam.
C. hirsuta Sw. St. brown-grey, densely hirsute. Lvs unequal, hirsute, larger to 12cm, oblong-elliptic to narrowly obovate, shallowly serrate, smaller 2–6cm, elliptic. Fls 1–3 per axil; cal. red or green, hirsute, seg. to 2cm, linear, remotely toothed; cor. to 5cm, strongly 2-lipped, red broadly banded yellow, tube enclosed by cal., upper lip to 2.5. Jam.
C. hirsutissima Morton. St. to 30cm, unbranched, red-hairy. Lvs markedly unequal, larger 6–10cm, oblong, acute, rounded or cordate at base, crenulate or serrulate, red-hairy, smaller to 1cm, ovate. Cal. to 1.8cm, lobes linear, red-hairy; cor. to 7.5cm, red, slightly spurred at base, hood to 2.5cm truncate. Panama.
C. hirta Klotzsch & Hanst. St. branched, pendent, red-pubesc. Lvs unequal, larger to 5.3cm, oblong, obtuse, sparsely toothed, pilose. Cal. green, erect, lobes to 1.5cm, lanceolate, toothed; cor. orange-scarlet, to 7.5cm, red-pilose, to 3cm. Costa Rica, Panama. var. *mortonii* (Raym.) Morley. Cal. lobes less deeply toothed. Panama. var. *pilosissima* (Standl.) Standl. St. with colourless hairs. Cor. to 8.2cm, lat. lobes reflexed not spreading. Hond.
C. hispida Sw. St. brown-grey, hispid. Lvs unequal, dark green above, pale green beneath, red-pubesc., larger to 16cm, elliptic or obovate, obtuse, toothed, smaller to 6cm. Fls to 3 per axil; cal. seg. to 1.5cm narrowly oblong; cor. to 2.5cm, dull orange-yellow, upper lip to 1.5cm. Jam.
C. illepida H.E. Moore = *Trichantha illepida*.
C. jamaicensis Urban = *C. repens*.
C. ×kewensis hort. (*C. glabra* ×*C. schiedeana*.) Intermediate

between parents. Gdn origin.

C. kienastiana Reg. Differs from *C. dodsonii*, in lvs larger, lanceolate; cal. lobes serrate; cor. to 5cm, red. Columbia.

C. kucyniakii Raym. Erect shrub, to 2m; st. tetragonal. Lvs to 25cm, ovate, maroon beneath, sparsely pilose. Fls many in pendent axillary cymes; cal. lobes marked maroon; cor. to 6cm, lemon yellow, inflated at middle, white-pubesc., with 2 red spots at base of lower lobe. Ecuad.

C. lehmannii Mansf. = *Trichantha lehmannii*.

C. lepidocaula Hanst. St. robust, brown, marked with age. Lvs to 8cm, succulent, elliptic or ovate, deep green. Fls 1 per axil; cal. seg. to 2.5cm, oblong-lanceolate; cor. to 7.5cm, orange, with yellow patches at throat and below, hood to 3cm. Costa Rica.

C. linearis Ørst. St. ascending or spreading. Lvs to 8.2cm, linear, lustrous dark green above, pubesc. beneath. Fls 1 per axil; cal. lobes to 2cm, ovate-lanceolate, often pink; cor. to 4.5cm, deep pink, finely pubesc., lower lip to 1.2cm. Costa Rica.

C. maculata Morton. St. woody, orange-pilose. Lvs markedly unequal, larger to 23cm, oblong-oblanceolate, lustrous dark green and pilose above, flushed pink and maroon beneath, smaller lf caducous. Fls 1 per axil; cal. lobes 1.7cm, ovate-lanceolate, ragged-toothed, marked pink or maroon, orange-pilose; cor. to 7cm, yellow-green to yellow banded and blotched red to black, pale yellow-pilose, hood to 1.7cm. Costa Rica, Panama.

C. magnifica Klotzsch & Hanst. ex Ørst. St. to 1.2m, erect, sparingly branched. Lvs to 11cm, oblanceolate or elliptic-oblanceolate, acute or acuminate, cuneate at base, entire, tinged red beneath, pilose above. Fls 1–3 per axil; cal. to 1.5cm, tinged red, lobes ovate-lanceolate, glandular-toothed; cor. to 7cm, scarlet, pilose, interior yellow, hood to 4×3cm, rounded, entire. Costa Rica, Panama

C. microcalyx Hanst. St. to 2m, pendent, shrubby, branching, red-strigose when young. Lvs to 3.2cm, ovate-elliptic, marked maroon, acute, rounded to cordate at base, pilose, red-ciliate. Fls 1 per axil; cal. lobes to 1.3cm, spreading, oblanceolate, hirsute, often flushed red; cor. to 7cm, pink or orange-red to maroon-purple, often marked yellow at base of lower lip and throat, red-pilose, hood to 2cm, truncate. Costa Rica.

C. microphylla Ørst. St. many, pendent, rusty-pilose. Lvs to 1cm, ovate to orbicular, often flushed red beneath, densely red-pilose. Fls 1 per axil; cal. lobes to 1cm, entire or sparsely dentate, often flushed red, pilose; cor. to 8cm, bright red with a yellow blotch below mouth and lower lobe, hood to 5cm. Costa Rica. 'Diminutifolia': st. slender; lvs v. small, ovate or nearly round, green or often tinged red, with dense red hairs; fls scarlet, with a yellow blotch at throat and at base of lower lip. 'Variegata': lvs grey-green edged cream.

C. minor (Hook.) Hanst. = *Trichantha minor*.

C. mira Morley = *Trichantha mira*.

C. moorei Morton = *Trichantha moorei*.

C. mortonii Raym. = *C. hirta* var. *mortonii*.

C. nicaraguensis Ørst. St. shrubby, robust, to 75cm, red-brown-pilose. Lvs markedly unequal, larger to 1.2cm, ovate to elliptic, coriaceous, short-acuminate, rounded to cordate at base, strigose, smaller minute, caducous. Fls 1 per axil; cal. lobes to 1.2cm, ovate, long-acuminate, tinged red at margins, dentate below; cor. to 6.5cm, red, white-hairy, hood broad, ovate, to 3cm. Costa Rica, Panama 'Marginata': lvs waxy, striped and edged white; fls 5cm carmine red.

C. oerstediana Klotzsch ex Ørst. St. to 1.2m, pendulous, branched, sparsely strigose. Lvs to 16cm, ovate, succulent, obtuse or acute, rounded at base, glab. above, thinly strigose beneath. Fls 1 per axil; cal. to 1.5cm, green, lobes ovate, long-acuminate; cor. to 7cm, scarlet, exterior sparsely pilose, hood to 3.5cm, truncate. Costa Rica, Panama

C. oxyphylla Hanst. St. pendent or arching, shrubby at base. Lvs narrowly lanceolate, long-acuminate, broadly rounded at base, sparsely strigose. Fls 1 per axil; cal. lobes linear-lanceolate, white-villous; cor. to 6.5cm, orange-red, tube bent, limb short. Costa Rica, Panama.

C. parviflora Morton = *Trichantha parviflora*.

C. percrassa Morton = *C. billbergiana*.

C. pilosissima Standl. = *C. hirta* var. *pilosissima*.

C. proctori Stearn. St. grey, hispid. Lvs unequal, hirsute, larger to 10cm, ovate to obovate, smaller 1–3.5cm, orbicular. Fls 1–3; cal. glandular-hirsute, seg. narrowly lanceolate, to 2cm; cor. to 5cm, pale yellow striped red, upper lip to 2cm. Jam.

C. pulchra (Wiehler) Skog = *Trichantha pulchra*.

C. purpureovittata (Wiehler) Morley = *Trichantha purpureovittata*.

C. quercetii Ørst. St. shrubby, erect, branching, brown-scaly, white-pubesc. Lvs markedly unequal, larger to 10cm, narrow, acute, dark green above, pale green spotted maroon beneath, glab. Fls 1–3 per axil; cal. lobes tinged maroon, oblong; cor. to 5cm, red-orange to orange or yellow, red-tomentose. Costa Rica.

C. raymondii Morton. St. to 40cm, to 5mm diam., shrubby. Lvs markedly unequal, oblanceolate, dark green above, yellow-green beneath, veins red-pilose, larger to 9cm, smaller to 1.5cm. Fls 1 per axil; cal. dentate, red toward apex, margin pilose; cor. to 6cm, deep red, with a yellow blotch on throat below and yellow lines on limb, tube to 3cm, hood to 3×2cm. Costa Rica.

C. repens (Hook.) Hanst. St. short, creeping, shrubby, grey. Lvs unequal, setose, dark green above, pale beneath, larger to 5.5cm, narrowly ovate, acuminate or acute, base cuneate, entire or remotely serrate, smaller to 3cm. Fls 1 per axil; cal. sparsely pilose, seg. to 1.5cm, narrowly ovate cor. to 3cm, bright red or orange-yellow, streaked red, upper lip to 1cm. Jam.

C. rubra Morton. St. scarcely branched, glabrescent. Lvs unequal, larger to 14cm, narrowly oblong or oblanceolate, acute, succulent, glab. above, strigose and red beneath; smaller lf caducous. Fls in pairs; cal. to 2cm, red, lobes linear-lanceolate, red-strigose; cor. to 6.5cm, yellow, dilating at throat, pilose, hood to 2.5cm. Panama

C. rubricaulis Standl. St. pendent to ascending, red-pilose; young shoots tinged red. Lvs in unequal pairs or whorls, to 6cm, linear-oblong, attenuate, glab. above, sparsely pilose beneath. Fls 1 per axil; cor. bright orange, pilose, hood to 2.5cm. Hond., Nic.

C. rutilans Sw. St. grey, red-strigose or tomentose, glabrescent. Lvs unequal, dark green and strigillose above, red-veined or red throughout and pilose beneath; larger 7–18cm, lanceolate, remotely toothed, smaller lf 2–4.5cm. Fls 1–4 per axil; cal. red-pilose, seg. to 2.5cm, pinnatifid; cor. to 5.5cm, red banded orange, upper lip to 3cm. Jam.

C. salmonea Raym. Br. robust, pendent or arching. Lvs to 2.5cm, ovate, sparsely pilose above, pale green with maroon-tinged, downy veins beneath. Fls 1 per axil, erect; cal. to 1.5cm, lobes entire, white-strigose; cor. to 5×1cm, salmon pink, pilose, hood to 2×2cm, quadrate. Costa Rica.

C. sanguinea (Pers.) Hanst. St. brown-pilose becoming somewhat woody and shrubby. Lvs markedly unequal, larger 11–24cm, oblong-lanceolate, acuminate, serrate, hirsute, blotched red beneath, smaller 2–4cm, lanceolate. Fls 1–4 per axil; cal. seg. to 2cm, lanceolate, toothed, pubesc.; cor. to 3×0.7cm, inflated at middle, pale yellow, densely hairy. Carib. var. *cubensis* Urban. Lvs unmarked beneath, less deeply toothed. Cuba.

C. sanguinolenta (Klotzsch ex Ørst.) Hanst. = *Trichantha sanguinolenta*.

C. scandens L. St. slender, creeping or cascading, becoming rather woody. Lvs to 6.5cm, oblong to narrowly oblong or ovate-elliptic, acute or obtuse, rounded to cuneate at base, strigose, red-ciliate. Fls 1–2 per axil; cal. lobes ovate, lanceolate or linear, entire or toothed; cor. to 8.5×1cm, funnel-shaped, inflated at middle, red or yellow, upper lobe to 1.4cm pilose. Lesser Antilles. 'Flava': fls bright yellow. 'Rubra': fls red. var. *tulae* (Urban) Wiehler. Lvs to 5×2cm, ovate-elliptic, pale green. Fls solitary; cor. yellow, pink or red, lobes smaller than in type. Puerto Rico, Dominican Rep., Haiti.

C. schiedeana Schltr. St. to 90cm, shrubby, maroon-villous at apex. Lvs unequal, lanceolate to oblong, acute to subacuminate, dark green and white-pilose above, tomentose beneath, remotely toothed. Fls 1–2; cal. lobes ovate, to 2cm, tinged red, remotely toothed, pubesc.; cor. yellow-brown blotched and banded dark red, to 6cm, hood to 2.5cm. Mex.

C. segregata Morley = *Trichantha segregata*.

C. spathulata Mansf. = *Pentadenia spathulata*.

C. splendens Paxt. = *Nematanthus crassifolium*.

C. stenophylla Standl. = *C. crassifolia*.

C. strigosa Benth. = *Pentadenia strigosa*.

C. subcordata Morton. St. grey-brown, hispid. Lvs unequal, white-hirsute-pilose, larger 14cm, oblong-elliptic, acuminate, subcordate at base, ciliate. Fls 1–4 per axil; cal. to 2.2cm, 2-lipped, hispid; cor. strongly 2-lipped, pale yellow, glandular-pilose, to 4.8cm, upper lip to 2.5cm. Jam.

C. sulfurea (Donn) Sm. St. red-brown, with long red hairs. Lvs unequal, oblong-elliptic, elliptic or obovate, larger 6–11cm, smaller 2–5cm, sparsely pilose, red or maroon beneath, often crenate. Fls 1–2; cal. long-pilose, seg. green or red, linear, to 2.8cm; cor. to 7cm, slightly bent, thinly pilose, bright yellow, hood to 1.5cm. Mex., Hond., Guat., Belize.

C. tenensis (Wiehler) Morley = *Trichantha tenensis*.

C. teuscheri (Morton) H.E. Moore = *Trichantha minor*.

C. tomentulosa Morton. Subshrub, often epiphytic, to 40cm; st. branched, tomentose. Lvs to 2.5cm, ovate, obtuse, broadly cuneate at base, entire, soft-tomentose. Fls 1 per axil; cal. lobes to 6mm, ovate-lanceolate, deeply toothed; cor. scarlet, tubular, pilose, hood to 1.5cm, oblong. Nic., Costa Rica, Panama.

C. tulae Urban = *C. scandens* var. *tulae*.

C. urbanii Stearn. St. climbing, pilose. Lvs clustered at br. tips, to 8cm, elliptic or rounded to obovate, obtuse at apex, pilose, strigose. Fls 1–2; cal. hirsute below, seg. to 2cm, lanceolate; cor. 2-lipped, to 5cm, yellow, hirsute, upper lip to 2.5cm. Jam.

C. ×*vedrariensis* Vilm. ex Mottet. (*C. magnifica* ×*C. schiediana*.) St. pendent or ascending, to 90cm. Lvs to 10cm, elliptic-lanceolate, midrib red, sparsely pilose. Fls 1–2; cal. lobes dentate, flushed red; cor. bright red marked yellow. Gdn origin.

C. verecunda Morton. St. to 80cm, fleshy, sparsely branched. Lvs unequal, larger to 11cm, oblong-lanceolate, acute, rounded at base, ± coriaceous, entire, red and strigose beneath. Fls several, clustered, cal. lobes to 1.5cm, linear-subulate, cor. to 3.5cm, pale-pubesc., yellow or orange-red, hood to 1.3cm. Costa Rica.

C. ×*vilmoriniana* Meuniss. (*C.* ×*vedrariensis* ×*C. gloriosa*.) St. slender, to 60cm. Lvs to 7cm, elliptic to ovate-oblong, tomentose. Fls 1–2; cor. scarlet, striped yellow from lower lip to middle of throat. Gdn origin.

C. woodii H.E. Moore. (*C. crassifolia* ×*C. nicaraguensis*.) Upright, suffrutescent perenn. Lvs ovate, fleshy. Fls 1–2 per axil; cor. dark red-orange, throat marked bright yellow, tube yellow below. Gdn origin.

C. zebranella Wiehler. Herb or subshrub; st. spreading or ascending, to 1m, pale brown, woolly. Lvs unequal, larger to 12cm, oblanceolate, acuminate, serrulate, glab. above, flushed pink and sericeous beneath, red-ciliate, smaller lf to 3cm. Fls 2–4 per axil; cal. pilose, lobes to 2cm, lanceolate, serrate, speckled maroon; cor. to 7.5cm, spurred, tube lemon yellow, streaked maroon, hood maroon, to 1.3cm, pilose. Panama.

C. zebrina Raym. St. pilose, pendent. Lvs unequal, larger to 13.5cm, oblanceolate, acute, green and glab. above, tipped maroon and sericeous beneath. Fls several per axil; cal. lobes to 2.2cm, ovate, remotely dentate, occas. tipped maroon; cor. to 5.8cm, red-pilose, yellow or orange-red with maroon stripes on lobes continuing to base of tube, hood truncate, to 2cm. Panama.

C. miscellaneous cvs and hybrids. 'Campus Sunset': lvs 5cm long, ovate, olive-green above, red beneath, pubesc. Fls yellow, orange to red. 'Cayugan': habit vigorously trailing. 'Cornellian': lvs narrow-elliptic, dark green, red beneath. 'Diminutifolia' = *C. microphylla* 'Diminutifolia'. 'Early Bird': habit spreading, but compact. 'Magnifica': fls large, fan-shaped, brilliant scarlet-red with yellow veins. 'Mary Ann': fls deep pink. 'Royal Tangerine': fls 8cm tubular, curved, bright tangerine-orange with red-orange hairs. 'Stavanger': fls cardinal-red, with a conspicuous, helmet-shaped upper lip. 'Superba': lvs velvety maroon; fls gaping, orange red. 'Variegata' ('Andenken an Rosalinde'): lvs 5–8cm, long-elliptic, glossy grey green, edged and striped pink and white, veined red-violet beneath; fls 5–6cm long, axill., 2-lipped, pubesc., vivid orange or scarlet.

Colutea L. Leguminosae (Papilionoideae). 26 decid., unarmed or spiny shrubs or small trees. Br. slender, hairy at first; bark exfoliating. Lvs pinnate or trifoliolate. Fls pea-like in rac. Fr. a legume, becoming grossly inflated, nacreous, translucent. Eur., Afr., C Asia.

C. arborescens L. BLADDER SENNA. To 5m. Lvs to 15cm; lfts to 4×2.5cm in 5–7 pairs, broadly elliptic to ovate, shortly acuminate, sparsely adpressed-pubesc. Infl. 3–8-fld, to 12cm; cor. to 2cm, yellow; standard streaked red. Fr. to 8×3cm, strongly inflated, pale green tinted red, becoming pearly green. Summer. S Eur. 'Bullata': low and dense; lfts to 1.5cm, puckered. 'Copper Beauty': fls bright orange-yellow; seed pods v. inflated strongly tinted red-brown. 'Crispa': small; lfts with wavy margins. 'Variegata': lvs variegated. Z5.

C. atlantica Browicz. Lvs to 5cm; lfts to 1.5×1cm, in 3–6 pairs, elliptic, mucronate, tomentose. Infl. to 6cm, 1–4-fld; cor. to 2cm yellow. Fr. to 6×3cm. NW Afr., SE Spain. Z6.

C. brevialata Lange = *C. arborescens*.

C. bushei (Boiss.) SHaparenko. Upright vigorous shrub to 5m. Lvs blue-green; lfts 7–9. Fls 2–7 per rac., large, golden-yellow. Fr. large, inflated. Summer–autumn. Iran.

C. cilicica Boiss. & Bal. To 5m. Lvs to 10cm; lfts to 3×2.5cm, 4–5 pairs, elliptic to obovate, obtuse, mucronate. Infl. 3–6-fld, to 8cm; cor. to 2cm, yellow. Fr. to 7×3cm, shiny. Turk., S Russia. Z6.

C. cruenta Ait. = *C. orientalis*.

C. gracilis Freyn & Sint. To 3m. Lvs to 8cm; lfts to 1×0.5cm, in 3–5-pairs, broadly elliptic or ovate, glab. above. Infl. to 5cm, 4–5-fld; cal. minutely black-hairy; cor. to 1.5cm, bright yellow. Fr. to 4.5×2cm, v. sparsely hairy. C Asia, Iran. Z6.

C. halepica Lam. = *C. istria*.

C. istria Mill. To 3m. Lvs 3–6cm; lfts to 11×0.5cm, in 3–6 pairs, elliptic or obovate, obtuse. Infl. 4-fld, to 8cm; cor. to 2cm, yellow. Fr. to 6×3cm, loosely hairy. Middle East. Z7.

C. longidata Koehne = *C. cilicica*.

C. ×*media* Willd. (*C. arborescens* ×*C. orientalis*.) Lfts in 3–6

pairs, elliptic, grey-green. Fls to 1.5cm, brown-red or orange. Gdn origin. Z6.

C. melanocalyx Boiss. & Heldr. Lvs to 7cm; lfts to 2cm, in 3–4 pairs, broadly elliptic, obtuse. Infl. 2–5-fld; cal. densely black-hairy; cor. to 2cm, golden. Fr. to 6.5×2.5cm. Turk. Z7.

C. multiflora Chaparenko ex Ali. Arching medium-sized shrub. Shoots purple-red. Lvs blue-green; lfts 11–15. Fls small, to 14 per rac., crimson in bud, opening brick red to orange. Summer. Nepal.

C. orientalis Mill. To 3m. Lvs 4–8cm; lfts to 2×1.5cm, in 3–4 pairs, obovate-cuneate, glab., blue-green. Infl. 3–5-fld, to 6cm; cor. to 1.5cm, orange-red with darker copper veins, standard spotted yellow at base. Fr. to 5×2cm. S Russia, N Iran. Z7.

C. persica Boiss. To 2m. Lvs to 6cm; lfts to 1×1cm, obovate, obtuse, blue-green, glab. above. Infl. to 5cm, 2–5-fld; cal. loosely black-hairy; cor. to 2cm, yellow. Fr. to 6cm, blunt-tipped. S Iran. Z7.

Coluteocarpus L. Cruciferae. 1 tufted perenn. herb, 4–20cm. Lvs oblong-lanceolate, glab., with 3–5 sharp teeth, in basal rosettes or on st. and entire. Fls numerous, golden yellow, in flat-topped cymes; pet. 6–11mm, 4, clawed. Fr. inflated, papery, 14–33×16–21mm. E Medit., Asia Minor. Z8.

C. reticulatus Boiss. = *C. vesicaria*.

C. vesicaria (L.) Holmb.

→*Alyssum*.

Colvillea Bojer ex Hook. Leguminosae (Caesalpinioideae). 1 tree to 15m. Crown spreading. Lvs to 80cm, bipinnate; pinnae 15–25 pairs; lfts to 1.5×0.7cm, 15–30 pairs, elliptic-oblong. Fls to 4.5cm diam. in large downy pyramidal rac.; pet. scarlet-orange, standard broad; sta. 10, declinate, showy, yellow. Autumn. Madag. Z10.

C. racemosa Bojer ex Hook.

Colysis Presl. Polypodiaceae. 30 terrestrial ferns. Rhiz. creeping or climbing. Fronds stipitate usually uniform, simple, lobed or divided; stipes distant, decurrent-winged. Afr., Asia, Jap., New Guinea, Aus. (Queensld). Z10.

C. hemionitidea (Wallich) Presl. Rhiz. long-creeping, to 4mm wide; scales dark brown. Fronds to 45×7cm, simple, broadly lanceolate, apex narrowly acute, base cuneate and decurrent, entire or slightly undulate, herbaceous, membranous to papery; stipes usually winged. India, Nepal to E Asia.

C. wrightii (Hook.) Ching. Rhiz. long-creeping, to 2.5mm wide; scales dark brown to black. Fronds to 40×6cm, simple, lanceolate, apex narrowly acute, base cuneate and v. long-decurrent, entire to undulate, stipes broadly winged. China, Taiwan, Korea to Vietnam.

→*Gymnogramme, Microsorium, Pleopeltis* and *Polypodium*.

Colza *Brassica napus*.

Comandra Nutt. BASTARD TOADFLAX. Santalaceae. 6 parasitic herbs; rhiz. woody, creeping. St. soft, ascending. Lvs alt. Infl. a term. pan. or cluster; sep. 4–5, petaloid; pet. 0; sta. 4–5. Fr. a nut or a drupe. N Amer., N Eur., Medit.

C. pallida DC. To 40cm. Lvs linear-lanceolate, glaucous, thick. Infl. paniculate; sep. to 5mm, dull white. W N Amer.

Comarostaphylis Zucc.

C. diversifolia (Parry) Greene = *Arctostaphylos diversifolia*.

Comb Fern *Schizaea*.

COMBRETACEAE R. Br. 20/500. *Combretum, Quisqualis, Terminalia*.

Combretum Loefl. Combretaceae. *c*250 trees or shrubs, some climbing. Rac. or pan. term. or axill.; cal. tube glab. or pubesc., lobes 4 or 5, filiform to deltoid; pet. 4 or 5, sometimes 0, exceeding cal. lobes, glab. or pubesc.; sta. 8 to 10, usually exserted. Fr. 4 or 5-winged, carinate or angled. Trop. (except Aus.). Z10.

C. apiculatum Sonder. Small tree, erect, much-branched. Lvs to 7.5cm, oblong to elliptic, apiculate, lepidote, green tinged red. Rac., equalling lvs; fls yellow. Fr. oblong-lanceolate, golden-yellow, 4-winged, glab., glossy. S Afr.

C. bracteosum (Hochst.) Brandis. HICCOUGH NUT. Small tree, shrub or climber to 8m. Lvs to 10cm, ovate, acuminate, rounded or narrowed at base, dull green above, pale green beneath. Rac. dense, short; fls small, bright red-scarlet; bracts large, leafy. Fr. ovoid or rounded, slightly 5-angled. S Afr.

C. celastroides Welw. ex Lawson. Small tree or shrub, often rambling, much-branched. Lvs to 6cm, broadly lanceolate or ovate, obtuse or emarginate, narrowed or rounded at base, chartaceous, lepidote and velutinous beneath. Rac. to 10cm, lax; fls yellow. Fr. small, subglobose, tinted bright red, winged. Angola.

C. coccineum (Sonn.) Lam. Shrub or climber, glabrescent. Lvs to 24cm, oblong, rac. or a pan. elongate; fls to 2.5cm, red; sta. red. Fr. to 0.8cm, orbicular, compressed, wings 4–5, papery. Madag.

C. comosum G. Don. Scandent shrub. Lvs oblong or elliptic, acute or acuminate, subcordate at base, glab. or pubesc. Pan. to 15cm; fls to 12mm, red. Fr. to 2cm, rose when young, with 4 papery wings. Sierra Leone.

C. decandrum Roxb. Everg. shrub, scandent; br. orange-brown pubesc. Lvs chartaceous, oblong to oblong-lanceolate, acuminate, glab. Pan. densely orange-brown-pubesc.; fls small, white; bracts to 3cm, white or pale green. Fr. to 2.5cm, oblong, 5-winged, glab. India, Burm.

C. erythrophyllum (Burchell) Sonder. BUSH WILLOW. Tree to 12m. Lvs to 13cm ovate or elliptic, acute, glab., dark glossy green, light red-green when young, red and gold in fall. Spike capitate, shorter than lvs; fls cream, yellow or green-yellow, slightly fragrant. Fr. to 1.3cm diam., green turning light brown, suborbicular to broadly elliptic, 4-winged. S Afr.

C. flagrocarpum Herb. ex C.B. Clarke. Scandent or straggling shrub, tomentose or villous when young. Lvs to 20cm, ovate or oblong-elliptic to lanceolate, glabrescent. Rac. or pan. to 15cm; fls yellow. Fr. to 4cm, rotund. Summer–winter. Burm., NE India.

C. grandiflorum G. Don. Scandent shrub. Lvs to 10cm, ovate-elliptic, acuminate, glab. or pubesc. Spikes short; fls red, large, showy. Fr. to 2cm, subrotund, emarginate. N Afr.

C. latifolium Bl. Branchlets glab., scaly, red when young. Lvs to 20cm, chartaceous to subcoriaceous, ovate-elliptic, acuminate, base cuneate to rounded. Pan. to 20cm; velvety; fls green-white. Fr. to 3cm diam., subrotund, 4-winged, viscid. India, Burm., Ceylon, Indochina, Thail., Malaysia, New Guinea.

C. microphyllum Klotzsch. FLAME CREEPER; BURNING BUSH. Small tree or scrambler. Lvs to 6cm, ovate, oblong or sub-rotund, apex rounded or apiculate, rounded at base, pubesc. Rac. axill., shorter than lvs; fls bright red, pubesc. Fr. to 2cm, yellow-green to red, ellipsoid, 4-winged. Moz.

C. paniculatum Vent. Everg. climber to 10m. Lvs to 18cm, elliptic-oblong, apex rounded or acuminate, subcordate to obtuse at base, chartaceous, glabrescent. Pan. term. or axill.; fls red. Fr. to 2.5cm, elliptic-oblong, slightly pubesc., 4 or 5-winged. Trop. Afr.

C. racemosum Beauv. Shrub to 4m, often scandent. Lvs to 10cm, elliptic-lanceolate, acuminate, rounded at base, glab. Pan. dense, fls red. Fr. to 2cm, elliptic, 4-winged. W Afr.

→Terminalia.

Comet Orchid Angraecum sesquipedale.
Comfrey Symphytum.

Commelina L. WIDOW'S TEARS; DAYFLOWER. Commelinaceae. 50–100 perenn. and ann. herbs, sometimes tuberous; st. usually slender, procumbent. Infl. ± enclosed by a folded, keeled, spathe (measurement given below for folded spathe); sep. 3, free, the outermost hooded; pet. 3, upper 2 clawed, lower reduced; fertile sta. 3, fil. glab.; staminodes 3–2. Mainly tropics and subtrop.

C. africana L. Lvs to 13cm, ovate to lanceolate. Infl. solitary; spathe margins free to base; fls yellow. Spring–autumn. Trop. Afr. Z9.

C. angustifolia Michx. = C. erecta var. angustifolia.

C. benghalensis L. St. creeping and rooting. Lvs 5–7cm, ovate-lanceolate, hairy, lf sheaths rusty-ciliate. Infl. solitary or clustered; spathe margins ± connate; fls 1.5cm upper pet. blue or violet, lower pet. small, colourless. Summer. Trop. Asia, Afr. 'Variegata': lvs variegated creamy white. Z9.

C. coelestis Willd. Perenn., erect to 1m+; roots tuberous. Lvs 8–18cm, cordate-ovate to oblong-lanceolate, rough with fine stiff hairs. Infl. crowded, stalked; spathe semi-ovate, subcordate and open basally, suffused or streaked purple-blue; fls 2–3cm diam., usually blue. Summer. C & S Amer. 'Alba': fls white. 'Variegata': lvs variegated cream. var. **bourgeaui** C.B. Clarke. More robust. Z9.

C. communis L. St. sprawling to 70cm, branching, sometimes rooting. Lvs 6–10cm, oblong-lanceolate, acute to acuminate, rounded and slightly stalked at base, subglabrous. Infl. stalks c2cm; spathe 2–3cm, semi-ovate, rounded and open basally; fls 2cm diam.; pet. blue. Summer–autumn. China, Jap., nat. S Eur. and E US. 'Aureostriata': lvs striped creamy white. Z7.

C. crispa Wooton = C. erecta var. angustifolia.

C. dianthifolia Delile. Tuberous-rooting perenn.; st. ± erect, branching but not rooting. Lvs linear, 9–13cm, glab. or short-pubesc. Infl. stalks usually 4–7cm, spathe to 8cm, semi-ovate,

caudate, often suffused purple, margins free; fls 1.5–3cm diam. similar to C. tuberosa. Summer. SW US, Mex. Z7.

C. diffusa Burm. f. St. prostrate to ascending, branching and rooting. Lvs 2.5–6cm, lanceolate or ovate-lanceolate, usually obtuse, rounded at base, nearly glab. Infl. stalk short; spathe 0.8–2cm, semi-ovate, acute or acuminate, glab. or ciliolate, margins rounded at the back, free; upper pet. 4–5mm, blue, lower pet. much reduced, pale blue or green-white. Spring–autumn. Widespread in the tropics and subtrop., US N to NJ. Z7.

C. elegans Kunth = C. erecta.

C. elliptica Kunth. Like C. tuberosa, but ± stemless. Lvs to 11cm, mostly basal, lanceolate. Infl. scapose, to 20cm; spathe to 4cm; fls blue or white. Summer. Mts of Mex. to Peru, Boliv. Z8.

C. erecta L. Erect or decumbent perenn. to 70cm; slenderly tuberous. Lvs 7–15cm, linear to lanceolate to ovate-lanceolate, acute or acuminate, rounded at the base, usually glab.; sheath with white hairs. Infl. short-stalked, solitary or 2–4 clustered at top of st.; spathe 2–3.5cm, semi-ovate, glab. or hairy, margins fused at the back; upper pet. 1–2.5cm, pale to deep blue, lower pet. much reduced, white. Summer–autumn. Widespread in the tropics and subtrop. var. **angustifolia** (Michx.) Fern.: lvs narrow. Z9.

C. hirtella Vahl = C. erecta.
C. lutea Moench = C. africana.
C. nudiflora Burm. f. non L. = C. diffusa.
C. orchioides Booth ex Lindl. = C. elliptica.
C. prostrata Reg. = C. benghalensis.
C. sellowiana Schldl. = C. diffusa.
C. sikkimensis hort. = C. coelestis.

C. tuberosa L. Procumbent, tuberous branching perenn. Lvs 6–9cm, narrowly lanceolate, hairy towards margins, sometimes with short, stiff hairs. Infl. stalks 3–6cm; spathe 2–3cm, ovate-lanceolate, obtuse or shortly beaked, cordate and open towards base, usually suffused or streaked dark purple-blue, hairy; pet. equal, blue or white. Summer. C & S Amer. Z8.

C. virginica auct. non L. = C. erecta.

COMMELINACEAE R. Br. 42/620. Aneilema, Callisia, Cochliostema, Coleotrype, Commelina, Cyanotis, Dichorisandra, Geogenanthus, Gibasis, Murdannia, Palisota, Siderasis, Tinantia, Tradescantia, Tripogandra, Weldenia

Commelinantia Tharp.
C. anomala (Torr.) Tharp. = Tinantia anomala.
C. pringlei (S. Wats.) Tharp. = Tinantia anomala.

Common Alder Alnus glutinosa.
Common Allamanda Allamanda cathartica.
Common Amsinckia Amsinckia intermedia.
Common Arrowhead Sagittaria sagittifolia.
Common Ash Fraxinus excelsior.
Common Bamboo Bambusa vulgaris.
Common Barberry Berberis vulgaris.
Common Basil Ocimum basilicum.
Common Bean Phaseolus vulgaris.
Common Bearberry Arctostaphylos uva-ursi.
Common Beech Fagus sylvatica.
Common Billy Buttons Craspedia glauca.
Common Birch Betula pendula.
Common Bird Cherry Prunus padus.
Common Bog Rosemary Andromeda polifolia.
Common Box Buxus sempervirens.
Common Bride's Bush Pavetta gardeniifolia.
Common Brier Rosa canina.
Common Broom Cytisus scoparius.
Common Burdock Arctium minus.
Common Calamint Calamintha sylvatica.
Common Camellia Camellia japonica.
Common Caper Capparis spinosa.
Common Carline Thistle Carlina vulgaris.
Common Catalpa Catalpa bignonioides.
Common Cat's Paw Anigozanthos humilis.
Common Cockscomb Celosia argentea var. cristata.
Common Coral Tree Erythrina crista-galli; E. lysistemon.
Common Corn Salad Valerianella locusta.
Common Correa Correa reflexa.
Common Cotton Grass Eriophorum angustifolium.
Common Dandelion Taraxacum.
Common Devil's Claw Proboscidea louisianica.
Common Dogbane Apocynum androsaemifolium.
Common Dogwood Cornus sanguinea.
Common Duckweed Lemna minor.
Common Elder Sambucus nigra.
Common English Ivy Hedera helix.
Common European Ash Fraxinus excelsior.

Common Evening Primrose *Oenothera biennis.*
Common Everlasting Flower *Helichrysum apiculatum.*
Common Fig *Ficus carica.*
Common Flat-pea *Platylobium obtusangulum.*
Common Foxglove *Digitalis purpurea.*
Common Gardenia *Gardenia augusta.*
Common Garden Cress *Lepidium sativum.*
Common Garden Verbena *Verbena ×hybrida.*
Common German Flag *Iris germanica.*
Common Ginger *Zingiber officinale.*
Common Grape Hyacinth *Muscari neglectum.*
Common Grape Vine *Vitis vinifera.*
Common Guava *Psidium guajava.*
Common Gum Cistus *Cistus ladanifer.*
Common Hackberry *Celtis occidentalis.*
Common Hair Grass *Deschampsia flexuosa.*
Common Hawthorn *Crataegus monogyna.*
Common Heath *Epacris impressa; E. obtusifolia.*
Common Holly *Ilex aquifolium.*
Common Honeysuckle *Lonicera periclymenum.*
Common Hop *Humulus lupulus.*
Common Horehound *Marrubium vulgare.*
Common Hornbeam *Carpinus betulus.*
Common Horsetail *Equisetum arvense.*
Common Houseleek *Sempervivum tectorum.*
Common Hyacinth *Hyacinthus orientalis.*
Common Ivy *Hedera helix.*
Common Jasmine *Jasminum officinale.*
Common Jujube *Ziziphus jujuba.*
Common Juniper *Juniperus communis.*
Common Kioki *Blechnum capense.*
Common Laburnum *Laburnum anagyroides.*
Common Large Monkey Flower *Mimulus guttatus.*
Common Lettuce *Lactuca sativa.*
Common Lilac *Syringa vulgaris.*
Common Lime *Tilia ×vulgaris.*
Common Lousewort *Pedicularis canadensis.*
Common Madia *Madia elegans.*
Common Maidenhair *Adiantum capillus-veneris.*
Common Maidenhair Fern *Adiantum aethiopicum.*
Common Mallow *Malva neglecta.*
Common Marigold *Calendula officinalis.*
Common Matrimony Vine *Lycium barbarum.*
Common Moonwort *Botrychium lunaria.*
Common Morning Glory *Ipomoea purpurea.*
Common Moss Rose *Rosa ×centifolia.*
Common Mountain Ash *Sorbus aucuparia.*
Common Mussaenda *Mussaenda glabra.*
Common Myrtle *Myrtus communis.*
Common Nardoo *Marsilea drummondii.*
Common Net-bush *Calothamnus quadrifidus.*
Common Nightshade *Solanum nigrum.*
Common Oak *Quercus robur.*
Common Olive *Olea europaea* var. *europaea.*
Common Osier *Salix viminalis.*
Common Palmetto *Sabal palmetto.*
Common Passion Flower *Passiflora caerulea.*
Common Pear *Pyrus communis.*
Common Pepper *Piper nigrum.*
Common Pimpernel *Anagallis arvensis.*
Common Pitcher Plant *Sarracenia purpurea.*
Common Plantain *Plantago major.*
Common Plum *Prunus ×domestica.*
Common Polypody *Polypodium vulgare.*
Common Privet *Ligustrum vulgare.*
Common Quaking Grass *Briza media.*
Common Quince *Cydonia oblonga.*
Common Rasp-fern *Doodia media.*
Common Red Ixora *Ixora javanica.*
Common Reed *Phragmites australis.*
Common Rose Mallow *Hibiscus moscheutos.*
Common Rue *Ruta graveolens.*
Common Rush *Juncus effusus.*
Common Sage *Salvia officinalis.*
Common Scarlet Sundew *Drosera glandulifera.*
Common Scurvy Grass *Cochlearia officinalis.*
Common Sickle Pine *Falcatifolium falciforme.*
Common Smokebush *Conospermum stoechadis.*
Common Snakeweed *Stachytarpheta jamaicensis.*
Common Snowberry *Symphoricarpos albus.*
Common Snowdrop *Galanthus nivalis.*
Common Speedwell *Veronica officinalis.*
Common Spindle Tree *Euonymus europaeus.*
Common Spotted Orchid *Dactylorhiza fuchsii.*
Common Spruce *Picea abies.*
Common Staghorn Fern *Platycerium bifurcatum.*

Common Stonecrop *Sedum acre.*
Common Sunflower *Helianthus annuus.*
Common Tarweed *Madia elegans.*
Common Teasel *Dipsacus fullonum.*
Common Thorn Apple *Datura stramonium.*
Common Toadflax *Linaria vulgaris.*
Common Tobacco *Nicotiana tabacum.*
Common Unicorn Plant *Proboscidea louisianica.*
Common Valerian *Valeriana officinalis.*
Common Verbena *Verbena officinalis.*
Common Vervain *Verbena officinalis.*
Common Vetchling *Lathyrus pratensis.*
Common Viper's Grass *Scorzonera hispanica.*
Common Watercress *Nasturtium officinale.*
Common White Dogwood *Cornus florida.*
Common White Sunray *Helipterum floribundum.*
Common Wolffia *Wolffia columbiana.*
Common Woodsia *Woodsia obtusa.*
Common Woollybush *Adenanthos cygnorum.*
Common Wormwood *Artemisia absinthium.*
Common Yellowwood *Afrocarpus falcatus.*
Comon Camassia *Camassia quamash.*
Compact Brome *Bromus madritensis.*

Comparettia Poepp. & Endl. Orchidaceae. 8 epiphytic orchids. Pbs small, ellipsoid, sheathed. Lvs solitary, oblong-elliptic, coriaceous, erect. Rac. basal, delicate, arching, sometimes branched; sep. narrow-elliptic to broadly lanceolate, lat. sep. fused below to form spur; pet. resembling dors. sep.; lip trilobed, wavy, midlobe reniform, cleft, callus with 2 spur-like projections, lat. lobes small, erect, rounded. Winter. Andes, W Indies, Mex. Z10.
C. coccinea Lindl. Fls to 2.25cm diam, scarlet; lip flattened, rounded, scarlet above, yellow below. Braz.
C. falcata Poepp. & Endl. Fls to 2cm diam., cerise, fading to rose or white at centre. Throughout genus range.
C. macroplectron Rchb. & Triana. Fls to 4cm diam., white, pale mauve or lilac, spotted purple; spur long (to 5cm). Colomb.
C. rosea Lindl. = *C. falcata.*

Compass Barrel Cactus *Ferocactus cylindraceus.*
Compass-plant *Silphium lacinatum.*

Comperia K. Koch. Orchidaceae. 1 terrestrial tuberous orchid to 60cm. Lvs to 15cm, oblong or oblong-ovate. Spike broadly cylindric; tep. maroon or green tinted purple, fused, forming a hood; lip broad, trilobed, midlobe cleft, convex, white or rose veined red with green or maroon apical fil. Eur., Middle E. Z8.
C. comperiana (Steven) Asch. & Gräbn.
C. karduchorum Bornm. & Kränzl. = *C. comperiana.*
C. taurica K. Koch = *C. comperiana.*
→*Orchis.*

COMPOSITAE Giseke. 1300/21,000. *Abrotanella, Achillea, Acmella, Acourtia, Acroclinium, Ageratina, Ageratum, Agoseris, Ainsliaea, Ajania, Alfredia, Allardia, Amberboa, Amellus, Ammobium, Anacyclus, Anaphalis, Andryala, Antennaria, Anthemis, Antheropeas, Aphanostephus, Arctanthemum, Arctium, Arctotheca, Arctotis, Argyranthemum, Argyroxiphium, Arnica, Artemisia, Aster, Asteriscus, Astranthium, Athanasia, Athrixia, Ayapana, Baccharis, Bahia, Baileya, Balsamorhiza, Barnedesia, Barrosoa, Bartlettina, Bedfordia, Bellis, Bellium, Berkheya, Bidens, Boltonia, Brachycome, Brachyglottis, Brachylaena, Brickellia, Buphthalmum, Cacalia, Cacaliopsis, Calendula, Callistephus, Calocephalus, Calomeria, Calotis, Carduncellus, Carduus, Carlina, Carthamus, Cassinia, Castalis, Catananche, Celmisia, Centaurea, Centratherum, Cephalipterum, Cephalorhynchus, Chaenactis, Chaetanthera, Chamaemelum, Cheirolophus, Chiliotrichum, Chromolaena, Chrysanthemoides, Chrysanthemum, Chrysanthemopsis, Chrysocoma, Chrysogonum, Chrysopsis, Chrysothamnus, Cicerbita, Cichorium, Cineraria, Cirsium, Cladanthus, Cnicus, Coleostephus, Conoclinium, Conyza, Coreopsis, Corethrogyne, Cosmos, Cotula, Cousinia, Craspedia, Cremanthodium, Crepis, Crossostephium, Crupina, Cyanopsis, Cynara, Dahlia, Delairea, Dendranthema, Dimorphotheca, Dolichoglottis, Dolichothrix, Dolomiaea, Doronicum, Dracopis, Dymondia, Echinacea, Echinops, Edmondia, Emilia, Encelia, Enceliopsis, Engelmannia, Ericameria, Erigeron, Eriocephalus, Eriophyllum, Espeletia, Eumorphia, Eupatorium, Euryops, Farfugium, Felicia, Fleischmannia, Gaillardia, Galactites, Gazania, Geraea, Gerbera, Gnaphalium, Grindelia, Guizotia, Gundelia, Gutierrezia, Gynura, Haastia, Haplocarpha, Haplopappus, Hazardia, Hebeclinium, Helenium, Helianthella, Helianthus, Helichrysum, Heliocauta, Heliopsis, Helipterum, Heteranthemis, Heteropappus, Heterorhachis, Heterotheca, Hidalgoa, Hieracium, Hippolytia, Homogyne, Hulsea, Hyalo-*

sperma, Hymenolepis, Hymenopappus, Hymenoxys, Hypochoeris, Inula, Ixodia, Jurinea, Jurinella, Kalimeris, Kleinia, Krigia, Lactuca, Lagenophora, Lasianthaea, Lasthenia, Layia, Leibnitzia, Leontodon, Leontopodium, Leptinella, Lessingia, Leucanthemella, Leucanthemopsis, Leucanthemum, Leucogenes, Leuzea, Liatris, Libanothamnus, Ligularia, Lindheimera, Lonas, Lucilia, Luina, Machaeranthera, Madia, Mairia, Marshallia, Matricaria, Melampodium, Mikania, Monolopia, Montanoa, Moscharia, Munnozia, Mutisia, Nabalus, Nannoglottis, Nassauvia, Nauplius, Neocabreria, Neomirandea, Nipponanthemum, Oldenburgia, Olearia, Oncosiphon, Onopordum, Osteospermum, Otanthus, Othonna, Ozothamnus, Packera, Paranephelius, Parthenium, Perezia, Pericallis, Petasites, Phaenocoma, Phalacraea, Phalacrocarpum, Picris, Pilosella, Piqueria, Pittocaulon, Pityopsis, Plagius, Plectocephalus, Plectostachys, Podachaenium, Podolepis, Polyarrhena, Prenanthes, Prionopsis, Pseudognaphalium, Pseudogynoxys, Pteropogon, Ptilostemon, Pulicaria, Pyrrocoma, Raoulia, Ratibida, Reichardia, Rhodanthe, Roldana, Rudbeckia, Santolina, Sanvitalia, Saussurea, Schoenia, Scolymus, Scorzonera, Senecio, Seriphidium, Serratula, Silphium, Silybum, Simsia, Sinacalia, Solanecio, Solidago, X Solidaster, Sonchus, Staehelina, Steirodiscus, Stenotus, Stevia, Stifftia, Stokesia, Synotis, Synurus, Tagetes, Tanacetum, Taraxacum, Telanthophora, Telekia, Tephroseris, Tetraneuris, Thelesperma, Thymophylla, Tithonia, Tolpis, Tonestus, Townsendia, Tragopogon, Tridax, Tripleurospermum, Triptilion, Tussilago, Urospermum, Ursinia, Verbesina, Vernonia, Viguiera, Vittadinia, Waitzia, Wedelia, Wulffia, Wyethia, Xanthisma, Xeranthemum, Zinnia.

Comptie *Zamia pumila.*

Comptonia Ait. Myricaceae. SWEET FERN. 1 decid., suckering shrub to 1m. Twigs hirsute at first. Lvs 6–12cm, fern-like, aromatic, linear to narrow-lanceolate, closely pinnatifid, dull green with rusty pubescence, lobes small, rounded. ♂ infl. red-brown, catkin-like, to 3.5cm; ♀ infl. brown, spherical, to 2.5cm diam. when fruiting. Summer. E US. Z4.
C. peregrina (L.) Coult. var. *asplenifolia* (L.) Fern. Compact, low-growing, with v. fine foliage.

Conandron Sieb. & Zucc. Gesneriaceae. 1 rhizomatous perenn. herb. Lvs to 30×5cm, elliptic-ovate, acuminate, shiny, bullate, dentate; petioles winged. Infl. 10–40-fld, cymose, scapose; cor. to 1.5cm diam., deeply 5-lobed, purple, rarely white, lobes narrowly deltoid, obtuse. Jap. Z9.
C. ramondioides Sieb. & Zucc. var. *pilosum* Mak. Lvs often pilose beneath. Scape pilose. Honshu.

Conanthera Ruiz & Pav. Liliaceae (Tecophilaeaceae). 4 cormous perenn. herbs. Lvs linear. Infl. a pan.; perianth seg. 6, united below in a short tube; anth. yellow, united to form a cone-like structure. Late spring–early summer. Chile. Z9.
C. bifolia Ruiz & Pav. Corms and st. base covered in coarse reticulate fibres. Lvs 25–45cm, basal. Fls in small, 5–10-fld pan., perianth seg. shortly united at base, reflexed, deep blue tinted purple. Chile.
C. campanulata Lindl. Lvs 25–30cm, sheathing flowering st. at base. Fls campanulate, to 10 in a lax pan.; perianth seg. joined in lower third, not reflexed, blue, white or dark purple-blue. Chile.
C. simsii Sweet = *C. campanulata.*

Conch Apple *Passiflora maliformis.*
Conchita *Centrosema virginianum.*

Condanthus Hassl.
C. puberulus Siebert. = *Anemopaegma puberulum.*

Cone Flower *Echinacea; Isopogon baxteri; Rudbeckia.*
Conessi *Holarrhena pubescens.*
Conesticks *Petrophila pulchella.*
Confederate Jasmine *Trachelospermum jasminoides.*
Confederate Rose Mallow *Hibiscus mutabilis.*
Confederate Vine *Antigonon leptopus.*

Congea Roxb. Verbenaceae. 7 scandent shrubs. Fls in small, capitate, involucrate cymes, usually in a term. pan.; cal. tubular, persistent, 5-toothed; cor. bilabiate, upper lip erect, 2-lobed, lower lip spreading, 3-lobed; sta. 4, long-exserted. SE Asia. Z10.
C. tomentosa Roxb. SHOWER ORCHID. Large shrub, short-tomentose. Lvs to 20cm, ovate to ovate-oblong, tomentose to subglabrous beneath. Infl. bracts to 2.5cm, white to lilac, ovate to elliptic oblong, short-tomentose; fls white. Burm., Thail.

Congoo Mallee *Eucalyptus dumosa.*

Conicosia N.E. Br. Aizoaceae. 10 small, shrubby, succulents. Lvs in tufted rosettes, spiralled, narrowly subulate-triquetrous. Fls on lat. shoots, long-pedicellate, malodorous. S Afr. Z9.
C. capitata (Haw.) Schwantes = *C. pugioniformis.*
C. elongata (Haw.) N.E. Br. = *Herrea elongata.*
C. pugioniformis (L.) N.E. Br. Shrubby, 15–30cm; st. 1–2cm thick. Lvs 15–20×1.2cm, acute, upper surface grooved, grey-green, tinged red below. Fls 7cm diam., glossy sulphur-yellow.

Coniogramme Fée. Adiantaceae. 20 clump-forming, terrestrial ferns. Rhiz. creeping. Stipe fairly rigid, pale stramineous. Lamina oblong-ovate, 1–3-pinnate, pinnae few, large, coriaceous. OW Trop., Hawaii, Mex. (1 sp.). Z10.
C. fraxinea (D. Don) Diels. Fronds to 1.2m, 1–2-pinnate, pinnae to 18–25×5cm, narrowly elliptic, caudate-acuminate, lower 2–4 pairs of pinnae often pinnate, glossy green, ultimate seg. narrowly elliptic, cordate-acuminate. Asia, Philipp., Fiji, Samoa.
C. intermedia Hieron. Fronds to 1m, 1–2-pinnate, lower pinnae often pinnate, linear-oblong, acuminate, dark green. Jap., China, Korea, N India.
C. japonica (Thunb.) Diels. BAMBOO FERN. Differs from above spp. in veins anastomosing, not free. There is a variegated form with a yellow stripe down each pinna. Jap., China, S Korea, Taiwan.

Conium L. Umbelliferae. 2–3 highly toxic glab. biennials. Lvs 2–4-pinnate. Umbels compound; involucre and involucel of few to several bracts and bracteoles; fls white. Eurasia.
C. maculatum L. HEMLOCK; POISON HEMLOCK; SPOTTED HEMLOCK; CALIFORNIA FERN; NEBRASKA FERN; WINTER FERN. To 2.5m; st. glaucous, spotted purple. Lvs to 50×40cm, ferny, foetid, ovate to deltate in outline, lobes oblong-lanceolate to deltate, to 2cm, toothed to pinnatifid, petioles long, spotted. Umbels to 5cm diam.; rays 10–20; bracts 5–6 reflexed. Summer. Eur., nat. US. Z5.

Connemara Heath *Daboecia cantabrica.*

Conoclinium DC. Compositae. 3 perenn. herbs. Cap. discoid, clustered in a rac. or pan. E US, Mex.
C. coelestinum DC. MISTFLOWER; AGERATUM. To 1m. Lvs to 10cm, ovate to oblong, often cuneate, crenate-serrate, puberulent. Cap. many, to 5mm diam.; flts c50, white, blue or violet. Summer–autumn. C & SE US, W Indies.
→*Eupatorium.*

Conopharyngia G. Don.
C. holstii (Schum.) Stapf = *Tabernaemontana pachysiphon.*

Conophyllum Schwantes.
C. chrysoleucum (Schltr.) Schwantes = *Monilaria chrysoleuca.*
C. mitratum (Marloth) Schwantes = *Mitrophyllum mitratum.*
C. moniliforme (Haw.) Schwantes = *Monilaria moniliformis.*
C. pisiforme (Haw.) Schwantes = *Monilaria pisiformis.*
C. scutatum (L. Bol.) Schwantes = *Monilaria chrysoleuca.*

Conophytum N.E. Br. Aizoaceae. c80 small succulent perennials, usually tufted and stemless. Lvs highly succulent, paired, opposite, fused forming a small fleshy body, obconic, globose, ovoid, oblong or subcylindric, apex convex, flat, depressed, notched or 2-lobed with a small fissure at centre or between lobes. Fls usually solitary, growing through central fissure; cal. with elongated, fleshy tube; cor. with a distinct slender or funnel-shaped tube and numerous pet. S Afr. (Cape Prov.), Nam. Z9.
C. admiraalii L. Bol. = *C. gratum.*
C. advenum N.E. Br. = *C. piluliforme.*
C. aggregatum (N.E. Br.) N.E. Br. = *C. piluliforme.*
C. albescens N.E. Br. = *C. bilobum.*
C. ampliatum L. Bol. = *C. bilobum.*
C. amplum L. Bol. = *C. bilobum.*
C. angustum N.E. Br. = *C. bilobum.*
C. anomalum L. Bol. = *C. meyeri.*
C. approximatum Lavis = *C. meyeri.*
C. asperulum L. Bol. A rough-textured form of *C. bilobum.*
C. auriflorum Tisch. Bodies 10–15×4–6mm, barrel-shaped to cylindric, dark green to red-green, shining unspotted or sparsely dotted, minutely pitted, covered with white raphides; fissure surrounded by a dark green band. Fls golden-yellow. W Cape.
C. avenantii L. Bol. = *C. wettsteinii.*
C. barbatum L. Bol. Bodies 12–15×4–6mm, clavate, apex truncate, surface deep green, ± unmarked, papillose fissure surrounded by longer barbate papillae. Fls pink. W Cape.

C. batesii N.E. Br. A plain-coloured form of *C. pictum*.

C. bilobum (Marloth) N.E. Br. Bodies 10–70×10–28×10–15mm, cuneate-oblong, laterally compressed to subcylindric, tips 3–25mm, terete to ovate in section, keel often tinged red to deep purple, surface white-green to deep blue-green, glossy to velvety, unmarked or heavily spotted, partially fenestrate; fissure ciliate. Fls pale yellow to deep golden-yellow tipped red, occas. white. W Cape.

C. blandum L. Bol. Bodies 17–30×10–15×6–10mm, oblong, bilobed, lf tips free, strongly keeled, apiculate, surface minutely and densely papillate, white-green, occas. flushed red, margins with pellucid dots; fissure ciliate. Fls strongly scented, white to rose-pink. W Cape.

C. braunsii Schwantes = *C. pearsonii*.

C. breve N.E. Br. Bodies 8–15×8–12mm, obconical, truncate or weakly convex at circular top, pale glaucous-green to pale yellow-green, reddened below, sometimes spotted; fissure dimpled at each end, surrounded by a reddened ring. Fls scented, yellow to ochre. W Cape.

C. brownii Tisch. A red to brown-green variant of *C. ectypum*.

C. burgeri L. Bol. Bodies 13–25×20–25mm, globose, broadened below, surface cells convex and translucent, pale grey-green to deep purple-red; fissure narrow. Fls sweetly scented, purple-rose. W Cape.

C. calculus (A. Berger) N.E. Br. Bodies 15–35×10–30mm, globose, v. firm, glab., unmarked, chalky green to pale yellow-green. Fls scented of clove, pale yellow to orange. W Cape.

C. calitzdorpense L. Bol. A dwarf variant of *C. truncatum*.

C. candidum L. Bol. A white-fld variant of *C. bilobum*.

C. catervum (N.E. Br.) N.E. Br. A variant of *C. viridicatum*, v. vigorous, body surface light grey-green.

C. christiansenianum L. Bol. A crenately lobed, papillose variant of *C. bilobum*.

C. compressum N.E. Br. A thin-bodied, 'compressed' variant of *C. bilobum*.

C. concavum L. Bol. Bodies 20–35×15–22×12–15mm, sub-obconic, concave above, soft-textured, pale green to dusky red-grey, velvety; fissure depressed, surrounded by a green-tinged pellucid zone. Fls strongly honey-scented, white to cream. W Cape.

C. connatum L. Bol. A variant of *C. bilobum* with nearly connate lobes.

C. corculum Schwantes. A tightly clustering variant of *C. meyeri*.

C. crassum L. Bol. A large form of *C. bilobum* with bodies 6–6.5cm tall.

C. craterulum Tisch. = *C. velutinum*.

C. cupreatum Tisch. Bodies 10–25×8–10×4–7mm, obconic to subcylindric, truncate to convex above, deep green to green-brown, subglabrous to papillose, partially fenestrate near fissure with 'islands' of yellow-orange to orange-tan colour and a slight metallic lustre. Fls white to pale rose-pink, rarely magenta. W Cape.

C. cupreiflorum Tisch. Probably a natural or artificial hybrid of *C. elishae* and *C. violaciflorum*. Some arising in cult. also show influence of *C. bilobum* and *C. velutinum*.

C. curtum L. Bol. = *C. bilobum*.

C. declineatum L. Bol. = *C. obcordellum*.

C. densipunctum L. Bol. Bodies 15–25×12–15×8–10mm, later-ally compressed, sharply keeled and bilobed at the top, lobes not diverging, pale yellow grey-green, densely spotted. Fls scented, white. Nam.

C. devium Rowley. Body 10–18×6×6mm, cylindrical, ± tuberculate, lobes 2–3.5mm high, erect, tips with translucent windows. Fls pink-white. W Cape.

C. discrepans G. Rowley = *C. maughanii*.

C. dolomiticum Tisch. = *C. bilobum*.

C. ecarinatum L. Bol. A white-fld variant of *C. bilobum*.

C. ecarinatum L. Bol. = *C. bilobum*.

C. ectypum N.E. Br. Bodies 8–25×4–10×3–10mm, conic to obovate or clavate, apex circular or elliptic, sometimes keeled, pale grey-green to red-brown or deep black-green, usually glossy or metallic, with translucent, often raised, green- or red-tinged striations, with white patches between them; fissure short, papillate. Fls white to pale pink, magenta, red-orange or yellow, sometimes white at base. W Cape.

C. elishae (N.E. Br.) N.E. Br. A variant of *C. bilobum*. To c27mm tall, maculate, compressed, shortly lobed, glab. Fls yellow. W Cape.

C. ernianum Loesch & Tisch. Possibly a ssp. of *C. taylorianum*. Surface finely wrinkled, with sunken stomata, level idioblasts, an irregularly retuse keel. Nam.: Great Namaqualand.

C. fibuliforme (Haw.) N.E. Br. Bodies 10–25×8–12mm, conic, apex truncate or slightly convex, not keeled, grey-green with long papillae, densely spotted; fissure zone densely papillate, slightly raised. Fls brilliant magenta with darker stripes. W Cape.

C. ficiforme (Haw.) N.E. Br. Bodies 20–30×10–15×8–12mm, depressed at apex, with two distinct lobes, grey-green or yellow-green, often flushed purple, much spotted, apex with grey to red dots or lines surrounding fissure. Fls carnation-scented, off-white, pale yellow, pink or rose-pink. SW Cape.

C. flavum N.E. Br. Bodies 8–35×10–30mm, obconic, apex convex, truncate or rarely concave, pale white-green to deep grey-green, translucent green spots usually numerous; fissure obscurely papillate, surrounded by a translucent ring. Fls yellow. W Cape.

C. fraternum (N.E. Br.) N.E. Br. Bodies 15–20×6–10×6–9mm, conic, apex truncate or, slightly depressed, circular, light yellow-green, slightly shining, with large, raised markings; fissure small, minutely papillate, surrounded by red streaks. Fls white to pale pink. W Cape.

C. friedrichiae (Dinter) Schwantes. Bodies 8–40×6–15×4–10mm, cylindric, bilobed, soft, rubbery, apex truncate or rounded, translucent, brown-green to red-green or grey-green, v. glossy when turgid, otherwise dull, shortly papillate; fissure often pustulate at base. Fls scented or unscented, white to mauve-pink. Namaqualand.

C. frutescens Schwantes. Shrubby. Bodies 25–50×20–30×10–15mm, long-cordiform, often bowed in the middle, bright green becoming orange in dormancy, usually un-spotted, keel red; fissure surrounded by a small translucent patch. Fls orange or cerise, often with darker streaks. W Cape.

C. fulleri L. Bol. Bodies 6–20×5–18mm, conic, apex convex or truncate, pale yellow-green to deep green or purple, with numerous papillate, translucent 'blisters' 0.5–2mm across; fissure small, papillate. Fls often scented, pink, rarely white. W Cape.

C. germanum N.E. Br. A small, finely marked variant of *C. obcordellum*.

C. giftbergense Tisch. Midway between *C. uvaeforme* and *C. obcordellum*.

C. gracilistylum (L. Bol.) N.E. Br. Close to *C. bilobum*. Bodies 15–30×10–15×9–12mm, oval to cordate, surface blue-green, spotted, lobes long, keel red, glab. Fls rose-pink. W Cape.

C. graessneri Tisch. A larger-bodied variant of *C. saxetanum*. S of River Orange.

C. gratum (N.E. Br.) N.E. Br. Bodies 12–30×6–20mm, turbini-form to subglobose, apex round, convex or rarely flattened, sides rounded, pale white-green to blue-green, sometimes yellow-green or purple-grey, rarely, papillate, spots many, obscure and apparently sunken or obvious; fissure sunken, slightly papillate, surrounded by red flecks. Fls pink, magenta or pure white. W Cape, Nam.

C. herrei Schwantes. A small-bodied, well marked variant of *C. minisculum*.

C. hians N.E. Br. Bodies 4–18×3–9×2–6mm, ovoid, shortly bilobed, pale grey-green to blue-green, papillose, keels often punctate; fissure gaping, with long white papillae. Fls sweetly scented, white, cream, pink or tinged red, often dark-tipped. W Cape.

C. hirtum Schwantes = *C. hians*.

C. impressum Tisch. = *C. obcordellum*.

C. intrepidum L. Bol. = *C. fibuliforme*.

C. johannis-winkleri (Dinter & Schwantes) N.E. Br. A pale blue-bodied, northern variant of *C. subrisum*.

C. julii Schwantes = *C. uvaeforme*.

C. karamoepense L. Bol. = *C. marginatum*.

C. kennedyi L. Bol. A green-bodied form of *C. lithopoides*.

C. khamiesbergense (L. Bol.) Schwantes. Bodies 8–15×4–8×2–5mm, obconic, lvs only partially fused, sharply cuneate, grey-green to ruddy, with numerous rough white 'warts', margins dentate, fissure wide-gaping, often pustulate. Fls scented of raspberries, white-pink to mauve. W Cape.

C. koubergense L. Bol. = *C. lithopoides*.

C. koupense Tisch. = *C. viridicatum*.

C. kubusanum N.E. Br. = *C. gratum*.

C. lambertense Schick & Tisch. Bodies 10–15×5–8×3–6mm, obconic, elliptic from above, apex slightly convex, surface grey-green to blue-grey, shiny, top surface with fine, dendritic red markings; fissure slightly sunken, finely papillate, surrounded by a dark line. Fls white to straw-coloured, rarely pink. W Cape. var. *conspicuum* Rawe. Bodies small, ornately marked and glossy.

C. latum L. Bol. = *C. meyeri*.

C. lavisianum L. Bol. = *C. bilobum*.

C. lavranosii Rawe = *C. taylorianum*.

C. laxipetalum N.E. Br. = *C. bilobum*.

C. leipoldtii N.E. Br. Close to *C. minusculum* with a papillose sur-face.

C. leviculum (N.E. Br.) N.E. Br. = *C. pictum*.

C. lilianum Littlew. = *C. pellucidum*.

C. limbatum N.E. Br. = *C. ectypum*.

C. **lithopoides** L. Bol. Bodies 10–30×8–15×6–10mm, ovate-cylindric, sometimes divided into 2 short lobes, apex truncate to slightly convex, oval to rounded or rounded-rectangular. Rusty brown or red-purple to yellow-green, glab. to slightly velvety-papillose, fenestration with mottled dendritic marking or unmarked; fissure slightly sunken, finely papillate, surrounded by a coloured line. Fls magenta, occas. with a white centre, rarely pale rose pink or carmine. W Cape.

C. **longibracteatum** L. Bol. = *C. bilobum.*

C. **longum** N.E. Br. Bodies 25–30×20×14mm, somewhat compressed cylindrical, smooth, grey-green, often slightly brown below; fissure extending from side to side, lobes truncate with a translucent, papillose surface. Fls white to v. pale pink. W Cape.

C. **luckhoffii** Lavis. Bodies 8–15×4–8×2–5mm, elongate-cordiform, lobes sharply keeled or rounded, grey-green to purple-brown, with prominent red spots and lines; fissure slightly sunken, densely papillate, surrounded by a coloured band. Fls magenta to carmine. W Cape.

C. **luisae** Schwantes. One of the smaller forms of *C. bilobum* with longer internodes, forming a small shrub with age.

C. **luteum** N.E. Br. = *C. flavum.*

C. **marginatum** Lavis. Bodies 15–30×4–8×3–6mm, elongate-cordiform, rounded to sharply keeled, white to yellow-green, velvety-papillate or glab., with green dots, lobe margins outlined in red; fissure slightly sunken, densely papillate. Fls slightly scented, magenta to carmine. W Cape.

C. **marlothii** N.E. Br. Differs from *C. fraternum* in longer, thinner st., bodies 8×5×5mm, surface blue-grey with dots level with surface with a distinct sheen.

C. **marnierianum** Tisch. & Jacobsen. (*C. ectypum* × *C. bilobum.*) Bodies 2.5–15×10mm, obcordate, lobes 8mm, truncate, with an acute, forked keel, surface red-brown to olive-green with prominent veins and dots on the body sides. Fls fiery red. W Cape.

C. **maughanii** N.E. Br. Bodies 20–35×15–30×15–25mm, cylindric to subglobose, slightly bilobed, soft and pulpy, top rounded, translucent to nearly opaque, surface yellow-green to orange or red-brown, glab. or shortly papillate with green idioblasts. Fls strongly scented, white to yellow or pale peach. W Cape.

C. **meleagris** L. Bol. = *C. uvaeforme.*

C. **meridianum** L. Bol. = *C. cupreatum.*

C. **meyerae** Schwantes. Close to *C. bilobum.* Lobes v. long, often flaring, fissure and body surface glab.

C. **meyeri** N.E. Br. Bodies 9–20×5–15×5–10mm, obovoid, slightly bilobed and keeled, dull green to pale white-green, glab. or velvety-papillose, sometimes partly surrounded by a green or red ring. Fls white to yellow.

C. **minusculum** (N.E. Br.) N.E. Br. Bodies 5–8×5–8×3–6mm, obovate, elliptic or round in outline, apex convex or truncate, brown-green becoming red or purple-brown at apex, with lines or dots; fissure surrounded by a translucent band, with dense papillae. Fls magenta to carmine, rarely white. Cape Prov.

C. **minutum** (Haw.) N.E. Br. Bodies 15–30×5–10×5–10mm, narrowly obovate, apex convex, truncate rarely concave, round or elliptic in outline, glab. or finely papillose, light blue-green to dark green or purple, occas. red on sides, dotted; fissure surrounded by a translucent band, depressed, papillose. Fls white magenta or pink. W Cape.

C. **miscellum** N.E. Br. = *C. saxetanum.*

C. **miserum** N.E. Br. = *C. hians.*

C. **muirii** N.E. Br. = *C. viridicatum.*

C. **multipunctatum** Tisch. = *C. truncatum.*

C. **mundum** N.E. Br. A dark-bodied, highly tuberculate variant of *C. obcordellum.*

C. **muscosipapillatum** Lavis = *C. bilobum.*

C. **nelianum** Schwantes. A large member of the *C. elishae/C. bilobum* complex.

C. **nevillei** (N.E. Br.) N.E. Br. = *C. obcordellum.*

C. **noctiflorum** (L. Bol.) Rowley = *C. maughanii.*

C. **novellum** N.E. Br. = *C. viridicatum.*

C. **novicum** N.E. Br. = *C. flavum.*

C. **nudum** Tisch. Close to *C. minutum.* Bodies 10×5×5mm, cylindrical, apex circular, flat to ± convex, surface immaculate, dark dull green to deep purple. Fls mauve-pink. W Cape.

C. **obconellum** (Haw.) Schwantes = *C. obcordellum.*

C. **obcordellum** (Haw.) N.E. Br. Bodies 8–20×5–20×5–20mm, obconical, apex convex or concave round, elliptical, reniform or hexagonal from above, surface sides red to purple, shiny, apex silvery pale green to blue-green, suffused with red or brown, glab. to short-papillose, usually with black-green lines and dots; fissure short, papillose. Fls strongly scented, white to yellow or pink. W Cape.

C. **obscurum** N.E. Br. Bodies 6–15×3–7×3–7mm, obconical, apex truncate, round or elliptical in outline, surface bright to

dark green or purple-brown rugose, shiny, marked with green dots; fissure short-papillose. Fls pale to lilac-pink or magenta. W Cape.

C. **orbicum** N.E. Br. ex Tisch. = *C. gratum.*

C. **orientale** L. Bol. = *C. truncatum.*

C. **ornatum** Lavis = *C. flavum.*

C. **oviforme** (N.E. Br.) N.E. Br. = *Oophytum oviforme.*

C. **ovigerum** Schwantes = *C. meyeri.*

C. **pageae** (N.E. Br.) N.E. Br. Bodies 8–10×6–10×5–9mm, obconical, apex slightly convex or flat, rounded in outline, surface glab., bright apple-green, sides and around fissure red to purple, fissure slightly protuberant. Fls strongly scented, yellow, ochre, rarely pink or ivory, tips red. W Cape.

C. **pardicolor** Tisch. = *C. pellucidum.*

C. **parviflorum** N.E. Br. = *C. obcordellum.*

C. **parvipetalum** N.E. Br. = *C. obcordellum.*

C. **pauxillum** (N.E. Br.) N.E. Br. = *C. pictum.*

C. **pearsonii** N.E. Br. Bodies 12–25×8–25×8–25mm, broadly obconical, apex overhanging, truncate or slightly convex, round in outline, surface glab., light blue-green to grey-green, almost unspotted; fissure often off-centre, surrounded by translucent band. Fls pink or magenta. W Cape.

C. **peersii** Lavis. An elongate-pyriform, sub-bilobed variant of *C. truncatum.*

C. **pellucidum** Schwantes. Bodies 10–25×6–12×4–6mm, cylindrical, apex convex flattened or grooved, generally divided into 2 short lobes, glab. or crystalline-papillose, coffee-brown, dull red, ochre or silvery grey, bullate, warted or smooth, spotted, sometimes blood red; fissure slightly sunken, papillose. Fls white to rose-pink, rarely yellow. W Cape.

C. **pictum** (N.E. Br.) N.E. Br. Bodies 8–15×7–12×6–9mm, obconical, apex truncate to slightly convex, elliptical, glab. to finely papillose, light grey-green to dull green, marked with lines and spots, not raised, not shining; fissure level or slightly sunken, papillose. Fls scented, white, pale yellow or slightly pink. W Cape.

C. **picturatum** N.E. Br. = *C. obcordellum.*

C. **pillansii** Lavis. Bodies 12–25×10–25×8–20mm, ± globose, apex flattened, divided into 2 short lobes or wholly fused, glab. or papillose, pale green to yellow or red, densely and finely marked, window prominent or reduced to patches beside the fissure. Fls slightly scented, pale to deep pink or magenta. W Cape.

C. **pilosulum** N.E. Br. = *Gibbaeum pilosulum.*

C. **piluliforme** (N.E. Br.) N.E. Br. Bodies 4–8×2–5×2–5mm, globose-obconical, truncate to slightly convex on top, pill-like seen from above, light grey-green to grass-green or purple-green marked with fine v. dark lines and spots. Fls strongly scented, dark maroon or purple. W Cape.

C. **piriforme** L. Bol. = *C. bilobum.*

C. **pisinnum** (N.E. Br.) N.E. Br. = *C. viridicatum.*

C. **plenum** N.E. Br. = *C. bilobum.*

C. **pluriforme** L. Bol. = *C. bilobum.*

C. **poellnitzianum** Schwantes = *C. subrisum.*

C. **polulum** N.E. Br. = *C. bilobum.*

C. **polyandrum** Lavis. Close to *C. velutinum.* Epidermis paler green, glab., fls pink to nearly white. W Cape.

C. **praecinctum** N.E. Br. = *C. pictum.*

C. **praecox** N.E. Br. A white-fld version of *C. fraternum.*

C. **praeparvum** N.E. Br. = *C. uvaeforme.*

C. **primosii** Lavis = *C. roodiae.*

C. **proximum** L. Bol. = *C. bilobum.*

C. **pulchellum** Tisch. = *C. obscurum.*

C. **pygmaeum** Schick & Tisch. = *C. breve.*

C. **quaesitum** (N.E. Br.) N.E. Br. Bodies 10–25×6–15×5–10mm, broadly ovoid to cylindrical, bilobed, apex acutely keeled or rounded, surface pale grey-green or yellow-green, sometimes marked, finely papillose, keels outlined with red or white; fissure sunken, papillose. Fls heavily scented, white, straw-yellow to rose-pink. W Cape.

C. **rarum** N.E. Br. = *C. gratum.*

C. **reconditum** A.R. Mitch. Bodies 6–15×3–7×2–4mm, short-cylindric to flask-shaped, lobes distinct, 4–5mm, triangular to terete, lobe tips truncate, fenestrate, densely tuberculate, grass-green when young, later grey-green-brown, grey-purple-red or bright green, papillate. Fls scentless, pure white or suffused with pale green-yellow or tawny-yellow. W Cape.

C. **regale** Lavis. Bodies 20–40×15–20×10–15mm, obcordate, soft, lobes 5–12mm, diverging, triangular in section, carinate, surface pale green or yellow-green, densely papillose, sparsely dotted, keels red; fissure surrounded by a large fenestrate zone. Fls lightly scented, rose-pink. W Cape.

C. **reticulatum** L. Bol. = *C. minusculum.*

C. **rubristylosum** Tisch. = *C. flavum.*

C. **rubrolineatum** Rawe. Close to *C. minusculum.* Bodies 14×7×7mm, cushion-forming with to 50 heads, long-conical, apex flat, circular to oval with silver and red glassy papillae forming lines and dots. Fls pink-violet. W Cape.

C. rufescens N.E. Br. Red-bodied variant of *C. maughanii*.

C. ruschii Schwantes. A small form of *C. wettsteinii*.

C. saxetanum N.E. Br. (N.E. Br.) Body 5–10×2–6×1–5mm, cylindrical, apex convex, often bilobed, surfaces smooth, green to grey-green, purple-red or faded orange, spotted, unspotted or with reticulate green lines; fissure surrounded with a translucent band with dense white papillae. Fls nocturnal, fragrant, white, cream-coloured, pink-orange or violet. Namib., Cape.

C. schwantesii Rowley = *C. friedrichiae*.

C. scitulum (N.E. Br.) N.E. Br. A globose, convex variant of *C. pictum* with elegantly looped markings.

C. semivestitum L. Bol. Bodies 22×14×7mm, turbinate, compressed and keeled towards the apex, somewhat lobed, keels and marins outlined with dark green confluent dots, pilose; fissure gaping, v. hairy. Fls diurnal, scented, rose-pink. W Cape.

C. signatum (N.E. Br.) N.E. Br. = *C. pictum*.

C. simile N.E. Br. = *C. bilobum*.

C. smorenskaduense Boer. Bodies 15–25×5–10×4–10mm, cylindrical, slightly tapered above, often sub-bilobed, v. soft, yellow-green, pustulate, pustules, sometimes coalescing at apex to form a quasi-window. Fls diurnal, bright magenta. W Cape. ssp. *hermarium* Hammer. Bodies 15–20×4–6×4–5mm cylindrical, tapering slightly to truncate to convex apex, bright yellow-green, smooth, shiny with translucent idioblasts; fissure short, ciliate. Fls smaller.

C. speciosum Tisch. A form of *C. wettsteinii* var. *ruschii* with showy fls.

C. spectabile Lavis. A form of *C. obcordellum*. Bodies large with branched, red lines. Fls large.

C. stenandrum L. Bol. A variant of *C. obcordellum*. Bodies silver-grey to red-brown or purple, with prominent scattered brown-red markings. W Cape.

C. stephanii Schwert. Bodies 7–15×4–8×4–8mm, obconical, convex to truncate at apex, deep to olive-green or red, covered by translucent white papillae; fissure short, hairy. Fls nocturnal, slightly scented, brown-yellow to maroon. E Cape.

C. stevens-jonesianum L. Bol. = *C. breve*.

C. steytlervillense Tisch. = *C. truncatum*.

C. subfenestratum Schwantes = *C. pillansii*.

C. subglobosum Tisch. = *C. truncatum*.

C. subrisum (N.E. Br.) N.E. Br. Bodies 20–30×15–25×15–25mm, turbiniform, apex truncate or slightly depressed, smooth pale green, chalky or yellow-green, occas. with scattered green spots; fissure glab. often eccentric, ringed red. Fls nocturnal, clove-scented, golden-yellow or white. W Cape.

C. sulcatum L. Bol. A variant of *C. ectypum*. Bodies sulcate olive-green.

C. swanepoelianum Rawe. Bodies 5–7×3–4×2mm or smaller, elongate-conical, apex surface flat to slightly concave, sometimes keeled or concave, smooth, grey-green, purple or black-green with numerous fine raised lines or wart-like points; fissure sunken with white papillae. Fls diurnal, yellow to magenta. W Cape.

C. taylorianum (Dinter & Schwantes) N.E. Br. Bodies 8–15×3–8×3mm, obconical, apex truncate to slightly keeled, slightly glossy, grey-green to purple, marked with green idioblasts; fissure rhomboid, papillate. Fls diurnal, white shading to lilac-pink. Nam.

C. terrestre Tisch. = *C. pellucidum*.

C. terricolor Tisch. = *C. pellucidum*.

C. tishleri Schwantes. A variant of *C. ectypum*. Bodies large, green with puffy white sheaths. Fls large and yellow. Cape Prov.

C. translucens N.E. Br. = *C. truncatum*.

C. truncatellum (Haw.) N.E. Br. = *C. truncatum*.

C. truncatum (Thunb.) N.E. Br. Bodies 6–30×3–25×3–25mm, obconical to cylindrical, truncate, apex concave or convex, occas. quasi-bilobed, smooth, glab. or finely papillose, white-green to chartreuse or red-grey-green, usually marked with green to pink idioblasts, sometimes arranged in fine lines or concetrated around the fissure; fissure sunken, papillose. Fls nocturnal, scented, white, pink or yellow. W Cape.

C. udabibense Loesch & Tisch. = *C. subrisum*.

C. ursprungianum Tisch. A variant of *C. obcordellum*. Bodies v. flat-topped, grey to chalky green, pale with dark lustrous spots. W Cape.

C. uvaeforme (Haw.) N.E. Br. Bodies 8–25×4–15×3–12mm, grape-shaped to long-cylindrical or globose, surface smooth or slightly rugose from translucent raised spots, often papillose, grey-green to red, often marked with red or dark green lines and spots; fissure impressed, papillose. Fls nocturnal, scented, white to pale pink or straw-coloured. W Cape.

C. vanbredai L. Bol. = *C. globosum*.

C. vanheerdei Tisch. Bodies 12–20×6–10×6–10mm, ovoid to cylindrical, apex rounded to slightly pointed, pale yellow-green, dull covered with large, glassy warts, occas. coalescing to form a window near apex; fissure papillose. Fls diurnal, white to dark purple. W Cape.

C. variabile L. Bol. = *C. bilobum*.

C. velutinum Schwantes. Bodies 12–20×6–15×6–15mm, cordiform, somewhat saddle-shaped above, papillose, sometimes spotted, dark grey to light grass-green, dull; fissure sunken, surrounded by a green band, densely papillose. Fls diurnal white shading to purple-pink. W Cape.

C. verrucosum (Lavis) Rowley. Body 27×15×22mm, cylindrical, lobed by a fissure 3–4.5mm deep, tips tuberculate, convex, window zone divided into smaller windows by warty tubercles, red-brown with numerous translucent spots. Fls diurnal. glossy white. W Cape.

C. villetii L. Bol. = *C. subrisum*.

C. viride Tisch. = *C. viridicatum*.

C. viridicatum (N.E. Br.) N.E. Br. Bodies 12–25×5–15×4–12mm, obconical, apex convex or centrally depressed, smooth or minutely; dull to grey-green, sometimes flushed red, spotted and lined with translucent markings; fissure papillose, often ringed with tannin spots. Fls nocturnal, scented, white to yellow or salmon-pink. W Cape.

C. vitreopapillum Rawe. A small-bodied variant of *C. obscurum*. W Cape.

C. wagneriorum Schwantes = *C. truncatum*.

C. wettsteinii (Berger) N.E. Br. Bodies 15×20–25×15–25mm, broadly obconical, narrowing below, apex truncate to concave, smooth, mat. pale or blue-green usually with green dots; fissure sometimes v. eccentrically placed, finely papillose, with a translucent border. Fls diurnal, magenta, pale pink, rarely pure white or pink with a white eye. W Cape.

C. wiesmannianum Schwantes = *C. fulleri*.

C. wiggettae N.E. Br. Close to *C. truncatum*, heavily marked with dense red dots.

C. wittebergense Boer. Close to *C. pictum* with larger, flatter bodies and wider maroon markings.

→*Berresfordia, Derenbergia, Lithops, Mesembryanthemum* and *Opthalmophyllum*.

Conospermum Sm. SMOKE BUSH. Proteaceae. *c*40 shrubs or trees. Lvs entire. Fls in dense spikes, subtended by a persistent bract; perianth tubular, 4-lobed, often woolly. Aus. Z8.

C. caeruleum R. Br. Low, weak shrub, 0.5–1m. Lvs 10×1–2cm, mostly basal, elliptic-oblong to lanceolate, on slender petiole. Pan. loose, spikes few, woolly, fls blue. Spring. W Aus.

C. crassinervium Meissn. TASSEL SMOKEBUSH. Short woody-based plant. Lvs basal, linear-lanceolate, to 5mm wide, with thick margins and midrib. Scape to 1.2m; fls woolly, white in short, dense; term. pan. Spring–summer. W Aus.

C. glumaceum Lindl. HOODED SMOKEBUSH. Glab., spreading shrub, 1–2m. Lvs 2–8cm, linear-lanceolate. Pan. loose and leafy, to 30cm, fls tiny, concealed by large cream bracts. Spring–summer. W Aus.

C. huegelii R. Br. SLENDER SMOKEBUSH. Subshrub with short shoots to 25cm. Lvs 2–10cm, narrow-linear. Scapes to 30cm, terminating in an ovoid spike of small blue fls. Spring. W Aus.

C. incurvum Lindl. PLUME SMOKEBUSH. Erect, branching shrub to 80cm. Lvs 1.5cm, terete, spreading at base becoming incurved, shorter and adpressed below infl. Infl. a dense raceme-like pan.; fls woolly, white. Spring. W Aus.

C. longifolium Sm. LONG-LEAF SMOKEBUSH. Low woody shrub, 30–100cm. Lvs to 25cm, oblanceolate to spathulate. Infl. a corymb, terminating a 30cm st.; fls white. Spring. E Aus.

C. stoechadis Endl. COMMON SMOKEBUSH. Upright, open shrub to 1.5m. Lvs 8–16cm, rigid, erect, terete or narrow-linear. Fls spikes few in a loose pan., fls densely woolly, white, black-tipped. Spring–early summer. W Aus.

C. taxifolium Sm. VARIABLE SMOKE BUSH. Variable erect shrub, 60–150cm. Lvs 0.6–3cm, crowded, narrow-linear to narrow-obovate. Fls in spike in upper lf axils forming a corymbose pan., white. Spring. E Aus. Hybrids with *C. longifolium* are common.

C. triplinervium R. Br. TREE SMOKEBUSH. Tall shrub to small tree, 3–7m. Lvs 4–7cm, lanceolate. Spikes in pan. held clear of foliage; fls densely woolly, white. Spring–early summer.

Conostephium Benth. Epacridaceae. 5 small shrubs. Lvs small. Fls solitary, stalked, in the axils of upper lvs, usually pendulous; cor. tube partially or fully enclosed by cal., apex conical, lobes small, erect. W Aus. Z9.

C. pendulum Benth. PEARL FLOWER. Erect, much branched, dwarf shrub to 50cm. Lvs to 2cm, narrowly obovate, pungent, revolute. Fls pendulous on long decurved pedicels, surrounded by many bracts, sep. broadly ovate, white; cor. tube to 1.7cm,

Conradina A. Gray. Labiatae. 7 low shrubs. Fls in axill. clusters; cal. curving at maturity, tube 13-nerved, 2-lipped; cor. exceeding cal., 2-lipped, upper lip erect, retuse, lower lip spreading, 3-lobed, middle lobe indented. US (Flor. and Tenn.).

C. grandiflora Small. Shrub to 1m. Lvs 1–3cm, narrowly spathulate, revolute, glandular-punctate, canescent beneath. Fls in small axill. cymes; cal. 6–7mm, finely pubesc.; cor. blue to pink. Flor. Z9.

C. verticillata Jennison. Undershrub; br. procumbent. Lvs to 1.8cm, linear, revolute, canescent beneath. Fls whorled; cal. 6–7mm, hirsute; cor. lavender, spotted purple within. Tenn. Z7.

C. cvs. 'Low Grey': habit low and spreading, wiry.

Consolea Lem. = *Opuntia*.

Consolida (DC.) S.F. Gray. LARKSPUR. Ranunculaceae. *c*40 ann. herbs close to *Delphinium*. St. erect, simple or branched. Lvs palmately laciniate. Infl. racemose or paniculate with dissected, leafy bracts; fls zygomorphic; sep. 5, petaloid, posterior sep. spurred; 2 upper pet. fused, appearing solitary, subentire to 3–5-lobed, with spur extending into spur of posterior sep., nectariferous; lower pet. 0. W Medit. to C Asia.

C. ajacis auct. = *C. ambigua*.

C. ambigua (L.) P.W. Ball & Heyw. St. to 1m, simple or sparsely branched. Lvs finely dissected, seg. oblong to linear. Infl. racemose, rarely paniculate; fls bright blue, sometimes pink or white or freaked blue and pink; sep. 1.5cm, spur to 18mm; pet. 3 lobed, upper lobe bifid. Summer. Medit. Dwarf Hyacinth Hybrids: compact; fls in shades of plum, violet, lilac, blue and white. Giant Double Hyacinth Hybrids: non-branching, early flowering.

C. armeniaca (Stapf ex Huth) Schrödinger. St. to 1m, simple or branched, hairy, to 40cm. Lvs linear-laciniate. Fls in lax rac., bright violet-blue; sep. to 1cm, spur curved, to 2.5cm; pet. to 1.5cm, 3-lobed, central lobe short and narrow. Summer. Turk.

C. orientalis (Gay) Schrödinger. Close to *C. ambigua*. St. to 1m, simple or branched. Lf seg. linear-oblong to linear. Infl. racemose; fls purple-violet; pet. 3-lobed, upper lobe bifid. Summer. N Afr., S & E Iberian penins., SE Eur., W Asia.

C. regalis S.F. Gray. St. branched, to 50cm, hairy. Lf seg. linear. Infl. paniculate; fls deep blue to pink or white; sep. to 15mm, spur to 25mm; upper lobe of pet. 2mm+ wide, entire to erose or bifid. Summer. Eur., Cauc.

C. cvs. 'Blue Bell': fls sky-blue. 'Blue Cloud': st. branching; fls bright blue. 'Blue Spire': fld deep blue tinged purple. 'Brilliant Rose': fls deep carmine pink. 'Carmine King': fls bright carmine. 'Dazzler': fls bright scarlet. 'Exquisite Rose': fls bright pink. Imperial Series: tall plants with long, closely branched spikes or rounded, spurred double fls in pink, blue, mauve, red and white; suitable for cutting. 'Lilac Spire': fls pale mauve. 'Miss California': fls salmon-pink. 'Pink Perfection': fls pale pink. 'Rosalie': fls dark pink. 'Salmon Beauty': fls bright salmon. 'White King': fls white.

→*Delphinium*.

Constantia Barb. Rodr. Orchidaceae. 3 dwarf, epiphytic orchids. Pbs, massed, globose to obpyriform, to 0.5cm. Lvs to 0.5cm, suborbicular to reniform, bright green, coarse. Fls to 0.75cm, term., solitary; tep. lanceolate to ovate, pet. smaller than sep. and forward-pointing. Winter–spring. Braz. Z10.

C. cipoensis Barb. Rodr. Fls green to yellow, tinted red-purple. Braz.

Consumptive's Weed *Eriodictyon californicum*.
Contra Hierba *Dorstenia contrajerva*.

Convallaria L. LILY OF THE VALLEY. Liliaceae (Convallariaceae). 1 rhizomatous herbaceous perenn. St. erect with green or red-purple sheaths. Lvs 3–23cm, 1–4 on upper part of st., ovate-lanceolate to elliptic, mid-green. Rac. scapose, arching, slender secund; fls strongly fragrant, pendent; perianth 5–11mm, rounded-campanulate, waxy, white to ivory, seg. 6, largely united, tips reflexed. Fr. a scarlet berry. N temp. regions. Z3.

C. majalis L. 'Albistriata': lvs dark green striped white. 'Aureovariegata' ('Lineata', 'Striata', 'Variegata'): lvs striped gold. 'Flore Pleno': fls white, double. 'Fortin's Giant' ('Fortins'): tall, to 30cm; lvs wide; fls large, well scented. 'Hardwick Hall': lvs wide, edged yellow-green; fls large, white. 'Prolificans': fls tiny, congested in a tightly branched pan., often slightly malformed. 'Vic Pawlowski's Gold': lvs dark green closely striped clear gold. var. *keiski* (Miq.) Maxim. Smaller, to *c*7.5cm. Lvs to 15cm, 2–3, elliptic-oblong. var. *rosea* Rchb. Fls

pink. f. *picta* Wilcz. Fil. spotted purple at base.
C. montana Raf. = *C. majalis*.

CONVOLVULACEAE Juss. 58/1650. *Argyreia, Calystegia, Convolvulus, Dichondra, Evolvulus, Ipomoea, Merremia, Porana, Stictocardia*.

Convolvulus L. BINDWEED. Convolvulaceae. *c*250 ann. or perenn., erect, climbing or scrambling herbs and shrubs. Lvs usually entire. Fls solitary or in clusters; pedicels with minute leaf-like bracteoles; cor. funnel-shaped, midpetaline areas often a different colour to limb; sta. included. Widely distrib. in most temp. and subtrop. regions, with a few trop. sp.

C. althaeoides L. Perenn. herb to 1m, pubesc.; st. slender, climbing or trailing. Lvs grey-green, ovate-cordate, cordate to sagittate, often deeply and finely lobed. Infl. axill., 1–3- 5-fld; cor. 2.5–4cm diam., pink to pink-purple, widely funnel-shaped. Summer. S Eur. ssp. *tenuissimus* (Sibth. & Sm.) Stace. Hairs dense, adpressed, silvery and soft. Lf lobes narrower and deeper. Fls often solitary. Summer. S Eur. Z8.

C. arvensis L. FIELD BINDWEED. Rampant perenn. herb to 2m. St. climbing or trailing, slender. Lvs linear to ovate or ovate-oblong, sagittate to hastate, usually entire. Infl. axill., 1–3-fld, cor. 1.5–2cm diam., white or pink with pink midpetaline areas. Summer–autumn. Eur., Asia, widely nat. elsewhere. Z5.

C. boissieri Steud. Cushion-forming perenn., to 7.5cm high. Lvs ovate, silver-grey. Fls large, rosy-white. Early summer. Spain ssp. *compactus* Stace. Lvs rhombic-obovate. Z8.

C. calvertii Boiss. Tuft-forming perenn. to 10cm high. Lvs to 30cm, broad-lanceolate, silver-grey-pubesc. Fls erect, pink. Summer. Crimea. Z7.

C. canariensis L. Woody climber to about 2m. Lvs 4–9cm, oval-oblong, densely hairy, with raised veins above. Infl. axill., 7–9-fld; cor. pale blue. Canary Is. Z9.

C. cantabricus L. Woody-based perenn., 10–50cm; st. erect, pubesc. Lvs oblanceolate to linear. Infl. 1- to several-fld, cor. 1.5–2.5cm diam., pink. Summer. S Eur. Z8.

C. cneorum L. SILVERBUSH. Erect or spreading woody-based perenn., 10–50cm, clothed in silver-grey, silky hair. Lvs to 4cm, oblanceolate to linear, base attenuate. Fls clustered; cor. 1.5–2.5cm diam., v. pale shell pink to white, midpetaline areas darker pink on dors. side. Summer. It. and Balk. to N Afr. Z8.

C. cyclostegius House = *Calystegia macrostegia* ssp. *cyclostegia*.
C. elegantissimus Mill. = *C. althaeoides* ssp. *tenuissimus*.

C. floridus L. f. Woody climber or shrub to 4m. Lvs 2–14cm, linear-lanceolate, oblong-linear to spathulate. Infl. term., paniculate, man-fld; fls about 1cm diam., white or pale pink. Canary Is. Z9.

C. humilis Jacq. Ann. or short-lived herbaceous perenn. to 40cm. Lvs ovate-oblong to oblanceolate, wavy. Infl. subsessile, 1-fld; cor. 7–12mm diam., blue or violet. Late spring–early summer. C & S Spain, SE Port., It. Z8.

C. imperialis hort. = *Ipomoea ×imperialis*.

C. incanus Vahl. Perenn. to 1m, prostrate or climbing, grey-silky. Lvs 2–5cm, hastate, oblong-ovate or linear-sagittate, basal lobes occas. forked or toothed. Infl. 1–3-fld; cor. 1–2cm, pink to white, acutely lobed. Spring, summer. US. Z4.

C. japonicus Thunb. = *Calystegia hederacea*.

C. lineatus L. Woody-based perenn., 3–25cm; st. ascending procumbent, sericeous. Lvs oblanceolate or elliptical to linear, base attenuate. Infl. 1- to several-fld, axill. or term.; cor. 1.2–2.5cm diam., pink. Summer. Fr. to SC Russia and Greece. Z7.

C. macrostegius Greene = *Calystegia macrostegia*.
C. major hort. = *Ipomoea purpurea*.
C. mauritanicus Boiss. = *C. sabatius*.
C. minor hort. = *C. tricolor*.
C. occidentalis A. Gray = *Calystegia occidentalis*.

C. ocellatus Hook. Erect to prostrate perenn., brown- to silver-pubesc. Lvs to 5cm, linear-oblong, occas. 5-lobed. Infl. axill., 1-fld; cor. pink, mauve or white with a maroon central spot. Summer. S Afr. Z8.

C. pellitus f. *anestius* Ledeb. = *Calystegia hederacea* 'Flore Pleno'.

C. pentapetaloides L. Prostrate ann. or short-lived perenn. to 30cm. Lvs oblanceolate to linear or oblong. Infl. 1-fld; cor. 7–10mm diam., blue with a yellow centre. Summer. Port. to Turk. Z8.

C. purpurea L. = *Ipomoea purpurea*.
C. randii Rendle = *C. ocellatus*.

C. sabatius Viv. Woody-based, shrubby perenn., 10–50cm, st. ascending to trailing, pubesc., herbaceous. Lvs oblong to orbicular, base cuneate to truncate, entire. Infl. axill., 1–3-fld, cor. 1.5–2.2cm diam., usually pale blue sometimes pink, tube usually paler, often yellow at base. Summer. It., N Afr. Z8.

C. scammonia L. SCAMMONY. Decid. glab. perenn.; st. angled, trailing. Lvs lanceolate-cordate to sagittate. Infl. 3-fld; fls campanulate, cream or pale red. E Medit., Asia Minor. Z7.

C. scoparius L. f.   Shrub to 1m+. Lvs 0.5–5cm, linear-filamentous, often caducous, with short hairs, gland. Infl. 5–6-fld, term. or axill.; cor. white or pink. Canary Is. Z9.

C. sepium L. = Calystegia sepium.

C. tenuissimus Sibth. & Sm. = C. althaeoides ssp. tenuissimus.

C. tricolor L. Ann. or short-lived bushy or climbing perenn. to 60cm. Lvs oblanceolate to obovate. Infl. 1-fld, axill.; cor. 1.5–5cm diam., light sky-blue to dark blue, tube white, golden-white at base inside. Summer. Port. to Greece and N Afr. 'Blue Ensign': cor. limb v. bright blue. 'Blue Flash': low bushy ann. with small saucer-shaped fls, deep blue with cream and yellow centre. 'Cambridge Blue': cor. limb pale blue. 'Crimson Monarch': cor. limb carmine to crimson. 'Lavender Rosette': cor. limb lavender-pink. 'Royal Ensign': cor. limb intense dark blue throat yellow below, white at rim. 'Royal Marine': fls deep royal blue with white throat. Z8.

C. tuguriorum Forst. f. = Calystegia tuguriorum.

C. undulatus Cav. = C. humilis.

Conyza Less. Compositae. c50 ann. and perenn. herbs, rarely shrubs. St. erect, branched, leafy. Cap. small, many, in elongated pan., ligulate; phyllaries imbricate; outer flts many, v. short, white, rarely pink; central flts usually yellow. N Amer., nat. Eur. Z7.

C. canadensis (L.) Cronq. HORSEWEED; MULE TAIL; CANADIAN FLEABANE. Ann. to 1.5m, sparsely hairy. Lvs many, to 10×1cm, linear-oblanceolate, entire or obscurely dentate. Cap. to 1cm diam., usually many; outer flts usually 25, ligules white or tinged purple. Summer–early winter. N & S Amer., widely nat.

→*Erigeron.*

Cooba Acacia salicina.
Coolibah Eucalyptus microtheca.
Coontie Zamia pumila.

Cooperia Herb.
C. drummondii Herb. = Zephyranthes drummondii.
C. pedunculata Herb. = Zephyranthes drummondii.
C. jonesii Cory = Zephyranthes jonesii.
C. smallii Alexander = Zephyranthes smallii.
C. traubii Hayw. = Zephyranthes traubii.

Cooper's Burma Rose Rosa laevigata.
Cootamundra Wattle Acacia baileyana.
Copall Pistacia mexicana.

Copernicia Mart. WAX PALM; CARANDA PALM. Palmae. 24 dwarf or tall palms. St. often swollen at base, clothed with persistent lf bases, sometimes bare and scarred. Lvs palmate to costapal-mate, dead lvs persisting in a thatch-like skirt round trunk; sheaths fibrous, margins armed with stout spines; blade cuneate or circular, divied in upper quarter to third, seg. single-fold, acuminate, thickened and rigid, margins often spiny, midrib tomentose or waxy. W Indies, S Amer. Z10.

C. alba Morong. CARANDAY; CARANDA.   8–30m. Petioles to 80cm, with spines to 2cm; seg. c48, median seg. to 75cm, usually waxy, spotted orange to red. Braz., Boliv., Parag., N Arg.

C. australis Morong ex Becc. = C. alba.

C. baileyana Léon. YAREY; YAREY HEMBRA; YAREYON.   10–15m. Petioles to 130cm sparsely spiny; seg. to 130, median seg. to 165cm, waxy, conspicuously spotted. Cuba.

C. berteroana Becc. YAREY; PALMA DE CANA; LATANIER CAYE. To 5m. Petiole to 90cm, spotted and with white tufts of hair; seg. to 100, median seg. to 115cm, spots conspicuous beneath, obscure or 0 above. Dominica and Haiti.

C. cerifera Mart. = C. prunifera.

C. glabrescens Wendl. ex Becc. GUANO; GUANO BLANCO; GUANO JATA. To 6m. Petiole to 90cm, spines irregularly spaced; seg. to 62, median seg. to 1m, waxy. Cuba.

C. holguinensis Léon = C. yarey.

C. hospita Mart. GUANO; CANA; GUANO ESPINOSO; GUANO HEDIONDO. To 8m. Petiole to 120cm, coarsely spiny; seg. to 76, median seg. to 115cm, grey-waxy. Cuba.

C. macroglossa Wendl. ex Becc. PETTICOAT PALM; JATA DE GUANBACOA. To 7m, with skirt of persistent dead lvs. Petiole 0; lf blades cuneate, seg. to 64, median seg. to 145cm, outer seg. spiny. Cuba.

C. nigra Morong ex Becc. = C. alba.

C. occidentalis Léon. GUANO BLANCO.   To 8m. Petiole to 130cm, coarsely spiny; seg. 78, median seg. to 125cm, usually waxless. Cuba.

C. prunifera (Mill.) H.E. Moore. CARNAUBA.   St. to 15m, lower 3m clothed with persistent petiole bases. Petiole to 115cm, with

irregularly spaced teeth to 1cm; seg. to 62, median seg. to 93cm, waxy. NE Braz.

C. ramosissima Burret = C. glabrescens.

C. ramulosa Burret = C. alba.

C. rubra Morong = C. alba.

C. sanctae-mariae Becc. = C. tectorum.

C. tectorum (HBK) Mart. COBIJA; PALMA DE SOMBRERO. To 10m. Petiole to 160cm, with spines to 2cm; seg. c40, median seg. to 1m, green spotted orange-white. NC Venez., Colombian coast.

C. torreana Léon = C. macroglossa.

C. xescazana Léon = C. hospita.

C. yarey Burret. YAREY HEDIONDO.   To 8m. Petiole to 130cm, with coarse spines; seg. to 80, median seg. to 1.2m. Cuba. var. **robusta** Léon.   To 10m. Petiole to 115cm; seg. to 62, median seg. to 1m. Cuba.

→*Arrudaria* and *Corypha.*

Copey Clusia rosea.

Copiapoa Britt. & Rose Cactaceae. c20 low-growing or mound-forming cacti; some with large taproot connected to st. by a slender neck; st. ribbed or tuberculate; apex often densely woolly; spines few to numerous. Fls usually yellow, rarely red, short-funnelform to campanulate, small. N Chile.

C. bridgesii (Pfeiff.) Backeb.   Similar to C. marginata; st. only 5–8cm diam., more woolly at apex; ribs 8–12; central spines more v. stout, slightly curved upwards. Fls 3–3.8cm. Summer. Z9.

C. calderana F. Ritter.   Resembling C. cinerascens, but less clump-forming; st. globose to short-cylindric, 5–10cm diam.; ribs 10–17, less tuberculate; spines 1–4cm. Summer. N Chile. Z9.

C. cinerascens (Salm-Dyck) Britt. & Rose).   Eventually cluster-ing; swollen taproot connected to st. by narrow neck; st. depressed-globose, 6–15cm diam., grey-green; ribs 12–20, obtuse, tuberculate above areoles; central spines 1–4, 1–2cm, subulate; radial spines 7–10, 0.5–1.5cm, stoutly acicular, straight, grey or off-white. Fls 2.7–5.5cm. Summer. var. **cinerascens**. St. 8–15cm diam.; ribs 15–20; central spines 1–4; radial spines 7–9. Fls 2.7–3.7cm. var. **grandiflora** (Ritter) A. Hoffm. St. 6–10cm diam.; ribs 12–19; central spines to 5cm, acicular; radial spines 7–10, to 3cm. Fls 3–5.5cm. Z9.

C. cinerea (Philippi) Britt. & Rose.   Simple or clustering and mound-forming; st. globose to cylindric, 10–70(–140)×6–25cm, powdery white or grey, apex with dense white or yellow wool (orange-brown in var. gigantea); ribs 12–47, low and rounded, somewhat tuberculate; central spines 0–4, 0.5–6cm; radial spines 0–12, to 4cm, acicular to subulate. Fls 2.5–4.5cm. Summer. var. **cinerea**. St. to 20cm diam.; ribs 12–20; spines 1–11, 0.5–4cm, black-brown, stout. var. **columna-alba** (F. Ritter) Backeb. St. to 20cm diam.; ribs 26–47, tuberculate; spines 0–11(–12), 0.5–2.5cm, black to yellow-brown. var. **giga-ntea** (Backeb.) N.P. Tayl. St. to 25cm diam., pale green, apex with orange-brown wool; ribs 14–37, rounded; spines 3–16, 1–4cm, yellow-brown, slender. Z9.

C. coquimbana (Ruempl.) Britt. & Rose.   Clustering; st. 5–14cm diam., green to blue-green; ribs 10–20, strongly tuberculate, central spines 0–3, to 6cm; radial spines 4–9, 1–5cm, stout, curved, black to grey. Fls 2.5–5.5cm. Summer. var. **coquimbana**. St. 7–12cm diam.; ribs 13–18; central spines 0–1; radial spines 5–7. Fls 3.5–5.5cm. var. **fiedleriana** (Schum.) A. Hoffm. St. 5–8cm diam.; ribs 15–20; central spines 0; radial spines 4–8. Fls 2.5–3cm. Z9.

C. echinoides (Lem. ex Salm-Dyck) Britt. & Rose.   Resembling C. marginata but st. depressed-globose to globose, 7–18cm diam., sometimes bronzed; ribs 11–17; central spines straight to curved, to 5cm; radial spines to 2.5cm. Fls 3.5–4cm. Summer. Z9.

C. fiedleriana Schum. = C. coquimbana var. fiedleriana.

C. gigantea Backeb. = C. cinerea var. gigantea.

C. grandiflora F. Ritter = C. cinerascens var. grandiflora.

C. haseltoniana Backeb. = C. cinerea var. gigantea.

C. humilis (Philippi) P.C. Hutchison.   Simple or clustering; tap-root large, connected to st. by neck; st. subglobose to globose, 3–10cm diam., green, olive-green or brown; ribs 9–17, often dis-solved into tubercles; central spines 0–1–3(–4), 1–3.5cm; radial spines 7–13, 0.8–2.5cm, shorter and adpressed in young plants. Fls 2.5–4cm. Summer. var. **humilis**. St. 3–9cm. diam.; ribs 10–14; central spines 1–4; radial spines 7–13. Fls 3–4cm. var. **taltalensis** (Werderm.) Looser. Looser. St. 5–10cm diam.; ribs 12–17; central spines 1–3; radial spines 8–10. Fls 2.5–4cm. Z9.

C. hypogaea F. Ritter.   Simple or clustering; taproot large, con-nected to st. by a slender neck; st. depressed-globose, 1–6.5cm diam., grey or bronze; ribs 10–16, ± dissolved into low spiralled tubercles; central spines 0–1, minute or to 1.5cm, nearly black; radial spines (0–1)1–10, 0.5–4(–5)mm. Fls 1.5–2.2cm. Summer.

var. *hypogaea* St. 3–6.5cm diam. Fls 20–22mm. var. *laui* (Diers) A. Hoffm. Dwarf form, st. 1–3cm diam.; ribs dissolved into tubercles. Fls 15–18mm. Z9.

C.krainziana F. Ritter. Clustering; st. globose to cylindric, 6–20cm diam., pale green-grey or somewhat powdery; ribs 13–24, acute to rounded; spines 12–30+, 1–3.5cm, acicular to hair-like, straight or curved and tangled, white, to grey-black. Fls 2–5–3.5cm. Summer. Z9.

C. laui Diers = *C. hypogaea* var. *laui*.

C. malletiana (Salm-Dyck) Backeb. Differs from *C. cinerea* var. *cinerea* in st. to 12(–16)cm diam.; ribs 15–33, higher and more acute; spines (0–)1–8, 1–6cm, black to light brown, stout. summer. Z9.

C. marginata (Salm-Dyck) Britt. & Rose. Simple or branched; st. 20–50×7–10cm, cylindric, grass-green; ribs 10–14, broad, scarcely tuberculate; central spines 1–3, 2.5–4cm, straight; radial spines 5–10, 1–1.5cm, stout, ± straight. Fls 2.5–3.5cm. Summer. N Chile. Z9.

C. megarhiza Britt. & Rose. Simple or somewhat clustering; tap-root large; st. depressed-globose to globose, 5–10cm diam., grey-green, v. spiny; ribs 10–21, slightly tuberculate; central spines 1–10, 1.5–4cm, straight; radial spines 7–12, 0.5–2.5cm, straight to curved, yellow, brown or black, later grey. Fls 2.5–4cm. Summer. Z9.

C. montana F. Ritter. Simple or clustering; taproot large, connected to st. by a slender neck; st. 4–20×4–10cm, depressed-globose to oblong, grey green to bronzed; ribs 10–17, tuberculate; central spines 0–3, 1–3cm, straight; radial spines 4–9, 0.5–2cm, straight or slightly curved, black, later grey. Fls 2.5–4. Summer. N Chile. Z9.

C.solaris (F. Ritter) Ritter. Clustering and forming mounds 1×2m in the wild; st. 8–12cm diam., cylindric, grey-green; ribs 8–12 to 3.5cm high, not tuberculate; central spines 2–5, 2–6cm; radial spines c7–10, 1.5–5cm, curved, stout. Fls 2.5–3cm. N Chile. Z9.

C. taltalensis Werderm. = *C. humilis* var. *taltalensis*.

C. tenuissima Ritter (invalid name). Differs from *C. humilis* in smaller st., 2–4(–5)cm diam.; ribs 13–16, dissolved into small spirally-arranged tubercles; central spines usually 0; radial spines 8–14, only 3–6mm. Fls 2–2.6cm. Summer. N Chile. Z9.

Copihue *Lapageria*.
Copper Beech *Fagus sylvatica* f. *purpurea*.
Copper Leaf *Alternanthera*; *Echeveria multicaulis*.
Copper Roses *Echeveria multicaulis*.
Copper Shield Fern *Dryopteris erythrosora*.

Coprosma Forst. Rubiaceae. *c*90 dioecious, everg. shrubs and small trees. St. erect or prostrate. Lvs minute to large, petiolate or subsessile, obovate to linear. Fls inconspicuous, solitary, or in clusters; cal. limb 4–5-toothed or -lobed or truncate or, in males, entirely 0; cor. funnel- or bell-shaped, lobes to 6, sta. 4 or 5, anth. exserted. Fr. a drupe, ovoid to globose, fleshy. Java and Borneo to Hawaii, S and E to Aus., NZ and Pacific Is. Z9.

C.acerosa Cunn. SAND COPROSMA. St. prostrate or suberect, to 2m high, wiry. Lvs to 1.5×0.1cm linear, green, glab. Fr. 8×6mm, globose, translucent, pale blue. Autumn. NZ. f. *brunnea* T. Kirk. Br. and branchlets fewer and shorter, dark brown. Lvs bronze. Z8.

C. alba Colenso = *C. propinqua*.

C.areolata Cheesem. St. erect to 5m. Lvs to 1.5cm, narrowly ovate to elliptic, pale green, acute to sharp-pointed, membranous, glab. above, pubesc. beneath on veins. Fr. globose, 5mm wide, black. Autumn. NZ.

C.atropurpurea Ckn. & Allan) L.B. Moore. Mat-forming. Br. tangled, prostrate, bearing short, erect branchlets. Lvs minute, dark green to bronze-purple. Fr. to 8mm diam., translucent, claret red. Summer. NZ.

C. aurantiaca Colenso = *C. rigida*.
C. australis (A. Rich.) Robinson = *C. grandifolia*.
C. autumnalis Colenso = *C. grandifolia*.

C.baueri Endl. Shrub or small tree, to 8m; br. glab.; branchlets minutely pubesc. Lvs to 8cm, obovate, obtuse and indented at apex, lustrous green, revolute. Fr. ovoid, to 8mm, yellow-orange. Autumn. NZ.

C. baueri hort. non Endl. = *C. repens*.
C. baueriana Hook. f. = *C. repens*.

C. 'Beatson's Gold'. A hybrid of obscure origin forming a robust, frost-hardy, spreading shrub with lvs to 16×8mm, emerald green splashed gold. Fr. bright red. Gdn origin.

C.billardieri Hook. f. NATIVE CURRANT. Shrub, erect, to 3m. Br. slender, 2-ranked, often terminating in spines. Lvs to 2cm, narrow-ovate or oblong to narrow-elliptic or lanceolate, narrowed at base, leathery. Fr. oblong, 7mm, lustrous orange to red. Aus. (Vict., NSW), Tasm.

C. 'Blue Pearl'. (*C. petriei* ×*C. acerosa* f. *brunnea*.) Br. rigid, spreading; branchlets short, lvs small. Fr. translucent Cambridge blue, to 8×6mm, becoming darker with age. Gdn origin.

C. brunnea (T. Kirk) Cheesem. = *C. acerosa* f. *brunnea*.

C.cheesemanii W. Oliv. Prostrate shrub. Lvs to 1.5cm, linear to narrow-oblong. Fr. to 0.5cm diam., orange-red. NZ.

C. 'Chocolate Soldier'. A ♂ selection of an obscure hybrid. Br. erect. Lvs brown, to 2cm. Gdn origin.

C. coffaeoides Colenso = *C. robusta*.

C.cuneata Hook. f. St. erect or spreading, to 2m. Lvs 1.5×0.3cm, densely clustered, wedge-shaped, or linear- or oblong-ovate, stiff, leathery, dark green. Fr. globose, 4mm wide, red. NZ.

C. cuneata auct. non Hook. f. = *C. pseudocuneata*.

C.×cunninghamii Hook. f. (*C. propinqua* ×*C. robusta*.) Br. few, ascending to 4m; branchlets glab. Lvs to 5×0.5cm, linear, linear-lanceolate, or linear-cuneate, acute to subacute at apex, leathery. Fr. oblong, 6mm long, pale yellow. NZ. Z8.

C. cuspidifolia DC. = *C. hirtella*.

C.depressa Colenso ex Hook. To 1m. Br. rooting, prostrate or trailing. Lvs to 0.8×0.3cm, opposite, in clusters, ovate or obovate or linear-lanceolate or -oblong, narrowed at base, stiff, leathery, sometimes ciliate. Fr. globose, 5mm wide, orange or red. NZ.

C.foetidissima Forst. Robust shrub, to 5m. Lvs to 4×2cm, mid-green, malodorous if crushed. Fr. large, ovoid, orange. NZ.

C. foetidissima Cunn. non Forst. = *C. ×cunninghamii*.

C.grandifolia Hook. f. Shrub or small tree, to 5m. Lvs to 20×9cm, oval-oblong to elliptic-oblong, acute at apex, narrowed at base, membranous or somewhat leathery, dull green, pale beneath. Fr. oblong, obtuse, 8mm long, orange-red. NZ.

C.hirtella Labill. Shrub, erect, stiff, to 2m. Lvs to 6×3cm, ovate, obovate, elliptic, or lanceolate, narrwly acute at apex, narrowed at base, leathery, rough or glab. above, pale beneath. Fr. globose, 6mm wide, red to brown or black. S & SE Aus.

C.×kirkii Cheesem. (*C. acerosa* ×*C. repens*.) Shrub, procumbent or suberect, occas. erect and spreading, to 1m. Br. tangled. Lvs to 3cm, linear or linear-oblong, narrowly obovate, or lanceolate, obtuse or acute at apex, narrowed at base, leathery. Fr. oblong, 6mm long, white, sometimes red-flecked. NZ. 'Brunette': habit sprawling; lvs glossy bronze; fr. orange. 'Green Girl': a seedling of 'Brunette'; lvs pale green, 2×0.8cm; fr. pale yellow. 'Kiwi Gold': lvs spattered yellow. 'Variegata': fast-growing, hardy, sprawling shrub; lvs to 2×0.6cm, pale green edged white; ♀ selection.

C. lentissima Colenso = *C. rigida*.

C.lucida Forst. & Forst. f. Shrub or tree, to 5m. Br. many, spreading. Lvs to 13×6cm, obovate or elliptic- to oblong or lanceolate, apex obtuse or abruptly acute, base narrow-cuneate, leathery, lustrous. Fr. oblong or oblong-obovoid, to 1.2cm, vivid orange-red. NZ. Z8.

C.macrocarpa Cheesem. Shrub or tree, to 10m. Br. spreading. Lvs to 13×8cm, broadly ovate- or elliptic-oblong, obtuse or acute and short-pointed at apex, narrowed at base, somewhat leathery. Fr. oblong or ovoid, to 2.5cm, orange-red. NZ.

C.moorei Rodway. Dwarf perenn., to 10cm; st. rooting, prostrate. Lvs to 0.5cm, ovate or ovate-lanceolate, acute or obtuse at apex, narrowed at base, lustrous. Fr. oblong or globose, 7mm, succulent, blue. Tasm.

C. multiflora Colenso = *C. areolata*.
C. myrtillifolia Hook. f. = *C. parviflora*.

C.nitida Hook. f. Shrub erect or prostrate to 2m. Br. many, stiff, often ending in spines. Lvs 0.5–1×0.3–0.5cm, elliptic to lanceolate, or oblong- or ovate-lanceolate, obtuse at apex, narrowed at base, leathery and lustrous. Fr. oblong or globose, 6mm, orange-red. Tasm., Aus. (Vict.). Z8.

C.parviflora Hook. f. Shrub or small tree, to 5m. Br. spreading. Lvs to 1.2×0.6cm clustered, linear-oblong or orbicular, obtuse or subacute at apex, narrowed at base, leathery. Fr. globose, to 6mm wide, translucent white or violet-blue to dark purple or black. NZ. Z8.

C. perpusilla Colenso = *C. repens*.
C. petriei var. *atropurpurea* Ckn. & Allan = *C. areolata*.

C.petriei Cheesem. Dwarf shrub, to 8cm. St. wiry, prostrate and creeping. Lvs to 0.6×0.3cm, in clusters, linear-oblong to -obovate, margins sometimes thickened, leathery, dark green, paler beneath. Fr. globose, to 12mm wide, white to sky blue or indigo. NZ. 'Lyn': compact, bearing bead-like white fruits. Z7.

C.propinqua Cunn. Shrub or small tree, to 6m. Br. divaricate; branchlets tangled, wiry. Lvs to obovate, obtuse or somewhat acute at apex, narrowed at base, leathery. Fr. globose, to 8mm wide, pale, translucent blue to opaque, dark blue or black. NZ. Z8.

C. 'Prostrata'. A ♂ selection of uncertain hybrid origin. Habit prostrate forming dense groundcover, lvs to 2×0.6cm, oblong-lanceolate, emerald green. Gdn origin.

C. pseudocuneata W. Oliv. Shrub, to 3m usually shorter. Br. spreading, obscurely 4-angled. Lvs to 2×0.6cm, in clusters, oblong to cuneate, or narrowly obovate, obtuse or somewhat acute at apex, narrowed at base, leathery, dark green above, pale beneath. Fr. oblong, to 6mm, orange-red to scarlet. NZ. Z8.

C. pubens Petrie non Gray = *C. depressa*.

C. pumila Hook. f. pro parte. = *C. petriei*.

C. quadrifida (Labill.) Robinson = *C. billardieri*.

C. ramulosa Petrie = *C. depressa*.

C. repens A. Rich. LOOKING-GLASS PLANT; MIRROR PLANT. Shrub or small tree, to 8m. Br. spreading, semi-prostrate, mat-forming. Lvs to 8×5cm, narrowly to broadly oblong or obovate, subobtuse to indented at apex, narrowed at base, revolute, lustrous and leathery or fleshy, dark green above, pale beneath. Fr. obovoid, to 10mm, yellow-orange to red. NZ, introd. S Aus. 'Argentea': lvs flecked silver-white. 'Brownie': a ♀ selection with erect br., small lvs bronze above, lime green below; fr. white or pale yellow. 'Coppershine': lvs glossy bronze. 'Exotica': a ♀ selection; lvs irregularly edged bright green with an ivory or golden centre; fr. large, orange. 'Marble King': slow-growing; lvs speckled lime green. 'Marble Queen': a ♂ selection; lvs cream-splashed and spotted green. 'Marginata': lvs edged yellow-white. 'Picturata': a ♂ selection, otherwise resembles 'Exotica'. 'Pink Splendor': lvs deep green edged yellow, later pink. 'Variegata': lvs bright green edged ivory to pale gold.

C. retusa Hook. f. = *C. repens*.

C. rhamnoides Cunn. Shrub, to 2m. Br. many, spreading, stiff. Lvs to 1.2cm, orbicular or ovate to ovate-oblong, occas. linear to lanceolate, rounded to acute at apex, narrowed at base, leathery glab. or minutely pubesc. Fr. globose, to 4mm wide, scarlet to crimson, occas. black. NZ. 'Tuffet': br. densely divaricate, tangled; fr. shiny black, produced in profusion.

C. rigida Cheesem. Shrub, erect, to 3m. Br. divaricate or 2-ranked, often tangled, branchlets rigid. Lvs to 2×1cm, usually smaller, oblong to obovate, obtuse or subretuse, narrowed at base, leathery to membranous, glab. Fr. oblong or obovoid, to 7mm, yellow-orange or white. NZ. Z8.

C. robusta Raoul. Shrub, erect, to 3m. Br. and branchlets spreading, glab. Lvs to 1.3×0.5cm, elliptic to elliptic-oblong or obovate, acute or obtuse at apex, narrowed at base, revolute, leathery, lustrous and dark green above, pale beneath. Fr. oblong or ovoid, to 9×5mm, orange-red to yellow. NZ. 'Variegata': a ♂ selection with a streak of golden yellow in the lf. 'Williamsii': lvs softer sea-green bordered ivory with dark green central mottling; fr. orange-red.

C. rotundifolia Cunn. Shrub, to 3m, occas. small tree, to 5m. Br. sparse, erect to spreading, divaricate; branchlets densely hairy. Lvs to 2.5cm, distantly paired, orbicular to ovate-oblong, obtuse or acute to sharp-pointed at apex, obtuse to cordate at base, membranous, pubesc., on veins and margins, dull green with maroon or brown patches. Fr. often paired or fused, globose or subglobose, 4mm wide, red. NZ.

C. rufescens Colenso = *C. rotundifolia*.

C. rugosa Cheesem. Variable shrub, erect, to 3m. Br. divaricate, rigid, tangling; branchlets 4-angled. Lvs to 1.3×0.2cm, linear to narrowly cuneate, leathery, dark green above, pale beneath. Fr. oblong to subglobose, to 8mm, pale, translucent white or blue. NZ.

C. serrulata Hook. f. ex Buch. Br. short, erect to 60cm. Lvs to 6×3cm, thickly coriaceous, dark green above, pale green beneath, serrulate. Fr. ovoid, orange-red. NZ.

C. spathulata Cunn. Shrub, to 2m. Br. and branchlets sparse. Lvs to 2cm, orbicular to oblong, obtuse or indented at apex, narrowed at base, revolute leathery, lustrous; petioles winged. Fr. globose to oblong, to 8mm, scarlet to black. NZ.

C. stockii Williams = *C. repens*.

C. tenuicaulis Hook. f. Br. and branchlets sparse. Lvs to 2cm, orbicular to oblong, obtuse or indented at apex, narrowed at base, revolute, leathery, lustrous; petioles winged. Fr. globose to oblong, to 8mm, scarlet to black. NZ.

C. tenuifolia Cheesem. Shrub or small tree, to 5m. Br. and branchlets sparse, spreading. Lvs to 10×4cm, ovate to oblong, or ovate- or elliptic-lanceolate, acute at apex, narrowed at base, undulate to crenulate, membranous or leathery, pubesc., green-brown. Fr. ovoid or oblong, to 9mm, orange. NZ.

C. turbinata Colenso = *C. rigida*.

C. virescens Petrie. Semi-prostrate, to 15m. Br. slender, interlacing. Lvs to 3mm diam.; suborbicular. Fr. amber. NZ.

Coptis Salisb. GOLDTHREAD; GOLDENTHREAD. Ranunculaceae. 10 low perenn. herbs, from slender, yellow-stained rhiz. Lvs everg., radical, often 1–2-ternate, or much divided; petioles long. Fls small, solitary or 2-many on scapes exceeding foliage;

sep. 5–8 petaloid linear-lanceolate; pet. 3–5–7, clawed, often hooded, smaller than sep.; sta. 12–25. N temp. regions.

C. asplenifolia Salisb. To 25cm. Lvs 2-ternate, lfts 3–5, pinnatifid, seg. lobed, cut or serrulate. Fls 2–3 per scape, green-white; sep. to 10mm; pet. dilated and hooded, clawed with gland at base. Spring. Alask. to BC. Z3.

C. groenlandica (Oeder) Fern. = *C. trifolia* ssp. *groenlandica*.

C. japonica (Thunb.) Mak. To 25cm. Lvs ternate, lfts ovate, pinnatisect or pinnate, petiolulate, toothed. Fls 1–3 per scape, white; sep. 8mm, pet. gland. at apex. Spring. Jap. Z7.

C. laciniata A. Gray. To 15cm. Lvs ternate, lfts 2–7cm, ovate, 3-parted, sharply toothed. Fls solitary or few on scape, green-white; sep. 6–10mm; pet. slender-clawed, gland. at base. Spring. W. U.S. Z8.

C. occidentalis (Nutt.) Torr. & A. Gray. Similar to *C. laciniata*; lfts 3–6cm, broad ovate to ovate-cordate, deeply 3-lobed, seg. entire, dentate, or lobed; petioles long. Fls 2–5 per scape, white tinged green or yellow, sep. *c*10mm; pet. not hooded. Spring. W. N.America. Z4.

C. orientalis Maxim. = *C. japonica*.

C. quinquefolia Miq. 10–25cm. Lvs palmate, lfts 1–2.5cm, 5, obovate or rhombic, toothed; petiole 10–12cm. Fls solitary, white; sep. to 1cm; pet. clawed gland. at apex. Jap., Taiwan. Z7.

C. trifolia (L.) Salisb. 5–15cm. Lvs trifoliolate; lfts 1–2cm, obovate, cuneate, leathery, crenate-dentate, sessile. Fls 0–15mm diam., solitary, white; pet. 3–5, club-shaped, fleshy, gland. at apex. Spring. NE Asia, Alask. ssp. *groenlandica* (Oeder) Hult. Lfts shortly petiolulate. Sep. smaller, not clawed; pet. broader than long. Spring–summer. NE N Amer., Greenland. Z2.

→*Chrysocoptis* and *Thalictrum*.

Coquieri Dicori *Syagrus coronata*.
Coquiero do Campo *Syagrus petraea*.
Coquito *Syagrus orinocensis*.
Coquito Palm *Jubaea*.
Coracan *Eleusine coracana*.
Coral Aloe *Aloe striata*.
Coral-bark Maple *Acer palmatum*.
Coral-bark Willow *Salix alba* var. *caerulea*.
Coral Beads *Cocculus carolinus*; *Sedum stahlii*.
Coral Bean *Erythrina herbacea*.
Coral Bells *Heuchera*.
Coralberry *Aechmea fulgens*; *Ardisia crenata*; *Symphoricarpos* (*S. orbiculatus*).
Coral Bush *Templetonia retusa*.
Coral Cactus *Rhipsalis cereuscula*.
Coral Drops *Bessera elegans*.
Coral Echeveria *Echeveria carnicolor*.
Coral Gem *Lotus berthelotii*.
Coral Gum *Eucalyptus torquata*.
Coral Heath *Epacris microphylla*.
Coral Honeysuckle *Lonicera sempervirens*.
Coral Lily *Lilium pumilum*.

Corallocarpus Welw. ex Hook. f. Cucurbitaceae. 13 tuberous climbing or trailing perenn. herbs. Tendrils simple. Lvs simple to palmate. ♂ infl. racemose, crowded at apex; fls small, green or yellow; cal. tube campanulate, lobed; pet. united at base; ♀ or solitary with staminodes 5 or 0. Fr. a berry, red. Afr., Madag., India. Z10.

C. boehmii (Cogn.) C. Jeffrey. St. sparsely to densely lanate, with papery bark below. Lvs pubesc., sinuate-toothed, 2–5×3–7cm, lobes 3. Fr. subspherical, beaked, minutely pubesc. Trop. Afr. Z10.

→*Kedrostis*.

Corallodiscus Batal. Gesneriaceae. 18 rhizomatous perenn. herbs. Lvs in a basal rosette, veins deeply impressed. Fls scapose, solitary or in clusters; cal. seg. 5; cor. tubular, upper lip 2-lobed, lower lip 3-lobed, lower lobes larger. Himal. to NW China and SE Asia. Z9.

C. kingianus (Craib) B.L. Burtt. Lvs to 11cm, broadly lanceolate to ovate-lanceolate, coriaceous, glab. above, orange-red-pilose beneath. Scape to 6cm; fls many; cor. to 15mm, blue or blue and white. Chungkian.

C. lanuginosus (DC.) B.L. Burtt. Lvs to 4cm, ovate, entire to bluntly toothed, rusty-pilose. Scape to 10cm; fls few; cor. to 12mm, pale purple or white. Himal.

→*Didissandra*.

Corallospartium J.B. Armstr. Leguminosae (Papilionoideae). 1 ± leafless shrub, rigid, erect to 2m. Br. thick, or strongly compressed, furrowed, to 1cm diam. terete. Lvs small, rarely seen, circular to oblong. Fls pea-like in dense clusters; cal. pubesc.; cor. to 8mm, cream-white. NZ.

C. crassicaule (Hook. f.) J.B. Armstr.

Coral Moss *Nertera granadensis*.
Coral Necklace *Illecebrum*.
Coral Pea *Adenanthera pavonina*; *Kennedia*.
Coral Plant *Berberidopsis*; *Jatropha* (*J. multifida*); *Russelia equisetiformis*.
Coral Root Bittercress *Cardamine bulbifera*.
Coral Spurge *Euphorbia corallioides*.
Coral Tree *Erythrina* (*E. caffra*; *E. corallodendrum*).
Coral Vine *Antigonon leptopus*; *Kennedia coccinea*.
Coralwood *Adenanthera pavonina*.
Corazón-de-jesús *Begonia fuchsioides*.

Corbularia Salisb.
C. bulbocodium (L.) Haw. = *Narcissus bulbocodium*.
C. hedraeanthus Webb & Heldr. = *Narcissus hedraeanthus*.

Corchoropsis Sieb. & Zucc. Sterculiaceae. 3 hairy, ann. herbs. Fls axill., solitary, small, subtended by 3 filiform bracts; sep. 5, persistent; pet. 5, slightly longer than the sep.; sta. 10–15, free or connate at base; staminodes 5, linear, exceeding sta. Korea, China, Jap. Z9.
C. crenata Sieb. & Zucc. = *C. tomentosa*.
C. tomentosa (Thunb.) Makino. Ann., to 1.2m, stellate-pubesc., much-branched. Lvs 4–8cm ovate, toothed. Fls on slender stalks to 3cm; sep. 6mm, linear-lanceolate; pet. 0.7–1cm, obovate; staminodes 1cm, linear. Jap., Korea, China.

Corchorus L. Tiliaceae. 40 usually ann. herbs or subshrubs. Lvs simple, serrate or lobed, often with bristly-tipped basal teeth. Fls small, yellow, solitary or in few-fld axill. rac.; pet. and sep. 5; sta. 7+, on a short androgynophore. Fr. a woody capsule. Trop., Aus. Z10.
C. capsularis L. Ann. to 3.6m erect, much-branched. Lvs 5–15cm, ovate-oblong to lanceolate, acuminate. Pet. 1.5cm. Fr. to 1.5cm diam., globose, crinkled, with copper-coloured seeds. China.
C. olitorus L. Differs from *C. capsularis* in taller habit and larger, deeper yellow fls. Fr. cylindrical, slender, with grey-green to deep blue seeds. India.

Cord Grass *Spartina*.

Cordia L. Boraginaceae. *c*300 decid. or everg. shrubs or trees, occas. climbers. Infl. term. – cymes, pan. spikes or heads; cal. usually 3–5-, rarely 10-lobed; cor. funnelform to campanulate, sometimes tubular, lobes 5, sometimes 4–18, limb sometimes unlobed. C & S Amer., trop. Afr. and through Middle East and Asia. Z10.
C. abyssinica R. Br. = *C. africana*.
C. africana Lam. MUKUMARIAUHI; WANZA; BA'GAMBIL; INDERAB; ZAN; JENNEB; THANNEB. Everg. tree, to 24m. Lvs 2.5–30×2.5–22.5cm, suborbicular to ovate-oblong, base truncate or rounded, apex acute, rough-pubesc. becoming glab. above, densely rusty pubesc. beneath, entire to crenate; petiole to 6cm, rusty-pubesc. Infl. a loose terminal pan. to 14×17cm; fls snow-white, fragrant; cor. 3×2.5cm, limb sinuous or crenate. Trop. Afr., Saudi Arabia, Yemen.
C. alba hort. = *C. dentata*.
C. alliodora (Ruiz & Pav.) Cham. ex DC. CYP; CYPRE; ECUADOR LAUREL; SALMWOOD. Branchlets developing gall-like swellings inhabited by ants. Lvs to 18×5cm, ovate, apex and base acuminate, glab. above, pubesc. beneath, entire; petiole 1.2cm, sparsely pubesc. Infl. a term. cyme; fls 1.2cm, cream-white; cor. lobes 5, oblong, truncate. Trop. Amer.
C. angiocarpa A. Rich. Decid. shrub or tree to 10m. Lvs 8–13×5–8cm, oval or suborbicular, apex rounded, base obtuse, entire or sinuous, rusty pilose and scabrous above. Cymes corymbose; fls to *c*6cm, orange. cor. lobes 14, oval-oblong, acute. Cuba.
C. boissieri A. DC. ANCAHUITA. Everg. tree to *c*8m. Lvs 14cm, elliptic-ovate, scabrid-velvety above, tomentose beneath, apex and base obtuse, entire to crenulate. Fls in term., paniculate cymes; cor. *c*2.5cm, 5-lobed, white with yellow centre. SW US, Mex.
C. collococca L. Decid. tree, to 22m. Lvs to 24×10cm, entire ovate, setose beneath, apex acuminate; petiole 1.2cm. Infl. precocious, crowded; fls white. Spring. Braz.
C. crenata Delile. Shrub to 7m. Young growth glab. or pubesc. Lvs 1.8–10.8×1.3–6.9cm, elliptic to ovate or obovate, rarely suborbicular or rhombic, base rounded to cuneate, apex obtuse, rounded, or truncate, pubesc. becoming glab., entire, serrate or crenate; petiole to 3.5cm, glab. or pubesc. Fls white in term.

pan. or in dichotomous cyme; cor. tube to 6mm, lobes 4–6, ovate-oblong or spathulate, to 6×2.5mm, acute or acuminate. NE Afr., SW Asia. ssp. *meridionalis* Warfa. EBITIOTHIN; GUETA; MUREBU. Young shoots and lvs densely pubesc. Kenya, Somalia, Uganda, N & C Tanz.
C. decandra Hook. & Arn. Everg. tree to 4m+. Lvs 3–5×0.4–0.7cm, simple, sessile, coriaceous, oblong-lanceolate, apex attenuate, glaucous green beneath, pubesc., entire, revolute. Fls white, in corymbose pan. at br. tips; cor. 2–2.5cm, funnelform, 10–12-lobed. Chile.
C. dentata Poir. Semi-evergreen, multi-stemmed shrub or tree, to 10m. Lvs to 10×7cm, elliptic to ovate, apex obtuse, acute or rounded, base obtuse to rounded, scabrous above, glab. to puberulent beneath, dentate or entire. Fls white to yellow, in pan. to 20cm diam.; cor. funnelform, *c*12mm, lobes 5, ovate, 4mm. Trop. Amer.
C. dichotoma Forst. f. Tree to 10m. Lvs 8–12×4–8cm, elliptic, ovate or obovate, base acute or rounded, apex often acuminate, glabrescent, entire, sometimes repand-sinuate toward apex; petiole to 4cm. Infl. cymose, dichotomously branched, to 8cm diam.; cor. to 1cm, lobes reflexed, to 6×2.5mm, tube to 6.5cm. Asia to NE Aus.
C. dodecandra DC. To 16m. Lvs to 15×8cm, oblong to suborbicular, scabrous and hispid beneath, base and apex rounded or obtuse, entire or sinuate; petiole velvety. Pan. compact term.; cor. 3.5×3.5cm, funnelform, 12–16-lobed, intense orange. Mex., Guat.
C. gerascanthus L. SPANISH ELM; LAUREL NEGRO; BARIA. Resembles *C. alliodora*, but lacking ant swellings and obvious stellate pubescence. Lvs oblong-lanceolate, apex and base acuminate. Pan. term., whorled cor. white, limb equal tube, lobes 5, oblong, truncate. Spring. Mex., W Indies.
C. greggii Poir. Compact shrub to 2.5m. Lvs *c*1.8cm, ovate, pubesc., dentate, pan. term.; fls 4–6, fragrant; cor. funnelform, pure white, lobes 5, rounded, to 3cm diam. US, New Mex., Calif.
C. leucosebestena Griseb. ANACAGUITA; ICACO CIMARRON. Shrub to 5m. Lvs 2.5–5cm, elliptic to elliptic-ovate, papery, bristly to glabrescent above, white-tomentose beneath, sometimes emarginate, entire. Fls in corymbose cymes; cor. white, spreading, lobes 5, ovate, obtuse. Cuba.
C. lutea Lam. Shrub or tree to 8m. Lvs 4–10×1.5–8cm, ovate, or obovate to elliptic, dark green and scabrous above, pale green pubesc. beneath, crenulate; petioles to 2.5cm, pubesc. Fls pale yellow, fragrant, in term. cymes; cor. funnelform, to 1.5cm across at apex, 5–8-lobed. Ecuad., Marquesas, Galapagos, Peru.
C. macrostachya (Jacq.) Roem. & Schult. Shrub to 2.5m. Lvs to 20×10cm, ovate-oblong to lanceolate, acute or obtuse, denticulate, glab. above with soft hairs on veins beneath; petiole to 3cm. Fls white, in spikes to 10cm; cor. to 5mm. Guyana.
C. monoica Roxb. MARER; MARER DEYLAB; MAREER DOCOL. Everg. tree or shrub to 8m. Lvs to 9.5×6.7cm, ovate-rotund, base cuneate to round, apex acute, rounded to emarginate, scabrous above, densely pubesc. beneath; petiole 1.26–2.5cm, tawny pubesc. pan. dense axill., tawny-pubesc.; fls pale yellow to white, fragrant; cor. tube to 15mm, pubesc. lobes 4–5, obovate. Trop. Afr., Asia, Arabia.
C. myxa L. non Forssk. ASSYRIAN PLUM; SELU. Everg., shrub or tree to 12m. Lvs ovate to suborbicular or cordate, sometimes cuneate, apex rounded, glab., repand-dentate; petiole to 3.5cm. Pan. loose, term.; fls white to cream; cor. tube to 4.5mm, lobes 5, elliptic, 5×2mm. Trop. Asia, Afr., Arabia.
C. myxa Forssk. non L. = *C. crenata*.
C. nitida Willd. RED MANJACK; INDIAN CHERRY. Tree to 20m. Lvs 4–14cm, elliptic to obovate-elliptic, papery, obtuse or acute, shining above, often pilose beneath, entire. Cymes corymbose *c*10cm diam.; cor. white, to 1.2cm across. Antilles.
C. nivea Fres. Shrub to 1.5m, downy. Lvs 7–11×3.5–5.5cm, ovate to lanceolate, base obtuse to rounded, apex acute to acuminate, strigose and pubesc. above, white-tomentose beneath; petiole to 2cm. Infl. capitate; cor. white or yellow, 1.5–6cm, funnelform, lobes shallow, emarginate, suborbicular. NE Braz.
C. polycephala (Lam.) I.M. Johnst. Shrub to 5m, often semi-scandent. Lvs to 12×5cm, ovate to lanceolate, tuberculate and sparsely strigose above, brown, often tomentose beneath, denticulate to entire; petiole to 1cm. Fls in subglobose, glomerate cymes; cor. to 0.5cm, white. W Indies and warm Amer.
C. rothii Roem. & Schult. Tree to *c*10m. Lvs to 4.5cm., lanceolate, apex obtuse and mucronate, scabrous at first, pubesc. on midrib beneath, entire or undulate; petiole *c*2cm. Infl. corymbose; cor. lobes 4, 0.4cm. N India.
C. sebestena L. GEIGER TREE. Everg. shrub or tree to 8m. Lvs to 20×12cm, ovate, apex acute, base rounded to obtuse, rarely cordate, scabrous above, glab. beneath except on veins, entire,

rarely undulate; petioles to 4.5cm, pubesc. Infl. cymose, 12cm diam.; cor. to 5.8cm funnelform, bright orange-red, lobes 5–7, ovate, c1cm. W Indies to Venez.

C. sebestena Forssk. non L. nec Poir. = *C. myxa*.

C. sebestena Poir. non L. nec Forssk. = *C. africana*.

C. subcordata Lam. MARER; MAREER. Tree to 15m. Lvs 8–20×5–15cm, base cuneate, rounded or acute, entire, rarely dentate, short-pubesc. above, pubesc. with veins tomentose beneath; petiole to 8cm. Infl. loose, term., to 20-fld; hirsute; fls white, orange or red; cor. glab., tube 2.5cm, lobes 5–7, to 15×13mm. Trop. Asia, Indian Ocean, S Pacific; E Afr.

C. superba Cham. Everg. tree to 6m. Lvs 20cm, oblong-lanceolate to obovate-elliptic, scabrid, strigose or lightly hairy beneath, apex mucronate, base acuminate to rounded, entire or dentate, sometimes pubesc. beneath. Cymes term.; cor. white, to 5cm, funnelform, 5-lobed. E Braz.

C. trichotoma (Vell.) Arráb. & Steud. Closely resembles *C. alliodora*, but fls larger and more abundant, indumentum thicker. Lvs glab. or minutely pubesc. above and yellow stellate-pubesc. beneath. Braz. & Parag. to Arg. and Boliv.

→*Calyptra, Cerdana,* and *Sebestena*.

Cordiada Vell.

C. trichotoma Vell. = *Cordia trichotoma*.

Cordyline Comm. ex R. Br. CABBAGE TREE. Agavaceae. 15 woody shrubs or trees. St. cane-like, simple to sparsely branched, ultimately large, much-branched above. Lvs crowded near br., persistent, lanceolate to linear. Infl. densely paniculate, term.; fls radially symmetric; tep. 6, united at base to form a short tube, lobes reflexed; sta. 6. Fr. a small berry. SE Asia, Australasia, Polyn., Hawaii. Z10.

C. australis (Forst.) Endl. CABBAGE TREE. Tree to 20m. Trunk slender, ultimately copiously branched above, massive. Lvs 30–100×3–6cm, arching, narrowly lanceolate to linear, bases dilated, clasping, light green. Pan. to 150×60cm, much-branched, axes almost hidden by fls; fls 5–6mm, crowded, creamy white, sweetly fragrant. NZ. Z9. 'Alberti': lvs dull green striped cream, centre red, margins flushed pink. 'Atropurpurea' ('Lentiginosa'): main vein beneath and lf bases purple. 'Atrosanguinea': lvs bronze tinted plum. 'Aureostriata': lvs with yellow lines. 'Cuprea': lvs dark copper. 'Doucetti': lvs dull green striped cream-white, margins flushed pink. 'Lineata': lvs broader than usual, sheathing base purple. 'Marginata': lvs dull green edged white. 'Purpurea' ('Purple Tower'): lvs broad, arching, rich deep plum. 'Torbay Dazzler': lvs variegated cream. 'Torbay Red': lvs red. 'Variegata': lvs striped creamy white. 'Veitchii': main vein beneath and lf bases bright crimson.

C. banksii Hook. Shrub to 4m. St. clustered, erect, occas. branched. Lvs 100–200×4–8cm, linear-lanceolate, green, petiolate, veins prominent above. Infl. to 2m, copiously branched axes visible; fls numerous, 1cm, v. fragrant, white. NZ. 'Purpurea': lvs purple tinted bronze.

C. baueri Hook. Tree to 3m. St. solitary, erect, slender. Lvs 15–60×5–6.5cm, arching, linear-lanceolate, tapered to base, light green, main vein broad. Infl. a large much-branched pan.; fls 9mm, white, sweetly fragrant. NZ.

C. congesta Endl. = *C. stricta*.

C. fruticosa (L.) A. Chev. = *C. terminalis*.

C. goldieana (Bull) De Vos = *Dracaena goldieana*.

C. haageana Koch. Small shrub to 1m+. Lvs 10–20×5–7cm, crowded, broadly lanceolate, abruptly contracted at base, green; petiole 7–10cm, channelled. Infl. sparingly branched, 30cm; fls 7mm, white within, tinged purple without. Aus.

C. hookeri T. Kirk = *C. indivisa*.

C. indivisa (Forst.) Steud. Shrub to 8m. St. scarcely branched, massive. Lvs 100–200×10–15cm, narrowly lanceolate, glaucous, main vein conspicuous, often red. Infl. to 160cm, compact, sparingly branched, axes hidden by fls; fls 7–8mm, crowded, white or off-white within, flushed purple without. NZ. 'Purpurea': lvs flushed purple-bronze. 'Rubra': lvs deep bronze.

C. pumilio Hook. f. Shrub to 2m, often flowering when smaller. St. arching, slender. Lvs 30–200×1–2cm, narrowly linear, base narrowed, green, coriaceous; petiole channelled. Infl. v. open, to 60cm; fls remote, 4–5mm; white or flushed pink. NZ.

C. rubra Kunth. Tree-like shrub, 3–5m. St. clustered, erect, simple or sparingly branched, slender. Lvs 30–40×2–5cm, oblanceolate, dull green, thick, main vein conspicuous; petiole broad, channelled, 10–15mm. Infl. pendulous branched; fls numerous, 8mm, pale mauve to lilac. Fr. red. Gdn origin.

C. stricta (Sims) Endl. Shrub to 4m. St. erect, slender. Lvs 30–60×1.5–2.3cm, linear-lanceolate, minutely dentate, apex acuminate, green, sessile. Infl. pyramidal, much-branched, to 60cm; fls 7mm, lilac to blue. Aus. 'Discolor': lvs dark purple-bronze. 'Grandis': larger; lvs highly coloured. 'Rubra': lvs flushed red-copper.

C. terminalis (L.) Kunth. TI. Shrub to 4m. St. clustered, erect, simple or somewhat branched, slender. Lvs 30–60×5–10cm, oblong-lanceolate, green or tinged purple or red, narrowing to grooved petiole. Infl. to 60cm, much branched, axes visible between fls; fls 6mm, white or tinged yellow or red. Trop. SE Asia, Aus., Hawaii. 'Amabilis': lvs broad, glossy green with bronze and red, becoming tinged and spotted with white and pink. 'Baby Ti': miniature, lvs green-copper edged red. 'Baptistii': lvs broad, recurved, deep green with pink and yellow stripes. 'Firebrand' ('Red Dracaena'): compact rosette; lvs deep burgundy. 'Guilfoylei': lvs tapered to both ends, recurved, with red, pink or white stripes, and petiole and basal part of lf white. 'Hawaiian Bonsai': compact; lvs darkest crimson. 'Imperialis': lvs deep green marked pink or red. 'Madame Eugene André': spreading; lvs broad, deep green-copper, edged red, new lvs pink. 'Margaret Storey': compact; lvs green-copper splashed pink and red. 'Mayi': Lvs red when young, becoming green with red margins when mature. 'Negri': lvs large, dark copper-maroon. 'Norwoodiensis': lvs green with yellow stripes, margins and petioles crimson.

→*Dracaena*.

Cordylophorum (Nutt. ex Torr. & A. Gray) Rydb. = *Epilobium*.

Corema D. Don. BROOM CROWBERRY. Empetraceae. 2 low-growing, everg., heath-like plants. Br. rigid, closely branched. Lvs linear. Fls small in short term. clusters; sep. 3–6, petaloid; pet. 0; sta. 3–4. Fr. a subglobose drupe. N Amer., Macaronesia, SW Eur.

C. album D. Don. To 30cm. Lvs to 0.5cm, gland-dotted, revolute. Fls white. Fr. white. SW Eur., Azores. Z8.

C. conradii (Torr.) Torr. ex Loud. POVERTY GRASS. To 20cm. Lvs to 0.7cm. Fls with purple fil. E N Amer. Z3.

Coreopsis L. TICKSEED. Compositae. c80 glab. or pubesc., ann. or perenn. herbs, usually branched. Lvs opposite, rarely alt., simple and entire, dentate or deeply lobed, or 1–3-ternate or pinnate. Cap. radiate, solitary, or in loose corymbose-paniculate infl. N & S Amer., esp. Mex. and S US.

C. angustifolia Dryand. = *C. linifolia*.

C. atkinsoniana Douglas ex Lindl. = *C. tinctoria* var. *atkinsoniana*.

C. auriculata L. Erect or ascending perenn., to 1.5m, with stolons. Lvs to 12cm, ovate-circular or elliptic-obtuse or somewhat acute, entire or 1–2 lobed. Cap. to 5×1cm, solitary, long-stalked; ray-florets c8, yellow; disc-florets yellow. Spring. SE US. 'Cutting Gold': fls vivid gold. 'Nana': dwarf to 25cm; lvs dark green; fls bright orange. 'Superba': fls bright yellow with central purple splash. Z4.

C. baccata L. f. = *Wulffia baccata*.

C. basalis (Dietr.) S.F. Blake. Erect ann. to 40cm. Lvs to 12cm, mostly 1–3 pinnate, lfts linear-lanceolate, elliptic-oblong or circular, entire and undulate. Cap. to 4.5×0.8cm, term., peduncles to 15cm; ray flts c8, yellow, base brown-red; disc flts dark red at least at apex. Late spring–summer. Tex., introd. elsewhere.

C. bigelovii (A. Gray) Voss. Erect ann. to 40cm. Lvs to 11cm, usually 1–2-pinnate, lfts linear. Cap. to 4×2×1cm, term., peduncles long; ray flts 8, yellow; disc flts yellow. Calif.

C. californica (Nutt.) H. Sharsm. Ann. to 45cm. Lvs to 15cm, erect, linear-filiform, entire or to 1 to few-lobed, lobes linear-filiform. Cap. to 3.5×1cm, peduncles long; ray flts 5–12, yellow; disc flts, yellow. S Ariz., S Calif., NW Mex.

C. calliopsidea (DC.) A. Gray. Ann. to 60cm. Lvs to 7cm, 1–2 pinnatifid, lobes linear, petioles to 5cm, winged. Cap. to 5×1–2cm, term., solitary, peduncles long; ray flts usually 8, yellow; disc flts yellow. S Calif.

C. cardaminifolia (DC.) ex Nutt. = *C. tinctoria* var. *atkinsoniana*.

C. coronata Hook. = *C. nuecensis*.

C. ×*delphinifolia* Lam. Perenn., to 1.5m. Lvs to 9cm, palmately 3-lobed, central seg. often 3–5 lobed, lat. seg. rarely 2-lobed, lobes linear. Cap. to 5×1cm; peduncles to 7cm; ray flts c8, yellow; disc flts brown at apex. S Carol., Georgia. Z8.

C. diversifolia Hook. = *C. basalis*.

C. douglasii (DC.) H.M. Hall. Glaucous ann. to 25cm. Lvs to 8cm, linear-filiform, entire, obtuse, red-tipped, rounded beneath, or with 1–2 lat. linear-filiform lobes. Cap. to 2.5×1cm, ray flts 5–8, golden-yellow; disc flts golden-yellow. Calif.

C. drummondii (D. Don) Torr. & A. Gray = *C. basalis*.

C. elegans hort. ex Wiegand = *C. tinctoria*.

C. gigantea (Kellogg) H.M. Hall. Erect woody-based, thick-stemmed perenn., to 3m. Lvs to 20cm, usually 2–3-pinnate, lfts linear-filiform, entire or laterally notched. Cap. to 8×1.3cm, in a corymbose infl.; peduncles to 20cm; ray flts 10–16, yellow; disc flts yellow. SW Calif. Z8.

C. grandiflora Hogg ex Sweet. Erect or ascending perenn. or ann. to 60cm. Lvs to 10cm, lower lvs simple or irregularly parted, seg. spathulate or lanceolate, upper lvs 3–5 parted, seg. linear or linear-lanceolate. Cap. to 6×1.2cm, peduncles to 15cm; ray flts usually 8, yellow; disc flts orange at apex. Late spring–early summer. C & SE US. 'Badengold': to 100cm; fls deep yellow. 'Domino': to 40cm; fls yellow. 'Early Sunrise': to 45cm; fls semi-double, light gold. 'Louis d'Or': to 90cm, fls double, deep gold. 'Mayfield Giant': to 100cm; fls large, single, bright yellow. 'Ruby Throat': fls yellow with dark claret throat. 'Schnittgold': fls vivid gold. 'Sunray': to 75cm; fls double, deep yellow. Z7.

C. lanceolata L. Perenn., to 60cm. Lvs to 15cm, spathulate, linear, lanceolate- or oblanceolate-linear, usually entire, rarely dissected. Cap. to 6×1.4cm; ray flts c8, yellow; disc flts yellow. Spring–summer. C & SE US. 'Baby Gold': to 40cm; fls pure gold. 'Baby Sun' ('Sonnenkind'): small to 30cm; fls gold. 'Brown Eyes': fls yellow with brown spots. 'Double Sunburst': fls double, bright yellow. 'Goldfink': small to 25cm; fls gold. 'Goldteppich': to 35cm; fls gold. 'Grandiflora': fls yellow, heads large. 'Lichtstad': fls yellow with rust spots. 'Rotkehlchen': to 30cm; fls yellow splashed with brown. 'Sterntaler': to 40cm; fls gold with brown rings. 'Sunburst': to 75cm; fls double, yellow. Z3.

C. linifolia Nutt. Pale, glab., perenn., to 70cm. Lvs to 10cm, margin hardened, entire, lower lvs spathulate or oblanceolate, rounded, upper lvs linear. Cap. to 3×0.7cm, few, in a paniculate-corymbose infl., peduncles to 7cm; ray flts c7–8, yellow; disc flts dark-purple. Late summer–autumn. Coast from Virg. to SE Tex. Z8.

C. major Walter. Erect, perenn., to 90cm. Lvs to 20cm, uppermost simple, lower tripartite, lobes oval-diamond-shaped, elliptic-to linear-lanceolate or lanceolate, entire, ± pubesc. Cap. to 5×0.9cm, in a somewhat corymbose infl.; peduncles to 8cm; ray flts c8, yellow; disc flts yellow. Late spring–early autumn. SE US. Z7.

C. maritima (Nutt.) Hook. f. Perenn., to 80cm. Lvs 10–15cm, 2–3-pinnate, lfts to 3cm, oblong-linear. Cap. to 13.5×1.5cm, few to many; peduncles to 40cm; ray flts 14–20, yellow; disc flts yellow. SW Calif. Z8.

C. marmorata hort. ex Wiegand = *C. tinctoria*.

C. mutica DC. Perenn., to 2m. Lvs to 17cm, simple or tripartite, broadly oblong ovate-lanceolate, serrate, often somewhat leathery. Cap. to 5×1.7cm, 5–60, in a paniculate-corymbose infl., peduncles to 4cm; ray flts 5, yellow; disc flts yellow. S Mex. to Guat. Z9.

C. nana hort. = *C. tinctoria*.

C. nudata Nutt. Glab. perenn., to 1.2m. Lvs to 40cm, simple, narrowly linear, ± terete. Cap. to 6×0.8cm, few, in a corymbose infl., peduncles long; ray flts c8, red; disc flts yellow. Spring. SE US. Z8.

C. nuecensis A.A. Heller. Ann., to 60cm. Lvs to 20cm, broadly oval or oblong-spathulate or pinnate, lfts to 5. Cap. to 4.8×1cm, peduncles to 30cm; ray flts c8, yellow base with large dark red or brown-red spots; disc flts yellow or purple at apex. Spring. SE Tex. Z8.

C. palmata Nutt. Perenn., to 50–90cm. Lvs to 7cm, rigid, thick, pedately or palmately tripartite, seg. entire or irregularly 2–3 lobed, oblong-linear. Cap. to 6×1.5cm, 1–6, peduncles to 4cm; ray flts c8, yellow; disc flts yellow. Summer. Minn. and Wisc. to extreme N Louisiana. Z4.

C. pubescens Elliott. Erect, pubesc. perenn., to 1.2m. Lvs to 10cm, oval, oblong-ovate or elliptic-lanceolate, 3–5 pinnate, lfts small, oblong to linear-lanceolate. Cap. to 5×1.1cm, peduncles, to 20cm; ray flts c8, yellow; disc flts yellow. Summer. C & SE US. Z7.

C. rosea Nutt. Erect, glab., ann. or perenn., to 60cm. Lvs to 5cm, ± connate and ciliate at base, entire or ± 2–3-partite, lobes linear. Cap. to 2.5×0.6mm, term., peduncles to 10cm; ray flts c8, red or white; disc flts yellow. Summer–early autumn. Nova Scotia to Maryland. 'Nana': dwarf. Z4.

C. senifolia Michx. = *C. major*.

C. stillmanii (A. Gray) S.F. Blake. Glab. ann., to 45cm. Lvs to 10cm, pinnately 3–7-partite, lfts sometimes lobed, narrowly linear-spathulate. Cap. to 3×0.9cm, solitary, peduncles long; ray flts c8, yellow; disc flts yellow. Calif.

C. tinctoria Nutt. Glab. ann. to 1.2m. Lvs to 10cm, entire or 1–2-pinnate, lfts linear or linear-lanceolate. Cap. to 3×0.6cm, numerous, in somewhat corymbose, infl., peduncles to 10cm; ray flts c7–8, yellow, brown-red at base; disc flts dark red. Late spring–early autumn. Much of N Amer., esp. C and E US. 'Nana': compact dwarf. var. *atkinsoniana* (Douglas ex Lindl.) H. Parker ex E.B. Sm. Basal lvs 1–3-pinnatisect. Peduncles to 15cm; disc flts purple-red. SW Canada to C & W US.

C. tripteris L. Pale, glab. or pubesc. perenn., to 3m. Lvs to 12cm, 3-partite, middle leaflet often 3-parted, seg. broadly elliptic-

linear or narrowly oblong-lanceolate. Cap. to 5×1cm, in subcorymbose infl., peduncles to 8cm; ray flts usually 7–8, yellow; disc flts yellow, becoming brown or purple. Summer–early autumn. C & SE US. Z4.

C. verticillata L. Glab. perenn., to 90cm. Lvs to 6cm, pinnately 3-parted, seg. 1–2 pinnate, apical seg. linear-filiform, pointed. Cap. to 5×0.9cm, few, in a corymbose infl., peduncles to 6cm; ray flts c8, yellow; disc flts yellow. Summer. SE US. 'Grandiflora' ('Golden Shower'): to 60cm; fls yellow, heads large. 'Moonbeam': to 50cm; fls lemon-yellow. 'Zagreb': to 30cm; fls gold. Z6.

→*Anacis, Bidens, Calliopsis, Chrysomelea, Chrysostemma, Coreopsoides, Diplosastera, Electra, Leachia, Leptosyne, Pugiopappus* and *Tuckermannia*.

Corethrogyne DC. Compositae. 3 perenn. herbs, sometimes woody at base, white-tomentose at first. Cap. solitary or in corymbs or pan., many-fld, radiate; ray flts violet to pink; disc flts yellow. Calif. Z8.

C. californica DC. St. 15–40cm, decumbent, woody at base. Lvs 2–4cm, linear-oblanceolate, entire or sparsely dentate, white-tomentose. Cap. usually solitary, 2–3.5cm diam.; involucre minutely glandular-pubesc., sometimes tomentose; ray flts violet-purple to lilac-pink. Spring–summer.

C. filaginifolia (Hook. & Arn.) Nutt. Subshrub, to 80cm; st. erect or ascending. Lvs 2–6cm, lanceolate to oblanceolate, sometimes sharply serrate, tomentose then glabrescent. Cap. c2.5cm diam., few, in a pan. involucre glab.; ray flts violet to purple. Summer–winter.

C. linifolia (H.M. Hall) Ferris. Like *C. filaginifolia* but persistently tomentose; lvs linear, to 5mm wide, entire, sometimes revolute; involucre tomentose; ray flts lavender. Summer–early autumn.

→*Aster*.

Coriander *Coriandrum sativum*.

Coriandrum L. Umbelliferae. 2 ann. herbs. Lower lvs lobed, seg. ovate, upper lvs 1–3 pinnate, seg. linear. Umbels compound; involucre 0; bracteoles few; fls white to pale purple; outer pet. larger, 2-lobed. W Medit.

C. sativum L. CORIANDER; CHINESE PARSLEY. Glab. ann. to 50cm, all parts strongly scented. Lower lvs with lobes to 1cm, ovate-cuneate, incised-serrate; petiole long; upper lvs 2–3 pinnate, seg. narrow-linear. Umbels with 2–5 rays, to 1.5cm. Summer–autumn. Eur.

Coriaria L. Coriariaceae. c30 herbs, shrubs or small trees with angular st. Br. usually frondose with lvs 2-ranked, colouring well in fall. Fls in terminal or axill. rac., small, green, 5-merous; pet. free, smaller than cal. in fl., ultimately accrescent and fleshy, coloured, enclosing fr. of single-seeded achenes. S Eur., E Asia, C & S Amer., NZ & Pacific Is. Z8.

C. japonica A. Gray. Subshrub to 2m. St. arching. Lvs 2.5–9cm, ovate-lanceolate, acuminate coloured amber-red in fall. Infl. 4–6.5cm from joints of previous year's shoots; cor. bright red, then purple-black in fr. Summer. Jap.

C. microphylla Poir. Herb, or subshrub with spreading rhiz. and frondose br. to 1.5m. Lvs to 2cm, ovate, crowded. Infl. to 10cm slender, pubesc.; cor. dark brown in fr., 3mm across. Summer. NZ, temp. S Amer.

C. myrtifolia L. Shrub to 3m. Br. curving. Lvs 3–6cm, ovate-lanceolate, acute of cuspidate, opposite or in whorls. Infl. axill. or term. on short lat. br., 2–5cm in fl. cor. dark red-brown in fr. Summer. SW Eur., N Afr.

C. nepalensis Wallich. Shrub with arching red-brown br. Lvs to 5cm, elliptic, rarely ovate-oblong, acuminate, serrulate, coloured well in fall. Infl. axill., 2.5–10cm; cor. black in fr., to 8mm across; sta. and styles red or dull purple, conspicuous. Spring. Himal. to SW China.

C. ruscifolia L. Shrub or small tree to 6m. Lvs 3.5–7.5cm, ovate, apex acute, base rounded to cordate. Infl. axill., slender, 10–30cm; cor. black in fr. Summer. NZ, temp. S Amer.

C. sinica Maxim. Coarse shrub to 6m; shoots tuberculate. Lvs 3.5–8.5cm, elliptic to ovate, apex acute, base rounded. Infl. axill. 2.5–5cm; cor. black in fr. sta. red. Summer. China.

C. terminalis Hemsl. Subshrub to 1.5m, spreading by rhiz. St. glandular-hairy. Lvs 3–7.5cm, ovate, acute, colouring well in fall. Infl. term., 10–15cm; cor. black in fr., 8mm across. Summer. Himal. to W China. var. *xanthocarpa* Rehd. & Wils. Fruiting cor. translucent yellow. Sikkim. f. *fructorubro* Hemsl. Fruiting cor. translucent currant-red. Origin unknown.

C. thymifolia Humb. & Bonpl. ex Willd. = *C. microphylla*.

CORIARIACEAE DC. See *Coriaria*.

Coris L. Primulaceae. 2 woody-based perenn. or bienn. herbs. St. to 35cm, erect. Lvs alt. Fls in a term. spike-like rac.; cal. campanulate, with 2 rows of teeth, cor. to 1.2cm diam., unequally 5-partite, tube short, lobes unequally bifid; sta. exserted. Summer. Eur., Somalia. Z7.

C. hispanica Lange. Lvs to 5×5mm, sinuate, revolute rarely spinose-dentate. Infl. lax; cal green outer teeth developed dorsally only, inner row of teeth with dark patches, cor. white or pale pink. SE Spain.

C. monspeliensis L. Lvs to 20x3mm, entire of sinuate, subrevolute, upper lvs, sometimes spinose-dentate, often with black spots on either side of midrib. Infl. dense; cal membranous tinged purple, outer teeth spinose, inner teeth with red or black patch, cor. pink, purple or blue. Distrib. as for the genus.

Corkbark Fir *Abies lasiocarpa.*
Cork-leaved Bayur *Pterospermum suberifolium.*
Cork Oak *Quercus suber.*
Corkscrew *Euphorbia mammillaris.*
Corkscrew-flower *Strophanthus speciosus*; *Vigna caracalla.*
Corkscrew Hazel *Corylus avellana* 'Contorta'.
Corkscrew Rush *Juncus effusus* 'Spiralis'.
Cork Tree *Erythrina latissima.*
Corkwood *Leitneria floridana*; *Musanga cecropioides.*
Corkwood Wattle *Acacia sutherlandii.*
Corn *Zea mays.*

CORNACEAE Dumort. 12/90. *Aucuba, Cornus, Corokia, Curtisia, Griselinia, Helwingia.*

Corn-cob *Euphorbia mammillaris.*
Corn-cockle *Agrostemma.*
Cornel *Cornus.*
Cornelian Cherry *Cornus mas.*
Cornflower *Centaurea cyanus.*
Cornish Elm *Ulmus carpinifolia* var. *cornubiensis.*
Cornish Heath *Erica vagans.*
Cornish Moneywort *Sibthorpia europaea.*
Corn Lily *Clintonia borealis.*
Corn Marigold *Chrysanthemum segetum.*
Corn Mint *Mentha arvensis.*
Corn Plant *Dracaena fragrans.*
Corn Poppy *Papaver rhoeas.*
Corn Salad *Valerianella.*
Corn Spurrey *Spergula arvensis.*

Cornus L. DOGWOOD; CORNEL. Cornaceae. c45 perenn., semi-woody herbs, shrubs or small trees, decid. or sometimes everg. Lvs opposite or sometimes alt., simple, entire, with prominent venation. Infl. of term. cymes, umbels, pan. or compact heads; bracts 1–4; fls usually ♂, white, green-white or yellow, small. Fr. a drupe, bilocular, 2-seeded. Temp. N hemis.; rare in S Amer. and Afr.

C. alba L. RED-BARKED DOGWOOD; TARTARIAN DOGWOOD. Decid., suckering shrub to 3m; st. erect; shoots glab., red in autumn and winter. Lvs 4–8cm, ovate-elliptic with short, slender point, dark green above, glaucous beneath. Fls in narrow cymes 3–5cm across, cream. Fr. white to light blue. Early summer. Sib., N China to Korea. 'Atrosanguinea': dwarf, st. crimson; 'Elegantissima': lvs grey-green edged white to cream. 'Kesselringii': st. purple-black, lvs open brown; 'Sibirica' ('Splendens') (SIBERIAN DOGWOOD): less robust; st. bright coral red. 'Westonbirt': st. dark coral pink. With variegated lvs: 'Argenteomarginata': lvs edged white; 'Aurea': lvs soft yellow-green; 'Behnschii': lvs variegated white and red; 'Gouchaltii' ('Froebelii'): lvs variegated yellow and pink; 'Spaethii': lvs edged yellow, bronzed on opening. Z3.

C. alba auct., non L. = *C. stolonifera.*
C. alba var. *sibirica* (Lodd.) Loud. = *C. alba* 'Sibirica'.

C. alternifolia L. f. PAGODA DOGWOOD; GREEN OSIER. Decid. tree or shrub to 8m flat-topped with tiered br. Lvs 6–12cm, ovate-elliptic, dark green above, glaucescent beneath. Fls small in cymes 5cm across, yellow-white. Fr. black, rarely yellow. Early summer. E N Amer. 'Argentea' ('Variegata'): habit dense; lvs marked white. 'Corallina': st. red. 'Ochrocarpa': fr. pale yellow. 'Umbraculifera': br. conspicuously tiered. 'Virescens': br. green. Z3.

C. amomum Mill. Compact decid. shrub to 4m. Lvs 5–12cm, ovate-elliptic, dull green above, lighter with silky down beneath pronounced and red-brown on vein pairs, lvs red in fall. Fls small, yellow-white in arched cymes to 6cm across. Fr. pale grey-blue. Summer. E N Amer. Z5.

C. ×arnoldiana Rehd. (*C. racemosa* ×*C. obliqua.*) Differs from *C. racemosa*, in habit more spreading, older br. purple; lvs felted beneath; infl. smaller; fr. blue. Z4.

C. aspera Wangerin = *C. bretschneideri.*

C. asperifolia Michx. Decid. shrub to 4m. Lvs to 7.5cm, oval, rough. Infl. to 5cm; sta. and fr. blue. Late spring. SE US. var. **drummondii** (C.A. Mey.) Coult. & W.H. Evans. Erect shrub or small tree to 6m; shoots red-brown. Lvs 5–10cm, ovate-elliptic, dark green and rough above, downy beneath. Fls yellow-white in loose cymes 8cm across. Fr. white, c6mm diam. Summer. E to Central N Amer. Z9.

C. australis C.A. Mey. Decid. shrub to 4m. Lvs 8cm, ovate, apex cuspidate, adpressed hairy, lower surface rough. Fls white, in dense cymes 5cm across. Fr. 5mm diam., dark purple. Summer. Asia Minor, around the Black and Caspian seas. var. **koenigii** (C. Schneid.) C. Schneid. Lvs to 13cm; fr. to 1cm diam. Z7.

C. baileyi Coult. & W.H. Evans = *C. stolonifera* 'Baileyi'.
C. brachypoda K. Koch non C.A. Mey. = *C. controversa.*
C. brachypoda C.A. Mey. non K. Koch = *C. macrophylla.*
C. brachypoda 'Variegata'. = *C. controversa* f. *variegata.*

C. bretschneideri (L.) Henry. Decid. shrub, similar to *C. alba*, to 5m. Young shoots downy, green-yellow, yellow to red above in winter. Lvs 5–10cm, ovate, gently undulate with long, acuminate apex, dull green above, grey-green and scabrid beneath. Fls cream, tips red in wide cymes 5–10cm across. Fr. blue-black. Early summer. N China. Z5.

C. ×californica C.A. Mey. (*C. occidentalis* ×*C. stolonifera.*) CREEK DOGWOOD. Shrub to 5m, st. smooth, dark red. Lvs 10cm, oval-elliptic, pointed, downy. Fr. white. Spring–summer. BC to Calif. Z8.

C. canadensis L. BUNCHBERRY; DWARF CORNEL; CRACKERBERRY; CREEPING DOGWOOD; PUDDING BERRY. Differs from *C. suecica* in lvs in term. whorls, not opposite and paired. Ground-covering perenn. with creeping rhiz. and erect ann. st. to 8cm. Lvs 2–4cm, ovate to lanceolate. Fls clustered in a term. umbel, green to red-violet, subtended by 4–6 large white bracts 1–2cm long. Fr. bright red. Summer. Greenland to Alask. Z2.

C. candidissima Mill. = *C. florida.*
C. candidissima Marshall non Mill. = *C. racemosa.*

C. capitata Wallich. BENTHAM'S CORNEL. Everg. to 16m. Br. horizontal. Lvs 5–12cm, ovate to lanceolate, thin to leathery, dark above, grey-green beneath. Fls white, v. small, crowded in clusters to 1.5cm across; bracts 2–4×4–8cm, obovate to oblanceolate, cream or white. Fr. a fleshy, strawberry-shaped, scarlet aggregate, 2.5cm diam. Summer. Himal., China. Z8.

C. chinensis Wangerin. Resembles *C. mas* and *C. officinalis* but fr. black, not red. Decid. upright tree to 10–20m. Lvs 14cm, ovate to elliptic, apex long tapered, conspicuously veined. Fls yellow in large unstalked clusters before lvs. Fr. black. Late winter. C & S China. Z8.

C. circinata L'Hérit. = *C. rugosa.*
C. coerulea Lam. = *C. amomum.*
C. comosa Raf. = *C. racemosa.*

C. controversa Hemsl. GIANT DOGWOOD. Resembles *C. alternifolia*, differing in greater height. Decid. tree to 17m; br. horizontal, tiered, shoots pruinose. Lvs 7–15cm, ovate to broadly elliptic, cuspidate, glab., dark glossy green above, glaucous beneath, colouring red in early fall but persisting. Fls white, 1.3cm across in flat, wide cymes 10–18cm diam. Fr. blue-black. Summer. Jap., China, Himal. 'Variegata' (WEDDING CAKE TREE): lvs lanceolate, with an uneven white-yellow margin. Z5.

C. coreana Wangerin. Closely related to *C. walteri.* Decid. tree to 20m; bark fissured and ridged, forming square plates, br. red at first. Lvs elliptic. Infl. 7–8cm wide. Korea. Z6.

C. drummondii C.A. Mey. = *C. asperifolia* var. *drummondii.*

C. 'Eddie's White Wonder'. (*C. florida* ×*C. nuttallii.*) Habit upright, pyramidal, br. drooping. Lvs orange-brown in fall. Infl. to 12cm diam.; bracts 4(-5-6), obovate-circular, overlapping, white. Gdn origin. Z6.

C. florida L. EASTERN FLOWERING DOGWOOD; COMMON WHITE DOGWOOD. Small, decid. tree or wide spreading shrub, to 10m. Br. spreading to ascending, cinereous at first. Lvs 7–15cm, broadly oval to ovate, dull green above, white-downy beneath, orange to red in fall. Fls small, green in a crowded head 1.2cm wide; bracts 4cm, 4, obovate, notched, white. Fr. scarlet. Spring. E N Amer. 'Apple Blossom': bracts apple-blossom pink. 'Bonnie': bracts white. 'Pendula': br. drooping. 'Pluribracteata': bracts 6–8, large, with smaller bracts in centre. 'Purple Glory': lvs purple; bracts red. 'Pygmaea': to 1m, bracts profuse. 'Rainbow': lvs variegated light and dark green and yellow, turning in autumn to lavender, reds and scarlet. 'Salicifolia': small tree, lvs narrow, willow-like. 'Spring Song': bracts large, flamingo pink with dark rose veins. 'Tricolor': lvs green, margin painted creamy-white, tinted rose, turning bronze to purple edged red in autumn. 'Welchii': lvs variegated red, yellow, often deformed. 'White Cloud': lvs bronzed; bracts white. 'Xanthocarpa': fr. yellow. Z5. f. **rubra** (Weston) Schelle. Bracts pale pink to red.

'Cherokee Chief': bracts deep rose. 'Royal Red': bracts deep red, profuse. 'Spring Song': bracts deep rose-red.

C. foemina Wangerin non A. Mill. = *C. racemosa.*

C. foemina A. Mill. non Wangerin = *C. stricta.*

C. glabrata Benth. WESTERN CORNEL; BROWN DOGWOOD. Decid. bushy shrub, slender, twiggy, often pendulous, to 6m. Lvs 3–8cm, lanceolate to elliptic, apex and base acuminate, glossy grey-green. Fls off-white in small cymes, 3cm across. Fr. white to blue-white. Summer. W N Amer. Z6.

C. hemsleyi Schneid. & Wangerin. Decid. shrub or small tree to 8m. Shoots downy then red and glab. Lvs 5–7.5cm, round-ovate, apex shortly tapered, stiffly hairy above, glaucous, downy beneath, midrib downy, brown. Fls small, white, in cymes 5–7cm across; anth. blue. Fr. blue-black. Summer. China. Z6.

C. hessei Koehne. Compact, slow, close-growing, decid. shrub, to 50cm. Lvs 3cm, elliptic-lanceolate, base cuneate, apex acute, adpressed hairy, dark almost black-green above, glaucous beneath, purple in fall. Fls pink-white; infl. cymose 3–4cm across. Fr. blue-white. Summer. Origin unknown, probably NE Asia. Z5.

C. japonica G. Don = *C. kousa.*

C. koenigii C. Schneid. = *C. australis* var. *koenigii.*

C. kousa (Buerger ex Miq.) Hance. KOUSA. Decid. tree or tall shrub to 7m. Br. erect. Lvs 5–9cm, ovate, apex acuminate, base cuneate, undulate, dark green above, blue green beneath, red in fall. Fls small in compact rounded heads; bracts 4, lanceolate, creamy white, spreading, acuminate. Fr. a fleshy, scarlet strawberry-like aggregate, 2cm diam. Summer. Jap., Korea, China. Z5. var. *chinensis* Osborn. Habit more tree-like and open, to 10m. Lvs lighter green, usually not undulate. Bracts larger, to 6cm, green at first, changing to white ageing pink. 'Elizabeth Lustgarten': habit weeping. 'Gold Star': lvs heart-shaped, marked with yellow. 'Milky Way': lvs bronze in autumn; fls profuse, white. 'Rubra': bracts pink. 'Snowboy': lvs grey-green deeply edged white. 'Summer Stars': lvs maroon in autumn; fls profuse; fr. cherry red. 'Variegata': lvs variegated. 'Xanthocarpa': fr. yellow.

C. latifolia Bray = *C. sanguinea.*

C. macrophylla Wallich. Decid. tree or tall shrub, to 15m, br. spreading, yellow-red. Lvs 10–17cm, elliptic-ovate to oblong, apex long-acuminate, dark lustrous green above, glaucous blue with silvery hairs beneath. Fls yellow-white, 1–1.5cm diam., in broad term. cymes 8–15cm diam. Fr. blue. Late summer. Himal., China, Jap. Z6.

C. macrophylla Koehne = *C. controversa.*

C. mas L. CORNELIAN CHERRY; SORBET. Decid. shrub with spreading habit, sometimes a small tree, to 5m. Young br. cinereous. Lvs 4–10cm, ovate, apex acute, base tapered or rounded, dark green, adpressed pubesc. Fls small, bright yellow in flat topped cymes 2cm diam., produced before lvs. Fr. bright red oblong. Spring. Eur., W Asia. f. *sphaerocarpa* Cretz. fr. globose. 'Alba': fr. white. 'Aurea': lvs yellow. 'Crispa': lvs puckered and rolled. 'Elegantissima': lvs edged yellow, flushed pink. 'Golden Glory': lvs and fr. large, fls larger, more profuse. 'Lanceolata': lvs narrow, edged white. 'Nana': dwarf spherical bush. 'Pyramidalis': growth upright and narrow. 'Variegata': lvs dark green deeply edged grey-green and cream. 'Violacea': fr. violet blue. 'Xanthocarpa': fr. yellow. Z5.

C. mas f. *aureomarginata* Schelle = *C. mas* f. *sphaerocarpa* 'Elegantissima'.

C. mascula L. = *C. mas.*

C. microcarpa Nash = *C. asperifolia.*

C. monbeigii Hemsl. Decid. shrub, 4–6m, related to *C. macrophylla.* Young st. brown. Lvs 10cm, elliptic to orbicular to ovate, base cordate to rounded, apex long acuminate, dull green above, grey-white beneath, softly pubesc veins tinged red. Fls 1.5cm across, white, in narrow downy term. cymes 8–12cm diam. Fr. black. Summer. China. Z7.

C. 'Norman Hadden'. (*C. kousa* × *C. capitata.*) Infl. bracts white, ageing pink; fr. persistent, large. Z5.

C. nuttallii Aud. MOUNTAIN DOGWOOD. Tree to 30m in the wild, decid. Shoots downy at first. Lvs 8–12cm, oval to obovate, apex short-acuminate, downy when young. Fls purple and green, in spherical heads; bracts to 7.5cm, 4–8, oval to obovate, green-white to cream, sometimes tipped green-red later with a pink flush. Fr. orange-red. Spring. W N Amer. 'Corego Giant': infl. to 15cm diam. 'Eddiei': mature lvs spotted yellow. 'Gold Spot': lvs mottled yellow. 'North Star': lvs purple when young; bracts long, narrow. 'Portlemouth': infl. large. Z7.

C. obliqua Raf. SILKY DOGWOOD. Differs from *C. amomum* in looser habit. Decid., open-growing shrub to 4m. Br. green to orange-purple. Lvs 5–8cm, oval-elliptic to oblong, apex tapering, dull grey-white beneath, veins brown-red-pubesc. Infl. white, to 5cm across. Fr. blue to white. Summer. E N Amer. Z4.

C. oblonga Wallich. Everg. shrub or small tree to 6m. Young shoots angular with yellow-brown down. Lvs 3–12cm, narrowly oval, apex acuminate, base cuneate, dark glossy green with adpressed hairs above, dull grey, downy beneath. Fls white or purple-tinged, 4mm wide, fragrant, in pyramidal pan. 7×7cm. Fr. black. Autumn. Himal., China. Z9.

C. occidentalis Cov. Similar to *C. stolonifera.* Decid. shrub, sometimes tree-like, 2–6m. Br. glab., dark purple. Lvs 4–10cm, ovate, apex blunt or pointed, dark green above, tomentose and glaucous beneath. Fls yellow-white packed in rounded, downy cymes 5cm across. Fr. white. Summer. E N Amer. Z6.

C. officinalis Sieb. & Zucc. JAPANESE CORNELIAN CHERRY; JAPANESE CORNEL. Differs from *C. mas* in red-brown tufts of hairs in vein axils of lf. undersides. Decid. tree or shrub, 10m+. Lvs to 12cm, ovate to elliptic, apex acuminate, turning red in autumn. Fls bright yellow, before lvs, in loose umbels 2cm or more across. Fr. bright red. Late winter. China, possibly Korea, Jap. Z6.

C. 'Ormonde'. (*C. nuttallii* × *C. florida.*) To 4m. Fls dark; bracts white with pink tip, freely produced. Z6.

C. paniculata L'Hérit. = *C. racemosa.*

C. paucinervis Hance. Decid. shrub to 3m. Young shoots angular. Lvs 4–10cm, narrowly oval to oblong-ovate, tapered at base and apex, deep green above, lighter beneath, adpressed-pubesc. Fls clcm diam., creamy white, in fragrant rounded cymes 6–8mm across. Fr. Black. Summer. China. Z5.

C. poliophylla C. Schneid. Shrub to 4m sometimes tree-like, differs from *C. monbeigii* in smaller stature and anth. blue. Z7.

C. pubescens Nutt. = *C. occidentalis.*

C. pumila Koehne. Decid. shrub to 2m, compact, slow-growing. Lvs 4–8cm, ovate-orbicular, dark green above, paler beneath, adpressed hairy. Fls white in long-stalked cymes. Fr. black. Summer. Origin unknown. Z5.

C. purpusii Koehne = *C. obliqua.*

C. quinquenervis Franch. = *C. paucinervis.*

C. racemosa Lam. PANICLED DOGWOOD. Decid. shrub to 5m, shoots glab. Lvs 5–10cm, ovate to lanceolate, apex long-acuminate, base cuneate, dark green above, pale blue beneath, adpressed pubesc. Fls small, white, in arched term. cymose pan. 6cm across. Fr. white; stalk red. Summer. E N Amer. 'Slavins Dwarf': habit dwarf, to less than 50cm. Z5.

C. rugosa Lam. ROUND-LEAVED DOGWOOD. Decid., upright, often tree-like, shrub to 3m. Br. and shoots green and warty, purple with age. Lvs 4–10cm, broad-oval to ovate, apex short-acuminate, grey-tomentose beneath. Fls white in slightly downy, arched cymes 5–7cm across. Fr. pale blue. Summer. N Amer. Z5.

C. sanguinea L. COMMON DOGWOOD; BLOOD-TWIG; PEGWOOD; DOGBERRY. Decid., erect shrub to 4m. Shoots dull brown-green flushed red. Lvs 4–10cm, broadly elliptic to ovate, apex slender-acuminate, red-purple in fall. Fls dull white, heavily scented, in dense, pubesc. cymes 5cm across. Fr. purple-black. Summer. Eur. 'Compressa': dwarf dense shrub to 1m, st. erect. 'Mietzschii': lvs variegated, grey, green and white, colouring well in autumn. 'Variegata': lvs variegated yellow and white. 'Viridissima': br. and fr. green. Z5.

C. sanguinea var. *australis* (C.A. Mey.) Koehne = *C. australis.*

C. sericea L. = *C. stolonifera.*

C. sessilis Torr. Similar to *C. mas* and *C. officinalis.* Decid. shrub to 3m. Young bark green, slightly pubesc. Lvs 5–7cm, ovate to oval, tapered, glab. above, adpressed-pubesc. beneath, vein axils downy tufted. Fls gold-yellow, precocious, small in sessile umbels. Fr. glossy purple-black. Spring. E N Amer. Z7.

C. sibirica Lodd. = *C. alba* 'Sibirica'.

C. × slavinii Rehd. (*C. rugosa* × *C. stolonifera.*) Lvs woolly beneath, as *C. rugosa*, habit more like that of *C. stolonifera*, though more upright. Fr. tinged blue, rarely white. Z5.

C. stolonifera Michx. f. RED OSIER DOGWOOD; AMERICAN DOGWOOD. Decid. shrub, 2–3m, vigorous, suckering freely. Main br. procumbent, young shoots dark purple-red to dark red, esp. in winter, glab. Lvs 5–10cm, oval to oval-lanceolate, apex long-acuminate, dark green above, glaucous blue-green beneath, with adpressed hairs. Fls dull white, small, in cymes 3–5cm across. Fr. white. Summer. E N Amer. 'Angustipetala': sep. small and pointed. 'Baileyi': shrub to 3m, not stoloniferous; br. short, shoots downy, red-brown in winter; lvs 5–12cm, ovate-lanceolate, downy when young colouring brilliantly in fall; fls small in woolly cymes to 3–5cm. 'Elongata': st. green; lvs 2.5× longer than wide. 'Flaviramea': vigorous, shoots yellow. 'Isanti': dwarf to 1m, st. close, bright red; fls white, profuse. 'Kelseyi' ('Nana'): mounded bush to 50cm; st. bright red. 'Nitida': lvs rather glossy; shoots green in winter. 'Pendula': low shrub, br. arching. 'White Gold' ('White Spot'): lvs edged white. Z2.

C. stolonifera var. *baileyi* (Coult. & W.H. Evans) Dresch. = *C. stolonifera* 'Baileyi'.

C. stricta Lam. STIFF DOGWOOD. Decid. shrub to 5m, erect. Br.

purple-brown. Lvs 3–7cm, oval-elliptic to lanceolate, apex tapered, pale green glab. above, with adpressed hairs. Fls white, in cymes 3–6cm across. Summer. W US. Z8.

C. suecica L. Similar to *C. canadensis* but without term. whorl of lvs. Herbaceous perenn., 10–15cm, with freely branching, creeping st. Lvs 2–4cm, paired, opposite, red in fall. Fls v. small, tinted red, in term. solitary umbels, surrounded by 4 white ovate bracts 1–1.5cm long. Fr. scarlet. Summer. N Eur. to N Jap. and N N Amer. Z2.

C. sylvestris Bubani = *C. sanguinea*.

C. tatarica Mill. = *C. alba*.

C. tomentulosa Michx. f. = *C. rugosa*.

C. ×unalaschkensis Ledeb. (*C. canadensis* ×*C. suecica*.) Intermediate form; lvs 6, whorled at st. apex and opposite, paired below. Greenland, Newfoundland, Alask. Z2.

C. walteri Wangerin. Related to *C. sanguinea*. Decid. tree, 10–12m. Young br. soon glab., green-yellow to green-red. Lvs 5–12cm, oval-elliptic, apex long-acuminate, base cuneate, dark green, adpressed-pubesc. Fls white, 1cm wide in cymes 5–7cm across. Fr. black. Summer. C & W China. Z6.

C. wilsoniana Wangerin. Differs from *C. walteri* in bark red; young br. glab.; lvs to 10cm, elliptic, gradually tapered. Summer. C & W China. Z6.

→*Benthamidia, Chamaepericlymenum, Dendrobenthamia, Swida* and *Thelycrania*.

Cornutia L. Verbenaceae. 12 everg. trees and shrubs, pubesc., often resinous and gland. Br. tetragonal, often winged; nodes ring-like. Lvs large and broad. Cal. cupuliform to campanulate, rim entire or minutely 4–5 toothed; cor. tubular, slightly curved, bilabiate, 4-parted, upper lip 3-lobed and smaller than lower lobe; sta. 4, 2 fertile exserted. Fr. drupaceous, black, subglobose. Trop. Amer. Z10.

C. grandifolia (Schldl. & Cham.) Schauer. Shrub or tree to 8m. Br. stout, obtusely tetragonal, villous. Lvs to 30×20cm, elliptic or elliptic-ovate, densely villous-tomentose, entire or toothed, dark green above, paler beneath. Infl. term., to 40×25cm, many-fld; bracts large and leafy; cor. pale blue, light violet, mauve or purple, to 9mm, 3 smaller lobes elliptic, blunt, largest lobe acute. C Amer.

C. pyramidata L. BOIS CASAVA. Shrub or small tree to 11m. Br. strongly tetragonal, winged, tomentose, gland. Lvs to 20×10cm, elliptic, or broadly ovate, membranous-chartaceous, entire, pubesc. Infl. term., paniculate, to 15×6cm; bracts linear-subulate; cor. blue, violet or pink, to 12mm, tube straight, to 11mm, lobes ovate, 3 smaller lobes acute, largest and lower lobe obtuse. Greater Antilles, Surinam.

C. quinata Lour. = *Vitex quinata*.

Coroa *Sicana odorifera*.
Coroba *Schinus lentiscifolius*.

Corokia Cunn. Cornaceae. 3 everg. trees or bushes. Br. slender, grey, cinereous becoming dark grey or black, often spiralling, tangled or zigzagging. Lvs alt. or in fascicles, entire, coriaceous, grey-green, silky beneath. Fls yellow, small star-like in pyramidal pan. or solitary. Fr. a small, orange-red drupe. NZ. Z8.

C. buddleioides Cunn. KOROKIO. To 4m. Lvs lanceolate, to 12×2cm, revolute, grey-green above, silver beneath. Spring. var. *linearis* Cheesm. Lvs narrowly linear.

C. cotoneaster Raoul. WIRE NETTING BUSH. To 2m. Br. densely tortuous. Lvs orbicular, to 2cm, maroon-green or bronze, silvery beneath. Late spring.

C. macrocarpa T. Kirk. To 3m. Lvs lanceolate, 8×3cm, grey-green to sage-green above, silver beneath. Early Summer.

C. ×virgata (Turrill) Metcalfe. (*C. buddleioides* ×*C. cotoneaster*.) Erect shrub, to 2m. Br. twisted, introverted at first, then ascending. Lvs sparse, bronze to silver-black, spathulate to oblanceolate, base narrowed and decurrent to petiole. Late spring. 'Bronze King': erect to 2.2m; lvs dark green suffused bronze. 'Bronze Knight': br. dense, twiggy; lvs green suffused bronze; more erect and branched than 'Bronze Lady'. 'Bronze Lady': br. v. dense, to 3m; lvs bronze above. 'Cheesemanii': erect to 3m; br. spreading; lvs alt., oblanceolate-elliptic, 4.5×1cm. 'Red Wonder': fr. deep red. 'Yellow Wonder': fr. yellow.

Coronaria L. = *Lychnis*.

Coronil *Ormosia panamensis*.

Coronilla L. Leguminosae (Papilionoideae). CROWN VETCH. 20 herbs and shrubs. Lvs imparipinnate, sometimes uni- or trifoliolate; lfts blue-green to dark green. Fls pea-like, radiating in long-stalked umbels. Eur., Asia, Afr.

C. cappadocica Willd. = *C. orientalis*.

C. coronata L. Perenn. herb, 30–70cm. Lvs pinnate, glaucous; lfts 1.5–3cm, obovate-elliptic, in 3–6 pairs. Fls 7–10mm, yellow, in 10–20-fld umbels. Summer. C & S Eur. Z6.

C. cretica L. Ann. herb, 10–70cm. Lvs pinnate, mid-green; lfts 0.5–2cm in 3–8 pairs, obovate-oblong. Fls 4–7mm, white or pink, in 3–6-fld umbels. SE Eur., S & E It. Z8.

C. elegans Pančić. Similar to *C. varia* but lfts 2–5cm, in 3–5 pairs, pruinose beneath. Fls 8–10mm, in 6–18-fld umbels. Albania to Czech. and Ukraine. Z6.

C. emeroides Boiss. & Sprun. = *C. emerus* ssp. *emeroides*.

C. emerus L. SCORPION SENNA. Everg. shrub, 30cm-2.5m. Branchlets somewhat glaucous, angled. Lvs 2.5–6cm, pinnate, emerald green; lfts 1–2cm, in 2–4 pairs, obovate, somewhat glaucous beneath. Fls 14–20mm, fragant, yellow, 2–3 in short-stalked axill. umbels; standard striped red at base. Fr. 5–11cm, segmented, like a scorpion's tail. Spring–autumn. C & S Eur. ssp. *emeroides* (Boiss. & Sprun.) Hayek. Lfts usually 7. Umbels longer-stalked, 4–8-fld. SE Eur. Z6.

C. glauca L. = *C. valentina* ssp. *glauca*.

C. iberica Steven = *C. orientalis*.

C. juncea L. Shrub to 1m. St. terete, rush-like, arching. Lvs pinnate; lfts 0.5–2.5cm, in 2–3 pairs, linear or narrow-oblong. Peduncles to 10cm; fls yellow, 6–12mm, in 5–12-fld umbels. W Medit. to S Port. and W Balk. Z8.

C. minima L. Sprawling, glaucous shrub to 30cm. Lfts 0.2–1.5cm, in 2–6 pairs, elliptic or obovate to rounded. Fls 5–8mm, yellow, fragrant, 5–12 per umbel. Summer. SW Eur. to NW Fr., SW Switz., E It. Z7.

C. montana Scop. = *C. coronata*.

C. orientalis Mill. Mill. Perenn., prostrate herb, 6–40cm. Lvs pinnate, glaucous; lfts to 2cm, cuneate, in 3–5 pairs, ciliate. Fls 12–18mm, yellow, 3–9 in umbels. Summer. Asia Minor. Z8.

C. scorpioides (L.) Koch. Ann. herb to 40cm. Lvs glaucous, simple or trifoliolate; term. leaflet largest to 4cm, elliptic to semi-orbicular. Fls yellow, 4–8mm, 2–5 per umbel. S Eur. Z7.

C. securidacea L. Ann. herb, 10–50cm. Lvs pinnate; lfts cuneate, in 5–8 pairs. Fls 8–17mm yellow. Medit., N Middle E, Cauc. Z8.

C. vaginalis Lam. Shrub to 50cm. Lfts 0.4–1cm, in 2–6 pairs. Fls 6–10mm, yellow, 4–10 per umbel. Mts of C Eur., It., Balk., Albania. Z6.

C. valentina L. Spreading everg. shrub to 1.5m. Young st. blue-green. Lvs 3–5cm; lfts 0.6–2cm, in 3–6 pairs, broadly obovate, mucronulate, vivid green above, glaucescent beneath. Fls 7–12mm, golden yellow, strongly fragrant, 7–12mm, 4–12 per umbel, on stalks to 7.5cm. Spring–summer. Medit., S Port. 'Citrina': fls pale milky yellow. 'Variegata': lvs strongly variegated creamy yellow; fls vibrant yellow. ssp. *glauca* (L.) Battand. Differs in 2–3 pairs of lfts, broadly obovate to obcordate, blue-green, glaucous. Fls lemon yellow. Winter–summer. Medit., Aegean, N Afr. 'Variegata': lvs and young st. variegated sea-green and creamy yellow. Z9.

C. varia L. CROWN VETCH. Perenn. herb, 20–120cm, ascending or prostrate. Lvs green; lfts 0.6–2cm, oblong or cuneate, in 3–14 pairs. Fls 10–15mm, white, purple or pink, 4–20 per umbel. Summer–autumn. C & S Eur. 'Emerald': vigorous, creeping st. to 2m long; fls pale pink. 'Penngift': habit neat, to 60cm tall; st. creeping; fls pink. Z6.

C. viminalis Salisb. Procumbent shrub. Lfts obovate, 13–21, emarginate. Fls 6–10 per umbel, white or rose; standard striped red. Summer. Alg. Z9.

→*Securigera*.

Correa Andrews. AUSTRALIAN FUCHSIA. Rutaceae. 11 everg. shrubs or trees. Lvs simple, coriaceous. Fls axillary or term., solitary or in few-fld cymes; cal. cupular, entire to 4-lobed; cor. tubular, 4-lobed, exterior often tomentose; sta. 8, usually exserted. Late summer to spring. Aus. Z9.

C. aemula (Lindl.) F. Muell. HAIRY CORREA. Spreading shrub to 2m; br. tomentose. Lvs to 4cm, ovate-lanceolate to orbicular, scabrous above, tomentose beneath. Fls to 3cm, dull green to blue-green or purple, pendent. Vict., S Aus.

C. alba Andrews WHITE CORREA. Spreading shrub to 2m; tomentose. Lvs to 4cm, ovate to orbicular, subglabrous above, white-tomentose beneath. Fls to 2cm, white, waxy. NSW, Vict., Tasm., S Aus. 'Pinkie': to 1.5m; fls pale pink.

C. backhousiana Hook. Dense, spreading shrub to 2m, orange-brown tomentose. Lvs to 3cm, ovate to elliptic, base rounded or cuneate, smooth above, tomentose beneath. Fls to 2.5cm, cream to pale green or orange-brown. Tasm., Vict.

C. ×bicolor Paxt. (*C. alba* ×*C. pulchella*.) Fls to 2.5cm, tubular, tube crimson, lobes and interior white. Gdn orig.

C. calycina J.M. Black. Shrub to 3m; br. sparsely tomentose. Lvs to 4cm, oblong to ovate-oblong, subglabrous above, pale green and slightly pubesc. beneath. Fls to 3cm, green, pendent. S Aus.

C. decumbens F. Muell. Spreading shrub to 1m; br. prostrate, tomentose. Lvs to 3.5cm, narrowly oblong, lustrous dark green and glab. above, grey to brown and tomentose beneath. Fls to 2.5cm, red tipped green, erect, tubular. S Aus. Z8.

C. × harrisii Paxt. (*C. pulchella* × *C. reflexa*). Fls to 3cm, tubular, scarlet. Gdn orig.

C. lawrenciana Hook. MOUNTAIN CORREA. Dense shrub or small tree to 8m; br. grey-tomentose. Lvs to 8cm, ovate to oblong, obtuse, downy beneath. Fls to 3cm, cream to green, sometimes red. NSW, Vict., Tasm.

C. neglecta Ashby = *C. pulchella*.

C. pulchella Mackay ex Sweet. Prostrate shrub to 1.5m. Lvs to 2cm, ovate; elliptic or oblong, glab., green. Fls to 2.5cm, orange to pink-red, sometimes white, pendent. S Aus.

C. reflexa (Labill.) Vent. COMMON CORREA. Erect or prostrate shrub to 3m. Lvs to 5cm, broadly ovate or lanceolate to ovate-oblong, subglabrous above, white-tomentose beneath. Fls to 4cm, white to green, pink or red, pendent. Aus. var. **cardinalis** (F. Muell. ex Hook.) Court. Lvs oblong. Fls bright red tipped green. Vict.

C. schlechtendalii Behr. Erect shrub to 2.5m; br. rusty-tomentose when young. Lvs to 4.5cm, broadly elliptic or ovate, aromatic, above, subglabrous or tomentose beneath. Fls to 2.5cm, red and green, tubular. S Aus.

C. cvs. 'Carmine Bells': fls carmine, tubular, nodding. 'Dusky Bells': fls dull red to pink. 'Ivory Bells': fls white, tubular, nodding. 'Marion's Marvel': fls pink at neck, suffused to lime green skirt, strongly pendulous.

C. speciosa Donn ex Andrews = *C. reflexa*.

Correosa *Rhus microphylla*.

Corryocactus Britt. & Rose. Cactaceae. 20 shrubby or tree-like cacti; st. erect, ascending or procumbent, cylindric; ribs 4–10; spines often fierce. Fls campanulate; tube short; floral areoles felted and spiny. Fr. globose, spiny. Peru, Boliv., Chile.

C. aureus (Meyen) P.C. Hutchison ex F. Buxb. Low shrub forming colonies; st. 10–20×3–5cm, usually not segmented, ±clavate; ribs 5–8, c1cm high; spines to 6cm, brown to almost black. Fls c4cm, yellow. N Chile, S Peru. Z9.

C. brachypetalus (Vaup.) Britt. & Rose. Shrub 2–4m, br. numerous, fastigiate, 6–10cm diam.; ribs 7–8; spines black at first, most to 1cm, longest 10–16cm. Fls c6cm; inner tep. deep orange. Fr. 6–7cm diam., green-yellow, edible. S Peru. Z9.

C. brevistylus (Schum. ex Vaup.) Britt. & Rose. Robust shrub, branching below, to 1.5–3(–5)m, sometimes with short trunk; st. segmented, 8–15cm diam.; ribs 6–9; spines to 10(–20)cm. Fls 8–11cm, yellow; throat expanded. S Peru. Z9.

C. erectus (Backeb.) Ritter. Erect or clambering to 3m; st. slender, 15–33mm diam.; ribs 5–11; spines 14–18, red-brown or tinged yellow. Fls 3–4cm, scarlet-pink or fiery red. S Peru. Z9.

C. maximus Backeb. = *C. squarrosus*.

C. melanotrichus (Schum.) Britt. & Rose St. erect, branching and clustering, 1–2m×3–6cm; ribs 7–9; spines 1.5–7cm. Fls 6–8cm, purple-red. Boliv. Z9.

C. pulquinensis Cárdenas. St. to 4m×4cm, sometimes clambering, 4–5-ribbed; 0.5–2cm. Fls to 7.5cm, orange-yellow. Boliv. Z9.

C. spiniflorus (Philippi) P.C. Hutchison = *Austrocactus spiniflorus*.

C. squarrosus (Vaup.) P.C. Hutchison. St. prostrate or suberect to 50cm, br. c25×2–2.5cm; ribs 7–8, compressed; central spine 1, strong; radial spines to 10, unequal. Fls 4–4.5cm, yellow to red. C Peru. Z9.

→*Erdisia*.

Corsican Curse *Soleirolia soleirolii*.
Corsican Heath *Erica terminalis*.
Corsican Mint *Mentha requienii*.
Corsican Pine *Pinus nigra* var. *maritima*.

Cortaderia Stapf. PAMPAS GRASS. Gramineae. 24 large tussock-forming perenn. grasses. St. robust, coarse. Lvs crowded at base, long, stiff, narrow-linear, glaucous, margins rough to v. sharp. Infl. showy, plumed, silver-white to pale rose or golden. Summer–autumn. S Amer., NZ, New Guinea. Z8.

C. argentea (Nees) Stapf = *C. selloana* 'Elegans'.
C. conspicua F. Forst. = *Chionochloa conspicua*.
C. fulvida (Buch.) Zotov. To 1.8m. Lvs long, curved, narrow, nerved, forming large tussocks. Pan. pale, tawny, 30–60cm. NZ.
C. jubata (Lemoine) Stapf. Stapf. Resembles *C. selloana* but infl. looser, br. nodding. To 3m. Lvs to 120cm, arching, scabrous, tough. Pan. to 60cm; br. nodding, yellow tinged red to purple. Autumn. W Trop. Amer. Sometimes misnamed *C. rudiuscula*.
C. quila (Nees & Mey.) Stapf = *C. jubata*.

C. richardii (Endl.) Zotov. TOE TOE; PLUMED TUSSOCK. To 3m. Lvs to 120cm, recurved. Infl. to 60cm, white, tinged yellow or silver. Summer–autumn. NZ.
C. rosea hort. = *C. selloana* 'Rosea'.
C. rubra hort. = *C. selloana* 'Violacea'.
C. selloana (Schult. & Schult. f.) Asch. & Gräbn. To 3m. Lvs narrow, to 270cm, arching, margins scabrous. Pan. oblong to pyramidal, to 120cm, silver-white, tinged red or purple. Autumn. Temp. S Amer. 'Albolineata' ('Silver Stripe'): compact, slow-growing; lvs edged white. 'Aureolineata' ('Gold Band'): small; lvs broadly edged rich yellow, later deep gold; hardy. 'Bertinii': dwarf to 1m; all parts miniature. 'Carminea Rendatleri': culms to 2.5cm high; weak; plumes pink flushed purple. 'Carnea': pan. soft pink. 'Elegans' ('Argentea'): pan. silvery white. 'Marabout': culms erect; pan. large, dense, pure white. 'Monstrosa': large, mound-forming, to 2m; st. to 3m; pan. to 70cm. 'Pumila': dwarf, to 1.5m, compact; floriferous. 'Roi des Roses': pan. flushed pink. 'Rosea' ('Rosa Feder'): pan. lightly tinted pink. 'Silver Beacon': lvs rigid, more erect, edged white; culms tinted purple. 'Silver Cornet': lvs striped cream; st. to 1.2m. 'Sunningdale Silver': habit large, culms to 3.5m; plumes dense, white; wind-resistant, sturdy. 'Variegata': lvs striped cream. 'Violacea': pan. tinted violet. 'White Feather': pan. to 2m high, white. Z5.

→*Gynerium* and *Arundo*.

Cortusa L. Primulaceae. 8 perenn. herbs. Lvs basal, long-petiolate, orbicular to cordate. Fls to 1cm diam., slender-stalked, nodding in scapose umbels subtended by leafy bracts; cal. 5-lobed; cor., 5-lobed, infundibuliform. Summer. Mts of C Eur. to N Asia. Z7.

C. matthioli L. Rusty-pubesc. throughout. Lvs to 25cm, reniform to suborbicular, with coarsely dentate lobes. Scapes to 35cm; bracts laciniate; cor. purple-violet to magenta. W Eur. f. **pekinensis** Richter. Lvs 7–9-lobed, deeply incised, densely hirsute. f. **pubens** (Schott, Nyman & Kotschy) Schur. Lvs deeply and broadly lobed coarsely dentate. Transylvania.

C. semenovii Herd. Lvs to 8cm, rounded or reniform, lobed, dentate, glab. except for hairy veins. Scapes to 10cm; bracts erose-denticulate; cor. pale yellow. Summer. C Asia.

Coryanthes Hook. HELMET ORCHID; BUCKET ORCHID. Orchidaceae. 12 epiphytic orchids. Pbs to 15cm, squat-cylindric to elongate-ovoid. Lvs to 60cm, broadly lanceolate, obscurely plicate, petiolate. Infl. basal, arching to pendulous; fls waxy, fragrant, short-lived; sep. broadly elliptic, wing-like; pet. reflexed, narrower and shorter than sep.; lip complex: hypochile a concave, saccate 'helmet', mesochile slender, tube-like expanding into bucket-shaped epichile; column stout, arched, winged. Summer. Trop. Amer. Z10.

C. biflora Barb. Rodr. Dors. sep. 4×5.5cm, translucent bronze, lat. sep. to 12×8cm, light brown spotted oxblood; pet. to 6×1.5cm, ivory, spotted or ringed blood red; epichile interior ivory spotted blood red, fading to orange, exterior yellow flushed red. Venez., Braz., Peru.

C. maculata Hook. Fls variable, to 9cm diam.; tep. membranous, yellow-ochre spotted purple or maroon, lip yellow spotted oxblood. Panama, Colomb., Venez., Guianas, Braz.

C. speciosa (Hook.) Hook. Tep. light bronze, spotted maroon, epichile ivory within, mottled maroon, exterior ivory or buff, flushed red-purple, interior spotting visible through translucent walls; dors. sep. to 2×2.5cm, lat. sep. to 6×4cm; pet. to 3.5×0.8cm; lip to 6cm. Guat. to Peru.

Corybas Salisb. Orchidaceae. c50 tuberous, terrestrial orchids. Lf solitary, rounded, ovate-cordate lying flat on surface of soil. Fl. solitary, unstalked; dors. sep. erect, forming a hood, lat. sep. and pet. linear, minute; lip erect, short-tubular, margin recurved denticulate or fringed. Spring–Summer. Indomal., Aus., NZ. Z9.

C. aconitiflorus Salisb. Fl. to 4cm; dors. sep. purple-brown, rounded, concave, lat. sep. to 5mm; lip white, marked purple or red, margin recurved. E Aus., Tasm., NZ.

C. diemenicus Lindl. Fl. to 2.5cm; dors. sep. narrow-ovate, concave, green-grey blotched and spotted purple to maroon, lat. sep. to 2mm; lip with a yellow or white channelled central plate, margins denticulate. C & S Aus., Tasm.

C. fimbriatus (R. Br.) Rchb. f. Fl. to 3cm, crimson to purple-red; dors. sep. cuneate transparent, spotted purple-red, lat. sep. linear, minute; lip purple, margins fringed. E Aus.

C. pruinosus (R. Cunn.) Rchb. f. Fls to 3cm, grey-green marked maroon; dors. sep. narrow, concave, projecting beyond lip, lat. sep. to 2mm, filiform; lip with red central patch, calli many. SE Aus.

→*Corysanthes*.

Corydalis Vent. Papaveraceae. *c*300 rhizomatous or tuberous ann. or perenn. herbs. Lvs basal and alt. on st., compound, usually biternate, triangular in outline; lfts often divided. Fls in rac.; cor. tubular, pet. 4, in pairs, outer pair with reflexed tips and basal spur, the inner pair convergent, enclosing sta. and style. N temp. regions, esp. the Sino-Himal. area, and S Afr.

C. ×*allenii* hort. ex W. Irv. non Fedde. Hybrid involving *C. bracteata*. Perenn. to 25cm. St. unbranched. Lvs to 25cm, glaucous, lfts oblong, obtuse. Fls racemose, cream, streaked purple, to 2cm, spur to 1cm. Late spring. Gdn origin. Z6.

C. allenii Fedde non hort. = *C. scouleri*.

C. ambigua Cham. & Schlecht. St. numerous. Lvs ternate, lobes entire glaucous. Fls azure, in dense, showy rac., inner pet. light blue, spur deltoid. Spring to summer. Jap. Z6.

C. angustifolia (Bieb.) DC. Tuberous perenn., to 20cm. St. single. Lvs 2–3, biternate, laciniate, lfts lanceolate-oblong. Fls to 2cm, racemose, pale yellow or white, spur strongly recurved, to 1cm. Early spring. Cauc. Z6.

C. aurea (Muhlenb. ex Willd.) Willd. To 60cm. Ann. or bienn. producing dense leafy rosette. St. many, glaucous. Lvs bipinnate, lobes dissected. Fls to 1.5cm, racemose, yellow, spur to 0.5cm, straight or downward-pointing. Spring. N Amer. Z6.

C. bracteata (Stephan) Pers. Tuberous perenn., to 35cm. St. unbranched. Lvs 2, biternate, lfts deeply divided into linear lobes. Fls 2.5–4.5cm, light yellow, in rac., spur to 1.5cm. Spring. C Sib. Z7.

C. bulbosa (L.) DC. Tuberous perenn. to 15cm. Lvs 2, bipinnate, lfts cuneate, lobed. Fls 2–2.5cm, 10–20 in erect rac., tubular, horizontal, violet, dull purple or white, spur curved downwards. Early spring. C Eur. 'Albiflora' ('Alba'): fls white. Z6.

C. cashmeriana Royle. Perenn. to 25cm. St. unbranched. Lvs ternate, bright green, lfts 1.5–2cm, oblong or elliptic. Fls 1–2cm, in dense, 3–8-fld rac., bright blue, apices dark blue, spur to 1cm, curved. Summer. Himal. Z5.

C. cava (L.) Schweig. & Körte = *C. bulbosa*.

C. chaerophylla DC. non Royle. Perenn., to 75cm. Lvs long-petioled, biternate, lfts pinnatifid. Fls to 1.5cm, bright yellow, racemose, spur to 1cm, straight or slightly curved downward. Spring. C Himal. Z5.

C. cheilanthifolia Hemsl. Perenn. Almost stemless. Lvs 15–45cm, brown-green, clustered in a dense rosette, long-petioled, ferny, 2–3-pinnate. Scapes to 45cm, simple or branched; fls to 1.5cm, bright yellow, spur straight. Early spring. C China. Z6.

C. chionophylla Czerniak. Lvs subsessile, lat. lfts entire. Fls white; lower outer pet. with a maroon patch at apex. Spring. Iran. Z8.

C. clavibracteata Ludlow & Stearn. To 10cm, forming cushions. Lvs oblong, crowded, finely dissected, appearing cristate, glaucous grey-green. Fls yellow, in erect or spreading rac.; lower outer pet. with a central brown band. Summer. W Nepal. Z6.

C. claviculata (L.) DC. CLIMBING CORYDALIS. Ann. St. to 1m, climbing, slender. Lvs long-petioled, 1–2-pinnate, lfts entire, reduced to a tendril at apex. Fls to 0.6cm, in axill. rac.; pale yellow, streaked with pink, inner pet. tipped dark red, spur short. Summer. Eur. Z6.

C. cornuta Royle. Differs from *C. vaginalis* in st. erect, inner pet. tipped purple. Spring. Himal. Z6.

C. diphylla Wallich. Lvs long-stalked; lobes linear-lanceolate, glaucescent. Fls 6–10 in a term. rac.; pet. white, outer pet. deep maroon at apex. Spring. W Himal. Z5.

C. flavula (Raf.) DC. Differs from *C. aurea*, in fls small with a high crest and v. short, downward-pointing spur. Spring. N Amer. Z6.

C. glauca Pursh = *C. sempervirens*.

C. glaucescens Reg. Branching from half way up st., glaucous. Fls nodding, broadly winged, pink to red, in erect, loose rac., spur straight. Spring to summer. C Asia. Z8.

C. gortschakovii Schrenk. Differs from *C. rupestris* in leaflet lobes 3 times larger, floral bracts deeply divided into many lobes. Spring. Himal. to NW China. Z6.

C. halleri (Willd.) Willd. = *C. solida*.

C. latiflora Hook. f. & Thoms. Lvs biternate, lobes obtuse, purple-grey, glaucous. Fls clustered in a spreading rac.; pet. broadly crested, blue-grey, tinged mauve at apex, strongly scented, outer pet. with a brown-black band, spur short, downward-curving. Summer. Himal. Z5.

C. lineariloba Sieb. & Zucc. Lvs pinnate; lobes ovate, acute. Fls few, to 2cm, white; outer pet. with light mauve, reflexed apical lips; not spurred, inner pet. tipped maroon. Summer. E Asia. Z9.

C. lutea (L.) DC. Bushy perenn., to 40cm. Lvs deltoid in outline, 2–3-pinnate, arching and ferny, green above, glaucous beneath. Fls in axill., rac.; cor. golden yellow; spur short, nearly straight. Late spring. Eur. 'Alba': fls white. Z6.

C. nariniana Lvs subsessile, lfts unequal, ternate or biternate, obtuse. Fls to 2cm, with a deep pink cor. tube,

white at apex, in a loose, erect rac.; outer pet. white and reflexed at apex, spur to 1.5cm. Summer. Cauc. Z5.

C. nobilis (L.) Pers. Perenn., to 80cm. Lvs ± sessile, glaucous, 2-pinnate at base, lfts cuneate. Fls in dense term. rac.; cor. 2–2.5cm, pale yellow, tipped brown and dark purple, spur short, downward-pointing. Spring. Sib. Z6.

C. ochotensis Turcz. Bienn. or ann., to 60cm. St. angular, winged. Lvs deltoid in outline, long-petioled, 2–3-pinnate. Fls 1.7–2cm, in simple or branched rac.; cor. yellow, maroon at tip, spur tapering, downward-curving. Summer–late autumn. N. China, Jap., Korea. Z7.

C. ochroleuca Koch. Perenn., to 45cm, similar to *C. lutea*. Lvs glaucous; petioles flattened. Fls to 1.5cm, pale yellow, in dense axill. rac., more sharply downward-curving than in *C. lutea*. Summer–late autumn. SE Eur. Z5.

C. ophiocarpa Hook. f. & Thoms. Perenn. to 75cm. Lvs in a dense rosette, 10–50cm, grey-green, bipinnate. Fls to 1.2cm, crowded in term. rac.; ivory, inner pet. tipped dark red, spur to 3mm, ascending. Spring. E Himal. Z6.

C. oppositifolia DC. To 8cm. Lvs pinnate ternate to biternate, grey-green. Fls to 3.5cm, pink, streaked purple, spur to 1.5cm. Spring. Anatolia, Kurdistan. Z8.

C. pallida (Thunb.) Pers. Perenn. to 45cm, clustered, leafy. Rac. many-fld, 2.5–12.5cm; fls 2.5cm, bright yellow, lip spotted brown, spur short. N & E China, Japan, Korea. Z6.

C. parnassica Orph. & Heldr. To 7cm. Lvs to 6cm, biternate; glaucous blue-green lobes obtuse. Fls light grey-mauve, in erect, dense rac.; outer pet. crested, inner pet. tipped maroon, spur downward-curving. Late summer. Greece. Z7.

C. persica Cham. & Schltr. Plants offered under this name are usually *C. nariniana*.

C. popovii Nevski. Lvs ternate, lobes ovate, glaucous, blue-green. Fls in erect rac.; pet. white, upper outer pet. dark maroon at apex, outer pet. with a maroon, concave lip, spurs downward-curving. Spring. C Asia. Z8.

C. ramosa Wallich = *C. vaginans*.

C. rosea Maxim. Perenn. to 60cm. St. branching. Fls to 10, in loose term. rac.; cor. to 2.5cm, pink to red, spur to 1cm. Spring. China. Z6.

C. rupestris Kotschy ex Boiss. Perenn. to 20cm. St. many. Lvs somewhat succulent, bipinnate, pinnules to 0.5cm. Fls in short, term. rac.; cor. yellow, outer pet. with broad wings at apices, spur short, swollen. Spring. Iran. Z6.

C. rutifolia Sibth. & Sm. Perenn. to 20cm. Lvs 2-ternate, lfts ovate, entire or trifid. Fls in 6–12-fld rac.; cor. to 2.5cm, violet with dark purple tips, spur ascending, inflated. Spring. Mts of Asia Minor, Eur. Z6.

C. saxicola Bunting. Perenn. to 30cm. Lvs to 37.5cm, shiny, pinnate, pinnae 5–7, 2.5–7.5cm, divided ×3 into ovate or obovate-cuneate lobes. Fls in spreading rac.; cor. yellow, to 2.5cm, lower pet. pouched, spur to 5mm. Spring–summer. C China. Z7.

C. scouleri Hook. Perenn. to 1m. St. much branched. Lvs grey-green, pinnatisect, lfts 3-pinnate, lobes entire. Fls 15–25 in rac.; cor. to 3cm, pink or white, spur slender. Early summer. N Amer. Z6.

C. sempervirens (L.) Pers. ROMAN WORMWOOD; ROCK HARLEQUIN. Glaucous ann. or bienn. to 40cm. Lvs ternately divided with few pairs of pinnae. Fls in loose rac.; cor. to 15mm, pale pink to purple, apex yellow, spur short, obtuse. Summer. NE US and Canada. 'Alba': fls white. 'Rosea': fls rose. Z6.

C. shanginii B. Fedtsch. To 20cm. Lvs biternate, lobes ovate, glaucous blue-green. Fls to 5cm, white, in long, dense rac.; inner pet. dark-tipped, spur downward-curving. Summer. C Asia. Z8.

C. sibirica (L. f.) Pers. Differs from *C. ochotensis* in lf lobes narrower. Fls to 9mm, yellow. Summer. N Asia. Z6.

C. solida (L.) Sw. FUMEWORT. Perenn., to 20cm. Lvs 2-ternate, lfts deeply and unevenly dissected, lobes lanceolate-oblong. Fls to 20 in erect rac.; cor. to 2cm, pale mauve pink to light red with dark tips, spur tapered. Often confused with *C. bulbosa*. Spring. N Eur., Asia. 'George P. Baker': fls deep red-salmon. Z6.

C. thalictrifolia Jameson ex Reg. = *C. cornuta*.

C. thalictrifolia Franch. non Jameson ex Reg. = *C. saxicola*.

C. tomentella Franch. Perenn. to 30cm. Lvs bipinnate, glaucous grey, downy, lfts ovate. Fls bright yellow, tipped green, in dense, erect rac. to 20cm. Summer. China. Z6.

C. transsylvanica hort. = *C. solida*.

C. vaginans Royle. Glaucous ann. or bienn. St. branching, often decumbent. Lvs 2–3-ternate, lfts deeply divided, term. seg. elliptic-obovate. Fls to 2cm in loose rac.; cor. yellow veined brown, darker at apex, outer pet. crested, spur tapered, downward-curving. Summer. NW Himal. Z5.

C. verticillaris DC. Perenn., to 15cm. Lvs to 10cm, trifid, lfts 3–4-pinnate, terminal seg. linear to narrow-elliptic. Fls to

2.5cm, in a term. rac., pale pink tipped maroon, spur downward-curving. Early spring. Iraq, Iran. Z6.

C. vesicaria (L.) Pers. Ann., climbing, to 1m. Lvs bipinnate, lfts entire or cut, elliptic, becoming reduced to tendrils. Fls to 0.5cm, in axill. rac.; pet. yellow, outer pet. broadly winged, spur short. Spring–summer. S Afr. Z8.

C. wendelboi Lvs in a basal rosette, biternate; lobes oblong, glaucous. Scape stout; fls to 2cm, pale pink to mauve, in crowded, arching rac.; inner pet. tipped dark purple. Summer. Turk. Z9.

C. wilsonii N.E. Br. Perenn. to 30cm. St. short. Lvs to 7.5cm, glaucous, pinnate, lfts entire or incised, oblong. Rac. several; fls to 2cm; pet. bright yellow, tipped yellow-green, spur to 0.5cm, blunt. Spring. C China. Z7.

C. zeaensis Mikhailova. To 25cm. Lvs biternate, lobes ovate-lanceolate, glaucous blue-green. Scapes red; fls to 3cm, facing downward, red, in branching rac., inner pet. tipped yellow, spur straight, tapering. Summer. E Sib. Z5.

→*Calocapnos, Cysticapnos* and *Fumaria.*

Corylopsis Sieb. & Zucc. WINTER HAZEL. Hamamelidaceae. 30 decid., usually spreading, shrubs or small trees. Br. slender, often downy when young. Lvs alt., petiolate, broadly ovate, veins pronounced. Fls fragrant in pendent rac., appearing before lvs, bracts colourless to translucent green to light brown; sep. 5; pet. 5, yellow; sta. 5. Bhutan to Jap. Z6 unless specified.

C. glabrescens Franch. & Savat. Shrub or small tree to 5m. Shoots glab. Lvs to 8cm, broadly ovate, acuminate, base cordate, glaucous beneath, veins to 12 pairs. Infl. 2.5cm, bracts usually glossy, downy; pet. v. pale yellow, to 8mm, orbicular to ovate; anth. yellow or purple. Spring. Jap., Korea.

C. gotoana Mak. = *C. glabrescens.*

C. griffithii Hemsl. Like *C. himalayana*, but more commonly cult. Lvs larger, to 20cm, to 17 pairs veins. Infl. to 9cm. Himal.

C. griffithii Hemsl. = *C. himalayana* var. *griffithii.*

C. himalayana Griff. Shrub or small tree to 5m. Shoots densely downy or stellate-pubesc. Lvs to 10cm, broadly ovate to lanceolate, acute, base cordate to cuneate, glab. or pilose to brown-tomentose beneath, veins woolly, 8–12 pairs. Infl. to 6cm; bracts glab. to silky, light brown; pet. to 6mm, palest yellow, obovate to elliptic. Early spring. Himal.

C. multiflora Hance. Shrub or small tree to 4m. Shoots stellate pubesc. Lvs to 15cm, ovate to obovate or broadly lanceolate to elliptic, acuminate, base cordate, usually glaucous and downy beneath. Infl. to 7×1.5cm; fls 10–20 pale yellow on softly hairy to woolly axis. Jap.

C. pauciflora Sieb. & Zucc. BUTTERCUP WITCH-HAZEL. Shrub to 3m. Shoots glab. Lvs to 6.5cm, ovate, base cordate, bright green above, glaucous beneath, veins to 9 pairs. Infl. to 3cm; fls large and open, fragrant; bracts glab. to glossy-downy; pet. primrose yellow, to 8mm, oblong-obovate; anth. light yellow. Early spring. Jap., Taiwan.

C. platypetala Rehd. & Wils. = *C. sinensis* var. *calvescens.*

C. sinensis Hemsl. Shrub to 5m. Shoots glab. or downy. Lvs to 12cm, obovate to oblong, acuminate, base rounded or cordate, glaucous and downy beneath, veins 7–12 pairs. Infl. to 8cm; bracts usually downy; pet. lemon yellow, to 8mm, rounded; anth. yellow. China. var. *sinensis.* Lf usually pubesc. between veins beneath, often with network of secondary veins. China. 'Spring Purple': young st. purple-violet. var. *calvescens* Morley & Chao. Lf petioles glab., lf surfaces glab. between veins beneath. Fls pale primrose, broad.

C. spicata Sieb. & Zucc. SPIKE WITCH-HAZEL. Shrub to 3m. Shoots pubesc. Lvs 4–11cm, ovate to obovate, acuminate, base rounded to cordate, glaucous and downy beneath, veins 6–7 pairs. Fls clustered at top of infl. to 6cm; bracts usually downy; pet. bright yellow, to 9mm, obovate; anth. red, brown or purple. Spring. Jap.

C. veitchiana Bean = *C. sinensis* var. *calvescens.*

C. willmottiae Rehd. & Wils. = *C. sinensis* var. *sinensis.*

C. wilsonii Hemsl. = *C. multiflora.*

C. yunnanensis Diels = *C. sinensis* var. *sinensis.*

Corylus L. HAZEL. Betulaceae (Corylaceae). 15 decid. shrubs or small trees. Shrubs often thicket-forming. Lvs usually ovate to obovate, double-serrate. ♂ catkins in clusters of 2–5, pendulous, to 7.5cm. ♀ catkins bud-like with protruding red styles. Fr. a hard brown nut, in clusters at br. tips, surrounded by 2 bracts. N temp. zone.

C. americana Marsh. AMERICAN HAZEL. Multistemmed shrub, to 3m. Young shoots glandular-pubesc. Lvs broadly ovate, cordate or rounded at base, short-acuminate, to 12cm, sparsely hairy above, downy beneath, biserrate; petiole glandular-pubesc. Fr. in groups of 2–6, ellipsoid-ovoid, to 1.5cm, bracts to 2.5cm, downy, jaggedly cut. Spring. E N Amer. Z4.

C. avellana L. HAZELNUT; COBNUT. Multistemmed shrub to 6m, rarely tree to 10m. Bark light grey-brown, peeling. Lvs orbicular, abruptly acuminate, to 10cm, with stiff hairs above, hairy on veins beneath, margins with acute teeth, scalloped toward base. Fr. in term. clusters of 1–4, ovoid, to 2cm, bracts overlapping, to 1cm, deeply jaggedly toothed or incised, sparsely hairy. Spring. Eur. 'Aurea': lvs yellow-green. 'Contorta' (CORKSCREW HAZEL; HARRY LAUDER'S WALKING STICK): br. and shoots strongly spiralling. Lvs contorted. 'Heterophylla' ('Quercifolia', 'Laciniata'): lvs ovate, with deep, deltoid lobes. 'Pendula': br. arching, forming a weeping, small tree. Z4.

C. chinensis Franch. CHINESE HAZEL. Tree, to 35m. Young shoots dark brown. Lvs ovate, acute, to 18cm, cordate at base, glab. above, hairy on veins beneath, serrate; petioles glandular-downy. Fr. in clusters of 3–6, finely hairy to glab.; bracts constricted above nut, cut into linear lobes. Spring. SW China. Z6.

C. colurna L. TURKISH HAZEL. Tree, to 30m. Bark buff-brown, corrugated. Crown pyramidal. Lvs broadly obovate, to 12.5cm, cordate at base, abruptly acuminate, lustrous dark green, bidentate to broadly shallow-lobed. Fr. closely clustered, to 2cm; bracts to 3cm, cut into linear lobes, finely glandular-bristly. Spring. SE Eur., Asia Minor, W Asia. Z5.

C. colurna var. *chinensis* (Franch.) Burkill = *C. chinensis.*

C. ×colurnoides Schneid. (*C. avellana* ×*C. colurna*) TRAZEL. Similar to *C. colurna.* Bark thinner, fissured. Lvs broader, more coarsely toothed. Fr. ovoid; bracts deeply lobed, glandular-hairy.

C. cornuta Marsh. BEAKED HAZEL. Multistemmed shrub, to 3m. Shoots slightly downy. Lvs ovate to obovate, cordate at base, acute, to 11cm, sparsely hairy above; downy on veins beneath, finely dentate, sometimes slightly lobed. Fr. occas. in pairs, to 1.5cm; bracts constricted past nut into a narrow tube to 3cm, downy with sparse bristles. Spring. N Amer. var. *californica* (A. DC.) Rose. Larger, to 8m. Lvs more downy beneath. Involucral tube shorter. W US. Z4.

C. davidiana Baill. = *Ostyropsis davidiana.*

C. ferox Wallich. Tree, to 10m. Young shoots pubesc. Lvs obovate, rounded to ovate at base, to 12cm, irregular biserrate. Fr. in clusters; bracts cup-like, densely spiny. Spring. Himal. Z8.

C. ferox var. *tibetica* (Batal.) Franch. = *C. tibetica.*

C. heterophylla Fisch. & Trautv. Shrub or small tree, to 7m. Br. glandular-hairy. Lvs ovate-round, abruptly acuminate, often abruptly obtuse, mucronulate, cordate at base, dentate, glab. above, downy beneath on veins. Fr. solitary or in pairs, bracts forming a campanulate tube to 2.5cm, incised with deltoid teeth to 1cm deep, or entire, glandular-hairy below. Spring. Jap., China. var. *sutchensis* Franch. Lvs glab. beneath, bract shorter than nut, lobed. C & W China. var. *yunnanensis* Franch. Lvs more densely arranged; petioles glandular-hairy. SW China. Z6.

C. jacquemontii Decne. Tree to 25m, similar to *C. colurna*, but new growth breaks up to one month earlier; lvs obovate, to 20cm, coarsely toothed; involucral bracts less densely glandular-pubesc. Spring. NW Himal. Z7.

C. mandschurica Maxim. & Rupr. = *C. sieboldiana* var. *mandschurica.*

C. maxima Mill. FILBERT. Habit as for *C. avellana.* Young shoots glandular-hairy, grey. Lvs slightly lobed, to 14cm, double-serrate in upper part. Fr. ovoid to oblong; bracts forming a nearly closed tube, deeply narrowly lobed, twice length of fr. Spring. SE Eur., Asia Minor. 'Purpurea' ('Atropurpurea'): lvs dark maroon-purple. Z5.

C. rostrata Ait. = *C. cornuta.*

C. rostrata var. *californica* A. DC. = *C. cornuta* var. *californica.*

C. sieboldiana Bl. JAPANESE HAZEL. Shrub to 5m. Lvs elliptic-oblong to obovate, to 10cm, often with a central rust-coloured patch, biserrate. Fr. 2–6 or solitary; bracts forming a tube to 3cm, constricted above fr. into a beak, bristly. Spring. Jap. var. *mandschurica* (Maxim. & Rupr.) Schneid. Lvs rounded to obovate, cordate at base, to 15cm, shallowly lobed above. Fr. conic; bracts to 5m, browny-hairy. Spring. China, Jap. Z6.

C. tibetica Batal. Shrub or tree to 15m. Young shoots glab. Lvs broadly ovate to obovate, cordate to rounded at base, to 12cm, veins downy beneath; petiole gland.-pubesc. Fr. in clusters of 3–6; bracts finely prickly. Spring. C China. Z7.

C. tubulosa Willd. = *C. maxima.*

C. ×vilmorinii Rehd. (*C. chinensis* ×*C. avellana.*) Tree, to 25m. Lvs smaller than in *C. chinensis*, less cordate at base, bracts not constricted above fr., regularly cut usually along one side. Spring. Gdn origin. Z5.

Corymborchis Thouars. Orchidaceae. 5 terrestrial orchids. Aerial st. reed-like, leafy. Fls white to green-white or yellow, often fragrant. Trop. Asia, Aus., S Pacific. Z10.

C. veratrifolia (Reinw.) Bl. To 1.5m. Lvs ovate, plicate. Fls clustered, fragrant; tep. green, linear to oblong-spathulate, dors. sep. concave, to 3×0.3cm, lateral sep. falcate, to 2.5×0.5cm, pet. recurved, undulate or crisped; lip white narrow, tublar below, apex expanded, ovate to suborbicular, undulate or crisped. Range as for the genus.

Corynabutilon (Schum.) Kearney.
C. vitifolium (Car.) Kearney = *Abutilon vitifolium*.

CORYNOCARPACEAE Engl. See *Corynocarpus*.

Corynocarpus Forst. & Forst. f. Corynocarpaceae. 4 everg. trees. Lvs alt., simple, entire. Fls small, 5-merous, in term. pan. Fr. a drupe. New Guinea, NE Aus., New Caled., Vanuatu, NZ.
C. laevigata Forst. & Forst. f. Upright to 50m. Lvs to 20cm, elliptic-oblong, coriaceous, glossy dark green. Fls green-white. Fr. to 3.25cm, orange. NZ. Z10.

Corypha L. Palmae. 8 giant monocarpic palms. St. solitary, erect. Lvs costapalmate; petiole thick, rigid, split at base, margins spiny; blade divided to half depth; seg. single-fold, rigid, undulate, shallowly divided at apex. Infl. term., pyramidal, branched ×4; rachillae in thousands, bearing a multitude of white to cream fls. Fr. *c.*3cm, globose, khaki to brown, smooth, 1-seeded. India, through Trop. Asia, Malay Archipel. and N Aus. Z10.
C. australis R. Br. = *Livistona australis*.
C. dulcis HBK = *Brahea dulcis*.
C. elata Roxb. = *C. utan*.
C. gembanga Bl. = *C. utan*.
C. minor Jacq. = *Sabal minor*.
C. obliqua Bartr. = *Serenoa repens*.
C. palma Bartr. = *Sabal palmetto*.
C. palmetto Walter = *Sabal palmetto*.
C. pumila Walter = *Sabal minor*.
C. repens Bartr. = *Serenoa repens*.
C. taliera Roxb. Trunk to 10m. Lf blades suborbicular or sub-peltate, shallowly divided into acuminate seg. Infl. about half length of trunk; rachillae *c*60cm, pendent.
C. tectorum HBK = *Copernicia tectorum*.
C. umbraculifera L. TALIPOT PALM. Trunk 12–24m to 60cm diam., ringed, but not furrowed. Lf blades to 4.8m; petiole to 3m, armed with short teeth. Infl. 6–8m; rachillae declinate, 15–35cm. Sri Lanka, S India.
C. utan Lam. GEBANG PALM. Trunk to 21m, to 75cm diam., ringed and furrowed. Lf blades to 6m, orbicular, seg. 80–100; petiole 2–4m, margins black with stout teeth. Infl. to 3m, conical rachillae to 40cm, spreading. Bengal, Burm., Philipp., Indo-china to N Aus.

Coryphantha (Engelm.) Lem. Cactaceae. 45 cacti; st. simple or clustering, globose to cylindric; spines normally developed, or sometimes modified into coloured glands. Fls funnelform or campanulate. SW US, Mex. Superficially like *Mammillaria*, but with grooved tubercles.
C. aggregata misapplied. = *Escobaria vivipara*.
C. alversonii (J. Coult. ex Zeissold) Orcutt = *Escobaria vivipara*.
C. andreae (Purpus & Boed.) A. Berger = *C. pycnacantha*.
C. arizonica (Engelm.) Britt. & Rose = *Escobaria vivipara*.
C. asperispina Boed. = *Escobaria missouriensis*.
C. asterias (Cels ex Salm-Dyck) Hubner = *C. ottonis*.
C. bella (Britt. & Rose) Fosb. = *Escobaria emskoetteriana*.
C. bergeriana Boed. St. simple, clavate, to 12×6cm, dark green; tubercles conic; central spines 4, upper 12mm, lower to 2cm; radial spines 17–20, upper 6–8 to 15mm, lower to 10mm. Fls 4×7cm; outer tep. olive-green with yellow margins; inner tep. yellow. Summer. Mex. Z9.
C. bisbeeana Orcutt = *Escobaria vivipara*.
C. bumamma (Ehrenb.) Britt. & Rose. Perhaps a var. of *C. elephantidens* or *C. sulcolanata*; spines all radial, 5–8; fls 5–6cm diam., pale yellow. Summer. SW Mex. Z9.
C. calcarata (Engelm.) Lem. = *C. sulcata*.
C. calochlora Boed. = *C. nickelsiae*.
C. chaffeyi (Britt. & Rose) Fosb. = *Escobaria dasyacantha* var. *chaffeyi*.
C. chihuahuensis (Britt. & Rose) A. Berger = *Escobaria chihua-huensis*.
C. chlorantha (Engelm.) Britt. & Rose = *Escobaria vivipara*.
C. clava (Pfeiff.) Lem. = *C. octacantha*.
C. clavata (Scheidw.) Backeb. Cylindric to clavate, to 7cm diam., dark blue-green; tubercles conic; central spines 0–1, yellow to brown; radial spines 8–9, 8–15mm, brown, dark-tipped. Fls to 5×4cm, pale yellow. Summer. C Mex. Z9.
C. compacta (Engelm.) Britt. & Rose. St. simple, depressed-globose, 3–6×5–8cm; tubercles 8mm; central spine 0, or straight, white; radial spines 14–16, 1–2cm, white, interlacing. Fls 2×2cm, yellow. Summer. NW Mex. Z9.

C. cornifera (DC.) Lem. St. simple, globose or ovoid, to 12cm, pale or glaucous green; tubercles pyramidal; central spine (0–)1, *c*1.5cm, decurved, dark; radial spines 16–17, 10–12mm. Fls to 6×7cm, yellow. Summer. C Mex. Z9.
C. daimonoceras (Lem.) Lem. = *C. scolymoides*.
C. dasyacantha (Engelm.) Orcutt = *Escobaria dasyacantha*.
C. delaetiana (Quehl) A. Berger. Clustering; st. 10×6cm, pale green; tubercles conic; central spines 3–4, black, 2–2.5cm; radial spines 10–15, unequal, 1–2cm, glassy white, black tipped. Fls with outer tep. yellow with brown midstripe; inner tep. yellow. Summer. N Mex. Z9.
C. deserti (Engelm.) Britt. & Rose = *Escobaria vivipara*.
C. difficilis (Quehl) Orcutt. Simple, depressed-globose, to 6×8cm, grey-green or blue-green; tubercles obtuse-conic; central spines 4, to *c*2cm, red-brown, darker tipped; radial spines 12–14, 1–2cm, off-white, often brown-tipped. Fls 4–5cm broad, yellow. Summer. N Mex. Z9.
C. duncanii (Hester) L. Bens. = *Escobaria dasyacantha* var. *duncanii*.
C. durangensis (Runge ex Schum.) Britt. & Rose. Simple or for-ming small clumps; st. short-cylindric, to 10cm, grey-green; tubercles compressed, initially woolly, central spine, 1, erect, black-brown; radial spines 6–8, to 1cm, spreading. Fls *c*2×2.5–4cm; outer tep. tinged purple, inner tep. pale yellow. Summer. NW Mex. Z9.
C. echinoidea (Quehl) Britt. & Rose = *C. glanduligera*.
C. echinus (Engelm.) Britt. & Rose. St. usually simple, depressed-globose, 3–5cm diam., ± concealed by spines; central spines 0, later 1 or 3–4, 12–17mm; radial spines 16–30, to 16mm, interlacing. Fls 2.5–5cm, yellow. Summer. SW US, N Mex. Z9.
C. elephantidens (Lem.) Lem. Simple, depressed-globose, to 14×19cm; tubercles large, gibbous, axils woolly; spines radial, *c*8, to 2cm, tinged yellow, tipped brown. Fls to 11cm, deep purple-pink or nearly white with red throat. Summer. SW Mex. Z9.
C. erecta (Lem. ex Pfeiff.) Lem. Simple at first, st. cylindric, to 30(–50)×5–8cm; tubercles conic; areoles with small yellow glands; central spines (2–4), to 2cm, amber-yellow; radials 8–14(–18), to 12mm. Fls 5–7cm, yellow. Summer. C Mex. Z9.
C. exsudans (Zucc.) Lem. = *C. ottonis*.
C. georgii Boed. = *C. ottonis*.
C. gladiispina (Boed.) A. Berger = *C. delaetiana*.
C. glanduligera (Otto ex Dietr.) Lem. St. simple, depressed-globose to obovate-ovoid, 3.5–6cm diam., dark grey-green, ± con-cealed by spines, apex woolly; tubercles conic; central spines 0–3, to 15mm, dark-tipped; radial spines to 20–25, to 15mm, white, dark-tipped. Fls 6–8cm diam., pale yellow or pink. Summer. Mex. Z9.
C. guerkeana (Boed.) Britt. & Rose. Simple, depressed-globose, *c*6×8cm, green; tubercles 1.5×2cm with wool and red glands; central spines 2–3, 1.5–2cm, v. stout, often 6-angled; radial spines usually 7, to 1.5cm, with bristly spines at top of areole. Fls as in *C. ottonis*. Summer. Z9.
C. hesteri Y. Wright = *Escobaria hesteri*.
C. macromeris (Engelm.) Lem. Clustering, sometimes forming mounds 50cm across; st. 5–20×5cm; tubercles cylindric, flabby; central spines to 4(–6), 2.5–5cm, thin, black-brown, brown or grey; radial spines 6–15, 2–2.5cm, thinner and paler than centrals. Fls 4.5–6×3–8cm; outer tep. fimbriate, inner tep. bright pink to red-purple. Summer. SW US, N Mex. var. *macromeris*. Tubercles 12–30mm; radial spines 9–15. Fls 6–8cm diam. var. *runyonii* (Britt. & Rose) L. Bens. Tubercles 10–20mm; radial spines 6–12. Fls 3–5cm diam. Z9.
C. maiz-tablasensis Backeb. St. clustering, depressed-globose, to 3×5.5cm, blue-green; tubercles *c*10×13mm; spines 6–7, to 12mm, all radiating, grey-white, black-tipped at first. Fls tinged yellow. Summer. E Mex. Z9.
C. marstonii Clover = *Escobaria missouriensis*.
C. minima Baird = *Escobaria minima*.
C. missouriensis (Sweet) Britt. & Rose = *Escobaria missou-riensis*.
C. muehlenpfordtii Britt. & Rose = *C. scheeri*.
C. nellieae Croizat = *Escobaria minima*.
C. neomexicana (Engelm.) Britt. & Rose = *Escobaria vivipara*.
C. nickelsiae (Brandg.) Britt. & Rose. Forming dense clusters; st. 7cm, pale green and glaucous, purple-green in older plants; tubercles low, almost hidden by the spines; spines radial, 14–16, 8–10mm, interlacing, yellow with dark tip. Fls 5–7cm diam., yellow with red throat. Summer. Mex. Z9.
C. octacantha (DC.) Britt. & Rose. St. simple, cylindric, to 30×12–15cm; tubercles elongate, somewhat 4-angled; axils woolly; central spines 1–2, 25mm, brown; radial spines 8, 10–12mm, dark-tipped. Fls *c*6cm, diam., yellow; sta. red. Summer. C Mex. Z9.
C. odorata Boed. St. clustering, ovoid, to 6×3cm; tubercles cylindric, flabby; central spines 3–4, 20–25mm, hooked, dark;

radial spines 7–9, 8–10mm, pale brown or off-white. Fls narrowly funnelform, 15–20×10mm; outer tep. tinged pink-brown, inner tep. creamy white. Summer. NE Mex. Z9.

C. ottonis (Pfeiff.) Lem. Simple, depressed-globose to cylindric, to 12×8cm, dark green; tubercles to 12mm; central spines 1–4, to 2cm, stout, straight or hooked; radial spines 6–12, to 12mm. Fls to 5cm diam., nearly white, pale yellow or light pink. Summer. C Mex. Z9.

C. pallida Britt. & Rose. Simple or clustering; st. globose, 12cm diam., blue-green; tubercles close-set, short, thick; central spines 3, tipped black or all black; radial spines 20+, white. Fls 7×6–7cm; outer tep. green-yellow with red midstripe, inner tep. pale lemon-yellow; sta. deep red. Summer. SE Mex. Z9.

C. palmeri Britt. & Rose, as to type. = *C. guerkeana*.

C. pectinata (Engelm.) Britt. & Rose = *C. echinus*.

C. poselgeriana (A. Dietr.) Britt. & Rose. Robust, unbranched plants; st. globose, 6.5–17cm diam., blue-green; tubercles large, conic-pyramidal; central spine 1, 2–4cm, stout; radial spines 9–13, the uppermost to 2cm, bristly. Fls to 6cm, yellow at first, with red throat, turning pink. Summer. N Mex. Z9.

C. pseudoechinus Boed. Simple or clustering; st. ovoid to short-cylindric, to 12×5.5cm; tubercles conic; central spine 1, 13–20mm, almost black; radial spines 18–25, 8–15mm. Fls 2–2.5cm, pink or purple with paler throat. Summer. N Mex. Z9.

C. pycnacantha (Mart.) Lem. St. offsetting, globose to cylindric, to 10×5–7cm, dark glaucous green; apex woolly; tubercles broad; central spines 3–4, to 25mm, recurved, black; radial spines 10–12, 10–16mm, slender. Fls 4–5×4–5cm, yellow. Summer. S Mex. Z9.

C. radians (DC.) Britt. & Rose. Simple, globose, to 7.5cm diam., apex woolly; tubercles conic; axils woolly; spines radial, 12–20, 10–12mm, pale, often dark-tipped. Fls to 7cm diam.; outer tep. tinged red, inner tep. lemon-yellow. Summer. C Mex. Z9.

C. radiosa (Engelm.) Rydb. = *Escobaria vivipara*.

C. ramillosa Cutak. Simple, globose to broadly obovoid, 6–7.5×6cm; tubercles 12–15mm; central spines 4, to 4cm; radial spines 9–20, to 2cm, white. Fls *c*6.5×5cm, pink, purple or crimson, throat white. Summer. SW US, N Mex. Z9.

C. recurvata (Engelm.) Britt. & Rose. Clustering; st. depressed-globose to short-cylindric, to 25×15cm; tubercles low; central spines 1(–2), 12–20mm; radial spines 15–20, 12–15mm, pectinate, adpressed, glassy yellow. Fls 2.5–4×2.5–4cm; outer tep. green edged yellow, inner tep. lemon-yellow. Summer. SW US, N Mex. Z9.

C. retusa (Pfeiff.) Britt. & Rose. Simple or clustering; st. depressed-globose, 5–10cm diam.; apex woolly; tubercles large, gibbous; spines radial, 6–12, adpressed and recurved, yellow or brown. Fls 3×4, yellow. Summer. S Mex. Z9.

C. robertii A. Berger = *Escobaria emskoetteriana*.

C. robustispina (Schott ex Engelm.) Britt. & Rose = *C. scheeri* var. *robusti spina*.

C. rosea Clokey = *Escobaria vivipara*.

C. roseana (Boed.) Moran = *Escobaria roseana*.

C. runyonii Britt. & Rose = *C. macromeris* var. *runyonii*.

C. salm-dyckiana (Scheer ex Salm-Dyck) Britt. & Rose. Simple or clustering, 10–15cm diam., glaucous; tubercles larger; central spine 1, to 5cm; porrect; radial spines 8–10, to 4cm, recurved, older areoles with a tuft of bristly spines. Fls 4cm; outer tep. green- or red-tinged, inner tep. yellow. Summer. N Mex. Z9.

C. scheeri Lem. Simple or clustering; st. oblong-ovoid or cylindric, 10–17×7.5–10cm, green; tubercles 12–20×12–25mm; central spines 1–5, to 4cm, straight to hooked; radial spines 6–16 to 3cm. Fls 5–6×5–7.5cm, yellow, pink or white. Summer. SW US, N Mex. var. *scheeri*. Simple; central spine 1, to 4cm, not strongly curved or hooked; radial spines 6–10(–11), to 2cm, inner tep. yellow, striped red. var. *robustispina* (Schott ex Engelm.) L. Bens. Forming clumps; central spine 1, to 3cm, curved and hooked; radial spines (6–)10–15, 19–22mm; inner tep. yellow, orange-pink or rarely white. var. *valida* (Engelm.) L. Bens. Simple; central spines 1–4(–5), to 4cm, not hooked; radial spines (9–)12–16, to 3cm, inner tep. yellow. Z9.

C. schwarziana Boed. = *C. glanduligera*.

C. scolymoides (Scheidw.) A. Berger. Clustering; st. depressed globose to ovoid, to 15cm diam., pale green; tubercles upcurved, imbricate; central spines 3, to 3.5cm or more, curved dark; radial spines 14–20, to 2cm, pale, dark-tipped. Fls over 5cm broad, yellow with red throat. Summer. C Mex. Z9.

C. similis (Engelm.) Britt. & Rose = *Escobaria missouriensis*.

C. sneedii (Britt. & Rose) A. Berger = *Escobaria sneedii*.

C. strobiliformis misapplied. = *Escobaria tuberculosa*.

C. sulcata (Engelm.) Britt. & Rose. Clustering, st. subglobose or ovoid, 4–13×4–13cm, green; tubercles lax; central spines 0 or 1–3, 9–12mm; radial spines 8–14, 8–18mm, white. Fls to 6×6cm, yellow with red throat. Summer. SW US, NE Mex. Z9.

C. sulcolanata (Lem.) Lem. Clustering; st. depressed-globose, *c*5×6.5cm, shining green; tubercles gibbous; central spines 0;

radial spines 9–10, 1.2–1.6cm, unequal, yellow-white, tipped purple, later dark, tipped black. Fls 6×8cm; outer tep. red, inner tep. yellow. Summer. S Mex. Z9.

C. unicornis Boed. Simple at first, later clustering; st. globose, to 8cm diam., shiny blue-green; tubercles conic; central spine 1, to 2cm; radial spines 7–9, to 1.5cm. Fls yellow. Summer. N Mex. Z9.

C. valida Purpus, invalid name. = *C. scheeri*.

C. varicolor Tiegel = *Escobaria tuberculosa*.

C. vaupeliana Boed. St. simple, globose, 7cm diam., dull blue-green; tubercles conic; central spines 4, 2cm, yellow-grey; radial spines *c*15, 8–12mm. Fls yellow. Summer. NE Mex. Z9.

C. vivipara (Nutt.) Britt. & Rose = *Escobaria vivipara*.

C. vivipara subvar. neomexicana Engelm. = *Escobaria vivipara*.

C. werdermannii Boed. St. simple, globose to ovoid, to 8×6cm, dull pale grey-green; tubercles pyramidal; central spines 4, to 22mm, yellow-brown to nearly white, darker tipped; radial spines 15–30, 6mm, grey-white. Fls 6cm diam.; outer tep. pale yellow, with red tip or midstripe, inner tep. pale yellow. Summer. N Mex. Z9.

C. wissmannii (Hildm. ex Schum.) A. Berger = *Escobaria missouriensis*.

C. zilziana Boed. = *Escobaria zilziana*.

→*Neolloydia*.

Corysanthes R. Br.

C. bicalcarata R. Br. = *Corybas aconitiflorus*.

C. cheesmanii Hook. f. ex T. Kirk = *Corybas aconitiflorus*.

C. pruinosa R. Cunn. = *Corybas pruinosus*.

Corytholoma (Benth.) Decne.

C. cooperi (Paxt.) Fritsch = *Sinningia cooperi*.

C. sellovii Mart. = *Sinningia sellovii*.

Cosmea Willd. = *Cosmos*.

Cosmetic Bark Tree *Murraya paniculata*.

Cosmibuena Ruiz & Pav. Rubiaceae. 6 trees or epiphytic shrubs. Lvs fleshy. Fls term. and solitary, or in clusters; cal. tube campanulate or turbinate, 5–6 toothed; cor. long-tubed, funnel- or salver-shaped, lobes 5–6, spreading. Trop. Amer. Z10.

C. grandifolia var. **latifolia** (Benth.) Steyerm. Tree to 6m. Lvs to 15cm, ovate to elliptic. Fls highly fragrant in terminal, cymose clusters; cor. white, to 8×1cm. Colomb.

C. obtusifolia Ruiz & Pav. = *C. grandiflora* var. *latifolia*.

Cosmidium Nutt.

C. burridgeanum Reg., Körn. & Rach = *Thelesperma burridgeanum*.

Cosmos Cav. Compositae. *c*26 ann. or perenn. herbs, rarely sub-shrubs, glab. or hairy. St. erect or ascending. Lvs undivided, lobed or 1–3-pinnatisect. Cap. usually radiate, long-stalked in loose corymbs. Trop. and warm Amer., esp. Mex.

C. atrosanguineus (Hook.) Voss CHOCOLATE COSMOS. Perenn. to 1m. Lvs 7–15cm, spathulate, mostly 1–2-pinnate, seg. rhomboid-ovate, cuneate, entire or serrate. Cap. vanilla-scented, solitary, to 4.2cm diam., on peduncles to 35cm; ray flts 8, obovate, deep velvety black-red to maroon. Summer. Mex. Z8.

C. bipinnatus Cav. Ann. to 2m. Lvs to 11cm, 2-pinnate, seg. narrowly linear or filiform. Cap. many, to 8cm diam., peduncle to 20cm; ray flts 8, obovate, rose-pink to lilac. Mex., S US. A large range of seed races and F1 hybrids are offered. Dwarfs include the bright red 'Ladybird Scarlet' to 25cm, the 60cm 'Sunny Red' and the 30cm semi-double 'Sunny Gold'; regular semi-double selections include the early-flowering Bright Lights Mixed and the deep sunset orange of 'Diablo'; the large-fld 'Gazebo' is v. early. Among the most colourful are the semi-dwarf 'Daydream' with pale pink fls and dark carmine centres, and the pink or white Sensation Series and 'Candy Stripe' with snow-white fls splashed or stippled with crimson.

C. dahlioides S. Wats. = *C. diversifolius*.

C. diversifolius Otto. Perenn. to 90cm. Lvs to 15cm, simple and spathulate, or pinnatisect, seg. cuneate-lanceolate or ovate. Cap. solitary, to 7cm diam.; peduncles 20–40cm; ray flts 8–10, rose-pink, violet or lilac; disc flts yellow. S Mex., Guat. Z9.

C. diversifolius var. **atrosanguineus** Hook. = *C. atrosanguineus*.

C. sulphureus Cav. Ann. to 2m+. Lvs to 35cm, 2–3-pinnatisect, seg. linear or lanceolate, membranous, faintly spinulose-ciliate, glab. or sparsely hispid. Cap. to 5.5cm diam., term. on 10–20cm peduncles; ray flts *c*8, rich orange or pale yellow-red, obovate. Mex., C Amer., N S Amer.

→*Bidens* and *Dahlia*.

Costmary *Tanacetum balsamita.*

Costus L. SPIRAL FLAG; SPIRAL GINGER. Zingiberaceae. 90 rhizomatous perenn. herbs. Lvs ± spirally arranged on reed-like st. Infl. a spike with overlapping bracts, terminating leafy st. or scapose; cor. tubular, pet. 3, lip funnelform, crêpe-like, ruffled. Trop. Z10.

C. afer Ker-Gawl. SPIRAL GINGER. To 1–4m. Lvs 15cm, lanceolate, acuminate, glab., spiralling. Fls in dense spikes term. on leafy shoots or scapose. Fls white, pellucid; lip white with a central deep yellow stripe. W Afr.

C. arabicus Rosemary M. Sm. To 1.2m, glab. Lvs 10–20cm, oblong to elliptic, green above, purple beneath; ligule with red hairs. Spike oval; bracts red and green; fls white; lip white and yellow. Braz.

C. cernuus Sw. ex Schult. = *Renealmia cernua.*

C. cuspidatus (Nees & Mart.) Maas. FIERY COSTUS. St. to 50cm, flushed purple-red. Lvs 10–20cm, oblong or oblong-lanceolate, deep green above, tinged red beneath. Fls few, orange. Braz.

C. cylindricus Jacq. = *C. scaber.*

C. discolor Roscoe = *C. arabicus.*

C. dubius (Afzel.) Schum. St. 1.5–3.5m. Lvs 24–36cm, elliptic, ciliate, midrib pubesc, beneath. Infl. term. on leafy shoots or scapes; fls white, pellucid, lip undulate, with central bright yellow spot. Trop. Afr.

C. elegans hort. = *C. malortieanus.*

C. englerianus Schum. Lvs 1 per st., 15cm, widely elliptic, fleshy, dark green. Fls few in a sessile spike, white with yellow throat. Trop. W Afr.

C. friedrichsenii Petersen = *C. villosissimus.*

C. igneus N. Br. = *C. cuspidatus.*

C. lucanusianus A. Braun & Schum. To 2m. St. stout, Lvs 12–25cm, lanceolate to oblong, silver-pubesc, beneath. Infl. term. on leafy shoots; fls white, pellucid, lip edged red with a central yellow stripe. Trop. W Afr. Differs from *C. afer* in hairy lf sheath.

C. malortieanus H. Wendl. SPIRAL GINGER; SPIRAL FLAG; STEPLADDER PLANT. St. stout. to 1m. Lvs 20cm, fleshy, broadly elliptic to obovate-obcordate, downy, pale green with dark stripes or mottling above. Fls in a dense spike term. on leafy shoot, golden yellow. lip yellow with red or brown stripes. Braz., Costa Rica.

C. musaicus = *C. malortieanus.*

C. pictus D. Don. To 45cm, erect. Lvs 20cm, oblong-lanceolate or oblanceolate, acuminate. Fls few, in an ovoid spike, yellow, lip marked purple and golden yellow. Midsummer. Mex.

C. pisonis Lindl. = *C. spiralis.*

C. pulverulentus C. Presl. To 3m. Lvs 30cm, narrow-elliptic or obovate, velvety blue-green veined silver, flushed red beneath. Infl. to 7.5×5cm, fusiform in outline, term. on leafy shoot; bracts red; fls red, lip red to yellow. Mex., C & W S Amer.

C. rumphii hort. = *C. malortieanus.*

C. sanguineus J.D. Sm. = *C. pulverulentus.*

C. scaber Ruiz & Pav. To 1–4m. Lvs oblanceolate, acute, to 20cm, sometimes yellow-ciliate. Fls in globose head, later loose; bracts red; fls white. W Indies, C & S Amer.

C. speciosus (J.G. Koenig) Sm. MALAY GINGER; WILD GINGER; CREPE GINGER. To 3m. Lvs 12–25cm, elliptic, acuminate. Infl. term. on leafy shoot, ovoid 12cm; bracts purple-red; fls white or pink, lip white with yellow-orange centre. India, SE Asia to New Guinea. 'Variegatus': lvs edged and striped pale cream or white.

C. spicatus (Jacq.) Sw. To 2.5m. Lvs 30cm, narrow-elliptic, or narrow-obovate. Infl. terminal on leafy shoot, cylindrical, 5–25cm; bracts green or glossy red, with yellow callus below tip; fls yellow to pink. Hispan.

C. spiralis Roscoe. To 1.2m, st. slender. Lvs 20cm, obovate-oblong, glossy, in a loose spiral. Infl. term. on leafy st., 25cm, conical; bracts red or green; fls rose to red, lip white flushed red, ruffled. W Indies, Ecuad.

C. unifolius N.E. Br. = *C. englerianus.*

C. villosissimus Jacq. To 2m, robust. Lvs 20cm, oblanceolate, downy. Fls in conical spike to 10cm; fls green-yellow, lip deep yellow, throat with red lines. C Amer.

C. zebrinus = *C. malortieanus.*

Cotinus Mill. SMOKEWOOD; SMOKE BUSH. Anacardiaceae. 3 decid. trees or shrubs; wood orange-yellow. Lvs simple, entire, membranous. Infl. a feathery term. pan.; fls small, 5-merous, many abortive, infl. axis thus becoming plumose. N Amer., S Eur. to E Himal. and C China. Z7.

C. americanus Nutt. = *C. obovatus.*

C. coggygria Scop. SMOKE TREE; VENETIAN SUMAC; WIG TREE. Shrub, 3–5m. Lvs to 7.5cm, broadly elliptic to oblong-ovate. Soft mid green, usually pink-bronze on emergence often with margins and midrib persistently red-tinted, base rounded to

truncate; petiole 2–4cm. Infl. 15–20cm, plume-like, purple-buff becoming smoky grey, highly branched. Summer. S Eur. to C China. 'Flame': lvs bright orange in autumn; possibly *C. coggygria* ×*C. obovatus.* 'Nordine': lvs plum, yellow to orange in autumn; infl. ruby red. 'Notcutts' Variety': lvs dark purple; infl. purple-pink. 'Pendulus': br. drooping; lvs green. 'Purpureus' ('Atropurpureus'): lvs purple; pan. dark purple pubesc., smoky pink. 'Red Beauty': lvs large, bright purple to dark red. 'Royal Purple': lvs deep maroon, margins becoming scarlet, ultimately colouring scarlet. 'Rubrifolius': lvs claret, later somewhat green; fls tinted red; infl. red to pink, softly haired. 'Velvet Cloak': lvs dark purple, purple and claret in autumn. fls purple. Z5.

C. coggygria var. *purpureus* (Dupuy) Rehd. = *C. coggygria* 'Purpureus'.

C. cotinoides (Nutt. ex Chapm.) Britt. = *C. obovatus.*

C. **Dummer Hybrids** (*C. coggygria* 'Velvet Cloak' ×*C. obovatus*). Large shrubs intermediate between parents with purple-pink infl. and purple-red lvs turning scarlet in autumn, the undersides ± downy as in *C. obovatus.* 'Grace' is an award-winning clone.

C. obovatus Raf. AMERICAN SMOKEWOOD; CHITTAMWOOD. Similar to *C. coggygria* but often a broad-crowned tree to 10m; lvs 6–12cm, broad-elliptic to obovate, base cuneate, sea green often spotted purple when young, turning gold, amber and scarlet in fall, ± hairy beneath; petiole red. S US. Z5.

→*Rhus.*

Cotoneaster Medik. Rosaceae. 70+ decid. or everg. shrubs or small trees. Lvs alt., simple. Fls small, solitary or in corymbs, usually white; pet. 5, erect or patent; sta. 10–20. Fr. a small, red or black pome. Eur., N Afr., E Asia, Sib., Himal.

C. acuminatus Lindl. Decid. upright shrub to 4m. Lvs to 6cm, elliptic-ovate, slender-pointed, dark dull green, sparsely-pubesc, or glab. beneath. Fls 1cm diam., white tinted pink. Fr. red. Summer. Himal. Z5.

C. acutifolius Turcz. Decid., bushy shrub, to 3m. Lvs 2.5–5cm, ovate to elliptic, dull green, sparsely pubesc, when young. Fls 2–5, in short corymbs, pink or tinged red. Fr. black. China. 'Nana': habit spreading, to 1.2m high. var. *villosulus* Rehd. & Wils. Vigorous; lvs larger, colouring purple and red in autumn. Fr. purple-black, brown-hairy. C & W China. Z4.

C. adpressus Bois. Scandent, spreading or prostrate, decid. shrub. Lvs to 1.5cm, broad-ovate or obovate, dull green, glab. or loose-pubesc, beneath, scarlet in autumn. Fls red with some white, solitary or paired. Fr. red. Summer. China. 'Little Gem': growth weaker, cushion-forming; lvs with little autumn coloration; fr. 0. Z4.

C. adpressus var. *praecox* Boiss. & Berth. = *C. nanshan.*

C. affinis Lindl. Decid. upright shrub. Lvs 2cm+, lanate. Fls usually 20–40-clustered. Fr. dark red to almost black. Summer. Himal. 'Anne Cornwallis': to 2.5m; fr. yellow stained apricot-orange. Z6.

C. affinis var. *bacillaris* (Wallich ex Lindl.) Schneid. = *C. bacillaris.*

C. ambiguus Rehd. & Wils. Shrub to 2m, close to *C. acutifolius.* Lvs 2.5–5cm, oval or ovate, acuminate, densely pubesc. beneath, pubesc. above when young. Fls white with red flush, in corymbs. Fr. black, glossy. China. Z5.

C. amoenus Wils. Everg. bushy shrub to 1.5m. Lvs to 2.5cm, oval to ovate, acuminate or acute, coriaceous, lustrous green, sparse-pubesc, above, white-tomentose beneath. Fls 5mm diam., white and rose-red, in compact, upright infl. Fr. red. Summer. China. Z6.

C. angustifolius Franch. = *Pyracantha angustifolia.*

C. apiculatus Rehd. & Wils. Decid. shrub to 2m, upright but often with br. pendent or spreading. Lvs to 1.3cm, suborbicular, contracted at apex to a short point, shiny green, glab. or loose-pubesc, beneath. Fls red with white, solitary. Fr. red. Summer. China. 'Blackburn': dense, compact; fr. numerous, larger, scarlet. 'Tom Thumb': compact miniature, to 10×25cm. Z4.

C. bacillaris Wallich ex Lindl. Decid. shrub to 5m, graceful, upright. Lvs to 8.5cm, lanceolate to oblanceolate, pointed. Fls in clusters to 5cm diam. Fr. purple-brown to black. Summer. Himal. Z6. cf *C. ignotus.*

C. bullatus Bois. Decid. shrub to 4m. Lvs to 7cm, ovate to oblong-elliptic, acuminate, dark green and bullate above, lanuginose beneath with fiery tints in autumn. Fls white tinted red, in clusters to 5cm diam. Fr. currant-red. Summer. China. 'Firebird': shrub to 3m, spreading; lvs 3cm, bullate, green above, hoary beneath; fr. dark orange to red, in dense clusters. Probably a new species. var. *floribundus* Rehd. & Wils. Lvs larger, shorter-stalked. Infl. abundant, 15–30-fld. Fr. larger and densely clustered. Z5.

C. bullatus var. *macrophyllus* Rehd. & Wils. = *C. rehderi.*

C. buxifolius Wallich ex Lindl. Everg. or semi-evergreen shrub, 2m. Lvs to 1.7cm, elliptic or obovate-grey-tomentose beneath.

Fls 2–20 per cluster. Fr. carmine. N India. f. *vellaceus* Franch. Procumbent shrub. Lvs 0.5–1cm, pubesc., coriaceous, obovate, slightly revolute, cano-tomentose beneath. Fls solitary. Z7.

C. buxifolius var. *marginatus* Loud. = *C. marginatus*.

C. cashmiriensis Klotz. Close to *C. microphyllus*; slow-growing, dense dwarf shrub; lvs 0.5–1cm, ovate-elliptical, deep glossy green above. Fr. small, bright red. Kashmir. Z7.

C. cavei Klotz. Decid. shrub to 80cm, erect to suberect. Lvs to 1.1cm, in 2 rows, elliptic, broad ovate- or obovate-elliptic, or orbicular, mucronulate, sparsely strigose-pilose. Fls solitary, nodding, pet. to 3mm, red. Fr. deep red. Sikkim-Himal. Z7.

C. cochleatus (Franch.) Klotz. Scandent, everg. or semi-evergreen shrub with rooting br. Lvs to 2cm, often in 2 rows, wide-elliptic, wide-obovate to rounded, coriaceous, dull green above, glab. or loose-pubesc. beneath. Fls to 10mm diam., usually solitary. Fr. crimson. China. Z7.

C. cochleatus hort. = *C. cashmiriensis*.

C. congestus Bak. Congested, spreading scandent or prostrate, everg. or semi-evergreen subshrub. Lvs to 1.1cm, often in 2 rows, obovate-elliptic or oblong-oblanceolate, coriaceous, dull green. Fls 6.5mm diam., white. Fr. to 9mm, carmine. Summer. Himal. 'Nanus': fls larger. Z6.

C. conspicuus Marq. Spreading scandent or prostrate everg. or semi-evergreen shrub, 1m. Lvs to 2cm, oblong or lanceolate, coriaceous, glab. or loose-pubesc. beneath. Fls to 1cm diam., white, solitary. Fr. shiny, scarlet. Summer. SE Tibet. 'Decorus': spreading, low-growing shrub, with dense foliage; fls and fr. abundant. 'Highlight': medium-size shrub, with a dense cluster of arching shoots; fls abundant, white; fr. orange-red. 'Flameburst': low-spreading, mat-forming; fr. orange-red. 'Red Glory': habit tall, elegant; fr. dark red. 'Red Pearl': habit low-spreading; fr. large, bright orange-red. 'Tiny Tim': mat-forming, low; fr. orange washed red. Z6.

C. cooperi Lange. Vigorous, open, decid. shrub to 2.5m. Lvs to 8cm, lanceolate, acuminate, glab. above, with white hairs beneath at first. Fls 1.75cm diam., white in numerous cymes to 3cm diam. Fr. purple-black. Bhutan. var. *microcarpus* Marq. Large shrub, br. slender, arched; fr. purple-red, smaller.

C. dammeri Schneid. Scandent to prostrate everg. shrub; shoots long. Lvs to 3cm, elliptic to obovate-oblong, dark glossy green, soon glab. Fls to 13mm diam., white, usually solitary. Fr. red. Summer. China. 'Coral Beauty': v. low-growing shrub; br. diffuse; fr. orange-red, abundant. 'Donnard Gem': habit low, spreading, rounded, to 20cm; lvs tiny, tinted grey; fr. red, long-lasting. 'Eichholz' ('Oakwood'): procumbent shrub, to 25cm; lvs 1.5–2cm; fr. large, carmine; held to be a hybrid of *C. dammeri* × *C. microphyllus* 'Cochleata'. 'Juergl': low-growing, to 50cm; br. broad-spreading, red-brown; lvs 1.5×0.9cm, bluntly elliptic, matt green above, light green and glabrescent beneath; fr. 6×9mm, light red, abundant. 'Lowfast': habit dense, branching; forms rapid groundcover. 'Major': strong-growing; lvs large. 'Minipolster': cushion-forming. 'Mooncreeper': fls large, white. 'Skogholm': to 60cm; br. rooting at tips, spreading to 2–3m wide; lvs elliptical, large, obtuse, dull dark green above, smooth; fls in groups of 2–6; fr. dull red. 'Smaragdpolster': as 'Coral Beauty' but dwarf; lvs dark green; fr. more abundant. 'Streibs Findling': lvs 0.8–1.5cm, small, broad-elliptic; perhaps a hybrid with *C. procumbens*. 'Tevlon Porter': habit creeping; fls white. 'Winter Jewel': habit prostrate, mat-forming, to 40cm; lvs v. dark green; fr. profuse, red; hybrid of 'Major' and 'Coral Beauty'. var. *radicans* Schneid. Lvs 1–1.5cm, ovate to obovate, apex rounded, often emarginate. Fls generally paired. Z5.

C. davidianus hort. ex Handl. = *C. horizontalis*.

C. dielsianus Pritz. ex Diels. Semi-evergreen shrub to 3m, graceful, loosely branching, arching-pendulous. Lvs to 2.5cm, rounded-oval, ovate or obovate, coriaceous, yellow-grey tomentose beneath. Fls pink, clustered. Fr. blood-red to currant-red. Summer. China. var. *elegans* Rehd. & Wils. Lvs to 1.5cm, almost orbicular, glabrescent above. Fr. coral-red, puberulent. var. *major* Rehd. & Wils. Lvs to 3×2.5cm. Infl. lax, long-stalked. Z5.

C. distichus Lange = *C. nitidus*.

C. distichus var. *parvifolius* T.T. Yu = *C. cavei*.

C. distichus var. *tongolensis* hort. non Schneid. = *C. splendens*.

C. divaricatus Rehd. & Wils. Spreading, decid. shrub, 2m. Lvs to 2cm, ovate-elliptic, glossy dark green, subglabrous. Fls white tinted red, clustered. Fr. currant-red. Summer. China. Z5.

C. floccosus (Rehd. & Wils.) Flinck & Hylmö = *C. salicifolius* var. *floccosus*.

C. foveolatus Rehd. & Wils. Decid., erect shrub to 3m; br. spreading, 2-ranked. Lvs to 8cm, elliptic to lanceolate, acuminate, matt and eventually glab. above, pubesc. beneath. Fls clustered, 7.5mm diam., pink and white. Fr. black. China. Z4.

C. franchetii Bois. Everg., slender shrub to 3m; br. arching. Lvs to 3cm, oval, somewhat pubesc., becoming glossy above, felted with mustard-coloured hairs beneath. Fls 5–15, white, tinged rose-pink. Fr. orange-scarlet. SW China, Tibet, and Burm. var. *cinerascens* Rehd. Tall-growing, to 4m. Lvs to 4cm, tomentose beneath. Infl. to 30-fld. Z6.

C. franchetii var. *sternianus* Turrill = *C. sternianus*.

C. frigidus Wallich ex Lindl. TREE COTONEASTER. Spreading decid. shrub or tree, to 18m. Lvs to 12cm, elliptic to elliptic-oblong or oblong-obovate, dull green, initially lanate beneath. Fls to 8.5mm diam., white clustered. Fr. light red. Summer. Himal. 'Notcutt's Var.': lvs large, dark green above, often red beneath. 'Fructuluteo' ('Xanthocarpus'): fr. creamy yellow. 'Pendulus': br. v. pendulous. Z7.

C. gamblei Klotz. Erect shrub or small tree to 6m. Lvs to 10.5cm, in 2 rows, elliptic-lanceolate or oblanceolate, obtuse-mucronulate, chartaceous or subcoriaceous, villous beneath, soon glabrescent. Fls to 1cm, in erect, 10–35 fld clusters. Fr. blood-red or black-red. Sikkim, Bhutan. Z7.

C. glabratus Rehd. & Wils. Everg. or semi-evergreen shrub to 5m. Young br. slightly angled. Lvs to 7cm, lanceolate or oblanceolate, coriaceous, bright green and glab. above, glaucous beneath. Fls in clusters to 4cm diam. Fr. orange-scarlet. Summer. China. Z6.

C. glaucophyllus Franch. Everg. shrub to 4m. Lvs oval, v. glaucous beneath, tawny-lanate when young, strongly veined. Fls in clusters to 2.5cm diam. Fr. orange. Summer. China. var. *vestitus* W.W. Sm. Strong-growing, to 3m. Lvs tomentose. Infl. smaller. Fls fewer. Z7.

C. glaucophyllus f. *serotinus* (Hutch.) Stapf = *C. serotinus*.

C. glomerulatus W.W. Sm. Medium-sized shrub. Br. slender, lax, graceful. Lvs undulate, glossy dark green, colouring well in fall. Fls clustered. Fr. crimson. SW China. Z6.

C. harrovianus Wils. Spreading everg. or semi-evergreen shrub to 4m. Lvs to 4.5cm, elliptic to elliptic-oblong, coriaceous, dark glossy green and glab. above, buff-pubesc. beneath. Fls many, in 4cm diam, corymbs. Fr. red. Summer. China. Z7.

C. harrysmithii Flink & Hylmö. Spreading decid. shrub to 2m. Lvs 1.7cm in 2 ranks, elliptic to elliptic-ovate, acute to acuminate, vivid green and pilose above, grey-white pubesc. beneath. Fls to 5×5mm, pink-red, usually clustered. Fr. brown-black to black. W China. Z6.

C. hebephyllus Diels. Decid. shrub to 3m. Lvs to 3cm, sub-orbicular to broad-oval, sparse-pilose above, villous beneath soon glab. Fls to 13mm diam., clustered. Fr. white to cardinal-red. Spring. China. var. *monopyrenus* W.W. Sm. Fr. large, rust-coloured. 'Hessei': habit creeping; lvs dark matt green, red in fall; fls tinged red; fr. pale red. Z6.

C. hjelmqvistii Flinck & Hylmö. Similar to a large *C. horizontalis*. A spreading small shrub; br. arching. Lvs to 2cm, broadly obovate to suborbicular, glossy green, red in fall. Fr. rosy red, abundant. W China. Z6.

C. henryanus (Schneid.) Rehd. & Wils. Everg. or semi-deciduous shrub to 3.6m; br. pendulous. Lvs to 11cm, narrow-obovate or oval, acute, somewhat rugose and dark green above, grey-woolly beneath when young. Fls in clusters to 5cm diam. Fr. deep crimson. China. Close to *C. salicifolius*. Z7.

C. horizontalis Decne. Decid. shrub of flat-growing habit. Branching herring-bone-like. Lvs to 1.3cm, often smaller, sub-orbicular to broad-elliptic, dark glossy green tinted bronze-red to scarlet in fall. Fls white stained red, solitary or paired. Fr. orange-red. Spring. W China. 'Ascendens': growth upright; lvs 1.2–1.6cm, ovate, acuminate; fr. crimson. 'Dart's Deputation': fr. clear bright red. 'Dart's Splendid': fr. profuse, brilliant red. 'Major': habit open and arching. 'Robusta': = *C. hjelmqvistii*. 'Saxatilis': weak-growing, with fan-like prostrate br.; lvs smaller. 'Variegatus': weak-growing; lvs variegated cream-white, sometimes tinted red in autumn. var. *perpusillus* Schneid. Dwarf shrub, short, congested br. Lvs 0.6–0.8cm, densely clustered. var. *wilsonii* Havemeyer ex Wils. To 1–2m, br. wide and ascending. Lvs larger. Fr. darker red. Z4.

C. humifusus Duthie ex J.H. Veitch = *C. dammeri*.

C. hummelii Flinck & Hylmö. Differs from *C. moupinensis* in narrow, more finely tapered, glossier lvs with less deeply impressed veins, tinted bronze at first; fr. longer, duller. China.

C. hupehensis Rehd. & Wils. Decid. shrub to 2m. Br. graceful, arching. Lvs to 3.5cm. elliptic to ovate, dark green, grey and thinly-langinose beneath. Fls 8.5mm diam., clustered. Fr. crimson. Spring–summer. China. Z5.

C. 'Hybridus Pendulus'. Everg. shrub, br. long, procumbent or weeping when grafted as a standard. Fr. brilliant red. abundant. Said to be a hybrid of *C. dammeri* with either *C. frigidus* or *C. salicifolius*. Z5.

C. ignavus Wolf. Decid. shrub to 2m. Lvs to 8cm, ovate or elliptic, rounded at base. Fls white tinted pink, clustered. Fr. nearly black. E Turkestan. Z6.

C. ignotus Klotz. Large erect shrub. Br. arching. Lvs broadly elliptic to obovate, blunt. Fr. black, pruinose, profuse. Himal.

Z6.

C. insignis Pojark. Decid. to semi-evergreen upright shrub to small tree to 6m. Lvs 5cm, rounded, tomentose or thick-pubesc, beneath. Fls 4–20-clustered. Fr. blue-black, pruinose. Iran, Afghan., Turkestan. Z6.

C. integerrimus Medik. Decid. shrub to 1.5m. Lvs to 4cm, acute or obtuse, membranous, dull or somewhat glossy and glab. above, tomentose or villous beneath. Fls 3–7-clustered. Fr. red. Spring. Eur., W Asia. Z6.

C. ingtegrifolius (Roxb.) Klotz. Dwarf, procumbent everg. Lvs narrow-oblong to obovate, obtuse to emarginate, glossy green above, hoary beneath. Fr. large, globose, dark pink. Himal., SW China. Commonly grown, usually as *C. microphyllus*.

C. koidzumii Hayata = *Pyracantha koidzumii*.

C. lacteus W.W. Sm. Everg. shrub to 4m. Lvs to 5cm, thick, broad-elliptic, coriaceous, wrinkled, glossy above, dark green. Fls milky white, in rounded corymbs to 6.5cm diam. Fr. red. Summer. China. Z6.

C. laxiflorus Lindl. To 2.5m. Lvs 2cm+, obtuse or rounded. Fls in clusters. Fr. black or black-red. Z7.

C. lindleyi Steud. Decid. shrub to 3.5m. Lvs to 4cm, rounded-oval to ovate, mucronate, grey-tomentose beneath. Fls 5–12-clustered. Fr. purple-black. Summer. Himal. Z6.

C. linearifolius (Klotz.) Klotz. Dwarf shrub often grown as *C. microphyllus* var. *thymifolius*. Lvs v. small, narrow, glossy, dark green. Fr. small, deep pink, persistent. Nepal.

C. lucidus Schldl. Decid. shrub to 2m. Lvs to 7cm, ovate-elliptic, shiny green and glab. above. Fls white, 5–15-clustered. Fr. shiny black. Spring–summer. Altai Mts. Z4.

C. marginatus Lindl. ex Schldl. Everg. shrub to 1m, erect or suberect. Br. yellow-green strigose, later glabrescent. Lvs to 1.6cm, spirally arranged, elliptic, obtuse-mucronate, coriaceous, sparse-strigose above, soon glab., yellow-green strigose-vilous beneath. Fls to 1cm diam., 2–8-clustered. Fr. crimson. Himal. Z7.

C. marquandii Klotz. Erect, decid. shrub. Br. divaricate. Lvs to 2cm in 2 rows, elliptic or broad obovate-elliptic, acuminate or cuspidate, subcoriaceous, glabrescent. Fr. deep red-orange. India. Z8.

C. melanocarpus Lodd. Decid. shrub to 2m, loosley erect, of spreading habit. Lvs to 8cm, ovate or elliptic, white-tomentose beneath. Fls pink-white, 3–15-clustered. Fr. black, pruinose. Spring–summer. Eur. to C & NE Asia. Z6.

C. melanocarpus var. *laxiflorus* (Lindl.) Schneid. = *C. laxiflorus*.

C. 'Merriot Weeper'. Habit arching, weeping, broader than high, to 1.5×2m+. Fr. red. Z6.

C. meyeri Pojark. Decid. shrub to 1.8m, habit spreading. Lvs to 3cm, oblong-elliptic, glab. above, sparsely pubesc, beneath when young. Fls 7–12 in corymbs. Fr. deepest purple. Z6.

C. microphyllus Wallich ex Lindl. Everg. subshrub to 1m. Lvs to 0.8cm, ovate to obovate, deep shiny green, white-grey strigose-pilose beneath. Fls 1–4-clustered. Fr. carmine. Spring–summer. Himal. Z5.

C. microphyllus f. *thymifolius* hort. = *C. linearifolius*.

C. microphyllus 'Cochleatus' = *C. cashmiriensis*.

C. moupinensis Franch. Decid. shrub to 3m, of upright habit. Lvs to 15cm, bullate. Fls pink, 10–25-clustered. Fr. purple-black. Summer. China. Z5.

C. multiflorus Bunge. Shrub, or small tree with arching or pendulous br., to 5m. Lvs to 4cm, ovate to round, obtuse. Fls 6–20-clustered. Fr. red. Spring. NW China. Z5. var. *calocarpus* Rehd. & Wils. Lvs elliptic, large; fr. profuse. var. *granatensis* (Boiss.) Wenz. Tall-growing lvs densely pubesc, beneath; infl. lax, pubesc. Z5.

C. nanchuenicus Reg. = *C. nanshan*.

C. nanshan Vilm.-Andr. Vigorous, decid. shrub similar to *C. adpressus*, to 60cm; br. arched to creeping. Lvs to 2.5cm, ovate, rounded, dark green above, lighter beneath, turning red. Fls 1–2, pink. 'Boer': br. more perpendicular, not arching. Z7.

C. 'Newryensis'. Medium to large, br. ascending; fr. orange-red. Said to be *C. franchetii* ×*C. simonsii*. Z6.

C. niger (Wahlenb.) Fries. Upright decid. shrub to 2m. Br. sprawling or nodding. Lvs to 5cm, usually 2-ranked, broad oval-oblong, obtuse or acute, dull dark green above, grey-villous beneath. Fls white with red, 2–12-clustered. Spring–summer. E Eur. to W Asia, E Mong. var. *commixtus* Schneid. Lvs ovate. Fls in groups of 8–15. var. *latiflorus* (Lindl.) Schneid. Lvs large. Fls in large, pendulous corymbs of 20–40. Z5.

C. nitens Rehd. & Wils. Decid. shrub to 2m, of dense habit. Lvs to 2cm frondose, round-oval, dark glossy green, sometimes scarlet in fall. Fls white with some red, usually 3-clustered. Fr. purple-black. Summer. China. Z6.

C. nitidifolius Marq. = *C. glomerulatus*.

C. nitidus Jacques. Everg. of semi-evergreen upright shrub. Lvs to 2cm, arranged in 2 ranks, coriaceous or thick-membranous,

glab. or loose-pubesc. beneath. Fls solitary, white with a pink flush. Fr. red. Summer. Himal., W China. Z6.

C. nummularius Fisch. & Mey. Shrub to 1.5m. Lvs to 2.5cm, broad-elliptic, obovate-elliptic or orbicular, rounded sparse-pilose above, dense-tomentose beneath. Fls to 9mm diam., 3–7-clustered. Fr. red. Asia Minor. Z7.

C. obscurus Rehd. & Wils. Decid. shrub to 3m. Br. sprawling, long, nodding. Lvs to 4cm, oval-elliptic, acuminate, dull green, thin-pubesc. above, grey-yellow tomentose beneath. Fls white or white with pink, 3–10-clustered. Fr. red or purple. Summer. W China. var. *cornifolius* Rehd. & Wils. Lvs large, 4–7cm, lanuginose above, lax pubesc. beneath. Fr. large, blood-red. Z5.

C. pannosus Franch. Everg. or semi-evergreen shrub to 3m. Br. long, slender. Lvs to 2.5cm, lanceolate-ovate or elliptic, sage green, white-tomentose beneath. Fls 8.5mm diam., 6–12-clustered. Fr. dull light red, lanuginose. China. Z7.

C. parneyi Poss. = *C. lacteus*.

C. permutatus Klotz. Everg. shrub erect to 1.5m. Lvs to 1.8cm, spirally arranged, oblong, oblong-oblanceolate or oblong-lanceolate, mucronate, coriaceous, sparse-pilose above, ash-grey villous beneath. Fls to 11mm diam., 1–2. Fr. deep red. Himal. Z7.

C. perpusillus (Schneid.) Flinck & Hylmö = *C. horizontalis* var. *perpusillus*.

C. polyanthemus auct. = *C. tomentosus*.

C. praecox Vilm.-Andr. = *C. nanshan*.

C. procumbens Klotz. Scandent to procumbent everg. or semi-evergreen shrub with rooting br. Lvs to 2cm, wide-elliptic, wide-obovate to rounded, coriaceous, glab. or loose-pubesc. beneath. Fls to 9mm diam., solitary. Fr. crimson. Summer. Himal. Z7.

C. prostratus Bak. Everg. semi-prostrate shrub. Br. long. Lvs to 1.3cm, elliptic or broad obovate-elliptic, rounded emarginate or obtuse, obtuse at base, coriaceous, shiny above, ash-grey strigose beneath. Fls to 11mm diam., solitary. Fr. crimson. Summer. Himal. 'Eastleigh': large, strong-growing shrub, many-branched; lvs dark green; fr. large, dark red. Z7.

C. prostratus hort. non Bak. = *C. procumbens*.

C. prostratus var. *lanatus* hort. = *C. marginatus*.

C. pyracantha (L.) Spach = *Pyracantha coccinea*.

C. pyrenaicus Chancerel = *C. congestus*.

C. racemiflorus (Desf.) Booth ex Bosse. Decid. shrub to 2m. Lvs to 3cm, oval-elliptic, obtuse and mucronate, pilose above, white-tomentose beneath. Fls to 9mm diam., 6–12-clustered. Fr. red. Spring–summer. S Eur., N Afr. to Himal. and Turkestan. var. *microcarpus* Rehd. & Wils. Fr. thin, waxy red. var. *royleanus* Dipp. Small, low-growing shrub. Lvs orbicular, to broad-obovate, obtuse or emarginate. Fls in cymes of 3–6. var. *songaricus* (Reg. & Herd.) Schneid. To 2m, br. arched. Lvs bluntly ovate, grey-green. Fls 3–12 in loose vertical infl. Fr. red. var. *veitchii* Rehd. & Wils. To 2m, br. diffuse. Lvs elliptic, acute, glabrescent above, grey-tomentose beneath. Fls larger, in clusters of 3–10. Fr. dark red. Z3.

C. radicans (Schneid.) Klotz. = *C. dammeri* var. *radicans*.

C. racemiflorus var. *nummularius* (Fisch. & Mey.) Dipp. = *C. nummularius*.

C. rehderi Pojark. Close to *C. bullatus*. Shrub to 5m, habit open. Lvs 5–15×8cm, dark green, veins impressed. Fr. deep red, profuse. W China. Z5.

C. rehderi Pojark. Close to *C. bullatus*. Shrub to 5m, habit open. Lvs 5–15×8cm, dark green, veins impressed. Fr. deep red, profuse. W China. Z5.

C. rhytidophyllus Rehd. & Wils. Spreading everg. shrub to 1.8m; br. arching. Lvs 3–8cm, oval-lanceolate, thickly-textured, rugose and dark shiny green above, covered in white- to yellow-tinged hairs beneath. Fls 10–15, in clusters 3cm diam. Fr. hairy when young, becoming orange-red. China. Z7.

C. roseus Edgew. Upright shrub. Lvs 2cm+ elliptic or ovate to oblong, acute or obtuse, glossy or dull and glab. above, glab. or sparse-pubesc, beneath. Fls 2–3-clustered, pink. Fr. red or dark red. NW Himal., Afghan. Z6.

C. rotundifolius Wallich ex Lindl. Everg. shrub of 2m, erect or suberect; br. erect or procumbent. Lvs to 2cm, broad-elliptic to broad obovate-elliptic, mucronulate or rounded, coriaceous, shiny above, yellow-green villous beneath. Fls to 13mm diam., usually solitary. Fr. crimson. Summer. C Himal. 'Ruby': to 1m; br. glab., outspread; lvs elliptic, obtuse, dark glossy green above, pale to blue-green beneath, somewhat hoary. Z6.

C. rubens W.W. Sm. Decid. to semi-evergreen shrub to 120cm. Lvs to 1.5cm, wide-elliptic to round, tomentose, lanate or villous beneath. Fls 1–3-clustered, pink. Fr. red. SW China. Z7.

C. rugosus E. Pritz. ex Diels. Everg. or semi-deciduous shrub; br. arching. Lvs to 8cm, elliptic-lanceolate, rugose and deep green above, with yellow wool beneath. Fls in clusters 5–6cm diam. Fr. red. China. Z6.

C. salicifolius Franch. Everg. shrub to 5m, of graceful habit. Shoots slender. Lvs to 8cm, elliptic-oblong to ovate-lanceolate, slender-pointed, coriaceous, glossy green, grey-tomentose beneath. Fls 5mm diam., in corymbs to 50mm diam. Fr. bright red. Summer. China. 'Autumn Fire' ('Herbstfeuer'): procumbent; lvs elliptic, glossy dark green above, sea-green, papillose and glab. beneath, with purple-red veins; fr. orange-red. 'Dekor': br. pendulous; lvs large, glossy green; fr. bright red. 'Emerald Carpet': habit dense, compact; lvs small; fls white; fr. red. 'Fructuluteo': fr. yellow. 'Gnom': procumbent, slow-growing; lvs 2cm, oblong, obtuse; fr. light red. 'Gracia': decid., dwarf shrub; br. arched; lvs shiny green, rugose, dull red in autumn; fruitless. 'Klampen': fast-growing, everg.; br. procumbent or ascending; lvs dark green, petioles red; fr. bright red. 'Parkteppich': like 'Gnom', but with longer br.; lvs larger; fr. light red in dense clusters. 'Perkeo': dwarf shrub, to 1m; br. dense, pendulous; lvs small. 'Red Flare': vigorous, prostrate to mound-forming; fr. bright red. 'Repens' ('Avonwood', 'Dortmundt'): prostrate shrub; br. not rooting; lvs narrowly elliptic, papillose, glabrescent, glossy green above, blue beneath; fr. small, light red. 'Saldam' (*C. salicifolius* var. *floccosus* × *C. horizontalis*): as 'Autumn Fire' but lvs paler green. 'Valkenburg': semi-deciduous shrub, to 1.7m, growth dense; br. arched; lvs glossy green; fr. not produced. var. *floccosus* Rehd. & Wils. Br. diffuse. Lvs smaller, lanceolate, floccose beneath. Fr. small, red, abundant. Z6.

C. serotinus Hutch. Everg. shrub to 4m, similar to *C. glaucophyllus*. Lvs to 7cm, elliptic or obovate-elliptic, dark green, glab. above, later glab. beneath. Fls in corymbs to 7.5cm diam. Fr. orange-red. Summer. China. Z6.

C. sherriffii Klotz. Medium to large decid. to semi-everg. shrub. Lvs small, broadly elliptic, grey-hairy beneath, purple in fall. Fr. turbinate, red, solitary or paired along branchlets. Tibet. Z6.

C. sikangensis Flinck & Hylmö. Decid. shrub to 3m, ascending. Lvs to 5cm, ovate to elliptic-ovate, acuminate, subcoriaceous, bullate, dark green, pilose, later subglabrous. Fls 6 per cyme. Fr. glossy red or vermilion. W China. Z7.

C. simonsii Bak. Decid. or semi-evergreen erect shrub to 4m. Lvs to 3cm, orbicular-ovate, dark glossy green, somewhat pubesc. above, paler and strigose beneath. Fls 8.5mm diam., 2–5-clustered, white with pink. Fr. scarlet. Summer. Himal., Nepal, Sikkim. Z5.

C. splendens Flink & Hylmö. Decid. shrub to 2m, ascending to decumbent. Lvs to 1.8cm, broad ovate-elliptic to suborbicular, acute, somewhat lustrous and pilose above, white-yellow pilose to tomentose beneath. Fls pink-red with rose margins, usually 3-clustered. Fr. bright orange. W China. Z5. 'Sabrina': berries freely produced.

C. sternianus (Turrill) Boom. Semi-evergreen shrub to 3m, somewhat stiff. Br. slightly spreading. Lvs to 3.5cm in 2 rows, elliptic, acuminate, dark green and glab. above, white-villous beneath. Fls 7–15-clustered, white tinted red. Fr. light red. Spring–summer. SE Tibet, N Burm. Z6.

C. suecicus Klotz. see *C. dammeri* 'Skogholm'.

C. tenuipes Rehd. & Wils. Decid. shrub to 2m, upright. Lvs to 4cm, acuminate or acute, glab. or sparse-pubesc, beneath. Fls 2–4-clustered. Fr. black or black-red. W China. Z7.

C. tomentellus Pojark. Small to medium, spreading shrub. Br. arching, young growth grey-hairy becoming purple-tinted. Lvs to 3.5cm, broadly elliptic to obovate, apex rounded, mucronate, grey-green, downy. Fr. bright red. China. Z7.

C. tomentosus Lindl. Decid. erect shrub to 3m. Lvs to 6cm, suborbicular to elliptic, densely white-woolly beneath. Fls pale pink, 3–7-clustered. Fr. brick-red. Spring. Eur. Z6.

C. turbinatus Craib. Shrub or pyramidal everg. tree to 4m. Lvs to 4.5cm, oblong-ovate to oblong, lanceolate, tapering at both ends, dull blue-green, grey-tomentose beneath. Fls 6.5mm diam., in hemispherical 5cm diam. clusters. Fr. red. Summer. China. Z7.

C. uniflorus Bunge. Decid. shrub to 1m. prostrate to erect. Lvs to 3cm, thin, elliptic to obovate, glab. above, pubesc. beneath when young. Fls solitary or paired, white with red or green tinge. Fr. red. C China. Z5.

C. verruculosus Diels. Decid. or semi-evergreen, upright shrub to 1.5m, young br. verruculose. Lvs to 1.4cm, in 2 rows, orbicular, broad-elliptic or -obovate, emarginate or mucronulate, shiny above, glab. beneath. Fls solitary, nodding, red to rose. Fr. dark red. SW China. Z6.

C. vestitus (W.W. Sm) Flinck & Hylmö = *C. glaucophyllus* var. *vestitus*.

C. villosulus (Rehd. & Wils.) Flinck & Hylmö = *C. acutifolius* var. *villosulus*.

C. vulgaris Lindl. = *C. integerrimus*.

C. wardii W.W. Sm. Everg. erect shrub to 3m. Lvs to 5cm, ovate, leathery, dark glossy green and rugose above, with white felt be-

neath. Fls 10–15, white or flushed pink. Fr. deep orange. SE Tibet. Z6.

C. × watereri Exell. (*C. frigidus* × *C. salicifolius* and *C. rugosus*.) Everg. or more often, semi-everg. shrub, sometimes procumbent. 'Aldenhamensis': narrowly upright, to 3m; br. slightly pendulous, dark brown; lvs 4–7cm, narrow, oblong-lanceolate, rugose above, villous beneath. Fls in small corymbs; fr. bright red. 'Cornubia': tall shrub, to 6m; br. rising diagonally; lvs 7–10cm, slightly acuminate, rugose and glabrescent beneath; fr. bright red, large and almost pendent. 'Exburiensis': similar to 'Rothschildianus', lvs large, glossy pale green above, rugose, downy beneath; fr. apricot-yellow, pink in winter. 'Glabratus': strong-growing, branching; lvs smaller; fr. small, dull red. 'Inchmery': tall and tree-like, resembling *C. frigidus*; fr. large, yellow becoming salmon-pink. 'John Waterer': strong-growing; br. long and arching; lvs 7–10cm, rugose and dark green above, glabrescent beneath; infl. broad; fr. abundant, red. 'Pendulus': fast-growing; br. long, procumbent or pendulous; lvs 4–7cm, glab. above; fls corymbose; fr. red. 'Pink Champagne': tall, vigorous shrub; br. deflexed; lvs narrow; fr. small, yellow clouded with pink. 'Rothschildianus': large, wide-spreading; fr. creamy yellow, in large clusters. 'Salmon Spray': medium-sized; as *C. henryanus* but fr. abundant, salmon-red. 'St Monica': large, strong-growing; lvs oblong-elliptic, 10–15cm; fr. in heavy pendent clusters, red. 'Vicaryi': strong-growing; upright; lvs to 10cm, rugose and green above, villous beneath; fr. purple-red, small. Z6.

C. wheeleri Exell. = *C. × watereri*.

C. wheeleri hort. = *C. buxifolius*.

C. zabelii Schneid. Decid., arching-spreading shrub to 2m. Shoots lanuginose. Lvs to 2.5cm, thin, oval to elliptic, rounded and emarginate or mucronate, dull pale green above, loosely greytomentose beneath. Fls pale pink, 4–10-clustered. Fr. red, lanuginose. Spring. China. Z7.

→*Mespilus*.

Cottendorfia Schult. f. Bromeliaceae. 17 rosette-forming perenn. herbs. Lvs tough, usually unarmed, white or grey-scaly. Infl. scapose; floral bracts and fls small; pet. elliptic. Guyana, Venez., NE Braz. Z10.

C. florida Schult. f. Lvs to 1m, grass-like, pungent. Infl. erect to 40cm with spreading br.; fls to 7mm, many, white. NE Braz.

Cotton *Gossypium*.
Cotton Bell *Espostoa lanata*.
Cotton Fern *Cheilanthes newberryi*.
Cotton Grass *Eriophorum*.
Cotton Lavender *Santolina*.
Cotton Palm *Washingtonia filifera*.
Cotton Rose *Hibiscus mutabilis*.
Cotton-seed Tree *Baccharis halimifolia*.
Cotton Thistle *Onopordum acanthium*.
Cottonweed *Froelichia*; *Otanthus maritimus*.
Cottonwood *Populus* (*P. fremontii*).
Cottony Jujube *Ziziphus mauritanica*.

Cotula L. BRASS BUTTONS. Compositae. *c*80 rhizomatous ann. to perenn. herbs. Lvs usually pinnate. Cap. solitary, disciform or discoid, long-pedunculate. Subcosmop., esp. S Hemis.

C. acaenoides (Hook. & Arn.) Albov. = *Leptinella scariosa*.

C. albida D. Lloyd = *Leptinella albida*.

C. atrata Hook. f. = *Leptinella atrata*.

C. atrata var. *dendyi* (Ckn.) Ckn. = *Leptinella dendyi*.

C. aurea L. = *Matricaria aurea*.

C. barbata DC. Tufted ann. Lvs to 8cm, pinnate above middle, seg. few, narrow, mucronate, softly villous. Cap. to *c*5mm diam., globose; flts yellow. S Afr.

C. coronopifolia L. BRASS BUTTONS. Ann. to perenn., to 30cm, glab., somewhat fleshy, ascending or decumbent. Lvs to *c*12cm, broadly linear, irregularly pinnatifid with few teeth or lobes or entire. Cap. 5–10mm diam.; phyllaries tinged purple; flts yellow. Winter. S Afr. 'Cream Buttons': infl. cream. Z7.

C. dendyi Ckn. = *Leptinella dendyi*.

C. dioica (Hook. f.) Hook. f. = *Leptinella dioica*.

C. goyenii Petrie = *Leptinella goyenii*.

C. hispida (DC.) Harv. Tufted rhizomatous perenn., to 40cm, often decumbent. Lower lvs to 3cm, narrowly ovate, 2-pinnate, villous, seg. linear, apiculate, petiole to 8cm, upper lvs smaller, pinnate, sessile. Cap. 10–15mm diam., globose; flts bright yellow to red. Winter–spring. S Afr. Z9.

C. lanata (Hook. f.) Hook. f. = *Leptinella lanata*.

C. lineariloba (DC.) Hilliard. Tufted perenn., sometimes matforming. Lower lvs *c*3cm, oblong, 1–2-pinnate, seg. linear, terete, obtuse, sericeous, petiole to 3.5cm, upper lvs smaller, pinnate to linear and bract-like. Cap. 1–2.5cm diam., globose; flts bright yellow to red. Winter–spring. S Afr. Z9.

C. muelleri T. Kirk = *Leptinella potentilla.*
C. pectinata Hook. f. = *Leptinella pectinata.*
C. perpusilla Hook. f. Tufted perenn., forming mats. St. creeping, white-hairy. Lvs to 3cm, narrowly oblong to obovate-oblong, finely pinnatisect, sericeous, seg. distant, entire, petiole to 1cm, slender, long-hairy. Cap. 3–7mm diam.; phyllaries edged purple. Winter. NZ. Z8.
C. pilulifera L. f. = *Oncosiphon piluliferum.*
C. plumosa (Hook. f.) Hook. f. = *Leptinella plumosa.*
C. potentillina (F. Muell.) Druce = *Leptinella potentillina.*
C. potentilloides hort. = *Leptinella potentilla.*
C. pyrethrifolia Hook. f. = *Leptinella pyrethrifolia.*
C. reptans Benth. = *Leptinella reptans.*
C. rotundata (Cheesem.) D. Lloyd = *Leptinella rotundata.*
C. scariosa (Cass.) Franch. = *Leptinella scariosa.*
C. sericea (T. Kirk) Ckn. & Allan = *Leptinella albida.*
C. squalida (Hook. f.) Hook. f. = *Leptinella squalida.*
C. traillii T. Kirk = *Leptinella traillii.*
→*Lancisia.*

Cotyledon L. Crassulaceae. 9 shrubs or shrublets. Lvs thickly fleshy, opposite or whorled, sessile. Pan. contracted, cymose, many-fld; fls usually nodding, bell-shaped; sep. 5, green, fused below; cor. fused below, lobes 5, triangular to linear; sta. 10, anth. exserted. Afr. Z10.
C. acutifolia Hemsl. non (Lindl.) Bak. = *Echeveria maxonii.*
C. acutifolia (Lindl.) Bak. non Hemsl. = *Echeveria acutifolia.*
C. adscendens R. A. Dyer. To 2m, sparsely branched. Lvs glab., 2–5×1–2.5cm, obovate, flattened sometimes concave above, convex beneath, tip triangular-acute, margin red. Flowering st. glab.; cor. red-orange, glab., tube, 12–15mm, lobes lanceolate. Summer. S Afr.
C. adunca Bak. = *Pachyphytum hookeri.*
C. agavoides Bak. = *Echeveria agavoides.*
C. aggregata Mak. = *Orostachys aggregata.*
C. alstonii Schönl. and Bak. f. = *Adromischus alstonii.*
C. atropurpurea Bak. = *Echeveria atropurpurea.*
C. ausana Dinter = *C. orbiculata* var. *orbiculata.*
C. barbeyi Schweinf. ex Bak. To 2m. Much-branched. Lvs gland. hairy to glab., green to brown, 4–16×1–4.5cm, obovate-linear, acute to mucronate, terete or flattened. Flowering st. glab. to gland.-hairy; cor. orange-red, tube 14–18mm, flask-shaped, gland. hairy, lobes linear. Winter. S Afr., E Afr. to Arabia.
C. batesii Hemsl. = *Villadia batesii.*
C. beckeri Schönl. & Bak. f. = *C. velutina.*
C. bracteolata (Link, Klotzsch & Otto) Bak. = *Echeveria bicolor.*
C. cacalioides (L. f.). = *Tylecodon cacalioides.*
C. caespitosa Haw. = *Dudleya caespitosa.*
C. californica Cav. = *Dudleya caespitosa.*
C. campanulata Marloth. To 50cm, branching below. Lvs yellow-green, glandular-hairy, 4–13×1–3.5cm, almost cylindrical or grooved above, lanceolate-linear, margin brown and wavy. Cor. yellow, tube 5–8mm, viscid, lobes reflexed. Summer. S Afr.
C. carnicolor Bak. = *Echeveria carnicolor.*
C. caryophyllacea Burm. f. = *Adromischus caryophyllaceus.*
C. clavifolia Haw. = *Adromischus cristatus* ssp. *clavifolius.*
C. coccinea Cav. = *Echeveria coccinea.*
C. corderoyi Bak. = *Echeveria agavoides* var. *corderoyi.*
C. crassifolia Salisb. = *Adromischus hemisphaericus.*
C. cristata Haw. = *Adromischus cristatus.*
C. cuneata Thunb. To 50cm, little-branched. Lvs yellow-green, 6–17×2.5–10cm, cuneate, flattened to terete, pungent or rounded. Flowering st. viscid; cor. yellow to green-yellow, tube 6–10mm, viscid, lobes reflexed. Summer. S Afr.
C. devensis N.E. Br. = *Echeveria acutifolia.*
C. erubescens (Maxim.) Franch. & Savat. = *Orostachys erubescens.*
C. farinosa Bak. = *Dudleya farinosa.*
C. filicaulis Ecklon & Zeyh. = *Adromischus filicaulis.*
C. flanaganii Schönl. & Bak. f. = *C. orbiculata* var. *flanaganii.*
C. gibbiflora (DC.) Bak. = *Echeveria gibbiflora.*
C. gracilis Haw. = *C. papillaris.*
C. grayi Bak. = *Echeveria paniculata.*
C. hemisphaerica L. = *Adromischus hemisphaericus.*
C. intermedia (Boiss.) Stef. = *Umbilicus horizontalis* var. *intermedius.*
C. iwarenge Mak. = *Orostachys iwarenge.*
C. jurgensenii Hemsl. = *Villadia jurgensenii.*
C. laciniata L. = *Kalanchoe laciniata.*
C. ladysmithiensis Poelln. To 30cm, freely branching subshrub. Lvs to 6×2cm, oblong-obovate, rounded with blunt teeth above, thickly fleshy, short-grey to golden-tomentose. Fls to 2cm, tubular, red-brown, nodding to 10 on stalk to 15cm. Cape Prov.
C. lanceolata Benth. & Hook. = *Dudleya lanceolata.*

C. leucophylla C. A. Sm. = *C. orbiculata* var. *oblonga.*
C. linearis Greene = *Dudleya linearis.*
C. macrantha De Smet. PIG'S EARS. Close to *C. orbiculata.* Lvs green, shiny, orbicular-obovate, flattened, mid green edged red. Fls red and yellow, larger. E Cape.
C. maculata Salm-Dyck = *Adromischus maculatus.*
C. mammillaris L. f. = *Adromischus mammillaris.*
C. marlothii Schönl. = *Adromischus filicaulis* ssp. *marlothii.*
C. meyeri Harv. = *C. papillaris.*
C. mollis Schönl. = *C. velutina.*
C. nodulosa Bak. = *Echeveria nodulosa.*
C. nuda (Lindl.) Bak. = *Echeveria nuda.*
C. nudicaulis Abrams non Lam. = *Dudleya densiflora.*
C. oppositifolia Ledeb. ex Nordm. = *Chiastophyllum oppositifolium.*
C. orbiculata L. To 1.5m, much-branched. Lvs green to grey-green, glab. to hairy, 3–16×1–9cm, obovate to linear, terete or somewhat flattened, apex rounded or pungent, margin often red. Infl. many-fld, sometimes hairy; cor. orange to deep red or purple, tube usually glab., lobes recurved, sometimes curled. Summer. S Afr. var. *orbiculata.* To 1m. Lvs opposite, apex mucronate to cuspidate, white-waxy upper margin red, horny. Cor. deep red often bloomed orange. var. *dactylopsis* Tölken. To 50cm. Lvs opposite, densely clustered. Cor. yellow, lobes long. var. *flanaganii* (Schönl. & Bak. f.) Tölken. To 1m. Lvs in whorls of three, terete. var. *oblonga* Tölken. St. branching at base, decumbent, occas. suberect. Lvs opposite, closely packed. Cor. red-orange. var. *spuria* (L.) Tölken. To 1.5m. Occas. decumbent. Lvs not tightly packed. Cor. pale yellow-orange occas. red.
C. ovata Mill. = *Crassula ovata.*
C. pachyphytum Bak. = *Pachyphytum bracteosum.*
C. paniculata (L. f.). = *Tylecodon paniculatus.*
C. pannosa Bak. = *Kalanchoe eriophylla.*
C. papillaris L. f. To 1m. St. much-branched, decumbent. Lvs yellow-green occas. glaucous, 1.5–6×0.4–1.3cm, linear to oblanceolate or elliptic, pungent, margin red. Cor. dark red to orange, tube 5–8mm, lobes reflexed. Summer. S Afr.
C. pendulina (DC.) Battand. = *Umbilicus rupestris.*
C. pillansii Schönl. = *C. cuneata.*
C. pinnata Lam. = *Kalanchoe pinnata.*
C. pringlei S. Wats. = *Echeveria pringlei.*
C. purpurea Thunb. = *C. orbiculata* var. *spuria.*
C. quitensis (HBK) Bak. = *Echeveria quitensis.*
C. reticulata L. f. = *Tylecodon reticulatus.*
C. roseata Bak. = *Echeveria rosea.*
C. rotundifolia Haw. = *Adromischus hemisphaericus.*
C. saxosa M.E. Jones = *Dudleya saxosa.*
C. schaeferiana Dinter = *Tylecodon schaeferianus.*
C. schaffneri S. Wats. = *Echeveria schaffneri.*
C. scheerii (Lindl.) Bak. = *Echeveria scheerii.*
C. secunda Bak. = *Echeveria secunda.*
C. simplicifolia hort. ex Gard. Chron. = *Chiastophyllum oppositifolium.*
C. sprucei Bak. = *Echeveria quitensis* var. *sprucei.*
C. spuria L. = *C. orbiculata* var. *spuria.*
C. stolonifera Bak. = *Echeveria stolonifera.*
C. strictiflora (A. Gray) Bak. = *Echeveria strictiflora.*
C. sturmiana Poelln. = *C. barbeyi.*
C. subrigida Robinson & Seaton = *Echeveria subrigida.*
C. teretifolia Thunb. = *C. campanulata.*
C. tomentosa Harv. To 50cm, much-branched. Lvs 2.5cm, grey-green, tomentose, ovate-oblong, compressed or terete. Infl. hairy; cor. red-orange to yellow, tube 12–16mm, hairy outside. Spring. S Afr.
C. transvaalensis Guill. = *C. barbeyi.*
C. triflora L. f. = *Adromischus triflorus.*
C. trigyna Burchell = *Adromischus trigynus.*
C. undulata Haw. SILVER CROWN; SILVER RUFFLES. Similar to *C. orbiculata.* Lvs broadly obovate, thickly grey-glaucous, margins strongly undulate. Cape Province.
C. van-der-heydenii hort. = *Adromischus cristatus* ssp. *clavifolius.*
C. velutina Hook. f. To 2m, few-branched. Lvs green to grey-brown, glab. to velvety-hairy, 5–11×2–4cm, oblanceolate, compressed, blunt, occas. mucronate, margin often red. Cor. orange to copper, edged yellow, occas. hairy on outside. Summer. S Afr.
C. virens Fedde = *Dudleya virens.*
C. viscida Wats. = *Dudleya viscida.*
C. wallichii Harv. = *Tylecodon wallichii.*
C. wickensii Schönl. = *C. barbeyi.*
C. woodii Schönl. & Bak. f. To 1.2m., much-branched. Lvs deep green, waxy, 2–3.2×0.6–1.5cm, obovate-lanceolate, narrowing below, apex pointed, red. Infl. glab.; cor. orange to red, tube 12–15mm, glab. Summer. S Afr.

Couch *Cynodon dactylon.*
Couch Honeypot *Dryandra nivea.*

Coudenbergia Marchal = *Aralia.*

Coulter Pine *Pinus coulteri.*
Council Tree *Ficus altissima.*
Country Borage *Plectranthus amboinicus.*
Country Fig *Ficus racemosa.*

Couralia Splitg.
C. rosea (Bertol.) Donnell-Sm. = *Tabebuia rosea.*

Courgette *Cucurbita pepo.*

Couroupita Aubl. Lecythidaceae. 3 trees. Lvs in apical whorls, simple. Rac. or pan. pendulous, borne on old wood. Fls large; sep. 6; pet. 6, oblong, unequal, spreading and incurved; androecium extending on one side into a large blade (androphore) bent over the ovary bearing many sta. on its inner surface. Fr. a large, round woody capsule; seeds numerous, embedded in pulp. Trop. Amer., W Indies. Z10.
C. guianensis Aubl. CANNONBALL TREE. Tree, to 35m. Lvs to 30cm, lanceolate-obovate, glab., entire, undulate or obscurely serrate. Rac. term. to 3.5m, growing from trunk; fls sweetly fragrant; pet. to 5cm, yellow-red outside, red inside; androphore red to pink, to 2cm diam. with *c*700 sta. Fr. to 24cm diam. N S Amer.

Cousinia Cass. Compositae. *c*600 perenn. herbs or shrubs, rarely annuals, usually spiny. Cap. discoid; phyllaries imbricate, usually with a term. spine, often appendaged, entire to spinulose. E Medit. to C Asia and W Himal.
C. hystrix C.A. Mey. = *C. pterocaulos.*
C. pterocaulos (C.A. Mey.) Rech. f. Tomentose perenn. herb to 50cm. Lvs pinnatilobed, seg. triangular-lanceolate, narrowing to a robust spine, coriaceous, sparsely hairy above, densely so beneath. Cap. to 5cm diam., solitary; phyllaries terminating in rigid spines; flts purple. Summer. NE Iran. Z7.

Coussapoa Aubl. Cecropiaceae. *c*35 lactiferous trees, shrubs, some epiphytes. Lvs spirally arranged, entire; stipules connate, amplexicaul. Fls small, unisexual, 3-merous, tubular, in dense bracteate heads. Mex. to S Braz. Z9.
C. microcarpa (Schott) Rizz. St. pubesc. Lvs to 12×6cm, dark green, revolute, subovate-elliptic, glaucescent; petiole long. Fl. head small, dense, paired, peduncle pubesc., to 2cm. Guyana, Braz.
C. schottii Miq. = *C. microcarpa.*
→*Brosimum.*

Coutarea Aubl. Rubiaceae. 5 everg. trees and shrubs. Lvs petiolate, opposite, thin-textured. Fls usually term., solitary, or few in cymose heads; cal. obovoid to turbinate, lobes 5–8; cor. funnel- to bell-shaped, tube curved, ventricose, lobes 5–8, spreading; sta. 5–8. Trop. Amer. Z10.
C. hexandra (Jacq.) Schum. To 6m. Lvs to 12cm, ovate to elliptic, glab. or puberulent, veins conspicuous. Fls fragrant, white or pale green or yellow and tinged purple; cor. to 5cm, lobes 6, ovate; sta. long-exserted. Mex. to Peru, Arg.
C. speciosa Aubl. = *C. hexandra.*
→*Portlandia.*

Coveniella Tind. Dryopteridaceae. 1 terrestrial fern. Rhiz. long-creeping, to 2cm diam., scales dark brown. Stipes erect, to 3×length of lamina; lamina 15–30cm, pinnate, chartaceous, golden-glandular-pubesc., scaly on veins beneath; pinnae 12–23cm, in 1–6 pairs, oblong or narrowly lanceolate, undulate or crenate, serrate toward apex. Aus. (NE Queensld). Z10.
C. poecilophlebia (Hook.) Tind.
→*Dryopteris.*

Coville *Larrea tridentata.*

Cowania D. Don ex Tilloch & Tayl. CLIFF ROSE. Rosaceae. 5 everg. shrubs or small trees. Lvs coriaceous, revolute, pinnatifid, gland. above, usually white-tomentose beneath. Fls rose-like, solitary pet. 5, obovate, spreading; sta. many, in 2 series. Achenes plumose in feathery seed-heads. SW N Amer. Z9.
C. mexicana D. Don. Mex., SW US. The form usually grown is var. *stansburiana* (Torr.) Jeps. Stiff shrub to 2m. Young br. red-brown, gland. Lvs to 1.5cm, obovate, lobes 3–5, linear. Fls fragrant, white to pale yellow, 2cm diam.
C. plicata D. Don. Shrub to 2m. Bark peeling; branchlets red, gland. and lanate. Lvs to 2.5cm, obovate, 5–9-lobed. Fls rich rose, 3cm diam. New Mex., SW US.
C. purpurea Zucc. = *C. plicata.*
C. stansburiana Torr. = *C. mexicana* var. *stansburiana.*

Cowberry *Vaccinium vitis-idaea.*
Cow-cockle *Vaccaria.*
Cowhage *Malpighia urens.*
Cow Horn *Euphorbia grandicornis.*
Cow-itch Cherry *Malpighia urens.*
Cow-itch Tree *Lagunaria patersonii.*
Cow Lily *Nuphar.*
Cow Okra *Parmentiera aculeata.*
Cow Parsley *Anthriscus sylvestris.*
Cowpea *Vigna unguiculata.*
Cowslip *Primula veris.*
Cowslip Orchid *Caladenia flava.*
Cow's Tail Pine *Cephalotaxus harringtonia.*
Cow-tongue Fern *Campyloneurum phyllitidis.*
Cow Tree *Brosimum.*
Crab Apple *Malus sylvestris.*
Crab Cactus *Schlumbergera truncata.*
Crab Grass *Digitaria* (*D. sanguinalis*); *Panicum.*
Crackerberry *Cornus canadensis.*
Crack Willow *Salix fragilis.*
Cradle Lily *Tradescantia spathacea.*
Cradle Orchid *Anguloa* (*A. clowesii*).
Crake Berry *Empetrum nigrum.*

Crambe L. Cruciferae. 20 often woody-based ann. or perenn. herbs. Lvs large, usually glab., thick-textured, basal, stout-stalked, ± bullate and undulate. Fls small, scented, numerous, in large branching rac.; pet. 4, white or sulphur-yellow. C Eur., Asia Minor, C Asia, Trop. Afr.
C. cordifolia Steven. Perenn. 1–1.5m. Lvs 13–31×14–28cm, reniform to ovate, base cordate, bullate, dark glossy green, toothed; petiole long, hairy. Infl. to 1.5m, massive, rounded, br. fine, v. numerous, spreading; pet. 6–7mm, white. Summer. Cauc. Z6.
C. hispanica L. Slender ann., to 1m. Lvs pinnatisect or lyrate, term. lobe large, round to cordate, lat. lobes small, paired. Infl. long, lax; pet. 3–4mm. Medit. Z7.
C. juncea Bieb. = *C. orientalis.*
C. koktebelica (Junge) Bush. To 2m, base, clothed with deflexed petioles, white-pubesc. Lvs to 30×18cm, lyrate, pinnatisect to entire, rounded, entire at base, subglabrous above, sparsely pilose on nerves beneath; petiole 1–10cm. Infl. v. large, densely and finely branched, far exceeding lvs; pet. to 6.5mm, white. Coasts of Black Sea and Sea of Azov, E Taurus, Transcauc. Z6.
C. kotschyana Boiss. Similar to *C. cordifolia* except to 5m, lvs hairy, pet. 7–11mm. Spring. Iran to W Tibet. Z7.
C. maritima L. SEA KALE. Perenn., 30–75cm. St. purple-grey. Lvs 12–30cm, fleshy, chalky blue-glaucous, elliptic or nearly round, undulate-crispate to irregularly pinnatifid. Infl. dense, corymbose to 0.5m; pet. 6–10mm, white. Coastal N Eur., Baltic and Black Seas. Z5.
C. orientalis L. Perenn., 75–150cm. St. erect, branching below. Lvs to 40cm, pinnately divided into 4–5 paired lobes and large term. lobe, hairy, irregularly toothed; petiole bristly, to 20cm. Infl. lax; pet. 3–5mm, white tinted lavender, rarely yellow. Turk., SW Asia. Z7.
C. tatarica Sebeók. Perenn., 30–90cm. St. erect, branching below. Lvs fleshy, grey-green, with red veins, deeply divided and toothed; petiole bristly. Infl. corymbose, dense at first, becoming lax; pet. 3–6mm. E Eur. Z5.

Crampbark *Viburnum opulus.*
Cranberry *Vaccinium macrocarpon*; *V. vitis-idaea*; *Viburnum trilobum.*
Cranberry Heath *Astroloma humifusum.*
Crane Flower *Strelitzia reginae.*
Cranesbill *Geranium.*
Crape Myrtle *Lagerstroemia indica.*

Craspedia Forst. f. BILLY BUTTONS; BACHELOR'S BUTTONS. Compositae. 8 ann. to perenn. herbs. Lvs in basal rosettes or cauline, entire. Cap. discoid, in spherical or cylindrical compound clusters or glomerules, on stiff, unbranched stalks, surrounded by leafy bracts. Aus., NZ. Z8.
C. alpina Backh. ex Hook. f. Densely white-woolly perenn. St. simple, erect, to 50cm. Basal lvs to 10cm, oblong-ovate to lanceolate, st. lvs lanceolate, smaller, amplexicaul. Glomerules to 3cm diam.; flts 6–8, yellow or white. Tasm., Vict.
C. chrysantha (Schldl.) Benth. GOLDEN BILLY BUTTONS; YELLOW DRUMSTICKS. Grey-woolly perenn., to 30cm. St. usually simple. Lvs to 2cm, linear. Glomerules to 1×2cm; flts 4–7, yellow. E Aus.
C. fimbriata var. *lanata* Hook. f. = *C. lanata.*

C. glauca (Labill.) Spreng. COMMON BILLY BUTTONS; BACHELOR'S BUTTONS. Tufted perenn. to 60cm. Lvs to 15cm, oblanceolate to linear, green and glab. to white-hairy. Glomerules to 3cm diam.; flts 6–8, yellow or cream. S Aus. var. *macrocephala* (Hook.) Benth. To 1m. Lvs hispid. Glomerules to 4cm diam.; flts 8–13, yellow.

C. globosa Benth. DRUMSTICKS. White-woolly perenn., to 1.5m. St. simple, rigid. Lvs to 30cm, broadly linear to lanceolate, acute. Glomerules to 2.5cm diam.; phyllaries tipped yellow; flts 4–6, yellow. W Vict., New S Wales.

C. incana Allan. Densely white-woolly perenn., to 30cm. Basal lvs to 10cm, obovate to spathulate, uppermost lvs bract-like. Glomerules to 3cm diam.; flts 4mm, yellow. NZ.

C. lanata (Hook. f.) Allan. White-woolly perenn., to 40cm. Basal lvs to 10cm, obovate to spathulate. Glomerules to 2cm diam.; flts to 4mm, yellow or white. NZ.

C. macrocephala Hook. = *C. glauca* var. *macrocephala*.

C. minor (Hook. f.) Allan. To 19m. Lvs to 8cm, ovate, tapering to short petiole, bristly-pubesc. Glomerules 2–3cm; flts light yellow. NZ.

C. richea Cass. = *C. glauca*.

C. uniflora Forst. f. BACHELOR'S BUTTONS; BILLY BUTTONS. Ann. to perenn., to 60cm. St. simple, erect. Basal lvs to 12cm, oblong-ovate, st. lvs lanceolate, amplexicaul. Glomerules to 4cm diam.; flts 5–10. S Aus., Tasm., NZ.

→*Calocephalus*.

Crassula L. Crassulaceae. *c*300 succulent perenn., bienn. and ann. herbs and small shrubs. St. and br. often woody. Lvs often fleshy with hydathodes on margins or spread over surfaces. Infl. 2–3-branched; fls tubular or stellate; sep. 5, occas. 4 or 8; pet. as many as sep., fused at base. Few cosmop., most restricted to S Afr. Z9.

C. alba Forssk. Perenn. or bienn., to 50cm. Lvs 0.6–1.7cm, in a basal rosette, spirally arranged, linear-lanceolate, sharply pointed, grooved, dark green-yellow, tinged purple, ciliate. Fls numerous; pet. 3–6mm, oblong, pointed, white to red; anth. dark brown. Widespread S Afr.

C. albiflora Sims. = *C. dejecta*.

C. alstonii Marloth. Perenn. St. short. Lvs 0.6–1cm, in 2 rows forming a dense rosette, 2–5cm across, round to transverse-obovate, tip erect, stiff-hairy beneath. Infl. term., rounded; pet. 2.5–3mm, lanceolate-oblong, yellow-cream, somewhat pointed; anth. brown-yellow. Autumn. Cape Prov.

C. aquatica (L.) Schönl. Aquatic ann., 2–5cm. St. horizontal. Lvs 0.3–0.6cm, sparse, linear, ± pointed, fleshy, fused below. Fls axill., solitary; pet. 4, ovate, white. N & C Eur., N Asia, N Amer.

C. arborescens (Mill.) Willd. SILVER JADE PLANT; SILVER DOLLAR; CHINESE JADE. Shrubby tree-like perenn. 1–2m. St. stout, branched, bark thin. Lvs 2–5cm, obovate to round, tip rounded, tapering below, blue-green, grey-bloomed, margin entire, tinged purple. Pet. 5–7, 7–10mm, lanceolate, hooded, cream, tinged red; anth. purple. Summer. Cape Prov.

C. archeri Compton = *C. pyramidalis*.

C. argentea Thunb. = *C. ovata*.

C. argyrophylla Diels. Close to *C. globularioides*. Lvs few, ± basal, 2–4cm, obovate, obtuse, thick, flattened, finely hairy. Infl. corymbose on scapes to 10cm.

C. atropurpurea (Haw.) Dietr. To 60cm. Lvs 0.8–6cm, sometimes restricted to a basal rosette, obovate to oblanceolate, blunt, flat to cylindrical, hydathodes scattered, hairy or glab., margin red. Infl. elongate; pet. 3.5–4.5mm, pandurate, cream, anth. yellow. Summer. Cape Prov. var. *purcellii* (Schönl.) Toelken. Lvs linear-elliptic, densely hairy, pointed.

C. barbata Thunb. Ann. or bienn., to 30cm. Lvs 1–4cm, erect, spirally arranged in basal rosette, obovate to orbicular, grey-green to green, ciliate. Infl. spike-like; pet. 4.5–6mm, oblong, white tinged pink; anth. black. Spring. Cape Prov.

C. barklyi N.E. Br. RATTLESNAKE CRASSULA. Perenn., 5–9cm. St. horizontal or erect, branching below. Lvs 0.3–0.4cm, adpressed to st. in a smooth column, transversely ovate, convex beneath, concave above, densely ciliate. Infl. somewhat hidden by upper lvs; pet. 9–11mm, oblong, cream, anth. yellow. Winter. Cape Prov.

C. basutica Schönl. = *C. dependens*.

C. brevifolia Harv. Shrubby perenn. to 50cm. Lvs 1.5–5cm, elliptic-oblong, sharply tapering to a bunt horny tip, spreading and upward-curved, convex or keeled, v. fleshy, grey-green, hydathodes on margins and upper surface. Infl. rounded; pet. 3–5mm, elliptic-oblong, anth. black to yellow. Nam., Cape Prov.

C. capensis (L.) Baill. Erect, rhizomatous perenn., 5–20cm. Lvs 2–8cm, obovate to round, tip blunt, base cordate or tapered, entire or with blunt teeth. Infl. usually flat-topped; pet. 3–8mm,

oblanceolate, pointed, white tinged red, anth. brown. Cape Prov.

C. capitella Thunb. Perenn., or bienn.,↑to 40cm. St. woody. Lvs 1–12cm, spirally arranged in a basal rosette, ovate to linear-lanceolate, pointed, glab. or hairy, grooved, often spotted red, hydathodes red, scattered, margins ciliate or papillose. Infl. glab. or hairy, spike-like; pet. 2–5mm, oblong-lanceolate, hooded, white tinged pink; anth. dark brown. S Afr. ssp. *nodulosa* (Schönl.) Toelken. Base tuberous. Lvs usually reflexed. Infl. hairy; sep. hairy. ssp. *thyrsiflora* (Thunb.) Toelken. Lvs glab., ciliate. Sep. glab., occas. toothed.

C. cephalophora Thunb. = *C. nudicaulis*.

C. clavifolia (E. Mey.) Harv. = *C. atropurpurea*.

C. coccinea L. Shrubby perenn., to 60cm. St. few-branched, concealed by lvs. Lvs 1.2–2.5cm, elliptic to ovate, pointed, green often tinged red, margin curved upwards, ciliate. Pet. 35–45mm, spathulate, recurved, red or white tinged red, anth. black. Summer. Cape Prov.

C. coerulescens Schönl. = *C. nemorosa*.

C. columella Marloth & Schönl. Similar to *C. elegans* except to 20cm; lvs 0.5–1cm, adpressed to st. forming a 4-angled column, often bristle-tipped, concave above, convex beneath. Summer. Cape Prov.

C. columnaris Thunb. Perenn., often monocarpic, 3–10cm. Lvs packed into an erect column 0.3–1cm, transversely ovate, blunt, grey or brown-green, dish-shaped, ridged, ciliate. Infl. ± hidden by lvs; pet. 7–13mm, oblong, rounded, white-yellow tinged red; anth. brown-yellow. Autumn. Cape Prov., Nam.

C. confusa Schönl. & Bak. f. = *C. nemorosa*.

C. congesta N.E. Br. Monocarpic. St. 5–20cm, simple. Lvs 1.5–3cm, lanceolate, pointed, flat above, convex beneath, tip terete, fleshy, grey-green to brown, sparsely ciliate below. Infl. somewhat hidden; pet. 9–13mm, oblong, hooded, cream tinged red; anth. yellow. Autumn. Cape Prov.

C. cooperi Reg. = *C. exilis* ssp. *cooperi*.

C. corallina Thunb. Perenn., to 8cm. Taproot often tuberous. St. sometimes woody. Lvs 0.3–0.5cm, obovate, tapering to tip and base, terete, warty, waxy. Fls solitary or clustered; pet. 2–3.5mm, obovate-oblong, cream; anth. yellow. SW Cape and Nam.

C. cordata Thunb. Perenn. to 25cm. St. horizontal or erect, rooting, usually woody. Lvs 1–3.5cm, ovate, blunt, base cordate, grey-green, hydathodes red, scattered, margin often tinged red. Pet. 4–5mm, lanceolate-aristate, light yellow-cream, tinged red; anth. yellow. Early spring. Cape Prov.

C. cultrata L. AIRPLANE PROPELLER PLANT; PROPELLER PLANT. Perenn. shrub, to 80cm. St. erect, branched, woody. Lvs 2.5–10cm, knife-shaped to oblanceolate, rounded to blunt, compressed, glab. or velvety, margin red. Infl. elongate loose; pet. 3.5–4.5mm, pandurate, cream; anth. black. Cape Prov., Natal.

C. cyclophylla Schönl. & Bak. f. = *C. spathulata*.

C. deceptor Schönl. & Bak. f. Perenn., to 15cm. Br. numerous, stout, covered in old lvs. Lvs 0.6–1.5cm, in 4 ranks, ± adpressed forming a square column, grey ovate, hydathodes conspicuous beneath. Infl. spreading; pet. 2–2.5mm, ciliate, elliptic-oblong, cream-brown; anth. brown. Summer. Cape Prov.

C. deceptrix Schönl. & Bak. f. = *C. deceptor*.

C. decipiens N.E. Br. = *C. tecta*.

C. dejecta Jacq. Shrubby perenn. to 40cm. St. much-branched, initially hairy. Lvs 0.5–2.5cm, elliptic or oblong-ovate, tip rounded, compressed, green-yellow, ciliate. Pet. 6–8mm, oblanceolate, pointed, white tinged red; anth. brown. Spring –summer. SW Cape Prov.

C. deltoidea Thunb. SILVER BEADS. Perenn. subshrub to 10cm. St. short, fleshy, branching. Lvs 1–2cm, oblanceolate-ovate or rhombic, fused below, blunt or pointed, flat above, convex beneath, grey-green, waxy. Infl. rounded, term.; pet. 3.5–5mm, oblanceolate-elliptic, cream-white, anth. black. SE Afr.

C. dentata Thunb. Tuberous perenn., to 15cm. St. horizontal, spreading. Lvs 0.5–1.5cm, whorled, long-stalked, broad-ovate to round, tip round or pointed, base cordate, serrate or entire. Infl. many-fld; pet. 2.5–3.5mm, lanceolate, pointed, white-cream; anth. yellow. Spring. Cape Prov.

C. dependens Bol. Perenn., 7–15cm. St. horizontal, many-branched, br. hairy when young. Lvs 0.5–2cm, sharply pointed, lanceolate, grey-green, ciliate. Infl. 2–3-branched; pet. 3–6mm, elliptic, narrow, pointed, with projections beneath, white-cream; anth. brown. Summer. NE Transvaal.

C. dichotoma L. Ann., 5–25cm. St. thin, tough, branching. Lvs 0.5–1.8cm, elliptic to linear or obovate, flat, green, hydathodes beneath. Infl. cymose, term.; pet. 7–20mm, elliptic-oblanceolate, orange-yellow; anth. yellow. Spring–summer. Cape Prov.

C. dielsii Schönl. = *C. dentata*.

C. drakensbergensis Schönl. = *C. vaginata*.

C. dregeana Harv. = *C. obovata* var. *dregeana*.

C. elata N.E. Br. = *C. capitella* ssp. *nodulosa*.

C. elegans Schönl. & Bak. f. Perenn., to 10cm, short-branched. Lvs 0.5–1.5cm, ovate, blunt or pointed, convex beneath, flat to convex above, closely packed, glab. to finely hairy, tinged red-brown, hydathodes scattered. Infl. hairy, spreading; pet. 2–2.5mm, elliptic-oblong, blunt, cream-white; anth. brown. Cape Prov., Nam.

C. ericoides Haw. Perenn., 15–40cm. St. usually erect, br. woody. Lvs 0.3–0.7cm, ovate-lanceolate, pointed. Infl. partly concealed by upper lvs; fls ± tubular; pet. 3–5mm, elliptic, pointed, white; anth. brown. Summer. Natal, Cape Prov.

C. excilis Harv. Cushion-forming perenn. or ann., to 10cm. Lvs spirally arranged, to 0.5cm, linear-elliptic, pointed, flat to terete, ciliate. Infl. term.; pet. 4–4.5mm, oblong-obovate, white tinged pink; anth. yellow. Cape Prov. ssp. *cooperi* (Reg.) Toelken. Cushions dense, spreading. Lvs oblanceolate, not v. fleshy.

C. falcata Wendl. = *C. perfoliata* var. *falcata*.

C. fascicularis Lam. Shrubby perenn., to 40cm. Lvs 1.5–3.5cm, linear-lanceolate, pointed, compressed, fleshy, tips reflexed, ciliate. Fls sessile; pet. 20–32mm, oblong, cream-yellow tinged red; anth. black. SW Cape Prov.

C. fusca Herre. Shrubby perenn. to 40cm. St. few-branched, covered with old lvs. Lvs 4–15cm, lanceolate, pointed, carinate, green-brown tinged red, hydathodes above, margins finely serrate at first. Infl. rounded; pet. 4–5mm, elliptic, pointed, white-cream, anth. black. Summer. Cape Prov., Nam.

C. gillii Schönl. = *C. montana* ssp. *quadrangularis*.

C. globularioides Britt. Perenn., to 25cm. St. erect, br. erect or drooping, woody. Lvs 0.8–7cm, in 4 ranks, obovate to elliptic, tips rounded, flat, hairy or glab., ciliate. Infl. term., flat-topped, hairy; pet. 3–5mm, oblong-oblanceolate, cream, tip pointed and reflexed; anth. yellow-brown. Summer. Transvaal, Swaz., Natal.

C. helmsii (T. Kirk) Ckn. Perenn. aquatic herb. St. simple or branched, erect. Lvs 0.4–2cm, linear to lanceolate, pointed, connate. Fls solitary, stalked; pet. 1.5–2mm, ovate, white-pink, blunt. Summer. Aus. and NZ, nat. N Eur.

C. hemisphaerica Thunb. ARAB'S TURBAN. Perenn., 5–12cm. Lvs 1–5cm, in rounded rosettes, obovate, blunt, bristle-tipped, flat, grooved, grey-green. hydathodes on margins and scattered above, ciliate. Infl. spike-like, glab.; pet. 2–3mm, oblong-lanceolate, cream-white; anth. black. Spring. Cape Prov.

C. impressa N.E. Br. = *C. schmidtii*.

C. indica Decne. = *Sinocrassula indica*.

C. justi-corderoyi Jacobs & Poelln. Herbaceous perenn., to 15cm. St. short, erect, branching below. Lvs c5cm, oblanceolate-elliptic, tapering to base, pointed, flat above, convex beneath, white, papillose. Infl. somewhat corymbose; pet. 5mm, pink. Known only in cult. 'Ken Aslet': habit bushy, v. small; lvs fleshy; fls pale pink.

C. lactea Sol. FLOWERING CRASSULA; TAILOR'S PATCH. Perenn., to 20cm. St. horizontal to scrambling, thick, to 40cm. Lvs 2.5–7cm, oblanceolate, tapering to base, apex abruptly pointed, terete, dull green, margin horny, yellow. Pet. 4–8mm, lanceolate, yellow-white, pink above; anth. purple. Autumn. Cape Prov.

C. lanuginosa Harv. Perenn., to 15cm. St. horizontal or drooping, rooting. Lvs 0.2–3.5cm, obovate to linear-lanceolate, pointed or blunt, terete, hairy, ciliate. Infl. term., indistinctly stalked; anth. black. Summer. Cape Prov.

C. lathispathulata Schönl. & Bak. f. = *C. spathulata*.

C. laxa Schönl. = *C. dependus*.

C. lineolata Ait. = *C. pellucida* ssp. *marginalis*.

C. lycopodioides Lam. = *C. muscosa*.

C. macowaniana Schönl. & Bak. f. Perenn. shrub. St. branched, sometimes prostrate, bark flaking. Lvs 2.5–8cm, linear-lanceolate, pointed, flat above, convex beneath, glab., brown-green. Infl. rounded; pet. 2.5–4mm, oblanceolate, rounded, white tinged pink, anth. black. Summer. Cape Prov., Nam.

C. marginalis Dryand. = *C. pellucida* ssp. *marginalis*.

C. marginata Thunb. = *C. pellucida* ssp. *marginalis*.

C. marnierana Huber & H.J. Jacobsen = *C. rupestris* ssp. *marnierana*.

C. mesembrianthoides Schönl. & Bak. f. = *C. elegans*.

C. mesembryanthemopsis Dinter. Differs from *C. susannae* in lvs cuneate, triangular in section, not grooved; infl. short-stalked, somewhat hidden by lvs; pet. 5–7mm; anth. yellow. Autumn. Cape Prov., Nam.

C. minima Thunb. = *C. dentata*.

C. montana Thunb. Cushion-forming perenn., 4–12cm. Lvs 0.4–3.5cm, 4-ranked in numerous rosettes, obovate to ovate, pointed, adpressed or spreading, green-brown, dark-spotted, hydathodes red, margin ciliate. Flowering st. to 10cm; infl. flat-topped, term.; pet. 3–6mm, oblong, blunt, reflexed, white, tinged pink, anth. black. Cape Prov. ssp. *quadrangularis* (Schönl.) Toelken. Lvs to only 20mm, rosette somewhat flat.

Infl. axill.

C. monticola N.E. Br. = *C. rupestris*.

C. montis-draconis Dinter = *C. brevifolia*.

C. multicava Lem. Perenn., to 40cm. St. horizontal or erect, thick, sparsely branched, swollen and rooting, woody below. Lvs 2–6.5cm, oblong-ovate or elliptic, tip blunt or notched, hydathodes conspicuous above, margin curled under; petiole 5–20mm, sheathing below. Infl. rounded or elongate; pet. 3–6mm, lanceolate, pointed, white or cream, tip red; anth. purple. Autumn. Cape Prov., Natal.

C. muscosa L. MOSS CYPRESS; PRINCESS PINE; RATTAIL CYPRESS; TOY CYPRESS; WATCH-CHAIN CYPRESS. Scrambling perenn., 10–80cm, resembling a miniature cypress or clubmoss. Br. woody, hidden by overlapping lvs. Lvs 0.2–0.8cm, 4-ranked, adpressed scale-like ovate to triangular, flat, pointed or blunt, glab., leathery, green tinged yellow, grey or brown. Infl. 1–8-fld; fls clustered; pet. ovate, triangular, yellow-green to brown; anth. yellow. Summer. S Afr.

C. namaquensis Schönl. Perenn., to 20cm. St. stout, covered in old lvs. Lvs 0.4–3.5cm, clustered, oblong to oblanceolate, blunt to pointed, convex beneath, flat above or terete, grey or blue-green, hairy. Infl. terminal; pet. 3–10mm, pandurate to elliptic, fine-pointed, cream; anth. black. Summer. Cape Prov. ssp. *comptonii* (Hutch. & Pill.) Toelken. Lvs blunt, oblanceolate, triangular or round in section. Pet. 3–5mm; anth. yellow.

C. nemorosa (Ecklon & Zeyh.) Endl. ex Walp. Tuberous perenn., 4–15cm. St. horizontal or erect, branched. Lvs 0.4–1.3cm diam., ovate to round, blunt at tip, cordate or blunt below, grey to brown-green, entire; petiole 0.3–1.5cm. Pet. 2–3.5mm, lanceolate with a fine point, green-yellow; anth. yellow. W Cape.

C. nodulosa Schönl. = *C. capitella* ssp. *nodulosa*.

C. nudicaulis L. Perenn. St. woody, hairy or glab. Lvs 2–9cm, in numerous rosettes, oblong-elliptic, sometimes linear or round, convex or flat above, convex beneath, hairy or glab. Infl. spike-like; pet. 3–5mm, pandurate with a projection, cream; anth. yellow. S Afr.

C. obliqua Sol. = *C. ovata*.

C. obovata Haw. Perenn. to 30cm. St. branched, woody. Lvs 0.5–4cm, in 4 ranks in basal rosettes, ovate-lanceolate or obovate, bluntly pointed, sometimes with adpressed hairs, flat, sometimes v. thick, often tinged brown, ciliate. Infl. with numerous bent hairs; pet. 5–8mm, oblong-lanceolate, pointed, hooded, white-cream; anth. purple. Cape Prov., Natal. var. *dregeana* (Harv.) Toelken. Rosette lvs spathulate, 0.3–0.5cm thick, densely hairy, ciliate.

C. obtusa Haw. Shrubby perenn., to 15cm. Br. horizontal, rooting. Lvs 0.5–2cm, oblong-elliptic, tip rounded, sessile, fleshy, green tinged red-brown, ciliate. Fls stalked; pet. 30–45mm, spathulate, fused for one-third length, white becoming red with age; anth. black. Summer. Cape Prov.

C. obvallata L. = *C. nudicaulis*.

C. odoratissima (André) Link = *C. fascicularis*.

C. orbicularis L. Perenn., 5–25cm. St. short, sometimes producing runners. Lvs 1.5–10cm, in basal rosettes, spirally arranged, elliptic to oblanceolate, pointed, hydathodes above and on margins, margin ciliate, sometimes tinged red. Infl. with scale-like lvs; pet. 2–5mm, oblanceolate, blunt or pointed, pale yellow-white, tinged pink, often with a dors. appendage; anth. yellow. Summer. Natal.

C. ovata (Mill.) Druce. DOLLAR PLANT; JADE PLANT; JADE TREE. Perenn., to 3m. St. many-branched, fleshy, thick, bark peeling. Lvs 2–4cm, elliptic, rounded to bluntly acute above, tapering below, shiny mid to dark green with scattered hydathodes, margin horny, red or pale green. Pet. 5–10mm, lanceolate, elliptic, ridged, white tinged pink, with a projection; anth. purple. Autumn. Cape Prov. 'Busutoland': fls white. 'Crosby's Compact': habit dwarf; lvs rounded, bronze-purple. 'Dwarf Green': lvs dark green, tipped burgundy. 'Sunset': lvs glossy green, striped yellow, edged red.

C. pachyphylla Schönl. = *C. congesta*.

C. peglerae Schönl. = *C. obovata*.

C. pellucida L. Perenn. or ann. herb, to 60cm. St. horizontal, rooting. Lvs 1–3.5cm, lanceolate to oblanceolate, sharp-pointed, flat, green, margin red or clear. Fls solitary, axill.; pet. 3–5mm, oblanceolate, white, striped pink; anth. purple-white. Spring. S Afr. ssp. *marginalis* (Dryand.) Toelken. PINK BUTTONS; TRAILING CRASSULA. Lvs broad-ovate, constricted and fused at base. Fls in small umbels.

C. perfoliata L. Perenn., to 1.5m. St. woody, erect, few-branched, papillose. Lvs 4–15cm, triangular-lanceolate, bases clasping to connate, apex blunt-pointed, concave above, convex beneath, powdery grey, sometimes almost flat, papillose. Infl. flat or rounded; pet. 3–7mm, oblanceolate, white to red, reflexed; anth. black. Summer–late summer. Cape Prov., Natal. var. *falcata* (Wendl.) Toelken. AIRPLANE PLANT; AIRPLANE

PROPELLERS; PROPELLER PLANT; SCARLET PAINT BRUSH; SICKLE PLANT. To 50cm. Lvs thick, grey, decussate-connate, broadly lanceolate, twisted like a propeller. Fls fragrant, bright red, in large clusters. Summer.

C. perforata Thunb. STRING OF BUTTONS. Shrubby or scrambling perenn. St. long, little-branched, covered in old lvs. Lvs 0.4–2cm, ovate, blunt or pointed, convex beneath, connate-perfoliate, hydathodes above, margins red-yellow, horny. Infl. long with adpressed bracts; pet. 2–2.5mm, yellow, oblong-elliptic; anth. brown. Cape Prov., Natal. 'Pagoda': habit rigid, erect; lvs rich green edged white.

C. perfossa Lam. = *C. perforata*.

C. plegmatoides Friedrich. Similar to *C. elegans* except to 15cm; unbranched or branched from base; lvs 0.5–1cm, adpressed to form a 4-angled column, somewhat pointed, papillate; pet. to 3mm. Cape Prov., Nam.

C. portulacaria L. = *Portulacaria afra*.

C. portulacea Lam. = *C. ovata*.

C. pseudocolumnaris Dinter = *C. plegmatoides*.

C. pseudolycopodioides Dinter & Schinz. = *C. muscosa*.

C. pubescens Thunb. Shrubby perenn., to 40cm. St. branched. Lvs obovate to elliptic, blunt or pointed, convex or flat, ± glab. Infl. rounded or elongate; pet. 2–3mm, pandurate to oblanceolate, tip bent inwards, pale yellow-white; anth. yellow. Summer. Cape Prov. ssp. *radicans* (Haw.) Toelken. Some br. drooping and rooting. Lvs to 3cm, glab., finely toothed.

C. purcellii Schönl. = *C. atropurpurea* var. *purcellii*.

C. pyramidalis Thunb. Perenn., 3–25cm. St. erect or horizontal, branched or simple. Lvs 0.4–1.2cm, sharply ovate, bluntly pointed, adpressed to form square column, margin horny. Infl. term., crowded; pet. 7–10mm, oblong, hooded, white-cream; anth. yellow. Spring. Cape Prov.

C. quadrangularis Schönl. = *C. montana* ssp. *quadrangularis*.

C. ramuliflora Link & Otto = *C. obovata*.

C. recurva (Hook. f.) Ostenf. non N.E. Br. = *C. helmsii*.

C. reversisetosa Bitter = *C. obovata*.

C. rhomboidea N.E. Br. = *C. deltoidea*.

C. rosularis Haw. = *C. orbicularis*.

C. rubicunda E. Mey. = *C. alba*.

C. rubricaulis Ecklon & Zeyh. Shrubby perenn., to 30cm. Lvs 1–3.5cm, oblanceolate to knife-shaped, blunt to rounded, convex beneath, flat above, margin ciliate, recurved, often red, hydathodes scattered. Pet. 4–5.5mm, white tinged red; anth. yellow. Summer. Cape Prov.

C. rupestris Thunb. BUTTONS ON A STRING; BEADVINE; NECKLACE VINE; ROSARY VINE. Shrubby perenn., to 50cm. Bark flaking. Lvs 0.3–1.5cm, ovate-lanceolate, rounded at tip, convex beneath, flat above, glab., brown-red. Infl. rounded; pet. 3–4mm, oblong-elliptic, tip rounded, white tinged red; anth. brown. Cape Prov. ssp. *marnierana* (Huber & H.J. Jacobsen) Toelken. Lvs fused for 4–6mm, closely packed; bracts large, spreading.

C. sarcocaulis Ecklon & Zeyh. Shrubby perenn., 20–60cm. St. usually erect, many-branched, thin-barked. Lvs 0.6–3cm, elliptic-lanceolate, pointed, red-tinted, compressed to terete. Infl. term., dense; fls malodorous, pet. 3–5mm, oblanceolate-oblong, white to rose, anth. brown. Late summer. S Afr. Z8.

C. sarmentosa Harv. Tuberous scrambling perenn., to 1m. St. sparsely branched, climbing or hanging. Lvs 2–6cm, ovate to elliptic, pointed, flat, green, hydathodes beneath, margin tinged red, serrate or entire. Infl. terminal, flat or rounded; pet. 4–8mm, linear-lanceolate, cream-white, tinged pink; anth. white tinged red. Winter. Cape Prov., Natal.

C. schmidtii Reg. Tuft-forming perenn., 5–15cm. Lvs 2.5–5cm, tapering to base, linear-lanceolate, fleshy, pointed, semiterete, green with dark spots, tinged red-brown, margin white, ciliate. Infl. ± corymbose; pet. 4mm, pink. Cape Prov.

C. sericea Schönl. Similar to *C. lanuginosa* except to 25cm; st. woody, robust; infl. distinctly stalked, erect; anth. brown. Summer. Cape Prov., Nam.

C. setulosa Harv. Cushion-forming perenn., to 25cm. St. often woody. Lvs 0.6–3.5cm, 4-ranked or spirally arranged in basal rosettes, pointed, flat, sometimes convex beneath, green tinged red, hydathodes on margins and upper surface, margin ciliate. Infl. hairy; bracts triangular; pet. 2.5–4mm, oblong, white tinged red, anth. yellow-brown. Summer. S Afr.

C. socialis Schönl. Differs from *C. montana* ssp. *quadrangularis* in its short reflexed style. Summer. Cape Prov.

C. spathulata Thunb. Prostrate perenn., to 20cm. St. rooting, sparsely branching. Lvs 2–3cm, ovate, blunt, somewhat cordate below, margin serrate, often tinged red. Pet. 3.5–5mm, linear lanceolate, somewhat hooded, white tinged pink; anth. purple-pink. Autumn. Cape Prov.

C. streyi Toelken. Differs from *C. multicava* in lvs sessile, tips pointed, veins purple beneath, hydathodes in 2 rows on margin beneath; anth. pale yellow. Autumn. Natal.

C. susannae Rauh & Friedrich. Perenn., 1–4cm. Lvs 0.6–1cm, 4-

ranked in rosettes, barely breaking soil surface, oblong, truncate, flat, fleshy, channelled, papillate. Infl. term., stalked, above lvs; pet. 2.5–3.5mm, sharply pointed, oblong, white; anth. black. Autumn. Cape Prov.

C. tecta Thunb. Perenn., to 20cm. St. much-branched. Lvs 2–3.5cm, oblong-oblanceolate, rounded, margin papillate above, ciliate below. Infl. rounded, term.; fls numerous; pet. 3–4mm, oblong-oblanceolate, blunt, white-cream; anth. yellow. Autumn. Cape Prov.

C. teres Marloth = *C. barklyi*.

C. tetragona L. BABY PINE OF CHINA; MINIATURE PINE TREE. Perenn., to 1m. St. branched, erect. Lvs 0.8–5cm, lanceolate, pointed, compressed to terete. Pet. 1–3mm, oblanceolate, elliptic, rounded, cream; anth. brown. Summer. Cape Prov.

C. thyrsiflora Thunb. = *C. capitella* ssp. *thyrsiflora*.

C. tomentosa Thunb. Similar to *C. barbata* except perenn. or bienn.; pet. pandurate to oblong, narrowing to a slender point, white-yellow. Cape Prov., Nam.

C. trachysantha (Ecklon & Zeyh.) Harv. = *C. elegans*.

C. turrita Thunb. = *C. capitella* ssp. *thyrsiflora*.

C. vaginata Ecklon & Zeyh. Rosette-forming perenn., to 50cm. Roots tuberous. Lvs 5–35cm, in basal rosettes, lanceolate-linear, often drying out at flowering, somewhat hairy, fused below, margin ciliate. Fls numerous; pet. 2.5–5mm, oblong, blunt, hooded, yellow-white; anth. yellow. Summer. S Afr. to Arabia.

C. yunnanensis Franch. = *Sinocrassula yunnanensis*.

→*Cotyledon, Grammanthes, Purgosea, Rochea, Sedum* and *Tillaea*.

CRASSULACEAE DC. 33/1500. *Adromischus, Aeonium, Aichryson, Chiastophyllum, Cotyledon, Crassula,* ×*Cremneria, Cremnophila, Dudleya, Echeveria, Graptopetalum,* ×*Graptophytum,* ×*Graptosedum,* ×*Graptoveria, Greenovia, Hylotelephium, Jovibarba, Kalanchoe, Lenophyllum, Monanthes, Orostachys, Pachyphytum,* ×*Pachyveria, Rhodiola, Rosularia,* ×*Sedadia, Sedum, Sempervivum, Sinocrassula, Thompsonella, Tylecodon, Umbilicus, Villadia.*

+**Crataegomespilus** Simon-Louis ex Bellair. BRONVAUX MEDLAR. Rosaceae. Graft hybrids bweteen *Crataegus* and *Mespilus*, differing from *Mespilus* in smaller fls clustered at the br. tips, sta. 14–18, and seeds 2–3, not viable; from *Crataegus* in the *Mespilus*-type fr. Gdn origin. Z6.

+ *C. dardarii* Simon-Louis. (*Crataegus monogyna* + *Mespilus germanica*.) BRONVAUX MEDLAR. Decid. tree to 6m. Branchlets spiny. Lvs to 15cm, narrowly oblong-elliptic, dark green, lanate beneath, entire or finely toothed. Fls 1.5cm diam., 5–8-clustered. Fr. to 2cm diam. 'Jules d'Asnières', a small, decid., bushy-headed tree. Br. pendulous; shoots lanate, sometimes spiny. Lvs to 7.5cm, obovate to broad-ovate, entire or deeply lobed Fls similar to those of the hawthorn but larger, white tinted rose. Fr. small, oblong, brown, lanuginose. 'Jouinii': earlier flowering than 'Jules d'Asnières'.

Crataegus L. HAWTHORN; THORN; THORN APPLE. Rosaceae. 100–200 decid. small trees or shrubs, usually thorny. Lvs simple, lobed or pinnatisect, and dentate. Fls white, rarely ageing pink, in term. corymbs or solitary; sta. usually 20. Fr. a small pome. Early summer. N hemis.

C. altaica (Loud.) Lange. ALTAI MOUNTAIN THORN. Small tree, spines sparse, robust to 2cm. Lvs to 5cm, ovate, almost pinnatisect, sharply serrate, bright green. Fls in open flattened corymbs. Fr. 8–10mm, globose, yellow. C Asia. Z5.

C. ambigua C.A. Mey. Shoots hiruste at first, purple; spines sparse, to 1cm. Lvs 6cm, with 4–7 deeply incised, slender lobes, slightly dentate toward apex. Fls 1.5cm diam., in clusters of 12–18; anth. red. SE Russia. Z5.

C. apiifolia (Marsh) Michx., non Medik. PARSLEY-LEAVED THORN. Shrub or small tree 3–7m; shoots pubesc.; spines to 2.5cm. Lvs 2.5–4cm, triangular-ovate to reniform, pinnately lobed, dentate, downy at first. Fls 2cm diam., in corymbose downy clusters of 12, anth. pink. Fr. 0.75cm, ovoid, scarlet. S US. Z7.

C. aprica Beadle. Shrub or small tree to 6m; br. curving; spines slender 2–3.5cm. Lvs 2–3.5cm, broad-ovate to oval, apex pointed or rounded, glandular-dentate, often shallowly lobed, coriaceous, deep purple with age. Fls 1.8cm diam., in corymbose downy clusters of 3–6; sta. 10, anth. yellow. Fr. 1.2cm, globose, orange-red. Late spring. SE US. Z6.

C. arborescens Elliot = *C. viridis*.

C. arkansana Sarg. Tree to 6m; thorns few, 0.5–1cm, or 0. Lvs 5–7cm, oblong-ovate to oval, shallowly lobed, dull green. Fls to 2.5cm diam. in pubesc. corymbs; anth. yellow. Fr. 1.5–2cm, subglobose, bright red. US (Ark.). Z5.

C. arnoldiana Sarg. Small tree, 7–10m; shoots stout, thorny, hirsute only at first. Lvs 4–5cm, broad-ovate, with 3–5 serrate lobes. Fls to 2cm diam., many, in loose, downy corymbs; sta. 10, anth. pale yellow. Fr. 1.5cm, globose, bright red, pitted, apex tufted. NE US. Z5.

C. aronia Bosc = *C. azarolus*.

C. azarolus L. AZAROLE. Small tree to 10m, shoots finely pubesc., spines sparse or 0. Lvs 3–7cm, obovate to rhomboid, pinnatisect lobes 3–5 pairs, entire or dentate; stipules strongly dentate. Fls 1.5–2.5cm, crowded, pubesc., corymbs to 8cm. Fr. 1.5–2.5cm, globose, orange-yellow, occas. white or red, with apple-like flavour. S Eur., N Afr., W Asia. var. *sinaica* (Boiss.) Lange. 2–5m, spines v. stout; lvs glab.; fls 5–8; fr. 6–7mm, ellipsoid, yellow-red. Sinai. Z6.

C. bibas Lour. = *Eriobotrya japonica*.

C. biltmoreana Beadle. Resembles *C. boyntonii*. Lvs scabrous serrate; fr. orange or red. E US. Z4.

C. boyntonii Beadle. Shrub or small tree to 7m, thorns few to 3cm, or 0. Lvs ovate or elliptic, with 3–4 pairs shallow finely toothed or biserrate lobes. Fls 1.5–2cm in diam., in clusters of 3–10. Fr. 0.5–1cm, red. US (NY to Alab.). Z5.

C. brachyacantha Sarg. & Engelm. POMMETTE BLEUE. Tree to 15m, crown rounded; thorns 8–15mm, stout, curved. Lvs 2–5cm, obovate or oval, shallowly crenate, downy above, soon lustrous dark green. Fls 8mm diam., in corymbs, white, becoming orange with age; sta. 15–20. Fr. 1cm, globose, bright blue, pruinose. S US. Z8.

C. calpodendron (Ehrh.) Medik. BLACK THORN; PEAR THORN. Erect tree to 6m, br. often crooked, thorns short or 0. Lvs 5–12cm, oval-oblong, shallowly lobed, biserrate, downy beneath. Fls in erect, loose, hirsute corymbs 6–12cm long; sta. 16–20, anth. pink. Fr. erect, 1cm, elliptic, yellow-red. Ont. to C US. Z2.

C. canbyi Sarg. Shrub or small tree to 6m, crown broad; thorns to 2.5cm+. Lvs 6cm, oblong-obovate or elliptic, often shallowly lobed, scabrous-serrate. Fls 0.5cm diam., long-stalked, in small glab. corymbs; 20, anth. pink. Fr. 0.5cm, subglobose, bright glossy red, pulp bright red. E US. Z6.

C. carrierei Vauv. ex Carr. = *C. ×lavallei* 'Carrierei'.

C. celsiana Dipp. non Bosc = *C. ×dippeliana*.

C. cerronis A. Nels. = *C. erythropoda*.

C. champlainensis Sarg. Closely related to *C. submollis*. Tree 5–6m; thorns 3–5cm. Lvs 5–7cm, ovate, base rounded or cordate, shallowly 5–7-lobed, dentate, blue-green glab. above, pubesc. on veins beneath. Fls 1.5cm diam. in sparse, pubesc. corymbs; sta. 10, anth. yellow. Fr. 1cm, obovoid, bright red. N US. Z6.

C. chlorosarca Maxim. Small tree, crown pyramidal; shoots stout, downy becoming dark red; thorns sparse, 10–12mm or 0. Lvs 5–9cm, broad ovate to triangular, abruptly acute, with 7–9 shallow, serrulate lobes, eventually glab. dark green above, hirsute beneath. Fls 1cm diam., in pubesc. corymbs 4–7cm. Fr. 1cm, subglobose, black, pulp green. Manch.

C. chrysocarpa Ashe. Tree to 6m; crown dense, spreading, shoots soon shiny brown; thorns slender to 5cm. Lvs 3–5cm, oval or obovate, with 3–4 shallow, glandular-biserrate lobes toward apex. Fls 2cm diam., in 5–7cm, glandular-hirsute corymbs; sta. 10, anth. yellow. Fr. pendulous, 1cm, globose, red, pulp yellow. NE US. var. *phoenicea* Palmer. Shoots and infl. glab. Fr. 1–1.2cm, dark red, glossy. Z5.

C. coccinea L. = *C. intricata* or *C. pedicellata*.

C. coccinea var. *mollis* Torr. & A. Gray = *C. mollis*.

C. coccinea var. *rotundifolia* (Moench) Sarg. = *C. chrysocarpa* var. *phoenicea*.

C. coccinoides Ashe. Large shrub or small tree to 8m, crown rounded; thorns 3–5cm, dark purple. Lvs 5–6cm, triangular to ovate, base rounded, margins with 4–5 pairs of acute, glandular-serrate lobes, red at first, subglabrous. Fls 2cm diam., 4–7 in corymbs; anth. pink. Fr. 1cm, subglobose, bright red. C US. Z5.

C. collina Chapm. Shrub or small tree to 8m, crown widespreading; thorns stout, on br. and trunk. Lvs obovate-elliptic, unevenly biserrate, yellow-green above, paler and glab. beneath. Infl. long-hirsute; sep. gland.-fringed; anth. yellow. Fr. 1cm, subglobose, dull red, pulp yellow, mealy. C & SE US. Z4.

C. coloradensis N. Nels. = *C. succulenta*.

C. colorata Sarg. = *C. macrosperma*.

C. columbiana Howell. Shrub or small tree to 5m, thorns robust, 2.5–5cm. Lvs 2.5–5cm, obovate, with 5–9 serrate lobes, slightly downy. Fls numerous, in subglabrous corymbs. Fr. red or purple. BC to Calif. Z5.

C. compta Sarg. Shrub or small tree to 6m, thorns slender. Lvs to 8cm, broad ovate with 3–5 pairs of biserrate lobes, glaucous beneath. Fls 1.5cm diam.; sta. 10, anth. red. Fr. 1cm, obovoid, bright crimson, slightly speckled. N Amer. Z3.

C. cordata Ait. = *C. phaenopyrum*.

C. crus-galli L. COCKSPUR THORN. Tree to 10m, crown widespreading, flat-topped; thorns stout, 3–8cm at first, later to 15cm

and branching. Lvs 2.5–10cm, obovate, apex rounded or abruptly acute, dentate, dark lustrous green, becoming orange-red in autumn. Fls 1.5cm diam., in glab. corymbs 5–7cm; sta. 10, anth. pink. Fr. 1cm, subglobose, deep red, persisting until spring. E US. 'Inermis': small thornless tree; lvs shiny dark green, rust and drought-resistant. 'Cruzam': to 5m, bark silvergrey; lvs glossy, thick; fls white; fr. 1.5cm; v. disease-resistant. 'Hooks' (*C. crus-galli* ×*C. prunifolia.*): 5–6.5m, blight-resistant; thorns fewer. 'Vaughan' ('Vaughnii') (*C. crus-galli* ×*C. phaenopyrum*): vigorous; lvs red in fall; fr. 0.5cm, profuse, long-lasting, bright orange-red. var. *arbutifolia* Bean. Lvs obovate to oval, v. variable 1.5–5cm+, glab. Fr. persistent. var. *capillata* Sarg. Infl. pubesc. var. *linearis* DC. Completely glab.; lvs narrow. var. *oblongata* Sarg. Smaller, horizontally branching tree with narrowly oblong-elliptic lvs and brightly coloured oblong fr. var. *pyracanthifolia* Ait. Lvs oblong-lanceolate; fr. smaller. var. *salicifolia* Ait. Lvs narrower than var. *pyracanthifolia*, oblanceolate, crown flattened. Z5.

C. crus-galli var. *splendens* Ait. f. = *C. ×prunifolia*.

C. cuneata Sieb. & Zucc. Shrub to 1.5m, shoots dense, slender, red, hirsute; thorns slender to 0.5cm. Lvs 2–6cm, obovate, apex rounded often shallowly serrate-lobed, pale green glab. above, faintly pubesc. beneath. Fls sparse in downy corymbs. Fr. globose, red. Jap., China. Z6.

C. cupulifera Sarg. Small tree or dense shrub rarely to 5–6m, br. glab. Lvs 5–7cm, obovate to rhomboidal with several biserrate lobes, crimson in fall. Fls 1.5cm diam., cupulate, in downy corymbs. Fr. 1cm, scarlet, in pendent bunches. US. Z5.

C. dahurica Koehne. Shrub or small tree, bark brown, armed, spines to 4cm. Lvs 2–5cm, oval-rhomboidal with sharp lobes, bright green, ageing russet-brown. Fls in lax corymbs. Fr. 8mm, rounded, pale brown. SE Sib. Z5.

C. diffusa Sarg. Tree to 10m, br. stoutly armed, spines to 3.5cm. Lvs to 5cm, slightly lobed, pale green. Fls to 1cm diam. Fr. 1cm, red. NE US. Z5.

C. ×dippeliana Lange. (*C. punctata* ×*C. tanacetifolia*.) Shrub or small tree. Lvs 4–7cm, broadly ovate, pinnatifid, lobes 7–11, sharply toothed, downy. Infl. a crowded, downy corymb; fls 2–2.5cm diam.; sta. 18–22, anth. red. Fr. 1.5cm, spherical, yellow or dull red. Gdn origin. Z5.

C. douglasii Lindl. Tree to 10m, crown globose, spines sparse to 3cm. Lvs 4–10cm, obovate to ovate, shallowly lobed toward apex, biserrate, occas. with a pair of deep lobes near base, dark lustrous green. Infl. a glab., 10–12-fld corymb. Fr. 0.75cm, ellipsoid, black. US. Z5.

C. dsungarica Zab. Tree closely resembling *C. altaica* but lvs 3–8cm, oval-rhomboid to broad ovate, with 3–7 deeply cleft lobes, lowest lobes largest, spreading, acute-dentate, soon glab. Infl. a glab., 5–7cm corymb; fls 1cm diam. Fr. 1cm, globose, black, glossy. SE Asia, N China. Z5.

C. dunbarii Sarg. Robust shrub to 4m; spines to 5cm, reflexed, red-brown. Lvs ovate or more rounded, shallowly 3–4-lobed and dentate, glab. or sparsely downy. Infl. a small tight 10–14-fld corymb; fls 1cm diam.; sta. 10, anth. red. Fr. 1–1.5cm, rounded, bright red, speckled. US. Z5.

C. ×durobrivensis Sarg. (*C. pruinosa* ×*C. suborbiculata*.) Shrub, 3–7m, br. glab.; thorns 3–5cm. Lvs 3–7cm, broadly ovate or oval, base cuneate, apex with 2–4 serrate lobes, soon glab., dark yellow-green. Fls 2–2.5cm diam., in small clusters; anth. pink. Fr. 1.5cm, globose, glossy, crimson, persistent. NE US. Z5.

C. eganii Ashe = *C. macrosperma*.

C. ellwangeriana Sarg. Tree to 6m, spines 3–5cm, sparse. Lvs 6–8cm, ovate to oval, lobes shallow, biserrate, upper surface rugose with short adpressed hair, lower surface shaggy at first. Fls 2cm diam., in broad clusters of 9–10; sta. 10, anth. pink. Fr. 1.5cm, oblong, red. E US. Z5.

C. erythropoda Ashe. Tree-like shrub to 5m, br. glab.; spines 2.5–3cm. Lvs 2.5–7.5cm, ovate to elliptic-ovate, unevenly sharply toothed. Infl. a glab. corymb; sta. sparse, anth. pink-purple. Fr. 0.5cm, red-black. W & SW US. Z5.

C. flabellata (Bosc) K. Koch. Tree or shrub to 6m; spines 4–10cm, stout, slightly hooked. Lvs 3–7cm, broad ovate or rhombic, with 4–6 pairs of acuminate serrate lobes, pubesc. above at first. Infl. a pubesc. or hirsute corymb; fls 1.5–2cm diam.; sta. 10 or fewer, anth. pink. Fr. 1cm, ellipsoid, bright red, pulp mealy. E N Amer. var. *grayana* (Eggl.) Palmer. Sta. 20. Fr. rounded. Z4.

C. flava Ait. SUMMER HAW; YELLOW FRUITED THORN; YELLOW HAW. Tree to 6m+, shoots glab., spines to 2.5cm. Lvs 2–5cm, obovate-oblong, base gland., apex acute with 3 biserrate lobes, coriaceous, light green glab.; stipules large, rounded. Infl. a sparse corymb 3–7-fld; sta. 10–20, anth. purple. Fr. 1cm, rounded or pyriform, dull green-yellow, edible. N Amer., Vancouver to Flor. Z6.

C. fontanesiana (Spach) Steud. Differs from *C. crus-galli* in sparse, short thorns (to 4cm); lvs elliptic-lanceolate, thinner, yellow-green; fls with 16–18 sta., anth. yellow. Fr. rounded-elliptic, red or green flushed red, flesh dry. E US. Z6.

C. grandiflora K. Koch = × *Crataemespilus grandiflora.*

C. × *grignonensis* Mouill. (*C. crus-galli* × *C. pubescens.*) Shrub, 3–4m; shoots glab., thorns sparse. Lvs to 7cm, ovate, with 2–4 crenate lobes, glossy green, shortly downy beneath, often persisting into winter. Fls many, in small clusters. Fr. 1.5cm, subglobose, red-brown speckled grey, persistent. Gdn origin. Z5.

C. heldreichii Boiss. Resembles a smaller *C. laciniata*, thorns to 1cm; lvs 1.5–3cm, lobes rounded, subentire, dull green above, paler beneath; fls small in erect coyrmbs; fr. 0.5cm, globose, red. Greece. Z6.

C. henryi Dunn. Tree 6–10m, or shrub, thornless. Lvs 3–7cm, larger on non-flowering shoots, narrow-elliptic to lanceolate, unlobed and finely serrate on flowering shoots, occas. 3-lobed and biserrate on vegetative shoots, adpressed-hairy becoming dark lustrous green. Fls 1cm diam., in crowded glab. corymbs to 5cm. Fr. 1.5cm, globose dull red. SW China. Z7.

C. heterophylla Fluegge. Shrub or small tree to 5m, crown rounded; shoots glab., sparsely thorned. Lvs on vegetative shoots 4–7cm, diamond-shaped, apex strongly lobed, lobes sharply unevenly dentate; lvs of flowering shoots smaller, oblong-obovate or oval, occas. 3-lobed or sparsely toothed, dark lustrous green, glab. Fls 2cm diam., in glab. 5–7cm corymbs; sta. 15–20. Fr. 1–1.5cm, slender, oval, red. Armenia. Z6.

C. holmesiana Ashe. Tree-like shrub to 10m; crown lax, open; thorns few, slender. Lvs 5–7cm, ovate or oval, thin, with 4–6 pairs of shallow, biserrate lobes. Fls 1.5–2cm diam., in glab. corymbs of 10 or more; sta. 5–10, anth. red. Fr. 1cm, oblong, red, flesh mealy. E US. Z5.

C. hupehensis Sarg. Tree to 5m; thorns 1.5cm. Lvs 10cm, ovate to oblong-ovate, apex tapered, with 3–4 glandular-serrate lobes toward apex. Fls 1–1.5cm diam., in many-fld glab. corymbs; sta. 20, anth. red. Fr. 2.5cm, dark red, edible. W China.

C. intricata Lange. Shrub 1–3m, br. erect or spreading; thorns 2–4cm, slender, curved. Lvs 3–5cm, ovate, shallowly acutely lobed, lobes biserrate, bright green, glab. Infl. a 3–7-fld corymb; bracts pubesc.; sta. 10, anth. yellow or pink. Fr. rounded-elliptic, red-brown. NE US. var. *straminea* Palmer. Fr. yellow-green to dull-orange. Z5.

C. jackii Sarg. Tree-like shrub to 3m, br. densely thorny. Lvs 2.5–3cm, oval-elliptic to ovate, lobes obscure, serrate. Fls 1.5cm diam., 5–10 in villous corymbs; sta. 5–10, anth. pale yellow. Fr. 12mm, broad-elliptic, dull dark red. Canada. Z4.

C. jonesiae Sarg. Large shrub or small tree to 6m, shoots downy, becoming lustrous orange-brown, thorns 5–7cm. Lvs to 10cm, elliptic-obovate, acutely lobed toward apex, lobes serrate, pub-esc. becoming glossy dark green. Fls 2.5cm diam.; sta. 10, anth. pink. Fr. 1.5cm, bright red, flesh juicy. NE US. Z5.

C. korolkowii Schneid. non L. Henry = *C. pinnatifida* var. *major.*

C. korolkowii L. Henry non Schneid. = *C. wattiana.*

C. laciniata Ucria. Tree to 7m, crown lax, shoots downy, sparsely thorny, spurs thorn-like. Lvs to 5cm, triangular to rhombic with 5–9 deep dentate lobes, deep green with ashy grey down. Fls 1.5cm diam., to 12 in downy corymbs. Fr. to 1.5cm, globose, downy, orange-red. SE Eur, W Asia.

C. laevigata (Poir.) DC. ENGLISH HAWTHORN; QUICK-SET THORN; WHITE THORN; MAY. Shrub or small tree to 2.5m, br. soon glab.; thorns to 2.5cm. Lvs 5cm, obovate, with 3(–5), shallow blunt serrate lobes, pale green beneath; stipules serrate. Fls 15–18mm, white to pink in corymbs of few to 10 blooms; anth. pink-purple. Fr. 1cm, ovate-globose, deep red. Eur., N Afr., India. 'Auriculata': lvs 3–5cm, asymmetrical, irregularly toothed; fr. dark red. 'Gireeoudii': second flush of lvs mottled pink and white. 'Candioplena': fls double, pure white, not fading. 'Masekii': fls double, pale rose. 'Paul's Scarlet' ('Coccinea Plena', 'Kermesiana Plena'): fls double, bright crimson. 'Plena': fls double, white, fading pink. 'Punicea': fls 2cm diam., deep pink, centre white. 'Rosea': fls pink, centre white. 'Rosea Flore Pleno': fls double, rose. 'Rubra Plena': fls double, deep pink. 'Aurea': fr. yellow. ssp. *laevigata.* Lvs to 3.5cm, glab. beneath. Cal. lobes hugging the fr., as long as wide. Fr. 8–10mm. ssp. *palmstruchii* (Lindm.) Franco. Lvs 3–5cm, tufted-hirsute in vein axils beneath. Fr. 10–12mm. Z5.

C. laevis Thunb. = *Photinia villosa* var. *laevis.*

C. × *lavallei* Henriq. ex Lav. (*C. stipulacea* × *C. crus-galli.*) Intermediate between parents. 'Carrierei': small tree to 7m; thorns to 5cm; lvs elliptic-oblong, irregularly toothed, sparsely hairy beneath; fls 2cm; anth. 5–10, pink; fr. 1.8cm, elliptic, long-lasting, orange-red. Z5.

C. leeana (Loud.) Bean = *C.* × *dippeliana.*

C. mackenzii Sarg. Tree to 6m, br. thorny. Lvs ovate to triangular, with 34 pairs of acute, subtriangular, serrate lobes. Fls 1.5cm diam., in sparse corymbs; anth. pink. Fr. 1cm, dull

red, bloomy. US (Iowa and Okl.). Z5.

C. macracantha Lodd. = *C. succulenta* var. *macracantha.*

C. macrosperma Ashe. Tree to 8m, thorns to 3cm. Lvs ovate to elliptic with 5 broad triangular sharply toothed lobes. Fls 1.5cm, 5–12 in glab. corymbs; sta. 10, anth. red. Fr. 0.5–1.5cm, obovoid to oblong, red. N Amer. Z5. 'Acutiloba': lvs broad, jaggedly serrate.

C. macrosperma Lindl. = *C. azarolus* var. *sinaica.*

C. marshallii Eggl. = *C. apiifolia.*

C. maximowiczii Schneid. Differs from *C. sanguinea* in lvs more strongly lobed, lower lf surfaces and infl. villous. NE Asia. Z5.

C. × *media* Bechst. (*C. monogyna* ssp. *nordica* × *C. laevigata* ssp. *laevigata.*) Lvs resembling those of *C. laevigata* but lobes acute or tapering, serrulate. Infl. glab. Fr. subglobose. Occurring with the parents. Z5.

C. mercerensis Sarg. Tree to 5m. Lvs oblong-obovate or elliptic, entire or with 2–4 pairs of shallow lobes above, glab. Fls 1cm diam., in sparse glab. corymbs; sta. 10, anth. white. Fr. 1cm, globose, orange-red. US. Z5.

C. mexicana DC. = *C. pubescens* f. *stipulacea.*

C. microcarpa Lindl. = *C. spathulata.*

C. missouriensis Ashe. Shrub or small tree, shoots grey-pubesc.; thorns slender to 5cm. Lvs 2.5–7cm, obovate, ovate or almost circular, sharply serrate, glossy green above, pubesc. beneath. Fls 1.5cm diam., in pubesc. corymbs of 3–8; anth. pink. Fr. 1cm, subglobose or pyriform, red. S US. Z5.

C. mollis (Torr. and A. Gray) Scheele. RED HAW. Tree 10–13m, crown spreading; br. grey, shoots white-hirsute at first; thorns 2.5–5cm. Lvs 5–10cm, broadly ovate, with 4–7 pairs of shallow acute glandular-toothed lobes, pubesc., upper surface becoming rugose. Fls 2.5cm diam., in tomentose corymbs; cal. lobes glandular-dentate; anth. yellow. Fr. 2–2.5cm, subglobose or pyriform, red, pubesc. C US. Z5.

C. monogyna Jacq. HAWTHORN; MAY; ENGLISH HAWTHORN. Arborescent shrub, 2–5m, occas. to 10m; thorns numerous, 2–2.5cm; shoots glab. or downy. Lvs broad-ovate to diamond-shaped, with 3–7 almost pinnatisect lobes, bright dark green above, white-green beneath, downy. Fls 1.5cm, white in glab. clusters of 6–12. Fr. 1cm, ovoid, globose or ellipsoid. GB, Denm. to Austria. Cvs range in habit from low and wide to narrow-ascending; br. ascending to pendulous and twisted; thorns few to many in fascicles; lvs green to yellow-green to variegated white, fan-shaped to deeply incised; fls white to pink, including bicoloured, sometimes double or repeat flowering; fr. dark red to yellow. 'Compacta': dwarf, br. stout, stiff, unarmed. 'Flexuosa': br. corkscrew-like. 'Pendula' ('Reginae'): br. pendulous. 'Stricta': br. tightly ascending. 'Lutescens': lvs yellow-green. 'Variegata' lvs variegated white. 'Bicolor': fls white, broadly edged pink. 'Biflora' GLASTONBURY THORN: lvs early, downy beneath; fls produced in spring and again in winter; fr. dark red. 'Rosea': fls pink. 'Semperflorens': slow-growing bush, repeat-flowering. 'Aurea': fr. yellow. ssp. *monogyna.* Lvs to 3.5cm, deeply 3-lobed, pale green, glab.; petiole 0.5–5cm. Fr. globose or cupulate, dark red. Carpath. and W Balk. to Fr. ssp. *azarella* (Griseb.) Franco. Lvs and shoots densely downy; lvs to 3cm, deeply 3–5- or 7-lobed. Fr. sub-globose, red-brown. Spain to Balk. and S Russia, Medit. ssp. *brevispina* (Kunze) Franco. Spines few and short. Lvs to 3cm, 3–5-lobed, coriaceous, blue-green, glab. beneath. Fr. globose, red. Iberian Penins. to Sardinia, W Medit. ssp. *nordica* Franco. Lvs to 5cm, lvs 3–5- or 7-lobed, glab. green beneath; petiole 2–2.5cm. Fr. subglobose, dark red. N & C Eur. Z5.

C. monogyna var. *bruantii* hort. = *C. monogyna* 'Semperflorens'.

C. monogyna var. *guimperi* Voss = *C. monogyna* 'Bicolor'.

C. monogyna var. *pauli* hort. = *C. laevigata* 'Paul's Scarlet'.

C. monogyna var. *praecox* Bean = *C. monogyna* 'Biflora'.

C. × *mordenensis* Boom. (*C. laevigata* × *C. succulenta.*) Differs from *C. laevigata* in large lvs and fls; differs from *C. succulenta* in shorter spines and more deeply lobed, smoother lvs, glab. infl., and eglandular cal. lobes. Gdn origin (Canada). 'Snowbird': lvs shallowly lobed, nearly entire, dark, glossy green; fls double; fr. 1cm, pink-red, few. 'Toba' (*C. laevigata* 'Paul's Scarlet' × *C. succulenta.*): small tree to 5m, trunk twisted; br. stout, erect, thorns to 1.5cm, stouter than *C. laevigata*; lvs 5–7cm, lobes 3, finely toothed, shiny dark green above, paler beneath; fls double, white, ageing pink; fr. few. Z5.

C. nigra Waldst. & Kit. HUNGARIAN HAWTHORN. Tree to 6m, crown rounded; br. stiff, grey-tomentose at first, later purple-brown; thorns to 1cm, sparse. Lvs 3–10cm, triangular to ovate, with 7–11 shallow, serrate lobes, dull green, pubesc.; stipules with large sharp serrations. Fls 1.5cm diam., white becoming pink, in small pubesc. corymbs; anth. yellow. Fr. 1cm, sub-globose, black, glossy, flesh soft. SE Eur., Hung. Z6.

C. × *nitida* (Engelm.) Sarg. (*C. viridis* × *C. crus-galli.*) Tree to 7m, crown globose, usually thornless. Lvs 2–8cm, elliptic-oblong, shallowly lobed, coarsely serrate, red-brown in fall. Fls

1.5cm diam., to 10 in corymbs; sta. 15–20, anth. yellow. Fr. 1cm, ovate, dull red, pruinose. S US. Z5.

C. odoratissima Lindl. = *C. orientalis.*

C. olivacea Sarg. = *C. fontanesiana.*

C. oliveriana (Dum.-Cours.) Bosc. Small tree, 3–4m; shoots grey-pubesc. at first; thorns v. sparse. Lvs 2.5–5cm, with 3–5 deep lobes, grey-pubesc. Fls 1.5cm diam, in compact, tomentose corymbs to 5cm. Fr. 0.5cm, ovoid, black-purple. SE Eur., W Asia. Z6.

C. orientalis Bieb. = *C. laciniata.*

C. orientalis var. *sanguinea* (Schräd.) Loud. = *C. schraderiana.*

C. oxyacantha 'Aurea' = *C. laevigata* 'Aurea'.

C. oxyacantha L. emend. Jacq. = *C. laevigata.*

C. oxyacantha var. *oliveriana* (Dum.-Cours.) Lindl. = *C. oliveriana.*

C. oxyacanthoides Thuill. = *C. laevigata.*

C. palmstruchii Lindm. = *C. laevigata* ssp. *palmstruchii.*

C. parviflora Ait. = *C. uniflora.*

C. pedicellata Sarg. SCARLET HAW. Tree to 7m, br. slender, thorns 3–5mm, straight or slightly curved. Lvs 5–10cm, broad-ovate, with 4–5 pairs of shallow biserrate lobes above, dark green, rugose above, glabrescent beneath. Fls 1.5–2cm diam. in long-tomentose, crowded corymbs; sta. 10, anth. pink-red. Fr. 1cm, pyriform, bright red, flesh dry. E US. Z5.

C. pedicellata var. *ellwangeriana* (Sarg.) Eggl. = *C. ellwangeriana.*

C. pentagyna Waldst. & Kit. Small tree to 5m; br. hairy at first; thorns sparse, to 1cm. Lvs 2–6cm, broadly ovate to obovate on flowering shoots, with 3–7 serrate lobes, dark green and slightly hirsute above, more hairy and paler beneath. Fls 1.5cm diam., in lax tomentose clusters 4–7cm diam.; anth. red. Fr. 1cm, oval, black-purple. SE Eur., Cauc., Persia. Z6.

C. pentagyna var. *oliveriana* (Dum.-Cours.) Rehd. = *C. oliveriana.*

C. peregrina Sarg. (Possibly a hybrid of *C. mollis.*) Tree to 5m. Lvs to 12cm, broad-ovate with 4–6 narrow lobes, downy beneath. Fls 1.5cm diam., in crowded long-tomentose corymbs. Fr. 1–2cm, dull purple. W Asia. Z6.

C. × persistens Sarg. (*C. crus-galli* × ?) Large shrub or small tree 3–4m, closely resembling *C. crus-galli*; crown spreading; thorns numerous, stout to 5cm. Lvs to 7cm, lanceolate to obovate, base cuneate, apex sharply toothed, dark lustrous green, persisting into winter. Fls 2cm diam.; sta. 15–20, anth. white. Fr. 1.5cm, ovate, crimson-speckled, long-persistent. Gdn origin. Z5.

C. phaenopyrum (L. f.) Medik. WASHINGTON THORN. Slender tree to 10m, crown dense, rounded; shoots glab., slender, thorns to 7cm, occas. branched. Lvs 2.5–7cm, triangular to broadly ovate, base rounded or cordate, apex acute, 3–5-lobed toward base, toothed, bright glossy green, orange-red in fall. Fls 1cm diam., in glab. corymbs to 7cm; anth. pink. Fr. 0.5cm, sub-globose, bright red, retained until spring. SE US. 'Fastigiata': habit narrow, upright. 'Washington': habit narrow, upright, st. many. Z5.

C. pinnatifida Bunge. Small tree to 6m; shoots glab., sparsely thorned. Lvs 5–10cm, broadly ovate-triangular, with 5–9 deep lobes, almost pinnatifid at the base, lobes biserrate. Fls 1.5cm diam., in lax downy corymbs to 7cm; anth. pink. Fr. 1.5cm, globose, red, pitted. N China. var. *major* N.E. Br. Vigorous; lvs larger, 7–20cm, thicker, lobes shallower, broader, veins flushed red. Fr. abundant, to 2.5cm, globose to pyriform, apex indented, deep glossy red, finely pitted. var. *pilosa* Schneid. Lvs glab., lobes narrower and more deeply cut, leafing out v. early and often damanged by frost; infl. glab. C Asia, Korea. Z6.

C. populifolia Walter = *C. phaenopyrum.*

C. pruinosa (Wendl.) K. Koch. Tree 5–6m; br. spreading; thorns to 3cm. Lvs 2.5–6cm, broad-ovate, sharply biserrate, often triangularly lobed toward apex, red-green at first becoming deep green above, blue-green beneath. Fls 1.5–2.5cm diam., in loose corymbs; anth. red. Fr. 1cm, globose, rather angular, bright green, flushed purple becoming dark red, glossy, punctate; flesh yellow, sweet. NE US. Z5.

C. × prunifolia (Poir.) Pers. (*C. crus-galli* × *C. macrantha.*) Tree to 6m, crown dense, spreading; shoots glab.; thorns stout, 3–7cm. Lvs 4–8cm, rounded-ovate, oval or obovate, coarsely serrate, rich crimson in fall. Fls 2cm diam., in dense rounded corymbs; pedicels hirsute; cal. lobes glandular-dentate; anth. pink. Fr. 1.5cm, globose, bright red. Origin unknown. Z5.

C. pubescens Loud. Shrub or tree to 1m, br. nearly glab.; thorns sparse. Lvs 4–8cm, elliptic to obovate, crenate and sharply toothed, felted beneath; stipules large, leaflike. Fls 2cm diam., 6–15 in tomentose corymbs. Fr. globose to pyriform, yellow-orange. Mex. Z7.

C. punctata Jacq. Tree, 6–10m, crown spreading, rounded, shoots soon glab.; thorns 5–7cm. Lvs 5–10cm, broad ovate, dentate, often lobed toward apex, downy becoming glab. Fls 2cm, white, in hirsute corymbs to 10cm; pink. Fr. numerous, 22.5cm, pyri-

form or subglobose, deep red, pale speckled, abscising early. US. 'Aurea' ('Xanthocarpa'): fr. and anth. yellow. 'Ohio Pioneer': to 8m, thornless; fr. brick red, spotted. Z4.

C. purpurea var. *altaica* Loud. = *C. altaica.*

C. putnamiana Sarg. Tree to 10m, shoots slender, glab., thorny. Lvs triangular to ovate, with 2–5 pairs of shallow, scabrous, serrate lobes. Fls 2cm diam., in loose corymbs; anth. red. Fr. 1cm, globose or rather angular, bright red. C US. Z5.

C. rivularis Nutt. Small tree to 4m, shoots glab. Lvs 4–8cm, elliptic to lanceolate, usually unlobed, biserrate, dark green above, paler beneath. Fls 1cm diam.; sta. 10, anth. pink-purple. Fr. 1cm, globose, red-black. W & SW US. Z5.

C. rivularis Nutt. = *C. douglasii.*

C. robesoniana Sarg. = *C. pedicellata.*

C. rotundifolia Lam. non Moench = *Amelanchier rotundifolia.*

C. saligna Greene. Tree to 6m, br. pendent at tips, red-brown; thorns 1.5cm. Lvs to 7cm, narrow-elliptic, crenate, pale green, orange and russet in fall. Fls small. Fr. 1cm, globose, plum-red becoming lustrous blue-black. US (Colorado). Z4.

C. sanguinea Pall. Tree to 7m, br. red becoming lustrous purple-brown; thorns sparse, to 3cm. Lvs 5–8cm, oval-rhombic to broad ovate, with 3, 5 or 7 shallow scabrous, serrate or biserrate lobes, lightly pubesc. Fls 1.5cm diam., in crowded, glab. corymbs; anth. purple. Fr. 1cm, globose, red. SE Russia, Sib. Z4.

C. sanguinea var. *villosa* Maxim. = *C. maximowiczii.*

C. schraderiana Ledeb. Similar to *C. laciniata*: a small, round-headed tree with slightly less downy and more broadly lobed grey-green lvs and profusely borne large, dark purple-red fr. Greece, Crimea.

C. sinaica Boiss. = *C. azarolus* var. *sinaica.*

C. × sorbifolia Lange. (*C. laevigata* × ?.) Medium shrub; thorns 1cm. Lvs 8cm, oval-elliptic, crenately lobed, dark lustrous green above, paler beneath, with short appressed hairs. Fls *c*12 in corymbs. Fr. oblong, scarlet. Origin unknown. Z5.

C. spathulata Michx. Shrub or small tree to 8m, crown spreading; shoots soon glab., red-brown; thorns sparse, to 3cm. Lvs 1–2.5cm on flowering shoots, 2.5–3.5cm, on vegetative shoots obovate or diamond-shaped, base narrowing to a winged petiole, apex 3-lobed with large blunt teeth. Fls numerous, 1cm diam., in corymbs to 3.5cm; sta. 16–20. Fr. small, 4–5mm, globose, red, persistent. S US. Z7.

C. stipulacea Loud. = *C. pubescens* f. *stipulacea.*

C. submollis Sarg. Large shrub or small tree 8–10m; shoots villous, when young, thorny. Lvs 4–8cm, ovate to oval, with 4–5 pairs of shallow, scabrous, serrate lobes, downy above, felted beneath, eventually glab. Fls 2cm diam., in loose many-fld tomentose corymbs; cal. lobes with red gland. bristles; anth. white-yellow. Fr. 1cm, obovoid to pyriform, pale red, downy, flesh dry. NE US. Z5.

C. succulenta (Link) Schräd. Tree to 6m; shoots glab. becoming purple-brown; thorns to 7cm. Lvs 5–7cm, rounded-obovate, with toothed lobes toward apex, veins deeply impressed. Fls 1.5cm diam., in hirsute corymbs to 8cm; anth. pink. Fr. 3.5cm, globose, deep bright red. E US. var. *macracantha* (Lodd.) Eggl. Thorns to 8cm; sta. 10, anth. white or yellow, occas. pink; fr. usually less than 1cm, soft. E US. Z4.

C. tanacetifolia (Lam.) Pers. TANSY-LEAVED THORN. Shrub or small tree to 10m, br. ascending, felted when young. Lvs 2.5cm, obovate to oval-rhombic, with 5–7 narrow-oblong, pinnatisect, glandular-serrate lobes, hirsute. Fls 2.5cm diam., fragrant, 6–8 in rounded felted corymbs; anth. red. Fr. 2–2.5cm, globose, yellow-red, aromatic, reminiscent of apples in scent and flavour, with incised bracts below. W Asia. Z6.

C. tanacetifolia var. *leeana* Loud. = *C. × dippeliana.*

C. tomentosa Duroi = *C. calpodendron.*

C. triflora Chapm. Shrub to 7m. Lvs 2–7cm, oval-elliptic, lobes sharply toothed, downy. Fls 2–3cm diam., white, downy in clusters of 3; anth. yellow. Fr. 1–1.5cm, globose, red, downy. Alab. Z7.

C. uniflora Moench. Lax shrub to 3m, shoots hirsute when young; thorns slender, 2.5–3cm. Lvs 4cm, obovate, base cuneate, apex rounded, finely crenate, dark lustrous green above, paler beneath. Fls 1.5–2cm, solitary or in clusters of 3, pedicels v. short, shaggy; anth. cream. Fr. 1cm, globose to pyriform, yellow or green-yellow. E US. Z5.

C. viridis L. Tree to 12m, br. spreading; shoots glab.; thorns few, slender, to 3.5cm. Lvs 2–6cm, ovate or oval, serrate, or slightly lobed. Fls 1.5cm diam., in glab. corymbs to 5cm; anth. pale yellow. Fr. few, 0.5–1cm, globose, bright red, persistent. E US. 'Winter King': vigorous, bark silver; lvs glossy, red in fall; fr. lasts long into winter, produced from an early age. Z5.

C. wattiana Hemsl. & Lace. Small tree, resembling *C. sanguinea.* Br. glossy red-brown; thorns short, few or 0. Lvs 5–9cm, ovate, base cuneate, with 3–5 pairs of pinnatifid serrulate lobes. Fls white in corymbs to 7cm; anth. white or pale yellow. Fr. 1cm, globose, yellow-orange, juicy, abscising early. C Asia. Z5.

C. wilsonii Sarg. Tree or shrub to 6m; thorns robust, 1–2.5cm. Lvs 5–10cm, ovate to obovate, shallowly lobed, lobes more pronounced on flowering shoots, finely serrate, dark glossy green. Fls 1cm diam., white, in crowded shaggy corymbs to 6cm. Fr. 1cm, elliptic, red, glossy. China. Z6.
→*Mespilus*.

✕ Crataemespilus Camus. Rosaceae. (*Crataegus* ✕ *Mespilus*.) Z6.

✕ C. gillotii Beck & Rchb. (*Crataegus monogyna* ✕ *Mespilus germanica*.) Resembles ✕ *C. grandiflora*, differing in lvs regularly lobed; fls smaller.

✕ C. grandiflora Camus. (*Crataegus laevigata* ✕ *Mespilus germanica*.) Domed shrub to small tree, br. arching. Lvs 3–7cm, ovate to obovate, irregularly toothed, lobed near apex, hairy beneath, orange-yellow in fall. Fls 2.5cm, white. Fr. 1.5cm, brown, hairy, resembling *Mespilus*. Late spring–summer.
→*Crataegus* and *Mespilus*.

Cratericarpium Spach = *Boisduvalia*.

Craterispermum Benth. Rubiaceae. 20 shrubs or trees. Fls in stalked, axill., subcapitate clusters; cal. tube turbinate or obconic, limb hemispheric or cup-shaped, subentire or 5-toothed; cor. funnel-shaped or salverform, tube usualy hairy at throat, lobes 5, spreading. Trop. Afr., Madag., Seych. Z10.

C. laurinum (Poir.) Benth. Shrub or tree to 8m. Lvs to 20cm, obovate-oval or -oblong or elliptic, leathery. Fls fragrant, in dense clusters to 2.5cm across; cor. 0.7cm, waxy, yellow-white, occas. tinged pink; anth. exserted. Fr. to 0.6cm diam., blue-black. Trop. Afr.
→*Coffea*.

Craterostemma Schum.
C. schinzii Schum. = *Brachystelma schinzii*.

Craterostigma Hochst. Scrophulariaceae. 20 small ± stemless perenn. herbs. Lvs in a basal rosette. Rac. or corymb erect, scapose; cal. 5-toothed; cor. tubular, 2-lipped, upper lip concave; stigma conspicuous. Summer. Trop. Afr., India, Madag. Z10.

C. plantagineum Hochst. BLUE GEM. Lvs ovate, obtuse, ciliate, glab. above, pubesc. beneath. Fls to 12mm, yellow, white, purple or blue. E Afr.

C. pumilum Hochst. Lvs broadly ovate, obtuse, narrowing to a short, broad petiole. Fls. 12–16mm, blue and white, throat yellow. E Afr.

Crateva L. Capparidaceae. 9 small trees or shrubs. Lvs trifoliolate; lfts oblong-obovate, subcoriaceous. Corymb term., erect; fls garlic-scented, long-stalked; sep. 4, ovate-spathulate; pet. 4, clawed, ovate to rhombic, subequal; sta. numerous, showy, fil. long, pink to white. Pantrop. Z10.

C. adansonii DC. To 9m. Petiole to 6.5cm; lfts to 7×3cm. Infl. short, many-fld; pet. to 17×10mm, white, sometimes tipped lilac; sta. 16–20, purple. Afr. ssp. *axillaris* (Presl) Jacobs. To 10m. Branchlets dull violet-black. Petiole to 8cm; lfts to 10×5cm. Infl. to 10cm; pet. to 25×22mm; sta. 16–25. Malesia. ssp. *odora* (Hamilt.) Jacobs. To 10m. Petiole to 9cm; lfts to 11×6cm. Infl. to 7cm; pet. to 18×15mm, yellow-white to green or pale pink; sta. 15–26, white to purple. India, Sri Lanka, Malaysia.

C. excelsa Bojer. To 8m. Petiole red-brown; lfts to 8×3cm. Fls several to many; pet. to 15×9mm white or cream to pink; sta. 10–15, fil. pink, anth. yellow or violet. Madag.

C. gynandra L. = *C. tapia*.

C. odora Hamilt. = *C. adansonii* ssp. *odora*.

C. religiosa Forst. f. TEMPLE PLANT. To 15m. Bark marked white. Petiole to 10cm; lfts to 16×10cm. Infl. to 5cm; pet. to 30×20mm, white or cream, sometimes orange, ovate to elliptic; sta. 13–18, dark red to violet. Asia to Aus. and Pacific.

C. religiosa auct. non Forst. f. = *C. adansonii*.

C. tapia L. To 15m. Petiole to 14cm; lfts to 14×6cm. Infl. to 40cm; pet. to 17×7mm, cream to white-green; sta. pink. Americas.
→*Crataeva*.

Crawfurdia Wallich.
C. bulleyana Forr. = *Gentiana bulleyana*.
C. japonica Sieb. & Zucc. = *Gentiana trinervis*.

Crazy-leaf Begonia *Begonia* 'Phyllomaniaca'.
Crazy Weed *Oxytropis*.
Creambush *Holodiscus discolor*.

Creamcups *Platystemon*.
Cream Nut *Lecythis pisonis*.
Cream Sacs *Orthocarpus lithospermoides*.
Cream Violet *Viola striata*.
Creashak *Arctostaphylos uva-ursi*.
Creek Dogwood *Cornus* ✕ *californica*.
Creek Plum *Prunus rivularis*.
Creeping Avens *Geum reptans*.
Creeping Banksia *Banksia repens*.
Creeping Berries *Senecio radicans*.
Creeping Blueberry *Vaccinium crassifolium*.
Creeping Blue Blossom *Ceanothus thyrsiflorus* var. *repens*.
Creeping Bluets *Hedyotis michauxii*.
Creeping Buttercup *Ranunculus repens*.
Creeping Button Fern *Pyrrosia nummulariifolia*.
Creeping Charlie *Pilea nummulariifolia*.
Creeping Dogwood *Cornus canadensis*.
Creeping Fig *Ficus pumila*.
Creeping Forget-me-not *Omphalodes verna*.
Creeping Gloxinia *Asarina erubescens*.
Creeping Jenny *Lysimachia nummularia*.
Creeping Juniper *Juniperus horizontalis*.
Creeping Lily *Gloriosa*.
Creeping Mint *Meehania cordata*.
Creeping Oxalis *Oxalis corniculata*.
Creeping Phlox *Phlox stolonifera*.
Creeping Rubber Plant *Ficus pumila*.
Creeping Sage *Salvia sonomensis*.
Creeping Shield Fern *Lastreopsis microsora*.
Creeping Snow-berry *Gaultheria hispidula*.
Creeping Soft Grass *Holcus mollis*.
Creeping Spike Rush *Eleocharis palustris*.
Creeping Thistle *Cirsium arvense*.
Creeping Vervain *Verbena bracteata*.
Creeping Wattle *Acacia aculeatissima*.
Creeping Willow *Salix repens*.
Creeping Windmill Grass *Chloris truncata*.
Creeping Wintergreen Checkerberry *Gaultheria procumbens*.
Creeping Yellow Oxalis *Oxalis corniculata*.
Creeping Zinnia *Sanvitalia procumbens*.

Cremanthodium Benth. emend. R. Good Compositae. *c*50 medium to dwarf herbs. Lvs mostly basal, often reniform, st. lvs bract-like. Cap. radiate or discoid, large, solitary or few in simple rac. or corymbs, usually nodding, often fragrant. Mts of Tibet, India and China.

C. arnicoides (Wallich) R. Good. To 1m. Basal lvs to 20cm, obovate, acute, dentate, petiolate. Cap. to 6cm diam., radiate, few in a loose rac.; phyllaries woolly below; ray flts yellow, deeply toothed; disc flts dark. W Himal. to S Tibet and Yunnan. Z6.

C. delavayi (Franch.) Diels ex A. Lév. To 90cm. St. white-arachnoid above. Basal lvs to 10cm, hastate, dentate, leathery, white-arachnoid, becoming glab. and dark green, long-petiolate. Cap. radiate or discoid, solitary, fragrant; phyllaries purple-green; disc flts dull orange. NE Burm., Yunnan. Z7.

C. nobile (Franch.) Diels in A. Lév. To 50cm. St. black-hairy. Basal lvs to 10cm, obovate to elliptic, mucronate, dentate, sessile. Cap. radiate; phyllaries black-hairy at centre; ray flts golden yellow; disc flts dull orange. SE Tibet, SW China. Z7.

C. oblongatum C.B. Clarke. To 30cm. Basal lvs broadly ovate-elliptic, truncate, coarsely dentate, glab., long-petiolate. Cap. radiate, solitary or in rac.; phyllaries arachnoid below; ray flts yellow. W Himal. to Tibet, Sikkim and Gansu. Z7.

C. reniforme (Wallich) Benth. To 90cm. Basal lvs to 20cm, reniform, with few shallow teeth, glab., petiole straw-like. Cap. 5cm diam., solitary; phyllaries black glandular-hairy; ray flts pale yellow. Sikkim, to Bhutan and Nepal. Z6.
→*Senecio*.

Cremastus Miers.
C. balbisianus (DC.) Miers = *Arrabidaea corallina*.

✕ Cremneria Moran. (*Cremnophila* ✕ *Echeveria*.) Crassulaceae. 3 gdn hybrids. Lvs in tight rosettes, turgid, waxy glaucous. Flowering st. erect, pendulous or trailing; infl. br. upright. Z9.

✕ C. expatriata (Rose) Moran. (*Cremnophila linguifolia* ✕ *Echeveria microcalyx*.) Lvs 3cm, 30–50, widest near pointed tip, entire, glaucous. Fls pink, held ± erect to somewhat decumbent. Spring–winter.

✕ C. mutabilis (Deleuil ex E. Morr.) Moran. (*Cremnophila linguifolia* ✕ *Echeveria carnicolor*.) Lvs 5–12.5cm, 20–40, wider near apex, tapering to fine, short-pointed tip, entire, shortly hairy, tinged pale purple. Infl. trailing, fls pale yellow to pink 1–5 per br.

×*C. scaphylla* (Deleuil ex E. Morr.) Moran. Lvs to 7cm, 60–100, somewhat wider toward tip, tapering to a short point, slightly indented above. Infl. pendent; fls pale yellow.

→*Echeveria.*

Cremnophila Rose. Crassulaceae. 2 perenn., rosette-forming succulent herbs. Mex. Z9.

C. linguifolia (Lem.) Moran. Lvs 3–10×1.5–5cm, crowded in dense rosette or more distant, broad, spathulate, oblong or ovate, thick, margin rounded, grey to red. Infl. nodding; fls to 14mm diam. pale green-white. Winter–spring. Mex.

C. nutans Rose. Lvs 2–10×0.7–1.7cm, crowded in dense rosette, broad, thick spathulate, oblong-obovate, widest toward apex, rounded above, grey to dull deep green. Infl. erect; fls to 14mm diam., sulphur yellow. Winter. Mex.

→*Echeveria* and *Sedum.*

Creosote Bush *Larrea* (*L. tridentata*).
Crepe Fern *Leptopteris fraseri; Todea barbara.*
Crepe Flower *Lagerstroemia indica.*
Crepe Gardenia *Tabernaemontana divaricata.*
Crepe Ginger *Costus speciosus.*
Crepe Jasmine *Tabernaemontana divaricata.*

Crepis L. HAWK'S BEARD. Compositae. *c*200 glab. to pubesc. ann. or perenn. herbs. Lvs radical or cauline, entire to pinnatifid, petiole often narrowly winged. Cap. ligulate, solitary or many in simple or compound rac., corymbs or pan. N. Hemis.

C. aurea (L.) Cass. Perenn. to 30cm. Radical lvs to 10cm, obovate to oblanceolate, dentate to pinnatifid, glab., mucronate. Cap. few to many; fls yellow or orange, outer face maroon. Summer–autumn. Alps, mts of It., S & W Balk. Z6.

C. barbata L. = *Tolpis barbata.*

C. biennis L. Bienn. to 120cm. Radical lvs to 25cm, oblanceolate, pinnatisect, acute, dentate, rough, petiole narrowly winged. Cap. 1–6, in a corymb; phyllaries grey or silky pubesc.; flts yellow. Summer. W & C Eur. Z6.

C. blattarioides (L.) Vill. = *C. pyrenaica.*

C. capillaris (L.) Wallr. Ann. or bienn. to 1m. Lvs glab. or sparsely pubesc., radical lvs to 30cm, lanceolate to oblanceolate, obtuse to acute, denticulate, runcinate-pinnatifid, lyrate, or 1–2 pinnatisect; petiole winged. Cap. many in a corymb; phyllaries grey-tomentose; flts deep yellow, outer surface maroon. Spring–autumn. W, C & S Eur. Z6.

C. conyzifolia (Gouan) A. Kerner. Perenn. to 50cm. Radical lvs to 30cm, oblanceolate, acute to obtuse, runcinate-denticulate to pinnatifid, rarely pinnatisect, petiole broadly winged. Cap. 1–10; phyllaries green-yellow hairy; flts yellow. Summer. SC Fr., Carpath., Pyren., SW Bulg. Z6.

C. hokkaidoensis Babc. Perenn. to 30cm. Radical lvs to 14cm, oblanceolate to elliptic, sinuately to runcinate or pinnatifid, entire or dentate, petiole winged. Cap. 4–12; phyllaries grey-tomentose; flts yellow. Summer. Mts Jap. Z7.

C. incana Sibth. & Sm. PINK DANDELION. Perenn. to 15cm. Lvs glab. or grey-tomentose; radical lvs 3–13cm, oblanceolate, acute, pinnatisect, seg. acutely lobed and dentate. Cap. few to many; phyllaries densely grey-tomentose, sometimes with black hairs; flts magenta-pink. Summer. S & SE Greece. Z8.

C. jacquinii Tausch. Perenn. to 40cm. Lvs to 15cm, oblanceolate to linear, entire to pinnatifid, glab. or sparsely hairy; petiole broad with narrow wing. Cap. 2–6; phyllaries glab. to tomentose; flts bright yellow. Summer. E Alps, Carpath., NW Balk. Z5.

C. macrorhiza Banks ex Hook. = *Tolpis macrorhiza.*

C. occidentalis Nutt. Perenn. to 40cm. Radical lvs to 35cm, elliptic, acute or acuminate, sinuate-dentate to runcinate-pinnatifid, lobes dentate, petiole winged. Cap. few to many, in a clustered corymb; phyllaries gland.; flts yellow. Summer. Saskatch., Mont., to BC, S Calif., Mex. Z4.

C. paludosa (L.) Moench. Perenn. to 1m. Lvs to 30cm, dark green, glab., radical lvs oblanceolate, early decid., sinuate-dentate or denticulate, petiole winged. Cap. to 25 in a corymb; phyllaries gland. hairy; flts yellow. Summer–autumn. N & C Eur., N Spain, S It., S Bulg., S & C Russia. Z6.

C. pannonica (Jacq.) Koch. Perenn., to 1.5m. Lvs ± hairy, imbricate, radical lvs to 30cm, oblanceolate to elliptic, acute, dentate, petiole winged. Cap. many, in a rac., pan. or corymb; flts yellow. Summer. E & C Eur. to C Czech., C Russia, NW Persia. Z6.

C. pygmaea L. Perenn., to 30cm. Lvs tomentose or glandular-pubesc., radical lvs to 11cm, lyrate-pinnatifid, term. seg. elliptic to orbicular to ovate, somewhat dentate; petiole narrowly winged. Cap. to 8 axillary phyllaries tomentose, ray flts yellow, outer surface maroon. Summer. W Eur., S Alps, S Apennines. Z6.

C. pyrenaica (L.) Greuter. Perenn. to 1m. Lvs with pale hairs, radical lvs to 20cm, early decid., oblanceolate, acute, dentate. Cap. 1–6; phyllaries hairy, flts yellow. Summer. Alps, N Apennines, Pyren., N & E Spain, S & E Fr. Z6.

C. rosea hort. = *C. incana.*

C. rubra L. Ann. or perenn. to 60cm. Lvs pubesc., radical lvs to 15cm, oblanceolate, base attenuate acute, denticulate or runcinate-pinnatifid, petiole slightly winged. Cap. 1 or 2; phyllaries glab. to strigose, flts pink or white. Spring–summer. S It., Balk., Crete. Z6.

C. sibirica L. Perenn. to 1.5m. Lvs hairy, esp. beneath; radical lvs, 10–40cm, ovate, oblong-lanceolate, acute, base cordate, sinuate-dentate, petioles winged, early decid. Cap. 1–6; flts yellow. Summer. Russia, C Rom., E Czech. Z5.

C. terglouensis (Hacq.) A. Kerner. Perenn. to 10cm. Lvs glab. or sparsely hairy, radical lvs to 8cm, oblanceolate, runcinate-dentate to pinnatifid, petiole winged. Cap. solitary; flts yellow. Summer. C & E Alps. Z5.

C. virgata Desf. = *Tolpis virgata.*

C. zacintha (L.) Babc. Ann. to 30cm. Lvs pale-hairy, radical lvs to 20cm, oblanceolate, lyrate-pinnatifid, early decid. Cap. many; phyllaries mostly glab., ray flts yellow, striped maroon on outer surface.

→*Lapsana* and *Leontodon.*

Crescentia L. Bignoniaceae. 6 sprawling small to medium trees or lianes. Lvs simple or 3-foliolate. Fls solitary or paired on old wood; cal. bilabiate; cor. tubular-campanulate, lobes deltoid, acuminate; sta. slightly exserted. Fr. a large spherical pepo or calabash, shell woody, pulpy within. Mex., W Indies to Braz. Z10.

C. aculeata Humb. = *Parmentiera aculeata.*

C. acuminata Humb. = *C. cujete.*

C. alata HBK. TECOMATE; JICARA; MORRO; CRUZ. To 8m. Lvs simple or 3-foliolate, lfts 1–4.5cm; petiole 2.7–11.5cm, winged. Fls musky-scented; cor. tan-brown, tube 2.8–4.2cm, lobes 1–1.5cm. Fr. 7–10cm diam. Mex. to Costa Rica.

C. angustifolia Willd. ex Seem. = *C. cujete.*

C. arborea Raf. = *C. cujete.*

C. coriacea Miers = *Amphitecna latifolia.*

C. cucurbitina L. = *Amphitecna latifolia.*

C. cujete L. CALABASH; WILD CALABASH; TREE CALABASH. To 10m. Lvs 1.5–26cm, simple, obovate, sessile. Cor. yellow to tan, lined purple, tube 2.8–4.5cm, lobes 2.5–3.1cm. Fr. to 30cm. C Amer., Mex.

C. cuneifolia Gardn. = *C. cujete.*

C. cuspidata Miers = *Amphitecna latifolia.*

C. edulis Desv. = *Parmentiera aculeata.*

C. elongata Miers = *Amphitecna latifolia.*

C. fasciculata Miers = *C. cujete.*

C. latifolia Mill. = *Amphitecna latifolia.*

C. lethifera Tussac = *Amphitecna latifolia.*

C. macrophylla Seem. = *Amphitecna macrophylla.*

C. nigripes Lind. = *Amphitecna macrophylla.*

C. obovata Benth. = *Amphitecna latifolia.*

C. ovata Burm. f. = *C. cujete.*

C. palustris Forsyth ex Seem. = *Amphitecna latifolia.*

C. pinnata Jacq. = *Kigelia africana.*

C. plectantha Miers = *C. cujete.*

C. regalis Lind. = *Amphitecna regalis.*

C. spathulata Miers = *C. cujete.*

Crested Beard-tongue *Penstemon eriantherus.*
Crested Callistemon *Callistemon lophanthus.*
Crested Euphorbia *Euphorbia lactea.*
Crested Hair Grass *Koeleria macrantha.*
Crested-tongued Penstemon *Penstemon eriantherus.*
Crested Wheatgrass *Agropyron cristatum.*
Crested Wood Fern *Dryopteris cristata.*
Cretan Brake *Pteris cretica.*
Cretan Dittany *Origanum dictamnus.*
Cretan Maple *Acer sempervirens.*

Cribbia Sengh. Orchidaceae. 1 epiphytic monopodial orchid. St. v. short. Lvs 3–4, 6–16cm, ligulate or oblanceolate. Rac. basal, equalling or slightly shorter than lvs, few-fld; fls 0.7–1cm diam., green-white or pale green-yellow, fragrant; dors. sep. lanceolate, lateral sep. falcate; pet. ovate; lip entire, ovate, acute; spur 4–6mm. W Afr., Sao Tomé, Zaire, Uganda, Kenya. Z10.

C. brachyceras Summerh.

→*Rangaeris.*

Cricket-ball Hakea *Hakea platysperma.*
Cricket-bat Willow *Salix alba* var. *caerulea.*
Crimean Linden *Tilia* 'Euchlora'.

Crimean Pine *Pinus nigra* var. *pallasiana*.
Crimson Bottlebrush *Callistemon citrinus*.
Crimson Bramble *Rubus arcticus*.
Crimson Clover *Trifolium incarnatum*.
Crimson Glory Vine *Vitis coignetiae*.
Crimson Mallee *Eucalyptus lansdowneana*.
Crinkled Hair Grass *Deschampsia flexuosa*.
Crinkle-leaf Plant *Adromischus cristatus*.
Crinkle Root *Cardamine diphylla*.

Crinodendron Molina. Elaeocarpaceae. 2 large everg. shrubs or small trees. Br. initially hirsute, lenticellate. Lvs leathery. Fls solitary or paired on slender, hanging pedicels; sep. 5, fused in a short, toothed ring; cor. tubular-campanulate to urceolate, pet. 5, thickly textured. Arg., Chile.

C. dependens (Ruiz & Pav.) Kuntze = *C. patagua*.

C. hookerianum C. Gay. CHILE LANTERN TREE. Tree to 9m or a multistemmed shrub to 4m. Branchlets thick. Lvs 5–10cm, narrowly elliptic to narrowly oblong-lanceolate, serrate, glossy dark green. Fls lantern-like, hanging below branchlets on pedicels to 5cm; cor. to 3cm, scarlet to carmine, strongly urceolate, fleshy, pet. cupped, ridged and valvate. Chile.

C. lanceolatum Miq. = *C. hookerianum*.

C. patagua Molina. Tree to 14m or shrub to 4m. Branchlets rather slender. Lvs 3–7cm, elliptic to oblong-ovate, apex usually rounded, sinuate to serrate, glossy deep green. Fls hanging below br. on pedicels to 3cm; cor. to 2.5cm, white, campanulate, pet. more slender and open than in *C. hookerianum*, giving the appearance of a fringed cup or bell. Chile.

→*Tricuspidaria*.

×**Crinodonna** Stapf.

×*Crinodonna corsii* Stapf = ×*Amarcrinum memoria-corsii*.
×*Crinodonna memoria-corsii* Ragion. = ×*Amarcrinum memoria-corsii*.

Crinum L. Amaryllidaceae. *c*130 everg. and decid. bulbous herbs. Bulb with an elongated neck. Lvs linear or lorate, usually broad, thick. Scape arising from bulb to one side of foliage, with 2 spathe valves; pedicels short; fls few or many in an umbel, often fragrant, actinomorphic or zygomorphic; perianth salverform or funnel-shaped, lobes 6; sta. 6, fil. long, curved, anth. versatile. Warm and trop. regions.

C. abyssinicum Hochst. ex A. Rich. Lvs to 3.5×2.5cm, linear, glaucous, denticulate. Scape to 60cm; perianth white, tube to 5cm, lobes oblong, acute, to 8cm; fil. less than 2.5cm. Ethiop. Z9.

C. acaule Bak. Lvs to 45×1.2cm, linear, glossy, channelled. Scape mostly buried, emerging to 5cm; perianth tube 10cm, lobes to 12×2cm, lanceolate, erect, recurved at one end, keeled, pale red; sta. half as long as lobes. S Afr. Z9.

C. amabile var. *augustum* (Roxb.) Herb. = *C. augustum*.

C. americanum L. FLORIDA SWAMP LILY; SOUTHERN SWAMP CRINUM. Lvs to 1.2m, curved, lorate, denticulate. Scape to 75cm; perianth creamy-white, tube to 13cm, tinged green or purple, equalling or exceeding lobes, lobes linear or linear-lanceolate, to 1.5cm across; sta. pink or red. S US. 'Miss Elsie': st. to 50cm; lvs wide; fls many, white, exterior tinted fox brown. 'Catherine': lvs erect, pointed; to 90cm; fls white, fil. purple. Z9.

C. amoenum Roxb. Lvs to 60×5cm, linear, spreading, bright green, undulate. Scape to 60cm, fls fragrant; perianth tube to 10cm, green, lobes to 8cm, lanceolate, white, tinged red outside; fil. bright red. India, Burm. Z9.

C. aquaticum Burchell = *C. campanulatum*.

C. arenarium Herb. WATER ISLAND SAND CRINUM. Lvs to 60×3.5cm, tapering, glaucous. Scape to 30cm; perianth tube to 10cm, pale green mottled red, curved, lobes 7cm, white, tipped green; fil. purple. NW Aus. Z10.

C. asiaticum L. POISON BULB. Lvs to 120×10cm, lorate, not channelled, arching, pale blue-green. Scape to 60cm; fls white, fragrant; perianth tube to 10cm, erect, tinged green, lobes to 8cm, drooping or curving downwards; fil. tinged red. Trop. Asia. var. *sinicum* Bak. ST. JOHN'S LILY. Lvs to 15cm across, undulate, forming a crown to 1.5m high. Scape to 1m; perianth tube and seg. longer than in type. China. var. *declinatum* Bak. Bud curving downwards, not erect; tips of perianth lobes tinged red. var. *procerum* Bak. Lvs to 150×15cm. Perianth tube and lobes to 13cm, lobes tinged red below. Rangoon. Z8.

C. asiaticum Roxb. = *C. defixum*.
C. asiaticum var. *bracteatum* (Willd.) Herb. = *C. bracteatum*.
C. asiaticum var. *japonicum* Bak. = *C. japonicum*.

C. augustum Roxb. Lvs to 75×10cm, few, canaliculate, green, purple at base. Scape equalling lvs, dark red-purple; fls fragrant, rose outside, striped inside; perianth tube to 13cm, curved, dark

red, lobes to 165cm, margins white, fil. purple. Maur., Seych. Z9.

C. balfouri Bak. Lvs to 30×5cm, lorate, bright green, denticulate. Scape to 60cm, compressed; fls fragrant; perianth tube 5cm, cylindric, green, erect, lobes lanceolate, white, to 1.2cm wide, equalling tube, spreading; style tinged red. Socotra. Z10.

C. blandum M. Roem. Differs from *C. arenarium* in lvs broader, scape longer, perianth limb broader, lobes to 6.5cm, red outside, fil. white. N Aus. Z10.

C. brachynema Herb. Lvs to 60×10cm, broadly lorate, bright green. Scape to 30cm; fls drooping, fragrant, pure white; perianth tube to 3.8cm, curved, slender, lobes to 3.8cm, spreading, elliptic-oblong; fil. white. India. Z10.

C. bracteatum Willd. Lvs to 45×13cm, spreading, striate. Scape to 30cm; fls white, fragrant; perianth tube 5cm, lobes equalling or slightly exceeding tube, outer lobes to 0.8cm wide, canaliculate-concave, the inner narrower; fil. blood-red. Maur., E India. Z10.

C. braunii Harms. Lvs to 100×5.5cm, linear, furrowed, margins white, finely dentate. Scape 70cm; fls erect, unscented; perianth tube to 15cm, furrowed, light green, upper part white, lobes to 10cm, linear, white, with pink margins; fil. dark red above. Madag. Z10.

C. brevifolium Roxb. = *C. bracteatum*.

C. bulbispermum (Burm.) Milne-Redh. & Shweick. Lvs ligulate, 60–90×7.5–11cm, channelled, reflexed, margins cartilaginous, dentate. Scape 50–90cm; fls fragrant, perianth tube curved, 7–15cm, green, tinged brown-red, lobes 7–13cm, white with pink or red streak. Summer–autumn. S Afr. 'Album': fls white. 'Cape Dawn': fls soft red to pink, in large umbels. 'Pam's Pink': fls large, rose. 'Roseum': fls pink. 'St. Christopher': fls cup-shaped, white. Some hybrids with *C.* ×*powellii*. Z6.

C. campanulatum Herb. Lvs to 1.2m, decid., linear, deeply channelled, dentate. Scape to 30cm; perianth tube red-green, to 8cm, limb campanulate, equalling tube, lobes oblong, obtuse, white suffused with pink. S Afr. Z9.

C. caribaeum Bak. Lvs to 30×10cm, lorate-oblong, tapering below. Fls erect; perianth tube to 10cm, straight, lobes to 0.4cm wide, white, linear, spreading. W Indies. Z10.

C. colensoi hort. = *C. moorei*.
C. crassifolium Herb. = *C. variabile*.

C. crassipes Bak. Lvs to 120×10cm, lorate, tapering to tip. Scape stout, to 30cm; perianth tube to 8cm, slightly curved, green, lobes oblanceolate, equalling tube, 1.2cm wide, white tinged red; fil. purple. Trop. Afr. Z10.

C. crispum Phillips = *C. lugardae*.

C. cruentum Ker-Gawl. Lvs to 120×4cm, dark green, canaliculate. Scape compressed or ancipitous; fls peach flushed purple, fragrant; perianth tube triangular, pale green, lobes elongate-lanceolate, striped green outside; fil. blood-red. C Amer. Z9.

C. declinatum Herb. = *C. asiaticum* var. *declinatum*.

C. defixum Ker-Gawl. Lvs to 100×2cm, erect, linear, semicylindrical, concave, shiny, margin hispid. Scape shorter than lvs, glaucous, tinged purple; fls fragrant at night; perianth tube cylindric, to 15cm, green tinged red, lobes to 8cm, recurved-appendiculate; fil. white, red above. E India. Z10.

C. douglasii Bail. Lvs to 75×12cm, dark green, blunt-tipped. Scape to 75cm, dark-mottled; perianth tube 13cm, outer lobes to 9cm, undulate, purple-red, inner lobes shorter and narrower. Aus. Z10.

C. erubescens Ait. Large aquatic herb. Lvs to 90×8cm, many, curved, strap-shaped, thick and succulent. Scape to 60cm; fls fragrant; perianth tube to 15cm, narrow, red, lobes lanceolate, reflexed, maroon outside, white inside; fil. red. Trop. Amer. Z10.

C. erubescens HBK non Ait. = *C. kunthianum*.

C. erythrophyllum Carey ex Herb. Lvs to 30×5cm, sprawling, curling, red. Scape to 30cm; perianth lobes to 10cm, white, linear-lanceolate. Burm. Z10.

C. flaccidum Herb. MURRAY LILY; MACQUARIE LILY; DARLING LILY. Lvs to 60×3cm, linear-lorate, channelled. Scape to 60cm; fls white, fragrant; perianth tube slightly curved, shorter than limb, limb funnel-shaped, to 8cm diam., lobes white with green hook, fil. green. Aus. Z10.

C. forgetii C.H. Wright. Lvs to 35×7cm, oblong-lanceolate, denticulate. Scape to 30cm; perianth tube 20×0.5cm, green, lobes 8–12cm, ligulate, acuminate, white, revolute; fil. red. Peru. Z9.

C. ×*herbertii* Sweet. (*C. zeylanicum* 'Album' × *C. bulbispermum*.) Lvs 12–15, ensiform-acuminate, 90–180cm, margins scabrid, deep green to slightly glaucous. Scape to 90cm; fls white to pink; perianth tube curved, 10cm, lobes 8.5cm, semi-elliptic, recurved. Gdn origin. 'Gulf Pride': fls white, keels marked pink, pet. broad and rounded. Z10.

C. hildebrandtii Vatke. Lvs to 60×7cm, lanceolate, tapering, bright green, firm. Scape slender, to 30cm; fls pure white, erect; perianth tube to 18cm, lobes to 8cm, oblanceolate, spreading, fil. bright purple. Comoro Is. Z10.

C. humile Herb. = *C. nubicum*.

C. intermedium Bail. Lvs blunt-tipped with longitudinal veins. Scape compressed, glaucous; perianth lobes white with apiculate yellow tips. Aus. Z10.

C. japonicum (Bak.) Hannibal. Lvs 45–60×5–12.5cm, succulent, somewhat channelled, ascending. Scape stout, 30–45cm; fls white; perianth tube straight, erect, to 7.5cm, seg. spreading, to 7.5cm. Summer–autumn. Jap. 'Variegatum': lvs bright green striped cream.

C. johnstonii Bak. = *C. macowanii*.

C. kirkii Bak. Lvs to 120×12cm, lorate, tapering to a point, margin bristly. Scapes 2–3 per bulb, to 45cm; perianth tube to 10cm, tinged green, lobes oblong, acute, equalling tube, white striped red. E Afr. 'P.F. Reasoner' (*C. kirkii* × *C. bulbispermum*): lvs to 1m; fls white with red keels. Z10.

C. kunthianum Roem. Lvs to 90×8cm, 20, strap-shaped, undulate. Scape to 30cm; fls pure white or tinged purple perianth tube to 20cm, lobes lanceolate, to 6cm; fil. red. C Amer. Z9.

C. latifolium L. = *C. zeylanicum*.

C. lineare L. f. Lvs to 60×36cm, linear, channelled, glaucous. Scape slender, to 30cm; perianth tube to 6cm, slender, curved, lobes to 8cm, white, tinged red in the centre, oblong or oblanceolate. S Afr. Z9.

C. longifolium Thunb. = *C. bulbispermum*.

C. lugardae N.E. Br. Lvs to 75×1.8cm, linear, deep green, concave, margins finely scabrous. Scape to 30cm; perianth tube to 10cm, cylindric, curved, lobes 9cm, lanceolate, white with light pink median stripe and green tip. Central S Amer. Z10.

C. mackenii hort. = *C. moorei*.

C. macowanii Bak. PYJAMA LILY. Lvs to 90×10cm, decid, strap-shaped, thin, bright green. Scape to 90cm, stout; fls nodding, fragrant, perianth tube to 10cm, curved, green at base, lobes equalling tube, to 3.5cm across, oblong, acute, pink or white, striped deep pink along middle, curving outwards at apex; sta. white. E, C & S Afr. Z9.

C. makoyanum Carr. = *C. moorei*.

C. mearsii Bedd. Lvs to 30×2.5cm. Scape to 13cm; fls white; perianth tube slender, to 13cm, lobes to 6cm, lanceolate. Upper Burm. Z10.

C. moorei Hook. f. Lvs to 90×10cm, decid., lorate, spreading. Scape to 90cm; fls pale to deep pink, or white, fragrant; perianth tube to 8cm, curved, green or tinged red, limb funnelform, equalling tube, lobes oblong, 3.5cm wide, white suffused pink; fil. pink. S Afr. 'Album': fls white. 'Roseum': fls pink. Z8.

C. natalense hort. = *C. moorei*.

C. nubicum Hannibal. Lvs to 30cm, linear, green, surface pitted. Scape to 30cm; perianth tube green, lobes 5cm, narrow linear-lanceolate, white; fil. purple. Trop. Asia. Z10.

C. ornatum (Ait.) Bury. = *C. zeylanicum*.

C. parvum Bak. Lvs to 23×1.4cm, linear. Scape slender, almost equalling lvs; fl. solitary; perianth tube to 8cm, cylindrical, erect, lobes to 8cm, narrow, white striped red. CS Afr. Z10.

C. pedicellatum Pax = *C. macowanii*.

C. pedunculatum hort. = *C. asiaticum* var. *sinicum*.

C. podophyllum Hook. f. = *C. lugardae*.

C. ×powellii L.H. Bail. (*C. bulbispermum* × *C. moorei*.) Lvs ensiform, 65–150×7.5–10cm+, tapering to slender apex, deeply channelled. Scape to 150cm+; fls pink, fragrant; perianth tube curved, to 10cm, lobes 7.5–12.5cm, apex recurved; style red. Gdn origin. 'Album': fls pure white. 'Krelagei': fls large, dark pink, in large umbels. 'Harlemense': fls soft pink, in large umbels. 'Roseum': fls pale pink. Z6.

C. pratense Herb. Lvs to 60×5cm, linear. Scape to 30cm; fls white; perianth tube to 10cm, tinged green, lobes lanceolate, nearly equalling tube, to 1.2cm wide; fil. bright red. India. Z10.

C. procerum Carey = *C. asiaticum* var. *procerum*.

C. purpurascens Herb. Lvs to 90×4cm, lorate, dark green, channelled, thin, undulate. Scape to 30cm; perianth tube to 15cm, slender, straight, green tinged purple, lobes lanceolate, half length of tube, white suffused pink or purple; fil. bright red. E Guinea. Z10.

C. pusillum Herb. Lvs to 30×1cm, erect, linear. Scape 2.5cm; fls few, erect; perianth tube 8cm; lobes linear. India (Nicobar Is.). Z10.

C. roozenianum O'Brien = *C. americanum*.

C. scabrum Herb. = *C. zeylanicum*.

C. schimperi Vatke ex Schum. Lvs to 50×3cm, lorate, erect, blue-green. Scape to 20cm; perianth tube to 11cm, white, lobes 7cm; anth. black. Ethiop. Z10.

C. schmidtii Reg. = *C. moorei*.

C. sinicum Roxb. = *C. asiaticum* var. *sinicum*.

C. submersum Herb. LAKE CRINUM. Lvs to 45×5cm, sharply

pointed, channelled, yellow-green. Scape 45cm; fls fragrant at night; perianth tube to 13cm, green-yellow; lobes to 10cm, white with pink stripes and pointed red tips, oval, channelled near the base; fil. red. Braz. Z10.

C. sumatranum Roxb. Lvs to 180×15cm, erect, broadly sublate, concave, stiff, margins white. Scape shorter than lvs; fls fragrant, white; perianth tube to 10cm, tinged red or green, lobes equalling tube, to 0.6cm wide. Sumatra. Z10.

C. toxicarium Roxb. = *C. asiaticum*.

C. undulatum Hook. Lvs to 45×2.5cm, ensiform. Scape shorter than lvs; perianth tube to 20cm, green, lobes to 7cm, undulate, fil. red. Peru, Braz. Z10.

C. variabile (Jacq.) Herb. Lvs linear, weak, outer lvs to 60×5cm. Scape to 45cm; perianth tube to 3.5cm, green, lobes to 8.5cm, oblong, acute, white, flushed red down the middle; fil. red. S Afr. (Cape). Z9.

C. wimbushii Worsley. Lvs to 120×63cm, deeply channelled, spreading. Scape to 45cm; fls subcampanulate, white flushed pink, fragrant; perianth tube to 9cm, slightly curved, outer lobes to 2cm wide, inner lobes to 2.5cm; fil. pink. C Afr. Z10.

C. woodrowii Bak. Lvs to 30×10cm, blunt, glab., bright green. Scape to 30cm; perianth tube to 8cm, cylindric, lobes white, lanceolate, equalling tube; fil. deep red. C India. Z10.

C. yucciflorum Salisb. = *C. zeylanicum*.

C. zeylanicum L. MILK-AND-WINE LILY. Lvs to 90×10cm, thin, sword-shaped, erect or spreading, margins undulate, scabrous or dentate. Scape to 90cm, fls fragrant; perianth tube to 10cm, round to 3-angled, curved, lobes to 10×2.5cm, oblanceolate, white with a broad violet-purple keel; fil. violet-purple. Trop. Asia, E Afr. Z10.

C. cvs. 'Ellen Bosanquet': lvs wide, fleshy; fls burgundy. 'Peach Blow': lvs dark; fls fragrant, lavender pink, interior pale, seg. recurving.

→*Amaryllis*.

Crithmum L. Umbelliferae. 1 succulent, perenn., maritime herb to 60cm, glab., slightly woody at base. Lvs biternate or triternate; lfts 1.25cm, fleshy, thick, linear, olive to dark green. Fls small yellow-white, in compound, flat-topped umbels. Summer. Eur. (Atlantic coast). Z7.

C. maritimum L. SEA SAMPHIRE; SAMPHIRE.

Crocanthemum Spach.
C. bicknellii (Fern.) Janch. = *Helianthemum bicknellii*.
C. canadense (L.) Britt. & A. Britt. = *Helianthemum canadense*.
C. majus Britt. & A. Britt. non Rydb. = *Helianthemum bicknellii*.
C. majus Rydb. non Britt. & A. Britt. = *Helianthemum canadense*.
C. scoparium (Nutt.) Millsp. = *Helianthemum scoparium*.

Crocanthus Klotzsch ex Klatt.
C. croceus (Jacq.) L. Bol. = *Malephora crocea*.
C. purpureocroceus (Haw.) L. Bol. = *Malephora crocea* var. *purpureocrocea*.
C. thunbergii (Haw.) L. Bol. = *Malephora thunbergii*.

Crocodile Jaws *Aloe humilis*.

Crocosmia Planch. MONTBRETIA. Iridaceae. Some 7 cormous perenn. herbs. Lvs linear-lanceolate, acuminate, sheathing base of flowering st., ribbed or plicate. Fls held above lvs, usually in 2 rows along simple or branching erect to horizontal spikes; perianth slender, tubular, curving downwards, lobes spreading, obtuse. Fr. a small bead-like capsule. S Afr. Z7.

C. aurea (Hook.) Planch. To 1m. Lvs to 85×2cm, ribbed, pale green, papery. Fls semi-opposite, on simple or branching spikes; perianth pale to burnt orange, straight-sided, to 5cm, opening to broad lobes, each to 2.5×0.5cm. Early summer. 'Flore Pleno': fls double. 'Imperialis': robust; fls large, brilliant orange-red. 'Maculata': perianth lobes with orange-brown basal spot. Z7.

C. ×crocosmiiflora (Burb. & Dean) N.E. Br. (*C. aurea* × *C. pottsii*.) Hybrid differing from *C. aurea* in upper part of perianth which is somewhat inflated and curved, and narrower lobes. Summer. Gdn origin. Z5.

C. masoniorum (Bol.) N.E. Br. To 1.25m. Lvs to 90×6cm, glab., plicate. Scape ascending then horizontal, simple or branching with fls semi-erect; perianth vermilion, to 5cm, narrow at base, widening to outspread lobes. Late summer. 'Firebird': fls fiery orange-red, throat tinged green. Z6.

C. paniculata (Klatt) Goldbl. To 1m. Lvs to 90×6cm, olive green, plicate, pubesc. Fls alt. on erect, branching spikes, axis flexuous; perianth deep orange, to 6cm, curving downwards, somewhat inflated with lobes spreading, to 2cm across. Summer.

C. pottsii (Bak.) N.E. Br. To 90cm. Lvs to 90×1.5cm, ribbed. Fls, horizontal or erect along one side of each br. of a branched spike; perianth to 3cm, widening sharply from narrow base, orange flushed red, lobes to 1×0.5cm. Z6.

C. cvs. 'Bressingham Blaze': fls widely funnel-shaped, fiery orange-red. 'Citronella': fls yellow with red-brown markings in centre. 'Emberglow': fls orange-brown, upward-arching. 'Emily McKenzie': fls nodding, dark orange with red splashes in paler throat. 'Fire Bird': fls orange-red outside, inside with a large yellow ring, margins and veins darker, throat tinged green. 'His Majesty': fls large, orange-scarlet. 'Jackanapes': fls small, bicoloured yellow and deep orange-red. 'James Coey': fls large, nodding, v. dark orange-red, interior paler. 'Lady Hamilton': fls large, soft orange-yellow, central zone apricot, with small maroon dots on lower perianth lobes, flushed maroon on upper lobes. 'Lucifer': fls large, flame-red. 'Solfatarre': fls apricot-yellow; lvs smoky bronze. 'Star of the East': to 90cm; fls v. large, soft apricot-yellow, throat paler, tips darker.

→*Antholyza, Curtonus, Montbretia* and *Tritonia.*

Crocus L. Iridaceae. 80 cormous perenn. herbs. Corms with tunics of various types. Lvs emerging with or after fls from bracts or cataphylls, linear to linear-lanceolate, usually with pale green or silver-white central stripe. Fls stemless 1–4 emerging from a sheath; perianth tube narrow, expanding to 6 lobes in 2 overlapping whorls; fil. 3; style trifid or divided further. Mid & S Eur., N Afr., Middle E, Central Asia.

C. abantensis Baytop & B. Mathew. Tunics finely reticulate-fibrous. Lvs to 1mm wide. Fls 1–2, tube mid to deep blue, throat yellow; style trifid, orange. Spring. Turk. Z7.

C. adanensis Baytop & B. Mathew. Tunics papery, parallel fibrous. Lvs to 3mm wide. Fls 1–2, tube white, throat white; interior of lobes lilac with cream base, exterior buff speckled violet at base; anth. yellow. Early spring. S Turk. Z8.

C. aerius Herb. Tunics papery, splitting lengthwise from base. Lvs to 2mm wide. Fls to 3, tube deep blue, often flushed royal blue from base of lobes, overlaid with darker feather veins; style trifid, vermilion to scarlet. Mid–late spring. N Turk. Z7.

C. aerius hort. non Herb. = *C. biflorus* ssp. *pulchricolor.*

C. alatavicus Semenova & Reg. Outer tunics parallel-fibrous, inner entire, papery. Lvs to 2mm wide. Fls to 5, tube white suffused violet, throat yellow, glab., interior white, exterior stained dark violet; style trifid, orange. Spring. Russia, W China. var. *albus* Reg. Fls white with throat yellow. var. *ochroleucus* Bak. Exterior of fls ivory to pale yellow. var. *porphyreus* Bak. Exterior flecked damson purple. Z4.

C. albiflorus Kit. ex Schult. = *C. vernus* ssp. *albiflorus.*

C. aleppicus Bak. Tunics papery at apex, otherwise parallel- or, rarely, reticulate-fibrous. Fls to 4, sweetly fragrant, exterior yellow flushed mauve; anth. yellow, purple-black at base or black throughout. Winter. Asia Minor. Z7.

C. algeriensis Bak. = *C. nevadensis.*

C. almehensis C. Brickell and B. Mathew. Differs from *C. chrysanthus* in lvs to 3mm wide; fls yellow to orange, suffused bronze outside. Spring. NE Iran. Z7.

C. ancyrensis (Herb.) Maw. Tunic reticulate-fibrous. Lvs to 1mm wide, grey-green. Fls 1–3, tube yellow or mauve; throat yellow, glab., lobes 1–3cm, vivid yellow to pale orange; style trifid, deep orange. Spring. Turk. 'Golden Bunch': bears up to 5 fls per corm. Z6.

C. angustifolius Weston. CLOTH-OF-GOLD CROCUS. Tunic reticulate-fibrous. Lvs to 1.5mm wide, dull green. Fls shorter than lvs, throat yellow, glab. or minutely pubesc., lobes yellow, exterior flushed or veined maroon; anth. yellow; style trifid, deep yellow to vermilion. Spring. SW Russia. Z4.

C. annulatus var. *chrysanthus* Herb. = *C. chrysanthus.*

C. antalyensis B. Mathew. Tunic papery, splitting lengthwise into fibres. Lvs 1–2.5mm wide, green or grey-green, slightly scabrid. Fls 1–3, scented, tube white or lilac above, throat yellow, pubesc., lobes 2–3.5cm, elliptic to oblanceolate, lilac-blue or white tinged blue or buff externally with violet flecks; styles 6–12-lobed, orange or yellow. Early spring. SW Turk. Z7.

C. aphyllus Ker-Gawl. = *C. nudiflorus.*

C. argenteus Sab. = *C. biflorus.*

C. asturicus Herb. = *C. serotinus* ssp. *salzmannii.*

C. asumaniae B. Mathew & Baytop. Tunic reticulate-fibrous. Lvs 0.5–1mm wide, grey-green. Fls 1–3, tube white, throat white or pale yellow, glab., lobes 2.5–3cm, oblanceolate or narrow-elliptic, white, veined darker at throat, occas. pale lilac; style trifid, red-orange. S Turk. Z8.

C. athous Bornm. = *C. sieberi* ssp. *sublimis.*

C. atlanticus Pomel = *C. nevadensis.*

C. aucheri Boiss. = *C. olivieri.*

C. aureus Sibth. & Sm. = *C. flavus.*

C. balansae Gay ex Bak. = *C. olivieri* ssp. *balansae.*

C. balcanensis Janka = *C. veluchensis.*

C. banaticus Gay. Tunics finely parallel-fibrous at base, reticulate at apex. Lvs to 6mm wide, dark green. Fls lilac-mauve, inner lobes to 3cm, erect, outer lobes to 5cm, spreading to deflexed, darker; anth. bright yellow; style much divided, feathery, violet. Autumn. N Rom., N Balk., SW Russia. Z4.

C. banaticus Heuff. non Gay = *C. vernus.*

C. biflorus Mill. ssp. *biflorus* Tunic papery, tough, splitting horizontally from base as rings. Lvs to 3mm wide, silvery green. Fl. throat white to golden yellow, glab., lobes to 3cm, white, lilac or pale blue with dark mauve veins; style trifid, deep yellow. Spring and autumn. S Eur., Asia Minor. ssp. *alexandri* (Velen.) B. Mathew. Fls white, exterior suffused deep violet. Spring. S Bulg., S Balk. ssp. *melantherus* (Boiss. & Orph.) B. Mathew. Fls flecked white and feathered grey-purple on exterior; throat pale yellow; anth. damson purple to black. Autumn. S Greece. ssp. *pulchricolor* (Herb.) B. Mathew. Fls indigo, most intense at base of lobes; throat bright yellow. Spring. NW Turk. ssp. *weldenii* (Hoppe & Für.) B. Mathew. Fls white flushed pale lilac at base or on undersides of lobes; throat white or pale blue. Spring. Balk., Albania. Z4.

C. biflorus var. *parkinsonii* Sab. = *C. biflorus.*

C. biliottii Maw = *C. aerius.*

C. boryi Gay. Tunics thin, papery, splitting longitudinally from base. Lvs to 3mm wide. Fls to 4, tube ivory, exterior sometimes veined or flushed mauve, lobes to 5cm, often smaller, obovate; anth. white; style multifid, burnt orange. Autumn. W & S Greece, Crete. Z8.

C. boulosii Greuter. Tunics splitting longitudinally, terminating in tuft of fibres. Lvs to 1mm wide, with a fine, silver-green stripe. Fls 1, throat dotted papillose-pubesc., lobes white, exterior stained pearl-grey to blue at base; anth. yellow flushed purple, to 1cm; style orange, multifid. Late winter. Libya. Z8.

C. byzantinus Herb. = *C. banaticus.*

C. caeruleus Weston = *C. vernus* ssp. *albiflorus.*

C. cambessedesii Gay. Lvs to 1mm wide, sometimes with a central white stripe. Fls 1–2, white to mauve, exterior feather-veined purple, interior flushed yellow; anth. deep yellow; style dark orange, trifid, br. widened and minutely lobed. Autumn–early winter. Balearic Is. Z8.

C. campestris Pall. ex Herb. = *C. pallasii.*

C. cancellatus Herb. ssp. *cancellatus* Tunics fine, openly reticulate-fibrous. Lvs to 2mm wide, somewhat silvery. Fls white to opal or lilac with purple veins; throat yellow, sometimes pubesc., lobes to 5.5cm; anth. pale yellow, style multifid, deep orange. Autumn. S Turk., W Syr., Leb., N Isr. ssp. *mazziaricus* (Herb.) B. Mathew. Lobes 3–5.5cm, oblanceolate, white to lilac sometimes stained yellow at base, usually veined violet and more cupped than in type. Autumn. Balk., Greece, Turk. Z5.

C. candidus Clark. Lvs 4–9mm wide, ciliate, dark glossy green. Fls to 3, white, tube stained purple-maroon, throat yellow, glab., outer lobes flushed and spotted violet-grey or blue; style 6-branched, deep yellow. Late winter, early spring. NW Turk. Z7.

C. carpetanus Boiss. & Reut. Lvs to 3mm wide, ciliate, grooved beneath, largely covered above by silver stripe. Fls 1, white flushing to lilac, usually with fine mauve veins, throat glab., white with yellow tint; style ivory or lilac, trifid, flattened and ruffled at tips. Spring. C & NW Spain, N Port. Z8.

C. cartwrightianus Herb. WILD SAFFRON. Tunics reticulate-fibrous, fine, gathering into neck at apex. Lvs to 1.5mm wide, dull green. Fls 1–5, fragrant; throat pubesc., lobes 1.4–3.2cm, white, lilac or mauve with darker veins and a stronger purple flush at base; style trifid, vermilion, br. club-shaped, 1–2.7cm. Autumn–early winter. Greece. Z8.

C. caspius Fisch. & C.A. Mey. Tunics papery, splitting longitudinally, fibres indistinct. Lvs to 2mm wide, grooved and prominently veined below. Fls 1–2, white to rose-lilac, tube white or pale yellow, throat pubesc., vivid yellow; style light orange, trifid, tips widened. Autumn. Russia, Iran. Z7.

C. chrysanthus (Herb.) Herb. Tunics tough, papery, splitting from base as whole or jagged rings. Lvs 0.5–2mm wide, dull green. Fls 1–4, scented, creamy yellow to golden, exterior occas. striped or stained bronze-maroon; anth. yellow or with basal lobes almost black; style trifid, deep yellow. Lat winter–mid spring. Balk., Turk. 'Advance': fls yellow, exterior violet. 'Blue Bird': fls large and rounded, white, exterior grey-blue. 'Blue Pearl': fls pearly blue, base bronze, interior silver-blue with rich orange styles. 'Blue Peter': fls soft blue inside with a golden throat, exterior rich purple-blue. 'Brassband': fls apricot yellow outside with a bronze green-veined blotch, inside straw-yellow with a tawny glow. 'Cream Beauty': fls rounded, on short 'stalks', creamy yellow. 'E.A. Bowles': lobes rounded, gold, throat dark bronze. 'Elegance': fls violet outside, edge paler, inner lobes with a deep blue blotch, inside pale violet with a bronze centre. 'Gipsy Girl': fls large, golden yellow, outer lobes striped and feathered purple-brown. 'Ladykiller': outer lobes rich blue, narrowly edge white, inner lobes white, blotched with inky blue, silver-white inside. 'Snow Bunting': fls white with golden throat, exterior feathered purple. 'Snow White': fls pointed, frost-white with a gold base. 'Zenith': fls glossy violet-blue, inside silver-blue, contrasting with gold anth. and throat. 'Zwanenburg Bronze': fls golden yellow, exterior dark bronze. Z4.

C. cilicicus Maw = *C. cancellatus*.

C. corsicus Vanucci. Tunics finely fibrous, reticulate above. Lvs 1–1.5mm wide, deep green. Fls 1, scented, interior lilac, exterior yellow-pink with 3 mauve, feathered veins per outer lobe; style deep orange, trifid, with flattened, pleated tips. Spring–summer. Corsica. Z7.

C. cretensis Körn. = *C. boryi*.

C. crewei hort. non Hook. = *C. biflorus* ssp. *melantherus*.

C. croceus K. Koch = *C. chrysanthus*.

C. cvijicii Košanin. Tunics finely reticulate-fibrous. Lvs to 3.2mm wide. Fls 1, yellow, rarely white, tube white or pale yellow, sometimes tinted purple, throat white, sometimes stained yellow, pubesc.; style trifid, yellow-orange, br. widened at tips. Late spring–early summer. S Balk., N Greece, E Albania. Z7.

C. cyprius Boiss. & Kotschy. Tunics splitting longitudinally and in rings from base. Lvs to 2mm wide, grooved beneath with fine white stripe above. Fls 1–2, scented, white-lilac, exterior flushed mauve, darkest at base of lobes and on tube, throat yellow; anth. yellow; style trifid, orange, tips enlarged. Late winter–early spring. Cyprus. Z8.

C. dalmaticus Vis. Differs from *C. reticulatus* in its more finely reticulate tunic fibres and wider perianth lobes, and from *C. sieberi* in its lvs to 3mm wide and single fls, the exterior pearly grey-mauve to biscuit and faintly striped purple. Late winter–spring. SW Balk., N Albania. Z7.

C. danfordiae Maw. Differs from *C. chrysanthus* and *C. biflorus* in its 1–4 diminutive fls, pale lemon or bronze-yellow, opal or white, exterior minutely flecked silver-purple. Late winter–early spring. C Turk. Z7.

C. dispathaceus Bowles = *C. pallasii* ssp. *dispathaceus*.

C. elwesii (Maw) Schwartz = *C. pallasii*.

C. etruscus Parl. Tunics reticulate-fibrous. Lvs 2–6mm wide. Fls 1–2, delicate lilac; tube white; throat pubesc. sulphur yellow; lobes 3–4cm, the outer whorl ivory, nacreous or tawny, feathered purple. Late winter–spring. N It. 'Zwanenburg': fls pale blue. Z6.

C. fimbriatus Lapeyr. = *C. nudiflorus*.

C. flavus Weston ssp. *flavus*. Tunics papery, splitting lengthwise into fibres. Lvs 2.5–4mm wide, green, margins ciliate or papillose. Fls 1–4, scented, light golden yellow to apricot-yellow, tube exterior and base of lobes sometimes striped or stained brown; style trifid, yellow. Spring. S Balk., C & N Greece, Bulg., Rom., NW Turk. ssp. *dissectus* Baytop & B. Mathew. Lvs, sometimes pubesc. throughout; style divided into 6–15 br. Spring. W Turk. Z4.

C. fleischeri Gay. Tunics composed of finely plaited fibres, enclosing developing cormlets. Lvs to 1mm wide. Fls 1–2, scented; throat pale yellow, lobes 1.7–3.1cm, oblanceolate, white flushed mauve or maroon at base, outer lobes sometimes with central purple stripe; style multifid, vermilion. Late winter–spring. S & W Turk., E Aegean Is. Z6.

C. fontenayi Reut. = *C. laevigatus*.

C. gaillardottii (Boiss. & Blanche) Maw = *C. aleppicus*.

C. gargaricus Herb. Tunics reticulate-fibrous. Lvs to 2mm wide. Fls 1, yellow-orange, throat glab.; style deep yellow, trifid, tips dilated, fimbriate. Spring. NW Turk. Z7.

C. gilanicus B. Mathew. Tunics thin, papery. Lvs 1.5–2.5mm wide, light green. Fls 1; tube white sometimes faintly veined mauve throat pubesc., white, lobes 2–3.5cm, narrow-elliptic, white veined purple, tips occas. tinted lavender. Autumn. W Iran. Z8.

C. 'Golden Yellow'. = *C.* × *luteus* 'Dutch Yellow'.

C. goulimyi Turrill. Tunics smooth, tough, split, jagged at base. Lvs 1–2.5mm wide. Fls 1–2, scented; tube white, throat pubesc., white, lobes 1.5–4cm, rounded, lilac to pale mauve, inner whorl paler; style trifid, white to orange. Autumn. S Greece. 'Albus': fls pure white. Z7.

C. granatensis Boiss. ex Maw = *C. serotinus* ssp. *salzmannii*.

C. graveolens Boiss. & Reut. ex Boiss. Tunics papery or tough, splitting longitudinally from base. Lvs 0.5–1.5mm wide, silvery green, margins rough. Fls 2–6, malodorous; tube yellow with bronze or maroon stripes and spots, throat yellow, lobes spreading-deflexed, golden, exterior marked as tube; style multifid, deep yellow. Late winter–spring. S Turk., NW Syr., Leb., N Isr. Z8.

C. hadriaticus Herb. Tunic fibrous, finely netted. Lvs to 1mm wide, ciliate. Fls 1–3; tube white, yellow, maroon or mauve; throat pubesc., yellow, sometimes white, lobes 2–4.5cm, elliptic, white suffused yellow, buff or lavender at base, occas. tinted lilac throughout; style trifid, orange. Autumn. W & S Greece. Z8.

C. hartmannianus Holmb. Differs from *C. cyprius* in tunics only splitting longitudinally, lvs well developed at flowering and anth. dark violet-maroon. Late winter. Cyprus. Z8.

C. hermoneus Kotschy ex Maw. Differs from *C. cancellatus* in parallel fibrous tunics, splitting lengthwise, subreticulate at apex and neck. Early winter. Isr., Jord. Z8.

C. heuffelianus Herb. = *C. vernus*.

C. hittiticus Baytop & B. Mathew = *C. reticulatus* ssp. *hittiticus*.

C. hybernus Friv. = *C. pallasii*.

C. hyemalis Boiss. & Blanche. Tunics papery, fibrous at apex, splitting longitudinally in bands. Lvs 2–2.5mm wide. Fls 1–4, scented, tube white sometimes flushed mauve, throat glab., pale yellow, lobes 2.4–4.2cm, white, outer whorl suffused or flecked purple below, sometimes with mauve central region; style orange, multifid. Late autumn–winter. Isr., Leb., Syr. Z8.

C. imperati Ten. ssp. *imperati*. Tunics parallel fibrous, sometimes subreticulate at apex. Lvs 2–3mm wide, shining dark green. Fls 1–2; tube 3–10cm, white, occas. yellow or mauve, throat glab., deep yellow, lobes obtuse, 3–4.5cm, bright purple within, exterior tawny with to 5 feathered violet stripes. Style orange-coral, trifid. Late winter–early spring. W It., Capri. 'de Jager': fls lilac inside, buff and purple outer stripes. ssp. *suaveolens* (Bertol.) B. Mathew. Fls smaller, each outer lobe marked with 3 purple stripes, the central stripe darkest and extending to tip. Late winter. W It. Z7.

C. incurvus Donn ex Steud. = *C. imperati* ssp. *imperati*.

C. insularis Gay = *C. corsicus* or *C. minimus*.

C. ionicus Herb. = *C. boryi*.

C. iridiflorus Rchb. = *C. banaticus*.

C. karduchorum Kotschy ex Maw. Tunics thin, papery, parallel-fibrous or subreticulate. Lvs to 2mm wide. Fls 1, fragrant; tube white, 4–9cm, throat white, pubesc., lobes 3–4cm, oblanceolate, pale violet fading to white at base with darker, delicate veins; style spreading, multifid. Autumn. SE Turk. Z8.

C. karduchorum hort. non Kotschy ex Maw. = *C. kotschyanus* ssp. *kotschyanus* var. *leucopharynx*.

C. kirkii Maw = *C. candidus*.

C. korolkowii Reg. ex Maw. CELANDINE CROCUS. Tunics papery, splitting, parallel-fibrous. Lvs 1–2.5mm wide, keel prominently veined. Fls 3–5, scented; tube 3–10cm, golden sometimes marked bronze or maroon, throat glab., yellow to metallic buff, lobes to 3cm, elliptic, golden yellow, outer lobes marked dark brown or maroon below; style trifid, orange, tips widened. Late winter–early spring. Afghan., N Pak., Russia. Z6.

C. kosaninii Pulev. Differs from *C. etruscus* in its finely parallel-fibrous tunics, reticulate only at apex, and fls with golden, glab. throat. Spring. Balk. Z6.

C. kotschyanus Koch ssp. *kotschyanus*. Tunics papery, fibres parallel at base, subreticulate at apex. Lvs to 4mm wide, keel nearly as wide as lamina. Fls 1, scented; tube to 13cm, white; throat pubesc., white tinted yellow with 2 golden splashes at base of each lobe, sometimes coalescing, lobes 3–4.5cm, pale lavender with darker, parallel veins; style trifid, ivory to pale yellow, tips expanded and subdivided. Autumn. C & S Turk., NW Syr., C & N Leb. var. *leucopharynx* B.L. Burtt. Fls blue-lavender, veined blue, with white throat, yellow markings 0; style pale cream. Turk. ssp. *cappadocicus* B. Mathew. Throat glab. Early autumn. Turk. ssp. *hakkariensis* B. Mathew. Perianth lobes lozenge-shaped. Autumn. SE Turk. ssp. *suworowianus* (K. Koch) B. Mathew. Unscented; throat glab. with pale yellow markings, lobes near-erect, cream with mauve veins, tone suffusing where veins converge. Early autumn. Russia, Turk. Z5.

C. lacteus Sab. = *C. flavus*.

C. laevigatus Bory & Chaub. Tunics tough splitting at base into narrow, pointed strips. Lvs to 2.5mm wide, deep green. Fls to 3, often fragrant; tube 2–8cm, white tinted yellow or mauve toward yellow, glab. throat, lobes 1.3–3cm, obovate to elliptic, white or pale rose-lilac above, outer lobes white, mauve, bronze or yellow, with up to 3 broad dark purple or maroon feathered lines, markings sometimes 0 or exterior wholly purple; style multifid, orange. Autumn–early spring. Greece, Crete. Z7.

C. lagenaeflorus Salisb. = *C. flavus*.

C. lazicus (Boiss. & Bal.) Boiss. = *C. scharojanii*.

C. leichtlinii (D. Dewar) Bowles. Tunics tough, splitting lengthwise. Lvs to 1mm wide. Fls to 4, fragrant; tube 4–6cm, white suffused yellow toward throat or tinted blue, appearing iridescent green, throat golden, glab., lobes to 3cm, narrow-oblanceolate, opal to sky blue, exterior deeper blue; style trifid, pale orange. Spring. SE Turk. Z8.

C. libanoticus Mout. = *C. pallasii*.

C. longiflorus Raf. Tunics finely reticulate-fibrous. Lvs 1–3mm wide, with white central stripe. Fls 1–2, scented; tube 5–10cm, pale yellow, striped violet; throat yellow, glab. or thinly pubesc., lobes 2–4.5cm, lilac, exterior with darker veins, sometimes shaded bronze; style trifid, vermilion, tips widened, crenate or subdivided. Autumn. SW It., Sicily, Malta. Z5.

C. lusitanicus Herb. = *C. capetanus.*

C. ×*luteus* Lam. (*C. flavus* × *C. angustifolius.*) Sterile gdn hybrids – the common large yellow spring crocus. Fls rich orange-yellow, paler externally, with 3 short olive-green stripes on outer lobes. 'Dutch Yellow' ('Golden Yellow', 'Yellow Giant', 'Yellow Mammoth'): fls large, deep yellow. 'Stellaris': resembling *C. flavus*, tunic coarsely reticulate; fls bright golden yellow, striped and feathered dark-brown externally. Early spring.

C. luteus Lam. = *C. flavus.*

C. maesiacus Ker-Gawl. = *C. flavus.*

C. malyi Vis. Tunics finely parallel-fibrous, sometimes subreticulate at apex. Lvs 1.5–2.5mm wide, slightly silver-green. Fls 1–2; tube 4–9cm, white, occas. flushed yellow, bronze or mauve, throat pubesc., yellow, lobes 2–4cm, white, often with grey-blue or bronze stain at base; style trifid, orange, tips expanded, notched. Spring. W Balk. Z7.

C. marathonisius Heldr. = *C. boryi.*

C. marcetii Pau = *C. nevadensis.*

C. maudii Maly = *C. sieberi* ssp. *sublimis.*

C. medius Balb. Tunics strongly reticulate-fibrous. Lvs 2.5–4mm wide, dark green with silver-white central stripe, sometimes ciliate. Fls 1; tube 8–20cm, white to mauve at apex, throat glab., white veined violet, lobes 2.5–5cm, obovate, pale blue-mauve, veined darker at base; style multifid, vermilion, br. recurved. Autumn. NW It., SE Fr. Z6.

C. michelsonii B. Fedtsch. Tunics smooth, reticulate. Lvs 1.5–2mm wide, silver-green, keel prominently veined, margins sometimes ciliate. Fls 1–2; tube 4–8cm, white suffused lilac, throat glab., white-lilac, lobes 2.5–4cm, oblanceolate, translucent white above, stained or spotted pale mauve below; style trifid, white, tips widening. Spring. Russia, Iran. Z7.

C. micranthus Boiss. = *C. reticulatus* ssp. *reticulatus.*

C. minimus DC. Tunics parallel-fibrous. Lvs 0.5–1mm wide. Fls 1–2; tube 4–11cm, white flushed mauve at apex, throat glab., white sometimes tinted pale yellow, lobes 2–3cm, oblanceolate, light mauve to deep purple, striped, veined or shaded darker below, on bronze background; style trifid, orange, tips crenate-lobed. Late winter–early spring. Sardinia, Corsica, Isles Sanguinaires. Z8.

C. moabiticus Bornm. & Dinsm. ex Bornm. Tunics finely parallel-fibrous, reticulate at apex. Lvs 1–2mm wide, silver-green, keel sparsely papillose. Fls to 5; tube 2–4cm, white, throat pubesc., white tinted mauve, lobes 1.5–2.5cm, narrow-elliptic, white veined purple; style deeply trifid, burnt orange. Early winter. N Jord. Z8.

C. montenegrinus Kerner ex Maw = *C. vernus* ssp. *albiflorus.*

C. mouradii Whittall = *C. flavus* ssp. *dissectus.*

C. multifidus Ramond = *C. nudiflorus.*

C. napolitanus Mord. de Laun. & Lois. = *C. vernus.*

C. neapolitanus Ten. = *C. imperati* ssp. *imperati.*

C. nevadensis Amo. Tunics finely parallel-fibrous, fibres often produced at apex as points or narrow neck. Lvs 1–2.5mm wide, ciliate or minutely denticulate. Fls 1, scented; tube 3–8.5mm, cream tinted mauve, throat pubesc., cream or pale yellow, lobes 2–4cm, obtuse, cream-lilac, veined purple, sometimes tinted green below; style trifid, white, br. short, flattened, ruffled. Late winter–spring. N Alg., Moroc., Spain. Z8.

C. niveus Bowles. tunics finely reticulate-fibrous, extended as neck. Lvs 1–2mm wide. Fls 1–2; tube 9–18cm, ivory to dull yellow, throat golden, pubesc., lobes 3–6cm, obovate, obtuse, white, sometimes stained lilac; style trifid, scarlet, tips flattened, lobed or fimbriate. Autumn. S Greece. Z6.

C. nudiflorus Sm. Tunics membranous, loosely parallel-fibrous. Lvs 2–4mm wide, appearing after fls. Fls 1; tube 10–22cm, white flushed mauve toward apex, throat white-mauve, glab. or papillose, lobes 3–6cm, obtuse, pale mauve to amethyst; style multifid, orange. Autumn. SW Fr., N & E Spain. Z5.

C. ochroleucus Boiss. & Gaill. Tunics thin, papery, parallel-fibrous, subreticulate at apex. Lvs 1–1.5mm wide. Fls 1–3; tube 5–8cm, white, throat pubesc. pale yellow-golden tone spreading to base of lobes, lobes 2–3.5cm, elliptic, ivory; style trifid, golden yellow. Autumn–winter. Z5.

C. odorus Biv. = *C. longiflorus.*

C. officinalis Martyn = *C. sativus.*

C. officinalis var. *sativus* (L.) Huds. = *C. sativus.*

C. olbanus Siehe = *C. pallasii.*

C. olivieri Gay. Tunics papery, parallel-fibrous, splitting, jagged at base. Lvs 2–5mm wide, ciliate, often pubesc. above. Fls 1–4; tube 5–7cm, yellow or maroon, throat yellow, lobes 1.5–3.5cm, yellow-orange, or striped bronze-maroon beneath and on tube; style divided ×6, pale orange. Late winter–spring. Balk., Turk. ssp. *balansae* (Gay ex Bak.) B. Mathew. Fls striped or stained brown bronze or maroon beneath; style divided ×12–15. Late winter–spring. W Turk., Aegean. Z7.

C. orbelicus Stoj. = *C. veluchensis.*

C. oreocreticus B.L. Burtt. Differs from *C. cartwrightianus* in lvs barely emerging at flowering, fls v. rarely white, usually mauve with bronze or pearly hue. Autumn–winter. Crete. Z8.

C. orphanidis Hook. f. = *C. tournefortii.*

C. pallasii Goldbl. ssp. *pallasii* Tunics reticulate-fibrous, forming a neck. Lvs 0.5–1.5mm wide. Fls 1–6, scented; tube 4–7cm, white or mauve, throat white or mauve, pubesc., lobes 2.5–5cm, inner whorl smaller, rose-mauve-indigo, faintly veined darker; style trifid, vermilion. Autumn. Balk., Middle E. ssp. *dispathaceus* (Bowles) B. Mathew. Perianth lobes strap-like, 0.4–0.7cm wide, dark rose-mauve; style pale yellow. Autumn–early winter. S Turk., N Syr. Z8.

C. pelistericus Pulev. Tunics finely reticulate-fibrous, forming a neck. Lvs 1–2mm wide. Fls 1; tube 3–4cm, purple, throat white, glab., lobes 2–3cm, obtuse, deep purple, lustrous with darker veins; style abruptly trifid, cream-orange, tips flattened, frilled. Late spring–early summer. S Balk., N Greece. Z7.

C. peloponnesiacus Orph. = *C. hadriaticus.*

C. pestalozzae Boiss. Differs from *C. biflorus* in lvs 0.5–1.55mm wide; fls smaller, white or blue-mauve, fil. stained black at base, not wholly yellow. Late winter–early spring. NW Turk. 'Caeruleus': fls slender, lilac blue; fil. spotted black, style threadlike. Z7.

C. pholegandricus Orph. = *C. tournefortii.*

C. praecox Haw. = *C. biflorus.*

C. pulchellus Herb. Differs from *C. speciosus* in its golden yellow perianth throat, gracefully incurving opal-blue lobes with lilac veins and cream anth. Autumn–early winter. Turk. 'Zephyr': fls to 20cm long, pale, pearly blue. Z6.

C. purpureus Weston = *C. vernus.*

C. pusillus Ten. = *C. biflorus.*

C. pyrenaeus Herb. = *C. nudiflorus.*

C. reticulatus Steven ex Adams ssp. *reticulatus.* Tunics reticulate-fibrous. Lvs 0.5–1.5mm wide, silver-green. Fls 1–2, scented; tube 3–6cm, white or mauve, throat glab. or papillose, cream-yellow, lobes 1.7–3.5cm, outer whorl white above, white, pale mauve or bronze tinted beneath with 3–5 purple, feathered veins, inner whorl shorter, wider, white-mauve beneath; style trifid, vermilion, tips widened, papillose. Spring. SE Eur., SW Russia, Turk. ssp. *hittiticus* (Baytop & B. Mathew). Anth. violet-black not yellow. Late winter–spring. S Turk. Z8.

C. robertianus C. Brickell. Tunics coarsely reticulate-fibrous. Lvs 4–6mm wide, dark green with strong central stripe, margins rough. Fls 1–2; tube 7–10cm, sometimes longer, ivory-mauve; throat glab. or pubesc., cream-yellow, lobes 3–6cm, lilac to blue tinted mauve; style trifid, burnt orange, tips widened, slightly fimbriate. Autumn. C & N Greece. Z8.

C. salzmannii Gay = *C. serotinus* ssp. *salzmannii.*

C. sativus L. SAFFRON. Sterile mauve to indigo-fld cultigen selected from *C. cartwrightianus*, differing chiefly in perianth lobes to 5cm and bright orange style br. to 3cm. Z6.

C. sativus var. *cartwrightianus* (Herb.) Maw = *C. cartwrightianus.*

C. scardicus Košanin. Tunics finely reticulate-fibrous, forming neck. Lvs 0.5–1mm wide. Fls 1; tube 2–4cm, mauve or white tinted violet, lobes 2–4cm, obtuse, lemon to golden yellow, exterior faded below and stained mauve; style abruptly trifid, pale orange, tips widening, ruffled or lobed. Late spring–early summer. Balk., Albania. Z6.

C. scepusiensis (Rehm & Wol.) Borb. = *C. vernus.*

C. scharojanii Rupr. Tunics papery, fibres parallel at base, subreticulate at apex. Lvs 1.5–3mm wide, persisting. Fls 1, seldom opening fully; tube to 10cm, yellow, throat glab., yellow, lobes 2.5–4cm, golden yellow to orange at tips; style trifid, orange. Summer–autumn. Russia, NE Turk. Z6.

C. serotinus Salisb. ssp. *serotinus.* Tunics reticulate-firbous, lattice-like. Lvs 0.5–2mm wide, appearing with fls. Fls, scented; tube 2–5cm, white to mauve, throat pubesc., white or ivory, lobes 2.5–4cm, obtuse, pale mauve to lilac blue, sometimes veined purple; style multifid, burnt orange. Autumn. Port. ssp. *clusii* (Gay) B. Mathew. Tunics finely reticulate-fibrous. Lvs emerging as fls fade. Perianth throat glab. or pubesc. Autumn. Port., NW & SW Spain. ssp. *salzmannii* (Gay) B. Mathew. Tunics papery, splitting longitudinally. Perianth tube to 11cm. Autumn–winter. N Afr., Spain, Gibraltar. Z6.

C. siculus Tineo = *C. vernus* ssp. *albiflorus.*

C. sieberi Gay ssp. *sieberi.* Tunics finely reticulate-fibrous. Lvs to 2mm wide. Fls to 3, scented; tube 2.5–5cm, white or mauve, usually deep yellow toward glab., golden yellow or orange throat; lobes 2–3cm, obtuse, white within, tinted purple, exterior of outer whorl striped, barred or suffused mauve; style trifid, yellow-orange, tips divided or ruffled. Spring–early summer. Crete. ssp. *atticus* (Boiss. & Orph.) B. Mathew. Corm tunic distinctly reticulate-fibrous, bulb neck present. Late winter–spring. Greece. 'Bowles White': fls with pure white pet., orange throat; style scarlet. 'Firefly': outer pet. nearly white, inner pet. violet, base yellow. 'Hubert Edelsten': fls deep purple, blotched white at tip. 'Violet Queen': fls rounded, violet-blue on short stalks. ssp. *nivalis* (Bory & Chaub.) B. Mathew. Perianth throat yellow, glab., lobes lilac. Late winter–early summer. Greece. ssp. *sublimis* (Herb.) B. Mathew. Perianth throat yellow, pubesc., lobes blue-mauve, darker at tips, sometimes white at base. Late winter–early summer. Greece, S Balk., S Albania. ssp. *sublimis* f. *tricolor* B.L. Burtt. Fls with 3 distinct bands of colour-lilac, pure white and golden yellow. Z7.

C. *sieheanus* Barr ex B.L. Burtt. Resembles *C. ancyrensis* and *C. chrysanthus*. Differs in papery, parallel-fibrous tunics, vermilion style held above sta., anth. pale yellow. Spring. Turk. Z7.

C. *skorpilii* Velen. = *C. chrysanthus*.

C. *speciosus* Bieb. ssp. *speciosus*. Tunics tough, splitting as rings from base. Lvs 3–5mm wide, margins sometimes ciliate or rough. Fls 1, scented; tube 5–20cm, white or pale mauve, throat glab., off-white, rarely, tinted yellow, lobes 3–6cm, mauve-blue above, exterior veined or spattered purple, sometimes on a paler, opal ground; style multifid, orange, far exceeding anth. Autumn. C Asia, Iran, Turk. 'Aitchisonii': large, pale lilac with feather veins; 'Albus': white; 'Artabir': pale lilac with strong veins; 'Cassiope': large, pale violet with yellow throat; 'Globosus': diminutive, fls lavender-blue, appearing inflated; 'Pollux': large, pale mauve with pearly exterior; 'Oxonian': indigo; 'Trotter': large, white. ssp. *xantholaimos* B. Mathew. Lvs 1–2.5mm wide. Perianth throat deep yellow, thinly pubesc., lobes 3–3.8cm; style much branched, shorter than anth. N Turk. Z4.

C. *stellaris* Haw. = *C.* ×*luteus* 'Stellaris'.

C. *suaveolens* Bertol. = *C. imperati* ssp. *suaveolens*.

C. *susianus* Ker-Gawl. = *C. angustifolius*.

C. *suterianus* Herb. = *C. olivieri*.

C. *thiebautii* Mout. = *C. pallasii*.

C. *thirkeanus* K. Koch = *C. gargaricus*.

C. *thomasii* Ten. Tunics finely reticulate-fibrous, forming neck. Lvs 0.5–1.5mm wide. Fls 1–3, scented; tube 3–6cm, white to mauve, throat pubesc., yellow, lobes 2–4cm, white to pale mauve, veined or suffused darker at base; style trifid, coral pink, widened at tips. Autumn. S It., W Balk. Z7.

C. *tommasinianus* Herb. Tunics finely parallel-fibrous, subreticulate at apex. Lvs 2–3mm wide, with conspicuous, silver stripe. Fls 1–2; tube 3.5–10cm, white, throat white, thinly pubesc., lobes 2–4.5cm, pale mauve to violet, occas. white or rose, darker at apex, sometimes with silver or bronze hue below; style trifid, orange flattened and fimbriate at tips. Late winter–spring. Balk., Hung., Bulg. 'Albus': fls white, exterior sometimes straw-coloured. 'Barr's Purple': outer lobes tinged grey, inner lobes rich purple-lilac. 'Pictus': outer lobes marked mauve or purple at apex. 'Roseus': fls pink-purple. 'Ruby Giant': probably a hybrid with *C. vernus*; fls dark red-purple. 'Whitewell Purple': fls purple-mauve externally, silver-mauve within. Z5.

C. *tomoricus* Markgr. = *C. veluchensis*.

C. *tournefortii* Gay. Tunics papery, splitting from base into fine fibres. Lvs 1–2.5mm wide, sometimes ciliate. Fls 1, sometimes scented; tube 3–10cm, white, rarely suffused purple, throat glab. or pubesc., yellow to ivory, lobes 1.5–3.5cm, pale lilac, often veined darker at base, rarely white throughout; style multifid, orange-crimson, br. arching, widening and lobed at tips. Autumn–winter. S Greece, Crete, Cyclades. Z8.

C. *vallicola* Herb. Fls 1, white; lobes veined mauve, with 2 yellow spots at base, apex finely acuminate. Late summer–autumn. Russia, Turk. Z7.

C. *vallicola* var. *suworowianus* (K. Koch) Maw = *C. kotschyanus* ssp. *suworowianus*.

C. *variegatus* Hoppe & Hornsch. = *C. reticulatus* ssp. *reticulatus*.

C. *veluchensis* Herb. Tunics finely reticulate-fibrous. Lvs 2–5mm wide. Fls 1–2, rarely scented; tube 2–10cm, white to blue-mauve; throat pubesc., white tinted mauve; lobes 2–4cm, pale lilac to purple, exterior darker at base and apex; style trifid, ivory, yellow or orange, widened and dissected at tips. Spring–early summer. Balk., Albania, Bulg., Greece. Z6.

C. *veneris* Tapp. ex Poech. Tunics papery, parallel-fibrous. Lvs 0.5–1mm wide, margins sometimes rough. Fls 1–2, fragrant; tube 3–4cm, white, throat pubesc., yellow, lobes 1.5–2.5cm, acute, white, exterior of outer lobe striped or feathered purple; style multifid, golden yellow. Late autumn–early spring. Cyprus. Z8.

C. *vernus* Hill ssp. *vernus*. Tunics finely parallel-fibrous, subreticulate toward apex. Lvs 4–6mm wide. Fls 1; tube 5–15cm, mauve or white; throat white, often suffused mauve, glab. or pubesc., lobes 3–5.5cm, obtuse, rarely emarginate, white, violet or blue-mauve, sometimes striped white or violet, usually with a darker, v-shaped marking near tips; style trifid, yellow-orange,

widened and fimbriate at tips. Spring–early summer. It., Austria, E Eur. 'Early Perfection': fls violet-purple to blue with dark edges. 'Enchantress': fls light amethyst purple, silvery base dark. 'Pickwick': fls white with deep lilac stripes, base deep purple. 'Remembrance': fls large, rounded, silver-purple, base flushed purple. 'Vanguard': fls pale blue, exterior grey, early-flowering. 'Glory of Limmen': fls v. large, rounded, white with short purple stripes at base. 'Haarlem Gem': fls small, silvery-lilac externally, pale-lilac-mauve within. 'Jeanne d'Arc': fls large, white, with 3 thin purple stripes, tinged violet at base. 'Kathleen Parlow': fls large, white, base and tube purple. 'Little Dorrit': fls v. large, rounded, pale silver-lilac. 'Paulus Potter': fls large, glossy red-purple. 'Purpureus Grandiflorus': fls large, deep glossy rich purple. 'Queen of the Blues': fls large, lavender-blue. 'Striped Beauty': fls pale silver-grey, striped deep mauve, base violet-purple. ssp. *albiflorus* (Kit. ex Schult.) Asch. & Gräbn. Fls usually white, sometimes marked purple. Spring–summer. Eur. Z4.

C. *versicolor* Ker-Gawl. Tunics papery, splitting, ultimately parallel-fibrous. Lvs 1.5–3mm wide, prominently veined below. Fls 1–2; tube 6–10cm, white or purple-striped; throat glab., lemon yellow or ivory; lobes 2.5–3.5×1cm, white-mauve, exterior striped darker, sometimes with bronze-yellow hue; style trifid, pale orange, tips widened, indented. Late winter–spring. S Fr. to W It., Moroc. 'Picturatus': fls white outside, feathered violet. Z5.

C. *vilmae* Fiala = *C. vernus* ssp. *albiflorus*.

C. *visianicus* Herb. = *C. thomasii*.

C. *vitellinus* Wahl. Tunics tough, papery, splitting longitudinally. Lvs 1.5–3mm wide. Fls 2–6, fragrant; tube 4–7cm, yellow, throat yellow, lobes 2–3cm, obtuse, inner whorl shorter than outer, spreading or recurved, golden yellow, sometimes striped or spotted maroon-bronze; style multifid, golden to vermilion. Late autumn–early winter. Turk., Syr., Leb. Z8.

C. 'Yellow Giant' = *C.* ×*luteus* 'Dutch Yellow'.

C. 'Yellow Mammoth' = *C.* ×*luteus* 'Dutch Yellow'.

C. *vittatus* Raf. = *C. reticulatus* ssp. *reticulatus*.

C. *zonatus* Gay = *C. kotschyanus*.

Crookneck Squash *Cucurbita moschata*.

Cropleaf Ceanothus *Ceanothus dentatus*.

Crosnes du Japon *Stachys affinis*.

Crossandra Salisb. Acanthaceae. *c*50 everg. shrubs or subshrubs. Lvs usually entire, loosely whorled. Infl. a 4-sided, term. or axill. spike; bracts conspicuous, densely overlapping; cal. lobes 5, unequal; cor. tube narrow, limb broad, spreading, 5-lobed, 2-lipped. Arabia, Trop. Afr., Madag., Indian subcontinent. Z10.

C. *infundibuliformis* (L.) Nees. FIRECRACKER FLOWER. To 1m; st. erect, slender, finely downy. Lvs 5–12cm, ovate to lanceolate, undulate, glossy deep green. Spikes to 10cm, narrowly conical to ellipsoid; bracts to 1.25cm, downy; cor. bright orange to salmon pink, tube to 2.5cm, incurved, lobes to 2.5cm obovate-flabellate. S India, Sri Lanka. 'Mona Walhead': compact, to 50cm; lvs lustrous vivid green; fls deep salmon pink.

C. *nilotica* Oliv. To 50cm. Lvs to 10cm, elliptic, finely tapering, pubesc., not undulate. Spikes 2.5–7cm, tightly packed, slender; bracts 1.25–2cm, downy; cor. brick-red to orange, tube 1.75–2cm, lobes to 1.25cm, obovate. Trop. Afr.

C. *pungens* Lindau. Dense subshrub to 60cm. Lvs oblong, dull green traced with pearly veins. Spikes congested; bracts bristly to spiny; cor. orange. Trop. Afr.

C. *undulifolia* Salisb. = *C. infundibuliformis*.

Cross-leaved Heath *Erica tetralix*.

Crossostephium Less. Compositae. 1 low, erect shrub, 10–40cm. St. densely leafy, branched, white-tomentose. Lvs alt., to 5.5×3cm, narrowly spathulate to obovate-oblanceolate or oblong-ovate, fleshy, white-tomentose, lower lvs trilobed or pinnatifid. Cap. 4–7mm diam., disciform, erect, in leafy racemose infl., white-tomentose; flts yellow. China, Jap. Z7.

C. *chinense* (L.) Mak.
→*Artemisia*.

Crossostigma Spach = *Epilobium*.

Cross-vine *Bignonia capreolata*.

Crosswort *Crucianella*.

Crotalaria L. Leguminosae (Papilionoideae). RATTLEBOX. *c*600 herbs or shrubs. Lvs simple or 1–3-foliolate. Rac. terminal or axill., rarely solitary or clustered; fls pea-like; cal. lobes usually 5; standard orbicular to ovate usually with 2 concealed basal teeth, keel beaked, wings oblong, corrugated. Widespread in trop. and warm regions. Z9.

C. agatiflora Schweinf. CANARY-BIRD BUSH. Subshrub or shrub, 1–10m. Twigs glab. or downy. Lfts 3, 2.5–7cm, narrow-elliptic to elliptic-ovate, pungent, glab. to hirsute. Rac. to 40cm, term.; standard pure yellow to olive green, ovate, keel 3.5–5.5cm, rounded, with a short protuberant beak tinted purple or green. Highlands of E & NE Afr.

C. ageratiflora auctt. = *C. agatiflora*.

C. anagyroides Kunth = *C. micans*.

C. brevidens Benth. Ann. or short-lived perenn. to 2m; br. sprawling, hirsute. Lfts 3, 4–10cm, filiform to narrow elliptic-oblong, downy beneath. Rac. term., 10–50cm; standard yellow or cream veined mahogany, elliptic or ovate, keel 1.2–2.5cm, rounded, with a long, protuberant beak, wings often with a dark basal patch. C to W Afr.

C. capensis Jacq. YELLOW PEA; CAPE LABURNUM. Small tree or bushy shrub, 1–6m tall. Br. pendulous. Lfts 3, 1.5–7cm, elliptic to obovate, apex rounded or mucronate, pale green, glab. to densely pubesc. above, blue green beneath. Rac. 10.2–15.2cm term. or lat.; fls scented; standard yellow marked red, elliptic or ovate, keel 2–2.4cm, rounded, beak short and obtuse. S Afr.

C. cunninghamii R. Br. GREENBIRD FLOWER. Shrub, 60cm–1.2m, br. sturdy, pubesc. Lft 1, small, oblong-ovate or ovate, softly pubesc., rounded at apex. Rac. 15.2cm; cor. olive green, lined purple, standard 3–4cm, ovate, reflexed, keel pointed, exceeding standard. NW & C Aus.

C. grevei Drake. Shrub, 1–4m. St. long and delicate, pubesc. Lfts 3, 3.6–5cm, narrowly oblong-lanceolate to ovate-oblong, thinly downy beneath. Rac. 8–10-fld; standard ovate, yellow with brick-red or purple markings, keel 3cm, ovate-elliptic, bright green or pale yellow, tapering to a sharp-tipped, somewhat curved beak. Madag.

C. juncea L. Erect ann. to 1.6m tall. St. slender, sericeous, ribbed, loosely branched. Lvs 6–15cm, simple, linear to oblong, apex rounded, finely brown-hirsute. Rac. term., 10–50cm; cor. vivid yellow, standard delicately marked red, elliptic to semi-orbicular, keel to 2cm, beak long, twisted. India, widely grown elsewhere.

C. micans Link. Shrub, 2–4m. Br. thickly downy. Lfts 3, 4–10cm, oblong-lanceolate to narrow elliptic, sharp-tipped, pubesc. beneath. Rac. term., 15–40cm; cor. yellow, standard circular-ovate, stained red with age, keel 1.2–1.4cm, beak somewhat incurved. Trop. Amer.

C. sericea Retz. = *C. spectabilis*.

C. spectabilis Roth RATTLEBOX. Erect ann. herb, 50cm–2m. St. stout, usually flushed purple, glaucous. Lvs 8–14cm, simple, oblanceolate to obovate, apex rounded, downy beneath. Rac. 15–50cm, term. or axill.; cor. yellow, standard 1.5–2.5cm, lined purple-red, semi-orbicular, emarginate, keel beak twisted and somewhat incurved. India.

C. verrucosa L. Erect, shrubby ann., 40cm–1m. Br. furrowed, somewhat sinuous, downy. Lvs 5–13cm, simple, ovate to elliptic, sparsely downy. Rac. term., 11–24cm; standard lemon yellow blotched blue, elliptic or elliptic-obovate, wings blue or purple, elliptic-obovate, exceeding keel, keel to 1.2cm, beak short and twisted. Trop. Asia; nat. throughout tropics.

Croton *Codiaeum variegatum*

Croton L.
C. pictum Lodd. = *Codiaeum variegatum*.

Crowberry *Empetrum*.
Crow Corn *Aletris farinosa*.

Crowea Sm. Verbenaceae. 3 woody perenn. herbs or shrubs. Br. angular. Lvs to 5cm, simple, glandular-dotted, glab. Fls axill. or term., solitary or sometimes paired; sep. 5; pet. 5, free; sta. 10. S Aus. Z10.

C. angustifolia Sm. Woody perenn. herb or shrub to 3m. Lvs linear or narrowly oblong, denticulate. Fls mostly solitary, axill.; pedicel to 5mm, glab.; pet. to 12mm, pink, ovate or oblong; disc purple. SW Aus.

C. exalata F. Muell. Shrub to 1m. Lvs elliptic-oblong to narrowly spathulate. Fls solitary, term.; pedicel to 4mm, puberulent; pet. to 12mm, pale mauve to pink, ovate or oblong; disc dark green. Vict., NSW.

Crowfoot *Ranunculus*.
Crowfoot Violet *Viola pedata*.
Crow Garlic *Allium vineale*.
Crown Bark *Cinchona officinalis*.
Crown Beard *Verbesina*.
Crown Daisy *Chrysanthemum coronarium*.
Crown Fern *Blechnum discolor*.

Crown Imperial *Fritillaria imperialis*.
Crown of Thorns *Euphorbia milii*.
Crown Vetch *Coronilla* (*C. varia*).
Crow's Foot *Heritiera trifoliolata*.
Crow's-nest Fern *Asplenium australasicum*.

Crucianella L. CROSSWORT. Rubiaceae. 30 ann. or perenn. herbs and dwarf shrubs; st. slender, tetragonal. Lvs whorled. Fls in bracteate spikes or clusters; cor. narrow, funnel-shaped or tubular, lobes 4–5, awned. S Eur. and Medit. to W & C Asia. Z8.

C. aegyptiaca L. Erect or spreading ann. to 40cm; st. bristly. Lvs to 2cm, in whorls of 4–6, subulate or linear-lanceolate to falcate, bristly, acute. Fls many, in term. and lat. clusters and spikes, to 10×1cm; cor. 5×1mm, tubular, cream or pale yellow, lobes 5, ovate, cucullate, awned. Spring–summer. Medit., N Afr. to Middle E.

C. angustifolia L. Ann.; erect to 50cm, glab. Lvs to 1.5cm in whorls of 6–8, lanceolate-linear, revolute, scabrous, glaucous. Fls in 4-angled spikes to 8cm; cor. pale yellow, 15×1mm, 4-lobed. Spring–summer. Medit.

C. angustifolia Koch ex Nyman non L. = *C. latifolia*.

C. glauca A. Rich. Suberect. Lvs in whorls of 4, linear, prickly, sharply pointed, glaucous, revolute. Fls yellow, spicate. Summer. W Asia (Iran).

C. graeca Boiss. Similar to *C. herbacea*. Decumbent or erect ann. Lvs ovate or elliptic, upper linear, scabrous, revolute, spikes longer than in *C. herbacea*. Greece.

C. herbacea Forssk. Ann., to 40cm, scaberulous; st. densely branching below. Lvs in whorls of 6, lower lvs elliptic, upper lvs linear, revolute. Fls in dense to lax, oblong or linear spikes to 15cm; cor. lobes ovate. Spring. S Medit. (Moroc. to Palestine and Leb.).

C. latifolia L. Ann., erect, to 50cm. St. bristly or subglabrous. Lvs in whorls of 4–6, lower lvs obovate-elliptic, upper lvs lanceolate to linear, to 3cm, glab. or sparsely bristly, revolute. Spike long-stalked, terminal, to 15cm; cor. tubular, 6×1mm, glab., cream or pale pink, lobes 4–5, ovate-oblong. Spring–summer. Medit.

C. maritima L. Perenn. to 40cm. St. procumbent to ascending. Lvs to 1cm, densely overlapping in whorls of 4, ovate-lanceolate, leathery, acute, blue-green, white-margined. Spikes, ovoid to cylindric, to 4cm; cor. tubular, to 10×2mm, yellow, lobes 5, oblong. Spring–summer. W Medit. to Iberian Penins.

C. rupestris Guss. = *C. maritima*.

C. stylosa Trin. = *Phuopsis stylosa*.

C. suaveolens C.A. Mey. Perenn.; st. erect, branched. Lvs in whorls of 6 or 8, linear, acute, margins bristly, revolute. Spikes dense; fls yellow. Summer. W Asia.

CRUCIFERAE Juss. 390/3000. *Aethionema, Alyssoides, Alyssum, Anastatica, Arabis, Armoracia, Aubrieta, Aurinia, Barbarea, Berteroa, Biscutella, Bornmuellera, Brassica, Braya, Bunias, Cakile, Camelina, Capsella, Cardamine, Cardaminopsis, Chorispora, Cochlearia, Coluteocarpus, Crambe, Degenia, Diplotaxis, Draba, Elburzia, Eruca, Erysimum, Farsetia, Fibigia, Fourraea, Heliophila, Hesperis, Hugueninia, Iberis, Ionopsidium, Isatis, Kernera, Lepidium, Lesquerella, Lobularia, Lunaria, Lutzia, Malcolmia, Matthiola, Megacarpaea, Moricandia, Morisia, Nasturtium, Neotchihatchewia, Notothlaspi, Orychophragmus, Parrya, Peltaria, Petrocallis, Phoenicaulis, Physaria, Pritzelago, Raffenaldia, Raphanus, Rhizobotrya, Ricotia, Rorippa, Schizopetalon, Schouwia, Selenia, Sinapis, Sisymbrium, Smelowskia, Sobolewskia, Stanleya, Stenodraba, Streptanthus, Subularia, Thelypodium, Thlaspi, Thysanocarpus, Turritis, Vella, Wasabia.*

Cruel Plant *Araujia sericofera*.

Crupina (Pers.) DC. Compositae. 3 ann. herbs. St. slender, erect, branched above. Lvs alt., pinnatisect or simple. Cap. discoid, cylindrical; flts purple. Medit., SW Asia.

C. vulgaris Cass. St. to 50cm, leafy. Basal lvs oblong to obovate, entire to dentate, seg. to 2mm wide, linear, minutely dentate. Cap. term. on small, leafless br.; phyllaries pale green, tipped purple. Summer. S Eur.

→*Centaurea*.

Crusaders' Spears *Urginea maritima*.

Crusea Schldl. & Cham. Rubiaceae. 13 low ann. or perenn. herbs. St. slender. Lvs oblong-lanceolate to subulate. Fls small, in term. or axill. glomerules; cal. lobes 2–4, often unequal; cor. salverform. S US, Mex., C Amer. Z9.

C. calocephala DC. Perenn., often grown as an ann., 10–25cm;

st. decumbent, rooting, hairy. Lvs to 9cm, ovate. Fls violet. Mex., C Amer.

Cruz *Crescentia alata.*
Cry-baby Tree *Erythrina crista-galli.*

Cryophytum N.E. Br.
C. arenarum N.E. Br. = *Mesembryanthemum inachabense.*
C. fenchelii (Schinz) N.E. Br. = *Mesembryanthemum guerichianum.*
C. framesii L. Bol. = *Mesembryanthemum intransparens.*
C. fulleri L. Bol. = *Mesembryanthemum inachabense.*
C. grandifolium (Schinz) Dinter & Schwantes = *Mesembryanthemum guerichianum.*
C. inachabense (Engl.) N.E. Br. = *Mesembryanthemum inachabense.*
C. velutinum L. Bol. = *Mesembryanthemum macrophyllum.*

Crypsinus Presl. Polypodiaceae. 40 epiphytic or lithophytic ferns. Rhiz. long-creeping. Fronds somewhat dimorphic (fertile narrower than sterile), simple to pinnatifid or pinnate, thickened, notched, and cartilaginous at margin, leathery; stipes remote. Trop. Asia, Aus. Z10.
C. simplicissimus (F. Muell.) S.B. Andrews. Fronds to 15cm, suberect to pendent, simple, caudate, entire, veins prominent; stipes wiry. Aus. (Queensld).
→*Phymatopsis.*

Cryptantha Lehm. WHITE FORGET-ME-NOT. Boraginaceae. c100 setose ann. or perenn. herbs. Lvs, entire. Fls in simple or branching cymes, usually bracteate; cal. 5-lobed; cor. infundibular or salverform, often minute, throat with 5 small appendages, lobes 5, rotund to oblong-obovate. W N Amer. Z8.
C. barbigera (Gray) Greene. To 40cm, hirsute. Lvs to 7cm, linear-lanceolate to oblong, hirsute. Infl. to 15cm, white-villous; cor. v. small, white. SW US.
C. celosioides (Eastw.) Pays. To 40cm, setose. Lvs to 5cm, spathulate to oblanceolate, white-tomentose. Infl. densely setose, to 20cm; cor. white, tube to 5mm. Washington State.
C. intermedia (Gray) Greene. To 50cm, hirsute. Lvs to 7.5cm, oblanceolate or lanceolate to linear, strigose or hirsute, often somewhat pustulate. Infl. to 15cm; cor. to 8mm diam., white or yellow. BC to Baja Calif.
C. sheldonii (Brand) Pays. To 35cm. Lvs to 5cm, oblanceolate to spathulate, hispid-pilose. Infl. to 9cm, hispid-pilose; cor. to 10mm diam., white. W N Amer.
→*Eritrichium* and *Oreocarya.*

Cryptanthus Otto & A. Dietr. EARTH STAR. Bromeliaceae. 20 ± stemless perenn., terrestrial herbs, suckering or stoloniferous. Lvs in a flattened rosette or ranked on st., tough, mostly narrowly triangular, sessile and sheathing, scaly beneath, wavy and toothed. Fls small white, in short term., ± stalkless corymbs. E Braz. Z9.
C. acaulis (Lindl.) Beer. GREEN EARTHSTAR; STARFISH PLANT. Lvs 10–20cm, 10–15, brightly coloured, in a small, flat rosette, narrowly lanceolate, scaly beneath, undulate, denticulate. var. *argenteus* Beer. Lvs green, silvery-scaly above. var. *ruber* hort. ex Beer. Lvs tinged red. Known only in cult.
C. beuckeri E. Morr. Lvs 5–15cm, petiolate in a loose rosette; petioles brown, 3–8cm; blades 8–13cm, broadly lanceolate to ovate, green or brown, with paler or white spots, often flushed pink or banded white, scaly beneath, remotely serrulate. Known only in cult.
C. bivittatus (Hook.) Reg. Lvs 18–25cm, in a dense, spreading rosette, narrowly lanceolate, dark green, with 2 longitudinal, broad, white or pink bands above, pale brown-scaly beneath, undulate, serrulate. var. *bivittatus.* Lvs mainly green. var. *atropurpureus* Mez. Lvs flushed red, banded red. Known only in cult.
C. bromelioides Otto & A. Dietr. RAINBOW STAR. Relatively long-stemmed, stoloniferous. Lvs 10–20cm, olive green or variegated, basally narrowed, thick, white-scaly, often faintly striped beneath, undulate, somewhat serrate. var. *tricolor* M.B. Fost. Lvs striped cream and light green, flushed rose pink.
C. fosterianus L.B. Sm. Lvs to 28cm in a flat rosette, purple-brown or copper-green, banded grey beneath, linear-lanceolate, basally narrowed, grey-scaly beneath, thick and fleshy, undulate, distant-serrulate, sheaths inflated.
C. lacerdae Antoine. SILVER STAR. Lvs to 8cm, bright green, in a dense, spreading, star-shaped rosette, subovate with 2 broad silver stripes, white-scaly beneath, coarsely scaly above, margins silver, slightly wavy, closely denticulate. Known only in cult.
C. × osyanus Witte. (*C. lacerdae* × *C. beuckeri.*) Smaller than *C. beuckeri* with subovate, basally narrowed, lvs white-scaly be-

neath, with more irregular white or pink blotches or crossbands, sometimes with obscure stripes. Gdn origin.
C. sinuosus L.B. Sm. Resembles *C. acaulis* except lvs 6–30cm, blades more leathery, strongly undulate.
C. undulatus Otto & A. Dietr. = *C. acaulis.*
C. zonatus (Vis.) Beer. ZEBRA PLANT. Lvs to 20cm, in a spreading, asymmetric rosette, dark green to chocolate, irregularly banded silver-grey to cream with a faint pink-brown flush, linear-lanceolate, undulate, denticulate. 'Viridis': lvs bright green below. 'Zebrinus': more robust, lvs maroon to chocolate brown with bold silver bands. f. *fuscus* (Vis.) Mez. Lf blades red-brown. Known only in cult.
C. cvs. 'Aloha': rosette to 25cm across; lvs with scalloped edges, brightly coloured. 'Bueno Funcion': rosette to 25cm across; lvs broad, dark green flushed grey. 'Cascade': lvs tinted red; stolons to 60cm. 'It': rosette to 25cm across; lvs stiff, green, brown and pink. 'Koko': to 20cm across; lvs bright green. 'Lubbersianus' (*C. bivittatus* × *C. beuckeri*): tall; lvs dark green flushed red. 'Makoyanus' (*C. acaulis* × *C. bivittatus*): lvs oblanceolate, marked with double band of light green. 'Minibel': rosette to 40cm across; lvs rose edged dull green, margins spined; fls white. 'Mirabilis' (*C. beuckeri* × *C. × osyanus*): lvs broad-ovate, wavy, mottled light and olive green, banded cream, and flushed pink. 'Pink Starlight': rosette to 15cm across; lvs in tight rosette, white and pink with central olive stripe. olive stripe. 'Ti': lvs rose with dull green stripe at margin.

× **Cryptbergia** hort. ex R.G. Wils. & C. Wils. (*Cryptanthus* × *Billbergia.*) Bromeliaceae. Gdn origin. Z9.
× *C. meadii* Mead ex Padilla. (*Cryptanthus beuckeri* × *Billbergia nutans.*) Suckering freely. Lvs to 30cm, mottled pink, linear, in a funnel-shaped rosette. Fls rarely produced.
× *C. rubra* hort. (*Cryptanthus bahianus* × *Billbergia nutans.*) Suckering freely. Lvs dark bronze-red in a funnel-shaped rosette. Fls small, white, shortly scapose. 'Red Burst' is a highly coloured selection.

Cryptocereus Alexander.
C. anthonyanus Alexander = *Selenicereus anthonyanus.*
C. imitans (Kimnach & Hutchison) Backeb. = *Weberocereus imitans.*

Cryptocarya R. Br. Lauraceae. c200 everg. trees and shrubs. Lvs leathery. Fls small, paniculate. Fr. small, dry enclosed in enlarged cal. tube. Trop. Z9/10.
C. rubra (Mol.) Skeels. Tree to 20m. Lvs 2.5–5cm, ovate, glab., glaucous beneath. Chile.

Cryptocoryne Fisch. ex Wydl. WATER TRUMPET. Araceae. c50 aquatic rhizomatous or cormous everg. perenn. herbs. Lvs basal, usually submerged, long-stalked, blade membranous, cordate to linear, sometimes bullate, often undulate. Spathe v. short-stalked, emergent, tube margins overlapping, limb erect or reflexed, sometimes contorted, verrucose or fimbriate, spadix included. Trop. Asia (India to New Guinea). Z10.
C. affinis N.E. Br. Lvs 5–20cm, narrow-ovate to lanceolate, cordate, bullate, tinged red beneath, wine-red beneath. Spathe to 20cm+, spirally contorted, black purple within. Malay Penins.
C. aponogetifolia Merrill = *C. usteriana.*
C. axelrodii Rataj = *C. undulata.*
C. balansae Gagnep. = *C. crispatula.*
C. beckettii Thwaites ex Trimen. Lvs to 15cm, narrow-ovate to ovate, obtuse-truncate to subcordate at base, undulate, olive green to dark brown, veins purple. Spathe to 12.5cm, limb twisted, dull yellow, purple-brown within. Sri Lanka. var. *ciliata* (Roxb.) Schott. Lvs often emergent, 15–50cm, narrow-ovate to linear, weakly undulate, plain green. Spathe 15–35cm, green externally, tube yellow within, limb purple, fimbriate. S & SE Asia. var. *latifolia* Rataj. Lvs broader.
C. bertelihansenii Rataj = *C. crispatula.*
C. blassii De Wit = *C. cordata.*
C. caudata N.E. Br. = *C. longicauda.*
C. ciliata (Roxb.) Fisch. ex Scholt. Lvs 15–40cm, lanceolate to linear-oblong, ± undulate, deep green with paler midrib, often emergent. Spathe 10–30cm, tube long, green, limb short, hooded, purple, margin fimbriate, throat yellow. SE Asia.
C. cordata Griff. Lvs to 10(–15)cm, narrow-ovate to ovate, obtuse, cordate to emarginate, juveniles oblong-lanceolate, ± bullate, green to brown-purple or mottled above, red-brown beneath. Spathe to 24cm, tube pale pink, limb short, caudate, purple, yellow within. Malay Penins.
C. crispatula Engl. Lvs linear, 10–70cm, smooth or bullate, sometimes dentate, green to red-brown. Spathe limb spirally contorted, white, streaked or lined purple. India to S China.
C. drymorrhiza Zipp. = *C. beckettii* var. *ciliata.*

C. elata Griff. = *C. beckettii* var. *ciliata*.

C. evae Rataj = *C. cordata*.

C. griffithii Schott. Lvs 4–8cm, ovate, cordate, coriaceous, green, marbled red. Spathe to 6.5cm, tube pink-red, limb ovate, cuspidate, recurved, papillose, dark livid red. Malay Penins.

C. griffithii misapplied. = *C. purpurea*.

C. haerteliana Milkuhn = *C. affinis*.

C. hejnyi Rataj = *C. purpurea*.

C. johorensis Ridl. = *C. longicauda*.

C. kerrii Gagnep. = *C. cordata*.

C. koenigii Schott = *Lagenandra koenigii*.

C. kwangsiensis Li = *C. crispatula*.

C. lancifolia Schott = *Lagenandra lancifolia*.

C. lingua Engl. Lvs to 12cm, obovate, fleshy, green. Spathe 7cm, limb long-caudate, dark purple externally, yellow spotted red within. Borneo, nat. Singapore.

C. longicauda Engl. Lvs to 15cm, ovate, cordate, crispate or crenate, sometimes bullate, green to dull purple, main veins prominent. Spathe to 25cm, tube white below, purple above, collar red-purple, limb ovate, rugose, dark purple or wine-red, long-caudate. Malaysia, Borneo.

C. longispatha Merrill = *C. crispatula*.

C. lucens De Wit = *C. × willisii*.

C. lutea Alston = *C. walkeri*.

C. minima Ridl. Lvs 2–4cm, ovate, cordate, undulate, sometimes marbled red above, red beneath, with red veins. Spathe 5cm, limb 1cm broad, incurved, verrucose, dull yellow spotted brown, glossy brown-black within. Malay Penins.

C. nevillii misapplied. = *C. × willisii*.

C. ovata (L.) Schott = *Lagenandra ovata*.

C. petchii Alston = *C. beckettii*.

C. pontederiifolia Schott. Lvs 5–10cm, ovate, cordate, acute, coriaceous, occas. marbled purple. Spathe tube short, limb erect, wrinkled, yellow, collar prominent. Sumatra.

C. purpurea Ridl. Lvs 4–8cm, ovate to elliptic-ovate, cordate, mucronate, marbled red above, red beneath with red veins. Spathe to 18cm, tube yellow to purple, limb ovate, caudate, verrucose, red to red-purple within, collar yellow. Malay Penins.

C. retrospiralis (Roxb.) Kunth. Lvs to 30cm, linear to lanceolate, tapering. Spathe to 20cm, tube v. slender, limb linear-lanceolate, spirally twisted, 7.5cm, green, streaked purple. India to Malaysia.

C. siamensis Gagnep. = *C. cordata*.

C. sinensis Merrill = *C. crispatula*.

C. spathulata Engl. = *C. lingua*.

C. spiralis (Retz.) Fisch. ex Wydl. Lvs 10–15cm, linear-lanceolate, bright green. Spathe to 24cm, limb linear-lanceolate, spirally twisted, becoming straight, purple and rugose within. India.

C. stonei Rataj = *C. cordata*.

C. sulphurea De Wit = *C. pontederiifolia*.

C. thwaitesii Schott. Lvs to 6.5cm, elliptic to ovate, cordate, crenate, olive-green to dull purple above, dull red beneath. Spathe to 6.5cm, limb linear, caudate, white, spotted red within. Sri Lanka.

C. tonkinensis Gagnep. = *C. crispatula*.

C. undulata Wendt. Lvs to 15cm, narrow-ovate to lanceolate, base truncate or cordate, undulate, red-brown to green, veins red. Spathe to 10cm, limb twisted, dull green-yellow to pale brown. Sri Lanka.

C. usteriana Engl. Lvs 20–100cm, narrow-ovate to linear-lanceolate, bullate, green-brown. Spathe to 10cm, limb erect, twisted, wrinkled, dirty flesh red. Philipp.

C. walkeri Schott. Lvs to 11cm, elliptic to ovate, obtuse, mucronate, stiff, dark green above, dull brown beneath. Spathe to 6.5cm, limb lanceolate, slightly twisted or recurved, yellow to green yellow, collar yellow. Sri Lanka.

C. wendtii De Wit. Lvs 5–25cm, narrow-ovate to oblong-lanceolate, cordate, undulate, green to brown or red-brown. Spathe to 7.5cm, limb lanceolate, obliquely twisted, yellow to brown or dull red, violet within, collar black-purple. Sri Lanka.

C. × willisii Reitz. (Hybrid complex between *C. parva*, *C. beckettii* and *C. walkeri*.) Lvs 1–3cm, narrow-ovate to ovate, base truncate, green; petioles tinged red. Spathe to 7.5cm, limb twisted or recurved, papillose and dark red-purple within, collar yellow to dark purple. Sri Lanka.

C. willisii Baum = *C. undulata*.

C. yunnanensis Li = *C. crispatula*.

Cryptogramma R. Br. ROCK-BRAKE; PARSLEY FERN. Pteridaceae (Cryptogrammataceae). 4 dwarf, decid. ferns with dimorphic fronds. Rhiz. erect or creeping. Fronds 1–3-pinnate, resembling parsley, sterile fronds spreading, glab., membranous, pinnules flat, obtuse, dentate or crenate, small; fertile fronds exceeding sterile, pinnules entire, narrow, margin revolute, covering sori

which appear inflated, pod-like. Temp. to subtrop. regions of the N and S hemispheres.

C. acrostichoides R. Br. AMERICAN ROCK-BRAKE; AMERICAN PARSLEY FERN. Fronds to 12cm, closely clustered; stipes slender, green; sterile fronds ovate to ovate-lanceolate, 2–3-pinnate, pinnae few, pinnules crowded, ovate, oblong, or obovate, crenate or incised; fertile fronds 10–30cm, pinnules linear-oblong, 6–12mm. N Amer. Z4.

C. brunoniana Wallich. Differs from *C. crispa* in fertile seg. broad-oblong, 6×2mm, margins spreading when mature, not strongly revolute. N India, NW Tibet. Z7.

C. crispa (L.) R. Br. EUROPEAN PARSLEY FERN; MOUNTAIN PARSLEY FERN. Fronds densely clustered; stipes to 7cm, straw-yellow to pale green with pale brown scales below; sterile fronds 4–6cm, blades ovate-deltoid, bipinnate-pinnatifid, pinnae 4–6 pairs, pinnules to 5mm, cuneate-elliptic, dentate, thick, opaque, veins ending in hydathodes; fertile fronds to 20cm, pinnules 9–12mm, linear, thin, pale yellow-green. Eur., Asia Minor. Z6.

C. crispa var. *acrostichoides* (R. Br.) C.B. Clarke = *C. acrostichoides*.

C. stelleri (S.G. Gmel.) Prantl. SLENDER CLIFF-BRAKE; FRAGILE CLIFF-BRAKE. Fronds few, scattered, nodding, conspicuously veined; stipes to 7cm, pilose, scaly and brown below; sterile fronds 3–6cm, blade ovate, bipinnate, pinnae 5 or 6 pairs, deltoid-ovate, membranous, pinnules 12mm, obovate, crenate or obscurely lobed; fertile fronds bipinnate to tripinnate, pinnules to 20mm, linear-lanceolate. N Amer. Z3.

Cryptomeria D. Don. JAPANESE CEDAR; SUGI. Cupressaceae. 1 everg. coniferous tree to 60m. Crown conical. Bole 1–2m diam.; bark red-brown, thick and fibrous, peeling. Br. tiered, branchlets pendent. Shoots glossy bright green, becoming brown. Lvs 0.7–1.5cm, in 5-ranked spirals around shoot, growing forward, subulate, acute, stomata in 4 longitudinal lines; juvenile lvs to 2.5cm, flatter, softer and more spreading. Cones globose, solitary, brown on ripening, 10–25mm; scales subpeltate, tipped with 2–5 spiny teeth. Jap., S China. Z6.

C. fortunei Billain ex Otto & Dietr. = *C. japonica* var. *sinensis*.

C. japonica D. Don. Typical plant described above. var. *sinensis* Miq. in Sieb. & Zucc. Branchlets slender. Lvs longer; cone scales shorter and softer toothed. S China. Hundreds of cvs are recorded, many of them Japanese with Western equivalents, eg. *C.* 'Hoo-Sugi' = *C.* 'Selaginoides'. They include forms with variegated foliage; flattened, spreading needles; soft fine juvenile needles; twisted br.; cristate growth ('Cristata'); dwarves with only short shoots; forms with sparse, long, filamentous shoots; globose and conical types. The commonest is 'Elegans', with soft slender juvenile lvs, green turning bronze to purple in winter; shrubby, to 20m with trunk often bowed or curved. Z6.

C. kawaii Hayata = *C. japonica* var. *sinensis*.

Cryptophoranthus Barb. Rodr..

C. atropurpureus (Lindl.) Rolfe = *Zootrophion atropurpureum*.

C. dayanus (Rchb. f.) Rolfe = *Zootrophion dayanum*.

Cryptostegia R. Br. Asclepiadaceae. 2 everg. twiners producing toxic latex, yielding rubber. Afr. to India.

C. grandiflora R. Br. RUBBER VINE. To 15cm. Lvs to 20cm, oblong-elliptic, obtuse, thick, glossy. Fls in term. cymes; cor. to 7cm diam., funnelform-campanulate, red-green to lilac or maroon, tube with 5 cleft scales covering anth. Afr.

Cryptostemma R. Br.

C. calendulaceum R. Br. = *Arctotheca calendula*.

C. forbesianum (DC.) Harv. = *Arctotheca forbesiana*.

C. niveum Nichols. = *Arctotheca populifolia*.

Cryptostylis R. Br. Orchidaceae. 15 terrestrial rhizomatous orchids. Lvs basal, ovate to lanceolate, erect, often marked, spotted or veined. Rac. erect, arising independently; tep. usually linear, pet. shorter; lip uppermost, entire, concave or convex, margins reflexed, calli ridged. Indomal., W Pacific, Taiwan, Aus. Z9.

C. arachnites (Bl.) Hassk. To 60cm. Lvs to 17cm, ovate, pale green with darker reticulate veins; petiole to 15cm, spotted purple. Tep. green, sometimes tinted red, linear-lanceolate; lip erect, basally concave, maroon, apex paler, velvety, spotted dark red or purple. Summer. Malaysia.

C. leptochila F. Muell. ex Benth. To 35cm. Lvs to 6cm, ovate, narrowing to petiole, green above, deep red, brown or purple beneath. Tep. filiform, green; lip red, wide at base, narrowing to linear, fleshy recurved tip with dark, glossy central lamina, margins bearing stellate calli. Winter–mid spring. SE Aus.

C. longifolia R. Br. = *C. subulata*.

C. subulata (Labill.) Rchb. f. St. to 90cm. Lvs to 4.5cm, narrow-ovate or oblong, sometimes red beneath; petiole 1–9cm. Tep. yellow or green, tapering to base; lip oblong, acute, bright red-brown, convex above, lamina with 4 pubesc. ridges, terminating in a dark, bilobed projection. Australasia.
→*Zosterostylis*.

Cryptotaenia DC. Umbelliferae. 4 branching, glab. annuals or perennials. Lvs ternate; petioles sheathing. Umbels compound; involucre and involucel 0 or reduced; fls small, white. N Temp., to African mts.
C. canadensis (L.) DC. HONEWORT; WHITE CHERVIL; MITSUBA. Perenn. to 1m. Lf blade to 13cm, oblong-ovate in outline; lfts 5–10cm, ovate, biserrate or 2–3-lobed; petiole to 14cm. Umbel rays 3–10, 1–6cm. Eur, N America, Asia.

Crystal Anthurium *Anthurium crystallinum*.
Crystal Tea *Ledum palustre*.

Ctenanthe Eichl. Marantaceae. 15 perenn., rhizomatous herbs with simple or branched aerial shoots and lvs in rosettes. Leave entire, basal lvs long-petioled, st. lvs short-petioled. Fls white to yellow, often with purple staminodes in short bracteate cymules on term. rac. Costa Rica, Braz. Z10.
C. amabilis (E. Morr.) H. Kenn. & Nicols. Lvs oblong-ovate, acuminate, silver-grey with narrow bands of dark and light green in direction of veins above; petiole long. Braz.
C. burle-marxii H. Kenn. St. to 40cm, tinged purple, pilose. Lvs to 14cm, ovate to obovate-oblong, pale green with dark green falcate markings over raised veins above, dark purple beneath; petiole to 11cm. Braz. var. *obscura* H. Kenn. To 55cm. Lvs deep grey-green with green falcate markings above, purple beneath.
C. compressa (A. Dietr.) Eichl. St. to 70cm, reed-like. Lvs to 35cm, linear-oblong or ovate-oblong, slender-pointed, waxy, green above, grey-green beneath; petiole about 12cm, pulvinus villous; sheath villous. SE Braz. var. *lushnathiana* (Reg. & Körn.) Schum. Less robust. Lvs light green with obscure feathering in a darker tone above.
C. glabra (Körn.) Eichl. To 1.2m. Stoloniferous. Lvs 35cm, oblong-lanceolate, abruptly acute, yellow-green with darker veins above, lustrous green beneath; petiole to 4cm, sheath tinged red. E Braz.
C. glazioui Benth. = *C. kummerana*.
C. kummerana (E. Morr.) Eichl. To 35cm. Stoloniferous. Lvs 14cm, ovate to oblong-lanceolate, deep green with white veins above, purple beneath, banded silver above in young specimens; petiole short. SE Braz.
C. lubbersiana (E. Morr.) Eichl. About 40cm, shoots widely branched. Lvs 18cm, linear-oblong, deep green with yellow variegation above, pale green beneath; petiole to 9cm with downy apical pulvinous. Braz.
C. lushnathiana (Reg. & Körn.) Eichl. = *C. compressa* var. *lushnathiana*.
C. oppenheimiana (E. Morr.) Schum. To 1m, robust and bushy. Lvs to 40cm, lanceolate, leathery, green with silvery-grey feathering above, wine red to purple beneath; petiole glab. to downy. E Braz. 'Tricolor' NEVER-NEVER PLANT: lvs blotched cream.
C. pilosa (Schauer) Eichl. To 50cm+, stoloniferous. Lvs to 22cm, linear-oblong to subovate-oblong, acuminate, cordate at base, variable in colour; petioles to 1.5cm. Braz.
C. setosa (Roscoe) Eichl. To 1.5m. Lvs oblong-lanceolate to oblong, tip crooked, occas. with cream marginal stripe above; petiole villous, to 16cm. SE Braz.
C. 'Stripe Star'. Lvs thinly ribbed grey with faint feathering.
→*Calathea, Maranta, Phrynium, Stromanthe* and *Thalia*.

Ctenitis C. Chr. Dryopteridaceae. 120 terrestrial ferns. Rhiz. erect, short, stout; stipes tufted, scaly. Fronds bipinnatifid to 4-pinnate to decompound, deltoid, membranous, rachis hairy. Pantrop. Z10.
C. decomposita (R. Br.) Copel. = *Lastreopsis decomposita*.
C. pentangularis (Colenso) Alston = *Lastreopsis microsora* ssp. *pentangularis*.
C. rhodolepis (Clarke) Ching = *C. subglandulosa*.
C. sloanei (Poepp. ex Spreng.) Morton. Stipes to 5cm, scales golden-brown. Fronds to 100×80cm, arching to spreading, 3-pinnate to pinnatifid at base, 2-pinnate to pinnatifid above, pale green; pinnae to 12 pairs, basal pinnae unequally deltate, middle pinnae, narrowly oblong, acuminate, 6–9cm broad, seg. oblong, obtuse, minutely crenate to lobed. Trop. and subtrop. Amer.
C. subglandulosa (Hance) Ching. Stipes to 70cm, straw-yellow, scales pale brown to rust. Fronds 4-pinnatifid, pentagonal; pinnae short-petiolate or sessile; pinnules to 5cm, oblong-ovate

to lanceolate, obtuse to subacute, crenate to lobed; rachis scaly above. China, India, Jap., Taiwan.
→*Alsophila*.

Cuban Bast *Hibiscus elatus*.
Cuban Holly *Begonia cubensis*.
Cuban Palmetto *Sabal parviflora*.
Cuban Royal *Roystonea regia*.
Cuban Spinach *Montia perfoliata*.
Cubeb, Cubeb Pepper *Piper cubeba*.
Cubeb Pepper *Piper cubeba*.
Cucharillo *Tabebuia dubia*.
Cuckoo Bread *Oxalis acetosella*.
Cuckoo Flower *Cardamine pratensis*.
Cuckoo-pint *Arum maculatum*.

Cucubalus L. BERRY-BEARING CATCHFLY. Caryophyllaceae. 1 hairy perenn. herb, differing from *Silene* in shining black, berry-like fr. St. brittle, to 80cm. Lvs ovate, acute. Fls in a loose cyme, somewhat drooping; cal. broadly campanulate, teeth 5, long, obtuse; pet. 6–10mm, deeply bifid, green-white. Widespread in Eurasia; also in N Afr. Z7.
C. baccifer L.

Cucumber *Cucumis sativus*.
Cucumberleaf Sunflower *Helianthus debilis*.
Cucumber Tree *Magnolia acuminata*.

Cucumeropsis Naudin. Cucurbitaceae. 1 herbaceous climber, to 4m. Lvs ovate-cordate or somewhat reniform, punctate, denticulate, obtuse or acute, sometimes obscurely lobed, 6–12×7–14cm; petiole 2–10cm. Fls in umbels or rac. (♂), or solitary (♀); cal. campanulate, pubesc. within, lobes lanceolate; pet. small, united at base, pale yellow. Fr. cylindric ellipsoid, cream-white, striped green, about 19×9cm. W Afr. Z10.
C. edulis (Hook. f.) Cogn. = *C. mannii*.
C. mannii Naudin.
→*Cladosicyos*.

Cucumis L. Cucurbitaceae. 30 herbs, scrambling or climbing, ann. or perenn. St. hispid or scabrid. Tendrils simple. Lvs simple, occas. divided, palmate, angled or 3–7-lobed, usually scabrid or hispid. ♂ fls solitary or in short, lat. clusters, yellow, 1–2cm diam.; cal. tubular, lobes filiform; pet. 5, joined near base; sta. 3; ♀ fls solitary, occas. clustered, staminodes 3. Fr. fleshy, smooth or spiky. Trop. Afr., Asia, introd. to New World Trop. Z10.
C. acutangula L. = *Luffa acutangula*.
C. africanus L. f. Ann. trailer. St. grooved, hirsute to scabrid, to 1m. Lvs 2–10cm, palmate, ovate, cordate, setose, lobes 3–5(–7), broadly elliptic to lanceolate, dentate to subentire, median lobe largest, often lobulate. Fr. ellipsoid to subcylindric, spiny, pale green with purple bands. S Zimb. to S Afr.
C. africanus Thunb. non L. f. = *C. zeyheri*.
C. anguria L. WEST INDIAN GHERKIN; BUR GHERKIN; GOAREBERRY; GOOSEBERRY GOURD. To 2.5m. St. slender, angled, rough, pubesc. Lvs to 8cm, broadly ovate, ovate, veins pubesc., lobes 3–5, rounded, often lobulate. Fr. ovoid or oblong, to 5×4cm, prickly, grey-green with green stripes, becoming yellow. Tanz. to the Transvaal. var. *longipes* (Hook. f.) Meeuse. Fr. concolorous, with dense subulate spines. W & S Afr.
C. cognatus Cogn. = *C. melo*.
C. colocynthis L. = *Citrullus colocynthis*.
C. dipsaceus Ehrenb. ex Spach. HEDGEHOG GOURD; TEASEL GOURD. Ann. St. slender, grey-green, hispid. Lvs 2–10cm, broad-ovate to reniform-ovate, scabrid-pubesc., occas. shallowly 3-lobed. Fr. firm, soft-spiny, ellipsoid, 2–5cm. Arabia, NE Afr.
C. erinaceus hort. = *C. anguria*.
C. flexuosus L. = *C. melo* ssp. *melo* var. *flexuosus*.
C. grossulariiformis hort. = *C. anguria*.
C. maderaspatanus L. = *Mukia maderaspatana*.
C. melo L. MELON. Ann. or perenn., trailing or prostrate. St. angular and hirsute to terete and glab. Lvs 5–15cm, membranous, subreniform, obtuse, 5-angled or shallowly 3–5-lobed, villous, lobes broad, rounded. Fr. highly variable in size, shape and colour. Cult. throughout warmer regions. ssp. *melo*. SWEET MELON; MUSK MELON. Ann. Lvs softly pubesc. Fr. subglobose to ellipsoid. The many edible cvs fall into the following groups –
Cantalupensis group. CANTALOUPE. Fr. medium-sized, rind hard, rough, not netted, flesh sweet, fragrant.
Chito group. MANGO MELON; ORANGE MELON; MELON APPLE; VINE PEACH. Fr. yellow or orange, lemon- or orange-shaped and sized, flesh white, scarcely edible.

Conomon group. ORIENTAL PICKLING MELON. Fr. smooth globose to club-shaped, fleshy white or green, rather hard; used for pickling.

Dudaim group. DUDAIM MELON; QUEEN ANNE'S POCKET MELON; STINK MELON. Fr. small, marbled, v. fragrant.

Inodorus group. HONEYDEW MELON; WINTER MELON. Fr. large, rind smooth or wrinkled, flesh white or green, somewhat fragrant.

Reticulatus group. MUSK MELON; NETTED MELON; PERSIAN MELON. Fr. medium-sized to large, rind with coarse netted markings, flesh orange and muskily fragrant.

var. *flexuosus* (L.) Naudin. SERPENT MELON; SNAKE MELON. Fr. elongated, furrowed, to 90cm. ssp. *agrestis* (Naudin) Greb. Ovary densely puberulous, with adpressed forward-pointing hairs. Cult. in India and Pak. var. *momordica* (Roxb.) Cogn. PHOOT; KACHRA; SNAP MELON. Fr. ovoid to cylindric, glab., yellow, 30–60×7–15cm.

C. melo var. *cultus* Kurz = *C. melo* ssp. *melo*.

C. metuliferus Naudin. AFRICAN HORNED CUCUMBER; KIWANO. Ann., climbing or trailing. St. hispid. Lvs 4–10cm, broadly ovate, cordate, lobes 3, serrate, long-pubesc., ovate-triangular. Fr. to 10cm, oblong, orange marked red, with blunt conical spines. Trop. Afr. to S Afr.

C. momordica Roxb. = *C. melo* ssp. *agrestis* var. *momordica*.

C. odoratissimus Moench = *C. melo*.

C. prophetarum L. GLOBE CUCUMBER. Climber or trailer to 2m. St. scabrid, somewhat thickened. Lvs 1–5cm, ovate to suborbicular, cordate to truncate, sinuate-toothed, usually deeply 3–5-lobed. Fr. subglobose to ellipsoid, 2–7cm. Trop. Afr. to Pak. and India. ssp. *dissectus* (Naudin) C. Jeffrey. To 1.4m. St. scabrid. Lvs to 9×8cm. Fr. softly aculeate. Zaire to NE Afr. and Arabia.

C. sacleuxii Paill. & Boiss. St. hairs irritant. Lvs 3–9cm, palmate, broadly ovate, densely pubesc., with irritant hairs beneath, serrate, lobes 5–7, triangular, acute to obtuse. Fr. obovoid to ellipsoid, terete, smooth except for scattered spines, green striped yellow, 6–8×4–5cm. E Afr., Madag.

C. sativus L. CUCUMBER; GHERKIN; KHIRA. Trailing. St. rough, hairy, angular. Lvs 12–18cm, triangular-ovate, often 3–8-lobed, hispid or scabrid, lobes acute. Fr. ultimately smooth, green, globose to oblong or cylindric, minutely tuberculate or prickly when young, highly variable in size and form.

C. zeyheri Sonder. Herbaceous perenn. trailer or climber. Base woody. St. decid., slender, angular, to 2m. Lvs 3–10cm, firm, palmate, ovate-elliptic to oblong, lobes 3–5, lanceolate to obovate, denticulate, median lobe often lobulate, scabrid or setose. Fr. ellipsoid, yellow, spiny. Angola, Zimb., S Afr.

Cucurbita L. Cucurbitaceae. 27 ann. or perenn. herbs, prostrate or climbing by tendrils. Lvs entire to lobed, large, scabrous to pubesc. Fls large, orange-yellow to yellow-white; cal. campanulate, 5-lobed; cor. campanulate, 5-lobed; ♂ solitary or clustered with 3 sta., anth. connate; ♀ solitary, on short peduncles with 3 staminodes. Fr. a berry (pepo), indehiscent, with tough, hard rind, variable in shape and colour, flesh thick, succulent, often edible. Trop. and Warm Amer. Z10 unless specified.

C. andreana Naudin. Ann. vine. St. long-running, to 20m. Lvs 3-lobed, green marbled white. Fr. obovoid, 6–15cm, green striped white and yellow. Urug., Arg.

C. argyrosperma hort. ex L.H. Bail. SILVER-SEED GOURD; CUSH-AW. Ann. St. long-running. Lvs c20cm, cordate-ovate or cordate-reniform, shallowly lobed, obtuse, scarious, slightly pubesc., denticulate. Fr. 15–20cm, globose to ovoid, rind hard, grey-white striped and marked green. Mex. Z9.

C. citrullus L. = *Citrullus lanatus*.

C. cordata S. Wats. Pubesc. perenn. St. slender, angled. Lvs 4–8cm, ovate, cordate, lobes 3–5, rounded or acute, lobulate, pubesc., toothed. Fr. globose, c8cm, green with 5 clear, pale stripes, and secondary stripes and marks. Summer. Baja Calif., Mex. Z9.

C. digitata A. Gray. Perenn. St. trailing, slender, angled, pilose. Lvs suborbicular, lobes 5, 5–10cm, linear-lanceolate, acuminate, 2 lateral lobes again divided, slightly hirsute above, hairy beneath, toothed or angled. Fr. 8–9cm, subglobose, dark green striped white-green. Ariz., New Mex., S Calif. Z4.

C. ficifolia Bouché. CIDRA; SIDRA; MALABAR GOURD. Perenn. vine. St. stout, setose to pilose, woody below. Lvs 15–25cm, subreniform to orbicular-ovate, shallowly to deeply lobed, or sinuate, basal sinus deep. Fr. 15–35cm, ovoid to globose, green striped white. Mex. to Chile.

C. foetidissima Kunth. CALABAZILLA; MISSOURI GOURD; BUFFALO GOURD; FOETID WILD PUMPKIN. Perenn. St. to 6m, rooting. Lvs 15–30cm, triangular-ovate, base cordate or truncate, acute, occas. lobed, grey-green, scabrous above, entire to sinuate-dentate. Fr. 6–7cm, oblong to globose, green striped and marked cream. Neb. to Calif., Mex.

C. hispida Thunb. = *Benincasa hispida*.

C. lagenaria L. = *Lagenaria siceraria*.

C. leucantha hort. = *Lagenaria siceraria*.

C. lundelliana L.H. Bail. Ann. to perenn., sparsely hirsute or glab. St. prostrate or scandent, simple. Lvs 5–9cm, broadly ovate, cordate, lobes 5, obtuse, short-pilose above. Fr. c7×6cm, globose-oblong, green or yellow-tinged. Guat., SE Mex., Br. Hond.

C. maxima Duchesne ex Lam. AUTUMN SQUASH; WINTER SQUASH; PUMPKIN. Ann. St. long-running, striate, hirsute or setose. Lvs orbicular to reniform, obtuse, occas. with rounded lobes, often sinuate. Fr. squat-globose, oblong or compressed-cylindric, yellow, red, orange, or green ribbed. Summer. S Amer., widely cult. Z9.

C. melanosperma A. Braun ex Gasparr. = *C. ficifolia*.

C. melopepo L. = *C. pepo*.

C. mixta Pang. = *C. argyrosperma*.

C. moschata (Duchesne ex Lam.) Duchesne ex Poir. PUMPKIN; CANADA PUMPKIN; CROOKNECK SQUASH; WINTER SQUASH. Ann. vine. St. softly hairy. Lvs broad-ovate to suborbicular, often shallowly 5-lobed, green marked white. Fr. v. variable, often oblong or crookneck. Spring–summer. US to S Amer.

C. okeechobeensis (Small) L.H. Bail. Ann. vine. St. slender, glabrescent. Lvs 12–20cm, suborbicular to reniform, base cordate, apex short-triangular, 5–7-angled, slightly pubesc. below, sharp-toothed. Fr. 7–8cm, subglobose, green, marked white, flesh white. Flor.

C. palmata S. Wats. Perenn. vine. St. sulcate, grey, hispidulous. Lvs 6–10cm diam., suborbicular in outline, cordate, lobes 5, narrow, canescent, short-hirsute. Fr. 8–9cm, subglobose, dull green, banded and marked green-white. S Calif.

C. pepo L. AUTUMN PUMPKIN; SUMMER PUMPKIN; AUTUMN SQUASH; SUMMER SQUASH; VEGETABLE MARROW; MARROW; COURGETTE; ZUCCHINI. Highly variable hispid ann. St. short or trailing, prickly to bristly or hairy. Lvs triangular or ovate-triangular, cordate, often deeply 5-lobed, lobes obtuse, large, hispid. Fr. variable in shape and size, oblong-cylindric to squat-globose, smooth to ribbed, glab. to hispid, orange to green when mature. Spring–summer. US, widely cult.

C. perennis (James) A. Gray = *C. foetidissima*.

C. siceraria Molina = *Lagenaria siceraria*.

C. sororia L.H. Bail. Climbing ann., resembling *C. texana*. Lvs 3-lobed or 3–5-angled, more scabrous beneath. Fr. longer than wide, mottled not striped. S Mex.

C. texana (Scheele) A. Gray. Climbing ann. St. slender, angled, pilose. Lvs 12–14cm, ovate-triangular in outline, base cordate, 5-lobed, scabrous above, denticulate. Fr. c6cm diam., variable, ovoid to pyriform, green, striped pale green; peduncle grooved. Tex.

→*Tristemon*.

CUCURBITACEAE Juss. 121/760. *Acanthosicyos, Actinostemma, Alsomitra, Apodanthera, Benincasa, Bryonia, Cephalopentandra, Ceratosanthes, Cionosicyos, Citrullus, Coccinia, Corallocarpus, Cucumeropsis, Cucumis, Cucurbita, Cyclanthera, Diplocystis, Ecballium, Echinocystis, Echinopepon, Gerrardanthus, Gurania, Gynostemma, Hodgsonia, Ibervillea, Kedrostis, Lagenaria, Luffa, Marah, Melothria, Momordica, Mukia, Neoalsomitra, Posadaea, Praecitrullus, Psiguria, Sechium, Seyrigia, Sicana, Sicyos, Solena, Telfairia, Thladiantha, Trichosanthes, Trochomeria, Xerosicyos, Zehneria, Zygosicyos*.

Cudrania Trécul. Moraceae. 5 trees or shrubs, decid. or everg., often thorny. Fls unisexual, minute, in small, axill., globose heads. Fr. a fleshy syncarp, resembling *Maclura*. E Asia.

C. tricuspidata (Carr.) Bur. ex Lav. CHINESE SILKWORM THORN. Decid. tree to 8m. Lvs 5–8cm wide at base, ± 3-lobed at apex, deep green. Fl. heads green, to 0.8cm diam. Fr. 2.5cm diam., orange-yellow, glossy, hard, edible. C China, Korea.

C. triloba Hance = *C. tricuspidata*.

→*Maclura* and *Vaniera*.

Cudweed *Artemisia ludoviciana*; *Gnaphalium*.

Cuitlauzina La Ll. & Lex. Orchidaceae. 1 epiphytic orchid. Pbs 5–10cm, ovoid, compressed. Lvs 15–30cm, broadly ligulate, coriaceous. Rac. pendulous, crowded, 40–100cm; fls to 5cm diam., lemon-scented, waxy; tep. white, tinged rose or lilac, sep. ovate-oblong, undulate, pet. slightly longer, elliptic, undulate; lip bright or pale mauve-pink with long yellow claw, reniform, emarginate, callus spotted rose. Late spring–autumn. Mex. Z9.

C. pendula La Ll. & Lex.

→*Odontoglossum* and *Oncidium*.

Culcita Presl. Dicksoniaceae. 7 bracken-like ferns. Rhiz. usually long-creeping. Fronds stipitate, blades angled horizontally, to 5× pinnate, deltoid; stipes erect. Trop. Amer., Malaysia to Aus. and Polyn.; SW Eur. and Atlantic islands. Z9.
C. dubia (R. Br.) Maxon. FALSE BRACKEN. Rhiz. to 1cm diam., long-creeping. Fronds to 150×75cm, 2–4-pinnate, deltoid to ovate, somewhat leathery, bright green; pinnae to 45cm, lanceolate to oblong, pinnules lanceolate, seg. oblong, toothed to pinnatifid or entire. Aus. (Queensld).
C. macrocarpa Presl. Rhiz. to 3cm diam., erect to ascending. Fronds to 90×70cm, to 3-pinnate, deltoid, leathery, lustrous; pinnae deltoid, pinnules ovate, seg. rhomboid to oblong, deeply toothed. Iberian Penins. and Atlantic islands.
→*Davallia* and *Dicksonia*.

Culén *Psoralea glandulosa*.
Culver's Root *Veronicastrum virginicum*.
Cumin *Cuminum cyminum*.

Cuminum L. Umbelliferae. 2 slender annuals. Lvs 2-ternate. Umbels compound; involucre of unequal bracts; bracteoles similar to bracts; fls white or pink. Medit., to Sudan and C Asia.
C. cyminum L. CUMIN. To 30cm. Lvs to 10cm, ovate in outline; seg. linear-filiform, 2–5cm. Umbels with 1–5 rays, to 2.5cm; bracts 2–4 filiform or ternately divided, to 5cm; bracteoles usually 3. Fr. ovoid-oblong, 4–5mm. Medit.

Cunham-hen *Syagrus cocoides*.

Cunila Royen ex L. Labiatae. 15 aromatic perenn. herbs or shrubs. Lvs simple, entire or serrate, sometimes spotted. Cal. campanulate, narrow, 5-lobed, pubesc. inside; cor. bilabiate, upper lip erect, lower larger, spreading, 3-lobed. N & S Amer.
C. mariana L. = *C. origanoides*.
C. origanoides (L.) Britt. Straggling herbaceous perenn. St. 20–40cm, glab., gland. Lvs 1.5–2.5cm, ovate-lanceolate, glab. or sparsely pubesc., serrate, ± sessile. Fls in loose cymes; cor. purple, lavender or white, 4–5mm, pubesc. E US. Z6.

Cunninghamia R. Br. CHINA FIR. Cupressaceae. 2 coniferous, everg. trees to 50m. Crown conical. Bark red-brown, thick, fibrous, deeply fissured. Br. in irregular whorls; branchlets in 2 ranks. Lvs narrow-lanceolate, stiff, flexible, sharply acuminate, densely arranged in 2 ranks in the same plane. Cones globose to ovoid-conical. China, Taiwan.
C. kawakamii Hayata = *C. konishii*.
C. konishii Hayata. Lvs 1–2cm lanceolate-ovate, grey to bright green with stomata on both surfaces, in 5–8 spiral rows, leathery; juvenile lvs found on cult. plants-similar to *C. lanceolata* but to 4cm, more slender and radially arranged. Cones 2cm; scales broadly obtuse, mucronate. Taiwan. Z9.
C. lanceolata (Lamb.) Hook. f. Lvs 3–7mm, spirally arranged, but twisted at base to appear densely 2-ranked around shoot, spreading, recurved, lanceolate, lustrous bright green, stomata virtually lacking above, and in 2 broad, green or white bands beneath, margins finely toothed. Cones 2.5–4cm; scales trullate, abruptly acute, finely serrate, mucronate. C China. 'Compacta': dwarf form with low apical dominance. 'Glauca': soft bright glaucous blue. Z7.
C. sinensis R. Br. = *C. lanceolata*.
C. unicanaliculata Wang & Liu = *C. lanceolata*.

Cunonia L. Cunoniaceae. 15 everg. trees. Lvs imparipinnate, coriaceous. Rac. axill., densely flowered; fls small; cal. 5-lobed; pet. 5; sta. 10, long, conspicuous. S Afr., New Caledonia.
C. capensis L. AFRICAN RED ALDER. Tree to 18m, bark dark, rough. Br. spreading. Lvs lustrous dark green, lfts 5–7, to 10×5cm, oblong to lanceolate, serrate. Rac. to 15cm, bottle brush-like; fls white to cream, sweetly fragrant. S Afr.

CUNONIACEAE R. Br. 24/340. *Bauera, Caldcluvia, Callicoma, Calycomis, Ceratopetalum, Cunonia, Geissois, Platylophus, Weinmannia*.

Cunure *Calliandra tweedii*.
Cup-and-saucer *Campanula medium*.
Cup-and-saucer Heath *Erica glauca*.
Cup-and-saucer Plant *Holmskioldia sanguinea*.
Cup-and-saucer Vine *Cobaea scandens*.

Cupania L.
C. edulis K. Koenig = *Blighia sapida*.
C. sapida Voigt = *Blighia sapida*.
C. subcineria A. Gray = *Alectryon subcinereus*.

Cupflower *Nierembergia*.

Cup Grass *Eriochloa*.
Cup Gum *Eucalyptus cosmophylla*.

Cuphea P. Browne. Lythraceae. 260 ann. or short-lived perenn. herbs or subshrubs. St. downy, viscid. Lvs ovate to linear. Rac. or pan. term. or axillary; fls 6-merous, zygomorphic, 1–3 per node; cal. tube cylindric, sometimes flared, lobes 6, sometimes alternating with appendages; pet. 0 or to 6, ± equal, alternating with cal. lobes; sta. 6 or 11, semi-exserted; style exserted. SE US, Mex., Guat., Boliv., S Braz.
C. bilemekii Koehne = *C. procumbens*.
C. brownei Jacq. = *C. viscosissima*.
C. coccinea DC. = *C. cyanea*.
C. cyanea Moc. & Sessé ex DC. Branching subshrub to 2m, glandular-hairy. Lvs ovate, to 8cm. Infl. branched, term.; cal. tube to 2.3cm, orange-red with yellow-green apex; pet. 2, small, purple-black. Mex. Z9.
C. emarginata Piergrossi = *C. lanceolata*.
C. eminens Planch. & Lind. = *C. micropetala*.
C. hyssopifola HBK. FALSE HEATHER; ELFIN HERB. Branched pubesc. subshrub to 60cm. Lvs to 2cm, dark green, glossy, linear-lanceolate, crenately toothed or entire. Fls axill.; cal. tube to 0.6cm, green; pet. to 0.5cm, 6, silky, crumpled pale lilac veined lavender, or pink or white. Summer–autumn. Mex., Guat. Z10.
C. ignea A. DC. FIRECRACKER PLANT; CIGAR FLOWER; RED-WHITE-AND-BLUE FLOWER. Short-lived shrublet to 60cm. Br. glab. Lvs oblong or lanceolate, to 8cm. Fls axill.; cal. tube to 2.6cm, scarlet, apex black edged white; pet. 2, black-purple. Summer–autumn. Mex., Jam. 'Variegata': lvs flecked cream and lime green. Z9.
C. jorullensis HBK. To 60cm. Lvs lanceolate, to 6cm. Infl. a leafy rac.; cal. tube 2.8cm, red, tipped green; pet. 6, white. Mex. Plants grown under this name are often *C. micropetala*. Z10.
C. lanceolata Ait. f. Ann. herb 65cm, unbranched, viscid, purple-haired. Lvs ovate-lanceolate, to 7.5cm. Infl. a leafy rac.; cal. tube to 2.5cm, lined purple, neck constricted, lobes unequal; pet. black-purple, unequal, upper 2 to 1.8cm, lower 4 to 0.5cm; 2 dors. sta. villous, in purple woolly mass at mouth of tube. Late spring to autumn. C Mex. Z7.
C. llavea La Ll. & Lex. Shrubby, to 90cm. Lvs ovate to lanceolate, to 7.5cm. Rac. terminal, cal. tube 3.8cm, green-violet, hirsute, upper lobe elongate; pet. 2, bright red; 2 longest sta. with violet hairs. Mex. var. *miniata* (Brongn.) Koehne. Smaller; st. hirsute, cal. tube 2.8cm. Z10.
C. micropetala HBK. Subshrub to 90cm. Lvs lanceolate, to 16cm, slightly scaly. Rac. terminal leafy; cal. tube red shaded green-yellow, to 3.25cm, pubesc., lowest cal. lobe longest; pet. minute, red, white or yellow. Summer–autumn. Mex. Z10.
C. miniata hort. non Brongn. = *C. ×purpurea*.
C. miniata Brongn. = *C. llavea* var. *miniata*.
C. ×neubertii hort. ex Biedenf. (*C. ignea ×C. llavea*.) Like *C. ignea* but cal. tube crimson, pubesc.; pet. violet-black. Z9.
C. platycentra Lem. = *C. ignea*.
C. procumbens Ortega. Herbaceous viscid ann. to 60cm with long spreading br. Lvs lanceolate to ovate, to 7cm. Rac. term. leafy, cal. tube to 2cm, flared, red-purple or green, ribs purple-villous, mouth woolly, dors. lobe largest with tawny hairs, appendages green with purple hairs. Summer–winter. Mex., S US, Boliv. Z10.
C. pubiflora Benth. = *C. cyanea*.
C. ×purpurea Lem. (*C. llavea ×C. procumbens*.) St. herbaceous, stiffly pubesc., to 1m. Lvs broadly lanceolate. Cal. tube tinted pink at apex; pet. red to pink, tinted opal or mauve. Gdn origin. 'Avalon': fls purple. 'Firefly': fls orange-red. Z9.
C. silenoides Nees = *C. lanceolata*.
C. strigulosa Lem. = *C. cyanea*.
C. strumosa Moc. & Sessé = *C. micropetala*.
C. viscosissima Jacq. BLUE WAXWEED; TARWEED; CLAMMY CUPHEA. Viscid ann. herb to 50cm; st. much-branched, purple-hairy. Lvs ovate to lanceolate, to 5cm, pubesc. Infl. a leafy rac. or pan.; cal. tube to 1.2cm, straight, deep purple to pale yellow, purple-hairy; pet. purple, upper 2 largest, to 5.5mm; 2 dors. sta. densely villous but not forming a woolly mass in mouth of tube. Summer–autumn. US. Z7.
C. viscosissima hort. non Jacq. = *C. lanceolata*.
C. zimpanii E. Morr. = *C. lanceolata*.
→*Lythrum*.

Cupid's Dart *Catananche*.
Cup-leaf Ceanothus *Ceanothus greggii* var. *perplexans*.
Cup-of-gold Vine *Solandra*.
Cup-plant *Silphium perfoliatum*.

CUPRESSACEAE Bartling. 17/113. *Actinostrobus, Athrotaxis, Austrocedrus, Callitris, Calocedrus, Chamaecyparis, Cryptome-*

ria, Cunninghamia, ✕Cupressocyparis, Cupressus, Diselma, Fitzroya, Fokienia, Glyptostrobus, Juniperus, Libocedrus, Metasequoia, Microbiota, Neocallitropsis, Papuacedrus, Platycladus, Sequoia, Sequoiadendron, Taiwania, Taxodium, Tetraclinis, Thuja, Thujopsis, Widdringtonia.

✕ Cupressocyparis Dallim. LEYLAND CYPRESS. (*Cupressus ✕Chamaecyparis*.) Cupressaceae. Everg. trees to 40m. Br. ascending; twigs in flattened pinnate or plumose sprays. Lvs scale-like, imbricate. Cones to 2cm; scales to 8m, umbonate; seeds to 5 or more per scale, mostly infertile.

✕ C. leylandii (Dallim. & A.B. Jackson) Dallim. LEYLAND CYPRESS. (*Cupressus macrocarpa ✕Chamaecyparis nootkatensis*.) Vigorous fast-growing tree to 35m+. Crown dense, columnar to pyramidal. Bark smooth, green-brown, shallow-fissured; br. pendent. Lvs in flat sprays, dark green tinged grey. Cones globose, 15–20mm diam.; scales 6–8, warty. 'Castlewellan Gold': slower-growing than green cvs; lvs yellow in summer, bronzed in winter, shoots plumose, commonest yellow cv. 'Green Spire': narrow-columnar, dense; lvs bright green. 'Golconda': narrowly conic., lvs v. bright gold. 'Haggerston Grey': br. open, spreading, semi-opposite, plumose on 2 planes, lvs tinted grey. 'Leighton Green': narrow-columnar with distinct central leader, branching irregular, dense, flat-pinnate on an even plane, bright green to olive green; cones profuse. 'Naylor's Blue': resembles 'Leighton Green' except in br. more open, plumose, tips of the youngest br. terete; lvs grey-green, glaucous in winter. 'Robinson's Gold': compact and conical, v. vigorous; lvs bronzed in spring, later lime-green, then gold. 'Rostrevor': similar to 'Leighton Green' but leading shoots with more widely spaced br. and denser foliage; v. vigorous. 'Silver Dust': habit large, narrow, conic, to 4.5✕3.5m; lvs green splashed with cream and silver-white. 'Stapehill 21': similar to 'Leighton Green', foliage with darker blue tint, esp. beneath; young shoots yellow-green, later orange-brown, then brown tinted purple. Z7.

✕ C. notabilis Mitch. (*Cupressus arizonica* var. *glabra ✕Chamaecyparis nootkatensis*.) NOBLE CYPRESS; ALICE HOLT CYPRESS. To 20m+. Crown conic, broader and more open than ✕C.leylandii; br. ascending, flattened, bipinnate; old shoots green tinged brown, becoming violet, pendulous. Lvs in sprays, bright blue-green. Cones globose, 12–18mm diam., pruinose; scales 4–8. Z6.

✕ C. ovensii Mitch. (*Cupressus lusitanica ✕Chamaecyparis nootkatensis*.) Habit close to *Chamaecyparis nootkatensis*, to 15m+. Br. in flat sprays, green, later suffused purple or rose. Lvs strong blue-green, with white stomatal lines beneath, lemon-scented if crushed. Cones globose, 10mm, heavily glaucous, ripening violet; scales 4–6, bract mucronate. Z7.
→*Cupressus.*

Cupressus L. CYPRESS. Cupressaceae. *c*20 everg. coniferous trees. Bark flaking in long ribbons or exfoliating in papery scales. Shoots tetragonal, terete or flattened. Lvs scale-like in decussate pairs, imbricate, forward-pointing, with a dors. gland often exuding a white resin spot. Cones globose to oval; scales peltate, in decussate pairs, woody, with umbonate central bract. SW US to C Amer., N Afr. to C China.

C. abramsiana Wolf. SANTA CRUZ CYPRESS. Closely related to *C.goveniana*. To 25m+ in cult., 10m in wild; bark grey, deeply split; br. horizontal; shoots maroon. Lvs to 1.5mm, yellow-green to deep green, obtuse. Cones 2–2.5cm, globose, becoming lustrous grey-buff, pale; scales 6, umbo to 2mm. Calif. Z8.

C. arizonica Green. ARIZONA CYPRESS; SMOOTH CYPRESS. To 25m. Crown broad ovoid-conic; shoots dense, branching angular. Lvs v. finely serrate. Cones ovoid, 16–32mm, with 6 or 8 grey-brown, rhombic to 5-sided rugose scales, with an often prominent central bract. var. *arizonica* (var. *bonita* Lemmon) has thick fibrous coarsely shredding grey-brown bark on trunk and stout br. of mature trees, smooth and exfoliating in papery red layers on br., and trunk of young trees; lvs dull grey-green, glands not secreting resin. SE Ariz. to W Tex. and adjacent N Mex. var. *glabra* (Sudw.) Little. SMOOTH ARIZONA CYPRESS. Bark always smooth, exfoliating in papery layers, purple to red; lvs bright blue-green, with obvious white resin glands. C Ariz. 'Aurea': lvs tinted gold in summer, paler in winter. 'Blue Ice': lvs ice-blue. 'Compacta': dwarf, globose to conic; lvs grey-green. 'Conica': broad ovoid-conic, to 4m after 10 years; br. ascending, branchlets profuse, loose, short and stiff; lvs ice-blue; cones freely produced. 'Crowborough': dwarf, globose; branchlets dense, ascending; lvs blue. 'Fastigiata': compact, narrowly upright; lvs grey tinted blue. 'Fastigiata Aurea': upright, loosely conic; branchlets and lvs sulphur-yellow. 'Glauca': dense, narrow, conic; lvs juvenile, strongly tinted blue. 'Hodgins': vigorous, erect tree with aromatic, resinous silvery grey foliage. 'Pyramidalis': similar to 'Conica', but

broader, foliage more glaucous. 'Sulphurea': columnar, upright, slow-growing; lvs grey-yellow. 'Variegata': conic, slow-growing; br. tips variegated white; lvs green tinted blue, stippled cream. var. *montana* (Wiggins) Little. Bark as type; lvs dark grey-green as type but resin glands obvious. N Baja Calif. var. *nevadensis* (Abrams) Little. Bark similar to type but thick and fibrous higher in crown and on smaller br.; lvs bright grey-green, resin glands obvious. Calif. var. *stephensonii* (Wolf) Little. Bark as var. *glabra*; lvs grey-green to blue-green, glands not secreting resin. SW Calif., N Baja Calif. Z7.

C. atlantica Gauss. = *C. sempervirens* var. *atlantica*.

C. bakeri Jeps. MODOC CYPRESS. To 30m; bark red-grey, cracking into small scales; crown ovoid-conical; shoots arranged around br., tetragonal. Lvs grey-green, aromatic, acute; resin gland conspicuous. Cones subglobose, green-grey ripening grey-brown, to 2cm diam.; scales 6–8, warty with resin blisters, bract knob-like. N Calif. ssp. *mathewsii* C.B. Wolf SISKIYOU CYPRESS. A taller, longer-branched tree, extending into Oregon. Z7.

C. benthamii Endl. = *C. lusitanica.* var. *benthamii.*
C. cashmeriana hort. = *C. himalaica* var. *darjeelingensis.*

C. chengiana Hu. To 30m; crown columnar; bark shallowly furrowed, splitting in long strips. Lvs to 5mm, acute, curved towards shoot, dull green, gland. below. Cones 1.4–2cm spherical or oval; scales 8–12, flattened apically. W China. Z7.

C. corneyana Carr. = *C. lusitanica.*
C. corneyana Franco non Carr. = *C. himalaica.*

C. duclouxiana Hickel. YUNNAN CYPRESS. To 50m; crown slender conic to columnar, br. erect. Shoots similar to *C. sempervirens*, dark green to blue-green, v. slender. Cones globose, 2–3cm, scales 8–10. SW China. Z8.

C. dupreziana Camus = *C. sempervirens* var. *dupreziana.*
C. forbesii Jeps. = *C. guadalupensis* ssp. *forbesii.*

C. funebris Endl. CHINESE WEEPING CYPRESS; MOURNING CYPRESS. To 25m, crown conic to columnar; br. level to ascending, branchlets pendulous, flat, shoots in one plane. Lvs bright yellow-green with a pale resin gland. Cones globose, 0.7–1.4cm, scales 8, glaucous dark green at first. China. Z8.

C. gigantea Cheng & L.K. Fu. TSANGPO CYPRESS. V. similar to *C. chengiana* but to 45m, crown narrowly columnar. Cult. trees tend to have acicular, 6mm, glaucous green juvenile lvs; adult lvs are diamond-shaped in section, with fewer dors. glands. Cones to 2cm, umbo pointing toward apex. SE Tibet. Z8.

C. glabra Sudw. = *C. arizonica* var. *glabra.*

C. goveniana Gordon. GOWEN CYPRESS. To 26m; crown ovoid-conic; bark grey-brown, flaking; shoots maroon-brown, tetragonal. Lvs obtuse, bright to dark green. Cones spherical, black-grey to brown-grey, 1–2.2cm diam.; scales 6, rarely 4 or 8, umbo pointing to apex. Calif. 'Bregeonii': shrub-like; br. slender, suffused blue; cones globose, ash-grey, to 1.5cm diam. 'Compacta': broadly conic, dense, regular. 'Pendula': br. long, nodding; lvs flattened, acuminate. var. *pygmaea* Lemmon. MENDOCINO CYPRESS. On poor soil to 3m, on better soil to 40m. Lvs dark green, longer. Calif. Z8.

C. goveniana var. *abramsiana* (Wolf) Little = *C. abramsiana.*
C. goveniana var. *sargentii* (Jeps.) Henry = *C. sargentii.*

C. guadalupensis S. Wats. GUADALUPE CYPRESS. To 20m; bark smooth, red or maroon, exfoliating in scales; crown conical, becoming broad and rounded with age. Lvs glaucous-blue, acute to obtuse, finely dentate. Cones spherical, brown, glaucous when young, 3–4cm diam.; scales 8–10, umbo straight, low, broadly rounded. W Mex. 'Glauca': lvs deeper blue. ssp. *forbesii* (Jeps.) Beauchamp. TECATE CYPRESS. To 12m. Lvs more sharply acute, bright green. Cones smaller, 2.5–3.5cm, scales 6–10. SW Calif. N Baja Calif. Z9.

C. himalaica Silba. BHUTAN CYPRESS. To 45m+, crown broad conic, bark red-brown, exfoliating in strips. Br. and shoots similar to *C. funebris*, similar lvs, in flat pendulous sprays with a white flecked resin gland. Sikkim, Bhutan, N Assam. var. *darjeelingensis* Silba. KASHMIR CYPRESS. A tall, slender tree with an open, tiered habit and long weeping, feathery branchlets of a vivid blue grey. Z9.

C. leylandii Dallim. & A.B. Jackson = ✕ *Cupressocyparis leylandii.*
C. lindleyi Klotzsch = *C. lusitanica.*

C. lusitanica Mill. MEXICAN CYPRESS; PORTUGUESE CYPRESS; CEDAR OF GOA. To 45m; bark brown, furrowed, exfoliating in strips; crown conical. Lvs acute, dark to blue-green. Cone spherical, 1–8cm diam., glaucous becoming brown; scales (4–)6–8, umbo conical, to 4mm, recurved or straight. Mex. to Hond. 'Chamaecyparissoides': br. whip-like; lvs blue. 'Coerulea': br. spreading, sparse, branchlets shorter vivid blue; cones blue. 'Flagellifera': br. and branchlets long, nodding, cord-like. 'Glauca': br. more flattened; lvs stronger blue. 'Glauca Pendula': to 20m+; crown spreading; br. and branchlets weeping, glaucous blue. 'Knightiana': v. similar to var. *benthamii*; young shoots and lvs slightly richer blue. 'Pendula': habit open and upright; br. ascending, branchlets weeping; lvs dark green, tips outspread. 'Variegata': lvs stippled yellow and green. var. *benthamii* (Endl.) Carr. Crown narrowly conical. Lvs flattened, in frond-like sprays, bright green, gland-pitted. NE Mex. Z9.

C. macnabiana Murray. Tree to 20m, broad, conical; bark maroon to grey, fissured; branchlets irregularly arranged, flattened. Lvs acute, grey-green, citrus-scented, resin gland at centre of lf. Cones 1.5–2.5cm grey-brown, angular-ovoid, in clusters; scales 6–8 peltate, umbo conical, straight or curving. Calif. 'Sulphurea': shoots with yellow tips when young. Z8.

C. macrocarpa Hartw. ex Gordon. MONTEREY CYPRESS. Tree to 45m; bark purple-brown or grey, thick, ridged; crown columnar to conical, becoming flat topped with age, with br. tiered. Lvs bright green to yellow-green, somewhat fleshy, acute, margins paler. Cones 1.8–4cm, globose to elliptic, maroon-brown to dark brown; scales 8–14, angular, usually convex, undulate, umbo short. Calif., Monterey Bay. 'Crippsii': br. short, stiff, tips tinted silver; lvs subulate; juvenile form. 'Donard Gold': tall and conical; lvs bright deep yellow. 'Fastigiata': narrowly columnar; br. narrowly upright. 'Globe': dwarf, flattened, globose. 'Goldcrest': narrowly columnar, dense and compact; lvs juvenile, rich yellow. 'Golden Pillar': v. narrowly conic; br. ascending; outside lvs gold, inside lvs green tinted yellow. 'Horizontalis Aurea': small, broad and flattened; lvs gold. 'Lutea' ('Aurea'): to 28m, broadly columnar; lvs yellow when young. 'Minima' ('Nisbet's Gem'): dwarf, globose, dense and slow-growing; lvs mostly juvenile, subulate. 'Pendula': conic, wide-spreading; br. tips nodding; lvs needle-form. 'Prostrate Gold': large, spreading, to 1m; flat-topped; lvs light gold. 'Pygmaea': dwarf, low, flat-globose, slow-growing; juvenile and adult lvs mixed, bright green. 'Variegata' ('Lebretonii'): lvs and young shoots stippled green and cream. Z8.

C. montana Wiggins = *C. arizonica* var. *montana*.
C. nevadensis Abrams = *C. arizonica* var. *nevadensis*.
C. nootkatensis D. Don = *Chamaecyparis nootkatensis*.
C. pendula Griff. = *C. himalaica* var. *darjeelingensis*.
C. pygmaea (Lemmon) Sarg. = *C. goveniana* var. *pygmaea*.

C. sargentii Jeps. SARGENT CYPRESS. To 26m, related to *C. goveniana* but bark fissured, stringy. Shoots thick, lvs 2mm, dark green, dors. gland not resinous. Cones brown globose to oblong, 2–2.5cm, scales 6–10. W Calif. Z8.

C. sempervirens L. ITALIAN CYPRESS. To 40m; bark grey-brown, shallowly ridged, scaly; wild trees (f. *horizontalis* (Mill.) Voss) conic, with open level to ascending br. and pendulous branchlets, cultivated trees usually fastigiate form (f. *sempervirens*) slender columnar with erect br. and branchlets. Shoots yellow-brown, becoming maroon. Lvs obtuse, grooved beneath, dark green. Cones ovoid, green becoming lustrous brown, 2.2–4.4cm, scales 8–14, margins finely wavy, umbo small. Crete, Rhodes, Turk. to Iran; nat. elsewhere in Medit. 'Glauca': narrowly columnar; lvs tinted blue. 'Gracilis': narrowly columnar, dense and compact. 'Stricta': narrowly columnar; lvs dark green. 'Swaine's Gold': compact, v. narrow, upright; lvs strongly tinted gold. var. *atlantica* (Gauss.) Silba. MOROCCAN CYPRESS. Lvs more glaucous with white resin spots on glands; shoots slightly flattened; cones globose, scales 8. Atlas Mts. var. *dupreziana* (Camus) Silba SAHARAN CYPRESS. Shoots flattened, with most branching in one plane; lvs with white resin spots on glands, fragrant. Cone scales 10–12. SE Alg. var. *indica* Royle ex Carr. Cones 1.5–2.5cm, globose, scales 8–10. Iran to NW Pak. Z7.

C. stephensonii Wolf = *C. arizonica* var. *stephensonii*.
C. torulosa D. Don. HIMALAYAN CYPRESS. Tree to 40m; bark brown, furrowed, curled, peeling in long ribbons; crown conical; br. horizontal; branchlets whip-like, ± pendulous, in regular plane, young shoots maroon. Lvs acute, curving inwards, light yellow-green, with dors. gland. Cones 1–1.7cm, spherical to ovoid, green, becoming brown; scales 8–10, umbo short, deltoid, often recurved. W Himal. 'Ericoides': open and bushy; lvs subulate, light brown in winter. 'Majestica': stronger, taller and hardier; br. yellow, thicker; branchlets thicker, curved; lvs congested, scale-like. Z8.
→*Chamaecyparis*.

Curare *Strychnos*.
Curarire *Tabebuia serratifolia*.

Curculigo Gaertn. Hypoxidaceae. 35 perenn. herbs. Tuber or rhiz. usually bristly. Lvs forming a clump, stalked, tough, plicate, sometimes hairy. Fls starry, lily-like in a dense bracteate rac. at ground level or below lvs. S hemis. Z10.

C. capitulata (Lour.) Kuntze. PALM GRASS. Lvs 60–90×5–15cm, oblanceolate, hairy. Infl. to 7cm, on scape to 20cm; bracts to 3cm, hairy, brown; perianth lobes 0.6–0.8cm, yellow, tube short. S & SE Asia to Malesia, Aus.

C. ensifolia R. Br. = *C. orchioides*.
C. hortensis Britt. = *C. capitulata*.
C. latifolia Dryand. Lvs 30–60×5–10cm, lanceolate to oblong lanceolate, hairy beneath. Infl. at ground level; bracts to 3.5cm, glab., green; perianth lobes 0.8–1.2cm, yellow exterior hairy tube distinct. SE Asia to W Malesia.
C. orchioides Gaertn. Lvs 15–30×0.6–2.4cm, lanceolate, glab. Rac. congested; perianth yellow, lobes 1.25–1.9cm, lanceolate, tube 2.5–7cm. Jap., Hong-Kong, Java, Aus., New Caledonia.
C. recurvata Dryand. = *C. capitulata*.
→*Molineria*.

Curcuma Roxb. Zingiberaceae. 40 perenn. herbs. Rhiz. thick, aromatic, roots swollen. St. reed-like. Lvs lanceolate or oblong. Infl. term. on short leafy shoot or scapose, cone-shaped, densely bracteate, upper bracts sterile, coloured differently from lower bracts; pet. 3, thin-textured, posterior erect, hooded, lat. pet. decurved; lateral staminodes petaloid; lip broad, base tubular. Trop. Asia. Z10.

C. aeruginosa Roxb. Lvs to 90cm. Fls in 20cm spike, appearing before lvs; bracts fleshy, red above, green below; cor. yellow. Burm., Thail.
C. albiflora Thwaites. St. to 30cm. Lvs 15cm. Infl. 10cm, terminating shoots or scapose; bracts green; cor. white; lip tinged yellow. Sri Lanka.
C. amada Roxb. MANGO GINGER. To 60cm. Tuber large, aromatic, yellow within. Lvs 40cm. Infl. 18cm, term. on leafy shoot; bracts striped green and white, upper bracts narrow pink; cor. white and yellow. Autumn. India.
C. angustifolia Roxb. INDIAN ARROWROOT; BOMBAY ARROWROOT. Root tubers used for arrowroot. St. to 45cm, slender. Lvs to 40cm. Infl. scapose; fls yellow; fertile bracts green; sterile bracts purple-pink. Himal.
C. aromatica Salisb. To 1m; rhiz. large, pale yellow within. Lvs 60cm, often banded light green, long-stalked. Infl. scapose, to 30cm; bracts white-pale green, upper bracts tinged pink; cor. yellow-white, tinged pink. Spring. India.
C. australasica Hook. f. To 75cm; rhiz. white within, scarcely-aromatic. Lvs 15cm. Infl. 15cm; bracts pale green, upper bracts oblong-lanceolate, rose; cor. yellow. N Aus.
C. cordata Wallich = *C. petiolata*.
C. domestica Val. = *C. longa*.
C. elata Roxb. To 1m+; rhiz. thick, pale yellow within. Lvs 120cm. Infl. scapose, 20cm; bracts 5cm, dark green, upper bracts violet; cor. yellow. Burm.
C. ferruginea Roxb. to 1m; st. and sheaths red-brown, rhiz. thick, yellow within. Lvs 45cm, with red-brown stripe above. Infl. 12cm, bracts green lined and edged red, upper bracts bright red; cor. red; lip and staminodes yellow. Spring. India.
C. gigantea hort. = *C. elata*.
C. heyneana Val. = *C. zedoaria*.
C. kunstleri Bak. = *Scaphochlamys kunstleri*.
C. latifolia Roscoe. To 3m; rhiz. large, pale yellow within. Lvs to 1m, broad, midrib purple, downy beneath. Spike 20cm cylindric; bracts green, striped red at tip, upper bracts oblong, bright red with white base; fls white. Spring. India.
C. leucorrhiza Roxb. Rhiz. large, cylindric or carrot-shaped, almost white within. Lvs 60cm. Spike 10cm cylindric; bracts green, upper bracts narrow, salmon pink; fls white. India.
C. longa L. TURMERIC. To 1m; rhiz. large, elliptic or cylindric, deep yellow within and aromatic. Lvs to 50cm. Infl. 20cm, term. on leafy shoot, cylindrical; bracts pale green to white, upper bracts rose; cor. yellow. India.
C. mangga Val. & Van Zijp = *C. zedoaria*.
C. pallida Lour. = *C. zedoaria*.
C. petiolata Roxb. QUEEN LILY. To 60cm; rhiz. pale yellow within. Lvs 25cm, narrow, long-stalked. Infl. 15cm, term. on leafy shoot; bracts pale or deep green tinted violet, upper bracts violet; fls yellow and white. Malaysia.
C. purpurascens Bl. = *C. longa*.
C. roscoeana Wallich. HIDDEN LILY. To 90cm; rhiz. white within. Lvs 15–30cm. Infl. 20cm, term. on leafy shoot; bracts orange-red to glossy red-purple; fls yellow. Malaysia. 'Jewel of Burma': bracts orange.
C. rubescens Roxb. Rhiz. large, aromatic, white within. Lvs 50cm, midrib red, petiole long, edged red. Spike 12cm loose; bracts pale green and red, sterile bracts few, pale red; cor. yellow with red lobes. India.
C. xanthorrhiza Roxb. = *C. zedoaria*.
C. zedoaria (Christm.) Roscoe. ZEDOARY. To 1m; rhiz. large, white or yellow within, camphor-scented with bitter, aromatic taste. Lvs 60cm with irregular maroon-brown band on either side of midrib; petioles long. Infl. 10cm, scapose; bracts tinged green, upper bracts red or purple; cor. white to pale yellow, tinged pink. India.
C. zerumbet Christm. = *C. zedoaria*.

Curcurita Palm *Maximiliana.*

Curima Cook.
C. calophylla Cook = *Aiphanes acanthophylla.*

Curled Pondweed *Potamogeton crispus.*
Curlew Berry *Empetrum nigrum.*
Curlflower *Clematis crispa.*
Curly Clematis *Clematis crispa.*
Curly-curly *Dipcadi brevifolium.*
Curly Grass *Schizaea pusilla.*
Curly-heads *Clematis ochroleuca.*
Curly Mesquite *Hilaria berangeri.*
Curly Palm *Howea belmoreana.*
Curly Water Thyme *Lagarosiphon.*
Currajong *Asterotrichion (A. discolor).*
Currant *Ribes.*
Currant Tomato*Lycopersicon esculentum* var. *pimpinellifolium.*
Currawang *Acacia doratoxylon.*
Curry Leaf *Murraya koenigii.*
Curry Plant *Helichrysum italicum.*
Curtain Fig *Ficus microcarpa.*

Curtisia Ait. Cornaceae. 1 everg. tree, to 15m. Br. dichotomous,
branchlets rusty-pubescent. Lvs to 11cm, ovate, coriaceous,
coarsely toothed, glossy above, tomentose beneath; petiole to
2cm, brown-tomentose. Fls small white, in term. hairy pan. S
Afr. Z9.
C. dentata C.A. Sm.

Curtonus N.E. Br.
C. paniculatus (Klatt) N.E. Br. = *Crocosmia paniculata.*

Curua *Sicana odorifera.*
Curuba *Passiflora mollissima; Sicana odorifera.*
Curved-fruit Hakea *Hakea cyclocarpa.*
Cushaw *Cucurbita argyrosperma.*
Cush-cush *Dioscorea trifida.*
Cushion Bush *Calocephalus.*
Cushion Calamint *Clinopodium vulgare.*
Cushion Penstemon *Penstemon caesius.*
Cushion Phlox *Phlox caespitosa.*
Cushion Pink *Silene acaulis.*

Cuspidaria DC. Bignoniaceae. 8 lianes. Lvs (1-)3-foliolate or
with 2 lfts and term. tendril. Thyrses axill. or term.; cal.
campanulate, 5-dentate; cor. funnelform-campanulate, limb
slightly oblique. S America. Z10.
C. floribunda (DC.) A. Gentry. Lfts 7.5cm, ovate, base
attenuate, apex acuminate, glab. Cor. 2.5cm crimson. Boliv.
C. pterocarpa (Cham.) DC. CIPO-CRUZ. Lfts 4–11cm, ovate-
lanceolate to ovate, base acute or rounded, apex acuminate,
veins pubesc. Cor. 3.5–5.5cm, lilac-pink or white. Braz., Parag.,
NE Arg.
→*Adenocalymma* and *Nouletia.*

Cussonia Thunb. CABBAGE TREE; KIEPERSOL; UMSENGE. Araliaceae. 20 everg. or decid. trees and shrubs. Lvs spirally arranged
in term. rosettes, long-stalked, lobed, palmatifid or digitately
compound. Infl. term., 1–2× compound; fls small, white to
yellow spicately or racemosely arranged, sometimes crowded.
Fr. drupaceous. Afr., Comoros Is. Z10.
C. paniculata Ecklon & Zeyh. Shrub or tree to some 4.6m, bark
rough, corky. Lvs digitately compound; lfts 7–12, oblong-
elliptic, in juvenile plants, coarsely pinnatifid, lobes ovate,
spine-tipped, in later lvs serrate or entire. Infl. paniculate,
2×compound; br. to 30cm+; fls spicate on secondary br. S Afr.
C. spicata Thunb. Tree to 17m pachycaul at first, then multi-
stemmed; bark fissured. Lvs digitately compound or palmatifid;
lfts 5–12, to 35cm, pinnately divided or falsely pinnately
compound, toothed. Infl. paniculate, 2×compound, umbel-like
in outline; fls aggregated, cob-like in the upper two-thirds of the
spike. S & E Afr., Comoros Is.
C. thyrsiflora Thunb. Shrub or small tree to 4m. Lf seg. 5–8, entire or toothed, lobed or 3-parted above. Infl. as in *C. spicata*,
but secondary br. or rac. only to 12.5cm. S Afr.
C. umbellifera Sonder = *Schefflera umbellifera.*

Custard Apple *Annona.*
Cutch *Acacia catechu.*

Cuthbertia Small.
C. rosea (Vent.) Small = *Callisia rosea.*

Cut-leaf Banksia *Banksia praemorsa.*
Cut-leaf Blackberry *Rubus laciniatus.*

Cut-leaf Dryandra *Dryandra praemorsa.*
Cut-leaved Bramble *Rubus laciniatus.*
Cut-leaved Penstemon *Penstemon richardsonii.*
Cut-leaved Plantain *Plantago coronopus.*
Cut-leaved Triloba *Viola triloba* var. *dilatata.*

Cyamopsis DC. Leguminosae. 3 ann. herbs. Lvs imparipinnate.
Fls small, pea-like in axillary rac. Fr. a flattened, ridged, many-
seeded pod. Trop., Afr., Arabia. Z10.
C. psoraloides DC. = *C. tetragonolobus.*
C. tetragonolobus (L.) Taub. CLUSTER BEAN; GUAR. Bushy erect
herb, 1–3m. Lfts 3, 5–7.5cm, elliptic, acute, dentate. Fls white
flushed purple, in short axill. rac. Fr. to 5cm, straight, fleshy,
pubesc. Cultigen known from India, probably originating from
E Afr.
→*Psoralea.*

Cyananthus Wallich ex Benth. TRAILING BELLFLOWER. Campanulaceae. *c*30 tufted, prostrate, perenn. herbs. Lvs usually entire. Fls usually term., solitary, pedicellate; cal. 5-lobed; cor.
broad campanulate to cylindric, 5-lobed. Himal., China.
C. barbatus Franch. = *C. delavayi.*
C. delavayi Franch. Decumbent; branchlets slender, pubesc. Lvs
to 0.5cm, reniform, hispid beneath. Cor. to 2.5cm, dark blue,
lobes narrow, hairy within. Autumn. SW China. Z7.
C. incanus Hook. f. & Thoms. Low, spreading. Lvs to 1cm, elliptic, entire or v. shallowly lobed, white-villous. Cor. to 1.5cm,
lobes oblong-acuminate, spreading, azure blue. Summer.
Sikkim. Z7.
C. integer Wallich ex Benth. Differs from *C. microphyllus* in lvs
larger, elliptic, base cuneate, white-tomentose, and cor. funnelform, minutely pubesc. W Himal. Z4.
C. lobatus Wallich ex Benth. Tufted, to 10cm. Lvs obovate, base
cuneate, deeply lobed, fleshy. Cal. brown to black-villous; cor.
to 3cm, funnelform, lobes obovate, spreading, bright purple to
blue, throat hairy. Autumn. Himal. Z5. 'Albus': fls white. 'Giganteus': fls showy, deep lilac-blue. Z5.
C. longiflorus Franch. St. long, trailing. Lvs to 1cm, narrow-
ovate, recurved, white-velutinous beneath. Cor. to 5cm, tube to
2.5cm, cylindric, lobes linear-obovate, dark blue to lilac, with
tufted white hairs within. Autumn. W China. Z7.
C. macrocalyx Franch. St. to 12cm, creeping or suberect. Lvs to
1cm, deltoid-lanceolate, obtuse, abruptly recurved, petiole
winged. Cal. enlarged in fr., tinged yellow; cor. tube cylindric,
lobes spreading, elliptic-oblong lime with violet streaks. Tibet,
China. Z7.
C. microphyllus Edgew. St. to 15cm, tufted, trailing, or ascending. Lvs to 0.8cm, oblong to elliptic, base cordate to obtuse. Fls
solitary; cor. violet-blue, funnelform, lobes lanceolate, tube
with tufts of white hairs within. Autumn. N India, Nepal. Z4.
C. neglectus Marq. Like *C. longiflorus*, but with cor. lobes shortly
ovate. St. trailing, to 25cm, hispid. Lvs narrow ovate, white-
velutinous beneath. Cor. tube to 1.5cm, blue, with tufts of hair
near base of lobes. China. Z7.
C. sherriffii Cowan. St. many slender creeping or ascending. Lvs
ovate to deltoid, blunt, entire, grey-pubesc. beneath. Cal. grey-
black-pubesc.; cor. campanulate, lobes revolute, densely
bearded, light blue, paler in throat. Autumn. Bhutan, S Tibet.
Z8.

CYANASTRACEAE Engl. See *Cyanastrum.*

Cyanastrum Oliv. Cyanastraceae. 6 perenn., everg. herbs. St.
partially buried, swollen, tuber-like grey-green. Lvs in basal
clumps, entire, glossy dark green, cordate, veins parallel, sunken; petiole solid, sulcate. Rac. short, congested, bracteate;
perianth lobes 6, equal, broadly lanceolate. Trop. Afr. Z10.
C. cordifolium Oliv. Petiole to 30cm; lf blade cordate-reniform,
to 20cm. Rac. to 17cm; bracts violet-green; fls to 3cm diam., indigo to dark blue; anth. golden yellow. var. *compactum* R.T.
Clausen. Lvs broadly cordate. Infl. to 8cm; fls sky blue.

Cyanella L. Amaryllidaceae. 8 cormous perenn. herbs. Lvs in a
basal rosette and lying flat. Rac. simple or much-branched
pedicels curved; tep. 6, spreading; sta. 6, 5 short and equal, 1
longer, anth. yellow. Spring. S Afr., Nam. Z9.
C. alba L. f. Lvs to 12.5cm. Flowering st. to 25cm; fls solitary,
2.5cm diam.; tep. white flushed pale yellow, outer acute, inner
rounded, slightly cup-shaped. S Afr
C. capensis L. = *C. hyacinthoides.*
C. hyacinthoides L. LADY'S HAND. Lvs 20–30cm, undulate.
Flowering st. to 30cm, branched, fls 8–10 per br., lightly fragrant; tep. pale lilac or blue-violet, often blotched carmine at
base. S Afr. (Cape Penins.).
C. lutea L. f. FIVE FINGERS. Lvs to 15cm, narrow, undulate.

Flowering st. to 30cm often branched; tep. yellow, outside of outer tep. with prominent brown veins. S Afr.

C. orchidiformis Jacq. Lvs 12cm, ±prostrate, green tinged grey. Flowering st. 30–40cm; fls to 16 per st.; tep. pale mauve with a dark carmine-mauve ring in the centre. S Afr. (Namaqualand).

Cyanococcus (A. Gray) Rydb.
C. atrococcus (A. Gray) Small = *Vaccinium atrococcum*.
C. corymbosus (L.) Rydb. = *Vaccinium corymbosum*.
C. elliottii (Chapm.) Small = *Vaccinium elliottii*.
C. fuscatus (Ait.) Small = *Vaccinium fragile*.
C. hirsutus (Buckl.) Small = *Vaccinium hirsutum*.
C. myrsinites (Lam.) Small = *Vaccinium myrsinites*.
C. pallidus (Ait.) Small = *Vaccinium pallidum*.
C. virgatus (Ait.) Small = *Vaccinium virgatum*.

Cyanopsis L. Compositae. 1 pubesc. ann. herb to 50cm. St. erect, furrowed, branched. Lvs oblong to ovate or oblong-lanceolate, obscurely toothed, basal lvs pinnately 3–5-lobed, petiolate, upper lvs sessile, entire or coarsely toothed. Cap. solitary, to 5cm diam.; phyllaries villous spine-tipped, pale yellow, edged black; flts tubular, the outermost ray-like, pink to purple. Summer. S Spain.
C. muricata (L.) Dostál.
C. radiatissima Cass. = *C. muricata*.
→*Amberboa* and *Centaurea*.

Cyanotis D. Don. Commelinaceae. *c*30 usually perenn., often tuberous-rooted herbs. Lvs narrow, often distichous, ±succulent, ciliate. Fls radially symmetric, ± stalkless in dense single, axill. cincinni subtended by a leaf-like or reduced bract, bracteoles, conspicuous; sep. 3; pet. 3; sta. 6, fil. nearly always bearded, tips often swollen. OW Trop.
C. kewensis (Hassk.) C.B. Clarke. TEDDY BEAR VINE. Prostrate perenn., creeping from its initial rosettre, internodes and lf sheaths brown-hairy. Rosette lvs lanceolate, to 5cm, those of side-shoots overlapping in 2 ranks, smaller, dark green above, purple beneath, velvety. Cincinni lax, to 3cm, with 8 fls *c*8mm diam., purple-pink. India. Z9.
C. nodiflora (Lam.) Kunth = *C. speciosa*.
C. somaliensis C.B. Clarke. Succulent perenn. rarely with non-flowering basal rosettes; shoots creeping to *c*25cm stolon-like. Lvs oblong-linear, mucronulate, to 12cm on rosettes, 1.5–4cm on lat. shoots, densely hairy beneath, sheaths inflated, becoming papery. Cincinni short, several-fld; fls *c*5mm diam., mauve-blue. Somalia. Z9.
C. speciosa (L.) Hassk. Perenn. succulent herb with basal rosettes and stolons to 50cm forming loose mats. Lvs narrowly oblong, channelled, to *c*10cm, clothed with white silky hairs, or glabrescent. Infl. spiciform, arching, to 30cm; fls blue to mauve or pink. Summer–autumn. S Afr. Z9.
→*Belosynapsis*.

Cyathea J. Sm. TREE FERN; SAGO FERN. Cyatheaceae. 600+ tree ferns. Caudex usually tall, erect, with dense adventitious roots and scales. Fronds 1- or 2-pinnate-pinnatifid, v. large. Pantrop. Z9.
C. arborea (L.) Sm. WEST INDIAN TREE FERN. Caudex to 15m. Fronds to 3.5m, ovate, acuminate, light green, glab.; pinnae alt., 40–80cm; pinnules to 2cm wide, lanceolate-oblong to elliptic-lanceolate, apex attenuate; seg. 25–32 pairs, to 3mm wide, narrowly oblong-subfalcate, serrate; stipes to 60cm, tinged yellow, with creamy scales below. Trop. Amer.
C. australis (R. Br.) Domin. ROUGH TREE FERN. Caudex 3–18m. Fronds to 4m; pinnae to 100cm; pinnules 10cm, lanceolate or linear, entire or obscurely crenate, sterile fronds often minutely serrate; stipes, with bright brown scales below. Aus. (Queensld, NSW, Vict., Tasm.).
C. baileyana (Domin) Domin. WIG TREE FERN. Caudex slender, to 5m. Fronds to 3m, dark glossy green; lower pinnae reduced to a much-branched dense of dense fil., green at first, later red; pinnules long-acuminate, serrate; stipes with black scales. Aus. (NE Queensld).
C. borbonica Desv. = *C. robusta*.
C. brevipinna Bak. Fronds to 1m; pinnae 15cm; pinnules to 2.5cm; seg. broad, entire or slightly lobed; rachis thick, scaly-hispid. Aus. (NSW, Lord Howe's Is.).
C. brownii Domin. NORFOLK ISLAND TREE FERN. Caudex slender, marked with scars of fallen fronds. Young fronds covered with pale brown scales. Norfolk Is.
C. capensis J. Sm. Caudex to 5m. Fronds 2–3m, submembranous; pinnae 30–45cm; pinnules 5–10cm, deeply cut; seg. narrowly oblong, acute; stipe to 60cm, brown-scaly when young. S Afr., S Amer.
C. celebica Bl. Caudex to 6m, covered with white or fawn silky scales. Fronds to 4m, dark green above, grey, silky beneath,

coriaceous; pinnae linear-lanceolate; pinnules linear-subfalcate, obtuse, crenulate. Indon. (Celebes, Ternate), Aus. (NE Queensld), New Guinea.
C. colensoi (Hook. f.) Domin. Caudex usually prostrate, to 1m+, 8cm diam. Fronds 60–100cm, broadly ovate, pale brown to yellow-green, membranous; pinnae 15–40cm, oblong-lanceolate; pinnules to 5cm; seg. oblong, dentate or lobulate, to 8mm. NZ.
C. cooperi (F. Muell.) Domin. Differs from *C. australis* in ±stellate scales on midribs of pinnules. Aus.
C. costaricensis (Klotzsch ex Kuhn) Domin. Fronds to 3m; pinnules acute-acuminate; seg. crenate-serrate, obtuse to acute ±, to 2.5mm wide; rachis pale brown to straw-yellow, ±glab.; veins with white to pale brown fimbriate scales; stipes slightly spiny below. Mex. to Costa Rica.
C. cunninghamii Hook. f. Caudex to 6m, slender. Fronds coriaceous, flaccid, with stellate hairs beneath; pinnae to 60cm; pinnules to 13cm, pinnatifid at apex, oblong, acuminate; seg. to 15cm, pinnatifid, linear, lobules entire; rachis straw-yellow; stipes slender, purple-black to dark brown, tubercled. Aus., Tasm., NZ.
C. dealbata (Forst. f.) Sw. Caudex to 10m, to 45cm diam. at base. Fronds 3cm, dark green above, pale green beneath when young, white or glaucous when mature, subcoriaceous; pinnae to 50cm, oblong-acuminate; pinnules to 10cm, oblong-lanceolate, attenuate; seg. subfalcate, crenate-serrate, slightly revolute; stipes stout, scales shining dark brown. NZ.
C. dregei Kunze. Caudex to 5m. Fronds arching, with tips turned upward, 2×1m, dark green above, paler beneath, firm; pinnae 12–20 pairs; pinnules lanceolate, acute, to 8cm, tomentose beneath; seg. subacute, entire or dentate; rachis tomentose. S Afr.
C. horrida J. Sm. Fronds to 3m, clothed in cobwebby tomentum; pinnae to 60cm, deeply pinnatifid, sessile, oblong-lanceolate; pinnules to 7.5cm, oblong-lanceolate, acuminate, pinnatifid with short obtuse lobes. W Indies.
C. howeana Domin. Caudex to 3m. Fronds scaly-hirsute with rusty hairs disappearing or leaving a few tubercles; pinnae to 8cm, lanceolate; pinnules deeply dentate or pinnatifid, to 2cm. Aus. (NSW, Lord Howe's Is.).
C. insignis D.C. Eaton. Caudex erect, to 6m, densely scaly. Fronds 2.5m, dark green above, pale or subglaucous beneath; pinnae, 45–75cm, oblong-lanceolate; pinnules 25–33, 7.5–10cm, linear-lanceolate, apex crenate-attenuate; seg. 17–20 pairs, 7–9mm oblong-subfalcate, entire or crenately incised; stipes to 60cm, densely scaly. W Indies.
C. leichhardtiana (F. Muell.) Copel. Resembles *C. australis*. Caudex slender, to 7m. Fronds to 4m; pinnae to 10cm; pinnules lanceolate or linear; seg. narrow, serrate; rachis loosely tomentose or glab. Aus. (Queensld, NSW).
C. lindeniana hort. = *C. mexicana*.
C. medullaris (Forst. f.) Sw. SAGO FERN; BLACK TREE FERN. Caudex to 15m+. Fronds 6m, dark green above, pale green beneath, coriaceous; pinnae to 1m, oblong-lanceolate, attenuate; pinnules to 15cm, narrow oblong-attenuate; seg. to 1cm, narrow-oblong, subfalcate, crenate-serrate to crenulately lobed, revolute; stipes to 1m, stout, black, tuberculate, with linear black scales below. NZ, Aus. (Tasm., Vict.), Pacific Is.
C. meridensis Karst. Fronds tripinnate; pinnules narrow-lanceolate; costae scaly beneath. Colomb.
C. mexicana Schldl. & Cham. Fronds bipinnate; pinnules to 10cm, lanceolate, glab.; seg. oblong, slightly subfalcate, serrate, somewhat obtuse. Mex.
C. microdonta (Desv.) Domin. Caudex to 1m, spiny above, scaly with dark brown scales. Fronds to 2m, ovate-oblong, acute to acuminate, light green, glab.; pinnules numerous; seg. 18–25 pairs, linear, slightly falcate, minutely crenate-serrate; stipes to 50cm, light brown with sharp conic spines and dark brown scales. Trop. Amer.
C. rebeccae (F. Muell.) Domin. Caudex v. slender, to 7m. Fronds to 3m, dark green, shiny; pinnules to 8cm, lanceolate, crenate or serrate; stipes with dark brown scales in central upper groove. Aus. (Queensld).
C. robertsiana (F. Muell.) Domin. Caudex v. slender, to 7m. Fronds to 2.5m, pale green, soft, hispid or with scattered rigid hairs beneath; pinnae to 8cm; pinnules to 1cm, deeply pinnatifid; stipes with brown scales below. Aus. (Queensld).
C. robusta Bojer. Fronds glab., indistinctly minutely tubercled; pinnae to 45cm, bipinnate to pinnatifid at apex, oblong, acuminate; pinnules to 3cm, oblong, entire or serrate. Maur.
C. sclerolepis Bak. = *C. vieillardii*.
C. smithii Hook. f. SOFT TREE FERN. Caudex to 8m+. Fronds to 2m+, oblong-lanceolate, bright green above, paler beneath, membranous; pinnae 15–40cm, lanceolate-oblong; pinnules to 6cm, narrow-oblong, crenate-serrate, subfalcate; rachis stout, pale yellow-green, muricate, covered in red hairs when young; stipes slender, to 30cm, dark, grooved, densely scaly below.

NZ.

C. spinulosa Wallich. Fronds flaccid, glab., membranous; pinnules lanceolate; seg. oblong, acute, serrulate, glab.; stipes and main rachises spiny, often dark purple. India, Jap.

C. tricolor Colenso = *C. dealbata*.

C. vieillardii Mett. Fronds smooth, to 30cm; pinnae to 30cm; pinnules to 5cm; seg. falcate, obtuse, entire; stipes pale grey, muricate, scaly at base with shining brown-black firm scales. New Caledonia.

C. walkerae Hook. Fronds large; pinnae to 45cm, thick, firm, v. coriaceous; pinnules remote, to 10cm; seg. oblong, entire or slightly crenate. Sri Lanka.

C. woollsiana (F. Muell.) Wakef. Differs from *C. leichhardtiana* in rachis densely tomentose. Aus.

→*Alsophila, Hemitelia* and *Sphaeropteris*.

CYATHEACEAE Kaulf. See *Cyathea*.

Cyathodes Labill. Epacridaceae. Some 15 heath-like shrubs or small trees. New growth often flushed pink or bronze. Lvs small, usually overlapping. Fls small, in terminal spikes or solitary with numerous bracts or small scales; cal. 5-partite; cor. tubular at base, lobes 5, spreading or recurved, glab. to bearded inside. Fr. a drupe. Aus., NZ, Tasm., Polyn.

C. acerosa (Gaertn.) R. Br. = *C. juniperina*.

C. articulata Colenso = *C. juniperina*.

C. colensoi (Hook. f.) Hook. f. Small shrub, prostrate to decumbent. Lvs to 1cm, narrow-oblong, ciliate, prominently nerved, glab., glaucous. Fls v. small, hairy, green-white in erect rac. Fr. white to pink or red. NZ.

C. empetrifolia Hook. f. V. low-growing shrub; br. wiry, pubesc. Lvs to 0.6cm, long-linear, coriaceous, blunt, upper surface convex, glaucous beneath, revolute, ciliolate. Fls small, fragrant, solitary or clustered, cream-white. Fr. white. NZ.

C. glauca Labill. CHEESE BERRY. Shrub to 1.5m or small tree to 12m. Lvs to 3cm, narrowly obovate, glaucous beneath. Fls to 0.9cm, white. Fr. pink or white. Winter. Tasm.

C. juniperina (Forst. & Forst. f.) Druce. Prostrate or upright shrub to 2m. Lvs to 1.5cm, linear to narrowly ovate, tightly revolute, ciliolate, coriaceous, pungent, glaucous beneath. Fls to 0.4cm, solitary, axill., white, green or pink. Fr. white, deep pink or purple. Spring, summer. Aus., NZ, Tasm.

C. laurina R. Br. ex Rudge = *Trochocarpa laurina*.

C. parviflora (Andrews) Allan. PINK MOUNTAIN BERRY. Upright shrub, to 2m. Lvs 1–2cm, narrowly ovate to oblanceolate, coriaceous, glaucous beneath, revolute, pungent. Fls to 0.3cm, white, in dense spikelets. Fr. pink ripening black. Winter–spring. NZ.

C. robusta Hook. f. Shrub to 5m, similar to *C. juniperina* but more robust. Lvs 1–2cm, linear-oblong to narrowly lanceolate, coriaceous, rigid, blunt, revolute. Fls to 0.4cm, green-white, solitary. Fr. red. Chatham Is.

→*Epacris, Leucopogon* and *Styphelia*.

Cybistax Mart. ex Meissn. Bignoniaceae. 3 small shrubs or trees. Lvs digitate. Thyrses term. appearing with young lvs; cal. slender but dilated at apex, campanulate or turbinate, 5-angled, lobes acuminate; cor. funnelform-campanulate, sparsely scaly or pubesc. outside, lobes spreading. Braz. to Parag.

C. antisyphilitica (Mart.) Mart. 3–10m. Lfts 4–15cm, 5–7, narrowly elliptic, apex attenuate or long-acuminate, papery, veins glab. or pubesc. scaly-punctate, entire. Infl. lax, puberulent; cor. 3–8.5cm, green-yellow or green. Braz., Peru, Boliv., Parag.

C. chrysea (S.F. Blake) Seib. To 20m. Lfts to 22cm, 5, ovate-elliptic to ovate-lanceolate, membranous, crenate, puberulent, veins pilose. Infl. a rac., 10cm; cor. 6–7cm, golden, membranous. Venez., Colomb.

C. donnell-smithii (Rose) Seib. PRIMAVERA. To 25m. Lfts to 25cm, 5–7, glab. except veins, entire or serrate. Infl. a lax pan.; cor. to 3.7cm, glandular-pubesc., yellow. Mex., Guat.

C. macrocarpa Benth. = *Godmania aesculifolia*.

→*Tabebuia* and *Yangua*.

Cybistetes Milne-Redh. & Schweick. Amaryllidaceae. 1 perenn. bulbous herb. Lvs to 35×1cm, in 2 ranks, glaucous, ligulate, curving. Scape to 20cm; fls fragrant, to 24 per umbel; perianth tube to 1cm; lobes to 7cm, oblanceolate, obtuse, spreading, glossy rose pink to magenta; sta. 6, exserted. Spring. S Afr. Z9.

C. longifolia (L.) Milne-Redh. & Schweick.

→*Amaryllis* and *Ammocharis*.

CYCADACEAE Pers. See *Cycas*.

CYCADS See *Cycadaceae, Stangeriaceae, Zamiaceae*.

Cycas L. CYCAD; SAGO; FALSE SAGO. Cycadaceae. *c*20 everg., 'palm-like' gymnosperms. St. usually unbranched, columnar and scarred by lf bases. Lvs pinnate, in term. whorls; pinnae felty, circinate on emergence, hardening linear-lanceolate, rigid to soft, ± glossy with conspicuous midvein. ♂ cone woolly, rusty-yellow; sporophylls rhombic, acuminate; ♀ a loosely arranged mass of modified lvs, each bearing ovules along its margins, apex laciniate, toothed or entire. Seeds ovoid, to 7cm hard-shelled, outer coat fleshy. OW Trop. and subtrop., from E Afr. to Jap.

C. basaltica Gardn. = *C. media* var. *basaltica*.

C. beddomei Dyer. St. v. short, stout. Lvs to 90cm; pinnae to 12×0.3cm, narrow linear, pungent, held at 30° to rachis, dark green above, rusty-tomentose beneath, midvein pale, margins v. revolute. ♀ sporophylls to 20cm, rusty pubesc., lamina long-acuminate, rhombic, shallowly toothed. S India, Java. Z10.

C. celebica Miq. = *C. rumphii*.

C. circinalis L. (in part). FALSE SAGO; FERN PALM; SAGO PALM. St. to over 5m. Lvs to 3m, hardening glossy grey-green; pinnae to 30×1.5cm, linear-lanceolate, subfalcate, pliant to semi-rigid, margins thickened rather than revolute. ♀ sporophylls to 30cm; lamina rhombic, to 4cm wide, flattened, upper margins shallowly dentate to crenulate, apex long-acuminate. SE India. Z10.

C. circinalis ssp. *papuana* (F. Muell.) Schust. = *C. papuana*.

C. comorensis Bruant = *C. rumphii*.

C. immersa Craib = *C. siamensis*.

C. kennedyana F. Muell. = *C. papuana*.

C. madagascariensis Miq. = *C. rumphii*.

C. media R. Br. AUSTRALIAN NUT PALM. St. to 5m. Lvs to 1.5m, hardening glossy dark green; pinnae, narrow-linear, to 25×0.7cm, pungent, revolute. ♀ sporophylls to 40cm, tomentose, stalk long, attenuate and twisting; lamina rhombic, to 4×2cm, scarcely acuminate with teeth reduced to ribs on wavy upper margins. Queensld. var. *basaltica* (Gardn.) Schust. St. to 2m, swollen basally; lvs smaller; pinnae to 20cm, v. rigid, margins thickened or slightly revolute. ♀ sporophylls densely rusty pubesc. except lamina, which is rhombic, glab., entire. W Aus. Z10.

C. miquelii Warb. = *C. taiwaniana*.

C. normanbyana F. Muell. St. short, swollen. Lvs to 1.5m; pinnae semi-erect, to 20×0.5cm, coriaceous, dull green, pungent. ♀ sporophylls to 15cm; lamina to 7×0.8cm, narrow-lanceolate, crenulate or slightly toothed. Aus. Z10.

C. papuana F. Muell. St. to 4m. Lvs to 1.5m; pinnae to 20×1cm, held at 45° to rachis, upwardly overlapping, rigid, linear-lanceolate, slightly falcate, grey-blue to pale green. ♀ sporophylls yellow-tomentose, to 25cm; lamina rhombic, to 2cm diam., apex narrow-acuminate, upper margins wavy or toothed, somewhat involute. New Guinea, Queensld. Z10.

C. revoluta Thunb. St. to 2m, sometimes branching. Lvs to 1.5m, hardening glossy, glab.; pinnae to 15×0.5cm, semi-rigid, shining dark green above, paler, minutely pubesc. beneath, linear-lanceolate, held densely at 45–60° to rachis, pungent, gracefully incurved, revolute, midvein sunken, yellow-green. ♀ sporophylls to 20cm, golden-tomentose; lamina 10cm wide, obovate, deeply pinnatifid with to 22 pinnae/spines per side, each to 3cm. S Jap. Dwarf, variegated and cristate clones are grown. Z9.

C. revoluta var. *taiwaniana* (Carruth.) Schust. = *C. taiwaniana*.

C. rumphii Miq. St. to 8m resembling *C. circinalis* but with growth larger and more lax. Lvs to 2m, arching; pinnae linear-falcate, to 30×2cm, softer than in *C. circinalis*, dull dark green, paler beneath, margins swollen or slightly revolute, base decurrent on rachis, midvein grooved. ♀ sporophylls long, narrow, to 30cm, tomentose, lamina attenuate, rhombic to lanceolate, serrate or crenulate, often involute, apex narrow acuminate, mucronate. Coastal SE Asia, Micronesia, Madag., E Afr. Z10.

C. siamensis Miq. St. to 1.5m, swollen at base. Lvs to 1.5m, emerging villous; pinnae to 80, to 15×0.8cm, linear-lanceolate, pungent, semi-rigid, somewhat glaucous above, paler beneath, revolute, held at 30° or less to rachis, abbreviated to a few spines at base. ♀ sporophylls spathulate, to 10cm, golden or rusty-tomentose; lamina to 6cm across, ovate, pectinate, with teeth fewer and more rigid than in *C. revoluta* and midvein produced as long, term. spine. Indochina. Z10.

C. taiwaniana Carruth. Differs from *C. revoluta* in pinnae grey-green at first, linear-lanceolate, slightly broader, more widely spaced and held at 60° to rachis, margins thickened or slightly revolute. S China, Taiwan. Z10.

C. thouarsii R. Br. = *C. rumphii*.

Cyclamen L. PERSIAN VIOLET; ALPINE VIOLET; SOWBREAD. Primulaceae. 19 tuberous perenn. herbs. Lvs radical, slender-stalked. Fls solitary, nodding on recurved pedicels; sep. 5, united; pet. 5, reflexed through 90–180°, twisted away from cal. and upwards. Eur., Medit. to Iran, 1 sp. Somalia.

C. africanum Boiss. & Reut. Lvs to 10cm, circular to reniform or cordate, crenate to serrate, dark green, lightly marked silver-grey, lustrous, light green beneath. Fls violet-scented, to 2.5cm; pet. slightly reflexed, auricled, ovate-lanceolate to lanceolate, pale pink to dark rose-pink, with a deep red patch at base. Autumn. Alg. Z9.

C. alpinum hort. = *C. trochopteranthum*.

C. balearicum Willk. Lvs to 9cm, narrowly ovate or cordate, acute, shallow-toothed, blue-grey above, heavily marked with silver-grey, crimson beneath, margins scalloped. Fls to 2cm, pink or white veined pink, v. fragrant; pet. lanceolate, undulate. Spring. Balearic Is., S Fr. Z8.

C. caucasicum (Koch) Willd. ex Boiss. = *C. coum* ssp. *caucasicum*.

C. cilicium Boiss. & Heldr. Lvs suborbicular, serrate to crenate, grey-green to dark green, with silver-grey and dark blotches, purple-red beneath. Fls 1–2cm; pet. obovate, acute, twisted, reflexed, white to deep pink, crimson blotch at base finely suffusing pet. Autumn. SW Turk. (Cilicia). 'Album': fls white. Z7.

C. cilicium var. *intaminatum* Meikle = *C. intaminatum*.

C. coum Mill. Lvs orbicular to reniform, 2.5–6cm diam., dark to light green, marked with lighter spots or a silver-green band above, red, green or green marked-red beneath. Fls to 2cm; cor. tube rimmed white or pink; pet. elliptic to ovate-elliptic, strongly reflexed, sometimes folded, off-white or light pink to deep carmine, with a dark blotch at base. Winter–early spring. Bulg., Turk., Cauc., Leb., Isr. 'Album': fls white, flushed pink at base. 'Atkinsii': hardy; fls rose pink. 'Roseum': pet. pink with purple spot. Pewter-leaved group: lvs silver-grey above. 'Maurice Dryden': lvs silver with dark green margin; fls white. 'Tilebarn Elizabeth': lvs small, silver with narrow green margin; fls pale pink below, darker at pet. apex, with dark basal blotch. ssp. *caucasicum* (Koch) Schwarz. Lvs cordate, dentate, with silver-grey markings. Cor. rim pale mauve, pet. acute. Cauc. Z6.

C. creticum (Dörfl.) Hildebr. Lvs acute, to 4cm diam., jagged-toothed, dark grey-green, spotted with light silver-grey, purple-red beneath. Fls fragrant; pet. lanceolate, white pale pink. Spring. Crete. Z8.

C. cyprium Kotschy. Lvs broadly cordate, sharply acute or ovate-lanceolate, acuminate, to 3.5cm diam., olive-green, blotched light green near margin, with a hastate inner pattern marked with grey-green, red beneath, v. shallowly lobed, lobes tipped yellow. Fls to 2.5cm; pet. sharply reflexed, folded near base, twisting toward apex, irregularly toothed, auricled, pure white or pale pink with a V-shaped pink-purple blotch at base. Autumn–early winter. Cyprus. 'E.S.': lvs heavily spotted white. Z9.

C. europaeum L. = *C. purpurascens*.

C. fatrense Halda & Sojak = *C. purpurascens*.

C. graecum Link. Lvs obcordate, acute, velvety dark green, with a silver-grey zone within margin, sometimes fainter, appearing chequered, beautifully veined lime green or silver-grey, light green or maroon beneath, teeth red-brown. Pet. much reflexed, to 1.5cm, not twisted, auricled, pale pink to deep carmine, with 2 maroon blotches at base, streaking across pet., auricles blue-mauve. Autumn–early winter. S Greece, Aegean Is., S Turk., Cyprus. Z9.

C. hederifolium Ait. Lvs ivy-like, 5–15cm, rounded to lanceolate, entire to shallowly lobed, dark green to light grey-green or silver-grey mottled or veined above, green or purple-red beneath, serrate or entire. Pet. to 2.5cm, ovate-lanceolate, acute, reflexed, constricted at base, light to deep pink, with dark red blotch at base, streaking across pet. in 2 lines, rarely pure white, mouth of cor. tube pentagonal. Late summer–early winter. S Eur. to Turk. 'Album': fls white. 'Bowles' Apollo': lvs heavily marbled; fls pink. Corfu form: fls pink, scented. 'Ellen Corker': fls white, with strong pink basal marking, turning deeper purple with age. 'Pink Pearls': fls slightly larger. Scented Strain: fls pink, sweetly scented. Silver-Leaved group: lvs predominantly silver-grey. Z6.

C. hiemale Hildebr. = *C. coum*.

C. hyemale Salisb. = *C. coum*.

C. ibericum Meikle = *C. coum* ssp. *caucasicum*..

C. intaminatum (Meikle) Grey-Wilson. Lvs to 4cm, suborbicular, obtuse, emarginate, green with light marbling above, light green beneath, occas. marked purple, shallowly crenate. Fls to 1cm; pet. white or pale pink, elliptic-oblanceolate, grey-veined. WC & SW Turk. Z8.

C. libanoticum Hildebr. Lvs rounded or obcordate, undulate, to 8cm diam., dull blue-green, dark-blotched, bright red beneath, hastate inner pattern dark green. Cor. tube campanulate, white-rimmed; pet. to 2.5cm, broadly ovate, acute, rarely

twisted, pale pink to carmine, with a light red mark at base. Winter–early spring. Syr., Leb. Z9.

C. mirabile Hildebr. Lvs suborbicular to reniform, obtuse, to 3.5cm across, dark green, zoned or marbled grey, pink or red above, purple beneath, minutely toothed. Fls comparatively large; pet. to 2.5cm, oblong to obovate, finely toothed and emarginate above, pale pink with a carmine blotch at base. Autumn. SW Turk. Z7.

C. neapolitanum Ten. = *C. hederifolium*.

C. orbiculatum Mill. = *C. coum*.

C. parviflorum Pobed. Lvs suborbicular, dull green, cordate at base, entire. Fls short-stalked; pet. to 1cm, spreading then abruptly reflexed and slightly twisted, mauve-pink with purple basal blotch. Winter. NE Turk. Z7.

C. persicum Mill. Lvs usually cordate, acute at apex, finely toothed, marbled or silver-grey, with a dark green central zone surrounded by a lighter or darker margin in a hastate pattern with small silver-grey spots, green, rarely maroon beneath. Fls fragrant; pet. 2–3cm, far reflexed, twisted, oblong-lanceolate, white, pale mauve, pale pink or deep pink, with a darker basal spot. Spring. E Medit., Rhodes, Crete, Libya. The florist's Cyclamen with many cvs ranging in habit from large and robust to dwarf and compact; lvs from large and fleshy to small and silver patterned; fls from small to v. large, white to scarlet through salmon to pale pink, from simple to 'double', ruffled, twisted, sometimes scented. Z9.

C. pseudibericum Hildebr. Lvs obcordate, to 6.5cm, dark green, marbled silver-grey above, red-maroon beneath, dentate. Fls fragrant; pet. to 2.5cm, broadly lanceolate to elliptic, mauve to bright magenta or pink, with cordate purple-brown blotch at base streaking across white cor. rim. Winter–spring. S Asia Minor. Z7.

C. purpurascens Mill. Lvs circular-ovate, base cordate, to 8cm, dark green, marbled silver-grey above, red-green beneath, usually denticulate. Fls v. fragrant; pet. to 2cm, oblong, reflexed, slightly twisted, pink to deep carmine, often veined dark pink with a deep carmine blotch at base, rarely white. Late summer–autumn. C & E Eur. ssp. *ponticum* (Albov) Grey-Wilson. Lf margin with cartilaginous teeth. Z6.

C. repandum Sibth. & Sm. Lvs broadly cordate, short-acuminate, to 12.5cm, dark green, hastate inner pattern bordered grey-silver, occas. speckled white, red-maroon beneath, margins lobed with mucronate teeth. Fls fragrant; pet. to 2cm, linear to oblong, white to deep carmine with a bright red basal spot; cor. tube red-rimmed. Spring. C & E Medit. ssp. *peloponnesiacum* Grey-Wilson. Lvs dark green, marked silver-grey, hastate pattern often 0. Pet. carmine, magenta at tube mouth, twisting. Greece (Peloponnese). f. *vividum* Grey-Wilson. Fls deep purple. ssp. *rhodense* (Meikle) Grey-Wilson. Lvs grey-green, marked with silver-grey. Pet. pale pink or white, subacute to obtuse, to 2.5cm. Rhodes. Z7.

C. rohlfsianum Asch. Lvs with buff-pink hairs when young, reniform-orbicular, 9×11cm, bright green, patterned silver-grey, maroon-red beneath, base cordate, apical ⅔ shallowly 5–8-lobed, finely toothed. Fls often fragrant; pet. to 2.5cm, lanceolate, acute, twisted, auricled, rose-pink with a crimson patch at base; sta. and stigma far exserted, forming a cone. Autumn. Libya. Z9.

C. somalense Thulin & Warfa. Lvs 3.5–10.5cm, broadly cordate, subobtuse, unevenly dentate, deep grey-green, with conspicuous silver hastate inner pattern, purple beneath. Pet. 1.2–1.5cm, pale carmine-pink, darker at mouth, narrow, somewhat twisted. Autumn to early winter. Somalia.

C. trochopteranthum Schwarz. Similar to *C. coum*. Lvs 2.5–5cm, reniform to broadly ovate, base cordate, apex truncate, dark green zoned with silver above, purple-red beneath. Fls scented, to 4cm diam., pale pink to carmine; pet. broad, twisted, with a dark basal blotch, scarcely reflexed thus perpendicular to ovary and propeller-like. Winter–spring. SW Turk., Cilician Taurus. Z7.

C. vernale K. Koch = *C. coum*.

CYCLANTHACEAE Dumort. 11/190. *Carludovica, Cyclanthus*.

Cyclanthera Schräd. Cucurbitaceae. 15 ann. or perenn. vines climbing by tendrils. Lvs lanceolate to orbicular, simple to lobed. ♂ fls small, in axill. rac. or narrow pan.; cor. 5-lobed, rotate, yellow-white or tinged green; ♂ fls larger, solitary. Fr. usually explosively dehiscent, spiny or setose, rarely smooth. Amer. Z10.

C. brachybotrys (Poepp. & Endl.) Cogn. Lvs 7–12cm diam., lobes 3, triangular to oblong, crenate, punctate-scabrous above, paler and scabrous beneath. Fr. to 3cm, slightly spiny. Peru.

C. brachystachya (Ser.) Cogn. Lvs 5–10cm diam., ovate to suborbicular, strongly 3–5-angled or -lobed, basal sinus deep, square, apex acute. Fr. 2–4cm, spiny. Summer. Mex. to

Colombia, Ecuador.

C. explodens Naudin = *C. brachystachya.*

C. pedata (L.) Schräd. Lvs 2.5–20cm, broadly ovate to orbicular, pedately lobed, lobes 5, lanceolate, glab., serrulate to dentate. Fr. to 16cm, indehiscent, sparsely setose. C & S Amer.

C. tonduzii Cogn. ex Dur. & Pittier. Lfts 4–12cm, 5, denticulate to crenate, often deeply lobed or 3-sect, punctate-scabrous above. Fr. 2–2.5cm, densely spiny. Costa Rica.

→*Momordica.*

Cyclanthus Poit. Cyclanthaceae. 1 clump-forming, stemless, palm-like perenn. Lf blade to 0.8m, obovate-flabellate, deeply cleft at apex, strongly plicate, composed of ± fused, lanceolate bright green, seg. with free tips; petioles to 2m. Fls small, fragrant, whorled on a large scapose, spadix subtended by 3–5 yellow spathes. Trop. Amer. Z10.

C. bipartitus Poit.

Cyclobalanopsis Ørst.

C. glauca (Thunb.) Ørst. = *Quercus glauca.*
C. neglecta Schottky = *Quercus bambusifolia.*
C. salicina (Bl.) Ørst. = *Quercus salicina.*

Cyclocarya Iljinsk. Juglandaceae. 1 decid. tree to 12m. Lvs to 25cm, imparipinnate; lfts 6–15cm, 7–9 per lf, oblong-ovate to broadly lanceolate, acute, serrulate, coriaceous. Fls small unisexual in an olive-green pendulous catkin to 25cm. Fr. single-seeded, encircled by a tough wing to 5cm diam. China. Z8.

C. paliurus (Batal.) Iljinsk.
→*Pterocarya.*

Cyclodium Presl. Dryopteridaceae. 2 ferns. Fronds pinnate; sterile pinnae broad; fertile pinnae contracted. Trop. Amer. Z10.

C. meniscioides (Willd.) Presl. Rhiz. ascending or creeping, stout, scaly. Fronds oblong; sterile pinnae, oblong, entire, sinuate or crenate, acuminate, cuneate at base, to 18cm; fertile pinnae oblong-lanceolate, entire or sinuate-dentate, smaller and narrower. Trin. to Braz., Peru, Ecuad.

→*Aspidium.*

Cyclopeltis J. Sm. Dryopteridaceae. 6 terrestrial ferns. Rhiz. erect, woody, scaly. Fronds clustered, arching; blades uniform, pinnate; pinnae elongate, subentire. SE Asia to Solomon Is. Z10.

C. semicordata (Sw.) J. Sm. Rhiz. to 3cm thick. Fronds to 1.5×0.3m; blades narrowly to broadly oblanceolate, abruptly acuminate; pinnae numerous, base auricled, entire or slightly sinuate, 1–2cm broad; stipes grooved, short. Trop. Amer.

→*Aspidium.*

Cyclosorus Link. Thelypteridaceae. 3 terrestrial ferns. Rhiz. long-creeping. Lamina 2-pinnate or -pinnatifid. Pantrop. and subtrop. in S hemis. Z10.

C. acuminatus (Houtt.) Nak. = *Christella acuminata.*
C. dentatus (Forssk.) Ching = *Christella dentata.*
C. gongylodes (Schkuhr) Link = *C. interruptus.*
C. interruptus (Willd.) H. Itô. Stipes to 75cm. Lamina 60–120×38–45cm, oblong to linear, glossy and glab. above, glab. to scaly beneath; pinnae to 30×2cm, spreading, to 25 pairs, narrow-oblong to linear-lanceolate, lobes shallow, deltoid to oblong. Trop.

C. parasiticus (L.) Farw. = *Christella parasitica.*
C. striatus (Schumacher) Ching. Stipes to 90cm. Lamina to 80×30cm, oblong to ovate; pinnae to 20×2.5cm, spreading, oblong, deeply lobed, lobes somewhat falcate, oblong to linear, entire to notched. Trop. Afr.

→*Dryopteris* and *Thelypteris.*

Cycnoches Lindl. SWAN ORCHID. Orchidaceae. 12 epiphytic or terrestrial orchids. Pbs to 25cm, elongate, fusiform, thick. Lvs 15–40cm, plicate, lanceolate. Rac. lateral, arching or pendent; fls fleshy, unisexual; staminate fls swan-like, borne on curving pedicels with a 'body' of reflexed tep. and the slender, arching swan's neck of the column. ♀ fls fewer, spreading and with a less conspicuous column. Trop. Amer. Z10.

C. barbatum Lindl. = *Polycycnis barbata.*
C. chlorochilon Klotzsch = *C. ventricosum* var. *chlorochilon.*
C. cucullata Lindl. = *C. loddigesii.*
C. egertonianum Batem. Tep. to 3×7cm, thin-textured, pale green to green-tan (rarely yellow or white), sometimes flushed deep purple, spotted purple, lanceolate or linear-lanceolate; lip to 1.5×0.6cm, white to pale green, marked rose-purple, obovate, concave, clawed, disc suborbicular, with elongate, clavate, rounded processes, column to 3cm, slender, strongly arching. Mex. and Guat. to Colomb., Peru & Braz.

C. loddigesii Lindl. Tep. light green-brown, blotched and veined maroon; dors. sep. 6.5–10×1–1.5cm, narrowly elliptic to linear-elliptic, acuminate, lat. sep. 5–7.5×1–2cm, narrowly elliptic, acute, recurved; pet. 4–6.5×1.5–2.25cm, lanceolate; lip to 7×2cm, white to pale pink, sometimes lightly spotted red-brown, convex, lanceolate, column maroon, to 8cm, slender, winged. Venez., Colomb., Braz., Guianas.

C. musciferum Lindl. & Paxt. = *Polycycnis muscifera.*
C. pentadactylon Lindl. Fls fragrant; tep. white to yellow-green, spotted and barred red-brown or chocolate-brown; sep. 3.75–5×0.75–1cm, lanceolate-ligulate, acuminate; pet. 3.5–4×0.8–1.5cm, oblong, acute, reflexed; lip white to green, spotted purple or chocolate-brown, fleshy, claw with erect, finger-like process, lamina 4-lobed, tip ligulate to lanceolate, column to 4.5cm, purple, slender. Braz.

C. pescatorei Lindl. = *Lueddemannia pescatorei.*
C. ventricosum Batem. Fls fragrant; tep. green; dors. sep. 4–6×0.75–1.5cm, linear-elliptic, lat. sep. obliquely lanceolate; pet. 4–6×1.5–2.5cm, elliptic to elliptic-lanceolate; lip to 5×2cm, white, ovate or ovate-lanceolate, convex, acute to acuminate, callus lunate, rounded, black, column to 3.5cm. Mex. to Panama. var. *chlorochilon* (Klotzsch) Allen. Fls large, dove-grey to pale green, lip white, not clawed.

C. ventricosum var. *egertonianum* (Batem.) Hook. = *C. egertonianum.*

Cydista Miers. Bignoniaceae. 4 lianes. Lvs simple or unijugate, sometimes tipped with simple tendril. Rac. or pan. axill. or term.; cor. tubular-funnelform. Americas. Z10.

C. aequinoctialis (L.) Miers. BEJUCO COLORADO; BEJUCO DE DANTA; VAQUERO BLANCO. Lfts 5.4–16.2cm, ovate, membranous or papery, lepidote, veins pubesc.; petioles 0.9–4.5cm. Infl. paniculate; fls fragrant; cor. white to lilac, lined chestnut, throat yellow, tube 1.9–5cm, lobes 0.6–2.6cm, glandular-lepidote outside, puberulent inside. Mex., W Indies, to Braz. var. *hirtella* (Benth.) A. Gentry. Lfts v. hairy on veins beneath. Mex. to N Colomb.

C. amoena Miers = *C. aequinoctialis.*
C. praepensa (Miers) Sandw. = *Mansoa difficilis.*
C. pubescens Blake = *C. aequinoctialis* var. *hirtella.*
C. sarmentosa (Bertol.) Miers = *C. aequinoctialis* var. *hirtella.*
C. spectabilis (Vahl) Miers = *C. aequinoctialis.*
→*Anemopaegma, Arrabidaea, Bignonia* and *Levya.*

Cydonia Mill. QUINCE. Rosaceae. 1 decid. shrub or small tree, thornless, to 6m. Lvs to 10cm, ovate-elliptic, entire, deep green above, grey-woolly beneath; stipules large, glandular-dentate. Fls solitary, 5cm diam., white to soft pink; sep. 5, persistent; pet. 5, rounded-obovate; sta. 20+, anth. yellow. Fr. a large, aromatic, obscurely pyriform pome, light golden-yellow. Spring–summer. W Asia. Z4.

C. cathayensis Hemsl. = *Chaenomeles cathayensis.*
C. japonica (Thunb.) Pers. = *Chaenomeles japonica.*
C. lagenaria (Lois.) Koidz. = *Chaenomeles speciosa.*
C. lusitanica Mill. = *C. oblonga* 'Lusitanica'.
C. maulei (T. Moore). = *Chaenomeles japonica.*
C. oblonga Mill. QUINCE; COMMON QUINCE. 'Lusitanica' PORTUGUESE QUINCE: fls large, pale rose, abundant. Fr. 10×9cm, tapering to the stalk, deep yellow, grey-lanuginose.
C. sinensis (Dum.-Cours.) Thouin. = *Pseudocydonia sinensis.*
C. speciosa Sweet = *Chaenomeles speciosa.*
C. veitchii Trabut = ×*Pyronia veitchii.*
C. vulgaris Pers. = *C. oblonga.*

Cylindrophyllum Schwantes. Aizoaceae. 6 mat- and clump-forming succulents. Lvs long, 4-ranked, thick, tapered, cylindric. Fls produced on bracteate pedicels, opening in the afternoon. Summer. S Afr. Z9.

C. calamiforme (L.) Schwantes. Lvs 5–7cm long, 0.8cm thick, curved, inclined, cylindric, obtuse, mucronate, grey-green with minute dots. Fls 5–7cm diam., yellow-white.

C. comptonii L. Bol. Lvs 9cm long, 1cm thick, dense, erect, cylindric, tapered, one side ± flattened. Fls 7.5cm diam., silvery white.

Cylindropuntia (Engelm.) F. Knuth = *Opuntia.*

Cymbalaria Hill. Scrophulariaceae. 10 herbaceous perennials, often short-lived. St. slender, trailing, rooting. Lvs small, reniform to suborbicular, petiolate. Fls solitary, axillary; cal. 5-lobed; cor. bilabiate, spurred, palate pubesc. Summer. W Eur. Z7.

C. aequitriloba (Viv.) A. Chev. Lvs orbicular to reniform, entire or with 3–5 rounded lobes. Cor. 8–13mm, pale violet, throat purple. S Eur. 'Alba': fls white. Z7.

C. hepaticifolia (Poir.) Wettst. As *C. pallida* but lvs glab.; cor. 15–18mm. Corsica. 'Alba': fls white. Z8.

C. muralis P. Gaertn., Mey. & Scherb. KENILWORTH IVY; COLISEUM IVY; PENNYWORT; IVY-LEAVED TOAD FLAX. Lvs reniform to semi-circular, glab., 5–9-lobed. Cor. 9–15mm lilac-blue to violet, palate yellow (rarely white). Nat. SW & C Eur. 'Alba': fls white. 'Albiflora': fls white, yellow-throated. 'Globosa Alba': clump-forming; fls white. 'Maxima': fls large. 'Nana Alba': to 5cm, fast-growing; fls white. Z3.

C. pallida (Ten.) Wettst. Lvs reniform to orbicular, entire, pilose beneath, lobes deltate, 0–5. Cor. 15–30mm, pale blue-violet, palate golden yellow. C It. Z7.

C. pilosa (Jacq.) Grande. Lvs reniform, lobes 5–11, rounded. Cor. 9–15mm, lavender to white, palate yellow. It. Z4.

→*Linaria.*

Cymbidiella Rolfe. Orchidaceae. 3 large terrestrial or epiphytic orchids. Pbs fusiform. Lvs strap-shaped, rigid. Infl. racemose or paniculate, arising from axils of lower lvs; tep. to 4.5cm, oblong-lanceolate, spreading, petal shorter and broader than sep.; lip 3–4-lobed. Summer. Madag. Z10.

C. falcigera (Rchb. f.) Garay. Pan. 80–100cm, many-fld; fls pale green; lip heavily marked with dark purple, to 3cm, trilobed, midlobe quadrate with reflexed, acute apex, undulate.

C. flabellata (Thouars) Rolfe. Rac. far exceeding lvs, 10–15-fld; fls yellow-green, pet. dotted red; lip spotted and edged red, 1.5–2cm, trilobed, midlobe broadly obovate or flabellate, apex cleft, strongly undulate.

C. humblotii (Rolfe) Rolfe = *C. falcigera.*

C. pardalina (Rchb. f.) Garay = *C. rhodocheila.*

C. rhodocheila (Rolfe) Rolfe. Rac. equalling lvs, many-fld; fls yellow-green or apple-green, with large dark green or purple spots on the pet.; lip red with a yellow throat, to 4cm, 4-lobed, fleshy, triangular, apical lobes rounded, thin, undulate.

→*Grammangis.*

Cymbidium Sw. Orchidaceae. *c*45 epiphytic or terrestrial orchids. Pbs ovoid or spindle-shaped; sometimes 0. Lvs strap-shaped, subcoriaceous grassy or succulent, sheathing pb. and 1–3 at apex. Rac. erect, arching or pendulous, borne basally; fls waxy, pet. usually narrower than sep.; lip trilobed, fleshy, lat. lobes embracing column, callus usually ridged. Asia to Aus. Z9.

C. affine Griff. = *C. mastersii.*

C. aloifolium (L.) Sw. Pbs v. small. Lvs to 60×3cm, ligulate, rigid, fleshy. Rac. to 90cm, pendent; fls to 5.5cm diam., tep. pale yellow to cream, central stripe maroon-brown, often dark-streaked, oblong to narrowly ligulate-elliptic, pet. narrow-elliptic; lip cream or white, base yellow, saccate, papillose or pubesc., lobes veined maroon, midlobe ovate, recurved, entire, callus yellow. Early spring–summer. India, S China to Java.

C. atropurpureum (Lindl.) Rolfe. Differs from *C. aloifolium* in fls scented of coconut; tep. maroon or dull yellow-green tinged maroon, revolute, lip yellow-white, blotched maroon. Spring–summer. Thail., Malaysia to Philipp.

C. bicolor Lindl. Pbs ellipsoid, to 5cm. Lvs ligulate, coriaceous, to 90×3cm. Rac. to 72cm, arched or pendent; fls to 4.5cm diam., fragrant; tep. pale yellow cream, with a central maroon stripe, oblong to oblong-ligulate, narrow, pet. elliptic to oblong, narrow; lip cream or white, base yellow, saccate, papillose or pubesc., midlobe elliptic to ovate, base white to yellow, dotted or blotched purple-brown or maroon, apex pointed, strongly recurved, margins cream, often undulate, callus dappled purple-brown or maroon. Spring–summer. Indochina to Malaysia. ssp. *pubescens* (Lindl.) Dupuy & Cribb. Rac. pendulous, crowded, to 25cm; tep. bronze to olive with a central maroon stripe; lip ivory, pubesc. within, midlobe pale gold streaked maroon, tip recurved, callus yellow.

C. canaliculatum R. Br. Pbs narrow-ellipsoid. Lvs to 65×4cm, coriaceous, linear, deeply grooved above. Rac. arching, crowded; fls to 4cm diam.; tep. lanceolate to elliptic, green, brown or maroon beneath, olive green to pale bronze, streaked or spotted red-brown above; lip ivory, spotted purple or red, minutely pubesc., midlobe ovate, acute, sometimes undulate, callus pale green or cream, pubesc. Autumn–winter. Aus. var. *sparkesii* (Rendle) Bail. Fls deep blood red; tep. longer.

C. dayanum Rchb. f. Pbs obscure. Lvs to 115×2.5cm, narrow-linear. Rac. to 35cm; fls fragrant, to 5cm diam.; tep. oblong-lanceolate to narrow-elliptic, cream or white, with a central maroon stripe, occas. tinged burgundy particularly below, lip white, marked maroon, base orange or yellow, midlobe ovate, entire, recurved, minutely downy, maroon with pale yellow triangular basal stripe, callus glandular-pubesc., lat. lobes, white, with maroon veins and margins. Summer. N India to China, Jap. to Sabah.

C. devonianum Lindl. & Paxt. Pbs v. small, ovoid. Lvs to 30×6cm, blade oblong to elliptic-spathulate, coriaceous; petiole slender. Rac. pendulous, to 44cm; fls to 3.5cm diam.; tep. ovate-elliptic to subrhombic, pale bronze to dull green, dappled maroon; lip garnet red, papillose, midlobe triangular-ovate, decurved, maroon with 2 purple basal spots, lateral lobes cream, dappled maroon. Spring–early summer. NE India to N Thail.

C. eburneum Lindl. Pbs ellipsoid to ovoid. Lvs to 60×2cm, ligulate, pliable. Rac. to 36cm; fls to 12cm diam., lilac-scented; tep. white, often tinged pink, waxy, oblong, pet. subfalcate; lip ovate, lat. lobes rounded, ivory, midlobe white to cream, triangular, undulate to crispate, minutely pubesc., centre and base golden yellow often dotted maroon, calli 3, yellow, velvety. Winter–spring. N India, Nepal, N Burm., China.

C. eburneum var. *parishii* (Rchb. f.) Hook. f. = *C. parishii.*

C. elegans (Bl.) Lindl. Pbs to 7cm, ovoid. Lvs to 80×2cm. Rac. slender, to 60cm; fls to 3cm diam., pendent, campanulate, slightly scented; tep. incurved, obovate, pale straw yellow to cream, occas. tinted pale pink, or pale bronze; lip triangular, pale green to cream, rarely with random red spots, midlobe bilobed, undulate, callus orange-yellow. Late autumn–mid winter. N India, Burm., China.

C. ensifolium (L.) Sw. Pbs v. small. Lvs grass-like, tufted, linear, to 95cm. Rac. to 70cm; fls 3–5cm diam., often scented; tep. spreading, straw yellow to green, lined red or red-brown; lip green or pale yellow, rarely white, midlobe ovate to triangular, papillose, blotched or spotted red, undulate, lat. lobes streaked and edged red. India, China to Philipp.

C. erythrostylum Rolfe. Pbs narrow-ovoid, to 6cm. Lvs linear, thin, arched. Rac. erect or arching, to 60cm; fls to 11cm diam.; sep. spreading, white; pet. forward-pointing, white with broken lines of pink near base; lip yellow-white, midlobe triangular, undulate, shortly pubesc., yellow, with deep red veins becoming blotched, toward apex, callus cream, dappled pink, downy. Spring–summer. Vietnam.

C. findlaysonianum Lindl. Pbs ovoid, small. Lvs tough, sword-like, grooved, to 85×6cm. Rac. to 140cm, pendent; fls to 6cm diam., slightly fragrant; tep. olive to yellow-green, tinted pink near centre, fleshy, sep. narrow-elliptic, pet. broader, incurved; lip white, papillose or sparsely pubesc., midlobe broad-elliptic, undulate, notched, triangular, blotched maroon or spotted red, callus yellow or claret, lateral lobes veined claret. Summer–autumn. Vietnam, Malaysia, Philipp.

C. floribundum Lindl. Pbs ovoid, to 2.5cm. Lvs linear, arched, to 55×2cm. Rac. arching, to 40cm; fls crowded, 3–4cm diam.; tep rusty brown or green edged yellow-green, oblong; lip white, papillose, midlobe ovate, broad, blotched maroon (rarely pink), base yellow, calli 2, bright yellow. Spring–summer. S China, Taiwan.

C. fragrans Salisb. = *C. sinense.*

C. giganteum Wallich ex Lindl. = *C. iridioides.*

C. giganteum var. *lowianum* Rchb. f. = *C. lowianum.*

C. goeringii (Rchb. f.) Rchb. f. Pbs small, ovoid. Lvs linear-elliptic, arched, often finely toothed, to 80×1cm. Rac. erect; fls to 5cm diam., sometimes fragrant; green to burnt sienna, tinted red at base, spreading, obovate-elliptic, margins incurved; lip entire to trilobed, papillose, midlobe ovate to oblong, recurved, cream marked red; lat. lobes erect, edged and spotted crimson with large discs of callus. Winter–spring. China, Jap., Taiwan.

C. grandiflorum Griff. = *C. hookerianum.*

C. hookerianum Rchb. f. Pbs ovoid, to 6cm. Lvs to 65cm, ligulate. Rac. to 70cm, erect; fls to 14cm diam., scented; tep. apple green, base spotted red, rarely tinged red-brown; lip cream, base bright yellow, spotted maroon, edged green, midlobe ovate-cordate, papillose, callus pubesc., lat. lobes fringed. Winter–early spring. N India, China.

C. insigne Rolfe. Pbs ovoid, to 8cm. Lvs linear-elliptic, to 100×1.8cm. Rac. to 150cm, arched; fls to 9cm diam., few; tep. white or pale pink, midvein and base often spotted red, obovate; lip white, papillose, veined and dotted maroon-red, midlobe triangular, undulate, centre and base blotched yellow, central blotches pubesc., callus densely pubesc. Late autumn–spring. Vietnam, China, Thail.

C. iridifolium Cunn. = *C. madidum.*

C. iridioides D. Don. Pbs elongate-ovoid, to 17cm. Lvs to 90×4cm, ligulate. Rac. to 90cm, suberect or horizontal; fls to 10cm diam., remote, scented; tep. olive green, irregularly striped rusty-red or maroon, margins cream, sep. obovate, concave, pet. narrower, falcate; lip trilobed, oblong, midlobe pubesc. above, wavy, ciliate, yellow spotted red; column ivory, streaked blood-red beneath. Summer. N India, Burm., SW China.

C. lancifolium Hook. Pbs narrow-ellipsoid, to 15cm. Lvs to 21×3cm, lanceolate-elliptic, semi-rigid. Rac. to 35cm, erect; fls to 6, remote, to 5cm diam., fragrant; sep. narrow-oblong, white to olive green, pet. shorter, white to green with broken claret midvein and scattered spots; lip papillose, midlobe decurved, white, banded purple-red at base with 2 purple lines near apex, lat. lobes, rounded, white, edged and marked red-purple; column green-white streaked maroon. Summer. N India to Jap., W Malaysia to New Guinea.

C. lowianum (Rchb. f.) Rchb. f. Resembling *C. iridioides* in habit. Rac. to 100cm+, ascending to arching, tep. olive to lime green, irregularly veined rusty-brown or blood-red, sep. narrow-obovate, pet. narrow-obovate, subfalcate; lip yellow to white, base orange or bright yellow, spotted red-brown, midlobe cordate, short-pubesc. at centre and base, with deep red, velvety V-shaped marking, undulate. Late winter–early summer. Burm., China, Thail. 'Concolor': tep. pale bronze to lime green; lip white.

C. madidum Lindl. Resembling *C. canaliculatum* in habit except lvs to 90×5cm, softer, not so deeply grooved. Rac. pendent; fls to 3cm diam., fleshy, faintly scented; tep. bronze to brown beneath, yellow-green above; lip minutely pubesc., primrose, with yellow stripe and 2 red-brown blotches at base, midlobe truncate, callus a central, shining, viscid line. Summer–winter. Aus.

C. mastersii Griff. ex Lindl. Pbs elongate-ellipsoid. Lvs to 65×2.5cm, ligulate, arched. Rac. to 30cm; fl. solitary, to 6cm diam., scented of almonds; tep. white or tinted pink, oblong-elliptic to narrowly obovate, concave; lip white, spotted and tinged maroon, midlobe to 1.3×1.3cm, ovate, rounded, base blotched yellow, callus bright yellow. Autumn–winter. N India, Burm., N Thail.

C. parishii Rchb. f. Differs from *C. eburneum* in lvs to 45×2.5cm, obscurely striped pale green; fls highly scented; lip broader, disc deeper golden yellow, callus not velvety on midlobe. Summer. Burm.

C. parishii var. *sanderae* Rolfe = *C. sanderae*.
C. pendulum (Roxb.) Sw. = *C. aloifolium*.
C. pendulum var. *atropurpureum* Lindl. = *C. atropurpureum*.
C. pubescens Lindl. = *C. bicolor* ssp. *pubescens*.
C. pumilum Rolfe = *C. floribundum*.

C. sanderae (Rolfe) Cribb & Dupuy. Differs from *C. parishii* in lvs to 50×2.5cm; fls to 8cm diam., tep. white, flushed pink beneath and spotted purple at base of pet.; lip cream, centre and base blotched yellow, pubesc., margin marked maroon. Winter–late spring. Vietnam.

C. sanderi O'Brien = *C. insigne*.
C. sikkimense Hook. f. = *C. devonianum*.

C. sinense (Jackson) Willd. Pbs ovoid, to 3cm. Lvs narrow-linear, glossy. Rac. to 80cm, erect; fls to 5cm diam., scented; sep. yellow veined oxblood, purple-brown, or v. dark, pet. paler, often dark-veined; lip cream or pale yellow, papillose or minutely pubesc., midlobe blotched and dotted dark red, oblong, undulate or kinked. Autumn–spring. Burm. to Hong Kong, Taiwan, Ryukyu Is.

C. tigrinum Parish ex Hook. Pb. to 6×3.5cm, ovoid-globose. Lvs to 25×3.5cm, coriaceous, lanceolate. Rac. erect, exceeding lvs; fls to 5cm diam., fragrant; tep. olive to yellow, faintly lined and spotted purple or red; lip white, lined and spotted purple, margins purple. Spring–mid summer. Burm., NE India.

C. tracyanum Rolfe. Differs from *C. iridioides* in scape to 120cm, fls to 12.5cm diam., tep. with stronger markings, lip cream to yellow, lined brown or maroon, lat. lobes fringed; column green-white ot olive-green, spotted red. Autumn–summer. China, Burm., Thail.

There are many hundreds of *Cymbidium* grexes and clones ranging in habit from miniature (*C.* Showgirl) to v. large (*C.* Beresford 'Jersey Giant') with erect, arching or pendulous spikes of fls in shades of white, rose, pink, wine red, chestnut brown, amber, ochre, green and yellow, often marked with red or brown, esp. on the lip which may be velvety with golden crests.

Cymbopogon Spreng. Gramineae. 56 aromatic, usually perenn. grasses. St. clumped, erect, with sheathing lf bases. Lvs linear to lanceolate; ligules membranous. Pan. narrow, spathaceous; rac. short, paired; spikelets paired, sessile, fertile, or stipitate, ♂; sessile spikelets awned. OW Trop., warm temp. Z9.

C. citratus (DC. ex Nees) Stapf. LEMON GRASS. Perenn. to 1.5m+, all parts strongly scented of lemon. St. often cane-like and sheathed. Lvs blue-green, to 90cm×1cm, sheaths coarsely pubesc., apex and base attenuate, midrib stout, margins rough. S India, Ceylon.

C. confertiflorus Stapf = *C. nardus*.

C. nardus (L.) Rendle. CITRONELLA; MANA GRASS. Lemon-scented perenn. to 2m+. St. robust, erect, smooth. Lvs to 90cm×1.8cm. Trop. Asia.

C. schoenanthus (L.) Spreng. Perenn., to 30cm. St. erect, glab. Lvs to 25cm, flexuous, filiform, semi-terete, roughly edged, glaucous. N Afr. to N India.
→*Andropogon*.

Cynanchum L. Asclepiadaceae. 100 lianes or non- or short-climbing dwarf plants with thick fleshy br. Lvs 0 or reduced to scales. Infl. small, capitate; fls small with corona lobes forming a pentagon. Trop. & Subtrop. Z10.

C. ampanihense Jum. & Perrier. St. to 1m, creeping or climbing; br. fusiform, 3–8×0.2–0.3cm, flushed purple-red. Infl. paired, 5-fld; cor. lobes 5, strongly reflexed, 2.5–3×1.5–2mm; corona 6×3mm, spiny. Madag.

C. aphyllum (Thunb.) Schltr. St. scrambling; br. 10–40×0.2–0.3cm. Fls in sparse umbels; corona green striped brown. S & trop. Afr., SW Madag.

C. compactum Choux. Stolons subterranean; st. 20–30×0.3–0.5cm, grey-green, sometimes red-violet, forming dense clumps. Fls to 8mm diam., in terminal clusters of 10–15, yellow-green; corona white. SC Madag. var. *imerinense* Descoings. St. more slender; fls smaller. Madag.

C. crispum Jacq. = *Fockea crispa*.
C. humbertii Choux = *C. ampanihensis*.

C. macrolobum Jum. & Perrier. Shrub to 40cm, branching irregularly; st. 6mm thick, verrucose due to peeling waxy surface. Infl. term., few-fld; fls green-maroon-brown, 1.3cm diam. SW Madag.

C. mahafalense Jum. & Perrier. St. v. slender, long, twining, grey. Fls 4–5mm diam., 3–5 together; cor. lobes beige, with 3 red veins; corona white. SC Madag.

C. marnieranum Rauh. Low, much-branched shrub; st. succulent, erect to creeping, 5–7mm thick, dark to olive green, covered with tubercles and white hairs. Infl. 3–5-fld; cor. lobes 5–6mm, bright yellow, at first erect with tips united; corona white. C Madag.

C. nodosum (Jum. & Perrier) Descoings. St. clambering, cylindric, 4–10mm thick, covered with thick, white, cracking layer of wax, internodes to 1cm. Fls 8–13 in small umbels. S Madag.

C. perrieri Choux. Shrub, branching from base, 80–160cm; st. erect, terete or slightly angular, 9–13mm thick, grey-green, smooth or rough, nodes prominent. Infl. usually 5-fld; fls small; cor. lobes insignificant; corona white. Madag.

C. pycneuroides Choux. Stolons creeping, subterranean; st. erect, unbranched, to 60×2.5cm, green. Lvs needle-like, persistent. Cor. lobes green-white, 4–6×2–3mm. C Madag.

C. rauhianum Descoings. St. to 80cm, 4-angled to subterete, 6–10mm thick, waxy, constricted at nodes, seg. 4–5cm. Infl. term., many-fld; cor. lobes 4.5–5×2mm, brown-green; corona white. SE Madag.

C. rossii Rauh. Forming mats of creeping growths; st. 4-angled, dark green, lanate. Fls solitary or paired; cor. lobes 4×2.5mm, olive green edged cream-white above, hairy at first. S Madag.

C. sarcostemmatoides Schum. = *C. aphyllum*.
→*Asclepias* and *Sarcostemma*.

Cynara L. Compositae. 10 perenn. herbs. Lvs basal or cauline, lobed, lobes spiny. Cap. discoid, solitary or many in a corymb; involucre globose to ovoid; phyllaries imbricate; receptacle fleshy; flts white to blue or purple. Medit., NW Afr., Canary Is.

C. cardunculus L. CARDOON. To 1m, woolly. Lvs to 50cm, leathery, bright green, silvery white-tomentose, st. lvs 1–2-pinnatifid, seg. ovate to linear-lanceolate, spiny. Involucre to 6×5.5cm; phyllaries ovate, apical spine to 50mm, glaucous or purple-tinged; flts purple. Early summer–autumn. SW Medit., Moroc. Z6.

C. horrida Ait. = *C. cardunculus*.

C. hystrix Ball. To 1m. Lvs sharply spiny, white-tomentose below, lower lvs pinnatisect to pinnatifid seg. linear, dentate, acute, spinescent. Involucre to 5×4cm; outer phyllaries adpressed, leaf-like cartilaginous; flts purple. Summer. Moroc. Z8.

C. scolymus L. GLOBE ARTICHOKE. Like *C. cardunculus* but st. to 2m, sparsely hairy. Lvs to 80cm, pubesc. above, grey-tomentose beneath, seg. unarmed. Involucre to 7×8cm; phyllaries fleshy, apical appendage to 4cm, not or scarcely spine-tipped. Autumn. N Medit. 'Glauca': lvs to 1.5m, deeply divided, silver; infl. purple. Z6.

Cynodon Rich. Gramineae. 8 creeping perenn. grasses. St. erect or ascending. Lvs flat, linear to filiform, ligules hyaline or a pubesc. fringe. Infl. term., umbellate, with 2–6 spikes; spikelets 1-fld, laterally compressed. Trop. and S Afr. widely nat.

C. dactylon (L.) Pers. BERMUDA GRASS; BAHAMA GRASS; KWEEK; DOOB; COUCH; STAR GRASS. St. slender; to 30cm. Lvs to 15cm×1.8cm, grey to grey-green; ligule a row of hairs. Infl. spikes 3–6, to 5cm. Summer–autumn. Cosmop. Z7.

C. transvaalensis Burtt-Davy. Differs from *C. dactylon* in its finer lvs, spikes to 2cm. S Afr., introd. US. Z8.

Cynoglossum L. HOUND'S TONGUE. Boraginaceae. *c*55 ann., bienn. or perenn. herbs. Lvs alt., simple, those on st. usually smaller, ± sessile. Fls in terminal scorpioid cymes; cal. deeply 5-lobed; cor. tube cylindrical to infundibular-campanulate, limb rotate, 5-lobed, faucal scales 5. Temp. regions.

C. amabile Stapf & J.R. Drumm. CHINESE FORGET-ME-NOT. Bienn. to 60cm, unbranched erect, long-pubesc. Basal lvs to 20cm, oblong to lanceolate or elliptic, petiolate. Fls to 5mm, white, pink or blue. E Asia. 'Firmament': dwarf, to 40cm; lvs tinted grey; fls intense blue. Z7.

C. anchusoides Lindl. = *Lindelofia anchusoides*.

C. apenninum L. = *Solenanthus apenninus*.

C. cappadocicum Willd. = *Omphalodes cappadocica*.

C. cheirifolium L. Bienn., to 40cm, tomentose to hirsute, lvs lanceolate, sessile, white-tomentose. Infl. bracteate; cor. to 8mm, pale purple becoming violet or deep blue. SW Eur. Z7.

C. coelestinum Lindl. Bienn. to 100cm, erect, sparsely pubesc. Basal lvs to 20cm, ovate-cordate, long-petiolate. Fls blue, sometimes edged white, 8mm diam. N India. Z8.

C. columnae Ten. Ann., to 45cm, densely pubesc. Basal lvs to 10cm, elliptic to oblong, obtuse, long-petiolate. Fls dusky red to deep blue, to 6mm. Eur. Z7.

C. creticum Mill. Bienn., to 80cm, hirsute to tomentose. Basal lvs to 12cm, narrowly lanceolate to elliptic, obtuse, densely pubesc. to tomentose; petiole to 1.5cm. Fls pink or white, becoming blue with dark blue reticulate veins, to 9mm. Eur. to W Asia. Z7.

C. denticulatum A. DC. = *C. wallichii*.

C. dioscoridis Vill. Bienn., to 40cm, hirsute. Lvs linear-lanceolate, pubesc. Fls deep blue, to 5mm. Eur. Z6.

C. furcatum Wallich = *C. zeylanicum*.

C. glochidiatum Wallich = *C. wallichii*.

C. grande Douglas. Perenn., to 80cm, erect, glab. Basal lvs to 15cm, ovate or elliptic, sparsely hirsute or glab. above, densely hirsute beneath, long-petiolate. Fls deep blue, sometimes with purple tube. W N Amer. Z8.

C. lanceolatum Forssk. Bienn., to 50cm, densely grey-strigose. Basal lvs to 7cm, narrowly oblong to oblong-lanceolate, acute, base acuminate, petiolate. Fls white or blue, limb to 3mm diam. NE Afr. through Asia to Philipp. Z8.

C. linifolium L. = *Omphalodes linifolia*.

C. lithospermifolium Lam. = *Paracaryum lithospermifolium*.

C. longiflorum Benth. = *Lindelofia longiflora*.

C. nervosum Benth. ex C.B. Clarke. Perenn. to 90cm, erect, white-pubesc. Basal lvs to 4cm, ovate or ovate-oblong, rounded, base attenuate, white-pubesc.; petiole to 4cm. Fls blue, to 8mm diam. W Pak., Kashmir, NW India. Z5.

C. officinale L. Bienn., to 90cm, erect, unbranched, hirsute. Basal lvs to 12×2.5cm, elliptic-oblong; petiole to 15cm. Fls dark purple, to 6mm. Eur. to W Asia. Z6.

C. pictum Ait. = *C. creticum*.

C. racemosum Schreb. = *Paracaryum racemosum*.

C. virginaticum L. HOUND'S TONGUE. Perenn. to 90cm, erect, un-branched, hirsute. Basal lvs to 20×10cm, ovate-oblong, petiolate. Fls white, pale blue or purple, to 10mm diam. N Amer. Z4.

C. wallichii G. Don. Bienn., to 90cm, erect, densely white-pubesc. Basal lvs to 17×3cm, obovate to lanceolate, subacute to obtuse, with prominent veins, white-pubesc., petiolate. Fls pale to dark blue, to 4mm. C & S Asia. Z6.

C. zeylanicum (Vahl) Thunb. ex Lehm. Bienn., to 85cm, erect, covered with yellow or brown adpressed hairs. Basal lvs to 20cm, elliptic to oblong, subacute to obtuse, pubesc.; petioles to 12cm. Fls blue, to 9mm diam. Afghan. to Ceylon and Jap. Z7.

→*Adelocaryum* and *Anchusa*.

Cynorchis Thouars. Orchidaceae. *c*130 terrestrial, tuberous herbaceous orchids. St. and infl. axis often glandular-hairy. Lvs mostly radical; cauline lvs sheath-like. Rac. term., few to many-fld; dors. sep. forming a hood with pet.; lat. sep. spreading; lip spurred, entire or lobed, often much larger than other perianth parts. Mainland Afr., Madag., Masc. Is. Z9.

C. compacta (Rchb. f.) Rolfe. To 20cm. Lf 1, to 8cm, ovate-oblong. Infl. glab.; fls white with red-purple spots on lip; sep. 4mm, ovate, convex; pet. 4mm; lip *c*9mm, 3–5-lobed, basal lobes much larger than apical lobes, all lobes rounded; spur 3mm. S Afr. (Natal).

C. fastigiata Thouars. 10–30cm. Lvs 1–2(–3), 6–20cm, narrowly lanceolate. Infl. glab.; fls about 3cm, purple; sep. 5–6mm, obtuse; pet. 5mm, narrowly oblong, obtuse; lip 10–15mm, with 4 ± equal lobes; spur 18–30mm. Madag.

C. gibbosa Ridl. 25–50cm. Lvs 1(–2), 10–20cm, oblong-lanceolate, often spotted. Infl. glandular-hairy; fls large, carmine-red or purple; dors. sep. 12mm, lat. sep. and pet. 15mm, pet. narrower; lip trilobed, lat. lobes slightly emarginate,

midlobe deeply bilobed, apiculate; spur 20–25mm, swollen at apex. Madag.

C. kassneriana Kränzl. 15–50cm. Lvs 1(–2), to 20cm, oblanceolate or elliptic, purple beneath. Infl. glandular-hairy; fls pink-purple with purple marks; dors. sep. 5–7mm, ovate, convex, lat. sep. 6–8mm, spreading, ovate; pet. 4.5–7.5mm, lanceolate; lip 5–10mm, trilobed, lobes ± triangular; spur 6–9mm, sometimes swollen at apex. Widespread in trop. Afr.; S Afr.

C. Kewensis. (*C. lowiana* ×*C. purpurascens*.) Lf 1, 30cm, lanceolate. Tep. to 10mm, lilac; lip bright lilac-purple with white and purple blotches at base, about 30mm, with 4 lobes, oblanceolate and truncate; spur 30mm. Spring. Gdn origin.

C. kirkii Rolfe. 10–50cm. Lvs 1(–2), 4.5–22cm, lanceolate. Infl. glandular-hairy; fls lilac-pink or mauve, lip paler than tep. with darker tips, sometimes yellow at base; dors. sep. 5mm, ovate, lateral sep. 5–6mm, elliptic; pet. 5mm, falcate; lip 10–20mm, 4-lobed, lobes 4mm wide, oblong or obovate, rounded or truncate; spur 20–30mm. Tanz., Malawi, Zimb., Moz.

C. lowiana Rchb. f. 10–16cm. Lf 1, 4.5–13cm, narrowly linear-lanceolate. Scape slender, 1–2-fld; tep. 8–10mm, green, tinged pink, lip carmine-red with darker spot, 22×27mm, 4-lobed; spur 25–45mm. Madag.

C. purpurascens Thouars. 25–50cm. Lf 1, 20–40cm, ovate or lanceolate. Infl. glab.; fls mauve; sep. 10mm, lat. sep. wider than dors.; pet. 7–10mm; lip 18–25mm, narrow with 4 subequal lobes, basal pair wider; spur 15–40mm. Madag., Masc. Is.

Cynosurus L. Gramineae. 7 ann. or perenn. grasses. St. clumped, slender. Lvs glab.; ligules membranous. Infl. paniculate, secund, spicate. Summer–autumn. Medit., Eur., N Afr. Z7.

C. echinatus ROUGH DOG'S TAIL GRASS. Ann., to 110cm. Lvs glab., to 20×1cm. Infl. ovoid to globose, to 8cm; spikelets to 14mm; glumes narrow-lanceolate, to 13mm; lemmas, long-awned.

C. elegans Desf. Resembles *C. echinatus*, but to 45cm. Lvs narrower. Infl. narrower, to 2.5cm, more lax; spikelets smaller; awns silky, longer than lemmas.

Cyp *Cordia alliodora*.

Cypella Herb. Iridaceae. 15 bulbous, perenn. herbs. Lvs plicate, linear-lanceolate. Fls ephemeral, term., solitary or corymbose; perianth seg. 6, outer seg. obovate, spreading, inner seg. smaller, erecto-patent, recurved at apex with a bearded claw, style br. often petal-like. Mex. to Arg. Z9.

C. armosa Ravenna. Flowering st. to 60cm, unbranched, fls 5–6.5cm diam., yellow; outer seg. pandurate-spathulate, reflexed; inner seg. recurved, 1.5cm, marked yellow-orange and brown-black; style orange. Arg., Parag.

C. coelestis (Lehm.) Diels. Flowering st. 50–80cm, unbranched; fls 6–8cm diam., leaden blue with a tawny flush and yellow-brown spots; outer seg. spreading, inner seg. erect, blotched yellow, claw bearded; style lilac. Late summer. Braz., Urug. to Arg.

C. curuzupensis Ravenna. Flowering st. to 40cm+, unbranched; fls to 4cm diam., yellow, marked dull green; outer seg. ovate, 2.3cm, inner seg. 1.5cm; style pale yellow. Parag.

C. herbertii (Lindl.) Herb. Herb. Flowering st. to 30cm, often branched; fls 4–6cm diam., outer seg. ovate-pandurate, claw slender, chrome yellow to pale bronze or apricot with a mauve stripe, inner seg. yellow spotted purple, reflexed. Summer. Braz., Urug., Arg. 'Pulchella': fls pale mauve.

C. peruviana Bak. Differs from *C. herbertii* in infl. unbranched, fls bright yellow with purple, maroon or chestnut spots or broken bands in cup formed by base of seg.; style chrome yellow. Winter. Peru, Boliv.

C. plumbea Lindl. = *C. coelestis*.

CYPERACEAE Juss. 115/3600. *Bolboschoenus, Carex, Cladium, Cyperus, Eleocharis, Eriophorum, Isolepis, Pycreus, Rhyncho-spora, Schoenoplectus, Schoenus, Scirpoides, Scirpus*.

Cyperus L. Cyperaceae. *c*600 ann. or perenn. rhizomatous herbs. Lvs grass-like, basal and sheathing scapes or 0. Spikelets linear, few- to many-fld, usually subtended by leaflike bracts in a simple or compound scapose umbel; fls v. small, in 2 rows in the axils of leaflike bracts. Cosmop., except v. cold regions.

C. albostriatus Schräd. Scape 20–50cm, thin, firm. Lvs numerous, equalling scape, 8–16mm wide, 3-nerved, nerves pale, prominent. Bracts 6–9, leaflike, exceeding infl., 16mm broad, spreading; umbel compound, lax, rays 8–24, 2.5–10cm. S Afr. Z9. 'Variegatus': lvs and bracts striped white.

C. alopecuroides Rottb. Scape to 120cm, 3-angled. Lvs 6–12mm wide, often exceeding scape, nerves 3, prominent above. Bracts

4–7, lower bracts exceeding infl; umbel compound; rays 5–10, 18cm. Trop. Afr. Z10.

C. alternifolius L. UMBRELLA PLANT. Scapes 45–90cm, numerous, erect, dark green, crowded. Lvs 0. Bracts 11–25, leaflike, 6–10mm wide, flat, longer than infl.; rays 20–25, 6cm; spikelets brown, 6–8×1.5–2mm. Madag. Z10. 'Gracilis': more slender than type. 'Variegatus': St., lvs and bracts striped and mottled white or wholly white.

C. compressus L. Ann. Scape 10–40cm. Lvs 3–5mm across, two-thirds scape length. Bracts leaflike, lowest exceeding infl.; umbels usually simple; spikelets in clusters of 3–10, 12–20-fld, 12–25×4–6mm, compressed. Trop. Afr. Z10.

C. congestus C.B. Clarke. Scape to 30cm. Lvs equal to or exceeding scape, 2–12mm wide. Infl. lax, compound or simple, rays 2–12, 8cm; spikelets 3–25-fld, 8–30mm, stalked, brown; bracts 4–6, exceeding infl. S Afr., Aus. Z9.

C. cyperoides (L.) Kuntze. Scape to 75cm, slender, 3-angled. Lvs two-thirds st. length, bright green. Umbel simple, 2–12cm across; rays 5–12, 2–10cm. Afr. (widespread). Z9.

C. diffusus hort. non Vahl. = *C. albostriatus*.

C. elegans hort. non L. = *C. albostriatus*.

C. eragrostis Lam. Scape 60–90cm, stout, roughly 3-angled above, leafy. Lvs equalling scape, 4–8mm wide, net-veined, margin rough. Bracts 5–8, exceeding infl.; umbel compound, spreading; rays 8–10, to 12mm. Summer. SW US and warm temp. S Amer. Z8.

C. erythrorrhizos Muhlenb. Ann. Scape 15–120cm, bluntly 3-angled. Lvs linear, 4–8mm wide, margin rough. Bracts 3–10, leaflike, exceeding infl.; umbel simple, sometimes compound; rays 3–12, 8cm. Summer. N Amer. Z7.

C. esculentus L. CHUFA. Ann. or perenn., occas. producing tubers. Scape to 90cm, solitary, rigid, 3-angled, often compressed. Lvs 3–10mm wide, rigid, bright green, shorter than or exceeding scape. Bracts 4–8, some exceeding infl.; umbel simple or compound; rays 4–10, to 10cm. S Eur. to India. var. *sativa* Boeck. Consistently tuberous. Fls rarely produced. Z8.

C. fertilis Boeck. Scape 4–10cm, 3-angled, compressed. Lvs lanceolate or linear-lanceolate, 8–14mm wide, prominently 3-nerved, v. finely toothed. Bracts 5–7, many times longer than infl.; umbel simple, lax; rays 5–8, 40mm. W Afr. Z10.

C. filicinus Vahl = *Pycreus filicinus*.

C. flabelliformis Rottb. = *C. involucratus*.

C. haspan L. Scape 10–50cm, 3-angled above. Lvs 3–5mm wide, linear, flat, smooth, much shorter than scape. Bracts 2–3, shorter than infl.; umbel compound; rays 4–12, 4–12cm. C Asia. Z8.

C. involucratus Rottb. Scape 0.5–2m, 3-angled to terete, pale green. Bracts 12–28, 6–40×1–8mm, finely grooved, tapering from base, apex pointed; rays 14–32, tapering, slender, 0.5–12cm. Afr., nat. elsewhere. Z9.

C. isocladus Kunth = *C. profiler*.

C. longus L. GALINGALE. Scape 0.6–1.5m, 3-angled, stiff. Lvs 2–3, 2–10mm wide, bright glossy green and grooved above, pale and sharply keeled beneath, margin rough. Bracts 2–6, some exceeding infl. Umbel lax; rays 2–10 to 35mm, brown. Eur., N Amer. Z7.

C. melanorhizus Delile = *C. esculentus*.

C. nuttallii Eddy = *Pycreus filicinus*.

C. papyrus L. PAPYRUS; EGYPTIAN PAPER REED. Scape 2–5m, dark green, bluntly 3-angled. Lvs 0. Bracts 4–10, 15mm wide, exceeded by infl.; umbel compound; rays 100–200, 12–30cm. Afr. Z9.

C. papyrus 'Nanus' = *C. prolifer*.

C. profiler Lam. MINIATURE PAPYRUS. Scape 30–75cm, triangular or round in section. Lvs 0. Bracts v. much shorter than infl. Umbel simple; rays 50–100, 2.5–10mm, slender. S Afr. Z9.

C. sumula hort. = *C. cyperoides*.

C. umbilensis C.B. Clarke ex Will. Wats. Scape 60–90cm, 3-angled, rough above. Lvs 6–8mm, wide, two-thirds scape length, midrib often rough beneath; bracts 4–8, 30–60cm. Umbel large, compound. S Afr. Z9.

C. vegetus Willd. = *C. eragrostis*.

→*Mariscus*, *Pycreus* and *Scirpus*.

Cyperus Sedge *Carex pseudocyperus*.

Cyphanthera Miers. Solanaceae. 9 shrubs. Fls zygomorphic; cal. campanulate to cupular, 5-lobed; cor. funnel-shaped to campanulate, tube striped, lobes 5 spreading. Aus. Z9.

C. albicans (Cunn.) Miers. GREY RAYFLOWER. Erect shrub, to 2.5m+, white-pubesc. Lvs ovate to oblong, to 13cm white young, later to 2.5cm. Fls to 2.5cm, glab. to pubesc. white occas., streaked purple, clustered in compact pan. SE Aus.

→*Anthocercis*.

Cyphomandra Mart. ex Sendt. Solanaceae. 30 herbs, shrubs, vines or trees, closely related to *Solanum*. Fr. a 2-chambered

berry, globose to oblong; seeds numerous. Trop. Amer. Z9.

C. betacea Miers = *C. crassicaulis*.

C. crassicaulis (Ortega) Kuntze. TREE TOMATO; TAMARILLO. Erect pubesc. shrub, to 3m+, sparsely branching. Lvs to 25cm, cordate to ovate, thinly fleshy, entire, apex acuminate. Infl. axillary, cymose, to 15cm; fls long-stalked, buff to pale pink, later tinged green. Fr. to 8cm, edible, ovoid-ellipsoid, brick- to orange-red. Peru, S Braz.

Cyphostemma (Planch.) Alston. Vitaceae. 150 shrubs, climbers and vines. St. usually swollen, caudiciform below with pale, papery, peeling bark; br. ± succulent. Lvs ± fleshy, glab. or felted, usually compound. Fls small, green-white in flat-topped cymes. Fr. a fleshy berry. S & E Afr., Madag. Z9.

C. bainesii (Hook. f.) Descoings. St. swollen, spherical to bottle-shaped, 60×25cm, divided above into thick br. Lvs usually tripartite, lfts 12×5cm, coarsely serrate, green, lanate. Fr. coral-red. Nam.

C. cirrhosa (Thunb.) Descoings. St. succulent, compressed, curved in different directions with tufted hairs. Lvs obovate, sharply serrate. Fr. green, hairy. S Afr.

C. cornigera Descoings. St. 2×0.4m, fleshy, succulent, v. sappy, br. climbing, gland. at first. Lvs tripartite, lfts 4.5–7.5×3.5cm, almost round, crenate, puberulous beneath. SW Cape.

C. cramerana (Schinz). Descoings = *C. currori*.

C. currori (Hook. f.) Descoings. Arborescent; st. 1–4m, thick, conic, branching freely. Lvs tripartite, lfts 15×10cm, ovate to ovate-oblong, coarsely dentate with raised raphides. Fr. yellow-red. W Cape, Nam., Angola.

C. hereroensis (Schinz) Descoings. Caudex thick, tuberous, to 70cm; st. 30–50cm, fleshy, prostrate, flexuous, shortly grey-papillose. Lvs 5–7-partite, lfts 8–10cm, lanceolate, crenate-serrate, grey-papillose beneath. Fr. yellow-green. Nam.

C. juttae (Dinter & Gilg) Descoings. St. 1–2m, pachycaul, conic with several thick br. above. Lvs tripartite; lfts 10–15cm, oval, serrate, glossy green to grey-green, often tinged red, waxy-pruinose, ribs beneath covered with translucent hairs. Fr. dark red or yellow. Nam.: Great Namaqualand. var. *ternatus* Jacobsen. Lfts 30–35cm, narrowing to a 3cm petiole, sharply serrate. Fr. scarlet.

C. laza Descoings. St. 1–2×0.7–1m, narrowly conic, fleshy, br. 3–5m, prostrate to clambering, white-felted when young. Lvs 7–16cm, pinnatifid. Fr. ovoid-globose, 1.5cm. Madag.

C. seitziana (Gilg & Brandt) Descoings = *C. bainesii*.

C. uter (Exell and Mend.) Descoings. Base of st. swollen, spherical to conic, dichotomously branched above, forming a low, broad, tree-like shape. Lvs 5-partite, leathery, lfts almost round, 8cm diam., serrate, prominently ribbed beneath. Fr. green. Angola.

→*Cissus* and *Vitis*.

Cypre *Cordia alliodora*.

Cypress *Chamaecyparis*; *Cupressus*.

Cypress Pine *Callitris*.

Cypress Spurge *Euphorbia cyparissias*.

Cypress Vine *Ipomoea quamoclit*.

Cyprian Plane *Platanus orientalis* var. *insularis*.

Cypripedium L. SLIPPER ORCHID; LADY'S SLIPPER ORCHID; MOCCASIN FLOWER. Orchidaceae. 35 terrestrial, rhizomatous herbaceous orchids. St. erect, slender, basally sheathed. Lvs basal or cauline, prominently veined, usually plicate. Fls 1 or to 12 in a slender-stalked term. rac., subtended by leafy bracts; pet. and dors. sep. free, outspread to erect, narrow-lanceolate to ovate-acute, lat. sep. usually fused in a concave synsepalum; lip strongly inflated, saccate with upper margin involute. N & C Amer., Eur., Asia.

C. acaule Ait. To 40cm. Lvs to 30cm, 2, broad-elliptic, puberulous, plicate-ribbed. Fl. 1; dors. sep. linear-oblong, falling forward, olive green to brown-purple; pet. lanceolate, falcate, olive green to brown-purple; lip v. inflated, oblong, white to deep rose pink. Spring–summer. E N Amer. Z5.

C. album Ait. = *C. reginae*.

C. arietinum R. Br. RAM'S HEAD. To 30cm. Lvs 3–4, elliptic-lanceolate, plicate, to 10cm. Fl. 1; dors. sep. ovate-lanceolate, green veined purple-brown, lat. sep. to 2cm, free, linear-lanceolate, twisted, incurved around lip, green to purple; pet. similar; lip shorter than pet., white veined purple. Late spring–early summer. CE & N US. Z4.

C. calceolus L. LADY'S SLIPPER ORCHID. To 50cm. Lvs 3–4, to 12cm, elliptic to ovate-oblong, prominently veined. Fl. 1; tep. purple-brown, sep. ovate to elliptic-lanceolate, pet. 4–6cm, linear-lanceolate; lip to 3.75cm, bright yellow sometimes spotted red within. Mid spring–mid summer. Eur., Medit. var. *parviflorum* (Salisb.) Fern. Fls 1 or 2, small, dors. sep., ovate-lanceolate, undulate, red to purple-brown, pet. linear-lanceolate, spiralled; lip golden yellow, spotted purple within. Mid spring–late summer. E N Amer. var. *pubescens* (Willd.) Correll. Tep. yellow-green dotted brown, dors. sep. to 8cm, ovate-lanceolate, undulate; pet. to 10cm linear-lanceolate, falcate; lip bright yellow. Spring–summer. N Amer., Jap. Z5.

C. californicum A. Gray. To 120cm. Lvs to 15cm, 5–10, pubesc., elliptic-lanceolate, plicate. Fls yellow-green, 1–12; dors. sep. to 2cm elliptic; pet. to 1.8cm lanceolate, spreading; lip to 1.8cm, white, suffused pink or spotted purple. Mid spring–mid summer. WC US. Z7.

C. debile Rchb. 5–10cm. Lvs to 5cm, ovate-cordate, 2, glossy veins sunken. Fl. 1, 1–2cm diam., solitary, on slender, nodding stalk, pale yellow-green marked red; dors. sep. ovate-lanceolate; pet. narrower, 1–1.5cm; lip to 1cm, green, paler within and veined maroon to garnet. Spring. Jap., China. Z7.

C. fasciculatum Wats. To 20cm. Lvs 5–12cm, elliptic, plicate. Fls to 4, clustered, maroon to green, pendent; dors. sep. 1.5–2cm, ovate-lanceolate, veined purple-brown; pet. ovate; lip dull yellow-green streaked or dappled purple. Mid spring–mid summer. WC & N US. Z8.

C. flavum P. Hunt & Summerh. To 45cm. Lvs 5–23cm, pubesc. Fl 1; tep. clear yellow; lip v. inflated, vivid yellow, dotted or blotched purple-brown. Summer. SW China. Z7.

C. guttatum Sw. To 50cm. Lvs 6–12cm, elliptic to elliptic-ovate, blue-green. Fls 1, white speckled purple; dors. sep. to 3cm, ovate, incurved; pet. oblong, dotted purple, spreading; lip white tinged yellow, spotted lilac. Mid spring–mid summer. Russia, China, Korea, Jap. var. *yatabeanum* (Mak.) Pfitz. St. 10–30cm. Lvs 7–15cm, 2, oblong. Fl. yellow-green chequered brown. Early summer. Jap. Z4.

C. henryi Rolfe. To 60cm. Lvs 10–18cm, 4–5, ovate-oblong, plicate. Fls 2–3, green to yellow-green; dors. sep. 3.5–5cm, ovate, acuminate, incurved; pet. 3.5–4cm, linear, broad, falcate, incurved. Spring. S China. Z7.

C. himalaicum Hemsl. To 30cm. Lvs to 8cm, ovate-elliptic to oblong. Fls to 6cm diam., purple-brown; sep. ovate-oblong, concave; pet. longer, spreading; lip pendent, aperture margins crenate, flushed and veined purple. Summer. Himal. Z5.

C. humile Salisb. = *C. acaule*.

C. irapeanum La Ll. & Lex. To 150cm. Lvs to 15cm, ovate-lanceolate, undulate. Fls bright yellow, 1–8; dors. sep. 3–6cm, ovate-lanceolate; pet. to 6.5cm, oblong; lip golden, spotted or blotched red. Summer–early autumn. Mex. Z8.

C. japonicum Thunb. To 50cm, pubesc. Lvs to 20cm, 2, fan-shaped, plicate. Fl. 1; sep. green spotted purple-maroon at base; pet. to 6cm; lip rose-pink spotted mauve, v. inflated, wrnkled. Early summer. Jap., China. Z8.

C. kentuckiense Reed. Similar to *C. calceolus* except larger. Lvs 5, broad-ovate, apex narrow, twisted. Fl. to 15cm diam., white to pale cream or amber. Late spring. US. Z6.

C. luteum Franch. non Ait. = *C. flavum*.

C. macranthum Sw. To 40cm. Lvs 8–20cm, 3–5, oblong, plicate. Fl. 1, white, veined pale pink; dors. sep. ovate, pointed, incurved; pet. ovate-lanceolate; lip v. inflated, white, lined and tinted rose pink. Early summer. Russia, Jap. var. *speciosum* (Rolfe) Koidz. Fl. pale pink, veined magenta. Early summer. Russia, China, Korea. var. *ventricosum* (Sw.) Rchb. f. Fls to 10cm diam., pale; lat. sep. not wholly fused, exceeding lip. Lip oblong-saccate. Early summer. Jap. Z6.

C. margaritaceum Franch. To 20cm. Lvs to 18cm, 2, broad-elliptic, plicate, spotted purple. Fl. 1, to 5cm diam.; tep. ovate, yellow-green spotted purple, exceeding lip; lip v. inflated, ovoid, tep. pale yellow, glandular-pubesc., spotted purple. Summer. China. Z7.

C. montanum Douglas. To 70cm. Lvs to 6, ovate-lanceolate, plicate. Fls 1–3; dors. sep. 3–6cm, ovate-lanceolate, undulate, suffused purple; pet. 4–7cm, linear-lanceolate, purple, twisted; lip basally veined or suffused pink or purple, interior spotted purple. Late spring–summer. W N Amer. Z5.

C. parviflorum Salisb. = *C. calceolus* var. *parviflorum*.

C. passerinum Richardson. To 35cm. Lvs 5–15cm, ovate-lanceolate, plicate, glandular-pubesc. Fl. 1; dors. sep. 1.5–2cm, suborbicular, concave, yellow-green; pet. to 2cm, linear-oblong, spreading, white; lip to 1.25cm, white sometimes flushed pink, spotted purple within. Summer. W & C N Amer. Z2.

C. pubescens Willd. = *C. calceolus* var. *pubescens*.

C. reginae Walter. SHOWY LADY'S SLIPPER. To 90cm. Lvs 10–25cm, 3–7, ovate-lanceolate, undulate, plicate. Fls 1–4; dors. sep. to 4.5cm, broad-elliptic to orbicular, white; pet. to 5cm, spreading, oblong, white; lip large, v. inflated, pink mottled white. Spring–summer. NE N Amer. var. *album* Ait. Fls cream to ivory. Z4.

C. speciosum Rolfe = *C. macranthum* var. *speciosum*.

C. tibeticum King & Pantl. To 30cm. Lvs to 4.5cm broadly ovate or elliptic, minutely pubesc. Fl. 1, dors. sep. tapering; pet. elliptic, equalling dors. sep. green-yellow streaked and dotted

maroon; lip, conspicuously veined. Summer. Tibet. Z6.

C. yatabeanum Mak. = *C. guttatum* var. *yatabeanum*.

C. yunnanense Franch. Resembles *C. macranthum* but smaller. Lvs elliptic to lanceolate or ovate, acuminate. Fls white, veined pink; pet. lanceolate, acuminate, twisted; lip 2.3–5cm. Summer. China. Z6.

Cyprus Cedar *Cedrus libani*.
Cyprus Turpentine *Pistacia terebinthus*.

Cyrilla Gdn ex L. Cyrillaceae. 1 glab. decid. or everg. shrub or small tree, 1–9m. Lvs 4–10cm, elliptic to obovate or oblanceolate, entire, tapering to base, tapering abruptly to apex or rounded, colouring well in fall. Fls small, white, 5-merous, crowded in slender, cylindric, axillary rac. to 15cm, in horizontal whorls at the base of the previous year's wood. Summer–autumn. SE US to W Indies, S to Braz. Z5.

C. parviflora Raf. = *C. racemiflora*.

C. racemiflora L. LEATHERWOOD; BLACK TITI; MYRTLE.

CYRILLACEAE Endl. 3/14. *Cliftonia, Cyrilla*.

Cyrtandra Forst. & Forst. f. Gesneriaceae. *c*350 shrubs or small trees. Lvs opposite or in whorls. Cymes axillary or cauliflorous on old st., occas. involucrate; cal. fusiform to campanulate, 5-lobed; cor. tube cylindric or barrel-shaped, straight or deflexed, glab. or pubesc., limb 2-lipped, upper lip 2-lobed, lower lip 3-lobed. Malesia and Pacific Is. Z10.

C. pendula Bl. St. creeping or ascending, to 75cm, tetragonal, brown-pilose. Lvs in markedly unequal pairs – large lf ovate-elliptic to ovate-oblong, 13–20cm, glab. above, veins densely pubesc. beneath, smaller lf stipule-like. Cymes axill., few-fld; peduncle rusty-pubesc., to 18cm; cor. white, tinted pink, villous, tube to 4cm. Java.

C. pritchardii Seem. Shrub or small tree to 4m. St. subtetragonal, glab. Lvs to 15cm, long-petiolate, elliptic to ovate, bluntly toothed, bright green above, pale green beneath, glab. Fls 1–3 in axill. cymes; cor. tube to 3cm, slightly incurved, white. Fiji Is.

Cyrtanthera Nees.
C. magnifica Nees = *Justicia carnea*.
C. pohliana var. *obtusior* Nees = *Justicia carnea*.

Cyrtanthus Ait. FIRE LILY. Amaryllidaceae. 47 bulbous perenn. herbs. Lvs linear or strap-shaped. Fls umbellate or solitary, scapose; perianth funnel-shaped, waxy, often fragrant, with a narrow tube, seg. 6, usually spreading at tips, subequal. Trop. Afr., S Afr.

C. angustifolius (L. f.) Ait. FIRE LILY. Everg. Lvs to 45×1.75cm. Scape to 45cm; fls 4–10, pendulous; perianth to 5cm, scarlet, expanding toward bluntly ovate, spreading seg. S Cape.

C. brachyscyphus Bak. DOBO LILY. Everg. Lvs to 25×0.5cm. Scape equalling lvs; fls 6–8; perianth fiery orange red to cinnabar to bright red, to 2.5cm, seg. oblong-lanceolate. S Afr.

C. breviflorus Bak. Decid. or everg. Lvs to 30×1.5cm. Scape to 30cm; fls 2–10; perianth yellow or white, tube to 1cm, seg. to 2cm. S Afr.

C. elatus (Jacq.) Traub. GEORGE LILY; SCARBOROUGH LILY. Everg. Lvs to 60×3cm. Scape to 1m, glaucous; fls 6–9, deep pink or, more commonly, bright scarlet; perianth erect, tube to 3.5cm, tinged green, seg. spreading, to 5×2.5cm. S Afr. 'Albus': fls white.

C. falcatus R.A. Dyer. Decid. Lvs 25×2–3cm, falcate. Scape 25–30cm, recurved and somewhat compressed below umbel; fls 6–10, pendulous; perianth red, tube 4cm, seg. 2cm, obovate-oblong. S Afr.

C. lutescens var. *cooperi* Bak. = *C. mackenii* var. *cooperi*.

C. mackenii Hook. f. IFAFA LILY. Everg. Lvs to 30×1cm. Scape to 30cm; fls 4–10, ivory-white, fragrant; perianth slender, to 5cm. var. *cooperi* (Bak.) R.A. Dyer. Fls yellow to ivory. S Afr.

C. obrienii Bak. Everg. Lvs to 30×1cm. Scape exceeding lvs; fls 7–8; perianth pale or bright scarlet, tube curved, 3.5cm+, seg. ovate, 0.4cm. S Afr.

C. obliquus (L. f.) Ait. Lvs strap-shaped, grey-green, ± twisted. Scape 20–60cm; fls to 12, pendent; perianth to 7cm, tubular, red and yellow.

C. parviflorus Bak. = *C. brachyscyphus*.

C. purpureus (Ait.) Herb. = *C. elatus*.

C. sanguineus (Lindl.) Hook. f. Decid. Lvs to 2.5×2cm. Scape to 25cm; fls 1–3; perianth to 10cm, bright scarlet, tube erect or curved, spreading widely at throat, seg. ovate, to 5cm. E Afr., Natal.

→*Anoiganthus, Gastronema* and *Vallota*.

Cyrtidium Schltr. Orchidaceae. 2 epiphytic orchids allied to *Maxillaria*. Summer. Venez., Colomb. Z10.

C. rhomboglossum (Lehm. & Kränzl.) Schltr. Rhiz. creeping. Pbs globose to ovoid, to 4cm. Lvs strap-shaped, to 10×2cm, apical or overlapping on st. Fls solitary, insect-like, borne in succession; tep. to 2×0.6cm, fleshy, tangerine to ochre, veined chocolate or maroon; lip to 1×0.8cm, sericeous, pale brown marked maroon with buff and violet-black hairs, midlobe minutely ciliate, disc smooth, bronze. Colomb.

Cyrtomium Presl. Dryopteridaceae. 20 terrestrial ferns. Rhiz. ascending to erect, densely scaly. Fronds pinnate, firm; pinnae mostly acuminate, usually falcate, commonly auriculate on anterior side, entire or dentate; stipes tufted. Hawaii, E Asia to S Afr., C & S Amer.
C. caryotideum (Wallich) Presl. Stipes to 40cm. Fronds 20–50×15–22cm; pinnae 8–25×3–7cm, 3–6 pairs, short-petiolate, oblong-ovate to ovate, long-acuminate, finely spine-toothed, usually prominently auricled on anterior side; term. pinnae large, 3- or 2-cleft. China to India, Hawaii. Z9.
C. falcatum (L. f.) Presl. JAPANESE HOLLY FERN. Stipes to 40cm. Fronds 20–60×10–25cm, lustrous, firmly coriaceous; pinnae 7–13×2.5–5cm, 3–11 pairs, short-stalked, ovate to oblong-ovate, apex acuminate, subentire, base rounded to broadly cuneate, oblique, falcate, with rufous scales when young. China, Malaysia, Taiwan, India to E & S Afr., Hawaii. Z9.
C. fortunei J. Sm. Stipes to 30cm. Fronds 30–60×10–15cm; pinnae 5–7×1–3cm, 12–26 pairs, subsessile, broadly lanceolate to narrowly ovate-oblong, gradually attenuate, subentire to minutely dentate, usually auriculate on anterior side, with hair-like scales when young. S & E China to Jap. & Korea. Z6.
C. juglandifolium (Humb. & Bonpl. ex Willd.) Moore = *Phanerophlebia juglandifolia*.
C. macrophyllum (Mak.) Tag. Stipes to 30cm. Fronds 20–50×15–25cm; pinnae 2–8 pairs, 10–20×4–7cm, uppermost short-stalked, ovate to oblong-ovate, abruptly acuminate, usually rounded at base, slightly unequal, subentire or mucronate-dentate, lower pinnae larger, term. entire or 3-cleft. China to Himal., Jap., Taiwan. Z8.
C. macrosorum (Bak.) Morton = *Phanerophlebia macrosora*.
→*Aspidium*, *Phanerophlebia* and *Polystichum*.

Cyrtopodium R. Br. Orchidaceae. 30 terrestrial or epiphytic orchids. Pbs thick, narrow-ellipsoid to cane-like, usually sheathed with bracts and sharp, dried lf bases. Lvs in 2 ranks, alt., linear-lanceolate, arching, somewhat grass-like in texture, ribbed or loosely plicate. Rac. erect to arching, exceeding lvs, produced with new growth, often branching; fls fleshy; tep. usually lanceolate-obovate, clawed, crispate and undulate, reflexed; lip rigid, strongly 3-lobed, crispate and often verrucose. Summer. Braz., Guyana, Venez., W Indies. Z10.
C. aliciae Lind. & Rolfe. Differs from *C. punctatum* in fls to 2.25cm diam., lip with reduced midlobe. Braz., Parag.
C. andersonii (Lamb. ex Andrews) R. Br. Pbs to 1.2m. Lvs to 75cm. Fls to 5cm diam., fragrant, fleshy; sep. bronze-yellow tinged green; pet. lemon yellow flushed lime green at apex; lip lemon yellow, disc golden to apricot. W Indies to Braz.
C. elegans Hamilt. = *Tetramicra canaliculata*.
C. punctatum (L.) Lindl. Pbs to 1m. Lvs to 75cm. Fls to 4cm diam.; sep. ochre, mottled and spotted maroon; lip midlobe truncate, crispate or ragged, maroon or amethyst with golden centre, lat. lobes reniform, erect, dark rust-brown. S Flor., W Indies, C & S Amer. to Arg.
C. virescens Rchb. f. & Warm. Pbs to 10cm. Lvs to 45cm. Fls to 4.75cm diam., spreading, bronze-green spotted chocolate; lip oxblood. Braz., Parag., Urug.

Cyrtorchis Schltr. Orchidaceae. 16 epiphytic monopodial orchids. Lvs tough, leathery or fleshy, 2-ranked. Rac. arising from st. or among lvs; fls 2-ranked, white to ivory, turning apricot with age, often scented, spurred; tep. triangular-lanceolate. Trop. and S Afr. Z9.
C. arcuata (Lindl.) Schltr. Lvs to 24×5cm, oblong or ligulate. Rac. to 18cm; all perianth parts lanceolate, acuminate, spreading, sep. 28–45mm, pet. 24–26mm, lip similar to pet.; spur 3–10.5cm, tapering, straight to sigmoid.
C. chailluana (Hook. f.) Schltr. Lvs 8–25×2–3.5cm, oblong. Rac. 15–24cm; all perianth parts triangular-lanceolate, acuminate, recurved; sep. 30–50mm; pet. slightly shorter and narrower; lip like pet. but slightly broader; spur 9–15cm, tapering. Nigeria, Cameroun, Gabon, Zaire, Uganda.
C. crassifolia Schltr. Lvs to 3×1cm, succulent, glaucous. Rac. 4cm; fls not opening wide; all perianth parts triangular-lanceolate, acute, sep. 14mm, pet. 10mm, lip 10mm; spur 1–2cm long, ± sigmoid. C Afr.
C. hamata (Rolfe) Schltr. Differs from *C. arcuata* in narrower lvs, slightly smaller fls with slender green spur hooked to rolled at tip. Ghana, Nigeria.

C. monteiroae (Rchb. f.) Schltr. Lvs 5–20×1.5–5cm, oblong-elliptic or oblanceolate. Rac. to 30cm; all perianth parts lanceolate, recurved, sep. 10–12mm, pet. slightly shorter, lip 8–10mm; spur 2.5–4.5cm, green or orange. W Afr., Zaire, Uganda, Angola.
C. praetermissa Summerh. Lvs 6–9×1cm, ligulate, thick, conduplicate. Rac. pendent; all perianth seg. triangular-lanceolate, recurved, sep. 8×3mm, pet. slightly shorter and narrower, lip 7–8×4mm; spur 3–4cm, slightly curved. Zaire to Uganda, S to Moz. and S Afr.
C. sedenii (Rchb. f.) Schltr. = *C. arcuata*.
→*Angraecum* and *Listrostachys*.

Cyrtosperma Griff. Araceae. 11 tuberous or rhizomatous marginal or aquatic herbs. Lvs to 60cm, hastate or sagittate; petioles long, warty or spiny. Peduncle prickly, shorter than petioles; spathe ovate-lanceolate, occas. twisted, sometimes convolute at base to form tube; spadix short, adnate to spathe or sessile, completely covered by hermaphrodite fls. Fr. a berry. New Guinea, SE Asia. Z10.
C. ferox L. Lind. & N.E. Br. = *C. merkusii*.
C. johnstonii (Bull) N.E. Br. Lvs to 60×45cm, oblong-sagittate, lobes equal, olive-green with pink veins above, coppery-black beneath; petiole to 1m+, mottled dark violet and rose, spines upward-pointing, clustered. Spathe to 17cm, incurved, brown to purple or dark violet. Solomon Is.
C. merkusii (Hassk.) Schott. Rhiz. short and slender to massive, weighing to 70kg. Lvs to 130×80cm, sagittate or hastate, lobes unequal; petioles to 3m, unarmed or with stout conical spines. Spathe to 30cm, erect to reflexed, white to green or purple. Malaysia to Papuasia, Oceania; widely cult.
→*Alocasia*.

Cyrtostachys Bl. Palmae. 9 palms. St. erect, smooth, ringed, solitary or clustered. Crownshaft distinct, waxy. Lvs pinnate; petiole channelled above, convex, or angled beneath; pinnae single-fold, regularly spaced along rachis, often rigid, midvein clothed with ramenta beneath. New Guinea, Solomon Is., Sumatra, Malaysia, Borneo. Z10.
C. lakka Becc. SEALING-WAX PALM; MAHARAJAH PALM; LIPSTICK PALM. St. clustered, to 10m, slender. Lvs to 1.5m; sheath, petiole and rachis glossy scarlet; pinnae 50 per side, to 45×3.75cm, grey-blue beneath. Malay Penins., Borneo, Sumatra. 'Duvivierana': crownshaft, petiole and rachis bright red.
C. renda Bl. = *C. lakka*.

Cyrtostylis R. Br. Orchidaceae. 1 terrestrial orchid. St. 5–19cm. Lf 1.5–4cm, solitary, orbicular-cordate. Fls 1–7 in term. rac., red-brown, rarely green; dors. sep. to 15mm, linear-lanceolate, incurved, lateral sep. and pet. spreading, linear; lip to 15mm, broad-oblong, with two dark basal protrusions. Spring–autumn. SE Aus. Z9.
C. reniformis R. Br.
→*Acianthus*.

Cystanthe Spach.
C. sprengelioides R. Br. = *Richea sprengelioides*.

Cysticapnos Mill.
C. africanus Gaertn. = *Corydalis vesicaria*.

Cystopteris Bernh. BLADDER FERN. Woodsiaceae. 18 small, ferns. Rhiz. short to creeping, with soft, brown scales. Fronds erect, delicate, 2–4-pinnate. Sori round with membranous indusia. Cosmop.
C. alpina (Roth) Desv. Resembling *C. fragilis*. Fronds to 20cm, oblong-lanceolate, 3-pinnatifid, largest pinna about 2.5–4×1cm, deltoid-lanceolate, pinnules ovate-rhomboid, slightly toothed. Eur., Asia Minor. Z6.
C. bulbifera (L.) Bernh. BERRY BLADDER FERN; BULBLET BLADDER FERN. Fronds to 75×13cm, linear-lanceolate or ovate-lanceolate, 2-pinnate, pinnae 20–40 pairs, lowest pair largest, pinnules 5–8cm, lanceolate, seg. linear-oblong, slightly toothed, bearing bulbils in axils of upper pinnae. N Amer. Z5.
C. dickieana Sim. Resembling *C. fragilis*. Lvs to 13cm, pinnae deflexed, overlapping, pinnules broad, obtuse, overlapping, crenate to crenately lobed. Eur. Z6.
C. fragilis (L.) Bernh. BRITTLE BLADDER FERN; BRITTLE FERN; FRAGILE FERN. Rhiz. short, much-branched. Fronds to 45cm, 2–3-pinnate, membranous, 4.5–30×2–10cm, oblong-lanceolate to ovate-lanceolate, acute or acuminate, pinnae to 5cm, about 30, ovate-lanceolate to oblong-lanceolate, 1–2-pinnate; pinnules not overlapping, ovate to oblong, decurrent, the lower larger, deeply pinnatifid to pinnately toothed, seg. acutely or obtusely toothed; stipe dark, fragile. Temp. N Hemis., S to Chile. Z2.

C. montana (Lam.) Desv. MOUNTAIN BLADDER FERN. Rhiz. creeping, little-branched. Fronds to 40cm, 3-pinnate, deltoid, deep green, sparsely gland.; pinnae *c*26, to 10cm, triangular-ovate, acute; pinnules to *c*5cm, ovate to oblong, base cuneate, pinnately lobed or pinnatifid, seg. usually apically bidentate and often with 1–2 teeth on margins. N hemis. Z4.

C. protrusa (Weatherby) Blasdell. LOWLAND FRAGILE FERN. Similar to *C. fragilis*, but with growing point prolonged beyond lf tuft; lowest pinnules of the larger pinnae cuneate at base, stalked. US. Z6.

C. regia (L.) Desv. = *C. alpina*.

C. spinulosum Maxim. = *Athyrium spinulosum*.

C. sudetica A. Braun & Milde. Differs from *C. montana* in lamina ovate-deltate, yellow-green, pinnae oblong-lanceolate. Eur. Z6.

C. ×tennesseensis Shaver. (*C. protrusa* ×*C. bulbifera*.) TENNESSEE BLADDER FERN. Fronds to 40cm, narrowly deltoid to sublanceolate, to 14cm wide at the base, acuminate, 1–2-pinnate, glab., pinnae to 7.5cm, deltoid to lanceolate, acute to acuminate, pinnate to pinnatifid, shortly stalked, seg. ovate or oblong, obtuse or acute, serrulate, bearing bulbils in or near axils of pinnae. US. Z6.

Cytisanthus Lang.

C. horridus (Vahl) Gams = *Genista horrida*.

C. radiatus Lang = *Genista radiata*.

Cytisophyllum Lang. Leguminosae. 1 decid. ascending shrub to 2m. Br. long, glab., flushed red at first. Lvs trifoliolate, ± sessile; lfts 0.8–2cm, obovate to broadly elliptic, pale green, glab. Rac. erect, term., 3–12-fld; fls pea-like, yellow, standard 11mm, suborbicular. Late spring–early summer. It., S Fr., E Spain.

C. sessilifolium (L.) Lang.
→*Cytisus*.

Cytisus L. BROOM. Leguminosae (Papilionoideae). 33 everg. or decid. shrubs, or small trees. Br. frequently ribbed. Lvs trifoliolate, more rarely simple or unifoliolate. Fls pea-like, in term. rac. or packed on axill. short shoots. N Afr., W Asia, Eur., Canary Is.

C. adamii Poit. = +*Laburnocytisus adamii*.

C. albus (Lam.) Link non Hacq. = *C. multiflorus*.

C. albus Hacq. non (Lam.) Link = *Chamaecytisus albus*.

C. alpinus Mill. = *Laburnum alpinum*.

C. ardoinii Fourn. Prostrate, decid. shrub, 20–60cm. Young br. pubesc., ridged, winged. Lvs 3-foliolate, lfts 4–10mm, obovate or oblong, pubesc. above. Fls rich yellow, axill., solitary or grouped 1–3 on short stalks; standard orbicular, 8–12mm. Spring. SW Alps, S Fr. 'Cottage': habit dense and clump-forming, to 40cm high; growth green tinted grey; fls creamy yellow. Z7.

C. austriacus L. = *Chamaecytisus austriacus*.

C. austriacus var. *heuffelii* (Wierzb. ex Griseb. & Schenk) C. Schneid. = *Chamaecytisus heuffelii*.

C. battandieri Maire = *Argyrocytisus battandieri*.

C. ×beanii Dallim. (*C. ardoinii* ×*C. purgans*.) Semi-procumbent, decid. shrub, to 40cm. Br. terete, hirsute when young. Lvs 12mm, linear, simple, hirsute. Fls rich yellow, axillary, single, paired or in 3's. Spring. Gdn origin. Z5.

C. biflorens Host = *Chamaecytisus supinus*.

C. biflorus L'Hérit. = *Chamaecytisus ratisbonensis*.

C. canariensis (L.) Kuntze = *Genista canariensis*.

C. candicans Lam. = *Genista canariensis*.

C. capitatus Scop. pro parte. = *Chamaecytisus rochelii*.

C. capitatus Scop. pro parte. = *Chamaecytisus supinus*.

C. caramanicus Nyman = *Podocytisus caramanicus*.

C. ×dallimorei Rolfe. (*C. multiflorus* ×*C. scoparius*.) Erect shrub to 2.4m, similar to *C. scoparius*. Lvs usually 3-foliolate, lfts to 19mm, elliptic to oblanceolate, pubesc. when young. Fls pink or mauve, solitary or paired, axill.; standard *c*16mm, roughly orbicular, wings crimson. Spring. Gdn origin. 'Lena': fls lemon yellow and cream, wings ruby-red. 'Lilac Time': dwarf; fls deep red tinted purple. 'Munstead': fls small, white flushed lilac, wings and buds purple. Z6.

C. decumbens (Dur.) Spach. Ascending or prostrate shrub, 10–30cm. Br. pubesc. when young. Lvs 6–20mm, simple, oblong to obovate, pubesc. Fls grouped 1–3, vivid yellow; standard 10–14mm, ovate. Late spring–early summer. S Eur. Z5.

C. demissus Boiss. = *Chamaecytisus hirsutus*.

C. elongatus Waldst. & Kit. = *Chamaecytisus glaber*.

C. emeriflorus Rchb. Dense shrub, prostrate to erect, 30–70cm, stiffly branched. Lvs 3-foliolate, lfts 10–20mm, obovate to lanceolate, sericeous beneath. Fls yellow, in 1–4-fld term. rac.; standard 10–12mm. Late spring–early summer. N It., Switz. Z6.

C. filipes (Webb & Berth.) Masf. Small shrub. Br. narrow, dense, spindly. Lfts oblanceolate to thinly obovate, subglabrous. Fls axill., single or paired, white, scented. Late winter–early spring. Canary Is. Z9.

C. fontanesii Spach. Shrub, 20–50cm, erect or ascending. Lvs 3-foliolate, lfts 4–9mm, linear, adpressed-pubesc. Fls yellow, usually grouped 2–4; standard 8–12mm, cordate. Spring. S & E Spain, Balearic Is. Z8.

C. fragrans Lam. = *C. supranubius*.

C. glaber L. f. = *Chamaecytisus glaber*.

C. glabrescens Sartorelli = *C. emeriflorus*.

C. grandiflorus (Brot.) DC. WOOLLY-PODDED BROOM. Shrub, ascending or erect, 2–3m. Young growth grey-pubesc. Lvs 1- and 3-foliolate (on young and mature twigs respectively), glab., caducous, lfts 6–12mm, obovate to elliptic-lanceolate. Fls vivid yellow, solitary or paired in leafy infl.; standard 18–25mm diam. Spring. S & C Port., S Spain. Z8.

C. hirsutus L. = *Chamaecytisus hirsutus*.

C. hirsutus ssp. *ciliatus* (Wahlenb.) Asch. & Gräbn. = *Chamaecytisus ciliatus*.

C. hispanicus hort. = *Genista hispanica*.

C. humifusus Nyman = *C. decumbens*.

C. ingramii Blakelock. Erect, thick-branched shrub to 2m. Br. pubesc. when young. Lvs 1–3-foliolate, lfts 20–30mm, elliptic-oblong to obovate, sericeous beneath. Fls axill., solitary; standard 22–23mm, cream-white, keel and wings yellow. Summer. N Spain. Z7.

C. ×kewensis Bean (*C. ardoinii* ×*C. multiflorus*.) Prostrate shrub, to 30cm, sometimes 1.8m diam. Lvs usually 3-trifoliolate, lfts pubesc., linear-oblong. Fls pale yellow or cream-white, single or grouped 2–3; standard 12mm diam. Late spring. Gdn origin. Z6.

C. leucanthus Waldst. & Kit. = *Chamaecytisus albus*.

C. linifolius (L.) Lam. = *Genista linifolia*.

C. maderensis Masf. = *Genista maderensis*.

C. monspessulanus L. = *Genista monspessulana*.

C. multiflorus (L'Hérit. ex Ait.) Sweet. WHITE SPANISH BROOM. Erect, many-branched shrub, 2–3m. Br. spindly; shoots striped, initially velvety later glab. Lvs 3-foliolate, lfts to 1cm, linear, silver-velvety. Fls white, 1–3 in bundles; standard 9–12mm. Late spring–early summer. Port., Spain. 'Albus': fls pure white. 'Durus': v. hardy. 'Pallidus': fls tinted yellow. 'White Gem': fls white, abundant. 'Toome's Variety': fls white faintly tinted pink, early-flowering; probably a hybrid involving *C. multiflorus*. Z6.

C. nigricans L. Erect shrub, 0.5–1.5m. Shoots slender, hirsute. Lvs 3-foliolate, lfts 10–30mm, oblong to obovate, deep green above, thinly pubesc. beneath. Fls yellow, in term., sericeous rac., 8–20cm long; standard 7–10mm. Summer. SE & C Eur. 'Cyni': habit dense and compact. Z5.

C. palmensis (Christ) Hutch. = *Chamaecytisus palmensis*.

C. perezii Hutch. = *Chamaecytisus proliferus* var. *perezii*.

C. ×praecox Wheeler ex Bean. (*C. multiflorus* ×*C. purgans*.) WARMINSTER BROOM. Similar to *C. multiflorus*, but with denser branchlets. Shrub, 70–150m. Br. slender, ash-green. Lvs 8–20mm, generally 1-foliolate, sericeous, caducous, lanceolate to linear-spathulate. Fls pale yellow, 1 or 2 in axils, numerous, small. Spring. Gdn origin. The typical clone is a small shrub with masses of creamy yellow fls. It has been named 'Warminster'. Other cvs include – 'Albus': fls white, abundant. 'Allgold': br. arching; fls deep gold, abundant, long-lasting. 'Frisia': habit wide; fls white, tinted purple, tinted pink inside. 'Goldspear' ('Goldspear', Canary Bird'): from a back cross of *C. ×praecox* and *C. purgans*; weak-growing; fls small, rich gold, abundant. 'Hollandia': fls pink-red, keel bordered off-white, wings cherry red. 'Kathleen Ferrier': habit elegant; fls cream. 'Luteus': habit dwarf. 'Osbornii' (possibly *C. ×praecox* ×*C. ×dallimorei*): fls faintly scented, late-flowering. 'Sneeuwwitje' (*C. ×praecox* ×*C. ×dallimorei*): habit bushy, broad and low; fls snow-white, late-flowering. 'Zeelandia' (*C. ×praecox* ×*C. ×beanii*): habit bushy; fls cream, sometimes lilac, wings tinted pink and cream, late-flowering. 'Zitronenregen' (*C. ×praecox* ×*C. ×beanii*): habit compact, to 1.5m; fls clear yellow, profuse. Z5.

C. procumbens (Willd.) Spreng. Prostrate, erect or decumbent shrub, 20–40cm. Br. terete, adpressed hairy. Young shoots rugose. Lvs 12–32mm, simple, oblong-lanceolate, pungent, adpressed villous beneath. Fls rich yellow, in cylindrical, leafy rac. 7.5–15cm; standard 12–15mm. Late spring–summer. SE Eur. Z5.

C. proliferus L. f. = *Chamaecytisus proliferus*.

C. prostratus Scop. = *Chamaecytisus supinus*.

C. pubescens Gilib. non Moench = *Chamaecytisus supinus*.

C. pubescens Moench non Gilib. = *Genista monspessulana*.

C. purgans (L.) Spach. Ascending or erect shrub, 30–100cm. Br. many, rigid, furrowed. Young shoots pubesc. Lvs 1-foliolate (lower 3-foliolate), caducous, lfts 6–12mm, oblanceolate, spathulate to linear-lanceolate, sericeous beneath. Fls rich yellow, fragrant, 1–2 per axil; standard 10–12mm. Spring–early summer. S Eur., N Afr. 'Aleida': elegant; fls v. profuse. Z5.

C. purpureus Scop. = *Chamaecytisus purpureus.*

C. racemosus hort. ex Marnock = *Genista ×spachiana.*

C. radiatus Koch = *Genista radiata.*

C. ramentaceus Sieber = *Petteria ramentacea.*

C. ratisbonensis Schaeff. = *Chamaecytisus ratisbonensis.*

C. rochelii Wierzb. = *Chamaecytisus rochelii.*

C. schipkaensis Dieck = *Chamaecytisus albus.*

C. scoparius (L.) Link. COMMON BROOM; SCOTCH BROOM. Erect shrub to 2m. Br. many, slender, green, glab. or sericeous at first. Lvs generally trifoliolate, lfts 6–20mm, thinly hirsute or glab., elliptic to obovate. Fls rich yellow, 1 or 2 per axil; standard 16–18mm diam. Late spring–early summer. Eur. Z5. ssp. *maritimus* (Rouy) Heyw. (var. *prostratus* (C. Bailey) A.B. Jacks). Dwarf spreading; fls large, golden. There are over 80 cvs and hybrids derived from *C. scoparius*, the crosses often involving *C. multiflorus* or *C. ×dallimorei*. Habit from low to slender or upright; lvs light green to white bordered; fls off-white through yellow to red to brown. 'Andreanus': fls marked brown crimson. 'Burkwoodii': standard carmine, wings rusty red edged gold. 'Cornish Cream': fls off-white, wings and keel cream. 'Diana': habit low; standard ivory, wings gold. 'Donard Gem': fls pink flushed red, profuse. 'Dragonfly': standard rich yellow, keel vibrant yellow, wings brown. 'Firefly': fls yellow, wings spotted rusty red. 'Golden Sunlight': fls large, clear yellow.

'Killiney Red' fls rich red, wings burgundy. 'Lord Lambourne': fls pale cream, outside flushed lilac, wings carmine edged gold. 'Moonlight': low and mounding; fls soft yellow, nodding. 'Radiance': standard and keel white, wings brown. 'Red Wings': standard and wings crimson, keel lilac. 'Sulphureus': fls cream, tinged red in bud, wing and keel sulphur. 'Variegatus': lvs tinted grey, edged white. 'Windlesham Ruby': fls large, ruby red.

C. sessilifolius L. = *Cytisophyllum sessilifolium.*

C. spachianus Kuntze = *Genista ×spachiana.*

C. stenopetalus (Webb) Christ = *Genista stenopetala.*

C. supinus L. = *Chamaecytisus supinus.*

C. supranubius (L. f.) Kuntze. TENERIFE BROOM. Erect shrub, 2–3m. Br. rigid, blue-green, initially pubesc. Lvs 3-foliolate, lfts 4–8mm, narrowly lanceolate to oblanceolate, caducous. Fls fragrant, white and pink tinged, 3–6 per axil, standard 8mm, obovate. Late spring. Canary Is. Z9.

C. sylvestris var. *pungens* Vis. = *Genista sylvestris.*

C. tenera Jacq. = *Genista tenera.*

C. tommasinii Vis. = *Chamaecytisus tommasinii.*

C. uralensis hort. ex Ledeb. = *Chamaecytisus ratisbonensis.*

C. ×versicolor (Kirchn.) Dipp. = *Chamaecytisus ×versicolor.*

C. villarsii Vis. = *Genista villarsii.*

C. virgatus Vukot. = *Genista tinctoria.*

C. weldenii Vis. = *Petteria ramentacea.*

→*Chamaecytisus, Chronanthus, Lembotropis* and *Spartocytisus.*

D

Daboecia D. Don. Ericaceae. 2 low, everg. shrubs, to 50cm. Lvs elliptic, 5–10mm, revolute, with scattered, gland-tipped bristles. Infl. terminal, nodding, loosely racemose; cor. to 12mm, 4-lobed; sta. 8. W Eur. to Azores, but not GB.

D. azorica Tutin & E.F. Warb. Dwarf. Lvs narrow, dark green above, silver-grey beneath. Fls campanulate, ruby red. Summer. Azores. Z8.

D. cantabrica (Huds.) K. Koch. CONNEMARA HEATH; ST. DABOEC'S HEATH. Straggling, to 50cm. Lvs dark green, silver-tomentose beneath. Fls strongly urceolate, rose-purple. Summer–early autumn. 'Alba': fls white. 'Atropurpurea' fls dark rose-purple. 'Bicolor': white, magenta and striped fls often on a single rac. 'David Moss': fls white. 'Donald Pink': v. pale pink, floriferous. 'Heather Yates': fls amethyst. 'Porter's Variety': dwarf, compact; fls small, magenta, narrow. 'Praegerae': dwarf, spreading; fls dark pink, narrowed. 'Snowdrift': fls white. Z6.

D. Scotica group. 'Bearsden': fls deep lilac-pink. 'Jack Drake': fls ruby. 'William Buchanan': v. floriferous, crimson.

D. polifolia (Juss.) D. Don = D. cantabrica.
→Menziesiá.

Dacrycarpus (Endl.) Laub. Podocarpaceae. 9 everg. coniferous shrubs or trees. Lvs spirally arranged, dimorphic; juvenile lvs falcate, bilaterally flattened, twisted at base to appear distichous; adult lvs short-subulate to scale-like. Juvenile and adult foliage often mixed. ♂ cones axill., cylindric to ovoid. ♀ cones subtended by involucral lvs; receptacle fleshy, warty, red. Malaysia & Philipp. to New Caledonia & Fiji, also NZ, N Is.

D. dacrydioides (A. Rich.) Laub. NEW ZEALAND DACRYBERRY; KAHIKATEA. Tree to 65m; bark brown suffused grey; br. drooping. Juvenile lvs to 6mm, green, tinged gold or red in winter; adult lvs to 2mm, imbricate, scale-like, keeled. NZ. Z9.

D. imbricatus (Bl.) Laub. JAVA DACRYBERRY. Tree to 30m+; bark dark brown to black, br. pendulous or spreading. Juvenile lvs to 17mm; adult lvs to 2mm, lanceolate, mucronate, imbricate. SE Asia to W Pacific. Z10.
→Podocarpus.

Dacrydium Sol. ex Forst. Podocarpaceae. 30 everg. trees or shrubs. Lvs linear to subulate when young; scale-like, adpressed, clothing branchlets, imbricate, and keeled on mature trees. ♂ cones axill., cylindric; ♀ cones terminal, erect; scales few. Seed on a cup-like fleshy receptacle. Subtrop. SE Asia, NZ, W Pacific Is.

D. araucarioides Brongn. & Griseb. Tree to 6m+. Crown candelabra-shaped; twigs short, cylindric, tinged purple when in fr. Juvenile lvs to 13mm, incurved; adult lvs linear, to 5×2mm, blunt. New Caledonia. Z10.

D. beccarii Parl. Shrub to 4m or tree to 35m. Bark smooth, fissured, brown; br. erect. Juvenile lvs to 2cm; adult lvs acicular, to 10×1mm, triangular or rhombic in section. SE Asia, Pacific. Z10.

D. beccarii var. **kinabaluense** Wasscher = D. gibbsiae.
D. beccarii var. **subulatum** Comm. = D. beccarii.
D. bidwillii Hook. f. ex Kirk = Halocarpus bidwillii.
D. biforme (Hook.) Pilger = Halocarpus biformis.
D. colensoi T. Kirk non Hook. = Halocarpus biformis.
D. colensoi Hook. non T. Kirk = Lagarostrobus colensoi.
D. cupressinum Sol. ex Forst. RED PINE; RIMU. Tree, to 40m. Crown slender conic, becoming rounded. Bark rust-brown or grey, branchlets long, narrow, weeping. Juvenile lvs to 6mm, dark green; adult lvs to 3mm. NZ. Z9.

D. elatum (Roxb.) Wallich. Tree to 30m+. Crown conic, becoming rounded; bark brown tinged red. Juvenile lvs to 12mm; adult lvs to 2×1mm, obtuse to subacute. Thail. to Vietnam, Malaysia, Philipp., Indon. Z10.

D. falciforme (Parl.) Pilger = Falcatifolium falciforme.
D. fonkii (Philippi) Benth. & Hook. f. = Lepidothamnus fonkii.
D. franklinii Hook. f. = Lagarostrobus franklinii.
D. gibbsiae Stapf. Tree to 10m+ or shrub to 2m. Twigs whip-like, to 8mm diam. including lvs. Juvenile lvs to 20mm, falcate; adult lvs to 7×2mm, flattened. Sarawak. Z10.

D. intermedium T. Kirk = Lepidothamnus intermedius.
D. junghuhnii Miq. = D. elatum.
D. kinabaluense (Wasscher) Laub. = D. gibbsiae.
D. kirkii F. Muell. ex Parl. non T. Kirk = Halocarpus kirkii.
D. laxifolium Hook. f. = Lepidothamnus laxifolius.

D. novo-guineense Gibbs. Tree to 10m. Br. rigid, ascending. Lvs acicular, triangular to lanceolate, to 12×1mm. Indon., Celebes, Moluccas, New Guinea. Z10.

D. pierrei Hickel = D. elatum.
D. taxoides Brongn. & Griseb. = Falcatifolium taxoides.
D. ustum Vieill. = Parasitaxus ustus.
D. westlandicum T. Kirk = Lagarostrobus colensoi.

Dactylis L. Gramineae. 1 perenn. grass to 1.5m. St. tufted. Lvs to 45cm, linear, flat or inrolled, green to grey-green; ligules papery, to 12mm; sheaths compressed. Infl. spicate, to 20cm, green-purple to yellow; spikelets short-stipitate, laterally compressed, in dense fascicles at br. apices, to 1cm. Summer to autumn. Eur., N Afr., temp. Asia. Z5.

D. glomerata L. COCKSFOOT; ORCHARD GRASS. 'Elegantissima': dwarf, hummock-forming, to 15cm; lvs striped white. 'Variegata': to 25cm; lvs striped green and white.

Dactylopsis N.E. Br. Aizoaceae. 2 dwarf, v. succulent perennials. Lvs cylindric, thick, enclosed by withered, papery sheath in dormant season. Fls solitary, white. S Afr. (Cape Prov.). Z9.

D. digitata (Ait.) N.E. Br. Forming dense mats. Lvs 8–12×2–2.5cm, digitately arranged, blunt, grey. Fls 15–20mm diam. W Cape.

D. littlewoodii L. Bol. Much smaller than D. digitata; st. producing stilt-like roots. Lvs variable, to 2.8×1.3cm, compressed, long-ovoid. Fls 14mm diam. W Cape.
→Mesembryanthemum.

Dactylorhiza Nevski. Orchidaceae. 30 tuberous terrestrial orchids. Lvs linear to lanceolate, sometimes spotted purple. Fls in subcylindric to rounded spikes with leaflike bracts; lat. sep., spreading dors. sep., forming a hood with pet.; lip entire or trilobed, spurred. Eur., Asia, N Amer., N Afr.

D. aristata (Fisch.) Soó. 10–40cm. Lvs sometimes spotted. Spike dense, fl. colour variable, usually maroon; lip trilobed to 25mm, spotted dark purple, spur to 25mm. Spring–mid summer. Jap., Korea, N Amer. Z7.

D. elata (Poir.) Soó. ROBUST MARSH ORCHID. 30–110cm. Spike lax or dense; fls pink to maroon; lip entire or trilobed. Spring–mid summer. Medit. Z6.

D. fistulosa (Moench) H. Baumann = D. majalis.
D. foliosa (Sol. ex Verm.) Soó. MADEIRAN ORCHID. 40–60cm. Spike dense; fls pink to light maroon; lat. sep. twisted; lip midlobe spreading, lanceolate; spur slender, long. Late spring–early summer. Madeira. Z7.

D. fuchsii (Druce) Soó. COMMON SPOTTED ORCHID. 20–60cm. Lvs spotted. Fl. pale pink to white or mauve spotted or lined deep red or purple; lip deeply trilobed. Late spring–early summer. Eur. Z6.

D. iberica (Willd.) Soó. 20–60cm. Spike ovoid or cylindric, lax; fls rose pink, spotted purple or magenta; lip flabellate, minutely pubesc., apical portion narrowly triangular, spur narrow, slender, marked white at base. Late spring–late summer. Eur., Asia, Middle E. Z7.

D. incarnata (L.) Soó. EARLY MARSH ORCHID. 15–80cm. Spike dense; fls pale rose, pink, cream or purple; lip entire or trilobed, revolute, with 1 or 2 inner patterns of red spots. Spring. Medit. Z7.

D. latifolia (L.) Soó = D. majalis.
D. maculata L. (Soó). 15–60cm. Lvs plain or spotted. Spike dense; fls white, rose-pink, red or mauve; sep. spreading or incurved; lip midlobe shorter, narrower than lat., marked deep purple, spur cylindric, shorter than or equalling ovary. Mid spring–late summer. Eur. Z6.

D. maculata ssp. **fuchsii** (Druce) Hylander = D. fuchsii.
D. maderensis hort. = D. foliosa.
D. majalis (Rchb. f.) P. Hunt & Summerh. BROAD-LEAVED MARSH ORCHID. 20–75cm. Lvs plain or spotted. Spike dense; sep. lilac to magenta, ovate-oblong, spreading, reflexed; lip spotted white and streaked purple, lat. lobes broad, midlobe smaller, triangular. Late spring–mid summer. C Eur., W Russia. Z6.

D. praetermissa (Druce) Soó. SOUTHERN MARSH ORCHID. 20–70cm. Spike dense, fls pale garnet; lip 10–14mm, spotted and streaked purple, lobes 3, shallow, equal. Summer. NW Eur., S GB. Z6.

D. purpurella (T. & T.A. Stephenson) Soó. NORTHERN MARSH ORCHID. To 40cm. Lvs often spotted toward apex. Fls pale claret to maroon; lip 10–14mm, shallowly trilobed or subentire, with central cluster of purple spots and lines. Mid–late summer. NW Eur., N GB. Z6.

D. romana (Sebast. & Mauri) Soó. 15–35cm. Fls yellow; lip mid-lobe oblong-rectangular, exceeding laterals, spur 12–25mm. Spring–summer. SW Eur. Z8.

D. saccifera (Brongn.) Soó. 30–50cm. Spike lax; fls pink; lat. sep. to 10mm, spreading; lip equally trilobed, spotted deep red, spur 7–13mm. Late spring–mid-summer. Medit. Z7.

D. sambucina (L.) Soó. ELDERFLOWER ORCHID. 10–30cm. Fls yellow or magenta, rarely bicolour; lip trilobed with minute brown spots, lobes ovate-triangular, short, spur 8–15mm. Early spring–mid summer. Eur. Z7.

D. sulphurea (Link) Soó = *D. romana*.

D. sulphurea ssp. *pseudosambucina* (Ten.) Franco = *D. romana*.

D. traunsteineri (Rchb.) Soó. IRISH MARSH ORCHID. Lvs spotted or plain. Spike lax; fls magenta to mauve; lip trilobed or entire, marked maroon, sometimes deflexed; spur conical. Mid–late summer. N & C Eur., Scand. Z6.
→*Orchis*.

Daffodil *Narcissus*.
Daffodil Garlic *Allium neapolitanum*.
Dagger Plant *Yucca aloifolia*.
Dahl *Cajanus cajan*.
Dahlberg Daisy *Thymophylla*.

Dahlia Cav. Compositae. *c*30 perenn. herbs or subshrubs, usually tuberous-rooted. Lvs pinnatifid or pinnate. Cap. radiate, usually on long slender peduncles; disc flts often replaced by ray flts in cvs. Mts of Mex. to Colomb.

D. arborea hort. ex Reg. = *D. imperialis*.

D. coccinea Cav. Perenn. herb to 3m often purple-tinged. Lvs to 40cm, simple to 3-pinnate, ovate to elliptic or ovate-lanceolate, dentate, dark green. Cap. few to many, in clusters of 2–3, erect or slightly nodding; ray flts yellow, orange or scarlet to dark maroon, sometimes many-coloured; disc flts yellow, occas. tipped scarlet. Summer–autumn. Mex. to Guat.

D. ×*cultorum* hort. = *D. hortensis*.

D. excelsa Benth. Perenn. herb or shrub, to 6m. Lvs to 80cm, 2-pinnatisect, seg. ovate, dentate, pale glaucous green beneath, acuminate. Cap. solitary, or 5–8 in a corymb; flts lilac; disc flts often ± ligulate. Mex.

D. gracilis Ortgies = *D. coccinea*.

D. hortensis Guillaum. (*D. pinnata* ×*D. coccinea?*) Perenn. herb, to 2m. Lvs to *c*30cm, simple or 1–2-pinnate, seg. 3–7, to 20cm, oblong to ovate or lanceolate, dentate. Cap. few, axill., in a corymb; disc flts red, white, yellow or orange, sometimes purple or mauve, often different colours combined in patterns.

D. imperialis Roezl ex Ortgies. Perenn. herb or subshrub to 9m. Lvs to 60cm, 2–3-pinnate; seg. to 40cm, to 15, ovate to elliptic, dentate, pubesc. above. Cap. numerous in clusters, erect or nodding; ray flts, yellow, occas. tipped red. Autumn–winter. Guat. to Columbia.

D. juarezii hort. non Van Der Berg ex Mast. = *D. hortensis*.

D. juarezii Van Der Berg ex Mast. non hort. = *D. coccinea*.

D. merckii Lehm. Perenn. herb, to 2m, usually tinged red. Lvs to 40cm, 1–2-pinnate, seg. to 16cm, *c*7, ovate to obovate. Cap. numerous in term. clusters on br.; ray flts white to purple; disc flts yellow, apex purple. Summer–autumn. Mex.

D. pinnata Cav. Perenn. herb to 2m, tinged purple. Lvs to 25cm, usually pinnatisect, seg. 3–5, to 14cm, ovate, pubesc. or strigose on veins. Cap. to *c*8, in clusters of 2 or 3, erect or nodding; ray flts pale purple, yellow or pink at base. Late spring–autumn. Mex.

D. pinnata hort. = *D. hortensis*.

D. rosea hort. non Cav. = *D. pinnata*.

D. scapigera (A. Dietr.) Knowles & Westc. Perenn. herb, to 50cm. Lvs crowded in a basal rosette, pinnate, seg. 3–7, to 4cm, ovate to lanceolate. Cap. few, usually solitary, slightly drooping; ray flts white to pale purple, base sometimes yellow; disc flts yellow, apex purple. Summer–autumn. Mex.

D. superflua (DC.) Ait. f. = *D. pinnata*.

D. tenuicaulis Sorensen. Subshrub or shrub, to 4m. Lvs to 45cm, 1–2-pinnate, seg. 3–7, to 18cm, ovate to obovate or lanceolate, dentate. Cap. many, usually in clusters of 12 per br.; ray flts lilac. Late summer–autumn. Mex.

D. variabilis hort. non (Willd.) Desf. = *D.* ×*hortensis*.

D. variabilis (Willd.) Desf. non hort. = *D. pinnata*.

D. yuarezii Mast. = *D. coccinea*.

D. zimapanii Roezl ex Ortgies = *Cosmos diversifolius*.

D. cvs. There are now 20,000 cvs listed in the International Register of Dahlia Names. The standard system of classification is based on ten Groups, divided according to the morphology of the head and the fls.

Group One. SINGLE-FLOWERED. Open-centred blooms with one or two complete outer rows of flts surrounding a disc, usually about 10cm in diameter, most grow only to about 30cm. Examples include 'Coltness Gem': a dwarf bedder, seed-sown, various colours; 'Inflammation' ('Red Lilliput'): v. small plants, fls red; ideal for pot culture or patio plantings.

Group Two. ANEMONE-FLOWERED. Blooms having one or more rows of ray flts surrounding a dense group of upward-pointing tubular flts 60–90cm high; blooms 7.5cm across. Examples include 'Comet': dark red; 'Scarlet Comet': a lighter red sport of 'Comet'.

Group Three. COLLERETTE (Collarette). Blooms with an open centre, surrounded by an inner ring of short flts, the 'collar', and one or two complete outer rows of usually flat ray flts. About 110cm high, blooms 10–15cm across. Many are sold as mixtures to raise from seed. Examples include 'Clair de Lune': yellow with a paler yellow colar; 'La Cierva': purple, tipped white on the outer flts with a white collar.

Group Four. WATERLILY or NYMPHAEA-FLOWERED. Fully double blooms, with broad and generally sparse ray flts, flat or with slightly incurved or recurved margins, the overall effect being of a flat or shallow bloom. 90–120cm high, blooms 10–12cm across. Examples include 'Peace Pact': pure white: 'Pearl of Heemstede': dark pink.

Group Five. DECORATIVE. Blooms fully double, showing no central disc, with broad, flat or slightly involute ray flts, sometimes slightly twisted and apex usually obtuse. 90–150cm high. Examples include 'Hamari Gold': a typical giant, golden bronze in colour; 'Nina Chester': small white. Decorative dahlias can have cut or fimbriate flt tips. In the US the decorative dahlias are split into two subgroups, the Formal Decoratives, with the ray flts in a regular arrangement, and the Informal Decoratives, in which the rays are generally long, twisted or pointed, and irregular in arrangement.

Group Six. BALL. Ball-shaped or globose, sometimes slightly flattened at the top, with ray flts blunt or rounded at the tips,and cupped for more than half the length of the flts. Small Ball Dahlias have blooms 10–15cm in diameter, those of the miniature Ball Dahlias up to 10cm across. Examples include 'Opal': a blend of pink and white; 'Wootton Cupid': a dark pink miniature.

Group Seven. POMPON. Sometimes referred to as 'drum-stick' dahlias, similar to the Ball Dahlias, but more globose, with flts involute for their entire length, and of miniature size, plants to 90cm high and flts to 5cm across. Examples include 'Moor Place': purple; 'Hallmark': dark pink flushed lilac.

Group Eight. CACTUS-FLOWERED. The cactus and semi-cactus groups are subdivided by size, as for the decorative groups. The cactus types have fully double blooms showing no disc, with long, pointed ray flts, finely quilled (i.e. strongly revolute) for over half their length. Examples include 'Banker': mid-red; 'Klankstad Kerkrad': pale lemon yellow blooms, 10–15cm across. As with decoratives, the flt ends are cut or fimbriate. In the US, this group is divided into the straight cactus types with straight, slightly incurved or recurved rays, and the incurved types, whose pointed rays curve towards the centre of the bloom.

Group Nine. SEMI-CACTUS-FLOWERED. Fully double blooms, with slightly pointed ray flts broad at base, revolute for less than half their length, and either straight or incurving. Plants about 120cm tall.

Group Ten. MISCELLANEOUS. A grouping of small, disparate classes. It includes the Orchid cvs, similar in form to the single dahlias except that their pet. are revolute for at least two-thirds of their length, such as 'Giraffe', banded yellow and bronze; the Star dahlias, with small incurving fls, formed by two or three rows of scarcely overlapping pointed rays, surrounding a central disc; the Chrysanthemum types, resembling incurved exhibition chrysanthemums, e.g. 'Akita'; and the tiny Lilliput series, with 2.5cm blooms. Other miscellaneous types include the Peony-flowered with two or more rows of flat, broad ray flts, and a centre open or partly covered by small twisted floral rays around the disc. This section is still considered distinct in the US and some other countries.

Dahoon *Ilex cassine*.
Dahurian Juniper *Juniperus davurica*.
Dahurian Larch *Larix gmelinii*.
Daily Dew *Drosera*.
Daimio Oak *Quercus dentata*.

Dais L. Thymelaeaceae. 2 decid. shrubs. Fls in term. heads; cor. tube cylindric, often curved; sta. 10, in 2 rows of unequal length, exserted. S Afr., Madag. Z9.

D. cotinifolia L. Lvs to 7×5cm, obovate, ovate or oblong, acute, glab., blue-green. Fls fragrant, to 15 per umbel; cor. lobes 5, spreading, 15mm diam., pale lilac, tube to 15mm. Summer. Range as for the genus.

Daiswa Raf. Liliaceae (Trilliaceae). 15 rhizomatous herbaceous perenn., related to *Paris* and *Kinugasa*. St. solitary. Lvs in an apical whorl, obovate to linear. Fls solitary, term.; sep. 4–8; pet. 4–8, often narrower and shorter than sep.; sta. to 20. Fr. a fleshy capsule, purple-green. Summer. Himal. to E Asia. Many spp. included in *Paris* (*Daiswa*) *polyphylla* at different times.

D. birmanica Takht. To 60cm. Differs from all other spp. in its conspicuous, broad, purple pet. Burm. Z10.

D. bockiana (Diels) Takht. To 40cm. Lvs 6–10, 7–12×2–4cm. Pedicel shorter than lvs; sep. 5–6; pet. 5–6, threadlike, 5–7cm. Burm., China. Z8.

D. chinensis (Franch.) Takht. To 1m. Lvs 6–8, obovate. Sep. 5–6, clawed, ovate-lanceolate, 2–5cm; pet. 5, showy, green-yellow, narrow at base, broadening toward tip, shorter than sep. Burm., China, SE Asia. Z9.

D. cronquistii Takht. To 55cm. Lvs 5, mottled dark green, ovate. Pedicel 20cm; sep. 5, ovate-lanceolate, tip attenuate, 5.5×2cm; pet. 5, threadlike, yellow-green, 4cm. China. Z9.

D. delavayi (Franch.) Takht. To 60cm. Lvs 6–8, oblanceolate. Pedicel shorter than lvs; sep. 4–5, 2–2.5cm, lanceolate, bronze-green; pet. 4–5, purple. China, Vietnam. Z8.

D. dunniana (Lév.) Takht. To 1m. Lvs 5–6. Pedicel to 70cm; sep. 5, 3–5cm, narrow-lanceolate, sessile; pet. 5, 1cm, green-yellow. China. Z9.

D. fargesii (Franch.) Takht. To 1m. Lvs 4–6, ovate, cordate. Pedicel almost equal to st.; sep. 4–6, 8–10×1–3cm, lanceolate, yellow-green, acuminate; pet. 4–6, threadlike, longer than sep. China, N Vietnam. Z9.

D. forrestii Takht. To 75cm. Lvs 5–6, oblong to obovate. Pedicel shorter than lvs; sep. 5–6, 2–3.5cm, broadly lanceolate narrowed at base; pet. to 3× longer than sep. Burm., China. Z9.

D. hainanensis (Merrill) Takht. To 2m. Lvs 6, obovate. Pedicel 50–150cm; sep. 6, 7cm, lanceolate; pet. 6, to 10cm, green, threadlike. China. Z10.

D. lancifolia (Hayata) Takht. Lvs 10–22, narrow lanceolate. Sep. 4–8, half length of lvs and as broad; pet. 3.5–8cm; threadlike. China, Tibet, Taiwan. Z8.

D. polyphylla (Sm.) Raf. To 1m. Lvs 6–12, oblong to oblanceolate. Sep. 4–6, 2.5–10cm, narrow-linear, sessile, green; pet. 4–6, green-yellow, threadlike, widening at tip, equalling sep. Himal., China, Taiwan, Burm., Thail. Z8.

D. pubescens (Hand.-Mazz.) Takht. To 45cm. Lvs 6–7, oblanceolate, undulate; petiole bronze, pubesc. Sep. 4–6, 2.5–5cm, oblanceolate; pet. green-yellow, equal or generally longer than sep. China. Z8.

D. thibetica (Franch.) Takht. To 80cm. Lvs 7–10, lanceolate. Sep. usually 5, lanceolate, sessile, half length of lvs; pet. threadlike, equal to or shorter than sep. China. Z8.

D. violacea (Lév.) Takht. To 20cm. Lvs 4–6, dark green with silver-white veins, lanceolate to oblanceolate. Pedicel 1–2cm; sep. 2–3cm, variegated, lanceolate; pet. threadlike, green-yellow. Himal. Z8.

D. yunnanensis (Franch.) Takht. To 80cm. Lvs 6–8, broadly lanceolate. Pedicel almost length of lvs; sep. 6–8, to 7cm, lanceolate; pet. 6–8, to 10×1cm, golden yellow. Summer. India, Burm., China, Tibet. Z8.
→*Paris*.

Daisy *Bellis.*
Daisy Bush *Olearia.*
Daisy-leaved Grape Fern *Botrychium matricariifolium.*
Daisy-star Aster *Aster bellidiastrum.*
Daisy Tree *Montanoa.*

Dalbergia L. f. Leguminosae (Papilionoideae). 100 lianes, shrubs and trees with beautifully coloured wood. Lvs imparipinnate or unifoliolate. Pan. axill. or term.; lobes 5, fls pea-like. Trop. Asia, Afr., Amer. Z9.

D. assamica Benth. Scandent shrub. Lvs to 25cm; lfts 15–21, as for *D. lanceolaria* but thinner, elliptic, obtuse. Trop. Himal.

D. cochinchinensis Pierre ex Lanessi. TRAC. Tree, to 25m. Lvs to 20cm; lfts to 5cm, 7–9, ovate, acute or short-acuminate; fls white; standard to 5mm. SE Asia, W India, Ceylon.

D. domingensis Pers. = *Lonchocarpus domingensis.*

D. lanceolaria L. Tree, to 20m. Lvs to 15cm; lfts to 5cm, 7–11, elliptic-ovate, leathery, emarginate. Fls pink; standard to 6mm wide. India, W Himal. to Ceylon.

D. latifolia Roxb. INDIAN BLACKWOOD; INDIAN ROSEWOOD; MAL-ABAR ROSEWOOD; BLACK ROSEWOOD; EAST INDIA ROSEWOOD. As for *D. sissoo*, but lvs to 22cm, lfts 5, suborbicular. Standard smaller. S India.

D. mammosa Pierre. Tree, to 20m. Lvs to 16cm; lfts to 4.5cm, 9–13, tapering, obtuse, leathery. Vietnam.

D. ooieinensis Roxb. = *Desmodium ooieinense.*

D. ougeinensis Roxb. ex Benth. = *Desmodium ooieinense.*

D. paniculata Roxb. As for *D. lanceolaria*, but lfts to 2.5cm, 9–13, midrib pubesc. Infl. less dense than in *D. lanceolaria*; fls to 6mm, subsessile, blue-white. C India, Burm.

D. sissoo Roxb. ex DC. SISSOO; SHISHAM. Tree, to 25m. Lvs to 18cm; lfts to 8cm, 4–6, suborbicular, thin, acuminate. Fls yellow-white; standard to 1cm wide. Summer. India.

Dalby Myall *Acacia stenophylla.*

Dalea L. Leguminosae (Papilionoideae). INDIGO BUSH. 160 perenn., monocarpic herbs and shrubs, glandular-punctate, appearing blistered. Lvs imparipinnate, rarely trifoliolate. Infl. a spike, or rac.; fls pea-like. Americas.

D. aurea Nutt. GOLDEN PRAIRIE CLOVER. Perenn. herb to 75cm. St. erect to ascending, sericeous. Lvs to 4cm; lfts to 2cm, 3–7, obovate to oblanceolate, obtuse. Infl. to 6×2cm, spicate, cone-like, many-fld; pet. pale yellow, standard to 1cm. Summer–autumn. S US.

D. candida (Michx.) Willd. WHITE PRAIRIE CLOVER. Perenn. herb, to 70cm. St. virgate. Lvs to 5cm, 5 or 7, obovate to linear-oblong. Infl. an ovoid-cylindric to subglobose spike 0.6–1cm diam.; cor. white, standard to 0.6cm. Summer. C US, Canada. var. *oligophylla* (Torr.) Shinn. To 70cm. Lfts to 2cm. Spikes lax.

D. enneandra Nutt. Erect, glab. perenn. herb to 120cm. St. densely leafy below, naked during flowering. Lvs to 2.5cm; lfts to 1.2cm, 6–12, narrowly oblanceolate to elliptic, obtuse. Infl. to 12cm, to 30-fld; fls 2-ranked; bracts persistent; cor. white, standard to 0.7cm. SW US.

D. frutescens J. Gray. Small slender shrub, to 80cm; br. erect to decumbent. Lvs to 2cm; lfts 8–20, obovate to oblanceolate. Infl. loose, to 30-fld, oblong; standard white with a yellow-green eye, wings and keel rose-purple or white. SW US.

D. gattingeri (A.A. Heller) Barneby. Perenn. herb to 35cm. St. sparse, short, decumbent, radiating. Lvs to 3.5cm; lfts to 1.8cm, 5–7, linear to elliptic. Infl. to 7.5×1cm, densely spicate, fls 3–4-ranked; cor. vivid rose purple, standard to 0.7cm. US (Tenn. to NW Alab.).

D. laxiflora Pursh = *D. enneandra.*

D. purpurea Vent. Perenn. herb, 20–90cm. St. usually slender, ascending, ribbed. Lfts 1–2.4cm, usually 5, rarely 3 or 7, tread-like, oblanceolate or elliptic, downy, glaucous or dark green. Rac. densely spicate, to 1.2cm diam.; cor. vivid rose-purple or carmine.

D. spinosa Gray = *Psorothamnus spinosus.*

D. villosa (Nutt.) Spreng. Perenn. herb 20–80cm, rough and leafy. St. costate, erect or spreading. Lvs 2–4cm, grey-green to dull silver; lfts 0.5–1.4cm, in 5–8 pairs, elliptic to elliptic-oblanceolate. Rac. to 1cm diam., spicate, crowded; cor. pale pink, rose-purple, or white. Summer. C US.
→*Petalostemon.*

Dalechampia L. Euphorbiaceae. Some 60 climbing or erect shrubs. Fls small, apetalous, in dense, rounded, hanging clusters, subtended by 2 conspicuous bracts. Trop. Z10.

D. roezliana Muell. Arg. Erect, much branched shrub, to 1.2m. Lvs 15cm, obovate-lanceolate, entire or coarsely toothed. Infl. yellow, borne on a slender stalk amid bracteoles and subtended by 2 broadly ovate, toothed, distinctly nerved, rose-pink bracts 5–6.5cm long. Mex.

Dallis Grass *Paspalum dilatatum.*
Dalmatian Iris *Iris pallida.*
Dalmatian Laburnum *Petteria.*
Dalmatian Pyrethrum *Tanacetum cinerariifolium.*
Dalmatian Toadflax *Linaria genistifolia* var. *dalmatica.*
Damask Violet *Hesperis matronalis.*

Damasonium Mill. Alismataceae. 6 aquatic, perenn. herbs. Lvs basal, floating, or emergent, long-stalked. Fls small, whorled in scapose umbels, rac. or pan. N hemis., Aus. Z7.

D. alisma Mill. Lvs to 8cm, oblong or ovate-oblong, base sub-cordate or truncate, apex obtuse or rounded. Pet. white, with a yellow spot at the base. W, S & SE Eur.

D. alismoides (L.) R. Br. = *Ottelia alismoides.*

D. californicum Torr. ex Benth. Lvs linear-oblong to ovate, to 10cm. Pet. white or pink. S US.

D. cygnorum Planch. = *Ottelia ovalifolia.*

D. minor Small. Lvs ovate, cordate to lanceolate. Pet. pale pink.

D. ovalifolium R. Br. = *Ottelia ovalifolia.*
→*Machaerocarpus.*

Dambala *Psophocarpus tetragonolobus.*
Dames Violet *Hesperis matronalis.*
Dammar Pine *Agathis.*

Dammera Laut. & Schum. = *Licuala*.

Damnacanthus Gaertn. f. Rubiaceae. 6 everg. spiny shrubs. Fls small, paired in axils; cor. funnelform, lobes 5, throat hairy. Asia. Z9.

D. indicus Gaertn. f. To 1m; branchlets v. slender, scurfy with needle-like spines to 2cm. Lvs to 2cm, ovate, apex pungent, base rounded. Fls to 2cm, white, fragrant. Fr. a berry, red to scarlet. Himalaya, China, Jap.

Dampiera R. Br. Goodeniaceae. Some 70 perenn. herbs or shrubs. Fls in pan., rac. or cyme, sometimes solitary; cal. 5-lobed; cor. tube deeply slit on upper side, 2 upper lobes deeply separated, unequally 2-winged, erect, 3 lower lobes broadly winged, spreading. Aus.

D. alata Lindl. Herb to 60cm. St. erect, 2-winged. Lvs to 5cm, obovate to oblong, coriaceous, entire or dentate. Infl. a cyme, stellate-pubesc.; cor. to 15mm, blue, with dark grey stellate hairs. W Aus.

D. brownii F. Muell. = *D. purpurea*.

D. coronata Lindl. Herb to 50cm. St. erect. Lvs to 4.5cm, obovate to narrowly oblong, dentate. Infl. a small cyme; cor. to 20mm, blue, with dark grey adpressed hairs, pubesc. W Aus.

D. discolor (De Vriese) Krause. Shrub to 2m, lanate. Lvs to 9.5cm, narrowly ovate to elliptic, subentire, white-pubesc. beneath. Infl. a term. rac. or pan., white to grey-pubesc.; cor. to 12mm, dark blue, exterior densely pubesc. Queensld.

D. diversifolia De Vriese. Perenn. herb, to 1m, prostrate. Lvs to 3cm, radical, lanceolate to oblong-spathulate, entire or minutely dentate. Fls solitary, cor. to 12mm, blue, exterior glab. W Aus.

D. fasciculata R. Br. Perenn. herb. St. to 1m, erect or decumbent, glab. or tomentose. Lvs to 5cm, oblanceolate or obovate to oblong-cuneate, entire or dentate. Infl. axill., usually stellate-tomentose, 1 or 2-fld; cor. blue, to 12mm. W Aus.

D. hederacea R. Br. Perenn. herb, procumbent, tomentose. Lvs to 4cm, ovate, cordate at base, entire to lobed, stellate-tomentose to glab. above, lanate beneath. Infl. a cyme, slender, surpassing lvs, cor. to 10mm, blue, sometimes, white, grey-pubesc. W Aus.

D. lanceolata A. Cunn. ex DC. Subshrub to 50cm, erect or procumbent, white-tomentose becoming glab. Lvs to 1.5cm, obovate-oblong to lanceolate, entire or slightly dentate, glabrescent. Infl. a cyme, exceeding lvs, white-tomentose; cor. to 14mm, blue, exterior stellate-tomentose. C E & SE Aus.

D. lavandulacea Lindl. Perenn. herb to 50cm, erect, initially white-tomentose. Lvs to 2cm, oblong, lanceolate or narrowly obovate, coriaceous, entire or dentate, white-tomentose beneath. Infl. a cyme, axill., few-fld, sometimes 1-fld, exceeding lvs; cor. to 12mm, blue or lilac, grey-pubesc. W Aus.

D. linearis R. Br. Perenn. herb to 50cm, erect, usually glab. Lvs to 4cm, coriaceous, obovate to elliptic, obtuse, entire to dentate. Fls in leafy cymes; cor. to 17mm, blue, exterior grey-pubesc. W Aus.

D. purpurea R. Br. Herb or shrub to 1m. Lvs to 7.5cm, ovate to elliptic-oblong, entire to dentate, glab. to stellate-pubesc. beneath. Infl. to 2.5cm, few-fld, pubesc.; cor. to 1.5cm, dark blue to violet, exterior white to grey-pubesc. E & SE Aus.

D. rosmarinifolia Schltr. WILD ROSEMARY. Shrub to 50cm, erect or procumbent, stellate-tomentose. Lvs to 2.5cm, linear-oblong or oblong, white-tomentose beneath. Infl. axill., white-tomentose; 1-fld; cor. to 14mm, blue-purple or pink, exterior stellate-tomentose. S Aus., Vict.

D. stricta (Sm.) R. Br. Herb or shrub to 60cm. Lvs to 3.5cm, ovate or obovate to elliptic, entire to dentate, glab. Infl. 1 to few-fld; cor. to 13mm, dark blue, exterior yellow-pubesc. S Aus.

D. teres Lindl. Shrub to 60cm. St. erect, lanate to glab. Lvs to 1.5cm, linear to terete. Infl. slender, a rac. or a pan.; cor. to 15mm, pale to deep blue, dark grey-pubesc. W Aus.

D. trigona De Vriese. Perenn. herb. St. erect or ascending, triquetrous, glab. Lvs to 5cm, narrowly elliptic to linear, entire to minutely dentate. Fls in large branched cymes; cor. to 15mm, blue or sometimes white, dark-grey pubesc. W Aus.

→*Goodenia* and *Linschotenia*.

Damson Plum *Chrysophyllum oliviforme*.

Danaë Medik. ALEXANDRIAN LAUREL. Liliaceae (Ruscaceae). 1 superficially shrub-like everg. perenn. herb, related to *Ruscus*. Rhiz. short. St. 60–120cm, clumped, branched, rigid. Cladophylls 3–7cm, ovate-lanceolate, tapering, lustrous green. Fls 5–8 in term. rac.; perianth 2–3.5mm, cream, seg. 6. Berry, 0.6cm diam., orange-red. Early summer. W Asia.

D. laurus Medik. = *D. racemosa*.

D. racemosa (L.) Moench.

Danaea Sm. Marattiaceae. 35 terrestrial ferns. Rhiz. prostrate; roots thick. Fronds pinnate, dimorphic: sterile fronds erect with swollen nodes, pinnae simple, thick, leathery; fertile fronds longer and narrower, pinnae contracted. Trop. of W Hemis. Z10.

D. alata Sm. Stipes 5–15cm. Sterile fronds to 45×20cm; pinnae to 12×2cm in 8–10 pairs, serrate. W Indies.

D. crispa Endress. Stipes and rachis winged; pinnae pinnatifid, undulate. Costa Rica.

D. nodosa (L.) Sm. Stipes to 1m, stout; sterile fronds to 1.5×0.7m; pinnae to 30×5cm, minutely serrate. Trop. Amer., W Indies.

Dancing-doll Orchid *Oncidium flexuosum*.
Dancing Lady *Oncidium varicosum*.
Dancing Orchid *Caladenia discoidea*.
Dandelion *Taraxacum*.
Dane's Elder *Sambucus ebulus*.
Danewort *Sambucus ebulus*.

Danthonia DC. Gramineae. 10 perenn. or ann. tufted grasses. Pan. crowded, compact, solitary; spikelets dimorphic: normal spikelets several-fld, cleistogamous spikelets 1–2-fld. Trop. Z10.

D. cunninghamia Hook. f. = *Chionochloa conspicua*.

D. purpurea (Thunb.) P. Beauv. ex Roem. & St. forming tussocks, to 22cm. Lvs to 3cm, curved, pubesc. Infl. purple-tinted. S Afr.

D. semiannularis (Labill.) R. Br. St. to 1m, clustered in tussocks. Lvs narrow, often inrolled. Aus., Tasm.

D. setacea R. Br. WALLABY GRASS. As for *D. semiannularis*, except to 30cm. Lvs setaceous. Aus.

Daphne L. Thymelaeaceae. Some 50 small everg. and decid. shrubs. Fls usually fragrant in term. or axill. heads or rac.; cal. a cylindrical fleshy tube with 4 spreading, ovate-oblong lobes ½ to 1× length of tube; pet. 0. Fr. a drupe. Eur., N Afr., Temp. & Subtrop. Asia.

D. acuminata Boiss. & Hohen. ex Stocks = *D. mucronata*.

D. acutiloba Rehd. Everg. to 1.5m; young shoots bristly. Lvs 5–10cm, lanceolate to oblanceolate, acuminate, leathery, smooth. Fls ± unscented in subterminal clusters of 6 or more, green, white, glab., to 2cm. Fr. bright red. Summer. China. Z6.

D. albowiana Woron. Differs from *D. pontica* in red fr. Cauc. Z6.

D. alpina L. Decid. to 45cm; shoots erect or prostrate, downy. Lvs 1–4cm, lanceolate to oblanceolate, pubesc., grey-green. Fls fragrant in terminal heads of 4–10, white, tube to 0.8cm, downy. Fr. red, yellow-orange, downy. Spring–early summer. S & C Eur. Z5.

D. altaica var. *longilobata* Lecomte = *D. longilobata*.

D. arbuscula Čelak. Everg., procumbent to 20cm. Lvs to 2cm, linear to oblanceolate, obtuse, glossy, coriaceous, sometimes pubesc. beneath. Fls v. fragrant in term. clusters of 3–8 or more, rose pink, downy, tube to 2cm. Fr. grey-white, not fleshy. Summer. Hung. Z6.

D. aurantiaca Diels. Everg., straggly, to 150cm. Lvs to 2cm, ovate to oblong or obovate to linear, tips pointed or blunt, leathery, deep green above, paler beneath. Fls fragrant, in groups of 2–4 in If axils, orange-yellow, smooth, tube to 10mm. Fr. yellow, thickly hairy. Spring. SW China. Z6.

D. bholua Buch.-Ham. ex D. Don. Everg. or decid., erect or spreading, 2–4m. Lvs 5–10cm, elliptic or oblanceolate, acute to acuminate, undulate to obscurely glandular-dentate, dull deep green, leathery. Fls v. fragrant, in clusters of 3–15, white to purple-pink, tube to 10mm, sericeous. Fr. black. Winter. E Himal. 'Gurkha': exceptionally hardy, decid. 'Jacqueline Postill': hardy, everg.; fls large, deep pink. Z8.

D. blagayana Freyer. Everg., procumbent, to 30cm. Lvs 3–5cm, oblong-obovate or obovate, blunt, smooth. Fls fragrant in dense term. heads of 20 or more; cream-white, tube to 13mm, sericeous. Fr. pink-white. Spring. N Greece, Balk., Bulg., Rom. Z5.

D. ×burkwoodii Turrill (*D. caucasica* ×*D. cneorum*.) Vigorous, upright, decid. to semi-everg. to 1.7×2m. Lvs 2.75–4cm, linear-oblanceolate to oblanceolate, apiculate or mucronate, bright green, glabrescent. Fls fragrant, in clusters of to 16 on term. branchlets, sparkling white flushing rose to mauve-pink. Spring. Gdn origin. 'Albert Burkwood': broad shrub to 1m; lvs to 3cm, linear-oblanceolate, apiculate; fls green flushed purple-pink, lobes white ageing to deep pink. 'G.K. Argles' vigorous; lvs broad, edged gold. 'Lavenirii': spreading shrub; lvs to 3cm, narrow-oblanceolate, apiculate; cal. tube dark purple pink, lobes light pink, throat deep pink. 'Somerset': lvs to 4cm, narrow-oblanceolate, mucronate to rounded; fls to 13mm diam.; cal. tube purple-pink, lobes light pink. 'Somerset Gold Edge': slow growth; lvs edged gold. 'Somerset Variegated': lvs variegated. 'Carol Mackie': lvs narrowly edged bright, pale gold. Z5.

D. cannabina Wallich pro parte = *D. bholua* or *D. papyracea*.

D. caucasica Pall. Robust, upright, decid., to 2m. Lvs 3–5cm, light green above, blue-green beneath, glab., oblanceolate or lanceolate, acute to rounded, minutely mucronate. Fls white, fragrant, in clusters to 20 on ends of short lat. shoots, tube to 10mm, sericeous. Fr. black or red. Late spring/early summer, often with second flush later. Cauc., Asia Minor. ssp. *altaica* (Pall.) Pall. Suckering vigorously, lvs wider, light green, elliptic. Cal. tube not so silky. Fr. yellow to black-red. Summer. Altai mts. ssp. *sophia* Kalen. Suckering, upright. Lvs obovate. Fr. bright red. Spring, often second flush. C Russia. Z6.

D. cneorum L. GARLAND FLOWER. Low-growing everg., to 40cm. Shoots pubesc. when young. Lvs 1–2.25cm, oblanceolate, acute to obtuse, smooth, deep green above, blue-green beneath. Fls fragrant, in dense term. clusters, light to deep rosy pink, tube downy, 10mm. Fr. yellow to brown. Spring and sometimes again in late summer. C & S Eur. (NW Spain to SW Russia). 'Alba': fls white to ivory. 'Albomarginata': lvs variegated. 'Major': lvs large. 'Eximia': lvs 1.5cm, fls large, tubes to 12mm, buds crimson. 'Ruby Glow': fls ruby red. var. *variegata* Knight. Lvs edged yellow. var. *pygmaea* Stoker. Smaller, more compact, to 15cm. Lvs smaller. Cal. tube exterior wrinkled. Alps (N It., SE Fr.). var. *verlotii* (Gren. & Godron) Meissn. Lower-growing, lvs pointed and narrow, cal. tube longer with narrower lobes. SE Fr. Z4.

D. collina Dickson ex Sm. = *D. sericea*.

D. collina var. *neapolitana* (Lodd.) Lindl. = *D. ×napolitana*.

D. dauphinii Loud. = *D. ×hybrida*.

D. farreri hort. = *D. cneorum* var. *verlotii*.

D. fioniana Dipp. = *D. ×hybrida*.

D. fortunei Lindl. = *D. genkwa*.

D. genkwa Sieb. & Zucc. Upright, slender, decid. to 1m. Lvs 3–6.5cm, lanceolate to ovate, acute, silky at first. Fls subtly fragrant, precocious in clusters of 2–7, amethyst, lilac, rose-purple or white, tube 10mm, sericeous near base. Spring. China. Z5.

D. giraldii Nitsche. Upright, decid., to 1.2m. Lvs 3–6cm, oblanceolate, blunt to abruptly acute. Fls fragrant in term. clusters of 3–8, golden-yellow, sometimes tinted purple in bud; tube to 9mm. Fr. red. Early summer. China. Z3.

D. glandulosa Spreng. = *D. oleoides*.

D. glomerata Lam. Everg., prostrate, suckering, to 30cm. Lvs 3.5–4cm, obovate-oblong to lanceolate, blunt or mucronate, shiny deep green. Fls sweetly fragrant, in term. heads of 2–30, cream-white, tube to 15mm, sometimes tinged pink. Fr. red. Summer. NE Turk., Cauc. Z6.

D. gnidioides Jaub. & Spach. Tall, everg. to 2m. Lvs 2.5–4cm, oblong-lanceolate, acuminate, coriaceous, grey-blue-green. Fls fragrant, to 8 in term. heads, sometimes in smaller groups in axils, white or pink, tube 6mm, pubesc. Fr. red-brown, dry. Late spring–early summer. S & W Turk., E Aegean Is. Z8.

D. gnidium L. Upright everg. to 2m. Lvs 2–5cm, spread out obovate-oblong to lanceolate, acute, coriaceous, shiny, dotted beneath. Fls sweetly fragrant in lax term. pan., cream-white to light pink, tube to 4mm, pubesc. Fr. red. Spring–summer. S Eur., Asia Minor, N Afr., Canary Is. Z8.

D. ×houtteana Lindl. & Paxt. (*D. laureola* ×*D. mezereum*.) Semi-evergreen to 1.3m. Lvs to 9cm, oblanceolate, acute, glossy dark green hued purple-red. Fls in clusters of 2–5 below lvs, deep to pale lilac, tube 5mm, glab. Spring. Gdn origin. Z6.

D. ×hybrida Colville ex Sweet. (*D. sericea* ×*D. odora*.) Bushy, everg. to 1.5×1m. Lvs 3–7cm, oblong to ovate, blunt to pointed or mucronate, shiny, leathery, pubesc. beneath when young. Fls v. fragrant, in term. clusters of to 15, dark pink-purple, tube to 1cm, hairy. Most of the year. Gdn origin. Z6.

D. japonica Thunb. = *D. odora*.

D. jasminea Sibth. & Sm. non Griseb. Dwarf upright or semi-prostrate everg. to 30cm. Lvs 0.7–1cm, oblong-lanceolate, mucronate, glab., blue-grey. Fls highly fragrant, in term. clusters of 2 or 3, interior white, exterior smoke red-purple, tube 10–12mm, usually glab. Spring. SE Greece. Z9.

D. jezoensis Maxim. ex Reg. Upright, summer-deciduous, to 50cm. Lvs 3–7cm, oblanceolate, rounded to mucronate, somewhat shiny above. Fls sometimes citrus-scented, in term. clusters of to 10, yellow, tube 8mm, green-tinged, glab. Fr. red. Winter–early spring. N Jap. Z6.

D. juliae Kos.-Poh. Resembles a dwarf *D. cneorum* with more crowded infl. S Russia.

D. kamtschatica Maxim. Upright, summer-deciduous to 50cm. Lvs oblong-lanceolate to oblanceolate, acute. Fls in dense axill. clusters, yellow-green. Late winter–early spring. Korea, E Russia, Jap. Z6.

D. kamtschatica var. *jezoensis* (Maxim. ex Reg.) Ohwi = *D. jezoensis*.

D. kiusiana Miq. Smaller than the closely related *D. odora*. Young br. pubesc. Fls white, cal. tube pubesc. Spring.

Jap.; Honshu. Z8.

D. kosaninii (Stoj.) Stoj. Everg. shrub, similar to *D. oleoides*, but taller, bark red-tinged, lvs smaller. Fls in heads, dark pink. SW Bulg. Z6.

D. laureola L. SPURGE LAUREL. Much-branched, everg. to 1.5m. Lvs 5–8cm, obovate-lanceolate or oblong, acute to obtuse, leathery, glossy. Fls fragrant in crowded axill. clusters, yellow-green, tube 3–8mm. Late winter–early spring. C, S & W Eur., W Asia. var. *latifolia* (Coss.) Meissn. Lvs broad-obovate. Summer. S Spain, Moroc. var. *cantabrica* (Willk.) Willk. Compact form. Cantab. Mts. ssp. *philippi* (Gren. & Godron) Rouy. Semi-prostrate, compact, to 40cm. Lvs obovate, pointed. Fls fragrant, smaller, yellow-green, often tinted violet. Pyren. Z7.

D. longilobata (Lecomte) Turrill. Everg. similar to *D. acutiloba*, but cal. tube pubesc. Infl. term. at first, but new growth soon arises below and surpasses infl. (in *D. acutiloba* new growth does not appear until the next year); fls white. Fr. red. Summer. SE Tibet, NW Yunnan. 'Peter Moore': shrub to 3m; lvs narrow, margined cream; fls white. Z6.

D. ×mantensiana Manten ex Taylor & Vrugtman. (*D. ×burkwoodii* ×*D. retusa*.) Gdn hybrid usually found as the clone 'Manten' – a dwarf, rounded everg. shrub with glossy dark lvs to 3.5cm. Fls v. fragrant in terminal clusters, tube dark rose-purple, interior deep lilac. Spring, summer and autumn.

D. mazelii hort. non Carr. = *D. blagayana*.

D. mazelii Carr. non hort. = *D. odora* 'Mazelii'.

D. mezereum L. MEZEREON; FEBRUARY DAPHNE. Short-lived, decid. to 1.75m. Br. few, usually simple, arising from short trunk. Lvs 3–8cm, oblanceolate, blunt or pointed, downy at first, soft grey-green. Fls sessile, fragrant, in lat. clusters on previous year's wood, lilac-pink to violet-red, sometimes white, tube 5–6mm, pubesc. Fr. bright red. Winter. Eur. f. *alba* (West) Schelle. Fls white. Fr. yellow. 'Alba Plena': fls double, white; fr. yellow-white. 'Bowles' White': fls pure white; fr. yellow. 'Paul's White': fls clear white. var. *autumnalis* hort. ex Rehd. Fls larger, bright purple. 'Grandiflora': shrub to 2m; fls large, dark. 'Rubra': fls deep red-purple. 'Rubra plena': double red-purple fls. 'Ruby Glow': habit upright, broad; fls purple-red, large, abundant. 'Rosea': fls rose-pink. 'Variegata': lvs variegated white. Z4.

D. mucronata Royle. Ungainly, upright, lax everg. to 3m. Young shoots glabrescent. Lvs to 7cm, narrow-oblanceolate, mucronate or acuminate, leathery, usually glab. Fls fragrant, in crowded term. clusters, cream-white, tube 6mm, thickly hairy. Fr. red-orange. Summer. E Turk., Afghan., NE Iraq, Kashmir and Punjab, Arabian Penins. Z8.

D. ×napolitana Lodd. (*D. sericea* ×*D. cneorum*.) Bushy, erect everg. to 75cm. Young br. lightly pubesc. Lvs 2–3.5cm, oblanceolate to narrow-obovate, obtuse or subacute, shiny above, glaucous beneath. Fls v. fragrant, in term. clusters, rose-lilac, tube to 1cm, white-downy. Spring, with further flushes in summer and autumn. Z8.

D. neopolitana hort. = *D. ×napolitana*.

D. odora Thunb. WINTER DAPHNE. Everg. to 2m. Br. few, erect. Lvs 5–8cm, narrow-ovate to lanceolate-elliptic, acute, shiny, leathery, slightly fleshy. Fls sweetly fragrant, in term. clusters, red-purple or white with red-purple exterior, and red-purple margin to limb, tube to 1cm, glab. Fr. red. Winter–spring. China, Jap. 'Mazelii': additional lat. infl. of pale pink fls with white insides. f. *alba* (Hemsl.) Hara. Fls white or cream-white. f. *marginata* (Miq.) Mak. Lvs variegated with yellow, white or cream margins. 'Aureomarginata': lvs margined yellow; fl. exterior red-purple, interior much paler. 'Variegata': lvs edged yellow; fls pale pink. f. *rosacea* (Mak.) Hara. Fl. exterior light pink, interior white. 'Rose Queen': lvs plain; fls dark carmine-red, in dense heads. 'Rubra': fls dark red. Z7.

D. odora var. *kiusiana* (Miq.) Keissler = *D. kiusiana*.

D. odorata Lam. = *D. cneorum*.

D. oleoides Schreb. Divaricately branched everg. to 50cm. Young shoots pubesc. Lvs 2–3cm, elliptic to obovate, blunt to pointed, glab. above, pubesc. beneath then glandular-punctate. Fls usually fragrant, to 8 in terminal clusters, usually cream-white, some red-pink forms, tube 8mm, pubesc. Fr. orange, pubesc. Summer. S Eur., N Afr., Asia Minor, Afghan., Himal. Z8.

D. papyracea Wallich ex Steud. emend Sm. & Cave. Upright, everg. to 1.5m. Young shoots hispidulous, bark becoming papery. Lvs 10–15cm, elliptic or oblanceolate, obtuse or obtuse-acuminate, leathery, dull green, glab. Fls ± unscented, in term. clusters of 12, white or green-white, tube 13mm, softly hairy. Fr. red. Winter. N India, Nepal. Z8.

D. petraea Leyb. Everg., mat-forming, to 15×30cm. Young shoots pubesc. Lvs 0.8–1.2cm, narrow-spathulate, obtuse or subacute, leathery, deep green. Fls fragrant, 3–6 in term. clusters, rose-pink, tube to 15mm, white, pubesc. Fr. green-brown, downy. Late spring–summer. N It. 'Flore Plena': fls double but seldom open. 'Grandiflora': fl larger, deeper pink. Z6.

D. pontica L. Everg. to 1.5m. Young shoots glab. Lvs 3–10cm, obovate or obovate-oblong, pointed, dark, shiny green. Fls fragrant, abundant, usually in pairs, clustered at base of new growth, pale yellow-white or green-yellow, tube to 12mm, glab. Fr. black. Spring–summer. Asia Minor, SE Eur., Cauc. Z6.

D. pseudomezereum A. Gray. Glab., summer-deciduous shrub, to 1.5m. Similar to *D. mezereum* but fls appearing at same time as lvs, tinged green, exterior sometimes purple. Fr. red. Spring. C & S Jap. Z6.

D. pygmaea hort. = *D. cneorum* var. *pygmaea*.

D. retusa Hemsl. = *D. tangutica*.

D. 'Rossetii'. (*D. laureola* ssp. *philippi* ×*D. cneorum*.) Naturally occurring hybrid. Low everg. to 20cm, narrow-oblanceolate, acute to apiculate, to 3cm. Fls green-yellow, exterior flushed red-purple. Pyren. Z6.

D. rupestris Facch. = *D. petraea*.

D. salicifolia Lam. = *D. caucasica*.

D. sericea Vahl. Small, many-branched everg. to 1m. Young br. sericeous. Lvs 1–5cm, oblanceolate, obovate or narrow-elliptic, acute to obtuse, glossy above, pubesc. beneath. Fls strongly scented, in clusters of to 15, dark rose, ageing to buff, tube to 12mm, sericeous. Fr. red or orange-brown. Spring, sometimes with a second flush in autumn. E Medit. Z8.

D. sinensis Lam. = *D. odora*.

D. sureil W.W. Sm. & Cave. Upright, everg. or decid., to 2.5m. Young shoots white-pubesc. Lvs 5–10cm, lanceolate to oblanceolate, acute to acuminate, light glossy green, glab. or tomentose beneath when young, thin and somewhat soft. Fls fragrant, in term. clusters of to 20, green-white, tube 14mm, downy. Fr. orange-red. Autumn–winter. Z8.

D. tangutica Maxim. Everg., upright and open, or rounded and densely branched to 1.75m. Young br. grey-hispidulous. Lvs 3.5–6cm, oblanceolate, oblong or elliptic, acute to rounded, glossy or leathery. Fls fragrant in crowded term. clusters 5–7cm diam., exterior rose-purple, interior white with purple suffusion, tube to 12mm. Fr. red. Early spring–summer. NW China. Z6.

D. ×thauma Farrer. (*D. striata* ×*D. petraea*.) Naturally occurring hybrid. Low, tufted everg. shrub, to 8×45cm. Lvs to 2cm, narrow-lanceolate to oblanceolate, acute, glab. Fls fragrant, in term. heads of 5–8, bright rose-purple, tube 14mm, downy. Fr. yellow. Summer. It. Z7.

D. 'Valerie Hillier' (*D. cneorum* ×*D. longilobata*.) Dwarf, spreading everg. shrub; branchlets downy. Lvs to 5cm, narrowly oblong-elliptic, glossy green. Fls fragrant, pink-purple fading to white edged pink. Spring to autumn. Z8.

D. verlotii Gren. & Godron = *D. cneorum* var. *verlotii*.

Daphne Heath *Brachyloma daphnoides*.

DAPHNIPHYLLACEAE Bl. See *Daphniphyllum*.

Daphniphyllum Bl. Daphniphyllaceae. 15 everg. shrubs or trees. Fls small, apetalous in dense axill. clusters, ♂ purple-red, ♀ green. Fr. a drupe, usually blue-black, to about 1cm. Asia.

D. glaucescens hort., non Bl. = *D. macropodum*.

D. humile Maxim. Glab., slow-growing shrub to about 2m, with greater spread. Lvs 5–12cm, ovate or obovate, glossy above, glaucous beneath. Jap., Korea. Z7.

D. jezoense Bean = *D. humile*.

D. macropodum Miq. Shrub or tree, to 15m, densely branched, rounded; young br. red-brown. Lvs 8–20cm, somewhat deflexed, oblong, leathery, dark glossy green above, glaucous beneath, petiole and midrib usually red. Late spring–early summer. Jap., Korea, China. Z6.

D. macropodum var. *humile* (Maxim.) K. Rosenth. = *D. humile*.

Dark-eye Sunflower *Helianthus atrorubens*.
Dark Mullein *Verbascum nigrum*.
Darling Lily *Crinum flaccidum*.
Darling Pea *Swainsona greyana*.

Darlingtonia Torr. COBRA LILY; CALIFORNIA PITCHER PLANT. Sarraceniaceae. 1 carnivorous perenn. herb. Lvs to 90×8cm in a basal rosette, ± erect, pitcher-like − a slender green tube at base, expanding and twisting to a rounded, incurved, inflated hood with an aperture on its underside and a forked, wing-like appendage, upper parts with translucent spots, often tinted red. Scape to 1m; fls pendulous; sep. 5, to 6.5cm, yellow-green; pet. 5, shorter, yellow-green veined dark red-purple. N Calif., S Oreg. Z7.

D. californica Torr.

Darmera Voss. Saxifragaceae. 1 perenn. herb. Rhiz. thick, creeping, flattened. Lvs peltate, to 60cm across, pubesc., orbicular and toothed, to 10–15-lobed, petioles slender, to 2m, pubesc. Infl. precocious, cymose; scape to 2m, stout, red-tinted; pet. 5, white to bright pink, oblong-ovate, 4.5–7mm; sta. 10. NW Calif. to SW Oreg. Z6.

D. peltata (Torr. ex Benth.) Voss. UMBRELLA PLANT; INDIAN RHUBARB. 'Nana': smaller in all respects.
→*Peltiphyllum*.

Darnel *Lolium*.

Darwinia Rudge. Myrtaceae. 60 dwarf to medium shrubs. Lvs usually decussate, aromatic. Fls small, in term. bracteate heads or pairs; cal. smooth or ribbed, with 5 glab. lobes; sta. 10, alternating with 10 staminodes; style often exserted. W Aus. Z9.

D. citriodora (Endl.) Benth. LEMON-SCENTED MYRTLE. Dwarf to small shrub. Lvs to 2cm, ovate-lanceolate, sometimes cordate, glaucous, lemon-scented. Fl. heads to 3cm across, erect to pendulous, outer bracts orange-red and green, fls ageing orange-red, style to 2cm, yellow to orange-red.

D. diosmoides (DC.) Benth. Small to medium, bushy shrub. Lvs to 6mm, trigonous, crowded, dark green, highly aromatic. Fl. heads 1–2cm across, white to pink, terminal, composed of many upturned fls.

D. fascicularis Rudge. Dwarf to small shrub. Lvs small, ± terete, grey-green to green, aromatic, in clusters. Fl. heads to 1.5cm across, initially white, becoming red with maturity, term., erect. ssp. *oligantha* Briggs. To 0.6m high; spreading br. layer themselves.

D. homoranthoides (F. Muell.) J.M. Black. Dwarf, spreading shrub. Br. self-layering. Branchlets often pink. Lvs 6–8mm, narrow, trigonous, grey-green, gland., aromatic. Fl. heads tubular, to 3cm, white to cream with green, initially upright.

D. hypericifolia (Turcz.) Domin. Dwarf shrub. Branchlets often red. Lvs to 2cm, oblong, revolute. Fl. heads to 3cm across, bell-shaped, narrow, pink to scarlet, pendent, terminal.

D. lejostyla (Turcz.) Domin. Dwarf, compact shrub. Lvs to 1cm, lanceolate, crowded, aromatic. Fl. heads bell-shaped, 3–4×2.5cm, red-pink and white, pendent.

D. macrostegia (Turcz.) Benth. MONDURUP BELL. Dwarf to small shrub. Branchlets often red. Lvs to 2cm, oblong to elliptical, minutely toothed. Fl. heads bell-shaped, to 6cm, term., pendent, bracts red with white blotches or all red.

D. oxylepis (Turcz.) N. Marchant & Keigh. Small upright shrub. Lvs *c*1cm, linear, trigonous to terete, scattered, glab. Fl. heads 3×2–3cm, bell-shaped, nearly all red with some white, term., pendent.

D. squarrosa (Turcz.) Domin. PINK MOUNTAIN BELL. Dwarf to small shrub. Lvs to 0.8cm, oblong to elliptical, keeled, crowded, fringed, sweetly aromatic. Fl. heads bell-shaped, 2×*c*1cm, pink, term., pendent, bracts fringed.

D. taxifolia Cunn. Dwarf to small shrub. Lvs to 1.2cm, linear to falcate, trigonous, decussate, grey-green. Fl. heads 2–4-fld to 1.5cm, white, ageing red, erect, axill., paired.

D. thymoides (Lindl.) Benth. Dwarf, spreading shrub. Br. spreading to cascading. Lvs to 1.2cm, linear-lanceolate, revolute, glab. Fl. heads to 2cm, white, term., erect.

D. vestita (Endl.) Benth. POM-POM DARWINIA. Dwarf shrub. Lvs to 0.4cm, heath-like, oblong to elliptic, adpressed, aromatic. Fl. heads globular, to 3cm across, white ageing pink to red, terminal.

Darwin's Barberry *Berberis darwinii*.
Darwin Woollybutt *Eucalyptus miniata*.
Dasheen *Colocasia* (*C. esculenta*).

Dasylirion Zucc. ex Otto & Dietr. SOTOL; BEAR GRASS. Agavaceae (Dracaenaceae). 18 arborescent, everg., perenn. herbs. St. single, ascending, thick. Lvs linear, in a term. rosette, usually spiny margined. Pan. scapose, densely flowered with spike-like br. bearing bract-like lvs. Fls campanulate, to 2cm, cream-white, tinted green; perianth seg. 6; sta. 6, exserted. S US to Mex. Z9.

D. acrotrichum (Schiede) Zucc. Trunk to 1.5m, robust. Lvs to 100×1–1.8cm, pale green, finely toothed between spines, spines to 2mm, hooked, pale yellow, tipped-brown, apex divided into 20–30 fibres. Infl. to 4.5m. Summer. Mex. var. *brevifolium* hort. Lvs shorter, to 60cm, not recurved.

D. bigelowii Torr. = *Nolina bigelowii*.

D. glaucophyllum Hook. Trunk to 30cm. Lvs to 120×1.2–2cm, glaucous, marginal spines 1–2mm, hooked, deep yellow, denticulate between spines, apex entire. Infl. 4–6m. Summer. E Mex. var. *latifolium* hort. More robust, lvs wider.

D. glaucum Carr. = *D. glaucophyllum*.

D. gracile (Lem.) Macbr. = *Nolina gracilis.*
D. gracile Planch. = *D. acrotrichum.*
D. graminifolium (Zucc.) Zucc. Trunk to 80cm. Lvs 90–120×1.3cm, bright green, glossy, finely toothed between spines, spines 1–2mm, horny, tinged yellow, 6–8 spreading fibres at apex. Infl. to 2.7m. Summer. Mex.
D. hartwegianum Hook. non Zucc. = *Nolina hookeri.*
D. hartwegianum Zucc. non Hook. = *Nolina hartwegiana.*
D. hookeri Lem. = *Nolina hookeri.*
D. juncifolium Rehn. = *D. longissimum.*
D. laxiflorum Bak. = *D. serratifolium.*
D. leiophyllum Engelm. Trunk to 80cm. Lvs to 100×2–3cm, glossy green or somewhat glaucous, margin with spines 3–4mm long and 1–1.5cm apart, recurved, yellow, becoming red, apex fibrous. Infl. to 3m. Summer. S Tex., New Mex., Mex.
D. longifolium Zucc. = *Nolina longifolia.*
D. longissimum Lem. Trunk to 3.6m. Lvs 1.2–1.8m×6cm, 4-angled (upper and lower surface raised to low keels), dull green, margin smooth, apex entire. Infl. to 5m. Summer. Mex.
D. quadrangulatum S. Wats. = *D. longissimum.*
D. serratifolium Karw. ex Schult. f. Almost stemless. Lvs to 100×1.5–3cm, glaucous, rough, finely toothed, spines 3mm, hooked, deep yellow, apex fibrous. Infl. to 30cm. Summer. SE Mex., Tex.
D. texanum Scheele. TEXAS SOTOL. To 5m; st. often buried. Lvs brush-tipped, to 1m×1–1.5cm, glossy green, marginal spines 2–3mm, yellow becoming brown. Tex., N Mex. 'Glaucum': lvs glaucous.
D. wheeleri S. Wats. Bushy tree, trunk to 1.5m. Lvs to 90×2.5–1cm, glaucous, denticulate, spines hooked, 2–5mm, yellow to rust-brown. Infl. 2.5–5m. Summer. SE Ariz., Tex.
→*Barbacenia* and *Yucca.*

Date *Phoenix dactylifera.*
Date Palm *Phoenix (P. dactylifera).*
Date Plum *Diospyros lotus.*

Datisca L. Datiscaceae. 2 large perenn. herbs. Lvs pinnately divided. Staminate fls in axill. fascicles; pet. 0; sep. 4–9; sta. 8–25. Pistillate fls in a rac.; styles 3, filiform, 2-branched. Asia Minor to India, Amer.
D. cannabina L. Hemp-like woody-based, perenn. herb to 2m. St. clumped, erect, unbranched, hollow. Lfts to 10cm, 7–13, lanceolate, serrate. Fls yellow, small, in tassel-like rac. Z6.

DATISCACEAE Lindl. See *Datisca.*

Datura L. THORN APPLE. Solanaceae. 8 ann. or short-lived perenn. shrubby herbs. Branching dichotomous. Fls extra-axillary or from forks in br., actinomorphic, erect or pendent, fragrant; cal. tubular, 5-lobed, circumscissile; cor. tubular to funnel-shaped. Fr. a usually spiny capsule, ovoid to spindle-shaped. S N Amer.
D. affinis Safford = *Brugmansia aurea.*
D. arborea L. = *Brugmansia arborea.*
D. aurea Safford = *Brugmansia aurea.*
D. candida (Pers.) Stapf = *Brugmansia ×candida.*
D. ceratocaula Ortega. Ann., to 90cm. St. tinged purple. Lvs ovate-lanceolate, dentate or pinnatifid, tomentose beneath. Fls white marked or flushed red-mauve, fragrant, trumpet-shaped, to 18cm, dark-veined, limb white, 10-toothed. Fr. to 4cm, ovoid, pendent, fleshy, smooth. Summer. C & S Amer. Z10.
D. chlorantha Hook. = *D. metel.*
D. cornigera Hook. = *Brugmansia arborea.*
D. cornucopia hort. = *D. metel.*
D. fastuosa L. = *D. metel.*
D. ferox L. LONGSPINE THORNAPPLE. Ann., to 1.5m, glab. to sparsely pubesc. St. red at base. Lvs rhombic to ovate, lobed. Fls white tinged opal to blue to 6cm, funnelform, white. Fr. to 8cm, ovoid, erect, spines to 60, 3cm, 2 pairs nearest apex larger. Summer. Eur., Asia. Z8.
D. gardneri Hook. f. = *Brugmansia suaveolens.*
D. guayaquilensis HBK = *D. innoxia.*
D. humilis Desf. = *D. metel.*
D. inermis Jacq. = *D. stramonium* f. *inermis.*
D. innoxia Mill. DOWNY THORN APPLE; INDIAN APPLE; ANGEL'S TRUMPET. Ann., to 1m, pubesc. Lvs broad-ovate, entire to sinuate. Fls pink or lavender, to 20cm, tubular, white to pink, veins green, limb undulate, 5-lobed but appearing 10-lobed. Fr. to 5cm, subglobose to ovoid, somewhat pendent, spines long, slender. C Amer., nat. OW. Z9.
D. laevis L. f. = *D. stramonium.*
D. macrocaulos Roth = *D. ceratocaula.*
D. metel L. HORN OF PLENTY; DOWNY THORN APPLE. Glab. ann. herb, to 1.5m. St. purple in purple-fld specimens. Lvs ovate, subentire, sinuate to coarsely sinuately serrate. Fls to 20cm,

frequently double or triple, exterior dark purple, white or yellow, interior pale violet, limb to 10-lobed. Fr. to 4cm diam., globose, spines conic, to 5mm. S China, widely nat. in Trop. 'Alba': fls white. 'Aurea': fls yellow. 'Caerulea', 'Huberana': fls blue. 'Cornucopea': double-fld. 'Flore Pleno': fls double, off-white to purple. Z9.
D. metel var. *quinquecuspida* Torr. = *D. wrightii.*
D. meteloides DC. ex Dunal = *D. innoxia.*
D. meteloides auct. non DC. ex Dunal = *D. wrightii.*
D. mollis Safford = *Brugmansia versicolor.*
D. pittieri Safford = *Brugmansia aurea.*
D. quercifolia HBK. Ann., to 1.5m. St. erect, purple, lightly pubesc. Lvs deeply pinnatifid, lightly pubesc., undulate. Fls to 7cm, 5-lobed, pale lavender. Fr. to 7cm, ovoid, spines sparse, to 13mm, more flexible than in *D. ferox*. SW US, Mex. Z8.
D. rosei Safford = *Brugmansia sanguinea.*
D. rubella Safford = *Brugmansia ×rubella.*
D. sanguinea Ruiz Pav. = *Brugmansia sanguinea.*
D. sinuata Sessé & Moc. = *D. ceratocaula.*
D. stramonium L. JIMSON WEED; JAMESTOWN WEED; COMMON THORN APPLE. Ann. to 2m, glab. to short-pubesc. Lvs elliptic to ovate, to acute, sinuate, dentate or lobed. Fls white or purple, to 10cm, funnelform. Fr. to 10cm, ovoid, 5-lobed, erect, spines to 1.5cm, slender. Americas, nat. Eur. f. *inermis* (Juss.) Hupka. Fr. unarmed. 'Horn of Plenty': fls single, lilac; pods spineless. Z7.
D. suaveolens Humb. & Bonpl. ex Willd. = *Brugmansia suaveolens.*
D. tatula L. = *D. stramonium.*
D. versicolor Safford = *Brugmansia versicolor.*
D. villosa Fern. = *D. quercifolia.*
D. wrightii Reg. Ann., to 1m+. St. grey-tomentose, spreading. Lvs ovate, entire to irregularly lobed. Fls white tinged purple to 20cm, white, margin purple, limb 5-lobed, lobes apiculate. Fr. to 3.5cm diam., globose, spines to 5mm. W Tex. to Colorado, Mex. Z9.

Daubentonia DC.
D. punicea (Cav.) DC. = *Sesbania punicea.*

Daubenya Lind. Liliaceae (Hyacinthaceae). 1 bulbous, perenn. herb. Lvs 5–15cm, 2, lying close to the ground, ovate or oblong, strongly veined. Scape v. short bearing an umbel-like head; fls of two kinds, outer fls to 6.5cm, red or yellow, sometimes orange, 2-lipped, with large lower lips forming periphery of infl., inner fls nearly radially symmetric, orange-yellow, tubes shorter. S Afr. Z9.
D. aurea Lindl.
D. fulva Lindl. = *D. aurea.*

Daucus L. Umbelliferae. *c*22 annuals or biennials. Lvs finely cut, 2–3-pinnate. Umbels compound; involucre and involucel of numerous bracts and bracteoles, often pinnatisect; fls white to pale yellow or tinged purple. Eur., C Asia, Trop. Afr., Aus., NZ, US.
D. carota L. WILD CARROT. Bienn. to 1m; st. striate or ridged. Lvs 2–3-pinnate, seg. linear, 0.5–3cm, serrate or pinnatifid. Umbels to 7cm diam.; involucral bracts 1–2-pinnatisect, lobes linear; bracteoles similar; fls white to purple-tinged, central fls often dark purple. Summer. Eur. to India. ssp. *sativus* (Hoffm.) Arcang. CARROT. Taproot fleshy, orange, edible.

Davallia Sm. HARE'S FOOT FERN. Davalliaceae. *c*40 semi-decid. terrestrial or epiphytic ferns. Rhiz. long-creeping, branching freely and interweaving, scales dense, chaffy. Fronds stipitate, uniform or with fertile seg. narrower than sterile, several times finely pinnate or pinnatifid. Warm temp., trop. and subtrop. OW. Z10 unless specified.
D. alata J. Sm. nom. nud., non Bl. = *D. decurrens.*
D. angustata Wallich, nom. nud.; Hook. & Grev. = *Humata angustata.*
D. barbata v.A.v.R. = *D. trichomanoides* f. *barbata.*
D. biflora Kaulf. = *Sphenomeris biflora.*
D. bullata Wallich. HARE'S FOOT FERN. Fronds to 30×20cm, 3-4-pinnate or -pinnatifid, somewhat membranous, fertile fronds markedly bullate above, primary pinnae, ovate, pinnules incised, lanceolate, to 8cm, lobes rhomboid to oblong, entire or pinnatifid, seg. falcate, linear, acute; stipes to 10cm. Trop. Asia.
D. bullata-mariesii hort. = *D. mariesii.*
D. canariensis Sm. CANARY ISLAND HARE'S FOOT FERN; DEER'S FOOT FERN. Fronds to 45×30cm, 4-pinnate, fertile fronds bullate above, pinnules to 8×2.5cm, deltoid to lanceolate, seg. ovate to oblong or rhomboid, not toothed at apex; stipes to 15cm. W Medit. to Atlantic Is. Z9.
D. ciliata Hook. = *Davallodes hirsutum.*
D. clavata (L.) Sm. = *Sphenomeris clavata.*

D. corniculata Moore. Fronds to 50×25cm, 3–4-pinnate, narrowly triangular in outline, pinnae distant, subopposite, to 9×3cm, pinnules approximate, lobed, lobes entire or toothed; stipes to 20cm. Malaysia.

D. decurrens Hook. Fronds to 60×35cm, 3–4-pinnatifid, deltoid, leathery, pinnae distant, lanceolate, pinnules to 10×3cm, lanceolate, incised, seg. linear or oblong, notched or toothed; stipes to 15cm. Philipp.

D. denticulata (Burm.) Mett. Fronds 60×60cm or longer, 3-pinnate, pinnae stalked, distant, pinnules lanceolate to deltoid, to 13×8cm, seg. deltoid or oblong, middle seg. lobed, upper seg. toothed, to 45×22mm, lobes notched; stipes to 40cm. Madag. and Trop. Asia to Aus., Polyn.

D. denticulata Luerssen, non (Burm.) Mett. = *D. epiphylla*.

D. dissecta J. Sm. = *D. trichomanoides*.

D. divaricata Bl. Fronds to 90×60cm, 3–4-pinnate or -pinnatifid, pinnae distant, deltoid, narrowly acute to 30×15cm, pinnules deltoid, caudate, seg. deltoid, lobes deltoid or elliptic (sterile), or linear or oblong (fertile), entire to dentate; stipes to 30cm. Trop. Asia.

D. dubia R. Br. = *Culcita dubia*.

D. elegans Sw. non Harrington = *D. denticulata*.

D. elegans Harrington, non Sw. = *D. embolostegia*.

D. embolostegia Copel. Fronds 1m, 4–5-pinnatifid, deltoid to ovate, leathery, pinnae narrowly acute, pinnules notched; stipes to 50cm. Indon. to Philipp.

D. epiphylla (Forst.) Spreng. Fronds to 50×50cm, 4–5-pinnate, deltoid to lanceolate, leathery, pinnae petiolate, pinnules lanceolate to ovate, entire, notched or incised, fertile seg. forked at apex; stipes to 50cm. Fiji to Tahiti.

D. epiphylla (Bl. non (Forst.) Spreng. = *D. corniculata*.

D. falcinella Presl = *Trogostolon falcinellus*.

D. fejeensis Hook. RABBIT'S FOOT FERN. Fronds 45×30cm, 4-pinnate, arching to horizontal, pinnae lanceolate, narrowly acute at apex, pinnules lanceolate to deltoid, fertile seg., linear, occas., bifid at apex, to 1mm wide; stipes to 25cm. Fiji. 'Dwarf Ripple': dwarf, fronds v. finely cut. 'Major': fronds with wider seg. 'Plumosa': fronds with narrower, feather-like seg.

D. fumarioides Sw. = *Odontosoria fumarioides*.

D. griffithiana Hook. = *Humata griffithiana*.

D. heterophylla Sm. = *Humata heterophylla*.

D. immersa Wallich = *Leucostegia immersa*.

D. inaequalis Kunze = *Saccoloma inaequale*.

D. jamaicensis Hook. = *Microlepia speluncae*.

D. lorrainii Hance = *D. trichomanoides* var. *lorrainii*.

D. mariesii Moore ex Bak. SQUIRREL'S FOOT FERN; BALL FERN. Fronds to 20×15cm, 3–4-pinnate, pinnae petiolate, oblong or deltoid to ovate, subacute at apex, to 12cm, pinnules lanceolate to oblong, subobtuse, entire or lobed, to 3mm wide, lobes 2–3; stipes to 13cm. China, Taiwan, Korea, Jap. Z9.

D. mooreana Mast. = *Leucostegia pallida*.

D. novae-zelandiae Colenso = *Leptolepia novae-zelandiae*.

D. pallida Mett. = *Leucostegia pallida*.

D. parvula (Wallich, nom. nud.) Hook. & Grev. = *Humata parvula*.

D. pectinata Sm. = *Humata pectinata*.

D. platyphylla D. Don = *Microlepia platyphylla*.

D. plumosa Bak. BLACK CATERPILLAR FERN. Rhiz. scales black. Fronds to 20×15cm, 2–3-pinnate or more, deltoid, pinnae lanceolate, narrowly acute, to 1cm wide, seg. oblique, oblong, occas. incised; stipes to 20cm. Samoa.

D. pycnocarpa Brackenr. = *Scyphularia pycnocarpa*.

D. pyxidata Cav. AUSTRALIAN HARE'S FOOT. Fronds to 70×30cm, 3–4-pinnate or pinnatifid, leathery, dark green, deltoid or lanceolate to ovate, fertile fronds bullate, primary pinnae to 28×20cm, petiolate, overlapping, rhomboid, acute, pinnules to 4×2cm, petiolate, seg. to 10×5mm, rhomboid or oblong, obtuse or acute, dentate; stipes to 30cm. Aus.

D. solida (Forst.) Sw. GIANT HARE'S FOOT. Fronds to 50×50cm, 3-pinnate or -pinnatifid, tough, shiny dark green, pinnae distant, deltoid, to 20×10cm, pinnules to 7×3cm, petiolate, acute, lobes elliptic, obtuse, notched; stipes to 30cm. Malaysia to Aus., Polyn. 'Ornata': pinnules broad. 'Ruffled Ornata': pinnules broad, crispate.

D. solida Luerssen non (Forst.) Spreng. = *D. fejeensis*.

D. speluncae (L.) Bak. = *Microlepia speluncae*.

D. stenolepis Hayata = *D. mariesii*.

D. tenuifolia Sw. = *Sphenomeris chinensis*.

D. trichomanoides Bl. SQUIRREL'S FOOT FERN; BALL FERN. Fronds to 30×30cm, finely 3–4-pinnate or -pinnatifid, pinnae petiolate, distant, rhomboid to ovate or sagitate, narrowly acute, to 5cm wide, pinnules oblong, seg. bifid (sterile) or toothed and horned (fertile), notched; stipes to 15cm. E Asia. var. *lorrainii* (Hance) Holtt. Scales dark. Fronds sparse. Malaysia.

D. tripinnata F. Muell. = *Oenotrichia tripinnata*.

→*Humata*.

DAVALLIACEAE Mett. ex Frank in Heunis. 10 genera. *Araiostegia, Davallia, Davallodes, Gymnogrammitis, Humata, Leucostegia, Rumohra, Scyphularia* and *Trogostolon*.

Davallodes (Copel.) Copel. Davalliaceae. 11 epiphytic ferns. Rhiz. creeping; scales brown or black. Fronds stipitate, uniform, pinnately divided, ± lanceolate, thin-textured and papery; rachis winged. Trop. Asia. Z10.

D. hirsutum (Presl) Copel. Rhiz. scales dark brown. Fronds to 45×18cm, to 3-pinnatifid, sagitate, pubesc., pinnae obtuse, notched or lobed, oblong; stipes to 10cm. Indon. to Philipp.

D. membranulosum (Wallich) Copel. Rhiz. scales pale brown. Fronds to 25×10cm, 1-pinnate, lanceolate, lower pinnae with many, oblong, dentate lobes; stipes to 8cm. Himal.

→*Davallia, Leucostegia* and *Microlepia*.

Davidia Baill. DOVE TREE; GHOST TREE; HANDKERCHIEF TREE. Nyssaceae (Davidiaceae). 1 decid. ± pyramidal tree to 20m. Lvs broadly ovate, to 16cm, serrate, base cordate, apex acuminate, veins impressed; petiole to 7.5cm. Fls minute, in a dense globose, purple-red, pendulous head to 2cm diam., subtended by 2 flaccid, leafy white bracts (the larger to 20cm). Fr. a subspherical to ovoid, hard brown drupe. SW China. Z6.

D. involucrata Baill. var. **vilmoriniana** (Dode) Wangerin. Lvs glossy pale green or glaucescent beneath, ± glab. The commonest form in cult.

D. vilmoriniana Dode = *D. involucrata* var. *vilmoriniana*.

David Pine *Pinus armandii*.
David's Peach *Prunus davidiana*.

Daviesia Sm. BITTER PEAS; BACON-AND-EGGS. Leguminosae (Papilionoideae). 110 shrubs or subshrubs. Lvs simple, or reduced to short prickles or teeth or 0. Fls pea-like in short axill. fascicles. Aus. and Tasm. Z9.

D. acicularis Sm. Small shrub; br. angular or terete. Lvs 1.5–3.5cm, linear, stiff, tightly inrolled. Fls solitary or clustered along branchlet ends, brown and yellow. Spring. Queensld, NSW.

D. cordata Sm. BOOKLEAF. Small shrub; br. densely angled. Lvs 5–10cm, cordate, acute, reticulate. Fls 5–12 in umbels; standard yellow, wings ruby-coloured; bracts increase in size after flowering to enclose fr. Spring. W Aus.

D. corymbosa Sm. Small shrub br. somewhat angular. Lvs 4–12cm, linear-lanceolate to ovate-attenuate, rounded or pointed. Fls yellow in dense corymbose rac. Spring. NSW.

D. horrida Preiss ex Meissn. HOP BITTER PEA. Small shrub; br. frequently glaucous; branchlets spiny. Lvs 3–15cm, linear to linear-lanceolate flat, pungent, glaucous. Fls in loose rac., on spiny branchlets, yellow. Spring. W Aus.

D. incrassata Sm. Small shrub; br. somewhat compressed or terete. Lvs 0.5–2.5cm, rigid, subterete or compressed and cuneate, upper margin rounded at apex, lower margin pungent. Fls orange-red, in smal clusters. Spring. W Aus.

D. latifolia R. Br. = *D. horrida*.

D. ulicifolia Andrews. GORSE BITTER PEA. Small, rigid, spiny shrub; br. angular, often spiny. Lvs 1–3cm, lanceolate or linear, pungent, flattened, rigid. Fls yellow, in axill. rac. Late spring. Aus.

D. ulicina Sm. = *D. ulicifolia*.

Davis Begonia *Begonia davisii*.
Dawn Redwood *Metasequoia glyptostroboides*.
Dayflower *Commelina*.
Day Jessamine *Cestrum diurnum*.
Daylily *Hemerocallis*.
Deadly Nightshade *Atropa belladonna*; *Solanum dulcamara*.
Dead Nettle *Lamium*.
Dead-sea Apple *Solanum linnaeanum*.

Deamia Britt. & Rose.
D. testudo (Karw. ex Zucc.) Britt. & Rose = *Selenicereus testudo*.

Deane's Boronia *Boronia deanei*.
Deane's Gum *Eucalyptus deanei*.
Deane's Wattle *Acacia deanei*.
Death Camas *Zigadenus* (*Z. nuttallii*; *Z. venenosus*).
Death Valley Penstemon *Penstemon fruticiformis*.

Debregeasia Gaudich. Urticaceae. 3 shrubs or small trees. Lvs finely toothed, usually coarsely hairy. Fls inconspicuous in axill., spherical, sessile or short-stalked clusters. Fr. a fleshy syncarp. Subtrop. & temp. Asia and Afr.

D. longifolia (Burm.) Wedd. To 3m. Br. slender, arching, hispidulous. Lvs to 10–20cm, linear to lanceolate, slender-acuminate, toothed, glabrate, above, tomentose beneath. Fr.

0.75–1.25cm diam., red-orange or yellow, in short-stalked heads. Summer. SE Asia, Himal.
D. velutina Gaudich. = *D. longifolia*.

Decabelone Decne.
D. angolense N.E. Br. ex H.J. Jacobsen = *Tavaresia barklyi*.
D. barklyi Dyer = *Tavaresia barklyi*.
D. elegans Decne. = *Tavaresia angolense*.
D. grandiflora Schum. = *Tavaresia barklyi*.
D. meintjesii (R.A. Dyer) G. Rowley = *Tavaresia meintjesii*.
D. sieberi Pfersd. = *Tavaresia angolense*.

Decaisnea Hook. & Thoms. Lardizabalaceae. 2 shrubs readily distinguished from other members of the Lardizabalaceae by their non-climbing habit, pinnate lvs and ♂ fls. E Asia.
D. fargesii Franch. Upright, decid. shrub, 3–5m, with stout st. Lvs 50–80cm, lfts 6–14cm, ovate to elliptic, glaucous beneath. Infl. a drooping pan., 20–45cm; fls pendulous, campanulate and apetalous; sep. 2.5–3cm, 6, petaloid, yellow-green, lanceolate. Fr. 5–10cm, pendent, cylindrical, bean-like, thick-skinned, leaden-blue, seeds black in white pulp. Summer. W China. Z5.
D. insignis Hook. f. & Thoms. Differs from *D. fargesii* in its yellow fr. to 8cm. Summer. Himal., Yunnan. Z8.

Decanemopsis Cost. & Gall.
D. aphylla Cost. & Gall. = *Sarcostemma madagascariense*.

Decaryia Choux. Didiereaceae. 1 shrub or small tree, 6–8m; st. straight; br. spreading with thorny, flexuous twigs. Lvs 5–3mm, fleshy, obcordate, borne below paired thorns. Fls small a bipartite cyme. SW Madag. Z10.
D. madagascariensis Choux.

Deccan Hemp *Hibiscus cannabinus*.
Deciduous Fig *Ficus superba* var. *henneana*.

Decumaria L. Hydrangeaceae. 2 decid. or semi-everg. shrubs climbing by aerial rootlets. Differing from *Hydrangea anomala* and *Schizophragma hydrangeoides*, in infl. composed wholly of small, fertile fls. W China, SE US.
D. barbara L. CLIMBING HYDRANGEA; WOOD VAMP. To 10m. Lvs 5–10cm, ovate to ovate-oblong, usually tapering and obscurely toothed toward apex, dark green above, puberulous beneath. Pan. 5–8cm diam., term., rather domed; fls white, sweetly fragrant. SE US. Z7.
D. sinensis Oliv. Seldom exceeding 4m. Lvs 3–7cm, sometimes persistent, obovate to orbicular, obtuse and sometimes serrate in apical half, matt mid-green. Pan. 3–8cm diam., term. or axill., flat-topped; fls white, muskily scented. C China. Z8.

Decussocarpus Laub.
D. falcatus (Thunb.) Laub. = *Afrocarpus falcatus*.
D. fleuryi (Hickel) Laub. = *Nageia fleuryi*.
D. gracilior (Pilger) Laub. = *Afrocarpus gracilior*.
D. mannii (Hook. f.) Laub. = *Afrocarpus mannii*.
D. nagi (Thunb.) Laub. = *Nageia nagi*.
D. vitiensis (Seem.) Laub. = *Retrophyllum vitiense*.
D. wallichiana (Presl) Laub. = *Nageia wallichiana*.

Deerberry *Vaccinium caesium*; *V. neglectum*; *V. stramineum*.
Deer Brush *Ceanothus integerrimus*.
Deer Cabbage *Nephrophyllidium crista-galli*.
Deer Clover *Lotus scoparius*.
Deer Fern *Blechnum spicant*.
Deer Grass *Rhexia*.
Deerhorn Cedar *Thujopsis*.
Deer Oak *Quercus sadleriana*.
Deer's Foot Fern *Davallia canariensis*.
Deer Tongue Fern *Blechnum spicant*.

Degenia Hayek. Cruciferae. 1 perenn. herb to 10cm. Lvs linear-lanceolate, rosulate, silvery-grey. Fls 4-merous, 10–12mm diam. yellow. NW Balk. Z7.
D. velebitica (Deg.) Hayek.

Deherainia Decne. Theophrastaceae. 2 everg. shrubs and small trees. Mex.
D. smaragdina Decne. Spreading shrub or tree to 4m; bark deep brown to black, twigs green-velutinous, hardening black. Lvs to 12cm, ovate-elliptic, dark green, glossy, downy beneath. Fls to 6cm diam., solitary or paired, heavily nectariferous, malodorous; cor. jade green, lobes 5, rounded, valvate, fleshy, united in a thick, campanulate tube at base. Mex.

Deimio Oak *Quercus dentata*.

Deinanthe Maxim. Hydrangeaceae. 2 robust perenn. herbs. St. erect, from a stout rootstock. Lvs ovate to elliptic, toward st. apex. Fls in term. clusters or pan., fertile fls numerous, large and nodding, sterile fls smaller. E Asia. Z7.
D. bifida Maxim. To 20cm. Lvs crinkly, coarse-textured and glossy, deeply lobed at apex. Fls white in term. clusters among lvs; sta. yellow. Jap.
D. caerulea Stapf. To 50cm. Lvs sharply toothed. Fls pale mauve to lilac-blue, in a terminal pan.; sta. blue. China.

Delairea Lem. Compositae. 1 succulent, climbing herb to 6m. Lvs to 10cm, deltoid to orbicular-reniform, lobed, lobes deltoid, acute; petioles to 11cm, with 2 winged auricles. Cap. discoid, in dense corymbs; flts yellow. Spring–summer. S Afr., nat. elsewhere. Distinguished from *Senecio scandens* by absence of ray flts. Z9.
D. odorata Lem. GERMAN IVY; PARLOUR IVY.
→*Senecio*.

Delarbrea Vieill. Araliaceae. 6 treelets or trees, unbranched or sparsely branched. Lvs in juvenile plants often finely divided, coarsely toothed; in adult plants imparipinnate. Infl. term., compound; fls small in umbels. Fr. drupaceous. E Malesia, Pacific. Z10.
D. collina auct., non Vieill. = *D. paradoxa*.
D. concinna Bull = *D. paradoxa*.
D. lauterbachii Harms = *D. paradoxa*.
D. michieana (F. Muell.) F. Muell. Similar to *D. paradoxa* but lvs in mature plants to 120cm, lfts long-acuminate, and infl. to 110cm, not corky; fr. steely blue, to 20mm. Spring. Aus. (Queensld).
D. paradoxa Vieill. To 10m. Juvenile lvs 1–2× compound, to 1m, arching, with 15–19 lfts, each with 3 pinnae or 3-lobed, toothed; lvs in mature plants compound, to 70cm, lfts 11–19 entire, oblong-elliptic to narrowly ovate, truncate to 22×8cm. Infl. to 60cm, corky; primary br. to 30cm. Fr. purple-black, to 10mm. Autumn–winter. E Malesia and SW Pacific, scattered. The name *D. spectabilis* has been applied to juveniles of this sp.
D. spectabilis Lind. & André = *D. paradoxa*.
→*Aralia*.

Delavay's Fir *Abies delavayi*.

Delonix Raf. Leguminosae (Caesalpinoideae). 10 everg. or decid. trees. Lvs bipinnate. Rac. ± corymbose; cal. deeply lobed; pet. 5, spreading, obovate-spathulate, ± equal, clawed; sta. 10, long, exserted. Trop. Afr., Madag., India.
D. regia (Bojer) Raf. FLAMBOYANT; PEACOCK FLOWER; FLAME TREE; ROYAL POINCIANA. Decid. tree, to 10m. Crown wide-spreading. Pinnae pairs 22–40; lfts to 15mm, 20–50, elliptic to oblong. Pet. to 7cm, scarlet to orange, standard yellow-white and scarlet, striped. Spring–summer. Madag. var. *flavida* Stehlé. Fls entirely golden yellow. Z9.
→*Poinciana*.

Delosperma N.E. Br. Aizoaceae. 150+ perennials, annuals or biennials, mat-forming, herbaceous or shrubby, or with ann. shoots from a tuberous caudex, lvs cylindric or flat. Fls 2.5–7cm diam., daisy-like. S & E Afr., Arabia. Z9 unless specified.
D. aberdeenense (L. Bol.) L. Bol. Small dense shrub with minutely papillose, often prostrate br. Lvs 0.4–1cm, semicylindric, acute. Fls purple-red. S Afr.
D. abyssinicum (Reg.) Schwantes. Erect shrub; br. slender, tinged red, papillose. Lvs 3–4cm, subcylindric, obtuse, soft, minutely papillose. Fls pink. Ethiop.
D. cooperi (Hook. f.) L. Bol. Freely branching, prostrate, papillose subshrub. Lvs to 5cm, cylindric, obtuse with papillae in longitudinal lines, soft. Fls purple-red. S Afr. Z6.
D. echinatum (Ait.) Schwantes = *D. pruinosum*.
D. ecklonis (Salm-Dyck) Schwantes. Br. prostrate, slender, with minute hairs at first. Lvs to 3cm, flat-compressed, triquetrous, acute, softly hirsute. Fls white. S Afr. var. *latifolia* L. Bol. Lvs to 2.7cm, oblong-oval, lanceolate or ovate. Fls purple-pink.
D. expersum (N.E. Br.) L. Bol. Shrubby, 15–30cm; br. thin, woody, ascending at first, tinged purple or brown. Lvs to 0.6cm, channelled-concave, papillose, off-white. Fls tinted red. W Cape. var. *decumbens* L. Bol. Br. prostrate. Lvs 10–20mm, narrowing toward tip. Fls purple-pink. SW Cape.
D. grandiflorum L. Bol. Shrubby, erect to clambering, 30–40cm; br. stiff. Lvs 2–3.5cm, channelled, narrowing toward obtuse tip, green, faintly papillose. Fls purple-pink. W Cape.
D. hallii L. Bol. Forming compact shrubs 10–15cm, br. 2-angled. Lvs to 4.6cm, fleshy, expanded midway, acute or obtuse, silvery grey to green, minutely tuberculate. Fls pink. Nam.
D. lehmannii (Ecklon & Zeyh.) Schwantes. Br. 10–25mm, 2-

angled, tinged red. Lvs to 2.5cm, triquetrous with convex sides, apiculate, grey to grey-green, smooth. Fls pale yellow. S Afr.

D. lineare L. Bol. Erect, slender shrub to 18cm; br. often prostrate, rough, papillose. Lvs 2–5cm, linear to semicyindric, acute, yellow-green. Fls white. Les.

D. lydenburgense L. Bol. Herbaceous; br. lax, to 20cm, minutely papillose. Lvs 3.5–5cm, linear, acute, flat to furrowed above. Fls purple-pink. Transvaal.

D. nubigenum (Schltr.) L. Bol. Prostrate, papillose subshrub. Lvs oblong-elliptic or linear, papillose. Fls orange-red. OFS.

D. pruinosum (Thunb.) J. Ingram. Bushy shrub to 30cm. Br. dichotomous with white papillae. Lvs to 1.3cm, ovate to hemispheric, upper surface flat, sap green with large, bristle-tipped white papillae. Fls white or tinged yellow. S Afr.

D. sutherlandii (Hook. f.) N.E. Br. Perenn. with napiform caudex. Shoots ann., rough-haired and papillose, 8–15cm. Lvs 5–8cm, slightly channelled above, with keel below, fresh green, minutely papillose, ciliate. Fls violet-pink. S Afr.

D. taylorii (N.E. Br.) L. Bol. Similar to *D. lehmannii* but more robust and lvs grey-green to grey-white. S Afr. var. *albanense* L. Bol. Lvs hemispheric, unequal, 0.4–0.7cm. Fls pale pink. E Cape.

D. tradescantioides (A. Berger) L. Bol. Dwarf, creeping, rooting at nodes. Lvs to 3cm, ovate, tapered, narrowed teretely at base, somewhat furrowed above with a keel below, minutely papillose. Fls white. S Afr.

→*Drosanthemum, Lampranthus, Mesembryanthemum* and *Schoenlandia*.

Delostoma D. Don. Bignoniaceae. 4 shrubs. Lvs simple. Rac. few-fld; cor. tubular-campanulate, slightly incurved, bilabiate, lobes 5, rounded, spreading. Andes. Z9.

D. dentatum D. Don. Lvs to 12cm, oblong, pubesc. beneath, serrate. Infl. to 7.5cm; fls 3.75cm, white tinged palest pink. Peru.

D. roseum Schum. Lvs to 15cm, ovate to orbicular, tomentose beneath. Infl. to 20cm; fls 3.75cm, pale pink. Ecuad., Colomb.

Delphinium L. LARKSPUR. Ranunculaceae. 250 ann., bienn. or perenn. herbs. St. erect, sometimes branching. Lvs petiolate to sessile, palmate or digitate. Infl. a spike or rac., sometimes paniculate; fls pedicellate, subtended by bracts and bracteoles, zygomorphic; sep. 5, petaloid, posterior sep. forming spur; pet. in 2 unequal pairs, sometimes darker and more downy than sep. and termed the 'bee', upper pair large with nectariferous spurs projecting into spur of posterior sep.; sta. numerous. N temp. zone, some isolated on mts in central Afr.

D. ajacis auct. = *Consolida orientalis* or *Consolida ambigua*.

D. alpinum Waldst. & Kit. = *D. elatum*.

D. altissimum Wallich. Perenn.; st. branched, sparsely hairy above, 60–120cm. Lvs to 15cm diam., lobes 5–7, further 3-lobed and toothed, cauline lvs 3-lobed or entire. Fls few in lax rac., deep blue or purple; sep. pubesc. outside, to 1.5cm, spur curved, to 22mm; upper pet. dark purple, toothed, lower pet. lobed, hairy. C to E Himal. Z6.

D. amabile Tidestr. = *D. parishii*.

D. andersonii A. Gray. Perenn.; st. 20–60cm, glab. Lvs 1–3cm diam., basal, lobes oblong, mucronate, slightly fleshy, glabrate. Fls 5–12 in rac.; sep. rich blue to purple; oblong-ovate, to 14mm, spur thick, ± straight, to 12mm; upper pet. white, emarginate, lower pet. rounded. Spring–summer. W US. Z5.

D. armeniacum Stapf ex Huth = *Consolida armeniaca*.

D. azureum Michx. = *D. carolinianum*.

D. barbeyi Huth. Perenn.; st. stout, pubesc., 30–100cm. Lvs 7–15cm diam., lower lvs with 5 lobes further dissected; upper lvs with 3, pubesc. above. Fls in dense rac., dark blue; sep. acuminate, yellow glandular-pubesc., to 2cm, spur straight to 2cm; upper pet. yellow, tinged blue, lower pet., blue, bifid. Summer. Rocky Mts. Z5.

D. ×belladonna hort. ex Bergmans. (*D. elatum* ×*D. grandiflorum*.) Close to *D. elatum*, but lacks distinct central rac. Sep. rich blue, spur to 3cm; pet. dull yellow. Summer. Gdn origin. 'Bellamosum': fls dark blue. 'Blue Bees': fls pale blue with white eye, abundant. 'Casablanca': fls white. 'Cliveden Beauty': fls sky blue. 'Lamartine': fls deep blue tinged purple, v. prolific. 'Moorheim': fls white. 'Orion': fls pale blue, repeat flowering. 'Piccolo': fls gentian-blue, free flowering. 'Volkerfrieden': st. tall, slender; fls deep blue. 'Wendy' ('Andenken an August Koenemann'): fls gentian-blue. Z3.

D. bellamosum hort. = *D. ×belladonna*.

D. bicolor Nutt. Perenn.; st. simple, 15–25cm, glab. to sparsely hairy. Lvs to 5cm diam., basal, subglabrous, with 5 lobes divided into linear seg. Fls 2–12 in rac., violet; sep. unequal, lower 2 to 1.5cm, equalling stout spur; upper pet., dull yellow or white, entire or emarginate. Spring–summer. W US, Canada.

Z4.

D. brownii Rydb. = *D. glaucum*.

D. brunonianum Royle. Hairy perenn.; st. to 20cm. Lvs 3–8cm diam., cordate to rounded, lobes 5, toothed, sometimes musk-scented. Fls few, clustered, blue to purple, conspicuously veined, hairy, appearing inflated; sep. 3–5cm, spur short; pet. black-purple, lower with golden hairs. Summer. Himal. Z4.

D. bulleyanum Forr. ex Diels. Perenn.; st. simple or branched above leafy, glab. except glandular-pubesc. infl., 30–140cm. Lvs 3–10cm diam., round-pentagonal, lobes 3–5, divided and toothed, sparsely pilose. Fls many in lax rac., deep blue-lavender to rich purple; sep. to 2cm, ovate, obtuse to acute, spur to 22mm, strongly curved, pet. blue, upper glab., emarginate, lower, bifid, ciliate. Summer. W China. Z7.

D. caeruleum Jacquem. Perenn.; st. branched from base, leafy, to 30cm. Lvs to 4cm diam., rounded, lobes 5–7, cuneate-oblong, incised or pinnatifid, seg. linear. Fls few in lax rac., or solitary, pale blue, hirsute, 2.5cm; sep. shorter than straight spur; pet. slightly hairy. Summer. Himal. Z7.

D. californicum Torr. & A. Gray. Perenn.; st. to 2m, simple, leafy. Lvs 5–15cm diam., palmate, lobes 5–7, divided and toothed. Fls in dense rac. to 50cm, dull blue or purple; sep. pale, tinged green or lavender, ovate, obtuse, pubesc., to 10cm, spur stout, arched, to 8mm; upper pet. beaked, villous, lower pet. hairy. Spring–summer. Calif. Z8.

D. candidum Hemsl. = *D. leroyi*.

D. cardinale Hook. Short-lived perenn.; st. to 2m, simple or branched. Basal lvs 5–20cm diam., lobes 5, further 3-lobed, dark green; cauline lvs 5–7-lobed, much divided. Fls in loose rac. or pan.; sep. to 16mm, scarlet, ovate, glab., spur stout, to 2cm, upper pet. yellow, tipped scarlet. Spring–summer. Calif., Baja Calif. Z8.

D. cardiopetalum DC. = *D. verdunense*.

D. carolinianum Walter. Perenn.; st. 40–120cm, simple or sparsely branched, leafy, glandular-bristly above. Lower lvs with 3–5 lobes deeply dissected, upper lvs less dissected. Fls in slender rac., deep blue or violet, 2.5cm; spur to 18mm; lower pet. bifid, hairy. Spring–summer. E US. Z4.

D. cashmerianum Royle. St. to 45cm. Basal lvs round, 3–5cm across, lobes 5–7, toothed. Infl. corymbose; fls 10–12, blue-purple, to 3.5cm, not as downy or inflated as in the related *D. brunonianun*; sep. obtuse, broad, spur curved, broad, to 1.5cm; upper pet. black-purple, lower pet. dull green. Summer. W Himal. 'Album': fls white. Z5.

D. caucasicum C.A. Mey. = *D. speciosum*.

D. cheilanthum Fisch. ex DC. Perenn.; st. glab., 30–100cm. Lvs large, round-cordate or -reniform, primary lobes 3, 3-lobed, dentate or entire, pubesc. beneath; upper lvs less dissected. Fls many in rac., blue; sep. ovate to elliptic, obtuse, pubesc., to 2.5cm, spur curved at apex, to 1.8cm; upper pet. blue or yellow, glab., lower pet. pubesc. Summer. Sib., E Asia. Z4.

D. chinense Fisch. = *D. grandiflorum*.

D. ciliatum Steven = *D. dictyocarpum*.

D. corymbosum Reg. Perenn.; st. branched, hairy and leafy below, 15–65cm. Lvs round-cordate, lobes 3, dissected, hairy; upper lvs linear, entire. Infl. corymbose; fls violet; sep. to 17mm, ovate, obtuse, long-hairy outside, spur curved, to 12mm; pet. v. dark, upper pair glab., entire, lower pair ciliate, bifid. Summer. C Asia. Z6.

D. crassifolium Schräd. & Reg. = *D. speciosum*.

D. ×cultorum Voss. Collective name for gdn hybrids.

D. dahuricum Besser = *D. cheilanthum*.

D. dasycarpum Steven = *D. elatum*.

D. decorum Fisch. & C.A. Mey. Perenn.; st. ± simple, 12–30cm, pubesc. Basal lvs 3–4cm across, fleshy, slightly pubesc., with 3 divisions, central lobe entire or trifid, lat. lobes sometimes bifid. Fls 2–5, villous, blue-purple; sep. oblong-ovate, obtuse to acute, to 16×8mm; upper pet. white, lobed, lower pet. blue, bifid. Spring. Calif. Z8.

D. delavayi Franch. Perenn.; st. simple, leafy, pubesc., 50–100cm. Lvs round-pentagonal, 3–10cm wide, pubesc., lobes 5–7, incised and toothed. Fls in dense rac., blue-violet to rich purple, pubesc.; sep. broadly ovate to elliptic-oblong, to 1.5cm, spur curved, to 2cm; upper pet. blue, entire, glab., lower pet. lobed, long-ciliate. Autumn. China. Z6.

D. denudatum Wallich ex Hook. f. & Thoms. Perenn.; st. branched, glab., to 1m. Basal lvs rounded, 5–15cm across, with 3–5 narrow divisions. Fls in spicate clusters, blue, 2.5cm across; sep. 12mm, spur 15mm; upper pet. white. Summer. W Himal. (Pak. to C Nepal). Z7.

D. depauperatum Nutt. ex Torr. & A. Gray. Perenn.; st. slender, bare glab., 6–30cm. Lvs few, basal, angular-rounded, 2–5cm across, with 3–5 entire or dissected lobes. Fls few, bright dark blue; sep. glab., oblong-ovate, 8mm, spur slender, straight, 15mm; upper pet. narrow, edged white, lower pet. orbicular-ovate, hairy. Spring–summer. W US. Z6.

D. dictyocarpum DC. Perenn.; st. glab. to hairy, branched above, 60cm–1m. Lvs round-cordate to -reniform, lobes 3–7, much dissected, seg. narrow, pubesc. beneath. Fls in dense rac., pale to dark blue; sep. ovate, glab., 1.5cm, spur straight, to 12mm; pet. pale blue to white, lower pair bifid, hairy. Summer. E Russia. Z6.

D. duhmbergii Huth. Perenn.; st. erect, long-hairy below, 30–65cm. Lvs orbicular-reniform, pubesc., lobes 5–7, cuneate, seg. narrow. Fls in dense rac., blue or white; sep. ovate, obtuse to 1.5cm, spur slightly curved, to 1.5cm; pet. v. dark. Summer. Sib. Z3.

D. elatum L. Variable perenn.; st. 40cm–2m, hairy below. Lvs 9×16cm, deeply 5–7-lobed, upper lvs with 3 divisions, much dissected, seg. to 7mm wide, acute. Fls in dense rac., blue, to 2.5cm long; sep. ovate, obtuse, glab., 15mm; pet. dull purple or yellow, lower pair with yellow hairs. Summer. S & C Eur. to Sib. Z3.

D. exaltatum Ait. Perenn.; st. glab. except above infl. axis 1–2m. Lvs large, lobes 3–5, much dissected. Infl. branched; fls numerous in long rac., blue or purple, puberulent; sep. ovate, 1cm, spur straight or curved, to 1.5cm; pet. dull yellow, lower pair bifid, hairy. Summer. E US. Z5.

D. exaltatum var. *californicum* (Torr. & A. Gray) Huth = D. californicum.

D. fissum Waldst. & Kit. Perenn.; st. glab. or pubesc., ± simple, 60–100cm. Basal lvs 7–18cm across, with many linear to lanceolate lobes. Fls in dense rac., blue, violet-blue to lilac, 2.5cm; spur straight; upper pet. lobed, lower pet. bifid. Summer. Balk., Turk. Z7.

D. formosum Boiss. & Huet. Perenn.; st. hairy or glabrescent, branched, 60–180cm. Lvs large, with 5–7 divisions, pinnately lobed and incised, glab. Fls many in rac., intense violet-blue; sep. glab. to puberulent without, pilose within, to 2.5cm, spur 2cm, straight, hooked; pet. purple-black, lower pair yellow-hairy. Summer. Turk., Cauc. Z3.

D. formosum hort. non Boiss. & Huet = D. ×belladonna.

D. geyeri Greene. Perenn.; st. leafy, esp. below, pubesc., 20–70cm. Lvs 5–8cm across, grey-strigose, much dissected. Fls in dense rac., bright blue; sep. oblong to oval, to 1.5cm, spur to 2cm; upper pet. yellow, tinged blue, entire, lower pet. blue, sinuate. Spring–summer. Rocky Mts. Z3.

D. glareosum Greene. Perenn.; st. simple, weakly glab., 20–40cm. Lvs basal, thick, 5–8cm across, shallowly 3-lobed, seg. ternate, obtuse. Fls in lax rac., dark blue or purple; sep. orbicular to oblong-ovate, to 1.5cm, spur slender, curved to 1.5cm; upper pet. white, lower pet. suborbicular, dark blue-purple, white-hairy. Spring–summer. W US. Z5.

D. grandiflorum L. Perenn. but often treated as an ann.; st. occas. simple, pubesc., 25–100cm. Lvs with 5 broad lobes dissected into nnarrow, acuminate seg., pilose. Fls in lax rac., blue, violet or white; sep. elliptic-ovate to -obovate, pubesc., to 2.5cm, spur upcurved, to 2cm; upper pet. sometimes with yellow apex, entire, lower pet. blue, hairy. Summer. Sib., E Asia (Mong., China, Jap.). 'Album': fls white. 'Azureum': habit dwarf. 'Blauer Spiegel' ('Blue Mirror'): to 1m; fls marine blue. 'Blauer Zwerg': to 20cm; fls gentian blue. 'Blue Butterfly': to 30cm; fls deep blue in loose spikes. Z3.

D. grandiflorum var. chinense (Fisch.) Fisch. ex DC. = D. grandiflorum.

D. hansenii (Greene) Greene. St. 40–90cm, pubesc. Basal lvs 4–9cm, palmatifid, divisions shallow; upper lvs smaller, pinnatisect. Fls in compact rac., dark purple to blue or purple-red; sep. oblong, obtuse, pubesc., to 8mm, spur curved to 1cm; upper pet. narrow, pale, striped, lower pet. dark, round, hairy. Spring. Calif. Z8.

D. hesperium A. Gray. Perenn. st. simple, slender, puberulent, 30–60cm. Lvs 2–4cm wide, 3–5-palmatifid, lobes with oblong seg., pubesc. Fls in dense rac., dark blue or blue-purple; sep. oblong-ovate, obtuse, to 12mm, spur ± straight, to 1.5cm; upper pet. white-edged, lower pet. rounded, hairy. Spring–summer. Calif. ssp. *cuyamacae* (Abrams) F. Lewis & Epling. Fls pale blue to violet; sep. to 8mm. S Calif. Z8.

D. hybridum Steven ex Willd. Perenn.; st. glandular-pubesc. above, 20–100cm. Lvs to 20cm diam., palmately lobed, lobes finely pinnatisect. Fls in dense rac., dark blue; sep. obtuse, strigulose, to 1cm, spur ascending, to 2cm, upper pet. blue, glab., shortly lobed, lower pet. hairy, bifid. Summer. N Turk., Transcauc. Z7.

D. hybridum hort. non Steven ex Willd. = D. ×cultorum.

D. incanum Royle = D. roylei.

D. intermedium Ait. = D. elatum.

D. laxiflorum DC. = D. villosum.

D. leiocarpum Huth = D. fissum.

D. leroyi Franch. ex Huth. Perenn.; st. pubesc., 50–150cm. Lvs orbicular-reniform, 15cm across, lobes 5, cuneate-obovate, dissected into 3 seg. Fls in pan., white or blue, scented; sep. broad

to 4cm, with green or brown swelling, spur to 4cm, hooked, upper pet. glab., emarginate, lower pet. 3-toothed, slightly hairy. Summer. E Afr. Z8.

D. leucophaeum Greene. Perenn.; st. slender, leafy, glab. below, 30–75cm. Lvs pentagonal, 4.5–9cm wide, lobes 3–5, pinnatifid or trifid, seg. short. Fls in lax rac., creamy white; sep. ovate, umbonate, puberulent outside, to 1.2cm, spur straight or upcurved, 1.2cm; upper pet. bright blue, lower pet. creamy white, emarginate. Spring–summer. W US. Z5.

D. likiangense Franch. Perenn.; st. simple, subglabrous, 10–50cm. Lvs basal, 3–6cm across, subglabrous, lobes 5, seg. linear. Fls 1–5, deep violet; sep. broad-ovate, obtuse to acute, strigulose, to 3cm, spur straight, to 2cm.; upper pet. blue, 2-toothed, lower pet. oblong-ovate, bifid, hairy. Summer. W China. Z7.

D. linarioides Boiss. Ann.; st. branched, pubesc., to 15cm, lvs 3–4-fid, seg. linear. Fls in lax rac., blue; spur blunt, incurved, slightly shorter than sep.; pet. 3-lobed, obtuse. Summer. Iran. Z8.

D. luteum Heller. Close to D. nudicaule. St. 20–40cm. Lvs 3–6cm across, with 3–5 divisions, seg. further lobed and toothed, pubesc. Fls in lax rac., yellow; sep. tipped purple, broad-ovate, 1.5cm, pubesc. Spring–summer. Coastal N Calif. Z8.

D. maackianum Reg. Perenn.; st. glab. or hairy, 55–80cm. Lvs round-reniform, to 8×16cm, lobes-3, dissected and toothed, glab. to strigose. Fls many, blue, in pan., subtended by brown-purple bracts; sep. ovate, exterior pilose, to 1.5cm, spur curved, to 2cm; pet. dark violet. Summer. Sib., Manch. Z3.

D. macrocentron Oliv. Perenn.; st. hairy below, branched above, to 2m. Lf lobes 3–7, much divided. Fls 3–10, nodding, pubesc., dark blue to turquoise or moss-green; sep. broad, spur to 5cm, curved upwards, blue to white; pet. oblong, white or pale blue with apex bright green. Summer. E Afr. Z8.

D. menziesii DC. St. 20–50cm, white-pubesc., lvs round-pentagonal, 3–6cm across, palmate with seg. lobed. Fls 3–10 in short rac., deep blue, hairy; sep. oblong-ovate, to 1.5cm, spur to 1.5cm; upper pet. pale, lower pet. rounded, dark blue, sometimes marked white. Spring. Calif. to BC. Z3.

D. moschatum Munro = D. brunonianum.

D. muscosum Exell & Hillc. Perenn.; st. much-branched from base, hairy, 10–15cm. Lvs suborbicular, 2–3cm across, seg. 3 divided into linear lobes. Fls solitary at ends of br., dark blue to dark violet; seg. elliptic to ovate, yellow-hairy outside, glab. within, to 2.5cm, spur slightly curved, 1.5cm; upper pet. narrow-elliptic, entire, lower pet. ovate, yellow- or white-hairy. Summer. Bhutan. Z7.

D. nelsonii Greene. Perenn. St. slender, puberulent, 20–50cm. Lvs to 5cm across, divided into many obtuse linear seg. Fls 6–10, blue-purple to pale blue; sep. oblong to ovate, obtuse, to 2cm, spur slender, 1.5cm; pet. white or dull yellow, upper entire to emarginate, lower pet. lobed. Spring–summer. W US. Z4.

D. nudicaule Torr. & A. Gray. Short-lived perenn.; st. glaucous, 20–60cm. Lvs 3–10cm across, divisions 3–5, shallowly lobed, glab. to sparsely pubesc. Fls in lax pan., orange-red; sep. ovate, glab., 1cm, spur to 2cm, straight; upper pet. yellow with red tips, ovate, toothed at apex, lower pet. narrow, bifid. Spring–summer. Calif. Z8.

D. nuttallianum Pritz. ex Walp. Perenn.; st. slender, pubesc. above, 10–30cm. Lvs few, orbicular, 3–5cm across, seg. 3–5, dissected into oblong obtuse lobes, glab. Fls few, nodding, bright blue to purple; sep. oblong-ovate, to 12mm, pubesc., spur straight, to 1.5cm; upper pet. white, lower pet. translucent, narrow-ovate, bifid. Spring–summer. BC to Calif., Utah. Z4.

D. orientale Gay = Consolida orientalis.

D. oxysepalum Borb. & Pax. Perenn.; st. pubesc. above, 10–50cm. Lf seg. 3–5, coarsely toothed. Fls numerous, deep blue to violet; sep. to 3cm, spur curved; pet. ciliate, to 1.5cm. Summer. Carpath. Z6.

D. pallasii Nevski = D. fissum.

D. parishii A. Gray. Perenn.; st. glaucous, glab. to pubesc., 15–60cm. Lvs 2–8cm across, seg.3, with linear to oblong lobes, subglabrous to pubesc. Fls 5–25 in lax or dense rac., lavender to light blue; sep. ovate, pubesc., 1cm, spur curved or straight to 13mm; upper pet. white, emarginate, lower pet. blue to violet, hairy. Spring–summer. Calif. Z9.

D. parryi A. Gray. Perenn.; st. slender, simple, puberulent, 30–90cm, lvs 2–8cm across, divisions 3–5, with linear lobes. Fls in lax rac., bright- to purple blue; sep. ovate, to 1.5cm, puberulent, spur to 1.5cm, straight; upper pet. exserted, white, lower pet. rounded, purple-blue, floccose. Spring. S Calif. Z9.

D. pauciflorum Nutt. ex Torr. & A. Gray (non D. Don). = D. nuttallianum.

D. peregrinum L. Ann. or bienn.; st. white-pubesc., branched, 30–80cm. Lvs palmatisect, seg. linear to linear-lanceolate, upper lvs entire. Fls in lax rac., dirty violet to blue-violet; sep. puberulent to 1cm, spur straight, to 2cm; pet. much exceeding sep., upper pet., lower pet. elliptic to obovate. Summer–autumn. C & E Medit. (It. to Turk.). Z7.

D. pictum Willd. Ann. or bienn. st. pubesc., to 1m. Lower lvs with 5–9 dissected lobes; upper lvs 3-lobed, seg. oblong or lanceolate. Fls in dense rac., pale blue, puberulent; sep. ovate, to 14mm, spur to 8mm, curved; upper pet. dull pale yellow, tipped blue, lower pet. suborbicular, abruptly clawed, blue. Summer. Balearics, Corsica, Sardinia, It. Z8.

D. przewalskii Huth. Perenn.; st. branched at base, pilose, 15–25cm. Lvs pilose beneath, lobes 3–5, laciniate into 2–3 seg. 2–6mm wide. Fls 1 to few in corymbose rac., deep blue; sep. ovate to elliptic-ovate, to 2.5cm, spur straight or curved, to 2cm; upper pet. dark brown, emarginate, cilliate, lower pet. dark brown at base, paler above, cleft, white-ciliate, yellow-hairy. Summer. W Mong. Z6.

D. pylzowii Maxim. ex Reg. Perenn.; st. leafy, sericeous, 25–30cm. Lvs orbicular to reniform, seg. oblong to linear, acute. Fls 1–3, large, deep purple; sep. broad ovate, hairy, 3cm, spur straight or curved to 3cm; pet. black-violet, upper entire, glab., lower hairy, bifid. Summer. NW China. Z6.

D. requienii DC. Ann. or bienn.; st. pubesc., sparsely branched, to 1m. Lvs 5–; st. pubesc., sparsely branched, to 1m. Lvs 5–9-lobed, dissected, upper lvs 3-lobed, seg. oblong to lanceolate. Fls in lax rac., blue, puberulent; sep. ovate, 1.5cm, spur curved, 8mm; upper pet. dull yellow, tinged blue, lower pet. obovate. Summer. S Fr., Corsica. Z8.

D. roylei Munz. Perenn.; st. leafy, hairy, simple or branching at base, 50–100cm. Lower lvs to 5cm across, seg. much dissected. Fls in dense rac., bright blue; sep. rounded, exterior pubesc., 1.5cm, spur straight, to 1.5cm. Summer. W Himal. Z7.

D. ×ruysii hort. ex Möllers. (*D. elatum × D. nudicaule.*) Short-lived perenn. to 1.5m, resembling *D. belladonna*, but fls pink. Summer–autumn. Gdn origin. Z6.

D. scabrifolium D. Don = *D. altissimum*.

D. schmalhausenii Alboff = *D. hybridum*.

D. scopulorum A. Gray. Perenn.; st. leafy, glab., to 1.6m. Lvs to 7.5cm across, seg. 5–7, cuneate to laciniate, toothed. Fls many in rac., violet-purple; sep. to 1cm, spur to 1cm. Summer. New Mex., Ariz. Z8.

D. semibarbatum Bien. ex Boiss. Perenn.; st. simple or few-branched, sparsely hairy below, 30–75cm. Lvs palmate, lobes 5, much dissected into linear seg. Fls pale clear yellow; sep. broad-elliptic, obtuse, glab. outside, 1.5cm, spur nearly straight, blunt, 1cm; lower pet. bifid, hairy. Spring–summer. Iran,C Asia. Z6.

D. speciosum Bieb. Perenn.; st. hairy, leafy, 35–75cm. Lvs 3–5-lobed, seg. broad, further lobed and coarsely toothed. Fls dense rac., blue; sep. broad-ovate, acuminate, white-hairy, to 3cm, spur straight curved, to 2cm; pet. dark purple, upper pair glab., lower pair gold-hairy, bifid. Summer. Cauc., C Asia. Z6.

D. staphisagria L. Bienn.; st. hairy, stout, leafy, branched above, 30–100cm. Lvs glossy dark green, pubesc., seg. 3–7, entire or 3-lobed, lobes ovate-lanceolate or oblong. Fls dense rac., smoky green-purple-blue, to 2cm; sep. obtuse, hairy outside, spur to 7mm; upper pet. white or dull pale yellow, exserted, lower pet. obovate, gradually narrowing to form claw, all glab. Spring–summer. Medit. Z8.

D. sulphureum hort. = *D. semibarbatum*.

D. sutchuense Franch. Perenn.; st. pubesc. to glab., 40–80cm. Lvs 6–9cm across, fine-pubesc., lobes 3–5, oblong, incised. Infl. branched; fls 2–6 in term. rac., violet-blue; sep. ovate-oblong, obtuse, strigulose, to 15mm, spur to 18mm, straight or slightly curved upwards; pet. blue, upper pet. emarginate, lower pet. oblong-ovate, bifid, hairy. Summer. W China. Z6.

D. tanguticum (Maxim.) Huth = *D. pylzowii*.

D. tatsienense Franch. Perenn. st. slender, simple or branched, subglabrous to strigulose, 20–60cm. Lvs 3–8cm across, lobes 3–5, incised into linear seg. Fls in open corymbs or short rac., brilliant blue; sep. ovate to oblong, obtuse, pubesc., to 2cm, spur straight, to 3cm; upper pet. blue, glab., lower pet. blue, emarginate, hairy. Summer. W China, E Tibet. 'Album': fls white. Z6.

D. tiroliense Kerner = *D. elatum*.

D. tricorne Michx. Perenn.; st. stout, rather succulent, simple, 20–60cm. Lvs basal, lobes 5, further dissected into narrow oblong-linear or cuneate seg. Fls few in lax villous rac., blue to violet, marked white; sep. to 1.5cm, spur curved upwards, to 2cm; upper pet. sometimes yellow, marked blue, lower pet. entire. Spring. E US. Z4.

D. triste Fisch. ex DC. Perenn.; st. pubesc., simple or sparsely branched, 30–70cm. Lvs hairy on margin and veins, deeply 3-lobed, further lobed and toothed. Fls in lax rac., dull, dark violet; sep. ovate or oblong-ovate, obtuse, densely white-hairy, to 2cm, spur straight, apex hooked, 1cm; pet. dark purple-brown, upper hairy at apex, lower pet. hairy, bifid. Summer. E Sib., Mong. Z3.

D. trolliifolium A. Gray. Perenn.; st. stout, leafy, glab. to pub-esc., 60–150cm. Lower lvs 10–15cm across, seg. 5–7, trifid, laciniately lobed, glab. Fls in lax rac., violet-purple; sep. ovate-lanceolate to elliptic, obtuse to acute, to 2.5cm, spur stout, hooked, to 2cm; upper pet. pale, narrow, lower pet. purple, oblong, villous. Spring–summer. Calif., Oreg. Z6.

D. variegatum Torr. & A. Gray. Perenn.; st. simple, leafy, sub-glabrous, 25–60cm. Lvs 1–5cm across, seg. 3, linear to rounded, puberulent to hirsute. Fls few in rac., light blue to rich blue-purple; sep. to 17mm, sparsely hairy, spur straight, to 1.5cm; upper pet. dull white or yellow, lower pet. rounded. Spring–summer. Calif. Z8.

D. verdunense Balb. Ann. or bienn.; st. slender, branched, pub-erulent, 10–40cm. Lvs small, dissected into linear-oblong seg. Fls 5–15 in short dense rac., deep blue-violet; sep. puberulent outside, to 12mm, spur straight or slightly curved, to 2cm; pet. blue, glab., lower pet. round-cordate. Summer. Fr., Iberia. Z8.

D. vestitum Wallich ex Royle. Perenn., all parts hairy; st. simple, to 1m. Lvs cordate, broad, lobes 5–7, cuneate. Fls many in elongate rac., dull purple to blue; sep. to 2.5cm, including short conic spur; pet. deep blue, lower pair bifid. Summer. Himal. (Pak. to E Nepal; Z7.

D. villosum Steven ex DC. Perenn.; st. glab. except in infl. 100–120cm. Lvs hairy on margins and veins, lobes 3–7, pinnate, seg. lanceolate, acute. Fls in lax rac., blue, hairy; sep. ovate, obtuse, to 1.5cm, spur curving upwards, to 2cm; pet. brown-purple, upper glab., lower yellow-hairy, bifid. Eur. Russia. Z6.

D. virescens Nutt. Perenn. st. pubesc. 40–120cm. Lvs deeply dis-sected, seg. 3–10mm wide, linear. Fls in dense rac., white, green- or blue-white; sep. 1cm, spur straight, to 1.5cm; lower pet. hairy, bifid. Summer. E N Amer. Z4.

D. viride Wats. Short-lived perenn.; st. slender, simple, glaucous, 75–100cm. Lvs 7–10cm, lobes 3, sharply toothed. Fls in lax rac. or pan., green-yellow; sep. lanceolate-ovate, pubesc., to 18mm, spur straight or slightly upcurved, to 22mm; pet. dark purple, upper emarginate, lower oblong-ovate, deeply bifid. Spring–summer. Mex. Z8.

D. wellbyi Hemsl. = *D. leroyi*.

D. yunnanense (Franch.) Franch. Perenn.; st. simple or branched, hairy below, 25–75cm. Lvs light green, pubesc. 4–12cm across, 5-lobed, further lobed and toothed. Fls few in lax rac., deep blue; sep. ovate, finely strigulose, to 12mm, spur straight, 2cm; upper pet. emarginate, lower pet. dull blue, shallowly lobed, long-ciliate. Summer. W China. Z6.

D. zalil Aitch. & Hemsl. = *D. semibarbatum*.

D. cvs. Dwarf. 'Baby Doll': to 130cm; mauve with pale yellow bee. 'Janice': to 1m, sturdy; pure white in pyramidal spike. 'Minstrel Boy': to 1m; blue tinged violet with black and gold bee. 'Betty Hay': sky blue, bee pure white. 'Junior': to 1.5m; pale blue with dark blue bee. 'Merlin': to 1.7m; light blue, bee white. 'Sommernachtstraum' ('Summer Night's Dream'): to 1.72cm; dark blue, dark bee. *Tall.* 'Boningale Glory': to 2.5m; semi-double, inner pet. mauve, outer pet. blue. 'Laura Fairbrother': pale purple with white bee, spike v. long. 'Mrs. J.S. Courtauld': to 2.5m; sky blue and mauve in large spikes. 'Silver Moon': to 190cm; silver-mauve with white bee covered in golden hair; spikes broad. spikes broad. PACIFIC HYBRIDS Tall, strong-stemmed varieties to 1.8m; large, semi-double or double in a range of colours from white, through pink semi-double or double in a range of colours from white, through pink and purple, to blue, single coloured strains now available. and purple, to blue, single coloured strains now available. 'Alice Artindale': dense, double, bright blue in narrow spikes. 'Astolat': shades of lilac and pink. 'Black Knight': dark violet with black bee. 'Blue Bird': clear blue with white bee. 'Guinivere': lavender tinged pink, bee white. 'King Arthur': violet with white eye. 'Summer Skies': shades of pale blue. 'Weisser Hercules' ('White Hercules'): white, bee black. UNI-VERSITY HYBRIDS Shades of red and orange.

Delta Maidenhair Fern *Adiantum raddianum*.

Dendranthema (DC.) Desmoul. Compositae. *c*20 strongly scented, perenn. herbs, sometimes woody at base. Lvs pinnatifid or entire. Cap. radiate, solitary or in loose corymbs. Eur., C & E Asia. Z6 unless specified.

D. arcticum (L.) Tzvelev = *Arctanthemum arcticum*.

D. boreale (Mak.) Ling. St. 1.5m, tufted, erect, branched above, white-pubesc. St. lvs to 7cm, oblong-ovate, pinnatifid, seg. in 2 pairs, oblong, dentate. Cap. to 15mm diam., numerous, in term. corymbs; ray flts to 7mm, yellow. Japan, Korea, Manchuria, N China.

D. coreanum (Lév. & Vaniot) Vorosh. St. striate, white-hairy. Basal lvs with elongate, acuminate, ± dentate lobes; st. lvs simple or toothed. Cap. solitary, large; ray flts white. Korea.

D. ×*grandiflorum* Kitam. FLORISTS' CHRYSANTHEMUM. Subshrub or perenn. herb to 1.5mm; st. branched, erect or spreading. Lvs to 12cm, ovate, pinnately lobed, toothed, fleshy, grey-hairy. Cap. to 30cm diam., clustered; ray flts in a v. wide range of shapes, configurations and colours. Cap. to 30cm diam., clustered; ray flts in a v. wide range of shapes, configurations and colours. Cultigen, probably raised in China from *D. indicum*. This is the Chrysanthemum of florists and gardeners – for a full discussion of types and cvs see Chrysanthemum in *The New RHS Dictionary*. Z4.

D. *indicum* (L.) Desmoul. Stoloniferous perenn. St. leafy, decumbent, pubesc. Mid-stem lvs to 5cm, obovate-oblong, cordate to truncate, coriaceous, pinnatifid with a term. lobe and 2 lat. pairs of linear lobes, dentate. Cap. 2.5cm diam., in corymbs, ray flts yellow, to 13mm. Autumn. Jap.

D. *indicum* hort. non (L.) Desmoul. = *D.* ×*grandiflorum*.

D. *japonicum* (Mak.) Kitam. St. to 80cm, branched. Lvs to 8cm, ovate, cuneate at base, 3-lobed or coarsely toothed, sparsely pubesc. above, long-hairy beneath. Cap. to 4cm diam., loosely arranged; ray flts white or rose, sometimes tubular. Autumn. Jap.

D. ×*koreanum* hort. = *D.* ×*grandiflorum*.

D. ×*morifolium* (Ramat.) Tzvelev = *D.* ×*grandiflorum*.

D. *naktongense* (Nak.) Tzvelev. St. to 1m. Lvs to 8cm, ovate, base truncate, pinnately lobed, seg. 4, toothed or lobed. Cap. to 8cm diam.; ray flts to 3cm. Summer–autumn. Korea, Jap., Manch.

D. *ornatum* (Hemsl.) Kitam. Stoloniferous herb. St. to 1.2m, branched, white-woolly. Lvs to 6cm, palmately lobed, lobes sinuate-toothed, white-hairy. Cap. to 5cm diam., many; ray flts to 2cm, white or pale pink. Autumn. Jap.

D. *pacificum* (Nak.) Rhizomatous perenn. to 40cm, silvery-tomentose above. Lvs 4–8cm, oblanceolate to obovate, pinnatifid, green above, silvery-tomentose beneath, lobes blunt, 1–2-toothed. Cap. to 1.5cm diam., crowded in corymbs; ray flts to 0.3cm, white or yellow. Jap. Z7.

D. *weyrichii* (Herbich) Tzvelev. Mat-forming; st. to 30cm, purple-green, sometimes branched. Lower lvs orbicular, palmately divided into 5 lobes, fleshy, upper lvs reduced, pinnatifid, or linear and entire. Cap. to 4cm diam.; ray flts white or pink. Summer–autumn. Jap. Z4.

D. *yezoense* (Maek.) D.J.N. Hind. Stoloniferous, to 50cm. Lvs to 4cm, ovate-cuneate, pinnately lobed or cleft, lobes oblong, fleshy. Cap. solitary, rarely to 3, long-peduncled; ray flts in 1 row, white, to 2cm. Autumn. Jap. Z3.

D. *zawadskii* (Herbich) Tzvelev. Rhizomatous perenn. to 60cm; st. sometimes branched, many-lvd, hairy. Lower lvs to 3.5cm, pinnatisect, lobes entire or dentate, thin; petiole winged. Cap. to 6cm diam., solitary or to 5 in a loose corymb; ray flts to 3cm, white, pink or purple. N & C Russia, Carpath., Urals.

D. *zawadskii* var. *latilobum* (Maxim.) Kitam. = *D. naktongense*.
→*Chrysanthemum* and *Matricaria*.

Dendrobenthamia Hutch.
D. *capitata* Hutch. = *Cornus capitata*.
D. *japonica* Hutch. = *Cornus kousa*.

Dendrobium Sw. Orchidaceae. 900–1400 epiphytic and terrestrial orchids. St. slender and branching or pseudobulbous. Pbs cane-like to ellipsoid. Lvs term. or 2-ranked. Fls in apical or axill. clusters or rac.; tep. unequal (diameter given below is that of fl. outspread); lip entire or trilobed, sometimes spurred. India, China, SE Asia, Jap., Malaysia, Philipp., New Guinea, Pacific Is., Aus., NZ. Z10.

D. *aduncum* Wallich ex Lindl. St. 40–60cm, slender, cylindrical, branched, pendent. Lvs 7–9cm, linear-lanceolate. Rac. about 7cm, 2–5-fld; fls to 3.5cm diam., pale pink or white with purple anther-cap; lip rounded, concave, hairy inside, with shiny callus. Spring. Burm., Sikkim, Indochina.

D. *aemulum* R. Br. Pbs to 30cm, often much shorter, linear to oblong. Lvs to 5cm, ovate or oblong. Rac. to 10cm, 2–12-fld; fls about 2.5cm diam., white, occas. pink-tinged, with yellow ridge on lip; tep. linear; lip midlobe with undulate yellow ridge. Aus.

D. *aggregatum* Roxb. Pbs 3–8cm, spindle-shaped, 1-lvd. Lf 5–16cm, oblong. Rac. 10–30cm, 5–15-fld, often pendent; fls to 4cm diam., scented, pale golden yellow, lip orange in throat, undulate. Assam, Burm., S China, Malaysia, Indochina.

D. *albosanguineum* Lindl. Pbs 12–28cm, cylindrical or club-shaped. Lvs 10–15cm, linear-lanceolate. Rac. 5–8cm, 2–3-fld; fls scented, 9cm diam., fleshy, cream-white or pale yellow; lip with 2 purple or crimson spots at base, obovate, undulate. Burm.

D. *amethystoglossum* Rchb. f. St. cane-like, 50–90cm. Rac. pendent, densely 15–20-fld; fls long-lasting, to 3cm diam., white with amethyst-purple lip. Winter. Philipp.

D. *amoenum* Wallich ex Lindl. = *D. aphyllum*.

D. *anceps* Sw. St. 30–60cm, somewhat flattened. Lvs about 3cm, lanceolate or ovate. Rac. short, axill.; fls 2cm diam., green or yellow. India.

D. *anosmum* Lindl. St. 60–120cm, arching or pendent. Lvs 12–18cm, oblong-elliptic. Infl. 1–2-fld; fls to 10cm diam., scented, pink to purple with purple throat. Philipp., Malay Penins., Laos, Vietnam, New Guinea.

D. *antelope* Rchb. f. = *D. bicaudatum*.

D. *antennatum* Lindl. Pbs 15–75cm, somewhat spindle-shaped. Lvs 4–15cm, oblong to elliptic. Rac. to 35cm, 3–15-fld; fls scented; sep. 1.5–2.5cm, white, dors. often spirally twisted; pet. 2.5–5cm, yellow-green, twisted once or twice; lip white with purple veins. New Guinea to Solomon Is. and NE Aus.

D. *aphyllum* (Roxb.) C. Fisch. Pbs to 90cm, narrow, pendent. Lvs 5–12cm, lanceolate or narrowly ovate. Infl. short, arising at nodes of old pbs, 1–3-fld; fls scented, thin-textured, 5cm diam.; tep. white or mauve-pink, lip cream or light yellow, marked with purple towards base, orbicular, erose. NE India and China, S to Malaya.

D. *atroviolaceum* Rolfe. Pbs to 30cm, spindle-shaped. Lvs to 13cm, oblong. Rac. short; fls scented, 7.5cm diam.; tep. primrose-yellow to green-white, spotted purple, lip green on outside, striped purple inside, apex purple. New Guinea.

D. *aurantiacum* Rchb. f. St. 30–60cm, slender. Lvs 5–8cm, linear-oblong. Rac. 1–3-fld; fls 3.5cm diam., golden-yellow to orange, base of lip sometimes streaked crimson, margins minutely fringed. Himal.

D. *aureum* Lindl. = *D. heterocarpum*.

D. *bellatulum* Rolfe. Pbs to 10cm, ovoid to spindle-shaped, ribbed. Lvs 3–5cm, ligulate or elliptic, with black hairs. Rac. 1–3-fld; fls to 5cm diam., scented, tep. cream-white, lip yellow, lat. lobes vermilion, disc with 5 red ridges. Burm., Yunnan, Vietnam, Thail.

D. *bensoniae* Rchb. f. St. to 1m, stout, cylindrical, suberect to pendent. Lvs 5–8cm, linear. Rac. short, 1–3-fld; fls about 6cm diam., white or pale yellow, lip yellow with 2 purple spots, pubesc. India, Burm.

D. *bicaudatum* Reinw. ex Lindl. Pbs to 40cm, cane-like. Lvs to 9cm, lanceolate. Rac. to 15cm, few-fld; fls to 4cm diam. green or yellow-green, sometimes flushed with red or brown, pet. linear, sometimes twisted; lip white or green, purple-veined; with a callus of 5 fleshy ridges, trilobed, apiculate. N Celebes, Sulu archipel., Moluccas.

D. *bigibbum* Lindl. Pbs to over 1m, cane-like. Lvs to 15cm, lanceolate. Rac. to 40cm, 2–20-fld; fls to 6cm, white, lilac-purple, mauve or pink; lip midlobe decurved with 5 hairy ridges. New Guinea, Aus. ssp. *bigibbum*. Fls about 5cm diam., light mauve, often with white patch on lip. ssp. *compactum* (C.T. White) Clements & Jones. Pbs to 2.5cm, spindle-shaped. ssp. *phalaenopsis* (Fitzg.) Clements & Cribb. Fls to 7cm diam., usually deep purple with broad lat. sep., slender pet. and a ± tubular, pointed lip. White and bicoloured forms occur.

D. *bracteosum* Rchb. f. Pbs 20–40cm, cylindrical. Lvs 4–8cm, ligulate. Rac. short, bracts almost as long as fls; fls to 4cm diam. scented, waxy, tep. white, pink or purple, lip orange-red, oblong-elliptic or spathulate, with shiny callus. Papua New Guinea, New Ireland.

D. *brymerianum* Rchb. f. Pbs 30–50cm, spindle-shaped. Lvs 10–15cm, oblong or lanceolate. Rac. to 11cm, 1- to few-fld; fls 5–6cm diam., yellow, and lip with orange lat. lobes, branched threads to 1.2cm long around the margin. Burm., Laos, Thail.

D. *bullenianum* Rchb. f. St. 25–60cm. Lvs 7–14cm, oblong, thin-textured. Infl. to 7cm, almost globose, many-fld; fls to 4cm diam. yellow to orange, striped red and purple; lip sub-spathulate, emarginate. Philipp. and W Samoa.

D. *canaliculatum* R. Br. Pbs 3–12cm, spindle-shaped or ovoid. Lvs to 20cm, linear, semi-cylindrical. Rac. 10–40cm, many-fld; fls scented, to 2.5cm diam., tep. ± twisted, yellow or brown, white at base, lip white with purple markings, trilobed, with 3 ridges, raised and undulate on midlobe. New Guinea, NE Aus.

D. *capillipes* Rchb. f. Pbs 10–15cm, spindle-shaped. Lvs 10–15cm, lanceolate or ligulate. Rac. 12–15cm, 1–4-fld; fls 3cm diam., yellow, orange in centre; lip reniform, short-clawed, undulate. Burm., China, Thail.

D. *capitisyork* M. Clements & D. Jones. Pbs to 40cm, almost pendent, cylindrical then 4-angled. Lvs to 8cm, ovate. Rac. to 2cm, 2–5-fld; fls to 10cm diam., yellow-green spotted with red, lip white with red lines on lat. lobes, trilobed, with basal callus of 3–5-ridges, midlobe narrow. Aus.

D. *cariniferum* Rchb. f. St. 15–25cm. Lvs 5–8cm, linear-oblong, the sheaths sparsely hairy. Rac. short, 2–3-fld; fls scented, pale buff, lip with golden-yellow streaks, occas. marked brick-red; trilobed, lateral lobes rounded, undulate midlobe obovate, disc fringed, edge crisped. India, Burm.

D. *chrysanthum* Wallich ex Lindl. St. 1–2m, pendent. Lvs 10–20cm, lanceolate-ovate. Infl. short, 1–3-fld; fls to 4cm diam., scented, golden-yellow, lip usually with 2 basal chestnut-brown spots, suborbicular, denticulate. E Himal. to Burm. and Thail.

D. *chryseum* Rolfe = *D. aurantiacum*.

D. chrysocrepis Parish & Rchb. f. Pbs 15–25cm, club-shaped. Lvs 5–8cm, lanceolate. Infl. single-fld; fls about 3cm diam., golden yellow, lip with red-brown hairs on disc, pyriform, inrolled. Burm.

D. chrysotoxum Lindl. Pbs 12–30cm, spindle-shaped. Lvs 10–15cm, lanceolate or oblong. Rac. to 20cm, pendent; fls scented, 4–5cm diam., golden-yellow, lip orange in centre, densely hairy, fringed. Assam, Burm., Thail., China, Laos.

D. coelogyne Rchb. f. = Epigenium coelogyne.

D. crepidatum Lindl. Pbs 15–50cm. Lvs 5–12cm, lanceolate. Infl. 1–3-fld; fls scented, to 4.5cm diam.; tep. white with pink tips, lip white, tip pink or magenta, disc orange, somewhat undulate. Assam, Sikkim, Burm.

D. cretaceum Lindl. Pbs 25–30cm, stout, curved. Lvs 5–8cm, lanceolate. Infl. single-fld; fls 4–5cm diam., white, lip with yellow disc and crimson veins, pubesc. funnel-shaped then orbicular, undulate and minutely fringed. SE Asia.

D. cruentum Rchb. f. Pbs about 30cm high, cylindrical. Lvs oblong. Infl. 1–2-fld; fls 3–5cm diam., green, lat. lobes, edge of midlobe and crest of lip crimson-red, midlobe apiculate, with 3 red ridges. Malay Penins.

D. crumenatum Sw. St. 60–90cm, spindle-shaped, tapered. Lvs 4–8cm, oblong. Infl. short; fls scented, short-lived, profuse, about 4cm diam., white, lip with primrose yellow disc and sometimes pink-veined, midlobe suborbicular, crisped or fimbriate. SE Asia.

D. crystallinum Rchb. f. Pbs 30–50cm, pendent, cylindrical. Lvs 10–15cm, curved-lanceolate. Rac. 1–3-fld; fls 5cm diam., white, the tep. purple-tipped, lip orange. Sikkim, Burm.

D. cucumerinum Macleay ex Lindl. St. spreading, branched, about 4mm diam. Lvs to 3.5cm, ovoid, swollen, tuberculate. Rac. to 5cm, 2–10-fld; fls about 1.2cm diam., green-white to cream, purple below, lip with dark red ridges. Aus.

D. cuthbertsonii F. Muell. Pbs globose or ovoid. Lvs to 4cm, linear to ovate, sometimes warty above. Infl. 1-fld fls to 4cm diam. red, sometimes purple, pink, orange, yellow, white or bi-coloured. New Guinea.

D. dalhousianum Wallich = D. pulchellum.

D. dearei Rchb. f. Pbs 60–90cm, erect, lf sheaths covered with black hairs. Lvs to 25cm, oblong. Rac. 8–18-fld; fls 5–6cm diam., white, lip yellow or lime green at base, midlobe ovate, crisped. Philipp.

D. densiflorum Wallich ex Lindl. Pbs 30–50cm, erect, almost 4-angled. Lvs to 16cm, lanceolate or ovate. Rac. to 26cm, pendent, many-fld; fls to 5cm diam., scented, yellow, lip orange at base, orbicular, fringed. Nepal, Assam, Sikkim, Burm.

D. devonianum Paxt. Pbs 60–100cm, cylindrical, pendent. Lvs 8–10cm, linear-lanceolate. Infl. 1–2-fld; fls 7–8cm diam., white or pale yellow, sep. and lip purple-tipped; lip shortly funnel-shaped, deeply fringed. India, Burm.

D. discolor Lindl. St. to 5m tall, cylindrical, sometimes purple-striped. Lvs 5–20cm, elliptical or ovate. Rac. to 60cm, arched; fls to 10cm diam., cream, yellow, bronze or brown, often flushed brown or purple; lip purple-veined, callus white; tep. twisted and crisped. Aus., New Guinea.

D. dixanthum Rchb. f. Pbs to 1m, cylindrical. Lvs to 17cm, lanceolate to ligular. Rac. to 5cm, 2–5-fld; fls to 6cm diam., yellow; lip striped red at base, suborbicular, undulate, serrate or fringed. Burm.

D. draconis Rchb. f. Pbs 30–45cm, spindle- or club-shaped, sheaths with black hairs. Lvs to 10cm, lanceolate or ligulate. Rac. 2–5-fld; fls scented, 6–7cm diam., ivory-white; lip orange or red at base, midlobe oblong, acute, undulate. Burm., Thail., Indochina.

D. falconeri Hook. St. 60–100cm, slender, branched, pendent. Lvs to 10cm, linear-lanceolate, acute. Infl. single-fld; fls 5–11cm diam., rose-pink or white with purple-tipped seg., lip purple and orange, ciliate. India, Upper Burm.

D. farmeri Paxt. Pbs 20–30cm, spindle-shaped, 4-angled. Lvs 8–18cm, ovate-lanceolate. Rac. 20–30cm, pendent, many-fld; fls to 5cm diam., white or lilac mauve, lip yellow, orbicular, finely serrate. Himal., Burm., Thail., Malaya.

D. fimbriatum Hook. Pbs to 120cm, spindle-shaped, erect or pendent. Lvs 8–15cm, oblong or lanceolate. Rac. to 18cm, pendent, to 15-fld; fls to 6cm diam., orange-yellow, lip darker, fringed. Nepal, Burm., Thail., India, China, Malaya.

D. formosum Roxb. Pbs to 45cm, erect, cylindrical. Lvs to 13cm, oblong, sheaths hairy, fls to 12cm diam., white with yellow lip, undulate. Nepal to Burm. and Thail.

D. fuscatum Lindl. = D. gibsonii.

D. fusiforme (Bail.) Bail. = D. jonesii.

D. gibsonii Paxt. St. slender, to 1m. Lvs lanceolate. Rac. pendent, many-fld; fls to 5cm diam., orange-yellow, lip with 2 brown blotches, suborbicular, ciliate and rolled back. Sikkim, Assam, Burm.

D. gouldii Rchb. f. Pbs 90–180cm, cane-like. Lvs to 18cm, oblong or elliptic. Rac. 30–70cm; fls 6–8cm diam., sep. white to yellow, pet. white, yellow, brown or violet, lip white to yellow with purple veining, midlobe subspathulate, apiculate, erose. Solomon Is., New Ireland, Vanuatu.

D. gracilicaule F. Muell. Pbs to 90cm, cylindrical. Lvs to 13cm, ovate. Rac. to 12cm, few- to many-fld; fls about 1.5cm diam., drooping, dull green, yellow or orange, blotched with red-brown outside; lip midlobe kidney-shaped. Aus.

D. gratiotissimum Rchb. f. Pbs to 90cm, swollen at nodes, usually pendent. Lvs 7–10cm, ligulate. Infl. 1–3-fld; fls to 7cm diam., white tipped purple-pink, lip orange in centre, ovate, funnel-shaped at base. Burm., Thail.

D. harveyanum Rchb. f. Pbs 15–25cm, erect, spindle-shaped. Lvs to 11cm, ovate-oblong. Infl. 2–6-fld; fls fragrant, about 5cm diam., canary yellow, lip orange in throat, orbicular to reniform, funnel-shaped, fringed. Summer. Burm., Thail., Vietnam.

D. hercoglossum Rchb. f. Pbs to 35cm, cylindrical. Lvs to 10cm, linear-lanceolate. Rac. 2–5-fld; fls 2–5cm diam., tep. magenta, lip white, apex magenta, orbicular, concave, apex lanceolate. Thail., Indochina.

D. heterocarpum Lindl. Pbs 40–150cm, spindle-shaped. Lvs to 18cm, oblong-lanceolate. Rac. 2–3-fld; fls scented, to 8cm diam., pale yellow with dark red blotch on lip; lip lanceolate-ovate, folded at base, finely toothed. Winter. Sri Lanka, India, Burm. and W to Philipp.

D. infundibulum Lindl. Pbs to 1m long, erect, sheaths with black hairs. Lvs 8.5cm, lanceolate or narrowly ovate. Rac. few-fld; fls to 8cm diam., white, lined with orange and red towards base of lip; lip ± tubular, midlobe emarginate, undulate and serrate. Burm., Thail.

D. jamesianum Rchb. f. = D. infundibulum.

D. japonicum Lindl. = D. moniliforme.

D. jenkinsii Wallich ex Lindl. Pbs 2–3cm, compressed, 1-lvd, forming dense tufts. Rac. pendent, 1–3-fld; fls large, golden yellow; lip suborbicular, emarginate. Assam.

D. johnsoniae F. Muell. Pbs 20–30cm, spindle-shaped. Lvs to 15cm, ovate. Rac. to 40cm, few- to many-fld; fls 7–12cm diam., white, streaked purple on lip. New Guinea, Bougainville.

D. jonesii Rendle. Pbs to 50cm, fusiform. Lvs to 15cm, ovate. Rac. to 40cm, arched, many-fld; fls to 4cm diam., scented, white or cream turning yellow, lip white with purple marks and a linear orange ridge towards base. Aus., New Guinea.

D. kingianum Bidwell ex Lindl. Pbs 6–35cm, narrowly conical. Lvs to 12cm, lanceolate, ovate or obovate. Rac. to 20cm, few- to 20-fld; fls to 4cm diam. white, pink, mauve, purple or red, lip sometimes with darker stripes. Aus.

D. lasianthera J.J. Sm. Pbs to 2.5m, cane-like. Lvs about 6cm, elliptic. Rac. to 50cm, fls to 8cm diam. pink or yellow, flushed purple or maroon; tep. spirally twisted; lip midlobe spathulate, apiculate. New Guinea.

D. lawesii F. Muell. Pbs to 45cm, subcylindrical, pendent, with maroon lf sheaths. Lvs distichous, 6–7cm, ovate-elliptic. Rac. v. short, 1–6-fld; fls to 4cm diam. pendent, white, red, orange, yellow or mauve; lip spathulate, finely toothed. New Guinea, Bougainville.

D. lindleyi Steud. = D. aggregatum.

D. lineale Rolfe. Pbs to 3m, cane-like. Lvs to 14cm, elliptic. Rac. to 75cm, many-fld; fls to 6cm diam., sep. and lip white or pale yellow, pet. white, pink, or blue-mauve, spathulate, half twisted or not twisted; lip purple-veined, midlobe, undulate and erose. New Guinea.

D. linguiforme Sw. Small, mat-forming with branched sts. Lvs to 4cm, oblong to obovate, fleshy, furrowed. Rac. to 15cm, to 20-fld; fls to 4cm diam., white or cream; tep. linear. Aus.

D. lituiflorum Lindl. Pbs 45–60cm, reed-like pendent. Lvs to 12.5cm, linear-lanceolate. Rac. 1–5-fld; fls scented, to 10cm diam., white, lilac or purple, lip maroon or purple at base, surrounded by white or yellow, trumpet-shaped. NE India, Burma, Thail.

D. loddigesii Rolfe. Pbs 10–17cm, pendent, cylindrical. Lvs 4–6cm, oblong. Fls solitary, 5cm diam., lilac-purple, lip purple-edged, orange in centre, suborbicular, fringed. Laos, S China.

D. longicornu Wallich. ex Lindl. Pbs 15–30cm, flexuous, covered with black hairs. Lvs 7cm, linear-lanceolate. Rac. 1–3-fld; fls fragrant, white, lip marked with red and yellow; lat. sep. to 5cm, almost triangular, forming a 2–3cm mentum. Nepal, Sikkim, Burm.

D. lyonii Ames = Epigenium lyonii.

D. maccarthiae Thwaites. Pbs 30–60cm, cylindrical, pendent. Lvs 4–10cm, lanceolate. Rac. 5–8cm, pendent; fls 8–9cm diam., not opening wide, rose-pink or violet-pink, lip maroon or purple in centre. Sri Lanka.

D. macranthum A. Rich. Pbs to 60cm, cane-like. Lvs 7–12cm, oblong or elliptic. Rac. to about 30cm, suberect, fls yellow, yellow-green or lime green, lip paler in middle with a lilac callus, purple-veined; lateral sep. 3.5cm, forming narrow, 1cm mentum. Santa Cruz Is., Vanuatu, New Caledonia.

D. macrophyllum A. Rich. Pbs to 50cm, club-shaped or spindle-shaped. Lvs 15–30cm, oblong. Rac. erect, to 40cm, fls yellow or yellow-green with purple spots or stripes on lip; sep. c2.5cm, hairy outside. Malaysia to New Guinea, Bougainville, Solomon Is., Fiji, Samoa.

D. macrophyllum Lindl. = *D. anosmum.*

D. mirbelianum Gaud. Pbs to 3m tall, cane-like. Lvs 8–12.5cm, oblong, elliptic or ovate. Rac. to 45cm, fls 5–10cm diam., yellow-green to olive-brown, lip with purple-brown veins and a white callus marked purple, midlobe recurved, ovate, acute, undulate and erose. Moluccas, New Guinea, Bismarck Archipel., Solomon Is., Aus.

D. mohlianum Rchb. f. St. to 50cm, cylindrical, sometimes pendent. Lvs 6–13cm, lanceolate. Rac. to 3cm, 4–6-fld; fls orange or red; lip obovate, hooded. Vanuatu, Solomon Is., Fiji, Samoa.

D. moniliforme (L.) Sw. Pbs 10–40cm, pendent, cylindrical, purple-brown with grey sheaths. Lvs 5–6cm, lanceolate. Infl. 2-fld; fls to 6cm diam. scented, white tinged with pink, base of lip yellow-green with brown spots. Jap., Korea, Taiwan.

D. moorei F. Muell. Pbs to 25cm cylindrical. Lvs to 12cm, oblong. Rac. to 8cm, 2–15-fld; fls to 3cm diam. white, somewhat drooping and not opening wide; lip midlobe crisped. Lord Howe Is.

D. moschatum (Buch.-Ham.) Sw. Pbs to 1.5m, cylindrical. Lvs about 15cm, elliptic or ovate. Rac. to 20cm, pendent, 8–10-fld; fls to 8cm diam., pale yellow or apricot, veined light purple, lip with 2 maroon blotches, hairy, concave, inrolled. Sikkim, Burm., Laos, Thail.

D. nardoides Schltr. Pbs to 2.5cm, ovoid or cylindrical, clustered. Lvs to 6cm, linear. Infl. 1–2-fld; fls to 4cm diam. purple-pink, lip apex scarlet. E New Guinea.

D. nobile Lindl. Pbs 30–50cm, erect, cylindric to club-shaped. Lvs 7–12cm, ligulate. Infl. short, 2–4-fld; fls scented, 6–8cm diam.; tep. mauve or pink, white at base, lip maroon in throat, edged yellow or white, funnel-shaped. NE India to China, Laos and Thail.

D. ochreatum Lindl. St. 15–25cm, stout, cylindrical, decumbent. Lvs 10–13cm, ovate-lanceolate. Rac. 2-fld; fls 7.5cm diam., golden yellow, disc red; lip funnel-shaped then orbicular, concave, pubesc., erose. India.

D. palpebrae Lindl. Pbs 15–50cm, subcylindrical. Lvs 7.5–15cm, lanceolate. Rac. to 10cm, many-fld; fls scented, to 6cm diam., pink or white, the lip with yellow or orange disc, ciliate. Sikkim, Burm., Thail., China.

D. papilio Loher. St. thin, grass-like. Lvs linear. Fls large, solitary, fragrant, pendent; tep. pale rose; lip yellow veined purple, undulate. Philipp.

D. parishii Rchb. f. Pbs to 50cm, cylindrical, arching to pendent. Lvs 5–10cm, elliptic. Rac. 2–3-fld; fls to 6cm diam., rose-purple, white towards base, lip with 2 purple blotches in throat, suborbicular, ± trilobed. Burm., Thail., Laos, Indochina, S China.

D. pendulum Roxb. Pbs 30–60cm, somewhat pendent. Lvs to 12cm, lanceolate. Infl. 1–3-fld; fls scented, long-lasting, to 7cm diam., white with purple tips to seg., lip yellow in throat, orbicular, pubesc. in middle. Assam, Burm., Thail.

D. phalaenopsis Fitzg. = *D. bigibbum.*

D. pierardii (Roxb.) C. Fisch. = *D. aphyllum.*

D. primulinum Lindl. Pbs 30–45cm, cylindrical, prostrate or pendent. Lvs to 10cm, oblong. Infl. 1–2-fld; fls scented, to 7cm diam., tep. pink, paler towards base, lip pale yellow, red in throat, funnel-shaped at base. Himal., SE Asia.

D. pulchellum Roxb. ex Lindl. Pbs 1–2m, slender, cylindrical, sheaths striped purple. Lvs 10–15mm, oblong. Rac. pendent, 5–12-fld; fls to 8cm diam., pink-buff to cream-yellow, lip white, yellow at base, with 2 maroon blotches. Assam, Burm., Thail., Malaysia, Indochina.

D. purpureum Roxb. Pbs to 50cm, subcylindrical 4-angled, pendent. Lvs to 14cm, oblong-lanceolate. Rac. short, 10–15-fld; fls to 3cm diam., rose-purple or white; lip saccate at base, apex erose. Vanuatu, Malaysia, New Guinea, Bougainville, Caroline Is., Fiji.

D. regale Schltr. = *Diplocaulobium regale.*

D. rhodostictum F. Muell. & Kränzl. Pbs to 25cm, club-shaped. Lvs to 11cm, lanceolate. Rac. erect or arched, few-fld; fls to 7cm diam., somewhat drooping, white, lip spotted purple, broadly obovate, obscurely trilobed, midlobe apiculate. Papua New Guinea and Solomon Is.

D. ruppianum A.D. Hawkes = *D. jonesii.*

D. sanderae Rolfe. Pbs to 80cm, subcylindrical, sheaths with black hairs. Lvs 5cm, ovate. Rac. 6cm, 3–4-fld; fls to 7cm diam., white, lip streaked red or purple. Philipp.

D. sanguinolentum Lindl. Pbs 60–100cm, pendent. Lvs 5–20cm, ovate or lanceolate, underside red. Rac. short, 3–5-fld; fls about 2.5cm diam., yellow, seg. violet-tipped, lip with red blotch, lip

lat. lobes rounded, midlobe subquadrate, emarginate. Malaysia.

D. scabrilingue Lindl. Pbs to 30cm, club-shaped, sheaths with black hairs. Lvs to 10cm, ligulate. Infl. v. short, 2-fld; fls to 4cm diam. scented, cream-white, mentum green, lip yellow in centre and marked with red on lat. lobes. Burm., Thail.

D. schuetzii Rolfe. Pbs 15–20cm, erect. Lvs 8.5cm, ovate. Rac. short, 3–4-fld; fls scented, to 9cm diam., white, disc green tinged with purple; lip lat. lobes incurved, forming tube, midlobe recurved, truncate, apiculate. Philipp.

D. sculptum Rchb. f. Pbs to 45cm. Fls to 5cm diam., 3 or 4 per spike; lip white with a square orange blotch in centre, base wrinkled. Borneo.

D. secundum (Bl.) Lindl. Pbs to 1m, spindle-shaped. Lvs 6–10cm, oblong, acute. Rac. to 12cm, many-fld; fls to 3cm diam., pink, purple or white, lip orange or yellow towards apex, spathulate. SE Asia, Pacific Is.

D. senile Parish ex Rchb. f. Pbs 5–10cm, almost club-shaped. Lvs 5–8cm, sickle-shaped, white-hairy. Infl. 1–2-fld; fls 5cm diam., golden yellow; lip apex slightly pubesc. Burm.

D. smilliae F. Muell. BOTTLE-BRUSH ORCHID. Pbs to 100cm, spindle-shaped, ribbed. Lvs to 20cm, oblong or lanceolate. Rac. to 15cm, packed; fls to 2cm diam. waxy, white, cream, green-white or pink, the apex of lip shiny bright green. New Guinea, Aus.

D. sophronites Schltr. = *D. cuthbertsonii.*

D. speciosissimum Rolfe = *D. spectatissimum.*

D. speciosum Sm. Pbs to 100cm, cylindrical or club-shaped. Lvs to 25cm, oblong, leathery. Rac. to 60cm, many-fld; fls to 8cm diam. scented, white, cream or yellow, lip marked red or purple, midlobe subquadrate or transversly oblong. E Aus.

D. spectabile (Bl.) Miq. Pbs to 40cm, cane-like. Lvs to 23cm, elliptic. Rac. 20–40cm, few to many-fld; fls to 8cm diam., yellow or cream, tep. speckled maroon, lip with maroon lines and white callus, all parts irregularly undulate; pet. twisted. New Guinea, Bougainville, Solomon Is.

D. spectatissimum Rchb. f. Pbs to 40cm, slender, covered with sparse black hairs; lvs also sparsely hairy. Rac. 1–2-fld; fls scented, long-lasting, 7–10cm diam., white with a red and yellow line on lip. Sabah.

D. stratiotes Rchb. f. Pbs to 1m tall, cane-like or spindle-shaped. Lvs 8–13cm, ovate or oblong. Rac. to 30cm, 4–8-fld; fls to 10cm diam., white, tep. green or yellow-green towards apex, lip purple-veined; pet. twisted 2–4-times. Moluccas, New Guinea.

D. strebloceras Rchb. f. Pbs to 1.5m tall, cylindrical. Lvs to 16cm, ovate or lanceolate. Rac. to 40cm, laxly 6–8-fld; fls to 8cm diam., fragrant, tep. pale yellow or green, tinged with dull purple or dark brown, lip marked with violet; pet. twisted about 3 times. Moluccas.

D. suavissimum Rchb. f. = *D. chrysotoxum.*

D. superbum Rchb. f. = *D. anosmum.*

D. taurinum Lindl. Pbs to 1.3m tall, cylindrical or spindle-shaped. Lvs to 15cm, oblong or elliptic. Rac. to 60cm, 20–30-fld; fls to 8cm diam., sep. yellow-green or green-white, pet. pink or purple to white at base, lip white tinged with purple; pet. twisted once. Philipp.

D. teretifolium R. Br. St. about 4mm diam., flexuous, branched, pendent to 3m. Lvs to 60cm, fleshy, terete. Rac. to 10cm, 10–15-fld; fls to 6cm diam., scented, cream or white, striped red or purple at base; lip midlobe ovate, acuminate, undulate. Aus. 'Aureum': fls yellow.

D. tetragonum Lindl. Pbs to 45cm, pendent, 4-angled. Lvs 3–10cm, ovate, often somewhat twisted. Rac. to 3cm, 1–5-fld; fls 3–6cm diam., green or yellow-green, sometimes edged with brown, or yellow blotched with purple-red. Aus.

D. tetragonum var. **giganteum** Gilbert = *D. capitisyork.*

D. thyrsiflorum Rchb. f. Pbs 30–50cm, erect, spindle-shaped. Lvs to 16cm, ovate. Rac. pendent, to 26cm; fls to 5cm diam., white or cream, lip golden yellow; pet. orbicular, toothed; lip orbicular, fringed. Nepal, Assam.

D. tigrinum Hemsl. = *D. spectabile.*

D. topaziacum Ames = *D. bullenianum.*

D. transparens Lindl. Pbs 30–60cm, cylindrical with yellow streaks. Lvs 8–11cm, linear-lanceolate, recurved. Rac. 2–3-fld, arising from large, translucent bracts; fls fragrant, 3–5cm diam., transparent white, tipped pink, lip with purple streaks. NE India, Burma, Nepal.

D. triflorum (Bl.) Lindl. = *Epigenium triflorum.*

D. trigonopus Rchb. f. Pbs 15–20cm, spindle-shaped, shiny brown-purple. Lvs to 10cm, ligulate, underside and sheaths hairy. Infl. 1–2-fld; fls 5cm diam., golden yellow, lip green-tinged in centre and with red lines on lateral lobes, midlobe oblong, obtuse, edge papillose. Burm., Yunnan, Laos, Thail.

D. undulatum R. Br. = *D. discolor.*

D. unicum Seidenf. Pbs to 25cm, subcylindrical, semi-erect or pendulous. Lvs to 6cm, lanceolate or elliptic. Rac. short, to 4-fld; fls to 6cm diam., bright orange, lip buff with darker veins;

elliptic-ovate, entire, with 3 ridges. Laos, Thail.
D. veitchianum Lindl. = *D. macrophyllum*.
D. velutinum Rolfe = *D. trigonopus*.
D. vexillare J.J. Sm. Pbs to 30cm, often much smaller, ovoid to
cylindrical. Lvs to 16cm, linear or elliptic, green or dark purple.
Rac. 2–5-fld; fls about 4cm diam., long-lasting, red, orange,
yellow, white, green, blue-green, blue, grey, lilac, purple or
pink, lip dark green, red or orange at apex. Moluccas, New
Guinea, Bismarck Archipel.
D. victoria-reginae Loher. Pbs 25–60cm, pendent, branched,
cylindrical, swollen at nodes. Lvs 3–8cm, oblong or lanceolate.
Rac. 3–12-fld; fls to 3cm diam., tep. violet-blue, white below, lip
with 5 violet lines in throat, obovate, somewhat concave.
Philipp.
D. wardianum Warner. Pbs to 120cm, cylindrical, thickened at
nodes. Lvs 8–15cm, oblong-lanceolate. Rac. short, 1–3-fld; fls
fragrant, to 10cm diam., white with purple-tipped seg., lip
yellow in throat with 2 maroon spots, ovate or suborbicular, en-
folding column at base. Assam, Burm., Thail.
D. williamsianum Rchb. f. St. to 3m, cane-like. Rac. erect or
arching, 3–10-fld, fls facing downwards, tep. mauve, purple-
veined, lip deep purple, the edge paler, ± orbicular. Papua
New Guinea.
D. williamsii Day & Rchb. f. Pbs 30–40cm, erect, spindle-shaped.
Lvs to 10cm, lanceolate, velvety, the sheaths with black hairs.
Infl. 1–2-fld; fls to 7.5cm, diam., fragrant, cream to pale yellow,
lip with large red or brown blotch, flabellate, trilobed, finely
toothed or ciliate, veins with long hairs, midlobe crisped.
Assam, Burm., Thail. There are many *Dendrobium* grexes with
fls in a wide range of colours. They usually fall into one of four
categories – the cool-growing Nobile and Formosum groups,
the *Antennatum* types with showy, long, twisted pet. and the
Phalaenopsis types, bred from *D. bigibbum*. The last make
extremely popular and durable cut fls.

Dendrocalamopsis (Chia & Fung) P.C. Keng.
D. oldhamii (Munro) Keng f. = *Bambusa oldhamii*.

Dendrocalamus Nees. Gramineae. 30 giant, clump-forming
bamboos. SE Asia. Z10.
D. giganteus Munro. KYO-CHIKU. Culms 15–40m×15–35cm, usually branchless below; sheaths v. large, caducous, rough, ligule
ciliate, blade small. Lvs 20–55×3–12cm, denticulate, glab.
above, glabrescent beneath. S Trop. Asia, China.
→*Sinocalamus*.

Dendrocereus Britt. & Rose = *Acanthocereus*.

Dendrochilum Bl. GOLDEN CHAIN ORCHID. Orchidaceae. 120
epiphytic orchids. Pbs ovoid to cylindrical. Lvs 1–2, apical,
lanceolate-elliptic, tough; petiole slender. Infl. racemose,
lateral, appearing from heart of emerging growths, v. slender,
long, ascending then pendulous, chain-like; fls crowded, 2-
ranked, small, fragrant, star-like. SE Asia, Malaysia. Z10.
D. cobbianum Rchb. f. Pbs to 8×2cm. Lf solitary, to 35×6cm.
Infl. to 50cm; fls to 1.8cm diam., tep. dull white; lip yellow to
orange, flabellate or cuneate. Philipp.
D. filiforme Lindl. Pbs to 2.5×1cm. Lvs 2, to 18×1cm. Infl. to
45cm; fls to 100+, to 0.6cm diam., fragrant, pale yellow; lip
faintly trilobed, sometimes golden. Philipp.
D. glumaceum Lindl. Pbs to 4×2cm. Lf solitary, to 45×4cm. Infl.
to 50cm; fls to 2cm diam., white to ivory, lip pale green; sep.
lanceolate; lip midlobe ovate to orbicular. Philipp.
D. longifolium Rchb. f. Pbs to 8×2cm. Lf usually solitary, to
40×7cm. Infl. to 40cm; fls to 1.6cm diam., pale green to bronze,
tipped chocolate; lip midlobe obovate-cuneate. Malaysia to
New Guinea.
D. uncatum Rchb. f. Resembles a diminutive *D. filiforme*. Lvs to
10×1.5cm. Infl. to 10cm, fls to 0.9cm, across; tep. ivory to
yellow-green, narrow-oblong; lip obtuse, bronze to sepia.
Philipp.

Dendromecon Benth. TREE POPPY; BUSH POPPY. Papaveraceae. 1
spreading everg. shrub or small tree, 3–6m. St. much branched,
smooth. Lvs to 10cm, lanceolate to ovate-lanceolate, acute,
tough, ± denticulate. Fls solitary, 2–7cm diam., fragrant; pet. 4,
yellow; sta. numerous. SW US, Mex. Z8.
D. harfordii Kellogg = *D. rigida* ssp. *harfordii*.
D. rhamnoides Greene = *D. rigida*.
D. rigida Benth. ssp. *harfordii* (Kellogg) Raven. To 6m. Lvs to
8cm, obovate to elliptic, entire. Pet. to 3cm.

Dendropanax Decne. & Planch. Araliaceae. 80+ slender-
branched trees or shrubs. Lvs simple, rarely palmately 3–5-
lobed. Infl. term., simple or compound, umbellate or paniculate
and then mostly umbelliform or racemiform; fls small; pet. 5–8;

sta. 5–8. Fr. drupaceous, round or ovoid, ripening black. Mex.,
C & S Amer., W Indies; E & S Asia to W Malesia.
D. arboreus (L.) Decne. & Planch. Shrub or tree to 12m.
Juvenile lvs 3–5-lobed, stalks to 40cm, lobes to 45cm diam.;
adult lvs with stalks to 23cm, blade simple, ovate to oblong, to
28cm, entire, undulate or obscurely toothed. Infl. paniculate to
10cm, with 5–20 umbelliferous, stalked br. each to 7cm; fls pale
yellow. Summer. New World trop. Z10.
D. chevalieri (R. Vig.) Merrill = *D. dentiger*.
D. dentiger (Harms ex Diels) Merrill. Similar to *D. trifidus* but lvs
simple or 3–5-lobed, entire or denticulate to 15cm. E & S
China, Taiwan, Vietnam. Z10.
D. japonicus (Jungh.) Seem. = *D. trifidus*.
D. pellucidopunctata Hayata = *D. dentiger*.
D. proteus (Champ.) Benth. Similar to *D. trifidus* but infl. usually
simple or with only 1–2 subsidiary umbels. Lvs simple or 3-
lobed, entire. S China, N Vietnam.
D. trifidus (Thunb.) Mak. ex Hara. Shrub or small tree. Juvenile
lvs long-petioled, to 20cm, usually 2–3-lobed or palmatifid; adult
lvs smaller, usually simple, rhomboid or ovate or elliptic, to
12.5cm, entire. Infl. simple or compound with 2–4 lat. umbels
arising from base of central umbel; fls yellow-green. Summer. S
Jap. The name *Aralia* (or *Fatsia*) *mitsde* represents the juvenile
form. Z8.
→*Arabia, Fatsia, Gilibertia* and *Textoria*.

Denea Cook.
D. forsteriana (C. Moore & F. Muell.) Wendl. & Drude = *Howea
forsteriana*.

Denmoza Britt. & Rose. Cactaceae. 2 globose then shortly
columnar cacti; st. simple, eventually many-ribbed. Fls arising
near apex, tubular, slightly zygomorphic, scarlet; tube slightly
curved and dilated above; floral areoles with numerous hair-
spines; perianth unexpanded; tep. short, erect; fil. and style
long-exserted. NW Arg.
D. erythrocephala (Schum.) A. Berger. Eventually to
1.5m×30cm, ribs 40–50. Spines 30+, to 6cm, needle- to hair-
like, ± curved, and with additional bristles at flowering areoles.
NW Arg. Z9.
D. rhodacantha (Salm-Dyck) Britt. & Rose. Eventually to
30×15cm or more, ribs 15–30. Spines 8–10, stout, spreading and
recurved, red-brown, to 3cm. Fls 6–7×1.5–2cm, flowering
areoles without extra bristles. NW Arg. Z9.

Dennstaedtia Bernh. Dennstaedtiaceae. 70 terrestrial or
epilithic ferns. Rhiz. creeping, woody. Fronds stipitate, uniform, 1–4-pinnate or -pinnatifid, glab. or pubesc. Trop. and subtrop. Z10 unless specified.
D. adiantoides (Humb. & Bonpl. ex Willd.)
Moore = *D. bipinnata*.
D. bipinnata (Cav.) Maxon. Rhiz. long-creeping, hairs dense,
viscid, red-brown. Fronds to 2×1m, 3–4-pinnate or -pinnatifid,
sparsely short-pubesc., lustrous, pinnae to 70×30cm, pinnules
ovate or linear to oblong, seg. rhomboid to oblong, obtuse,
toothed, to obtusely 2–4-lobed; stipes to 1m, grooved, pubesc.
above, brown. Trop. Amer.
D. cicutaria (Sw.) Moore. Rhiz. short-creeping, glab. to sparsely
short-pubesc. Fronds to 1.5×2m, 3–4-pinnate or -pinnatifid,
deltoid, apex narrowly acute, sparsely pubesc., pinnae, oblong,
secondary pinnae, linear to oblong, narrowly acute, pinnules
lanceolate or oblong, acute or obtuse, seg. deltoid or oblong,
toothed; stipes to 2m, grooved, short-pubesc. at base, straw-
coloured to brown. Trop. Amer.
D. cornuta (Kaulf.) Mett. = *D. dissecta*.
D. dissecta (Sw.) Moore. Rhiz. short-creeping, rough, glab. to
sparsely pubesc. Fronds to 2×1m, 3-pinnate-pinnatifid (occas.
2–4 -pinnate or -pinnatifid), deltoid, narrowly acute, pinnae
overlapping, lanceolate to oblong, apex caudate and
proliferous, seg. falcate, base cuneate, notched; stipes to 1m,
grooved above, rough and sparsely short-pubesc. at base,
brown. Trop. Amer.
D. globulifera (Poir.) Hieron. Rhiz. long-creeping; hairs dense,
red-brown. Fronds to 2m, 3–4-pinnate or -pinnatifid, ovate to
deltoid, pinnae to 65×30cm+, ovate, narrowly acute, secondary
pinnae, deltoid or linear to oblong, narrowly acute, pinnules
ovate to lanceolate or deltoid, or oblong, subacute to obtuse,
base winged, seg. ovate or trapeziform to oblong, obtuse to
truncate, toothed; stipes to 1m, grooved above, pubesc. at base,
straw-coloured to brown. Trop. Amer.
D. obtusifolia (Willd.) Moore. Rhiz. rough and glab. Fronds to
2×1m, 3-pinnate or -pinnatifid, deltoid, narrowly acute, pinnae,
lanceolate to oblong, apex caudate and proliferous, seg. occas.
falcate, lanceolate to oblong; stipes to 1m, grooved above.
Trop. Amer.
D. ordinata (Kaulf.) Moore = *D. obtusifolia*.

D. punctilobula (Michx.) Moore. HAY-SCENTED FERN.   Rhiz. long-creeping. Fronds to 75×20cm, 2–3-pinnate or -pinnatifid, deltoid or lanceolate to elliptic, base truncate, pinnae lanceolate to oblong, pinnules ovate to rhomboid, acute, notched to lobed, scented of hay when dried; stipes to 45cm. E N Amer. Z3.

D. rubiginosa (Kaulf.) Moore = *D. cicutaria.*

D. scabra (Wallich) Moore. Rhiz. long-creeping, pubesc. Fronds to 70×50cm, 3–4-pinnate, deltoid to hastate, sparsely pubesc. to bristly, esp. beneath, pinnae hastate, seg. toothed; stipes 45cm, rough and densely pubesc. at base, red-brown. Trop. Asia.

→*Dicksonia, Paradennstaedtia* and *Sitolobium.*

DENNSTAEDTIACEAE Lotsy. 18 genera. *Blotiella, Dennstaedtia, Histiopteris, Hypolepis, Leptolepia, Lindsaea, Lonchitis, Microlepia, Odontosoria, Oenotrichia, Paesia, Pteridium, Saccoloma* and *Sphenomeris.* ·

Dense Claw-flower *Calothamnus pinifolius.*
Dense Silky Bent *Apera interrupta.*

Dentaria L.
D. bulbifera L. = *Cardamine bulbifera.*
D. digitata Lam. = *Cardamine pentaphyllos.*
D. enneaphyllos L. = *Cardamine enneaphyllos.*
D. glandulosa Waldst. & Kit. = *Cardamine glanduligera.*
D. heptaphylla Vill. = *Cardamine heptaphylla.*
D. laciniata (Muhlenb.) = *Cardamine laciniata.*
D. pentaphyllos L. = *Cardamine pentaphyllos.*
D. rotundifolia (Michx.) Greene = *Cardamine rotundifolia.*

Deodar *Cedrus deodara.*

Deparia Hook. & Grev. Woodsiaceae. 5 terrestrial ferns. Rhiz. long-creeping, branched. Fronds stipitate, uniform, 2–3-pinnate to -pinnatifid, thin-textured. Amer., Asia, Aus., Polyn. Z9.
D. acrostichoides (Sw.) Kato. Fronds to 60×30cm, 2-pinnate to -pinnatifid, lanceolate, pinnae to 15×3cm, sessile, linear, pinnules elliptic to oblong, subentire; stipes to 30cm. N Amer., E Asia (Indochina).
D. japonicum (Thunb.) Bedd. = *D. petersenii.*
D. nephrodioides Bak. = *Lastreopsis nephrodioides.*
D. petersenii (Kunze) Kato. JAPANESE LADY FERN.   Fronds to 35×15cm, 2-pinnate to -pinnatifid, ovate or lanceolate to oblong, pinnae to 6×2cm, sessile to short-stalked, linear to lanceolate, pinnules elliptic to oblong, subentire to toothed or notched; stipes to 25cm. Indochina to Taiwan, Jap., to Aus. and NZ, Polyn.
→*Asplenium, Athyrium, Diplazium, Dryopteris.*

Deplanchea Vieill. Bignoniaceae. 5 robust trees. Lvs simple, whorled at end of br. Fls crowded into term. thyrses; cal. with 2–5 regular or irregular lobes; cor. tubular-ventricose, bilabiate, lobes fringed; sta. 4, exserted. Malesia, Aus., New Caledonia. Z10.
D. hirsuta (Bail.) Stenis. = *D. tetraphylla.*
D. tetraphylla (R. Br.) F. Muell. Tree to 25m, bark grey, corky. Lvs 11–60cm, obovate, yellow-velvety beneath. Infl. to 25cm, branched; cor. yellow, tube 1–1.25cm, to 1.3cm wide at apex; sta. to 4.5cm. Summer–autumn. NE Queensld.
→*Diplanthera.*

Deptford Pink *Dianthus armeria.*

Derenbergia Schwantes.
D. cryptopodia (Kensit) Schwantes = *Gibbaeum cryptopodium.*
D. nuciformis (Haw.) Schwantes = *Gibbaeum cryptopodium.*
D. quaesita (N.E. Br.) Schwantes = *Conophytum quaesitum.*

Dermatobotrys Bol. Scrophulariaceae. 1 straggling, epiphytic, glab. shrub. Lvs 5–15cm, ± fleshy, ovate or oblong, dentate. Fls whorled at nodes; cor. tubular, to 5cm, coral pink to carmine, apricot within, curved, lobes 5 spreading. Winter. S Afr. Z10.
D. saundersii Bol.

Derris Lour. Leguminosae (Papilionoideae). Some 40 woody climbers, trees or shrubs. Lvs imparipinnate or trifoliolate. Fls pea-like in term. or axill. rac. or pan. OW Trop. Z9.
D. elliptica (Wallich) Benth. TUBA ROOT; DERRIS ROOT.   Climber to 20m. Lvs to 25cm, emerging bronze, hardening bright green; lfts to 10cm, to 11, obovate, coriaceous. Rac. to 18cm; fls white tinted rose-mauve. Burm. to New S Wales.
D. scandens Benth. MALAY JEWEL VINE.   Climber to 20m. Lvs 34–76cm; lfts to 5cm, to 19, coriaceous, oblong or obovate-oblong. Rac. to 60cm; fls pale rose. E India to Malay Penins., China, N Aus.

Derris Root *Derris elliptica.*

Deschampsia Palib. HAIR GRASS. Gramineae. Some 50 tufted, perenn. grasses. St. slender, erect, unbranched. Lvs threadlike to linear. Infl. paniculate, axis pubesc.; spikelets laterally compressed, 2-fld, occas. tinged purple. Temp. zones. Z5.
D. caespitosa (L.) P. Beauv. TUFTED HAIR GRASS; TUSSOCK GRASS.   To 1.5m. St. slender to robust, smooth. Lvs to 60cm, rigid, rough; ligules acute, to 1.5cm. Infl. to 45×20cm, arching; spikelets pendulous, tinged silver, purple or variegated; awns to 0.4cm, straight. Summer. Temp. Eurasia, trop. Afr., Asia (mts). 'Bronzeschleier' ('Bronze Veil'): pan. large, tinted bronze. 'Fairy's Joke' (var. *vivipara*): long culms weighted down with tiny plantlets borne instead of seed. 'Goldgehänge' ('Gold Shower'): pan. golden yellow, late-flowering. 'Goldschleier' ('Gold Veil'): pan. bright yellow tinted silver. 'Goldstaub' ('Gold Dust'): pan. yellow. 'Schottland' ('Scotland'): tufted mound, to 40cm high; lvs dark green. 'Tardiflora': small; pan. tufted silver, late-flowering. 'Tautraeger' ('Dew Carrier'): small and slender. var. *parviflora* (Thuin) Coss. & Germain. Lf blades narrow; spikelets smaller.
D. flexuosa (L.) Trin. CRINKLED HAIR GRASS; WAVY HAIR GRASS; COMMON HAIR GRASS.   To 90cm. St. smooth, slender, wiry. Lvs to 20cm, glab., wavy, threadlike; ligules blunt, to 0.3cm. Infl. to 12cm×7.5cm, shiny; spikelets tinged purple, brown or silver; awns 0.8cm, twisted. Summer. Eur., Asia, NE & S Amer. 'Mückenschwarm' ('Fly Swarm'): spikelets dark and abundant. 'Tatra Gold' ('Aurea'): tuft-forming, to 50cm; lvs needle-like, bright yellow-green, arching; flowerheads soft bronze.
→*Aira.*

Desert Almond *Prunus fasciculata.*
Desert Apricot *Prunus fremontii.*
Desert Baeckea *Baeckea crassifolia.*
Desert Banksia *Banksia ornata.*
Desert Boronia *Boronia inornata.*
Desert Broom *Baccharis.*
Desert Candle *Eremurus.*
Desert Carrot *Monizia edulis.*
Desert Evening Primrose *Oenothera deltoides.*
Desert Fan Palm *Washingtonia filifera.*
Desert Fig *Ficus brandegeei; Ficus palmeri.*
Desert Five-spot *Eremalche rotundifolia.*
Desert Hakea *Hakea muelleriana.*
Desert Holly *Atriplex hymenelytra.*
Desert Honeysuckle *Anisacanthus.*
Desert Ironwood *Olneya.*
Desert Kumquat *Eremocitrus.*
Desert Kurrajong *Brachychiton gregorii.*
Desert Lily *Hesperocallis undulata.*
Desert Mallow *Sphaeralcea ambigua.*
Desert Marigold *Baileya.*
Desert Olive *Forestiera neomexicana.*
Desert Pea *Clianthus formosus.*
Desert Penstemon *Penstemon pseudospectabilis.*
Desert Poppy *Arctomecon merriamii.*
Desert Privet *Peperonia magnoliifolia.*   ·
Desert Rose *Adenium; Rosa stellata.*
Desert Sage *Salvia dorrii.*
Desert Selaginella *Selaginella eremophila.*
Desert Senna *Senna covesii.*
Desert Sumac *Rhus microphylla.*
Desert Sunflower *Geraea canescens.*
Desert Willow *Chilopsis; Pittosporum phillyreoides.*

Desfontainia Ruiz & Pav. Loganiaceae. 1 bushy, everg. shrub to 3m. Lvs holly-like, to 4cm, oval-ovate, glossy dark green, spiny to dentate. Fls waxy, solitary; cal. 5-lobed, green; cor. 1.5–9cm, tubular-funnelform, crimson to scarlet-orange with 5 yellow, shallow lobes. Summer–autumn. Chile, Peru. Z8.
D. spinosa Ruiz & Pav. 'Harold Comber': fls to 5cm, of a brighter vermilion.

Desmanthus Willd. Leguminosae (Mimosoideae).   Some 25 procumbent perenn. herbs or subshrubs. Lvs bipinnate. Fls in tight mimosa-like heads; cal. campanulate to short-cylindric, short-toothed; pet. joined, later free; sta. 5–10, exserted. Warm Amer.
D. illinoensis (Michx.) MacMill. ex Robinson & Fern. PRAIRIE MIMOSA; PRICKLEWEED.   Herbaceous perenn. to 130cm. Lvs to 15cm; pinnae 14–30; lfts to 3mm, 30–60, paired, oblong. Infl. to 1cm diam., tinged white. Spring–summer. US. Z4.
→*Mimosa.*

Desmidorchis Ehrenb.
D. crenulata Decne. = *Caralluma crenulata.*

D. pauciflora Decne. = *Caralluma pauciflora*.
D. umbellata Decne. = *Caralluma umbellata*.

Desmodium Desv. BEGGARWEED; TICK-TREFOIL. Leguminosae (Papilionoideae). Over 300 decid. shrubs, subshrubs, or herbs. Lvs pinnate, trifid or 3-foliolate with term. lft larger, broader. Fls pea-like, small, in axill. or terminal, loose rac. or pan. Trop. and subtrop.

D. canadense (L.) DC. Erect perenn. to 1.2m. Lfts to 7.5cm, 3, oblong-lanceolate, nearly glab. Fls red-purple, in rac. or pan. US. Z2.

D. concinnum DC. Shrub to 1.5m. Lvs 7cm. Lfts 3, elliptic to narrow-obovate, basally rounded, downy beneath. Fls purple, in term. or axill. rac. Bhutan. Z8.

D. elegans DC. Shrub, to 1.5m. Lfts 3, to 6cm, minutely pointed, dark green and pubesc. above, grey-downy beneath, obovate-rounded. Infl. 20cm, terminal; fls rosy-carmine, in whorls. China, Himal. Z6.

D. floribundum (D. Don) G. Don = *D. multiflorum*.
D. gyrans (L. f.) DC. = *Codariocalyx motorius*.
D. motorium (Houtt.) Merrill = *Codariocalyx motorius*.
D. multiflorum DC. Shrub to 1.5m. Lfts 3, to 7cm, tapering, rounded, glab. and deep green above, grey beneath. Fls deep pink, in large term. pan. China, Himal. Z8.

D. ooieinense (Roxb. Ohashi. Tree, to 12m. Lfts 3, leathery, stiff to 9cm, broadly rhombic-elliptic, lat. lfts ovate. Fls white-pink or tinted purple, in densely clustered rac. India, W Nepal. Z9.

D. penduliflorum Benth. = *D. concinnum*.
D. praestans Forr. = *D. yunnanense*.
D. spicatum Rehd. = *D. elegans*.
D. tiliifolium (D. Don) G. Don = *D. elegans*.
D. yunnanense Franch. Shrub, to 4m. Lfts 1(–3), 10–20cm, broadly ovate, obtuse basally truncate, pale green above, grey-green and downy beneath. Fls purple-pink, in term., downy pan. to 40cm. SW China. Z9.
→*Dalbergia* and *Ougeinia*.

Desmond Mallee *Eucalyptus desmondensis*.
Deurmekaarbos *Ehretia hottentotica*.

Deuterocohnia Mez. Bromeliaceae. 7 short-stemmed, xerophytic perennials. Lvs leathery, forming a rosette, sheaths large, blades narrow-triangular, margins densely spinose. Fls in remontant, scapose term. pan. amid green-brown bracts. S Amer. Z9.

D. longipetala (Bak.) Mez. Lvs to 40cm. Pet. yellow with green apical spot. N Peru.

D. meziana Kuntze ex Mez. Lvs 40cm+. Pet. yellow, orange or red. SE Boliv., SW Braz., Parag.

D. schreiteri Cast. Lvs to 20cm. Pet. yellow. Arg. *D. longipetala* is sometimes incorrectly named as *D. schreiteri*.
→*Dyckia*.

Deutzia Thunb. Hydrangeaceae. 60 decid. or everg. shrubs with peeling bark. Lvs usually short-stalked, sometimes toothed. Fls in rac., cymes, pan. or corymbs, or solitary; cal. teeth 5; pet. 5; sta. in 2 series of 5; fil. winged and toothed. Temp. Asia, C Amer.

D. albida Batal. Bushy, to 3m. Lvs 5–10cm, ovate-lanceolate, acuminate, finely toothed, dark green above with scattered hairs, beneath densely white-hairy, veins bristly. Fls pure white, 1–1.3cm diam., in pan. 5–7cm wide. Summer. N China. Z5.

D. amurensis (Reg.) Airy Shaw = *D. parviflora* var. *amurensis*.

D. calycosa Rehd. To 2m. Lvs 2–7cm, ovate, thinly hairy above, lower surface moderately to densely hairy. Infl. a dense cyme, 4–10cm, borne on a v. short shoot. Fls white with purple exterior, *c*2cm across. Spring. SW China. Z6.

D. ×*candelabra* (Lemoine) Rehd. (*D. gracilis* ×*D. scabra*.) Like *D. gracilis* but with larger, many-fld pan., coarser and more spreading growth. Early summer. Gdn origin. 'Candelabra': the type of the cross. 'Erecta': growth upright; lvs small, dark green; fls white in pan. 'Fastuosa': similar to 'Candelabra' except growth more upright. Z5.

D. ×*candida* (Lemoine) Rehd. (*D.* ×*lemoinei* ×*D. scabra*.) Upright. Lvs 3.5–5cm, ovate, serrate, slightly rough, hairy beneath. Fls numerous in pan., white, *c*2cm across. Summer. Gdn origin. var. *compacta* Lemoine. More compact, with smaller fls. 'Boule de Neige': compact habit, with denser infl. of larger creamy-white fls. Z5.

D. ×*carnea* (Lemoine) Rehd. (*D.* ×*rosea* 'Grandiflora' ×*D. scabra*.) Differs from *D. gracilis* in its broad, loose pan. of pink fls with sep. tinged purple. Spring–early summer. Gdn origin. 'Densiflora': fls large, milky white; buds pink. 'Lactea': lvs narrower, light green; fls white in large pan. 'Stellata': pet. narrow, light to dark carmine. Z6.

D. chunii Hu = *D. ningpoensis*.

D. compacta Craib. Young shoots at first densely stellate-hairy. Lvs to 7cm, lanceolate to ovate-lanceolate, base rounded, apex acuminate, finely toothed, dark green above with scattered hairs, grey-green beneath. Fls in compact corymbose pan. to 2cm across; cor. white, to 1.2cm diam. Summer. China. 'Lavender Time': fls lilac, fading pale lavender. Z6.

D. coreana Lév. To 2m, young shoots rough with small warts. Lvs elliptic-lanceolate, sharply toothed, dark green above; paler beneath, with scattered hairs throughout. Fls white, solitary, on short, leafless shoots. Summer. Korea. Z6.

D. corymbosa R. Br. To 2m. Lvs 6–10cm, ovate, acuminate, toothed, hairs sparse, but often denser above. Infl. corymb-like, borne on a shoot 10–18cm; fls 1–1.5cm across, white, hawthorn-scented. Early summer. W Himal. Z8.

D. corymbosa var. *hookeriana* Schneid. = *D. hookeriana*.

D. crenata Sieb. & Zucc. To 2.5m. Lvs 3–6cm, ovate to ovate-lanceolate, obscurely crenate, much larger on non-flowering shoots, hairy. Infl. a rac. or narrow pan., 10–15cm; fls 1.5–2cm across, white. Spring. Jap.; SE China. Much confused with *D. scabra*, from which it differs in its stalked lvs subtending the infl. 'Nakaiana': dwarf shrub to 30cm, br. arching. 'Nikko': lvs burgundy in autumn; fls double, white, profuse; often listed under *D. gracilis*. Z6.

D. discolor Hemsl. Arching, 1–2m. Lvs 4–11cm, thin, narrowly ovate-oblong, serrulate, densely hairy beneath with veins villous. Cymes loose; fls white to pink, 1.3–2.5cm wide. Spring. China. 'Major': fls with pink exterior. Z5.

D. discolor var. *purpurascens* Henry = *D. purpurascens*.

D. ×*elegantissima* (Lemoine) Rehd. Upright to 1.5m. Lvs ovate to oblong-ovate, irregularly and sharply toothed, sparsely hairy beneath. Cymes loose; fls pink, *c*2cm wide. Early summer. Gdn origin. Distinguished from *D. purpurascens* by its broader, more abruptly acuminate lvs. 'Conspicua': fls large, pure white, profuse; buds pink. 'Arcuata': br. arching; fls white in rounded heads; buds pink. 'Elegantissima': growth upright; lvs wrinkled, dark green; fls wide opening; pet. pale pink, edged carmine; anth yellow; the type of the cross. 'Fasciculata': habit rounded; fls wide opening, pale pink, darker outside, floriferous. 'Rosalind': fls deep carmine. Z6.

D. ×*excellens* (Lemoine) Rehd. (*D.* ×*rosea* 'Grandiflora' ×*D. longifolia*.) Like *D. longifolia* but lvs 3–6cm, ovate-oblong, margins with fine, forwardly-pointing teeth, upper surface rough with short hairs, lower surface grey-white. Fls in broad, loose corymbs 4–6cm across, white. Summer. Gdn origin. Z5.

D. globosa Duthie. Small, with red-brown, exfoliating bark. Lvs 5–9cm, ovate-lanceolate to elliptic, somewhat acute, toothed, rough above, tinged white beneath with rather denser hairs. Fls in almost spherical pan., yellow-white, to 1.5cm across. Summer. C China. Z6.

D. glomeruliflora Franch. To 3m, with arching br. Lvs to 4cm, lanceolate to ovate, acuminate, with fine forward-pointing teeth, lower surface densely hairy. Cymes numerous, few-fld, borne on shoots 2.5–5cm long; fls white, *c*2cm wide. Spring. W China. Z5.

D. gracilis Sieb. & Zucc. Erect, decid., 1–2m. Lvs 3.5–10cm, v. thin, bright green, lanceolate to ovate, minutely serrulate, thinly hairy. Fls in rac. or narrow pan. 40–80cm long; pedicels long and slender; fls pure white, 1–2cm across, strongly scented. Spring–early summer. Jap. 'Alba': fls white. 'Aurea': fls yellow. 'Grandiflora' (*D. gracilis* ×*D. sieboldiana*): larger in all parts. 'Marmorata': lvs mottled yellow. 'Pink': fls pink. var. *nagurae* (Mak.) Mak. Fls smaller (*c*5mm across). Z4.

D. grandiflora Bunge. 1.5–2m, young shoots grey-hairy. Lvs to 5cm, margins with fine forwardly pointing teeth, white beneath with dense hairs. Fls 1–3 on short leafy shoots, white, 2.5–3cm across. Early spring. N China. The earliest flowering sp., with the largest fls; the 1–3-fld infl. is distinctive. Z5.

D. hookeriana (Schneid.) Airy Shaw. To 2m, like *D. corymbosa* except for narrower lvs; fls sometimes tinged pink. Himal. to W China. Z5.

D. ×*hybrida* Lemoine. (*D. longifolia* ×*D. discolor*.) Like *D. longifolia* but lvs 6–10cm; fls larger and wider with pet. pink with wavy edges, anth. bright yellow. Early summer. Gdn origin. 'Contraste': br. arching; fls mid-pink, exterior streaked purple. 'Joconde': lvs acuminate; fls pale lilac-white, exterior streaked purple. 'Magician': pet. mid-pink, edged white, exterior darker with purple streak. 'Mont Rose' ('Montrose'): habit upright, lvs serrate; fls wide opening, mid pink; anth. yellow. 'Perle Rose': fls small, mid-pink, long-lasting, v. profuse. 'Pink Pompon' ('Pom Pom'): fls double, rose pink in dense heads. 'Reuthe's Pink': fls pink.

D. hypoglauca Rehd. = *D. rubens*.

D. ×*kalmiiflora* Lemoine. (*D. purpurascens* ×*D. parviflora*.) Like *D. purpurascens* but arching, to 1.5m, less densely hairy and with finely toothed lvs 3–6cm, flowering shoots 10–30cm, fls to 2cm across, deep pink outside, white inside, in upright, umbel-like pan. Early summer. Gdn origin. Z5.

D. ×lemoinei Lemoine. (*D. gracilis* ×*D. parviflora*.) Upright to 2m. Lvs 3–6cm, elliptic-lanceolate, long-pointed. Fls abundant in pan. or pyramidal corymbs. Early summer. Gdn origin. Z4.

D. longifolia Franch. 1.5–2m, young shoots sparsely hairy. Lvs 5–7cm lanceolate, acuminate, thick and with prominent veins, serrulate, dull green above, pale green, ± hairy beneath. Cymes broad, loose or compact, c8×6cm; fls 2–2.5cm across, white, usually with a purple-pink stripe outside. Early summer. W. China. 'Elegans': br. drooping; fls 2cm wide, pink-purple outside, in loose pan. 'Veitchii': lvs narrow; fls and flowering st. purple. var. **macropetala** Zaik. Lvs 6–11cm; fls 2.5–3cm across. The name *D. vilmoriniae* has been applied to a variant in which the pet. are pure white. Z6.

D. ×magnifica (Lemoine) Rehd. (*D. crenata* ×*D. longifolia*.) To 2m, similar to *D. crenata*, with strong, upright growth and stout br. Lvs 4–6cm, ovate-oblong, sharply but finely toothed, rough above and with dense hairs beneath. Fls white, single or double, in dense pan. 4–6cm long. Early summer. Gdn origin. 'Azaleiflora': v. early-flowering. 'Eburnea': fls bell-shaped, in loose pan. 'Emineus' ('Mirabilis'): pan. large. 'Formosa': fls double; pet. crinkled, incurved. 'Latiflora': fls 3cm, wide opening; pan. erect. 'Longiflora': pet. narrow. 'Longipetala': lvs narrow; fls in dense umbellate pan.; pet. narrow, fringed. 'Macrothrysa': tall, fls in umbellate pan. all along br. 'Staphyleoides': fls large in drooping pan.; pet. reflexed. 'Superba': lvs deep green; fls large, wide-opening. 'Suspensa': pan. drooping; pet. reflexed; fls v. profuse. Z5.

D. ×maliflora Rehd. (*D. ×lemoinei* ×*D. purpurascens*.) Like *D. purpurascens* but upright, to 2m. Lvs 2.5–4cm, ovate-oblong, acuminate, finely serrulate with scattered hairs. Fls tinged red outside, c1.5cm across, in corymbs 5–6cm broad. Gdn origin. 'Boule Rose': fls white edged pink, pink outside, profuse. 'Fleur de Pommier' (*D. myriantha* 'Fleur de Pommier'): habit upright; fls 2cm diam., bright pink outside, borne in dense heads all down the br. Z6.

D. maximowicziana Mak. To 2m, young shoots tinged brown, stellate-hairy. Lvs 3.5–9cm, narrowly oblanceolate to ovate-lanceolate, acuminate, inconspicuously toothed, densely white-hairy beneath. Fls in narrow pan. to 5cm long, white, to 1.8cm across. Late spring. Jap. Z6.

D. mollis Duthie. To 2m. Lvs large, to 9cm, coarsely biserrate, densely velvety-hairy beneath. Infl. paniculate or corymb-like, to 12×13cm, borne on shoots 9–20cm long; fls white, c1cm across. China. Z6.

D. monbeigii W.W. Sm. 1–1.5m, with slender br. Lvs 1.5–3cm, ovate-lanceolate, serrate, white-hairy beneath. Infl. corymb-like or cyme-like, c6×4cm; fls to 1.4cm across, white. Spring–summer. SW China. Z6.

D. ×myriantha Lemoine. (*D. parviflora* ×*D. setchuenensis*.) Upright to 1m. Lvs 4–6cm, oblong-lanceolate, finely toothed, rough-hairy. Fls white, c2cm across. Early summer. Gdn origin. Z5.

D. myriantha 'Fleur de Pommier'. = *D. ×maliflora* 'Fleur de Pommier'.

D. ningpoensis Rehd. To 2m. Lvs 3.5–7cm, ovate, generally entire, with dense hairs beneath. Infl. a narrow pan. to 10cm; fls white or pink, densely crowded, 5–10mm across. Summer. E China. Z5.

D. parviflora Bunge. To 2m. Lvs 3–11cm, ovate, ovate-lanceolate or elliptic, coarsely serrate, ± densely hairy above, thinly so beneath. Infl. broadly corymbose; fls white, c1–1.5cm across, with orange disc. Early summer. N China. var. **amurensis** Reg. Lacks the simple hairs on the lf veins beneath. N China, Korea. Z4.

D. pulchra Vidal. 2–4m. Lvs 5–10cm, lanceolate to narrowly ovate, entire or toothed, thick, with moderately dense hairs above and v. dense hairs beneath. Flowering shoot term. or almost so, bearing a few-fld pan. to 12×7cm; fls white. Spring. Philipp. and Taiwan. Z6.

D. purpurascens (Henry) Rehd. Slender, arching, to 1.5m. Lvs 4–7cm, ovate to ovate-lanceolate, serrate, hairy throughout. Cymes on short shoots of 4–6cm (rarely to 12cm); fls white inside, purple outside, c2cm across. Spring–summer. W China. Z6.

D. reflexa Duthie. To 1m, young shoots glab., shining. Lvs 5–10cm, narrowly ovate-lanceolate, acuminate, densely white-hairy beneath. Fls in densely corymbose pan. to 5cm wide, white, to 1.6cm across; pet. somewhat reflexed. Late spring. C China. Z6.

D. rehderiana Schneid. To 2m with densely stellate-hairy young shoots. Lvs ovate to ovate-lanceolate, acute or obtuse, finely toothed, 1–1.5cm, upper surface rough, dark green. Fls in rac. of 3–5 at the ends of short lat. shoots, white, to 1.3cm across. Spring. W China. Z6.

D. ×rosea (Lemoine) Rehd. Dwarf, arching to 1m. Lvs elliptic or oblong to lanceolate, serrate, scattered-hairy. Fls in short, broad pan., tinged red outside, white inside. Gdn origin. 'Campanulata': fls white, in dense pan. 'Carminea': fls red-pink. 'Eximia': fls pale pink, white inside. Z5.

D. rubens Rehd. Erect to 2m, young shoots stellate-hairy. Lvs 4–7cm, thin, oblong to ovate-oblong, acuminate, minutely toothed, with sparse hairs above and sparse to dense hairs beneath. Infl. cymose; fls pink, 8–25mm across. Early summer. C China. Z6.

D. scabra Thunb. To 2.5m. Lvs 3–8cm, broadly ovate, stalked except for those subtending the infl., coarsely serrate. Pan. broadly pyramidal, loose; fls c1–1.5cm across, white, honey-scented. Summer. Jap. Sometimes confused with *D. crenata*, from which it differs in its unstalked lvs subtending the pan. 'Angustifolia': lvs narrow. 'Candidissima' ('Wellsii'): fls white. 'Codsall Pink' ('Godsall', 'Godsall Pink'): br. peel orange-brown with age. 'Fortunei' ('Macropetala'): fls large. 'Marmorata': lvs mottled yellow, white and shades of green. 'Plena' ('Rosea Plena', 'Flore Plena'): vigorous, erect, fls double, pale pink. 'Pride of Rochester': fls double, white-pink. 'Punctata': lvs dotted white. 'Rosea' fls rose. 'Thunbergii': fls with orange centre. 'Variegata': lvs splashed white. 'Watereri': fls carmine outside. Z5.

D. schneideriana Rehd. 1–2m. Lvs 9–11cm, ovate or lanceolate-ovate, finely serrate, densely hairy beneath. Infl. corymbose, 9–11×4–6cm; pet. white, narrowly lanceolate, c1cm. Summer. China. var. **laxiflora** Rehd. Infl. looser and broader, pet. larger (1.2–1.4cm). Z6.

D. setchuenensis Franch. 1.5–2m. Lvs c6cm, ovate, long-acuminate, finely serrate, ± hairy. Infl. composed of loose corymbs; fls white, to 1cm across. Summer. W China. var. **corymbiflora** (Lemoine) Rehd. Lvs 3–11cm. Fls c1.5cm across, in larger corymbs, more commonly found in cult. Z6.

D. sieboldiana Maxim. = *D. scabra*.

D. staminea Wallich. 1m (rarely to 2m). Lvs ovate, acuminate, finely serrulate, densely hairy beneath. Infl. a pan. or rarely corymbose, c5cm wide; fls white or pink, c1.5cm across. Early summer. Himal. var. **brunoniana** Hook. & Thoms. Larger fls and styles longer than sta. Z8.

D. taiwanensis (Maxim.) Schneid. To 2m, young shoots stellate-hairy. Lvs 5–10cm, ovate to ovate-lanceolate, apex acute, base ± rounded, finely toothed. Fls in narrow pan. 7–12cm long, terminating leafy shoots, white, to 1.2cm across. Summer. Taiwan. Z7.

D. vilmoriniae Lemoine see *D. longifolia*.

D. ×wilsonii Duthie. To 2m. Lvs 7–11cm, acuminate, serrate, densely hairy. Fls in loose broad corymbs, white, c2cm across. Early summer. Gdn origin. Z6.

Devil Flower *Tacca chantrieri*.
Devil-in-a-bush *Nigella*.
Devil Lily *Lilium lancifolium*.
Devil Nettle *Cnidoscolus urens*.
Devil's Apples *Mandragora officinarum*.
Devil's Backbone *Pedilanthus tithymaloides*.
Devil's Bit *Chamaelirion*.
Devil's Claw *Ibicella*; *Martynia*; *Proboscidea*.
Devil's Club *Oplopanax horridus*.
Devil's Darning-needle *Clematis virginiana*.
Devil's Fig *Argemone mexicana*; *Solanum hispidum*.
Devil's Herb *Plumbago scandens*.
Devil's Ivy *Epipremnum aureum*.
Devil's Pins *Hovea pungens*.
Devil's Tongue *Amorphophallus* (*A. rivieri*).
Devil's Walking-stick *Aralia spinosa*.
Devil's Weed *Tribulus terestris*.
Devil Tree *Alstonia scholaris*.
Devilwood *Osmanthus*.
Dewberry *Rubus caesius*; *R. flagellaris*.
Dew-thread Sundew *Drosera filiformis*.
Dhak *Butea monosperma*.
Dhal *Cajanus cajan*.

Diacalpe Bl. Dryopteridaceae. 1 fern. Rhiz. fasciculate, subterranean. Fronds to 60cm, deltoid, 3-pinnate, hairy when young, primary pinnae alt., pinnules oblong-cuneate, lobed, decurrent, ultimate seg. linear. Trop. Asia. Z9.

D. aspidioides Bl.

Diacrium Benth.
D. amazonicum Schltr. = *Caularthron bicornutum*.
D. bicornutum (Hook.) Benth. = *Caularthron bicornutum*.
D. bigibberosum Hemsl. = *Caularthron bilamellatum*.

D. indivisum Broadway = *Caularthron bilamellatum*.
D. venezuelanum Schltr. = *Caularthron bilamellatum*.

✕**Dialaelia**. (*Diacrium* (*Caularthron*) ✕*Laelia*.) Orchidaceae. Gdn hybrids intermediate between parents.

Diamond-leaf Pittosporum *Pittosporum rhombifolium*.
Diamond Maidenhair *Adiantum trapeziforme*.
Diamond Milfoil *Myriophyllum aquaticum*.

Dianella Lam. FLAX LILY. Liliaceae (Phormiaceae). 25–30 fibrous-rooted, perenn. herbs. St. often becoming erect, slender, bearing a term. fan of lvs. Lvs radical or on st., 2-ranked; linear-ensiform, sheathing. Infl. loosely paniculate, spreading; tep. free, 2 whorls of 3. Fr. a globose or oblong-ovoid berry, to 2cm. OW Trop. Z9.

D. caerulea Sims. St. to 60cm, sometimes branched. Lvs to 90cm, margins and keel rough. Infl. to 30cm; tep. blue to white, to 8mm; anth. pale yellow, to 3× length of fil. Early summer. NSW.

D. ensifolia (L.) DC. UMBRELLA DRACAENA. St. to 180cm. Lvs to 30cm, margins and keel rough. Infl. to 60cm; tep. blue to white, to 8mm; anth. yellow, longer than fil. Fr. yellow, ripening blue-purple. Summer. Range as for the genus.

D. intermedia Endl. Lvs to 150cm, margins slightly rough, keel rough. Infl. to 60cm; tep. green-white or purple-white, 5–8mm across; anth. yellow. Summer. NZ, Norfolk Is., Fiji. 'Variegata': lvs striped cream.

D. laevis R. Br. To 90cm. Lvs to 45cm, margins and keel smooth. Infl. to 50cm; tep. blue, the outer 5-lined, the inner 3-lined; anth. yellow, twice length of fil. Spring–summer. NSW.

D. longifolia R. Br. = *D. revoluta*.
D. nemorosa Lam. = *D. ensifolia*.

D. nigra Colenso. NEW ZEALAND BLUEBERRY. V. similar to *D. intermedia* but st. narrower and tep. less than 5mm across. Fr. blue-black. Summer. NZ.

D. revoluta R. Br. St. to 120cm. Lvs to 90cm, margins revolute, keel smooth. Infl. to 60cm; tep. to 1cm, deep blue; anth. yellow, brown or black, to 3× length of fil. Summer. Tasm., NSW.

D. tasmanica Hook. f. St. to 150cm. Lvs to 120cm, margins with small, sharp teeth. Infl. to 60cm; tep. 2cm across, pale blue; anth. brown, equal to or shorter than fil. Fr. dark blue. Summer. Tasm., SE Aus.

→*Dracaena*.

Dianthus L. CARNATION; PINK. Caryophyllaceae. ± 300 mostly perenn. herbs, a few truly suffruticose, many somewhat woody at base; rarely ann. Lvs usually linear, often glaucous. Flowering st. often swollen at nodes; fls solitary or in few- to many-fld infl., sometimes capitate with involucral bracts; cal. usually cylindric, with 1–3 pairs of epical. bracts; pet. free, clawed, limb wide-spreading, often toothed or cut, often bearded below; sta. 10; styles 2. Mostly Eurasia; a few spp. in the African mts, 1 sp. arctic N Amer.

D. 'Allwoodii' see *D. alpinus* and *D. plumarius*.
D. alpester Balb. = *D. furcatus*.

D. alpinus L. Tufted, glab. perenn. to 15cm. Lvs linear-lanceolate to oblong-lanceolate, obtuse, shiny. Fls solitary, large, on st. to 10cm; pet. limb 1.5–2cm, obovate, toothed, bearded, deep pink with crimson-purple spots on white 'eye'. Early summer. E Alps. Colour-variants, including white and salmon-pink, are available. The plants usually sold as 'Allwoodii alpinus' are the products of back-crosses of the Allwoodii group of hybrids (see *D. plumarius* and *D. alpinus*). Z3.

D. amurensis Jacq. Glab. perenn. to 40cm. Lvs to 5cm, lanceolate, acute, bright green. Fls solitary or in 3-fld dichasia at ends of stem-branches; pet. limb 15–20mm, deeply toothed, bearded, rose-purple with dark 'eye', more rarely white. Summer. E Asia. Differs from *D. chinensis* in its perenn. habit and often solitary, purple-pink fls. Z3.

D. anatolicus Boiss. Mat-forming perenn. to 35cm. Lvs to 5cm, linear, long-acuminate. Fls solitary or in groups of 2 or 3; pet. limb c3mm, linear-oblong, entire, not bearded, white. Summer. Turk. Z6.

D. andrzejovskianus (Zapał.) Kulcz. = *D. capitatus*.
D. arboreus L. nom. ambig. = *D. fruticosus*.

D. arenarius L. Tufted, grass-green, glab. perenn. to 30cm with slender st. Lvs to 4cm, linear. Fls usually solitary at the ends of br.; pet. limb c12mm, deeply laciniate, bearded, white or pale pink. Summer. N & E Eur. Z3.

D. armeria L. DEPTFORD PINK. Hairy bienn. (sometimes ann.) to 40cm, with a rosette of narrowly oblong, obtuse basal lvs. Fls sessile in dense involucrate heads; pet. limb c5mm, narrowly ovate, toothed, bearded, pink with pale dots. Summer. Eur.; W Asia. Z6.

D. ✕*arvernensis* Rouy & Foucaud see *D. monspessulanus*.

D. atrorubens All. = *D. carthusianorum*.
D. banaticus Heuff. ex Griseb. & Schenk = *D. giganteus*.

D. barbatus L. SWEET WILLIAM. Short-lived perenn. to 70cm, ± glab. with smooth, robust st. Lvs lanceolate-elliptic to 10cm. Fls sessile in large, dense involucrate heads; cal. with narrow, pointed teeth; pet. limb c1cm, bearded, red-purple with pale dots near base. Summer. Native in S Eur. from the Pyren. to the Carpath. and Balk., widely nat. Crossed with other *Dianthus* to give hybrid groups such as 'Sweet Wivelsfield' produced by crossing to *D.* ✕*allwoodii* (see *D. plumarius*), following this, even more complex hybrids such as *D.* 'Loveliness' have been bred. Z4.

D. bebius Vis. ex Rchb. = *D. petraeus*.

D. biflorus Sibth. & Sm. Loosely tufted, glab. perenn. to 40cm. Lvs linear. Fls usually in a 2–4-fld head, rarely more or solitary, subtended by 2–4 long-pointed bracts; pet. limb 8–16mm, obovate, toothed, red-purple above, tinged yellow beneath. Summer. Greece. Z9.

D. boissieri Willk. = *D. sylvestris*.
D. boydii hort. = *D. callizonus*.
D. brachyanthus Boiss. = *D. subacaulis*.

D. brevicaulis Fenzl. Cushion-forming, glaucous perenn. to 12cm. Lvs to 20mm, linear, minutely-toothed. Fls solitary, on short stalks; pet. limb 4–7mm, toothed, ± bearded, deep pink, tinged yellow beneath. Summer. Turk. Z7.

D. caesius Sm. = *D. gratianopolitanus*.
D. ✕*calalpinus* hort. = *D. callizonus*.

D. callizonus Schott & Kotschy. Loosely mat-forming, glab. perenn. to 20cm. Basal lvs linear-lanceolate, obtuse, shorter than the st. lvs. Fls solitary; pet. limb 1–1.5cm, ± triangular, deeply toothed, bearded, lavender pink with a purple-spotted 'eye'. Summer. S Carpath. Z5.

D. calocephalus auct. = *D. cruentus*.

D. campestris Bieb. Perenn. to 40cm, usually hairy, with a stout stock and numerous branched st. Lvs linear, acute. Fls solitary or in pairs at tips of br.; pet. limb c6mm, toothed, bearded, pink or purple-pink, yellow-green beneath. Summer. SE Eur., Cauc., Sib. Z3.

D. capitatus DC. Loosely tufted, ± glaucous perenn. to 60cm. Lvs to 15cm, linear. Fls in dense heads surrounded by ovate, hairy, pointed bracts; cal. hairy, red purple; pet. limb 5–8mm, toothed, usually bearded, crimson or deep purple. Summer. Balk. Penins. Z7.

D. carthusianorum L. Perenn. to 60cm, usually glab., with ± branched, 4-angled st. Lvs linear, usually pale green with long sheaths. Fls in dense involucrate heads; pet. limb 1–1.5cm, obovate, toothed, bearded, purple or pink, rarely white. Summer. S & C Eur. ssp.*atrorubens* (All.) Pers. Fls deep red-purple. Z3.

D. caryophyllus L. CARNATION. Loosely tufted, glaucous perenn. to 80cm, with branched, woody stock. Lvs to 15cm, linear, flat and soft, with conspicuous sheaths. Fls 1–5 in loose cymes on stiff, ascending st., strongly fragrant; pet. limb 1–1.5cm, irregularly toothed, not bearded, bright pink-purple. Summer. Medit. area; native range not known. The presumed parent of all gdn carnations. Z8.

D. chinensis L. Bienn. or short-lived perenn. to 70cm, usually somewhat hairy. St. lvs lanceolate, acute. Infl. a loose cluster of to 15 fls; pet. limb c1.5cm, obovate, deeply toothed or cut, pink-lilac with purple eye. Summer. China. Long cultivated there. In gardens *D. chinensis* is represented by a range of showy cvs treated as annuals. 'Heddewigii': compact, v. free-flowering cvs derived from this sp. Z7.

D. cinnabarinus Sprun. ex Boiss. = *D. biflorus*.
D. croaticus Borb. = *D. giganteus*.

D. cruentus Griseb. Loosely tufted, glaucous perenn. to 60cm; st. 4-angled. Lvs to 15cm, linear. Fls in dense involucrate heads; cal. c2cm hairy, usually red-purple; pet. limb 5–8mm, toothed, usually bearded, bright crimson to deep purple. Summer. Balk. Penins. Z7.

D. deltoides L. MAIDEN PINK. Tufted or mat-forming, hairy perenn. to 45cm, green or glaucous. Non-flowering shoots prostrate with narrowly oblanceolate lvs; flowering shoots erect with linear lvs. Fls solitary (rarely 2 or 3), terminal; pet. limb c8mm, obovate, toothed, bearded, pale to deep pink with pale spots in dark 'eye'. Summer. Eur. and temp. Asia. Z3.

D. erinaceus Boiss. Prickly cushion- or mat-forming perenn. to 15cm. Lvs small, hard, squarrose. Fls usually solitary, sometimes paired; pet. limb 5–6mm, oblong, toothed, bearded, pink. Summer. Turk. Z7.

D. freynii Vandas. Densely tufted, glab. perenn. to 10cm. Lvs small, rigid, linear. Fls usually solitary on short st.; pet. limb 5–9mm, shallowly toothed, bearded, pale pink or white. Summer. C Balk. Z6.

D. friwaldskyanus Boiss. = *D. gracilis*.

D. fruticosus L. Small shrub to 50cm, with tortuous br. Lvs linear to elliptical or oblanceolate, obtuse, fleshy, glaucous. Fls ± aggregated; pet. limb c10mm, toothed, bearded, pink. Summer. S & W Greece; S Aegean region. Z9.

D. furcatus Balb. Loosely tufted, glab., and glaucous perenn. to 30cm. Lvs linear-lanceolate, mostly basal. Fls usually solitary, slightly pendent on long stalks, fragrant; pet. limb 5–10mm, entire or toothed, not bearded, pink, rarely white. Summer. SW Eur. Z7.

D. gallicus Pers. Loosely tufted, glaucous perenn. to 50cm, somewhat hairy toward base. Lvs linear-lanceolate, obtuse or subacute. Fls 1–3 together at ends of stem-branches, fragrant; pet. limb 1–1.5cm, cut into narrow seg., bearded, pink. Summer. Atlantic coasts of Eur. from Port. to NW Fr. Z9.

D. gelidus Schott., Nyman & Kotschy = D. glacialis.

D. giganteus Urv. Robust perenn. to 1m, like *D. cruentus*, but larger, and differing in involucral and epical. bracts which have only v. short term. points (long in *D. cruentus*). Fls purple-pink. Summer. Balk. Penins. Z5.

D. glacialis Haenke. Densely tufted, usually glab. perenn. to 10cm. Lvs linear, obtuse, glossy, soft. Fls usually solitary, on short st.; pet. limb 8–12mm, finely toothed, bearded, pink with a white 'eye' and pale beneath. Summer. E Alps, Carpath. A white-fld cv. is available. ssp. *gelidus* has larger, darker fls. Z5.

D. gracilis Sibth. & Sm. Loosely tufted, woody-based, glab. perenn. to 40cm; st. lvs 4–6 pairs. Fls solitary, or in small, short-stalked clusters; pet. limb 10mm, obovate, toothed, bearded, deep pink above, yellow- or purple-tinged beneath. Summer. Balk. Penins. Z7.

D. graniticus Jordan. Tufted, almost glab. perenn. to 30cm, with slender branching st. Lvs narrowly linear, dark green. Fls usually in clusters; pet. limb 4–6mm, ovate, toothed, bearded, bright pink to pink-purple. Summer. SC Fr. Z6.

D. gratianopolitanus Vill. CHEDDAR PINK. Compact, woody-based, mat-forming, glaucous perenn. to 20cm. Lvs to 5cm, linear, almost flat. Fls usually solitary, strongly fragrant, on erect st.; pet. limb 1–1.2cm, obovate, toothed, sometimes slightly bearded, pink or red. Summer. W & C Eur. Z3.

D. haematocalyx Boiss. & Heldr. Tufted, glab. perenn. to 30cm. Lvs linear, acute, marginally thickened. Fls solitary or in clusters of 2–4; cal. usually red-purple; pet. limb 6–12mm, obovate, toothed, sparsely bearded, deep pink-purple, tinged yellow beneath. Summer. Balk. Penins. ssp. *pindicola* (Vierh.) Hayek. Cushion denser, fls almost sessile. Z8.

D. 'Heddewigii' see *D. chinensis*.

D. hispanicus Asso see *D. pungens*.

D. holzmannianus Heldr. & Hausskn. = D. cruentus.

D. hoppei Portenschlag = D. plumarius.

D. hungaricus Pers. = D. plumarius.

D. inodorus L. Gaertn. = D. sylvestris.

D. kitaibelii Janka = D. petraeus.

D. knappii (Pant.) Borb. Hairy perenn. to 40cm, with long, straggling st. Lvs linear-lanceolate. Fls sessile in small involucrate clusters; pet. limb c7mm, bright yellow with purple spot near base. Summer. W Balk. Z3.

D. lateritius Hal. = D. cruentus.

D. lumnitzeri Wiesb. = D. plumarius.

D. microlepis Boiss. Dense, grey-green, cushion-forming perenn. with v. short st. with 1 or 2 pairs of scale-like st. lvs; basal lvs to 2cm, linear. Fls solitary; pet. limb 6–7mm, toothed, bearded, clear pink (rarely white). Summer. Bulg. Z5.

D. monspessulanus L. Loosely tufted, glab. perenn. to 60cm, with slender st., branching above. Lvs linear to linear-lanceolate, acuminate; soft-textured. Fls in groups of 2–7, or solitary, on short stalks, fragrant; pet. limb 1.2–2cm, cut into narrow seg., pink or white. Summer. Mts of S & C Eur. ssp. *sternbergii* (Sieber) Hegi Fls mostly solitary, rather glaucous lvs, habit more compact. The hybrid with *D. seguieri*, *D.* ×*arvernensis* Rouy & Foucaud, has a compact cushion habit. Z4.

D. musalae (Velen.) Velen. = D. microlepis.

D. myrtinervius Griseb. Densely mat-forming, glab. perenn. with st. to 5cm. Lvs small, elliptic-oblong, obtuse. Fls solitary on v. short stalks; pet. limb 4–6mm, obovate, toothed, sparsely bearded, bright pink. Summer. Macedonian border of Greece and Balk. Z7.

D. nardiformis Janka. Tufted perenn. to 10cm with slender, branched st. Basal lvs c1cm, bristle-like. Fls usually solitary; pet. limb c5mm, ovate, toothed, bearded, pink. Summer. E Bulg.; Rom. Z6.

D. neglectus auct. non Lois. = D. pavonius.

D. nitidus Waldst. & Kit. Like *D. alpinus* but to 30cm, and more loosely tufted, often with branching st. bearing 2 or more, rather smaller fls. Summer. W Carpath. Z6.

D. nitidus auct. non L. = D. scardicus.

D. noeanus Boiss. = D. petraeus.

D. pavonius Tausch. Densely tufted or mat-forming, glab.

perenn. to 15cm, usually grey-green. Basal lvs to 4cm, narrowly linear, acuminate. Fls usually solitary; pet. limb 1–1.5cm, toothed, bearded, crimson to pale pink, buff beneath. Summer. SW Alps (Fr., It.). Z4.

D. petraeus Waldst. & Kit. Mat-forming or loosely tufted, glab. perenn. to 30cm. Basal lvs to 2.5cm, linear, often rigid, tapering to a long point. Fls solitary or in loose clusters, fragrant; pet. limb 4–10mm, divided, toothed or almost entire, sometimes bearded, white (rarely pink). Summer. SE Eur. & SW Asia. Z4.

D. pindicola Vierh. = D. haematocalyx.

D. pinifolius Sibth. & Sm. Dense cushion-forming perenn. Basal lvs bristle-like. Flowering st. to 40cm; infl. a rather compact involucrate head; pet. limb 5–10mm, toothed, sometimes bearded, purple, pink or lilac. Summer. Balk. Penins. Z7.

D. plumarius L. PINK. Loosely tufted, rather glaucous perenn. to 40cm. Basal lvs to 10cm, linear, keeled, acute. Fls fragrant, usually solitary at the ends of br. in a loose irregular cyme; pet. limb 1.2–1.8cm, triangular-obovate, divided into narrow lobes, usually bearded, pink or white, often with a darker 'eye'. Summer. Native in EC Eur. widely nat. 'Allwoodii' is a range of hybrids produced by crossing this sp. with Perpetual-Flowering Carnations derived from *D. caryophyllus*; see cvs at end. Z3.

D. praecox Kit. ex Schult. = D. plumarius.

D. pruinosus Boiss. & Orph. = D. haematocalyx.

D. pungens L. Like *D. furcatus* but with broader, rigid, rough, pointed lvs and long-acuminate spreading epical. bracts. Summer. E Pyren. These and other closely related taxa, including *D. hispanicus* Asso, are endemic to the Pyrenees and Iberian peninsula. Z7.

D. sanguineus Vis. = D. carthusianorum.

D. saxifragus L. = Petrorhagia saxifraga.

D. scardicus Wettst. Like *D. alpinus* but a cushion plant, with st. not exceeding 10cm, pet. limb 7–8mm, pink. Summer. Mts of Balk. Z6.

D. seguieri Vill. Loosely tufted, glab. perenn. to 60cm. Lvs linear-lanceolate, grass-green. Infl. 1- to few-fld; pet. limb 7–17mm, obovate, deeply toothed, bearded, pink with a pale purple spotted band near base. Summer–autumn. SW Eur. Z7.

D. serratus Lapeyr. = D. pungens.

D. simulans Stoj. & Stef. Densely caespitose, cushion-forming, blue-grey perenn. Lvs small, narrowly triangular-lanceolate, rigid, in dense rosettes. Fls solitary on st. to 6cm; pet. limb 5–7mm, toothed, bearded, pink with pale spots. Summer. Mt Orvilos on the Greek-Bulgarian frontier. Z7.

D. 'Sinensis'. = D. chinensis.

D. speciosus (Rchb.) Rchb. = D. superbus.

D. spiculifolius Schur. Like *D. petraeus* but with pink, deeply cut, strongly bearded pet. limb up to 15mm. Summer. E Carpath. Z6.

D. squarrosus Bieb. Tufted, glab. perenn. to 20cm. Lvs to 3cm, linear, rigid, recurved, grass-green. Fls fragrant, at ends of infl. br.; pet. limb deeply cut, bearded, white. Summer. C Ukraine to W Kazakstan. Z6.

D. sternbergii Sieber = D. monspessulanus.

D. strictus Sibth. & Sm. non Banks & Sol. = D. petraeus.

D. subacaulis Vill. Densely tufted, glab., deep green perenn. to 10cm. Basl lvs lanceolate; crowded, somewhat recurved. Fls solitary; pet. limb c8mm, entire or finely toothed, not bearded, deep pink. Summer. Mts of SW Eur. Z5.

D. superbus L. Robust, glab. perenn. to 80cm, with st. decumbent below, branched above. Basal lvs linear-lanceolate, to 8cm. Fls fragrant, usualy solitary at the ends of br.; pet. limb 1–3cm, narrow, v. deeply cut into almost filiform lobes, bearded, pink or purple-pink. Summer. Most of Eur., widespread in Asia. ssp. *alpestris* Kablik ex Čelak. Shorter, with large fls. Z4.

D. sylvaticus Hoppe = D. seguieri.

D. sylvestris Wulf. Densely tufted, nearly glab. perenn. to 40cm. Lvs to 10cm, wiry, long-pointed. Fls 1–3 together on erect st. ± scentless; pet. limb 6–15mm, entire or toothed, not bearded, usually pink. Summer. S Eur. Z5.

D. tenuifolius Schur = D. carthusianorum.

D. zonatus Fenzl. Tufted perenn. to 30cm. Lvs to 8cm, linear. Fls solitary; pet. limb c1.2cm, deep pink, tinged yellow beneath. Summer. Mts of Turk. and Syr. Z7.

D. cvs.

BORDER CARNATIONS. (a) *Selfs* – fls of one colour throughout. 'Clarinda': fls salmon-pink. 'Edenside White': habit compact, strong; fls pure white. 'Fiery Cross': habit vigorous; fls brilliant scarlet. 'Lord Gray': fls French grey, overlaid with silver. (b) *Fancies* – fls of one colour, overlaid with spots, flecks, blotches or stripes of another. 'Alice Forbes Improved': fls white, with even, rose-mauve stripes. 'Bookham Fancy': habit strong; fls yellow, edged and ticked vivid carmine-purple. 'Harmony': fls French grey, striped cerise. 'Orange Maid': fls apricot, flaked bronze. 'Catherine Glover': fls rich yellow, barred scarlet. (c) *Picotees* – fls of one colour, delicately edged with another; different varieties classified as 'broad-edged', 'medium-edged', and 'wire-edged'. 'Dot Clark': fls deep yellow, with a broad edge of rose-pink. 'Eva Humphries': fls white, with a wide edge of purple. 'Santa Claus': fls yellow, with a medium edge of purple. (d) *Clove-scented*. 'Book-ham Perfume': fls deep burgundy. 'Candy Clove': fls large, white, striped rose-red. 'Lavender Clove': fls lavender. 'Leslie Rennison': fls orchid-purple, tinged rose. 'Violet Clove': fls deep violet.

PERPETUAL-FLOWERING CARNATIONS. (a) *Selfs* – fls white, through cream and yellow, to pink, rose, scarlet, and crimson. 'Allwood's Crimson': fls large, crimson, fragrant. 'Cardinal Sim': fls vivid scarlet. 'Dusty Sim': fls pastel pink. 'White Sim': fls pure white. 'William Sim': fls scarlet. (b) *Fancies* 'Arthur Sim': fls white, striped red. 'Doris Allwood': fls French grey, marked rose-pink, fragrant. 'Red Edged Skyline': fls dull orange, edged scarlet. 'Ron's Joanne': fls flecked pink. 'Spotlight': fls yellow, flecked pink. (c) *American Spray Carnations* – fls borne 5 or 6 per shoot. 'Elegance': fls rose-pink, edged off-white. 'Exquisite': fls violet, edged white. 'Rony': fls scarlet. 'Tibet': fls white.

PINKS. Gdn pinks (*D. plumarius*) – habit compact; fls with serrate pet. 'Earl of Essex': fls double, rose-pink. 'Excelsior' ('Pink Mrs Sinkins'): fls pink; pet. large. 'Fair Folly': fls raspberry, blotched white. 'Mrs Sinkins': fls double, white, fringed, v. fragrant. 'Sam Barlow': fls large, double, with a purple-black centre. (a) *Allwoodii Pinks* (*D. ×allwoodii*). (a) *Selfs*. 'Bovey Belle': fls double, purple. 'Diane': fls deep salmon-red. 'Joy': fls salmon-pink. 'Oliver': fls rose-cerise. (b) *Bicolours* 'Doris': fls pale pink, with a maroon centre. 'Maria': fls double, rose bengal with pink centre. 'Monica Wyatt': fls double, phlox-pink with a ruby-red centre. (c) *Fancies* 'Daphne': fls large, single mauve-pink with a dark centre. Laced pinks – fls edged with same colour as centre; pet. rounded. 'Dad's Favourite': fls double, white with red-brown lacing and a dark centre. 'Gran's Favourite': fls white, laced rose-red. 'Laced Hero': fls white, with deep red lacing and black centre. 'Laced Monarch': fls double, petunia-pink, laced chestnut-red. 'London Brocade': fls semi-double, pale pink, with dark red lacing. Show and Imperial pinks – habit extremely compact; fls large, double. 'Freckles': fls salmon-pink, with delicate red blotches. 'Iceberg': fls white. 'Show Aristocrat': fls with pink buff centre. 'Show Distinction': fls crimson-cerise. 'Show Satin': fls shell-pink, fragrant. 'Winsome': fls deep pink with a crimson centre. Alpine and rock gdn pinks – habit dwarf. 'Cornish Snow': habit v. compact, bushy; fls white. 'Little Jock': fls single, pink. 'Mars' ('Brigadier'); fls semi-double, bright crimson-magenta. Annuals and biennials (crosses from *D. chinensis*, *D. barbatus*, *D. superbus*). 'Brilliancy' (*D. 'Maiden Pink' ×D. sinensis*) fls vivid red; ann. 'Heddewigii' (from *D. chinensis*): habit dwarf; fls large, range of colours. 'Rainbow Loveliness' (*D. allwoodii ×D. superbus*): fls white, pink, and lavender, exceedingly fragrant; bienn. 'Sweet Wivelsfield' (*D. allwoodii ×D. barbatus*): fls single or double, range of colours; infl. looser than sweet william. Sweet william (*D. barbatus*) 'Auricula-eyed': fls large, with conspicuously darker centre. 'Harlequin': fls ball-shaped, pink and white. 'Nigrescens': fls deep crimson. Round-about Mixed: fls bicoloured white, through pink and rose.

Diapensia L. Diapensiaceae. 4 low-growing, tufted, everg. sub-shrubs. Fls solitary, terminal; cal. seg. 5, broad; cor. tubular, lobes 5, spreading; sta. 5. Himal., W China, circumboreal.

D. lapponica L. Creeping subshrub to 7.5cm. Lvs 0.75–1.25cm, crowded, spathulate to linear-oblong, apex rounded, base contracted to a short petiole, coriaceous, red in winter. Cor. tube to 0.75cm, green-white within, limb to 2cm across, lobes broad, obtuse, spreading, white. Circumboreal. var. *obovata* F.-Schmidt. Lvs obovate. Alask., N Asia, Jap. Z2.

D. obovata (F.-Schmidt) Nak. = *D. lapponica* var. *obovata*.

DIAPENSIACEAE Lindl. 3/13. *Diapensia, Galax, Shortia*.

Diaphananthe Schltr. Orchidaceae. 40 epiphytic monopodial orchids. Lvs leathery, 2-ranked on st. Rac. arching or pendent, arising from old lf scars; pet. often shorter and rounder than sep.; lip spurred, usually entire but sometimes trilobed at apex. Trop. & S Afr. Z9.

D. bidens (Sw.) Schltr. St. to 1m or more, scandent. Lvs 5–14cm, oblong-lanceolate or ovate. Rac. 5–18cm, pendent, many-fld; fls salmon pink, yellow-pink, flesh-coloured or white; sep. 3–5mm, lanceolate, acute; pet. narrower; lip 3.5–5mm, quadrate, un-dulate, midlobe a small apiculus; spur 5–6mm. Trop. Afr.

D. fragrantissima (Rchb. f.) Schltr. St. elongating with age. Lvs to 30cm, pendent, sword-shaped. Rac. to 35cm, fls in opposite pairs, translucent yellow or yellow-green; sep. 12–14mm, lanceolate; pet. shorter; lip 8–10mm, quadrate or broadly ovate, lat. margins undulate, apex apiculate; spur 10mm. Ethiop., Sudan, Zaire, E Afr. to S Afr. and Angola.

D. kamerunensis (Schltr.) Schltr. St. short. Lvs 20–50cm, narrowly oblanceolate, succulent. Rac. 10–30cm, several-fld; fls pale green; sep. and pet. 15–20mm; lip 17–19mm, obovate with a tooth-like callus in the mouth of the spur, denticulate, shortly apiculate; spur 15–16mm. Cameroun, Uganda, Zam.

D. pellucida (Lindl.) Schltr. St. pendent. Lvs to 70cm, fleshy, lanceolate. Rac. arising below lvs, 60–80cm, pendent; fls translucent, pearly white often tinged with green or yellow; sep. and pet. 9–11mm, lanceolate, acute, pet. ciliate; lip 9–10mm, quadrate or transversely oblong, fimbriate; spur 9–10mm. W Afr. to Uganda.

D. pulchella Summerh. St. to 10cm, erect or pendent. Lvs 5–12cm, ligulate, falcate. Rac. arching or pendent, to 8cm; fls translucent, white or creamy yellow; sep. 8mm, obovate; pet. elliptic; lip 10mm, oblong, erose with tooth in mouth of spur; spur 10mm. E Afr.

D. rutila (Rchb. f.) Summerh. St. to 30cm, pendent. Lvs 7–15cm, ligulate or oblanceolate, sometimes tinged purple. Rac. some 12cm; fls khaki-purple or creamy white; dors. sep. 3mm, broad-ly ovate; pet. 2mm, orbicular; lip 2–3mm, fan-shaped; spur 8–12mm. Trop. Afr.

D. stolzii Schltr. St. 50–60cm, pendent. Lvs to 5cm, oblong. Rac. to 4cm; fls creamy white or green-white, scented, esp. in even-ing; dors. sep. 9mm, ovate, lat. sep. narrower, deflexed; pet. 9mm, ovate, apiculate; lip 10mm, fan-shaped, with tooth in mouth of spur, undulate and somewhat erose; spur 18–25mm. Tanz., Malawi, Zimb.

D. tenuicalcar Summerh. St. 7–16cm, often pendent. Lvs 4–5cm, curved oblong-lanceolate. Rac. 10–17mm; fls white; dors. sep. 4.5mm, oblong-elliptic, rounded, lat. sep. 5mm, ligulate, slightly curved, obtuse; pet. 4.5mm, ovate; lip 7.5mm with tooth-like callus in mouth of spur, fan-shaped, emarginate, apiculate; spur 25mm. Uganda.

D. xanthopollinia (Rchb. f.) Summerh. St. v. short, or to 30cm. Lvs 4–8cm, fleshy, linear or ligulate. Rac. 4–10cm; fls translucent creamy yellow, lilac-scented; sep. 3–5mm, oblong, obtuse; pet. 2mm, rounded; lip 3mm, fan-shaped with no tooth in mouth of spur; spur 5–7mm. E Afr., Zam., Zimb., Angola, S Afr.

→*Angraecum*.

Diascia Link & Otto. Scrophulariaceae. 50 ann. and perenn. herbs. St. erect or decumbent. Lvs elliptic to ovate, serrate. Fls in term. rac., with lat. spurs containing dark glands, cor. with tube ± 0, limb 5-lobed, bilabiate, with a 'window'. Summer. S Afr. Z8.

D. anastrepta Hilliard & B.L. Burtt. Perenn. St. decumbent, to 40cm. Lvs glab., 2.5×2cm. Fls nodding, deep pink, 2 upward-curving spurs at right angles to tube, tips spotted inside with dark purple glands, window marked with purple blotch. Summer.

D. barberae Hook. f. TWINSPUR. St. erect or decumbent to 30cm, gland. and pubesc. near infl. Lvs glab., rounded at base. Fls rose-pink; lat. spurs incurved, containing dark glands, outer face of palate bears 2 small black glands, window concave, yellow portion fringed and blotched dark maroon. Early summer–early autumn. 'Katherine Sharman': lvs variegated. 'Pink Queen': fls rose-pink with yellow throats, in abundant clusters. 'Ruby Field': fls profusely over a long period.

D. cordata hort. = *D. barberae*.

D. fetcaniensis Hilliard & B.L. Burtt. Perenn., compact to 23cm, glandular-pubesc. Lvs ovate, pubesc. Fls rose-pink, 2 lat. spurs to 7mm, incurved with dark sessile glands, window concave. Summer–early autumn.

D. integerrima Benth. Perenn. to 45cm. Lvs glab., grey, entire, or toothed. Fls iridescent rose-pink, on erect rac.; keel of cor. unmarked, or covered in dark sessile glands; 2 downward-pointing lat. spurs incurved, lined with dark sessile glands, window concave. Summer.

D. lilacina Hilliard & B.L. Burtt. Sprawling perenn. to 16cm; lvs and st., pubesc. Lvs gland. Fls small, solitary, lilac-pink, lat. spurs 0, window yellow and maroon forming a hollow cone. Summer.

D. megathura Hilliard & B.L. Burtt. Perenn. St. decumbent or ascending to 45cm. Lvs thick, glandular-pubesc. beneath. Fls rich pink; lat. spurs 2, to 8mm with area of dark sessile glands at right angles to tube. Summer.

D. rigescens Hilliard & B.L. Burtt. St. glab., erect or decumbent, to 55cm. Lvs glab., ageing red-brown. Fls rose-pink, 2 downward-pointing lat. spurs incurved, each with dark sessile glands, window concave. Summer. 'Forge Cottage': to 45cm high, vigorous; lvs lightly speckled with yellow when young; fls copper-pink, in tall spikes.

D. stachyoides Hiern. Perenn., to 40cm. Habit similar to *D. lilacina*. Lvs slightly serrate. Infl. with serrate, leafy bracts;

fls deep rose-pink; 2 spurs pointing down and outward. Summer.

D. vigilis Hilliard & B.L. Burtt. Perenn. to 50cm. Lvs fleshy, glab., lustrous. Fls soft pink, lateral spurs slightly gland. descending, incurved dark, gland. within. Early summer–early winter.

D. cvs. 'Jack Elliot': fls large, pink. 'Rupert Lambert': fls pink.

Diastema Benth. Gesneriaceae. 40 usually downy perenn. herbs from creeping, scaly rhiz.; st. to 15cm, branching. Fls in axill. or term. clusters; cal. lobes 5, spreading; cor. tubular or funnel-shaped, somewhat angled downward, limb 5-lobed. Trop. Amer. Z10.

D. maculatum (Poepp.) Benth. ex Walp. Lvs to 8.5cm, ovate, dentate, bullate, strigose. Cor. to 2cm, tube cream-yellow, purple-striate, limb spreading, lobes rounded, violet at centre, upper 2 lobes with mauve margins, lower 3 lobes with white margins. Peru.

D. pictum Reg. = **D. vexans**.

D. quinquevulnerum Planch. & Lind. Lvs to 7.5cm, ovate-elliptic, acute-dentate, lustrous. Cor. tube to 2cm, white to cream, deeply 3-grooved below, upper 2 lobes erect, lower 3 lobes with a basal patch of purple or rose. Summer. Venez.

D. rupestre Brand. Lvs to 8cm, coarsely toothed, pale green. Cor. to 1.2cm, tube somewhat compressed, cream-yellow, 2-grooved below, grooves purple, lobes rounded, white. Mex.

D. vexans H.E. Moore. Lvs to 7.5cm, ovate to lanceolate, dentate, pubesc. Cor. tube to 1.8cm, white spotted with purple-brown, lobes to 0.4cm, with a purple-brown spot at base. Colomb.

Diaz Blue Stem *Dichanthium annulatum.*

Dicentra Bernh. BLEEDING HEART. Fumariaceae. 19 ann. or perenn. herbs, from taproots, tubers or rhiz. Stemless or with st. erect, ascending or climbing. Lvs in basal rosette or on upright st., usually fern-like, ternately decompound and long-petioled. Fls in scapose or axill. pan., rac., corymbs, or solitary, pendulous, heart-shaped in outline, laterally compressed; sep. 2, rudimentary; pet. 4 in 2 opposed pairs; outer pair spurred at base and usually pouched, tips reflexed; inner pair tongue-shaped, with convex inner faces and crested apices. Asia, N Amer.

D. canadensis (Goldie) Walp. SQUIRREL CORN. To 30cm. Lvs basal, triangular in outline, 10–30×4–18cm; lfts linear-elliptic to linear-obovate. Rac. 10–33cm; cor. white, tinged mauve; outer pet. 10–20mm, spurs 2–8mm. Spring. S Quebec, Minn., N Carol., Tenn., Missouri. Z5.

D. chrysantha Hook. & Arn. GOLDEN EARDROPS. To 1.5m. Lvs scattered on st., 10–45×3–16cm; lfts oblong-acute. Fls to 75 in pan., with pungent odour; cor. golden yellow, cordate to oblong; outer pet. 10–22mm, inner pet. purple-tipped. Spring–summer. S Calif. Z8.

D. cucullaria (L.) Bernh. DUTCHMAN'S BREECHES. To 40cm. Lvs glaucous beneath, triangular in outline, 10–36×4–18cm; lfts linear to linear-elliptic. Rac. to 40cm; cor. white to pink, tipped yellow; outer pet. 10–20mm, spurs 3–23mm. Early spring. Nova Scotia, N Carol. W to Kans. Z5.

D. eximia (Ker-Gawl.) Torr. TURKEY CORN; STAGGERWEED. To 65cm. Lvs basal, glaucous beneath, triangular in outline, 10–55×5–30cm; lfts lanceolate to oblong or ovate, incised. Fls in a nodding pan.; cor. magenta to pink, rarely white, outer pet. 15–30mm. Spring–summer. US. 'Alba': scattered white fls in late autumn; lvs light green. 'Bountiful': deep rosy-red fls, glaucous lvs. 'Adrian Bloom': deeper red, larger fls than 'Bountiful'. 'Silversmith': fls creamy-white, flushed pink. Z5.

D. formosa (Haw.) Walp. WILD BLEEDING HEART. Lvs basal, triangular in outline, 15–55×8–35cm, glaucous beneath; lfts oblong, incised. Pan. 2–30-fld; cor. rose-purple to yellow, rarely white, cordate; outer pet. 12–24mm, spurs 2–3mm. Early summer. W N Amer. ssp. *formosa* Walp. Fls rose-purple to pink, usually white. 'Alba': fls white. ssp. *oregana* (Eastw.) Munz. Glaucous throughout. Cor. cordate to sagittate; outer pet. cream, inner pet. pink-tipped. Calif., Oreg. Z5. 'Adrian Bloom': to 35cm, v. vigorous. Lvs dark. Fls large, cerise. 'Bountiful': to 25cm, lvs silver-grey. Fls dark pink. 'Silversmith': lvs silver-grey. Fls pure white.

D. glauca nom. nud. = **D. formosa**.

D. nevadensis Eastw. Lvs variably glaucous, 10–30×5–18cm; lfts linear-oblong, with 3 coarse teeth. Fls 2–20; outer pet. white, cream or rose-tinted, 12–18mm, spur 1–2mm, inner pet. white, tipped yellow. Summer. C Calif. Z6.

D. occidentalis (Rydb.) Fedde = **D. cucullaria**.

D. ochroleuca Engelm. Glaucous, perenn., st. 1–2m. Lvs sparse on st., tripinnate, 12–50×5–35cm; lfts linear-lanceolate. Fls in term. pan., straw-yellow to cream; outer pet. purple-tipped,

15–30mm, spurs 1mm; innner pet. purple. Spring–summer. Calif. Z7.

D. oregana Eastw. = **D. formosa** ssp. *oregana*.

D. pauciflora S. Wats. Lvs 7–16×3–10cm; lfts linear-lanceolate. Fls 1–3 per scape; cor. white to pink; outer pet. 15–25mm, spurs 4–5mm, inner pet. purple. Summer. Calif. Z7.

D. peregrina (Rudolph) Mak. To 15cm. Lvs glaucous, broadly triangular basal, deeply and finely cut, 4–16×1–4cm; lfts deeply divided into linear seg. Fls semi-erect; cor. white to purple; outer pet. 15–25mm, spurs 2–3mm; inner pet. purple-tipped. Summer. E Sib., China, Jap. Z5.

D. plumosa nom. nud. = **D. formosa** ssp. *formosa* 'Alba'.

D. pusilla Sieb. & Zucc. = **D. peregrina**.

D. scandens (D. Don) Walp. St. scrambling 3–4m. Term. lfts tendril-like, others ovate to lanceolate. Fls in 2–14-fld rac.; cor. yellow or white, tipped pink or light purple; outer pet. 13–22mm, spur 1–5mm. Summer. Himal. Z5.

D. schneideri Fedde = **D. formosa** ssp. *oregana*.

D. spectabilis (L.) Lem. BLEEDING HEART. To 140cm. Lvs 15–40×10–20cm; lfts with lanceolate lobes. Fls pendent 3–15 per rac.; outer pet. rose-purple to pink, rarely white, 20–30mm; inner pet. white. Spring–summer. Sib., Jap. 'Alba': fls white. Z6.

D. thalictrifolia Wallich = **D. scandens**.

D. torulosa Hook. f. & Thoms. Ann. St. 2–4m. Lvs biternately decompound; term. lfts often tendril-like; lfts entire. Fls pendent in 2–6-fld corymbs; cor. lemon-yellow; outer pet. 10–14mm, spur 2mm. Summer. Nepal to SE China.

D. uniflora Kellogg. STEER'S HEAD. Lvs basal, pubesc. bi- to triternately decompound, 4–10×1–4cm; lfts usually oblong. Fls solitary, nodding to erect; cor. pink to white; outer pet. 7–20mm; inner pet. purple tipped. Spring–summer. Washington, Idaho and S to Calif. Z5.

Dichaea Lindl. Orchidaceae. Some 40 small epiphytic or lithophytic orchids. Pbs 0. St. leafy, slender, elongated, tufted, sprawling, closely sheathed with overlapping lf bases. Lvs distichous, carinate, fleshy, short-stalked, axill.; tep. subequal, free; lip concave, usually 3-lobed. Trop. Amer. Z10.

D. glauca (Sw.) Lindl. St. to 60cm, ascending or pendulous. Lvs to 7cm, semi-erect, linear-oblong, glaucous. Fls to 2cm diam., vanilla-scented; tep. grey-white spotted mauve and amber; lip more heavily marked, anchor-shaped with slender, erect lobules. W Indies, Mex., Costa Rica, Guat.

D. graminoides (Sw.) Lindl. St. to 30cm, sprawling, often branching. Lvs 2–4cm, linear-elliptic, ciliate, sap-green. Fls to 1cm diam., white; tep. pandurate. Guat., Colomb.

D. morrisii Fawcett & Rendle. St. to 10cm, rigid, pendulous. Lvs to 2cm, oblong-elliptic, olive green, glab. or coarsely puberulent. Tep. 0.8cm, bronze-green, or white; lip white, flabellate with lat. lobules often attenuate and incurved. W Indies, Hispan., Costa Rica to Boliv.

D. muricata (Sw.) Lindl. St. to 22cm, branching, sprawling. Lvs to 1.2cm, oblong-lanceolate, scabrid to puberulent, olive-green; sheaths sometimes spotted. Sep. to 1.2cm, olive to orange, spotted or banded oxblood, often verrucose beneath; pet. bronze to orange, spotted lavender-blue; lip indigo, fleshy at base, sagittate. C Amer.

D. panamensis Lindl. Differs from *D. graminoides* in its semi-erect, clumped habit, glaucous lvs, green-white fls spotted garnet or violet, and sagittate, not pandurate, lip. Mex. to Peru.

D. pendula (Aubl.) Cogn. St. to 50cm clumped, pendulous. Lvs to 4cm, papery, soft, olive green. Tep. 0.6cm, bronze to yellow, mottled lilac near apex, softly ciliate; lip obscurely 3-lobed, ciliate, lilac mottled indigo. W Indies, Costa Rica, Venez., Colomb.

D. picta Rchb. f. St. to 18cm, erect or sprawling and ascending. Lvs to 1.5cm, olive green, oblong-lanceolate. Tep. to 0.6cm, bronze-green mottled pink to mauve; lip white flecked garnet. Guyana, Venez., Trin.

D. robusta Schltr. = **D. morrisii**.

D. trulla Rchb. f. St. to 50cm, pendulous. Lvs to 8cm, deep green, soft, glossy, linear-lanceolate. Tep. to 1cm, pale ochre; lip obscurely hastate, ciliate, green to violet at apex. Costa Rica, Panama, Venez., Colomb., Braz., Guyana. White-fld forms occur.

Dichaelia Harv.

D. elongata Schltr. = *Brachystelma elongatum*.

D. natalensis Schltr. = *Brachystelma sandersonii*.

D. pygmaea Schltr. = *Brachystelma pygmaeum*.

Dichanthium Willem. Gramineae. 20–30 ann. or perenn. grasses. Lvs flat or inrolled; ligules membranous. Infl. racemose. Trop. Z10.

D. annulatum (Forssk.) Stapf. DIAZ BLUE STEM; RINGED BEARD GRASS; BRAHMAN GRASS; KLEBERG GRASS. Perenn. to 1m, twisting, ascending. Lvs to 30×0.7cm. Rac. 1–15 per infl., to 7cm; peduncles glab. India, China, introd. subtrop. var. *papillosum* (A. Rich.) De Wet & Harlan. Lower glume of sessile spikelet with a fringe of bulbous-based hairs below apex.

D. aristatum (Poir.) C. Hubb. ANGLETON GRASS; ANGLETON BLUE-STEM. Perenn. to 1m. Lvs to 25×0.5cm. Rac. to 8cm, pubesc. India to SE Asia.

D. caricosum (L.) A. Camus. As for *D. annulatum*, sheaths flattened; ligule membranous, ciliate. India.

→*Andropogon*.

Dichelostemma Kunth Liliaceae (Alliaceae). 7 cormous perenn. herbs. Lvs long-linear, grassy. Fls in slender-scapose umbels; perianth campanulate; fertile sta. 3–6, inserted on inner perianth lobes; staminodes 3, inserted on outer lobes. Summer. W US.

D. californicum (Torr.) Alph. Wood = *D. volubile*.

D. congestum (Sm.) Kunth OOKOW. Scape 30–90cm; spathe valves pale mauve; pedicels short, bowed-ascending to erect, bases fused forming a stalk; perianth 1.4–2cm, blue-violet, tube 6-angled, somewhat constricted at throat, lobes spreading, equalling tube. W US. Z8.

D. ida-maia (Wood) Greene. FIRECRACKER FLOWER. Scape 30–90cm; spathe valves tinged red; pedicels slender, curving; perianth scarlet (sometimes yellow), tube 2–2.5cm, lobes much shorter than tube, pale green. W US. Z7.

D. multiflorum (Benth.) Heller. WILD HYACINTH. Scape 20–80cm; spathe valves tinged purple; pedicels erect; perianth violet, rarely white, 1.6–2.1cm, lobes as long as tube, widely spreading, tube waisted above ovary, not angled. W US. Z7.

D. pulchellum (Salisb.) Heller. BLUE DICKS; WILD HYACINTH. Scape 30–60cm; spathe valves purple-tinted; pedicels erect; perianth 1.2–1.8cm, white to violet, tube not constricted at throat or angled, lobes equalling or exceeding tube, not widely spreading. W US. Z5.

D. volubile (Kellogg) A.A. Heller. SNAKE LILY; TWINING BRODIAEA. Scape to 150cm, twining; pedicels slender, spreading or pendent in fl.; perianth to 2cm, pale to rose pink, tube 6-angled. Calif.

→*Brevoortia* and *Brodiaea*.

Dichondra Forst. & Forst. f. Convolvulaceae. 10 prostrate, perenn. herbs, rooting at nodes. Lvs cordate-reniform, entire. Fls axill., solitary; cor. minute, deeply 5-lobed, ± equalling cal. Trop. and subtrop.

D. micrantha Urban. St. to 50cm, creeping, slender, hairy. Lvs 0.5–3cm, forming a close mat, pubesc. Cor. 2–2.5mm, white, green or yellow-green. Summer–autumn. E Asia, nat. W Eur., S US. Z10. Used as a lawn plant. *D. carolinensis* Michx. and *D. repens* Forst. & Forst. f. are also offered, but plants grown under these names are likely to be *D. micrantha*.

Dichorisandra Mikan Commelinaceae. 25 stout perenn. herbs. St. ± erect. Lvs spirally arranged or 2-ranked. Infl. raceme-like thyrses, term. or rarely axill.; sep. 3, free, the upper-most longest, cucullate, often coloured like pet.; pet. 3, free or slightly united at base; sta. 6–5, fil. glab. Trop. Amer.

D. albomarginata hort. = *Tradescantia zanonia* 'Mexican Flag'.

D. musaica var. *undata* (K. Koch & Lind.) W. Mill. = *Geogenanthus poeppigii*.

D. reginae (L. Lind. & Rodigas) hort. ex W. Ludw.). St. erect to 30cm, simple, bare below. Lvs to 18cm, elliptic, acuminate, almost glab., striped or flecked silvery above and often flushed purple. Infl. compact; sep. 1cm, blue-green; pet. to 1.3cm, broadly obovate, white, blue-violet toward apex. Summer–autumn. Peru. Z9.

D. thyrsiflora Mikan. St. erect, to 2.5m. Lvs 20–30cm, elliptic-lanceolate, acuminate, glab. Infl. c20cm, dense; sep. 1cm, violet with darker veins; pet. c1.2cm, violet, white at base, suborbicular. Autumn. SE Braz. Z9.

Dichotomanthes Kurz. Rosaceae. 1 everg. shrub or small tree to 6m, differing from *Cotoneaster* in the dry fr. surrounded by fleshy cal. Br. woolly at first, arching. Lvs to 10cm, elliptic, glossy above, silky-pubesc. beneath. Infl. term., corymbose, to 5cm diam.; fls white, to 6mm diam. SW China. Z8.

D. tristaniicarpa Kurz.

Dichrostachys (DC.) Wight & Arn. Leguminosae (Mimosoideae). 12 decid. shrubs or small trees. Lvs bipinnate; stipules thorn-like. Infl. spicate; pet. 0; staminodes 10, slender; sta. 10, short. OW Trop. and Subtrop. Z10.

D. cinerea (L.) Wight & Arn. Thorny suckering shrub or tree to 6m. Pinnae 8–36, paired; lfts many, linear. Infl. nodding, compact, rose-purple at base, fading to yellow-white at tip. Afr., India. ssp. *nyassana* (Taub.) Brenan. Lfts oblong. Afr.

D. glomerata (Forssk.) Chiov. = *D. cinerea*.
D. nutans Benth. = *D. cinerea*.
D. nyassana Taub. = *D. cinerea* spp. *nyassana*.
→*Cailliea*.

Dicksonia L'Hérit. Dicksoniaceae. 25 terrestrial ferns. Rhiz. usually erect, massive, trunk-like, covered in fibrous roots. Fronds stipitate, spreading in crowns, 2–4-pinnate or -pinnatifid, fertile pinnae smaller than sterile. Amer., SE Asia, Australasia, Polyn.

D. aculeata Spreng. = *Hypolepis repens*.
D. adiantoides Humb. & Bonpl. ex Willd. = *Dennstaedtia bipinnata*.
D. altissima Sm. = *Dennstaedtia globulifera*.
D. antarctica Labill. SOFT TREE FERN. Rhiz. 60cm+ diam. to 15m high. Fronds to 2m, 2–3-pinnate, rhomboid, pinnae to 45cm, pinnules, linear, seg. oblong, toothed (sterile), or lobed (fertile); stipes to 2m, sparsely pubesc. to scaly, grey to brown. Aus., Tasm. Z8.
D. anthriscifolia Jenman non Kaulf. = *Dennstaedtia dissecta*.
D. berteroana Brackenr. non Hook. = *D. brackenridgei*.
D. bipinnata Cav. = *Dennstaedtia bipinnata*.
D. brackenridgei Mett. Rhiz. to 3m high. Fronds to 1.2m, 3-pinnate-pinnatifid, deltoid to rhomboid, sterile pinnae to 40cm, lanceolate to oblong, pinnules lanceolate, seg. lanceolate to oblong, subentire to notched; stipes to 60cm, rough and densely red-brown pubesc. Fiji, Samoa. Z10.
D. cicutaria Sw. = *Dennstaedtia cicutaria*.
D. cornuta Kaulf. = *Dennstaedtia dissecta*.
D. dissecta Jenman pro parte, non Sw. = *Dennstaedtia globulifera* and *Dennstaedtia obtusifolia*.
D. dissecta Sw. = *Dennstaedtia dissecta*.
D. exaltata Kunze = *Dennstaedtia globulifera*.
D. fibrosa Colenso. Rhiz. to 60cm diam., to 6m high, sometimes prostrate. Fronds to 2m, 2–3-pinnate, pinnae to 30cm, lanceolate to oblong, pinnules linear, seg. deltoid, entire or toothed; stipes smooth, scaly, pubesc. at base, brown. NZ. Z9.
D. fragilis Trev. = *Woodsia fragilis*.
D. ghiesbreghtii Maxon = *D. sellowiana*.
D. gigantea Karst. = *D. sellowiana*.
D. globulifera (Poir.) Kuntze = *Dennstaedtia globulifera*.
D. globuligera Desv. = *Dennstaedtia bipinnata*.
D. gracilis Colenso = *D. squarrosa*.
D. karsteniana (Klotzsch) Karst. = *D. sellowiana*.
D. laevis Heward = *D. lanata*.
D. lanata Colenso. Rhiz. to 5cm diam. and prostrate, or to 20cm diam., 2m high, erect, branched. Fronds to 50cm or more, 2–3-pinnate, ovate to deltoid or rhomboid, pinnae to 25cm, lanceolate to oblong, pinnules lanceolate, seg. ovate to oblong, notched or lobed; stipes to 60cm, brown-pubesc., especially at base. NZ. Z9.
D. lobulata Christ = *D. sellowiana*.
D. macrocarpa L'Hérit. = *Culcita macrocarpa*.
D. obtusifolia Willd. = *Dennstaedtia obtusifolia*.
D. ordinata Kaulf. = *Dennstaedtia obtusifolia*.
D. punctilobula Michx. = *Dennstaedtia punctilobula*.
D. rubiginosa Kaulf. = *Dennstaedtia cicutaria*.
D. scabra Wallich = *Dennstaedtia scabra*.
D. sellowiana Hook. Rhiz. to 25cm diam., to 10cm high. Fronds to 3m, 2–3-pinnate or -pinnatifid, lanceolate, glab. to sparsely pubesc. beneath, pinnae to 40cm, pinnules linear, seg. deltoid to oblong; stipes densely pubesc. Trop. Amer. Z10.
D. squarrosa (Forst. f.) Sw. Rhiz. to 10cm diam., 6m or more high, much branched. Fronds to 1.2cm, 2–3-pinnate, deltoid or lanceolate to oblong, pinnae to 50cm, ovate or deltoid to oblong, pinnules linear, seg. suborbicular to lanceolate, obtuse; stipes to 30cm, rough, densely pubesc. and scaly, brown to black. NZ. Z9.
D. umbrosa Liebm. = *Dennstaedtia cicutaria*.
D. youngiae C. Moore. BRISTLY TREE FERN. Rhiz. to 20cm diam., 4m+ high, bristly. Fronds 3-pinnate, deltoid to oblong, lustrous and leathery, pinnae to 30cm, lanceolate to oblong, pinnules lanceolate, seg. lanceolate, notched or lobed; stipes to 25cm, pubesc., lustrous, brown. Aus. Z10.

DICKSONIACEAE (C. Presl) Bower. 7 genera. *Cibotium, Culcita, Dicksonia, Lophosoria* and *Thyrsopteris*.

Dickson's Golden Elm *Ulmus carpinifolia* 'Dicksonii'.

Dicliptera Juss. Acanthaceae. 150 ann. and perenn. herbs, subshrubs, shrubs and lianes. St. usually 6-angled. Lvs opposite, entire. Fls in bracteate term. clusters; cor. bilabiate, tube slender, expanding toward throat, limb narrow. Trop. and warm temp. regions. Z10.

D. suberecta (André) Bremek. Grey-velvety perenn. herb or sub-shrub. St. slender, erect to pendent. Lvs to 7cm, ovate. Fls to 3.5cm, rusty red. Urug.
→*Justicia*.

Dicranopteris Bernh. Gleicheniaceae. 10 terrestrial ferns. Rhiz. creeping, branched. Fronds often scrambling and forming dense thickets, dichotomously branching, ultimate br. terminating in 2 pinnate blades subtended by 2 smaller frond-like blades ('stipules') in a bird's foot arrangement. Pantrop. Z10.
D. linearis (Burm.) Underw. 60–120cm. Rhiz. slender, ferruginous-setose; stipes slender, smooth, polished, ultimate blades linear-lanceolate; pinnules linear. Pantrop.
→*Gleichenia*.

Dicranostigma Hook. f. & Thoms. Papaveraceae. 3 perenn. or ann. herbs differing from *Glaucium* in having seeds *not* embedded in spongy tissue. Summer. Himal., W & C China. Z6.
D. franchetianum (Prain) Fedde. Ann., to 60cm. Basal lvs 7.5–30cm, 4–6-lobed. Fls term., yellow, to 2.5cm diam. W China.
D. lactucoides Hook. f. & Thoms. To 60cm. Basal lvs 12.5–25cm, 4–6-lobed. Fls term., orange, to 5cm diam. Himal. Differs from the other 2 spp. described here in its obtuse buds and downy fr.
D. leptopodum (Maxim.) Fedde. Perenn., to 60cm. Basal lvs to 15cm, 4–6-lobed. Fls term., to 3cm diam., yellow. China.

Dictamnus L. DITTANY; BURNING BUSH. Rutaceae. 1 aromatic, erect, woody-based perenn. herb, 40–80cm. Lvs imparipinnate with pellucid punctate glands, lfts 3–8cm, in (2)3–6 pairs, lanceolate to ovate, serrulate. Rac. terminal, erect, darkly glandular-pubesc.; fls zygomorphic; sep. 5, lanceolate; pet. 5, elliptic-lanceolate, 2–2.5cm, white, pink, red or lilac, sometimes with darker veins or dotted red, lower 2 projecting downwards; sta. 10. SW Eur., S & C Asia to China and Korea.
D. albus L. 'Purpureus': fls dark purple; 'Ruber': fls rosy-purple. var. **caucasicus** (Fisch. & Mey.) Rouy. Rac. to 60cm; fls larger, dark pink. 'Albiflorus': fls white veined yellow. Z3.
D. caucasicus Fisch. & Mey. = *D. albus* var. *caucasicus*.
D. fraxinella Pers. = *D. albus*.
D. gymnostylis Steven = *D. albus*.

Dictymia J. Sm. Polypodiaceae. 4 epiphytic ferns. Rhiz. creeping, scaly at first. Fronds uniform, stipitate, simple, linear or lanceolate, entire or undulate, ± leathery; costa prominent. Oceania. Z10.
D. brownii (Wikstr.) Copel. Fronds to 45×2cm, linear-elliptic to strap-shaped, apex acute or obtuse, base cuneate, lustrous and dark green; stipes to 18cm, smooth to rough, straw-coloured. Oceania.
→*Polypodium*.

Dictyosperma H.A. Wendl. & Drude. PRINCESS PALM. Palmae. 1 palm to 20m. St. solitary, to 10cm diam., erect, occas. swollen at base, brown to grey, ringed and cracked. Crownshaft white-grey to red-brown lanate. Lvs to 3m, pinnate, arched; petioles to 30cm, scaly and convex beneath; pinnae to 70 per side, lanceolate, often divided, midrib downy beneath, prominently 1–2-veined on either side, veins tinted when young; rachis slightly twisted. Maur., Réunion Is. Z10.
D. album (Bory) H.A. Wendl. & Drude ex R. Scheff. var. **aureum** Balf. f. Petiole glab., orange-yellow above, with a yellow stripe beneath extending to rachis; pinnae with yellow midrib. Rodrigues Is. var. **conjugatum** H.E. Moore & Guého. Pinnae connected towards apices by persistent fil. Round Is.
D. album var. **rubrum** L.H. Bail. = *D. album*.
D. furfuraceum var. **aureum** (Balf. f.) Becc. = *D. album* var. *aureum*.
→*Areca* and *Linoma*.

Dictyoxiphium Hook. Dryopteridaceae. 1 fern. Rhiz. fasciculate, erect, subterranean. Fronds to 60×7.5cm, simple, tufted, linear-lanceolate, entire, decurrent on stipe. C Amer.
D. panamense Hook.

Didder *Briza media*.

Didierea Baill. Didiereaceae. 2 decid. perennials, tree-like with age, thorny; st. simple or branched, with tuberculate short shoots terminating in a radial arrangement of thorns. Lvs rosulate, growing from thorns. Fls small, crowded, cymose; cor. cup-shaped, reticulate. SW Madag. Z10.
D. ascendens Drake = *Alluaudia ascendens*.
D. madagascariensis Baill. Perenn. shrub to small tree, 4–8m; st. v. woody, forming a column to 40cm thick, tip sometimes curv-

ing over, densely covered with 2–4cm shoots which terminate in a whorl of 4 v. stout, 4–10cm thorns. Lvs non-succulent, 7–15cm, narrow-linear.
D. mirabilis Baill. = *D. madagascariensis*.
D. procera Drake = *Alluaudia procera*.
D. trollii Capuron & Rauh. St. initially prostrate, forming a dense bush, producing 1 or more erect adult st. with horizontally projecting tuberculate br.; thorns 5 at tips of short shoots, thin, 2–4cm. Lvs 1–2cm, fleshy, ovate, elliptic or oblong.

DIDIEREACEAE Drake. 4/11. *Alluaudia, Alluaudiopsis, Decaryia, Didierea*.

Didiscus DC.
D. coeruleus DC. = *Trachymene coerulea*.
D. pusillus F. Muell. = *Trachymene pilosa*. .

Didissandra C.B. Clarke.
D. lanuginosus (DC.) C.B. Clarke = *Corallodiscus lanuginosus*.

Didymaotus N.E. Br. Aizoaceae. 1 succulent perenn. St. producing a single pair of lvs. Lvs thick, v. fleshy, upperside triangular, 15–20×30mm, flat or slightly concave, lower surface pulled forward over the tip like a pointed chin, carinate, white grey-green, rough. Fls white with a pink or red centre. S Afr. Z9.
D. lapidiformis (Marloth) N.E. Br.
→*Mesembryanthemum*.

Didymochlaena Desv. Dryopteridaceae. 1 subarborescent fern. Rhiz. erect. Stipes tufted, densely scaly. Fronds 60–150×30–60cm, 2-pinnate, glossy, coriaceous, emerging rose-bronze; pinnae lanceolate; pinnules obliquely ovate-rhomboid, short-petiolate, apex rounded, gently incurved, base obscurely lobed on upper margin. Trop. Afr. and Amer., Polyn.
D. truncatula (Sw.) J. Sm. TREE MAIDENHAIR FERN. Z10.
→*Aspidium*.

Didymopanax Decne. & Planch.
D. morototonii (Aubl.) Decne. & Planch. = *Schefflera morototonii*.

Didymosperma H.A. Wendl. & Drude ex Hook. f.
D. caudatum (Lour.) H.A. Wendl. ex Salomon = *Arenga caudata*.
D. distichum (Anderson) Hook. f. = *Wallichia disticha*.
D. engleri (Becc.) Warb. = *Arenga engleri*.
D. hastatum Becc. = *Arenga hastata*.
D. porphyrocarpa (Bl.) H.A. Wendl. & Drude ex Hook. f. = *Arenga porphyrocarpa*.

Dieffenbachia Schott. DUMB CANE; MOTHER-IN-LAW'S TONGUE; TUFTROOT. Araceae. c25 everg., erect, perenn. herbs. St. stout, fleshy, to 2.5m, bearing lvs toward apex. Lvs entire, often marked with white or yellow spots, or larger zones; petioles sheathing. Fls on a long spadix; spathe blade, green, convolute, boat-shaped, shorter than tube. Trop. Amer. Z10.
D. amoena Bull. V. robust, to 2m; st. thick. Lvs to 50cm, elliptic-oblong, base ± truncate, dark green with cream-white zones along lat. veins; petiole to 30cm, broadly winged. Origin obscure. Often treated as a form of *D. seguine*.
D. barraquiniana Versch. & Lemmon = *D. maculata* 'Barraquiniana'.
D. ×bausei Reg. (*D. maculata* × *D. weirii*.) Lvs to 30cm, broad-lanceolate, base subtruncate, yellow-green marked with few, large green blotches and smaller white spots. Gdn origin.
D. bowmannii hort. ex Veitch. Lvs to 75cm, narrowly ovate-elliptic, unequal, basally truncate, with irregular, intermingled light and dark green, parallel markings. E Braz.
D. brasiliensis hort. (Veitch). = *D. maculata*.
D. chelsonii hort. ex Bull. Lvs dark green with satin-like lustre, oblong, truncate at base, with yellow-green blotches and leathery grey stripe along midrib. Colomb.
D. costata Klotzsch ex Schott. Lvs to 22cm, ovate, deep velvety-green spotted with oblong ivory-white blotches, midrib ivory white, base blunt, undulate. Colomb.
D. daguensis Engl. Lvs to 45cm, obovate, bright green with many wide, spreading, lat. veins; petioles v. short. Colomb.
D. delecta Nichols. Lvs to 25cm, elliptic-lanceolate, spreading, satiny green with white variegation. Colomb. Material cultivated under this name has pendent, narrow lvs with a narrow zone along midrib.
D. eburnea Bull non Lind. = *D. maculata* 'Lancifolia'.
D. exotica hort. = *D. maculata* 'Exotica'.
D. fosteri hort. = *D. oerstedii* 'Fosteri'.

D. fourneri hort. Lvs to 40cm, broadly oblong-lanceolate, base truncate, leathery black-green, spotted and blotched white. Colomb.

D. hoffmannii hort. = *D. maculata* 'Hoffmannii'.

D. imperialis Lind. & André. Lvs to 60cm, elliptic-ovate, basally obtuse or subcordate, leathery, 60cm, dark green with yellow spots, midrib silvery. S Amer.

D. jenmannii hort. (Veitch). = *D. maculata* 'Jenmannii'.

D. latimaculata Lind. & André. Not in cult. Material offered under this name is probably *D. bowmannii*.

D. leonii nom. nud. = *D. maculata* 'Leonii'.

D. leopoldii Bull. Lvs to 35cm, broadly elliptic to ovate, base truncate, dark green, midrib ivory. Costa Rica.

D. longispatha Engl. & K. Krause. Lvs to 55cm, pure green, elongate-oblong-lanceolate, basally obtuse, leathery. Panama, Colomb.

D. macrophylla Poepp. = *D. costata*.

D. maculata (Lodd.) Bunting. Lvs oblong or lanceolate, narrower, acuinate, often heavily spotted white. C Amer., NS Amer. 'Angustior': robust; lvs lanceolate, dark green, thick, veins sunken. 'Barraquiniana': lvs 15–30cm, oblong, acuminate, basally obtuse, bright, light green, irregularly spotted white, midrib white. 'Camilla': mutation of 'Exotica Perfection'; dense; lvs to 25cm, ovate, compact, cream with white veins and lush green edge. 'Exotica': compact; lvs to 25cm, ovate, dark green, heavily variegated with white or green-white, some areas pure green, midrib variegated green and white. 'Exotica Alba': mutation of 'Exotica Perfection'; as 'Camilla' but lvs cream with white veins and green edge. 'Exotica Arvida': dense and upright; lvs small, ovate pointed, thick, heavily variegated creamy white. 'Exotica Perfection': dense; lvs to 20cm, thick, boldly variegated white-green with wide, matt green margin. 'Gigantea': large; lvs wide, glossy green, base cordate, veins indented, midrib and petiole lighter and marbled. 'Hoffmannii': similar to 'Exotica' to 35cm, broadly oblong-lanceolate, midrib white, variegated green only at the base. 'Janet Weidner': sport of 'Superba'; tall; lvs heavily variegated white. 'Jenmannii': lvs to 25cm, oblong, basally obtuse, pea green with long, white blotches along primary lat. veins from middle almost to margin. 'Lancifolia': lvs to 25cm, narrowly elliptic, acuminate, densely white spotted; petioles red. 'Leonii': lvs to 25cm, elliptic to oblong, basally truncate, dark green, variegated, with large, irregular yellow spots and blotches, white along midrib. 'Magnifica': lvs broadly ovate-lanceolate, glossy green, lightly blotched white, veins depressed, glaucous beneath. 'Mars': tall, similar to *D. compacta*. 'Mary Weidner': sport of 'Superba'; dense; lvs dotted cream, petioles marbled off-white. 'Pia': lvs large, pale green to white, edged deep green; offspring of 'Superba'. 'Rudolph Roehrs' (YELLOW-LEAF DIEFFENBACHIA): lvs ovate to elliptic, basally cordate, mostly creamy white, faintly spotted white, margins green. 'São Antonio': lvs broad, fresh green with chartreuse marks along midrib, dotted white; petioles marbled. 'Shuttleworthii': lvs narrowly elliptic, basally obtuse or truncate, midrib ivory with broad silvery stripe. 'Superba': lvs heavily splotched cream-white, margins and midribs green. 'Tropic Snow' ('Tropic Topaz', 'Hi-colour'): dense, tall; lvs thick, variegated cream and sage green. 'Tropic White': lvs large, stiff, blotched white. 'Veerie': lvs green-yellow with white blotches. 'Viridis': lvs green, oblong, basally subcordate. 'Wilson's Delight': lvs to 40cm, deep green with wide cream-marked midrib and end feathering.

D. × memoria-corsii Fenzl. Lvs blades elliptic to oblong, blotched with grey-silver esp. along the midrib, with a few white spots.

D. oerstedii Schott. To 1m. Lvs to 25cm, unequal, lanceolate-oblong to ovate, basally truncate or notched. Fr. red. Mex. to Costa Rica. 'Fosteri': lvs satiny. 'Variegata': midribs of lvs and bases of petioles white.

D. parlatorei Lind. & André. Lvs 60cm, broadly oblanceolate, deep green, blotched green-white, leathery; petioles v. short. Colomb. 'Marmorea': lvs with large irregular blotches of white, spotted green, midribs streaked white.

D. picta Schott = *D. maculata*.

D. picta var. **barraquiniana** (Versch. & Lemmon) Engl. = *D. maculata* 'Barraquiniana'.

D. picta var. **jenmannii** hort. = *D. maculata* 'Jenmannii'.

D. pittieri Engl. & K. Krause. Lvs to 22.5cm, oblique-oblong, basally obtuse to subacute, irregularly blotched pale green or white. Panama. Some material under this name has lvs elliptic to oblong, dull dark green, irregularly marked with white or light green.

D. regina hort. = *D. bowmannii*.

D. rex hort. ex Gent. Lvs to 50cm, elliptic to lanceolate, unequal, pale green near edge of narrower side, thickly covered with white blotches to within 1cm of margin, some green veins and patches of green throughout. S Amer.

D. roehrsii hort. = *D. maculata* 'Rudolph Roehrs'.

D. seguine (Jacq.) Schott. DUMB CANE. Lvs to 40cm+, oblong to elliptic to lanceolate or ovate, basally truncate to acute, glossy dark green above or variegated with pellucid white spots. This sp. is v. variable and there is little evidence that *D. seguine* and *D. maculata* differ. 'Liturata': If blades elliptic to oblong, basally obtuse-truncate, midrib white, bordered by a narrow, cream stripe on either side. 'Nobilis': If blades elliptic, with many white and emerald green splotches almost to the margins.

D. seguine 'Amoena' = *D. amoena*.

D. seguine 'Barraquiniana'. = *D. maculata* 'Barraquiniana'.

D. shuttleworthiana Bull = *D. maculata* 'Shuttleworthii'.

D. × splendens Bull. (*D. leopoldii* × *D. maculata*.) Lvs to 30cm, elliptic, base truncate, finely undulate, bottle green with white-green blotches widely dispersed, midrib broad, white. Colomb.

D. triumphans hort. ex Engl. Lvs 30cm, ovate to lanceolate, narrow-acuminate, dark green with irregular, angular, yellow-green blotches. Colomb.

D. weirii Berkl. Dwarf, to 40cm. Lvs bright green, oblong, attenuate at base. Braz.

Dierama K. Koch. ANGEL'S FISHING RODS; WAND FLOWER; AFRICAN HAIRBELL. Iridaceae. 44 perenn., cormous, everg. herbs. Lvs linear, grassy, grey-green, mostly basal, reduced to bracts on st.; fls pendulous on slender, strongly arching spikes exceeding lvs, usually funnel-shaped or bell-shaped, tube short, tep. 6, silky, with a diamond-shaped mark just above the base. Summer. Trop. and S Afr. Z9 unless specified.

D. adelphicum Hilliard. St. 60–120cm. Lvs 35–60cm×3–5mm. Fls 1.5–2cm, pale mauve-pink to magenta-pink, rarely white. S Afr.

D. cooperi N.E. Br. St. 60–2m. Lvs 30–70cm×3–5mm. Fls c1.5–2.5cm, bright pink or white. S Afr.

D. dracomontanum Hilliard. St. 30–100cm. Lvs 30–65cm×3–6mm. Fls 2–3cm, pale to deep rose pink, mauve, purple-pink, pale coral pink or coral red. S Afr., Les.

D. grandiflorum Lewis. St. 135–150cm. Lvs 60–90cm×4–8mm. Fls usually 5–7cm, tube blue-purple, tep. deep pink. S Afr.

D. igneum Klatt. St. 45–135cm. Lvs 30–90cm×2.5–9mm. Fls 1.5–3.5cm, pale to deep lilac or pink, sometimes almost white. S Afr.

D. insigne N.E. Br. St. 65–150cm. Lvs 35–75cm×2–6mm. Fls c2–3.5cm, pale pink or magenta-pink, occas. white. S Afr., Swaz.

D. jucundum Hilliard. St. 80–95cm. Lvs 45–65×5–7mm. Fls c2.5–3cm, openly bell-shaped, pale mauve. S Afr., Les.

D. luteoalbum Verdoorn. St. 65–110cm, lvs 35–60cm×3–4mm. Fls 3–5cm, white or creamy-yellow. S Afr., Natal.

D. pendulum (L. f.) Bak. St. 1–2m. Lvs 60–90cm×4–9mm. Fls c3–5cm, widely bell-shaped, usually purple-pink. S Afr. 'Album': fls white. 'Puck': habit dwarf; fls madder-pink. 'Roseum': fls rose-pink. 'Titania': habit dwarf, fls light pink. Z7.

D. pulcherrimum (Hook. f.) Bak. St. 90–180cm. Lvs 50–90×0.5–1cm. Fls narrowly bell-shaped, 3.5–5.5cm, pale to deep magenta-pink or deep red-purple, occas. white. S Afr. 'Album': fls white. Z7.

D. pumilum N.E. Br. = *D. dracomontanum*.

D. reynoldsii Verdoorn. St. 1–2m. Lvs 45–95cm×4–6mm. Fls 2–3cm, deep wine-red. S Afr.

D. robustum N.E. Br. St. 70cm–2m. Lvs 40–120cm×3–10mm. Fls c2.5–3.5cm, creamy-white, pale pink or mauve-pink, rarely deeper pink. S Afr., Les.

Diervilla Mill. BUSH HONEYSUCKLE. Caprifoliaceae. 3 spreading, suckering, decid. shrubs. Fls in small, axill. clusters sometimes grouped into term. cymes; cor. to 1.5cm, tubular, narrow, bilabiate, 5-lobed; sta. 5, exserted. N Amer.

D. amabilis Carr. = *Weigela coraeensis*.

D. canadensis Willd. = *D. lonicera*.

D. coraeensis (Thunb.) DC. = *Weigela coraeensis*.

D. decora Nak. = *Weigela decora*.

D. floribunda Sieb. & Zucc. = *Weigela floribunda*.

D. florida (Bunge) Sieb. & Zucc. = *Weigela florida*.

D. grandiflora Sieb. & Zucc. = *Weigela coraeensis*.

D. hortensis Sieb. & Zucc. = *Weigela hortensis*.

D. japonica (Thunb.) DC. = *Weigela japonica*.

D. lonicera Mill. BUSH HONEYSUCKLE. To 1m. Br. glab. Lvs 5–12.5cm, oblong-lanceolate to oval-lanceolate, acute, serrate, pubesc. Fls green-yellow, 3-grouped at axils or 5 per term. cyme. Summer. E N Amer. Z3.

D. lutea Pursh = *D. lonicera*.

D. middendorffiana Carr. = *Weigela middendorffiana*. a

D. middendorffiana var. **maximowiczii** S. Moore = *Weigela maximowiczii*.

D. praecox Lemoine = *Weigela praecox*.

D. rivularis Gatt. To 1m. Br. terete, pubesc. Lvs to 7cm, ovate to oblong-lanceolate, acuminate, serrate, pubesc., colouring well in autumn. Fls lemon-yellow, becoming red-yellow, in crowded cymes forming term. pan. Summer. SE US. Z3.

D. sessilifolia Buckley. BUSH HONEYSUCKLE. Resembles *D. rivularis* except br. tetragonal; lvs to 15cm, glab. except midrib beneath, veins flushed red; fls sulphur-yellow, paired in short term. clusters. Summer. SE US. Z4.

D. ×splendens (Carr.) Kirchn. (*D. sessilifolia* ×*D. lonicera.*) Resembles *D. sessilifolia* but lvs with veins green beneath. Gdn origin. Z3.

D. trifida Moench = *D. lonicera*.

D. venusta Stapf = *Weigela florida* var. *venusta*.

→*Weigela*.

Dietes Klatt. Iridaceae. 6 perenn. herbs. Rhiz. creeping or ascending. Lvs linear to ensiform, leathery, equitant. Flowering st. erect, branching, leafy below, spathaceous above; fls ephemeral; perianth radially symmetric, seg. 6, outer 3 larger with claws semi-erect, blades outspread, nectar guide conspicuous; style br. flattened, petal-like. Afr., 1 sp. Lord Howe Is. Z9.

D. bicolor (Steud.) Klatt. Flowering st. 60–100cm; fls yellow, outer perianth seg. 3–4cm, blotched dark brown at base of blade, claw bearded, spotted orange. Spring–summer. S Afr.

D. grandiflora N.E. Br. WILD IRIS. Flowering st. 1–1.25cm; fls white; outer perianth seg. 4–6cm, nectar guide yellow, claw with a yellow beard, inner seg. marked brown at base; style br. tinted lilac. Spring–summer. S Afr.

D. iridioides (L.) Klatt. Flowering st. 30–60cm; fls white, outer perianth seg. 2–3.5cm, downy and papillose in the centre, nectar guide yellow, claw spotted deep yellow or brown; style br. white suffused pale blue or mauve, or blue. Spring–summer. S Afr. through E Afr. to Kenya. 'Johnsonia': lvs erect, flowering st. taller, fls to 10cm diam. Oakhurst Hybrids: habit spreading; fls rounded, cream-white, blotched brown-yellow, with purple centre.

D. robinsoniana (F. Muell.) Klatt. Flowering st. to 2m; fls pure white; outer perianth seg. 4–5cm, nectar guide orange; style br. white. Spring–summer. Aus. (Lord Howe Is.).

D. vegeta auct. = *D. iridioides*.

→*Moraea*.

Digger Pine *Pinus sabiniana*.
Digger's Speedwell *Parahebe perfoliata*.

Digitalis L. FOXGLOVE. Scrophulariaceae. Some 20 bienn. or perenn. herbs. Lvs basal, rosulate and cauline. Term. rac. erect, secund, sometimes branched, bracteate; cor. tube inflated, campanulate, limb obliquely spreading, 4-lobed, upper lip shorter than lower. Summer. Eur., NW Afr. to C Asia.

D. alba Schrank = *D. purpurea* 'Alba'.

D. ambigua Murray = *D. grandiflora*.

D. aurea Lindl. = *D. ferruginea*.

D. campanulata hort. = *D. purpurea* 'Campanulata'.

D. canariensis L. = *Isoplexis canariensis*.

D. chinensis Hook. & Arn. = *Adenosma grandiflorum*.

D. davisiana Heyw. Perenn. to 70cm. Lvs linear-lanceolate, glab., serrulate or subentire. Rac. lax; peduncle glandular-pubesc.; cor. pale yellow veined orange. E Medit. Z8.

D. dubia Rodr. Perenn., to 50cm. Lvs rugose, villous beneath, entire or shallowly dentate. Rac. few-fld; cor. to 4cm, purple, inside heavily spotted. Spain, Balearics. Z8.

D. ferruginea L. RUSTY FOXGLOVE. Bienn. or perenn., to 120cm. Lvs glab. or ciliate. Rac. long, dense, many-fld; peduncle glab.; cor. c3.5cm, golden brown tinted rusty red, dark-veined inside. Capsule glab. S Eur., W Asia. 'Gigantea': fls larger. ssp. **schischkinii** (Ivanina) Werner. Cor. 1.2–1.8cm.

D. ferruginea auct. non L. = *D. ferruginea* ssp. *schischkinii*.

D. ferruginea var. *parviflora* Lindl. = *D. ferruginea* ssp. *schischkinii*.

D. gloxinioides Carr. = *D. purpurea* 'Gloxinoides'.

D. grandiflora Mill. LARGE YELLOW FOXGLOVE. Bienn. or perenn. to 100cm. Lvs ovate-lanceolate, finely toothed, sparsely pubesc. beneath. Rac. fairly dense; peduncle glandular-pubesc.; cor. 4–5cm, pale yellow, netted with brown veins. Eur. 'Glory of Roundway': fls apricot pink. 'Temple Bells': fls large.

D. laevigata Waldst. & Kit. Glab. perenn., to 90cm, lvs obovate, to linear-lanceolate, slightly toothed. Rac. sparsely fld; cor. to 3.5cm, yellow veined brown-purple, glab., lower lip white, ciliate. S Eur.

D. lanata Ehrh. GRECIAN FOXGLOVE. Bienn. or perenn. Lvs narrowly lanceolate, sessile, entire, glab. beneath. Peduncle to 20cm, villous; cor. to 3cm, off-white to pale fawn, finely veined brown, tube distended. Balk., Hung., Rom., Euro-Siberia. ssp. **leucophaea** Sibth. & Sm. GRECIAN FOXGLOVE. Cor. 1.5cm, dingy yellow-white, veined dark purple, tube slightly inflated. Turk., NE Greece.

D. lutea L. STRAW FOXGLOVE. Perenn. 60–100cm, ± glab. Lvs oblanceolate, obscurely serrate. Rac. fairly dense, many-fld; cor. 1–2.5cm, pale yellow to white. Eur. and NW Afr.

D. ×mertonensis Buxton & C. Darl. (*D. grandiflora* ×*D. purpurea.*) Perenn., 50–75cm. Lvs mid-green, lanceolate. Cor. to 5cm, strawberry pink. Gdn origin. True-breeding tetraploid.

D. monstrosa hort. = *D. purpurea* 'Monstrosa'.

D. obscura L. WILLOW-LEAVED FOXGLOVE. Perenn. subshrub, to 60cm, decumbent to erect. Lvs narrowly linear-lanceolate, entire, glab., coriaceous, shiny. Rac. elongate; cor. yellow veined or spotted bright red inside, tube v. short. Spain. ssp. **laciniata** (Lindl.) Maire. Lvs deeply cut.

D. orientalis Mill. = *D. grandiflora*.

D. parviflora Jacq. Perenn., to 60cm. Lvs obovate to oblanceolate, entire or slightly dentate. Rac. dense, cylindric, peduncle tomentose; cor. to 1.2cm, tube red brown veined violet, limb white-tomentose, lower lip purple-brown. N Spain.

D. purpurea L. COMMON FOXGLOVE. Bienn. or perenn. to 180cm. Lvs ovate to lanceolate, hairy. Rac. simple or sparsely branched, many-fld; cor. 4–5cm, purple to pale pink or white, usually heavily marked inside with white-edged darker purple spots, ciliate inside. W, SW, WC Eur. 'Alba': fls white. 'Apricot': fls apricot. 'Campanulata': upper fls united, forming large cupped bloom with many seg. 'Dwarf Sensation': dwarf; fls v. large, closely packed. Excelsior Hybrids: to 2m; fls pastel shades. Foxy Hybrids: to 75cm, fls carmine, pink, cream, and white, heavily spotted maroon. 'Gelbelanze': fls gold. 'Giant Shirley': fls v. large, open-faced, mottled, in shades of pink. 'Gloxinoides': more robust, rac. longer, fls v. large, wide open, varying in colour and marking. 'Monstrosa': fls almost double, term. fl. regular. 'Sutton's Apricot': fls creamy pink. 'The Shirley' (*D. purpurea* var. *gloxiniiflora*): to 1.5m; fls open, white, pink or magenta.

D. sceptrum L. = *Isoplexis sceptrum*.

D. schischkinii Ivanina = *D. ferruginea* ssp. *schischkinii*.

D. thapsi L. Perenn. 30–60cm, yellow-villous, gland. Lvs ovate lanceolate or oblong, rugose, crenate. Rac. lax, usually branched at base; cor. 2.5–5cm, purple, throat paler, spotted red, pubesc. outside. E Port., C & W Spain.

D. viridiflora Lindl. Perenn., 50–80cm, minutely pubesc. Lvs oblanceolate, denticulate. Cor. green-yellow, distinctly veined. Balk. Penins.

Digitaria Haller. FINGER GRASS; CRAB GRASS. Gramineae. 230 ann. or perenn. grasses. Lvs linear to lanceolate; ligules papery. Infl. spicate, digitate, secund, slender; spikelets overlapping to diffuse, lanceolate or elliptic. Cosmop. Z7.

D. sanguinalis (L.) Scop. HAIRY FINGER GRASS; CRAB GRASS. Ann. to 30cm, often tinged purple. St. slender, ascending. Lvs to 10×1cm, pubesc. Rac. at st. apex, to 15cm, slender, spreading, to 10 per infl.; spikelets paired, to 0.3cm, elliptic. Autumn.

→*Panicum*.

Digraphes Trin.

D. arundinacea (L.) Trin. = *Phalaris arundinacea*.

Dill *Anethum graveolens*.

Dillenia L. Dilleniaceae. *c*60 everg. trees and shrubs. Lvs large, lustrous, simple with conspicuous veins; petioles usually winged. Fls solitary and terminal or in rac. or pan.; pet. 5, rounded, spreading; sta. numerous. Fr. fleshy, star-shaped, enclosed in swollen cal. Asia, Indian Ocean, Aus.

D. burbidgei (Hook. f.) Gilg = *D. suffruticosa*.

D. indica L. CHULTA. Shrub or tree to 15m. Lvs to 36cm, elliptic-oblong, toothed, with 25–50 veins. Fls to 20cm diam., solitary, white. India to Java.

D. ovata Wallich ex Hook. f. & Thoms. Differs from *D. indica* in lvs to 25cm, with 18–25 veins; fls to 15cm diam., golden yellow. SE Asia.

D. speciosa Thunb. non hort. = *D. indica*.

D. suffruticosa (Griff.) Martelli. Spreading shrub to 10m. Lvs to 25cm, elliptic to obovate with 12–20 veins. Fls to 10cm diam., yellow, in 5–15-fld rac. Malay Archipel.

→*Wormia*.

DILLENIACEAE Salisb. 12/300. *Dillenia, Hibbertia*.

Dillwynia Sm. Leguminosae (Papilionoideae). 10–15 compact everg. shrubs. Habit heath-like. Lvs linear to acicular, terete, grooved above. Fls pea-like in axill. or terminal rac. or corymbs, or solitary. Aus., Tasm. Z9.

D. cinerascens R. Br. GREY PARROT PEA. Br. glab. or greypubesc. Lvs 0.5–1.2cm, cylindrical, grey-green, obtuse tips often recurved. Fls 3–8 in loose term. clusters or corymbs; cor. to

0.7cm diam., yellow and orange. Vict.

D. ericifolia Sm. = *D. floribunda.*

D. floribunda Sm. Br. glab. or pubesc. Lvs 0.5–1.2cm, tough, tubercular, pubesc. when young obtuse. Fls 1–3, axill., forming a crowded leafy spike; cor. to 1.4cm yellow, flecked or splashed red. Autumn–early winter. SE Aus.

D. glaberrima Sm. = *D. floribunda.*

D. juniperina Lodd. Br. slender, hairy. Lvs 0.6–1.3cm, finely filiform, carinate beneath, pungent. Fls in term. clusters of 4–9; standard orange, red at base, wings and keel red. Spring. Aus.

D. obovata Labill. = *Eutaxia myrtifolia.*

Dimerandra Schltr. Orchidaceae. 1 epiphyte. Rhiz. short. Pbs to 35cm, clumped, cane-like, jointed at lf insertions, sheathed with papery lf bases below. Lvs to 12×1cm, remote, in 2 ranks, ligulate to lanceolate, semi-rigid. Rac. short, term; fls to 3cm diam., rose madder to magenta; sep. elliptic-lanceolate, pet. elliptic-obovate; lip obscurely obcordate, marked white at base and on callus. W Indies, C & S Amer. Z9.

D. emarginata (Mey.) Hoehne.

D. rimbachii (Schltr.) Schltr. = *D. emarginata.*

D. stenopetala (Hook.) Schltr. = *D. emarginata.*

→*Epidendrum.*

Dimerocostus Kuntze. Zingiberaceae. 2 rhizomatous perenn. herbs. St. cane-like. Lvs fleshy, spirally arranged, narrowly elliptic, acuminate. Spike term. cone-like; bracts leathery, overlapping, green to yellow; cal. lobes 3; cor. seg. subequal; lip large; lat. staminodes 0; fertile sta. 1, fil. petaloid. C Amer. Z10.

D. strobilaceus Kuntze. 2–6m. Lvs 12–50cm, puberulent. Infl. 10–40cm; bracts 2–6cm; pet. 6.5–8cm, white or yellow, obovate, lip 7–9cm; flushed orange, crispate. ssp. *gutierrezii* (Kuntze) Maas. Bracts only partly sheathing infl. axis.

Dimocarpus Lour. Sapindaceae. 5 trees or shrubs. Lvs pinnate, rarely unifoliate. Infl. often term., sparsely branched, cymose; pet. to 5, oblanceolate, pubesc., slightly 5-lobed, densely hairy; sta. 8. Fr. globose to ellipsoid, warty, smooth or long-spiny, purple or brown when ripe; seeds black-brown, arillate. SE Asia to Aus. Z10.

D. longan Lour. LONGAN; LUNGEN. Tree to 40m, sometimes buttressed. Pinnae to 45×10cm in 2–4 pairs, entire. Infl. 8–40cm; fls 3–5 per cyme, yellow-white. Fr. globose, 2.5cm diam., almost smooth, yellow-brown, arillate pulp white, sweet. Summer. India.

→*Euphoria, Nephelium* and *Pseudonephelium.*

Dimorphanthus Miq.

D. elatus Miq. = *Aralia elata.*

Dimorphorchis Rolfe. Orchidaceae. 2 epiphytic, monopodial orchids. St. erect. Lvs ligulate, 2-ranked, coriaceous. Infl. pendent; fls dimorphic; tep. linear-oblong; lip saccate with a fleshy finger-like projection. Borneo. Z10.

D. lowii (Lindl.) Rolfe. St. to 2m. Lvs to 90cm. Infl. to 3m; lower fls to 7.5cm diam., tawny-yellow, spotted cinnabar-brown, broad, fleshy, upper fls narrow, deep red or chocolate, tipped yellow; tep. undulate; lip ± inflated, with yellow appendage.

→*Arachnis* and *Vanda.*

Dimorphotheca Vaill. ex Moench SUN MARIGOLD. Compositae. 7 glab. to gland.-hairy herbs or shrubs. Lvs entire to pinnatisect. Cap. radiate, usually solitary, term. S & Trop. Afr. Z9.

D. annua Less. = *D. pluvialis.*

D. aurantiaca hort. = *D. sinuata.*

D. aurantiaca DC., non hort. = *Castalis tragus.*

D. barberiae Harv. = *Osteospermum barberiae.*

D. calendulacea Harv. = *D. sinuata.*

D. chrysanthemifolia (Vent.) DC. Shrub or subshrub, to 1m. Lvs to 7cm, obovate to oblanceolate, coarsely dentate to pinnatisect. Cap. to 7cm diam.; peduncle to 6cm; ray flts yellow or golden, sometimes tinged red beneath; disc flts yellow. S Afr.

D. cuneata (Thunb.) Less. Shrub, to 1m. Lvs to 2cm, obovate to oblanceolate, denticulate to pinnatifid. Cap. to 5cm diam.; peduncle to 4cm; ray flts white above, blue-violet beneath, often flecked copper or white; disc flts yellow, many. S Afr.

D. ecklonis DC. = *Osteospermum ecklonis.*

D. jucunda E. Phillips = *Osteospermum jucundum.*

D. nudicaulis (L.) DC. = *Castalis nudicaulis.*

D. pinnata (Thunb.) Harv. = *Osteospermum pinnatum.*

D. pluvialis (L.) Moench. WEATHER PROPHET. Ann., to 40cm. Lvs to 10cm, obovate to oblanceolate, dentate or pinnatifid. Cap. to 6cm diam.; peduncle to 15cm; ray flts white, base dark purple above, blue-violet flecked copper and white beneath; disc flt tube white. S Afr., Nam.

D. sinuata DC. Ann. herb, to 30cm. Lvs to 10cm, oblongoblanceolate, coarsely dentate or denticulate to pinnatifid. Cap. peduncle to 12cm; ray flts golden, apex and base deep violet; disc flt tube white, tipped violet, lobes yellow. S Afr.

D. spectabilis Schltr. = *Castalis spectabilis.*

→*Calendula.*

Dinema Lindl.

D. polybulbon (Sw.) Lindl. = *Encyclia polybulbon.*

Dinner-plate Aralia *Polyscias scutellaria.*

Dinner-plate Fig *Ficus dammaropsis.*

Dinteranthus Schwantes. Aizoaceae. 6 ± stemless, highly succulent plants, branched or mat-forming. Lvs short and thick, upper surface flat, lower surface v. rounded, keeled toward tip. Fl. solitary, large, yellow. S Afr., Nam. Z9.

D. inexpectatus Jacobsen. V. compact. Lvs smaller and more rounded than in *D. microspermus* with an acute and prominent keel, surface smooth, grey with translucent green dots. Nam.

D. margaretae (Schwantes) Schwantes = *Lapidaria margaretae.*

D. microspermus (Dinter & Derenb.) Schwantes. Solitary to multi-headed. Lvs united to midway, free part 2.5–3cm long on upper surface, 3cm across, lower surface hemispherical, chinlike, minutely granular, rough, red-tinged to grey-violet, young lvs chalky white to grey-olive green. Nam.

D. pole-evansii (N.E. Br.) Schwantes. Usually solitary. Lvs united to midway, 4.5cm long, 2cm thick, v. rounded below, keel virtually 0, wrinkled, minutely gland., dove grey, sometimes tinged yellow or red. W Cape.

D. puberulus N.E. Br. Mat-forming. Lvs to 3×1.5cm, scarcely keeled beneath, minutely granular and hirsute, velvety, browngreen to grey-green with numerous green dots. W Cape.

D. punctatus L. Bol. = *D. puberulus.*

D. vanzylii (L. Bol.) Schwantes. Lf pairs clump-forming, almost completely united to form a body 4cm tall, hemispheric on lower surface, grey-green, rarely with faint red dots and lines. W Cape.

D. wilmotianus L. Bol. Solitary. Lvs united for half their length, 5–5.7cm long, 1.7–2cm wide, tapered above, rounded beneath, doubly carinate toward the tip, grey-pink with dark violet spots. W Cape.

→*Lithops, Mesembryanthemum* and *Rimaria.*

Dion Lindl. = *Dioön.*

Dionaea Sol. ex Ellis. VENUS' FLY TRAP; VENUS' MOUSE TRAP. Droseraceae. 1 low-growing, carnivorous, perenn. herb, to 45cm in fl. Lvs in basal rosette, to 16cm; petioles leafy, broadly winged, obhastate to spathulate; blade of 2 rounded, hinged lobes, snapping shut on prey, becoming glossy and red in bright sunlight, margins fringed with semi-rigid cilia. Fls in scapose umbel-like cymes; pet. 5, white, obovate, to 1cm. SE US. Z8.

D. muscipula Ellis.

Dionysia Fenzl. Primulaceae. 41 tufted or cushion-forming alpine subshrubs, often aromatic. St. with persistent dead lvs. Lvs spirally arranged, widely spaced or whorled, forming rosette at apex, often woolly-farinose esp. beneath. Fls solitary, sessile or in scapose umbels, sometimes whorled; cor. salver-shaped, with long tube, limb flat, with 5 lobes, entire to deeply emarginate. Turk., E to Afghan. and S Russia, Oman.

D. afghanica Grey-Wilson. Forming dense, deep green cushions; br. short, covered by overlapping, withered lvs. Lvs 2.5–3.5mm, oblanceolate to spathulate, entire, glandular-pubesc. Infl. 1-fld, subsessile; cor. violet-pink with darker eye, to 7mm diam., tube to 8mm, lobes obovate, emarginate. NW Afghan.

D. archibaldii Wendelbo. Loosely tufted, often mealy, cushionplant; br. covered by withered lvs in distinct whorls. Lvs revolute, 4–8mm, oblong to elliptic, glandular-pubesc., entire or crenulate. Fl. solitary, sessile; cor. violet, to 1cm diam., tube to 14mm, lobes narrow, deeply notched. Summer. Iran (mts).

D. aretioides (Lehm.) Boiss. Forming low, dense, grey cushions. Lvs flat or revolute, oblong to narrowly spathulate, to 7mm, pubesc., yellow- or white-farinose beneath, bluntly toothed above. Infl. 1-fld; cor. pale or deep yellow, to 1cm diam., tube 1–2cm, lobes narrow or broad-obcordate. Spring. N Iran.

D. balsamea Wendelbo & Rech. f.. Forming loose, rounded tufts. Lvs broad-ovate, 2.5cm, pubesc., crenate, apex rounded; longstalked. Infl. 1–4 superposed, verticils 3–5-fld; cor. to 18mm diam., tube 25mm, lobes obovate. Late spring. Mts of Iran, W & C Afghan.

D. bryoides Boiss. & Buhse. Forming compact cushions. Lvs broad-ovate to spathulate, 2–3mm, covered by minute glands. Infl. 1-fld; cor. pink with a pale eye, to 6mm diam., tube to 10mm, lobes broad-obcordate. Spring. S Iran.

D. curviflora Bunge. Forming compact, grey or green cushions. Lvs to 3mm, spathulate to oblong, hairy above. Infl. 1-fld; cor. pink, rarely white, eye yellow, to 6mm diam., tube 12mm, lobes narrow to broad-obcordate. Spring–early summer. S Iran.

D. demawendica Bornm. = *D. aretioides*.

D. denticulata Wendelbo. Forming loose tufts. Lvs 4–8mm, narrow-lanceolate to oblong or spathulate, minutely gland., denticulate above. Infl. 1-fld; cor. yellow, to 8mm diam., tube to 1cm, lobes narrow, suborbicular, emarginate. Early summer. C Afghan.

D. freitagii Wendelbo. Forming dense deep green cushions. Lvs to 5–8mm, elliptic to subrhombic, glandular-pubesc. veins prominent. Infl. 1-fld; cor. violet to purple-violet with dark eye, 8–12mm, diam., tube 13–16mm, lobes broad-obovate, emarginate. N Afghan.

D. involucrata Zapr. Forming deep green tufted cushions. Lvs 4–12mm, obovate to broadly spathulate, bluntly toothed above, minutely gland., veins conspicuous. Infl. 3–5-fld umbel; cor. lilac with eye white when young, becoming dark, rarely white, 7–14mm diam., tube 20–30mm, lobes broad-obcordate. Early summer. Russia.

D. janthina Bornm. & Winkl. Forming compact grey cushions. Lvs 2–3mm, oblong-spathulate, entire, densely pubesc., apex rounded. Infl. 1-fld; cor. pink, eye yellow, to 6mm diam., tube to 10mm, lobes broad-obcordate. Spring. S Iran.

D. lamingtonii Stapf. Forms compact, dense cushions. Lvs to 3mm, oblong to spathulate, densely pubesc., entire, acute to obtuse. Infl. 1-fld; cor. yellow, to 5mm diam., tube 10–15mm, lobes suborbicular, emarginate. Iran.

D. michauxii (Duby) Boiss. Forms dense, rounded, grey cushions. Lvs to 3mm, oblong to oblong-elliptic, entire, pubesc. Infl. 1-fld; cor. yellow, to 6mm diam., tube to 1cm, lobes obovate, emarginate. Spring. S Iran.

D. microphylla Wendelbo. Forms dense, compact, grey-green tufts. Lvs 1.5mm, yellow-farinose beneath, entire, often apiculate. Infl. 2–4 superposed, 4-fld verticils, or a 2–4-fld umbel; cor. violet to purple-violet at base of lobes, eye white, to 1cm diam., tube 12mm, lobes broad-obcordate. Early summer. N Afghan.

D. mira Wendelbo. Subshrub, forming loose tufts to 80cm diam. Lvs 2.5–8cm, oblong to lanceolate or oblanceolate, dentate or bidentate, pubesc. and gland., white-farinose beneath. Infl. 1 or 2–3 per rosette, or 3–7 superposed, 5–7-fld verticils; cor. yellow, to 9mm diam., tube 15–18mm, lobes oval to ovate, entire or emarginate. Oman.

D. paradoxa Wendelbo. Forming loose clumps. Lvs to 45mm, obovate, spathulate, dentate. Infl. 2–7cm, with 2–4 whorls, each 2–4-fld; cor. yellow, 12mm diam. E Afghan.

D. revoluta Boiss. Subshrub, forming loose, deep green tufts to 70cm diam. Lvs to 18mm, narrow-oblong or elliptic or linear, revolute, toothed, white-hairy and minutely gland., white- or yellow-farinose beneath. Infl. 2–4, or 1-fld; cor. yellow, 10–12mm diam., tube 15–18mm, lobes obcordate, deeply notched. SW Iran. ssp. *canescens* (Boiss.) Wendelbo. Plants grey-canescent. CW & SW Iran.

D. tapetodes Bunge. Forms densely tufted cushions. Lvs 2–4mm, obovate to spathulate, covered by tiny glands, entire or slightly crenulate above, often white- or yellow-farinose beneath. Infl. 1-fld; cor. yellow, to 6mm diam., tube 1–1.5cm, lobes obovate or suborbicular. Late spring–early summer. S Russia, N E Iran, C Afghan., W Pak.

D. teucrioides P.H. Davis & Wendelbo. Dwarf tufted subshrub, 10–15cm. Lvs 8–27mm, revolute or flat, blunt-toothed, pilose, oblong to oblanceolate, white-farinose beneath. Infl. 1–3-fld umbel, occas. with 1-fld, superposed vertical; cor. yellow, to 7mm diam., tube to 18mm, lobes ovate. Late spring. SE Turk.

D. viscidula Wendelbo. Forms loosely tufted cushions. Lvs 5–8mm, elliptic to spathulate, somewhat pointed, viscid, covered with small glands, entire. Infl. 1-fld; cor. violet with a white eye, to 1cm diam., tube 8–10mm, lobes obovate, emarginate. Late spring–early summer. NW Afghan.

Dioön Lindl. Zamiaceae. 10 arborescent cycads. St. usually simple, columnar, with petiole remnants and scars. Lvs in a term. whorls, pinnate, coriaceous. ♂ cones cylindric. ♀ cones elliptic-ovoid, massive, woolly. Mex., C Amer. Z10.

D. edule Lindl. St. to 1.5–0.75m, napiform-columnar. Lvs to 1.5m, semi-erect, emerging glaucous, lanuginose, hardening glossy, often glab.; pinnae to 13×1.5cm, linear-lanceolate, acuminate, pungent, grey-green, entire (except in juveniles and varieties), rigid, base decurrent, spreading. Mex. var. *imbricatum* (Miq.) A. DC. Pinnae to 0.6cm wide, spiny-serrulate, strongly overlapping; petioles woolly, erect. f. *lanuginosum* (Wittm.) Schust. Lvs v. stiffly erect, lanuginose, pinnae serrulate, upwardly overlapping to one-third of width.

D. mejiae Standl. & L.O. Williams. Similar to *D. spinulosum* but more robust, lvs more rigidly erect or outspread, pinnae lanceolate-subulate, widest at base and broadly decurrent, finely toothed, densely lanuginose. Hond.

D. spinulosum Dyer. St. to 10m+, slender, columnar. Lvs to 2m, semi-erect to arching, emerging woolly, later glab.; pinnae to 15×4cm, lanceolate, broadly acuminate, pungent, spiny-serrulate, decurrent, initially glaucous, later dark green, coriaceous. Mex.

Diopogon Jordan and Fourr.

D. allionii Jordan and Fourr. = *Jovibarba hirta* ssp. *allionii*.

Dioscorea L. YAM. Dioscoreaceae. 600 tuberous, scandent herbs. St. twining. Lvs simple or palmately compound, often cordate, axils sometimes bearing bulbils. ♂ fls in small, axill. rac., perianth campanulate, sta. 6; ♀ fls in spikes or spike-like rac., opening widely, perianth deeply 6-lobed. Trop. and subtrop. regions. Z10.

D. alata L. WHITE YAM; WATER YAM. Tubers to 2.5m. St. 4-winged or 4-angled, frequently with small axill. tubers. Lvs ovate to oblong, base cordate, glab., 7–9-veined. India to Malay Penins.

D. amarantoides Presl. St. somewhat angled. Lvs to 10cm, alt., ovate-lanceolate to cordate, 7-veined. Peru.

D. balcanica Košanin. Tuberous roots to 2cm diam. St. to 150cm, cylindrical. Lvs to 7cm, usually alt., sometimes subopposite, cordate or ovate, shortly acuminate, 9-veined, long-petiolate. SW Balk., N Albania. Z6.

D. batatas Decne. CHINESE YAM; CINNAMON VINE. Tuberous roots to 90cm, clavate or cylindrical. St. somewhat angled, bearing small axill. tubers. Lvs to 8cm, opposite, ovate, base cordate, 7–9-veined, short-petiolate. Temp. E Asia nat. US. Z5.

D. bulbifera L. AIR POTATO. Tuberous roots small, globose, sometimes 0. St. to 6m, bearing axill. tubers. Lvs to 25cm, usually alt., ovate, base cordate, cuspidate; petiole to 14cm. Trop. Afr. and Asia.

D. cotinifolia Kunth. Tuberous roots to 9×5cm. Lvs to 8cm, usually alt., broadly ovate, subcordate or truncate at base; petiole to 3cm. S Afr.

D. discolor Kunth. Tuberous roots to 7cm diam. St. slightly angled. Lvs to 15cm, alt., ovate or cordate, cuspidate, mottled velvety dark and light green above with a silvery white midrib, red-purple beneath. Trop. S Amer.

D. elephantipes (L'Hérit.) Engl. ELEPHANT'S FOOT; HOTTENTOT BREAD. Tuberous base to 90cm diam., woody, facetted, fissured. St. to 6m. Lvs to 6cm broad, alt., suborbicular-cordate to reniform, shortly mucronate, 7–9-veined. S Afr.

D. hastifolia Nees. Tuberous roots to 12×3cm. St. to 9m, cylindrical. Lvs to 8cm, alt., linear to linear-lanceolate or hastate. W Aus.

D. macrostachya Benth. Tuberous roots to 20cm diam., deeply corrugated. St. somewhat angled. Lvs to 20cm, alt., ovate, acuminate, base cordate, long-petiolate. C Amer.

D. trifida L. f. CUSH-CUSH; YAMPEE. Tuberous roots small. St. sharply angled or narrowly winged. Lvs to 25cm, lobed, cordate, puberulent above, veins pilose beneath. S Amer., W Indies.

→*Testudinaria*.

DIOSCOREACEAE R. Br. 8/630. *Dioscorea*.

Diosma L. Rutaceae. 28 aromatic shrubs. Lvs simple, sessile or short-petiolate, glandular-dotted. Fls term., solitary or in few-fld cymes or rac.; pet. 5, lanceolate to orbicular, spreading; sta. 5. S Afr. Z9.

D. alba Thunb. = *Coleonema album*.

D. calycina Steud. = *Coleonema calycinum*.

D. ciliata L. = *Agathosma ciliata*.

D. crenulata L. = *Agathosma crenulata*.

D. cupressina L. To 1m; branchlets glab. or minutely puberulent. Lvs oblong-lanceolate, glab., slightly ciliate. Fls term., usually solitary; pet. oblong, acuminate, white or cream.

D. ericoides L. BREATH OF HEAVEN; BUCHU. To 80cm; branchlets many, glab. Lvs to 0.6cm, oblong, crowded, erect, apex blunt, recurved. Fls white, v. fragrant.

D. hirsuta L. To 50cm; branchlets densely pubesc., yellow when young. Lvs to 2cm, linear-lanceolate, glabrescent. Fls in term. rac.; pet. to 2.5mm, white, ovate.

D. hirta Lam. = *Agathosma hirta*.

D. oppositifolia L. To 1m; branchlets sparsely pubesc., yellow. Lvs to 1cm, linear or lanceolate, glab. Infl. subterminal with fls in opposite pairs; pet. to 3mm, white, elliptic-oblong.

D. ovata Thunb. = *Agathosma ovata*.

D. pulchella L. = *Agathosma pulchella*.

D. purpurea hort. ex Bartling & Wendl. = *Agathosma corymbosa*.
D. tetragona L. f. = *Acmadenia tetragona*.

Diosphaera Buser.
D. asperuloides (Boiss. & Orph.) Buser = *Trachelium asperuloides*.
D. dubia Buser = *Trachelium rumelianum*.
D. jacquinii (Sieber) Buser = *Trachelium jacquinii*.

Diospyros L. Ebenaceae. 475 decid. and everg. trees and shrubs. Wood hard, sometimes black. Lvs entire. Fls usually unisexual: ♂ 2–5 per short-stalked cyme, ♀ solitary; cal. 4-lobed, persistent, accrescent in fr.; cor. urn- to bell-shaped, with 4 spreading or recurved lobes. Fr. a fleshy berry. S Eur., N & S Amer., Afr. and Asia, particularly in the tropics.
D. armata Hemsl. Tall everg. tree. Branchlets grey, thorn-tipped. Lvs 2–5cm, elliptic, dark glossy green above. Fls white, scented, in short rac. Fr. 1.5cm diam., yellow, bristly. China. Z8.
D. kaki L. f. KAKI; PERSIMMON; JAPANESE PERSIMMON. Decid. tree to 14m with grey bark. Young shoots downy. Lvs to 20cm, ovate to obovate, dark glossy above, orange-red in fall. ♂ fls with cor. to 13mm; ♀ fls pale yellow, with cor. to 15mm. Fr. waxy, globose to oblong, with persistent, accrescent cal. to 7.5cm diam., yellow to orange or red. Not known in the wild. Z8.
D. lotus L. DATE PLUM. Similar to *D. kaki* but in warm countries to 25m. Lvs to 12cm, lanceolate to elliptic, oblong or ovate, coriaceous, pubesc. at first, usually falling when green. ♂ fls with cor. to 6mm, white with yellow to pink lobes; ♀ fls with cor. to 5mm, brown. Fr. globose to ovoid, to 2cm diam., yellow, red or blue-black, pruinose. Summer. Temp. Asia, from Asia Minor to China. Z5.
D. virginiana L. AMERICAN PERSIMMON: POSSUMWOOD. Tree to 20m. Lvs to 12cm, elliptic to ovate or oblong, deep glossy green above, glab. except midrib beneath, red in fall. ♂ and ♀ fls with cor. to 10mm, white with yellow lobes. Fr. 2.5–1mm diam., orange. E US. Z4.

Diostea Miers. Verbenaceae. 3 decid. shrubs or small trees. Lvs simple, sessile. Fls in small rac. or spikes; cal. tubular or campanulate, 4 or 5-toothed; cor. tubular, 5-lobed, somewhat labiate, tube cylindrical or curved. S Amer. Z9.
D. juncea (Gillies & Hook.) Miers. Small tree or shrub to 6.5m. br. slender, rush-like. Lvs to 2.5cm, oblong or ovate-oblong, slightly dentate. Fls white or lilac, to 8mm. Chile, Arg.

Diotostemon hort.
D. glauca hort. = × *Pachyveria glauca*.

Dipanax Seem.
D. kavaiensis (H. Mann) A.A. Heller = *Tetraplasandra kavaiensis*.

Dipcadi Medik. Liliaceae (Hyacinthaceae). 55 bulbous perenn. herbs. Lvs narrow, glab., sheathing lower part of st. Fls narrowly bell-shaped or tubular, in long-stemmed loose rac.; tep. 6, slightly fleshy; sta. included. N Afr., S Afr., SW Eur., E Indies. Z8.
D. brevifolium (Thunb.) Fourc. BROWN BELLS; CURLY-CURLY. Lvs to 30cm, narrow-triangular to linear. Scape to 60cm; fls pale to emerald-green tinged ruby-red on outer tep. Spring–summer. S Afr.
D. fulvum (Cav.) Webb & Berth. Lvs 5–20cm, keeled. Scape to 45cm; fls pink, tinged with brown. Autumn. S Spain, Moroc., Canary Is.
D. serotinum (L.) Medik. Lvs to 30cm, linear, shorter than scape. Scape to 45cm; fls green to ochre or bronze, sometimes rusty-red or dull orange. Spring–summer. SW Eur., N Afr.
D. umbonatum Bak. = *D. viride*.
D. viride Moench. Lvs rolled. Scape to 45cm, exceeding lvs. Fls green to bronze. Spring–summer. S Afr.

Dipelta Maxim. Caprifoliaceae. 4 decid. shrubs allied to *Weigela*. Fls tubular-campanulate, large, solitary or 2–8-clustered; pedicels slender, surrounded by 2–4 peltate bracts which persist and dilate after fertilization. C & W China. Z6.
D. floribunda Maxim. Multistemmed shrub to 4.5m, branchlets glandular-pubesc. at first. Lvs 4.5–10cm, ovate to oval-lanceolate, acuminate, soon glab., entire to serrate. Fls fragrant, in 1–6-fld term. and axillary clusters; bracts 4, to 2cm, shield-like, green-white; cor. funnelform, to 3cm, white flushed shell pink, yellow in throat. Spring–summer. C & W China.
D. ventricosa Hemsl. To 2.25cm in cult. Branchlets downy to bristly. Lvs to 15cm, lanceolate-elliptic, acuminate, glab. except nerves beneath, sometimes sparsely toothed, often undulate, ciliate. Fls 1–3 per axill. cluster; bracts cordate-obtuse to 1.7cm;

cor. to 3cm, broadly tubular, flesh pink to lilac, interior pale rose or white marked deep yellow in throat, lobes tipped white. Summer. W China.
D. yunnanensis Franch. Spreading shrub, 2–4m. Young shoots 4-angled, downy. Lvs 5–12cm, ovate-lanceolate, acuminate, entire, downy beneath. Fls in short clusters; bracts cordate, membranous; cor. tubular at base, to 2.5cm, cream to white stained pink, throat orange. Spring. SW China.

Diphylleia Michx. Berberidaceae. 3 perenn. herbs. Rhiz. thick, creeping. Lvs peltate, radical, 2-lobed, long-petioled; flowering st. lvs 2. Cyme term.; sep. 6, petaloid; pet. 6, 10–15mm, ovate; sta. 6. Fr. a globose berry. E N Amer., Jap.
D. cymosa Michx. UMBRELLA LEAF. To 1m. Radical lvs 30–60cm across, cleft, seg. 5–7-lobed, toothed; flowering st. lvs deeply 2-lobed, 10–40cm across. Fls white, *c*10; pedicel red in fr. Berries blue, 12mm across. Spring–summer. E US. Z7.
D. pleiantha = *Podophyllum pleianthum*.

Diplacus Nutt.
D. aurantiacus (Curtis) Jeps. = *Mimulus aurantiacus*.
D. glutinosus (Wendl.) Nutt. = *Mimulus aurantiacus*.
D. puniceus Nutt. = *Mimulus puniceus*.

Dipladenia A. DC.
D. × *amabilis* hort. Buckl. = *Mandevilla* × *amabilis*.
D. boliviensis Hook. f. = *Mandevilla boliviensis*.
D. sanderi Hemsl. = *Mandevilla sanderi*.
D. splendens (Hook. f.) A. DC. = *Mandevilla splendens*.

Diplandra Hook. & Arn. = *Lopezia*.

Diplanthera Banks & Soland.
D. hirsuta Bail. = *Deplanchea tetraphylla*.
D. tetraphylla R. Br. = *Deplanchea tetraphylla*.

Diplarrhena Labill. Iridaceae. 2 rhizomatous perenn. herbs. Lvs basal or a few on st., linear, equitant. Flowering st. erect, usually simple; fls in a term. cluster subtended by 2 or more valves; perianth seg. 6, outer seg. larger, 1 enlarged; style br. 3, flattened. SE Aus. and Tasm.
D. latifolia Benth. Distinguished from *D. moraea* by lvs to 90cm, fls 5–12cm diam., lilac and yellow, 5–6 per spathe. Summer. Tasm. Z8.
D. moraea Labill. Lvs to 45cm. Flowering st. to 65cm; fls to 4cm diam., scented, 2–3 per spathe; outer perianth seg. white, broad, spreading, inner perianth seg. erect, narrower, white suffused or veined mauve-blue or yellow toward apex. Summer. SE Aus., Tasm. Z7.

Diplazium Sw. Woodsiaceae. 350 terrestrial or epiphytic ferns. Rhiz. short and erect, arborescent or creeping, often covered with roots and scales. Fronds stipitate, uniform, 1–3-pinnate-pinnatifid or simple, usually glab. Trop. regions. Z10 unless specified.
D. arboreum (Willd.) Presl = *D. shepherdii*.
D. australe (R. Br.) Wakef. AUSTRAL LADY FERN. Rhiz. short, erect and eventually trunk-like. Stipes to 60cm. Fronds to 120–90cm, 2–3-pinnate to -pinnatifid, erect to arched, ovate to deltoid, membranous, pinnae ovate or lanceolate to oblong, pinnules lanceolate, seg. lanceolate to oblong, toothed. Aus., Tasm., NZ. Z8.
D. bantamense Bl. Rhiz. short and suberect. Stipes to 30cm. Fronds to 60×25cm, pinnate, apex caudate and proliferous, firm-textured, pinnae, attenuate to acute, base obtuse to cuneate, decurrent, entire to toothed. Trop. Asia.
D. camptocarpon Fée = *D. franconis*.
D. caudatum (Cav.) Jermy. Rhiz. short-creeping. Stipes to 30cm. Fronds to 70×50cm, 2–3-pinnate to -pinnatifid, ovate to lanceolate, pinnae lanceolate, narrowly acute to caudate, pinnules lanceolate, toothed to notched. Azores.
D. celtidifolium Kunze. Rhiz. short and erect, robust. Stipes to 30cm. Fronds to 120×45cm, pinnate to pinnatifid, ovate to lanceolate, leathery; pinnae lanceolate, subentire to toothed or lobed. Trop. Amer.
D. cristatum (Desr.) Alston = *D. shepherdii*.
D. dietrichianum (Luerssen) C. Chr. Rhiz. short and erect, trunk-like. Stipes fleshy. Fronds to 2m×80cm, 2–3-pinnate to -pinnatifid, erect to arched, pinnae opposite to alt. pinnules to 15cm, lanceolate, notched to lobed. Aus.
D. dilatatum Bl. Rhiz. short and erect to ascending. Stipes to 50cm. Fronds to 80×40cm, 2-pinnate to 3-pinnatifid, deltoid, leathery, pinnae, lanceolate to deltoid, pinnules lanceolate to oblong, apex narrowly acute, base truncate to cordate, toothed to lobed, lobes entire to toothed. E Asia to Aus., Polyn.

D. esculentum (Retz.) Sw. VEGETABLE FERN. Rhiz. short and erect, occas., trunk-like, to creeping. Stipes to 50cm. Fronds to 1m×50cm, 1–2-pinnate, or 3-pinnatifid, ovate to deltoid, thin-textured, leathery, pinnae linear or oblong to lanceolate, pinnules, lanceolate, apex acute, base auriculate, seg. oblique. SE Asia to Polyn.

D. franconis Liebm. Rhiz. to 3cm wide, short and erect. Stipes to 80cm. Fronds to 1m×70cm, 2–3-pinnate to -pinnatifid, deltoid, leathery to papery, pinnae lanceolate, pinnules lanceolate, notched to lobed, lobes oblong, toothed. C Amer., Mex.

D. hookerianum Koidz. = *Athyrium decurrenti-alatum.*

D. japonicum (Thunb.) Beddome = *Deparia petersenii.*

D. lanceum (Thunb.) Presl, non Bory. Rhiz. to 2mm wide, creeping. Stipes to 15cm. Fronds to 30×3cm, simple, lanceolate to linear, attenuate, entire to undulate, leathery, glab. India, Sri Lanka to China, Taiwan, Jap.

D. latifolium Moore = *D. dilatatum.*

D. otophorum (Miq.) C. Chr. = *Athyrium otophorum.*

D. plantagineum (L.) Sw. = *D. plantaginifolium.*

D. plantaginifolium (L.) Urban. Rhiz. to 2cm distant, short and erect to ascending. Stipes to 30cm. Fronds to 30×7cm, simple, lanceolate to linear or oblong, acute to cuspidate, entire to toothed and undulate or deeply notched, leathery, glab. Trop. Amer.

D. proliferum (Lam.) Kaulf. Rhiz. short and erect occas. arborescent. Stipes to 60cm. Fronds to 1m×40cm, pinnate to pinnatifid, arched, ovate to deltoid, leathery, pinnae notched to shallowly lobed, lobes entire to toothed; rachis proliferous above. Trop. Afr., Asia, Polyn.

D. pycnocarpon (Spreng.) Broun = *Athyrium pycnocarpon.*

D. shepherdii (Spreng.) Link. Rhiz. to 2cm wide, short and erect to ascending. Stipes to 40cm. Fronds to 45×35cm, pinnate to pinnatifid, ovate or deltoid to oblong, thin-textured pinnae, subfalcate, ovate to lanceolate, attenuate to acute, base auriculate, notched to deeply lobed, lobes somewhat notched. Trop. Amer.

D. sibiricum (Turcz. ex Kunze) Jermy. Rhiz. short-creeping, much-branched. Stipes to 30cm. Fronds to 40×30cm, 2–3-pinnate to -pinnatifid, deltoid, pubesc. on veins, pinnae lanceolate, pinnules lanceolate, seg. oblong, toothed to notched. NE Eur. to Asia.

D. subsinuatum (Wallich ex Hook. & Grev.) Tag. = *D. lanceum.*

D. sylvaticum (Bory) Sw. Rhiz. short-creeping, fleshy. Stipes to 30cm. Fronds to 60×20cm, pinnate to pinnatifid, ovate to lanceolate, apex occas. proliferous, thin-textured, pinnae somewhat lobed. Trop. Asia to Aus.

D. thelypteroides Presl = *D. australe.*

D. werckleanum C. Chr. Rhiz. to 2cm wide, short suberect. Stipes to 18cm. Fronds to 40×10cm, pinnate to pinnatifid at apex, deltoid to lanceolate, thick-textured and leathery, glab., pinnae, lanceolate, auriculate, subentire to notched and undulate, or lobed, lobes minutely notched. Mex., C Amer.

→*Allantodia, Asplenium, Athyrium, Hemionitis* and *Tectaria.*

Diplocaulobium (Rchb. f.) Kränzl. Orchidaceae. 70 small epiphytic orchids. Pbs clustered, dimorphic, attenuate-pyriform or (in flowering growths) narrow except for swollen base. Lvs solitary, apical. Rac. apical, fls ephemeral. Malaysia to W Pacific. Z10.

D. regale (Schltr.) A.D. Hawkes Lvs oblong-ligulate, to 20cm. Fls rose pink; sep. oblong-ligulate, to 4cm; pet. elliptic; lip midlobe triangular, lat. lobes round. New Guinea.

→*Dendrobium.*

Diplocyclos (Endl.) T. Post & Kuntze. Cucurbitaceae. 4 fleshy-rooted climbing, perenn. herbs; tendrils 2-fid. Lvs palmate. Fls small, axill., ♂ fls clustered, ♀ fls solitary; cal. campanulate, 5-lobed; cor. 5-lobed, campanulate. Fr. a berry, solitary or clustered, fleshy, thin-walled. Trop. Afr. to Trop. Asia and Pacific Is. Z10.

D. palmatus (L.) C. Jeffrey. St. slender, becoming ridged and white-spotted. Lvs 4–14cm, glab., lobes 3–5, linear-lanceolate to elliptic. Fls white or pale yellow. Fr. green or red, with white stripes, ovoid, 1.5×2.5cm. Trop. Afr., Trop. Asia to N Aus.

→*Bryonia* and *Bryonopsis.*

Diplomeris D. Don. Orchidaceae. 3 tuberous terrestrial orchids. Lvs solitary or few. Infl. erect; fls 1–2; sep. spreading; pet. larger; lip trilobed or entire, spurred. Himal. Z9.

D. hirsuta (Lindl.) Lindl. Lf oblong-elliptic, sessile, solitary. Fl. 3.5–4cm diam.; sep. ovate-oblong, white; pet. orbicular-reniform; lip yellow, suborbicular, midlobe acute, spur to 4.5cm.

Diplopterygium (Diels) Nak. Gleicheniaceae. 20 scandent, thicket-forming, terrestrial ferns. Rhiz. long-creeping, wiry.

Primary pinnae to 2m, bipinnatifid; pinnules elongate, pinnatifid. Trop. and warm temp. Asia to W Pacific. Z10.

D. longissimum (Bl.) Nak. GIANT SCRAMBLING FERN. Large scrambling fern; stipes 30–100cm, glossy. Fronds rusty-scaly when young; primary pinnae 60–100cm; pinnules rounded, dark green above, glaucous beneath. Pacific region, Aus. to China.

→*Gleichenia.*

Diplosoma Schwantes. Aizoaceae. 2 small, ± stemless, highly succulent perennials. Lvs 2, opposite, united on one side to form an asymmetrical body, free parts divaricate, upper surface flat, furrowed with translucent windows, underside rounded. Fls to 2cm diam., term., sessile, solitary, purple-pink. S Afr. Z9.

D. luckhoffii (L. Bol.) Schwantes. Lvs 16×8mm forming a semi-cylindric body, soft, semi-translucent, papillose.

D. retroversa (Kensit) Schwantes. Lvs to 25×9mm, united by one edge to midway, with rounded tip and several translucent dots. *D. leipoldtii* L. Bol. is a smaller form of this sp.

→*Maughaniella.*

Diplotaxis DC. WALL ROCKET. Cruciferae. Some 25 ann. or perenn. herbs. Lvs mostly basal, st. lvs sessile. Fls 4-merous in term. rac. Eur. to NW India. Z8.

D. acris (Forssk.) Boiss. Ann., 4–60cm. Lvs obovate-oblong, petiolate, obtuse, toothed or lobed, st. lvs finely toothed. Pet. 12–22mm, obovate, lilac-white. Middle East.

D. erucoides (L.) DC. WHITE ROCKET. Similar to *D. acris* but lvs lyrate, pinnatifid. Pet. 7–12mm, blade white, claw violet. SW Eur.

D. saxatilis DC. = *Brassica repanda.*

→*Hesperis, Moricandia* and *Sinapis.*

Dipodium R. Br. Orchidaceae. 22 terrestrial orchids. St. short, slender, with bracts, or elongated, scandent, leafy and rooting. Rac. erect, axill.; pet. and sep. almost equal; lip trilobed with pubesc., ridged callus. Malaysia to New Caledonia. Z9.

D. ensifolium F. Muell. St. elongating. Lvs 6–28cm, linear. Fls to 3.5cm diam., rose to mauve, spotted red or deep mauve; tep. oblong-lanceolate; lip midlobe ovate-oblong. Mid autumn–mid winter. NE Aus.

D. hamiltonianum Bail. Rhiz. subterranean, swollen. St. to 60cm, leafless, spotted red, with overlapping bracts, fls to 5cm diam., bright yellow to dull yellow-green, spotted or streaked red; sep. oblong; pet. narrower; lip midlobe ovate. Late autumn–late winter. SE Aus.

D. pictum (Lindl.) Rchb. f. St. elongating. Lvs to 2.5cm, linear-lanceolate. Fls to 2cm, tep. pale yellow, blotched purple beneath, narrow; lip midlobe obtuse, striped purple at base, white pubesc. at tip. Summer–autumn. Malaysia.

D. punctatum (Sm.) R. Br. = *D. hamiltonianum.*

Dipogon Liebm. Leguminosae (Papilionoideae). 1 woody-based perenn. vine. Lfts to 4cm, rhomboid, glaucous beneath. Fls pea-like, to 1.25cm, in pendulous axill. clusters of 3–6, rose to mauve or white. Fr. to 2.5cm, glab., tinged brown. S Afr. Z9.

D. lignosus (L.) Verdc. AUSTRALIAN PEA.

→*Dolichos.*

Dipper *Lagenaria siceraria.*

DIPSACACEAE Juss. 8/250. *Cephalaria, Dipsacus, Knautia, Pterocephalus, Scabiosa, Succisa.*

Dipsacus L. TEASEL. Dipsacaceae. 15 bienn. or short-lived perenn. herbs. St. tall, slender, erect, arising from a basal rosette; st. lvs opposite, usually basally connate and cup-forming. Flowerheads term. on long stalks, oblong-ovoid to semi-globose, cone-like; involucral bracts slender, semi-rigid; fls small, packed, subtended by sharp bracteoles. Eur., Asia, N Afr.

D. fullonum L. COMMON TEASEL. Bienn. to 2m. Sts ridged, prickly. Basal lvs oblanceolate, crenate, toothed, spiny-pustular, st. lvs lanceolate, entire, strongly connate. Infl. oblong-ovoid, exceeded by unhooked bracts; fls lilac. Eur., Asia, nat. N Amer. Z3.

D. fullonum auct. non L. = *D. sativus.*

D. laciniatus L. Bienn. to 2m. Sts ridged, prickly. Lvs pinnatifid, laciniate. Infl. ovoid, seldom exceeded by bracts; fls white to pink. Eur., W Asia. Z3.

D. sativus (L.) Honck. FULLER'S TEASEL. Bienn. Differs from *D. fullonum* in entire lvs and infl. cylindrical exceeded by hooked bracts. Widespread in Eur., N Afr. and W Asia, also nat. US. Z5.

D. sylvestris Huds. = *D. fullonum.*

Dipteranthus Barb. Rodr. Orchidaceae. 8 dwarf epiphytic orchids. S America. Z10.
D. planifolius (Rchb. f.) Garay. Rhiz. slender, creeping. Pbs to 0.3cm, ovoid, with papery sheaths. Lvs to 4cm, linear-oblong to narrow-lanceolate. Rac. to 9cm, erect to pendulous, angled; fls to 0.8cm diam., tawny, white or green; sep. broadly lanceolate; pet. broadly ovate, slightly crisped; lip amber to olive, glossy, concave and white viscid-pubesc.; column golden, sigmoid. Venez.
→*Ornithocephalus.*

Dipteronia Oliv. Aceraceae. 2 decid. trees. Lvs pinnate. Pan. term., erect; sep. 5; pet. 5, shorter; sta. about 8. Schizocarps paired, winged, turning red. C & S China. Z8.
D. sinensis Oliv. Tree to 10m or a bushy shrub. Lvs 20–27cm; lfts 7–11, ovate or lanceolate, to 9cm, serrate. Pan. pyramidal; fls pale green; sta. white. C China.

Dipterosperma Hassk.
D. personatum Hassk. = *Stereospermum personatum.*

Dirca L. LEATHERWOOD. Thymelaeaceae. 2 decid. shrubs, tree-like in habit. Br. scarred; bark fibrous. Lvs entire, thin. Fls precocious, 3–4 per axill. cluster; cal. 4-lobed, yellow; pet. 0; sta. 8, protruding. Fr. a small drupe. N Amer.
D. occidentalis A. Gray. Similar to *D. palustris* but fls sessile, bud scales thickly pubesc.; cal. distinctly lobed. Calif. Z7.
D. palustris L. WICOPY; ROPEBARK. Shrub to 2m. Br. tinged yellow. Lvs 3–7cm, obovate to elliptic, initially pubesc. beneath. Fls subsessile, bud scales thinly pubesc.; cal. pale yellow, obscurely lobed. Fr. green to red. Spring. E US. Z4.

Disa Bergius. Orchidaceae. *c*100 tuberous terrestrial orchids. Lvs cauline or basal, narrowly elliptic to lanceolate, bract-like on st. Rac. terminal; dors. sep. spurred, usually forming hood, laterals usually spreading; pet. smaller, often lying inside hood; lip usually narrow. Trop. and S Afr., Madag. and Masc. Is. Z10.
D. cardinalis L. 30–60cm. Basal lvs, 5–10cm. Rac. 8–40-fld; fls bright red, dors. sep. 10–15×8–10mm, forming a hood 6–8mm deep with conical, obtuse spur 4mm long. S Afr.
D. crassicornis Lindl. To 1m. Basal lvs to 14cm. Rac. 5–25-fld; fls fragrant, white or cream spotted with pink or purple; dors. sep. 20–40×15–30mm, forming hood 10–15mm deep narrowing to a cylindric, decurved spur 30–40mm long, tip slightly inflated. S Afr.
D. grandiflora L. f. = *D. uniflora.*
D. Kewensis. Small fls in various shades of pink and orange.
D. Langleyensis. Tall spikes of pale pink fls.
D. racemosa L. f. 30–100cm. Basal lvs to 10cm. Rac. 2–12-fld; sep. pale to mid pink with darker veins, pet. and lip white to yellow, pet. with horizontal purple bars; dors. sep. 17–24×13–20mm, forming dish-shaped hood 5–8mm deep, spur almost obsolete. S Afr.
D. sagittalis (L. f.) Sw. 7–30cm. Basal lvs to 9cm. Rac. few to many-fld; fls white or mauve, pet. often darker than sep.; dors. sep. 6–13×8–12mm, forming shallow hood, half-moon-shaped toward apex with the lat. extensions reflexed; spur 2–7mm, slender. S Afr.
D. tripetaloides (L. f.) N.E. Br. 10–60cm. Basal lvs to 14cm. Rac. to 25cm; fls white or pink or bright yellow; dors. sep. 5–12mm forming hood 3–5mm deep; spur conical, rarely cylindrical. S Afr. ssp. *tripetaloides* Fls white to pink. ssp. *aurata* (Bol.) Lind. Fls bright yellow.
D. uniflora Bergius. 15–60cm. Lvs to 25cm. Rac. usually 1–3-fld; lat. sep. and lip usually carmine red, hood orange inside with red veining, pet. light carmine red at base, the blade yellow with red spots; yellow and pink forms also occur; dors. sep. 20–60×15–20mm, forming hood 15mm deep with lower margins incurved; spur 10–15mm, conical. S Afr.
D. Veitchii. Tall spikes of bright orange-red fls.
D. Watsonii. Fls light magenta, spotted, on tall spikes.

Disanthus Maxim. Hamamelidaceae. 1 decid. shrub to 4×2m. Shoots slender, spreading, with pale lenticels. Lvs to 10cm, entire, ovate to orbicular, base cordate, palmately veined, blue green above, lighter beneath, turning red with orange tints in fall, glab. Fls inconspicuous, paired back to back in lf axils; pet. 5, narrow, dark purple. Late autumn. China, Jap. Z8.
D. cercidifolius Maxim.

Discaria Hook. Rhamnaceae. 12 decid. shrubs or small trees, with long thorns. Lvs small. Infl. axill., dense, fasciculate; fls 4- or 5-merous, fragrant, pet. often 0. Temp. S Amer., Aus. and NZ. Z8.
D. chacaye (G. Don) Tortosa. Shrub to 2m, with decussate, 1–3cm spines, twigs in pairs below them. Lvs 1–1.4cm, elliptic to

oblanceolate, leathery, dark green, obtuse to emarginate, toothed and gland. Fls 2–3mm diam., in short axill. clusters, white. Late spring–early summer. S Chile and Arg.
D. crenata (Clos) Reg. Shrub or small tree to 5m, br. long, slender, pendulous, with paired spines to at least 2cm. Lvs 1.2–2.5cm, ovate-oblong, glab., crenate, shiny. Fls in crowded fascicles, 3mm diam., green-white. Early summer. C & S Chile, S Arg.
D. discolor (Hook.) Dusén = *D. chacaye.*
D. serratifolia (Vent.) Benth. & Hook. Shrub or small tree to about 5m, with slender, pendulous br., thorns to *c*2cm, paired. Lvs 1.2–2.5cm, ovate-oblong, glab., toothed, shiny. Fls in crowded fascicles, 3mm diam., green-white. Early summer. S Chile, Arg.
D. toumatou Raoul. WILD IRISHMAN. Shrub or small tree to 5m, twigs green, terete, flexuous, slender, spines many 2.5–5cm, opposite, horizontal. Lvs produced below spines, 1–2cm, leathery, obovate to ovate-oblong, blunt, glossy above. Fls solitary or few in cymose fascicles, 3–5mm diam., green to white. Late spring. NZ.
→*Colletia.*
Disc-leaved Hebe *Hebe pinguifolia.*

Discocactus Pfeiff. Cactaceae. 8 cacti; st. mostly simple, depressed-globose to globose, spiny; ribs distinct or strongly tuberculate. Flowering-zone (cephalium) apical, depressed, densely woolly and ± bristly; fls white tubular-salverform, nocturnal; tube slender, scaly. Braz., E Boliv., N Parag.
D. alteolens Lem. ex Dietr. = *D. placentiformis.*
D. hartmannii (Schum.) Britt. & Rose. Resembling *D. heptacanthus*, but ribs 15–22, resolved into conic, gibbous, tubercles; spines to 2cm, thick, not flattened. Cephalium with white wool and red-brown bristles; fls to 7.5(–10)×4cm. Summer. N Parag., Braz. Z9.
D. heptacanthus (Rodr.) Britt. & Rose. St. simple, depressed-globose to globose, to 7.5×15cm; ribs 9–14, divided into large tuercles; spines to 4cm, ± curved and flattened. Cephalium with wool and brown bristles; fls to 7×5cm. Summer. E Boliv., Braz. Z9.
D. horstii Buining & Brederoo. St. to 4×6(–7)cm, purple-brown; ribs 15–22, narrow, not tuberculate; spines 3–3.5mm, pectinate, addressed, chalky white. Cephalium with wool and bristles, ringed by spines; fls to 7.5×6cm. Summer. E Braz. Z9.
D. insignis auctt. non Pfeiff. = *D. pseudoinsignis.*
D. placentiformis (Lehm.) Schum. St. depressed-globose, to 10×12–25cm, light to dark green or blue-green, sometimes offsetting; ribs usually 9–26, not or not strongly tuberculate; spines 3–8, to 4cm, recurved and often flattened. Cephalium with white wool and bristles; fls *c*4.5–8.5×4–8cm. Summer. E Braz. Z9.
D. pseudoinsignis N. Tayl. & Zappi. St. 7–9×12–21cm, light to dark green; ribs 12–13, not tuberculate; spines grey to almost black, to 4cm. Cephalium white-woolly, usually with dark brown bristles; fl. *c*7.5–6cm. E Braz. Z9.
D. subviridigriseus Buining & Brederoo. St. 6–7×12–18cm, grey-green, sometimes offsetting; ribs 13–15, not tuberculate; spines to 3.5cm, strongly recurved, dark grey. Cephalium to 3.5cm diam., with white wool and occasional brown bristles at edge; fl. 4.5–7×3–5.5cm. E Braz. Z9.
D. tricornis Monv. ex Pfeiff. & Otto = *D. placentiformis.*
D. zehntneri Britt. & Rose. St. depressed-globose to globose, to 10×12cm, covered with interlacing spines; ribs 12–21, usually spiralled, divided into tubercles; spines to 7cm, terete, recurved. Fls 3.5–4.5×4–5.5cm. Summer. E Braz. Z9.

Diselma Hook. f. Cupressaceae. 1 low-growing shrubby everg. conifer to 4m. Br. irregularly arranged, whip-like in young plants. Lvs to 8×2mm, in pairs, scale-like or shortly subulate, pointing towards shoot tip, closely addressed, crowded, imbricate, keeled, dark green with 2 white stomatal bands. Cones minute, globose. W Tasm. Z8.
D. archeri Hook. f.

Dishcloth Gourd *Luffa cylindrica.*
Dish Fern *Pteris.*

Disocactus Lindl. Cactaceae. 12 shrubby epiphytic cacti; st. flattened, leaf-like, or dimorphic, with main st. terete and the lat. st. flattened, crenate or serrate, with areole, subtended by a vestigial lf in each sinus; spines minute, or 0. Fls usually 1 per areole, tube usually slender; limb erect to spreading or rotate. Fr. berry-like. Amer.
D. alatus (Sw.) Kimnach. St. pendent, up to 5m; cladodes broadly linear to lanceolate or oblong, 20–40×3–6cm, crenate-undulate. Fls 14–17mm; outer tep. pale yellow or tinged green, inner white. Fr. yellow-green. Winter. Jam. Z9.

D. biformis (Lindl.) Lindl. St. to 20cm or more; cladodes linear or narrowly oblong, 5–8×1–2cm, serrate. Fls magenta, c5×5cm. Fr. deep red. Spring. Guat. Z9.

D. eichlamii (Weber) Britt. & Rose. St. to 75cm×4–7mm, flat towards apex; lat. st. terete at base, flat above, linear or narrowly lanceolate, to 40×1.5–5cm, crenate or obtusely serrate. Fls solitary or up to 5, narrowly tubular-funnelform, 6–8×1cm; pericarpel and tube, maroon-red; outer tep. scarlet, inner tep. magenta-scarlet. Fr. red. Spring. Guat. Z9.

D. himantocladus (Roland-Goss.) Kimnach. St. flat, linear, 40–50×1–3cm, shallowly serrate. Fls tubular-salverform, c2.5×2cm; pericarpel and tube tinged purple; tep. white. Winter. Costa Rica. Z9.

D. macranthus (Alexander) Kimnach & Hutch. St. to 90cm, base terete, blade flat, to 4.5cm wide, tapering to apex, crenate. Fls solitary, c6.5×7cm, musk-scented; outer tep. pale orange-brown, pink-purple at base, inner lemon-yellow. Fr. red. Autumn–winter. Mex. Z9.

D. nelsonii (Britt. & Rose) Lindinger. St. pendulous, to 1.6m, flat at apex; lat. st. flat, oblanceolate, to 40×2–6cm, serrate or crenate. Fls solitary, 9–11×5–7cm; pericarpel and tube green, tinged brown at base; tep. pink. Fr. brown-red. Late winter–spring. S Mex. to Hond. Z9.

D. quezaltecus (Standl. & Steyerm.) Kimnach. St. to 80cm, terete below, flat above; lat. st. flat, linear-lanceolate, 10–35×1.5–6cm, obtusely serrate to crenate. Fls solitary, 8.5–9cm×9–11mm; pericarpel and tube, purple-red; limb pink. Fr. purple-red. Spring. Guat. Z9.

D. ramulosus (Salm-Dyck) Kimnach. St. to 70×2–5mm, terete below, flat above; lat. st. flat, linear to lanceolate, to 23×0.5–3cm, with petiole-like base, crenate or obtusely serrate, often suffused purple. Fls 7–12×10–14mm, yellow-white, tinged pink or green. Fr. white to pale pink. Spring. W Indies, Trop. Amer. Z9.

→Bonifazia, Chiapasia, Pseudorhipsalis, Rhipsalis, Wittia and Wittiocactus.

Disperis Sw. Orchidaceae. 70–80 tuberous terrestrial and epiphytic orchids. St. erect, slender, with 1 to few lvs. Fls small, solitary or in rac.; dors. sep. joined to pet., forming hood, lat. sep. usually spurred; lip complex, folded back over column and extended into a straight or reflexed limb bearing a simple or bilobed appendage. Trop. & S Afr., Masc. Is., India and E to New Guinea. Z10.

D. capensis (L. f.) Sw. 15–30cm. Lvs 1–2, to 7×1.5cm, lanceolate. Infl. 1–2-fld; fls mainly yellow-green; pet. sometimes rose purple; dors. sep. to 3cm; lat. sep. 2.5–3cm, reflexed, narrowly lanceolate, acuminate, with blunt sac 2–3mm long near base; lip mostly hidden inside hood. Winter. S Afr. (Cape Prov.).

D. fanniniae Harv. GRANNY'S BONNET. 10–20cm. Lvs 3–4, to 8×3cm, lanceolate, base cordate, dark glossy green, purple beneath. Rac. several-fld; fls white, often tinged purple; dors. sep. 9–10mm, lat. sep. 8mm, deflexed, lanceolate, acuminate, with blunt sac about half-way along; pet. with rounded lobe on outer margin, often spotted with green or purple; lip hidden inside hood. S Afr.

D. johnstonii Rolfe. 4–15cm. Lvs 1–3, 2–3×1.5–2cm, ovate, base cordate, purple beneath. Rac. 1–5-fld; dors. sep. and pet. yellow or mauve, lateral sep. white, sometimes tinged mauve; dors. sep. 8–12mm, lat. sep. 8–14mm, semi-orbicular, apiculate, with sac-like spur to 1mm; lip lying inside hood bearing 2-lobed papillose appendage. W & E Afr. to Natal.

Disphyma N.E. Br. Aizoaceae. 3 mat-forming, creeping, succulent perennials. Lvs united at base, linear, semicylindric or triquetrous, papillose or with translucent spots. Fls 1–3 together, pedicellate. Australasia, S Afr. Z9.

D. australe (Ait.) J.M. Black. Lvs 2×10cm, triquetrous, fresh green, faintly spotted, bluntly tapered. Fls 2cm diam., pink. Coast of NSW and Tasm., NZ, Chatham Is.

D. crassifolium (L.) L. Bol. Lvs 2.5–3.5×0.5cm, obtusely triquetrous, shortly tapered, dark green with faint translucent spots. Fls 4cm diam., pink-red. S Afr.

→Mesembryanthemum.

Disporum D. Don. Liliaceae (Colchicaceae). 10–20 perrennial, rhizomatous herbs. St. spreading or erect, leafy, sparingly branched. Lvs ovate or lanceolate, alt., sessile or shortly stalked. Fls solitary or in few-fld umbels, terminal, usually nodding; tep. 6, often slightly swollen at the base; sta. 6. US, Himal., E Asia.

D. cantoniense (Lour.) Merrill. To 90cm. Lvs 5–15cm, lanceolate, glab. Fls white to purple, in clusters of 3–6; tep. to 2.5cm. Fr. red. Himal., China, E Indies. Z8.

D. hookeri (Torr.) Nichols. 30cm–1m. Lvs 3–14cm, lanceolate to ovate, base cordate-amplexicaul, rough or minutely pubesc. on margins and veins beneath. Fls 1.5cm, in umbels of 1–3, green-white; tep. 0.9–2cm. Fr. scarlet. var. oreganum (S. Wats.) Q. Jones Differs in lvs long-acuminate, anth. exserted, ovary pubesc. NW US. Z8.

D. lanuginosum (Michx.) Nichols. To 90cm. Lvs 3–12cm, ovate-lanceolate, acuminate, minutely pubesc. beneath, with marginal hairs. Fls in clusters of 1–3, yellow-green; tep. 1–2cm. Fr. red. EC US. Z5.

D. sessile (Thunb.) D. Don. To 60cm. Lvs 5–15cm, oblong or oblong-lanceolate, glab. Fls white, tips tinged green, solitary or in clusters of 1–3; tep. 2.5–3cm. Fr. blue-black. Jap. 'Variegatum' lvs broadly striped cream. Z7.

D. smithii (Hook) Piper. FAIRY LANTERN. To 1m. Lvs to 12cm, ovate to lanceolate-ovate, rounded to cordate at base. Fls white, to 2.5cm, 1–5 per umbel. Fr. orange to red. BC to Calif. Z6.

→Uvularia.

Dissotis Benth. Melastomataceae. 60–100 ann. or perenn. herbs and small shrubs, usually hairy. Lvs opposite, short-stalked, conspicuously 3–5-veined. Fls solitary or in term. heads or pan.; cal. lobes alternating with hairy appendages; pet. 4–5, rose, purple or violet; sta. 8–10. Afr. Z10.

D. canescens (Graham) Hook. f. Subshrub to 90cm; st. 4-angled, purple, hairy. Lvs 2.5–7.5cm, linear to oblong, obtuse, grey-green, pubesc. Infl. a leafy, subterminal pan.; fls 2cm diam., rose-purple. Trop. Afr.

D. grandiflora Benth. in Hook. Perenn. 60–90cm, woody, swollen-tuberous at base, br. 4-angled, hispid. Lvs 5–9cm, narrowed at apex, toothed, sparsely hairy. Infl. a few-fld term. rac.; fls 5–8cm diam., purple-pink. Senegal, Gambia, Sierra Leone.

D. incana (E. Mey. ex Hochst.) Triana = D. canescens.

D. irvingiana Hook. f. Ann., 30–90cm; st. erect, 4-angled. Lvs 5–8cm, linear-oblong or oblong-lanceolate, acute. Fls 2.5–3.5cm diam., red-purple, solitary or 2–5 in axill. and term. cymes. Upper Guinea.

D. mahonii Hook. f. = D. plumosa.

D. plumosa Hook. f. Perenn. woody at base; br. terete, procumbent, bristly at nodes. Lvs 0.8–3.5cm, broadly ovate. Fls solitary, purple. Sierra Leone.

Distaff Thistle Carthamus lanatus.

Distictis Mart. ex Meissn. Bignoniaceae. 9 lianes. Br. hexagonal. Lvs 2-foliolate, often with trifid terminal tendril. Fls few, in term. rac. or pan., sometimes scented; cal. cupular, truncate or 5-toothed, margin gland.; cor. tubular or tubular-campanulate, pubesc. outside. Mex., W Indies. Z9.

D. buccinatoria (DC.) A. Gentry. Lfts 10cm, ovate-lanceolate, glab. above, minutely white-scaly beneath. Cor. 7.5–8cm, tubular-funnelform, purple-red yellow at base, yellow-tomentose. Mex.

D. cinerea (DC.) Greenman = D. laxiflora.

D. lactiflora (Vahl) DC. Lfts to 6cm, ovate, glab., scaly beneath. Cor. 2.5cm, white, throat yellow. W Indies, San Domingo, Puerto Rico.

D. laxiflora (DC.) Greenman. Lfts 2–7cm, ovate-elliptic, scaly puberulent to glabrescent above, puberulent beneath. Cor. 4.5–7.5cm, tubular-campanulate, purple in bud, then lavender, fading to white, puberulent. Spring–summer. Mex., Nic.

D. 'Rivers'. Lvs dark green. Fls dark mauve with gold throat, late-flowering.

→Bignonia, Phaedranthus and Pithecoctenium.

Distylium Sieb. & Zucc. Hamamelidaceae. 12 small, everg. trees and shrubs. Lvs alt., stipulate, entire or toothed. Fls in axill. rac. with small bracts; sep. 3–5, sometimes 0; pet. 0; sta. 2–8, spathulate. Jap., China, N India. Z8.

D. racemosum Sieb. & Zucc. ISU TREE. Broadly spreading shrub to 25m in the wild. Lvs to 7cm, elliptic to obovate, coriaceous, dark green and glossy above. Infl. to 7.5cm, stellate-pubesc.; sta. red, conspicuous. Spring. SW Jap.

Dita Bark Alstonia scholaris.
Ditchmoss Elodea.
Dittany Dictamnus.
Dittany of Crete Origanum dictamnus.

Diuris Sm. DOUBLE TAILS. Orchidaceae. c40 terrestrial tuberous orchids. Lvs grassy, often paired, above them a few sheathing bracts. Rac. tall, erect; pet. usually erect and clawed; dors. sep. hooded, lat. sep. long, narrow, strongly decurved; lip equalling or exceeding dors. sep., callus strongly ridged. Java, Aus. Z9.

D. alba R. Br. As *D. punctata* except fls white often tinged or spotted purple, fragrant. SE Aus.

D. aurea Sm. To 60cm. Fls to 8, dors. sep. recurved, ovate, golden spotted or stained brown, lat. sep. bronze-green, often widened at tips and overlapping; pet. golden or orange, claws spotted brown; lip to 22mm, deflexed, midlobe suborbicular, lat. lobes spotted maroon, erect, crisped. E Aus.

D. corymbosa Lindl. Fls 1–8, yellow to red-brown tinted purple; dors. sep. ovate, incurved, lat. sep. to 25mm, green, deflexed, parallel or crossed; pet. broadly ovate; lip projecting or deflexed, midlobe to 10mm, lateral lobes recurved, entire. SW & E Aus.

D. cuneata Fitzh. = *D. punctata* var. *longissima*.

D. lanceolata Lindl. SNAKE ORCHID. Fls 1–4, nodding, lemon yellow, exterior with darker markings; dors. sep. ovate, incurved, often recurved, lat. sep. linear, deflexed; pet. elliptic, claw red-brown; lip deflexed, midlobe ovate, lateral lobes irregularly dentate. SE Aus.

D. laxiflora Lindl. Fls 1–4, yellow, markings dark brown (esp. on lip and pet.); dors. sep. to 7mm, ovate, lat. sep. decurved, brown; pet. erect or recurved; lip deflexed, midlobe flabellate, lat. lobes spreading, undulate or entire. SW Aus.

D. longifolia R. Br. Fls 1–8, purple and mauve, dors. sep. and lip tinted yellow; dors. sep. to 12mm, ovate, lat. sep. 18–25mm, linear, tips widened, parallel or crossing; pet. ovate or elliptic, recurved or spreading; lip to 10mm, deep brown suffused yellow or mauve, midlobe cuneate, recurved, lat. lobes spreading or recurved, wavy or entire. W Aus.

D. maculata Sm. Fls 2–8, yellow, spotted dark brown; dors. sep. ovate, lat. sep. linear, parallel or crossed, green marked dark purple; pet. broadly ovate, yellow, dotted brown, darker below, claw red-brown; lip 6–7mm, midlobe cuneate, folded, lat. lobes spreading or recurved. SE Aus.

D. palustris Lindl. Fls 1–4, yellow, blotched dark brown with a spicy fragrance; dors. sep. ovate, to 8mm, lat. sep. linear, green or bronze, 15–18mm; pet. with a purple claw, recurved; lip 6–10mm, ovate, forward pointing, lobes oblong, dentate, interior yellow, exterior blotched brown. SE Aus.

D. punctata Sm. Fls 2–10, purple with darker blotches, rarely yellow or white; dors. sep. ovate, erect or apically recurved, lat. sep. narrow-linear, pendulous, crossed or curved, to 9cm; pet. elliptic-oblong to 15mm; lip to 2cm, midlobe flabellate often folded. E Aus. var. *longissima* Benth. Fls 2–6, pale lilac with darker spots and stripes; lat. sep. narrow, to 10mm, green; pet. narrow, elliptic, to 12mm; lip striped purple. SE Aus.

D. punctata var. *alba* (R. Br.) Docker = *D. alba*.

D. sulphurea R. Br. Fls 3–7, fragrant, yellow, marked dark brown; dors. sep. to 22mm, ovate, often recurved, with two central brown dots, lat. sep. linear, bronze-green, parallel or crossed; pet. elliptic, spreading; lip deflexed, yellow marked dark brown, midlobe rectangular, lat. lobes recurved, irregularly dentate. C & SE Aus.

D. tricolor Fitzh. Fls 3–6, suffused purple; dors. sep. ovate, erect, red-dotted, lateral sep. narrow, deflexed to 30mm, often crossed; pet. elliptic, spreading; lip deflexed, midlobe ovate, broad, lat. lobes obtuse, entire, upcurved. SE Aus.

Divi-divi *Caesalpinia coriaria*.

Dizygotheca N.E. Br.

D. elegantissima (Veitch ex Mast.) R. Vig. & Guillaum. = *Schefflera elegantissima*.

D. elegantissima auct., non (Veitch ex Mast.) R. Vig. & Guillaum. = *Schefflera veitchii*.

D. kerchoveiana hort., non (Veitch ex W. Richards) N. Tayl. = *Schefflera elegantissima* or *Schefflera veitchii*.

D. kerchoveiana (Veitch ex W. Richards) N. Tayl. = *Schefflera kerchoveiana*.

D. veitchii (Veitch ex Carr.) R. Vig. & Guillaum. = *Schefflera veitchii*.

Dobo Lily *Cyrtanthus brachyscyphus*.

Dobrowskya C. Presl.

D. tenella (Thunb.) Sonder = *Monopsis unidentata*.

Dock *Rumex*.
Dockmackie *Viburnum acerifolium*.

Docynia Decne. Rosaceae. 2 everg. or decid. shrubs or small trees, sometimes spiny. Lvs to 10cm, simple, dentate or entire. Fls subsessile, 2–3 per cluster; cal. downy, lobes lanceolate; pet. 5, to 1.5cm, white (pink in bud); sta. 30–50. Fr. quince-like with a persistent, downy cal. SE Asia. Z8.

D. delavayi (Franch.) Schneid. Tree to 10m. Lvs persistent, oblong, entire, white-tomentose beneath. Fr. yellow, 4cm diam.

S China.

D. docynioides Rehd. = *D. indica*.

D. indica (Wallich) Decne. Shrub to 5m. Lvs falling, lanceolate, dentate, downy beneath at first. Fr. yellow-green, to 5cm diam. W Himal., N Burm., N Thail., N Vietnam, SW China.

D. rufifolia (Lév.) Rehd. = *D. indica*.

→*Eriolobus* and *Pyrus*.

Dodan-tsutsuji *Enkianthus perulatus*.
Dodder-like Saxifrage *Saxifraga cuscutiformis*.

Dodecatheon L. SHOOTING STAR; AMERICAN COWSLIP. Primulaceae. 14 usually glab., perenn. herbs. Lvs in a basal rosette. Infl. a scapose, term. umbel; fls (4–)5-merous, long-stalked, nodding, cyclamen-like; cor. lobes strongly reflexed, tube v. short, thickened at throat; sta. inserted at throat, fil. united into a tube; style filiform, exserted. N Amer., Bering Straits. Z6.

D. alpinum (A. Gray) E. Greene. To 40cm. Lvs to 15cm, linear-oblong, apex acute, base tapering gradually. Fls deep red or purple, tube yellow, throat with purple ring; sta. deep purple. Calif. Z6.

D. amethystinum (Fassett) Fassett = *D. pulchellum*.

D. clevelandii E. Greene. To 50cm. Lvs to 6cm, rather fleshy, spathulate-ovate, irregularly toothed. Fls purple, tube yellow, deep purple spots in throat; sta. purple. Calif. Z6.

D. conjugans E. Greene. Lvs to 13cm, obovate and elliptical, obtuse, entire; petiole distinct. Fls purple, pink or white. Wyom., Oreg. Z3.

D. cruciatum E. Greene. To 40cm tall. Lvs to 7cm, ovate, thick, entire, rounded; petiole winged. Fls deep red or purple, base with purple ring and yellow spots. W US. Z6.

D. cusickii E. Greene. Similar to *D. pulchellum* but lvs gland., viscid, sometimes dentate or crenate. W US. Z3.

D. dentatum Hook. To 10cm. Lvs to 8cm, oblong-lanceolate, stalked, sometimes denticulate, obtuse or abruptly acute. Fls white; anth. yellow tinted black. Washington, N Oreg. to Idaho. Z5.

D. frigidum Cham. & Schldl. To 10cm. Lvs ovate, to 5cm, apex subacute to subobtuse, base subcuneate to truncate, nearly entire or irregularly sinuate-dentate; petiole slightly winged. Fls lilac to magenta; anth. large, black, tinged yellow. Bering Straits. Z3.

D. hendersonii A. Gray. SAILOR-CAPS; MOSQUITO-BILLS. To 40cm. Lvs to 6cm, oblong-ovate, rather fleshy, rounded, sometimes mucronate, often erose, gradually tapering to petiole. Fls violet, anth. edged yellow. Calif. Z6.

D. hugeri E. Greene = *D. meadia*.

D. integrifolium Michx. To 25cm. Lvs to 12cm, obovate to spathulate, base tapering gradually; petiole as long as lamina. Fls purple. BC. Z5.

D. jeffreyi Van Houtte. SIERRA SHOOTING STAR. Slightly viscid, to 50cm. Lvs to 30cm, oblanceolate, erect, entire, mucronate. Fls deep red to deep purple; sta. deep purple, free. Calif. Z5.

D. latifolium (Hook. Piper = *D. hendersonii*.

D. latilobum (A. Gray) Elmer ex Knuth. = *D. dentatum*.

D. macrocarpum (A. Gray) Knuth. = *D. pulchellum*.

D. meadia L. SHOOTING STAR; AMERICAN COWSLIP. To 50cm. Lvs to 25cm, oblong to ovate or oblanceolate, entire or toothed, apex obtuse, base narrowing to winged petiole. Fls purple with white base, sometimes wholly pink or white; anth. red tinged yellow, connective purple. E US. 'Album': fls white. 'Queen Victoria': to 30cm; fls lilac pink. 'Splendidum': fls dark rose. Z3.

D. pauciflorum (Dur.) E. Greene non hort. = *D. meadia*.

D. pauciflorum hort. = *D. pulchellum*.

D. poeticum L.F. Henderson. To 30cm. Lvs to 13cm, oblanceolate, glandular-pubesc. Fls bright rose-purple to lilac, sta. dark. S Washington to N Oreg. Z6.

D. puberulum Nutt. Piper = *D. pulchellum*.

D. pulchellum (Raf.) Merrill. To 35cm. Lvs glab. to glandular-pubesc., ova te-spathulate, to 20cm, somewhat wavy. Fls rose-purple to lilac; anth. yellow with purple-black connectives. W N Amer. to Mex., nat. E US. 'Album': fls white. 'Red Wings': scapes to 20cm; fls pale carmine. Z5.

D. radicatum E. Greene = *D. pulchellum*.

D. redolens (H.M. Hall) H.J. Thomps. To 38cm. Lvs to 32cm, oblanceolate, glandular-pubesc. Fls magenta to mauve, tube yellow; fil. dark. SW US. Z8.

D. tetrandrum Suksd. ex E. Greene = *D. jeffreyi*.

D. uniflorum Rydb. = *D. pulchellum* ssp. *watsonii*.

D. viscidum Piper = *D. conjugans*.

D. vulgare (Hook.) Piper = *D. pulchellum*.

Dodonaea Mill. Sapindaceae. 50 everg. shrubs and trees, covered with fine, yellow, gland. dots. Lvs simple or pinnate. Infl. cymose; fls inconspicuous. Fr. a membranous, 3-winged capsule. Trop. and subtrop., esp. Aus. Z9.

D. attenuata Cunn. = *D. viscosa*.
D. cuneata (L.) Jacq. = *D. viscosa*.
D. dioica DC. = *D. triquetra*.
D. hirtella F. Muell. non Miq. = *D. multijuga*.
D. laurifolia Sieber ex Loud. = *D. triquetra*.
D. laurina Sieber ex A. Spreng. = *D. triquetra*.
D. longipes G. Don. = *D. triquetra*.
D. multijuga G. Don. To 1.5m. Lvs 2–5cm; lfts 16–28, oblong to broadly ovate to obtriangular, rarely linear, pubesc., term. lft lobe-like. Capsule to 2cm, broadly winged. Aus.
D. triquetra Wendl. To 3m. Lvs to 12cm, elliptic, lanceolate or ovate, simple, entire or serrate, glab. Capsule to 16cm, broadly winged. Aus.
D. viscosa (L.) Jacq. NATIVE HOPS. To 2m. Lvs to 13cm, yellow-green, simple, elliptic, revolute, resinous. Capsule to 2cm, narrowly winged. S Afr., Aus., Mex. 'Purpurea': foliage purple-red.

Dogbane *Apocynum*.
Dogberry *Ardisia escallonioides*; *Cornus sanguinea*; *Ribes cynosbati*.
Dogbramble *Ribes cynosbati*.
Dog Brier *Rosa canina*.
Dog Fennel *Anthemis*.
Dog Grass *Agropyron*.
Dog Hobble *Leucothoë fontanesiana*.
Dog Rose *Rosa canina*.
Dog's-tooth Violet *Erythronium*.
Dogtooth Pea *Lathyrus sativus*.
Dog Violet *Viola canina*; *V. riviana*.
Dogwood *Cornus*.

Dolichandra Cham. Bignoniaceae. 1 glab. liane. Lvs bifoliolate, sometimes with a term. trifid tendril; lfts 3–7cm, oblong-lanceolate mucronate, dark, leathery, crispate. Cyme 1–6-fld to 1.5cm; bracts and bracteoles leafy; cal. 2cm, slender; cor. 5–7cm, tubular, decurved, vermilion to purple-vermilion, interior yellow, obliquely bilabiate; sta. exserted. Braz., Parag., Urug., Arg. Z10.
D. cynanchoides Cham.

Dolichandrone (Fenzl) Seem. Bignoniaceae. 9 shrubs or trees. Lvs pinnate, rarely simple. Rac. term., rarely axill.; fls few, white (unless qualified below), fragrant; cor. tube narrow, inflated to throat, lobes 5, crisped. Afr., Asia, Malesia to New Caledonia. Z10.
D. alba (Sim) Sprague. TSANI. Tree, 8–12m. Pinnae to 10cm, 8, ovate to elliptic, waxy, entire, undulate or serrulate. Cor. tube 4–5cm, cylindrical, slightly expanded at base, lobes 2.5×2cm, undulate, reflexed. Winter–spring. Moz.
D. alternifolia (R. Br.) Seem. Shrub to 5m. Lvs 2–6cm, simple, coriaceous, ovate to lanceolate, long-acuminate. Cor. 2.5–3cm. NE Aus.
D. arcuata (Wight) C.B. Clarke = *D. atrovirens*.
D. atrovirens Sprague. Tree to 20m. Pinnae 9–11, to 7.5cm, oblong, becoming glab. Cor. to 7.5cm, lobes reniform, curled. India.
D. crispa (Buch.-Ham.) Seem. = *D. atrovirens*.
D. filiformis (DC.) Fenzl. Shrub or tree, 3–8m. Pinnae 4–8, 10–25cm, filiform. Cor. to 3cm, white to pale yellow; lobes to 1.3cm. N Aus.
D. heterophylla (R. Br.) F. Muell. Tree to 6m. Lvs dimorphic; simple lvs 2.5–12cm, grey-green, coriaceous, pinnate lvs with pinnae, 3–13, linear-lanceolate. Cor. to 4cm, lobes short, crisped. Queensld and N Territ.
D. hildebrandtii Bak. = *Markhamia lutea*.
D. hirsuta Bak. Tree. Br. pubesc. pinnae in 2–3 pairs, to 3.7cm, oblong, apex obtuse, often densely pubesc. Cor. to 2.5cm long, 0.8cm diam., funnelform. SC Afr.
D. lutea Benth. ex Hook. & Jackson = *Markhamia lutea*.
D. obtusifolia Bak. Shrub or tree. Pinnae to 10cm, 7–9, oblong, obtuse, pubesc. Cor. 5cm, creamy yellow, campanulate. E Afr.
D. obtusifolia Bak. = *Markhamia obtusifolia*.
D. serrulata (DC.) Seem. Tree to 15m. Pinnae 3–8cm, 4–10, elliptic to oblong-elliptic, long-acuminate, entire to dentate. Fls resemble *D. spathacea*. SE Asia.
D. spathacea (L. f.) Schum. To 20m. Pinnae 6–16cm, 6–8, oblong-ovate to lanceolate-elliptic, entire, acuminate. Cor. tube 12–18cm, to 12cm diam. at mouth. Trop. SE Asia to New Guinea and Pacific Is.
→*Bignonia* and *Spathodea*.

Dolichoglottis R. Nordenstam. Compositae. 2 perenn. herbs. St. erect, leafy, base woody, covered with persistent lf bases. Lvs parallel-veined. Cap. radiate, in terminal corymbs; ray flts white, yellow or pink; disc flts campanulate, 4–5-lobed. NZ. Z8.

D. scorzoneroides (Hook. f.) R. Nordenstam. To 50cm. St. simple, softly hairy. Basal lvs to 20cm, lanceolate, glandular-pubesc., fleshy. Cap. to 6cm diam. NZ.
→*Senecio*.

Dolichos L.
D. biflorus auct. = *Macrotyloma uniflorum*.
D. lablab L. = *Lablab purpureus*.
D. lignosus L. = *Dipogon lignosus*.
D. sondanensis hort. = *Lablab purpureus*.

Dolichos Bean *Lablab purpureus*.

Dolichothele Britt. & Rose.
D. albescens (Tiegel) Backeb. = *Mammillaria albescens*.
D. balsasoides (Craig) Backeb. = *Mammillaria beneckei*.
D. baumii (Boed.) Werderm. & F. Buxb. = *Mammillaria baumii*.
D. beneckei (Ehrenb.) Backeb. = *Mammillaria beneckei*.
D. camptotricha (Dams) Tiegel = *Mammillaria camptotricha*.
D. decipiens (Scheidw.) Tiegel = *Mammillaria decipiens*.
D. longimamma (DC.) Britt. & Rose = *Mammillaria longimamma*.
D. melaleuca (Karw.) ex Salm-Dyck) Boed. = *Mammillaria melaleuca*.
D. surculosa (Boed.) F. Buxb. = *Mammillaria surculosa*.
D. uberiformis (Zucc.) Britt. & Rose = *Mammillaria longimamma*.
D. zephyranthoides (Scheidw.) Backeb. non (A. Dietr.) Britt. & Rose. = *Mammillaria zephyranthoides*.
D. zephyranthoides (A. Dietr.) Britt. & Rose non (Scheidw.) Backeb. = *Mammillaria sphaerica*.

Dolichothrix Hilliard & Burtt. Compositae. 1 small shrub, to 50cm. Lvs to 1mm, heath-like, adpressed, margins incurved, hairy above. Cap. discoid, to 6mm diam., 1–3 at br. apices; phyllaries white, dull yellow below; flts tubular, red. S Afr. Z9.
D. ericoides (Lam.) Hilliard & B.L. Burtt. 'Goldkind' ('Golden Boy'): to 25cm; vivid gold.
→*Helichrysum*.

Doll's Eyes *Actaea alba*.
Dolly Bush *Cassinia aculeata*.

Dolomiaea DC. Compositae. 14 stemless perenn. herbs. Lvs in a basal rosette, entire to pinnatifid or pinnate. Cap. discoid, solitary or numerous and clustered in corymbs. Himal., Tibet.
D. macrocephala DC. Lvs numerous, in a basal rosette, to 50cm, oblanceolate, pinnatifid or pinnate, seg. sometimes crisped, woolly above, white-tomentose beneath. Cap. to 2.5cm diam., ± unstalked, flts mauve. Autumn. W Himal. Z7.
→*Jurinea*.

Dombeya Cav. Sterculiaceae. *c*200 decid. or everg. shrubs or small trees. Bark grey to black; branchlets usually hairy. Lvs petiolate, stipulate, usually cordate, lobed or unlobed. Fls often candy or toffee-scented, in long-stalked, dense nodding umbellate cymes; bracts usually 3, foliaceous, below cal. or on pedicels; cal. 5-lobed; pet. 5, persistent and becoming scarious. Afr. and Madag. to Masc. Is. Z10.
D. acutangula Cav. Shrub or small tree to 8m; young br. pubesc. to glabrescent. Young lvs 5–9-lobed, adult lvs 3–5-lobed or -angled, or unlobed, 6–20×5–15cm, crenate-serrate or dentate, glab. above, minutely pubesc. beneath; petioles 2–13cm. Fls in term., double-scorpioid, many-fld cymes; peduncle 4–12cm; pedicels 0.7–1.8cm; pet. 1–1.8cm, white, rarely pink. Tanz., Zanzibar, Moz., Malawi, Zam., Madag. and Masc. Is.
D. ameliae Guill. Tree to 12m, br. glab. Lvs to 17.5×17.5cm, suborbicular, lobes 3–5, triangular, long-acuminate, denticulate-crenate; petiole to 20cm, glandular-pubesc. below blade. Fls in axill., many-fld, umbellate cymes; peduncle to 25cm, simple, glab.; pedicels 2.5–3.5cm; pet. 1.5–2cm, white. Madag.
D. angulata Cav. = *D. acutangula*.
D. burgessiae Gerrard ex Harv. Shrub to 4m; young br. densely pubesc. to glabrescent. Lvs 11–22×8–18cm, simple or with lobes 3–5 acuminate, crenate or dentate, villous to pubesc.; petioles 7–12cm. Fls in many-fld, axill., corymbose, bi-umbellate or sub-umbellate cymes; bracts usually 3, foliaceous, below cal. or more; peduncles equalling petioles; pedicels to 3cm; pet. 1.5–2.5cm, white or pink, sometimes with darker veins. C & S Afr.
D. calantha Schum. = *D. burgessiae*.
D. ×cayeuxii André. Differs from *D. wallichii* in smaller infl. bracts. St. bristly-hairy. Lvs large, cordate, acute, toothed, dark green; petioles 10–15cm. Fls pink, finely veined, in axill., pendent, many-fld umbellate cymes.

D. dawei Sprague = *D. burgessiae.*

D. dregeana Sonder = *D. tiliacea.*

D. elegans Cordm. Shrub or small tree to 6m; br. glab. Lvs 5–12×5–9cm, cordate or tricuspidate, acuminate, dentate, glab.; petioles 3–10cm. Fls in umbellate cymes; peduncles 5–10cm; pedicels 2–2.5cm; pet. 1–1.4cm, rose or white. Réunion.

D. goetzenii Schum. = *D. torrida.*

D. mastersii Hook. f. = *D. burgessiae.*

D. mollis Hook. Tree to 12m; densely stellate-pubesc. Lvs to 35×25cm, broadly ovate-cordate, lobes 3, acuminate, denticulate-serrate; petioles to 13.5cm, hirsute. Fls on axill. peduncles to 20cm, 3–4-branched at the apex, each br. with many-fld umbellate cymes; pedicels 0.2–1cm, recurved. Madag.

D. nairobensis Engl. = *D. burgessiae.*

D. natalensis Sonder = *D. tiliacea.*

D. nyasica Exell = *D. burgessiae.*

D. populnea (Cav.) Bak. Small tree to 10m; adult lvs 6–12×4–7cm, unlobed, ovate-cordate, acuminate, crenulate to entire, glab., petiole 3–10cm; juvenile lvs deeply dissected or lobed. Fls in irregularly branched cymes, on peduncles 3–7cm; pet. 6mm, white or pale rose. Masc. Is.

D. serrata (Bojer) Arènes = *Trochetia triflora.*

D. spectabilis Bojer. Shrub or tree to 15m, all parts with red pubescence. Lvs to 18×13cm, unlobed, ovate to suborbicular, coriaceous, apex emarginate to rounded or truncate-mucronate, entire to dentate; petiole 1–4.5cm. Fls in paniculate axill. cymes, appearing before lvs; pedicels 0.3–1.5cm; pet. 0.7–1.3cm, white to pink. Madag.

D. tanganyikensis Bak. = *D. burgessiae.*

D. tiliacea (Endl.) Planch. Small tree to 8m; young br. puberulous to glabrescent. Lvs 7–12×2–9cm, usually shallowly 3-lobed, acute, coarsely crenate; petiole 2–6cm. Fls in axill. umbellate 2–6-fld cymes; peduncle 3–8cm; pedicels 1–2cm; pet. to 2cm, white to pale pink. S Afr.

D. tiliifolia Cav. = *D. acutangula.*

D. torrida (J.F. Gmel.) Bamps. Tree to 20m; young br. pilose-hispid to glabrescent. Lvs to 28×20cm, unlobed, acuminate, serrulate, with tufts of hairs at base of main nerves; petiole 3.5–20cm. Fls on axill., subumbellate, many-fld br.; peduncle 2.5–13cm; pedicels 1–4cm; pet. to 1.9–2.8cm, pink or white, with or without red veins. Yemen and Tanz. to Ethiop.

D. triflora (DC.) Arènes = *Trochetia triflora.*

D. viburniflora Bojer. Tree to 12m; young and flowering br. covered with dense brown indumentum. Lvs to 30×24cm, ovate to suborbicular, lobes 0–3–5, triangular, acuminate, crenulate-denticulate; petiole to 30cm, brown-hairy. Infl. axill., many-fld, branched, umbellate; peduncle to 25cm; pedicels 1.2–2cm; pet. to 1.4cm, white. Madag. and Comoros.

D. viscosa Lign. & Bey. = *D. ameliae.*

D. wallichii (Lindl.) B.D. Jackson. Shrub or small tree to 8m; br. pubesc. Lvs 16–20×15–25cm, broadly ovate to ovate-orbicular, sometimes 3-angled; base cordate, apex acuminate, dentate, pubesc. beneath; petiole 7–17cm. Fls in a simple, many-fld dense umbellate cyme; peduncle 13–16cm; pedicels 1–2cm; pet. to 2.5cm, deep pink or red. E Afr. and Madag.

D. ×wallichii (Lindl.) Benth. & Hook. f. = *D. ×cayeuxii.*
→*Astrapaea.*

Domingoa Schltr. Orchidaceae. 2 epiphytic orchids allied to *Laelia* but superficially resembling *Pleurothallis*. Winter. Cuba, Hispan., Puerto Rico. Z10.

D. hymenodes (Rchb. f.) Schltr. Pbs to 3.25cm, v. slender, cylindrical. Lf to 7cm, narrow-obovate to elliptic, thin. Infl. term. to 12.5cm, slender; fls to 2.5cm diam., fragrant; tep. broadly lanceolate, translucent, green-white, often faintly lined violet or maroon; lip obovoid, cream marked maroon.

Donax Lour. Marantaceae. 6 tuft-forming perenn. herbs. St. slender, erect, partially lignified, petioles terete, bases sheathing. Infl. pendulous, branching; bracts narrow, keeled; fls 2 or 4 per bract; sep. narrow, exceeding cor.; cor. tubular, lobulate; staminodes tubular; anth. petaloid. Indomalesia. Z10.

D. canniformis (Forst.) Schum. To 5m. St. branching. Lf blades to 20×12cm, oblong to elliptic, slightly glaucous. Infl. to 20cm; bracts lanceolate, to 3cm; cor. white; staminode yellow. Burm. to Indochina.

D. cuspidata (Roscoe) Schum. = *Marantochloa cuspidata.*

D. purpurea (Ridl.) Schum. = *Marantochloa purpurea.*
→*Thalia.*

Donia R. Br.

D. ciliata Nutt. = *Prionopsis ciliata.*

D. squarrosa Pursh = *Grindelia squarrosa.*

Donkey's Tail *Sedum morganianum.*

Doob *Cynodon dactylon.*

Doodhi *Lagenaria siceraria.*

Doodia R. Br. Blechnaceae. 11 terrestrial ferns. Rhiz. short, suberect, tufted, bearing stout, black roots. Fronds pinnate; pinnae sharply dentate. Asia; Australasia. Z9.

D. aspera R. Br. HACKSAW FERN; PRICKLY RASP-FERN. Fronds 45×5–10cm, oblong-lanceolate, pinnatifid, scabrous; pinnae 2.5–5cm, linear, strongly dentate, reduced toward apex and base of blade. Australasia.

D. blechnoides A. Cunn. = *D. maxima.*

D. caudata (Cav.) R. Br. SMALL RASP-FERN. Fronds 8–30×2–5cm, dimorphic, lanceolate, acuminate, membranous, apex often entire; sterile fronds shorter and fewer than fertile, often decumbent; pinnae oblong or oblong-linear, obtuse, serrate; fertile fronds usually erect, harsher and more rigid, pinnae narrow-linear, term. pinna long, caudate. Aus., NZ, Polyn.

D. dives Kuntze. Fronds dimorphic; sterile fronds 30×8–12cm, oblong-lanceolate, pinnae linear-oblong, obtuse, undulate, serrate, base dilated; fertile fronds longer, pinnae connected by a broad wing to rachis. Sri Lanka, Java.

D. linearis C. Moore = *D. caudata.*

D. lunulata R. Br. = *D. media.*

D. maxima J. Sm. Fronds, 38×15cm, oblong-lanceolate; pinnae numerous, becoming smaller toward base, ultimately auricle-like, erose to serrulate at apex. Aus. (NSW).

D. media R. Br. COMMON RASP-FERN. Fronds 30–45×4–10cm, lanceolate, pinnate in lower half to two-thirds, pinnatifid above, coriaceous; pinnae linear or linear-lanceolate, spinulose-dentate, term. pinna often elongated. Aus., NZ, New Caledonia.

D. rupestris Kaulf. = *D. caudata.*

Dorcapteris Presl = *Polybotrya.*

✕Doritaenopsis. (*Doritis* ×*Phalaenopsis.*) Orchidaceae. Gdn hybrids intermediate between the parents in habit with ± erect, branching spikes of small to large fls in shades of white, pink, red and mauve, often marked yellow.

Doritis Lindl. Orchidaceae. 2 epiphytic, monopodial orchids. Lvs coriaceous, fleshy, semi-rigid, 2-ranked, sheathing short st., elliptic to broad-lanceolate. Pan. or rac. lat.; tep. oblong-obovate, unequal, spreading, lat. sep. forming a spur-like projection with column base; lip trilobed, lat. lobes erect, disc with a bilobed plate or callus. Indo-Malaya. Z9.

D. pulcherrima Lindl. Lvs to 15cm. Infl. 20–60cm, erect, often branched, flowering continuously; fls to 4cm diam., deep magenta, with lip midlobe deep mauve, lat. lobes red, disc lined white.

D. taeniale (Lind.) Hook. f. = *Kingidium taeniale.*

D. wightii (Rchb. f.) Benth. & Hook. f. = *Kingidium delicosum.*
→*Phalaenopsis.*

Doronicum L. LEOPARD'S BANE. Compositae. *c*35 perenn. tuberous or rhizomatous herbs. Cap. radiate, long-stalked, solitary or in term. corymbs; ray flts yellow; disc flts yellow. Eur., SW Asia, Sib.

D. altaicum Pall. To 30cm. Lvs broadly ovate-elliptic, serrate, basal and lower cauline lvs narrowed into petiole, upper cauline lvs amplexicaul. Spring–summer. Sib. Z2.

D. austriacum Jacq. To 120cm. Basal lvs obtuse, to 13cm, lower cauline lvs ovate-oblong, panduriform, amplexicaul, upper cauline lvs entire or denticulate, pubesc. Cap. 12, 3.5–6cm across, in term. corymbs. Spring. C & S Eur. Z5.

D. calcareum Vierh. = *D. glaciale* ssp. *calcareum.*

D. carpetanum Boiss. & Reut. ex Willk. To 80cm. Basal and lower cauline lvs 4–7cm, ovate to orbicular, entire to crenate-dentate, upper cauline lvs shortly petiolate or amplexicaul. Cap. 2–3, to 5cm across. Summer. N & C Spain and Port. Z7.

D. caucasium Bieb. = *D. orientale.*

D. clusii (All.) Tausch. To 35cm. Lvs thin, villous, lacking glands on the margin, basal lvs to 4.5cm, oblong to ovate-elliptic, narrowing to petiole, entire to sinuate-dentate, cauline lvs elliptic to lanceolate, short-petioled or amplexicaul. Cap. solitary, to 7.5cm across. Summer. E Alps, Carpath., Pyren. Z6.

D. columnae Ten. To 60cm. Basal lvs to 8cm, ovate to cordate, crenate-dentate, cauline lvs ovate-lanceolate, amplexicaul. Cap. solitary, 2–6cm across; peduncles glandular-pubesc. Spring. S Eur., W Asia. Z5.

D. cordatum hort. non Lam. = *D. columnae* and *D. orientale.*

D. cordatum Lam. = *D. pardalianches.*

D. corsicum (Lois.) Poir. To 120cm, glandular-hairy above. Lvs ovate to lanceolate, glab. or lightly pubesc., sinuate-dentate, basal lvs 9–16cm, short-petioled, cauline lvs amplexicaul. Cap.

3–8, to 4.5cm across, in term. corymbs. Summer. SW Fr. to S Port. Z7.

D. falconeri Clarke. To 45cm. Lvs obovate to spathulate, to 15cm, glab., petiolate, denticulate. Cap. 1–2, to 7.5cm across. Spring. Kashmir, Tibet. Z7.

D. glaciale (Wulf.) Nyman Like *D. clusii* but to 20cm, basal lvs to 4.5cm, thick. Cap. to 4.5cm across; phyllaries not villous. Summer. Alps, Carpath. ssp. *glaciale.* Lf margin with long eglandular and short gland. hairs. Range as for genus except NE Alps. ssp. *calcareum* (Vierh.) Hegi. Lf margin without short gland. hairs. Phyllaries with long gland. hairs. Z6.

D. grandiflorum Lam. To 35cm, pubesc. Basal lvs to 9cm, pubesc., dentate or subentire, cauline lvs petiolate to amplexicaul, panduriform. Cap. solitary, to 6.5cm. S Eur., N Spain, Corsica, Albania, Alps. Z5.

D. macrophyllum Fisch. ex Hornem. To 1m. Basal lvs cordate, 18cm, dentate, petioles to 30cm, upper lvs amplexicaul, elliptic. Cap. 4–6, in term. corymbs; peduncle 6–12cm; ray flts to 2.5cm. Spring. Iran. Z8.

D. orientale Hoffm. Like *D. columnae* but 30–60cm, conspicuously tufted, st. sparsely pubesc.; basal lvs 10cm, weakly crenate; cap. 1. Cauc., Leb., SE Eur. 'Finesse': to 50cm, cap. long-stalked, ray flts slender, yellow; comes true from seed. 'Frühlingspracht': to 40cm; fls double, golden yellow. 'Gerhard': lemon yellow, centre green. 'Goldkranz': cap. large, double, deep yellow; later-blooming. 'Goldzwerg': dwarf; fls golden. 'Magnificum': to 50cm, large-fld. Z5.

D. orphanidis Boiss. = *D. austriacum.*

D. pardalianches L. GREAT LEOPARD'S BANE. To 90cm, pubesc. Basal lvs 7–12cm, ovate, denticulate, pubesc. Cap. 2–6, 3–5cm across in a term. corymb. Spring. W Eur. to SE Germ., It. 'Goldstrauss': more floriferous. Z6.

D. plantagineum L. To 80cm. Basal lvs 3–11cm elliptic, narrowing to petiole, entire or subdentate, cauline lvs ovate to lanceolate. Cap. solitary, to 5cm across; peduncles to 10cm. W Eur. to N Fr. 'Excelsum': to 60cm; fls to 10cm across. 'Strahlengold': mildew-resistant, floriferous. Z6.

D. stiriacum (Vill.) Dalla Torre = *D. clusii.*

→*Arnica* and *Aronicum.*

Doronoki *Populus maximowiczii.*

Dorotheanthus Schwantes. Aizoaceae. 6 branching succulent annuals. Lvs basal or alt., narrow or lanceolate, covered in crystal-like papillae. Fls large, long-pedicellate. S Afr.

D. bellidiformis (Burm. f.) N.E. Br. LIVINGSTONE DAISY. Lvs 2.5–7cm, obovate to spathulate, narrowed toward base, fleshy, rough, glistening-papillose. Fls 3–4cm diam.; pet. white, pale pink, red, orange or white with red tips. The Livingstone daisies of horticulture are probably hybrids between *D. bellidiformis* and *D. gramineus.*

D. gramineus (Haw.) Schwantes. Lvs 3–5cm, linear, v. papillose, fresh green. Fls 2–2.5cm diam., brilliant crimson with a darker centre. 'Albus': fls white. 'Roseus': fls pink.

→*Cleretum, Mesembryanthemum* and *Micropterum.*

Dorrigo Oak *Oreocallis pinnata.*
Dorset Heath *Erica ciliaris.*

Dorstenia L. Moraceae. 170+ everg. perenn. herbs; rhiz. slender, or tuber-like. Aerial st. slender or pachycaul, or 0. Lvs petiolate, occas. subsessile, entire, dentate, or lobed. Fls minute, embedded in the spongy surface of an expanded dish-like receptacle, peltate on a long or short stalk, its margins commonly produced as finger-like lobes. Trop. Afr. and Amer., a few spp. in India.

D. argentata Hook. = *D. turnerifolia* var. *argentata.*

D. barkeri Bur. Herb to 60cm. St. erect from creeping base, slightly fleshy. Lvs 12.5–17.5cm, obovate-elliptic to elliptic, shortly acuminate, wavy or entire, glab.; petiole to *c*1.25cm. Infl. solitary; peduncle 1.25–1.9cm, puberulous; receptacle convex or flattened, orbicular, 2.5–4.4cm diam., margin broad, and membranous, prolonged into *c*15 unequal lobes to 1.9cm. Upper Guinea. var. *barkeri.* Infl. face suborbicular to orbicular, margins usually narrower. Cameroun, Fernando Po, SE Nigeria. var. *multiradiata.* Infl. face angulate to stellate. Cameroun, Nigeria.

D. bornimiana Schweinf. Lvs and peduncles springing from depressed-globose tuber. Lvs 5–7.5cm, cordate-ovate, blunt, undulate or obtusely dentate, sometimes 3-lobed, puberulous at first; petiole 15cm+. Peduncles similar to petiole or longer; receptacle narrowly oblong, sometimes linear with narrow margin passing into linear-tapering lobes. S, C & N Afr.

D. bowmanniana Bak. To *c*15cm. St. leafy. Lvs 7.5–12.5cm, lanceolate, scarcely toothed, smooth above, white along midrib and lower half of main veins. Receptacle round, irregularly toothed, purple beneath. Braz.

D. bowmannii hort. = *D. bowmanniana.*
D. brasiliensis Lam. = *D. tubicina.*

D. contrajerva L. CONTRA HIERBA; TORN'S HERB. Rhiz. creeping. Lvs to 20cm, deeply pinnately lobed except at palmately lobed base, scabrous to puberulent; petioles to 25cm. Receptacles ± 4-angled to irregularly lobed, to 5cm diam., long-peduncled. Carib.

D. convexa De Wildeman. St. to 30cm+, ascending, pubesc. Lvs 3.75–12.5cm, obovate-elliptic, occas. subcordate, undulate or dentate, glab.; petiole 0.6–1.7cm. Infl. short-stalked in upper lf axils; receptacle to 3.75×1.6–2.3cm, elliptic-oblong, convex, lobes many, *c*2.25mm, linear, green-yellow. S Central Afr.

D. crispa Engl. = *D. foetida.*

D. cuspidata A. Rich. Tuberous herb, 10–15cm. St. unbranched, puberulous. Lvs 1.5–12cm, elliptic to oblong or subovate, occas. lanceolate to linear, crenate to dentate, or repand to subentire, puberulous; petiole to 2.5cm. Infl. solitary or paired; peduncle 0.8–7cm; receptacle 0.7–2.2cm diam., discoid to broadly turbinate, irregularly stellate to subquadrangular subcircular or triangular, lobes in 2 rows, ovate to triangular, occas. filiform. Senegal to Ethiop., S to Zam., Moz., Zimb., and Madag. var. *cuspidata.* Receptacle widely turbinate stellate with 3–14 lobes and 3–14 appendages. var. *brinkmaniana* Hijman. Receptacle discoid, subtriangular to angular or subcircular, with 3–10 appendages. N Zam.

D. foetida (Forssk.) Schweinf. Undershrub to 15cm. St. succulent, periderm flaking, lf scars prominent. Lvs 3.5–14cm, thinly fleshy oblong to narrowly lanceolate or elliptic, crenate to dentate or subentire; petiole to 2.5cm. Infl. solitary; peduncle 1–3cm; receptacle 0.5–1cm diam., disc-shaped, flowering face substellate; lobes in 2 rows, outer row 2mm, twice length of inner, filiform. Kenya, Tanz. ssp. *lancifolia* Friis. Lvs lanceolate. Kenya.

D. gigas Schweinf. To *c*1.4m; st. pachycaul, to 45cm diam. Lvs 10–15cm, oblanceolate short-petioled, clustered at br. tips. Infl. short-stemmed, with *c*7 lobes. Socotra.

D. hildebrandtii Engl. St. 15–20cm, erect, fleshy. Lvs 3–75cm, sessile, lanceolate, fleshy, shortly sinuate-dentate. Peduncle 0.6–1cm, minutely puberulous; receptacle 0.6cm diam., suborbicular, dark purple; lobes 5–7, linear-tapering, unequal with intervening triangular teeth. N Afr.

D. holtziana Engl. = *D. zanzibarica.*

D. lujae De Wildeman. St. leafy, petioles and peduncles hairy. Lvs 9.4–12.5cm, obovate or narrowly obovate, slightly undulate, ± glab., narrowing below to v. short petiole. Infl. in upper lf axils, solitary; receptacle polygonal to orbicular, 1.9cm diam., lobes many triangular, to narrow-linear to 1.6cm. S Central Afr.

D. maculata Lem. = *D. contrajerva.*

D. mannii Hook. St. 30–60cm, erect, unbranched, slightly flexuous, hirtellous. Lvs 10–20cm, broadly elliptic, acuminate above, obtuse or subcordate below, entire or sinuate-dentate, glab.; petioles 0.6–2.5cm, hirtellous. Infl. in axils of fallen lvs, solitary; peduncle 1.25–2.25cm; receptacle 1.25–2.5cm diam., suborbicular or irregularly stellate, green, back-pubesc., convex, lobes 10–15, slender, 1.25–5cm, thickened toward tip. Upper Guinea.

D. multiradiata Engl. = *D. barkeri* var. *multiradiata.*
D. phillipsiae Hook. = *D. foetida.*

D. psilurus Welw. Herb to 75cm; rhiz. creeping, fleshy with long slender roots. St. simple, erect, slightly succulent. Lvs 10–15cm, cuneate and entire, occas. obtuse or obovate-elliptic to acuminate and slightly toothed, or obovate and deeply cut toward apex; petioles to 5cm, pubesc. Infl. solitary, long-stalked; receptacle to 3.75cm, linear-lanceolate, tapering into long erect lobe, base with curling appendage. C & SC Afr., India.

D. tetractis Peter = *D. cuspidata.*

D. tubicina Ruiz & Pav. Herb *c*75cm tall. Root strongly aromatic, large, woody. Lvs cordate, oblong, dentate; petiole equals blade. Receptacle wineglass-shaped, with margin curved inwards. Trin.

D. turnerifolia Fisch. & Mey. Small. Lvs toothed, obovate, concave, rounded. Infl. lobes 0. Trop. Amer. var. *argentata.* St. erect, tinged purple, tomentose. Lvs to 12.5cm, lanceolate, silver-white, margins green. Receptacle ringed with purple tubercles. S Braz.

D. unyika Engl. & Warb. = *D. cuspidata.*
D. volkensii Engl. = *D. zanzibarica.*
D. walleri Hemsl. = *D. cuspidata.*

D. yambuyaensis De Wildeman. St. erect, 30–60cm, woody below. Lvs 7.5–15cm, obovate-elliptic to elliptic, narrowing towards subcordate base, entire or waxy, occas. toothed, glab.; petiole 4.5–13.5mm, pubesc. Infl. solitary in upper lvs axils; peduncles 2.5–3.9cm; receptacle discoid or polygonal lobes 6,

5–10cm, narrow-linear, margin pectinate. Upper & Lower Guinea, SC Afr.

D. zanzibarica Oliv. Herb to 75cm, rhizomatous, occas. tuberous. St. ascending or erect. Lvs 1–21cm, oblong to subovate, lanceolate or elliptic, crenate-dentate, occas. repand, puberulous; petiole to 3cm. Infl. frequently clustered; peduncle to 1.3cm; receptacle discoid to broadly turbinate to subtriangular, 0.5–2cm diam., lobes in 2 rows, outer row longer, triangular. Kenya, Tanz., Zanzibar.

Doryalis Warb. = *Dovyalis*.

Doryanthes Corr. SPEAR LILY. Agavaceae. 3 tall herbs. Basal lvs sword-shaped, arching, fleshy, ribbed. Scapes erect, tall, clothed with reduced lvs; fls large, in short spikes compressed into a large term. globose head or along thyrse, sometimes bearing bulblets; perianth seg. 6. E Aus. Z10.

D. excelsa Corr. GLOBE SPEAR LILY. Basal lvs to 1.2m. Scape to 6m; fls in a term. globose head to 30cm diam.; bracts coloured; perianth seg. red, to 10cm, oblong-linear. NSW.

D. guilfoylei Bail. QUEENSLAND LILY. Resembling *D. palmeri*, but lvs to 3m; perianth seg. crimson, to 10cm. N Queensld.

D. palmeri W. Hill. Basal lvs to 2m. Scape to 2.5m; fls in oblong term. thyrse to 0.5m; bracts red-flushed; perianth seg. rich red, oblong-lanceolate, to 5cm, pale or white inside below. Queensld.

Dorycnium Mill. Leguminosae (Papilionoideae). 15 perenn. herbs and subshrubs. St. usually villous, spreading, densely branched. Lvs trifoliolate, appearing 5-parted due to enlarged stipules. Fls pea-like in axill. umbels. Medit.

D. broussonetii (Choisy) Webb and Berth. Shrub to 1.5m. Lfts 2–4cm, obovate to oval. Fls white tipped pink or purple, 5–8 per infl. Canary Is. Z9.

D. germanicum (Gremli) Rikli = *D. pentaphyllum* ssp. *germanicum*.

D. herbaceum Vill. = *D. pentaphyllum* ssp. *herbaceum*.

D. hirsutum (L.) Ser. HAIRY CANARY CLOVER. Subshrub, to 50cm; st. silvery-pubesc. Lfts 0.7–2cm, oblong to obovate, grey-green, thickly white-pilose. Fls cream flushed shell pink, 4–10 per umbel. Summer–autumn. Medit., S Port. Z8.

D. jordanii Loret & Barr. = *D. pentaphyllum* ssp. *gracile*.

D. pentaphyllum Scop. Perenn. herb or shrub, 10–80cm, lfts linear to obovate-oblong. Fls white 1.5–25 per infl. C & S Eur. ssp. ***pentaphyllum***. To 50cm, pubesc. lfts 0.6–1.2cm, narrowly oblanceolate. SW Eur. ssp. ***germanicum*** (Gremli) Gams. Lfts 0.8–2cm, oblong-obovate. Eur., Balk. ssp. ***gracile*** (Jordan) Rouy. To 80cm, lfts 1–2cm. Infl. 12–20-fld. Spain, Fr. ssp. ***herbaceum*** (Vill.) Rouy. 20–65cm, pubesc. lfts 0.5–2cm, oblong-obovate. C & SE Eur. Z8.

D. rectum (L.) Ser. Perenn., pubesc. herb or shrub, 0.3–0.5m. Lfts 0.7–3.5cm, ovate to reniform or obovate to oblong-obovate. Infl. with 20–40 white or pink fls. Medit. Z8.

D. suffruticosum Vill. = *D. pentaphyllum* ssp. *pentaphyllum*.

→*Bonjeanea* and *Lotus*.

Doryopteris J. Sm. Adiantaceae. 25 small to medium tufted ferns. Rhiz. erect or creeping, covered in dark scales. Stipe slender, black, shiny. Pantrop. Z10.

D. concolor (Langsd. & Fisch.) Kuhn. Stipes 15–20cm, winged; fronds pedate, 5–15cm, irregularly lobed with prominent dark veins beneath. Pantrop.

D. ludens (Wallich ex Hook.) J. Sm. Stipes 7.5–15cm on sterile fronds, longer on fertile fronds; sterile fronds to 10cm, ovate-cordate or with five unequal lobes, broadly deltoid in outline, to 18cm, fertile fronds cut into 3–5 narrow-lanceolate lobes, all or some forked. India, Malaysia, Philipp., Indon., New Guinea, Aus.

D. nobilis (T. Moore) C. Chr. Stipes to 30cm. Mature fronds palmate-pedate with proliferous buds at the base, tips of fertile seg. with many small teeth. Braz., Arg., Colomb., Boliv. 'Variegata': marked with silver.

D. palmata (Willd.) J. Sm. = *D. pedata* var. *palmata*.

D. pedata (L.) Fée. HAND FERN. Stipes 10–30cm; fronds coarsely lobed to finely palmatifid, seg. sometimes pinnatifid. Trop. Amer. var. ***palmata*** (Willd.) Hicken. Lobes markedly palmate, fewer, broader. Mex.

D. sagittifolia (Raddi) J. Sm. Stipes 10–15cm; fronds 10–15cm, hastate-lanceolate or subtriangular, basal lobes triangular, acuminate, entire, midrib black. S Braz., Venez.

→*Cheilanthes*.

Double Coconut *Lodoicea*.
Double Common Snowdrop *Galanthus nivalis* 'Flore Pleno'
Double Tails *Diuris*.
Double Yellow Rocket *Barbarea vulgaris* 'Flore Pleno'.

Doub Palm *Borassus flabellifer*.
Douglas Fir *Pseudotsuga menziesii*.

Douglasia Lindl. Primulaceae. 6 tufted, often stoloniferous herbs, rarely suffruticose. Lvs rosulate, usually crowded into globes, often imbricate. Infl. a bracteate umbel; cor. infundibuliform or salverform. Summer. US. Z5.

D. biflora A. Nels. = *D. montana*.

D. dentata S. Wats. = *D. nivalis*.

D. laevigata A. Gray. Densely tufted. Lvs to 1cm, oblong-lanceolate or lanceolate, glab., grey-green, imbricate. Infl. 2–4-fld; cor. pink, lobes round-obovate. E US.

D. montana A. Gray. Tufted. Lvs linear to ligulate, glab. except for downy margin. Infl. 1–2-fld; cor. pink, lobes obovate. Mont., Wyom.

D. nivalis Lindl. Rather loosely tufted. Lvs to 1cm, linear-ligulate, in loose rosettes, stellate-hairy. Infl. 3–7-fld; cor. flesh-pink, lobes obovate. BC.

D. vitaliana (L.) Hook. f. = *Vitalina primuliflora*.

Douglas Mulesfoot Fern *Marattia douglasii*.
Doum Palm *Hyphaene coriacea*.
Dove Tree *Davidia*.

Dovyalis E. Mey. Flacourtiaceae. 15 shrubs or small trees, sometimes spiny. Lvs alt., simple, glossy, with a short petiole and small stipules. Fls apetalous, unisexual, inconspicuous, green. Fr. a globose-ovoid berry. Afr., India, Sri Lanka.

D. abyssinica (A. Rich.) Warb. Shrub to 3.5m, with or without spines. Lvs to 8cm, ovate. Fr. 2.5cm diam., with the colour and flavour of apricots. Ethiop. Z10.

D. caffra Warb. KEI APPLE; UMKOKOLA. Vigorous shrub or small tree, to 6m, with spines. Lvs to 6cm, oblong-ovate. Fr. to 4cm diam., bright yellow, smelling like apricots. S Afr. Z9.

D. hebecarpa Warb. KITEMBILLA; CEYLON GOOSEBERRY. To 6m, with long sharp spines. Lvs to 10cm, lanceolate to ovate, entire or slightly toothed. Fr. 2.5cm diam., maroon-purple with sweet purple pulp tasting like gooseberry. India, Sri Lanka. Z10.

Dowerin Rose *Eucalyptus pyriformis*.

Downingia Torr. Campanulaceae. 11 somewhat fleshy ann. herbs of pools and marshy places. Lvs often dimorphic, submersed lvs linear to filiform, emersed lvs lanceolate. Fls solitary, axill., sessile; cor. bilabiate, lower lip spreading or recurved, upper lip of 2 erect lobes; staminal column usually curved, exserted. W US, mostly Calif.

D. cuspidata (Greene) Greene ex Jeps. Erect to 30cm. Lvs linear to lanceolate. Cor. pale purple-blue, occas. white, lower lip with conspicuous yellow ridges at base, and a broad white area with a central yellow patch. S Calif.

D. elegans (Douglas) Torr. BLUE CALICO FLOWER. Erect simple-stemmed or divaricately branched. Lvs linear to lanceolate. Cor. blue to purple, pink or occas. white, lower lip with central white spot, yellow ridges near base, tube often with 3 purple spots at base below. Summer. Washington to Idaho, Nevada and Calif.

D. immaculata Munz & Johnst. = *D. cuspidata*.

D. pulchella (Lindl.) Torr. Erect to 40cm. Lvs oblong-elliptic to ovate, crenulate. Cor. campanulate, dark blue, lower lip with a broad white spot enclosing 2 yellow spots alternating with 3 purple spots. Summer. Calif.

D. pulchella var. ***arcana*** Jeps. = *D. cuspidata*.

Downton Elm *Ulmus* 'Pendula'.
Down-tree *Ochroma*.
Downy Birch *Betula pubescens*.
Downy Black Poplar *Populus nigra* var. *betulifolia*.
Downy Cherry *Prunus tomentosa*.
Downy Ground Cherry *Physalis pubescens*.
Downy Manzanita *Arctostaphylos tomentosa*.
Downy Oak *Quercus pubescens*.
Downy Swamp Huckleberry *Vaccinium atrococcum*.
Downy Thorn Apple *Datura innoxia*; *D. metel*.
Downy Wattle *Acacia pubescens*.
Downy Willow *Salix lapponum*.
Downy Woundwort *Stachys germanica*.
Downy Yellow Violet *Viola pubescens*.

Doxantha Miers.
D. acutistipula Miers. = *Macfadyena unguis-cati*.
D. adunca Miers. = *Macfadyena unguis-cati*.
D. capreolata Miers. = *Bignonia capreolata*.
D. dasyonyx (Blake) Blake = *Macfadyena unguis-cati*.
D. exoleta (Vell.) Miers. = *Macfadyena unguis-cati*.
D. lanuginosa Miers. = *Macfadyena unguis-cati*.

D. mexicana Miers = *Macfadyena unguis-cati*.
D. praesignis Miers = *Macfadyena unguis-cati*.
D. serrulata Miers = *Macfadyena unguis-cati*.
D. tenuicula Miers = *Macfadyena unguis-cati*.
D. unguis (L. emend. DC.) Miers = *Macfadyena unguis-cati*.

Draba L. Cruciferae. 300 ann. or perenn., cushion-forming herbs. Bases often woody. Lvs small, rosette-forming. Infl. term., simple or branched, flg st. naked or leafy; sep. 4; pet. 4, entire, sta. 6. N temp. and boreal regions, S American mts. All described below are perenn. unless stated otherwise.

D. acaulis Boiss. Cushion-forming, to 2cm. Tufts rounded, 10cm diam. Lvs 3–4mm, in rosettes, linear-obovate, soft, fine, white-stellate hairy above, ciliate. Flg st. v. short, hairy. Fls 1–3; pet. 5mm, yellow. Spring. Turk. Z7.

D. aizoides L. Tufted, 5–10cm. Lvs to 1.5mm wide, in rosettes, narrow-linear, ridged, ± incurved, bristle-tipped, sparsely ciliate. Flg st. to 10cm, glab., erect. Fls 4–18; pet. 4–6mm, yellow. C & S Eur., GB. 'Compacta': habit dense. Z4.

D. aizoon Wahlenb. = *D. lasiocarpa*.

D. alpina L. Tufted, to 20cm. Lvs in dense rosettes, elliptic-lanceolate, hairy, ciliate. Flg st. downy, to 20cm. Fls 4–10 in corymbose rac.; pet. 3.5–5mm, bright yellow. N Eur., Iceland. Z6.

D. altaica (C.A. Mey.) Bunge. Tufted to 5cm. Lvs 5–11mm, linear-lanceolate, hairy, ciliate, entire or toothed. Flg st. 2–5cm, naked or with a few broad lvs. Fls 8–15; pet. *c*2mm, white. N Asia, Himal. Z6.

D. andina Philippi non Nutt. = *Stenodraba colchaguensis*.

D. androsacea Wahlenb. = *D. lactea*.

D. arabisans Michx. Diffuse, to 45cm. Lvs to 7mm, oblanceolate-spathulate, thin, sparsely or hairy, entire or toothed. Flg st. to 45cm, simple or branched, with scattered, serrate lvs. Fls in loose rac.; pet. white. E N Amer. Z6.

D. armata Schott, Nyman & Kotschy = *D. aspera*.

D. aspera Bertol. Similar to *D. aitzoides* but lvs to only 1mm wide. S Eur. (mts). Z4.

D. aurea Vahl. To around 20cm. Lvs oblanceolate-spathulate, acute, pubesc. often red beneath. Flg st. tall, simple or branched, leafy. Fls in dense rac.; pet. yellow. Greenland, Alask. Z4.

D. bertolonii Nyman = *D. aspera*.

D. borealis DC. Loosely tufted, to 22cm. Lvs 10–30mm, narrow obovate-oblong, tapering below, densely hairy, ciliate, entire or 1–2-toothed. Flg st. 4–22cm, simple or forking, lvs ovate, toothed. Rac. dense, 8–18-fld; pet. 4–5.5mm, white, ciliate. Arc., Asia, N Amer. Z4.

D. bruniifolia Steven. Cushion- or mat-forming, to 10cm. Lvs 5mm, linear, obtuse, keeled, woolly to glab.; margin bristly. Flg st. 1–10cm, glab. Fls 8–16 in a loose corymb; pet. 5mm, bright golden yellow. Medit. ssp. *olympica* (Sibth. ex DC.) Coode & Cullen. Flowering st. hairy, 3–8-fld. Turk. Z7.

D. bryoides DC. = *D. rigida* var. *bryoides*.

D. calycosa Boiss. & Bal. = *D. cappadocica*.

D. cappadocica Boiss. & Bal. Tuft-forming, to 2cm. Lvs linear-obovate, overlapping, soft, densely covered in white hairs. Fls 5–8; pet. 4mm, yellow. Turk., Anatolia, Kurdistan. Z7.

D. cinerea Adams. Similar to *D. daurica* but densely white pubesc. throughout. Arc. Eur. Z4.

D. compacta Schott, Nyman & Kotschy. Similar to *D. lasiocarpa* but v. dwarf. Fls 5–20, pale yellow. E Carpath., N Balk. Penins. Z7.

D. cranoides Boiss. & Huet = *D. rigida*.

D. cretica Boiss. & Heldr. Similar to *D. hispanica* but v. densely tufted. Lvs oblong, obtuse. Fls 3–6; pet. 3.5–4.5mm. Crete. Z9.

D. cuspidata Bieb. Densely tufted. Lvs linear, blunt, glossy, 1cm, bristle-tipped. Flg st. pilose. Fls 5–12 in a loose rac.; pet. 6.5–8mm, yellow. Crimea. Z6.

D. daurica DC. Robust, to 25cm. Lvs to 2cm, narrow-lanceolate, acute, occas. toothed at apex, densely hairy. Flg st. flexuous, hairy near base, with (0–)4 toothed lvs. Fls 8–20 in a corymb; pet. 5mm, ivory. Arc. Eur., Scand. Z4.

D. dedeana Boiss. & Reut. To 75mm, cushion-forming. Base v. woody. Lvs in dense rosettes, wide-linear, 5mm, blunt, bristle-tipped, ciliate. Flg st. to 7.5cm, hairy. Fls 3–10, in a dense corymb; pet. 4–6mm, white, pale violet at base. Pyren. var. *mawii* Hook. f. Lvs smaller, flowering st. much shorter, fls 3–5. Z7.

D. diversifolia Boiss. = *D. bruniifolia*.

D. dubia Suter. Laxly tufted, to 20cm. Lvs narrow-obovate, in tight rosette, hairy. Flg st. with to 3 entire, hairy lvs. Fls in loose rac.; pet. 3–5mm, white. C & S Eur. Z6.

D. elegans Boiss. To 10cm; tufts small, to 4cm wide. Lvs *c*8mm in dense rosettes, oblong, blunt, entire, covered in stiff hairs. Flg st. 5–9cm, naked, downy at base. Fls 8–25 in a corymb; pet.

6–6.5mm, golden yellow. Z7.

D. falklandica Hook. = *D. magellanica*.

D. fladnizensis Wulf. Tufted, to 10cm, tufts to 5cm diam. Lvs *c*6mm, oblong, tightly packed, entire, hispid. Flg st. to 10cm, usually naked. Fls 2–12, crowded; pet. 2–4, white tinged green. Eur. and C Asia. Z5.

D. glacialis Adams. V. similar to *D. alpina* but lvs densely ciliate, pet. sulphur yellow, around 5mm. Arc. Norway and Russia. Z5.

D. grandiflora C.A. Mey. = *Parrya microcarpa*.

D. haynaldii Stur. Similar to *D. lasiocarpa* but v. dwarf, to 6cm. Lvs to 1mm wide. Fls 3–8. S Carpath. Z7.

D. hirta L. Tufted, to 40cm, tufts around 5cm across. Lvs 8–40mm, narrow-lanceolate, acute, grey-hairy, entire or sparsely toothed. Flg st. 4–27cm, elongating in fr., lvs (0)–6, oblong-ovate, toothed. Fls 4–36; pet. 4–5.5mm, white. Arc. Eur., Greenland, Sib. Z4.

D. hirta auct. non L. = *D. daurica*.

D. hispanica Boiss. Tufted, to 5cm. Lvs linear, keeled, roughly hairy above, ciliate. Flg st. to 5cm, naked, bristly. Fls 6–15 in corymbose rac.; pet. 5–9mm, yellow. Spain. Z7.

D. hispida Willd. To 20cm; tufts 1.5–4cm wide. Lvs in dense rosette, obovate, petiolate, blunt, thin, hispidulous, ciliate, 1–3-toothed. Flg st. 20cm, hairy at base. Fls in a crowded corymb; pet. 4–6mm, golden yellow. Cauc. Z5.

D. hoppeana Rchb. Similar to *D. aizoides* but v. dwarf. Fls 2–9, pale yellow. Alps. Z7.

D. incana L. Bienn. or perenn. Lvs 16–24mm, lanceolate-obtuse, hairy, withering at flowering time, occas. toothed. Flg st. lvs numerous, shorter and wider than basal lvs. Fls 10–40 in a densely-hairy rac.; pet. 4–5mm, white. Eur. var. *confusa* (Ehrh.) Lilja. Fr. downy. Z3.

D. incerta Pays. Loosely tufted, to 13cm. Lvs 12mm, oblanceolate-linear, hairy, ciliate beneath. Flg st. naked, or with 1 lf, hairy. Fls 3–14 in a loose rac.; pet. *c*5cm, yellow. W N Amer., Alask. Z4.

D. kotschyi Stur. Similar to *D. dubia* but tufts looser, lvs often toothed; st. lvs ovate. S Carpath., Austria. Z6.

D. lacaitae Boiss. Densely tufted, to 15cm. Lvs 1.5–2×8mm, broadly linear, blunt, bristly, ciliate. Fls 6–18, in dense, corymbs, becoming lax; pet. *c*4mm, white tinged yellow. Greece. Z8.

D. lactea Adams. Loosely tufted, to 11cm. Lvs 5–15mm, lanceolate-linear, stellate-hairy, entire. Flg st. 2–11cm, naked, or with 1 lf. Fls 3–10, in compact rac.; sep. dark lilac; pet. 3.5–4mm, white. Arc., Sib., Eur., Scand. Z5.

D. lapponica Willd. = *D. lactea*.

D. lasiocarpa Rochel. Densely tufted, to 20cm. Lvs to 4mm wide, broadly linear-lanceolate, acute, ciliate. Flg st. to 20cm, naked, smooth. Fls 10–15; pet. 4–4.5mm, deep yellow. Alps, Carpath., Balk. Penins. Z5.

D. loiseleurii Boiss. Similar to *D. hispanica* but lvs broad-linear, blunt. Fls 5–10. Corsica. Z9.

D. longirostra Schott, Nyman & Kotschy = *D. aspera*.

D. longisiliqua Schmalh. To 9cm, tufts to 25cm across. Lvs 3–6mm, obovate-ovate, densely grey-hairy, entire. Flg st. 3–9cm, naked, usually glab. Fls 2–14 in a loose rac.; pet. 5.5–7mm, bright yellow. Cauc. Z6.

D. magellanica Lam. Cushion-forming to 30cm. Base erect, branching. Lvs 10–30mm, in dense clusters, oblanceolate-spathulate. Flg st. 1.5–30cm, simple or sparsely branched, erect, bearing 1–5 small, sessile lvs. Fls 8–21 in rac.; pet. 4–5mm, white. Arg., Chile, Falkland Is. Z6.

D. mollissima Steven. Cushion-forming, to 8cm. Lvs 3–6mm, oblong, blunt, entire, hoary. Flg st. 2–8cm, naked, glab. or hairy below. Fls 4–14 in tight rac., elongating in fr.; pet. 4–5mm, yellow. Cauc. Z6.

D. nivalis Lilja. Tuft-forming, to 5cm. Lvs 6mm, obovate, hairy, entire or few-toothed. Flg st. to 5cm, often leafy, hairy. Fls in dense rac.; pet. *c*3mm, white. Arc. Eur. and N Amer. Z3.

D. norvegica Gunnerus. Tufted, to 20cm. Lvs oblong-lanceolate, hairy, entire or with few teeth, ciliate. Flg st. with to 3 lvs. Rac. dense, 5–15-fld, becoming lax in fr.; pet. 3mm, white. NW Eur., Greenland. Z6.

D. ochroleuca Bunge. Loosely matted, to 24cm. Lvs 5–20mm, oblanceolate-obovate, somewhat fleshy, glab., ciliate, entire or with 1–6 teeth near tip. Flg st. 2–24cm, glab., naked or with 1–2 entire or toothed lvs. Fls 3–13 in compact rac.; pet. 4.5–6.5mm, yellow-white. W Sib. Z5.

D. oligosperma Hook. Cushion-forming, matted, to 10cm. Lvs 3–11mm, linear-lanceolate to oblanceolate, overlapping, hairy, ciliate. Flg st. 1–10cm, naked, glab., occas. hairy at base. Rac. 3–15-fld; pet. 3–4.5mm, yellow. WN Amer. Z4.

D. olympica Sibth. ex DC. = *D. bruniifolia* ssp. *olympica*.

D. oxycarpa Boiss. Tufts around 2.5×4cm. Lvs 5–8mm, wide-linear or oblong-obtuse, ciliate. Flg st. hispidulous, slender. Fls 5–12 in a close corymb; pet. yellow. Leb. Z7.

D. parnassica Boiss. & Heldr. Similar to *D. hispanica* but lvs blunt. Rac. to 22-fld. Balk. Penins. Z8.

D. polytricha Ledeb. Cushion-forming, to 4cm. Lvs 5mm, oblong-spathulate, blunt, white-hairy, entire, marginal hairs to 2mm. Flg st. to 4cm, pilose. Fls 4–10 in a corymb; pet. 3.5–4mm, bright yellow. Armenia, Turk. Z7.

D. pyrenaica L. = *Petrocallis pyrenaica*.

D. reuteri Boiss. & Huet = *D. polytricha*.

D. rigida Willd. Tufts 8cm across. Lvs 3–6mm, wide-linear to oblong-elliptic, tips spreading, ciliate. Flg st. 2–10cm, smooth. Fls 5–20, in a dense corymb, becoming lax; pet. 4.5–5mm, yellow. Armenia, Turk. var. **bryoides** (DC.) Boiss. Lvs to 2mm, tips inflexed. Z7.

D. rosularis Boiss. Similar to *D. acaulis* but lvs much larger, 8–20mm. Flg st. much longer, to 10cm. Turk., Lazistan to Kurdistan. Z6.

D. rupestris R. Br. = *D. norvegica*.

D. sauteri Hoppe. Loosely tufted; st. decumbent. Lvs 5–8mm, in loose rosettes, linear-spathulate or oblong, obtuse, glossy, ciliate. Flg st. thread-like, to 3cm. Fls 3–5, in loose corymb; pet. 4–5mm, yellow. E Alps. Z6.

D. scabra C.A. Mey. Tufted, to 8cm. Lvs 6–10cm, linear-lanceolate, bristle-tipped, glab., ciliate. Flg st. 4–8cm, naked, glab. Fls 5–10 in dense rac., elongating in fr.; pet. 4–6mm, yellow. Cauc. Z6.

D. sibirica (Pall.) Thell. St. long, ± prostrate. Lvs oblong-lanceolate, acute, entire, pubesc. Flg st. erect, with few lvs at the base. Fls 8–20, in a loose corymb; pet. 4–6mm, yellow, veins brown. Sib., Greenland. Z1.

D. siliquosa Bieb. Tufted, to 18cm. Lvs 7–15mm, oblong-lanceolate, hairy, ciliate, entire or sparsely toothed. Flg st. 2–18cm, hairy-glabrous, with (0–)1–2 entire lvs. Rac. compact; pet. 2.5–3.5mm, white. Cauc. Z6.

D. subamplexicaulis C.A. Mey. Similar to *D. daurica* but tufts often only 2cm across, lf hairs long. Pet. 3–4.5mm. Sib., C Asia. Z5.

D. tomentosa Clairv. Similar to *D. dubia* but v. densely stellate-hairy throughout. C & S Eur. Z6.

D. tomentosa Hegi non Clairv. = *D. dubia*.

D. ussuriensis Pohle. Loosely tufted, to 20cm. Lvs 7–14mm, obovate-oblong, tapering to a petiole, grey-hairy, entire to toothed. Flg st. glab. or hairy at base, naked or with few lvs. Fls 7–17 in a loose rac.; pet. 4–6mm, white to yellow-white. NE Asia. Z6.

D. ventosa A. Gray. Tufted. Base of st. covered with dead petioles. Lvs 6mm, oblanceolate to suborbicular, thick. Flg st. naked. Fls 3–20 in a rac.; pet. 4.5mm, yellow. N Amer. Z5.

D. vesicaria Desv. Similar to *D. acaulis* but lvs grey-stellate hairy. Fls 3–10; pet. 6mm. Leb. Z7.

D. violacea DC. Suffruticose, to 18cm. Lvs 6mm, crowded, overlapping, obovate or elliptic, white-hairy. Flg st. to 18cm, branched, erect, hairy. Fls 4–15 in a crowded rac.; pet. 8–9mm, violet. Andes. Z7.

Dracaena Vand. ex L. Agavaceae (Dracaenaceae). Some 40 glab. herbaceous perenn. herbs, shrubs or trees; st. slender to v. stout. Lvs ensiform or broad, smooth, glossy, coriaceous, usually spirally arranged, sometimes in false whorls. Pan. term.; fls 2 or more per bract, small, short-lived, subsessile; perianth lobes 6, united into a tube; sta. 6 inserted at the top of the tube. OW, esp. W Afr. to Canary Is., 1 sp. Amer. Z9.

D. amabilis hort. = *Cordyline terminalis* 'Amabilis'.

D. americana J.D. Sm. Tree to 11m, trunk to 30cm diam. Br. few. Lvs to 40×1cm, ensiform, bright green, soft. Infl. dense, ovoid, to 30cm; fls white or creamy white. Mex. to Costa Rica.

D. arborea (Willd.) Link. TREE DRACAENA. Tree to 20m with distinct trunk, branching at top. Lvs 50–150×4–7cm, linear to ensiform with prominent midrib beneath. Infl. to 2m, pendulous, short-branched; fls creamy white or green. Spring–summer. Trop. W Afr., S to Angola.

D. australis Forst. = *Cordyline australis*.

D. baptisii hort. = *Cordyline terminalis* 'Baptisii'.

D. beuckelarii Koch = *Cordyline banksii*.

D. bicolor Hook. Shrub to 1.5m, unbranched. Upper lvs to 10×50cm, oblanceolate, cuspidate, narrowing to a petiole, lower lvs to 35×50cm, oblong-lanceolate. Infl. erect, dense; fls white tinged purple; bracts purple. W Afr.

D. cincta Bak. Trunk slender, unbranched. Lvs 38×1.5cm, linear-ensiform, margins red-brown; some plants cult. as *D. marginata* may belong here. Origin obscure. 'Tricolor': lvs striped cream and edged red.

D. concinna Kunth. Shrub to 1.8m, compact. St. purple-tinged. Lvs to 90×7.5cm, oblanceolate, dull green, margins purple-red. Some material cult. as *D. marginata* may belong here. Maur.

D. congesta anon. = *Cordyline stricta*.

D. cylindra Hook. f. = *D. bicolor*.

D. deremensis Engl. Shrub to 4.5m. Lvs to 70×5cm, linear-lanceolate, dark green, spreading, narrowed to a petiole-like base. Infl. cylindric; fls dark red outside, white within. Trop. E Afr. 'Bausei': lvs with a central white band. 'Compacta': dense; lvs corrugated. 'J.A. Truffaut': lvs broad, wide central white stripe. 'Janet Craig': upright, loose-growing; lvs dark green, edges crinkled, corrugated lengthwise. 'Lemon and Lime': lvs lime green with pale yellow central stripe and edges. 'Longii': lvs pointed, hanging, central white stripe, corrugated lengthwise. 'Roehrs Gold' ('Roehrsii'): lvs with central pale yellow stripe with paler edges. 'Souvenir de Schriever' ('Warneckii'): lvs variegated with 2 white stripes. 'Yellow Stripe': lvs green with rich yellow central stripe and edges.

D. draco (L.) L. DRAGON TREE. Tree to 10m or more. Trunk v. thick, silvery grey, ultimately branching massively in a broad, domed crown. Lvs in dense rosettes at the ends of br., to 30–60×4cm, linear-lanceolate, glaucous, base clasping br., lf scars yield dark red resin. Infl. erect, much-branched; fls white, tinged green. Canary Is.

D. elliptica Thunb. Shrub to 2m, erect with spreading br. Lvs 6–20×4–7cm, leathery, glossy, spreading, ovate to lanceolate, abruptly rounded into short petiole, green spotted yellow marked with close parallel lines. Infl. elongate; fls yellow-green. India, Indon., Malaysia. 'Maculata': lvs spotted yellow.

D. ensifolia L. = *Dianella ensifolia*.

D. fragrans (L.) Ker-Gawl. Shrubby tree to 15m or more, branching above. Lvs to 100×10cm, lanceolate, flaccid, base attenuate then flared, glossy pale green, spreading or recurving, keeled. Infl. erect-arching or pendulous, axis flexuous, fls yellow v. fragrant. Sierra Leone to Malawi. 'Lindenii': lvs with creamy white marginal stripes. 'Massangeana' (CORN PLANT): lvs recurved, striped cream to yellow in centre. 'Victoriae': lvs wide, drooping, central silver streak, edged yellow.

D. godseffiana Mast. = *D. surculosa*.

D. goldieana Bullen ex Mast. & Moore. 60cm. St. slender, erect. Lvs to 20×12cm tapering to a distinct petiole, ovate-lanceolate, dark green with silvery blotches forming broken bands, sometimes tinged pink when young, midrib tinged yellow. Infl. appearing sessile; fls white. W & C Afr.

D. gracilis hort. non Salisb., non Wallich = *D. cincta*.

D. hookeriana K. Koch. Shrub, erect to 1.8m, occas. branched. Lvs to 75×11cm, lanceolate, somewhat congested toward summits of st., semi-erect, recurved, base attenuate then flared, keeled, margins narrow and white-translucent, rarely tinged red. Fls white tinged green. SE Afr. 'Gertrude Manda': lvs thick and wide, to 10cm wide, edges translucent; robust. 'Latifolia': lvs to 9cm across. 'Variegata': lvs white striped.

D. hybrida hort. Veitch. = *Cordyline terminalis*.

D. indivisa Forst. = *Cordyline indivisa*.

D. latifolia Reg. = *D. hookeriana*.

D. marginata Lam. Plants grown under this name are often *D. cincta* or *D. concinna*.

D. marmorata Bak.. Lvs crowded, lanceolate, recurved, ridged, bright green marbled white. Infl. narrow, to 60cm, fls green-white. Spring. Malaysia.

D. phrynioides Hook. Shrub; st. to 10cm covered by overlapping lf sheaths, unbranched. Lvs to 25×9cm, ovate, acuminate, dark green spotted yellow above, paler below, narrowed to an erect petiole. Infl. capitate, often pendulous. Fls white often tinged red, sometimes abruptly tapered into long tails. Trop. W Afr.

D. reflexa (Decne.) Lam. SONG OF INDIA. Shrub or small tree, slender, branched, erect, to 5m. Lvs to 20×5cm, dark green, narrow-lanceolate to elliptic, clothing st., spreading and recurved, tapering toward petiole, convex beneath. Infl. br. long, racemose; fls green tinged outside, white within. Madag., Maur. 'Honoriae': lvs narrow, striped yellow-white. 'Song of India' has been applied specifically to a graceful form with deeply white-edged lvs.

D. rubra hort., non Noronha = *Cordyline rubra*.

D. rumphii (Hook.) Reg. = *D. hookeriana*.

D. sanderiana hort. Sander ex Mast. BELGIAN EVERGREEN. Slender shrub, branched at base, to 1.5m. Lvs 18–26×1.5–4cm, spreading, narrowly lanceolate, acuminate, glossy green with silver-white stripes, tapering to a strap-shaped clasping petiole. Cameroun. 'Borinquensis': habit stiff; lvs pale green centre, surrounded by 2 white stripes and edged deep green. 'Celes': lvs narrow, erect, edged white. 'Margaret Berkely': lvs lanceolate, to 12cm, dark green with central white band.

D. smithii Bak. = *D. fragrans*.

D. surculosa Lindl. GOLD DUST DRACAENA; SPOTTED DRACAENA. Woody shrub, 1–4m. St. slender. Lvs 2–6×5–20cm, in false whorls, usually elliptic, acute, abruptly tapered to distinct petiole, dark green, with small, white or yellow dots and blotches. Infl. to 18cm; fls white. Trop. W Afr. 'Florida Beauty': lvs leathery, heavily blotched off-white. 'Friedmanii': st. thin; lvs elliptic, paired, olive with broad off-white central splash and spotting. 'Kelleri': lvs thicker, more spotted and marbled with ivory. var. *capitata* Hepper. Infl. capitate not racemose.

D. terminalis L. = *Cordyline terminalis*.

D. thalioides hort. Makoy ex E. Morr. Low shrub. Lvs lanceolate. Infl. with short lat. spikes; fls white, flushed red, to 3cm. Trop. Afr.

D. umbraculifera Jacq. Shrub or tree to 10m, erect, unbranched. Lvs to 60–100×5cm, linear-lanceolate, sessile, in a dense umbrella-like term. rosette, base attenuate, clasping, then flared, midrib distinct, margins undulate near base. Infl. capitate; fls tinged red. Maur.

→*Aletris, Cordyline, Pleomele* and *Sanseviera*.

Dracaena Fig *Ficus pseudopalma*.

Dracocephalum L. Labiatae. 45 ann. or perenn. herbs and dwarf shrubs. Lvs opposite, entire, dentate or incised; bracts usually, leafy. Fls whorled in terminal or axill. spikes or rac.; cal. 15-veined, 2-lipped; cor. tubular, 2-lipped, widening towards throat, upper lip 2-lobed, lower 2-lobed; sta. 4, in 2 pairs, seldom exceeding cor. Summer. Chiefly Eurasia, some N Afr., N US. Z7 unless specified.

D. argunense Fisch. ex Link. Perenn., to 75cm. Lvs to 5cm, linear-lanceolate, entire. Fls blue or white, 4cm, in pubesc., leafy spikes. Closely related to *D. ruyschianum*. NE Asia.

D. austriacum L. Perenn. 25–32cm, erect. Lvs pinnatisect, seg. 20–30mm, linear-lanceolate, revolute. Fls in 2–6-fld verticillasters in dense, oblong spikes; cor. 35–40mm, funnel-shaped, blue-violet. SE Fr. to WC Ukraine. Z4.

D. botryoides Steven. Decumbent, villous everg. St. to 15cm, woody at base. Lvs to 2cm, ovate, 3–5-pinnatisect, seg. oblong, pilose above, floccose beneath. Fls 15mm, lavender-pink, pilose, whorled in dense oblong spike. Cauc. Z5.

D. bullatum Forr. ex Diels. Purple-tinted robust perenn. St. erect to 25cm, grey-pubesc. Lvs 5cm, ovate-elliptic, subglabrous. Fls in dense rac. to 9cm; cor. 3–3.5cm, abruptly pouched, blue-violet, dark purple marks on lower lip. SW China.

D. calophyllum Hand.-Mazz. Tufted perenn. to 50cm. St. loosely branched, pilose. Lvs to 4.5cm, broadly pinnatifid, 7–5 linear seg. Fls bright purple-blue in short-pilose, spike-like, 10cm rac.; cor. pilose within. SE China, SE Tibet. var. *smithianum* Keenan. Lvs with 7–11 seg.; infl. floccose. Yunnan.

D. canescens L. = *Lallemantia canescens*.

D. chamaedryoides Balb. = *Lepechinia chamaedryoides*.

D. forrestii W.W. Sm. St. to 50cm, erect, slender, simple, densely leafy. Lvs pinnatisect or 3-partite, tightly inrolled, seg. to 2cm, linear. Fls deep purple-blue, white-pilose, in spike-like rac. of 10–30, 2–4-fld verticillasters. W China. Plants in cult. under this name are usually *D. calophyllum* var. *smithianum*. Z8.

D. govanianum Wallich ex Benth. = *Nepeta govaniana*.

D. grandiflorum L. St. 15–30cm, erect. Radical lvs oblong, to 3cm wide, crenate, long-stalked; st. lvs ovate, sessile. Fls 5cm, in oblong spikes to 7.5cm; cor. intense dark blue, hooded, lower lip with darker spots. Sib. Plants in cult. under this name are usually *D. rupestre*. Z3.

D. hemsleyanum Prain ex Marq. & Airy Shaw. Tufted perenn. St. 45cm, hairy, erect, branched, leafy. Lvs to 5cm, oblong or elliptic-oblong, entire, sessile. Fls purple-blue, 3cm, in 3–7-fld whorls in loose spike to 20cm. SE Tibet.

D. heterophyllum Benth. St. decumbent or ascending. Basal lvs 12–25mm, reniform or broadly ovate, obtuse, crenate. Verticillasters few-fld in short, dense spikes; cor. 25mm, cream, pilose. C Asia.

D. ibericum Bieb. = *Lallemantia iberica*.

D. imberbe Bunge. Lax perenn. herb to 25cm. Lvs broadly cordate, deeply crenate. Fls 4cm, pale blue. Sib. Z3.

D. inderiense Less. = *Lallemantia royleana*.

D. isabellae Forr. St. 30–50cm, densely white-lanate. Lvs almost digitate, seg. 15–20mm, 5–7, entire, linear. Fls to 4cm, deep violet in 4–6-fld whorls in close spike-like rac. to 10cm. W China. Z8.

D. maierei hort. non Lév. = *D. renatii*.

D. moldavicum L. Fragrant, branching, ann. herb. St. 15–25cm, erect, glab. or sparsely hairy. Lvs to 3.5cm, oblong-lanceolate, obtuse, serrate-crenate. Verticillasters 6–10-fld; cor. 2–2.5cm, white or violet, pilose. E & EC Eur., C Asia, Sib., nat. NE US. 'Album': fls white.

D. nutans L. Rhizomatous perenn. or bienn., short-pubesc., erect to 70cm, lower lvs to 4cm, ovate, coarsely crenate, glab., upper lvs to 7cm, ovate-oblong. Fls lilac-blue in elongated leafy rac. to 15cm; cor. 1.7–2.2cm. N & E Russia. var. *alpinum* Karel. & Kir. To 30cm, compact. Z3.

D. parviflorum Nutt. Ann. or bienn. to 90cm. Lvs to 8cm, lanceolate to lanceolate-ovate, serrate. Fls in spikes; cor. pale blue to violet, 1.2–2cm. NE US to New Mex. and Ariz.

D. peltatum L. = *Lallemantia peltata*.

D. peregrinum L. Perenn. St. to 75cm, decumbent, br. ascending. Basal lvs to 4cm, 2–4-toothed, short-petiolate; upper lvs linear-lanceolate, subsessile. Fls in few-fld verticillasters, infl. to 15cm; cal. to 1.2cm, purple-red, spine-tipped; cor. to 4cm, dark blue, red or white. C Asia, Sib.

D. prattii (Lév.) Hand.-Mazz. = *Nepeta prattii*.

D. purdomii W.W. Sm. Perenn. St. to 20cm, erect. Basal lvs ovate-oblong, to 2cm wide, crenate; petioles to 4cm; upper lvs subsessile. Infl. compact, hirsute; cor. blue-violet with purple markings on lower lip, 2.5cm. NW China.

D. renatii Emberger. Low perenn., densely grey-pilose. St. to 25cm, ascending. Lvs 2.5cm, ovate-oblong, entire, short-petiolate. Fls in spikes; cor. 2cm, creamy white, tube flushed red. Moroc.

D. royleanum Benth. in Wallich = *Lallemantia royleana*.

D. rupestre Hance. Perenn. St. to 35cm. Lvs in dense clumps; petioles to 8cm; basal lvs broadly cordate, 4–5cm wide, obtuse, crenate, upper lvs ovate. Fls dark blue-violet in short, dense, hirsute spikes; cor. 3.5–5cm. W China. Z5.

D. ruyschianum L. Perenn. St. to 60cm, erect or ascending, glab. or short-pilose. Lvs 2–7cm, linear-lanceolate, entire, obtuse, glab., revolute. Verticillasters 2–6-fld in dense term. spike; cor. 2–3cm, blue to violet, rarely pink or white. C Eur. and Russia. var. *japonicum* A. Gray. To 60cm. Cor. white, midlobe with blue border and white spots. Jap. Z3.

D. ruyschianum var. *speciosum* Ledeb. = *D. argunense*.

D. tanguticum Maxim. Perenn. aromatic herb to 50cm. Lvs 5–7-pinnapartite, seg. linear. Cor. 2.5–3cm, violet-blue. SW China.

D. urticifolium Miq. = *Meehania urticifolia*.

D. veitchii Dunn = *Nepeta veitchii*.

D. wallichii Sealy. Lax perenn. herb. St. 40–60cm. Basal lvs broadly cordate, 4cm+ wide, erect, petioles to 30cm. Fls in 2–4 dense whorls, ± secund; cor. blue-violet, with dark purple spots on lip. Summer. Himal.

D. wilsonii Dunn = *Nepeta wilsonii*.

Dracontium L. Araceae. 13 massive to slender cormous herbs. Lvs solitary, rarely paired, compound, major lobes 3, lfts sessile; petiole sometimes verrucose, often marbled. Infl. emerging with or preceding lf; peduncle stout, usually shorter than petiole, mottled; spathe campanulate to hooded or erect, convolute below; spadix much shorter than spathe, strongly malodorous. Trop. Amer. Z10.

D. asperum K. Koch. Lvs to 1m across, major lobes 3, pseudo-dichotomously lobed then pinnatipartite, seg. oblong or oblong-lanceolate; petiole to 3m, verrucose, mottled with brown or purple. Peduncle 10cm; spathe to 25cm, oblong, incurved above, coriaceous, externally brown-green, dark violet within. Braz.

D. carderi Hook. f. Lvs with major lobes twice pseudo-dichotomous, seg. oblong, rachis winged; petiole to 1m, flesh-coloured spotted brown. Peduncle to 1.8m; spathe to 30cm, lanceolate, lurid green externally, red-purple within. Colomb.

D. foecundum Hook. f. Lvs to 1.6m across, major lobes pinnate, seg. lanceolate to ovate-lanceolate; petiole to 1.8m, mottled grey. Peduncle 60–100cm; spathe oblong-lanceolate, cymbiform, deep purple within. E S Amer.

D. gigas Engl. Lvs to 3m across, major lobes bipinnate, seg. obliquely ovate to ovate-oblong; petiole to 4m, spiny, glossy green, mottled brown. Peduncle to 50cm; spathe to 60cm, erect, deep violet externally, brown-red within. Nic.

D. polyphyllum L. Lvs to 80cm across, major lobes much divided, seg. obliquely oblong, acute; petiole to 1m+, purple marked green-white. Peduncle v. short, later elongating; spathe to 15cm, oblong, cuspidate, deep violet. E S Amer.

Dracophilus Schwantes. Aizoaceae. 4 cushion-forming succulents. Lvs crowded, decussate, v. fleshy, connate at base, triquetrous, often with a few marginal teeth, blue-green, rough. Fls solitary, term. Summer. S Afr., Nam. Z9.

D. dealbatus (N.E. Br.) Walg. Lvs 23–45×15×15mm, light green, flat above, rounded, margins and keel entire. Fls 2.5–3cm diam., pink, rarely white. W Cape, Nam.

D. delaetianus (Dinter) Dinter & Schwantes. Lvs 20–30×10–15×10–15mm, broadly triangular above, with 5–6 teeth, keel with 2–3 teeth, off-white or tinged blue. Fls 2–2.2cm diam., violet-pink. Nam.

D. montis-draconis (Dinter) Dinter & Schwantes. Lvs 30–50×10–15mm, obtusely triquetrous, slightly curved upwards, with 1–2 flat tubercles at tip, blue-green, minutely rough. Fls 2.5–3cm diam., white or light pink. Nam.

D. proximus (L. Bol.) Walg. Lvs 40–50×14–14mm, flat to convex above, sides, margins and keel rounded, v. smooth, blue-green. Fls 2.5cm diam., pink. W Cape, Nam.

→*Juttadinteria*.

Dracophyllum Labill. Epacridaceae. Some 48 erect or prostrate shrubs or small trees; br. with annular lf scars. Lvs *Dracaena*-like, bases imbricate or sheathing at ends of br. Fls solitary or in term. pan., rac. or spikes; cor. cylindric or campanulate, lobes 5, spreading. Aus., NZ, New Caledonia, Antarc. Z8.

D. capitatum R. Br. Small, sparsely branched shrub to 1m. Lvs 1.25–2.5cm, narrowly obovate to linear-lanceolate, finely pointed, bases concealing branchlets. Fls in dense term. pan.; cor. white, limb to 1.25cm diam. Summer. W Aus.

D. frondosum Gaertn. = *D. longifolium*.

D. gracile R. Br. Narrowly upright or semiscandent shrub, to 1m. Br. wiry. Lvs 0.7–1cm, narrow-lanceolate, pungent, recurved. Fls fragrant in ovoid heads 2–5cm long; cor. white, limb to 1.25cm diam. Summer. W Aus.

D. longifolium (Forst. & Forst. f.) R. Br. Shrub to 3m, slender, erect. Lvs to 20cm, narrow-linear, st. clasping, coriaceous, stiff, serrulate, ciliolate. Cor. white, to 0.5cm. Summer. NZ, S Aus.

D. lyallii Hook. f. = *D. longifolium*.

D. paludosum Ckn. Prostrate shrub, to 2m; br. slender, bark almost black. Lvs 2.5–3.5cm, acuminate, with sheathing bases, ciliolate. Fls solitary or in 2–4 fld spike-like rac., cor. white, to 0.5cm. Chatham Is.

D. rosmarinifolium R. Br. = *D. paludosum*.

D. secundum (Poir.) R. Br. Dwarf to small shrub, to 1.5m, spreading or erect. Lvs 5–15cm, linear-lanceolate, tapering from sheath to a narrow point, glab., serrulate. Fls in narrow-cylindric, term. rac. to 15cm; cor. white, *c*1cm. Spring. SW Aus.
→*Epacris*.

Dracopis Cass. Compositae. 1 ann. herb to 1m. Lvs to 10cm, oblong to ovate, amplexicaul, acute or acuminate, sinuate to dentate. Cap. radiate, 1 to few, terminal; receptacle columnar, lengthening to 3cm after anthesis; disc flts yellow; ray flts 1–3cm, yellow to orange-purple, reflexed. Summer. N Amer. Z8.

D. amplexicaulis (Vahl) Cass.
→*Rudbeckia*.

Dracula Luer. Orchidaceae. 60 tufted epiphytic or lithophytic orchids distinguished from *Masdevallia* by their often pendulous fls with lips divided into epichile and hypochile. The epichile may be saccate, concave, convex or flat, the hypochile hinged and mobile. C Amer., Colomb., Ecuad., Peru. Z10.

D. bella (Rchb. f.) Luer. Rac. to 20cm, basal, arching to pendulous; fls solitary, nodding; sep. to 12×2.5cm, triangular, buff or olive, spotted oxblood, with a dark, slender, tails to 14cm, bases fused to form a sepaline cup to 5×1.5cm; pet. to 8mm, ivory spotted chocolate or red; epichile to 2cm diam., reniform, concave, white, sometimes lined blood-red. Colomb.

D. chestertonii (Rchb. f.) Luer. Infl. to 20cm, pendulous, bearing fls singly in succession; sep. to 3×2cm, spreading, ovate, sulphur-green spotted and bordered with violet-blue warts, abruptly caudate, tails to 1.5cm, black, lat. sep. fused along central axis; pet. to 5mm, orange spotted black; epichile to 2cm across, broadly reniform, involute, ochre to rust-red and lined with oxblood veins. Colomb.

D. chimaera (Rchb. f.) Luer. Infl. erect, to 55cm; fls to 6; sep. to 6cm, spreading and twisting, obscurely triangular, tapering to violet tails some 18cm long, buff to olive-green, flecked and stained maroon or violet-black, coarsely hairy, warty, inner margins of lat. sep. basally fused for some 3cm; pet. to 6mm, cream marked violet; epichile to 2cm, pouch-like, cream to fleshy pink. Colomb.

D. erythrochaete (Rchb. f.) Luer. Infl. to 20cm, descending; fls produced in succession, nodding; sep. to 6cm, spreading, broadly ovate, fused to form a broad cup to 0.8cm deep, cream to grey-pink, minutely spotted maroon, white-pubesc. above, tails maroon to 4cm; pet. 3mm, pale brown-yellow with an oxblood blotch; epichile to 1cm, inrolled, somewhat inflated, white or buff. Guat., Nic., Costa Rica, Panama.

D. vampira (Luer) Luer. Infl. creeping to pendulous, to 45cm; fls to 6, produced in succession; sep. to 5cm, ovate, tapering to tails to 10cm, the laterals connate to two-thirds of interior margins, yellow to sulphur-green veined violet-black, tails black; pet. to 8mm, white flecked violet; epichile to 2cm, reniform, concave, white veined pink. Ecuad.
→*Masdevallia*.

Dracunculus Mill. DRAGON ARUM. Araceae. 3 tuberous herbaceous perennials. Lvs basal; petioles erect with overlapping mottled sheaths forming a pseudostem enveloping peduncle; blade pedately divided. Peduncle long, stout; spathe convolute at base, limb large, flat; spadix nearly equalling spathe, v. malodorous, term. appendix long. Medit., Madeira, Canary Is.

D. canariensis Kunth. Peduncle to 60cm+, spotted; spathe 25–35×5–6cm, white above, green beneath, undulate; spadix

appendix to 25cm, slender, yellow. Early summer. Madeira, Canary Is. Z9.

D. crinitus Schott = *D. muscivorus*.

D. muscivorus (L. f.) Parl. HAIRY ARUM; DRAGON'S MOUTH. Peduncle short, spotted; spathe limb to 35×30cm, broadly, ovate-lanceolate, spreading to reflexed green-white streaked purple-brown beneath, purple-red mottled dull purple-grey above with red hairs toward base and in tube; spadix to 15cm, dark green or yellow, stinking of carrion, with red-brown fil. covering appendix. Early summer. W Medit. Is. Z9.

D. vulgaris Schott. DRAGON ARUM. Peduncle to 1m, mottled; spathe to 100×20cm, broadly ovate-lanceolate, acuminate, glab., dull green beneath, dark red-purple above (occas. green, white or yellow), undulate; spadix appendix nearly equalling spathe, black-red, swollen at base, tapering above, v. malodorous. Early summer. C & E Medit. Z9.
→*Arum* and *Helicodiceros*.

Dragon Arum *Dracunculus* (*D. vulgaris*).
Dragon Bones *Euphorbia lactea*.
Dragon Flower *Huernia*.
Dragon Mouth *Horminum*.
Dragon's Claw Willow *Salix matsudana* 'Tortuosa'.
Dragon's Head *Dracocephalum*.
Dragon's Mouth *Arethusa bulbosa*; *Dracunculus muscivorus*.
Dragon Spruce *Picea asperata*.
Dragon Tree *Dracaena draco*.

Drakaea Lindl.
D. irritabilis (F. Muell.) Rchb. f. = *Arthrochilus irritabilis*.

Drakensberg Cycad *Encephalartos ghellinckii*.

Drapetes Lam. Thymelaeaceae. 4 low-growing tufted shrubs. Lvs overlapping, entire. Fls sessile, in small term. heads, each head subtended by a circle of hairs; cal. tube funnel- to bell-shaped, lobes 4, petal-like; pet. 0. S Amer., Fuegia and Falkland Is., Australasia, Borneo, New Guinea, Tasm. Z7.

D. tasmanica Hook. f. Small prostrate, tufted shrub to 30cm diam. Lvs 2.5mm, almost erect, narrow-linear, young lvs fringed with hairs near tips. Fls white, silky-hairy, in term. heads of 4–6; tube 1.5mm, lobes as long as tube; sta. longer than lobes. Tasm.

Dregea E. Mey. Asclepiadaceae. 3 *Hoya*-like climbing shrubs. Warm regions of OW.

D. sinensis Hemsl. To 3m. Lvs to 10cm, broadly ovate, cordate, grey-felted beneath. Fls fragrant, starry, 1.5cm diam., in long-stalked, downy umbels to 9cm diam., white marked pink. China. Z9.
→*Wattakaka*.

Drejerella Lindau.
D. guttata (Brandg.) Bremek. = *Justicia brandegeana*.

Drepanostachyum Keng f. Gramineae. 15 clumping bamboos. Culms tall, hollow, terete, glab.; sheaths thin, lacking auricles or bristles, blades v. small; br. bushy. Lvs almost hairless; sheaths glab., ligule long. Himal. Z8.

D. falcatum (Nees) Keng f. Culms 2–6m×1.5–2.5cm, slender, often white-powdery at first. Lvs 11–35×1–2.5cm. E Himal.

D. falconeri (Hook. ex Munro) J.J.N. Campbell ex D. McClintock. Culms 5–10m×2–3cm, thin-walled, yellow-green, with a purple-flushed ring below nodes. Lvs 7–16×0.8–2.7cm. C Himal.

D. hookerianum (Munro) Keng f. Culms rather stout, erect, to 9–12m×5cm, white-powdered when young, streaked green and yellow and, later, pink. Lvs 7–30×1–4cm. India, Sikkim, Bhutan.

→*Arundinaria*, *Chimonobambusa*, *Himalayacalamus*, *Sinarundinaria* and *Thamnocalamus*.

Drepanostemma Jum. & Perr.
D. luteum Jum. & Perr. = *Sarcostemma decorsei*.

Dressleria Dodson. Orchidaceae. 4 epiphytic or lithophytic orchids. Pbs clumped, fusiform to narrow-cylindric, clothed by sheathing lf bases. Lvs obscurely plicate, lanceolate-elliptic, acuminate, in 2 alt. ranks, emerging as a lat. fan. Infl. erect, racemose or subcapitate, lat.; fls fleshy; sep. reflexed, narrow-lanceolate; pet. reflexed, elliptic-ovate, lip entire, apical margin often swollen, rigid and involute, basally concave. C Amer. Z10.

D. dilecta (Rchb. f.) Dodson. Infl. subcapitate; fls tan to cream; lip to 2.5cm, yellow to ochre, waxy, lustrous, margins translucent. Costa Rica, Nic., Panama, Venez., Colomb., Ecuad.

D. eburnea (Rolfe) Dodson. Infl. racemose; fls pale green-yellow; lip to 4cm, lacking callus or rigid, pouched apical margin. Colomb., Ecuad.

D. suavis (Ames & Schweinf.) Dodson. Infl. racemose; fls olive-green, ochre or cream; lip to 2cm, with an erect, translucent margin around cavity and callus formed by swelling of sides of cavity. Nic., Costa Rica, Panama.

→*Catasetum*.

Drimia Willd. Liliaceae (Hyacinthaceae). 15 bulbous perenn. herbs. Lvs 1 to many, narrow-lanceolate, flattened, grass-like. Scape erect, terete; rac. many-fld elongate; perianth seg. 6, connate at base, reflexed, united into a short tube; sta. 6. S Afr. Z9.

D. apertiflora Bak. = *Ledebouria apertiflora*.

D. cooperi Bak. = *Ledebouria concolor*.

D. haworthioides Bak. Bulb 2–3cm high, lying on surface of soil, loosely covered with stalked scales giving it a diameter of 5–6cm. Lvs 6–8×1–1.5cm, usually downy and fleshy. Scape 20–40cm, glaucous; fls green or green-brown; 1–1.5cm; sta. exserted. Winter.

D. maritima (L.) Stearn = *Urginea maritima*.

D. ovalifolia Schräd. = *Ledebouria ovalifolia*.

D. undulata Jacq. = *Ledebouria undulata*.

Drimiopsis Lindl. Liliaceae (Hyacinthaceae). 7 perenn. bulbous herbs. Lvs 2–4, ovate to ovate-oblong, often spotted. Scape exceeding lvs; rac. many-fld, ebracteate, spiciform; fls small; perianth seg. shortly united into a tube, tips slightly spreading, hooded; sta. 6, anth. exserted. Trop. & S Afr.

D. kirkii Bak. Lvs to 15cm, oblong, narrowing toward base, pale green with dark blotches above. Scape to 30cm; perianth 0.6cm, white. Summer. Zanzibar. Z10.

D. maculata Lindl. & Paxt. Lvs 10cm, ovate or ovate-oblong to cordate-oblong, bright green above, blotched deep green; petioles as long as blade. Scape 20–40cm; perianth to 0.4cm, white to green white. Spring. S Afr. Z9.

Drimys Forst. & Forst. f. Winteraceae. 30 glab. everg. trees and shrubs. Lvs aromatic, alt., entire, dark green, sometimes with red petioles. Infl. term., cal. 2–3-lobed, caducous; pet. 2 or more, spreading; sta. numerous. Fr. a berry. S Amer., Malesia, Australasia. Z8.

D. aromatica (R. Br.) Muell. non Murray = *D. lanceolata*.

D. aromatica Murray non (R. Br.) Muell. = *D. winteri*.

D. axillaris Forst. & Forst. f. = *Pseudowintera axillaris*.

D. chilensis DC. = *D. winteri* var. *chilensis*.

D. colorata Raoul = *Pseudowintera colorata*.

D. lanceolata (Poir.) Baill. PEPPER TREE. Shrub or small tree to 3m, rarely taller. Branchlets dull red to purple-red. Lvs to 12.5×1–4cm, narrow-lanceolate to oblong-lanceolate, subcoriaceous. Fls in pseudoumbels; sep. to 5mm; pet. 2–8, pale brown to green-white. Fr. black. Aus.

D. winteri Forst. & Forst. f. Tree or shrub to 20m. Bark aromatic. Lvs 2.5–20×1–8cm, elliptic to oblong-lanceolate, coriaceous, glaucous to white-pruinose beneath. Fls fragrant, in pseudoumbels; sep. to 6mm, red; pet. 5–7, white to cream. Fr. glossy black. Chile, Arg. var. *andina* Reiche. Seldom exceeding 1m. Fls solitary or 2–4 per pseudoumbel; pet. 4–9. Chile, W Arg. var. *chilensis* (DC.) Gray. 3–15m. Fls 15–40 per pseudoumbel; pet. 6–14. C Chile. The variant most frequently encountered in gardens; eventually forms an erect multistemmed tree.

Drooping Brome *Bromus tectorum.*
Drooping Coneflower *Ratibida pinnata.*
Drooping Juniper *Juniperus flaccida.*
Drooping Laurel *Leucothoë fontanesiana.*
Drooping Star-of-Bethlehem *Ornithogalum nutans.*
Drop-flower *Nabalus.*
Dropseed *Sporobolus.*
Drop-tongue *Schismatoglottis.*
Dropwort *Filipendula vulgaris.*

Drosanthemum Schwantes. Aizoaceae. 90 erect or prostrate succulent perenn. shrubs. Lvs decussate, compressed, triquetrous to cylindrical, papillose. Fls term. on lateral short shoots, solitary or in threes. S Afr., Nam.

D. candens (Haw.) Schwantes. Prostrate shrub; br. rooting, with short hairs. Lvs 8–12mm, ± cylindrical, obtuse, minutely papillose. Fls 12mm diam., white. Cape.

D. expersum (N.E. Br.) Schwantes = *Delosperma expersum*.

D. floribundum (Haw.) Schwantes. Cushion-forming; br. filiform, creeping, roughly hirsute. Lvs 12–14mm, ± curved, cylindric, thickened, blunt. Fls profuse, 18mm diam., pale pink. W Cape, Nam.

D. hispidum (L.) Schwantes. Freely branching shrub to 60cm tall and over 1m across; st. erect, then drooping and rooting, with rough white hairs. Lvs 15–25mm, cylindric, obtuse, light green to red-tinged with large transparent papillae. Fls to 3cm diam., deep purple-red. W Cape, Nam.

D. kolbei hort. = *Jacobsenia kolbei*.

D. luderitzii (Engl.) Schwantes = *D. paxianum*.

D. micans (L.) Schwantes. Erect, freely branched shrub to 80cm; st. erect, slender, papillose-glossy at first, becoming rough with white spots. Lvs 12–25mm cylindric, flattened above, crystalline-papillose. Fls 12–15mm diam., purple to tinged yellow. W Cape.

D. paxianum (Schltr. & Diels) Schwantes. Dense, mat-forming shrub, 10–15cm; st. spreading, densely leafy. Lvs 10mm, cylindric to lanceolate, subacute, papillose. Fls 15mm diam., pale pink. Cape Prov.

D. pruinosum (Thunb.) Schwantes = *Delosperma pruinosum*.

D. speciosum (Haw.) Schwantes. Shrub to 60cm; st. erect, papillose becoming rough-spotted. Lvs 12–16mm, semicylindric, curved, obtuse, crystalline-papillose. Fls to 5cm diam., deep orange-red with a green centre. W Cape.

D. stokoei L. Bol. Br. dense, projecting, rough-haired. Lvs 10–20mm, channelled above, semicylindric, obtuse, papillose. Fls 17mm diam., pink. S Cape.

D. striatum (Haw.) Schwantes. Erect to 30cm; st. bristly. Lvs 20–25mm, cylindric, obtuse, green with large transparent papillae, tipped with minute bristles. Fls 2.5–3cm diam.; pet. pink with red median stripe. S Cape.

→*Mesembryanthemum*.

Drosera L. DAILY DEW; SUNDEW. Droseraceae. Some 100 mostly perenn. carnivorous herbs to 45cm. St. a rhiz. or corm, sometimes elongated scrambling, persistent or ann. Lvs alt. or whorled, frequently in basal rosettes, round to linear, often long-stalked, covered and fringed with gland-tipped, usually red hairs above, trapping and digesting insects. Fls solitary or several in simple or branched, often secund infl.; sep. and pet. usually 5, sometimes 4 or 8; sta. as many as pet. Cosmop.

D. adelae F. Muell. St. to 10cm. Lvs 10–25cm, crowded, narrow-lanceolate, light green, membranous with pronounced midrib, sparsely gland. above and on margins. Scape 25–30cm; fls 3mm diam. cream to beige or red-brown. Summer. N Aus. Z10.

D. aliciae Raym. & Hamet. Lvs in a basal rosette to 5cm across, cuneate, obtuse, dark green with brilliant red gland. hairs. Scape 45cm; fls light purple pink, 1.3cm diam. S Afr. Z9.

D. anglica Huds. GREAT SUNDEW; ENGLISH SUNDEW. St. to 5cm. Lvs 1.3cm, basal, erect, linear-oblanceolate, pale green, glands bright red; petiole 5–10cm. Scape 10–25cm; fls white, 5–7.5mm diam. Early summer. N Eurasia, N N Amer. Z5.

D. arcturi Hook. Rhiz. elongated, clothed in old lvs. Lvs to 10cm, sessile, broadly linear, upper half gland. Fls solitary; pet. white, to 1.5cm. Spring–summer. SE Aus., NZ. Z9.

D. auriculata Backh. ex Planch. To 30cm. St. erect. St. lvs peltate, auricled; basal lvs reduced or in a rosette, petiole flat, blade orbicular. Scape to 10cm; fls pink; pet. to 5mm. Summer. SE Aus., NZ. Z8.

D. binata Labill. About 50cm high. Lvs basal, erect; petiole to 35cm; blade deeply cut into 2–14 linear to filiform lobes, with long tentacles. Scape to 50cm, branched; fls many, white, occas. pink to 2cm diam. Summer. SE Aus., NZ. 'Extrema': If much divided, forming a 14–36-point pattern. 'Giant Type': lvs 2–8-lobed, to 58cm, lobed portion spanning 18cm. 'Multifida': If blade 3 or often 4 or more times divided giving a pattern of 6–36 points. 'Pink Form': fls pink. 'Small Type': lvs 4-lobed, to 30cm×2.5mm. 'T Form': lvs clumped, forked once, to 30×2.5mm. Z9.

D. brevifolia Pursh. St. v. short. Lvs to 1cm, in a dense basal rosette, held close to ground, obovate; petiole to 1cm. Scape 7.5–15cm; fls white or pink; pet. 1–1.5cm. Spring–summer. US to S Amer. Z9.

D. bulbosa Hook. Tuberous. Lvs to 2cm, in a flat basal rosette, maroon to purple-tinged, spathulate-obovate; petiole cuneate. Fls 1 or 2 on 1–10 scapes to 3cm; pet. white, 0.5–1cm. Summer. W Aus. Z9.

D. burkeana Planch. St. 2–3cm. Lvs 1–2cm, in a basal rosette, broadly spathulate or orbicular; petiole to 2.5cm. Fls pink or purple; pet. 0.5–1cm. Spring to summer. S Afr., Madag. Z9.

D. burmanii Vahl. St. 1–3cm. Lvs in a tight basal rosette; petiole flat, to 3.5cm; blade circular, to 3.5cm diam., tinted maroon, outer tentacles long. Scape 7.5–15cm; fls white, 1cm across. Spring to summer. India to Jap., S to N Aus. Z9.

D. capensis L. St. becoming woody, retaining dead foliage. Lvs 3–6cm in a loose rosette, linear-oblong to spathulate-linear; petiole to 10cm. Scape 20–30cm; fls rosy-pink, 2cm across. Summer. S Afr. Z9.

D. capillaris Poir. PINK SUNDEW. St. short. Lvs 3–6mm in a basal rosette, broadly spathulate to orbicular; petiole to 2.5cm. Scape to 40cm; fls usually pink, rarely white; pet. 0.5cm. Summer. SE US, W Indies, Mex. to N S Amer. Z9.

D. cistiflora L. St. upright, to 30cm. Lvs 5–10cm, linear. Fls 5cm diam., usually solitary, scarlet, violet or white; pet. obovate, margin ragged. Summer. S Afr. Z9.

D. cuneifolia L. St. short. Rosette 2.5cm across. Lvs in a basal rosette, cuneate, fringed with non-glandular cilia; petiole indistinct. Scape 5–25cm; pet. purple, to 1.5cm. Summer. S Afr. Z9.

D. dichotoma Banks and Sol. = *D. binata*.

D. dichrosepala Turcz. St. erect to 5cm, clothed with old lvs. Lvs 2.5mm, oblong to oval, tinged red; petiole 4–5mm. Fls 2–7 per scape, cream or white; pet. 4–5mm. Summer. SW Aus. Z9.

D. dielsiana Exell & Laundon. Lvs in compact basal rosette, sessile, to 2cm, apex rounded, tapering to base. Scape 10–20cm, fls seldom opening, pink, mauve, violet or white; pet. 7mm. S Afr. Z9.

D. erythrorrhiza Lindl. RED INK SUNDEW. Tuberous. Lvs 2–5cm, in a basal rosette, broadly spathulate; petioles short. Scape to 4cm; fls white, 2.5cm across. Summer. W Aus. Z9.

D. filiformis Raf. DEW-THREAD SUNDEW; THREAD-LEAVED SUNDEW. To 30cm. St. rhizomatous. Lvs 10–25cm, filiform, with purple, gland. hairs; petioles much shorter than blade. Scape 5–22.5cm; fls rose-pink; pet. to 1.5cm. Summer. US. var. *tracyi* Diels. Larger, lvs with green gland. hairs. Z8.

D. gigantea Lindl. Tuberous. St. slender, scrambling to 1m. Lvs 4–6mm diam., cup-shaped, peltate. Fls numerous, in rac., white, 1.5cm diam. Summer. W Aus. Z8.

D. glandulifera Lehm. COMMON SCARLET SUNDEW. Ann. to 10cm. Rosette convex. Lvs 5mm diam., transversely oval, concave; petioles to 8mm. Scapes 3–5cm; fls red with black centres; pet. 4–5mm. Summer. W Aus., S Aus. Z9.

D. hamiltonii C.R.P. Andrews. Rosette-forming; rhiz. branched, corky. Lvs to 2.5cm, cuneate, narrowing below, apex obtuse, tinged red, sparsely gland. Scape to 45cm; fls lilac-purple, to 3.5cm across. Summer. S W Aus. Z8.

D. heterophylla Lindl. Erect, to 36cm. Lvs 0.5cm, scattered, reniform, shallow-lobed, peltate, tinged red; petiole 1–5cm. Fls 1–5, white, 2cm across. Summer. W Aus. Z9.

D. 'Highland Red' = *D. slackii*.

D. hilaris Cham. & Schldl. St. erect, unbranched, decumbent, covered by withered lvs. Lvs in irregular rosette or closely imbricate, narrow-oblanceolate, to 7cm. Scape to 25cm; fls magenta to red-purple; pet. 10–15mm. S Afr. Z9.

D. huegelii Endl. Tuberous. St. erect, flexuous, to 74cm. Upper lvs 1cm diam., conical, pendent; petiole 1–1.5cm. Fls 3–10 in pan.; pet. white or pink, 12–15mm. W Aus. Z9.

D. indica L. St. to 50cm, unbranched, lax. Lvs cauline, scattered, narrow-linear, to 10cm, narrowing to short petiole. Infl. racemose, to 15cm; pet. pink, orange or white, 5–12mm. Trop. OW N to China & Jap., Australasia. Z10.

D. intermedia Hayne. LOVE NEST SUNDEW. St. to 15cm. Lvs forming a basal rosette or scattered on st., 5mm, obovate; petiole to 3cm, slender. Scape 2.5–20cm; pet. white 5mm. Early summer. N Eurasia, S N Amer., W Indies, N S Amer. Z6.

D. leucantha Shinn. = *D. brevifolia*.

D. leucoblasta Benth. St. to 15mm, erect; rosette convex. Lvs 3–5mm diam., orbicular, petiole slightly flattened, 5–7mm. Scape to 12cm; fls white, pink, crimson or orange in 4–15-fld pan.; pet. 5–10mm. Spring–summer. W Aus. Z8.

D. linearis Goldie. Lvs erect in lax basal rosette, linear, 2–5cm; petiole 3–7cm, flattened. Scape 6–13cm; fls 1–4, pet. white 6mm. Summer. NE N Amer. Z3.

D. macrantha Endl. Tuberous. Climbing st. to 130cm. Lvs in groups of 3, with petiole 3–5cm, blades orbicular, concave, to 1cm diam. Fls term.; pet. white or pink, 6–14mm. Summer. W Aus. Z8.

D. macrophylla Lindl. Tuberous. Lvs 10cm, in low rosette, spathulate to obovate, sessile. Scape to 15cm; pet. white, 8–10mm. Summer. W Aus. Z9.

D. madagascariensis DC. St. thin, somewhat decumbent, to 25cm. Lvs alt. or clustered, obovate to spathulate, 1–1.5cm; petiole erect, 3cm. Scape 20–40cm; pet. pink obovate, 8mm. Trop. & S Afr., Madag.

D. menziesii R. Br. ex DC. Tuberous. St. erect or climbing to 1m+. Lvs in groups of 3, one of the three with petiole to 4cm, others 5–8mm red to purple, blades peltate, 3mm across, concave. Fls 2.5cm diam., pink to dark red, term., sometimes solitary. Summer. W Aus. Z9.

D. miniata Diels = *D. leucoblasta*.

D. natalensis Diels. St. ascending, v. short. Lvs in basal rosette, sessile, cuneate to spathulate, to 2cm, rounded, tapering towards base. Scape to 25cm; fls 1–10, seldom opening, white pink or purple; pet. 5mm. S Afr. Z9.

D. neesii Lehm. St. erect, to 50cm. Lvs in groups of 3, one with petiole 3–5cm, others 1–1.5cm; blade reniform, peltate. Fls in pan., white, yellow, pink or red; pet. 9–12mm. Summer. SW W Aus. Z9.

D. nitidula Planch. St. v. short, erect. Lvs 10–20 in convex rosette, suborbicular, 1–2mm diam., petioles 5–7mm. Scape to 2.5cm; fls 4–7 pet. white, 3–4mm. W Aus. Z9.

D. paleacea DC. St. erect, 10–25mm. Lvs in dense, convex rosettes, suborbicular, 2–3mm diam., tapering into 5–7mm petioles. Scapes 2–4, 1.5–5cm; fls 5–12, pet. bright pink, 3–4mm. Summer. W Aus. Z9.

D. peltata Sm. St. erect, to 10–25cm, lower lvs 3mm across, rosette-forming, orbicular and peltate, st. lvs cupped, terminating in narrow lobes. Fls 5–10 per rac., pink, 1.3cm diam. Summer. India to Jap., S to Aus. var. *foliosa* (Hook. ex Planch.) Benth. Fls white. Z9.

D. petiolaris R. Br. ex DC. St. short, covered by withered lvs. Lvs many in rosette, orbicular, concave, 2–5mm diam., petiole flattened, 1.5–5cm. Scapes to 12cm; fls 10–35, pale to deep pink; pet. 7mm. N Aus., Papua New Guinea. Z9.

D. platypoda Turcz. Tuberous. St. to 50cm. Lvs to 1.5cm, in a basal rosette and alt. on st., fan-shaped, clasping st. Fls 5–10, white, to 2cm across, term. or scapose. W Aus. Z9.

D. platystigma Lehm. BLACK-EYED SUNDEW. St. erect, to 15mm. Lvs in convex rosette, suborbicular, 2–3mm diam.; petiole to 7mm. Scape solitary; 3–7, dark red-orange marked with black at base; pet. 5–8mm. W Aus. Z9.

D. prolifera C.T. White. Lvs 1.5cm in a semi-erect basal rosette, reniform petiole 5cm. Fls 2–6, pink to red, small, on trailing stoloniferous and proliferous scapes. Summer. W Aus. Z9.

D. pulchella Lehm. Rhiz. short. Lvs *c*3mm diam. in a basal rosette, held close to the ground, orbicular; petiole 6mm, winged. Scape 10–18cm; fls pink, to 8mm across. Summer. SW Aus. Z9.

D. pygmaea DC. Lvs 1.6mm diam., in a dense basal rosette, round, dish-shaped, subpeltate; petioles to 5mm, flat. Scape 2.5cm; fl. solitary, white, pet. 1.6mm across. Spring–summer. SE Aus., NZ. Z8.

D. ramellosa Lehm. Tuberous. 1 or more foliage st. Lvs to 6mm, yellow-green, fan-shaped, alt. on st. or in basal rosette; petiole to 5mm. Scape to 3cm; fls 1–4, white; pet. 5–7mm. Spring–summer. W Aus. Z9.

D. regia Stephens. GIANT SUNDEW. Rhiz. to 5cm, clothed in dead foliage, producing a rosette of lvs. Lvs to 70cm, erect, linear, widening at centre, narrowing to apex. Scape to 70cm; fls pale pink to purple, to 3.5cm across. Summer. S Afr. Z9.

D. rotundifolia L. ROUND-LEAVED SUNDEW. Ann., to 10cm. Lvs 0.5–1cm, in a basal rosette, orbicular; petiole 1cm, flat. Scape 5–30cm; fls 1–25, white to pink; pet. 6mm. Summer. Circumboreal. Z6.

D. schizandra Diels. Lvs to 13cm, in a basal rosette, membranous, cuneate, obtuse or emarginate, midrib conspicuous, gland. hairs sparse, green; petioles to 3cm. Scape to 15cm; fls 10–12, bright pink; pet. 6mm. Summer. N Aus. Z9.

D. scorpioides Planch. St. erect or ascending, 1–6cm, branched, with withered lvs. Lvs numerous, elliptic, concave, 4–6mm; petiole slender, to 15mm. Scapes to 4cm; fls many, white or pink; pet. to 6mm. W Aus. Z9.

D. slackii Cheek. St. short, erect, with withered lvs. Lvs forming basal rosette, red-tinted, broad-spathulate, 2–3.5cm; petiole broad. Scape 12–25cm, somewhat curved; fls 6–15, pink; pet. to 10×14mm. S Afr. Z9.

D. spathulata Labill. SPOON-LEAF SUNDEW. Perenn. 4.5cm high. Lvs 1–2cm, in a basal rosette, oblong-spathulate; petioles 2.5cm. Scape to 20cm; fls 1–15, white to pink; pet. 3–6mm. Summer. S Jap., E China, s to NZ. Z9.

D. stolonifera Endl. Tuberous. Lvs usually fan-shaped to reniform, in whorls of 3–4 on st. and in a basal rosette; petiole 0.5–3cm. Fls white, borne on a branching scape or at st. apex; pet. 5–10mm. Summer. W Aus. Z8.

D. sulphurea Lehm. = *D. neesii*.

D. tracyi Macfarl. = *D. filiformis* var. *tracyi*.

D. whittakeri Planch. Tuberous. Lvs forming flat rosette, spathulate, 1.5–3.5cm, sessile. Scapes to 5cm; fl. solitary, white, fragrant; pet. to 1.2cm. S Aus., Vict. Z9.

D. zonaria Planch. PAINTED SUNDEW. Tuberous. Lvs 2.5cm, forming a dense basal rosette, reniform, margins crimson; petioles 5–8mm, flat. Scape to 2cm; fls white or pale yellow, to 2.5cm across. Summer. W Aus. Z8.

DROSERACEAE Salisb. 4/85. *Aldrovanda, Dionaea, Drosera, Drosophyllum.*

Drosophyllum Link. Droseraceae. 1 carnivorous perenn. to 30cm. St. slender, woody, sometimes branched, covered by withered lvs. Lvs to 20×3cm, numerous, linear-filiform, covered by gland. hairs secreting adhesive fluid for capture and digestion of insects. Cyme corymbose, bearing 5–15 fls; pet. 18–25mm, 5, bright yellow. Spring–summer. Port., S Spain, Moroc. Z9.

D. lusitanicum (L.) Link.

Drummond Maple *Acer rubrum* var. *drummondii.*
Drummond Phlox *Phlox drummondii.*
Drummond's Dryandra *Dryandra drummondii.*
Drummond's Wattle *Acacia drummondii.*
Drumstick Primula *Primula denticulata.*
Drumsticks *Craspedia globosa.*
Drunkard's Dream *Hatiora salicornioides.*

Dryadella Luer. Orchidaceae. Some 25 dwarf epiphytes and lithophytes closely resembling *Masdevallia* and bearing usually solitary fls amid tufted, dark green linear-lanceolate lvs. C & S Amer. Z10.

D. edwallii (Cogn.) Luer. Infl. to 2cm; sep. to 1cm, triangular to ovate, caudate (tails to 1cm), spreading or forward-projecting, ochre to golden yellow, spotted or banded oxblood; pet. to 0.3cm; lip to 3mm, maroon. Braz.

D. simula (Rchb. f.) Luer. Infl. to 1cm; sep. 1.5cm, ovate-oblong, acuminate, forward-projecting, white marked purple; pet. 0.35cm, white marked maroon; lip to 0.5cm, white to maroon. C Amer., Colomb.

D. zebrina. (Porsch) Luer. Infl. to 2cm; sep. to 1cm, adnate-cupped to spreading, caudate, cream densely spotted or banded violet-black to ash-grey; pet. to 0.3cm, cream to maroon; lip to 0.5cm, grey-white. Braz.
→*Masdevallia* and *Trigonanthe.*

Dryandra R. Br. Proteaceae. *c*60 shrubs or small trees, sometimes with a lignotuber. Lvs dentate or lobed, coriaceous, often pubesc. beneath. Fls in a terminal or lat. head, subtended by a persistent involucre; perianth with a linear claw, limb concave; anth. sessile, in limb concavity. W Aus. Z9.

D. armata R. Br. Much-branched shrub, 1–2m. Lvs 5–8cm, deeply pinnatifid, narrow, rigid and flat, lobes triangular, pungent. Flowerheads yellow, term. Winter–early summer. W Aus.

D. calophylla R. Br. Low shrub with thick almost prostrate st. Lvs 30cm, erect, broad, with triangular lobes to midrib. Flowerheads term., straw-coloured. Spring–early summer. W Aus.

D. carduacea Lindl. PINGLE. Tall shrub to 4m. Lvs 6–10cm, linear-cuneate to lanceolate, lobes pungent. Flowerheads term., yellow-green, bracts scarcely exceeding fls. Winter–spring. W Aus.

D. carlinoides Meissn. PINK DRYANDRA. Erect, stout shrub, 0.5–1.0m. Lvs 2–3cm, linear to linear-lanceolate, entire or with sparse teeth. Flowerheads term., pink, cream to yellow-brown, heavily scented. Spring. W Aus.

D. cirsioides Meissn. Prostrate prickly shrub, 65cm–1.5m. Lvs deeply pinnatifid, lobes recurved, green-white beneath. Flowerheads golden-yellow, axill. enclosed by densely hairy bracts. Autumn–spring. W Aus.

D. cuneata R. Br. WEDGE-LEAVED DRYANDRA. Shrub to 2m. Lvs 4–6cm, wedge-shaped, prickly-tooothed. Flowerheads yellow, term. Autumn–spring. W Aus.

D. drummondii Meissn. DRUMMOND'S DRYANDRA. Stemless, 50–70cm high. Lvs 30cm, broad, lobes incised to midrib. Flowerheads sessile, produced at ground level. Late winter to spring. W Aus.

D. foliosissima C. Gardn. Dense shrub, 2–3m high with sort spreading br. Lvs 8–18(23)cm, linear, lobes triangular, 3mm. Flowerheads yellow, terminal, sessile. Mid–winter to spring. W Aus.

D. formosa R. Br. SHOWY DRYANDRA. Shrub, 1–2m. Lvs 10–20cm, soft, triangular-lobed, tomentose beneath. Flowerheads large, term., golden-orange. Mid–winter–early summer. W Aus.

D. fraseri R. Br. Graceful shrub, 60cm–1m, sometimes decumbent. Lvs 5–10cm, feathery, rigid, grey-blue, lobes recurved. Flowerheads small, term., yellow. Winter–spring. W Aus.

D. hewardiana Meissn. Erect shrub, 1–2m. Lvs 8–30cm, lobes triangular, not contiguous, white beneath. Flowerheads yellow, on short axill. peduncles. Spring. W Aus.

D. kippistiana Meissn. Erect, densely branched shrub to 1.3m. Lvs 3–5cm, narrow brown-white beneath, revolute. Flowerheads pale yellow, on axill. peduncles. Winter–spring. W Aus.

D. longifolia R. Br. Tall, dense shrub, 1.5m–2m. Lvs 15–30cm, narrow, lobes triangular, revolute. Flowerheads large on short axill. br., yellow with long bracts. Winter–early spring. W Aus.

D. nivea (Labill.) R. Br. COUCH HONEYPOT. Low, prostrate shrub. Lvs 10–20cm, almost erect, lobes regular, triangular, near base, falcate toward apex, revolute. Flowerheads yellow-brown, on short st. Mid–winter–spring.

D. nobilis Lindl. GOLDEN DRYANDRA. Erect, much-branched shrub, 2–4m. Lvs 15–20cm, lobes broad, dissected to midrib. Flowerheads on v. short lat. br., yellow to honey-brown; bracts densely hairy. Late winter–spring. W Aus.

D. polycephala Benth. MANY-HEADED DRYANDRA. Erect shrub to 3m with slender, glab. br. Lvs 5–15cm, spreading or recurved, lobes short. Flowerheads yellow, numerous, small, terminating lat. br. Mid–winter to early summer. W Aus.

D. praemorsa Meissn. CUT-LEAF DRYANDRA. Shrub to 3.5m with erect br. Lvs 4–7cm, oak-like, oblong-cuneate, truncate, undulate, white beneath. Flowerheads terminal, golden-yellow. Winter–spring. W Aus.

D. proteoides Lindl. KING DRYANDRA. Shrub, 1–2m. Lvs 10–20cm with triangular lobes, almost concealing fls. Flowerheads large, yellow, bracts prominent orange to black, 2–8cm, glab. Mid–winter to spring. W Aus.

D. pteridifolia R. Br. TANGLED HONEYPOT. Tufted shrub with densely hairy short, thick st. Lvs 30cm, pinnately divided, seg. 2–5cm, revolute, white-hairy, reticulate. Flowerheads large, term., buried in lvs, yellow-cream; bracts with rusty-red hairs. Spring–early summer. W Aus.

D. quercifolia Meissn. OAK LEAVED DRYANDRA. Shrub, 1–2m. Lvs 7–10cm, oblong-cuneate to oblong-obovate, flat, undulate, prickly toothed. Flowerheads large, term., yellow bracts equalling fls. Early winter–late spring. W Aus.

D. sessilis (Knight) Domin. PARROT BUSH. Bushy, prickly shrub, 1–3m. Lvs 4–6cm, obovate to cuneate, sessile, sometimes green-blue. Flowerheads yellow, term.; bracts short. Mid-winter–late spring. W Aus.

D. speciosa Meissn. SHAGGY DRYANDRA. Shrub, 30cm–1.5m. Lvs 8–13cm, narrow linear, entire, revolute. Flowerheads red-brown to yellow, on short lat. br.; bracts, grey-brown, feather-like, to 5cm. Winter–spring. W Aus.

D. stuposa Lindl. Tall shrub to 3.5m. Lvs 5–15cm, lobes acute, not pungent. Flowerheads large, 7cm diam., yellow; bracts villous. Mid-winter–mid-spring. W Aus.

Dryandra-leaved Banksia *Banksia dryandroides.*

Dryas L. MOUNTAIN AVENS. Rosaceae. 3 everg., procumbent shrublets. Lvs simple, coriaceous, rugose above, usually white-tomentose beneath. Fls solitary on long peduncles; cal. 7–10-lobed; pet. 7–10, spreading; sta. numerous. Summer. Arctic-alpine regions.

D. alaskensis Pors. = *D. octopetala* ssp. *alaskensis.*

D. chamaedrifolia S.F. Gray = *D. octopetala.*

D. drummondii Richardson. Lvs to 4cm, elliptic to obovate, light green above, dull, white-tomentose beneath, rounded, coarse-crenate. Fls on stalks to 20cm; cal. black-glandular-pubesc.; pet. yellow, to 1.3cm. Summer. N Amer. var. *tomentosa* (Farr) Williams. Lvs grey-tomentose throughout. Z3.

D. hookeriana Juz. = *D. octopetala* ssp. *hookeriana.*

D. integrifolia Vahl. Lvs to 2.5cm, lanceolate to elliptic, acute, v. glossy above, tomentose beneath, toothed only at base. Fls white, to 2.5cm diam.; pedicels to 10cm. Labrador, Greenland. Z2.

D. lanata Stein ex Correv. = *D. octopetala* var. *argentea.*

D. octopetala L. MOUNTAIN AVENS. Lvs to 4cm, oblong to ovate, crenate, dull green and glab. above, densely white-tomentose beneath. Fls erect, pedicel to 20cm; cal. black-pubesc.; pet. white, to 1.5cm. N hemis. 'Minor': dwarf form. var. *argentea* Blytt. Lvs tomentose throughout. E Alps. ssp. *alaskensis* (Pors.) Hult. Lvs large, strongly ribbed, with several deeply incised beneath, often subglabrous beneath. Alask. ssp. *hookeriana* (Juz.) Hult. Lvs broadest at middle, tapering toward apex, shallow-toothed. BC to Colorado. Z2.

D. pentapetala L. = *Geum pentapetalum.*

D. ×suendermannii Kellerer ex Sünderm. (*D. octopetala* ×*D. drummondii.*) Vigorous. Fls nodding, white (ivory in bud).

D. tenella Pursh = *D. integrifolia.*

D. tomentosa Farr = *D. drummondii* var. *tomentosa.*

D. vestita hort. = *D. octopetala* var. *argentea.*

Dryepondt Fig *Ficus dryepondtiana.*
Dryland Berry *Vaccinium pallidum.*
Dryland Blueberry *Vaccinium vaccillans.*

Drymoglossum Presl. Polypodiaceae. 6 epiphytic ferns. Rhiz. long-creeping, wiry. Fronds sessile and jointed to rhiz., or short-stipitate, dimorphous, simple, fleshy and lustrous; sterile fronds generally wider and shorter than constricted fertile fronds. Madag. to Trop. Asia, New Guinea. Z10.

D. carnosum (Presl) Hook. = *Lemmaphyllum carnosum.*

D. carnosum var. *minor* (Presl) Hook. = *Lemmaphyllum microphyllum.*

D. microphyllum (Presl) C. Chr. = *Lemmaphyllum microphyllum*.

D. niphoboloides (Luerssen) Bak. Stipes to 2cm. Sterile fronds to 10×1cm, ovate to elliptic-oblong, obtuse, briefly stellate-pubesc., fertile fronds to 10×0.5cm, linear. Madag.

D. piloselloides (L.) Presl. Stipes to 1cm. Sterile fronds to 6×2cm, suborbicular or ovate to elliptic, obtuse, sparsely stellate-hairy, fertile fronds to 12×0.8cm, oblong to linear. India to New Guinea.

→*Microgramma* and *Taenitis*.

Drymonia Mart. Gesneriaceae. Some 30 scrambling shrubs or lianes, often epiphytic. Lvs in opposite pairs. Fls axill., solitary or in clusters; sep. 5, often coloured; cor. usually yellow-white, funnel-shaped, spurred at base, lobes 5, obtuse, upper 3 lobes larger than lower 2. Trop. Amer. Z10.

D. macrophylla (Ørst.) H.E. Moore. Lvs to 30cm, elliptic. Cor. to 3cm, pale yellow, marked with 2 purple-red stripes inside. Costa Rica, Guat.

D. mollis Ørst. Lvs to 12.5cm, oblong, pubesc. Cor. pale yellow, lobes fimbriate. Costa Rica.

D. parviflora Hanst. Lvs to 30cm, elliptic to obovate, denticulate. Cal. marked red; cor. to 3cm, yellow, puberulent. Costa Rica.

D. serrulata (Jacq.) Mart. Lvs to 15cm, oblong, tapered at base, shallowly dentate, pubesc. Cor. to 6.3cm, white, red- or purple-striate, pubesc., lower lip fimbriate. Mex. to Braz.

D. spectabilis (HBK) Mart. = *D. serrulata*.

D. stenophylla (J.D. Sm.) H.E. Moore. Lvs in v. unequal pairs, the smaller often reduced to a stipule, the larger to 25cm, elliptic to linear, glab. Cor. to 2.5cm, cream, throat pink, lobes fimbriate. Costa Rica.

D. strigosa (Ørst.) Wiehler. Lvs to 22.5cm, broadly oblong-elliptic to rhombic, acuminate, slightly toothed, sparsely hairy. Cal. red, sparsely hairy, toothed; cor. inflated toward base, S-shaped in upper part, to 3cm. S Mex.

Drymophloeus Zipp. Palmae. 15 palms. St. erect, solitary, smooth, with remote annular scars. Crownshaft clothed with rusty scales. Crown sparse; lvs pinnate, arching; petiole channelled above, convex beneath, scaly and tomentose; pinnae alt. to opposite, single-fold, cuneate or broadly lanceolate, term. pair sometimes fused, apex emarginate or praemorse. Moluccas to Solomon Is. Z10.

D. beguinii (Burret) H.E. Moore. Lvs to 4.5m. Lvs to 1.8m; pinnae 11–13 per side, to 40×15cm, apical pair united in a cleft fan. Moluccas.

D. oliviformis (Giseke) Mart. To 6m. Lvs to 2.4m; pinnae 10–11 per side, to 45×19cm, apical pair united in a cleft fan. Moluccas.

Drymotaenium Mak. Polypodiaceae. 1 epiphytic fern. Rhiz. short-creeping with dark scales. Fronds to 45×4mm, simple, narrowly linear, stipitate, revolute, glab. and leathery. China, Taiwan, Jap. Z8.

D. miyoshianum Mak.
→*Taenitis*.

Drynaria (Bory) J. Sm. Polypodiaceae. *c*20 large or giant ferns. Rhiz. long-creeping, much branched, stout and woody, scaly. Fronds dimorphic; sterile fronds ('nest leaves') erect or inclined towards support, short, broad, lobed, sessile, becoming brown and papery, collecting debris; fertile fronds erect, pinnate or pinnately lobed, green, on long stipes. Afr., Asia, China, India, Himal., Aus. Z10.

D. fortunei (Kunze) J. Sm. Sterile fronds 5–8×3–5cm, ovate, deeply dentate, brown; fertile fronds 25–40cm, deeply pinnatifid, bright green, coriaceous. China.

D. fortunei Moore = *Microsorum fortunei*.

D. mollis Bedd. Sterile fronds ovate, cut three-quarters of way to rachis into obtuse lobes, glab.; fertile fronds 22–42×4–12cm, lanceolate, cut to rachis into lanceolate seg., finely pubesc. Himal., China.

D. propinqua (Wallich) J. Sm. Sterile fronds 10–15×8–12cm, cut to three quarters into entire, acute lobes, subcoriaceous; fertile fronds, 30–50×8–12cm, cut almost to rachis, glab., lobes obscurely serrate. S China, N India, SE Asia.

D. quercifolia (L.) J. Sm. Sterile fronds to 40×30cm, narrowed from base, obtusely lobed in distal part; fertile fronds, to 100×30cm, long-stipitate, cut almost to rachis, lobes entire. S China, Asia, Aus., Fiji.

D. rigidula (Sw.) Bedd. BASKET FERN. Sterile fronds cut half way to rachis into obtuse lobes, to 36×8cm; fertile fronds to 1.5×0.5m, irregular, pinnate, long-stipitate, pinnae irregularly dentate. Asia, Aus., Polyn.

D. scandens (Forst. f.) Fée = *Microsorum scandens*.

D. sparsisora (Desv.) Moore. Sterile fronds to 25cm, generally broadest toward middle, fertile fronds to 70cm, lobes acute, stiff. Sri Lanka, Malaysia, Trop. Aus., Fiji.
→*Polypodium*.

Drynariopsis (Copel.) Ching. Polypodiaceae. 1 large epiphytic or lithophytic fern. Rhiz. stout, long-creeping, densely scaly with woolly rust-red roots. Fronds to 2.5×0.8m, sessile, erect, lanceolate, deeply pinnatifid, scarious, glab. and coriaceous with a stout midrib, base winged, clasping, seg. oblong-acute, undulate. Malaysia to New Guinea, Philipp. Z10.

D. heraclea (Kunze) Ching.
→*Aglaomorpha*.

DRYOPTERIDACEAE Ching. 50 genera. *Arachniodes, Coveniella, Ctenitis, Cyclodium, Cyclopeltis, Cyrtomium, Diacalpe, Dictyoxiphium, Didymochlaena, Dryopteris, Fadyenia, Hemigramma, Hypoderris, Lastreopsis, Olfersia, Peranema, Phanerophlebia, Polybotrya, Polystichum, Psomiocarpa, Quercifilix* and *Tectaria*.

Dryopteris Adans. WOOD-FERN; BUCKLER FERN; SHIELD FERN; MALE FERN. Dryopteridaceae. 150+ terrestrial ferns. Rhiz. short-creeping to erect, woody, generally stout, covered by old stipe bases; stipes stout, scaly. Fronds erect to spreading, 1–3-pinnate. Cosmop.

D. acuminata Houtt. = *Christella acuminata*.

D. adiantiformis (Forst. f.) Kuntze = *Rumohra adiantiformis*.

D. aemula (Ait.) Kuntze. Rhiz. erect or ascending, scales pale brown. Stipes matt, dark purple-brown at base. Blade 15–80cm; triangular-ovate, bright green, fragrant, pinnules triangular-ovate to oblong, seg. pinnatifid, margins upturned. W Eur. Z5.

D. affinis (Lowe) Fraser-Jenkins. GOLDEN SHIELD FERN. Rhiz. erect, covered with golden scales. Stipes with orange-brown scales. Blade 30–125×15–30cm, elliptic to narrowly elliptic, pinnae darkened at junction with rachis, pinnules oblong, lobed, dentate or toothed above. Eur., Asia. 'Crispa': dwarf, 20cm; a crisped, congested form. 'Crispa Barnes': 70–80cm; robustly crisped. 'Congesta Cristata': 15–25cm; congested and crested. 'Cristata' ('The King'): 100cm; pinnae and frond crested. 'Cristata Angustata': 80cm; pinnae short, hence a narrow form of 'Cristata'. 'Polydactyla Mapplebeck': a robust crested form 100cm, with wide polydactylous crests, really a grandiceps form. 'Pinderi': 70cm; a simple narrow form. 'Polydactyla Dadds': 80cm; somewhat flattened term. crests, resembles 'Polydactyla Mapplebeck' but less robust. 'Revolvens': 60cm; pinnae curved backwards giving frond a subtubular appearance. Z6.

D. africana (Desv.) C. Chr. = *Stegnogramma pozoi*.

D. amabilis (Bl.) Kuntze = *Arachniodes amabilis*.

D. amurensis Christ. Rhiz. short-creeping, scales pale brown. Stipes 20–50cm, stramineous, often darker brown toward base, scales as on rhiz. Blade 15–20cm, deltoid, pinnae to 5–8 pairs, narrowly deltoid, broader on posterior side, acuminate, stalked, pinnules ovate-oblong, pinnatipartite, softly bristle-toothed. Jap., NE Asia. Z6.

D. angustifolia (Willd.) Urban = *Meniscium angustifolium*.

D. arguta (Kaulf.) Watt. Rhiz. stout, short-creeping, scales bright chestnut brown. Stipes 10–25cm, scales as on rhiz. Blade 25–65×10–30cm, deltoid-lanceolate to oblong, pinnae oblong-lanceolate, long-acuminate, pinnules oblong, obtuse, biserrate to incised-pinnate. Pacific US. Z7.

D. atrata (Wallich ex Kunze) Ching. Rhiz. short, stout, scales brown-black to black tinged purple. Stipes 20–45cm, pale brown. Blade 40–60×15–25cm, oblanceolate to oblong-lanceolate, long-acuminate, pinnae to 20–30 pairs, broadly linear, broadly mucronate. NE Asia. Z7.

D. atrata hort. non (Wallich ex Kunze) Ching = *D. cycadina*.

D. austriaca hort. = *D. dilatata*.

D. austriaca var. *intermedia* (Muhlenb.) Morton = *D. intermedia*.

D. baileyi Maid. & Betche = *Lastreopsis munita*.

D. ×bootii (Tuckerm.) Underw. *D. intermedia* ×*D. cristata*. Similar to *D. intermedia* but with blades narrower and more entire, seg. less strongly spinulose. Z4.

D. campyloptera Clarkson. Stipes 10–35cm, scales beige to pale ferruginous. Blades 15–60cm, ovate-lanceolate, acute to acuminate at apex, pinnate; pinnule lobes and seg, finely minutely spinose. NE Amer. Z3.

D. carthusiana (Vill.) H.P. Fuchs. Rhiz. procumbent or creeping, scales pale brown; stipes 5–30cm, scales as on rhiz. Blades 6–30cm, stiffly erect, lanceolate or ovate-lanceolate, pale green to light lime-green, glandular-pubesc. beneath; pinnae 15–25 per side, triangular-ovate, pinnules pinnate or pinnatifid. Eur. Z5.

D. caucasica (A. Br.) Fraser-Jenkins. Rhiz. erect to procumbent, scales brown. Stipes pale, sparsely clothed in scales. Blade

50–80×25–10cm, ovate-lanceolate to elliptic; pinnae lanceolate or elliptic with attenuated apex, pinnules narrowly lanceolate, acute, deeply lobed to entire, toothed. Turk., Cauc., Iran. Z7.

D. celsa (W. Palmer) Small. LOG FERN. Stipes 30–50cm, scales pale with rusty central stipe. Blades 35–60cm, oblong, pinnate to pinnatifid, acuminate, seg. few, subentire to distantly serrate or serrately lobed, slightly minutely spinose. E US. Z5.

D. championii (Benth.) C. Chr. ex Ching. Rhiz. short, scales brown. Stipes 20–50cm, densely scaly. Blades 30–50×20–30cm, oblong-ovate to ovate, caudate-acuminate, pinnae in 10–13 pairs, deltoid-lanceolate, acuminate, broadest at base, shortly petiolate, pinnules oblong-ovate to ovate, shortly auriculate at base, dentate. Jap., S Korea, China. Z7.

D. chinensis (Bak.) Koidz. Rhiz. creeping, short, scales brown; stipes 15–30cm, slender, pale green to brown, scales as on rhiz. Blades 15–25×10–22cm, broadly ovate, 5-angled, pinnae in 5–6 pairs; deltoid-ovate, acuminate, herbaceous, stipitate, pinnules ovate-oblong, pinnately lobed to -parted, oblong, dentate. Jap., China, Korea. Z7.

D. clintoniana (D.C. Eaton) Dowell. Perhaps a fertile hybrid of D. cristata × D. goldiana. Rhiz. short-creeping, thick, scales dark and glossy; stipes to 35cm, scales as on rhiz. Blades to 95×20cm, lanceolate, acuminate, pinnae to 10–15 pairs, oblong-lanceolate, acuminate, shortly stipitate, seg. oblong, united by a narrow wing, spiny-serrate. NE Amer. Z4.

D. × complexa (D. filix-mas × D. affinis.) 'Grandiceps Askew': 30–40cm; small grandiceps form. 'Ramosissima Wright': 50cm; rachis branched with terminals crested; only reproduced by division; can revert to coarse form. 'Stableri': 70cm; tall, narrow, uncrested form.

D. crassirhizoma Nak. Rhiz. short, stout, scales lustrous brown. Stipes 10–25cm, stout, stramineous. Blades 40–100×15–25cm, oblanceolate, tapered to base, with hair-like scales, pinnae numerous, linear-lanceolate, pinnules narrowly oblong, rounded, crenate. NE Asia. Z6.

D. cristata (L.) Gray. CRESTED WOOD FERN. Rhiz. short-creeping, scales dull brown. Stipes 15–35cm, scales as on rhiz. Blades 20–50×7–15cm, narrowly lanceolate, acuminate, pinnae in 10–20 pairs, lanceolate, seg. ovate-oblong, united by a narrow wing, obtuse, incurved-serrate or biserrate; fertile fronds erect, decid. N Amer., Eur. Z4.

D. cycadina (Franch. & Savat.) C. Chr. Rhiz. erect, thick. Stipes 30cm+, densely paleate. Blades 60–90×20–40cm, pinnae 10–20×2cm, obtusely lobed, lobes 6–12mm. China, Jap., Malaya. Z6.

D. cystolepidota (Miq.) C. Chr. = D. erythrosora.

D. decomposita (R. Br.) Kuntze = Lastreopsis decomposita.

D. decursive-pinnata (Van Hall) Kuntze = Phegopteris decursive-pinnata.

D. dentata (Forssk.) C. Chr. = Christella dentata.

D. dickinsii (Franch. & Savat.) C. Chr. Rhiz. ascending to erect, scales with dark brown band, membranous. Stipes 10–25cm, slender, stramineous. Blades 40–70×12–20cm, lanceolate to oblanceolate, acuminate, pinnae in 2–30 pairs, linear-lanceolate, truncate to v. broadly cuneate at base, dentate and lobulate, short spine at base of veins above, lowermost pinnae deltoid-lanceolate, deflexed. China, Jap. Z7.

D. dilatata (Hoffm.) A. Gray. BROAD BUCKLER FERN. Rhiz. erect or ascending, scales pale brown, darker in centre. Stipes half to equal length of lamina. Blades 7–100×4–10cm, triangular-ovate, dark green, sparsely gland. beneath, pinnae 15–25 each side, triangular-ovate, stipitate, pinnules ovate to oblong, dentate or pinnately lobed. Eur. except extreme S, E to C Russia. 'Crispa Whiteside': 40cm; fronds uniformly crisped. 'Grandiceps': 50cm; fronds with heavy term. crests. 'Lepidota Cristata': 40–50cm; pinnules narrow, frond crested, small red-gold scales scattered over frond. 'Standishii': 40cm; pinnules narrowed, uncrested, rare. Z5.

D. effusa (Sw.) Urban = Lastreopsis effusa.

D. erythrosora (Eaton) Kuntze. JAPANESE SHIELD FERN; COPPER SHIELD FERN. Rhiz. ascending, stout, scales, brown to black. Stipes 30–60cm, red-brown, scales as on rhiz. Fronds 30–70×15–35cm, broadly ovate to oblong, acuminate, pinnae in 8–12 pairs, acuminate, pinnules narrowly oblong to linear-lanceolate, dentate or pinnately lobed. E Asia. Z8.

D. erythrosora var. cavalierei Rosenst. = D. championii.

D. erythrosora var. purpurascens H. Itô = D. purpurella.

D. expansa (Presl) Fraser-Jenkins & Jermy. Rhiz. ± erect. Stipes 10–40cm, scales beige often with darker central line. Blades 20–60×15–30cm, lanceolate to triangular-ovate, 3 2-pinnate-pinnatifid, acuminate at both ends, seg. and lobes minutely spinose. N temp. regions. Z3.

D. filix-mas (L.) Schott. MALE FERN. Rhiz. erect, thick, scales brown. Stipes 6–25cm, scales as on rhiz. Blades 30–90×30cm, decid., lanceolate acuminate, pinnae in 20–30 pairs, oblong-lanceolate, sharply acuminate, seg. oblong, obtuse, those above

base decurrent, serrate or slightly biserrate. N Amer., Greenland, Eurasia. 'Barnesii': 100cm, tall narrow form. 'Bollandiae': 60–80cm; plumose form, somewhat depauperate. 'Crispa': 50cm; frond crisped. 'Crispa Cristata': 30–50cm; frond crisped and crested. 'Cristata Jackson': 60cm; tall crested form, all crests large. 'Cristata Martindale': 60cm; tall crested form, all crests small, pinnae all curve towards apex of frond, distinctive. 'Decomposita': 60–80cm; large foliose form almost bipinnate. 'Depauperata Padley': 20–40cm; pinnae become confluent toward tip of frond, dark green. 'Grandiceps Willis': 50–70cm; large ramose term. crests, pinnae narrow with small crests. 'Linearis': 60–70cm; all pinnae narrowed with a crisped hard texture, often with polydactylous cresting to frond and pinnae. 'Lux-lunea': 50cm; a crested form with variegated foliage. Z2.

D. filix-mas var. setosa Christ = D. crassirhizoma.

D. floridana Kunze = D. ludoviciana.

D. fragrans (L.) Schott. Rhiz. short, clothed in withered fronds. Stipes 2–8cm, stramineous, darker below. Blades 8–20×2.5–4cm, scented, broadly lanceolate to oblanceolate, acuminate at both ends, scaly on veins beneath, pinnae lanceolate, obtuse, firmly herbaceous, pinnules elliptic to oblong, crenate-dentate. N Eurasia, N Amer. Z3.

D. fuscipes C. Chr. Rhiz. ascending, short, scales brown. Stipes 20–40cm, stramineous or tinged brown, densely scaly. Blades 25–50×15–30cm, oblong-ovate to deltoid-ovate, pinnae in 10–13 pairs, lanceolate, long-acuminate, pinnules broadly lanceolate to oblong, entire or crenately mucronate-dentate, occas. auriculate. Jap., Taiwan, China. Z8.

D. glabella (A. Cunn.) Christ = Lastreopsis glabella.

D. glanduligera (Kunze) Christ = Parathelypteris glanduligera.

D. goldiana (Hook.) Gray. GOLDIE'S SHIELD FERN; GOLDIE'S WOOD FERN. Rhiz. stout, short-creeping, scales dark glossy brown in centre; stipes to 40cm, scales as on rhiz. Blades to 80×35cm, ovate, abruptly acuminate, pinnae in 12–16 pairs, oblong-lanceolate, acuminate, short-stalked, seg. oblong, decurrent-confluent, serrate to biserrate. NE Amer. Z3.

D. gymnosora (Mak.) C. Chr. Rhiz. short, scales slender, brown to black. Stipes 30–50cm, slender, stramineous, often brown tinged purple on underside, scales as on rhiz. Blades 25–40×20–30cm, ovate, occas. subdeltoid, acuminate, pinnae lanceolate-deltoid, caudate-acuminate, broadly lanceolate, pinnately lobed to parted, -dentate. Jap., China.

D. hexagonoptera (Michx.) C. Chr. = Phegopteris hexagonoptera.

D. hirtipes (Bl.) Kuntze. Rhiz. erect, scales dull brown. Stipes to 35cm, densely scaly as rhiz. at base. Blades to 50×20cm, lanceolate, light green, pinnae to 15×1.5cm, with rounded crenate lobes, apex obliquely incised, acuminate. SE Asia. Z9.

D. hirtipes hort. = D. cycadina.

D. hispida (Sw.) Kuntze = Lastreopsis hispida.

D. intermedia (Muhlenb.) Gray. FANCY FERN. Rhiz. stout, sub-erect. Stipes to 40cm, stramineous or tinged green, densely scaly. Blades to 70×30cm, ovate-lanceolate, abruptly acuminate, bright green, gland., pinnae at 10–15 pairs, acuminate, minutely stipitate, pinnules in many pairs, seg. oblong, obtuse, minutely spinose-dentate. N Amer. Z3.

D. lacera (Thunb.) Kuntze. Rhiz. erect, short, stout, scales ferruginous to dark brown, lustrous. Stipes 7–25cm, with scales as rhiz. Blades 30–15×15–25cm, oblong, shortly acuminate, tough, pinnae oblong-lanceolate, pinnate at base, pinnatifid above, short-stalked, tinged white beneath, sterile pinnules, broadly lanceolate, crenate-serrate, fertile pinnules much reduced. NE Asia. Z7.

D. lanciloba (Bak.) Kuntze = Lastreopsis decomposita.

D. lepidopoda Hayata. Stipes 12–25cm, scales black to brown, dense. Blades 25–40×15–20cm, pinnae v. short-stalked, pinnules obtuse, sharply serrate, veins sparsely black-scaly. Himal., W China, Taiwan. Z6.

D. linnaeana C. Chr. = Gymnocarpium dryopteris.

D. ludoviciana (Kunze) Small. SOUTHERN WOOD FERN. Rhiz. short-creeping, stipes 15–40cm, beige to bronze. Blades 25–90×10–22cm, rhombic to rhombic-lanceolate, acute to acuminate, (fertile pinnae contracted), seg. subentire to remotely serrate, not spinulose. S US. Z8.

D. marginalis (L.) Gray. Rhiz. stout, erect, massive, scales pale brown darker near base. Stipes 10–30cm, densely scaly as rhiz. Blades 25–75×10–20cm, lanceolate, coriaceous, pinnae in 15–20 pairs oblong-lanceolate, substipitate, seg. oblong, obtuse, sub-entire to crenate. N Amer. Z4.

D. maximowiczii (Bak.) Kuntze = Arachniodes maximowiczii.

D. megaphylla (Mett.) C. Chr. = Sphaerostephanos penniger.

D. mutica (Franch. & Savat.) C. Chr. = Arachniodes mutica.

D. nevadensis (Bak.) Underw. = Parathelypteris nevadensis.

D. nigra Ching = D. lepidopoda.

D. novaeboracensis (L.) A. Gray = Parathelypteris novae-boracensis.

D. oreades Fomin. MOUNTAIN MALE FERN. Rhiz. ascending, much branched. Stipes short, scales pale brown. Blades oblong-lanceolate to narrowly lanceolate, pinnae linear-lanceolate, long-attenuate, lowermost oblong, obtuse, pinnules oblong, obtuse, obtusely dentate, veins extending into teeth. Cauc. 'Crispa': 30cm; pinnae undulate. 'Cristata Barnes': 60–80cm; frond and pinnae lightly crested. Z6.

D. oregana C. Chr. = *Parathelypteris nevadensis*.

D. oreopteris (Ehrh.) Maxon = *Oreopteris limbosperma*.

D. oyamensis (Bak.) C. Chr. = *Gymnocarpium oyamense*.

D. parasitica (L.) Kuntze = *Christella parasitica*.

D. patens (Sw.) Kuntze = *Christella patens*.

D. pennigera (Forst. f.) C. Chr. = *Pneumatopteris pennigera*.

D. pentheri (Krasser) C. Chr. Stipes 30cm+ with dense chestnut scales at base. Blades 30–60×20–30cm, ovate-deltoid, pinnae 15–20×5–8cm, pinnules lanceolate, dissected almost to rachis, seg. oblong, spinose-serrate. S Afr. Z9.

D. podophylla (Hook.) Kuntze. Rhiz. prostrate to erect, stout, scales almost black. Stipes to 30cm, scaly below. Blades 30–45×20–30cm, coriaceous, pinnae 2–8 each side, widely spaced, lanceolate to linear-lanceolate, subentire to deeply crenate. S China. Z9.

D. poecilophlebia (Hook.) C. Chr. = *Coveniella poecilophlebia*.

D. purpurella Tag. Similar to *D. erythrosora*, but with rachis and stipes suffused purple. Jap. Z8.

D. queenslandica Domin = *Lastreopsis munita*.

D. reptans (Gmel.) C. Chr. = *Goniopteris reptans*.

D. resinifera (Desv.) Weatherby = *Amauropelta resinifera*.

D. reticulata (L.) Urban = *Meniscium reticulatum*.

D. robertiana (Hoffm.) C. Chr. = *Gymnocarpium robertianum*.

D. sabae (Franch. & Savat.) C. Chr. Rhiz. short, erect, scales brown. Stipes 15–30cm, deep brown, lustrous above, scaly below. Blades 20–40×15–25cm, ovate, abruptly acuminate, pinnae in 5–7 pairs, oblong-ovate, lowest deltoid-ovate, acuminate, short-stalked, pinnules deltoid-oblong to deltoid-lanceolate, pinnately parted to lobed, glab. Jap. Z8.

D. setigera (Bl.) Kunze = *Macrothelypteris setigera*.

D. setosa (Christ) Kudô = *D. crassirhizoma*.

D. sieboldii (Moore) C. Chr. Rhiz. stout, short-creeping, scales, dark brown. Stipes 30–60cm, stout. Blades 20–50×20–35cm, broadly ovate, pinnae in 2–5 pairs, linear to oblong-lanceolate, coriaceous-chartaceous, pubesc. beneath, sterile pinnae crenate to mucronate-dentate, fertile pinnae, subentire to crenate. Jap., Taiwan. Z8.

D. simulata Davenp. = *Parathelypteris simulata*.

D. sparsa (Hamilt. ex D. Don) Kuntze. Rhiz. short, scales pale brown. Stipes 20–60cm, maroon-brown, scales as on rhiz. Blades 30–50×15–25cm, narrowly ovate to oblong-ovate, pinnae to 7–10 pairs, deltoid-ovate to -lanceolate, pinnules broadly lanceolate to oblong-ovate, mucronate-dentate, pinnately parted to lobed, seg. narrowly oblong. E Asia. Z8.

D. spinulosa Watt = *D. carthusiana*.

D. standishii (Moore) C. Chr. = *Arachniodes standishii*.

D. striata (Schumacher) C. Chr. = *Cyclosorus striatus*.

D. submontana (Fraser-Jenkins & Jermy) Fraser-Jenkins. RIGID BUCKLER FERN; LIMESTONE BUCKLER FERN. Rhiz. semi-erect. Stipes tufted c⅓ length of blade; blade 20–60cm, 3-pinnate-pinnatifid, fragrant, pinnules ± concave, seg. dentate, dull grey-green and mealy, covered with stalked yellow glands. W. Eur. Z7.

D. ×tavelii Rothm. (*D. filix-mas* × *D. borreri*.) Like *D. filix-mas*, but with scales of rhiz. and stipes tinged chestnut-brown, seg. minutely dentate near apex only. S & W Eur. This name is also applied to *D. affinis* and to *D. ×complexa*. Z5.

D. tetragona (Sw.) Urban = *Amauropelta tetragona*.

D. thelypteris (L.) A. Gray = *Thelypteris palustris*.

D. ×triploidea Wherry. (*D. intermedia* × *D. spinulosa*.) Similar to *D. spinulosa* but with dense glands of *D. intermedia*, blades often larger and pinnules dentate or serrate. N Amer. Z4.

D. uniformis (Mak.) Mak. Rhiz. erect, short, stout, scales black tinged brown; stipes stout, 15–30cm, scaly as rhiz. Blades 40–60×15–22cm, broadly lanceolate to oblong-ovate, truncate at base, pinnae numerous, lanceolate, pinnules oblong to broadly oblong-lanceolate, rounded to obtuse. NE Asia. Z7.

D. varia (L.) Kuntze. JAPANESE HOLLY FERN. Rhiz. stout, scales narrow, black to brown; stipes 20–60cm, scales as on rhiz. Blades 25–50×20–30cm, broadly ovate to oblong, base subtruncate, apex deltoid-lanceolate, pinnae in 6–9 pairs, broadly linear, pinnules oblong to linear-oblong, falcate, remotely dentate, occas. lobulate or pinnatifid, usually auricled. Jap., China to Indochina, Philipp., Taiwan. Z6.

D. velutina (A. Rich.) Kuntze = *Lastreopsis velutina*.

D. villarii (Bellardi) Woyn. ex Schinz & Thell. Rhiz. procumbent or ascending, scales chestnut-brown; stipes 5–20cm, lime green above, black at base, scales as on rhiz. Blades 10–25cm, lanceolate to deltoid-lanceolate, with yellow glandular-pubescence, fragrant, pinnae 15–25 each side, ovate-lanceolate,

pinnules pinnatifid to subpinnate. C, S & W Eur. Z4.

D. wallichiana (Spreng.) Hylander. Rhiz. erect, stout, scales dark brown with darker striations; stipes 30–40cm, brown, scales as rhiz. Blades 1–2m×30–40cm, lanceolate, gradually narrowed to base, pinnae linear-lanceolate, long-acuminate, subcoriaceous, pinnules narrowly oblong, rounded to subtruncate, cartilaginous-dentate. NE Asia. Z6.

→*Aspidium* and *Nephrodium*.

Drypis L. Caryophyllaceae. 1 glab. perenn. herb. St. stiff, tetragonal, much-branched. Lvs glossy, spiny, subulate. Infl. subcapitate, with numerous small fls surrounded by spiny bracts; pet. v. small and narrow, white or pink, bifid. S Eur. Z8.

D. spinosa L.

Dubia Philodendron *Philodendron radiatum*.

Duchesnea Sm. INDIAN STRAWBERRY; MOCK STRAWBERRY. Rosaceae. 2 stoloniferous perenn. herbs. Lvs basal, 3–5-foliolate, dentate; petioles with adnate stipules. Fls yellow, solitary; cal. tube short, seg. 5, alternating with toothed bracts; pet. 5, obovate; sta. 20–30. Fr. strawberry-like, dry, inedible. E & S Asia. Z6.

D. chrysantha (Zoll. & Moritz) Miq. Lfts to 3.5cm, ovate to ovate-orbicular, double- or incised-dentate, thinly pubesc., lat. lfts often bilobed. Pet. to 1cm. Fr. pale red; achenes rough. Spring–summer. Korea, Manch., China to Malaysia.

D. indica (Andrews) Focke. Lfts to 7cm, obovate, crenate, sericeous beneath. Pet. 0.8cm. Fr. bright red; achenes nearly smooth. Spring. Jap., to India, nat. Jam. and E N Amer.

→*Fragaria*.

Duckmeat *Lemna*.

Duck Plant *Sutherlandia frutescens*.

Duck Potato *Sagittaria latifolia*.

Duckweed *Lemna*; *Spirodela*.

Dudleya Britt. & Rose. Crassulaceae. 40 succulent perennials. Base usually short and thick. Lvs chiefly in basal rosettes, withering but persistent. Flowering st. erect or ascending, axill., with clasping, shorter, broader lvs; fls paniculate, tubular or stellate; sep. 5, linear-lanceolate; pet. 5, fused at the base, erect or spreading; sta. 10. W N Amer. Z8.

D. abramsii Rose. Delicate tufted perenn. Lvs 2.5–8cm in a dense rosette, oblong-lanceolate, pointed. Flowering st. 5–20cm. Infl. a branched rac.; pet. 7–12mm, light yellow, flecked red. Spring. S Calif.

D. albiflora Rose. Tufted, to 50cm. Base thick, densely branched. Tufts 20–30cm across. Lvs in term. rosettes, 20–45cm, linear-lanceolate, pointed, glaucous, tinged red with age. Pet. 9–15mm, erect, white. Spring. S Baja Calif.

D. aloides Rose = *D. saxosa* ssp. *aloides*.

D. arizonica Rose. Base thick. Lvs 5–15cm, spathulate to obovate, in solitary rosettes to 20cm across, mealy. Flowering st. 20–60cm; pet. 12–14mm, red, sometimes yellow. Late spring–summer. Nevada, W Ariz., NW Mex., SE Calif.

D. attenuata (S. Wats.) Moran. Tufted; base short or elongate. Lvs 2.5–10cm, linear-oblanceolate, glaucous, in a basal rosette. Flowering st. 10–25cm; cauline lvs ovate-lanceolate, pointed. Infl. 2–3-branched; pet. 6–12mm, yellow. Late spring. S Calif. ssp. *orcuttii* (Rose) Moran. Pet. white flushed rose.

D. brittonii Johans. Lvs 7–25cm crowded, finely pointed, dusted white in a usually solitary rosette. Flowering st. 30–90cm. Pet. erect, 7–12mm, yellow to green. Spring. Baja Calif.

D. caespitosa (Haw.) Britt. & Rose. Base long, branched, erect. Lvs 5–20cm, lanceolate-ovate, pointed, glaucous to yellow-green. Flowering st. 30–60cm; infl. a lax cyme; pet. 10–15mm, erect, yellow-white or red. Late spring–summer. S & C Calif.

D. candelabrum Rose. Lvs 10–15cm, lanceolate-oblong, in a solitary basal rosette. Flowering st. 30cm, stout. Infl. to 20cm, branched; pet. 5–9mm, erect, pale yellow. Spring–early summer. Santa Cruz, Calif.

D. candida Britt. Base to 6cm. Lvs 5–7cm, linear to oblong, numerous, mealy, short-pointed in clustered rosettes. Flowering st. 30cm. Infl. 6cm across, dense; pet. pale yellow. Spring. S Calif.

D. collomiae Rose = *D. saxosa* ssp. *collomiae*.

D. cultrata Rose Tufted. Lvs 6–10cm, in several rosettes, linear, cultrate, thick, terete, pointed. Flowering st. 30cm; infl. a number of compact rac.; pet. 13mm, yellow; anth. orange. Spring. S Calif.

D. cymosa (Lem.) Britt. & Rose. Lvs 2.5–15cm, oblanceolate, sharp-pointed, green dusted white. Flowering st. 10–30cm; infl. cymose; pet. 7–12mm, red-yellow. Spring–early summer. Calif. ssp. *minor* (Rose) Moran. A dwarf form, lvs rhombic.

D. densiflora (Rose) Moran. Base branching. Lvs 5–10cm, linear, pointed, glaucous, subterete. Flowering st. 15–30cm; infl. 3- or more branched, dense; pet. 5–10mm, white tinged pink. Summer. S Calif.

D. edulis (Nutt.) Moran. Base short and thick. Lvs 5–15cm, linear, pointed, somewhat glaucous. Flowering st. 15–50cm; infl. elongate, lax; pet. 7–10mm, white-cream. Early summer. S Calif.

D. farinosa (Lindl.) Britt. & Rose. Base horizontally branching. Lvs 2.5–5cm, oblong-ovate, pointed, green to mealy white. Flowering st. 15–30cm, stout; infl. a lax cyme; pet. 9–15mm, lemon yellow. Summer. Coastal Calif. to S Oreg.

D. grandis hort. = *D. brittonii*.

D. greenei Rose. Base thick and short. Lvs 6–7cm, linear, in basal rosettes, poiinted, glaucous, leathery. Flowering st. 30–40cm; infl. many-branched; pet. 8–10mm, pale yellow. Santa Cruz, Calif.

D. ingens hort. non Rose = *D. brittonii*.

D. lanceolata (Nutt.) Britt. & Rose. Lvs 10–15cm, lanceolate, long fine-pointed crowded in a usually solitary rosette, glaucous green. Flowering st. stout, 40–90cm; infl. a cyme, to 10cm across; pet. 12–16mm, red-yellow. Spring. S Calif., Baja Calif.

D. lanceolata var. *aloides* hort. = *D. saxosa* ssp. *aloides*.

D. linearis (Greene) Britt. & Rose. Caudex fleshy. Lvs 3–7.5cm, in a solitary rosette, linear, finely pointed, thick. Flowering st. 10–15mm; infl. a rac., 2–3-branched, compact; pet. 8–9mm, yellow-green. Spring. Baja Calif.

D. lurida Rose = *D. lanceolata*.

D. minor Rose = *D. cymosa* ssp. *minor*.

D. nevadensis (S. Wats.) Britt. & Rose = *D. cymosa*.

D. plattiana (Jeps.) Britt. & Rose = *D. cymosa*.

D. pulverulenta (Nutt.) Britt. & Rose. CHALK LETTUCE. To 1m; base thick, short. Lvs 7–30cm, oblong to obovate-spathulate, pointed, in a large solitary rosette. Flowering st. stout with long br.; fls pendent or spreading, in ascending rac.; pet. 12–18mm, red. Late spring–summer. Calif.

D. rigida Rose. Base woody, thick. Lvs numerous, 5–7cm, oblong, finely pointed, glaucous. Flowering st. with long thin br.; infl. of secund rac.; pet. 13mm, red. S Calif.

D. saxosa (M.E. Jones) Britt. & Rose. Tufted. Lvs 5–15cm, pointed, glaucous, semi-terete, in few or solitary rosettes. Flowering st. 10–25cm, tinged red; infl. 2–3-branched; pet. 10–12mm, yellow, drying red. Spring. S Calif. to Ariz. ssp. *aloides* (Rose) Moran. Flowering st. 15–35cm. Pet. erect, 7–15mm. S Calif. ssp. *collomiae* (Rose) Moran. Flowering st. to 40cm. Pet. 6–18mm. Ariz.

D. septentrionalis Rose = *D. farinosa*.

D. sheldonii Rose = *D. cymosa*.

D. stolonifera Moran. Base slender, stoloniferous. Lvs 3–7cm, in rosettes, obovate-oblong, green tinged purple. Flowering st. 8–20cm; infl. with a number of br. 1–6cm long; pet. 10–11mm, yellow. Late spring–summer. S Calif.

D. virens (Rose) Moran. ALABASTER PLANT. Base thick, short or elongate, to 30cm. Lvs 4–25cm, linear, pointed, glaucous-green. Flowering st. 10–50cm; infl. corymbose, flat-topped or elongate; pet. 7–10mm, white. Spring. Coastal S Calif.

D. viscida (Wats.) Moran. Base short. Lvs 6–10cm, deltoid-linear, dark green, sticky, in a basal rosette. Flowering st. 20–30cm; infl. somewhat elongate; pet. 6–9mm, white with red-pink markings. Late spring. S Calif.

→*Cotyledon*, *Echeveria*, *Sedum* and *Stylophyllum*.

Duff's Sword Fern *Nephrolepis cordifolia* 'Duffii'.

Duggena Weston.
D. spicata Standl. = *Gonzalagunia spicata*.

Duke Cherry *Prunus* ×*gondouinii*.
Duke of Argyll's Tea Tree *Lycium barbarum*.
Dull-coloured Linaria *Linaria tristis*.
Duma Yaka *Arenga tremula*.
Dumb Cane *Dieffenbachia* (*D. seguine*).
Dumpling Cactus *Lophophora williamsii*.
Dune Bride's Bush *Pavetta revoluta*.
Dune Manzanita *Arctostaphylos pumila*.
Dunkeld Larch *Larix* ×*marschlinsii*.
Dun Pea *Pisum sativum* var. *arvense*.
Dupont Rose *Rosa* 'Dupontii'.
Durand Oak *Quercus durandii*.
Durango Juniper *Juniperus durangensis*.
Durango Pine *Pinus durangensis*.

Duranta L. Verbenaceae. 30 trees or shrubs, sometimes spiny. Lvs simple, entire or serrate-dentate. Infl. a rac. or pan., term. or axill.; cal. tubular-campanulate, 5-dentate, accrescent in fr.;

cor. salverform, limb 5-lobed; sta. 4, short. Fr. a drupe, enclosed by persistent cal. Trop. Amer.

D. erecta L. PIGEON BERRY; SKY FLOWER; GOLDEN DEWDROP. Shrub or small tree to 6m, sometimes spiny. Lvs to 7.5cm, ovate-elliptic, entire or serrate, glabrescent. Rac. to 15cm, erect or recurved, many-fld; cor. white, lilac, blue or purple, limb to 9mm diam. Fr. to 11mm diam., yellow. Trop. Amer.

D. plumieri Jacq. = *D. erecta*.

D. repens L. = *D. erecta*.

D. stenostachya Tod. BRAZILIAN SKY FLOWER. Shrub to 5m. Lvs to 20cm, oblong-lanceolate, entire or toothed. Fls to 1.5cm diam., lilac. Fr. yellow. Brazil.

Durian *Durio* (*D. zibethinus*).

Durio Adans. DURIAN. Bombacaceae. 27 large everg. trees, trunk sometimes buttressed. Lvs simple, entire, coriaceous. Fls in cymose clusters, often cauliflorous; epical. present; cal. usually deeply 5-lobed; pet. 4–6+, sta. numerous, free or in 5 fascicles. Fr. a massive malodorous green capsule borne on trunks, rind with large prismatic thorns, with fleshy edible white pulp. Burm. to Indon. Z10.

D. zibethinus Murray. DURIAN. Large tree with buttressed trunk. Lvs to 18cm, elliptic to oblong, silvery beneath. Fls cauliferous, 3–30 per cyme; pet. to 6.5cm, pink to yellow- or green-white. Fr. ellipsoid to globose, to 40cm. Malaysia, Indon.

Durmast Oak *Quercus petraea*.
Dusky Coral Pea *Kennedia rubicunda*.
Dusty Miller *Artemisia stelleriana*; *Lychnis coronaria*; *Tanacetum ptarmiciflorum*.
Dutch Case-knife Bean *Phaseolus coccineus*.
Dutch Clover *Trifolium repens*.
Dutch Crocus *Crocus vernus*.
Dutch Elm *Ulmus* ×*hollandica*.
Dutch Irises *Iris* ×*hollandica*, *I. xiphium*.
Dutch Mice *Lathyrus tuberosus*.
Dutch Rush *Equisetum hyemale*.
Dutchman's Breeches *Dicentra cucullaria*.
Dutchman's Pipe *Aristolochia* (*A. macrophylla*).

Duvalia Haw. Asclepiadaceae. Some 19 perenn. herbs. St. succulent prostrate, 4–6-angled, angles toothed. Lvs scale-like, caducous. Fls on basal half of young st., clustered or solitary; cor. tube fleshy, annular, lobes 5, ciliate, corona stalked, outer whorl a 5–10-lobed disc, inner whorl of 5 free, lobes. Afr. Z10.

D. andreana Rauh = *Huernia andreana*.

D. angustiloba N.E. Br. St. 1.5–2cm, subspherical, teeth tuberculate. Cor. 2cm diam., dark brown, lobes 8–10mm, narrow-lanceolate, base inconspicuously hairy, annulus only slightly prominent. S Afr.

D. caespitosa (Haw.) = *D. reclinata*.

D. compacta Haw. St. 1.5–5cm, brown. Cor. 2cm, dark chocolate-brown, tube glab. to hairy, lobes lanceolate, acute, ciliate at base only; outer corona red-brown, inner whorl dark red-orange. S Afr.

D. corderoyi (Hook. f.) N.E. Br. St. 1.5–3cm, often purple, thick. Cor. 3–5cm diam., olive green, tube purple-pubesc., lobes red-brown near apex, often folded, with purple hairs at margin bases, otherwise glab.; outer corona brick red, inner whorl buff. S Afr.

D. eilensis Lavranos. St. 20–30cm, erect, with dark spots. Cor. to 2.5cm diam., annulus thick, lobes replicate, slightly ascending, inside tinged yellow, heavily spotted brown-purple, densely tuberculate, with stiff papillate hairs. Somalia.

D. elegans (Masson) Haw. St. 2–4cm, angles blunt, often flushed red. Cor. 2cm diam., dark violet or purple or almost black, densely purple-hairy within, lobes triangular-ovate, acute; outer corona ring-like, red-brown, inner whorl yellow-brown. S Afr.

D. maculata N.E. Br. St. 1.5–3cm, dark green, oblong, teeth sharply acute. Cor. 1.5–2cm diam., dark red or olive-brown, tube white spotted maroon, lobes acute, folded, basally ciliate; corona yellow. Nam. var. *immaculata* Luckh. Fls deep purple, unspotted, larger. S Afr.

D. modesta N.E. Br. St. to 2.5cm, glab., ovate or oblong. Cor. dark maroon, tube 0.5cm diam., glab., 5-angled, lobes purple-hairy at base, ovate, acute, margins strongly recurved. S Afr.

D. parviflora N.E. Br. St. 25×12mm, rounded, oblong, spotted red or grey-green. Cor. 1–1.4cm diam., green-yellow, lobes tipped purple, replicate. S Afr.

D. pillansii N.E. Br. St. to 2.5cm, cylindrical, teeth few, green or flushed red. Cor. 2cm diam., exterior green, interior smooth, brown-purple, tube yellow, lobes triangular, deeply furrowed beneath, red calli at base of margin. S Afr.

D. polita N.E. Br. St. 6–8cm, furrowed, angles blunt. Cor. 2.5–3cm diam., dark green to purple-brown, tube paler, hairy, lobes smooth, broadly triangular, with shiny basal region, slightly ciliate between lobes; outer corona red to chocolate brown, inner orange-red. Angola and Moz. to S Afr.

D. procumbens R.A. Dyer = *Huernia procumbens*.

D. propinqua A. Berger = *D. reclinata*.

D. pubescens N.E. Br. St. 2–5cm, teeth 2–4mm. Cor. 2.5cm diam., dark chocolate-brown, densely hairy within, esp. tube, tube 0.8cm diam., lobes projecting, margins reflexed, apex recurved. Nam.

D. radiata (Sims) Haw. St. 4–5cm, teeth stout, conical. Cor. 2.5–3cm diam. dark chocolate or maroon, tube fleshy, glab., large, lobes curved, erect to projecting; outer corona rusty brown, inner yellow, sometimes tinged red. S Afr.

D. reclinata (Masson) Haw. St. 2.5–10cm, erect or ascending, angles sharp. Cor. 2–2.5cm diam., tube green-brown, shiny, large, fleshy, hairy, lobes dark chocolate brown, strongly reflexed, ciliate; outer corona orange-brown, inner orange. S Afr. var. *angulata* N.E. Br. Outer corona 10-faceted. S Afr.

D. somaliensis Lavranos. St. 3–5cm long, clavate, glaucous. Cor. to 3.6cm diam., campanulate, glab., tube v. short, red-brown, covered in tiny calli, lobes ovate-triangular, yellow, with convex, irregular, rusty brown lines and spots, longitudinally furrowed. N Somalia.

D. sulcata N.E. Br. St. 2.5–6.5cm, thick, pale with purple spots. Fls 1–3-fascicled, cor. 4.5cm diam., red-brown, tube densely red-pubesc., lobes ovate, 5-furrowed, apices rough, clavate, basal hairs motile. Arabia. var. *seminuda* Lavranos. Lobes with marginal purple hairs; annulus glab. SW Arabia.

D. tanganyikensis Bruce & Bally = *Huernia tanganyikensis*.

D. velutina Lavranos. St. 2.5–6.5cm, green-white spotted purple. Cor. 4–5cm diam., inner surface densely felty, brown-red. Saudi Arabia.

Duvaliandra M. Gilbert. Asclepiadaceae. 1 succulent perenn. herb. St. creeping or ascending, to 10cm, pale or brown-green, angles toothed. Fls solitary or paired; cor. fleshy, round, to 5cm diam., ivory within, exterior pale green, verruculose, lobes ovate-triangular, sparsely covered in maroon hairs; corona pale pink, simple. S Yemen. Z10.

D. dioscoridis (Lavranos) M. Gilbert.
→*Caralluma*.

Duvaua Kunth.

D. pleuropogon Turcz. = *Lithrea caustica*.

Duvernoia E.H. Mey ex Nees. Acanthaceae 4 shrubs. Lvs entire. Fls in term. spikes; bracts small; cor. short-tubular, 2-lipped, upper lip entire, lower lip larger, 3-lobed. Afr. Z10.

D. adhatodoides E.H. Mey ex Nees. SNAKE BUSH. To 3m. Lvs to 15cm, elliptic. Fls fragrant, to 2.5cm, white marked purple. S Afr.

Dwarf Amazon Sword Plant *Echinodorus magdalenensis*.
Dwarf Apple *Angophora hispida*.
Dwarf Bearded Iris *Iris pumila*.
Dwarf Bilberry *Vaccinium caespitosum*.
Dwarf Birch *Betula nana*.
Dwarf Black Juniper *Juniperus pseudosabina*.
Dwarf Boerboon *Schotia capitata*.
Dwarf Cape Gooseberry *Physalis pruinosa*.
Dwarf Chaparral-broom *Baccharis pilularis*.
Dwarf Chinkapin Oak *Quercus prinoides*.
Dwarf Cornel *Cornus canadensis*.
Dwarf Daisy *Antheropeas*.
Dwarf Dandelion *Krigia*.
Dwarf Elder *Aralia hispida*; *Sambucus ebulus*.
Dwarf Erythrina *Erythrina humeana*.
Dwarf Fan Palm *Chamaerops humilis*.
Dwarf Fern-leaf Bamboo *Pleioblastus pygmaeus*.
Dwarf Flowering Almond *Prunus glandulosa*.
Dwarf Geebung *Persoonia chamaepeuce*.
Dwarf Ginger Lily *Kaempferia roscoeana*; *Siphonochilus decorus*.
Dwarf Ginseng *Panax trifolius*.
Dwarf Golden Chinkapin *Chrysolepis sempervirens*.
Dwarf Gorse *Ulex minor*.
Dwarf Kafferboom *Erythrina humeana*.
Dwarf Kangaroo Paw *Anigozanthos gabrielae*.
Dwarf Kumquat *Fortunella hindsii*.
Dwarf Lemon *Citrus limon*; *C. meyeri*.
Dwarf Lycopod *Selaginella rupestris*.
Dwarf Mountain Butterweed *Senecio fremontii*.
Dwarf Mountain Palm *Chamaedorea elegans*.
Dwarf Mountain Pine *Pinus mugo*.
Dwarf Palmetto *Sabal minor*.
Dwarf Pine *Pinus mugo*.

Dwarf Pomegranate *Punica granatum* var. *nanum*.
Dwarf Red Whortleberry *Vaccinium scoparium*.
Dwarf Russian Almond *Prunus tenella*.
Dwarf Siberian Pine *Pinus pumila*.
Dwarf Snapdragon *Chaenorrhinum*.
Dwarf Spanish Heath *Erica umbellata*.
Dwarf Spurge *Euphorbia exigua*.
Dwarf Sumach *Rhus copallina*.
Dwarf Whitebeam *Sorbus chamaemespilus*.
Dwarf White-striped Bamboo *Pleioblastus variegatus*.
Dwarf Whitewood Lily *Trillium nivale*.
Dwarf Willow *Salix herbacea*.

Dyakia Christenson. Orchidaceae. 1 epiphytic, monopodial orchid, to 8cm. Lvs 2-ranked, oblong-ligulate, rigid, to 10cm. Rac. dense, ascending; fls to 2.5cm diam.; sweetly scented, sparkling rose madder to magenta; dors. sep. elliptic, lat. sep. oblong; lip small, midlobe triangular; spur oblong-ligulate. Borneo. Z10.

D. hendersoniana (Rchb. f.) Christenson
→*Ascocentrum*.

Dyckia Schult. f. Bromeliaceae. 104 stemless, rosette-forming perenn. herbs. Lvs large, rigid, lanceolate, acuminate, covered with grey scales, margins sharply spinose. Infl. erect, scapose, bracteate, branching; fls numerous, small; pet. fused at base with fil. forming tube. Spring. Central S Amer. Z9.

D. acaulis (Mart. ex Schult. f.) Bak. = *Navia acaulis*.

D. altissima Lindl. To over 1m. Lvs linear-ensiform, glab. above, pale and scaly beneath. Infl. a stout, much-branched pan.; pet. bright yellow. Braz.

D. altissima Bak. non Lindl. = *D. encholirioides*.

D. argentea Nichols. = *Hechtia argentea*.

D. brevifolia Bak. 40–110cm. Lvs to 20cm, lanceolate-triangular. Infl. simple, many-fld, usually lax; pet. bright yellow. Braz.

D. choristaminea Mez. Resembles *D. cinerea* but smaller; 15–25cm. Lvs to 15cm. Infl. white-scaled; pet. yellow, fil. free above tube. S Braz.

D. cinerea Mez. To 1m. Lvs to 50cm, v. grey-scaly. Infl. grey-scaly, compound; pet. orange. SE Braz.

D. coccinea Mez = *D. tuberosa*.

D. desmetiana Bak. = *Hechtia desmetiana*.

D. distachya Hassl. To 1.3m. Lvs 14–20cm, narrowly triangular, glab. above, white-scaly beneath. Infl. to 50cm, simple or few-branched; pet. yellow-orange. S Braz., E Parag.

D. elata Mez. To 1m+. Lvs to 40cm, narrowly triangular, ± glab. Infl. loosely paniculate, many-fld; pet. orange. Braz.

D. encholirioides (Gaudich.) Mez. To 2m. Lvs 30–100cm, narrowly triangular, with pale grey scales beneath, glab. above. Infl. many-fld, simple or much-branched, rusty-tomentose; pet. red or yellow. Coastal S Braz. var. *rubra* (Wittm.) Reitz. Infl. axes and sep. red. Braz.

D. fosteriana L.B. Sm. Rosettes forming cushion-like clumps, 10–45cm in fl. Infl. simple, lax. Braz.

D. frigida (Lind.) Hook. f. Pan. much-branched, rusty-pubesc.; pet. yellow. Late winter–early spring. Braz.

D. gemellaria E. Morr. ex Mez = *D. brevifolia*.

D. gigantea K. Koch = *D. altissima*.

D. grisebachii Bak. = *Abromeitiella brevifolia*.

D. hebdingii L.B. Sm. Stemless, to 1m. Lvs 15cm, narrowly triangular, covered with ash-grey scales. Infl. lax with numerous spikes, covered in red-brown hairs; pet. yellow. Braz.

D. 'Lad Cutak'. (*D. brevifolia* × *D. leptostachya*.) Lvs 15–25cm, roughly triangular, maroon-green, glab., straight-toothed. Infl. a spike, lax, simple, 60–100cm, many-fld; pet. yellow-orange. A vigorous, frost-resistant hybrid, may produce several spikes per flowering season. Gdn origin.

D. laxiflora hort. ex Bak. = *D. altissima*.

D. lemaireana hort. = *D. altissima*.

D. leptostachya Bak. 50–150cm. Lvs 40–100cm, narrowly triangular, bulbous below, covered with ash-grey scales. Infl. simple or with few br., axis sparsely hairy or glab.; pet. red-orange. Throughout range.

D. longipetala Bak. = *Deuterocohnia longipetala*.

D. marnier-lapostollei L.B. Sm. Lvs 12cm, thick, triangular. Infl. simple, glab., few-fld, to 20cm; pet. yellow. Braz.

D. microcalyx Bak. 40cm–2m. Infl. many-fld; pet. orange. S Braz., Parag., NE Arg.

D. minarum Mez. 25–75cm. Lvs abruptly acute and thickened at apex, often glab. above. Infl. simple, lax, white-scaly; pet. orange-yellow. SE Braz.

D. niederleinii Mez. Resembles *D. leptostachys* but lvs more frequently glab. above, not bulb-forming. Infl. glab., pedicel stout; pet. orange. S Braz.

D. platyphylla L.B. Sm. To 80cm. Lvs to 23cm, succulent, thick, narrowly triangular, glab. above, white-scaly beneath. Infl. to

28cm, simple, many-fld, slender-stalked; pet. yellow. Braz.

D. princeps hort. ex Mez in part, non Lem. = *D. brevifolia*.

D. ramosa hort. ex K. Koch = *D. altissima*.

D. rariflora Schult. f. 50cm. Lvs 14cm, tapering sharply; sheaths large, ovate, not bulb-forming. Pet. orange. Braz.

D. rariflora Lindl. non Wittm. = *D. remotiflora*.

D. rariflora Wittm. non Lindl. = *D. brevifolia*.

D. regalis Lind. & Morr. ex Bak. = *D. frigida*.

D. remotiflora Otto & Dietr. Resembles *D. cinerea* but lvs 10–25cm, recurved, dark green, glab. Infl. simple and sparsely hairy; pet. dark orange. S Braz., Urug.

D. rubra Wittm. = *D. encholirioides*.

D. spectabilis (Mart. ex Schult. f.) Bak. = *Encholirium spectabile*.

D. sulphurea K. Koch = *D. brevifolia*.

D. tuberosa (Vell.) Beer. 35–100cm. Lvs 15–50cm, curved, narrowly triangular, glab. above, grey-scaly beneath, bases bulbous. Infl. lax, simple, glab.; pet. orange-red. SE Braz.

D. ursina L.B. Sm. Lvs to 60cm, linear, glab. Infl. simple, lax, brown-pilose; pet. orange. Braz.

D. velascana Mez. To 1m, forming dense colonies. Lvs scaly beneath. Pan. lax, densely fld, grey-scaly, hairy; pet. sulphur-yellow with brown basal hairs. NW Arg.

D. vestita Hassl. Infl. to 60cm+, compound, bracts ovate, yellow-hairy; pet. pale yellow. N Parag.

Dye Fig *Ficus tinctoria*.
Dyer's Buckthorn *Rhamnus saxatilis*.
Dyers' Chamomile *Anthemis tinctoria*.
Dyer's Greenweed *Genista tinctoria*.
Dyer's Woad *Isatis tinctoria*.
Dyer's Woodruff *Asperula tinctoria*.

Dymondia Compton. Compositae. 1 prostrate, mat-forming perenn. herb, to 50cm diam. Lvs in terminal rosettes, to 5cm, linear, obtuse, dark green above, tomentose beneath, margins 2–3 dentate each side, inrolled. Cap. radiate, few, surrounded by lvs; phyllaries many, ray flts 8–13, to 1.5×0.5cm, elliptic, yellow. S Afr.

D. margaretae Compton.

Dyschoriste Nees. Acanthaceae. 65 ann. or perenn. herbs, sub-shrubs or shrubs. Lvs opposite, usually entire, small. Fls solitary or clustered; cal. lobes 5, almost free; cor. bilabiate, tube slender at base, inflated toward throat. Americas, Afr., SE Asia. Z10.

D. thunbergiiflora (S. Moore) Lindau. MUSHUGUSHUGU. Shrub to 3m. Lvs to 2.5cm, obovate. Fls axill., bracteate; cor. to 5cm, mauve marked or tinted purple. Trop. E Afr.

Dyssochroma Miers. Solanaceae. 2 climbing shrubs or small trees. Lvs *c*10cm, elliptic, acuminate, entire, leathery. Fls large, pendulous at ends of branchlets; cal. lobes 5, narrow; cor. funnelform, with 5 long-lanceolate, recurved lobes. Braz. Z10.

D. eximia Benth. & Hook. f. Fls paired; cor. to 15cm, yellow-green; sta. slightly exceeding tube. Braz.

D. viridiflora (Miers) Sims. Fls solitary; cor. to 10cm, green; sta. exserted to 4.5cm beyond tube. Braz.

→*Markea* and *Solandra*.

Dyssodia Cav.

D. tenuiloba (DC.) Robinson = *Thymophylla tenuiloba*.

E

Eared Willow *Salix aurita.*
Ear-leaved Umbrella Tree *Magnolia fraseri.*
Early Black Wattle *Acacia decurrens.*
Early Blue Violet *Viola palmata.*
Early Buttercup *Ranunculus fascicularis.*
Early-flowering Catalpa *Catalpa speciosa.*
Early Hair Grass *Aira praecox.*
Early Marsh Orchid *Dactylorhiza incarnata.*
Early Nancy *Wurmbea dioica.*
Early Purple Orchid *Orchis mascula.*
Early Red Maidenhair *Adiantum pedatum.*
Early Sand-grass *Mibora.*
Early Spider Orchid *Ophrys sphegodes.*
Early Sweet Bilberry *Vaccinium vaccillans.*
Early Winter Cress *Barbarea verna.*
Early Yellow Violet *Viola rotundifolia.*
Earth Chestnut *Lathyrus tuberosus.*
Earth-nut Pea *Lathyrus tuberosus.*
Earth Star *Cryptanthus.*
East African Laburnum *Calpurnia aurea.*
East Bhutan Pine *Pinus bhutanica.*
Easter Cactus *Hatiora gaertneri.*
Easter Daisy *Townsendia exscapa*; *T. hookeri.*
Easter Ledges *Polygonum bistorta.*
Easter Lily *Lilium longiflorum.*
Easter Lily Cactus *Echinopsis.*
Easter Lily Vine *Beaumontia grandiflora.*
Eastern Camass *Camassia scilloides.*
Eastern Catalpa *Catalpa bignonioides.*
Eastern Cottonwood *Populus deltoides.*
Eastern Flowering Dogwood *Cornus florida.*
Eastern Hemlock *Tsuga canadensis.*
Eastern Hop Hornbeam *Ostrya virginiana.*
Eastern Pasque Flower *Pulsatilla patens.*
Easter Redbud *Cercis canadensis.*
Eastern Redcedar *Juniperus virginiana.*
Eastern Round-leaved Violet *Viola rotundifolia.*
Eastern Water Violet *Viola lanceolata.*
Eastern White Cedar *Thuja occidentalis.*
Eastern White Pine *Pinus strobus.*
Easter Tree *Holarrhena pubescens.*
East Indian Arrowroot *Tacca leontopetaloides.*
East Indian Fig Tree *Ficus benghalensis.*
East Indian Rosebay *Tabernaemontana divaricata.*
East Indian Wine Palm *Phoenix rupicola.*
East India Rosewood *Dalbergia latifolia.*
Eastwood Manzanita *Arctostaphylos glandulosa.*
Eaton's Firecracker *Penstemon eatonii.*
Eau de Cologne Mint *Mentha ×piperita.*

EBENACEAE Gürke. 2/485. *Diospyros.*

Ebenopsis Britt. & Rose.
E. flexicaulis (Benth.) Britt. & Rose = *Pithecellobium flexicaule.*

Ebenus L. Leguminosae (Papilionoideae). 18 perenn. herbs or small shrubs. Lvs imparipinnate or trifoliolate. Rac. or fl. head axill., subtended by membranous bracts; fls pea-like. E Medit. to C Asia. Z8.
E. cretica L. Everg. subshrub to 50cm, new growth finely silver-pubesc. Lfts to 3cm, 3 or in 2 pairs, appearing digitate, linear to elliptic-oblong. Fls vivid pink, streaked with dark lines. Summer. Crete.
E. sibthorpii DC. Erect herb to 30cm. Lfts to 1.8cm, in 2–4 pairs, elliptic-oblong to obovate, adpressed silver-pubesc. Fls red-purple. SE Greece.

Ebitiothin *Cordia crenata.*
Ebony Spleenwort *Asplenium platyneuron.*

Ebracteola Dinter & Schwantes. Aizoaceae. 2 lf succulents. Roots thickened to tuberous. St. low-growing and mat-forming. Lvs elongated-triquetrous, prismatic or cylindric, sometimes carinate. Fls term. Summer. Nam. Z9.
E. candida L. Bol. Lvs 3–4.5cm, linear-tapered on upper surface, laterally compressed and carinate on lower surface, sides con-

vex, tip obliquely rounded, blue-green, minutely tuberculate. Fls 3–4cm diam., white.
E. derenbergiana (Dinter) Dinter & Schwantes. Lvs 3–4cm, bluntly triquetrous, obtuse with the sides hatchet-shaped above, light blue-green, densely spotted. Fls 2–2.5cm diam., light pink.
E. montis-moltkei (Dinter) Dinter & Schwantes. Lvs 2–3cm, acutely triquetrous, tip navicular, curved upwards, keel some-what distorted, grey-green, densely spotted. Fls 1.5cm diam., light violet-pink.
→*Bergeranthus, Mesembryanthemum* and *Ruschia.*

Ecballium A. Rich. EXPLODING CUCUMBER; SQUIRTING CUCUMBER. Cucurbitaceae. 1 trailing or bushy herbaceous hispid perenn. Lvs palmately lobed, coarsely pubesc. above, pale and tomentose beneath, 4–15cm, lobes 5, shallow, sinuate. Fls to 2cm, yellow: ♂ in rac., ♀ solitary. Fr. 3–5cm, ovoid to short-cylindric, blue-green, coarsely white-hispid, shooting away from plant if touched and squirting seeds in a sticky mass. Medit. to S Russia. Z9.
E. elaterium (L.) A. Rich. SQUIRTING CUCUMBER.
→*Momordica.*

Eccremocactus Britt. & Rose.
E. bradei Britt. & Rose = *Weberocereus bradei.*
E. imitans (Kimnach & Hutchison) Kimnach = *Weberocereus imitans.*
E. rosei Kimnach = *Weberocereus rosei.*

Eccremocarpus Ruiz & Pav. GLORY FLOWER. Bignoniaceae. 5 everg. or herbaceous vines to 3m. Lvs to 7cm, bipinnate or twice pinnatisect, with term. tendrils. Rac. term.; cal. 5-lobed, campanulate; cor. tube long, narrow, throat swollen, contracted at mouth, limb entire or bilabiate. Chile and Peru. Z9.
E. **Anglia Hybrids.** Fls yellow, orange, pink, scarlet and crimson.
E. longiflorus Humb. & Bonpl. Pinnae entire, rarely notched at apex. Infl. long; cor. longer than in *E. scaber*, yellow, limb green. Summer. Peru.
E. scaber Ruiz & Pav. Pinnae entire or dentate. Infl. to 15cm; cor. to 2.5cm, scarlet to orange. Summer. Chile. 'Aureus': fls golden yellow. 'Carmineus': fls deep red. 'Roseus': fls bright pink to red.

×**Echephytum** Gossot = ×*Pachyveria.*

Echeveria DC. Crassulaceae. 150 succulent, everg. or occas. decid. herbs and subshrubs. St. usually short, simple. Lvs scattered or in dense low rosettes, usually entire and sessile. Rac. or pan. on long lateral stalks, fls on upper side of cymose br. with coiled tips; pet. 5, fused into a 5-angled tube at base, usually tapering to mouth then free. C & S Amer. Z8.
E. acutifolia Lindl. St. to 30cm, simple. Lvs 30×8cm, obovate-oblong, bristle-tipped or pointed, tinged red. Infl. to 100cm, paniculate, cor. 12mm, red, tube contracted at mouth. Winter. S Mex.
E. adunca (Bak.) Otto = *Pachyphytum hookeri.*
E. affinis Walth. St. to 10cm, simple. Lvs 5×2cm, oblanceolate-oblong, short-pointed, terete, bright green, darker in the sun. Infl. to 30cm, 2–5-branched; cor. 10mm, bell-shaped, red. Summer. W Mex.
E. agavoides Lem. St. v. short. Lvs few, 3–8×3cm in a solitary rosette or tuft-forming, ovate-triangular, sharply pointed, waxy, margins transparent. Infl. 2-branched; cor. 10–12mm, pink-orange outside, yellow within. Spring–early summer. Mex. var. *prolifera* Walth. Lvs numerous, 10–12×3cm. Pet. to 16mm. var. *corderoyi* (Bak.) Poelln. Lvs numerous, ovate, 6.5×3.5cm. Infl. 3-branched; pet. to 9mm. 'Carunculata': lvs with basal, warty excrescence above. 'Metallica' (*E. metallica*): lvs purple-lilac, turning olive-bronze. 'Pallida' (*E. pallida*): lvs pale green.
E. albicans Walth. St. ± 0. Lvs 3–5×1.5–2.5cm, in solitary, eventually tufted rosettes, overlapping, oblong-ovate, thickest near tip, small-pointed, white. Infl. usually unbranched, around 20cm high, secund; cor. 15–18mm, ± turbinate, pink outside, yellow inside. Summer. Mex.
E. albida (Rose) A. Berger = *Dudleya virens.*
E. amoena De Smet. Mat-forming. Lvs 20×6–8mm in dense ros-ettes, spathulate-oblanceolate, pointed, terete, somewhat clavate, grey-green, tip maroon. Infl. 10–20cm, erect, 6–12 fld;

bracts numerous; fls nodding; cor. to 9mm, pink to rose-red, margins yellow, thin. Spring. Mex.

E. amphoralis Walth. Subshrub, hairy throughout, to 20cm. Lvs 35×20mm, in loose rosettes, cuneate to obovate, bristle-tipped. Infl. to 20cm, racemose, few-fld; cor. to 24mm, amphora-shaped, red at base, yellow above and inside. Summer. Mex.

E. angusta Poelln. = *E. subrigida*.

E. atropurpurea (Bak.) E. Morr. St. 10–15cm high, 2.5cm thick. Lvs 10–12×0.5cm, in dense rosettes, oblong or spathulate-obovate, dark purple-green, glaucous. Infl. 30–60cm, racemose, 20–25-fld; cor. 12mm, red. Mex.

E. australis Rose. Subshrub. St. to 30cm, little-branched. Lvs 7×2cm, crowded at ends of br., cuneate to obovate, rounded, bristle-tipped, thin, keeled, lime green tinged purple. Infl. over 25cm, paniculate or racemose, dense; cor. 11–14mm, red outside, pink inside. Spring–summer. Costa Rica, Hond.

E. bella Alexander. St. v. short, branching. Lvs 28×5mm, in dense rosettes of 20–30, linear-oblanceolate, pointed, subterete. Infl. to 25cm, racemose, red, 12-fld; cor. 10mm, seg. bristled below apex, red-yellow. Spring. S Mex.

E. bergeriana hort. = × *Pachyveria sodalis*.

E. bicolor (HBK) Walth. St. to 60cm, 2cm thick, branched from base. Lvs 9×3.5cm in ill-defined rosettes, cuneate to obovate, rounded, bristle-tipped, green. Infl. to 50cm, racemose, 25-fld, sturdy; cor. to 15mm, seg. fine-pointed, yellow outside, orange-yellow inside. Winter. Venez., Colomb.

E. bifida Schldl. St. short, not branched. Lvs 35×100×12–25mm, oblanceolate-rhombic, pointed, bristle-tipped, glaucous, tinged red. Infl. 25–60cm, a 2-branched rac., 20–30-fld; cor. 12mm, keeled, urn-shaped, pink-orange outside, yellow inside. Summer. Mex.

E. bracteolata Link, Klotzsch & Otto = *E. bicolor*.

E. bracteosa Lindl. & Paxt. = *Pachyphytum bracteosum*.

E. buchtienii Poelln. = *E. whitei*.

E. carnicolor (Bak.) E. Morr. CORAL ECHEVERIA. St. ± 0. Lvs 5–7×1.5cm, 20 per rosette, oblanceolate to spathulate, blunt, thick, concave above, papillose. Infl. to 25cm, racemose, 6–20-fld; cor. 10mm, straight, thick, pink-orange outside, buff-yellow inside. Winter. E Mex.

E. chiapensis Rose ex Poelln. Subshrub. St. little-branched, to 30cm. Lvs 4–7×1.5–2.5cm, scattered or in loose rosettes, oblanceolate-ovate, thin, bristle-tipped. Infl. to 50cm, ascending 15–20-fld; sep. pink-red; cor. 10mm, seg. thin, yellow. Autumn. Mex.

E. chihuahuaensis Poelln. St. 0. Lvs 4–6×3–4cm, numerous, obovate to oblong, blunt, short-pointed, thin, white-glaucous, tip red-purple. Infl. to 20cm, simple or several-branched; cor. 14mm; red outside, orange within. Spring–summer. Mex.

E. chilonensis (Kuntze) Walth. St. short, to 5cm, branching. Lvs 7×1.5cm, 20 per rosette, linear to oblanceolate, ascending, fine-pointed or bristle-tipped. Infl. to 60cm, racemose, sometimes branching, 10–25-fld; cor. 13mm, urceolate, seg. pale yellow-green. Summer. Boliv.

E. ciliata Moran. Hairy throughout. St. to 7cm. Lvs to 5cm, 30–70 per rosette, cuneate to obovate, bristle-tipped. Infl. 4–14cm, simple, secund, racemose, 4–7-fld; cor. 10mm, hairy, yellow-red. Summer. Mex.

E. clavifolia hort. ex Walth. = × *Pachyveria clavata*.

E. coccinea (Cav.) DC. Densely hairy throughout. St. to 60cm, branching. Lvs 6–8×2cm, subterminal, oblanceolate, concave above. Infl. 30cm, a spike, 25-fld; cor. 10–12mm, cylindrical, red outside, orange inside. Autumn–winter. Mex. 'Recurvata': lvs short, broad, recurved.

E. columbiana Poelln. = *E. quitensis*.

E. corallina Alexander = *E. sessiliflora*.

E. corderoyi (Bak.) E. Morr. = *E. agavoides* var. *corderoyi*.

E. cotyledon (Jacq.) Nels. and Macbr. = *Dudleya caespitosa*.

E. craigii Walth. St. short, little-branched. Lvs 75–110×12–18mm, dense, lanceolate-elliptic, pointed, glaucous, tinged purple. Infl. 30–45cm, paniculate, few-fld; cor. 9mm, red. Autumn. W Mex.

E. crenulata Rose. St. 10cm, branching at base. Lvs 10×7cm, in a loose rosette, obovate-rhomboid, pointed, with or without a bristle tip, green, margins wavy or flat, brown. Infl. 50cm, several, paniculate; cor. 18mm, straight, pink outside, yellow inside. Winter. Mex. 'Roseo-grandis': lvs rich green, waxy, edged burgundy. 'Roseo-grandis Blue Giant': lvs broad, grey-blue, tipped red. 'Roseo-grandis Buettner Hybrid': lvs green, overlaid with blue-grey, edged red.

E. cuspidata Rose. Lvs 6×3.5cm, in a dense basal rosette, oblong-obovate, flat, rather thin, blunt with a small point, grey-green, somewhat glaucous, tip red. Infl. secund, racemose, 15-fld; cor. 14mm, conical, pink outside, orange inside. Spring–summer. Mex.

E. dactylifera Walth. St. v. short or 0. Lvs 25×9cm, in a crowded rosette, oblong-elliptic, pointed, keeled at base, green, margins

folded upwards from midrib, red. Infl. to 1m, paniculate, br. few-fld; pink; sep. lavender; cor. to 30mm, 5-angled, pink outside, yellow inside. Winter–spring. Mex.

E. derenbergii Purpus. St. short, much-branched. Lvs 2–4×2–2.5cm, in dense tuft-forming rosettes, cuneate to obovate, thick, bristle-tipped, pale green, margin red. Infl. to 10cm, racemose, few-fld; sep. red on margins; cor. 12–15mm, ± campanulate, erect, yellow, keel and tip red. Spring–summer. Mex.

E. desmetiana E. Morr. = *E. peacockii*.

E. discolor Bak. = *E. nodulosa*.

E. edulis (Nutt.) A. Berger = *Dudleya edulis*.

E. elegans Rose. MEXICAN SNOW BALL; WHITE MEXICAN ROSE; MEXICAN GEM. St. short. Lvs in rounded rosettes, thick, spathulate-oblong, 3–6×1–2cm, convex beneath, bristle-tipped, margins translucent. Infl. 10–15cm, unbranched, 5–10-fld; cor. 12mm, pink outside, yellow-orange within. Spring–summer. Mex. 'Kesselringii': lvs grey-blue in a globose rosette. var. *simulans* (Rose) Poelln. Rosettes somewhat flat. Lvs to 7×4cm, white. Infl. sometimes 2-branched; cor. 12–15mm, deep pink.

E. elegans (Rose) Berger = *E. harmsii*.

E. elegans var. *kesselringiana* Poelln. = *E. albicans*.

E. ×expatriata Rose = × *Cremneria expatriata*.

E. farinosa Lindl. = *Dudleya farinosa*.

E. fimbriata C. Thomps. St. to 50cm. Lvs 15–20×6–7cm, in a loose rosette, rounded with a bristle tip, somewhat hairy at first. Infl. to 60cm, branched 2–3 times; sep. light blue to grey-green; cor. to 15mm, pink-red outside, ochre inside. Winter. Mex.

E. ×fruticosa Rollins = × *Pachyveria glauca*.

E. fulgens Lem. St. to 30cm, occas. branched. Lvs 8–15×4–7cm, in rosettes, spathulate-obovate, glaucous, blunt with a bristle tip, undulate. Infl. to 90cm, few-branched, red, 20–30 fld; cor. to 15mm, red outside, orange inside. Winter. Mex.

E. fusifera hort. = × *Pachyveria sobrina*.

E. gibbiflora DC. St. to 30cm, erect, not branching. Lvs 15–35×10–25cm, rosulate, obovate-spathulate, pointed, tinged purple, margin wavy. Infl. to 1m, paniculate, many-branched; sep. lavender; cor. to 16mm, cylindrical to campanulate, red outside, buff inside. Autumn–winter. Mex.

E. gigantea Rose & Purpus. St. to 50cm, not branching. Lvs 15–20×8–10cm, in a loose rosette, spathulate-obovate, rounded and notched at apex, purple on margins. Infl. to 2m, paniculate; cor. 12–17mm, rose red. Winter. Mex.

E. ×gilva Walth. GREEN MEXICAN ROSE; WAX ROSETTE. (*E. agavoides* × *E. elegans*.) St. short, branching. Lvs 5–8×2–2.5cm, in a dense rosette, oblong, short-pointed, surface crystalline, margin translucent. Infl. to 25cm, racemose; cor. 9mm, pink below, yellow above. Spring. Gdn origin.

E. glauca Bak. = *E. secunda* var. *glauca*.

E. gloriosa Rose = *E. rubromarginata*.

E. goldiana Walth. St. v. short. Lvs 4×2.5cm, in dense rosettes, obovate, concave above, blunt with a small point, shiny green. Infl. to 40cm, racemose, 8–10-fld; fls nodding; cor. 13mm, pink, yellow at apex. Spring–summer. Mex.

E. goldmanii Rose = *Dudleya cymosa* ssp. *minor*.

E. gracilis Rose ex Walth. Subshrub. St. to 10cm. Lvs 25–30 ×12mm, scattered or in a loose rosette, oblong-clavate, curving upwards. Infl. 20cm, racemose, 10- or more fld; cor. 10mm, thick, red outside, orange within. Mex.

E. ×graessneri Van Keppel. (*E. derenbergii* × *E. pulvinata*.) St. to 15cm. Lvs 5×3cm, spathulate-obovate, bristle-tipped, margins red. Infl. to 15cm, few-branched; cor. 18mm, orange, red on keel. Summer. Gdn origin.

E. grandifolia Haw. Similar to *E. gibbiflora* except lvs 30×12cm, oblanceolate, margins curved upwards, pointed and bristle-tipped. Autumn–winter. Mex.

E. grayi (Bak.) E. Morr. = *E. paniculata*.

E. ×haageana hort. = *E. ×graessneri*.

E. halbingeri Walth. Lvs 25×13mm, in dense basal rosettes, obovate, blunt, with a small point, tip triquetrous, glaucous. Infl. to 12cm, racemose, 6–9-fld; cor. 16mm, urceolate, orange-chrome outside, light orange within. Summer. Mex.

E. harmsii J.F. Macbr. Short-haired throughout. St. to 30cm, branching. Lvs 2–5×1cm term. clusters, oblanceolate, pointed. margins red. Infl. to 20cm, several to many, few-fld; cor. 33mm, urceolate, red, margins and inside yellow. Summer. Mex.

E. heterosepala Rose. St. to 6cm, unbranched. Lvs 24–40× 9–15mm, numerous, oblanceolate-rhombic, tapering to point, glaucous. Infl. to 45cm, racemose, 8–15-fld; cor. 10mm, straight, green, tinged red. Spring–summer. S Mex.

E. holwayi Rose = *E. acutifolia*.

E. hookeri (Salm-Dyck) Lam. = *Pachyphytum hookeri*.

E. humilis Rose. St. short, branching. Lvs 4–7×2.5cm, in dense, elongate rosettes, lanceolate-ovate, bristle-tipped, convex beneath. Infl. to 20cm, racemose, occas. branched, wavy; cor. to 13mm, campanulate to urceolate, orange outside, orange-yellow within. Late summer. Mex.

E. hyalina Walth. St. 0. Lvs 6×3.5cm, in tufted rosettes, obovate, blunt with a small point, thin, crystalline, blue-green. Infl. to 30cm, racemose, nodding; cor. 11mm, urceolate, pink below, yellow-pink above, green inside. Winter–spring. Mex.

E. johnsonii Walth. St. to 10cm, branched. Lvs 35–9mm, crowded near end of br., clavate or oblanceolate, subterete, faintly purple on edges. Infl. 10cm, spike-like, 10-fld; cor. 11mm, straight, buff, red on keel, orange-yellow inside. Ecuad.

E. lagunensis Munz = *Dudleya arizonica*.

E. lanceolata Nutt. = *Dudleya lanceolata*.

E. laui Moran & Meyrán. Pruinose. St. to 10cm, simple. Lvs 5–9×3–4cm, 30–50 per dense rosette, convex beneath, tinged red. Infl. 6–10cm, 9–17-fld; cor. 13–16mm, red, seg. yellow. Mex.

E. laxa Lindl. = *Dudleya caespitosa*.

E. laxa auct. non Lindl. = *Dudleya cymosa*.

E. leucotricha Purpus. Hairy subshrub. St. branching, red, to 15cm. Lvs 60–80×20–25mm, in loose rosettes, oblong-lanceolate, blunt, bristle-tipped, upcurved, tip red. Infl. to 40cm, spike-like or paniculate, 12–15-fld; cor. 18mm, orange, red on keel. Spring. Mex.

E. lindsayana Walth. Lvs 5–9×3–4cm, in dense rosettes at first, oblong to obovate, tip red, blunt or bristle-tipped, slightly keeled. Infl. to 50cm, tinged pink, 2-branched, *c*14-fld; cor. 10mm, pink, yellow-orange at tips and inside. Spring–summer. Origin thought to be Mex.

E. linguifolia Lem. = *Cremnophila linguifolia*.

E. longissima Walth. St. short, unbranched. Lvs 6×3cm, in dense rosettes, cuneate to obovate, bristle-tipped, thick, red on margins. Infl. 30cm, secund, racemose, 4–12-fld; cor. 30mm, narrow, green-yellow below, green above. Summer. Mex.

E. lozanii Rose. Lvs 10–15×2–4cm, few, in a basal or short-stalked rosette, linear to oblanceolate, thick, pointed. Infl. 30–45cm, paniculate; cor. 10–15mm, copper. Mex.

E. lurida Haw. = *E. racemosa*.

E. lutea Rose. St. v. short. Lvs 11×3cm, in a crowded rosette, oblong-oblanceolate, pointed, up-curved, somewhat keeled, tinged purple. Infl. 30–60cm, simple or 2-branched, 12–30-fld; cor. to 17mm, yellow. Summer. E Mex.

E. macdougallii Walth. Subshrub to 12cm. Lvs 3×1cm, in loose apical rosettes, v. thick, obovate-clavate, subterete, glaucous green with red markings. Infl. 10–25cm, racemose, few-fld; cor. to 18mm, red, yellow on upper edges and inside. Mex.

E. maculata Rose. St. short or 0. Lvs 7–15×2–3cm, oblanceolate-obovate, fine-pointed, glaucous, up-curved. Infl. 30–90cm, spike-like or paniculate; cor. 16mm, narrowly urceolate, yellow. Spring–summer. Mex.

E. maxonii Rose. St. 30–80cm, little-branched. Lvs 3–10×3cm, scattered or in loose rosettes, spathulate-oblanceolate, blunt, bristle-tipped or pointed, concave above, papillose. Infl. to 60cm, racemose, 25-fld; cor. 10mm, red. Winter. Guat.

E. megacalyx Walth. St. short, branching. Lvs 10×2.5cm, in dense rosettes, thin, oblong-spathulate, margin thin, transparent. Infl. to 45cm, racemose, nodding; sep. 8–10mm, leaflike; cor. 8mm, green-yellow. Summer–autumn. S Mex.

E. microcalyx Britt. & Rose = *E. amoena*.

E. minima Meyrán. St. short. Lvs 8–20×5–9mm, in solitary dense rosettes, cuneate-obovate, convex beneath, glaucous, tip red. Infl. to 50cm, 3–9-fld; cor. 8–11mm, pink below, red above. Early summer. Mex.

E. minutiflora Rose = *Thompsonella minutiflora*.

E. mirabilis Delile = × *Pachyveria mirabilis*.

E. montana Rose. Similar to *E. nuda* except lvs broader, blunter, bearing a v. small bristle; cor. to 13mm, seg. not spreading at tips. Summer. Mex.

E. moranii Walth. St. 2–3cm. Lvs 6×3cm, in a dense rosette, cuneate-obovate, thick, concave above, bristle-tipped, papillose, green spotted and edged maroon. Infl. 20–50cm, racemose, 15-fld; cor. 13mm, conical, red outside, orange-buff inside. Summer. S Mex.

E. mucronata Schldl. St. short, subterranean. Lvs 7–9×2.5cm, few, oblanceolate, pointed, spotted red. Infl. a spike, to 50cm, 20-fld; sep. with bristle-like tips; cor. 12–16mm, urceolate, yellow, tinged red. Summer. Mex.

E. multicaulis Rose. COPPER LEAF; COPPER ROSES. St. much-branched, to 1m. Lvs 3–4×1.5–3cm, in term. rosettes, cuneate-obovate, blunt, bristle-tipped, flat, margins red. Infl. 25cm, racemose, 6–15-fld; upper bracts orange; sep. red; cor. 10mm, scarlet, orange-yellow inside. Winter–spring. Mex.

E. × mutabilis Deleuil ex E. Morr. = × *Cremneria mutabilis*.

E. navicaulis De Smet = *E. nuda*.

E. nodulosa (Bak.) Otto. St. to 20cm, branching. Lvs 5×1.5cm, in loose rosettes or scattered, cuneate-obovate, thick, concave above, deep red on margins and keel. Infl. to 30cm, racemose, 8–12-fld; cor. 16mm, red, yellow inside and on margins

Autumn. Mex.

E. nuda Lindl. St. 30–60cm, branched. Lvs 6–13×2.5–5cm, in loose terminal rosettes, spathulate-obovate, blunt with a bristle tip or pointed, thin, pruinose at first, margins red. Infl. to 40cm, later spike-like, 20-fld; cor. 8mm, red at base, green above. Summer. Mex.

E. nuda Botteri non Lindl. = *E. rubromarginata*.

E. nuda var. *montana* (Rose) Poelln. = *E. montana*.

E. nudicaulis (Abrams) A. Berger = *Dudleya densiflora*.

E. obscura (Rose) Poelln. = *E. agavoides*.

E. obtusifolia Rose. St. short. Lvs 4–8×2.5–3.5cm, in a rosette, spathulate-oblanceolate, margins red, apex round, with a bristle. Infl. 20–35cm, red, 2–3-branched; cor. 12mm, orange. Winter. Mex.

E. pachanoi Rose = *E. quitensis*.

E. pachyphytum (Bak.) Morr. = *Pachyphytum bracteosum*.

E. palmeri hort. non Rose = *E. rubromarginata*.

E. palmeri Rose = *E. subrigida*.

E. paniculata A. Gray. Lvs 10×3cm, to 40 per basal rosette, spreading, oblanceolate, fine-pointed. Infl. to 50cm, paniculate, br. 2–6-fld; cor. 12mm, conical, yellow, red at base. Summer. W Mex.

E. parrasensis Walth. = *E. cuspidata*.

E. peacockii Crouch. St. short. Lvs 5–6×2–3.5cm, numerous, in solitary rosettes, obovate-oblanceolate, pointed or bristle-tipped, convex beneath. Infl. 30cm, 20-fld, secund; cor. 11mm, not constricted at mouth, red-pink. Summer. Mex.

E. perelegans Berger = *E. elegans*.

E. pilosa Purpus. Pilose throughout; st. short, unbranched. Lvs 7×2cm, in loose rosettes, oblanceolate, tapering to the point, concave above. Infl. several to 30cm, paniculate below, spike-like above; cor. 12mm, orange, keels red, tips and inside yellow. Spring–summer. Mex.

E. pinetorum Rose. St. short, simple. Lvs 25–50×18mm, 10–15 per rosette, oblanceolate, fine-pointed, margins transparent, sometimes finely toothed. Infl. 20–50cm, spike-like; cor. 9mm, urceolate, red, tips yellow. Summer. S Mex.

E. pittieri Rose. St. branching, to 10cm. Lvs 4–10×2cm, in loose rosettes, oblanceolate-elliptic, pointed, slightly concave above, green, brown at tip. Infl. to 20cm, a dense spike; sep. green-purple; cor. 12–13mm, campanulate, red outside, pink within. Winter. Guat., Nic., Costa Rica.

E. platyphylla Rose. St. subterranean. Lvs 55×22mm, few in a basal rosette, obovate, semi-deciduous. Infl. to 40cm, 15-fld spike; cor. to 14mm, urceolate, white below, rich yellow above. Summer. Mex.

E. potosina Walth. Similar to *E. elegans* except lvs to 3cm across, thickest at apex, often tinged purple. Spring–early summer. Mex. 'Alba': fls white.

E. pringlei (S. Wats.) Rose. Densely hairy throughout. St. to 10cm, branching. Lvs 4×2cm, in loose rosettes or scattered, obovate-oblanceolate, pointed. Infl. to 20cm, a simple rac.; cor. to 15mm, urceolate, red outside, buff inside. Mex.

E. prolifica Moran & Meyrán. St. short, stoloniferous. Lvs 2–4×1–1.6cm, in dense rosettes, cuneate-obovate, blunt, with a small point. Infl. 15–25cm, becoming horizontal, cymose; cor. 5–6mm, yellow. Spring. Mex.

E. proxima Meyrán. = *E. moranii*.

E. pubescens Schldl. = *E. coccinea*.

E. pulchella Berger. St. ± elongate, to 6cm. Lvs 35×15mm, spathulate-oblong, ascending, thick, concave above, bristle-tipped, flushing red in sun. Infl. to 20cm, 10–18-fld, 2–3-branched; cor. 6mm, thin, red. Spring–summer. Mex.

E. pulidonis Walth. Lvs 5×1.5cm, numerous in a basal rosette, ascending, oblong-ovate, bristle-tipped, margin and tip red. Infl. to 18cm, simple, racemose, secund; fls nodding at first; cor. 10mm, lemon yellow. Spring–summer. Mex.

E. pulverulenta Nutt. = *Dudleya pulverulenta*.

E. pulvinata Rose. PLUSH PLANT; CHENILLE PLANT. Densely hairy. St. to 20cm. Lvs 25–65×18–35mm, lax, spathulate-obovate, fine-pointed. Infl. 20–30cm, racemose, 15-fld; cor. 12–18mm, urceolate, yellow, keel red. Winter–spring. S Mex. 'Ruby': lvs bright red, densely pubesc.

E. pumila Schldl. = *E. secunda* var. *pumila*.

E. purpusii (Schum.) Wittm. = *Dudleya cymosa*.

E. purpusorum Berger. Lvs 3–4×2cm, thick, in a dense rosette, ovate, tip sharply pointed, convex beneath, cuticle thick, spotted red and brown. Infl. to 20cm, racemose, 6–9-fld; cor. 12mm, fused only near base, thick, pink-red outside, yellow within. Early summer. Mex.

E. pusilla Berger = *E. amoena*.

E. quitensis (HBK) Lindl. St. short, branching. Lvs 1–6× 0.5–3cm, in loose rosettes or scattered, obovate-lanceolate, thin, keeled, blunt, notched or bristle-tipped, red on margins. Infl. 10–25cm; cor. 8–15mm, 5-sided, not constricted at mouth, yellow at base, red above, yellow inside. Ecuad., Colomb.,

Venez. var. *sprucei* (Bak.) Poelln. Lvs to 6mm wide.

E. racemosa Schldl. & Cham. St. 0 or short. Lvs 5–8×3.5cm, in a dense rosette, oblanceolate-rhomboid, pointed, slightly concave above, margins often cut. Infl. to 50cm, erect, thick, racemose; cor. 12mm, conical or urceolate, red-orange outside, orange-buff inside. Autumn. Mex.

E. rauschii Van Keppel. St. to 5cm, branched. Lvs 40–70× 8–15mm, 10–15 per rosette, triangular-oblanceolate, pointed, margins red.Infl. 10–25cm, tinged red, racemose; cor. straight, orange-red outside, orange-yellow inside. Early autumn. Boliv.

E. recurvata L. Carruth. St. short, occas. branched. Lvs 8×3cm, to 4mm thick, 30 per rosette, obovate, bristle-tipped, dark green, pruinose. Fls not known. Venez.

E. retusa Lem. = *E. fulgens*.

E. rosea Lindl. Subshrub, often epiphytic. St. little-branched, thin, horizontal. Lvs 5–9×1.5–2cm, oblanceolate-oblong, up-turned, pointed. Rac. to 20cm, spike-like; sep. pink-purple; cor. 13mm, straight, yellow, red at tips. Winter–spring. Mex.

E. rosei Nels. & Macbr. = *E. subrigida*.

E. rubromarginata Rose. St. short, unbranched. Lvs 11–17× 7–9cm in tufted rosettes, oblanceolate-obovate, bristle-tipped, glaucous, green-purple, margins bright red. Infl. 1m, paniculate; cor. to 14mm, red outside, chrome-yellow inside. Autumn. Mex.

E. runyonii Rose ex Walth. St. 0 or short. Lvs 6–8×3–4cm, in open rosettes, cuneate-spathulate, blunt, sometimes notched, glaucous. Infl. 2-branched, racemose, nodding at first; cor. to 20mm, erect, red-pink. Mex. var. **macabeana** Walth. Lvs pointed or bristle-tipped.

E. rusbyi (Greene) Kearney & Peebles = *Graptopetalum rusbyi*.

E. sanchez-mejoradae Walth. Tufted. Lvs 6×1.5cm, numerous in several rosettes, oblanceolate-obovate or linear, tip rounded with a small point. Infl. to 50cm, 10-fld, secund; cor. 11mm, urceolate, pink-green. Spring–summer. Mex.

E. sanguinea hort. = *E. atropurpurea*.

E. sayulensis Walth. Rosettes on short, branching st., to over 25cm across. Lvs 15×7cm, crowded, spathulate-obovate, blunt with a fine point, glaucous. Infl. to 36cm, branched, around 30-fld; cor. to 17mm, pink outside, yellow inside. Winter–spring. Mex.

E. ×scaphophylla hort. ex A. Berger = ×*Cremneria scaphylla*.

E. ×scaphylla Deleuil ex E. Morr. = ×*Cremneria scaphylla*.

E. schaffneri (S. Wats.) Rose. St. short. Lvs 6–10×2cm, in dense rosettes, oblanceolate-oblong, with a small abrupt point, margins red. Infl. to 20cm, 2-branched, 8–24-fld; cor. 14–17mm, not contracted at mouth, seg. sharply keeled, red outside, orange within. Winter–spring. Mex.

E. scheerii Lindl. St. to 10cm, sometimes branched. Lvs 9×4cm, in a crowded rosette, obovate, sides ascending, pointed, glaucous. Infl. to 50cm, 2–3-branched, 12–20-fld; cor. to 25mm, campanulate, orange-pink outside, yellow inside. Summer. Mex.

E. scheideckeri De Smet = ×*Pachyveria scheideckeri*.

E. scopulorum Rose = *E. obtusifolia*.

E. secunda W.B. Booth. St. short, offsetting. Lvs 25–75× 12–35mm, in dense basal rosettes, spathulate-cuneate, blunt, bristle-tipped, keeled, glaucous, margin often red. Infl. to 30cm, simple, 5–15-fld; cor. 7–12mm, red outside, yellow inside. Mex. var. **glauca** (Bak.) Otto. Lvs thin. var. **pumila** (Schldl.) Otto. Lvs to only 15mm across.

E. sedoides Walth. = *E. macdougallii*.

E. semivestita Moran. St. unbranched, short. Lvs 10–14× 1.5–3cm, in a rosette, lanceolate-oblanceolate, margins curved upwards, tinged red. Infl. to 55cm, paniculate; sep. green-purple, glaucous; cor. 13mm, pink-red outside, yellow-red inside. Mex.

E. sessiliflora Rose. St. short, 2–3cm, branched. Lvs 6–8× 1.5–1.6cm, in term. rosettes, oblanceolate, pointed, glaucous, margins brown-red. Infl. 40–50cm, pink, 20–25-fld; cor. 14mm, conical. Mex.

E. setosa Rose & Purpus. MEXICAN FIRECRACKER. Long-haired throughout; st. 0. Lvs 4–5×1.8–2mm, numerous, oblanceolate, ± convex beneath, pointed, bristle-tipped. Infl. to 30cm, racemose, 10-fld; cor. 10–12mm, urceolate, yellow with red markings, yellow inside. Summer. Mex.

E. shaviana Walth. St. short or 0. Lvs 5×1.5–2.5cm, in crowded rosettes, obovate, somewhat spoon-shaped, glaucous, undulate, toothed near apex. Infl. to 12cm, simple, secund, nodding; cor. 10–13mm, pink. Summer. Mex.

E. simulans Rose. St. short. Lvs 50–75×18–35mm, 9mm thick, cuneate-obovate, bristle-tipped, margin transparent. Infl. 15–30cm, racemose; cor. 6–15mm, urceolate, pink, yellow above. Winter–spring. Mex.

E. skinneri Walth. St. branched, to 30cm. Lvs 4×2cm, scattered, obovate-cuneate, concave above, margins red. Infl. 15–20cm, racemose; cor. 17–20mm, urceolate to conical, red outside,

yellow within and on edges. Spring–early summer. Mex.

E. ×sobrina Berger = ×*Pachyveria sobrina*.

E. ×sodalis Berger = ×*Pachyveria sodalis*.

E. spectabilis Alexander. Subshrub, 10–60cm. St. much-branched. Lvs 5–7×2.5–3cm, in loose rosettes or scattered, spathulate-obovate, bristle-tipped, flat, papillose, margin red. Infl. to 70cm, racemose, 10-fld; cor. 24mm, pouched at base, red-orange, yellow on margins and inside. Summer. Mex.

E. spilata Kunze = *E. secunda*.

E. sprucei (Bak.) Berger = *E. quitensis* var. *sprucei*.

E. stolonifera (Bak.) Otto. Tuft-forming. St. 5–10cm, branching, stoloniferous. Lvs 5–8×2–4cm, obovate-spathulate, bristle-tipped, concave above, keeled, glaucous when young. Infl. 6–10cm high; cor. 14mm, red outside, yellow within. Summer. Mex.

E. strictiflora A. Gray. St. 0 or short. Lvs 7–9×1.5–2cm, in a loose rosette, ascending, obovate-rhombic, tip pointed, thin, margins curled upwards, glaucous. Infl. to 20cm, secund 10–15-fld; cor. to 15mm, lobes sharply keeled, red outside, orange-red inside. Summer. Tex. to Mex.

E. subrigida (Robinson & Seaton) Rose. St. to 10cm, long, thick. Lvs 15–25×5–10cm, in dense rosettes, obovate to oblanceolate, pointed, margins red, upturned, crenulate. Infl. 60–90cm, paniculate, 6–15-branched; sep. grey-purple; cor. to 25mm, red, bloomed white outside, yellow-red inside. Summer. Mex.

E. subspicata (Bak.) Berger = *E. bicolor*.

E. tenetifolia Kunze = *E. bifida*.

E. tepeacensis V. Poelln. = *Thompsonella minutiflora*.

E. tolucensis Rose = *E. secunda*.

E. turgida Rose. Lvs 50×25mm, in a dense basal rosette, curving upwards, ± keeled near tip, blunt with a small point, grey-green, red-pruinose on margins. Infl. to 20cm, secund, racemose, 10-fld; cor. 12mm, conical, pink outside, yellow within. Spring–summer. Mex.

E. vanvlietii Van Keppel. St. to 5cm. Lvs 4–8×1–2cm, 20–25 per dense rosette, oblanceolate-oblong, with a small point, convex beneath, grey-green, tinged bronze. Infl. 20–50cm, racemose, 15–40-fld; cor. 12mm, creamy white. Summer. Boliv.

E. venezuelensis Rose. St. to 10cm. Lvs 8×4.5cm, in a dense term. rosette, cuneate to oblanceolate, rounded with a bristle tip, glaucous. Infl. 30–40cm, many-fld, racemose; sep. purple-green; cor. 10mm, urceolate, pink. Venez.

E. virens Berger = *Dudleya virens*.

E. viscida Berger = *Dudleya viscida*.

E. walpoleana Rose. St. 0. Lvs 5–9×2cm, in a dense rosette, lanceolate-obovate, carinate, pointed, green spotted red. Infl. to 1m, paniculate; sep. red; cor. 14mm, urceolate or conical, pink, spotted red at tips, yellow-orange inside. Summer. Mex.

E. waltheri Moran & Meyrán. St. to 90cm, horizontal to erect. Lvs 25–75×12–25mm, ovate-spathulate, abruptly pointed, margins red. Infl. 30–60cm, many-fld spikes; cor. 9mm, white below, red above. Autumn–winter. Mex.

E. weinbergii hort. ex Rose = *Graptopetalum paraguayense*.

E. whitei Rose. St. short, branching. Lvs 3–5×0.8–2cm, 35 per rosette, spathulate, bristle-tipped, rounded beneath, glaucous green-brown. Infl. to 30cm, sometimes secund, branched; cor. 10–15mm, urceolate, red. Winter–spring. Boliv.

→*Cotyledon, Oliverella, Pachyphytum*, ×*Pachyveria, Sedum* and *Urbinia*.

Echidnopsis Hook. f. Asclepiadaceae. *c*20 succulent, leafless, perenn. herbs, to 30cm. St. angled, prostrate to erect, ribs divided into hexagonal tubercles giving a tessellated appearance. Lvs short-lived, sometimes persisting as white spines on tubercles. Fls small in clusters, usually apical; cor. fleshy, tube short or 0, lobes 5, triangular-ovate to linear; corona brown, red or yellow with outer whorl 0 or cup-shaped and 5–10-lobed inner whorl. S Arabia, Trop. E Afr. Z9.

E. adamsonii Bally = *E. watsonii*.

E. angustiloba Bruce & Bally. St. 10–11-angled. Fls 1–1.5cm diam., rotate or slightly campanulate, yellow to yellow-lobed with red-yellow centre, setulose inside; lobes ovate-triangular with margins revolute above. Kenya.

E. archeri Bally. St. 8-angled. Fls 5–8×5–6mm, deeply cup-shaped; exterior purple to red-purple, occas. red-pink, interior dark purple to crimson; lobes erect with folded margins, tip acute, reflexed. Kenya.

E. ballyi (Marn.-Lap.) Bally. St. 6–8-angled. Fls pyriform-urceolate, 1–1.5cm long, 8–10mm wide narrowing to 2mm at the mouth, dark purple-red, lobes deltoid, erect to spreading, yellow patched red on inner face. Somalia.

E. bihendulensis Bally. St. 16-angled. Fls 6–7.5mm diam., exterior glab., pale green, interior setulose, yellow to red-brown, lobes deltoid, erect or spreading, margins and apex reflexed. Somalia.

E. cereiformis Hook. f. St. 8-angled. Fls 1cm diam., bright yellow or brown-yellow, rough within, lobes ovate-lanceolate to ovate, acute, incurved to campanulate. Ethiop., Somalia, Saudi Arabia.

E. chrysantha Lavranos = *E. scutellata* ssp. *planiflora*.

E. chrysantha var. *filipes* Lavranos = *E. scutellata* ssp. *planiflora*.

E. ciliata Bally = *E. sharpei* ssp. *ciliata*.

E. columnaris (Nel) R.A. Dyer & Hardy = *Notechidnopsis columnaris*.

E. dammanniana Spreng. Fls 9mm diam., tube yellow spotted purple-brown, lobes dark purple-brown, ovate, acute, projecting, covered by small calli. N Ethiop.

E. ericiflora Lavranos. St. 6–8-angled. Fls 5–8mm, urceolate, exterior wine red, glab., interior red to dark red in tube base, tube narrowing to less than 2mm at the mouth, lobes yellow at tips, reddening toward base, deltoid, erect. Kenya.

E. framesii (Pill.) A. White & B.L. Sloane = *Notechidnopsis tessellata*.

E. golathii Schweinf. = *Caralluma penicillata*.

E. insularis Lavranos. St. 6-angled. Fls v. fleshy, 9.5–11mm long, 4mm across at base, 3mm at mouth of tube, urceolate, exterior green-yellow, glab., interior green-yellow with thin purple lines, lobes erect, deltoid. Socotra.

E. leachii Lavranos. St. 6-angled. Fls 4×4–5mm, short-campanulate, exterior dark purple-pink, interior tinged yellow, lobes ovate-deltoid, ascending, slightly reflexed, bright purple-pink. Tanz.

E. malum (Lavranos) P.V. Bruyns. St. rooting. Fls broad-ellipsoidal, 14–16×13–15mm, exterior minutely and densely papillose, interior deep purple-red, tube mouth star-shaped. Somalia, Ethiop., Kenya.

E. mariae Lavranos = *E. scutellata* ssp. *australis*.

E. mijerteina Lavranos. St. 8–10-angled. Fls 1.5–2.5cm, cylindric, curved, exterior hispid, white to pale brown, interior setulose, red-purple, veined, tube narrowing then widening again at the mouth, transversely ribbed for most of the length. Somalia.

E. modesta Bally nom. nud. = *E. watsonii*.

E. montana (R.A. Dyer & E.A. Bruce) Bally. St. 6-angled. cor. lobes linear, 9–11mm, yellow-green, apex pale purple, acute. S Ethiop.

E. nubica N.E. Br. = *E. cereiformis*.

E. planiflora Bally. St. many-angled. Fls 7.5mm diam., pale yellow-green, cup-shaped, glab., lobes revolute and maroon at apex. Ethiop.

E. planiflora Bally = *E. scutellata* ssp. *planiflora*.

E. radians Bleck. = *E. watsonii*.

E. repens R.A. Dyer & Verdoorn. St. 8–10-angled. Fls solitary, 9mm diam., wine-red, tube slightly hairy, lobes ovate, margins recurved, hairy, minutely papillose. Tanz.

E. repens Dyer & Verdoorn = *E. scutellata* ssp. *repens*.

E. scutellata (Deflers) A. Berger. St. 8-angled. Fls 10mm+ diam., rotate to campanulate, pale to bright yellow, often with purple mottling on exterior; lobes deltoid to ovoid-deltoid. Yemen. ssp. *australis* P.V. Bruyns. St. 8–11 angled. Fls 6–9mm diam., rotate to rotate-campanulate, pale yellow-brown, exterior pale green. Kenya. ssp. *dhofarensis* P.V. Bruyns. St. 8-angled. Fls 9–10mm diam., pale yellow; tube cupular, adpressed to side of staminal column; lobes deltoid-ovate. Oman. ssp. *planiflora* (Bally) P.V. Bruyns. St. 8–15-angled. Fls 7–10mm diam., rotate to rotate-campanulate, brown to brown suffused yellow toward centre to bright yellow or green, exterior pale green. Ethiop., Somalia, Djibouti.

E. seibanica Lavranos. St. 6–8-angled. Fls 6–7mm diam., shallowly campanulate, exterior finely papillate, cream, interior setulose, sulphur yellow with red spots in the tube and on lower part of lobes; lobes twice as long as wide, rounded. S Yemen. ssp. *ciliata* (Bally) P.V. Bruyns. St. 8-angled. Fls 10–15mm diam., exterior green spotted purple, interior densely hairy, dark purple; lobes deltoid. Somalia. ssp. *repens* (Dyer & Verdoorn) P.V. Bruyns. St. creeping. Fls 7–9mm diam., exterior green, interior deep wine red, scattered hairs at the margins; lobes ovate-deltoid or ovate, sometimes yellow-tipped. Kenya, Tanz.

E. serpentina (Nel) A. White & B.L. Sloane = *Notechidnopsis tessellata*.

E. sharpei (Nel) A. White & B.L. Sloane. St. 8-angled. Fls 1cm diam., base red, apex grey-purple, exterior striped red, interior crimson, tube glab., lobes ovate, sparsely rose-ciliate. Kenya.

E. squamulata (Decne.) Bally. St. 6–9-angled. Fls 11–18mm long, 2–3mm wide at mouth, urceolate, pentagonal, exterior shiny red-brown, interior red-brown to dark purple or yellow speckled red-brown; lobes speckled pale yellow lobes outside. Yemen.

E. stellata Lavranos. = *E. virchowii* Schum.

E. urceolata Bally. St. 18–20-angled. Fls 10–18mm, urceolate, tube constricted to 3–4mm near mouth, exterior pale yellow, flushed purple toward base, interior dark purple-red, deeply

pentagonal, lobes deltoid, pale green-yellow. Kenya, Ethiop.

E. virchowii Schum. St. usually 8-angled. Fls 8–11mm diam., rotate, exterior setose, grey-green, interior purple-brown speckled with yellow-green, covered with spherical-stalked, often translucent white papillae, lobes ovate-deltoid to lanceolate-deltoid. Somalia.

E. watsonii Bally. St. 8–12-angled. Fls obpyriform to cupular, 1.5–11mm long, 2–3mm wide at mouth, exterior glab., dark purple-red, interior setulose, yellow to yellow-white, lobes linear-subulate. N Somalia, Kenya.

→*Caralluma, Ceropegia, Pseudopectinaria, Stapeliopsis, Trichocaulon* and *Virchowia*.

Echinacea L. CONE FLOWER. Compositae. 9 rhizomatous perenn. herbs, to 2m. St. simple. Lvs simple, radical and cauline. Cap. radiate, solitary or few, ray flts drooping, purple to rose-pink or white, rarely pink or yellow; disc flts yellow to orange. E US.

E. angustifolia DC. To 1.5m. Lvs to 15cm, lanceolate, hispid. Cap. solitary; ray flts to 2.5cm, light purple or rose-pink. Summer. Z3.

E. pallida (Nutt.) Nutt. To 1m. Lvs to 20cm, linear-lanceolate to elliptic, entire. Cap. solitary; ray flts 2–8cm, purple. Late summer. Z5.

E. purpurea (L.) Moench. To 1.5m. Lvs to 15×10cm, ovate-lanceolate, denticulate, rarely entire. Cap. 1 to few; ray flts 3–8cm, red-purple, shaded green at apex; disc flts orange. Summer–autumn. 'Abendsonne': small; cerise. 'Alba': white. 'Magnus': purple, dark orange boss. 'Monk's Silver': from 'White Lustre'; flts tinted silver. 'Leuchtstern' ('Bright Star'): purple red. 'Nana': dwarf. 'Robert Bloom': rich crimson washed with mauve. 'Rubinstern': to 100cm; large, dark carmine, dark orange boss. 'The King': large, deep carmine. 'White Lustre': to 80cm; clear white with darker centre. 'White Swan': large to 50cm, pure white, honey-scented. Z3.

Echinocactus Link & Otto. Cactaceae. 5 discoid, globose or shortly columnar cacti; st. strongly ribbed; areoles large, forming a broad woolly crown; spines stout, radials shorter than centrals. Fls apical, shortly funnelform to campanulate; pericarpel and tube short. Summer. SW US, Mex. Z9.

E. acanthodes auct., non Lem. = *Ferocactus cylindraceus*.

E. asterias Karw. ex Zucc. = *Astrophytum asterias*.

E. brevihamatus Engelm. = *Sclerocactus brevihamatus*.

E. concinnus Monv. = *Parodia concinna*.

E. coptonogonus Lem. = *Stenocactus coptonogonus*.

E. cornigerus DC. = *Ferocactus latispinus*.

E. corynodes Otto ex Pfeiff. = *Parodia erinacea*.

E. cylindraceus (Engelm.) Engelm. = *Ferocactus cylindraceus*.

E. diguetii F.A. Weber = *Ferocactus diguetii*.

E. durangensis Runge = *Sclerocactus unguispinus*.

E. echidne DC. = *Ferocactus echidne*.

E. electracanthus Lem. = *Ferocactus histrix*.

E. emoryi Engelm. = *Ferocactus emoryi*.

E. eyriesii Turpin = *Echinopsis eyriesii*.

E. gibbosus Haw. = *Gymnocalycium gibborus*.

E. glaucescens DC. = *Ferocactus glaucescens*.

E. glaucus Schum. = *Sclerocactus glaucus*.

E. grandis Rose = *E. platyacanthus*.

E. grusonii Hildm. GOLDEN BARREL CACTUS. St. to 130×80cm, globose, eventually elongating and sometimes offsetting; green; ribs few, tuberculate in young plants, eventually 30–40 or more, high and even-edged; central spines 4, to 3–5cm, angular, golden to pale yellow, sometimes white. Fl. to 6×3–5cm; tep. narrow, yellow, tapering to a brown point. C Mex.

E. haselbergii Ruempl. = *Parodia haselbergii*.

E. heteracanthus Muehlenpf. = *Stenocactus ochoterenanus*.

E. horizonthalonius Lem. St. to 10(–15)×10–20cm, depressed-globose to semi-globose, blue-green or grey-green; ribs 7–13, tuberculate or nearly even-edged, low, broadly convex; central spines 1–5, to 3cm, 2–3mm thick at base, somewhat curved, grey to nearly black, conspicuously ridged. Fl. 5–6×5–7cm; tep. pale pink to magenta, darker near base. N Mex. and SW US.

E. ingens Zucc. = *E. platyacanthus*.

E. johnsonii Engelm. = *Sclerocactus johnsonii*.

E. latispinus (Haw.) C.F. Först. = *Ferocactus latispinus*.

E. lecontei Engelm. = *Ferocactus cylindraceus*.

E. leeanus Hook. = *Gymnocalycium leeanum*.

E. longihamatus Gal. ex Pfeiff. = *Ferocactus hamatacanthus*.

E. mackieanus Hook. = *Gymnocalycium gibbosum*.

E. mammulosus Lem. = *Parodia mammulosa*.

E. multiflorus Hook. = *Gymnocalycium multiflorus*.

E. obvallatus DC. = *Stenocactus obvallatus*.

E. orcuttii Engelm. = *Ferocactus viridescens*.

E. ornatus DC. = *Astrophytum ornatum*.

E. ottonis (Lehm.) Link & Otto = *Parodia ottonis*.

E. oxygonus Link = *Echinopsis oxygona*.

E. palmeri Rose = *E. platyacanthus*.

E. pectinatus Scheidw. = *Echinocereus pectinatus*.

E. pectiniferus Lem. = *Echinocereus pectinatus*.

E. peninsulae F.A. Weber = *Ferocactus peninsulae*.

E. pentlandii Hook. = *Echinopsis pentlandii*.

E. pfeifferi Zucc. & Pfeiff. = *Ferocactus glaucescens*.

E. pilosus Gal. ex Salm-Dyck = *Ferocactus pilosus*.

E. platyacanthus Link & Otto. St. to 3×1m, smaller in cult., green but glaucous and sometimes purple-banded when juvenile; ribs 5–20 in young plants, increasing to 30–60 or more, at first strongly tuberculate, later high and even-edged; spines 4–12, c1–8cm, yellow or brown. Fl. 3–6×3–8cm; tep. yellow, the outer brown-apiculate. C & N Mex.

E. polyancistrus Engelm. & Bigelow = *Sclerocactus polyancistrus*.

E. polycephalus Engelm. & Bigelow. Simple or commonly offsetting; st. globose to cylindric, to 30(–60)×10–20cm, grey-green; ribs 13–21, ± tuberculate; central spines 4, to 7.5cm. Fl. c5×5cm; scales of tube spine-tipped; outer tep. yellow with pink midrib, inner tep. yellow. SW US, NW Mex. var. *polycephalus*. Forming many-stemmed clumps to 60cm×1.2m; spines ashy, the surface fraying and peeling. var. *xeranthemoides* J. Coult. Simple or forming smaller clumps than var. *polycephalus*; spines scarcely peeling, thus glab.

E. pottsii Salm-Dyck = *Ferocactus pottsii*.

E. pringlei (J. Coult.) Rose = *Ferocactus pilosus*.

E. rhodophthalmus Hook. = *Thelocactus bicolor*.

E. roseanus Boed. = *Escobaria roseana*.

E. saglionis Cels = *Gymnocalycium saglionis*.

E. schilinzkyanus Haage f. ex Schum. = *Frailea schilinzkyana*.

E. scopa (Spreng.) Link & Otto = *Parodia scopa*.

E. sinuatus A. Dietr. = *Ferocactus hamatacanthus* var. *sinuatus*.

E. spiralis Karw. ex Pfeiff. = *Ferocactus latispinus* var. *spiralis*.

E. texensis Hopffer. Simple, depressed-globose or discoid, to 12–20×30cm, light to dark green; ribs 13–27, acute; central spine 1, to 7.5cm, angular-flattened, directed downwards and strongly incurved at apex, red-brown. Fl. 5–6×5–6cm; pericarpel and tube with woolly scales; tep. pink, to orange-red in the throat, margins paler, lacerate-fimbriate. SE US, NE Mex.

E. trollietii Rebut ex Schum. = *Sclerocactus unguispinus*.

E. tubiflorus (Pfeiff.) Hook. = *Echinopsis tubiflora*.

E. turbiniformis Pfeiff. = *Strombocactus disciformis*.

E. uncinatus Gal. ex Pfeiff. & Otto = *Sclerocactus uncinatus*.

E. viridescens Torr. & A. Gray = *Ferocactus viridescens*.

E. visnaga Hook. = *E. platyacanthus*.

E. williamsii Lem. ex Salm-Dyck = *Lophophora williamsii*.

E. wislizeni Engelm. = *Ferocactus wislizeni*.

E. xeranthemoides (J. Coult.) Engelm. ex Rydb. = *E. polycephalus* var. *xeranthemoides*.

→*Homalocephala*.

Echinocarpus Bl.

E. hemsleyanus Itô = *Sloanea hemsleyana*.

E. sinensis Hemsl. = *Sloanea hemsleyana*.

E. sterculiaceus Benth. = *Sloanea sterculiacea*.

Echinocereus Engelm. Cactaceae. 45 low-growing shrubby cacti; st. simple or clustering, procumbent or clambering, globose to cylindric, ribbed. Fls developing on upper edge of st. areoles or breaking through above them, funnelform; floral areoles with spines, bristles and sometimes wool. Mex. and SW US.

E. acifer (Salm-Dyck) F.A. Haage = *E. polyacanthus* var. *densus*.

E. adustus Engelm. Simple, or sparingly clustering, depressed-globose to short cylindric, to 19×5–8(–12)cm; ribs 11–16, slightly tuberculate. Central spines 0–1(–5), to 32mm. Fl. purple, (3–)8×4–7cm. Spring. NW Mex. Z9.

E. aggregatus (Engelm.) Rydb. = *E. triglochidiatus* var. *melanacanthus*.

E. albispinus Lahman = *E. reichenbachii* var. *baileyi*.

E. amoenus (A. Dietr.) Schum. = *E. pulchellus*.

E. angusticeps Clover = *E. papillosus*.

E. arizonicus Rose ex Orcutt = *E. triglochidiatus* var. *arizonicus*.

E. baileyi Rose = *E. reichenbachii* var. *baileyi*.

E. barthelowanus Britt. & Rose. Resembling *E. ferreirianus*, but st. more slender; central spines up to 9, similar to the radials. Fl. 5–7cm diam. NW Mex. Z9.

E. berlandieri (Engelm.) hort. F.A. Haage. St. prostrate, 1.5–2.5cm diam.; ribs 5–7; areoles 8–20mm apart; spines 7–12, to 3cm, ± terete. Fl. broadly funnelform, purple without paler centre. Summer. S Tex., NE Mex. Z9.

E. blankii hort. = *E. berlandieri*.

E. bonkerae Thornber & Bonker = *E. fendleri* var. *bonkerae*.

E. boyce-thompsonii Orcutt = *E. fendleri* var. *boyce-thompsonii*.

E. brandegeei (J. Coult.) Schum. Clustering freely; st. erect or decumbent, cylindric to 1m×6cm, pale green; ribs 8–10, tubercles ± hexagonal; central spines 4 in cross-formation, 3–10(–13)cm, sword-like, white, yellow or brown. Fl. to

6.5×7cm, floral areoles with long white wool and spines; tep. pale pink to lavender-purple, crimson in throat. Summer. Baja Calif. Z9.

E. bristolii W.T. Marshall = *E. pseudopectinatus*.

E. bristolii var. *pseudopectinatus* N.P. Tayl. = *E. pseudopectinatus*.

E. caespitosus (Engelm.) Engelm. = *E. reichenbachii*.

E. chisoensis W.T. Marshall. Simple or rarely branching; st. cylindric or tapered toward the apex, sometimes constricted annually, to 5–25×3–5cm; ribs (10–)11–16, strongly tuberculate; central spines (1–)2–6, to 17mm, porrect, v. fine, dark brown. Fl. to 6–9.5×5–5.2cm, funnelform; floral areoles v. woolly, and with fine bristles; tep. v. numerous, thin and delicate, pink to magenta with white throat. SW US, NW Mex. Z9.

E. chloranthus (Engelm.) hort. F.A. Haage. St. simple, cylindric, 7.5–20(–25)×5–7.5cm; ribs 10–18. Fl. to 3.9cm diam., often not opening widely, not lemon-scented (cf. *E. viridiflorus*) yellow-green or tinged brown or red. Spring. N Mex., US (W Tex., S New Mex.). Z8.

E. cinerascens (DC.) Lem. Clustering to form clumps or mounds; st. sprawling, cylindric, 10–30(–60)×1.5–12cm; ribs 5–10(–12), tuberculate or not; spines 7–16, to 4.5cm, terete. Fl. 6–10×6–12cm, pink-magenta, paler to white or green in the throat. Summer. E & NE Mex. var. *cinerascens*. St. 4–10(–12)cm diam.; ribs 6–12; central spines equalling or shorter than the st. diam., pale yellow to brown. var. *ehrenbergii* (Pfeiff.) Bravo. St. 1.5–4(–6)cm diam.; ribs 5–6; central spines longer than the st. diam., glassy white to pale yellow. Z9.

E. coccineus Engelm. = *E. triglochidiatus* var. *melanacanthus*.

E. conglomeratus C.F. Först. ex Schum. = *E. stramineus*.

E. conoideus (Engelm. & Bigelow) Ruempl. = *E. triglochidiatus* var. *melanacanthus*.

E. ctenoides (Engelm.) Ruempl. = *E. pectinatus* var. *dasycanthus*.

E. dasycanthus Engelm. = *E. pectinatus* var. *dasycanthus*.

E. dasyacanthus Engelm. = *E. pectinatus*.

E. davisii Houghton = *E. viridiflorus* var. *davisii*.

E. delaetii (Gürke) Gürke. Branching from base to form lax clumps; st. decumbent, cylindric, to 30×4–8cm, almost covered by spines; ribs 14–24, narrow, tuberculate; central spines 4–5 to 10cm long, straight and bristly, or hair-like and shaggy. Fl. 6–10×6–12.5cm, bright pink-purple, white in throat, tep. fimbriate. N Mex. Z9.

E. dubius (Engelm.) Ruempl. = *E. enneacanthus*.

E. ehrenbergii (Pfeiff.) Ruempl. = *E. cinerascens* var. *ehrenbergii*.

E. engelmannii (Parry ex Engelm.) Lem. Clustering, st. cylindric, 5–60×4–8.7cm; ribs 10–13, not obviously tuberculate; spines (8–)10–21, (2–)4–7 central, 2–7cm, angular. Fl. to 9×9cm, purple-red to magenta or lavender. Summer. NW Mex., SW US. Z8.

E. enneacanthus Engelm. Clustering; st. mostly cylindric and partly prostrate, to 60×(3.5–)5–15cm diam.; ribs 7–10, scarcely tuberculate or tubercles large but flat; spines 7–17, to 4–8cm, terete or partly flattened and angled. Fl. to 8×10cm, magenta deepening to crimson in the throat. Spring–summer. N & NE Mex., SW US. Z9.

E. fasciculatus (Engelm. ex B.D. Jackson) L. Bens. = *E. fendleri* var. *fasciculatus*.

E. fendleri (Engelm.) F. Seitz. Simple or clustering; st. 7.5–50×4–8cm, ovoid to cylindric, erect; ribs 8–18(–22), strongly to weakly tuberculate; areoles 1–2.5cm apart; spines (2–)5–16(–18), terete. Fl. (5–)6–11×5–12cm, purple-magenta to white, darkening towards the sometimes green-tinged centre. Spring–summer. SW US, NW Mex. var. *fendleri*. St. 1–2(–5), 7.5–15(–25)cm; ribs 8–10; spines 5–10, (0–)1 central, to 3.8cm, curved upward. Fl. large. SW US, N Mex. var. *bonkerae* (Thornber & Bonker) L. Bens. St. 5–35, to 20cm; ribs (11–)13–16; spines 12–15, 1(–3) central, less than 1cm. Fl. small. US (Ariz.). var. *boyce-thompsonii* (Orcutt) L. Bens. St. 3–12, to 25cm; ribs (12–)14–18(–22). Spines 13–17, 3, central, the lowermost to 5(–10)cm, strongly deflexed, v. slender. SW US. var. *fasciculatus* (Engelm. ex B.D. Jackson) N.P. Tayl. St. 5–20, 17.5×45cm; ribs 8–13; spines 10–15, 1–3 central, the lowermost to 7.5cm, porrect to slightly deflexed. Ariz., SW New Mex., NW Mex. var. *kuenzleri* (Castetter et al.) L. Bens. St. 1–4(–8), to 25(–30)cm; ribs 9–10(–12); spines 2–6(–7), v. stout, 0(–1) central, to 2.9cm. Fl. v. large. New Mex., N Mex. (N Chihuahua). var. *ledingii* (Peebles) N.P. Tayl. St. 4–12, to 50cm; ribs 12–14(–16); spines 10–13(–16), all yellow, 1–3(–5) central, the principal one to 2.5cm, strongly recurved. US (SE Ariz.). var. *rectispinus* (Peebles) L. Bens. St. 1–10, to 18(–25)cm; ribs 9–10; spines 8–10, 1 central, to 3.8cm, porrect. Fl. large. SW US, NW Mex. Z9.

E. ferreirianus H. Gates. St. simple or branched at base, globose to cylindric, to 30(–40)×4–10cm, green grey-green or tinged blue or purple; ribs (9–)11–14, deep somewhat tuberculate; central spines 4–7, 5–10cm, up to 2.5mm thick, terete, red at first, later brown to black. Fl. 6–10×4–9.5cm; floral areoles with wool and bristly spines; tep. purple-pink, orange or red in throat. Baja Calif. var. *ferreirianus* Branching; st. 30(–40)×8cm; central spines usually 4. var. *lindsayi* (Meyrán) N.P. Tayl. Unbranched; st. to 13×10cm, eventually taller in cult., central spines 4–7. Z9.

E. fitchii Britt. & Rose = *E. reichenbachii* var. *fitchii*.

E. gentryi Clover = *E. scheeri* var. *gentryi*.

E. glycimorphus Ruempl. = *E. cinerascens*.

E. gonacanthus Engelm. & Bigelow = *E. triglochidiatus* var. *gonacanthus*.

E. grandis Britt. & Rose. St. simple or sparingly branched, cylindric, to 50×12cm; ribs 18–25; central spines 8–12, 3–6mm, dull white or pale yellow. Fl. 5–7×c5–8cm; floral areoles dense, with white wool and long, bristly spines; tep. white, pale yellow pale pink, green toward base. NW Mex. Z9.

E. hempelii Fobe = *E. fendleri* var. *kuenzleri*.

E. huitcholensis (F.A.C. Weber) Gürke = *E. polyacanthus* var. *huitcholensis*.

E. knippelianus Liebner. Simple or clustering; st. 3–8cm diam., depressed-globose, dark green; ribs 5–8 low and broad. Fl. 2.5–4×4–6.5cm, pink-lavender, purple or white. Spring. NE Mex. Z9.

E. kuenzleri Castetter et al. = *E. fendleri* var. *kuenzleri*.

E. laui G. Frank. Clustering; st. cylindric, to 10×4cm, covered with dense spines; ribs 14–16, low, finely tuberculate; central spines 4, to 30mm. Fl. 3–5×3–6.5cm, pink. Spring. NW Mex. Z9.

E. ledingii Peebles = *E. fendleri* var. *ledingii*.

E. leonensis Mathsson = *E. pentalophus* var. *leonensis*.

E. leucanthus N.P. Tayl. Branching near base; st. ascending, cylindric, v. slender, to 30cm×3–6mm; ribs 8, v. low; central spines 2–3 or more, minute, almost black. Fl. 2–4×4cm; inner tep. white, sometimes with pale pink mid-stripe, pale brown in throat. Summer. NW Mex. Z9.

E. lindsayi Meyrán = *E. ferreirianus* var. *lindsayi*.

E. longisetus (Engelm.) Lem. Clustering; st. erect or decumbent, to 30–50×3.5–6(–7.5)cm, covered with spines; ribs 11–17, tuberculate; central spines 4–9, to 7.5cm, slender, deflexed, glassy white or tinged yellow.Fl. 5.6–7×6–7.2cm; tep. pink-purple with darker mid-stripes, throat white. NE Mex. Z9.

E. longisetus var. *delaetii* (Gürke) N.P. Tayl. = *E. delaetii*.

E. longispinus Lahman = *E. reichenbachii* var. *baileyi*.

E. mamillatus (Engelm.) Britt. & Rose = *E. brandegeei*.

E. maritimus (M.E. Jones) Schum. Caespitose, branching to form clusters or mounds to 40cm×1–2m; st. 5–30×5–7cm; ribs 8–10, acute, deep; spines 14–20, red at first, later dirty yellow to grey, the central and upper to 3–6cm, strongly flattened and angled. Fl. to 6cm; outer tep. tinged brown or red, inner tep. bright yellow, fading to orange-pink. NW Mex. Z9.

E. melanocentrus Lowry, invalid. = *E. reichenbachii* var. *fitchii*.

E. merkeri Hildm. ex Schum. = *E. enneacanthus*.

E. mojavensis (Engelm. & Bigelow) Ruempl. = *E. triglochidiatus* var. *mojavensis*.

E. octacanthus (Muehlenpf.) Britt. & Rose. Possibly an older name for *E. triglochidiatus*.

E. oklahomensis Lahman = *E. reichenbachii* var. *baileyi*.

E. pacificus Engelm. = *E. polyacanthus* var. *pacificus*.

E. palmeri Britt. & Rose. Simple or few branched; st. ovoid to cylindric, 3–8×2–3cm, dark green, constricted annually; ribs 6–10, scarcely tuberculate; central spines 1–2, 1–2cm, slender, ascending, dark brown, tipped darker; fls to 4–7×5–11.6cm, fragrant; outer tep. tinged brown, inner tep. lavender-pink to purple with darker mid-stripe, paler towards base. N Mex. Z9.

E. papillosus Linke ex Ruempl. Clustering sparsely or freely; st. cylindric, 4–10(–30)×2–5(–7)cm, brown-green; ribs (6–)7–10, strongly tuberculate; spines 7–12, to 2cm. Fl. 8–12cm diam.; perianth broadly urceolate, yellow, red at base. Spring. US (S Tex.). var. *papillosus*. Clustering sparsely; st. to 10×3–5cm or larger. var. *angusticeps* (Clover) W.T. Marshall. Clustering freely; st. 4–8×2–3cm. Z9.

E. pectinatus (Scheidw.) Engelm. Simple, or eventually sparingly branched; st. globose to cylindric, to 8–35×13cm; ribs 12–23, divided into low tubercles; central spines (0–)1–5 or more, minute or to 15(–25)mm, radial spines pectinate. Fl. (5–)6–12(–16)cm diam.; broadly urceolate, white or maroon in the throat, green at base. Spring. SW US, N Mex. var. *pectinatus*. Fl. pink to lavender. var. *dasyacanthus* (Engelm.) N.P. Tayl. Fl. yellow to nearly white. Z9.

E. pensilis (K. Brandg.) Purpus. St. elongate, arching, prostrate or pendulous, 1–4m×2–5cm, producing aerial roots; ribs 8–11, rounded; spines initially 6–10, increasing to 70 or more, to 2.5cm, pale yellow. Fls to 6.9×4.5cm; floral areoles with white wool and spines; tep. orange-red with darker mid-stripe. Spring–summer. NW Mex. Z9.

E. pentalophus (DC.) Lem. Clustering; st. cylindric, sprawling or

erect, 20–60(–200)×1–6cm; ribs (3–)4–8; spines 3–10, v. short or to 6cm. Fl. 8–12×10–15cm, bright pink-magenta, white or yellow in the throat, rarely entirely white. Summer. E to NE Mex., S Tex. var. *pentalophus*. St. erect or prostrate, cylindric, branching above ground, green or suffused red-purple; ribs (3–)4–5; spines 3–7. var. *leonensis* (Mathsson) N.P. Tayl. St. ± erect, often tapered, grey-green, often branching by underground rhiz.; ribs 5–8; spines up to 9. Z9.

E. perbellus Britt. & Rose = *E. reichenbachii* var. *perbellus*.

E. polyacanthus Engelm. Caespitose or forming large clumps; st. erect or ascending, cylindric, to 20cm or more ×2–6(–10)cm, bright to dark green; ribs (9–)10–11(–14), tuberculate or not; central spines to 2.5cm, yellow-brown to nearly black. Fl. scarlet to crimson, variable in size; pericarpel and tube 2–8×c1cm diam.; floral areoles finely woolly with numerous bristly dark-tipped spines. Spring. NW Mex., SW US. var. *polyacanthus*. Fl. 4–7(–8)×3–4cm. var. *densus* (Reg.) N.P. Tayl. St. 5–8cm diam.; ribs 10–15, high; central spines to 10cm. Fl. 8–14×7cm. W and C N Mex. var. *huitcholensis* (F.A.C. Weber) N.P. Tayl. St. 2–5(–6)cm diam.; ribs to 13, low; central spines to 1.5cm. Fl. 5.5–15×4.5×8cm. W Mex. var. *pacificus* (Engelm.) N.P. Tayl. Forming large clumps to 1.3m diam. Fl. 3–5×2–3cm. NW Mex. Z9.

E. poselgeri Lem. St. clambering, weak, slender-cylindric, to 60(–120)×1–1.5(–2)cm; ribs 8–10, v. low; spines 9–17, to 9mm, adpressed. Fl. to 7.5×7.5cm, bright pink-magenta, darker in throat. Summer. NE Mex., US (S Tex.). Z9.

E. poselgerianus Linke = *E. berlandieri*.

E. procumbens (Engelm.) Lem. = *E. pentalophus*.

E. pseudopectinatus (N.P. Tayl.) N.P. Tayl. Simple or clustering; st. cylindric, to 20×5cm, ± obscured by spines; ribs 15–19; central spines 1–5, to 10(–15)mm. Fl. to 11×13cm; floral areoles woolly with few stout spines; tep. light magenta, paler or green-tinged near base. NW Mex., SE Ariz. Z9.

E. pulchellus (Mart.) Schum. Simple or clustering; st. 2.5–13cm diam., globose or hemispheric, grey to blue-green; ribs 9–17, tuberculate; central spines 0; radial spines inconspicuous. Fl. 3–6×3–8cm, pink, magenta or white. Spring. N & S Mex. var. *pulchellus*. St. 2.5–5cm diam.; ribs 9–12. var. *sharpii* N.P. Tayl. St. dark green; ribs 11–17. Fl. white or v. pale pink. var. *weinbergii* (Weingart) N.P. Tayl. St. 6–13cm diam.; ribs 11–15; spines conspicuous. Z9.

E. purpureus Lahman = *E. reichenbachii*.

E. rectispinus Peebles = *E. fendleri* var. *rectispinus*.

E. reichenbachii (Walp.) F.A. Haage. Simple, more rarely clustering; st. globose to cylindric, erect, to 30(–40)×10cm, ± obscured by spines; ribs (10–)11–19, narrow, with low tubercles; spines 12–40 or more, rather short, pectinate. Fl. to 5–12×6–16cm; floral areoles with dense wool and fine bristles; tep. v. numerous, thin and delicate, pink to purple. Spring–summer. NE Mex., SW US. var. *reichenbachii*. Central spines 0, radial spines 18–30 or more, to c6mm. Perianth white or deep magenta in throat. var. *armatus* (Poselger) N.P. Tayl. Central spines (0–1)1–2, to 20mm, radial spines to 23, to 8mm. Perianth pale in throat, green at base. NE Mex. var. *baileyi* (Rose) N.P. Tayl. Central spines 1–3, to 3mm, radial spines to 14, to 12(–25)mm. Perianth as in var. *reichenbachii*. var. *fitchii* (Britt. & Rose) L. Bens. Central spines 1–7, to 9mm, radial spines to 22m, to 7.5mm. Perianth deep crimson in throat. var. *perbellus* (Britt. & Rose) L. Bens. Central spines 0–1, 1mm, radial spines to 16(–20), to 6mm. Perianth crimson at base. Z8.

E. rigidissimus (Engelm.) F.A. Haage. Simple, v. rarely branched, globose to cylindric, 6–18(–30)×4–9(–11)cm, obscured by spines; ribs 15–23; central spines 0, radials 15–23(–35), pectinate, adpressed. Fl. 5–7×6–9cm; floral areoles with wool and short, stiff spines; tep. brilliant pink-red to magenta, white in the throat and at base. Summer. NW Mex., SE Ariz. Z9.

E. rosei Wooton & Standl. = *E. triglochidiatus* var. *neomexicanus*.

E. russanthus Wenig. = *E. chloranthus*.

E. salm-dyckianus Scheer = *E. scheeri*.

E. salmianus Ruempl. = *E. scheeri*.

E. sarissophorus Britt. & Rose = *E. enneacanthus*.

E. scheeri (Salm-Dyck) Scheer. St. cylindric, decumbent or prostrate, 10–60(–100)×1.5–3(–4)cm, branching; ribs 4–12(–14); areoles 2–6(–7)mm apart; central spines 0–4, 1–20mmm, white to dark brown; radial spines 0–13, 1–7mm, pale brown or white. Fl. buds sharply pointed; fls to 14×8cm, narrowly tubular-funnelform, scarlet, orange or pink. Spring. NW Mex. var. *scheeri*. Ribs (6–)7–10, tuberculate; spines 9–13, conspicuous. Fl. orange, pink or scarlet; floral areoles with spines to 8mm. var. *gentryi* (Clover) N.P. Tayl. Ribs 4–5(–7), scarcely tuberculate; spines 0 or minute. Fl. pink with pale or orange throat; floral areoles with spines to 3mm. Z9.

E. schmollii (Weingart) N.P. Tayl. Simple or sparingly branched; rootstock tuberous; st. ascending, cylindric, to

15(–25)cm×11mm; ribs 8–10, tuberculate; areoles 1.5–2mm apart; spines c35, to 7mm, bristle- or hair-like and giving the st. a woolly appearance. Fl. 3.5–5×5–6cm, funnelform; tep. bright pink. Summer. E Mex. Z9.

E. sciurus (K. Brandg.) Dams. Caespitose, forming clumps to 60cm across; rootstock somewhat tuberous; st. cylindric or tapering, to 20×3–5cm, covered with spines; ribs 12–17, 3–5mm high, finely tuberculate; areoles to 7mm apart; spines to c22, 3–16mm, slender, brown to nearly white with dark tips, centrals not differentiated or up to 6. Fl. to 8×7–10cm, funnelform; outer tep. with brown mid-stripe, inner tep. bright pink-purple with darker mid-stripe, paler at base. NW Mex. Z9.

E. scopulorum Britt. & Rose. Usually unbranched; st. cylindric 10–40× less than 10cm, covered with spines; ribs 13–15, 5×15mm; central spines (3–)6–10, shorter than the radials, porrect, radial spines c20, adpressed, 8–14mm. Fl. to 8.5×10cm, funnelform, fragrant; tep. oblanceolate-spathulate, pale to deep pink, throat white, base white. NW Mex. Z9.

E. stoloniferus W.T. Marshall. Clustering, usually branching by underground stolons; st. ovoid to cylindric, 9–30×3–6(–8)cm, deep olive-green; ribs 11–16, low, narrow; areoles 3–9mm apart; central spines 1–5, to 2(–2.5)cm, radial spines (8–)10–13, to 1.5cm. Fl. to 10×15cm, short-funnelform. Summer–autumn. NW Mex. Z9.

E. stramineus (Engelm.) F. Seitz. Clustering and forming mounds; st. to 45×8cm, tapering gradually towards apex; ribs 11–17, somewhat tuberculate; areoles 7–15(–18)mm apart; spines 9–18, the largest 4–9cm, mostly glassy white, terete to somewhat flattened. Fl. 6–12.5×6–12.5cm or more, broadly funnelform, bright pink-magenta. Summer. N Mex., SW US. Z8.

E. subinermis Salm-Dyck ex Scheer. Simple or sparingly clustering; st. depressed globose to cylindric, erect, 4–25(–32.5)×4–15cm, grey to dark blue-green; ribs 5–11, high, acute, not tuberculate; areoles circular to elliptic, 6–20mm apart; central spines 0–1(–4), minute or to 20mm, radial spines 0–10, 1–20(–30)mm. Fl. 10×13cm, funnelform, yellow. Summer. NW Mex. Z9.

E. subterraneus Backeb., invalid. = E. sciurus.

E. triglochidiatus Engelm. Simple or clustering, sometimes forming v. large clumps; st. 5–30(–40)×5–15cm, ovoid to cylindric, extremely variable; ribs 5–12, high and acute to low and tuberculate, sometimes spiralled, areoles 6–12mm apart with persistent wool; spines (1–)3–16(–22), 1–7cm, terete or angled, usually straight. Fl. 3–7(–9)×2.5–7cm, tubular-funnelform, brilliant scarlet, rarely pink, paler in the throat, remaining open day and night, unscented. Spring. SW US and adjacent N Mex. var. **triglochidiatus.** St. simple or sparsely offsetting, to 30×7.5cm; ribs 5–8; spines 3–4(–7), to 2.5cm, 3-angled, with 0.1 central. var. **arizonicus** (Rose ex Orcutt) L. Bens. Resembling var. *neomexicanus* but st. few, to 40cm; spines 6–14, the radial often slightly curved, the central 1–13, to 1.5mm thick at base. var. **gonacanthus** (Engelm. & Bigelow) Boissev. St. few to numerous, to 12.5×5–7.5cm; spines 6–9(–11), the central 0–2, to 4.4cm, 3–6-angled. var. **melanacanthus** (Engelm.) L. Bens. Forming mounds of up to 500 st., individually 7.7(–15)×2.5–6cm; ribs 8–10; spines 6–14, the central 1–3, to 6cm, rarely angled, straight. var. **mojavensis** (Engelm. & Bigelow) L. Bens. Resembling var. *melancanthus*; ribs 9–10; spines 6–10, the central 1–2, to 7cm, terete or angled, curving or twisting. var. **neomexicanus** (Standl.) W.T. Marshall. Forming clumps of up to 45 st., individually to 30×7.5–10cm; ribs 8–12; spines 11–22, the 4 centrals much longer, to 4cm, 1mm thick at base, terete, ± straight. Z8.

E. viridiflorus Engelm. St. simple or rarely branched, erect, globose, ovoid, or cylindric, 2.5–12.5×2.5–5cm; ribs 6–14, tuberculate; areoles circular to elliptic, 3–6mm apart; central spines 0–3(–4), radial spines 8–24. Fl. to 3×3cm, funnelform, opening widely, green to yellow-green, lemon-scented (cf. *E. chloranthus*). Spring. SC US (SW Dak. to Tex.). var. *davisii* (Houghton) W.T. Marshall. Dwarf, st. only 1.2–2.5×0.9–1.2cm. SW US. Z8.

E. websterianus G. Lindsay. Caespitose, forming clumps to 60cm across; st. cylindric, to 60×8cm; ribs 18–24, to 5mm high; areoles 6–9mm apart; spines golden yellow, later brown, to 1cm, 6–8 porrect, 14–18 spreading. Fl. 6×3–4cm, pink. NW Mex. Z9.

E. weinbergii Weing. = E. pulchellus var. weinbergii.

→*Cereus, Echinocactus, Mammillaria, Morangaya* and *Wilcoxia*.

Echinochloa Palib. Gramineae. 30 ann. or perenn., tufted or stoloniferous grasses. St. stout, sometimes succulent. Lvs linear to narrow-lanceolate, flat, glab., midrib prominent, ligules ciliate or 0. Infl. racemose or paniculate, spicate; spikelets usually in 4 rows, 2-fld; glumes membranous, often stiffly hairy. Cosmop.

E. crus-galli (L.) Palib. COCKSPUR; BARNYARD GRASS; BARNYARD MILLET. Ann., to 120cm. St. clumped, erect to spreading or decumbent. Lvs to 2cm diam., ligules 0. Infl. erect or pendent, lanceolate to ovate, to 25cm, tinged purple. Summer–autumn. Distrib. as for the genus. Z6.

E. polystachya (HBK) A. Hitchc. Creeping perenn., to 180cm. St. coarse, pubesc., hairs adpressed. Lvs to 2.5cm diam.; ligule stiff yellow-pubesc. Infl. a slender, dense pan., pendent, to 30cm. Summer. Americas. Z8.

→*Panicum.*

Echinocitrus Tan.
E. brassii (White) Tan. = *Triphasia brassii*.

Echinocystis (Michx.) Torr. & A. Gray. Cucurbitaceae. 1 climbing, tuberous, perenn. herb to 6m. Tendrils 2–3-fid. Lvs palmate, 3–5-lobed. Fls green white, lobes 6, slender, to 5mm; ♂ in axill. pan., ♀ solitary or paired. Fr. 5cm ellipsoid or globose, spiny. N Amer.

E. fabacea Naudin = *Marah fabacea*.
E. lobata (Michx.) Torr. & A. Gray. WILD CUCUMBER; WILD BALSAM APPLE; MOCK CUCUMBER; PRICKLY CUCUMBER.
E. macrocarpa Greene = *Marah macrocarpus*.
E. oregana (Torr. & A. Gray) Cogn. = *Marah oreganus*.
E. wrightii (A. Gray) Cogn. = *Echinopepon wrightii*.

Echinodorus (L.) Engelm. Alismataceae. 30 aquatic, ann. or perenn. herbs, often stoloniferous. Lvs radical, submerged or raised above water, mostly basal, long-petiolate, linear-lanceolate to cordate. Scapes long, terminating in pan. with whorls of 3–6 br.; pet. 3, white or pink, rarely yellow. Summer. Americas, Afr. Z9.

E. andrieuxii (Hook. & Arn.) Small. Lvs erect, long-petiolate, narrow-lanceolate to elliptic or ovate, base decurrent on petiole, to 25×8cm. Infl. racemose or paniculate, scape often winged between whorls, 50–100cm; fls in 6–13 whorls; pet. to 8mm. Trop. & subtrop. Amer. Z10.

E. berteroi (Spreng.) Fassett. Submerged lvs ribbon-like, emersed lvs ovate to cordate, to 15cm, pellucid lines conspicuous. Scape erect, lower br. compound; fls to 25mm wide. S US, W Indies. Z9.

E. bracteatus Micheli. Lvs erect, ovate, to 40cm, base cordate. Infl. branched to 3m, axis narrowly winged, with slender bracts. C Amer. Z9.

E. brevipedicellatus (Kuntze) Buchenau. Perenn. Submerged lvs linear, to 35–40cm, emersed lvs narrow-lanceolate, to 20–30cm, acuminate, with pellucid markings. Fls 1–2cm diam., in 4–6 whorls. Braz. Z10.

E. cordifolius (L.) Griseb. TEXAS MUD BABY. Lvs broadly ovate, 10–20cm, base cordate to truncate; petioles 5–15cm. Scape usually with long triangular bracts; fls 12–18mm diam. in 2–6 whorls. S, C & E US, Mex. Z9.

E. grandiflorus Griseb. Lvs erect, long-petiolate, ovate to broadly ovate, to 27cm, cordate at base, pellucid markings conspicuous. Infl. simple or branched; fls whorled. S Amer. Z9.

E. grisebachii Small. Lvs lanceolate to oblong-ovate, to 12cm, pellucid dots numerous. Scape simple or slightly branched, with close verticels of subsessile fls. N S Amer. Z10.

E. intermedius (Mart.) Griseb. PYGMY CHAIN SWORD PLANT. Similar to *E. parviflorus* but with larger fls and no pellucid lines. Lvs linear, to 14×2cm, membranous, crisped. Braz. Z10.

E. longistylis Buchenau = *E. andrieuxii*.

E. magdalenensis Fassett. DWARF AMAZON SWORD PLANT. Freely stoloniferous. Lvs lanceolate to narrowly ovate, 4–8cm; petioles 5–10cm. Scape to 30cm; fls 5mm diam., 4–7 per whorl. Colomb. Z10.

E. martii Micheli = *E. intermedius*.
E. muricatus Griseb. = *E. grandiflorus*.
E. nymphaeifolius (Griseb.) Buchenau. Lvs ovate, to 15cm, cordate at base. Scape to 1m; infl. 2–4× compound, in erect ovate or conical pan. N S Amer. Z10.

E. palaefolius (Nees & Mart.) Macbr. Lvs 5–25cm, base cordate, truncate or decurrent, without pellucid markings. Fls on winged erect or prostrate scapes. S & C Amer. Z10.

E. paniculatus Micheli. AMAZON SWORD PLANT. Lvs linear-lanceolate to elliptic, sometimes subfalcate, 25–45cm, base cuneate to truncate; petiole 5–15cm, winged. Infl. usually branched; fls 1–2cm diam., in 10–15 whorls. N S Amer. Z10.

E. radicans (Nutt.) Engelm. = *E. cordifolius*.
E. ranunculoides (L.) Engelm. = *Baldellia ranunculoides*.
E. rostratus (Nutt.) Engelm. = *E. berteroi*.
E. tenellus (Mart.) Buchenau. Mat-forming, stoloniferous. Submerged lvs to 10cm, linear-lanceolate to oblong, emersed lvs to 2–3cm, slightly fleshy; petioles to 5cm. Scape to 12cm; fls to 1cm diam., 3–6 in a single whorl. Americas. Z9.

Echinofossulocactus Britt. & Rose, non Lawrence.

Echinofossulocactus albatus sensu Britt. & Rose = *Stenocactus vaupelianus*.

Echinofossulocactus arrigens (Link ex A. Dietr.) Britt. & Rose = *Stenocactus obvallatus*.

Echinofossulocactus caespitosus Backet. = *Stenocactus obvallatus*.

Echinofossulocactus coptonogonus (Lem.) Lawrence = *Stenocactus coptonogonus*.

Echinofossulocactus crispatus (DC.) Lawrence pro parte = *Stenocactus crispatus*.

Echinofossulocactus crispatus (DC.) Lawrence pro parte = *Stenocactus multicostatus*.

Echinofossulocactus lamellosus (A. Dietr.) Britt. & Rose = *Stenocactus crispatus*.

Echinofossulocactus lancifer (A. Dietr.) Britt. & Rose = *Stenocactus crispatus*.

Echinofossulocactus lloydii Britt. & Rose = *Stenocactus multicostatus*.

Echinofossulocactus multicostatus (Hildm. ex Schum.) Britt. & Rose = *Stenocactus multicostatus*.

Echinofossulocactus obvallatus (DC.) Lawrence = *Stenocactus obvallatus*.

Echinofossulocactus ochoterenanus (Tiegel) Whitm. = *Stenocactus ochoterenanus*.

Echinofossulocactus pentacanthus (Lem.) Britt. & Rose = *Stenocactus obvallatus*.

Echinofossulocactus phyllacanthus (A. Dietr.) Lawrence = *Stenocactus phyllacanthus*.

Echinofossulocactus vaupelianus (Werderm.) Whitm. = *Stenocactus vaupelianus*.

Echinofossulocactus violaciflorus (Quehl) Britt. & Rose = *Stenocactus obvallatus*.

Echinofossulocactus zacatecasensis Britt. & Rose = *Stenocactus multicostatus*.

Echinomastus Britt. & Rose.

E. durangensis (Runge) Britt. & Rose = *Sclerocactus unguispinus*.

E. erectocentrus (J. Coult.) Britt. & Rose = *Sclerocactus erectocentrus*.

E. intertextus (Engelm.) Britt. & Rose = *Sclerocactus intertextus*.

E. macdowellii (Quehl) Britt. & Rose = *Thelocactus macdowellii*.

E. mapimiensis Backeb. = *Sclerocactus unguispinus*.

E. mariposensis Hester = *Sclerocactus mariposensis*.

E. unguispinus (Engelm.) Britt. & Rose = *Sclerocactus unguispinus*.

Echinopanax Decne. & Planch. nom. nud.

E. elatus Nak. = *Oplopanax elatus*.

E. horridus (Sm.) Decne. & Planch. = *Oplopanax horridus*.

E. japonicus Nak. = *Oplopanax japonicus*.

Echinopepon Naudin. Cucurbitaceae. 12 slender annuals. St. hairy at nodes. Tendrils bifid. Lvs lobed, base cordate. ♂ fls in pan. or rac. from axils; cor. white, rotate; ♀ fls solitary; cor. larger than in ♂. Fr. glab. or downy, spiny, dry. N Amer.

E. wrightii (A. Gray) S. Wats. Climbing, pubesc. Lvs to 10cm, reniform, base cordate, denticulate to 3–5-lobed or -angled. ♂ fls in long rac.; cor. rotate, 6–8mm diam., lobes 5, triangular-ovate. Fr. beaked, to 2×1.5cm, spines to 15mm. Summer. W Tex., Ariz. to N Mex.

→*Echinocystis*.

Echinops L. GLOBE THISTLE. Compositae. *c*120 erect perenn., bienn. or ann. herbs. Lvs simple, 1–3-pinnatifid. Cap. unifloral, grouped into 1 or more globose infl. (pseudocephalia), subtended by small, laciniate, basal bracts; fits tubular, blue or grey-green to white, anth. blue-grey. Eur., Medit. to C Asia and trop. Afr. (mts).

E. bannaticus Rochel ex Schräd. Perenn. 50–120cm. Lvs glandular-hairy, sparsely strigose and arachnoid above, margin densely scabridulous, white-tomentose beneath, ovate to elliptic, subentire to 2-pinnatisect, seg. triangular, with few, slender spines. Pseudocephalia 2.5–5cm diam., blue or grey-blue; flts grey-blue. SE Eur. to Czech. 'Blue Globe' ('Blue Ball'): to 1m; dark blue. Z3.

E. chantavicus Trautv. Perenn. 50–100cm. Lower lvs green and hirsute above, white-tomentose beneath, eglandular, 30–40cm, deeply pinnately lobed, lobes ovate, with unequal, spiny teeth. Pseudocephalia 3–4cm diam., solitary, dark blue; flts dark blue. C Asia. Z5.

E. commutatus Juratzka = *E. exaltatus*.

E. exaltatus Schräd. Perenn., 40–200cm. Lvs sparsely strigose above, tomentose beneath, margin densely scabridulous, ovate to elliptic, 1–2-pinnatifid, lobes triangular, with few, short,

slender spines. Pseudocephalia 3.5–6cm diam., white to grey, rarely tinged green; flts white or grey. E Eur. to Russia. Z3.

E. giganteus A. Rich. Shrubby perenn. 2–5m. Lvs setose-hispid above, white-tomentose beneath, lanceolate, unequally pinnatifid, seg. incised-dentate, spiny. Pseudocephalia to 20cm diam., solitary, or many and much smaller. Ethiop. Z9.

E. gmelinii Turcz. Ann., 15–30cm. Lvs green, gland. hairy, to 5cm, oblong, entire or slightly lobed, semi-amplexicaul, margin spiny. Pseudocephalia to 3cm diam., solitary at ends of br., white. C Asia, Mong., China. Z5.

E. graecus Mill. Perenn. 25–70cm. Lvs arachnoid above, white-tomentose beneath, or glab., elliptic, 2-pinnatisect, seg. linear-lanceolate, margins with slender, short spines. Pseudocephalia 3–4cm diam., shiny silver-white; flts blue. Greece. Z8.

E. horridus auct. = *E. orientalis*.

E. humilis Bieb. Perenn., 7–30cm. Basal lvs rosulate, numerous, thinly white-tomentose, to 7cm, lyrate-pinnately lobed, lobes ovate, obtuse, st. lvs with lobes, spiny-toothed. Pseudocephalia 3–4cm and somewhat smaller; flts light blue. Sib. Z3.

E. latifolius Tausch. Perenn., 30–60cm. Lvs sparsely arachnoid above, ± tomentose beneath, bipinnately divided to pinnatifid, spiny-toothed or -lobed, 10–15cm. Pseudocephalia 4–6cm diam., dark-blue. E Sib., Mong. Z3.

E. nivens Wallich & DC. Perenn., to 1m. Lvs white tomentose beneath, 7–20cm, lanceolate or elliptic, pinnately divided, seg. numerous, linear, spiny, revolute. Pseudocephalia 3.5–8cm diam., pale blue. W Himal. Z7.

E. orientalis Trautv. Perenn., 50–80cm. Lvs densely glandular-pubesc. above, white-tomentose beneath, broadly oblong, 2-pinnatisect, seg. linear-lanceolate to triangular, spiny-dentate. Pseudocephalia 4.5–7cm diam., grey-green; flts green-white. SE Eur., Caspian region. Z3.

E. paniculatus Jacq. f. = *E. sphaerocephalus*.

E. ritro L. non hort. Perenn., 20–60cm. Lvs glandular-hairy, with few simple hairs, or slightly arachnoid above, white-tomentose beneath, elliptical, 1–2-pinnatisect, seg. linear-triangular, revolute, with spines. Pseudocephalia 3.5–4.5cm diam., blue; flts blue, rarely white. C & E Eur. to C Asia. 'Blue Glow': vigorous and hardy, to 1m; delicate light blue. 'Taplow Blue': v. vigorous to 1m; strong blue. 'Veitch's Blue': to 80cm; vivid mid-blue. Z3.

E. ritro hort. non L. = *E. bannaticus*.

E. ritro ssp. *ruthenicus* (Bieb.) Nyman = *E. ruthenicus*.

E. ruthenicus Bieb. 20–90cm. Lvs dark green and glab. above, densely white-lanate beneath, revolute, shortly and sparsely spiny, to 45cm, oblanceolate to elliptic, deeply 1–2-pinnatisect, seg. usually narrow. Pseudocephalia 1–8, to 4.5cm diam., blue; flts deep blue. SE Eur. and S Russia to E China. Z6.

E. sphaerocephalus L. Perenn., 50–200cm. Lvs glandular-pubesc., or with eglandular and gland. hairs above and white-tomentose beneath, oblong-elliptic to ovate, amplexicaul, 1–2-pinnatifid, seg. triangular to lanceolate, revolute, with short, slender spines. Pseudocephalia 3–6cm diam., grey or white; flts white or grey. S & C Eur. to Russia. 'Niveus': infl. grey-white. Z3.

E. spinosissimus Turra. Perenn., 50–80cm. Lvs glandular-hairy above, white-tomentose and often glandular-hairy on veins beneath, ovate-lanceolate, usually 2-pinnatisect, seg. broadly lanceolate to triangular with short, slender spines. Pseudocephalia 3.5–7cm diam., grey, green or green-blue; flts white or pale blue. E Medit. to It. Z7.

E. 'Tenuifolius' = *E. ruthenicus*.

E. tournefortii Ledeb. ex Trautv. Perenn., 50–100cm. Lvs arachnoid-glandular or eglandular above, lanate beneath, with gland. hairs on veins, linear-elliptic, usually 1–2-pinnatisect, margin spiny. Pseudocephalia to 8cm diam., pale blue or white; flts pale blue or white. Transcauc. Z6.

E. tschimganicus B. Fedtsch. Perenn., 10–30cm. Basal lvs densely gland. above, oblong, deeply pinnatisect, seg. linear, entire, revolute. Pseudocephalia *c*3cm diam., solitary; flts light blue. C Asia. Z6.

E. viscosus DC. = *E. spinosissimus*.

Echinopsis Zucc. Cactaceae. 50–100 shrubby, tree-like or columnar cacti; st. erect, procumbent or v. low, simple, branched or clustering, slender-cylindric to columnar, to globose, usually distinctly ribbed, v. spiny to nearly spineless. Fls lat. or subapical, elongate-funnelform to subcampanulate; floral areoles ± densely hairy; sta. numerous; fil. often fused below in ring. Central S Amer.

E. albispinosa Schum. = *E. tubiflora*.

E. ancistrophora Speg. Simple or offsetting, flattened globose, to 8cm diam.; ribs 15–20, divided into small tubercles; central spines 1–2cm, bent or hooked, radial spines recurved. Fl. 10–16cm, white, sometimes tinged pink outside. W Arg. Z9.

E. arachnacantha (Buining & Ritter) Friedrich. Clustering; st. flattened globose, to 2×4cm, often violet-tinged; ribs *c*14; central spine 5mm, black, upcurved, radial spines pale, splayed like spider's legs. Fl. 5–6cm diam., yellow to orange. Boliv. Z9.

E. aurea Britt. & Rose. Simple or clustering; st. globose to elongate, to 10–40×4–12cm; ribs straight, 11–16; central spines 1(–4), to 3cm, radial spines to 1cm. Fl. 5.5–9×4–8cm, lemon yellow, darker inside. Arg. Z9.

E. ayopayana Ritter & Rausch. = *E. comarapana*.

E. backebergii Werderm. ex Backeb. Simple or clustering, globose to obovoid, *c*4–5cm diam.; ribs *c*15, incised above areoles; spines radial, red-brown, later grey, 0.5–5cm, thin, sometimes hooked. Fl. 4–9cm diam., carmine-red or violet, throat pale. E Boliv., S Peru. Z9.

E. bertramiana (Backeb.) Friedrich & G. Rowley. Branching below or from a short trunk; st. to 2m×25cm; ribs *c*20, acute deep; spines unequal, to 10cm, sometimes bristly, glassy white to yellow-brown. Fl. 10–14×*c*10cm, purple or pale yellow to almost white. Boliv. Z9.

E. bruchii (Britt. & Rose) Cast. & Lelong. Usually simple, depressed-globose, reaching 50cm diam., glossy dark green; ribs 50+, somewhat inflated between areoles; spines to 3cm, yellow or brown. Fl. 4–5×5cm, deep red; floral areoles woolly. Spring–summer. Arg. Treated by Rausch as a var. of *E. (Lobivia) formosa*. Z9.

E. cachensis Speg. = *E. saltensis*.

E. calochlora Schum. Clustering; st. subglobose, 6–9cm diam., shiny pale green; ribs *c*13; central spines slightly thicker and darker than radials, radial spines 5–10mm, straw-yellow. Fl. 16×10cm, white. Summer. Braz. Z9.

E. calorubra Cárdenas. To 6–7×14cm; ribs 16; central spine to 2.5cm, radial spines somewhat curved. Fl. to 15cm diam.; inner tep. orange-red above, pink, tinged blue, towards base. Boliv. Z9.

E. camarguensis (Cárdenas) Friedrich & G. Rowley. Resembling *E. strigosa*, but later with spines always yellow at first. St. ascending, cylindric, to 50cm; ribs 14; central spines to 5cm, radial spines to 3cm. Fl. to 20cm diam., white. Boliv. Z9.

E. campylacantha Pfeiff. = *E. leucantha*.

E. candicans (Gillies ex Salm-Dyck) F.A. Weber ex D. Hunt. Branching near base to form large clumps; st. cylindric, eventually decumbent, to 60×14cm, light green; ribs 9–11, low; spines subulate, brown-yellow, central spines 3–11cm. Fl. 18–23×11–19cm; tubular funnelform, white, fragrant. W Arg. Z9.

E. chalaensis (Rauh & Backeb.) Friedrich & G. Rowley. Shrub, to 4m; st. fastigiate, erect, to 15cm diam.; ribs 8, broad, furrowed above areoles; central spines to 5cm, dark brown at first, or tipped black. Fl. 17×10cm; tube with black hair-spines; outer tep. wine-red, inner tep. white. S Peru. Z9.

E. chamaecereus Friedrich & G. Rowley. PEANUT CACTUS. Freely branching to form clumps or mats, offsets 2–3cm, shaped like an unshelled peanut; st. weak, slender-cylindric, decumbent, to 30×1–1.5cm; ribs 6–9, v. low; spines 1–2mm, bristly, white or tinged brown. Fl. 4–7cm diam.; tep. orange-scarlet. Summer. Arg. Z9.

E. chilensis (Colla) Friedrich & G. Rowley. Large shrub or small tree, to 4(–8)m, branching below; st. erect, 12–15cm diam.; ribs 12–16, ± tuberculate; central spine 6–7(–12)cm. Fl. 14cm, outer tep. tinged maroon, inner tep. white. Chile. Z9.

E. chiloensis = *E. chilensis*.

E. chrysantha Werderm. St. simple, depressed-globose to short-cylindric, 4–6×6–7cm, violet-tinged in strong light; ribs 8–26; spines radial, 7–15mm, black. Fl. to 5.5cm diam., campanulate-funnelform yellow to orange with darker throat; stigmas purple. N Arg. Z9.

E. chrysochete Werderm. St. simple or offsetting below, depressed globose, to 20cm diam.; ribs to 25m, tuberculate-crenate between areoles; spines to 10cm, bristly, yellow to brown. Fl. *c*5×4cm, orange-red to red with yellow or paler throat. N Arg. Z9.

E. cinnabarina (Hook.) Labouret. St. simple, depressed-globose to globose, to 15cm diam.; ribs *c*20, irregular, acutely tuerculate; central spines somewhat curved, radial spines 6–12mm, slender, recurved. Fl. 4–8×4–6cm, scarlet, tube short. Spring–summer. Boliv. Z9.

E. comarapana Cárdenas. Resembling *E. leucantha* but smaller; st. short-cylindric, 10–15×4–8cm; ribs 8–12; central spines 15–20(–50)mm, radial spines 5–11mm. Fl. 13–15cm diam., white. Boliv. Z9.

E. coquimbana (Molina) Friedrich & G. Rowley. Shrub 1–2m, forming clumps several metres across; st. ascending or prostrate, 7–8cm diam.; ribs 12–13; areoles large; central spines 3–4, often 7–8cm, radial spines 8–12, 1–2cm. Fl. *c*10–12cm diam., campanulate-funnelform; floral areoles, with black hairs; perianth white. Fr. green, edible. Chile. Z9.

E. chiloensis = *E. chilensis*.
E. cordobensis Speg. = *E. leucantha*.
E. cristata Salm-Dyck = *E. obrepanda*.

E. cuzcoensis (Britt. & Rose) Friedrich & G. Rowley. Tall shrub, 5–6m, much branched, somewhat spreading; ribs 7–9, low, rounded; spines to 7cm, stout, swollen at base. Fl. 12–14cm diam., fragrant; tube 5–6cm, green; inner tep. white. Peru, near Cuzco. Z9.

E. decaisneana (Lem.) Lem. = *E. eyriesii*.
E. densispina Werderm. = *E. kuehnrichii*.

E. deserticola (Werderm.) Friedrich & G. Rowley. Shrub 1–1.5m; st. 4–7cm; ribs 8–12, deeply incised; central spines to 12(–18)cm, radial spines irregular, 1–3cm, dark brown, later grey. Fl. 7–12×7–9cm, fragrant; tube with dark woolly hairs; outer tep. pink, inner tep. white. Chile. Z9.

E. eyriesii (Turp.) Zucc. ex Pfeiff. & Otto Globose becoming short-cylindric, offsetting and clustering; main st. to 15(–30)×10(–15)cm; ribs 11–18; spines v. short, almost black. Fl. 20–25×5–10cm, white. Summer. S Braz. to N Arg. Z9.

E. ferox (Britt. & Rose) Backeb. St. unbranched, to 20×30+cm; ribs to 30, spiralled; areoles *c*3cm apart; central spines 3–4, to 15cm, upcurved, radial spines 10–12, to 6cm. Fl. 7–10cm diam., white or rarely pink. Boliv. to N Arg. Z9.

E. fiebrigii Gürke = *E. obrepanda* var. *fiebrigii*.

E. formosa (Pfeiff.) Jacobi ex Salm-Dyck St. usually simple, globose becoming cylindric, to 50(–200)×12.5–20(–40)cm, pale grey-green; ribs 15–35, obtuse, repand; central spines to 7cm, red-brown to white, radial spines yellow-white. Fl. 6–8cm diam., yellow, campanulate-funnelform, tube to 2.5cm, laxly hairy. W Arg. Z9.

E. fulvilana (Ritter) Friedrich & G. Rowley = *E. deserticola*.
E. grandiflora Linke = *E. tubiflora*.

E. haematantha (Speg.) D. Hunt. St. simple, depressed-globose to globose, 5–10×6–7cm, dark green; ribs 8–16, somewhat tuberculate, obtuse; spines to 8cm, radial spines 0.2–5cm, slender to stout. Fl. 4–8×4–8cm, dark red to orange or yellow, throat paler; floral areoles with long hairs. N Arg. Z9.

E. hamatacantha Backeb. Resembling *E. ancistrophora*; st. to 7×15cm; ribs to 27, acutely tubercled; spines 4–12mm, yellow-white to horn-coloured, 1 curving to crown and bent or hooked. Fl. 20cm diam., white, scented. Arg. Z9.

E. hertrichiana (Backeb.) D. Hunt. St. to 10cm diam., simple at first, later clustering; ribs 11–22, rounded to acute; spines to 3cm. Fl. *c*5×4–6cm, bright red. SE Peru. Z9.

E. herzogiana (Cárdenas) Friedrich & G. Rowley. St. simple, or branching, to 2.2m, erect, columnar, to 20cm diam., deep green; ribs *c*21, acute; central spine directed downwards, pale yellow, tipped brown, radial spines to 4cm, white, tipped brown. Fl. creamy white. Boliv. Z9.

E. huascha (F.A. Weber) Friedrich & G. Rowley. Branching below; st. to 1m×4–5(–10)cm, ascending or decumbent; ribs 14–17, low; central spines 2–7cm, radial spines 1.5cm, dark yellow to brown. Fl. *c*10×6–7cm, red, orange or yellow, funnelform-campanulate; floral areoles densely hairy. Summer. Arg. Z9.

E. intricatissima Speg. = *E. leucantha*.
E. kermesina Krainz = *E. mamillosa* var. *kermesina*.

E. knuthiana (Backeb.) Friedrich & G. Rowley. Becoming a small tree, with trunk 3m; st. to 10cm diam., glaucous; ribs *c*7, obtuse, broad; areoles felted; central spine to 10cm. Fl. large, white. Peru. Z9.

E. kratochviliana Backeb. Resembling *E. ancistrophora*; st. depressed-globose, to 6cm diam.; ribs to 18, acute, tuberculate; spines to 5cm. Fl. 5cm diam. or less, white; floral areoles with dark hairs. Arg. Z9.

E. kuehnrichii (Fric) Friedrich & Glaetzle. Resembling *E. haematantha*; st. simple, ovoid, 8×5.5cm; ribs *c*17, grooved between areoles; central spines to 1.5–2cm, dark, tipped black, radial spines to 8mm. Fl. *c*8.5cm diam., golden yellow, sometimes orange; stigmas green. N Arg. Z9.

E. lageniformis (C.F. Först.) Friedrich & G. Rowley. Shrub, 2–5m; st. to 15cm diam., somewhat glaucous; ribs 4–8, obtuse; spines 2–6, to 10cm, shorter in cult. Fl. 18cm diam., white. Boliv. Z9.

E. lamprochlorus (Lem.) F.A. Weber ex Friedrich & Glaetzle. Name used in different senses. The plant usually grown as *E. lamprochlorus* resembles *E. candicans*.

E. lateritia Gürke. St. simple, globose to cylindric, to 25×10cm, glaucous; ribs 16–20, acute, deep; central spine to 3(–5)cm, upcurved, radial spines, 10mm, pale brown. Fl. 4–5cm diam., short-funnelform, scarlet to brick red. Boliv. Z9.

E. lecoriensis Cárdenas = *E. longispina*.

E. leucantha (Gillies ex Salm-Dyck) Walp. Usually simple; st. globose to cylindric 30–150×10–15cm; ribs 10–14; central spine to 10cm, curved, dark brown, radial spines to 2cm, curved, pale brown. Fl. 15–17×10cm, white or pale pink. Arg. Z9.

E. leucomalla (Wessner) H. Friedrich = *E. aurea*.

E. leucorhodantha Backeb. = *E. ancistrophora*.

E. litoralis (Johow) Friedrich & G. Rowley. Resembling *E. chilensis*, but shrubby, forming wide clumps 1–2m tall; st. erect or decumbent, 8–12cm diam.; ribs 15–22, ± tuberculate; central spines 1.5–2.5cm, radial spines short and weak. Fl. as in *E. chilensis*. Chile. Z9.

E. longispina (Britt. & Rose) Backeb. Resembling *E. ferox*; st. globose to elongate, to 30×25cm; ribs 25–50; spines over 8cm, hooked on new growth, yellow, brown or black. Fl. to 10cm diam., white, yellow, orange, pink or red. N Arg. Z9.

E. macrogona (Salm-Dyck) Friedrich & G. Rowley. Arborescent; st. cylindric, 2(–6)m×9cm, blue-green; ribs usually 7, low and rounded; central spines to 5cm, downward-pointing, radial spines to *c*2cm. Fl. to 18×7cm, nocturnal, white. Origin unknown. Z9.

E. mamillosa Gürke. Simple, rarely clustering; st. broadly globose, to 12×10–25cm; ribs 17–32, tubercles rounded; central spines to 1cm, pale yellow, brown above, radial spines 5–10mm. Fl. 13–18× to 8cm, white, sometimes tinged pink. S Boliv., N Arg. var. *ritteri* (Boed.) Ritter St. 10–25cm diam.; radial spines 1–2.5cm. S Boliv. (Tarija). var. *kermesina* (Krainz) Friedrich. St. semi-globose, to more than 15cm diam.; ribs 15–23; radial spines to 12mm. Fl. to *c*18×9cm, carmine or paler. N Arg. Z9.

E. marsoneri Werderm. Simple, depressed-globose to short-cylindric, 4–6×3–9cm; ribs 7–20, acute, crenately tuberculate; central spines to 7cm, often somewhat hooked, radial spines 1–3cm, thin, adpressed. Fl. 5–7×5–6.5cm, campanulate-funnelform, yellow, orange, pink or red with dark throat; staminal throat-circle prominent; fil. usually dark violet. N Arg. Z9.

E. maximiliana Heyder ex A. Dietr. Clustering; st. depressed-globose to obovoid, *c*7.5×5cm; ribs *c*17, acute, crenately tuberculate; central spines to 7cm, upcurved, radial spines to 3–5cm, curved, brown-yellow. Fl. 5–8cm diam., scarlet with orange-yellow throat, inner tep. sometimes darker-tipped, somewhat reduced and erect. S Peru, N Boliv. Z9.

E. mirabilis Speg. Usually unbranched, cylindric, to 15×2.5cm, dark brown-green; ribs *c*11; central spine 10–15mm, stout, porrect, dark, minutely velvety, radial spines 3–5mm, bristly. Fl. 6–12×3–5cm, white, nocturnal; floral areoles woolly. Arg. Z9.

E. mistiensis Werderm. & Backeb. = *E. pampana*.

E. multiplex (Pfeiff.) Pfeiff. & Otto = *E. oxygona*.

E. nigra Backeb. = *E. longispina*.

E. nigrispina Backeb. = *E. kuehnrichii*.

E. obrepanda (Salm-Dyck) Schum. Simple at first, depressed-globose, to 20cm diam.; ribs *c*13–16, acute; central spines to 4–5cm, bent at tip, radial spines to 1cm, mostly pectinate. Fl. 10–20cm diam., white, scented of parsley; tube somewhat curved. Summer. Boliv. var. *fiebrigii* (Gürke) Friedrich. Fl. scented but not of parsley; tube straight. Z9.

E. orurensis (Cárdenas) Friedrich & G. Rowley = *E. bertramiana*.

E. oxygona (Link) Zucc. ex Pfeiff. & Otto Clustering; st. globose, eventually 25–30×12–15cm; ribs 13–15; spines to 2.5cm, yellow-brown. Fl. *c*25×10cm; tube green tinged red; perianth pink. Summer. S Braz., N Arg. Z9.

E. pachanoi (Britt. & Rose) Friedrich & G. Rowley. Shrub, to 7m, branching from base; st. erect, 6–11(–15)cm diam., often glaucous at first; ribs 6–8, broad and rounded, creased above areoles; spines 2–8(–30)mm, brown. Fl. 19–24×20cm, funnel-form, nocturnal, fragrant, white; tube with black hairs. Ecuad., Peru. Z9.

E. pampana (Britt. & Rose) D. Hunt. Clustering; st. globose, 5–7cm diam.; ribs 17–21, undulate; areoles white-felted when young; spines 5cm ± curved dense in wild plants, ± 0 in cult. S Peru. Z9.

E. pasacana (F.A. Weber ex Ruempl.) Friedrich & G. Rowley. Resembling *E. terscheckii* but with fewer br.; ribs 20+; spines more numerous and flexible. N Arg., S Boliv. Z9.

E. pecheretianus (Backeb.) Friedrich & G. Rowley = *E. huascha*.

E. pelecyrhachis Backeb. = *E. ancistrophora*.

E. pentlandii (Hook.) Salm-Dyck. Clustering from base; st. globose to obovoid, *c*12cm diam.; ribs 13–15, crenately tuberculate; central spines 3–10mm, radial spines to 1.5cm, somewhat recurved. Fl. 5–7×4–5cm, purple-pink, red, orange or yellow, often with paler throat; tube relatively stout. Spring–summer. S Peru, N Boliv. Z9.

E. pereziensis Cárdenas = *E. comarapana*.

E. peruvianus (Britt. & Rose) Friedrich & G. Rowley. Large shrub to 4m; st. 15–20cm diam., glaucous when young; ribs 6–8; spines to 4cm, brown. Peru. Possibly a form of *E. pachanoi* with stronger spines.

E. polyancistra Backeb. Resembling *E. ancistrophora*; st. usually less than 6cm diam.; ribs 17–30, narrow, ± rounded and tuberculate; central spines curved to hooked, to 12mm, radial

spines bristly. Fl. to 10cm diam., white, scented; tube v. slender. Arg. Z9.

E. pugionacantha Rose & Boed. Usually simple, to 15cm diam.; ribs 15–30; spines to 2.5cm+, dagger-like. Fl. 4.5–6cm diam., yellow or orange-yellow to dark red. Boliv. Z9.

E. purpureopilosa (Weing.) Friedrich & G. Rowley. Resembling *E. strigosa*; branching from base; st. to 30×6.5cm; ribs 12, low; central spines 3–7mm, radial spines to 7mm. Fl. 21.5×14cm red, white within with pink sheen. Arg. Z9.

E. rhodotricha Schum. Simple or offsetting; st. globose to short-columnar, to 80×9cm; ribs 8–13; central spine to 2.5cm, radial spines *c*2cm, pale yellow, tipped brown. Fl. 15cm diam., white. Summer. Parag., NE Arg. Z9.

E. ritteri Boed. = *E. mamillosa* var. *ritteri*.

E. rowleyi Friedrich = *E. huascha*.

E. saltensis Speg. Simple at first, later sparsely clustering, globose or somewhat depressed, to 5cm diam., ribs (9–)17–18, low, somewhat tuberculate; central spines 10–12mm, thin, radial spines to 6mm. Fl. 4–5cm diam., urceolate-campanulate, red. Arg. Z9.

E. sanguiniflora (Backeb.) D. Hunt. Simple; st. depressed-globose, to 8cm diam.; ribs 18(–24), tuberculate; central spines to 25mm, brown at first, radial spines 10–15mm, adpressed. Fl. (3–)5×5cm, red with white throat. N Arg. Z9.

E. santiaguensis (Speg.) Friedrich & G. Rowley = *E. spachiana*.

E. schickendantzii F.A. Weber. Low shrub, branching below, forming clumps 1–2m across; st. oblong to cylindric, to 25×6cm, ribs 14–18, low, subacute; spines 5–10mm, slender, pale yellow. Fl. 20–22cm diam., tubular-funnelform, white, not fragrant; floral areoles with black hairs. Fr. edible. W Arg. Z9.

E. schieliana (Backeb.) D. Hunt. Clustering; st. globose, 3–6cm diam., to oblong-cylindric, dark green; ribs 13–21, straight or twisted; spines white to yellow or brown, 2–15(–50)mm. Fl. 4–5×4–5cm, red or yellow. Boliv. Z9.

E. schreiteri (Cast.) Werderm. Forming cushions *c*30cm diam.; individual st. 1.5–3cm diam., dark green; ribs 9–14, tuberculate; central spines to 1cm, radial spines 6–8, 5–10mm. Fl. to 3cm diam., orange to dark red, with dark purple throat and sta. Arg. Z9.

E. shaferi Britt. & Rose = *E. aurea* or *E. leucantha*.

E. silvestrii Speg. Resembling *E. tubiflora* but smaller, with grey spines and broader tep. Arg. Not to be confused with *E. chamaecereus*, commonly known as *Chamaecereus silvestrii*. Z9.

E. smrziana Backeb. Branching to form groups up to 1.5m across; st. globose to cylindric and decumbent, to 50×14cm, dark green; ribs 11–13, *c*2cm high, acute; central spine to 3cm, radial spines 1–2.5cm. Fl. 12×12cm, white. N Arg. Z9.

E. spachiana (Lem.) Friedrich & G. Rowley. Shrub to 1m+, branching from base; st. 5–10cm diam.; ribs 10–15, low; spines straight, yellow-brown at first; central spine 1–2cm, radial spines 4–10mm. Fl. 18–20×15cm, white; floral areoles densely hairy. Arg. Authors have considered *E. santiaguensis* (Speg.) Friedrich & Rowley to be conspecific, though this is an arborescent sp. with a trunk 4–7m×16–20cm. Z9.

E. spegazziniana Britt. & Rose = *E. leucantha*.

E. spiniflora (Schum.) A. Berger. Simple; globose to short cylindric, eventually to 60×15cm; ribs *c*16–20, acute; spines to 4cm, needle-like, pale yellow to brown, darker tipped. Fl. 4–5×4cm, erect, tubular-campanulate; tube green; scales spine-tipped, brown; perianth pale mauve, pink or white; sta. incurved lowermost staminodial, hair-like. W Arg. Z9.

E. strigosa (Salm-Dyck) Friedrich & G. Rowley. Shrubby, forming clumps 1m across; st. to 60×5–6cm; ribs 15–18, low; spines nearly white to yellow or red-brown and darker-tipped; central spines to 7cm, radial spines 1–5cm. Fl. *c*20×5cm, funnelform, nocturnal, white to salmon-pink. W Arg. Z9.

E. tacaquirensis (Vaupel) Friedrich & G. Rowley = *E. pasacana*.

E. taquimbalensis (Cárdenas) Friedrich & G. Rowley. St. simple or branching below, to 2.5m×15cm; ribs 9; central spine to 6cm, porrect or downward-pointing, radial spines to 2cm, subulate. Fl. 23cm diam., white. Boliv. Z9.

E. tarijensis (Vaupel) Friedrich & G. Rowley. Simple or branched; st. columnar, to 5m×40cm, ribs about 25; areoles densely felted; spines dense, 1–8cm, pale brown to almost white. Fl. *c*12×9cm, subapical, funnelform; tube *c*8cm; floral areoles with dense hairs; outer tep. brown-green, inner tep. usually red, sometimes pink or cream. S Boliv., N Arg. Z9.

E. tegeleriana (Backeb.) D. Hunt. Usually simple; st. globose, to 10cm diam.; ribs 16–20, acutely crenate-tuberculate; spines 1–2cm, ± curved, horn-coloured, tipped darker, longest sometimes hooked. Fl. *c*4×1.5cm, tubular-funnelform, yellow, orange or red, throat pink-orange. Central Peru. Z9.

E. terscheckii (Parmentier ex Pfeiff.) Friedrich & G. Rowley Arborescent, 10–12m; br. fastigiate, columnar, 10–20cm diam.; ribs 8–18, obtuse, deep; areoles with dense brown tomentum;

spines 1–7cm+, yellow to brown. Fl. 15–20×12.5cm, campanulate-funnelform; tube green; floral areoles with dense hairs; outer tep. dark red to green, inner tep. white. N Arg. Z9.

E. thelegona (F.A. Weber ex Schum.) Friedrich & G. Rowley. Simple or sparsely branched; st. procumbent or decumbent, elongate, to 2m×7–8cm; ribs c13, low, tubercles subhexagonal areoles at apices of tubercles; spines honey-yellow at first, tipped brown, 2–4cm, protruding. Fl. c20×15cm, funnelform; floral areoles with dull red bristles and hairs. W Arg. Z9.

E. thelegonoides (Speg.) Friedrich & G. Rowley. Resembling *E. thelegona*, but st. thicker, more branched; ribs 15–16, not tuberculate, but furrowed between the areoles. N Arg. Z9.

E. thionantha (Speg.) Werderm. Simple, globose to cylindric, 12(–50)×10(–15)cm; ribs 9–15, rounded; central spines 0 or 1–4, 5–20mm, subulate, at first brown or black, later grey or horny, radial spines 5–10. Fl. to 5×5cm; scales spine-tipped; floral areoles with hairs and bristles; perianth bright yellow to red or white; sta. erect; staminodial hairs pale brown. NW Arg. Z9.

E. tiegeliana (Wessner) D. Hunt. Simple or offsetting; st. depressed-globose to globose, to 7cm diam., ribs 18–30, dissolved into tubercles; central spines to 15mm, radial spines adpressed. Fl. 4–5×5.5cm, deep red or purple-pink. Boliv. Z9.

E. toralapana Cárdenas. Resembling *E. obrepanda*, but differing in fl. to 14cm diam., magenta. Boliv. Z9.

E. torrecillasensis Cárdenas. St. numerous, globose, 1–2cm diam.; ribs 16; spines to 1cm, curved. Fl. 8cm, red to salmon red. Boliv. Sometimes considered a var. of *Lobivia arachnacantha*. Z9.

E. trichosa (Cárdenas) Friedrich & G. Rowley. St. simple, columnar and somewhat clavate, to 1m; ribs 9, 2cm high, broad, obtuse; central spine 1, to 7cm, porrect, radial spines 1–3.5cm, subulate. Fl. 23cm diam., white. Boliv.

E. tubiflora (Pfeiff.) Schum. Simple or clustering; st. to 12cm diam., dark green; ribs 10–12, prominent; central spines 1–2cm, nearly black, radial spines shorter and weaker. Fl. 20–24×10cm, white. Summer. Arg. Z9.

E. turbinata (Pfeiff.) Zucc. ex Pfeiff. & Otto = *E. eyriesii*.

E. uyupampensis (Backeb.) Friedrich & G. Rowley. St. prostrate to pendent, to 2m×3.5cm; ribs 9, low, shallowly tuberculate; spines 2–6mm, slender. Fl. c16cm diam.; outer tep. tinged red, inner tep. white. S Peru. Z9.

E. volliana (Backeb.) Friedrich & G. Rowley. Resembling *E. spachiana*, but st. more shiny, spines more open; st. to 10cm diam.; ribs 13, 5mm high; central spine to 2.5cm, radial spines 7mm, thin, sharp. Fl. to c12cm, white. Boliv. Z9.

E. walteri (Kiesling) Friedrich & Glaetzle. Clustering; st. to 16×16cm; ribs c11; spines 1–2.5cm, yellow. Fl. 7–9.5cm diam., campanulate-funnelform, yellow. Arg. Z9.

E. werdermannianus (Backeb.) Friedrich & G. Rowley = *E. pasacana*.

E. winteriana Ritter = *E. backebergii*.

E. wrightiana Backeb. = *E. backebergii*.

→*Acanthocalycium*, *Arthrocereus*, *Cereus*, *Chamaecereus*, *Echinocactus*, *Eriosyce*, *Helianthocereus*, *Lobivia*, *Pseudolobivia*, *Setiechinopsis*, *Soehrensia* and *Trichocereus*.

Echinospartum (Spach) Fourr.
E. horridum (Vahl) Rothm. = *Genista horrida*.

Echinospermum Sw. ex Lehm.
E. floribundum Lehm. = *Hackelia floribunda*.

Echinus L. Bol.
E. apiculatus (Kensit) L. Bol. = *Braunsia apiculata*.
E. geminatus (Haw.) L. Bol. = *Braunsia geminata*.
E. mathewsii (L. Bol.) N.E. Br. = *Braunsia geminata*.

Echioides Ortega.
E. griffithii (Boiss.) Rothm. = *Arnebia griffithii*.
E. linearifolium (A. DC.) Rothm. = *Arnebia linearifolia*.

Echium L. Boraginaceae. 40 ann., bienn. or perenn. herbs or shrubs, hispid-setose. Basal lvs rosulate, petiolate; cauline lvs narrower sessile or subsessile. Infl. of numerous scorpioid cymes, term., often forming a pan. in some giant spp. exceptionally highly branched, spire-like with leafy bracts; cal. deeply 5-lobed; cor. zygomorphic, infundibular, annulus with several tufts of hairs, interior glab.; sta. 5, included or exserted. Eur., Canary Is., Afr., W Asia.

E. albicans Lagasca & Rodr. Perenn., to 75cm, erect, white-pubesc., setose. Lvs to 7cm, linear-lanceolate to linear-oblong. Fls rose to violet to 26mm, with 2 or 3 exserted sta. Spain.

E. benthamii Wallich ex G. Don = *Arnebia benthamii*.

E. boissieri Steud. Bienn., to 250cm, erect, usually unbranched, hispid. Basal lvs to 25cm, linear-lanceolate, white-hispid. Infl. a

dense spike; fls rose-pink 18mm; sta. long-exserted. Spain, Port.

E. bourgaeanum Webb = *E. wildpretii*.

E. callithyrsum Webb ex Bolle. Robust, woody shrub, hispid. Lvs ovate to lanceolate, setose above. Infl. short, a branching spike; fls pale red to deep blue. Canary Is.

E. candicans L. f. PRIDE OF MADEIRA. Bienn. shrub to 2.5m. St. white-pubesc., br. stout, leafy near apex. Lvs lanceolate, silvery-pubesc. Infl. a term., cylindrical pan. to 30cm; fls white or blue streaked white, red-purple in bud; sta. exserted. Madeira.

E. creticum L. Bienn. to 90cm, erect, hispid. Basal lvs to 18cm, narrowly oblanceolate, setose. Infl. a pan.; fls red-purple, sometimes becoming blue or blue-purple to 40mm, with 1 or 2 sta. exserted. Eur.

E. fastuosum Jacq. = *E. candicans*.

E. giganteum L. Giant simple-stemmed shrubs to 2.5m. Lvs to 20cm, oblanceolate or lanceolate, hispid or hirsute. Fls white; sta. exserted. Canary Is.

E. lusitanicum L. Perenn., erect or ascending, branched above, softly pubesc. Basal lvs to 45cm, broadly lanceolate, adpressed-setose. Infl. a spike; fls white-blue, with violet veins to 10mm; sta. all exserted, fil. red. Eur.

E. lycopsis L. = *E. plantagineum*.

E. petraeum Tratt. = *Moltkia petraea*.

E. pininana Webb & Berth. Closely resembles *E. simplex* except st. larger. Lvs narrower, elongate, rough. Infl. to 4m; fls blue and rose. Canary Is. Hybrids with *E. wildpretii* are hardier plants producing compact spires of fls to 1.8m in blue, mauve, rose and apricot.

E. plantagineum L. Ann. or bienn., to 60cm, erect, white-pubesc. Basal lvs to 14cm, ovate to lanceolate, adpressed-setose. Infl. a pan.; fls red to blue-purple to 30mm, with 2 exserted sta. Eur.

E. pomponium Boiss. = *E. boissieri*.

E. rubrum Jacq. non Forssk. = *E. russicum*.

E. russicum J.F. Gmel. Bienn., to 60cm, erect, simplle, hispid-setose. Lvs to 10cm, linear-lanceolate, densely adpressed-setose. Infl. to 30cm, a pan.; fls dark red to crimson to 12mm, with 4 or 5 long-exserted sta. Eur. 'Burgundy': fls in long spikes, dark red.

E. simplex DC. PRIDE OF TENERIFE. Short-lived simple-stemmed giant perenn. or bienn. to 2m. Lvs elliptic-lanceolate or ovate-lanceolate, densely silvery-hispid. Infl. cylindrical; fls white; sta. exserted. Canary Is.

E. vulgare L. VIPER'S BUGLOSS. Bienn., to 90cm, erect, usually simple, hispid-setose. Lvs white-hispid-setose, to 15cm, narrowly oblong to linear-lanceolate. Infl. a spike or a pan.; fls blue or blue-violet, sometimes pink or white to 18mm; sta. all long-exserted. Eur. 'Blue Bedder': to 30cm high; fls bell-shaped, blue. Dwarf Hybrids: to 30cm high; fls bell-shaped, purple, lilac, pink, rose and white.

E. wildpretii H. Pearson ex Hook. f. Giant simple-stemmed bienn., to 2m, softly pubesc. Lvs to 20cm, narrowly linear-lanceolate, densely setose. Infl. a pyramidal pan.; fls pale red; bracts slender, decurved; sta. long-exserted. Canary Is.

Ecuador Laurel *Cordia alliodora*.

Edelweiss *Leontopodium* (*L. alpinum*).

Edgeworthia Meissn. PAPER BUSH. Thymelaeaceae. 3 decid. or semi-evergr. shrubs to 2.5m. Br. thick, ascending, grey-brown, with papery bark. Lvs to 10cm, lanceolate to oblong, simple, entire, tough, usually hairy, clustered at br. tips. Fls precocious, fragrant, in dense, stalked heads; cal. tube cylindrical, lobes 4, spreading; pet. 0; stigma elongate. Fr. a dry drupe. Early summer. Nepal to China, introd. Jap. Z8.

E. chrysantha Lindl. To 1.5m. Fls yellow (orange-red in f. *rubra*) fragrant, silky. China.

E. gardneri (Wallich) Meissn. Differs from *D. papyrifera* in lvs persistent; fls stained yellow; ovaries wholly pubesc. Nepal, Sikkim.

E. papyrifera Sieb. & Zucc. PAPERBUSH. Fls white. China, introd. Jap.

Edging Lobelia *Lobelia erinus*.

Edible Banana *Musa* ×*paradisiaca*.

Edible Olive *Olea europaea* var. *europaea*.

Edible-podded Pea *Pisum sativum* var. *macrocarpon*.

Edible Prickly Pear *Opuntia ficus-indica*.

Edithcolea N.E. Br. Asclepiadaceae. 1 succulent perenn. herb to 30cm. St. to 2.5cm diam., mat-forming, ridges 5, spiny-toothed. Lvs scale-like, caducous. Fls apical, usually solitary; cor. 10–12.5cm across, lobes 5, triangular-ovate, pale yellow, spotted and striped purple or rusty-brown, margins hairy,

purple; outer corona lobes pouch-like, inner lobes erect, fleshy. Somalia, Ethiop., E Afr., S Yemen. Z10.
E. grandis N.E. Br. PERSIAN CARPET FLOWER. var. *baylissiana* Lavranos & Hardy. St. to 75cm, 4-angled. Fls 8–10cm diam., lobes broadly ovate-deltoid. Tanz.

Edjujongo *Fernandoa adolfi-friderici.*

Edmondia Cass. Compositae. 3 subshrubby perenn. St. tufted, usually simple, spreading, erect, densely leafy. Lvs rigid, erect or adpressed, imbricate, narrowly lanceolate to awl-shaped, often involute, white-tomentose above, glab. and shining beneath. Cap. discoid or disciform, solitary, or rarely 2 to several in term. corymbs; phyllaries many, overlapping, radiating, 'everlasting'; flts numerous, yellow. S Afr. Z9.
E. pinifolia (Lam.) Hilliard. Lvs elongated, dorsally rounded, lower lvs flat. Cap. c3cm diam.; phyllaries white or pale to deep pink. SW Cape (mts).
E. sesamoides (L.) Hilliard. Lvs of sterile shoots mostly 2–5cm, ascending, lvs of fertile shoots 0.5–0.7cm, adpressed, both kinds with a raised dors. nerve. Cap. c2.5cm diam.; phyllaries white, cream, primrose yellow or pink, often partly or wholly pale to dark brown or pink. W & SW Cape.
→*Helichrysum* and *Xeranthemum.*

Edraianthus A. DC. GRASSY BELLS. Campanulaceae. Some 24 tufted perenn. herbs, similar to *Wahlenbergia*. Lvs narrow, basal. Fls in term. heads or solitary, surrounded by leafy bracts. Medit. to Cauc.
E. caricinus Schott, Nyman & Kotschy = *E. graminifolius.*
E. caudatus (Vis.) Rchb. f. = *E. dalmaticus.*
E. croaticus (A. Kern) A. Kern = *E. graminifolius.*
E. dalmaticus (A. DC.) A. DC. St. to 7cm, ascending. Lvs linear, basally ciliate. Fls several, exceeded by broadly ovate-acuminate bracts; cor. to 2cm, blue to violet. Summer. Balk. 'Albus': fls white. Z6.
E. dinaricus (A. Kerner) Wettst. Differs from *E. pumilio*, in taller st. sparsely leafy above. Lvs to 5cm, pubesc. above. Fls usually solitary, term., blue to violet. Balk. Z7.
E. graminifolius (L.) A. DC. Low, tufted, rosulate perenn.; flowering st. ascending. Lvs linear. Fls in globose term. clusters; bracts ovate, acuminate, usually shorter than fls; cor. to 2cm, blue to violet, rarely white. Summer. E Eur. 'Albus': fls white. Z8.
E. intermedius Deg. = *E. graminifolius.*
E. kitaibelii (A. DC.) A. DC. = *E. graminifolius.*
E. parnassicus (Boiss. & Sprun.) Hal. Tufted, woody-based perenn., st. ascending. Lvs irregularly crenate, oblanceolate to spathulate. Fls 3–4, violet in globose, short-stalked clusters; bracts ovate-mucronate. Macedonia, C Greece. Z8.
E. pumilio (Portenschlag) A. DC. V. dwarf perenn. with densely leafy st. Lvs linear, to 1mm wide, grey-tomentose. Fls solitary, violet to blue. Z6.
E. serbicus Petrović. Similar to *E. dalmaticus*, habit erect, to 20cm, st. hirsute. Lvs to 9cm. Fls purple, exceeding or equalling outer bracts. Balk., Bulg. Z6.
E. serpyllifolius (Vis.) A. DC. Tufted perenn. Lvs spathulate, blunt or emarginate, almost rosulate, usually glab. Fls solitary, term., deep violet, exceeding blunt bracts. Balk. 'Major': fls larger. Z7.
E. tenuifolius (Waldst. & Kit.) A. DC. Compact, to 15cm, tufted. Like *E. graminifolius*, but lvs v. narrow, ciliate to apex. Fls blue-violet, shorter than elliptic bracts in heads to 15. Balk. 'Albus': fls white. Z7.
E. wahlenbergia var. *serpyllifolius* (Vis.) G. Beck = *E. serpyllifolius.*
E. wettsteinii Hal. & Bald. Similar to *E. pumilio*. Lvs to 2mm wide. Fls usually solitary, pubesc. Albania, Balk. Z7.
→*Wahlenbergia.*

Edwardsia Endl.
E. chilensis Miers. = *Sophora macrocarpa.*
E. macnabiana Curtis = *Sophora microphylla.*

Edwinia A.A. Heller.
E. californica Small = *Jamesia americana* var. *californica.*

Eel Grass *Vallisneria* (*V. spiralis*).

Egeria Planch. Hydrocharitaceae. 2 submerged aquatic herbs; st. elongate, branching. Lvs opposite or whorled, linear to narrow-oblong. Cyme, subtended by tubular spathe; ♂ fls 2–5 per spathe, opening above water; sep. 3, green; pet. 3, white to yellow; sta. 9, in 3 whorls; ♀ fls with staminodia 3, ovary inferior. S Amer., nat. elsewhere. Z9.

E. densa Planch. St. 1–3mm diam. Lvs 22×3mm, in whorls of 4. ♂ spathes 7–12×1–4mm, 2–4 fld; fil. clavate, densely papillose. S Amer., widely nat. elsewhere.
E. naias Planch. St. 1–1.5mm diam. Lvs 15×1.5mm in whorls of 5 often curved. ♂ spathes, 2–9×1–2mm, 2–3 fld; fil. elongate, slightly papillose. S Amer.
→*Elodea.*

Eggfruit *Pouteria campechiana.*
Egg-plant *Solanum melongena.*
Eglantine *Rosa rubiginosa.*
Egyptian Bean *Lablab purpureus.*
Egyptian Honesty *Ricotia lunaria.*
Egyptian Lupin *Lupinus albus.*
Egyptian Mimosa *Acacia nilotica.*
Egyptian Paper Reed *Cyperus papyrus.*
Egyptian Pea *Cicer arietinum.*
Egyptian Rose *Scabiosa atropurpurea.*
Egyptian Star-cluster *Pentas lanceolata.*
Egyptian Sycamore *Ficus sycomorus.*
Egyptian Thorn *Acacia nilotica.*
Egyptian Water Lily *Nymphaea lotus.*

Ehretia P. Browne. Boraginaceae. 50 decid. or everg. trees or shrubs. Infl. a term. pan.; fls usually small, sometimes fragrant; cal. 5-toothed, tube short; cor. 5-lobed, tubular-campanulate, lobes spreading or reflexed; sta. 5, usually exserted. Fr. a subglobose, glab. drupe to 2cm, red to yellow-orange ripening black. Afr., Asia, Americas.
E. acuminata R. Br. KODO WOOD. Decid. tree to 10m; br. grey. Lvs to 16cm, obovate, leathery, glossy, rigid-pubesc. above, paler and glab. beneath, serrate. Infl. few-branched, slender, to 15cm, crowded; cor. white, lobes exceed tube. Coastal E Aus., Jap., China, Philipp. var. *serrata* (Roxb.) I.M. Johnst. Lvs sharply serrate. Summer. Himal. Z7.
E. anacua (Terán & Berl.) I.M. Johnst. Everg. or semi-evergreen tree, 3–10m; branchlets puberulent, becoming furrowed and red scaly. Lvs 2–9cm, elliptic or ovate, scabrous above, scabrous to puberulent beneath, entire, often revolute, rarely serrate. Fls fragrant, in term. cymes to 6cm; cor. to 7.8mm, white, puberulent outside. SE Tex., Mex. Z8.
E. bourreria L. = *Bourreria succulenta.*
E. buxifolia Roxb. = *Carmona retusa.*
E. ciliata Miers = *E. anacua.*
E. dentata Courch. = *Carmona retusa.*
E. dicksonii Hance. Decid. tree to 12m; branchlets rigid, serose. Lvs to 18cm, oblong-elliptic, leathery, glossy, rough-setose above, velvety-pubesc. beneath, serrate to 12cm broad. Fls white tinged yellow, fragrant; cor. 6mm. Summer. China, Taiwan, Ryukyu Is. Z7.
E. elliptica DC. = *E. anacua.*
E. exasperata Miers = *E. anacua.*
E. havanensis Roem. & Schult. = *Bourreria succulenta* var. *revoluta.*
E. heterophylla (Cav.) Spreng. = *Carmona retusa.*
E. hottentotica Burchell CAPE LILAC; PUZZLE BUSH; DEURMEKAARBOS. Shrub or small tree to 3.6m; br. pale grey, glab., punctate, tangled. Lvs 1.3–5cm, ovate to lanceolate, apex rounded, entire, scabrid. Fls lilac, fragrant, clustered on bare br. Summer–autumn. S Afr., Bots. Z9.
E. laevis Roxb. Tree to 10m. Lvs to 18cm, apex and base rounded to obtuse, shining above, minutely gland. and pubesc. to glab. beneath, entire or dentate. Infl. dichotomously branched, axis tawny-tomentose; cor. white, to 3.5mm. Indochina, India, Burm. Z9.
E. lancifolia Sessé & Moc. = *E. anacua.*
E. macrophylla Wallich. Decid. shrub or tree to 6m. Lvs ovate, 15cm, dentate, bristly above and more so beneath. Pan. globose; cor. white, tube twice as long as cal. Himal. to China. Z9.
E. macrophylla Shiras. non Wallich = *E. dicksonii.*
E. microphylla Lam. = *Carmona retusa.*
E. ovalifolia Hassk. = *E. acuminata.*
E. scabra Kunth & Bouché = *E. anacua.*
E. sulcata Miers = *E. tinifolia.*
E. thyrsiflora (Sieb. & Zucc.) Nak. = *E. acuminata.*
E. tinifolia L. Everg. tree to 15–25m; branchlets glab. Lvs 5–16.5cm, elliptic, apex obtuse to rounded, glab., shining above. Pan. to 15cm diam.; cor. white, tubular-campanulate, to 5mm. Mex., W Indies. Z9.

Ehrharta Thunb. Gramineae. 25 ann. and perenn. grasses. St. erect to scandent, spreading. Lvs flat, linear; ligules membranous, occas. ciliate. Infl. usually paniculate, narrow; spikelets laterally flattened, 3-fld. Afr., Masc. Is., NZ. Z8.

E. erecta Lam. Perenn. to 90cm. St. ascending, branched. Lvs to 15×0.9cm; ligules membranous. Infl. to 20cm, pale green. Autumn. S Afr.

Eichhornia Kunth. WATER HYACINTH; WATER ORCHID. Pontederiaceae. 7 perenn. aquatic herbs. St. short, tufted, floating, proliferating and detaching or stoloniferous and anchored in mud. Lvs glossy, erect amid rounded basal sheaths in a crowded rosette, if free-floating, with ciliate roots below; petioles narrow-cylindric if immersed or embedded, if floating, ellipsoid, inflated. Infl. usually spicate; perianth lobes 6, spreading, connate at base. Trop. S Amer. Z10.

E. azurea (Sw.) Kunth. St. thick, floating or rooting into mud. Petioles not inflated; lf blades round-cordate to rhomboid, to 20cm across; submerged lvs linear. Fls bright pale blue, interior deep purple spotted yellow; inner seg. narrower, fringed. Summer. Subtrop. & Trop. Amer.

E. crassipes (Mart.) Solms-Laub. WATER HYACINTH; WATER ORCHID. St. thick, floating or anchored. Petioles v. inflated at base; lf blades orbicular to ovate, to 12cm across. Fls 3cm across, violet-blue, with central violet and yellow blotch. Selections have been made with rose- and yellow-tinted fls. Trop. S Amer., widely nat. throughout tropics and subtrop.

E. martiana Seub. = *E. paniculata*.

E. paniculata (Spreng.) Solms-Laub. St. not floating, soft, terete, to 1m. Lf blades broadly cordate, acuminate, with deep, narrow basal sinus, exceeding petioles. Infl. compound; fls 2.5cm across; lower 3 seg. purple, upper 3 smaller, blue, with central white and yellow spot. Summer. Trop. S Amer.

E. speciosa Kunth = *E. crassipes*.

ELAEAGNACEAE Juss. 3/45. *Elaeagnus, Hippophaë, Shepherdia.*

Elaeagnus L. OLEASTER. Elaeagnaceae. *c*45 decid. or everg. shrubs or trees, st. often spiny. Lvs and branchlets often covered with minute silvery or brown scales. Fls few, clustered in axils, small, often fragrant, unisexual; cal. petaloid, 4-lobed, tubular or campanulate. Drupe 1-seeded, edible. Asia, S Eur., N Amer.

E. angustifolia L. RUSSIAN OLIVE; OLEASTER; WILD OLIVE; SILVER BERRY. Decid. shrub or tree to 7m; bark dark grey-brown, thin; twigs tinted red, covered with silvery scales, sometimes spiny. Lvs 4.5–9cm, narrow-ovate to lanceolate, dark green above, silver scales beneath. Fls fragrant, to 1cm, yellow within, exterior silver. Fr. 1cm, yellow-brown, covered in silvery scales. Summer. W Asia. 'Red King': vigorous growth to 7m. Z2.

E. angustifolia var. *caspica* Sosn. = *E.* 'Quicksilver'.

E. argentea hort. = *E.* 'Quicksilver'.

E. argentea Moench non Pursh = *E. angustifolia*.

E. argentea Pursh non Moench = *E. commutata*.

E. commutata Bernh. SILVER BERRY. Decid., stoloniferous shrub to 5m; bark grey-brown; twigs red-brown, unarmed. Lvs 3–6cm, broadly elliptic, lustrous, silvery. Fls fragrant, exterior silvery, interior yellow. Fr. silvery, mealy. Late spring. N Amer. Z2.

E. crispa Thunb. = *E. umbellata*.

E. ×*ebbingei* Boom. (*E. macrophylla* ×*E. pungens*.) Shrub to 3m, usually everg. Lvs to 11.5cm, elliptic, dark, glossy or metallic sea-green above, silvery-scaly beneath. Fls small, white-cream, waxy, intensely fragrant. Autumn–winter. Gdn origin. 'Albert Doorenbos': lvs large to 12cm long. 'Gilt Edge': lvs with narrow golden margin. 'Limelight': lvs variegated yellow. 'Salcombe Seedling': fls white, fragrant, abundant. 'The Hague': upright; lvs narrow. Z6.

E. edulis Carr. = *E. multiflora*.

E. glabra Thunb. Semi-scandent everg. shrub to 6m; twigs thornless, young shoots with shiny, brown scales. Lvs with lustrous metallic brown scales beneath. Fls fragrant. Autumn. China, Jap., Korea. Z8.

E. latifolia L. OLEASTER; WILD OLIVE. Erect shrub or climber. Lvs to 13cm, ovate to broadly-elliptic, with silver or brown metallic scurfy scales beneath. Fr. red. India, China. Z9.

E. longipes A. Gray = *E. multiflora*.

E. loureirii Champ. Unarmed shrub. Lvs to 9cm, ovate to elliptic-oblong, red-brown scales beneath, glab. above. Hong Kong.

E. macrophylla Thunb. Spreading everg. shrub to 3m. Br. unarmed, covered in silvery-white scales when young. Lvs 5–12cm, broadly ovate to elliptic, with silvery scales throughout when young, becoming glossy above. Fls to 1.2cm, cream, highly fragrant, silver-scaly. Fr. red, scaly. Autumn. Jap., Korea. Z8.

E. multiflora Thunb. Decid. shrub to 3m. Young br. covered in red-brown scales. Lvs 3–10cm, ovate-oblong to elliptic, deep green and glabrescent above, silvery with numerous brown scales beneath. Fls to 1.5cm, fragrant. Fr. dark red to brown, edible, on slender stalks to 3cm. Spring. Jap., China. 'Giga-

ntea': fls large; fr. deep red. var. *ovata* (Maxim.) Servettaz. Fr. pendulous brown on long stalks. Jap. Z6.

E. parvifolia Wall. ex Royle = *E. umbellata* var. *parvifolia*.

E. philippinensis Perrott. Everg. shrub to 3m. Lvs elliptic, covered with silvery scales beneath. Fls fragrant. Fr. dull pink with silvery scales. Philippine Is. Z10.

E. pungens Thunb. Everg. shrub to 4m, often spiny. Young br. covered in brown scales. Lvs 4–8cm, tough, oval to oblong, undulate or crispate, lustrous above, dull silvery-white and dotted with brown scales beneath. Fls fragrant, silvery-white. Fr. brown, becoming red. Autumn. Jap. 'Dicksonii': lvs edged deep yellow. 'Dicksonii': lvs with wide golden margin, some with upper third entirely yellow. 'Frederici' ('Frederici Variegata'): lvs narrow, centred yellow with thin margin of dark green. 'Fruitlandii': habit dense; lvs round with wavy edges, rich green scaled silver, white and brown scales beneath. 'Golden Rim': lvs with variable golden yellow margin. 'Maculata' ('Aureomaculata'): lvs large, splashed yellow in centre. 'Marginata': lvs edged silver. 'Nana': habit dwarf. 'Reflexa': lvs dark brown and scaly below. 'Rotundifolia': lvs tinged silver. 'Simonii': lvs occas. variegated yellow and white tinged pink, silver beneath. 'Tricolor': lvs green with somewhat yellow and pale rose-pink coloration. 'Variegata': lvs margined white tinged yellow. Z7.

E. pungens var. *reflexa* (Morr. & Decne.) Schneid. = *E.* ×*reflexa*.

E. ×*pyramidalis* Wróbl. (*E. commutata* ×*E. multiflora*.) Compact, somewhat pyramidal shrub to 2.5m, producing short branchlets. Lvs 3–4cm, apex obtuse or abruptly acute, silvery green above, silver beneath. Z5.

E. 'Quicksilver' Tall, suckering, ± pyramidal shrub with oblong-lanceolate grey-blue lvs, densely silver-scurfy. Possibly a hybrid of *E. angustifolia* and *E. commutata*.

E. ×*reflexa* Morr. & Decne. (*E. pungens* ×*E. glabra*.) Br. long, sparsely thorny. Lvs ovate-lanceolate, lustrous above, with brown scales beneath, margins lack the wavy margin of *E. pungens*. Retains the semi-scandent habit of *E. glabra*. Z7.

E. ×*submacrophylla* hort. = *E.* ×*ebbingei*.

E. umbellata Thunb. Decid. shrub or small tree, 4–10m. Young br. golden-brown, silvery or covered with brown scales, usually thorny. Lvs 4–10cm, elliptic to ovate-oblong, often wavy-margined, bright green above, with silver and some brown scales beneath. Fls yellow-white, fragrant. Fr. to 8mm diam., silver to bronze, ripening red. Autumn. Himal., China, Jap. 'Cardinal': habit large; lvs powder green; fr. amber. 'Titan' ('Tizam'): habit dense, upright branching; lvs olive green tinged silver; fls golden-yellow, abundant, fragrant; fr. deep red. var. *parvifolia* (Royle) C. Schneid. Shrub to 5m. Br. sparse, erect, silvered, thorny. Lvs 3–7cm, elliptic lanceolate, silvery. Fr. silvered at first, ripening brown. Z3.

Elaeis Jacq. Palmae. 2 palms. St. to 18m, solitary, erect or procumbent, clothed with lf bases, becoming bare and obliquely scarred. Crown dense. Lvs pinnate, marcescent, sheath fibrous; petiole channelled above, angled beneath, tomentose, margin armed with spine-like fibres below and jagged spines; pinnae crowded, single-fold, held in differing planes along rachis, linear, acute, sometimes scaly, midribs prominent. Fr. 1-seeded, ovoid, angled at base; mesocarp thick, oily, fibrous, endocarp black, hard. Trop. Afr. and Amer. Z10.

E. guineensis Jacq. OIL PALM; AFRICAN OIL PALM; MACAW FAT. Lvs to 4.5m; pinnae crowded, grouped in clusters and in several planes along rachis. Afr.

E. melanococca Gaertn. non hort. = *E. oleifera*.

E. melanococca hort. non Gaertn. = *E. guineensis*.

E. oleifera (HBK) Cortés. AMERICAN OIL PALM. Lvs to 3m; pinnae crowded, regularly spaced in one plane along rachis. C & S Amer.

→*Corozo*.

ELAEOCARPACEAE DC. 10/520. *Aristotelia, Crinodendron, Elaeocarpus, Muntingia, Sloanea, Vallea.*

Elaeocarpus L. Elaeocarpaceae. 60 everg. trees or shrubs. Lvs entire or toothed. Fls fragrant, small, in axill. rac., with 3–5 toothed or fringed pet.; sta. numerous. Fr. a drupe, to 2cm diam. E Asia, Indomal., Australasia, Pacific. Z9.

E. cunninghamii Raoul = *E. dentatus*.

E. cyaneus Sims. Tree to 18m or more, usually a shrub in cult., glab. throughout. Lvs 10–15cm, oblong-elliptic or oblong-lanceolate, serrate. Rac. shorter than lvs, lax; fls small, ivory; pet. fimbriate. Fr. blue. Aus.

E. dentatus (Forst. & Forst. f.) Vahl. Tree to 18m, usually a shrub in cult. Branchlets initially sericeous. Lvs 5–10cm, oblong to obovate, entire or bluntly toothed, or sinuate, coriaceous, glossy above, downy beneath. Rac. to 10cm, pendulous; pet. white, 3–5-lobed. Fr. purple-grey. NZ.

Elaeodendron

E. ganitrus Roxb. = *E. sphaericus*.
E. reticulatus Sm. = *E. cyaneus*.
E. sphaericus (Gaertn.) Schum. BEAD TREE OF INDIA. Tree to 15m, usually less in cult. Lvs 12.5–15cm, elliptic to oblong, acuminate, serrulate, vein axis gland. beneath. Rac. pendulous; pet. white, tinted purple in bud. Fr. purple. India, Malaysia.

Elaeodendron Jacq. f.
E. australe Vent. = *Cassine australis*.
E. capense (L.) Ecklon & Zeyh. = *Cassine papillosa*.
E. glaucum Pers. = *Cassine glauca*.
E. laneanum A.H. Moore = *Cassine laneana*.
E. laurifolium Harv. = *Cassine laurifolia*.
E. orientale Jacq. f. = *Cassine orientalis*.
E. papillosum Hochst. = *Cassine papillosa*.
E. sphaerophyllum (Ecklon & Zeyh.) Presl = *Cassine sphaerophylla*.

Elaeophorbia Stapf. Euphorbiaceae. 4 woody or succulent shrubs or trees producing latex. Lvs simple, alt., thick, Infl. pedunculate, axill.; cyathium a whorl of 5 lobes interspersed with 5 glands. Fr. drupaceous. Trop. & S Afr. Z10.
E. drupifera (Thonn.) Stapf. Prickly tree to 15m. Br. 4–6-sided, becoming terete, woody. Lvs oblong-cuneate to obovate, to 25×9cm, often emarginate, glab., fleshy. Peduncles 3, forked; involucre cupulate, to 1cm diam. Fr. exserted from sta. remains, yellow.
E. grandifolia (Haw.) Croizat. As for *E. drupifera* but lvs to 30×7.5cm.

Elaphoglossum Schott ex J. Sm. Lomariopsidaceae. At least 400 mostly epiphytic ferns. Rhiz. creeping or short-erect, usually scaly. Sterile fronds linear to nearly round, ± tongue shaped, entire, often hairy; stipe usually scaly; fertile fronds differing in length and size or shape of blade. Pantrop. Z10.
E. caudatum Moore = *E. petiolatum*.
E. coniforme (Sw.) Schott. Fronds 10–15×2.5cm, ligulate, obtuse, rounded or tapering at base, undulate, thickly coriaceous, glab.; stipe to 15cm, nearly white, glab. S Afr.
E. crinitum (L.) Christ. ELEPHANT-EAR FERN; ELEPHANT'S EAR. Sterile fronds 17–48×8–25cm, elliptic-oblong to ovate, acute or obtuse at apex, truncate or rounded or shallowly cordate at base, usually hairy; stipes to 33cm, hairy; fertile fronds 12–22×4–10cm, ovate to lanceolate-ovate, acute, always smaller than the sterile fronds. Trop. Amer.
E. hirtum (Sw.) C. Chr. Sterile fronds often pendent, 6–50×2–5cm, linear or narrowly elliptic, long-acuminate, caudate, attenuate at base, papery, densely scaly and black-hairy; stipes to 22cm, scaly; fertile fronds narrowly lanceolate or elliptic, always smaller than sterile. Azores, Madeira, Jam., Hispan., Mex., C Amer.
E. latifolium (Sw.) J. Sm. Sterile fronds 15–48×3–10cm, lanceolate to narrowly elliptic, short-acuminate, attenuate and slightly decurrent at base, thick, scaly, stipes to 24cm, narrowly winged, slightly scaly; fertile fronds narrowly lanceolate or elliptic, always smaller than sterile. Trop. Amer.
E. lingua Raddi in Brackenr. Sterile fronds 15–23×5–7.5cm, acute, base narrowed abruptly, margins thickened, coriaceous, glab.; stipe erect, to 30cm, glab.; fertile fronds much narrower than sterile. W Indies to Braz. and Peru.
E. longifolium (Jacq.) J. Sm. Sterile fronds 30–75×6cm, lanceolate, sharply acuminate, gradually attenuate at base, membranous, stipe to 23cm; fertile fronds half as long and narrower than sterile. Trop. Amer.
E. peltatum (Sw.) Urban = *Peltapteris peltata*.
E. petiolatum (Sw.) Urban. Sterile fronds 8–28×1–2.5cm, linear, acute or abruptly acuminate, attenuate at base, thick, glandular-punctate, scaly above and on abaxial midrib, stipe to 16cm, glandular-punctate, scaly; fertile fronds always exceeding sterile, linear. Trop. Amer.
E. squamosum (Sw.) J. Sm. = *E. hirtum*.
E. villosum (Sw.) J. Sm. Sterile fronds 6–20×1.5–3.5cm, linear to oblong or narrowly elliptic, caudate or long-acuminate, short-attenuate at base, papery, covered with tiny gland. hairs and hair-like scales, stipes to 14cm, with minute gland. hairs and rufescent hair-like scales; fertile fronds shorter than fertile, linear or narrowly elliptic, caudate. C Amer., W Indies.
E. viscosum (Sw.) J. Sm. = *E. petiolatum*.

ELATINACEAE Dumort. 2/32. *Elatine*.

Elatine L. Elatinaceae. 50 aquatic or terrestrial herbs. St. erect to prostrate, rooting, somewhat succulent. Lvs opposite or whorled, entire, stipulate. Fls small, axill., usually solitary; sep. 3 or 4, membranaceous, free or connate at base, obtuse; pet. 3 or 4, membranaceous; sta. 2–8. Cosmop. Z8.

E. alsinastrum L. Ann. or perenn. herb to 80cm. St. robust, hollow. Lvs whorled, sessile, in aquatic plants lvs to 18 in a whorl, ovate to linear, in terrestrial plants lvs to 3 in a whorl, ovate to lanceolate. Fls green. N Afr., Eurasia.
E. hexandra (Lapierre) DC. Ann. or short-lived perenn. St. to 20cm, prostrate to decumbent. Lvs opposite, spathulate, short-petiolate. W & C Eur.
E. hydropiper L. Ann. herb to 16cm, slender. Lvs to 2cm, opposite, ovate-oblong, often long-petiolate. Fls pale red. N Afr., Eurasia.
E. macropoda Guss. Ann. to 16cm. Lvs to 2cm, opposite, lower lvs petiolate, upper lvs sessile. Fls pale red. S Eur.
E. triandra Schkuhr. Ann. to 18cm. St. decumbent. Lvs to 1cm, opposite, ovate to lanceolate, short-petiolate. Fls white to rose. Eurasia, S Amer.

Elatostema Forst. & Forst. f.
E. repens (Lour.) Hall = *Pellionia repens*.

Elburzia Hedge. Cruciferae. 1 low, cushion-forming, woody-based perenn. herb to 10cm. Lvs to 15mm including petiole, blue-green, tinged purple beneath, slightly fleshy, 3-lobed to entire, oblong-linear. Rac. corymbose; pet. 4, 5mm, clawed, white, almost round. Summer. NW Iran. Z8.
E. fenestrata (Boiss.) Hedge.
→*Petrocallis*.

Eldar Pine *Pinus brutia*.
Elder *Sambucus*.
Elderberry *Sambucus* (*S. nigra*).
Elderberry Panax *Polyscias sambucifolia*.
Elderflower Orchid *Dactylorhiza sambucina*.
Elecampne *Inula helenium*.
Election Posies *Castilleja coccinea*.
Elegant Penstemon *Penstemon concinnus*.

Eleocharis R. Br. SPIKE RUSH. Cyperaceae. 150 tufted ann. or perenn. grass-like herbs. St. slender; rhiz. stoloniferous, sometimes tuberous. Lvs reduced to bladeless sheaths or short blades. Spikelet solitary, term.; fls v. small, glumes present, perianth reduced to bristles or 0. Cosmop.
E. acicularis (L.) Roem. and Schult. NEEDLE SPIKE RUSH; SLENDER SPIKE RUSH; HAIR GRASS. Perenn., 5–30cm. Rootstock thin, mat-forming. Lf sheaths blunt. Spikelets 3–10-fld; glumes pale green with brown bands on either side of midrib; bristles 3–4, short. Summer. Widespread N Amer., Eur., Asia. Z7.
E. dulcis (Burm.) Trin. ex Hens. CHINESE WATER CHESTNUT. Perenn. 40–120cm. Rootstock red-brown, tuberous. Lf sheaths red-brown, pointed, membranous. Spikelets 50-fld; glumes straw-yellow to grey, bristles light brown. Asia. Z9.
E. palustris (L.) Roem. and Schult. CREEPING SPIKE RUSH. Perenn., 30–160cm. Roots horizontal. Lower lf sheaths brown, sometimes bearing a short blade, upper sheaths lacking blade. Spikelets many-fld; glumes pale green to brown with a green midrib; bristles slender, barbed. Late summer. N Amer., Eur., Asia.
E. parvula (Roem. & Schult.) Link ex Bluff, Nees & Schauer. Tuft-forming perenn., to 8cm. Stolons thin, producing white tubers. Lf sheaths v. thin, pale brown. Spikelets 3–8-fld; green; lowest glume large, blunt. Eur., SE Russia. Z8.
E. pygmaea Torr. = *E. parvula*.
E. vivipara Link. Perenn., 10–30cm. Rootstock stout, vertical, deep brown. Lf sheaths yellow, purple at base, tip pointed, often tinged purple. Spikelet, many-fld, viviparous, glumes dark brown, margin white; bristles barbed, red-brown. SE US. Z9.
→*Scirpus*.

Elephant Apple *Limonia acidissima*.
Elephant Bush *Portulacaria afra*.
Elephant-ear Wattle *Acacia dunnii*.
Elephant-foot Tree *Nolina recurvata*.
Elephant Hedge Bean Tree *Schotia latifolia*.
Elephant's-ear *Caladium*; *Elaphoglossum crinitum*; *Enterolobium cyclocarpa*.
Elephant's Ear Fern *Platycerium elephantotis*.
Elephant's-ear Plant *Alocasia*.
Elephant's Food *Portulacaria*.
Elephant's Foot *Dioscorea elephantipes*.
Elephant's Grass *Xerophyta equisetoides*.
Elephant's Milk Bush *Euphorbia hamata*.
Elephant Tree *Bursera microphylla*.
Elephant-tusk *Ibicella*; *Martynia*; *Proboscidea*.
Elephantwood *Bolusanthus speciosus*.
Elephant Yam *Amorphophallus paeoniifolius*.

Elettaria Maton. Zingiberaceae. 4 thickly rhizomatous aromatic perenn. herbs. St. erect, reed-like. Lvs 2-ranked. Infl. a basal, scapose spike with dense bracts; pet. 3, equal; lip oblong-ovate, emarginate, sometimes forming a hood; lat. staminodes small, not petaloid. Capsule dry, thin-walled, globose or ellipsoid. India, Sri Lanka, Malaysia, Sumatra. Z10.

E. cardamomum (L.) Maton. CARDAMOM; CEYLON CARDAMOM; MALABAR CARDAMOM. To 3m. Lvs 60×10cm, linear-lanceolate, acuminate. Spike loose 60cm, cor. 2cm, white; lip striped with pink, lilac or violet with yellow edge. Fr. aromatic. India.

E. speciosa Bl. = *Etlingera elatior*.
→*Amomum*.

Eleusine Gaertn. Gramineae. 9 ann. or perenn. stoloniferous grasses. St. tufted. Lvs linear, flat or folded; sheaths compressed, ligule membranous, ciliate. Infl. term., spikes digitately arranged. E, NE Afr., S Amer. Z9.

E. barcinonensis Costa = *E. tristachya*.

E. coracana (L.) Gaertn. FINGER MILLET; CORACAN; KURAKKAN; RAGI; AFRICAN MILLETT. Ann. to 1.5m. Lf blades to 50×1.5cm. Infl. 1–11-spicate, to 8×1cm. OW Trop.

E. indica (L.) Gaertn. YARD GRASS; WIRE GRASS; GOOSE GRASS. Ann. to 1.5m. Infl. 2–5-spicate, to 30×0.8cm. Lf blades to 17×0.5cm. Summer. OW Trop., nat. elsewhere.

E. oligostachya Link = *E. tristachya*.

E. tristachya (Lam.) Lem. Similar to *E. indica* but smaller with narrower lf blades. Spikes usually 3. OW Trop.

Eleutherine Herb. Iridaceae. 2 perenn. bulbous herbs. Lvs plicate, lanceolate, basal and 1 on st. Fls clustered, subtended by a pair of short spathes, white, star-like, opening in the evening; style br. 3, filiform. C & S Amer.; nat. Asia. Z10.

E. anomala Herb. = *E. bulbosa*.

E. bulbosa (Mill.) Urban. 15–75cm. Infl. axis much-branched; tep. 10–18mm. SE Braz. and Boliv. to Venez. and W Indies; nat. Philipp. and Indochina.

E. latifolia (Standl. & Williams) Ravenna. To 20cm. Infl. axis simple; tep. 12–14mm. Mex. to C & S Amer.

E. plicata (Sw.) Klatt = *E. bulbosa*.

Eleutherococcus Maxim. Araliaceae. *c*30 generally decid. and often bristly or prickly shrubs or trees, sometimes sprawling. Lvs digitately (1–)3–5-foliolate, petiole bases sheathing twigs. Infl. term., simple or compound; fls small, 5-merous, in umbels or heads. Fr. drupaceous, black or purple-black. S & E Asia.

E. divaricatus (Sieb. & Zucc.) S.Y. Hu. Open growing, early decid. shrub to 4m; twigs sometimes with pairs of spines at nodes. Petiole long, sometimes with one or more prickles; lfts 3–5, to 7×4cm, elliptic to obovate, hairy beneath, serrate. Infl. paniculate, downy; term. fls in an umbel, lat. fls in few to several heads on elongate peduncles subtended by a leafy bract; pet. brown to purple. Fr. blue-black to black, *c*8mm. Late summer. E China; Jap. Z6.

E. giraldii (Harms) Nak. Shrub to 3m, sometimes sprawling; br. densely covered with bristle-like prickles, or unarmed. Petiole to 8cm, often bristly-spiny; lfts 3–5, to 5×2.5cm, v. thin, glab. when mature, oblong-obovate to obovate to oblanceolate, biserrate. Infl. on main and short shoots term., usually a solitary umbel, axis to 2cm, with or without long hairs or bristles; pet. white tinged green. Fr. black, 8mm diam. Summer. NC China. Differs from *E. senticosus* in larger lvs with stalked lfts. Z6.

E. gracilistylus (W.W. Sm.) S.Y. Hu. Slenderly twiggy, scandent or prostrate armed shrub to 3m, similar to *E. sieboldianus* but with lfts more finely toothed; twigs unarmed or with a few prickles at nodes. Fls green. Summer. China, Vietnam. Sometimes confused with *E. spinosus*. Z6.

E. henryi Oliv. Sturdy armed shrub to 3m, twigs initially rough-hairy; prickles recurved, scattered. Lvs rough to the touch, petiole to 7cm; lfts 3–5, to 10×4cm, elliptic or obovate, base decurrent, brown-hairy beneath, biserrate. Infl. a congested cluster of umbels to 3cm diam. Fr. blue-black to black, to 8mm. Late summer. C China. 'Nanus': more compact. Z6.

E. lasiogyne (Harms) S.Y. Hu. Round-headed large shrub or small tree to 6m, glab. except for infl.; twigs with paired spines at nodes. Petiole to 7.5cm, unarmed; lfts 3, to 6×4.5cm, somewhat glossy, oblong or obovate, the middle often rhombic, thinly coriaceous, entire or toothed toward apex. Infl. simple or compound, fairly compact, umbels solitary or in clusters on both long and short shoots, white-hairy or glab.; pet. white. Fr. black, 7–9mm. Later summer–autumn. W China. Z6.

E. leucorrhizus Oliv. Shrub to 4m, usually with prickles at nodes or scattered on older wood. Petiole to 7cm, sometimes with 1–2 prickles; lfts 3–5, to 12×4cm, glab. at maturity, oblong to obovate to narrowly obovate, chartaceous or thinner, glaucous beneath, biserrate, teeth bristle-tipped. Infl. glab., usually

compound, term. umbel with pseudowhorls or clusters of lat. umbels and up to 5cm diam.; main axis to 10cm. Fr. blue-black or black, to 7mm. Summer. C & W China. Z6.

E. rehderianus (Harms) Nak. Scandent shrub to 3m, superficially similar to *E. sieboldianus* but with infl. appearing at ends of both long and short shoots; lfts sessile or subsessile, crenate-serrate above. Infl. simple, commonly with 2 accessory fls on peduncle below. Fr. black, 5mm. C China. Z6.

E. senticosus Rupr. & Maxim. SIBERIAN GINSENG. Shrub to 7m usually smaller, st. erect, sparingly branched, bristly, prickly or unarmed (f. *inermis* Komar.). Petioles to 12cm, finely prickly or unarmed; lfts 3–5, to 13×7cm, elliptic-obovate to oblong, dark green above, paler beneath with brown hairs on veins. Infl. simple or compound; umbels solitary or in clusters of 2–4, lat. glab.; ♀ fls green, ♂ and perfect fls purple to lilac. Fr. to 8mm. Summer. NE Asia. Z3.

E. sessiliflorus (Rupr. & Maxim.) S.Y. Hu. WANGRANGKURA. Vigorous spreading shrub to 5m with sprawling br., eventually pyramidal. Petiole to 12cm, sometimes with one or more prickles; lfts 3–5, obovate, to 18×7cm, glab., serrate. Infl. simple or compound, compact, term. umbel head-like, solitary or surrounded by a cluster of 2–4 similar umbels, hairy; pet. dull purple. Fr. black, 10–15mm, crowded together on v. short stalks. Late summer. NE Asia. Z4.

E. setchuensis (Harms) Nak. Glab. shrub to 4m, similar to *E. leucorrhizus*; unarmed or with a few prickles. Lvs usually 3-foliolate, lat. lfts serrate, teeth not bristle-tipped. Infl. usually compound but laterally contracted, main axis to 10cm. Summer. W China. Z6.

E. sieboldianus (Mak.) Koidz. Scandent shrub to 3m, with slender arching, cane-like br. armed at nodes. Lvs (3–)5(–7)-foliolate, rhombic-elliptic, toothed. Infl. simple, umbels solitary on long glab. stalks; fls green-white. Fr. black, 6–8mm across. Late spring to early summer. E China; Jap. (introd.). 'Variegatus': lfts edged creamy-white. Z4.

E. simonii (Schneid.) Hesse. Weakly growing, bushy armed shrub to 3m; twigs glab., sometimes green, with strong spines clustering around nodes and scattered, long prickles elsewhere. Petioles to 7cm; lfts 3–5, to 12×4cm, narrowly elliptic or obovate, bristly-hairy, biserrate. Infl. simple or compound, relatively small and compact; term. umbel to 3cm diam.; main axis to 7–8cm, glab.; pet. green. Fr. black, 5–6mm diam. Early summer. C China. Z6.

E. spinosus (L. f.) S.Y. Hu. Shrub to 3.5m, similar to *E. sieboldianus*, but with smaller lvs and shorter infl. Lfts cuneiform, entire, wavy or shallowly and sparsely toothed. Summer. Jap.

E. trichodon (Franch. & Savat.) Ohashi. Strongly branching shrub to 3m, superficially resembling *E. sieboldianus* but with infl. at ends of both long and short shoots; st. ± unarmed. Petiole minutely spiny; lfts bristly-biserrate; infl. simple, axis purple-red, to 5cm, glab.; fr. purple-black, 6–7cm. Jap. Z6.

E. trifoliatus (L.) S.Y. Hu. Scandent or erect armed shrub to 7m, prickles scattered; br. grey. Petioles short, prickly; lfts 3, to 8×4.5cm, rhombic to obovate to oblanceolate, toothed, midrib beneath often bristly. Infl. term., paniculate, sometimes partly leafy, main axis elongate. Fls green. Fr. laterally compressed, to 4mm long. S & E Asia, Taiwan, Philipp., China. Z7.

E. wilsonii (Harms) Nak. Similar to *E. giraldii* but br. unarmed or with bristly spines only at the nodes and lfts simple-serrate. Umbels solitary. Fr. black, 6–7mm across. W China. Z5.
→*Acanthopanax* and *Aralia*.

Eleven-o'clock *Portulaca grandiflora*.
Elfin Herb *Cuphea hyssopifola*.
Elim Heath *Erica regia*.

Elisena Herb.
E. longipetala Lindl. = *Hymenocallis longipetala*.

Elk *Pyrularia pubera*.
Elk Clover *Aralia californica*.
Elk Grass *Xerophyllum tenax*.
Elkhorn *Euphorbia lactea*.
Elkhorn Fern *Platycerium* (*P. bifurcatum*).
Elk Sedge *Cladium mariscus*.
Elkwood *Magnolia tripetala*.

Elleanthus Presl. Orchidaceae. 50 epiphytic or terrestrial orchids. St. reed-like, leafy, tufted. Lvs alt., plicate, fls in dense term., conspicuously bracteate heads or spicate rac.; sep. free, erect, pet. narrower and thinner; lip simple or somewhat trilobed, usually erose-fimbriate. C & S Amer. Z10.

E. aurantiacus. (Lindl.) Rchb. f. To 1m. Lvs to 12cm, lanceolate, mucronate. Infl. to 10cm, usually shorter; fls bright orange, edged red. Venez., Colomb., Ecuad., Peru.

E. capitatus (R. Br.) Rchb. f. To 150cm. Lvs to 23cm, lanceolate to lanceolate-elliptic, long-acuminate. Infl. to 8.5cm, gummy; fls pink-white. Summer. Widespread throughout genus range.

E. caravata (Aubl.) Rchb. f. To 60cm. Lvs to 16cm, lanceolate, subverrucose above. Infl. a dense rac.; fls pale to bright yellow. Autumn. Venez., Guyana, Fr. Guiana.

E. furfuraceus (Lindl.) Rchb. f. To 50cm. Lvs to 14cm, lanceolate or elliptic-lanceolate, long-acuminate. Fls 4–16, magenta, base white. Summer. Guyana, Venez., Colomb., Ecuad., Peru.

E. linifolius Presl. To 30cm. Lvs to 10cm, linear. Infl. to 3.5cm; floral bracts, imbricate, largely concealing fls; fls white, tipped pale green. W Indies, Mex., C Amer. to Peru.

E. longibracteatus (Lindl.) Fawcett. To 90cm. Lvs to 20cm, lanceolate to elliptic-lanceolate, acuminate. Infl. to 8cm; floral bracts to 3cm; fls cream to pale yellow. W Indies, Colomb., Ecuad., Boliv.

E. xanthocomus Rchb. f. To 30cm. Lvs to 17.5cm, lanceolate to oblong-lanceolate, acuminate. Infl. to 7.5cm; floral bracts yellow, green at apex; fls numerous, bright yellow. Spring. Peru.

Elliottia Muhlenb. ex Elliott. Ericaceae. 1 decid. shrub, 1–3m, or small tree to 6m. Young br. slender, pubesc. Lvs 5–12cm, oval or obovate, entire, acuminate, thin-textured, dull above, paler and thinly hirsute beneath. Fls fragrant, in pan. or erect term. rac. 10–25cm long; pedicels white, delicate; cal. lobes 3–5, short; cor. irregularly rotate, pet. 6–16mm, 4(–5), free, white, oblong, reflexed, ciliate; sta. 8, shorter than pet. Summer. SE US. Z8.

E. bracteata (Maxim.) Benth. & Hook. f. = *Tripetaleia bracteata*.
E. paniculata (Sieb. & Zucc.) Benth & Hook. f. = *Tripetaleia paniculata*.
E. pyroliflora (Bong.) Brim & Sterens = *Cladothamnus pyroliflorus*.
E. racemosa Elliott. GEORGIA PLUME.

Elm *Ulmus*.

Elmera Rydb. Saxifragaceae. 1 pubesc., perenn. herb to 25cm. Lvs mostly basal, reniform, palmatifid, to 6cm wide, bronze or red-tinted, pubesc., gland. above, bicrenate; petioles long. Fls small, in lax, term., 10–35-fld rac. on leafy st.; sep. 5, green-yellow, fused below to form a cup; pet. 5, small, white, crenate, equalling sep. Summer. NW US. Z5.

E. racemosa (S. Wats.) Rydb.
→*Heuchera* and *Tellima*.

Elm-leaf Begonia *Begonia ulmifolia*.
Elm-leaf Fig *Ficus ulmifolia*.
Elm-leaved Sumac *Rhus coriaria*.

Elodea Michx. WATERWEED; PONDWEED; DITCHMOSS. Hydrocharitaceae. 12 submerged freshwater perenn. herbs. St. erect or creeping, slender, terete, sometimes producing turions, rooting. Lvs cauline, in whorls of 3. Infl. spathaceous, minute. N Amer. to subtrop. S Amer., widely nat.

E. callitrichoides (Rich.) Caspary. Turions not developing. Lvs 1–2mm wide near base, linear to narrowly lanceolate or narrowly triangular, flat and spreading. Temp. S Amer., widely nat. Eur.

E. canadensis Michx. CANADIAN PONDWEED. Developing turions. Lvs 5–12×2–5mm, oblong to ovate, flat, spreading, dark green, translucent. N Amer., widely nat. Eur.

E. crispa hort. = *Lagarosiphon major*.
E. densa (Planch.) Casp. = *Egeria densa*.
E. ernstae St. John = *E. callitrichoides*.
E. naias (Planch.) Casp. = *Egeria naias*.
E. nuttallii (Planch.) St. John. Lvs to 1.5mm wide, linear to lanceolate, folding along midrib, recurved, light green. N Amer., nat. Eur.
E. richardii St. John = *E. callitrichoides*.
E. verticillata (L. f.) F. Muell. = *Hydrilla verticillata*.

Elsholtzia Willd. Labiatae. 38 shrubs and ann. or perenn. herbs. Fls in dense verticils, sometimes secund; floral bracts persistent; cal. 5-veined, 5-toothed; cor. small, 2-lipped; tube straight, upper lip hooded, lower lip 3-lobed. C & E Asia, NE Afr.

E. ciliata (Thunb.) Hylander. Ann., erect to 60cm, glab. and puberulent. Lvs 5–10cm, ovate-elliptical, crenate-serrate, softly pubesc. Infl. dense, secund, terminal and axill.; bracts to 6mm, obovate-orbicular, often tinged purple; cor. pale rose or lilac. Jap., China, nat. C, S & E Eur. Z5.

E. cristata Willd. = *E. ciliata*.

E. fruticosa (D. Don) Rehd. Aromatic, erect, subshrub, 1–1.75m. St. pubesc. Lvs 4–8cm, ovate-lanceolate, pubesc.,

serrate. Infl. subpaniculate forming a linear spike of dense whorls of fls with small bracteoles; cor. white or pink. Nepal, China. Z5.

E. patrinii (Lepech.) Garcke = *E. ciliata*.
E. polystachya Benth. = *E. fruticosa*.
E. stauntonii Benth. Subshrub 1–1.75m, branched. St. finely pubesc. Lvs 5–15cm, ovate-elliptic, coarsely serrate, glab. Infl. secund, spike-like, forming a branched pan.; bracts linear; cor. dark pink. China. 'Alba': fls white. Z4.
→*Perilla*.

Elymus L. WILD RYE; LYME GRASS. Gramineae. 150 tufted or rhizomatous perenn. grasses. St. slender to stout, usually erect. Lvs linear, flat or rarely rolled; ligules membranous. Infl. linear, stout to slender, spicate, bristled; spikelets sessile, laterally flattened. N temp. Asia.

E. angustus Trin. = *Leymus angustus*.
E. aralensis Reg. = *Leymus multicaulis*.
E. arenarius L. = *Leymus arenarius*.
E. canadensis L. CANADA WILD RYE. St. to 180cm. Lf blades to 20mm diam., flat or rolled, scabrous or slightly hispid, green to glaucous green. Infl. spikes pendent, densely arranged, bristled, to 25cm; spikelets in groups to 4, 2–5-fld, to 16mm. Summer–autumn. N Amer. Z3.
E. chinensis (Trin.) Keng. = *Leymus chinensis*.
E. condensatus Presl & Presl = *Leymus condensatus*.
E. elongatus (Host) Runem. St. to 90cm. Lvs scabrous above, flat becoming involute, rigid. Spikelets borne in 2 rows, with 4–8 fls. Eurasia. Z5.
E. farctus (Viv.) Runem. ex Melderis. St. 30–60cm, rigid, glab. Lf blades 2–5mm diam., convolute or flat with inrolled margins, rigid, glaucous-green, pubesc. on ribs above, glab. beneath. Spike to 25cm. Turk., Medit. Z5.
E. giganteus Vahl = *Leymus racemosus*.
E. glaucifolius Muhlenb. = *E. canadensis*.
E. glaucus Buckley = *Leymus secalinus*.
E. hispidus (Opiz) Melderis. INTERMEDIATE WHEATGRASS. St. to 1.2m. Lvs hispid, involute. Spikelets 3–8-fld. Eurasia. Z5.
E. junceus Fisch. = *E. farctus*.
E. mollis Trin. = *Leymus mollis*.
E. multicaulis Karel. & Kir. = *Leymus multicaulis*.
E. racemosus Lam. = *Leymus racemosus*.
E. sibiricus L. St. to 90cm, slender, erect, nodes black. Lvs to 23×1.3cm, scabrous, thin, finely pointed. Spikes pendent, dense; spikelets in pairs, 3–7-fld, to 2.5cm, green or green tinged purple. Summer. E Eur., temp. Asia. Z5.
E. spicatus (Pursh) Gould. St. to 90cm, erect. Lf sheaths glab.; blades less than 2mm diam., pubesc. above, flat to loosely involute. Spikes to 15cm, slender; spikelets mostly 6–8-fld. US. Z5.
E. trachycaulos (Link) Gould ex Shinn. SLENDER WEATHGRASS. St. over 90cm, erect. Lf sheaths usually glab., rarely pubesc.; blades to 2mm diam. Spikes to 25cm, slender, erect to nodding; spikelets slightly overlapping, few-fld. US. Z5.
E. virginicus L. VIRGINIA WILD-RYE. St. erect, to 1.2cm. Lf sheaths glab.; blades to 15mm diam., flat, scabrous. Spike to 15cm, erect, tinged yellow. N Amer. Z3.
→*Clinelymus* and *Agropyron*.

Elythranthera (Endl.) A.S. George. ENAMEL ORCHID. Orchidaceae. 2 terrestrial orchids to 30cm. Lf basal, solitary, lanceolate, glandular-pubesc. Scape erect; tep. iridescent, glossy above, spreading, oblong-lanceolate; lip membranous, recurved or sigmoid with 2 mobile basal calli. Late summer–mid winter. SW W Aus. Z9.

E. brunonis (Endl.) A.S. George. Lf 2–8cm, oblong-oblanceolate. Fls 1–3; tep. purple, paler above, blotched deeper purple; lip white, lanceolate, entire, base marked purple.
E. emarginata Lindl. Lf 6–10cm, linear-lanceolate to lanceolate. Fls 1–4, rose pink, spotted below; lip marked rose-purple, linear to narrow oblong, emarginate.
→*Glossodia*.

Emblic *Phyllanthus emblica*.

Embothrium Forst. & Forst. f. Proteaceae. 8 everg. shrubs or trees. Lvs coriaceous, entire. Fls in terminal and axill. clusters or rac.; perianth narrow-tubular, splitting into 4 narrow, twisted lobes; style long-exserted. C & S Andes.

E. coccineum Forst. & Forst. f. CHILEAN FIREBUSH; CHILEAN FLAMEFLOWER. Shrub or tree to 10m. St. ascending, clumped. Lvs to 12cm, oblong to narrow-lanceolate, glab., pale or dark green. Rac. to 10cm, crowded; pedicels red-green; fls to 4.5cm, sealing wax red to vivid scarlet. Late spring–summer. Chile. Z8. 'Eliot Hodgkin': fls bright yellow. 'Longifolium': lvs longer, oblong-lanceolate. Z8. var. *lanceolatum* Ruiz & Pav. Lvs narrower. 'Norquinco Valley': lvs linear-lanceolate; fls in clusters along br., bright scarlet. Z8.

Emerald Creeper *Strongylodon macrobotrys.*
Emerald Fern *Asparagus densiflorus.*
Emerald-ripple Pepper *Peperomia caperata.*

Emilia Cass. Compositae. *c*24 ann. herbs to 80cm. Lower lvs lanceolate-oblong or lyrate, sessile or with a winged petiole; upper lvs oblong to ovate, amplexicaul. Cap. discoid, solitary or few in a term. corymb. India, Polyn., Trop. Afr. Z9.
E. coccinea (Sims) D. Don. TASSEL FLOWER. Glab. or scabrous. Lvs to 14cm, oblong-lanceolate, sessile, entire to dentate. Cap. in a term. corymb; phyllaries much shorter than flts; flts scarlet. Summer–autumn. Trop. Afr.
E. flammea hort. = *E. coccinea.*
E. javanica hort. non (Burm. f.) Robinson = *E. coccinea.*
E. javanica (Burm. f.) Robinson = *E. sonchifolia.*
E. sonchifolia (L.) Moench. Glab., often glaucous. Lvs to 10cm, lyrate, base winged, auriculate; dentate. Cap. in a term. corymb; phyllaries equal to flts; flts purple-red. Trop. Asia and Afr. 'Lutea': flts yellow.
→*Cacalia.*

Eminium Schott. Araceae. 7 tuberous, perenn. herbs, resembling *Biarum* and *Dracunculus*, the former particularly in respect of fls and fr., the latter in respect of foliage. Spathe v. short-stalked or partially buried, expanding into a broad blade, often reflexed or lying flat on soil surface. Fruiting heads often developing below ground. E Medit. to C Asia. Z8.
E. alberti Reg. Lvs to 25cm, ovate-lanceolate, usually simple, sometimes lobed. Spathe equalling lvs, tube short, base green-yellow, blade broadly ovate-lanceolate, undulate, reflexed, deep velvety blood red above; spadix appendage, fleshy green-brown, ± equalling spathe blade. C Asia.
E. intortum (Banks & Sol.) Kuntze. Lvs to 15cm, ovate-lanceolate to hastate, strongly divided and undulate. Spathe equalling lvs, erect, blade undulate, inrolled, hooded, dark velvety purple above, green below; spadix appendage to half length of spathe blade, purple-black. S Turk., Syr., Iraq.
E. lehmannii Kuntze. Lvs to 15cm, simple, lanceolate to sub-sagittate. Spathe velvety black above, green below; spadix black. Fr. white, breaking the soil surface to ripen red to violet. Iran.
E. rauwolfii (Bl.) Schott. Lvs narrow-lanceolate to obscurely sagittate, sometimes spotted and flecked white or grey-green. Spathe equalling lf petioles, base squat, bright green, blade erect, ovate-lanceolate, velvety purple-black; spadix appendage club-like, glossy black. E & S Turk., Syr.
E. spiculatum (Bl.) Schott. Lvs to 25cm, erect, strongly undulate and pinnatifid. Spathe 10–22cm (far smaller in ssp. *negevense*), tube usually buried, blade ovate-lanceolate, reflexed, purple-black, corrugated, above; spadix black, erect, to half length of spathe. Iraq, Syr., Turk., Negev, Sinai Penins.

Emmenanthe Benth. Hydrophyllaceae. 1 viscid ann. herb to 30cm, usually smaller. St. simple or intricately branched. Lvs to 7cm, oblong, pinnatifid, ± sessile. Infl. of loose scorpioid cymes; cor. to 1.25cm, cream, yellow or pale pink, strongly campanulate, lobes 5–10, spreading. SW N Amer. Z9.
E. penduliflora Benth. YELLOW BELLS; GOLDEN BELLS; WHISPERING BELLS.

Emmenopterys Oliv. Rubiaceae. 2 decid. trees. Lvs opposite, petiolate, entire, somewhat leathery. Fls in corymbose, term. pan.; cor. funnel- or bell-shaped, lobes 5, spreading, ovate, downy; cal. lobes 5, ovate, ciliate, 1 lobe sometimes developed into enlarged wing- or leaflike bract. China, SE Asia.
E. henryi Oliv. To 26m; bark dark grey, rough; branchlets grey or purple, glab. Young growth red-bronze. Lvs to 20cm, elliptic-ovate to oblong-ovate, acute, lustrous dark green above, pale and pubesc. beneath; petioles red to purple. Pan. to 18cm; cor. white, 3×2.5cm; enlarged cal. lobe to 5×3.5cm, white, claw to 5cm. Summer. C & W China, Burm., Thail. Z8.

Emory Oak *Quercus emoryi.*

EMPETRACEAE 3/5. *Corema, Empetrum.*

Empetrum L. CROWBERRY. Empetraceae. 2 low-growing, in-tricately branched heath-like everg. shrubs. Lvs suberect, whorled, narrow. Fls small, purple-red, solitary or clustered; sep. 3; pet. 0. Drupe edible, glossy, succulent, globose. N temp. regions, S Andes, Falklands. Z3.
E. eamesii Fern. & Wiegand. ROCKBERRY. To 15cm. Br. prostrate; branchlets hoary. Lvs to 3mm, narrow-oblong to

linear-elliptic. Fr. to 4mm, rose to red. E N Amer. ssp. *herma-phroditum* (Hagerup) D. Löve. Branchlets glab. or brown-tomentose. Fls hermaphrodite. Fr. purple-black. N Amer., Eur-asia.
E. hermaphroditum Hagerup = *E. eamesii* ssp. *hermaphroditum.*
E. nigrum L. BLACK CROWBERRY; CRAKE BERRY; CURLEW BERRY; MONOX. To 30cm, usually shorter. Br. decumbent; branchlets initially gland. Lvs to 4mm, linear-oblong. Fr. to 8mm, glossy black. N Amer., Eurasia. The names *atropurpureum*, var. *purpureum* and var. *rubrum* are of doubtful application and, in gardens, may refer to *E. eamesii.* 'Lucia': new growth cream.
E. pinnatum Lam. = *Margyricarpus pinnatus.*

Empress Candle Plant *Senna alata.*
Empress Tree *Paulownia.*

Enallagma (Miers) Baill.
E. cucurbitina (L.) Baill. ex Schum. = *Amphitecna latifolia.*
E. latifolia (Mill.) Small = *Amphitecna latifolia.*
E. macrophylla (Seem.) Lund. = *Amphitecna macrophylla.*

Enamel Orchid *Elythranthera.*

Encelia Adans. Compositae. *c*15 low, branched shrubs and perenn. herbs. Cap. radiate or discoid, solitary or in pan.; ray flts yellow; disc flts yellow or purple. SW US to Mex., Peru, Chile and Galapagos Is. Z8.
E. actonii Elmer = *E. virginensis.*
E. californica Nutt. Subshrub, forming broad, rounded clumps, to 1.5m. Lvs to 6cm, lanceolate to ovate, acute, green, pubesc. Cap. radiate, solitary; ray flts to 3cm, golden-yellow; disc flts purple. Calif.
E. calva (Engelm. & A. Gray) A. Gray = *Simsia calva.*
E. canescens Cav. Subshrub, to 50cm. Lvs to 7cm, broadly ovate, obtuse, entire, grey-hairy. Cap. solitary to few; flts orange. Summer. Peru.
E. farinosa A. Gray. BRITTLE BUSH; INCIENSO. Fragrant rounded shrub to 1m. Lvs to 8cm, narrowly to broadly ovate, entire or toothed, silvery-tomentose. Cap. radiate, solitary or few in cymes, stalks long often nodding in fr.; ray flts to 1.2cm, orange-yellow; disc flts yellow or red-brown. Spring. SW US.
E. fructescens (A. Gray) A. Gray. Rounded, much-branched shrub, to 1.5m. Lvs to 2cm, lanceolate-oblong to ovate, base truncate, entire, or with a pair of teeth near base. Cap. usually discoid, solitary, on long stalks; disc flts yellow. Spring. Mojave and Colorado Deserts to Ariz.
E. scaposa A. Gray. Herbaceous perenn., to 50cm. Lvs to 10cm, linear, in basal tufts. Cap. to 4cm diam., on long stalks. New Mex.
E. virginensis Nels. Like *E. fructescens* but st. scabrous, lvs larger, ovate, sometimes canescent and gland., ray flts to 1cm. Late spring. SW US.

Enceliopsis (A. Gray) Nels. SUNRAY. Compositae. 4 scapose, often silvery, xerophytic, perenn. herbs. Lvs radical, entire, petiolate, canescent. Cap. radial, large, yellow, long-stalked. SW US. Z8.
E. argophylla (D.C. Eaton) Nels. Tufted, tomentose, to 1m. Lvs to 10cm, rhombic-ovate, petiole short, broadly-winged, silvery-velutinous. Scapes to 50cm; cap. to 13cm diam.; ray flts to 4cm. Spring–summer. S Utah, S Nevada, NW Ariz.
E. covillei (Nels.) S.F. Blake. PANAMINT DAISY. Like *E. argophylla* except ray flts to 5cm, and fr. puberulent or glabrate not silky-villous. S Calif.
E. grandiflora Nels. = *E. covillei.*
E. nudicaulis (Gray) Nels. Like *E. argophylla* except less robust, shorter and densely tomentose to canescent, often with tufts of wool in lf axils. Lvs obovate or suborbicular, petiole long. Ray flts shorter. Spring. Ariz., Utah, Idaho.

Encephalartos Lehm. Zamiaceae. 25 cycads. St. usually arborescent, stout, simple, columnar, rarely short or buried. Lvs pinnate, whorled in term. crowns; rachis usually tomentose and armed toward base; pinnae linear to ovate-lanceolate, rigid, thick, leathery, often spiny-toothed. ♂ cones stalked, sub-cylindric, with scales spirally placed; ♀ cones usually broader and heavier; seed coat red to yellow or brown, fleshy. S & C Afr. Z9.
E. altensteinii Lehm. PRICKLY CYCAD. St. 4–7m. Lvs to 3.5m, straight or recurved; pinnae to 15cm, linear-oblong, rigid, fresh green, with 1–3 spiny teeth along each margin. S Afr.
E. arenarius R.A. Dyer. St. to 1m. Lvs to 1.5m, distinctly recurved; pinnae to 16cm, rigid, mid-green, occas. blue with 3 or 4 flat lobes. S Afr.
E. barteri Carruth. ex Miq. St. to 15m. Lvs to 1.5m; pinnae to 17.5cm, linear-lanceolate, entire or with few spiny teeth, dark

olive green. C Afr.

E. brachyphyllus Lehm. = *E. caffer*.

E. caffer (Thunb.) Lehm. KAFFIR BREAD. St. ± subterranean, crown woolly. Lvs to 1m; pinnae to 10cm, linear-lanceolate, entire or with 1–2 teeth near apex, fresh green. S Afr.

E. cycadifolius (Jacq.) Lehm. St. to 1m, densely woolly. Lvs to 1.2m; pinnae to 15cm, ovate-lanceolate, mostly overlapping, tinged grey or silver, margin entire, thickened. S Afr.

E. eugene-maraisii Verdoorn WATERBERG CYCAD St. to 4m. Lvs to 1.5m; pinnae to 20cm, blue-green, broadly lanceolate, entire or with 1–2 small teeth on lower margin. S Afr.

E. ferox Bertol. St. to 1m. Lvs to 1.8m; pinnae oblong-ovate, glossy dark green, with 2–4 broad sharp spiny teeth along each margin. S Afr.

E. friderici-guilielmi Lehm. WHITE-HAIRED CYCAD. St. to 4m. Lvs to 1.5m; pinnae to 18cm, woolly beneath when young, narrowly linear, entire, v. sharply pointed, overlapping, dark green with age. S Afr.

E. ghellinckii Lehm. DRAKENSBERG CYCAD. St. to 3m; crown golden-woolly. Lvs to 1m, spirally twisted; pinnae to 14cm, entire, strongly revolute, almost acicular, densely grey-woolly when young, becoming bright green. S Afr.

E. gratus Prain. St. to 1m, ± ovoid. Lvs to 1.8m; pinnae to 25cm, ovate-lanceolate, grey-green or olive, rigid, curved, with 1–4 teeth on lower margin. Trop. Afr.

E. heenanii R.A. Dyer. WOOLLY CYCAD. St. to 3m, covered above with golden-brown wool. Lvs to 1.3m, curving gently upwards, woolly, pale silver-green; pinnae to 15cm, oblong-lanceolate, acuminate, densely brown-woolly, with a white tinged bloom when young, entire, rarely with 1 or 2 small teeth. S Afr., Swaz.

E. hildebrandtii A. Br. & Bouché. St. to 6m. Lvs to 2.7m; pinnae to 10cm, linear-lanceolate, woolly becoming glab., grey-green, with 2–4 teeth on each margin. Trop. E Afr.

E. horridus (Jacq.) Lehm. St. exposed to 50cm or subterranean. Lvs to 1m, arching; pinnae to 10cm, deeply cut with 2–3 large spine-tipped, revolute, glaucous blue-green lobes. S Afr.

E. humilis Verdoorn. St. subterranean or exposed to 30cm. Lvs to 50cm, twisted, recurved; pinnae to 13cm, linear-lanceolate, finely pubesc. when young, deep green. S Afr.

E. inopinus R.A. Dyer LYDENBURG CYCAD. St. to 3m, reclining. Lvs to 1.5m, with brown wool covering bases when young; pinnae to 20cm, linear-lanceolate, falcate, blue-green. S Afr.

E. laevifolius Stapf & Davy. St. to 3m. Lvs to 1.5m, occas. twisted toward apex; pinnae to 15×7cm, entire, blue-green, tinged grey when young, becoming dark green. S Afr.

E. lanatus Stapf & Davy. CLIFANTS RIVER CYCAD. St. to 1.5m. Lvs to 1m, recurved above; pinnae to 14cm, lanceolate, soft green, overlapping, entire. S Afr.

E. latifrons Lehm. ALBANY CYCAD. St. to 3m. Lvs to 1.5m, sharply recurved above; pinnae to 15cm, ovate to ovate-lanceolate, overlapping, finely velvety when young, becoming glab., dark glossy green, with 3–4, curled lobes on lower margin. S Afr.

E. laurentianus De Wild. St. to 9m. Lvs over 6m; pinnae to 50cm, linear-lanceolate, grey-green, with 6–10 teeth along both margins. W Afr.

E. lebomboensis Verdoorn. LEBOMBO CYCAD. St. to 4m, erect. Lvs 1–3m; pinnae to 17cm, lanceolate, overlapping, bright green, with 2–4 teeth along both margins. S Afr.

E. lehmannii Lehm. KAROO CYCAD. St. to 2m, often reclining. Lvs to 1.5m, recurving slightly at apex, with swollen yellow bases; pinnae to 18cm, blue-grey when young, becoming green, lanceolate, falcate, entire or occas. with 1 or 2 small teeth on the lower margin. S Afr.

E. longifolius (Jacq.) Lehm. SUURBERG CYCAD. St. to 4m. Lvs to 2m, arching; pinnae to 20cm, lanceolate, overlapping, dark glossy green, occas. glaucous blue, entire or with 1–3 teeth along the lower margin. S Afr.

E. manikensis (Gilliland) Gilliland. RHODESIAN CYCAD. St. to 2.5m. Lvs to 2m; pinnae to 20cm, ovate-lanceolate, glaucous, with 2–4 teeth along both margins at base. Zimb.

E. natalensis R.A. Dyer & Verdoorn. NATAL CYCAD. St. to 4m. Lvs to 3.5m, straigh; pinnae to 25cm, broadly lanceolate, dark green, entire or with 1–4 teeth along one or both margins. S Afr.

E. ngoyanus Verdoorn. St. mostly subterranean, swollen. Lvs to 1.25m, straight; pinnae to 10cm, well spaced, dark green, lanceolate, occas. entire, otherwise with 1 or more teeth along lower margin. S Afr.

E. paucidentatus Stapf & Davy BARBERTON CYCAD. St. to 6m. Lvs to 2.5m, straight; pinnae to 25cm, reflexed, widely spaced, glossy dark green, lanceolate, with 1–3 small teeth along both margins. S Afr.

E. princeps R.A. Dyer. KEI CYCAD. St. to 3m, reclining. Lvs to 1.3m, decurved above; pinnae to 15cm, silver-blue when young,

dull green with age, lanceolate, entire or with a few teeth along lower margin. S Afr.

E. transvenosus Stapf & Davy. MODJADJI CYCAD. St. to 13m. Lvs to 2.5m; pinnae to 25cm, deflexed, glossy dark green, broadly lanceolate, with 2–5 small teeth along the upper margin, 1–3 along lower margin. S Afr.

E. trispinosus (Hook.) R.A. Dyer. St. subterranean or exposed to 1m. Lvs to 1.25m, recurved; pinnae 10–18cm, narrower than in *E. horridus* and less glaucous, with 1 or 2 strongly recurved lobes along the lower margin. S Afr. Has hybridized with *E. horridus*.

E. umbeluziensis R.A. Dyer. St. subterranean, to 25cm diam. Lvs to 2m, straight, finely pubesc. when young, becoming glossy bright green with age; pinnae to 20cm, with 1 or 2 teeth along 1 or both margins. S Afr.

E. villosus Lem. St. subterranean. Lvs to 3m, recurved; pinnae to 25cm, dark green, narrowly lanceolate, with 1–3 teeth along both margins or entire, slightly recurved, obscurely villous beneath and on teeth. S Afr.

E. woodii Sander. WOOD'S CYCAD. Resembling *E. natalensis* but with broader pinnae. St. to 6m. Lvs to 2.5m; pinnae to 20×5cm, dark green, distinctly toothed in juveniles, adults entire. ♂ only known. S Afr.

Encholirium Mart. ex Schult. f. Bromeliaceae. 12 short-stemmed perenn. herbs. Lvs in a dense rosette, with large sheaths and narrowly triangular blades, margins spiny, coarsely toothed. Infl. scapose, simple or sparsely branched. NE Braz. Z9.

E. spectabile Mart. ex Schult. f. To 5m in fl. Lvs to 60cm, scaly, beneath; teeth to 1cm or longer. Infl. densely racemose, br. few; floral bracts linear; fls to 2.5cm, yellow-green.

→*Dyckia* and *Puya*.

Encyclia Hook. f. Orchidaceae. *c*150 epiphytic and lithophytic orchids. Pbs ovoid to fusiform, 1–4-leaved at apex. Lvs oblong to ligulate, fleshy to coriaceous. Infl. a term. rac. or pan.; sep. free, spreading or reflexed, subequal; pet. largely similar to sep.; lip simple or trilobed. Subtrop. and Trop. Americas W Indies. Z10.

E. adenocaula (La Ll. & Lex.) Schltr. Pbs to 8×6cm, ovoid-conical. Lvs to 35cm, ligulate, glossy, hard. Pan. to 100cm, many-fld; peduncle verrucose; fls to 9cm diam., slender, spreading, pale rose-pink to pale purple sometimes streaked dark rose; lip spreading, paler with dark markings. Spring–summer. Mex.

E. adenocaula var. *kennedyi* (Fowlie & Withner) Hagsater & Gonzalez = *E. kennedyi*.

E. alata (Batem.) Schltr. Pbs to 12×6cm, ovoid to pyriform. Lvs to 55cm, linear-lanceolate, tough, often flushed red-purple. Infl. to 150cm, usually branching; fls to 6cm diam., slender, spreading pale green or yellow-green marked purple or red-brown, lip usually white veined maroon. Summer. Mex. to Nic.

E. ambigua (Lindl.) Schltr. Pbs to 8×4cm, ovoid-conical. Lvs to 37cm, linear-ligulate. Pan. to 80cm; peduncle minutely verrucose; fls to 3.5cm diam., fragrant, cream-yellow or green-yellow, sometimes tinged pale brown, lip cream to straw-yellow spotted and streaked red, undulate-crisped. Summer. Hond., Guat., Mex.

E. aromatica (Batem.) Schltr. Pbs to 8×5cm, conical to sub-spheric, often dark. Lvs to 30cm, linear-ligulate or elliptic-ligulate. Pan. to 90cm, fls to 4cm diam., cream, pale yellow or yellow-green, often suffused red-brown, lip cream or yellow veined red-brown, strongly undulate, verrucose, triangular. Mostly spring. Guat., Mex.

E. baculus (Rchb. f.) Dressler & Pollard. Pbs to 30×2cm, fusiform-cylindrical. Lvs to 30cm, linear-elliptic. Infl. to 7cm, erect, 2 to 3-fld; fls to 3cm diam., fragrant, white-cream to pale yelow-green, lip white or cream striped maroon to violet. Spring–summer. Mex., Braz., Colomb., Nic., Hond., Guat., El Salvador.

E. belizensis (Rchb. f.) Schltr. Pbs to 4.5×2cm, ovoid-conical. Lvs to 50cm, elliptic-lanceolate to linear, coriaceous. Infl. to 90cm, often branched; fls to 4cm diam., fragrant, long-lived, pale yellow to olive green, the tip white to cream streaked red-brown, midlobe suborbicular, obtuse, undulate. Spring–summer. Belize, Hond., Mex.

E. bicamerata (Rchb. f.) Dressler & Pollard. Pbs to 7×3cm, ovoid. Lvs to 25cm, elliptic-oblong. Infl. to 40cm, many-fld; fls to 2.5cm diam., fragrant, tawny-brown or chestnut-brown; the lip white stained ochre at base and spotted purple on callus, midlobe transversely oblong to subreniform. Spring–summer. Mex.

E. boothiana (Lindl.) Dressler. Pbs to 3.5×2.5cm, subglobose. Lvs to 17cm, oblanceolate, rigid. Infl. to 25cm, loosely few-fld; fls to 3cm diam. yellow blotched deep red-brown, lip yellow-green marked white, midlobe apex fleshy-thickened. Winter. Flor., Mex., W Indies, Belize.

E. bractescens (Lindl.) Hoehne. Pbs to 3.5×2cm, conical or ovoid-conical. Lvs to 27cm, ligulate to linear-lanceolate. Infl. to 30cm, sometimes branched, fls to 6cm diam., tep. yellow-brown to brick-red; lip white-yellow with red-purple veins, midlobe, suborbicular-obovate to transversely oblong, retuse, undulate-crenulate. Winter–summer. Mex., Guat., Hond., Belize.

E. brassavolae (Rchb. f.) Dressler. Pbs to 20×5cm, ovoid to pyriform. Lvs to 28cm, oblong-elliptic to oblong-lanceolate. Infl. to 50cm, simple, erect; fls to 7cm diam.; tep. green-yellow to olive-tan, narrow; lip rose-purple, cream at base, narrow, acuminate. Summer–autumn. C Amer., Mex. to Panama.

E. bulbosa (Vell.) Pabst. Pbs to 9×1.5cm, fusiform. Lvs to 21cm, coriaceous, ligulate. Infl. to 12cm, erect; fls to 5cm diam., cream-white, the lip marked purple, simple, acuminate.

E. calamaria (Lindl.) Pabst. Pbs to 5×1cm, fusiform. Lvs to 11cm, narrowly oblanceolate. Infl. to 6cm, few-fld; fls to 3cm diam., white-cream to pale yellow-green, the lip streaked purple, simple, ovate to cordate, acute. Braz.

E. campylostalix (Rchb. f.) Schltr. Pbs to 12×4cm, ovoid-oblong to ellipsoid, compressed. Lvs to 30cm, subcoriaceous, elliptic to oblong. Infl. to 38cm, sometimes branched, erect; fls to 5cm diam., pendent, red-purple lined yellow, grey-green below, lip white spotted red at base, midlobe obovate to suborbicular, sub-apiculate or rounded. Guat., Panama, Costa Rica.

E. candollei (Lindl.) Schltr. Pbs to 8×3.5cm, ovoid-conical to globose. Lvs to 35cm, coriaceous, elliptic-ligulate to narrowly lanceolate. Pan. to 90cm, loosely many-fld; fls to 4cm diam. yellow-green or yellow brown to chocolate, the lip white to cream streaked purple, midlobe suborbicular to flabellate, acute to shortly acuminate. Spring–summer. Guat.

E. ceratistes (Lindl.) Schltr. Pbs to 7×2.5cm, ovoid to ovoid-pyriform. Lvs to 45cm, linear-ligulate. Infl. to 1m, branched, suberect to pendent; fls to 4cm diam.; tep. cream to pale green or green-yellow; lip white to yellow-cream, midlobe lined dark purple, suborbicular to ovate-triangular, acute. Spring–autumn. Venez., Colomb., C Amer., Mex.

E. chacaoensis (Rchb. f.) Dressler & Pollard. Pbs to 10×5cm, ovoid to fusiform. Lvs to 30cm, elliptic. Infl. to 10cm, 2 to 7-fld; fls to 4cm diam., white, cream or green-cream, lip uppermost, striped maroon or purple, broadly ovate to suborbicular, sub-truncate. Spring–summer. C Amer., Venez., Colomb.

E. chondylobulbon (Rich. & Gal.) Dressler & Pollard. Pbs to 25×2.5cm, slightly compressed, fusiform. Lvs to 40cm, linear-lanceolate. Rac. to 13cm, few-fld; fls to 7cm diam., white or yellow-cream, lip striped purple, ovate-cordate, long-acuminate. Summer–autumn. Mex., Guat., El Salvador.

E. citrina (La Ll. & Lex.) Dressler. Habit strongly pendulous. Pbs to 6×3cm, ovoid to fusiform. Lvs to 26cm, elliptic-lanceolate, glaucous grey-green. Infl. short, 1 or 2-fld, pendulous; fls to 6.5cm long, highly fragrant, appearing only partially open; tep. fleshy, lemon-yellow to golden, often some-what glaucous, lip deeper with pale margins and callus and orange-flushed midlobe and veins. Spring–early summer. Mex.

E. cochleata (L.) Lemée. COCKLE ORCHID; CLAMSHELL ORCHID. Pbs to 25×4cm, pyriform to ellipsoid. Lvs to 40cm, elliptic-lanceolate to linear-lanceolate. Infl. to 50cm, erect, simple; fls to 9cm diam., opening over many seasons, sep. and pet. yellow-green to lime green, linear-lanceolate; lip uppermost, deep purple to black, white toward base with deep purple veins, concave above, orbicular-cordate, broadly acute. Colomb., Venez., Flor., W Indies, C Amer.

E. concolor (La Ll. & Lex.) Schltr. Pbs to 6×3cm, ovoid to globose. Lvs to 19cm, narrowly lanceolate or elliptic-lanceolate. Infl. to 45cm, sometimes branched; fls to 3cm diam., green-brown, yellow-brown or ochre, lip white to pale yellow, midlobe transversely oblong or obcordate, retuse or mucronate. Winter–early summer. Mex.

E. cordigera (HBK) Dressler. Pbs to 11×8cm, conical-ovoid. Lvs to 45cm, linear-lanceolate. Infl. to 70cm; fls to 7cm diam., brown, purple-brown or purple-green, lip cream streaked or flushed rose to magenta, midlobe suborbicular to ovate, emarginate, undulate. Mostly spring. C Amer., Colomb., Venez., Mex.

E. diota (Lindl.) Schltr. Pbs to 8×4cm, ovoid-conical. Lvs to 40cm, elliptic-ligulate. Pan. to 95cm; fls to 2.5cm diam., sweet-scented, green-yellow to cinnamon, often edged yellow, the lip yellow or orange streaked deep brown, midlobe ovate-cordate, acute, undulate. Spring–early summer. Guat., Hond., Nic., Mex. Plants with large, fleshy-pink and chestnut marked fls are sometimes offered as ssp. *atrorubens*.

E. doeringii Hoehne = *E. cordigera*.

E. fragrans (Sw.) Lemée. Pbs to 13cm, fusiform to ellipsoid. Lvs to 30cm, oblong-ligulate to elliptic. Infl. to 17cm, few-fld; fls to 2cm, fragrant, white, cream or green-white, lip uppermost, striped violet or maroon, orbicular-ovate, abruptly acuminate. Mostly summer. C Amer., N S Amer., W Indies.

E. ghiesbreghtiana (Rich. & Gal.) Dressler. Pbs to 6×2.5cm, ovoid to ellipsoid. Lvs to 20cm, lanceolate to elliptic-ligulate. Infl. to 12cm, usually 2-fld; fls to 5cm diam., pale green striped or spotted brown, lip white faintly marked mauve at base, sub-orbicular to subquadrate, retuse. Winter–spring. Mex.

E. gravida (Lindl.) Schltr. Pbs to 4×3cm, ovoid-conical. Lvs to 28cm, linear-ligulate. Infl. to 35cm, sometimes branched, few-fld; fls to 4cm diam.; tep. olive to ochre; lip lat. lobes green, veined purple, midlobe suborbicular to subrhombic, white veined purple, acute. Mostly autumn–winter. Trop. Amer.

E. guatemalensis (Klotzsch) Dressler & Pollard. Pbs to 5×3.5cm, conical to ovoid. Lvs to 32cm, linear-ligulate.Infl. to 60cm, often branched; peduncle sometimes verrucose; fls to 4cm diam., green, tinged red-brown or chocolate-brown, lip white or yellow veined purple, midlobe suborbicular, acute, undulate. Spring–summer. Guat., Hond., El Salvador, Nic., Mex.

E. guttata (Rich. & Gal.) Schltr. = *E. maculosa*.

E. hanburyi (Lindl.) Schltr. Pbs to 8×4cm, ovoid-conical. Lvs to 23cm, linear-elliptic to oblong-elliptic. Infl. to 1m, sometimes branched, many-fld; fls to 5cm diam., dull purple-brown to yellow-brown streaked purple, lip white to rose veined purple-red, midlobe subreniform to suborbicular, undulate, retuse or obtuse. Spring–summer. Mex.

E. hastata (Lindl.) Dressler & Pollard. Pbs to 5×2cm, ovoid to ellipsoid. Lvs to 16cm, linear-elliptic. Infl. to 25cm, 1- to several-fld; fls to 3cm diam., purple-brown or green-brown, veined dark purple, lip pure white, suborbicular to subquadrate, obtuse. Spring. Mex.

E. insidiosa (Rchb. f.) Schltr. = *E. diota*.

E. kennedyi (Fowlie & Withner) Hagsater. Differs from *E. adenocaula* in fls deeper red, lip with prominent midvein. Summer. Mex.

E. kienastii (Rchb. f.) Dressler & Pollard. Pbs to 11×2cm, narrowly fusiform or cylindrical. Lvs to 15cm, oblong-lanceolate to oblong-elliptic. Infl. to 37cm, sometimes branched; fls to 5cm diam., light rose-pink veined dark purple, lip white to pale rose veined purple, midlobe obovate-oblong, acute, slightly un-dulate. Spring. Mex.

E. lancifolia (Pav. ex Lindl.) Dressler & Pollard. Pbs to 14×5cm, fusiform-ellipsoid or pyriform. Lvs to 28cm, elliptic. Infl. to 12cm, several-fld; fls 4cm diam., cream or green-white to yellow-white, lip green or yellow green, streaked or striped purple, suborbicular to ovate-triangular. Summer–autumn. Mex.

E. livida (Lindl.) Dressler. Pbs to 10×2cm, fusiform. Lvs to 22cm, elliptic to elliptic-ligulate. Infl. to 15cm, few to several-fld; fls to 1.5cm diam., pale green suffused brown, lip ivory to pale yellow veined purple, midlobe suborbicular to sub-quadrate, undulate-crisped. Flowering throughout year. Mex. to Panama, Venez., Colomb.

E. luteorosea (Rich. & Gal.) Dressler & Pollard. Pbs to 7×2.5cm, ovoid-fusiform. Lvs to 28cm, narrowly linear to elliptic-ligulate. Infl. to 45cm, usually branched; fls to 2.5cm diam., yellow-green or yellow-brown, tinged brown distally, lip ivory marked purple, obcordate to obovate, retuse. Mostly spring–autumn. C Amer. to Venez., Peru.

E. maculosa (Ames, Hubb. & Schweinf.) Hoehne. Pbs to 12×2.5cm, ovoid-fusiform to ovoid-conical. Lvs to 30cm, ellip-tic to linear-oblong. Infl. to 20cm, erect; fls to 5cm diam., fra-grant, orange or orange-brown, sometimes spotted red-brown, lip white spotted purple or maroon, midlobe ovate-oblong, obtuse. Spring–summer. Mex.

E. mariae (Ames) Hoehne. Similar to *E. citrina* in habit, but not so completely pendulous. Infl. arching weakly or pendulous; tep. to 4cm, spreading, lime- to olive-green, lip brilliant white tinted or lined green, subpandurate to oblong-elliptic, ± funnel-form, retuse, slightly undulate. Summer. Mex.

E. meliosma (Rchb. f.) Schltr. Pbs to 9×7cm, subspherical to ovoid-conical. Lvs to 36cm, ligulate to elliptic-ligulate. Infl. to 1m, branched, many-fld; fls to 4cm diam., yellow to yellow-green streaked and tinged red-brown, lip cream to yellow veined red-brown, midlobe elliptic-ovate to rhombic-ovate, acuminate. Spring–summer. Mex.

E. michuacana (La Ll. & Lex.) Schltr. Pbs to 8×4cm, ovoid to pyriform. Lvs to 60cm, elliptic-lanceolate to ligulate. Infl. to 2m, branched, many-fld; fls to 3.5cm diam., red-brown or green-brown, lip cream or pale yellow, often spotted purple, midlobe suborbicular, triangular-ovate or transversely oblong. Flowering throughout year. Mex., Guat., Hond.

E. microbulbon (Hook.) Schltr. Pbs to 4×2.5cm, ovoid-conical. Lvs to 12cm, linear to elliptic-ligulate. Infl. to 45cm, sometimes branched; fls to 4cm diam., green, veined red-brown, lip white sometimes spotted red, midlobe ovate to suborbicular, dentate-undulate. Winter–summer. Mex.

E. nemoralis (Lindl.) Schltr. = *E. adenocaula*.

E. ochracea (Lindl.) Dressler. Pbs to 10×1cm, ovoid-cylindrical or narrowly ovoid.Lvs to 25cm, linear-ligulate or linear-lanceolate. Infl. to 20cm, many-fld; fls to 3cm diam. yellow-brown, lip white or yellow spotted red, midlobe quadrate-oblong or triangular-oblong, obtuse or retuse, undulate-crisped. Flowering throughout year. Mex. to Cost Rica.

E. ovula (Lindl.) Schltr. = *E. microbulbon*.

E. panthera (Rchb. f.) Schltr. Pbs to 9×1.5cm, ovoid-fusiform. Lvs to 22cm, linear-ligulate. Infl. to 22cm, many-fld; fls to 2cm diam., olive green to yellow-orange blotched and spotted deep red-brown, the lip white to ivory, midlobe quadrate, undulate, retuse. Winter–spring. Guat., Mex.

E. polybulbon (Sw.) Dressler. Pbs to 2cm, ovoid to ovoid-cylindrical. Lvs to 8cm, ovate-elliptic to elliptic-oblong. Fl. solitary to 3cm, pale yellow flushed brown, lip yellow-white, suborbicular-ovate to cordate, denticulate, undulate. Mostly autumn–winter. Mex. to Hond., Cuba, Jam.

E. prismatocarpa (Rchb. f.) Dressler. Pbs to 30cm, pyriform to cylindrical. Lvs to 37cm, ligulate. Rac. to 35cm, many-fld, erect; fls to 5cm diam., fragrant; tep. yellow-green spotted dark purple-brown or black, lanceolate; lip lilac-purple, yellow-green at base, margins white, midlobe lanceolate. Costa Rica to Braz.

E. pseudopygmaea (Finet) Dressler & Pollard. Resembles *E. pygmaea* except pbs regularly to 10cm, narrowly fusiform. Lvs to 15cm, narrowly lanceolate. Fls larger, numerous. Winter. C Amer. to Panama, Mex.

E. pygmaea (Hook.) Dressler. Pbs to 10cm, typically far smaller, ovoid, ellipsoid or fusiform. Lvs to 10cm, narrowly ovate to elliptic. Fls to 1.5cm diam., usually solitary, fleshy, pale green tinged lavender; lip midlobe minute, triangular. Trop. Americas.

E. radiata (Lindl.) Dressler. Pbs to 11×3cm, narrowly fusiform to ellipsoid-ovoid.Lvs to 35cm, elliptic-lanceolate. Infl. to 24cm, few to many-fld; fls to 4.5cm diam., fragrant, cream or pale green-white, lip uppermost, striped purple or maroon, triangular-reniform to ovate-cordate, undulate-crenate. Spring–summer. Guat., Hond., Mex.

E. selligera (Lindl.) Schltr. Pbs to 10×5cm, ovoid. Lvs to 30cm, linear- or elliptic-ligulate.Infl. to 1m, usually branched, many-fld; fls to 5cm diam., fragrant, pale green or green-brown suffused red-brown, lip white, cream or pink, veined purple, midlobe suborbicular-obovate or ovate, undulate-crisped. Winter–spring. Guat., Mex.

E. spondiada (Rchb. f.) Dressler. Pbs to 16×1.5cm, cylindrical to narrowly ovoid. Lvs to 30cm, ligulate to elliptic. Infl. to 11cm, few-fld; fls to 4cm diam., yellow-green, tinged red-purple at tips of pet. and sep., suborbicular-reniform to cordate, apiculate. Winter. Jam., Costa Rica, Panama.

E. tampensis (Lindl.) Small. Pbs to 8cm, ovoid to suborbicular. Lvs to 42cm, linear to linear-lanceolate, coriaceous. Infl. to 75cm, sometimes branched; fls to 4cm diam., fragrant, ochre to olive sometimes flushed rose or garnet, lip white blotched and veined purple or magenta, midlobe suborbicular, slightly undulate. Spring–winter. Flor., Bahamas.

E. tenuissima (Ames, Hubb. & Schweinf.) Dressler. Pbs to 1.5×1cm, ovoid to ovoid-spherical. Lvs to 8cm, linear. Infl. to 15cm, sometimes branched; fls to 2.5cm diam yellow to yellow-orange; lip obovate, obtuse. Winter–early summer. Mex.

E. trachychila (Lindl.) Schltr. = *E. ambigua*.

E. tripunctata (Lindl.) Dressler. Pbs to 4×2cm, usually far smaller, ovoid. Lvs to 6–20cm, linear-elliptic, grassy. Infl. short, few-fld; fls to 1.5cm diam., pale green to yellow-green, lip white and the column a distinctive purple with yellow teeth. Spring–summer. Mex.

E. tuerckheimii Schltr. Pbs to 6×3cm, ovoid. Lvs to 40cm, ligulate to linear-lanceolate. Infl. to 70cm, sometimes branched, erect, peduncle verrucose; fls to 5.5cm diam., green to yellow-brown or bronze; lip midlobe, elliptic-oblong to elliptic-obovate, acuminate, undulate-crisped. Late spring–summer. Mex., Guat. to Costa Rica.

E. varicosa (Lindl.) Schltr. Pbs to 20cm, ovoid-fusiform or ovoid-elliptic at base, slender above. Lvs to 30cm, elliptic-oblong to elliptic-lanceolate. Infl. to 60cm; fls to 3.6cm diam., fragrant, green-brown or red-brown, lip cream to yellow, sometimes tinted green, often spotted red or purple, midlobe transversely oblong or obreniform, retuse. Mostly winter. Mex. to Panama.

E. venosa (Lindl.) Schltr. Pbs to 8×2cm, ellipsoid to fusiform. Lvs to 22cm, narrowly elliptic-oblong to elliptic-ligulate. Infl. to 12cm, few-fld; fls to 4cm diam., pale green or yellow-green, sometimes striped red-brown, lip snow white veined purple on lat. lobes, midlobe triangular-cordate. Spring–autumn. Mex.

E. vespa (Vell.) Dressler. Pbs to 20×5cm, ovoid-fusiform or ellipsoid to cylindric. Lvs to 40cm, elliptic-oblong to linear-oblong. Infl. to 35cm; fls to 1.5cm diam., fleshy cream-green or yellow-green, spotted or blotched maroon-purple, lip white to yellow marked pink, transversely elliptic to ovate-cordate,

acute. Mostly spring. Trop. Amer.

E. virens (Lindl. & Paxt.) Schltr. = *E. belizensis*.

E. vitellina (Lindl.) Dressler. Pbs to 6cm, ovoid-conical. Lvs to 25cm, usually shorter, lanceolate, grey-green. Infl. to 40cm; fls to 5cm diam., vermilion to scarlet, lip orange to yellow, elliptic to elliptic-oblong, acute. Spring–summer. Mex., Guat.

E. wendlandiana (Kränzl.) Schltr. = *E. venosa*.

→*Cattleya, Dinema* and *Epidendrum*.

Endive *Cichorium endivia*.
Endlicher's Pine *Pinus rudis*.

Endoloma Raf.
E. purpurea Raf. = *Amphilophium paniculatum*.

Endymion Dumort.
E. hispanicus (Mill.) Chouard = *Hyacinthoides hispanica*.
E. non-scriptus (L.) Garcke = *Hyacinthoides non-scripta*.
E. patulus Dum.-Cours. = *Hyacinthoides hispanica*.

Engelhardia Leschen. ex Bl. Juglandaceae. 8 trees. Young twigs brown-tomentose. Lvs pinnate, usually red when young, midrib keeled above. Infl. lat. or term. catkins; fls fused to 3-lobed bract; ♂ fls with reduced perianth, sta. 4–13; ♀ fls with 4-lobed perianth. Fr. an indehiscent drupe; bract accrescent, forming a conspicuous 3-lobed wing. W Himal. to S China, Indochina, Malaysia, Taiwan, Philipp., C Amer. Z9.

E. aceriflora Bl. = *E. spicata*.
E. chrysolepis Hance = *E. roxburghiana*.
E. fenzelii Merrill = *E. roxburghiana*.
E. formosana Hayata = *E. roxburghiana*.
E. pterococca O.K. Rev. = *E. roxburghiana*.
E. roxburghiana Wallich. To 20m, sometimes with low buttress. Bark scales golden yellow, later brown. Rachis to 14cm; lfts coriaceous, glab., 10–16×3–5cm, bluntly acuminate, brown glandular-scaly beneath. ♂ catkins 8–12cm; ♀ catkins 12–22cm. NE India, S China, Indochina, Malaysia.
E. spicata Leschen. ex Bl. To 36m, occas. with small buttress. Rachis black, 20–30cm; lfts firm to coriaceous, to 30×80cm, usually much smaller, acuminate, with domatia or grey scales beneath. ♂ catkins 10–18cm; ♀ catkins 21–40cm. N India, Tibet, S China, Indochina, Malaysia, Philipp.
E. wallichiana (Lindl. ex Wallich) C. DC. = *E. roxburghiana*.
→*Juglans* and *Pterilema*.

Engelhardtia C. DC. = *Engelhardia*.

Engelmannia Torr. & A. Gray. Compositae. 1 erect, pilose, perenn. herb, to 1m. Lvs to 15cm, oblong, deeply pinnatisect, lobes pinnatifid to dentate. Cap. radiate, in a cymose pan., on slender stalks; ray flts 8 to 10, golden-yellow. Spring–autumn. S & C US. Z8.
E. pinnatifida Torr. & A. Gray.

Engelmann Spruce *Picea engelmannii*.
Engelmann's Vervain *Verbena ×engelmannii*.

Englerophoenix Kuntze.
E. regia (Mart.) Kuntze = *Maximiliana maripa*.

English Babytears *Nertera granadensis*.
English Bean *Vicia faba*.
English Bluebell *Hyacinthoides non-scripta*.
English Elm *Ulmus procera*.
English Hawthorn *Crataegus laevigata*; *C. monogyna*.
English Holly *Ilex aquifolium*.
English Iris *Iris latifolia*.
English Ivy *Hedera helix*.
English Laurel *Prunus laurocerasus*.
English Lavender *Lavandula angustifolia*.
English Oak *Quercus robur*.
English Plantain *Plantago lanceolata*.
English's Fig *Ficus rigo*.
English Sundew *Drosera anglica*.
English Tree *Tamarix anglica*.
English Violet *Viola odorata*.
English Walnut *Juglans regia*.
English-weed *Oxalis pes-caprae*.

Enkianthus Lour. Ericaceae. 10 decid. or everg. shrubs. Br. ± tiered, slender. Lvs simple, entire or serrate, short-stalked. Fls in drooping, term. umbels or corymbose rac.; cal. lobes 5, persistent; cor. waxy, campanulate to urceolate, teeth 5, entire or jagged, short; sta. 10, included. Himal. to Jap.
E. campanulatus (Miq.) Nichols. FURIN-TSUTSUJI. Decid. shrub, 4–5m. Lvs 3–7cm, obovate-elliptic, sharp-tipped, serrate, thinly

brown-hirsute to glab. above, loosely soft-hirsute to glab. beneath, dull green, vivid red in fall. Fls 5–15 in term., drooping corymbose rac.; pedicels 10–25mm; cor. campanulate, *c*5mm diam., pale cream to pale pink with faint salmon, peach or rust veins. Late spring–summer. Jap. 'Albiflorus': fls off-white. 'Donardensis': fls large, limb broad, deeper red. 'Hiraethlyn': fls cream with mulberry venation. 'Red Bells': habit small; lvs red in autumn; fls red, in hanging clusters. var. *longilobus* (Nak.) Mak. Lvs elliptic to broadly elliptic. Cor. deeply 5-toothed. Jap. var. *palibinii* (Craib) Bean. Lvs obovate to broadly ovate, ferruginous-downy on midrib. Summer. Jap. Z5.

E. cernuus (Sieb. & Zucc.) Mak. Decid. shrub, 1.5–3m. Lvs 2–5cm, elliptic to ovate-rhombic, acute, serrate, soft-hirsute and bright green above, brown-downy on veins beneath. Fls 5–12 in drooping, downy rac.; pedicels 7–15mm; cor. 6×*c*6mm, broadly campanulate, white, teeth jagged and unequal. Late spring–summer. Jap. f. *rubens* (Maxim.) Ohwi. Fls deep rich red. var. *matsudae* (Komatsu) Mak. Lvs broadly lanceolate to narrowly ovate, roughly serrate, soft brown hirsute on midrib beneath. Cor. deep red. Spring. Jap. Z6.

E. chinensis Franch. Shrub, 2.4–3.6m. Lvs 5–7.5cm, elliptic to elliptic-oblong, apex acuminate, sharp-tipped, blunt-toothed, bright green and pubesc. along midrib above, glaucous and glab. beneath. Fls 12–24 in drooping rac. 7.5–12.5cm long; cor. *c*9mm, campanulate, yellow-cream with rosy markings, broader at mouth, lobes tinted pink, recurved. C & W China. Z7.

E. deflexus (Griff.) Schneid. Shrub or small tree, 1.8–9m; young br. red. Lvs 2.5–7.5cm, lanceolate, obovate or oval, acuminate, hirsute. Fls 8–20 in a terminal umbel or rac.; pedicel 18–32mm; cor. broad-campanulate, 15mm diam., yellow-red and marked with dark lines, lobes deltoid, darker. Late spring–early summer. Himal., W China. Z6.

E. himalaicus Hook. f. & Thoms. = *E. deflexus*.

E. japonicus Hook. f. = *E. perulatus*.

E. longilobus (Nak.) Ohwi = *E. campanulatus* var. *longilobus*.

E. matsudae Komatsu = *E. cernuus* var. *matsudae*.

E. perulatus (Miq.) Schneid. DODAN-TSUTSUJI. Decid. shrub, 90cm–2m; young br. red, glab. Lvs 2–5cm, obovate or elliptic-ovate, acute, serrate, downy beneath on midrib, yellow and scarlet in fall. Fls 3–10 in term., drooping umbels; pedicels *c*12mm; cor. 6–8mm, white, urceolate, with 5 basal swellings, lobes reflexed, rounded. Spring. Jap. Z6.

E. quinqueflorus Lour. Decid. or semi-evergreen shrub, 90–180cm. Lvs 5–10cm, entire, narrow oval or obovate, coriaceous, acute, initially red, later deep green. Fls usually 5, in term., umbellate clusters; pedicels 12–25mm; cor. campanulate, 9–12mm, pink or pink with white, with 5 basal nectaries, lobes reflexed, pale. Spring. SE China, Hong Kong. Z8.

E. serrulatus (Willd.) Schneid. Similar to *E. quinqueflorus*. Decid. shrub or small tree to 6m. Lvs 3.8–8cm, less coriaceous than in *E. quinqueflorus*. Fls to 6 in drooping umbels; cor. pure white, campanulate, *c*12mm, lobes small, reflexed. C & W China. Z6.

E. sinohimalaicus Craib = *E. chinensis*.

E. subsessilis (Miq.) Mak. Erect shrub, 90cm–3m. Lvs 2–3cm, obovate to elliptic, acute, sharp-tipped, finely dentate, white downy on midrib above, paler and loosely brown-downy beneath, ± sessile. Fls 5–10 in drooping, hirsute rac. 20–50mm long; pedicels 10–25mm; cor. white, *c*5mm, urceolate, lobes short, recurved. Jap. Z6.

Ensete Horan. Musaceae. 7 giant everg. perenn. herbs, close to *Musa* but with stouter pseudostems formed of loosely concentric paddle-shaped lvs and dry inedible fr. OW Trop. Z10.

E. gilletii (De Wildeman) E.E. Cheesm. Pseudostem short, barely distinct, purple-brown. Lvs to 3.8×0.6m held erect in pseudorosette, narrow-elliptic, long-acuminate, bright green, midrib sunken, bright red. Afr.

E. superbum (Roxb.) E.E. Cheesm. Pseudostem to 4m, basally swollen, almost conical. Lvs 1.5–3×0.45–1m, bright green. Infl. nodding to pendent, formed of 30cm bracts, green without, dull red within. India.

E. ventricosum (Welw.) E.E. Cheesm. ABYSSINIAN BANANA; ETHIOPIAN BANANA. Pseudostem 8–12m, trunk-like, flushed purple, somewhat bulbous at base. Lvs 3–6×1–1.5m, clustered at the top of the pseudostem, olive green with maroon midrib. Infl. 1m+, erect to nodding; bracts large buff. Afr. 'Maurelii': fast-growing; st. tall; lvs large, broad, in compact rosettes, tinged red. 'Montbeliardii': st. tall, slender; lvs narrow, midrib shaded black.
→*Musa*.

Entelea R. Br. Tiliaceae. 1 everg. shrub or tree to 6m with v. light wood. Lvs 10–20cm, cordate, apex long-acuminate, double-toothed, with small triangular lobes above; petiole to

20cm. Infl. cymose, to 12cm diam.; pet. to 2.5cm, white, 4–5; sta. numerous, anth. yellow. NZ.
E. arborescens R. Br.

Enterolobium Mart. Leguminosae (Mimosoideae). 5 trees closely allied to *Albizia*. Lvs bipinnate; rachis gland. Fls in dense heads, solitary or in clustered rac.; cal. dentate; cor. funnel-shaped, lobes subequal; sta. showy, exserted. Fr. spiralling, flattened. Trop. Amer. Z9.

E. contortisiliqua (Vell.) Morong. As for *E. cyclocarpa*, but pinnae 6–28; lfts 20–30; fr. larger, glaucous at first. Braz.

E. cyclocarpa (Jacq.) Griseb. ELEPHANT'S EAR. Tree to 30m; crown spreading. Pinnae 16–24; lfts 30–50. Infl. heads to 1.5cm diam., white, in term. fascicles. Fr. forming a woody circle to 10cm diam., brown, shiny. Trop. Amer.
→*Mimosa*.

Eomecon Hance. SNOW POPPY. Papaveraceae. 1 perenn. rhizomatous herb. St. branched; sap orange. Lvs to 10cm across, cordate-reniform to sagittate, coriaceous, slightly succulent, dull green beneath, undulate; petioles to 30cm. Peduncles to 40cm, erect; fls in sparse term. pan.; pet. 1–2cm, 4, elliptic, white; sta. 70. Spring. E China. Z7.
E. chionantha Hance.

Eora Cook.
E. cheesmanii (Becc.) Cook. = *Rhopalostylis cheesmanii*.

EPACRIDACEAE. R. Br. 34/400. *Acrotriche, Andersonia, Astroloma, Brachyloma, Conostephium, Cyathodes, Dracophyllum, Epacris, Leucopogon, Pentachondra, Prionotes, Richea, Styphelia, Trochocarpa*.

Epacris Cav. AUSTRALIAN HEATH. Epacridaceae. 35 heath-like shrubs. Lvs alt. or scattered, usually crowded and overlapping, ovate to linear, ± sessile. Fls axill., usually forming term. rac.; bracts numerous; cor. tube cylindric to campanulate, limb 5-lobed. E & SE Aus., Tasm., NZ and New Caledonia. Z9.

E. acuminata Benth. Erect, bushy dwarf shrub to 1m. Lvs to 1cm, ovate-lanceolate, apex pungent, base cordate or obtuse sheathing st., concave above. Fls few to 1.5cm, white-pink. Autumn. Tasm.

E. grandiflora Willd. = *E. longiflora*.

E. heteronema Labill. Erect dwarf shrub to slender tree. Lvs to 1cm, ovate-cordate to lanceolate, thick, pungent, margins translucent, serrulate. Fls to 0.7cm, white, forming a dense term. rac. Autumn. SW Aus., Tasm.

E. impressa Labill. COMMON HEATH. Spindly, erect shrub, to 1m. Lvs to 1.5cm, linear-lanceolate to narrow ovate, base truncate or rounded, tip mucronate to pungent, minutely pubesc. Fls nodding in slender, erect term. rac., white to rose or purple-red to 1.8cm. Winter–spring. S Aus., Tasm.

E. juniperina Forst. & Forst. f. = *Cyathodes juniperina*.

E. lanuginosa Labill. WOOLLY HEATH. Erect shrub, to 1m; new growth tomentose. Lvs to 1.5cm, narrowly ovate to linear-lanceolate, pungent, sometimes overlapping, glab. Fls white, to 1cm, clustered in upper lf axils, forming a showy rac. Autumn–winter. SW Aus., Tasm.

E. longiflora Cav. FUCHSIA HEATH. Erect or diffuse shrub, to 1.5m; new growth tomentose. Lvs 1cm, broadly ovate to ovate-lanceolate, pungent, veins prominent. Fls solitary to 2cm, scarlet to carmine, limb, white. Summer. SW Aus.

E. longifolia Forst. & Forst. f. = *Dracophyllum longifolium*.

E. microphylla R. Br. CORAL HEATH. Erect shrub, to 2.5m; branchlets pubesc. Lvs 0.5cm, broadly ovate, acuminate, concave above, base stem-clasping. Fls fragrant arranged in leafy, cylindrical spikes 3–10cm long, white to cream, often tinged pink in bud. Summer. SW Aus., Tasm.

E. miniata Lindl. = *E. longiflora*.

E. mucronulata R. Br. Related to *E. acuminata*. Lvs to 1.2×0.2cm, narrow-elliptic, apex acuminate, mucronulate, margins finely serrulate. Fls to 1cm, white, borne in upper axils; cor. lobes relatively large. Winter. Tasm.

E. nivalis Lodd. = *E. impressa*.

E. obtusifolia Sm. COMMON HEATH; BLUNT-LEAF HEATH. Erect shrub 0.3–1.5m; branchlets pubesc. Lvs 1.5cm, elliptic to oblong-lanceolate, apex blunt, broad. Fls fragrant to 1.2cm, waxy, ivory, sta. tinted red. Autumn. Queensld, SW Aus., Tasm.

E. onosmiflora A. Cunn. = *E. purpurascens*.

E. paludosa R. Br. ALPINE HEATH; SWAMP HEATH. Narrowly upright shrub, to 1.5m; br. pubesc. Lvs 1cm, linear-lanceolate, acuminate, erecto-patent, pungent, thick, serrulate to scabrid, glab. Fls white in capitate clusters. Autumn–winter. SW Aus., Tasm.

E. pulchella Cav. Erect, much-branched shrub to 75cm; branchlets pubesc. Lvs to 1cm, broadly ovate, base cordate, concave, almost imbricate. Fls to 0.8cm, many white suffused red. SW Aus. Often confused with *E. microphylla*.

E. pungens Cav. = *E. purpurascens*.

E. purpurascens R. Br. PORT JACKSON HEATH. Narrowly upright shrub to 1m. Lvs 0.5–1.5m, crowded, lanceolate, base amplexicaul, apex pungent, concave above. Fls usually spicate, to 1.2cm, white suffused pink, colour deepening to magenta or rosy purple with age. Autumn. S & W Aus.

E. reclinata Cunn. ex Benth. Upright or procumbent shrub to 1m; br. initially downy. Lvs 0.6cm, ovate-cordate, crowded, acuminate-pungent, dark, glossy above, ciliolate. Fls to 1.6cm, nodding, pale pink to red, rarely white, many in upper axils. Summer. SW Aus.

E. rigida Sieb. ex Spreng. KEELED HEATH. Bushy shrub to 1.5m; br. rigidly erect, many. Lvs to 0.5cm, ovate to ovate-oblong, acuminate, blunt, midrib prominent beneath. Fls to 0.6cm, white, short-stalked. Autumn. SW Aus.

E. rosmarinifolia Forst. f. = *Dracophyllum paludosum*.

E. serpyllifolia R. Br. THYME HEATH. Prostrate or erect, much branched shrub to 1.5m. Lvs 0.6cm, ovate-acuminate, thick, almost imbricate. Fls to 1cm, white, in dense clusters forming slender, cylindrical spikes. Autumn. SW Aus., Tasm.

Epaulette Tree *Pterostyrax.*
Epazote *Chenopodium ambrosioides.*

Ephedra L. JOINT FIR. Ephedraceae. *c*40 horsetail-like shrubs or climbers. Br. slender, jointed, whorled, cylindric, green, becoming woody. Lvs much reduced, scale-like. Fls yellow, small, unisexual, apetalous in bracteate, cone-like clusters to 1cm. Fr. fleshy, red, to 1cm. S Eur., N Afr., Asia, subtrop. Amer.

E. americana Humb. & Bonpl. Shrub, procumbent, to 2m+, or small tree, to 4m. Br. and branchlets arching downwards. Andes (Ecuad. to Patagonia). var. *andina* (Poepp. ex C.A. Mey.) Stapf. Young shoots green, finely ridged, smooth to scabrous. Z6.

E. andina Poepp. ex C.A. Mey. = *E. americana* var. *andina*.

E. chilensis Miers = *E. americana* var. *andina*.

E. distachya L. Shrub to 1m, usually less, sometimes procumbent, with subterranean rhiz.; br. stiff, dark green or green tinged blue, striped, straight or arched, to 2mm diam. S Eur. to Sib. var. *monostachya* (L.) Stapf. Low shrub. Br. to 1mm diam. ssp. *helvetica* (C.A. Mey.) Asch. & Gräbn. To 50cm. Br. deep green. Z4.

E. fragilis Desf. Shrub, climbing to 5m, sometimes procumbent. St. woody; br. flexible, brittle. Medit. Z8.

E. gerardiana Wallich. Creeping shrub. Br. dark green, thin. China, Himal. var. *sikkimensis* (hort.) Stapf. Taller, more robust. Z7.

E. helvetica C.A. Mey. = *E. distachya* ssp. *helvetica*.

E. intermedia Schrenk ex C.A. Mey. Shrub to 1m. St. erect or sprawling; br. rigid, to 3mm diam., green tinged yellow, or glaucous, striped, scabrous or smooth. C Asia. Z6.

E. major Host. Shrub, to 2m. St. wiry, erect, diffusely branched; br. occas. opposite, green, chalky, glaucous. Medit. to Himal. ssp. *procera* (Fisch. & C.A. Mey.) Markgr. Erect shrub. Br. smooth. Z6.

E. minima Hao. Dwarf, creeping, to 3cm. St. wiry. China. Z7.

E. monostachya (L.) Guss. = *E. distachya* var. *monostachya*.

E. nebrodensis Tineo = *E. major*.

E. peruviana Brot. = *E. americana* var. *andina*.

E. procera Fisch. & C.A. Mey. = *E. major* ssp. *procera*.

E. sikkimensis hort. = *E. gerardiana* var. *sikkimensis*.

E. viridis Cov. Erect shrub, to 1m. Br. stiff, thin, vivid green, striped, surface rough. W US. Z9.

E. vulgaris Rich. = *E. distachya*.

EPHEDRACEAE Dumort. See *Ephedra*.

✕**Epicattleya**. (*Epidendrum* ✕ *Cattleya*.) Orchidaceae. Gdn hybrids – usually compact, *Cattleya*-type plants with clusters of fls in shades of red, mauve and green.

Epidendrum L. Orchidaceae. 500+ epiphytic or terrestrial orchids. St. long-pseudobulbous or cane-like, thick or slender, simple or branched, 1- to many-leaved. Lvs terete or flattened, distichous and sheathing st. or term., fleshy or coriaceous. Rac. or pan. usually term. and long-stalked; sep. spreading, subequal; pet. similar to sep.; lip clawed, entire or trilobed, smooth or callose. Trop. Americas. Z10.

E. adenocaulum La Ll. & Lex. = *Encyclia adenocaula*.

E. adolphii Schltr. = *Oerstedella endresii*.

E. alatum Batem. = *Encyclia alata*.

E. aloifolium Batem. = *E. parkinsonianum*.

E. ambiguum Lindl. = *Encyclia ambigua*.

E. anceps Jacq. St. tufted, erect, leafy. Lvs to 20cm, linear-elliptic to oblong, coriaceous, often flecked purple. Rac. subcapitate, term.; peduncle elongate; fls to 1.5cm diam.; tep. green-brown to chocolate, fleshy, glossy; lip pale green flushed pink, midlobe transversely oblong, apiculate. Flor., Mex. to Panama, W Indies, N S Amer.

E. aromaticum Batem. = *Encyclia aromatica*.

E. atropurpureum auct. = *Encyclia cordigera*.

E. aviculum Lindl. = *Lanium aviculum*.

E. baculus Rchb. f. = *Encyclia baculus*.

E. basilare Klotzsch = *E. stamfordianum*.

E. belizense Rchb. f. = *Encyclia belizensis*.

E. bicameratum Rchb. f. = *Encyclia bicamerata*.

E. bicornutum Hook. = *Caularthron bicornutum*.

E. bidentatum Lindl. = *Encyclia boothiana*.

E. bilamellatum Rchb. f. = *Caularthron bilamellatum*.

E. boothianum Lindl. = *Encyclia boothiana*.

E. boothii (Lindl.) L.O. Williams = *Nidema boothii*.

E. bractescens Lindl. = *Encyclia bractescens*.

E. brassavolae Rchb. f. = *Encyclia brassavolae*.

E. bulbosum Vell. = *Encyclia bulbosa*.

E. cajamaracae Schltr. = *E. geminiflorum*.

E. calamarium Lindl. = *Encyclia calamaria*.

E. calocheilum Hook. = *Encyclia alata*.

E. campylostalix Rchb. f. = *Encyclia campylostalix*.

E. candollei Lindl. = *Encyclia candollei*.

E. caroli Schltr. St. clumped, to 9cm, clavate. Lvs to 8cm, toward st. apex, elliptic to oblong, coriaceous. Rac. simple or, rarely, branched, slender, few-fld; fls to 1cm diam.; tep. green-brown or purple-brown; lip yellow, fleshy, ovate-cordate. Guat.

E. catillus Rchb. f. & Warsc. St. to 1m, simple, leafy toward apex. Lvs to 7.5cm, ovate to oblong-lanceolate, fleshy-coriaceous. Rac. or pan. erect, few- or many-fld; peduncle elongate; fls to 3cm diam.; cinnabar red, violet-red or violet; lip vermilion, ovate-triangular, deeply 3-lobed, callus yellow. Colomb., Ecuad., Peru.

E. ceratistes Lindl. = *Encyclia ceratistes*.

E. chacaoense Rchb. f. = *Encyclia chacaoensis*.

E. chioneum Lindl. St. to 65cm, erect or ascending, usually branched. Lvs to 9cm, coriaceous, ovate-lanceolate. Rac. term., to 8cm, arcuate to pendent, usually subcapitate; fls often fleshy, fragrant, to 2cm diam., white, yellow or yellow-green, midlobe obovate-subquadrate or subquadrate, retuse and apiculate. Colomb., Venez., Ecuad.

E. chondylobulbon Rich. & Gal. = *Encyclia chondylobulbon*.

E. ciliare L. Pbs tufted, oblong-compressed, to 16cm. Lvs to 28cm, oblong-ligulate, coriaceous. Rac. to 30cm, erect, few-fld; peduncle with large sheaths; fls to 12cm diam.; fragrant, white to green or pale yellow with white lip; lip lat. lobes deeply lacerate-fimbriate, midlobe linear-filiform, rigid. Mex. to Panama, Venez. to Boliv., W Indies, Guyana, Braz.

E. cinnabarinum Salzm. ex Lindl. St. to 1.25m, cane-like, simple. Lvs to 11cm, 2-ranked, oblong to elliptic-oblong, fleshy-coriaceous. Rac. or pan. term., held clear of lvs, few- to many-fld; fls to 6cm diam., opening over a period of several seasons, bright scarlet, crimson or orange-red; lip lateral lobes dentate, midlobe triangular-lanceolate, disc yellow spotted red. Mostly spring. Braz.

E. citrinum (La Ll. & Lex.) Rchb. f. = *Encyclia citrina*.

E. claesianum Cogn. = *E. chioneum*.

E. cochleatum L. = *Encyclia cochleata*.

E. concolor La Ll. & Lex. = *Encyclia concolor*.

E. confusum Rolfe = *Encyclia baculus*.

E. conopseum R. Br. GREEN-FLY ORCHID. St. to 20cm, slender, compressed. Lvs to 9cm, rigid, narrowly oblong to linear-lanceolate. Rac. to 16cm; fls to 2cm diam., fragrant, grey-green, often tinged purple; lip cordate-reniform, lat. lobes subrotund, midlobe narrower. SE US.

E. coriifolium Lindl. St. to 25cm, strongly compressed. Lvs to 30cm, elliptic-oblong to linear-oblong, rigid, coriaceous. Rac. to 30cm; fls to 4cm diam., fleshy green or yellow-green, often tinged red or purple, subtended by conspicuous, fleshy green, bracts; lip cordate reniform, cleft and apiculate, entire or erose. Mex. to Panama, Venez., Ecuad., Braz.

E. coronatum Ruiz & Pav. St. to 90×1cm, subterete. Lvs closely 2-ranked, to 17cm, elliptic to lanceolate, fleshy-coriaceous. Rac. to 40cm, pendent, many-fld; tep. to 2cm, cream to yellow-green, sometimes tinged brown, rose or violet at base; lip ivory tinted lime or grey-green, slightly undulate, lat. lobes suborbicular, midlobe bilobulate, rounded. C Amer., N S Amer., Trin.

E. corymbosum Ruiz & Pav. = *E. secundum*.

E. cristatum Ruiz & Pav. St. stout, simple. Lvs to 25cm, coriaceous, elliptic-lanceolate to elliptic-oblong. Rac., to 60cm, pendent; fls to 6cm diam., sometimes fragrant, long-stalked, fleshy; sep. and pet. yellow to pale green, spotted or streaked red-brown or purple; lip lat. lobes lacerate-fimbriate to dentate, midlobe bilobulate. C & S Amer., W Indies.

E. difforme Jacq. St. to 30cm, cane-like, flexuous. Lvs to 11cm, ovate-elliptic to oblong-lanceolate, fleshy to coriaceous. Infl. subumbellate, short; fls to 5cm diam., pale green, green-yellow or white; lip to midlobe transversely oblong, entire to bilobed, truncate. Flor., W Indies, Mex. to Braz., Peru, Ecuad.

E. diguetii Ames = *Encyclia tripunctata*.

E. diotum Lindl. = *Encyclia diota*.

E. dipus Lindl. = *E. nutans*.

E. discolor (Lindl.) Benth. = *Nanodes discolor*.

E. eburneum Rchb. f. St. to 60cm, slender. Lvs to 14cm, elliptic to lanceolate, lustrous. Rac. term., few-fld; peduncle strongly fractiflex; fls to 7cm diam., fragrant, waxy; tep. slender, white, ivory or yellow-green; lip white, cordate-orbicular to sub-quadrate, often apiculate. Autumn–winter. Panama.

E. endresii Rchb. f. = *Oerstedella endresii*.

E. falcatum Lindl. = *E. parkinsonianum*.

E. flavidum Lindl. = *E. leucochilum*.

E. floribundum HBK. St. to 2.5m, terete, slender to stout. Lvs to 25cm, ovate-elliptic to linear-lanceolate, subcoriaceous, often tinged purple beneath. Rac. or pan. loose, far exceeding lvs; fls to 2.5cm diam., fragrant; white-green to rose-purple; lip usually white, sometimes spotted red, lateral lobes erose, midlobe short, usually bilobulate, erose. Mostly summer. Trop. Americas.

E. fragrans Sw. = *Encyclia fragrans*.

E. friederici-guilielmi (Lindl.) Rchb. f. St. 60–150cm, thick, cane-like. Lvs to 30cm, distichous, obovate-oblong to elliptic. Rac. term., to 43cm, erect to pendent; fls to 5cm diam., deep purple or light carmine red; lip midlobe porrect, ligulate, acute, callus white. Peru.

E. fuscatum Sm. = *E. anceps*.

E. geminiflorum HBK. St. to 90cm, subpendent, much-branched. Lvs to 6cm, oblong-elliptic, coriaceous. Rac. short, 2- or 3-fld; fls to 3cm diam., yellow-green or maroon-green; lip midlobe ovate-triangular. Venez., Colomb., Ecuad., Peru.

E. ghiesbreghtianum Rich. & Gal. = *Encyclia ghiesbreghtiana*.

E. globosum Jacq. = *Jacquiniella globosa*.

E. gravidum Lindl. = *Encyclia gravida*.

E. guatemalense Klotzsch = *Encyclia guatemalensis*.

E. guttatum Rich. & Gal. = *Encyclia maculosa*.

E. hanburyi Lindl. = *Encyclia hanburyi*.

E. hastatum Lindl. = *Encyclia hastata*.

E. ibaguense HBK. St. to 2m, slender, scrambling, rooting freely at nodes, producing plantlets. Lvs to 12cm, 2-ranked, oblong to lanceolate, coriaceous. Rac. term., subpyramidal, erect, to 70cm; fls to 4cm diam., orange-yellow to dark red or white-rose; lip uppermost, cruciform, lat. lobes lacerate-dentate, midlobe oblong-cuneate, bilobulate, lacerate-dentate, disc usually yellow. Mex. to Panama, Venez., Colomb., Peru, Guyana.

E. ibaguense var. *schomburgkii* (Lindl.) C. Schweinf. = *E. schomburgkii*.

E. imatophyllum Lindl. St. erect, to 1m, slender. Lvs to 20cm, oblong-ligulate to linear-lanceolate, coriaceous. Rac. term., simple or branched, to 25cm, erect, many-fld; fls to 4cm diam., rose to deep purple; lip uppermost, obscurely 3-lobed, lat. lobes subentire to fimbriate. Mex. to Peru and Braz., Trin.

E. imetrophyllum Paxt. = *E. imatophyllum*.

E. incumbens Lindl. = *Encyclia aromatica*.

E. inversum Lindl. = *Encyclia bulbosa*.

E. kennedyi Fowlie & Withner = *Encyclia kennedyi*.

E. kienastii Rchb. f. = *Encyclia kienastii*.

E. lamellatum Westc. ex Lindl. = *Dimerandra emarginata*.

E. lancifolium Pav. ex Lindl. = *Encyclia lancifolia*.

E. lanipes Lindl. Differs from *E. purum* in pubesc. pedicels and ovaries and yellow to bronze fls. Peru, Colomb., Boliv.

E. latifolium (Lindl.) Garay & Sweet. St. to 50cm, terete, erect. Lvs to 15cm, suborbicular to elliptic. Fls to 10cm, diam., solitary, yellow-green to yellow-brown; lip white; midlobe tinged yellow-green at apex, linear-filiform. W Indies, Venez., Trin., Braz. Cf. *E. nocturnum*.

E. latilabrum Lindl. = *E. difforme*.

E. laucheanum Rolfe ex Bonhof. St. to 22cm, slender, erect. Lvs to 19cm, linear-lanceolate, coriaceous. Rac. to 50cm, arching or pendent, bearing to 100 fls; fls to 2.5cm diam.; tep. pink-brown or purple to purple-green; lip rigidly fleshy, yellow-green, suborbicular, plicate, often undulate. Guat., Hond., Nic., Costa Rica, Colomb.

E. leucocardium Schltr. = *E. eburneum*.

E. leucochilum Klotzsch. St. slender, erect to 80cm. Lvs to 25cm, coriaceous, oblong to narrowly elliptic.Infl; to 40cm, 3–15-fld; fls to 7.5cm diam.; tep. pale green; lip ivory-white, lat. lobes dolabriform; midlobe lanceolate. Venez., Colomb.

E. lindleyanum (Batem. ex Lindl.) Rchb. f. = *Barkeria lindleyana*.

E. lineare Ruiz & Pav. = *Encyclia luteorosea*.

E. lividum Lindl. = *Encyclia livida*.

E. longipetalum Lindl. & Paxt. = *Encyclia alata*.

E. luteo-roseum Rich. & Gal. = *Encyclia luteorosea*.

E. macrothyrsodes Rchb. f. = *E. sceptrum*.

E. maculosum Ames, Hubb. & Schweinf. = *Encyclia maculosa*.

E. mariae Ames = *Encyclia mariae*.

E. medusae (Rchb. f.) Veitchen. = *Nanodes medusae*.

E. meliosmum Rchb. f. = *Encyclia meliosma*.

E. michuacanum La Ll. & Lex. = *Encyclia michuacana*.

E. microbulbon Hook. = *Encyclia microbulbon*.

E. microphyllum Lindl. = *Lanium microphyllum*.

E. micropus Rchb. f. = *Encyclia tripunctata*.

E. mosenii Barb.-Rodr. = *E. strobiliferum*.

E. musciferum Lindl. = *E. anceps*.

E. nemorale Lindl. = *Encyclia adenocaula*.

E. nocturnum Jacq. A highly variable sp. St. to 1m, slender or stout. Lvs to 14cm, narrow-oblong to elliptic, coriaceous. Rac. sometimes branched, 1- to few-fld; fls fragrant, to 6cm diam., slightly nodding; tep. narrow, white to yellow-green, often flushed pale amber with age; lip white, lateral lobes obliquely ovate usually entire, midlobe long-acuminate. Trop. Americas.

E. nocturnum var. *latifolium* Lindl. = *E. latifolium*.

E. nutans Sw. St. to 60×1cm, erect to arching, terete. Lvs to 28cm, coriaceous, oblong to oblong-lanceolate. Infl. drooping, to 50cm, many-fld, branched at base; fls to 2cm diam., fragrant; tep., soft green; lip white tinted green, entire to erose, lat. lobes subrotund, midlobe smaller, bilobulate. Venez., Braz., Jam., Trin.

E. O'Brienianum. An early orchid hybrid common in cult. with tall, vigorous reed-like st. and term. clusters of rosy crimson fls.

E. ochraceum Lindl. = *Encyclia ochracea*.

E. oerstedii Rchb. f. Related to and resembling *E. ciliare*, *E. nocturnum* and *E. parkinsonianum*; differs from the first in entire lat. lobes to lip, from the second by its stouter pbs and tougher lvs, and from the last in its erect habit. Costa Rica, Panama.

E. ottonis Rchb. f. = *Nidema ottonis*.

E. ovulum Lindl. = *Encyclia microbulbon*.

E. palpigerum Rchb. f. = *E. imatophyllum*.

E. paniculatum Ruiz & Pav. = *E. floribundum*.

E. panthera Rchb. f. = *Encyclia panthera*.

E. papyriferum Schltr. = *Encyclia panthera*.

E. parkinsonianum Hook. Rhiz. thick, branching; st. short, decurved, 1–2-lvd. Lvs to 50cm, lanceolate-falcate, fleshy, pendulous, clustered, lobster claw-like. Rac. short, pendent, 1–5-fld; fls to 15cm diam.; tep. white, pale yellow or yellow-green, becoming darker with age, narrow; lip white or pale yellow-orange, lat. lobes obtriangular, denticulate, midlobe linear, acuminate. Mostly summer-autumn. Mex., Guat., Hond., Costa Rica, Panama.

E. patens Sw. St. to 50cm, slender, ± pendent. Lvs to 10cm, oblong to oblong-lanceolate. Infl. to 13cm, pendent, few- to many-fld; fls to 3cm diam., fragrant; tep. pale yellow or yellow-green fading to white; lip cream-white, midlobe ovate, obtuse, sometimes bilobulate. Mostly summer. W Indies, Braz., Venez.

E. pentotis Rchb. f. = *Encyclia baculus*.

E. piliferum Rchb. f. = *E. floribundum*.

E. polybulbon Sw. = *Encyclia polybulbon*.

E. porpax Rchb. f. = *Nanodes mathewsii*.

E. prismatocarpum Rchb. f. = *Encyclia prismatocarpa*.

E. pseudepidendrum (Rchb. f.) Rchb. f. St. to 1m, robust, simple. Lvs 2-ranked, to 20×4.5cm, linear-oblong or oblanceolate, coriaceous. Rac. loose, to 15cm; tep. to 3cm, lustrous apple green; lip bright orange or orange-red, sub-quadrate, undulate, retuse, finely fimbriate, disc yellow, sometimes crimson edged orange ('Auratum'). Summer-autumn. Costa Rica, Panama.

E. purum Lindl. St. elongate-fusiform, to 50cm. Lvs to 22cm, linear-lanceolate, coriaceous. Pan. spreading, many-fld; fls to 2cm, campanulate, fragrant, white or green-white. Venez. to Boliv.

E. pygmaeum Hook. = *Encyclia pygmaea*.

E. quadratum Klotzsch = *Encyclia varicosa*.

E. radiatum Lindl. = *Encyclia radiata*.

E. radicans Pav. ex Lindl. = *E. ibaguense*.

E. ramosum Jacq. St. to 90cm, slender, simple to much-branched, often flexuous. Lvs to 12cm, 2-ranked, linear to oblong-elliptic. Rac. v. short; fls to 1cm diam., inconspicuous, cream-white to pale green or yellow-green, sometimes tinged red. Mex. to Panama, W Indies to Venez., Braz., Peru.

E. raniferum Lindl. = *E. cristatum*.

E. reflexum Ames & Schweinf. = *E. floribundum*.

E. rigidum Jacq. St. to 25cm, erect. Lvs to 8.5cm, ligulate-oblong to elliptic-oblong, coriaceous. Rac. to 15cm, erect or arching; fls loosely 2-ranked, minute, fleshy, green or yellow-green, sometimes concealed by bracts. C & S Amer., W Indies.

E. sceptrum Lindl. Rhiz. creeping; pbs to 30cm, narrowly fusiform. Lvs to 30cm, coriaceous, oblong to lanceolate. Infl. to 55cm, erect or arching, many-fld; tep. to 2cm, yellow or yellow-brown spotted dark purple; lip white at base, strongly marked dark purple, rhomboid to subrotund, acute to apiculate. Venez., Colomb., Ecuad.

E. schlechterianum Ames = *Nanodes discolor*.

E. schomburgkii Lindl. St. to 75cm. Lvs to 20cm, 2-ranked, oblong, fleshy-coriaceous. Rac. erect, far exceeding lvs; fls to 3.5cm diam., long-lived, rich vermilion-scarlet to bright orange; lip deeply 3-lobed, lat. lobes incurved, lacerate, midlobe cuneate, bilobulate, dentate, disc yellow. Mostly winter. Colomb., Venez., Guianas, Peru, Braz.

E. schumannianum Schltr. = *Oerstedella schumanniana*.

E. schweinfurthianum Correll = *Oerstedella schweinfurthiana*.

E. secundum Jacq. St. to 1m, terete. Lvs to 14cm, ovate-oblong to ovate-lanceolate. Infl. simple or rarely branched, to 75cm, many-fld at apex; fls to 3cm diam., white to orange or rose-pink; lip deeply 3-lobed, lat. lobes rounded, dentate to lacerate, midlobe large, broadly cuneate, dentate to lacerate. W Indies, Trop. S Amer.

E. selligerum Batem. ex Lindl. = *Encyclia selligera*.

E. skinneri Batem. ex Lindl. = *Barkeria skinneri*.

E. spectabile (Batem. ex Lindl.) Rchb. f. = *Barkeria spectabilis*.

E. spectatissimum Rchb. f. = *E. leucochilum*.

E. sphenoglossum Lehm. & Kränzl. = *E. sceptrum*.

E. splendens Schltr. = *E. schomburgkii*.

E. spondiadum Rchb. f. = *Encyclia spondiada*.

E. stamfordianum Batem. Pbs to 25cm, fusiform. Lvs to 24cm, linear-oblong to elliptic-oblong, coriaceous. Rac. or pan. to 60cm lat.; fls to 4cm diam, fragrant; tep. pale yellow-green to pale bronze mottled red-brown or purple; lip white, sometimes tinted or flushed rose, midlobe, bilobulate, deeply emarginate, erose. Mex. to Panama, Venez., Colomb.

E. stenopetalum Hook. = *Dimerandra emarginata*.

E. strobiliferum Rchb. f. St. clustered, simple to much-branched. Lvs to 4cm, distichous, fleshy, elliptic to linear-lanceolate. Rac. to 3.5cm, few-fld; fls to 0.8cm diam., green to white, sometimes lined red. C & S Amer. (from Flor. to Peru), W Indies.

E. tampense Lindl. = *Encyclia tampensis*.

E. tenuissimum Ames, Hubb. & Schweinf. = *Encyclia tenuissima*.

E. teretifolium Sw. = *Jacquiniella teretifolia*.

E. tesselatum Batem. ex Lindl. = *Encyclia livida*.

E. trachychilum Lindl. = *Encyclia ambigua*.

E. tridens Poepp. & Endl. = *E. nocturnum*.

E. tripunctatum Lindl. = *Encyclia tripunctata*.

E. trulla Rchb. f. = *Encyclia lancifolia*.

E. tuerckheimii (Schltr.) Ames, Hubb. & Schweinf. = *Encyclia tuerckheimii*.

E. umbellatum Sw. = *E. difforme*.

E. varicosum Batem. ex Lindl. = *Encyclia varicosa*.

E. variegatum Hook. = *Encyclia vespa*.

E. venosum Lindl. = *Encyclia venosa*.

E. verrucosum Sw. = *Oerstedella verrucosa*.

E. vespa Vell. = *Encyclia vespa*.

E. vinosum Schltr. = *E. catillus*.

E. violascens Ridl. St. to 14cm, terete, simple or branched.Lvs to 2cm, coriaceous, rigid, oblong-lanceolate. Pan. term., to 20cm; peduncle maroon, filiform; bracts maroon; fls to 1cm diam., red-purple fleshy; lip light yellow-green, transversely elliptic to rounded-subreniform, erose. Venez., Braz., Guyana.

E. virens Lindl. & Paxt. = *Encyclia belizensis*.

E. virgatum Lindl. = *Encyclia michuacana*.

E. viridipurpureum Hook. = *E. anceps*.

E. viscidum Lindl. = *E. ciliare*.

E. vitellinum Lindl. = *Encyclia vitellina*.

E. wallisii Rchb. f. = *Oerstedella wallisii*.

E. wendlandianum Kränzl. = *Encyclia venosa*.

E. xanthinum Lindl. = *E. secundum*.

E. xipheres Rchb. f. Pbs to 3×1cm, ovoid. Lvs to 26cm, narrowly linear, conduplicate, coriaceous. Rac. or pan. to 36cm, few-fld; fls to 3cm diam., spreading, long-lived; ovaries echinate; tep. red-brown, usually edged and marked yellow or green-lavender; lip dull yellow striped lavender, midlobe undulate. Spring–summer. Mex., Guat., Hond.

E. yucatanense Schltr. = *E. xipheres*.

→*Pseudepidendrum*.

Epigaea L. Ericaceae. 3 small, creeping, everg. shrubs. Br. rusty-hirsute. Lvs entire, tough, prominently veined; petioles short. Fls in short, axillary or term. fascicles or rac., scented; cor. funnelform or tubular-campanulate, lobes 5. N Amer., Asia.

E. asiatica Maxim. Lvs 3.5–10×2–4.5cm, oblong to elliptic, base cordate, apex acute, ciliate, dark green and glossy above, paler beneath. Fls 3–6 in short pendulous rac.; cor. c1cm, tubular-campanulate, white tinted pale rose, tube downy inside at base, lobes rounded, recurved. Spring. Jap. Z4.

E. gaultherioides (Boiss. & Bal.) Takht. Lvs 8–12cm, ovate to oblong, apex acute, base round, margin and veins bristly. Fls 1–3 per cluster, to 5cm diam., open-campanulate, soft pink. Spring. NE Turkey.

E. ×intertexta Mullig. (*E. asiatica* × *E. repens*.) Lvs 6×4cm, dark green, sinuate. Fls larger than those of *E. repens*, 3–9, in fascicles; cor. downy, pink, inside of tube white, limb pale crimson. Late winter–spring. 'Apple Blossom': fls clear pink. 'Aurora': fls pink, limb pale pink, tube white inside. Z3.

E. repens L. TRAILING ARBUTUS; MAYFLOWER. Lvs 2–8×2–5cm, ovate-oblong, apex rounded or terminating in a short point, base cordate, dark glossy green, sparsely setaceous-hirsute. Fls fragrant, 4–6 in dense, racemose clusters; cor. 1.2–1.5cm, white to pink, inside of tube hairy, lobes ovate. Spring. N Amer. 'Plena': fls double. 'Rosea': fls pale pink. 'Rubicunda': fls dark pink. Z2.

→*Orphanidesia*.

Epigeneium Gagnep. Orchidaceae. 35 epiphytic orchids. Rhiz. long, creeping. Pbs usually remote, ovoid, or ellipsoid, 4-angled and tapering basally. Lvs 2, to 15cm, apical, spreading, tough, oblong. Rac. term.; fls fragrant, waxy; sep. and pet. widely spreading, often in a vertical plane, narrow-oblong, long-acuminate, sometimes linear, twisted and recurved; lip broad, trilobed, motile. Asia, Malesia. Z10.

E. coelogyne (Rchb. f.) Summerh. Pbs to 7cm. Fls usually solitary, to 9cm diam., waxy, fragrant; tep. linear-lanceolate, twisted, yellow to deep yellow below, pale ochre above, spotted maroon; lip midlobe fleshy, channelled, dark maroon to violet-black, lat. lobes ivory marked purple. Burm., Thail.

E. cymbidioides (Bl.) Summerh. Pbs to 4cm, clustered. Infl. to 12-fld; fls to 4cm diam.; tep. ligulate, cream to ochre; lip white to pale yellow, midlobe streaked purple at base. Java, Philipp.

E. lyonii (Ames) Summerh. Pbs to 6cm. Rac. to +15-fld; fls to 12cm diam.; tep. triangular, white to yellow, flushed garnet to maroon, tipped yellow or green; lip to 3cm, red-purple, lat. lobes dark red at base. Philipp.

E. triflorum (Bl.) Summerh. Pbs to 2cm. Rac. 2–6-fld; tep. yellow, to 3cm; lip deep yellow, margins white, broad, basally dark brown, spotted red, lat. lobes white dappled brown-red. Java.

→*Dendrobium*.

Epilobium L. Onagraceae. c200 perenn., rarely ann. herbs and subshrubs. Fls solitary in lf axils, or clustered into leafy infl., actinomorphic, sometimes zygomorphic with or without conspicuous tube; sep. 4; pet. 4, apex usually notched; sta. 8, exserted; stigma capitate, club-shaped or 4-lobed. Summer. Temp. climates, esp. W N Amer., Arc., trop. mts. Summer.

E. alpinum auct. mult. non L. = *E. anagallidifolium*.

E. alsinifolium Vill. Stolons long. St. 10–30cm, with pubesc. lines. Lvs to 5cm, ovate to lanceolate-ovate, glab., finely serrate. Fls actinomorphic with floral tube; pet. 7–11mm, rose purple. Eur. mts, Arc. lowlands. Z3.

E. alsinoides A. Cunn. Perenn.; stolons leafy. St. to 36cm, strigulose, branched. Lvs 0.5–2cm, ovate-lanceolate, blue-green, mostly glab., finely serrate. Fls with floral tube; pet. 2.8–6×1.8–4.5mm, apex notched, white becoming tinged pink. NZ. Z8.

E. anagallidifolium Lam. Perenn.; stolons leafy. St. 2–10cm, with lines of strigulose hairs. Lvs 1–2.5cm, ovate to elliptic, entire. Infl. cernuous; pet. 3–4.5mm, apex notched, pale purple. N Eur., S to mts of Balk. and Corsica. Z6.

E. angustifolium L. GREAT WILLOWHERB; FRENCH WILLOW; ROSEBAY WILLOWHERB; FIREWEED; WICKUP. Perenn. St. erect, to 2.5m. Lvs 2.5–20cm, linear-lanceolate, sometimes undulate. Fls in rac., zygomorphic, floral tube 0; pet. to 1.5cm, pale pink to purple-pink, entire. N Hemis. 'Album': fls white. 'Isobel': fls pale pink, cal. crimson. Z3.

E. antipodum Petrie = *E. crassum*.

E. brevipes Hook. f. Perenn. St. branched, to 40cm, mostly glab. Lvs 1.3–2.6cm, glab., shining, coriaceous, elliptic-lanceolate, with few fine teeth. Infl. erect; fls with floral tube; pet. 6.7–7.4×3.8–4.6mm, white becoming tinged pink, apex notched. NZ. Z8.

E. caespitosum Hausskn. = *E. pedunculare*.

E. canum (Greene) Raven ssp. **canum** HUMMING BIRD'S TRUMPET; CALIFORNIA FUCHSIA. Shrublet to 60cm, much branched, pubesc. Lvs 1.25–3.75cm, linear to oblong, grey-tomentose to silky white-pubesc. Fls funnelform, to 3.75cm diam., vermilion to scarlet; pet. obcordate. SW US to Mex. 'Album': fls white.

'Dublin' ('Glasnevin'): to 20cm; fls long, tubular, bright orange-red. 'Solidarity Pink': fls pale pink. ssp. *garrettii* (A. Nels.) Raven. To 30cm. Lvs 2–3cm, hairy, leathery, elliptic to ovate, with a few small teeth. Fls deep red, tips green. ssp. *latifolium* (Hook.) Raven. Shorter. Lvs to 1.5cm wide, linear to broad-ovate, gland. Style and sta. strongly exserted. Z8.

E. canum ssp. *septentrionale* (Keck) Raven = *E. septentrionale*.

E. chloraefolium Hausskn. Perenn. St. 7–45cm, clustered, branched, strigulose. Lvs 1–3cm, ovate to broad-ovate, finely serrate. Infl. erect; fls with floral tube; pet. 7–11×5–8mm, white, notched. NZ. Z8.

E. chloraefolium var. *kaikourense* Ckn. = *E. chloraefolium*.

E. chloraefolium var. *verum* Ckn. = *E. chloraefolium*.

E. crassum Hook. f. Prostrate, glab. perenn. St. to 10cm. Lvs 1.2–4cm, shining, ascending, narrowly obovate, obtuse, entire or with few fine teeth. Fls with floral tube; pet. 5.1–7.5×2.7–5.2mm, white veined pink becoming tinted pink, notched. NZ. Z8.

E. dodonaei Vill. Rootstock woody. St. to 1.1m, erect. Lvs 2–2.5cm, linear, strigulose. Infl. loose, fls, zygomorphic; pet. deep rose-purple. C & S Eur. to W Asia. Z6.

E. erubescens Hausskn. = *E. glabellum*.

E. fleischeri Hochst. Closely resembles *E. dodonaei*. Rootstock thick, woody. St. 8–45cm, decumbent. Lvs 1.5–4cm, lanceolate, glab. Fls light to dark purple. Eur. Alps. Z5.

E. glabellum Forst. f. Perenn. forming tangled, bushy mat. St. 5–40cm, with lines of strigulose hairs, often tinted red. Lvs 0.5–2cm, elliptic to ovate, finely serrate. Infl. erect; fls with floral tube; pet. 3–18×2–12mm, white or rose-violet, notched. NZ. 'Roseum': fls pink. 'Sulphureum': fls sulphur-yellow. Z8.

E. hectori Hausskn. Perenn. St. 2–25cm, branched, forming clumps, with lines of strigulose hairs. Lvs 0.3–2cm, blue-green, elliptic, apiculate, entire to finely serrate. Infl. erect; fls with floral tube; pet. 2.5–8.6×1.8–5.5mm, notched, white to pink. NZ. Z8.

E. hirsutum L. CODLINS AND CREAM. Stolons below ground. St. to 2m, erect, tomentose. Lvs 2–12cm, oblanceolate, partly clasping st., finely serrate. Pet. 6–16mm, bright rose-purple. Eurasia, N Afr., nat. in US. Z8.

E. inornatum Melville = *E. komarovianum*.

E. komarovianum A. Lév. Prostrate, mat-forming perenn. St. glab. or hispid-pubesc. Lvs 0.2–1.2cm, tinged bronze-pink, dull, oblong-ovate to orbicular, entire or with few teeth, sometimes hispid-pubesc. Fls with floral tube; pet. 2–5×0.9–3mm, white, notched. NZ. Z8.

E. krulleanum Hausskn. = *E. hectorii*.

E. latifolium L. RIVER BEAUTY. Roots thick, woody. St. to 45cm, decumbent. Lvs ovate-elliptic, alt., dull blue-green. Fls 1.25–2.1cm diam., zygomorphic; pet. entire, white to pink-purple, like *E. angustifolium* but duller. N Eurasia, N Amer. Z5.

E. linnaeoides Hook. f. = *E. pedunculare*.

E. luteum Pursh. St. to 40cm, simple or branched. Lvs to 7.5cm, overlapping, oblanceolate to ovate, glab., serrate. Fls 3cm; pet. yellow, notched. N Calif. to Alask. Z3.

E. nerterioides sensu Petrie = *E. komarovianum*.

E. nerterioides var. *minimum* (T. Kirk) Ckn. = *E. komarovianum*.

E. nummularifolium ssp. *nerterioides* (A. Cunn.) T. Kirk pro parte = *E. komarovianum*.

E. nummularifolium var. *brevipes* Hook. f. = *E. komarovianum*.

E. nummularifolium var. *caespitosum* (Hausskn.) T. Kirk = *E. pedunculare*.

E. nummularifolium var. *minimum* T. Kirk = *E. komarovianum*.

E. nummularifolium var. *nerterioides* (A. Cunn.) Hook. f. pro parte = *E. komarovianum*.

E. nummularifolium var. *pedunculare* (A. Cunn.) Hook. f. pro parte = *E. pedunculare*.

E. pedunculare A. Cunn. Creeping perenn., forming mats to 50cm. St. with lines of strigulose hairs. Lvs 0.25–1.5cm, ovate to suborbicular, green tinged bronze-pink, serrate. Fls solitary, erect; pedicels to 5cm; floral tube present; pet. 3–5×1.9–2.6mm, notched, white. perenn. NZ. Z8.

E. pedunculare sensu Hausskn. pro parte. = *E. komarovianum*.

E. perplexum T. Kirk = *E. chloraefolium*.

E. purpuratum Hook. f. Almost prostrate perenn. St. 4–20cm, purple-black. Lvs 0.4–1.6cm, elliptic to suborbicular, obtuse, dull green, weakly serrulate. Fls solitary, nodding; pedicel to 3.5cm; pet. 4.5–9×3–4mm, white, veined pink, becoming tinged pink, notched. NZ. Z8.

E. rosmarinifolium Haenke = *E. dodonaei*.

E. rubromarginatum Ckn. = *E. glabellum*.

E. septentrionale (Keck) Raven. HUMBOLDT COUNTY FUCHSIA. Densely white pubesc. matted perenn. to 20cm, base shrubby. Lvs 1–2.5cm, lanceolate to ovate, green, gland., hairy. Infl.

gland.; pet. to 1.5cm, orange-red. Close to *E. canum*. W US. Z8.

E. simulans Allan = *E. hectori*.

E. spicatum Lam. = *E. angustifolium*.

E. vernicosum Cheesem. = *E. glabellum*.

→*Chamaenerion, Pyrogennema* and *Zauschneria*.

Epimedium L. BISHOP'S HAT; BISHOP'S MITRE. Berberidaceae. 25 herbaceous, rhizomatous perennials. Rhiz. slender, branching irregularly, creeping. Lvs 2-ternately divided, basal, rarely simple or more divided; petiole slender, delicate, lfts cordate at base, pointed at tip. Scape naked to 6-leaved. Infl. few- to many-fld, simple or branching; fls nodding on slender stalks; sep. in 2 sets of 4, inner set petaloid, spreading; pet. 4, nectariferous, short, spurred. Medit. to Asia.

E. acuminatum Franch. 25–50cm. Lvs 3-foliolate; lfts 3–18cm, obliquely lanceolate, long-acuminate, emerging pink tinted maroon, leathery, spiny-toothed; flowering st. with 2 lvs. Infl. 10–55-fld; fls pale violet-rose, white or yellow; outer sep. 3–4.5mm, inner sep. 8–12mm; pet. 15–25mm. W & C China. Z7.

E. alpinum L. 6–30cm. Lvs 2-ternate; lfts to 13cm, ovate, apex acuminate, bright green, margin spiny, tinged red at first; flowering st. bearing a single lf. Infl. 8–26-fld; outer sep. 2.5–4mm, grey with red spots, inner sep. 3–7mm, dull red; pet. 4mm, slipper-shaped, yellow. S Eur. Z5.

E. alpinum var. *pubigerum* DC. = *E. pubigerum*.

E. ×cantabrigiense Stearn. (*E. alpinum* ×*E. pubigerum*.) 30–60cm in fl., lfts 7–17, to 10cm, ovate, apex acute or short-acuminate, margins with few spines, persistently pubesc. beneath.Infl. lax, gland., with red-tipped hairs; fls 1cm diam., outer sep. caducous, inner sep. dull red, to 6mm; pet. pale yellow. Gdn origin. Z5.

E. citrinum Bak. = *E. ×versicolor* 'Sulphureum'.

E. concinnum Vatke = *E. ×youngianum* 'Roseum'.

E. diphyllum Lodd. 10–20cm. Lvs 2-foliolate; lfts ovate-triangular, blunt at apex, thin, light green, 2–5cm, margin spineless or nearly so; flowering st. bearing a single lf. Rac. 4–9-fld; fls pendulous, bell-shaped, white; outer sep. 3mm, inner sep. 6mm; pet. 7mm. Spring. Jap. Z5.

E. diphyllum Yoshino non Lodd. = *E. setosum*.

E. grandiflorum Morr. 12–35cm. Lvs 2- to 3-ternately divided, 30cm long; lfts 3–13cm ovate, membranous, light green, bronze at first, margin spinose, toothed; flowering st. bearing a single lf. Infl. 4–16-fld; fls white, violet to deep rose red; outer sep. 4–5mm, suffused red, inner sep. 8–18mm, pointed; pet. exceeding sep., spurs to 25mm. Spring–summer. Jap., S Manch., N Korea. 'Album': fls white. 'Elfkönig': fls cream. 'Lilafee': fls lavender-violet. 'Normale': outer pet. red, inner violet, nectaries white. 'Rose Queen': fls crimson-carmine; pet. paler than inner sep.; spur tips long, becoming white. f. *flavescens* Stearn. Inner sep. and pet. yellow. The names *E. flavescens* hort., *E. sulphurellum* Nak. and *E. koreanum* Nak. and *E. creneum* hort. appear to belong here. f. *violaceum* (Morr.) Stearn. Innermost sep. and pet. pale violet. Z5.

E. hexandrum Hook. = *Vancouveria hexandra*.

E. leptorrhizum Stearn. 12–30cm in fl. Rhiz. scaly. Lvs rarely 1-foliolate; petiole red-pubesc.; lfts narrow, ovate, apex long-acuminate, densely spiny-serrate, papillose beneath, veins red-pubesc. Infl. gland., 4–8-fld; fls white, tinged pale or deep rose; pet. long-spurred, exceeding inner sep. China. Z7.

E. lilacinum Donck. = *E. ×youngianum* 'Roseum'.

E. niveum Vilm.-Andr. = *E. ×youngianum* 'Niveum'.

E. ×perralchicum Stearn. (*E. perralderianum* ×*E. pinnatum*.) Similar to *E. pinnatum* except lvs occas. simple, bronze when young, densely spiny-toothed. Gdn origin. 'Fröhnleiten': lvs everg.; fls bright golden yellow. 'Wisley': lvs bold, everg., to 50cm; infl. to 55cm; fls large, bright yellow. Z8.

E. perralderianum Coss. Similar to *E. pinnatum* except lvs not more than trifoliate, rarely simple, bronze when young, margins densely spiny-toothed. Outer sep. green. N Afr. Z7.

E. pinnatum Fisch. 20–30cm. Lvs usually 2-ternate, sometimes pinnate or 3-foliolate, white- or red-hairy, becoming glab.; lfts 8cm, becoming somewhat leathery, spiny-toothed; flowering st. naked. Rac. 12–3-fld; outer sep. 3–5mm, brown, inner sep. 8mm, yellow, veins red; pet. 2mm, yellow. N Iran. ssp. *colchicum* (Boiss.) Busch. To 40cm. Lvs usually 3–5-foliolate, sparsely spiny to entire. Z6.

E. pinnatum var. *sulphureum* (Morr.) Bergmans = *E. ×versicolor* 'Sulphureum'.

E. pinnatum var. *perralderianum* (Coss.) Wehrh. = *E. perralderianum*.

E. pubigerum (DC.) Morr. & Decne. 20–75cm. Lvs usually 2-ternate; lfts ovate to round, cordate at base, hairy beneath, spinose. Infl. lax, 12–30-fld. Flowering st. bearing one lf, outer sep. 3mm, green, tinged red, inner sep. 5–7mm, pale rose to white; pet. 3.5–4mm, bright yellow. Turk., SE Eur. Z5.

E. roseum Vilm.-Andr. = *E.* ×*youngianum* 'Roseum'.

E. ×*rubrum* Morr. (*E. alpinum* ×*E. grandiflorum.*) 25–35cm. Lvs 2-ternately divided, sometimes more; lfts 14cm, ovate, pointed, thin, bright red at first, spiny-toothed; flowering st. bearing a single lf. Infl. 10–23-fld, lax; outer sep. 3–4mm, grey with red spots, inner sep. 10mm, bright crimson; pet. 10mm, yellow, slipper-shaped. Gdn origin. Z5.

E. sagittatum (Sieb. and Zucc.) Maxim. 25–50cm. Lvs 3-foliolate; lfts 5cm, sometimes much larger, lanceolate to ovate, base sagittate, leathery, hairy beneath, spiny-toothed; flowering st. bearing 2, rarely 3 lvs. Infl. 20–60-flld; outer sep. 4.5mm, white spotted purple, inner sep. 4mm, white; pet. 2–4mm, yellow-brown. C China, nat. Jap. Z6.

E. sempervirens Nak. ex Muekawa. As *E. grandiflorum* except lvs everg., more glaucous beneath. Fls white, sometimes tinged purple. Jap., Korea. Z7.

E. setosum Koidz. Lvs biternately palmate or bipinnate; lfts pub-esc. at first, somewhat glaucous beneath, ovate-cordate, abruptly acute, base sagittate to auriculate, margin bristly; petiole villous. Infl. a slender pan. or rac.; pet. white. Jap. Z7.

E. sulphureum Morr. = *E.* ×*versicolor* 'Sulphureum'.

E. sutchuenense Franch. 15–30cm in fl. Lvs trifoliolate; lfts ovate to narrow-ovate, abruptly long-acuminate, papillose beneath, sparsely grey-hirsute above. Infl. gland., 4–8-fld; fls mauve-purple or rose; inner sep. 1.5–1.7cm; pet. equalling or exceeding inner sep. China. Z7.

E. ×*versicolor* Morr. (*E. grandiflorum* ×*E. pinnatum* ssp. *colchicum.*) Similar to *E. grandiflorum* except flowering st. sometimes naked. Fls smaller; pet. spurs shorter, pet. only just exceeding, or slightly shorter than sep. Gdn origin. 'Cupreum': inner sep. copper-red. 'Neosulphureum': lvs with 3–9 lfts, tinged brown when young, narrow, ovate, to 9×7cm; infl. simple, lax, 7–16-fld; fls pale yellow, outer sep. tinged purple, inner sep. pale sulphur-yellow; pet. pale yellow, enveloping the sta.; spurs upcurved, tinged brown. 'Sulphureum': lfts 5–11, sometimes mottled red or brown, to 6×8cm; infl. 8–20-fld; inner sep. pale yellow, pet. brighter. Z5.

E. ×*warleyense* Stearn. (*E. alpinum* ×*E. pinnatum* ssp. *colchicum.*) 20–55cm. Lvs 5–9-foliolate; lfts 13×9cm, ovate, tip acute, hairy beneath, sparsely spiny-toothed; flowering st. bearing a single lf or naked. Infl. 10–30-fld; outer sep. 3–4mm, green-suffused purple, inner sep. 8mm, yellow to brick red; pet. shorter, yellow. Spring. Gdn origin. Z5.

E. ×*youngianum* Fisch. & C.A. Mey. (*E. diphyllum* ×*E. grandiflorum.*) 10–30cm. Lfts 2–9, thin, becoming glab. beneath; flowering st. bearing a single lf. Infl. 3–12-fld; fls white, sometimes rose; inner sep. 8–11mm; pet. 7–10mm, ± spurless. Gdn origin. 'Niveum': as 'Roseum' except lfts blunt, 2–9; infl. more lax, fls white; spur shorter than inner sep., often 0. 'Roseum': 10–30cm in fl.; lvs variable, 2–9-foliolate; lfts ovate, blunt, margins spiny-serrate; infl. lax, 4–12-fld; fls shades of purple-mauve. 'Yenomato': as 'Roseum' except fls white, spur straight, slender, to 1.2cm. Z5.

→*Aceranthus* and *Bonsteddtia.*

Epipactis Zinn. Orchidaceae. 24 rhizomatous herbaceous orchids. St. solitary or many. Lvs lanceolate to ovate, 2-ranked or spiralling, usually ribbed. Spike lax or dense, erect or nodding; bracts leafy; pet. and sep. spreading or incurved; lip spurless, constricted, basally cupped, apically spreading, ridged. Summer. N Temp. Zone, Trop. Afr., Thail., Mex.

E. atrorubens (Bernh.) Besser. BROAD-LEAVED HELLEBORINE. To 1m. Lvs 3–10, ovate to ovate-lanceolate. Spike 7–25cm, pub-esc.; tep. ruby red, sometimes amber; lip 5.5–6.5mm, apex edged deep green and spotted red. Spring–summer. Eur. Z6.

E. falcata Thunb. = *Cephalanthera falcata.*

E. gigantea Douglas. To 90cm. Lvs 4–12, ovate to lanceolate. Spike to 15-fld, lax; sep. bright green veined purple; pet. rose-pink ageing green; lip 14–18mm, red-verrucose, lat. lobes yellow, veined purple to brown, apical lobe orange-yellow tipped pink. Spring–summer. N Amer. 'Serpentine Night': lvs and st. deep wine red. Z6.

E. helleborine (L.) Crantz. To 100cm. Lvs 3–10, ovate to elliptic, acuminate. Spike secund, 15–50-fld; sep. green tinted purple; pet. pale green to violet; lip interior green, apex cream-yellow, pink or purple. Summer. Eur. Z6.

E. palustris (L.) Crantz. MARSH HELLEBORINE. To 50cm. Lvs oblong to oblong-lanceolate. Spike lax, secund; sep. maroon to grey-green, interior red; pet. cream, flushed or lined garnet or maroon; lip undulate, veined pink to mauve, spotted orange, apex cream or white with yellow stripe at base. Summer–early autumn. Eur. Z6.

E. purpurata Sm. VIOLET HELLEBORINE. 20–90cm. Lvs 5–10, ovate-lanceolate to lanceolate. Spike 15–30cm, dense; fls nodding; tep. green below, white above, rarely tinted pink; lip

exterior green, interior dappled violet, apex white with pink callus. Late summer–early autumn. NW & C Eur. Z6.

E. thunbergii A. Gray. 30–70cm. Lvs to 3–10, ovate-lanceolate. Fls golden-bronze; pet. spotted maroon above. Summer. Jap., China, Korea. Z8.

E. veratrifolia Boiss. & Hohen. SCARCE MARSH HELLEBORINE. 20–150cm. Lvs 8–20, ovate-lanceolate to lanceolate. Spike lax, arching, with long floral bracts; fls nodding; tep. olive to buff, dappled deep red or purple-brown; lip base purple with brown projections, apex buff with a red-brown band. Late spring–late summer. E Medit., SW & E Asia, Somalia. Z8.

×Epiphronitis. (*Epidendrum* ×*Sophronitis.*) Orchidaceae. Gdn hybrids. Small plants with upright st. and term. clusters of orange-red and yellow fls.

Epiphyllanthus A. Berger.

E. obovatus Britt. & Rose = *Schlumbergera opuntioides.*

E. obtusangulus (Schum.) A. Berger = *Schlumbergera obtusangula.*

E. opuntioides (Loefgr. & Dusen) Moran = *Schlumbergera opuntioides.*

Epiphyllum Haw. Cactaceae. ORCHID CACTUS. 15 mostly epiphytic cacti; st. terete becoming 2-ribbed, flat, leaf-like, margins crenate, serrate, sinuate or pinnatisect; spines 0, or present on terete st. Fls funnelform; tube elongate. C & S Amer.

E. ackermannii Haw. = *Nopalxochia ackermannii.*

E. anguliger (Lem.) G. Don. FISHBONE CACTUS. St. flattened, linear or narrowly lanceolate, obtuse or acute, to 100×4–8cm, deeply and acutely lobed. Fl. 15–18×10–13cm, scented; outer tep. lemon or golden yellow, inner tep. white. Late autumn. S Mex. Z9.

E. caudatum Britt. & Rose. Similar to *E. oxypetalum*, but fls much smaller; lat. st. 15–20×3–4cm, flattened, elliptic-acuminate and cuneate, undulate-crenate. Fl. 12–15cm diam. Mex. Z9.

E. chrysocardium Alexander. Lat. st. to 1m, pinnatifid, elliptic overall, lobes oblong, curved toward apex, thinly leathery. Fl. c32×20cm; tube 16×1.25cm, lower part pale green, dull purple above; outer tep. dull purple, inner white. Winter. Mex. Z9.

E. crenatum (Lindl.) G. Don ex Loud. St. flattened, to 50×3.5cm, rather thick, crenate. Fl. 20–29×10–20cm; outer tep. pale yellow, inner tep. white. S Mex. to Hond. Z9.

E. darrahii (Schum.) Britt. & Rose = *E. anguliger.*

E. gaertneri (Reg.) Schum. = *Hatiora gaertneri.*

E. guatemalense Britt. & Rose = *E. hookeri.*

E. hookeri Haw. Resembling *E. phyllanthus*, but fls much broader. S Mex. to Costa Rica. Z9.

E. lepidocarpum (Weber) Britt. & Rose Flattened st., 3–5.5cm broad, truncate-serrate. Fl. 20cm diam., white, nocturnal. Nic. to Panama. Z9.

E. macropterum Lem. An unidentifiable sp. See Kimnach in *Cact. Succ. J.* (US) 37: 162–163 (1965).

E. oxypetalum (DC.) Haw.. Lat. st. 30×10–12cm, flattened, elliptic-acuminate, thin, undulate-crenate, green. Fl. 25–30×12–17cm; outermost tep. narrow, red, inner tep. to 2.5cm broad, white; fil. white. Summer. S Mex. to Hond. Widely cult. in trop. Z9.

E. phyllanthoides (DC.) Sweet = *Nopalxochia phyllanthoides.*

E. phyllanthus (L.) Haw. Lat. st. flattened except at base, linear, obtuse or acute, 25–30×3–10cm, stiff, crenate, midrib prominent. Fl. 20–29×4–9cm; outer tep. tinged green or red, inner 3–10mm broad, white. Trop. S Amer. Z9.

E. pittieri (F.A. Weber) Britt. & Rose = *E. hookeri.*

E. pumilum (Vaupel) Britt. & Rose. Habit v. similar to *E. caudatum* and *E. oxypetalum* but the fls only 8–12cm diam. S Mex., Guat. Z9.

E. speciosum Haw. = *Nopalxochia phyllanthoides.*

E. stenopetalum (C.F. Först.) Britt. & Rose = *E. hookeri.*

E. strictum (Lem.) Britt. & Rose = *E. hookeri.*

E. thomasianum (Schum.) Britt. & Rose. Resembling *E. oxypetalum*, but lat. st. thicker, oblanceolate to elliptic, obtuse, margins green or brown. Fl. 28–34×20–26cm; outer tep. tinged red, inner tep. creamy white; fil. yellow. S Mex. to Nic.

E. truncatum Haw. = *Schlumbergera truncata.*

E. cvs. Orchid cacti are available in shades of pink, rose, red and orange-red.

→*Marniera.*

Epipremnum Schott. Araceae. 8 everg. lianes, to 30m+, with juvenile and adult phases; adhesive roots emerging from st. Lvs entire to pinnate, occas. perforated, coriaceous. Peduncle short, solitary; spathe to 30cm, cymbiform, not forming tube, yellow to green or purple; spadix short, stout, included. SE Asia to W Pacific. Z10.

E. aureum (Lind. & André) Bunting. GOLDEN POTHOS; DEVIL'S IVY; HUNTER'S-ROBE. St. climbing or sprawling, green, striped yellow or white. Juvenile lvs 15–30cm, ovate, cordate, bright green, variegated yellow or white; adult lvs to 80cm, ovate to ovate-oblong, cordate, irregularly pinnatisect, variegated, short-stalked. Solomon Is. 'Marble Queen': lvs green boldly streaked white and moss green, petioles white; st. white streaked green. 'Tricolor': lvs boldly variegated white, petioles and st. off-white.

E. giganteum Schott. Lvs 30–60cm, entire, oblong, obtuse, cordate, coriaceous, glossy bright green, long-stalked. Malaysia, Thail.

E. mirabile Schott. TONGA PLANT. Lvs 30–50cm, entire when juvenile, pinnatifid when adult, cordate, perforated along midrib, seg. 4–10 per side, dark green; petiole to 38cm. Malaysia, Polyn. to Aus.

E. pinnatum (L.) Engl. Juvenile lvs oblong-lanceolate, entire or pinnatifid or perforate; adult lvs to 100cm, elliptic-oblong, perforate or with translucent spots along midrib, irregularly pinnatifid. Malaysia to New Guinea.

E. cvs. 'Exoticum': lvs oblique-lanceolate, to 20cm, thin, matt dark green, splashed silver.

→*Monstera, Pothos, Raphidophora* and *Scindapsus*.

Episcia Mart., emend. Wiehler. Gesneriaceae. 6 terrestrial or epiphytic herbs, creeping and stoloniferous, sometimes suffrutescent. Lvs in pairs. Fls axill., solitary, fasciculate or in rac.; sep. 5, green or coloured, free or connate; cor. funnel-shaped, spurred at base, limb spreading, lobes 5. S Amer. Z10.

E. adenosiphon Leeuwenb. = *Nautilocalyx adenosiphon*.

E. bicolor Hook. = *Nautilocalyx bicolor*.

E. bractescens (Hook.) Hanst. = *Nautilocalyx bracteatus*.

E. chontalensis (Seem.) Hook. f. = *E. lilacina*.

E. cupreata (Hook.) Hanst. Stolons hirsute, to 50cm. Lvs to 8.5×5.5cm, ± bullate, dark green, paler at midrib, purple beneath. Fls clustered; cor. to 6cm, villous, scarlet with a yellow ring and occas. purple-spotted at throat. Colomb., Venez., Braz. 'Acajou': lvs dark mahogany with contrasting veins and central colouring of bright metallic silver-green. 'Chocolate Soldier': lvs v. large, soft brown with median silver-grey band. 'Frosty': lvs minutely pubesc., emerald-green with copper-tinted margins and median silver-white blotches. 'Metallica': lvs copper marked silver. 'Silver Sheen': lvs crinkled, pubesc., bright silver-grey with copper-green margins; fls yellow through lilac to red. 'Tetra': fls large, orange-red, lobes wavy, orange-yellow inside. 'Tropical Topaz': fls yellow.

E. dianthiflora H.E. Moore & R.G. Wils. = *Alsobia dianthiflora*.

E. fimbriata Fritsch. Lvs oblong-lanceolate, bullate, purple at margin. Fls solitary or clustered; cor. to 4cm, white, often marked with mauve. Peru, Braz.

E. fulgida (Lind.) Hook. = *E. reptans*.

E. hirsuta (Benth.) Hanst. Creeping herb; st. hirsute. Lvs to 13×8cm, oblong-elliptic, bullate, often red- to purple-beneath, paler along mid-rib above. Fls 1–6 per infl.; cor. to 7cm, trumpet-shaped, tube white, limb pale mauve or lavender. Guyana Highlands. 'Argentea': lvs bronze green, with median silver-green shading; fls pale lilac.

E. lilacina Hanst. Creeping, villous herb. Lvs to 5×3cm, ovate, crenate, villous, pilose and purple beneath. Fls 1–4 in sessile infl.; cor. to 4.5cm, lilac, pilose, tube narrowly cylindric, lobes orbicular. Costa Rica. 'Cuprea': lvs deep bronze-velvet, with inconspicuous median silver-green shading; fls lavender-blue with pale centre. 'Lilacina': lvs pubesc., dark copper with prominent silver-green veins; fls 3cm, lavender-blue. 'Mrs Fanny Haage': lvs with paler veins; 'Panama': lvs narrow, pubesc., copper-green with inconspicuous median stripe. 'Viridis': lvs broad, downy, emerald-green with pale, glossy silver markings; fls light blue.

E. lucianii Fourn. = *Nautilocalyx lucianii*.

E. melittifolia (L.) Mart. = *Nautilocalyx melittifolius*.

E. panamensis (Seem.) Morton = *Nautilocalyx panamensis*.

E. picta (Hook.) Hanst. = *Nautilocalyx pictus*.

E. reptans Mart. Creeping, stoloniferous herb to 20cm; st. hirsute. Lvs to 15×10cm, elliptic, bullate, dark green above with a pale green area above midrib, purple-tinged beneath. Fls solitary or in clusters; cor. to 4cm, trumpet-shaped, scarlet, pale at throat, lobes serrulate. Colomb., Guyana, Braz. 'Lady Lou': lvs bronze-green with slender silver veins, and rose-pink, occas. white or grey stripes.

E. splendens (Lind.) Hanst. = *E. cupreata*.

E. tessellata hort. ex Lem. = *Nautilocalyx bullatus*.

E. villosa HBK = *Nautilocalyx villosus*.

E. cvs. 'Catherinae': habit robust; lvs green, flecked with silver and veined pale green. 'Chocolate Velour': lvs thickly-textured, black, luxuriant. 'Ember Lace': lvs quilted, dark bronze-brown, blotched vivid rose-pink; fls rose-pink. 'Filigree': lvs to 15cm,

flattened, sparsely pubesc., copper to olive-green with conspicuous silver-green veins, tinged purple beneath; fls numerous, red. 'Fire N' Ice': lvs large, bronze, velvety, overlaid with pink veins; fls bright red. 'Helen O': lvs large, bronze, velvety, overlaid with pink veins; fls bright red. 'Moss Agate': lvs black-green with silver etching, puckered; fls scarlet. 'Pink Panther': lvs lime-coloured; fls v. large, tubular, rose-pink. 'Pink Ric-Rac': lvs large, dark bronze, with pink etching. 'Pinkiscia': lvs metallic brown-bronze, with silver-green veins and pink pubescence; fls orange-yellow with rose flecks inside tube and broad rose-pink limb. 'Shimmer': lvs to 10cm, chocolate-brown, overlaid with a silver-green sheen, borne in a rosette; fls orange-red.

Epithelantha Britt. & Rose Cactaceae. 1 variable, dwarf cactus; st. globose to obovoid, simple or clustering, 1–7.5cm diam.; tubercles minute, often obscured by off-white to yellow initially clavate spines. Fls 3–12mm diam., at woolly stem-apex, campanulate, almost white or pale orange to pink. SW US, NE Mex.

E. micromeris (Engelm.) Britt. & Rose. SW US, NE Mex. var. *micromeris*. Simple or clustering; st. 1.3–3 8(–6)cm diam.; ± obscured by spines; spines *c*20, 1–3mm, the uppermost much longer and clavate. Fl. *c*6×3–4.5mm. SE Ariz. to NE Mex. var. *bokei* (L. Bens.) Glass & Fost. Simple or clustering, 2.5–5cm diam., obscured by spines; spines 35–38, longest to 4.5mm, tightly adpressed.Fl. to 12×12mm. var. *greggii* (Engelm.) Borg. Simple or clustering; st. 5–7.5cm diam., ± obscured by spines; spines 1–4mm, the upper ones longer, not strongly adpressed, giving the st. a bristly appearance. var. *pachyrhiza* W.T. Marshall. Rootstock carrot-like, connected to the st. by a narrow neck; st. occas. branching dichotomously; spines strongly adpressed, pectinate. var. *polycephala* (Backeb.) Glass & Fost. Clustering; st. slender, to 70×15(–20)mm; spines 0.5–2mm, yellow-orange, darker tipped. Fl. 11×5mm. var. *unguispina* (Boed.) Backeb. Clustering; st. 3–5cm diam., not obscured by spines; longest spines to *c*5mm, not adpressed. Z9.

E. pachyrhiza (W.T. Marshall) Backeb. = *E. micromeris* var. *pachyrhiza*.

E. polycephala Backeb. = *E. micromeris* var. *polycephala*.

→*Mammillaria*.

EQUISETACEAE Rich. ex DC. See *Equisetum*.

Equisetum L. HORSETAIL; SCOURING RUSH. Equisetaceae. 25 perenn., rush-like, flowerless herbs. Rhiz. invasive. Aerial st. usually clumped, erect, cylindric, fluted, simple or with jointed br. whorled at the solid sheathed nodes. Lvs minute, black or brown, forming a ring of teeth at nodes. Strobili grey to buff, term., formed of peltate sporophylls. Widely distrib., except Aus. and NZ.

E. arvense L. COMMON HORSETAIL; FIELD HORSETAIL. Sterile st. to 60cm, prostrate to erect, 6–14-furrowed, slightly rough, green; br. in dense whorls, usually simple, 3- to 4-angled. Fertile st. to 25cm, erect, smooth, light brown, soon withering; internodes 2–8. Strobilus lanceolate-ovoid, pedunculate, 2–3cm. Eurasia, Greenland, N Amer. Z2.

E. fluviatile L. SWAMP HORSETAIL. St. ann., to 1m+, to 8mm diam., 9–25-ridged, ridges smooth; internodes to 5cm, often developing 6–8-angled st.; br. none, or few, 4- or 5-angled, arcuate-ascending, with rough low-winged angles, to 15cm, nearly smooth. Strobili pedunculate, cylindric, to 2cm. Eurasia, N Amer. Z2.

E. hyemale L. DUTCH RUSH; SCOURING RUSH; ROUGH HORSETAIL. St. to 1.5m, everg., 18–40-ridged, ridges broad, rounded, with prominent bands of silica; internodes to 12cm; br. 0 or few. Strobili short-peduncled, apiculate, 8–15mm. Eurasia (rare in Medit.), N Amer. var. *robustum* (A. Br.) Eaton. To 3m. Z5.

E. maximum auct. = *E. telmateia*.

E. robustum A. Br. = *E. hyemale* var. *robustum*.

E. scirpoides Michx. St. 16×0.1cm, ascending or prostrate, slender or filiform, flexuous, 3- or 4-ridged, ridges broad and deeply sulcate; internodes to 3cm; br. 0 or irregular and elongate. Strobili small, subsessile, apiculate. Eurasia, Greenland, N Amer. Z2.

E. sylvaticum L. St. 60×0.4cm, ann. Sterile st. mostly solitary, ridges 10–18 with 2 rows of hooked spinules; internodes 3–6cm; br. numerous, 4- or 5-angled, simple or with filiform, triangular branchlets. Fertile st. green or light brown, br. 0 or whorled, compound. Strobilus 15–25mm, long-peduncled. Eurasia (except S Russia, rare in Medit.), N Amer. Z2.

E. telmateia Ehrh. Sterile st. erect, 50–200×1–2cm, ivory white or pale green, ridges smooth, grooves fine, 20–40; internodes 2–9cm, br. regular and abundant, simple, 4–6-angled, rough with bands of silica. Fertile st. simple, 25–60×1–2.5cm, white or pale brown, smooth, succulent, soon withering. Strobilus stoutpedunculate, 40–80mm. Eurasia (except extreme N and most of Russia), N Afr., N Amer. (BC to Calif.). Z6.

E. variegatum Schleich. St. 10–30×0.1–0.2cm, 5–10-ridged, ridges sulcate, with 2 rows of siliceous tubercles; internodes 15–30mm; br. 0 or from near base. Strobilus subsessile, strongly apiculate, 5–10mm. Eurasia (N & C Eur. S to Pyren., N Apennines and S Urals), Greenland, N Amer. Z2.

Eragrostis Wolf. LOVE GRASS. Gramineae. 250 ann. or perenn. grasses. St. clumped. Lvs narrow, flat or rolled; sheaths often gland.; ligules ciliate, occas. papery. Infl. paniculate, open or dense; spikelets closely overlapping, 2- to many-fld, laterally compressed; glumes convex, keeled. Trop., subtrop., N & S Amer., S Afr., Aus.

E. abyssinica (Jacq.) Link = *E. tef.*

E. amabilis (L.) Wight & Arn. = *E. tenella.*

E. capillaris (L.) Nees. St. to 50cm. Lvs to 3mm diam., erect, flat, pilose above. Pan. oblong or elliptic, open, diffuse, with capillary br. US. Z7.

E. chloromelas Steud. Perenn. St. erect, to 90cm. Lvs elongate, involute. Pan. to 20cm, dark olive. S Afr. Z9.

E. cilianensis (All.) Lutat. Ann. St. to 30cm, ascending or spreading. Lvs to 7mm diam., flat. Pan. to 20cm, open, erect, dark grey-green, with ascending br. US, Mex., W Indies, S to Arg. Z9.

E. curvula (Schräd.) Nees. WEEPING LOVE GRASS; AFRICAN LOVE GRASS. Perenn. St. to 120cm. Lvs to 30cm×0.3cm+, scabrous above. Pan. erect to pendent, to 30cm; spikelets dark olive-grey. Summer–autumn. S Afr. Z7.

E. elegans Nees = *E. tenella.*

E. interrupta Palib. = *E. tenella.*

E. japonica (Thunb.) Trin. Ann. St. to 60cm erect. Lvs to 20×0.4cm, glab. Pan. open, ovoid-cylindric to ovoid-oblong, to 25cm, stiff, br. whorled, spreading; spikelets tinged purple, delicate. Summer–autumn. Trop. Asia, Aus. Z9.

E. mexicana (Hornem.) Link. MEXICAN LOVE GRASS. Ann. St. to 90cm, erect or ascending. Lvs to 23×0.6cm, flat, scabrous above. Infl. oblong to ovoid, to 38×20cm; spikelets tinged purple or grey. Summer–autumn. US, Mex. Z8.

E. namaquensis Nees = *E. japonica.*

E. obtusa Munro ex Stapf. Perenn. St. to 45cm. Lvs to 23×0.6cm, flat, scabrous above. Infl. oblong to ovoid, to 38×20cm; spikelets tinged purple or grey. Summer–autumn. S Afr. Z7.

E. pellucida Steud. = *E. pilosa.*

E. pilosa (L.) Palib. SOFT LOVE GRASS. Ann. St. to 45cm. Lvs to 15×0.3cm, margins usually inrolled. Pan. ovoid, open to compressed, to 18×8cm; spikelets resemble those of *Briza maxima.* Autumn. Warm temp. regions. Z7.

E. plumosa (Retz.) Link = *E. tenella.*

E. spectabilis (Pursh) Steud. Perenn. St. to 60cm, erect to spreading. Lvs to 8mm diam., flat or folded, rigid, ascending, glab. or pilose. Pan. to 40cm, diffuse, bright purple. US. Z6.

E. tef (Zucc.) Trotter. TEFF. Ann. St. to 1.5m, upright to spreading. Lvs glab., to 45×1cm, flat. Infl. pendent, loose, open or contracted, to 60cm; br. flimsy; spikelets green, white or violet. Summer–autumn. NE Afr., Ethiop., SW Arabia. Z9.

E. tenella (L.) Palib. Ann. St. flimsy, erect or sprawling, to 60cm. Lvs to 10×0.3cm, flat, glab., narrow-acuminate. Infl. ovoid to oblong, to 13×0.4cm; spikelets tinged green or purple. Summer–autumn. OW Trop. Z9.

E. tenuissima Schräd. = *E. japonica.*

E. trichodes (Nutt.) Alph. Wood. Perenn. St. to 120cm. Lvs to 60×0.6cm, flat. Infl. loose, open, oblong to elliptic, to 60cm; spikelets green or purple. Summer–autumn. US. 'Bend': infl. bronze. Z9.

E. unioloides (Retz.) Nees ex Steud. Perenn. St. to 45cm. Pan. graceful, loose or dense, lanceolate to ovoid, to 15×6cm; spikelets tinged green to purple. Autumn. Trop. Asia. Z9.

→*Briza* and *Poa.*

Eranthemum L. Acanthaceae. Some 30 perenn. shrubby herbs and shrubs. Lvs usually entire. Infl. a conspicuously bracteate spike or pan.; cor. tube slender, curved, limb 5-lobed, lobes suborbicular. Trop. Asia. Z10.

E. atropurpureum auct. non Hook. f. = *Pseuderanthemum atropurpureum.*

E. elegans (P. Beauv.) R. Br. ex Roem. & Schult. = *Lankesteria elegans.*

E. igneum Lind. = *Xantheranthemum igneum.*

E. nervosum (Vahl) R. Br. = *E. pulchellum.*

E. pulchellum André. BLUE SAGE. Everg. shrub to 1.25m. Lvs 10–20cm, elliptic, sometimes broadly toothed, glossy green with veins sunken above. Spike to 7cm, sometimes clustered; bracts to 1.25cm, elliptic, green feathered with white; cor. to 3cm, deep blue. India, nat. elsewhere.

E. reticulatum Hook. f. = *Pseuderanthemum reticulatum.*

E. wattii (Bedd.) Stapf. St. straggling, shorter and less robust than in *E. pulchellum.* Lvs to 10cm, ovate, rugose. Fls deep purple. India.

Eranthis Salisb. WINTER ACONITE. Ranunculaceae. 7 tuberous perenn. herbs. Basal lvs petiolate, peltate, deeply palmately lobed; st. lvs dissected forming an involucral whorl below scapose, solitary fl.; perianth seg. in 2 whorls, petaloid cal. seg. 5–8 as outer whorl, inner whorl of tubular, entire or 2–4-lipped nectaries; sta. numerous. Eur., Asia, nat. N. Amer.

E. cilicica Schott & Kotschy. Lvs tinged bronze on emergence; involucral lvs finely dissected. Fls shiny golden yellow, larger and emerging later than *E. hyemalis.* Winter. Turk. to Afghan. Z4.

E. hyemalis (L.) Salisb. To 15cm. Basal lvs to 8cm diam., emerging after fls, lobes with further divisions. Fls 2–3cm diam., yellow; sep. 6, narrowly ovate. Winter. S Fr. to Bulg. var. **bulgaricus** Stef. Lvs and bracs more divided resembling *E. cilicica.* Bulg. 'Aurantiaca': fls yellow-orange. Z5.

E. keiskei Franch. & Savat. = *E. pinnatifida.*

E. longistipitata Reg. Resembling *E. hyemalis* but much smaller. Basal lvs 3–5-lobed. Flowering st. 5cm; involucral seg. linear; pedicel elongating in fr.; fls yellow, 1.5cm diam.; sep. 5–6, elliptic. Spring. C Asia. Z6.

E. pinnatifida Maxim. To 15cm. Basal lvs 4cm wide, lobes 3, pinnatifid. Fls white, to 2cm across; sep. 5, ovate; nectaries yellow. Spring. Jap. Z4.

E. sibirica DC. Close to *E. longistipitata.* Basal lvs with lobes 3–5, tripartite. Flowering st. 5cm; involucral seg. linear; pedicels elongating in fr.; fls yellow, 1.5cm diam.; sep. 5–6, elliptic or oval. Spring. Sib. Z3.

E. ×tubergenii Bowles. (*E. cilicica* × *E. hyemalis.*) Lvs tinged bronze on emergence. Fls large, golden, appearing later than *E. hyemalis*; nectaries more numerous than in parents. Winter. Gdn origin. 'Guinea Gold': bracts deeply cut, lobes narrow; fls deep golden yellow, fragrant, long-lasting. Z5.

E. uncinata Turcz. = *E. sibirica.*

Ercilla A. Juss. Phytolaccaceae. 2 everg. climbers with adventitious roots with disc-like holdfasts. Lvs thick, leathery, entire. Fls small in axill. spikes; cal. 5-lobed. Fr. a berry. Americas, S Afr. Z8.

E. spicata Moq. To 6m. Lvs to 5cm, ovate-cordate to oblong, fleshy, glossy, dark green. Fls in spikes to 4.5cm; cal. purple or green; pet. 0; sta. white. Fr. dark purple. Peru, Chile.

E. volubilis Juss. = *E. spicata.*

→*Bridgesia* and *Phytolacca.*

Erdisia Britt. & Rose.

E. erecta Backeb. = *Corryocactus erectus.*

E. melanotricha (Schum.) Backeb. = *Corryocactus melanotrichus.*

E. meyenii Britt. & Rose = *Corryocactus aureus.*

E. spiniflora (Philippi) Britt. & Rose = *Austrocactus spiniflorus.*

E. squarrosa (Vaup.) Britt. & Rose = *Corryocactus squarrosus.*

Erect Sword Fern *Nephrolepis cordifolia.*

Eremalche Greene. Malvaceae. 4 ann. herbs. Lvs suborbicular, entire or palmately lobed, stellate-hairy. Epical. seg. 3; sep. united at base; pet. clawed; staminal column glab. SW US. Z8.

E. rotundifolia (A. Gray) Greene. DESERT FIVE-SPOT. Erect to 60cm; st. simple or branched, hispid. Lvs 2–5cm, unlobed, crenate; petioles 2–10cm, hairy. Fls in corymbose clusters; cor. almost globose, pet. rose-pink to lilac, each with a darker spot at base. Calif., Colorado, Ariz., Nevada.

→*Malvastrum.*

Eremochloa Buse. Gramineae. Some 10 perenn., creeping grasses. Lvs stiff. Spikelets enclosing a solitary ♂ flt, dorsally flattened, sessile. SE Asia.

E. ophiuroides (Munro) Hackel. CENTIPEDE GRASS; LAZY MAN'S GRASS. Forming dense clumps; st. to 10cm. Rac. spicate, obovoid on a slender, compressed rachis to 6cm. SE Asia.

Eremocitrus Swingle. AUSTRALIAN DESERT LIME; DESERT KUMQUAT. Rutaceae. 1 xerophytic small tree or large shrub, twigs glaucous, green, spines in axils. Lvs 2.5–4cm, falling in dry conditions, held vertically, oblong, glaucous, coriaceous with grey hairs (slender cataphylls produced by juveniles). Fls white, solitary or clustered, 3–5-merous, 5–8mm diam. Fr. ovoid or pyriform, 1cm, full of acid juice, peel thick and fleshy, with oil glands. Aus. (Queensld, NSW). Z9.

E. glauca (Lindl.) Swingle.

→*Triphasia.*

Eremophila R. Br. Myoporaceae. 180 perenn., everg. trees and shrubs. Lvs simple, entire. Infl. axill.; cal. 5-lobed; cor. tubular, limb 2-lipped and 5-lobed. Aus. Z9.

E. maculata F. Muell. Shrub 1–2.5m. Lvs to 1.8cm, linear- to ovate-lanceolate, glab. at maturity. Fls solitary, on curved, 2cm peduncles; cor. 2–3.5cm, red or pink, yellow-spotted, hairy inside; sta. exserted. NE to SW Aus.

Eremostachys Bunge. Labiatae. Some 60 tuberous perenn. herbs. St. erect, ± simple, stoloniferous. Lvs sessile or basal and petiolate. Fls in distant verticillasters, on dense, term. spikes or cap.; cal. tubular to bell- or funnel-shaped, teeth 5; cor. 2-lipped, tube included, upper lip hooded, lower lip spreading, 3-lobed, lat. lobes reduced; sta. 4, anth. exserted. W to C Asia. Z8.

E. laciniata (L.) Bunge. To 1m+. St. glab. to tomentose. Lvs to 35×20cm, pinnate-pinnatifid, elliptic to oblong; seg. margin obtusely lobed, lobes toothed to notched; cor. to 4cm, white or cream to pink, upper lip pubesc. to tomentose. Summer. W to C Asia.

E. nerimanii Stapf = *E. laciniata*.

E. superba Royle ex Benth. To 1m. St. ± glab., purple. Lvs 25×14cm, pinnate-pinnatifid, ovate, margin notched to lobed; cor. to 8cm, primrose yellow, interior glab. Summer. W Himal.

Eremurus Bieb. DESERT CANDLE; FOXTAIL LILY. Liliaceae (Asphodelaceae). 40–50 stoutly rhizomatous perenn. herbs. Lvs narrow, basal, forming tufts or rosettes. Scape erect, rac. dense, tapering; tep. 6, sometimes fused at base; sta. 6, sometimes exserted. W & C Asia. Z7.

E. aitchisonii Bak. Lvs narrowly lanceolate, to 8cm wide, glossy green, margins rough. Scape to 2m, glab.; rac. lax; tep. 18–25mm, pale pink to white, 1-nerved. Summer. C Asia, E Afghan. 'Albus': fls white. Z6.

E. altaicus (Pall.) Steven. Lvs 15–22×1.5cm, ligulate, glab. Scape to 1.2m, rac. dense; tep. yellow, incurved. Summer. C Asia. Z4.

E. anisopterus (Karel. & Kir.) Reg. As for *E. bucharis* except scape glab. throughout, lvs with smooth margins, tep. shorter, concave. Summer. Iran, C Asia. Z6.

E. aurantiacus Bak. = *E. stenophyllus* ssp. *aurantiacus*.

E. bucharicus Reg. Lvs linear, to 5mm wide, glab. or finely pubesc., glaucous, margins rough. Scape to 1m, sometimes pubesc. at base; rac. lax; tep. 13–15mm, white to pale pink, 1-nerved; sta. included. Summer. Afghan., C Asia. Z4.

E. bungei Bak. = *E. stenophyllus*.

E. caucasicus hort. = *E. spectabilis*.

E. comosus O. Fedtsch. As for *E. turkestanicus* except lvs to 1.5cm wide, pubesc., glaucous; scape to 1.8m; tep. dusky rose; fr. closely pressed to scape. Summer. C Asia to W Pak. Z5.

E. elwesianus hort. = *E. aitchisonii*.

E. elwesii Micheli = *E. aitchisonii*.

E. griffithii Bak. = *E. kaufmannii*.

E. hilariae Popov & Vved. Lvs linear, to 40cm, glaucous, grey-pubesc., keel and margins scabrous; tep. 12–16mm, white, yellow at base. Summer. C Asia. Z5.

E. himalaicus Bak. Lvs ligulate, to 4cm wide, glab. Scape to 2.5m glab.; rac. dense, to 90cm; tep. 17–20mm, white, 1-nerved; sta. equal to tep. Late spring–summer. Afghan., NW Himal. Z3.

E. 'Himrob'. (*E. himalaicus* × *E. robustus*.) Early blooming. Lvs blue-green. Fls v. pale pink. Z4.

E. inderiensis (Steven) Reg. Lvs 8–15mm wide, pubesc. Scape to 1.2m, finely pubesc.; tep. 11–12mm, red-brown, nerves 3–5, olive green. Summer. C Asia, Afghan., Iran. Z5.

E. ×*isabellinus* hort. (Vilm.) (*E. stenophyllus* ×*E. olgae*.) To 1.5m. Fls orange, pale yellow, pink, white to copper yellow. Gdn origin. Shelford Hybrids: 1.25m, fls yellow, orange, pink or white suffused yellow; include 'Isobel': (pale yellow, 'Rosalind': bright pink. Early summer. Highdown Hybrids: orange to buff, late-flowering, include dwarf forms. 'Feuerfackel' (Flame Torch): fls flaming orange to red. 'Moonlight': fls pale yellow. 'Schneelanze': fls pale green to white. 'White Beauty': fls pure white. Ruiter's hybrids: to 2m, brightly coloured. 'Cleopatra': fls deep orange; 'Fatamorgana': fls white to cream; 'Image': clear yellow; 'Obelisk': fls white; 'Parade': fls clear pink; 'Pinokkio': fls orange; 'Romance': fls tinted red; 'Sahara': fls copper. Z5.

E. kaufmannii Reg. Lvs to 3.5cm wide, pubesc., glaucous. Scape 0.6–1m, pubesc.; tep. 15–22mm, 1-nerved, white, base yellow. Summer. Afghan., C Asia. Z5.

E. korolkowii Reg. = *E. anisopterus*.

E. lactiflorus O. Fedtsch. Lvs linear, to 45cm, glab., glaucous. Scape to 1m, glab.; rac. laxly fld; tep. golden yellow in bud, opening white with yellow base, revolute; sta. slightly exserted. Summer. C Asia. Z5.

E. olgae Reg. Lvs narrowly linear, 1–1.5cm wide, glab., margin rough. Scape to 1m, pubesc. at base; tep. 12–16mm, pink, rarely

white with yellow base, 1-nerved. Late summer–autumn. C Asia to N Iran. Z6.

E. regelii Vved. To 2m. Lvs linear, glab. Tep. brown, 2.5cm wide, margins white; sta. exserted. C Asia. Z5.

E. robustus (Reg.) Reg. Lvs ligulate, to 4cm wide, glaucous. Scape to 1m, glaucous; rac. to 1m, densely fld; tep. 18–21mm, pink, 1-nerved; sta. equal tep. Summer. C Asia, Afghan. Z6.

E. robustus var. *elwesii* (Micheli) Leichtlin = *E. aitchisonii*.

E. ×*shelfordii* hort. = *E.* ×*isabellinus*.

E. sogdianus (Reg.) Benth. & Hook. Lvs to 1.5cm wide. Scape to 1.5m pubesc. at base; tep. 10–14mm, outer tep. elliptic to narrowly ovate, sulphur green, 1-nerved, inner tep. broader, white, 3-nerved, nerves green; sta. exserted. Summer. C Asia to N Afghan. Z6.

E. spectabilis Bieb. Lvs linear-ligulate, to 4.5cm wide, glaucous, margins sometimes rough. Scape to 1m, glab.; rac. to 80cm; tep. 1cm, pale yellow suffused green, 3-nerved; sta. twice length of tep., anth. brick-red, fil. orange-red near base, yellow above. Late spring–summer. Asia Minor to W Pak. Z6.

E. spectabilis var. *marginatus* O. Fedtsch. = *E. regelii*.

E. stenophyllus (Boiss. & Buhse) Bak. Lvs to 12mm wide, linear, sometimes pubesc., margins rough. Scape 0.3–1.5m, glab. to pubesc.; rac. dense; tep. 9–12mm, 1-nerved, clear yellow ageing brown; sta. exceeding tep., anth. orange. Summer. C Asia to W Pak. ssp. *stenophyllus*. Lvs and scape glab. ssp. *aurantiacus* (Bak.) Wendelbo. Lvs scabrous-pubesc. Tep. orange-yellow. Z5.

E. tauricus hort. = *E. spectabilis*.

E. ×*tubergenii* Tuberg. (*E. stenophyllus* ×*E. himalaicus*.) To 2.5m. Fls pale yellow. Gdn origin. Z6.

E. turkestanicus Reg. Lvs broad-linear, glab. Scape to 1m, glab.; rac. 40–60cm; tep. 1cm, outer tep. sulphur yellow with brown central stripe, 5-nerved, inner tep. white with sulphur yellow stripe, 3-nerved; sta. exserted. Summer. C Asia. Z6.

E. unaniensis Gilli = *E. kaufmannii*.

E. ×*warei* hort. Reuthe. (*E. stenophyllus* ×*E. olgae*.) To 2.5m. Rac. slender. Fls small, orange. Early summer. Gdn origin.

Erepsia N.E. Br. Aizoaceae. 27 erect succulent shrubs. St. 2-angled. Lvs somewhat united at base, compressed-triquetrous, keel cartilaginous. Fls to 4cm diam., to 3 together on a pedicel to 5cm long with 2 bracts. Autumn. S Afr. Z9.

E. aperta L. Bol. Mat-forming; st. 15cm. Lvs 0.5–2.5mm, ± falcate, with a few indistinct spots. Fls solitary, pink. SE Cape.

E. gracilis (Haw.) L. Bol. Shrub to 60cm; st. v. slender. Lvs 2cm, fresh green, minutely dotted. Fls purple-pink. Cape Prov.

E. haworthii (Donn) Schwantes = *Lampranthus haworthii*.

E. heteropetala (Haw.) Schwantes. St. erect to spreading. Lvs 2cm, falcate, compressed, upper surface somewhat furrowed, keel dentate, spotted green, blue-pruinose. Fls tinged red or white. SE Cape.

E. inclaudens (Haw.) Schwantes. St. to 20cm, curved-ascending or prostrate. Lvs 1.5–2.5cm, sabre-shaped, glossy green to red-tinged, with large translucent dots, keel denticulate toward the tip. Fls glossy purple-violet. S Cape.

E. montana (Schltr.) Schwantes = *E. heteropetala*.

E. mutabilis (Haw.) Schwantes. Erect shrub; st. curved. Lvs 1.5–2cm, angles straight or undulating, tip minutely cartilaginous, awned, grey-green. Fls pink, centre pale yellow. S Cape.

→*Mesembryanthemum*.

Eria Lindl. Orchidaceae. 350 epiphytic or terrestrial orchids. Pbs ellipsoid to narrow-cylindric, often sheathed. Rac. term. or axill.; sep. almost equal, lateral sep. sometimes fused below, forming a small spur or sac; pet. smaller; lip trilobed or entire, often with calli or keels. Indopacific. Z9.

E. convallarioides Lindl. = *E. spicata*.

E. coronaria (Lindl.) Rchb. f. Pbs narrow-cylindric, stalk-like, to 14cm. Lvs 2, term., to 14.5cm, broadly lanceolate, thinly fleshy. Infl. a short term. rac., semi-erect; fls to 7, to 2.5cm diam., waxy, slightly fragrant; tep. sparkling white; lip midlobe bright yellow, lat. lobes erect, veined maroon to violet-black. Himal., Burm., Thail., Malaysia.

E. dasyphylla Parish & Rchb. f. = *Trichotosia dasyphylla*.

E. ferox (Bl.) Bl. = *Trichotosia ferox*.

E. floribunda Lindl. Pbs narrow-ellipsoid, stem-like, to 50cm. Lvs 2–5, borne apically, linear-lanceolate to elliptic, soft, to 25cm. Infl. a crowded rac., arching, to 20cm; peduncle pubesc.; fls to 0.6cm diam., white, tinted pink; column tipped violet. Malaysia.

E. hyacinthoides (Bl.) Lindl. Pbs oblong, to 10cm. Lvs to 40cm, paired at apex, narrow-lanceolate. Infl. erect, canescent, to 18cm; fls many, to 2cm diam., scented, white; lip lat. lobes maroon or violet. Java.

E. javanica (Sw.) Bl. Rhiz. long. Pbs ovoid to compressed pyriform, to 15cm. Lvs 2, to 30×8cm, lanceolate, thick, obscurely grooved with dark scurf when young. Infl. erect, exceeding lvs, narrow-cylindric; fls numerous, to 4cm diam., star-like, cream to white, sometimes flecked or lined maroon. Summer. Across range.

E. meirax (King & Pantl. N.E. Br. = *Porpax meirax*.

E. ornata (Bl.) Lindl. Rhiz. long. Pbs elliptic-oblong to lanceolate, to 11×5cm. Lvs usually 4, to 20cm, thick, elliptic. Rac. to 45cm, ascending to arching, rusty tomentose; bracts orange or red-brown; fls 1–5cm diam.; sep. pale yellow-green, pubesc.; pet. streaked and dotted purple; lip white marked purple with crispate, violet margins. Java.

E. rigida Bl. Pbs stem-like, to 1m+, curved, hanging. Lvs coriaceous, narrow-lanceolate, to 14cm. Infl. many, lat.; bracts red-green; fls solitary, to 1.5cm diam., white; column base with orange papillae. Borneo.

E. rosea Lindl. Pbs ovoid or conic. Lvs linear-lanceolate to oblong, coriaceous, to 22cm. Fls 3–4, rose or white suffused rose; lip crenate and undulate. China, Hong Kong.

E. rugosa Lindl. = *E. javanica*.

E. spicata (D. Don) Hand.-Mazz. Pbs to 20cm, oblong or broadly ellipsoid. Lvs 4, apical, fleshy, lanceolate, to 20cm. Infl. to 15cm, arching; fls crowded, white to straw-coloured, glab. or sparsely softly pubesc., lightly fragrant, seldom opening fully. Nepal, N India, Burm.

E. stellata Lindl. = *E. javanica*.

E. suavis (Lindl.) Lindl. = *E. coronaria*.

E. velutina Lodd. ex Lindl. = *Trichotosia velutina*.

E. vestita Lindl. = *Trichotosia vestita*.

→*Trichosma*.

Eriastrum Wooton & Standl. Polemoniaceae. 14 ann. or perenn. herbs, sparsely hairy to woolly or arachnoid. Fls in clusters surrounded by bracts; cal. lobes 5, subulate, pungent, sinuses filled by a hyaline membrane; cor. funnelform to sub-hypocrateriform, 5-lobed; sta. 5, exserted or included. W US. Z8.

E. densifolium (Benth.) H.L. Mason. Woody-based, erect perenn. to 1.2m. Lvs 2–5cm, entire or pinnatifid, lobes linear, pungent. Infl. term., sessile, arachnoid, many-fld; bracts needle-shaped; cor. 1.5–2.5cm, blue, tube white to yellow; sta. exserted. S Coastal Calif., Baja Calif. ssp. *densifolium* To 30cm tall, (sub)glabrous. Fl. heads usually 25-fld or more; cor. 2.2–2.5cm, limb dark blue. Late spring–early autumn. ssp. *austromontanum* (Craig) H.L. Mason. To 40cm, subglabrous. Fl. heads usually *c*20-fld; cor. 1.5–1.9cm, limb dark blue. Late spring–early autumn. ssp. *elongatum* (Benth.) H.L. Mason. To 1m, woolly. Fl. heads to 20-fld; cor. 1.5–1.6cm, limb blue-violet to dark blue. Late spring–early autumn.

→*Gilia*.

Erica L. HEATH; HEATHER. Ericaceae. 735 woody everg. prostrate subshrubs to small trees. Lvs whorled, rarely opposite, needle-like, revolute. Fls in pseudoterminal 1–30-fld heads or, more commonly, 1–3 per axil on short lat. br., the whole often resembling a pan. or clustered rac.; cor. campanulate to urceolate, free lobes short, 4–5. Afr., Madag., Middle E, Eur., Atlantic Is.

E. annectens Guthrie & Bol. Erect, spreading shrub, to 1m; younger br. finely hairy. Lvs 6–10mm, in whorls of 4–6. Fls 2–6, term. or subterminal; cor. 20–24mm, tubular, orange-red. Summer. S Afr. Z9.

E. arborea L. TREE HEATH. Arborescent shrub, to 4m+. St. hairy. Lvs to 5mm, in whorls of 4, occas. 3, dark green. Fls in lax pyramidal rac. to 40cm, fragrant; cor. to 4mm, campanulate, white tinged grey. Late spring. SW Eur., Medit., N Afr., C E Afr. (mts). 'Albert's Gold': to 1.2m; lvs golden throughout year; fls white. 'Alpina': to 2m, hardier, fls rather later in denser rac. 'Estrella Gold': to 90cm; lvs golden; fls white,. fragrant. 'Spring Smile': lvs light green tipped pink-yellow in winter; fls white. Z7.

E. australis L. SPANISH HEATH. Erect shrub, to 2m. Br. soft-hairy when young. Lvs to 6mm, in whorls of 4. Fls 4–8 in short lat. br.; cor. to 9mm, tubular to campanulate, red-pink, lobes reflexed; anth. barely exserted. Spring–summer. W Iberian Penins., Tangier. 'Aragonensis': to 1.5m high; lvs fine, densely arranged; fls smaller, pink-red, more abundant. 'Holehird': fls dark, lilac-pink. 'Mr Robert': lvs light green; fls white. 'Riverslea': narrower habit, lvs dark green; fls slightly larger lilac-pink. 'Wishanger Pink': fls purple-pink. Z9.

E. axilliflora Bartling. Erect, to 50cm, sparsely branched. Lvs 4–8mm, in whorls of 4–6, erect, overlapping. Fls at ends of short lat. branchlets clustered up main br.; cal. small, red; cor. 5–7mm, bell-shaped, deep red-pink, slightly sticky. Late summer. S Afr. Z9.

E. azorica Hochst. = *E. scoparia* ssp. *azorica*.

E. baccans L. Erect, much-branched, to 2m. Lvs 5–7mm, in whorls of 4, erect, overlapping. Fls in whorls of 4 at ends of branchlets, scattered over the shrub; cal. large, pink; cor. 5–6mm, globose, bright rose-pink. Winter–spring. S Afr. Z10.

E. bauera Andrews. BRIDAL HEATH. Open, sparsely branched, to 1.5m. Lvs in whorls of 4, spreading, blue-green, 4–5mm. Fls pendent, in compact pseudospikes; cal. small, white or pink; cor. 15–20mm, tubular, inflated, white or pale pink. All year, mainly summer. S Afr. Z10.

E. bergiana L. Erect, to 0.5m, br. hairy. Lvs 3–6mm, in whorls of 4, spreading, hairy. Fls subpendent in whorls of 4 at ends of lat. branchlets; cal. small, pink; cor. 3.5–7mm, globose, deep purple-pink. Summer. S Afr. Z9.

E. blandfordia Andrews. Erect to 1m, br. finely hairy. Lvs 3–4mm, in whorls of 4, erect to spreading. Fls subpendent, mostly in whorls of 4 at ends of br.; cal. small, green; cor. 5–8mm, tubular, conical, yellow. Winter–early summer. S Afr. Z9.

E. blenna Salisb. CHINESE LANTERN HEATH. Erect shrub, to 1.2m, br. finely hairy to glab. Lvs 8–10mm in whorls of 3. Fls subpendent, in whorls of 3 at ends of short lateral branchlets; cal. small, green; cor. 9–15mm, ovoid-conical, sticky, bright orange with green tips. Mainly winter and spring. S Afr. var. *grandiflora* Bol. Rather sparse, finely branched shrublet, to 0.5m. Fls usually solitary; cor. 16–20mm, conical. Z9.

E. bowiena Lodd. = *E. bauera*.

E. bryantha Thunb. = *Bryanthus gmelinii*.

E. caffra L. Erect to 4m, br. hairy. Lvs 8–12mm, in whorls of 3, grey, hairy. Fls pendent, in whorls of 3 or subumbellate; cal. small, green; cor. 5–7mm, conical, finely hairy, white to pale green. Spring–early summer. S Afr. Z10.

E. campanularis Salisb. Compact, wiry, to 0.5m. Lvs 3–5mm, in whorls of 3. Fls subpendent at ends of lat. branchlets; cal. small, green; cor. 5–7mm, bell-shaped, bright yellow. Late winter–spring. S Afr. Z9.

E. campanulata Andrews = *E. campanularis*.

E. canaliculata Andrews. Erect, to 2m, br. grey, hairy. Lvs 4–10mm, in whorls of 3. Fls whorled at ends of branchlets; cal. small, white; cor. to 3.5mm, cup-shaped, purple-pink, dark anth. visible at mouth; style far exserted. Through the year. S Afr. 'Rosea': fls rosy-pink. Z8.

E. carnea L. WINTER HEATH. Dwarf shrub, to 25cm. St. procumbent. Lvs to 8mm, in whorls of 4, linear. Rac. to 10cm, term., somewhat secund, leafy; cor. to 6mm, cylindric, purple-pink; anth. exserted. Late winter–early spring. E Eur. (C Alps, NW It., NW Balk.). 'Adrienne Duncan': vigorous, longer flowering period; lvs dark tinged bronze; fls deep rose. 'Amy Doncaster': fls salmon-pink. 'Atrorubra': growth somewhat prostrate; lvs green tinged blue; fls carmine, late-flowering. 'Aurea': lvs golden throughout year; fls lilac-pink. 'Cecilia M. Beale': habit low, globose, to 15cm; br. erect; fls pure white. 'Challenger': lvs dark green; fls deep magenta. 'December Red': fls red. 'Foxhollow': vigorous to 20cm; lvs yellow-green; fls white fading to pink. 'Gracilis': habit open, elegant; lvs fine, deep green; fls pale pink. 'Loughrigg': to 15cm; lvs light green often shaded blue; fls bright purple, abundant. 'Myretoun Ruby': fls intense rosy pink; lvs dark green. 'Pink Spangles': strong grower, to 30cm; fls dark pink-red, abundant, large. 'Praecox Rubra': to 15cm, widely branching; fls dark pink, long-lasting. 'Queen of Spain': habit open; lf tips deflexed; fls pale pink. 'R.B. Cooke': lvs mid-green; fls lavender, v. abundant. 'Ruby Glow': fls carmine red; lvs dark green, bronzed in autumn. 'Springwood Pink': long br.; fls clear pink, abundant. 'Springwood White': lvs bright green; fls pure white. 'Vivelli': lvs dark green with bronze hue; fls deep rose-pink. 'Wentwood Red': habit compact; lvs dark; fls magenta deepening with age. 'Winter Beauty': habit dense and compact to 15cm; lvs dark; fls deep pink, v. abundant. Z5.

E. casta Guthrie & Bol. Erect to 0.5m. Lvs 6–12mm, in whorls of 6, erect, crowded. Fls in pseudospikes below ends of main br.; cal. dark red; cor. 10–14mm, tubular, white, occas. pink, slightly sticky. Winter–spring. S Afr. Z9.

E. cerinthoides L. Erect, to 1.5m. Lvs to 16mm, in whorls of 4–6, gland., hairy. Fls in umbels; cal. small, red; cor. 22–36mm, tubular, inflated, bright red, occas. pale pink or white, gland., hairy. Throughout the year. S Afr., Swaz. var. *barbertona* (Galpin) Bol. Cor. 12mm, broadly tubular. Z10.

E. chamissonis Klotzsch ex Benth. GRAHAMSTOWN HEATH. Erect, to 0.6m, br. finely hairy. Lvs 3–5mm, in whorls of 3, erect to spreading, rough-hairy. Fls in whorls of 3 at ends of br., crowded over plant; cal. small, white, finely hairy; cor. 3.5–5mm, cup-shaped, glab., purple-pink with dark anth. visible. Spring. S Afr. Z10.

E. ciliaris L. DORSET HEATH. Spreading shrub, to 80cm. Lvs to 4mm, in whorls of 3(–4), ovate to lanceolate, usually gland., ciliate, revolute. Infl. term., racemose; cor. to 12mm, long-urceolate, curved above, deep pink-red; anth. included. Late summer–autumn. SW Eur., SW Engl., Eire. 'Aurea': lvs yellow; fls pink, sparse. 'Camla': growth broad, bushy; lvs coarse; fls pink-red, large, abundant. 'Corfe Castle': to 30cm; lvs mid-green, bronze-green in winter; fls rose-pink. 'David McClintock': to 40cm; fls base white, lips purple. 'Egdon Heath': lvs grey-green; fls pink. 'Globosa': fls large, lilac-pink. 'Maweana': to 30cm, strong, upright, narrow; fls large, dark flesh-pink. 'Mrs C.H. Gill': to 30cm, compact, bushy; lvs dark green; fls red. 'Stapehill': to 25cm; br. long-flowering; fls off-white turning purple. 'Stoborough': lvs mid-green; fls white. 'Storbaye': fls white. 'White Wings': lvs dark grey-green; fls white. 'Wych': to 45cm, fls cream flushed pink in long heads. Z7.

E. cinerea L. BELL HEATHER. Low shrub, to 60cm. Young twigs short-hairy. Lvs to 5mm+, in whorls of 3, linear, revolute. Rac. or umbel term.; pedicel downy; cor. 5-7mm, red, pink or white, urceolate; anth. included. Summer. W Eur. 'Apricot Charm': habit neat, compact; lvs pale yellow turning to apricot-orange in winter; fls mauve, sparse. 'Cairn Valley': habit broad; fls pink fading to near white. 'Eden Valley': habit tidy, prostrate; fls lavender fading to white at base of cor. 'Foxhollow Mahogany': broad, open habit; br. somewhat pendulous; fls dull magenta, abundant. 'Frances': strong, upright habit, providing neat cover; fls dusky rose. 'Golden Drop': habit mat-like; new growth tinged copper, later yellow-brown, coppery red in winter; fls lilac-pink. 'Hermann Dijkhuizen': to 35cm, tall, vigorous habit; lvs dark green; fls purple. 'Mrs Dill': dwarf to 10cm, habit nearly hemispherical; lvs bright green; fls dark pink. 'Pink Ice': habit dwarf, twiggy to 15cm; fls rose-pink. 'Sherry': habit compact; fls ruby. 'Alba Minor': habit neat, dense to 15cm; fls white, abundant. 'Atrorubens': to 20cm, broad; lvs grey-green; fls deep magenta, abundant. 'C.D. Eason': to 20cm; lvs deep green, fls glowing pink. 'C.G. Best': fls salmon-pink on long upright rac. 'Domino': to 20cm; br. pale grey turning green; fls off-white with brown anth. turning black. 'Jack London': lvs yellow-green throughout the year; fls pale mauve. 'Katinka': to 30cm; lvs dark green; fls black-purple. 'Knap Hill Pink': lvs dark green; fls magenta. 'Pallas': to 35cm; fls pure lilac, abundant. 'Pink Foam': fls delicate pink. 'Pink Ice': to 20cm; lvs deep green, bronzed when young and in winter; fls large, pure soft pink. 'Robert Michael': habit erect to 30cm; fls deep pink. 'Schizopetala': to 35cm; fls v. deeply split with 4 lobes, pale lilac. 'Velvet Night': lvs v. dark; fls purple-black. 'Windlebrooke': lvs yellow turning orange-red in winter; fls purple. Z5.

E. coccinea L. Erect, to 1.2m, with numerous short, lat. branchlets. Lvs 4-8mm, in whorls of 3. Fls pendent, in pseudospikes; cor. 6-17mm, tubular, red to orange or yellow or green, or yellow and black, glab. or sticky; anth. far-exserted. S Afr. Z9.

E. codonodes Lindl. = *E. lusitanica.*

E. colorans Andrews. Erect, compact, to 1.5m, br. hairy. Lvs 3-4mm, in whorls of 4, glab. Fls on short lat. br. crowded into long spike-like clusters; cal. small, white; cor. 14-16mm, tubular with distinct swelling below mouth, white ageing deep pink. Mostly spring. S Afr. Z9.

E. conica Lodd. Erect, to 0.5m. Lvs 8-12mm, in whorls of 4-6, erect. Fls in pseudospicate clusters; cal. green; cor. 6-12mm, narrowly funnel-shaped to bell-shaped, slightly sticky, deep red-pink. Winter–spring. S Afr. Z9.

E. corsica DC. = *E. terminalis.*

E. cruenta Sol. Erect, to 1m. Lvs 5-8mm, in whorls of 3. Fls pendent or spreading at ends of lat. branchlets; cal. green; cor. 20-24mm, curved tubular, wine red, shiny. Summer–winter. S Afr. Z9.

E. cubica L. Erect, wiry, to 0.5m. Lvs 4-10mm, in whorls of 4. Fls pendent on 4-8mm stalks and in dense subumbels; cal. large, pink; cor. 3-6.5mm, cup-shaped, purple-pink, smooth; anth. with apical crests. Mainly spring–early summer. S Afr. Z9.

E. curviflora L. Erect to 1.6m, hairy. Lvs 3-7mm, in whorls of 4. Fls usually solitary on lat. br.; cal. green; cor. 20-38mm, tubular, sparsely hairy, red, pink, orange or yellow. Summer–winter. S Afr. Z9.

E. curvirostris Salisb. Low, compact, to 0.5m, br. finely hairy. Lvs 4-6mm, in whorls of 4, glab. Fls fragrant, in whorls of 3; cal. small, red; cor. 3-4.5mm, bell-shaped, pink. Late summer. S Afr. Z9.

E. daphniflora Salisb. Erect to 1m. Lvs 4-6mm, in whorls of 4. Fls in whorls of 4; cal. small, green; cor. 6-15mm, globose to conical-tubular, deep pink to white or yellow. Summer. S Afr. Z9.

E. ×darleyensis Bean. (*E. erigena* ×*E. carnea*.) As for *E. carnea*, but a more vigorous, bushy, multi-stemmed shrub, to 60cm. Lvs to 13mm. Fls white to rose pink. Winter–spring. 'Ada S. Collings': habit compact; lvs dark green; fls white. 'Arthur Johnson': infl. to 20cm; fls lilac-pink. 'Darley Dale': habit

broad, upright, open; lvs tipped cream in spring; fls pink. 'Erecta': habit bushy, open, upright; fls lilac-pink. 'Furzey': to 45cm; fls deep rosy pink. 'George Rendall': new growth pink and green. 'Ghost Hills': lvs light green tipped cream in spring; fls pink. 'Jack H. Brummage': lvs yellow throughout year; fls heliotrope. 'J.W. Porter': young shoots tipped red; fls red-purple. 'Kramer's Rote': lvs tinged bronze; fls magenta. 'Margaret Porter': habit neat; fls lilac. 'Silberschmelze' ('Molten Silver'): lvs deep green, tinged red in winter; fls silver-white. Z6.

E. densifolia Willd. Erect to 1.5m, br. slightly hairy. Lvs 3-5mm, in whorls of 3, densely crowded. Fls in densely packed pseudospicate clusters; cal. red; cor. 24-30mm, curved tubular, hairy, somewhat sticky, dark red with green-yellow mouth. Summer. S Afr. Z9.

E. denticulata L. SCENTED HEATH. Like *E. daphniflora* but fls usually white and scented of carnations. Spring. S Afr. Z9.

E. erigena R. Ross. IRISH HEATH. As for *E. carnea*, but erect, to 2m. Spring. Tangier, Iberian Penins., SW Fr., Eire. 'Alba Compacta': habit compact, neat; fls pure white. 'Brian Proudley': to 90cm, vigorous, erect; lvs bright green; fls white, abundant in long rac. 'Brightness': to 50cm; strongly branched; lvs tinged purple in winter, lightening to sea-green; buds deep bronze; fls red-purple. 'Coccinea': to 90cm; buds deep bronze; fls dark mauve tinged pink. 'Golden Lady': to 20cm, slow-growing; lvs golden yellow; fls white, sparse. 'Irish Dusk': lvs dark grey-green; fls rose-pink from salmon buds. 'Mrs Paris Lavender': habit upright to 45cm; fls mauve-blue. 'Nana': habit dense, compact to 45cm; lvs dull grey-green; fls pale pink. 'Superba': to 1.8m, strong, densely branched; lvs dark green; fls pale pink deepening with age, heavily scented. 'W.T. Rackliff': compact to 50cm; lvs rich green; fls white, abundant. Z8.

E. fairii Bol. Erect, stoutly branched, to 0.6m. Lvs 4-5mm, in whorls of 4-6, thick, coriaceous, minutely toothed. Fls pendent at ends of br., stalks like a swan's neck; cal. green; cor. 25-30mm, tubular, sticky, pink with green tips. Spring–early winter. S Afr. var. *imperialis* (Andrews) Bol. Smaller. Fls with inflated cor. Spring. Z9.

E. fastigiata L. FOUR SISTERS HEATH. Tightly erect, to 0.5m. Lvs 5-7mm, in whorls of 4. Fls erect, in whorls of 4 at ends of br.; cal. green; cor. 8-15mm, narrow-tubular, wine red with large, spreading, pale lobes with red ring in centre. Spring–early summer. S Afr. Z9.

E. formosa Thunb. Erect to 1m. Lvs 2-3mm, in whorls of 3, spreading, thick. Fls pendent, in whorls of 3 at ends of br.; cal. white; cor. to 4mm, globose, fluted, white, sticky. Winter–early summer. S Afr. Z9.

E. gilva Wendl. see *E. mammosa.*

E. glandulosa L. Erect to sprawling, to 1.5m, covered with gland. hairs. Lvs 4-10mm, in whorls of 4, on lat. branchlets. Fls spreading, 2-5 at ends of br.; cor. 18-26mm, tubular, curved, pink-orange with darker stipes and paler mouth. Throughout the year. S Afr. Z9.

E. glauca Andrews. CUP-AND-SAUCER HEATH. Erect, to 2m. Lvs in whorls of 3, somewhat glaucous. Fls spreading to subpendent, pseudo-umbellate; bract and bracteoles enlarged, wine-red; cal. saucer-like, wine-red; cor. 8-10mm, flask-shaped, plum-red with brown tips. Summer. S Afr. var. *elegans* (Andrews) Bol. PETTICOAT HEATH. To 1m. Fls pendent, in heads surrounded by enlarged pale pink bracts; cal. large, pale pink, obscuring pale green cor. Spring. SW Cape. Z9.

E. glomiflora Salisb. Erect to 1.5m, br. with v. short hairs. Lvs 2-6mm, in whorls of 3. Fls crowded toward ends of main br.; cal. green; cor. 5-8mm, ovoid, white tinged pink, shiny, sometimes sticky. Spring, early summer. S Afr. Z9.

E. gracilis Wendl. Compact, finely branched, to 0.5m. Lvs 2-4mm in whorls of 4. Fls in whorls of 4 at ends of br.; cal. green or red; cor. 3-4mm, ovoid, glab., pale to deep pink. Summer. S Afr. 'Glasers Rote': lvs adpressed; fls dark red, luminous. 'Globularis': fls in several colours, small, abundant, long-lasting. Z10.

E. grandiflora L. f. Erect to 1.5m, br. slightly hairy. Lvs 16-20mm, in whorls of 6. Fls in pseudospicate clusters; cal. green; cor. 24-28mm, tubular, with spreading lobes, dry and shiny to slightly sticky, orange to red. Summer–winter. S Afr. var. *exsurgens* (L. f.) E. Oliv. Lvs longer. Fls yellow. Summer–early winter. S Afr. Z9.

E. halicacaba L. Erect, sometimes procumbent, to 0.5m. Lvs 8-14mm, in whorls of 3, closely set. Fls pendent, in whorls of 1-3 cal. broad, white; cor. 16-22mm, ovoid, green-cream to white. Spring. S Afr. Z9.

E. hebecalyx Benth. V. similar to *E. speciosa*, *E. dichrus* and *E. diaphana*, but cal. woolly and cor. sometimes uniformly green. Summer. S Afr. Z9.

E. herbacea L. = *E. carnea.*

E. hibernica (Hook. & Arn.) Syme = *E. erigena.*

E. ×*hiemalis* hort. FRENCH HEATHER; WHITE WINTER HEATHER. Small shrub, to 60cm. Lvs to 5mm, in whorls of 4, linear, light green. Rac. term.; fls 2–8 at br. apices; cor. to 1.5cm, tubular, white suffused pink; anth. dark brown. Winter. Origin unknown; name often used for hybrids produced in the UK. 'Prof. Diels': fls long, tubular, scarlet with grey-blue shading. 'Inspector Vorwerk': cor. long, tubular, purple with white crown. 'Osterglocken': fls long, tubular, dark pink. 'Ostergruss': habit compact; fls tubular, long, pink-purple. Z8.

E. *hirtiflora* Curtis. Erect to 0.5m. Lvs in whorls of 4, hairy. Fls semi-pendent, in whorls of 4 at ends of br.; cal. green; cor. 3–4mm, ovoid, purple-pink, hairy. Spring–summer. S Afr. Z9.

E. *lateralis* Willd. Erect to slightly spreading, to 1m, br. hairy. Lvs 4–8mm, in whorls of 4. Fls in whorls of 4 at ends of br.; cal. small, green to red; cor. 4–8mm, ovoid, glab., pale to deep pink. Winter–spring. S Afr. Z9.

E. *longifolia* Ait. Erect to 1m. Lvs 8–20mm, in whorls of 6, mostly erect to spreading. Fls in subterminal pseudospikes; cal. green; cor. 12–22mm, tubular, red, pink, white, green, yellow or bicoloured pink and white or red and yellow, glab. to sparsely hairy or sticky. Throughout the year. S Afr. Z9.

E. *lusitanica* Rudolphi. PORTUGUESE HEATH. As for *E. arborea*, but less stout, to 3.5m, unbranched when young. Lvs to 7mm; cor. 5mm, narrow-campanulate, pink in bud, later white. Spring–early summer. W Iberian Penins. to SW Fr., nat. SW Engl. 'George Hunt': lvs yellow; fls white. Z8.

E. *mackaiana* Bab. Shrub, to 50cm. Decumbent to erect, young br. hirsute. Lvs in whorls of 4, oblong lanceolate, slightly revolute, usually gland. Infl. term., umbellate; cor. to 7mm, urceolate, pink; anth. included, anth. appendages long. Spain, Ireland. 'Ann D. Frearson': to 10cm, habit broad, compact; fls semi-double, lilac-pink. 'Donegal': fls larger. 'Dr Ronald Gray': to 15cm; fls white. 'Lawsoniana': to 15cm; lvs short, wide, dark green; fls pale pink. 'Maura': to 15cm; lvs grey-green; fls semi-double, heliotrope, abundant. 'Plena': to 15cm; fls double, magenta. 'Shining White': lvs dark green; fls clear white. Z3.

E. *mackaii* Hook. = **E.** *mackaiana*.

E. *macowanii* Cufino. Erect, to 2m, br. hairy. Lvs 6–9mm, in whorls of 4, erect-incurved. Fls often crowded into pseudospikes; cal. green; cor. 20–24mm, tubular, with a bulge below apex, sparsely and shortly hairy, dark red tipped yellow-green or plain yellow-green. Spring and early summer. S Afr. Z9.

E. *mammosa* L. Erect, to 1.5m, br. finely hairy. Lvs 6–10mm, in whorls of 4. Fls pendent in subterminal pseudospikes; cal. green; cor. 15–20mm, tubular, sometimes curved, with 4 distinctive indentations near base, dark wine red to orange pink or pale green. Summer–winter. S Afr. Z9. *E. gilva* is v. similar but with green-white fls and much longer pseudospikes. Z9.

E. *manipuliflora* Salisb. As for *E. vagans*, but lvs short, in whorls of 3. Fls in pseudowhorls. SE It., Balk. 'Aldburgh': habit upright; lvs dark on white st.; fls lilac-pink in short terminal clusters, fragrant. 'Ian Cooper': habit broad, spreading; lvs small, grey-green; fls pale pink. 'Korcula': habit broad, open; fls white tinged pink, large, in long sprays. Z9.

E. *mariae* Guthrie & Bol. Erect to 1m, glab. Lvs 6–10mm, in whorls of 6. Fls in dense pseudospike clusters; cal. red; cor. 20–24mm, tubular, with glab., shiny, dark red. Spring, summer. S Afr. Z9.

E. *mauritanica* L. Erect, compact, to 0.5m, br. finely hairy. Lvs 2–4mm, in whorls of 4, erect. Fls erect at ends of branchlets; cal. green or red; cor. 2–3mm, cup-shaped, with a depression below sinus of lobes, pale pink. Winter. S Afr. Z9.

E. *mediterranea* L. non hort. = **E.** *carnea*.

E. *mediterranea* auct. non L. = **E.** *erigena*.

E. *mediterranea* var. *hybrida* hort. = **E.** ×*darleyensis*.

E. *melanthera* L. Erect, to 0.6m, br. finely pubesc. Lvs 2–4mm in whorls of 3, thick. Fls pendent, in small groups at ends of lat. branchlets; cal. white; cor. 3.5–4mm, cup-shaped, pale pink to deep red-pink; anth. black. Spring, early summer. S Afr. Z8.

E. *melanthera* Lodd. non L. = **E.** *canaliculata*.

E. *monsoniana* L. f. Erect, to 1.5m, br. dendroid, hairy. Lvs 4–6mm, in whorls of 3, erect, infl. lvs often expanded and tinged white. Fls pendent, in compact pseudospikes; cal. large; cor. 18–20mm, elongate-ovate, white. Winter–spring. S Afr. Z9.

E. *multicaulis* Salisb. = **E.** *terminalis*.

E. *multiflora* L. Not cultivated; plants grown under this name are a form of *E. vagans*.

E. *nana* Salisb. Compact, low to 15cm. Lvs 4–8mm, in whorls of 4. Fls pendent, in whorls of 3; covering whole plant; cal. green; cor. 20–22mm, tubular, yellow, waxy. Spring. S Afr. Z9.

E. *oatesii* Rolfe. Erect, to 1.5m, br. hairy. Lvs 6–9mm, in whorls of 3 or 4, roughly hairy. Fls subumbellate on ends of lat. br.; cal. green; cor. 10–13mm, ovoid-tubular, smooth or finely hairy, pink to scarlet. Autumn–winter. S Afr., Les., Swaz. Z9.

E. *pageana* L. Bol. Erect to 0.5m with finely hairy br. Lvs 5–8mm, in whorls of 4, packed. Fls in groups of 3–4 at ends of

lat. branchlets; cal. green; cor. 6–8mm, tubular-campanulate, finely hairy, yellow. Spring. S Afr. Z9.

E. *parilis* Salisb. Erect, to 0.6m, br. stout, hairy. Lvs 5–8mm, in whorls of 3–6. Fls spreading to pendent, in pseudospicate clusters; cal. green; cor. ovoid, bright yellow, smooth; anth. dark. Summer. S Afr. Z9.

E. *patersonia* Andrews. Erect, to 0.5m. Lvs 8–12mm, in whorls of 4, erect, incurved. Fls in densely packed pseudospikes; cal. green; cor. 14–18mm, tubular, waxy, golden yellow with small, darker lobes. Winter. S Afr. Z10.

E. *persoluta* L. = **E.** *subdivaricata*.

E. *perspicua* Wendl. PRINCE OF WALES HEATH. Much-branched, fastigiate, to 2m. Lvs 3–4mm, in whorls of 3 or 4. Fls in loose pseudospikes to 30cm; cal. green; cor. 16–24mm, tubular; white or pale pink to deep mauve-pink with white tips, finely hairy. Spring–early summer. S Afr. Z10.

E. *peziza* Lodd. Erect to 1.5m, br. woolly. Lvs 3–4mm, in whorls of 3. Fls pendent, crowded over whole plant; cal. green; cor. 3–5mm, cup-shaped, white, hairy. Spring. S Afr. Z10.

E. *pinea* Thunb. Erect to 1.5m. Lvs 12–16mm, in whorls of 6, densely erect to incurved. Fls in dense pseudospicate clusters near ends of br.; cal. green; cor. 20–24mm, tubular, glab., green-yellow, mouth white, pale yellow or white; anth. dark, visible. Late summer. S Afr. Z9.

E. *plukenetii* L. Erect to 0.6m. Lvs 12–16mm, incurved and densely overlapping. Fls pendent, in subterminal pseudospikes; cor. 12–20mm, tubular-ovoid to tubular, glab., red to pink, rarely white; anth. far-exserted. Spring–summer. S Afr. Z10.

E. ×*praegeri* Ostenf. = **E.** ×*stuartii*.

E. *quadrangularis* Salisb. Compact to 0.5m, br. finely hairy. Lvs 1.5–3mm, in whorls of 4. Fls in whorls of 4 at ends of br.; cal. green to red; cor. 2–2.5mm, bell-shaped, deep to pale pink or white, glab. Late winter, summer. S Afr. Z9.

E. *regia* Bartling. ELIM HEATH. Erect, much-branched, to 1m, br. finely hairy. Lvs 6–12mm, in whorls of 6. Fls in dense subterminal pseudospikes; cal. red; cor. 14–18mm, tubular, waxy, white with upper third red and purple band between. Spring. S Afr. Z10.

E. *regia* var. *variegata* Bol. = **E.** *regia*.

E. *scoparia* L. BESOM HEATH. Slender, erect shrub, to 6m. Lvs in whorls of 3–4, linear, to 7mm, shiny. Infl. narrow, racemose, leafy; cor. to 3mm, campanulate, green tinged red; anth. included. SW Fr., Spain, N Afr., Canary Is. 'Lionel Woolner': habit loose, open, erect; lvs light green; fls small, magenta. 'Minima': habit neat; lvs light green; fls green tinged brown, small, sparse. 'Pumila': habit dense, to 30cm; lvs glossy. ssp. *scoparia*. To 2.5m. Cor. to 3mm; stigma included. ssp. *azorica* (Hochst.) D.A. Webb. To 6m. Cor. to 3× cal. length; stigma exserted. Z9.

E. *sessiliflora* L. f. Erect to 2m. Lvs 4–14mm, in whorls of 6. Fls in dense subterminal pseudospikes to 60mm; cal. green; cor. 16–30mm, tubular, pale green, glab. Fruiting 'heads' protected by subsucculent sep. Autumn–spring. S Afr. Z9.

E. *sitiens* Klotzsch. Erect to 1m, br. finely hairy. Lvs 3–8mm, in whorls of 4. Fls spreading to subpendent, at ends of lat. branchlets; cal. green; cor. 6–8mm, elongate bell-shaped, glab., white to pink or deep red-pink with white tips. Summer. S Afr. Z9.

E. *sparsa* Lodd. Erect, to 0.5m, br. covered with short, grey hairs. Lvs 2–3mm, in whorls of 3. Fls crowded over whole plant; cal. large, broad, pink; cor. 1.5–2mm, cup-shaped, smooth, pale purple-pink; anth. dark. Spring–autumn. S Afr. Z9.

E. *speciosa* Andrews. Erect, to 1.5m. Lvs 4–9mm, in whorls of 3, suberect to spreading, hairy. Fls in whorls of 3, occas. solitary; cal. green; cor. 20–30mm, tubular, shiny, sometimes sticky, orange to pink-red with green mouth. Throughout the year. S Afr. Z10.

E. *spumosa* L. Erect to 0.3m, br. wiry, finely hairy. Lvs 2–3mm, in whorls of 3. Fls in nodding, 3-fld heads; cal. large, pink, papery; cor. 3–3.5mm, ovoid, just visible, pale pink; anth. dark, exserted. Spring. S Afr. Z9.

E. *stricta* Donn ex Willd. = **E.** *terminalis*.

E. ×*stuartii* Linton. (*E. mackaiana* ×*E. tetralix*.) As for *E. mackaiana*, sep. hairy, ovary shortly hairy. Summer–autumn. W Ireland. 'Connemara': habit dense to 15cm; fls magenta, abundant. 'Irish Lemon': fls pale mauve, large, new growth tipped lemon in spring. 'Irish Orange': lvs dark green tinged orange in spring; fls clear pink. 'Charles Stewart' ('Stuartii'): lvs grey-green tipped coral in spring; fls pale pink tipped maroon. Z9.

E. *subdivaricata* Berg. Erect to 0.5m, br. thin, finely hairy. Lvs 3–4mm, in whorls of 4, erect to spreading. Fls in whorls of 4, at ends of br., profusely borne over the plant; cal. green; cor. 3–4mm, bell-shaped, white, rarely rosy. Late summer. S Afr. Z10.

E. *taxifolia* Ait. Erect, rounded, to 0.6m, br. finely hairy. Lvs 8–12mm, in whorls of 3, slightly blue-green. Fls erect, in subumbellate clusters; cal. large, pink; cor. 6–9mm, ovoid, pale pink with darker lobes soon becoming brown. Summer. S Afr. Z9.

E. *tegulifolia* Salisb. Erect, to 1m, br. stout, hairy. Lvs in whorls of 3, closely adpressed, 3–6mm. Fls pendent, in whorls of 3; cal. large, pink to dark red; cor. 5–7mm, ovoid, pink to dark red. Spring. S Afr. Z9.

E. *terminalis* Salisb. CORSICAN HEATH. To 2.5m. Br. suberect, slightly hairy when young. Lvs in whorls of 4, linear, dark green, puberulent when young. Infl. appearing umbellate; cor. rose-pink, urceolate, to 7mm, anth. included. Summer. SW Medit. 'Thelma Woolmer': fls darker pink. Z9.

E. *tetralix* L. CROSS-LEAVED HEATH. Dwarf shrub, to 35cm; branchlets puberulent. Lvs to 6mm, in whorls of 4, lanceolate to linear oblong, ciliate. Infl. umbellate; cal. villous; cor. to 9mm, pale pink. Summer–autumn. Iberian Penins., Fr., GB. 'Alba Mollis': vigorous; lvs silver-grey; fls white, abundant. 'Con Underwood': to 20cm; lvs grey-green, fls large, crimson. 'George Fraser': vigorous to 35cm; lvs grey-green; fls deep rose, abundant. 'Hookstone Pink': to 30cm, vigorous; lvs persistently silver-grey; fls clear pink. 'Ken Underwood': habit broad, upright, to 30cm; lvs grey-green; fls dusky cerise, abundant. 'Melbury White': to 20cm; lvs greyish; fls pure white in large clusters. 'Pink Star': habit wide, loose, low-growing to 15cm; lvs grey-green; fls dark pink, held upright. 'Rubra': v. compact, to 20cm; fls red. 'Ruby's Variety': fls bicoloured, white with purple tips. 'Silver Bells': fls white ageing to pale pink. Z3.

E. *tetralix* var. *praegeri* hort. = E. ×*stuartii*.

E. *thomae* L. Bol. Erect, to 1m, br. long, stout, grey-hairy. Lvs 15–20mm, in whorls of 7, erect to incurved. Fls in subterminal pseudospicate clusters; cal. green; cor. 25–30mm, tubular, v. sticky, white to maroon. Summer. S Afr. Z9.

E. *umbellata* L. DWARF SPANISH HEATH. Dwarf, to 80cm. Young branchlets hairy. Lvs to 4mm, in whorls of 3, linear. Infl. umbellate; cor. to 6mm, campanulate to ovoid, rose pink-purple; anth. exserted, chocolate brown. Late spring–early summer. W Iberian Penins., Tangier. Z9.

E. *vagans* L. CORNISH HEATH. Erect shrub, to 80cm, decumbent to ascending. Lvs in whorls of 4 or 5, to 11mm. Cor. to 4mm, cylindric to campanulate, lilac pink to white; anth. exserted, brown tinged purple. W Fr., Spain, Cornwall, Ireland. 'Alba': fls white, anth. dark brown. 'Cornish Cream': fls off-white in long, narrow, tapering spikes. 'Cream': lvs dull green, young shoots bright; fls white, anth. red to brown. 'Diana Hornibrook': habit dense, compact; fls red, abundant. 'Fiddlestone': robust; lvs dark; fls deep cerise. 'George Underwood': fls salmon-pink. 'Grandiflora': to 7cm, habit loose, vigorous; fls pink fading with age. 'Kevernensis Alba': to 30cm; fls white, in compact heads. 'Lyonesse': vigorous, compact; br. pale grey-yellow; fls white, anth. pale-brown, in dense rac. 'Mrs D.F. Maxwell': to 45cm; lvs dark green, fls deep rose in long rac. 'Nana': dwarf to 20cm, dense; lvs tinged yellow in winter; fls cream. 'Rubra': habit broad, bushy; fls dark maroon in long rac. 'St Keverne': to 45cm, bushy; fls more bell-shaped, bright-pink. 'Valerie Proudley': habit broad, upright; lvs light yellow; fls white, insignificant. 'Viridiflora': fls small, both blue-green and mauve. Z5.

E. ×*veitchii* Bean. (E. *arborea* ×E. *lusitanica*.) Shrub, to 2.2m. Habit as for E. *arborea*, but more vigorous; young br. hairy. Lvs similar to E. *lusitanica* in colour, cor. cylindric-globose; stigmas flattened, tinged pink; sta. pink. Spring. Gdn origin. 'Exeter': 1.9m; fls white, sweet scented, abundant, stigmas pink. 'Gold Tips': young shoot tips golden, fading to pale green. Z8.

E. *ventricosa* Thunb. Compact, much-branched, to 0.5m. Lvs 12–16mm, in whorls of 4, margins hairy. Fls in subumbellate clusters; cal. green; cor. 12–16mm, flask-shaped, waxy pink with paler lobes. Spring. S Afr. 'Grandiflora': fls large, pink-purple. Z10.

E. *versicolor* Wendl. Close to E. *speciosa*. Erect, to 2.5m. Lvs 4–7mm, in whorls of 3, erect to spreading. Fls in whorls of 3 at ends of lat. br.; cal. green; cor. 22–28mm, tubular, slightly curved, with small, spreading lobes, glab., sometimes sticky. Spring–early summer. S Afr. Z10.

E. *verticillata* Berg. Erect, to 1m with long br. from a bushy base. Lvs 4–6mm, in whorls of 4–6, dense. Fls in pseudospicate clusters; cor. 14–20mm, tubular, finely hairy, purple-pink. Summer. S Afr. Z9.

E. *verticillata* Forssk. non Berg = E. *manipuliflora*.

E. *vestita* Thunb. Erect, bushy, to 1m. Lvs 12.5–33mm, in whorls of 6, erect to spreading, tremulous. Fls in compact pseudospicate clusters; cal. green; cor. 17–25mm, trumpet-shaped, faintly hairy, white to crimson. Summer. S Afr. Z10.

E. ×*watsonii* Benth. (E. *ciliaris* ×E. *tetralix*.) As for E. *mackaiana*, but lvs. sep. and ovary hairy. Infl. a condensed rac.; anth. included. 'Ciliaris Hybrida': fls lilac-pink, new growth yellow. 'Cherry Turpin': lvs tinged grey; fls pale pink in

long rac. 'Dawn': to 20cm; foliage tinged yellow-orange at first; fls large, rich rose pink. 'Down': new growth red. 'F. White': fls v. pale pink, small, abundant. 'Gwen': to 15cm; lvs often tinged copper; fls pale pink with hint of lilac. 'H. Maxwell': tall to 30cm; young shoots golden orange; fls pink. 'Rachel': to 25cm; lvs dark green; fls dark pink. 'Truro': to 20cm; almost prostrate in habit, fls large, pink to crimson. Z5.

E. ×*williamsii* Druce. (E. *vagans* ×E. *tetralix*.) Habit as for E. *vagans*, to 75cm. Br. dense; young shoots soft hairy, new foliage yellow. Lvs 8mm, in whorls of 4, linear, margin short gland. hairy. Infl. a leafy rac., or an umbellate fascicle; cor. to 3mm diam., campanulate, rose pink, sta. included, anth. brown. SW GB. 'Gwavan': to 30cm; shoot tips golden yellow in spring; fls pale pink. 'P.D. Williams': to 30cm; shoot tips yellowish green in spring; fls pink. Z5.

E. *cvs*. 'Elegant Spike' (E. *manipuliflora* ×E. *vagans*): habit vigorous, upright; fls rose in long spikes. 'Pres. Carnot': st. woody; cor. tubes long, deep pink tipped white. 'Valerie Griffiths' (E. *manipuliflora* ×E. *vagans*): tall, bushy habit; lvs yellow deepening to gold in winter; fls pale pink. 'Ville de Cherbourg': small, growth starry; lvs narrow; fls ivory, jug-like. 'Wilmorei': lvs narrow, erect, in threes; fls large, in long leafy rac., tubular, rose tipped with white, long-lasting.

ERICACEAE Juss. 103/3350. *Agapetes, Agarista, Andromeda, Arbutus, Arcterica, Arctostaphylos, Bejaria, Bruckenthalia, Bryanthus, Calluna, Cassiope, Cavendishia, Chamaedaphne, Cladothamnus, Daboecia, Elliottia, Enkianthus, Epigaea, Erica, Gaultheria, Gaylussacia, Kalmia, Kalmiopsis, Ledum, Leiophyllum, Leucothoë, Loiseleuria, Lyonia, Macleania, Menziesia, Oxydendrum,* ×*Phylliopsis, Phyllodoce, Pieris, Rhododendron, Rhodothamnus, Tripetaleia, Tsusiophyllum, Vaccinium, Zenobia.*

Ericameria Nutt. Compositae. c7 everg. shrubs and subshrubs. Lvs narrowly linear and heath-like, rarely obovate to oblanceolate, entire, resinous-punctate. Cap. radiate or discoid, in term. pan., cymes or rac.; involucre turbinate; phyllaries leathery or papery; flts yellow. S & W N Amer.

E. *cuneata* (A. Gray) McClat. Shrub, to 1.5m. Lvs to 1cm, oblanceolate to obovate, obtuse, mucronate, base attenuate, dark green. Cap. radiate or discoid, solitary or in compact cymes; flts to 5m, or 0. Sierra Nevada.

E. *ericoides* (Less.) Jeps. MOCK HEATHER. Compact shrub, to 1m. Lvs crowded or in fascicles, to 5mm, linear-terete, sparsely pubesc. Cap. radiate, in corymbose pan.; flts to 5. Calif.

E. *parishii* (Greene) H.M. Hall. Subshrub or shrub, to 1m. Lvs to 5cm, oblanceolate or linear, acute, base attenuate. Cap. discoid, in term. cymes to 5cm high; flts 10–12. Calif.

Erigenia Nutt. Umbelliferae. 1 low, tuberous perenn. to 20cm. Lvs 6–11cm, 1–3-ternate, seg. linear to spathulate, to 12mm, glab.; petioles to 2cm. Umbels to 6cm diam. with 3–6 rays; involucral bracts 1 to few, simple to 5cm; bracteoles entire to deeply lobed, exceeding fls; pet. white, entire; sta. maroon. Spring. NE US.

E. *bulbosa* (Michx.) Nutt. HARBINGER-OF-SPRING; PEPPER-AND-SALT.

Erigeron L. FLEABANE. Compositae. c200 ann. and perenn. herbs. Lvs radical and cauline, usually shorter, narrower and ± sessile on st., entire to divided. Cap. radiate, rarely discoid, scapose, solitary, or in small clusters; disc flts yellow. Cosmop., esp. N Amer.

E. *acer* L. BLUE FLEABANE. Ann. to bienn. herb, erect to 2cm. Lower lvs to 8cm, obovate-lanceolate, entire, shortly petiolate. Cap. to 2cm diam., several, in a corymbose pan.; ray flts erect, pale purple. Summer. Temp. N hemis.

E. *acris* L. = E. *acer*.

E. *alpinus* L. Coarsely hairy perenn. herb, to 40cm. Lower lvs to 8cm, narrow-elliptic to spathulate, acute, shortly petiolate, hispid. Cap. to 3.5cm diam., usually solitary; ray flts slender, lilac. Summer. Mts S & C Eur. Z5.

E. *annuus* (L.) Pers. Erect perenn. herb, to 1m. Lower lvs spathulate, scabrous above, st. lvs to 9cm, dentate, to entire and lanceolate, sessile. Cap. few to many, in an irregular corymb or pan.; ray flts white. N Amer., widely nat. Z3.

E. *aphanactis* (A. Gray) Greene. Spreading, hirsute, perenn. herb, to 30cm. Basal lvs to 8cm, linear-oblanceolate to spathulate, long-petiolate, ray flts 0. Cap. solitary, or several. SW N Amer. Z4.

E. *arenarius* Greene = E. *bellidiastrum*.

E. *asper* Nutt. = E. *glabellus*.

E. *asperugineus* (Eaton) A. Gray Pubesc. spreading to erect perenn. herb, to 20cm. Lower lvs to 8cm, obovate or elliptic, long-petiolate. Cap. solitary; ray flts 10–25, deep blue to red-purple. NW US. Z4.

E. atticus Vill. Glandular-hairy erect perenn. herb to 50cm. Lower lvs to 25cm, oblong-lanceolate, mucronate, hispid, gland. hairy, base tapered to petiole. Cap. 3–10+, in a branched, corymbose pan.; ray flts many, purple. Mts Eur. Z6.

E. aurantiacus Reg. ORANGE DAISY. Mat-forming, velvety, perenn. herb, to 30cm. Lower lvs to 9.5cm, spathulate-oblong, petiolate, entire. Cap. to 5cm diam., solitary, on stout scapes; ray flts bright orange-yellow. Summer. Turkestan. Z6.

E. aureus Greene. Perenn. herb, to 20cm. Lvs finely, or villous-hirsute, to 8cm, broadly elliptic to obovate, petiolate. Cap. solitary; ray flts to 1cm, 25–70, yellow. Summer. NW N Amer. Z5.

E. barbellatus Greene. Perenn. herb, to 20cm. Lvs to 4cm, in a basal tuft, oblanceolate, obtuse or rounded, finely strigose, petioles of lowest lvs enlarged, lustrous, tinged purple. Cap. solitary; ray flts to 12mm, 15–35, pale blue or purple. Calif. Z6.

E. basalticus Hoover. Perenn. herb, to 30cm, spreading or pendulous. Lvs to 4cm, cuneate to obovate, petiolate, trilobed, lobes entire or 1–2-dentate. Cap. to 12mm diam., term.; ray flts to 7.5mm, 25–30, lilac. NW US. Z5.

E. bellidiastrum Nutt. Ann. herb, to 50cm. Lvs to 4cm, oblanceolate to linear, entire or apex 3-toothed, petiole to 4cm. Cap. numerous; ray flts to 6mm, 30–70, pink or white. C US. Z4.

E. bellidifolius Muhlenb. ex Willd. = *E. pulchellus*.

E. bloomeri A. Gray. Perenn. herb, to 20cm, glab. to white-strigose, much-branched, slender. Lvs to 7cm, linear. Cap. discoid, solitary. W US. Z4.

E. borealis (Vierh.) Simmons. ALPINE FLEABANE. Perenn. herb, to 30cm. Lvs to 5cm, narrowly spathulate, rounded, glab., petiolate. Cap. to 1.5cm diam., solitary, occas. 2–3; ray flts numerous, lilac. Summer. NW Eur. Z6.

E. caespitosus Nutt. Perenn. herb, to 40cm, sometimes decumbent. Lvs to 12cm, oblanceolate to spathulate, obtuse, 3-nerved, grey-pubesc., petiole to 12cm. Cap. solitary or few; ray flts numerous, white, pink or blue. W & C N Amer. Z4.

E. canadensis L. = *Conyza canadensis*.

E. capensis Houtt. = *Vernonia capensis*.

E. caucasicus Steven. Perenn. herb, to 40cm. Lvs to 25cm, oblanceolate or spathulate, entire. Cap. to 3.5cm diam., solitary or few in a corymb; ray flts numerous, white-lilac. Turk. to Iran. Z7.

E. cinereus Hook. & Arn. Perenn. herb, to 50cm, erect, densely hispid. Lower lvs to 10cm, in a loose basal rosette, oblanceolate-spathulate, pubesc., tapered to petiole, entire. Cap. solitary, or few in a loose pan.; ray flts white or pink. Andes. Z8.

E. compositus Pursh. Perenn. herb, to 30cm. Lvs gland.-hirsute, basal lvs 3–4-ternately lobed or dissected. Cap. solitary, on erect scapes; ray flts to 12mm, (0–)20–60, white, pink or blue. Greenland, W N Amer. var. *glabratus* Macoun. Lvs 2–3-ternate, lobes linear-oblong. NW US. var. *discoideus* A. Gray. Lvs 1-ternate. 'Albus': fls white. Z5.

E. concinnus (Hook. & Arn.) Torr. & A. Gray. = *E. pumilis* ssp. *concinnoides*.

E. coulteri Porter. Perenn. herb, to 70cm. Lvs hirsute, dentate, to 15cm, oblanceolate to elliptic, petiolate. Cap. 1–3; ray flts to 2.5cm, numerous, white. Summer. Rocky Mts. Z5.

E. delicatus Cronq. Slender perenn. herb, to 40cm. Lower lvs to 3cm, oblanceolate, obtuse or rounded, glab., petiole to 4cm. Cap. 1 or 2; ray flts c40, blue. Calif. Z7.

E. delphinifolius Willd. Stout-stemmed, short-lived perenn. herb, to 1m. Lvs deeply pinnatifid with narrow lobes, hirsute, often gland., most upper eglandular. Cap. several, in an open corymb; ray flts to 13mm, numerous, white. CS US. ssp. *neomexicanus* (A. Gray) Cronq. St. hairs spreading. Ray flts wider. CS US, New Mex. Z8.

E. divaricatus Nutt. = *E. divergens*.

E. divergens Torr. & A. Gray. Ann. to short lived perenn. herb to 80cm. Lvs hirsute, to 2.5cm, oblanceolate to spathulate, petiole to 5cm, usually entire. Cap. several; ray flts to 1cm, numerous, blue or pink to white. Late spring–summer. C & SW US. Z4.

E. eatonii A. Gray. Perenn. herb, to 30cm, usually decumbent. Lower lvs to 15cm, linear. Cap. usually solitary; ray flts 20–50, white, occas. pink or blue. NW US. Z4.

E. elatior (A. Gray) Greene. Perenn. herb, to 65cm. Lower lvs entire, acute, villous to 10cm, oblanceolate to narrowly elliptic, petiolate. Cap. usually solitary. ray flts numerous, pink to purple. WC US. Z4.

E. elegantulus Greene. Perenn. herb, to 20cm. Lvs to 6cm, in a basal rosette, narrow-linear, with enlarged bases, sparsely strigose. Cap. solitary; ray flts 15–20, blue or pink. W US. Z6.

E. elongatus Ledeb. = *E. acer*.

E. eriocephalus Vahl = *E. uniflorus* ssp. *eriocephalus*.

E. eucephaloides Greene = *E. speciosus* var. *macranthus*.

E. filifolius Nutt. Perenn. herb, to 50cm. Lvs to 8cm, linear to linear-filiform. Cap. solitary to several; ray flts several to numerous, blue, pink or white. W US. Z4.

E. flagellaris A. Gray. Bienn. to short lived perenn., trailing, stoloniferous. Lvs hirsute or strigose with adpressed hairs, lower lvs to 5cm, oblanceolate, obtuse or acute, petiolate, entire to pinnately lobed. Cap. solitary; ray flts to 1cm, numerous, white, pink or blue. C US. Z4.

E. flettii G.N. Jones. Perenn. herb, to 20cm, usually erect. Lvs to 5cm, mostly basal, oblanceolate or spathulate, rounded, glab. to hirsute, petiolate, ciliate. Cap. solitary; ray flts to 2.5mm, many, white. NW US. Z5.

E. foliosus Nutt. Perenn. herb, erect to 15cm. Lvs to 8cm, linear-filiform to narrowly oblong. Cap. several or numerous; ray flts to 1.5cm, many, blue. W US. var. *confinis* (Howell) Jeps. To 30cm. Lvs crowded, glab. or minutely hairy. Z5.

E. formosissimus Greene. Perenn. herb, to 40cm, slender, ± decumbent, gland. Lvs to 15cm, mostly basal, oblanceolate to spathulate or elliptic, rounded or obtuse, tapered to winged petiole. Cap. 1–6; ray flts numerous, blue, pink or rarely white. S Rocky Mts. Z6.

E. frigidus Boiss. ex DC. Tufted, densely pubesc. perenn. herb, to 10cm. Lower lvs to 3.5cm, narrow-spathulate, long- and short gland. hairy, entire. Cap. to 13mm diam., solitary; ray flts to 8mm wide, in 2–3-series, lilac. Summer. S Spain. Z8.

E. gilliesii hort. = *E. cinereus*.

E. glabellus Nutt. Bienn. to perenn. herb, to 50cm. Lower lvs to 15cm, oblanceolate, acute or obtuse, rarely rounded. Cap. 1–15; ray flts to 1.5cm, numerous, blue, pink, or white. Summer. Alask. to WC US. ssp. *pubescens* (Hook.) Cronq. St. hairs usually long, coarse, spreading. Z2.

E. glabratus Hoppe & Hornsch. ex Bluff & Fingerh. Slender perenn. herb, to 40cm. Lower lvs to 7cm, narrowly spathulate, sparsely ciliate to subglabrous, petiole attenuate. Cap. to 2cm diam., 1–2; ray flts spreading, lilac, rarely white. Summer–early autumn. S & C Eur. Z6.

E. glaucus Ker-Gawl. SEASIDE DAISY; BEACH ASTER. Perenn. herb, to 50cm, tufted succulent. st. stout, sprawling. Lvs to 15cm, basal, broadly spathulate to obovate, rounded, tapered to winged petiole. Cap. 1–15; flts numerous, lilac to violet. Summer. W US. 'Albus': fls white. 'Elstead Pink': fls dark pink. 'Roseus': fls pink. Z3.

E. grandiflorus Hook. Perenn. herb, to 30cm. Lvs hirsute-pilose, to 9cm, oblanceolate, acute, occas. obtuse, base narrowed to petiole. Cap. solitary; ray flts numerous, blue or white. Midsummer. Rocky Mts. Z5.

E. hispidus Nutt. = *E. glaucus*.

E. howellii A. Gray. Perenn. herb, to 50cm. Lvs mucronate, glab., ciliate, occas. dentate, to 8cm, elliptic to orbicular; petiole to 12cm. Cap. solitary; ray flts many, white. Oreg. Z6.

E. humilis Graham. Perenn. herb, to 20cm. Lvs villous to villous-hirsute at first, to 8cm, oblanceolate to spathulate. Cap. solitary; ray flts to 6mm, numerous, white to purple. Arc. and subarc. Z2.

E. × hybridus hort. A name applied to an extremely variable hybrid group, probably originating from crosses between *E. atticus* × *E. aurantiacus*. Perenn. herbs, to 30cm. Cap. to 2.5cm diam.; ray flts apricot to violet rose. *E. × hybridus* has been crossed in turn with various spp. including *E. elatior*, *E. coulteri*, *E. peregrinus* ssp. *callianthemus*, *E. speciosus* var. *macranthus*, giving rise to leafy perenn. herbs with ray flts of various shades of pink and blue to lilac. See *E. speciosus*. Z6.

E. hyperboreus Greene = *E. caespitosus*.

E. hyssopifolius Michx. Perenn. herb, to 40cm. Lvs to 3cm, linear or linear- to lanceolate-oblong, acute or obtuse, glab., entire, ciliate. Cap. solitary scapose; ray flts to 8mm, many white or pink. NE N Amer. Z4.

E. karvinskianus DC. Woody-based perenn. herb or subshrub, to 80cm, st. slender, decumbent. Lvs to 4cm, elliptic-lanceolate or obovate-cuneate, acute, thinly pubesc., entire to finely toothed or slightly pinnatifid. Cap. solitary, or in a loose pan. of 2–5; ray flts numerous, white or pink, becoming red-purple. Mex. to Panama. Z7.

E. leiomerus A. Gray. Perenn. herb, to 10cm. Lower lvs to 7cm, spathulate to oblanceolate or obovate, glab., petiolate. Cap. solitary; ray flts several to many, blue to nearly white. Rocky Mts. Z3.

E. linearis (Hook.) Piper. Perenn. herb, to 25cm. Lvs to 9cm, linear to linear-oblanceolate, strigose. Cap. solitary, occas. 2–3; ray flts to 11mm, yellow. WC & SW US. Z4.

E. macranthus Nutt. = *E. speciosus* var. *macranthus*.

E. mairei Braun-Blanquet. Tufted perenn. to 7.5cm, st. hairy. Lvs to 5cm, mostly basal, linear-oblong. Cap. to 1.5cm diam., solitary; ray flts to 3mm, lilac. N Afr. Z8.

E. melanocephalus (Nels.) Nels. Perenn. herb, to 20cm. Lvs to 6cm, mostly basal, oblanceolate or spathulate, glab. or slightly hirsute. Cap. solitary; phyllaries purple-villous; ray flts many, to 11mm, white or pink. SW US. Z8.

E. miyabeanus Tatew. & Kitam. Densely pubesc. perenn. herb, to 20cm. Basal lvs 3.5cm, elliptic, rounded or obtuse. Cap. to 3.5cm diam., solitary; ray flts to 13mm, blue-purple. Summer. Jap. Z6.

E. montanensis Rydb. = E. ochroleucus.

E. mucronatus DC. = E. karvinskianus.

E. multifidus Rydb. = E. compositus var. glabratus.

E. multiradiatus (Lindl.) C.B. Clarke. HIMALAYAN FLEABANE. Perenn. herb, to 30cm. Lower lvs to 6cm, oblanceolate to lanceolate, narrowed to petiole, entire or coarsely toothed. Cap. to 5cm diam., solitary or few; ray flts long, slender, pink-purple. Summer. Himal. from Pak. to Bhutan. 'Roseus': flts pink. Z6.

E. myosotis Pers. Perenn. herb, to 30cm. Lower lvs to 10cm, oblanceolate, hirsute, tapered to petiole, entire. Cap. 1–6; ray flts to 6mm, numerous, white or lilac. Patagonia. Z8.

E. nanus Nutt. Tufted perenn. herb, to 10cm. Lvs to 4cm, in a tufted, basal cluster, linear-oblanceolate. Cap. solitary; ray flts several, violet or purple. WC US. Z3.

E. neomexicanus A. Gray = E. delphinifolius ssp. neomexicanus.

E. nudicaulis Michx. = E. vernus.

E. ochroleucus Nutt. Perenn. herb, to 40cm. Lower lvs to 12cm, linear to linear-oblanceolate, strigose to subglabrous. Cap. solitary or few; ray flts few to many, blue, purple or white. WC US to SW Canada. var. **scribneri** (Canby ex Rydb.) Cronq. To 10cm. Lower lvs to 6cm. Involucre rarely to 7mm; phyllaries barely purple-tinged. Z4.

E. oharai (Nak.) Botsch. Perenn. herb, to 4cm, st. slightly woody. Lower lvs 7.5cm, rosulate at first, obovate or orbicular, gland.-pubesc., petiole to 4.5cm, winged, obtusely toothed to entire. Cap. solitary and terminal; ray flts to 12mm; many, white-purple or -blue. Summer–early autumn. Jap., Korea. Z7.

E. oreganus A. Gray. Perenn. herb, to 15cm, decumbent or weakly erect, gland., viscid-villous. Lower lvs to 9cm, tufted, spathulate to obovate, gland., coarsely toothed or incised, short-petiolate to sessile. Cap. 1 to several; ray flts several to many, pink or white. NW N Amer. Z6.

E. peregrinus (Pursh) Greene. Perenn. herb, to 70cm. Lower lvs to 20cm, linear-oblanceolate to oblanceolate or spathulate, petiolate. Cap. commonly solitary, occas. to 8; ray flts several to many, white to purple. Mts of W N Amer. ssp. **callianthemus** (Greene) Cronq. St. robust, leafy. Ray flts several, rose-purple. Z2.

E. philadelphicus L. Bienn. to short lived perenn. herb, to 80cm. Lower lvs to 15cm, oblanceolate to obovate, rounded, crenate or lobed. Cap. 1 to several in corymbs; ray flts to 1cm, numerous, pale red-purple. Summer. N US and Canada. Z2.

E. pinnatisectus (A. Gray) Nels. Tufted perenn. herb, to 10cm. Lvs mostly basal, linear, pinnatifid, petioles bristly-ciliate. Cap. solitary; ray flts to 12mm, several to many, blue or purple. C US. Z4.

E. poliospermus A. Gray. Perenn. herb, to 20cm, hispid-hirsute, gland. Lower lvs to 8cm, linear-oblanceolate to spathulate. Cap. solitary; ray flts few to several, pink or purple to deep violet, occas. inconspicuous. NW N Amer. Z4.

E. pulchellus Michx. ROBIN'S PLANTAIN. Bienn. to short-lived perenn. herb, to 70cm. Lower lvs to 12cm, spathulate, entire or toothed. Cap. 1–6, in a corymb; ray flts blue, pink or rarely white. E & SC US. Z4.

E. pumilis Nutt. Perenn. herb, to 50cm. Lvs to 8cm, oblanceolate to linear-oblanceolate, hirsute. Cap. 1 to several; ray flts many to numerous, white, occas. pink to blue. C US. ssp. **concinnoides** Cronq. Cap. several; ray flts commonly pink or blue. W US. Z4.

E. purpuratus Greene. Perenn. herb, to 10cm, finely gland. Lvs to 3cm, oblanceolate or spathulate, villous at first, entire to 3-toothed or 3-lobed. Cap. solitary; ray flts to 6mm, many, white, becoming purple-tinged. W Canada, Alask. Z3.

E. radicatus Hook. Perenn. herb, to 10cm. Lvs to 2cm, mostly in basal rosette, oblanceolate or linear-oblanceolate, glab. to sparsely hairy, ciliate. Cap. solitary; ray flts several, white. Rocky Mts. Z5.

E. roylei DC. Robust, hispid perenn. herb, to 15cm. Lvs to 8cm, oblong-spathulate, mucronate, ciliate. Cap. to 5cm diam., many in a loose corymb; ray flts purple. India. Z9.

E. salsuginosus auctt. = E. peregrinus ssp. callianthemus.

E. scribneri Canby ex Rydb. = E. ochroleucus var. scribneri.

E. simplex Greene. Tufted perenn. herb, to 30cm, st. viscid-villous. Lower lvs to 7.5cm, oblanceolate or spathulate, glab. to moderately hirsute, ciliate. Cap. solitary; ray flts numerous, blue, pink or white. WC US. Z4.

E. speciosus (Lindl.) DC. Perenn. herb, to 80cm. Lvs mostly

glab., entire, ciliate, basal and lower lvs to 15cm, oblanceolate to spathulate, tapered to winged petiole. Cap. solitary to few; ray flts numerous, blue or rarely white. Mts of NW US. 'Adria': to 60cm, large, bright violet-blue. 'Charity': pale lilac. 'Darkest of All' ('Dunkelste Aller'): to 45cm; dark violet. 'Dignity': to 45cm; pink. 'Dimity': to 30cm; pink and orange. 'Förster's Darling' ('Förster's Liebling'): semi-double, dark pink. 'Lilofee': to 60cm, semidouble, dark lilac. 'Märchenland' ('Fairyland'): to 60cm, large, soft pink, semi-double. 'Pink Jewel': pale lilac-pink. 'Quakeress': to 70cm, white flushed pink. 'Rosa Triumph': to 60cm, bright pink, semi-double. 'Rotes Meer': deep red. 'Schneewittchen': pure white. 'Schwarzes Meer': dark violet. 'Sincerity': to 75cm; lilac. 'Sommerneuschnee': white to pale pink. 'Strahlenmeer' ('Shining Sea'): to 70cm, light violet. 'Violetta': to 70cm, dark violet, v. double. 'Wuppertal': semi-double, light violet. ssp. **macranthus** (Nutt.) Cronq. Phyllaries glab. not gland.-hairy. Z3.

E. subtrinervis Rydb. Perenn. herb, to 1m, st. pubesc. Lower lvs 3-nerved, pubesc., entire, ciliate, to 13cm, oblanceolate, tapered to petiole. Cap. 1–21; ray flts numerous, blue or rose-purple. NW N Amer. to SC US. Z4.

E. thunbergii A. Gray. Perenn. herb, to 40cm, st. densely pubesc. Lower lvs 8cm, spathulate-oblong, ± glab., occas. few-toothed. Cap. to 3.5cm diam., solitary; ray flts to 1.5cm, in 3-series, blue-purple. Late spring–early summer. Jap. Z7.

E. trifidus Hook. = E. compositus var. discoideus.

E. turneri Greene = E. glabellus ssp. pubescens.

E. tweedyi Canby. Perenn. herb, to 20cm. Lvs grey, silky-strigose-pubesc., lower lvs to 2.5cm, ovate to elliptic or ± orbicular, petioles to 4cm. Cap. 1–4; ray flts several, blue to purple, occas. white. NW US. Z3.

E. uniflorus L. Perenn. herb, to 15cm, st. hairy. Lower lvs to 5cm, spathulate, rounded, sparsely pubesc. at first. Cap. to 1.5cm diam., solitary; ray flts white to pale lilac. Summer–early autumn. Circumpolar and mts of Eurasia. ssp. **eriocephalus** (Vahl) Cronq. To 35cm. Lower lvs oblanceolate, occas. spathulate. Phyllaries red-purple. Arc. Z2.

E. ursinus Eaton. Perenn. herb, to 30cm. Lvs glab. to sparsely hirsute-strigose, lower lovs to 12cm, oblanceolate, petiolate, ciliate. Cap. solitary; ray flts several to numerous, blue, occas. pink-purple. NW US. Z3.

E. vagus Pays. Perenn. herb, to 30cm, spreading-hirsute to densely gland. Lvs to 2cm, crowded, commonly 3-lobed, petiolate. Cap. solitary, on scapes to 5cm; ray flts to 7mm, several, pink or white. W US. Z4.

E. vernus (L.) Torr. & A. Gray. Bienn. to short-lived perenn., to 50cm. Lower lvs to 10cm, oblanceolate to orbicular, glab., denticulate, petiole short, winged. Cap. several, in a loose corymb; ray flts to 8mm, several to many, white. Z8.

E. villarsii Bellardi = E. atticus.

→Aster, Haplopappus and Vittadinia.

Erinacea Adans. Leguminosae (Papilionoideae). 1 everg., mound-forming shrub, to 30cm, branchlets thorn-like. Lvs dark, 1–3-foliolate, lfts to 0.5cm, narrow-oblanceolate. Fls to 2cm, pea-like, 2–4 per cluster, pale blue, indigo or purple. Summer. W Medit. to E Pyren. Z8.

E. anthyllis Link. HEDGEHOG BROOM; BRANCH THORN; BLUE BROOM.

E. pungens Boiss. = E. anthyllis.

→Anthyllis.

Eringoe Eryngium.

Erinus L. Scrophulariaceae. 2 perenn. herbs. Lvs entire. Rac. term.; cal. lobes 5; cor. tube cylindric, lobes 5, acute. Summer. N Afr., S & C Eur. Z6.

E. alpinus L. ALPINE BALSAM; LIVER BALSAM. To 30cm, carpeting, tufted, sticky. Lvs 5–20mm, oblanceolate to cuneate, crenate-serrate. Cor. 6–10mm diam., purple, sometimes white, 2 upper lobes narrower than lower. Summer. S & C Eur. 'Albus': fls white. 'Carmineus': fls red. 'Dr Hahnle': fls deep crimson. 'Lilacinus': fls violet. 'Mrs Charles Boyle': fls pink. 'Pikos de Europa': to 13cm high; lvs v. small; fls light pink. 'Roseus': fls pink.

Eriobotrya Lindl. Rosaceae. 10 everg. shrubs or trees. Lvs simple, coriaceous, dentate, veins impressed; petiole short. Fls small, white, 5-merous, with many sta., in broad pyramidal, usually dense, hairy panicle., term. pan. Fr. an obovoid to globose pome, with persistent cal. teeth at apex; seeds v. large. E Asia.

E. buisanensis (Hayata) Mak. & Nemoto = E. deflexa var. buisanensis.

E. deflexa (Hemsl.) Nak. Tree to 10m. Lvs to 25cm, obovate-oblong to elliptic, obtuse, coarsely toothed, glab., dark green above, paler beneath, veins in 13–15 pairs. Infl. rusty brown-pubesc. Fr. ellipsoid, to 2.5cm, tomentose. China, Taiwan. 'Bronze Improved': lvs vivid bronze when young, later rich green. var. *buisanensis* (Hayata) Kanehira & Sasaki. Lvs to 15cm, oblong to lanceolate, apex usually acuminate-acute or obtuse. Taiwan. var. *koshunensis* Kanehira & Sasaki. Lvs to 15cm, obovate-oblong, obtuse at apex. Taiwan. Z9.

E. grandiflora Rehd. & Wils. Tree to 10m. Lvs to 16cm, elliptic-oblong, apex obtuse or cuspidate, tomentose, later glab., with 10–12 pairs of veins. Pan. to 10cm, tomentose. Fr. subglobose, 2.5cm diam., red-orange. W China. Z9.

E. hookeriana Decne. Small tree. Lvs to 30cm, elliptic-lanceolate, apex short-acuminate or acute, sharply toothed, 15–30 pairs of veins, glab. or woolly beneath. Pan. to 15cm, tomentose. Fr. ellipsoid, to 2cm, yellow. E Himal. Z9.

E. japonica (Thunb.) Lindl. LOQUAT; JAPANESE LOQUAT; JAPANESE MEDLAR; NISPERO. Tree to 7m. Br. stout, with pale golden, coarse, downy when young. Lvs to 25cm, broadly oblanceolate to narrow-obovate, apex acuminate, sometimes toothed, deep green, lanate-pubesc. above, later glossy, scurfy beneath. Fls in erect, crowded pan. Fr. globose to pyriform, to 4cm diam., yellow. Autumn–winter. China, Jap. 'Variegata': lvs variegated white. Z7.

E. prinoides Rehd. & Wils. Tree to 10m. Lvs to 12cm, elliptic, apex obtuse or subacute, glab. above, with grey down beneath, 10–12 pairs of veins. Pan. to 10cm, tomentose. Fr. ovoid to 1cm diam. SW China. Z9.

E. prionophylla Franch. = *Photinia prionophylla*.
→*Crataegus, Mespilus* and *Photinia*.

ERIOCAULACEAE Desv. 14/1200. *Eriocaulon*.

Eriocaulon L. Eriocaulaceae. 400 perenn., aquatic or marginal herbs. Lvs in a dense basal spiral clump, rush-like, linear, narrow. Fls small, in solitary, compact, woolly heads on erect, slender scapes. Trop., Subtrop., Jap., N Amer., Ireland, Hebrides.

E. aquaticum (Hill) Druce. PIPEWORT. Lvs to 10cm, tapering to a point. Scape to 60cm; rac. button-like, white, to 2cm diam. with grey involucre. N Amer., Ireland, Hebrides. Z5.

E. decangulare L. Lvs to 45cm, tapering bluntly. Scape to 110cm; rac. button-like, white, to 2cm diam., involucre white-hairy, reflexed. US. Z7.

Eriocephalus L. KAPOK BUSH. Compositae. 27 much-branched, rigid, often aromatic and silvery-pubescent shrubs. Lvs mostly linear. Cap. radiate, globose to cylindrical, solitary or in racemose or umbellate cluster. Seed heads cottony. S Afr.

E. africanus L. To 1m. Lvs to 2.5cm, linear or lobed, obtuse, channelled, pubesc., thick. Cap. in a term. umbellate cluster; ray fls 3–5, broad, white; disc fls deep purple. Winter–early spring. S Afr. Z9.

Eriocereus Riccob.
E. adscendens (Gürke) A. Berger = *Harrisia adscendens*.
E. bonplandii (Parmentier ex Pfeiff.) Riccob. = *Harrisia pomanensis*.
E. guelichii (Speg.) A. Berger = *Harrisia guelichii*.
E. jusbertii (Rebut ex Schum.) Riccob. = *Harrisia jusbertii*.
E. martinii (Labouret) Riccob. = *Harrisia martinii*.
E. pomanensis (F.A. Weber) A. Berger = *Harrisia pomanensis*.
E. regelii Weingart = *Harrisia regelii*.

Eriochilus R. Br. Orchidaceae. 5 terrestrial tuberous orchids. Lf basal, solitary, ovate-lanceolate. Scape slender; fls 1–6; dors. sep. erect, lanceolate, lat. sep. clawed, deflexed or spreading; pet. erect, shorter than or equalling sep.; lip apex sharply recurved, mid-lobe pubesc. Aus. Z9.

E. cucullatus (Labill.) Rchb. f. To 25cm. Lf to 3.5cm. Fls pale to bright pink or white; lat. sep. 1–1.7cm elliptic-lanceolate. Winter–mid spring. Aus. (except W Aus.).

E. dilatatus Lindl. To 15cm. Lf to 6cm. Fls white; lat. sep. 1.3–1.5cm, oblong-lanceolate; pet. dilated at red tip; lip blotched red. Early–mid summer. SW & W Aus.

Eriochloa HBK. CUP GRASS. Gramineae. Some 30 ann. or perenn. grasses. St. clumped. Infl. racemose or paniculate; spikelets 2-fld, solitary to clustered, elliptic, pubesc., with a beadlike structure at base. S US, Mex.

E. villosa (Thunb.) Kunth. HAIRY CUP GRASS. Ann., to 60cm. St. loosely clumped. Rac. 3–15, to 2cm; spikelets elliptic, pubesc., to 6mm; infl. axis conspicuously pubesc. Asia. Z9.

Eriodendron DC. = *Ceiba*.

Eriodictyon Benth. Hydrophyllaceae. 8 everg. shrubs, woolly or glab. and viscid. Lvs alt., simple. Infl. of scorpioid cymes; cal. lobes 5, often gland.; cor. funnelform, lobes 5. SW N Amer., Baja, Mex. Z8.

E. californicum (Hook. & Arn.) Torr. CONSUMPTIVE'S WEED; YERBA SANTA. Viscid shrub to 2.25m. Lvs to 15cm, lanceolate, entire, undulate or serrate, thickly viscid above, woolly-white beneath. Fls to 1.25cm, deep lilac to white. Calif., Oreg.

E. crassifolium Benth. Woolly shrub to 3m, often v. much shorter. Lvs to 15cm, lanceolate-elliptic, crenate to coarsely toothed. Fls mauve; cal. eglandular. S Calif.

E. crassifolium var. *niveum* (Eastw.) Brand = *E. tomentosum*.

E. lanatum (Brand) Abrams. Distinguished from *E. trichocalyx* by its pubesc. branchlets, hoary lvs and glandular-viscid cal. S Calif. to Baja and Mex.

E. niveum Eastw. = *E. tomentosum*.

E. tomentosum Benth. Woolly shrub to 2m. Lvs to 6.25cm, oblanceolate to elliptic, entire or toothed, thickly tomentose. Fls pale mauve to white; cal. gland. Calif.

E. trichocalyx A.A. Heller. Viscid, subglabrous shrub to 2m. Lvs to 10cm, lanceolate or ovate-lanceolate, serrate, resinous above, puberulent beneath. Fls lilac, mauve or white; cal. densely pubesc., eglandular. S Calif. to Baja Calif.

E. trichocalyx var. *lanatum* (Brand) Jeps. = *E. lanatum*.

Erioglossum Bl.
E. edule Bl. = *Lepisanthes rubiginosa*.
E. edule Bl. = *Lepisanthes rubiginosa*.
E. rubiginosum Bl. = *Lepisanthes rubiginosa*.
E. rubiginosum Bl. = *Lepisanthes rubiginosa*.

Eriogonum Michx. WILD BUCKWHEAT; UMBRELLA PLANT; ST. CATHERINE'S LACE. Polygonaceae. 150 ann. or perenn. herbs and small shrubs. Lvs in basal rosettes or cauline. Fls small, in heads, clusters, or umbels with a cup-like involucre of 4–10, toothed to lobed bracts. Fr. a 3-angled achene. US.

E. allenii S. Wats. UMBRELLA PLANT. Perenn. herb, 50–80cm, lvs ovate to oblong, long-petiolate; st. lvs whorled 3–5 at nodes, uppermost reduced. Fls many in flat-topped, branched clusters, bright yellow; involucre tomentose. Late summer–autumn. Virg. Z5.

E. annuum Nutt. White-tomentose ann. to 90cm. Lvs 3–5cm, oblong, slightly revolute, st. lvs reduced. Infl. an open, much-branched or compact flat-topped cyme; fls white to rose. Summer. S Dak. to Tex. Z4.

E. arborescens Greene. Shrub to 1.5m; st. thick, branchlets tomentose when young. Lvs linear or oblong, 2–3cm, revolute, white-tomentose beneath. Infl. dense, leafy, term. 5–15cm across; fls white to pale rose-pink; involucre tomentose. Calif. Z9.

E. auriculatum Benth. = *E. latifolium* ssp. *auriculatum*.

E. bakeri Greene = *E. jamesii* var. *bakeri*.

E. caespitosum Nutt. Mat-forming perenn. herb or subshrub. Lvs 0.5–1.5cm, elliptic to oblong-spathulate, revolute, densely white-tomentose. Fls in term. heads on 3–8cm, tomentose leafless st., yellow to red-tinged. Summer. W US. ssp. *douglasii* (Benth.) S. Stokes. Lvs 1–2cm, oblong to spathulate, not revolute. Fls larger, cream in round heads with an involucral whorl of leaf-like bracts midway on st. Washington to Calif. Z7.

E. cinereum Benth. Shrub, 60–150cm, white-tomentose. Lvs 1.5–3cm, ovate, obtuse, tomentose beneath, cinereous above, margin crisped. Infl. laxly branched, composed of numerous white to pink fl. heads and subtended by involucral lvs. Summer–autumn. Coastal S Calif. Z8.

E. compositum Douglas ex Benth. Perenn. herb or subshrub to 45cm, with woody rootstock; br. matted. Lvs 5–15cm, basal, oblong-ovate, hairy beneath; petiole long. Fls white, rose or pale yellow in simple or branched heads on leafless st. Summer. Washington to N Calif. Z5.

E. corymbosum Benth. Shrub 30–100cm; br. white-tomentose. Lvs 2–3cm, lanceolate, elliptic to rounded, white-tomentose beneath. Fls white tinged red or green to yellow-white in broad umbels; involucre tomentose. Summer–early autumn. Wyom., Colorado. Z5.

E. crocatum Davidson. SAFFRON BUCKWHEAT. Perenn. herb or subshrub to 20cm. Base woody with low, dense br. Lvs 1.5–3.5cm, broadly ovate or elliptic, white-felty. Fls sulphur-yellow in dense cymes to 8cm diam. Late spring–summer. Coastal S Calif. Z9.

E. depauperatum Small = *E. ovalifolium* var. *depauperatum*.

E. depressum (Blank.) Rydb. = *E. ovalifolium* ssp. *vineum* var. *depressum*.

E. douglasii Benth. = *E. caespitosum* ssp. *douglasii*.

E. elatum Douglas ex Benth. Perenn. woody-based herb, st. stout, to 80cm, villous. Lvs 7.5–20cm basal, lanceolate to lanceolate-ovate, loosely tomentose beneath. Fls white to pink, in scattered heads on a laxly branched infl. Summer. Washington to N Calif. and W Nevada. Z4.

E. fasciculatum Benth. CALIFORNIA BUCKWHEAT. Low rounded shrub, spreading to 90cm. Lvs 5–15mm, in tufts or clusters on br., margins inrolled. Fls in leafless, term. loosely arranged heads, white to pink-tinged. Summer. Calif., Utah, Nevada. 'Dana Point': habit low, fast-growing; lvs deep green. ssp. **foliolosum** (Nutt.) S. Stokes Pubesc. throughout. Calif., Baja Calif. ssp. **poliifolium** (Benth.) S. Stokes. 20–50cm, st. and lvs cinereous. Summer–autumn. Desert regions Calif., Utah, Nevada. Z7.

E. flavum Nutt. Hairy, low perenn. herb to 20cm, woody at base. Lvs 2–5cm, basal, obovate to oblanceolate, slightly hairy above to densely woolly beneath. Fls yellow in scapose, involucrate umbels. Manit. to Colorado and Idaho. ssp. **piperi** (Greene) S. Stokes. To 30cm. Lvs to 10cm, in mat-forming rosettes, lanceolate to spathulate, white-silky beneath. Fls yellow to green-yellow, often tipped scarlet, densely pubesc. Washington. Z5.

E. giganteum S. Wats. ST. CATHERINE'S LACE. Rounded shrub to 2.5m, central trunk to 10cm diam. Lvs 3–10cm, oblong to oblong-ovate, leathery, grey-white hairy above, white-tomentose beneath. Flowering st. 2–3-forked, fls white fading rusty red, white-woolly heads some 30cm across. Summer. Santa Barbara Is., S Calif. Z9.

E. glaberrimum Gand. = **E. umbellatum** var. **subalpinum**.

E. gracilipes S. Wats. = **E. kennedyi** var. **gracilipes**.

E. grande Greene = **E. latifolium** ssp. **grande**.

E. heracleoides Nutt. Loosely branched perenn. herb to 40cm. Lvs 3–8cm, linear-lanceolate or oblanceolate, loosely floccose above, white-tomentose beneath. Fls in compound umbel with lvs whorled below; white or tinged rose. NW US. Z6.

E. incanum Torr. & A. Gray = **E. marifolium** var. **incanum**.

E. jamesii Benth. Tufted or mat-forming perenn. herb with woody rootstock. Lvs in a basal rosette, spathulate to ovate, tomentose beneath, undulate. Fls white, cream or yellow, downy, in heads subtended by leafy bracts. Colorado, Utah, New Mex. var. **bakeri** (Greene) S. Stokes. Lvs elliptic-lanceolate. Fls yellow. Z4.

E. kennedyi Porter in S. Wats. SULPHUR FLOWER. Dense, woody-based, mat-forming. Lvs to 0.6cm, lanate, revolute. Flowerheads 1cm, white veined red, on stalks to 15cm. Sierra Nevada. ssp. **alpigenum** (M. & J.) S. Stokes. Lvs to 0.3cm. Flowerheads 2cm, red-tinted. ssp. **austromontanum** (M.E. Jones) S. Stokes. Lvs to 1cm. Flowerheads green-white on floccose stalks. ssp. **gracilipes** (S. Wats.) S. Stokes. Lvs 2cm, oval to oval-lanceolate. Flowerheads white-pink on stalks to 10cm. Z5.

E. kennedyi ssp. **pinorum** Stokes = **E. kennedyi** ssp. **austromontanum**.

E. latifolium Sm. Perenn. woody-based herb to 60cm; st., much-branched, densely leafy, withered lvs persisting. Lvs 2.5–5cm, oblong-ovate to orbicular, glab. above, white-woolly beneath, often crisped. Fls cream to white tinted rose, glab. or downy, in dense heads to 3cm diam. on leafless forked st. Summer. Oreg. to Calif. var. **rubescens** (Greene) S. Stokes. Lower and more sprawling; lvs large; fls clustered, rose-red. Calif. ssp. **auriculatum** (Benth.) S. Stokes. Lvs 3–7cm, elliptic to ovate, shorter than petioles. Fls usually cream-pink, occas. tinged yellow. Summer. Calif. ssp. **grande** (Greene) S. Stokes. Shrubby. Lvs 3–10cm, oblong-ovate, strongly undulate-crisped, white-woolly beneath; petiole exceeding lvs; fls white to pale pink. Summer–early autumn. S Calif. ssp. **nudum** (Douglas ex Benth.) S. Stokes. To 1m. Lvs 3–7cm, elliptic-ovate to oblong, undulate, usually shorter than petioles. Fls white, pink or yellow. Summer–early autumn. Calif. Z8.

E. lobbii Torr. & A. Gray. Low perenn. herb with stout rootstock, br. short, densely leafy, with persistent dead lvs. Lvs 1.5–3cm, ovate to rounded, white-tomentose becoming hirsute; petiole long. Fls white or rose, in umbels on 15–20cm st., subtended by leafy bracts. Calif., W Nevada. Z5.

E. marifolium Torr. & A. Gray. Low, mat-forming perenn. herb; br. leafy, glab. Lvs 2–4cm, elliptic, grey-tomentose beneath. Fls yellow fading to red in a term., scapose compound umbel, 2–20cm tall. Oreg. to Calif. var. **incanum** (Torr. & A. Gray) M.E. Jones. Forming a dense, woolly mat. Calif. Z6.

E. microthecum Nutt. Laxly branched subshrub to 30cm+. Lvs 10–25mm, linear to narrow-obovate, tomentose beneath. Fls yellow, white or pink in flat-topped heads to 6cm diam. Summer. N Amer. Z6.

E. niveum Douglas ex Benth. Perenn. to 30cm; rootstock woody, sparsely branched. Lvs 1.5–2.5cm, tufted, oblong-ovate, white-tomentose; petioles equal lvs. Fls cream, pink, or yellow in compound umbels. Summer. BC to Calif., Idaho. Z5.

E. nudum Douglas ex Benth. = **E. latifolium** ssp. **nudum**.

E. ochrocephalum S. Wats. Mat-forming tufted perenn. Lvs

1–3cm, oblanceolate or ovate, silvery-tomentose; petiole long. Fl. heads, scapose, yellow (rarely cream), 6–8-lobed tubular involucre. Summer. Idaho, Oreg., Calif. Z4.

E. ovalifolium Nutt. Silvery hairy mat-forming perenn. Lvs 5–15mm, broad-oblanceolate to elliptic. Scapes to 20cm; fl. heads to 2cm diam., spherical, cream to purple. Summer. NW US. ssp. **vineum** (Small) S. Stokes. Lvs 7–12mm, rounded-ovate. Scapes to 10cm; fls rose. Oreg., Calif. to Nevada. var. **depressum** Blank. Dwarf. Lvs to 1.5cm. Fls white with dark or rose midvein. Mont. to Oreg., Canada. var. **depauperatum** (Small) S. Stokes. Cushion-forming dwarf. Lvs slender, woolly. Fls pink in heads on short stalks. Z4.

E. parvifolium Sm. Resembling **E. fasciculatum** in habit. Lvs 5–15mm, ovate to oblong, tomentose beneath, revolute. Fls white or rose-tipped in heads or umbels, on st. to 5cm. Calif. Z9.

E. piperi Greene = **E. flavum** ssp. **piperi**.

E. poliifolium Benth. = **E. fasciculatum** ssp. **poliifolium**.

E. polyanthum Benth. = **E. umbellatum** var. **polyanthum**.

E. purpusii Brandg. = **E. kennedyi**.

E. pyrolifolium Hook. Perenn. woody-based herb. Lvs to 3cm, basal, round to obovate, leathery, smooth or woolly; petiole long. Fls white or rose in umbels on scapes to 10cm; involucre large, toothed. Summer. Mont. to Calif. Z4.

E. racemosum Nutt. Compact, sparsely branched herb. Lvs 2.5–3.5cm, basal, ovate to oblong-ovate, white-hairy beneath; petiole occas. longer than lf. Fls cream-white in a spike-like infl. on st. to 20cm. Summer. Nevada to New Mex. Z5.

E. rubescens Greene = **E. latifolium** var. **rubescens**.

E. saxatile S. Wats. Perenn. herb to 45cm. Lvs 1–2.5cm, crowded at base, rounded ovate to obovate, leathery, white-hairy. Flowering st. to 30cm, branching, leafless, tomentose; fls white to rose or yellow. Summer. S Calif. Z8.

E. speciosum Drew = **E. umbellatum**.

E. sphaerocephalum Douglas ex Benth. Shrubby perenn. to 25cm, erect or decumbent. Lvs 1–3cm, narrow-oblanceolate, white-tomentose beneath, often revolute. Fls cream-white in spherical involucrate clusters on a scape to 10cm. Washington to Calif. and Nevada. Z5.

E. subalpinum Greene = **E. umbellatum** var. **subalpinum**.

E. thymoides Benth. THYME-LEAVED ERIOGONUM. Subshrub to 5cm, much-branched, decumbent or erect. Lvs 0.3–1.5cm, linear-spathulate, white-tomentose beneath. Scapes 1–7cm, with whorl of bracts near midlobe; fls tomentose, pale yellow to pink or red. Early summer. NW US. Z5.

E. tomentosum Michx. Erect perenn. herb to 1m. Basal lvs 7–12cm, elliptic to oblong, tomentose beneath; petioles 5–7cm; st. lvs whorled. Fls in heads of 10–20, white to pink. Summer to early autumn. S Carol. Z8.

E. torreyanum A. Gray = **E. umbellatum** var. **torreyanum**.

E. umbellatum Torr. SULPHUR FLOWER. Perenn. herb or subshrub, low and spreading, rarely to 1m. Lvs to 2cm, in rosettes, spathulate to obovate, tomentose beneath; petiole equalling lf. Fls sulphur or cream in lax involucrate umbels, on scapes to 30cm. Summer. E Rocky Mts, SW Canada. var. **monocephalum** Torr. & A. Gray. More compact. Umbels simple. var. **polyanthum** (Benth.) M.E. Jones. Fls deep yellow to red-tinged. Calif. var. **stellatum** (Benth.) M.E. Jones. Fls in compound umbels. var. **subalpinum** (Green) M.E. Jones. Fls cream, rose with age. Rocky Mts, BC. Z3. var. **torreyanum** (A. Gray) M.E. Jones. Lvs dark green, glab. N Calif. to S Oreg. Z7.

E. vimineum Douglas ex Benth. Erect ann., 10–30cm; st. floccose-below. Lvs 1–2cm, usually basal, round-ovate, tomentose beneath, long petiole. Fl. heads along br., white to rose or tinged yellow. Summer. Washington, Oreg., Calif., Ariz. Z6.

E. vineum Small = **E. ovalifolium** ssp. **vineum**.

E. wrightii Torr. ex Benth. Low, branched subshrub to 40cm. Lvs 0.5–1.5cm, oblanceolate to elliptic, white-tomentose. Fls white or pink in tight heads arranged in a spike, on scapes to 25cm. Summer. Calif., Colorado to Tex. Z4.

Eriogynia Hook.
E. caespitosa S. Wats. = *Petrophytum caespitosum.*
E. hendersonii Canby = *Petrophytum hendersonii.*
E. uniflora S. Wats. = *Kelseya uniflora.*

Eriolobus M. Roem.
E. delavayi Schneid. = *Docynia delavayi.*
E. tschonoskii Rehd. = *Malus tschonoskii.*

Eriophorum L. COTTON GRASS. Cyperaceae. 20 perenn., grass-like herbs. St. tufted, leafy, 3-angled. Lvs slender, flat. Spikelets in a dense term. umbel or solitary; sep. and pet. represented by numerous soft, pale, cotton-like hairs, elongating in fr. to aid dispersal. Summer. Eur., N Amer., S Afr.

E. alpinum L. 15–40cm. St. triangular in section, scabrid above. Spikelets 8–12-fld, ellipsoid-lanceolate; glumes brown-yellow, oblong-lanceolate, blunt; bristles 4–6, white, to 2.5cm. Summer. N N Amer., N & C Eur. Z7.

E. angustifolium Honck. COMMON COTTON GRASS. 15–75cm. St. subterete, 3-angled at apex. Infl. an umbel; spikelets 3–7, drooping; glumes brown-red, dark at tip, lanceolate-ovate, hairs showy, white, cotton- or down-like, densely tufted, to 5cm. N Eur., N Amer., inc. Sib. and Arc. regions. 'Heidelicht': showy; glumes white. Z4.

E. chamissonis C.A. Mey. 10–80cm. St. subterete. Infl. a single term. spikelet, 15–20mm; glumes blunt, brown to dark grey, margins broad, white; hairs red-tinged to tawny, to 5cm. W N Amer. var. *albidum* (Nyl.) Fern. Hairs white. Z7.

E. latifolium Hoppe. BROAD-LEAVED COTTON GRASS. Similar to *E. angustifolium* except st. 3-angled, lvs 3–8mm wide. Eur., Turk., Sib., N Amer. Z8.

E. paniculatum Druce = *E. latifolium*.

E. ×polystachion L. (*E. angustifolium* × *E. latifolium*.) Similar to *E. angustifolium* except to 30cm, infl. hairs 3–4cm. Eur., Sib., N Amer. Z6.

E. scheuchzeri Hoppe. Similar to *E. vaginatum* except to 40cm, st. terete, lvs to 2mm wide, infl. hairs to 3cm. N Eur. to the Urals, C Eur. Z6.

E. vaginatum L. Tussock-forming, 30–80cm. St. terete at base, thereafter 3-angled. Lvs around 1mm wide. Infl. a simple term. spikelet, 2cm at flowering; hairs around 2cm, white. N Temp. regions. Z7.

E. viridicarinatum (Engelm.) Fern. 20–90cm. Lvs 2–6mm across, folded from mid-point to tip. Spikelets 2–10; glumes 4–10mm; bristles bright white. Summer. N N Amer., Eurasia. Z7.

Eriophyllum Lagasca. WOOLLY SUNFLOWER. Compositae. c12 tomentose, ann. to perenn. herbs and shrubs. Lvs alt., usually toothed or pinnatifid, in annuals often entire. Cap. usually radiate, in leafy cymose or corymbose clusters; ray flts usually yellow; disc flts usually yellow. W N Amer.

E. artemisiifolium Kuntze = *E. stoechadifolium*.

E. caespitosum Douglas ex Lindl. = *E. lanatum*.

E. confertiflorum (DC.) A. Gray. Subshrub to 60cm, branched below, erect above, slender. Lvs 1–4cm, 1–2-pinnatifid, lobes linear. Cap. sessile or subsessile, in term. clusters on br.; ray flts 2–4mm, few or 0. Spring–summer. Calif. to Baja Calif. Z8.

E. integrifolium (Hook.) Greene = *E. lanatum* var. *integrifolium*.

E. lanatum (Pursh) Forbes. Perenn., loosely tomentose. St. 20–60cm, erect or decumbent, stout. Basal lvs to 15cm, spathulate or oblanceolate, entire or lobed, st. lvs pinnatifid, upper lvs narrow, entire, glabrate above, white-lanate beneath. Cap. solitary or loosely corymbose; ray flts 1–2cm, 8–12, yellow. Late spring–summer. BC to N Calif. and W Mont. var. *integrifolium* (Hook.) Smiley. Lower lvs entire or apically 3–5-toothed or -lobed, st. lvs pinnatifid or pinnatisect with 3 seg. Ray flts 0.6–1cm. Calif. to Wyom. and Nevada. var. *lanceolatum* (Howell) Jeps. Lvs entire or coarsely serrate, lanate. Ray flts 0.7–1cm. Oreg. to Calif. Z5.

E. lanceolatum Howell = *E. lanatum* var. *lanceolatum*.

E. leucophyllum Rydb. = *E. lanatum* var. *integrifolium*.

E. monoense Rydb. = *E. lanatum* var. *integrifolium*.

E. multiflorum Rydb. = *E. lanatum* var. *integrifolium*.

E. nevinii A. Gray. Shrubby perenn. St. to 2m, decumbent, stout, leafy, tomentose. Lvs 8–20cm, broadly ovate, pinnatifid, 8–20cm, lobes narrow, tomentose. Cap. radiate, clustered in corymbose pan.; ray flts to 2mm. Spring–early autumn. Calif. Z8.

E. pedunculatum A.A. Heller = *E. lanatum*.

E. stoechadifolium Lagasca. Much-branched perenn., often forming a rounded shrub, to 1.5m. Lvs linear to linear-oblanceolate, entire or with few linear lobes, glab. above, densely tomentose beneath, revolute. Cap. in dense, branched clusters; ray flts 3–5mm, elliptic, sometimes 0. Spring–autumn. Calif. Z8.

E. wallacei A. Gray = *Antheropeas wallacei*.

→*Actinella, Bahia* and *Tricophyllum*.

Eriopsis Lindl. Orchidaceae. 6 epiphytic orchids. Pbs basally sheathed. Lvs 2–3, borne apically, lanceolate to oblanceolate, prominently veined beneath. Rac. basal; sep. subequal, fleshy, lanceolate to elliptic, dors. concave, lat. spreading; pet. narrower, spreading; lip obscurely obcordate, 3-lobed, disc crested. Trop. Amer. Z10.

E. biloba Lindl. Pbs to 45cm, cylindric to compressed-ovoid. Lvs to 40×8cm. Rac. to 1m; tep. 12–25mm, ivory to tawny yellow flushed oxblood; lip 12–23mm, lat. lobes yellow to tan flushed and veined oxblood, midlobe cream spotted maroon. Costa Rica to Peru.

E. rotudibulbon Hook. = *E. biloba*.

E. schomburgkii Rchb. f. = *E. biloba*.

Eriostemon Sm. Rutaceae. 33 subshrubs, shrubs or small trees. Branchlets glandular-punctate. Lvs simple, entire, glandular-punctate, sessile or short-petiolate. Fls in cymes or rac. or solitary in axils; sep. usually 5, persistent; pet. usually 5, free, overlapping; sta. usually 10, incurved, fil. woolly. Aus. Z10.

E. angustifolius P.G. Wils. Undershrub. Branchlets glandular-verrucose. Lvs to 10mm, clavate or terete, glab., canaliculate above. Umbels term., sessile; fls white; pet. to 9mm, elliptic or ovate, exterior glab., interior papillose; fil. to 3mm, densely lanate-ciliate. S Aus., NSW, Queensld. ssp. *montanus* P.G. Wils. Lvs to 4mm, obovate, strongly glandular-bullate. Pet. interior glab. Vict.

E. australasius Pers. Erect shrub to 2m. Branchlets angular, minutely stellate-pubesc. Lvs to 70mm, coriaceous, narrowly elliptic or oblong to obovate, glabrescent. Fls term., pink or red, sometimes white; pet. to 18mm, elliptic; fil. to 6mm. NSW, Queensld.

E. buxifolius Sm. Undershrub to 130cm. Branchlets terete, hispid. Lvs to 12mm, coriaceous, orbicular to elliptic, rounded, gland. beneath, glabrescent. Fls solitary, white, sometimes tinged pink; pet. to 15mm, broadly elliptic, glab.; fil. to 3.5mm, sparingly pilose above. NSW.

E. lanceolatus Gaertn. f. = *E. australasius*.

E. myoporoides DC. Shrub to 2m. St. verrucose; branchlets terete, glandular-verrucose. Lvs to 110mm, elliptic or oblong to broadly obovate, glandular-verrucose. Fls in axill. cymes, white or white-rose; pet. to 8mm, broadly elliptic, carinate, glab.; fil. to 5mm, lanate to pilose. Queensld, NSW, Vict.

E. neriifolius Sieb. ex Spreng. = *E. myoporoides*.

E. obovalis A. Cunn. Shrub to 1m. Branchlets terete, minutely tomentose. Lvs to 7mm, coriaceous, obcordate, minutely verrucose beneath, glab. Fls solitary, white or pale rose; pet. to 6mm, elliptic, glab.; fil. to 3.5mm, somewhat pilose. NSW.

E. salicifolius Sm. = *E. australasius*.

E. scaber Paxt. Undershrub to 60cm. Branchlets terete, sometimes verrucose, slightly hispid. Lvs to 20mm, linear, concave above, verruculose beneath, ± glab., dark green. Fls solitary, white to rose; pet. to 8mm, elliptic, glab.; fil. to 3mm, ciliate. NSW.

E. spicatus A. Rich. Woody perenn. to 60cm, erect. Branchlets glab. to lanate. Lvs to 20mm, elliptic to linear, concave above, glab. to sparsely lanate. Fls in term. rac. to 15cm, white to pink or blue, somewhat lanate; pet. to 4.5mm, elliptic, glab.; fil. to 2.5mm, apex gland. W Aus.

E. trachyphyllus F. Muell. Small tree or shrub to 7m. Branchlets terete, glab., verrucose. Lvs to 55mm, chartaceous, elliptic to obovate-oblong, glab., rugulose. Fls usually solitary, white to pink; pet. to 7mm, elliptic, glab.; fil. to 5.5mm, pilose. NSW, Vict.

E. verrucosus A. Rich. Shrub to 2m. Branchlets terete, glab., verrucose. Lvs to 15mm, coriaceous, obcordate, glandular-verrucose beneath. Fls axill., white; pet. to 6mm, elliptic, glab.; fil. to 3.5mm, slightly lanate. S Aus., Vict., Tasm.

Eriosyce Philippi. Cactaceae. 2 barrel-shaped cacti; st. simple, globose to shortly columnar, ribbed; spines numerous. Fls arising in the woolly apex, campanulate, floral areoles with matted white hair-spines; perianth limb short. Chile.

E. aurata (Pfeiff.) Ritter = *E. sandillon*.

E. ausseliana Ritter, invalid = *E. sandillon*.

E. ceratistes Britt. & Rose, misapplied = *E. sandillon*.

E. ihotzkyanae Ritter = *E. sandillon*.

E. korethroides Werderm. = *Echinopsis bruchii*.

E. lapampaensis Ritter = *E. sandillon*.

E. sandillon (Rémy) Philippi. St. globose, to 55cm diam., with densely woolly apex; ribs eventually 24–40; spines 9–20, 2.5–3.5cm, straight or curved, yellow to black. Fls 3.5–5cm, numerous, orange-red. Chile. Z9.

Eritrichium Schräd. ALPINE FORGET-ME-NOT. Boraginaceae. 30 low-growing, tufted perenn. herbs. Lvs simple. Cyme short racemose; cal. deeply 5-lobed; cor. subrotate or funnelform, lobes 5, spreading, throat usually with crested swellings. Temp. N Hemis.

E. barbigerum Gray = *Cryptantha barbigera*.

E. canum (Benth.) Kitam. Tufted, low-growing, adpressed-sericeous; flowering st. to 20cm. Lvs to 3.25cm, linear. Fls to 7mm diam., blue. W Himal. Z5.

E. elongatum (Rydb.) W. Wight. To 7.5cm, densely tufted, mat-forming. Lvs to 0.7cm, oblanceolate, woolly. Fls to 7mm diam., blue, crest yellow. W US. Z7.

E. howardii (A. Gray) Rydb. Densely mat-forming, strigose; st. to 12.5cm. Lvs to 1.5cm, linear-oblanceolate. Fls to 9mm diam., dark blue. Mont., Wyom. Z3.

E. intermedium Gray = *Cryptantha intermedia.*

E. nanum (L.) Schräd. ex Gaudin. Densely tufted, silvery-lanate; st. to 5cm. Lvs to 1cm, elliptic or oblanceolate to linear, sericeous. Fls to 8mm diam., sky blue, crests yellow. Eur. Alps. Z6.

E. nipponicum Mak. = *Hackelia nipponica.*

E. nothofulvum Gray = *Plagiobothrys nothofulvus.*

E. primuloides Decne. = *Mertensia primuloides.*

E. rupestre Bunge = *E. canum.*

E. strictum Decne. = *E. canum.*

Erman's Birch *Betula ermanii.*

Ernodea Sw.
E. montana Sibth. & Sm. = *Putoria calabrica.*

Erodium L'Hérit. STORKSBILL; HERON'S BILL. Geraniaceae. 60 perenn. and ann. herbs and subshrubs, similar to *Geranium*, but with only 5 fertile sta. (*Geranium* has 10). Fls slender-stalked, actinomorphic or zygomorphic, in scapose umbels or rarely solitary; sep. 5; pet. 5. Ripe fr. splits into 5 1-seeded parts, the awn attached to each mericarp twists in a corkscrew fashion. Eur., C Asia, Temp. Aus., Trop. S Amer.

E. absinthoides Willd. Tufted perenn. to 20cm. Lvs to 5cm, oblong, bipinnate, lfts lanceolate or oblong, sparsely gland. hairy. Fls in umbels of 2–8, 2cm diam., violet, pink or white. Summer. SE Eur., Asia Minor. Z6.

E. absinthoides var. *amanum* (Boiss. & Kotschy) Brumh. = *E. amanum.*

E. absinthoides var. *cinereum* Boiss. & Heldr. = *E. cinereum.*

E. absinthoides var. *sibthorpianum* Sibth. & J.E. Sm. = *E. sibthorpianum.*

E. acaule (L.) Bech. & Thell. Stemless perenn. to 20cm, silver-hairy. Lvs 4–9cm, pinnate, lfts ovate, serrate, sparsely white hairy. Fls to 9 in umbels; pet. to 7cm, lilac to purple. Medit. Z7.

E. alpinum (Burm. f.) L'Hérit. Grey-hairy and gland. perenn. to 15cm. St. short, bristly. Lvs to 5cm wide, narrow-oblong, bipinnate, lfts broad, 3–7-toothed. Fls 1cm diam., 2–10 per umbel, purple-violet. Early summer. S It. Z6.

E. amanum (Boiss. & Kotschy. Similar to *E. absinthoides* but smaller and covered in short white-grey hairs, st. slender and short, lvs many, fls white, larger.

E. carvifolium Boiss. & Reut. Perenn. to 35cm. Lvs basal, 5–16cm, bipinnate, midrib white-hairy. Fls in umbels of 4–10; pet. to 9mm, bright red. Spring. C Spain. Z7.

E. cedrorum Schott & Kotschy. Perenn. to 17cm, glandular-hairy. St. much-branched, often short. Basal lvs 2.5–5cm, bipinnatisect, seg. linear wedge-shaped, deeply cut. Fls to 25mm diam., 3–7 per umbel; pet. violet to white, lower ones spotted. Summer. Asia Minor. Z7.

E. chamaedryoides (Cav.) L'Hérit. = *E. reichardii.*

E. cheilanthifolium Boiss. Tufted stemless perenn., densely white-hairy, gland. Lvs 2–5cm, oblong-lanceolate, bipinnate, lfts to 3mm. Fls to 17mm diam., 2–4 per umbel; pet. white to pale pink, veins red, upper 2 stained dark red at base. Summer. S Spain, Moroc. 'Rachel': compact; lvs tinged silver; fls many, small, rounded, pet. lightly veined, upper pet. blotched. 'Stephanie': robust; fls 2 per umbel, large, white, upper pet. blotched. Z6.

E. chrysanthum L'Hérit. Tufted perenn., spreading to 40cm. St. thick, branching. Lvs 3.5cm, bipinnate, seg. wide, obtuse, silvery. Fls 20mm diam., saucer-shaped, 2 to 5 per umbel, sulphur or cream yellow. Summer. Greece. Z7.

E. cinereum Boiss. & Heldr. Similar to *E. absinthoides* but taller, grey-hairy, lf seg. narrow, acute. Armenia. Z6.

E. corsicum Léman. Mat-forming perenn. to 20cm, spread 23cm, similar to *E. reichardii* but with longer st. and silvery downy lvs. Lvs ovate, crumpled, crenate. Fls 1–3 per umbel, saucer-shaped, 20mm diam., rose-pink, veins red. Spring–summer. Corsica, Sardinia. 'Album': lvs grey, softly haired; fls white. Z8.

E. daucoides Boiss. Stemless perenn. to 10cm. Lvs to 5cm, lanceolate to triangular, hairy, bipinnate, seg. linear-lanceolate, 1mm; fls 14mm diam., rose, 2–6 per umbel. S Spain. Z8.

E. foetidum (L. & Nath.) L'Hérit. Perenn. to 15cm. Lvs basal, softly hairy, pinnate, rachis toothed. Fls 20mm diam., 2–7 per umbel, veined red. Summer. Pyren., S Fr. Z6.

E. glandulosum (Cav.) Willd. Tufted perenn. to 23cm, aromatic. Lvs basal, bipinnate, veins glandular-hairy. Fls 25mm diam., saucer-shaped, 5 per scape; pet. lilac, upper 2 with deeper patches at base. Summer. Pyren. 'Roseum': fls deep pink blotched purple. Z6.

E. gruinum (L.) L'Hérit. Ann. or bienn. to 45cm. St. stout. Lowest lvs entire, upper lvs ovate-cordate, deeply 3- to 5-lobed, toothed. Fls large, 3–5, pedunculate; pet. violet with deeper eye. Spring. Sicily, N Afr. to Iran. Z8.

E. guicciardii Heldr. Tufted perenn. to 20cm, silver-silky. St. leafy, forked. Lvs to 10cm, oblong, bipinnate, silver-hairy. Fls 2–3cm diam., 2–7 per umbel; pet. rose to violet. Summer. N Greece. Z7.

E. gussonii Ten. = *E. nervulosum.*

E. guttatum (Desf.) Willd. Clump-forming woody-based perenn., to 15cm. Lvs to 2.5cm, ovate to cordate, slightly lobed, crenate, silky. Fls to 25mm diam., 2–3 per umbel; pet. pale pink-lilac, upper 2 with deeper patch at base, veins darker. Summer. SW Eur. Z8.

E. × *hybridum* Sünderm. (*E. daucoides* × *E. manescavii.*) Resembles *E. manescavii*, but lvs more finely divided, fls smaller and paler. Gdn origin. Z7.

E. hymenodes L'Hérit. = *E. trifolium.*

E. × *kolbianum* Sünderm. ex Knuth. (*E. glandulosum* × *E. rupestre.*) Lvs more lax than in *E. rupestre*; fl. colour variable, pale to white rose, veins dark, but fine. Gdn origin Z6.

E. leucanthum Boiss. Perenn. subshrub to 14cm. St. ± upright, gland. hairy. Basal lvs to 5cm, long-stalked, st. lvs sessile, oblong or triangular, 2–3-pinnatisect, seg. to filiform. Fls 10mm diam., 2–5 per umbel; pet. white. Summer. Asia Minor. Z6.

E. × *lindavicum* Sünderm. (*E. amanum* × *E. chrysanthum.*) Lvs similar to *E. chrysanthum*, white-grey to silver hairy. Fls dull yellow. Gdn origin. 'Charter House': lvs tinged silver; fls in rounded heads of 7–8, white, veined green. Z7.

E. macradenum L'Hérit. = *E. glandulosum.*

E. manescavii Coss. Perenn. to 40cm. Lvs basal, to 30cm, lanceolate to ovate-lanceolate, hairy, pinnate, seg. ovate, toothed. Fls to 35mm diam.; pet. purple-red, upper 2 darker-spotted. Summer. Pyren. Z6.

E. moschatum (L.) L'Hérit. WHITE STEMMED FILAREE; MUSK CLOVER. Ann. to bienn. to 50cm. Lvs broad-ovate, pinnate, lightly pubesc., lfts toothed. Umbels 6–13-fld; pet. violet to pink-purple. Eur., nat. Americas. Z6.

E. mouretii Pitard. Similar to *E. gruinum*, but glandular-hairy. Pet. white or rose, veins purple, upper 2 with dark blotch at base. Moroc. Z8.

E. nervulosum L'Hérit. To 25cm, ± decumbent, base woody. Basal lvs falling early, stalked, upper lvs to 5cm, sessile, ovate-cordate, deeply lobed. Early summer. S It. Z8.

E. pelargoniiflorum Boiss. & Heldr. Perenn. St. to 30cm, woody at base. Basal lvs to 4cm, ovate-cordate, lobed, round-toothed, petioles to 10cm. Fls 2cm diam., 4–10 in umbels; pet. white, upper 2 spotted purple. Summer. Anatolia. Z6.

E. petraeum (Gouan) Willd. = *E. foetidum.*

E. petraeum ssp. *glandulosum* (Cav.) Bonnier. = *E. glandulosum.*

E. reichardii (Murray) DC. ALPINE GERANIUM. Mat-forming perenn. to 8cm. Lvs to 1.5cm cordate, crenate, dark green; petioles 3cm. Fls solitary, 8mm diam., white, veins rose. Summer. Majorca, Corsica. Z7.

E. romanum (Burm. f.) Ait. = *E. acaule.*

E. rupestre (Pourr.) Guitton. Perenn. to 10cm. Lvs 20–60mm, basal, ovate or oblong, bipinnate, silver hairy above, green beneath; petioles longer than lamina. Fls 2–4, 15mm diam., pet. white. Summer. Pyren. Z6.

E. ruthenicum Bieb. Perenn., 20–40cm, white-hairy. Basal lvs 7cm, ovate triangular, deeply dissected, ferny, hairy. Fls 3–10 per stalk, deep violet. Cauc. Z6.

E. sebaceum Delile. Perenn. with tallow smell. St. branching. Lvs to 23cm in rosettes at br. end, bipinnate, bristly white and gland. hairy; petiole long, winged, bristly, green or dull purple. Scapes to 27cm, gland.; pet. 13mm, magenta at tips, white below, veins pink, red streaked at base. Moroc., Atlas Mts. Z8.

E. serotinum Steven = *E. ruthenicum.*

E. supracanum L'Hérit. = *E. rupestre.*

E. tordylioides (Desf.) L'Hérit.). Ann. or bienn. to 50cm. St. few or solitary, leafy, often v. short. Basal lvs with soft hairs, oblong to ovate-oblong, pinnate. Scapes 10cm, woolly; pet. violet with deeper base. Spring. S Moroc., Spain. Z9.

E. trichomanefolium L'Hérit. ex DC. Lvs basal, 3–10cm, oblong to linear oblong, bipinnate, bristly hairy, seg. linear; petioles with spreading gland. hairs. Fls to 10mm diam., 2–7 per umbel, pet. pink or white, veins red. Summer. Syr., Leb. Z6.

E. trifolium (Cav.) Cav. Perenn. or bienn. to 35cm upright, shrubby. Lvs 3-lobed, blunt, deeply toothed. Fls 25mm diam., 4–11 per umbel; pet. pink, upper pet. spotted brown at base. Atlas Mts. Z8.

E. × *variabile* Leslie. (*E. corsicum* × *E. reichardii.*) Intermediate between parents. 'Album': fls white. 'Bishop's Form': to 60cm; st. branched, low; fls bright pink. 'Roseum': to 3cm; fls pink veined crimson. 'Flore Pleno': fls double, deep pink. Z7.

E. × *willkommianum* Sünderm. ex Knuth. (*E. cheilanthifolium* × *E. glandulosum.*) Lvs a little longer than in *E. cheilanthifolium*, hairs finer but more abundant. Z6.

E. cvs. 'Charm': mound-forming; lvs v. small; fls pink. 'County

Park': lvs bright green; fls pink. 'David Crocker': lvs tinged silver; fls white blotched pink at centre. 'Merthsham Pink': to 22cm; fls pink, abundant. 'Pickering Pink': (*E.* 'Merthsham Pink' × *E. glandulosum*): pet. pink, blotched.

Eruca Mill. ARUGULA; ROCKET SALAD; ROQUETTE; ITALIAN CRESS. Cruciferae. 5 ann. to perenn. herbs. Lvs pinnatisect. Infl. racemose; sep. 4, oblong, slightly saccate; pet. 4, long-clawed. Medit. Z7.
E. sativa Mill. The edible form, scarcely distinct from *E. vesicaria*.
E. vesicaria (L.) Cav. Pungently flavoured ann., 20–100cm. Lvs lyrate or pinnatisect with 2–5 pairs of lat. lobes and a large term. lobe ± glab., dark green. Pet. 15–20mm, yellow-white, veins white.

Ervatamia Stapf.
E. coronaria (Jacq.) Stapf = *Tabernaemontana divaricata*.
E. cumingiana (A. DC.) Markgr. = *Tabernaemontana pandacaqui*.
E. divaricata (L.) Burkill = *Tabernaemontana divaricata*.

Ervum L.
E. lens L. = *Lens culinaris*.

Erycina Lindl. Orchidaceae. 2 epiphytic orchids allied to *Oncidium*. Mex. Z10.
E. diaphana (Rchb. f.) Schltr. Differs from *E. echinata*, in its smaller lip, with slender, clavate, spreading lat. lobes and an obscurely quadrate, retuse midlobe.
E. echinata (HBK) Lindl. Pbs to 5cm, clustered, oval, stalked. Lvs to 10cm, to 5 per bulb, narrow-oblong, 2-ranked. Infl. to 15cm, racemose, arching; fls to 2cm diam., cupped; tep. yellow to green, narrow-ovate, lip to 1×0.8cm, golden yellow, lat. lobes flabellate, rounded, incurved, midlobe orbicular to reniform, apiculate; column white; anth. cap. red.
E. major Schltr. = *Erycina echinata*.
→*Oncidium*.

Eryngium L. ERYNGO; ERINGOE; SEA HOLLY. Umbelliferae. 230 perennials, biennials and annuals. Flowering st. ascending and branching. Lvs mostly basal, entire to 3-pinnatisect, linear-lanceolate to ovate, leathery or membranous, petiolate or sessile, variably spiny. Cap. hemispherical to cylindrical, solitary or in loosely candelabriform cymes or rac.; fls small, packed; involucral bracts spiny; sep. 5 stiff; pet. shorter than sep., emarginate. Cosmop.
E. agavifolium Griseb. Glab. perenn. to 1m; st. erect, branching. Basal lvs 10–35×5–25cm, sword-shaped, rosulate, coarsely spinose-dentate. Cap. numerous, to 5cm, green-blue; bracts 5–7mm, entire to spinose-dentate. Arg. Often sold as *E. bromeliifolium*. Z7.
E. alpinum L. Perenn. to 60cm. Basal lvs 8–1.5cm, blade ovate to triangular-cordate, spiny-toothed, soft, petiole exceeds blade; upper lvs palmately lobed, tinged blue. Cap. to 4×2cm, steel blue or white cylindrical-ovoid; bracts to 6cm, 25 or more, pinnatifid, softly spiny. Summer. Eur. (W & C Balk.). 'Amethyst': flowerheads small, dark violet; lvs more finely divided. 'Holden Blue': strong growth; flowerheads large, blue. 'Opal': infl. silver lilac. 'Superbum': to 60cm; lvs tinged blue; infl. large, dark blue.
E. amethystinum L. Perenn. to 70cm. Basal lvs to 15cm, obovate, upper lvs palmatisect, seg. 2–3-pinnatisect, final seg. linear-lanceolate, spiny, leathery; petiole equals blade. Cap. numerous on a silver-blue st., electric blue to amethyst, globose to ovoid, to 2cm; bracts 5–9, to 5cm, with 1–4 pairs of spines. Summer. It., Sicily, Balk.
E. aquaticum L. Perenn. to 120cm. Basal lvs 15–35×0.5–7cm, linear to oblong-lanceolate, entire to spiny-toothed, or laciniate, petioles to 30cm; st. lvs linear-lanceolate. Cap. numerous in cymes, ovoid-elipsoid, 8–12mm diam., white, bracts reflexed 8–10, to 2.5cm, white tinged purple. Summer. E US. Plants labelled as *E. aquaticum* in commerce are often *E. yuccifolium*.
E. biebersteinianum Nevski = *E. caucasicum*.
E. billardieri Delaroche. Perenn. to 75cm. Basal lvs 5–20cm, triangular to suborbicular in outline, ternate, seg. 1–2-pinnatifid, leathery, spinose-dentate, petiole unarmed; st. lvs reduced, spiny or 3-parted, spinose. Infl. pale blue or amethyst; cap. globose, to 15mm diam.; bracts 3–9, sharp, exceeding cap. Summer. Orient.
E. billardii hort. = *E. billardieri*.
E. bourgatii Gouan. Perenn. to 15–45cm. Lf blades to 7cm, suborbicular, 3-parted, seg. 1–2-pinnatifid, spiny, leathery dark green with silver venation; petioles exceeding blades. Cap. to 7, in a sky blue/silver infl., ovoid-globose, 1.5–2.5cm diam.; bracts 10–15, to 5cm, entire or spiny-toothed. Summer. Spain, Pyren. 'Oxford Blue': flowerheads dark silver-blue. ssp. *heldreichii*

(Boiss.) P.H. Davis. To 45cm. Cap. 3–13, 12–15mm diam.; bracts 7–12, longer than cap., entire or sparsely spiny. Summer. Leb., Anti-Lebanon, E Medit. Z5.
E. bromeliifolium hort. non Delaroche = *E. monocephalum*.
E. bromeliifolium Delaroche. Perenn. to 1m. Sword-shaped linear-lanceolate, spiny-toothed. Cap. ovoid or ovoid-cylindrical, *c*2.5cm, blue-white; bracts many rigid, sharp, longer than cap. Summer. Mex. Confused with *E. eburneum* or *E. agavifolium*. Z7.
E. caeruleum Bieb. = *E. caucasicum*.
E. campestre L. Glaucous perenn. to 60cm. Basal lvs 5–20cm, triangular-ovate in outline, ternate, seg. 2-pinnatifid, spiny-serrate, leathery, petiole equals lf. Cap. numerous in corymbose pan., ovoid, to 1.5cm diam., white to blue, bracts 5–8, to 4.5cm, entire or with spines. Summer. Eur. to SW Asia. Z6.
E. carlinae Delaroche f. Perenn., 10–25cm. Basal lvs 3–10cm, oblanceolate, obtuse, spiny-serrate to pinnatifid, petioles winged, to 2cm. Cap. ovoid, 6–10×5–7mm, blue, violet or white; bracts 8–12, ovate to oblanceolate, *c*1.5cm, blue-green below, white above, entire to spinose-serrate. Mex. Z8.
E. caucasicum Trautv. Perenn., 40–60cm. Basal lvs 2–6cm, not persistent, cordate-ovate or with 3 oblong, grass-like lobes, spiny-toothed, petiole long; st. lvs palmatipartite, spiny-toothed. Cap. blue, several, subglobose, *c*1cm diam.; involucral bracts 4–6, 3–5cm, spiny. Summer. Cauc., S Russia, N & NW Iran. Z4.
E. coeruleum auct. = *E. planum*.
E. corniculatum Lam. ONE-HORNED ERYNGIUM. Ann. or bienn., 15–60cm. Basal lvs 2–5cm, ovate-oblong, entire or obscurely toothed, petiole long, segmented; st. lvs 5-parted, spiny. Infl. spreading, tinted blue; cap. numerous, blue, subglobose, 0.5–1cm diam. with an apical spine; bracts 5–6, to 3cm, entire, spiny. Summer. Port., SW Spain. Z7.
E. creticum Lam. Perenn., bienn. or ann. to 60cm, branched above. Basal lvs 5–15cm, short-lived, crenate, dentate or 3-parted with spiny teeth, petiole unwinged, exceeding lf; upper lvs palmatifid, seg. spiny, sessile. Cap. globose, blue-purple, to 1cm diam., numerous in glaucous blue infl.; bracts 5, to 3cm, with 1–2 pairs of spines. Summer. Balk. Penins., Aegean. Z7.
E. decaisneanum Urban = *E. pandanifolium*.
E. dichotomum Desf. Perenn., some 60cm. Basal lvs 3.5–6cm, decid., cordate, oblong, leathery, serrate, petiole exceeds lf; upper lvs 5-parted, spiny. Cap. subglobose, 1–1.5cm diam., blue, in blue-tinged infl.; bracts 6–7, with spiny teeth. Summer. S Eur. Z7.
E. ebracteatum Lam. Perenn. to 2m, glab. Basal lvs 20–100cm, linear, entire with few spines. Cap. in loose corymbs, cylindrical, 5–30×2–5mm, wine-coloured; bracts 0 or 5–7 to 2mm. S Amer. Z8.
E. eburneum Decne. Perenn. to 2m; upper st. branched. Basal lvs 100×2.5cm, linear to sword-shaped entire, with stout spines. Cap. in pan., ovoid, 1–2×0.8–1.3cm, ivory; bracts linear-lanceolate, to 2cm, apex spiny. S Amer. Z8.
E. elegans Cham. & Schldl. Erect perenn., 5–10cm. Basal lvs 5–30cm, oblanceolate to linear-lanceolate, coarsely ciliate and spiny-toothed. Cap. white, globose, to 1cm diam.; bracts 6–10, linear, 4–10mm, spiny-dentate. S Amer. Z8.
E. giganteum Bieb. MISS WILLMOTT'S GHOST. Robust short-lived perenn., to 1.5m. Basal lvs 7–16cm, cordate-triangular, sub-coriaceous, irregularly crenate-dentate, petioles to 20cm; st. lvs 3-fid, incised-spinose. Cap. 3–9, electric blue to pale green, ovate to oblong, to 4cm; bracts 6–10, spinose, to 6cm. Summer. Cauc. 'Silver Ghost': to 60cm; fls small, white, sta. blue, bracts grey-white, in large heads. Z6.
E. glaciale Boiss. Alpine perenn. to 20cm. Basal lvs 3–5cm, lobes 3, lanceolate-acuminate, spiny-toothed; petiole with spiny wing above. Stalk blue; cap. 3, globose blue, 1–1.5cm diam.; bracts 7–8, narrow, spine-tipped, with 1–2 pairs of lat. spines, to 5cm. Summer. S Spain. Z7.
E. heldreichii Boiss. = *E. bourgatii* ssp. *heldreichii*.
E. humile Cav. Glab. perenn.; st. 0 or to 60cm. Lvs ovate-oblong to obovate, 2–15cm, veins reticulate, spinose-crenate-serrate. Cap. ovoid, 0.5–1cm, white or blue, solitary and long-stalked, or subsessile, or in 3-branched infl. with central stalk to 12cm; bracts *c*10 oblanceolate, silvery above, entire to slightly spiny-serrate. Peru. Z8.
E. lasseauxii Decne. = *E. pandanifolium* var. *lasseauxii*.
E. leavenworthii Torr. & A. Gray. Perenn. to 1m, red-purple. Lower lvs 3–6×1–2cm, oblanceolate, petiole short; upper lvs ovate to orbicular, palmatifid, seg. pinnatifid, spiny. Cap. purple, ovoid-cylindric, 15–25mm diam. with an apical tuft of spiny bracteoles; bracts *c*8, spinose-pinnatifid, to 4cm, purple-crimson. Summer. Tex. Z5.
E. maritimum L. SEA HOLLY; SEA HOLM; SEA ERYNGIUM. Vividly glaucous, short-lived perenn. to 60cm, silver or blue-grey throughout. Lvs to 10cm, suborbicular, rigidly coriaceous with

to 5 sharply spined lobes. Cap. pale blue, subglobose, *c*2.5cm diam.; bracts ovate to ovate-lanceolate, to 4cm, spiny, resembling lvs. Summer. Eur., nat. E coast US. Z5.

E. monocephalum Cav. Glab. perenn., *c*1.5m. Basal lvs 10–50cm, sword-shaped to linear-lanceolate, resembling a bromeliad, glossy, spinose-serrate. Cap. often solitary or few, ovoid, yellow-green, 1–2.5×1–1.5cm; bracts 12–30 spiny; 3–8cm. Mex. Z8.

E. ×*oliverianum* Delaroche f. (*E. alpinum* ×*E. giganteum* ?). 60–100cm. Lower lvs cordate-ovate, slightly 3-lobed, spinose-serrate, dark green with conspicuous veins, petiole long; upper lvs 3-lobed to palmately, 4–5-parted, spinose-serrate. Cap. cylindrical-ovoid, vivid blue, to 4cm; bracts 10–15, linear, purple, spinose-serrate. Late summer. Gdn origin. Z8.

E. palmatum Pančić & Vis. Perenn. to 75cm, glab. Basal lvs 5–9cm, reniform-orbicular, palmatisect, seg. oblanceolate, 3-lobed, leathery, serrate. Cap. 10 in green infl. hemispherical, 1–1.5cm diam.; bracts 5–7, 2–4cm, with 1–5 pairs of spiny teeth. Summer. Balk. Z6.

E. pandanifolium Cham. & Schldl. Perenn. to 2.5m. Basal lvs 1–1.5m, linear to sword-shaped, weakly spined. Cap. in pan., globose-ovoid, 7–10×3–6mm, purple-red; bracts ovate, shorter than cap. Summer. Braz. to Arg. var. *lasseauxii* (Decne.) Mathias & Constance. Lvs spinose-ciliate, with spines commonly paired or grouped. Cap. green-white. Summer. S Amer. Z8.

E. paniculatum Cav. & Domb. ex Delaroche. Perenn. to 1m. Basal lvs 5–35×0.8–1.5cm, linear to linear-lanceolate, spinose-serrate. Cap. in pan., globose, 0.8–1.5cm diam., white; bracts *c*10, leathery. Patagonia, Chile. Z8.

E. paniculatum hort. non Cav. & Domb. ex Delaroche = *E. eburneum*.

E. planum L. Perenn. to 75cm. Lower lvs 5–10×3–6cm, oblong to ovate-oblong, serrate, base cordate, slightly leathery, dark green, petiole equalling blade; upper lvs palmatifid, lobes spinulose, tinted blue. Cap. numerous, deep blue, globose-ovoid, 10–15mm diam.; bracts 6–8, linear, to 2.5cm, spiny. Summer. C & SE Eur. 'Azureum': cap. azure. 'Blauer Zwerg' ('Blue Dwarf'): dwarf, to 50cm, intense blue. 'Roseum': cap. tinted lilac-rose. Z4.

E. prostratum Nutt. Prostrate or ascending perenn. to 70cm. Basal lvs 15–55×0.7–2.5cm, ovate or elliptic, entire to dentate, simple to palmately lobed, petiole to 8cm. Cap. numerous, blue on filiform peduncles, ovoid-cylindric, 3–4mm diam.; involucral bracts 5–10, reflexed, equal to cap. Summer. C & E US. Z6.

E. proteiflorum Delaroche f. Perenn., *c*1m. Basal lvs 10–30× 1–2.5cm, rosulate, linear-lanceolate, spiny-lobed. Cap. ovoid-cylindrical, pale blue, 2–7×1.5–4cm; bracts 15–30, linear to lanceolate, sharp, to 12cm, silver-white, spiny. Autumn. Mex. Z8.

E. serbicum Pančić. Perenn. to 75cm; st. slender, tinted blue. Basal lvs palmatisect, seg. 10–25cm, 5–7, linear, entire, soft-spined, petiole long, winged; st. lvs with narrower, spiny seg. Cap. numerous, hemispherical, 1–1.5cm diam.; bracts 5–7, narrow-linear, 1–4cm, with 1–2 pairs of spiny teeth. Balk. Z6.

E. serra Cham. & Schldl. Perenn. to 2m. Basal lvs 30–60×2–5cm, linear-lanceolate to sword-shaped, acute, spiny-toothed, ciliate. Cap. in pan., globose white, to 10mm diam.; bracts 6–9, lanceolate, 4–5mm, spiny-toothed. Autumn. Braz. to Arg. Z8.

E. spinalba Vill. Perenn. 20–35cm. Basal lvs suborbicular, spiny-white-toothed, base cordate, 4–5-parted, seg. pinnatifid, rigid, petiole longer than blade. Cap. blue-white, ovoid-cylindrical, 4–6×2–3cm; bracts 15–30, rigid, 6–9cm, often 3-fid, spiny-toothed. Summer. Alps. Z6.

E. tricuspidatum L. Perenn. to 75cm. Basal lvs 2–6×1.5–5cm, oblong-ovate to suborbicular, cordate, simple to 3-lobed, crenate-dentate; petiole longer than blade. Cap. 2–8, in green infl., hemispherical, *c*1cm diam.; bracts 5–7, to 5cm, with 4–8 pairs of spiny teeth. Summer. SW Spain. Z8.

E. ×*tripartitum* Desf. Parentage unknown. To 120cm; st. blue above. Basal lvs 3-lobed, middle lobe obtuse, dark green, spinose; st. lvs 3-parted, seg. lanceolate, coarsely spiny-toothed. Cap. metallic blue, globose, *c*1cm; bracts 6–9, narrow-lanceolate, blue-green, exceeding cap. Summer. Probably Medit. Z5.

E. triquetrum Vahl. Perenn. to 40cm. Basal lvs *c*4cm, 3-lobed or -parted, spiny-toothed, seg. palmatifid to 2-pinnatifid, petiole longer than blade; st. lvs 3–5-partite. Cap. in corymbs, blue, hemispherical, *c*5mm diam.; bracts 3–4, sharp, linear-lanceolate, 1.5–3cm, keeled, entire. Summer. S It., Sicily. Z8.

E. variifolium Coss. Everg. perenn. to 45cm, with silver-blue st. Lvs in basal rosette, oblong-orbicular, base cordate, dark green, marbled white, toothed. Cap. to 2cm diam., rounded; bracts white-blue, exceeding cap., with 1–2 pairs of spines. Summer. N Afr. Z7.

E. virginianum Lam. = *E. aquaticum*.

E. yuccifolium Michx. RATTLESNAKE-MASTER; BUTTON-SNAKEROOT. Glab. perenn. to 180cm. Basal lvs 15–100cm, broadly linear to sword-shaped, bristly-spiny. Cap. 1–2.5cm diam., white to pale blue, globose-ovoid; bracts 6–10 to 1.5cm, cuspidate, bracteoles. Summer. US. Z4.

E. ×*zabelii* Christ ex Bergmans. (*E. alpinum* ×*E. bourgatii*.) Perenn. to 45cm. Basal lvs suborbicular, 3-parted, seg. 3-lobed, spinose-toothed. Cap. globose-cylindrical, deep blue-purple, to 2.5cm; bracts long, rigid, spinose-serrate. Summer. Gdn origin. 'Jewel': to 60cm; lvs rich green; cap. rich blue, bracts large, finely cut. 'Violetta': fls large, blue. Z5.

Eryngo *Eryngium*.

Erysimum L. Cruciferae. 80 ann. or perenn. herbs often woody-based. Lvs usually narrow. Rac. usually corymbose, term., ± erect; fls often fragrant; sep. 4, erect, the inner pair saccate at base, outer sep. often with a horny projection below tip; pet. 4, long-clawed. Eur. to W & C Asia, N Afr. and N Amer.

E. ×*allionii* hort. SIBERIAN WALL FLOWER. Parentage probably includes *E. perofskianum*. Tuft-forming perenn., grown as a bienn., 50–60cm. Lvs 5–8cm, lanceolate, coarsely toothed. Fls large, bright orange, in a corymbose rac. Gdn origin. Z7.

E. alpinum hort. non Pers. = *E. hieraciifolium*.

E. arbuscula (Lowe) Snogerup. Shrub to 45cm. Lvs linear-oblanceolate, grey-green, obtuse. Fls strongly scented, white to grey-orange, soon lilac, with dark veins. Winter–spring. Madeira. Z8.

E. arkansanum Nutt. ex Torr. & A. Gray = *E. asperum*.

E. asperum (Nutt.) DC. WESTERN WALL FLOWER. Bienn. or short-lived perenn., 30–100cm, rarely branched. Lvs 3–12cm, linear to lanceolate, short-haired, slightly toothed to entire. Fls crowded, bright yellow-orange. Early summer. BC to Washington, Minn. and Kans. Z4.

E. asperum var. *perenne* S. Wats. ex Cov. = *E. perenne*.

E. aurantiacum (Leyb.) Leyb. = *E. sylvestre* ssp. *aurantiacum*.

E. aureum Bieb. Ann. or perenn. 60–130cm, often branching. Lvs lanceolate-oblong, slender-pointed, branched-hairy, wavy to sharply toothed. Fls lightly fragrant; golden yellow, back hairy. Early summer. C & S Russia. Z7.

E. bicolor DC. Shrub, 60–90cm, freely branching. Lvs lanceolate or oblanceolate, distantly sharp-toothed, narrowly pointed. Fls lightly fragrant; cream to pale yellow or bronze, soon pale lilac. Spring. Madeira, Canary Is. Z9.

E. 'Bowles Mauve' ('E.A. Bowles'). Bushy shrub or perenn., to 75cm. Lvs to 5cm, narrowly lanceolate, grey-green. Fls small, rich mauve. Late winter–early spring.

E. californicum Greene = *E. capitatum*.

E. capitatum (Douglas) Greene. COASTAL WALL FLOWER. Bienn., 30–60cm, erect, downy, sometimes branching. Lvs 4–15cm, oblong-oblanceolate or linear, entire or wavy-toothed. Fls pale yellow-cream or brown-maroon. W N Amer. Z7.

E. cheiranthoides L. WORMSEED MUSTARD. Ann., 30–120cm, branching. Lvs lanceolate-oblong, sparsely hairy, entire or sparsely toothed. Fls bright yellow, back hairy. Summer. Widespread, Eur. Z5.

E. cheiri (L.) Crantz. WALLFLOWER. Perenn. subshrub, cultivated as a bienn., 25–80cm. Lvs 4–22cm, lanceolate to obovate-lanceolate, pointed, somewhat hairy, usually entire. Fls bright yellow-orange, striped red-purple. S Eur. Z7.

E. concinnum Eastw. = *E. suffrutescens*.

E. decumbens (Schleich. ex Willd.) Dennst. = *E. ochroleucum*.

E. elatum Nutt. = *E. capitatum*.

E. helveticum (Jacq.) DC. Clump-forming, tufted perenn. to 10cm. Lvs linear to linear-lanceolate, dark to grey-green. Fls small, fragrant, bright yellow in flat heads opening from purple-tinted buds. Spring–summer. C & E Eur. Z6.

E. hieraciifolium L. Bienn. or perenn., 30–120cm. St. hairy. Lvs 2.5–9cm, oblong-lanceolate, hairy above, wavy to toothed. Fls yellow, back hairy. Summer. C & N Eur. Z7.

E. humile Pers. = *E. ochroleucum*.

E. ×*kewense* hort. (*E. cheiri* ×*E. bicolor*.) Habit and foliage similar to *E. bicolor*. Fls large, on a spike-like rac., fragrant, orange-yellow to bronze, turning purple. Winter–summer. Gdn origin. 'Aurora': fls apricot, bronze, orange and mauve. 'Harpur Crewe': fls double, strong yellow, v. fragrant. 'Variegatum': lvs variegated cream. Z7.

E. kotschyanum Gay. Densely tufted perenn., 5–10cm. Lvs *c*1cm, densely crowded, linear, pale green, usually toothed. Fls orange-yellow to yellow. Summer. Turk. Z6.

E. linifolium (Pers.) Gay. Perenn., 12–70cm. Base woody, branching. St. numerous, slender. Lvs 2–9cm, oblong, wavy; flowering st. lvs linear-lanceolate, pointed, entire. Fls purple or violet. Spring. Spain and N Port. 'Bicolor': fls white and pink-violet on same rac. 'Variegatum': lvs variegated white. Z6.

E. marschallianum Andrz. Similar to *E. hieraciifolium* but bienn.; lvs to only 4cm, linear-oblong, entire to finely toothed. C & E Eur. Z6.

E. ×*marshallii* hort. = *E.* ×*allionii*.

E. murale Desf. = *E. cheiri*.

E. mutabile (Broussonet ex Sprengel) Boiss. & Heldr. = *E. bicolor*.

E. ochroleucum (Schleich.) DC. Mat-forming perenn., to 40cm. Lvs 2–8cm, in rosettes, oblanceolate-linear, finely toothed to entire. Fls yellow. SW Alps. Z6.

E. pachycarpum Hook. f. and Thoms. Similar to *E. perofskianum* but robust, to 60cm. Rac. few-fld. Summer. Himal. Z7.

E. perenne (S. Wats. ex Cov.) Abrams. Short-lived perenn., to 30cm, petiole bases persistent. Lvs 3–5cm, spathulate to oblanceolate. Fls yellow. Summer. Sierra Nevada. Z8.

E. perofskianum Fisch. and Mey. Bienn. or perenn., cult. as an ann., 15–40cm. Lvs 5–10 in a rosette, elliptic-oblong, finely toothed to entire. Fls red-orange. Summer. Afghan., Pak. Z8.

E. pulchellum (Willd.) Gay. Tuft-forming perenn., to 40cm. Lvs in rosettes, spathulate-oblong, lyrate, toothed. Fls bright golden yellow. Early summer. E Eur. to Asia Minor. Z6.

E. pumilum hort. = *E. helveticum*.

E. purpureum Asch. Erect, woody-based perenn., to 30cm. Lvs oblanceolate-linear, narrow, grey-hairy. Fls violet. Turk., W. Syr. Z8.

E. pycnophyllum Gay = *E. thyrsoideum*.

E. repandum L. Ann., to 60cm. St. branched. Lvs 1–7cm, linear-lanceolate, tip recurved, wavy-toothed to entire, fls 7–10mm, yellow, back hairy. Spring. C & S Eur. Z6.

E. scoparium (Brouss. ex Willd.) Snogerup. Similar to *E. bicolor* except lvs grey-green; fls white, becoming purple. Canary Is. Z8.

E. semperflorens (Schousb.) Wettst. Subshrub, 22–60cm. Lvs narrow, lanceolate-oblanceolate, grey-green, entire or remotely toothed. Fls white. Winter. Moroc. Z8.

E. suffrutescens (Abrams) Rossbach. Shrubby, woody-based, long-branched perenn. to 60cm. Lvs 3–7cm, linear-lanceolate, succulent. Fls yellow. Spring. Coastal Calif. Z9.

E. suffruticosum Spreng. = *E. cheiri*.

E. sylvaticum Bieb. = *E. aureum*.

E. sylvestre (Crantz) Scop. Woody-based perenn., 10–65cm. Lvs 2–12cm, in rosettes, linear-lanceolate, entire to remotely toothed. Fls yellow, sometimes hairy. Alps, NW Balk. ssp. *aurantiacum* (Leyb.) P. W. Ball. Flowering st. violet at base; pet. always glab. Z6.

E. thyrsoideum Boiss. Similar to *E. kotschyanum* except bienn. St. winged. Lvs light grey-hairy. Fls larger. Turk. Z8.

E. torulosum Piper. Bienn., 15–45cm. St. few, erect, occas. branched. Lvs 3–8cm, spathulate, pointed, hairy, toothed to nearly entire. Fls yellow. W N Amer. Z7.

E. wahlenbergii (Asch. and Engl.) Borlás. Similar to *E. hieraciifolium* except lvs hairy beneath; fls larger. W Carpath. Z6.

E. witmannii Zawadzski. Bienn., to 50cm. Lvs 2–7cm, oblanceolate-linear, wavy-toothed, rarely entire. Fls yellow to green-yellow, back hairy. Carpath. Z6.

E. cvs. 'Blood Red': fls deep magenta, fragrant. 'Bredon': lvs tinted blue; fls rich yellow. 'Butterscotch': fls orange. 'Cloth of Gold': fls large, gold, fragrant. 'Covent Garden': fls deep magenta, fragrant. Double Dwarf Mixed: fls double, wide colour range. Early Wonder Mixed: fls mahogany and gold; spring-flowering. 'Eastern Queen': fls salmon red. Fair Lady Mixed: fls red and pastel-coloured. 'Fire King': fls flaming orange. Glasnost Mixed: fls fragrant, in shades of cream, lemon, apricot, gold and lilac. 'Golden Gem': fls deep yellow. 'Jacob's Jacket': fls orange washed lilac and bronze. 'Jubilee Gold': fls golden. 'Primrose': habit low, dense; fls yellow. 'Rufus': fls orange. 'Scarlet Bedder': fls rich red. 'Sprite': habit v. low; fls pale yellow. 'Tom Thumb Mixed': dwarf; fls bright coloured. 'Wenlock Beauty': fls yellow tinted bronze. 'White Dame': fls cream.

→*Cheiranthus*.

Erysium L.

E. barbarea L. = *Barbarea vulgaris*.

Erythea S. Wats.

E. aculeata Brandg. = *Brahea aculeata*.

E. armata var. *microsperma* Becc. = *Brahea armata*.

E. brandegeei C.A. Purpus = *Brahea brandegeei*.

E. edulis (H.A. Wendl. & S. Wats.) S. Wats. = *Brahea edulis*.

E. roezlii Becc. = *Brahea armata*.

Erythraea Borkh.

E. massonii hort. = *Centaurium scilloides*.

E. scilloides (L. f.) Chaub. ex Puel = *Centaurium scilloides*.

E. venusta A. Gray = *Centaurium venustum*.

Erythrina L. CORAL TREE. Leguminosae (Papilionoideae). 108 decid. or everg. shrubs, trees or perenn. herbs, usually with conical thorns or curved prickles. Lvs pinnate; lfts entire, usually stalked. Fls solitary, paired or fasciculate, in erect rac.; cal. tubular-campanulate, slit beneath, 5-lobed; standard always longer than other cor. seg., erect and folded enclosing keel, wings and sta. or spreading. Fr. a legume; seeds often scarlet. Pantrop. Z10 unless specified.

E. abyssinica Lam. ex DC. RED HOT POKER TREE. Tree or shrub, to 14m with much-branched, spreading crown, br. spiny. Petiole and petiolules prickly; lfts to 14cm, elliptic or suborbicular, rounded, woolly when young, prickly beneath. Fls scarlet to brick-red, in robust rac.; standard to 4.5×1.6cm. Trop. Afr., Himal.

E. acanthocarpa E. Mey. Thicket-forming, stiff shrub to 2m. Lfts to 2.5cm, elliptic, obtuse or short-acuminate, glaucous. Fls scarlet, green-tipped on short peduncles; standard to 5×4cm. S Afr. Z9.

E. americana Mill. NAKED CORAL TREE. Spiny shrub or small tree to 7m, slightly prickly, densely rufous-villous. Lfts ovate to triangular, term. lft to 11cm, deltoid to ovate. Fls brilliant red to rose in short dense or open rac., standard to 7×2cm. Mex., Ariz. Z9.

E. arborea Small = *E. herbacea*.

E. arborescens Roxb. Tree to 6m, somewhat prickly. Lfts to 30.5cm, broad, membranous, acuminate. Fls bright red in short, dense rac.; standard to 4.5×2cm. India, Nepal, Burm., China.

E. berteroana Urban. Tree to 6m+. Lfts to 15cm diam., rhombic-ovate, acute to acuminate, waxy. Fls orange-red in rac. to 12.5cm, sometimes longer; standard to 10×1.6cm. C & S Amer., W Indies.

E. ×*bidwillii* Lindl. (*E. crista-galli* ×*E. herbacea*) Woody-based perenn. herb or shrub to 4m, intermediate between parents. Fls dark red, in threes and axill., or in term. rac.; standard to 5×1.5cm. Z8.

E. caffra Thunb. CAPE KAFFERBOOM; CORAL TREE; LUCKY BEAN TREE; KORAALBOOM. Semi-everg., spreading tree to 18m. Br. sometimes prickly; bark grey. Petiole prickly; term. lft to 9cm, broad-ovate, subacute. Fls usually orange-scarlet, occas. cream, in short rac.; standard 5.5×3.5cm. Seed coral-red, glossy with a black spot. E S Afr. 'Flavescens': fls cream.

E. constantiana Micheli = *E. caffra*.

E. corallodendrum L. CORAL TREE. Decid. shrub or small tree to 3m, prickly. Petiole without prickles; lfts broad, rhombic-ovate. Fls deep scarlet-red, in rac. to 30cm; standard 5cm. Spring–summer. Jam., Haiti.

E. coralloides A.DC. = *E. americana*.

E. crista-galli L. COMMON CORAL TREE; COCKSPUR CORAL TREE; CRY-BABY TREE. Erect shrub or small tree, 9m. Br. with stout spines. Petioles to 19cm, spiny; lfts to 12cm, coriaceous, ovate-to oblong-lanceolate, sometimes with small prickles beneath, term. lft. Fls dark scarlet-red, solitary or clustered or in large, leafy term., rac.; standard to 5.5×3cm. Summer–autumn. S Amer. E of the Andes. Z8.

E. falcata Benth. Resembles *E. crista-galli*, but with fls in leafless lat. rac. S Peru, E Braz., Parag., N Arg.

E. flabelliformis Kearney. Shrub or small tree to 6m. Lfts chartaceous, suborbicular to triangular, term. lft to 7.5cm, usually rounded. Fls bright red, narrow, in short rac.; standard to 7.5×2cm. N Amer. Z9.

E. fulgens Lois. = *E. americana*.

E. fusca Lour. SWAMP IMMORTELLE. Decid. tree to 26m. Trunk crooked, with blunt spines to 2cm. Petiole to 19cm; lfts to 20cm, coriaceous, elliptic, glaucous beneath, term. lft smaller. Infl. to 13cm; standard to 7×6cm, bright orange-red, wings and keel green-cream, apex often purple. SE Asia, New Guinea, Fiji, Madag., W Indies, C & S Amer. Z8.

E. gibbsae Bak. f. = *E. latissima*.

E. glauca Willd. = *E. fusca*.

E. herbacea L. CARDINAL-SPEAR; CHEROKEE BEAN; CORAL BEAN. Perenn. herb to 1m or shrub or small tree. St. often single. Lfts ovate or slightly hastate, term. lft to 12.5cm, hastate, long-acuminate. Fls deep scarlet, in rac. to 60cm; standard to 5cm. Seeds scarlet, with a black line. Summer–autumn. SE US, Mex.

E. herbacea var. *arborea* Chapm. = *E. herbacea*.

E. hondurensis Standl. Resembles *E. flabelliformis*, but term. lfts acuminate, pubesc. Seeds wholly scarlet, lacking black line. Hond., Nic.

E. humeana Spreng. DWARF KAFFERBOOM; DWARF ERYTHRINA; KLEINKORAALBOOM. Decid. shrub or small tree to 4m. Bark grey, prickly. Lfts ovate, tapering, entire or sinuate, dark shiny term. lft to 20cm, triangular, acuminate, with spines beneath.

Fls nodding, in slender, term. rac. to 50cm; standard 4×2cm, scarlet-red. Summer. S Afr., Moz. Z9.

E. indica Lam. = *E. variegata.*

E. insignis Tod. = *E. caffra.*

E. latissima E. Mey. BROAD-LEAF KAFFERBOOM; HAIRY KAFFERBOOM; CORK TREE; ROYAL KAFFERBOOM. Tree to 9m. Bark corky, rough, brown; br. with formidable prickles, thick-pubesc., later glab. Lvs large and broad; lat. lfts to 21cm, ovate, grey-velutinous, later coriaceous, occas. prickly, term. leaflet to 30cm. Fls rich crimson, in heads to 11cm. S Afr., Moz.

E. livingstoniana Bak. Tree to 25m, of spreading habit. Bark thick, furrowed; st. v. spiny. Petiole to 20cm; lfts to 17cm, palmately 3-lobed, term. lobe triangular, lat. lobes truncate, occas. almost bilobed. Fls brilliant scarlet, large, in rac. to 20cm long; standard to 4×4cm. Moz., Malawi, Zimb.

E. lysistemon Hutch. COMMON CORAL TREE; LUCKY-BEAN TREE; TRANSVAAL KAFFERBOOM. Semi-evergreen tree, to 10m. Bark dary grey to grey-brown, not corky. Petiole sometimes uncinate-prickly; lfts to 17cm, ovate, tapering. Fls clear scarlet, in densely compact infl. to 20cm; standard to 6×2cm. S Afr. Z9.

E. macrophylla A. DC. Resembles *E. americana*, but rac. to 25.5cm. Pedicels and cal. densely brown-pubesc. C Amer.

E. mitis Jacq. Resembles *E. berteroana*, but rac. to 10cm, cal. campanulate, asymmetric, convex at margin, standard to 7.5×2cm and keel pet. separate. Venez.

E. monosperma Gaudich. = *E. tahitensis.*

E. mulungu Mart. = *E. verna.*

E. ovalifolia Roxb. = *E. fusca.*

E. poeppigiana (Walp.) Cook. MOUNTAIN IMMORTELLE. Tree to 18m, prickly. Lfts to 20.5cm, rhombic-ovate to suborbicular. Fls orange; standard to 6.5×2.5cm. C & N S Amer.

E. princeps A. Dietr. = *E. humeana.*

E. pulcherrima Tod. = *E. crista-galli.*

E. sandwicensis Deg. = *E. tahitensis.*

E. ×sykesii Barneby & Krukoff. (*E. lysistemon* ×?) Br. ascending. Lvs tinted blue. Fls flaming orange, in spikes.

E. tahitensis Nad. Large decid. tree. Fls red to salmon or pink to white; standard 4cm, broad. Tahiti, Hawaii.

E. tomentosa R. Br. ex A. Rich. = *E. abyssinica.*

E. umbrosa HBK = *E. mitis.*

E. variegata L. Decid. tree to 27m. Br. thick, with large prickles. Bark grey-green or grey, furrowed. Petioles to 20cm; lfts to 19.5cm, ovate to broadly rhomboid, soon glab., occas. variegated light green and yellow. Fls scarlet or crimson, rarely white, in dense, many-fld, tomentose infl. to 20cm; standard to 7cm. Tanz., Indian Ocean Is., China, Taiwan, India, Malesia and parts of Polyn. 'Alba': fls white.

E. velutina Willd. Large tree to 9m. Br. spreading spiny; branchlets stout. Petioles to 27cm, initially stellate-pubesc.; lfts chartaceous, initially stellate-pubesc., term. leaflet to 16cm, subdeltoid to subrotund, emarginate, truncate to subcordate at base. Fls orange-red; standard to 5.5×3cm. W Indies, N Venez., N Colomb., W Ecuad., W Peru, E Braz.

E. verna Vell. Resembles *E. poeppigiana*, but cal. broader than long, and standard to 4.5×2.5cm. C & S Braz., E Boliv.

E. vespertilio Benth. Slender tree to 13m. Lvs to 10.5cm, v. variable, v. broad-emarginate or broad-convex, cuneate at base. Fls red in infl. to 24cm long; standard to 4×2.5cm. Aus.

E. zeyheri Harv. PRICKLY CARDINAL. Small shrub to 1m, v. spiny. Petioles and lfts with many prickles beneath; lfts broad-ovate or elliptic, prominently veined. Fls red. S Afr. Z9.

→*Micropteryx.*

Erythrocoma Greene.

E. ciliatum Greene = *Geum triflorum* var. *ciliatum.*

Erythronium L. DOG'S-TOOTH VIOLET; ADDER'S TONGUE; TROUT LILY; FAWN LILY. Liliaceae (Liliaceae). Some 20 perenn. bulbous herbs, often stoloniferous. Lvs ovate-elliptic, entire, basal, mottled or plain. Fls nodding, solitary to many on scape; perianth seg. 6, free, sometimes strongly reflexed; sta. 6. Spring–early summer. N US, Eur. and Asia.

E. albidum Nutt. WHITE DOG'S-TOOTH VIOLET; BLONDE LILIAN. Lvs usually mottled to 3.5cm wide. Fls solitary, white inside, yellow centre, exterior tinted blue or pink; anth. ivory. S Canada to Tex. var. *mesochoreum* (Kuerr) Rickett. Lvs narrower, unmottled. Z4.

E. americanum Ker-Gawl. YELLOW ADDER'S TONGUE; TROUT LILY; AMBERBELL. Lvs mottled brown and white. Fls solitary, yellow exterior marked brown or purple, interior spotted; anth. yellow, purple or brown. E N Amer. Z3.

E. californicum Purdy. FAWN LILY. Resembling the related *E. helenae*, *E. oregonum*, *E. citrinum* and *E. howellii.* Lvs mottled brown-green. Fls 1–3, creamy white with ring of orange-brown; anth. white; stigma trifid. Calif. Z5.

E. californicum var. *bicolor* Purdy = *E. helenae.*

E. citrinum S. Wats. Similar to *E. californicum* but inner seg. yellow-green at centre, basally appendaged, stigma entire. NW Calif., SW Oreg. Z4.

E. dens-canis L. Lvs mottled pink-chocolate. Fls solitary, rose to mauve; anth. lilac; stigma lobed. Eur. and Asia. 'Album': fls white. 'Carneum': fls flesh pink. 'Frans Hals': lvs mottled; fls large, pale plum. 'Lilac Wonder': fls lavender, to rich purple with brown spot at base. 'Niveum': fls white. 'Pink Perfection': fls large, clear pale pink, early-flowering. 'Purple King': lvs heavily mottled; fls large, rich plum, centre mottled brown and white. 'Rose Queen': lvs mottled; fls deep pink. 'Roseum': fls rose. 'Snowflake': lvs mottled; fls pure white. 'White Splendour': fls white, centre dark, early-flowering. Z3.

E. giganteum Lindl. = *E. grandiflorum.*

E. grandiflorum Pursh. AVALANCHE LILY. Differs from other yellow-fld plain-lvd spp. in 3-lobed stigma. W US. 'Album' ('Candidum'): fls white, centre yellow. 'Robustum': tall; fls large, gold. Z5.

E. hartwegii S. Wats. = *E. multiscapoideum.*

E. helenae Appleg. Fls white to yellow. Differs from *E. oregonum* in narrow, not flattened fil., from *E. californicum* in yellow anth. and tep. base. NW Calif. Z5.

E. hendersonii S. Wats. Lvs dark green, mottled, margins crisped. Fls to 10 per st., lilac-pink with purple centre; anth. purple. SW Oreg., NW Calif. Z5.

E. howellii S. Wats. Distinguished from *E. californicum* by its entire, not trifid stigma. SW Calif., SW Oreg. Z3.

E. montanum A. Wats. AVALANCHE LILY. To 30cm or more. Lvs to 15cm, ovate-lanceolate. Fls 1 to several, 38mm, white, orange at base inside, tep. slightly recurved; anth. white. NW Amer.

E. multiscapoideum (Kellogg) Nels. & Kellogg. Lvs mottled. Scapes several per bulb; fls solitary, white, interior pale green or yellow at base; anth. white. Sierra Nevada. Z5.

E. obtusatum Goodd. = *E. grandiflorum.*

E. oregonum Appleg. Differs from *E. californicum* in fls with yellow centres and anth. Oreg. to BC. Z5.

E. purdyi hort. = *E. multiscapoideum.*

E. purpurascens S. Wats. Lvs plain bright green. Fls to 8 per rac.; white or cream with yellow centre flushing purple with age; anth. white. Calif. Z5.

E. revolutum Sm. Lvs mottled, margins crisped. Fls 1–3 per st., deep pink with yellow centre; anth. yellow. N Calif., Vancouver Is. Z5. 'Citronella': to 25cm; lvs mottled; fls lemon yellow. 'Pagoda': to 40cm, vigorous; lvs marbled bronze; fls pale sulphur yellow, with brown centre, 3–5 per plant; hybrid of 'White Beauty'. 'Pink Beauty': fine rose fls. 'White Beauty': to 15cm; lvs heavily mottled; fls large, white, centre yellow. var. *johnsonii* (Bolander) Purdy. Fls dark pink. Z5.

E. smithii Orcutt = *E. revolutum.*

E. tuolumnense Appleg. Lvs plain green. Fls solitary, small, bright yellow veined green; anth. yellow. C Calif. Sometimes confused with *E. nudopetalum* (Appleg.), which lacks basal appendages to the perianth seg. and has white anth. Z5.

E. cvs. 'Jeanette Brickell': fls white, free-flowering. 'Jeannine': to 30cm; fls large, clear sulphur, central pale brown ring paler with age. 'Kondo': lvs lightly mottled; fls light yellow, centre brown. 'Miss Jessop': lvs mottled chestnut; fls pale pink.

Erythropsis Lindl. ex Schott. & Endl.

E. barteri (Mast.) Ridl. = *Hildegardia barteri.*

Erythrorhipsalis A. Berger.

E. pilocarpa (Loefgr.) A. Berger = *Rhipsalis pilocarpa.*

Escabon *Chamaecytisus proliferus.*

Escallonia Mutis ex L. f. Grossulariaceae. 50–60 mostly everg. ± aromatic, viscid shrubs and small trees. Lvs ± sessile, mostly glandular-toothed. Pan. or rac. term.; cor. funnel-shaped, 5-lobed. S Amer.

E. alpina DC. Glab. shrub to 1.5m, squat, shoots angled. Lvs 1.5–3cm, obovate to oblanceolate, shiny green. Infl. to 10cm, a straight pan.; fls deep pink or red to maroon. Chile. Z9.

E. bellidiflora Lindl. = *E. ×stricta.*

E. berteroana DC. = *E. pulverulenta.*

E. bifida Link & Otto Small tree, glab., not sticky. Lvs 3–7cm, narrow, elliptic, finely toothed. Pan. to 15cm, rounded, rather flattened; fls white, style and sta. protruding. Braz., Parag., Uraguay, Arg. Z9.

E. ×exoniensis hort. (*E. rosea* ×*E. rubra.*) Shrub 4–6m, br. gland., downy, ribbed. Lvs 2cm, oval, shiny above, pale beneath. Infl. to 7cm, paniculate; fls white or pink. Gdn origin. 'Balfourii': fls blush, tinted white. 'Frades': fls carmine in term. clusters. Z8.

E.floribunda HBK. Shrub to 2.5m, sometimes tree-like, br. glab., sticky. Lvs 3–10cm, obovate to narrow oval, toothed to entire, resinous-spotted, glab. beneath. Pan. to 20×12.5cm; fls white, fragrant. Summer. Venez., Columbia. Confused with *E. bifida*. Z9.

E.floribunda hort. non HBK = *E. bifida*.

E. fonkii Philippi = *E. alpina*.

E.×franciscana Eastw. (*E.illinita ×E.rubra* var. *macrantha*.) Intermediate form. Lvs resinous-spotted. Fls white, fragrant. Gdn origin. Z8.

E. glaberrima Philippi = *E. alpina*.

E.grahamiana Gillies. Upright shrub, arching, with sessile glands. Lvs to 5cm, oval obovate to oblong, finely toothed, glossy above, resinous-dotted beneath. Infl. pyramidal; fls white. Chile. Often found under the names *E. alba*, *E.floribunda*, *E. bifida* and *E. virgata*. Z9.

E. grahamiana Hook. & Arn. = *E. illinita*.

E.illinita C. Presl. Shrub 2–2.5m, shoots glandular-resinous. Lvs to 2–6cm, obovate to oval, apex rounded, resinous beneath when young. Infl. to 10cm, terminal, bracted, resinous, pyramidal; pet. forming a tube, tips spreading. Summer. Chile. Z8.

E.laevis (Vell.) Sleumer. Shrub to 1.5m, br. angled, glab. and glandular-resinous. Lvs 5–7cm, narrow obovate to oval, dark above, pale beneath, finely toothed, often red-tinged. Pan. 5–7cm, term., rounded; fls pale rose, darker in bud. Braz.

E.×langleyensis hort. (*E.rubra ×E.virgata*.) Semi-evergreen arching shrub to 3m. Lvs 1–2.5cm, narrow oval to obovate, glandular-resinous beneath. Fls solitary or in small rac., pink or red. Gdn origin. 'Apple Blossom': sturdy to 1.2m, lvs large; fls profuse, pale pink with white eye. 'Donard Gem': compact, fls pink, fragrant. 'Donard Scarlet': upright, narrow to 2m, fls scarlet. 'Donard White': fls white, pink in bud. 'Edinensis': fls light red, darker in bud. 'Pride of Donard': to 1.5m, fls v. large, scarlet pink. 'Slieve Donard': arching, to 1.5m, fls pink-red. Z8.

E.leucantha Rémy. Large shrub to small tree to 12m, br. hairy. Lvs to 2.5cm, obovate to oblanceolate, dentate. Rac. to 5cm, on lat. shoots; fls white. Summer. Chile, Arg. Z9.

E. macrantha Hook. & Arn. = *E. rubra* var. *macrantha*.

E. montana Philippi = *E.rosea*.

E. montevidensis (Cham. & Schldl.) DC. = *E. bifida*.

E. organensis Gardn. = *E. laevis*.

E. philippiana (Engl.) Mast. = *E. virgata*.

E. pterocladon Hook. = *E. rosea*.

E.pulverulenta (Ruiz & Pav.) Pers. Shrub to 4m, br. angled, downy, sticky. Lvs 5–10cm, oblong, finely toothed, glossy above, shortly pubesc. beneath. Infl. 10–20cm, dense; fls white. Summer–autumn. Chile. Z9.

E. punctata DC. = *E. rubra*.

E.revoluta (Ruiz & Pav.) Pers. Shrub or small tree to 8m, br. angled, grey-felted. Lvs to 5cm, obovate, unevenly toothed, grey-felted, revolute. Pan. term. 3–7cm; fls 1cm, white. Chile. Z9.

E.×rockii Eastw. (*E.bifida ×E.rubra* var. *macrantha*.) Most closely resembling *E. bifida*, lacking gland. hairs on infl. Z8.

E.rosea Griseb. Shrub 2–2.5m, br. angled, downy, tinged red. Lvs 1–2.5cm, lanceolate, toothed, glossy above. Pan. loose to 2cm, on short side shoots; fls white or red, fragrant; pet. united in a long tube. S Amer., Patagonia. Z9.

E.rubra (Ruiz & Pav.) Pers. Shrub to 4m, br. glandular-downy, tinged red. Lvs 2.5–5cm, obovate to lanceolate, long-tapered, gland. resinous beneath. Pan. sparse, fls pink-red. Summer. Chile. 'Crimson Spire': upright to 1.8m, lvs v. dark, glossy; fls red. Suitable for hedging. 'Woodside' ('Pygmaea'): v. dense spreading dwarf to 0.5m, fls intense red. var. *macrantha* (Hook. & Arn.) Reiche. Dense vigorous shrub 1.5–4m. Lvs 2.5–7cm, obovate to broad ovate, double toothed. Pan. term.; fls 1.5cm, deep pink-red. Summer–autumn. 'C F Ball': erect to 3m, open habit; lvs small, deep green; fls large, deep red. 'Ingramii': narrowly upright 2–4m; lvs large, narrow; fls rose pink. 'William Watson': medium sized, compact; fls bright red produced over a long period. Z8.

E. sanguinea hort. = *E. rubra* var. *macrantha*.

E.sellowiana DC. Shrub to 6m, br. thin, glab. Lvs 2–5cm, oblanceolate, apex rounded, toothed, gland. resinous beneath. Pan. to 6cm, dense term.; fls white. Braz. Z9.

E.×stricta Rémy ex C. Gay. (*E.leucantha ×E.virgata*.) Shrub to 1.5m, br. thin. Lvs small. Fls small, white. Chile, Arg. Grown as 'Harold Comber'. Z7.

E.tucumanensis Hosseus. Erect decid. shrub to 6m. Lvs to 5cm, oblong, long tapered, finely toothed. Pan. loose, pet. large, white, claws forming a tube. NW Arg. Z9.

E.virgata (Ruiz & Pav.) Pers. Decid. shrub to 2m, br. arching, finely downy, tinged red. Lvs 8–15mm, lanceolate to obovate, finely toothed, shiny above. Rac. 5cm; fls 1cm, white or pale pink. Chile, Arg. 'Gwendolyn Anley': dwarf to 1.5m, lvs small;

fls flesh pink; hardy. Z7.

E. virgata var. *philippiana* Engl. = *E. virgata*.

E.viscosa Forbes. Resembles *E. illinita*, differs in stronger aroma and one-sided pan. Lvs 2.5–7cm, obovate, finely toothed, shiny with resinous glands. Infl. 12–15cm, pendulous; fls white. Summer. Chile. Z9.

E.cvs. 'Bantry Bay': fls pale pink. 'C.H. Beale': robust, fls crimson, freely produced. 'Compacta Coccinea': v. erect, fls red. 'Dart's Rosy Red': fls deep pink. 'E.G. Cheesman': (a hybrid with *E.revoluta*): vigorous; lvs ovate to rounded obovate, grey-green; infl. term., leafy; fls 12mm, bell-shaped, deep red. 'Glasnevin Hybrid': vigorous to 4m; fls deep red. 'Iveyi': (*E. bifida ×E.×exoniensis*): lvs to 6cm, elliptic, deep green; fls white, buds pink, fragrant. 'Newryensis': (*E.rosea ×E.×langleyensis*): vigorous, upright; fls white tinged pink. 'Pink Elf': compact; fls bright pink. 'Pink Pearl': br. arching; lvs small; fls 2cm in dense rac., pale pink with darker marking. 'Red Elf': compact; fls red. 'Red Hedger': similar to 'Crimson Spire', lvs larger, fls crimson. 'Rubricalyx': a selected form of *E.×franciscana*. 'St Keverne': br. arching; lvs small; fls large, deep pink, profuse.

Eschscholzia Cham. Papaveraceae. 8–10 ann. or perenn. herbs, producing clear sap, basally branching. Lvs mostly basal, usually glaucous and deeply dissected. Fls solitary, on long peduncles; sep. 2 forming a cap; pet. 4–8, broad, silky; sta. 16 or more; stigma 4–6-lobed. NW Amer., nat. in Eur.

E.caespitosa Benth. TUFTED CALIFORNIA POPPY. Ann. to 25cm, branching from base. Lvs finely divided, obtuse-lobed. Fls bright yellow, to 5cm across. C Calif. 'Sundew': forming compact tufts, fls single, pale yellow, abundant. Z7.

E.californica Cham. CALIFORNIA POPPY. Cotyledon bifurcate. Ann. or short-lived perenn. to 60cm, sometimes pubesc., matforming, glaucous. St. leafy. Fls to 7cm across, yellow to orange. W US, India, nat. Eur. 'Alba': to 35cm; fls single, creamy white. 'Aurantiaca': fls single, orange. 'Ballerina': fls double, pet. fluted. 'Carmine King': to 35cm; fls single, carmine-rose. 'Compacta': habit compact. 'Crocea': fls deep orange and more freely produced. 'Golden West': to 35cm; fls single, bright yellow with orange centre. 'Mikado': fls single, orange-crimson. 'Milky-White': fls single, cream with orange centre. 'Mission Bells': fls double and semi-double. Monarch Hybrids: fls single and semi-double, cerise, carmine, orange, yellow and red; seed race. 'Orange King': fls single, bright orange. 'Purple Glean': fls single, purple-violet. 'Purple-Violet': fls single, mauve. 'Red Chief': fls single, deep red. 'Rosea': fls single, salmon. Thai Silk Hybrids: fls single and semi-double, tinged bronze. Z6.

E. californica var. *parvula* Gray = *E. mexicana*.

E. crocea Benth. = *E. californica* 'Crocea'.

E. cucullata Greene = *E. californica*.

E. douglasii Torr. = *E. mexicana*.

E. glauca Greene = *E. californica*.

E.hypecoides Greene. LITTLE LEMMON'S CALIFORNIA POPPY. V. glaucous, pubesc. or glab. St. leafy and branched, smaller than *E. californica*. Pet. bright yellow with orange spotting at base or wholly orange. S Calif. coast. Z7.

E.lobbii Greene. FRYING PANS; Usually glab. ann. to 30cm, not glaucous, lvs only sparsely acutely lobed. Fls yellow, to 4.5cm across. C Calif. Z7.

E. maritima Greene = *E. californica*.

E. mexicana Greene. MEXICAN GOLD. Cotyledon simple. Usually smaller than *E.californica*. Lvs basal, less dissected than in other sp. Fls usually dark orange, occas. pale yellow. Ariz. to W Tex. Z7.

E. pulchella Greene = *E. lobbii*.

E. tenuifolia Benth. non Hook. = *E. caespitosa*.

E. tenuifolia Hook. non Benth. = *E. lobbii*.

Escobaria Britt. & Rose. Cactaceae. 17 low-growing cacti, simple or clustering; st. depressed-globose to cylindric, tuberculate; spines present. Fls arising at upper edge of areoles; pericarpel naked; tube short; outer tep. usually ciliate. Fr. berry-like. W US, S Canada, N Mex. and Cuba.

E.aguirreana (Glass & Fost.) N.P. Tayl. St. simple to 7cm diam., depressed-globose to globose, bronzed-green; spines 8–15(–20)mm, pale brown. Fl. 18×18mm, yellow or tinged red; stigmas 5–6, yellow. Fr. 1.2cm, tinged bronze. Summer. NE Mex. Z9.

E.albicolumnaria Hester. Usually simple, to 25×6cm, cylindric; spines 1–2.5cm, pale. Fl. 1.5–3×1–2.5cm, pale pink to magenta; stigmas white or pale pink. Fr. yellow-green to pink. SW US. Z9.

?E. bella Britt. & Rose = *E. emskoetteriana*.

E. chaffeyi Britt. & Rose = *E. dasyacantha* var. *chaffeyi*.

E. chihuahuensis Britt. & Rose. St. simple or clustered, to 8cm diam., globose to cylindric, variable in size and shape; spines mostly adpressed. Fl. to 2×2cm, pale pink to purple; stigmas 5–6, white. Fr. green. Spring. N Mex. Z9.

E. dasyacantha (Engelm.) Britt. & Rose. St. simple, rarely 2–3-branched, subglobose to cylindric, 7.5–17.5×5–7.5cm; spines 25–50. Fl. 1–3×1–2.5cm, pink to pale brown. Fr. 1–2cm, bright red to deep pink. Spring. S New Mex., W Tex., N Mex. var. **duncanii** (Hester) N.P. Tayl. St. only 2.5–6×2.5–3.5cm; spines to 74. Fl. 3cm diam. S New Mex., W Tex. var. **chaffeyi** (Britt. & Rose) N.P. Tayl. Spines finer and more uniform. Fl. 1.5cm diam., pink, brown-tinged or sometimes green (then the fr. green also). N Mex. Z9.

E. emskoetteriana (Quehl) Borg. Clustering; st. to 5×2–4cm, globose to short-cylindric; central spines 6–8, radials 15–30. Fl. 1.5–3×2–3cm, off-white, yellow-green or pale purple; outer tep. with darker or brown mid-stripe. Fr. to 9mm, pink, red or purple. Summer. NE Mex. Z9.

E. henricksonii Glass & Fost. Resembling *E. chihuahuensis* but clustering more freely; st. to 3cm diam. cylindric; spines v. dense, more tightly adpressed. Fl. to 2.5cm diam., stigmas 1–2. Fr. 8mm, tinged red. Spring. N Mex. Z9.

E. hesteri (Y. Wright) F. Buxb. Clustering; st. 2.5–4cm, globose; central spines 0–4, radial spines 12–22. Fl. to 2.3×2.5cm, light purple; stigmas 3–4, white. Fr. 6–7mm. Summer. W Tex. Z9.

E. leei Boed. = *E. sneedii* var. *leei*.

E. lloydii Britt. & Rose. Clustering; central spines several, 2cm, stout, radial spines c20, white. Fl. 2.5cm diam.; inner tep. white with green tinge; stigmas green. Fr. 6–12mm, red. N Mex. Z9.

E. minima (Baird) D. Hunt. Simple or clustering; st. 1–2cm diam. globose to cylindric; spines c20–25, adpressed, flattened and truncate, pale yellow, pale pink or grey. Fl. c2cm, bright pink to red-purple. Fr. 5mm, green. SW US. Z9.

E. missouriensis (Sweet) D. Hunt Clustering, rarely simple; st. to 10cm diam., depressed-globose; central spines 0–1, radial spines 8–20, to 2cm, pubesc. Fl. 1.5–6cm diam., tep. green-tinged, yellow or pink, or cream with brown-pink mid-stripe. Fr. to 2×2cm, bright red. Spring. US, NE Mex. Z9.

E. muehlbaueriana (Boed.) F. Knuth = *E. emskoetteriana*.

E. roseana (Boed.) Schmoll ex F. Buxb. Clustering, rarely simple; st. 3–5cm diam., globose to cylindric, bright green; spines c20, to 15mm, yellow. Fl. to 2×2cm; tep. pale yellow with darker red-tinged and mid-stripe; stigmas 6–7. Fr. 1–1.5cm, pale green. Summer. NE Mex. Z9.

E. runyonii Britt. & Rose = *E. emskoetteriana*.

E. sneedii Britt. & Rose. Densely clustering; st. 2.5–7.5× 1.2–2.5cm, cylindric, nearly hidden by the spines; spines 3–15mm, white. Fl. 1–2×1–2cm, pale pink to magenta; stigmas 3–5, v. short. Fr. to 15×6mm. SW US. var. **leei** (Boed.) D. Hunt Spines recurved towards st. Fl. pink, tinged brown. SW US. Z9.

E. strobiliformis misapplied = *E. tuberculosa*.

E. tuberculosa (Engelm.) Britt. & Rose. Simple or clustering; st. 5–12(–20)×2.5–7.5cm; ovoid to cylindric, spines numerous, white, some strongly projecting, dark-tipped. Fl. to 2.5×3.5cm, pale pink to nearly white, sweetly scented; stigmas 4–7. Fr. to 2cm, deep pink to dull red, or green with red tinge. Summer. N Mex., SW US. Z9.

E. varicolor invalid = *E. tuberculosa*.

E. vivipara (Nutt.) F. Buxb. Clustering or simple, v. variable; st. depressed-globose to cylindric; central spines 2–12, radial spines 12–40. Fl. 2.5–5×2.5–6cm, pink to purple, or yellow, tinged green, orange or brown, occas. white; stigmas 5–10. Fr. 12–25mm, green. Spring. S Canada, US, N Mex. Z9.

E. zilziana (Boed.) Backeb. Clustering; st. to 10×3cm, cylindric; central spines 0–1 or more, radials 16–22, to 15mm. Fl. to 2.5×3cm; tep. pale yellow, olive-green or nearly white with pink mid-stripe. Fr. to 2cm, bright pink or red. Summer. N Mex. Plants in cult. are commonly misidentified as *E. tuberculosa* or *E. muehlbaueriana* (i.e. *E. emskoetteriana*). Z9.

→*Coryphantha, Echinocactus, Gymnocactus, Mammillaria, Neobesseya* and *Thelocactus*.

Escobita *Orthocarpus purpurascens*.

Escontria Britt. & Rose Cactaceae. 1 small candelabriform tree to 4m; trunk to 40cm diam.; st. to 20cm diam.; ribs 7–8, shallowly crenate; areoles close-set; central spines 3–5, one to 7cm, radial spines 10–15, to 1cm. Fls 3cm, subapical, tubular-campanulate; tube short with imbricate, scales; tep. pale yellow. S Mex. Z9.

E. chiotilla (F.A. Weber ex Schum.) Rose.

Esmeralda Rchb. f. Orchidaceae. 3 scrambling, monopodial, epiphytic orchids allied to *Vanda*. Lvs to 16cm, strap-shaped,

tough, folded when young. Rac. axillary; tep. spreading; lip mobile, midlobe ovate, basally saccate, longitudinal ridges 3–5, lat. lobes oblong, erect. Himal., SE Asia. Z10.

E. bella Rchb. f. Fls to 6cm diam., dors. sep. linear, lat. sep. and pet. oblong, cuneate, ochre, barred cinnamon; lip broad, basal callus white, spotted brown, lat. lobes striped purple-brown. Himal.

E. cathcartii (Lindl.) Rchb. f. Fls 4.5–8cm diam.; tep. ovate to broadly elliptic, yellow banded chocolate; lip white, striped red, margins yellow, undulate, dentate. Spring–summer. E Himal.

E. clarkei Rchb. f. Fls to 7cm diam., fragrant; tep. yellow, striped brown; sep. oblong; pet. narrower; lip fleshy, banded brown, apex rounded, minutely serrate, lat. lobes erect, square, papillose. Autumn–winter. Nepal.

E. sanderiana (Rchb. f.) Rchb. f. = *Euanthe sanderiana*. →*Vanda*.

Esparcet *Onobrychis viciifolia*.

Esparto Grass *Stipa tenacissima*.

Espeletia Humb. & Bonpl. Compositae. 30 to 80 herbs, shrubs or trees. Lvs mostly alt., often rosulate at trunk apex. Cap. radiate, solitary or in pan. or rac. Venez., Colomb., N Ecuad. Z10.

E. argentea Humb. & Bonpl. Shrub. St. short, erect, or apparently 0. Lvs in a term. cluster, to 45cm, linear, densely silvery adpressed-pubesc. Cap. to 3cm diam., in a term. corymb; phyllaries silvery-pubesc.; ray flts yellow; disc flts brown. Summer. Colomb.

E. grandiflora Humb. & Bonpl. Shrub. St. to 3m, covered with persistent dead lvs. Lvs to 50cm, elliptic to oblong, densely grey- to rust-lanate. Cap. to 4cm diam., in a dense term. pan.; ray flts golden-yellow; disc flts brown. Colomb.

E. neriifolia Schultz-Bip. ex Wedd. = *Libanothamnus neriifolius*.

E. schultzii Wedd. Perenn. herb. St. erect, to 1m, densely lanate. Lvs to 40cm, mostly opposite, oblong to oblong-lanceolate, grey-lanate. Cap. to 2.5cm diam. on 1–4cm peduncles; phyllaries yellow-lanate; ray flts, to 15mm. Venez.

Esperance Wax *Chamelaucium axillare*.

Espostoa Britt. & Rose. Cactaceae. 10 shrubs or small trees; st. columnar, many-ribbed, spiny. Cephalium present. Fls usually nocturnal; tube short; tep. short, spreading to recurved; lowermost sta. inserted on a diaphragm partially closing the nectar chamber. S Ecuad., Peru, Boliv.

E. blossfeldiorum (Werderm.) F. Buxb. Simple or branched below, to 2–3m; st. to 5–7cm diam.; ribs 18–25; central spines to 3cm, 1–4, brown or nearly black, radial spines 5–10mm, 20–25, glassy white. Cephalium with dense pale yellow wool and dark bristles. Fl. 6–7×5cm; inner tep. creamy yellow. N Peru. Z9.

E. huanucoensis Johnson ex Ritter = *E. lanata*.

E. lanata (Kunth) Britt. & Rose. Shrubby or tree-like, to 4–7m; st. up to 10–15cm diam.; ribs 20–30; non-flowering areoles with long silky hairs; central spines 1–2, 2–5cm, yellow, brown or black, radial spines numerous, 4–7mm, pale yellow. Cephalium white, pale yellow brown; fls 4–8cm diam, white to purple. S Ecuad., Peru. Z9.

E. melanostele (Vaupel) Borg. Shrub to 2m, branching from base; st. to 10cm diam.; ribs c25; non-flowering areoles with dense white or pale brown hairs clothing the whole st.; spines yellow, later black, central spines 1–3, 4–10cm, radial spines 40–50, 5–10mm. Cephalium white, yellow or brown. Fl. 5–6×5cm, white. Central Peru. Z9.

E. senilis (Ritter) N.P. Tayl. Shrub 2–4m, few-branched from or towards base; st. 4–6cm diam., fastigiate, covered by spines; ribs 17–18; central spines 0–2, bristly, longer and darker than the radials, radial spines 60–80, c1cm, white. Cephalium covering 6–12 ribs. Fl. 4.5–6×3–4cm, purple. Peru. Z9.

E. sericata (Backeb.) Backeb. = *E. lanata*.

E. ulei (Gürke) F. Buxb. = *Facheiroa ulei*.

→*Binghamia, Cephalocereus, Pseudoespostoa* and *Thrixanthocereus*.

Espostoopsis F. Buxb. Cactaceae. 1 shrub, 2–4m, branching; st. 4–10cm diam., cylindric; ribs 22–33, non-flowering areoles with white hairs covering whole st.; central spines 1–3, 1–3cm, pale yellow, red or brown, radial spines 5–8mm, concealed by the areolar hair. Cephalium or fleece on one side of stem-apex; fls c4cm diam., shortly tubular-campanulate, nocturnal; tep. short, white. E Braz. Z9.

E. dybowskii (Roland-Goss.) F. Buxb.

→*Austrocephalocereus* and *Cephalocereus*.

Esrog *Citrus medica*.

Estragon *Artemisia dracunculus*.

Ethiopian Banana *Ensete ventricosum.*
Ethiopian Cabbage *Brassica carinata.*

Etlingera Giseke. Zingiberaceae. 57 rhizomatous, perenn. herbs. St. cane-like. Infl. scapose, torch-like; bracts thick, waxy, lowermost largest, decurved, remainder ± erect and tightly overlapping in a cone; fls small, ± concealed, lip tubular. Sri Lanka to New Guinea.
E. elatior (Jack) Rosemary M. Sm. TORCH GINGER; PHILIPPINE WAXFLOWER. 5–6m. Lvs to 85cm, linear-lanceolate. Scape to 1.5m; infl. to 30cm; bracts 8–12cm, deep pink; lip deep crimson, margin white or yellow. Malesia.
→*Alpinia, Elettaria, Nicolaia* and *Phaeomeria.*

Etrog *Citrus medica.*
Etruscan Honeysuckle *Lonicera etrusca.*

Euanthe Schltr. Orchidaceae. 1 monopodial, epiphytic orchid. St. tall, robust. Lvs to 40cm, ligulate, leathery, 2 ranked. Rac. axill.; fls 6–10cm diam.; sep. ovate to suborbicular, dors. sep. rose, tinged white, lateral sep. tawny-yellow, veined or flushed rose; pet. ovate-rhombic, with tawny basal blotch, dotted red; lip honey-coloured, streaked or veined red, midlobe oblong, fleshy, basally saccate, with 3 ridges, lat. lobes round, erect. Philipp. Z10.
E. sanderiana (Rchb. f.) Schltr.
→*Esmeralda* and *Vanda.*

Eucalyptus L'Hérit. Myrtaceae. Over 500 aromatic, oily trees, shrubs or mallees. Bark flaking, smooth, fibrous, stringy or tessellated. Juvenile lvs alt. or opposite, amplexicaul to pairedperfoliate; adult lvs mostly alt., usually petiolate, lanceolate, often falcate, pendulous, rarely erect, tough. Infl. of umbel-like condensed dichasia, sometimes single or paired in lf axils, or in term. pan.; cal. and/or cor. forming a cap, shed at anthesis; sta. numerous, usually creamy-white or yellow, occas. red, borne on a cup-like turbinate to globose hypanthium. Fr. usually woody, cylindrical, globose or urceolate. Aus., Malesia, Philipp. Z10 unless specified.
E. acaciiformis var. *linearis* Deane & Maid. = *E. nicholii.*
E. acervula Sieber ex DC. = *E. eugenioides.*
E. acmenoides Schauer. WHITE MAHOGANY. Tree to 60m. Bark fibrous, somewhat stringy, thick, grey-brown. Juvenile lvs opposite, ovate, shining, acuminate; adult lvs 8–12.5cm, alt., lanceolate to broadly lanceolate, sometimes falcate, acuminate, thin, green. Infl. axill., simple, 7–11-fld umbels. Queensld, NSW.
E. acutangula Turcz. = *E. tetraptera.*
E. agglomerata Maid. BLUE-LEAVED STRINGY BARK. Tree to 40m. Bark fibrous, stringy, furrowed grey. Juvenile lvs usually alt., ovate; adult lvs 7.5–12cm, alt., lanceolate to broadly lanceolate, acuminate, green or blue-green. Infl. axillary, simple; umbels 11–15-fld or more; fls to 1.5cm diam. white. NSW, Vict.
E. aggregata Deane & Maid. BLACK GUM. Tree to 18m. Bark rough, fibrous, hard, furrowed, grey, persistent. Juvenile lvs opposite, elliptic to ovate or broadly lanceolate, dull green, leathery; adult lvs 5–13cm, alt., lanceolate to narrowly lanceolate, acuminate, bright to dark green. Infl. axill.; umbels 4–7-fld; fls about 1cm diam., white. NSW, Vict.
E. agnata Domin = *E. occidentalis.*
E. alba Reinw. ex Bl. WHITE GUM. Tree to 20m, ± decid. Bark pink-red to white or cream, smooth. Juvenile lvs alt., broadly ovate, grey-green, leathery; adult lvs 7–21cm, alt., lanceolate or ovate, acuminate, thin, green. Infl. axill., simple; umbels 7-fld; fls white, fragrant. W Aus., N Territ., Queensld; also in Timor and New Guinea.
E. albens Benth. WHITE BOX. Tree to 25m. Bark rough, fibrous, light grey or somewhat bleached on trunk, then smooth and white above. Juvenile lvs alt., ovate to suborbicular, sometimes cordate, grey-green to blue-green; adult lvs 10–16cm, alt., lanceolate, acuminate, glaucous or grey-green. Infl. term., paniculate, also axill.; umbels 7-fld. NSW, Vict., Queensld, S Aus.
E. alpina Lindl. GRAMPIANS GUM. Mallee to 2m, or tree to 10m. Bark fibrous, grey on st. and smooth, grey-white above, or smooth throughout. Juvenile lvs opposite, quickly becoming alt., elliptic to ovate, grey green, paler beneath, lower lvs stellate-pubesc.; adult lvs 7.5–10cm, alt., broadly lanceolate to ovate, mucronate, thick, dark green. Infl. axill., simple; umbels 3–7-fld; fls 2cm diam., white to cream. Vict. Z9.
E. ambigua DC. = *E. stricta.*
E. amplifolia Naudin. CABBAGE GUM. Tree to 30m. Bark smooth throughout, white, grey, blue-grey or grey-green. Juvenile lvs alt., broadly lanceolate to orbicular, stalked; adult lvs 10–20cm, alt., lanceolate to broadly lanceolate, acuminate, firm. Infl.

axill., simple; umbels usually 7-fld; fls c2cm diam., white, numerous. NSW.
E. amygdalina Labill. PEPPERMINT. Tree 15–30m, or a mallee to 10m. Bark finely fibrous, grey-brown on larger br., smooth, salmon pink or white to grey above. Juvenile lvs opposite and sessile, becoming alt. and shortly stalked, green to grey-green, paler beneath; adult lvs 7–12cm, alt., narrowly lanceolate to linear, falcate, acuminate or uncinate, thin, dull green, scented of peppermint. Infl. axill., simple; umbels with 11–15 or more fls; fls to 1.5cm diam., cream. Tasm. Z9.
E. amygdalina var. *latifolia* Deane & Maid. = *E. dives.*
E. amygdalina var. *regnans* F. Muell. = *E. regnans.*
E. andreana Naudin = *E. elata.*
E. andrewsii Maid. NEW ENGLAND BLACKBUTT. Tree to 45m. Bark fibrous, grey to brown-grey on trunk and larger br. Juvenile lvs subopposite, ovate to ovate-lanceolate, stalked, dull blue-green, sometimes glaucous; adult lvs 10–16cm, alt., lanceolate, often falcate, acuminate, oblique, green or blue-green. Infl. axill., simple; umbels 11–15-fld; fls to 1cm diam., white. Queensld, NSW. ssp. *campanulata* (R. Bak. & H.G. Sm.) L. Johnson & Blaxell. NEW ENGLAND ASH. Tree to 25m. Adult lvs 9–18cm. Fls campanulate.
E. angulosa Schauer. RIDGE-FRUITED MALLEE. Mallee to 4.5m. Bark smooth, grey to light brown, sometimes rough at base. Juvenile lvs opposite, elliptic-ovate to lanceolate, stalked, pale green; adult lvs 6–10cm, alt., lanceolate, sometimes elliptic, uncinate, green. Infl. axill., simple; umbels 3–7-fld; fls ± 2cm diam., pale yellow. W & S Aus.
E. angustifolia (Turcz.) Desf. ex Link = *E. viminalis.*
E. archeri Maid. & Blakely. ALPINE CIDER GUM. Mallee or small tree to 9m. Bark smooth, tinged grey, decid., leaving white to pink-grey new bark. Juvenile lvs opposite, becoming alt., ovate, sessile, amplexicaul; adult lvs 5–8cm, alt., elliptic to ovate, acuminate, stalked, thick, green. Infl. axill., simple; umbels 3-fld; fls over 1cm diam., white to cream. Tasm. Z9.
E. argillacea W. Fitzg. Tree to 14m, mallee-like. Bark rough, fibrous, grey. Juvenile lvs ± opposite, ovate to almost circular, short-stalked, leathery; adult lvs 8–14cm, alt., lanceolate, acute, light or grey-green. Infl. term., sometimes axill.; umbels 3–7-fld; fls c1.2cm diam., white, showy. W Aus., N Territ., Queensld.
E. astringens (Maid.) Maid. BROWN MALLET. Tree to 24m, sometimes a mallee. Bark smooth, light brown to grey, with small patches of curly exfoliating bark. Juvenile lvs alt., ovate, green or grey-green; adult lvs 7–11cm, alt., lanceolate, acuminate. Infl. axill., simple; umbels usually 7-fld; fls to 3cm diam., creamy yellow. W Aus.
E. aurantiaca F. Muell. = *E. miniata.*
E. australiana R. Bak. & H.G. Sm. = *E. radiata.*
E. baueriana Schauer. BLUE BOX. Tree to 20m. Bark fibrous, flaky, pale grey on large br., then smooth, white to grey above, rough and persistent on smaller br. Juvenile lvs opposite, becoming alt., suborbicular to broadly ovate, emarginate, stalked, thin, pale green; adult lvs 6–10cm, alt., ovate to broadly lanceolate, acuminate, stalked, pale green or slightly glaucous. Infl. term.; paniculate; umbels 8-fld; fls to 1.5cm diam., white to creamy, numerous. NSW, Vict.
E. behriana var. *purpurascens* F. Muell. ex Benth. = *E. lansdowneana* ssp. *albopurpurea.*
E. bicolor Cunn. ex Mitch. = *E. largiflorens.*
E. bicostata Maid., Blakely & J. Simmonds = *E. globulus* ssp. *bicostata.*
E. blakelyi Maid. Tree to 25m. Bark smooth, white or grey with grey-blue, pink or cream-yellow patches. Juvenile lvs alt., ovate to suborbicular, grey-green; adult lvs 9–16cm, alt., lanceolate, acuminate, moderately thick. Infl. axill., simple; umbels 7–11-fld; fls c1.5cm diam., white or pink. NSW, Queensld and Vict.
E. blaxlandii Maid. & Cambage. BLAXLAND'S STRINGYBARK. Tree to 35m. Bark usually fibrous, stringy, furrowed, greybrown. Juvenile lvs alt., ovate, short-stalked, slightly hairy beneath, thin-textured; adult lvs 7–12cm, alt., broadly lanceolate, apiculate to acuminate, shining, green. Infl. axill., simple; umbels 7–11-fld; fls c1.5cm diam., white. NSW.
E. bosistoana F. Muell. BOSISTO'S BOX; COAST GREY BOX. Tree to 60m. Bark rough, finely fibrous, grey below, or rather smooth and grey-white. Juvenile lvs alt., ovate or orbicular; adult lvs 10–20cm, alternate, lanceolate to narrowly lanceolate, sometimes falcate, acuminate. Infl. usually axill., simple, sometimes term., paniculate; umbels 7-fld. NSW, Vict.
E. botryoides Sm. BANGALAY; SOUTHERN MAHOGANY. Tree to 40m. Bark fibrous or flaky-fibrous, brown to grey-brown, on larger br., smooth, grey-white on smaller br. Juvenile lvs opposite, becoming alt., ovate; adult lvs 10–16cm, alt., broadly lanceolate, long-acuminate. Infl. axill., simple; umbels 7–11-fld. NSW, Vict.
E. bowmannii F. Muell. ex Benth. = *E. fibrosa.*
E. brachypoda Turcz. = *E. rudis.*

E. bridgesiana R. Bak. APPLE BOX. Tree to 22m. Bark rough, fibrous, flaky, tessellated, grey-brown. Juvenile lvs ± opposite, orbicular to broadly ovate, amplexicaul, crenulate, glaucous; adult lvs 12–20cm, alt., lanceolate or narrowly lanceolate, acuminate, dark green. Infl. axill., simple; umbels 7-fld. Queensld, NSW, Vict. Z9.

E. bridgesiana var. *amblycorys* (Blakely) Cameron = *E. bridgesiana*.

E. burdettiana Blakely & Steedman. BURDETT'S GUM. Mallee or shrub to 3.5m. Bark smooth, green-brown to light brown. Juvenile lvs opposite becoming alt., elliptic to ovate or lanceolate; adult lvs 6–9cm, alt., lanceolate, acuminate, shining. Infl. axill., simple; umbels 7–11-fld. W Aus.

E. burracoppinensis Maid. & Blakely. BURRACOPPIN MALLEE. Mallee to 6m, diffuse. Bark smooth, grey, except lower trunk where rough, persistent. Juvenile lvs opposite, soon alt., petiolate, lanceolate; adult lvs 8–11cm, alt., lanceolate, acuminate, light green. Infl. axill., simple; umbels 3-fld. W Aus.

E. caerulescens Naudin = *E. melliodora*.

E. caesia Benth. GUNGURRU. Mallee to 10m. Bark at first smooth, red-brown, later falling in curling flakes. Juvenile lvs opposite becoming alt., petiolate, orbicular or cordate, shining; adult lvs 7–12cm, alt., lanceolate, acute or acuminate, sometimes falcate, grey-green. Infl. axill., simple; umbels 3-fld, pendulous; sta. red. W Aus. ssp. *magna* Brooker & Hooper. SILVER PRINCESS. Mallee to 10m. Adult lvs 15–24cm, acuminate. Z9.

E. calophylla R. Br. ex Lindl. MARRI. Tree to 60m. Bark tessellated, grey-brown. Juvenile lvs opposite, soon alt., petiolate, peltate, ovate; adult lvs 9–14cm, alt., ovate to broadly lanceolate, acuminate; thick, shining, dark green. Infl. term., corymbose pan.; umbels 3–7-fld; fls cream (rarely pink). W Aus.

E. calycogona Turcz. GOOSEBERRY MALLEE. Mallee or small tree, to 8m. Bark smooth, grey throughout, often with ribbons or flakes of shedding bark on lower trunk. Juvenile lvs opposite, becoming alt., narrowly lanceolate to ovate, grey-green; adult lvs 6–10cm, alt., narrowly lanceolate to lanceolate, uncinate, shining, green, with conspicuous oil glands. Infl. axill., simple; umbels 7-fld. W Aus., S Aus., NSW, Vict.

E. camaldulensis Dehnh. RIVER RED GUM. Tree to 45m. Bark smooth, white, grey, brown or red. Juvenile lvs opposite, soon alt., ovate to broadly lanceolate, grey-green or blue-green; adult lvs 8–30cm, alt., lanceolate to narrowly lanceolate, thick, grey-green. Infl. axill., simple; umbels 7–11-fld. Aus. Z9.

E. campanulata R. Bak. & H.G. Sm. = *E. andrewsii* ssp. *campanulata*.

E. campaspe S. Moore. SILVER-TOPPED GIMLET. Tall shrub or tree to 11m. Bark smooth, copper-brown to dark red-brown. Juvenile lvs opposite, becoming alt., broadly lanceolate, grey-green; adult lvs 8–11cm, alt., lanceolate, stalked, glaucous, grey-green. Infl. axill., simple; umbels 7-fld; fls to 2.5cm diam., cream, v. conspicuous. W Aus.

E. camphora R. Bak. MOUNTAIN SWAMP GUM. Tree to 22m. Bark smooth throughout, decorticating at base, grey to almost black. Juvenile lvs subopposite, becoming alt., ovate, spathulate or elliptic; adult lvs 6–13cm, alt., ovate to broadly lanceolate, sometimes emarginate, shining. Infl. axill., simple; umbels 7-fld. NSW and Vict. Z9.

E. cannonii R. Bak. = *E. macrorhyncha* ssp. *cannonii*.

E. capitellata Sm. BROWN STRINGYBARK. Tree to 20m. Bark usually fibrous, stringy, furrowed, grey-brown. Juvenile lvs usually alt., broadly lanceolate, shortly stalked, undulate, the lower ones stellate hairy; adult lvs 8–17cm, alt., lanceolate, falcate, mucronate to acuminate, thick, shining, green. Infl. axill., simple; umbels 7–11-fld or sometimes more. NSW.

E. carnea R. Bak. = *E. umbra* ssp. *carnea*.

E. cephalocarpa Blakely. MEALY STRINGYBARK. Tree 8–24m. Bark rough, fibrous grey-brown, fissured. Juvenile lvs opposite, sessile, amplexicaul, orbicular to ovate, grey-green or glaucous; adult lvs 12.5–20cm, alt., lanceolate, grey-green. Infl. axill., simple; umbels 7–11-fld. NSW, Vict.

E. cinerea F. Muell. ex Benth. ARGYLE APPLE. Tree to 16m. Bark rough, fibrous, red-brown on larger br., smooth and red-brown or grey above, or rough throughout. Juvenile lvs opposite, ± sessile, amplexicaul, orbicular to cordate, glaucous; juvenile or intermediate lvs usually persist on adult trees; adult lvs 7.5–11.5cm, alt., broadly lanceolate, acuminate, thick, glaucous. Infl. axill., simple; umbels 3-fld. NSW, ACT, Vict. 'Pendula': growth pendulous; lvs rounded, silver.

E. cinerea var. *multiflora* Maid. = *E. cephalocarpa*.

E. citriodora Hook. LEMON-SCENTED GUM. Tree 25–50m. Bark white, powdery, sometimes pink, red or blue-grey. Juvenile lvs alt., narrow to broadly lanceolate often peltate, sometimes setose; adult lvs alt., 8–16cm, lanceolate, lemon-scented when crushed. Infl. term. or sometimes axillary, corymbose pan.; umbels 3-fld. Queensld.

E. cladocalyx F. Muell. SUGAR GUM. Tree to 35m. Bark smooth, grey-white, yellow or blue-grey. Juvenile lvs opposite, becoming alt., petiolate, orbicular, dark green; adult lvs 11–15cm, alt., lanceolate, acuminate, shining, dark green. Infl. axill., simple; umbels 11–15-fld. S Aus. Z9.

E. clavigera Cunn. ex Schauer. APPLE GUM; CABBAGE GUM. Tree to 10m. Bark tessellated, grey, smooth above. Juvenile lvs ± opposite, ovate to cordate, stalked, setulose on veins beneath; adult lvs 11–19cm, mostly alt., petiolate, lanceolate, acute, usually rounded, thick, grey-green. Infl. axill., compound; umbels to 11-fld. W Aus., N Territ.

E. cloeziana F. Muell. GYMPIE MESSMATE. Tree to 55m. Bark fissured or tessellated, brown, grey or grey-yellow on trunk and larger br.; smaller br. smooth, grey-white or yellow. Juvenile lvs alt., ovate or broadly lanceolate, short-stalked, pale green; adult lvs 8–13cm, alt., lanceolate, acuminate. Infl. axill., paniculate; umbels 7-fld. Queensld.

E. coccifera Hook. f. TASMANIAN SNOW GUM. Shrub or tree to 10m. Bark smooth, white-grey, yellow or pink when fresh. Juvenile lvs opposite becoming alt., broadly elliptic or orbicular, apiculate, sessile, subglaucous; adult lvs 5–10cm, alt., elliptic or lanceolate, uncinate, thick, grey-green, with peppermint scent. Infl. axill.; umbels 3(–9)-fld. Tasm. Z8.

E. coccifera var. *parviflora* Benth. = *E. coccifera*.

E. conoidea Benth. = *E. erythronema*.

E. consideniana Maid. YERTCHUK. Tree to 30m. Bark fibrous, grey. Juvenile lvs opposite, soon alt., elliptic-ovate, sessile, becoming petiolate, blue-green; adult lvs 8–14cm, alt., lanceolate, acuminate, often oblique. Infl. axill., simple; umbels 11–15-fld. NSW, Vict. Z9.

E. coolabah Blakely & Jacobs = *E. microtheca*.

E. cordata Labill. SILVER GUM. Shrub to 3m, or tree to 21m. Bark smooth, white, grey, green or yellow-green and purple. Juvenile lvs opposite, sessile, amplexicaul, orbicular or cordate, crenulate, glaucous, usually persisting on mature trees; adult lvs usually only in upper parts of large tree, 7.5–13cm, alt., lanceolate, acute, dull, glaucous. Infl. axill., simple; umbels 3-fld. Tasm. Z8.

E. coriacea Cunn. ex Schauer = *E. pauciflora*.

E. cornuta Labill. YATE. Tree to 25m, sometimes a mallee to 10m. Bark rough, hard, deeply furrowed, dark grey on larger br., smooth, grey or grey-brown above. Juvenile lvs alt., petiolate, orbicular to broadly lanceolate; adult lvs 8–14cm, alt., lanceolate to broadly lanceolate, acuminate, shining. Infl. axill., simple; umbels usually 11–15-fld. W Aus. Z9.

E. corymbosa Sm. = *E. gummifera*.

E. corynocalyx F. Muell. = *E. cladocalyx*.

E. cosmophylla F. Muell. CUP GUM. Mallee to 2m or tree to 10m. Bark smooth, matt, white or blue-grey. Juvenile lvs alt., lanceolate, stalked; adult lvs 7.5–15cm, alt., lanceolate, leathery. Infl. axill., simple, occas. apparently term., umbels 3-fld. S Aus.

E. costata F. Muell. & Behr ex F. Muell. = *E. incrassata*.

E. crebra F. Muell. NARROW-LEAVED IRONBARK. Tree to 30m. Bark rough throughout, dark grey to black. Juvenile lvs usually alt., linear to narrowly lanceolate, green to grey-green; adult lvs 6.5–15cm, usually alt., lanceolate, acuminate, dull, green or grey-green. Infl. term., paniculate; umbels 7–11-fld. Queensld, NSW.

E. crucis Maid. SILVER MALLEE. Mallee to 15m, spreading or erect. Bark at first smooth, red-brown, later curling in flakes. Juvenile lvs oppposite, sessile, orbicular or ovate, grey-green, mucronate, with black oil dots; adult lvs alt., lanceolate, sometimes 0. Infl. axill., simple; umbels 7-fld. W Aus. ssp. *lanceolata* Brooker & Hooper. Mallee to 15m, erect. Adult lvs 5–10cm.

E. cuspidata Turcz. = *E. angulosa*.

E. dalrympleana Maid. MOUNTAIN GUM. Tree to 40m. Bark smooth, blotched white and grey to yellow-white, and sometimes pink, green to olive. Juvenile lvs opposite, sessile, occas. amplexicaul, orbicular to ovate, light green to subglaucous; adult lvs 10–20cm, alt., narrowly lanceolate, acuminate, sometimes undulate, often shining. Infl. axillary, simple; umbels 3- or 7-fld. NSW, Vict. and Tasm. ssp. *heptantha* L. Johnson. Tree to 30m. Adult lvs 10–22cm. Umbels 7-fld. Z8.

E. daphnoides Miq. = *E. coccifera*.

E. dealbata Cunn. ex Schauer. TUMBLEDOWN GUM. Tree to 15m. Bark smooth, grey or white. Juvenile lvs alt., broadly ovate, stalked, usually glaucous; adult lvs 7.5–11.5cm, alt., lanceolate, acuminate, glaucous. Infl. axill., simple; umbels 7–11-fld. Queensld, NSW, Vict.

E. deanei Maid. DEANE'S GUM. Tree to 65m. Bark smooth, white and blue-grey. Juvenile lvs alt., ovate to suborbicular stalked, dark green; adult lvs 8–12.5cm, alt., lanceolate, long-acuminate. Infl. axill., simple; umbels 7–11-fld. Queensld, NSW.

E. decepta Blakely = *E. siderophloia*.

E. deglupta Bl. MINDANAO GUM; BAGRAS. Tree to 70m. Bark

peeling in thin ribbons, freshly exposed surface bright green gradually changing through blue to purple to brick-red, inner bark off-white. Lvs simple, alt., 7.5–15cm, lanceolate, acuminate, slightly leathery, aromatic when crushed. Infl. axill. and term., many-fld umbels. Philipp., Bismarck Archipel., New Guinea, Celebes.

E. delegatensis R. Bak. ALPINE ASH. Tree to 40(–90)m. Bark fibrous, grey to brown below, smooth and white above, usually with insect 'scribbles'. Juvenile lvs alt., elliptic to ovate or broadly lanceolate, oblique, becoming stalked, dull-green or glaucous; adult lvs 9–22cm, alt., lanceolate, falcate, oblique, shining. Infl. (5)–11(–27)-fld. NSW, ACT, Vict. and Tasm. ssp. *tasmaniensis* Boland. Juvenile st. warty with conspicuous oil glands; juvenile lvs orbicular with a short drip-tip. Adult lvs 5–17. Z9.

E. desertorum Naudin = *E. foecunda.*

E. desmondensis Maid. & Blakely. DESMOND MALLEE. Mallee, slender, willowy, to 4.5m. Bark smooth, powdery white. Juvenile lvs alt.; adult lvs 7.5–10cm, alt., lanceolate to elliptic, acuminate, stalked, grey-green. Infl. axill., simple; umbels 11–15-fld; sta. lemon to yellow opening from bronze-red buds. Restricted to Mt Desmond, W Aus. Z9.

E. dextropinea R. Bak. = *E. muelleriana.*

E. diptera C.R.P. Andrews. TWO-WINGED GIMLET. Tree or mallee to 8m; trunk spirally fluted. Bark coppper-brown, shining. Juvenile lvs alt., lanceolate, stalked; adult lvs 6–9cm, alt., narrowly lanceolate, acuminate. Infl. axill., simple, 7-fld umbels. W Aus.

E. divaricata McAulay & Brett ex Brett = *E. gunnii.*

E. diversicolor F. Muell. KARRI. Tree to almost 90m. Bark smooth, orange-yellow, bronze or white, often patterned. Juvenile lvs alt., broadly ovate or orbicular, stalked; adult lvs 9–12cm, alt., broadly lanceolate, acuminate. Infl. axill., simple, 7-fld umbels. W Aus.

E. diversifolia Woolls = *E. macarthurii.*

E. dives Schauer. BROAD-LEAVED PEPPERMINT. Tree to 25m. Bark fibrous, grey-brown on larger br., smooth and grey above. Juvenile lvs opposite, ovate-cordate, sessile, amplexicaul, sometimes connate, usually glaucous; adult lvs 7–15cm, alt., broadly lanceolate, acuminate, thick, shining, green, with peppermint scent. Infl. axill., simple; umbels with 11–15 or more fls. NSW, ACT, Vict.

E. dorrienii Domin = *E. falcata.*

E. dumosa Cunn. ex Oxley. WHITE MALLEE; CONGOO MALLEE. Mallee to 8m, or rarely a tree to 13m. Bark smooth, white or yellow-white, flaky below. Juvenile lvs alt., ovate, stalked, grey-green; adult lvs 7–10cm, alt., lanceolate, uncinate, thick, dull, yellow-green to grey-green. Infl. axill., simple; umbels to 40-fld. S Aus. and NSW.

E. elata Dehnh. RIVER PEPPERMINT. Tree to 30m. Bark fibrous to *c*10m, compact, dark grey, fissured, then smooth, grey or white above. Juvenile lvs opposite, lanceolate, sessile, amplexicaul; adult lvs 10–14cm, alt., narrowly lanceolate, acuminate, thin, with peppermint scent. Infl. axill., simple; umbels to 40-fld. NSW, Vict.

E. eremophila (Diels) Maid. TALL SAND MALLEE. Shrub to 4.5m. Bark smooth, light brown or yellow-brown to grey-white. Juvenile lvs alt., ovate; adult lvs 6–8cm, alt., narrowly lanceolate to elliptic-lanceolate, acuminate or uncinate. Infl. axill., simple; umbels 7-fld. W Aus.

E. erthyrocalyx Oldfield & F. Muell. = *E. pyriformis.*

E. erythrocorys MF. Muell. ILLYARRIE; RED CAP GUM. Mallee or small tree to 8m. Bark smooth, grey to grey-brown, flaking to leave white to grey new bark. Juvenile lvs opposite to alt., ovate, stalked, pubesc., tinged grey; adult lvs 12–25cm, opposite, narrowly lanceolate, usually falcate, acuminate or cinate, stalked, glab.; leathery, thick, bright green. Infl. axill., simple; umbels 3-fld; fls to 5cm diam., with bright yellow sta. opening from bright red bud. W Aus.

E. erythronema Turcz. RED-FLOWERED MALLEE. Mallee or small tree to 6m. Bark almost white turning red, smooth, white, grey, red or pink-brown, usually powdered. Juvenile lvs alt., narrow-lanceolate, stalked, slightly glaucous; adult lvs 6–8cm, alt., narrowly lanceolate, uncinate, shining. Infl. axill., simmple; umbels 3–7-fld; sta. deep red. W Aus. var. *marginata* (Benth.) Domin. Umbels 3-fld, rim of open bud expanded, becoming wing-like in fr.

E. eugenioides Sieber ex Spreng. THIN-LEAVED STRINGYBARK; WHITE STRINGYBARK. Tree to 30m. Bark usually stringy, furrowed, grey to brown. Juvenile lvs usually alt., ovate-lanceolate, acuminate, short-stalked, dark green, lower ones stellate-hairy; adult lvs 10–14cm, alt., lanceolate, acuminate, green. Infl. axill., simple; umbels 7–11-fld, sometimes more. Queensld, NSW, Vict.

E. ewartiana Maid. EWART'S MALLEE. Mallee to 6m. Bark at first smooth, red-brown, later curling. Juvenile lvs alt., petiolate,

ovate, green; adult lvs 5–9cm, lanceolate to ovate-lanceolate, uncinate, dull grey- or yellow-green, gland. Infl. axill., simple; umbels 7-fld. W Aus.

E. eximia Schauer. YELLOW BLOODWOOD. Tree, usually 12(–20)m. Juvenile lvs alt., petiolate, oblong-lanceolate, blue-green; adult lvs 13–20cm, alt., lanceolate, falcate, acuminate, thick. Infl. term., corymbose pan.; umbels 7-fld. NSW.

E. fabrorum Schldl. = *E. obliqua.*

E. falcata Turcz. SILVER MALLET. Tree to 9m or mallee to 3.5m. Bark smooth grey-brown. Juvenile lvs usually alt., broadly lanceolate, grey-green; adult lvs 8–9.5cm, alt., lanceolate-ovate, sometimes falcate, uncinate, grey-green. Infl. axill., simple; umbels 7–15-fld; buds cream. W Aus.

E. falcifolia Miq. = *E. obliqua.*

E. fastigata Deane & Maid. BROWN BARREL. Tree to 45m. Bark rough, furrowed, shedding in long strips above, leaving smooth white upper br. Juvenile lvs alt., petiolate, ovate to broadly lanceolate, oblique, green adult lvs 8–15cm, alt., lanceolate, acuminate. Infl. axill., simple; umbels paired, 11–15-fld. NSW, Vict.

E. fergussonii R. Bak. = *E. paniculata.*

E. fibrosa F. Muell. BROAD-LEAVED IRONBARK. Tree to 35m. Bark rough, grey-black to black. Juvenile lvs usually alt., orbicular to ovate; adult lvs 14–18cm, usually alt., lanceolate, acuminate. Infl. term., paniculate, with some axill. umbels; 7–11-fld. Queensld, NSW. ssp. *nubila* (Maid. & Blakely) L. Johnson. BLUE-LEAVED IRONBARK. Juvenile lvs glaucous; adult lvs 11–18cm, lanceolate, glaucous.

E. ficifolia F. Muell. RED-FLOWERING GUM. Tree to 10m, straggly. Bark rough, fibrous, grey. Juvenile lvs usually alt., ovate to broad-lanceolate, stalked, bristly; adult lvs 7.5–15cm, alt., sometimes opposite, broadly lanceolate or ovate, acuminate, thick, glossy, dark green above. Infl. term., corymbose pan.; umbels 3–7-fld; fls crimson. W Aus. Z9.

E. flocktoniae (Maid.) Maid. Tree or mallee, to 12m. Bark smooth, grey to light brown or red-brown. Juvenile lvs opposite, sessile, decurrent, elliptic to broadly lanceolate, glaucous; adult lvs 8–11cm, alt., lanceolate, uncinate, dark green, shining, gland. Infl. simple, axill.; umbels 7–11-fld. W & S Aus.

E. floribunda Hueg. ex Endl. = *E. marginata.*

E. foecunda Schauer. Mallee to 5m, or tree to 8m. Bark smooth, grey to brown. Juvenile lvs opposite, lanceolate, sessile; adult lvs 4–8cm, alt., lanceolate, moderately thick, shining, often with prominent oil glands. Infl. axill., simple; umbels 7–13-fld. W Aus., S Aus., NSW and Vict.

E. formanii C. Gardner. FORMAN'S MALLEE. Mallee or small tree to 11m. Bark rough, grey, flaky, persistent below, smooth, grey, decid. above, exposed new bark grey-brown. Juvenile lvs alt., linear, densely clustered, glaucous; adult lvs 5–9cm, alt., linear, thick, yellow green. Infl. axill., simple; umbels 7–11-fld; fls to 1.5cm diam., cream, showy. W Aus.

E. forrestiana Diels. FUCHSIA GUM. Tree or shrub to 5m. Bark smooth, grey to light brown. Juvenile lvs usually alt., ovate, stalked; adult lvs 6–9cm, alt., lanceolate, apiculate, shining, deep green, gland. Infl axill., simple; umbels 1-fld, rarely 3-fld. Fr. red, pyriform, quadrangular. W Aus.

E. forsythii Maid. = *E. melliodora.*

E. fraxinoides Deane & Maid. WHITE MOUNTAIN ASH. Tree to 40m. Bark fibrous, compact, dark grey, smooth and white above, usually with insect 'scribbles'. Juvenile lvs alt., ovate to broadly lanceolate, sessile to stalked, light grey or blue-green; adult lvs 8–16cm, alt., lanceolate, falcate, acuminate or uncinate, usually oblique. Infl. axill., simple; umbels 7–11-fld. NSW, Vict. Z9.

E. gigantea Hook. f. non Desf. = *E. delegatensis* ssp. *tasmaniensis.*

E. gigantea Desf. non Hook. f. = *E. globulus.*

E. glandulosa Desf. = *E. amygdalina.*

E. globoidea Blakely. WHITE STRINGYBARK. Tree to 30m. Bark usually fibrous, stringy, furrowed grey. Juvenile lvs usually alt., ovate, undulate, stalked, discolorous; adult lvs 7.5–12.5cm, alt., lanceolate, acuminate. Infl. axill., simple; umbels 7–11-fld or sometimes more. NSW, Vict.

E. globoidea var. *subsphaerica* Blakely = *E. globoidea.*

E. globulus Labill. TASMANIAN BLUE GUM; BLUE GUM. Tree to 45(70)m. Bark usually smooth, white to cream, yellow or grey. Juvenile lvs to ovate, sessile, amplexicaul, paired-connate, grey-green to glaucous; adult lvs 12–25cm, lanceolate sometimes falcate, acuminate, green. Infl. axill., simple; umbels 1-, 3- or 7-fld. NSW, Vict., Tasm. 'Compacta': habit extremely dense, compact; trunk tinged grey; lvs to 30cm, ovate, deep glaucous-blue when young, becoming falcate, dark glossy green, to 30cm with age; fls white. ssp. *bicostata* (Maid., Blakely & J. Simmonds) Kirkpatr. EURABBIE; SOUTHERN BLUE GUM. Adult lvs 14–25cm, acuminate, thick. Umbels 3-fld. ssp. *maidenii* (F. Muell.) Kirkpatr. MAIDEN'S GUM. Adult lvs 12–28cm, acuminate, thick. Umbels 7-fld. ssp. *pseudoglobulus* (Naudin ex

Maid.) Kirkpatr. VICTORIAN EURABBIE. Tree to 45m. Adult lvs 13–25cm, acuminate, thick. Z9.

E. globulus var. *stjohnii* R. Bak. = *E. globulus* ssp. *pseudoglobulus*.

E. gomphocephala DC. TUART. Tree to 40m. Bark rather fibrous, finely fissured, grey. Juvenile lvs alt., petiolate, ovate, often cordate, pale green; adult lvs 9–16cm, alt., lanceolate, acuminate. Infl. axill.; umbels 7-fld. W Aus. Z9.

E. goniocalyx var. *nitens* Deane & Maid. = *E. nitens*.

E. grandis W. Hill ex Maid. FLOODED GUM; ROSE GUM. Tree to 55m. Bark smooth, white, blue-white or blue-grey, with some flaky bark below. Juvenile lvs alt., ovate to lanceolate, short-stlked; adult lvs 10–16cm, alt., lanceolate, long-acuminate. Infl. axill., simple; umbels 7–11-fld. Queensld, NSW.

E. grasbyi Maid. & Blakely = *E. longicornis*.

E. grossa F. Muell. ex Benth. COARSE-FLOWERED MALLEE. Mallee to 3m, straggly tree to 6m. Bark rough, grey, fissured. Juvenile lvs oppposite to alt., elliptic, stalked; adult lvs 9–13cm, opposite, subopposite or alt., broadly lanceolate to ovate, shining. Infl. axill., simple; umbels 7-fld, pendulous; sta. lemon-yellow. W Aus.

E. gullickii R. Bak. = *E. mannifera* ssp. *gullickii*.

E. gummifera (Sol. ex Gaertn.) Hochr. RED BLOODWOOD. Tree to 35m. Bark tessellated, grey-brown or brown. Juvenile lvs alt., petiolate, elliptic to ovate, stalked, setose; adult lvs 10–14cm, alt., lanceolate, acuminate, thick, shining, dark green above. Infl. term., corymbose pan.; umbels 7-fld. Queensld, NSW, Vict.

E. gunnii Hook. f. CIDER GUM. Tree to 25m. Bark smooth white, grey-green, sometimes flaky at trunk base. Juvenile lvs perfoliate to paired-connate or opposite, ovate, amplexicaul, crenulate, emarginate, grey-green; adult lvs 5–8cm, alt., elliptic or ovate to broadly lanceolate, acuminate or apiculate, grey-green. Infl. axill., simple; umbels 3-fld. Tasm. Z8.

E. gunnii var. *acervula* (Labill.) Deane & Maid. = *E. ovata*.

E. gunnii var. *maculosa* (R. Bak.) Maid. = *E. mannifera* ssp. *maculosa*.

E. gunnii var. *montana* Hook. f. = *E. gunnii*.

E. gunnii var. *ovata* (Labill.) Deane & Maid. = *E. ovata*.

E. haemastoma Sm. SCRIBBLY GUM. Tree to 15m. Bark smooth, white, grey or yellow-white, with insect 'scribbles'. Juvenile lvs alt., broadly lanceolate or ovate, falcate, shortly stalked, blue-green; adult lvs 12–15cm, alt., lanceolate, acuminate, oblique, thick, shining. Infl. axill., umbels 7–15-fld, 6–8mm. NSW. var. *capitata* Maid. Habit low, bushy. Lvs narrow-to-broad-lanceolate. Umbels 10–20-fld.

E. haemastoma var. *inophloia* C.T. White = *E. andrewsii*.

E. hemilampra F. Muell. = *E. resinifera*.

E. hemiphloia F. Muell. = *E. moluccana*.

E. hemiphloia var. *albens* (Benth.) Maid. = *E. albens*.

E. hemiphloia var. *purpurascens* (F. Muell. ex Benth.) Maid. = *E. lansdowneana* ssp. *albopurpurea*.

E. heterophylla Miq. = *E. obliqua*.

E. hypoleuca Schauer in Lehm. = *E. marginata*.

E. incrassata Labill. LERP MALLEE. Mallee to 4.5m. Bark smooth, grey to light brown. Juvenile lvs usually alt., lanceolate, stalked, grey-green; adult lvs 6–9cm, alt., lanceolate, acuminate to uncinate, shining. Infl. axill., simple; umbels 3–7-fld. W Aus., S Aus., NSW and Vict.

E. incrassata Sieber ex DC. = *E. pilularis*.

E. incrassata var. *angulosa* (Schauer) Benth. = *E. angulosa*.

E. incrassata var. *costata* (F. Muell. & Behr ex F. Muell.). = *E. incrassata*.

E. incrassata var. *dumosa* (Cunn. ex Oxley) Maid. = *E. dumosa*.

E. insignis Naudin = *E. tereticornis*.

E. johnstonii Maid. TASMANIAN YELLOW GUM. Tree to 40m. Bark smooth, orange-red or yellow-green to grey or yellow-bronze. Juvenile lvs opposite, elliptic, sessile to alt., petiolate, orbicular, shining, dark green; adult lvs 8–12cm, alt., lanceolate, sub-crenulate, acuminate, shining, dark green. Infl. axill., simple; umbels 3-fld. Tasm. Z8.

E. kruseana F. Muell. BROOKLEAF MALLEE. Mallee to 2.5m. Bark smooth, grey-brown, flaking, new bark yellow-brown. Juvenile lvs opposite, ovate to orbicular; adult lvs 1.5–2cm, opposite, sessile, orbicular. Infl. axill., simple; umbels 7-fld; sta. yellow. W Aus.

E. lactea R. Bak. = *E. mannifera* ssp. *praecox*.

E. laevopinea var. *minor* R. Bak. = *E. eugenioides*.

E. lamprocarpa F. Muell. ex Miq. = *E. dumosa*.

E. lanepoolei Maid. SALMONBARK WANDOO. Tree to 12m. Bark smooth, white or pink-yellow, often with red-brown flakes. Juvenile lvs opposite, becoming alt.; adult lvs 7.5–13cm, alt., lanceolate, falcate, uncinate, green to grey-green. Infl. axill., simple; umbels 3–7-fld. W Aus.

E. langii Maid. & Blakely = *E. cladocalyx*.

E. lansdowneana F. Muell. & J.E. Br. CRIMSON MALLEE. Mallee to 6m or small tree to 9m. Bark rough, grey-brown on larger br., then smooth and white-grey above. Juvenile lvs opposite becoming alt., lanceolate, stalked; adult lvs 8–14cm, alt., lanceolate, acute, grey-green to yellow-green. Infl. term., paniculate, or axill., simple; umbels 7-fld; fls crimson. S Aus. ssp. *albopurpurea* Boomsma. PORT LINCOLN MALLEE. Adult lvs 7–11cm, lanceolate, dull green to dark green; fls usually mauve.

E. lansdowneana var. *leucantha* Blakely = *E. lansdowneana* ssp. *albopurpurea*.

E. largiflorens F. Muell. BLACK BOX. Tree to 20m. Bark rough, fibrous, dark grey on larger br., smooth and white above. Juvenile lvs opposite to alt., linear to narrowly lanceolate, blue-green, short-stalked; adult lvs 9–18cm, alt., narrowly lanceolate to lanceolate, acute, dull, green or grey-green. Infl. usually term.; umbels 7–11-fld. S Aus., Vict., Queensld, NSW.

E. lehmannii (Schauer) Benth. BUSHY YATE. Mallee to 3m. Bark smooth, grey-brown or grey-red. Juvenile lvs opposite to alt., ovate or orbicular, stellate-hairy, stalked; adult lvs 5–7cm, alt., elliptic to lanceolate, apiculate. Infl. axill., simple; umbels 7–22-fld. W Aus. Z9.

E. leptophylla F. Muell. ex Miq. = *E. foecunda*.

E. leucadendron Reinw. ex Vriese = *E. alba*.

E. leucophylla Domin = *E. argillacea*.

E. leucoxylon F. Muell. YELLOW GUM; BLUE GUM; WHITE IRONBARK. Tree to 16m, or mallee. Bark rough, fibrous to 2m, grey to dark grey, then smooth, white, grey, yellow and/or blue. Juvenile lvs opposite, broadly lanceolate to ovate or orbicular, cordate, sessile, sometimes connate; adult lvs 9–13cm, alt., lanceolate, acuminate, dull green to glaucous. Conflorescences axill.; umbels 3-fld; sta. white, pink or red. S Aus., Vict., NSW. 'Rosea': sta. pink. 'Purpurea': sta. bright purple. ssp. *megalocarpa* Boland. Tree to 10m. Juvenile lvs sessile, ovate to broadly lanceolate; adult lvs 10–15cm. Peduncle 10–18mm; pedicels 8–17mm. ssp. *pruinosa* (F. Muell. ex Miq.) Boland. Mallee or tree to 15m. Juvenile lvs sessile, sometimes connate, orbicular, cordate, glaucous; adult lvs 9–14cm, grey-green or glaucous. ssp. *petiolaris* Boland. Tree to 13m. Juvenile lvs petiolate, broadly lanceolate to ovate, green; adult lvs 8–13cm. Z9.

E. leucoxylon ssp. *angulata* Benth. = *E. leucoxylon*.

E. leucoxylon ssp. *erythrostema* F. Muell. ex Miq. = *E. leucoxylon*.

E. leucoxylon ssp. *macrocarpa* J.E. Br. = *E. leucoxylon* ssp. *megalocarpa*.

E. leucoxylon ssp. *pauperita* J.E. Br. = *E. leucoxylon* ssp. *pruinosa*.

E. leucoxylon ssp. *rugulosa* F. Muell. ex Miq. = *E. leucoxylon*.

E. leucoxylon var. *minor* Benth. = *E. sideroxylon*.

E. leucoxylon var. *pallens* Benth. = *E. sideroxylon*.

E. lindleyana var. *stenophylla* Blakely = *E. elata*.

E. longicornis (F. Muell.) F. Muell. ex Maid. Tree to 30m. Bark rough, flaky or fibrous, grey on lower br., smooth, red-grey or grey-brown above. Juvenile lvs apparently in threes or spirally arranged, sessile, elliptic, grey-green, decurrent; adult lvs 7–12cm, alt., narrowly lanceolate, uncinate or acuminate, dark, shining, gland. Infl. simple, axill.; umbels 7–13-fld. W Aus.

E. longifolia Link. WOOLLYBUTT. Tree to 35m. Bark subfibrous, ridged and cracked, grey on larger br., smooth, light brown or grey-green above. Juvenile lvs opposite, ovate to broadly lanceolate, stalked, grey-green; adult lvs 11–24cm, alt., lanceolate, falcate. Infl. axill., simple, occas. apparently term.; umbels 3-fld, long-stalked. NSW.

E. luehmanniana F. Muell. YELLOW-TOP MALLEE ASH. Mallee to 6m. Bark smooth, white. Juvenile lvs alt., oblong or elliptic, stalked, shining, green; adult lvs 15–18cm, alt., lanceolate, acuminate or mucronate, oblique, leathery, shining green. Infl. axill., simple; umbels 7–11-fld. NSW.

E. macarthurii Deane & Maid. CAMDEN WOOLLYBUTT. Tree to 40m. Bark rough, fibrous, grey-brown on larger br., smooth and grey oon smaller br. Juvenile lvs opposite, sessile, broadly lanceolate to ovate or suborbicular, amplexicaul, dull green; adult lvs 8.5–19cm, alt., narrowly lanceolate, sometimes falcate, acuminate. Infl. axill., simple; umbels 7-fld. NSW. Z8.

E. macrandra F. Muell. ex Benth. LONG-FLOWERED MARLOCK. Mallee to 3m, or tree to 6m. Bark smooth, light brown to grey. Juvenile lvs alt., lanceolate; adult lvs 7.5–10cm, alt., lanceolate. Infl. axill., simple; umbels to 15-fld; sta. yellow-green to cream. Z8. W Aus.

E. macrocalyx Turcz. = *E. pyriformis*.

E. macrocarpa Hook. MOTTLECAH. Mallee to 5m, spreading or sprawling. Bark smooth, grey. Juvenile lvs opposite, ± sessile, broadly elliptic to suborbicular, grey-green or glaucous; adult lvs 8–12cm, opposite, sessile, broadly ovate to elliptic-ovate, apiculate, glaucous. Infl. axill., simple; umbels 1-fld; sta. red, rarely pink or cream. W Aus.

E. macrocera Turcz. = *E. cornuta*.

E. macrorhyncha F. Muell. RED STRINGYBARK.   Tree 12–35m. Bark fibrous, stringy, furrowed, grey-brown. Juvenile lvs alt., ovate, oblique, ± sessile, the lower ones stellate-hairy; adult lvs 9–14cm, alt., lanceolate, green, uncinate, stalked. Infl. axill., simple; umbels 3–11-fld. NSW, Vict., S Aus. ssp. *cannonii* (R. Bak.) L. Johnson & Blaxell. CANNON'S STRINGYBARK.   Tree to 12(–25)m. Adult lvs 10–18cm. Umbels 3–7-fld.

E. macrorhyncha var. *minor* Blakely = *E. macrorhyncha.*

E. maculata Hook. SPOTTED GUM.   Tree to 45m. Bark cream, pink-grey or blue-grey, mottled in several colours, dimpled. Juvenile lvs opposite, soon alt., ovate, some peltate, setose becoming glab.; adult lvs alt., 12–21cm, lanceolate to narrowly lanceolate, acuminate. Infl. term. or sometimes axill., corymbose pan.; umbels 3-fld. Queensld, NSW, Vict.

E. maculata var. *citriodora* (Hook.) Bail. = *E. citriodora.*

E. maculosa R. Bak. = *E. mannifera* ssp. *maculosa.*

E. mahoganii F. Muell. = *E. marginata.*

E. maidenii F. Muell. = *E. globulus* ssp. *maidenii.*

E. mannifera Mudie. MOTTLED GUM.   Tree to 25m. Bark smooth, white, cream, grey, sometimes with patches of red, usually powdery. Juvenile lvs linear to lanceolate, opposite soon becoming alt., petiolate; adult lvs alt., 10–18cm, lanceolate, acuminate, dull, blue-green to grey-green. Infl axill., simple; umbels 7-fld. NSW. ssp. *elliptica* (Blakely & McKie) L. Johnson. BRITTLE GUM.   Tree to 20m. Juvenile lvs orbicular or ovate to broadly lanceolate, subglaucous; adult lvs 15–25cm, lanceolate, green. ssp. *gullickii* (R. Bak. & H.G. Sm.) L. Johnson. MOUNTAIN SPOTTED GUM.   Tree to 18m. Juvenile lvs elliptic to broadly lanceolate, pale green; adult lvs 10–14cm, lanceolate, sometimes falcate, green. ssp. *maculosa* (R. Bak.) L. Johnson. BRITTLE GUM.   Tree to 18m. Juvenile lvs elliptic to narrowly lanceolate, blue-green to glaucous; adult lvs 6–15cm, lanceolate, dull, grey-green. ssp. *praecox* (Maid.) L. Johnson. Tree to 10m. Juvenile lvs orbicular, slightly glaucous; adult lvs 8–14cm, lanceolate, pale green. Z9.

E. marginata Donn ex Sm. JARRAH.   Tree to 40m; trunk to 2m diam. Bark fibrous, red-brown or brown, ageing grey. Juvenile lvs alt., ovate, dark green; adult lvs 8–13cm, alt., lanceolate, sometimes falcate, uncinate or acuminate, dark green, shining. Infl. axill., simple; umbels 7–11-fld. W Aus.

E. megacarpa F. Muell. BULLICH.   Tree to 30m, or mallee to 5m. Bark smooth, white or yellow-white. Juvenile lvs opposite, becoming alt., petiolate, ovate; adult lvs 8.5–14cm, alt., falcate or lanceolate, acuminate, dull, green. Infl. simple, axill.; umbels 3-fld. Fr. to 3cm diam. W Aus.

E. megacornuta C. Gardn. WARTY YATE.   Tree to 12m. Bark smooth, grey-brown to grey-red. Juvenile lvs ovate to lanceolate, opposite becoming alt. grey-green to green; adult lvs 6–8.5cm, alt., elliptic to lanceolate, acuminate. Infl. axill., simple; umbels 7-fld. W Aus.

E. melissiodora Lindl. = *E. citriodora.*

E. melliodora Cunn. ex Schauer. YELLOW BOX. YELLOW BOX.   Tree to 30m. Bark fibrous, grey, yellow or red-brown, then smooth, white-yellow above. Juvenile lvs opposite becoming alt., petiolate, ovate or elliptic, grey-green; adult lvs 6.5–14cm, alt., lanceolate, acuminate, green or grey-green. Infl. axill.; umbels 7-fld. Queensld, NSW, Vict.

E. micrantha DC. = *E. racemosa.*

E. microcorys F. Muell. TALLOW-WOOD.   Tree to 60m. Bark rough, softly fibrous red-brown. Juvenile lvs opposite becoming alt., petiolate, ovate, often crenulate; adult lvs 8–13cm, alt., ovate, often crenulate. Infl. axill.; umbels 7–9-fld. Queensld, NSW.

E. microtheca F. Muell. COOLIBAH.   Tree to 20m. Bark smooth and white or grey to rough, fibrous, grey to grey-black on trunk and larger br. Juvenile lvs opposite becoming alt., lanceolate, stalked, green to grey-green or glaucous; adult lvs 8–17cm, alt., lanceolate, acute, dull, green or grey-green. Infl. term., sometimes axill.; umbels 7-fld. Aus.

E. miniata Cunn. ex Schauer. DARWIN WOOLLYBUTT.   Tree to 30m. Bark stringy, spongy, fissured, grey or rusty red below, smooth and white above. Juvenile lvs elliptic, short-stalked, opposite, stellate-hairy; adult lvs 9–16cm, alt., sometimes falcate, acute or acuminate, green. Infl. axill.; umbels 7-fld; sta. orange or scarlet. W Aus., N Territ., Queensld.

E. mitchelliana Cambage. BUFFALO MALLEE.   Tree to 15m. Bark smooth, white to grey. Juvenile lvs opposite to alt., elliptic, lanceolate, subsessile, dark green; adult lvs 7.5–13cm, alt., lanceolate, moderately thick. Infl. axill., simple; umbels 7–11-fld. Vict.

E. moluccana Roxb. GREY BOX.   Tree to 30m. Bark rough, fibrous, grey below, smooth, sometimes shining, grey or white above, hanging in ribbons. Juvenile lvs alt., ovate, sometimes suborbicular; adult lvs 8.5–14cm, alt., broadly lanceolate to lanceolate, acuminate, shining green. Infl. term., paniculate, often also with axill., simple umbels; umbels 7-fld. Queensld,

NSW.

E. morrisonii Maid. = *E. kruseana.*

E. muelleri Miq. non Naudin = *E. dumosa.*

E. muelleri Naudin non Miq. = *E. ovata.*

E. muelleriana A. Howitt. YELLOW STRINGYBARK.   Tree to 40m. Bark fibrous, stringy, furrowed thick, grey-brown. Juvenile lvs usually alt., ovate, often oblique, short-stalked, green, lower lvs stellate-hairy; adult lvs 8–13cm, alt., lanceolate-acuminate, green. Infl. axill., simple; umbels 7–11-fld. NSW, Vict.

E. multiflora Rich. non Poir. = *E. deglupta.*

E. multiflora Poir. non Rich. = *E. robusta.*

E. naudiniana F. Muell. = *E. deglupta.*

E. neglecta Maid. OMEO GUM.   Tree to 6m. Bark rough, fibrous, grey below, smooth and green or green-grey above. Juvenile lvs opposite, sessile, broadly elliptic to suborbicular, grey-green, glaucous on midrib; adult lvs 7.5–15cm, alt., lanceolate, acute, thin, green. Infl. axill., simple; umbels 7–15-fld. Vict.

E. nervosa F. Muell. ex Miq. = *E. obliqua.*

E. nicholii Maid. & Blakely. NARROW-LEAVED PEPPERMINT; NICHOL'S WILLOW-LEAFED PEPPERMINT.   Tree to 15m. Bark rough, fibrous, yellow-brown. Juvenile lvs alt., crowded, sessile to shortly petiolate, linear, grey-green; adult lvs 6–13cm, alt., narrowly lanceolate, acuminate, blue- to grey-green, peppermint-scented. Infl. axill., simple; umbels 7-fld. NSW. Z8.

E. niphophila Maid. & Blakely = *E. pauciflora* ssp. *niphophila.*

E. nitens (Deane & Maid.) Maid. SHINING GUM.   Tree to 70(–90)m. Bark smooth, yellow-white or grey, or rough, flaky, grey to black below. Juvenile lvs opposite, sessile, broadly lanceolate to ovate, amplexicaul, glaucous; adult lvs 13–24cm, alt., lanceolate to narrowly lanceolate, acuminate, shining, green. Infl. axill., simple; umbels 7-fld. NSW and Vict. Z8.

E. nubila Maid. & Blakely = *E. fibrosa* ssp. *nubila.*

E. nutans F. Muell. RED-FLOWERED MOORT.   Mallee to 2.5m. Bark smooth, light brown to grey. Juvenile lvs alt., lanceolate; adult lvs 5–6.5cm, alt., lanceolate, acuminate to uncinate, shining, green. Infl. axill., simple; umbels 7-fld; sta. usually red-pink. W Aus.

E. obcordata Turcz. = *E. platypus.*

E. obliqua L'Hérit. MESSMATE; MESSMATE STRINGYBARK.   Tree to 90m. Bark fibrous, stringy, furrowed, grey to red-brown. Juvenile lvs opposite, becoming alt., ovate, oblique, often shortly acuminate, stalked, shining; adult lvs 10–15cm, alt., broadly lanceolate, acuminate, oblique, dark green, shining. Infl. axill., simple; umbels with 11 or more fls. Queensld, NSW, Vict., Aus., Tasm. Z9.

E. obliqua var. *alpina* Maid. = *E. delegatensis.*

E. obliqua var. *degressa* Blakely = *E. obliqua.*

E. obliqua var. *megacarpa* Blakely = *E. obliqua.*

E. occidentalis Endl. FLAT-TOPPED YATE; SWAMP YATE.   Tree to 20m. Bark rough, flaky, fibrous below, smooth, grey above. Juvenile lvs alt., ovate, stalked, green, discolorous; adult lvs 7–16cm, alt., lanceolate, uncinate. Infl. axill., simple; umbels usually 7-fld; sta. yellow-green to cream. W Aus.

E. occidentalis var. *astringens* Maid. = *E. astringens.*

E. occidentalis var. *eremophila* Diels = *E. eremophila.*

E. oldfieldii F. Muell. Mallee to 6m or tree. Bark smooth, grey-brown. Juvenile lvs alt., petiolate, lanceolate-ovate, pale green; adult lvs 7–10cm, alt., lanceolate to broadly lanceolate, acuminate, dull, grey-green. Infl. axill., simple; umbels 3-fld. W Aus.

E. oleosa F. Muell. ex Miq. = *E. foecunda.*

E. oleosa var. *flocktoniae* Maid. = *E. flocktoniae.*

E. oleosa var. *longicornis* F. Muell. = *E. longicornis.*

E. orbifolia F. Muell. ROUND-LEAVED MALLEE.   Mallee or tree to 6m. Bark at first smooth, red-brown, later decid. in longitudinally curling flakes. Juvenile lvs opposite, petiolate, suborbicular, grey-green; adult lvs 2.5–3.8cm, alt., sometimes opposite, suborbicular, retuse or emarginate, grey-green. Infl. axill., simple; umbels 7-fld. W Aus., N Territ., S Aus.

E. ovalifolia R. Bak. = *E. polyanthemos.*

E. ovata Labill. SWAMP GUM.   Tree to 30m. Bark smooth, white, grey or pink-grey, often rough and decorticating below. Juvenile lvs alt., elliptic to ovate, dull, green; adult lvs 8–15cm, alt., broadly lanceolate, undulate, acuminate, shining. Infl. axill., simple; umbels 7-fld. S Aus., Vict., NSW and Tasm. Z8.

E. ovata var. *aquatica* Blakely = *E. camphora.*

E. ovata var. *camphora* (R. Bak.) Maid. = *E. camphora.*

E. pallens DC. = *E. obliqua.*

E. paludosa R. Bak. = *E. ovata.*

E. paniculata Sm. GREY IRONBARK.   Tree to 50m. Bark rough, light grey. Juvenile lvs opposite becoming alt., ovate to broadly lanceolate, stalked, green; adult lvs 9.5–15cm, alt., lanceolate, acuminate, green. Infl. term., paniculate; umbels 7-fld. NSW.

E. papuana F. Muell. GHOST GUM.   Tree to 15m. Bark smooth, decid., white or grey-white. Juvenile lvs opposite to sub-opposite, oblong or elliptic to broadly lanceolate, acute, short-stalked, glab. or sparsely bristly, undulate, blue-grey; adult lvs 5–18cm, alt., narrowly to broadly lanceolate, stalked, light yellow-green to deep glossy green. Infl. axill., occas. term. and paniculate; umbels 7–11-fld; sta. white to tinged green. Queensld, W Aus., N Territ.

E. parvifolia Cambage. KYBEAN GUM. Tree to 9m. Bark smooth, dull, grey, grey-green or sometimes pink. Juvenile lvs opposite, sessile, elliptic, green, often persisting on mature trees; adult lvs 5–7cm, subopposite, lanceolate, acute. Infl. axill., simple; umbels 7-fld. NSW. Z8.

E. patentiflora Miq. = *E. melliodora*.

E. pauciflora Sieber ex Spreng. SNOW GUM; GHOST GUM. Tree to 20m, or mallee. Bark smooth, white to light grey or sometimes brown-red, shedding in irregular patches or strips, giving a mottled appearance, sometimes with 'scribbles'. Juvenile lvs opposite quickly becoming alt.; adult lvs 7–16cm, alt., lanceolate to broadly lanceolate or narrowly ovate, acute to acuminate, oblique, petiolate. Infl. axill., simple; umbels 7–15-fld. Queensld, NSW, Vict., S Aus., Tasm. Z8. ssp. *niphophila* (Maid. & Blakely) L. Johnson & Blaxell. SNOW GUM. Straggly small tree or shrub to 6m. Juvenile lvs ovate, dull, blue green; adult lvs 5–8cm, broadly lanceolate to narrowly ovate, uncinate, thick, green to blue-green. Umbels usually 7–11-fld. Z7. ssp. *debeuzevillei* (Maid.) L. Johnson & Blaxell. JOUNAMA SNOW GUM. Many-stemmed shrub or a crooked tree, 9(–18)m. Juvenile lvs lanceolate, dull, blue-green; adult lvs 7.5–15cm, lanceolate, uncinate, thick. Umbels 7–11-fld. Z8.

E. perriniana F. Muell. ex Rodway. SILVER DOLLAR GUM; SPINNING GUM; ROUND-LEAFED GUM. Mallee to 6m or straggly tree to 9m. Bark smooth, bronze, white-green or grey, often a short stocking of persistent bark at trunk base. Juvenile lvs perfoliate, orbicular, glaucous; adult lvs 8–13cm, alt. or subopposite, lanceolate, acuminate, dull, grey-green or blue-green. Infl. axill., simple; umbels 3-fld. NSW, ACT, Vict. Z8.

E. persicifolia Lodd. = *E. pilularis*.

E. phellandra R. Bak. & H.G. Sm. = *E. radiata*.

E. phlebophylla F. Muell. ex Miq. = *E. pauciflora*.

E. phoenicea F. Muell. SCARLET GUM; GNAINGAR. Tree to 12m. Bark flaky, fibrous, yellow to yellow-brown, smooth and cream or white above. Juvenile lvs subopposite becoming alt., ovate, short-stalked, setose at first; adult lvs 8–12cm, alt., lanceolate, acuminate, grey-green. Infl. simple, axill.; umbels many-fld; sta. orange or scarlet. W Aus., N Territ., Queensld.

E. pilularis Sm. BLACKBUTT. Tree to 70m. Bark fibrous, grey-brown on most of trunk, then smooth, white or yellow-grey above, often with insect 'scribbles'. Juvenile lvs opposite, sessile, oblong to narrow-lanceolate, green above, often purple beneath, glab.; adult lvs 9–16cm, alt., lanceolate. Infl. simple, axill.; umbels 7–15-fld on long flattened peduncles, 3–6mm. Queensld.

E. piperita Sm. SYDNEY PEPPERMINT. Tree to 20–30m. Bark fibrous, grey below, smooth and white or grey above. Juvenile lvs opposite becoming alt., sessile, ovate, falcate; adult lvs 10–16cm, alt., lanceolate, falcate, acuminate, oblique, green or blue-green, dull, peppermint-scented. Infl. axill., simple, 7–15-fld umbels. NSW. ssp. *urceolaris* (Maid. & Blakely) L. Johnson & Blaxell. Tree to 30m. Adult lvs 6–18cm. Fr. urceolate not ovoid.

E. piperita var. *laxiflora* Benth. = *E. piperita*.

E. platyphylla F. Muell. POPLAR GUM. Tree to 20m, decid. Bark white, grey or tan, often powdery. Juvenile lvs alt., broadly lanceolate to ovate, short-stalked; adult lvs 7–13cm, alt., orbicular, cordate or rhomboid, rarely lanceolate, rounded or apiculate, thin, green. Infl. axill., simple; umbels 3–7-fld. Queensld.

E. platypus Hook. ROUND LEAFED MOORT. Tree or mallee to 9m. Bark smooth, brown-pink or grey. Juvenile lvs alt., ovate; adult lvs 4–6.5×2–3.9cm, alt., usually orbicular, sometimes obovate, often retuse, undulate, or lanceolate to spathulate, olive green. Infl. axill., simple; umbels 7-fld. W Aus.

E. polyanthemos Schauer. RED BOX; SILVER DOLLAR GUM. Tree to 25m. Bark fibrous, grey-brown, or ± smooth throughout, grey, cream or pink. Juvenile lvs alt., orbicular, emarginate, stalked, dull, grey-green; adult lvs 5.5–9cm, alt., ovate to broadly lanceolate, apiculate, grey or glaucous. Infl. term., paniculate; umbels 7-fld. NSW, Vict. Z9.

E. populnea F. Muell. BIMBLE BOX; POPLAR BOX. Tree to 20m. Bark rough, fibrous, grey to brown or often bleached below, smooth and brown to grey-brown above. Juvenile lvs alt., ovate to orbicular, stalked, shining, green; adult lvs 5–10cm, alt., ovate, broadly lanceolate or rhombic, acute, shining green. Infl. term.; umbels 7–15-fld. Queensld, NSW.

E. praecox Maid. = *E. mannifera* ssp. *praecox*.

E. preissiana Schauer. BELL-FRUITED MALLEE. Mallee to 2.5m. Bark smooth, grey. Juvenile lvs opposite, sessile, ovate to elliptic, concolorous; adult lvs 7–12cm, opposite or subopposite,

ovate to elliptic, obtuse, broadly cuneate, sessile, thick, grey-green. Infl. simple, axill.; umbels 3-fld; sta. yellow opening from ovoid-campanulate red buds. W Aus.

E. procera Dehnh. = *E. obliqua*.

E. pruinosa Turcz. = *E. pyriformis*.

E. pseudoglobulus Naudin ex Maid. = *E. globulus* ssp. *pseudoglobulus*.

E. ptychocarpa F. Muell. SPRING BLOODWOOD. Tree to 20m. Bark somewhat tessellated or fibrous, grey-brown. Juvenile lvs opposite, lanceolate, stalked, occas. peltate; adult lvs 20–30cm, mostly alt., narrowly ovate to lanceolate, acute or acuminate, thick, green or grey-green. Infl. term., corymbose pan.; umbels 3–7-fld. W Aus., N Territ., Queensld.

E. pulchella Desf. WHITE PEPPERMINT. Tree to 21m. Bark smooth, yellow to white and grey. Juvenile lvs initially opposite, linear, sessile; adult lvs 5–10cm, alt., linear, acuminate or uncinate, thin, with peppermint scent. Infl. axill., simple; umbels with 15+ fls. Tasm.

E. pulverulenta Sims. SILVER-LEAVED MOUNTAIN GUM. Tree to 9m, or mallee to 5m. Bark smooth, bronze to grey. Juvenile lvs opposite, sessile, amplexicaul, orbicular to ovate, glaucous, usually persisting on mature plants; adult lvs rarely seen, 5–10cm, alt., lanceolate or oblong, apiculate, glaucous. Infl. axill., simple; umbels 3-fld. NSW. Z9.

E. punctata DC. GREY GUM. Tree to 35m. Bark grey, usually smooth with a matt surface, cream to orange, weathering to grey or grey-brown. Juvenile lvs alt., narrowly lanceolate to lanceolate; adult lvs 8–15cm, opposite becoming alt., lanceolate, slightly falcate, stalked, shining above. Infl. axill., simple, occas. apparently term.; umbels 7-fld. NSW. Z9.

E. punctata var. *didyma* R. Bak. & H.G. Sm. = *E. punctata*.

E. purpurascens var. *petiolaris* DC. = *E. gummifera*.

E. pyriformis Turcz. DOWERIN ROSE; PEAR-FRUITED MALLEE. Mallee to 4.5m. Bark smooth, grey to light brown. Juvenile lvs alt., petiolate, ovate-lanceolate, sometimes orbicular; adult lvs 6–8cm, alt., lanceolate to ovate-lanceolate, acuminate, light green. Infl. axill., simple; umbels 3-fld, pendulous; sta. red, pink, yellow or ivory from large pyriform buds. W Aus. Z9.

E. pyriformis var. *elongata* Maid. = *E. pyriformis*.

E. racemosa Cav. SCRIBBLY GUM; SNAPPY GUM. Tree to 15m. Bark smooth, white or yellow-white, with insect 'scribbles'. Juvenile lvs alt., narrowly lanceolate; adult lvs 7–14cm, alt., lanceolate, acuminate, oblique, thin, green. Infl. axill., simple; umbels 7–15-fld. NSW.

E. radiata Sieber ex DC. NARROW-LEAVED PEPPERMINT. Tree 10–50m. Bark fibrous, grey-brown or with smaller br., smooth. Juvenile lvs amplexicaul; adult lvs 7–15cm, alt., linear to lanceolate, acuminate, thin, with peppermint scent. Infl. axill., simple; umbels 7–23-fld. NSW, ACT, Vict. ssp. *robertsonii* (Blakely) L. Johnson & Blaxell. Tree to 50m. Juvenile lvs grey-green or blue-grey; adult lvs 7.5–13cm, lanceolate to narrowly lanceolate, acuminate, thin, grey-green or subglaucous. Z9.

E. radiata var. *subexserta* Blakely = *E. radiata*.

E. radiata var. *subplatyphylla* Blakely & McKie = *E. radiata*.

E. raveretiana var. *jerichoensis* Domin = *E. microtheca*.

E. redunca Schauer. BLACK MARLOCK. Mallee to 4.5m. Bark smooth, light brown to grey or grey-brown. Juvenile lvs alt., lanceolate, stalked; adult lvs 5.5–8cm, alt., lanceolate, sometimes falcate, apiculate, dull green. Infl. axill., simple; umbels 11–15-fld; sta. lemon or cream. W Aus.

E. regnans F. Muell. MOUNTAIN ASH. Tree 75(–100)m. Bark rough up to 15m on trunk, smooth, white or grey-green above, often shedding in strips. Juvenile lvs opposite becoming alt., petiolate, ovate to broadly lanceolate, oblique, green; adult lvs 9–14cm, alt., lanceolate or broadly lanceolate, acuminate. Infl. axill., simple; umbels paired, 9–15-fld. Vict., Tasm. Z9.

E. resinifera Sm. RED MAHOGANY. Tree to 45m. Bark fibrous, red-brown, brown or grey. Juvenile lvs alt., ovate to broadly lanceolate, stalked; adult lvs 10–17cm, alt., broadly lanceolate, long-acuminate. Infl. axill., simple; umbels 7–11-fld. Queensld, NSW.

E. resinifera var. *grandiflora* Benth. = *E. resinifera*.

E. resinifera var. *hemilampra* (F. Muell.) Domin = *E. resinifera*.

E. rhodantha Blakely & Steedman. ROSE MALLEE. Mallee to 3m. Bark smooth, grey-brown. Juvenile lvs opposite, sessile, ovate to orbicular, grey-green; adult lvs 6–8cm, opposite, sessile, clasping, orbicular, cordate, acuminate, silvery-glaucous. Infl. axill., simple; umbels usually 1-fld, rarely 3-fld; sta. red. W Aus.

E. risdonii Hook. f. RISDON PEPPERMINT. Shrub, mallee or tree to 8m. Bark smooth, grey to cream-white, sometimes with grey-pink patches. Juvenile lvs opposite, orbicular, ovate or broadly lanceolate, becoming connate, glaucous, persisting on mature trees; adult lvs 6.5–10cm, alt., lanceolate, acuminate, firm, subglaucous or green, scented of peppermint. Infl. axill., simple; umbels 7–15-fld. Tasm.

E. risdonii var. *elata* Benth. = *E. delegatensis* ssp. *tasmaniensis*.

E. robertsonii Blakely = *E. radiata* ssp. *robertsonii*.

E. robusta Sm. SWAMP MAHOGANY. Tree to 30m. Bark rough, spongy, subfibrous, red-brown. Juvenile lvs alt., ovate, stalked; adult lvs 10–16cm, alt., broadly lanceolate, long-acuminate. Infl. axill., simple; umbels 9–15-fld. Queensld, NSW.

E. rostrata Schldl. = *E. camaldulensis*.

E. rudis Endl. FLOODED GUM. Tree to 20m. Bark rough, fibrous, grey below, smooth and grey above. Juvenile lvs alt., ovate or orbicular, dull, grey-green; adult lvs 9–14cm, alt., lanceolate, acuminate, moderately thick, green. Infl. axill., simple; umbels 7-fld. W Aus.

E. salicifolia Cav. = *E. amygdalina*.

E. saligna Sm. SYDNEY BLUE GUM. Tree to 55m. Bark smooth, white or blue-grey, with rough, brown-grey, flaky bark at base. Juvenile lvs opposite, becoming alt., ovate to broadly lanceolate, stalked; adult lvs 9–17cm, alt., lanceolate, long-acuminate. Infl. axill., simple; umbels 7–11-fld. Queensld, NSW.

E. saligna var. *parviflora* Dean & Maid. = *E. deanei*.

E. saligna var. *protrusa* Blakely & McKie = *E. saligna*.

E. salmonophloia F. Muell. SALMON GUM. Tree to 24m. Bark smooth throughout, salmon-coloured or pink-brown to grey or grey-brown, changing colour with the seasons. Juvenile lvs opposite to alt., shortly petiolate, elliptic to lanceolate; adult lvs 6–12cm, alt., uncinate, shining green. Infl. simple, axill.; umbels 7–11-fld. W Aus.

E. salubris F. Muell. GIMLET GUM. Tree to 15(–24)m; trunk strongly spirally fluted. Bark smooth, shining, red-brown or copper-coloured. Juvenile lvs opposite to alt., lanceolate; adult lvs 4.5–10.5cm, alt., narrowly lanceolate, shining green, gland. Infl. axill., simple; umbels usually 7-fld. W Aus. var. *glauca* Maid. Adult lvs glaucous.

E. sargentii Maid. SALT RIVER GUM. Tree to 11m. Bark rough, flaky, black below, smooth, maroon above. Juvenile lvs opposite, linear-lanceolate, stalked, grey-green; adult lvs 10cm, alt., narrowly lanceolate, acuminate, stalked, thin, pale green. Infl. axill., simple; umbels 7-fld; sta. cream opening from brown to yellow-red buds. W Aus.

E. semicorticata F. Muell. = *E. pilularis*.

E. sepulcralis F. Muell. WEEPING GUM. Mallee or slender tree to 8m; br. pendulous, branchlets pruinose. Bark smooth, white to grey-brown. Juvenile lvs opposite, sessile, elliptic, becoming alt., petiolate, oblong-lanceolate, grey-green; adult lvs 7–9cm, alt., linear-lanceolate. Infl. axill., simple; umbels 7-fld, pendulous; sta. pale yellow. W Aus.

E. siderophloia Benth. NORTHERN GREY IRONBARK. Tree to 45m. Bark rough, sometimes smooth above, grey to grey-black. Juvenile lvs opposite to alt., ovate to broadly lanceolate, stalked, green; adult lvs 8–15cm, usually alt., lanceolate to broadly lanceolate, acuminate, dull, green or grey-green. Infl. term., paniculate; umbels 7-fld. Queensld, NSW.

E. siderophloia var. *glauca* Deane & Maid. = *E. fibrosa* ssp. *nubila*.

E. sideroxylon Cunn. ex Woolls. RED IRONBARK; PINK IRON BARK; MUGGA. Tree to 35m. Bark hard, black, deeply furrowed throughout or below, smooth, white on upper br. Juvenile lvs opposite becoming alt., petiolate, linear to lanceolate or ovate, green or grey-green; adult lvs 7–14cm, alt., lanceolate, acuminate or uncinate, green, grey-green or blue-green. Infl. simple, axill.; umbels 3- or 7-fld; sta. white, cream, pink or red. Queensld, NSW, Vict. ssp. *tricarpa* L. Johnson. Juvenile lvs lanceolate to ovate; adult lvs 9.5–22cm, green. Umbels 3-fld. Z9.

E. sieberi L. Johnson. SILVERTOP ASH. Tree usually to 35(–45)m. Bark fibrous, hard, furrowed, dark grey to black below, smooth and white above. Juvenile lvs opposite, becoming alt., ovate, grey- or blue-green; adult lvs 9–15cm, alt., lanceolate, acuminate, shining. Infl. axill., simple; umbels 7–15-fld. NSW, ACT, Vict., Tasm. Z9.

E. sieberiana F. Muell. = *E. sieberi*.

E. smithii R. Bak. GULLY GUM. Tree to 45m. Bark rough, fibrous, grey or brown below, smooth and white or cream above. Juvenile lvs opposite, sessile, lanceolate, amplexicaul, green, st. sometimes glaucous; adult lvs 10–18cm, alt., narrowly lanceolate, acuminate. Infl. axill., simple; umbels 7-fld. NSW, Vict.

E. spathulata Hook. SWAMP MALLET. Tree or mallee to 12m. Bark smooth, red-brown to grey. Juvenile lvs opposite, to alt., narrowly lanceolate; adult lvs 5–6cm, alt., linear-lanceolate or narrowly elliptic, often uncinate, stalked, gland. Infl. axill., simple; umbels 3–7-fld. W Aus. ssp. *grandiflora* L. Johnson & Blaxell. Tree or mallee to 4.5m. Adult lvs 5–6cm, narrowly elliptic, acuminate or uncinate, green or grey-green. Fls larger.

E. splachnicarpon Hook. = *E. calophylla*.

E. staigeriana F. Muell. ex Bail. LEMON-SCENTED IRONBARK.

Tree to 21m. Bark rough, dark grey to black, deeply fissured. Juvenile lvs alt., ovate to elliptic, stalked green; adult lvs 4–10cm, usually alt., lanceolate to elliptic, obtuse, apiculate, strongly lemon-scented. Infl. axill. and term., paniculate; umbels 7–11-fld. Queensld.

E. stannariensis Bail. = *E. cloeziana*.

E. steedmanii C. Gardn. STEEDMAN'S GUM. Small tree to 12m. Bark smooth, red-brown. Juvenile lvs opposite, to alt., broadly lanceolate or ovate, stalked; adult lvs 4.5–6.5cm, alt., narrowly elliptic or lanceolate, apiculate. Infl. axill., simple; umbels 3-fld. W Aus.

E. stellulata Sieber ex DC. BLACK MALLEE; BLACK SALLY. Tree to 15m. Bark rough, dark grey on lower half, decid. above, smooth, brown to olive-green. Juvenile lvs opposite, orbicular to ovate, ± sessile; adult lvs to 9cm, alt., elliptic to broadly lanceolate, thick, stalked green. Infl. axill., simple; umbels 7–23-fld; sta. white to cream.

E. stjohnii (R. Bak.) R. Bak. = *E. globulus* ssp. *pseudoglobulus*.

E. stowardii Maid. FLUTED HORN MALLEE. Tree or mallee to 8m. Bark smooth, yellow-brown to grey or grey-pink. Juvenile lvs opposite to alt., broadly lanceolate to ovate, stalked, green; adult lvs 8–11.5cm, alt., lanceolate, acuminate. Infl. axill., simple; umbels usually 7-fld; sta. yellow-green to cream. W Aus.

E. stricklandii Maid. STRICKLAND'S GUM. Tree to 11m. Bark smooth, red-brown to grey, with flaky grey-black rough bark below. Juvenile lvs opposite becoming alt., elliptic to ovate, stalked; adult lvs 10–13cm, alt., lanceolate, shining. Infl. axill., simple; umbels 7-fld; sta. yellow green-yellow. W Aus. Z9.

E. stricta Sieber ex Spreng. BLUE MOUNTAINS MALLEE. Mallee to 5m. Bark smooth, white or grey. Juvenile lvs opposite to alt., lanceolate, thick; adult lvs 6–10cm, alt., narrowly lanceolate, acuminate, oblique, thick. Infl. axill., simple; umbels 7-fld, sometimes more. NSW. Z9.

E. stuartiana F. Muell. ex Miq. = *E. bridgesiana*.

E. stuartiana var. *amblycorys* Blakely = *E. bridgesiana*.

E. subcrenulata Maid. & Blakely. TASMANIAN ALPINE YELLOW GUM. Tree to 18m. Bark smooth, grey to white or yellow-green. Juvenile lvs opposite, alt., ± sessile, elliptic or ovate to orbicular, crenulate, green; adult lvs 6–10cm, alt., lanceolate to broadly lanceolate, subcrenulate, acuminate, shining, green. Infl. axill., simple; umbels 3-fld. Tasm. Z9.

E. submultiplinervis Miq. = *E. pauciflora*.

E. subulata Cunn. ex Schauer = *E. tereticornis*.

E. tasmanica Blakely = *E. delegatensis* ssp. *tasmaniensis*.

E. tenuiramis Miq. SILVER PEPPERMINT. Tree to 25m. Bark smooth, white to grey or somewhat yellow. Juvenile lvs initially opposite, sessile, elliptic, becoming connate, ovate, glaucous; adult lvs 5.5–13cm, alt., broadly lanceolate to elliptic-lanceolate, acuminate or uncinate, usually thin, grey-green or glaucous, with a peppermint scent. Infl. axill., simple; umbels with 11–15 or more fls. Tasm. Z9.

E. tereticornis Sm. FOREST RED GUM. Tree to 50m. Bark smooth, white, grey or grey-blue. Juvenile lvs alt., ovate, dull, green to blue-green; adult lvs 10–20cm, alt., narrowly lanceolate to lanceolate, acuminate, thick, shining. Infl. axill., simple; umbels 7–11-fld. Queensld, NSW, Vict.

E. tereticornis var. *brachycorys* Benth. = *E. punctata*.

E. tetragona (R. Br.) F. Muell. TALLERACK. Mallee to 3m. Bark light brown to white or grey. Juvenile and mature lvs similar, 7–15cm, opposite, broadly elliptic, apiculate, thick, glaucous or green. Infl. axill., simple; umbels 3-fld; buds quadrangular; sta. in 4 bundles. W Aus.

E. tetraptera Turcz. Mallee to 3m. Bark smooth, grey to light brown, sometimes rough at base. Juvenile lvs opposite to alt., broadly elliptic, green; adult lvs 13–18cm, alt., broadly lanceolate or elliptic, apiculate, bright green. Infl. axill., simple; umbels 1-fld; buds with 4 wings. W Aus.

E. torquata Luehm. CORAL GUM. Tree to 11m. Bark to 4m rough, dark grey, slightly fissured, then smooth, grey-brown above. Juvenile lvs opposite to alt., lanceolate, stalked; adult lvs 9–12cm, alt., lanceolate, sometimes falcate, acuminate or uncinate, dull, grey-green. Infl. axill., simple; umbels 7-fld; sta. pink or red. W Aus.

E. tropica Cambage ex Maid. = *E. argillacea*.

E. umbellata (Gaertn.) Domin = *E. tereticornis*.

E. umbra R. Bak. BROAD-LEAVED WHITE MAHOGANY. Tree to 25m, or shrub to 4m. Bark fibrous, somewhat stringy, thick, grey to grey-brown. Juvenile lvs opposite, ovate, sessile, amplexicaul, dark green, shining; adult lvs 10–14cm, alt., lanceolate, somewhat falcate, acuminate, oblique, thick, green. Infl. axill., simple, 7–11-fld umbels. ssp. *carnea* (R. Bak.) L. Johnson. Tree to 25m. Adult lvs 8–12cm, blue green.

E. uncinata var. *rostrata* Benth. = *E. foecunda*.

E. urnigera Hook. f. URN GUM. Tree to 12m. Bark smooth, white-grey or yellow-brown. Juvenile lvs opposite, to alt., sessile, orbicular, crenulate, amplexicaul, often emarginate, shining; adult lvs 5–9cm, alt., lanceolate, acute, thick, green or slightly glaucous. Infl. axill., simple; umbels 3-fld; buds urceolate. Tasm. Z8.

E. variegata F. Muell. = *E. citriodora*.

E. vernicosa Hook. VARNISHED GUM. Dwarf shrub to 1m, or mallee to 3.5m. Bark smooth, grey. Juvenile lvs opposite, sessile, elliptic to ovate, crenulate, mucronate, shining, green; adult lvs 1.5–2.5cm, opposite, elliptic to ovate, mucronate, shining green. Infl. axill., simple; umbels 3-fld. Tasm. Z8.

E. viminalis Labill. MANNA GUM. Tree to 50m. Bark smooth, grey, white or yellow-white, or rough, fibrous on lower or whole trunk and on larger br. Juvenile lvs opposite, sessile, lanceolate, cordate, or amplexicaul, green; adult lvs 12–20cm, alt., lanceolate or narrowly lanceolate, acuminate. Infl. axill., simple; umbels 3- or 7-fld. S Aus., Queensld, Vict. ssp. *cygnetensis* Boomsma. ROUGH-BARKED MANNA GUM. Bark rough, thick, fibrous below, grey-brown, then smooth and grey-white above. Adult lvs 12–18cm. Umbels 7-fld. Z8.

E. viminalis var. *pedicellaris* F. Muell. ex Deane & Maid. = *E. smithii*.

E. viminalis var. *rhynchocorys* F. Muell. ex Maid. = *E. viminalis*.

E. virgata var. *fraxinoides* (Deane & Maid.) Maid. = *E. fraxinoides*.

E. virgata var. *stricta* (Sieber ex Spreng.) Maid. = *E. stricta*.

E. whittingehamei Landsborough = *E. gunnii*.

E. wiburdii Blakely = *E. eugenioides*.

E. wilkinsoniana R. Bak. = *E. eugenioides*.

E. wilkinsoniana var. *crassifructa* Blakely = *E. eugenioides*.

E. woodwardii Maid. LEMON-FLOWERED GUM. Tree to 15m, sometimes straggly. Bark smooth, grey or pink-white, sometimes scaly below. Juvenile lvs opposite to alt., oblong or broadly lanceolate, stalked, grey-green; adult lvs 10–15cm, alt., lanceolate, acuminate, thick. Infl. axill., simple; umbels 7-fld; sta. lemon-yellow. W Aus.

E. woollsii F. Muell. = *E. longifolia*.

E. yangoura Blakely = *E. globoidea*.

Eucharis Planch. & Lind. Amaryllidaceae. 17 bulbous, everg. perennials. Lvs ovate or elliptic to lanceolate, glossy, narrowing to a long petiole. Umbel scapose; spathe valves 2; fls pedicellate, drooping, white to ivory, often tinted green at base, somewhat fleshy, often fragrant; perianth tube short-cylindrical, somewhat ribbed; perianth lobes 6, spreading; sta. 6, broadened at base and fused to form a cup. S Amer. Z10.

E. amazonica Lind. ex Planch. Lvs to 40×18cm, long-elliptic, tip acuminate, base subcordate, undulate; petiole to 30cm. Scape to 70cm; perianth tube white, curved, to 6×2cm at throat, lobes ovate, spreading to 9cm diam., white; staminal cup to 14×30mm, cylindrical, dentate; style protruding by up to 1.5cm. NE Peru.

E. amazonica hort. non Lind. = *E.* ×*grandiflora*.

E. bakeriana N.E. Br. Lvs to 55×20cm, elliptic, rather succulent, smooth. Scape to 80cm; perianth tube to 40mm, lobes spreading to 6cm diam.; staminal cup to 16×15mm, subcylindrical to campanulate, dentate; style just exceeding anth. Peru.

E. bouchei Woodson & Allen. Lvs to 25×10cm, broadly elliptic, slightly succulent, smooth, seldom undulate; petiole to 25cm. Scape to 55cm; fls unscented; tube to 45mm, curved, lobes to 32×17mm; staminal cup to 12×15mm, subcylindrical, dentate or divided; style exceeding anth. by up to 1cm. C Amer.

E. candida Planch. & Lind. Lvs to 35×11.5cm, elliptic, dark green above, deeply plicate, undulate; petiole to 30cm. Scape to 60cm; unscented; tube to 35mm, lobes spreading, to 6cm diam., sometimes recurved; staminal cup to 11×16mm, lobed or dentate; style exceeding anth. by up to 1cm. Ecuad., N Peru, SE Colomb.

E. ×*grandiflora* Planch. & Lind. AMAZON LILY; EUCHARIST LILY; STAR OF BETHLEHEM. Naturally occurring hybrid involving *E. amazonica*. Lvs to 33×16cm, ovate or elliptic, deeply plicate, undulate; petiole to 30cm. Scape to 50cm; perianth tube curved to 55mm, lobes to 40mm, ovate, undulate, slightly overlapping; staminal cup to 0.7×2.5cm, dentate; style far exceeding cup. Colomb.

E. lowii Bak. = *E.* ×*grandiflora*.

E. mastersii Bak. = *E.* ×*grandiflora*.

E. sanderi Bak. Lvs to 37×17cm, ovate or elliptic, base subcordate, deeply plicate, bright green, undulate; petiole to 5cm. Scape to 55cm; tube to 6cm, curved, lobes to 3.7cm, somewhat overlapping, subequal; staminal cup to 24mm diam., protruding slightly; style far exceeding cup. W Colomb.

E. subedentata (Bak.) Benth. & Hook. Lvs 21×12.5cm, oblong, coriaceous; petioles to 30cm. Scape to 45cm; perianth tube 3.5cm, urceolate above, lobes 2cm, slightly recurved, corona 0;

staminal cup 0, sta. half length lobes, style included. Colomb. →*Caliphruria* and *Urceolina*.

Eucharist Lily *Eucharis* ×*grandiflora*.

Euclinia Salisb. Rubiaceae. 3 decid. shrubs or trees. Fls term. and solitary; cal. tubular, lobes usually 5, spreading; cor. cylindric to funnel-shaped, base and, occas., interior pubesc., lobes twisted in bud. Trop. Afr., Madag. Z10.

E. longiflora Salisb. St. climbing, to 6m. Lvs to 30cm, obovate-oblong, acuminate, pubesc. beneath. Fls term. and solitary, white to cream or light yellow and tinged red at tips; cor. tube to 24cm, lobes oblong to elliptic, to 5cm. Trop. Afr.

→*Gardenia, Randia* and *Rothmannia*.

Eucnide Zucc. Loasaceae. 8 ann. or bienn. herbs, covered in stinging hairs. Fls solitary, axill.; cal. tube oblong, limb 5-lobed; pet. 5, united at base, yellow or white; sta. numerous in a dense showy boss, usually exceeding pet. SW US and N Mex.

E. bartonioides Zucc. ROCK NETTLE. To 35cm, procumbent to ascending, grey-green. Lvs 2–3cm, ovate, acute, lobed and toothed. Fls to 2.5cm diam., pet. ovate to obovate, lemon-yellow, sometimes denticulate.

Eucodonia Hanst. Gesneriaceae. 2 small perenn. herbs. St. ± succulent; rhiz. scaly. Lvs in pseudowhorls. Fls solitary, long-stalked; cor. campanulate to funnelform. C Amer.

E. andrieuxii (DC.) Wiehler. St. pink-tomentose, short. Lvs elliptic, to 12.5cm, crenate, densely pale-tomentose beneath, peduncles to 6.5cm. Cor. to 2×1.5cm, violet, throat white, spotted purple. S Mex.

→*Achimenes* and *Gloxinia*.

Eucomis L'Hérit. PINEAPPLE LILY. Liliaceae (Hyacinthaceae). 15 bulbous perenn. herbs. Lvs in a basal rosette, strap-shaped, glossy, light green flecked purple, appearing with fls. Scape terete; infl. cylindrical, composed of dense rac. of star-shaped green fls, crowned by a coma of leafy bracts. S Trop. Afr., mainly S Afr. Z8.

E. albomarginata Barnes = *E. autumnalis* ssp. *clavata*.

E. amaryllidifolia Bak. = *E. autumnalis* var. *amaryllidifolia*.

E. autumnalis (Mill.) Chitt. To 50cm. Lvs to 45cm, margins wavy. Rac. 5–15cm; fls white or olive green at first, becoming deeper green; bracts 10–45, oblong to lanceolate, 2.5–8cm with wavy edges. Late summer. ssp. *autumnalis*. Lvs to 30cm. Rac. to 30cm; perianth lobes to 1.3cm; bracts oblong 3–7cm. S Afr., Zimb., Malawi. ssp. *clavata* (Bak.) Reyneke. Lvs to 60cm, rac. 8–15cm; perianth lobes 1.2–1.7cm; bracts ovate, 5–8cm. S Afr., Swaz., Bots. ssp. *amaryllidifolia* (Bak.) Reyneke. Lvs linear to 50cm. Infl. loosely obconical, 6–23cm; perianth lobes 6–8mm; bracts lanceolate, 2.5–8cm. Late summer. S Afr.

E. bicolor Bak. Lvs 30–50cm, undulate. Scape to 60cm, often flecked maroon; perianth lobes with purple margin; bracts ovate, 5–8cm, margins purple, undulate. Late summer. S Afr. 'Alba': perianth uniformly green-white.

E. clavata Bak. = *E. autumnalis* ssp. *clavata*.

E. comosa (Houtt.) Wehrh. Lvs to 70cm with purple spots beneath, undulate. Scape 45–70cm, spotted purple; rac. to 30cm; perianth purple; bracts lanceolate, to 8cm, margins sometimes purple. Late summer. S Afr. var. *striata* (Houtt.) Wehrh. Lf and bract spotting merges to form stripes.

E. nana Ait. Lvs to 60cm, base flushed purple. Rac. 7–10cm; fls green maroon on stout stalk, spotted purple. Summer. S Afr.

E. pallidiflora Bak. Lvs to 70cm, tightly crispate. Scape 45–75cm; rac., 24–43cm; perianth white-green, bracts narrow-elliptic, 3–4cm, crispate. Summer. S Afr.

E. pole-evansii N.E. Br. Differs from *E. pallidiflora* in larger lvs, taller scape 90–180cm, and larger bracts.

E. punctata var. *concolor* Bak. = *E. pallidiflora*.

E. robusta Bak. = *E. autumnalis* ssp. *clavata*.

E. undulata Ait. = *E. autumnalis* ssp. *autumnalis*.

E. zambesiaca Bak. Lvs 30–60cm, margin ± flat, not spotted or striped below. Scape 15–25cm; rac. 10–20cm, dense, oblong; perianth green; bracts small, ovate. Malawi.

Eucommia Oliv. Eucommiaceae. 1 decid. tree to 20m, crown broadly domed. Branchlets hollow, pith lamellate. Lvs 7–15cm, narrowly ovate to elliptic, acuminate, serrulate, initially pubesc., leathery, exuding latex if torn. Fls solitary, apetalous, in axill. clusters, borne with or before lvs; males with 6–12 narrow sta., anth. red-brown. C China. Z5.

E. ulmoides Oliv. GUTTA-PERCHA TREE.

EUCOMMIACEAE Oliv. See *Eucommia*.

Eucrosia Ker-Gawl. Amaryllidaceae. 7 bulbous perennials. Lvs usually paired, ovate or elliptic, long-petiolate. Umbel scapose, spathaceous; fls pendulous; perianth narrowly campanulate, with 6 subequal lobes in 2 rows, fused basally to form a tube; sta. 6, long-exserted. Ecuad. and Peru. Z10.

E. aurantiaca (Bak.) Pax. Lvs to 40×22cm. Scape to 90cm; fls 7–13; perianth to 4cm, yellow, rarely orange or pink, tube to 7mm, lobes to 2.9cm, 3 inner lobes forming a lip-like structure; sta. to 11cm. Ecuad.

E. bicolor Ker-Gawl. Lvs to 24×11cm. Scape to 70cm; fls 5–10; perianth tube to 10mm, lobes to 2.6cm, pale red tipped and stained yellow, 2 ascending and the others spreading laterally; sta. to 6.5cm, fused below into a staminal cup, yellow or red. Ecuad., Peru.

E. eucrosioides (Herb.) Pax. Lvs to 26×21cm. Scape to 73cm; fls 7–12; perianth to 3cm, tube to 0.5cm, lobes spreading to 1.4cm, keeled, otherwise orange-scarlet; sta. to 9cm, strongly curved. SW Ecuad., N Peru.

E. eucrosioides var. *rauhinia* (Traub) Traub = *E. aurantiaca*.

E. morleyana Rose = *E. aurantiaca*.

E. stricklandii (Bak.) Meerow. Lvs 21–23×11cm. Scape 40–45cm; fls 6–7, 3–4cm long; perianth funnel-shaped-tubular, red or pink, tube 1cm, lobes to 1.8cm lanceolate-spathulate; sta. shortly exserted. Ecuad.

→*Callipsyche* and *Phaedranassa*.

Eucryphia Cav. Eucryphiaceae. 6 everg. trees or shrubs (*E. glutinosa* decid. in cult.). Lvs leathery, simple or pinnate, dark green with caducous interpetiolar stipules. Fls fragrant, solitary in lf axils; sep. usually 4, forming a cap over pet. in bud; pet. usually 4, white; sta. numerous, with pink anth. Chile, SE Aus.

E. billardieri Spach = *E. lucida*.

E. cordifolia Cav. ROBLE DE CHILE; ULMO. Columnar tree to 20m. Lvs to 7×4cm+, simple, oblong, cordate to rounded at base, sinuate, crenate to serrate, glab. above, grey and downy beneath. Fls 5cm diam. Late summer–early autumn. C & S Chile. Z9.

E. glutinosa (Poepp. & Endl.) Baill. NIRRHE. Upright tree or shrub to 10m. Lvs to 5×2–3cm, lfts (3)–5, elliptic-oblong serrate, appressed-pubesc. Fls bloom. Late summer. C Chile. Z8. 'Camelliflora': fls pure white, pet. reflexed; anth. crimson. 'Daisy Hill': fls semi-double, anth. brown, intermixed with pet. 'Nana': dwarf bush as high as wide, fls over whole surface. Plena group: fls semi-double or double.

E. ×hillieri Ivens. (*E. lucida* ×*E. moorei*.) Tree to 10m or more, similar to *E. moorei* but lvs with usually 3–7 shortly mucronate lfts, sometimes simple and then like *E. lucida*. Fls to 3.5cm diam. Summer. Gdn origin. 'Winton' is the form usually grown.

E. ×hybrida Bausch. (*E. lucida* ×*E. milliganii*.) Lvs to 2.5×1cm, sometimes trifoliate on vigorous shoots. Fls 2–2.5cm diam. Summer. Tasm. Some plants grown as *E. milliganii* belong here. Pink forms are recorded.

E. ×intermedia Bausch. (*E. glutinosa* ×*E. lucida*.) Upright tree similar to *E. lucida* but differs in bearing both simple and pinnate lvs with 3(–5) lfts., green or only slightly glaucous beneath. Summer. Gdn origin. Z8. 'Grayswood': anth. yellow. 'Rostrevor': the form usually grown, described above.

E. lucida (Labill.) Baill. LEATHERWOOD; PINKWOOD. Upright tree to 8m; buds, young lvs and shoots resinous, appressed-pubesc. when young. Lvs to 5×1.5cm, simple, narrow-oblong to oblong-lanceolate, entire (trifoliolate in juveniles), appressed-pubesc. and glossy above, glaucous beneath. Fls nodding, 3–5cm diam. Summer. Tasm. Z8. 'Leatherwood Cream': lvs edged cream. 'Pink Cloud': fls pink with crimson centre. A new form, as yet unnamed, has variegated lvs and pink new growth.

E. lucida var. *milliganii* (Hook. f.) Summerh. = *E. milliganii*.

E. milliganii Hook. f. Similar to *E. lucida* but differs in slower growth, to 6m, columnar, sometimes v. narrowly so. Lvs to 1.5×0.7cm, glab. or with appressed hairs above, glab. beneath, emarginate. Fls cup-shaped, 2–2.5cm diam. Summer. Tasm. Z8.

E. moorei F. Muell. STINKWOOD; PINKWOOD; PLUM TREE. Everg. tree to 15m. Young shoots densely pubesc, buds glutinous. Lvs to 7×1.5cm, with to 15 narrowly oblong, entire, mucronate lfts ± pubesc., glossy above, pale green to glaucous beneath. Fls 2.5cm diam. Late summer. SE Aus. (NSW, Vict.). Z9.

E. ×nymansensis Bausch. (*E. cordifolia* ×*E. glutinosa*.) Vigorous columnar tree of dense habit, to 15m. Lvs glossy above, pale beneath, simple lvs to 6cm, elliptic-oblong or elliptic-lanceolate, serrate, compound lvs with usually 3 serrate lfts to 8×3.5cm. Fls to 7.5cm diam. Late summer–autumn. Gdn origin. Z7. 'Nymansay': the most commonly grown form, described above. 'Mount Usher': similar to 'Nymansay', shy-flowering and prone to doubling.

E. 'Penwith' (*E. cordifolia* ×*E. lucida*.) Similar to *E. lucida* but young shoots with spreading hairs. Lvs to 6.5×3cm, oblong,

sinuate, slightly cordate at base, glaucous and downy on midrib beneath, sometimes, trifiolate. Fls 5cm across. Summer. Gdn origin. Z9.

E. pinnatifolia Gay = *E. glutinosa*.

EUCRYPHIACEAE Endl. See *Eucryphia*.

Eudianthe (Rchb.) Rchb.
E. coeli-rosa (L.) Rchb. = *Silene coeli-rosa*.

Eugenia L. STOPPER. Myrtaceae. 1000 everg. trees or shrubs. Lvs simple, firm and glossy. Fls usually in short lat. rac.; cal. lobes 4; pet. 4 or 5, white, spreading; sta. many. Fr. a berry, 1- or 2-seeded, crowned by the persistent cal. lobes, sometimes edible. Mostly from the Americas with a few in Afr., Asia and the Pacific. Z10.

E. aggregata (Vell.) Kiaerskov. CHERRY-OF-THE-RIO-GRANDE. Shrub or small tree to 5m. Bark peeling. Lvs to 8cm, narrow-elliptic, thick, glossy green. Fr. oblong or obovoid berry to 2.5cm long, orange-red at first, later deep purple-red. Braz.

E. alternifolia Benth. Small tree. Lvs obovate. Colomb., Ecuad.

E. aquea Burm. f. = *Syzygium aqueum*.

E. aromatica Kuntze = *Syzygium aromaticum*.

E. atropunctata Steud. Shrub to small tree, to 6m. Lvs 7–11.5cm, oblong or lanceolate-oblong, acuminate, chartaceous. Fr. round, 7mm diam., black. Braz.

E. australis J.C. Wendl. ex Link = *Syzygium paniculatum*.

E. brasiliensis Lam. BRAZIL CHERRY. Tree to 17m. Lvs to 13cm, elliptic to obovate-oblong, leathery. Fr. cherry-sized, dark red, later black, edible. Braz.

E. buxifolia (Sw.) Willd. = *E. foetida*.

E. caryophyllus (Spreng.) Bullock & S. Harrison = *Syzygium aromaticum*.

E. cauliflora DC. = *Myrciaria cauliflora*.

E. confusa DC. RED STOPPER; IRONWOOD. Tree with scaly bark. Lvs to 5cm, ovate or elliptic-ovate, slender-acuminate, leathery. Fr. subglobose, 1cm diam. Flor., W Indies.

E. coronata Schumach. & Thonn. Shrub or small tree to 7m. Lvs to 7.5cm, elliptic or ovate-elliptic, leathery. Fr. to 2.5cm, ovoid-ellipsoid, blue-black. Trop. W Afr.

E. cumini (L.) Druce = *Syzygium cumini*.

E. darwinii Hook. = *Amomyrtus luma*.

E. densiflora (Bl.) Miq. = *Syzygium pycnanthum*.

E. edulis Vell. = *Myrciaria edulis*.

E. floribunda West ex Willd. = *Myrciaria floribunda*.

E. foetida Pers. SPANISH-STOPPER. Shrub or small tree; bark scaly. Lvs to 4cm, oblong, pale beneath. Fr. ovoid, to 5cm long, black. Flor., W Indies.

E. garberi Sarg. = *E. confusa*.

E. gayana Barnéoud = *Luma chequen*.

E. grandis Wight = *Syzygium grandis*.

E. jambos L. = *Syzygium jambos*.

E. javanica Lam. = *Syzygium samarangense*.

E. klotzschiana O. Berg. Shrub. Lvs to 6.5cm, oblong-lanceolate, leathery. Fr. pyriform, to 4cm, yellow. Braz.

E. ligustrina (Sw.) Willd. Shrub or small tree. Lvs to 5cm, elliptic to elliptic-oblong, leathery. Fr. globose, 5cm diam., black or scarlet, sweet, edible. W Indies to Braz.

E. luschnathiana Klotzsch & O. Berg. PITOMBA. Shrub. Lvs to 6cm, oblong-lanceolate, leathery, pale beneath. Fr. globose, 2.5cm diam., orange-yellow. Braz.

E. malaccensis L. = *Syzygium malaccense*.

E. michelii Lam. = *E. uniflora*.

E. monticola (Sw.) DC. Shrub or tree, to 11m. Lvs to 4cm, ovate to narrowly lanceolate. Fr. globose, 7mm diam., black. W Indies.

E. myriophylla Casar. = *Myrciaria myriophylla*.

E. myrtoides Poir. = *E. foetida*.

E. natalitia Sonder. Much-branched shrub. Lvs to 4cm, ovate to elliptic, pale beneath. Fr. ellipsoid, c15mm, purple. S Afr.

E. oblata Roxb. = *Syzygium oblatum*.

E. oleosa F. Muell. = *Syzygium oleosum*.

E. operculata Roxb. = *Syzygium nervosum*.

E. orbiculata Lam. Shrub, 2–3m. Lvs 1.5–6cm, oval, orbicular, or broadly obovate, thick and leathery. Maur.

E. paniculata (Gaertn.) Britten = *Syzygium paniculatum*.

E. pitanga (O. Berg) Kiaerskov. PITANGA. Low shrub, young growth red-pubesc. Lvs to 7.5cm, elliptic-oblong. Fr. globose, c1.5cm diam., red, 8-nerved, edible. Braz., Arg.

E. polycephaloides C. Robinson = *Syzygium polycephaloides*.

E. polycephalum Miq. = *Syzygium polycephalum*.

E. supra-axillaris Spring. Tree to 8m. Lvs to 7.5cm, elliptic-oblong, glossy. Fr. globose to obovate, to 2.5cm diam. Braz.

E. ugni (Mol.) Hook. & Arn. = *Ugni molinae*.

E. uniflora L. SURINAM CHERRY. Shrub or small tree, 3–10m. Lvs

2.5–6cm, ovate to ovate-lanceolate. Fr. depressed-globose, 8-ribbed, 2.5–3cm diam., red, edible.

E. uvalha Cambess. Small tree, branchlets pubesc. Lvs to 3cm, oblong. Fr. the size and shape of small pear, yellow, aromatic, edible. Braz.

E. zeyheri Harv. Shrub or small tree, 3–5m; br. grey-white. Lvs 1.5–3.5cm, oblong, ovate, elliptic or obovate. Fls sometimes pink. Fr. globose, 5–12mm diam., purple or bright red. S Afr.

→*Jossinia* and *Phyllocalyx*.

Euklisia Rydb.

E. hyacinthoides (Hook.) Small = *Streptanthus hyacinthoides*.

Eulalia *Miscanthus sinensis*.

Eulophia R. Br. ex Lindl. Orchidaceae. 100 terrestrial orchids with pbs, tubers or fleshy roots. Lvs lanceolate to linear, sometimes plicate, sometimes fleshy. Rac. scapose; lip usually spurred, usually trilobed, crested. Trop. and S Afr., Madag., W Indies, trop. Amer., S US. Z9.

E. alta (L.) Fawcett & Rendle. Cormous. Lvs 4–6, to 100cm, linear-lanceolate, plicate. Scape 40–150cm; fls green and dull purple-maroon; dors. sep. 18×6mm, oblanceolate, lat. sep. 23×7–8mm, oblanceolate; pet. 13×7mm, obovate; lip trilobed, 11–17mm long, undulate. W & C Afr., trop. Amer., Flor., W Indies.

E. congoensis Cogn. = *E. guineensis*.

E. cristata (Sw.) Steud. Tuberous. Lvs about 50×2–6cm, lanceolate. Scape to 1m; fls pink-lilac, lip purple; sep. 18–24mm, oblong, lat. sep. slightly longer; pet. almost twice as wide; lip 13–24mm, midlobe elliptic-ovate, obtuse. W & C Afr., Sudan, Ethiop., Uganda.

E. cucullata (Sw.) Steud. Tuberous. Lvs 30–50×1cm, linear-lanceolate, ribbed. Scape to 1m; sep. green, tinged purple, pet. and lip pale to deep pink or purple, yellow or white in throat; sep. 15–30×3–12mm, ovate; pet. 14–25mm, orbicular, overlying column; lip 20–35×40mm, obscurely trilobed. Afr., Comoros Is.

E. euglossa (Rchb. f.) Rchb. f. Pbs elongate. Lvs 20–30cm, lanceolate. Scape 40–200cm; fls pale green, lip white with pink or purple veins; sep. and pet. 12–14mm, oblong-lanceolate; lip 12mm, trilobed, crenulate. W Afr., Zaire, Uganda.

E. gracilis Lindl. Pseudobulbous at base. Lvs 30–45×1–5cm, linear-lanceolate. Scape to 1m; sep. 10–12mm, lanceolate; pet. smaller; lip 7–8mm, funnel-shaped, truncate, fimbriate. W Afr., Zaire, Angola.

E. guineensis Lindl. var. **guineensis**. Pseudo-bulbous at base. Lvs 10–45×4–10cm, obovate or elliptical, plicate. Scape 40–90cm, tep. green to purple-green, lip pale to deep lilac with magenta blotch in throat; tep. 20–30×4–6mm, linear-lanceolate, curled back; lip 20–40mm, ± acute. W Afr., Zaire, Uganda, Tanz., Angola. var. **purpurata** Rchb. f. ex Kotschy. Midlobe of lip rounded or emarginate at apex. W Afr., C Afr., Sudan, Ethiop., E Afr. to Zimb.

E. horsfallii (Batem.) Summerh. Pseudobulbous. Lvs to 250×10cm, everg., lanceolate, ribbed. Scape to 1.5m; sep. shiny olive green, pet. pink, lip purple, lat. lobes green, veined purple; sep. 25×10mm, erect, spathulate; pet. 30mm, ovate, overlying column; lip 35mm, midlobe with 3 fringed, cream lamellae. Trop. Afr.

E. lurida (Sw.) Lindl. = *Graphorkis lurida*.

E. macra Ridl. Pseudobulbous. Lvs 40–60cm, narrowly linear. Scape 60–120cm; pan. laxly many-fld; fls dull-coloured; sep. 6mm, lanceolate; pet. slightly shorter and wider; lip 8×5mm, entire, fimbriate. Madag.

E. paivaeana (Rchb. f.) Summerh. = *E. streptopetala*.

E. petersii (Rchb. f.) Rchb. f. Pseudobulbous. Lvs 20–30cm, linear-lanceolate, stiff, succulent, margins finely toothed. Scape to 2m; tep. pale green tinged with purple-brown, lip white with purple lamellae, lat. lobes green with purple veins; sep. 20–30mm, linear erect, apex curled; lip 16–30mm, midlobe undulate. Arabian peninsula; E Afr. from Ethiop. to S Afr.

E. porphyroglossa (Rchb. f. Bol. = *E. horsfallii*.

E. pulchra (Thouars) Lindl. = *Oeceoclades pulchra*.

E. quartiniana A. Rich. = *E. guineensis* var. *purpurata*.

E. saundersiana Rchb. f. = *Oeceoclades saundersiana*.

E. scripta (Thouars) Lindl. = *Graphorkis scripta*.

E. speciosa (R. Br. ex Lindl.) Bol. Tuberous. Lvs 2–3, fleshy, lanceolate. Scape to 1.5m; sep. green, pet. and lip bright shiny yellow with faint purple lines; sep. 7–10mm, reflexed, ovate, apiculate; pet. 16–20mm, spreading, suborbicular; lip 25mm, midlobe oblong, obtuse, with 3–7 ridges. Widespread in E Afr. from Kenya to S Afr.

E. streptopetala Lindl. Pseudobulbous. Lvs 30–75cm, lanceolate, acute, pleated. Scape to 2m; sep. green, blotched with purple-brown, pet. bright yellow on outer surface, creamy yellow in-

ner, lip yellow, lat. lobes purple; sep. 10–20mm, obovate, erect and spreading; pet. 10–20mm, suborbicular, lying parallel to column; lip 10–20mm, midlobe elliptic, convex, with 3 crests. Ethiop., Kenya, Uganda, S to S Afr.

E. taitensis Cribb & Pfennig. Pseudobulbous. Lvs arranged in fan, to 45cm, green, rigid, serrate. Scape to 1m; fls malodorous; tep. green-white with maroon marks, lip white to cream with purple veins; sep. about 25mm; lip 22×20mm, midlobe undulate. Kenya.

E. zeyheri Hook. f. Tuberous. Lvs to 55cm, lanceolate, ribbed. Scape to 40cm; fls primrose yellow, midlobe of lip with orange blotch, lat. lobes with large purple blotch; sep. 38–40mm, elliptic, projecting forwards; lip 30×22mm, midlobe obovate. Nigeria, Zaire, E Afr. from Sudan to S Afr.

→*Lissochilus*.

Eulophiella Rolfe Orchidaceae. 3 epiphytic orchids with long pbs. Lvs 3–6, plicate, lanceolate. Rac. lat.; fls large; lat. sep. adnate to column-foot; lip not spurred, trilobed, suborbicular, with crests or lamellae. Madag. Z10.

E. elizabethae Lind. & Rolfe. Pbs 10–15×2.5cm, fusiform to oblong, 4–5-lvd. Lvs 45–(60)cm. Rac. 35–45cm, arching, 12–15-fld; fls 3–4cm diam., white, sep. tinged with rose-pink outside, lip with a large yellow blotch.

E. peetersiana Kränzl. = *E. roempleriana*.

E. perrieri Schltr. Similar to *E. elizabethae*, differing mainly in erect infl. with smaller fls (2cm diam.), white, tinged with red on outside, lip with a red spot at base of column and 2 yellow blotches.

E. roempleriana (Rchb. f.) Schltr. Pbs 8–30×2–4cm, narrowly ovoid, 4–8-lvd. Lvs 90–120cm. Rac. erect, to 120cm, 15–25-fld; fls to 6cm diam., pale to deep pink.

E. 'Rolfei' (*E. elizabethae* × *E. roempleriana*.) Rac. erect, to about 30-fld. Fls 6cm diam., pale to deep rose-pink, pale pink to almost white in centre, the lip with orange crests. Gdn origin.

Eulychnia Philippi. Cactaceae. 8 shrubs or small tree-like cacti; spines robust, long. Fls borne near tips of br., small, broadly campanulate; tube short; floral areoles with woolly hairs and bristly spines. Chile, Peru.

E. acida Philippi. Shrubby or arborescent, 1–4m or more; st. 9–12cm diam.; ribs 10–16, broad; spines up to c12, radiating, 1cm or more, 1–2 central, to 20cm. Fl. 5–7×4–6cm; tep. white, usually with pink midstripe. Chile. Z9.

E. breviflora Philippi. Shrubby or arborescent, much branched, to 5m; st. 6–10cm diam.; ribs 10–13, rounded; central spines 3–6, 5–15cm, radial spines 10–22 to 3cm. Fl. 7–8×5–6cm; tep. white, often pink above. Chile. Z9.

E. castanea Philippi. Shrubby, forming clumps up to 20m across; st. erect, later spreading to 50–100×6–8cm, ribs 8–13, low; central spines 1–2, 3–10cm, radial spines 6–10, 5–20mm, fl. 5–5.5×4–5cm; inner tep. white or pale pink. Chile. Z9.

E. iquiquensis (Schum.) Britt. & Rose. Shrubby or arborescent, 2–4(–7)m, branching below or with short trunk to 1.5m; st. 7–10cm diam., dark grey-green; ribs (10–)12–14, somewhat tuberculate; spines 10–20, v. unequal, longest to 12cm. Fl. 5.5–6.5×5–6cm; tep. short, white. Chile. Z9.

E. ritteri Cullmann. Shrub or small tree, 2–4m, densely branched; st. 6–8cm diam., grey-green; ribs 13–20, c15mm high; areoles white-woolly; spines numerous, v. unequal, longest to 8cm, black-brown at first. Fl. 2×1.5cm, pink. S Peru. Z9.

E. saint-pieana Ritter. Shrub or small tree, 2–4m; st. 7–10cm diam., dark green or grey-green; ribs 10–15; areoles white-woolly then felted. Fl. 6–7.5×5–7.5cm; tep. white, usually with pink midstripe. N Chile. Z9.

E. spinibarbis misapplied = *E. breviflora*.

→*Philippicereus*.

Eumong *Acacia stenophylla*.

Eumorphia DC. Compositae. 4 shrubs of heath-like habit. Lvs crowded, small, linear. Cap. radiate, often solitary and term. or in a many-clustered corymb. S Afr. Z9.

E. sericea Wood & M. Evans. To 50cm, much-branched. Br. grey-hairy when young, densely leafy. Lvs to 1cm, linear or 3-lobed, loosely grey-hairy. Cap. solitary and term.; ray flts to 8mm, white or rose-pink; disc flts yellow. Summer. S Afr.

Eunomia DC.

E. iberidea Boiss. = *Aethionema iberideum*.

Euodia Forst. & Forst. f. = *Tetradium* (see *Evodia*).

Euonymus L. Celastraceae. 170 decid. or everg., erect, procumbent or scandent shrubs or trees. Fls small, yellow-green in cymes or solitary, slender-stalked. Fr. a capsule, 3–5-valved, sometimes winged; seeds ± enclosed in an aril, endosperm fleshy. Asia, Eur., N & C Amer., Madag., Aus.

E. alatus (Thunb.) Sieb. WINGED SPINDLE TREE. Decid. shrub, much-branched, to 2m+; br. with 4 thin, wide, corky wings. Lvs to 2–7cm, ovate-elliptic, serrate, bright deep red in autumn. Fr. narrowly obovoid, 1–4-lobed, to 8mm, pale red, 1-seeded; seeds enclosed in an orange-vermilion aril. Summer. NE Asia to Middle China. 'Angelica Compactus': v. dense and compact. 'Compactus': compact, dwarf; br. corky, winged; lvs scarlet to purple in autumn. 'Monstrosus': a v. vigorous form. 'Nordine': branching lower; lvs large, tinted orange; fr. abundant. 'October Glory': compact, bushy; br. winged; lvs brilliant red in autumn. var. *apterus* Reg. Habit lax; br. ± unwinged. Z3.

E. americanus L. STRAWBERRY BUSH. Upright decid. shrub to 2.5m; twigs 4-angled. Lvs to 8cm, narrowly ovate to lanceolate, ± coriaceous, persisting well into autumn. Fr. 3–5-lobed, pink, with warty prickles; seeds white tinged yellow, aril bright red. Summer. E US. Z6.

E. aquifolium Loes. Everg. shrub to 3m; br. 4-sided. Lvs to 7cm, ovate to oblong, spiny sinuate-dentate. Fr. flat-globose, 4-lobed, to 1.5cm wide; seeds purple, aril orange. W China. Z9.

E. atropurpureus Jacq. WAHOO; BURNING BUSH. Decid. shrub, narrowly upright, to 2.5m. Lvs to 12cm, ovate-elliptic, finely serrate, yellow-red in autumn. Fr. deeply 4-lobed, to 1.5cm wide, crimson; aril scarlet. Summer. N Amer. Z4.

E. bungeanus Maxim. Decid. shrub to 4m; br. thin, rod-like. Lvs to 10cm, ovate-elliptic, long-acuminate, finely serrate. Fr. deeply 4-lobed, 12mm wide, yellow tinged pink; seeds white to tinged red, aril orange. Summer. China, Korea. 'Pendulus': br. pendulous. var. *semipersistens* (Rehd.) Schneid. Foliage semi-evergreen elliptic. Fr. turbinate, pink. China. Z4.

E. carlesii hort. = *E. fortunei* 'Carlesii'.

E. carrierei Vauv. = *E. fortunei* 'Carrierei'.

E. chinensis Lindl. Everg. shrub. Lvs obovate, obscurely dentate, coriaceous. China. Z9.

E. colorata hort. = *E. fortunei* 'Coloratus'.

E. cornutus Hemsl. Everg. shrub. Lvs 6–11cm, narrow-lanceolate, long-acuminate, serrate, coriaceous. Fr. tinted pink, with 4 narrow horn-like wings, (5–6 in var. *quinquecornutus* (Comber) Blakel). China. Z9.

E. echinatus Wallich. Everg., procumbent shrub. Lvs to 7cm, elliptic-ovate to lanceolate, long-acuminate, serrate. Fr. 8mm wide, covered with prickles. Himal. Z9.

E. europaeus L. COMMON SPINDLE TREE. Decid. shrub to 7m; br. with corky stripes. Lvs to 8cm, ovate-elliptic to oblong, crenate, acute. Fr. 4-lobed, to 2cm wide, pink to bright red; seed white, aril orange. Spring. Eur. to W Asia. 'Albus': to 3m; fr. white. 'Aldenhamensis': upright, v. vigorous; lvs red in autumn; fr. pink. 'Aucubifolius': lvs variegated, yellow and white, maroon in autumn; fr. scarlet. 'Argenteovariegatus': lvs variegated white. 'Atropurpureus': lvs narrow lanceolate, purple, red to violet in autumn. 'Atrorubens': fr. dark pink-red. 'Burtonii': compact; fr. red tinged orange. 'Chrysophyllus': lvs yellow tinged green, turning greener. 'Haematocarpus': fr. crimson. 'Microphyllus': lvs 2–3×1–1.8cm. 'Pumilus': dwarf, dense and erect; lvs lanceolate. 'Red Cascade': forming small tree; lvs oval, green tinged red in autumn; fr. orange-red. Z3.

E. europaeus var. *latifolius* L. = *E. latifolius*.

E. fimbriatus Wallich. Decid. shrub to 5m; br. long, rod-like. Lvs to 10cm, elliptic-oblong, short-acuminate, finely double serrate to fimbriate, thin. Fr. light red, with long, acute wings. Himal. Z8.

E. fortunei (Turcz.) Hand.-Mazz. Everg. climbing shrub to 5m, or procumbent along the ground; br. warty. Lvs to 6cm, ovate-elliptic, acute, finely serrate, thinly coriaceous. Fr. to 6mm wide, ivory to yellow; seeds orange to pink. Summer. China. 'Berryhill': to 70cm, strong, erect; lvs green. 'Carlesii': upright shrub, to 1m; lvs coarse, thick, glossy; fr. abundant. 'Carrierei': bushy, low, climbing when supported; lvs elliptic-oblong, acute, to 5cm, glossy; fr. v. abundant. 'Coloratus': climbing to 8m; lvs rather coarsely serrate, to 5cm, thin, deep purple in autumn. 'Dart's Blanket': lvs thick, leathery, bronze to crimson in winter. 'Dart's Carpet': to 35cm; br. procumbent; lvs small, dark green tinged bronze-red in winter. 'Dart's Dab': to 35cm; br. spreading; lvs small, dull green. 'Emerald Charm': habit erect; lvs glossy green; fr. yellow-white, seeds orange. 'Emerald Gaiety': hardy, compact shrub; lvs green margined silver. 'Emerald 'n' Gold': lvs variously variegated, green, gold, and pink. 'Golden Prince' ('Gold Tip'): small, compact shrub; tips of young br. gold; lvs green tinged yellow. 'Gracilis': br. ascending; lvs variegated white, yellow or pink or combinations of these. 'Kewensis': st. slender prostrate; lvs minute. 'Marginatus': trailing or climbing, dense; lvs small, ovate, margined cream; fr. pink. 'Minimus': procumbent, rooting along br., forming dense mats; br. erect, dense, thin, usually not more than 5cm high; lvs to 6mm, elliptic to rounded.

'Pulchellus': lvs narrow-oblong to lanceolate-oblong, small. 'Reticulatus': lvs veined white. 'Robustus': upright; lvs large, pale green. 'Silver Gem': tall, compact; lvs edged white, speckled red. 'Silver Queen': compact; lvs large, later tinged pink, broad cream margin. 'Uncinatus': lvs small, oval, margins serrate, grey-green with grey veins. 'Vegetus': broad and bushy, occas. climbing; br. thick, lvs elliptic to rounded, crenate, dull light green, thick; fr. abundant. var. *radicans* (Miq.) Rehd. St. trailing. Lvs to 3.5cm, ovate-elliptic, shallowly toothed. The commonest form in cult. Z5.

E. fortunei var. *vegetus* (Rehd.) Rehd. = *E. fortunei* 'Vegetus'.

E. frigidus Wallich. Everg. shrub to 4m; young br. 4-sided. Lvs to 12cm, oblong to lanceolate, long-acuminate, finely serrate, dark green, glossy. Fr. pendulous, carmine, with 4 wings; seeds white, aril orange-red. NE Asia. Z9.

E. glaber Roxb. Small tree. Lvs to 17cm, elliptic to ovate, crenate-serrate toward. E Bengal. Z9.

E. grandiflorus Wallich ex Roxb. Semi-evergreen shrub or small tree, to 5m. Lvs to 10cm, linear-lanceolate or narrow-elliptic, acuminate, finely dentate, glossy, purple in autumn. Fls green to yellow, to 2cm diam. Fr. 4-sided, 15mm wide, light pink; seeds black, aril scarlet. N India to W China. *F. salicifolius* Stapf. & F. Ballard. Form usually cult. Lvs longer, narrower. Z8.

E. hamiltonianus Wallich. Decid. shrub to small tree, similar to *E. europaeus* but with br. terete. Lvs oblong-lanceolate, short-acuminate, tougher, thicker. Fr. obcordate, 4-lobed, pink. Himal. to Jap. 'Coral Charm': lvs pale yellow in fall. Fr. pale pink, profuse with red arils. 'Coral Chief': erect. 'Fiesta': lvs blotched cream, purple in fall. 'Red Elf': fr. deep pink, arils bright red. var. *lanceifolius* (Loes.) Blakelock. Shrub or tree, to 10m. Lvs to 14cm, broad-lanceolate to elliptic-oblong, crenate, tough. Fr. 4-lobed, light pink; seed pink, aril orange. Spring–summer. C & E China. ssp. *maackii* (Rupr.) Komar. Round shrub to 5m. Lvs 5–8cm, lanceolate, long-acuminate, scabrous and finely serrate. Fr. pink; seed red, aril orange. Summer. N China to Korea, Jap. ssp. *sieboldianus* (Bl.) Hara. Shrub to small tree, to 4m. Lvs to 12cm, oblong, sometimes ovate-oblong or elliptic, acuminate to abruptly acute, crenate, red in autumn; petioles to 20mm. Fr. pink; seeds blood-red, aril orange. Summer. Jap., Korea. Z4.

E. ilicifolius Franch. Everg. shrub to 2m; br. angular at first. Lvs to 7cm, elliptic, coarsely spiny, coriaceous. Fr. to 1.2cm across, subglobose, not lobed, grey-white; aril scarlet. W China. Z9.

E. intermedius Gaudich. = *E. europaeus*.

E. japonicus Thunb. Everg. shrub or small erect tree to 8m, glab.; br. rather thick. Lvs to 7cm, elliptic or ovate, obtusely serrate, glossy above, coriaceous. Fr. globose, not lobed, to 8mm long; pink; seeds white, aril orange. Summer. China, Jap., Korea. 'Albomarginatus': to 5m, dense; br. erect; lvs small, oval, dark green edged white. 'Argenteovariegatus': lvs oval, bright green, broad white margin. 'Aureomarginatus': upright, dense; lvs golden-green with bright gold margin. 'Aureus': lvs yellow edged dark green. 'Calamistratus': lvs curled and twisted, dark green. 'Crispus': lvs curly, marbled green and white, edged white. 'Duc d'Anjou': lvs green, variegated yellow and grey-green. 'Fastigiatus': erect; lvs narrow elliptic. 'Giganteus': lvs large, dark glossy green. 'Grandifolius': upright, compact; lvs large, deep green. 'Latifolius Albomarginatus': lvs broad and oval with wide, white margin. 'Longifolius': br. often hanging; lvs 4.5–8cm, oblanceolate, dark green. 'Macrophyllus': lvs large. 'Medio Pictus': lvs oval, st., petiole and centre yellow, green at margin. 'Microphyllus': small, compact, box-like shrub with small, narrow lvs. 'Microphyllus Albovariegatus': lvs narrow, variegated white. 'Microphyllus Aureovariegatus': lvs narrow, variegated yellow. 'Microphyllus Gold Pillar': compact, erect; lvs variegated with gold. 'Microphyllus Pulchellus': lvs v. small, variegated with gold. 'Microphyllus Variegatus': dwarf, compact and dense; br. erect; lvs dark green edged white. 'Ovatus Albus': lvs broad, margined and suffused green, grey-green and white. 'Ovatus Aureus': lvs oval, blotched and margined yellow. 'Pictus': dwarf; lvs bright green. 'President Gauthier': lvs large, dark green blotch in centre, grey-green middle with broad cream margin. 'Punctatus': lvs dotted yellow. 'Pyramidalis': dense, upright; lvs broad elliptic. 'Robustus': v. hardy; lvs thick, round, packed in dense stiff growth. 'Rugosus': lvs oblong, irregular veining above, deep green. 'Silver King': dense, upright; lvs large, narrow, green with silver-white margin. 'Sulphureovariegatus': lvs edged dark green with light yellow middle. 'Tricolor': lvs yellow tinged green and pink. 'Variegatus': dense; lvs small, variegated with silver. 'Yellow Queen': lvs oval, margin yellow. Z7.

E. kiautschovicus Loes. Everg., or semi-evergreen shrub, creeping or broadly upright, to 2m. Lvs 5–8cm, broadly ovate, crenate. Fr. not lobed, to 1cm wide, pink; seeds brown, aril orange. Summer. China. 'Jewel': hardy, compact, dense; lvs bright green. 'Dupont': dense; lvs small. 'Newport': v. dense habit. 'Manhattan': to 2m, upright; lvs serrate, dark green. 'Pauli': exceptionally hardy. 'Vincifolius': upright, spreading shrub; lvs *Vinca*-like. Z6.

E. koopmannii Lauche = *E. nanus*.

E. lanceifolius Loes. = *E. hamiltonianus* var. *lanceifolius*.

E. lanceolatus Yatabe. Small shrub, creeping; br. obscurely 4-striate. Lvs 7–12cm, broadly oblanceolate to broadly lanceolate, long-acuminate, minutely serrate, deep green above. Fr. globose, to 8mm wide, smooth. Summer. Jap. Z8.

E. latifolius (L.) Mill. Upright shrub or small tree, decid., to 5m; br. long, rod-like. Lvs to 12cm, oblong-elliptic, finely crenate, deep green. Fr. pendulous, 4- or 5-winged, to 2.5cm wide, light carmine-red, wings to 7mm; seed white, aril orange. S Eur. to Asia Minor. Z5.

E. latifolius Marshall = *E. atropurpureus*.

E. lucidus D. Don. Tall everg. shrub or small tree. Lvs 5–12cm, pendent, narrow-ovate to lanceolate, lustrous dark green, regularly and deeply serrate, new growth glossy red to pink-bronze. Fr. deeply 4-lobed, to 12mm wide; aril orange. Spring. Himal., N Assam. Z9.

E. maackii Rupr. = *E. hamiltonianus ssp. maackii*.

E. macropterus Rupr. Decid. broad shrub, to 2.5m+. Lvs to 9cm, obovate or elliptic, long-acuminate, finely serrate, glossy. Fr. 4-winged, wings acuminate, to 10mm, pink; aril deep red. Spring. NE Asia. Z5.

E. melananthus Franch. & Savat. Decid. shrub, rather small, glab.; br. 4-striate. Lvs to 8cm, ovate, sometimes broadly lanceolate, abruptly acuminate and subacute, mucronate-serulate. Fls to 7mm diam., purple. Fr. globose, to 1cm wide, smooth. Summer. Jap. Z8.

E. monbeigii W.W. Sm. Decid. shrub or tree to 8m, differing from *E. sanguineus*, in lvs ovate to oblong, densely serrate. Fr. with triangular wings to 5mm. Spring. China, SE Tibet. Z9.

E. monstrosus hort. = *E. alatus* 'Monstrosus'.

E. myrianthus Hemsl. Everg. shrub to 3m, glab. Lvs to 10cm, elliptic-lanceolate to oblong-vate, long-acuminate, sparsely and obtusely serrate, dull green above. Fr. turbinate, 4-sided, tinged yellow. W China. Z9.

E. nanoides Loes. & Rehd. Decid. shrub, to 1m; br. sharply 4-sided to narrow-winged. Lvs 8–20mm, linear-lanceolate, obtuse. Fr. flat-globose, lobed to the middle, 1cm wide, usually only 2 fertile chambers; seeds dark purple, aril orange. W China. Z3.

E. nanus Bieb. Decid. shrub, procumbent-ascending, to 80cm; br. angular, rod-like. Lvs to 4cm, linear-lanceolate, sparsely dentate, revolute. Fr. 4-lobed, pink to rose-red; seeds brown, aril red. Spring–summer. E Eur., W Russia, Cauc., E Turkestan to W China. 'Turkestanicus': upright; lvs long, narrow, red-bronze in autumn; seeds pink. Z2.

E. nikoensis Nak. = *E. hamiltonianus ssp. sieboldianus*.

E. obovatus Nutt. RUNNING STRAWBERRY BUSH. Decid. shrub, prostrate, glab., self-rooting, climbing if supported. Lvs to 6cm, obovate-elliptic, crenate, light green. Fr. usually 3-lobed, to 18mm wide, carmine-red, warty; aril red. N Amer. 'Variegatus': trailing; lvs green and white. Z3.

E. occidentalis Nutt. WESTERN BURNING BUSH. Decid. shrub or small tree, to 5m, closely related to *E. atropurpureus*. Lvs to 10cm, ovate to elliptic-lanceolate, abruptly acuminate, finely serrate. Fr. red-purple; aril red. N Amer. var. *parishii* (Trel.) Jeps. Branchlets tinged white. Lvs generally ± obtuse. S Calif. Z5.

E. oresbius W.W. Sm. Decid. shrub to 1.5m, glab.; br. 4-sided, narrowly winged. Lvs to 2cm, linear to oblanceolate, obtuse, serrulate. Fr. 12mm wide, with 4 winged lobes, pink-red; seeds dark purple, aril scarlet. Summer. W China. Z5.

E. oxyphyllus Miq. Decid. shrub or small tree to 7m, glab.; br. terete. Lvs 7×3–4cm, oval-oblong, acuminate, finely serrate, red in autumn, membranous. Fr. globose, with 4–5 ribs, to 12mm wide, dark red; seed scarlet. Spring. China, Jap., Korea. Z5.

E. parishii Trel. = *E. occidentalis* var. *parishii*.

E. patens Rehd. = *E. kiautschovicus*.

E. pauciflorus Maxim. Decid. shrub to 2m, similar to *E. verrucosus*; br. densely warty. Lvs to 6cm, elliptic to obovate, acuminate, finely serrate, densely pubesc. beneath. Fr. 4-lobed, red; seeds black, aril red. NE Asia. Z5.

E. pendulus Wallich = *E. lucidus*.

E. phellomanus Loes. Decid. shrub to 5m, glab.; br. 4-sided, with broad corky wings. Lvs to 10cm, oval-oblong to oblong-lanceolate, crenate. Fr. 4-lobed, pink; seed nearly black, aril deep red. N & W China. Z5.

E. planipes (Koehne) Koehne. Decid. shrub to 5m, similar to *E. latifolius*, but lvs more coarsely dentate; petioles not furrowed above; fr. more conical at the apex, lobes 4–5, not so wing-like. Jap., Korea, NE China. Z4.

E. planipes Koehne = *E. sachalinensis*.

E. pulchellus Carr. = *E. fortunei* 'Pulchellus'.

E. rosthornii Loes. = *E. myrianthus*.

E. sachalinensis (F. Schmidt) Maxim. Shrub to 4m. Lvs to 12cm, obovate, short-acuminate, crenate-serrate. Fr. 5-angled, to 18mm wide, carmine red; aril orange. NE Asia. Z5.

E. sacrosanctus Koidz. = *E. alatus*.

E. sanguineus Loes. ex Diels. Decid. shrub or small tree to 5m; br. rod-like, tinged red when young. Lvs to 10cm, oval-oblong to broad-elliptic, scabrous and densely serrate, new growth tinged red, turning red and persisting in autumn. Fr. somewhat lobed, to 2.5cm wide, wings to 8mm, outspread; seeds black, aril orange. Spring. China, SE Tibet. Z5.

E. sargentianus Loes. & Rehd. = *E. myrianthus*.

E. semenovii Reg. & Herd. Decid. shrub to 2m; br. smooth. Lvs to 4.5cm, lanceolate, finely crenate, rather thick. Fr. with seeds green tinged purple, aril orange. Turkestan, China. Z8.

E. semiexsertus Koehne = *E. hamiltonianus* ssp. *sieboldianus*.

E. semipersistens Sprague = *E. bungeanus* var. *semipersistens*.

E. sieboldianus Bl. = *E. hamiltonianus* ssp. *sieboldianus*.

E. subtriflorus Bl. = *E. alatus*.

E. tingens Wallich. Everg. shrub or small tree to 5m; br. angular. Lvs to 7cm, narrow-ovate to lanceolate, attenuate, glossy. Fr. 4–5-lobed, to 15mm wide, dark pink; aril scarlet. Spring. Himal., W China. Z9.

E. ussuriensis Maxim. = *E. macropterus*.

E. velutinus (C.A. Mey.) Fisch. & Mey. Decid. shrub differing from *E. europaeus* in young br., lf undersides and infl. densely tomentose. Cauc., Armenia, N Iran, Transcaspian. Z6.

E. verrucosoides Loes. Decid. shrub, v. closely related to *E. alatus*, but lvs more crenate, venation beneath not so elevated. Seeds black, v. conspicuous. SE Tibet, China. Z6.

E. verrucosus Scop. Decid. shrub, upright to 2m; br. covered with fine black warts. Lvs to 6cm, ovate-lanceolate, acuminate, crenate, pale lilac to yellow in autumn. Fr. deeply 4-lobed, 6mm wide, red tinged yellow; seeds black, aril red. S Eur., W Asia. Z6.

E. vincifolius hort. = *E. kiautschovicus* 'Vincifolius'.

E. wilsonii Sprague. Everg. shrub, climbing to 6m. Lvs to 14cm, lanceolate, acuminate, shallowly dentate. Fr. 4-lobed, 2cm wide, with awl-shaped spines; aril yellow. Summer. W China. Z9.

E. yedoensis Koehne = *E. hamiltonianus* ssp. *sieboldianus*.

→*Celastrus*.

Eupatorium L. Compositae. *c*40 perenn. herbs, subshrubs or shrubs. St. usually simple or branched above. Lvs opposite or whorled. Cap. discoid, clustered in a term., often loose, pan. or corymb. E US, Eurasia.

E. adenophorum Spreng. = *Ageratina adenophora*.

E. ageratoides L. f. = *Ageratina altissima*.

E. album L. Perenn. herb, to 1m, rough-hairy. Lvs opposite, to 5cm, oblong lanceolate, coarsely dentate. Cap. clustered in a corymb; flts *c*5, white. Late summer. E US. Z4.

E. altissimum L. TALL THOROUGHWORT. Perenn. herb, to 2m, downy. Lvs mostly opposite, to 13cm, lanceolate, tapered, entire or toothed above. Cap. in a dense corymb; flts *c*5, white. CE & SE US. Z4.

E. araliifolium Less. = *Neomirandea araliifolia*.

E. aromaticum L. = *Ageratina aromatica*.

E. atrorubens Nichols. = *Bartlettina sordida*.

E. cannabinum L. HEMP AGRIMONY. Perenn. herb, to 2m, puberulent. St. lvs opposite, to 12cm, palmatifid, lobes lanceolate to oblong-lanceolate, coarsely serrate-dentate. Cap. in a fairly dense pan.; flts white, red or mauve. Late summer–autumn. Eur. 'Album': white. 'Flore Pleno': infl. rose, double. Z5.

E. chinense L. Perenn. herb, to 2m, pubesc. Lvs to 18cm, ovate-oblong to elliptic, short-acuminate, gland. beneath. Cap. in a loose corymb; flts 5, often white, or variously tinged. Autumn. E Asia. Z7.

E. coelestinum L. = *Conoclinium coelestinum*.

E. conspicuum Kunth & Bouché = *Ageratina grandifolia*.

E. dubium Willd. ex Poir. Perenn. herb, to 2m, sparsely pubesc. Lvs in whorls, to 20cm, lanceolate to oblong-ovate, acuminate, finely crenate-dentate. Cap. in a spreading, hemispherical to pyramidal pan.; phyllaries purple tinged; flts 3–8, pale pink or white. Late summer–early autumn. E US. Z4.

E. frasieri Poir. = *Ageratina altissima*.

E. glabratum hort. = *Ageratina modesta*.

E. glandulosum Kunth = *E. album*.

E. glechonophyllum Less. = *Ageratina glechonophylla*.

E. grandifolium Reg. = *Ageratina grandifolia*.

E. herbaceum (A. Gray) E. Greene = *Ageratina herbacea*.

E. hidalgense Robinson = *Ageratina hidalgensis*.

E. hirsutum Hook. & Arn. = *Chromolaena hirsuta*.

E. hyssopifolium L. Perenn. herb, to 60cm, minutely pubesc. Lvs opposite, to 5cm, linear to linear-lanceolate, entire or toothed, apex obtuse. Cap. clustered in a corymb; flts *c*5, white. CE US.

Z5.

E. ianthinum (Hook.) Hemsl. = *Bartlettina sordida*.

E. incarnatum Walter = *Fleischmannia incarnata*.

E. japonicum Thunb. = *E. chinense*.

E. kirilowii Turcz. = *E. lindleyanum*.

E. lasseauxii (Carr.) Wittm. = *Barrosoa candolleana*.

E. ligustrinum DC. = *Ageratina ligustrina*.

E. lindleyanum DC. Perenn. herb, to 70cm, puberulent. Lvs opposite, to 13cm, lanceolate to linear-lanceolate, sometimes deeply divided, mucronulate, gland. beneath. Cap. clustered in a corymb; flts 5, white. Autumn. Jap., SE China, Taiwan. Z7.

E. maculatum L. JOE PYE WEED. Perenn. herb, to 2cm, st. speckled or blotched purple. Lvs in whorls, to 25cm, lanceolate to lanceolate-elliptic or ovate, often incised and coarsely serrate. Cap. in a ± flat-topped cymose pan.; phyllaries purple-tinged; flts 15, pale- or rose-purple. NE to SC US. 'Atropurpureum': foliage purple-tinted; infl. wine red. Z5.

E. megalophyllum (Lem.) Klatt = *Bartlettina sordida*.

E. micranthum Less. = *Ageratina ligustrina*.

E. modestum (Kunth). = *Ageratina modesta*.

E. occidentale Hook. = *Ageratina occidentalis*.

E. odoratum L. = *Chromolaena odorata*.

E. perfoliatum L. BONESET; THOROUGHWORT. Perenn. herb, to 1.5m. Lvs opposite, to 20cm, lanceolate, connate-perfoliate, widely spreading acuminate, serrate, wrinkled, downy beneath. Cap. in a v. large, compound corymbs; flts 10–40, white, often purple-tinged. Late summer–autumn. SE US. Z3.

E. petiolare Moc. & Sessé ex DC. = *Ageratina petiolaris*.

E. probum N.E. Br. = *Ageratina proba*.

E. purpureum L. TRUMPET WEED; JOE PYE WEED. Perenn. herb, to 3m, purple-tinged. Lvs in whorls, to 25cm, elliptic-ovate to ovate or lanceolate, acuminate, finely serrate-dentate, vanilla-scented when bruised. Cap. in a hemispherical to pyramidal corymb or pan.; phyllaries purple; flts 5–15, pale pink to green-yellow or rose-purple. Late summer–autumn. E US. Z4.

E. purpusii Brandg. = *Ageratina purpusii*.

E. raffillii Hemsl. = *Bartlettina sordida*.

E. riparium Reg. = *Ageratina riparia*.

E. rugosum hort. = *Ageratina altissima*.

E. serrulatum DC. = *Neocabreria serrulata*.

E. sessilifolium L. UPLAND BONESET; Perenn. herb, to 2m, smooth. Lvs to 15cm, oblong- to ovate-lanceolate, apex pointed, serrate. Cap. in a v. compound corymb; flts 5–8, white. NE US to C & SC US. Z5.

E. sordidum Less. = *Bartlettina sordida*.

E. triplinerve Vahl = *Ayapana triplinervis*.

E. urticifolium Reichard = *Ageratina altissima*.

E. vernale Vatke & Kurtz = *Ageratina vernalis*.

E. verticillatum Lam. = *E. dubium*.

Euphorbia L. SPURGE. Euphorbiaceae. Some 2000 ann., bienn. or perenn. herbs, shrubs or trees, many succulent, with milky-white latex. Lvs of succulent spp. often reduced or caducous; those of herbaceous perenn. spp. borne on ann. st. Infl. of ♀or unisexual cyathia, solitary or in pseudocymes or pseudoumbels; infl. lvs sometimes differing in form and colour from ordinary lvs; cyathia usually enclosed in a ± 5-lobed involucre bearing glands or nectaries and often subtended by 2 or more enlarged, sometimes brightly coloured bract-leaves. Cosmop.

E. abyssinica J.F. Gmel. Succulent leafless tree, to 10m. St. 5–8-angled, jointed, angles winged, sinuate; spines short. Infl. crowded, term. inconspicuous. Ethiop., Eritrea, Somalia. Z10.

E. acanthothamnos Heldr. & Sart. ex Boiss. Cushion-forming, glab. shrub to 35cm. St. with spines derived from buds, umbellate rays. St. lvs to 2×0.5cm, elliptic-ovate. Infl. yellow. E Medit., Aegean. Z8.

E. acrurensis N.E. Br. = *E. abyssinica*.

E. actinoclada S. Carter. Tufted succulent perenn.; main st. 5×2cm. Br. erect, often spreading, produced from apex in succession, to 15cm, cylindric, dark green with paler stripes; teeth shallow, in 5 series; spines to 2cm with short prickles. Lvs deltoid, to 1mm. Kenya, S Ethiop. Z10.

E. adenoptera Bertol. Perenn. herb, to 30cm, prostrate, pubesc. Lvs elliptic-ovate, to 6mm. Infl. white. W Indies, SE, US. Z7.

E. aeruginosa Schweick. Dwarf succulent, to 15cm. Main st. thickened, subterranean, br. ascending, 4–5-angled, bronze-green; spines to 2cm, red, with 2 smaller spines above and 1 solitary prickle below. S Afr., Zimb. Z7.

E. aggregata A. Berger. PINCUSHION EUPHORBIA. Resembles *E. ferox*, but clumps formed from br. produced at or near ground level. Dwarf succulent, cushion-forming bush, to 8cm. Br. to 3cm diam., 8–9-angled, green, brown below; spines solitary, red to plum-purple. Lvs to 0.2cm, linear. S Afr. var. **alternicolor** (N.E. Br.) A. White, R.A. Dyer & B.L. Sloane. Br. banded buff to pale white-green. Z7.

E. albertensis N.E. Br. Low succulent. Main st. cylindric,

10×3.7cm, br. in upper part erect or ascending, cylindric, 2×0.8cm, spineless but remains of peduncles persistent, tubercles small, rhomboid. Lvs linear-lanceolate, to 3mm, caducous. S Afr. (Cape Prov.). Z9.

E. alcicornis hort. = *E. ramipressa*.

E. alluaudii Drake. Succulent tree, to 4m; br. dense, cylindric, to 15mm diam. Madag. ssp. **oncoclada** (Drake) Friedman & Cremers. Br. seg. fusiform. Z10.

E. alternicolor N.E. Br. = *E. aggregata* var. *alternicolor*.

E. altissima Boiss. TALL SPURGE. Resembles *E. orientalis*, but taller, to 2.5m. St. lvs linear-ensiform, occas. somewhat pendent, soft pubesc. Transcauc. Z9.

E. ammak Schweinf. Succulent tree, to 10m. St. grey-green, 3–5-sided; br. to 15cm diam., segmented, ridges undulate; spines paired, to 5mm; lvs oblanceolate, soon abscising. Infl. pale yellow. S Arabia. Z10.

E. ampliphylla Pax. Tree to 30m. Bole to 90cm diam.; bark grey, rough, young br. fleshy, triangular to rhombic, to 17cm diam., winged, dark green; spines attenuate. Lvs large, semi-persistent. E Afr. Z10.

E. amygdaloides L. WOOD SPURGE. Perenn. herb, to 85cm. St. clumped, tinged violet, lvs spathulate to obovate, to 8cm+, entire, obtuse, glossy green. Infl. yellow to lime-green. Spring–summer. Eur., SW Asia. 'Purpurea': lvs purple-red; fl. heads bright lime green. 'Rubra': habit compact, bushy; lvs flushed purple-red, particularly in winter and new growth. 'Variegata': lvs margined cream, centre pale; st. and winter lvs tinged pink. var. **robbiae** (Turrill) Rad.-Sm. Robust. Lvs broader, dark green, in rosettes. Infl. yellow-green. Z7.

E. anacantha Ait. = *E. tridentata*.

E. androsaemifolia Willd. = *E. esula*.

E. anoplia Stapf. Shrub, to 18cm. St. 7–19-angled, to 6cm, ridges tuberculate; tubercles pyramidal; br. short, 5-angled. Lvs soon abscising, subulate; spines 0. S Afr. (Cape Prov.). Z9.

E. antiquorum L. Succulent shrub, to 4m. St. bluntly 4–5-angled; br. triangular, segmented; seg. sinuate; spines to 7mm, grey. Lvs ovate-spathulate to rounded. S India. Z10.

E. antiquorum E. Mey. = *E. hamata*.

E. antisyphilitica Zucc. CANDELILLA. Succulent, spineless shrub, to 1.5m. St. woody, to 4mm diam.; br. erect, slender, cylindric, pruinose, terete; nodes purple. Lvs to 5mm, linear, crimsoon. Infl. red. SW US. Z8.

E. aphylla Brouss. ex Willd. Succulent, spineless, compact shrub, to 1m. St. slender; br. segmented, cylindric, whorled or dichotomous, to 8cm×6mm, grey-green; lf scars circular. Lvs linear, obtuse. Canary Is. Z9.

E. arida N.E. Br. Low succulent. Main st. to 5×5cm+, br. many erect to spreading cylindric to 3.5cm, spineless but remains of peduncles persistent, tubercles prominent, rhomboid, dull dark green. Lvs linear, to 3mm. S Afr. (Cape Prov.). Z9.

E. armata Thunb. = *E. loricata*.

E. armena Prokh. = *E. woronowii*.

E. atrispina N.E. Br. Dwarf, cushion-forming, succulent, to 20cm. St. branching basally; br. cylindric, to 2cm diam., 6–9-angled, angles rounded, crenate, waxy; spines to 12mm+, branched, black. Lvs to 1mm, dark brown. S Afr. (Cape Prov.). var. **viridis** A. White, R.A. Dyer & B.L. Sloane. Br. 6–8-angled; spines green, tinged yellow. Z7.

E. atropurpurea Brouss. Succulent shrub, to 1.5m+. St. to 2cm diam., glaucous, brown tinged grey. Lvs 5–9cm, at br. tips, oblong-spathulate, obtuse, grey-green. Infl. branched, purple-red. Canary Is. Z9.

E. austriaca A. Kerner = *E. villosa*.

E. avasmontana Dinter. Succulent shrub to 2m, branching from base; br. many, erect, to 8cm diam., usually pentagonal; seg. to 13cm, green tinged yellow, pruinose; spines 10mm, rigid. Nam., SW Cape. Z7.

E. baga A. Chev. Perenn. herb; rootstock stout, st. short, erect, subterranean or partially exposed, with lvs and fls at apex. Lvs few, oblanceolate, to 14cm. Infl. red. W trop. Afr. Z10.

E. baioensis S. Carter. Succulent perenn.; br. from base, erect or decumbent, cylindric, 8–10-sided, to 30×2cm; spines to 10mm, red, turning black. Lvs deltoid, to 1mm, later forming prickles. Kenya. Z10.

E. balearica Poir. ex Klotzsch & Garcke = *E. pithyusa*.

E. ballyana Rauh. Succulent perenn., branching from base. Br. erect, cylindric, 30–50×0.7–1cm, grey-green with dark stripes; teeth v. obscure; spines to 1.5cm. Lvs deltoid, 1.5mm. Kenya. Z10.

E. balsamifera Ait. Shrub, to 2m. St. spineless, many-branched, grey, gnarled. Lvs in rosettes, oblong-spathulate to 2.5cm, obtuse to acute. NW Afr., Canary Is., Somalia. ssp. **balsamifera**. Lvs linear-lanceolate. ssp. **adenensis** (Deflers) Bally. Compact. Z9.

E. barnhartii Croizat. Succulent. Shrub. Br. triangular, pale green, wavy-angled. Lvs to 6×3cm, spathulate, ovate to narrow-lanceolate, base cuneate; spines to 1cm. India. Z9.

E. barteri N.E. Br. = *E. kamerunica.*

E. basutica Marloth = *E. clavarioides.*

E. baumii Pax = *E. monteiroi.*

E. baylissii Leach. Succulent shrub to 1.5m+. St. usually solitary, 4-sided, segmented; br. segmented, green, striped white when young, angles wavy, winged, spines to 5mm, stout. Lvs soon abscising. Infl. orange, tinged pink. Moz. Z9.

E. beaumeriana Hook. f. & Coss. Resembles *E. echinus*, but st. 9–10-angled. Moroc. Z9.

E. beharensis Leandri. Succulent, spiny, compact shrub. St. branched; br. to 5mm diam., grey tinted red; spines to 1.5cm, occas. tinged red when young. Lvs to 5mm, decid. Infl. white, red, pink or yellow. SW Madag. Z10.

E. bergeri N.E. Br. Resembles *E. caput-medusae*, but br. more slender; lvs to 12mm. Dwarf succulent, to 20cm. St. subglobose; br. cylindric, curved, to 23cm×18mm. Lvs narrow-lanceolate to spathulate; lf scars diamond-shaped; spines 0. Distrib. unknown. Z10.

E. biglandulosa Willd. = *E. burmannii.*

E. biglandulosa Desf. non Willd. = *E. rigida.*

E. bilocularis N.E. Br. = *E. candelabrum.*

E. biumbellata Poir. Perenn. herb, to 50cm+. St. glab., branching from base. Lvs linear-lanceolate to 5cm+. W Medit. Z8.

E. bivonae Steud. Herbaceous shrub, to 130cm+. St. glab., lvs 0 at base. Lvs linear-lanceolate to ovate-lanceolate, acute or acuminate, entire. C Medit. Z8.

E. bojeri Hook. = *E. milii.*

E. bougheyi Leach. Succulent tree, to 7m. Crown umbrella-shaped, to 3m diam.; st. to 9-sided; spines to 8mm. Lvs triangular-ovate. Moz. Z9.

E. bracteata Jacq. = *Pedilanthus bracteatus.*

E. bravoana Svent. Close to *E. atropurpurea.* St. succulent, dark brown. Lvs at ends of st., linear-lanceolate, to 10cm, glaucous, those below infl. tinged purple. Infl. dark red-purple. Canary Is. Z9.

E. breviarticulata Pax. Succulent tree-like shrub, to 4.5m+. Br. erect to spreading, triangular to rhombic, to 12cm diam., winged, blue-green, streaked yellow-green, seg. to 8cm, undulate, dentate; spines to 8cm. Lvs to 2.5mm, deltoid. Infl. gold-yellow. S Ethiop., S Somalia, Kenya, Tanz. Z9.

E. brevitorta Bally. Densely tufted succulent perenn. to 15cm; root tuberous. St. subterranean, giving rise to secondary plants, forming a cushion to 1m across. Br. to 12cm, 3-angled to 2.5cm diam., often spirally twisted, conspicuously toothed, spines to 9mm. Lvs deltoid, 2mm. Infl. yellow. Kenya. Z10.

E. brittingeri Opiz ex Samp. Woody-based pubesc. lax perenn., herb to 40cm+. Lvs obovate to oblong-elliptic, serrate, to 3.5cm. Infl. yellow, becoming green, occas. green tinged purple. C & W Eur., N Balk. Z7.

E. bubalina Boiss. BUFFALO EUPHORBIA. Succulent, spineless shrub, to 1.3m. St. over 2cm diam., dark green, tubercles spirally arranged, br. cylindric. Lvs to 10cm, oblong-lanceolate, persistent. Infl. often scarlet or green, margins scarlet. S Afr. Z9.

E. bupleurifolia Jacq. Dwarf succulent to 20cm. St. globose to ovoid, to 7cm diam. Br. usually 0; tubercles spirally arranged. Lvs at st. apex, lanceolate, to 7cm. Infl. green, becoming red. S Afr. Z7.

E. burmannii E. Mey. Succulent shrub, to 2m. St. spineless, woody at base, succulent above, branching. Lvs spathulate, to 3mm. Infl. buff green tinged yellow. S Afr. (Cape Prov.). Z7.

E. buruana Pax. Dwarf succulent perenn., to 30cm. St. subterranean; br. to 50cm, undulate, ascending or creeping, triangular to rhombic, grey-green; seg. obovoid; spines to 2cm. Lvs deltoid, to 1.5mm. Infl. yellow. E Afr. Z10.

E. bussei Pax. Tree to 10m+. Bole to 30cm diam. with 6 rows of spines; br. spreading, to 5m; branchlets triangular to rhombic, to 15cm diam., winged, fleshy; seg. ovoid, to 15cm+; spines to 2cm. Lvs ovate, to 2mm. E Afr. var. *kibwezensis* (N.E. Br.) S. Carter. Br. seg. subcircular; wings 3–4, with horny margin and robust spines. E Afr. Z10.

E. buxoides Radc.-Sm. Small tree or shrub to 6m; br. stiff, erect. Lvs obovate, 3–6.5cm, slightly revolute, coriaceous, dark green above, paler beneath. New Guinea (known only in cult.) Z10.

E. cactus Ehrenb. ex Boiss. Succulent shrub to 3m. St. branched, 3–5-angled, segmented, grey-green, mottled yellow; seg. to 30cm, to 10cm diam., ovoid, ridges flattened, undulate, margin bony; spines paired, to 4mm. S Arabia, Sudan, Eritrea. 'Aureovariegata': br. twisted, marked yellow. Z10.

E. caerulescens Haw. NOORS. Succulent shrub to 1.5m+. Rhiz. spreading; br. to 5cm diam.; seg. to 10cm, rhombic to hexagonal, glaucous, sombre green tinged blue, leafless; spines paired, to 13mm, chestnut. S Afr. (Cape Prov.). Z7.

E. calycina N.E. Br. = *E. candelabrum.*

E. canariensis L. Succulent arborescent shrub to 12m+. St.

many, ascending, fresh green; ridges acute, toothed; spines curved, 4–6-angled to 5mm. Infl. green tinged red. Canary Is. var. *spiralis* Bolle. Br. tinged red; ridges spiralling. var. *viridis* Kunkel. Fr. green, not red-brown. Z10.

E. candelabrum Kotschy. Succulent tree, to 20m. Crown candelabriform, rounded; bark grey, cracked; br. ascending, 3–5-sided, to 10cm diam., seg. oblong; ridges deep dentate; spines to 5mm, rust-red brown. Lvs deltoid, soon abscising. Infl. golden green. S Afr. to NE Afr. Z9.

E. caniculata Lam. = *E. clava.*

E. caniculata Lodd. = *Pedilanthus tithymaloides.*

E. capitulata Rchb. Herbaceous perenn. to 10cm. St. procumbent, glab., densely leafy, lvs obovate, to 1cm, overlapping, obtuse. Infl. glands lavender. Balk. Z8.

E. cap-saintemeniensis Rauh. As for *E. decaryi* but cyathia erect; involucral lvs ovate, acute, green, margin red. Madag. Z10.

E. caput-medusae non L. = *E. bergeri.*

E. caput-medusae L. MEDUSA'S HEAD. Similar to *E. inermis*, but involucral raylet lvs not soft pubesc. Dwarf, succulent, perenn. shrub to 30cm. St. globose, partly subterranean; br. radial, crowded, to 75cm, to 25mm diam.; tubercles conic. Lvs linear, to 5mm, fleshy. S Afr. (Cape Prov.). Z7.

E. caput-medusae L. in part. = *E. clava.*

E. caput-medusae L. in part = *E. tridentata.*

E. carniolica Jacq. Woody-based glab. to pubesc. perenn., to 40cm+. St. clumped. Lvs obovate-oblong, to 7cm. Rays 3–5. Cyathia long-stipitate; glands yellow brown. C & SE Eur. Z6.

E. carpatica Wol. = *E. villosa.*

E. ceratocarpa Ten. Perenn. herb, to 1m+. St. erect, glab., base tinged red. Lvs linear-lanceolate to oblong, pale green, wavy. Rays 5–6, forking; raylet lvs elliptic-ovate, connate, green tinged yellow. S It., Sicily. Z9.

E. cereiformis L. MILK BARREL. Succulent shrub to 1m+, br. basal to term., erect, to 5cm diam., matt green with tubercles on 9–15 straight angles; spines to 1cm, red-brown, later grey. Possibly S Afr.; known only in cult., possibly of hybrid origin. Z7.

E. cereiformis Schumann non L. = *E. fimbriata.*

E. cereiformis var. *submammillaris* A. Berger = *E. submammillaris.*

E. cervicornis Boiss. = *E. hamata.*

E. characias L. Perenn. woody-based herb, to 1.5m+. St. clumped, erect, tomentose, tinged purple. Lvs linear to obovate, to 13cm, dark grey-green. Rays to 20; involucre yellow-green, suborbicular to semicircular, pubesc.; glands deep purple. W Medit., Port. Z8. 'Blue Hills': lvs blue-grey; infl. large, yellow. ssp. *wulfenii* (Hoppe & Koch) Rad.-Sm. To 2m; glands yellow. Balk., Eur. Turk. 'H.E. Bates': lvs glaucous, shoot tips purple in winter; infl. lime green, abundant. 'Humpty Dumpty': habit bushy; infl. large, rounded, lime with red glands. 'John Tomlinson': infl. large, rounded, bright yellow-green. 'Lambrook Yellow': spreading; lvs grey-green; fl. heads large, pale green-yellow. 'Lambrook Gold': infl. golden yellow. 'Perry's Winter Blusher': to 120cm; st. and fl. heads flushed purple-red. Z7.

E. clandestina Jacq. THE SOLDIER. Dwarf succulent, to 60cm. St. usually simple, to 4cm diam., tubercles spirally arranged, to 8mm. Lvs apical, to 37mm, linear to linear-oblanceolate, fleshy. Cyathia sessile; bracts purple, inner bracts green; glands yellow. S Afr. (Cape Prov.). Z7.

E. classenii Bally & S. Carter. Succulent shrub, to 1m, branched from base; br. 6–8-angled, to 3cm diam., fresh green; ridges wavy-dentate; spines grey, to 8mm. Lvs deltoid, to 1mm. Infl. golden yellow. Kenya. Z9.

E. clava Jacq. As for *E. bubalina*, but st. stouter, to 1m, often clavate, to 6cm diam.; tubercles more prominent. S Afr. (Cape Prov.). Z7.

E. clava E. Mey. non Jacq. = *E. bubalina.*

E. clavarioides Boiss. LION'S SPOOR. Dwarf succulent, compact cushion-forming, to 8×30cm; br. to 5cm, tubercles 4–5 sided; spines 0. Lvs ovate to lanceolate, abscising, to 2mm, fleshy. S Afr. var. *truncata* (N.E. Br.) A. White, R.A. Dyer & B.L. Sloane. Cushions of growth flat not domed; br. truncate. Z7.

E. clavata Salisb. = *E. clava.*

E. clivicola R.A. Dyer. Succulent perenn., to 15cm. St. to 15×3cm, branched below ground; br. to 3×1.5cm, rhombic, warty, clearly ribbed, yellow-green; spines to 5mm; lvs reduced. Infl. yellow. S Afr. Z7.

E. colliculina A. White, R.A. Dyer & B.L. Sloane. Dwarf succulent, to 15cm+. St. largely subterranean, br. to 12cm×7mm; tubercles rhombic to hexagonal. Infl. glands brilliant red. S Afr. (Cape Prov.). Z7.

E. columnaris Bally. Succulent shrub, to 1.3m. St. solitary, erect, to 8cm diam., 10–13-sded, angles dentate; spine shields pale yellow; spines 18mm. Cymes to 30, forked. N Somalia. Z10.

E. commelinii DC. = *E. caput-medusae.*

E. condylocarpa Bieb. Herbaceous perenn., to 40cm, with swollen root-tubers. St. simple or branched. St. lvs oblong, apex obtuse, base cordate. Rays 2–5; ray lvs rhombic. Spring––summer. Turk., Cauc., N Iran. Z8.

E. confertiflora Volkens = *E. candelabrum*.

E. confinalis R.A. Dyer. As for *E. triangularis* in habit, but more robust, to 1m+; br. less conspicuously winged. S Afr. Z7.

E. cooperi N.E. Br. Succulent tree, to 5m+. Bole to 20cm diam.; br. arching upward, pentagonal to hexagonal; seg. to 15×7.5cm, obcordate in outline; spines paired, to 8mm. E S Afr., Moz., S Zimb., Zam. Z7.

E. cooperi A. Berger = *E. ingens*.

E. corallioides L. CORAL SPURGE. Perenn., herb to 60cm. St. flimsy, clumped, shaggy, lvs oblong to oblanceolate, soft-pubesc., green suffused violet when young. Rays to 3+; ray lvs as for st. lvs but wider involucral lvs green, occas. suffused red. C & S It., Sicily; nat. SE Engl. Z8.

E. corollata L. WILD SPURGE; FLOWERING SPURGE; TRAMP'S SPURGE. Perenn. herb, erect to 90cm. Lvs elliptic to ovate or linear, to 6cm. Rays 3–7, forking; involucre campanulate; gland. processes petaloid, white, conspicuous. US. Z5.

E. coronata Thunb. = *E. clava*.

E. cotinifolia L. Small tree or shrub to 3m. Lvs usually in whorls of 3, broad-ovate, obtuse, 5–12cm, copper-red. Infl. small with cream petaloid appendages. Mex. to S Amer.; nat. elsewhere in Trop. Z10.

E. cotinoides Miq. Shrub 2–6m; br. erect. Lvs broad- to elliptic-ovate, somewhat peltate, olive-green above, glaucous beneath. Involucral bracts obovate-oblong to lanceolate. Surinam, Peru, Guyana. Z10.

E. crispa (Haw.) Sweet. Tuberous perenn. herb. Lvs lanceolate to elliptic, 1.2–5cm, folded inwards along midrib, undulate. Infl. umbellate; rays 2–5 to 3.5cm; involucre cup-shaped, glands toothed and ciliate. S Afr. (Cape Prov.). Z9.

E. cryptospinosa Bally. Succulent shrubby perenn. St. much branched, erect, from 20cm, to 1cm diam. 5–10-ribbed; spines grey-brown, v. fine, on young growth, bases forming long-itudinal strips covering st. in older plants. Lvs linear, to 3mm. Cymes solitary, bright crimson. Kenya, S Ethiop., S Somalia. Z10.

E. cuneata Vahl. Woody shrub to 4m, bark peeling. Br. with spine-tipped branchlets to 12cm. Lvs cuneate-spathulate, to 4.5cm. Cyathia solitary or in 2–4-branched umbels; glands yellow. S Arabia. Z10.

E. curvirama R.A. Dyer. As for *E. triangularis*, but to 7m; br. more curved at base, dark green; seg. more robust, angles thick-er; spines stouter. S Afr. (Cape Prov.). Z7.

E. cyathophora Murray. PAINTED LEAF; FIRE ON THE MOUNTAIN; MEXICAN FIRE PLANT. Non-succulent, ann. shrub to 70cm+. St. erect; lvs ovate to linear or pandurate, entire to dentate becom-ing red toward st. summit. Infl. bracts bright red, lf.-like. US, E Mex. Frequently cult. as '*E. heterophylla*'. Z9.

E. cylindrifolia Marn.-Lap. & Rauh. Perenn., to 15cm. St. clumped; stolons subterranean. Lvs to 2.5cm, cylindric, fleshy, apex often falcate. Involucre green, tinged violet above; glands yellow. Madag. Z10.

E. cyparissias L. CYPRESS SPURGE. Perenn. herb, to 40cm+. St. slender, branched above; st. lvs dense, linear, to 40mm. Ray lvs 9–11, linear-oblong; raylet lvs rhombic to suborbicular, to 1mm, yellow-green, becoming lilac to red-tinged; glands yellow. W, C & S Eur., nat. N Amer. 'Baby': habit small. 'Bush Boy': br. feather-like in appearance. 'Orange Man': infl. in shades of orange. 'Tall Boy': to 50cm tall. Z4.

E. davyi N.E. Br. Dwarf succulent, to 4cm. St. ± buried, conic or obovate, to 5.5cm diam.; br. erect, in whorls to 3, to 15cm, pale green, brown at sides, tubercles rhombic. Lvs to 3cm, linear-lanceolate, fleshy, folded. S Afr. Z7.

E. dawei N.E. Br. Succulent tree 15–25m, with rounded crown. Trunk simple, to 60cm diam., bark fissured, with 4(–5) rows of persistent spines and pit-scars. Br. horizontal, to 4m, densely rebranched; branchlets fleshy, 2–3-angled, 4–10cm diam., con-stricted into 5–40cm long seg.; angles toothed; spines to 6mm. Lvs obovate, to 6mm. E Afr. Z10.

E. decaryi Guillaum. Succulent perenn.; stolons subterranean; st. prostrate or curved, to 12×1.2cm diam. Lvs at br. apices, tinged red to 5cm, ovate to lanceolate, undulate, rough. Involucre yellow-green, margin red, white below. SE Madag. Z10.

E. decepta N.E. Br. Low succulent to 8cm. Main st. partially underground, globose, 6–10cm thick, marked into flattened areas with tubercle at centre. Br. to 3.7×0.8cm, cylindric, covering top and sides of main st., peduncle remains spiny, spir-ally tuberculate. Lvs to 1.5mm. Involucre green tinged purple. S Afr. (Cape Prov.). Z9.

E. decidua Bally & Leach. Dwarf succulent, to 30cm; br. prostrate or ascending, clumped, to 12×0.6cm, 2–4-sided, twisted, decid.; spines to 3mm. Lvs to 3mm, acute. SC Afr.

Z10.

E. decipiens Boiss. & Buhse. Perenn. herb, glaucous in all parts. St. ascending, unbranched, short, thick, with lvs at apex. Lvs many, linear-lanceolate, 12–18mm, subacute, subcoriaceous. Iran. Z10.

E. deightonii Croizat. Succulent shrub or tree, to 6m. Br. triangular or rhombic to hexagonal; ridges winged; spines paired, to 18mm. Lvs to 3mm, obovate to scale-like, soon abscising. W trop. Afr. Z9.

E. delphinensis Ursch & Leandri. Succulent perenn. to 10cm. St. cylindric, to 8mm diam.; br. to 14cm diam.; spines to 18mm. Lvs to 2cm, obovate, coriaceous, undulate. Madag. Z10.

E. dendroides L. Shrub, to 2–3m. Crown rounded; st. glab.; branching dichotomous. Lvs to 6cm, linear to elliptic, mucronate; lf scars prominent. Rays 5–8, forking; raylet lvs yellow-green. Spring. Medit. Z8.

E. desmondii Keay & Milne-Redh. Arborescent succulent shrub, to 6m. Bole to 10cm diam.; br. triangular to rhombic, to 35mm diam.; angles undulate, segmented; spines to 7mm, rust-brown to black. Lvs spathulate to obcordate, to 12cm, fleshy, leathery, notched. Infl. glands dull crimson. Cameroun, Nigeria. Z9.

E. discreta N.E. Br. = *E. woodii*.

E. dregeana E. Mey. Succulent shrub to 2m. St. frequently fascia-ting; br. to 5cm diam., erect, white-green; spines 0. Lvs decid., reduced. Nam., S Afr. (Cape Prov.). Z7.

E. dulcis L. Perenn. herb; rhiz. thick, fleshy. St. slender, pubesc., st. lvs oblong to oblanceolate, to 7cm, green. Rays 4–8, spread-ing; raylet lvs triangular-ovate to rhombic, green, becoming red, later purple; glands tinged red or yellow. W, C & S Eur. to Macedonia. 'Chameleon': lvs rich purple; fl. heads yellow-green flushed purple in summer. Z6.

E. duvalii Lecoq & Lamotte. Woody-based perenn. herb, to 30cm. St. glab., scaly near base. Lvs obovate to lanceolate serrate, apex obtuse, base cordate. S Fr. Z8.

E. echinata Salm-Dyck = *E. cereiformis*.

E. echinus Hook. f. & Coss. Succulent shrub, to 1.5m+. St. multi-branched, hexagonal. Spine shields forming ribs, grey, horny; spines 13mm, grey or red, spreading. Moroc. Z8.

E. edulis L. = *E. neriifolia*.

E. elastica Marloth = *E. dregeana*.

E. elliptica Thunb. = *E. silenifolia*.

E. enneagona A. Berger = *E. aggregata*.

E. enopla Boiss. As for *E. atrispina*, but bushy, to 1m high. St. branched at or above base; spines to 6cm. Involucres dark red. S Afr. (Cape Prov.). var. *viridis* Spines green, tinged yellow. A. White, R.A. Dyer & B.L. Sloane Z7.

E. enopla A. Berger = *E. heptagona*.

E. enormis N.E. Br. Dwarf succulent, to 15cm+. St. and root a conic, tuberous body, to 10cm diam.; br. to 20, subterranean, re-branching above ground, 4–5-angled, sometimes spiraling, tuberculate; spines to 6mm. Lvs reduced. S Afr. Z9.

E. enterophora Drake = *E. xylophylloides*.

E. ephedroides E. Mey. Succulent, to 50cm+. St. slender, branched from base; br. to 7cm, to 5mm+ diam., dichotomous; spines 0. Lvs subulate, abscising. S Afr. (Cape Prov.). Z7.

E. epithymoides Jacq. non L. = *E. polychroma*.

E. erosa Willd. = *E. cereiformis*.

E. erosa A. Berger non Willd. = *E. fimbriata*.

E. erubescens Boiss. = *E. macrostegia*.

E. esculenta Marloth. Dwarf succulent, to 50cm diam., br. in a rosette around a central area to 4cm diam., ascending to spread-ing, to 20×2cm, glab., tuberculate. S Afr. (Cape Prov.). Z7.

E. esula L. LEAFY SPURGE; WOLF'S MILK. Similar to *E. cyparissias* but to 1m+, st. lvs more distant, to 8.5cm, oblanceolate. Rays 5–17, forking; raylet lvs rhombic to reniform, sessile. Eur., nat. in NE N Amer. Z5.

E. esula ssp. *tommasiniana* (Bertol.) Nyman = *E. waldsteinii*.

E. evansii Pax. As for *E. grandidens*, but to 10m. Br. less crowded, secondary br. 4–5-angled. Lf margins slightly un-dulate; warts never bearing basal prickles. S Afr. Z7.

E. excelsa A. White, R.A. Dyer & B.L. Sloane. Succulent tree, to 10m; br. whorled, to 1m, decid., rhombic to square in sec-tion, to 3cm diam.; seg. to 15cm; spines to 8mm. S Afr. Z7.

E. exigua L. DWARF SPURGE. Glaucous ann. St. often much branched from base, 5–35cm. Lvs linear, 0.5–3cm. Infl. umbellate; rays 4–5, much-branched; raylet lvs obliquely triangular-ovate. Summer. Eur.

E. falsa N.E. Br. = *E. meloformis*.

E. fasciculata Thunb. Dwarf succulent, to 30cm. St. solitary, to 8cm diam., unbranched; tubercles spirally arranged, hexagonal. Cyathia 3–5; fertile peduncles robust, curved persistent, borne in a triangular hollow in tubercle surface; involucre cupulate, fimbriate. S Afr. (Cape Prov.). Z7.

E. fasciculata N.E. Br. = *E. schoenlandii*.

E. ferox Marloth. PINCUSHION EUPHORBIA. Dwarf, clump-forming succulent, to 15cm, branching underground, br. to 25×4.5cm,

9–12-angled, pale buff-green; spines to 3cm+ brown, becoming grey. Lvs rudimentary, abscising. Cyathia solitary; bracts 6–9, brown; involucre purple, dotted white. S Afr. (Cape Prov.). Z7.

E. filiflora Marloth. Succulent, 20–30cm. Main st. erect, subclavate to subcylindric, 7.5–10cm thick, tuberculate. Br. from upper part of main st., cylindric, 5–8×0.8–1.8cm, spirally tuberculate. Lvs linear, 2–3mm. Involucre to 1×1.2cm, glands 5, divided into linear seg., green-yellow. S Afr. (Cape Prov.). Z9.

E. fimbriata Scop. As for *E. mammillaris*, but taller; br. more slender; spines to 4mm, or 0; involucre to 6mm, lobe margins fimbriate. S Afr. (Cape Prov.). Z7.

E. 'Flamingo' (*E. lophogona* × *E. milii* var. *splendens*.) Robust, woody. Br. stout, thorny. Lvs long, obovate. Infl. flesh pink in long clusters. Z10.

E. flanaganii N.E. Br. Dwarf succulent. St. subcylindric to conic, to 5cm; br. in 4 series, ascending, to 4cm, tubercles tiny. Lvs to 1cm, decid. S Afr. (Cape Prov.). Z7.

E. fluminis S. Carter. Succulent perenn., subscandent, to 2m. St. and br. to 1cm diam., angles 4, toothed, mottled, variegated or striped; spines to 1.5cm, forked at tip. Lvs deltoid, 1mm. Kenya. Z10.

E. fortissima Leach. Spiny succulent candelabriform tree, not exceeding 5m with rounded crown, branching close to base; br. 3(–4)-winged; seg. spheric or ellipsoid, 10×9cm at apex; spines paired, divergent, to 7mm. Cyathia yellow, arranged vertically. S Afr. Z9.

E. fournieri hort. = *E. leuconeura*.

E. fragifera Jan. Close to *E. polychroma*. Herbaceous pubesc. perenn. St. to 30cm, woody below. Lvs lanceolate to obovate, 1–2cm, base rounded, entire. Rays 4–5, ray lvs ovate, raylet lvs broadly so. Balk., Albania. Z6.

E. franckiana A. Berger. Resembles *E. caerulescens* but to 1m+, branching. St. frequently triangular; ridges acute. Cyathia borne midway between spine pairs. S Afr. Z7.

E. francoisii Leandri. Perenn., dwarf succulent. Lvs to 6cm, somewhat succulent, oblong-linear to ovate, green variegated silver-grey, pink or white, midrib frequently red, undulate, dark green. Involucre yellow-green. SE Madag. Z10.

E. franksiae N.E. Br. As for *E. woodii*, but peduncles longer, to 18mm; glands green tinged yellow; margin slightly crenate. S Afr. (Natal). var. *zuluensis* A. White R.A. Dyer & B.L. Sloane. St. tapering to apex; br. stem-like. Involucral glands green. Z7.

E. frickiana N.E. Br. = *E. pseudoglobosa*.

E. fructuspina Sweet = *E. bergeri*.

E. fructus-pini Mill. = *E. caput-medusae*.

E. fruticosa Forssk. Succulent shrub, to 50cm. St. to 10cm diam., branched from base; br. cylindric to clavate, to 7.5cm diam., 10–13-sided, tinged grey; spines to 18mm, red-brown, later black to grey. Lvs inconspicuous. Involucre yellow; glands yellow, fringed. S Arabia. Z10.

E. fulgens Karw. ex Klotzsch. SCARLET PLUME. Shrub to 2m. St. slender, branched; br. arching. Lvs narrow-lanceolate, to 10cm, dark green. Cyathia in axill. cymes; involucral glands 'flower'-like with rounded scarlet petaloid processes. Mex. 'Alba': fls cream, long-lasting. 'Albatross': br. long, arching; lvs blue-green, pendulous; fls pure white, star-shaped. 'Purple Leaf': lvs deep burgundy purple; fls bright orange. Dark red, pink and golden forms are also grown. Z10.

E. fusca Marloth. Low succulent, st. ± globose, 30×20cm, covered by br. Br. cylindric, 2–15cm, tubercles rhomboid-hexagonal. Lvs caducous, v. small, Cyathia glands with 5–7 narrow processes on outer margin, rich brown, lobes 5–6, fimbriate. S Afr. (Cape Prov.), Nam. Z9.

E. fusiformis Haw. ex D. Don. Low glab. herb. Lvs radical, subsessile, obovate or oblanceolate, acute to obtuse. Cymes from apex of rootstock, dichotomous; bracts ovate, 3-lobed. N India. Z10.

E. gemmea Bally & S. Carter. Succulent perenn. St. rhizomatous to weakly erect, to 45cm; br. quadrilateral, to 1cm diam., spotted green, ridges dentate; spines to 12mm. Lvs rudimentary. Cymes solitary; cyathia wide-funneliform; glands deep red. Kenya. Z10.

E. geniculata Ortega = *E. heterophylla*.

E. gerardiana Jacq. = *E. seguieriana*.

E. 'Giant Christ Thorn'. Slow-growing. St. to 6cm thick, grey, thorns brown. Lvs green tinged blue, arranged in clusters. Infl. pink with paler sheen. Z10.

E. gilberti A. Berger = *E. micracantha*.

E. glauca Forst. SHORE SPURGE. Erect rhizomatous herb to 40cm+. Lvs to 10cm, glaucous, blue-green, entire; lf scars linear. Rays 5–6; involucral glands 4–5, dark purple. NZ. Z9.

E. globosa (Haw.) Sims. Dwarf succulent, to 8cm, forming thick mats. St. subglobose, to 3cm diam.; br. to subcylindric, to 6cm×14mm, tubercles to 1cm. Lvs lanceolate, to 3mm; spines 0. Cyathia solitary; peduncles threadlike, involucre to 2cm

diam., lobes rhombic. S Afr. (Cape Prov.). Z7.

E. glochidiata Jex-Blake non Pax = *E. meridionalis*.

E. glomerata hort. ex A. Berger = *E. globosa*.

E. gmelinii Steud. = *E. esula*.

E. goldei Prokh. = *E. nicaeensis*.

E. gorgonis A. Berger. Succulent, to 10cm. St. subterranean, globose to obconic; br. radial in 3–5 series, around branch-free centre, tubercles to 5mm, sometimes tinged purple. Lvs reduced, abscising. Cyathia solitary, involucre dull purple; glands ruby to brown-purple. S Afr. (Cape Prov.). Z9.

E. gossypina Pax. Shrub, sprawling to 12.5m or scrambling to 4m. Br. spreading, succulent, 1cm diam., with dark brown lf scars. Lvs lanceolate to linear-lanceolate, 4cm, caducous. Umbel 4–8-branched around central sessile cyathium, rays to 3cm; bracts green or red. E Afr. Z10.

E. graciliramea Pax. Tufted succulent to 15cm, in clumps 30–60cm diam. St. to 25×1cm, cylindric; teeth in 4 series; spines solitary, 2cm. Lvs deltoid, 1mm. Kenya and Tanz. Z10.

E. graminea Jacq. Perenn. herb. St. sprawling to1.5m, terete, branching from base. Lvs oblong-elliptic to sublinear or ovate, 2–8×0.5–5cm. Cyathia term. on dichotomizing upper br.; glands with or without large white appendage. S Mex. to N S Amer. Z9.

E. grandialata R.A. Dyer. Succulent shrub to 2m, br. produced at base, arching upwards, 3–4-angled, to 13cm diam.; seg. 7–15cm, pyramidal, angles wing-like, to 8cm across; spines doubly paired. Cymes clustered, to 3; involucre yellow; glands yellow. S Afr. Z7.

E. grandicornis Goebel. BIG HORNED EUPHORBIA; COW HORN. Succulent shrub to 2m, branching from base; br. 3-angled, erect to ascending, to 15cm diam. seg. irregular, to 12cm edges horny; spines paired, to 7cm. Cyathia borne between spine pairs, short-stipitate, tinged yellow. S Afr. Z7.

E. grandidens Haw. BIG TOOTH EUPHORBIA; NABOOM. Shrub, later a succulent tree, to 20m+. Bole cylindric; br. ascending, whorled, seg. 0, angles 3, deeply toothed; spines to 6mm, grey, frequently bearing prickles. Lvs reduced. Cymes solitary; involucre pale green, fringed. S Afr. Z7.

E. grandidens Goebel = *E. grandicornis*.

E. grandidens Adlam = *E. ingens*.

E. grantii Oliv. As for *E. monteiroi*, but stouter bush to small tree, to 9m; tubercles 0; lvs linear-lanceolate to spathulate, to 30×3cm, coriaceous. Trop. Afr. Z9.

E. greenwayi Bally & S. Carter. Succulent perenn., to 30cm. Br. rhombic in section, blue-green, sides striped, ridges dentate; spines slender, to 1cm; prickles to 5mm. Lvs deltoid, to 1mm. Tanz. Z10.

E. griffithii Hook. f. Rhizomatous perenn. herb to 90cm. Sts erect. Lvs to 13cm, linear-oblong or linear-lanceolate, dark green with a pale or pink midrib; upper lvs flushing pink to orange-red. Involucre campanulate, pink-red to orange; cyathia copper to orange or red. E Himal. 'Dixter': compact, lvs dark, luxuriant, tinged red, grey-pink beneath; infl. orange. 'Fire-glow': infl. bright fiery red. 'Wickstead's Form': young growth richly coloured; infl. dark orange. var. *griffithii*. Lvs glab. var. *bhutanica* (Fisch.) Long. Lvs softly pubesc. beneath. Z5.

E. griseola Pax. Succulent shrub to 70cm+ branching at base; br. slender, to 1.5cm diam., angles (4–)5(–6) tuberculate, undulate, spines to 8mm, grey. Lvs to 6mm, ovate, decid. Cymes solitary; involucre green to yellow-green. SC Afr. Z7.

E. groenewaldii R.A. Dyer. As for *E. tortirama*, but br. fewer, not spiralling, shorter, to 7cm, unsegmented, more toothed. S Afr. Z7.

E. hadramautica Bak. Small succulent herb. St. erect to ascending, cylindric, 3–12×1–2cm, with persistent spiral lf scars. Lvs at apex, linear- to broad-ovate, 2–10cm, entire to somewhat undulate. Cyathia white-hairy, green; glands green or pink. Arabia. Z10.

E. halipedicola Leach. Succulent, arborescent shrub to 10m. Bole cylindric to hexagonal; br. spreading, later erect, appearing whorled above, winged, segmented, margin undulate, horny seg. to 40×20cm, ovoid to cordate; spines to 15mm. Lvs to 0.3mm, ovate to circular. Moz. Z10.

E. hamata (Haw.) Sweet. ELEPHANT'S MILK BUSH. Succulent shrub to 35cm+, to 45cm diam. St. branched from base, to 12mm diam., somewhat 3-angled, glaucous, tubercles recurved. Lvs to 17mm, ovate to lanceolate. Cyathia green tinged yellow; glands yellow to red. S Afr. (Cape Prov.), Nam. Z7.

E. handiensis Burchd. Small shrub to 80cm, densely branched. St. succulent, 8–14-ribbed, with paired straight 2–3cm long spines, and cluster of spines at apex. Cyathia red. Z10.

E. havanensis hort. = *E. lactea*.

E. hedyotoides N.E. Br. Small shrub. Br. and st. thin. Lvs opposite at st. forks, or at br. ends, linear, to 2cm. Cyathia 1–3 in lf axils, glands with fimbriate appendages. Madag. Z10.

E. heldreichii Orph. ex Boiss. As for *E. amygdaloides*, but st. lvs subtending rays whorled; raylet lvs only partly joined. Greece, S Albania. Z8.

E. helicothele Lem. = *E. nivulia*.

E. helioscopia L. SUN SPURGE. Glabrescent ann.; st. solitary, erect, 10–50cm. Lvs obovate-spathulate, 1.5–3cm, serrulate above. Infl. 5-rayed, bracts similar to lvs but more rounded, yellow-green; glands green. Eur. Z6.

E. heptagona L. MILK BARREL. As for *E. atrispina*, but bush to 130cm, branched at base. St. thicker above; br. 5–10-angled, to 22×3cm; spines to 3cm, brown. S Afr. (Cape Prov.). Z7.

E. heptagona A. Berger non L. = *E. pentagona*.

E. hermentiana Lem. = *E. trigona*.

E. heteracantha Pax = *E. subsalsa*.

E. heterochroma Pax. As for *E. griscola*, but taller, to 2m; br. thicker, to 25mm diam., slightly constricted, at intervals 2–10cm, 4–5-angled. Kenya, Tanz. Z8.

E. heterophylla L. JAPANESE POINSETTIA; MOLE PLANT; PAINT LEAF. Ann. or perenn., to 80cm+. St. erect, simple or branched. Lvs to 12cm, variable in shape, upper lvs pandurate, often variegated, frequently scarlet or white at base, entire to dentate, sometimes undulate. Infl. bracts scarlet. US, C Amer., Boliv., Hawaii, nat. in Trop. Z7. Material labelled as *E. heterophylla* in cult. is often *E. cyathophora*.

E. hierosolymitana Boiss. Non-succulent shrub, to 3m. St. spine-less, glab., ray lvs elliptic to obovate, to 4.5cm, mucronate. Rays 5, to 3 times forking; raylet lvs elliptic-obovate, yellow-green. E Medit., Cyprus, W Syr. Z8.

E. himalayensis (Klotzsch ex Klotzsch & Garcke) Boiss. Perenn. herb to 60cm. St. erect; br. ascending. Lvs oblong to oblong-lanceolate, to 4cm; upper lvs whorled. Rays to 4cm; involucre campanulate, glands brown. Himal. to Laos. Z9.

E. hislopii N.E. Br. As for *E. milii* but taller. St. to 6cm diam., 8–10-sided; spines to 25mm. Lvs ovate-lanceolate, to 18mm; involucral lvs pink to red. Madag. Z10.

E. horrida Boiss. AFRICAN MILK BARREL. Succulent shrub, to 1.5m+; br. clumped, to 10cm diam., angles 7 to 20-winged to 1.5cm, undulate; spines to 5cm. Lvs reduced. Cyathia 3 in each cyme; glands plum purple. S Afr. (Cape Prov.). var. *striata* A. White, R.A. Dyer & B.L. Sloane. Br. grey-green; angles wavy, sides horizontally striated; spines shorter. var. *noorsveldensis* A. White R.A. Dyer & B.L. Sloane More glaucous, spines longer. var. *major* A. White, R.A. Dyer & B.L. Sloane. Larger. Z7.

E. hottentota Marloth. Succulent shrub to 2m. Br. at base, later ascending, to 4cm diam., 5–6-angled, sometimes segmented, glaucous; spines to 5mm. S Afr. Z7.

E. hyberna L. IRISH SPURGE. Perenn., herb to 60cm; rhiz. stout. St. lvs elliptic-oblong, broad, dark green, apex obtuse to emarginate. Rays typically 5; raylet lvs ovate yellow. W Eur. ssp. *canuti* (Parl.) Tutin. Rays 1 or 0. ssp. *hyberna* Briq. Rays to 5. ssp. *insularis* (Boiss.) Briq. Rays many. Z9.

E. hydnorae E. Mey. = *E. mauritanica*.

E. hystrix Jacq. = *E. loricata*.

E. impervia A. Berger = *E. heterochroma*.

E. inconstantia R.A. Dyer. Succulent shrub to 1.5m+. St. solitary to many, to 8cm diam.; upper br. to 5cm diam., 7–10-angled; spines derived from peduncles. Lvs reduced, soon abscising. S Afr. (Cape Prov.). Z7.

E. inermis Mill. Dwarf succulent, similar in habit to *E. caput-medusae*. Br. to 15mm diam., to 30cm, tubercles conic, to 10×6mm, 6-sided, spirally arranged. Lvs soon abscising; spines derived from peduncles. Infl. showy, involucral glands bearing numerous white processes. S Afr. (Cape Prov.). var. *huttonae* (N.E. Br.) A. White, R.A. Dyer & B.L. Sloane. Involucral gland white, lacking processes. Z7.

E. inermis var. *laniglans* N.E. Br. = *E. esculenta*.

E. infausta N.E. Br. = *E. meloformis*.

E. infesta Pax = *E. triaculeata*.

E. ingens E. Mey. CACTUS EUPHORBIA; NABOOM. Tree to 12m. Crown crowded, lower br. persisting; br. straight, succulent, 4–5-angled; spines 0 or rudimentary. S Afr. to Kenya. Z7.

E. inornata N.E. Br. Low succulent. Main st. subglobose, to 10cm+ diam., covered by many closely placed ascending br., except for depressed tubercular apical area. Br. cylindric, to 7.5×1cm, tubercular, tinged purple. Lvs broad-ovate, 1.5mm. Infl. involucre to 7mm diam., green with red dots. S Afr. Z9.

E. intisy Drake. Shrub or small tree, to 7m; br. cylindric, dichotomous, grey-green. Lvs reduced, borne on projections, br. thus appearing nodular, glab.; spines 0. Madag. Z10.

E. isacantha Pax. Succulent perenn., to 25cm, to 1m diam. St. branching from base; br. decumbent, to 50cm, sharply 4-sided, to 10mm diam., ridges entire; spines to 5mm, brown. Lvs to 1mm. Malawi, Tanz. Z10.

E. jacquemontii Boiss. Perenn. herb. St. to 45cm, pubesc. Lvs lanceolate, 5–6.5cm, tinged red, conspicuously veined. Infl. umbellate; rays 5, v. short, ray lvs 3, ovate, obtuse; involucre campanulate, glands undulate. W Himal. Z8.

E. jacquiniiflora Hook. = *E. fulgens*.

E. jansenvillensis Nel. Dwarf succulent, to 30cm. St. sub-terranean; br. erect, to 16cm×15mm, ridges 5, warty. Lvs fleshy, to 2mm. Cyathia solitary; involucre narrow-lobed, red; glands green tinged yellow. S Afr. (Cape Prov.). Z7.

E. johnsonii auct. non Pax = *E. knuthii*.

E. kamerunica Pax. Tree to 6m. St. branched; br. succulent, spiny, 3–5-sided; shoots 4-sided, to 6cm diam.; spines to 6mm. Equat. Guinea, Cameroun. Z10.

E. kibwezensis N.E. Br. = *E. bussei* var. *kibwezensis*.

E. knuthii Pax. Dwarf succulent. St. branching at ground level; br. to 15cm×12mm, suffused grey, angles 3–4, undulate, tubercles pale green. Lvs reduced, soon abscising; spines to 8mm, spreading, brown, bearing grey, bearing a pair of prickles at base. Moz., Swaz., E Transvaal, Natal. Z10.

E. kotschyana Fenzl. Stout perenn., to 70cm+. St. glaucous to subglabrous, base woody. St. ray lvs to 8cm, narrow-oblanceolate to elliptic-oblong, shiny above, dull beneath. Rays 5, forking to ×3, involucre cupulate, to 4cm diam., yellow-green; glands horned. Summer. Turk., W & S Anatolia. Z8.

E. lactea Haw. MOTTLED SPURGE; CANDELABRA CACTUS; FALSE CACTUS; HAT-RACK CACTUS; DRAGON BONES. Candelabriform succulent, arborescent shrub, to 5m. Br. to 5cm diam., mottled green, banded with white lines running toward 3–4, sinuate angles; spines to 5mm, brown. Lvs inconspicuous, soon abscising. India, nat. in W Indies, US (Flor.). 'Cristata' (CRESTED EUPHORBIA; FRILLED FAN; ELKHORN): br. crested, fan-shaped, forming a cluster. Z10.

E. lagascae Spreng. Glab. ann., 30–45cm. Lower lvs ovate, upper oblong-lanceolate, obtuse, entire or weakly sinulate. Rays 3, ray lvs ovate-lanceolate or triangular-ovate, base subcordate, apex mucronate, raylet lvs ovate-rhombic. Spain, Sardinia. Z8.

E. lambii Svent. Shrub to 1.5m; st. light brown with conspicuous scars. Lvs clustered at branch-ends, narrow-lanceolate, retuse. Infl. simple or compound umbelliform, green-yellow; bracts large, fused. Canary Is. Z9.

E. laro Drake = *E. tirucalli*.

E. lateriflora Schum. & Thonn. Scrambling succulent perenn., to 1m. St. terete, to 90cm; br. to 7mm diam. Lvs sessile, linear to linear-lanceolate. Equat. Guinea, N Nigeria. Z10.

E. lathyris L. CAPER SPURGE; MYRTLE SPURGE; MOLE PLANT. Bienn. herb, to 1.5m+. St. glaucous. St. lvs decussate, to 15cm, oblong-lanceolate, leathery, blue-green. Rays 2 or 4, forking to ×8; ray lvs ovate-lanceolate; raylet lvs ovate-lanceolate, yellow-green. Fr. caper-like. Native location uncertain, cosmop. weed. Z6.

E. laxiflora Kuntze = *E. bubalina*.

E. ledienii A. Berger. As for *E. coerulescens* but to 2m; seg. irregular, 4–7-angled; spines less conspicuous. S Afr. (Cape Prov.). var. *dregei* N.E. Br. Raylet lvs forming a narrow, funneliform involucre. Z7.

E. leucocephala Lotsy. PASCUITA; SNOWS OF KILIMANJARO. As for *E. pulcherrima*, but lower lvs lanceolate-ovate, in whorls, to 8cm, apiculate, upper lvs oblanceolate, entire, pink to white. Infl. with white, petaloid appendages. C Amer. Z9.

E. leucodendron Drake = *E. alluaudii*.

E. leuconeura Boiss. Arborescent shrub to 0.5m+; br. angles 4, fringed. Lvs oblong-obovate, to 12cm, obtuse. Madag. Z10.

E. leviana Croizat = *E. cereiformis*.

E. lignosa Marloth. Dwarf rounded shrub to 25cm+. St. robust, rigid; br. succulent, becoming rigid term. twigs, spiny. Lvs to 1.5cm, lanceolate to linear-lanceolate, folded. Namaqualand. Z10.

E. ligularia Roxb. = *E. neriifolia*.

E. lombardensis Nel = *E. micracantha*.

E. ×*lomii* Rauh. (*E. lophogona* ×*E. milii*.) GIANT CROWN OF THORNS. Closely resembling *E. milii* in habit, but st. much stouter. Lvs ovate, 15cm, succulent, becoming red in sun. Involucral bracts v. large, rose-carmine to red. Cult. origin. Z10.

E. longibracteata Pax = *E. monteiroi*.

E. longifolia D. Don. As for *E. griffithii*, but red colouring 0. Lvs to 11cm, oblong-linear-lanceolate; involucral bracts to 2cm, ovate, yellow. Bhutan. Z7.

E. longituberculosa Boiss. Glab. perenn. herb to 30cm. St. swollen, to 8×4cm, with br. to 8cm, tuberculate or smooth, somewhat succulent. Lvs linear-lanceolate, to 5cm. E Afr., Yemen. Z10.

E. lophogona Lam. Succulent upright shrub to 45cm, br. pentagonal, ridged; ridges spiny. Lvs to 20cm, term., obovate or lanceolate-obovate, coriaceous, revolute, involucre sub-orbicular, to 7mm diam., white or pink, petaloid, fimbriate, glands yellow. Madag. Z10.

E. loricata Lam. Succulent shrub to 100cm. Br. cylindric, tubercles spirally arranged; secondary br. to 12mm diam., spines derived from peduncles to 5cm. Lvs to 7.5cm, linear-lanceolate, blunt. S Afr. (Cape Prov.). Z7.

E. lyttoniana R. Dexter = *E. pseudocactus* var. *lyttoniana*.

E. macrantha Stephan ex Willd. = *E. stricta*.

E. macrostegia Boiss. Herbaceous perenn., to 60cm. St. robust. St. lvs to 11cm, obovate to oblong-lanceolate, reduced above. Rays 3–5, forking; involucre to 4cm diam. W Syr., S Turk., Leb., W & S Iran. Z9.

E. magnidens Haw. ex Salm-Dyck = *E. grandidens*.

E. malevola Leach. Succulent shrub to 1.5m+. Br. spreading, ascending, to 2cm diam., 4–5-sided; spines to 2mm. Involucre funnelform, to 6×3mm; lobes 5, subfimbriate. S Zimb. Z10.

E. mamillosa Lem. = *E. squarrosa*.

E. mammillaris L. CORN COB; CORKSCREW. Dwarf succulent, to 18cm+. St. small, erect; br. clustered, erect, to 6cm diam., polygonal, tubercles hexagonal, with an apical lf scar, separated by transverse lines; spines to 1cm, derived from peduncles. S Afr. (Cape Prov.). 'Variegata': br. columnar, green-white marked bright green tinted pink. Z7.

E. mammillaris Haw. = *E. fimbriata*.

E. 'Manda's Cowhorn' (*E. pseudocactus* × *E. grandicornis*.) Br. ascending, fan-like, uppermost with long, spine-tipped tubercle, bright green edges undulate, grey-brown set with pairs of spines. Z7.

E. 'Manda's Zigzag' (*E. grandicornis* × *E. pseudocactus*.) St. upright, 3-angled, br. zig-zagged, dark green herringbone olive, edged undulate, grey-brown set with pairs of spines. Z7.

E. marginata Pursh. SNOW ON THE MOUNTAIN; GHOST WEED. Ann. to 1m. St. erect, softly pubesc. above. St. lvs to 8cm, ovate to obovate or oblong, pale green, margins of upper lvs edged white. Rays 3; ray and raylet lvs petaloid, elliptic-ovate, edged or entirely white. Autumn. N Amer. 'Summer Icicle': dwarf; lvs green and white. 'White Top': erect to 90cm; upper lvs variegated white. Z4.

E. marlothiana N.E. Br. Low succulent. Main st. a continuation of taproot, forming a clavate or elongate-obconic body. Br. several, erect or ascending, 7.5–40×1–2.5cm, tuberculate. Lvs oblong or linear, to 6mm. S Afr. (Cape Prov.). Z9.

E. marlothii Pax = *E. monteiroi*.

E. × martinii Rouy. Natural hybrid of *E. amygdaloides* × *E. characias*. Variable, resembles either parent. Z7.

E. mauritanica L. YELLOW MILK BUSH; MELKBOS; JACKAL'S FOOD. As for *E. dregeana*, but st. to 1m+; br. thinner, green suffused yellow. Cyathia solitary, yellow. S Afr. Z7.

E. media N.E. Br. = *E. tirucalli*.

E. medusae Thunb. = *E. caput-medusae*.

E. melanostica E. Mey. = *E. mauritanica*.

E. melapetala Gasparr. = *E. characias*.

E. mellifera Ait. As for *E. dendroides*, but to 3m+. St. lvs narrow-lanceolate, larger, dark green. Infl. term., scented. Madeira. Z10.

E. meloformis Ait. MELON SPURGE. Dwarf succulent, to 10cm+. St. subglobose, to 10cm diam., apex sunken, 8–12-angled, occas. banded pale green, purple brown or darker green; angles occas. spiralling; br. variable in number. Lvs soon abscising. S Afr. (Cape Prov.). 'Prolifera': habit well-branched. Z7.

E. melonoformis Link = *E. meloformis*.

E. memoralis R.A. Dyer. Succulent, perenn. shrub, to 3m. St. cylindric, 5–7-sided, to 10cm diam., segmented; seg. to 15cm, winged, margin horny; spines to 6mm; lvs oblong-lanceolate, linear, to 2cm, or scale-like, to 2mm. S Zimb. Z10.

E. meridionalis Bally & S. Carter. Succulent perenn., to 1m. St. branching from base; br. to 15mm diam.; ridges 4, striped dark green, glaucous, becoming green tinged purple, dentate; spines solitary, to 2cm, apex forking. Cyathia to 6mm, bright carmine. Kenya, Tanz. Z10.

E. micracantha Boiss. As for *E. squarrosa*, but br. generally 4-angled; tubercles less prominent; spines more slender, to 6mm, grey. S Afr. (Cape Prov.). Z7.

E. milii Desmoul. CROWN OF THORNS; CHRIST THORN; CHRIST PLANT. Scrambling shrub to 1m. St. spiny, grey, irregularly branched, to 120cm×9mm, 5–6-sided; spines to 3cm. Lvs to 3.5cm, obovate, apex truncate, base attenuate. Peduncles to 5cm, red; involucral bracts 2, ovate, scarlet. Madag. 'Koeniger's Aalbäumle': habit dwarf; lvs obovate, deep green; fls bright red. White, yellow, carmine and deep scarlet forms are also grown. var. *splendens* (Bojer ex Hook.) Ursch & Leandri. To 180cm. Lvs to 5cm. Peduncles tacky; involucral lvs brilliant red. Z10.

E. milii var. *hislopii* (N.E. Br.) Ursch & Leandri = *E. hislopii*.

E. misera Benth. Irregularly branched shrub, 30–90cm; st. grey, puberulent when young. Lvs in whorls, round-ovate, 4–15mm; stipules fimbriate. Cyathia solitary, 2–3mm; glands purple with white crenulate appendage. Spring–summer. W N Amer. Z6.

E. mlanjeana Leach. Succulent shrub to 1m; br. 3–5-sided, to 60×3cm, segmented, base attenuate; spines to 4.5mm. Lvs to 4mm, ovate. Malawi. Z10.

E. mogadorensis hort. = *E. resinifera*.

E. monteiroi Hook. f. Succulent shrub, occas. arborescent, to 1m.

St. simple or branched; br. spirally arranged, cylindric, to 5cm diam., tubercles spirally arranged. Lvs to 15cm, borne near apex, oblong to linear. Peduncles to 30cm; involucre bell-shaped, red-brown to dark brown; glands with 3–6 fingers. Nam., S Angola, Bots. Z7.

E. morinii A. Berger = *E. heptagona*.

E. mucronata Clarke = *E. hierosolymitana*.

E. muirii N.E. Br. Dwarf succulent, sometimes to 45cm, branching below ground; primary br. erect, to 18cm, tuberculate. Lvs linear, to 2cm. Cyathia solitary; peduncles to 2cm; involucre to 15mm diam., lobes vivid red; glands with yellow fingers. S Afr. (Cape Prov.). Z7.

E. mulennae Rendle = *E. grantii*.

E. multiceps A. Berger. Many-headed, conical, succulent shrub to 60cm. Br. spreading, basal br. to 8×3cm, tubercles spirally arranged; spines derived from peduncles, to 7cm. Lvs to 12mm, soon abscising. S Afr. (Cape Prov.). Z7.

E. multiflora Willd. ex Klotzsch & Garcke = *E. adenoptera*.

E. multiramosa Nel. Low succulent. Main st. subglobose, 20×12cm, covered by br. except for small apical area, often with spiny peduncle remains. Br. 4–11×0.5–1.5cm, tapering upwards, tuberculate, blue-green. Lvs clustered at br. tips, linear, 10mm, fleshy. Cyathia solitary; bracts fleshy, spathulate, white-hairy, glands 5, erect, yellow-green, lobes fimbriate. S Afr. (Cape Prov.). Z9.

E. murielii N.E. Br. = *E. candelabrum*.

E. myrsinites L. Perenn. glaucous herb. St. several, stout, trailing to 25cm+. Lvs spirally arranged, obovate to suborbicular, fleshy, blue-grey, mucronate. Rays 5–12, bright green; raylet lvs sulphur yellow. Spring. S Eur., Asia Minor. 'Washfield': infl. tinged red. Z6.

E. namibensis Marloth. Low succulent. Main st. subglobose or ovoid, 7.5–20×7.5–15cm, partly subterranean. Br. numerous, erect or spreading, cylindric or tapering, 2–5(–9)×1.1.5cm, spirally tuberculate, with spiny peduncle remains. Lvs linear, to 3.7cm. Nam. Z10.

E. natalensis hort. ex A. Berger = *E. ingens*.

E. neriifolia L. HEDGE EUPHORBIA; OLEANDER SPURGE. Succulent erect shrub to small tree, to 6m+. St. terete, leafy toward ends; br. whorled to spirally arranged, to 4cm diam., ridges 5, spirally arranged; spines black. Lvs obovate-spathulate, to 12cm, coriaceous; lf scars conspicuous. Spring. W India to Moluccas and S New Guinea. 'Variegata Cristata': st. crested, bright green variegated off-white. Z10.

E. neriifolia hort. non L. = *E. undulatifolia*.

E. nesemannii R.A. Dyer. Spiny succulent. Main st. v. short, combined with tuberous main root. Br. clustered at apex, 8–40×1–3cm, 6–14-angled, tuberculate on young br. only; spines solitary. Lvs minute, caducous. S Afr. Z9.

E. nicaeensis All. Bushy perenn., to 80cm. St. glaucous, frequently suffused red; stock woody. Lvs to 7.5cm, lanceolate to oblong, grey-green, leathery, obtuse. Rays to 18, forking; ray lvs yellow, mucronate to ovate-elliptic. S, E & C Eur. ssp. *glareosa* (Pall. ex Bieb.) A.R. Sm. Less glaucous. Rays 7–8. Z6.

E. niciciana Borb. ex Novák = *E. seguieriana* ssp. *niciciana*.

E. nigrispina N.E. Br. Succulent shrub. Br. to 8mm diam.+, 4-angled, glaucous; spines to 16mm, black; prickles 2, inconspicuous. Lvs not produced. Somalia, Ethiop. Z10.

E. nivulia Buch.-Ham. Perenn. succulent shrub. St., br. terete; br. whorled to 2.5cm diam.; somewhat segmented; spines stout. Lvs obovate, notched. Penins. India. Z10.

E. nubica N.E. Br. Succulent perenn. shrub to 1.5m+. Br. scrambling, slender cylindric, green. Lvs lanceolate, to 18mm, soon abscising; spines 0. Rays 3–7, to 2cm. Sudan, Ethiop., Somalia. Z10.

E. nubigens Leach. Succulent perenn., to 25cm. St. branched at base; br. to 15mm diam., quadrangular; spines brown. Cyathia bright yellow. Angola. var. *rutilans* Leach. Infl. vivid red. Z10.

E. nyikae G. Reynolds non Pax = *E. halipedicola*.

E. nyikae auct. non Pax = *E. buruana*.

E. obesa Hook. f. GINGHAM GOLF BALL; LIVING BASEBALL. Dwarf succulent. St. to 20×9cm, subglobose, becoming squat-cylindric, broadly hexagonal, green, obscurely banded purple. S Afr. (Cape Prov.). Z7.

E. oblongifolia (K. Koch) K. Koch. Pubesc. or subglabrous rhizomatous perenn. St. erect, to 85cm. Lvs broadly ovate-lanceolate or -oblanceolate to ovate, 3–13cm, obtuse to sub-acute, base rounded, truncate or shallowly cordate. Turk. Z8.

E. obovalifolia auct. non Rich. = *E. ampliphylla*.

E. obovalifolia A. Rich. = *E. abyssinica*.

E. obtusifolia Poir. Succulent shrub, to 2m. Br. in whorls of 3, straight, slender. Lvs linear, to 7cm, obtuse to short-acute. Canary Is., Moroc. Z10.

E. obtusifolia var. *regis-jubae* (Webb & Berth.) Maire = *E. regis-jubae*.

E. odontophylla Willd. = *E. cereiformis*.

E. officinarum L. Succulent shrub to 90cm+. St. erect; br. whorled, 9–13-sided, to 8mm diam., angles acute, margin horny; spines unequal, paired, to 16mm, pale grey or white-grey. Lvs soon abscising. Infl. yellow. Moroc. Z9.

E. oncoclada Drake = *E. alluaudii* ssp. *oncoclada*.

E. orientalis L. Perenn., to 50cm+. St. branched, red. Lvs lanceolate, to 12cm, tomentose, blue-green, mucronate. Infl. yellow-green. Cauc., E Turk., N Iraq, Iran, also Taiwan. Z7.

E. ornithopus Jacq. BIRD'S FOOT EUPHORBIA. Resembles *E. tridentata*, but cyathia often borne in cymes; peduncles to 10cm; involucral glands with white-edged processes. S Afr. (Cape Prov.). Z7.

E. oxystegia Bak. non Boiss. = *E. bubalina*.

E. palustris L. Similar to *E. polychroma*. Perenn., to 1m+. St. clumped, pale green. St. lvs eliptic to oblong-lanceolate, to 6cm; axill. shoot lvs narrower, becoming red in autumn. Rays forked to ×3; raylet lvs ovate-suborbicular, lime to bright yellow. Spring–summer. Eur. (S Scand., Spain, E to W Cauc.). Z5.

E. pannonica Host = *E. nicaeensis*.

E. paralias L. SEA SPURGE. Glaucous perenn., to 70cm. St. tufted; lvs fleshy. St. lvs overlapping, oblong to ovate, to 2.5cm+. Rays forked to ×3; ray lvs ovate to ovate-lanceolate, raylet lvs kidney- to bowl-shaped; glands orange. Macaronesia, W Eur., Medit. and Black Sea coast; introd. Aus. Z8.

E. parvimamma Boiss. = *E. bergeri*.

E. passa N.E. Br. = *E. woodii*.

E. patula Sweet = *E. ornithopus*.

E. pentagona Haw. Succulent shrub to 3m. St. erect; br. some-what whorled, erect, to 4cm diam., usually 5-angled, vivid green, becoming grey; spines to 2cm, green tinged grey. Lvs rudimentary, to 7mm. Involucre cupulate, to 4mm diam., buff-lavender. S Afr. (Cape Prov.). Z7.

E. persistens R.A. Dyer. Dwarf succulent. St. subterranean; br. many, erect to ascending, to 20cm, glaucous, angles 3–5, to 1.5cm, segmented; spines to 15mm, pale brown. S Afr. Z7.

E. persistentifolia Leach. Succulent arborescent shrub to 3m+. St. robust; br. whorled, erect, to 5cm diam., 4–5-angled occas. winged, seg. to 40cm, margin horny, white; spines paired, to 7mm; lvs narrow-elliptic, to 10cm, fleshy. S Zimb., Zam. Z10.

E. petraea S. Carter. Spreading succulent shrub, to 60cm. St. branched from base; br. decumbent, 4–5-sided, to 2cm diam., ridges sinuate-dentate; spines to 8mm. Lvs ovate, to 1mm. Uganda. Z10.

E. pfersdorfii hort. = *E. submammillaris*.

E. phymatoclada Boiss. = *E. mauritanica*.

E. pillansii N.E. Br. As for *E. stellaespina*, but smaller, to 30cm; br. 7–9-angled; spines more robust, diverging, grey. S Afr. (Cape Prov.). var. *ramosissima* A. White, R.A. Dyer & B.L. Sloane. Br. many, thinner, darker green. var. *albovirens* A. White, R.A. Dyer & B.L. Sloane. Br. white-green. Z7.

E. pilosa L. Glab. or pubesc. perenn. herb. St. many, erect, to 90cm, branched above. Lvs linear to oblong, to 1.5cm wide, acute. Rays 5–9, long or short, raylet lvs orbicular or broad-ovate, acute, bright yellow; involucre villous within. C Asia to W Himal. Z7. Much confused with *E. villosa*.

E. pinea L. Perenn., to 0.5m. St. branching from base. St. lvs densely spirally arranged, linear-lanceolate, to 3cm. Rays 5, forking; raylet lvs yellow, rhombic, obtuse, base cuneate to heart-shaped. SW Eur. Z6.

E. piscidermis M. Gilbert. Succulent perenn., to 4cm. St. sub-globose; tubercles scale-like (feature unique to this sp.). Somalia. Z10.

E. pithyusa L. Suffrutescent, glaucous perenn., to 50cm, branched at base. St. lvs linear to oblanceolate, to 3cm, reflexed, imbricate below, ± glaucous. SW Eur., N Afr. Z8.

E. platyclada Rauh. Shrub to 50cm. Br. erect or decumbent, jointed, rebranching, succulent, with conspicuous lf scars, grey-green, mottled red and black. Madag. Z10.

E. platymammillaris Croizat = *E. fimbriata*.

E. plumerioides Teijsm. ex Hassk. Shrub or small tree, 3–6m. Lvs alt., linear-oblanceolate to oblong-oblanceolate, to 15cm, dull beneath. Cyathia in small pseudocymes, not exceeding lvs. New Guinea, Philipp., Indon. var. *acuminata* J.J. Sm. Lvs acute to acutely acuminate at apex, glossy. Pseudocymes exceeding lvs. New Guinea. Z10.

E. poissonii Pax. Succulent shrub to 1.6m, br. cylindric, to 4cm diam., grey-green; spines often 0 on older growth. Lvs obovate, borne towards st. apices, to 14cm, emarginate; petiole stout, fleshy. Involucre to 8mm diam., funnelform; sta. crimson. W Afr. Z10.

E. polyacantha Boiss. FISHBONE. Succulent shrub to 1.5m. Br. to 4cm diam., slightly segmented, ridges 4–5, crenately dentate; spines to 6mm, sombre grey. Lvs minute, scaly, caducous. Ethiop. Z10.

E. polycephala Marloth. Dwarf succulent, similar in habit to

E. globosa. St. compact, densely branched; br. conic, warty; spines 0. Lvs to 1cm, ovate to lanceolate. S Afr. Z7.

E. polychroma Kerner. Clump-forming perenn., to 60cm. St. robust, pubesc. St. lvs 5.5cm, obovate to elliptic-oblong, some-times tinged purple, obtuse. Rays 5, forked ×3; raylet lvs elliptic-ovate, to 2cm, yellow-green occas. tinged red to violet. C & SE Eur., Asia Minor. 'Emerald Jade': habit small, elegant; autumn colours attractive. 'Midas': infl. bright yellow. 'Major': mound-forming; infl. bright yellow. 'Purpurea': lvs purple; fls sulphur yellow. 'Sonnengold': infl. bright yellow. Z6.

E. polygona Haw. Succulent shrub toClose to var. *plumerioides*, but 1.5m+. St. branching from base, to 10cm diam., 7-sided when young, becoming 12–20-angled, ridges deep, undulate; spines to 1cm, or 0. Lvs caducous, reduced. S Afr. (Cape Prov.). Z7.

E. polygona Marsilio ex Scop. = *E. fimbriata*.

E. polygonata Lodd. = *E. cereiformis*.

E. pomiformis Thunb. = *E. meloformis*.

E. portlandica L. PORTLAND SPURGE As for *E. pinea*, but slightly smaller, to 18cm, occas. 40cm; st. lvs oblanceolate, to 2.5cm, brighter green, tinged grey, mucronate. W Eur. Z7.

E. primulifolia Bak. Tuberous perenn. Lvs to 11cm, in term. fascicles of 6–12, linear or lanceolate, flat or undulate. Cyathia 2–4 on peduncles to 4cm; involucral bracts pink to white. C Madag. Z10.

E. procumbens Sweet = *E. pugniformis*.

E. procumbens Meerb. = *E. stellata*.

E. procumbens N.E. Br. = *E. woodii*.

E. proteifolia Boiss. = *E. bupleurifolia*.

E. pseudocactus A. Berger. Succulent shrub to 1m, branching from base; br. (3–)4-5-angled; seg. irregular, 2–15cm, with green, yellow-tinged, wedge-shaped markings; spines at teeth apices, to 1cm+, brown, becoming grey. S Afr. var. *lyttoniana* (R. Dexter) R.A. Frick. Spines 0. Z7.

E. pseudoglobosa Marloth. Dwarf succulent. St. subterranean, cylindric to globose, br. borne from apex, globose, to 1.5cm diam., hexagonal, tubercles conic; br. of ♀ plants 5–6-ridged, becoming 5–7-angled, to 2cm diam., buff-green, tubercles flush. S Afr. (Cape Prov.). Z7.

E. pseudotuberosa Pax. Perenn. herb. Main root tuberous, produced into elongated, fleshy subterranean st. Ann. br. few to many, 1–5cm. Lvs linear or lanceolate, 12–37mm, infolded, glaucous. S Afr. Z8.

E. ×pseudovirgata (Schur) Soó. (*E. esula* ×*E. waldsteinii*.) Glab. perenn., 30–80cm; rhiz. creeping. St. numerous, erect. Lvs linear-lanceolate, 2–8cm, acute. Infl. umbelliform, broad, 6–12-rayed; glands with long horn-like appendages. Summer. Eur. (widely nat.). Z6.

E. pteroneura A. Berger. Succulent shrub, to 50cm. St. to 45cm×8mm; br. segmented, 5–6-angled; spines 0. Lvs to 4cm, lanceolate-ovate caducous, bases decurrent. Cymes umbellate; raylet lvs 2, reniform, yellow-green. Mex. Z9.

E. pubescens Vahl. Hairy perenn. herb. St. many, erect, to 80cm. Lvs oblong-oblanceolate to ovate-lanceolate, 2–5cm, base cordate-auriculate, minutely serrulate. Medit. to N Iraq. Z9.

E. pubiglans N.E. Br. Low succulent, 8–30cm. Main st. simple or branching below, 3.7–5cm, diam., tapering upwards, with tubercles in 13 spiral rows, spiny peduncle remains persistent. Lvs linear, 2–3.7cm, margins inrolled or adpressed. Cyathia solitary, pedunculate with whorl of large bracts below involucre to 2.5cm diam., dull purple. S Afr. (Cape Prov.). Z9.

E. pugniformis Boiss. As for *E. woodii*, but smaller. St. sub-globose; br. tapering. S Afr. (Cape Prov.). Crested forms occur. Z7.

E. pugniformis Bak. non Boiss. = *E. woodii*.

E. pulcherrima Willd. ex Klotzsch. POINSETTIA. CHRISTMAS STAR; CHRISTMAS FLOWER; PAINTED LEAF; LOBSTER PLANT; MEXICAN FLAMELEAF. Slender shrub to 3m. Lvs lanceolate to ovate-elliptic, occas. pandurate, to 15cm+, entire or dentate to sinuately lobed. Cymes umbellate; bracts large leaf-like, spread-ing, scarlet; glands yellow. W Mex. 'Annette Hegg': habit compact; freely branching; lvs ovate, hardy; bracts broad, smooth, vivid red. 'Barbara Ecke Supreme': more freely branching; st. heavy; lvs deep green; bracts broad, flexible, bright blood red. 'Ecke's White': st. wiry; lvs bright green, ovate; bracts membranous, cream. 'Henrietta Ecke': bracts broad, horizontal, vermilion, crown 'double'. 'Oakleaf': vigorous, tall; lvs lobed; bract on long stalks, narrow, dark red. 'Plenissima': bracts narrow, bright red, forming almost globe-shaped infl. 'Rosea': lvs pale, ovate, petioles and veins darker; bracts obovate, pale pink, darkly veined. 'Ruth Ecke': dwarf, compact; lvs small; bracts small, deep red. Z9.

E. pulvinata Marloth. PINCUSHION EUPHORBIA. As for *E. ferox*, but to 30cm+: br. clumped, produced at or slightly below ground level; spines to 12mm. S Afr. Z7.

E. punicea Sw. Shrub to 3m, or tree to 10m. Br. thick, terete, with conspicuous lf scars. Lvs narrow-oblong to obovate, 4–15cm. Bracts 2–7, elliptic to obovate, brilliant scarlet, crimson or pink-orange. Jam. Z10.

E. pyriformis N.E. Br. = *E. meloformis*.

E. quercifolia hort. = *E. undulatifolia*.

E. radiata Boiss. non Thunb. = *E. clava*.

E. radiata Thunb. = *E. stellata*.

E. ramipressa Croizat. Resembles *E. grandidens*, but br. generally more 2-angled. Known only in cult. Z7.

E. reflexa F.nek = *E. seguieriana* ssp. *niciciana*.

E. regis-jubae Webb & Berth. Succulent shrub to 2m. St. pale brown. Lvs narrow-oblong, acute to obtuse, caducous. Canary Is., Cape Verde Is. Z9.

E. reinhardtii Volkens = *E. candelabrum*.

E. resinifera A. Berger. Succulent shrub, to 60cm+, to 2m or more wide. St. branched from base; br. ascending, pale greygreen; ridges 4, indented; spines paired, to 6mm, brown. Lvs inconspicuous, green tinged brown. Moroc. Z8.

E. restituta N.E. Br. Succulent shrub to 24cm+, branched below; br. cylindric, 6mm thick, with 20 spiral rows of prominent tubercles, peduncle remains persistent. Lvs oblanceolate-spathulate, 2.5cm, caducous. S Afr. (Cape Prov.). Z9.

E. restricta R.A. Dyer. Dwarf succulent. St. to 8cm diam.; br. many, to 16×3cm; seg. to 2cm; angles 4–6, acute, margin horny; spines 10mm. S Afr. Z7.

E. rhipsaloides Welw. = *E. tirucalli*.

E. rigida Bieb. Perenn., to 40cm+. St. v. glaucous, erect-ascending. St. lvs lanceolate, fleshy, acute; ray lvs to 12, obovate, notched; raylet lvs jointed, lobes yellow, ovate, ciliate. Spring. Port. through Medit. to Crimea, W Cauc. Resembles an upright *E. myrsinites*, occas. sold labelled as *E. biglandulosa*. Z8.

E. robbiae Turrill = *E. amygdaloides* var.*robbiae*.

E. robecchii Pax. Juveniles to 1m, unbranched, succulent, 4–5-angled, angles pale green mottled with dark green. Young plants with br. ascending, then drooping, obtusely 3–4-angled, to 1.5cm thick, toothed. Mature tree 3–10m, with rounded crown; trunk to 40cm diam. Br. to 5m, ascending, then spreading. Lvs deltoid, 5×3mm. E Afr. Z10.

E. royleana Boiss. Succulent, erect shrub to 3m, or tree, to 8m. St. branched, to 40–50cm diam.; br. whorled, to 7cm diam., ridges 4–5, wavy, wings to 2cm wide; spines conic, paired, pointing downwards. Lvs obovate, to 11cm, obtuse, apiculate. Spring. Bhutan. Z9.

E. samburensis Bally & S. Carter. Succulent perenn., to 90cm diam. St. clumped, to 2cm diam., grey-green, ridges dentate; spines robust, to 2.5cm, red becoming pale grey. Lvs to 1.5mm, deltoid. Kenya. Z10.

E. sansalvador hort. = *E. resinifera*.

E. sarawschanica Reg. Resembles *E. palustris* and may be in cult. Turkestan.

E. sauliana Boreau ex Boiss. = *E. palustris*.

E. saxorum Bally & S. Carter. Succulent perenn. St. many, creeping, to 8mm diam., dark green with purple green patches, angles 4, shallow-dentate; spines to 1cm, black. Lvs to 1.5mm, deltoid. Cymes solitary, simple, subsessile, deep crimson. Kenya. Z10.

E. schillingii Radc.-Sm. Glab. perenn. herb. St. erect to 1m. Cauline lvs elliptic-oblong or oblong-oblanceolate, to 13cm, obtuse, deep green with conspicuous white veins. Infl. broad; ray-lvs 2–3 per node, rhombic-suborbicular, 2.5cm, rounded, yellow. Nepal. Z5.

E. schimperi Presl. Not widely cultivated. Material labelled as such in cult. is *E. nubica*. Z10.

E. schinzii Pax. As for *E. aeruginosa*, but br. olive green, more conspicuously 4-angled; spines in 2 pairs. Infl. vivid yellow-green. S Afr., S Zimb., Bots. Z7.

E. schoenlandii Pax. As for *E. fasciculata* but stouter, to 1.3m, st. to 20cm diam., unbranched; spines derived from sterile peduncles. S Afr. (Cape Prov.). Z7.

E. scolopendria Donn = *E. stellata*.

E. scoparia N.E. Br. = *E. tirucalli*.

E. scopolifolia Steud. = *E. fimbriata*.

E. segetalis ssp. *pinea* (L.) Hayek = *E. pinea*.

E. segetalis var. *littoralis* Lange = *E. portlandica*.

E. seguieriana Necker. Perenn. herb to 50cm+. St. clumped, glaucous; base woody. St. lvs linear to oblong-linear, to 4cm, glaucous, apex acute. Rays to 30, forked to ×5; ray lvs to 38, ovate to linear-lanceolate; raylet lvs yellow, ovate to rhombic, to 15mm. Nonseasonal. C & W Eur. E to Sib., Cauc., Pak. ssp. *seguieriana* Rays to 10; lvs erect. ssp. *niciciana* (Borb. ex Novák) Rech. f. Axill. rays to 30. Lvs patent. Z5.

E. sekukuniensis R.A. Dyer Succulent candelabriform tree to 7mm; main trunk stout, with small head of slender br. Br. 1m long, to 2cm diam., 4–5-angled; spines paired, 8mm, spine shields forming horny margin. Infl. yellow-green. S Afr. Z9.

E. semiverticillata Hal. = *E. heldreichii*.

E. semivillosa Prokh. = *E. villosa*.

E. septentrionalis Bally & S. Carter. Succulent, densely clumped perenn. St. branched from base, erect, to 15cm or decumbent, to 1m×8mm, cylindric, grey-green with dark green stripes; br. with teeth in 4 stripes; spines grey, to 15mm. Lvs ovate, inconspicuous. Uganda, Kenya. Z10.

E. serpentina hort. = *E. inermis*.

E. serrata L. Perenn. to 50cm. St. glab. to glaucous. St. lvs linear-lanceolate or oblong, pale grey-green, finely-serrate, blunt to obtuse. Rays 3–4, forking; raylet lvs ovate-deltoid to reniform, pale yellow-green. W Medit., Fr. Z8.

E. serrulata Thuill. = *E. stricta*.

E. sikkimensis Boiss. As for *E. griffithii*, but young shoots and lvs tinted coal pink, veined ruby red; raylet lvs yellow. Summer. E Himal. Z6.

E. silenifolia (Haw.) Sweet. Succulent perenn. St. indistinct from root in an ellipsoid tuberous organ, to 5cm diam. Lvs linear to elliptic-lanceolate, to 10cm, occas. folded, decid., tinged blue above. S Afr. Z7.

E. similiramea S. Carter. V. close to *E. graciliramea*, differing in br. 30×1.5cm, with teeth more acute and prominent, usually in 5 spiral series. Kenya and Tanz. Z10.

E. similis A. Berger = *E. ingens*.

E. sipolisii N.E. Br. Succulent shrub; br. 4-sided glab., angles convex, grey-green; seg. to 11cm. Lvs triangular, caducous. Infl. bracteate; involucre campanulate, glab., 5–6-lobed, lobes fimbriate. Braz. Z10.

E. soongarica Boiss. Perenn., to 60cm. St. robust, glab. Lvs to 11cm, linear-lanceolate, acuminate, serrate above. Rays 5–10, to 35mm; ray lvs ovate, to 3cm; raylet lvs obscuring umbel, rhombic-ovate, to 10mm. Temp. C Asia, E Russia. Z7.

E. spinosa L. As for *E.acanthothamnus* but to 20cm; br. persistent, resembling spines; st. lvs linear-lanceolate, to 2cm. Rays 1–3; raylet lvs ovate or obovate. C Medit. Z7.

E. splendens Bojer ex Hook. = *E. milii* var. *splendens*.

E. squamosa Masson ex A. Berger = *E. bupleurifolia*.

E. squarrosa Haw. Dwarf succulent, to 10cm diam. St. subterranean; br. borne at ground level, to 15×2.5cm, angles usually 3, straight to twisted, tubercles slender, to 1cm high; spines to 6mm, red-green, becoming grey-brown. S Afr. Z7.

E. stapfii Berger Succulent shrub to 4m, much-branched; br. 1.5cm thick, green, angles 4, straight to shallowly undulate, spines paired, to 6mm. Lvs deltoid, to 2mm. Uganda. Z10.

E. stellaespina Haw. STAR-SPINE. Succulent shrub, to 45cm. St. branching from base; br. to 8cm diam., 10–16-angled; ridges tuberculate; spines to 1cm, with to 5-branches. S Afr. (Cape Prov.). var. *atrispina* (N.E. Br.) A. White, R.A. Dyer & B.L. Sloane. Spines 4–6-branched. Z7.

E. stellaespina E. Phillips non Haw. = *E. pillansii*.

E. stellata Willd. Dwarf, succulent perenn. St. largely subterranean; br. to 15×1.4cm, procumbent, spreading, concave above, tuberculate; spines borne on tubercle apices at 2 angles, to 4mm. Lvs 0. S Afr. (Cape Prov.). Z7.

E. stenoclada Baill. Small shrub to 1m; br. becoming spines. Madag. Z10.

E. stepposa Zoz ex Prokh. = *E. nicaeensis*.

E. stolonifera Marloth. Rhizomatous succulent small shrub to 40cm+. St. subterranean, many-branched; br. subcylindric, to 1cm diam., pruinose, dark green, occas. tinged yellow. Infl. as for *E. mauritanica*. S Afr. (Cape Prov.). Z7.

E. stricta L. UPRIGHT SPURGE; TINTERN SPURGE. Ann. to 30cm, occas. to 120cm. St. slender, shiny, wiry, red. St. lvs oblanceolate, auriculate, serrate. Rays 5, raylet lvs ovate, base rounded or cuneate. Eur. to SW Asia. Z6.

E. stuhlmanii Schweinf. ex Volkens = *E. heterochroma*.

E. stygiana H. Wats. Low glab. shrub to 1.5m. St. erect or ascending, branched. Lvs oblong, 15cm, mucronate, apple-green with white midrib and lat. veins, sometimes red in autumn and winter. Azores. Z10.

E. subapoda Baill. = *E. primulifolia*.

E. submammillaris (A. Berger) A. Berger. As for *E. mammillaris*, but br. thinner, more numerous, to 25mm diam., 5–8-angled; spines less conspicuously whorled; angles dentate. Peduncles to 2cm, red, becoming brown. Probably S Afr. 'Pfersdorfii': br. many, fewer-angled. Z7.

E. subsalsa Hiern. Succulent shrub to 1m+. St. branching from base; br. to 12mm diam., 4-angled, pale green, tuberculate; spines to to 12mm. Infl. yellow. Angola. Z10.

E. subtilis Prokh. = *E. esula*.

E. supina Raf. Prostrate pubesc. ann., much-branched from base; br. 10–45cm. Lvs elliptic or obovate-oblong, to 10mm, obtuse, serrulate, usually with red-brown mark in centre. Cymes axill.; cyathia few; glands red-brown with small white or pink petaloid appendages. E Amer., but now widely nat. Z5.

E. susannae Marloth. Dwarf succulent. St. subterranean; br.

globose to cylindric, to 8cm, 12–16-angled. frequently appearing as green discs at ground level, tuberculate. Lvs appearing as bristles at apices of young tubercles. S Afr. (Cape Prov.). Z7.

E. sylvatica L. = *E. amygdaloides*.

E. symmetrica A. White, R.A. Dyer & B.L. Sloane. As for *E. obesa*, but to 10×17cm. S Afr. Z7.

E. taruensis S. Carter. Succulent perenn. to 20cm, to 45cm in cult., branched from base; br. 4-sided, to 8mm diam., variegated fresh green, ridged to 1mm. Lvs deltoid. Kenya. Z10.

E. tauricola Prokh. = *E. villosa*.

E. tenuirama A. Berger non Schweinf. Succulent shrub. St. erect, (4–)5-angled; br. to 2.5cm diam., triangular, slightly segmented, fresh green; spines to 6mm, pale grey. Known only in cult. Z10.

E. terracina L. GERALDTON CARNATION WEED; FALSE CAPER. Perenn., to 70cm. St. occas. branched from base. St. lvs to 2.5cm, oblanceolate to elliptic-lanceolate, entire to minutely dentate, acute. Rays 3–5, forked to ×5; ray lvs lanceolate to ovate-lanceolate; raylet lvs to 15mm, glab.; glands horned. Canaries, Madeira, Moroc. E to Transcauc.; nat. Mex. Z8.

E. tessellata Sweet = *E. caput-medusae*.

E. tetragona Haw. NABOOM. Succulent tree, to 10m+. Bole to 15cm diam., 6–8-angled; br. to 5-angled, ascending, term. branchlets whorled, to 5cm+ diam., 4–5-ridged, tuberculate; spines to 12mm. Lvs reduced, caducous. S Afr. Z7.

E. tetragona Bak. non Haw. = *E. micracantha*.

E. tetragona Sim non Haw. = *E. pentagona*.

E. tirucalli L. MILK BUSH; TIRU-MALU; RUBBER EUPHORBIA; FINGER TREE; PENCH TREE. Succulent tree, to 9m. St. branched, term. br. clustered, to 7mm diam., cylindric, pale green. Lvs to 12mm, linear to linear-lanceolate, soon abscising. Trop. & S Afr., India E to Indon. Z7.

E. tirucalli Thunb. non L. = *E. burmannii* or *E. mauritanica*.

E. tithymaloides L. = *Pedilanthus tithymaloides*.

E. togoensis Pax = *E. lateriflora*.

E. tortirama R.A. Dyer. Dwarf succulent. St. and root in a tuberous body, to 30×15cm, apex branched; br. to 50, to 30×4.5cm, triangular, spirally contored, tuberculate; spines to 2cm, grey. S Afr. Z7.

E. trapifolia A. Chev. Shrub, to 2m. Br. terete, ascending, to 2cm diam. Lvs to 3cm, obovate to fan-shaped, fleshy, bifid; st. tubercles in 5–8 spirally arranged rows; spines to 8mm. W Sudan. Z10.

E. triaculeata Forssk. Succulent perenn. shrub to 45cm. St. 3–5+sided; ridges notched, dentate; spines solitary, to 3cm. Arabia, Ethiop. var. *triacantha* (Boiss.) N.E. Br. Br. 3–5-sided. Z10.

E. triangularis Desf. Succulent tree, to 20m. Bole cylindric, br. to 120cm×10cm, fastigiate, (3–)4(–5)-angled, seg. to 30cm, margins sometimes tuberculate; spines to 8mm, brown, later grey. Lvs to 7mm, variably cordate, caducous. S Afr. Z7.

E. trichadenia Pax. Perenn. herb. Root tuberous with elongated woody st. to 10cm long. St. ann. herbaceous, prostrate or erect, to 10cm. Lvs linear-lanceolate, to 6.5cm, acute; bracts smaller than lvs, lanceolate, sometimes ciliate. Infl. cymose; involucre cup-shaped, to 1cm diam., glands 5, divided into filiform seg. Angola, S Afr. Z9.

E. tridentata Lam. As for *E. globosa*, but less closely addressed to ground; br. less globose, tapering to apex. S Afr. Z7.

E. triflora Schott, Nyman & Kotschy. Herbaceous perenn., to 15cm+. St. glab., glaucous. St. lvs to 1.5cm, oblong to ovate-deltoid. Rays 3–5, forking; ray lvs as for st. lvs; raylet lvs rhombic to ovate. SE Eur. Z8.

E. trigona Mill. Succulent, arborescent shrub; br. erect, to 6cm diam., seg. 15–25cm apart, dark green, mottled white, furrows banded white; ridges 3–4, undulate-dentate, somewhat winged; spines to 15mm, red-brown. Lvs to 3–5cm, spathulate. Origin not known Z9.

E. trigona Roxb. non Mill. = *E. barnhartii*.

E. truncata N.E. Br. = *E. clavarioides* var. *truncata*.

E. tuberculata Jacq. Succulent herb. St. obconic, robust; br. to 75×4cm, apical, erect to decumbent, tuberculate, buff-green. Lvs to 4cm, linear. Cyathia solitary; glands fingered, processes cream, tipped scarlet. S Afr. var. *macowanii* (N.E. Br.) A. White, R.A. Dyer & B.L. Sloane. Br. to 20cm. Involucre pub-esc. Z7.

E. tuberculatoides N.E. Br. As for *E. tuberculata*, but br. to 2cm diam. Lvs to 1cm. Involucre smaller, to 1cm diam., purple. S Afr. (Cape Prov.). Z7.

E. tubiglans Marloth ex R.A. Dyer. Succulent, dwarf perenn. St. subterranean, turnip-shaped; br. in fascicles of 2–5, 5–6-sided, to 12cm in cult., to 18mm diam., constricted at base; ridges obtuse, tuberculate. Lvs caducous, bases persistent; spines 0. S Afr. (Cape Prov.). Z7.

E. turbiniformis Chiov. As for *E. piscidermis*, but st. smooth, red-brown; tubercles delineated by shallow grooves; infl.

smaller. Somalia. Z10.

E. uliginosa Welw. ex Boiss. Perenn., to 60cm from a stout woody stock. St. slender, base robust. Lvs to 2cm, linear-oblong, obtuse, serrulate, leathery. Rays 2–5; ray lvs linear-lanceolate to obovate; raylet lvs triangular. SW Eur. Z9.

E. uncinata DC. = *E. stellata*.

E. undulatifolia Janse. WAVY-LEAVED SPURGE. Shrub or tree to 3m+. Bole to 12cm diam.; br. pentagonal, later terete, ridges sinuate, somewhat spiral, dark green. Lf scars orbicular; spines dark. Lvs in a term. rosette, obovate, to 18cm, soon abscising, undulate. India? (known only in cult.). Z10.

E. valida N.E. Br. Dwarf succulent, to 20cm+. St. subglobose, to 13cm diam., hexagonal, glab., buff-green, banded pale green, occas. branching from base, ridges sometimes spirally arranged. S Afr. (Cape Prov.). Z7.

E. vallaris Leach. Succulent tree, to 12m. Bole cylindric; br. to 90×5.5cm, tubercles prominent; spines purple-brown, to 7mm. Lvs to 15cm, narrow-ovate to elliptic. Angola. Z10.

E. vandermerwei R.A. Dyer. Dwarf succulent, to 20cm. St. sub-terranean; br. simple to 2, sometimes more; secondary br. to 30×2cm, 4–5-angled, straight to spiralling, green, tuberculate; spines to 1cm. S Afr. Z7.

E. varians Haw. = *E. nivulia*.

E. variegata Sims = *E. marginata*.

E. veneta var. Willd. = *E. characias* ssp. *wulfenii*.

E. verrucosa L. 1759, non L. 1758. = *E. brittingeri*.

E. viguieri M. Denis. Shrub, to 1.5m. St. clavate, green, to 3cm diam., hexagonal, ridges bearing triangular lf scars; spines stipular, to 5mm, persistent, branched. Lvs clustered at br. apices, lanceolate-ovate, vivid red, midrib pale green. Peduncles to 4cm, involucral bracts yellow-green, occas. tinged red. W Madag. var. *tsimbazazae* Ursch & Leandri. To 150cm. Peduncles to 10cm. var. *ankarafantsiensis* Ursch & Leandri. Lvs mucronate. Z10.

E. villosa Waldst. & Kit. ex Willd. Rhizomatous perenn., to 1m+. St. robust; st. and lvs sometimes pubesc. St. lvs usually 5, to 6cm, elliptic to oblong, mucronate. Rays (4–)5 or more; ray lvs ovate; raylet lvs smaller, wider than ray lvs, green tinged yellow. SE to C Eur., N to NW Fr. Z5.

E. viminalis Burm. f. = *E. burmannii*.

E. viperina A. Berger = *E. inermis*.

E. virosa Willd. Succulent shrub to 2m+. St. almost sub-terranean, spirally angled; br. to 5cm diam., occas. re-branched, 5–8-angled; seg. 5–8cm long; spines to 1cm, dark red, shiny, becoming buff-grey. Lvs caducous. Nam., SW Cape, SW Angola. Z7.

E. virosa Boiss. = *E. caerulescens*.

E. volgensis Krysht. = *E. nicaeensis*.

E. wakefieldii N.E. Br. Tree, to 7m. Br. to 1m; bole to 15cm diam., simple or sparingly branched; br. fleshy when young, 3 to 4-sided, to 20mm diam., ridges dentate; spines to 8mm, black. Lvs to 1mm. Kenya. Z10.

E. waldsteinii (Soják) Radc.-Sm. As for *E. esula*, but lvs lanceolate to linear, base rounded, apex acute; umbel rays 5–9. SE, E, C Eur. Z5.

E. wallichii Hook. f. Perenn. herb to 50cm; st. erect, clumped. Lvs 7–12cm, linear to elliptic-oblong, spreading, ± glab., dark green with purple-tinted margins and white midvein. Infl. yellow-green, glands large, green. W & C Himal. Z7.

E. waterbergensis R.A. Dyer. Spiny, succulent shrub, to 1.5m+. St. branching near base; br. erect to spreading, 4–6-sided, to 25mm diam., seg. to 20cm, glaucous to dark green, margin grey, horny; spines to 5mm. Summer–autumn. S Afr. Z7.

E. wildii Leach. Succulent shrub or small tree to 3m. Trunk cylindric, 7.5–10cm diam., spirally tuberculate. Br. ascending, c5cm diam., with persistent peduncle remains towards apex. Lvs clustered at br. ends, narrow-elliptic, or -obovate, to 12cm. Zimb. Z10.

E. wilmaniae Marloth. Dwarf succulent, to 1m diam., but only to 5cm tall. St. subterranean, spreading; br. clavate, short, stubby, tuberculate. S Afr. (Cape Prov.). Z7.

E. winkleri Pax = *E. ampliphylla*.

E. woodii N.E. Br. Dwarf succulent. St. to 12cm diam.; br. to 40, borne in 2 series, cylindric, to 20cm, to 1.5cm diam., vivid green; spines 0; tubercles to 1cm, bearing lvs; lvs rudimentary, linear. S Afr. (Natal). Z7.

E. woronowii Grossh. As for *E. myrsinites*, but rays fewer. Transcauc. Z6.

E. wulfenii Hoppe ex Koch = *E. characias* ssp. *wulfenii*.

E. xantii Engelm. Shrub to 2m. Br. strongly ascending, wand-like. Lvs opposite or in whorls. Baja Calif. Z9.

E. xylophylloides Brongn. ex Lem. Succulent shrub or tree to 1.8m; st. branching from base and above; br. irregularly whorled, 2-angled, flattened; seg. to 15cm, ridges slightly crenate. Lvs small, rounded, caducous. S Madag. Z10.

E. zhiguliensis Prokh. = *E. esula*.

EUPHORBIACEAE Juss. 321/7950. *Acalypha, Aleurites, Andrachne, Antidesma, Bischofia, Breynia, Cnidoscolus, Codiaeum, Dalechampia, Elaeophorbia, Euphorbia, Hevea, Homalanthus, Hura, Jatropha, Mallotus, Manihot, Margaritaria, Monadenium, Pedilanthus, Phyllanthus, Ricinus, Sapium, Synadenium.*

Euphoria Comm. ex Juss.
E. litchi Desf. = *Dimocarpus longan.*
E. longan (Lour.) Steud. = *Dimocarpus longan.*
E. malaiensis Radlk. = *Dimocarpus longan.*
E. sinensis Gmel. = *Dimocarpus longan.*
E. verruculosa Salisb. = *Dimocarpus longan.*
E. verticillata Wallich = *Lepisanthes senegalensis.*

Euphrasia L. EYEBRIGHT. Scrophulariaceae. 450 herbs, semiparasites, usually of grasses. Lvs small, opposite, often glandular-pubesc. toothed. Rac. spike-like, terminal; cal. 4-lobed, tubular or campanulate; cor. tubular, 2-lipped, lower lip 3-lobed, usually spotted yellow and marked yellow in throat. Cosmop. Z6.
E. hectori Petrie = *Ourisia caespitosa.*
E. montana Jordan. Erect, to 20cm, 4-branched. Cor. 9–13mm, upper lip lilac or purple. Eur.
E. officinalis L. EYEBRIGHT. Erect, to 50cm, 8–12-branched. Cor. 7–13mm, upper lip lilac, lower lip white. Eur.

Euploca Nutt.
E. convolvulacea Nutt. = *Heliotropium convolvulaceum.*

Euptelea Sieb. & Zucc. Eupteleaceae. 3 decid. trees and shrubs, usually broadly pyramidal; br. somewhat lenticelled. Lvs alt., serrate, petiolate, usually tinted red on emergence. Fls apetalous, produced before lvs in clusters along shoots; sta. numerous, anth. red. Fr. stalked, whorled, winged samaras. E Asia.
E. davidiana Baill. = *E. pleiosperma.*
E. franchetii Tieghem = *E. pleiosperma.*
E. pleiosperma Hook. & Thoms. To 10m. Lvs 5–10cm, broadly ovate, apex attenuate, acuminate, base cuneate, with shallow regular teeth, sometimes glaucous beneath, colouring red in autumn. W China. Z6.
E. polyandra Sieb. & Zucc. To 7m; lvs 7–12cm, broadly ovate to subcircular with deep, somewhat irregular teeth, colouring red and yellow in autumn. Jap. Z6.

EUPTELEACEAE Wilhelm. See *Euptelea.*

Eupteron Miq. = *Polyscias.*

Eurabbie *Eucalyptus globulus.*
Eureka Lily *Lilium occidentale.*
European Alder *Alnus glutinosa.*
European Bean *Vicia faba.*
European Beech *Fagus sylvatica.*
European Black Currant *Ribes nigrum.*
European Brooklime *Veronica beccabunga.*
European Cranberry *Vaccinium oxycoccos.*
European Cranberrybush *Viburnum opulus.*
European Dewberry *Rubus caesius.*
European Dune Grass *Leymus arenarius.*
European Elder *Sambucus nigra.*
European Fan Palm *Chamaerops humilis.*
European Feather Grass *Stipa pennata.*
European Field Elm *Ulmus carpinifolia.*
European Hop *Humulus lupulus.*
European Hornbeam *Carpinus betulus.*
European Larch *Larix decidua.*
European Linden *Tilia × vulgaris.*
European Nettle Tree *Celtis australis.*
European Parsley Fern *Cryptogramma crispa.*
European Raspberry *Rubus idaeus.*
European Red Elder *Sambucus racemosa.*
European Silver Fir *Abies alba.*
European White Birch *Betula pendula.*
European White Lily *Nymphaea alba.*
European White Lime *Tilia tomentosa.*

Eurya (Thunb.) Mak. Theaceae. 70 mostly everg. trees and shrubs. Br. dense with lat. growth in herringbone pattern. Lvs simple, crenate-serrate; petiole short. Fls small, unisexual, short-pedicellate, solitary or in clusters; sep. 5; pet. 5, connate at base; sta. 5–20 or more. Fr. a many-seeded berry. S & E Asia, Pacific Is.
E. chinensis R. Br. Shrub or tree, branchlets pubesc. at first. Lvs to 6cm, obovate, bluntly acuminate, sharply serrate. Fls white. Fr. 4–5mm diam., globose. S China, Taiwan. Z9.
E. emarginata (Thunb.) Mak. Shrub or small tree, branchlets yellow-brown, ascending-pilose. Lvs 2–3.5cm, obovate to oblong-obovate, obtuse, emarginate, crenate-serrate, coriaceous, glab. Fls pale yellow-green. Fr. 5mm diam., purple-black. E Asia. var. *microphylla* Mak. Lvs to 0.8mm, obovate-orbicular. Jap. Z7.
E. japonica Thunb. Shrub or tree to 10m; br. glab. or thinly ascending-pilose. Lvs 3–8cm, oval to obovate, bluntly acute, coriaceous, glossy dark green. Fls white. Fr. 4–5mm diam., black. Asia. 'Variegata': lvs dark glossy green edged cream-white. 'Winter Wine': habit small, spreading; lvs burgundy in autumn. Z9.
E. latifolia hort. ex K. Koch = *E. japonica.*

Euryale Salisb. FOX NUTS. Nymphaeaceae. 1 giant aquatic rhizomatous perenn. herb. Lvs 0.6–1.5m diam., floating, circular, peltate, margins flat, olive-green, puckered and sparsely spiny above, purple-red with prominent prickly veins beneath. Fls to 6cm diam., partially submerged to emersed; stalks and cal. prickly; pet. many, red, purple or lilac; sta. numerous. Fr. berry-like, prickly, many-seeded. N India, China, Jap., Taiwan. Z8.
E. ferox Salisb.

Eurybia Cass.
E. ciliata Benth. = *Olearia ciliata.*
E. ericoides Steetz = *Olearia ericoides.*
E. floribunda Hook. f. = *Olearia floribunda.*
E. hookeri F. Muell. ex Sonder = *Olearia hookeri.*
E. megalophylla F. Muell. = *Olearia megalophylla.*
E. nummularifolia Hook. f. = *Olearia nummularifolia.*
E. obcordata Hook. f. = *Olearia obcordata.*
E. persoonioides DC. = *Olearia persoonioides.*
E. pinifolia Hook. f. = *Olearia pinifolia.*
E. solandri Hook. f. = *Olearia solandri.*
E. subrepanda DC. = *Olearia phlogopappa* var. *subrepanda.*
E. traversii F. Muell. = *Olearia traversii.*
E. virgata Hook. f. = *Olearia virgata.*

Eurychone Schltr. Orchidaceae. 2 monopodial epiphytic orchids. St. short. Lvs closely 2-ranked. Rac. axill., pendent; fls large, scented; tep. free; lip broad, funnel-shaped, somewhat trilobed, narrowing into a spur. Trop. Afr. Z10.
E. galeandrae (Rchb. f.) Schltr. Lvs 7–17×1–3cm, narrowly cuneate. Rac. to 15cm; fls to 4cm diam. white or pale pink with maroon-red streaks. Zaire, Gabon.
E. rothschildiana (O'Brien) Schltr. Lvs 6–20×1.5–7cm, broadly oblanceolate or oblong. Rac. to 9cm; fls c6cm diam., tep. white, tinged pale green, lip white, green in centre, with chocolate-brown or purple blotch at base. W Afr., Zaire, Uganda.
→*Angraecum.*

Eurycles Salisb. ex Schult. & Schult. f.
E. alba (R. Br.) F. Muell. = *Proiphys alba.*
E. cunninghamii Ait. ex Lindl. = *Proiphys cunninghamii.*
E. sylvestris Salisb. ex Schult. & Schult. f. = *Proiphys amboinensis.*

Euryops Cass. Compositae. *c*100 shrubs and herbs. Lvs alt., sessile, often ± overlapping, sometimes rosulate or fascicled. Cap. radiate or discoid, pedunculate; disc flts usually yellow. S Afr. to Arabia and Sokotra.
E. abrotanifolius (L.) DC. Much-branched, erect shrub, to 2m. Lvs to 8cm, linear-filiform, pinnatisect to entire, lobes to 7cm, 1–8 per side, green to glaucous, coriaceous to fleshy. Cap. term., solitary or few together, peduncles to 20cm; ray flts to 25mm, oblong, yellow, sometimes red below. Winter–early spring. S Afr. Z9.
E. acraeus M.D. Henderson. Dense, rounded shrub to 1m. St. forked. Lvs to 3cm, erect, linear, flattened, tip bluntly 3-toothed, glaucous and white-striate above, green beneath, coriaceous. Cap. axill., solitary or 2–3 together, peduncles to 4cm; ray flts to 10mm, oblong, yellow. Spring–summer. S Afr. Z7.
E. athanasiae DC. = *E. speciosissimus.*
E. chrysanthemoides (DC.) R. Nordenstam. Bushy shrub, to 2m. Lvs to 10cm, pinnately lobed, lobes to 2cm, 3–10 per side, ovate to lanceolate, mucronate. Cap. term., often several together, peduncles to 20cm; ray flts to 20mm, narrowly obovate to oblanceolate, yellow. S Afr. Z9.
E. euryopoides (DC.) R. Nordenstam. Erect shrub, to 1.5m. Lvs 1–3cm, usually 3-lobed from middle, sometimes entire, lobes to 1.5cm, linear. Cap. term., solitary or few together, peduncles to

5cm; ray flts to 20mm, narrowly oblong to linear, yellow. S Afr. Z9.

E. evansii Schltr. Few-branched shrub or subshrub, to 2m. Lvs to 10cm, linear-lanceolate to narrowly oblong, apex 3-toothed, entire to minutely sinuate-dentate. Cap. term., 1–5 together, shortly pedunculate; ray flts to 16mm, elliptic-oblong, yellow. S Afr. Z9.

E. pectinatus (L.) Cass. Vigorous shrub, to 2m, often densely tomentose. Lvs to 10cm, pinnatisect to pinnately lobed, lobes to 2cm, 4–10 each side, linear, entire to rarely pinnatifid, grey-tomentose. Cap. terminal, solitary or few together, shortly pedunculate; ray flts to 22mm, oblanceolate, yellow. Summer. S Afr. Z8.

E. spathaceus DC. Much-branched, erect shrub, to 1.5m, glab. Lvs to 10cm, subterete to linear, apiculate, coriaceous to fleshy, axils hairy. Cap. lat., many on upper br., peduncles to 7cm; ray flts to 15mm, lanceolate to narrowly oblong, yellow. Summer. S Afr. Z9.

E. speciosissimus DC. Resinous shrub to 3m. Lvs to 20cm, pinnatipartite to entire, coriaceous, seg. to 7–8 each side, to 15cm, linear-filiform. Cap. term., solitary or 2 together, peduncles to 40cm, stout, erect; ray flts to 20mm, oblong, yellow. S Afr. Z9.

E. virgineus (L. f.) DC. Much-branched, compact shrub, to 4m. Lvs to 1.2cm, usually imbricate, obovate to oblanceolate, cuneate, coriaceous, 3–7-lobed, lobes to 0.4cm, lanceolate, acute and apiculate. Cap. lat. in upper lf axils, forming a racemose cluster, on peduncles to 3cm; ray flts to 6mm, oblanceolate, yellow. Spring. S Afr. Z9.

Euscaphis Sieb. & Zucc. Staphyleaceae. 1 small decid. tree. Lvs 15–25cm, odd-pinnate, lfts 5–10cm, 7–11, ovate-lanceolate, slender-pointed, finely toothed. Fls 5-merous, 0.5cm diam., green or yellow, in long-stalked pan. Fr. 1–3 coriaceous, dehiscent follicles, red, each with dark blue seeds. Spring. China, Jap.

E. japonica (Thunb.) Kanitz.

Eustephia Cav. Amaryllidaceae. 6 bulbous herbs. Lvs basal, erect, linear to narrow-lanceolate. Scape erect; fls drooping, in an umbel; perianth tube short, narrowly funnel-shaped, lobes 6, long, erect; sta. 6, fil. winged. Andes. Z10.

E. coccinea Cav. Scape 30cm; fls horizontal or drooping, 2–8; perianth lobes to 3.5cm, bright red, with pale margins, green-tipped, upper quarter with a green keel. Peruvian Andes.

E. jujuyensis hort. Undescribed plant known in horticulture by this name. Scape 45–60cm; fls brilliant orange-red. N Arg.

E. macleanica Herb. = *E. coccinea*.

E. pamiana Stapf. Scape to 40cm; fls 6, nodding; perianth lobes to 3.5cm, pink at base, green outside and above with red tips. Arg.

E. yuyuensis hort. = *E. jujuyensis*.

Eustoma Salisb. Gentianaceae. 3 ann., bienn. or perenn. herbs. St. glaucous, leafy. Lvs opposite, sessile, sometimes amplexicaul. Fls long-stalked, solitary or in pan.; cor. showy, funnel-shaped to campanulate, deeply 5–6-lobed, lobes twisted; sta. 5–6, recurved at maturity; anth. yellow. S US to N S Amer. Z9.

E. exaltatum (L.) Griseb. Glaucous ann. or short-lived perenn. to 60cm+. St. branched above. Lvs to 9cm, obovate to oblong-elliptic. Pedicels to 10cm; cor. blue to white or pale purple, occas. tinged yellow, lobes to 2.5cm, tube to two-fifths length of lobes. Summer–winter. S US, Mex., C Amer., W Indies.

E. grandiflorum (Raf.) Shinn. PRAIRIE GENTIAN. Erect, thickly glaucous ann. or perenn., to 60cm+. St. branched above. Lvs to 8cm, thinly fleshy, ovate to elliptic-linear. Pedicels to 6cm; cor. lobes 5–6cm, white, blue, pink or purple with darker central patch, satiny, tube short, paler than lobes. Summer. US, Mex. f. *grandiflorum*. Fls purple-blue. 'Double Deep Purple': fls double, dark purple. 'Prairie Blue': fls dark blue with a darker centre. 'Prairie Deep Blue': fls dark blue. 'Texas Blue': fls light blue. f. *bicolor* (Standl.) Shinn. Fls white, lobes tinged purple. f. *fischeri* (Standl.) Shinn. Fls white. 'California White': fls snow white. 'Prairie White': fls ivory. f. *flaviflorum* (Cockerell) Shinn. Fls yellow. f. *roseum* (Standl.) Shinn. Fls pink. 'Double Pink Pearl': fls double, pearly pale rose. 'Double Prima Donna': fls double, blushing pink. 'Prairie Rose': fls salmon pink with a darker centre. 'Florida Pink': fls flamingo pink.

E. russellianum (Hook.) G. Don ex Sweet = *E. grandiflorum*.

E. silenifolium Salisb. = *E. exaltatum*.

→*Gentiana* and *Lisianthius*.

Eutaxia R. Br. Leguminosae (Papilionoideae). 8 dwarf to medium shrubs. Lvs small, decussate, simple, sometimes spiny-tipped. Fls pea-like, 1–4, per axill. cluster, often forming

terminal, leafy, compound rac. Aus. Z9.

E. diffusa F. Muell. = *E. microphylla*.

E. empetrifolia Schldl. = *E. microphylla*.

E. empetrifolia hort. = *E. myrtifolia*.

E. microphylla (R. Br.) J.M. Black. MALLEE BUSH-PEA. To 1m. Lvs to 0.7×0.2cm, oblong or linear, grey-green. Fls to 1cm, yellow-red, standard usually purple-streaked or red-veined, keel blotched, purple. Late summer–early autumn. W Aus.

E. myrtifolia (R. Br.) Sm. To 1.5m. Lvs to 2×0.4cm, overlapping, narrow-elliptic to oblanceolate, grey- to light-green. Fls 0.8cm, yellow and orange. Autumn. W Aus.

E. obovata (Labill.) Gardn. = *E. myrtifolia*.

→*Dillwynia* and *Sclerothamnus*.

Euterpe Mart. ASSAI PALM; MANACO. Palmae. 28 palms. St. erect, solitary or clustered, pale grey, ringed, sometimes swollen at base. Crownshaft slender, green. Lvs pinnate; pinnae pendent, linear-lanceolate, tapered, in symmetrical rows, midrib with tattered scales above. Fr. to 1cm diam., globose, purple-black. S Amer. Z10.

E. aculeata (Willd.) Spreng. = *Aiphanes aculeata*.

E. acuminata Waby = *Roystonea regia*.

E. carbiaea Spreng. = *Roystonea oleracea*.

E. edulis Mart. ASSAI PALM. St. solitary, to 30m. Crownshaft green, to 1.2m. Lvs to 2.7m; pinnae pendent, to 2.5cm diam., 60–75 each side of rachis. ♂ fls with pet. purple. Braz.

E. jenmannii C.H. Wright = *Roystonea jenmanii*.

E. macrospadix Ørst. St. solitary, to 21m. Crownshaft green, to 1.2m. Lvs to 2.7m; pinnae pendent, to 2.5cm diam., 60–75 each side of rachis. ♂ fls with pet. white tinged pink. Belize to Peru.

E. oleracea Mart. ASSAI PALM. St. usually clustered, to 18m. Crownshaft tinged red, to 1m. Lvs to 2.7m; pinnae 50–80 each side of rachis. ♂ fls with pet. purple-red. Braz. to Venez., Guyana.

E. ventricosa C.H. Wright = *Roystonea regia*.

Eutoca R. Br.

E. viscida Benth. ex Lindl. = *Phacelia viscida*.

E. wrangeliana Fisch. ex C.A. Mey. = *Phacelia divaricata*.

Evening Primrose *Oenothera*.
Evening Snow *Linanthus dichotomus*.
Evening Trumpet Flower *Gelsemium sempervirens*.
Everglades Palm *Acoelorraphe*.
Evergreen Blueberry *Vaccinium myrsinites*.
Evergreen Candytuft *Iberis sempervirens*.
Evergreen Grape *Rhoicissus*.
Evergreen Huckleberry *Vaccinium ovatum*.
Evergreen Kangaroo Paw *Anigozanthos flavidus*.
Evergreen Maidenhair *Adiantum venustum*.
Evergreen Oak *Quercus ilex*.
Evergreen Pear *Pyrus kawakamii*.
Evergreen Pittosporum *Pittosporum crassifolium*.
Evergreen Rose *Rosa sempervirens*.
Evergreen Sumac *Rhus virens*.
Evergreen Violet *Viola sempervirens*.
Evergreen Wisteria *Millettia*.
Everlasting *Antennaria*; *Gnaphalium*.
Everlasting Flower *Acroclinium*; *Helichrysum*.
Everlasting Pea *Lathyrus grandiflorus*.
Everlastings *Helipterum*.

Evodia Forst.

E. bodinieri Dode = *Tetradium ruticarpum*.

E. henryi Dode = *Tetradium daniellii*.

E. hupehensis Dode = *Tetradium daniellii*.

E. meliifolia (Hance ex Walp.) Benth. = *Tetradium glabrifolium*.

E. velutina Rehd. & Wils. = *Tetradium daniellii*.

Evodiopanax (Harms) Nak.

E. evodiifolius (Franch.) Nak. = *Gamblea evodiifolia*.

E. innovans (Sieb. & Zucc.) Nak. = *Gamblea innovans*.

Evolvulus L. Convolvulaceae. 100 ann. or perenn. herbs or subshrubs, never climbing. Infl. axill. or term., 1- to several-fld; sep. 5, small; cor. small, funnel-shaped to rotate with a short tube, entire or lobed. N US to S Arg., 2 sp. in OW Trop.

E. glomeratus Nees. & Mart. Herb or subshrub to 50cm, prostrate to decumbent. Lvs 1–3cm, spathulate or oblanceolate to ovate-oblong, downy, esp. beneath. Fls clustered 1–1.5cm diam., bright blue. Summer. Braz. Z8.

E. nuttallianus Roem. & Schult. = *E. pilosus*.

E. pilosus Nutt. To 20cm decumbent or prostrate, with dense, silky hairs. Lvs 0.7–1cm, silky-grey, appressed. Fls solitary, 1–2cm diam., lavender-pink. Summer. US. 'Blue Daze':

compact; lvs elliptic-ovate, white-tomentose; fls bright blue with white centres. Z7.

Ewart's Mallee *Eucalyptus ewartiana.*

Exacum L. Gentianaceae. Some 25 ann., bienn. or perenn. glab. herbs. St. erect, branched. Lvs sessile to short-stalked, simple, entire. Infl. cymose, leafy, forking or fls solitary; cal. 4–5-lobed; cor. salverform to rotate, tube cylindric, lobes 4–5, ovate to oblong; sta. protruding, yellow. OW Trop. and subtrop. Z9.

E. affine Balf. f. GERMAN VIOLET; PERSIAN VIOLET.   Ann. or short-lived perenn. to 60cm. Br. subterete to quadrangular. Lvs 1–3cm, ovate to elliptic. Fls 0.8–2cm diam., fragrant sky blue to pale violet or rich purple. S Yemen, widely nat. elsewhere in OW. 'Elfin': rounded and compact in growth; fls violet with gold sta., highly fragrant. 'Midget Blue': dwarf and compact; fls dark lavender, sweetly fragrant; free-flowering. 'Rosendal Blue': to 2.5cm diam.; fls Oxford blue with purple zone and bright yellow sta. Rosendal Mixed: a seed race producing plants with blue, pink and white fls. var. *atrocaeruleum* Farringt. Fls dark lavender.

E. macranthum Arn. = *E. trinervium* ssp. *macranthum.*
E. ovale Griseb. = *E. trinervium* ssp. *macranthum.*
E. trinervium (L.) Druce. Bienn. to 1m. Br. cylindric to quadrangular, angles winged. Lvs to 7.5cm, elliptic to lanceolate. Fls to 3.2cm diam., blue or violet. Sri Lanka. ssp. *macranthum* (Arn.) Kramer. To 1m. Lvs to 9.5cm. Fls violet to blue-purple to 3.5cm. Sri Lanka.
E. zeylanicum Roxb. = *E. trinervium.*
→*Chironia* and *Lisianthius.*

Exarrhena R. Br.
E. colensoi T. Kirk = *Myosotis colensoi.*
E. macrantha Hook. f. = *Myosotis macrantha.*

Exbucklandia R.W. Br. Hamamelidaceae. 2 everg. trees, to 30m. Lvs stipulate, alt., ovate, sometimes 3-lobed, leathery; stipules in pairs, large; petioles long. Fls in capitate groups of 4; cal. tubular, 5-lobed; ♂ fls with variable pet.; sta. 10–14; ♀ fls with 4 rudimentary pet., sta. 0. E Himal., S China, Malesia. Z7.
E. populnea R.W. Br. Lvs 10–15cm, ovate to cordate, shiny above, young lvs red beneath, veins red; petioles red, to 7.5cm. E Himal. to Java.
→*Bucklandia.*

Exeter Elm *Ulmus glabra* 'Exoniensis'.

Exochorda Lindl. PEARLBUSH. Rosaceae. 4 decid. shrubs. Lvs alt., entire or serrate, pale green, usually softly pubesc. Rac. term., elongate; cal. constricted in the middle, 4–5-lobed; pet. 5, white, large, obovate, rather crumpled; sta. 15–30. China
E. alberti Reg. = *E. korolkowii.*
E. alberti var. *macrantha* Lemoine = *E.* ×*macrantha.*
E. giraldii Hesse.   To 3m, spreading. Lvs to 8cm, oblong to obovate, entire, v. rarely crenate, pale green, veins tinged red; petiole red. Fls to 2.5cm diam., 6–8 in term. rac., sessile near apex of rac., short-stalked below. NW China. Z5. var. *wilsonii* (Rehd.) Rehd. Habit more upright. Lvs larger, narrower, coarsely toothed above, petioles green. Fls 5cm diam. C China.
E. grandiflora (Hook.) Lindl. = *E. racemosa.*
E. korolkowii Lav. To 4.5m, erect. Lvs to 9cm, obovate, tapering and serrate above, olive or lime green above, grey to yellow-green beneath. Fls 4cm diam., sessile, in erect, 5–8-fld rac. to 10cm. Spring. Turkestan. Z6.
E. ×*macrantha*   (Lemoine)   Schneid.   (*E. korolkowii* ×*E. racemosa.*)   Erect. Fls 3cm diam., in 6–10-fld, erect to spreading rac. to 10cm. Spring. Gdn origin. 'Irish Pearl' ('The Pearl'): flowering shoots v. long; lvs light green above, tinted blue beneath; fls grouped to 10. 'The Bride': habit dense and compact; br. nodding; fls large, profuse. Z5.
E. racemosa (Lindl.) Rehd.   To 3m, dense, rounded. Lvs to 7.5cm, narrow-obovate, short-cuspidate or obtuse, entire or serrate above, light green above, darker beneath, glab. Fls to 4cm diam., on erect, 6–10-fld rac. to 10cm. Spring. N China. Z4.
E. racemosa var. *wilsonii* Rehd. = *E. giraldii* var. *wilsonii.*
E. serratifolia Moore. To 2m. Lvs to 7cm, elliptic, serrate above, somewhat pubesc. beneath. Fls 4cm diam., in lax rac.; pet. emarginate. Spring. Manch., Korea. Z5.
E. tianschanica Gontsch. = *E. korolkowii.*
→*Amelanchier* and *Spiraea.*

Exotic Fig *Ficus benjamina.*
Exploding Cucumber *Ecballium.*
Explorer's Gentian *Gentiana calycosa.*
Eyebright *Euphrasia* (*E. officinalis*).
Eyelash Begonia *Begonia bowerae.*
Ezo-yama-hagi *Lespedeza bicolor.*

F

Faber's Fir *Abies fabri.*

Fabiana Ruiz & Pav. Solanaceae. 25 heath-like shrubs, often viscid. Fls subsessile, crowded at tips of br.; cal. tubular to campanulate, lobes short; cor. tube elongate, limb short, lobes 5. Warm temp. S Amer. Z8.
F. imbricata Ruiz & Pav. PICHI. Everg., to 2.5×2.5m. St. erect, lat. br. short, downy. Lvs small, overlapping, triangular to acicular. Cor. to 1.3cm, white to pale rose pink, lobes obtuse, reflexed. Summer. Chile. 'Violacea': fls pale mauve to blue-violet. 'Prostrata': low-growing; fls white.

Facheiroa Britt. & Rose. Cactaceae. 3 or more shrubby or tree-like cacti; st. cylindric; ribs low, narrow. Fls tubular, nocturnal; tep. short. Fr. globose, fleshy. Braz.
F. pubiflora Britt. & Rose = *F. ulei.*
F. ulei (Gürke) Werderm. Arborescent, to 5m; st. 5–7cm diam; ribs 15–20; areoles brown-felted; central spines 2–4, 1–3cm, radial spines 10–15, 1–1.5cm. Flowering zone fleece-like, with dense, red-brown bristly hairs; fl. 3cm, white. E Braz. Z9.
→*Espostoa.*

Fadyenia Hook. Dryopteridaceae. 1 small terrestrial fern, forming colonies. Rhiz. ascending, short, scaly. Fronds sessile, clustered; sterile fronds 4–7×1.5–2cm, obovate-spathulate, ± prostrate or 10–25×1.5–3cm, lanceolate to narrowly elliptic with attenuate, proliferous apex, rooting at tips; fertile fronds 8–15×0.5–1cm, erect, ligulate-spathulate. W Indies. Z10.
F. hookeri (Sweet) Maxon.
→*Aspidium.*

FAGACEAE Dumort. 7/1050. *Castanea, Castanopsis, Chrysolepis, Fagus, Lithocarpus, Nothofagus, Quercus.*

Fagara L.
F. ailanthoides (Sieb. & Zucc.) Engl. = *Zanthoxylum ailanthoides.*
F. capensis Thunb. = *Zanthoxylum capense.*
F. clava-herculis (L.) Small = *Zanthoxylum clava-herculis.*
F. fagara (L.) Small = *Zanthoxylum fagara.*
F. fruticosum (A. Gray) Small = *Zanthoxylum clava-herculis* var. *fruticosum.*
F. horrida Thunb. = *Gleditsia japonica.*
F. piperita L. = *Zanthoxylum piperitum.*
F. schinifolia (Sieb. & Zucc.) Engl. = *Zanthoxylum schinifolium.*

Fagopyrum Mill.
F. dibotrys (D. Don) Hara = *Polygonum dibotrys.*
F. esculentum Moench = *Polygonum fagopyrum.*
F. sagittatum Gilib. = *Polygonum fagopyrum.*

Fagraea Thunb. Loganiaceae. 35 trees or epiphytic shrubs. Lvs ochreate, large, leathery, entire. Fls solitary or in cymes, fragrant, showy; cor. funnelform with 5 (-6–7), overlapping lobes. Fr. a many-seeded berry. E Asia, Malesia, W Pacific. Z10.
F. auriculata Jack. Epiphytic shrub. Lvs 9–40×4–25cm, narrowly obovate to oblong. Fls 4.5–15cm, term., in threes, yellow. Burm. to Philipp. and Indon.
F. berterana A. Gray ex Benth. Usually a small tree to 15m. Lvs obovate or ovate, 9–16×4.5–12cm. Fls 3–15cm, in branched cymes, white. Pacific Is., Aus.
F. ceilanica Thunb. Erect shrub to 15m. Lvs ovate to obovate, 4.5–35×1.5–9cm. Fls 3–17 per infl., white; cor. tube 2–5cm. Sri Lanka.
F. fragrans Roxb. Tree or shrub 8–25m. Lvs elliptic, 4–15×1.5–6cm. Fls few to 100, white, fragrant, in branched cymes; cor. tube 1–2.5cm. India, Malaysia.
F. obovata Wallich ex Roxb. Shrub or small tree to 3.5m. Lvs to 15cm, obovate or ovate. Fls to 10cm, term., in threes, fragrant, white. Sri Lanka.
F. zeylanica Murr = *F. ceilanica.*

Fagus L. BEECH. Fagaceae. 10 decid. trees. Crown spreading; bark smooth, grey. Shoots slender; buds narrowly ellipsoid. Lvs alt., entire to dentate, shiny. ♂ fls in long slender heads, perianth 4–7-lobed, sta. 8–16; ♀ fls 2–3 together, perianth 4–6-lobed, ovary 3-chambered. Fr. solitary, cupule spiny, splitting

open in 4 sections; nuts ovoid-acute, triangular in section. N temp.
F. americana Sw. = *F. grandifolia.*
F. crenata Bl. JAPANESE BEECH. To 40m. Lvs 7–13×5–6.5cm, elliptic-ovate to rhombic, short-acuminate, shallow-crenate, veins in 7–10 pairs, soft pubesc. when young. Fr. glossy mid-green, paler beneath, peduncle 1–2cm, short-pubesc.; cupule scaly bristled. Jap. Z4.
F. engleriana Seemen. CHINESE BEECH. To 20m, branching from base. Lvs 13×4–6cm, lanceolate to elliptic-ovate, short-acuminate, undulate to remotely dentate, veins in 10–14 pairs, pubesc., yellow-green above, blue-green beneath. Fr. on slender, glab. peduncles to 6cm; cupule 1.5cm, bracteate, linear-foliose at base. C China. Z6.
F. grandifolia Ehrenb. AMERICAN BEECH. To 35m. Lvs 6–15×4–7cm, obovate to oblong, blue green above, paler beneath, serrate, veins in 10–15 pairs. Fr. on peduncle to 2.5cm, short-pubesc.; cupule short-pubesc., scales curved or straight. E N Amer. var. *caroliniana* (Loud.) Fern. & Rehd. Lvs shorter, ovate, less obviously toothed. Cupule with shorter scales. Z4.
F. japonica Maxim. JAPANESE BLUE BEECH. To 25m. Lvs 5–13×4–6cm, elliptic-ovate to ovate, acute, ± crenate to sub-entire, glaucous beneath, midrib somewhat downy, veins in 9–15 pairs. Fr. on a 2.5–3cm peduncle; cupule short, to 0.8cm. Jap. Z5.
F. latifolia (Moench) Sudw. = *F. grandifolia.*
F. longipetiolata Seemen. To 2.5m. Lvs 6–14×4–7cm, ovate to oblong-ovate, dentate, acuminate, bright green above, downy and glaucous beneath, veins in 9–12 pairs. Fr. on 4–5cm peduncle; cupule to 2.5cm, short-pubesc., scales slender, reflexed. C & W China.
F. lucida Rehd. & Wils. Tree to 15m. Lvs 5–10×2.5–5cm, narrow-ovate, veins in 8–10 pairs, ending in teeth, otherwise shallow-crenate. Fr. on slender peduncle to 7cm, slender, glab.; cupule scales somewhat triangular, recurved. W China. Z6.
F. ×moesiaca (Maly) Czeczot (*F. sylvatica* × *F. orientalis*). Lvs longer, narrower than *F. sylvatica* with 6–11 pairs of veins, but fr. as *F. sylvatica.* Probably natural hybrids. Balk. Penins. Z5.
F. orientalis Lipsky. To 40m. Lvs 8–17×5–8cm, elliptic-oblong to obovate, dentate, veins in 7–13 pairs. Fr. on 2–3cm peduncle; cupule to 2cm, basal scales spathulate. SE Eur., SW Asia, N Iran, Cauc. Z5.
F. sieboldii Endl. = *F. crenata.*
F. sinensis Oliv. = *F. longipetiolata.*
F. sylvatica L. COMMON BEECH; EUROPEAN BEECH. To 48m; bark smooth, grey. Lvs 5.5–11×3.5–6.5cm, elliptic-ovate, undulate-crenate, often remotely denticulate, ciliate, veins in 5–9 pairs, soft-pubesc. Fr. on peduncle to 2.5cm; cupule to 2.5cm+, scales narrow, subulate, spreading. C Eur. to Cauc. f. *tortuosa* (Pépin) Hegi. Br. twisted. f. *purpurea* (Ait.) Schneid. (COPPER BEECH) covers the many purple-leaved clones, f. *pendula* (Loud.) Schelle (WEEPING BEECH) the pendulous clones, and f. *laciniata* (Pers.) Domin (CUT-LEAF BEECH; FERN-LEAF BEECH) the clones with deeply cut lvs. 'Dawyck' (DAWYCK BEECH) is fastigiate and 'Zlatia' (GOLDEN BEECH) has lvs golden in spring. Most traits are now available in combination; 'Rohan Obelisk' is a purple, cut-leaf, fastigiate tree. Z5.
F. sylvatica var. *macrophylla* Hohen. = *F. orientalis.*
F. sylvatica var. *orientalis* (Lipsky) Greuter & Burdet = *F. orientalis.*

Fairies' Thimbles *Campanula cochleariifolia.*
Fair Maids of France *Ranunculus aconitifolius; Saxifraga granulata.*
Fair Maids of Kent *Ranunculus aconitifolius.*
Fairway Crested Wheatgrass *Agropyron cristatum.*
Fairy-carpet Begonia *Begonia versicolor.*
Fairy-duster *Calliandra eriophylla.*
Fairy Elephant's Feet *Frithia pulchra.*
Fairy Fans *Clarkia breweri.*
Fairy Lantern *Calochortus.*
Fairy Lily *Zephyranthes.*
Fairy Moss *Azolla.*
Fairy Primrose *Primula malacoides.*
Fairy Rose *Rosa chinensis.*
Fairy Wand *Chamaelirion luteum.*
Fairy Washboard *Haworthia limifolia.*

Fairy Water Lily *Nymphoides aquatica.*
Falcate Yellowwood *Podocarpus henkelii.*

Falcatifolium Laub. Podocarpaceae. 5 everg. conifers. Lvs linear, falcate, twisted at base in 2 ranks. ♂ cones to 3cm, cylindric clustered. ♀ cones solitary, pendent; receptacle red with a swollen, thorny, basal appendage; seeds 1. Malaysia, Philipp., New Guinea, New Caledonia. Z10.
F. falciforme (Parl.) Pilger COMMON SICKLE PINE; MALAYSIAN SICKLE PINE. Tree to 10m+. Bark brown tinged purple, fibrous. Lvs thick, 2–6×0.5–0.8cm. Indon., Malaysia, to the Moluccas.
F. taxoides (Brongn. & Griseb.) Laub. YEW-LEAF SICKLE PINE. Shrub or tree, to 15m, bark brown tinged red, fibrous. Lvs narrow-ovate, to 3×0.6cm, prominently keeled. C New Caledonia. Host of the parasitic conifer, *Parasitaxus ustus.*
→*Dacrydium* and *Podocarpus.*

Falling Stars *Campanula isophylla.*

Fallopia Adans.
F. aubertii (L. Henry) Holub = *Polygonum aubertii.*
F. baldschuanica (Reg.) Holub = *Polygonum baldschuanicum.*

Fall Phlox *Phlox paniculata.*

Fallugia Endl. APACHE PLUME. Rosaceae. 1 decid. shrub to 2.5m. Br. slender, bark pale, exfoliating; branchlets white-lanuginose. Lvs to 2cm, downy beneath, finely pinnatifid with 3–7 linear lobes. Fls to 2cm diam., forming rac. at the ends of br.; cal. cup lanuginose, lobes ovate, cuspidate, alternating with 5 small epical. seg.; pet. 5, white, spreading; sta. many. Seed heads with conspicuous plumose appendages. SW US, Mex. Z5.
F. paradoxa (D. Don) Endl.
→*Sieversia.*

False Acacia *Robinia pseudoacacia.*
False Anemone *Anemonopsis.*
False Aralia *Schefflera elegantissima.*
False Asphodel *Tofieldia.*
False Baby's Breath *Galium aristatum*; *G. mollugo.*
False Banyan *Ficus altissima.*
False Bird of Paradise *Heliconia.*
False Bishop's Weed *Ammi majus.*
False Blind-grass *Agrostocrinum.*
False Bracken *Culcita dubia.*
False Buckthorn *Bumelia lanuginosa.*
False Bugbane *Trautvetteria carolinensis.*
False Cactus *Euphorbia lactea.*
False Caper *Euphorbia terracina.*
False Chamomile *Boltonia.*
False Cypress *Chamaecyparis.*
False Dayflower *Tinantia.*
False Dogwood *Sapindus saponaria.*
False Dragon Head *Physostegia.*
False Fiddle-leaf Fig *Ficus sagittifolia.*
False Foxglove *Aureolaria.*
False Garlic *Allium vineale*; *Nothoscordum.*
False Goatsbeard *Astilbe biternata.*
False Heather *Cuphea hyssopifolia*; *Hudsonia ericoides.*
False Holly *Osmanthus heterophyllus.*
False Hop *Justicia brandegeana.*
False Indigo *Baptisia.*
False Ipecac *Psychotria emetica.*
False Jalap *Mirabilis jalapa.*
False Jasmine *Gelsemium sempervirens.*
False Jerusalem Cherry *Solanum capsicastrum.*
False Lily of the Valley *Maianthemum bifolium.*
False Lupine *Thermopsis macrophylla.*
False Mallow *Sphaeralcea.*
False Mistletoe *Phoradendron.*
False Mitrewort *Tiarella.*
False Nettle *Boehmeria.*
False Oat *Arrhenatherum elatius.*
False Olive *Cassine orientalis.*
False Payapa *Ficus forstenii.*
False Rue Anemone *Isopyrum.*
False Saffron *Carthamus tinctorius.*
False Sago *Cycas* (*C. circinalis*).
False Sarsparilla *Hardenbergia violacea.*
False Sea Onion *Ornithogalum longibracteatum.*
False Solomon's Seal *Smilacina.*
False Spikenard *Smilacina racemosa.*
False Spiraea *Sorbaria.*
False Tamarisk *Myricaria.*
False Vervain *Stachytarpheta.*
Fameflower *Talinum* (*T. paniculatum*).

Fan Aloe *Aloe plicatilis.*
Fancy Fern *Dryopteris intermedia.*
Fan Fern *Sticherus flabellatus.*
Fan Hakea *Hakea baxteri.*
Fan Palm *Trachycarpus.*
Fanwort *Cabomba caroliniana.*
Farewell to Spring *Clarkia.*

Farfugium Lindl. Compositae. 2 rhizomatous everg. perenn. herbs. Lvs in basal tufts, cordate, reniform or flabellate, long-stalked. Cap. radiate, in loose corymbs. E Asia.
F. japonicum (L.) Kitam. Lvs 4–15×6–30cm, basal, reniform, mucronate-dentate to subentire, thick, lustrous above; petiole long. Cap. 4–6cm diam., scape to 75cm long; flts yellow. Autumn–winter. Jap. 'Argentea' ('Albovariegata', 'Variegata'): lvs irregularly stippled dark green, grey-green and cream. 'Aureomaculata': lvs with yellow spots. 'Crispata' ('Cristata'): lvs green, crumpled, crisped at margins.
→*Ligularia, Senecio* and *Tussilago.*

Fargesia Franch.
F. maling (Gamble) Simon ex D. McClintock = *Yushania maling.*
F. murielae (Gamble) Yi = *Thamnocalamus spathaceus.*
F. nitida (Mitford) Keng f. & Yi = *Sinarundinaria nitida.*
F. spathacea Franch. = *Thamnocalamus spathaceus.*

Farkleberry *Vaccinium arboreum.*
Farley Maidenhair Fern *Adiantum tenerum.*
Farrer Spruce *Picea farreri.*
Farrer's Threepenny-bit Rose *Rosa elegantula.*

Farsetia Turra. Cruciferae. 20 herbs and subshrubs. Lvs entire, opposite, downy. Fls in rac.; sep. 4; pet. 4; sta. 6. Fr. a silique, compressed, hairy. Moroc. to NW India and mts of Trop. Afr.
F. aegyptica Turra. To 60cm, shrubby. Lvs narrow-linear; pet. 15mm, white suffused yellow. Fr. broadly oblong-elliptic, 10–20×6mm. N Sudan. Z8.
F. clypeata (L.) R. Br. = *Fibigia clypeata.*
F. eriocarpa DC. = *Fibigia eriocarpa.*
F. incana (L.) R. Br. = *Berteroa incana.*
F. lunarioides R. Br. = *Fibigia lunarioides.*

Fascicularia Mez. Bromeliaceae. 5 stemless or short-stemmed, perenn., xerophytic herbs. Lvs in a dense, flat rosette, rigid, linear, toothed and spinose, pungent. Infl. dense, embedded in the rosette centre; fls ± sessile; sep. free, hairy and scaly; pet. elliptic, fleshy, free, blunt, with 2 small basal scales. Chile. Z8.
F. bicolor (Ruiz & Pav.) Mez. Lvs to 50cm, innermost bright crimson at flowering, blades rigid, linear, brown-scaly beneath, spiny-toothed. Infl. corymbose or capitiform; outer bracts longer than fls, ivory white; floral bracts toothed; pet. 20mm, pale blue, scales tiny, fleshy. Summer.
F. pitcairniifolia (hort. Berlin ex Verl.) Mez. Lvs to 1m, innermost bright red at flowering, pale-brown, with short, brown, spreading spines, blade glaucous, leathery, linear, sometimes scaly beneath. Infl. densely capitate, outer bracts shorter than fls; floral bracts fimbriate; pet. 22–24mm, blue or bright violet. Summer.
→*Hechtia.*

Fat-hen *Chenopodium bonus-henricus.*
Fat Pork Tree *Clusia major.*

✗ **Fatshedera** Guill. (*Fatsia japonica* 'Moseri' ✗ *Hedera hibernica.*) Araliaceae. Everg. shrub of loose sprawling habit, to 1.2m. Lvs palmately and deeply 5-lobed, glossy above; young lvs and petioles rusty-pubesc. Fls small, sterile, green-white, umbellate in pan. Autumn. Gdn origin. Z7.
✗ *F. lizei* Guill. 'Pia': lvs undulate. 'Anna Mikkels': lvs variegated yellow. 'Variegata': lvs variegated cream.

Fatsi *Fatsia japonica.*

Fatsia Decne. & Planch. Araliaceae. 3 unarmed, pachycaul, everg. shrubs or small trees with foliage crowded towards br. tips. Lvs large, leathery, palmately lobed. Infl. term., exceeding lvs, usually twice compound; fls in umbels; pet. 5; sta. 5. Fr. drupaceous, usually round. E Asia.
F. japonica (Thunb.) Decne. & Planch. FATSI; JAPANESE FATSIA; GLOSSY-LEAVED PAPER PLANT. Shrub to 6m+, widely spreading; br. stout, with prominent lf scars. Lvs to 90×40cm, long-petioled, dark green above; lobes 7–11, narrowly oblong-elliptic, mostly toothed. Infl. creamy-white, glabrescent, with several br.; umbels 2.5–3.7cm across. Fr. at first green, then black, 8–9mm wide. Autumn. Jap. 'Aurea': lvs variegated with gold. 'Marginata': lvs grey-green edged off-white, deeply lobed.

'Moseri': more compact; of vigorous growth; lvs larger. 'Variegata': lf lobes deeply margined cream at tips. Z8.

F. oligocarpella (Nak.) Koidz. Lf lobes strongly narrowed. Z9. Bonin Is. (introd. Hawaii)

F. mitsde (Sieb.) Vriese = Dendropanax trifidus.

F. papyrifera (Hook.) Miq. ex Witte = Tetrapanax papyrifer. →Aralia.

Fat Solomon Smilacina racemosa var. amplexicaulis.

Faucaria Schwantes. TIGER JAWS. Aizoaceae. 30+ succulent, mat-forming perennials. Lvs 4–6 on one shoot, decussate, united at the base, thick-fleshy, semicylindric at base, lower surface carinate-triquetrous toward tip, rhombic, spathulate or lanceolate, margins cartilaginous with hooked teeth, firm-textured, usually with raised spots. Fls sessile, 3–5cm diam. Late summer–late autumn. S Afr. Z9.

F. acutipetala L. Bol. = F. felina.

F. albidens N.E. Br. Lvs 25×6–7mm, tapering triangularly, angles with 3–5 pale, awn-like teeth, with scattered spots. Fls golden yellow.

F. bosscheana (A. Berger) Schwantes. Lvs 30×10mm, narrow-lanceolate or acute-rhombic, glossy, angles irregularly dentate, with 2–3 teeth. Fls golden yellow.

F. britteniae L. Bol. Lvs 35×15mm, rhombic-ovate in outline, margins with 3–4 hair-like teeth midway. Fls white.

F. candida L. Bol. Lvs 25×15mm, ± rhombic in outline, marginal teeth 6–7, 2mm long, pink-tipped. Fls white.

F. cradockensis L. Bol. = F. felina.

F. duncanii L. Bol. = F. lupina.

F. felina (Weston) Schwantes ex Jacobsen. Lvs 4–5cm×15–20cm, oblong-rhombic, long-tapered, with distinct white dots, margins with 3–5 pointed fleshy teeth. Fls golden yellow.

F. grandis L. Bol. = F. britteniae.

F. haagei Tisch. = F. bosscheana.

F. jamesii L. Bol. ex Tisch. = F. felina.

F. kendrewensis N.E. Br. = F. albidens.

F. longidens L. Bol. = F. felina.

F. lupina (Haw.) Schwantes. Lvs lanceolate in outline, triangularly tapering, with tiny rough dots, margins with 7–9 fine teeth. Fls yellow.

F. militaris Tisch. = F. felina.

F. peersii L. Bol. Clump-forming. Lvs to 4×2cm, rhomboid to rounded in outline, keel and margins white, entire or with few teeth lacking bristles. Fls yellow tinted red beneath.

F. ryneveldiae L. Bol. = F. lupina.

F. subintegra L. Bol. Lvs 20–25×13–10mm, thick and swollen, ovate in outline above, rounded or rarely subacute, square in the lower part, margins entire or with 1–3 teeth. Fls golden yellow.

F. tigrina (Haw.) Schwantes. Lvs 3–5×1.6×2.5cm, rhombic to ovate, short-tapered, lower surface v. rounded, grey-green with humerous dots in rows, margins with 9–10 stout, hair-tipped teeth. Fls golden yellow.

F. tuberculosa (Rolfe) Schwantes. Lvs 2cm×16mm, rhombic to triangular on the upper surface with teeth-like tubercles, with 3 stout marginal teeth and several rudimentary teeth. Fls yellow.

Fauria Franch.

F. crista-galli (Menz. ex Hook.) Mak. = Nephrophyllidium crista-galli.

F. japonica Franch. = Nephrophyllidium crista-galli.

Fawn Lily Erythronium (E. californicum).
Feather Duster Palm Rhopalostylis sapida.
Feathered Bush Lysiloma.
Feathered Hyacinth Muscari comosum 'Plumosum'.
Feather Flower Verticordia (V. plumosa).
Feather Geranium Chenopodium botrys.
Feather Grape Hyacinth Muscari comosum 'Plumosum'.
Feather Grass Stipa.
Feather-leaved Banksia Banksia brownii.
Feather Reed Grass Calamagrostis ×acutiflora.
Feathertop Pennisetum villosum.
Feathery Cassia Senna artemisioides.
February Daphne Daphne mezereum.

Fedia Gaertn. Valerianaceae. 2–3 ann., erect herbs. Lvs opposite, simple. Fls in small, terminal cymes; cal. usually v. small, with 4 teeth; cor. with 5 unequal lobes, tube cylindrical; sta. 2. Fr. with 1 fertile and 2 sterile cells. Medit.

F. cornucopiae (L.) Gaertn. AFRICAN VALERIAN; HOUSE-OF-PLENTY. To 30cm, glab. Lvs spathulate to elliptic, lower to 15cm, entire, upper smaller, denticulate, cor. to 1.6cm, red marked pink on limb. Medit., S Port.

Fe'i Banana Musa troglodytarum.

Feijoa O. Berg.

F. sellowiana (O. Berg) O. Berg = Acca sellowiana.

Felicia Cass. BLUE MARGUERITE; BLUE DAISY; KINGFISHER DAISY. Compositae. 83 ann. to perenn. herbs, dwarf subshrubs and shrubs. Lvs simple, entire to dentate. Cap. radiate, often solitary, long pedunculate; disc flts yellow. Trop. & S Afr., Arabia. Z9.

F. abyssinica A. Rich. Tufted shrub, to 50cm. Lvs to 2cm, linear, entire or minutely bristly serrate, crowded. Cap. to 2cm diam., solitary, term.; peduncles to 8cm; ray flts violet-blue. Trop. Afr., Arabia.

F. adfinis (Less.) Nees = F. dubia.

F. aethiopica (Burm. f.) Adams & Salt. Shrub to 60cm. Lvs to 2cm, elliptic to obovate, glab. Cap. to 3cm diam., solitary; peduncles gland.; ray flts blue. S Afr.

F. amelloides (L.) Voss. BLUE DAISY; BLUE MARGUERITE. Hairy subshrub to 60cm; st. slender, trailing to erect. Lvs to 3cm, ovate to obovate, subentire, sessile. Cap. 4cm diam., solitary; peduncles to 18cm; ray flts light blue. Summer. S Afr. 'Read's Blue': to 30cm; fls large, blue with gold eye. 'Read's White': to 30cm; fls white with gold eye. 'Santa Anita': to 30cm; fls large, blue. 'Santa Anita Variegata': to 30cm; lvs stippled; fls large, blue.

F. amethystina hort. = F. 'Snowmass'.

F. amoena (Schultz-Bip.) Levyns. Downy ann. or perenn. herb to 50cm; st. slender, shrubby. Lvs to 3cm, elliptic to linear. Cap. 3.5cm diam., solitary; peduncles to 12cm; ray flts bright blue. S Afr. 'Variegata': to 15cm; lvs variegated cream and green; fls blue.

F. bergeriana (Spreng.) O. Hoffm. KINGFISHER DAISY. Villous, mat-forming ann. to 25cm. Lvs to 4cm, lanceolate, hairy, toothed to entire. Cap. to 3cm diam., solitary, shortly pedunculate; ray flts bright blue. Summer. S Afr.

F. dubia Cass. Hairy ann. to 50cm. Lvs to 3cm, obovate to oblong, base truncate, entire. Cap. 2cm diam., usually solitary; ray flts blue. S Afr.

F. echinata (Thunb.) Nees. Subshrub to 60cm. Lvs to 2cm, oblong to lanceolate, ciliate or spiny. Cap. to 4cm diam., in groups of 1–6; peduncle and phyllaries densely hispid; ray flts lilac to white. S Afr.

F. elongata (Thunb.) O. Hoffm. Subshrub to 80cm. Lvs to 2cm, linear to lanceolate, entire, silvery-hairy. Cap. 5cm diam., solitary; peduncles to 30cm; ray flts white to mauve or pink with maroon base. S Afr.

F. fragilis Cass. = F. tenella.

F. fruticosa (L.) Nichols. Shrub to 1m. Lvs to 2cm, densely arranged, alt., linear, entire. Cap. to 3cm diam., solitary, peduncles to 10cm; ray flts white, pink or purple. S Afr.

F. heterophylla (Cass.) Grau. Ann. to 50cm. Lvs to 5cm, oblanceolate, entire to dentate. Cap. solitary; peduncle to 20cm; ray flts usually blue. S Afr. (Cape Prov.).

F. hyssopifolia (Berger) Nees. Often densely tomentose straggling subshrub to 50cm. Lvs to 105cm, linear. Cap. solitary; ray flts mauve or blue. S Afr.

F. linifolia (Harv.) Grau. Shrub or subshrub to 60cm. Lvs 2cm alt., linear to lanceolate. Peduncles to 10cm; ray flts blue. S Afr.

F. natalensis Schultz-Bip. ex Walpers. = F. rosulata.

F. pappei (Harv.) Hutch. = F. amoena.

F. petiolata (Harv.) N.E. Br. Prostrate perenn. Lvs to 3cm, lanceolate, sparingly lobed. Cap. 2cm diam., solitary; ray flts white to violet. S Afr.

F. reflexa (L.) DC. = Polyarrhena reflexa.

F. rosulata Yeo. Perenn. herb to 40cm, rhizomatous. Lower lvs to 10cm, rosulate, elliptic to obovate, hairy; st. lvs smaller, lanceolate. Cap. to 3cm diam., solitary; ray flts blue. S Afr.

F. rotundifolia G.C. Tayl. = F. amelloides.

F. 'Snowmass'. Small, to 8cm. Lvs feathery. Fls v. soft violet.

F. tenella (L.) Nees. Hairy ann. or perenn. subshrub to 60cm. Lvs to 5cm, linear, pubesc. Cap. to 2cm diam., solitary; few to numerous; ray flts violet to white. Summer. S Afr.

F. uliginosa (Wood & M. Evans) Grau. ± procumbent perenn. Ray flts lilac. S Afr.

→Aster, Charieis and Kaulfussia.

Felt Fern Pyrrosia.
Feltleaf Ceanothus Ceanothus arboreus.
Felwort Gentianella.

Fendlera Engelm. & A. Gray. Hydrangeaceae. 3 arching decid. shrubs. Lvs opposite, entire, sessile. Fls 1–3 on short side-shoots; cal. and cor. 4-parted; sta. 8, yellow to pink. N Amer. Z5.

F. rupicola A. Gray. 0.5–1m. Br. intricate, spreading, initially tawny and downy, bark exfoliating in ragged strips. Lvs 1.75–3.25cm, lanceolate to narrow-oblong, 3-veined, coarsely hairy. Fls to 3cm diam., fragrant; pet. white sometimes flushed rose, ovate-orbicular, long-clawed. SW US.

F. wrightii (A. Gray) Heller. Close to *F. rupicola* but with lvs woolly-white beneath. SW US, Mex.

Fendler Globe Mallow *Sphaeralcea fendleri.*

Fenestraria N.E. Br. Aizoaceae. 2 stemless succulent perennials. Lvs to 3cm, glab., opposite, crowded, cylindric-clavate, apex flattened with a translucent window. Nam. Z10.

F. aurantiaca N.E. Br. Fls 3–7cm diam., golden yellow.

F. rhopalophylla (Schltr. & Diels) N.E. Br. BABY'S TOES. Fls 1.8–3cm diam., white.

Fennel *Foeniculum vulgare.*
Fennel Flower *Nigella* (*N. hispanica*).
Fennel Pondweed *Potamogeton pectinatus.*
Fen Orchid *Liparis loeselii.*
Fen Pondweed *Potamogeton coloratus.*
Fen Rose *Kosteletzkya.*
Fenugreek *Trigonella foenum-graecum.*

Ferdinanda Lagasca.
F. eminens Lagasca = *Podachaenium eminens.*

Ferdinandia Welw. ex Seem.
F. superba hort. ex Seem. = *Amphitecna macrophylla.*

Fernandoa Welw. ex Seem. Bignoniaceae. 13 trees. Lvs pinnate, pinnae decreasing in size from apex, glab. or tomentose. Infl. thyrsiform, term. or lat.; cal. tubular or campanulate, 2–5 lobed; cor. tubular-campanulate, lobes crenate; sta. 4, unequal, with fifth sterile staminode. Fr. a linear capsule. Afr., Madag., Indomalesia.

F. adenophylla (G. Don) Steenis. Tree 4–20m, young parts and infl. rusty hairy. Lvs to 50cm; pinnae to 24cm, 2–4 pairs, circular to elliptic. Fls to 7cm, tan, white or green-yellow. S & SE Asia, Penins. Malaysia.

F. adolfi-friderici (Gilg & Mildbr.) Heine. EDJUJONGO. To 25m. Lvs 6.3cm, pinnae 3–7, dentate. Fls yellow. Cameroun to Zaire.

F. magnifica Seem. Shrub or tree. Lvs to 30cm; pinnae to 12.5cm, 9–13, ovate to oblong. Fls to 7.5cm, rich orange. E Afr. →*Haplophragma*, *Heterophragma* and *Spathodeopsis*.

Fern Asparagus *Asparagus filicinus.*
Fern Begonia *Begonia foliosa.*
Fern-leaf Aralia *Polyscias filicifolia.*
Fern-leaf Beech *Fagus sylvatica* f. *laciniata.*
Fern-leaf Geranium *Pelargonium denticulatum.*
Fern-leaf Wandering Jew *Tripogandra.*
Fern-leaf Yarrow *Achillea filipendulina.*
Fern-leaved Begonia *Begonia foliosa.*
Fern-of-the-desert *Lysiloma.*
Fern Palm *Cycas circinalis.*
Fern Pine *Podocarpus gracilior.*
Fern Rhapis *Rhapis excelsa.*

Ferocactus Britt. & Rose. Cactaceae. 23 cacti, unbranched or clumped; st. often large, depressed-globose to cylindric, ribbed; areoles with nectar-secreting glands; spines often fierce. Fls funnelform or campanulate; tep. and sta. separated by a ring of hairs. Fr. globose to oblong, thick-walled, dry or juicy. Summer. SW US, Mex. Z10.

F. acanthodes Britt. & Rose, misapplied. = *F. cylindraceus.*

F. alamosanus (Britt. & Rose) Britt. & Rose = *F. pottsii* var. *alamosanus.*

F. chrysacanthus (Orcutt) Britt. & Rose. St. simple, globose to short cylindric, to 100×30cm; ribs tuberculate; central spines c10, yellow or red, flattened and twisted, to c5cm, radial spines 12 or more, finer. Fls 4.5cm, yellow to orange; tep. with red-tinged mid-stripe. NW Mex.

F. coloratus H.E. Gates = *F. gracilis.*

F. cornigerus (DC.) Kreutz. = *F. latispinus.*

F. covillei Britt. & Rose = *F. emoryi.*

F. crassihamatus (F.A. Weber) Britt. & Rose = *Sclerocactus uncinatus.*

F. cylindraceus (Engelm.) Orcutt. Simple; st. to 3m×40(–50)cm; cylindric or barrel-shaped; ribs tuberculate; central spines 4–7, red orange or yellow, 7–17cm, sometimes hooked, often recurved, radial spines 15–25, fine or stout. Fl. 3–6cm, green, yellow, or tinged red. NW Mex., SW US.

F. diguetii (F.A. Weber) Britt. & Rose. Resembling *F. emoryi*,

but even larger, to 4m×60cm; spines of juvenile plants (those cult.) yellow. Fl. 4×4cm, red. NW Mex.

F. echidne (DC.) Britt. & Rose. Simple or clustering; st. subglobose to cylindric or clavate, to 35(–100)×20(–30)cm; areoles well separated; central spine 1, 5–10cm, radial spines 7–9. Fl. 2–4.5cm, yellow. E & NE Mex.

F. electracanthus (Lem.) Kreutz. = *F. histrix.*

F. emoryi (Engelm.) Orcutt. Simple; st. globose to cylindric to 1.5(–3)m×45–60(–100)cm; ribs strongly tuberculate; central spine 1, red or brown, 4–10cm, rarely to 25cm, hooked or straight, radial spines 7–9, to 8cm, red or almost white. Fl. to 6–7.5cm, yellow or red. NW Mex., SW Ariz.

F. flavovirens (Scheidw.) Britt. & Rose. Clustering; st. to 30–40×20cm; areoles widely spaced; central spines 4–6, to 8cm, light brown, radial spines 12–20, light brown to grey, some bristle-like. Fl. to 3.5cm, red; tep. narrow. S Mex.

F. fordii (Orcutt) Britt. & Rose. Simple; st. to 25cm diam., depressed-globose to globose; ribs tuberculate, low; central spines 4–7, red or grey, lowermost to 4–7cm, flattened, hooked, sometimes twisted, radial spines c15, to 3cm, paler. Fl. c4cm, lilac to purple, produced on young plants. Baja Calif.

F. gatesii G. Lindsay = *F. gracilis.*

F. glaucescens (DC.) Britt. & Rose Simple or clustering; st. globose to cylindric, to 45(–70)×50(–60)cm, ± glaucous; areoles close-set in adults; spines 4–6(–8), almost equal, to 2.5(–3.5)cm, yellow. Fl. 2–4.5cm, yellow. E Mex.

F. gracilis H.E. Gates. Simple; st. globose, then cylindric, to 1.5–3m×30cm; central spines 4–12, red, twisted and tangled, the larger upper and lower ones flattened, to 7cm, occas. hooked, radial spines c8–12, slender, pale. Fl. 4–6cm, red. Baja Calif.

F. haematacanthus (Salm-Dyck) H. Bravo ex Backeb. & F. Knuth. Simple; st. globose to cylindric, to 30×120×26–36cm, glaucous when young; areoles confluent in old plants; spines blood-red with yellow tips; central spines 4, 4–8cm, radial spines 6(–7). Fl. 6–7cm, purple-pink. E Mex.

F. hamatacanthus (Muehlenpf.) Britt. & Rose Simple, or clustering; st. to 60×30cm, hemispheric to cylindric; ribs rounded and strongly tuberculate; central spines 4–8, lowermost recurved to hooked, to 8cm, radial spines 8–20, 1.5–4(–8)cm long. Fl. 6–10cm, yellow. N & NE Mex., SW US. var. *sinuatus* (A. Dietr.) L. Bens. Sometimes confused with *Thelocactus setispinus* but has fls lacking a red throat. var. *sinuatus* (A. Dietr.) L. Bens. Mature when only 10cm diam.; ribs c13, narrow, more acute; central spines flattened above, radial spines 8–12, some flattened.

F. herrerae Gonzalez = *F. wislizeni* var. *herrerae.*

F. histrix (DC.) G. Lindsay. Simple: st. depressed-globose to short-cylindric, to 110×80cm. Usually much smaller; areoles almost confluent in old plants; spines yellow, red or brown at base; central spines 1–4, uppermost 2–3 to 3.5cm, lowermost to 9cm, projecting and often slightly decurved, except in young plants, radial spines 6–9. Fl. 2–3cm, yellow. NC Mex.

F. horridus Britt. & Rose = *F. peninsulae.*

F. johnsonii (Parry ex Engelm.) Britt. & Rose = *Sclerocactus johnsonii.*

F. latispinus (Haw.) Britt. & Rose. Usually simple; st. typically depressed-globose or flattened, to 10–40×16–40cm; ribs acute, sometimes spiralled; central spines 4, lowermost recurved, v. broad and flattened above, radial spines typically 9–15, acicular. Fl. c4cm, purple-pink, or yellow; tep. narrow. C & S Mex. var. *spiralis* (Karw. ex Pfeiff.) N. Tayl. St. globose to cylindric, to 40(–100)×35cm; ribs 13–16; radial spines fewer, 5–7, stout. Fl. to 5cm; tep. white with pink or purple mid-stripe. S Mex.

F. lecontei (Engelm.) Britt. & Rose = *F. cylindraceus.*

F. macrodiscus (Mart.) Britt. & Rose. Simple; st. depressed-globose or flattened, to 10×30–40cm; ribs crenate between areoles; central spines 4, to 3.5cm, radial spines 6–8, c2–3cm. Fl. 3–4cm, purple-pink. C & S Mex. Z9.

F. mathssonii (Berger ex Schum.) N. Tayl. = *Sclerocactus uncinatus.*

F. melocactiformis Britt. & Rose = *F. histrix.*

F. nobilis sensu Britt. & Rose = *F. latispinus* var. *spiralis.*

F. orcuttii (Engelm.) Britt. & Rose = *F. viridescens.*

F. peninsulae (F.A. Weber) Britt. & Rose. Resembling *F. wislizeni*, esp. in spination and fl.; simple; st. globose, ovoid or clavate, to 70–250×50cm, much smaller and flowering when c10–13cm diam. var. spines 12–20, acute. Baja Calif.

F. pilosus (Gal. ex Salm-Dyck) Werderm. Usually simple in cult., but in nature sometimes forming clumps; st. eventually cylindric, to 3m×50cm; ribs acute in young plants; central spines 6–12, to 5cm, nearly straight, red, radial spines bristly, glassy white. Fl. to 4cm, orange-red; tep. erect. N Mex.

F. pottsii (Salm-Dyck) Backeb. Simple, rarely clustering; st. globose to short cylindric, to 100×15–50cm, grey-green; ribs rather broad and obtuse; central spine 1, to 3(–7.5)cm, straight or slightly upward-curved, radial spines 3–8, to 4.5cm, often v. short. Fl. to 4.5cm, yellow. NW Mex. var. *alamosanus* (Britt. & Rose) G. Unger. St. globose, 15–30cm diam., green; ribs acute and narrow; radial spines dense and yellow. NW Mex.

F. pringlei (J. Coult.) Britt. & Rose = *F. pilosus*.

F. rafaelensis (Purpus) Borg = *F. echidne*.

F. rectispinus (Engelm.) Britt. & Rose = *F. emoryi*.

F. recurvus sensu Borg = *F. latispinus* var. *spiralis*.

F. reppenhagenii G. Unger. Resembling *F. pottsii* var. *alamosanus*; st. simple, globose to short-cylindric, to 30(–80)×9–24cm; ribs obtuse; areoles confluent on old plants; spines yellow, central spine 1, 2.8–8cm, straight, radial spines (6–)7–9(–11), to 4cm. Fl. 2–3cm, yellow or orange. SW Mex.

F. robustus (Otto ex Pfeiff.) Britt. & Rose. Clustering freely, forming mounds up to 1×5m; st. globose to cylindric, to 12cm diam.; ribs acute; areoles widely spaced; central spines 4–7, to 6cm, straight or curved, angled or flattened, radial spines 10–14, bristle-like, nearly white. Fl. 3–4cm, yellow. S Mex. Z9.

F. schwarzii G. Lindsay. Resembling *F. glaucescens*; st. simple, globose to obovoid, to 8×0.5m, flowering when 10cm diam., dark green; areoles confluent; spines (0–)1–4(–5), 0.5–5.5cm, yellow. Fl. to 5cm, yellow. W Mex.

F. setispinus (Engelm.) L. Bens. = *Thelocactus setispinus*.

F. stainesii (Salm-Dyck) Britt. & Rose = *F. pilosus*.

F. tortulispinus H.E. Gates = *F. cylindraceus*.

F. townsendianus Britt. & Rose = *F. peninsulae*.

F. uncinatus (Gal. ex Pfeiff. & Otto) Britt. & Rose = *Sclerocactus uncinatus*.

F. viridescens (Torr. & A. Gray) Britt. & Rose. Simple, rarely clustering; st. globose to short cylindric, to 30(–130)×18–30(–40)cm, bright green; ribs tuberculate, low; central spines 4–9, to 5cm, yellow or red, some flattened, curved, hooked in young plants, radial spines to 19 or more, some bristle-like, others stouter. Fl. to 5cm; tep. green, sometimes the outer tinged red. Baja Calif., SW Calif.

F. viscainensis H.E. Gates = *F. gracilis*.

F. wislizeni (Engelm.) Britt. & Rose. Simple; st. globose to barrel-shaped or cylindric, tapering towards apex, to 1.6(–3)m×45–80cm; ribs high and acute; central spines 4(–8), brown to grey, uppermost 3 terete, lowermost to 10cm, flattened, usually recurved or hooked, radial spines 12–30, bristle-like to acicular. Fl. 5–7.5cm, yellow, orange or red. SW US, NW Mex. var. *herrerae* (Gonzalez) N. Tayl. St. to 2m×45cm; central spines not flattened, straight, radial spines few or 0. NW Mex.

→*Echinocactus* and *Hamatocactus*.

Feronia Corr. Serr.

F. elephantum Corr. Serr. = *Limonia acidissima*.

F. limonia (L.) Swingle = *Limonia acidissima*.

Ferraria Burm. Iridaceae. 10 small, cormous perenn. herbs. Basal lvs few, linear-lanceolate, somewhat rigid, st. lvs shorter, 2-ranked, ovate-lanceolate, clasping. Flowering st. branched, bearing short bracteate cymes; fls short-lived, malodorous; perianth radially symmetric, seg. 6, ovate-lanceolate, ± equal, spreading or slightly deflexed, long-clawed; fil. forming a tube; style br. expanded, petal-like, fringed. Spring. Trop. & S Afr.

F. crispa Burm. Flowering st. 18–45cm; perianth seg. to 2.2cm, deep chestnut spotted and lined in a paler shade or yellow to tan spotted and lined brown, strongly undulate. S Afr.

F. divaricata Sw. Flowering st. to 20cm+; fls sweetly scented or foetid, yellow, green, grey-green, orange-yellow or brown, often marked purple-green or purple-blue, with crisped margins. S Afr.

F. ferrariola (Jacq.) Willd. Flowering st. to 30cm; fls 5–6cm diam., green-white to green-blue, sweetly scented; outer seg. with dark streaks; inner seg. narrow; style br. pale-hairy. S Afr.

F. undulata L. = *F. crispa*.

Ferula L. GIANT FENNEL. Umbelliferae. 172 usually glab., aromatic, robust perennials, from thick rootstock. Lower lvs 3–4-pinnate or ternate, upper lvs reduced to sheathing base. Umbels compound; involucre 0; involucel sparse or 0; fls small, yellow or yellow-white. Medit. to C Asia.

F. assa-foetida L. ASAFOETIDA. To 2m. Lower lvs 30–35×15–25cm, 2-4-ternate to pinnatisect, seg. entire to pinnatisect, to 2.5cm, pubesc. Umbels in a compact pan.; rays 10–50, to 5cm; fls yellow. Summer. Iran. Z8.

F. communis L. GIANT FENNEL. 2–3m. Lvs 25–45×20–30cm, seg. linear to linear-filiform, to 5cm. Term. umbels large, overtopped by long-stalked lat. umbels; rays 20–30; fls yellow. Early summer. Medit. Bronze- and purple-lvd forms occur. 'Gigantea': to 4m; stalk thick, tinted purple; lvs dark green; fls yellow. ssp. *glauca* (L.) Rouy & Camus. Lf seg. linear, glaucous beneath. Medit. Z8.

F. foetida (Bunge) Reg. To 1m. Lower lvs 40×35cm, 2-pinnate, seg. oblong to lanceolate, to 8cm, softly pubesc. beneath, entire. Umbels in loose pan.; rays 25–35; fls *c*15 per umbellule, white to pale yellow. Spring–summer. Russia, C Asia, Afghan., Pak., Iran. Z8.

F. galbaniflua Boiss. & Buhse = *F. gumosa*.

F. glauca L. = *F. communis* ssp. *glauca*.

F. gumosa Boiss. To 1m. Lower lvs to 30×20cm, 3–4-pinnatisect, seg. crowded, narrow-linear, entire to pinnatisect, pubesc. Umbels with 10–20 rays; fls pale yellow. Summer. Iran.

F. jaeschkeana Vatke. = *F. narthex*.

F. linkii Webb & Berth. To 3m. Lower lvs finely divided, seg. linear to filiform, lobes shorter than in *F. communis*. Term. umbels large, surrounded by smaller lat. umbels; rays to 20; fls yellow. Summer. Tenerife, Gran Canaria. Z9.

F. narthex Boiss. Pubesc., aromatic to 2m. Lower lvs 22–40×12.5–10cm, 2-pinnatisect, seg. linear, to 20cm, pubesc. beneath, entire to finely toothed. Umbels with 15–25 rays to 5cm; fls *c*20 per umbellule, pale yellow. Summer. Afghan., Pak. Z8.

F. orientalis L. To 1.5m. Lower lvs 30–50×20–30cm, 4-pinnate, seg. filiform, *c*5mm. Umbels with 7–15 rays, central umbel ± sessile. Fls 8–18 per umbellule, pale yellow. Summer. S Ukraine, SE Bulg., Iran, Iraq. Z7.

F. persica Willd. To 1m. Lower lvs 30–35×25cm, 3–4-pinnate, seg. pinnatisect, 0.4–2cm, pubesc. beneath, entire to toothed. Umbels 17–25-rayed, term. umbel 8–10cm diam.; fls 15 per umbellule, pale yellow. Spring–summer. Iran, Cauc. Z7.

F. sumbul Hook. f. To 2.5m, strongly aromatic. Lower lvs deltoid, 3-pinnate, seg. slightly pinnatifid, lobes cuneate, crenate, glaucous beneath. Umbels compound, to 6cm diam., forming a pan.; rays 7–10; fls yellow. Summer. Turkestan. Z9.

F. tingitana L. To 2m. Lower lvs 30–50×20–45cm, 4-pinnate, seg. ovate, pinnatisect, lobes oblong to lanceolate, to 6mm, glaucous, revolute. Central umbel short-stalked; rays 15–40, unequal; fls 12–25 per umbellule, yellow. Summer. Asia Minor, N Afr. Z9.

Ferulago Koch. Umbelliferae. 47 erect perennials. Basal lvs triangular-ovate to linear in outline, 2–4-pinnate; st. lvs reduced to sheathing bases. Umbels clustered, central fertile, lat. umbels often sterile; involucre and involucel composed of well-developed, persistent bracts and bracteoles. Medit. to C Asia.

F. galbanifera (Mill.) Koch. Glab., to 1m. Basal lvs 20–35×15–30cm, 4–5-pinnate, seg. linear, to 1cm. Infl. paniculate to corymbose; rays 4–8, to 5cm; bracts lanceolate, to 5mm. Fls yellow. Summer. S Eur., C & S Russia, Cauc. Z6.

Fescue *Festuca*.

Festuca L. FESCUE. Gramineae. 300 perenn. grasses, rhizomatous or tufted. Lvs flat, folded or rolled; ligules translucent, papery. Fls in a dense or loose pan.; spikelets flattened laterally. Summer. Cosmop. Z5.

F. alpina Suter. To 28cm. Lvs glab., to 0.5mm diam. Pan. to 3.5cm; spikelets 6mm, 2–4-fld, yellow-green, sometimes violet-tinged. Alps, Pyren.

F. amethystina L. TUFTED FESCUE. To 1m. St. flimsy, forming dense tussocks, flushed mauve. Lvs v. narrow, to 25cm. Pan. to 10cm, flexuous, hispidulous, tinged violet; spikelets to 3cm. C Eur. 'Aprilgrün': lvs olive green. 'Bronzeglanz': lvs tinted bronze. 'Klose': lvs olive. 'Superba': lvs blue; st. amethyst when flowering.

F. arundinacea Schreb. = *F. elatior*.

F. arvensis Augier, Kerguelen & Markgr. = *F. glauca*.

F. capillata Lam. = *F. tenuifolia*.

F. cinerea Vill. To 35cm, densely tufted. Lvs somewhat hard, to 1mm diam., glaucous, usually scabrous. Pan. dense to 6cm; br. glab. or short-pubesc.; spikelets to 7.5mm, glaucous, violet-tinged. S Fr., NW It.

F. crinum-ursi hort. non Rum. = *F. gautieri*.

F. elatior L. MEADOW FESCUE. Perenn. to 120cm, short-rhizomatous or stoloniferous. Lvs flat, narrow-linear, to 8mm diam. Pan. erect or pendulous at apex, to 20cm; br. ascending, scabrous, bearing spikelets almost to the base; spikelets pale green, to 12mm. Summer. Eur., Sib., introd. to Calif. from Eur.

F. eskia Ramond ex DC. To 45cm. St. flimsy, from creeping rhiz., forming compact cushions. Lvs filiform to 20cm, stiff, terete, glab. Pan. to 10cm; loose, pendent, ovoid, spikelets narrowly ovate, to 1cm, green, marked yellow and orange. Pyren.

F. gautieri (Hackel) K. Richt. St. to 50cm. Lvs glab., pungent-often curved, to 0.5mm diam. Pan. dense to 7cm; br. short-pubesc.; spikelets few, to 12mm, yellow-green to stramineous. SW Fr., NE Spain. 'Pic Carlit': dwarf.

F. gigantea (L.) Vill. GIANT FESCUE. To 1.5m. St. tufted. Lvs bright green, glab., flat, linear, to 60×2cm, arching, occas.

scabrous above. Pan. to 50cm, loose, nodding, lanceolate to ovate, spikelets to 2cm. Eur., temp. Asia, N Afr.

F. glacialis Miégev. To 15cm. St. flimsy, forming dense tussocks, clothed at base with old lf sheaths. Lvs filiform, obtuse, glab., grey-green, pan. to 2.5cm; narrow, branched spikelets usually solitary, to 0.5cm. Pyren. and Alps.

F. glauca Vill. BLUE FESCUE; GREY FESCUE. To 40cm. St. upright, densely tufted, blue-green. Lvs glab., glaucous, blue-green, filiform, terete. Pan. to 10cm, dense, obovate, shortly branched, erect, blue-green; rachis glab.; spikelets elliptic to oblong, to 0.5cm. Often confused with *F. cinerea*. Eur. 'Azurit': tal, to 30cm. 'Blaufink' ('Blue Finch'): tall, to 15cm; lvs dull blue. 'Blauglut' ('Blue Ember'): lvs intense silver-blue. 'Blausilber' ('Blue Silver'): lvs strong blue silver. 'Caesia': lvs more slender, vivid blue. 'Daeumling' ('Tom Thumb'): dwarf, to 10cm; lvs blue. 'Frühlingsblau' ('Spring Blue'): lvs strong blue. 'Harz': lvs dark olive, sometimes tinted plum at tips in summer. 'Meerblau' ('Sea Blue'): lvs blue-green; strong-growing. 'Palatinat': lvs blue tinted green. 'Seeigel' ('Sea Urchin'): lvs v. fine, green. 'Silberreiher' ('Silver Heron'): lvs silvery blue. 'Soehrenwald': tall, to 20cm; lvs olive green. 'Bergsilber', 'Glaucantha' and 'Kentucky Blue' are also listed.

F. mairei St Yves. ATLAS FESCUE. To 1.2m, clump-forming. Lvs to 60×0.5cm, flat, semi-rigid, scabrous-serrate, grey-green. Pan. sparsely branched, slender. Moroc. Z7.

F. nigrescens Lam. To 90cm, densely tufted. Lvs soft, usually glab., dark green, to 1mm diam. Pan. to 10cm, secund; br. scabrous; spikelets to 9.5mm. S, W, & C Eur.

F. ovina L. SHEEP'S FESCUE. To 60cm forming dense tussocks. Lvs glab. to scabrous, green or slightly glaucous, filiform, closely infolded, rigid to 25cm. Pan. to 12cm, erect, lanceolate to narrowly oblong, tinged-purple; spikelets borne mainly on one side of rachis, elliptic, to oblong, to 1cm. N temp. regions. 'Glauca Minima': lvs intensely glaucous blue.

F. ovina var. *glauca* (Vill.) Hackel = *F. glauca*.

F. paniculata (L.) Schinz & Thell. To 1m. St. erect, densely tufted. Lvs rigid, long, to 0.5cm, wide. Pan. to 15cm, ovate to obovate; spikelets broadly ovate, to 0.5cm, rust-brown tinted purple. S Eur.

F. pumila (Vill.) = *F. quadriflora*.

F. punctoria Sm. To 30cm. St. rigid, tufted. Lf blades tightly inrolled, terete, filiform, to 7.5cm, v. glaucous, blue-grey. Pan. to 5cm, lanceolate to narrowly obovate, dense; spikelets obovate, to 1cm. N Turk.

F. pyrenaica Reut. To 32cm, loosely tufted. Lvs to 0.5mm diam., soft, slightly pubesc., somewhat pink below. Pan. to 3.5cm; spikelets to 6.5mm, grey-violet. C & E Pyren.

F. quadriflora Honck. To 30cm. St. scabrous. Lvs slightly pungent, to 1mm diam. Pan. lax, erect to 4cm; br. scabrous; spikelets few, to 1cm, usually glaucous, violet. Eur.

F. rubra L. RED FESCUE. To 110cm. Loosely caespitose, usually long-rhizomatous. Lvs to 1mm diam. when folded, pubesc., somewhat pink below. Pan. lax to 14cm, br. glab. or pubesc.; spikelets to 1cm, bright green or glaucous or plum-tinted. Eur.

F. rupicola Heuff. Densely tufted. St. to 65cm, scabrous above. Lvs to 32.5cm×1mm, scabrous. Pan. to 9.5cm, lax; br. scabrous; spikelets green, to 8mm. C Eur., Balk.

F. scoparia A. Kerner ex Nyman non Hook. f. = *F. gautieri*.

F. sulcata (Hackel) Nyman = *F. rupicola*.

F. tenuifolia Sibth. To 55cm, densely caespitose. St. usually scabrous above. Lvs to 0.5mm diam. Pan. lax to 8cm; br. scabrous; spikelets to 6.5mm, somewhat green, occas. proliferating. W & C Eur.

F. valesiaca Schleich. ex Gaudin. To 50cm. St. scabridulous above. Lvs to 0.5mm diam., scabrous, pruinose. Pan. somewhat interrupted, to 7cm; br. scabridulous; spikelets glaucous, to 6.5mm. Eur. 'Silbersee' ('Silver Sea', 'Seven Seas'): dwarf and compact; lvs silvery blue.

F. varia Haenke. To 55cm. St. scabrous above. Lvs pungent, glab., to 1mm diam. Pan. to 9cm lax; br. densely short-pubesc.; spikelets few, to 11mm, glaucous, violet-tinted. E Alps.

F. vivipara (L.) Sm. V. similar to *F. ovina* except spikelets producing small plantlets instead of flts. N Eur. 'In': v. dwarf, to 5cm.

Fetter Bush *Lyonia lucida; Pieris floribunda.*
Fever Bush *Garrya fremontii.*
Feverfew *Tanacetum parthenium.*
Fever Root *Triosteum perfoliatum.*
Fever Tree *Pinckneya pubens.*
Feverwort *Triosteum.*

Fevillea L.
F. pedata Sims = *Telfairia pedata.*

Few-flowered Leek *Allium paradoxum.*

Fibigia Medik. Cruciferae. 14 perenn. herbs, to 75cm. Lvs simple, densely pubesc. Fls 4-merous in term. rac. Fr. a silicle, elliptic-oblong, septum membranous. Eur. to Afghan.

F. clypeata (L.) Medik. 30–75cm. Lvs oblong-lanceolate, woolly, usually entire. Pet. 8–13mm, yellow. Fr. 14–28×9–13mm, oblong-elliptic, short stellate-pubesc. Eur. to Iran. Z7.

F. eriocarpa (DC.) Sibth. & Sm. Similar to *F. clypeata* except lvs linear-oblong, usually toothed. Fr. simple- and stellate pubesc. Greece, Cauc. Z8.

F. lunarioides (Willd.) Sibth. & Sm. 5–30cm. St. much-branched, woody at base. Lvs lanceolate-obovate or spathulate, tomentose, entire. Pet. to 16mm, bright yellow. Fr. 12–22×9–18mm, obovate-elliptic, pointed at both ends, hairy. Aegean Is. Z7.

F. triquetra (DC.) Boiss. ex Prantl. Similar to *F. lunarioides* but lvs with adpressed, hoary pubescence. Fr. less than 8mm wide. W Balk. Z6.
→*Alyssum* and *Farsetia.*

Ficus L. FIG. Moraceae. 800 decid. or everg. lactiferous trees, shrubs, and woody root-climbing or strangling vines; stipules enclosing buds at first leaving ring-like scars at nodes. Lvs simple (rarely palmately or pinnately lobed and then mostly in saplings), thin to thick. Fls minute, unisexual, wholly enclosed within a fleshy receptacle (syconium or 'fig'), entered by an apical orifice and pollinated by fig wasps. Trop. and subtrop. Z10 unless specified.

F. acuminata auct. non Roxb. = *F. parietalis.*
F. acuminata Roxb. = *F. subulata.*
F. afzelii G. Don ex Loud. = *F. saussureana.*
F. altissima Bl. COUNCIL TREE; FALSE BANYAN; LOFTY FIG. Large, spreading tree to 23m or more. Like *F. benghalensis* but with fewer aerial roots; crown to 40m or more across. Lvs glab., to 25×15cm, ± thick, elliptic to ovate, apex rounded or obtuse, tip shortly acuminate, base broad, rounded, venation palmipinnate. Figs ovoid, sessile, glabrescent, to 1.5cm diam., yellow, ripening scarlet. S & SE Asia to Malesia.

F. americana Aubl. WEST INDIAN LAUREL FIG; JACQUINIA-LEAVED FIG; WERCKLE'S RUBBER TREE. Glab. shrub or tree to 30m, with few aerial roots on lower trunk. Lvs to 5×2.5cm, subcoriaceous, oblong, elliptic or more usually obovate, apex rounded or obtuse, base usually narrowed, venation finely pinnate. Figs paired, globose, to 0.7cm diam., glab., green with scattered white or pale green flecks. Bahamas, Antilles and C Amer. to S Amer. Some plants in trade are *F. microcarpa*. Z9.

F. amplissima Sm. BAT TREE; TSIELA. Large glab. tree, similar to *F. rumphii* but with ovate, elliptic or elliptic-lanceolate lvs. Figs purple. Penins. India, Maldive Is., Sri Lanka.

F. angustifolia Miq., non Roxb. = *F. citrifolia.*

F. arnottiana (Miq.) Miq. PARAS PIPAL. Large glab. shrub or small tree, often epiphytic. Lvs thinly textured, broadly ovate, apex acute, tip shortly acuminate, base cordate; basal veins widely spreading. Fig 5–8mm across (10mm across in var. *subcostata*). S Asia (Himal. southwards), Sri Lanka.

F. aspera Forst. f. Decid. or everg. tree to 20m. Lvs pinnately lobed to coarsely dentate to crenate or entire, slightly rough to the touch above, hairy beneath, to 32×15.5cm, thin, ovate or oblong-ovate to elliptic, obtusely subacuminate, tip to 4cm in sapling lvs, base v. oblique; venation palmipinnate, lat. veins prominent. Figs usually rami- or cauliflorous, spherical, pubesc. to 25mm diam., yellow ripening red. Vanuatu. Usually grown as one or other of the following cvs. 'Canonii': lvs dark bronze-red above, vinous-purple or red beneath, petioles and midrib bright red; figs ripening scarlet. 'Parcellii': (CLOWN FIG; MOSAIC FIG): lvs marbled, speckled or dotted ivory white on dark green; figs ripening pink to purple.

F. aurea Nutt. GOLDEN FIG; STRANGLER FIG; FLORIDA STRANGLER FIG. Semi-decid. tree to 20m, often starting as an epiphyte and strangling support, becoming somewhat buttressed, growing aerial roots. Lvs dark green above, paler beneath, glab. (save for small rusty hairs on either side of the midrib beneath), to 17×8cm, ± thick, elliptic to oblong or obovate, apex obtuse or subacute, tip small, shortly acuminate, base subacute to slightly cordate; venation pinnate, midrib elevated beneath. Figs usually paired, subglobose, somewhat puberulent, to 0.8cm diam., ripening orange-yellow. S Flor., Carib. Not as finely veined as *F. citrifolia.*

F. auriculata Lour. ROXBURGH FIG. Relatively low, thick-stemmed, spreading everg. (or briefly decid.) tree sometimes to 18m across. Lvs initially maroon or mahogany becoming bright green, slightly toothed or entire, glab. above, pubesc. along main veins beneath, to 40×34cm on more, thin, ovate, acute or obtuse, base cordate; venation palmipinnate, prominent. Figs rami- or cauliflorous, aggregated, depressed-globose to pyriform, silky-hairy, green to red-brown with conspicuous white or rusty flecks. Himal. to Thail., Indochina and S China.

F. australis hort. non Willd. = *F. obliqua*.

F. australis Willd. non hort. = *F. rubiginosa* 'Australis'.

F. barbata Miq. = *F. villosa*.

F. barteri Sprague. Glab. shrub or small tree, sometimes beginning life as an epiphyte and later strangling its host. Lvs bright green above, paler beneath, 10–30×1.5–7cm, coriaceous, oblong to linear elliptic, tip sharply caudate-acuminate, base acute; venation finely pinnate. Figs axillary, solitary or paired, all but glab., orange-yellow to orange, to 1.1(–2.5)cm diam. W & C Trop. Afr.

F. belgica hort. = *F. elastica* 'Belgica'.

F. bellingeri C. Moore & Betche = *F. watkinsiana*.

F. benghalensis L. BANYAN TREE; EAST INDIAN FIG TREE; INDIAN BANYAN. V. large tree, epiphytic when young, eventually reaching 30m in height and in spread to 200m diam. with many buttresses and aerial roots. Lvs bronze when young, later green, glab. above, velvety-pubesc. to glab. beneath, to 25×17cm, rather leathery, broadly ovate to elliptic, tip blunt or shortly acuminate, base rounded or truncate or subcordate; lat. veins 5–7 per side. Figs in axill. pairs globose, puberulous, to 1.8cm diam., orange-red ripening to scarlet, with indistinct white flecks. S Asia. 'Krishnae'; (KRISHNA FIG; KRISHNA'S CUP): lf blades inrolled and fused, cup-shaped.

F. benjamina L. BENJAMIN TREE; WEEPING FIG; TROPIC LAUREL; JAVA TREE; SMALL-LEAVED RUBBER PLANT; WARINGIN. Graceful shrub or tree, epiphytic when young, eventually attaining at least 30m; br. drooping, aerial roots, few from br. or forming trunk. Lvs glab., to 13×6.3cm, thinly leathery, ovate-elliptic, tip cuspidate base obtuse to rounded; lat. veins 8–12 per side. Figs in pairs, globose to slightly oblong, to 1.1×0.8cm, green maturing orange-red to red or scarlet and finally purplish-black. S & SE Asia through Malesia to N Aus. and SW Pacific. 'Exotica'; (EXOTIC FIG): tree with slender drooping br. and long-tipped lvs with twisting tips. 'Golden King': habit pyramidal, tall, narrow. 'Golden Princess': small tree; lvs elliptic. 'Hawaii': small tree, br. short, curving upward; lvs glossy, elliptic. 'Indica': br. spreading; lvs narrow elliptic. 'Major': lvs large, elliptic. 'Rysenhout': br. spreading upward. 'Variegata': lvs rich green with white variegation. var. *nuda* (Miq.) Barrett. Lvs narrower, tip longer, more slender; figs off-white or red-brown, with twisted, narrowed base. The foliage also forms tufted masses.

F. benjamina var.*comosa* (Roxb.) Kurz = *F. benjamina* var. *nuda*.

F. bennettii Seem. = *F. habrophylla*.

F. binnendykii (Miq.) Miq. NARROW-LEAF FIG. Glab. shrub or tree. Lvs in young plants 18–26×3–4.5cm, linear-lanceolate, later to 9×3–3.5cm and elliptic to oblong-lanceolate, tip long-acuminate, base broadly acute; venation palmipinnate. Figs solitary or in pairs, ovoid or subglobose, to 10mm across. SE Asia to Philipp. 'Amstelveen': habit narrow. Lvs to 12cm, oblong-lanceolate, tapering finely, semi-rigid with a slightly depressed centre.

F. brandegeei Standl. BRANDEGEE'S FIG; DESERT FIG. Tree or shrub. Lvs pale green above, glaucescent beneath, glab., to 10.5×8cm, coriaceous, broadly deltoid-ovate, obtuse, base subcordate or cordate; venation somewhat palmipinnate. Figs globose, glab., 1.5cm diam. Baja Calif.

F. brassii R. Br. ex Sab. = *F. sur*.

F. brevifolia Nutt. = *F. citrifolia*.

F. buxifolia De Wildeman = *F. lingua*.

F. callosa Willd. CALLOSE-LEAVED FIG; SHINY-LEAVED FIG. Decid. tree to 30m or more; buttresses short. Lvs slightly rough to touch below; sapling lvs distinctly lobed, sometimes toothed toward base, to 75×20cm; ordinary lvs smaller, entire, pale beneath, to 28×15cm, rather leathery, elliptic to oblong-elliptic, apex obtuse to rounded, base rounded to cordate; venation pinnate, elevated beneath. Figs ripening green-yellow, 2cm across. S & SE Asia to Moluccas, Sulawesi and the Philipp.

F. calophylloides Elmer = *F. subcordata*.

F. canonii (Bull) N.E. Br. = *F. aspera* 'Canonii'.

F. capensis Thunb. = *F. sur*.

F. carica L. BROWN TURKEY FIG; COMMON FIG; FIG. Decid. shrub or tree to 9m. Crown rounded. Lvs 3(–5)-lobed, rough above, pubesc. beneath, to 20(–30)×18cm across, broadly ovate to orbicular, lobes elongate, dentate or crenate. Figs solitary, pyriform or ± globose, glab., green to maroon or brown, 2–5cm diam. Cyprus, Turk. and Cauc. to Turkmen Rep. and Afghan. Z7. All figs in cult. are ssp. *carica* of which there are many edible cvs. Wild plants with ♂ fls have been referred to var. *caprificus* Tausch & Rav.

F. caulocarpa (Miq.) Miq. Semi-deciduous, frequently multi-stemmed and spreading strangler-tree to 20m. Aerial roots numerous. Lvs glab., to 22×8.5cm, rather thin, narrowly oblong-elliptic to oblong-ovate, apex obtuse, tip acuminate, base rounded to obtuse; venation pinnate, slightly raised below. Figs axill. crowded, in fascicles of 2–4, pedunculate, globose,

maturing dull grey-purple, to 0.6cm across. Sri Lanka and SE Asia to the Philipp. and Solomon Is.

F. cavronii Carr. Erect, robust. Lvs bright green above, rusty beneath with a yellow-white midrib and raised venation, narrowly obovate, to 45×24cm or more, apex rounded, base attenuate. Figs not reported. Reputedly from Brazil, but only young plants have been described and it may properly be a stage of the African *F. saussureana*.

F. cerasiformis Desf. = *F. parietalis*.

F. chrysocoma Bl. = *F. drupacea*.

F. citrifolia Mill. SHORTLEAF FIG; JAMAICA CHERRY. Smooth, somewhat open-growing tree to 16m or a shrub; aerial roots few. Lvs glab. 2.5–20×1.5–12cm, thin, lanceolate to ovate to oblong-ovate to elliptic, tip cuspidate or acuminate, base rounded to subcordate; venation slightly palmipinnate, midrib elevated beneath. Figs usually in pairs, pedunculate, globose to pyriform, glab., scarlet when mature, sometimes with white flecks, to 1.2(–1.5)cm diam. Bermuda, S Flor., Bahamas, Antilles, Mex. and C Amer. S to Parag.

F. columnaris C. Moore = *F. macrophylla* ssp. *columnaris*.

F. comosa Roxb. = *F. benjamina* var. *nuda*.

F. confusa Elmer = *F. subulata*.

F. cordata Thunb. Lvs ovate to elliptic, base cordate to rounded. S Afr. to Angola. ssp. *salicifolia* (Vahl) C. Berg. WILLOW-LEAVED FIG. Shrub or small tree. Lvs glab., to 15×5cm, v. thin to somewhat coriaceous, narrowly ovate-lanceolate or oblong-lanceolate, apex gradually narrowing, acuminate, base rounded or subcordate; venation slightly palmipinnate. Figs solitary or in pairs shortly pedunculate, glab., globose, ripening red, to 0.7cm across. Trop. Afr. N to the Sahara (entering Alg., Libya and Egypt), Socotra and S Arabian Penins.

F. cunia Hamilt. ex Roxb. = *F. semicordata*.

F. cyathistipula Warb. Much-branched tree to 15m, sometimes beginning life as an epiphyte. Lvs glossy or dull green, glab., to 20(–22)×7cm, rather leathery, obovate to oblanceolate, apex obtuse, tip shortly acuminate, base attenuate to cuneate, venation pinnate, widely spaced. Figs axillary, solitary or in pairs or threes, pedunculate, globose or obovoid, shortly white- or brown-pubesc., rough to touch, pale green to pale yellow, 2–3cm across. Trop. W, C & E Afr., S to Angola, Zam. and Malawi.

F. dammaropsis Diels. DINNER-PLATE FIG. Straggly-branched open shrub or small tree to 10(–13)m. Lvs strongly rugose and undulate, grey-green and glab. above with deep channels, paler beneath with elevated, often red venation, usually pubesc., often rough to the touch, to 70(–90)×60cm, v. thick, broadly ovate, apex obtuse, tip shortly acuminate, base obtuse or rounded; venation pinnate. Figs axill., solitary or in pairs, entirely enclosed in a basket of overlapping scales, ripening purple, the whole to 10×15cm. New Guinea.

F. decora hort. = *F. elastica* 'Decora'.

F. dekdekena (Miq.) A. Rich. = *F. thonningii*.

F. deltoidea Jack. MISTLETOE FIG; MISTLETOE RUBBER PLANT. Largely glab. shrub or small tree to 7m, sometimes epiphytic. Lvs bright green above and ferruginous to olive-brown or ochre beneath, entire, to 8×7.5cm, stiffly coriaceous, broadly spathulate to obovate, apex rounded or deltoid, base usually cuneate. Lvs in young plants narrowly elliptic to lanceolate, acute, penninerved (feature retained in adults of var. *diversifolia* (Bl.) Corner). Figs axill., paired, pedunculate, subglobose to ellipsoid, ripening through dull yellow and orange to red, to 10mm across. S Thail. to Sumatra, Java, Borneo and Palawan.

F. diversifolia Bl. = *F. deltoidea* var. *diversifolia*.

F. diversifolia var. *lutescens* (Desf.) King = *F. deltoidea* var. *diversifolia*.

F. doescheri hort. = *F. elastica* 'Doescheri'.

F. drupacea Thunb. BROWN-WOOLLY FIG; PAYAPA. Large, spreading, usually everg. strangler-tree to 20m or more. Lvs smooth brown-hairy, then glab., to 26(–35)×14–16cm, coriaceous, narrowly elliptic to oblong-elliptic to obovate, apex usually obtuse, passing into a broad, short, acuminate tip, base usually narrowed or cordate; venation distinctly raised, palmipinnate. Figs in pairs, sometimes crowded, glab., ripening from yellow-ochre through orange to red, to 35×20cm. SE Asia. var. *pubescens* (Roth) Corner. MYSORE FIG. Buds usually rusty-pubesc.; fig often hairy at first, with basal bracts to 6×8mm. S & SE Asia, Sri Lanka.

F. dryepondtiana Gentil DRYEPONDT FIG. Epiphytic shrub, later strangling its support and developing into a large tree. Lvs somewhat rugose, green above, red-purple or bronze beneath (at least in young plants), entire or undulate, glab. save for fine puberulence on veins below, to 16(–32.5)×6(–15)cm, papery to leathery, oblong or elliptic to ovate or obovate, apex acute, tip caudate-acuminate, base rounded to cordate; venation pinnate, strongly elevated beneath. Figs in clusters on old wood, globose or slightly pyriform, pedunculate, slightly pubesc., yellow-brown with white flecks, 3–5cm diam. C Trop. Afr. Z11.

F. eburnea hort. = *F. septica*.

F. edulis Bur. = *F. habrophylla*.

F. eetveldiana André. Tree with grey bark. Lvs bright green above, paler beneath, glab., to 30×20cm, rather thin, broadly ovate to elliptic, apex obtuse to rounded, tip v. shortly acuminate, base tapered to slightly cordate; venation pinnate, well-spaced, raised beneath. Figs not reported. C Afr.

F. elastica Roxb. ex Hornem. INDIA RUBBER TREE; INDIA RUBBER FIG; RUBBER PLANT; SNAKE FIG; ASSAM RUBBER. Initially epiphytic, ultimately a giant banyan to 60m with a spreading crown, high buttresses and aerial roots. Stipules united, pink to scarlet, to 20cm. Lvs glab., glossy dark green above, hardly paler beneath, to 30(–45)×15cm (diminishing as plants age), coriaceous, oblong to elliptic, apex rounded, tip acuminate or abruptly apiculate, base rounded; venation finely pinnate, midrib red or pale, strongly raised beneath. Figs in pairs, or crowded, sessile with the bract bases forming a persistent thickened pseudostalk, oblong, glab., green with darker flecks, later yellow, to 1.1×0.7cm. E Himal. to N Malay Penins., Sumatra and Java. 'Belgica': lvs slightly corrugated. 'Burgundy Knight': lvs dark vinous red, midribs scarlet. 'Decora': broad-lvd, surfaces shining; midrib creamy white, red beneath (possibly more than one variant grown under this name). 'Doescheri': lvs variegated green, grey-green, creamy yellow, or white; petioles and midrib pink. 'Foliis Aureomarginata': lvs with golden margins to 2.5cm wide, most prominent in autumn. 'Rubra': lvs distinctly maroon-red when young, midribs on older lvs red. 'Schrijveriana': lvs broad, variegated green, grey-green, creamy yellow and white; petioles red. Vigorous. 'Tricolor': lvs grey-green, variegated pink and creamy white; midrib red. 'Variegata': lvs pale green with white or yellow margin.

F. elastica var. *belgica* L.H. & E.Z. Bail. = *F. elastica* 'Belgica'.

F. elastica var. *decora* Guillaum. = *F. elastica* 'Decora'.

F. elastica var. *rubra* L.H. & E.Z. Bail. = *F. elastica* 'Rubra'.

F. elastica var. *variegata* (Gentil) Nehrl. = *F. elastica* 'Variegata'.

F. erecta Thunb. Large, many-stemmed straggling shrub or small tree to 4.5m. Lvs flat, entire save for some teeth near apex, slightly rough, to 20×10cm, v. thin, obovate to narrowly obovate, apex acute to obtuse, passing into an acuminate tip, base obtuse or rounded; venation slightly palmipinnate. Figs solitary, usually pedunculate, glab., globose or pear-shaped, to 1.7cm diam. China, Taiwan, Ryukyu Is., Jap. and Korea. Includes *F. sieboldii* (Miq.) Corner, with linear to oblong-lanceolate lvs. var. *beecheyana* (Hook. & Arn.) King. HEAVENLY FAIRY FRUIT. Differs in hispid-villous pubescence of most parts and rougher lf surface, the bases are also more angular and commonly subcordate, and the figs larger (to 2.5cm across). China, Ryukyu Is., Taiwan.

F. eriobotryoides Kunth & Bouché = *F. saussureana*.

F. eugeniifolia (Liebm.) Hemsl. = *F. americana*.

F. eugenioides (Miq.) F. Muell. ex Miq. = *F. obliqua*.

F. eximia Schott = *F. citrifolia*.

F. exotica hort. = *F. benjamina* 'Exotica'.

F. fairchildii Backer = *F. subcordata*.

F. falcata Thunb. = *F. punctata*.

F. forstenii Miq. FALSE PAYAPA. Resembles *F. drupacea*, but lvs relatively broader for their length and of 'heavier' appearance with prominent main veins. Large tree with widely spreading br. Lvs initially puberulent beneath, to 22×8.5cm, v. thick, elliptic to obovate, tip abruptly cuspidate. Figs axill., base surrounded by triangular bracts, smooth, green at first, later scarlet, to 2.3×1.5cm. Malaya, Borneo, Sulawesi, Philipp.

F. foveolata Wallich ex Miq. = *F. sarmentosa*.

F. foveolata var. *nipponica* (Franch. & Savat.) King = *F. sarmentosa* var. *nipponica*.

F. garciniifolia Miq. = *F. subcordata*.

F. gemella Wallich ex Miq. = *F. neriifolia*.

F. gibbosa Bl. = *F. tinctoria*.

F. glabella Bl. = *F. virens* var. *glabella*.

F. glomerata Roxb. = *F. racemosa*.

F. glomerata auct. non Roxb. = *F. virens*.

F. gnaphalocarpa (Miq.) A. Rich. = *F. sycomorus*.

F. habrophylla G. Bennett ex Seem. Tree to 12m with rounded crown. Lvs to 30×21cm, coriaceous, smooth, broadly, shortly acuminate, base narrowly acute, cordate or panduriform, entire except sometimes for minute teeth around base; lateral veins prominent beneath. Figs to 40mm across stalks to 24mm long, glabrescent, ripening red to purple-black. New Caledonia, Loyalty Is.

F. hauilii Blanco = *F. septica*.

F. hemsleyana Standl., non King = *F. citrifolia*.

F. henneana Miq. = *F. superba* var. *henneana*.

F. hillii Bail. = *F. microcarpa* var. *hillii*.

F. hispida L. f. ROUGH-LEAF FIG; BRISTLY FIG; ROUGH RUBBER TREE. Bushy shrub or small tree. Lvs finely serrate, hispid

above, rough beneath, to 30.5×15cm, thin, narrowly elliptic to obovate or oblanceolate, apex obtuse, tip blunt to cuspidate, base rounded to subcordate; venation prominent. Figs clustered, sometimes in branching sprays to 1m long, pedunculate, oblate or spherical, densely pubesc., dull green with flecks of white and sometimes scale-bracts, later yellow, to 2.5×2.5cm. SE Asia to S New Guinea and Aus.

F. hookeri Miq., non Sweet = *F. hookeriana*.

F. hookeriana Corner. Large glab. tree, giving off aerial roots later forming pillar-stems. Lvs to 28×16cm, thinly coriaceous, usually broadly elliptic or ovate, apex obtuse to rounded, tip broadly and shortly acuminate, base broad, obtuse to subcordate; venation pinnate. Figs in pairs, base surrounded by a cup of fused bracts, ovoid, to 2.5cm diam. E Himal. to Yunnan.

F. indica L. non auct. = *F. benghalensis*.

F. indica auct., non L. = *F. sundaica*.

F. infectoria auct., non Willd. = *F. virens*.

F. jacqiniifolia A. Rich. = *F. americana*.

F. jaliscana S. Wats. = *F. petiolaris*.

F. japonica Bl. = *F. erecta*.

F. krishnae C. DC. = *F. benghalensis* 'Krishnae'.

F. lacor auct., non Hamilt. = *F. virens*.

F. laevigata Vahl = *F. citrifolia*.

F. leprieurii Miq. = *F. natalensis* ssp. *leprieurii*.

F. lingua Warb. ex De Wildeman & T. Dur. BOX-LEAVED FIG Epilithic or epiphytic shrubs, becoming stranglers, sometimes developing into big trees. Lvs glab., to 4.5(–5.5)×1.5(–3)cm, thinly coriaceous, obovate to narrowly obdeltoid, apex obtuse to emarginate, base cuneate to obtuse; venation pinnate. Figs solitary or in pairs, pedunculate, globose, sparsely pubesc., white to yellow to deep red, to 0.5cm diam. Moz. to Kenya and Uganda across C Afr. to Cameroun; also in W Afr.

F. longifolia hort. = *F. binnendykii*.

F. lutea Vahl. LAGOS RUBBER TREE; VOGEL'S FIG; ZULU FIG; NEKBUDU. Epiphytic shrub, later strangling, ultimately a tree to 21m or more with a large trunk and spreading br., sometimes producing aerial roots. Lvs glab. above, pubesc. beneath, veins beneath, to 20(–45)×10(–20)cm, coriaceous, oblong, elliptic or oblong-obovate, tip blunt or shortly acuminate, base rounded or cordate; venation pinnate, distinctly raised beneath. Figs sometimes in clusters on ramiflorous short shoots, usually paired, aggregated, subglobose but often angular, initially woolly-pilose but later silky-pubesc., at first green, later yellow or orange and finally dark red or tan, 2×2cm, with basal bracts. Cape verde Is., Trop. and S Afr., Madag., Seych.

F. lutescens Parmentier ex Desf. = *F. deltoidea* var. *diversifolia*.

F. lyrata Warb. FIDDLE-LEAF FIG; FIDDLE-LEAF; BANJO FIG. Coarsely-leaved tree to 12m, sometimes starting as an epiphyte and strangling its host; buttresses and aerial roots 0. Lvs glossy green and puckered above, initially finely hairy, later glab., to 45×30.5cm, coriaceous, obovate to lyrate-pandurate, broadly rounded; venation pinnate, fairly prominent. Figs solitary or in pairs, globose, sometimes oblique, finely hairy, green with white flecks, 2.5–3cm or more diam. Trop. W & C Afr.

F. macrocarpa Hueg. ex Kunth & Bouché = *F. macrophylla*.

F. macrocarpa Bl., non Hueg. ex Kunth & Bouché = *F. punctata*.

F. macrophylla Desf. ex Pers. MORETON BAY FIG; AUSTRALIAN BANYAN. Tree to 55m, sometimes beginning as an epiphyte and later overwhelming host, crown spreading with enormous pale br., snake-like buttresses and aerial roots. Lvs green and glab. above, paler beneath, 10–25×7–12cm, coriaceous, oblong to elliptic or ovate, apex obtuse or broadly acute, base rounded to cordate; venation finely pinnate. Figs usually paired, ovoid to oblong-ellipsoid, glab. to puberulent, green to purple with large, yellow-green flecks, to 1.8cm; peduncles 2–2.5cm, swollen. Aus. (Queensld, NSW). ssp.*columnaris* (C. Moore) P. Green LORD HOWE ISLAND BANYAN. multi-stemmed, wide-spreading, lvs relatively broad for their length, and lvs and figs somewhat smaller; adult lvs remain rusty-pubesc. beneath. Young plants superficially resemble *F. elastica*, but the lvs appear less leathery.

F. magnolioides Borzi = *F. macrophylla*.

F. mallotocarpa Warb. = *F. sur*.

F. microcarpa L. f. INDIAN LAUREL; CURTAIN FIG; MALAY BANYAN; CHINESE BANYAN; GLOSSY-LEAF FIG. Large glab. banyan to 25m, ultimately with a spreading crown to 30m or more across and festoons of aerial roots forming 'curtains'. Lvs usually glab., to 12×9cm, coriaceous, often slightly asymmetric, narrowly to broadly elliptic to obovate (var.*latifolia*), apex acute to obtuse, base cuneate to rounded, venation finely pinnate, prominent pair of basal veins; lat. veins 7–12 with strong development of veins. Figs usually paired, sessile (shortly pedunculate in var. *naumannii*), ± globose, glab. or hairy, ripening purple to black, 9–12mm diam. Ryukyu Is. and S China, S & SE Asia to Aus. and Pacific Is. Sometimes grown under the misapplied names *F. retusa* or *F. nitida*. Var., *crassifolia*, has been listed (also known as 'Panda'). 'Hawaii': lvs shiny, leathery, variegated. 'Variegata': habit small; lvs variegated white. var. *hillii* (Bail.) Corner. Lvs to 11×6cm, narrow, the base cuneate, the basal veins less prominent and elongated. Aus. (Queensld), New Caledonia and S Malesia.

F. microcarpa Vahl, non L. f. = *F. thonningii*.

F. microcarpa var. *rigo* (Bail.) Corner = *F. rigo*.

F. microphylla hort., non Desf. = *F. rubiginosa*.

F. mildbraedii Hutch. = *F. barteri*.

F. montana Burm. f. OAKLEAF FIG. Lax shrub or half-climber. Lvs wavy or irregularly indented or lobed, glab. and smooth or slightly scabrous above, scabrous beneath, to 15×7.5cm, thin, oblong, apex acute, base rounded or subcordate; venation prominent beneath. Figs solitary or in pairs, pedunculate, urn-shaped, green, surface rough with white flecks and tubercular scales, to 0.8×0.5cm. SE Asia to Java and Borneo. The related *F. heteropoda* (Philippines, Sulawesi and Moluccas) and *F. copiosa* (Sulawesi to Micronesia, Solomon Is. and Australia) are occas. cultivated; the lvs are usually opposite not alt.

F. mysorensis Heyne ex Roth = *F. drupacea* var. *pubescens*.

F. mysorensis var. *pubescens* Roth = *F. drupacea* var. *pubescens*.

F. natalensis Hochst. NATAL FIG. Epiphytic or terrestrial shrub or tree, sometimes a strangler. Lvs glab., to 10×5cm or more, coriaceous, elliptic to obovate to obdeltoid, apex acute to obtuse, base acute to obtuse; venation pinnate. Figs solitary or in pairs, pedunculate globose, glab. to puberulent, to 1.5cm diam. Trop. and S Afr. ssp. *leprieurii* (Miq.) C. Berg. Lvs ± broadly obdeltoid to obovate with midrib disappearing well before the apex and relatively small figs. NW Zam. to Senegal. 'Westland': habit upright; lvs drooping, pale green when young, turning dark.

F. nekbudu Warb. = *F. lutea*.

F. nemoralis Wallich ex Miq. = *F. neriifolia* var. *nemoralis*.

F. neriifolia Sm. Small glab. tree, briefly decid. in early spring. Lvs entire or undulate, initially red, later green above, paler beneath and rough to touch, glab., to 15(–22.5)×5(–7.5)cm, chartaceous, narrowly elliptic, apex acute, passing into a distinct acumen, base rounded or subcordate; venation pinnate, raised beneath. Figs solitary or in pairs, ripening red, to 0.75cm diam. Himal. (Nepal eastwards) to SW China (Yunnan). var. *nemoralis* (Wallich ex Miq.) Corner. Figs ± sessile. Himal. Plants in cult. may be *F. celebensis* Corner, a sp. from N. Sulawesi with lanceolate lvs closely related to *F. tinctoria* and *F. subulata* (but without the pseudostrangling habit and aerial roots of those spp.) and previously known as *F. irregularis* Miq. Z9.

F. neumannii Cels ex Kunth & Bouché = *F. lutea*.

F. nipponica Franch. & Savat. = *F. sarmentosa* var. *nipponica*.

F. nitida Thunb. non auct. = *F. benjamina*.

F. nitida auct. non Thunb. = *F. microcarpa*.

F. nota (Blanco) Merrill. TIBIG. Tree to 9m high or crooked shrub. Lvs coarsely serrate to almost entire, rough, pubesc. on veins above, silky-pubesc. beneath, to 25×15cm or more, chartaceous, ovate, apex acuminate, base obtuse to subariculate, venation palmipinnate, prominent. Figs in fascicles on naked br. to 20cm long arising from the ground upwards along trunk, globose to oblate, pubesc. but glossy, maturing yellow, then scarlet, to 3.5×4cm. Philipp., N Borneo.

F. nymphaeifolia Mill. Glab. tree to 35m, sometimes with buttress-like aerial roots. Stipules to 4cm, pink. Lvs dark green above, off-white beneath, to 17.2(–30)×13.5(–20)cm, thinly coriaceous, broadly ovate or oblong-ovate or oblong, apex acute to rounded, mucronate, base usually deeply cordate with a distinct sinus; venation palmipinnate. Figs paired, sessile to shortly pedunculate, globose, green with purple spots, minutely puberulent to glaucous, to 2.5cm diam. Trin.; Costa Rica to N S Amer. (E to the mouth of the Amaz.).

F. obliqua Forst. f. NATIVE FIG; SMALL-LEAVED MORETON BAY FIG. Tree to 15(–30)m, aerial roots sometimes produced. Lvs alt., glab., to 15×6cm, subcoriaceous, elliptic, apex obtuse to acute, base sometimes narrowed, rounded; venation finely pinnate. Figs in pairs, pedunculate, spherical to ovate, mostly glab., initially green, often spotted, to 0.8cm diam. Sulawesi to Pacific Is. and Aus. var. *petiolaris* most commonly cultivated, has figs 10–15mm diam. on peduncles to 1cm; petioles to 5cm.

F. oppositifolia Roxb. = *F. hispida*.

F. ovata Vahl. Shrub to tree with broad crown, sometimes scrambling, frequently epiphytic when young. Lvs dull, glab. above, pubesc. at least on veins beneath, to 30×20cm, chartaceous or thinly coriaceous, ovate, elliptic or oblong, apex broadly acute to obtuse, tip acuminate, base rounded to slightly cordate; venation raised, pinnate. Figs usually in pairs, surrounded in early stages by a red involucre of triangular bracts, spherical or somewhat laterally compressed, maturing maroon or brown, to 5.5×4cm. W, C & E Trop. Afr., S to Angola.

F. padifolia Kunth = *F. pertusa*.

F. palawanensis Merrill = *F. forstenii*.

F. palmata Forssk. Shrub or small tree. Lvs variable, entire to 3(–5- or even 7)-lobed, bluntly toothed, rough and scabrous, to 20×12.5cm, thinly chartaceous, ovate to orbicular, tips acuminate, base rounded, truncate or cordate; venation palmate. Figs solitary, pedunculate, subglobose or pyriform, puberulous or scabrous, to 2.5cm diam. NE Afr. and Arabia to Afghan., NW India and Nepal. V. closely related to the common fig (*F. carica*), but with smaller figs and lvs lobed only in juvenile phase.

F. palmeri S. Wats. DESERT FIG; ANABA. Small to large spreading tree with white to yellow bark. Lvs glaucous, initially densely white-pubesc. later glab. usually except for veins beneath, to 14(–17.5)×11.5(–13)cm, coriaceous, usually broadly ovate-deltoid, apex rounded to obtuse, shortly acuminate, base truncate to deeply cordate; venation pinnate with prominent basal veins. Figs in pairs on stout peduncles, pyriform, initially densely soft-pubesc., white, to 1.5cm diam. Baja Calif. A 'semi-succulent' fig related to *F. brandegeei* and *F. petiolaris*. Z9.

F. parcellii Veitch). = *F. aspera* 'Parcellii'.

F. parietalis Bl. SHARP-POINTED FIG. Initially an epiphytic shrub, later a climber with thick coiling st. or, arborescent to 15m. Lvs glab. above, rough-pubesc. beneath, to 18×9cm, thinly coriaceous, elliptic, distinctly caudate, base obtuse; venation palmipinnate, raised beneath. Figs solitary, globose or ovoid, pendent on a stipe, to 2×2.2cm, warty, yellow to bright orange, hispid-tomentose. SE Asia to Philipp.

F. payapa Blanco = *F. drupacea*.

F. perforata L. = *F. americana*.

F. pertusa L. f. CENTRAL AMERICAN BANYAN. Epiphytic shrub, later superceding its host and free-standing with broad crown, aerial roots and prop-trunks. Lvs glab., bright green, to 12×4.7cm, coriaceous, sometimes slightly curved, narrowly oblong to elliptic-oblong to lanceolate, apex acute, tip blunt or shortly acuminate, base obtuse to rounded, venation finely pinnate, midrib prominent. Figs in pairs, pedunculate, turbiniform to obovoid to subglobose, glab. to slightly puberulent, ripening brown, the apex jug-like, protruding, 0.8×0.7–1.1cm. Jam., Mex., C & S Amer. to Parag.

F. petiolaris Kunth. PETIOLATE FIG. Tree with stout, thick br.; suckers sometimes freely produced. Lvs pale green above, paler beneath, glab. except for tufts of long white hairs in axils of veins beneath, to 10(–15)cm, orbicular, apex rounded, tip abruptly acuminate, base deeply cordate, the lobes sometimes overlapping; venation pinnate. Figs in pairs, pedunculate, globose, densely fulvous-villous when young, usually pink- or white-spotted, to 15mm diam. Mex. Distinguished from *F. brandegeei* and *F. palmeri* by orbicular lvs with large basal lobes, sometimes overlapping.

F. philipensis Bonard ex Héricnq = *F. septica*.

F. philippinensis hort., non Miq. = *F. stricta*, *F. benjamina* var. *nuda* or *F. virens*.

F. philippinensis Miq. = *F. virgata*.

F. pilosa Reinw. ex Bl. = *F. drupacea*.

F. platyphylla Del. BROADLEAF FIG. Tree to 25m, often originating as an epiphyte. Lvs glab. above, sometimes slightly pubesc. beneath, to 25×17(–20)cm, thinly coriaceous, oblong-elliptic to broadly elliptic to ovate, apex broadly acute to obtuse, base deeply cordate; venation pinnate. Figs solitary or in clusters, pedunculate, glab. or nearly so, ripening red, to 2cm diam. W, C & E Trop. Afr. Sometimes united with the similar *F. umbellata*.

F. platypoda var. *petiolaris* Benth. = *F. obliqua* var. *petiolaris*.

F. populnea Willd. = *F. citrifolia*.

F. porteana Reg. = *F. callosa*.

F. pseudocarica Miq. = *F. palmata*.

F. pseudopalma Blanco PALM-LIKE FIG; DRACAENA FIG; PHILIPPINE FIG. Multistemmed, sometimes unbranched palm-like shrub or small tree to 6m. St. thick. Lvs in term. rosettes, prominently and coarsely dentate above, almost entire below, glab., to 100×15cm, coriaceous, narrowly oblanceolate, mucronate, base auriculate; venation pinnate, prominent. Figs in pairs oblong-obovoid, ribbed, green-purple with raised white flecks, to 4×2.3cm. Philipp.

F. pumila L. CREEPING FIG; CLIMBING FIG; CREEPING RUBBER PLANT. Root-climber spreading over large surfaces. Juvenile lvs glab., entire, to 5×3cm, thinly coriaceous, ovate to elliptic, blunt, base oblique, cordate. Adult phase erect or spreading; lvs entire ± glab. with prominent venation, to 10.5×5cm, coriaceous, oblong to elliptic to ovate, apex narrowly rounded to obtuse, tip blunt, base rounded to slightly cordate; venation palmipinnate, strongly reticulate. Figs mostly solitary, pyriform to oblong or cylindrical on thick stalks, green with white flecks, maturing purple, densely hairy, to 6.2×4cm. E Asia. 'Minima': v. slender, small, slow-growing; lvs to 1cm. 'Quercifolia': lvs pinnately lobed. 'Sonny': v. small, spreading; lvs round to oval, irregularly waved, with variable cream margins. 'Variegata': vigorous, tufted; lvs marbled white to cream. Z9.

F. punctata Thunb. SICKLE-LEAVED FIG. Much-branched everg. creeping shrub or root-climber, broadly resembling *F. pumila*. Juvenile lvs distichous, glab. paler and tessellated beneath, to 0.8×0.6cm, coriaceous, oblong-lanceolate to elliptic-obovate, falcate, apex tip blunt, base rounded, midrib to one side; intermediate and adult lvs developing on rootless, lat. shoots, larger otherwise not strongly distinct from juveniles. Figs on short leafless shoots to 3.5cm, globose to pyriform, beaked, velvety-hispid, peach-pink, to 11×8cm. S Thail. to Java, Borneo and Sulawesi.

F. quercifolia Roxb. = *F. montana*.

F. racemosa L. CLUSTER FIG; RED-WOODED FIG; COUNTRY FIG; GULAR. Decid. rami- and cauliflorous small to medium tree to 20m with a spreading crown to 10m wide with thin plank buttresses. Lvs glab. or slightly hairy, to 15(–20)×6(–8.5)cm, stiff, chartaceous to thinly coriaceous, ovate to ovate-lanceolate, apex acute, base obtuse to rounded; venation strongly raised beneath. Figs in clusters on much-divided leafless br., subglobose, initially green with white flecks, later scarlet, puberulent, to 3.5(–4)cm across. Sri Lanka, S China (Yunnan), S & SE Asia and locally in Malesia to S New Guinea and N Aus. S of Queensld.

F. radicans Desf. = *F. sagittata*.

F. ramentacea Roxb. = *F. sagittata*.

F. religiosa L. BO TREE; PEEPUL; SACRED FIG. Decid. or semi-deciduous tree to 7.5m or more, fast-growing, potentially strangling support trees. Lvs aspen-like, entire or wavy-margined, glab., to 17×12.5cm, thinly coriaceous, broadly triangular, tip markedly acuminate, to 6.2cm, base broad, rounded or truncate; venation pinnate; petiole slender, 7.5–10cm. Figs paired sessile, glab., oblate, green to purple with scarlet flecks, to 1.25cm diam. Himal. foothills to SW China, N Thail. and Vietnam. An allied sp. sometimes planted in India is *F. tsjahela* Burm. f. with elliptic lvs and figs in clusters.

F. repens auct. non Willd. = *F. pumila*.

F. reticulata (Miq.) Miq. = *F. sarmentosa*.

F. retusa auct. non L. = *F. microcarpa*.

F. rhynchocarpa Mildbr. & Burret = *F. cyathistipula*.

F. rigo Bail. ENGLISH'S FIG. Tree to 15m; br. arising at a low level, sometimes becoming trunk-like. Lvs glab., to 15–7.5cm, coriaceous, oblong or obovate, apex abruptly acute, blunt or emarginate, base cuneate; venation pinnate. Figs solitary or paired, sessile, glab., initially green with white flecks, ripening yellow to orange with red spots, 10–15mm across; basal bracts 3, relatively large. New Guinea.

F. rostrata auct. non Lam. = *F. sagittata*.

F. roxburghii Wallich ex Miq. = *F. auriculata*.

F. rubiginosa Desf. ex Vent. PORT JACKSON FIG; RUSTY FIG; LITTLE-LEAF FIG; BOTANY BAY FIG. Tree to at least 12m; br. spreading, sometimes supported by root-stems. Lvs tinted red above, later smooth and glab., initially rusty-pubesc. beneath, to 17.2×6.2cm, coriaceous, oblong to elliptic to ovate; venation finely pinnate. Figs usually in pairs, pedunculate, globose, rusty-pubesc. to glabrescent, warty green-brown, to 1.25cm diam. Aus. (NSW). 'Variegata': lvs variegated cream-yellow. 'Australis': lvs glab. in both young and mature trees, to 8×6cm.

F. rubra hort. non Roth = *F. elastica* 'Rubra'.

F. rubra Roth non hort. = *F. microcarpa*.

F. rumphii Bl. Superficially similar to *F. religiosa*, but with lvs narrower, tip less elongated, and base slightly decurrent, not truncate or shallowly cordate; venation evidently palmipinnate. S & SE Asia through Java to Moluccas.

F. sagittata Vahl. Wiry climbing or trailing everg. creeper with rooting st., later climbing or free-standing. Juvenile lvs soon glabrescent, not bullate, to 8cm, ovate, shallowly cordate; adult lvs glab. except initially for the veins, surface finely reticulate, to 20cm or more, ovate or oblong-lanceolate, apex acuminate, base rounded or slightly cordate; venation pinnate. Figs solitary or paired, globose, initially pubesc., ripening red, to 1.4cm across. Himal., S China, SE Asia. 'Variegata': lvs grey-green with creamy-white variegation.

F. sagittifolia Warb. FALSE FIDDLE-LEAF FIG. Similar to *F. lyrata*, differing chiefly in narrowly oblanceolate-sagittate lvs to 45×15cm with 13–17 (not 3–5) lateral veins on each side. W & C Trop. Afr.

F. salicifolia Vahl = *F. cordata* ssp. *salicifolia*.

F. salicifolia Miq. non Vahl. = *F. subulata*.

F. sarmentosa Hamilt. ex Sm. Dimorphic climber, similar to *F. pumila* but differing in more limited development of basal veins, sharper lf apices and figs generally in pairs; juvenile lvs star-shaped, to 2×2cm; adult lvs to 15×6cm, narrowly lanceolate. Nepal to China, Taiwan, Ryukyu Is., Jap. and Korea. Plants in cult. are var. *nipponica*, (Franch. & Savat.)

Corner, with fr. v. short-stalked. 'Variegata': lvs irregularly margined cream.

F. saussureana DC. NONKO; OLD CALABAR FIG; LOQUAT-LEAVED FIG. Tree to 20m or more, sometimes beginning life as strangler. Lvs spirally arranged in loose rosettes, glab. above, puberulous beneath, to 50×17cm, coriaceous, oblong-obovate, tip acuminate, base narrowed; venation pinnate, prominent beneath. Figs in pairs, crowded, globose, densely yellow-villous, to 4cm diam. W, C & E Trop. Afr., not Braz.

F. scabra Jacq. = *F. hispida*.

F. scandens Lam. = *F. pumila*.

F. schlechteri Warb. = *F. microcarpa* var. *hillii*.

F. semicordata Hamilt. ex Sm. WEDGELEAF FIG KHANYU. Tree to 6m. Lvs distichous, entire to serrate, sericeous beneath, sometimes glabrescent above, to 20×8.5cm+, irregularly elliptic to ovate, apex acute, tip acuminate to cuspidate, base rounded auriculate; venation pinnate, strongly raised beneath. Figs on long trailing or hanging, naked br. to 3m+ emanating from the trunk from the base upwards, pedunculate, oblong or globose, hispid, brown, to 1.8×1.8cm. S China, S & SE Asia to N Malay Penins.

F. septica Burm. f. WAVY-LEAF FIG; IVORY FIG. Tree, branching near ground and spreading. Lvs alt. (rarely opposite), entire or wavy, glab., glossy above, slightly paler beneath, to 30(–37.5)×22.5cm, broadly oblong to ovate, apex obtuse to broadly acute, tip bluntly acute to cuspidate, base rounded to subcordate; venation prominent, ivory-white and somewhat raised beneath. Figs axill. among lvs or in clusters on tubercles on br. and trunk, pedunculate, glab., smooth to ribbed, to 1.5×2cm, green with white (later rusty) flecks, ripening red-brown. Sumatra and Borneo to the Philipp., Vanuatu and Aus.

F. sintenisii Warb. = *F. americana*.

F. stipulata Thunb. = *F. pumila*.

F. stipulosa Miq. = *F. caulocarpa*.

F. stricta (Miq.) Miq. Tall glab. tree. Lvs somewhat glossy above, to 17×5cm, coriaceous, elliptic, apex acute, tip acuminate or cuspidate, base rounded; venation finely pinnate. Figs axill., in pairs, globose, smooth, yellow when mature, about 1.8cm across; basal bracts conspicuous. SW China & SE Asia to Java, Sulawesi and the Philipp. Differs from *F. subcordata* and *F. benjamina* in the conspicuous bracts under the figs.

F. stricta hort. = *F. pertusa*.

F. subcordata Bl. Epiphytic shrub developing into an erect strangler-tree with multi-buttressed trunk and aerial roots to 30m with widely spreading crown. Lvs glab., to 17.5×7.5cm, thinly coriaceous, elliptic to lanceolate, apex acute to obtuse, tip acuminate to shortly cuspidate, base rounded; venation finely pinnate. Figs mostly in pairs, sessile, bracteate, oblong-ellipsoid, green to yellow, later red to almost black, pustulate to 2.5cm. SE Asia.

F. subpanduraeformis auct. non Miq. = *F. sagittifolia*.

F. subulata Bl. Largely semiscandent, epiphytic or straggling basket-rooted shrub. Lvs dark green, glab., 10–25cm, elliptic-lanceolate, apex narrowed, acute, tip caudate-acuminate, base acute to obtuse; venation pinnate. Figs solitary or in pairs, almost sessile, becoming orange-red, to 1.25cm diam. E Himal. and S China through SE Asia and Malesia to Solomon Is.

F. sundaica Bl. Large everg. tree, initially an epiphyte but later strangling its host and developing a vast crown with stilt-roots. Lvs glab., to 23×11cm, stiffly coriaceous, elliptic or oblong-obovate, apex obtuse to rounded, abruptly acuminate or caudate, base narrowed, broadly acute to ± obtuse; venation palmipinnate, raised beneath. Figs paired, sessile, glab., wider than long, ripening bright red, to 13×19mm, base with 3 large bract-scales. E India and SE Asia to Java and Borneo.

F. superba (Miq.) Miq. SEA FIG. Briefly decid. large tree, with some aerial roots. Lvs pink when young, later fresh green, to 25×13cm, elliptic, base rounded or nearly cordate. Figs clustered, pedunculate, pyriform, dull purple, scurfy-pubesc. when young, to 2cm diam. Jap., China and S & SE Asia to Moluccas. *F. concinna*, with thinner twigs, lvs 1–4cm wide and smaller, axill. figs, is grown in the Philippines. var. *henneana* (Miq.) Corner. CEDAR FIG; DECIDUOUS FIG. Smaller. Twigs to 0.6cm diam. Lvs to 10cm wide. N Aus.

F. sur Forssk. CAPE FIG; BUSH FIG. Decid. shrub or tree of alder-like habit to 25(–30)m. Lvs wavy-margined, crenate or sub-entire, glab. above, glab. to sparsely pubesc. beneath, to 20(–32)×13(–16)cm, thinly coriaceous, elliptic or ovate, apex acute or just obtuse, tip shortly acuminate, base obtuse, rounded or subcordate; venation palmate or subpalmate, prominent. Figs pedunculate, on leafless, divaricating br. to 50cm long arising from old wood, globose or obovoid, ripening orange or red, 0.5–3.3cm diam. Cape Verde Is., Afr., Yemen.

F. surinamensis Miq. = *F. citrifolia*.

F. sycomorus L. SYCAMORE; SYCAMORE FIG; MULBERRY FIG; EGYPTIAN SYCAMORE. Thick-branched, sometimes buttressed, briefly decid. tree to 25m, forming a large spreading crown. Lvs deep green above, paler beneath, entire, undulate or slightly repand-dentate, sandpaper-like to the touch above, to 15×10cm or larger; subcoriaceous, broadly ovate to almost orbicular, apex obtuse or rounded, tip blunt, base cordate; venation palmate, prominent. Figs axill. or on naked br. to 10cm long, globose or obovoid, velvety-tomentose or puberulent, yellow, orange or red, to 3.7cm broad. Afr., Arabian Penins.; cult. N of Sudan. The biblical Sycomore; allied to *F. racemosa* and *F. sur*.

F. tanensis Seem. = *F. habrophylla*.

F. thonningii Bl. Sometimes multi-trunked and much-branched shrub or tree to 21m (or more); aerial roots often present. Lvs dark green above, glab., to 12(–18)×6(–7)cm, coriaceous, elliptic, oblong-elliptic or oblong-obovate, apex and base obtuse; venation pinnate. Figs crowded in pairs, subglobose, yellow or red, puberulous or glab., to 8mm across; basal bracts persistent. Cape Verde Is., Afr.

F. thonningii hort. non Bl. = *F. natalensis*.

F. tinctoria Forst. f. DYE FIG; HUMPED FIG; HUMPED FIG TREE. Shrub or tree, developing many slender aerial roots, but without prop-roots. Twigs initially flexuous. Lvs mid- to light green above, glab. or rough or hairy, to 18×7cm, rather angular to 4-sided, thinly coriaceous, obliquely oblong-ovate to oblong-elliptic, apex acute to obtuse, tip shortly acuminate or cuspidate, base narrowed to rounded; veins repandly pinnate. Figs axill., solitary or in pairs, ± sessile, pyriform-globose, green to yellow and then red-orange, glab. or v. slightly pubesc., to 1.1cm diam. S China, S & SE Asia to Polyn.

F. triangularis Warb. = *F. natalensis* ssp. *leprieurii*.

F. tsiela Roxb. = *F. amplissima*.

F. ulmifolia Lam. ELMLEAF FIG. Shrub or small tree to 4.5m+. Juvenile lvs to 16cm long but often only 1.1cm wide, linear, usually with 2 small basal lobes; adult lvs coarsely toothed to subentire, sandpaper-like to the touch, to 20×7.5cm, subcoriaceous, ovate to elliptic, apex ± acute, tip acuminate to caudate, base rounded, often oblique; venation pinnate to subplamate, with 1 sometimes prominent pair of basal veins. Figs axill. near ends of twigs, solitary or in pairs, sometimes crowded, globose to pyriform, green ripening orange-red to scarlet, initially hispid, to 1.1cm diam. Philipp. V. variable, *F. odorata*, grown in the Philippines, differs in its more strongly asymmetric, distichous lvs, fragrant when dry.

F. umbellata Vahl. Tree to 10m, sometimes beginning as epiphyte. Juvenile lvs palmately lobed; ordinary lvs often wavy-margined, glab., smooth, to 26(–30)×19(–20)cm, coriaceous, elliptic to ovate to orbicular, apex acute to obtuse, tip acuminate, base shallowly cordate; venation pinnate. Figs in fascicles, globose to obovoid, velvety, becoming yellow to dark brown with light flecks, to 3cm diam. W & C Trop. Afr. Plants in cult. may be *F. platyphylla*.

F. utilis Sim = *F. lutea*.

F. variegata Bl. RED STEM-FIG. Medium-sized to large everg. or briefly decid. tree to 25m+, ultimately with buttresses and rounded, dense crown. Lvs entire or, in saplings, coarsely toothed, glab. above, initially silky-pubesc. along veins beneath, to 32×15cm, chartaceous, broadly ovate, apex obtuse to acute, tip acuminate, base rounded to truncate or shallowly cordate; venation prominent, palmate. Figs found all over trunk and br. in clusters on twigs to 8cm long, globose to pyriform, velvety to glab., light green ripening rose-red with, sometimes, longitudinal stripes or variegations, to 3.5cm diam. India and S China to Solomon Is.

F. verrucosa Hemsl., non Miq. = *F. citrifolia*.

F. vesca Miq. = *F. racemosa*.

F. villosa Bl. VILLOUS FIG. Trailing or scandent shrub or high-climbing liane. Twigs stout, purple-brown, densely villous. Juvenile lvs hairy beneath, to 17×9.5cm, thin, broadly ovate, apex acute, tip slightly acuminate, base cordate; adult lvs dark green, to 25.5×13cm, leathery, oblong to ovate, densely villous beneath, sparsely hairy or almost glab. above, apex obtuse or acute, tip acuminate, base rounded to cordate; venation pinnate, raised beneath. Figs fascicled, globose or apically flattened, beaked, moderately hairy, green to orange-yellow, about 1cm diam. Malaysia, Indon. and the Philipp.

F. virens Ait. GREY FIG; SPOTTED FIG; JAVA WILLOW. Briefly decid., heavy-limbed spreading tree to 15m. Br. somewhat drooping, with aerial and pillar-roots. Young foliage scarlet or bronze. Lvs slightly poplar-like, green, entire or somewhat undulate, to 17×7.5cm, thin, elliptic to ovate, apex obtuse to acute, abruptly passing into a long, narrow tip, base broad, rounded to truncate; venation pinnate, prominent. Figs axill. usually in pairs, globose, slightly beaked, finely hairy or glabrescent, initially green later white, commonly with scarlet dots, 0.7–1.1cm diam. India to the Solomon Is. and N Aus. *F. lacor* differs in its densely hairy twigs and stipules; *F. virens* proper is at most sparsely hairy, *F. concinna* is sometimes in-

cluded here, is also distinct var. *glabella* (Bl.) Corner. Lvs smaller, obovate or oblanceolate; figs sessile or on short wood burrs behind lvs. S Thail. to Sumatra, Java and Borneo.

F. virgata Reinw. ex Bl. Glab. basket-strangler resembling *F. tinctoria*. Lvs oblong, narrower than *F. tinctoria*, cuspidate. Figs axill., small, ripening red. Ryukyu Is., Taiwan, Philipp. and E Malesia through New Guinea to Aus.

F. vogelii (Miq.) Miq. = *F. lutea*.

F. watkinsiana Bail. WATKINS FIG; BELLINGER RIVER FIG. Resembles *F. macrophylla*, but with less massive buttresses, glab. lvs to 30×10.5cm and figs globose or oblong, finely pubesc., green to rusty, to 2.5×1.8cm, with apex protruding. Aus.

F. wightiana auct., non (Miq.) Benth. = *F. superba*.

F. wildemaniana Warb. ex De Wildeman & T. Dur. Tree. Lvs green and glossy above, much paler and aureous beneath, glab., to 20×11.5cm, coriaceous, narrowly oblong-oblanceolate, apex obtuse, tip acuminate, base narrow, cordate, venation pinnate, raised beneath. Figs subglobose, glab., about 3cm diam. C Afr.

F. wilsonii Warb. = *F. americana*.

→*Artocarpus*.

Fiddleheads *Osmunda cinnamonea*.
Fiddle-leaf Fig *Ficus lyrata*.
Fiddle-leaf Philodendron *Philodendron bipennifolium*.
Fiddleneck *Amsinckia; Phacelia tanacetifolia*.
Fiddlewood *Citharexylum*.
Field Balm *Glechoma hederacea*.
Field Bean *Vicia faba*.
Field Bindweed *Convolvulus arvensis*.
Field Brome *Bromus arvensis*.
Field Garlic *Allium oleraceum*.
Field Gladiolus *Gladiolus italicus*.
Field Horsetail *Equisetum arvense*.
Field Lupine *Lupinus albus*.
Field Madder *Sherardia arvensis*.
Field Maple *Acer campestre*.
Field Marigold *Calendula arvensis*.
Field Mustard *Brassica rapa*.
Field Pansy *Viola arvensis; V. rafinesquii*.
Field Pea *Pisum sativum* var. *arvense*.
Field Poppy *Papaver rhoeas*.
Field Rose *Rosa arvensis*.
Field Wood-rush *Luzula campestris*.
Fiery Costus *Costus cuspidatus*.
Fiery Spike *Aphelandra aurantiaca*.
Fiesta Flower *Pholistoma auritum*.
Fig *Ficus* (*F. carica*).
Fig-leaved Gourd *Cucurbita ficifolia*.
Figwort *Scrophularia*.
Fiji Fan Palm *Pritchardia pacifica*.
Filazel *Corylus avellana* × *C. cornuta*.
Filbert *Corylus maxima*.

Filipendula Mill. MEADOWSWEET; DROPWORT. Rosaceae. 10+ rhizomatous perenn. herbs, sometimes tuberous. Lvs usually pinnate, large pairs of lfts alternating with smaller ones, terminal lfts large, serrate-palmatifid, lat. lfts small, often 0 on cauline lvs. Fls many, small in cymose corymbs; cal. 4–5-lobed; pet. 4–5, orbicular; sta. 20–40, fil. filiform. Fr. a head of 8–12 achenes or follicles, glab. or ciliate. N Temp. regions.

F. hexapetala Gilib. = *F. vulgaris*.

F. kamtschatica (Pall.) Maxim. To 3m. St. erect, angled, hairy. Lvs large; term. lft orbicular, to 25cm diam., 3–5-palmatifid, biserrate, green, hispid. Fls to 8mm diam., white to pale pink, in large corymbs. Summer–autumn. Jap., Manch., Kamchatka. Z3.

F. multijuga Maxim. To 1m. Term. lfts broad, rounded, to 10cm diam., 5–7-pinnatifid, dentate. Fls usually rose, to 5mm diam., in terminal, many-fld, glab. corymbs. Summer. Jap. Z6.

F. palmata (Pall.) Maxim. To 1m. Lvs pink-tomentose beneath; lfts 3–5-palmatifid. Fls white, small, in term. corymbs; anth. red. Summer. Jap. to China, Mong., Sib., Kamchatka. 'Alba': vigorous; fls white. 'Digitata Nana': to 60cm; fls deep rose. 'Elegantissima': to 90cm; fls dark rose; seed heads bronze. 'Rosea': fls pink. 'Rubra': fls dark red. Z2.

F. palmata hort. non Pall. = *F. purpurea*.

F. purpurea Maxim. To 130cm. St. grooved, often purple, glab. Lvs gland. above; terminal lfts ovate, to 25cm diam., 5–7-palmatifid, fine glandular-serrate. Fls purple-red or pink. Summer. Jap. 'Alba': fls white. 'Purpurascens': lvs strongly tinted purple. Z6.

F. rubra (Hill) Robinson. QUEEN OF THE PRAIRIE. To 2.5m. Lfts pubesc. only on veins beneath; term. lft to 20cm diam., 3-lobed, lobes lanceolate-oblong, incised. Fls deep peach-blossom pink, in a large, congested corymbs. Summer. E US. 'Venusta' ('Magnifica'): to 2m; fls deep rose. Z2.

F. ulmaria (L.) Maxim. MEADOW SWEET; QUEEN OF THE MEADOWS. To 2m. St. tomentose, term. lft ovate-oblong, to ovate-suborbicular, to 8cm, dentate or shallow-lobed. Fls creamy white, in corymbs to 25cm. Summer. W Asia, Eur. 'Aurea': lvs vivid gold, later dark cream. 'Flore Pleno': fls double. 'Rosea': fls soft pink. 'Variegata' ('Aureo-Variegata'): lfts with a central yellow stripe. Z2.

F. vestita (Wallich ex G. Don) Maxim. To 1m. St. finely pubesc. lfts to 10cm, dentate. Fls cream, in much-branched, oblong corymbs. Himal. Z6.

F. vulgaris Moench. DROPWORT. To 80cm. St. glab.; roots bearing ovoid tubers, lfts to 2cm, ciliate, pinnatisect, narrow-dentate. Fls white flushed red or purple, in corymbs to 10cm. Eur., N & C Asia. 'Flore Pleno': to 60cm; fls double, in drooping pan., cream. 'Grandiflora': fls large. 'Rosea': fls light pink. Z3.
→*Spiraea.*

Filmy Fern *Hymenophyllum; Trichomanes.*
Filmy Maidenhair *Adiantum diaphanum.*
Fine-leaved Vetch *Vicia tenuifolia.*
Finger Grass *Chloris; Digitaria.*
Finger Lime *Microcitrus australasica.*
Finger Millet *Eleusine coracana.*
Fingernail Plant *Neoregelia spectabilis.*
Finger of God *Aechmea orlandiana.*
Finger Tree *Euphorbia tirucalli.*
Finocchio *Foeniculum vulgare var. azoricum.*
Fir *Abies.*
Firebird *Heliconia bihai.*
Firebush *Hamelia patens; Streptosolen jamesonii.*
Firecracker Flower *Crossandra infundibuliformis; Dichelostemma ida-maia.*
Firecracker Plant *Cuphea ignea; Russelia equisetiformis.*
Firecracker Vine *Manettia cordifolia; M. luteorubra.*
Fire Fern *Oxalis alstonii.*
Fire-king Begonia *Begonia goegoensis.*
Fire-leaved Ivy *Parthenocissus quinquefolia.*
Fire Lily *Cyrtanthus (C. angustifolius); Lilium bulbiferum.*
Fire on the Mountain *Euphorbia cyathophora.*
Firethorn *Pyracantha (P. coccinea).*
Fire-tree *Nuytsia.*
Fireweed *Epilobium angustifolium; Ixodia.*
Firewheels *Gaillardia pulchella.*
Firewheel Tree *Stenocarpus sinuatus.*
Firewood Banksia *Banksia menziesii.*

Firmiana Marsili. Sterculiaceae. 9 trees or shrubs. Lvs entire or palmately lobed. Fls in pan. or rac.; cal. campanulate, 5-dentate; pet. 0; androgynophore well developed; sta. united in a column; anth. 10–15, sessile. Fr. 4–5 papery follicles, dehiscing into leaf-like carpels. E Asia, 1 sp. E Afr.

F. barteri (Mast.) Schum. = *Hildegardia barteri.*
F. colorata (Roxb.) R. Br. Decid. tree, to 25m, with basal buttresses. Lvs to 30cm diam., ovate to palmately 3–5-lobed. Cal. 2.5–3cm, tubular, rusty-tomentose, lobes short. Follicles to 8cm, glab. India to Java. Z10.
F. platanifolia (L. f.) Marsili = *F. simplex.*
F. simplex (L.) W. Wight. CHINESE PARASOL TREE; CHINESE BOTTLETREE; JAPANESE VARNISH TREE; PHOENIX TREE. Decid. tree, to 20m, with green smooth bark. Lvs 30–40cm diam., 3–7-lobed. Cal 1.2–1.5cm, lemon-yellow, lobes often reflexed, longer than cal. tube. Follicles 8–12cm, densely pilose. E Asia, from Ryukyus to Vietnam. 'Variegata': lvs mottled white. Z9.
→*Sterculia.*

Fir Tree Kalanchoe *Kalanchoe laciniata.*
Fishbone *Euphorbia polyacantha.*
Fishbone Cactus *Epiphyllum anguliger.*
Fishbone Water Fern *Blechnum nudum.*
Fish Fuddle *Piscidia piscipula.*
Fish Grass *Cabomba.*
Fishpole Bamboo *Phyllostachys aurea.*
Fishtail Camellia *Camellia japonica.*
Fishtail Fern *Nephrolepis falcata* f. *furcans.*
Fishtail Hoya *Hoya polyneura.*
Fishtail Lawyer Cane *Calamus caryotoides.*
Fishtail Palm *Caryota.*

Fittonia Coëm. Acanthaceae. 2 low, stem-rooting, downy, everg. perenn. herbs. Lvs colourfully veined; petioles short. Fls small, barely exceeding overlapping bracts in erect term. spikes; cor. tubular, bilabiate. S Amer. Z10.

F. argyroneura Coëm. = *F. verschaffeltii var. argyroneura.*
F. verschaffeltii (Lem.) Coëm. MOSAIC PLANT. St. to 8cm. Lvs 6–10cm, oval to elliptic, downy, deep olive green with a dense network of ruby to scarlet veins. Fls white in slender, 4-angled spikes to 8cm, largely concealed by bracts. Peru. var. *argyroneura* (Coëm.) Nichols. NERVE PLANT; SILVER NET PLANT; SILVER FITTONIA; SILVER NERVE; SILVER THREADS. Lvs emerald green closely net-veined silver-white. var. *pearcei* Nichols. SNAKESKIN PLANT. Lvs larger and more thinly textured, sage to olive green net-veined carmine, somewhat glaucous beneath.

Fitzroya Hook. f. Cupressaceae. 1 everg. conifer to 45m or shrubby at altitude. Bark rusty red, fissured, branchlets pendulous. Lvs in lax whorls of 3, 2–4mm, oblong, imbricate, convex, incurved, dark green with paler midrib and 2 white bands. ♂ cones solitary toward tips of br. ♀ cones term., solitary, globose; scales subulate, resinous, 9 in 3 decussate whorls; fertilized cones globose green, ripening brown, 6–8mm diam., opening to 9–13mm across; scales swollen, with a broad, triangular bract. C Chile, N Patagonia. Z8.

F. cupressoides (Molina) Johnson. PATAGONIAN CYPRESS.
F. patagonia Hook. f. = *F. cupressoides.*

Five-finger *Potentilla; Pseudopanax arboreus.*
Five-fingered Maidenhair Fern *Adiantum pedatum.*
Five Fingers *Cyanella lutea.*
Five Spot *Nemophila maculata.*
Five-spot Baby *Nemophila maculata.*

Flacourtia Comm. ex L'Hérit. Flacourtiaceae. 15 shrubs or small trees, often spiny. Lvs simple. Fls yellow-green to white, small, in clusters, ♀ fls often solitary; cal. with 4–7 lobes; pet. 0; sta. numerous. Fr. a fleshy berry. Trop. Afr., trop. Asia, China, Masc. Is. 10.

F. cataphracta Roxb. = *F. jangomans.*
F. indica (Burm. f.) Merrill BATOKO PLUM; GOVERNOR'S PLUM; RAMONTCHI; MADAGASCAR PLUM. Decid. shrub or tree to 14m with spines to 5cm. Lvs to 9×6cm, elliptic, crenate, leathery, glab. or pubesc. Fls solitary or few in short infl. term. or on naked, lat. shoots and thorns; style 5–7, short. Fr. to 2.5cm diam., red-black, becoming translucent. S Asia, Madag., Zam.; nat. in parts of Flor.
F. jangomans (Lour.) Rausch. RUKAM; PANIALA. Tree to 10m; st. densely spiny below, upper br. unarmed. Lvs to 10×3cm, ovate to lanceolate, emerging red, becoming dark green, thin, dentate or entire. Fls in small clusters; style single, 4-lobed. Fr. 2.5cm diam., dark brown, with yellow-green pulp. Wild state unknown, probably a cultigen originating in India; nat. on E coast of Aus.
F. ramontchi L'Hérit. = *F. indica.*
F. rukam Zoll. & Moritzi. RUKAM. Small tree to 15m; br. spiny at base. Lvs to 18×6cm, elliptic, crenate, thin. Fls in axill. clusters; styles 4–8, short, thick, in a circle. Fr. to 2.5cm diam., rose tinted green, ripening mauve to blood red. Malaysia.
F. sepiaria Roxb. = *F. indica.*

FLACOURTIACEAE DC. 89/875. *Azara, Berberidopsis, Carrierea, Dovyalis, Flacourtia, Hydnocarpus, Idesia, Kiggelaria, Oncoba, Poliothyrsis, Scolopia, Xylosma.*

Flag *Iris.*
Flagroot *Acorus calamus.*
Flaky Fir *Abies squamata.*
Flaky Juniper *Juniperus squamata.*
Flamboyant *Delonix regia.*
Flamboyant Tree *Caesalpinia pulcherrima.*
Flame Azalea *Rhododendron calendulaceum.*
Flame Bush *Templetonia retusa.*
Flame Coral Tree *Erythrina coralloides.*
Flame Creeper *Combretum microphyllum.*
Flame Flower *Tropaeolum speciosum.*
Flamegold *Koelreuteria elegans.*
Flame Kurrajong *Brachychiton acerifolius.*
Flame Nasturtium *Tropaeolum speciosum.*
Flame of the Forest *Butea monosperma.*
Flame of the Woods *Ixora coccinea.*
Flame Tree *Brachychiton acerifolius; B. australis; Delonix regia; Nuytsia.*
Flame Vine *Pyrostegia venusta.*
Flame Violet *Episcia cupreata.*
Flaming Katy *Kalanchoe blossfeldiana.*
Flamingo Flower *Anthurium (A. andraeanum).*
Flamingo Plant *Hypoestes phyllostachya; Justicia carnea.*
Flaming Poppy *Stylomecon.*
Flaming Sword *Vriesea splendens.*
Flanders Poppy *Papaver rhoeas.*
Flannel Bush *Fremontodendron; Solanum lasiophyllum.*
Flannel Flower *Actinotus.*
Flat Pea *Lathyrus sylvestris; Platylobium formosum.*

Flat-topped Yate *Eucalyptus occidentalis.*
Flat Wattle *Acacia glaucoptera.*
Flawn *Zoysia matrella.*
Flax *Linum* (*L. usitatissimum*).
Flaxleaf Paperbark *Melaleuca linariifolia.*
Flax Lily *Dianella*; *Phormium.*
Flax Wattle *Acacia linifolia*; *A. longissima.*
Fleabane *Erigeron*; *Pulicaria.*
Fleawort *Plantago psyllium.*
Fleece Vine *Polygonum.*

Fleischmannia Schultz-Bip. Compositae. *c*75 ann. or perenn. herbs or subshrubs. Lvs usually opposite. Cap. discoid, in a laxly branched cyme or densely branched corymb. N Amer., W S Amer. Z10.
F. incarnata (Walter) R. King & H. Robinson. Pubesc. perenn. to 1m. Lvs to 6cm, ovate to ovate-deltoid, coarsely serrate, apex acute to acuminate; petioles to 6cm. Cap. cylindrical, to 4mm; flts white to pale mauve. S US, N Mex.
→*Eupatorium.*

Fleur de Dieu *Petrea kohautiana.*
Fleur-de-lis *Iris.*

Flickingeria A.D. Hawkes. Orchidaceae. 70 epiphytic orchids. Rhiz. tufted with branched, erect aerial st. bearing 1-lvd pbs. Infl. bracteate, pseudoterminal; fls small, short-lived, produced in succession, fragrant; tep. spreading; lip midlobe fringed, lat. lobes almost enveloping column. Trop. Asia to Oceana. Z9.
F. comata (Bl.) A.D. Hawkes. Lvs elliptic to obovate, coriaceous. Fls to 25mm diam., cream often spotted purple; lip to 20mm, basal margins undulate-crispate, apically pubesc., midlobe tapering, blunt, lat. lobes dentate. NE Aus., New Guinea, Indon., Malaysia.
F. convexa (Bl.) A.D. Hawkes. Lvs ovate, fleshy. Fls to 15mm diam., cream, lip yellow and red; sep. triangular, overlapping pet. base; lip to 10mm, forward-pointing, concave, midlobe bilobed. NE Aus., Indon., Malaysia.

Floating Fern *Ceratopteris.*
Floating Heart *Nymphoides.*
Floating Stag's-horn Fern *Ceratopteris.*
Floating Water Plantain *Luronium natans.*
Flooded Gum *Eucalyptus grandis*; *E. rudis.*
Floradora *Stephanotis floribunda.*
Flor de Muerto *Lisianthius nigrescens.*
Florence Fennel *Foeniculum vulgare* var. *azoricum.*
Florida Arrowroot *Zamia pumila.*
Florida Bean *Mucuna pruriens* var. *utilis.*
Florida Chinkapin *Castanea alnifolia* var. *floridana.*
Florida Fiddlewood *Citharexylum fruticosum.*
Florida Orange *Citrus nobilis.*
Florida Silver Palm *Coccothrinax argentata.*
Florida Strangler Fig *Ficus aurea.*
Florida Strap Fern *Campyloneurum phyllitidis.*
Florida Swamp Lily *Crinum americanum.*
Florida Thatch *Thrinax radiata.*
Florida Yew *Taxus floridana.*
Florists' Chrysanthemum *Dendranthema* ×*grandiflorum.*
Florist's Cineraria *Pericallis* ×*hybrida.*
Florists' Gloxinia *Sinningia speciosa.*
Florist's Verbena *Verbena* ×*hybrida.*
Florist's Willow *Salix caprea.*
Floss Silk Tree *Chorisia speciosa.*
Flowering Almond *Prunus triloba.*
Flowering Ash *Fraxinus ornus.*
Flowering Banana *Musa ornata.*
Flowering Cherry *Prunus.*
Flowering Crabapple *Malus.*
Flowering Currant *Ribes sanguineum.*
Flowering Dogwood *Cornus florida.*
Flowering Fern *Anemia*; *Helminthostachys*; *Osmunda regalis.*
Flowering Flax *Linum grandiflorum.*
Flowering Gum *Eucalyptus ficifolia.*
Flowering Inch Plant *Tradescantia cerinthoides.*
Flowering Maple *Abutilon.*
Flowering Oak *Chorizema cordata.*
Flowering Onion *Allium neapolitanum.*
Flowering Pepper *Peperomia fraseri.*
Flowering Quince *Chaenomeles.*
Flowering Raspberry *Rubus odoratus.*
Flowering Rush *Butomus.*
Flowering Senna *Senna corymbosa.*
Flowering Spurge *Euphorbia corollata.*
Flowering Stones *Lithops.*
Flowering Tobacco *Nicotiana alata.*

Flowering Wintergreen *Polygala paucifolia.*
Flower of an Hour *Hibiscus trionum.*
Flower of Tigris *Tigridia.*
Flowery Rata Vine *Metrosideros perforatus.*
Flumine Mississippi *Vallisneria americana.*
Fluted Horn Mallee *Eucalyptus stowardii.*
Fly Honeysuckle *Lonicera canadensis.*
Fly Orchid *Ophrys insectifera*; *Trichoceros parviflorus.*
Fly Poison *Amianthum muscitoxicum.*
Foam Flower *Tiarella cordifolia.*
Foam of May *Spiraea arguta.*

Fockea Endl. Asclepiadaceae. 10 perenn. caudiciform succulents. St. tuberous or napiform, br. usually thin, twining or erect. Lvs oblong, undulate. Fls borne in lf axils, solitary or in dense clusters, starfish-like. S Afr. (Angola to the Karroo).
F. angustifolia Schum. Caudex large; st. erect or climbing, minutely hairy. Lvs 1.5–10cm, linear. Fls in clusters of 2–6, lobes green. Cape Prov.
F. capensis Endl. = *F. crispa.*
F. crispa (Jacq.) Schum. Puberulous throughout. Caudex napiform, large, almost entirely subterranean; st. twining or prostrate. Lvs 2–3cm, strongly undulate, oval acuminate. Fls 2–3 together, green-grey with small brown blotches. S Afr.
F. dammarana Schltr. Caudex ± thickened; br. felty when young. Lvs 1.2–2.3cm, linear-lanceolate. Fls few. Nam.
F. edulis (Thunb.) Schum. Caudex large. Lvs oblong to elliptical. Fls solitary or in groups of 2–3, lime green; corona white with long lobes. S Afr.
F. glabra Decne. = *F. edulis.*
F. multiflora Schum. Caudex large; br. stout, gnarled. Lvs small, flat, white-felted beneath. Fls numerous, in clusters. S Angola.
→*Cynanchum.*

Fodder Turnip *Brassica rapa.*

Foeniculum Mill. Umbelliferae. 1 glaucescent, aromatic perenn. or bienn. to 2m; st. soft, hollow, finely grooved. Lvs to 30cm, triangular in outline, 3–4-pinnate, v. finely cut, seg. filiform to 5cm; petiole bases ribbed, sometimes thick, sheathing. Umbels compound, 10–40-rayed, lacking involucre and involucel; fls yellow. Summer. Eur., Medit. Z5.
F. dulce DC. non Mill. = *F. vulgare* var. *dulce.*
F. dulce Mill. non DC. = *F. vulgare* var. *azoricum.*
F. piperitum (Ucria) Sweet = *F. vulgare* ssp. *piperitum.*
F. vulgare Mill. FENNEL. 'Purpurascens': st. and lvs flushed dark maroon, later bronze-green. var. *azoricum* (Mill.) Thell. FLORENCE FENNEL; FINOCCHIO. Lf bases enlarged and massively swollen, imbricate. var. *dulce* (DC.) Battand. & Trabut. Lf bases not thickened. ssp. *piperitum* (Ucria) Cout. Lf seg. rarely to 1cm, fleshy, petiole bases v. large and sheathing. Medit.

Foetid Adder's Tongue *Scoliopus bigelowii.*
Foetid Bugbane *Cimicifuga foetida.*
Foetid Currant *Ribes glandulosum.*
Foetid Pothos *Symplocarpus.*
Foetid Wild Pumpkin *Cucurbita foetidissima.*

Fokienia Henry & Thom. Cupressaceae. 1 everg. conifer, to 15m, usually a shrub to 3m in cult. Crown conic. Branchlets in 1 plane. Juvenile lvs bright green, arranged in false whorls, facial pairs small, obovate, acute, mucronate, with a wide, white, stomatal band either side of a central ridged, lat. pairs out-spread, each overlapping the pair above, giving shoots a jointed appearance; adult lvs smaller. Cones spherical, 1.7–2.5cm across; scales 12–16. S China, N Vietnam. Z8.
F. hodginsii (Dunn) Henry & Thom.

Folhado *Clethra arborea.*
Foliage Flower *Phyllanthus angustifolius*; *P. arbuscula.*

Folotsia Costantin & Bois. Asclepiadaceae. Leafless succulents. St. climbing or shrubby, smooth, segmented, terete. Infl. term.; fls numerous; corona lobes united at base, forming a pentagon. Madag. Z10.
F. aculeatum (Descoings) Descoings. St. to 30–40cm, trailing, thin, branching from the base, white-powdery. Fls few; cor. large, papillose within, white, tube 3.5mm, lobes triangular-oblong bifid. S Madag.
F. floribundum Descoings. Br. intricately entwined to 3m long, 1.5cm thick, intense green. Fls rose-scented, lobes 8–9mm long, 4mm wide at base, off-white, corona forming a pentangle with its edges opposite the sep. N Madag.
F. grandiflorum (Jum. & H. Perrier) Jum. & H. Perrier. Trailing, br. green, becoming white. Fls *c*20 in sessile umbels at nodes;

cor. round, large, lobes 7×2mm, triangular, pointed. Madag. →*Prosopostelma*.

Fontanesia Labill. Oleaceae. 1 spreading decid. shrub to 3m. Lvs to 2cm, oval to lanceolate, serrulate or coarse-margined, dull green. Fls numerous in axill. rac. or term. pan., small, green-white; pet. 4; sta. 2, longer than pet.; ovary superior, 2-chambered; style short. Fr. a thin, flat samara. Near East; China. Z6.

F. fortunei Carr. = *F. phillyreoides* ssp. *fortunei*.
F. phillyreoides Labill. ssp. *fortunei* (Carr.) Yaltirik. Shrub to 3m, upright. Lvs to 10cm, lanceolate, long-acuminate, entire, glossy, persisting to early winter. Fls small, white. Early summer. China. 'Nana': dwarf.

Fonteinbos *Psoralea aphylla*.

FONTINALACEAE W. Schimp. See *Fontinalis*.

Fontinalis L. ex Hedw. WATER MOSS. Fontinalaceae. 55 submerged aquatic mosses, forming loose mats. Lvs small in 3 rows on long st., usually ovate to lanceolate or suborbicular. Cosmop.

F. antipyretica L. ex Hedw. St. to 80cm, slender, erect-ascending dark olive-green. N Amer., Eurasia, N Afr. Z5.

Fool's Huckleberry *Menziesia ferruginea*.
Foothill Penstemon *Penstemon heterophyllus*.
Footsteps-of-spring *Sanicula arctopoides*.
Forest Bluegrass *Poa chaixii*.
Forest Boronia *Boronia muelleri*.

Forestiera Poir. Oleaceae. 20 usually decid. privet-like small trees or shrubs. Fls in axill. clusters or rac., insignificant. N & C Amer. Z6.

F. acuminata (Michx.) Poir. Shrub 1.5–2m or small tree, br. smooth. Lvs 3–10cm, ovate-oblong to lanceolate, acuminate, ± serrate above, dull green. Fls green-white; ♂ clustered, ♀ paniculate. Fr. to 1.2cm, purple. US. Z5.

F. neomexicana A. Gray. DESERT OLIVE. Shrub to 3m; br. slightly armed. Lvs to 5cm, ovate to lanceolate, crenulate, dull green, glab. Fls before lvs, yellow-white, clustered. Fr. 4mm, pruinose. Spring. SW US.

Forest Red Gum *Eucalyptus tereticornis*.
Forget-me-not *Myosotis* (*M. scorpioides*).
Fork Fern *Psilotum*.
Forman's Mallee *Eucalyptus formanii*.
Formosan Cherry *Prunus campanulata*.
Formosan Fir *Abies kawakamii*.
Formosan Gum *Liquidambar formosana*.

Forstera L. f. Stylidiaceae. 5 mat-forming perenn. herbs. Lvs imbricate, entire, leathery. Fls solitary or 2–5 on a slender, erect, term. peduncle; cal. 5–6-lobed; cor. 5–9-lobed. NZ, Tasm. Z9.

F. sedifolia L. f.. St. to 30cm, few-branched. Lvs 0.7cm, ovate to oblong-obovate. Fls 1.3cm diam., white, peduncles to 5cm. NZ.

Forsteronia G. Mey. Apocynaceae. 50 woody climbing vines with milky sap. Fls in dichasial or thyrsiform infl.; cor. funnel-form, limb flared; sta. carried on cor. tube, anth. exserted. Fr. a pair of follicles. Trop. Amer.

F. corymbosa (Jacq.) G. Mey. To 6m+. Lvs to 7.5cm, obovate to elliptic, coriaceous. Fls many; cor. red to salmon pink, tube 2–3mm, lobes 4–5mm. Fr. 10–15cm, robust. Cuba, Hispan.

Forster Sentry Palm *Howea forsteriana*.

Forsythia Vahl. Oleaceae. 6 decid. shrubs. Br. with chambered pith, sometimes hollow, golden-green, covered with lenticels. Fls yellow, borne before lvs, singly or clustered from scaly buds; cal. 4-lobed, green; cor. deeply divided into 4, basally united as short tube; sta. 2. E Asia, C Eur.

F. 'Arnold Dwarf'. (*F. intermedia* ×*F. japonica* var. *saxatilis*.) Prostrate. Lvs small, ovate, rarely 3-lobed, serrate. Fls seldom produced, green-yellow. Z5.

F. europaea Deg. & Bald. Related to *F. viridissima*, differs in its ovate lvs and loose habit, to 2m. Lvs to 8cm, ovate, simple, entire or sparsely serrate. Fls solitary; cal. lobes broad-ovate, green; cor. lobes narrow-oblong, deep yellow. Early spring. Albania, Balk. Z6.

F. fortunei Lindl. = *F. suspensa* var. *fortunei*.
F. giraldiana Lingl. To 4m. Br. dark grey, muricate. Lvs to 12cm, elliptic to lanceolate-oblong, acuminate, entire or serrulate, grey-green above, slightly downy beneath. Fls solitary; cor. pale yellow with short tube, bell-shaped to 2cm diam. Early spring (the first sp. to fl.). NW China. Z5.

F. ×intermedia Zab. (*F. suspensa* ×*F. viridissima*.) To 3m erect, spreading. Br. green-gold. Lvs ovate-lanceolate, serrate, simple or 3-lobed. Fls in clusters; cor. dark yellow, lobes spreading, somewhat revolute, twisted. Spring. 'Arnold Giant': fls large, golden, nodding. 'Beatrix Farrand': erect habit; fls single, 6cm wide, golden; one of the Farrand Hybrids. 'Charming': foliage variegated white; mutation in Lynwood Hybrids. 'Densiflora': broadly arching habit; fls single, large, crowded pale yellow; lobes reflexed. 'Karl Sax': vigorous, free-flowering; br. to 3m, laxer than 'Beatrix Farrand'; fls deep yellow, to 4.5cm wide, throat marked orange. 'Lynwood': a mutation of 'Spectabilis'; semi-erect; fls larger than 'Spectabilis'. 'Primulina': upright to 2m; lvs scabrous, serrate towards tip; fls single, like 'Densiflora' but with narrower lobes; profusely flowering, mid-spring. 'Spectabilis': upright to 2.5m; fls densely packed, dark yellow, lobes twisted; cor. divisions 5–6. 'Vitellina': vigorous, erect, then pendent; fls profuse, egg-yellow, small; cor. lobes reflexed. Z5.

F. japonica Mak. Related to *F. ovata* but more robust. Shrub to 1.5m. Lvs to 10cm, broad-ovate, closely serrate, downy beneath. Fls solitary, 1.5cm. Spring. Jap. Z6.

F. koreana (Rehd.) Nak. = *F. viridissima* var. *koreana*.
F. ovata Nak. KOREAN FORSYTHIA. To 1m, domed, compact. Br. grey-gold, twisted. Lvs to 6cm, ovate, entire or serrulate. Fls small, singly or in pairs, bright yellow. Mid-spring. 'French's Florence': to 1.5m; fls smaller, paler and more frost-resistant. 'Ottawa': hardier and more vigorous in growth, erect, strongly branched; fls profuse. 'Robusta': vigorous. 'Tetragold': bushy and low-growing to 1m; fls large, to 3cm across, deep yellow, early. Z5.

F. suspensa (Thunb.) Vahl. To 3m. Lvs often trifoliolate. Fls slender-stalked. Early spring. China. var. *fortunei* (Lindl.) Rehd. Shrub to 3m, erect, arching as growth matures. Lvs to 9×5cm, simple or 3-lobed, ovate, serrate. Fls clustered; cor. deep yellow, lobes deflexed, twisted. Mid-spring. China. var. *sieboldii* Zab. Shrub to 2.5m, semi-pendent, sometimes creeping. 'Atrocarpa': branchlets dark purple. 'Atrocaulis': v. vigorous, upright, branchlets and bark tinted dark purple-red or maroon; fls small, pale yellow. 'Aurea': lvs yellow. 'Decipiens': erect; fls solitary, long-stalked, numerous, deep yellow; cor. lobes spreading, margins involute. 'Nymans': close to 'Atrocaulis', fls larger, bright pale yellow; later than most. 'Pallida': ± upright, fls pale yellow, solitary. 'Variegata': lvs variegated yellow, fls sparse, deep yellow. Z5.

F. suspensa f. *atrocaulis* Rehd. = *F. suspensa* 'Atrocaulis'.
F. ×variabilis Seneta. (*F. ovata* ×*F. suspensa*.) 'Volunteer': vigorous shrub with dark brown br.; fls crowded, golden.

F. viridissima Lindl. To 3m, erect. Br. remain green for several seasons, tetragonal in section. Lvs to 8cm, lanceolate, v. seldom divided ×3, serrate above, flushing purple at fall. Fls clustered; cor. bright yellow with green stain, lobes narrow-oblong, to 1.5cm (late spring). China. 'Bronxensis': dwarf to 30cm; internodes v. short; lvs to 4cm, ovate; fls abundant. 'Robusta': vigorous, lvs long to 12cm, fls large. 'Variegata': lvs stippled white. var. *koreana* Rehd. To 2.5m, erect, spreading. Lvs to 12cm, ovate-oblong, violet-brown in autumn. Fls larger, pale yellow. Korea. Z5.

Fort Bragg Manzanita *Arctostaphylos nummularia*.
Forteventura *Lonchocarpus latifolius*.
Fortnight Lily *Dietes*.

Fortunaea Lindl.
F. chinensis Lindl. = *Platycarya strobilacea*.

Fortunearia Rehd. & Wils. Hamamelidaceae. 1 spreading shrub, to 10m. Young shoots stellate-pubesc., bark grey-brown. Lvs to 15×7cm, obovate, unequally toothed, abruptly acute, basally rounded, coriaceous, veins pubesc. beneath. Fls green, in term. rac.; cal. 5-lobed; pet. 5, narrow, minute, shorter than sep.; ♂ infl. almost catkin-like; ♀ fls open with the lvs, to 5cm. C & E China.

F. sinensis Rehd. & Wils. Z8.

Fortunella Swingle. KUMQUAT. Rutaceae. 4–5 shrubs or small trees, sometimes spiny. Lvs ovate, densely glandular-punctate beneath; petioles winged or margined. Fls solitary or in clusters, generally 5-merous, waxy, fragrant, white; sta. 16 or 20, in irregular bundles. Fr. ovoid or globose, small, seg. 3–7; peel thick, aromatic, with large immersed oil glands. S China.

F. crassifolia Swingle. MEIWA KUMQUAT. Twigs almost spineless. Lvs thick. Fr. 2.5–3.5×2.5cm, broadly ovoid to subglobose, seg. generally 7, with irregularly thickened walls, some seedless; peel v. thick, sweet. China. Z9.

F. hindsii (Champ.) Swingle. HONGKONG WILD KUMQUAT; DWARF KUMQUAT. Twigs spiny. Lvs ovate-elliptic, acuminate, dark green above; petioles winged. Fr. 1–1.5cm diam., bright tangerine-orange to flame-orange when ripe. Hong Kong, China. Z9.

F. japonica (Thunb.) Swingle. ROUND KUMQUAT; MARUMI KUMQUAT. V. similar to *F. margarita*, except lvs smaller, lighter green. Fr. ovoid, peel sweeter. S China. 'Meiwa': dwarf; fr. small, round, golden yellow. 'Sun Stripe': lvs variegated creamy yellow; fls white, scented; fr. yellow and striped green. Z9.

F. margarita (Lour.) Swingle. OVAL KUMQUAT; NAGAMI KUMQUAT. Small spiny tree, 3–4m. Lvs lanceolate, obtuse, dark glossy green above; petioles v. narrowly margined. Fr. 3–4×2–2.5cm, obovoid-oblong, golden yellow, peel spicy, sharp. S China. 'Nagami': dwarf; fr. small, oblong, bright orange. Z8.
→*Atalantia* and *Citrus*.

Fortune's Plum Yew *Cephalotaxus fortunei.*

Fosterella L.B. Sm. Bromeliaceae. 13 stemless perenn. herbs, to 80cm in fl. Lvs to 40cm, few, soft, forming a rosette, entire or weakly toothed. Pan. scapose, term.; floral bracts inconspicuous; fls small, white. C & S Amer. Z9.

F. micrantha (Lindl.) L.B. Sm. Lvs lanceolate. Infl. with a cobweb-like coating, much-branched; pet. narrow-elliptic. S Mex., Guat., El Salvador.

F. penduliflora (C.H. Wright) L.B. Sm. Lvs linear-lanceolate. Infl. lax, paniculate, glab.; pet. lanceolate-oblong. C Peru to NW Arg.

Fothergilla L. Hamamelidaceae. 2 decid. shrubs, to 3m. Lvs turning crimson or orange-yellow in autumn. Fls fragrant, precocious, apetalous in bottle brush-like, terminal heads or spikes, made up of about 24 long sta., anth. yellow. SE US.

F. alnifolia L. f. = *F. gardenii.*
F. alnifolia var. *major* (Lodd.) Sims = *F. major.*
F. carolina Britt. = *F. gardenii.*
F. gardenii Murray. Young shoots hairy-tomentose. Lvs to 6.5cm, obovate or oval, base cordate, margins unequally toothed in upper half. Fls in cylindrical spikes; fil. white, 2.5cm. Spring. SE US. A form exists with dark pink fls. Z5.
F. major Lodd. Young shoots white stellate-pubesc. Lvs to 10cm, round-oval or broadly ovate, nearly entire with a few teeth in upper half, stellate-pubesc. on veins beneath. Fls sweetly fragrant, in erect spikes; fil. to 2cm, white tinged pink. Early summer. Alleghany Mts. Z5.
F. monticola Ashe = *F. major.*
F. parvifolia Kearney = *F. gardenii.*

Fountain Bamboo *Sinarundinaria nitida.*
Fountain Flower *Ceropegia sandersonii.*
Fountain Grass *Pennisetum alopecuroides; P. setaceum.*
Fountain Plant *Russelia equisetiformis.*

Fouquieria HBK. Fouquieriaceae. 11 spp. ranging from small, columnar-stemmed succulents and spiny shrubs to trees. Lvs decid.; petioles becoming spinose; secondary lvs usually clustered in axils along st., somewhat fleshy. Fls showy in bracteate rac. or pan.; sep. 5, free; cor. tubular or campanulate, lobes 5, overlapping, spreading; sta. 10–17, exserted. Mex., SW US. Z9.

F. columnaris (Kellogg) Kellogg. BOOJUM TREE. St. columnar to 20m, erect, tapering, simple or with br. slender, glab., green to yellow, spiny, held at right angles; smaller br. arranged spirally; periderm dull green to light yellow. Lvs 22–40mm, elliptic to spathulate; secondary lvs elliptic-obovate. Pan. elongate, pseudoterminal; fls honey-scented; cor. creamy-yellow, 6–7mm. Summer–autumn. Mex., SW Calif.

F. diguetii (Tieghem) I.M. Johnst. Shrub to 4m, trunk branching basally, to 5 ascending st., periderm bronze, thin. Lvs to 44mm, ovate; secondary lvs to 26×12mm, broadly obovate to ovate. Pan. conical; cor. red, green-white below, waxy, to 20mm. Winter. Mex., SW Calif., Baja Calif.

F. fasciculata (Willd. ex Roem. & Schult.) Nash. Shrub or small tree, trunks 1–3, swollen, to 5m, 25–60cm diam., shiny green, succulent within, narrowing abruptly above. Lvs 25–55mm, oblanceolate to elliptic; secondary lvs 40×15mm. Pan. short; fls fragrant; cor. white to yellow, to 10mm. Winter–spring. Mex.

F. purpusii Brandg. Shrub to small tree, to 5m. Trunks 1–4, conical, tapering, 20–60cm diam.; br. numerous, slender, spiny, shiny except for patches of grey periderm. Lvs 35–50mm, elliptic to linear; secondary lvs 5–9, to 33×3mm, darker green above, entire. Pan. dense; cor. 7.5–9mm. Spring. Mex.

F. spinosa Torr. = *F. splendens.*

F. splendens Engelm. COACH-WHIP; OCOTILLO; JACOB'S STAFF; VINE CACTUS. Shrub to 10m. St. numerous, ascending, sometimes pendulous and branched; candelabriform; trunk stocky, basal diam. 15–25cm. Lvs 30–50mm, elliptic to oblanceolate; secondary lvs to 35×11mm, linear-spathulate to broad-obovate. Pan. pyramidal; cor. vermilion, 10–28mm. Winter–spring. New Mex. and Tex. to S Calif. and Baja Calif.

F. splendens HBK non Engelm.. = *F. fasciculata.*
→*Idria.*

FOUQUIERIACEAE DC. 1/11.
Fouquieria.

Four-angled Bean *Psophocarpus tetragonolobus.*
Four-o'-clock *Mirabilis jalapa.*

Fourraea Greuter & Burdet. Cruciferae. 1 perenn. herb to 4m. Lvs simple, ovate, entire; petiole long or 0 in narrower st. lvs. Fls 4-merous, racemose; pet. 4, pink or white, 4–7mm. S & SW Eur. Z7.
F. alpina (L.) Greuter & Burdet.
→*Arabis* and *Brassica.*

Four Seasons Rose *Rosa ×damascena* var. *semperflorens.*
Four Sisters Heath *Erica fastigiata.*
Foxberry *Vaccinium vitis-idaea.*
Foxglove *Digitalis.*
Foxglove Tree *Paulownia tomentosa.*
Fox Grape *Vitis labrusca; V. rotundifolia.*
Fox Nuts *Euryale.*
Fox's Brush *Centranthus ruber.*
Fox-tail Barley *Hordeum jubatum.*
Foxtail Fern *Asparagus densiflorus* 'Myersii'.
Foxtail Grass *Alopecurus.*
Foxtail Lily *Eremurus.*
Foxtail Millet *Setaria italica.*
Foxtail Orchid *Rhynchostylis.*
Foxtail Pine *Pinus balfouriana.*

Fragaria L. STRAWBERRY. Rosaceae. 12 stoloniferous, perenn. herbs. Lvs radical, petiolate, ternate; lfts dentate. Fls white, 5-merous, in 1–10-fld cymes; epical. present; cal. persistent; pet. 5–8; sta. 10–30. Fr. many small achenes on the surface of an enlarged, conical, fleshy, red receptacle. N Temp. zones, Chile.

F. alpina hort. = *F. vesca* 'Semperflorens'.
F. ×ananassa Duchesne. GARDEN STRAWBERRY; CULTIVATED STRAWBERRY. (*F. chiloensis* ×*F. virginiana.*) Stolons numerous; rhiz. somewhat stout. Lfts to 8×6cm, broad-ovate or obovate, glaucous and glab. above, white and adpressed-pubesc. beneath, dentate-serrate. Fls to 3.5cm diam., 5–15 per scape. Eur. 'Variegata': to 15cm; lvs variegated cream and green.

F. californica Cham. & Schlecht. Rootstock slender, short. Lfts to 5cm, rounded-obovate, obtuse, coarsely serrate, subglabrous above, sericeous beneath. Fls 2cm diam. in few-fld infl. Receptacle to 1.5cm diam., achenes superficial. Calif.

F. chiloensis Duchesne. BEACH STRAWBERRY. Rootstock short, thick. Lfts to 5cm, obovate, blunt, dentate, coriaceous, wrinkled, glossy above, sericeous-tomentulose beneath. Fls to 3cm diam. on thick, sericeous stalks. W US, S Amer. Z4.

F. chrysantha Zoll. & Moritz = *Duchesnea chrysantha.*
F. collina Ehrh. = *F. viridis.*
F. daltoniana Gay. Rootstock stout. Lfts to 2.5×2cm, obovate, coarsely dentate, adpressed or patent pubesc. beneath. Fls 1.5cm diam., occas. splotched red. Receptacle globose, later conical, to 2.5×1.5cm, pink or white. N India.
F. elatior Ehrh. = *F. moschata.*
F. indica Andrews = *Duchesnea indica.*
F. moschata Duchesne. HAUTBOIS STRAWBERRY; PLYMOUTH STRAWBERRY. Stolons few or 0. Lfts to 6cm, ovate or obovate to rhombic, coarsely serrate, corrugated-plicate, sparsely pubesc. above. Fls 2cm diam. scape exceeding lvs. Receptacle red, glab., lacking achenes near base. C Eur. Z6.
F. rubiginosa Lacaita = *F. daltoniana.*
F. sikkimensis Kurz = *F. daltoniana.*
F. vesca L. WILD STRAWBERRY. Stolons long, rooting. Lfts to 6cm, ovate, obovate or rhombic, serrate, bright green and sparse-pubesc. above, canescent beneath. Fls to 1.8cm diam., scape to 30cm, 2–7-fld. Receptacle to 1cm, glab.; achenes uniformly scattered over and projecting from the receptacle. Spring–summer. Eur. 'Alexandria': fr. small, sweet. 'Alpine Yellow': fr. yellow, small, sweet. 'Baron Solemacher': fr. small, acid to sweet. 'Rügen': fr. large, aromatic; v. productive. 'Semperflorens' (ALPINE STRAWBERRY, FRAISE DU BOIS): to 25cm, almost without runners; fls and fr. small; fls early summer and again in autumn. 'Variegata': lvs variegated cream and

grey-green. var. *monophylla* Duchesne. SINGLE LEAF STRAW-BERRY. Lvs 1–3-foliolate. Z5.

F. virginiana Duchesne. SCARLET STRAWBERRY. Stolons many, somewhat coriaceous, blue-green, subglabrous above. Fls often unisexual, ♀ fls much smaller than ♂; scapes to 25cm. Receptacle 2cm, deep red; achenes deeply sunken, 0 near the base. Spring. N Amer., E Eur. f. *alba* (Ehrh.) Rydb. Fr. less succulent, pale pink or green-white. The parent of 'Alpine', 'Everbearing' and 'Perpetual'. Z3.

F. viridis Duchesne. Resembles *F. vesca*, but stolons short, fili-form, lfts appressed-pubesc. or glab. above, fls cream-white, scape to 20cm, receptacle lacking achenes near its base. Spring–summer. Eur., Canary Is., Cauc., N & C Asia. Z6.

Fragile Cliff-brake *Cryptogramma stelleri*.
Fragile Fern *Cystopteris fragilis*.
Fragrant Agrimony *Agrimonia procera*.
Fragrant Epaulette Tree *Pterostyrax hispida*.
Fragrant Fern *Microsorium scandens*.
Fragrant-flowered Garlic *Allium ramosum*.
Fragrant Myall *Acacia omalophylla*.
Fragrant Olive *Osmanthus fragrans*.
Fragrant Orchid *Gymnadenia conopsea*.
Fragrant Snowball, Fragrant Snowbell *Styrax obassia*.
Fragrant Sumac *Rhus aromatica*.
Fragrant Waterlily *Nymphaea odorata*.
Fragrant Woodsia *Woodsia ilvensis*.

Frailea Britt. & Rose Cactaceae. *c*20 cacti; st. small tufted or solitary, depressed-globose to cylindric, usually weakly ribbed or tuberculate. Fls shortly funnelform, yellow, opening only briefly and in bright weather, or cleistogamous; floral areoles with dense wool and bristles. Fr. thin-walled, dry. E Boliv., S Braz., Parag., Urug. and N Arg.

F. albicolumnaris F. Ritter. Resembling *F. pygmaea*; st. shortly cylindric, 4–6×2–2.6cm; ribs finely tuberculate, without purple markings; areoles minute; spines 2–5mm, partly interlacing, nearly white. Fl. *c*4×5cm, stigmas 11. S Braz. Z9.

F. asterioides Werderm. = *F. castanea*.

F. caespitosa (Speg.) Britt. & Rose = *Parodia caespitosa*.

F. castanea Backeb. Simple; rootstock napiform; st. depressed-globose, 1–2×4.5cm, chocolate brown to dark green; ribs flat to slightly convex, scarcely tuberculate; areoles brown or nearly white, conspicuous; spines 0.5–5mm, stout, usually all directed downwards, ± adpressed, slightly or not interlacing, shiny brown becoming dull to almost black. Fl. 3–4×3–5cm, stigmas 8–11. NE Arg., S Braz., N Urug. Z9.

F. cataphracta (Dams) Britt. & Rose. Simple or sometimes clustering; st. depressed-globose, 1–3.5×2.5–4cm, dull deep green or bronzed; ribs low with almost flat tubercles; areoles white to brown, often with dark crescent-shaped markings be-neath; spines to 4mm, mostly adpressed or partly decid. Fl. 2–3.8×2–4cm, stigmas 5–9. E Boliv., Braz., S & E Parag. var. *cataphracta*. Areolar wool brown or almost 0; spines to 2mm, persistent, pale yellow or glassy-white, brown at base, strongly adpressed. Parag. var. *duchii* Moser. Areolar wool conspic-uous, white; spines to 4mm, decid. or persistent, yellow-grey or red-brown to almost black. E Boliv., Braz., S & E Parag. Z9.

F. chiquitana Cárdenas. Simple, rarely offsetting; st. 2–3×2.5–3.5cm, depressed-globose to globose, rarely short-cylindric, yellow- or blue-green or tinged with pink to red; ribs well defined but broken up into conspicuous, blunt tubercles, often with pronounced red markings beneath; areoles large, with persistent white wool; spines to 3mm, not or slightly inter-lacing, nearly white or dark. Fl. 1.7–3.2×2.2–4cm; stigmas 5–7. E Boliv. Z9.

F. colombiana (Werderm.) Backeb. Resembling *F. pumila*; st. 6×4cm, depressed-globose to short-cylindric, green; ribs tuberculate; spines to 6mm, interlacing, brown, yellow or yellow tipped brown, v. dense. Fl. to 2.5×2–2.5cm; stigmas *c*7. Colomb. (introd.?), S Braz., Urug. Z9.

F. curvispina Buining & Brederoo. Simple or clustering; st. to 5×3cm, grey-green; ribs finely tuberculate; spines 4–6mm, glassy white to pale yellow, curved and twisted, interlacing and obscuring the st. Fl. *c*3×2.6cm; stigmas 8. S Braz., Urug. Z9.

F. gracillima (Lem.) Britt. & Rose. Simple; st. 6–10×1.5–3cm, erect, cylindric, grey-green; ribs tuberculate; central spines 2–5, 4–10mm, dark red-brown to black-brown, radial spines 8–13, 2–4mm, white. Fl. to 3.5–4×3.5–4cm, densely woolly and bristly; stigmas *c*9–10. N Urug., S Braz. Z9.

F. grahliana (F.A. Haage, Jr. ex Schum.) Britt. & Rose. Cluster-ing, forming mounds; st. to 1.75–3×2.5–4cm, depressed-globose, dark green or bronzed; ribs conspicuously tuberculate; areoles with white to yellow wool; spines to 3.5–5mm, scarcely interlacing, pale yellow at first. Fl. to 3.5×4cm; stigmas 7–8, *c*2.5mm. S Parag., N Arg. Z9.

F. horstii Ritter. Resembling *F. gracilima*; st. to 18×2–2.5cm, eventually sprawling and branching; central spines 3–6, yellow-to red-brown, radial spines 15–20. Fl. to 4.3×5cm. S Braz. Z9.

F. ignacionensis Buining & Moser. Resembling *F. pumila*; st. simple depressed-globose, 2.5–3×4–4.5cm, green; ribs ± dis-solved into conspicuous, spiralled tubercles; spines to 4–5mm, mostly interlacing, nearly white to pale brown. Fl. 2.4–3×2–4.5cm; stigmas 5. Parag. Z9.

F. knippeliana (Quehl) Britt. & Rose. Resembling *F. pumila*; st. *c*4×2cm, simple or branching when old, short-cylindric, grass-green; ribs conspicuously tuberculate; spines to 5mm, interla-cing, yellow; central spines *c*2, radial spines 12–14. Fl. to 2.5×4.5cm; stigmas 6. Parag. Z9.

F. lepida Buining & Brederoo. Resembling *F. gracilima*; st. to 5×1–1.5cm, erect, grey to black-green; ribs sometimes marked purple below tubercles; spines 1.5–3mm. Fl. 1.5–2×2.2cm; stigmas 5–6. S Braz. Z9.

F. mammifera Buining & Brederoo. Simple, rarely branching; st. *c*3×2.5cm, globose or somewhat elongate, shiny, dark green; tubercles conspicuous, blunt, *c*2.5mm diam., with pronounced red-purple markings beneath; areoles minute, wool evanescent; spines to 5mm, slightly interlacing, golden yellow at first. Fl. 2.2–2.5×2.6cm; stigmas 5–8. S Braz., E Arg. Z9.

F. moseriana Buining & Brederoo. Resembling *F. grahliana*; clustering and mound-forming; st. 2.5–4×3–4cm, depressed-globose to globose, green; ribs strongly tuberculate; areoles large and woolly; spines to 5mm, partly interlacing, yellow-white, darker tipped. Fl. 2.4–3×2.1–3.5cm; stigmas 4–7. Parag. Z9.

F. perumbilicata F. Ritter. Resembling *F. pygmaea*; st. 1.5–3cm diam., simple, globose, dark or somewhat grey-green; ribs flat and scarcely tuberculate; areoles minute; spines 2–3mm, not or partly interlacing, light to dark brown. Fl. 3.5–4×4–5cm; stigmas 7–10. S Braz. Z9.

F. phaeodisca (Speg.) Speg. Simple; st. 1.5–3×1.5–3.5cm, pale to dark green or dark brown; ribs completely flat, separated by a dark, vertical line; areoles violet-black, with dark crescent-shaped markings beneath in young plants; spines to 2.5mm, not interlacing, white, brown-black at base. Fl. 2.2–3.5×2.2–4cm; stigmas 6–7. S Braz., Urug. Z9.

F. pulcherrima (Arech.) Speg. = *F. pygmaea*.

F. pumila (Lem.) Britt. & Rose. Simple or clustering sparsely when old; st. to 3×3–5cm, depressed-globose to globose, dark green or tinged red; ribs tuberculate; spines to 5mm, ± interla-cing, yellow, brown or red-brown. Fl. 1.8–2.7×2–3.5cm; stigmas 7–11. S Parag., S Braz., Urug. Z9.

F. pygmaea (Speg.) Britt. & Rose. Simple, sometimes clustering when old, st. 1–7×1–2.5cm, globose to shortly cylindric, light to dark or grey-green; ribs composed of minute, nearly flat tubercles, often with dark red-purple, crescent- or V-shaped markings beneath; areoles minute, with white, grey or brown wool; spines 1–4mm, bristly, not or partly interlacing, usually ± adpressed, white, yellow or brown at first. Fl. 3.5–5×3.5–5cm; stigmas 7–12. Arg., S Braz., Urug. Z9.

F. schilinzkyana (F.A. Haage, Jr. ex Schum.) Britt. & Rose. Usually clustering; st. 2–4×2–4cm, deprsesed-globose to globose, bright green; ribs ill-defined or dissolved into low but conspicuous, spirally-arranged tubercles; spines to 3mm, not interlacing, brown to nearly black. Fl. 2–3.5×2.5–3.5cm; stigmas 5–7. S Parag., N Arg. Z9.

→*Echinocactus*.

Fraise du Bois *Fragaria vesca*.
Framboise *Rubus idaeus*.
Franceschi Palm *Brahea elegans*.

Francoa Cav. BRIDAL WREATH. Saxifragaceae. 5 perenn. everg. herbs, 90–150cm. Lvs basal, obovate to broadly-lanceolate, usu-ally pinnatisect, lobes rounded, net-veined, bristly and gland. Rac. dense, terminal, scapose spike-like; fls small, white-pink; sep. 4; pet. 4, oblong with dark spots at base of claw; sta. 8. Summer. Chile. Z7.

F. appendiculata Cav. Infl. to 68cm, sparingly branched, compact; fls shell pink, occas. spotted.

F. glabrata DC. = *ramosa*.

F. ramosa D. Don. BRIDAL WREATH. Infl. to 90cm, axis downy, much-branched; fls white.

F. sonchifolia Cav. Lvs with broadly winged petioles. Infl. to 60cm; fls pink with darker spotting or blotches.

Frangipani *Plumeria*.

Frangula Mill.
F. alnus Mill. = *Rhamnus frangula*.
F. californica A. Gray = *Rhamnus californicus*.

F. caroliniana (Walter) A. Gray = *Rhamnus carolinianus*.
F. rupestris (Scop.) Schur = *Rhamnus rupestris*.

Frankenia L. Frankeniaceae. 40 usually prostrate, halophytic, everg. subshrubs or perenn. herbs. St. wiry. Lvs small, heath-like, revolute, pubesc. Fls 4–6-merous, to 5mm diam., term. or from forks of br.; cal. tubular, ribbed; pet. overlapping. Temp. and subtrop. coastal regions.
F. laevis L. SEA HEATH. Everg. shrublet to 15cm. Br. wiry, becoming tinged red, finely pubesc. Lvs clustered, linear, ciliate at base, glab. above. Fls pink, solitary at ends of shoots and in forks of br. S & W UK to Medit. and Asia Minor.
F. thymifolia Desf. Everg. subshrublet; st. to 15cm, creeping, densely tufted. Lvs opposite, downy, thick, oblong. Fls rose, solitary or in small groups. Spain to N Afr.

FRANKENIACEAE Gray. 3/30. *Frankenia*.

Franklandia R. Br. Proteaceae. 2 shrubs. Lvs alt., lobed, petiolate. Rac. term.; fls few, subtended by minute bracts; perianth tube slender, lobes spreading; fil. inserted below tube apex. W Aus. Z9.
F. fucifolia R. Br. LANOLIN BUSH. Slender shrub to 1.6m. Lvs 3–6cm, glandular-punctate, seg. divergent, erect, terete. Rac. 8–12-fld to 15cm; fls yellow, spotted red, lanolin-scented, perianth tube 2–4cm. All year. W Aus.
F. triaristata Benth. PLUMED LANOLIN BUSH. Erect shrub to 1m. Lvs 20cm, less divided than *F. fucifolia*. Rac. 5–9-fld; fls chocolate-scented; perianth off-white, chocolate-brown beneath, tube 5–6cm, lobes undulate. Late winter to spring. W Aus.

Franklinia Marshall. Theaceae. 1 decid. shrub or tree to 10m. Br. erect; young shoots silky. Lvs 10–15cm, obovate-oblong, sparsely serrate, dark glossy green, pubesc. beneath, bright red in fall. Fls to 8cm diam., cup-shaped, solitary or paired in axils; pet. 5, obovate, crenulate, white. Fr. a woody rounded capsule to 2cm diam. SE US (Georgia). Z8.
F. alatamaha Bartr. ex Marshall.
→*Gordonia*.

Frasera Walter. GREEN GENTIAN; COLUMBO. Gentianaceae. 15. Robust, erect, taprooted, bienn. or perenn. herbs. Lvs mostly basal, opposite or whorled, entire. St. solitary, simple; fls crowded in paniculate clusters; cor. rotate, 4-merous, each lobe bearing 1–2 fringed basal glands. Summer. N Amer.
F. albicaulis Douglas ex Griseb. To 60cm. Lvs to 30cm, narrow-oblanceolate to spathulate, margin white, pubesc. Fls tinted blue-green. W N Amer. Z5.
F. caroliniensis Walter. To 2.5m. Lvs to 15cm, oblong. Fls cream, dotted dark purple. E N Amer. Z2.
F. montana Mulf. To 90cm. Basal lvs to 20cm, linear-lanceolate, lvs reduced, margins narrow, white. Fls white to cream. Idaho. Z4.
F. nitida Benth. = *F. albicaulis*.
F. parryi Torr. To 1.2m. Basal lvs to 30cm oblanceolate to obovate, st. lvs narrow. Fls white, often stained green, flecked purple-black near glands. S Calif. Z8.
F. speciosa Douglas ex Griseb. GREEN GENTIAN. To 2m. Lvs to 30cm, oblanceolate to obovate. Fls white flushed green, dotted purple. NW US. Z3.
F. umpquaensis Peck & Appleg. To 90cm. Lvs to 30cm, oblanceolate. Fls white flushed green to pale yellow. Oreg. Z4.
→*Swertia*.

Fraser River Douglas Fir *Pseudotsuga menziesii* var. *caesia*.
Fraser's Boronia *Boronia fraseri*.

Fraxinus L. ASH. Oleaceae. 65 mostly decid. trees. Lvs opposite, pinnate. Fls often insignificant, in pan. or rac. before lvs; cal. small, 4-lobed or 0; cor. with, usually, 4 pet., sometimes 0. Fr. a 1-seeded samara with long, flattened, wing. Temp. Eur., Asia, N Amer., a few in Trop.
F. acuminata Lam. = *F. americana* 'Acuminata'.
F. alba Marsh = *F. americana*.
F. albicans Buckley = *F. texensis*.
F. americana L. Tree to 40m, crown spreading, bark grey, furrowed; buds dark brown. Lfts to 9, to 15×9cm, petiolate, oblong-lanceolate, acute, entire or serrate, glab. above, slightly downy beneath. Fr. wing oblong, 3–5cm. Spring. NE US. 'Acuminata': lvs long-acuminate, entire, glossy dark green above, almost white beneath, tinted purple in autumn. 'Asciidiata': lvs long-acuminate, more ovate. 'Autumn Blaze': habit oval; lvs purple in fall. 'Autumn Applause': trunk straight, crown rounded, dense and vigorous; autumn lvs deep red to mahogany. 'Autumn Purple': fall foliage purple to chocolate

brown, mottled mauve and bronze, persistent. 'Champaign County': strong and straight, crown dense; lvs lustrous, dark green, bronzed in autumn. 'Pendula': br. and branchlets pendulous. 'Rosehill': fast-growing, br. sparse with strong central leader, lvs dark green above, tinted white beneath, bronzed in autumn. var. *microcarpa* A. Gray. Fr. much smaller. Z3.
F. americana var. *biltmoreana* (Beadle) J. Wright = *F. biltmoreana*.
F. americana f. *texensis* Gray = *F. texensis*.
F. angustifolia Vahl. Tree to 25m. Lfts to 13, sessile, oblong-lanceolate, to 7cm, narrow-acuminate, serrate, dark green above, paler beneath, glab. Fr. wing elliptic-oblong, to 4cm, rounded at base. S Eur., N Afr. 'Elegantissima': small to 8m, lfts to 6×1cm, light green. 'Monophylla': lvs simple or 3-lobed at br. bases, to 12cm, ovate to lanceolate, serrate, bright green above, pubesc. beneath. 'Pendula': br. thin, pendulous. 'Raywood': vigorous with strong leader and loose feathery crown; lvs slender, glossy, dark green, colouring plum-violet in autumn. var. *australis* (Gay) Schneid. Lvs puberulous beneath. S Eur., N Afr. var. *lentiscifolia* Henry. Lvs widely spaced. ssp. *syriaca* (Boiss.) Yaltirik. Lvs crowded in whorls; pinnae slender. Asia Minor. Z6.
F. anomala Torr. UTAH ASH. Tree to 8m. Br. winged; buds dark grey-tomentose. Lfts 5, blunt, ovate, to 6cm, entire or crenulate, dark green above; rachis russet, downy at first. Fr. wing obovate to 2cm. SW US. Z6.
F. berlandierana DC. Tree to 10m. Lfts to 5, term. lft oblanceolate, others obovate, to 10cm, basal portion cuneate, entire or sparsely serrate, veins pubesc. beneath. Fr. wing ovate to spathulate, to 3.5cm. Tex., Mex. Z8.
F. biltmoreana Beadle. BILTMORE ASH. Tree to 15m. Lfts to 11, obovate, sometimes falcate, to 15cm, entire or slightly crenate, glab., dark green above, pubesc., blue-green beneath, autumn colour maroon-yellow. Fr. wing emarginate, to 4cm. E US. Z4.
F. bungeana DC. Shrub to 5m. Lfts to 7, stalked, obovate, acuminate, crenulate, glab., to 4cm; rachis pubesc., sulcate. Fls pubesc., in showy pan. to 7cm. Fr. wing narrow-oblong to 3cm, emarginate. Late spring. N China. Z5.
F. bungeana Hance non DC. = *F. chinensis* var. *rhyncophylla*.
F. caroliniana Mill. SWAMP ASH. Small tree to 15m. Lfts to 7, stalked, oval, acuminate, serrate, dark green above, pale beneath with conspicuous veins, white-downy. Fr. wing obovate, to 5×1.8, broadly winged. SE US. Z6.
F. chinensis Roxb. Not widely cultivated, differs from var. *rhyncophylla* in ± equal lfts. var. *acuminata* Lingl. has slender, acuminate lfts. var. *rhyncophylla* (Hance) Hemsl. Tree to 25m. Lfts 5, obovate, short-acuminate, term. lft 6–15cm, others short-er, near-sessile, crenate, dark green, glab. above, slightly downy beneath, dark hair fascicles at juncture of pinnae and rachis, purple-tinted in fall. Fls fragrant in term. pan. to 15cm. Fr. wing oblanceolate, 3×0.5cm. Summer. Korea, China. Z6.
F. coriacea S. Wats. = *F. velutina*.
F. densiflora Lingl. = *F. paxiana*.
F. dipetala Hook. & Arn. Small tree to 5m. Br. flushed red at first. Lfts to 7, obovate, oval to cuneate in term. lft, 2–6cm, entire or crenate, obtuse, pale green. Fls off-white with pet., 2, in pan. to 10cm, showy. Late spring. Calif. Z8.
F. dippeliana Lingl. = *F. bungeana*.
F. excelsior L. COMMON EUROPEAN ASH. Tree to 40m. Dormant buds black. Lfts to 11, sessile, obovate, serrate, dark green above, paler beneath, glab. Fr. wing oblong, to 4cm. Spring. Eur. to Cauc. 'Angustifolia': pinnae narrow. 'Argenteovariegata': lvs white, variegated. 'Aurea': lvs yellow, slow-growing. 'Aurea Pendula': pendulous, branchlets golden. 'Aureovariegata': lvs yellow, variegated. 'Crispa': Lfts crispate. 'Diversifolia': lvs simple or trifoliate, habit erect. 'Erosa': lvs narrow, undulate. 'Heterophylla Pendula': lvs simple, habit pendulous. 'Jaspidea': lvs yellow, vigorous. 'Nana': low, domed. 'Pendula': br. pendulous. 'Pendulifolia Purpurea': pendulous, maroon shoots. 'Spectabilis': habit upright, pyramidal. 'Westhof's Glorie': tall with spreading crown; young growth deep brown, appearing late; lfts to 13, lf base 2-lobed. Z4.
F. floribunda Wall. HIMALAYAN MANNA ASH. Related to *F. ornus*, differs in larger, long-acuminate lfts. Tree to 40m. Young br. mauve, punctate; lfts to 9, sessile, oval-oblong, to 15cm, coarsely toothed, long-acuminate, glab. above, pubesc. beneath; rachis winged. Fls in showy pan. to 30cm, white. Fr. wing spathulate, emarginate, 3cm. Early summer. Himal. Z8.
F. floridana (Wenz.) Sarg. = *F. caroliniana*.
F. formosana Hayata = *F. griffithii*.
F. griffithii Clarke. Tree to 7m. Bark grey. Young shoots brown, downy, square in section. Lfts entire to 7, to 8cm, elliptic-oblong, short-acuminate, pale shiny green above with silvery pubesc. veins beneath, coriaceous. Fls white, showy, in term.

silvery pan. SE Asia. Z8.

F. holotricha Koehne. Tree to 10m. Growth densely pubesc. Dormant buds brown. Lfts to 13, short-petiolate, lanceolate, to 7cm, coarsely serrate, acuminate, hoary. Balk. 'Moraine': br. spreading at first, then erect to incurved; bark silver-grey; lvs persist into autumn. Z6.

F. juglandifolia Lam. = *F. americana*.

F. lanceolata Borkh. = *F. pennsylvanica* var. *subintegerrima*.

F. latifolia Benth. OREGON ASH. Related to *F. pennsylvanica*, from which it differs by sessile, lat. lfts. Tree to 20m. Young growth rusty-pubesc., muricate. Lfts to 9, ovate-oblong, to 15cm, acute, slightly pubesc. beneath. Fr. wing to 5cm. W US. Z6.

F. longicuspis hort. = *F. sieboldiana*.

F. mandshurica Rupr. MANCHURIAN ASH. Related to *F. nigra*, differs in lf veins sunken above, prominent beneath. Tree to 30m. Lfts sessile, to 11, obovate or lanceolate, to 12cm, coarsely toothed, matt green, pubesc. above with veins sunken, vein axils rusty-pubesc. beneath, rachis winged. Fr. wing lanceolate, to 3cm. N Asia. 'Mancana': vigorous to 2.25m, crown globose; lvs large. Z6.

F. mariesii Hook. f. = *F. sieboldiana*.

F. moorcroftiana Brandis = *F. xanthoxyloides*.

F. nigra Marsh. BLACK ASH. Related to *F. mandshurica* from which it differs in having pinnae basally rounded with v. shallow teeth. Tree to 25m. Lfts to 11, sessile, oblanceolate to 12cm, serrulate, veins brown, downy beneath. Fr. wing oblong, obtuse, to 4cm. N Amer. 'Fallgold': lvs gold in autumn. Z7.

F. obovata Schneid. = *F. chinensis* var. *rhyncophylla*.

F. oregona Nutt. = *F. latifolia*.

F. ornus L. MANNA ASH; FLOWERING ASH. Tree to 8m, buds grey-brown. Lfts to 7, obovate, petiolate, to 7cm, term. lft obovate, serrulate, dark-green above, paler beneath, midrib somewhat pubesc. Fls white, fragrant, in showy term. pan. Fr. wing narrow-oblong, to 2.5cm. Spring. S Eur., Asia Minor. var. *rotundifolia* (Lam.) Ten. Lfts more rounded. S Medit. 'Pendula': br. mostly pendulous. Z6.

F. oxycarpa hort. = *F. angustifolia* 'Raywood'.

F. oxycarpa Bieb. ex Willd. = *F. angustifolia*.

F. oxycarpa var. *angustifolia* (Vahl) Lingl. = *F. angustifolia*.

F. oxyphylla Bieb. = *F. angustifolia*.

F. oxyphylla var. *oligophylla* Boiss. = *F. angustifolia* ssp. *syriaca*.

F. paxiana Lingl. Shrub or small tree, to 20m. Winter buds rusty-tomentose. Lfts to 9, ovate, to 18cm, sessile, crenulate, glab., long-acuminate. Fls showy, white, fragrant. Early summer. China, Himal. Z5.

F. pennsylvanica Marsh. RED ASH. Tree to 18m. Bark fissured, brown. Lfts to 9, lanceolate, acuminate, entire or serrulate toward apex, olive green, midrib sunken, petiolules sulcate, 7–15×3–5cm. Fr. wing usually spathulate-lanceolate. N Amer. 'Aucubifolia': pinnae dappled yellow-green. 'Bailey': to 20m, seedless, trunk straight, br. regular; hardy. 'Bergeson': to 20m, straight and fast-growing, br. sparse when young, later dense; lvs glossy. 'Dakota Centennial': to 17m, crown globose, seedless. 'Emerald': to 12m, bark rough, corky, crown ellipsoid, lvs dark green. 'Kindred': hardy and erect, later spreading; lvs glossy dark green. 'Marshalls Seedless': vigorous; lvs glossy dark green; seedless; disease-resistant. 'Newport': improved seedless form, trunk straight, br. regular. 'Patmore': vigorous, fastigiate; lvs shiny, lasting into autumn; good pest resistance. 'Summit': ♀, pyramidal when young, later broadening, autumn lvs tinted gold. 'Urbanite': broadly pyramidal; lvs lustrous, thick, bronzed in autumn, tolerant of city conditions, resistant to sun scorch. 'Variegata': lvs silvery, bordered and marked ivory. var. *subintegerrima* (Vahl) Fern. (var. *lanceolata*): the Green Ash with bright green, glab. shoots and glab., narrowly lanceolate lfts. Z4.

F. pistaciaefolia Torr. = *F. velutina*.

F. platycarpa Michx. = *F. caroliniana*.

F. platypoda Oliv. Tree to 20m, bark iron-grey, finely furrowed. Lfts to 11, oval-oblong or lanceolate, minutely serrate, narrow-acuminate, base cuneate, 8–14×3–5cm, dark green, glab. above, papillose beneath, midrib downy. Infl. to 30cm. Fr. wing oblong, tapered toward end, 2.5cm, wings red-green. China. Z5.

F. platypoda sensu Dallim. = *F. spaethiana*.

F. potamophila Herd. Tree to 10m. Lfts to 9, rarely 11, petiolate, ovate-elliptic, 2.5cm, cuneate, serrate, glab. Fr. wing elliptic-oblong, 3–5cm. Turkestan. Z6.

F. pubescens Lam. = *F. pennsylvanica*.

F. pubinervis Bl. = *F. sieboldiana*.

F. quadrangulata Michx. BLUE ASH. Tree to 25m. Young shoots square in section; dormant buds hoary. Lfts to 11, short-petiolate, ovate-lanceolate, 6–12cm, cuneate at base, coarsely serrate, yellow-green above, glab. beneath, midrib pubesc. Fr. wing to 5cm, oblong, crenate at apex. N Amer. Z4.

F. regelii Dipp. = *F. potamophila*.

F. rhyncophylla Hance = *F. chinensis* var. *rhyncophylla*.

F. rotundifolia Lam. = *F. ornus* var. *rotundifolia*.

F. sambucifolia Lam. = *F. nigra*.

F. sieboldiana Bl. Tree to 8m. Young growth slender, grey, downy. Lfts to 7, to 3.5cm wide, ovate, abruptly acuminate, serrate or entire, near-sessile except apical lft, glab., midrib downy. Fls white in pan., to 15cm. Early summer. Jap., China. Z6.

F. sogdiana Dipp. = *F. angustifolia* ssp. *syriaca*.

F. spaethiana Lingl. Tree to 10m. Br. grey, glab., buds black. Lfts to 9, sessile, ovate-lanceolate, abruptly acuminate, to 16cm, crenate, coriaceous, dark green, glab. above, paler, sparsely pubesc. beneath; rachis red brown, swollen at base. Fls white, apetalous in glab. pan. Fr. wing oblanceolate, obtuse, to 3cm. Jap. Z6.

F. stenocarpa Koidz. = *F. spaethiana*.

F. suaveolens W.W. Sm. = *F. paxiana*.

F. subintegerrima Vahl. = *F. pennsylvanica* var. *subintegerrima*.

F. syriaca Boiss. = *F. angustifolia* ssp. *syriaca*.

F. tamariscifolia Vahl = *F. angustifolia*.

F. texensis (A. Gray) Sarg. Tree to 15m. Lfts 5, 3–8cm, v. coriaceous, obtuse, crenate, terminal lft acute, dark green above, pale beneath with woolly vein axils and reticulate venation. Tex. Z6.

F. tomentosa Michx. f. PUMPKIN ASH. Possibly *F. pennsylvanica* ×*F. americana* (tetraploid form). Tree to 40m, trunk swollen at base with protruberances. Young br. tomentose at first. Lfts to 9, lanceolate, elliptic, to 11×4cm, entire or uneven-serrate, leathery, deep olive green above, paler, pubesc. beneath. Fr. wing to 7cm, oblong-elliptic, obtuse or emarginate. Spring. E US. Will tolerate wet situations Z6.

F. toumeyi Britt. = *F. velutina* var. *toumeyi*.

F. turkestanica Carr. = *F. angustifolia* ssp. *syriaca*.

F. uhdei (Wenz.) Lingl. SHAMEL ASH. Everg. tree or shrub; buds rusty brown. Lvs 10–18cm. Lfts to 7, oblong-lanceolate, long-attenuate, serrate, glab.; rachis and petiole silver-tomentose. Fls dense in pan. to 17cm. Fr. wing elliptic, to 3×0.5cm. C Amer. 'Majestic Beauty': v. large, vigorous and strongly-branched, crown rounded; lvs glossy dark green. 'Tomlinson': small, crown narrow, br. ascending; lvs leathery, serrate. Z8.

F. velutina Torr. ARIZONA ASH. Shrub or small tree. Lfts to 7, lanceolate-elliptic, to 7cm, coarsely serrate and dull green above, pubesc. beneath. SW US. 'Fan-Tex': fast-growing, well-proportioned; lvs larger, deep green, uniform, leathery; seedless. 'Von Ormi': vigorous, seedless, lvs narrow. Z7. var. *coriacea* (S. Wats.) Rehd. Lvs more coriaceous and glab. Calif. var. *toumeyi* (Britt.) Rehd. Habit dense. Lvs smaller, lfts 3–5, downy. Ariz., NW Mex.

F. verecunda Koidz. = *F. spaethiana*.

F. xanthoxyloides (G. Don) DC. AFGHAN ASH. Small tree to 6m. Lfts to 9, 2–4cm, sessile or short-stalked, narrow- to broad-elliptic, obtuse, crenate, midrib pubesc. beneath; rachis winged, downy. Fr. wing spathulate, emarginate with cal. persistent. Himal. to Pak., N Afr. (Atlas Mts) var. *dumosa* (Carr.) Lingl. Shrubby, dwarf, globose with tangled br. Lfts ovate, to 1cm, thick, rigid. Z8.

Freckle Face *Hypoestes phyllostachya*.

Freesia Ecklon ex Klatt. Iridaceae. 11 perenn. cormous herbs. Lvs linear-lanceolate, conduplicate, ribbed, arranged in a fan. Flowering st. simple or branched, flexuous; infl. a secund spike; bracts green or scarious; fls irregular, sometimes only slightly so, sometimes 2-lipped; perianth tube slender at base, tep. 6; sta. inserted on tube throat; style filiform, 3-branched. S Afr. Z9.

F. alba (G.L. Mey.) Gumbl. St. 12–40cm, usually branched; spike 2–8-fld; fls 25–60mm, erect, almost regular, sweetly scented, white, sometimes flushed purple outside and lined with purple in throat, sometimes with a yellow mark on lowest tep. Winter–spring.

F. armstrongii Wats. = *F. corymbosa*.

F. corymbosa (Burm. f.) N.E. Br. St. to 50cm with several br.; spikes 3–10-fld; fls 25–35mm, scented or unscented, ivory, pale yellow with the lower tep. bright yellow, or pink with a yellow throat (*F. armstrongii*). Usually late winter–spring.

F. ×hybrida L.H. Bail. = *F. cvs.*

F. ×kewensis hort. = *F. cvs.*

F. leichtlinii Klatt. St. usually 8–20cm, simple or with 1–2 br.; spike 2–8-fld; fls 25–40mm, bilabiate scented, cream or pale yellow, the lower tep. orange yellow, the upper tep. sometimes flushed with purple-brown on outside. Late winter–early spring.

F. muirii N.E. Br. = *F. leichtlinii*.

F. odorata Ecklon ex Klatt = *F. corymbosa*.

F. ×ragioneri hort. = *F. cvs.*

F. refracta (Jacq.) Klatt. St. (8–)20–45cm; spike 5–12-fld; fls 25–40mm bilabiate, with a spicy scent, pale yellow, yellow-brown, green or purple with orange marks on lower tep., veined with purple in throat. Winter–early spring.

F. refracta 'Leichtlinii'. = *F. leichtlinii*.

F. refracta var. *alba* G.L. Mey. = *F. alba*.

F. sparmannii (Thunb.) N.E. Br. St. 12–18cm; spikes 3–8-fld; fls 30–40mm, scentless, tube and outside of tep. purple-flushed, inside white with yellow spot on lower tep. and at junction of narrow and wide parts of tube. Early spring.

F. cvs. The florist's freesias are complex hybrids involving *F. alba*, *F. corymbosa*, *F. refracta* and *F. leichtlinii*. L.H. Bailey grouped them under the hybrid epithet *F.* ×*hybrida*; several hybrids within the complex but of more determined parentage had also been named, including *F.* ×*kewensis*, an accidental cross between *F. leichtlinii* and a pink form of *F. corymbosa* that arose toward the end of the 19th century, *F.* ×*ragioneri*, derived from *F. alba* and *F. leichtlinii*, and *F.* ×*tubergenii*, derived from *F. corymbosa* and *F. alba*. The cvs range in height from 10cm to 30cm, in habit from the neat and tufted to the tall and graceful, in infl. from short and semi-erect to long, sparsely branched and horizontal; the fls may be single or 'double', scarcely to sweetly scented, and vary in colour from silvery white (e.g. 'Miranda') to ivory (i.e. 'Fantasy', with fls double), yellow or bronze; from soft pink (e.g. 'Aphrodite': fls double) to red (e.g. 'Pallas': fls fragrant) and mauve (e.g. 'Romany': fls double; 'Apothoase': fls pale mauve, throat white) blue and indigo (e.g. 'Uchida': fls semi-double with a yellow throat). These colours are sometimes combined, particularly as bronze, pearly or lavender flushing on the exterior or as a pale yellow or white throat.

F. ×*tubergenii* hort. = *F.* cvs.

Fremontia Torr.

F. californica Torr. = *Fremontodendron californicum*.

F. mexicana (Davidson) Macbr. = *Fremontodendron mexicanum*.

F. napensis Eastw. = *Fremontodendron californicum* ssp. *napense*.

Fremontodendron Cov. FLANNEL BUSH; CALIFORNIA BEAUTY. Sterculiaceae. 2 ± everg. shrubs, tawny-stellate-pubescent. Lvs leathery, unlobed or palmately 3-, 5-, or 7-lobed. Fls solitary, on short pedicels; cal. waxy petaloid, 5-lobed, with glandular-pitted nectaries at base inside; bracts usually 3, at the base of the cal.; pet. 0; staminal tube divided into 5. SW N Amer.

F. californicum (Torr.) Cov. Shrub to 7m, br. spreading. Branchlets spurlike. Lvs to 5cm, suborbicular to elliptic-ovate, unlobed to 3-lobed, dull green and sparsely stellate-pubesc. above, densely tawny-stellate beneath. Fls fully visible, opening all at once 3.5–6cm diam., shining golden yellow, nectaries hairy. Calif., W Ariz., N Baja Calif. ssp. *napense* (Eastw.) Munz. Habit shrubbier. Lvs to 2.5cm, thinner; fls to 3cm diam., often rose-tinged. Calif.

F. mexicanum Davidson. Close to *F. californicum*, differing in 5-lobed lvs and narrower cal. lobes. Shrub to 6m. Lvs 2.5–7cm, suborbicular, cordate and 5–7-lobed, sparsely stellate-pubesc. above, densely tawny-tomentose beneath. Fls partly hidden by lvs, successional 6–9cm diam., shallowly campanulate, orange-yellow, becoming red at base outside, nectaries glab. or glabrate. S Calif. and N Baja Calif. Z9. 'California Glory' (*F. californicum* ×*F. mexicanum*): hardier than either parent, growth strong; fls flat, lemon tinged red on exterior, nectaries softly haired. 'Ken Taylor': dwarf; fls orange-yellow. 'Pacific Sunset': vigorous, to 6m; lvs angularly lobed; cal. bright yellow with tail-like tips. 'San Gabriel': like 'California Glory' but with deeply cut almost maple-like lvs.

→*Fremontia*.

Fremont's Crowfoot *Clematis fremontii*.
French Bean *Phaseolus vulgaris*.
French Heather *Erica* ×*hiemalis*.
French Honeysuckle *Hedysarum coronarium*.
French Hybrid Ceanothus *Ceanothus* ×*delilianus*.
French Lavender *Lavandula stoechas*.
French Marigold *Tagetes patula*.
French Plantain *Musa* ×*paradisiaca*.
French Rose *Rosa gallica*.
French Rye *Arrhenatherum elatius*.
French Sorrel *Rumex scutatus*.
French Tarragon *Artemisia dracunculus*.
French Thyme *Plectranthus amboinicus*.
French Tree *Tamarix gallica*.
French Weed *Thlaspi arvense*.
French Willow *Epilobium angustifolium*.

Frenela Mirb. = *Callitris*.

Frerea Dalz. Asclepiadaceae. 1 succulent, perenn. herb; st. to 10cm, glab., decumbent or pendulous, green or grey, to 2cm thick. Lvs to 60mm, fleshy, oblong or ovoid. Fls solitary or in pairs, apical, 20mm diam.; cor. maroon, lobes deltoid, with a small yellow central spot, margins purple-ciliate; corona purple. E India. Z10.

F. indica Dalz.
→*Caralluma*.

Freshwater Cord Grass *Spartina pectinata*.

Freycinetia Gaudich. Pandanaceae. 175 climbing or scrambling tall everg. shrubs. St. slender, ringed with persistent lf bases, sometimes producing aerial roots. Lvs *Dracaena* like, decussate to spiralling, linear-lanceolate, slightly concave above, recurved, tip finely acuminate, base sheathing, leathery, dark green, veins parallel. Fls unisexual, apetalous in cylindrical spadices subtended by tough, pointed, overlapping coloured bracts. Sri Lanka to SE Asia, Aus., NZ, Pacific Is. Z10.

F. banksii Cunn. Lvs to 90×2.5cm, minutely toothed. Infl. bracts thick, white or pale lilac, fleshy. NZ.

F. multiflora Merrill. Lvs to 30×2cm, smooth. Infl. bracts orange to brick-red, boat-shaped, waxy. Philipp.

Freylinia Colla. Scrophulariaceae. 4 glab., everg. shrubs. Lvs entire, sessile. Fls in pan. or rac.; cal. lobes 5, elliptic or lanceolate; cor. tube straight, throat pubesc., lobes 5, ovate or oblong, fertile sta. 4, rarely protruding. Trop. & S Afr. Z9.

F. cestroides Colla. = *F. lanceolata*.

F. lanceolata (L. f.) G. Don. HONEY BELLS. To 3m. Lvs linear. Pan. to 10cm; fls scented; cor. 12×3–6mm, tube exterior white or cream, interior deep yellow, lobes rounded, often tipped pink.

F. oppositifolia Colla. = *F. lanceolata*.

F. rigida G. Don. = *F. undulata*.

F. undulata Benth. To 1.8m. Lvs ovate to ovate-lanceolate. Rac. 8–13cm; cor. lilac, tube to 2cm, limb to 0.8cm diam., lobes rounded.

→*Capraria*.

Friar's Cap *Aconitum napellus*.
Friar's Cowl *Arisarum vulgare*.
Friendship Plant *Billbergia nutans*; *Pilea involucrata*.
Friendship Tree *Crassula ovata*.
Frijol *Phaseolus vulgaris*.
Frijolito *Sophora secundiflora*.
Frilled Fan *Euphorbia lactea*.
Fringebell *Shortia soldanelloides*.
Fringe Cups *Tellima*.
Fringed Brome *Bromus canadensis*.
Fringed Everlasting *Helichrysum baxteri*.
Fringed Galax *Shortia soldanelloides*.
Fringed Gentian *Gentianopsis*.
Fringed Polygala *Polygala paucifolia*.
Fringed Poppy Mallow *Callirhoë digitata*.
Fringed Synthyris *Synthyris schizantha*.
Fringed Violet *Viola fimbriatula*.
Fringed Water Lily *Nymphoides peltata*.
Fringed Wattle *Acacia fimbriata*.
Fringed Wormwood *Artemisia frigida*.
Fringepod *Thysanocarpus*.
Fringe Tree *Chionanthus*.

Frithia N.E. Br. Aizoaceae. 1 cushion-forming stemless succulent. Lvs erect, clavate to subcylindrical, 2cm, papillose, dark purple-green with a transparent 'window' on the flattened tip. Fls solitary, sessile, 9–23mm diam., crimson to purple-white with a white centre, occas. pure white. S Afr. Z9.

F. pulchra N.E. Br. FAIRY ELEPHANT'S FEET.

Fritillaria L. Liliaceae (Liliaceae). 100 bulbous perenn. herbs. Lvs lanceolate to linear, a solitary basal lf and several alt. or whorled st. lvs. Fls usually pendulous, tubular to campanulate subtended by leaflike bracts; tep. 6, in 2 whorls, those of inner whorls broader; nectaries ± conspicuous, 1 per tep.; sta. 6; style solitary, ± equal to sta., entire or bifid. Temp. regions of N Hemis., esp. Medit., SW Asia, W N Amer.

F. acmopetala Boiss. St. 15–45cm. Lvs 7–11, alt., linear. Fls solitary or 3 together, broadly campanulate; tep. 2.5–4cm, lanceolate to oblanceolate, inner acute, recurved, green with ferruginous markings; nectaries 5–11×2–4mm, ovate to ovate-lanceolate, green or tinged black. W Asia, E Medit. (Cyprus, Leb., Syr., S Turk.). Z7.

F. affinis (Schult.) Sealy. RICE-GRAIN FRITILLARY. St. 15–20cm. Lvs 3–15, in whorls, linear-lanceolate to ovate. Fls 1–4, occas. to

12, campanulate; tep. 2–4cm, lime-green to purple, tessellated; nectaries 1–2cm, triangular to ovate-lanceolate. NW Amer. Z5.

F. agrestis Greene. STINK BELLS. St. 30–60cm. Lvs 5–11cm, 5–12, oblong-lanceolate to linear-lanceolate, glaucous. Fls 1–5, campanulate, malodorous; tep. 25–30mm, white tinged green, ± purple-brown spotted within; nectaries oblong, small, green. Calif. Z8.

F. alburyana Rix. St. 4–10cm. Lvs 3–4, alt., lanceolate. Fls 1–2, cupular to almost flat; tep. 2–3cm, pale pink, tessellated; nectaries 1mm, basal, elliptic, green. NE Turk. Z7.

F. alfredae Post. ssp. **glaucoviridis** (Turrill) Rix. St. 10–35cm. Lvs 9–11, often opposite, oblanceolate to ovate. Fls 1–3, narrowly campanulate; tep. 12–30mm, inner spathulate, green and glaucous without, lime-green within, unmarked; nectaries 5×2mm, basal, ovate, green. S Turk. Z8.

F. armena Boiss. St. 10–20cm. Lvs 3–4, alt., lower lanceolate, upper linear. Fls solitary, conic; tep. to 2cm, elliptic-lanceolate, ciliate, deep red to dark purple-brown, tessellated; nectaries 3–5mm, basal, oblong to linear-lanceolate, hirsute. NE Turk. Z7.

F. askabadensis Micheli = *F. raddeana*.

F. assyriaca Bak. St. 4–20cm. Lvs 3–9cm, 4–12, alt., linear, often canaliculate. Fls 1-5, narrowly campanulate; tep. 12–25mm, obtuse or acute, tinged dull green or purple-brown; nectaries 2–4×1mm, linear-lanceolate. Turk. Z8.

F. assyriaca hort. non Bak. = *F. uva-vulpis*.

F. atropurpurea Nutt. St. 15–60cm. Lvs 5–9cm, 7–14, alt. or whorled, linear to lanceolate. Fls 1–4, openly campanulate; tep. 10–20mm, oblong to rhombic, purple-brown, spotted yellow or white, with yellow apical tuft; nectaries circular, yellow tinged brown. NW Amer. Z4.

F. aurea Schott. St. 4–15cm. Lvs 3.5–8cm, 5–8, alt., lanceolate to ovate-lanceolate, glaucous. Fls solitary, broadly campanulate; tep. 2–5cm, ovate to oblong, yellow with orange or red-brown tessellations; nectaries to 7mm, rhomboid. Turk. Z7.

F. biflora Lindl. MISSION BELLS; BLACK FRITILLARY. St. 15–40cm. Lvs mostly basal, ovate-lanceolate, glossy green. Fls 1–6, campanulate; tep. 2–3.5cm, with longitudinal ridges within, brown tinged black to purple, flushed with green; nectaries linear. Calif. 'Martha Roderick': fls rusty red and white. Z8.

F. bithynica Bak. St. 8–20cm. Lvs 5–12, opposite, oblanceolate to ovate. Fls 1 to 4, narrowly campanulate; tep. 17–27mm, inner obovate and cuneate, lime-green or glaucous without, occas. with purple markings, lime-green within; nectaries 3×1mm, lanceolate, brown or green. Spring. W Turk., Greek Is. Z8.

F. bornmuelleri Hausskn. = *F. aurea*.

F. bucharica Reg. St. 10–35cm, papillose. Lvs opposite or alt., lanceolate to ovate. Fls 1–10, cupulate; tep. 14–20mm, lanceolate, white or off-white with green veins; nectaries 3mm, deeply indented. C Asia, NW Afghan. Z5.

F. burnatii Planch. = *F. meleagris* ssp. *burnatii*.

F. camschatcensis (L.) Ker-Gawl. BLACK SARANA. St. 15–75cm. Lvs whorled below, alt. above, lanceolate. Fls 1–8, broadly campanulate to cupulate; tep. 20–30mm, acute, ridged within, purple-brown to black, occas. tinged yellow-green; nectaries narrowly oblong. Late spring. NE Asia to NW Amer. Z4.

F. carduchorum Rix = *F. minuta*.

F. carica Rix. St. 5–15cm. Lvs 3–7.5cm, 4–8, alt., lanceolate or oblanceolate, glaucous, margins papillose, upper lvs twisted. Fls 1–3, narrowly campanulate; tep. 13–20mm, ovate to lanceolate, obtuse, yellow fading to orange; nectaries 2–4×1mm, narrowly ovate, tinged black. SW Turk. Z8.

F. caucasica Adams. St. 15–40cm. Lvs 3–4, alt., lower oblong-ovate, upper narrowly lanceolate. Fls solitary, campanulate to conic; tep. 18–25mm, elliptic-lanceolate, dark red-violet to purple-brown, exterior cinereous; nectaries 3–5mm, linear-lanceolate. NE Turk., Cauc. Z7.

F. caussolensis Goaty & Pons ex Ardoino = *F. montana*.

F. chitralensis Wallich. Like *F. imperialis* except fls 1–4, smaller, conic, buttery yellow. N India. Z6.

F. cirrhosa D. Don. St. 20–60cm. Lvs whorled, usually linear. Fls 1–4, broadly campanulate; upper bracts tendril-like; tep. 3.5–5cm, narrowly elliptic, tinged purple, green or white, variously marked; nectaries ovate. Late spring. E Himal., China. Z5.

F. citrina Bak. = *F. bithynica*.

F. collina Adams. St. 4–35cm. Lvs 5–9, alt., linear to lanceolate, glossy green. Fl. solitary, broadly campanulate to turbinate; tep. 3.5–5cm, incurved at apex, dark maroon, with yellow tessellations, exterior glaucous, inner tep. fringed; nectaries narrowly ovate, deeply indented. S Russia, Georgia. Z8.

F. contorta hort. ex Bak. = *F. meleagris* ssp. *burnatii* 'Contorta'.

F. crassifolia Boiss. & Reut. St. 6–20cm. Lvs generally 4, alt., lanceolate. Fls 1–3, broadly campanulate; tep. 18–24mm, tinged yellow or green, with small brown tessellations, generally with an indistinct green central stripe; nectaries linear. Anatolia. ssp.

kurdica (Boiss. & Noë) Rix. Lvs 5–7, linear, glaucous; inner tep. obtuse; nectary forming longitudinal ridge. Z7.

F. dasyphylla Bak. = *F. bithynica*.

F. davisii Turrill. St. 10–20cm. Lvs 3.5–11cm, 7–10, alt., or opposite, upper narrower than lower, glossy green. Fls 1–3, broadly campanulate; tep. 18–24mm, green, with brown or black tessellations; nectaries lanceolate. S Greece. Z8.

F. delphinensis Gren. & Godron = *F. tubaeformis*.

F. drenovskyi Deg. & Stoj. St. 10–30cm. Lvs 6–7cm, 4-9, alt., narrowly lanceolate, glaucous. Fls 1–4, narrowly campanulate; tep. 15–25mm, dark dull purple to red-brown, tinged green within, glaucous without; nectaries linear-lanceolate, green. NE Greece, SW Bulg. Z6.

F. eduardi Reg. Similar to *F. imperialis* but lacking characteristic odour. St. 50–150cm. Lvs in 3–4 whorls, oblong-lanceolate to ovate-lanceolate. Fls in a crowded umbel, erect or conic to broadly campanulate; tep. 45–50mm, oblong-lanceolate, bright red; nectaries circular. Tadzhikistan, S Kashmir. Z7.

F. eggeri Bornm. = *F. persica*.

F. ehrhartii Boiss. & Orph. St. 8–20cm. Lvs 2.5–7cm, 6–10, opposite below, alt. above, oblong-lanceolate to ovate. Fls 1 to 4, narrowly campanulate; bracts 3, whorled; tep. 17–27mm, outer narrowly ovate or oblong, inner obovate-cuneate, dark purple-brown and yellow at apex without, lime-green within; nectaries lanceolate, brown or green. Greece. Z8.

F. elwesii Boiss. St. 15–55cm. Lvs 4–8, alt., linear, glaucous. Fls 1–4, narrowly campanulate; tep. 20–30mm, purple-brown with a clear green stripe; nectaries lanceolate. S Turk. Z7.

F. gibbosa Boiss. St. to 6–30cm, densely papillose below at first. Lvs 3–7cm, 4–10, ovate or lanceolate, upper much narrower. Fls to 25mm diam., 1–10, open saucer-shaped; tep. 15mm, pink or rosy-purple, darker at base, spotted or blotched; nectaries deeply impressed. NE Iran, Afghan. Z8.

F. glauca Greene. SISKIYOU-LILY. St. 12–18cm. Lvs 2–4cm, mostly basal, alt., glaucous. Fls 1–4 together, pendulous, broadly campanulate; tep. 15–20mm, yellow mottled with brown, occas. all brown; nectaries lanceolate to elliptic. W US. Z7.

F. glaucoviridis Turrill = *F. alfredae* ssp. *glaucoviridis*.

F. gracilis (Ebel) Asch. & Gräbn. = *F. messanensis* ssp. *gracilis*.

F. gracillima Smiley = *F. atropurpurea*.

F. graeca Boiss. & Sprun. St. 6–20cm. Lvs 3.5–11cm, 7–10, alt., or opposite, glaucous. Fls 1–3, broadly campanulate; tep. 18–24mm, green, with brown or black tessellations, with a clear green central stripe; nectaries lanceolate. S Greece. ssp. **thessala** (Boiss.) Rix. Larger; lvs not glaucous; bracts in a whorl of 3; tep. 28–38mm, green, lightly tessellated. S Albania, Balk., NW Greece. Z7.

F. graeca var. **gussichiae** Deg. & Dörfl. = *F. gussichiae*.

F. guicciardii Heldr. & Sartori = *F. graeca*.

F. gussichiae (Deg. & Dörfl.) Rix. St. 20–30cm. Lvs 5–8, alt., ovate to lanceolate, v. glaucous. Fls 1–3 in a long rac., broadly campanulate; tep. 30mm, green, ferruginous-marked (not tessellated); nectaries ovate, green. Mid Balk. Z6.

F. hermonis Fenzl in Kotschy ssp. **amana** Rix. St. 10–35cm. Lvs 5–6, alt., lanceolate or oblong. Fls 1 or 2, broadly campanulate; tep. 25–35mm, green, faintly brown- or purple-tessellated or yellow; nectaries ovate, green or black. S Turk. to Leb. Z8.

F. hispanica Boiss. & Reut. St. 10–50cm. Lvs 5–7.5cm, generally 6–9, alt., linear to narrowly lanceolate. Fls 1–3, broadly campanulate; tep. 20–40mm, sometimes recurved, green to brown without, tinged yellow within, with brown markings or tessellations. Spain and Port. Z8.

F. imperialis L. CROWN IMPERIAL. Muskily scented. St. 50–150cm. Lvs in 3–4 whorls of 4–8, lanceolate. Fls 3–5 in an umbel, broadly campanulate; bracts 10–20 in a term. coma; tep. 40–55mm, orange or red; nectaries circular, white. S Turk. to Kashmir. 'Argenteovariegata': lvs edged white; fls rusty orange, pendent. 'Aureomarginata': lvs edged gold. 'Aurora': fls bright red-orange. 'Crown on Crown': fls red-orange, two whorls of fls one above the other. 'Lutea': fls golden yellow. 'Lutea Maxima': tall; fls large, butter yellow. 'Orange Brilliant': fls orange, tinted brown. 'Rubra Maxima': tall; fls large, orange tinted red. 'Sulphurino': fls pale tangerine. 'The Premier': fls orange tinted yellow, veins tinged purple. Z4.

F. imperialis ssp. **inodora** Reg. = *F. eduardi*.

F. involucrata All. St. 15–25cm. Lvs 7–10, opposite, linear-lanceolate to linear. Fls solitary, broadly campanulate; bracts in a whorl of 3; tep. 25–40mm, green, sometimes tessellated purple-brown; nectaries ovate, blackened. SE Fr., NW It. Z7.

F. karadaghensis Turrill = *F. crassifolia* ssp. *kurdica*.

F. kurdica Boiss. & Noë = *F. crassifolia* ssp. *kurdica*.

F. lanceolata Pursh = *F. affinis*.

F. latifolia Willd. St. 4–35cm. Lvs 5–9, alt., ovate to lanceolate, glossy green. Fls solitary, broadly campanulate to turbinate; tep. 35–50mm, incurved, dark maroon, with yellow tessellations within, somewhat glaucous without; nectaries narrowly ovate, impressed. NE Turk., Cauc., NW Iran. The related *F. nobilis* Bak. from Caucasus and Turkish Armenia, has dull purple olive-yellow chequered fls. Z6.

F. libanotica (Boiss.) Bak. = *F. persica*.

F. liliacea Lindl. WHITE FRITILLARY. St. 15–35cm. Lvs 2–20, mostly basal, lower opposite, oblong-lanceolate to ovate, glossy green. Fls 2–8, conic to campanulate; tep. 12–25mm, white, tinged green or yellow at base; nectaries oblong, lime-green, occas. with purple spots. Calif. Z9.

F. lusitanica Wilkstr. = *F. hispanica*.

F. lutea Bieb. non Mill. = *F. collina*.

F. macrandra Bak. = *F. tuntasia*.

F. meleagris L. SNAKE'S HEAD FRITILLARY; GUINEA-HEN FLOWER; CHEQUERED LILY; LEPER LILY. St. 12–30cm. Lvs 6–13cm, 4–6, alt., linear to linear-lanceolate. Fl. solitary or 2 together, broadly campanulate; tep. 30–45mm, white or pink tinged and blood red- to purple-tessellated, to pure white; nectaries linear, green. Spring–early summer. Eur. (S Engl. to N Balk., Rom., W Russia). 'Alba': fls white. 'Aphrodite': fls white, large. 'Artemis': fls checked with deepest purple. 'Charon': fls dark purple. 'Emperor': fls checked grey and violet. 'Pomona': fls checked white and violet. 'Poseidon': fls purple-pink. 'Saturnus': fls pale violet tinted red. ssp. *burnatii* (Planch.) Rix. Lvs smaller; tep. purple. S & W Alps. 'Contorta': fl. contracted to a narrow bell to 5cm long, and tep. joined in lower part. Z4.

F. messanensis Raf. St. 15–45cm. Lvs 7–10, lowest opposite, linear. Fls 1–3, broadly campanulate; bracts in a whorl of 3; tep. 22–42mm, inner recurved green, ferruginous-tessellated; nectaries ovate-lanceolate, green. C Medit. var. *atlantica* Maire. Lvs shorter, v. glaucous. Atlas Mts, Moroc. ssp. *gracilis* (Ebel) Rix. Bracts generally alt.; tep. not recurved, plain green. Balk., Albania. Z9.

F. michailovskyi Fomin. St. 6–24cm. Lvs 5–9, alt. or lowest opposite, lanceolate. Fls 1–4, ± umbellate, broadly campanulate; tep. 20–30mm, purple-brown or tinged green without, tipped yellow; nectaries linear, prominent, yellow. NE Turk. Z7.

F. micrantha Heller. BROWN BELLS. St. 40–90cm, light green. Lvs 5–15cm, on upper part of st., whorled, linear. Fls 4–10, broadly campanulate; tep. 12–20mm, tinged purple or white tinged green, occas. faintly mottled, with tuft of white hairs at apex; nectaries oblong-lanceolate. Calif. Z8.

F. minor Ledeb. = *F. ruthenica*.

F. minuta Boiss. & Noë. St. 10–20cm. Lvs generally 5–7, alt. or whorled above, lanceolate 7–10cm, shining green. Fls 1–3, narrowly campanulate; tep. 16–22mm, lanceolate, acute, yellow tinged purple or red-brown, sometimes blotched; nectaries lanceolate. SE Turk. Z8.

F. montana Hoppe. St. 15–40cm. Lvs 8–20, alt. or whorled, linear. Fls 1–3, broadly campanulate; tep. 18–26mm, elliptic, green, with heavy tessellations in dark red or purple to black, or brown; nectaries linear. S Eur. Z6.

F. multiflora Kellogg = *F. micrantha*.

F. mutica Lindl. = *F. affinis*.

F. neglecta Parl. = *F. messanensis* ssp. *gracilis*.

F. nigra hort. non Mill. = *F. montana*.

F. nigra Mill. non hort. = *F. pyrenaica*.

F. nobilis Bak. see *F. latifolia*.

F. obliqua Ker-Gawl. St. 10–20cm. Lvs to 13cm, 8–11, alt. or opposite, lanceolate, glaucous. Fls 1–4, conic to campanulate, narrowed at mouth; tep. 20–30mm, v. dark purple tinged black, glaucous without; nectaries linear, green. S Greece. Z8.

F. olivieri Bak. St. 20–30cm. Lvs 5–8, alt., narrowly lanceolate, green. Fls 1–3 in long rac., broadly campanulate; tep. 3cm, green, ferruginous-marked (not tessellated); nectaries ovate, green. Iran. Z6.

F. oranensis Pomel = *F. messanensis* var. *atlantica*.

F. orientalis Adams. St. 15–40cm. Lvs 4–13cm, 6–10, opposite or whorled, linear. Fls solitary, broadly campanulate; tep. to 30mm, oblong-elliptic, tinged green, with heavy dull purple-brown tessellations; nectaries linear, tinged green. S Eur. Z7.

F. pallidiflora Schrenk. St. 10–80cm. Lvs opposite or alt., broadly lanceolate, glaucous. Fls v. broadly campanulate; tep. 25–45mm, pale yellow tinged green, with faint red-brown tessellations; nectaries deeply indented, ovate. Spring–early summer. E Sib., NW China. Z3.

F. parviflora Torr. = *F. micrantha*.

F. persica L. St. 20–50cm, leafy. Lvs alt., lanceolate, grey-green. Fls 7–20+ in an erect, term. rac., narrowly campanulate; tep. 15–20mm, tinged with black, grey, purple-maroon or green; nectaries triangular to rectangular. W Asia, Middle East. 'Adiyaman': tall, to 1m; fls dull maroon. Z5.

F. pinardii Boiss. St. 6–20cm. Lvs 3–8, alt., lanceolate, glaucous. Fls 1 to 4, narrowly campanulate; tep. 15–25mm, tinged grey or purple and glaucous without, orange, yellow or green within; nectaries linear-lanceolate. Turk. Z7.

F. pineticola Schwarz = *F. bithynica*.

F. pinetorum Davidson. St. 10–30cm, glaucous. Lvs 5–15cm, 12–20, somewhat whorled, linear, glaucous. Fls 3–9, ± erect; tep. 14–1mm, purple, mottled with yellow-green; nectaries indistinct. SW US. Z5.

F. pluriflora Torr. ADOBE-LILY; PINK FRITILLARY. St. 18–40. Lvs 6–13, alt., mostly basal, oblong-lanceolate. Fls 1–12; tep. 20–35mm, obovate, pink or somewhat tinged purple; nectaries linear. Calif. Z5.

F. pontica Wahlenb. St. 15–45cm. Lvs about 8, opposite or sub-opposite, lanceolate to linear-lanceolate. Fls solitary or 2 together, broadly campanulate; bracts in a whorl of 3; tep. 25–45mm, green, usually ferruginous-marbled; nectaries circular, blackened. Balk., N Greece, NW Turk. Z6.

F. pterocarpa Stocks = *F. gibbosa*.

F. pudica (Pursh) Spreng. YELLOW FRITILLARY. St. 8–30cm. Lvs 2–7, lowest generally opposite, upper alt., linear to narrowly lanceolate. Fls 1–6, narrowly campanulate; tep. 10–25mm, yellow or orange tinged, nectaries dark. W N Amer. Z3.

F. purdyi Eastw. St. 10–40cm. Lvs mostly basal, rosulate, elliptic to oblong-lanceolate, sinuate. Fls 1–4, (to 14) campanulate; tep. 15mm, off-white or tinged pale green, strongly veined and mottled purple-brown; nectaries oblong. Calif. Z8.

F. pyrenaica L. St. 15–30cm. Lvs 4.5–11cm, 7–10, alt., lanceolate to linear-lanceolate. Fls solitary or 2 together, broadly campanulate; tep. 25–35mm, recurved at apex, dark purple tinged black or brown, heavily tessellated without, green tinged yellow within and brown tessellated in basal half; nectaries triangular to ovate-lanceolate. S Fr., NW Spain. Z5.

F. racemosa Ker-Gawl. = *F. montana*.

F. raddeana Reg. St. 50–150cm. Lvs to 15cm, alt., or whorled, lanceolate, pale lustrous green. Fls 6–20 in an umbel, broadly campanulate to conic; bracts 10–20, linear, in a term. coma; tep. 40–55mm, oblong-lanceolate or inner lanceolate-rhomboid, pale yellow or tinged green with yellow-green veins, with apical white hairs; nectaries circular. NW Iran, Turkmenia. Z4.

F. recurva Benth. SCARLET FRITILLARY. St. 20–90cm. Lvs 9–25, in whorls, linear to linear-lanceolate, often glaucous. Fls 3–12, in a rac., narrowly campanulate; tep. 20–35mm, recurved, orange-red to scarlet, with yellow tessellations; nectaries lanceolate. Calif., S Oreg. Z7.

F. rhodocanakis Orph. ex Bak. St. 6–20cm. Lvs 3.5–11cm, 7–10, alt., or opposite, glaucous. Fls 1–3, broadly campanulate; tep. 18–25mm, inner obtuse, dark purple or purple-brown, yellow at apex and along margins, or yellow tinged green throughout; nectaries lanceolate. S Greece. Z8.

F. roylei Hook. f. St. 20–60cm. Lvs 4–5 in each of 6–7 whorls, linear-lanceolate. Fls 1–4, broadly campanulate; tep. 35–50mm, narrowly ovate, green tinged yellow, spotted or streaked dull purple; nectaries ovate. Late spring. Kashmir, Punjab. Z5.

F. ruthenica Wikstr. St. 20–50cm. Lvs 6–9cm, 6–12, opposite, alt. or in whorls, linear. Fls 1–3, broadly campanulate; bracts coiled; tep. 18–26mm, elliptic, blackened without, yellow tinged green within, with purple-brown tessellations; nectaries linear. Russia, W Sib. Z4.

F. schliemannii Sint. = *F. bithynica*.

F. sewerzowii Reg. St. 15–20cm. Lvs alt. or opposite, lanceolate. Fls 4–12, in a rac., or solitary, narrowly campanulate, widely flared at mouth; bracts to 7×2cm, solitary at base of each fl. stalk; tep. 25–35mm, green to livid purple without, and yellow to brick-red at base and within; nectaries linear, grooved. C Asia, NW China. Z5.

F. sibthorpiana (Sm.) Bak. St. 20–30cm. Lvs 9–17cm, 2–3, alt., ovate-lanceolate. Fls solitary, narrowly campanulate; tep. 18–22mm, lanceolate, yellow; nectaries linear-lanceolate, green. Greece, SW Turk. Z8.

F. stenanthera (Reg.) Reg. St. 10–30cm, papillose. Lvs opposite, ovate and alt., lanceolate to linear. Fls 1–10, generally 4–7, in a rac., conic, flared at mouth; bracts 2 at the base of each fl. stalk; tep. 14–20mm, lanceolate, tinged pink; nectaries visible as bulges on outside. Soviet Asia. Z7.

F. syriaca Hayek & Siehe = *F. pinardii*.

F. tenella Bieb. = *F. orientalis*.

F. thessalica Sprun. & Nyman = *F. graeca* ssp. *thessala*.

F. thunbergii Miq. St. 30–80cm. Lvs numerous, opposite, alt. or whorled, linear. Fls 1–6 broadly campanulate to cupulate; bracts tendril-like; tep. 23–35mm, off-white, faintly tessellated or green-veined; nectaries linear-lanceolate. C China. Z8.

F. tristis Heldr. & Sartori = *F. obliqua*.

F. tubaeformis Gren. & Godron. St. 4–35cm. Lvs 5–9, alt., lanceolate to linear-lanceolate, glaucous. Fl. solitary, broadly campanulate to turbinate; tep. 35–50mm, incurved, dark maroon tinged glaucous grey without, with yellow tessellations within; nectaries ovate, impressed. SW Alps. ssp. *moggridgei* (Boiss. & Reut.) Rix. Tep. yellow tinged green; nectaries linear-lanceolate. SW Alps. Z6.

F. tuntasia Heldr. St. 10–35cm. Lvs to 13cm, 8–25, alt. or opposite, lanceolate, upper smaller, glaucous. Fls 1–6, conic to campanulate, somewhat narrowed at mouth; tep. 20–30mm, dark purple tinged black, exterior glaucous; nectaries linear, green. Greece. Z8.

F. uva-vulpis Rix. St. 10–35cm. Lvs 3–5, alt., lanceolate, shining green. Fls solitary or 2 together, narrowly campanulate; tep. 20–28mm, grey-purple and glaucous without, tinged yellow within; nectaries ovate, large. W Asia. Z7.

F. verticillata Willd. St. 20–60cm. Lvs lowest opposite, others in whorls of 3–7, narrowly lanceolate to linear. Fls 1–5, broadly campanulate; bracts tendril-like; tep. to 45mm, oblong to oblong-obovate, concave, off-white or tinged pale yellow, dark-striped without, faintly mauve-tessellated within; nectaries linear-lanceolate, indented. C Asia, W Sib. Z5.

F. verticillata var. *thunbergii* (Miq.) Bak. = *F. thunbergii*.

F. walujewii Reg. St. 20–70cm. Lvs numerous, opposite, alt. or whorled, linear-lanceolate. Fls 1–6, broadly campanulate to cupulate; bracts tendril-like; tep. to 50mm, oblong-elliptic, white tinged green to pink without, white or flushed with red to purple-brown and faintly spotted or tessellated within; nectaries orbicular to lanceolate. Tadzhikistan, NW China. Z7.

F. wanensis Freyn = *F. crassifolia* ssp. *kurdica*.

F. whittallii Bak. St. 10–20cm. Lvs 8–12cm, 6–7, alt., linear. Fls 1–2, broadly campanulate, tep. 25–32mm, narrowly ovate, green, with brown tessellations; nectaries ovate to circular. Spring–early summer. Turk. Z8.

→*Korolkowia*.

Froelichia Moench. COTTONWEED. Amaranthaceae. 26 ann., bienn. or perenn. herbs. St. erect to procumbent; br. hairy, viscid above. Lvs to 15cm, opposite, ovate, linear oblong or spathulate, canescent above, tomentose beneath. Spikes opposite and term., with woolly bracts; lat. fls inconspicuous, subtended by a scarious bract and 2 bracteoles; cal. tubular; sta. 5, fused into a long tube. Americas.

F. drummondii Moq. Erect ann., to 1.2m. Br. brown-silky to woolly. Spikes 1–6cm; bracts ovate, fuscous or stramineous; cal. tube winged, ridged, wings erose. Okl., Tex. Z7.

F. floridana Moq. Erect, ann. to 1.8m. Br. white or yellow, lanate to tomentose. Spikes to 10cm, white-woolly; bracts rotund, black; cal. tube 6mm, woolly, with 2 lat. wings. Indiana to Minn. to Tex. Z6.

F. gracilis (Hook.) Moq. Erect or procumbent ann., to 60cm. Br. villous to tomentose. Spikes 1–3c; cal. to 4mm, v. woolly, with 2 rows of spines. Iowa to Colorado, S to Tex. Z6.

Frogbit *Hydrocharis* (*H. morsus-ranae*).
Frogfruit *Phyla*.
Frog Orchid *Coeloglossum*.
Frog's Buttons *Lemna*.
Frog's Lettuce *Groenlandia*.
Frost Grape *Vitis cordifolia, V. riparia, V. vulpina*.
Frostweed *Helianthemum canadense; Verbesina virginica*.
Frosty Wattle *Acacia pruinosa; A. schinoides*.
Fruiting Quince *Cydonia oblonga*.
Fruta da Catey *Bourreria succulenta*.
Frying Pans *Eschscholzia lobbii*.

Fuchsia L. LADY'S EARDROPS; LADIES' EARDROPS. Onagraceae. 105 shrubs or small trees. Fls solitary and axill., or in term., racemose, paniculate or involucrate infl.; pedicels slender, often pendulous; perianth actinomorphic, tube cylindrical to campanulate; sep. 4, spreading to recurved; pet. 4 or 0, rolled together or spreading; sta. 8 in 2 unequal ranks, often strongly exserted, anth. dorsifixed; ovary inferior, 4-locular; stigma usually exserted. Fr. a berry. C & S Amer., NZ, Tahiti.

F. affinis Cambess. = *F. regia* ssp. *serrae*.

F. alpestris Gardn. Climbing shrub, 1–5m. Lvs 6–14cm, apex acute to acuminate, base rounded to cordate, entire or denticulate, lightly pubesc. above, densely so beneath. Fls solitary; pedicel 2.5–4cm; perianth tube 0.5–1cm, pubesc.; sep. 1.8–2.6cm, red to purple-pink; pet. 1–1.4cm, obovate, violet; fil., anth. and style red. Fr. 1.4–1.6cm, ellipsoid, purple. Braz. Z10.

F. ampliata Benth. Erect to twining shrub to 3m. Lvs 4–9cm, apex acute to acuminate, base acute to cuneate, entire to finely dentate, strigose above, paler and more villous beneath, venation purple red. Fls sparse; pedicels 1.5–3.5cm; perianth tube 4–5cm, strigose; sep. 1.6–2.3cm, oblong-elliptic, vermilion; pet. 1–1.8cm, ovate to orbicular; sta. shorter than or just exceeding sep., fil. red, anth. white, style red. Fr. 1.4–1.6cm, red, ellipsoid. Ecuad., S Colomb. Z10.

F. aprica Lundell = *F. microphylla* ssp. *aprica*.

F. arborea Sessé & Moc. = *F. arborescens*.

F. arborescens Sims. Shrubs or small trees, 3–8m. Lvs 10–21cm, apex acute to acuminate, base acute to cuneate, entire, dark green above, paler beneath. Fls in term. pan.; pedicels 0.9–1.8cm, erect; perianth tube 3.5–6mm, pink-purple; sep. 4–11mm, oblong to lanceolate, pink-purple; pet. 4–9mm, lanceolate-oblong or elliptic, light purple; sta. purple-pink in 2 unequal pairs; style pink. Fr. 0.8–1.2cm subglobose, purple. Mex. Z10.

F. ayavacensis Munz non Humb. = *F. ampliata*.

F. × *bacillaris* Lindl. (*F. microphylla* × *F. thymifolia*.) Erect or spreading shrub to 2m. Lvs 0.7–2.7cm, lanceolate to ovate, entire to finely serrate, ciliate. Fls solitary; perianth tube to 0.9cm, rose-pink to red; sep. 0.25–0.5cm, lanceolate, rose-pink to red; pet. 0.2–0.4cm, elliptic to suborbicular, pink to deep red. Fr. 0.5–1.5cm, subglobose, glossy black-purple. Mex. 'Cottinghamii': taller, fls smaller, fr. glossy purple-brown. 'Reflexa': lvs minute, fls small, cerise, becoming darker; fr. black. Z9.

F. boliviana Carr. Erect shrubs or small trees 2–4.5(6)m. Lvs 5–20cm, narrowly elliptic to broadly ovate, finely glandular-toothed, glab. to pubesc. above, pale and grey-puberulent or canescent beneath, venation often flushed red. Fls in pendent rac. or pan.; perianth tube 3–6cm, pubesc., pale pink to vermilion; sep. 1–2cm, lanceolate, pale pink to vermilion, rarely white; pet. 0.8–1.6cm, oblong-elliptic, crispate, scarlet; sta. red with white anth. Fr. 1–2.6cm, oblong-ellipsoid, terete, deep purple, strigose. N Arg. to Peru, nat. elsewhere. 'Alba': lvs pale green; fl. tube pure white. Z10.

F. canescens sensu Munz = *F. ampliata*.

F. chiapensis Brandg. = *F. microphylla* ssp. *aprica*.

F. cinnabarina E. McClintock = *F.* × *bacillaris*.

F. coccinea Dryand. Erect shrub to 1.5m, or climbing to 7m. Lvs 1.5–5.5cm, ovate, apex acute to acminate, base rounded usually serrulate, light green, glab. to sparsely puberulent. Fls solitary; perianth tube 0.5–1cm, subglabrous to puberulent; sep. 1.5–2.5cm, narrowly lanceolate, pubesc., red to deep pink; pet. 0.7–1cm, obovate, violet; sta. and anth. red-purple, strongly exserted; style red. Fr. 1.4–1.7cm, ellipsoid, purple. Braz. Z9.

F. × *colensoi* Hook. f. (*F. excorticata* × ?.) Shrub. Br. long, trailing. Lvs 1.25–5cm, ovate to rounded-ovate, base rounded or cordate, entire or subentire, thin-textured. Fls like those of *F. excorticata* but shorter with smaller sep. Summer. NZ. Z9.

F. colensoi Hook. f. = *F.* × *colensoi*.

F. colimae Munz = *F. thymifolia* ssp. *thymifolia*.

F. conica Lindl. = *F. magellanica*.

F. cordifolia Benth. = *F. splendens*.

F. corymbiflora Ruiz & Pav. Erect or climbing shrub 1–4m. Lvs 6–12cm, oblong-elliptic, acute to acuminate, entire or glandular-denticulate, dull green. Fls in terminal rac. or pan.; perianth tube 4–6.5(7)cm, narrow, base bulbous, pale pink to vermilion; sep. 1.2–1.5cm, lanceolate-oblong, pale pink to vermilion; pet. 1.2–1.7cm, oblong, darker red; sta. pink to red with white anth.; style pink. Fr. 1–1.2cm subglobose, red. Peru. Z10.

F. cuspidata Fawcett & Rendle = *F. boliviana*.

F. denticulata Ruiz & Pav. Erect to twining shrubs to 4m, or trees to 10m. Lvs 4–17cm, elliptic to narrowly lanceolate, acute to acuminate, denticulate, firm-textured, dark green above, paler and glab. or strigose on veins beneath. Fls clustered toward apex of br.; pedicel to 4.5cm; perianth tube 3.6–4.7cm, pink to light red, glab. to puberulent outside, densely hairy within; sep. 1.7–2.6cm, lanceolate, pink to light red tipped green-white, sometimes green-white throughout; pet. 1.4–1.8cm, lanceolate-oblong, slightly wavy, orange to vermilion; sta. pale pink to red with white anth.; style pale pink to red. Fr. 2–2.6cm, green to purple red. Peru and Boliv. Z10.

F. discolor Lindl. = *F. magellanica*.

F. 'Dominiana'. (*F. denticulata* × *F. macrostigma*.) Fls long, red, pendent.

F. elegans Salisb. = *F. coccinea*.

F. excorticata (Forst. & Forst. f.) L. f. Shrub or small tree to 12(13)m, with papery, red-brown, peeling bark. Lvs 5–10cm, ovate-lanceolate, slender-pointed, entire or subentire, green above, paler beneath. Fls 2–3cm, solitary, on slender pedicels; perianth tube 1.5cm, gibbous at base, green flushed maroon, shining; sep. green flushed maroon; sta. exserted, anth. blue; style exceeding sta. Spring. NZ. 'Purpurascens': lvs purple, white tinged silver beneath. Z9.

F. fulgens DC. Shrubs 0.5–3m. Subterranean parts tuberous. Young branchlets flushed red. Lvs 9–15cm, ovate to cordate, with fine red teeth, gland., flushed red beneath. Fls in pendent term. rac.; perianth tube 5–6.5cm, hairy, pink to red; sep. 1.2–1.7cm, lanceolate, pale red, tips green-yellow; pet. 0.6–0.9cm, ovate-elliptic; sta. light red, anth. white; style pink. Fr. 2–3cm, oblong-ellipsoid, deep purple. Mex. 'Rubra Grandiflora': tube orange-scarlet, sep. green, pet. orange-scarlet, long-flowering. Z10.

F. fulgens var. *pumila* Carr. = *F. fulgens*.

F. globosa Lindl. = *F. magellanica*.

F. gracilis Lindl. = *F. magellanica*.

F. hemsleyana Woodson and Seib. = *F. microphylla* ssp. *hemsleyana*.

F. heterotricha Lundell = *F. microphylla* ssp. *aprica*.

F. hidalgensis (Munz) Breedlove. Bushy shrub to 2m. Lvs 0.6–2.5cm, serrate in upper two-thirds. Fls white, sep. reflexed. Mex. ssp. *quercetorum* Breedlove. Bushy shrub to 2.5m. Lvs 0.6–3cm, margin entire, revolute. Fls small, red. Mex. to Guat. Z10.

F. integrifolia Cambess. = *F. regia* ssp. *regia*.

F. intermedia Hemsl. = *F. splendens*.

F. killipii I.M. Johnst. = *F. venusta*.

F. lampadaria J. Wright = *F. magdalenae*.

F. leptopoda K. Krause = *F. denticulata*.

F. longiflora Benth. = *F. macrostigma*.

F. lycioides Andrews. Shrub to 3m. Lvs to 4.5cm, ovate, acute-acuminate. Fls solitary; perianth tube 1.25cm, constricted at base, bright pink-red; sep. bright pink-red; pet. erect, slightly pinker than sep.; sta. just exserted. Summer. Chile. Z10.

F. macrostema Ruiz & Pav. = *F. magellanica*.

F. macrostigma Benth. Shrub to 1.5m. Lvs 6–27cm, elliptic to obovate or ovate, acute or acuminate, remotely glandular-toothed, subglabrous to velutinous, paler or flushed red with pubescence on veins beneath. Fls solitary, pedicels to 3cm, ascending, perianth tube 5–8cm, light to dark red, glab. or hairy; sep. 1.4–2.3cm, oblong-elliptic, fleshy, red tipped green; pet. 1.2–1.8cm, orbicular to ovate, waxy; sta. red; style pink, sparsely hairy to subglabrous; stigma 3.5×4.6mm, lobes 4, large, sticky, white to pink. Fr. 2–2.2cm, ellipsoid, warty. Colomb., Ecuad. Z10.

F. magdalenae Munz. Shrub 2–5m. Lvs 2.5–8.5cm, elliptic to ovate, entire or finely dentate, firm-textured, glab. above, paler beneath with hairs on margins, veins purple. Fls solitary; pedicels red, 1.5–6cm; perianth tube 4.2–6cm, vermilion, base purple; sep. 1.3–1.8cm, lanceolate, glossy orange-red tipped green; pet. 1.1–1.9cm, orange-red, margin sometimes irregular; sta. light red with cream anth.; style orange-red, exceeding anth. Fr. 2–2.4cm, ellipsoid, deep purple. Colomb. Z10.

F. magellanica Lam. Erect or semi-climbing shrub, 0.5–3(5)m. Lvs 1.5–5.5cm, ovate-elliptic, glab., venation sometimes strigulose, sometimes tinted red beneath, crenate-dentate. Fls solitary or paired; pedicels pendent; perianth tube 0.7–1.5cm, glab. to strigulose; sep. 1.7–2.5cm, oblong-lanceolate, deep crimson, rarely white or pale pink; pet. 1.1–2cm, obovate, rounded, purple, rarely pale pink; sta., anth. and style purple-red, exserted. Fr. 1.5–2.2cm, red-purple, oblong. Chile, Arg., nat. in S Amer., E Afr., NZ, Ireland, Hawaii. 'Conica' ('Globosa'): buds globe-shaped. 'Longipedunculata': pedicel v. long, fl. tube and sep. red, pet. mauve-lilac, long. 'Pumila': dwarf to 30cm, hardy; fls red and blue. 'Thompsonii': habit bushy; lvs short and relatively narrow; fls small, abundant. 'Variegata': lvs margined cream, otherwise as for var. *gracilis*. 'Versicolor' ('Tricolor'): lvs grey-green tinted silver, some partially margined white, young growth with red-purple hue, variegation bright red. var. *gracilis* (Lindl.) L.H. Bail. A highly floriferous shrub with a slender habit, lvs usually paired and small scarlet and violet fls. Pale-coloured variants of *F. magellanica* are grown as *F. magellanica* var. *molinae* Espin. (fls pale shell pink) and *F. magellanica* var. *eburnea* Pisano ('Alba': fls white). var. *molinae* includes cv. Sharpitor, with lvs grey-green edged white. *F. magellanica* 'Riccartonii': a commonly grown shrub robust, hardy; cal. darker than in type with broader sep.; possibly of hybrid origin. Z6.

F. meridensis Steyerm. = *F. venusta*.

F. microphylla HBK. Bushy or climbing shrub, 0.5–5m. Lvs 0.6–4cm, lanceolate to oblanceolate, acute, entire or toothed, margin and venation sometimes pubesc. Fls solitary, on pedicels 0.3–1.6cm long; perfect fls with perianth tube 0.4–1.3cm, white to red-purple; sep. 0.2–0.6cm, white to red-purple; pet. 0.15–0.6cm, elliptic to suborbicular, white to purple; sta. equal or unequal, 2 just exceed perianth tube, 2 included in it; style exceeds sta., pistillate fls slightly smaller and sta. v. short, all included. Fr. 0.5–1.5cm, ellipsoid, black-purple. Mex. to Costa Rica and Panama. Z10. ssp. *microphylla*. Bushy shrub 0.5–3m. Lvs 0.8–3(4)cm, elliptic, margin serrate in upper half. Fls purple-red with slightly paler pet. Mex. ssp. *aprica* (Lundell) Breedlove. Shrub to 3m. Lvs 0.12–0.4cm, thin-textured, entire, or thick-textured, serrate. Perianth tube 0.7–1.3cm, red to purple-red; sep. 0.4–0.6cm, red to purple-red; pet. 0.3–0.5cm, rounded to emarginate, sparsley pubesc. red to pale purple-red. Mex., Guat., El Salvador, Hond. ssp. *hemsleyana* (Woodson & Seib.) Breedlove. To 3m. Fls resemble those of ssp. *aprica*, but perianth tube generally shorter, sep. reflexed not spreading to

erect. Costa Rica, N Panama. Z10.

F. minimiflora Hemsl. = *F. thymifolia* ssp. *minimiflora*.

F. minutiflora Hemsl. = *F. microphylla* ssp. *microphylla*.

F. minutiflora var. *hidalgensis* Munz = *F. hidalgensis*.

F. mixta Hemsl. = *F. microphylla* ssp. *microphylla*.

F. mollis Krause = *F. alpestris*.

F. montana Cambess. = *F. coccinea*.

F. munzii J.F. Macbr. = *F. corymbiflora*.

F. notarisii Lehm. = *F. microphylla* ssp. *microphylla*.

F. paniculata Lindl. Shrubs or small trees, 3–8m. Lvs 5–15.5cm, elliptic to narrowly lanceolate, serrate, dark shining green above, paler beneath. Fls in pan.; pedicels erect to 1.2cm; perianth tube 4–8mm, mauve-pink; sep. 0.5–1cm, lanceolate, mauve-pink; pet. 0.4–1cm, pale purple; sta. pink; style shorter than or exceeding anth., stigma pale purple. Fr. 4–9mm, subglobose, purple, glaucous. Mex. to Panama. Z10.

F. parviflora hort. = *F. bacillaris*.

F. pendula Salisb. = *F. coccinea*.

F. pringlei Robinson & Seaton = *F. thymifolia* ssp. *thymifolia*.

F. procumbens A. Cunn. Slender, prostrate shrub. Lvs 6–18mm, suborbicular, cordate. Fls 1.2–1.8cm, erect; perianth tube pale orange, lobes green at base, tips purple; pet. 0; sta. exserted, anth. blue. Fr. 1.8cm, bright red, glaucous. NZ. Z9.

F. pubescens Cambess. = *F. regia* ssp. *reitzii*.

F. pulchella Woodson and Seib. = *F. microphylla* ssp. *hemsleyana*.

F. pyrifolia C. Presl = *F. regia* ssp. *regia*.

F. racemosa Sessé & Moc. non Lam. = *F. fulgens*.

F. racemosa Lam. non Sessé & Moc. = *F. triphylla*.

F. radicans Miers = *F. regia* ssp. *serrae*.

F. regia (Vell.) Munz. Erect to climbing shrub to 15m. Lvs 2–14cm, elliptic to ovate, entire or glandular-toothed, membranous to leathery, glab. to hairy. Fls solitary or paired; pedicels 1–5.5cm, pendent; perianth tube 0.5–1.6cm, glab. or hairy; sep. 1.5–4.5cm, red to rose-pink; pet. 1–2.5cm, obovate to oblong, purple; sta. purple-red, exserted, style exserted beyond sta. Fr. 1–2.7cm, ellipsoid or subglobose, deep purple. Braz. ssp. *regia*. Lvs dull, subentire. Fls large; sep. 2.4–4.5cm. ssp. *reitzii* P. Berry. Lvs dull, glandular-serrate. Fls smaller than ssp. *regia*, sep. 1.7–2.8cm. ssp. *serrae* P. Berry. Lvs shining. Fls with sep. fused for more than ¼ length. Z10.

F. regia var. *typica* Munz = *F. regia* ssp. *regia*.

F. 'Riccartonii' = *Fuchsia magellanica*.

F. serratifolia Ruiz & Pav. = *F. denticulata*.

F. simplicicaulis Ruiz & Pav. Climbing shrub 2–5m. Lvs 8–15cm, linear-lanceolate to ovate, subentire, glab. above, glab. or sparsely pilose beneath. Fls 3–4 per whorl, in pendent infl., subtended by large membranous bracts; perianth tube 4–5cm, base bulbous, hairy, light pink-red; sep. 1.6–2mm, lanceolate, puberulent, light pink-red; pet. 9–13mm, elliptic, red. Fr. 11–13mm, ellipsoid, puberulent. C Peru. Z10.

F. siphonata K. Krause = *F. denticulata*.

F. skutchiana Munz = *F. thymifolia* ssp. *minimiflora*.

F. spectabilis Hook. ex Lindl. = *F. macrostigma*.

F. splendens Zucc. Shrub, 0.5–2.5m. Lvs 3.5–13cm, ovate to cordate, serrate, glab. or hairy above, often flushed red and pubesc., beneath. Fls solitary on slender, spreading to pendent pedicels; perianth tube 2–4.6(6.4)cm, pubesc., rose-pink to red; sep. 0.8–2cm, lanceolate, green, base red; pet. 0.6–1.2cm, ovate, olive-green; sta. exserted, yellow-green, anth. yellow; style pale green. Fr. 2–4cm, green to deep purple, warty. Mex. to Costa Rica. 'Karl Hartuneg': growth upright; lvs large; tube short, scarlet, sep. short, virtually erect, yellow and green, pet. pale green. Z9.

F. tacanensis Lundell = *F. thymifolia* ssp. *thymifolia*.

F. tacsoniiflora K. Krause = *F. denticulata*.

F. thymifolia HBK. Erect shrub to 3m. Lvs 0.8–6.5cm, elliptic to ovate, entire or finely serrate, pubesc. Fls solitary on pendent pedicels 0.4–2.6cm long, perfect fls with perianth tube 0.25–0.7cm, pubesc., green-white to pink; sep. 0.25–0.5cm, lanceolate, green-white to pink; pet. 0.2–0.4cm, elliptic to suborbicular, white to pink fading dark purple, pubesc.; one pair of sta. slightly exserted from perianth tube; style exceed sta.; pistillate fls smaller, sta. all included, anth. sterile. Fr. 0.5–1.5cm, oblanceolate to ellipsoid, glossy black-purple. Mex. to N Guat. ssp. *thymifolia*. To 2.2m. Lvs 0.8–3cm, elliptic to ovate. Perfect fls on pedicels to 1.2cm; perianth tube 0.4–0.7cm; sep. 0.2–0.5cm; pet. 0.2–0.4cm. Mex. ssp. *minimiflora* (Hemsl.) Breedlove. Shrub to 3m. Lvs 2.2–6.5cm, elliptic to narrowly ovate. Perianth tube shorter and broader than in ssp. *thymifolia*; sep. 0.15–0.2cm in pistillate fls. Mex., Guat. Z9.

F. tillettiana Munz. Shrub to 5m. Lvs 3–10cm, oblong-ovate or elliptic, entire to finely serrate, thin, glab. to pruinose or puberulent above, glab. to puberulent beneath. Fls clustered at br. tips, pendent; pedicels 2.5–5cm; perianth tube 3.6–4.6cm, pubesc., light pink to pink-red; sep. 1.9–3.3cm, lanceolate, light pink to shocking pink-red; pet. 0; sta. pink to deep purple, with yellow anth., exserted; style pink, exceeding anth. Fr. 1.8–2.1cm, oblong-ellipsoid, green-purple to glossy red, puberulent. Venez., possibly also Colomb. Z10.

F. triphylla L. Shrub or subshrub 0.3–2m. Lvs 2.5–10cm, elliptic or oblanceolate, subentire or finely denticulate, mid- to dark green and strigulose above, paler and usually tinged purple beneath. Fls in erect to nodding rac.; perianth tube 2.5–4cm, base bulbous, orange to coral; sep. 1–1.3cm, lanceolate, orange to coral; pet. 6–9mm, orange to coral; sta. orange-red with cream anth.; style orange-red. Fr. 1.5–1.8cm, subglobose to oblong-ellipsoid, strigose, red-purple. Hispan. Z10.

F. uniflora Sessé and Moc. = *F. microphylla* ssp. *microphylla*.

F. velutina I.M. Johnst. = *F. corymbiflora*.

F. venusta Humb. Erect to twining shrub to 3m. Lvs 5–11.5cm, elliptic, subentire, membranous to leathery, shining above, paler, glab. or venation pubesc. beneath. Fls solitary or in term. subracemose infl. to 2cm; pedicels arching to pendent; perianth tube 3.5–6cm, glab. to puberulent outside; sep. 1.4–2cm, lanceolate, orange-red, shining; pet. 1.5–2.2cm, oblanceolate, orange to vermilion, crispate or waxy; fil. red, anth. cream; style villous, red. Fr. 0.8–2cm, subglobose to ellipsoid, green to deep purple. Colomb., Venez. Z10.

Fuchsia cvs. There are only a few clear-cut subdivisions within the range of hybrids, notably those of 'hardy' and 'basket' types. The basic shape is that of the 'bush' or 'shrub', although training can produce of number of v. different shapes; habit ranges from trailing, spreading and loose to upright and compact with varying degrees of hardiness; lvs golden-yellow through pale to dark, glossy green, some variegation, small to large, often serrate, young growth occas. tinged red; fls single, semi-double and double, made up of tube, sep. and cor. which can all display individual variation in shape, size and colour, predominantly white, red and purple with tremendous range of shading. *Single:* 'Achievement': habit upright, vigorous; lvs green tinged yellow; tube pink-red, medium length, sep. pink-red, long and thin, cor. purple tinged red shading to scarlet at base. 'Alice Hoffman': small shrub; lvs densely clustered, purple-tinged; fls small, cal. scarlet, cor. white. 'Brenda White': lvs pale green; fls small, tube and sep. red, cor. white veined pink. 'Brilliant': small shrub; fls large, cal. rose-scarlet, cor. broad, rose-purple. 'Chillerton Beauty': small shrub; fls medium-sized, cal. white flushed rose, cor. soft violet. 'Corallina' ('Exoniensis'): vigorous, robust shrub; lvs large, deep green; fls scarlet and violet. 'Countess of Aberdeen': habit upright, bushy, self-branching; lvs somewhat small; tube short, cream, sep. white, slightly upturning, cor. small, white. 'Display': small shrub; fls large, cal. carmine, cor. rose-pink, sta. long-exserted. 'Eleanor Leytham': habit erect; lvs small, pale, ruffled; fls v. small, tube white, sep. white tinged pink, cor. pale pink. 'Genii': dwarf; shoots red; lvs lime-yellow; fls small, cal. cerise, cor. violet becoming purple-red. 'Graf Witte': small; fls single, borne in profusion; cal. carmine, cor. purple tinted rose-mauve. 'Mrs Popple': small bush, large-fld; cal. scarlet, spreading, cor. violet; sta. and style crimson, long-exserted. 'Mrs W.P. Wood': fls single, borne in profusion; cal. pale pink, sep. slender, upturned; cor. white. 'Pixie': sport of 'Graf Witte'; erect to 90cm; lvs yellow-green; fls single, cal. carmine, cor. mauve veined carmine. 'Playford': growth strong; tubes short, green tinged red, sep. short, pink, cor. blue shaded mauve. 'Snowcap': dwarf; fls to 5cm, cal. red, cor. white veined red; suitable for bedding. 'Swanley Gem': habit bushy, upright; lvs small; tube scarlet, sep. lifting to become horizontal, bright red, cor. deep violet somewhat veined red. 'Tennessee Waltz': low, arching; cal. glossy scarlet; cor. intense purple-violet. 'Tom Thumb': highly floriferous dwarf; cal. rose-scarlet, pet. violet. *Semi-double:* 'Aurora Superba': habit bushy; fls medium, tube and sep. pale apricot, cor. deep orange-salmon. 'Continental': habit upright; tubes and sep. white flushed pink, cor. pink with rose, picotee edges. 'Dipton Dainty': habit bushy; tube short, pink, cor. pale mauve-blue, flecked bright pink. 'Lady Thumb': dwarf, bushy; fls borne profusely, semi-double; cal. pale red, cor. white veined red. *Double:* 'Blue Gown': dwarf, compact, v. floriferous; fls double, cal. scarlet, cor. deep purple. 'Dollar Princess': habit upright, bushy, vigorous; lvs serrate, medium-sized; tube small, cerise, sep. reflexing to tube, cerise, cor. small, purple turning deep pink at base. 'Elsa': small shrub; fls large, cal. white tinted pink, cor. double, violet-rose. 'Flirtation Waltz': habit upright, bushy, vigorous; lvs pale, serrate, tube short, thick, white, sep. white tipped green, pink beneath, cor. fully double, compact, pale pink. 'Joe Kusber': habit upright, bushy; fls abundant, v. full, tube short, somewhat thick, white, sep. long, white tipped pink, cor. blue tinged purple, pet. variegated with pink. 'Swingtime': habit upright, lax, vigorous; lvs dark green veined red, finely cut; fls large, full, tube scarlet, sep. broad, reflexing, scarlet, cor. white veined bright red. 'Texas Longhorn': habit trailing; lvs veined red, serrate; tube

long, scarlet, sep. long, drooping, scarlet, cor. v. long, white veined cherry red. Z9.

BASKET TYPES. These are normally of trailing or pendulous habit. *Single:* 'Auntie Jinks': habit pendulous; lvs small; tube pink-red, sep. white edged rich pink, cor. purple shaded white. 'Marinka': habit bushy, vigorous; lvs dark green veined red; tube long, red, sep. short and broad, opening to slightly below horizontal, red, cor. compact, deeper red. 'Tom West': habit spreading; lvs cream and green tinged red; tube and sep. red, cor. purple, small, compact. *Semi-double:* 'Belsay Beauty': habit trailing, bushy; lvs pale green, smooth; tube and sep. rhodamine pink, cor. violet, anth. pale pink. 'La Campanella': habit trailing, spreading; lvs small; tube white, sep. white tinged pink, cor. imperial purple. 'Thunderbird': semi-double to double; habit trailing, vigorous; lvs serrated; tube and sep. rose-red, long and slender, cor. vermilion paler at base. *Double:* 'Applause': growth spreading; tube and sep. flesh pink, cor. salmon-pink. 'Cheers': habit spreading, vigorous; tube orange-pink, sep. broad, sharply pointed, streaked orange-pink, cor. orange to flame red. 'Haute Cuisine': habit spreading; fls large, tubes and sep. dark red, cor. dark aubergine. 'Humboldt Holiday': habit trailing; lvs golden-yellow veined deep pink, magenta red beneath, turning pale green with age, st. magenta red; tube white tinged pink, thin, sep. white tinged pink, frosted pink beneath, cor. large, violet splashed pink fading to white at base. Z9.

'HARDY' TYPES. These normally withstand winters in Zone 7. *Single:* 'Beacon Rosa': habit upright, bushy; lvs dark green, heavily serrated; tubes and sep. rose-red, cor. pink, lightly veined red. 'Hawkshead': habit upright, bushy; lvs small, serrate; tube and sep. white tinged green, cor. pure white, rounded. 'White Pixie': habit upright, bushy; lvs shaded golden-yellow, veined red; tube red, short, thin, sep. red, short and broad, cor. white veined rose-red. *Semi-double:* 'Abbé Farges': habit upright, vigorous; lvs small, glossy, lightly serrate; tubes and sep. cherry red, cor. rosy lilac. 'Lena': habit lax bush, vigorous; lvs pale green, serrate; tube short, flesh pink, sep. flesh pink on top, darker shade beneath, tipped green, cor. purple paling towards base. 'Snowcap': habit upright, bushy, vigorous; lvs small, serrate; tube and sep. scarlet, cor. loose, white veined red. *Double:* 'Constance': habit upright, bushy; tube pale pink, sep. pale pink tipped green, cor. mauve, tinted pink at base. 'Mauve Beauty': habit upright, bushy; lvs serrate, young growth tinged red near petiole; tube short, bright red, sep. bright red curling towards tube, cor. loose, mauve turning pale purple, veined red. 'Prosperity': habit upright, vigorous; lvs dark green, glossy, serrate; tube thick, crimson, sep. long, crimson, cor. neyron rose, tinged and veined rose-red. Z8.

TRIPHYLLA HYBRIDS: all are single flowered. 'Andenken an Heinrich Henkel': habit spreading vigorous; lvs dark olive green veined dark pink; tube pale rose, sep. long, thin, small, sep. and cor. deep pink. 'Billy Green': growth vigorous, upright; lvs olive-green; tube long, fls salmon-pink. 'Bornemann's Beste': tube and sep. orange tinged red, cor. tangerine. 'Gartenmeister Bonstedt': growth vigorous, upright; lvs dark bronze tinged red above, purple-red beneath; tube long, thin, red-brown, sep. small, cor. short, both red-brown. 'Madame Cornelissen': large-fld *F. magellanica* hybrid; cal. red, cor. white. 'Mantilla': habit trailing, bushy; lvs green tinged bronze; tube long, thin, sep. short, pointed, cor. compact, small, all rich carmine. 'Mary': habit upright; lvs dark green veined red-purple, tinged purple beneath; tube long, sep. short, cor. short-petalled, brilliant scarlet. 'Stella Ann': habit upright, vigorous; lvs olive green; tubes long, broad, poppy red, sep. orange-pink tipped green, cor. orange. 'Thalia': habit upright, vigorous; lvs olive veined and ribbed deep pink; tube long, orange-red, sep. small, pointed, cor. compact, both flame red. 'Trumpeter': habit trailing; lvs green tinged blue; fls with long tubes, sep. and cor. pale geranium lake. Z9.

ENCLIANDRA GROUP. A large number of cvs, mostly distinguished by their miniature fls and v. small lvs; growth normally slender; fls mostly pendulous. After flowering black seed pods appear, increasing the ornamental value of the plants. 'Fuksie Foetsie': habit upright, bushy, vigorous; lvs pale green, small, serrate; tube small, thick, sep. v. small, entire bloom off-white shading to pink. 'Mendocini Mini': habit trailing; lvs v. small, serrate; tube thin, short white, back of sep. white, front pink, v. small, cor. small, white becoming dark pink, sta. blood red, pistil white. 'Neapolitan': fls relatively large, separately in white, pink and red, sep. reflexing to tubes, cor. opening to become flat. 'Oosje': habit upright; lvs small, serrate; tube and sep. red darkening with age, cor. white-red turning to dark red, v. small. 'Rading's Inge': habit spreading; fls tiny, tube rose-pink, sep. cream, cor. orange. 'Ri Mia': habit bushy, spreading; fls small, tube, sep. and cor. pale lilac. Z9.

F. venusta var. *huilensis* Munz = *F. venusta*.

F. virgata Sweet = *F. magellanica*.

Fuchsia Begonia *Begonia fuchsioides.*
Fuchsia Eucalyptus *Eucalyptus forrestiana.*
Fuchsia-flowered Currant *Ribes speciosum.*
Fuchsia Gum *Eucalyptus forrestiana.*
Fuchsia Heath *Epacris longiflora.*
Fuji Cherry *Prunus incisa.*
Fukanoki *Schefflera heptaphylla.*
Fuller's Teasel *Dipsacus sativus.*
Full Moon Maple *Acer japonicum.*

Fumana (Dunal) Spach. Cistaceae. 9 sprawling shrublets. Lvs grey-hairy slender, clothing st. Sep. 5, inner whorl larger than outer, prominently veined; pet. 5, yellow; sta. many, slender, outermost sterile. Early–late summer. Medit., N Afr., Asia Minor. Z8.
F. ericoides (Cav.) Gand. To 35cm, shortly glandular-pubesc. Lvs to 1.2cm, linear. Fls solitary or in clusters, scattered on st. Medit.
F. laevipes (L.) Spach. To 30cm. Lvs to 0.8cm, linear, bright green to blue-grey, glab. or sparsely glandular-pubesc. Infl. term., 3–8-fld. N Afr., Medit.
F. nudifolia (Lam.) Janch. = *F. procumbens.*
F. procumbens (Dunal) Gren. & Godron. To 40cm, pubesc. Lvs 0.8–2cm, linear. Fls to 2cm diam., solitary, on nodding stalks. Medit.
F. spachii Gren. & Godron = *F. ericoides.*
→*Cistus* and *Helianthemum.*

Fumaria L.
F. africana Lam. = *Rupicapnos africana.*
F. angustifolia Bieb. = *Corydalis angustifolia.*
F. bracteata Stephan ex Willd. = *Corydalis bracteata.*
F. capnoides L. = *Corydalis lutea.*
F. cava Mill. = *Corydalis cava.*
F. claviculata L. = *Corydalis claviculata.*
F. fungosa (Ait.) Greene ex BSP = *Adlumia fungosa.*
F. lutea L. non Thunb. = *Corydalis lutea.*
F. nobilis L. = *Corydalis nobilis.*
F. sempervirens L. = *Corydalis sempervirens.*
F. sibirica L. f. = *Corydalis sibirica.*

FUMARIACEAE DC. 18/450. *Adlumia, Dicentra, Hypecoum, Pteridophyllum, Rupicapnos, Sarcocapnos.*

Fumewort *Corydalis solida.*

Funkia Spreng.
F. coerulea Andrews = *Hosta ventricosa.*
F. fortunei Sieb. non Bak. = *Hosta tokudama.*
F. fortunei Bak. non Sieb. = *Hosta fortunei.*
F. japonica var. *lancifolia* Honda = *Hosta longissima.*
F. lancifolia var. *angustifolia* Reg. = *Hosta longissima.*
F. lancifolia (Thunb.) Spreng. = *Hosta lancifolia.*
F. latifolia (Miq.) Andrews = *Hosta ventricosa.*
F. longipes Franch. & Savat. = *Hosta longipes.*
F. ovata var. *minor* Bak. = *Hosta minor.*
F. ovata Spreng. = *Hosta ventricosa.*
F. sieboldiana var. *condensata* Miq. = *Hosta tokudama.*
F. sieboldiana Hook. = *Hosta sieboldiana.*
F. sieboldii Lindl. = *Hosta sieboldiana.*
F. subcordata Spreng. = *Hosta plantaginea.*
F. tardiflora W. Irv. = *Hosta tardiflora.*
F. undulata Otto & Dietr. = *Hosta undulata.*

Funnel-crest Rosebud Orchid *Cleistes divaricata.*

Furcraea Vent. Agavaceae. 20 succulent herbs; st. thick, fleshy. Lvs sword-shaped, usually rigid, spinose-serrate, in term. rosettes. Infl. term., paniculate, scapose, far exceeding lvs; fls green white; perianth tube short, cylindrical, seg. 6, oblong; sta. 6; ovary inferior, 3-chambered, often producing bulbils. Mex., C Amer. Z9.
F. albispina hort. ex Bak. Lvs 15–20, to 50×5cm, marginal spines green-white, deltoid. Fls white tinged green, pendulous, in rhomboid pan. to 1.5m. Winter. C Amer.
F. bedinghausii K. Koch. Lvs 50+, to 120×10cm, glaucous, denticulate. Infl. to 5m, often bulbiliferous; br. long, drooping. Summer. Mex.
F. cubensis (Jacq.) Haw. = *F. hexapetala.*
F. elegans Tod. Lvs 40–50, to 2.5m, marginal spines curving forward, dull green with purple margins. Infl. to 7.5m, br. to 1.65m; perianth seg. pale green within, exterior tinted purple, turning brown. Mex.
F. flavoviridis Hook. Lvs 20–30, to 75cm, bright green, smooth above, rough beneath, margins with horny, deltoid, hooked spines. Pan. 3.6–4.5m. Mex.
F. foetida (L.) Haw. MAURITIUS HEMP; GREEN ALOE. Lvs 40–50, to 180×15cm, rigid, entire or armed with sparse, hooked spines.Infl. to 7.5m; fls strongly scented, milk-white inside. C Amer. 'Mediopicta': lvs spineless, variegated cream.
F. gigantea Vent. = *F. foetida.*
F. hexapetala (Jacq.) Urban. Lvs c30 per rosette, to 75cm, bright green, grooved above, apex brown, convolute, rough beneath, margins with deltoid, hooked spines 3mm. Pan. loose to 1.8m, lower br. compound; fls faintly scented. Cuba.
F. lindenii Andrew = *F. selloa* var. *marginata.*
F. longaeva Karw. & Zucc. Lvs in a dense rosette, to 150×12cm, opaque green, recurved, keel rough beneath, denticulate. Infl. to 12m, br. spreading or drooping, compound, to 4m; perianth seg. off-white. Mex.
F. macdougalii Matuda. Lvs to 210×6cm, fleshy, linear-oblong, toothed. Infl. to 9m. Mex.
F. pubescens Tod. Lvs c30, to 60×7cm, rigid, concave, smooth, pungent, armed with broad, hooked spines. Pan. tall. Trop. Amer.
F. pugioniformis hort. = *F. elegans.*
F. roezlii Andrew = *F. bedinghausii.*
F. selloa K. Koch. Lvs 30–40 in dense rosette, to 120×10cm, rigid, bright green, margin with large brown, horny spines 6mm. Scape 2.4–3m; pan. to 1.8m, br. simple; fls faintly scented, flushed green. Mex., Guat. var. *marginata* Trel. Lvs bordered white or yellow.
F. stricta Jacobi. Lvs to 30, to 75×7cm, bright green, deeply grooved, spines large, distant. Infl. to 2.7m; fls to 2.5cm. Trop. Amer.
F. tuberosa (Willd.) Ait. f. Lvs 30, 60–90cm, bright green, firm, smooth beneath, rough above, marginal teeth to 5mm. Infl. to 9m, br. compound; fls sweetly scented. W Indies, Trop. Amer.
F. watsoniana hort. = *F. foetida* 'Mediopicta'.
→*Agave* and *Yucca.*

Furin-tsutsuji *Enkianthus campanulatus.*

Furrowed Saxifrage *Saxifraga exarata.*

Furze *Ulex europaeus.*

Fushige-chigaya *Imperata cylindrica.*

Fustic *Chlorophora.*

Fustic-tree *Chlorophora tinctoria.*

Fustuq *Pistacia vera.*

Fyfield Pea *Lathyrus tuberosus.*

G

Gagea Salisb. Liliaceae (Liliaceae). 50 small, bulbous perenn. herbs. Lvs linear or linear-lanceolate, hollow, solid or flat. Infl. scapose; fls solitary, racemose or umbellate; perianth cylindric-campanulate to rotate, seg. free; sta. 6. Eur., C Asia, N Afr.

G. arvensis (Pers.) Dumort. = *G. villosa.*

G. fibrosa (Desf.) Schult. & Schult. f. Basal lvs 2, linear, flat or channelled, 2–4mm wide; st. lvs 3–5, whorled. Infl. an umbel, 1–6-fld; pedicels woolly, 2–8cm; seg. yellow inside, green outside, lanceolate, acuminate, 15–25mm. Medit., N Afr., Aegean, Cauc. Z8.

G. fistulosa (Ramond ex DC.) Ker-Gawl. Basal lvs 1 or 2, linear, hollow, glab., 6–20×0.3–0.5cm; st. lvs 2, opposite, broadly lanceolate. Infl. an umbel, 2–4(–6)-fld; pedicels usually hairy, 1.5–5cm; seg. yellow, narrowly ovate, 10–18mm. Spring–summer. Eur., Cauc., Iran, Iraq. Z7.

G. graeca (L.) A. Terracc. Basal lvs 2–4, linear, 4–12×0.1–0.2cm, flat; st. lvs 3, alt., linear-lanceolate. Fls 1–5; seg. 7–16mm, oblanceolate, white with 3 purple stripes. Spring. Greece, Crete, E Medit. Z8.

G. liotardii (Sternb.) Schult. & Schult. f. = *G. fistulosa.*

G. lutea (L.) Ker-Gawl. Basal lf solitary, linear-lanceolate, flat, 7–15mm wide; st. lvs 2, opposite, lanceolate, ciliate. Infl. an umbel, to 10-fld; pedicels glab. or hairy; seg. yellow, tinged green, oblong-linear, 15–18mm. Spring. Eur., Russian Asia. Z6.

G. minima (L.) Ker-Gawl. Basal lf solitary, lanceolate, flat, 1–2mm wide; st. lvs 1–2, opposite, lanceolate. Fls 1–7; pedicels glab. or slightly pubesc.; seg. yellow, linear-lanceolate, acuminate, 10–15mm. Spring. Eur. Z6.

G. peduncularis (Presl & C. Presl) Pascher. Basal lvs 2, linear, glab., channelled, 6–30×0.1–0.2cm; st. lf 1, lanceolate, acuminate. Infl. a pan., 3–14cm, 1–7-fld hairy or glab.; pedicels densely woolly above, 3–4cm; seg. yellow, narrowly ovate or oblanceolate, 8–16mm, woolly at base outside. Spring. N Afr., Balk., Aegean. Z7.

G. pratensis (Pers.) Dumort. Basal lf solitary, linear, flat or channelled, 3–15×0.2–0.4cm; st. lvs 1–2, opposite, lanceolate, sometimes ciliate. Infl. an umbel 1–7-fld; pedicels 10–20mm; seg. yellow inside, green outside, linear-lanceolate, acuminate, 9–16mm. Spring. Eur., Crimea, Turk. Z7.

G. stenopetala Rchb. = *G. pratensis.*

G. sylvatica (Pers.) Loud. = *G. lutea.*

G. villosa (Bieb.) Duby. Basal lvs 2, linear, D-shaped in section, glab. or hairy, 16×0.1–0.3cm; lvs with bulbils in their axils often present; st. lvs opposite, to 9mm wide. Infl. 1–15-fld, sub-umbellate, hairy or glab.; seg. yellow, narrowly ovate, 7–10cm, sometimes hairy at base outside. Eur., N Afr., Turk., Iran. Z7.

Gai Choi *Brassica juncea.*

Gaillardia Foug. BLANKET FLOWER. Compositae. 30 ann., bienn. and perenn. herbs. Lvs alt. or often radical, entire, toothed or pinnatifid, base petiolate or sessile, ± clasping, pubesc. Cap. radiate, solitary; ray flts yellow to red, tipped with yellow or red-purple; disc flts purple. S US, Mex., S Amer.

G. acaulis Pursh = *Tetraneuris acaulis.*

G. amara Raf. = *Helenium amarum.*

G. amblyodon Gay. Hairy ann., to 50cm. Lvs 3–7cm, oblong-lanceolate, sessile. Cap. to 5cm diam.; peduncle to 10cm; ray flts to 2cm, dark red to purple-brown. Summer. SW US. Z8.

G. aristata Pursh. Hairy perenn. to 70cm. Lvs to 20cm, oblanceolate to lanceolate, entire to toothed or lobed, densely hairy. Cap. *c*10cm diam.; peduncle to 20cm; ray flts 2.5cm, yellow or yellow with red to base. Summer–autumn. N Amer. (E Rocky Mts). Z8.

G. bicolor Lam. = *G. pulchella.*

G. comosa A. Gray. Hairy perenn. to 25cm. Lvs to 12cm, basal or on lower third of st., oblong to lanceolate, entire or lobed. Cap. to 5.5cm diam.; ray flts to 1.5cm, yellow-pink, purple-veined. Summer. Mex. Z8.

G. drummondii DC. = *G. pulchella.*

G. ×grandiflora Van Houtte. (*G. aristata* × *G. pulchella.*) Like *G. aristata* but larger and more vigorous. Gdn origin, nat. SW US. 'Summer Fire': 35cm, ray flts yellow, red-zoned; 'Red Plume': 35cm, brick red; 'Kobold' ('Goblin'): 40cm, ray flts red, bordered yellow; 'Chloe', 'Sunset', 'Aurea', 'Goldkobold' and 'Yellow Queen': to 60cm, flts yellow; 'Burgundy': to 60cm, flts

red; 'Bremen', 'Baby Cole', 'Attraction': ray flts yellow, zoned red; 'Tokajer': to 75cm, ray flts vivid dark orange. Seed races include the Portola Giants, blooming all summer with large, bronzed scarlet, gold-tipped fls, and the variously coloured Gaiety Mixed and Stokes Royal Monarch Hybrids. Z4.

G. lanceolata Michx. Perenn. to 70cm. Lvs to 10cm, ± entire, gland., shortly hairy, oblanceolate to linear. Cap. to 6cm diam.; peduncles to 20cm, ray flts to 2cm, red or yellow. Spring–summer. SE US. Z7.

G. lorenziana hort. = *G. pulchella* 'Lorenziana'.

G. multiceps E. Greene. Pubesc. subshrub to 30cm, compactly branched, minutely pubesc. Lvs to 8cm, linear-oblanceolate, punctate, hairy. Cap. to 6.5cm diam.; peduncle to 10cm; ray flts to 2cm, yellow, with brown hairs. Mex., SW US (Ariz., New Mex., Tex.). Z6.

G. parryi E. Greene. Hairy perenn. to 25cm. Lvs to 4cm, basal, obovate to ovate, gland., succulent. Cap. lemon yellow; ray flts to 1.5cm, yellow. SW US. Z8.

G. picta Sw. = *G. pulchella* var. *picta.*

G. pinnatifida Torr. Perenn. to 40cm. Lvs to 10cm, on basal half of st.; oblanceolate, usually pinnatifid, hairy. Cap. to 6cm diam. peduncle to 18cm; ray flts to 1.5cm, yellow, tinged pink or red at base, purple or red-veined. Summer. S US, Mex. Z8.

G. portola hort. = *G. ×grandiflora.*

G. pulchella Foug. INDIAN BLANKET; BLANKET FLOWER; FIREWHEELS. Hairy ann., sometimes suffruticose, to 60cm. Lvs to 8cm, oblong to oblanceolate, lobed, coarsely toothed or entire, hairy. Cap. to 6cm diam.; peduncle to 15cm; ray flts to 2cm, red with yellow tips or entirely yellow or red. Summer–autumn. E & SC US, Mex. Largely represented in cult. by cv. Lorenziana, with disc flts numerous, enlarged, funnel-shaped, red, yellow or bicoloured. var. *picta* (Sweet) A. Gray. To 50cm: robust, forming compact rounded bushes, much-branched, secondary br. widely spreading. Lvs rather succulent. Mex., Tex. Z8.

G. suavis (A. Gray & Engelm.) Britt. & Rusby. Perenn. to 1m. Lvs to 15cm, basal, spathulate or oblanceolate and entire, slightly toothed or lyrate-pinnatifid, slightly hairy. Cap. to 4.5cm diam.; peduncle to 80cm; ray flts to 6mm, yellow or red-brown. SC US. Z6.

Galactites Moench. Compositae. 3 white-tomentose, ann. herbs. Lvs alt., pinnatifid and spiny to toothed. Cap. discoid, solitary or in corymbose cymes or clusters; phyllaries spine-tipped; flts white to purple, outer larger. Canaries and Medit.

G. tomentosa Moench. To 1m. Lvs to 20×8cm, basal lvs lanceolate to oblanceolate, serrate, white-veined or variegated above, tomentose beneath, st. lvs usually pinnatifid, spiny. Cap. arachnoid-pubesc. Summer. Medit.

Galamai-amo *Schefflera elliptica.*
Galangal *Alpinia galanga.*

Galanthus L. SNOWDROP. Amaryllidaceae. 15 bulbous perennials. Shoot surrounded by sheathing tube; vernation flat, convolute or reduplicate; lvs paired, occas. 3, ligulate to elliptic-oblong, usually shorter than scape at flowering. Scape terminated by a spathe of 2 membranous bracteoles; fls solitary, pedicel short slender; perianth seg. 6, 3 outer oblanceolate to oblong-elliptic, acute to rounded, usually pure white, 3 inner much shorter, cuneate, emarginate, marked green at apex. Anth. 6, yellow, fil. short. W Eur. to Iranian Cauc. and Caspian Sea.

G. allenii Bak. Vernation convolute; lvs broad, somewhat glaucous, 6×2cm at flowering, concave at apex. Scape to 12cm; fls almond-scented; outer seg. obovate, 2×1.5cm, inner seg. 9mm, marked green at apex. Winter. Cauc., NW Iran. Z6.

G. alpinus Sosn. Vernation reduplicate; lvs broad, lanceolate-spathulate, acute, to 9×2cm, dark green, glaucous. Scape to 8cm; fls scented of bitter almonds; outer seg. spathulate, 1.5–2cm, inner seg. 7mm, with small apical green spot. Winter.

G. bortkewitschianus Koss. Close to both *G. alpinus* and *G. caucasicus*. Lvs narrow, glaucous deep green, strongly hooked at apex. Fls to 1.5cm, with marking on inner seg. narrow. Sterile triploid of v. restricted range. Cauc. Z6.

G. bulgaricus Velen. = *G. gracilis.*

G. byzantinus Bak. = *G. plicatus* ssp. *byzantinus.*

G. cabardensis Voss = *G. lagodechianus.*

G. caucasicus (Bak.) Grossh. Vernation convolute; lvs oblong, to 15×2cm+ glaucous. Scape to 14cm; outer seg. obovate, to 2cm+, inner seg. 9mm, marked green at apex. Winter. Cauc. var. **hiemalis** Stern. Fls smaller. Flowering late autumn and early winter. 'Lady Beatrix Stanley': probably a hybrid involving *G. caucasicus*; lvs glaucous pale green, erect; fls double; outer seg. narrow, 'claw-like', inner seg. minutely green-spotted at apex. 'Straffan': vigorous, often with 2 scapes per shoot. Z5.

G. cilicicus Bak. = *G. nivalis* ssp. *cilicicus*.

G. corcyrensis (G. Beck) F. Stern see *G. reginae-olgae*.

G. elswesii ssp. *minor* D.A. Webb = *G. gracilis*.

G. elwesii Hook. f. Variable. Vernation convolute; lvs broad, oblong or wider, 7.5–9.5×1–3cm at flowering, expanding later, glaucous, hooded at apex. Scape c10cm when fl. appears; fls honey-scented; outer seg. broad-obovate or rounded, often widely flared, to 3cm, inner seg. half length outer, marked green at apex and base. Winter. Balk., W Turk. 'Colesborne': probably *G. elwesii* ×*G. caucasicus*; scape short; fls large; inner seg. green from apex to base. Z6.

G. fosteri Bak. Vernation convolute; lvs broad, to 25×2.6cm, deep green, recurved. Scape to 20cm; fls small from immature plants, larger when older; outer seg. oblong-spathulate, to 2.5cm, inner seg. marked green at apex and base. Winter. S Turk., Leb. Z5.

G. gracilis Čelak. Vernation flat; lvs narrow, twisted, about 6cm×7mm at flowering, glaucous. Scape to 10cm; fls sometimes violet-scented; outer seg. obovate, to 2.5cm, inner seg. marked green at apex and base. Winter. Bulg., Greece, Turk. Z6.

G. graecus hort. non Boiss. = *G. gracilis*.

G. ×grandiflorus Bak. see *G. plicatus*.

G. ikariae Bak. Variable, formerly split into several taxa including the broad-leaved ssp. *latifolius* (Rupr.) Stearn. Vernation convolute; lvs ligulate to broad, to 16×3cm, bright glossy green. Scape to 15cm; fls variable in size; outer seg. oblong-spathulate, to 3cm, inner seg. emarginate, with apical green mark. Winter. Aegean Is., Turk., Cauc. Z6.

G. imperati Bertol. = *G. nivalis* ssp. *imperati*.

G. kemulariae Kuth. = *G. lagodechianus*.

G. ketzhovellii Kem.-Nat. = *G. lagodechianus*.

G. krasnowii Khokhrj. Differs from *G. ikariae* in inner cor. seg. not emarginate. Z6.

G. lagodechianus Kem.-Nat. Similar to *G. rizehensis* but lvs a brighter glossy green. Winter. Cauc. Z6.

G. latifolius Rupr. non Salisb. = *G. ikariae*.

G. maximus Velen. = *G. elwesii*.

G. 'Merlin' (*G. elwesii* ×*G. plicatus*.) Vernation convolute. Fls large; inner seg. deep green all over. Various progeny of this cross, many of them named.

G. nivalis L. SNOWDROP. Vernation flat; lvs linear, 9×0.6cm at flowering, somewhat glaucous. Fls faintly honey-scented; outer seg. oblong, 1.5–2cm, inner seg. with apical green mark. Winter. Eur. 'Atkinsii': vigorous, to 25cm; fls large, elongated; another clone, 'Atkinsii Backhouse', usually has one outer seg. deformed. 'Flore Pleno', ('Plenus'): fls double, with inner seg. irregular and untidy to regular and neat; sterile, spreading by prolific offsets. Several clones. 'Lady Elphinstone': fls double; inner seg. marked yellow, sometimes temporarily reverting to green. 'Lutescens': small plants; scape yellow-green; ovary and marking on inner seg. yellow. 'Magnet': vigorous, tall; fls large, held on long slender pedicels. 'Poculiformis': inner seg. lack green markings, equalling length of outer seg. 'S. Arnott' ('Sam Arnott', 'Arnott's Seedling'): vigorous, strongly scented; fls large, rounded, on stout scapes. 'Scharlokii': bracteoles long, leafy, free, resembling long ears; outer seg. marked green toward apex. 'Viridiapicis': bracteoles united by membrane; outer seg. marked green toward apex. ssp. *cilicicus* (Bak.) Gottl.-Tann. Lvs glaucous, 16–18cm at flowering. Marking on inner tep. more elongated. Winter. (earlier than ssp. *nivalis*). S Turk., Leb. ssp. *imperati* (Bertol.) Bak.. Fls larger, elongated. Winter. It. Z4.

G. nivalis ssp. *reginae-olgae* (Orph.) Gottl.-Tann. = *G. reginae-olgae*.

G. nivalis var. *lutescens* Harpur-Crewe. = *G. nivalis* 'Lutescens'.

G. olgae Orph. ex Boiss. = *G. reginae-olgae*.

G. platyphyllus Traub & Mold. = *G. ikariae* ssp. *latifolius*.

G. plicatus Bieb. Vernation reduplicate. Lvs broad, 10×1cm at flowering, dull green, glaucous in centre of lamina, slightly undulate above. Scape to 20cm; fls variable in size; outer seg. oblong, to 2.5cm, inner seg. marked green at apex only. Winter. E Eur. 'Warham': lvs apple green *G. plicatus* ×*G. nivalis* = *G. ×grandiflorus* Bak. Several hybrids between *G. plicatus* and *G. nivalis* 'Plenus', collectively termed Greatorex doubles. Most are vigorous gdn plants, including 'Ophelia' and 'Jacquenetta': fls double, inner pet. form a rosette, heavily marked green. ssp. *byzantinus* (Bak.) D.A. Webb. Inner seg. marked green at apex and base. N Greece, W Turk. Z6.

G. rachelae Burb. = *G. reginae-olgae*.

G. reginae-olgae Orph. Differing from *G. nivalis* in autumnal flowering and glaucous-lined lvs. Lvs linear, with central glaucous stripe, to 14×1cm, produced after fls; vernation flat. Scape to 10cm; fls faintly scented; outer seg. to 2.5cm, inner seg. marked green at apex. Autumn. Sicily, Greece, SW Turk. Plants from Corfu and Sicily flowering in late autumn with their lvs showing have been named *G. corcyrensis* (G. Beck) F. Stern or *G. reginae-olgae* ssp. *corcyrensis* (G. Beck) G. Kamari. ssp. *vernalis* G. Kamari. Lvs with central glaucous stripe, to 7cm, present at flowering. Winter. Balk. Z7.

G. rizehensis F. Stern. Vernation flat; linear, dull deep green, 10×0.5cm, obtuse. Scape to 13cm; outer perianth seg. oblong-oval, to 2cm, inner seg. marked green at apex only. Winter. NE Turk. Z6.

G. sandersii hort. = *G. nivalis* 'Lutescens'.

G. schaoricus Kem.-Nat. = *G. alpinus*.

G. transcaucasicus Fomin = *G. rizehensis*.

G. woronowii A. Los. = *G. ikariae*.

Galax Sims. WANDFLOWER; WANDPLANT; BEETLEWEED; GALAXY; COLTSFOOT. Diapensiaceae. 1 tufted, everg. perenn. herb. Rootstock thick, creeping. Lvs 2.5–7.5cm diam., circular-cordate, toothed, glossy becoming bronze; petioles slender, ascending. Scape to 45cm, erect; rac. spike-like to 25cm; fls white, 0.4cm across; cal. lobes 5; sta. 5, united with 5 cor. lobes into a 10-toothed tube. SE US. Z5.

G. aphylla auct. non L. = *G. urceolata*.

G. urceolata (Poir.) Brummitt.

Galaxia Thunb. Iridaceae. 12 perenn. cormous herbs. St. shortly emerging or buried, elongating in fr. Lvs linear, ensiform or oblong-ovate. Fls solitary, short-lived, to 5cm, scarcely exceeding lvs; perianth funnelform, tube slender, lobes 6, subequal, spreading, oblong-cuneate; fil. partly or wholly fused in a narrow tube. SW S Afr. Z9.

G. fugacissima (L. f.) Druce. Distinguished from *G. ovata* by its narrower lvs, scented fls, fil. sometimes free toward apex, anth. divergent. Summer. SW Cape.

G. graminea Thunb. = *G. fugacissima*.

G. ovata Thunb. Lvs oblong-ovate, coarse, ribbed, minutely ciliate. Fls yellow; fil. united. Late spring–summer. SW Cape.

G. ovata var. *purpurea* Ker-Gawl. = *G. versicolor*.

G. versicolor Klatt. Lvs lanceolate, somewhat undulate, ciliate. Fls mauve to rose-pink (throat yellow); fil. free at apices. Summer. SW Cape.

Galaxy *Galax*.

Galeandra Lindl. & Bauer. Orchidaceae. 8 terrestrial and epiphytic orchids. Pbs clustered, clothed with coarse, grey sheaths. Lvs plicate, narrow-lanceolate, grassy, bases sheathing st. and articulate. Rac. few-fld, term., nodding; sep. free, equal, spreading, lanceolate; pet. oblanceolate, reflexed, lip entire or obscurely 3-lobed, folded-tubular, spurred. C & S Amer. Z10.

G. batemanii Rolfe = *G. baueri*.

G. baueri Lindl. Pbs narrow-fusiform, to 30cm. Lvs to 20cm, linear-lanceolate. Tep. to 2cm, ochre to chocolate brown; lip to 5cm, pale rose purple, base white or tan, margins crenate, spur to 2cm. Mex. to Panama and Surinam.

G. beyrichii Rchb. f. St. to 90cm, slender, pseudobulbous at base. Lvs reduced. Fls to 4.5cm diam., pale green, lip white edged crimson and nerved lime green at base, pubesc. within. Flor., W Indies, Hispan., S Amer. to Peru.

G. devoniana Lindl. Pbs to 75cm, narrow-fusiform. Lvs to 20cm, linear-lanceolate. Tep. to 4.5cm, elliptic-lanceolate, olive green or pale brown stained or lined chocolate; lip to 5cm, white veined rose or garnet above, margin undulate, spur to 1.5cm. Guyana, Venez., Braz.

G. viridis Barb. Rodr. = *G. beyrichii*.

Galega L. GOAT'S RUE. Leguminosae (Papilionoideae). 6 erect, perenn. herbs. Lvs imparipinnate. Fls pea-like in axill. rac. S Eur. to Asia Minor, trop. E Afr.

G. bicolor Hausskn. = *G. officinalis*.

G. bicolor var. *hartlandii* hort. ex K. Först. = *G. officinalis* Hartlandii group.

G. ×hartlandii Hartland = *G. officinalis* Hartlandii group.

G. officinalis L. GOAT'S RUE. To 1.5m. Lfts to 5×1.5cm, 4–8 pairs, oblong, elliptic or lanceolate, mucronate, glab. or sparsely pubesc. beneath stipules to 1cm, subsagittate. Cor. white to lavender, standard 1cm, equalling wings. Summer. C & S Eur., Asia Minor. Hartlandii group: once held to be the progeny of *G. bicolor* ×*G. officinalis* (now treated as synonyms); st. long; fls white or lavender, wing and keel pet.

white, lilac-tinged. 'Alba': fls white. 'Her Majesty': fls white and mauve-pink. 'Lady Wilson': fls lilac blue in fine spikes. Z4.

G. orientalis Lam. Resembles *G. officinalis*, but to 0.5m, lfts in 6–12 pairs, larger and tapering; stipules to 1.5cm, ovate or ovate-orbicular. Cor. blue-violet, standard to 1.5cm, exceeding wings. Cauc. Z6.

G. persica Pers. = *G. officinalis*.

G. tricolor Hook. = *G. officinalis*.

Galeobdolon Adans.

G. argentatum hort. = *Lamium galeobdolon* 'Variegatum'.

G. luteum Huds. = *Lamium galeobdolon*.

Galeopsis L. Labiatae. 10 erect, ann. herbs. Verticillasters dense, uppermost crowded, lower distant; cal. tubular-campanulate, teeth 5, spinose with a ring of hairs within; cor. distinctly 2-lipped, upper lip hooded, lower lip 3-lobed with 2 bluntly conical protuberances at base. Eur.

G. dubia Leers = *G. segetum*.

G. galeobdolon L. = *Lamium galeobdolon*.

G. intermedia Vill. = *G. ladanum*.

G. ladanum L. St. to 40cm with curled and gland. hairs. Lvs ovate-lanceolate to broadly ovate, dentate. Cor. 15–28mm, deep pink with yellow blotches. Eur.

G. ochroleuca Lam. = *G. segetum*.

G. pubescens Besser. St. to 50cm, angles sparsely setose, sides densely pubesc. Lvs ovate, dentate. Cor. 20–25mm, bright pink-red, usually with yellow blotches, middle lobe of lower lip broadest. C Eur.

G. segetum Necker. St. to 50cm with curled and gland. hairs. Lvs lanceolate to ovate, dentate. Cor. usually pale yellow, rarely pink or lilac with purple blotches. Eur.

G. speciosa Mill. St. to 1m, angles setose. Lvs ovate to ovate-lanceolate, dentate. Cor. 22–34mm, yellow, lower lip with large purple blotch. Eur.

G. ×tetrahit L. (*G. speciosa* ×*G. pubescens*.) Cor. 15–30mm, pink or rarely pale yellow or white, with purple markings. Eur. A distinct natural hybrid.

G. versicolor Curtis = *G. speciosa*.

Galeottia Nees.

G. grandiflora A. Rich. = *Mendoncella grandiflora*.

G. jorisiana (Rolfe) Schltr. = *Mendoncella jorisiana*.

Galingale *Cyperus longus*.

Galinsoga Ruiz & Pavon.

G. trilobata Cav. = *Tridax trilobata*.

Galium L. BEDSTRAW; CLEAVERS. Rubiaceae. *c*400 ann. or perenn. herbs. St. erect, climbing, or creeping and weak, 4-angled or cylindrical, prickly-adhesive, pubesc. or glab. Lvs sessile, opposite or whorled. Fls solitary and axill. or term. or in pedunculate pan. or cymes; cor. cylindric to campanulate, lobes 3–5, usually 4, limb rotate; sta. 3–5, anth. exserted. Sub-cosmopolitan. Z8.

G. adriaticum Ronn. = *G. corrudaefolium*.

G. aetnicum Biv. To 60cm. St. 4-angled, ascending, rough, frosted and glaucous, glab. Lvs to 2cm×2mm, linear or spathulate to oblanceolate, glab. Fls loose, term. pan., white. Summer. It., Sardinia, Sicily. Often confused with *G. corrudaefolium*.

G. aparine L. GOOSE GRASS; CLEAVERS; SPRING CLEAVERS. Ann. to 1.5m. St. 4-angled or terete, ascending or creeping and scrambling, pubesc. to bristly. Lvs to 7×1cm, whorled, linear to lanceolate or oblanceolate, rough and ciliate. Fls to 3 per axill. cyme, white. Spring–summer. N Amer., Eur., Asia.

G. aristatum L. FALSE BABY'S BREATH. Perenn., to 80cm. St. 4-angled, glab. Lvs to 65×5mm, lanceolate, toothed, rough, usually glaucous beneath. Fls white in loose, rounded, many-fld pan. W Eur. (Pyren. to Alps). Z6.

G. aureum Vis. = *G. firmum*.

G. baldense Spreng. Perenn., to 10cm. St. 4-angled, ascending to creeping, tufted, glab. Lvs to 10×1mm, linear to oblanceolate, thick-textured. Fls white to yellow, in pyramidal, many-fld pan. C Eur. (Alps). Z6.

G. boreale L. NORTHERN BEDSTRAW. Perenn., to 80cm. St. terete or 4-angled, erect and stiff, glab. or short-pubesc. Lvs 0.6–3cm, whorled, linear to lanceolate, ciliate, coarse, glab. to short-pubesc. Fls white, in dense, terminal pan. or cymes. Summer. N Amer., Eur., Asia. Z2.

G. corrudaefolium Vill. To 40cm. St. 4-angled, erect, sparsely branched, short-pubesc. Lvs to 11×1mm, linear, leathery, margin rough, revolute. Fls white to cream or yellow in pan. Eur. (Medit.). Z7.

G. firmum Tausch. Perenn., to 1m. St. erect, much-branched, short-pubesc. Lvs to 25×5mm, whorled, elliptic to oblanceolate, mucronate, leathery. Fls in loose or dense, ovoid pan., yellow. Eur. (Balk.). Z6.

G. humifusum Bieb. Perenn., to 1.5m. St. 4-angled, ascending to creeping, rough and papillose, glab. to pubesc. Lvs to 22×4mm, whorled, linear to oblanceolate, toothed, rough, somewhat leathery, glab. to sparsely pubesc. Fls white to cream or yellow, axill. and solitary or in elongate-thyrsoid or paniculate cymes. SE Eur. to C Asia. Z6.

G. longifolium (Sibth. & Sm.) Griseb. Perenn. to 1m. St. terete to obscurely 4-angled, erect to ascending, initially frosted and glaucous. Lvs to 50×6mm, whorled, linear or oblong to lanceolate, toothed and papillose, leathery above, frosted and glaucous beneath. Fls white in loose, rounded pan. Turk. Z7.

G. mollugo L. WHITE BEDSTRAW; WHITE MADDER; FALSE BABY'S BREATH. Perenn., to 1.5m. St. 4-angled or terete, erect to ascending, weak, glab. or pubesc., spreading. Lvs to 25×7mm, whorled, linear or oblong to lanceolate, attenuate to cuspidate, margin rough, thin-textured. Fls white and purple-flecked in loose, term., many-fld pan. or cymes, brown. Summer–autumn. N Amer., Eur. Z3.

G. odoratum (L.) Scop. WOODRUFF; SWEET WOODRUFF. Perenn., to 45cm. St. 4-angled, erect, pubesc. on internodes, stolons creeping, subterranean, dried shoots strongly scented of hay. Lvs to 50×14mm, whorled, elliptic to oblanceolate, margin rough and ciliate to prickly, stiff. Fls white in term., umbellate, cymes. Spring–summer. Eur., N Afr. Z5.

G. olympicum Boiss. Perenn., to 3cm. St. 4-angled or terete, tufted, glab. Lvs to 8×1mm, whorled, overlapping, linear to subulate, margin somewhat thickened, rough and glab. to minutely ciliate. Fls white in few-fld pan. or cymes. E Medit. Z8.

G. paschale Forssk. = *G. longifolium*.

G. rubrum L. To 50cm. St. 4-angled or terete, stoloniferous, pubesc. to prickly. Lvs to 25×3mm, whorled, oblanceolate. Fls purple in ovoid to oblong, crowded pan. or cymes. Eur. (Alps, Apennines). Z6.

G. septentrionale Roem. & Schult. = *G. boreale*.

G. triandrum Hylander = *Asperula tinctoria*.

G. vaillantii DC. = *G. aparine*.

G. verum L. YELLOW BEDSTRAW; OUR LADY'S BEDSTRAW. Perenn., to 1.2m. St. terete to 4-angled, erect to ascending, becoming somewhat woody at base, glab. or short-pubesc., stolons creeping. Lvs to 30×2mm, whorled, filiform to oblanceolate, margin rough, revolute. Fls yellow in dense, paniculate cymes. Summer–autumn. N Amer., Eur., Asia. Z3.
→*Asperula*.

Gallberry *Ilex glabra*.

Galleta *Hilaria jamesii*.

Gallito *Viola pedunculata*.

Gall-of-the-earth *Nabalus serpentarius*.

Galpinsia Britt. = *Calylophus*.

Galtonia Decne. Liliaceae (Hyacinthaceae). 3 bulbous perenn. herbs. Lvs basal, rather fleshy, linear-lanceolate to lorate, usually flattened-conduplicate. Fls nodding, in a scapose, cylindric to conical, term. rac.; perianth exceeding tube, lobes spreading; sta. 6, shorter than lobes. Late summer. E S Afr.

G. candicans (Bak.) Decne. SUMMER HYACINTH. Lvs 50–100×5cm. Scape to 120cm; rac. slender, to 15-fld; fls fragrant; bracts to 4cm, ovate-lanceolate, acute; perianth 3cm, snow-white faintly tinged green at base of tube. OFS, Natal, Les. Z5.

G. princeps (Bak.) Decne. Similar to *G. candicans* but lvs 40×4cm; scape to 90cm; fls fewer in shorter, broader rac.; perianth tube green, lobes tinted green, only slightly longer than tube. Natal, Transkei. Z8.

G. viridiflora Verdoorn. Lvs to 60×10cm. Scape to 1m; rac. 15–30-fld; bracts to 3cm, lanceolate, acuminate; perianth 2–5cm, pale green, lobes edged white. OFS, Natal, Les. Z8.
→*Hyacinthus*.

Galvezia Domb. ex Juss. Scrophulariaceae. 6 shrubs. Lvs entire, in whorls. Rac. term.; sep. 5; cor. tube 2-lipped, pouch-like, throat almost closed by palate; sta. 4. Summer. Is. off Calif., Mex., Ecuad., Peru. Z8.

G. speciosa (Nutt.) A. Gray. Everg. scrambling shrub to 2.1m. Lvs to 4cm, elliptic to ovate. Fls scarlet, to 2.5cm. Is. off Calif. 'Firecracker': small shrub; lvs tomentose; fls bright red.
→*Antirrhinum*.

Gambel Oak *Quercus gambelii*.

Gamblea C.B. Clarke. Araliaceae. 4 everg. or decid. unarmed trees or shrubs. Lvs usually palmately compound, clustered toward br. tips. Infl. yellow-green, term., usually compound-umbellate; cal. rim minute or 0. S, SE & E Asia.

G. evodiifolia (Franch.) Frodin. Decid. to 16m. Lfts 3–5, oblong-ovate to ovate-lanceolate, chartaceous to thinly coriaceous, to 10×3cm, glab. except for tomentose vein axils beneath, entire or ciliate-toothed. Infl. compound-umbellate, br. bearing stalked lat. umbels; pet. and sta. 5. Fr. black, round, 3–4mm diam. C & W China to Vietnam. Z7.

G. innovans (C.B. Clarke) Frodin. TAKA-NO-TSUME; IMO-NO-KI. Decid. to 6m. Lfts 1–3, rhomboid-ovate, membranous, to 15×8cm, glab., entire or ciliate-toothed. Infl. uniaxial, axis elongate with 1–5 stalked, lat. umbels; pet. and sta. 4. Fr. black, round, 7–8mm diam. Jap. Z7.

→*Acanthopanax, Evodiopanax* and *Kalopanax*.

Gamboge *Garcinia xanthochymus.*
Ganagra *Rumex hymenosepalus.*
Gandergoose *Orchis morio.*
Gand Flower *Polygala vulgaris.*
Ganja *Cannabis.*
Gaping Penstemon *Penstemon breviflorus.*
Garbanzo *Cicer arietinum.*

Garcinia L. MANGOSTEEN. Guttiferae. 200 everg. trees and shrubs. Lvs decussate, entire, coriaceous, usually glossy. Fls solitary or few, term. or axill.; sep. 4–5, occas. 2, valvate; pet. 4–5, overlapping, sta. 8–many; ovary 2–12-locular; stigma lobed, flattened. Fr. a leathery indehiscent berry; seeds with succulent arils. Trop. Asia, Polyn., S Afr.

G. aristata (Griseb.) Borh. Shrub or small tree, to 10m. Lvs elliptic, acuminate, to 7.5cm, glossy. Fls clustered on side shoots, white to 15mm across. Fr. to 7mm diam. Cuba.

G. cambogia Lam. = *G. gummi-gutta.*

G. cornea L. Tree to 7m. Lvs oblong to oblong-lanceolate, 10–15cm. ♂ fls in term. clusters; ♂ fls solitary, all pale green, to 20mm across. Fr. 8cm diam., bright red, pericarp spongy; aril white, sour. India to Malaysia.

G. dulcis (Roxb.) Kurz. Tree to 7m. Lvs oblong, 15cm+. Fls clustered, creamy-white. Fr. smooth, yellow, apple-sized; arils yellow, edible. Winter. Moluccas.

G. gummi-gutta (L.) N. Robson. Tree to 14m. Lvs elliptic to lanceolate, to 13cm. ♂ fls 3–4, axillary, yellow; ♀ fls larger, in axils of term. If pair. Fr. globose, grooved, on 2.5cm, stalks, orange or yellow, to 8cm diam.; aril red or white. Indon.

G. humilis (Vahl) C. Adams. Shrub to 2.5m or tree to 10m. Lvs elliptic 10–18cm, cordate at base. Fls clustered, creamy-yellow or white, to 2.5cm across. Fr. ellipsoid, beaked, yellow, to 6cm. Year-round. Carib.

G. livingstonei Anderson. Tree to 11m. Lvs oblong to elliptic, to 13cm, undulate. Fls solitary or in clusters, pale green, white or pale yellow, vanilla-scented, 7mm. Fr. globose, orange-yellow to red, 2.5cm diam. Trop. S Afr.

G. mangostana L. MANGOSTEEN. Tree to 10m. Lvs elliptic, 25cm, coriaceous. Fls solitary or paired, rose-pink to yellow, 5–6cm across. Fr. large, deep purple-black, 7.5cm diam.; aril white. Malesia.

G. morella Desr. Tree to 15m. Lvs oblong-elliptic to lanceolate, to 10cm. Fls axillary, yellow, clustered or solitary ♂. Fr. cherry-shaped, 2cm diam., sep. persistent. SE Asia.

G. spicata Hook. f. Tree to 10m. Lvs broad-elliptic, to 20cm. Fls 7mm across. Fr. globose, to 2.5cm diam., dark green. India, Sri Lanka.

G. xanthochymus Hook. f. ex Anderson. GAMBOGE. Tree to 13m. Lvs linear-oblong to oblong-lanceolate, to 45cm, glossy. Fls white, to 2cm across, 4–8 in axill. clusters. Fr. globose, apple-sized, dark yellow. Summer. N India, W Himal.

→*Rheedia.*

Garden Angelica *Angelica archangelica.*
Garden Balsam *Impatiens balsamina.*
Garden Burnet *Sanguisorba minor.*
Garden Currant *Ribes × koehneanum; R. silvestre.*
Gardener's Garters *Phalaris arundinacea.*
Garden Forget-me-not *Myosotis sylvatica.*
Garden Heliotrope *Valeriana officinalis.*
Garden Huckleberry *Solanum melanocerasum.*

Gardenia Ellis. Rubiaceae. *c*250 shrubs and trees. Lvs leathery, petiolate. Fls axillary or term., solitary or in few-fld cymes, fragrant; cal. short-tubular, limb truncate, toothed or lobed; cor. showy, campanulate; to salverform, lobes 5–12, spreading; sta. 5–12, inserted at throat of cor. tube. Fr. a berry, leathery or fleshy. Trop. OW.

G. augusta (L.) Merrill. GARDENIA; JASMIN; CAPE JESSAMINE. Everg. shrub or tree, to 12m. Lvs 5–15cm, ovate, lanceolate or elliptic to oblong, acute, leathery glossy dark green. Fls white to ivory, intensely fragrant, usually double, solitary or in short-stalked, few-fld cymes; cal. tube to 15mm, prismatic to cup-shaped, lobes to 3cm×6mm; cor. cylindric, tube to 3cm, lobes to 3cm, obovate. China, Taiwan, Jap. 'August Beauty': bushy; lvs rich green; fls double, soft white, long-lasting. 'Belmont' ('Hadley'): vigorous, well-branched; lvs to 15cm long, glossy; fls double, large, rose-shaped, creamy white, yellowing later, strongly scented. 'Fortuniana': br. woody; lvs large, leathery, shiny; fls large, white, yellowing later, scented. 'Mystery': bushy and compact; lvs dark green, glossy; fls semi to double, creamy white, scented. 'Radicans': miniature, low mounding habit; lvs small, glossy green; fls small, white. 'Radicans Variegata': as for 'Radicans', but lvs tinted grey and edged off-white. 'Veitchii': habit upright and compact; lvs small, bright green; fls small, pure white, fully double, sweetly fragrant. 'Veitchii Variegata': as for 'Veitchii', but lvs streaked white.

G. capensis (Montin) Druce = *G. thunbergia.*

G. carinata Wallich. Everg. tree, to 6m or more. Lvs to 45×20cm, obovate to oblanceolate, narrowly acute to cuspidate, lustrous and leathery above, pubesc. beneath. Fls solitary or in few-fld cymes, cream to yellow or orange; cal. to 3cm, limb truncate to acutely 5–6-lobed, pubesc.; cor. tube to 5cm, lobes 6–9, obovate. India, Malaysia.

G. citriodora Hook. = *Mitriostigma axillare.*

G. cornuta Hemsl. NATAL GARDENIA. Shrub or tree, to 5m. Lvs to 5×3cm, obovate, apex attenuate to obtuse, entire to undulate, lustrous above. Fls white to yellow, fragrant; cal. to 18mm, 2-lipped, lobes 6, with cylindrical appendages; cor. tube to 6cm, slender, lobes to 3cm, 5–6, spreading. S Afr.

G. florida L. non Forst. f. = *G. augusta.*

G. florida Forst. f., non L. = *G. taitensis.*

G. formosa L. f. = *Randia formosa.*

G. fortunei (Lindl.) hort. Shrub, to 2m. Lvs elliptic to lanceolate, apex and base attenuate, lustrous and glab. Fls white, axill., solitary; cor. salverform.

G. genipa Sw. = *Genipa americana.*

G. globosa Hochst. = *Rothmannia globosa.*

G. grandiflora Lour. = *G. augusta.*

G. imperialis Schumacher. Shrub or tree, to 12m. Lvs to 50×25cm, obovate to elliptic, narrowly acute or obtuse, lustrous above, somewhat pubesc. beneath. Fls solitary, white to pink and crimson or brown-flushed; cal. tube to 15mm, ellipsoid to oblong, sticky, limb ribbed, lobes to 1cm, 5; cor. tube to 25cm, flared, exterior rough, papillose and gland., lobes to 6×4cm, 5, spreading, ovate to oblong, papillose and somewhat downy. Trop. Afr.

G. jasminoides Ellis = *G. augusta.*

G. jasminoides var. *fortuniana* Lindl. = *G. fortunei.*

G. jovis-tonantis (Welw.) Hiern = *G. ternifolia* ssp. *jovis-tonantis.*

G. latifolia Ait. Shrub or tree to 6m. Lvs to 30×25cm, obovate to elliptic to orbicular, apex obtuse pubesc. or glandular-pubesc. beneath. Fls white to yellow, fragrant, solitary; cal. tube campanulate, mealy and pubesc., lobes 5–9, lanceolate, hair-tipped, pubesc.; cor. funnelform, tube to 8cm, pubesc., lobes to 12cm, 5–9, obovate. Trop. Asia.

G. macrantha Schult. = *Euclinia longiflora.*

G. manganjae Hiern = *Rothmannia manganjae.*

G. radicans Thunb. = *G. augusta.*

G. rothmannia L. f. = *Rothmannia capensis.*

G. spatulifolia Stapf & Hutch. V. close to *G. volkensii*, but smaller, to 5m. Lvs to 6cm, obovate to rhombic-obovate. Fls to 5cm diam., white tinted green, fading yellow, faintly scented. S Afr.

G. spinosa Thunb. = *Catunaregam spinosa.*

G. taitensis DC. Shrub or tree, to 6m or more. Lvs to 25×12cm, obovate to elliptic. Fls white and green-flecked, axill. and solitary; cal. lobes to 3cm, 4, ovate to oblong; cor. tube to 4cm, glab., lobes to 3cm, 6–8, obovate. Polyn.

G. ternifolia Schumacher & Thonn. Shrub or tree, to 6m. Lvs to 20×10cm, elliptic to obovate or oblanceolate, apex acute or obtuse, leathery, glab. to pubesc. Fls solitary, white to yellow; cal. tube to 1cm, rough, glab. to pubesc., lobes to 15×5mm, linear to spathulate; cor. cylindric, tube to 11cm, glab. to pubesc., lobes to 6×3cm, 6–9, oblong to obovate or elliptic. Trop. Afr. ssp. *jovis-tonantis* (Welw.) Verdc. Lvs to 12.5cm, obovate. Fls to 7.5cm diam., ivory, fragrant; cor. tube to 7.5cm, cylindrical, lobes 8–9.

G. thunbergia L. f. WHITE GARDENIA. Shrub or tree, to 5m. Lvs to 14×6cm, elliptic, apex attenuate to obtuse, lustrous, gland. on veins. Fls white to cream, term. and solitary, fragrant; cal. tube to 25mm, appendaged; cor. tubular to salverform, tube to 7cm, lobes to 25mm, 8, spreading, overlapping, obtuse. Winter to spring. S Afr.

G. tubifera Wallich. Shrub, to 2m, or tree, to 15m. Lvs to 25×12cm, elliptic to obovate or oblanceolate, apex narrowly acute to cuspidate, glab. to minutely pubesc. on veins beneath. Fls white turning yellow to orange, solitary, cal. tube to 18mm, limb to 12mm, truncate; cor. cylindric, tube to 10cm, lobes to 24×8mm, 6–9, oblong, obtuse. Trop. Asia (Malaysia, Indon.).

G. urcelliformis Hiern = *Rothmannia urcelliformis*.

G. volkensii Schumacher. Shrub or tree, to 10m. Lvs to 10×5cm, obovate or lanceolate to rhomboid, acute or obtuse, thin-textured and rough, glab. to pubesc. Fls white to cream or yellow, solitary, fragrant; cal. tube to 1cm, oblong, pubesc., lobes to 20×8mm filiform to spathulate, sometimes connate; cor. cylindric, tube to 12cm, glab., lobes to 5×3cm, 6–9, obovate to elliptic. Trop. Afr.

Garden Lettuce *Lactuca sativa*.
Garden Loosestrife *Lysimachia punctata*.
Garden Monkshood *Aconitum napellus*.
Garden Myrrh *Myrrhis odorata*.
Garden Nasturtium *Tropaeolum majus*.
Garden Pea *Pisum sativum*.
Garden Rhubarb *Rheum* ×*cultorum*.
Garden Sorrel *Rumex acetosa*; *R. scutatus*.
Garden Strawberry *Fragaria* ×*ananassa*.
Garden Violet *Viola odorata*.
Garden Wolfsbane *Aconitum napellus*.
Garget *Phytolacca americana*.
Gari *Manihot esculenta*.
Garland Flower *Daphne cneorum*; *Hedychium coronarium*.
Garland Lily *Calostemma purpureum*; *Hedychium*.
Garland Spiraea *Spiraea* ×*arguta*.
Garlic *Allium sativum*.
Garlic Chives *Allium tuberosum*.
Garrocha *Tecoma garrocha*.

Garrya Douglas. SILK TASSEL; TASSEL TREE. Garryaceae. 18 everg. trees or shrubs. Br. roughly tetragonal, pubesc. when young. Lvs leathery; petioles short. Fls inconspicuous, in pendulous bracteate catkins; ♂ catkins stalked, clustered in br. axils, sep. 4, often joined, sta. 4; ♀ catkins subsessile, solitary; cal. 0 or bilobed. Fr. a round, dry dark, 2-seeded berry. W US, Mex., W Indies.

G. buxifolia A. Gray. Shrub, to 1.5m. Lvs oblong-elliptic, to 4.5cm, shiny dark green or olive-green above, pubesc. beneath. ♂ catkins in clusters of 2–4, 5–8cm; ♀ catkins to 9cm. N Calif. to SW Oreg. Z8.

G. congdonii Eastw. Shrub to 2m. Lvs ovate to elliptic, to 7cm, yellow-green, pilose beneath. ♂ catkins to 8cm; ♀ catkins to 5cm. Calif. Z8.

G. elliptica Lindl. Shrub or small tree to 4m. Lvs to 8cm, oblong-elliptic, undulate to sinuate, glossy grey-green to matt dark green, tomentose becoming glab. beneath. ♂ catkins to 20cm in subterminal clusters, grey. ♀ infl. to 10cm. Winter–spring. W US. 'Evie': lvs strongly undulate; catkins to 30cm. 'James Roof': lvs dark sea green; catkins to 20cm, silver-grey, in dense clusters. Z8.

G. fadyenii Hook. Shrub to 5m. Lvs to 8cm, elliptic to oblong, mucronate, glossy above, hairy beneath. ♂ catkins branched, hairy, to 3cm; ♀ catkins simple, tomentose, to 5cm. Spring. Jam., Cuba. Z9.

G. flavescens S. Wats. Shrub to 2.5m. Lvs to 6cm, elliptic to oblong, yellow-green, almost glab. above, thickly pubesc. beneath. ♂ and ♀ catkins dense, pendulous, to 3cm. SW Amer. var. *pallida* Eastw. Lvs with a glaucous or waxy white bloom above. Calif. Z9.

G. fremontii Torr. FEVER BUSH; SKUNK BUSH; QUININE BUSH. Shrub to 3m. Lvs broad-elliptic, to 6cm, dark glossy green and hairy above and beneath at first. Catkins clustered terminally; ♂ catkins to 20cm, yellow; ♀ catkins to 5cm, woolly. Spring. Calif., Oreg. Z7.

G. ×*issaquahensis* Nel. (*G. elliptica* ×*G. fremontii*.) Shrub or tree to 5m. Lvs 6cm, elliptic to ovate, mucronate, undulate, glossy dark green above, light green and sparsely hairy beneath. ♂ catkins mauve when young, becoming paler, to golden when mature. ♀ catkins rigid. 'Pat Ballard': ♂ lvs bright green, margins less undulate; catkins to 20cm.

G. laurifolia Benth. Shrub or tree to 5m. Lvs to 15cm, broadly elliptic, obtuse to abruptly acute. var. *macrophylla* Benth. Robust shrub or small tree to 3m. Lvs to 15cm, oblong, often mucronate, dark glossy above, tomentose beneath. ♂ catkins to 7cm, usually branched; ♀ catkins to 12cm. Early summer. Mex. Z8.

G. ×*thuretii* Carr. (*G. elliptica* ×*G. fadyenii*.) Fast-growing shrub to 5m. Lvs to 10cm, narrow-oblong, tapering, mucronate, shiny above, pubesc. beneath. Catkins nearly erect, to 8cm, hairy. Summer. Gdn origin. Z8.

G. veitchii Kellogg. Shrub to 3m. Lvs to 8cm, lanceolate to ovate-elliptic, acuminate, flat or undulate, downy, particularly beneath. ♂ catkins to 10cm, dense; ♀ catkins to 5cm. Calif. Z8.

G. wrightii Torr. Shrub to 2m. Lvs to 5cm, elliptic or elliptic-ovate, acute or mucronate, ± glab. beneath, bright green. Catkins slender, to 7cm. Summer. SW US. Z8.

GARRYACEAE Douglas ex Lindl. See *Garrya*.

Garuga Roxb. Burseraceae. 10 decid. trees. Lvs imparipinnate; lfts crenate or serrate. Pan. term., produced before lvs, tomentose; cal. tube campanulate, tomentose, 5-lobed; pet. 5, inserted in cal. tube; disc thin, fleshy, 5- or 10-lobed; sta. 10, fil. pubesc. Fr. a drupe. SE Asia, Philippine Is., Melanesia, N Aus.

G. pinnata Roxb. To 25m. Lvs to 20cm, tomentose when young; lfts oblong or oblong-lanceolate. Infl. to 15cm; cal. tube to 4mm, lobes to 2mm; pet. to 6×2mm, cream or yellow, oblong or lanceolate. Fr. to 1.5×1cm, oblong, corniculate, yellow-green. India, Burm. Z10.

✕ **Gasteraloe** Guill. (*Aloe* ×*Gasteria*.) Liliaceae (Aloeaceae). 24 hybrid succulents. St. short or indistinct. Lvs in spiral rosettes. Infl. a loose rac. or few-branched pan.; perianth tube, cylindrical, sometimes slightly swollen at base. Gdn origin. Z9.

✕*G. beguinii* (Radl) Guill. (*Aloe aristata* ×*Gasteria carinata* var. *verrucosa*.) Lvs 7–8×2.5–3cm, triangular, acute, dark green, often flushed purple, banded with purple spots, margins and keel white-denticulate. var. *chludowii* (Radl) G. Rowley. Lvs to 16cm, strap-shaped. var. *perfectior* Guill. Lvs longer and paler.

✕*G. pethamensis* (Bak.) G. Rowley. (*Aloe variegata* ×*Gasteria carinata* var. *verrucosa*.) Lvs 7.5–10×1.8–2cm, lanceolate, deep green often tinged purple with large white tubercles, margin and keel rough-tuberculate.

→*Aloe* and *Gasteria*.

✕ **Gasterhaworthia** Guill. (*Gasteria* ×*Haworthia*.) Liliaceae (Aloeaceae). 5. Small, clump-forming, succulent perennials. Lvs 2-ranked, spiralling in tight rosettes, stiff, usually covered in pale tubercles. Pan. racemose; fls usually orange-pink; perianth tube slightly inflated at base. Gdn origin. Z9.

✕*G. bayfieldii* (Salm-Dyck) G. Rowley. Lvs 10–14×2.5–3cm, triangular, brittle concave above, convex beneath, keeled toward apex, dark green with scattered paler spots, sparsely toothed. Pan. to 80cm; fls ascending, 1.3cm, pink.

✕*G. holtzei* (A. Berger) Guill. Lvs 9×3cm, lanceolate to triangular, short-acuminate, concave above, obliquely keeled, covered in white tubercles.

✕*G.* 'Royal Highness'. Resembling *Haworthia margaritifera* but more robust. Lvs to 10×3.5cm, triangular to lanceolate, stout, dark green, conspicuously white-tubercled. Pan. to 1m or taller; fls green-white, to 2cm.

✕*G. squarrosa* (Bak.) G. Rowley. Lvs to 13×2.5cm, concave above, convex beneath, sparsely green-white-tubercled, margins scabrous, pungent. Pan. to 80cm; fls to 18mm.

→*Aloe* and *Gasteria*.

Gasteria Duval. Liliaceae (Aloeaceae). 14. Compact, v. short-stemmed perenn. succulents. Lvs ligulate, dark green, distichous to spirally arranged in compact rosettes, flat or keeled. Infl. racemose simple or branched; fls usually pendulous, tubular, base inflated; tep. 6, pink to vermilion, apex green. S Afr. (Cape Prov. to Nam.). Z9.

G. acinacifolia (Jacq.) Haw. Lvs 22–60×4.5–10cm, sometimes falcate, linear-lanceolate to ligulate, obliquely keeled beneath, dark green, smooth, densely spotted white, serrulate. E Cape.

G. angulata Haw. = *G. carinata*.

G. angustiarum Poelln. Lvs with incurved tips, lorate to triangular-lanceolate, asperulous at first, later smooth and shiny, dark green, obscurely banded with white spots, margins tuberculate, crenate, serrulate toward tip. W Cape. var. *bayeri* Jaarsv. Lvs to 5cm, apex obtuse or truncate.

G. apicroides Bak. = ✕ *Gastroloba apicroides*.

G. batesiana G. Rowley. Lvs 5–18×1.5–4cm, triangular to linear, keeled, dark green to black-green, green- and white-tuberculate above and beneath, denticulate to serrulate. N Natal, NE Transvaal.

G. baylissiana Rauh. Lvs 2.5–10×2–2.5cm, short-lorate, apex truncate, densely white-tuberculate throughout, margins tuberculate. E Cape.

G. beckeri Schönl. = *G. nitida*.

G. bicolor Haw. Lvs 3–22×1.5–5cm, lorate to linear, smooth when mature, dark green, spotted white in obscure crossbands, margins thickened, tuberculate, denticulate, apex with an eccentric mucro. E Cape. var. *liliputana* (Poelln.) Jaarsv. Miniature; lvs to 6cm, with white spots.

G. caespitosa Poelln. = *G. bicolor*.
G. candicans Haw. = *G. acinacifolia*.
G. carinata (Mill.) Duval. Lvs 3–12×1–5cm, triangular to lanceolate or lorate, ± keeled beneath, almost covered in pale tubercles, margins thickened, tubercule or finely toothed. S Cape. var. **retusa** Jaarsv. Lvs 5–9×2.5–3.5cm, distichous, lorate, not keeled, truncate or retuse, crenate. var. **verrucosa** (Mill.) Jaarsv. Lvs 5–7×1.5–3cm, linear-lanceolate, not keeled, heavily white-tuberculate, acute or obtuse, entire.
G. ×cheilophylla Bak. (*G. carinata* var. *verrucosa* ×*G. obliqua?*) Lvs 22–30×2.5–4cm, linear, acute, sometimes obliquely keeled, inclined to spreading, smooth, densely white-tubercled, glossy dark green, margins thickened with raised spots. Origin unknown.
G. colubrina N.E. Br. = *G. bicolor*.
G. croucheri (Hook.) Bak. Lvs 20–36×3–10cm, linear-lanceolate, sharply and obliquely keeled, dark green, smooth, densely spotted white, denticulate to serrulate.
G. decipiens Haw. = *G. nitida*.
G. disticha (L.) Haw. Lvs 6–17×3–4.5cm, lorate, asperulous, banded with dense white spots, obtuse, rarely truncate, mucronate, undulate. W Cape.
G. excavata Haw. = *G. carinata*.
G. excelsa Bak. Lvs 10–40×10–18cm, forming dense rosettes, triangular to lanceolate, obliquely keeled below, dark green, obscurely banded with white spots, margins thickened, sharply serrulate. E Cape.
G. fuscopunctata Bak. = *G. excelsa*.
G. glabra Haw. = *G. carinata*.
G. herreana Poelln. = *G. bicolor*.
G. laetepuncta Haw. = *G. carinata*.
G. liliputana Poelln. = *G. bicolor* var. *liliputana*.
G. maculata Haw. = *G. bicolor*.
G. marmorata Bak. = *G. bicolor*.
G. minima hort. = *G. bicolor* var. *liliputana*.
G. neliana Poelln. = *G. pillansii*.
G. nigricans Duval = *G. disticha*.
G. nitida (Salm-Dyck) Haw. Lvs 2–18×2.5–8cm, short-triangular to broad-lanceolate, acute, ± obliquely keeled, dark green, smooth, glossy, indistinctly spotted white, margins thickened, entire. SE Cape. var. **armstrongii** (Schönl.) Jaarsv. Retaining juvenile habit, with squat, distichous, tuberculate, prostrate lvs. Eur.
G. obliqua (DC.) Duval. Lvs 24–36×2.5–4cm, sometimes falcate, linear, tapering, acuminate, semiterete or triangular, dark green, smooth, banded with dense white spots, serrulate. E Cape.
G. obtusifolia Haw. = *G. disticha*.
G. pethamensis Bak. = × *Gasteraloe pethamensis*.
G. picta Haw. = *G. bicolor*.
G. pillansii Kensit. Lvs 7–20×1.5–5cm, ligulate, asperulous, obscurely banded with immersed tubercles, margins thickened, tuberculate or crenulate, mucro acute to obtuse. Namaqualand.
G. planifolia Bak. = *G. bicolor*.
G. pulchra Haw. = *G. obliqua*.
G. rawlinsonii Oberm. Lvs 6–8×2–2.5cm, linear, ligulate, mucro obtuse, maturing dark green, sparsely spotted, asperulous, finely serrate, spines to 2mm. SE Cape.
G. retata Haw. = *G. bicolor*.
G. spiralis Bak. = *G. bicolor*.
G. squarrosa Bak. = × *Gasterhaworthia squarrosa*.
G. stayneri Poelln. = *G. nitida*.
G. subcarinata Haw. = *G. carinata*.
G. subverrucosa Haw. = *G. carinata* var. *verrucosa*.
G. sulcata Haw. = *G. carinata*.
G. verrucosa Duval = *G. carinata* var. *verrucosa*.
G. vlokii Jaarsv. Lvs 5–9×2–3cm, lanceolate to triangular-falcate, short-ligulate, obliquely keeled, green, spotted white in obscure bands, minutely tuberculate. E Cape.

Gastonia Comm. ex Lam. Araliaceae. 9 trees, some at least of palm-like habit when young, later developing a rounded crown. Lvs in term. rosettes, imparipinnate, compound. Infl. term., paniculate; fls in umbels; cal. rim ± prominent; pet. 4–14, discrete and valvate or fused; sta. 7–100. Fr. drupaceous, usually round. Madag., Masc. Is., Seych., Malesia, Solomon Is.
G. cutispongia Lam. BOIS D'EPONGE. Tall smooth tree covered with spongy bark. Lvs 5–9-foliolate, ovate, obtuse, leathery. Pan. to 30cm; pet. 10–14, distinct. Fr. depressed-globose with low, spreading styles. Masc. Is. (Réunion). Z10.
G. palmata Roxb. ex Lindl. = *Trevesia palmata*.

Gastrochilus D. Don. Orchidaceae. 20 monopodial, short-stemmed, epiphytic orchids. Lvs coriaceous, alt., 2-ranked, ligulate to oblong. Rac. axill.; sep. and pet. similar, spreading;

lip basally saccate, the sides fused to the column wings, mid-lobe forward-pointing, entire or fringed. Asia. Z10.
G. acutifolius (Lindl.) Kuntze. Lvs oblong-lanceolate, to 15cm. Fls to 2cm diam., yellow or pale green, tinged and dotted dull brown; tep. oblong-lanceolate, fleshy; lip midlobe, papillose-pubesc., margins jagged. N India to Thail.
G. bellinus (Rchb. f.) Kuntze. Lvs lorate, 10–20cm. Fls fragrant, to 4cm diam., yellow, blotched red to maroon; tep. obovate-oblong, fleshy; lip yellow, apex irregularly incised, callus papillose. Burm.
G. calceolaris (Buch.-Ham. ex Sm.) D. Don. Lvs linear-oblong, to 30cm. Fls to 1.7cm diam., pale green, speckled red-brown, waxy, slightly fragrant, spur yellow; dors. sep. ovate-oblong, lat. sep. narrower, falcate; pet. oblong-ovate; lip midlobe, fringed, callus pubesc. Himal., Indochina to Malaysia.
G. dasypogon (Sm.) Kuntze. Lvs oblong, to 20cm. Fls to 2.5cm diam., bright yellow, spotted maroon; tep. oblong-lanceolate; lip midlobe, fleshy, margins narrowly divided. Winter. India.
→*Aerides* and *Saccolabium*.

× Gastrolea Walth. = × *Gasteraloe*.

× Gastroloba Cunn. (*Astroloba* ×*Gasteria*.) Liliaceae (Aloe-aceae). 2 compact, everg., perenn. succulents with spotted lvs as in *Gasteria*, but spirally arranged as in *Astroloba* and with ascending fls.
×G. apicroides (Bak.) G. Rowley. St. to 15cm. Lvs 10–15×2.5–3cm, deep green with scattered spots, margins pale, tuberculate. Infl. 60–90cm, with 4–6 br.; fls pale red.
→*Gasteria*.

Gastrolobium R. Br. POISON PEAS. Leguminosae (Papilionoideae). 45 toxic everg. shrubs. Lvs simple, entire, usually rigid, v. short-petioled. Fls pea-like, racemose. W Aus. Z10.
G. bilobum R. Br. HEART-LEAVED POISON; HEART-LEAF POISON. To 4m. St. erect; branchlets angular, sericeous. Lvs to 4×1cm, oblong, cuneate. Fls 1cm diam., standard yellow marked red, wings mostly yellow, keel red. Spring. W Aus.
G. grandiflorum F.J. Muell. To 2m; branchlets sericeous, numerous. Lvs to 6×3cm, ovate to oblong, obtuse or emarginate. Fls to 1.5cm diam., standard red to deep red; keel red, becoming purple, much incurved. W Aus.
G. pyramidale T. Moore. To 2m; branchlets pubesc. or loosely villous. Lvs 2.5–6.5×3–4cm, ovate, rarely obovate-oblong, rounded or cordate at base, glabrescent, whorled. Fls 1.5cm diam., bright orange-yellow with a red keel. W Aus.

Gastronema Herb.
G. sanguineum Lindl. = *Cyrtanthus sanguineus*.

× Gaulnettya Marchant. Ericaceae. (*Gaultheria* ×*Pernettya*) The parent genera are now united in *Gaultheria*. See *Gaultheria* ×*wisleyensis*.

Gaultheria Kalm. ex L. Ericaceae. c170 everg. shrubs. Lvs shortly petiolate. Fls short-stalked, solitary in axils, racemose or paniculate, cal. (4–) 5-parted, sometimes enlarging to enclose fr. in pseudoberry; cor. campanulate or urceolate, lobes (4–)5, shallow, sta. 10. Fr. a dry capsule, enclosed by fleshy cal., or a spherical berry (*Pernettya*), both often scented of wintergreen. Amer., W Indies, Jap. to Australasia.
G. adenothrix (Miq.) Maxim. Dwarf procumbent shrub. Lvs ovate to elliptic, somewhat serrate toward apex, acute or obtuse, 1–3×0.5–2cm, coriaceous, hispid near margin. Fls solitary, pendent; cor. ovoid-urceolate, to 10mm, white. Fr. globose, 6mm diam., bright red, pubesc. Late spring. Jap. Z9.
G. antarctica Hook. f. Low spreading shrub to 10cm high. Lvs ovate to oblong, ± serrate, acute, 6×3mm, coriaceous, ± pubesc. Fls solitary; cor. campanulate, 4–7mm, white. Fr. pyriform to globose, 6–8mm, white to pink. Spring. Patagonia and Falkland Is. Z9.
G. antipoda Forst. f. Shrub procumbent, to 10cm or erect, to 2m. Lvs rounded-obovate to oblong-lanceolate, undulate to serrate, 8–15mm, thick, glab. Fls solitary, cor. campanulate to urceolate, 3mm, white. Fr. globose, to 12mm, white or red. Summer. NZ. Z9. 'Adpressa': plant procumbent.
G. caudata Stapf. Shrub to 2.5m, similar to *G. forrestii* except br. rufescent; lvs less closely dentate, more finely acuminate; infl. of axillary rac.; bracteoles more distant from cal. SW China. Z6.
G. codonantha Airy Shaw. Shrub to 2m; br. arching. Lvs ovate to lanceolate, irregularly dentate, acute, 5–15×2–12cm, hispid between veins beneath, glab. above when mature. Corymbs axill., 4–7b-fld; cor. cupulate, to 2cm diam., white tinged green, often flushed red. Fr. depressed-globose, to 2cm diam., purple-black. Late autumn. Assam.

G. cumingiana Vidal. Small shrub. Lvs ovate, long-acuminate at apex, rounded to somewhat cordate at base, serrate, 5–8×1.5–2.5cm, glab., thick. Rac. 3–5-fld; cor. campanulate, 7mm, white. Fr. globose, 7mm diam., purple-black. S China to Philipp. Z10.

G. cuneata (Rehd. & Wils.) Bean. Dwarf compact shrub 20–30cm. Lvs ovate-oblong to obovate, attenuate, glandular-serrate, 1–3×0.5–1cm, coriaceous. Rac. short; cor. urceolate, 6mm, white. Fr. globose, 6mm, white. Summer. W China. Z6.

G. depressa Hook. f. Dwarf cushion-forming shrub to 30cm. Lvs rounded-oval to broadly obovate, obtuse to sub-acute, bristly toothed when young, 4–8×3–4mm, bronze in autumn, coriaceous. Fls solitary; cor. campanulate, 3mm, white or flushed pink. Fr. globose, 8–15mm, scarlet or white. Late spring–early summer. NZ. Z9.

G. eriophylla (Pers.) Sleumer Shrub to 90cm; young br. pink, brown pilose. Lvs ovate-oblong to broadly elliptic, apiculate, to 6×3cm, lanate then subglabrous above. Rac. axill., sometimes grouped into pan.; cor. urceolate, 6mm, pink to red, white-pubesc. within. Fr. black. SE Braz. Z10.

G. ×*fagifolia* Colenso. (*G. antipoda* ×*G. oppositifolia*.) Shrub low and spreading to suberect, 0.5–2.5m. Lvs oblong to ovate-oblong, acute or subacute at apex, generally cordate at base, bristly-serrate, 1–2.5cm, coriaceous. Rac. and pan. axill. and term.; cor. ovoid-campanulate, 4mm, white. Summer. NZ.

G. forrestii Diels. Bush to 1m, rounded. Lvs narrowly ovate to oblong or oblanceolate, acute, bristly serrate, 5–9×1–4cm, sparsely hispid, becoming glab. and brown-punctate, coriaceous. Rac. axill. distributed along previous year's growth; cor. small, broadly urceolate, fragrant, 4–5mm, milky white. Fr. rather few, globose to ovoid, 6mm diam., blue. Late spring–early summer. SW China. Z6.

G. fragrantissima Wallich. Large shrub or small tree, 1m+. Lvs ovate to narrowly elliptic, glandular-mucronate at apex, bristly-toothed, 3–10×2–5cm, bright green above, bristly then brown-punctate beneath, coriaceous. Rac. dense, axill., pendulous; cor. campanulate to globose-urceolate, 6–8mm, yellow tinged green to white, v. fragrant. Fr. ovoid to globose, 8mm, blue. Spring. India. Z9.

G. hirtiflora Benth. Everg. shrub. Lvs triangular-ovate, obtuse or acute at apex, deeply cordate at base, finely serrate, 3–9cm, minutely pubesc. to glab. Cor. 6–7cm, pink to red. Fr. 4–5mm. Mex. to Guat. Z9.

G. hispida R. Br. SNOW-BERRY; WAXBERRY. Shrub, 0.5m, erect to spreading. Lvs oblong to narrowly ovate-lanceolate, shortly apiculate, finely dentate to bristly-serrate, 2.5–5cm, hispid, coriaceous. Rac. 3–7cm; cor. broadly campanulate to ovoid-urceolate, 4mm, white. Fr. globose, 10–12mm, snowy white. Aus. and Tasm. Z9.

G. hispidula (L.) Muhlenb. ex Bigelow. CREEPING SNOW-BERRY; MOXIE PLUM; MAIDENHAIR BERRY. Procumbent shrublet; br. matted, rough-hairy. Lvs rounded-ovate, entire, 4–10mm, hispid beneath. Fls solitary; cor. urceolate-campanulate, 4mm, white. Fr. globose, 6mm, white, hairy. Late spring–summer. N N Amer. and Jap. Z6.

G. hookeri C.B. Clarke. Shrub, 70–150cm, broadly erect. Lvs ovate to obovate or elliptic, bristly-dentate, rounded at base, glandular-mucronate, 5–10×2–4cm, hispid on veins beneath, coriaceous. Rac. 2–5cm, dense, pubesc.; cor. ovoid-urceolate to tubular, 4–6mm, pink. Fr. globose or turbinate, 5mm, violet, pruinose. Spring. E Himal., Sikkim. Z6.

G. humifusa (Graham) Rydb. ALPINE WINTERGREEN. Shrublet 7–10cm high, bushy, creeping. Lvs elliptic to rounded, obtuse to subacute, bristly-serrate, 1–2×0.5–1cm, glossy above, thin. Fls solitary; cor. campanulate, 5mm, white to pink. Fr. depressed-globose, 6mm, scarlet. Summer. W N Amer.

G. insana (Molina) Middleton. Erect shrub to 50cm. Branchlets tomentose. Lvs 2.5–5×1.2–2.5cm, apex acuminate, base tapered or truncate. Rac. short, axill.; cor. 0.6–0.9cm, white, urceolate. Fr. brown-red. S Chile, Arg. Z6.

G. itoana Hayata. Shrublet 10–15cm; br. wiry. Lvs lanceolate to oblong-obovate, acute, glandular-serrate ± revolute, acute, 10–15×3–7mm, thin and tough, glab. Rac. subterminal, 2cm; cor. tubular-ovoid to ovoid-urceolate, 5mm, white. Fr. globose, 6mm, white or flushed pink. Late spring. China and Taiwan. Z6.

G. lanceolata Hook. f. Small, erect shrub. Lvs c17×4–5mm, oblong-elliptic. Fls solitary; cor. white, shortly campanulate. Fr. ± entirely enclosed by enlarged cal. Tasm. Z7.

G. laxiflora Diels = *G. yunnanensis*.

G. leucocarpa f. *cumingiana* (Vidal) Sleumer = *G. cumingiana*.

G. macrostigma (Colenso) Middleton. Prostrate, diffuse shrub. 50–70cm. Lvs 12–14×2–3mm, narrowly elliptic, oblong or linear, apex acute and downward-curving, setose-crenulate, thinly downy above, glab. beneath. Fls solitary; cor. c3mm, white. Fr. flat, c6mm diam., pink, enclosed in enlarged, fleshy cal. Spring.

NZ. Z8.

G. merilliana hort. = *G. itoana*.

G. microphylla hort. non Hook. f. = *G. antarctica*.

G. miqueliana Tak. Shrub to 30cm. Lvs ovate to obovate, rounded to subacute at apex, 2–4×1–2cm, glandular-serrate, glab., glandular-punctate beneath. Rac. small in upper lf axils; cor. campanulate-urceolate, 4mm, white. Fr. globose, 1cm, white or pale pink. Late spring–summer. Jap. Z6.

G. mucronata (L. f.) Hook. & Arn. Stiff, thickly branched, suckering shrub, 50cm–1.5m. Lvs 8–18×4–6mm, oval-elliptic to oblong-elliptic, acute, mucronate, dentate, coriaceous, rigid. Fls solitary, nodding; cor. white to pink, c6mm, oval-urceolate. Fr. 8–12mm diam., white, rose or lilac to crimson to purple-black, spherical. Late spring–early summer. Chile, Arg. 'Alba': fr. white. 'Bell's Seedling': hermaphroditic; young shoots tinged red; lvs deep green, v. lustrous; fr. large, persistent, crimson. 'Cherry Ripe': fr. cherry-red. 'Crimsonia': habit broad, robust; fr. carmine-red, 14–16mm thick. 'Edward Balls' ('E.K. Balls'): young growth upright, stiff, tinged red, bristly; lvs broadly oval. 'Lilian': habit broad; fr. red-lilac, 14–16mm thick. 'Mulberry Wine': fr. large, maroon turning dark purple. 'Parelmoer': habit somewhat broad; fr. pale, 13–15mm thick. 'Rosalind': habit broad; fr. carmine pink, 12–14mm thick. 'Rosie': young growth tinged red; lvs dark, shaded blue; fr. pink with darker markings. 'Sneeuwwitje' ('Snow White'): habit broad, shoots few, protuberant; fr. in long clusters, virgin white, speckled with red spots, 10–12mm thick. 'Stag River': habit small, neat; lvs small, glossy; fr. large, pink, abundant. 'Wintertime': somewhat compact; fr. virgin white, late ripening, long-persistent, 10–12mm thick. var. *angustifolia* (Lindl.) Middleton. Lvs larger, oblong-elliptic, thinner, tapering to base and apex. Fls smaller. C Chile. var. *rupicola* (Phillips) Middleton. Twigs finely downy. Lvs thinner, 8–12×4mm, narrowly elliptic, sharply acute, 2–5-toothed on each side, lustrous. Fls white tinged pink. C China. Z6.

G. myrsinites Hook. = *G. humifusa*.

G. myrsinoides HBK. Prostrate or creeping shrub, c15cm. Lvs 4–7×1.8–2.5mm, elliptic to oblong elliptic, sharp-tipped, setose-crenulate. Fls solitary; cor. white, 5–6mm diam., urceolate. Fr. blue-black, to 15mm thick, subglobose, with enlarged cal. Spring–summer. Costa Rica to C Chile. ssp. *pentlandii* DC. To 50cm. Shoots downy, somewhat setose. Lvs 20–30×5–9mm, oblong-ovate, lustrous and glab. above, paler beneath, shallowly serrate. Cal. slightly fleshy, tinged purple; cor. white, 3–5mm, urceolate. Fr. coloured like cal. Costa Rica to N Chile. Z9.

G. nummularioides D. Don. Prostrate shrublet; br. interwoven, hispid. Lvs rounded, ovate to elliptic, bristly-serrate, glandular-mucronate, 6–15mm, dull green above, paler and hispid beneath, rugose. Fls solitary, concealed in foliage; cor. conic-urceolate, 6mm, white to pink or tinged red-brown. Fr. ovoid, 8mm, blue-black. Summer. Himal. Z9.

G. oppositifolia Hook. f. Broadly erect, shrublet, to 2.5m. Lvs ovate or oblong to ovate-lanceolate, acute or obtuse at apex, cordate at base, bristly-serrate, 3–6cm, glab. above, somewhat hispid beneath. Infl. paniculate; cor. campanulate, 4mm, white. Fr. a dry capsule, 4mm. Late spring–summer. NZ. Z9.

G. ovatifolia A. Gray. Shrub, procumbent or broadly spreading, 15–30cm high. Lvs broadly ovate to suborbicular, acute to obtuse at apex, truncate to cordate at base, shallowly bristle-toothed, 1.5–2.5cm, glossy, rugose, thin. Fls solitary; cor. campanulate, 5mm, white to pink. Fr. depressed-globose, 6mm, scarlet. Summer. BC to Calif. and Idaho. Z6.

G. parvula Middleton. Dwarf shrub, decumbent, erect, 25–75mm. St. narrow, wiry. Lvs 3–6×1–2mm, ovate, sharp-tipped, coriaceous, setose-crenulate, glandular-downy above. Fls solitary; cor. enlarging and becoming fleshy during fruiting, lobes ovate. Fr. depressed 4–15mm thick, flushed red. Spring. NZ. Z9.

G. phillyreifolia (Pers.) Sleumer. Everg. shrub 0.5–2m; br. finely pubesc. Lvs lanceolate, scabrous-dentate, tips prickly, 1–2cm, glab. Rac. axill. 3–10-fld; cor. urceolate, 3–4mm, white. Fr. red-brown. Arg. Z6.

G. procumbens L. WINTERGREEN; CHECKERBERRY; TEABERRY; MOUNTAIN TEA; CREEPING WINTERGREEN CHECKERBERRY; SPICY WINTERGREEN CHECKERBERRY. Shrublet, stoloniferous, creeping. Lvs elliptic to elliptic-obovate, acute and glandular-mucronate, crenate to bristly-serrate, 2–5×1–2cm, glossy, glab. Fls solitary or in small rac.; cor. conic to urceolate, 7mm, white to pale pink. Fr. globose, 8–15mm, red, v. aromatic when crushed. Summer. E N Amer. Z4.

G. pumila (L. f.) Middleton. Diffuse, prostrate shrub. Lvs 5–6×c1.5mm, ovate or ovate-lanceolate, dense, blunt or rounded, sparsely dentate, coriaceous, glab., lustrous. Fls solitary, drooping; cor. white, c6×5mm, campanulate. Fr. 12–22mm diam., white to red-tinted. Spring. Falkland Is.,

Patagonia, Tierra del Fuego. 'Harold Comber': fr. large, deep pink. var. *leucocarpa* (DC.) Middleton. Fr. white. S Chile. Z7.

G. pyrolifolia C.B. Clarke = *G. pyroloides*.

G. pyroloides Miq. emend. Tak. Shrublet, stoloniferous, ground-covering, 10–15cm high; br. slightly pubesc. Lvs obovate to sub-orbicular, minutely mucronate, dentate particularly toward apex, 1.5–3.5cm, glab. above, sparsely pubesc. beneath, coriaceous. Rac. short pubesc.; cor. ovoid-urceolate, 5mm, white flushed pink. Fr. rounded-ellipsoid, 8mm, blue-black. Late spring–summer. Himal. Z6.

G. pyroloides var. *cuneata* Rehd. & Wils. = *G. cuneata*.

G. repens Raf. = *G. procumbens*.

G. rupestris (Forst.) G. Don. Shrub procumbent to erect to 1m. Lvs oblong-lanceolate, obtuse to subacute, bristly-serrate, 10–25×3–8mm. Rac. near br. tips; cor. ovoid-campanulate, 4mm, white. Fr. a dry capsule, depressed-globose, 4mm. Summer. NZ. Z7.

G. semi-infera (C.B. Clarke) Airy Shaw. Shrub to 2m, far lower in cult; branchlets conspicuously hairy at first. Lvs elliptic, acuminate, finely crenate, 6–7×2cm, glab. above, laxly setose then punctate beneath. Rac. axill., 2.5–4cm; cor. urceolate, 4mm, white. Fr. somewhat pyriform, 8mm, blue, fleshy. Sikkim to NW Yunnan. Z9.

G. serpyllifolia (Pursh) Salisb. = *G. hispidula*.

G. shallon Pursh. SALAL; SHALLON. Shrub, stoloniferous, to 60cm. Lvs broadly ovate, acute at apex, cordate at base, bristly-serrate, 5–10×4–8cm. Rac. pendulous, several-fld, 5–10cm; cor. broadly urceolate, 5mm, white tinged pink. Fr. rounded or obconic, 1cm, red ultimately tinged black, glandular-pubesc. Late spring–summer. Alask. to Calif. 'Acutifolia': lvs more acuminate.

G. sinensis Anthony. Shrub, compact to procumbent, 10–15cm high; ferruginous-hispid. Lvs oblong to obovate-oblong, obtuse, bristly-serrate, 1–1.5×0.5cm, ± glab. Fls solitary; cor. open-campanulate, 6mm, white. Fr. top-shaped, 1cm, blue, pink or white. Spring. Upper Burm., Yunnan, Tibet. Z9.

G. stapfiana Airy Shaw. Shrub, somewhat rounded, stiff, 60–100cm, branchlets bristly then punctate. Lvs elliptic, obtuse to acute, bluntly serrate, 6–10×2–3cm, smooth above, paler and darkly hispid or punctate beneath, coriaceous. Rac. 2–4cm; cor. urceolate, 5mm, soft pink. Fr. depressed-globose, 5–7mm, lilac-blue. Late spring–summer. SW China, Upper Burm., N Assam. Z9.

G. tasmanica (Hook. f.) Middleton. Divaricately branching shrub forming cushion-like mats. Lvs 6–8×3–4mm, oblong, acute, somewhat crenate, coriaceous, lustrous. Fls solitary; cor. white, *c*6mm, campanulate. Fr. *c*10mm diam., with a vivid red enlarged fleshy cal. Spring. Tasm. Z7.

G. tetramera W.W. Sm. Shrub, erect or procumbent, 30–50cm. Lvs broadly elliptic to lanceolate or obovate, shortly mucronate, bristly-serrate, 3–7×1–2.5cm, coriaceous, hispid-punctate beneath. Rac. axillary, 2.5cm; cor. ovoid-urceolate, 5mm, white tinged pink. Fr. 6mm, blue, fleshy. Late spring. Tibet, W China. Z9.

G. thymifolia Stapf. Dwarf shrub, 10–15cm; br. v. slender, almost filamentous, finely hispid. Lvs oblanceolate, bristly-serrate in distal subacute, ± revolute, 5–10×1.5–3mm, glab. Fls solitary; cor. campanulate, v. small, white or red-tinted. Fr. 1cm, pale blue. Summer. Upper Burm. Z6.

G. tricophylla Royle. Low-growing shrub, cushion-forming; br. v. slender, wiry, hispid. Lvs elliptic to ovate-elliptic or narrowly oblong, subacute, bristly-serrate, 8–10×6mm; cor. campanulate, 4mm, red to pink or white. Fr. to 1cm, pale blue. Late spring. W China, Himal. Z8.

G. veitchiana Craib. Shrub, procumbent, dense; shoots hispid. Lvs ovate to obovate, glandular-mucronate, bristly-serrate, 5–7.5×2–4cm, hispidulous then glandular-punctate beneath, coriaceous. Fl. clusters dense, pendulous; cor. ovoid-urceolate, 4–6mm, white. Fr. subglobose, 6mm, bright to dark blue, fleshy. Late spring. W & C China.

G. wardii Marq. & Airy Shaw. Shrub, low and spreading, 70–100cm; br. somewhat arching, bristly. Lvs oblong to lanceolate, acute at apex, rounded to subcordate at base, bristly-serrate, 3–8cm, coarsely hispid with veins sunken above. Rac. compact, to 2cm; cor. urceolate, 5mm, white. Fr. globose, 5mm, blue, pruinose, not fleshy. Late spring–summer. SE Tibet. Z6.

G. willisiana C.R. Davie = *G. eriophylla*.

G. × wisleyensis (*G. shallon* × *G. mucronata*.) Hybrids formerly held to be intergeneric (× *Gaulnettya*). 'Pink Pixie': dwarf suckering shrub; fls white tinged pink; fr. purple-red; late spring. 'Ruby': small vigorous shrub forming dense thickets; lvs to 2.5cm, dark green, coriaceous; fls white in crowded terminal and axill. rac.; fr. ruby red with swollen cal. remnant. 'Wisley Pearl': small shrub with matt dark green lvs to 3.8cm; fr. large, purple-red in crowded bunches in autumn and winter. Z6.

G. yunnanensis (Franch.) Rehd. Shrub to 1m+; br. nodding, glab. Lvs oblong to elliptic or lanceolate, subacute to acuminate at apex, cordate at base, finely serrate, 5–10cm, coriaceous, glab. to glandular-hispid beneath. Rac. slender; fls also sometimes solitary; cor. broadly campanulate, 4–6mm, white tinged green, often with brown markings. Fr. depressed-globose, 6mm, black. Late spring–summer. SW China. Z6.

→*Chiogenes* and *Pernettya*.

× **Gaulthettya** Camp see × *Gaulnettya* and *Gaultheria*.

Gaura L. Onagraceae. 21 ann., bienn. or perenn. herbs. Lvs mostly basal, rosulate, pinnatifid, term. lobe largest, round, petiole winged. Fls in a leafless spike, bracteate, usually 4-merous, rarely 3-merous, zygomorphic with pet. in upper half, or actinomorphic, ephemeral; floral tube narrow; pet. clawed, opened out flat; sta. twice as many as sep. N Amer. Z4.

G. biennis L. Ann. or bienn. to 180cm, branched, villous, and gland. above. Basal lvs to 40cm, irregular in outline, cauline lvs 1.5–1.3cm, narrow-elliptic, entire to undulate-denticulate. Fls zygomophic, opening at dusk; floral tube 6–12.5mm; pet. white becoming red, 6.5–12×2–6mm. C & E US, Ont.

G. filiformis var. *munzii* Cory = *G. lindheimeri*.

G. lindheimeri Engelm. & Gray. Robust, villous, perenn. St. branched, to 150cm, forming a clump. Lvs 0.5–9mm, narrow-elliptic to oblanceolate, with a few large teeth. Fls zygomorphic, opening at dawn; floral tube 4–9mm; pet. 10.5–15×5–10mm, white becoming suffused pink. Spring–summer. Tex., Louisiana.

Gauridium Spach = *Gaura*.

Gaussia H.A. Wendl. Palmae. 4 unarmed palms. St. supported on mass of roots, sometimes swollen at base or middle. Lvs pinnate, pinnae linear-lanceolate, single-fold, tapered, waxy. Infl. branched ×2–3; fls orange or yellow to white. Fr. globose to obpyriform, orange to black, red or brown, 1-seeded, to 2cm. C Amer. Z10.

G. attenuata (Cook) Becc. LLUME PALM. Trunk to 20m, narrow, swollen at base to 25cm diam., supported by prop roots. Lvs to 2m; pinnae suberect, in 2 rows, to 50×4cm. Puerto Rico.

G. maya (Cook) Quero & Read. Trunk to 20m×15cm, columnar, with visible roots. Lvs to 3m; pinnae in 4 rows, to 70×4cm. Guat., Belize, Mex.

G. princeps H.A. Wendl. PRIMA DE SIERRA. To 18m. Trunk swollen at base, suddenly constricted above, ringed, on thick, terete, prop roots. Lvs to 2.5m, pinnae in 4 rows, with conspicuous swellings, to 70×3cm. Cuba.

→*Opsiandra*.

Gaya Kunth.

G. lyallii (Hook. f.) Bak. f. = *Hoheria lyallii*.

Gay Feather *Liatris*.

Gaylussacia Kunth. Ericaceae. 40 decid. or everg. shrubs. Fls few, 5-merous, in axill. rac.; cal. 5-lobed; cor. tubular, urceolate or campanulate; sta. 10. Fr. a berry-like drupe. Americas.

G. baccata (Wangenh.) K. Koch. BLACK HUCKLEBERRY. Erect, decid. shrub to 1m. Lvs to 5cm, elliptic-oblong, pale green above, resinous. Rac. drooping; cor. urceolate, 5mm, dull red. Fr. to 8mm, black, glossy, edible. E US.

G. brachycera (Michx.) Torr. & A. Gray. BOX HUCKLEBERRY. Creeping, stoloniferous, everg. shrublet to 45cm. Lvs to 2.5cm, ovate, oval or oblong, slightly revolute, shallowly dentate, gland., leathery. Rac. short; cor. tubular-urceolate, 5mm, white with red-tinged stripes. Fr. to 1.25cm, black, flavourless. E US.

G. resinosa Torr. & A. Gray = *G. baccata*.

Gay-wings *Polygala paucifolia*.

Gazania Gaertn. TREASURE FLOWER. Compositae. 16 perenn. to ann. herbs with milky sap. Lvs crowded toward base or cauline, variable. Cap. radiate, usually large, solitary, v. showy. Trop. and S Afr. Z9.

G. jurineifolia DC. Dwarf perenn. Lvs 2.5cm, entire to pinnatisect, lobes in 2–5 pairs, linear, entire or base 1–2-lobed, spinose-mucronate, revolute, glab. above, white beneath. Cap. on peduncles to 2.5cm; ray flts white; disc flts yellow. S Afr.

G. krebsiana Less. St. 0. Lvs to 9×1cm, linear-lanceolate, entire or occas. pinnatifid, lobes in 2–3 pairs, decurrent, revolute, petiolate, white-lanate beneath, glab. above. Cap. on peduncles to 5cm; ray flts pale yellow with a deep yellow band near base; rose-violet below; disc flts golden-yellow. S Afr. ssp. *serrulata* (DC.) Roesler is a smaller, neater plant.

G. leucolaena DC. = *G. rigens* var. *leucolaena*.

G. linearis (Thunb.) Druce. Perenn., with woody rootstock. Lvs 5–6cm, lanceolate to elliptic-oblong, entire or pinnatisect with linear-lanceolate lobes, glab. to sparsely minutely hispid above, white-lanate beneath, petiolate. Cap. on peduncles to c8cm; ray flts golden-yellow; disc flts orange-brown. Natal.

G. longiscapa DC. = G. linearis.

G. montana Spreng. = G. krebsiana ssp. serrulata.

G. pygmaea Sonder = G. krebsiana ssp. serrulata.

G. rigens (L.) Gaertn. TREASURE FLOWER. Decumbent perenn. to 30cm; st. short and densely leafy. Lvs to 12–1cm, oblong-spathulate, entire or pinnatifid, obtuse, petiolate, green and glab. above, white beneath; margins reflexed. Cap. on peduncles to 20cm; flts orange with black eye-spot at base; disc flts orange-brown. S Afr. 'Aureo Variegata': to 30cm; lvs variegated green and gold; fls orange. 'Torquay Silver': lvs tinted silver; fls orange. 'Variegata': lvs variegated gold and cream; fls orange. var. *uniflora* (L. f.) Roessler. Cap. smaller; ray flts yellow. yellow. Summer. var. *leucolaena* (DC.) Roessler. White-tomentose throughout. Cap. smaller; ray flts yellow.

Cvs and hybrids. Carnival Hybrids: vigorous, to 30cm; fls to 7cm diam., yellow, arrays, rose and scarlet. 'Chansonette': vigorous to 20cm; fls single, early-flowering, colours variable, rose, bronze, salmon, red, orange and yellow, many with rings and dark centres. centres. 'Cream Beauty': lvs grey-green, fls cream. Daybreak Hybrids: dwarf; fls orange, yellow, pink and white; early-flowering. 'Flash': lvs silver; fls orange with basal black rings highlighted by white spots. spots. Harlequin Hybrids: to 40cm; bright yellow, orange, pink and red, mostly with vivid zones. 'Magenta Green': fls deep purple. Mini-Star Series: dwarf to 20cm; lvs tinted silver; fls white, gold, tangerine and russet, some with vivid rings. 'Orange Beauty': fls rich orange. Pinata Series: to 30cm; lvs tinted silver or bright green; fls large, single, yellow, red and gold bicolours, orange and red. 'Silver Beauty': lvs bright silver; fls pale yellow. 'Silver Filigree': lvs light silver; fls clear yellow. 'Snuggle Bunny': compact, to 15cm; fls rusty orange with brown centre. 'Sunbeam': fls rich yellow. Sunshine Giants Hybrids: to 30cm; fls yellow, gold and red bicolours, yellow and gold. 'Tangerine': fls soft orange. 'Vimmer's Variegated': to 25cm; lvs broadly edged yellow; fls orange. 'Yellow Buttons': fls small, yellow.

G. ringens hort. = G. rigens.

G. splendens hort. = G. rigens.

G. uniflora Sims = G. rigens var. uniflora.

Gean Prunus avium.

Gebang Palm Corypha utan.

Geebung Persoonia.

Geiger Tree Cordia sebestena.

Geissois Labill. Cunoniaceae. 20 trees or shrubs. Lvs opposite, digitate; stipules large. Rac. axill.; fls small, stalked; cal. red, 4- or 5-lobed, valvate; pet. 0; sta. numerous, fil. red, elongate. Fr. a capsule, coriaceous. Aus., New Caledonia, Fiji Is. Z10.

G. benthamii F. Muell. Tree to 30m, base often buttressed. Lvs trifoliate, lfts to 18×7cm, elliptic or ovate, serrate, glab.; stipules to 2.5cm diam.; petioles to 4cm. Infl. yellow, br. to 15cm; sep. to 3mm. Fr. to 15mm, orange-brown pubesc. Queensld.

→*Weinmannia*.

Geissorhiza Ker-Gawl. Iridaceae. 80 cormous perenn. herbs. Lvs 1 to several. St. ± erect, simple or branched. Infl. spicate, subtended by two bracts; fls usually regular, sometimes slightly zygomorphic, usually with short perianth tube and spreading tep.; style long, slender, exceeding tube, with 3 recurved br. Winter. S Afr. Z8.

G. aspera Goldbl. Lvs usually 3, linear, erect or curved. St. 8–35cm, simple or 1–3-branched, rough to the touch; fls star-like, white, pale to deep blue or purple; tube 1–2mm, tep. 11–15×4–6mm, obovate. Cape Penins.

G. erosa (Salisb.) R. Fost. = G. inflexa.

G. fulva Ker-Gawl. ex Bak. Lvs 3, terete with 4 longitudinal grooves. St. 7–18cm erect, slighty bent below lowest fl.; spike 1–3-fld; fls star-like, deep golden yellow; tube to 5mm, tep. 15–28×15mm, obovate. SW Cape.

G. hirta (Thunb.) Ker-Gawl. = G. inflexa.

G. humilis (Thunb.) Ker-Gawl. Lvs 2–3, almost linear with 4 longitudinal grooves. St. to 14cm, usually simple; fls star-like, bright yellow; tube 5–6mm, tep. to 22×14mm, obovate. Cape Penins. and Cape Flats.

G. inflexa (Delaroche) Ker-Gawl. Lvs 2–3, almost linear but with edges extended outwards at right angles and midrib winged, the edge and midrib pubesc. St. 12–30cm, usually simple; fls star-like, pink, red or purple, or white, cream or pale yellow tinged red; tube 1–2.5mm, tep. 10–18×8–10mm, rarely to 24mm, obovate. SW Cape.

G. ovata (Burm. f.) Asch. & Gräbn. Lvs 2–3, ovate-oblong, the edge and sometimes veins ciliate, often with minute dots. St. to 15cm; fls white or pale pink, marked with red in centre and dark red outside; tube 10–30mm, tep. spreading but slightly cup-shaped, 10–13×5–7mm, lanceolate or obovate. SW Cape.

G. radians (Thunb.) Goldbl. Lvs 3, linear. St. to 16cm, erect, simple or with 1 br. Fls slightly zygomorphic, tep. concave, red at base, the apical half deep blue-violet, the colours separated by a white band, each tep. also with a dark, pitted mark in the centre; tube 6–8mm, tep. 15–22×12–15mm. W Cape Flats.

G. rochensis (Ker-Gawl.) Ker-Gawl. = G. radians.

G. secunda Ker-Gawl. = G. aspera.

G. splendidissima Diels. Lvs 3, linear with 4 grooves, slightly sticky. St. 8–20cm, rough to touch, simple or 1–2-branched; fls deep violet-blue, dark toward base of tep., yellow in throat, cup-shaped, slightly zygomorphic, tube 2–4mm, tep. 15–22×8–13mm, ovate. Late winter–early spring. W Cape.

→*Hesperantha*.

Gelasine Herb. Iridaceae. 4 perenn. cormous herbs. Lvs plicate. Fls several in a terminal cluster, regular, short-lived; perianth tube v. short; seg. subequal, obovate; fil. united to form a short column; style br. 3, linear. S Amer. Subtrop. S Amer. Z9.

G. azurea (Herb.). = G. elongata.

G. elongata (Graham) Ravenna. St. 50–60cm. Lvs basal, to 60×3cm, narrowly lanceolate. Fls cup-shaped; seg. c2cm, cuspidate, bright blue with a white blotch at the base. Urug., S Braz.

G. punctata Herb. = Alophia drummondii.

Gelibia Hutch. = Polyscias.

Gelsemium Juss. YELLOW JESSAMINE; CAROLINA JASMINE. Loganiaceae. 3 perenn., everg., twining, glab. shrubs. Fls 5-parted, solitary or in clusters; cor. funnelform, lobes short, overlapping. Americas, SE Asia.

G. rankinii Small. Similar to G. sempervirens but lf base rounded not narrow; fls unscented on stalks scaly only at base; sep. acuminate, persistent. SE US. Z8.

G. sempervirens (L.) St.-Hil. FALSE JASMINE; EVENING TRUMPET FLOWER. To 6m. Lvs to 5cm, oblong to ovate-lanceolate, glossy. Fls sweetly scented on scaly stalks; sep. obtuse, falling in fr.; cor. to 3×2.5cm, yellow with an orange centre. S US, Mex., Guat. Z9.

Geniostoma Forst. & Forst. f. NEW ZEALAND PRIVET. Loganiaceae. 20 shrubs or small trees. Fls in axill. cymes or clusters; cal. 5-lobed; cor. tubular-campanule, lobes 5, sta. 5, attached to the cor. tube between lobes. Fr. a dry capsule. Malaysia, Jap., S Sea Is., Australasia.

G. ligustrifolium Cunn. HANGEHANGE; PIGWOOD. Privet-like glab. shrub to 3.5m. Lvs to 8cm, ovate, acuminate, glossy. Fls 3mm diam., scented, white tinged green, in many, few-fld axill. cymes. Capsule globose, the 2 black outer halves of the capsule persisting. Spring. NZ. Z9.

Genipa L. Rubiaceae. 8 everg. shrubs or trees. Lvs stipulate. Fls in axill. or terminal, few-fld cymes; cal. tube turbinate to campanulate, limb truncate or 5–6-lobed; cor. salverform, tube glab. or pubesc. at throat, lobes 5–6, spreading, acute or obtuse, leathery; sta. 5–6, anth. exserted. Fr. a subglobose, juicy berry, crowned by persistent cal. Trop. Amer.

G. americana L. GENIPAP; GENIPAP FRUIT; JAGUA; MARMALADE BOX. Tree, to 14m. Lvs to 35×19cm, rhomboid or lanceolate to oblong or obovate, apex acute, leathery or papery, glab. to minutely pubesc. beneath. Fls on pedicels to 4cm in dense, axill. cymes or corymbs; cor. white to yellow, tube to 3cm, sericeous at throat, lobes to 3cm, oblong, obtuse. Fr. to 8cm, green with dark purple juice, edible. Mex. to Peru. var. *caruto* (HBK) Schum. Tree, to 6m. Lvs obovate, densely pubesc. beneath. Fls white, in terminal, to 3-fld cymes. W Indies, Mex., central to N S Amer.

G. caruto HBK = G. americana var. caruto.

G. oblongifolia Ruiz & Pav. Tree, to 6m. Lvs oblong-ovate, apex obtuse, margins revolute, pubesc. beneath, esp. on veins. Fls white then yellow, short-pedicellate, in dense, term. cymes. Fr. to 3.75cm diam., yielding a blue dye. Peru.

G. pubescens DC. = Genipa americana.

→*Gardenia*.

Genipap Genipa americana.

Genipap Fruit Genipa americana.

Genipe Melicoccus bijugatus.

Genista L. BROOM; WOADWAXEN. Leguminosae (Papilionoideae). 90 shrubs, or small trees, sometimes spiny mostly decid., appearing everg. due to green, flattened branchlets. Lvs simple or trifoliolate, sometimes 0. Fls pea-like, yellow, in term. rac. or heads. Fr. a legume, linear-oblong or ovate, convex or turgid. Eur., Medit. to W Asia.

G. acanthoclada DC. Erect shrub, to 50cm. Br. terminating in a small spine. Lvs trifoliolate; lfts to 10×3mm, narrow-oblanceolate, sericeous. Fls solitary, near br. tips; standard to 10mm, rhombic, yellow, sericeous, shorter than keel, wings as long as standard. Fr. 9mm, ovoid, acuminate, sericeous, 1–2-seeded. Greece and Aegean region, Syr., Libya. ssp. *echinus* (Spach) Vierh. Standard to 12mm, equal to or longer than keel. SW & S Turk., Rhodes, Syr. Z9.

G. acanthoclada var. *fasciculata* Knoche = G. lucida.

G. aetnensis (Raf. ex Biv.) DC. MT ETNA BROOM. Shrub to 6m; br. weeping. Lvs to 13mm, linear, sparse or 0. Fls in loose rac. 13mm diam.; golden yellow; standard 10mm, broad- or angular-ovate, shorter than keel, subglabrous, wings as long as standard. Fr. to 13mm, ovoid-acuminate, beaked, subglabrous, 2–3-seeded. Summer. Sardinia, Sicily (slopes of Mt Etna). Z8.

G. albida Willd. Low spreading shrub, initially white-downy. Lvs to 10mm, elliptic to obovate, white-pubesc. throughout or glab. above. Fls in short rac., yellow; standard to 12mm, broadly ovate, equal to wings and keel. Fr. narrow oblong, densely pubesc., 3–8-seeded. Summer. E Balk., S Ukraine. Z6.

G. alpestris Bertol. = G. tinctoria.

G. alpini Spach = G. acanthoclada.

G. andreana Puiss. = Cytisus scoparius.

G. anglica L. NEEDLE FURZE; PETTY WHIN. Decumbent to erect, glab. shrub to 60cm, with numerous spines to 2cm. Lvs to 7mm, often fasciculate, ovate-lanceolate, pungent. Fls in short rac.; standard to 8mm, ovate, acute, usually shorter than keel and glab., keel glab., wings equalling standard. Fr. 15mm, falcate inflated, glab., 1–12-seeded. Summer. W Eur. 'Cloth of Gold': habit mat-forming, to 10cm; st. woody; lvs tinted grey; fls gold. var. *subinermis* (Legrand) Rouy. Almost unarmed. Scotland, C Fr. Z6.

G. anxantica (Ten.) Fiori = G. tinctoria.

G. arcuata Koch = G. sylvestris.

G. armeniaca Spach = G. albida.

G. aspalathoides Lam. Erect, spiny shrub, to 30cm. Lvs trifoliolate, lfts to 12mm, narrow-oblanceolate, with appressed grey hairs. Fls paired or clustered in loose rac. on young br., bright yellow; standard to 12mm, broadly ovate, equal to keel, sericeous. Fr. to 15mm, narrow-oblong, sericeous , 1–5-seeded. Summer. Sicily, Pantellaria, Alg., Tun. Z8.

G. aspalathoides auctt. non Lam. = G. lobelii.

G. baetica var. *pumila* Debeaux & Reverchon = G. pumila.

G. baetica var. *tejedensis* Porta & Rigo = G. lobelii.

G. berberidea Lange. Resembles *G. falcata* and *G. anglica*, but young br. and cal. densely pubesc., stipules thorny. Erect shrub. Lvs to 12mm, narrow-elliptic; standard to 10mm, keel to 11mm, wings 6mm. Fr. to 15mm, with sparse patent hairs along the sutures, 4–6-seeded. Summer. NW Spain, N Port. Z9.

G. boissieri hort. non Spach = G. horrida.

G. bruguieri Spach = G. acanthoclada.

G. canariensis L. To 2m, everg. Lvs trifoliolate, white-hairy, lfts to 13mm. Infl. term. on lat. shoots, 5–12-fld; fls 1.5cm, bright yellow, fragrant; standard reflexed, hairy outside. Fr. to 25mm, hairy. Canary Is. Z9.

G. candicans L. = G. canariensis.

G. cinerea (Vill.) DC. Erect shrub to 3m. Br. long, slender, grooved, sericeous. Lvs to 13mm (smaller and fasciculate on older br.), narrow-elliptic, oblanceolate or obovate, acute to pungent, sericeous beneath. Fls 13mm, bright yellow, mostly paired or in clusters in irregular rac. to 20cm; standard to 13mm, broad ovate, equal to wing and keel, emarginate, glab. or with a median ridge of hairs. Fr. to 17mm, narrow-oblong, sericeous, 2–5-seeded. Summer. SW Eur., N Afr. ssp. *leptoclada* (Willk.) P. Gibbs. Br. with a dense, white, appressed-sericeous to farinose indumentum. Spain (Mallorca). Z7.

G. cinerea hort., non DC. = G. tenera.

G. corsica (Lois.) DC. Resembles *G. scorpius*, but fls not borne directly on spines and fr. to 2cm. Spines to 1.5cm. Lvs to 5mm, narrowly obovate. Fls in congested rac.; standard to 11mm. Fr. 3–8-seeded, glab. Corsica, Sardinia. Z9.

G. dalmatica Bartling & H.L. Wendl. = G. sylvestris.

G. decipiens Spach = G. tournefortii.

G. decumbens (Durande) Willd. = Cytisus decumbens.

G. delphinensis Vill. = G. sagittalis.

G. depressa Bieb. = G. tinctoria.

G. echinus Spach = G. acanthoclada ssp. echinus.

G. elatior Koch = G. tinctoria.

G. ephedroides DC. Erect shrub to 1m, young shoots virgate, pendulous, finely grooved, downy. Lvs to 15mm, trifoliolate at the base of the shoots, simple towards the tips, v. few, sparsely sericeous. Fls in loose, term. rac.; standard to 10mm, shorter than keel, broad to angular ovate, sparsely sericeous, wings equalling standard. Fr. 10mm, ovoid-acuminate, sericeous, seeds 1–2, black shining. Spring. Sardinia, Sicily, Corsica, Alg. Z9.

G. erinacoides (Lois.) Vierh. = G. lobelii.

G. falcata Brot. Erect shrub with stout often branched spines to 5cm, usually downy. Young br. rigid, furrowed, pilose-sericeous. Lvs to 14mm, narrow-oblanceolate, glab. above. Fls to 10mm, in clusters of 2–5 at ends of lat. br., or in narrow pan.; standard 9mm, somewhat acute, glab. or with a narrow median ridge of hairs, keel 10mm, subglabrous with a few hairs along the ventral suture. Spring. W Spain, Port. Z9.

G. fasselata Decne. Erect shrub to 1.5m, with stout, recurved spines. Lvs to 15mm, simple or trifoliolate, narrow-oblanceolate, sericeous. Fls solitary or loosely clustered on spines and br.; standard to 7mm, broad, angular-ovate, glab., shorter than keel, keel sparsely sericeous, wings equalling standard. Fr. ovoid acuminate, sparsely sericeous, 1–2-seeded. S Aegean region, Isr. Z9.

G. ferox (Poir.) Poir. Erect shrub with stout spines. Lvs to 12mm, trifoliolate or simple, narrow-oblanceolate or obovate, acuminate, sericeous beneath; stipules spiny. Fls in term. rac.; standard 12mm, broad-ovate, glab., equalling keel and wings. Fr. 15mm, narrow-oblong, sericeous, 3–6-seeded. N Afr. Z9.

G. florida L. Erect shrub, to 2.5m. Br. curving. Lvs to 25mm, elliptic to oblanceolate or linear, adpressed-sericeous. Fls in rac. to 8cm; standard to 12mm, broad-ovate, subglabrous, keel and wings equalling standard. Fr. 2cm, narrow oblong, sericeous, 3–8-seeded. Spain, Port.,Morocco. Z9.

G. germanica L. Erect shrub to 50cm, with axill. spines. Lvs to 2cm, elliptic-oblong, dark green, with long subpatent hairs beneath and on margins. Fls in loose term. rac. to 5cm on the young shoots; standard 8mm, ovate, acute, shorter than keel, glab. or sparsely sericeous, wings equalling standard. Fr. 10mm, ovoid acuminate, subglabrous, 1–2-seeded. Summer. C & W Eur. var. *inermis* Koch. Spines 0. Z5.

G. glabrescens Briq. = Cytisus emeriflorus.

G. grandiflora Spach = Cytisus grandiflorus.

G. hirsuta Vahl = Chamaecytisus hirsutus.

G. hispanica L. SPANISH GORSE. Erect shrub to 70cm, with axill. spines, young br. with patent hairs. Lvs to 10mm, ovate-oblong, obtuse, downy beneath, present only on flowering br. Fls 2–12 in crowded subterminal rac., golden-yellow; standard to 8mm, broad-ovate, shorter than or equalling keel, glab., apex slightly retuse, keel subglabrous, wings equalling standard. Fr. 10mm, oblong, acute, sparsely sericeous, 1–2-seeded. Summer. S Fr., N Spain. 'Compacta': habit dense. 'Nana': habit dwarf. ssp. *occidentalis* Rouy. Br. and lvs adpressed-sericeous. Standard to 11mm. SW Fr., W Pyren., N Spain. Z6.

G. hispanica var. *hirsuta* Willk. = G. hispanica.

G. hispanica var. *villosa* Willk. = G. hispanica ssp. occidentalis.

G. horrida (Vahl) DC. Dense, cushion-forming, rigid, spiny shrub to 60cm, usually shorter. Lvs trifoliolate; lfts 8mm, linear, pubesc. Fls to 15mm, 1–3, in term. heads, yellow; standard glab. Fr. 25mm, oblong, silky-tomentose. Pyren. Z7.

G. humifusa Vill. non L. = G. villarsii.

G. humilior (Bertol.) Schneid. = G. tinctoria.

G. humilis Ten. = G. tinctoria.

G. hungarica Kerner = G. tinctoria.

G. involucrata auct. non Spach = G. albida.

G. januensis Viv. GENOA BROOM. Erect or prostrate shrub, to 30cm; br. usually triangular-winged. Lvs to 12mm on flowering br., elliptic to obovate, on sterile br. to 40mm, elliptic to lanceolate, glab., minutely dentate. Fls in short rac., bright yellow; standard 10mm, broad-ovate, equalling keel and wings, glab., keel glab. Fr. 1.5cm, narrow-oblong, glab., 3–8-seeded. Late spring–early summer. It., Balk. Z8.

G. jaubertii Buchegger non Spach = G. sessilifolia.

G. juncea (L.) Scop. = Spartium junceum.

G. kewensis hort. = Cytisus × kewensis.

G. leptoclada Gay ex Spach = G. florida.

G. leptophylla Spach = G. lydia.

G. linifolia L. Everg. or semi-evergreen shrub to 3m. Br. erect, adpressed silky-pubesc. Lvs trifoliolate, lfts 1–2.5cm, lanceolate, adpressed pubesc. beneath. Infl. congested term. rac.; fls golden; standard 1–1.8cm, ovate, pubesc. Spain, N Afr., Canary Is. Z9.

G. lobelii DC. Dwarf or prostrate spiny shrub, to 40cm; young br. pubesc. and furrowed. Lvs 3.5mm, elliptic to obovate, pulvinulate, adpressed sericeous beneath. Fls single, rarely paired, bright yellow; standard to 10mm, broad-ovate, densely sericeous, keel and wings equalling standard. Fr. to 1.5cm, narrow-oblong or lanceolate-ovate, sericeous, 1–5-seeded. Summer. SE Fr., SE Spain. Z9.

G. lobelii var. *pumila* (Debeaux & Reverchon) Deg. & Herv.-Bass. = *G. pumila*.

G. longipes Pau = *G. lobelii*.

G. lucida Cambess. Erect shrub with stout spines. Lvs to 8mm, narrow-elliptic, sericeous beneath, stipules spiny. Fls in term. rac., standard 10mm, ovate, shorter than keel, somewhat acute, subglabrous, wings equalling standard. Fr. ovoid, acuminate, sparsely sericeous, 1–2-seeded. Balearic Is. (Mallorca). Z9.

G. lydia Boiss. Prostrate shrub, to 30cm. Br. ascending, with prickly tips, grey-green. Lvs to 10mm, sometimes fasciculate, linear-elliptic, subglabrous. Fls few, on short rac. at ends of br., golden-yellow; standard to 12mm, broad ovate, glab., keel and wings equalling standard, keel glab. Fr. to 2cm, narrow-oblong, flat, glab., 3–8-seeded. Late spring–early summer. E Balk., Syr. var. *rumelica* (Velen.) Bornm. Erect shrub, to 1m, loosely branched. Greece, Bulg. Z7.

G. maderensis Lowe. Everg. shrub or tree to 6m. Young branchlets silver-pubesc. Lvs crowded, trifoliolate, long-stalked; lfts 6–9mm, oblong-obovate to lanceolate, pubesc. beneath. Rac. term., 6–12-fld; fls fragrant, golden; standard glab.; keel densely pubesc. Fr. 2.5cm, compressed, pubesc. Madeira. Z9.

G. mantica Pollini = *G. tinctoria* var. *humilior*.

G. micrantha Ortega. Low, unarmed, spreading shrub. Lvs 12mm, narrow-elliptic, subglabrous. Fls in term. rac.; standard to 7mm, triangular, base truncate to obtuse, shorter than keel, keel sparsely sericeous along ventral suture, wings equalling standard. Fr. 6mm, ovoid-acuminate, sericeous, 1–2-seeded. NW Spain, N Port. Z8.

G. monosperma (L.) Lam. = *Retama monosperma*.

G. monspessulana (L.) O. Bolós & Vigo. Everg., much branched shrub to 2.5m. Branchlets pubesc. Lvs trifoliolate, stalked; lfts 12–20mm, obovate, sometimes incised, pubesc. beneath. Rac. or clusters term., 3–9-fld; fls yellow; standard elliptic; keel subglabrous. Fr. 2–3cm, pubesc. or scaly, straight or curved. S Eur.: Port. to Asia Minor. Z8.

G. montbretii Spach = *G. albida*.

G. mugronensis Vierh. = *G. pumila*.

G. nissana Petrovic. Resembles *G. sessilifolia*, but br., lvs and standard densely pubesc., and lfts to 6mm diam., linear-oblanceolate to elliptic, not involute. Summer. S Balk. Z6.

G. numidica Spach = *G. ephedroides*.

G. ovata Waldst. & Kit. = *G. tinctoria*.

G. peloponesica Spach = *G. acanthoclada*.

G. pilosa L. Prostrate to erect shrub, to 45cm. Br. ascending, downy. Lvs to 15mm, oblanceolate, adpressed sericeous beneath, deep green above. Fls 1–3 in loose rac. to 14.5cm, golden-yellow; standard 8mm, broad-ovate, sericeous, keel and wings subequal to standard. Fr. to 2cm, narrow-oblong, sericeous, 3–8-seeded. Late spring–early summer. W & C Eur. 'Goldilocks': strong grower, broad and bushy, to 60cm, but much wider, flat globose; fls v. numerous, golden-yellow. 'Procumbens': st. prostrate. 'Superba': habit shrubby, to 45cm high; lvs mid-green; fls yellow. 'Vancouver Gold': habit spreading, prostrate, mound-forming, to 45cm tall; lvs dark green; fls gold, April. 'Yellow Spreader' ('Emerald Spreader'): low, spreading; fls bright yellow, June. Z5.

G. polygalifolia DC. = *G. florida*.

G. polygaliphylla Brot. = *G. florida*.

G. pomelii Marès & Vigin. = *G. lucida*.

G. procumbens hort. = *G. pilosa* 'Procumbens'.

G. procumbens Waldst. & Kit. = *Cytisus procumbens*.

G. pulchella Gren. & Godron non Vis. = *G. villarsii*.

G. pumila (Debeaux & Reverchon) Vierh. Resembles *G. lobelii*, but br. thick and stout, fls usually in short rac. Lvs to 5mm. Fr. 3–5-seeded. Mts of EC Spain. Z8.

G. purgans L. = *Cytisus purgans*.

G. radiata (L.) Scop. Erect unarmed shrub, to 80cm. Br. strongly ridged, pulvinate. Lvs to 20mm, trifoliolate, lfts narrow-oblanceolate, sericeous beneath. Fls 4–12, in term. clusters; standard to 14mm, broad-ovate, glab. or with a narrow median line of silky hairs, equal to or shorter than keel, wings as long as standard. Fr. to 12mm, ovoid-acuminate or slightly flattened, densely sericeous, 1–2-seeded. Late spring–early summer. SW Fr., S Alps, It., Greece, Asia. Z6.

G. raetam Forssk. = *Retama raetam*.

G. ramosissima (Desf.) Poir. Resembles *G. cinerea*, but fls more villous, and sessile or v. shortly stalked. Erect shrub to 1m. Lvs 5mm. Fr. 3–6-seeded. N Afr., SE Spain. Z9.

G. repens Lam. = *G. pilosa*.

G. rigidissima Vierh. = *G. pumila*.

G. rumelica Velen. = *G. lydia* var. *rumelica*.

G. sagittalis L. Prostrate shrub, to 15cm. Br. green with two broad wings giving the whole a leafy, everg. appearance. Lvs to 20mm, lanceolate, few, subglabrous. Fls in short term. rac. to 4cm, golden-yellow; cor. to 13mm, standard usually glab. Fr. to 2×0.5cm, sericeous, 4–6-seeded. Late spring–early summer. S

& C Eur., Balk. Z4.

G. scariosa Viv. = *G. januensis*.

G. scoparius (L.) Lam. = *Cytisus scoparius*.

G. scorpioides Spach = *G. triacanthos*.

G. scorpius (L.) DC. Erect shrub to 2m, with stout spines. Lvs to 11mm, narrow-elliptic to narrow-oblanceolate or -obovate, sparsely sericeous beneath. Fls single, paired or fascicled, toward br. tips and on spines; standard to 12mm, broad-ovate, glab., keel and wings equalling standard, keel glab. Fr. to 4cm, narrow-oblong, subglabrous; seeds 2–8. Early summer. SW Fr., E Spain. Z9.

G. scythica Pacz. = *G. albida*.

G. sericea Wulf. Shrub to 30cm; br. ascending, adpressed pubesc. Lvs to 25mm, narrow-elliptic or obovate, white, sericeous beneath, bright green above, short-mucronate. Fls 2–5, in crowded term. rac., golden-yellow; standard to 14mm, broad-ovate, sericeous, keel and wings equalling standard. Fr. to 1.5cm, narrow-oblong with dense patent hairs, 3–8-seeded. Late spring–early summer. S Alps. Z8.

G. sessilifolia DC. Erect shrub. Br. sparse. Lvs trifoliolate, subsessile, lfts to 15mm, v. narrowly oblanceolate, sericeous beneath, revolute. Fls in loose rac.; standard 10mm, ovate, acute, sericeous, keel to 11mm, densely sericeous, wings shorter than keel. Fr. to 10mm, ovoid-acuminate, 1-seeded. N Balk., Turk. Z7.

G. sibirica Falk non Hohen. ex Boiss. = *G. tinctoria*.

G. × spachiana Webb. (*G. stenopetala* × *G. canariensis*.) Everg. shrub 3–6m. Young branchlets pubesc., grooved. Lvs trifoliolate, stalked; lfts 8–18mm, obovate, rounded, dark green above, silky beneath, rac. 5–10cm, downy; cor. 1.25cm, yellow. Z9.

G. spathulata Spach = *G. januensis*.

G. sphacelata Spach = *G. fasselata*.

G. sphaerocarpa (L.) Lam. = *Retama sphaerocarpa*.

G. spiniflora Lam. = *G. scorpius*.

G. stenopetala Webb & Berth. To 3m. Young branchlets white-sericeous. Lvs trifoliolate, distinctly stalked; lfts to 3cm, narrowly elliptic to oblanceolate, silky-pubesc. Rac. to 11cm, 1-sided, silky-pubesc.; fls bright yellow; standard 0.5cm across, glab. Fr. 2.5cm, adpressed hairy. Spring. Canary Is. Z9.

G. sylvestris Scop. Subshrub to 20cm, densely branched, spiny or subspinescent. Lvs to 20mm, narrow-oblong, puberulent beneath. Fls in term. rac., bright to golden-yellow; standard to 8mm, triangular, subglabrous, shorter than keel, keel subglabrous, wings as long as standard. Fr. 6mm, ovoid-acuminate, sparsely sericeous, 1–2-seeded. Summer. SE Eur. Z6.

G. tenella Willk. = *G. micrantha*.

G. tenera (Jacq.) Kuntze. Resembles *G. cinerea*, but br. shorter, stouter, becoming more twiggy and producing fls near ends of short lat. branchlets, not in small lat. clusters. Shrub to 2m+. Lvs grey-green, revolute. Rac. to 5cm. Fr. to 2.5cm, 3–5-seeded. Summer. Madeira, Tenerife. 'Golden Showers': fls esp. abundant, golden-yellow. Z9.

G. teretifolia Willk. Low shrub. Young br. adpressed-sericeous. Lvs to 9mm, v. narrow-oblanceolate, sericeous. Fls in loose term. rac.; standard 9mm, broad-ovate, sericeous, keel and wings equalling standard. Fr. narrow-oblong, sericeous, 3–6-seeded. NW Spain. Z8.

G. tinctoria L. DYER'S GREENWEED. Variable erect or ascending, non-spiny shrub, to 2m. Lvs to 5cm, elliptic, lanceolate or oblanceolate, bright green, glab., ciliate. Fls many, in term. simple or branched rac., golden-yellow; standard to 12mm, broad-ovate, glab., keel and wings equalling standard, keel glab. Fr. to 2.5cm, narrow-oblong, usually glab., 4–10-seeded. Summer. Most of Eur., to Asia Minor and the Ukraine; 0 from most islands, but found in Sicily. var. *anxantica* (Ten.) Fiori. Glab. dwarf form. S Ital. var. *humilior* (Bertol.) Schneid. St. erect, downy, red-tinted. Fls deep yellow. var. *prostrata* Bab. To 20cm. Lvs usually to 10mm. Fls few. Eur. (esp. maritime NW Eur.). f. *angustata* (Schur) Rehd. Lvs to 20mm elliptic to narrow-oblong. Fls in short rac. f. *latifolia* (DC.) Rehd. Lvs to 35mm, broad-elliptic. var. *ovata* (Waldst. & Kit.) Arcang. Erect or ascending, usually 20cm+. Lvs usually 10mm+ and pubesc. Fr. pubesc. SC Eur. var. *depressa* (Bieb.) P. Gibbs. Prostrate, to 20cm. Lvs to 10mm, usually pubesc. Fls few. Fr. pubesc. Balk. 'Golden Plate': habit spreading, tight; br. falling; fls clear yellow. 'Royal Gold': habit low; st. erect to 80cm; fls rich yellow, abundant, long-lasting. 'Plena': procumbent dwarf shrub; fls double. Z3.

G. tournefortii Spach. Erect shrub, with spines. Lvs to 18mm, lanceolate, with long hairs beneath ± glab. Fls in crowded term. rac., occas. subacapitate; standard to 11m, broadly ovate, subglabrous, somewhat retuse, shorter than keel, keel sparsely sericeous, wings equalling standard. Fr. 8mm, ovoid-acuminate, sparsely pilose, 1–2-seeded. S & C Spain, Port., Moroc. Z9.

G. triacanthos Brot. Erect shrub, with spines. Young br. sparsely

pubesc. Lvs to 7mm, trifoliolate, lfts narrow-oblanceolate, subglabrous. Fls in loose terminal, or intercalary, rac.; standard to
7mm, triangular, glab., shorter than keel, keel glab., wings
equalling standard. Fr. 7mm, ovoid-acuminate, sparsely sericeous, 1–2-seeded. W & SW Spain, Port., Moroc., Alg. Z9.

G. triangularis Willd. = *G. januensis*.

G. trifoliata Janka = *G. sessilifolia*.

G. triquetra Waldst. & Kit. non hort. = *G. lydia*.

G. triquetra hort. non Waldst. & Kit. = *G. januensis*.

G. versicolor hort. non Wallich ex Royle = *Chamaecytisus versicolor*.

G. villarsiana Jordan = *G. villarsii*.

G. villarsii Clementi. Procumbent shrub, occas. forming spiny
hummocks. Br. downy. Lvs to 9mm, narrow-elliptic, usually
clustered, with long hairs. Fls in short, subterminal rac.;
standard to 11mm, broad-ovate, densely sericeous, keel and
wings equalling standard. Fr. 12mm, narrow-oblong, densely
sericeous, 2–6-seeded. Late spring–early summer. Mts of SE Fr.
and Croatia. Z6.

G. villosa Lam. = *G. germanica*.

G. virgata (Ait.) Link non Lam. nec Willd. = *G. tenera*.

G. virgata Willd. non (Ait.) Link nec Lam. = *G. tinctoria*.

→*Chamaespartium*, *Cytisanthus*, *Cytisus*, *Echinospartium*, *Genistella*, *Spartium* and *Voglera*.

Genistella L.
G. sagittalis (L.) Gams = *Genista sagittalis*.

Genlisea A. St.-Hil. Lentibulariaceae. 16 rootless, semi-aquatic
carnivorous herbs. Rhizoids present, emerging from base of st.
Lvs either forming dense rosettes at base of st., long-petiolate,
entire, spathulate to suborbicular, or modified into traps
(utricles) consisting of stalk and slender tube, swollen in middle,
passing into 2 long, spirally twisted arms, with transverse bands
of stiff reversed hairs on inner side, together with digestive
glands. Rac. scapose, sometimes branched; cal. deeply 5-lobed;
cor. 2-lipped, upper lip erect, entire or emarginate, lower lip
larger, palate raised, ± 2-gibbous, margin deflexed, 3-lobed,
spur present. Trop. Amer., Afr., Madag.

G. africana A. St.-Hil. Lvs to 7×3mm, spathulate-cuneate.
Utricles variable in size, tube to 1.5cm. Scape to 30cm,
glandular-puberulous; fls 3–6; cor. to 0.6cm, pale purple.
Angola.

G. hispidula Stapf in Dyer. Lvs to 20×7mm, obovate-spatulate.
Utricles on long stalks, tube to 1.5cm, arms 2cm. Scape to
30cm, glab. or sparsely bristled; fls 3–5; cor. to 1cm, yellow to
white with yellow spots on palate. Moz., Malawi, S Afr.

Genoa Broom *Genista januensis*.
Genogeno *Lonchocarpus domingensis*.
Gentian *Gentiana*.

Gentiana L. GENTIAN. Gentianaceae. 400 ann., bienn. or
perenn. herbs. Lvs cauline and opposite or in whorls or tufted in
basal rosettes. Fls solitary or in elongate to capitate cymes, axill.
or term.; cal. tubular or campanulate, lobes 4–8; cor. rotate,
campanulate, tubular, funnel-shaped, salverform or clavate,
4–7-lobed, with interstitial plicae, tube sometimes pleated.
Cosmop. except Afr.

G. acaulis L. Tufted perenn. Lvs 2–3.5cm, elliptic or lanceolate
to obovate in basal rosette. Fls solitary, term., usually stalked;
cor. to 5cm, campanulate, dark blue, spotted green within tube,
lobes ovate, spreading, acute, plicae shorter than lobes,
triangular. Calcifuge. Spring–early summer. Eur. (Spain to
Balk.). 'A.G. Weeks Form': fls less heavily spotted green within; usually flowering twice per season. 'Alba': st. short; fls
white. 'Belvedere': v. vigorous, forming a wide-spreading mat,
free-flowering; fls deep blue. 'Coelestina': fls cambridge blue.
'Gedanensis' ('Danzig'): fls large, 4.0–4.5cm across, clear ultramarine. 'Holzmannii': st. 10–12cm; fls dark azure, 4.5–5cm,
with olive green anthers in spring and autumn. 'Krumrey': to
10cm; fls dark blue. 'Rannoch': dwarf, to 5cm; fls deep blue
with darker throat, striped green and white. 'Trotter's Variety'
('Trotter's Form'): free-flowering in spring and autumn. 'Undulatifolia': upper lvs undulate; free-flowering, fls dark blue;
sometimes listed under *G. clusii*. Z3.

G. acaulis 'Dinarica'. = *G. dinarica*.

G. adscendens Pall. = *G. decumbens*.

G. affinis Griseb. ex Hook. Perenn. to 30cm. St. clustered, erect
or somewhat decumbent. Lvs 2–3cm, paired lanceolate-ovate.
Fls in upper axils; cor. 2–3cm, azure to indigo, narrowly funnelform, lobes 3–5mm, spreading, ovate, green below, plicae 2–3-
toothed, shorter than lobes. Summer. W N Amer. Z5.

G. alba Muhlenb. Herbaceous perenn. to 60cm. St. stout, simple.
Lvs to 12cm, cauline, ovate to oblong-lanceolate, base cordate.
Fls clustered, term. or axillary; cor. 3cm, tubular, white tinged

yellow-green, lobes ovate, twice length of irregularly lobed
plicae. Summer. Central N Amer. (prairies). Z5.

G. albiflora Britt. see *G. andrewsii*.

G. algida Pall. Perenn. to 20cm; st. erect, simple. Basal lvs to
12.5cm, rosulate, linear to linear-lanceolate, glossy. Fls 1–3,
term., stalked; cor. 3–3.5cm, tubular-campanulate, white,
spotted and veined blue-green, lobes erect, triangular, acute,
plicae entire or toothed. Summer. NE Asia, W N Amer. Z5.

G. alpina Vill. Tufted perenn. Lvs basal to 2cm, elliptic to suborbicular, leathery, dull green, rosulate. Fls solitary, often
sessile; cor. to 4.5cm, funnelform, deep blue, tube spotted
green within, lobes rounded, plicate irregular, triangular. Early
summer. Eur. (Alps, Pyren., Spain). Z6.

G. altaica Laxm. Perenn. to 5cm. St. erect, tufted, simple.
Basal lvs to 2.5cm, linear, in a loose rosette. Fls solitary, term.
on short st.; cor. 3.5cm, funnelshaped, deep blue, tube paler
within, lobes rounded-ovate, plicae rounded, serrated, half
length of lobes. Spring. EC Asia (Sib., Mong.). Z3.

G. amoena C.B. Clarke. Perenn. St. forming mats 2.5cm high.
Lvs to 1.25cm, in basal rosette, broadly-ovate, truncate. Fls
solitary, sessile on longer shoots; cor. 2.5cm, campanulate, pale
to deep blue, banded white, lobes sometimes tinged purple,
ovate, plicae triangular, entire. Autumn. Himal. Z7.

G. andrewsii Griseb. CLOSED GENTIAN; BOTTLE GENTIAN. Herbaceous perenn. to 60cm. St. leafy, erect. Lvs 5cm, paired,
narrowly ovate to lanceolate. Fls sessile, term. or in upper axils;
cor. 3.5cm clavate, closed at mouth, white (*G. albiflora* Britt.)
or blue with white, lobes ovate, plicae deeply cleft, larger than
cor. lobes. Summer. E N Amer. Z6.

G. angustifolia Vill. Tufted perenn. to 10cm. Basal lvs 5cm,
rosulate, linear-lanceolate to oblanceolate. Fls solitary on short
stalks; cor. 5cm, funnel-shaped, deep sky-blue, paler and
spotted green within tube, lobes ovate, acute, plicae irregular,
obtuse. Summer. Eur. (SW Alps, Jura, Pyren.). Z7.

G. angustifolia Michx. non Vill. = *G. autumnalis*.

G. arvernensis hort. = *G. pneumonanthe* var. *depressa*.

G. asclepiadea L. WILLOW GENTIAN. Herbaceous perenn. to
60cm. St. leafy, arching. Lvs 5–7.5cm, cauline, ovate-
lanceolate, acute, prominently 3–5-veined. Fls sessile in axill.
clusters of 2–3; cor. 3.5cm, narrowly campanulate, azure,
spotted purple within, throat striped white or cor. entirely white
('Alba), lobes ovate, pointed, plicae short, entire. Summer.
Eur., Asia Minor. 'Knightshayes': small to dwarf; cor. throat
white. 'Nymans': st. arching; lvs dark green, fls with large spots
in throat. 'Phyllis': vigorous, to 70cm; fls pale blue. Z6.

G. austromontana Pringle & Sharp. Upright perenn. to 45cm,
resembling *G. andrewsii*. Lvs paired, ovate to lanceolate, glossy
green. Fls term., clustered; cor. clavate, constricted at mouth,
deep blue-violet. Autumn. E US. Z6.

G. autumnalis L. PINE BARRENS GENTIAN. Herbaceous perenn. to
45cm. St. solitary or 2–3, simple. Lvs 4–6.5cm, paired, linear to
oblanceolate, thick. Fls term., solitary on long stalk; cor. to
5cm, funnel-shaped, bright blue, lobes ovate, acute, narrowed
at base, plicae many-cleft, half length of cor. lobes. Autumn. E
US. f. *albescens* (Fern.) Fern. Fls white. Z6.

G. bavarica L. Mat-forming perenn. to 15cm. Basal lvs 1–1.5cm,
held loosely, obovate to spathulate, cauline lvs similar, in 3–4
pairs. Fls solitary; cor. tube to 2.5cm, lobes spreading, dark
blue, plicae bilobed, short. Summer. Eur. (S Alps to Carpath.,
Apennines.) Z5.

G. bellidifolia Hook. f. Ann. or short-lived perenn. to 15cm.
Basal lvs 2.5–3.25cm, spathulate to linear-spathulate, obtuse, ±
fleshy, in loose rosettes, cauline lvs linear-obovate, in 2–3 pairs.
Fls stalked, in terminal umbels; cor. to 2.2cm diam., white,
open-campanulate, lobes oblong, obovate, rounded, plicae
minute. NZ. Z7.

G. bernardii hort. = *G.* ×*stevenagensis* 'Bernardii'.

G. bigelovii A. Gray = *G. affinis*.

G. boryi Boiss. Tufted, creeping perenn. to 10cm. Lvs 0.5cm,
ovate to orbicular, fleshy. Fls term., solitary; cor. 1.25cm,
purple to brown outside, fading toward lobes, white within,
lobes pale blue, rounded, plicae white, toothed. Summer.
Spain. Z8.

G. brachyphylla Vill. Close to *G. verna* but smaller and more
compact, lvs closely overlapping, slender, acute, and fls more
slender, saucer-shaped, deep azure. Eur. ssp. *favratii* (Rittner)
Tutin. Lvs blunt and rounded, not slender and acute, cor. lobes
broad. Z4.

G. brevidens Franch. & Savat. = *G. triflora*.

G. bulleyana (Forr.) Marq. Climbing perenn. to 7m. Lvs
2.5–7.5cm, ovate-cordate, apex slender-acuminate. Fls solitary
in axils; cor. to 5cm, pale indigo, throat dark indigo,
campanulate to broadly funnelform, lobes triangular; plicae
short, rounded. Autumn. Burm. Z8.

G. burseri Lapeyr. Robust herbaceous perenn. to 1m. St. erect,
simple. Basal lvs 15–25cm, elliptic-ovate, cauline lvs 5–7.5cm,

rounder, sessile. Fls in axill. whorls and term. clusters; cor. 4cm, narrowly campanulate, yellow tinged green at base (deeply spotted in var. *villarsii*), lobes ovate-oblong, acute sometimes spotted brown, plicae entire, triangular, small. Summer. Eur. (Pyren., W Alps). Z7.

G. cachemirica Decne. Rosette-forming perenn. St. to 25cm, prostrate. Basal lvs 2.5–5cm, narrow-ovate, glaucous, cauline lvs to 1.5cm, broader. Fls term., sessile, solitary or few; cor. to 4cm, campanulate, clear blue striped yellow-white and darker blue, lobes round-ovate, plicae shorter than lobes, fringed. Summer. Kashmir to Pak. Z8.

G. calycosa Griseb. EXPLORER'S GENTIAN. Herbaceous perenn. St. to 30cm, tufted. Lvs 2–4cm, cauline, paired, ovate to suborbicular. Fls term., subtended by paired bracts; cor. 4cm, campanulate, deep blue, tube paler within, spotted green, lobes ovate, somewhat erect, plicae small, triangular, many-cleft. Summer. BC to Calif. Z4.

G. ×caroli hort. (*G. farreri* ×*G. lawrencei*.) Trailing perenn. resembling *G. lawrencei* in growth. Fls terminal, solitary; cor. to 5cm, funnel-shaped, copper-sulphate blue, striped outside, lobes oblong, plicae acute, bifid. Autumn. Gdn origin. 'Coronation': st. to 8cm, leafy, mostly prostrate; fls cobalt-blue, exterior striped green. Z4.

G. catesbaei Andrews non Walter = *G. andrewsii*.

G. catesbaei Walter non Andrews = *G. saponaria*.

G. cephalantha Franch. Perenn. to 40cm. St. arising from basal rosettes, branched. Basal lvs to 15cm, lanceolate, tapering to long petiole, glaucous beneath; cauline lvs to 7.5cm, paired. Fls term., 6–10 in a cluster; cor. 2cm, funnel-shaped, pale blue, lobes ovate, acute, plicae darker blue, less than half length of cor. lobes, unequal, bifid. Autumn. SW China. Z8.

G. cerina Hook. f. Perenn. St. to 35cm, leafy, trailing, then ascending. Basal lvs 1–4cm, oblong- to obovate-spathulate, obtuse, leathery, cauline lvs smaller, short-stalked. Fls term. on br., corymbose, sessile or on slender pedicels; cor. 2cm, broadly rotate-campanulate, white veined red or purple, lobes oblong, obtuse. Summer. NZ. Z8.

G. ×charpentieri Thom. (*G. lutea* ×*G. punctata*.) Naturally occurring hybrid. Fls long-stalked; cal. entire; cor. yellow, lobes obtuse, shorter than tube, plicae present. Summer. Eur. Z7.

G. ciliata Gunnerus = *Gentianopsis detonsa*.

G. clausa Raf. CLOSED GENTIAN. Herbaceous perenn. to 65cm, similar to *G. andrewsii*, differing in larger fls with cor. lobes equalling 2–3-cleft plicae. Summer. E N Amer. Z4.

G. clusii Perrier & Song. Tufted perenn. to 15cm. Basal lvs 2.5cm, rosulate, elliptic to elliptic-lanceolate, acute, bright green, leathery, margin papillose, cauline lvs smaller, sharply acute. Fls term., solitary; cor. 5cm, funnelform or campanulate, deep azure, paler and spotted olive-green within, lobes rounded, acute, plicae irregular, rounded. Summer. C & S Eur. 'Ovyd Strain': v. free-flowering fls slate blue. Z6.

G. cordifolia Koch = *G. septemfida* var. *cordifolia*.

G. costei Braun-Blanquet = *G. clusii*.

G. crassicaulis Duthie ex Burkill. Coarse perenn. to 60cm. St. thick, hollow. Basal lvs to 30cm, elliptic-ovate. Fls clustered, term., surrounded by 4 bracts; cor. to 2cm, funnelform, green-white, spotted, lobes ovate, erect, plicae small, triangular. Summer. W China. Z8.

G. crinita Froelich = *Gentianopsis crinita*.

G. cruciata L. Erect, leafy perenn., 10–40cm. St. emerging from basal rosette. Basal lvs 10–20cm, ovate-lanceolate, glossy; cauline lvs decussate, connate at base. Fls sessile, clustered, axill. and term.; cor. 2–2.5cm, clavate, azure, dull blue or green outside, lobes 4, ovate, acute, plicae bifid, less than half length of lobes. Summer. Eur., W & C Asia. Z5.

G. dahurica Fisch. Perenn. 15–30cm. St. branched, erect or ascending. Basal lvs 15–20cm, narrow-lanceolate, obtuse, cauline lvs in 2–3 pairs. Fls clustered, axill. and stalked, or term. and sessile; cor. to 3.5cm, narrowly funnelform, deep blue, paler within, lobes ovate, acute, plicae triangular, toothed. Summer. Asia Minor to N China. Z4.

G. ×davidii Franch. (*G. lawrencei* ×*G. prolata*.) St. to 4cm, branched. Lvs resemble *G. prolata*. Fls solitary, term., stalked pale blue; cor. tube to 3.5cm, narrowly funnelform, plicae short, acute. Late summer. Gdn origin. Z5.

G. decumbens L. f. Perenn. St. branched, prostate then ascending to 25cm. Basal lvs 7–12cm, rosulate, linear-lanceolate; cauline lvs in 2–3 pairs, connate at base. Fls in clusters, term. and axill., sessile or short-stalked; cor. 3cm, campanulate, deep blue to purple-blue, lobes round-ovate, acute, plicae entire, short. Summer. Himal. to Sib. Z4.

G. dendrologii Marq. Erect or ascending perenn. to 35cm. St. branching above. Basal lvs 10–20cm, lanceolate to linear, cauline lvs in 4–5 pairs, broader. Fls in clusters, stalked and axill. or term. and sessile; cor. to 3.5cm, cylindric, white, lobes ovate, obtuse, plicae short, truncate. Summer. W China. Z8.

G. depressa D. Don. Low, glaucous, mat-forming perenn. Lvs on sterile shoots to 1.5cm, forming rosette, obovate, overlapping, lvs on fertile shoots to 2cm, broadly ovate, subtending cal. Fls term., sessile; cor. 2–3cm, broadly campanulate, pale blue to green-blue, streaked white on plicae, white spotted purple within, lobes triangular, suberect, acute, plicae equalling lobes, triangular, entire. Autumn. Himal. (C Nepal to SE Tibet). Z5.

G. detonsa Rottb. = *Gentianopsis detonsa*.

G. dinarica G. Beck. Tufted perenn.; st. erect, unbranched to 12cm. Basal lvs 3.5cm, stiff, broadly-elliptic; cauline lvs smaller, elliptic-lanceolate. Fls solitary, term.; cor. 5cm, funnelform to campanulate, deep blue, unspotted, lobes cordate, apices tapering, plicae irregular, broadly triangular. Summer. SW Balk., Albania, C It. 'Harlin': vigorous. Z6.

G. elegans Nels. = *Gentianopsis thermalis*.

G. elwesii C.B. Clarke. Ann. or perenn., forming rosettes. St. erect, 15–35cm. Basal lvs 2.5–5cm, elliptic to ovate, obtuse. Fls several, stalked, term.; cor. to 3cm, tubular, inflated in middle; mouth closed, pale blue above, white below, lobes short, ovate, obtuse, plicae short, triangular, paler than lobes. Autumn. E Nepal to SE Tibet. Z7.

G. exaltata L. = *Eustoma exaltatum*.

G. excisa C. Presl = *G. acaulis*.

G. 'Farorna' = *G. 'Devonhall'*.

G. farreri Balf. f. Perenn. St. 10–15cm, branched, slender, trailing. Lvs linear-lanceolate, those at base to 3.5cm, rosulate, those on st., 1.5–3.5cm, paired, recurved. Fls solitary, term. subsessile; cor. 5–6.5cm, narrowly funnel-shaped, Cambridge blue tinged green, tube white within, striped violet and white on exterior, lobes broadly-ovate, acute, recurved, plicae shorter than lobes, truncate, sometimes fringed. Autumn. NW China. Z5.

G. favratii Rittener = *G. brachyphylla* ssp. *favratii*.

G. fetisowii Reg. & Winkl. Perenn. St. erect to 40cm, simple, arising from basal rosettes. Basal lvs to 16cm, narrow-lanceolate, cauline lvs in 2–3 pairs, decussate, smaller. Fls clustered at apex, sessile; cor. to 3.5cm, tubular-campanulate, purple-blue, white spotted brown within, lobes spreading, ovate, acute, recurved, plicae a quarter length of lobes, obtuse. Summer. C Asia to NW China. Z4.

G. flavida A. Gray = *G. alba*.

G. forwoodii A. Gray = *G. affinis*.

G. freyniana Bornm. ex Freyn. Herbaceous perenn. St. to 30cm, ascending, leafy. Lvs to 2.5cm, paired, connate at base, linear-lanceolate, obtuse. Fls term., solitary, sessile; cor. to 3cm, campanulate to clavate, purple-blue, lobes ovate, acute, plicae one-third length of lobes, bifid, acute. Summer. Turk. Z7.

G. frigida Haenke. Perenn. St. to 15cm, tufted erect or ascending. Basal lvs to 7.5cm, forming rosettes, linear to linear-oblong, sometimes undulate, cauline lvs shorter. Fls term., solitary, sessile; cor. 5cm, campanulate, yellow, spotted and veined blue, lobes short, ovate, obtuse, plicae small, entire, acute. Summer. E Eur. (Carpath., Alps of C Austria, SW Bulg.). Z5.

G. froelichii Jan ex Rchb. Low, tufted perenn. Lvs 2.5–3cm, forming loose rosettes, oblong to spathulate, thick, cauline lvs in 1–2 pairs, basally connate. Fls terminal on 2.5–5cm st., solitary; cor. 3cm, narrow-campanulate, pale-blue, unspotted, lobes erect, ovate, acute, plicae entire, triangular, less than half length of lobes. Summer. SE Alps. Z6.

G. gebleri Ledeb. = *G. decumbens*.

G. gelida Bieb. Perenn. St. to 30cm, ascending, leafy, sometimes branched above. Lvs to 3.5cm, scale-like below, ovate to linear-lanceolate above. Fls clustered, term. or in upper axils; cor. 3cm, clavate or campanulate, yellow to white, lobes broadly ovate, obtuse, plicae entire or bifid. Summer. W Asia (Turk. to Iran, Cauc.). Z6.

G. gentianella hort. = *G. acaulis*.

G. gilvo-striata Marq. Glaucous, tufted perenn. St. prostrate, rosette-forming. Basal lvs 0.7cm, oblanceolate, obtuse, cauline lvs grouped below fls. Fls solitary, term., sessile; cor. 3cm, funnel-shaped, sea blue, paler and spotted purple-blue within, tube striped purple-brown outside, lobes broadly ovate, plicae ovate, obtuse, shorter than lobes. Autumn. Upper Burm., Tibet. Z8.

G. glauca Pall. Tufted rhizomatous perenn. St. to 10cm. Basal lvs 1–1.25cm, rosulate, ovate to obovate, fleshy, glaucous, st. lvs smaller. Fls terminal and sessile, or stalked and 1–3 per axil; cor. to 2cm, blue, lobes ovate, blunt, plicae entire or cleft. N Amer., E Asia. Z4.

G. gracilipes Turrill. Perenn. St. to 25cm, branched, decumbent. Basal lvs 15cm, rosulate, narrow-lanceolate, cauline lvs shorter, in 2–4 pairs. Fls solitary, terminal, long-stalked; cor. 3.5cm, narrow-campanulate, deep purple-blue, green outside, lobes spreading, ovate-triangular, obtuse, plicae entire, half length of lobes. Summer. NW China. Z6.

G. grandiflora Laxm. = *G. altaica*.

G. grombczewskii Kuzn. Loosely tufted perenn. St. to 40cm, erect or ascending. Basal lvs 15–30cm, oblong-lanceolate, cauline lvs paired. Fls term., densely clustered, sessile; cor. to 2.5cm, tubular to funnel-shaped, pale yellow, lobes ovate-oblong, obtuse, plicae lanceolate to narrowly subulate, entire or bifid, almost equaling lobes. Summer. C Asia. Z7.

G. × hexa-farreri hort. (*G. hexaphylla* × *G. farreri*.) Vigorous gdn hybrid. St. trailing. Lvs 1.5–2cm, oblong to lanceolate, 2–5 per whorl. Fls solitary, term.; cor. 4.5cm, campanulate, deep sky blue, lobes triangular, mucronate, plicae triangular, acute. Summer. Gdn origin. 'Aberchalder': st. 8–10cm; fls deep azure blue; summer-autumn. 'Alpha': vigorous and free-flowering; cor. striped within; throat with white centre. 'Inez Weeks': vigorous seedling; fls to 14 per st., paler blue. 'Omega': like 'Alpha', but without white centre in throat. Z6.

G. hexaphylla Maxim. ex Kuzn. Tufted perenn. St. to 15cm, trailing. Lvs 1.2cm, linear, in whorls of 6. Fls term., solitary; cor. 3.5cm, funnel-shaped, pale blue, spotted green within, striped blue outside, lobes 6, broadly ovate, acuminate, plicae half length of lobes. Summer. Tibet. Z5.

G. holopetala (A. Gray) T. Holm = *Gentianopsis holopetala*.

G. hopei hort. = *G. trichotoma*.

G. igarashii Miyabe & Kudô = *G. algida*.

G. imbricata Froelich = *G. terglouensis*.

G. interrupta Sims non Greene = *G. ochroleuca*.

G. jesoana Nak. = *G. trinervis*.

G. kesselringii Reg. Perenn. St. to 25cm, erect, thick. Basal lvs 7.5cm, rosulate, lanceolate to linear-lanceolate, cauline lvs smaller, in 3–4 pairs, basally connate. Fls term. in a dense bracteate cluster; cor. to 2.5cm, tubular, with a swelling above middle, white to cream, spotted purple, lobes ovate, plicae bifid, acuminate. Summer. C Asia. Z5.

G. kochiana Perrier & Song. = *G. acaulis*.

G. kurroo Royle. Perenn. St. to 20cm, suberect, branched, from basal rosette. Basal lvs 10cm, lanceolate, cauline lvs 2.5cm, linear, 2–6 pairs, connate at base. Fls term., solitary, stalked; cor. 3.5cm, narrowly campanulate, deep blue, white spotted green within, lobes large, ovate, acute, plicae much smaller than lobes, deeply bifid. Autumn. Kashmir, NW Himal. Z7.

G. lagodechiana (Kuzn.) Grossh. ex Möllers = *G. septemfida* var. *lagodechiana*.

G. latifolia Jakow. = *G. acaulis*.

G. lawrencei Burkill. Perenn. St. 10–15cm, prostrate, from basal rosette. Basal lvs to 3.5cm, linear, recurved, cauline lvs paired. Fls solitary, term., long-stalked; cor. 4cm, tubular, turquoise-blue, paler to white within, banded blue with green-white panels outside, lobes triangular, plicae acute. Summer. Sib. Z5.

G. lhassica Burkill. Perenn. St. to 15cm, decumbent, branched. Basal lvs 7.5–10cm, in an open rosette, lanceolate; cauline lvs paired, smaller. Fls terminal, solitary, sessile; cor. 2cm, narrow-campanulate, deep violet, paler within, lobes round-ovate, plicae ovate, acute. Autumn. Tibet. Z7.

G. linearis Froelich. Leafy perenn. to 45cm. St. simple, erect or ascending. Lvs 3.5cm, narrow-lanceolate to linear. Fls term., clustered, or solitary in upper axils; cor. 2.5–3.5cm, narrowly funnel-shaped, blue to purple-blue, lobes erect, rounded, plicae almost equalling lobes, entire to bifid. Summer. E N Amer. Z3.

G. loderi Hook. f. Perenn. St. 10cm, prostrate then ascending. Lvs 1.5cm, in many pairs, broadly-elliptic, rounded, thick. Fls term., solitary, sessile; cor. to 3cm, tubular-campanulate, pale blue, lobes round-ovate, plicae half length of lobes, erect, fimbriate. Summer. Kashmir. Z8.

G. lutea L. GREAT YELLOW GENTIAN. Robust perenn. to 2m. St. thick, hollow. Basal lvs 30cm, broadly ovate, strongly ribbed, cauline lvs paired, connate at base. Fls 3–10 in clusters in each axil, long-stalked; cor. 2.5cm, rotate, yellow, tube short, lobes deep, oblong, plicae 0. Summer. Eur. (mts, Pyren. to Carpath.). Z5.

G. × macaulayi hort. (*G. sino-ornata* × *G. farreri*.) Vigorous perenn. St. branched, often rooting. Lvs as in *G. farreri*. Fls term., solitary, short-stalked; cor. 6.5cm, widely funnel-shaped, deep blue, striped violet and panelled green-white outside, lobes broadly triangular, plicae short. Summer-autumn. Gdn origin. 'Blue Bonnets': fls sky blue with white throat, striped pale yellow and dark blue. 'Edinburgh': habit somewhat straggly; fls mid-blue; late-flowering. 'Elata': fls mid-blue. 'Kidbrooke Seedling': v. strong grower; fls large, v. deep blue. 'Kingfisher': vigorous; foliage dark green; fls large. 'Praecox': like 'Elata' but flowering up to three weeks earlier. 'Wells Variety': reverse cross; fls pale blue. Z4.

G. makinoi Kuzn. Perenn. St. simple, erect to 60cm. Lvs to 5cm, largest above, lanceolate to lanceolate-ovate, paired. Fls term., clustered, also borne in upper axils; cor. 3.5cm, tubular-campanulate, pale blue, heavily spotted, lobes ovate, acute, plicae short, entire. Summer. Jap. 'Royal Blue': fls strong blue.

Z6.

G. menziesii A. Gray = *G. sceptrum*.

G. microdonta Franch. ex Hemsl. Rhizomatous perenn. St. erect to 60cm, simple. Basal lvs to 15cm, rosulate, spathulate, cauline lvs 5cm, ovate-oblong. Fls 2–3 in axillary clusters; cor. to 2.5cm, tubular, deep azure, lobes ovate, plicae irregular, ovate, one-third length of lobes. Summer. W China. Z8.

G. moorcroftiana Wallich ex G. Don = *Gentianella moorcroftiana*.

G. newberryi A. Gray. Dwarf, mat-forming perenn. St. 4–12cm. Basal lvs 2–6cm, loosely revolute, broadly spathulate, cauline lvs 1.5cm, obovate to lanceolate, paired. Fls term., solitary, occas. paired; cor. 2–3cm, funnel-shaped, v. pale blue to white, striped green-brown outside, lobes ovate, acute, plicae narrow, bifid. Summer-autumn. W US. Z7.

G. nikoensis Franch. & Savat. = *G. algida*.

G. nipponica Maxim. Perenn. Sterile st. trailing, branched, flowering st. 5–12cm, erect. Lower lvs 0.7cm, ovate to ovate-lanceolate, thick, revolute, upper lvs smaller, narrower. Fls 1–3, term., subsessile; cor. to 2cm, funnel-shaped, purple-blue, lobes ovate to obovate, obtuse, plicae triangular, entire. Summer. Jap. Z7.

G. nivalis L. Slender ann. 3–15cm. St. erect, branched. Basal lvs 0.2–0.5cm, ovate to obovate, obtuse, cauline lvs similar, acute. Fls term., solitary, deep blue; cor. 1–1.5cm × 0.8cm, subcylindric, lobes spreading, ovate, acute, plicae white, bifid. Summer. Eur. to Cauc., Arc. N Amer., Greenland. Z5.

G. nopcsae Jáv. = *G. pneumonanthe*.

G. nubigena Edgew. Perenn. St. 7–15cm, erect, simple, from basal rosettes. Basal lvs to 5cm, oblong-linear, obtuse, cauline lvs paired, shorter. Fls terminal, 1–3 on short stalks; cor. to 4cm, funnel-shaped, yellow, striped blue outside, lobes blue, erect, ovate, acute, plicae irregular, triangular, entire, shorter than lobes. Autumn. Himal. Z8.

G. obtusifolia hort. = *G. brachyphylla* ssp. *favratii*.

G. ochroleuca Froelich. Stout perenn. to 30cm. St. erect, sometimes branched, leafy 2.5–7.5cm. Lvs obovate to oblong, narrowing to base. Fls term., occas. axill., clustered; cor. to 3.5cm, claviform, green-white, tinged purple, lobes triangular, acute, plicae irregular, entire or toothed. Autumn. E US. Z6.

G. olivieri Griseb. Perenn. St. to 23cm, arising from rosettes. Basal lvs 10cm, spathulate; cauline lvs 1–2-paired, shorter. Fls in a term. cyme, stalked or sessile; cor. to 3cm, campanulate, deep blue, lobes-narrow-oblong, plicae regular, triangular, bifid, half length of lobes. Summer. W Asia. Z7.

G. oregana Engelm. ex A. Gray = *G. affinis*.

G. orfordii T.J. Howell = *G. sceptrum*.

G. ornata Wallich. Perenn. St. to 10cm, prostrate, leafy, tinged red. Lvs to 2.5cm, linear, acute. Fls term., solitary; cor. 2.5–3.5cm, broadly campanulate, pale blue, striped purple-blue with white panels outside, lobes ovate to broadly triangular, plicae ragged, nearly equalling lobes. Autumn. C Nepal to SW China. Z6.

G. pannonica Scop. Stout erect perenn. to 60cm. Basal lvs to 20cm, elliptic, cauline lvs to 10cm, paired, connate at base. Fls term., in upper axils, clustered, sessile; cor. to 3.5cm, campanulate, purple-brown, darker-spotted, lobes ovate to elliptic, plicae small, obtuse. Summer. C Eur. Z5.

G. parryi Engelm. Leafy perenn. to 40cm. St. erect or ascending. Lvs 1.5–4cm, cauline, linear-lanceolate to ovate, paired, connate at base, somewhat succulent and glaucous. Fls 1–6, term., sessile; cor. 4cm, campanulate, bright blue to purple-blue, lobes obovate, acute, plicae bifid, dentate, shorter than lobes. Summer-autumn. US (Rocky Mts). Z4.

G. patula Cheesem. Perenn. to 50cm. St. ascending, branched. Basal lvs 2.5–7.5cm, oblong- to lanceolate-spathulate, leathery, cauline lvs in 1–5 pairs. Fls in a term. umbel or cyme, few to many; cor. 2.5cm across, campanulate, white, lobes oblong, obtuse, plicae bifid, half length of lobes. Summer. NZ. Z7.

G. phlogifolia Schott & Kotschy = *G. cruciata*.

G. phyllocalyx C.B. Clarke. Ann. or bienn., occas. perenn., to 15cm. St. erect, simple. Basal lvs 1.5cm, rosulate, broadly-obovate, cauline lvs paired, smaller. Fls term., solitary, occas. to 4; cor. 3 × 0.7cm, tubular, inflated at middle, pale to deep blue, lobes ovate, plicae irregular, dentate, shorter than lobes. Summer-autumn. C Nepal to SW China. Z8.

G. platypetala Griseb. Perenn. St. to 40cm, stout, leafy. Lvs to 4cm, elliptic to ovate. Cal. split with 2 rosy spathes, half as long as cor., with v. small teeth; cor. to 4cm, blue. NW N Amer.

G. pneumonanthe L. MARSH GENTIAN; CALATHIAN VIOLET. Perenn. St. to 30cm, slender, ascending, leafy. Lvs to 3.5cm, linear, revolute. Fls term. and axill., sessile or stalked; cor. to 5cm, funnel-shaped, deep blue with 5 stripes of green spots, lobes ovate, acute, plicae triangular, entire. Summer. Eur., Asia, Cauc. var. *depressa* Bourg. St. to 23cm, prostrate or ascending. Fls deep blue. 'Alba': fls white. 'Styrian Blue': to

45cm, more robust; fls rich deep blue. Z4.

G. porphyrio Gmel. = *G. autumnalis*.

G. procera T. Holm = *Gentianopsis procera*.

G. prolata Balf. f. Prostrate perenn. St. to 15cm, slender, leafy. Lvs to 1.5cm, elliptic-lanceolate to oblong, acute. Fls term., solitary, sessile; cor. to 3.5cm, tubular-funnelform, blue, outside banded purple and white, lobes triangular, acute, plicae erect, toothed, shorter than lobes. Summer. C Nepal to SE Tibet. Z6.

G. propinqua Richardson = *Gentianella propinqua*.

G. przewalskii Maxim. Perenn. erect to 28cm. Basal lvs to 7.5cm, loosely rosulate, narrow-spathulate to lanceolate, cauline lvs paired, connate at base. Fls 1–3, term., stalked; cor. 5cm, clavate to obconic, white to pale yellow, striped blue, lobes blue, broadly deltoid, plicae irregular, entire, half length of lobes. Summer. W China, NE Tibet. Z7.

G. pseudo-pneumonanthe Schult. = *G. linearis*.

G. pterocalyx Franch. ex F. Forbes & Hemsl. To 30cm+, branched. Lvs to 2.5cm, cordate-ovate. Fls solitary; cor. 5cm+, deep azure, sometimes tinted yellow.

G. puberula auct. non Michx. = *G. puberulenta*.

G. puberula Michx. = *G. saponaria*.

G. puberulenta Pringle. Erect, leafy perenn. to 60cm. Lvs 5cm, oblong-lanceolate to linear. Fls 1–6, term., sessile, subtended by involucral lvs; cor. 3.5cm, narrowly campanulate, blue to purple-blue, white below, lobes ovate to obovate, spreading, plicae triangular, many-cleft. Summer–autumn. Central N Amer. (prairies). Z5.

G. pumila Jacq. Tufted perenn. St. to 7.5cm. Basal lvs to 1.5cm, rosulate, linear-lanceolate, cauline lvs paired. Fls term., solitary; cor. 1.5–2cm diam., saucer-shaped, deep blue, lobes ovate-lanceolate, acute, emarginate, plicae bifid, much shorter than lobes. Summer. Eur. Z6.

G. punctata L. SPOTTED GENTIAN. Stout taprooted perenn. to 60cm. St. erect, angled. Basal lvs to 10cm, elliptic; cauline lvs narrower. Fls in term. or axill. whorls, sessile; cor. 3.5cm, campanulate, pale yellow, spotted purple, lobes ovate, obtuse, plicae irregular, v. short. Summer. C Eur. Z5.

G. purdomii Marq. = *G. gracilipes*.

G. purpurea L. Stout perenn. to 60cm. St. erect, simple, angled. Basal lvs 20cm, ovate-oblong, cauline lvs paired, narrower. Fls term. and in upper axils, sessile; cor. to 3.5cm, campanulate, purple-red, paler within, spotted, striped green on tube, lobes obovate, obtuse, widest at middle, plicae short, truncate. Summer. Eur. (Alps to Norway), Cauc. Z5.

G. pyrenaica L. Dwarf, tufted perenn. to 7.5cm. Lvs to 1.5cm, rosulate, elliptic to linear-lanceolate, glossy. Fls term., solitary, stalked; cor. to 3.5cm, funnel-shaped, violet to indigo, green outside, lobes ovate, obtuse, plicae nearly equalling lobes, rounded, toothed. Summer. Eur. (Pyren., Carpath.), W Asia (Cauc., Iran). Z4.

G. quadrifolia Bl. Lvs to 1cm, ovate to elliptic-obovate. Fls solitary, term.; cor. to 1cm, tubular-campanulate, dark blue. Java. Z9.

G. quinqueflora L. emend Sm. = *Gentianella quinquefolia*.

G. quinquefolia L. = *Gentianella quinquefolia*.

G. regelii Kuzn. = *G. tianschanica*.

G. rigescens Franch. ex Hemsl. Erect perenn. to 40cm. St. tinged purple, simple. Lvs to 5cm, oblong-ovate, paired. Fls term. and in upper axils, sessile, clustered; cor. to 3cm, tubular to funnel-shaped, purple-rose to purple-blue, spotted green, lobes broadly ovate, acuminate, plicae irregular, ovate, entire, short. Autumn. W China. Z7.

G. rochellii A. Kerner = *G. clusii*.

G. romanzovii Ledeb. = *G. algida*.

G. rostanii Reut. Tufted perenn. St. 10–15cm. Lvs on sterile shoots 1.5cm, linear-lanceolate to linear, cauline lvs in 2–4 pairs, smaller. Fls terminal, sessile; cor. saucer-shaped, 1.7cm diam., deep blue, lobes obovate, obtuse, plicae bifid, short. Summer. Eur. (Alps). Z6.

G. rubricaulis Schwein. Perenn. similar to *G. linearis*. St. 30–60cm, leafy, red to purple. Lvs to 7.5cm, lanceolate to ovate, slightly succulent, pale green. Fls term., 1–15 in clusters; cor. 3.5cm, tubular, pale violet to white. Summer. N Amer. (Hudson Bay to Great Lakes). Z5.

G. sabauda Boiss. & Reut. = *G. angustifolia*.

G. saponaria L. Erect, leafy perenn. 30–90cm. Lvs to 6.5cm, ovate to oblong to lanceolate. Fls term., or in upper axils, 1–8 in a cluster; cor. 5cm, clavate, closed at mouth, blue, spotted green within, lobes erect, rounded, short, plicae irregular, bifid to multifid, nearly equalling lobes. Summer–autumn. N Amer. Z5.

G. saxosa Forst. f. Tufted perenn. St. to 7cmm, prostrate then ascending. Basal lvs to 3.5cm, rosulate, spathulate to linear-spathulate, tinged brown-purple, fleshy. Fls term., solitary or 2–5 in cymes; cor. 2cm, open-campanulate, white, veined

purple-brown, lobes deep, oblong, obtuse, plicae 0. Summer. NZ. Z8.

G. scabra Bunge. Erect to suberect perenn. to 30cm. St. leafy. Lvs to 3.5cm, paired, basally connate, ovate to lanceolate. Fls in term. clusters or axillary pairs, sessile; cor. 2.5cm, campanulate, deep blue, often spotted, lobes broadly ovate, plicae entire, acute, small. N Asia, Jap. var. *buergeri* (Miq.) Maxim. To 45cm. Lvs 7.5cm, ovate-lanceolate. Fls larger; cor. narrow-campanulate, to 3.5cm, brighter blue. Forms with white-spotted fls sometimes named var. *bungeana*. var. *fortunei* has slender, ascending st. and more heavily spotted fls. Z5.

G. scarlatina Gilg. Monocarpic. St. 4–7cm, branched. Basal lvs to 3cm, lanceolate to oblong-spathulate, fleshy, cauline lvs smaller. Fls term.; cor. to 2cm, obconic to open-campanulate, yellow, exterior scarlet, lobes obovate, acute. Spring. Peru. Z8.

G. sceptrum Griseb. KING'S GENTIAN. Stout perenn. to 90cm. St. erect, leafy. Lvs 2–6cm, ovate to lanceolate-ovate. Fls in term. clusters or 2–3 in upper axils, stalked; cor. to 5cm, clavate to campanulate, blue-purple, spotted green, lobes rounded, plicae entire, subtruncate. Summer. BC to Calif. Z6.

G. septemfida Pall. Erect or ascending perenn. 15–30cm. St. several to many, simple, leafy. Lvs 2.5–3.5cm, paired, ovate. Fls term., clustered, 1–8; cor. 3.5cm, narrowly campanulate, deep blue with pale spots, paler within, lobes ovate, acute, plicae deeply laciniate, half length of lobes to nearly equalling them. Summer. W & C Asia. var. *cordifolia* (Koch) Boiss. St. short, decumbent. Lvs broader, semi-orbicular to broadly cordate. Fls solitary or few. var. *lagodechiana* Kusn. St. branched. Fls solitary. Confusion surrounds the many named forms of *G. septemfida*, *G.* ×*hascombensis* may be a selection of a cross between *G. septemfida* sens. strict and *G. septemfida* var. *lagodechiana* and might more acceptably be styled *G. septemfida* var. *lagodechiana* 'Hascombensis'. Amid so many colour and habit variants, the precise application of this name is unclear. 'Doeringiana': to 15cm; fls deep blue. 'Latifolia': lvs broad. Z3.

G. septemfida var. *procumbens* hort. = *G. septemfida* var. *cordifolia*.

G. setigera A. Gray. Perenn. to 30cm. St. erect or ascending. Lvs 2.5–6cm, paired, basally connate, ovate to rounded. Fls 1–4, term., short-stalked, subtended by paired bracts; cor. 3–4cm, campanulate, blue, lobes 8–12mm, spreading, plicae laciniate, shorter than lobes. Summer. Calif. to Oreg. Z7.

G. setulifolia Marq. Low perenn.; sterile shoots many, prostrate, short, fertile shoots erect, 10–15cm. Lvs to 1.5cm, in whorls of 7, linear, acute, ciliate. Fls term., solitary, sessile; cor. 3.5cm, funnel-shaped, sea-blue, tube paler striped dark blue, lobes ovate, acute, plicae short, toothed. Autumn. Burm.–Tibet borders. Z8.

G. sikkimensis C.B. Clarke. Mat-forming perenn. St. to 20cm. Lvs 2.5cm, paired, oblong, glossy. Fls term., clustered above whorl of bracts; cor. 2.5cm, tubular to claviform, blue, white within, lobes ovate, obtuse, short, plicae irregular, bifid, much shorter than lobes. Summer. E Himal. to Yunnan. Z8.

G. sikokiana Maxim. Slender perenn. to 30cm. St. erect, 4-angled, leafy. Lvs 7.5cm, paired, elliptic, acute, margin cartilaginous. Fls term. and in upper axils, in clusters of 3; cor. funnel-shaped, purple-blue, spotted white, lobes broadly ovate, plicae entire, triangular, much shorter than lobes. Summer. Jap. Z6.

G. sino-ornata Balf. f. Prostrate perenn. St. 15–20cm, rooting. Basal lvs forming loose rosettes, cauline lvs to 3.5cm, paired, linear-lanceolate. Fls terminal, solitary, sessile; cor. 5.5cm, funnel-shaped, deep blue, paler within, outside with 5 bands of deep purple-blue, panelled green-white, lobes broadly ovate, acute, plicae entire or emarginate. Autumn. W China, Tibet. 'Alba': fls white. 'Angel's Wings': fl. colour v. unstable, usually blue randomly splashed with white, sometimes all blue or all white, even on the same plant. 'Ann's Special': vigorous; fls mid-blue. 'Brin Form': st. long, climbing. 'Blauer Dom': vigorous; fls deep blue; autumn. 'Edith Sarah': v. hardy; fls deep blue; autumn. 'Leslie Delaney': weak grower; fls pale blue, autumn. 'Mary Lyle': to 10cm; fls white, plicae tinged blue; autumn. 'Praecox': fls stalked; cor. tubular to funnel-shaped; fls earlier. 'Woolgreaves' ('Woolgreave's Variety'): vigorous, long-flowering; fls rich blue; autumn. Z6.

G. siphonantha Maxim. ex Kuzn. Upright perenn. to 30cm. Basal lvs to 24cm, linear-lanceolate, acute, cauline lvs similar, 10–15cm, in 4–5 pairs. Fls clustered, terminal and in upper axils, sessile; cor. to 2.5cm, tubular to funnel-shaped, blue to purple-blue, lobes ovate-oblong, acute, plicae entire, subulate, half length of lobes. Summer. Tibet, NW China. Z8.

G. speciosa (Wallich) Marq. Twining or scandent perenn. to 3m. St. slender. Lvs 5–8cm, opposite, elliptic to ovate, acuminate, undulate, dentate. Fls, pendulous, axill., in clusters of 1–3; cor. 5cm, tubular-campanulate, deep blue-purple, lobes widely spaced, spreading, triangular, plicae short. Autumn. C Himal.

to SE Tibet, Burm. Z9.

G. squarrosa Ledeb. Ann. or bienn. to 10cm. Basal lvs 1–4cm, rosulate, rhombic-ovate to narrowly rhombic-ovate, with hair-like point, silvery. Fls terminal, short-stalked; cal. lobes aristate; cor. 1.2–1.7cm, pale blue, plicae shorter than lobes, sometimes 2-fid. Spring–summer. NE Asia, Himal. Z8.

G. ×stevenagensis hort. ex F. Barker. (*G. sino-ornata* ×*G. veitchiorum.*) Lvs longer than in *G. veitchiorum*. Fls term. on branched st., short-stalked; cor. to 6.5cm, funnel-shaped, deep purple-blue, spotted and striped green-yellow within, plicae narrow, acute. Autumn. Gdn origin. The reverse cross produced *G.* ×*stevenagensis* 'Bernadii' (*G. bernardii* hort.) similar but fls deeper purple-blue, esp. purple on plicae. 'Frank Barker': fls deep blue, almost purple. Z5.

G. stictantha Marq. Erect perenn. to 25cm. St. arising from basal rosettes, simple. Basal lvs 10–15cm, narrowly lanceolate. Fls term. and axill., clustered; cor. to 3cm, narrowly funnel-shaped, yellow-white, spotted and striped violet-blue, lobes ovate, plicae irregular, obtuse, minute. Autumn. SE Tibet. Z8.

G. stragulata Balf. f. & Forr. Mat-forming perenn. St. to 7.5cm, decumbent. Basal lvs to 2cm, obovate, cauline lvs to 1.5cm, paired, elliptic to ovate, obtuse. Fls 1–3 in a term. cluster, sessile; cor. 5cm, tubular, constricted at throat, purple-blue, lobes deltate, plicae bifid, shorter than lobes. Summer. W China. Z8.

G. straminea Maxim. Stout perenn. to 30cm. St. ascending. Basal lvs to 12.5cm, rosulate, linear-lanceolate, cauline lvs in 2–3 pairs, connate at base. Fls several, term., long-stalked; cor. 3cm, obconic, green-white to straw yellow, lobes ovate, spreading; plicae deltate, bifid, one-third length of lobes. Summer. NE Tibet, NW China. Z5.

G. stylophora C.B. Clarke = *Megacodon stylophorus.*

G. tenuifolia Petrie. Ann. to 35cm. St. simple, slender. Basal lvs 7.5–12.5cm, oblong-obovate to obovate-spathulate, thin-textured, st. lvs narrow. Fls crowded in umbels; cor. to 1.25cm, white, lobes, acute. NZ.

G. tergestina G. Beck = *G. verna.*

G. terglouensis Hacq. TRIGLAV GENTIAN. Dwarf, tufted perenn. St. 2–4cm, erect. Basal lvs 0.3–0.5cm, ovate-lanceolate, overlapping. Fls term., solitary, sessile; cor. 1.8–2.4cm diam., saucer-shaped, sky blue, lobes rounded, emarginate, plicae bifid, much shorter than lobes. Summer. Eur. (S & SE Alps). Z6.

G. ternifolia Franch. Trailing perenn. St. to 20cm, decumbent then ascending. Basal lvs to 1.6cm, loosely rosulate, linear-lanceolate, cauline lvs in whorls of 2–3, incurved at tips. Fls term., solitary; cor. 4cm, funnel-shaped to campanulate, sky blue, paler within, minutely spotted, green-white striped deep blue outside, lobes ovate, acute, plicae broadly triangular, emarginate. Autumn. W China. Z8.

G. thermalis Kuntze = *Gentianopsis thermalis.*

G. tianschanica Rupr. Upright perenn. to 25cm. Basal lvs to 8cm, rosulate, linear-lanceolate, cauline lvs to 5cm, paired, basally connate, oblong. Fls clustered, term. and in upper axils, stalked; cor. 2.5cm, tubular to funnel-shaped, blue to violet, lobes ovate-oblong, acute, plicae deltate, entire or bifid. Summer. C Asia, Himal. Z8.

G. trichotoma Kuzn. Erect perenn. to 60cm. St. branched. Basal lvs to 10cm, linear-lanceolate to lanceolate, cauline lvs broader. Fls in clusters of 3, stalked, axill. and term.; cor. 3cm, cylindric to clavate, deep blue, paler and spotted within, lobes deltate, plicae irregular, bifid to crenate, paler blue. Summer. W China. Z8.

G. triflora Pall. Erect perenn. to 45cm. St. slender, branched, leafy. Lvs to 6cm, decussate, narrow-lanceolate. Fls term. and sessile, or axill. and stalked; cor. 3cm, narrow-campanulate, deep blue to purple-blue, banded white outside, lobes erect, rounded-ovate, obtuse, plicae minute. Summer–autumn. NE Asia. var. *japonica* (Kuzn.) Harrer. Lvs ovate to ovate-lanceolate becoming narrow-lanceolate toward summit of st. Fls to 5cm, 1–2 axil, mauve-blue. Jap. Z5.

G. trinervis (Thunb.) Marq. Scandent perenn. to 1.5m. Lvs 7.5cm, narrow-cordate, acute, conspicuously 3-veined, long-petiolate. Fls axill., solitary or paired, pendulous; cor. 2.5cm, funnel-shaped, white to purple, lobes ovate, acute, plicae short. Summer. Jap., China, Himal. Z8.

G. tubiflora Wallich. Low, tufted perenn. to 5cm. Basal lvs to 0.7cm, spathulate to oblong, forming tight rosettes, cauline lvs narrower. Fls term., solitary; cor. 2.5cm, narrow-tubular, deep blue, lobes triangular to ovate, erect, plicae irregular, entire, short. Summer. Himachal Pradesh to SE Tibet. Z6.

G. utriculosa L. Ann. to 30cm. St. erect, slender, branched. Basal lvs to 1cm, elliptic, acute; cauline lvs recurved. Fls term., solitary; cal. 1–2cm, broadly winged; cor. to 1.8cm diam., rotate, deep blue, lobes ovate, plicae bifid. Summer. Eur. Z6.

G. veitchiorum Hemsl. Trailing perenn. St. to 12cm, many, branched. Basal lvs to 3.5cm, rosulate, linear-oblong, thick, cauline lvs paired, basally connate. Fls term., solitary; cor. 5cm, funnel-shaped, deep royal blue, outside banded green-yellow, lobes deltoid, spreading, plicae short. Summer–autumn. W China. Z6.

G. venusta (G. Don) Griseb. Tufted, stoloniferous perenn. to 8cm. Lvs of sterile shoots 0.6cm, broadly spathulate, lvs on flowering st. to 1cm, broader. Fls terminal, 1–5, sessile; cor. 2.5cm, tubular, blue, exterior yellow, lobes round to ovate, plicae toothed, shorter than lobes. Summer–autumn. Himal. (Pak. to C Nepal). Z8.

G. verna L. SPRING GENTIAN. Low, tufted perenn. Flowering st. to 10cm. Basal lvs 1.5–3cm, rosulate, elliptic-lanceolate, cauline lvs 1–3-paired, spathulate. Fls term., solitary; cal. winged; cor. 1.8–3cm diam., rotate, brilliant blue, occas. pale blue, pink- to red-purple, throat white, lobes ovate, obtuse, plicae bifid, striped white, becoming blue, much shorter than lobes. Spring–summer. Eur. 'Angulosa': vigorous, to 6cm, forming neat clumps; fls profuse, vivid blue. Z5.

G. villosa L. Erect perenn. to 45cm. St. simple. Lvs 2.5–7.5cm, obovate to oblong, pale green. Fls term., clustered; cor. 3.5cm, clavate, green-white, occas. tinged blue-violet, lobes triangular, plicae irregular, entire or rarely dentate. Autumn. E N Amer. Z6.

G. vulgaris L. Keller = *G. clusii.*

G. waltonii Burkill. Perenn. St. to 45cm, ascending or decumbent. Basal lvs to 15cm, rosulate, linear-lanceolate, acute, cauline lvs to 6cm. Fls term. and axill., sessile and stalked; cor. 3.5cm, narrowly campanulate, sky-blue to purple-blue, lobes broadly ovate, plicae triangular, entire, half length of lobes. Summer. Tibet. Z7.

G. wutaiensis Marq. Decumbent perenn. St. to 20cm. Basal lvs to 15cm, strap-shaped, cauline lvs 5cm, lanceolate to linear-lanceolate. Fls term. and axillary, sessile, clustered; cor. to 2.5cm, tubular-campanulate, deep blue, paler within tube, lobes ovate to rounded, plicae deltoid, acute, entire. Summer. China. Z7.

G. yakushimensis Mak. Perenn. St. erect to 30cm, leafy, simple. Lvs linear-lanceolate, in whorls of 4, white beneath. Fls term., solitary; cor. to 5cm, tubular-campanulate, deep blue to blue-purple, lobes 6–8, erect, triangular, acute, plicae toothed, short. Summer. Z7.

G. zollingeri Fawcett. Bienn., 5–10cm. Basal lvs small, st. lvs 0.5–1.5cm, ovate, abruptly pointed, often red-purple beneath, with a thick off-white margin. Fls few, ± sessile; cor. 1.8–2.5cm, blue. Korea, Jap., China, Sakhalin.

Hybrids and cvs.

'Apollo' (*G.* 'Inverleith' ×*G. ornata*): 'Barbara Lyle': lvs v. dark green; fls large, dark velvet blue. 'Blauer Edelstein': small, to 10cm; fls deep azure. 'Blue Flame': seedling from 'Inverleith'; fls large, trumpet-shaped, vivid dark-blue; autumn. 'Blue Heaven': to 8cm; fls well-formed, trumpet-shaped, dark blue; summer. 'Christine Jean': fls dark violet with vivid purple sheen; autumn. 'Devonhall' (*G. ornata* ×*G. farreri*): tufted, compact perenn. with improved vigour; fls solitary, term.; cor. 5cm, widely funnel-shaped, pale blue, paler and spotted green within, lobes triangular, plicae short; autumn. 'Farorna', with fls azure and exterior striped, is derived from the reverse cross. Drake's Strain Hybrids (*G. ornata* ×*G. farreri*): compact, to 6cm; fls broad, vivid sea-blue, throat usually white. 'Ida K': compact. 'Orphylla': neat and compact; fls pale blue; cal. tube white. 'Orva' (*G. ornata* ×*G. veitchiorum*): compact; fls deep cobalt-blue, exterior streaked purple; long-flowering.

'Edina' (*G. ornata* ×*G. prolata*): fls several per st., cor. 4cm, funnel-shaped, deep sky blue, lined and spotted on tube, lobes narrow-triangular, plicae short, obtuse; autumn. 'Eleanor': multi-headed; st. tinged red; fls large, trumpet-shaped, mouth pale blue, throat white. 'Elizabeth Brand': similar to 'Inverleith'; st. mahogany, shorter; fls to 5×3.5cm, electric blue; autumn. 'Excelsior': fls large, to 8cm, deep blue, throat white; summer–autumn. 'Fasta Highlands' (*G. farreri* ×*G. stevenagensis*): vigorous; fls large, pale to deep blue. 'Glendevon' (*G. ornata* ×*G. sino-ornata*): resembling *G. ornata* in habit but less compact; st. branched; fls term., solitary; cal. tube 1.5cm, lobes longer, tips recurved; cor. 3.5–4.5cm, narrow-campanulate, deep blue, exterior tinged purple, lined and spotted purple, lobes broadly triangular, plicae small; autumn.

Inshriach Hybrids: ('Kingfisher'): to 8cm, carpet-forming; fls vivid clear blue. 'Inverleith' (*G. veitchiorum* ×*G. farreri*): vigorous hybrid; st. to 24cm, procumbent, straggly; lvs linear-lanceolate, recurved, longer than in *G. veitchiorum*; fls term., solitary, stalked; cal. tube 1.5–2cm, lobes recurved, equalling tube; cor. to 6.5cm, funnel-shaped, intense Cambridge blue, striped darker outside, lobes broadly triangular, plicae short, sometimes bifid; autumn. 'Marion Lyle' ('Marianne Lyle'): similar to *G. sino-ornata*, vigorous; fls 5 per st., vivid ultramarine; late summer.

'Midnight': seedling from 'Inverleith'; fls deep dark blue, with no bands or spots; autumn. 'Royal Highlander': seedling from 'Devonhall', carpet-forming, floriferous; fls 4 per st., bright blue, remaining open on dull days. 'Sensation': fls dark azure, exterior imperial purple, conspicuously striped; autumn. 'Sinora' (*G. sino-ornata* ×*G. ornata*): neat and compact; fls similar to shape to *G. sino-ornata*, deep shiny butterfly blue; autumn. 'Strathmore': fls large, sky blue, exterior with silver stripe. 'Susan Jane': to 8cm, early-blooming, vigorous; fls vivid sea-blue, trumpet-shaped, throat white; autumn. 'Thunersee': fls light sapphire blue, throat white; autumn. 'Vorna' (*G. tianschanica* ×*G. ornata*): st. long; lvs dark green; fls dark blue; long-flowering; autumn. 'Wealdensis': similar to *G. sino-ornata*, fls deeper blue, lobes reflexed; autumn. 'Zauberland': fls large, grey-blue; autumn.
→*Crawfurdia*.

GENTIANACEAE Juss. 74/1200. *Canscora, Centaurium, Chironia, Eustoma, Exacum, Frasera, Gentiana, Gentianella, Gentianopsis, Halenia, Lisianthius, Megacodon, Orphium, Sabatia, Sebaea, Swertia*.

Gentianella Moench. FELWORT. Gentianaceae. 125 ann., bienn. or perenn. glab. herbs. St. often 4-angled. Lvs opposite, paired, often in basal rosettes in first year. Infl. term., usually cymose; fls usually 5-merous; cal. tubular, lobed; cor. tube cylindric, funnel-shaped or campanulate, lobes spreading, lacking plicae (cf. *Gentiana*). N Eur., temp. Asia, N & S Amer., NZ.
G. moorcroftiana (Wallich ex G. Don) Airy Shaw. Slender ann. to 20cm; st. much-branched. Basal lvs 1.5–3cm, oblong to elliptic, withered by flowering time, cauline lvs lanceolate. Cyme lax; cor. 1.5–3cm, funnel-shaped, pale blue to dark mauve; anth. yellow, conspicuous. Summer. W Himal.
G. propinqua (Richardson) J.M. Gillett. Ann. to 35cm. Basal lvs to 3cm, elliptic to spathulate, cauline lvs shorter. Fls solitary or in sparse cymes; cor. 2cm, tubular to narrowly funnel-shaped, pale lilac or violet. Summer. Canada, Alask.
G. quinquefolia (L.) Small. AGUE WEED. Ann. or bienn. to 60cm; st. branched. Lvs to 3.5cm, ovate, acuminate, connate at base. Fls 3–5 per cyme; cor. to 2cm, clavate, purple-blue. Summer. E N Amer.
→*Gentiana*.

Gentianopsis Ma. FRINGED GENTIAN. Gentianaceae. 25 erect ann. or bienn. herbs. Lvs opposite. Fls borne singly on long stalks, 4-merous; cal. tubular, 4-angled, lobes with membranous margins; cor. funnel-shaped to campanulate, lobes spreading, usually fimbriate. N Amer., Eurasia.
G. crinita (Froelich) Ma. Ann. or bienn. to 1m. Lvs ovate to lanceolate, base amplexicaul. Fls one or many; cor. to 5cm, bright blue, lobes obovate, fringed all round. Summer. E N Amer. Z3.
G. detonsa (Rottb.) Ma. Ann. or bienn. to 60cm. Basal lvs to 3.5cm, obovate-elliptic to spathulate, cauline lvs to 5cm, linear to lanceolate. Fls many; cor. 3.5cm, pale blue to blue-purple, lobes ovate, sparsely fringed, toothed at apex. Summer. Circumboreal. Z3.
G. holopetala (A. Gray) Iltis. Ann. to 40cm. Lvs to 3.5cm, mostly on lower parts of st., obovate to linear. Fls solitary, term.; cor. 5cm, blue, lobes oblong, only slightly, or not fringed. Summer. Calif. Z7.
G. procera (T. Holm) Ma. Resembles *G. crinita*, but with lvs linear-lanceolate, cor. lobes fringed only on sides, short-toothed at apex. Summer. E N Amer. Z3.
G. thermalis (Kuntze) Iltis. Ann. to 30cm. Basal lvs 1–3cm, spathulate to obovate, obtuse, cauline lvs 2–4cm, sessile. Fls solitary; cor. to 5cm, deep blue, streaked paler blue, lobes obovate-oblong, fimbriate on sides, apex toothed. Summer. W US (Rocky Mts). Z5.
→*Gentiana*.

Geobalanus Small.
G. oblongifolius (Michx.) Small = *Licania michauxii*.

Geodorum Jackson. Orchidaceae. 16 terrestrial orchids. Pbs subterranean. Lvs to 35cm, lanceolate to oblong-elliptic, stalked, plicate. Indomal., W Pacific. Z10.
G. citrinum Jackson. Fls green-yellow, lip apex striped red-purple; sep. to 2.5cm; pet. to 1cm diam.; lip carinate, notched, disc with rows of wrinkles and papillae. Burm., Thail., Malaysia.
G. densiflorum (Lam.) Schltr. Fls white, pink or purple, lip white striped purple; sep. to 1.2cm, linear-oblong to oblanceolate; pet. broader; lip with 2 round apical lobes, tip veined or warty. Burm., Malaysia, Indon.
G. purpureum R. Br. = *G. densiflorum*.

Geoffroea Jacq. BASTARD CABBAGE TREE; CHANAR; CHANAL. Leguminosae (Papilionoideae). 3 decid. trees or shrubs. Lvs pinnate, lfts subcoriaceous; stipules present. Fls pea-like, few, in simple rac. Trop. & subtrop. S Amer.
G. decorticans (Hook. & Arn.) Burkart. Tree or shrub to 10m, with thorns to 2cm. Lvs to 7cm; lfts to 3.5cm, 3–13, elliptic or obovate, entire, glab. to sericeous. Rac. to 8cm, 2–5-fld, slender, from spurs on thorny br. and branchlets; fls to 1cm, orange or yellow, striped red. Fr. to 3.5cm, ovoid or globose, red or pink, glab. Spring. Chile, Arg., S Peru.
→*Gourliea*.

Geogenanthus Ule. Commelinaceae. 4 perenn. herbs with short or creeping st. Lvs few, at st. apex, broad, stalked. Cymes with few fls, borne near st. base; fls long-stalked; sep. 3, free; pet. 3, free; sta. 5, unequal, 3 shorter, bearded, 2 longer, hairless.
G. poeppigii (Miq.) Faden. SEERSUCKER PLANT. To 15–25cm. Lvs 6–12cm, orbicular and subcordate, puckered, transversely wavy, dark green above with several longitudinal silver stripes, tinted purple-red beneath, finely hairy. Fls *c*2.5cm diam., violet. Spring. Braz., Peru. Z9.
G. undatus (K. Koch & Lind.) Mildbr. & Strauss = *G. poeppigii*.
→*Dichorisandra*.

George Lily *Cyrtanthus elatus*.
Georgia Bark *Pinckneya pubens*.
Georgia Blueberry *Vaccinium melanocarpum*.
Georgia Oak *Quercus georgiana*.
Georgia Plume *Elliottia racemosa*.

Geraea Torr. & A. Gray Compositae. 2 ann. to perenn. herbs to 1m. Lvs to 10cm, alt., simple, usually toothed, hairy. Cap. radiate or discoid, few, showy, in pan.; flts yellow, disc flts 5-lobed. SW US, Mex. Z8.
G. canescens Torr. & A. Gray. DESERT SUNFLOWER. Ann. white-hairy. Lvs ovate to lanceolate or oblanceolate, entire to dentate, petiole with a white margin. Cap. radiate, to 5cm diam.; phyllaries white-ciliate. Summer. Utah, S California, Nevada, Arizona, New Mexico.
G. viscida (A. Gray) S.F. Blake. Short-lived perenn., hairy and downy. Lvs oblong-ovate, irregularly dentate, clasping at base. Cap. discoid, to 2.5cm diam.; phyllaries gland. Summer. S Calif.

Geraldton Carnation Weed *Euphorbia terracina*.
Geraldton Wax Flower *Chamelaucium uncinatum*.

GERANIACEAE Juss. 14/730. *Biebersteinia, Erodium, Geranium, Monsonia, Pelargonium, Sarcocaulon*.

Geranium L. CRANESBILL. Geraniaceae. 300 mostly perenn. herbs and subshrubs. Lvs usually palmately divided, divisions often lobed and toothed, basal lvs usually in a loose rosette from which arises forking flowering st., st. lvs usually smaller with fewer divisions. Infl. diffuse, or umbel-like; fls stalked, solitary, paired, or in cymules; sep. 5, free carinate to triangular, pointed; pet. usually 5, overlapping, equal; sta. 10, rarely 5, ± united at base, in 2 whorls; carpels 5, base of the style grows after fertilization forming a long beak with the carpels attached below; when ripe this beak dries and splits longitudinally, 5 strips peel away from bottom upwards dispersing the seeds in the process. Cosmop. in temp. regions.
G. aconitifolium L'Hérit. = *G. rivulare*.
G. albanum Bieb. Perenn. with gland. and sometimes eglandular hairs. Basal lvs round in outline, cut to about the middle into 7 or 9 divisions, lobed and toothed at apex. Infl. diffuse; fls 25mm diam.; pet. lightly notched, bright pink, veins dark magenta; fil. magenta; anth. blue; stigma pink. Summer. SE Cauc., Iran. Z7.
G. albiflorum Ledeb. Much-branched perenn. to 60cm. Lvs 5–20cm wide, lobes 7, sometimes blunt and sparsely toothed, edged purple-brown. Infl. lax; fls facing upwards, broadly funnel-shaped; pet. notched, white or light mauve, veins violet, to 8mm; stigma light pink. Summer. N & C Asia, NE Russia. Z6.
G. anemonifolium L'Hérit. = *G. palmatum*.
G. argenteum L. Perenn., similar to *G. cinereum* but lvs silver, silky-hairy, cut into 7, 3-lobed toothless divisions. Fls few; pet. to 15mm, notched, light pink, veins netted; fil. green or white; anth. orange-pink stigmas 1.5mm, yellow. Fr., Alps, N It., Balk. Z6.
G. aristatum Freyn. Grey-pubesc. perenn. to 60cm. Basal lvs to 20cm wide, divided into 7–9 divisions, pale green, coarsely lobed, dentate. Cymules often 3-fld; fls pendent; pet. to 16mm, white or lilac-pink, reflexed, oblong, veins lilac-pink; fil. pink at base; anth. cream. S Albania, Balk., Greece. Z7.
G. armenum Boiss. = *G. psilostemon*.

G. asphodeloides Burm. f. Perenn. Lvs cut into 5 or 7, widest above mid-point; st. glandular-hairy. Infl. diffuse; fls starry, to 35mm diam., pet. white or light to dark pink, veins dark; stigma red. Summer. S Eur., eastwards from Sicily, N Iran, Turk. Z8.

G. biuncinatum Kokw. Closely resembles *G. ocellatum* except pet. to 10.5mm, overlapping, basal triangle with a fine white border. E Afr., Arabian Penins. Z9.

G. brutium Gasparr. Ann. to 50cm. Similar to *G. pyrenaicum* but lvs not as deeply divided; to 25mm diam., bright rose-pink. Summer. S It., Sicily, Balk., Turk. Z7.

G. caffrum Ecklon & Zeyh. Clump-forming sprawling, downy perenn. St. to 60cm, woody at base, upper parts grey glandular-hairy. Lvs to 8cm, wide, divisions 3–5, pinnately lobed and deeply toothed at apex, to 2mm wide, green above, paler beneath. Fls white to deep pink; pedicels long; pet. 13mm, obovate, notched. Summer. S Afr. Z9.

G. canariense Reut. Short-lived everg. perenn. to 30cm. Lvs to 25cm wide, in rosettes, succulent, cut into 5 pinnately lobed, toothed divisions; petioles brown to purple. Infl. to 45cm, purple, glandular-hairy; pet. to 25mm, clawed, blade narrow, dark pink; anth. red; style white; stigma white or pink. Spring–summer. Canary Is. Z9.

G. candicans hort. = *G. lambertii*.

G. × cantabrigiense Yeo. (*G. macrorrhizum* × *G. dalmaticum*.) Plant to 30cm, creeping. Basal lvs to 9cm wide, divided into 7 divisions, lobed, light green, dentate. Fls to 28mm diam., similar to *G. macrorrhizum*; pet. bright pink or white, tinged pink at base. Z5.

G. cataractum Coss. Dwarf, aromatic, glandular-hairy perenn., to 30cm. Lvs to 10cm wide, cut into 5 stalked, deeply pinnately lobed and bluntly toothed divisions. Infl. dense; fls facing upwards, funnelform; pet. 15mm, light pink, clawed; fil. pink, anth. yellow, style red, stigma pink and white. Summer. S Spain, Moroc. Z8.

G. chinense hort. = *G. eriostemon*.

G. cinereum Cav. Rosette-forming perenn. to 15cm. Basal lvs to 5cm diam., round in outline, green-grey, cut into 5–7 wedge-shaped divisions, lobed at apex. Infl. with few or no lvs; fls few, 2.5cm diam., upright, white or light to bright pink, veins purple or white. Late spring and summer. Pyren. var. *cinereum* Fls 3cm diam., white or light pink with network of pink-purple or white veins; fil. white; anth. yellow; stigma green. 'Album': fls white. 'Artistry': fls clear pink with darker veins. 'Ballerina': lvs somewhat grey; fls pink tinged purple veined dark red, shaded at base, pet. notched. 'Lawrence Flatman': habit vigorous; fls similar to 'Ballerina' but usually with darker triangle of ground colour at apex. var. *obtusilobum* (Bornm.) Yeo. Lvs bright green, to 3cm wide. Fls bowl-shaped, pet. white, flushed pink, veins feathery. Summer. var. *subcaulescens* (L'Hérit. ex DC.) Knuth. Lvs deep green. Fls larger; pet. carmine, black 'V' at base. It., Balk., Turk. 'Giuseppii': pet. broad, rounded to slightly notched, nearly magenta, fading just above darker base. 'Splendens': pet. broad, rounded, somewhat notched, brilliant iridescent purple-red with darker veins, basal blotch black-red with white margins. Z5.

G. clarkei Yeo. Perenn. to 50cm. Basal lvs with 7 deeply cut divisions, lobes deep, pinnate, margins sparsely toothed. Infl. diffuse; fls many, facing upwards, cup-shaped; stalks to 8cm; pet. 29–22mm, purple-violet or white with mauve-pink veins. Summer. Kashmir. 'Kashmir Blue': to 60cm; fls pale blue. 'Kashmir Pink': fls large, clear pink. 'Kashmir Purple': lvs finely cut; fls deep lilac-purple. 'Kashmir White': to 60cm; fls white, pet. veined pale lilac. Z7.

G. collinum Willd. Bushy perenn. Basal lvs to 20cm wide, cut into 7 divisions, often yellow and flushed pink when young, deeply lobed, dentate, pubesc. Peduncle to 14cm; pet. to 20mm, rounded, pale or darker pink, veins sometimes red; fil. fringed with hairs at base, apex lilac or pink; anth. yellow or pink. S Eur., C and W Asia to Himal. Z7.

G. columbinum L. Ann. Basal lvs to 5cm wide, with 5–7 divisions, deeply lobed, dentate. Cymules longer than lvs; fls infundibular; pet. to 12mm, pale to deep red-pink, base white; fil. slightly pubesc.; anth. blue. Eur., W Asia. Z7.

G. cristatum Steven = *G. albanum*.

G. dalmaticum (Beck) Rech. Dwarf plant to 15cm, trailing. Basal lvs to 4cm wide, glab., with 5–7 divisions, glossy green. Infl. few-fld; pet. to 18mm, bright pink, rounded, clawed; anth. red. SW Balk., Albania. 'Album': fls white. Z5.

G. delavayi Franch. Closely resembles *G. sinense* except lf divisions broader, overlapping; pet. downy, paler. SW China. Z9.

G. dissectum L. Low-growing ann. Basal lvs to 5cm wde, divisions 7, narrow; st. lvs to 10cm wide, divisions 5, pinnately lobed, toothed. Infl. dense; peduncles to 5cm; sep. to 6mm, mucronulate; pet. to 6mm, deep or pale pink, deeply notched; anth. blue. Eur., W Asia. Z7.

G. donianum Sweet. Perenn, sometimes dwarf, to 40cm. Lvs to

10cm wide, marbled, deeply cut into 5 or 7 palmately and narrowly lobed divisions, sparsely toothed, overall shape somewhat reniform. Infl. diffuse; fls upright or facing upwards, funnelform; pet. to 20mm, rounded or notched, rich red-purple, hairy; fil. deep purple. Himal., SW China and Tibet. Z7.

G. endressii Gay. Hairy everg. perenn. St. to 50cm. Lvs 5–15cm diam., divisions 5, lobed, toothed. Infl. somewhat crowded; fls erect, funnel-shaped, 30–40mm diam.; pet. notched, bright pink deepening with age, paler below, veins netted, darker pink; fil. white flushed pink, anth. yellow or purple; stigma pink or red. Summer–flowering over a long period. Pyren. 'Wargrave Pink': habit vigorous; lvs small in dense tufts; fls small, salmon-pink, abundant. Z5.

G. endressii var. *thurstonianum* Turrill = *G. × oxonianum* 'Thurstonianum'.

G. erianthum DC. Perenn. to 50cm; rootstock compact. Lvs colouring in autumn; basal lvs 5–20cm wide, with 7–9, acutely lobed and freely toothed divisions; upper lvs of 5 or 7 narrower divisions, veins hairy beneath. Infl. dense, umbel-like; fls flat (not nodding), 25mm diam.; pet. almost triangular, pale to dark-blue violet, veins dark; fil. black-purple, base white, anth. deep purple. Early summer often with later flushes. E Sib., Jap., Sakhalin, Aleutian Is., Alask. to N BC. Z3.

G. eriostemon Fisch. ex DC. Hairy perenn. to 50cm. Similar to *G. erianthum* but lower st. hairs spreading, not adpressed. Lf divisions broad, less deeply cut, narrowed to apex, lobes shallow, teeth fewer shallower; upper lvs with 3 or 5 divisions. Fls nodding; pet. to 16mm, rounded or lobed, pale violet fading to white below. Late spring–early summer, often with a second flush. E Sib., Korea, Jap., W China. Z5.

G. farreri Stapf. Dwarf, taprooted alpine perenn. to 12cm. St. somewhat sprawling or erect; petioles and lf margins red. Basal lvs 5cm wide, round or reniform, deeply cut into 7 divisions, 3-lobed at apex, sparsely toothed; st. lvs smaller. Fls 35mm diam.; peduncles 4cm, pet. rounded, light pink-mauve, margin wavy; anth. blue-black; stigma pink. Early summer. W China. Z4.

G. flanaganii Knuth. Similar to *G. ornithopodon* but with large fls. pet. to 16×11mm, pale to deep pink, veins darker. S Afr. Z9.

G. fremontii Gray. Perenn. with thick rootstock, glandular-hairy except petioles of basal lvs and upper lf surfaces. Basal lvs to 10cm wide, cut into 5 or 7, apically lobed and toothed divisions. Infl. diffuse, v. branched, cymules may be 3-fld; fls to 40mm diam., similar to *G. nervosum*, but pet. 16mm+, hairy, occas. notched. Summer. W US. Z4.

G. gracile Nordm. Perenn. to 40cm, rootstock branched, thick; similar to *G. nodosum*, but upper parts gland. hairy; lvs pale green, surfaces wrinkled with 5 or 7 divisions, margins serrate. Summer. NE Turk., S Cauc., N Iran. Z7.

G. grandiflorum Edgew. = *G. himalayense*.

G. grevilleanum Wallich = *G. lambertii*.

G. himalayense Klotzsch. Carpet-forming, hairy perenn. with upper st. gland. hairy, basal lvs to 20cm wide, with 7 divisions, lobes broad, sparsely obtusely toothed, with spreading hairs beneath. Infl. diffuse; fls saucer-shaped, to 60mm diam.; peduncles to 18cm; pet. rounded, dark blue, base often pink and white; fil. pink; anth. deep blue; stigma pink-purple. Summer, flowering for long periods. Himal. 'Irish Blue': fls to 3.5cm diam., pale blue, with larger shaded purple centre. 'Gravetye' ('Alpinum'): habit spreading, growth slow; lvs smaller, lobes sharper and narrower; fls clear blue. 'Plenum' ('Birch Double'): less vigorous; lvs small, lobes rounded; fls double, deep blue-purple. Z4.

G. ibericum Cav. Perenn. to 50cm, similar to *G. platypetalum*, basal lvs 10cm wide, cut into 9 or 11 pinnately lobed and toothed, overlapping divisions. Fls to 45mm diam., facing upwards; pet. rich lavender blue, veins purple, feathered. Summer. Cauc., Turk., N Iran. 'Album': fls white. Z6.

G. ibericum var. *platypetalum* (Fisch. & Mey.) Boiss. = *G. platypetalum*.

G. incanum Burm. f. Bushy perenn. to 1m. St. branched. Lvs solitary or paired, fragrant, cut into 5 linear divisions with linear pinnate lobes and teeth, all seg. less than 1mm wide, white downy beneath. Infl. diffuse; peduncles 14cm, pedicels to 7cm; pet. to 18mm, cordate, dark magenta, white 'v' at base, veins darker; fil. pink, base white; anth. cream and purple; stigma pink, hairy. Summer–autumn. S Afr. Z9.

G. incisum (Torr. & A. Gray) Brewer & Wats. = *G. nervosum*.

G. kishtvariense Knuth. Bushy, bristly-hairy perenn. rhiz. creeping, st. nodes and petioles swollen, basal lvs to 9cm wide, lowest lvs single, others paired, with 5 shallowly lobed toothed divisions, tips and teeth acute, bright green, wrinkled; upper lvs 3 lobed; peduncles to 6cm; fls facing upwards; pet. 20mm, rounded, dark purple-pink with white 'v' at base, margins and surface of base hairy; fil. black-red, base white. Kashmir. Z8.

G. lambertii Sweet. Trailing perenn. St. procumbent, basal lvs few; st. lvs to 15cm wide, reniform, hairy, with 5 divisions, narrowed to both ends from above middle, apex 3-lobed and acutely toothed. Infl. diffuse; pedicels glandular-hairy; fls shallow, inverted or nodding; pet. to 20mm, pink to white, base marked purple, apex rounded; fil. white, hairy toward base; anth. black. Summer. Himal. 'Swansdown': lvs marbled lighter and darker green; fls large, nodding, cup-shaped, white stained red-purple at centre. Z8.

G. lanuginosum Lam. Sprawling ann., glandular-pubesc., similar to *G. bohemicum*, lvs not wrinkled, marbled, lobes and teeth finger-like. Pet. to 9mm, blue, pale pink-white toward fringed base. Medit. Z8.

G. libani P.H. Davis. Perenn. to 40cm, close to *G. peloponnesiacum* but without gland. hairs. Leafy in winter, basal lvs deeply cut into 5 or 7 divisions, lobed and toothed above midpoint, glossy above. Pet. violet, to 20mm, veins leathery, beak to 35mm. Spring. Leb., W Syr., S Turk. Z8.

G. libanoticum (Boiss.) Boiss. = *G. libani*.

G. × lindavicum Sünderm. ex Knuth. (*G. argenteum* × *G. cinereum*.) Lvs deeply lobed, somewhat silky. Infl. trailing; pet. to 19mm, rounded or notched, densely net-veined, white or pink. 'Apple Blossom' ('Jenny Bloom'): habit low; lvs silver grey, divisions 3-lobed; fls off-white, faintly veined, stigmas almost white. 'Alanah' ('Purpureum'): lvs with less of a silver hue; fls bright crimson-purple, abundant. 'Gypsy': low-growing; lvs grey-green; pet. irregularly lobed or with narrow notch, bright cerise fading to white above butterfly-shaped, maroon blotch at base. 'Lisadell': lvs silver; fls rich wine colour. Z6.

G. lucidum L. Erect ann. to 50cm, st. red, succulent, lvs to 5cm wide. Divisions 5, glossy, succulent, apex 3-lobed, fls erect; pet. to 9mm, deep pink. Eur., N Afr., SW & C Asia. Z7.

G. macrorrhizum L. Foetid, gland.-hairy perenn. to 50cm; rootstock long and thick, basal lvs to 20cm wide, divisions 5–7, narrowed to both ends, lobed and toothed. Infl. dense; fls facing horizontally, in pairs or umbels; cal. pink to purple-red; pet. magenta to dark purple-red, pink or white; fil. purple-red, anth. orange to red; style purple-red, stigma yellow. Summer. S Eur. 'Album': pet. white; sep. tinged red. 'Bevan's Variety': fls intense deep magenta, sep. deep red. 'Czakor': habit low, clump-forming to 30cm; lvs scented; fls magenta, sep. dark. 'Ingwersen's Variety': lvs light green and glossy; fls light pink. 'Spessart': cal. dark pink, pet. white-pink. 'Variegatum': lvs irregularly variegated cream; fls purple-pink. Z4.

G. macrostylum Boiss. Similar to *G. tuberosum* but with narrower rootstock, upper parts red glandular-hairy, lvs smaller. Fls smaller; pet. 8mm, light pink or pink-blue with feathered veins, base darker. Early summer. NE Medit. Z7.

G. maculatum L. Perenn. to 75cm, upper parts hairy, basal lvs to 20cm wide, deeply cut into 5 or 7 widely spaced divisions, acutely lobed and deeply toothed. Infl. umbel-like; fls facing upwards, saucer-shaped; pet. 20mm, tip rounded or slightly notched, light to deep pink; fil. pink, anth. grey; stigma pink. Spring–summer. NE US. 'Album': pet. pure white. Z4.

G. maderense Yeo. Perenn. to 1.5m. St. stout, to 60cm, lvs in rosette on st. Petioles light brown, blades to 60cm wide, deeply lobed and toothed. Infl. much-branched, from centre of rosette, purple-hairy; pet. to 21mm, nearly as wide as long, dark magenta, veins paler; fil. purple or deep red, clawed. Winter, spring, summer. Madeira. Z9.

G. × magnificum Hylander. (*G. ibericum* × *G. platypetalum*.) Sterile hybrid perenn. to 70cm+. Differs from *G. ibericum* in pedicels glandular-hairy and from *G. platypetalum* in having long eglandular as well as gland. hairs on pedicels, fls rich violet purple. Summer. Gdn origin. Z5.

G. malviflorum Boiss. & Reut. Perenn., tubers of rootstock connected by narrow sections, basal lvs to 15cm wide, deeply cut, divisions 7, narrowly pinnately lobed and toothed; fls to 45mm diam., shallow; pedicels v. hairy; pet. cordate, blue-violet, veins dark; fil. purple, base dilated, hairy, anth. cream, edges blue to black; stigma dark red. Spring. S Spain, NW Afr. Z8.

G. meeboldii Briq. = *G. himalayense*.

G. × monacense Harz. (*G. phaeum* × *G. reflexum*.) Intermediate between parents. Pet. 14mm, reflexed, sometimes lobed at tips, deep purple red or pink-mauve, base white, blue-violet between. Summer. Gdn origin. Sometimes sold in nurseries as *G. punctatum*, a name of no botanical standing. 'Muldoon' ('Variegatum'): lvs boldly blotched. Z5.

G. napuligerum hort. non Franch. = *G. farreri*.

G. nepalense Sweet. Weedy, bushy perenn.; rootstock slender, st. slender. Lvs persisting in winter, to 10cm wide, deeply cut into 5 or 7 diamond-shaped, lobed and toothed divisions, deep green, brown-hued above, sparsely hairy beneath, often somewhat marbled. Infl. diffuse, cymules 1- or 2-fld; fls small, many; pet. to 8mm, notched or rounded, white to rose pink, veins purple; anth. blue-mauve; stigma red. Summer. Himal., China, India.

Z7.

G. nervosum Rydb. Perenn., upper parts glandular-hairy and sticky; rootstock thick and woody. Lvs to 20cm wide, divisions 5–7, broad, palmately lobed, acutely toothed. Infl. diffuse, fls upright, flat; peduncles to 3cm; pet. 22mm, hairy, sometimes notched, light to dark pink, base white, veins dark, branching, fil. just longer than sep. diverging, pink, coarsely hairy; anth. yellow, edges pink or purple. Early summer–autumn. N US. Z4.

G. nodosum L. Perenn. with elongated rhiz. St. to 50cm. Lvs 5–20cm diam., shiny with sparsely lobed and unevenly toothed divisions: 5 on basal lvs elliptic, 3 on st. lvs lanceolate. Infl. diffuse; fls erect, funnel-shaped; pet. conspicuously notched, 16mm+, wedge-shaped, bright purple-pink, veins sparse, carmine at base; fil. hairy for some of length, white; anth. blue; style red, stigma glab., red, 2mm. Summer. C Fr. to Pyren., C It., C Balk. Z6.

G. ocellatum Cambess. Ann. Lvs to 10cm wide, divisions 5–7, profusely lobed, dentate. Fls to 18mm diam.; pet. to 10mm, deep pink with black triangle at base; sta. black; stigmas dark red. Afr., Arabian Penins., Himal., SW China.

G. oreganum Howell. Perenn. to 60cm; rootstock compact. Basal lvs to 20cm wide, divisions 7, deeply lobed, dentate. Fls upwardly inclined; peduncles to 11cm; pet. to 23mm, deep pink-purple, with a dense tuft of hairs at base; fil. pink, anth. yellow edged purple. W US. Z7.

G. orientalitibeticum Knuth. Dwarf alpine perenn., similar to *G. pylzowianum* but taller, to 35cm; tubers larger, to 10×5cm. Basal lvs to 10cm wide, lf divisions broader, marbled. Fls 25mm diam., flat with bowl-shaped centre; pet. dark pink-purple, base white and hairy, not clawed. Summer. SW China. Z8.

G. ornithopodon Ecklon & Zeyh. Clump-forming, much-branched, spreading perenn., all parts with white hairs; rootstock woody and thick. St. to 90cm. Lvs to 8cm wide, cut into 5 pinnately lobed divisions; petioles 10cm. Fls nodding, small; pedicels slender, densely downy, to 45mm; pet. to 8mm, white, veins red, or light pink with deeper veins. S Afr. Z8.

G. ornithopodum auctt. = *G. ornithopodon*.

G. × oxonianum Yeo. (*G. endressii* × *G. versicolor*.) Perenn., to 80cm. Lvs similar to *G. versicolor*, but with deeper lobes as in *G. endressii*, 5–20cm wide, somewhat wrinkled, sometimes blotched brown. Fls funnel-shaped; pet. to 2.6cm, pink, notched, veins usually deeper, netted. 'A.T. Johnson': fls pink tinged silver. 'Claridge Druce': vigorous, hairy, tall plant; lvs dark, somewhat glossy; fls rose-pink with darker veins, basal part of veins fade with age. 'Hollywood': fls pale pink, darkly veined. 'Rose Clair': to 35cm; fls purple-pink. 'Southcombe Star' ('Southcombe Double'): vigorous; fls small, pink, star-shaped, sta. occas. petaloid. 'Thurstonianum': pet. narrow strap-shaped, purple, colour due to crowded veins; sta. petaloid. 'Winscombe': to 40cm; fls v. pale pink darkening with age with darker veins; abundant. Z5.

G. palmatum Cav. Perenn. to 45cm, similar to *G. canariense*, but differs in st. only developed in older plants; lvs to 35cm wide, central division stalked; infl. to 120cm; fls facing horizontally; fil. dark pink-red, anth. cream-yellow; stigma purple-red; pet. 30mm, purple-pink to purple-red at base. Summer. Madeira. Z9.

G. palustre L. Eglandular, stiffly hairy perenn. to 40cm. Basal lvs 5–20cm wide, deeply cut into 7 roughly pinnately lobed divisions, lobes with 1–3 teeth. Infl. diffuse, peduncles to 7cm; pedicels long, hairy; fls broadly trumpet-shaped; pet. 18mm, rounded, bright dark magenta, base white, veins feathered, deep purple, hairy above and at margins; fil. as for pet. or paler, anth. cream to violet; stigma flesh to deep red. Summer. E & E Eur. Z6.

G. peloponnesiacum Boiss. Thickly rhizomatous gland. perenn. to 60cm becoming dormant after flowering. Lvs present in winter; basal lvs to 20cm wide, deeply cut into 7 diamond-shaped lobed and toothed divisions. Infl. diffuse, fls facing upwards, in umbel-like groups on long pedicels; pet. blue-violet, to 25mm, notched, veins dark, netted; fil. purple-pink; anth. off-white; edges blue. Late spring. Greece. Z8.

G. phaeum L. BLACK WIDOW. Tall perenn. to 80cm; rootstock stout. Lvs present in winter, basal lvs to 20cm wide, shallowly cut into 9 toothed lobes often marked purple at base. Infl. lax, branched, 1-sided; fls nodding; pet. to 14mm, spreading, v. deep purple-black, deep maroon, blue-red or light mauve, with a white spot at base, tips notched or with a point; fil. long, hairy near base; stigma yellow-green. Late spring to summer. S, C & W Eur. 'Album': fls larger, white. 'Langthorn's Blue': fls violet-blue. 'Lily Lovell': fls large, lvs light green; deep mauve. 'Variegatum': lvs irregularly margined pale yellow, also with dark blotches; fls purple. var. **phaeum.** Fls v. deep silky purple-black, with white star-shaped centre. var. *lividum* (L'Hérit.) Pers. Lvs usually plain; pet. pale blue, pink or mauve with white base, with blue interstices. 'Majus': fls large, pale lilac. Z5.

G. platyanthum Duthie = *G. eriostemon*.

G. platypetalum Fisch. & Mey. Hairy perenn. to 40cm; rootstock thick, compact. Basal lvs to 20cm wide, round, cut to middle into 7 or 9 broad, lobed and toothed divisions. Infl. dense; fls flat; peduncles reduced; pedicels gland. hairy; pet. to 22mm, notched, deep violet, veins deep violet-red, forking; fil. hairy, colour as pet. base paler; anth. blue-black; stigma 2.5mm, deep red. Summer. Cauc., Turk. Z6.

G. pogonanthum Franch. Perenn. with compact rootstock. Basal lvs to 10cm, deeply cut into 5 or 7 palmate to pinnate, acutely toothed divisions, marbled above. Infl. diffuse; fls inverted; pedicels to 8mm; pet. to 20mm, rounded, recurved, pink to pink-white; fil. purple-red, anth. black-blue. Mid-late summer. SW China, Burm. Z8.

G. polyanthes Edgew. & Hook. f. Perenn. to 45cm; rootstock thick and bumpy. Lvs deeply lobed, to 5cm wide, petioles long and hairy. Infl. umbel-like; pet. to 15mm, rounded, bright pink-purple, veins delicate, base lighter; anth. yellow; stigma yellow tipped pink. Summer. Himal., SW China. Z8.

G. pratense L. MEADOW CRANE'S BILL. Perenn. to 120cm; rootstock compact. Basal lvs to 20cm wide, divisions 7–9 deeply cut, narrow, pinnately lobed, lobes bent outwards, toothed, adpressed-hairy above, veins hairy beneath, petioles hairy. Infl. dense, peduncles to 10cm, fls saucer-shaped; pet. to 22mm, rounded, blue-violet to white, veins sometimes pink; fil. dark pink, hairy at base, anth. dark. C Asia, NW Himal., C & W Eur. 'Albiflorum': fls white. 'Bittersweet': to 75cm; lvs tinged purple; fls pink-mauve with pale veining, anth. dark. 'Blue Chip': to 75cm; fls pale blue tinged pink on opening, anth. dark. 'Galactic': to 75cm; infl. flat-topped, pet. white with translucent veins, overlapping, sometimes slightly notched. 'Mrs Kendall Clark': fls light violet blue, with pale translucent veins. 'Plenum Album': fls small, double, white. 'Plenum Caeruleum': fls small, double, light blue-mauve. 'Plenum Violaceum': fls small, double, dark violet-blue. 'Silver Queen': habit tall to 130cm; fls large, white slightly tinged palest violet; anth. blue-black. 'Striatum': pet. white with streaks and spots of violet-blue. 'Wisley Blue': to 60cm; fls large, blue, abundant. Z5.

G. procurrens Yeo. Perenn. with long, trailing, rooting st.; glandular-hairy on upper parts. Basal lvs few, to 10cm wide, cut into usually 5 divisions, narrowed to both ends, 3-lobed at apex, toothed. Peduncles to 8cm, pedicels 4.5cm; pet. 18mm, dark purple-pink, black 'V' at base, veins black; sta. black; stigma black. Late summer–autumn. Himal. Z7.

G. psilostemon Ledeb. Short-hairy and gland. upright perenn. to 120cm, rootstock compact. Basal lvs large, to 20cm+, divisions 7 deeply cut, acutely lobed. Acutely toothed; st. lvs with 5 divisions. Infl. erect, lax; fls erect, to 35mm diam., shallow bowl-shaped; pet. slightly notched or rounded at tips, magenta, base and veins black, 18mm; sta. black; stigma purple-red. Summer. NE Turk. 'Bressingham Flair': shorter; fls less intensely coloured, deep lilac-pink. Z6.

G. pulchrum N.E. Br. Coarse subshrub to 1.3m. St. upright or procumbent, woody at base. Lvs to 12m wide, divisions 5–7 elliptic, shallowly lobed near apex and bluntly toothed near bse, acute with mucro, adpressed hairy above, silver-felted, beneath. Peduncles and pedicels covered in white gland. hairs, pedicels to 6cm; pet. 20mm, obovate, notched, pale purple to dark pink. Summer. S Afr. Z9.

G. punctatum hort. = *G. ×monacense*.

G. pylzowianum Maxim. Perenn. to 25cm; rootstock of pea-like tubers joined by filiform stolons. Lvs to 5cm wide, deeply cut into narrowly lobed, toothed, wedge-shaped divisions. Fls few, broad trumpet-shaped; peduncles to 10cm; pet. to 23mm, clawed, rounded or slightly notched, pink to dark pink, base white, veins darker; fil. white tipped pink, anth. cream and blue. W China. Z5.

G. pyrenaicum Burm. f. Everg. minutely hairy perenn. to 60cm. Basal lvs round, to 10cm wide, cut to below mid-point into 5, 7 or 9 lobed and sometimes toothed divisions. Infl. diffuse on procumbent st.; fls 20mm diam.; pet. to 10mm, pink-purple to violet, deeply notched, base clawed, white, veins deeper. Spring–autumn. SW & W Eur. Z7.

G. rectum var. *album* hort. = *G. clarkei* 'Kashmir White'.

G. reflexum L. Similar to *G. phaeum* except fls to 16mm diam., inverted, rose-pink, blue band above white base. Summer, often with second flush. Fr., It., Balk., Greece. Z6.

G. regelii Nevski. Similar to *G. pratense*. Basal lvs to 10cm wide, lobes broad. Infl. small; fls few. C Asia, NE Afghan., N Pak. Z6.

G. renardii Trautv. Clump-forming perenn. to 20cm. Basal lvs to 10cm wide, round, cut to midway into 5 lobed, toothed, round divisions, soft, deep grey to olive green above, veins impressed. Infl. dense, umbel-like; fls flat; pet. white to pale lavender,

wedge-shaped, notched, to 18mm, veins violet, branching. Summer. Cauc. 'Whiteknights': fls white with pale blue-lilac ground colour, darker veins.

G. richardsonii Fisch. & Trautv. Perenn to 60cm, rootstock thick. Basal lvs to 10cm wide, green, somewhat shiny, cut into 5 or 7 lobed and sparsely toothed divisions narrowed to both ends. Infl. diffuse, fls to 2.8cm diam.; peduncles to 6cm, pedicels to 2cm; pet. rounded, white or light pink, veins v. light purple or 0; fil. base dilated, hairy, anth. mauve to grey; stigma green to yellow. Early summer onwards. W US.

G. × *riversleaianum* Yeo. (*G. endressii* × *G. traversii*.) Sterile hybrid. Creeping perenn. covered in short adpressed hairs. Rhiz. thick and short. Lvs of 7 lobed divisions, sparsely blunt toothed. Infl. diffuse; fls erect, broad funnel-shaped, to 32mm diam.; pet. slightly notched, base and margins lightly hairy, light pink to dark magenta, veins simple, darker than ground colour; fil. hairy, white, shorter than sep., anth. purple or yellow; stigma pink to deep red. Summer. Gdn origin. 'Chapel End Pink': fls 2.5cm diam., shell-pink. 'Chapel End Red': fls crimson. 'Mavis Simpson': medium pink, paler in centre, with slightly brown marks in lf notches. 'Russell Prichard': fls 3cm diam., rich magenta, lvs sharp toothed. Z7.

G. rivulare Vill. Upright perenn. to 45cm; rootstock compact. Lvs of 7–9 deeply cut, narrow-lobed divisions, acutely toothed. Infl. crowded; fls erect, funnelform, to 25mm diam.; pet. white, veins violet; stigma dark pink. Summer. Eur. (Alps). 'Album': fls white. Z6.

G. robertianum L. HERB ROBERT. Ann. or bienn. to 25cm, often tinted brown or red, hairy. Basal lvs to 11cm wide, cut to base into 5 stalked divisions, divisions pinnately lobed and bluntly and mucronately toothed. Infl. diffuse; peduncles slender; pet. 14mm, dark pink, veins pale at base, claws shorter than blades; anth. red to peach. Summer–autumn. Eur., E US, NW Afr., W Asia, Canary Is., Himal., SW China. 'Album': trailing, lvs and st. red-brown; fls large, white. 'Celtic White': dwarf; fls small, white. Z6.

G. robustum Kuntze. Subshrub to 1m. St. upright, woody at base. Lvs to 5cm diam., divisions 3–7 finely pinnately lobed, silvery silky-hairy above, tomentose beneath. Infl. of groups of cymes; gland. and eglandular hairy; pedicels 6cm; pet. 18mm, lightly notched, pale purple with white base. Summer. S Afr. Z9.

G. rubescens Yeo. Bienn. similar to *G. robertianum*, but much larger; st. to 60cm, thicker, crimson at base; lf petioles crimson; lamina to 25cm wide, teeth acute with prominent mucros; pet. clawed, 20mm, bright pink-purple, veins paler at base. Summer. Madeira. Z9.

G. rubifolium L. Similar to *G. kishtvariense*, but with compact rootstock, stout, upright, fewer st. to 1.5m; basal lvs to 15cm wide, shallowly lobed; pet. smaller, to 18mm, purple violet to violet with white 'V', tips lightly notched. Summer. Kashmir. Z8.

G. sanguineum L. BLOODY CRANES BILL. Bushy perenn. with somewhat spreading rhiz. Basal lvs few, not as deeply cut as st. lvs; st. lvs rounded in outline, v. deeply cut into 5 or 7, sparsely toothed, trilobed divisions, outer lobes splayed, 5–10cm wide. Infl. diffuse, cymules 1-fld; fls mostly upright; peduncles 7cm; pet. 21mm, cordate, usually notched, deep purple-red to bright carmine, base white, veins deeper; fil. coloured as pet.; anth. blue; stigma red or flesh. Summer. Eur., N Turk. 'Album': fls white. 'Alpenglow': low-growing to 25cm; lvs dark; fls vivid rose-red. 'Cedric Morris': to 45cm; fls rose-magenta. 'Elspeth': to 20cm; fls v. large, bright purple, pedicel and cal. covered with long hairs. 'Glenluce': habit dense; fls clear pink. 'Holden': habit spreading; lvs small; fls bright rose-pink. 'Jubilee Pink': habit compact; fls to 38mm wide, magenta-pink. 'Minitum': habit compact, dwarf; lvs to 2.5cm; fls to 3cm wide. 'Nanum': habit low, compact; fls rose red. 'Shepherd's Warning': habit compact; fls bright rose-pink. var. *striatum* Weston. Dwarf habit, fls light flesh pink, heavily veined. Early summer. GB (Walney Is., Cumbria). 'Splendens': taller, to 45cm; pet. slightly serrated, pale pink, darkly veined. Z5.

G. sanguineum var. *lancastriense* Nichols. = *G. sanguineum* var. *striatum*.

G. sanguineum var. *prostratum* (Cav.) Pers. = *G. sanguineum* var. *striatum*.

G. schlechteri Knuth. Perenn. glandular-hairy herb. St. sprawling, to 1m. Lvs to 6cm wide, divisions 5 elliptic, lobed and toothed, sparsely adpressed-hairy above, spreading long hairs beneath. Pedicels to 4cm; pet. to 12mm, obovate, sometimes lightly notched, white to pink, rose or white with pink veins. Summer. S Afr. Z9.

G. sessiliflorum Cav. Dwarf perenn.; rootstock stout, compact. Basal lvs 1.5–3cm wide, rounded, divided into 5–7 shallowly lobed, seldom toothed divisions. Infl. diffuse, fls erect, funnel-shaped; pet. 6.5–7mm, white; fil. white. NZ. 'Nigricans': lvs olive green or bronze as they unfold, becoming orange as they die. Z8.

G. shikokianum Matsum. Bushy perenn. to 40cm, rootstock compact. Basal lvs to 10cm wide, marbled above, glossy beneath, divisions 5 or 7 acutely toothed, lobed. Infl. diffuse, peduncles to 15cm; fls funnelform; pet. 18mm, rounded, narrowed to base, pink, base white, veins red; fil. white, tips pink; anth. blue. Summer, for long periods. S Jap., Korea. Z8.

G. sibiricum L. Sprawling perenn.; rootstock slender. Basal lvs few; st. lvs to 10cm wide, narrowly divided, pale green, many-lobed, lower lvs dentate. Infl. diffuse; fls solitary; pet. to 7mm, white or pale pink with purple veins, rounded or notched; anth. violet-blue; stigmas pink. E & C Eur. Z6.

G. sinense Knuth. Perenn. with compact rootstock. Basal lvs deeply cut into 5 or 7 elongated lobed and/or toothed divisions, to 20cm wide, strong green. Infl. diffuse; fls inverted; pet. 10mm, rounded with irregular lobes at tip, velvety dark maroon, base pink; green nectary present; fil. deep red. Late summer. SW China. Z8.

G. soboliferum Komar. Small compact perenn.; rootstock compact. Basal lvs with 7 divisions, narrowly lobed, dentate. Infl. dense; peduncles to 6cm. Fls to 30mm diam.; pet. deep red-purple, rounded, with a basal tuft of hairs; fil. deep red-purple, anth. blue; style red. Russia, Manch. Z6.

G. stapfianum 'Roseum'. = *G. orientalitibeticum*.

G. striatum L. = *G. versicolor*.

G. subcaulescens DC. = *G. cinereum* var. *subcaulescens*.

G. sylvaticum L. Upright perenn. to 70cm, glandular-hairy above. Lf lobes 7–9 deeply cut, acute, lobed, acutely toothed; basal lvs 10–20+cm wide. Infl. crowded; fls erect, saucer-shaped, to 30mm diam.; pet. rounded or lightly notched, base hairy, blue to purple-violet with white base, or white or pink; fil. pink, anth. blue; stigma purple. Summer. Eur., N Turk. 'Album': fls white, lvs pale. 'Birch Lilac': fls rich lilac. 'Mayflower': fls rich violet-blue, with distinct small white centre. 'Silva': lvs dark green; fls pale blue. f. *albiflorum* A. Blytt. Pet. white. f. *roseum* Murray. Pet. pink. var. *wanneri* Briq. Pet. light rose, veins bright rose. Z4.

G. thunbergii Lindl. & Paxt. Sprawling perenn. pubesc. Lvs to 10cm+ diam., with 5 broad divisions, mostly light green, shallowly lobed, dentate. Infl. diffuse, cymules 2-fld; pet. to 11mm, white or pale to deep pink-purple, purple veined, rounded or slightly notched; anth. violet-blue. N China, Jap., Taiwan. Z7.

G. transbaicalicum Serg. Resembles *G. pratense*. St. to 25cm, darkly pigmented. Lvs edged red or brown, basal lvs to 20cm wide, with numerous narrow lobes and teeth. Pet. darker than in *G. pratense*. Sib. Z3.

G. traversii Hook. f. Plants in cult. are var. *elegans* Ckn. Perenn., low growing, silvery throughout, basal lvs many, circular in outine, to 10cm wide, deeply cut into 5 or 7 divisions with 3 broad, few-toothed lobes. Infl. diffuse, cymules 1-fld; pet. broad 13mm, rounded, cloudy pink, veins darker; fil. white, anth. yellow, edges pink; stigma pink. Summer. Chatham Is. Z8.

G. tuberosum L. Upright, perenn. to 40cm. Tubers to 15mm wide joined by filiform rhiz. Lvs to 10cm diam., deeply cut into 7, narrowly pinnately lobed, toothed divisions, none wider than 3mm. Infl. mostly unstalked, pet. 17mm, notched, purple-violet, veins darker, forked; fil. hairy, anth. deep blue; stigma crimson. Summer. Medit. 'Charlesii': habit low, spreading; lvs divided; fls deep pink. Z8.

G. versicolor L. Low-growing bristly perenn. to 60cm. Basal lvs to 20cm wide; divisions 5, pinnately lobed, dentate. Infl. diffuse; pet. to 16mm, white with magenta venation, notched, base sparsely hairy; sta. white with pink apices, sparsely hairy, anth. blue. It., Balk. Penins. Z6.

G. viscosissimum Fisch. & Mey. Similar to *G. nervosum* but st. glandular-hairy and sticky throughout (not just upper parts). Lvs larger. Infl. umbel-like; pedicels longer. Summer. W US. Z7.

G. wallichianum D. Don. Perenn. St. decumbent. Lvs in pairs with 3 or 5 quite deeply cut, lobed divisions, margins acutely toothed. Infl. lax, leafy; peduncles to 15cm; fls facing upwards, almost flat to shallow bowl-shaped; pet. to 17mm, cordate or triangular, notched, dark to purple-pink, base often white, tuft of hairs on either side at base with line of hairs joining them; sta., stigma, and style black. Summer–early autumn. Himal. (NE Afghan. to Kashmir). 'Buxton's Variety' ('Buxton's Blue'): habit dense, compact, creeping; lvs small, marbled; fls china blue, centre white, delicately veined. 'Syabru': fls purple-pink, not paler at centre. Z7.

G. wilfordii hort. non Maxim. = *G. thunbergii*.

G. wlassovianum Fisch. ex Link. Bushy perenn. to 30cm, softly hairy; rootstock compact, basal lvs to 15cm wide, short-stalked, shallowly cut into 7 divisions, coarsely pinnately lobed at tips, outline round reniform. Infl. diffuse; peduncles to 8cm; pet. to

22mm, rounded, dark to pale purple-violet, veins feathered, deep violet, base white; fil. base dilated, purple-violet; stigma dark red to pink. Summer. Sib., Mong., E Russia, N China. Z3.

G. yesoense Franch. & Savat. Bushy perenn. to 40cm; rootstock compact. Basal lvs 5–10cm wide, shiny with spreading hairs beneath, deeply cut into 7 pinnately lobed narrow divisions, deeply acutely toothed at apices. Infl. lax; pet. 20mm, pink or white, veins darker; style red, stigma pink or red. Summer. Jap., Kuril Is. Z8.

G. yunnanense Franch. Similar to *G. pogonanthum*, but lvs with fewer lobes and teeth; fls nodding, fewer in number, bowl-shaped; pet. not recurved. Midsummer. SW China, Burm. Z8.

Cvs of hybrid origin. 'Ann Folkard' (*G. procurrens* ×*G. psilostemon*): habit sprawling; lvs golden-green, esp. when young; fls purple centred black. 'Johnson's Blue' (*G. himalayense* ×*G. pratense?*): shortly creeping; lvs with narrow divisions; fls 50mm wide, deep blue; pet. entire. 'Maxwelton' (*G.* ×*oxonianum* ×*G. psilostemon*): to 70cm; fls rose magenta, centre dark red. 'Robert Burns' (*G.* ×*oxonianum* ×*G. traversii* var. *elegans*): lvs widely divided, silver-hairy; pet. blunt, pink centred white with margin of prominent veins between colours. 'Salome' (*G. lambertii* ×*G. procurrens*): habit trailing; fls dark violet and white. 'Walter's Gift': new growth brown tinged orange; fls pale pink, heavily veined, abundant.

Geranium *Pelargonium* ×*hortorum*.
Geranium Aralia *Polyscias guilfoylei*.

Gerardia L.
G. delphiniifolia L. = *Sopubia delphiniifolia*.
G. pedicularia L. = *Aureolaria pedicularia*.
G. purpurea L. = *Agalinis purpurea*.
G. tenuifolia Vahl. = *Agalinis tenuifolia*.
G. virginica (L.) BSP = *Aureolaria virginica*.

Gerbera L. TRANSVAAL DAISY; BARBERTON DAISY. Compositae. 40 hairy, stemless, perenn. herbs. Lvs ascending or spreading in a basal rosette, entire to dentate or pinnately lobed, petiolate, hairy beneath. Cap. radiate, solitary, long-stalked. Afr., Madag., Asia, Indon.

G. anandria Schultz-Bip. = *Leibnitzia anandria*.
G. asplenifolia (Lam.) Spreng. = *G. linnaei*.
G. aurantiaca Schultz-Bip. HILTON DAISY; TRANSVAAL DAISY. Lvs to 6.5cm, elliptic, broadly acute, tapering to base, entire to denticulate, tomentose, becoming glab. beneath; petiole short, narrowly winged. Cap. to 20×35mm; peduncles to 50cm; outer ray flts to 42cm crowded, usually crimson, dull below, inner ray flts pink or red; disc flts pink or red. Winter. S Afr.
G. jamesonii Bol. ex Adlam. BARBERTON DAISY. Lvs to 70×14cm, spreading, oblong-spathulate, pinnatifid, dark green above, paler and sparsely tomentose beneath, undulate; petiole to 40cm. Cap. to 22×48mm; peduncles to 70cm; outer ray flts yellow, orange to dark red, white or pink, dull below. Winter. S Afr., Swaz. Much material in cult. is *G. jamesonii* ×*G. viridifolia*. Over 15 seed selections are produced by US nurseries, mostly double, all in bright colours; single-fld rac. include the large (to 60cm), multi-coloured California Mixed and the 45cm early-flowering Parade Mix, with single and double fls lasting two weeks after cutting; doubles include the early Festival Mixture and Pandora Series and the large-fld (to 10cm across) Sunburst Mixture and Happipot Mixture with conspicuous dark green lvs; Fantasia Double Strain has v. large fls, to 12cm across, with quilled centres. Z8.
G. kunzeana hort. = *Leibnitzia anandria*.
G. linnaei Cass. Lvs 30×2cm, lanceolate, pinnatifid to deeply pinnatisect, lobes quadrate to rounded, apical lobe triangular or sagittate, often dentate, sinuate, green, glab. to sparsely villous, sometimes rugose above, yellow-brown- or grey-brown-tomentose beneath; petiole to 10cm. Cap. to 26×38mm; peduncles to 54cm; ray flts white or white above, purple, red-brown or yellow below; disc flts dark. Summer, winter. S Afr. Z8.
G. viridifolia (DC.) Schultz-Bip. Lvs to 50×12cm, lanceolate to broadly lanceolate, elliptic or oblong, obtuse or subacute, base often cuneate, sometimes narrowly cordate, entire to shallowly lobed, often toothed, hairy, becoming glab.; petiole to 30cm. Cap. to 22×37mm; peduncles to 70cm; ray flts usually white above, pink below, occas. pink, red, purple or yellow; disc flts white, yellow or tinged green, rarely violet. S Afr., E Afr., Cameroun. Z8.

German Chamomile *Matricaria recutita*.
Germander *Teucrium*.
Germander Speedwell *Veronica chamaedrys*.
German Garlic *Allium senescens*.
German Ivy *Delairea odorata*.

German Onion *Ornithogalum longibracteatum.*
German Primrose *Primula obconica.*
German Rampion *Oenothera biennis.*
German Violet *Exacum affine.*

Gerrardanthus Harv. ex Hook. f. Cucurbitaceae. 5 semi-tuberous perenn. climbers. St. often succulent, becoming partially lignified. Tendrils bifid. Lvs simple or lobed. Cor. rotate, seg. 5. Fr. obconical, dry, coriaceous, trigonous. C, E & S Afr. Z9.

G. macrorhiza Harv. ex Benth. & Hook. f. St. swollen at base, to 50cm diam., becoming woody; br. climbing freely. Lvs glab., 3–7-lobed, 3–8cm. Fr. yellow-brown, somewhat ribbed, to 7cm. S & E Afr.

Gesneria L. Gesneriaceae. 47 perenn. herbs, subshrubs or tree-lets. Fls in a compound cyme or solitary; peduncles glab. to pilose, often red-tinged; cal. 5-lobed; cor. tubular, cylindric or campanulate, limb 5-lobed, occas. 2-lipped; sta. usually 4, sometimes exserted, with an infertile staminode. Trop. Amer. Z10.

G. acaulis L. Subshrub; st. erect or decumbent, to 30cm. Lvs 4–24cm, oblanceolate to obovate, acuminate, membranous, crenate, serrate to lobulate, villous or glab. above, red- or green-hairy and resinous beneath. Fls many; cor. tube to 3.5cm, cylindric, bent, outside red, pink or orange, occas. tinged yellow, inside yellow or pink, limb dark red-orange. Jam.

G. aggregata Ker-Gawl. = *Sinningia aggregata.*
G. bulbosa Ker-Gawl. = *Sinningia bulbosa.*
G. calycina Sw. Shrub; st. erect, branching from enlarged nodes. Lvs 12–22cm, crowded at br. tips, elliptic to oblanceolate to obovate, membranous to subcoriaceous, slightly crenate to dentate, green and glab., cymes, 2–4-fld axill., long-stalked; cor. subcampanulate, tube to 1.2cm, green, glab. Jam.
G. calycosa (Hook.) Kuntze. Shrub or tree; st. to 5m, woody. Lvs 9–17.5cm, elliptic to oblong, acuminate, membranous, serrate-crenate. Fls axill., solitary; cor. subcampanulate, tube to 2cm, outside yellow-green to cream, glab., inside pale green. Jam.
G. canescens Mart. = *Sinningia canescens.*
G. cardinalis Lehm. = *Sinningia cardinalis.*
G. christi Urban. Subshrub; st. to 12cm, woody, erect or spreading. Lvs to 27cm, closely spaced, narrowly obovate or oblanceolate, membranous, acute, undulate-lobulate, lobules serrate or dentate, sparsely white-hairy above, red-veined beneath. Fls 1–3, axill.; cal. red-veined and pilose; cor. tube inflated in middle, to 3.7cm, outside yellow-orange to red with darker veins, inside yellow or red, glab., lobes darker than tube with light spots, gland. Haiti.
G. citrina Urban. Subshrub; st. to 1m, pendent or decumbent. Lvs to 6cm, obovate or spathulate, coriaceous, obtuse to acute, glossy above, glab. beneath, veins often red-brown, margin ± ciliate. Fls in axill. cymes; cor. tube to 2cm, curved, nearly cylindric, outside orange to yellow, densely puberulent, inside pale yellow, glab. Puerto Rico.
G. cubensis (Decne.) Baill. Shrub or small tree to 5m; br. erect. Lvs 1–7cm, or restricted to br. apices, elliptic to obovate or oblanceolate, obtuse to acuminate, serrate or crenate above. Fls 1–3 in axill. clusters; cor. tube to 2.7cm, ventricose, outside red from yellow base, inside pink or yellow, upper lobes rounded. Cuba.
G. cuneifolia (DC.) Fritsch. St. to 15cm, herbaceous, occas. woody, erect or decumbent, pilose and resinous above. Lvs 2–14cm, clustered at br. apices, oblanceolate or obovate, membranous, acute or obtuse, crenate or dentate, glab. or pilose. Fls 1–3, in pendent cymes; cal., green to dark red; cor. 1.6–2.6cm, tubular, expanded at middle, outside pink to dark red with darker veins, inside yellow or pink, lobes orbicular to ovate. Puerto Rico.
G. hirsuta HBK. = *Kohleria hirsuta.*
G. humilis L. Subshrub; st. to 50cm, erect or pendent. Lvs to 18cm, narrowly oblanceolate to obovate or ovate, acute to acuminate, serrate to lobulate, sparsely pilose. Fls 1 to many in axill. cymes, sometimes long-stalked; cor. tube to 2cm, narrowly campanulate, slightly constricted at mouth, pale green to yellow, glab., lobes patent to reflexed. Cuba.
G. libanensis Lind. ex Morr. Subshrub; st. to 60cm, erect or pendent, pilose above, resinous. Lvs to 16cm, whorled, oblanceolate, glabrescent above, with sparse red hairs beneath, serrate, occas. lobulate-undulate. Fls 1–5 on short stalks; cor. tube to 3.6cm, outside yellow at base, red toward apex, pilose, inside red or yellow, upper lobes suborbicular. Cuba.
G. pauciflora Urban. Stemless or suffruticose to 30cm, erect or decumbent. Lvs 0.9cm, narrowly ovate, acuminate, base, subentire at base, serrate-crenate toward apex, glossy above, pilose beneath. Fls 1 to few, long-stalked; cal. red-tipped; cor. to

2.3cm, tubular, curved, outside yellow-orange, densely pilose, inside yellow, glab., lobes broadly elliptic. Puerto Rico.
G. pedicellaris Alain. Subshrub; st. to 75cm, erect or pendent, resinous, red or green. Lvs to 16.5cm, clustered at st. apex, oblanceolate or obovate, membranous, apex acute, base cordate, white-hairy above, villous on red veins beneath, crenate to serrate. Fls 1–4 in long, villous-stalked cymes; cor. tube to 3.5cm, curved downward, inflated at middle, outside yellow at base, red-orange at middle, red at limb, inside yellow-orange, glandular-pubesc. Hispan.
G. pedunculosa (DC.) Fritsch. Shrub or tree to 5m, erect, much-branched. Lvs to 11cm, crowded at br. apices, elliptic to obovate, acute, subentire to dentate, glossy above. Fls 2–4 in long-stalked cymes; cor. to 2cm, campanulate, outside yellow-green to light pink, inside yellow-green, lobes reflexed, occas. marked purple. Puerto Rico.
G. pumila Sw. St. to 1m, pendent or erect. Lvs to 15cm, crowded at st. apices, oblanceolate to subspathulate or obovate, membranous to coriaceous, dentate to deeply serrate, pilose to glab. above, pilose to subglabrous beneath. Fls few to many; peduncles to 5cm; cor. 1.5–1.8cm, cylindrical, red. Jam.
G. reticulata (Griseb.) Urban. Subshrub; st. to 20cm, soft branching at base. Lvs to 11.4cm, oblanceolate, ovate, obovate or spathulate, apex acute, base cordate, margin entire to deeply dentate. Fls in 1–3-fld infl.; cal. lobes ovate, red-tinged; cor. tube to 2.7cm, cylindric, slightly bent, outside red-orange or yellow, inside yellow to orange, lobes emarginate. Hispan., Puerto Rico.
G. ventricosa Sw. Shrub or small tree; st. to 3m. Lvs to 22cm, ovate to oblanceolate, membranous to subcoriaceous, apex acute to rounded, margin denticulate to serrate. Fls 1 to many in long-stalked cymes; cal. lobes filiform to deltoid; cor. tube to 3.2cm, curved, inside yellow, gradually intensifying to red at mouth, glab. to sparsely pilose. Lesser Antilles.

GESNERIACEAE Dumort. 146/2400. ×*Achimenantha, Achimenes, Aeschynanthus, Agalmyla, Alloplectus, Alsobia, Ancylostemon, Asteranthera, Besleria, Boea, Briggsia, Bucinellina, Capanea, Chirita, Chrysothemis, Codonanthe, Columnea, Conandron, Corallodiscus, Cyrtandra, Diastema, Drymonia, Episcia, Eucodonia, Gesneria, Gloxinia, Haberlea, Isometrum, Jankaea, Koellikeria,* ×*Koellikohleria, Kohleria, Loxostigma, Lysionotus, Mitraria, Monopyle, Nautilocalyx, Nematanthus, Neomortonia, Niphaea, Opithandra, Oreocharis, Paliavana, Paraboea, Pentadenia, Petrocosmea, Phinaea, Ramonda, Rehmannia, Saintpaulia, Sinningia, Stauranthera, Streptocarpus, Titanotrichum, Trichantha.*

Gethyllis L. Amaryllidaceae. 32 fleshy-rooted, bulbous, herbaceous perennials. Lvs developing from a long neck after fruit-set, usually flat and slender, often spiralling. Fls usually solitary, ± scapose, scented; perianth cylindric-salverform, tep. 6; sta. 6(+). Fr. claviform, succulent, colourful, fragrant. Summer. S Afr. Z9.
G. afra L. Lvs to 5cm, linear, spirally twisted, ribbed, glab. Tep. to 5×2cm, white striped red, oblong to oblanceolate; style longer than sta. Fr. yellow.
G. ciliaris L. Lvs to 15cm, linear, spirally twisted, ciliate. Tep. to 7.5×1.5cm, oblong-lanceolate, white; style equals sta. Fr. red.

Geum L. AVENS. Rosaceae. 50 perenn. herbs and subshrubs; rhiz. thick, short, sometimes stoloniferous. Lvs radical (rosulate) and cauline (alt. and reduced), pinnate or lyrate; veins often impressed above, pubesc. beneath; stipules large or linear and small, adnate to petioles. Fls solitary or in cymes; cal. with a short obconic tube, lobes 5, alternating with 5 epical. seg.; pet. 5; sta. numerous, free. Fr. a head of achenes, each with a persistent plumose style. Eur., Asia, NZ, N & S Amer., Afr.
G. aleppicum Jacq. YELLOW AVENS. St. erect, patent-hipsid. Radical lvs 5–11-foliolate; lat. lfts with minute accessory seg., term., lfts to 10cm, rhombic-ovate to orbicular, acute to rounded, irregularly dentate. Fls to 2cm diam., in 3–10-fld cymes; pet. orange to deep yellow, rounded, patent. Summer–autumn. E Eur., Asia Minor, Sib., China, Korea, N Amer. Z3.
G. anemonoides Willd. = *G. pentapetalum.*
G. atrosanguineum hort. = *G. chiloense.*
G. ×borisii Kellerer ex Sünderm. (*G. bulgaricum* ×*G. reptans.*) Clump-forming. Fls bright yellow, nodding. Bulg. Z3. *G. 'Borisii'* is a name applied to plants of *G. coccineum* (esp. cv. Werner Arends) with compact habit and freely produced orange-scarlet fls. The true natural hybrid is seldom cultivated. Balk. Z4.
G. borisii hort. non Kellerer ex Sünderm. = *G. coccineum* 'Werner Arends'.

G. bulgaricum Pančić. To 50cm. Rhiz. thick. Lvs grey-green, downy, lyrate; term. lft to 15cm, cordate-reniform. Fls to 2.5cm diam., campanulate, nodding; pet. white to pale yellow or orange, triangular, emarginate. Balkans. *G. bulgaricum* of gardens with erect yellow or pale orange fls is probably a selection of *G. ×heldreichii*. Z4.

G. calthifolium Sm. To 30.5cm. St. hirsute, radical lvs lyrate-pinnatifid; term. leaflet large, round-reniform, with a deep, narrow sinus, lobed and double-serrate, lat. lfts to 1cm, few, greatly reduced. Fls 2.5cm+ diam., solitary or a few, ascending; pet. yellow or bright orange, broad-ovate to suborbicular, outspread. Summer. Alask., E Asia. 'Dilatum': fls far larger. Z6.

G. canadense Jacq. WHITE AVENS. To 80cm. Radical lvs 3-foliolate or pinnately divided, seg. dentate and lobed, cauline lvs 3–5-lobed or divided; lfts rhombic, serrate. Fls to 1.6cm diam.; pet. white, oblong. Summer. N Amer. Z3.

G. chiloense Balb. ex Ser. To 60cm. Radical lvs large, cordate, lobed, term. lobe crenate, lateral lobes 2.5cm, almost equalling term. lobe. Fls scarlet-red, large, in erect cymes. Summer. Chile. Some of the following cvs may be hybrids. 'Bernstein': to 50cm; fls light gold. 'Dolly North': to 50cm; fls large, yellow washed orange. 'Fire Opal': to 75cm; st. purple; fls semi-double, orange washed scarlet. 'Georgenberg': to 25cm; fls orange washed gold. 'Lady Stratheden' ('Goldball'): to 60cm; fls double, warm yellow. 'Mrs Bradshaw': to 60cm; fls semi-double, bright brick red. 'Mrs Bradshaw Improved': as 'Mrs Bradshaw', but fls twice the size. 'Princess Juliana': to 45cm; fls double, brilliant orange. 'Rijnstroom': to 50cm; fls single, copper washed orange. 'Rubin': to 40cm; fls semi-double, crimson.

G. ciliatum Pursh = *G. triflorum* var. *ciliatum*.

G. coccineum Sibth. & Sm. To 45cm. St. erect, branched, radical lvs short-pubesc., lyrate, 5–7-foliolate; term. leaflet reniform, 8cm. Fls erect, in 2–4-fld cymes; pet. to 18mm, red, rounded, cupped to spreading. Summer–autumn. Balk. 'Coppertone': to 25cm, clump-forming; lvs fresh green; fls wide open, translucent apricot, abundant, on short st., early-flowering. 'Fuermeer': to 40cm; fls vibrant red tinted orange, flowering twice a year. 'Prince of Orange': fls brilliant orange. 'Red Wings': to 70cm; fls large, semi-double, scarlet, abundant, on tall, well branched st., early-flowering. 'Werner Arends': fls semi-double, orange tinted red, profuse. Z5.

G. coccineum hort. non Sibth. & Sm. = *G. chiloense*.

G. dryadioides (Sieb. & Zucc.) Franch. & Savat. = *G. pentapetalum*.

G. elatum Wallich ex G. Don. To 30cm. Radical lvs to 30cm, 21–31-foliolate; lfts to 2.5×2cm, broad-elliptic, acute or obtuse, crenate-dentate, ciliate or sparse-pubesc. Infl. 1–3-fld; cal. tube maroon, pubesc.; pet. to 1.5cm, yellow, suborbicular or obovate. Himal.

G. ×heldreichii hort. ex Bergmans. (*G. coccineum ×G. montanum.*) To 30cm. Fls large, orange-red. Summer–autumn. Gdn origin. 'Georgenberg': to 25cm, hummock-forming; lvs bright green, rounded, pubesc.; fls single, pale-golden orange, early-flowering. 'Magnificum': fls 40mm wide, semi-double orange. 'Sisiswang': fls brilliant orange flushed red. 'Uferschmuck' ('Bank Jewel'): fls orange-red. The last two both possibly showing influence of *G. rivulare*. Z5.

G. heterocarpum Boiss. To 50cm. St. branched, soft-pubesc. Radical lvs lyrate; term. leaflet cordate, 6cm, lobed. Fls 1cm diam., campanulate, in 5–10-fld infl.; pet. pale yellow, elliptic or obovate. Spring–summer. E & S Spain, SE Fr., C It., Albania. Z7.

G. hybridum hort. A name applied to the many hybrid progeny of *G. chiloense*, *G. coccineum* and others; floriferous, orange to red-fld plants with silvery-pubesc. foliage.

G. ×intermedium Ehrh. (*G. urbanum ×G. rivale.*) Nat. hybrid intermediate betwen parents. Z3.

G. iyoanum Koidz. = *G. japonicum*.

G. ×jankae G. Beck. (*G. coccineum ×G. rivale.*) Nat. hybrid intermediate between parents. Mts. Z4.

G. japonicum Thunb. Rhiz. short; st. simple or somewhat branched, velvety. Lvs puberulent, occas. sparsely long-pilose, radical lvs 3–5-foliolate; lat. lfts small, sometimes obsolete, often with accessory lfts, term. leaflet to 6×6cm, orbicular to broad-ovate, rounded to obtuse, subcordate at base, dentate, usually 3-lobed. Fls 1.5cm diam., long-stalked, yellow, few, loosely arranged. Summer–autumn. China, Jap. Z7.

G. kolbianum Obrist. & Stein ex Stein = *G. ×rhaeticum*.

G. leiospermum Petrie. To 20cm. Radical lvs to 5cm, pinnate, pubesc., 11–21-foliolate; lateral lfts small, incised, term. leaflet to 2cm, broad-ovate to suborbicular, serrate-dentate. St. simple to few-branched, erect, pubesc.; fls few, to 1cm diam.; pet. white, 5–6, suborbicular. NZ. Z7.

G. macrophyllum Willd. YELLOW AVENS. To 1m, erect, pubesc., radical lvs lyrate, long-petiolate; stipules lanceolate, incised; lat. lfts small, term. leaflet large, 3–5-lobed, cordate-reniform. Fls

yellow, 1.6cm diam., in 4–9-fld cymes. E Asia, N Amer. Z4.

G. magellanicum Lechl. ex Scheutz = *G. parviflorum*.

G. molle Vis. & Pančić. St. to 40cm, erect, dense soft-pubesc. radical lvs pinnate, 5–7-foliolate; term. leaflet to 6cm, orbicular, subcordate, crenate. Fls erect, in 3–5-fld infl.; pet. to 1.2cm, pale yellow, elliptic, patent. Balk., C & S It. Z6.

G. montanum L. ALPINE AVENS. Rhiz. thick, creeping. Radical lvs lyrate; term. leaflet 6cm. St. to 30cm; fls to 4cm diam., golden-yellow, in 1–3-fld infl. Spring. C & S Eur. Z6.

G. parviflorum Sm. To 30cm. Rhiz. stout, woody, basal lvs to 5×6cm, orbicular to oblong-cordate, bicrenate, pilose, veins impressed, lat. lfts to 1.5cm, few or to 15 pairs, uppermost longest, serrate-crenate. Flowering st. stout, villous; fls 1cm diam., in small cymes; pet. white, ovate to obovate, claw sometimes ciliate. Chile, Arg., NZ. Z9.

G. peckii Pursh. To 40cm. St. glab. Radical lvs lyrate-pinnatifid, ciliate; terminal leaflet to 13cm diam., round-reniform, truncate at base or with a v. shallow-rounded sinus, lobed and biserrate, lat. lfts few, to 1cm. Fls 1–5, ascending; pet. to 1.5cm, yellow or orange, broad-obovate to suborbicular. N Amer. Z4.

G. pentapetalum (L.) Mak. Everg. subshrub. Br. prostrate. Lvs to 6cm, 7–9-foliolate; lfts to 1.5cm, broad-oblanceolate to obovate, acute, incised, occas. obscurely trilobed, tough, lustrous. Flowering st. to 20cm, erect, subtended by a 3–5-lobed lf; fls to 3cm diam., solitary; pet. white, orbicular. Summer. Kamchatka, Jap. Z8.

G. pyrenaicum Mill. Rhiz. short, thick; st. erect, radical lvs lyrate, 9–13-foliolate; lateral lfts unequal, term. leaflet 10cm, rounded, crenate, lobed. Fls large, erect, in 1–5-fld infl.; pet. to 1.5cm, bright yellow, rounded, patent. Pyren. Z6.

G. reptans L. CREEPING AVENS. Rhiz. thick, terminating in a stoloniferous lf rosette. Radical lvs pinnate, seg. deeply incised. Flowering st. to 10cm; fls to 4cm diam., bright yellow, usually solitary. Alps, Carpath., Balk. Z6.

G. ×rhaeticum Brügger. (*G. montanum ×G. reptans.*) To 20cm. St. numerous, radical lvs to 13cm, interruptedly pinnate; terminal leaflet large, cordate, lobed, lat. lfts ovate, entire or 3-dentate. Fls 2.5cm diam., golden-yellow. Summer. It. Z6.

G. rhodopeum Stoj. & Stef. To 45cm. Radical lvs 7–13-foliolate; term. leaflet to 8cm, reniform. Infl. 2–4-fld; erect; fls to 4cm diam., yellow. Balk. Z6.

G. rivale L. WATER AVENS; INDIAN CHOCOLATE; PURPLE AVENS; CHOCOLATE ROOT. Rhiz. short, thick; st. branched. Radical lvs to 35cm, pinnate, 7–13-foliolate; lat. lfts unequal, term. leaflet to 5cm, rounded, incised or lobed. Fls campanulate, nodding, in 2–5-fld cymes; cal. dark brown-purple; pet. to 1.5cm, cream to pink to pale orange streaked red, erect, long-clawed, emarginate. Spring–summer. Eur. 'Album': fls nodding, pale off-white, cal. light green. 'Leonardii' ('Leonard's Variety', 'Leonard's'): stalks tinged mahogany; fls faintly bell-shaped, nodding, copper-pink tinted orange. 'Leonardii Double': as 'Leonardii', but fls double. 'Lionel Cox': to 30cm, clump-forming; lvs soft green; fls nodding, cal. brown, pet. undulate, primrose tinted apricot. Z3.

G. rivale var. *leonardii* Bergm. = *G. rivale* 'Leonardii'.

G. rossii (R. Br.) Sev. Perenn. herb to 25cm. Radical lvs pinnate, glab., to 17-foliolate; lfts 3-lobed, cuneate, incised-dentate, ciliate. Fls 4cm diam., usually solitary; pet. yellow, orbicular, spreading. Summer. Alask., Yukon, Asia. Z2.

G. sikkimense Prain. Radical lvs to 15cm, 11–21-foliolate; term. leaflet to 5×5cm, broad-ovate or suborbicular, rounded, deeply cordate at base, crenate or shallow-lobed, lat. lfts to 1×1cm, broad-elliptic. Flowering st. to 50cm, 1–2-fld; cal. tube yellow, lobes green or brown, pubesc.; pet. to 1cm, white or pink, obovate. Summer. Bhutan, Sikkim. Z8.

G. sylvaticum Pourr. To 40cm. Rhiz. usually short and thick. Radical lvs lyrate, 3–5-foliolate; term. leaflet to 5cm, ovate, lobed. Fls 2cm diam., erect, in 1–3-fld infl.; pet. yellow, suborbicular, patent. SW Eur. Z7.

G. ×tirolense Kern. (*G. montanum ×G. rivale.*) St. erect or ascending, usually branched. Radical lvs interruptedly pinnate; term. leaflet v. large, round or cordate-reniform, lateral lfts much smaller, ovate. Fls yellow, nodding or somewhat erect. Summer. Carpath., Bosnia. Z6.

G. triflorum Pursh. PURPLE AVENS; LION'S-BEARD; OLD MAN'S WHISKERS; GRANDFATHER'S-BEARD; PRAIRIE SMOKE. Lvs to 15cm, oblong to obovate, to 30-foliolate; lfts unequal, linear or oblong, puberulent, hirsute or pilose, grey. Flowering st. to 40cm; fls in 1–9-fld cymes; cal. maroon to pink or almost yellow, turbinate to cup-shaped; pet. to 0.5cm, light yellow to maroon-tinged, erect to convergent, elliptic or elliptic-obovate. Achenes with styles to 5cm, purple, straight or tortuous, strongly plumose. Summer. N Amer. Z1. var. *ciliatum* (Pursh) Fassett. St. soft-pubesc. and fine-glandular, radical lvs to 20cm, 9–19-foliolate; lfts obovate, cleft into linear or cuneate, dentate seg. Fls in 1–3-fld cymes; cal. lobes to 1cm, maroon; pet. to 1cm, yellow or purple-tinged. Spring–summer. Calif. var. *campanulatum* (Greene) C.L. Hitchc. is also grown. Z7.

G.turbinatum Rydb. Close to *G. rossii*. Lvs with 11–33 seg. oblanceolate to obovate, 3–5 dentate. Fls to 1.2cm diam., yellow. Rocky Mts. Z2.

G. umbrosum Boiss. non Dumort. = *G. heterocarpum*.

G.uniflorum Buch. To 25cm. Rhiz. stout, somewhat woody, creeping, to 50cm. Radical lvs to 10cm, glab. to pilose, 3–5-foliolate; term. leaflet to 4×3cm, broadly ovate to oblong-cordate, crenate, margins densely ciliate to golden-pubesc.; lat. lfts minute, dentate or entire. Scapes to 15cm, villous; fls 2.5cm diam., solitary; pet. white, broadly ovate. NZ. Z8.

G.urbanum L. HERB BENNET; CLOVEROOT; WOOD AVENS. To 60cm. Rhiz. short, thick; st. erect, branched, pubesc. Cauline lvs large, 3–5-lobed, radical lvs to 35cm, 3–11-foliolate; lat. lfts unequal, term. leaflet to 10cm, rounded, deeply lobed. Fls to 1.5cm diam., long-pedicelled, erect, in 1–5-fld cymes; pet. pale yellow, obovate or oblong, outspread. Achenes to 6mm, 70, forming a globose head, pubesc. Eur. Z6.

G. versipatella Marq. = *G. sikkimense*.

G. vidalii Franch. & Savat. = *G. aleppicum*.

G.virginianum L. VIRGINIA AVENS. To 90cm. Radical lvs and lower cauline lvs usually pinnatifid to pinnate, seg. oval-lanceolate. Fls 0.6cm diam., pale or green-yellow. Summer. US (Virg.). Z6.

G.cvs. 'Ewenii': to 60cm; fls semi-double, orange and terracotta; spring–autumn. 'Lemon Drops': to 38cm; lvs rich green; fls in drooping heads, single, green tinted yellow, cal. green and red; sta. orange; chance seedling. 'Rijnstroom': fls orange flushed brass. 'Starker's Magnificum': to 40cm; fls double, apricot blushing orange. 'Tangerine': habit dwarf, tufted, to 12cm; fls deep orange.

→*Dryas, Erythrocoma* and *Sieversia*.

Gevuina Molina. CHILE NUT; CHILEAN HAZELNUT. Proteaceae. 1 everg. shrub or tree to 12m. Br. rusty-tomentose at first. Lvs pinnate or bipinnate, 20–42cm; lfts 3–30, to 16×7cm, ovate-elliptic, acute, glab., coriaceous, coarsely toothed. Rac. to 12cm, axill., narrow-cylindric; perianth tubular, to 2.5cm, ivory to pale buff, lobes splitting, narrow-lanceolate, recurved. Fr. drupaceous, red ripening black. Summer. Chile. Z9.

G. avellana Molina.

Gherkin *Cucumis anguria*.
Ghost Bramble *Rubus thibetanus*.
Ghost Gum *Eucalyptus papuana; E. pauciflora*.
Ghost Plant *Graptopetalum paraguayense*.
Ghost Tree *Davidia*.
Ghost Weed *Euphorbia marginata*.
Giant Bellflower *Ostrowskia magnifica*.
Giant Bracken *Pteris tripartita*.
Giant Burmese Honeysuckle *Lonicera hildebrandtiana*.
Giant Buttercup *Laccopetalum giganteum*.
Giant Chain Fern *Woodwardia fimbriata*.
Giant Chincherinchee *Ornithogalum saundersiae*.
Giant Cowslip *Primula florindae*.
Giant Crown of Thorns *Euphorbia* × *lomii*.
Giant Dogwood *Cornus controversa*.
Giant Elephant's Ear *Alocasia macrorrhiza*.
Giant Fennel *Ferula (F. communis)*.
Giant Fern *Angiopteris*.
Giant Fescue *Festuca gigantea*.
Giant Finger Grass *Chloris berroi*.
Giant Fir *Abies grandis*.
Giant Garlic *Allium scorodoprasum*.
Giant Granadilla *Passiflora quadrangularis*.
Giant Groundsel *Ligularia wilsoniana*.
Giant Hake's Foot *Davallia solida*.
Giant Hogweed *Heracleum mantegazzianum*.
Giant Hollyfern *Polystichum munitum*.
Giant Honeysuckle *Lonicera hildebrandtiana*.
Giant Hyssop *Agastache*.
Giant Knotweed *Polygonum sachalinense*.
Giant Larkspur *Consolida ambigua*.
Giant Leather Fern *Acrostichum danaeifolium*.
Giant Lemon *Citrus ponderosa*.
Giant Lily *Cardiocrinum giganteum*.
Giant Maidenhair *Adiantum formosum; A. trapeziforme*.
Giant Mallow *Hibiscus*.
Giant Orchid *Barlia robertiana*.
Giant Pineapple Flower *Eucomis pallidiflora; E. pole-evansii*.
Giant Pineapple Lily *Eucomis pallidiflora; E. pole-evansii*.
Giant Potato Creeper *Solanum wendlandii*.
Giant Redwood *Sequoiadendron giganteum*.
Giant Reed *Arundinaria gigantea; Arundo*.
Giant Rhubarb *Gunnera manicata*.

Giant Scabious *Cephalaria gigantea*
Giant Scrambling Fern *Diplopterygium longissimum*.
Giant Sequoia *Sequoiadendron*.
Giant Spaniard *Aciphylla scott-thomsonii*.
Giant Stapelia *Stapelia gigantea*.
Giant Stock Bean *Canavalia ensiformis*.
Giant Sundew *Drosera regia*.
Giant Sunflower *Helianthus giganteus*.
Giant Taro *Alocasia macrorrhiza*.
Giant Timber Bamboo *Phyllostachys bambusoides*.
Giant Velvet Rose *Aeonium canariense*.
Giant Water Lily *Victoria*.
Giant Wild Rye *Leymus condensatus*.

Gibasis Raf. Commelinaceae. 11 ann. or perenn. herbs, often tuberous. Cincinni individually stalked, in pairs or umbels, bracts usually inconspicuous, fertile part of cincinni usually many-fld, with 2 rows of v. small bracteoles; fls actinomorphic; sep. and pet. 3, free; sta. 6, equal, connectives broadly triangular, versatile. Trop. Amer.

G.geniculata (Jacq.) Rohw. Decumbent villous perenn. to 60cm, freely branched, rooting at nodes. Lvs 3–11cm, ovate to oblong-elliptic, acute, base subcordate, ± sessile, green to dark maroon. Infl. often gland., cincinni paired; fls 6–7mm diam., white. Flowering sporadic over year. Martinique; Mex. to Parag. and N Arg., W Indies. Z9.

G.karwinskyana (Schult. f.) Rohw. Suberect tuberous-rooted, sparsely branched glab. perenn. Lvs to 14cm, lanceolate, acute, rounded or subcordate above sheath, subsucculent, pale glaucous green. Cincinni 4–12 in an umbel; fls *c*2cm diam., purple-pink or paler, rarely white. Summer. Mex. Z9.

G.linearis (Benth.) Rohw. Slender, usually unbranched, tuberous-rooted perenn. Lvs to 30cm, narrowly linear, channelled to the hooded tip, semi-rigid, green not glaucous. Infl. about 5–30cm, scape-like or with 1 to several lvs; cincinni typically 2-nate but often 3 to several; fls 12–20mm diam., purple-pink. Summer–autumn. W Mex. Z8.

G.oaxacana D. Hunt. Erect or decumbent, branching, glandular-villous perenn. Lvs to 9cm, ovate-lanceolate to ovate-elliptic, acuminate, petiolate or subpetiolate above the sheath, thin, green or deep purple, with viscid hairs above. Cincinni paired or 3–8 in a small umbel, fls *c*8mm diam., white. Winter. S Mex. Z9.

G.pellucida (Martens & Gal.) D. Hunt. BRIDAL VEIL. Decumbent or creeping perenn., branching and rooting at the nodes, glab. or sparsely hairy. Lvs 1–10cm, narrowly oblong-lanceolate to ovate, acute or acuminate, sessile, ± 2-ranked, thin, green, sometimes tinged purple beneath. Cincinni paired; fls 7–14mm diam., white. Winter–spring. Mex. Z9.

G.venustula (Kunth) D. Hunt. Resembles *G. linearis*. Erect or sprawling, glab. tuberous-rooted perenn. Lvs 5–30cm, linear, attenuate-acuminate, subsucculent, glaucous, flaccid. Infl. to 50cm, cincinni 2–8-nate; fls 12–25mm diam., clear blue, rarely pale pink or white. Summer. E Mex. Z9.

→*Tradescantia*.

Gibbaeum Haw. ex N.E. Br. Aizoaceae. 20 highly succulent perennials. Lvs unequal, ± united at base, forming a rounded or elongated body often emerging from persistent lf remains on woody br. Fls 6-partite, cal. lobes and pet. sometimes united into a v. short tube, stalked. S Afr. Z9.

G.album N.E. Br. Lvs rounded to chin-like, v. unequal, united to form an obliquely ovoid body 20–25mm long, 12–14mm wide, fissure later ± gaping, surface densely white-pubesc. Fls white or pink. W Cape.

G.angulipes (L. Bol.) N.E. Br. Lvs united for 7–9mm at the base and 9mm wide, 23 and 26mm long, rounded-carinate beneath, ± tapered above, blue-green, minutely velvety. Fls pink-purple. SW Cape.

G.argenteum N.E. Br. = *G. pubescens*.

G.cryptopodium (Kensit) L. Bol. Shoots with ± spherical to ovoid bodies, 16–22×10–16×9–14mm, lobes acute, ± carinate beneath, glossy pale green to flushed red. Fls 25mm diam., purple-pink to pink. W Cape.

G.dispar N.E. Br. Clump-forming. Lvs united to form an ovoid body with a v. deep fissure, free parts sometimes obtusely carinate, thick, grey-green tinged red, slightly glossy, minutely velvety. Fls mauve-red. W Cape.

G. dubium (N.E. Br.) Jacobsen = *G. heathii*.

G.fissoides (Haw.) Nel. Clump-forming; st. short, woody, rooting. Lvs flat above, carinate beneath, obtuse, ± tuberculate, grey-green to red-tinged, smooth or rugulose. Fls light red. Karroo.

G.geminum N.E. Br. V. dwarf, forming cushions. Lf pairs 2–3 on one shoot, the larger 15mm long, 6mm thick, terete with a distinct ridge over rounded tip, the smaller 4–6mm, light grey-green with minute hairs. Fls red. W Cape.

G. gibbosum (Haw.) N.E. Br. Branching, forming dense clumps 3–6cm high, 6–15cm across. Lvs v. unequal, the longer curved slightly inwards, semi-cylindric, ± flattened above, underside with 2 keels, rounded at the tip, the smaller with its upperside at first lying in the triangular part of the upperside of the larger lf, fissure small, smooth, deep green. Fls pink-purple. S Cape.

G. haagei Schwantes. ± acauline, prostrate. Lvs triquetrous, acutely carinate, somewhat carinate above, sheathed, the longer lf to 4cm, the shorter lf with the chin pulled forward, blue-green-hirsute. Fls red. SE Cape.

G. heathii (N.E. Br.) L. Bol. Mat-forming from a long rootstock. Lvs forming a ± spherical body, 2–6cm×15–20mm, often un-equal, united to midway fissure gaping, smooth, grass green to white-green. Fls white, cream to pink. W Cape.

G. helmiae L. Bol. = *G. cryptopodium*.

G. marlothii N.E. Br. = *G. gibbosum*.

G. molle N.E. Br. = *G. cryptopodium*.

G. muirii N.E. Br. = *G. gibbosum*.

G. muirii (N.E. Br.) Schwantes = *G. schwantesii*.

G. nebrownii Tisch. Stemless, clump-forming. Lf bodies 2–8 together, 12–15×8–16mm with a fissure across the entire width, lobes convex, soft, surface smooth with minute hairs, deep grey-green or green-brown, lobe tips ± translucent. Fls pink. Mid-autumn. W Cape.

G. nelii Schwantes = *G. fissoides*.

G. pachypodium (Kensit) L. Bol. Many radiating br., forming cushions, remains of old lvs persisting. Lvs shortly united at base, triquetrous to semi-cylindric, slightly carinate beneath toward the rounded or acute tip, 6–10cm×5–15mm, the smaller lf 2.5–8×4–10mm. Fls pink to pink-red. W Cape.

G. perviride (Haw.) N.E. Br. = *G. gibbosum*.

G. perviride var. *luteoviride* (Haw.) N.E. Br. = *G. luteoviride*.

G. petrense (N.E. Br.) Tisch. Mat- or clump-forming, v. dwarf. Lvs 1–2 pairs per shoot, united for one-third of their length, lower surface round at first, free part acutely carinate, 6–10×0.4–0.5cm, smooth, firm, white-green to grey-green. Fls pink-red. SW Cape.

G. pilosulum (N.E. Br.) N.E. Br. Mat-forming. Bodies obovoid, 25×16–18mm, fissure 10–11mm in a notch 3–4mm deep, slightly glossy, light green with fine, lax, white hairs. Fls mauve-red. W Cape.

G. pubescens (Haw.) N.E. Br. Br. short, woody. Lf pairs 2–3 per br., longer lf 3cm long, to 15mm thick, cylindric, laterally compressed and abruptly carinate above with hook-like tip, the shorter only one-third as long, obtuse, white-grey with minute, felty, white hairs. Fls violet-red. W Cape. ssp. *shandii* (N.E. Br.) H.F. Glen. Body surface yellow-green or grey-felty. Fls tinged red.

G. schwantesii Tisch. Similar to *G. velutinum*, lvs longer, less obliquely keeled, the larger lf 5–6×2–3cm, triangular-acute above, underside deeply carinate, smaller lf 3–5×0.6–0.8cm, lf pair closed together at first, velvety, dark green to green-brown or grey. Fls white. SW Cape.

G. shandii (N.E. Br.) N.E. Br. = *G. pubescens* ssp. *shandii*.

G. velutinum (L. Bol.) Schwantes. Mat-forming. Lvs basally united, broadly divaricate, resting on the soil, longer lf 5–6cm long, 2.5–3cm across below, hooked, carinate, shorter lf 4cm, triquetrous, acute, keel pulled forward over the side, light grey to grey-green, pale velvety. Fls pink. W Cape.

→*Conophytum, Derenbergia, Imitaria, Mentocalyx,* and *Rimaria*.

Gidgee Myall *Acacia omalophylla*.
Giles Net-bush *Calothamnus gilesii*.

Gilia Ruiz. & Pav. Polemoniaceae. 25 ann. or perenn. herbs. Lvs usually pinnately lobed, basal or reduced on erect slender flowering st. Fls hypocrateriform to tubular-funnelform. SW US, S S Amer. Z8.

G. achilleifolia Benth. Ann. to 70cm, often glandular-pubesc. above. Lvs 4–10cm, mostly bipinnate. Infl. a dense, fan-shaped cluster of cymes; cor. 1–2cm, blue-violet, lobes oval. Summer. S Calif., Baja Calif. Z8. ssp. *multicaulis* (Benth.) V. & A.D. Grant. Infl. laxly cymose; fls in groups of 2–7; cor. 5–10mm.

G. aggregata Spreng. = *Ipomopsis aggregata*.

G. aggregata ssp. *attenuata* A. Gray = *Ipomopsis aggregata* ssp. *attenuata*.

G. androsacea Steud. = *Linanthus androsaceus*.

G. aurea Nutt. = *Linanthus aureus*.

G. californica Benth. = *Leptodactylon californicum*.

G. capitata Sims. Ann., 20–80cm, glab. to gland. or floccose. Lvs 4–10cm, bipinnate. Infl. a term. head 1.4–4cm diam., 25–100-fld, usually glab., never gland.; cor. 6–8mm, lobes linear, pale violet-blue. Summer. BC to Calif. Z8.

G. caruifolia Abrams. Glab. ann., 30–60(–120)cm, with scapose st. Lvs 3–7(–30)cm, bi- or tripinnate, seg. deeply cut. Infl. cymose, glandular-hairy towards apex; fls in pairs; cor. 1.5–2cm diam., pale blue-violet, tube v. pale inside with yellow spots, lobes often with pairs of purple spots at base. Summer. S Calif., Baja Calif. Z8.

G. cephaloidea Rydb. = *Ipomopsis spicata*.

G. coronopifolia Pers. = *Ipomopsis rubra*.

G. densiflora (Benth.) Benth. = *Linanthus grandiflorus*.

G. densifolia (Benth.) Benth. = *Eriastrum densifolium*.

G. dianthoides Endl. = *Linanthus dianthiflorus*.

G. dichotoma Benth. = *Linanthus dichotomus*.

G. globularis Brandg. = *Ipomopsis spicata* ssp. *capitata*.

G. grandiflora Steud. = *Linanthus grandiflorus*.

G. incisa Benth. Glandular-pubesc. ann. to perenn. to 50cm. Lvs to 6cm, long-petiolate, subentire to deeply toothed or lobed, often pinnate at base. Infl. a lax pan. or fls solitary; cor. lavender to pale blue or white, to 1cm diam. Spring. SW Tex., New Mex., N Mex. Z8.

G. latiflora (A. Gray) A. Gray Ann., 10–30cm, glab. at base, glandular-pubesc. towards apex; st. 1 to many. Lvs 2–7cm, ligulate, pinnately lobed to sinuately toothed, slightly cobwebby. Infl. a lax, subcymose pan.; cor. 1.5–2.2cm, tube slender, purple, limb dilated, lobes pale violet at apex, white at base. Summer. S Calif. Z8.

G. latifolia S. Wats. Ann. 10–30cm, glandular-hairy. Lvs 2–8cm, rounded to oval, laciniate with mucronate teeth or coarsely serrate. Infl. a corymb-like pan., many-fld; cor. 6–11mm, narrowly funnelform, bright cerise inside, buff outside. Spring. S Calif. to Utah. Z8.

G. leptomeria A. Gray. Ann. herb, 5–20cm, glandular-hairy; st. 1 to many. Lvs 2–5cm, broadly ligulate, in a dense basal rosette, pinnatifid to coarsely paniculate. Infl. corymbose-paniculate; cor. 4.7–6.5mm, tubular, white to pale pink, lobes often tridentate, streaked purple in centre. Late spring–early summer. Calif. to Wyom. and Ariz. Z7.

G. liniflora Benth. = *Linanthus liniflorus*.

G. longiflora (Torr.) G. Don = *Ipomopsis longiflora*.

G. lutea Steud. = *Linanthus androsaceus* ssp. *luteus*.

G. micrantha Steud. = *Linanthus androsaceus* ssp. *micranthus*.

G. nuttallii A. Gray = *Linanthus nuttallii*.

G. punctata (Cov.) Munz = *Langloisia punctata*.

G. pungens (Torr.) Benth. non Douglas = *Leptodactylon pungens*.

G. pungens Douglas non (Torr.) Benth. = *Navarretia squarrosa*.

G. rubra (L.) A.A. Heller = *Ipomopsis rubra*.

G. spicata Nutt. = *Ipomopsis spicata*.

G. tricolor Benth. BIRDS EYES. Ann., 10–40cm, glab. to floccose at base, glandular-hairy above, divaricately branched. Lvs 1–4cm, lobed or bipinnate, seg. narrow. Infl. a 2–5-fld glomerule or fls 1.1–1.6cm, pale to dark violet-blue, tube orange to yellow, with 2 purple spots in throat at base of each lobe. Late spring–early summer. Calif. Z7.

G. valdiviensis Griseb. Ann., glandular-hairy, esp. towards infl. Lvs bipinnatisect to pinnatisect, seg. linear or lanceolate, acute. Infl. a 2–3-fld cyme; cor. c1–1.6cm, blue, throat paler, lobes oblong, acuminate. Spring. Chile. Z7.

Gilibertia Ruiz & Pav. non J.F. Gmel.

G. arborea (L.) Marchal = *Dendropanax arboreus*.

G. chevalieri R. Vig. = *Dendropanax dentiger*.

G. dentigera Harms. ex Diels = *Dendropanax dentiger*.

G. japonica (Jungh.) Harms = *Dendropanax trifidus*.

Gillenia Moench. Rosaceae. 2 rhizomatous perenn. herbs; st. to 1.2m, erect to arching, branching. Lvs subsessile, trifoliolate, stipulate; lfts incised-serrate. Fls in loose pan.; cal. persistent, narrow, teeth 5, margins gland., overlapping; pet. 5, oblanceolate to linear-lanceolate; sta. 10–20, fil. short, anth. large. E, C & SE N Amer.

G. stipulata (Muhlenb. ex Willd.) Baill. AMERICAN IPECACUANHA. Stipules to 2.5cm, ovate to orbicular, incised; lfts to 8cm, lanceolate, acuminate, deeply biserrate. Pet. to 1.5cm, white or pink. Spring–summer. SE US. Z5.

G. trifoliata (L.) Moench. BOWMAN'S ROOT; INDIAN PHYSIC. Stipules to 0.8cm, subulate, usually entire; lfts to 7cm, ovate-oblong, serrate. Pet. to 1.2cm, white, sometimes tinged purple. Spring–summer. NE US, Canada. Z4.

→*Spiraea*.

Gilliesia Lindl. Liliaceae (Alliaceae). 4 bulbous, perenn. herbs. Lvs few, basal, linear. Fls in terminal scapose umbels; perianth seg. 6, 2 sometimes united, green; fil. united into a tube split on one side, fertile anth. 3. Chile.

G. graminea Lindl. Lvs 30cm, channelled. Scape weak,

decumbent; fls small, drooping, in a few-fld, spreading umbel; spathe 2-valved, erect, persistent. Chile.

Gill-over-the-ground *Glechoma hederacea.*
Gillyflower *Matthiola.*
Gimlet Gum *Eucalyptus salubris.*
Ginger *Zingiber.*
Gingerbread Palm *Hyphaene thebaica.*
Ginger Lily *Alpinia*; *Hedychium.*
Gingermint *Mentha* × *gracilis.*
Gingham Golf Ball *Euphorbia obesa.*

Ginkgo L. Ginkgoaceae. 1 decid., dioecious tree to 40m. Bark grey, furrowed. Crown narrow, becoming wider with age; older br. arching. Lvs fan-shaped, 5–12cm across, tough, yellow-green above, paler beneath, bright yellow in autumn, apical margin irregular, often cut into 2, rarely more lobes, cuneate at base, tapering into petiole. ♂ infl. catkin-like, pendulous, yellow, to 8cm. Fr. on slender stalks, single or in pairs, ovoid to globose, to 2.5cm, light yellow decaying to purple-black, fleshy outer layer enclosing 2cm-long, ovoid, ridged nut. Spring. China. Z4.
G. biloba L. MAIDENHAIR TREE. 'Aurea': slower-growing than type; lvs yellow throughout the summer. 'Autumn Glory': habit rounded; lvs green, vivid yellow in autumn. 'Autumn Gold': broadly conic, regular, ♂; lvs gold in autumn. 'Fairmount' ('Fairmont'): strong-growing, dense, conic; br. v. close set; ♂. 'Fastigiata': narrowly conic to columnar; br. semi-erect; ♂. 'Horizontalis': v. low-growing; br. lat., almost prostate. 'Laciniata': vigorous, conic; lvs large, more deeply divided and toothed than type. 'Lakeview': conic; lvs green, yellow in autumn. 'Mayfield': habit narrowly columnar; lvs green, yellow in autumn; ♂. 'Ohazuki' ('Epiphylla'): fr. stalk adnate to lf petiole. 'Pale Alto': habit broadly spreading; lvs green, yellow in autumn. 'Pendula': small, domed; br. and branchlets almost weeping. 'Tremonia': habit narrowly columnar. 'Variegata': lvs streaked cream.

GINKGOACEAE Engl. see *Ginkgo.*

Ginseng *Panax*; *P. ginseng.*
Gippsland Palm *Livistona australis.*
Gladdon Iris *Iris foetidissima.*
Glade Fern *Athyrium pycnocarpon.*
Glade Mallow *Napaea* (*N. dioica*).

Gladiolus L. Iridaceae. 180 cormous perenn. herbs. Lvs linear or ensiform, sometimes equitant. Infl. a spike, usually simple and secund; fls zygomorphic, sometimes scented; perianth tubular or funnel-shaped, usually curved, lobes 6, subequal or unequal. 3; style 3-branched. Afr., Madag., Eur., Arabia, W Asia. Z9 unless specified.
G. abbreviatus Andrews. 30–65cm. Lvs X-shaped in cross-section. Spike 3–8-fld; fls red, dark red, brown-red or orange-red; tube 38–56mm, abruptly widening with a nectar-sac at the midpoint; topmost tep. 22–28mm, upper laterals 8–10mm, lower 3 much smaller. S Afr.
G. alatus L. 8–35cm. Lvs linear, usually scabrous. Spike 1–10-fld; fls scented, brick-red to orange, lower lobes mostly yellow or lime green; lobes clawed, uppermost 30–48mm, sometimes hooded, upper laterals 20–30mm, spreading, lower lobes spathulate, deflexed, shorter and narrower. Late winter–spring. S Afr.
G. angustus L. LONG-TUBED PAINTED LADY. 20–75cm. Lvs linear. Spike 2–10-fld; fls funnel-shaped, white, cream or pale yellow, sometimes pink-tinged, with red or purple diamond- or spade-shaped marks on lower lobes; tube 4–7cm, straight or slightly curved; uppermost lobe hooded, 25–35mm, oblong, the 3 lower lobes 18–28mm, elliptic. Spring–summer. S Afr.
G. arcuatus Klatt. To 35cm. Lvs linear, curved. Spike 2–9-fld, rachis twisted; fls scented, 2-lipped, mauve or purple, the basal half of the lower lobes yellow or lime green; tube 12–14mm, slightly curved; lobes clawed, elliptic, dors. 23–33mm, upper laterals and 3 lower lobes somewhat shorter and narrower. Late winter–early spring. Namaqualand, Nam.
G. atroviolaceus Boiss. 35–70cm. Lvs narrowly linear, grass-like. Spike densely 4–10-fld; fls deep violet-purple, almost black; tube curved. Spring–summer. Greece, Turk., Iraq, Iran. Z7.
G. aureus Bak. GOLDEN GLADIOLUS. St. 50–60cm. Fls pale to golden yellow. Winter–spring. S Afr.
G. blommesteinii L. Bol. St. 30–70cm. Lvs ± equalling st., v. narrow. Spike 1–4-fld; fls funnel-shaped, pale to deep pink, mauve or blue-mauve, the basal half of the lower lobes yellow or cream with red or purple striations; tube 14–20mm, curved; lobes elliptic, 25–35mm, dors. slightly larger than others, tip of lower lobes deflexed, upper 3 13–19mm wide, lower 3 8–12mm wide. Late winter–spring. S Afr.

G. bonae-spei Goldbl. & De Vos. 30–70cm. Basal lf linear, pub-esc. Spike 2–6-fld; fls gold, orange-red or red; tube 28–47mm, with a small nectar-sac where tube widens abruptly; tep. obovate, apiculate, the topmost 18–25mm, the other slightly smaller. S Afr. var. *aureus* Lewis. Fls golden-yellow or orange-yellow, sometimes tinged with red. Spring. var. *merianellus* (Devos) Goldbl. & De Vos. Fls red or orange-red.
G. brevifolius Jacq. 15–65cm. Basal lf linear, spirally twisted; st. lvs 1–3, sheathing. Spike 3–20-fld; fls sometimes scented, 2-lipped, pale to deep pink or mauve, rarely white, dull yellow or brown, green-brown or grey-blue and yellow, lower lobes usually with yellow and pink, red or mauve marks; tube 10–15mm, funnel-shaped, curved; dors. lobe hooded, 20–30mm, obovate, upper lat. lobes slightly shorter and narrower, lower 3 lobes somewhat recurved, sometimes clawed, 15–25mm, joined at base. Autumn. S Afr. var. *brevifolius.* St. less than 60cm. Spike 3–10-fld; fls not or v. slightly scented, over 3cm long, pink, mauve or white. var. *minor* Lewis. St. usually less than 30cm. Fls scented, less than 3cm, pink, mauve, occas. white. var. *obscurus* Lewis. To 75cm. Fls small, dull yellow-grey or brown, green-brown or grey-blue and yellow. var. *robustus* Lewis. St. usually over 60cm; spike 12–20-fld. Fls pink, mauve-pink, or white.
G. brevitubus Lewis. 15–50cm. Lvs narrowly linear. Spike 2–6-fld; fls small, scented, almost regular, pale to deep salmon-pink, orange or brick red, sometimes yellow in centre, or with a yellow mark on lower lobes; tube funnel-shaped, 3mm; lobes spreading, 12–22mm oblong or obovate. Spring–summer. S Afr.
G. bullatus Thunb. CALEDON BLUEBELL. 35–70cm. Lvs sheathing st. with a short, free blade. Spike 1–2-fld; fls bell-shaped with lower lobes longer and projecting forwards, pale to deep mauve-blue, lower lobes with yellow transverse marks and purple spots below; tube 10–13mm, funnel-shaped, curved; 3 upper lobes, obovate to orbicular, lower lobes 30–40mm, spathulate, joined at base. Late winter–spring. S Afr.
G. byzantinus Mill. = *G. communis* ssp. *byzantinus.*
G. callianthus Marais. 70–100cm. Lvs linear, about half as long as st. Spike 2–10-fld; fls scented, white with dark red or purple marks in throat; tube 18cm, slender, slightly curved; lobes 2–3cm, subequal, spreading. Early autumn. E Trop. Afr.
G. cardinalis Curtis. WATERFALL GLADIOLUS; NEW YEAR LILY. 60–115cm. Lvs sword-shaped. Spike 5–12-fld; fls crimson or scarlet with a white or cream diamond-shaped mark bordered, mauve on lower 3 lobes, occas. on upper lat. lobes; tube 3–4cm, becoming funnel-shaped; dors. lobe hooded, others spreading, upper lobes 40–55cm, dors. wider than laterals, lower lobes 35–48mm, elliptic to oblong-spathulate, joined at base. Summer. S Afr.
G. carinatus Ait. 20–100cm. Lvs linear, grass-like. Spike laxly 2–9-fld; fls sometimes scented, funnel-shaped, bell-shaped or bilabiate, pale to deep blue or violet-mauve, pale to deep pink or pale to deep yellow, lower lobes with an irregular yellow band with purple spots; tube 12–18mm, curved; dors. lobe 25–38mm, hooded, obovate, upper laterals slightly smaller, lower lobes clawed, spathulate, 25–35mm. Winter–spring. S Afr.
G. carmineus C.H. Wright. HERMANUS CLIFF GLADIOLUS. 16–60cm. Lvs linear, grass-like, glaucous. Spike 2–6-fld; fls deep pink or carmine red with white or cream mark bordered with darker pink on lower lobes; tube 30–45mm, straight or somewhat curved; lobes 35–58mm, dors. hooded, others spreading. Later summer–autumn. S Afr.
G. carneus Delaroche. PAINTED LADY. 20–100cm. Lvs linear or sword-shaped. Spike laxly 3–12-fld, sometimes branched; fls funnel-shaped, white, cream, mauve or pink, usually with yellow, red or purple markings on lower lobes, or with dark blotches in throat; tube 2–4cm, slender, curved, widening near throat; lobes usually spreading, equalling tube, ovate, upper 3 larger than lower 3. Spring–summer. S Afr.
G. caryophyllaceus (Burm. f.) Poir. 50–75cm, rarely branched. Lvs 1–2cm wide, sparsely hairy. Spike secund or distichous, 2–8-fld; fls scented, bell-shaped or funnel-shaped, pale to deep pink or mauve, lower lobes spotted or streaked with red or pink, exterior with a darker line; tube 35–50mm, curved; lobes obovate, dors. 30–40mm, others 25–35mm, the lower 3 joined at base. Late winter–spring. S Afr.
G. citrinus Klatt. 6–25cm. Lvs sometimes hispid, rigid, semiterete. Spike 1–3-fld; fls ± regular, erect, funnel-shaped, bright yellow, purple-maroon in throat, flushed with purple on outer lobes; tube 14–20mm; lobes 20–35mm, subequal, oblong or obovate, blunt. Late winter–spring. S Afr.
G. × *colvillei* hort. (*G. tristis* × *G. cardinalis.*) A group of hybrids from which were later derived the Nanus Hybrids. Early spring. 'Albus': fls white, lowest tep. striped yellow; anth. tinged blue. 'Roseus': fls pale pink. 'Ruber': fls carmine-red. Z8.
G. communis L. 50–100cm. Lvs linear. Spike usually with 2–3 br., 10–20-fld. Fls pink, the lower lobes usually streaked or blotched

with white or red; tube somewhat curved. S Eur. ssp. *byzantinus* (Mill.) A. Hamilt. BYZANTINE GLADIOLUS. 50–100cm. Spike sometimes with 1–2 br.; fls 4–5cm long, deep purple-red with narrow, paler marks outlined in dark purple on lower lobes. Spring–summer. S Spain, Sicily. 'Albus': fls white. 'Ruber': fls vivid cerise. Z6.

G. comptonii Lewis. To 75cm. Lvs linear, minutely hispid. Spike 1–3-fld; fls funnel-shaped, bright yellow with red-brown streaks and dots in the throat; tube curved, 10–14mm; lobes lanceolate or ovate-lanceolate, reflexed, dors. lobe 36–46mm, others slightly smaller. Winter. S Afr.

G. crassifolius Bak. To 1m. Lvs equitant, linear, stiff. Spike many-fld, sometimes with a basal br.; fls narrowly bell-shaped, white, pink, mauve, purple, red or orange, lower lat. lobes with a dark mark near apex; tube 8–15cm, curved; upper lobes ± hooded, to 30mm, oblong or obovate, lower lobes about 15mm. Autumn. E S Afr., Les., Zimb., Moz., Malawi.

G. cruentus Moore. 30–90cm. Lvs 2-ranked, sword-shaped. Spike 3–10-fld, secund or distichous. Fls bell-shaped, scarlet, tube paler on outside, pale yellow flecked with red in throat, lower lobes marked white; tube 35–40mm, ± curved; lobes spreading, subequal, 30–50mm, obovate or spathulate. Summer. S Afr. Z8.

G. cunonius (L.) Gaertn. 15–50cm. Lvs distichous, spirally twisted toward apex. Spike 3–8-fld; fls crimson, the 3 lower lobes yellow; tube 15mm, topmost lobe clawed, 35–42mm, upper lat. lobes 14mm, erect, obtuse or emarginate, lower 3 lobes 4–5mm. Spring. S Afr.

G. dalenii van Geel. V. variable to 1.5m, occas. branched. Lvs equitant, linear or sword-shaped. Spike few to many-fld; fls green, yellow, orange, red, pink or purple, self-coloured or striped or mottled with another colour; tube 25mm, curved; upper lobes forming hood, dors. covering mouth of fl., 30–50mm long, ovate or obovate, lower lobes smaller, recurved, lanceolate. Summer. Trop. Africa; S Africa. 'Hookeri': v. tall, fls large, yellow; v. late.

G. debilis Ker-Gawl. PAINTED LADY. 30–65cm. Lvs linear. Spike 1–4-fld; fls trumpet-shaped, white or pale pink spotted or streaked red in throat, tube sometimes dark red; tube 10–20mm, straight, lobes spreading, upper one 15–35mm, ovate, lower 3 slightly smaller. Spring. S Afr.

G. dracocephalus Hook. f. = *G. dalenii*.

G. equitans Thunb. 15–45cm. Lvs equitant, sword-shaped or oblong. Spike 3–9-fld, rachis twisted; fls scented, orange or vermilion, basal part of lower lobes yellow or lime green, dors. lobe with 2 white papillate ridges bordered red; tube 12–16mm, curved, slender, dors. lobe 33–45mm, arched, concave, obovate, the upper laterals slightly shorter and narrower, lower lobes 30–35mm, deflexed, spathulate, joined at base. Late winter–spring. S Afr.

G. floribundus Jacq. 15–55cm, sometimes branched. Lvs linear or sword-shaped, bases mottled purple-red. Spike 2–14-fld, secund or distichous; fls variable in size and shape, white, pink, salmon or mauve with dark median line on lobes and sometimes purple marks on lower lobes and throat; tube short and curved or long and straight, lobes 20–50mm long, oblong to ovate, subequal or upper ones slightly larger. Spring. S Afr. ssp. *floribundus* Fls white, cream, pale pink or mauve; lower perianth lobes much smaller than upper. ssp. *fasciatus* (Roem. & Schult.) Oberm. Fls pink or pink and white in arching spray, spike usually with 1–2 br.; tube short, lobes crisped and undulate. ssp. *milleri* (Ker-Gawl.) Oberm. Fls cream or pale yellow, flushed pink or mauve on outside and with purple or red median line on basal half of lobes; perianth almost regular. ssp. *miniatus* (Ecklon) Oberm. Fls salmon-pink; perianth regular, tube slender, not funnel-shaped. ssp. *rudis* (Lichtenst. ex Roem. & Schult.) Oberm. Fls with purple, arrow-shaped marks on lower lat. lobes.

G. × gandavensis hort. (*G. dalenii × G. oppositiflorus*.) A group of hybrids; at first claimed to be between *G. dalenii* and *G. cardinalis*.

G. garnieri Klatt. 30–50cm, dormant in winter; lvs several, linear. Fls pale salmon pink, usually with yellow blotch on lower lobes. Summer. Madag.

G. gracilis Jacq. 20–75cm. Lvs mainly sheathing with a short, free blade, usually subterete, but sometimes flat. Spike 1–8-fld; fls usually scented, funnel-shaped or somewhat 2-lipped with the lower lip projecting, pale blue, mauve or pale pink with a band of yellow or cream dotted and streaked with purple on lower lobes; tube 14–17mm, curved; upper lobes 20–35mm, obovate, lower lobes slightly longer, spathulate. Winter–spring. S Afr.

G. grandis Thunb. = *G. liliaceus*.

G. huttonii (N.E. Br.) Goldbl. & De Vos. 25–85cm. Lf X-shaped in cross-section. Spike 2–7-fld; upper red or orange-red, lower tep. yellow, orange-yellow or red with yellow mid-line, the 3 upper 25–38mm, the topmost the largest, the 3 lower 10–22mm. Winter–early spring. S Afr.

G. illyricus Koch. 25–50cm. Lvs glaucous, sword-shaped. Spike 3–10-fld; distichous, sometimes with 1 br.; fls 4–5cm, magenta-purple; lobes 25–30mm, obovate the lower 3 with white, lanceolate marks; tube curved. Spring–summer. W Eur., N to S Engl., Medit., Asia Minor, Cauc. Z6.

G. imbricatus L. 30–80cm. Lvs sword-shaped. Spike densely 4–12-fld; sometimes with 1–3 br. Fls pale crimson to red-purple or magenta, lower lobes with a white, lanceolate mark outlined in purple; tube curved near apex; lobes overlapping, tips reflexed. Spring–summer. C & S Eur. Z6.

G. inflatus Thunb. TULBAGH BELL. 25–60cm. Lvs ± terete, apex spine-like. Spike 1–6-fld; fls usually bell-shaped, pale to deep pink, blue-mauve, grey-blue, rarely almost white, with a cream or yellow mark outlined in purple on lowest lobe, sometimes also with dark or yellow mark on lower lat. lobes; tube 9–25mm, curved; upper lobes 18–30mm, dors. largest, obovate, laterals elliptic, lower lobes 20–30mm, spathulate. Spring–summer. S Afr. ssp. *inflatus* Perianth 2–3cm, pink, not opening wide; tube short and curved or long and almost straight. ssp. *intermedius* Lewis. Perianth 2–4cm, blue to mauve or grey-mauve, opening wide; tube short and curved.

G. × insignis hort. (*G. carneus × G. cardinalis*.) A group of richly coloured, early-flowering hybrids.

G. italicus Mill. FIELD GLADIOLUS. 40–110cm. Lvs sword-shaped. Spike laxly 5–15-fld; fls 3–4cm, purple-pink to magenta, lower lobes with a pink, lanceolate blotch outlined in purple; tube slightly curved; lobes spreading, lanceolate. Spring–summer. S Eur. Z6.

G. liliaceus Houtt. LARGE BROWN AFRIKANER. 25–90cm. Lvs linear. Spike laxly 1–5-fld; fls strongly scented at night, usually dull yellow flecked with brown, pink, red or purple, occas. green-cream, sometimes with red in throat changing to deep mauve or blue; tube 4–6cm, curved; lobes spreading, recurved, 33–35mm. Late winter–summer. S Afr.

G. maculatus Sweet. 30–80cm. Basal lf filiform; st. lvs mostly sheathing. Spike laxly 1–4-fld; fls scented, narrowly bell-shaped, dull yellow, pink or brown flecked red, purple or dark brown, or pink or white, sometimes spotted in throat; tube 3–5cm, curved, slender below; lobes of similar length to tube, ovate, sometimes undulate, dors. largest, hooded. Autumn–winter. S Afr.

G. natalensis (Ecklon) Reinw. ex Hook. = *G. dalenii*.

G. nebulicola Ingram = *G. dalenii*.

G. nerineoides Lewis. 35–40cm. Basal lf 1, linear, hairy; st. lvs mainly sheathing, the lowest minutely hairy. Spike 4–7-fld; fls salmon-pink to rich orange-red; tube 30mm, straight or slightly curved; lobes equal, somewhat recurved, 18–20mm, oblong. Summer–autumn. S Afr.

G. ochroleucus Bak. 45–100cm, sometimes with 1 br. Lvs distichous, sword-shaped. Fls white, cream, yellow, pink or mauve, often veined with a darker colour; tube 15–35mm, curved, becoming funnel-shaped; lobes spreading, of similar length to tube but outer lobes slightly longer, oblong, ovate or lanceolate. Autumn. S Afr. var. *ochroleucus*. Fls 4–5cm, white, cream, yellow or pink. var. *macowanii* (Bak.) Oberm. Fls 7–9cm long, pale to deep pink with darker throat; lobes lanceolate.

G. odoratus L. Bol. 30–80cm. Basal lf sword-shaped; st. lvs sheathing for most of their length. Spike 3–13-fld; fls scented, dull yellow or yellow-brown, spotted and striped with purple or red; tube 20–25mm, curved, funnel-shaped; lobes 20–30mm, slightly crisped, dors. lobe hooded, obovate. Autumn–winter. S Afr.

G. oppositiflorus Herb. To 1.5m. Lvs forming a fan, linear, minutely pubesc. Spike 10–35-fld, secund or distichous, sometimes branched. Fls funnel-shaped, somewhat 2-lipped, white or pale to deep pink, with dark blotches in throat and dark median line on each lobe; tube spreading, c5cm, equalling curved tube, ovate-lanceolate, acute or acuminate. Summer–autumn. S Afr.

G. orchidiflorus Andrews. Lvs distichous, grass-like. Spike sometimes branched, 5–15-fld; fls scented, 2-lipped, green, yellow-green or cream, usually tinged and blotched with purple, lobes with purple median line; tube slender, curved dors. lobe 20–35mm long, arched, almost linear, the others somewhat spathulate, spreading or recurved. Winter–spring. S Afr.

G. ornatus Klatt. PINK BELL. 30–60cm. Lvs linear or subterete. Spike laxly 1–4-fld; fls funnel-shaped or bell-shaped, pale to deep pink, the lower lobes with yellow, spar-shaped marks outlined in red; tube 15–20mm, curved; lobes 25–35mm, upper 3, elliptic, lower 3 spathulate. Winter–spring. S Afr.

G. palustris Gaud. 25–50cm. Lvs linear. Spike laxly 1–6-fld; fls magenta-purple; tube curved. Spring–summer. C Eur. Z6.

G. papilio Hook. f. 50–90cm. Lvs distichous, sword-shaped. Spike laxly 3–10-fld, secund or distichous; fls funnel-shaped or bell-shaped, yellow, usually tinged purple on outside and on lower lobes, or dull purple, lower lobes edged yellow-green; tube 15–25mm, curved; lobes 25–33mm, upper 3 obovate, dors.

largest, the lower 3 narrower, spathulate. Summer–autumn. E S Afr. Z8.

G. primulinus Bak. = *G. dalenii*.

G. priorii (N.E. Br.) Goldbl. & De Vos. 30–80cm. Basal lf narrowly linear. Spike usually 2–3-fld; fls bright red or pink-red, yellow in throat; tube 40–50mm, abruptly expanded; tep. ovate, acuminate, the 3 upper 20–35mm, the topmost largest, 3 lower 20–30mm. Winter. S Afr.

G. pritzelii Diels. 30–50cm. Lvs v. slender, usually hairy. Spike 1–3-fld; fls scented, nodding, bell-shaped, lower lobes projecting, yellow with dark yellow or brown patches on lower lobes, often tinged red or grey; tube 7–12mm, sharply curved; lobes 20–30mm, cuspidate, dors. lobe hooded, upper laterals rhomboid, lower lobes obovate or spathulate. Winter–spring. W Cape.

G. psittacinus Hook. = *G. dalenii*.

G. punctatus Schrank. 25–80cm. Lvs slender, glab. or hairy. Spike 1–8-fld; fls 4–5cm, funnel-shaped, pale to deep pink or mauve, lower 3 lobes streaked with orange, red or purple, the lower laterals usually white or yellow in basal half; tube 12–30mm, curved; lobes 20–30mm, obovate, lower 3 slightly longer and narrower than upper 3. Winter–spring. S Afr. var. *autumnalis* Lewis. Autumn flowering.

G. purpureoauratus Hook. f. = *G. papilio*.

G. quadrangularis (Burm. f.) Ait. 50–90cm. Basal lf slender, X-shaped in cross-section. Spike 3–10-fld; fls pale to bright red, occas. pink; tube with narrow basal part 13–15mm, widening abruptly to an upper part 20–30mm long, with a small nectar sac where it widens; tep. ovate, acute, 3 upper 18–30mm, topmost largest, 3 lower 9–18mm. Spring. S Afr.

G. quadrangulus (Delaroche) Barnard. 15–30cm, v. slender. Lvs linear with a long sheathing base. Spike 1–7-fld; fls scented, regular, tube yellow, lobes pale lilac, pale blue, pale mauve or almost white with small dark dots at the base; tube 7–10mm, funnel-shaped; lobes subequal, 16–20mm, oblong, obtuse. Winter–spring. S Afr.

G. recurvus L. 30–50cm. Lvs almost terete. Spike laxly 1–4-fld; fls scented, cream, pale yellow, pale grey-green or grey-mauve, lower lobes often paler, with purple streaks and spots; tube 28–33mm, curved, narrow; lobes recurved, undulate, dors. 25–30mm, obovate, concave, other lobes 20–26mm, oblong or obovate. Winter–spring. S Afr.

G. rogersii Bak. 30–65cm+. Lvs linear. Spike usually 1–5-fld, rarely branched; fls nodding, bell-shaped, pale to deep blue, mauve or purple with dark streaks and yellow marks on lower lobes; tube 9–20mm, sharply curved, funnel-shaped towards throat, dors. lobe 20–30mm, hooded, broadly obovate or almost orbicular, upper laterals slightly smaller; lower lobes narrower, spathulate. Winter–spring. S Afr.

G. saccatus (Klatt) Goldbl. & De Vos. 25–80cm. Fls bright red, v. irregular; topmost tep. 40mm long, upper laterals short and narrow, forming pouch-like spur with 3 lower tep. Winter. S Afr., Nam.

G. saundersii Hook. f. 40–90cm. Lvs distichous, sword-shaped. Spike laxly 3–12-fld; fls large, salmon-red, scarlet or vermilion, the 3 lower lobes white or cream below; tube 30–40mm, curved then funnel-shaped; upper lobes 35–70mm, elliptic, lower lobes shorter and narrower. Summer–autumn. S Afr., Les. Z8.

G. schweinfurthii (Bak.) Goldbl. & De Vos. Basal lvs lanceolate, soft-textured. Bracts large, 2.5–3.5cm, partly enclosing fls; exposed part of fl. red, enclosed part pale; topmost tep. 18–25mm, upper laterals smaller, lower 3 much reduced. Ethiop., Somalia, SW Arabia.

G. scullyi Bak. 10–70cm, sometimes branched. Lvs linear. Spike 2–10-fld, rachis twisted; fls scented, tube and basal half of lobes cream, yellow or lime green, apical halves pale to deep mauve, blue, pink, red or maroon-purple; tube erect, 11–17mm, slender then funnel-shaped; upper 3 lobes forming hood, 25–35mm, claw short, the blade ovate, lower lobes 19–32mm including claw 5–10mm long. Winter–spring. S Afr.

G. segetum Ker-Gawl. = *G. italicus*.

G. sempervirens Lewis. 40–50cm. Lvs lanceolate or sword-shaped, distichous, usually everg. Spike 4–8-fld; fls bright scarlet with white, diamond-shaped marks on lower lobes; tube 25–50mm, curved; upper lobes 50–65mm, broadly elliptic, acute, lower lobes 50–55mm, elliptic, acute. Late summer–autumn. S Afr.

G. sericeovillosus Hook. f. To 2m. Lvs forming fan, linear, sometimes hairy. Spike to 40-fld, sometimes branched; fls 2-lipped, cream, yellow, pink, mauve or maroon, sometimes speckled, with yellow or green marks outlined in a darker colour on lower lobes; tube 20mm, curved; upper lobes 25–30mm, lanceolate, dors. somewhat hooded, lower lobes slightly shorter and narrower. Summer–winter. S Afr., Swaz.

G. splendens (Sweet) Herb. 50–60cm. Lvs lanceolate. Fls bright red; topmost tep. c40mm, upper laterals smaller; low-er 3 much reduced in size. Winter–early spring. S Afr.

G. stefaniae Oberm. 40cm. Lvs linear. Spike 2–3-fld; fls ± regular, red, the lower 3 each with a white line; tube 4cm, funnel-shaped; dors. lobe 65mm, ovate-lanceolate, other lobes slightly smaller. Similar to *G. sempervirens*, but decid. and with fewer lvs and fls. Autumn. S Afr.

G. stellatus Lewis. 15–75cm. Sometimes branched. Lvs linear or subterete. Spike 3–18-fld, secund or distichous; fls scented, rather star-shaped, almost regular, white to pale blue, mauve or grey-mauve, sometimes with mauve median line; tube 4–6mm, straight; lobes subequal, 13–20mm, shortly clawed then lanceolate, acute or acuminate. Winter–spring. S Afr.

G. tenellus Jacq. 10–45cm. Lvs rigid, ± terete, glab. or minutely hairy. Spike 1–4-fld; fls suberect, scented at night, funnel-shaped, white, cream or pale to bright yellow, often tinged purple, mauve or red on outside, with purple or red lines on lower lobes, and often yellow in centre; tube 13–24mm, slightly curved; upper lobes 20–42mm, oblong or elliptic, lower lobes narrower, sometimes clawed, joined for 2–3mm at base. Winter–spring. S Afr.

G. tristis L. MARSH AFRIKANER. 40–150cm. Lvs cruciform in cross-section, often spirally twisted near apex. Spike 1–20-fld; fls scented at night, narrowly bell-shaped, white, cream or pale yellow, often tinged with green, usually flushed or dotted with mauve, red,-brown or purple, and with basal half of lower lobes yellow-green; tube 4–6cm, curved; lobes 30–33mm, dors. elliptic, others slightly narrower. S Afr. var. *tristis*. Spike 1–8-fld; fls cream or pale yellow heavily marked dark green, brown or purple. Late winter–spring. var. *aestivalis* (J. Ingram) Lewis. SUMMER MARSH AFRIKANER. To 1.5m high; spike to 20-fld, fls funnel-shaped. Summer. var. *concolor* (Salisb.) Bak. Spike 1–8-fld; fls cream or pale yellow, sometimes tinged green. Spring. Z7.

G. undulatus L. 30–100cm. Lvs linear or sword-shaped. Spike 4–9-fld, sometimes with a short br.; fls bell-shaped from a long, tapering tube; white, green-white, cream or pink, lower lobes marked deep pink or red; tube 5–7cm, straight or slightly curved; lobes shorter than tube, lanceolate or ovate, acuminate, dors. hooded, the lowest recurved. Spring–summer. S Afr.

G. varius L. Bol. To 1m. Lvs distichous, linear. Spike densely 3–14-fld; fls funnel-shaped or bell-shaped, pale to bright pink with lilac-purple mid line on lower lobes; tube 10–50mm; lobes to 40mm, lanceolate or ovate. Late summer–autumn. S Afr., Swaz. var. *varius*. Fls magenta-pink, to 7cm long; tube long, slender and curved. var. *micranthus* (Bak.) Oberm. Fls white or pink, to 4cm; tube short.

G. versicolor Andrews = *G. liliaceus*.

G. vigilans Barnard. 20–40cm. Lvs terete. Spike 1–3-fld; fls funnel-shaped, oblique, rose-pink with pale spade-shaped mark on lower lobes; tube to 40mm, slender; upper lobes to 25mm, ovate, dors. somewhat wider than laterals, lower lobes much smaller, spreading and recurved. Early summer. S Afr.

G. virescens Thunb. 10–30cm, sometimes branched. Lvs linear or terete. Spike 1–7-fld; fls sometimes scented, 2-lipped, dull yellow-green with brighter yellow patch on basal half of lower lobes, usually with upper lobes brown- or purple-veined, or white, cream, pink or mauve with darker veins; tube 10–13mm; lobes v. unequal, dors. 30–40mm, spathulate, upper laterals 19–27mm, ovate from a short claw, lower lobes 22–28mm, spathulate. Late winter–spring. S Afr.

G. watermeyeri L. Bol. 10–40cm, sometimes branched. Lvs linear or sword-shaped. Spike 1–6-fld; fls scented, 2-lipped, upper lobes cream or pale green flushed and veined with purple, lower lobes lime green, apices cream; tube 12–14mm; lobes unequal, dors. 26–35mm, ovate, arched, upper laterals 20–25mm, broadly ovate, somewhat spreading, lower lobes deflexed, 20–28mm, lowest ovate, lower laterals spathulate. Winter–spring. S Afr.

G. watsonioides Bak. Infl. several-fld; bracts large; fls bright red, slightly drooping; perianth tube 30–40mm, slender, curved; tep. subequal, 20–30mm. Kenya, Tanz. (mts).

G. watsonius Thunb. 40–100cm. Basal lf with midrib and margins thickened. Spike 2–6-fld; fls bright red or orange-red, yellow in throat; tube 40–50mm with a small nectar-sac about halfway along, where it abruptly widens, upper 3 lobes 25–35mm, topmost widest, 3 lower 20–35mm. Spring. S Afr.

G. xanthus Lewis = *G. dalenii*.

G. cvs. *Miniature Hybrids*: 50–90cm; fls to 5cm in diameter, usually frilled, closely arranged. 'Amanda Mahy': fls orange-pink, lower tep. flecked pale mauve. 'Charm': fls pink with broad yellow-green blotches. 'Hot Sauce': fls heavily frilled, light red with yellow markings. 'Nymph': fls white-pink, blotches cream, edged china rose. 'Robineau': fls bright red, edged cream on lowest tep. *Butterfly Hybrids*: to 1.2m; fls to 10cm in diameter, often conspicuously blotched on throat, densely arranged. 'Chartres': fls purple with darker blotches. 'Georgette': fls cherry red with rich yellow centre. 'Mme Butterfly': fls shell-pink with salmon and purple throat. 'Mykonos': fls salmon-yellow blotched red. *Primulinus Hybrids*: to 90cm; fls to 7.5cm in diameter, top pet. hooded, loosely arranged. 'Lady Godiva': fls white. 'Joyce': fls pale cerise with yellow throat. 'Pegasus': fls yellow; pet. tipped red. 'Red Star': fls star-shaped, vivid purple-orange with paler centre. *Large Flowered Hybrids*: habit vigorous, erect to 1.2m; fls to 18cm in diameter, somewhat triangular, borne in spikes to 50cm; extremely wide range of colours. colours. 'Applause': fls pink. 'Blue Conqueror': fls deep violet-blue with paler centres. 'Ebony Beauty': fls velvety black-red with white sta. 'Fidelio': fls purple. 'Hunting Song': fls orange-red. 'Jacksonville Gold': fls bright yellow. 'Minuet': fls clear white. 'Vesuvius': fls bright scarlet-red. 'White Friendship': fls pure white. For fuller discussion of hybrids and cvs, see *The New RHS Dictionary of Gardening*.

→*Acidanthera, Antholyza, Homoglossum* and *Petamenes*.

Gladwyn *Iris foetidissima*.
Gland Bellflower *Adenophora*.

Glandularia J.F. Gmel.
G. bipinnatifida Nutt. = *Verbena bipinnatifida*.

Glandular Labrador Tea *Ledum glandulosum*.
Glastonbury Thorn *Crataegus monogyna*.

Glaucidium Sieb. & Zucc. Paeoniaceae. 1 perenn., rhizomatous herb to 40cm, white-pubesc. when young. Lvs 2 at summit of rigid st., to 20cm, reniform to cordate-orbicular, palmately lobed, lobes 7–11, irregularly toothed, often incised; petioles to 15cm. Fls solitary, term., to 8cm across; sep. 4, petaloid, spreading, broadly ovate, mauve to pale lilac; sta. many. Summer. Jap. Z6.
G. palmatum Sieb. & Zucc. 'Leucanthemum' ('Album'): fls white.
G. paradoxum Mak. = *G. palmatum*.

Glaucium Mill. HORNED POPPY. Papaveraceae. 25 ann., bienn. or perenn. glaucous herbs. Base sometimes woody, st. erect or ascending; latex orange. Lvs in a basal rosette or sessile on st., pinnately lobed or dissected, seg. toothed. Fls in loose, broadly branched term. pan., cup-shaped; sep. 2; pet. 4. Fr. a narrow, cylindric, tapering capsule, horn-like. Summer. Eur., N Afr., C & SW Asia. Z7.
G. corniculatum (L.) Rudolph. Bienn. to 45cm. St. sparsely branched, hairy. Lvs pinnate, hoary, glaucous, seg. narrowly oblong, toothed to sinuate. Fls to 5cm diam., orange, yellow or tawny red, spotted with orange or red at base. Fr. to 20cm, slender, curved, scabrous, slightly hairy. Eur., SW Asia.
G. flavum Crantz. YELLOW HORNED POPPY. Bienn. or perenn. to 1m. St. branching, slightly hairy. Lvs deeply pinnatifid, glab., blue-green, scabrous, lobes incised or toothed. Fls to 5cm diam., golden yellow. Fr. to 30cm, linear, curving, bumpy, scabrous. Eur., N Afr., W Asia.
G. grandiflorum Boiss. & Reut. Perenn. to 50cm. St. un-branched, scabrous. Lvs pinnatisect. Fls 6–10cm diam., yellow to red, with darker basal spots. Fr. to 15cm, pilose. Turk., Iraq, W Iran.
G. leiocarpum Boiss. = *G. oxylobum*.
G. oxylobum Boiss. & Buhse. Perenn. or bienn. to 50cm. Lvs lyrate-pinnate, seg. dentate-sinuate. Fls yellow. Fr. to 15cm, glab., subtorulose, bumpy at base. Medit., SW Asia.
G. phoenicium Crantz = *G. corniculatum*.
G. squamigerum Karel. & Kir. Ann. to 45cm. St. many, un-branched, glab. Basal lvs lyrate-pinnate, seg. narrowly ovate, toothed, st. lvs sessile, few, trifid, minute. Fls to 5cm diam., yellow or orange. Fr. to 20cm, scaly, sparsely hispid. C Asia.
G. tricolor Bernh. = *G. corniculatum*.

Glaucothea Cook.
G. aculeata (Brandg.) Johnst. = *Brahea aculeata*.
G. brandegeei (C.A. Purpus) Johnst. = *Brahea brandegeei*.
G. elegans (Fenzi ex Becc.) Johnst. = *Brahea elegans*.

Glaucous Bristle Grass *Setaria glauca*.
Glaucous Maidenhair Fern *Adiantum latifolium*.
Glaucous Meadowgrass *Poa glauca*.

Glechoma L. Labiatae. 12 perenn. herbs. St. creeping, stoloniferous. Lvs petiolate, opposite, incised. Fls 2–6 in secund verticils; bracts leafy; cal. tubular to campanulate, 2-lipped, 15-veined; cor. tubular, distended toward apex, 2-lipped, upper lip erect or suberect, entire to emarginate or bifid, lower lip spreading, 3-lobed, middle lobe emarginate. Eur., nat. N Amer.
G. hederacea L. GROUND IVY; ALEHOOF; FIELD BALM; GILL-OVER-THE-GROUND; RUNAWAY ROBIN. Flowering st. ascending to

30cm, non-flowering st. rhizomatous, straggling and mat-forming, glab. to pubesc. Lvs to 3cm, ovate, apex obtuse or acute, base cordate or truncate, toothed. Verticillaster 4–6-fld; cor. to 2cm, violet to mauve or lilac, occas. white or pink, exterior downy. Summer. Eur. to Cauc., nat. N Amer. 'Rosea': to 20cm high, vigorous; fls large, pale pink, abundant. 'Variegata': lvs green with broken edges and zones of white and silver-grey.
G. urticifolia (Miq.) Mak. = *Meehania urticifolia*.
→*Nepeta*.

Gleditsia L. HONEY LOCUST. Leguminosae (Caesalpinioideae). 14 decid. trees, usually with stout, simple or branched thorns on trunks and br. Lvs bipinnate on new growth, pinnate on estab-lished wood. Fls small, green-white, in axill. rac.; cal. 3–5-lobed, short-campanulate; pet. 3–5, slightly larger than cal.; sta. 6–10, exserted. Fr. a legume, often pulpy. C & E Asia, N & S Amer., Iran, trop. Afr.
G. amorphoides (Griseb.) Taub. Thorns cylindric, simple or slightly branched. Bipinnate lvs with 4–8 pinnae, pinnate lvs 10–18-foliolate; rachis to 15cm, pubesc. when young; lfts to 3.5cm, elliptic to elliptic-oblong, glossy, glab. Rac. to 4cm. Fr. to 10×3cm, short, oblong-falcate, flat, thick. N & S Amer. Z6.
G. amorphoides hort. non (Griseb.) Traub. = *G. triacanthos*.
G. aquatica Marsh. WATER LOCUST; SWAMP LOCUST. To 18m. Thorns to 10cm, branched. Young br. with conspicuous lenticels. Lvs to 20cm, bipinnate lvs with 6–10 pinnae; pinnate lvs 12–24-foliolate; lfts to 4cm, oval-oblong, rounded or emarginate, finely crenate in apical half, subglabrous. Rac. to 15cm. Fr. 8×2cm, oblique rectangular, flat. Summer. SE US. Z6.
G. caspica Desf. CASPIAN LOCUST. To 12m. Trunk with formid-able, branched, slightly flattened thorns, to 15cm+. Lvs usually pinnate, to 25.5cm, 12–20-foliolate, glab., shining green, rachis pubesc.; lfts to 5cm, ovate to oval, rounded and minutely bristle-tipped, finely crenate. Rac. to 10cm. Fr. 20×3cm, falcate, thin. Summer. N Persia, Transcauc. Z6.
G. delavayi Franch. To 10m. Thorns to 25cm, branching, flattened at base coarse. Pinnate lvs 8–18-foliolate, bipinnate lvs with 4–6 pinnae; rachis to 25cm; lfts to 6cm, elliptic-ovate, irregularly arranged, entire to crenulate, usually emarginate, dark, glossy above, downy beneath. Rac. fascicled, to 30cm. Fr. to 60×7cm, oblong, straight to subfalcate, flat, thin. N Amer., SE China. Z8.
G. ferox Desf. To 10m. Thorns v. thick, branching, coarse. Lfts to 5cm, 16–30, oval-oblong to -lanceolate, glossy green above, paler beneath, crenate. Rac. long, densely grey-sericeous. Fr. to 11cm, curved, thin, leathery. China. Z6.
G. fontanesii Spach = *G. macracantha*.
G. hebecarpa McCoy = *G. ×texana*.
G. heterophylla Bunge. To 3m, closely resembling *G. microphylla*. Thorns simple or tripartite, thin. Pinnate lvs 20–28-foliolate, bipinnate lvs with 3–4 pinnae, each 12–20-foliolate; lfts to 3cm, oblique-oblong, obtuse, entire, grey-green and pubesc. beneath. Racs downy, usually tightly clustered. Fr. to 5cm, obliquely elliptic, thin. NE China. Z6.
G. horrida hort. non Willd. nec Mak. = *G. japonica* or *G. triacanthos*.
G. horrida Willd. non Mak. = *G. sinensis*.
G. inermis Mill. non L. = *G. aquatica*.
G. inermis L. non Mill. = *G. triacanthos* f. *inermis*.
G. japonica Miq. To 20m. Trunk and br. formidably armed with branched, slightly flattened thorns to 8cm. Lvs to 30cm, clustered; bipinnate lvs with 2–12 pinnae, pinnate lvs 14–24-foliolate; rachis glab.; lfts to 4cm, oblong to lanceolate, entire to sparsely crenate, glossy above, midrib finely pubesc. or glab. be-neath. Fr. to 30×1cm, falcate, often twisted. Jap., China, in-trod. E US and Calif. Z6.
G. macracantha Desf. To 18m. Thorns branched, cylindric, v. large. Pinnate lvs to 20-foliolate, bipinnate lvs with 2–6 pinnae; rachis to 20cm, glab. or sparsely puberulent; lfts to 8cm, oval-oblong, finely crenate, glab. except for the pubesc. midrib. Rac. downy, simple, slender, to 15cm. Fr. to 35×1cm, not twisted, slightly bowed, finely punctate. Spring. C China. Z6.
G. microphylla Gordon ex Isely. Close to *G. heterophylla*. Thorns simple or slightly branched, cylindric. Pinnate lvs 20-foliolate, bipinnate lvs with 4 pairs pinnae; rachis to 10cm; lfts to 2cm, elliptic to oblong, entire. Rac. to 8cm. Fr. to 6.5×2cm, ovate-oblong, flat. China. Z6.
G. monosperma Walter = *G. aquatica*.
G. sinensis Lam. To 12m. Thorns branched, terete, to 20cm. Lvs mostly pinnate, 8–18-foliolate, to 30cm, (some bipinnate lvs, with 2–6 pinnae): rachis glab. or sparsely puberulent; lfts to 8cm, ovate or ovate-lanceolate, obtuse, dull-yellow green above, crenulate, glab. beneath except for midrib. Rac. pendulous, downy, to 9cm. Fr. to 25×3cm, oblong, straight, flat

but thick. China, Mong., introd. US. Z5.

G. sinensis hort. non Lam. = *G. triacanthos.*

G. ×texana Sarg. (*G. triacanthos* ×*G. aquatica.*) To 36.5m. Thorns 0. Lvs to 20cm, bipinnate lvs with 6–7 pairs pinnae, pinnate lvs 12–32-foliolate; lfts to 2.5cm, oblong-ovate, rounded, shallow-dentate, lustrous dark green. Rac. glab., to 10cm, staminate fls dark orange-yellow. Fr. to 15×3cm, oblong, flat, apiculate. S & SW US. Z6.

G. triacanthos L. HONEY LOCUST. To 45m. Trunk and br. armed with stout, sharp, simple or branched, flat thorns. Lvs to 20cm, bipinnate lvs with 4–16 pairs pinnae, pinnate lvs 14–32-foliolate; lfts to 4cm, oblong-lanceolate, rounded at apex, sparsely crenulate, bright green, downy then glab., pinnately nerved. Fls on downy rac. to 7cm. Fr. to 15×4cm, flat, falcate, twisted. Summer. C & E N Amer.; introd. temp. OW. Z3. 'Bujotii' ('Pendula'): elegant, pendulous tree. Br. and branchlets v. slender; lfts narrower than in the type, often mottled white. 'Continental': vigorous, crown narrow, to 22m; br. stout, thornless; lvs large, finely cut, dark green tinted blue. 'Elegantissima': to 8m dense, shrubby habit with elegant foliage. f. *inermis* (L.) Zab. This name covers the many thornless cvs of *G. triacanthos.* 'Aurea': see 'Sunburst'. 'Emerald Cascade': habit weeping, to 5m high and wide; br. arching to weeping; lvs finely divided, deep emerald, rich yellow in autumn; a ♂ selection. 'Green Glory': habit broadly pyramidal, dense, vigorous; lvs dark green. 'Halka': habit erect, rounded, compact, to 12m tall and wide, vigorous; br. somewhat horizontal; lvs v. feathery. 'Imperial': to 10m, opencrowned, broad-globose, with a dominant central leader; br. widespreading. Lvs bright-green. 'Majestic': to 20m, growth straight, upright, oval, open crowned, symmetric; br. horizontally ordered, upper br. ascending; lvs deep-green. 'Moraine': tall tree with broad crown; middle and upper br. slightly ascending, lower ones horizontal to horizontally; v. densely leafy; ♂ selection. 'Nana': to 18m. 'Rubylace': young foliage dark-red becoming bronze-green. 'Shademaster': tall tree, erect habit, but v. broadly crowned, br. tips somewhat nodding; lvs deepgreen, foliage persists late into autumn. 'Skyline': to 15m; crown broadly conical, v. symmetric; upper br. ascending, middle and lower ones flatter to almost horizontal. Lvs dark-green, golden-yellow in autumn. 'Skymaster': habit pyramidal, uniform branching; lvs dark green, lfts large. 'Summerlace': stronggrowing; lvs light green when young, later darkening. 'Sunburst' ('Aurea'): fast-growing, to 12m; broadly conical habit; br. spreading horizontally or slightly ascending, young shoots and lvs golden-yellow in spring, usually becoming lime-green later; fr. 0; the most popular selection in cult. today. 'Trueshade': habit rounded, to 15m high, to ×15m; bark dark and shiny; lvs light green, bright gold in autumn.

G. triacanthos var. *nana* Henry = *G. triacanthos* 'Nana'.

→*Fagara.*

Gleichenia Sm. Gleicheniaceae. 10 bracken-like ferns. Rhiz. dichotomously branched, widely creeping, clad with hairs and scales. Stipes slender, erect; fronds slender, usually dichotomously branched, by arrestment of term. bud and elongation of lat. pinnae, bipinnate or more decompound, pinnules bead-like. S Afr. and Masc. to Malaysia and NZ. Z10.

G. acutifolia Hook. = *G. quadripartita.*

G. alpina R. Br. To 30cm. Pinnae narrowly linear, pinnules to 1mm, suborbicular, rusty-hairy and scaly beneath. NZ, Tasm., Samoa.

G. circinata Sw. = *G. dicarpa.*

G. dicarpa R. Br. To 50cm. Pinnae narrowly linear, pinnules to 1mm, suborbicular, somewhat revolute, densely hairy to glabrate and concave beneath. Malaysia to Australasia.

G. flabellata R. Br. = *Sticherus flabellatus.*

G. laevigata (Willd.) Hook. = *Sticherus lobatus.*

G. linearis (Burm.) Clarke = *Dicranopteris linearis.*

G. longissima Bl. = *Diplopterygium longissimum.*

G. microphylla R. Br. Freely scrambling; fronds to 3m, attractively tiered. Pinnules 30–50 per pinna, oblong-triangular, obtuse, flat to slightly concave, to 3mm, often glaucous beneath. NZ, Aus., Malaysia.

G. quadripartita (Poir.) Moore. Fronds few, once-forked, each br. dichotomously flabelliform; pinnae 10–15cm, lanceolate, pectinate-pinnatifid, falcate, acuminate, seg. narrowly linear, subfalcate, margins slightly revolute. Extreme S Amer., Tierra del Fuego.

G. rupestris R. Br. Fronds to 2m, pinnae deeply lobed, pinnules, rounded or obtusely subquadrangular, not concave, margins thickened, revolute, v. deep green above, subglaucous beneath. Aus., New Caledonia.

G. semivestita Labill. = *G. microphylla.*

GLEICHENIACEAE (R.Br.) C. Presl. *Dicranopteris, Diplopterygium, Gleichenia* and *Sticherus.*

Gliricidia Kunth. Leguminosae (Papilionoideae). 6 unarmed trees and shrubs. Lvs imparipinnate. Fls pea-like in axill. rac. S & C Amer. Z10.

G. maculata (Kunth) Steud. = *G. sepium.*

G. robinia var. *sepium* Jacq. = *G. sepium.*

G. sepium (Jacq.) Kunth ex Walp. MADRE DE CACAO; NICARAGUAN COCAO-SHADE. Decid. tree to 10m. Br. ± tortuous. Lfts to 7×3cm, 5–19, oblong-lanceolate to ovate or elliptic. Rac. dense, to 15cm; cor. to 2cm, pink and lilac to white. Trop. Amer., Carib. Lvs, bark and seeds poisonous. Z10.

→*Lonchocarpus* and *Robinia.*

Globba L. Zingiberaceae. 70 perenn. rhizomatous herbs with ann. reed-like leafy st. Lvs 2-ranked, with sheathing bases. Rac. usually pendulous, terminal, bracts showy; fls in cincinni on slender branchlets, lower fls often replaced with bulbils; pet. 3, small, subequal, posterior pet. spurred; lip fused into tube with sta., 2-lobed; lateral staminodes petaloid; fertile sta. 1, fil. long and curved. SE Asia. Z9.

G. atrosanguinea Teijsm. & Binnend. To 75cm, st. flushed purple. Lvs 20cm, elliptic-lanceolate, acuminate, glab. above, downy with yellow margin beneath. Infl. 7cm, erect; bracts bright red; fls yellow; bulbils not produced. Borneo.

G. bulbifera Roxb. = *G. marantina.*

G. japonica Thunb. = *Alpinia japonica.*

G. marantina L. To 75cm. Lvs 20cm, elliptic, hairy beneath. Infl. to 10cm, becoming pendent; bracts to 1.5cm, pale green, often bearing white bulbils; fls yellow, with lip yellow spotted orange or red at base. Autumn. SE Asia.

G. schomburgkii Hook. f. = *G. marantina.*

G. winitii C.H. Wright. To 1m. Lvs to 20cm, lanceolate, cordate at base, hairy beneath. Infl. to 15cm, pendent; bracts 3.5cm, pink to mauve or purple; fls yellow. Thail.

Globe Amaranth *Gomphrena globosa.*

Globe Artichoke *Cynara scolymus.*

Globe Daisy *Globularia.*

Globe Flower *Trollius* (*T. europaeus*).

Globe Lily *Calochortus.*

Globe Mallow *Sphaeralcea.*

Globe Spear Lily *Doryanthes excelsa.*

Globe Thistle *Echinops.*

Globe Tulip *Calochortus.*

Globularia L. GLOBE DAISY. Globulariaceae. 22 usually everg. herbs or shrublets. Lvs leathery, entire or with a few sharp teeth. Fls small, blue, in stalked cap.; cor. 2-lipped, upper lip usually 2-lobed, lower lip 3-lobed, larger; sta. and style exserted. Cape Verde Is., Canaries, Eur., Asia Minor.

G. alypum L. Dwarf shrublet. Lvs oblanceolate to obovate, mucronate or 3-dentate, with copious calcareous secretion, v. coriaceous, shortly petiolate, scattered on main st., fasciculate on short, non-flowering lat. br. Cap. 1–2.5cm diam., sometimes with sessile axill. cap. below; involucral bracts broadly ovate, obtuse or mucronate, ciliate, imbricate. Medit.

G. aphyllanthes auct. non Crantz = *G. punctata.*

G. bellidifolia hort. = *G. meridionalis* or *G. cordifolia.*

G. cordifolia L. Dwarf creeping shrublet; flowering st. 1–10cm, leafless or with 1–3 small lvs. Rosette-lvs spathulate, usually emarginate, sometimes mucronate or 3-dentate, petiolate. Cap. 1–2cm diam.; involucral bracts numerous, ovate-lanceolate to ovate, acuminate. Mts of C & S Eur., from the Carpath. to NE Spain and S Bulg. 'Alba': fl. heads white. 'Rosea': fl. heads rose-pink. Z6.

G. cordifolia ssp. *bellidifolia* Wettst. = *G. meridionalis.*

G. cordifolia ssp. *meridionalis* Podp. = *G. meridionalis.*

G. dumulosa Sw. Low bushy subshrub, to 75cm across. Lvs congested towards tips of br., nearly orbicular, abruptly narrowed below into petiole. Cap. subsessile, to 2.5cm diam.; involucral bracts aristate-acute, minutely villous. Turk. Z7.

G. elongata Hegetschw. = *G. punctata.*

G. incanescens Viv. St. 3–10cm, with slender rhiz. Lvs orbicular to lanceolate, obtuse or emarginate, often mucronate, ± erect, the lower long-petiolate, the uppermost subsessile, grey-green due to calcareous secretion. Cap. *c*1.5cm diam.; involucral bracts usually 5, linear-lanceolate, ciliate. Medit.

G. meridionalis (Podp.) O. Schwarz. Similar to *G. cordifolia* but more robust. Lvs 2–9cm, lanceolate to oblanceolate, acute or slightly emarginate. Involucral bracts ovate, almost cuspidate. SE Alps, Balk. Penins., C & S Apennines. Z5.

G. nana Lam. = *G. repens.*

G. nudicaulis L. Tufted herb; st. to 30cm. Lvs 6–12cm, ± erect, crowded at base of st., oblanceolate to obovate, obtuse. Cap.

1.5–3cm diam.; involucral bracts numerous, lanceolate to ovate, acuminate. Alps, Pyren., N Spain. Z5.

G. orientalis L. Glab. perenn. with tortuous, br. ascending from a woody base. Lvs oblong or obovate spathulate, narrowed to stalk, upper lvs narrower. Cap. 5–7 in a loose spike on fragile, sparsely leafy shoots; involucral bracts obovate, 3-nerved. N Syr. Z8.

G. punctata Lapeyr. Tufted herb; st. to 30cm. Lower lvs rosulate, obovate to spathulate, rounded or weakly emarginate; cauline lvs lanceolate to oblong, sessile. Cap. *c*1.5cm diam.; involucral bracts numerous, lanceolate, acuminate. N Fr. to N Spain, S It., NE Greece, Czech., S, C & E Russia. Z5.

G. repens Lam. Like *G. cordifolia* but smaller; lvs acute, folded; cap. usually subsessile; involucral bracts lanceolate, shortly acuminate, acuminate. SW Eur. (mts).

G. stygia Orph. ex Boiss. Dwarf shrub with slender, creeping woody st. and subterranean stolons. Rosette lvs suborbicular, obtuse, rarely emarginate, petiolate. Cap. subsessile; involucral bracts numerous, oblong-lanceolate, acuminate. Greece (N Peloponnese). 'Suendermannii': far more floriferous than the rather sparsely flowered type. Z8.

G. trichosantha Fisch. & C.A. Mey. Stolons to 30cm; st. *c*20cm. Lower lvs forming a flat rosette, obovate, obtuse to emarginate, sometimes mucronate, cauline lvs elliptical, sessile. Cap. to 2.5cm diam.; involucral bracts numerous, oblong-lanceolate, aristate. E Balk. Penins. Z6.

G. vulgaris L. To 20cm. Lvs lanceolate to elliptic, 3-dentate, margin flat; petiole usually longer than lamina. Cap. *c*2.5cm diam.; involucral bracts lanceolate, acuminate. Mts of Spain, S Fr. and Sweden. Z6.

G. wilkommii Nyman = *G. punctata*.

GLOBULARIACEAE DC. 10/250. *Globularia*.

Gloriosa L. GLORY LILY; CLIMBING LILY; CREEPING LILY. Liliaceae (Colchicaceae). 1 tuberous, perenn. herb climbing by means of tendrils at lf tips. St. to 2.5m, 1–4 per tuber, slender, twining, bright green. Lvs 5–8cm, ovate-lanceolate to oblong, acuminate, glossy bright green, soft, tendril 3–5cm. Fls solitary, axill., long-stalked, usually angled downwards; tep. 6, 4–10×2.5–3cm, oblong-lanceolate, acuminate, free, spreading, gently reflexed at tip, yellow to red or purple or bicoloured, margins often incurved, undulate or crisped; sta. 6, slender, spreading, anth. to 1cm, versatile; style 3-branched, bent at base at right angle to ovary. Summer–autumn. Trop. Afr. and Asia. Z9.

G. abyssinica Rich. = *G. superba* 'Abyssinica'.

G. carsonii Bak. = *G. superba* 'Carsonii'.

G. rothschildiana O'Brien = *G. superba* 'Rothschildiana'.

G. simplex L. = *G. superba* 'Simplex'.

G. superba L. 'Abyssinica': st. 45–60cm; tep. 5–7.5cm, red centrally banded gold, especially at base, not crisped. 'Carsonii': st. to 90cm; tep. purple-red, yellow toward centre, strongly reflexed, undulate, not crisped. 'Rothschildiana': st. to 250cm; tep. 7.5–10cm, scarlet fading to ruby or garnet, yellow at base and in central stripe, strongly recurved – the largest and finest form. 'Citrina': tep. citron yellow tinted or striped claret. 'Simplex': st. to 120cm; tep. spathulate, deep orange and yellow, not crisped. 'Grandiflora': like 'Simplex', but tep. larger, golden-yellow. 'Superba': st. to 180cm; tep. narrow, deeply undulate and crisped, reflexed, deep rich orange and red. 'Verschuurii': st. to 150cm; tep. reflexed, undulate, crimson, yellow at margins and edge.

G. verschuurii Hoog = *G. superba* 'Verschuurii'.

Glory Bower *Clerodendrum philippinum*.
Glory Bush *Tibouchina*.
Glory Fern *Adiantum tenerum*.
Glory Flower *Clerodendrum bungei*; *Eccremocarpus scaber*.
Glory Lily *Gloriosa*.
Glory of the Snow *Chionodoxa*.
Glory of the Sun *Leucocoryne ixioides*.
Glory Pea *Clianthus formosus*; *C. puniceus*.
Glory Vine *Eccremocarpus scaber*.
Glory Wattle *Acacia spectabilis*.

Glossodia R. Br. Orchidaceae. 5 terrestrial tuberous orchids. St. slender. Lf solitary, lying flat on ground, oblong to lanceolate. Infl. erect, 1- or 2- flowered; tep. subequal, spreading; lip clawed, simple, entire, bicallose at base; column winged, incurved. E Aus. Z10.

G. brunonis Endl. = *Elythranthera brunonis*.

G. major R. Br. To 38cm. Fls purple or mauve to white; tep. to 2.5cm, lanceolate, often dotted purple, glandular-pubesc.; lip to 1.2×0.5cm, ovate-lanceolate, base white, pubesc., calli large, linear, erect, purple.

G. minor R. Br. Resembles *G. major* except smaller. Fls deep blue-violet, sometimes white; tep. broadly lanceolate, obtuse; lip ovate, base deep blue-violet, calli, clavate. Aus.

Glossy Ixora *Ixora lobbii*.
Glossy-leaf Fig *Ficus microcarpa*.
Glossy-leaved Paper Plant *Fatsia japonica*.

Glottiphyllum Haw. ex N.E. Br. Aizoaceae. 50+ highly succulent perennials. St. semi-prostrate, dichotomously branching. Lvs densely arranged, ± distichous or decussate, upper surface somewhat swollen and blister-like at base, semi-cylindric to subcylindric or obliquely linguiform, paired, soft and v. fleshy, fresh glossy green or white-green, sometimes suffused purple. Fls solitary. Autumn–late winter. S Afr. Z9.

G. cultratum (Salm-Dyck) A. Berger = *G. latum* var. *cultratum*.

G. depressum (Haw.) N.E. Br. Shoots prostrate with 3–4 pairs of lvs. Lvs 10×2.5×1–1.2cm, prostrate, distichous, elongate, tip curved upwards, obliquely carinate, green. Fls 5.5cm diam., yellow. Cape.

G. fragrans (Salm-Dyck) Schwantes. Lvs 6–8×2.5×1.2cm, obliquely linguiform, convex on one side, the other surface extended into a keel, obtuse at apex. Fls 8–10cm diam., glossy golden-yellow, scented. W Cape.

G. latum (Salm-Dyck) N.E. Br. Lvs unequal, 7–9×2.5cm, linguiform, falcate and decurved, thicker and obliquely truncate at apex, dark green. Fls 5–6cm diam., golden-yellow. SW Cape. var. *cultratum* Salm-Dyck. Lvs 8×2.5cm, only slighly curved or not curved, margins acute, obtuse above.

G. linguiforme (L.) N.E. Br. Lvs distichous, 5–6×3–4cm, linguiform, curved slightly upwards above, lower angle obliquely thickened, tip bluntly rounded, fresh green, glossy. Fls 7cm diam., golden-yellow. SW Cape. Most plants in cult. under this name are hybrids.

G. longum (Haw.) N.E. Br. Lvs 7–10×2cm, ± erect, linguiform, somewhat tapered toward obtuse tip, flat on the upper side. Fls 6–8cm diam., golden-yellow. E Cape.

G. nelii Schwantes. Forming rounded clumps. Lvs distichous, ± erect, longer lf of pair 4–5×2×1.2cm with the tip rounded and hooked, smaller lf shorter and rounded at the tip, upper surface flat, lower surface obliquely carinate, light green with translucent angles. Fls 4cm diam., golden-yellow. SW Cape.

G. obliquum (Willd.) N.E. Br. = *G. latum*.

G. oligocarpum L. Bol. Br. prostrate, creeping. Lvs distichous, unequal, 4–4.5×2.2×1cm, tip obtuse or broadly rounded, white-ovate-green with prominent dots, minutely velvety. Fls 5–6cm diam., yellow. SW Cape.

G. parvifolium L. Bol. Lvs 3–4×1–2×1–1.2cm, ± erect, oblong, somewhat obliquely semi-cylindric, acute and apiculate, carinate on the lower surface toward the tip, green. Fls 8cm diam., glossy golden-yellow. W Cape.

G. pustulatum (Haw.) N.E. Br. = *G. longum*.

G. regium N.E. Br. Shoots erect, each with 2 pairs of lvs, forming clumps. Lvs ultimately divaricate, one 2.5–10cm long, 1–1.5cm wide and thick at the base, the other shorter, thinner, rounded on the lower surface, chin-like above, smooth, light green. Fls 4cm diam., yellow. SW Cape.

G. semicylindricum (Haw.) N.E. Br. Developing a short st. with age; br. stiffly projecting. Lvs 4–5×0.5–0.6×0.5–0.6cm, prostrate, slightly incurved, semicylindric, compressed-carinate at tip, margins with small teeth-like projections, fresh glossy green with faint dots. Fls 4cm diam., golden-yellow. E Cape.

→*Mesembryanthemum*.

Gloxinia *Sinningia speciosa*.

Gloxinia L'Hérit. Gesneriaceae. 8 terrestrial scaly-rhizomatous herbs or subshrubs. St. erect, mostly simple. Lvs opposite, paired. Fls axill., solitary or in pairs; sep. united at base, oblong; cor. funnelform to campanulate, limb oblique, spreading, lobes 5, unequal, obtuse; sta. 4, inserted. C & S Amer.

G. guttata (Lindl.) Mart. = *Sinningia guttata*.

G. gymnostoma Griseb. Lvs to 7.5×4.3cm, ovate, pubesc. Fls solitary; cor. to 3.4cm, rose-pink, limb spotted. Arg.

G. micrantha Martens & Gal. = *Eucodonia andrieuxii*.

G. perennis (L.) Druce. CANTERBURY BELLS. Lvs of the same pair connected by transverse ridges, to 20×15cm, ovate-cordate, serrate-crenate, green and hispid above, pale red and glab. beneath. Lower fls solitary, upper fls forming rac.; cor. to 4cm, pale purple. Colomb. to Peru.

G. 'Redbird': st. tall, grey, square; lvs ovate, dark green, glossy; fls tubular, inflated, orange-red, spotted red on yellow inside.

G. speciosa Lodd. = *Sinningia speciosa*.

→*Achimenes*.

Glyceria R. Br. SWEET GRASS; MANNA GRASS. Gramineae. 16 perenn. aquatic or marsh grasses. Rhiz. creeping; st. pithy, reed-like. Lvs with folded blades, becoming flat; sheaths tubular. Fls in open or contracted, deltoid pan. N Temp., Aus., NZ, S Amer.

G. aquatica L. = *G. maxima.*

G. maxima (Hartm.) Holmb. REED SWEET GRASS; REED MEADOW GRASS. To 2.5m. St. erect, forming large stands. Lvs with tesselated venation; blades narrowly strap-shaped, acute, 30–60×2cm, with a central keel. Pan. to 45cm, much-branched, often tinged purple. Summer. Temp. Eurasia. var. *variegata* Boom & Ruys. Lf blades striped green and cream, flushed pink on emergence. 'Pallida': lvs boldly variegated off-white. Z5.

Glycine *Solanum seaforthianum.*

Glycine L. Leguminosae (Papilionoideae). 9 erect or sprawling herbs. Lvs 3(–5–7)-foliolate. Rac. axillary; cal. 5-lobed, the upper 2 lobes somewhat united, slightly shorter than cor. Fr. oblong or linear, septate; seeds 2–4. Asia to Aus. Z8.

G. apios (L.) = *Apios americana.*

G. hispida (Moench) Maxim. = *G. max.*

G. max (L.) Merrill. SOYA BEAN; SOJA BEAN; SOYBEAN. Erect to 2m. All parts stiffly red-brown-pubesc. Lfts to 15cm, ovate-elliptic. Infl. to 8-fld+; fls white to violet or pink to 7mm. Fr. to 8cm, pendent; seeds 2–4, globose or flattened, to 11mm. Throughout genus range and widely nat. elsewhere.

G. soja Sieb. & Zucc. = *G. max.*

→*Soja.*

Glycosmis Corr. Serr. Rutaceae. 50 shrubs or small trees, un-armed, most parts initially rusty-pubesc. Lvs simple, 3-foliolate or odd-pinnate; lfts ± coriaceous, petiolulate. Infl. compound, often densely racemose; fls small, fragrant, 5-merous; cal. lobed to middle; cor. white; sta. 10, disk annular or cylindric. Fr. a berry, dry or juicy. SE Asia to NE Aus. Z10.

G. arborea Corr. Serr. Shrub or small tree to 6m. Lvs 5-foliolate, lfts elongate, obscurely dentate. Infl. cymose, paniculate or racemose; fil. v. long. Late spring–late summer. India, SE Asia.

G. citrifolia (Willd.) Lindl. = *G. parviflora.*

G. parviflora (Sims) Little. CHINESE GLYCOSMIS. Shrub or small tree to 2m. Lvs 1–3-foliolate, rarely to 5-foliolate, lfts elliptic or oblong-elliptic. Fl. 11–13mm, subglobose, translucent white or flushed pink. Throughout the year. S China to Thail.; nat. in W Indies and warm Amer.

G. pentaphylla (Retz.) Corr. JAMAICA MANDARIN ORANGE. Shrub or small tree; bark white. Lvs generally 5-foliolate; lfts elliptic, dark glossy green. Fr. globose, translucent, watery white or flushed flesh-pink or crimson, edible. Summer. India, Sri Lanka, Burm., Malaysia, Philipp.

Glycyrrhiza L. Leguminosae (Papilionoideae). 20 clammy perenn. herbs. Lvs imparipinnate or trifoliolate; stipules membranous, caducous. Fls pea-like, racemose. Summer. Eurasia, Aus., Americas.

G. echinata L. To 130cm. Lfts 5–13, lanceolate to obovate, mucronate. Infl. short, capitate; cor. to 6mm, purple. SE Eur. Z8.

G. glabra L. LICORICE; LIQUORICE; SWEETWOOD. To 1m+; deep-rooting, stoloniferous. St. and petioles pubesc., occas. rough. Lfts 9–17, oblong to elliptic-ovate, blunt, occas. mucronate. Infl. elongate, loose; cor. to 12mm, pale blue to violet. Medit. to SW Asia. Z8.

G. glandulifera Waldst. & Kit. = *G. glabra.*

G. inermis Boiss. = *G. echinata.*

G. macedonica Boiss. = *G. echinata.*

Glyptostrobus Endl. CHINESE SWAMP CYPRESS; CHINESE DECID-UOUS CYPRESS. Cupressaceae. 1 decid., coniferous tree to 25m. Found in wet or flooded places but lacking 'knees'. Bark weakly furrowed, brown-grey. Crown conic to columnar. Shoots green, turning brown. Lvs on persistent branchlets scale-like, imbricate, 3mm with 5–10mm decurrent base; lvs on decid. branchlets in 2 opposed ranks; on young plants, 15–20×2mm, flat, linear, soft, bright grass-green; on decid. shoots of older plants, 8–15mm×0.5–1mm, falcate, subulate, flat, slightly hard-er, glaucous; all becoming red-brown in autumn. Cones erect, pear-shaped, 1.5–2.5×1cm. SE China to N Vietnam. Z8.

G. heterophyllus Brongn. = *G. pensilis.*

G. lineatus (Poir.) Druce = *G. pensilis.*

G. lineatus hort. = *Taxodium ascendens* 'Nutans'.

G. pensilis (Staunton) Koch.

→*Taxodium.*

Gmelina L. Verbenaceae. 35 trees or shrubs, often scandent when young, and armed with axill. spines. Fls cymose or racemose, often arranged in a terminal pan.; cal. persistent, obconical-campanulate, truncate or 4 to 5-dentate, often with large glands; cor. tube infundibular, limb bilabiate, upper lip entire or 2-lobed, lower lip 3-lobed; sta. 4, usually included. Fr. a succulent drupe. Afr., Masc., Australasia and Indomal. Z10.

G. arborea Roxb. Decid. tree to 20m. Lvs to 25×15cm, ovate, acuminate, base cordate, entire, pubesc. beneath, with 2 to several basal glands. Pan. to 30cm; cor. to 2.5cm diam., yellow tinged brown. Fr. to 2cm, yellow. India.

G. asiatica L. Shrub to 10m, often spiny. Lvs to 10×7cm, ovate or ovate-elliptic to obovate, acute or obtuse, entire or lobed, villous beneath. Rac. term., to 6cm, slightly pendent; cor. to 5cm, yellow, exterior sparsely pubesc., interior densely glandular-pubesc. Fr. to 5cm, yellow. India, Ceylon.

G. elliptica Sm. = *G. asiatica.*

G. hystrix Schult. ex Kurz = *G. philippensis.*

G. leichthardtii (F. Muell.) Benth. WHITE BEACH; GREY TEAK. Tree to 40m, light brown-tomentose. Lvs to 18×8cm, ovate, acute or acuminate, base rounded or cuneate, entire, tomentose beneath. Cor. white marked purple, tube to 10mm, lobes to 7mm. Fr. to 2.5cm, blue. Australasia.

G. philippensis Cham. WILD SAGE. Shrub; br. pendent or sub-scandent. Lvs to 10×6cm, ovate-elliptic to obovate, acute or obtuse, with peltate scales beneath, veins pubesc. Rac. to 20cm, many-fld; bracts large, red-purple; cor. yellow, to 5.5cm, exterior pubesc. India, Philipp.

→*Vitex.*

Gnaingar *Eucalyptus phoenicea.*

Gnaphalium L. CUDWEED; EVERLASTING. Compositae. c150 ann., bienn. or perenn. herbs, lanate, often aromatic. Lvs alt., entire, often narrow and decurrent. Cap. small, discoid, usually term. in dense cymes; phyllaries imbricate, scarious; flts yellow, white or tinged with red or purple. Cosmop.

G. andicola Kuntze = *Lucilia chilensis.*

G. californicum DC. GREEN EVERLASTING. Erect bienn. to 30cm, glandular-pilose and often thinly grey-lanate, sweet-scented. Lvs to 10×2.5cm, oblanceolate to linear-oblong, green and gland., occas. sparsely grey-lanate. Cap. subglobose, in a corymbose pan.; phyllaries pearly white, stramineous or pink. Summer. Oreg. to Baja Calif. Z8.

G. decurrens A. Gray = *G. californicum.*

G. eximium L. = *Helipterum eximium.*

G. hoppeanum K. Koch. Ann. to 15cm. Lvs to 5×0.4cm, lanceolate-spathulate to linear-lanceolate. Cap. broadly ovoid, shortly pedunculate. SC Eur.

G. japonicum Thunb. Erect ann., to 40cm, adpressed-lanate. Lvs to 5×1cm, narrowly spathulate to oblanceolate, tapered to slender petiole, revolute, thick, tomentose beneath. Cap. cylindrical in a dense capitate cluster; phyllaries linear, tawny or tinged purple, hyaline. Spring–early summer. Jap., introd. to E Asia, Aus. and N Amer.

G. leontopodium L. = *Leontopodium alpinum.*

G. margaritaceum L. = *Anaphalis margaritacea.*

G. nivale Ten. = *Leontopodium alpinum* ssp. *nivale.*

G. norvegicum Gunnerus. Erect perenn. to 60cm, sparsely lanate. Lvs to 6×1.6cm, linear or narrowly oblanceolate, sub-glabrate. Cap. 10 to many, in a narrow spiciform or thyrsoid infl.; phyllaries rounded, stramineous, scarcely lanate, margins dark brown. Summer. Canada and circumpolar regions. Z2.

G. obtusifolium L. = *Pseudognaphalium obtusifolium.*

G. palustre Nutt. Erect or diffuse ann. to 30cm, loosely grey-lanate. Lvs to 5×1cm, spathulate or oblanceolate to oblong, obtuse and apiculate, narrowed to base. Cap. usually exceeded by subtending lvs; phyllaries linear, tinged green, lanate, apices shining, white tinged brown. Spring–autumn. W N Amer.

G. ramosissimum Nutt. PINK EVERLASTING. Erect bienn. to 1.5m, thinly grey-lanate to glabrate, v. fragrant. Lvs to 6.5×1cm, line-ar to lanceolate, acuminate, often revolute and waved, decurrent, glandular-pubesc. Cap. narrowly campanulate to turbinate, clustered in an elongate or pyramidal pan.; phyllaries usually pink, occas. becoming white, thinly scarious. Summer–early autumn. Calif. Z8.

G. sieboldianum Franch. & Savat. = *Leontopodium japonicum.*

G. supinum L. Dwarf perenn. to 10cm, sparsely lanate. Lvs to 2.5×0.3cm, mostly basal, tufted, linear or linear-oblanceolate. Cap. 1–8 in a terminal, spiciform or subcapitate infl.; phyllaries tan or tinged light green, dark brown on margins and apex. Summer–early autumn. E N Amer. and circumpolar regions. Z2.

G. sylvaticum L. Erect perenn. to 60cm, sparsely lanate. Lvs to 7×1cm, linear or narrowly oblanceolate, subglabrate. Cap. in a narrow spiciform or thyrsoid infl., with leafy bracts; phyllaries stramineous, sometimes tinged green toward base, often with dark brown mark above middle, apices transparent.

Summer–early autumn. E N Amer. and circumpolar regions. Z4.

G. traversii Hook. f. Caespitose perenn. to 10cm, softly white-tomentose. Lvs to 5×0.5cm, mostly basal, linear to obovate-spathulate, ascending, st. lvs bract-like, linear. Cap. solitary; phyllaries linear, outermost floccose. Summer–early autumn. Aus., NZ. Z8.

G. trinerve Forst. f. = *Anaphalis trinerve*.

G. viscosum Kunth. Erect ann., to 80cm, glandular-pubesc., becoming lanate, fragrant. Lvs to 10×1cm, numerous, linear-lanceolate, decurrent, glandular-pubesc. above, lanate or sometimes glandular-pubesc. beneath. Cap. many, in a branched, often elongate infl.; phyllaries white tinged yellow, lanate near base. Summer–early autumn. N Amer. Z4.

GNETACEAE Lindl. See *Gnetum*.

Gnetum L. Gnetaceae. 28 lianes, shrubs or trees. Lvs opposite, entire, coriaceous; veins clearly reticulate. Infl. spicate; fls small, unisexual: ♂ crowded, below ring of sterile ♀, stalked, cal. 2-lobed, sta. 1; ♀ fl. an erect ovule surrounded by 3 envelopes. Seeds ovoid, outer envelope a pulpy rind. Most in Indomal., few in Amazonia & trop. W Afr. Z10.

G. brunonianum Griff. = *G. gnemon*.

G. gnemon L. Everg. tree to 18m. Crown pyramidal. Bark grey. Branchlets divaricate, nodes pulvinate. Lvs 8–20cm, broadly elliptic to rhombic, emerging bronze, ultimately glossy dark green. Fr. 2–4cm, yellow, ripening red, tinged orange. Asia.

Gnidia L. Thymelaeaceae. 140 everg. shrubs often with upright, heath-like habit. Fls in terminal clusters or solitary in lf axils; cal. cylindrical, lobes 4 or 5, petal-like; pet. insignificant or 0. S & Trop. Afr., Madag., Arabia, India, Sri Lanka. Z9.

G. anthylloides Gilg. Shoots densely woolly at first. Lvs to 2.5cm, alt. closely set, oblong-lanceolate, sericeous. Fls in term. heads 5–8cm diam., yellow, to 4cm, slender, densely hairy. Early autumn. S Afr.

G. denudata Lindl. 1–4m, heath-like. Shoots densely hairy. Lvs 1–2cm, opposite, ovate-oblong, downy. Fls in term. clusters on short lateral shoots, pale yellow, to 2.5cm, hairy. Spring. S Afr.

G. eriocephala Meissn. To 60cm. Young br. downy. Lvs to 1.8cm, thickly set, linear, triquetrous, glab. Fls in woolly term. heads to 7.5cm diam., to 1.6cm, silky. Summer. S Afr.

G. oppositifolia L. To 4m. Shoots slender, spreading, glab. Lvs to 1.2cm, opposite, ovate to ovate-lanceolate. Fls to 1.2cm, pale yellow, hairy, in term. clusters. Summer. S Afr.

G. pinifolia L. To 70cm+. Shoots glab. Lvs 1–2cm, alt., crowded, linear. Fls 1.4cm, white, fragrant, many, in term. clusters. Spring–summer. S Afr.

G. polycephala (C.A. Mey.) Gilg. To 70cm. Br. glab. Lvs to 1.5cm, alt. Fls to 2.5cm, silky, rich yellow in term. heads of 4–8. S Afr.

Goa Bean *Psophocarpus tetragonolobus*.
Goareberry *Cucumis anguria*.
Goat Grass *Aegilops* (*A. kotschyi*).
Goat Nut *Simmondsia chinensis*.
Goat's Beard *Aruncus* (*A. dioicus*); *Tragopogon* (*T. pratensis*).
Goat's Foot *Oxalis caprina*.
Goat's Rue *Galega* (*G. officinalis*); *Tephrosia virginiana*.
Goat Willow *Salix caprea*.

Godetia Spach.
G. amoena (Lehm.) G. Don = *Clarkia amoena*.
G. decumbens (Douglas) Spach = *Clarkia purpurea* ssp. *quadrivulnera*.
G. grandiflora Lindl. = *Clarkia rubicunda*.
G. rubicunda Lindl. = *Clarkia rubicunda*.
G. vinosa Lindl. = *Clarkia amoena*.

Godmania Hemsl. Bignoniaceae. 2 small to medium trees. Lvs palmately compound, long-stalked. Pan. term.; cal. small, narrowly campanulate, 5-lobed; cor. urceolate, bilabiate, upper lip 2-lobed, lower lip 3-lobed; sta. 4. Fr. a linear capsule. Mex. to Braz. and Boliv. Z10.

G. aesculifolia (HBK) Standl. Tree to 13m. Lfts 5–9, 8.2–16.5cm, obovate to lanceolate, acute, membranous, veins puberulent and gland. beneath. Pan. puberulent; cor. yellow to orange-brown, tube to 1cm, upper lobes 2–3mm, lower lobes 3–4mm, pubesc. Fr. to 1m, ribbed, twisted, puberulent. Spring. Mex., Braz., Boliv.

G. macrocarpa (Benth.) Hemsl. = *G. aesculifolia*.
G. uleana Kränzl. = *G. aesculifolia*.
→*Cybistax*, *Tabebuia* and *Tecoma*.

God's Eye *Veronica chamaedrys*.

Goethea Nees. Malvaceae. 2 everg. shrubs. St. slender, erect and sparsely branched. Lvs alt., petiolate, simple, conspicuously stipuled. Fls in short, axill. clusters, or borne directly on older bare st.; epical. seg. 4–5, showy; sep. 5; cor. tube-like; sta. united in a tubular, exserted column with 5-toothed apex, fil. spreading; style spreading into 10 br. Braz.

G. cauliflora Nees = *G. strictiflora*.
G. makoyana (E. Morr.) Hook. f. = *Pavonia makoyana*.
G. semperflorens Nees = *Pavonia semiserrata*.
G. strictiflora Hook. To 1.2m. Lvs to 20cm, ovate to ovate-elliptic, leathery, initially downy beneath, sinuate-dentate toward apex. Fls to 2.5cm; epical. white-yellow, veined or flushed red; cal. to 1.2cm, lobes ovate-acuminate, white or light green; pet. to 1cm, white flushed crimson, obcordate, veined. Braz.

Gokizuru *Actinostemma tenerum*.
Gold-and-silver Flower *Lonicera japonica*.
Gold Birch *Betula ermanii*.
Gold Coast Bombax *Bombax buonopozense*.
Gold Dust Dracaena *Dracaena surculosa*.
Gold-dust Wattle *Acacia acinacea*.
Golden Alexanders *Zizia aurea*.
Golden Apple *Spondias dulcis*.
Golden Arum Lily *Zantedeschia elliottiana*.
Golden Aster *Chrysopsis*.
Golden Ball Cactus *Parodia leninghausii*.
Golden Bamboo *Phyllostachys aurea*.
Golden Barrel Cactus *Echinocactus grusonii*.
Golden Bells *Emmenanthe penduliflora*.
Golden Billy Buttons *Craspedia chrysantha*.
Golden Buttons *Tanacetum vulgare*.
Golden Chain *Laburnum anagyroides*.
Golden Chain Orchid *Dendrochilum*.
Golden Chalice Vine *Solandra maxima*.
Golden Chervil *Chaerophyllum aureum*.
Golden Chestnut *Chrysolepis*.
Golden Chinkapin *Chrysolepis* (*C. chrysophylla*).
Golden Club *Orontium*.
Golden Crown Beard *Verbesina encelioides*.
Golden Cup *Hunnemannia*.
Golden Currant *Ribes aureum*.
Golden Dewdrop *Duranta erecta*.
Golden Dryandra *Dryandra nobilis*.
Golden Eardrops *Dicentra chrysantha*.
Golden Elder *Sambucus nigra* 'Aurea'.
Golden Everlasting *Helichrysum bracteatum*.
Golden-eyed Grass *Sisyrinchium californicum*.
Golden Fairy Lantern *Calochortus amabilis*.
Golden-feathered Palm *Chrysalidocarpus lutescens*.
Golden Fern *Pityrogramma calomelanos* var. *aureoflava*.
Golden Fig *Ficus aurea*.
Golden Flame Lily *Pyrolirion aureum*.
Golden Flax *Linum flavum*.
Golden Fleece *Thymophylla tenuiloba*.
Golden Foxtail *Alopecurus pratensis*.
Golden Gladiolus *Gladiolus aureus*.
Golden Globe Tulip *Calochortus amabilis*.
Golden Gram *Vigna radiata*.
Golden-groove Bamboo *Phyllostachys aureosulcata*.
Golden Groundsel *Packera aurea*.
Golden Hardhack *Potentilla fruticosa*.
Golden Heather *Hudsonia ericoides*.
Golden Hedgehog Holly *Ilex aquifolium* 'Ferox Aurea'.
Golden Hurricane Lily *Lycoris aurea*.
Golden Knee *Chrysogonum*.
Golden Larch *Pseudolarix*.
Golden Maidenhair *Polypodium vulgare*.
Golden Mimosa *Acacia baileyana*.
Golden Oak *Quercus alnifolia*.
Golden Oats *Stipa gigantea*.
Golden Paper Daisy *Helipterum molle*.
Golden Pea *Thermopsis macrophylla*.
Golden Polypody *Phlebodium aureum*.
Golden Pothos *Epipremnum aureum*.
Golden Prairie Clover *Dalea aurea*.
Golden Ragwort *Packera aurea*.
Golden Rain Tree *Koelreuteria*.
Golden Rain Wattle *Acacia prominens*.
Golden-rayed Lily of Japan *Lilium auratum*.
Goldenrod *Solidago*.
Golden Saxifrage *Chrysosplenium*.
Golden Seal *Hydrastis* (*H. canadensis*).
Golden Shield Fern *Dryopteris affinis*.
Golden Shower Tree *Cassia fistula*.
Golden Spaniard *Aciphylla aurea*.

Golden Spider Lily *Lycoris aurea.*
Golden Spray *Viminaria.*
Golden Star *Hypoxis hygrometrica.*
Golden Thistle *Scolymus hispanicus.*
Goldenthread *Coptis.*
Golden-tongued Penstemon *Penstemon miser.*
Golden Top *Lamarckia.*
Golden Trumpet *Allamanda cathartica.*
Golden Trumpet Tree *Tabebuia chrysotricha.*
Golden Vine *Stigmaphyllon ciliatum.*
Golden Wattle *Acacia pycnantha.*
Golden Weather Grass *Hypoxis hygrometrica.*
Golden Willow *Salix alba* var. *vitellina.*
Golden Wonder *Senna splendida.*
Golden Wreath Wattle *Acacia saligna.*
Golden Yellow Palm *Chrysalidocarpus lutescens.*
Gold Fern *Pityrogramma chrysophylla.*
Goldfish Plant *Columnea gloriosa.*

Goldfussia Nees.
G. isophylla Nees = *Strobilanthes isophyllus.*

Gold Guinea Plant *Hibbertia scandens.*
Goldie's Shield Fern, Goldie's Wood Fern *Dryopteris goldiana.*
Goldilocks *Aster linosyris.*
Gold-of-pleasure *Camelina sativa.*
Goldthread *Coptis.*

Gomesa R. Br. Orchidaceae. 20 compact, epiphytic or lithophytic orchids. Pbs oblong-ovoid. Lvs strap-shaped, 2–4 per pb., 1–2 borne apically, the others basally sheathing. Rac. lat., densely many-fld, fls small, fragrant; dors. sep. and pet. subsimilar, free, spreading, lat. sep. free or connate; lip simple to trilobed, lat. lobes erect, midlobe spreading or reflexed, disc bicallose. Braz.
G. crispa (Lindl.) Klotzsch ex Rchb. f. Infl. to 22cm, pendent; fls fragrant, yellow, lime, olive or sea-green edged yellow, most parts strongly undulate; sep. to 10×2mm, oblong or oblong-ligulate, acute; pet. to 10×3mm, oblong or oblong-spathulate, subacute; lip to 8×4mm, broadly oblong, obtuse, recurved, disc bicarinate, undulate-dentate sometimes v. much paler or tinted rusty red. Braz.
G. laxiflora (Lindl.) Klotzsch & Rchb. f. Similar to *G. crispa* except fls smaller, tep. not undulate, lateral sep. connate. Braz.
G. planifolia (Lindl.) Klotzsch & Rchb. f. Infl. to 25cm, arching, fls yellow-green, highly fragrant; dors. sep. to 9×4mm, subspathulate, obtuse, lat. sep. to 9×6mm, oblong-ligulate, acute, connate, crispate; pet. to 9×4mm, oblong-spathulate, crispate; lip to 9×6mm, ovate, acute, concave, crispate-undulate, disc 2-crested, undulate-denticulate with 2 oblong tubercles. Braz.
G. recurva R. Br. Infl. to 35cm, pendent; fls yellow-green, fragrant; sep. to 12×4mm, narrowly oblong-spathulate, acute, spreading, lat. sep. connate; pet. to 11×4mm, oblong-spathulate, apiculate or rounded; lip to 10×6mm, ovate, acute or obtuse, strongly recurved, disc prominently bicarinate. Braz.
G. sessilis Barb. Rodr. Infl. to 35cm; fls yellow-green; sep. to 8×2mm, linear-ligulate, acute or acuminate, lat. sep. connate; pet. to 7×2mm, narrowly ligulate, acute or acuminate, undulate; lip to 6×3mm, ovate-oblong, acute, undulate, disc prominently 2-crested, denticulate. Braz.
→*Odontoglossum.*

Gomphocarpus R. Br.
G. fruticosus (L.) R. Br. = *Asclepias fruticosa.*
G. physocarpus E. Mey. = *Asclepias physocarpa.*

Gompholobium Sm.
G. hendersonii Paxt. = *Burtonia hendersonii.*
G. scabrum Sm. = *Burtonia scabra.*

Gomphrena L. Amaranthaceae. 90 ann. or perenn. herbs. St. erect or prostrate, simple to much-branched, usually hairy. Lvs opposite, entire. Infl. dense, capitate, spicate or glomerate, subtended by 2 sessile lvs; fls small, hermaphrodite, bracts 2, with excurrent midrib; bracteoles mucronate, navicular; tep. 5, erect, almost free, lanceolate, lanate; sta. 5, forming a tube with entire to bilobed teeth. Trop. Amer., Aus. Zone 7 if treated as a half-hardy ann., otherwise Z9.
G. aurantiaca hort. = *G. haageana.*
G. celosioides Mart. = *G. decumbens.*
G. coccinea Decne. = *G. haageana.*
G. decumbens Jacq. Ann. to 50cm, ascending to erect, much-branched; young br. lanate. Lvs to 4.5×1.3cm, narrow-oblong to oblanceolate, glab. or thinly pilose above, with dense white hairs along margins and beneath; petiole barely distinct. Spikes to 7cm, white or purple, occas. in clusters; bracts to 4mm;

bracteoles with dentate wing along upper third of midrib; tep. to 5mm, 1-nerved, green. S Braz. to Arg., W Indies.
G. globosa L. GLOBE AMARANTH; BACHELOR'S BUTTON. Ann., ascending or erect, to 60cm, branched, densely white-pubesc. when young. Lvs to 15×6cm, thinly pilose, mucronate; petiole to 1cm. Spikes cylindric, solitary, occas. clustered, pink to deep red; bracts to 5mm, persistent, ovate, acuminate; bracteoles to 12mm, midrib dentate, white, purple, pink or variegated; tep. to 7mm, 1-nerved. Panama, Guat. In addition to the following cvs, seed races are offered with white, pink, rose and purple-red flower-heads. 'Aurea-superba': fls orange-yellow, with red-tinged bracts. 'Buddy': habit compact, globular; fls deep purple, long-lasting. 'Dwarf White': fls clear-white, everlasting. Mixed: fls white, pink, rose, and red-purple. 'Nana': 12cm high; fls dark red. 'Rubra': lvs edible. 'Strawberry Fields': to 45cm; fls scarlet to crimson.
G. haageana Klotzsch. Perenn., cult. as an ann., to 70cm, erect, simple to much-branched. Lvs 3–8×0.3–1cm, acute to blunt, finely pilose. Spikes globose, to 6cm, pale red to rust; bracts to 5mm; bracteoles with midrib crested, dentate; tep. yellow, to 5mm. S US, Mex.
G. tuberifera Torr. = *G. haageana.*

Gongora Ruiz & Pav. Orchidaceae. 25 epiphytic orchids. Pbs ovoid, cylindric-pyriform, or ovoid-conical. Lvs 30–60cm, oblong to elliptic-lanceolate, acuminate, loosely plicate, narrowing to a grooved petiole. Rac. basal, long, arching or pendulous; fls strongly scented, alt. or opposite in 2 ranks along slender straight or flexuous axis, resembling a swan in outline or a hovering insect; pedicels slender, strongly incurved; dors. sep. usually adnate to column, erect-spreading; lat. sep. spreading or reflexed, wider than dors.; pet. smaller than sep., adnate to column, erect and spreading above; lip fleshy-waxy, narrow, hypochile erect, corniculate or aristate, epichile gibbous-saccate to laterally compressed, apex bilobed, acute or acuminate; column slender, arched, winged above. W Indies, Mex. to Peru & Braz. Z10.
G. armeniaca (Lindl. & Paxt.) Rchb. f. Infl. elongate, pendent, few to many-fld; fls waxy, salmon-pink, yellow or orange, sometimes spotted purple-brown, dors. sep. 1–1.8cm, broadly oblong to elliptic-oblong, erect, concave, lat. sep. 1–1.7cm, ovate, acute, obtuse or apiculate, spreading or reflexed; pet. to 0.6cm, lanceolate, tips recurved; lip short-clawed, to 1.2cm, inflated, calciform, obtuse, epichile erect, linear-lanceolate. Costa Rica, Panama, Nic.
G. bufonia Lindl. = *G. quinquenervis.*
G. cassidea Rchb. f. Infl. to 30cm, pendulous, loosely few-fld; fls green-brown to pink-brown; dors. sep. 1.75–2.5cm, elliptic to subrotund, cucullate, slightly narrower than lat. sep.; pet. to 1.2cm, recurved, obliquely oblong-lanceolate, aristate; lip to 2.5cm; hypochile saccate, bilobulate, lobules erect, cuneate-obovate, epichile 0.9–1.3cm, base gibbous, centre linear, apical lobules 2, linear-lanceolate. Guat., Hond., Nic.
G. galeata (Lindl.) Rchb. f. Infl. 15–28cm, arching to pendent, many-fld; fls yellow-brown to cream-green; sep. 2–2.5cm, ovate to ovate-oblong, concave, spreading, obtuse; pet. to 0.6cm, oblong-falcate, bidentate; lip to 1.25cm, hypochile large, recurved, epichile short, saccate. Mex.
G. jenischii hort. ex Rchb. f. = *G. quinquenervis.*
G. maculata Lindl. = *G. quinquenervis.*
G. quinquenervis Ruiz & Pav. Infl. to 90cm, pendent; fls thin-textured, except for lip, pale yellow, variously spotted and banded red or red-brown spotted pale yellow, dors. sep. 2–2.3cm, elliptic-lanceolate, strongly revolute, lat. sep. to 3cm, ovate-lanceolate, reflexed, revolute; pet. to 1.2cm, lanceolate or linear-lanceolate, recurved; lip to 2cm, laterally compressed, hypochile saccate, bearing 2 basal tubercles; epichile laterally compressed, basally gibbous, sulcate above, apex spur-like. Mex., C Amer., N S Amer., Trin.
G. sanderiana Kränzl. Infl. to 30cm, pendulous, few-fld; ivory to amber spotted rose, dors. sep. 2.75–4cm, ovate or ovate-elliptic, concave, lat. sep. 3.75–4.5cm, broadly ovate; pet. 4–5cm, fleshy, linear; lip to 2.8cm, clawed; hypochile linear, expanded as 2 quadrate, erect lobes with a fleshy tubercle between epichile, linear. Peru.
G. scaphephorus Rchb. f. & Warsc. Infl. to 70cm, pendulous; fls yellow or yellow-white to red-brown, spotted dull purple; dors. sep. 1–1.5cm, ovate-elliptic, concave, lateral sep. 1.75–2cm, semiorbicular, concave; pet. small, obliquely triangular; lip to 2.5cm, hypochile compressed, base with 2 erect, oblong lobules, epichile to 1cm, navicular or ovate, acuminate, base with an erect, quadrate keel. Peru.
G. tricolor Rchb. f. = *G. quinquenervis.*
→*Acropera.*

Goniolimon Boiss. Plumbaginaceae. 20 woody-based perenn. herbs. Lvs in basal rosettes, tapering to a petiole. Infl. a slender-stemmed pan. or corymb, composed of spikes bearing mucronate bracts usually on angled or winged br.; spikelets 2–6-fld; cal. funnelform, scarious, limb broad, sometimes distinctly lobed; cor. annular, seg. joined at base; sta. 5, free; styles downy. Eur. to C Asia, NW Afr.

G. callicomum (C.A. Mey.) Boiss. 10–50cm. Lvs 5–10cm, occas. longer, fleshy, oblong-elliptic to lanceolate, grey-green, mucronate. Flowering st. terete, occas. puberulous; br. sometimes winged; spikes 2–8cm, spikelets about 8mm, 3–4-fld; fls rose. Early summer. Sib. Z3.

G. collinum (Griseb.) Boiss. = *G. incanum*.

G. elatum (Fisch. & Spreng.) Boiss. To 80cm, somewhat pubesc. Lvs 5–15cm, obovate to oblanceolate, obtuse or emarginate, mucronate. Spikes about 2cm, spikelets 2–4-fld; fls blue. SE Russia. Z5.

G. eximium (Schrenk) Boiss. 30–70cm, glaucescent; infl. br. terete, pubesc. Lvs 5–12cm, occas. longer, oblong to obovate, obtuse, abruptly mucronate, somewhat crispate. Spikes capitate, dense, spikelets 4–6-fld, lax; fls pink to lilac, tipped white. Summer. C Asia to Mong. var. *album* Hubb. Fls white. Z5.

G. incanum (L.) Hepper. 20–45cm. Lvs 4–12cm, lanceolate to oblong-lanceolate, smooth, mucronate. Infl. to 60cm, winged; spikes densely overlapping, spikelets 1-fld; fls purple-pink, white or cream. Turk. Z4.

G. speciosum (L.) Boiss. = *G. incanum*.

G. tataricum (L.) Boiss. STATICE; TARTARIAN STATICE. To 30cm, flowering st. subangular. Lvs 2–15cm, obovate to lanceolate-spathulate, mucronate, white-punctate above. Spikes 1–1.5cm, dense; spikelets 1–2-fld; fls maroon to mauve. SE Eur. to S Russia. Z4.

→*Limonium* and *Statice*.

Goniophlebium (Bl.) Presl. Polypodiaceae. 20 epiphytic ferns. Rhiz. creeping, fleshy and thick; scales usually lanceolate. Fronds uniform, arching or pendent, pinnate or pinnatifid, pinnae jointed to rachis, herbaceous, veins prominent; stipes distant, jointed to phyllopodia. Asia. Z10.

G. amoenum (Wallich) J. Sm. Rhiz. to 4mm wide; scales entire, brown to black. Fronds to 65cm, ovate; pinnae to 15cm, horizontal, sword-shaped, apex narrowly acute, entire or toothed to notched, lower 2 deflexed; stipes erect, straw-like, to 30cm. N India (Himal.) to China, Taiwan.

G. areolatum (Humb. & Bonpl. ex Willd.) Presl = *Phlebodium aureum* var. *areolatum*.

G. lepidotrichum Fée = *Polypodium lepidotrichum*.

G. pectinatum (L.) J. Sm. = *Pecluma pectinata*.

G. persicifolium (Desv.) Bedd. Rhiz. to 5mm wide; scales toothed, pale to dark brown. Fronds to 2m, pendent, ovate to oblong; pinnae to 15cm, stalked, spreading, elongate-lanceolate, apex narrowly acute, base cuneate, distinctly toothed; stipes to 30cm. N India to China, Malaysia, Indon., Philipp.

G. pyrrholepis Fée = *Polypodium pyrrholepis*.

G. subauriculatum (Bl.) Presl. Rhiz. eventually chalk-white; scales dull, white to 1m+, pendent, oblong to lanceolate, pinnae to 15cm, ± sessile and jointed to rachis, linear to lanceolate, apex narrowly acute, base rounded, cuneate, truncate, or auricled, entire, toothed, or notched; stipes erect, to 30cm, lustrous. Trop. Asia (N India, China, Malaysia) to Aus., Polyn. 'Knightiae': fronds arching, narrower, pinnae broader, deeply incised, occas. overlapping, with linear, pointed lobes.

→*Polypodium*.

Goniopteris Presl. Thelypteridaceae. 70 terrestrial ferns. Rhiz. erect or ascending to creeping, covered with massed roots and sparse, pubesc. scales. Fronds uniform or dimorphous, 1–2-pinnatifid to pinnate, rarely simple, pubesc. and, occas. gland.; rachis and costa proliferous, pubesc.; stipes approximate and clustered, pubesc. Trop. Amer. Z10.

G. reptans (Gmel.) Presl. Rhiz. suberect to short-creeping, scales stellate-pubesc., red-brown. Stipes 2–25cm. Lamina to 30×10cm, elliptic or lanceolate to oblong or linear, stellate-pubesc., sterile fronds proliferous, creeping and rooting, fertile fronds erect; pinnae to 2×1cm, ovate to oblong or linear, obtuse or narrowly acute at apex, entire or notched or obtusely lobed. Flor., W Indies, Mex. to NS Amer. Z10.

G. tetragona (Sw.) Small Rhiz. short-creeping, scales with forked hairs, red-brown. Stipes to 50cm. Lamina to 45×25cm, lanceolate or deltoid to ovate or oblong; rachis with minute forked and simple hairs; pinnae to 20×3cm, linear-oblong, apex acuminate to attenuate. W Indies, C & S Amer.

→*Dryopteris* and *Thelypteris*.

Gonzalagunia Ruiz & Pav. Rubiaceae. 20 shrubs or small trees. Fls in term. pan., rac., or spikes; cal. tube campanulate spherical, lobes 4–5; cor. salver- or funnel-form, soft-haired, lobes 4–5, spreading, rounded. Fr. berry-like. S Amer. Z10.

G. hirsuta Schum. = *G. spicata*.

G. spicata (Lam.) Maza. To 4m, br. sericeous at first. Lvs to 18×8cm, ovate, oblong, elliptic-oblong, or lanceolate, membranous, glabrescent. Rac. to 40cm; cor. to 15mm, white, hairy, lobes 4, obtuse, to 7mm. Fr. subglobose, to 4mm wide, blue or white. C & N S Amer., W Indies.

→*Duggena*.

Goodenia Sm. Goodeniaceae. 170 shrubs and herbs. Lvs alt. or radical, usually stalked. Infl. term. or axill., a rac., pan. or cyme; cal. tube 5-lobed; cor. tube adnate to ovary, sometimes spurred, slit on upper side, 5-lobed, lobes winged; sta. free. Aus., New Guinea, SE Asia. Z9.

G. affinis (De Vriese) De Vriese. Small lanate perenn. Lvs to 10×1.5cm, usually radical, oblong-lanceolate or oblanceolate to obovate, entire or denticulate, with stellate hairs beneath. Infl. radical or axill., equalling or exceeding lvs; cor. to 20mm, yellow, exterior pubesc. W & S Aus.

G. albida Sm. = *Scaevola albida*.

G. albiflora Schltr. Perenn., erect, mostly glab. St. to 60cm, angular. Lvs to 9×4cm, lanceolate or ovate-lanceolate, dentate. Infl. cymose; axillary, 2- or 3-fld; cor. to 25mm, white, exterior glandular-pubesc., basally saccate. S Aus.

G. amplexans F. Muell. Subshrub to 1m, glandular-pubesc., erect. Lvs to 9×2.5cm, oblong-lanceolate to ovate, dentate, clasping st., auriculate. Infl. short, axill., 1- or 2-fld; cor. to 18mm, yellow, exterior pubesc., upper lobes winged. S Aus.

G. calendulacea Andrews = *Scaevola calendulacea*.

G. decurrens R. Br. Perenn. St. to 55cm, erect or ascending, usually glab. Lvs to 10cm, decurrent, oblong, glab., coarsely serrate. Infl. term., a rac. or pan., 1–5-fld; cor. to 2cm, yellow, upper lobes unequally winged. NSW.

G. grandiflora Sims. Herb or subshrub to 1m, erect, glandular-pubesc., often viscid. St. angular. Lvs to 7×5cm, alt., ovate, dentate or serrate, truncate to cordate at base, sometimes slightly lobed along petiole. Infl. to 4cm, axill., 1–3-fld, glandular-pubesc.; cor. to 3cm, yellow, exterior pubesc., interior villous, lobes broadly winged. Aus.

G. hederacea Sm. Rosette-forming or stoloniferous herb. Lvs to 8×4cm, elliptic to obovate or suborbicular, cuneate or rounded at base, entire to serrate, sometimes glaucous, lanate to glab. beneath; petiole to 6.5cm. Infl. to 10cm, axill., 1–3-fld; cor. to 18mm, yellow, exterior pubesc. Queensld, Vict., NSW.

G. heteromera F. Muell. Perenn. herb. St. slender, to 20cm, prostrate or procumbent. Lvs to 4×1cm, basally rosulate or clustered at nodes, lanceolate to narrowly obovate, entire to minutely denticulate, sometimes pinnatifid, glab. to adpressed-pubesc. Infl. to 3.5cm, pubesc., 1-fld; cor. to 10mm, yellow, exterior pubesc., upper lobes unequally winged. S Aus., Queensld, NSW, Vict.

G. heterophylla Sm. Herb to 1m. St. decumbent or ascending. Lvs to 4.5×2cm, broadly ovate to ovate, subcordate to truncate at base, deeply dentate or crenate, pubesc. Infl. to 4cm, axill., pubesc., 1-fld; cor. to 2cm, yellow, exterior pubesc. Queensld, NSW.

G. humilis R. Br. Dwarf herb. Lvs to 4×1cm, radical, ovate-lanceolate to linear-lanceolate, glab. to pubesc., subentire. Infl. short, 1- to few-fld and paniculate; cor. to 12mm, yellow, exterior pubesc., upper lobes unequally winged. S Aus., Vict.

G. ovata Sm. Shrub to 1.5m, erect, slender, usually glab. Lvs to 8×4cm, alt., ovate, lanceolate or ovate-cordate, serrate to denticulate, rounded to cuneate at base. Infl. to 1.5cm, slender, axill., 1 to 3-fld; cor. to 20mm, yellow, exterior glab. E & SE Aus.

G. paniculata Sm. Rosulate herb, glab. or pubesc. Lvs to 13×4cm, obovate to linear-obovate, attenuate at base, entire to deeply serrate, usually glab. Pan. to 45cm, term.; cor. to 1.5cm, yellow, exterior pubesc. Queensld, NSW.

G. phylicioides F. Muell. Shrub to 55cm, erect, branching, white-lanate. Lvs to 2.5cm, linear to oblong-lanceolate, coriaceous, obtuse, entire, revolute, white-green beneath. Fls clustered in term. heads; cor. white, spreading, exterior tomentose-pubesc. W Aus.

G. pinnatifida Schltr. Rosette-forming herb to 40cm, pubesc. Basal lvs to 5.5×2.5cm, pinnatifid to pinnatisect, oblong-obovate in outline, long-attenuate at base. Infl. to 14cm, axill., glandular-pubesc.; cor. to 25mm, yellow, usually glab., upper lobes unequally winged. Aus.

G. rotundifolia R. Br. Perenn. herb. St. ascending or procumbent, slightly pubesc. Lvs to 4.5×4.5cm, broadly ovate, cordate to cuneate at base, coarsely dentate, minutely tomentose, bright green above. Infl. to 4cm, slender, axill., 1- to few-fld; cor. to 18mm, yellow, exterior pubesc., lobes winged. Queensld, NSW.

G. scaevolina F. Muell. Subshrub to 1m, viscid-pubesc. or hirsute. Lvs to 7.5cm, often shortly decurrent, oblanceolate to obovate-oblong, coarsely serrate. Infl. cymose, axill., 3–7-fld, sometimes 1-fld; cor. to 2.5cm, blue, exterior pubesc. to hirsute, upper lobes unequally winged. W Aus.

G. stelligera R. Br. Rosette-forming herb. Lvs to 37×1cm, linear to linear-obovate, entire to minutely dentate, glab. Infl. to 1m, a rac. or pan.; cor. to 1.5cm, yellow, exterior with stellate hairs. Queensld, NSW, Vict.

G. stricta Sm. = Dampiera stricta.

G. varia R. Br. Prostrate or ascending subshrub, sometimes viscid. Lvs to 5×3.5cm, ovate-lanceolate or obovate to suborbicular, entire or denticulate. Infl. cymose, axill., 1- to several-fld; cor. to 18mm, yellow, exterior glab. W Aus., S Aus., NSW, Vict.

GOODENIACEAE R. Br. 16/430. Dampiera, Goodenia, Leschenaultia, Scaevola.

Good King Henry Chenopodium bonus-henricus.
Good Luck Leaf, Good Luck Plant Oxalis tetraphylla.
Good's Banksia Banksia goodii.

Goodyera R. Br. Orchidaceae. 40 everg. or herbaceous, largely terrestrial orchids. St. creeping and rooting. Lvs in a loose spiral or rosette, thinly fleshy, minutely to velvety-papillose above, often with a network of coloured veins. Fls mostly small in erect, narrow, term. spikes; tep. hooded; lip saccate, tip recurved. Spring–autumn. Temp. zones except Afr.

G. biflora (Lindl.) Hook. f. St. 5–7.5cm, tinted red. Lvs ovate, obtuse or subacute, green with white reticulate veins above, mauve-green beneath. Spike hairy; tep. white; lip blotched pink or yellow, undulate. Summer. Asia. Z9.

G. biflora var. **macrantha** (Maxim.) Hashim. = G. macrantha.

G. discolor Ker-Gawl. = Ludisia discolor.

G. foliosa (Lindl.) Benth. St. 15–30cm. Lvs ovate-lanceolate, 3–5-veined. Spike glandular-pubesc., 5–7.5cm; tep. pink often tinted orange; lip with orange and white apical lobe. Summer. Asia. Z9.

G. grandis (Bl.) Bl. St. 50–100cm. Lvs 13–15cm, ovate-oblong, pale green, undulate. Spike 10–20cm, glandular-pubesc.; fls purple. Summer. Aus., SE Asia, Jap. Z8.

G. hachijoensis Yatabe. St. 10–25cm, tinted red. Lvs to 6cm, green, oblong-ovate, veins white, reticulate with a central silver flash. Spike dense; sep. white stained brown-pink; lip dull yellow. Autumn. Jap. Z8.

G. japonica Bl. St. to 35cm. Lvs oblong-ovate, flushed rose pink at first, later green tinted ginger to chocolate, midrib silver-striped. Spike lax; fls white. Summer. China, Jap. Z8.

G. macrantha Maxim. St. 4–10cm. Lvs 2–4cm, ovate, acuminate, often undulate, deep red-green to copper, midrib silver. Fls large (2–3cm), 1–3, pale red; dors. sep. linear-oblong; pet. linear; lip lanceolate, recurved. Summer. Jap., Korea. Z7.

G. oblongifolia Raf. St. to 45cm. Lvs to 7cm, elliptic-oblong, dark blue-green with paler midrib and netted veins, sometimes undulate. Spike to 30-fld, secund; dors. sep. pale green; pet. white with green midvein. Mid summer–early autumn. N Amer. Z7.

G. picta Boxall & Naves = G. macrantha.

G. pubescens (Willd.) R. Br. RATTLESNAKE PLANTAIN. St. 40–50cm, pubesc. Lvs 3–9cm ovate-oblong, blue-green, veins reticulate, silver-white. Spike dense; tep. white with a green midvein. Summer. N, C & E Eur. Z6.

G. repens (L.) R. Br. LESSER RATTLESNAKE PLANTAIN. Rhiz. creeping. Lvs to 3cm, elliptic-ovate, dark green, sometimes obscurely net-veined white. Spike secund; fls small, white, rounded. N Amer., N Eurasia. Z4. var. **ophioides** Fern. WHITE BLOTCHED RATTLESNAKE; NETLEAF; SQUIRREL EAR. Lvs distinctly veined white. N Amer.

G. schlechtendaliana Rchb. f. St. 12–25cm. Lvs 2–4cm, in basal rosette, ovate-lanceolate, pale blue-green with darker blotches. Spike secund; fls pale red, to 10. Late summer. China, Korea, Taiwan, Jap. Z9.

G. tesselata Lodd. St. to 35cm, densely pubesc. Lvs 2–8cm, in basal rosette, ovate-lanceolate to elliptic-lanceolate, blue-green net-veined white. Spike secund or cylindric; fls to 40, white. Summer. NE Amer. Z7.

G. velutina Maxim. St. to 20cm, purple-brown. Lvs 2–4cm, ovate, acuminate, velvety, dark green with white midrib above, maroon beneath. Fls pale red-brown. Autumn. Jap., S Korea, Taiwan. Z9.

Goodyer's Elm Ulmus angustifolia.
Goora Nut Cola acuminata.

Gooseberry Ribes (R. grossularioides; R. uva-crispa).
Gooseberry Gourd Cucumis anguria.
Gooseberry Mallee Eucalyptus calycogona.
Gooseberry Tree Phyllanthus acidus.
Goose Foot Acer pensylvanicum; Chenopodium (C. bonushenricus).
Goose Grass Eleusine indica; Galium aparine; Potentilla anserina.
Gooseneck Loosestrife Lysimachia clethroides.
Goose Plum Prunus americana.
Goose Tansy Potentilla anserina.

Gordonia Ellis. Theaceae. 70 everg. trees and shrubs. Lvs alt. Fls solitary, axill., long-stalked; sep. 5, short; pet. elliptic-obovate; sta. many in groups of 5. Fr. a woody capsule. SE Asia, warm N Amer.

G. alatamaha (Marshall) Sarg. = Franklinia alatamaha.

G. anomala Spreng. = G. axillaris.

G. axillaris (Ker.-Gawl.) Endl. Shrub or tree to 12m. Lvs 6–17cm, oblanceolate to oblong, shallowly toothed or entire, dark glossy green, coriaceous. Fls to 15cm diam., solitary, ± sessile; pet. 5–6, deeply notched, creamy white; sta. orange-yellow. Winter to spring. China, Taiwan. Z8.

G. chrysandra Cowan. Shrub 3–10cm; branchlets tinted red, downy at first. Lvs 6–11cm, obovate-elliptic, dark glossy green, sparsely crenate. Fls short-stalked, to 6cm diam.; pet. 6–7, white tinted yellow; sta. golden yellow. Winter. China. Z8.

G. lasianthus (L.) Ellis. LOBLOLLY BAY. Shrub or tree to 20m. Lvs obovate-lanceolate, shallowly serrate, deep glossy green above. Fls 6–8cm diam., long-stalked; pet. 5, concave, white; sta. yellow. Summer. SE US. Z9.

G. sinensis Hemsl. & Wils. Shrub or tree to 10m. Lvs to 11cm, elliptic-ovate, crenate, leathery glossy green. Fls white on stalks to 2cm. China. Z9.

Gordon's Pine Pinus gordoniana.

Gorgasia Cook.
G. maxima Cook = Roystonea oleracea.

Gorgon's Head Euphorbia gorgonis.

Gormania Britt. = Sedum.

Gorse Ulex europaeus.
Gorse Bitter Pea Daviesia ulicifolia.

Gorteria L.
G. barbata L. = Berkheya barbata.

Gosan-chiku Phyllostachys aurea.
Gosford Wattle Acacia prominens.
Gossamer Wattle Acacia floribunda.

Gossypium L. COTTON. Malvaceae. 39 ann. or perenn. herbs, subshrubs, shrubs and small trees, stellate-pubesc. or glabrate, gland-dotted. Lvs petiolate, slightly lobed or deeply parted, with foliar nectaries; stipules subulate to falcate. Fls axill., solitary, rarely clustered; epical. seg. 3, foliaceous, cordate, laciniate or dentate, persistent in fr.; cal. truncate or 5-dentate; cor. campanulate or funnelform, pet. 5; staminal tube included, 5-toothed, anth. numerous; style single. Fr. a capsule, glab., ovoid, splitting to release seeds bedded in dense white fine fibres (cotton). Warm temp. and trop. regions.

G. arboreum L. TREE COTTON. Subshrub or shrub to 5m. Lvs deeply 3-, 5-, or 7-lobed, lobes obovate to linear. Epical. to 2.5cm, seg. ovate, entire or sparsely-laciniate; pet. pale yellow to deep red-purple, usually spotted purple-red at base. Capsule to 2.5cm, oblong-acute, profusely glandular-pitted, 3-celled. Trop. & subtrop. Asia.

G. barbadense L. SEA ISLAND COTTON. Shrub or small tree to 3m, sparsely stellate-pubesc. to glabrate. Lvs to 20cm, 3-, 5-, or 7-lobed, lobes ovate to lanceolate. Epical. 2–6cm, seg. broadly-ovate, cordate, laciniate; pet. to 8cm, yellow, with a dark red spot at base. Capsule 3.5–6cm, narrowly ovoid, gradually tapering to an acute tip, 3-celled, prominently pitted. Trop. S Amer., introd. to cult. in many regions of the world.

G. herbaceum L. LEVANT COTTON. Ann. or perenn. herb to 1.5m, sparsely pubesc. Lvs broadly 3-, 5-, or 7-lobed to middle. Epical. to 2.5cm, seg. broadly ovate to triangular, sharply 6–13-dentate; pet. to 5cm, yellow, with purple centre. Capsule c2.5cm, subglobose, beaked, 3–4-celled, with few oil glands. S Afr., cult. in Middle E, Afr. and India.

G. hirsutum L. UPLAND COTTON. Ann. or perenn. herb or shrub to 2m. Lvs 4–10cm, densely pubesc. to glab., cordate, weakly 3- or 5-lobed, or unlobed. Epical. 2–5cm, seg. ovate, 3–19-laciniate; pet. 3–7cm, cream or pale yellow, with or without a dark spot at base, fading pink-purple. Capsule 2–4cm, broadly ovoid or subglobose, beaked, 3–5-celled. C Amer., widely nat. elsewhere. var. *punctatum* (Schumacher) J.B. Hutch. St. woody, to 3m. Fls smaller, almost tube-like below. C Amer., Gulf Coast of Flor. to W Indies.

G. indicum Tod. = *G. arboreum.*
G. mexicanum Tod. = *G. hirsutum.*
G. obtusifolium Roxb. = *G. arboreum.*
G. peruvianum Cav. = *G. barbadense.*
G. punctatum Schumacher = *G. hirsutum* var. *punctatum.*
G. religiosum L. = *G. hirsutum* var. *punctatum.*
G. sturtianum Willis. STURT'S DESERT ROSE. Shrub to 3m, glaucous, glab.; st. much-branched, black-tuberculate. Lvs orbicular to ovate, often folded or rolled, unlobed or shallowly 3-lobed. Epical. to 1.5cm, seg. ovate to triangular, entire or slightly laciniate; pet. mauve with purple centre. Capsule 1.2cm, ovoid, acute, black-punctate, 3–4-celled. Aus.
G. sturtii Muell. = *G. sturtianum.*
G. thurberi Tod. ARIZONA WILD COTTON. Shrub to 4m, glabrate, much-branched. Lvs palmately 3-, 5-, or 7-lobed, lobes lanceolate, acuminate, upper lvs sometimes unlobed, lanceolate. Epical. to 1cm, seg. linear, entire or few-toothed at apex; pet. 1.5–2.5cm, cream, light purple below. Capsule 1–1.5cm, ovoid, mucronate, 3–4-celled. Ariz. and New Mex.
G. vitifolium Lam. = *G. barbadense.*
→*Thurberia.*

Gourliea Gillies ex Hook. & Arn.
G. decorticans Hook. & Arn. = *Geoffroea decorticans.*
G. spinosa (Molina) Skeels non Jacq. = *Geoffroea decorticans.*

Gout Plant *Jatropha* (*J. podagrica*).
Goutweed *Aegopodium podagraria.*
Gouty Geranium *Pelargonium gibbosum.*
Governor's Plum *Flacourtia indica.*
Gowen Cypress *Cupressus goveniana.*

Grabowskia Schldl. Solanaceae. 6 divaricately branched shrubs, armed with short spines in lf axils. Lvs alt., entire. Fls solitary or in corymbs 5-merous; cal. campanulate, 5- or rarely 10-dentate; cor. infundibuliform, tube short, limb spreading; sta. attached at base of cor., exserted. S Amer. Z10.
G. boerhaaviifolia Schldl. Shrub, 2–3m, scrambling or broadly spreading, decid.; branchlets often sharp and spine-like; spines in lf axils 6mm. Lvs 2.5–4cm, suborbicular to broadly obovate, succulent, glaucous. Fls solitary or in rac.; cor. tube to 1cm, limb to 1cm diam., pale blue or white. Late spring to early summer. Braz. and Peru.
G. duplicata Arn. Shrublet or shrub to 3m. Lvs 2–5cm, narrowly elliptic to ovate, obtuse, sometimes undulate, v. glaucous. Fls in clusters; cor. tube to 0.6cm, limb to 0.7cm diam., white tinted green. Summer. S Braz., NW Arg.
G. glauca hort. = *G. boerhaaviifolia.*

Graceful Wattle *Acacia decora.*
Grace Garlic *Nothoscordum.*

Grahamstown Heath *Erica chamissonis.*
Graham's Willow *Salix ×grahamii.*
Grain Oak *Quercus coccifera.*
Grains of Paradise *Aframomum melegueta.*
Grama Grass *Bouteloua.*

GRAMINEAE Juss. 635/9000. *Aegilops, Agropyron, Agrostis, Aira, Alopecurus, Ammophila, Ampelodesmos, Andropogon, Anthoxanthum, Apera, Arrhenatherum, Arundinaria, Arundinella, Arundo, Avena, Bambusa, Bothriochloa, Bouteloua, Brachiaria, Brachypodium, Briza, Bromus, Buchloe, Calamagrostis, Cenchrus, Chasmanthium, Chimonobambusa, Chionochloa, Chloris, Chusquea, Coix, Cortaderia, Cymbopogon, Cynodon, Cynosurus, Dactylis, Danthonia, Dendrocalamus, Deschampsia, Dichanthium, Digitaria, Echinochloa, Ehrharta, Eleusine, Elymus, Eragrostis, Eremochloa, Eriochloa, Festuca, Glyceria, Gynerium, Hakonechloa, Helictotrichon, Hibanobambusa, Hilaria, Holcus, Hordeum, Hyparrhenia, Hystrix, Imperata, Indocalamus, Koeleria, Lagurus, Lamarckia, Leymus, Lolium, Melica, Mibora, Milium, Miscanthus, Molinia, Neyraudia, Oplismenus, Oryza, Oryzopsis, Otatea, Panicum, Paspalum, Pennisetum, Phalaris, Pharus, Phleum, Phragmites, Phyllostachys, Pleioblastus, Poa, Polypogon, Pseudosasa, Rhynchelytrum, Rostraria, Saccharum, Sasa, Sasaella, Sasamorpha, Schizachyrium, Semiarundinaria, Setaria, Shibataea, Sinarundinaria, Sinobambusa, Sorghastrum, Sorghum, Spartina, Spodiopogon, Sporobolus, Stenotaphrum, Stipa, Stipagrostis, Thamnocalamus, Themeda, Thysanolaena,* *Trichloris, Tricholaena, Uniola, Vetiveria, Yushania, Zea, Zizania, Zoysia.*

Grammangis Rchb. f. Orchidaceae. 2 epiphytic orchids. Pbs bearing 3–5 lvs at apex. Lvs flat, fleshy. Rac. basal; fls large, spreading; median sep. free, lat. sep. and pet. joined at base; lip trilobed, with crests or calli inside. Madag. Z9.
G. ellisii (Lindl.) Rchb. f. Pbs 8–20cm, 4-angled, fully developed by flowering time. Lvs 15–40cm, oblong. Rac. 15–20-fld; fls yellow, with glossy mahogany- to green-bronze markings, lip striped red and yellow; dors. sep. 4cm, obovate, undulate, lat. sep. slightly narrower; pet. smaller; lip 1.8×1.8cm, lat. lobes sickle-shaped, midlobe narrower, callus large, bifid, keel prominent dividing into 3 short crests.
G. falcigera Rchb. f. = *Cymbidiella falcigera.*
G. fallax Schltr. Similar to *G. ellisii* but pbs not fully developed until after flowering; sep. longer, yellow-green with violet-black apex; pet. obovate white with dull red apex, lip smaller, with rounded lobes, white, dull red between calli.
G. pardalina Rchb. f. = *Cymbidiella rhodocheila.*

Grammanthes DC.
G. gentianoides (Lam.) DC. = *Crassula dichotoma.*

Grammatophyllum Bl. Orchidaceae. 12 large epiphytic or terrestrial orchids. Pbs stoutly cane-like, clustered. Lvs 2-ranked, linear or ligulate. Infl. a basal rac., sometimes branched, many-fld; fls showy; sep. and pet. free, spreading; lip small, erect, concave, lat. lobes embracing column, midlobe short, recurved-spreading. SE Asia & Indon. to New Guinea, Philipp., Polyn. Z10.
G. scriptum (L.) Bl. Pbs 0.5–2m, narrowly ellipsoid. Lvs to 55×7cm, linear-ligulate. Infl. to 1.25m; fls to 4.5cm diam., tep. oblanceolate, falcate, undulate, waxy, yellow-green, blotched dark brown; lip lateral lobes white-yellow veined brown, erect, pubesc. below, midlobe yellow-white, veined dark brown, callus yellow and white, spotted and lined brown, sulcate. New Guinea, Philipp., Borneo, Celebes, Moluccas, Solomon Is.
G. speciosum Bl. Pbs to 3m, subcylindrical. Lvs to 60×3cm, linear-ligulate. Infl. to 2m; fls to 12cm diam.; tep. elliptic-oblong, slightly undulate, dark red-brown; lip white-yellow, striped yellow and red-brown, lat. lobes narrowly oblong, erect, midlobe ovate, acute or obtuse, disc tricarinate, lined red. Malaya and Sumatra to Philipp.

Grammitis Sw.
G. augustifolia (Sw.) Heward = *Campyloneurum augustifolium.*
G. longifolia Bl. = *Paragramma longifolia.*
G. rutifolius R. Br. = *Pleurosorus rutifolius.*

Grampians Grevillea *Grevillea confertifolia.*
Grampians Gum *Eucalyptus alpina.*
Granadilla *Passiflora edulis; P. ligularis; P. quadrangularis.*
Granadina *Passiflora subpeltata.*
Grandfather's-beard *Geum triflorum.*
Grand Fir *Abies grandis.*
Granite Banksia *Banksia verticillata.*
Granite Boronia *Boronia cymosa.*
Granite Bottlebrush *Melaleuca elliptica.*
Granite Gilia *Leptodactylon pungens.*
Granny's Bonnet *Aquilegia vulgaris; Disperis fanniniae.*
Grape *Vitis vinifera.*
Grape Fern *Botrychium.*
Grapefruit *Citrus ×paradisi.*
Grape Honeysuckle *Lonicera prolifera.*
Grape Hyacinth *Muscari.*
Grape Ivy *Cissus.*
Grape-leaf Begonia *Begonia dregei.*
Grapevine Begonia *Begonia ×weltoniensis.*

Graphorkis Thouars. Orchidaceae. 2–3 epiphytic orchids. Pbs well developed, lvs appearing after flowering. Infl. paniculate; sep. and pet. similar; lip trilobed, usually spurred. Trop. Afr., Madag., Masc. Is., Comoros Is. Z9.
G. lurida (Sw.) Kuntze. Pbs 3–9cm, cylindrical, conical or ovoid. Lvs to 40cm, lanceolate. Pan. 30–60cm; tep. 5–8mm, oblong-spathulate, dull purple-brown; lip of similar length, yellow, lat. lobes obtuse or rounded, midlobe broadly obovate, somewhat emarginate or bifid; spur 4mm, bent forwards. W & C Afr., Uganda.
G. scripta (Thouars) Kuntze. Pbs 3–14cm, ovoid-conical. Lvs 8–11cm, grasslike. Pan. 22–65cm; fls yellow marked with red; tep. 12–15×6–8mm; lip of similar length, lat. lobes rounded, midlobe obovate, crenulate or emarginate; spur 3mm, straight. Madag., Masc. Is., Comoros Is.
→*Eulophia.*

Graptopetalum Rose. Crassulaceae. 12 succulent perenn. herbs and shrubs to 2m. Lvs mainly in rosettes, fleshy. Infl. cymose; sep. usually 5, adpressed to pet.; pet. usually 5, fused towards base, spreading from centre; sta. 10. Parag., Mex. to Ariz. Z9.

G. amethystinum (Rose) Walth. JEWEL-LEAF PLANT. Subshrub, 15–30cm, branching from base. Lvs 3–7cm, in lax rosettes, oblong-ovate, blunt, margin rounded, green-blue, lavender to purple. Infl. 3–10-branched; fls 12–15mm across, green-yellow banded with red dots. Spring–early summer. Mex.

G. filiferum (S. Wats.) Whitehead. Clumps of rosettes to 5cm across. Lvs 1–5cm, crowded, spathulate, tip bristle-like, rich green, white towards winged margin. Infl. 2–5-branched; fls 12–18mm across white, banded with red dots. Spring. NW Mex.

G. grande Alexander. Shrub, 30cm–2m tall, st. erect, thick. Lvs 5–8cm, spathulate, rather thin, flat, glaucous when young. Infl. 8–15-branched, stalk twisted; fls to 2.5cm across yellow, with red dots. Winter. S Mex.

G. macdougalii Alexander. Herb arising from stolon, forming clumped stemless rosettes. Lvs 0.8–4cm, oblong, slightly convex above, short-acuminate. Infl. an umbel-like pan.; fls to 18mm across white to yellow-green, brown-tipped. Winter–early spring. Ariz.

G. mexicanum Matuda = Thompsonella minutiflora.

G. pachyphyllum Rose Trailing herb, rosette-forming. Lvs 1–2cm, 20–50, glaucous, red toward tip, club-shaped. Infl. 1–4-branched; fls 12–18mm across, banded with red dots. Early summer. Mex.

G. paraguayense (N.E. Br.) Walth. GHOST PLANT; MOTHER OF PEARL PLANT. Decumbent herb to 30cm. Lvs 3.5–5cm, obovate-spathulate, stiff, thick, short-pointed, glaucous, young lvs pale mauve. Infl. 2–6-branched; fls to 18mm across, occas. spotted red. Late winter–early spring. Mex.

G. rusbyi (Greene) Rose. Tufted herb. Lvs 1–5cm, spathulate, short-pointed, hairy. Infl. 2–3-branched; fls to 1.5mm across, with bands of red dots. Spring. Ariz. and Mex.

G. weinbergii (Rose) Walth. = G. paraguayense.

→Byrnesia, Echeveria, Pachyphytum and Sedum.

Graptophyllum Nees Acanthaceae. 10 everg., glab. shrubs. Lvs opposite, usually entire and painted or spotted. Infl. a short rac. or pan.; cor. tubular, bilabiate. Fr. a capsule. Australasia, SW Pacific. Z10.

G. hortense hort. = G. pictum.

G. pictum (L.) Griff. CARICATURE PLANT. Lax shrub to 2m. Lvs to 15cm, oval-elliptic, subcoriaceous, glossy dark green blotched or marbled cream in central zone. Infl. a rac.; fls crimson. Widespread as an escapee in SE Asia; origin uncertain, possibly New Guinea. 'Igneum': lvs painted red. 'Luridosanguineum': lvs flushed purple, veined crimson. 'Tricolor': lvs oval, acute, purple-green mottled yellow and rose, midrib and petiole flushed red.

✕**Graptophytum** Gossot. (Graptopetalum ✕Pachyphytum.) Crassulaceae. Small rosette-forming succulents, similar to Graptopetalum except fls closer to Pachyphytum, more cup-shaped and not always spotted.

✕**G. 'Anita'.** (Graptopetalum filiferum ✕Pachyphytum oviferum.) Clump-forming. Lvs in rosettes to 10cm diam., broadly obovate, acuminate, flat above, rounded beneath, v. fleshy, glaucous, with pink tips. Infl. lat., around 15cm, pet. dark red, pointed. Spring.

✕**Graptosedum** G. Rowley. (Graptopetalum ✕Sedum.) Crassulaceae. Small subshrubs and rosette-forming succulents, fleshy.

✕**G. 'Heswall'.** (Graptopetalum bellum ✕Sedum suaveolens.) Lvs in rosettes 12–17cm diam., broadly obovate, acuminate, grey-green and glaucous, margins pink. Infl. lat., dome-shaped; pet. 5, white, tips recurved. Spring.

✕**Graptoveria** Gossot. (Graptopetalum ✕Echeveria.) Crassulaceae. Succulents with rosette habit of Echeveria and urn-shaped, yellow to pink fls of Graptopetalum.

Grass Aloe Aloe myriacantha.
Grass Fern Asplenium septentrionale.
Grass Haworthia Haworthia graminifolia.
Grass-leaved Daylily Hemerocallis minor.
Grass-leaf Hakea Hakea francisiana.
Grassnut Triteleia laxa.
Grass of Parnassus Parnassia.
Grass Pansy Viola pedunculata.
Grass Tree Xanthorrhoea.
Grass Vetchling Lathyrus nissolia.
Grass Widow Olsynium douglasii.
Grassy Bells Edraianthus.

Grassy Death Camas Zigadenus venenosus var. gramineus.
Grassy Rush Butomus.

Gratiola L. HEDGE HYSSOP. Scrophulariaceae. 25 erect or creeping, glab. or glandular-pubesc. herbs. Lvs small, usually sessile. Fls solitary, axill.; cal. deeply 5-lobed, subtended by 2 bracteoles; cor. tube wide, limb spreading, upper lip entire or 2-lobed, lower lip larger, 3-lobed. Cosmop.

G. officinalis L. GRATIOLE. Rhizomatous perenn. to 60cm. St. 4-angled. Lvs 2–2.5cm, linear-lanceolate, apex dentate, glandular-punctate. Cor. 10–18mm, tube yellow-white, lobes spreading, white veined purple-red. Summer. Eur. Z6.

Gratiole Gratiola officinalis.
Gravel Bottlebrush Beaufortia sparsa.
Greasewood Adenostoma fasciculatum; Sarcobatus.
Great Alpine Rockfoil Saxifraga cotyledon.
Great Basin Violet Viola beckwithii.
Great Burdock Arctium lappa.
Great Burnet Sanguisorba officinalis.
Great Comb Caladenia dilatata.
Great Double White Rose Rosa ✕alba.
Great Duckweed Spirodela polyrrhiza.
Greater Bird's Foot Trefoil Lotus uliginosus.
Greater Bladderwort Utricularia vulgaris.
Greater Burnet Saxifrage Pimpinella major.
Greater Butterfly Orchid Platanthera chlorantha.
Greater Celandine Chelidonium majus.
Greater Evergreen Saxifrage Saxifraga cotyledon.
Greater Knapweed Centaurea scabiosa.
Greater Masterwort Astrantia major.
Greater Periwinkle Vinca major.
Greater Pond Sedge Carex riparia.
Greater Quaking Grass Briza maxima.
Greater Spearwort Ranunculus lingua.
Greater Water Parsnip Sium latifolium.
Greater Woodrush Luzula maxima.
Great-leaved Macrophylla Magnolia macrophylla.
Great Leopard's Bane Doronicum pardalianches.
Great Lobelia Lobelia siphilitica.
Great Maple Acer pseudoplatanus.
Great Millet Sorghum bicolor.
Great Purple Monkey Flower Mimulus lewisii.
Great Quaking Grass Briza maxima.
Great Rose Mallow Hibiscus grandiflorus.
Great Solomon's Seal Polygonatum biflorum.
Great Sundew Drosera anglica.
Great Water Dock Rumex hydrolapathum.
Great White Cherry Prunus 'Taittaku'.
Great Willowherb Epilobium angustifolium.
Great Yellowcress Rorippa amphibia.
Great Yellow Gentian Gentiana lutea.
Grecian Fir Abies cephalonica.
Grecian Foxglove Digitalis lanata.
Grecian Strawberry Tree Arbutus andrachne.
Grecian Urn Plant Quesnelia marmorata.
Greek Basil Ocimum basilicum.
Greek Clover Trigonella foenum-graecum.
Greek Fir Abies cephalonica.
Greek Hay Trigonella foenum-graecum.
Greek Juniper Juniperus excelsa.
Greek Maple Acer heldreichii.
Greek Valerian Polemonium caeruleum; P. reptans.
Green Alder Alnus viridis.
Green Almond Pistacia vera.
Green Aloe Furcraea foetida.
Green Arrow Arum Peltandra virginica.
Green Ash Fraxinus pennsylvanica var. subintegerrima.
Green Bark Ceanothus Ceanothus spinosus.
Green Bean Phaseolus vulgaris.
Greenbird Flower Crotalaria cunninghamii.
Green Bottlebrush Callistemon viridiflorus.
Green Bristle Grass Setaria viridis.
Green Cliff Brake Pellaea viridis.
Green Douglas Fir Pseudotsuga menziesii.
Green Earthstar Cryptanthus acaulis.
Green Everlasting Gnaphalium californicum.
Green Fivecorner Styphelia viridis.
Green-flowered Wintergreen Pyrola chlorantha.
Green-fly Orchid Epidendrum conopseum.
Green Gentian Frasera (F. speciosa).
Green Gram Vigna radiata.
Greenheart Guettarda scabra.
Green Hellebore Helleborus viridis.
Greenhood Pterostylis.
Green Kangaroo Paw Anigozanthos viridis.

Green Manzanita *Arctostaphylos patula.*
Green Mexican Rose *Echeveria × gilva.*
Green Osier *Cornus alternifolia.*

Greenovia Webb & Berth. Crassulaceae. 4 tuft-forming perenn. herbs. St. short, producing off-sets. Lvs in dense rosettes, fleshy. Flowering st. leafy. Infl. secund, simple or few-branched; sep. 20–32, fused at base, green; pet. 20–32, narrow lanceolate-obovate; sta. twice as many as sep. Canary Is. Z8.

G. aizoon Bolle. Tuft-forming, many-branched. Lvs 3–4cm, glandular-hairy, spathulate-oblong in a flat, dense rosette. Flowering st. to 15cm; fls 12mm across, yellow; sep. 4mm, c20; pet. 6–7mm, c20, oblanceolate, pointed. Spring.

G. aurea (Christ) Webb & Berth. Similar to *G. aizoon* except rosettes several; lvs glaucous; fls 30, to 25mm across; sep. and pet. 35.

G. diplocycla Webb = *G. aurea.*
G. gracilis C. Bolle. = *G. aurea.*

Greenowia Christ = *Greenovia.*

Green Pepper *Capsicum.*
Green-ripple Pepper *Peperomia caperata.*
Green Rose *Rosa chinensis.*
Green-scaled Willow *Salix chlorolepis.*
Green Spleenwort *Asplenium viride.*
Greenthreads *Thelesperma.*
Greentip Kaffir Lily *Clivia nobilis.*
Green Wattle *Acacia decurrens.*
Green-winged Orchid *Orchis morio.*

Grevillea R. Br. ex Knight. SPIDER FLOWER. Proteaceae. Some 250 everg. trees or shrubs. Lvs often dentate or deeply lobed. Rac. or pan. term., fls paired, subtended by a bract; perianth tubular; anth. subsessile; nectary a broad gland. Aus., New Caledonia. Z9.

G. acanthifolia Cunn. Spreading shrub to 3m high. Lvs 8cm, rigid, seg. 3–5 pointed. Fls pink in one-sided, 10cm rac. Spring–early summer. E Aus.

G. acerosa F. Muell. Erect, shrub to 2m, young shoots silky-hairy. Lvs 1–3cm, terete, rigid, pungent, revolute. Fls white, woolly, in umbel-like rac. Spring. W Aus.

G. alpina Lindl. Prostrate to erect shrub to 2m. Lvs 1–3cm, linear to rounded. Fls in short crowded rac., red to pink to white. Winter–spring. E Aus. A variable sp. with red, pink, green, yellow and white fls; many different forms are in cult. 'Coral': to 1m, with clusters of deep pink fls in a spidery head. 'Grampians Gold': fls golden yellow, perianth covered in rusty brown hairs. 'Olympic Flame': dense, rounded shrub to 1m high and wide; lvs pointed; fls profuse, pink-red and cream in pendulous clusters.

G. annulifera F. Muell. PRICKLY PLUME GREVILLEA. Glaucous, straggling shrub, 2–4m. Lvs 1.5–2.5cm, seg. 5–7 narrow-linear, pungent, revolute. Fls in erect showy pan., white to cream, becoming pink with age. Mid-winter–spring. W Aus.

G. aquifolium Lindl. Shrub, prostrate to erect, to 3m. Lvs to 7cm, ovate, holly-like, hairy beneath. Fls 5cm, term. or on short lat. br., green with white hairs; style red. Spring. E Aus. Often confused with *G. ilicifolia.*

G. arenaria R. Br. Rounded woody shrub to 3m. Lvs 4cm, oblong, grey-green, hairy beneath. Fls 2–3, in term. rac., pink to green. Winter–spring. E Aus.

G. aspera R. Br. Compact, rounded shrub to 1m. Lvs 4cm, lanceolate to oblong, hairy beneath. Fls in term., 40cm rac., red and cream. All year. E Aus.

G. asplenifolia Knight. Spreading shrub 3–4m high. Lvs 25cm, linear to linear-lanceolate, entire or incised, hairy beneath. Fls in one-sided term. 5cm, rac., red and green. Late winter–spring. E Aus.

G. 'Audrey' (Purported hybrid of *G. juniperina × G. victoriae.*) Rounded shrub to 2m. Lvs 2.5cm, broad-linear. Fls in dense clusters, orange-red. All year. Gdn origin.

G. 'Australfora Canterbury Gold' (Probably *G. aquifolium × G. acanthifolia.*) Spreading, prostrate. Lvs divided, young growth copper-coloured. Fls in one-sided rac., pink. Gdn origin.

G. australis R. Br. Prostrate to erect, to 2m. Lvs linear and 1cm long to oblanceolate and 3cm long. Fls insignificant in clusters, off-white with rust colouring towards base of perianth. Summer. E Aus.

G. banksii R. Br. RED FLOWERED SILKY OAK. Shrub to 4m. Lvs 25cm, pinnatifid, lobes 15cm, linear, silky grey beneath. Fls red, in cylindrical 10cm rac.; style prominent. All year. E Aus. A variable sp. with several prostrate forms. 'Albiflora': fls white. 'Kangaroo Slippers': sport of *G. banksii* with 'capped' fls; perianth tube, is released from the base, remains attached to the style.

G. bipinnatifida R. Br. Diffuse, decumbent, prickly shrub to 1m. Lvs 7–10cm, deeply pinnatifid, with broad prickly lobes, bright green to grey-green. Fls downy, red to dull yellow, in loose pendent rac., to 15cm. Mid-winter and spring. W Aus.

G. biternata hort. = *G. curviloba.*

G. 'Boongala Spinebill' (Purported hybrid of *G. bipinnatifida × G. caleyi.*) Spreading shrub 2m high. Lvs 12cm, toothed; young growth tinged red. Fls in toothbrush-like term. rac., perianth green, style deep red. Most of the year.

G. brachystylis Meissn. Loosely branched shrub, 30–60cm; young shoots hairy. Lvs 4–8cm, linear-lanceolate, entire. Fls red in umbel-like clusters, pollen presenter with a horny appendage. Spring. W Aus.

G. bracteosa Meissn. Slender shrub to 1.5m. Lvs 2–8cm, narrow-linear, entire or 3-fid. Fls pale pink to purple in globose rac. on leafless flowering br.; floral bracts large. Spring. W Aus.

G. 'Bronze Rambler' Spreading shrub to 30cm. Lvs 10cm, lobes linear, young growth bronze-red. Fls red to deep pink, in one-sided rac. to 8cm. All year.

G. caleyi R. Br. Spreading shrub to 3m high. Lf lobes to 2.5cm, narrow-oblong, revolute. Fls pink-grey, in term., one-sided rac. to 6cm. Spring. E Aus.

G. 'Canberra Gem' (*G. juniperina × G. rosmarinifolia.*) Vigorous rounded shrub to 2.5m high. Lvs 3cm, linear, pungent. Fls in clusters, bright pink, waxy. Most of the year, esp. winter and spring.

G. candelabroides C. Gardn. Shrub to small spruce-like tree to 5m. Lf seg. 8–9 narrow-linear, 8–20cm. Fls creamy white in erect term. pan. of narrow. Summer. W Aus.

G. 'Cascade'. (Purported variant in the *G. triloba–G. tridentifera–G. vestita* group.) Vigorous shrub 3m high by 10m across. Lvs variably lobed. Fls white, in short, slender axill. rac. Spring.

G. 'Clearview David'. (*G. rosmarinifolia × G. lavandulacea.*) Vigorous, compact shrub 2.5m. Lvs 3×0.3cm. Fls rose-red in large spidery clusters. Winter and spring.

G. confertifolia F. Muell. GRAMPIANS GREVILLEA. Upright to spreading shrub, to 1.5m high. Lvs 3cm, narrow-linear, pungent. Fls purple in dense rac. Spring. E Aus.

G. crithmifolia R. Br. Bushy, spreading shrub, to 1.5m. Lvs 1.5–2cm, seg. 3 narrow-linear. Fls fragrant pinky mauve, ageing white, in short, sessile rac. subtended by hairy bracts. Spring. W Aus.

G. 'Crosbie Morrison' (*G. lanigera × G. lavandulacea.*) Low, spreading shrub to 1.5m high. Lvs 1.5cm, linear, grey-green, revolute. Fls red and cream, in dense spidery rac. Winter to early summer.

G. curviloba McGillivray. Erect to prostrate shrub to 2m or more, lf seg. 2cm, narrow-linear, pinted. Fls white, sweetly scented, in loose axill. clusters. Spring. W Aus.

G. depauperata R. Br. Prostrate or spreading shrub, to 1m. Lvs 1–3cm, ovate to narrow-lanceolate, white silky-hairy beneath. Fls red, in few-fld umbel-like rac. Mid-winter and spring. W Aus.

G. dielsiana C. Gardn. Open shrub to 2m high, intricately branched. Lvs 4–5cm, linear-terete, trichotomously divided into 1cm seg. Fls orange or red, in 5–10cm pendulous rac. Mid-winter to spring. W Aus.

G. drummondii (W. Fitzg.) McGillivray. Erect, compact shrub to 2m. Lvs 3–5cm, broad-lanceolate or elliptic, scattered-pubesc. Fls yellow to orange red in pendent terminal rac. Winter and spring. W Aus.

G. endlicheriana Meissn. Straggling shrub to 2m. Lvs 2–8cm, entire, linear to linear-lanceolate, recurved. Fls pink or white in dense, oblong rac., on arching leafless br. Mid-winter and spring. W Aus.

G. fasciculata R. Br. Spreading open shrub to 0.5m. Lvs 0.5–4.5cm, linear-lanceolate. Fls red, hairy, racemose. Winter and spring. W Aus. Many yellow-fld forms in cult.

G. glabrata (Meissn.) McGillivray. Glab. shrub with slender br. Lvs 4.6cm, split into 3 lanceolate, lobed seg. Fls white, in axill. rac. Spring. W Aus.

G. 'Glen Pearl' (Probably *G. victoriae × G. juniperina.*) Erect shrub to 2m high. Lvs 5cm, narrow. Fls salmon-pink, in large clusters. Winter–summer.

G. gordoniana C. Gardn. Tall shrub or small tree to 7m. Lvs to 20cm, terete, grey-green. Fls yellow, numerous in sub-umbellate clusters at the ends of leafless pan. br. Summer. W Aus.

G. hilliana F. Muell. Tall tree to 30m. Lvs 20–30cm, lobed to entire with undulate margins, silver beneath. Fls creamy white in dense, 30cm rac. Winter–early summer. E Aus.

G. hookeriana Meissn. RED TOOTHBRUSHES. Erect shrub, 1–3m, with hairy br. Lvs 15–20cm, seg. 8–9 linear, revolute. Fls white-green in one-sided, spike-like rac.; styles red. Spring. W Aus. 'Hookeriana' (sic) (Purported hybrid of *G. hookeriana* and unknown parent.): rounded dense shrub to 3m high, br. ± horizontal; lvs 5cm, lobes narrow-linear, 3cm; fls bright red in one-sided rac. about 7cm.

G. ilicifolia R. Br. Spreading to erect shrub, to 1.5m. Lvs 2.5–6cm, entire and prickly lobed to pinnatisect. Fls red to yellow in one-sided term. rac. Winter and spring. E Aus.

G. intricata Meissn. Open shrub, 1–3m. Lvs long, slender, ternately divided, seg. terete. Fls yellow to white in slender term. or lat. rac. Mid-winter and spring. W Aus.

G. 'Ivanhoe' (*G. longifolia* × *G. caleyi ?*) Vigorous, dense shrub to 3m. Lvs to 10cm, deeply toothed. Fls red, in one-sided 5cm rac.

G. johnsonii McGillivray. Rounded open shrub to 4m. Lvs 12–25cm, dark green and shiny, seg. narrow-linear. Fls red-cream, waxy, in erect clusters on a red stalk. Late winter and spring. E Aus.

G. juniperina R. Br. Dense rounded shrub, 2m high. Lvs 1–2cm, narrow-lanceolate to narrow-linear. Fls green to yellow to pink, in nodding clusters. Winter to summer. f. *sulphurea* (A.M. Cunn.) I.K. Ferg. Dense rounded shrub, 2m high. Lvs 1–2cm, narrow-lanceolate to narrow-linear. Fls green to yellow to pink, in nodding clusters. Winter to summer. E Aus.

G. lanigera A.M. Cunn. ex R. Br. Rounded shrub 1.5 high. Lvs to 2.5cm, narrow-oblong, green, hairy, revolute. Fls usually yellow, sometimes green or cream to pink and cream in clusters. Winter and spring. E Aus. Z9. Hybridizes with *G. alpina* and *G. rosmarinifolia*.

G. laurifolia Sieber ex Spreng. Prostrate shrub to 5m diam.; young growth tinged red. Lvs to 12cm, oblong, hairy beneath. Fls red, in one-sided 50cm term. rac. Winter and spring. E Aus.

G. lavandulacea Schldl. Low, upright or spreading shrub to 1.2m. Lvs 2.5cm, grey-green, oblong-linear to lanceolate, revolute. Fls red and cream in spidery clusters. Winter and spring. E Aus. Many different forms in cult; hybridizes with *G. alpina*.

G. leucopteris Meissn. Rounded shrub, 2–4m. Lvs 30cm, seg. 8–15 narrow-linear, 8–25cm. Fls white to cream, strong-smelling, in term. pan. raised above, lvs on arching canes. Flowering spring. W Aus.

G. linearifolia (Carr.) Druce. Small open shrub 1m high to medium-sized rounded shrub to 3m. Lvs 2–9cm, linear, revolute. Fls pink or white in slender term. clusters. All year. E Aus.

G. longifolia R. Br. Spreading shrub. Lvs 10–25cm, broadly linear to narrow ovate-elliptic, with coarse teeth. Fls red in one-sided 5cm rac. Winter and spring. E Aus.

G. macrostylis F. Muell. Straight-stemmed, prickly shrub to 2m. Lvs 2–3cm with 3 broad, triangular, lobes, silver beneath. Fls red-orange, few, in axill. or terminal rac. Winter and spring. W Aus.

G. 'Mason's Hybrid' (*G. bipinnatifida* × *G. banksii*.) Bushy shrub to 1.5m high. Lvs with broad-linear seg. Fls orange in loose, almost pendulous rac. to 12cm. All year.

G. miqueliana F. Muell. Erect open shrub to 2m high. Lvs to 6cm, silver beneath. Fls pale with rust red hairs, in pendulous rac., style red. Winter and spring. E Aus.

G. 'Misty Pink' (*G. banksii* × *G. sessilis*.) Erect, bushy shrub to 3m. Lvs pinnate. Fls pale pink in erect, terminal, 15cm, cylindrical rac. All year.

G. mucronulata R. Br. Spreading shrub to 1.5m. Lvs to 3cm, ovate to elliptic, pungent, densely hairy beneath. Fls green in spidery clusters; perianth hairy; style purple-hairy. Winter and spring. E Aus.

G. nudiflora Meissn. Rounded shrub to 40cm or prostrate shrub to 4m wide. Lvs 5–15cm, narrow-linear, revolute. Fls red and yellow on 50cm leafless br., often prostrate. Spring. W Aus.

G. obtusifolia Meissn. = *G. thelemanniana* ssp. *obtusifolia*.

G. ornithopoda Meissn. Glab. shrub to 3m; br. slender, drooping. Lvs to 10cm, pale green, apex deeply 3-lobed, lobes to 3cm, linear, curved outwards. Fls white in dense drooping crowded rac. W Aus. Z10.

G. **Poorinda Hybrids.** 'Poorinda Annette': derived from *G. juniperina*; compact shrub 1m high and 70cm across; lvs broader than in *G. juniperina*. Fls apricot and pink in term. clusters. 'Poorinda Constance' (*G.* 'Constance') (Purported hybrid between *G. juniperina* and the red-fld form of *G. victoriae*.): large rounded shrub to 4m high; lvs 3cm, oblong, pungent, revolute; fls red in spidery clusters on short lat. br.; winter and spring. 'Poorinda Golden Lyre' (Purported hybrid of *G. alpina* × *G. victoriae*.): low, spreading shrub to 1m; lvs 3cm narrow-elliptic, revolute; fls yellow, in clusters on short lat. br.; winter and spring. 'Poorinda Peter' (Purported hybrid of *G. acanthifolia* × *G. longifolia*.): tall spreading shrub 3m high and 4m wide; lvs 15cm, pinnate, occas. bipinnate with new foliage purple to bronze; fls purple-red in one-sized term. rac.; spring and summer. 'Poorinda Pink Coral' (Purported hybrid between *G. juniperina* × *G. victoriae*.): similar to *G. juniperina*; medium-sized shrub 1.5m high, 2m wide; lvs to 3cm, linear,

crowded; fls deep pink and green, in clusters on short br. 'Poorinda Queen' (Purported hybrid between *G. juniperina* × *G. victoriae*.): medium-sized to tall shrub to 4m, usually 2m high, 3m wide; lvs 3cm, broad linear, pungent; fls apricot-pink in large clusters; most of the year. 'Poorinda Royal Mantle' (Purported hybrid of *G. laurifolia* × *G. willisii*): vigorous, prostrate; lvs variable, entire and broadly lanceolate to divided with 11cm long lobes, silver beneath; fls red-brown in one-sided rac.; winter to autumn.

G. paniculata Meissn. Glab., often glaucous shrub, 2–2.5m. Lvs 2.5–4cm, slender, rigid, pungent, twice divided into terete seg. Fls white, sweetly scented, in rac. Spring. W Aus.

G. parallela Knight. SILVER OAK. Small, slender tree to 8m. Lvs 30cm, entire or divided, grey-green pendulous. Fls white or cream in term. branching sprays of 3–5 rac. 10cm long. All year. N Aus.

G. petrophiloides Meissn. Shrub, 1–1.5m, with rigid, erect br. Lvs 10–20cm, erect, ternately or pinnately divided, into linear-terete, 3–5cm seg. Fls red in 10cm, spike-like rac. Mid-winter and spring. W Aus.

G. pinaster Meissn. = *G. thelemanniana* ssp. *pinaster*.

G. 'Pink Lady' (Purported hybrid of *G. juniperina* × *G. rosmarinifolia*.) Low spreading shrub 30cm high and 2m wide. Lvs 1.5cm, linear, revolute. Fls pale pink, in spidery clusters. Winter and spring.

G. 'Pink Surprise' (Purported hybrid of *G. banksii* × *G. whiteana*.) Large shrub to 6m. Lvs grey-green, resembling *G. banksii* except lf sep. narrower. Fls pale-pink, in term. cylindrical rac. to 22cm.

G. pteridifolia Knight. Variable, from a slender tall tree to a prostrate shrub. Lvs 40cm, pinnate, seg. numerous 15cm narrow-linear. Fls golden orange, in terminal or upper axill. rac. 15cm long; style prominent, orange. Winter and spring. N Aus.

G. quercifolia R. Br. Shrub to 1m high, glaucous. Lvs 3–10cm, sinuate-pinnatifid, lobes pungent. Fls purple in dense rac. Spring–early summer. W Aus.

G. repens F. Muell. ex Meissn. Prostrate shrub. Lvs 5cm, ovate, undulate with prickly teeth. Fls maroon to red/pink, in one-sided term. 4cm. rac. Late spring and summer. E Aus.

G. robusta A.M. Cunn. ex R. Br. SILKY OAK. Fast-growing tree to 35m. Lvs 30cm, bronze to dark green, pinnatifid, segs with incised, rounded lobes, silky-hairy beneath. Fls orange in 12cm, one-sided rac. produced singly or in clusters; style prominent, 2cm. Spring. E Aus.

G. rosmarinifolia A. Cunn. Variable shrub, usually 2m high and wide, sometimes dwarf. Lvs 3cm, grey-green, ± rigid, linear to lanceolate, revolute. Fls pink/red with cream, in clusters style smooth, 15cm. Winter and spring. E Aus. 'Lutea': small shrub 40cm high and 50cm wide; lvs 2cm, linear; fls creamy yellow, waxy; late winter and spring. 'Noellii': rounded shrub, 1.5×1.5m. Z8.

G. saccata Benth. Loose spreading shrub, 30–40cm; villous to woolly at first. Lvs 1–2cm, linear to lanceolate. Fls bright red in term. clusters, perianth saccate at the base with 2 hairy ribs. Mid-winter and spring. W Aus.

G. 'Sandra Gordon' (*G. sessilis* × *G. pteridifolia*.) Tall, open, slender shrub to 5m. Lvs 20cm, pinnate, lobes numerous to 7cm with silvery hairs beneath. Fls yellow, woolly in cylindrical rac. to 12cm. Most of the year.

G. × *semperflorens* F.E. Briggs ex Mullig. (*G. thelemanniana* × *G. juniperina* f. *sulphurea*.) Medium shrub to 2m, br. arching. Lvs 4.5cm, divided, occas. entire, seg. 3.5cm, linear. Fls orange-yellow and red, in one-sided pendulous rac. to 3cm, style red. Autumn and winter. Z8.

G. sericea (Sm.) R. Br. Small to medium shrub, to 1.5m. Lvs 6cm, broad-linear to ovate, silky hairy, revolute. Fls pink, occas. white, in term., spidery clusters. All year. E Aus.

G. shiressii Blakely. Medium shrub, 4×3m. Lvs 16cm, lanceolate, undulate, prominent-veined. Fls inconspicuous, green, blue-purple and brown, in axillary clusters. Winter and spring. E Aus.

G. 'Sid Cadwell'. (Chance hybrid of unknown parentage.) Spreading shrub, 1.5m high. Lvs 7cm, variously lobed with broad-linear, pungent seg. Fls red in one-sided, 60cm rac.

G. speciosa (Knight) McGillivray. RED SPIDER. Shrub, low and bushy, to 1m or narrow and 3m high. Lvs 1.5–5cm, narrow-elliptic to ovate, silky beneath. Fls red in spidery clusters; perianth densely hairy. All year. E Aus.

G. 'Starfire' (Seedling selection of a purported hybrid *G. banksii* × *G. pteridifolia*.) Medium shrub 3×2m. Lvs 30cm, pinnate, seg. narrow-linear, grey-green beneath. Fls coppery brown ageing red, in 15cm term., cylindrical rac. All year.

G. sulphurea (A.M. Cunn.) Benth. = *G. juniperina* f. *sulphurea*.

G. synapheae R. Br. Low growing shrub, 30–60cm. Lvs 5–10cm, 3-lobed, 3-toothed. Fls yellow-white, fragrant in 1–2cm, oblong rac., on long peduncles. Mid-winter and spring. W Aus.

G. thelemanniana Endl. Prostrate to low shrub, 1.5m high. Lvs to 5cm, from hirsute grey-green to green, pinnate with narrow-linear seg. Fls pink with green tips, in one-sided term. rac. Late winter and spring. W Aus. ssp. *obtusifolia* (Meissn.) McGillivray. Lvs 2cm, oblong-linear or linear cuneate, obtuse. Spring. ssp. *pinaster* (Meissn.) McGillivray. Erect shrub 1–1.8m high with fls red-white. Clones with grey and blue green foliage are also in cult.

G. thyrsoides Meissn. Semi-prostrate to spreading shrub, 30cm high. Lvs rigid, pinnate, seg. narrow-linear 6–14 pairs. Fls red, hairy in dense, 5–10cm rac. borne on leafless flowering st. Winter. W Aus.

G. triloba Meissn. Medium spreading shrub, 2m high. Lvs 5cm, linear-cuneate, lobes 3, 3cm, revolute. Fls white, sweetly scented on axill. or term. rac. Winter. W Aus.

G. vestita (Endl.) Meissn. Erect, bushy, rhizomatous shrub to 3m, villous. Lvs 4cm, cuneate, apex lobed, lower lvs oblanceolate, sometimes entire. Fls white, prolific, fragrant, in umbel-like clusters. Winter and spring. W Aus.

G. victoriae F. Muell. Variable shrub, usually to 2m. Lvs to 10×2.5cm, grey-green, lanceolate to oblanceolate, silver hairy beneath. Fls red in 7cm, pendulous, term. rac. Winter and spring. E Aus. 'Murray Queen': lvs bright green. 'Waverley Ghost': lvs variegated cream and green.

G. whiteana McGillivray. Usually tall shrub to 5m high, occas. a tree. Lvs to 16cm, silver-green, pinnate, lobes narrow-linear. Fls cream, rarely honey-coloured (*G.* 'Honeycomb'), in 7–12cm cylindrical rac. Winter and spring. E Aus.

G. 'White Wings'. (Purported hybrid of *G. curviloba* ×*G. phanerophlebia*.) Spreading shrub 3m high. Lvs to 4cm, rigid, lobed, seg. linear. Fls white, slender, fragrant. Winter and spring.

G. wickhamii McGillivray. ssp. *aprica*. Large shrub to 5m. Lvs to 8cm, obovate, grey-green, with prickly teeth and coarse venation. Fls red, in 8cm pendulous rac.; perianth with a swollen base. Autumn to spring. N Aus.

G. wilsonii A.M. Cunn.. Erect, open shrub, 1–15m high, glab. Lvs to 5cm, ternately divided, pungent, revolute. Fls scarlet, waxy in short, erect, terminal rac.; style 3.5cm, prominent, red. Mid-winter and spring. W Aus.

Grewia L. Tiliaceae. 150 climbers, shrubs or trees; br. stellate-tomentose. Lvs simple, entire or serrate; stipules persistent. Fls solitary, or in few-fld cymes; sep. 5, stellate-tomentose; pet. 5, usually with nectariferous claws; sta. numerous, distinct. Fr. a small drupe, fleshy or fibrous, sometimes lobed. S & E Asia, Afr., Aus. Z10 unless specified.

G. asiatica L. PHALSA. Subherbaceous shrub to 1.2m. Lvs to 12.5cm, suborbicular, cordate, short-tomentose beneath. Fls less than 2cm diam. Fr. red, small. Asia.

G. biloba D. Don. Decid. shrub to 2.5m. Lvs 5–12cm, ovate to rhombic-ovate, densely stellate-pubesc. beneath, serrate, occas. 3-lobed. Fls to 1.5cm diam., cream-yellow, in pubesc., umbels. Fr. red or orange, mostly 2-lobed, to 1cm diam. E China, Korea. Z6.

G. biloba var. *parviflora* (Bunge) Hand. & Mazz. = *G. biloba*.

G. caffra Meissn. Spreading or climbing everg. shrub, 2–3m. Lvs to 8cm, glabrate, acute or acuminate. Fls 4cm diam., axill., pale lavender pink; sta. yellow, prominent. Fr. globose, without lobes, glab. or sparsely pubesc. E & S Afr.

G. columnaris Sm. = *G. orientalis*.

G. damine Gaertn. Shrub or small tree. Lvs to 7.5cm, elliptic-oblong, obtuse or acute, serrate, grey-hairy beneath. Fls in cymes. Fr. glab. with two lobes. India, Sri Lanka.

G. flavescens Juss. Shrub to 4.5m. Lvs to 10cm, oblanceolate to suborbicular, cordate, densely pubesc. Fls in cymes, yellow; sep. to 2cm. Fr. yellow-brown, flattened, globose, stellate-pubesc., mostly 2-lobed. Afr., Arabia, India.

G. occidentalis L. Shrub or small tree to 2.7m. Lvs to 10cm, lanceolate to rhombic-ovate, glab. or pubesc. above. Fls to 3cm diam., in slender, stalked, fascicles; sep. to 2cm, linear, pink-purple inside; pet. pink, mauve or white. Fr. to 2cm diam., red-mauve, glossy, mostly with 4 lobes. Afr.

G. oppositifolia Roxb. Small, decid. tree. Lvs 6–10cm, ovate, bluntly toothed, pubesc. beneath, base rounded. Fls to 3cm diam., tinged yellow, in stalked fascicles of 8–20; sep. to 2cm, linear. Fr. tinged black, pea-sized. Himal. Z9.

G. orientalis L. Trailing or erect shrub. Lvs 7.5cm, ovate to oblong, shortly acuminate, scabrous beneath. Fls in cymes; sep. to 1cm, yellow; pet. white or yellow. Fr. to 1.5cm diam., tinged purple, with 4 shallow lobes. India.

G. parviflora Bunge = *G. biloba*.

G. parviflora var. *glabrescens* (Benth.) Rehd. & Wils. = *G. biloba*.

G. retinervis Burret. Close to *G. flavescens*, but differing in its shorter and cylindrical habit, glab. lvs, and glossy red-brown minutely pubesc. fr. without lobes. E Afr.

G. rothii DC. Close to *G. damine*, but differing in its acuminate, almost serrate lvs, longer peduncles and white-tomentose fr. without lobes. India.

G. salviifolia Roxb. = *G. damine*.

G. similis Schum. Climbing shrub to 4.5m. Lvs to 10cm, ovate to ovate-elliptic. Fls in cymes, mauve. Fr. deep orange, 4-lobed. India.

G. tiliifolia Vahl. Small tree. Lvs to 10cm, ovate to orbicular. Fls in cymes; sep. to 1.5cm. Fr. tinged black, lobes 2 or 0. India.

Grey Alder *Alnus incana*.
Grey Ball Sage *Salvia dorrii*.
Grey Birch *Betula populifolia*.
Grey Box *Eucalyptus moluccana*.
Grey Douglas Fir *Pseudotsuga menziesii* var. *caesia*.
Grey Fescue *Festuca glauca*.
Grey Fig *Ficus virens*.
Grey Goddess *Brahea armata*.
Grey Gum *Eucalyptus punctata*.
Grey-head Coneflower *Ratibida pinnata*.

Greyia Hook. & Harv. NATAL BOTTLEBRUSH. Greyiaceae. 3 shrubs or small trees. Lvs clustered at st. tips. Rac. short, terminal, fls small, showy; sep. and pet. 5; disc fleshy; sta. 10, elongate. S Afr. Z9.

G. radlkoferi Szyszyl. Closely resembles *G. sutherlandii* except larger in all parts. Lvs tomentose beneath when young. Pet. narrowed at base.

G. sutherlandii Hook. & Harv. To 4.5m. Lvs to 7cm, sub-orbicular to oblong, base cordate, deeply dentate, glab. Infl. to 10×5cm; fls red; pet. oblong, fil. red.

GREYIACEAE Hutch. See *Greyia*.

Grey Ironbark *Eucalyptus paniculata*.
Greyleaf Cherry *Prunus canescens*.
Grey Mulga *Acacia brachybotrya*.
Grey Parrot Pea *Dillwynia cinerascens*.
Grey Pea *Pisum sativum* var. *arvense*.
Grey Poplar *Populus* ×*canescens*.
Grey Rayflower *Cyphanthera albicans*.
Grey Sally *Acacia prominens*.
Grey Sunray *Helipterum corymbiflorum*.
Grey Teak *Gmelina leichthardtii*.
Grey Willow *Salix cinerea*.

Grias L. Lecythidaceae. 6 everg. trees. Lvs grouped at ends of br., sessile or long-stalked, large, leathery, usually glab. Fls fragrant, borne on trunk or br., in fascicles, or rac.; pedicels with a single bract and 2 bracteoles; cal. 2–4-lobed or entire; pet. 4, fleshy; sta. numerous, incurved, in 3–5 concentric rings. Fr. 1-seeded, indehiscent, fusiform or pyriform, ribbed. C Amer., Jam., NW S Amer. Z10.

G. cauliflora L. ANCHOVY PEAR. To 30m, trunk 45cm diam. Lvs to 110×28cm, oblanceolate, acuminate, entire. Fls 2.5–5cm diam., in fascicles of 2–4; cal. entire or splitting; pet. white or cream; sta. 85–150. Fr. to 9×4cm, brown. Jam., Guat. and Belize to Colomb.

G. foetidissima Dugand = *G. neuberthii*.
G. grandifolia Pilger = *G. peruviana*.
G. loretensis Knuth = *G. neuberthii*.
G. maranoensis Knuth = *G. peruviana*.

G. neuberthii Macbr. To 20m. Lvs to 120×22cm, oblanceolate, entire, apex acuminate, base attenuate. Fls 5–8cm diam., in rac. to 35cm; cal. 4-lobed; pet. yellow tinged pink or red; sta. to 210. Fr. to 13×6cm, brown. S Colomb., E Ecuad., N Peru.

G. peruviana Miers. To 30m. Lvs to 118×35cm, elliptic or oblanceolate, entire or serrulate, apex acuminate or attenuate. Fls 3.5–7cm diam., in rac. to 12cm; cal. entire or splitting; pet. yellow or white; sta. 90–180. Fr. to 13×7cm, brown with yellow flesh. NW Ecuad. to Peru.

G. tessmannii Knuth = *G. peruviana*.

Griegia Reg. Bromeliaceae. 26 perenn. herbs. Lvs overlapping along st. (rosettes not dying after flowering), linear or narrowly triangular, toothed. Infl. lat., short-stemmed dense; fls small, fleshy. S Mex. to C Peru, S Chile.

G. mulfordii L.B. Sm. 30–150cm. Lvs 80cm, brown-scaly, linear. Infl. 6–7cm, flattened, many-fld; bracts dark brown with green margins, broadly elliptic, slightly toothed; floral bracts 3cm, lanceolate, dark brown and leathery, base and margins pale-membranous, apex acuminate; pet. 35mm, pale lilac. Colomb., Ecuad.

G. oaxacana L.B. Sm. To 90cm. Lvs to 90cm, drooping, glab. above, white-scaly beneath, linear, teeth prominent. Infl. few-fld, ± compound; bracts dark brown, narrowly ovate, lower bracts pale-margined, upper with green, toothed, densely scaly apices; floral bracts 2.1cm, dark brown toward mucronate apex, linear-lanceolate; pet. 25mm, white tipped pale lavender. S Mex.

Griffinia Ker-Gawl. Amaryllidaceae. 7 bulbous perenn. herbs. Lvs broad, usually petiolate. Fls in scapose umbels; perianth 6-lobed, funnel-shaped, 3 upper seg. broader, directed upwards, 2 lower seg. spreading, the third directed downwards. Braz. Z10.

G. blumenavia K. Koch & Bouché ex Carr. = Hippeastrum blumenavium.

G. dryades M. Roem. To 45cm. Lvs 12–15cm, oblong to lanceolate; petiole 15–20cm. Fls 10–13 per umbel, purple, lilac, white at centre. Early summer. S Braz.

G. hyacinthina Ker-Gawl. To 60cm. Lvs 15–22.5cm, ovate to oblong; petiole 15–22.5cm. Fls to 4.5cm diam., 9–10 per umbel, white sometimes tipped blue or tinted. Early summer. Braz. 'Micrantha': fls to 2.5cm. 'Maxima': lvs broadly ovate to oblong; fls 10–12 per umbel, 12.5cm diam., white, tipped deep blue.

G. intermedia Lindl. To 30cm. Lvs oblong, acute, narrowing into a long petiole. Fls 6–10 per umbel, to 3.5cm, pale lilac. Early summer. Braz.

G. liboniana Lem. To 30cm. Lvs 7.5–10cm, oblong-acute, sessile. Fls 2.5–3cm, 6–8 per umbel, pale lilac. Early summer. C Braz.

G. ornata T. Moore. To 45cm. Lvs to 30cm, elliptic to oblong; petiole short. Fls 20–24 per umbel, opalescent to nearly white. Early summer.

G. parviflora Ker-Gawl. To 30cm. Lvs to 15cm, oblong, acute; petiole 15cm. Fls 2–3cm, 10–15 per umbel, pale lilac. Early summer. Braz.

G. rochae G.M. Morel. To 25cm. Lvs to 12cm, oblong, acute; petiole 5–6cm. Fls to 3cm, 6–8 per umbel, bright lilac. Braz.
→*Amaryllis*.

Grindelia Willd. GUM PLANT; TARWEED; ROSIN-WEED. Compositae. c60 ann. or perenn. herbs, rarely shrubs. Lvs ± resinous-punctate. Cap. usually radiate, several or numerous, fairly large; involucre producing white gum; ray flts yellow; disc flts yellow. W N & S Amer.

G. arenicola Steyerm. = G. stricta ssp. venulosa.

G. arguta A. Gray = G. inuloides.

G. camporum Greene. Ann. or perenn. to 1.5m; st. erect, simple or openly branched, glab. Lvs 2–8cm, narrowly oblong to broadly oblanceolate, dentate, glab. or scabrous, subcoriaceous, resinous. Cap. 2.5–4cm diam., phyllaries elongate, tips green, recurved or hooked; ray flts to 1.5cm, 18–35. Summer–autumn. Calif. Z8.

G. chiloensis (Cornelisson) Cabr. Suffruticose perenn. to 1m; st. ascending, branched from base, glab., resinous. Lvs to 10cm, mostly basal, oblanceolate to obovate, entire or serrate. Cap. to 5cm diam., phyllaries lanceolate, glab.; ray flts to 1.3cm, 20–30. Summer. Patagonia. Z6.

G. glutinosa (Cav.) Dunal. Everg. subshrubby perenn. to 60cm; st. erect, branching, viscid above. Lvs to 10cm, obovate-oblong, dentate, viscid. Cap. to 4.5cm diam.; phyllaries linear-acuminate, aristate; ray flts to 1.5cm, 13–30. Winter. Peru. Z8.

G. grandiflora Hook. = G. squarrosa.

G. humilis Hook. & Arn. MARSH GRINDELIA. Shrubby perenn. to 1.5m; br. subcorymbose, glab. to villous. Lvs 2–8cm, cuneate-oblanceolate to oblong-lanceolate, minutely serrate, coriaceous, scarcely resinous. Cap. 3–5cm diam., phyllaries lanceolate, erect, tips short, flat, reflexed; ray flts to 1.8cm, 16–34. Summer–autumn. Calif. Z8.

G. integrifolia DC. Perenn. to 80cm; st. several, erect or ascending, glab. or somewhat villous. Lvs to 35cm, lanceolate to oblanceolate, entire or serrate, membranous, occas. auriculate-amplexicaul above. Cap. 2.5–4cm diam., phyllaries with slender green tips, loose or gently recurved; ray flts to 1.5cm, 10–35. Summer–early autumn. W US and Canada. Z7.

G. inuloides Willd. Perenn. herb to 50cm; st. erect or ascending, villous or minutely pubesc. Basal lvs to 18cm, elliptic, serrate to pinnatifid, st. lvs narrower, often amplexicaul, entire to distinctly serrate. Cap. to 5cm diam.; phyllaries graduate, linear to oblong-lanceolate, innermost broader; ray flts to 1.8cm, 20–30. Summer. Mex. Z8.

G. lanceolata Nutt. Bienn. herb to 1.5m; st. branched above, usually glab. Lvs to 11cm, linear or oblong-lanceolate, with bristle-tipped teeth, occas. entire. Cap. to 5cm diam.; phyllaries loose, subequal; ray flts to 1.5cm, 15–30. Summer–autumn. SC US. Z5.

G. latifolia Kellogg. COASTAL GUM-PLANT. Succulent perenn. herb, to 60cm; st. stout, decumbent or ascending. Lvs to 8cm, mostly cauline, lanceolate-ovate to broadly oblong, serrate to

dentate, base amplexicaul to subcordate, thick, scabrous, ciliate. Cap. 5cm diam.; phyllaries leaflike, outermost with green squarrose tips; ray flts to 1.5cm, 30–45. Summer. Calif. Z8.

G. maritima (Greene) Steyerm. Perenn. herb to 80cm; st. slender, erect, laxly branched. Lvs to 18cm, narrowly oblanceolate, minutely serrate, petiolate, st. lvs smaller, amplexicaul. Cap. 4cm diam.; phyllaries mostly erect, green, with short tips; ray flts to 1.3cm, 30–40. Late summer–early autumn. Calif. Z8.

G. robusta Nutt. Perenn. herb to 1.2m; st. few, erect, stout, corymbosely branched above, glab. Lvs to 18cm, oblanceolate, entire to sharply dentate or finely serrate. Cap. to 5cm diam.; phyllaries with green, strongly recurved tips; ray flts 25–45, 8–15mm. Spring–autumn. Calif., Baja Calif. Z7.

G. rubicaulis var. **maritima** Greene = G. maritima.

G. rubicaulis var. **robusta** DC. = G. robusta.

G. speciosa Lindl. & Paxt. = G. chiloensis.

G. squarrosa (Pursh) Dunal. Bienn. or perenn. to 1m; st. branched above, sometimes at base. Lvs to 7cm, ovate or oblong to oblanceolate,, entire or finely serrate, or lower lvs coarsely bluntly dentate or pinnatifid, punctate. Cap. to 3cm diam.; phyllaries with green, squarrose-reflexed tips; ray flts to 1.5cm, 20–35, or 0. Summer–autumn. W & C N Amer. Z3.

G. stricta DC. PACIFIC GRINDELIA. Perenn. herb to 90cm; st. simple or branched, decumbent to ascending, occas. gland. Lvs to 25cm, oblong to oblanceolate, entire to minutely serrate above, base attenuate, petiolate; st. lvs amplexicaul. Cap. 4–5cm diam.; phyllaries linear-lanceolate, erect, with slender, recurved tips; ray flts to 2cm, 10–35. Summer–early autumn. W N Amer. ssp. **venulosa** (Jeps.) Keck. St. procumbent to decumbent. Lvs shorter, broader and more succulent, rounded. Phyllaries with reflexed or coiled tips. SW US. Z8.

G. venulosa Jeps. = G. stricta ssp. venulosa.
→*Aster, Donia* and *Hoorebekia*.

Grisebachia Wendl. & Drude.
G. belmoreana C. Moore & F. Muell. = Howea belmoreana.

Griselinia Forst. Cornaceae. 6 everg. trees and shrubs. Lvs alt., coriaceous. Fls insignificant, 5-merous in axill. pan. or rac. Late spring. NZ, Braz., Chile.

G. littoralis Raoul. Dense, everg. shrub or small tree, to 8m. Br. dark gold to brown-yellow. Lvs 9×4.5cm, ovate to oblong, apple green, glossy, slightly fleshy, ± undulate. NZ. Z7. 'Dixon's Cream': splashes of creamy white. 'Variegata': blotched or zoned white.

G. lucida Forst. Erect, branching shrub to 4m. Br. brown-black. Lvs larger than in G. littoralis, to 18×10cm, mid-green, glossy; petioles longer, to 2.5cm. var. **macrophylla** Hook. Lvs orbicular or subcordate. NZ. Z8. 'Variegata': lvs marked yellow-cream and dull green.

Grobya Lindl. Orchidaceae. 3 epiphytic orchids. Rhiz. short. Pbs short. Lvs narrow, plicate. Rac. basal; fls large; dors. sep. free, erect, lateral sep. shortly connate, spreading; pet. broader, erect to spreading; lip small, articulated, erect, 3-lobed, disc callose. Braz. Z10.

G. amherstiae Lindl. Pbs to 3.5cm, tufted, ovoid to subglobose, 4 to 6-lvd at apex. Lvs to 40cm, linear-lanceolate, rigid. Infl. to 15cm; tep. to 2cm, obovate to elliptic, pale green to yellow tinged and spotted purple; lat. sep. twisted; lip to 7×8mm, pale yellow, lat. lobes subrotund, midlobe transversely elliptic, callus dull purple. E Braz.

Groenlandia Gay. FROG'S LETTUCE. Potamogetonaceae. 1 aquatic herb. St. to 30cm, branching above. Lvs submerged, 2×1cm, lanceolate, sessile, in opposite pairs or a whorl of 3. Fls 4 on a short erect stalk, strongly recurved after flowering. W Afr., Asia, Eur. Z7.

G. densa Fourr.
→*Potamogeton*.

Gromwell's Puccoon *Lithospermum*.

Gronophyllum R. Scheff. Palmae. 3 tall palms. St. erect, solitary or clustered, bare, ringed. Crownshaft prominent, densely scurfy and hairy. Lvs pinnate; petiole channelled above; pinnae regularly spaced or clustered, ribs minutely scaly and scurfy. Infl. at base of crownshaft, arching, much-branched; rachillae straight or flexuous, bearing 2 rows of white to cream fls in triads (2 ♂ and 1 ♀). Fr. smooth, globose to ellipsoid. Celebes, Moluccas, New Guinea, N Aus. Z10.

G. ramsayi (Becc.) Moore. NORTHERN KENTIA PALM. To 35m. St. to 25cm diam., ringed dark grey. Crownshaft to 1m, pale yellow, pruinose. Lvs to 2.5m; pinnae to 70×5cm, grey-green, linear, acuminate. Infl. to 40cm. Fr. to 1.5cm, bright waxy red. N Aus.

Grosourdya Rchb. f. Orchidaceae. 10 monopodial epiphytic orchids. Lvs linear-oblong, 2-ranked along st. Sep. oblong-ligulate, apex broad, pointed; pet. narrower; lip clawed, linear-subulate, abruptly expanded; midlobe 3-toothed, keels 2, inflated, filamentous. Malaysia, Indon. Z10.
G. muscosa (Rolfe) Garay. Rac. short, axill.; fls few, dull yellow, tep. spotted red-brown at base, lip white, spotted and streaked purple near spur aperture; spur apex pale yellow. Andaman Is.
→*Sarcochilus*.

Grossularia Mill. = *Ribes*.
G. ×*robusta* (Jancz.) A. Berger = *Ribes* ×*robustum*.

GROSSULARIACEAE DC. 23/340. *Anopterus, Carpodetus, Escallonia, Itea, Quintinia* and *Ribes*.

Ground Ash *Aegopodium podagraria*.
Ground Cedar *Lycopodium complanatum*.
Ground Cherry *Physalis* (*P. pubescens*).
Ground Elder *Aegopodium podagraria*.
Ground Ivy *Glechoma hederacea*.
Groundnut *Arachis hypogaea; Panax trifolius*.
Ground Pine *Ajuga chamaepitys; Lycopodium clavatum; L. complanatum; L. obscurum*.
Ground-pink *Linanthus dianthiflorus*.
Ground Plum *Astragalus crassicarpus*.
Ground Rattan *Rhapis excelsa*.
Ground Rose *Protea pudens*.
Groundsel Tree *Baccharis halimifolia*.
Grouseberry *Vaccinium scoparium*.
Grub Fern *Polypodium formosanum*.
Gru Gru *Acrocomia aculeata*.

Grumilea Gaertn.
G. capensis (Ecklon) Sonder = *Psychotria capensis*.

Grusonia Schum. ex Britt. & Rose.
G. bradtiana (Coult.) Britt. & Rose = *Opuntia bradtiana*.
G. santamaria Baxter = *Opuntia santamaria*.

Guaba *Inga vera*.
Guadalupe Cypress *Cupressus guadalupensis*.
Guadalupe Palm *Brahea edulis*.

Guaiacum L. Zygophyllaceae. 6 resinous, everg. trees or shrubs, often with swollen nodes. Lvs opposite, pinnate, ± coriaceous. Fls in clusters or solitary, stipulate; sep. 4 or 5, free; pet. 4 or 5, free; sta. 8–10, fil. with basal glands. Fr. a capsule, orange to yellow, *c*2cm, obovoid. C & S Amer. Z10.
G. officinale L. LIGNUM VITAE. Tree to 9m. Lvs about 9cm; lfts 1–5cm, elliptic to broadly obovate glab., 2–4 pairs; stipules *c*1mm, pubesc. Fls in clusters; stalks and sep. with pale down; pet. *c*1.2cm, obovate, blue, tomentose at apex. S C Amer. to N S Amer., Carib.
G. sanctum L. Tree or shrub to 10m. Lvs 4–10cm; lfts 1.5–3.5cm, oblong to obovate to lanceolate, glab., 2–5 pairs; stipules 2–3mm, pubesc. Fls solitary or in clusters, stalks hairy; pet. *c*1cm, blue or purple, glab. Flor. to N S Amer. and Carib.

Guamá *Inga laurina*.
Guanabana *Annona muricata*.
Guano *Coccothrinax argentea; Copernicia glabrescens; Copernicia hospita*.
Guano Blanco *Copernicia glabrescens; C. occidentalis*.
Guano Cana *Sabal parviflora*.
Guano Espinoso *Copernicia hospita*.
Guano Hediondo *Copernicia hospita*.
Guano Jata *Copernicia glabrescens*.
Guapiruvu *Schizolobium*.
Guar *Cyamopsis tetragonolobus*.
Guaramaco *Brownea latifolia*.
Guaran Colorado *Tecoma garrocha*.
Guariroba do Campo *Syagrus comosa*.
Guava *Psidium* (*P. guineense*).
Guayacan *Tabebuia serratifolia*.
Guayacan Polvillo *Tabebuia serratifolia*.
Guayiga *Zamia pumila*.
Guayule *Parthenium argentatum*.
Guelder Rose *Viburnum opulus*.
Guernsey Lily *Nerine sarniensis*.
Gueta *Cordia crenata*.

Guettarda L. Rubiaceae. 50 or more shrubs or small trees. Lvs stipulate. Fls ± sessile in axill., often secund, bifurcate cymes, or solitary; cal. tube ovoid or globose, limb tubular, cup- or bell-shaped, truncate, irregularly dentate, decid.; cor. salverform or funnel-shaped, lobes 4–9; sta. 4–9, anth. included. Fr. a drupe, globose or ovoid. Trop. Amer. Z10.
G. coccinea Aubl. = *Isertia coccinea*.
G. odorata (Jacq.) Lam. Shrub to 4m. Lvs to 7×4cm, oval or elliptic-oblong, narrowly acute at apex, obtuse or narrowed at base, membranous, glossy above, paler and hairy beneath. Fls to 2cm, many, in axill. cymes, pale red or white, fragrant. Fr. to 0.6cm diam., woolly. Summer. C Amer.
G. scabra (L.) Lam. ROUGH VELVET-SEED; VELVET-BERRY; GREEN-HEART. To 10m. Lvs to 15×10cm, oblong to oblong-ovate to oblong or elliptic, obtuse to mucronate at apex, obtuse or sub-cordate at base, leathery, scabrous above, pubesc. beneath. Fls to 2.5cm, few, in cymes, white, occas. tinged pink. Fr. to 0.8cm diam., red, pubesc. Flor. to Braz., W Indies.
G. speciosa L. To 5m. Lvs 20×15cm, broadly obovate or ovate, acute or obtuse at apex, obtuse or cordate at base, glab. above, pubesc. beneath. Fls to 4cm, in dense axill. cymes, white. Fr. to 2.5cm diam., white to brown. Summer. E Afr., Trop. Asia to Aus. and Polyn.
→*Matthiola*.

Guiana Chestnut *Pachira aquatica*.

Guichenotia Gay. Sterculiaceae. 6 everg., stellate-hairy shrubs. Lvs narrow, revolute; stipules similar to lvs but shorter. Fls in rac.; cal. conspicuous, 5-lobed with raised ribs; pet. 5, small, scale-like; sta. 5, connate at base or free. SW Aus. Z10.
G. ledifolia Gay. To 1.5m. Lvs 3–6cm, linear, densely stellate-hairy. Rac. 3–6-fld; cal. 0.6–0.7cm, mauve, densely stellate-hairy, lobes narrowly ovate, slightly longer than tube; sta. 4–5mm, anth. longer than fil. SW Aus.
G. macrantha Turcz. To 2m. Lvs 3–10cm, linear, becoming glab. above. Rac. 2–4-fld; cal. 1.5–2.2cm, pink to mauve, stellate-hairy, lobes triangular, equalling tube; sta. 5–8mm, anth. dark-purple, much longer than fil. SW Aus.

Guilandina L.
G. echinata (Lam.) Spreng. = *Caesalpinia echinata*.

Guilelma auctt.
G. gasipaes (HBK) L.H. Bail. = *Bactris gasipaes*.
G. utilis Ørst. = *Bactris gasipaes*.

Guindo Beech *Nothofagus betuloides*.
Guinea Cubeb *Piper guineense*.
Guinea Gold Vine *Hibbertia*.
Guinea Grains *Aframomum melegueta*.
Guinea-hen Flower *Fritillaria meleagris*.
Guinea Pepper *Xylopia aethiopica*.
Guinea-wing Begonia *Begonia albopicta*.

Guizotia Cass. Compositae. 6 ann. or perenn. herbs or shrubs. St. leafy, branched. Lvs simple, uppermost alt., basally fused, often leathery, entire to serrate, lower lvs opposite. Cap. erect, radiate; ray flts yellow, elliptic, apex truncate, 3-lobed; disc flts yellow. W & E Afr.
G. abyssinica (L. f.) Cass. Erect, glab. or glandular-pubesc. ann. to 2m. St. branched, occas. purple-stained. Lvs to 15cm, entire to serrate, ampelixcaul. Cap. many, 1–2cm diam.; peduncles 1–2cm, densely hairy beneath head; ray flts 6–15, *c*2mm. Ethiop., nat. India.
→*Verbesina*.

Gular *Ficus racemosa*.
Gulf Vervain *Verbena xutha*.
Gully Gum *Eucalyptus smithii*.
Gum Arabic Tree *Acacia nilotica; A. senegal; A. seyal*.
Gumbo *Abelmoschus esculentus*.
Gum Lac *Schleichera oleosa*.
Gummy Gooseberry *Ribes lobbii*.
Gum Plant *Grindelia*.
Gum Tree *Eucalyptus*.
Gundablue Wattle *Acacia victoriae*.

Gundelia L. Compositae. 1 thistle-like, perenn. herb with milky sap, to 1m. St. erect, branching. Lvs to 30cm, alt., lanceolate, pinnatisect, dentate, sessile or decurrent into st. wings. Cap. discoid, to 5×4cm term., solitary, subtended by a bract; phyllaries united into a turbinate cupule, prickly; flts 4–8, yellow, green, white, maroon or purple. SW Asia to Iran.
G. tournefortii L.

Gungurru *Eucalyptus caesia.*

Gunnera L. Gunneraceae (Haloragidaceae). 40–50 stoutly rhizomatous or creeping, giant or diminutive perenn. herbs. Lvs round to ovate, often cordate and lobed, usually toothed with long petioles and conspicuous stipules. Fls minute, packed in brush-like scapose spikes or pan. Fr. clustered, drupaceous. Summer. Australasia, S Afr., S Amer., Pacific region N to Hawaii. Z8.

G. albocarpa (T. Kirk) Ckn. Mat-forming. Lvs 1–2cm wide, long-stalked, deep green, rounded to reniform, 3–5-lobed, coarsely toothed and sparsely hairy. Fr. 2–3mm, white. NZ.

G. arenaria Cheesem. Mat-forming. Lvs 1cm, short-stalked, deep green, sometimes, tinted grey, ovate to oblong, coarsely crenate. Fr. 4–6mm, yellow to pale red. NZ.

G. brasiliensis Schindl. = *G. manicata.*

G. chilensis Lam. = *G. tinctoria.*

G. densiflora Hook. f. Mat-forming. Lvs 1.5–3.5cm long-petiolate, deep green, broadly ovate, coarsely toothed. Fr. 3mm, deep red. NZ.

G. dentata T. Kirk. Mat-forming. Lvs to 2.5cm, long-petiolate, deep green, sometimes grey-green, broadly-ovate to elliptic-oblong, irregularly toothed, sometimes lobed. Fr. 3–5mm, orange to red. NZ.

G. flavida Colenso. Mat-forming. Lvs to 2.5cm, long-petiolate, brown or coppery green, broadly elliptic to oblong, shallow-crenate. Fr. 3–5mm, pale yellow or white. NZ.

G. hamiltonii T. Kirk ex Hamilt. Cushion-forming. Lvs to 3cm, usually slate-green, triangular-ovate, crenulate. Fr. 3mm. NZ (Stewart Is.).

G. magellanica Lam. Mat-forming. Lvs 5–9cm diam., erect, stalks 8–15cm; blades reniform, somewhat cupped, deep green, crenate. Fr. 5mm, orange to red. S S Amer., Falkland Is.

G. manicata Lind. ex André. GIANT RHUBARB. Clump-forming, eventually exceeding 4–wam across. Lvs with stout prickly stalks 1.5–2.4m tall; blades rounded to reniform, 1.5–2m diam. sometimes more, palmately lobed, sharply toothed, with v. prominent, prickly veins beneath. Fls in stiff, 1–2m conical pan., green or rusty red. Fr. 2–3mm, not fleshy, red-green. S Braz., Colomb.

G. monoica Raoul. Mat-forming. Lvs to 1.5cm, long-petioled, clear deep green, broadly ovate to reniform with a cordate base and several toothed lobes. Fr. to 2mm diam., white. NZ.

G. prorepens Hook. f. Mat-forming. Lvs to 3cm+, short-petiolate, ovate, purple-green, crenate. Fr. 3–4mm, deep red. NZ.

G. scabra Ruiz & Pav. = *G. tinctoria.*

G. tinctoria (Molina) Mirb. Much like *G. manicata* but differs in forming smaller clumps; lf blades shorter, blades 60–150cm wide, rounded in outline with sharply pointed lobes; pan. shorter, more cylindrical; fls and fr. usually more strongly red-tinted. Chile.

GUNNERACEAE Meissn. See *Gunnera.*

Gunpowder Plant *Pilea microphylla.*

Gurania Cogn. Cucurbitaceae. 75 ann. or perenn. herbs climbing by simple tendrils. ♂ infl. a rac. or cap.; receptacle tubular; sep. narrow, tinged red, exceeding pet.; pet. ligulate, yellow; sta. 2; ♀ fls solitary or clustered, similar to ♂ except staminodes 0–2. Fr. long, cylindric, fleshy. Trop. Amer. Z10.

G. makoyana (Lem.) Cogn. Hairy perenn. climber. Lvs sub-orbicular, 15–35×18–4cm, lobes 3, rounded, acuminate, denticulate. ♂ infl. capitate, ♀ infl. a few fld cluster; sep. *c*2cm, shorter in ♀ fls; pet. to 0.8cm, fused. Fr. green. Guat., Hond.

Guriry *Syagrus petraea.*

Gustavia L. Lecythidaceae. 41 everg. trees. Lvs clustered at the ends of br. Fls showy in term. or axill. rac.; pedicels bracteolate, long; cal. entire or 4–6-lobed; pet. 6 or 8; sta. numerous, fused into a ring, anth. yellow. Fr. berry-like. C & S Amer. Z10.

G. augusta L. To 22m, sometimes shrub-like. Lvs to 48×13cm, obovate to oblanceolate, entire to serrulate. Fls 9–20cm diam., in rac. of 1–8, usually above lvs; pet. 6–9, white, tinged pink below. Guianas, Amazonia.

G. gracillima Miers. Small slender tree. Lvs to 46×3.5cm, narrow elliptic or lanceolate, serrulate. Fls axill. or on st., 10cm diam.; pet. 8, narrowly obovate or oblanceolate, pink or purple. W Colomb.

G. hexapetala (Aubl.) Sm. To 20m. Lvs to 24×12cm, elliptic, oblanceolate or obovate, entire or serrulate. Fls 1–4, in axils of uppermost lf or bract, 6–9cm diam.; pet. 5–8, white. Amazonia, Guianas and N Venez.

G. insignis Hook. = *G. augusta.*

G. pterocarpa Poit. = *G. hexapetala.*

G. speciosa (Kunth) DC. To 20m. Lvs to 44×18cm, narrowly elliptic, oblanceolate or narrowly ovate, entire or serrulate. Rac. 3–10-fld, to 7cm, above lvs; fls 13–14cm diam.; pet. 6 or 8, white, exterior sometimes tinged rose. Colomb., Ecuad.

G. superba (Kunth) Berg. To 20m. Lvs to 128×25cm, oblanceolate, serrate. Rac. to 7cm, 3–12 fld; fls 10–15cm diam., bracteoles fused to form a cup; pet. 7–9, white, tipped and speckled pink. SW Costa Rica to NW Colomb.

→*Pirigara.*

Gutierrezia Lagasca. BROOMWEED; SNAKEWEED; MATCHWEED. Compositae. 19 viscid, perenn. herbs and subshrubs. St. many, slender. Lvs alt., linear to oblanceolate, entire, glab. Cap. radiate, numerous, small, in cymes or pan.; flts few, yellow. W N Amer. & warm S Amer.

G. sarothrae (Pursh) Britt. & Rusby. Subshrub to 1m. Lvs to 8cm, linear-lanceolate. Cap. few, turbinate, term. Summer–autumn. W N Amer.

Gutta-percha Tree *Eucommia ulmoides.*

GUTTIFERAE Juss. 47/1350. *Calophyllum, Clusia, Garcinia, Hypericum, Mammea, Mesua.*

Guzmania Ruiz & Pav. Bromeliaceae. 126 ± stemless perenn., epiphytic herbs. Lvs forming a rosette, entire. Infl. simple or bipinnate, br. with fls in many rows, scapose, with brightly coloured bracts. S US, Mex., W Indies to Braz., Boliv., Peru. Z10.

G. angustifolia (Bak.) Wittm. To 20cm in fl. Lvs 8–12cm, erect, narrowly lanceolate, green to red, grey scaly beneath. Infl. sparse, simple-spicate, tip arched and sterile; floral bracts red, enclosing sep.; pet. bright yellow. Costa Rica, Panama, Ecuad., Columbia.

G. bulliana André = *G. angustifolia.*

G. caulescens Mez & Sodiro = *G. angustifolia.*

G. dissitiflora (André) L.B. Sm. To 90cm in fl. Lvs to 90cm, base dark brown, elliptic, blades linear, sparsely scaly beneath. Infl. lax, simple, 7–15-fld; scape short, with bright red overlapping bracts; floral bracts like upper scape bracts; pet. white. Costa Rica, Panama, Colomb.

G. lindenii (André) Mez. To 4m in fl. Lvs to 70cm, base red-brown, blade green, with fine green or brown crossbands. Infl. slender, tripinnate at base becoming bipinnate; bracts green, finely banded, densely overlapping; floral bracts green; pet. white. C & N Peru.

G. lingulata (L.) Mez. To 30cm in fl. Lvs 45cm, dark brown at base, sometimes with fine, violet, stripes above, ligulate, green, sparsely scaly. Infl. 10–50-fld, simple, corymbiform; bracts leaflike, upper red, orange or pink, lanceolate, forming a star-shaped involucre; floral bracts linear, hooded; pet. white. Belize and W Indies to Braz., Boliv. var. *splendens* (Planch.) Mez. Lvs with longitudinal maroon stripes, sometimes wholly maroon beneath. Many-fld; involucral bracts erect, purple, red or pink; floral bracts strongly hooded. W Indies, Guyana. var. *cardinalis* (André) André ex Mez. Lvs green. Many-fld; involucral bracts spreading, bright scarlet; floral bracts strongly hooded. Colomb., Ecuad. var. *minor* (Mez) L.B. Sm. Lvs pale green. Few-fld; involucral bracts erect, red; floral bracts weakly hooded. Guat. to Colomb. and NE Braz. *Guzmania* 'Magnifica', a hybrid between this var. and the typical plant, attains 75cm and carries a red infl. low in the crown, with spreading bracts.

G. melionis Reg. 20–25cm in fl. Lvs 30–50cm, base green striped red, blades broadly acute or obtuse and apiculate, pale green-red, undersides grey scaled. Infl. simple, 8–10cm, subcylindric; scape concealed by imbricate red bracts; floral bracts red; pet. yellow or white. Fr. Guiana, Colomb., Ecuad., Peru, Boliv.

G. minor Mez = *G. lingulata* var. *minor.*

G. monostachia (L.) Rusby ex Mez. To 40cm in fl. Lvs to 60cm, base brown, scaly, sometimes with longitudinal green and white stripes, ligulate, yellow-green, paler beneath. Infl. a spike, 8–15cm, with fls in many rows; scape with pale green, ovate bracts; lower floral bracts green with fine, brown-black stripes, upper bracts bright scarlet or white; pet. white. Throughout range.

G. musaica (Lind. & André) Mez. To 50cm in fl. Lvs to 70cm, sparsely scaly, with dark brown or green, fine, irregular cross-bands, often flushed purple beneath, brown at base, broadly linear. Infl. to 25-fld, subglobose, simple; scape with bright pink, bracts; floral bracts bright pink; fls subsessile; sep. yellow, enclosing pet. Panama, Colomb.

G. 'Orangeade'. Large plants. Lvs sulphur green. Infl. flaming orange red.

G. patula Mez & Werckle. 50–60cm in fl. Lvs 25–40cm, elongated, base red-striped, brown-scaly.Infl. simple or bipinnate, spikes cylindric 2cm in diam.; floral bracts coriaceous; pet. 20mm, white or yellow-green. Costa Rica, Venez., Ecuad., Columbia, Braz.

G. peacockii (E. Morr.) Mez = *G. lingulata* var. *splendens*.

G. sanguinea (André) André ex Mez. To 20cm in fl. Lvs 25–35cm, ligulate, all or inner only bright red or orange-yellow when in fl. Infl. corymbiform, simple, 7–12-fld, sunken in centre of rosette; floral bracts thin; pet. to 75mm, yellow. Costa Rica, Colomb., Ecuad., Trin. & Tob.

G. 'Symphonie' (*G. zahnii* × *G. lingulata* var. *splendens*.) To 75cm. Lvs olive green with copper-red stripes. Fls yellow in large, star-shaped head with pointed red bracts.

G. tricolor Ruiz & Pav. = *G. monostachia*.

G. vittata (Mart. ex Schult. f.) Mez. To 55cm in fl. Lvs 40–60cm, linear, dark green or banded purple beneath. Infl. 3–4cm, simple and globose or digitate and broadly ovoid; bracts pale green, spotted purple, lanceolate, imbricate; br. spicate, sessile, 10–15-fld, dense; floral bracts leathery; pet. white. Amazonian Braz. and Colomb.

G. wittmackii (André) André ex Mez. To 50cm in fl. Lvs to 85cm, sparsely scaly. Infl. bipinnate; scape with bright red, leaflike, imbricate bracts; infl. bracts to 4cm, leaflike, spreading; floral bracts bright red; pet. creamy-white. S Colomb., Ecuad.

G. zahnii (Hook. f.) Mez. To 50cm in fl. Lvs to 60cm, linear, with fine, dark red stripes at base; blades ligulate, maroon, sometimes green at apex with fine, red-brown stripes. Infl. to 25cm, bipinnate, pyramidal or short-thyrsoid; scape red to yellow with bright scarlet bracts; infl. bracts tipped purple; br. 5–12-fld, to 5cm; floral bracts broad convex; pet. yellow. Costa Rica, Panama.

→*Caraguata*.

Gymnadenia R. Br. Orchidaceae. 10 tuberous terrestrial orchids. St. leafy. Spike cylindric, dense; lateral sep. spreading, oblong-ovate, the dors. forming a hood with pet.; lip recurved, trilobed, lobes shallow; spur conspicuous. N Amer., temp. Eurasia. Z6.

G. conopsea (L.) R. Br. FRAGRANT ORCHID. St. 15–65cm. Lvs 4–8, linear-lanceolate, keeled beneath, light green, reduced toward summit of st. Spike dense, 6–16cm; fls fragrant; pink, lilac or red, rarely white or purple; pet. and sep. 4–5mm; lip lobes equal; spur to 18mm. Spring–summer. Eur.

G. odoratissima (L.) Rich. SHORT-SPURRED FRAGRANT ORCHID. As *G. conopsea* except st. 15–30cm; pet. and sep. 2.5–3mm; lip midlobe exceeding lat. lobes; spur 4–5mm. Late spring–late summer. Eur., Russia.

Gymnandra Pall.
G. stolonifera K. Koch = *Lagotis stolonifera*.

Gymnocactus Backeb.
G. aguirreanus Glass & Fost. = *Escobaria aguirreana*.
G. roseanus (Boed.) Glass & Fost. = *Escobaria roseana*.

Gymnocalycium Pfeiff. Cactaceae. 50+ low-growing, globose cacti, mostly unbranched; st. often depressed, or globose to short-cylindric, umbilicate at apex; ribs sometimes spiralling. Fls usually subapical, funnelform to campanulate, diurnal; pericarpel and tube scales broad, obtuse. Braz., Parag., Boliv., Urug., Arg. Z10.

G. albiareolatum Rausch. (as '*alboareolatum*'). Simple; st. to 2×6–9cm, depressed-globose; grey-green; ribs 9–13; tubercles low, separated by transverse furrows; spines all radial, 5–7(–9), 5–8mm, slightly recurved, nearly white, pink at base. Fl. 5.5–6.5×5–6cm, slender, white, red in throat. Arg.

G. ambatoense Piltz = *G. tillianum*.

G. andreae (Boed.) Backeb. Clustering; st. to 4.5cm diam., globose, lustrous dark blue- or black-green; ribs c8, nearly flat; central spines 1–3, to 8mm, acicular, often curved, dark brown, radial spines similar to the centrals but dull white, brown at base. Fl. 3×4.5cm, funnelform outer tep. pale yellow-green with darker mid-stripe inside, inner tep. yellow. N Arg.

G. anisitsii (Schum.) Britt. & Rose. St. globose, 5.5×8×7.5–10cm, becoming short cylindric, bronzing in full sun; ribs 8–11, acute, strongly tubercled; spines 5–7(–9), usually all radial and c2.5cm, tortuous, nearly white, darker-tipped. Fl. 4×4cm, funnelform; outer tep. tinged green, edged red, inner tep. white. Parag.

G. asterium Y. Itô = *G. stellatum*.

G. baldianum (Speg.) Speg. Simple; st. 2.5–4×4–7cm, depressed-globose, dark blue- to grey-green; ribs 9–11, obtuse, with small tubercles; spines radial, 3–7, 7–12mm, bristly, adpressed, straight or curved, pale-tipped, becoming brown. Fl. 3.5–4×5–5.5cm, deep pink to crimson or purple-red. NW Arg.

G. bodenbenderianum (Hosseus) A. Berger = *G. quehlianum*.

G. bruchii (Speg.) Hosseus. Forming clumps 10–15cm diam.; individual st. 1–2×1–2cm, subglobose, dull green; ribs c10, low, flat, tubercles indistinct, central spines 0–3, 2–5mm, white to pale brown, radial spines 12–17, 2–5mm, slender, recurved and adpressed, white, sometimes brown at base. Fl. 1.5–2(–4)×1.5–2cm, campanulate, sometimes faintly scented; tep. pale pink with darker mid-stripe. N Arg.

G. buenekeri Swales. St. to 10cm or more diam., hemispheric becoming short-cylindric, matt mid-green; ribs 5–6, rounded and broadly triangular; tubercles indistinct; spines radial 3(–5), to 2.5cm or more, usually shorter, curved and outstanding, pale yellow darkening to pale brown. Fl. 4.5×6.5cm, rose-pink, throat somewhat deeper pink. S Braz.

G. calochlorum (Boed.) Y. Itô. Usually simple; st. 4×6cm, depressed-globose, shining pale green; ribs 9–11, broad, flat; spines radial to 9, c9mm, often interlacing, slender, pink at first, later grey-white. Fl. 5–6×5–6cm; tube leaf-green; scales white; throat carmine, outer tep. pink with grey-green tip, inner tep. pale pink with darker mid-stripe and grey pink. N Arg.

G. capillaense (Schick) Backeb. St. to 4–5×10cm, depressed-globose, dull blue-green; ribs 8–11; tubercles blunt; areoles elliptic with yellow wool at first; spines radial (3–)5(–7), 10–25mm, radiating or adpressed, at first pale horn-coloured, later grey. Fl. to 10×6–7cm; pericarpel scales white to pale pink; outer tep. ivory-white with darker mid-stripe, inner tep. white to pale pink with pink mid-stripe; throat red. Arg.

G. cardenasianum Ritter. St. 5–20×12–23cm, depressed-globose, grey-green; ribs c8, broad, flat, straight; tubercles indistinct; spines v. dark to pale brown, later grey; central spines 1–2, to 8cm, radial spines 3–6, 3–6cm, strong and curved. Fl. 5×8–9cm, tube short; tep. pale purple, with rust-red mid-stripe; throat dull red. S Boliv.

G. castellanosii Backeb. Simple; st. to 15×10cm, globose to short-cylindric, velvety blue-green; ribs 10–12, broad; tubercles rounded; central spines 0–1, radial spines 5–7, to 2.5cm, robust, slightly curved, white, tipped darker. Fl. c4.5cm diam., campanulate to funnelform, white with pink sheen. Arg.

G. chiquitanum Cárdenas. Simple; st. 2–4×6–9cm, depressed-globose, bronzing in full sun; ribs 6–7, rounded, furrowed between tubercles; central spines 0–1, 1.8cm, tipped dark brown, radial spines to 6, 1.5–2.3cm, somewhat curved. Fl. to 6cm, funnelform, v. pale lilac-pink; throat magenta. S Boliv.

G. chubutense (Speg.) Speg. = *G. gibbosum*.

G. cumingii P.C. Hutchison. = *Rebutia neocumingii*.

G. damsii (Schum.) Britt. & Rose = *G. anisitsii*.

G. deeszianum Dölz. A name of uncertain application.

G. delaetii (Schum.) Hosseus = *G. schickendantzii*.

G. denudatum (Link & Otto) Pfeiff. St. 5–10×5–15cm, sub-globose, lustrous; ribs 5–8, rounded, transversely furrowed; spines radial 5–8, 8–17mm, bristly, sinuous, adpressed, pale yellow, later white. Fl. 5–7.5×6cm, sometimes scented; outer tep. white, tinged grey, inner tep. white, sometimes tinged green. S Braz.

G. fidaianum Backeb. = *Rebutia fidaiana*.

G. fleischerianum Backeb. Simple or offsetting; st. to 6–7×10cm, globose to subcylindric, glossy green; ribs to 8m, rounded, tubercles indistinct; spines to c20, to 2.5cm, uniform, bristly, pale yellow at first. Fl. to 4×3.5cm, funnelform, white; throat deep pink. N Parag.

G. friedrichii (Werderm.) Pazout = *G. mihanovichii* var. *friedrichii*.

G. gibbosum (Haw.) Pfeiff. Simple, or offsetting; st. to 20×10–15cm, glaucous, globose becoming clavate-cylindric, brown-green; ribs 12–19, convex; tubercles small, prominent; spines straight or slightly curved, mostly brown, later grey; central spines usually 1–3, 3cm, often 0 in young plants, radial spines 7–10(–14), 2–3(–3.5)cm. Fl. 6–6.6×3–5cm, pure white, or outer tep. with pale pink mid-stripe outside. Arg.

G. horstii Buining. Simple; st. to 7×11cm, depressed-globose, glossy green; ribs 5–6, v. broad, rounded; tubercles indistinct; spines radial usually 5, to 3cm, rigid, straight, pale yellow to almost white. Fl. to 11×11cm, often smaller outer tep. deep pink, inner tep. lilac-pink to white with deeper pink mid-stripe. S Braz.

G. hossei A. Berger, misapplied. = *G. mazanense*.

G. hybopleurum (Schum.) Backeb. Simple; st. broadly globose, dull blue- to grey-green; spines radial usually 9, to 3cm, interlacing, red-brown at first, later grey. Fl. c4cm; outer tep. white with green mid-stripe, inner white, tinged green; throat pink-green. N Arg.

G. intertextum Backeb. ex Till = *G. moserianum*.

G. izozogsii Cárdenas = *G. pflanzii*.

G. kieslingii Ferrari = *G. albiareolatum*.

G. kurtzianum (Gürke) Britt. & Rose = *G. mostii*.

G. lafaldense Vaupel = *G. bruchii*.

G. leeanum (Hook.) Britt. & Rose. Simple or offsetting; st.

3–6cm diam., depressed-globose to globose, glaucous; ribs c14, obtuse, prominently tubercled; central spines 0–1, radial spines 8–11, to c12mm, brown at first. Fl. 4.5×4.5cm, campanulate-funnelform; outer tep. with broad purple-green mid-stripe, inner tep. pale yellow. Urug.

G. leptanthum (Speg.) Speg. A name of uncertain application. Plants grown under this name are probably *G. albiareolatum*.

G. loricatum Speg. = *G. spegazzinii*.

G. marsoneri Fric ex Y. Itô. Simple; st. depressed-globose, bronzing in full sun; ribs 10–15, dissolved into large, spirally-arranged tubercles; spines radial c7, 2–3cm, brown above, lighter below at first, later darker. Fl. 3–3.5×3–4.5cm, campanulate to funnelform, white or tinged pale green. Parag.

G. mazanense (Backeb.) Backeb. St. depressed-globose, matt grey-green or tinged brown; ribs 10–14, low, rounded, tuberculate; areoles felted; spines ± curved, pink-tinged, later grey; central spines 0–1, to 3.5cm, radial spines 7, to 3cm. Fl. c4cm diam.; tube short; tep. pale pink to almost white, darker in throat. N Arg.

G. megalothelos (Sencke ex Schum.) Britt. & Rose. Simple then offsetting; st. to 10–16cm diam., depressed-globose to short-cylindric, bronzing in full sun; ribs (6–)10–12, pronounced, deeply furrowed between large tubercles; areoles 1–1.5cm apart; spines yellow at first, central spine 1, radial spines 7–8, to 15mm, straight or curved. Fl. 3–4cm, campanulate-funnelform; outer tep. purple-green, inner white, tinged pink. Parag.

G. mesopotamicum Kiesling. Usually simple; st. to 2.5×4cm, depressed-globose, dark green; ribs 7–9, low, tubercles rather indistinct; spines radial, 9–12, unequal, 2–9mm, bristly, adpressed, red-brown at first, later pale brown. Fl. 5.5×6.5cm, white, throat tinged red. NE Arg.

G. michoga Itô, invalid. = *G. schickendantzii*.

G. mihanovichii (Fric & Gürke) Britt. & Rose. Variable; st. to 8cm or more diam., depressed-globose, short-cylindric, dark olive-green with cross-banding; ribs 8, prominent, acute, scarcely tuberculate; spines radial, 5–6, to 1cm, sometimes lost, dull yellow tipped brown, later grey. Fl. 4–4.5cm, campanulate to funnelform, outer tep. yellow-green, tipped red, inner tep. not spreading, green. N Parag. var. *friedrichii* Werderm. Inner tep. spreading, deep pink. N Parag. Japanese cvs such as 'Red Cap' ('Hibotan'), 'Pink Cap' and 'Gold Cap' are often sold. These lack chlorophyll and have bright red, pink and yellow st. To survive, they must be grafted.

G. monvillei (Lem.) Britt. & Rose. Usually simple; st. to 22cm diam., depressed-globose to columnar, glossy yellow-green; ribs 13–17, divided into pentagonal tubercles with pronounced 'chin'; spines radial 12–13, to 4cm, bright yellow, red-brown at base. Fl. to 8×8cm, broadly funnelform; outer tep. white with broad green mid-stripe outside, inner tep. white, tinged pink. Arg.

G. moserianum Schütz. Simple; st. to 10×15cm, depressed-globose, dark green or grey-green; ribs c10–15, ± strongly tuberculate and cross-furrowed; areoles 2cm apart, thickly felted at first; spines 3–5(–7), to 25mm, sometimes twisted, dark brown towards base, paler above. Fl. white with red throat. N Arg. Not to be confused with the plant known as *G. friedrichii* var. *moserianum*.

G. mostii (Gürke) Britt. & Rose. St. depressed-globose, dark green or blue-green; ribs 11–14, vertical, or spiralling; tubercles distinct; areoles with pale yellow wool at first; spines strong, slightly recurved, horn-coloured, glossy; central spine 18–20mm, radial spines 7.6–22mm. Fl. 7–8cm diam.; pericarpel short, shiny blue-green; tep. rose-pink with somewhat darker base. N Arg.

G. multiflorum (Hook.) Britt. & Rose. Simple; st. to 9×6cm or more, depressed-globose, blue-green; ribs indistinct; tubercles large, obscurely angled; areoles woolly; spines 5, c2.5cm, recurved, horn-coloured, purple at base. Fls. c5–6cm, funnelform, several open at once; pericarpel scales suffused dull purple; outer tep. green, inner tep. almost white, with narrow pink mid-stripe. Unknown (Parag). Most plants grown as *G. multiflorum* are *G. monvillei*.

G. multiflorum hort. non Hook. = *G. monvillei*.

G. neocumingii (Backeb.) P.C. Hutchison = *Rebutia neocumingii*.

G. netrelianum (Monv. ex Labouret) Britt. & Rose = *G. leeanum*.

G. neumannianum (Backeb.) P.C. Hutchison = *Rebutia neumanniana*.

G. nidulans Backeb. = *G. mostii*.

G. nigriareolatum Backeb. = *G. hybopleurum*.

G. occultum Fric ex Scheutz = *G. quehlianum*.

G. ochoterenae Backeb. = *G. quehlianum*.

G. oenanthemum Backeb. = *G. tillianum*.

G. ourselianum Monv. = *G. multiflorum*.

G. paraguayense (Schum.) Scheutz. St. to 4–5×6cm, globose to columnar, bronzing in full sun; ribs 8–12+, angular, tuberculate

and cross-furrowed; spines radial usually 5, unequal, upper c1cm, remainder to 2cm, somewhat curved and adpressed, honey yellow fading to white. Fl. 4–5×4–5cm, white with wine-red throat. Parag.

G. pflanzii (Vaupel) Werderm. Simple; st. to 50cm, usually shorter, depressed-globose, dull green; ribs indistinct, spiralling, divided into large tubercles; spines to 2.5cm, red-brown, later rough pink-grey, dark-tipped; central spines 1, erect, radial spines 6–9, somewhat curved. Fl. c4×4cm, fading from pale peach through pale pink to white, with wine-red throat. SE Boliv.

G. platense (Speg.) Britt. & Rose. St. to 10×12cm, globose, dark olive green to purple-green; ribs (10–)13(–18); spines radial, 5–7, 0.5–1.5cm, subulate, base swollen, dark, powdery white to grey-purple or nearly black above. Fls 5–6.5×5–6.5cm; outer tep. white with pale pink mid-stripe, inner tep. pure white. Arg.

G. quehlianum (Haage f. ex Quehl) A. Berger. St. to 3.5×7cm, depressed-globose, bronzing in full sun; ribs 8–11, strongly tuberculate; spines radial usually 5, to 5mm, adpressed, almost bristly, horn-coloured, red-brown towards base. Fl. 3–4×3–4cm; tep. white; throat red. N Arg.

G. ragonesei Cast. St. 1.5–2.5×3–5cm, depressed-globose, purple-brown to almost brick-red; ribs c10, flat, with low tubercles separated by shallow transverse grooves; spines radial (5–(6(–7), small, bristly, spidery, white. Fl. 3.5–4cm, funnelform; outer tep. grey with white margins, inner tep. white, often with light grey mid-stripe; throat dull red. N Arg.

G. saglionis (Cels) Britt. & Rose. Simple; st. to 30cm diam., depressed-globose, green or blue-green; ribs 13–32, spiralling, often indistinct, divided into large tubercles; spines ± curved, red-brown to black; radial spines to 4cm. Fl. to 3.5cm, in a ring at apex, broadly funnelform; outer tep. pale green, inner tep. white or pale pink. NW Arg.

G. schickendantzii (F.A. Weber) Britt. & Rose. Simple; st. to 10–15×30cm, broadly depressed-globose, bronzing in full sun; ribs 7–14 on older plants, somewhat spiralled; tubercles moderately large; spines radial 6–7, 2–3cm, flattened and recurved, grey-red to horn-coloured, often darker-tipped. Fl. to 5cm, in a ring at apex, or almost lat., campanulate to funnelform; pericarpel blue-green; outer tep. pale green or red-tinged, inner tep. white, tinged pink. N Arg.

G. schroederianum Osten. St. to 7×14cm, depressed-globose, dark grey-green; ribs 24, broad, obtuse, with v. prominent, broad, tubercles; spines radial, usually 7, pale yellow soon ash-grey, red at base. Fl. 7×5.5cm; pericarpel slender; scales olive green with white margin; tep. almost white with pale green base. Urug., Arg.

G. sigelianum (Schick) A. Berger = *G. capillaense*.

G. spegazzinii Britt. & Rose. St. to 20×18cm, simple, sub-globose, blue- or grey-green to brown; ribs 10–15 or more, broad, with low tubercles; central spines 0–1, radial spines 5–7, to 5.5cm curved, ± adpressed, dark brown to nearly black at first. Fl. to 7×5cm; tep. nearly white to pale pink, often with broad red mid-stripe; throat pale purple. N Arg.

G. stellatum Speg. V. variable; st. to 2.5–5×10cm, depressed-globose, bronze in full sun; ribs indistinct; tubercles small; spines radial 3–5, 5–10mm, ± projecting, dark grey-brown. Fl. 4–5cm, broadly funnelform; tep. white; throat red. Arg.

G. sutterianum (Schick) A. Berger = *G. capillaense*.

G. tillianum Rausch. St. to 10–12cm diam., depressed-globose, grey-green to blue-green; ribs 10–13, broad, obtuse, prominently tuberculate; spines radial 5–7, to 1.5–2cm, stout, slightly curved, pink at first, later grey. Fl. to 5×4.5cm, wine-red or deep salmon-pink. N Arg.

G. urselianum auct. = *G. multiflorum*.

G. uruguayense (Arech.) Britt. & Rose. St. depressed-globose; ribs 12–14; tubercles pronounced; spines 3(–7), 1.5–2cm, stout, recurved and adpressed. Fl. 4×5.5–6cm; outer tep. pale yellow-green, inner tep. white with pink mid-stripe. Urug.

G. vatteri Buin. St. to 4×9cm, depressed-globose, bronzing in full sun; ribs c11, large, tuberculate; spines 1–3(–5), 1–2(–3)cm, strong, adpressed or projecting, horn-coloured or darker. Fl. 5×4cm; tep. white; throat red. N Arg.

G. venturianum (Fric) Backeb. = *G. baldianum*.

G. weissianum Backeb. = *G. mazanense*.

→*Echinocactus*.

Gymnocarpium Newman Woodsiaceae. 5 decid., terrestrial ferns. Rhiz. slender, creeping and branching freely, covered with scales and bristles. Fronds arising singly, triangular, 2–3-pinnate, basal pinnae enlarged; stipes erect, longer than lamina, scaly and dark brown towards the base. Eur., N Amer., SE Asia.

G. dryopteris (L.) Newman. OAK FERN. Fronds to 40cm; stipe glab. with few scales; lamina broadly triangular, 3-pinnate, bright yellow-green, thin, glab.; pinnae opposite, about 6 pairs, the lowest triangular, 2-pinnate, long-stalked, the second pair oblong-lanceolate, pinnate, other pinnae pinnate to pinnatifid, becoming decurrent, sessile; pinnules ovate to oblong, rounded at the apex, entire, crenate, or pinnately toothed. Eur., Asia Minor, N Asia, China, Jap., Canada, US. 'Plumosum': all lf parts enlarged and overlapping. Z3.

G. oyamense (Bak.) Ching. Fronds to 35cm, pinnatifid; stipe slender, pale green with thin brown scales, to 20cm; lamina to 15×12cm, ovate-deltoid, acute, cordate, blue-green, glab., somewhat glaucous; pinnules in 7–12 pairs, oblong to oblong-lanceolate, crenate, the lowest lanceolate, to 2cm wide, deflexed. Jap., China. Z8.

G. robertianum (Hoffm.) Newman. LIMESTONE FERN; NORTHERN OAK FERN. Fronds to 55cm, fragrant when bruised; stipe sparsely gland.; lamina triangular, 2–3-pinnate, dull yellow-green, mealy-glandular; pinnae opposite, about 5–10 pairs, the lowest largest, triangular, pinnate or 2-pinnate at the base, stalked, the second pair pinnate or pinnatifid, often long-stalked; pinnules pinnate or deeply pinnatifid; seg. entire or crenate at apex. Eur., Balk., Afghan., N N Amer. Z4.

→*Dryopteris, Phegopteris* and *Thelypteris*.

Gymnocereus Backeb.

G. microspermus (Werderm. & Backeb.) Backeb. = *Browningia microsperma*.

Gymnocladus Lam. Leguminosae (Caesalpinioideae). 5 unarmed decid. trees. Lvs bipinnate. Fls in short term. pan. or rac.; cal. 5-lobed; pet. oblong, 5, equal; sta. 10, pet. Fr. a large legume, ultimately woody; seeds glossy flat, hard. US, China.

G. canadensis Lam. = *G. dioica*.

G. chinensis Baill. SOAP TREE. To 10m. Lvs 30–90cm; lfts 2–4cm, 20–24 per pinna, oblong, pubesc. Fls precocious, lilac, in downy rac. Fr. 7–10×3.8cm, thick, pulpy. China. Z9.

G. dioica (L.) K. Koch. KENTUCKY COFFEE TREE; CHICOT. To 25m; bark coarsely fissured; branchlets thick. Lvs 30–80cm, emerging pale pink; lfts 2–5cm, ovate, 8–14 per pinna, pubesc. Fls dull green-white, downy, in clustered or single rac. to 10cm. Fr. 6–15×3–4cm, brown or maroon, thick, succulent becoming woody. Summer. C & E N Amer. 'Variegata': lfts variegated cream. Z4.

Gymnogramma Desv.

G. argentea (Willd.) Mett. ex Kuhn = *Pityrogramma argentea*.

G. canescens (Kunze) Klotzsch. = *Jamesonia canescens*.

G. decurrenti-alata Hook. = *Athyrium decurrenti-alatum*.

G. fendleri (Kunze) Mett. = *Cheilanthes fendleri*.

G. muelleri Hook. = *Paraceterach muelleri*.

G. pearcei Moore = *Pityrogramma pearcei*.

G. pulchella Moore = *Pityrogramma pulchella*.

G. rutifolia (R. Br.) Hook. & Grev. = *Pleurosorus rutifolius*.

G. sulphurea (Sw.) Desv. = *Pityrogramma sulphurea*.

G. wilsonii J. Sm. ex Jenman = *Pityrogramma sulphurea*.

G. wrightii Hook. = *Colysis wrightii*.

Gymnogrammitis Griff. Davalliaceae. 1 epiphytic fern. Rhiz. wide-creeping; scales lanceolate, hair-tipped. Fronds 3-pinnate, ovate to deltoid, to 45×30cm; pinnae short-stalked, lanceolate to oblong, pinnules incised, to 3cm, seg. spathulate, entire; stipes to 15cm, lustrous brown. Z10.

G. dareiformis (Hook.) Ching.

Gymnopetalum Arn.

G. japonicum Miq. = *Trichosanthes kirilowii* var. *japonica*.

Gymnopteris Bernh. Adiantaceae. 5 small to medium-sized ferns. Rhiz. creeping to erect, scales linear, tawny. Stipes brown, hairy and scaly below; frond blades pinnate, thin. Trop. Amer., India, China. Z10.

G. decurrens Hook. = *Hemigramma decurrens*.

G. flagellifera Bedd. = *Bolbitis heteroclita*.

G. latifolia (Meyen) Presl = *Hemigramma latifolia*.

G. nicotianifolia (Sw.) Presl = *Bolbitis nicotianifolia*.

G. portoricensis (Spreng.) Fée = *Bolbitis portoricensis*.

G. rufa (L.) Bernh. Rhiz. short, erect. Stipes to 15cm. Fronds 30–45cm, pinnate, pinnae about 10 each side, ovate-oblong, occas. cordate at base, or terminal pinnae with 2 basal lobes, chestnut-brown-pubesc. Trop. Amer.

G. variabilis Bedd. = *Leptochilus decurrens*.

G. vestita (Wallich) Underw. Rhiz. short-creeping. Stipes 10–14cm. Fronds 15–30cm, pinnate, pinnae in 5–8 pairs, ovate to ovate-cordate or oblong, entire, densely ferruginous velvety-pubesc. SW China, Himal., Pak., Taiwan.

Gymnospermium Spach. Berberidaceae. 4 tuberous perenn. herbs. Lvs mostly basal, ternately divided; lfts pinnately lobed,

glab. Rac. term., sep. 6, petaloid, yellow; pet. 6, v. small, nectary-like; sta. 6, longer than pet. Eur. to C Asia. Z7.

G. alberti (Reg.) Takht. 20–25cm. Basal lvs long-petioled; flowering st. lvs short, subsessile. Rac. 5–15-fld; pedicels 6–13mm; fls 12–18mm across; sep. oblong-elliptic, veins red-brown on back; ovary stalked. Spring. C Asia. Z4.

G. altaicum (Pall.) Spach. Similar to *G. alberti* except 5–20cm, sep. plain yellow, ovary not stalked. Black Sea. Z4.

→*Leontice*.

Gymnosporia Hook. f.

G. cassinioides Masf. = *Celastrus cassinioides*.

G. serratus (Hochst. ex A. Rich.) Loes. = *Maytenus serratus*.

Gymnothrix Spreng.

G. caudata Schräd. = *Pennisetum macrurum*.

G. latifolia (Spreng.) Schult. = *Pennisetum latifolium*.

Gympie Messmate *Eucalyptus cloeziana*.

Gynandriris Parl. Iridaceae. 9 perenn. cormous, *Iris*-like herbs. Lvs narrow and channelled, usually 1–2 per corm. Fls in term. and axill. cymes, short-lived; perianth seg. free, tube 0; sta. partly united; style br. 3, petaloid, concealing anth. S Afr., Medit., E to Pak.

G. monophylla Boiss. & Heldr. ex Klatt. To 5cm. Lvs 1, rarely 2, narrow, prostrate or coiling on the ground. Infl. unbranched; fls 1–2.5cm diam., 1–several per cyme, pale slate-blue, falls with orange-yellow stripe bordered with white. Spring. E Medit. Z8.

G. pritzeliana (Diels) Goldbl. 7–25cm. Lvs coiled, prostrate, with white line on inner surface. Infl. branched from base, fls solitary, mauve-blue, falls with white stripe, yellow at base. S Afr. Z9.

G. setifolia (L. f.) R. Fost. 5–20cm. Lvs linear spreading. Infl. unbranched; fls 1–4, sessile, yellow, pale blue or lilac, falls with yellow stripe. Winter. S Afr. Z9.

G. simulans (Bak.) R. Fost. 10–45cm. Lvs 1–2, linear, erect. Infl. br. short, or fls sessile on main axils; fls lilac with white spots. S Afr. Z9.

G. sisyrinchium (L.) Parl. 10–40cm. Lvs flexuous, usually prostrate. Infl. 1–4 compact cymes; fls 1–6 per cyme, violet blue to lavender, falls with a white or white and orange patch. Spring. Port., Medit. to SW Asia and Pak. Z8.

→*Iris*.

Gynandropsis DC.

G. gynandra (L.) Briq. = *Cleome gynandra*.

Gynatrix Alef. Malvaceae. 1 ± scabrous shrub or small tree to 5m. Lvs 3–10cm, ovate to lanceolate, crenate; petioles 2–5cm. Fls unisexual in small dense pan. or rac.; epical. 0; ♂ on short pedicels; cal. campanulate, lobes 2–4mm, broadly triangular; pet. 3–6mm, cream-white; sta. 20–30; ♀ sessile; cal. ovoid to globose; sta. small and abortive, on a short staminal column. SE Aus. and Tasm.

G. pulchella (Willd.) Alef. HEMP BUSH. S Aus., NSW, Vict., Tasm.

→*Plagianthus*.

Gynerium Willd. Gramineae. 1 large perenn., aquatic reed. St., coarse, erect, tufted, to 2.5cm diam. Lvs forming a fan, at st. apex, flat, scabrous to 2m×10cm. Pan. plumose, to 1m, grey-green to grey. Early autumn. Trop. Amer., W Indies. Z9.

G. jubatum Lemoine = *Cortaderia jubata*.

G. saccharoides Humbert & Bonpl. = *G. sagittatum*.

G. sagittatum (Aubl.) P. Beauv. UVA GRASS.

Gynopleura Cav.

G. linearifolia Cav. = *Malesherbia linearifolia*.

Gynostemma Bl. Cucurbitaceae. 2 trailing sometimes woody-based herbs. Tendrils usually bifid. Lvs usually palmate. Infl. an axill. pan. or rac.; cal. small, rotate, 5-lobed; cor. rotate, lobes 5. Fr. a globose berry. Asia. Z8.

G. pentaphyllum (Thunb.) Mak. SWEET TEA VINE. Ann. or perenn. to 8m. Tendrils simple. Lvs long-stalked, lfts 3–7, to 8cm, lanceolate to ovate, serrate. Infl. to 15cm, pubesc.; fls yellow-green. Fr. to 8mm diam., dark green to black, smooth, with white line. Jap.

Gynura Cass. VELVET PLANT. Compositae. 50 perenn. herbs and subshrubs. Cap. discoid, solitary or few to many in corymbs at the ends of br.; flts yellow, red or purple, malodorous. OW Trop.

G. aurantiaca (Bl.) DC. VELVET PLANT; PURPLE VELVET PLANT; ROYAL VELVET PLANT. Robust perenn. herb, to 2.5m, violet velvety hairy. St. upright at first, clambering later. Lvs to 20cm, ovate to broad elliptic, base cordate, truncate, cuneate or attenuate, coarsely toothed, veins purple. Cap. in loose corymbs; phyllaries violet-hairy; flts yellow, becoming purple, exceeding phyllaries. Winter. Java. 'Purple Passion' ('Passion Purple', 'Sarmentosa'): st. slender, decumbent; lvs to 14×5cm, v. purple-hairy.

G. bicolor (Roxb. ex Willd.) DC. Erect to spreading perenn. herb to 4m. Lvs to 15cm, ovate to broadly lanceolate to oblanceolate, entire, toothed or lobed, acute, base cuneate, purple or green beneath, glab. or hairy on veins only. Cap. in loose or tight corymbs; phyllaries glab., apex purple; flts orange-yellow, shorter than phyllaries. Himal.

G. procumbens (Lour.) Merrill. Subglabrous perenn. herb, erect at first, later climbing or trailing. Lvs to 12.5cm, ovate to broad-lanceolate, acute, base cuneate or attenuate, entire or slightly toothed, green above, tinged purple beneath, shortly hairy to glab. Cap. in loose corymbs; phyllaries purple, glab.; flts orange-yellow, shorter than phyllaries. Trop. W Afr., Malaysia, China, Vietnam, Thail.

G. sarmentosa (Bl.) DC. = *G. procumbens*.

G. sarmentosa hort. = *G. aurantiaca* 'Purple Passion'.

G. scandens O. Hoffm. Climbing, glandular-hairy shrub, to 6m. Lvs to 9cm, ovate to elliptic, obtuse or acute, base cuneate, cordate or truncate, lobed to entire or dentate. Cap. in crowded corymbs; flts orange-yellow, exceeding phyllaries. Trop. E Afr.

Gypsophila L. Caryophyllaceae. 100 ann. or perenn. herbs. St. sometimes arising from a woody stock. Lvs opposite, linear or lanceolate, often somewhat fleshy or glaucous. Fls usually numerous and small in spreading pan.; cal. 5-toothed, with membranous tissue separating the 5 veins; pet. 5; sta. 10. Eurasia, 1 sp. nat. Aus. and NZ.

G. aretioides Boiss. Cushion-forming perenn. Lvs v. small, fleshy, oblong, triangular in section. Fls usually solitary, sessile, sometimes in few-fld infl. to 4cm; pet. small, white, entire. Summer. Mts of N Iran and the Cauc. 'Caucasica': extremely dense; lvs grey-green. Z5.

G. carminea hort. = *G. elegans* 'Carminea'.

G. cerastioides D. Don. Loose, grey-hairy, mat-forming perenn. Lower lvs spathulate, long-stalked, upper lvs obovate, nearly sessile. Fls to 2cm diam. in loose corymbs; pet. white or lilac with pink veins. Summer. Himal. Z5.

G. dubia Willd. = *G. repens*.

G. elegans Bieb. Glab. ann. to 50cm, branching above. Lvs oblong-lanceolate to linear. Infl. a loosely branched pan. with numerous fls on long slender pedicels; pet. 8–15mm, white (in wild plant) with pink or purple veins. Summer. Asia Minor, Cauc., S Ukraine, but widely cult. and occas. nat. elsewhere in Eur. 'Carminea': fls carmine rose. 'Covent Garden': fls large,

white. 'Giant White': fls v. large, white. 'Grandiflora Alba': fls large, white. Improved Mixed: fls white, pale pink, rose and carmine; seed race. 'Purpurea': fls somewhat purple. 'Red Cloud': fls carmine to pink, profuse. 'Rosea': fls pale rose pink.

G. imbricata Rupr. = *G. aretioides*.

G. nana Bory & Chaub. Tufted, viscid-pubesc. perenn. Flowering st. not exceeding 5cm. Lvs narrowly oblong. Fls to 10, on pedicels mostly twice as long as cal.; pet. 8–10mm, pale purple. Summer. Mts of S Greece and Crete.

G. pacifica Komar. Glab., much-branched perenn. to 1m. Lvs ovate-lanceolate, sessile, somewhat fleshy. Infl. many-fld, loosely paniculate; pet. 5–8mm, pink. Summer. E Sib., Manch. Z3.

G. paniculata L. BABY'S BREATH. Rhizomatous, diffusely branched perenn. to 120cm, usually glab. and glaucous. Lvs linear-lanceolate. Infl. a many-fld, loose pan.; pet. 2–4mm, white or pink. Summer. C Asia and C & E Eur., widely cult. and nat. 'Bristol Fairy': fls double, pure white, long-lasting. 'Compacta': habit dense. 'Compacta Plena': dwarf; fls double, white. 'Double Snowflake': fls pure white, many double. 'Early Snowball': fls double, white, early-flowering. 'Flamingo': bushy; fls double, pale pink. 'Perfecta': fls v. large, double, white. 'Pink Fairy': to 45cm; fls double, clear pale pink. 'Pink Star': to 60cm; spreading; fls large, double, deep pink. 'Plena': to 70cm; fls double, white. 'Red Sea': fls small, pink to red. 'Rosenschleier' ('Rosy Veil'; *G. paniculata × G. repens*): to 30cm; fls palest pink. 'Snow Flake': to 60cm; fls double, white. 'Viette's Dwarf': compact, to 35cm; fls fully double, blush pink. 'Virgo': to 100cm; fls white, many double. Z4.

G. petraea (Baumg.) Rchb. Densely tufted perenn. St. to 20cm, unbranched, pubesc. above. Lvs linear, glab. Infl. ± capitate, surrounded by large, ovate bracts; pet. 3–6mm, white or pale purple, narrowly ovate. Summer. Mts of SE Eur. Z7.

G. repens L. Mat-forming, ± glaucous perenn. sterile shoots long, arching, flowering st. ascending, to 20cm. Lvs linear, often falcate. Infl. a loose, subcorymbose pan.; fls to 25; pet. 6–8mm, narrowly ovate, white, pink or pink-purple. Mts of C & S Eur. from N Spain to the Carpath. 'Alba': fls white. 'Bodgeri': double-fld. 'Dorothy Teacher': habit neat; lvs blue-grey; fls soft pink, darker with age. 'Dubia': dwarf; st. dark red; lvs dark; fls white flushed pink. 'Letchworth Rose': fls pink. 'Rosa Schönheit' ('Rose Beauty'): fls rich rose pink. 'Rosea' ('Pink Baby'): fls pink, deep rose in bud. Z4.

G. tenuifolia Bieb. Tufted, glab. perenn. Flowering st. to 20cm. Lvs basal, numerous, narrowly linear. Infl. few-fld, corymbose, sometimes subcapitate; pet. 8–10mm, obovate, white to pink. Summer. Cauc., mts of NE Turk. Z5.

Gypsyweed *Veronica officinalis*.

Gypsywort *Lycopus europaeus*.

H

Haageocereus Backeb. Cactaceae. 5–10 shrubby or arborescent cacti; st. ribbed, spiny. Fls nocturnal, tubular-funnelform; tube stout, fleshy; perianth spreading, relatively narrow; sta. in a single series; style exserted. Fr. globose to ovoid, fleshy, sparsely scaly and hairy. Deserts of Peru and N Chile.

H. acranthus (Vaup.) Backeb. = *H. limensis.*

H. albispinus (Akers) Backeb. = *H. multangularis.*

H. australis Backeb. = *H. decumbens.*

H. chosicensis (Werderm. & Backeb.) Backeb. = *H. multangularis.*

H. chrysacanthus (Akers) Backeb. = *H. multangularis.*

H. decumbens (Vaup.) Backeb. St. to c1m×4–8cm, decumbent or pendent; ribs 12–22; central spines 1–5, 1–5cm, v. stout, dark. Fl. 6–8×5–6cm; tube brown- or red-green; tep. white. S Peru. Z9.

H. dichromus Rauh & Backeb. = *H. multangularis.*

H. laredensis (Backeb.) Backeb. = *H. multangularis.*

H. limensis (Salm-Dyck) Ritter. St. to 2m×7–10cm, erect or ascending, branching from base; ribs 12–14, somewhat tuberculate; central spines 1–3, 2–6cm, v. stout. Fl. 6–8×5–6cm; tube green; tep. white or pale pink. Central Peru. Z9.

H. multangularis (Willd.) Ritter St. to 1.5m×(4–)6–10cm, erect or ascending, branching from base; ribs 18–26; central spines 1–4 up to 8cm, v. stout. Fl. 4–8×2.5–4cm; tube dull red, brown or green; tep. red, pink or white. Central Peru. Z9.

H. olowinskianus Backeb. = *H. limensis.*

H. pacalaensis (Backeb.) Backeb. = *H. multangularis.*

H. platinospinus (Werderm. & Backeb.) Backeb. & F. Knuth. = *H. decumbens.*

H. pseudomelanostele (Werderm. & Backeb.) Backeb. = *H. multangularis.*

H. superbus Cullmann = *H. decumbens.*

H. versicolor (Werderm. & Backeb.) Backeb. St. slender, erect, branching from the base to 1.5m×5cm; ribs 16–22; central spines 1–2, 1–4cm, variable in colour. Fl. 6–8×4–6cm; tube light green; tep. white. N Peru. Z9.

H. viridiflorus (Akers) Backeb. = *H. multangularis.*

H. weberbaueri (Schum. ex Vaup.) D. Hunt. Large shrub or small tree, to 6m, much-branched below; st. 6–15cm diam.; ribs 15–35; central spines to 8, to 10cm, fierce. Fl. 6–11×2–4.5cm; tube curved, dull red, brown or green; tep. not widely spreading, pink or white with brown or green tinge. S Peru. Z9.

→*Binghamia, Borzicactus, Trichocereus* and *Weberbauerocereus.*

Haastia Hook. f. VEGETABLE SHEEP. Compositae. 3 cushion-forming perenn. herbs or subshrubs. Lvs broad, imbricate, concealing st. Cap. disciform, solitary, large, sessile; involucre cupulate to broadly campanulate; phyllaries numerous, linear, usually lanate. Summer. NZ. Z7.

H. pulvinaris Hook. f. VEGETABLE SHEEP. Cushions dense, to 2m diam. Lvs to 1×1cm, strongly imbricate, broadly obcuneate, crenulate, densely tawny long-hairy above and beneath, or beneath only.

H. recurva Hook. f. Procumbent, 25cm, branchlets hidden by persistent lf bases. Lvs to 2×1cm, loosely imbricate, obovate, strongly recurved from middle, rugose, densely tawny to red-brown or white above and beneath, except at base above.

H. sinclarii Hook. f. Decumbent or suberect, to 30cm. Lvs to 3.5×1.5cm, spreading, oblong-obovate, apex subacute to rounded, not recurved, rather rugose, tawny to buff tomentose except at base.

Habenaria Willd. Orchidaceae. c600 terrestrial tuberous orchids. Lvs basal or sheathing st. Rac. term., 1- to many-fld; dors. sep. often forming a hood with pet.; lat. sep. spreading or reflexed; pet. entire or bilobed; lip entire or trilobed, lat. lobes sometimes with fringed margins, spurred at base. Trop. and subtrop. Z9.

H. bonatea L. f. = *Bonatea speciosa.*

H. macrandra Lindl. 15–55cm. Basal lvs 3–7 with petiole to 7cm, blade to 24×6cm, lanceolate, acute, dark green. Rac. laxly 2–11-fld; fls green and white, occas. white; sep. 15–30×3–5mm, lanceolate; pet. 16–36mm, narrowly linear; lip midlobe 20–45mm, lat. lobes 30–55mm, all lobes filiform but midlobe slightly broader; spur 5–7.5cm. Trop. Afr. (widespread).

H. macrantha A. Rich. 20–50cm, lvs 5–7, to 12×5cm, lanceolate, acute. Rac. laxly 2–9-fld; fls green or green and white; sep.

20–25×7–10mm, lanceolate; pet. 20–25mm, curved lanceolate, papillose-hairy.; lip midlobe 14–23×1–2mm, linear, obtuse, lat. lobes slightly longer, outer edge divided into 6–10 narrow threads; spur 2–3.5cm. Arabian Penins., Ethiop., Uganda, Kenya.

H. procera (Sw.) Lindl. To 60cm, lower lvs to 30×5.5cm, lanceolate or ovate, with sheathing bases. Rac. to 35-fld; fls white, tep. green at the tips; sep. to 12×7mm, ovate; pet. oblong; lip midlobe to 18×2mm, lat. lobes much narrower, to 27mm; spur 7–8cm. W Afr., Zaire, Uganda.

H. pusilla Rchb. f. = *H. rhodocheila.*

H. radiata Thunb. = *Pecteilis radiata.*

H. rhodocheila Hance. 20–30cm. Lvs to 12×2cm, green with network of darker veins. Rac. about 10-fld; sep. and pet. green, lip yellow, orange or scarlet; dors. sep. and pet. forming hood 9mm long, lat. sep. spreading or deflexed, twisted, 10mm; lip midlobe 15×12mm, obovate, bilobed at apex, lobes rounded, lat. lobes about 10mm, rounded; spur 5cm. S China and Indochina, S to Penang.

H. splendens Rendle. 35–70cm, lvs to 20×6cm, ovate, acute, loosely funnel-shaped at base. Rac. laxly 4–20-fld; sep. green, pet. and lip white; dors. sep. 23–30mm, ovate; pet. 20–30mm, falcate; lip densely pubesc., midlobe 15–23×1mm, linear, lat. lobes with 8–12 thread-like br. on outer margin; spur 2.5–5cm. E C Afr.

H. susannae (L.) R. Br. = *Pecteilis susannae.*

Haberlea Friv. Gesneriaceae. 2 perenn., stemless herbs. Lvs rosulate. Infl. scapose, umbellate; pedicels pendulous, with pair of linear-lanceolate bracts at base; cal. 5-lobed, purple-brown-pubesc.; cor. unequally bilabiate, tube ± cylindric, lobes 5, rounded; sta. 4, included. Balk.

H. ferdinandi-coburgi Urum. Similar to *H. rhodopensis* except lvs subglabrous above; cor. lilac, tube darker above, throat yellow-spotted. C Bulg.

H. rhodopensis Friv. Lvs 3–8×2–4cm, obovate to ovate-oblong, obtuse, coarsely crenate, softly hirsute; petiole short. Scapes several, 8–15cm, 1–5-fld; cor. 1.5–2.5cm pale blue-violet. C & S Bulg., NE Greece. 'Virginalis': fls white.

Habranthus Herb. Amaryllidaceae. 10 perenn. bulbous herbs. Lvs linear, often appearing after fls. Fls solitary or paired, scapose; spathe sheathing the pedicel; perianth zygomorphic, infundibuliform, tube short, lobes subequal; sta. 6, declinate, 4 different lengths, with a corona of scales between them. S Amer. Z9.

H. andersonii Herb. = *H. tubispathus.*

H. andicola (Poepp.) Herb. = *Rhodophiala advena* or *R. andicola.*

H. bagnoldii Herb. = *Rhodophiala bagnoldii.*

H. brachyandrus (Bak.) Sealy. Lvs to 30cm. Scape slender, to 30cm; fls 9cm, solitary, nearly erect, brilliant or pale pink, tube short, deep red-black at base, lobes oblong-lanceolate, acute, 1.2cm wide. S Braz.

H. cardinalis (C.M. Wright) Sealy = *Zephyranthes bifolia.*

H. concolor Lindl. Lvs to 30×1.5cm. Scape 15–30cm, v. stout; fl. to 6.5cm long, pale green-white or creamy-white, green in throat; perianth seg. erect, to 2.5cm wide. Spring-summer. Mex.

H. gracilifolius Herb. Lvs to 45cm, subterete. Scape to 45cm; perianth to 5.5cm, tube short, green; lobes acuminate, pink or white, corona of scales between the sta. closing the tube. Urug., Arg.

H. juncifolius Traub & Hayward. Lvs to 75cm, terete. Fls 2–4, to 5.5cm, tube short, red-green, lobes white flushed pink. Arg.

H. longipes (Bak.) Sealy. Lvs linear, glab. Scape fragile, to 30cm; fls pale red, to 8cm, tube short, narrowly funnelform, lobes lanceolate, spreading. Urug.

H. phycelloides Herb. = *Phycella phycelloides.*

H. plumieri (Hume). Lvs to 22.5cm×1.5mm. Scape 10–20cm, slender; perianth 5–6cm, pink, funnel-shaped, tube slender, to 1.5cm. Spring. W Indies.

H. robustus Herb. ex Sweet. Lvs 4mm broad. Scape to 30cm, fls 1 or 2, declinate, to 7cm, tube green, lobes subequal, to 1.2cm wide, elliptic, pink. Arg., S Braz.

H. texanus (Herb.) Herb. ex Steud. = *H. tubispathus.*

H. tubispathus (L'Hérit.) Traub. Lvs to 15cm. Scape to 15cm, tinged red; fls solitary, perianth to 3.5cm, tube to 3mm, lobes obovate, cuspidate, orange, yellow or golden above, grey-pink, with darker stripes beneath. Arg., S Braz., Urug., S Chile.

H. versicolor Herb. Lvs to 30×0.6cm. Scape to 12cm, red fading to green; fls 5cm, rose, fading to white suffused with rose, red at the tip and streaked with red below, lobes to 1.8cm wide, with a red stripe on each side of midrib near base and a green central nerve, tube closed by a bearded or dentate membrane. Urug., Braz.

→*Amaryllis*, *Hippeastrum* and *Zephyranthes*.

Hachijo-giboshi *Hosta rupifraga.*
Hackberry *Celtis* (*C. occidentalis*).

Hackelia Opiz. STICKSEED; BEGGAR's LICE. Boraginaceae. Some 45 ann., bienn. or perenn. herbs. Lvs basal and cauline. Infl. term. or axill., often a pan.; cal. deeply lobed; cor. infundibular, campanulate, cylindrical or subrotate, faucal appendages usually conspicuous; sta. included. N Amer., Eur., Asia. Z7.
H. floribunda (Lehm.) Johnst. Bienn. or perenn. St. to 120cm, erect, solitary or few, strigose to velutinous. Basal lvs to 21×2.5cm, narrowly elliptic to oblanceolate, petiolate. Floral bracts usually 0; cor. to 7.5mm diam., blue or white. W N Amer.
H. jessicae (McGreg.) Brand = *H. micrantha.*
H. micrantha (Eastw.) J.L. Gentry. Perenn. St. to 110cm, several to numerous, erect, pubesc., hirsute or strigose. Basal lvs to 28×3cm, narrowly elliptic to oblanceolate, long-petiolate. Cor. to 10mm diam., blue or white. W N Amer.
H. nipponica (Mak.) Brand. Perenn., grey-strigose. St. to 20cm, tufted, decumbent then ascending. Basal lvs to 6×0.6cm, rosulate, linear-lanceolate sessile. Floral bracts to 7mm, linear; cor. to 8mm diam., blue. Asia.
→*Echinospermum*, *Eritrichium* and *Lappula.*

Hackmatack *Populus balsamifera.*
Hacksaw Fern *Doodia aspera.*

Hacquetia Necker ex DC. Umbelliferae. 1 clump-forming, perenn. herb to 7cm. Lvs radical, palmatifid, semi-orbicular in outline, glab., lobes 3, 2–3-cleft. Fls minute, yellow, in a scapose umbel subtended by 5–7 leafy bracts to 2cm, giving the overall impression of a single, green-petalled fl. with golden sta. Spring. Eur. Z7.
H. epipactis (Scop.) DC.

Hadrodemas H.E. Moore.
H. warszewiczianum (Kunth & Bouché) H.E. Moore. = *Callisia warszewicziana.*

Haemanthus L. Amaryllidaceae. 21 bulbous herbs. Lvs distichous, ligulate to elliptic. Umbels scapose; spathe to 13-valved, fleshy or scarious; fls actinomorphic; perianth tube cylindrical or campanulate, lobes oblong to lanceolate, fil. usually strongly exserted. Fr. clustered, ovoid to globose berries. S Afr., Nam. Z9.
H. albiflos Jacq. Lvs erect, oblong, ligulate or elliptic, to 40×11.5cm, flat sometimes spotted white, usually pubesc., margins ciliate. Scape to 35cm, green, glab. or pubesc.; umbel to 7cm diam.; spathe to 8-valved, white veined green, stiff, rigid, ciliate; fls to 50, white; pedicels to 1cm, green; perianth to 2.3cm; tep. to 1.8cm. Fr. white, orange or red. S Afr.
H. albomaculatus Bak. = *H. albiflos.*
H. carinatus L. = *H. coccineus.*
H. coarctus Jacq. = *H. coccineus.*
H. coccineus L. CAPE TULIP. Lvs recurved to prostrate, ligulate to elliptic, to 45×15cm, flat or channelled, fleshy, sometimes barred maroon, green or white, glab. or pubesc. Scape to 37cm, cream to pale red streaked dark red; umbel to 10cm across; spathe 6–9-valved, coral, vermilion or scarlet, fleshy; fls to 100, coral to scarlet with white markings; pedicels to 2cm, white to pale red; perianth to 3cm, tep. to 2.5cm. Fr. white to deep pink. Late summer. S Afr.
H. coccineus Forssk. non L. = *Scadoxus multiflorus* ssp. *multiflorus.*
H. humilis Jacq. Lvs prostrate to erect, elliptic to lanceolate, to 30×15cm, pubesc. Scape to 30cm, pale green or maroon, pubesc.; umbel to 12cm across; spathe 5–10-valved, pink, scarious; fls to 120, white to pink; pedicels to 3cm, green; perianth to 2.5cm, tep. to 2cm. Fr. green-white to orange. Summer. S Afr. ssp. **humilis**. Spathe to 7-valved; fls white to pink, perianth to 1.5cm, lobes to 1cm. Summer. ssp. *hirsutus* (Bak.) D. Snijman. Lvs pubesc., fls pale pink to white, perianth to 2.6cm, lobes 2.1cm. Early summer.
H. insignis Hook. = *Scadoxus puniceus.*
H. kalbreyeri Bak. = *Scadoxus multiflorus* ssp. *multiflorus.*

H. katherinae Bak. = *Scadoxus multiflorus* ssp. *katherinae.*
H. longitubus Wright = *Scadoxus multiflorus* ssp. *longitubus.*
H. lynesii Stapf. = *Scadoxus multiflorus* ssp. *multiflorus.*
H. magnificus (Herb.) Herb. = *Scadoxus puniceus.*
H. mannii Bak. = *Scadoxus multiflorus* ssp. *longitubus.*
H. natalensis Poepp. = *Scadoxus puniceus.*
H. nelsonii Bak. = *H. humilis* ssp. *humilis.*
H. orientalis Thunb. = *Brunsvigia orientalis.*
H. pubescens L. f. Lvs prostrate or recurved, later than fls, ligulate to oblong, to 20×4.5cm, flat or striate, glab. or white-pubesc. above, glab. or sparsely villous beneath, margin ciliate. Scape to 28cm, red, glab.; umbel to 6cm across; spathe to 5-valved, fleshy red, apex white; pedicels to 0.3cm, white or red; perianth to 3cm, tep. to 2.5cm. Fr. white to pink. Autumn.
H. rouperi hort. = *Scadoxus puniceus.*
H. sacculus Phillips = *Scadoxus multiflorus* ssp. *multiflorus.*
H. sanguineus Jacq. Lvs prostrate, elliptic to oblong, to 40×28cm, flat, coriaceous, scabrid above, glossy beneath, margin red or hyaline, smooth or denticulate. Scape to 27cm, furrowed, claret red; umbel to 8cm across; spathe to 11-valved, red-pink; fls 25, red to salmon pink marked white; pedicels to 3.2cm; perianth to 3.2cm, tep. to 2.4cm, acute. Fr. glassy white to claret. Late summer.
H. tenuiflorus Herb. = *Scadoxus multiflorus* ssp. *multiflorus.*
H. tigrinus Jacq. = *H. coccineus.*

Haemaria Lindl. = *Ludisia.*

Haematoxylum L. Leguminosae (Caesalpinioideae). 3 spiny glab. shrubs or trees. Lvs imparipinnate or bipinnate. Rac. axill.; fls many, yellow, sep. 5, subequal; pet. 5, oblong; sta. 10, free fil. pilose. Trop. Amer., Nam. Z9.
H. campechianum L. LOGWOOD; CAMPEACHY; BLOODWOOD TREE. Shrub or tree to 7.5m becoming buttressed. Br. spiny; twigs white-lenticellate. Lvs emerging red, bipinnate; lfts in 2–4 pairs, cuneate-obovate, notched. Infl. to 12cm; fls to 1.8cm diam., fragrant. W Indies, Mex., C Amer.

HAEMODORACEAE R. Br. 16/85. *Anigozanthos.*

Hag Taper *Verbascum thapsus.*
Hair Grass *Aira*; *Deschampsia*; *Eleocharis acicularis.*
Hairpin Banksia *Banksia spinulosa.*
Hairy Arum *Dracunculus muscivorus.*
Hairy Begonia *Begonia decora.*
Hairy Boronia *Boronia pilosa.*
Hairy Buttonbush *Cephalanthus occidentalis* var. *pubescens.*
Hairy Canary Clover *Dorycnium hirsutum.*
Hairy Correa *Correa aemula.*
Hairy Cup Grass *Eriochloa villosa.*
Hairy Darling Pea *Swainsona greyana.*
Hairy Finger Grass *Digitaria sanguinalis.*
Hairy-fruited Blueberry *Vaccinium hirsutum.*
Hairy Germander *Teucrium occidentale.*
Hairy Golden Aster *Heterotheca villosa.*
Hairy Honeysuckle *Lonicera hirsuta.*
Hairy Huckleberry *Vaccinium hirsutum.*
Hairy Jugflower *Adenanthos barbigerus.*
Hairy Kafferboom *Erythrina latissima.*
Hairy Lace Fern *Oenotrichia tripinnata.*
Hairy Manzanita *Arctostaphylos columbiana.*
Hairy-pod Wattle *Acacia glandulicarpa.*
Hairy Verbena *Verbena hispida.*
Hairy Vervain *Verbena hispida.*
Hairy Wattle *Acacia vestita.*
Hairy Wood-rush *Luzula pilosa.*
Hakama-giboshi *Hosta helenioides.*

Hakea Schräd. PINCUSHION TREE. Proteaceae. 110 shrubs or small trees. Lvs rigid-coriaceous, sometimes dentate or lobed. Fls paired in short axill. bracteate rac. or clusters, perianth straight below, limb ovoid or globose, seg. concave; anth. sub-sessile, inserted in the concavity of the lamina; nectary a broad gland; style protruding. Fr. a large woody bivalved capsule. W Aus. Z9.
H. amplexicaulis R. Br. PRICKLY HAKEA. Glab., erect, straggling shrub, 3–4m. Lvs 10–20cm, ovate-oblong, undulate-sinnate, base expanding into prickly-toothed auricles. Fls creamy-white, ageing pink in dense axill. clusters; perianth glab., 5mm. Late winter–spring. W Aus.
H. auriculata Meissn. Erect shrub to 1m. Lvs to 5cm, cuneate to narrow-linear, prickly toothed, with two prickly auricles clasping st. Fls white to dark purple, in small clusters in the upper axils; perianth tube 4mm. Winter and spring. W Aus.
H. bakeriana F. Muell. & Maid. Rounded shrub 2m high and

wide. Lvs 7cm, terete. Fls pink in clusters; perianth 1cm. Winter–early spring. E Aus.

H. baxteri R. Br. FAN HAKEA. Erect, stiff shrub, 1.5–3m. Lvs 4–7cm, flabellate, thick and leathery, undulate, prickly-toothed. Fls brown, in clusters; perianth 6mm. Winter–spring. W Aus.

H. bucculenta C. Gardn. RED POKERS. Erect shrub to 4m. Lvs 12–17×0.1–0.2cm, entire, rigid, erect. Fls red in elongated, rac. to 15cm; perianth glab., 6mm. Late winter-spring. W Aus.

H. ceratophylla (Sm.) R. Br. Erect spreading shrub, 1–2m. Lvs 6–10cm, irregularly and deeply divided in upper half into 3 toothed lobes, tinged red when young. Fls in small clusters; perianth 5mm, pink with rusty-brown hairs. Spring. W Aus.

H. cinerea R. Br. Rigid shrub, 2–2.5m. Lvs 6–12cm, flat, leathery, rigid, linear-cuneate or oblanceolate, prominently 3 nerved. Fls yellow in globular, 5cm diam, clusters. Late winter–spring. W Aus.

H. conchifolia Hook. Stout, erect shrub, 3–5m. Lvs shell-like, 4cm wide, margins with short prickly teeth. Fls white or pale pink in clusters. Mid-winter–spring. W Aus.

H. coriacea Maconochie Erect shrub, 3–4m. Lvs 14–17×0.5–0.6cm, linear coriaccous. Fls pink to red in a 8–12cm spike; perianth glab. Late winter–early spring. W Aus.

H. corymbosa R. Br. CAULIFLOWER HAKEA. Much-branched, stout, flat-topped shrub, 30–60cm. Lvs 3–6cm, linear-cuneate, fiercely pungent, erect, rigid. Fls yellow-green in dense clusters; perianth glab., straight, 12mm. Mid-winter–spring. W Aus.

H. costata Meissn. RIBBED HAKEA. Erect shrub, 1–2m, clothed in long fine hairs. Lvs 1cm, linear-lanceolate, glab., 1-veined, pungent. Fls white-cream in small dense clusters, giving a spike-like effect. Mid-winter–spring. W Aus.

H. crassifolia Meissn. Shrub, 4–6m, rigid, erect. Lvs 4–8cm, oblong, mucronate, rusty brown when young. Fls large, creamy in short axill. rac.; perianth with rusty hairs, 10mm. Spring. W Aus.

H. cristata R. Br. Erect shrub, 2–3m. Lvs 4–9cm, broadly oblong to obovate, prickly toothed, undulate. Fls small, white in short axill. rac.; perianth 3mm. Winter. W Aus.

H. cucullata R. Br. SCALLOPS. Erect, straggly shrub, 3–5m. Lvs 4–8cm, undulate, sometimes slightly crenulate, rusty brown when young. Fls cream-pink in axill. clusters. Mid-winter–spring. W Aus.

H. cyclocarpa Lindl. CURVED FRUIT HAKEA. Straggling, sparse shrub, 1–2m. Lvs 6–18cm, oblong, lanceolate or cuneate, thick, obscurely 3-veined. Fls white in clusters; perianth hairy, 10mm. Late winter-spring. W Aus.

H. dactyloides (Gaertn.) Cav. Variable shrub to 5m. Lvs 10cm, slightly sickle-shaped, narrow-lanceolate, to oblong to obovate, with 3 prominent veins, young growth bronze. Fls white in clusters. Spring. E Aus.

H. elliptica (Sm.) R. Br. Shrub to 3m, densely leafy. Lvs 4–8cm, broadly ovate to elliptic, young growth bronze. Fls white in clusters; perianth glab. Late winter-spring. W Aus.

H. epiglottis Labill. Erect or spreading shrub to 4m. Lvs 2–10cm, terete, pungent, curved. Fls yellow in clusters, perianth hairy, 5mm. Spring. E Aus.

H. eriantha R. Br. TREE HAKEA. Bushy shrub to 4m. Lvs 12cm, narrow-lanceolate to lanceolate, young growth red. Fls white in clusters; perianth woolly, 6mm. Spring. E Aus.

H. falcata R. Br. Erect shrub, 1.5–3m. Lvs 8–14cm, broadly linear-lanceolate, occas. falcate, 3-veined. Fls white to pale yellow, scented, in loose axill. rac.; perianth 4mm. Spring. W Aus.

H. ferruginea Sweet. Slender shrub, 1–3m. Lvs 2–3cm, cordate-ovate to ovate-lanceolate, glab. or villous, shortly acuminate, young lvs covered in rusty red hairs. Fls white, in clusters; perianth glab., 6mm. Spring. W Aus.

H. flabellifolia Meissn. Low, erect shrub to 2m. Lvs to 7cm, thick, coarsely toothed, fan-shaped. Fls purple-brown in small clusters; perianth adpressed-hairy, 6mm. Late autumn–spring. W Aus. Similar to H. baxteri, but lvs narrower.

H. florida R. Br. Erect, stiff shrub, 1–2m. Lvs 2.5–4cm linear-lanceolate to lanceolate, acute and pungent, margins prickly toothed. Fls small, white in clusters. Spring. W Aus.

H. florulenta Meissn. Low shrub to 1(–3)m. Lvs 10(–15)cm, broadly oblanceolate to oblong-obovate. Fls white, in clusters, sweetly scented; perianth glab., 8mm. Spring. E Aus.

H. franciziana F. Muell. GRASS LEAF HAKEA. Tall shrub, 3–4m. Lvs 8–18cm, linear, with 5–7 parallel veins. Fls pink-red, in densely-fld, cylindrical rac. 3–9cm long. Winter–spring. W & E Aus.

H. gibbosa (Sm.) Cav. Erect prickly shrub to 3m. Lvs 5cm, terete, stiff, pungent. Fls cream in few-fld clusters; perianth glab., 6mm. Winter. E Aus.; nat. S Afr.

H. gilbertii Kipp. ex Meissn. Open, spreading shrub with 1–2 st. to 70cm with clumped br. Lvs 5cm, divaricate to recurved, with 5–6 longitudinal grooves. Fls cream, rarely suffused pink with

sickly aroma, in dense globular clusters. Mid-winter to spring. W Aus.

H. invaginata B.L. Burtt. Shrub to 2m. Lvs 2cm, grey-green, terete, with 5 longitudinal grooves. Fls pink, rarely cream, in dense clusters; perianth glab., 5mm. Mid-winter and spring. W Aus.

H. laurina R. Br. PINCUSHION HAKEA. Tall, sometimes straggling shrub to 6m. Lvs to 15cm, flat, oblong-lanceolate. Fls cream, ageing red in large globular clusters. Late autumn to mid-winter. W. Aus.

H. lehmanniana Meissn. BLUE HAKEA. Bushy shrub to 1.5m. Lvs 2–6cm, linear, terete, roughly triangular in section with a wide shallow channel between striae. Fls pale blue, in dense axill. clusters. Mid-winter–spring. W Aus.

H. leucoptera R. Br. NEEDLEWOOD. Suckering shrub to small tree to 5m. Lvs 7cm, terete, pungent. Fls creamy white in clusters. Spring–summer. C & E Aus.

H. linearis R. Br. Erect bushy shrub to 3m. Lvs 3–5cm, linear-lanceolate, entire to sparsely prickly toothed. Fls white in dense clusters; perianth 6cm. Mid-winter to summer. W Aus.

H. lissocarpha R. Br. HONEY BUSH. Densely branched, spreading, rigid shrub, 1.5m. Lvs 2–4cm, pinnate, seg. 3–7, divaricate, pungent. Fls small, white or pink, sweetly scented in clusters. Early winter–spring. W Aus.

H. lissosperma R. Br. NEEDLE BUSH. Shrub to 3m high, to small tree to 6m. Lvs 10cm, terete, pungent, tending to curve upwards. Fls white in clusters. Summer. E Aus.

H. megalosperma Meissn. LESUEUR HAKEA. Rigid, many-stemmed shrub to 1m. Lvs 4–8cm, obovate-oblong, thick. Fls white-pink to deep red in clusters. Late autumn–early winter. W Aus.

H. microcarpa R. Br. Small to medium shrub to 1.5m. Lvs 7cm, rigid, terete to linear, pungent. Fls cream to white, in clusters; perianth, 6mm. Spring–summer. E Aus.

H. minyma Maconochie. Erect shrub, 2×1.5m. Lvs to 15cm, broad-linear to oblong, leathery. Fls pale pink to cream in 5cm cylindrical rac.; perianth 9mm. Spring. C & W Aus.

H. muelleriana J.M. Black. DESERT HAKEA. Erect rounded shrub to 4m. Lvs 12cm, terete to narrow-linear, triangular in section. Fls creamy white, in clusters; perianth 4mm. Late spring–early summer. E Aus.

H. multilineata Meissn. Tall shrub or small tree to 5m. Lvs 10–13cm, erect, grey-green, linear-oblong or linear-cuneate. Fls pink-purple in dense 3–7cm spikes. Mid-winter and spring. W Aus. Confused with H. franciziana but fls are a much brighter colour.

H. myrtoides Meissn. Low, diffuse or spreading shrub to 1m. Lvs to 1–2cm, entire, lanceolate to cordate, glossy, flat, 1-veined, pungent. Fls deep pink to purple-mauve, rarely apricot, in dense clusters; perianth 4mm. Winter to early spring. W Aus.

H. neurophylla Meissn. Robust shrub to 2m. Lvs 7–12cm, ovate-elliptic to oblong-lanceolate, slightly acuminate, 3–5-veined. Fls rose-pink to red. Winter. W Aus.

H. nitida R. Br. Densely branched, erect and prickly shrub to 3m high. Lvs 4–10cm, oblanceolate to obovate, sometimes entire, mostly with prickly toothed or slightly lobed margins. Fls white in loose, globular, clusters. Late winter and spring. W Aus.

H. nodosa R. Br. Medium, spreading shrub to 3m. Lvs to 4cm, terete. Fls yellow, in clusters; perianth glab., 3 mm. Late autumn and winter. W Aus. Forms with yellow st. and blue-green foliage have been recorded.

H. obtusa Meissn. Spreading shrub, 0.5–2m. Lvs 3–7cm, elliptic or oblong-lanceolate, 3-veined, blunt. Fls cream-white becoming pink, in dense clusters. Winter. W Aus.

H. oleifolia (Sm.) R. Br. Shrub or small tree to 7m. Lvs 2.5–6cm, thick, oblong-lanceolate to cuneate-oblong, 1-veined. Fls white in short clusters or rac.; perianth glab., 4mm. Late winter–spring. W Aus.

H. orthorrhyncha F. Muell. Rounded shrub to 3m. Lvs 7–15cm, narrow-linear, thick, flat, mostly entire, sometimes pinnate. Fls red in clusters; perianth silky. Mid-winter–spring. W Aus.

H. pandanicarpa R. Br. Erect, rounded shrub to 2m. Lvs to 10cm, oblong-cuneate narrowing into a short petiole. Fls white in clusters among upper lvs; perianth 10mm, covered in short rusty hairs. Mid-winter–late spring. W Aus.

H. petiolaris Meissn. Shrub to 6m. Lvs 7–12cm, elliptic, rigid and thick, slightly undulate, grey-green, with 3 prominent nerves. Fls pink to red, rarely cream, in clusters or rac.; perianth glab., 6mm. Autumn–winter. W Aus.

H. platysperma Hook. CRICKET BALL HAKEA. Rigid, erect shrub with spreading br., 1.5–4m. Lvs 8–13cm, thick, terete, smooth, pungent. Fls yellow or creamy, sweet-scented in clusters; perianth minutely silky. Mid-winter and spring. W Aus.

H. propinqua A. Cunn. Variable shrub open, 3m high and wide, to narrowly erect. Lvs 4–6cm, terete, pungent. Fls creamy white in clusters. Late autumn–winter. E Aus.

H. prostrata R. Br. Shrub or small tree to 4m. Lvs to 7cm, broad-oblong or obovate, entire or with prickly teeth. Fls white, cream, pink to purple, sweetly scented in clusters; perianth 5mm. Late winter–spring. W Aus.

H. purpurea Hook. Erect shrub to 3m. Lvs 2–10cm, rigid, terete, rarely occas. 3-fid, pungent. Fls pink to red, purple, in clusters. Winter–spring. E Aus.

H. pycnoneura Meissn. Straggling shrub to 2m with br. and lvs covered in minute, silver hairs. Lvs 8–20cm, linear, flat. Fls large, mauve-purple in dense rac.; perianth 4cm, glab. Winter. W Aus.

H. recurva Meissn. Stout, rigid, glab. shrub or small tree to 7m. Lvs 5–10cm, terete, thick, spreading or recurved, pungent. Fls white or light yellow, in axill. clusters or dense rac. Winter––spring. W Aus.

H. rhombales F. Muell. Medium shrub to 2m. Lvs 5–17cm, terete, pungent. Fls deep pink or red in clusters, malodorous; perianth 10mm. Winter. C & W Aus.

H. ruscifolia Labill. Erect, densely bushy shrub, 2–3m. Lvs 1–2cm, crowded, elliptic-lanceolate, pungent. Fls small, white, honey-scented, in dense clusters terminating short, leafy br. Summer. W Aus.

H. salicifolia (Vent.) B.L. Burtt. Shrub to small tree, to 5m. Lvs 10–15cm, lanceolate to oblong-elliptic. Fls creamy-white in clusters. Spring. E Aus.

H. scoparia Meissn. Erect, many-stemmed shrub to 1–2m. Lvs 6–20cm, terete, star-shaped in section, striate and grooved, pungent. Fls pale yellow to deep pink. Mid-winter and spring. W Aus.

H. sericea Schräd. Bushy to open shrub, 3m. Lvs 5cm, terete, pungent. Fls white to pink, in clusters. Late winter–spring. E Aus., widely nat.

H. suaveolens R. Br. Erect shrub, 1.5–2m. Lvs 7–20cm, pinnate, seg. erect, 2–5cm, pungent. Fls cream in dense rac. Winter. W Aus.

H. subsulcata Meissn. Erect shrub, 1–2m. Lvs 3–11cm, erect, terete, with 10–12 striae. Fls cream to mauve, in clusters; perianth glab. Late winter–spring. W Aus.

H. sulcata R. Br. Erect, many-stemmed shrub, 0.5–15m. Lvs 6–12cm, flat, linear-oblanceolate. Fls cream, in clusters. Late winter–early spring. W Aus.

H. teretifolia (Salisb.) Britten. Variable, prickly shrub to 3m. Lvs to 5cm, terete, rigid and pungent. Fls creamy-white, in clusters; perianth hairy. Spring–summer. E Aus.

H. trifurcata (Sm.) R. Br. Densely branched shrub to 3m. Lvs 3–6cm, entire and terete to divided-terete or flat, oval, oblong or lanceolate. Fls white in clusters; perianth 6mm, silky hairy. Mid-winter–spring. W Aus.

H. varia R. Br. Erect, spreading or diffuse shrub, 1–3m. Lvs 2.5–4(7)cm, entire to dissected, cuneate, narrow-lanceolate or linear-oblong. Fls small, white green-white or yellow, in clusters. Mid-winter–spring. W Aus.

H. verrucosa F. Muell. Shrub to 2m. Lvs 4–8cm, rigid, terete, pungent. Fls purple-red (creamy in bud), in short rac.; perianth glab. Mid-winter and spring. W Aus.

H. victoria J. Drumm. Columnar to bushy shrub to 3m. Lvs to 12cm diam., green near base, variegated higher up, white when young, ageing orange then red. Fls cream to pink in clusters; perianth 10mm. Late winter–spring. W Aus.

Hakea-leaf Wattle *Acacia hakeoides.*

Hakonechloa Mak. ex Honda Gramineae. 1 rhizomatous perenn. grass to 75cm. St. ascending or spreading, flimsy. Lvs smooth, linear-lanceolate, acute, to 25×1.5cm. Fls in a loose, lanceolate to ovoid, nodding pan. to 18cm; spikelets stalked, oblong, somewhat flattened, 3–5-fld, to 2cm, pale green. Autumn. Jap. (mts). Z5.

H. macra (Munro) Mak. 'Alboaurea': lvs striped off-white and gold. 'Albovariegata': lvs striped white. 'Aureola' ('Urahajusa Zuku'): lvs yellow, striped with narrow, green lines.

Hako-tsutsuji *Tripetaleia bracteata.*
Halberd Fern *Tectaria heracleifolia.*
Halberd-leaved Marsh Mallow *Hibiscus militaris.*
Halberd-leaved Rose Mallow *Hibiscus militaris.*
Halberd-leaved Violet *Viola hastata.*
Halberd-willow *Salix hastata.*

Halenbergia Dinter.
H. hypertrophica (Dinter) Dinter = *Mesembryanthemum hypertrophicum.*

Halenia Borkh. SPURRED GENTIAN. Gentianaceae. 70 ann., bienn. or perenn. herbs. Lvs basal, (rosulate) and cauline, (opposite), entire. Infl. cymose; fls 4-merous; cor. campanulate,

tube v. short, lobes spurred at base. Summer. Eurasia, N & S Amer. Z7.

H. elliptica D. Don. Erect, glab., to 60cm; st. narrowly winged. Basal lvs 1.5cm, elliptic, cauline lvs 2.5–5cm, narrow-elliptic. Fls clustered on axillary br. or term.; cor. 8mm diam., pale blue, campanulate, deeply 4-lobed, with spurs to 7mm. Himal.

H. perrottetii Griseb. Differs from *H. elliptica* in cor. clear blue with lobes more than twice lenght of spurs. India (Nilgiri Hills).

Halesia Ellis ex L. SILVERBELL TREE; SNOWDROP TREE. Styracaceae. 4–5 decid. small trees or shrubs. Br. stellate-pubesc., later glab. Fls pendulous, in axill. clusters; cal. tube obconical with 4 minute teeth, slightly 4-ribbed; cor. broadly campanulate, 4-lobed; sta. 8–16, fil. hairy below; style slender, pubesc. to glab. Drupe oblong, dry, 2–4-winged. China, E N Amer.

H. carolina L. = *H. tetraptera.*

H. carolina var. *monticola* Rehd. = *H. monticola.*

H. diptera Ellis. Large shrub or small tree, rarely to 8m. Lvs 6–12cm, oval or obovate, cuneate or rounded at base, minutely and distantly toothed, abruptly acuminate, young foliage pubesc. Fls 3–6 per fascicle; cal. v. downy; cor. white, 2–2.5cm; sta. usually 8. Fr. 2-winged. Spring. SE US. var. *magniflora* Godfrey. Fls to 3cm, more numerous. Z6.

H. fortunei Hemsl. = *Alniphyllum fortunei.*

H. monticola (Rehd.) Sarg. Tree to 28m. Lvs 8–16cm, elliptic to oblong-obovate, remotely serrate, acuminate, cuneate at base, soon glab. except on veins beneath. Fls 2–5 per fascicle; cal. glab. or pubesc.; cor. white, 1.5–2.5cm; sta. 10–16. Fr. 4-winged. Spring. SE US. 'Rosea': fls pale rose. var. *vestita* Sarg. Lvs to 12cm, white-tomentose beneath when young, base more rounded; fls 3–5 per fascicle, sometimes tinted rose. N Carol., Ark. Z5.

H. parviflora Michx. = *H. tetraptera.*

H. tetraptera Ellis. Small tree or shrub, to 6m. Lvs 5–16cm, ovate-lanceolate, rounded or cuneate at base, acute or acuminate, serrulate, glab. above, grey stellate-pubesc. beneath. Fls 2–6 per fascicle; cal. glab. or tomentose; cor. white, 1–1.5cm; sta. 10–16. Fr. 4-winged. Spring. S US. 'Meehanii': lvs broader, wrinkled, pubesc. beneath; fls smaller, cor. lobes more deeply cut, fil. hairless; pedicel shorter. Fr. 2-winged. f. *dialypetala* (Rehd.) Schneid. Cor. split almost to base. var. *mollis* (Lange) Perkins. Lvs broader, short-acuminate, downy above, densely villous or tomentose beneath. Cor. larger; sta. 8–12. Z5.

✕**Halimiocistus** Janch. Cistaceae. Hybrids between *Cistus* and *Halimium*, some occurring in the wild. S Eur. Z8.

✕*H.* 'Ingwersenii'. (*Halimium umbellatum* ✕*Cistus hirsutus.*) To 50cm. Lvs 2–3cm, linear-lanceolate, obtuse, sessile, dark green above, downy. Fls in sparse, long-stalked branching cymes; pet. white. Early–late summer. Port.

✕*H. revolii* (Coste & Soulié) Dansereau. (*Halimium alyssoides* ✕*Cistus salviifolius.*) To 50cm. Lvs 0.6–1.8cm, elliptic to broad-elliptic, pubesc. beneath, grey-green. Fls in term. cymes; pet. white to pale yellow, base pale to deep yellow. Early–late summer. S Fr.

✕*H. sahucii* (Coste &Soulié) Janch. (*Halimium umbellatum* ✕*Cistus salviifolius.*) To 1m. Lvs 1.5–2.5cm, linear to linear-oblanceolate, pubesc. above, densely pubesc. beneath. Fls 3–5 per cyme; pet. white. Mid summer. S Fr.

✕*H. wintonensis* Warb. & E.F. Warb. (*Halimium ocymoides* ✕*Cistus salviifolius.*) To 60cm. Lvs to 5cm, elliptic-lanceolate, acuminate pubesc. Fls in long-stalked, lax, 2–4-fld cymes; pet. white, often deepening to yellow at base with a strong maroon basal blotch. Early–late summer. Gdn origin. 'Merrist Wood Cream': fls. deep cream to primrose yellow with a dark maroon basal spot; mid spring–late summer.

→*Cistus* and *Helianthemum.*

Halimium (Dunal) Spach. Cistaceae. 12 everg., low-growing, grey-pubesc. shrubs and subshrubs. Fls in rac. or umbellate cymes; sep. 3–5; pet. 5, broad, thin-textured. Medit., SW Eur., N Afr., Asia Minor. Z8.

H. alyssoides (Lam.) K. Koch. To 1m. Lvs 0.8–3cm, obovate to ovate-lanceolate, dark green above, white-pubesc. beneath, sometimes above also. Infl. cymose, short downy; fls to 1.5cm diam.; pet. yellow, not spotted. Late spring–late summer. SW Eur.

H. atriplicifolium (Lam.) Spach. To 2m. Lvs 2–5cm, ovate-lanceolate or rhombic to elliptic, covered with dense hairs and peltate scales. Infl. to 20cm, cymes paniculate, leafless, rigid, with scattered purple hairs overlaying white; fls to 4cm diam.; pet. yellow, basal spot brown. Late spring–early summer. SC Eur.

H. commutatum Pau. To 50cm. Lvs 1–3.5cm, linear, revolute, glab. above, grey-pubesc. beneath. Fls solitary or to 5 in a term.

cyme; pet. pale yellow, not spotted. Late spring–early summer. SW Eur.

H. eriocephalum Willk. = *H. lasianthum*.

H. formosum (Curtis) Dunal = *H. lasianthum*.

H. halimifolium (L.) Willk. & Lange. To 1m. Lvs 1–4cm, oblong to obovate-lanceolate, initially white-pubesc., hardening grey-green, silver-scaly above. Fls to 3cm diam., long-stalked, in erect, paniculate cymes; pet. golden with maroon basal spot. Late spring–early summer. SW Eur. ssp. *multiflorum* (Salzm. ex Dunal) Maire. Exceptionally floriferous. Late spring–early summer. SW Eur., N Afr.

H. lasianthum (Lam.) Spach. To 70cm. Lvs to 2.5cm, oval, obtuse, pubesc., usually revolute. Fls to 4cm diam.; stalks downy; pet. golden with red basal spot. Early–mid summer. SW Eur. 'Concolor': fls unspotted. ssp. *formosum* (Curtis) Heyw. Fls 4–6cm diam., basal spot higher up pet. 'Sandling': pet. with conspicuous maroon blotches.

H. libanotis Lange in part. = *H. commutatum*.

H. multiflorum (Salzm. ex Dunal) Willk. = *H. halimifolium* ssp. *multiflorum*.

H. occidentale Willk. in part. = *H. lasianthum*.

H. ocymoides (Lam.) Willk. & Lange. 1m. Lvs 1.2–3cm, obovate-lanceolate, grey-pubesc. Fls few, long-stalked in erect, term. pan. forming broad infl.; pet. golden, typically with wide maroon spot at base. Early–late summer. SW Eur. 'Susan': habit compact; lvs broad.

H. rosmarinifolium (Pourr. pro parte) Spach = *H. commutatum*.

H. umbellatum (L.) Spach. To 40cm. Lvs to 3cm, linear-lanceolate, leaf-green, pale green above, hoary pubesc, beneath. Fls 2cm diam., 3–6 per term., subumbellate pan.; pet. white stained yellow at base. Early–late summer. Medit.

→*Cistus* and *Helianthemum*.

Halimodendron Fisch. ex DC. Leguminosae (Papilionoideae). 1 spiny shrub, to 2m. St. grey-blue. Lvs silvery at first, pinnate; rachis persistent, spine-tipped; lfts to 3.5cm, in 1–2 pairs. Rac. to 4cm, axill., 1–3-fld; fls pea-like, to 2cm, pale purple. Summer. Eur., Turk. to C & SW Asia. Z2.

H. argenteum (Lam.) DC. = *H. halodendron*.

H. halodendron (Pall.) Voss. SALT TREE. 'Purpureum': fls vibrant pink flushed purple and white.

Halleria L. Scrophulariaceae. 4 everg. shrubs or trees. Fls in term. cymes or solitary; cal. campanulate, 4–5-lobed; cor. tube 4–5-lobed. Fr. a berry. Summer. Trop. & S Afr., Madag. Z9.

H. lucida L. AFRICAN HONEYSUCKLE. Straggling, everg. shrub or tree to 9m. Lvs to 8cm, ovate, serrulate, acuminate. Fls to 2.5cm, nodding to pendulous, curving; cor. scarlet, 2-lipped. Fr. violet-black. Trop. & S Afr.

Halocarpus Quinn. Podocarpaceae. 3 everg., coniferous trees or shrubs. Juvenile lvs linear, thin, spirally arranged; adult lvs overlapping, spirally arranged, scale-shaped, keeled. ♂ cones solitary, term.; ♀ cone borne near br. apices, with limp, spreading scales. Seeds pendulous, receptacle fleshy. NZ.

H. bidwillii (Hook. f. ex Kirk) Quinn. TARWOOD; NEW ZEALAND; MOUNTAIN PINE. Shrub to 4×6m. St. prostrate to erect; twigs cylindric, flecked white, to 2mm diam. Juvenile lvs to 1cm; adult lvs to 2mm. Seed receptacle white. NZ. Z7.

H. biformis (Hook.) Quinn. Tree to 15m, or a shrub to 1m at higher altitudes. Twigs tetragonal, to 3mm diam., obscured by sheathing lvs. Juvenile lvs resembling *Taxus*, distichous, 1–2cm; adult lvs to 2mm. Seed receptacle white. NZ. Z8.

H. kirkii (F. Muell. ex Parl.) Quinn. MONOAO. Tree to 25m; twigs cylindric, to 2mm diam. Juvenile lvs to 4cm, adult lvs to 4mm. Seed receptacle orange. NZ. Z9.

→*Dacrydium*.

HALORAGIDACEAE R. Br. 9/120. *Myriophyllum*, *Proserpinaca*.

Haloxylon Bunge. Chenopodiaceae. 10 small trees or shrubs; st. brittle, jointed. Lvs reduced or obsolete. Fls v. small, solitary, in axils of scale-like bracts on short twigs; perianth seg. 5, membranous, sta. 5, fil. exserted. Fr. a nutlet bearing wings of persistent perianth. W Medit. to Burm. and C Asian deserts.

H. ammodendron (C.A. Mey.) Bunge. Shrub to 2m, bark pale grey; young shoots green or glaucescent, ± succulent. Lvs reduced to pubesc. tubercles. Fr. wings to 1cm across, cordate. Early summer. C Asia, Mong.

H. persicum Bunge ex Boiss. & Buhse. Tree to 5m; st. tuberculate; bark light grey, shoots pale green becoming white-tinged. Lvs scale-like, aristate, appressed. Fr. wings to 1cm across, suborbicular, often twisted. C Asia to Iran.

→*Anabasis* and *Arthrophytum*.

HAMAMELIDACEAE R. Br. 28/90. *Corylopsis, Disanthus, Distylium, Exbucklandia, Fortunearia, Fothergilla, Hamamelis, Liquidambar, Loropetalum, Parrotia, Parrotiopsis, Rhodoleia, Sinowilsonia,* ×*Sycoparrotia, Sycopsis*

Hamamelis L. WITCH-HAZEL. Hamamelidaceae. 5 decid. shrubs or small trees. Br. and buds tomentose. Lvs alt., ovate to obovate, toothed, base oblique, turning yellow with tints of red and orange in autumn. Fls fragrant in dense, axill. clusters; cal. shortly 4-lobed, tomentose, interior red; pet. 4, to 2cm, strap-like. Autumn–winter. N Amer., Jap., E Asia.

H. angustifolia Nieuwl. = *H. virginiana*.

H. arborea hort. Ottol. ex Mast. = *H. japonica*.

H. ×intermedia Rehd. (*H. japonica* ×*H. mollis.*) Shrub to 4m. Lvs broad-ovate to obovate, narrower than *H. mollis*, 10–15cm. Fls to 3cm diam., pet. crumpled. Winter. Gdn origin. 'Advent': earliest flowering; fls bright yellow. 'Allgold': medium-sized, br. ascending; lvs elliptic to ovate, 11–18cm, yellow in autumn; fls butter-yellow, pet. narrow, twisted; cal. red. 'Arnold Promise': fls densely clustered; pet. deep sulphur-yellow, to 1.5cm; cal. interior red-green. 'Carmine Red': pet. to 2cm, narrow, twisted, pale bronze, tips suffused copper; late flowering. 'Diane': vigorous; autumn colour intense yellow and scarlet; pet. straight, to 17mm, carmine; cal. interior violet. 'Hiltingbury': large broad or ascending shrub; lvs circular to ovate, to 12×10cm; autumn colour red, orange and copper; fls pale copper-red; cal. interior purple. 'Jelena' ('Copper Beauty'): large ascending shrub; lvs ovate, to 17×15cm, autumn colour scarlet, bronze, red and orange; fls densely clustered, yellow suffused deep copper-red; pet. twisted, undulate, to 2cm; cal. interior burgundy. 'Magic Fire' ('Feuerzauber', 'Fire Charm'): erect, medium-sized shrub; lvs ovate to broad-elliptic, to 17×10cm, autumn colour yellow; pet. copper-orange, suffused red, to 2cm, twisted. 'Moonlight': medium to large shrub, br. ascending; lvs circular, to 18×12cm, autumn colour yellow; fls highly fragrant, densely clustered, pale sulphur-yellow, basal blotch burgundy. 'Nana': pet. to 3cm, deep yellow. 'Orange Beauty': erect shrub; lvs as *H. mollis*, more acute, autumn colour yellow; pet. to 1.5cm, golden yellow to orange-yellow; cal. interior green-brown becoming brown-red. 'Primavera': fls densely clustered; pet. to 2cm, sickle-shaped, primrose yellow. 'Ruby Glow' ('Rubra Superba', 'Adonis'): medium shrub, br. ascending to erect; lvs round to ovate, to 16×12cm, autumn colour orange, bronze and scarlet; pet. to 2cm, copper-red. 'Sunburst': early-flowering; fls sulphur yellow. 'Winter Beauty': vigorous; fls as 'Orange Beauty' but larger, pet. base brown-red. Z5.

H. japonica Sieb. & Zucc. JAPANESE WITCH-HAZEL. Shrub or tree to 3m; br. spreading. Lvs to 15cm, broad-ovate to obovate, tip acute, base oblique, stellate-hairy when young. Fls yellow; cal. interior green or purple; pet. to 20mm. Spring. Jap. 'Arborea': vigorous, to 5m, spreading to horizontal; lvs obovate, often broad, short-acuminate, crenate, autumn colour yellow; pet. yellow, crispate, to 1.5cm; cal. brown. 'Sulphurea': br. ascending, later spreading; lvs broadly obovate to subcircular, crenate, autumn colour yellow; pet. to 1.5cm, sulphur yellow. 'Zuccariniana': br. erect, later spreading; lvs obovate to rounded, crenate, autumn colour yellow; pet. to 1.2cm, twisted, crispate, sulphur yellow; cal. interior green to green-yellow. var. *flavopurpurascens* (Mak.) Rehd. Large, spreading, with many small sulphur fls tinted red at base. Lvs gold in fall. Z5.

H. macrophylla Pursh. See *H. virginiana*.

H. mollis Oliv. CHINESE WITCH-HAZEL. Shrub or small tree to 5m; young shoots pubesc., br. spreading. Lvs round to broad-obovate, to 16cm, tip short-acuminate, base cordate, margins round-toothed, stellate-hairy above, tomentose beneath. Fls sweetly fragrant; cal. interior red-purple; pet. golden yellow tinged red at base, straight, to 17mm. Winter–early spring. W & WC China. 'Brevipetala' ('Aurantiaca'): larger, erect; lvs blue-green, persisting longer in winter; pet. to 1cm, orange-yellow; cal. interior yellow-green to pale brown; early flowering. 'Coombe Wood': large, broad habit; lvs almost oval, autumn colour yellow; fls few; pet. to 2cm, flat, apex inrolled, golden yellow, base suffused red. 'Goldcrest': large shrub, br. ascending; autumn colour yellow; pet. to 2cm, apex crispate, golden, basal blotch burgundy; cal. interior purple-red. 'Pallida': medium shrub, br. ascending; autumn colour yellow; fls covering br., sulphur yellow. 'Westerstede': late flowering; fls pale yellow. Z6.

H. orbiculata Nieuwl. = *H. virginiana*.

H. vernalis Sarg. Upright suckering shrub to 2m. Similar to *H. virginiana* except lvs to 12cm, paler cal. lobe interior red; pet. yellow to red. Winter. SC US. 'Carnea': pet. and cal. interior pale pink. 'Lombart's Weeping': br. pendulous; lvs blue-green; fls pale red. 'Red Imp': pet. bases claret, copper at apex. 'Sandra': young foliage violet-purple, becoming green, flushed

purple beneath, autumn colour red, scarlet and orange; fls
cadmium yellow. 'Squib': pet. cadmium yellow; cal. green. Z5.
H. virginiana L. VIRGINIAN WITCH-HAZEL. Shrub or small tree, to
5m. Lvs obovate, to 15cm, coarsely round-toothed above middle, pubesc. on veins beneath, yellow in autumn. Cal. lobes
green or brown inside; pet. 17mm, crinkled, golden yellow.
Late autumn. E US. 'Rubescens': pet. bases suffused red; cal.
interior green, tinged yellow or brown. *H. macrophylla* from the
SE US has lvs generally larger, sinuately lobed with superb
autumn colour, the fls are small, crinkled and pale yellow, opening in late autumn and winter. Z5.
H. zuccariniana (hort. Ottol. ex Mast.) Gumbl. = *H. japonica*
'Zuccariniana'.

Hamatocactus Britt. & Rose.
H. crassihamatus (F.A.C. Weber) F. Buxb. = *Sclerocactus uncin-
atus*.
H. hamatacanthus (Muehlenpf.) F. Knuth = *Ferocactus hamata-
canthus*.
H. setispinus (Engelm.) Britt. & Rose = *Thelocactus setispinus*.
H. uncinatus (Gal. ex Pfeiff. & Otto) Orcutt = *Sclerocactus uncin-
atus*.

Hamburg Parsley *Petroselinum crispum* var. *tuberosum*.

Hamelia Jacq. Rubiaceae. 40 everg. shrubs or small trees. Fls in
2–3-branched, secund, term. cymes; cal. ovoid to turbinate,
lobes 5; cor. bell-shaped or tubular, 5-angled, lobes 5, spreading
or erect; sta. 5, anth. short-exserted or included. Fr. a berry,
ovoid to cylindric, 5-lobed. Trop. & subtrop. Amer. Z10.
H. coccinea Sw. = *H. patens*.
H. erecta Jacq. = *H. patens*.
H. grandiflora L'Hérit. = *H. patens*.
H. patens Jacq. SCARLET BUSH; FIREBUSH; COLORADILLO. Shrub
or small tree. 3–7m; branchlets 4-angled, pubesc. to glab. Lvs to
15×7cm, elliptic to obovate to lanceolate, acute or acuminate at
apex, pubesc., veins 7–10, pink; petioles pubesc., red. Fls
orange to scarlet or crimson; cor. to 2cm, pubesc., lobes ovate,
2mm. Fr. to 8×6mm, yellow-green, then red to purple and
black. Summer. Flor., W Indies, Mex. S to Boliv., Parag., Braz.
H. sphaerocarpa Ruiz & Pav. = *H. patens*.
H. ventricosa Sw. PRINCE WOOD; SPANISH ELM. Shrub or tree, to
6m. Branchlets 4-angled, glab. Lvs to 15×5cm, elliptic,
narrowly acute at apex, glab. above, minutely pubesc. beneath,
8–10-veined; petioles ± glab. Fls yellow; cor. to 5cm, lobes
ovate, 6mm. Fr. to 12mm, crimson. Summer–autumn. Jam.

Hamiltonia Roxb.
H. oblonga (Bunge) Franch. = *Leptodermis oblonga*.
H. suaveolens Roxb. = *Spermadictyon suaveolens*.

Hammock Fern *Blechnum occidentale*.
Hand Fern *Doryopteris pedata*.
Handkerchief Tree *Davidia*.
Hangehange *Geniostoma ligustrifolium*.
Hanging Geranium *Pelargonium peltatum*.

Haplocarpa Less. Compositae. *c*10 mat-forming, perenn.
herbs. Lvs rosulate. Cap. radiate, solitary, subsessile to shortly
pedunculate; involucre campanulate; ray flts yellow, 3-toothed;
disc flts tubular, 5-lobed. Afr. Z9.
H. nervosa (Thunb.) Beauv. Lvs 1–6cm, oblong to ovate, apex
subacute to rounded, attenuate to a broad, half-clasping petiole,
glab. to thinly or coarsely hairy above. Cap. several, to 5cm
diam.; peudncle to 8cm; ray flts *c*20×5mm, pale yellow, sometimes tinged green outside; disc flts pale yellow. Autumn–
spring. S Afr.
H. rueppellii (Schultz-Bip.) Beauv. Like *H. nervosa* but lvs v.
variable in shape, glab. above or loosely tomentose, cap.
*c*2–3cm diam. Throughout the year. Mts of E Afr., Ethiop.

Haplopappus Cass. Compositae. *c*160 ann. to perenn. herbs,
subshrubs or shrubs. Cap. usually radiate, few to several,
solitary or loosely clustered; ray flts yellow or purple; disc flts
yellow, 5-lobed. N & S Amer. Z9 unless specified.
H. acaulis (Nutt.) A. Gray = *Stenotus acaulis*.
H. apargioides A. Gray = *Pyrrocoma apargioides*.
H. armerioides (Nutt.) A. Gray = *Stenotus armerioides*.
H. blephariphylla A. Gray = *Machaeranthera blephariphylla*.
H. brandegei A. Gray = *Erigeron aureus*.
H. canus (A. Gray) S.F. Blake = *Hazardia cana*.
H. ciliatus (Nutt.) DC. = *Prionopsis ciliata*.
H. clementis (Rydb.) S.F. Blake = *Pyrrocoma clementis*.
H. coronopifolius (Less.) DC. = *H. glutinosus*.
H. croceus A. Gray = *Pyrrocoma crocea*.
H. cuneatus A. Gray = *Ericameria cuneata*.

H. cuneifolius Nutt. Caespitose ann. to perenn., to 15cm. St.
ascending or somewhat prostrate, often rooting, glab. Lvs to
1.5×1cm, cuneate-obovate to oblong-spathulate, obtuse, entire
or apex obscurely denticulate, sessile. Cap. solitary, peduncles
to 5cm; phyllaries papery, mostly pink. Winter. Chile, Arg.
H. ericoides (Less.) Hook. & Arn. = *Ericameria ericoides*.
H. eximius H.M. Hall = *Tonestus eximius*.
H. glutinosus Cass. Caespitose perenn., to 15cm, often forming
cushions. St. spreading or erect, glab., viscid. Lvs to 4×1cm,
oblong or elliptic, lobed to pinnatisect, seg. 1–4, linear, acute
apex often sharply dentate, attenuate to a short petiole. Cap.
solitary, on peduncles to 16cm. Winter. Chile, Arg.
H. gracilis (Nutt.) A. Gray. Ann., to 30cm. St. erect, branched
below. Lvs to 3×0.3cm, linear, dentate to pinnate, teeth or
lobes bristle-tipped, apex obtuse, usually sessile, lower lvs
sometimes lanceolate-spathulate, 1–2-pinnatifid and petiolate.
Cap. solitary or clustered, shortly pedunculate. Summer. SW
US, N Mex.
H. lanuginosus A. Gray = *Stenotus lanuginosus*.
H. lanuginosus ssp. *andersonii* (Rydb.) H.M. Hall = *Stenotus
andersonii*.
H. lyallii A. Gray = *Tonestus lyallii*.
H. parishii (Greene) S.F. Blake = *Ericameria parishii*.
H. phyllocephalus DC. CAMPHOR DAISY. Ann., to 1m. St. often
striate, grey or tinged red, gland., hairy. Lvs to 5×1cm, oblong
to spathulate-oblong, remotely dentate, teeth with bristles, or
lobes gland., scabrid, sessile. Cap. solitary, term. and ± sessile,
or clustered in cymes, on peduncles to 10cm; ray flts pale
yellow, sometimes red-tinged. Summer–autumn. S US, Mex.
H. pulchellus DC. Ann. or perenn., to 1m. St. woody below,
erect, much branched, glab. or minutely pubesc., glutinous. Lvs
to 6×1cm, lanceolate, apex and base acuminate, acutely
dentate. Cap. solitary or clustered in corymbs, on peduncles to
12cm. Chile.
H. pygmaeus (Torr. & A. Gray) A. Gray = *Tonestus pygmaeus*.
H. spinulosus (Pursh) DC. Perenn. to 60cm. St. erect or ascending, striate, glab. to scabrid or tomentose, usually gland. Lvs to
6×1cm, oblong- to linear-spathulate, ± entire, dentate or 1–2-
pinnatifid, teeth and lobes bristle-tipped, sessile. Cap. solitary,
on peduncles to 16cm. Summer–autumn. W N Amer. Z2.
H. tortifolia Torr. & A. Gray = *Machaeranthera tortifolia*.

Haplophragma Dop.
H. adenophyllum (DC.) Dop = *Fernandoa adenophylla*.

Hapuu, Hapuu-ii *Cibotium chamissoi*.
Haragiri *Kalopanax septemlobus*.
Harbinger-of-spring *Erigenia bulbosa*.
Hard Beech *Nothofagus truncata*.

Hardenbergia Benth. Leguminosae (Papilionoideae). 3 vines
and subshrubs. Lvs with a single lft or imparipinnate. Fls pea-
like in pairs or small clusters in long, axill. rac. Aus., Tasm. Z9.
H. comptoniana Benth. WESTERN AUSTRALIA CORAL PEA. Everg.
vine to 3m. St. slender, twining. Lvs 3–5-foliolate; lfts 6×3cm,
narrow-lanceolate to ovate. Fls in dense rac. to 12.5cm long,
blue to purple, standard with white, green-spotted blotch at
base. Summer. W Aus.
H. monophylla (Vent.) Benth. = *H. violacea*.
H. violacea (Schneev.) F.C. Stearn. VINE LILAC; PURPLE CORAL
PEA; FALSE SARSAPARILLA. Everg. climbing shrub to 2m+. St.
twining, or prostrate. Lvs 8×2.5cm, unifoliolate, ovate to
lanceolate, leathery. Fls in pendulous rac., purple, white, pink,
or lilac, standard, spotted yellow or green at centre. Spring. E
Aus., Tasm. 'Rosea': fls pink. 'Violacea': habit low, mounding,
vining; lvs lustrous; fls bright lavender with primrose eye,
spring. 'White Crystal': fls pure white, late winter.

Hard Fern *Blechnum* (*B. spicant*); *Pellaea calomelanos*.
Hard Hack *Spiraea tomentosa*.
Harding Grass *Phalaris aquatica*.
Hard-leaf Wattle *Acacia sclerophylla*.
Hard Rush *Juncus inflexus*.
Hardy Begonia *Begonia grandis*.
Hardy Catalpa *Catalpa speciosa*.
Harebell *Campanula rotundifolia*.
Hare's-foot Fern *Davallia* (*D. bullata*); *Phlebodium aureum*.
Hare's Tail *Lagurus*.
Haricot *Phaseolus vulgaris*.
Harmal *Peganum harmala*.

Harpagophytum DC. ex Meissn.
H. pinnatifidum Engl. = *Pterodiscus speciosus*.

Harpephyllum Bernh. ex K. Krause. Anacardiaceae. 1 everg.
tree to 10m. Lvs pinnate; lfts 5–17, 5–10cm, lanceolate, dark

shiny green. Fls cream to yellow-green in small spikes; cal. 4–5-lobed; pet. 4–5; sta. 7–10, conspicuous. Fr. oblong, thinly fleshy, to 2.5cm, red. Late summer. S Afr. Z9.
H. caffrum Bernh. ex K. Krause. KAFFIR PLUM; WILD PLUM.

Harpullia Roxb. Sapindaceae. 26 shrubs or trees. Lvs spirally arranged, paripinnate, rachis sometimes winged; pinnae alt., rarely opposite, glossy, thinly coriaceous, entire. Fls to 2.5cm diam. in bracteate rac. or pan.; cal. 5-merous; pet. 5, oblong-ovate, sessile or clawed; sta. 5–8, exserted. Fr. a capsule, lobes 2–3, inflated, leathery; seeds black, shiny. Trop. Asia to Aus. and Madag. Z10.
H. arborea (Blanco) Radlk. Tree to 33m. Pinnae 6–11, 10–20×3–9cm. Fls yellow-green, often with red margins. Fr. orange-yellow to red; seeds black, mahogany or dark purple, with an orange aril. Fls throughout year. Indomal., Philipp.
H. cupanoides auct. non Roxb. = H. arborea.
H. pendula Planch. ex F. Muell. TULIP-WOOD TREE. Tree to 15m. Young shoots red-brown, bark sometimes rough and irregularly flaked, light grey to cream coloured. Pinnae 8–10, 4–11×2–4cm. Fls pale yellow to pale green, faintly scented in pendulous pan. Fr. bright orange; seeds black with a yellow aril. Spring. Coastal NE Aus., Indomal., Philipp.
H. tomentosa Ridl. = H. arborea.
→Streptostigma.

Harrisia Britt. Cactaceae. c20 succulent shrubs, some tree-like, or scandent; st. usually slender, ribbed, seldom segmented. Fls nocturnal, funnelform, white. SE US, Carib., Braz., Boliv., Parag., Arg. Z9.
H. aboriginum Small = H. gracilis.
H. adscendens (Gürke) Britt. & Rose. Shrub, woody at base; st. much branched or clambering to 5–8m×2–5cm; ribs 7–10, tubercles elongate; leaf-rudiments present; spines usually 10, 2–3cm, stout. Fl. 15–18cm. E Braz.
H. bonplandii (Parmentier ex Pfeiff.) Britt. & Rose = H. pomanensis.
H. earlei Britt. & Rose. Prostrate shrub; st. 2–3m, eventually 4–6cm diam.; ribs 5–7, dark green; spines 5–8, 4–5cm, ascending. Fl. c20cm. Cuba.
H. eriophora (Pfeiff.) Britt. Like H. gracilis. Ribs 9–12. Spines 8–15, the longest 1.2–4.4cm. Fl. 15–17.5×7.5–10cm. Summer. Cuba, SE US (Flor.).
H. fragrans Small = H. eriophora.
H. gracilis (Mill.) Britt. Erect or sprawling shrub; st. 1–5×2.5–4cm; ribs 9–11; spines 7–16, to 2.5cm, rigid. Fl. 15–20×10–20cm, inner tep. toothed. Summer. Jam., SE US (Flor.).
H. guelichii (Speg.) Britt. & Rose. Clambering shrub, to 25m; st. 3–5cm diam., segmented, 3–4 angled; spines c6, 1 stouter and longer than the rest. Fl. large. Summer. N Arg.
H. jusbertii (Rebut ex Schum.) Borg. St. suberect; ribs 4–6, broad; spines c7–11, less than 5mm. Fl. 18cm. Possibly a hybrid or a variant of H. pomanensis. Known only in cult., used as a grafting stock.
H. martinii (Labouret) Britt. & Rose. Sprawling or clambering shrub, to 2m or more; st. 1.5–2.5cm diam.; ribs 4–5; tubercles broad, central spine 1, 2–4cm, stout, radial spines 1–3, to 3mm. Fl. 15–22×15–17cm, inner tep. sometimes pale pink. Summer. Arg.
H. nashii Britt. Slender shrub to 2–3m; st. divergent, 3–4cm diam.; ribs 9–11, rounded; spines 3–6, to 15mm. Fl. 16–20cm. Hispan.
H. pomanensis (F.A. Weber) Britt. & Rose. St. erect then sprawling or clambering to 3m or more, 3–8cm diam., 4(–5)-angled, jointed, glaucescent; spines rigid, pink-tinged at first, later nearly white, tipped almost black; central spine 1, 1–2.5cm, radial spines 5–8, c1cm. Fl c15cm. Summer. S Braz. to N Arg.
H. portoricensis Britt. Slender shrub to 2–3m; st. suberect, 3–4cm diam.; ribs 11, rounded; spines 13–17, to 3cm. Fl. c15cm. Puerto Rico.
H. regelii (Weingart) Borg. Perhaps a var. of H. martinii.
H. simpsonii Small = H. gracilis.
H. tetracantha (Labouret) D. Hunt. Shrub or small tree to 4m; st. 6–10cm diam., blue- or grey-green; ribs 7–9, somewhat tubercled; central spine 1, radial spines 4–7. Fl. 18–22cm. Boliv.
H. tortuosa (Forbes ex Otto & A. Dietr.) Britt. & Rose. Intermediate between H. pomanensis and H. martinii; st. 2–4cm diam., 6–7-ribbed what tuberculate, grooves slightly zig-zag; central spine 1. 3–4cm, radial spines 5–10, to 2cm. Fl. 12–15cm; inner tep. white to pale pink. Summer. Arg.
→Eriocereus, Roseocereus and Trichocereus.

Hart's Tongue Fern Asplenium scolopendrium.

Hartwegia Lindl.
H. purpurea Lindl. = Nageliella purpurea.
H. purpurea var. angustifolia Booth ex Lindl. = Nageliella angustifolia.

Harvest-lice Agrimonia.
Haryob Syagrus macrocarpa.

Hatiora Britt. & Rose. Cactaceae. 4 epiphytic or saxicolous cacti; st. cylindric, angled, winged or flat, segmented; spines 0 or soft, bristly. Fls campanulate; pericarpel angled or terete, naked; tube short; perianth spreading. Fr. small, obovoid, naked. SE Braz.
H. bambusoides F.A. Weber = H. salicornioides.
H. clavata (F.A.C. Weber) Moran = Rhipsalis clavata.
H. cylindrica Britt. & Rose = H. salicornioides.
H. gaertneri (Reg.) Barthlott. EASTER CACTUS. Stem-seg. mostly flat, oblong or elliptic, truncate, 4–7×2–2.5cm, shallowly crenate; areoles with 1-few fine, decid., brown bristles. Fl 4.5×4–7.5cm, intense scarlet. Fr. oblong, red. Spring. E Braz. Z9.
H. ×graeseri (Werderm.) Barthlott. (H. rosea ×H. gaertneri.) Fl. 4–6cm diam., intermediate between those of its parents and with a range of fl. colours. Spring. Gdn origin. Z9.
H. rosea (Lagerh.) Barthlott. Stem-seg. flat or 3–5-angled, oblong or narrowly oblanceolate, 2–4×c1cm; areoles with fine, brown bristles. Fl. 3–4×3–4cm, pink. Fr. depressed-globose, yellow, weakly angled. Spring. SE Braz. (Parana). Z9.
H. salicornioides (Haw.) Britt. & Rose. BOTTLE CACTUS; BOTTLE PLANT; DRUNKARD'S DREAM. Small shrub, much-branched; mains st. erect or pendent, cylindric to 1cm diam.; stem-seg. cylindric-clavate, 1.5–5cm×3–5mm, arising in whorls, resembling inverted bottles. Fl. to 13×10mm, yellow to orange. Fr. globose, white. SE Braz. Z9.
→Epiphyllum, Rhipsalidopsis, Rhipsalis and Schlumbergera.

Hat-rack Cactus Euphorbia lactea.
Hat Tree Brachychiton discolor.
Haumakaroa Pseudopanax simplex.
Hautbois Strawberry Fragaria moschata.

Hauya Moc. & Sessé ex DC. Onagraceae. 2 trees or shrubs. Fls large, solitary, 4-merous; cal. tybe cylindrical, elongate, sep. reflexed with age; sta. 8. C Amer.
H. ruacophila J.D. Sm. & Rose. 2–10m, downy. Lvs 5–12.5cm, round-cordate to oblong-ovate, entire. Cal. tube 5–10cm; pet. 3.5–4.5cm, ovate, white. Guat.

Havardia Small = Pithecellobium.

Hawaiian Hibiscus Hibiscus rosa-sinensis.
Hawaiian Tree Fern Cibotium chamissoi.
Hawkbit Leontodon.
Hawk's Beard Crepis.
Hawkweed Hieracium.

Haworthia Duval. Liliaceae (Aloeaceae). Over 70 dwarf, perenn., everg., ± stemless succulents. Lvs soft or rigid, spirally packed into a flat or extended rosette, sometimes in 3 twisting series, triangular and tapering to almost club-shaped, frequently with translucent patches or lines, smooth or with pearly tubercles, entire or dentate. Fls small in simple or sparsely branched rac., tubular, oblique-limbed, with 6 fleshy tep. united at the base, white or tinged green, yellow or pink, often with dark midveins. S Afr., extending to Nam., Swaz. and Moz. Z9.
H. aegrota Poelln. = H. arachnoidea.
H. affinis Bak. = H. cymbiformis.
H. agavoides Zantner & Poelln. = H. sordida.
H. albanensis Schönl. see H. angustifolia.
H. albicans Haw. = H. marginata.
H. altilinea Haw. Stemless, clustering. Rosette 6–8cm diam. Lvs about 35, incurved to ascending, 4×1.2×1.2cm, oblanceolate to oblong, v. inflated and juicy, smooth, pellucid in the upper part, with longitudinal flecks, finely toothed; apical awn to 8mm. E Cape.
H. angustifolia Haw. Stemless, clustering. Rosette 2–7cm diam. Lvs 12–40, ascending to recurved, to 10×1.5×0.4cm, lanceolate, tapering, acuminate, dull to tawny green, plump, slightly mottled, margins with scattered minute teeth; awn 2–3mm, white. Cape Prov. H. albanensis is a tetraploid variant of this sp.
H. arachnoidea (L.) Duval COBWEB ALOE. Stemless, clustering. Rosettes 2–13cm diam. Lvs 50–60, arachnoid, ascending to incurved, to 7×1.2×0.6cm, oblong to lanceolate, green, soft and juicy, semi-translucent flecked, aristate, longitudinally lined,

margins and upper part of keel with white to pale brown teeth; awn to 6mm. Cape Prov.

H. aranea (A. Berger) M. Bayer. Probably a variant of *H. bolusii*, with larger, flatter, saucer-shaped lvs.

H. archeri W. Barker ex M. Bayer. Close to *H. pulchella* and *H. marumiana*, but non-proliferous in habit.

H. argyrostigma Bak. = *H. attenuata*.

H. aristata Haw. Differs from *H. mucronata* in the firmer and longer-pointed lvs. Cape Prov. *H. helmiae* Poelln. is a compact variant of *H. aristata* with more lvs.

H. armstrongii Poelln. Intermediate between *H. coarctata* and *H. glauca*, and probably a hybrid between them. Cape Prov.

H. asperiuscula Haw. see *H. viscosa*.

H. asperula Haw. Rosette stemless, 2–7cm diam. Lvs about 12, erect to recurving, firm, to 3.5×2×1.5cm, with a slightly concave triangular pellucid end area to 2cm, rough from clear tubercles as if dusted with sugar, 7–9-lined. Cape Prov.

H. atrofusca G.G. Sm. = *H. magnifica*.

H. atrovirens (DC.) Haw. = *H. arachnoidea*.

H. attenuata Haw. Stemless or short-stemmed with basal offsets. Lvs erect or slightly curving, to 8×1.7×0.7cm, dark green, flexible, narrow-triangular, acuminate, rough from white tubercles, in bands on underside. Cape Prov. 'Variegata': lvs variegated. *H. clariperla* Haw., a widely grown plant with orange, pearl-dotted lvs, is a variant of this sp.

H. badia Poelln. = *H. mirabilis*.

H. batesiana Uitew. Stemless, forming compact many-headed tufts. Rosettes *c*4cm diam. Lvs *c*30, erect to spreading, 2–2.3×0.6×0.3cm, ovate to oblong, acuminate, soft and plump, pale green, translucent and longitudinally lined, smooth; awn 2mm. E Cape.

H. batteniae Scott = *H. bolusii*.

H. baylissii Scott = *H. angustifolia*.

H. beanii G.G. Sm. = *H. viscosa*.

H. bijliana Poelln. = *H. mucronata*.

H. bilineata Bak. = *H. cymbiformis*.

H. blackbeardiana Poelln. = *H. bolusii*.

H. blackburniae W. Barker. Tufts of smooth, linear, glaucous, green, grass-like lvs 1.5–2×0.2–0.5cm arising from a clump of tuberous roots to 1.2cm thick. W Cape.

H. bolusii Bak. Similar to *H. arachnoidea*, but lvs more incured, translucent toward the tip and with more numerous bristles. SE Cape.

H. brevis Haw. = *H. minima*.

H. britteniana Poelln. = *H. attenuata*.

H. broteriana Res. see *H. coarctata*.

H. browniana Poelln. = *H. fasciata*.

H. bruynsii M. Bayer. Similar to *H. emelyae* in vegetative features, but fl. tube curved, abruptly widened at base, whereas fl. tube shaped like an inverted club with trigonous base in *H. emelyae*. Cape Prov.

H. caespitosa Poelln. = *H. turgida*.

H. carissoi Res. = *H. glauca*.

H. cassytha Bak. = *H. ×rigida* 'Cassytha'.

H. chatwinii Marloth & Berger = *H. coarctata*.

H. chloracantha Haw. Close ally of *H. angustifolia*, distinguished by the smaller lvs. W Cape.

H. clariperla Haw. see *H. attenuata*.

H. coarctata Haw. St. to 20cm, offsetting, densely clothed in spirally arranged incurving, tawny to yellow-green lvs to 4.5×2.1×1cm, triangular, firm and stiff, keeled, covered in white or pale green tubercles. E Cape. *H. baccata* G. G. Sm. is a variant of this sp. *H. broteriana*, Res. *H. revendettii* and Uitew, *H. sampaiana* Res., are most likely gdn hybrids between tetraploid and hexaploid races.

H. ×coarctatoides Res. & Viv. Probably *H. coarctata* ×*H. reinwardtii*, and intermediate in appearance.

H. columnaris Bak. = *H. cooperi*.

H. comptoniana G.G. Sm. Larger than *H. emelyae*, the smooth lvs having the end area reticulate and somewhat translucent. W Cape.

H. concava Haw. = *H. cymbiformis*.

H. concinna Haw. = *H. viscosa*.

H. confusa Poelln. = *H. minima*.

H. cooperi Bak. Stemless, clustering. Rosette 4–8cm diam. Lvs 45–60, incurved to ascending, 2–4.5×1.3–1.6×0.5–0.8cm, tapered-oblong, pale to purple, green, inflated and juicy, with a translucent tip and longitudinal flecks, margins and uppermost part of keel with fine white 1–3mm teeth; awn 5–14mm. Karroo.

H. cordifolia Haw. = *H. viscosa*.

H. correcta Poelln. = *H. emelyae*.

H. curta Haw. Doubtfully referable to *H. nigra*.

H. ×cuspidata Haw. Probably *H. cymbiformis* ×*H. retusa*, and intermediate in general appearance. SE Cape.

H. cymbiformis (Haw.) Duval. Stemless (except *f. ramosa*), offsetting freely. Rosette 2.5–10cm diam. or more. Lvs about 30,

incurved to spreading, 1–5×1–5×0.5–0.8cm, ovate, acute, pale green sometimes flushed pink, turgid and soft, nearly translucent with ± clear striate tips, smooth or finely toothed; awn 3mm. E Cape. Many varieties and forms are recognized, *H. gracilidentata* Poelln.: rosettes small, lvs incurving, mainly translucent. *H. planifolia* Haw.: lvs broader, flatter; *H. ramosa* G.G. Sm.: branched; small rosettes on elongated st.; *H. umbracticola* Poelln.: lvs obtuse.

H. decipiens Poelln. = *H. pearsonii*.

H. dekenahii G.G. Sm. = *H. retusa*.

H. denticulata Haw. = *H. aristata*.

H. dielsiana Poelln. = *H. cooperi*.

H. distincta N.E. Br. = *H. venosa* ssp. *tessellata*.

H. divergens M. Bayer = *H. angustifolia*.

H. diversifolia Poelln. = *H. nigra*.

H. eilyae Poelln. = *H. glauca*.

H. emelyae Poelln. Rosette stemless, 6–9cm diam. Lvs to 20, erect to recurved, 3–4×1.2–2.5×1.1–1.6cm, with a retuse, flat or convex, pellucid end area 1.7–2.5×1–2cm, minutely tuberculate, 3–8 lined. E Cape. 'Robusta': habit broad.

H. engleri Dinter = *H. venosa* ssp. *tessellata*.

H. erecta Haw. = *H. margaritifera*.

H. expansa Haw. = *H. ×rigida* 'Expansa'.

H. fallax Poelln. = *H. coarctata*.

H. fasciata (Willd.) Haw. ZEBRA HAWORTHIA. Similar to *H. attenuata* but with shorter lvs that are smooth on the upper side with bands of white tubercles beneath. SE Cape. 'Ovatolanceolata': lvs irregularly striped beneath. 'Sparsa': lvs to 5cm, stiped and faintly banded beneath. 'Subconfluens': tubercles beneath white, somewhat confluent in bands. 'Vanstaadensis': tubercles irregularly striped below.

H. fergusoniae Poelln. = *H. mucronata*.

H. floribunda Poelln. Differs from *H. angustifolia* in the ± non-clumping habit, smaller marginal teeth and blunter lf tips. SE Cape.

H. fouchei Poelln. see *H. retusa*.

H. fulva G.G. Sm. = *H. coarctata*.

H. geraldii Scott see *H. retusa*.

H. gigas Poelln. = *H. arachnoidea*.

H. glabrata (Salm-Dyck) Bak. Differs from *H. attenuata* in the fatter, fleshier lvs of uniform dull green with a smooth but slightly pustulate surface. Cape.

H. glauca Bak. Stem-forming, 5–20cm, sparingly branched at base. Lvs spirally packed, erect, grey- to blue-green, 2.5–5×0.8–1.5×0.4–0.6cm, narrow-triangular, stiff and sharp-pointed, smooth or sparsely tuberced, faintly dark-lined longitudinally. OFS, Cape. *H. jacobseniana* Poelln.: miniature, clump-forming variant with blue-green lvs.

H. globosiflora G.G. Sm. see *H. nortieri*.

H. gordoniana Poelln. = *H. cymbiformis*.

H. gracilidentata Poelln. see *H. cymbiformis*.

H. gracilis Poelln. = *H. translucens*.

H. graminifolia G.G. Sm. GRASS HAWORTHIA. Lvs extremely long grass-like 30–45×0.3cm, a single tuft on a short st. arising from a cluster of tuberous roots to 1.2cm diam. W Cape.

H. granata Haw. = *H. minima*.

H. granulata Marloth = *H. venosa*.

H. greenii Bak. = *H. coarctata*.

H. guttata Uitew. = *H. reticulata*.

H. haageana Poelln. = *H. reticulata*.

H. habdomadis Poelln. = *H. mucronata*.

H. heidelbergensis G.G. Sm. Differs from *H. retusa* in its shorter, narrower lvs with fewer longitudinal lines. SE Cape.

H. helmiae Poelln. = *H. aristata*.

H. henriquesii Res. = *H. coarctata*.

H. herbacea (Mill.) Stearn = *H. arachnoidea*.

H. herrei Poelln. = *H. glauca*.

H. hilliana Poelln. = *H. cymbiformis*.

H. hurlingii Poelln. see *H. reticulata*.

H. hybrida (Salm-Dyck) Haw. = *H. ×rigida* 'Hybrida'.

H. icosiphylla Bak. = *H. ×rigida* 'Icosiphylla'.

H. inconfluens (Poelln.) M. Bayer = *H. mucronata*.

H. incurvula Poelln. = *H. cymbiformis*.

H. indurata Haw. = *H. viscosa*.

H. inermis Poelln. = *H. bolusii*.

H. integra Poelln. Differs from *H. cymbiformis* and *H. reticulata* in more slender, lanceolate lvs with red veins. W Cape.

H. intermedia Poelln. = *H. reticulata*.

H. isabellae Poelln. = *H. translucens*.

H. jacobseniana Poelln. see *H. glauca*.

H. janseana Uitew. = *H. ×rigida* 'Janseana'.

H. jonesiae Poelln. = *H. reticulata*.

H. kewensis Poelln. Cultigen possibly of hybrid origin. St. 15cm or more, clothed in ovate-acuminate or cuspidate dull green ascending lvs 3–3.5×1.5–3×1.5cm, covered in conspicuous green-white tubercles.

H. kingiana Poelln. Distinct from *H. margaritifera* by the bright yellow-green lvs and flatter, less conspicuous tubercles. SE Cape.

H. koelmaniorum Oberm. & Hardy. Similar to *H. limifolia*, but forms a squat fibrous base and few offsets, and the lf tubercles do not coalesce into lines. Transvaal.

H. krausii Haage & Schmidt = *H. × rigida* 'Krausii'.

H. **'Kuentzii'**. Cultigen of unknown origin, assigned on general looks to *H. attenuata*, of which it is perhaps a hybrid.

H. laetevirens Haw. = *H. turgida*.

H. laevis Haw. = *H. marginata*.

H. lateganiae Poelln. = *H. starkiana*.

H. leightonii G.G. Sm. = *H. cooperi*.

H. lepida G.G. Sm. = *H. cymbiformis*.

H. limifolia Marloth. FAIRY WASHBOARD. Stemless, stoloniferous. Rosette to 12cm diam. Lvs to 20, erect to spreading 3–10×2–4×0.6cm, green, tawny or yellow, broadly triangular, firm and sharp-pointed, rarely smooth but more often with conspicuous transverse wavy ridges. Natal, Transvaal, Moz., Swaz.

H. limpida Haw. = *H. mucronata*.

H. lisbonensis Res. & Poelln. = *H. × rigida* 'Lisbonensis'.

H. lockwoodii Archibald. Lvs flat, soft, pale green, 6×2.5cm, the ends dying back to give white papery tips like a scaly bulb. W Cape.

H. longiana Poelln. Forms large clumps. Lvs v. long, ascending, narrowly triangular, to 30×2.8×0.4cm, stiff, shining green, minutely tubercled, mainly on lower surface. In cult., the lvs tend to die back from the tips. W Cape.

H. longiaristata Poelln. = *H. xiphiophylla*.

H. longibracteata G.G. Sm. = *H. retusa*.

H. luteorosea Uitew. = *H. arachnoidea*.

H. maculata (Poelln.) M. Bayer = *H. asperula*.

H. magnifica Poelln. Differs from *H. asperula* in the smooth or lightly tubercled end area of the lf. W Cape.

H. major (Haw.) Duval = *H. margaritifera*.

H. × mantelii Uitew. (*H. × cuspidata × H. truncata.*) Spiralled rosette of soft, broad, flattened lvs with ± truncate windowed tips reminiscent of *H. truncata*.

H. maraisii Poelln. = *H. asperula*.

H. margaritifera Haw. PEARL HAWORTHIA. Largest of the genus, with ± stemless usually solitary rosette to 10–18cm diam., 15cm or more tall, of around 50 tightly packed, incurved to ascending, fat, rigid, dark or purple-green lvs with sharp red-brown tips, covered in large, rough, pearly white tubercles. W Cape. 'Variegata': lvs variegated.

H. marginata (Lam.) Stearn Habit of *H. margaritifera*, but stemless, lvs tough, horny-edged, uniformly green with few or no tubercles. W Cape.

H. marumiana Uitew. Differs from *H. pulchella* in the small, clear pustules from with the teeth arise. W Cape.

H. maughanii Poelln. Plant body below soil level with only the flat, translucent window tip of each lf exposed. W Cape.

H. maxima (Haw.) Duval = *H. margaritifera*.

H. mclarenii Poelln. Narrow-lvd ally of *H. mucronata*. SE Cape.

H. mcmurtryi Scott = *H. asperula*.

H. minima (Ait.) Haw. Smaller than *H. margaritifera* with less rigid lvs and smaller but more numerous white tubercles. W Cape.

H. minor (Ait.) Duval = *H. margaritifera*.

H. minutissima Poelln. = *H. venosa* ssp. *tessellata*.

H. mirabilis Haw. Closely linked to the *H. asperula* group, but distinguished by the slender fl. buds exceeding 12mm with brown rather than green veins. SW Cape.

H. monticola Fourc. = *H. angustifolia*.

H. morrisiae Poelln. = *H. scabra*.

H. mucronata Haw. Stemless, clustering. Rosette 3–7cm diam. Lvs 40–50, incurved to spreading, 2.5–8×1.2×0.3–0.6cm, tapered oblong to oblanceolate, pale to yellow-green, soft and juicy, ± translucent, longitudinally lined, smooth, margins rough or finely toothed; awn brown, to 8mm. W Cape.

H. multifaria Haw. = *H. mirabilis*.

H. multilineata G.G. Sm. = *H. retusa*.

H. mundula G.G. Sm. = *H. mirabilis*.

H. musculina G.G. Sm. = *H. coarctata*.

H. mutabilis Poelln. = *H. minima*.

H. mutica Haw. Smooth-lvd ally of *H. asperula*. SW Cape.

H. nigra (Haw.) Bak. Close to *H. viscosa*; differs in the larger, flatter tubercles on the v. dark green trifariously arranged lvs. C & S Cape.

H. nitidula Poelln. = *H. mirabilis*.

H. nortieri G.G. Sm. Rosette stemless, usually solitary, 5–8cm diam. Lvs 40–45, erect to incurved, 3.7–4.5×1.2–1.5×0.6cm, ovate to obovate, acute, flushed purple, pellucid-flecked longitudinally, margins and lower surface with fine white 1–1.5mm teeth; awn to 4mm, white. W Cape. *H. globosiflora* G.G. Sm. is

a variant with fls more globose and inflated lf tips.

H. notabilis Poelln. Doubtfully considered an ecotype of *H. magnifica*. W Cape.

H. obtusa Haw. = *H. cymbiformis*.

H. **'Ollasonii'**. Apparently *H. cooperi × H. retusa*.

H. otzenii G.G. Sm. = *H. mutica*.

H. pallida Haw. = *H. arachnoidea*.

H. papillosa (Salm-Dyck) Haw. = *H. margaritifera*.

H. paradoxa Poelln. = *H. asperula*.

H. parksiana Poelln. Dwarf. Rosette rarely above 2.5cm diam. Lvs fairly numerous, 1.5–2×0.6–0.7×0.3cm, packed closely recurving, ovate, pointed, dark dull green, rough with tiny tubercles. Cape Prov.

H. paynei Poelln. = *H. arachnoidea*.

H. pearsonii Wright. Differs from *H. arachnoidea* by the broader, flatter lvs with wider teeth. W Cape.

H. pehlemanniae Scott. Doubtfully distinct sp., having the rosettes of *H. translucens* but the squat fls of *H. globosiflora* (G.G. Sm.).

H. pellucens Haw. = *H. translucens*.

H. × perplexa Poelln. Natural hybrid intermediate between *H. angustifolia* and *H. cymbiformis*. E Cape.

H. picta Poelln. = *H. emelyae*.

H. pilifera Bak. = *H. cooperi*.

H. planifolia Haw. see *H. cymbiformis*.

H. poellnitziana Uitew. Differs from *H. margaritifera* in its elongated grey-green lvs and yellow tips to the tep. SE Cape.

H. polyphylla Bak. = *H. mucronata*.

H. pseudogranulata Poelln. = *H. venosa* ssp. *tessellata*.

H. pseudotessellata Poelln. = *H. venosa* ssp. *tessellata*.

H. pseudotortuosa (Salm-Dyck) Haw. = *H. viscosa*.

H. pubescens M. Bayer = *H. asperula*.

H. pulchella M. Bayer. Stemless, solitary or sparingly branched. Rosette c4cm diam. Lvs about 35, ± curved, 2.7×0.7×0.15cm, lanceolate, acuminate, striate, with fine white teeth to 1mm on the keel and margins, tip 1mm. Cape Prov.

H. pumila (Ait.) Duval = *H. margaritifera*.

H. pygmaea Poelln. = *H. asperula*.

H. radula (Jacq.) Haw. Differs from *H. attenuata* in the plumper lvs with smaller, more numerous white tubercles. W Cape.

H. ramifera Haw. = *H. marginata*.

H. ramosa G.G. Sm. see *H. cymbiformis*.

H. recurva Haw. Probably referable to *H. venosa*. W Cape.

H. reinwardtii (Salm-Dyck) Haw. Differs from *H. coarctata* in the thinner st., broader lvs and tubercles on the underside larger and less prominent. SE Cape.

H. resendeana Poelln. = *H. reinwardtii*.

H. reticulata Haw. Stemless, clustering. Rosette 3–8cm diam. Lvs c40, erect to ascending, 6×2×0.3cm, ovate, acute, white-green, smooth, soft and pulpy, ± pellucid dotted towards the tip and finely lined, awn 2mm. S Cape. *H. hurlingii* Poelln.: a dwarf, highly succulent variant.

H. retusa (L.) Duval. V. variable. Rosette stemless, to 14cm diam. Lvs 15–30, ascending to recurved, to 8×1.5–3×0.7–2cm, acute, with a flat to slightly convex, shining, smooth or minutely tuberculate end area 1.5–3×1.5–2.5cm, longitudinally 4–12-lined, with or without an awn. S Cape. *H. fouchei* Poelln.: freely clustering variant with narrower, more erect lvs. *H. geraldii*: is a clump-forming variant with paler foliage.

H. revendettii Uitew. see *H. coarctata*.

H. × rigida (Lam.) Haw. Complex of gdn hybrids apparently derived from *H. glabrata* and *H. tortuosa*. 'Cassytha': possibly a hybrid between 'Lisbonensis' and *H. tortuosa*. 'Expansa': smaller than *H. × rigida*; lvs shorter, 5×1.5cm, rough, glossy. 'Hybrida': st. short; lvs flat at base, lower surface with a single keel, long tapered. 'Icosiphylla': short-stemmed; rosettes 7–8cm diam. with c20 spiralled, lanceolate-triangular lvs, 3–4×2×0.3cm, upper surface concave, lower surface convex and carinate, green to red, tuberculate, rough. 'Janseana': stemless, clump-forming; rosettes 4.5–5cm diam.; lvs numerous, 2.5×0.8–1cm, ovate-lanceolate, tapering, pale grey-green, with many longitudinal lines, upper surface grooved, lower surface convex-carinate, margins and keel irregularly and minutely dentate, teeth 0.6mm; awn 2mm. 'Krausii' ('Krausiana'): possibly a hybrid between *H. glabrata* and *H. tortuosa*. 'Lisbonensis': st. to 12cm, basally branching; lvs in spiral rows, 3–4.5×1–2×0.2–0.6cm, ovate-lanceolate, tapering, both surfaces with 2 distinct keels and minutely rough tuberculate, dark green with a lighter tip. 'Tisleyi': rosettes 7–8cm diam.; lvs 30–40, 2.5–3×1.5×0.6cm, lanceolate-triangular, upper surface flat, lower surface convex and obliquely carinate, dark green, often red, rough with concolorous tubercles.

H. rossouwii Poelln. = *H. mirabilis*.

H. rubrobrunnea Poelln. Differs from *H. coarctata* in lvs narrower.

H. rugosa (Salm-Dyck) Bak. = *H. radula*.

H. rycroftiana M. Bayer. Variant of *H. mucronata*.

H. ryneveldii Poelln. = *H. nigra*.

H. sampaiana Res. see *H. coarctata*.

H. scabra Haw. Habit of *H. starkiana*, but lvs covered with large, smooth tubercles, those on the underside confluent into transverse rows. W Cape.

H. schmidtiana Poelln. = *H. nigra*.

H. schuldtiana Poelln. = *H. asperula*.

H. semiglabrata Haw. = *H. margaritifera*.

H. semimargaritifera (Salm-Dyck) Haw. = *H. margaritifera*.

H. semiviva (Poelln.) M. Bayer. Differs from *H. bolusii* only in the papery lf tips. reminiscent of *H. lockwoodii*. W Cape.

H. setata Haw. = *H. arachnoidea*.

H. smitii Poelln. Intermediate between *H. scabra* and *H. starkiana* and possibly a natural hybrid. SW Cape.

H. sordida Haw. Similar to *H. starkiana*, but lvs with conspicuous scattered pearly tubercles. SE Cape Prov.

H. springbokvlakensis Scott. Slow-growing ally of *H. emelyae* with clear, inflated lf tips and slightly viscid surfaces. SE Cape.

H. starkiana Poelln. Stemless or short-stemmed, clustering from the base. Rosette c15cm diam. Lvs c30, incurved to ascending, triangular, averaging 7×2×1cm, v. firm with a sharp brown tip, smooth, uniform dark or yellow-green. SW Cape.

H. stayneri Poelln. = *H. cooperi*.

H. subattenuata (Salm-Dyck) Bak. = *H. margaritifera*.

H. sublimpidula Poelln. = *H. asperula*.

H. submaculata Poelln. = *H. arachnoidea*.

H. subregularis Bak. = *H. reticulata*.

H. subrigida Bak. = *H. tortuosa*.

H. subulata (Salm-Dyck) Bak. = *H. radula*.

H. ×*tauteae* Archibald. Natural hybrid intermediate between *H. scabra* and *H. viscosa*.

H. tenera Poelln. = *H. translucens*.

H. tessellata Haw. = *H. venosa* ssp. *tessellata*.

H. tisleyi Bak. = *H.* ×*rigida* 'Tisleyi'.

H. torquata Haw. = *H. viscosa*.

H. tortella Haw. = *H. tortuosa*.

H. tortuosa Haw. Varied complex of cultigens combining features of *H. nigra* and *H. viscosa*.

H. translucens Haw. Differs from *H. arachnoidea* by the elongated pellucid markings near the lf tips, and the shorter marginal teeth. E Cape.

H. triebneriana Poelln. = *H. mirabilis*.

H. truncata Schönl. Similar to *H. maughanii* with flatter, broader lvs in 2 series like the pages of an open book. W Cape.

H. tuberculata Poelln. = *H. scabra*.

H. turgida Haw. Widespread, extremely variable sp. with plump, soft, pale green lvs combining features of *H. reticulata* and *H. retusa*. S Cape.

H. ubomboensis Verdoorn = *H. limifolia*.

H. uitewaaliana Poelln. = *H. marginata*.

H. umbraticola Poelln. see *H. cymbiformis*.

H. unicolor Poelln. = *H. aristata*.

H. variegata L. Bol. Distinct from *H. angustifolia* by the softer, greener, narrower lvs. W Cape.

H. venosa (Lam.) Haw. V. variable complex; ± stemless, stoloniferous. Rosette to 10cm diam. Lvs 10–20, ascending to spreading, 5–8×1.5–3×0.3–0.6cm, rigid, triangular, tawny to grey-green with the upper surface checkered with pale lines, rough from fine tubercles. E Cape. ssp. *tessellata* (Haw.) M. Bayer Lvs shorter, broader, glossy with sharp tubercles. S Afr., Nam.

H. venteri Poelln. = *H. aristata*.

H. virescens Haw. = *H. marginata*.

H. viscosa (L.) Haw. Stem-forming to 20cm, with lvs tightly packed in 3 usually spiralled series, proliferous from base. Lvs to 4.3×1.9×0.7cm, sheathing, triangular, channelled, keeled below, dark to purple-green, scabrous from minute tubercles, horny with a sharp tip. SW Cape. *H. asperiuscula* is a thick-lvd variant.

H. vittata Bak. = *H. cooperi*.

H. whitesloaneana Poelln. = *H. asperula*.

H. willowmorensis Poelln. = *H. mirabilis*.

H. wittebergensis W. Barker. Rosette solitary or slowly offsetting, stemless, c3cm diam. Lvs 15 or more, ascending, 7×0.7×0.25cm, linear-lanceolate, grey to purple-green, leathery, finely tuberculate with marginal teeth, dying back at tips in drought. W Cape.

H. woolleyi Poelln. Reminiscent of *H. venosa*, but lvs v. dark green, thinner and more erect, with finely toothed margins. SE Cape Prov.

H. xiphiophylla Bak. Differs from *H. arachnoidea* in the longer, narrower, opaque lvs with fewer and larger teeth. SE Cape.

H. zantneriana Poelln. Differs from *H. variegata* in the smooth lf margins and larger pale spots. E Cape.

→*Aprica*.

Hawthorn *Crataegus* (*C. monogyna*).

Hawthorn Leaved Gooseberry *Ribes oxyacanthoides*.

Hawthorn Maple *Acer crataegifolium*.

Haylockia Herb.

H. pusilla Herb. = *Zephyranthes pusilla*.

Hay Rattle *Rhinanthus minor*.

Hay-scented Fern *Dennstaedtia punctilobula*.

Hazardia E. Greene. HOARY GOLDENBUSH. Compositae. 5 usually resinous, glab. to tomentose shrubs and subshrubs. St. erect, much branched. Cap. radiate or discoid, sessile or shortly pedunculate; ray flts yellow, sometimes becoming red-purple, or 0; disc flts yellow, sometimes becoming red-purple. W US, Mex.

H. cana (A. Gray) E. Greene. Shrub, to 2m. Lvs to c12×4cm, oblanceolate, obtuse, serrulate to entire, membranous, glab. above, densely tomentose beneath, petiole to 1cm. Cap. radiate; flts yellow, becoming red-purple. Summer–autumn. Calif., San Clemente Is., Guadelupe Is.

→*Haplopappus*.

Hazel *Corylus*.

Hazel Alder *Alnus serrulata*.

Hazelnut *Corylus avellana*.

Heal-all *Prunella*.

Heartleaf Manzanita *Arctostaphylos andersonii*.

Heart-leaf Philodendron *Philodendron cordatum*; *P. scandens*.

Heart-leaf Poison *Gastrolobium bilobum*.

Heart-leaved Everlasting *Helichrysum cordatum*.

Heart-leaved Flame Pea *Chorizema cordata*.

Heart-leaved Poison *Gastrolobium bilobum*.

Heart-leaved Triptilion *Triptilion cordifolium*.

Heartnut *Juglans ailanthifolia*.

Heart of Flame *Bromelia balansae*.

Heart Pea *Cardiospermum halicacabum*.

Heart's-ease *Viola tricolor*; *V.* ×*wittrockiana*.

Heartseed *Cardiospermum grandiflorum*.

Hearts Entangled *Ceropegia linearis* ssp. *woodii*.

Hearts on a String *Ceropegia linearis* ssp. *woodii*.

Heath *Erica*.

Heather *Calluna*; *Erica*.

Heath-leaved Banksia *Banksia ericifolia*.

Heath Violet *Viola canina*.

Heavenly Bamboo *Nandina*.

Heavenly Fairy Fruit *Ficus erecta* var. *beecheyana*.

Hebe Comm. ex Juss. Scrophulariaceae. 75 everg. shrubs, dwarf and procumbent to erect and bushy, to tree-like; branchlets with distinct lf scars. Lvs 2-ranked or decussate, in some spp. spreading, petiolate or sessile, rounded to lanceolate, often somewhat fleshy, in others scale-like and closely adpressed (the Whipcord Hebes). Fls in axill. or subterminal rac. or heads; cor. short-tubular, limb expanded, 4-lobed; sta. 2, exserted. NZ, Aus., temp. S Amer. Z8 unless specified.

H. albicans (Petrie) Ckn. Compact spreading or rounded shrub to 60cm. Br. thick, intricate. Lvs to 2×1.5cm, spreading to imbricate, ovate to oblong, glaucous, fleshy. Rac. to 6cm: fls white; anth. purple. Summer. NZ. 'Cranleigh Gem': low domed shrub to 60cm; lvs grey, lf buds large; fls white in short broad rac.; anth. dark, conspicuous. 'Pewter Dome': v. compact; lvs small, dull grey-silver. 'Red Edge': lvs edged red; fls mauve. 'Sussex Carpet': hardy; to 30cm spreading; lvs glaucous; infl. short. 'Trixie': lvs green; fls white. Z8.

H. '**Alicia Amherst**'. Robust with deep green, lustrous lvs and showy rac. of strong purple fls. Similar to *H.* 'Royal Purple' and *H.* 'Veitchii', cf *H. speciosa*.

H. allionii hort. = *Veronica allionii*.

H. amplexicaulis (J.B. Armstr.) Ckn. & Allan. Decumbent shrub to 50cm. Br. stout, semi-rigid, encircled by lf scars. Lvs to 1.5×1.2cm, overlapping, concave, broad-oblong, fleshy, glaucous, apex obtuse, base cordate. Fls white to pink, forming a dense head. NZ. Z9.

H. '**Amy**'. Lvs purple-tinted when young. Fls dark mauve in erect rac., borne over a long period, cf. *H. speciosa*.

H. ×*andersonii* (Lindl. & Paxt.) Ckn. (*H. salicifolia* ×*H. speciosa*.) Spreading shrub to 1.6m. Lvs to 10×3cm, ovate to lanceolate, obtuse, deep green. Fls crowded on spikes to 10cm, violet. 'Variegata': vigorous, soon attaining 2m; lvs dark green, mottled or graded with grey-green, irregularly edged white to ivory; fls lilac. Z9.

H. angustifolia (A. Rich.) Ckn. & Allan = *H. parvifolia* var. *angustifolia*.

H. anomala J.B. Armstr. see *H. odora*.

H. armstrongii (J.B. Armstr.) Ckn. & Allan. Erect shrub to 1m. Br. whipcord, spreading then ascending, terete, yellow-green, particularly in winter. Lvs to 1.8mm, closely adpressed apex truncate to rounded, margins yellowing. Fls white, to 6 in each erect term. infl. NZ. Commonly confused with *H. ochracea* in cult., from which it differs in its yellow-green (not ochre) br. and less arching habit.

H. armstrongii hort. non (J.B. Armstr.) Ckn. & Allan = *H. ochracea*.

H. astonii (Petrie) Ckn. & Allan = *H. subsimilis* var. *astonii*.

H. **'Autumn Glory'**. To 80cm. Internodes flushed dark red, glab. Lvs to 3cm, broadly obovate, dark green edged red when young. Fls violet-blue in long, sometimes branching rac. Z8.

H. barkeri (Ckn.) Ckn. Similar to *H. dieffenbachii*, from which it differs in its more erect habit and juvenile purple-stained internodes. Erect shrub to 1.2m. Lvs to 5×1.2cm, spreading, lanceolate to oblong-lanceolate, fleshy, pale green, dull beneath, apex subacute. Infl. erect, simple; fls mauve.

H. **'Bowles Hybrid'**. Low-growing, to 50cm. Nodes flushed red, internodes long, green, puberulent. Lvs to 3cm, narrowlanceolate to oblong, purple-green, somewhat glossy above. Fls lilac in lax, branching rac. Various clones are grown under this and similar names.

H. brachysiphon Summerh. Rounded spreading shrub to 1.3m. Branchlets finely pubesc., green. Lvs to 2.5×0.5cm, erect to spreading, ovate to lanceolate, light green, apex reflexed, margin minutely pubesc.; petioles winged, occas. twisted. Fls white, in lat., simple or branched rac. to 5cm. Summer. NZ. 'White Gem': low-growing with dark br.; lf sinus 0; possibly a selection of *H. brachysiphon* or *H. brachysiphon* ×*H. pinguifolia*. Z7.

H. buchananii (Hook. f.) Ckn. & Allan. Shrub to 20cm, forming clumps to 90cm across. Br. tortuous, black. Lvs 0.7×0.5cm, spreading, ovate and concave, thick, glaucescent, dull dark green, midrib distinct. Fls white, erect, crowded in simple infl. to 2cm. Summer. NZ. 'Minor': smaller and more compact, forming a hummock of minute green lvs. Z7.

H. buxifolia (Benth.) Ckn. & Allan. Erect shrub to 1m. Lvs to 1×0.3cm, oblong-obovate, concave, dark green above, punctate beneath, apex acute, margins yellow. Fls white in crowded infl. to 2.5cm, often corymbose. Summer. NZ. *H. buxifolia* of gardens is likely to be *H. odora*. Z7.

H. buxifolia hort. non (Benth.) Ckn. & Allan = *H. odora*.

H. buxifolia var. *pauciramosa* Ckn. & Allan = *H. pauciramosa*.

H. **'Caledonia'**. Erect, to 50cm. Internodes flushed red. Lvs to 1.25cm, oblong-lanceolate, somewhat glaucous, margins and midrib tinted red. Fls violet.

H. canterburiensis (J.B. Armstr.) L.B. Moore. Low shrub to 1m. Branchlets pubesc. Lvs to 1.7×0.5cm, loosely overlapping, distichous, elliptic to obovate, subcoriaceous, glab. above, petiole and margin pubesc., apex acute. Infl. to 2.5cm, crowded, lat., simple; fls white. Summer. NZ. Z9. 'Prostrata': procumbent, to 30cm; internodes flushed red; lvs bright green, twisted back and overlapping; fls white, on sporadically produced, short rac. Possibly referable to *H. vernicosa*.

H. 'Carl Teschner' = *H.* 'Youngii'.

H. **'Carnea'**. Dense, glab., to 1m. Lvs to 6.25cm, narrow-oblong to lanceolate, green faintly tinted red at margins and midrib. Rac. 6–8cm; fls pink fading to white, giving a 2-tone appearance to infl.

H. **'Carnea Variegata'**. Close to *H.* 'Carnea' but with lvs irregularly bordered cream and edged red.

H. carnosula (Hook. f.) Ckn. & Allan. Shrub to 40cm, forming leafy tufts of erect shoots. Lvs to 2×1.6cm, closely overlapping, decussate, obovate, concave, thick, somewhat glaucous. Fls white, sessile, in term. rounded infl. to 1.5cm diam.; anth. purple. Summer. NZ. Commonly mistaken for *H. pinguifolia*, from which it can be distinguished by its less glaucous lvs. Z6.

H. catarractae (Forst. f.) Allan = *Parahebe catarractae*.

H. chathamica (Buch.) Ckn. & Allan. Prostrate shrub to 25cm, by 1m across. Br. straggling. Lvs to 3.6×1.2cm, usually smaller, elliptic to obovate-oblong, fleshy, pale green, apex obtuse to subacute. Infl. lat., simple, compact; fls pale violet fading to white. Chatham Is.

H. cheesemanii (Buch.) Ckn. & Allan. Densely branched greygreen whipcord, 6–30×30–45cm. Branchlets tetragonal, not grooved. Lvs to 2×1.5mm, erect, closely adpressed, broadovate, concave, apex slightly keeled, ciliate. Infl. to 5cm, crowded; fls white. Summer. NZ.

H. ciliolata (Hook. f.) Ckn. & Allan. Decumbent semi-whipcord to 30cm. Lvs 0.4×0.1cm, narrow-oblong, green, margins raised, ciliate. Infl. to 6mm, with to 3 pairs of white fls. NZ.

H. colensoi (Hook. f.) Ckn. Low shrub to 50cm. Lvs to 2.5×1cm, usually smaller, erecto-patent, obovate, initially strongly glaucous, later dark green, acuminate, midrib prominent. Rac. crowded, to 2.5cm, usually lateral (appearing term.); fls white. Summer. NZ. 'Glauca': compact; lvs highly glaucous. Z6.

H. cookiana hort. = *H. stricta* var. *macroura*.

H. **'C.P. Raffill'**. Erect to 1m. Internodes long, yellow-green, nodes flushed dark purple. Lvs to 7cm, similar to *H.* 'Spender's Seedling' but somewhat broader with margins and midrib pubesc. Fls white in rac. to 10cm.

H. cupressoides (Hook. f.) Ckn. & Allan. Cypress-like whipcord with dense, rounded or open habit, to 1.5×2m. Branchlets glaucous, puberulent, sometimes glutinous and aromatic. Juvenile lvs linear, sometimes lobed, mature lvs to 0.15cm, scale-like, closely adpressed but not hiding st., narrow-ovate to triangular, subacute, ciliate. Fls to 8 per infl., v. pale blue; anth. red-brown. Summer. NZ. 'Boughton Dome': to 30×50cm, forming a broad and densely branched dome of fine grey-green branchlets clothed with both juvenile (spreading, lobed) and adult (small, scale-like, adpressed) lvs. Z6.

H. cupressoides var. *variabilis* N.E. Br. = *H. propinqua* 'Major'.

H. darwiniana hort. = *H. glaucophylla*.

H. decumbens (J.B. Armstr.) Ckn. & Allan. Decumbent densely branching shrub to 50cm. Branchlets tinged purple. Lvs 0.8–2cm, dense, spreading, elliptic, usually concave, fleshy or coriaceous, dark green, subacute to obtuse, margins tinted red and minutely pubesc. Rac. to 2.5cm, simple, crowded, sometimes, paired; fls white, anth purple. Summer. NZ. Often labelled *H.* 'Robin' in cult. Z5.

H. dieffenbachii (Benth.) Ckn. & Allan. Shrub to 1.2m, strongly spreading. Branchlets pale green. Lvs to 9×3cm, spreading, elliptic to oblong, thick, pale green, grey-green beneath, glab. or sparsely pubesc., apex obtuse, base auriculate, margin cartilaginous. Infl. crowded, lat., simple; fls purple-tinged to white. NZ. Z9.

H. diosmifolia (A. Cunn.) Ckn. & Allan. Erect shrub to 1.5m. Br. glab. to floccose. Lvs to 3×0.6cm, dense, linear to lanceolate, acute, glab., dark green above, shallowly incised. Rac. to 2.5cm, cymose; fls light blue to white. Summer. NZ. Z7.

H. 'Dorothy Peach' = *H.* 'Watson's Pink'.

H. 'E.B. Anderson' = *H.* 'Caledonia'.

H. **'E.A. Bowles'**. Close to *H.* 'Mrs Winder', but somewhat taller and of looser habit, lacking internode pubescence, lvs not colouring so strongly in cold weather. Fls blue, late into the season.

H. **'Edinensis'**. Spreading, low-growing plant to 30cm. Internodes green, almost concealed by small vivid green lvs adpressed at base, reflexed and spreading at tips. Spikes to 3cm, white faintly tinted mauve. A hybrid of obscure parentage, between a whipcord and a small-lvd sp., possibly *Parahebe lyalli*.

H. elliptica (Forst. f.) Pennell. Shrub to small tree to 5m, usually about 1.5m. Br. slender, terete. Lvs 2.4cm, spreading, often oriented in one direction, elliptic to oblong, coriaceous, keeled, lustrous dark green, apex mucronate to apiculate, margin ciliate. Rac. grouped as corymbs at br. tips; fls mostly white to violet or pink. NZ, Terra del Fuego, Falkland Is. Salt-tolerant. Z7.

H. epacridea (Hook. f.) Ckn. & Allan. Low-growing shrub to 40cm. Lvs to 7×6mm, spreading, ovate-oblong, usually recurved, strongly keeled, rigid, coriaceous, glab. or minutely pubesc., deep matt green, subacute to cuneate, base adpressed. Infl. to 3×2cm, compact, compound; fls white. Summer. NZ. Z7.

H. 'Eversley Seedling' = *H.* 'Bowles Hybrid'.

H. **'Fairfieldii'**. (*H. hulkeana* ×*H. lavaudiana*?) Compact, upright to 60cm. Close to *H. hulkeana* but with br. rigidly erect, duller lvs, shorter, stout infl. and larger lilac fls. Late spring. Z7.

H. **'Fairlane'**. (*H. pinguifolia* ×*H.* 'Youngii'.) Dwarf, spreading bush, seldom exceeding 30cm; internodes short, dark. Lvs slightly glaucous, edged red at first. Fls mauve in short rac. Early summer.

H. ×*franciscana* (Eastw.) Souster. (*H. elliptica* ×*H. speciosa*.) Shrub to 1.3m, habit rounded, dense. St. glaucous. Lvs to 6×2.5cm, larger, duller than *H. elliptica*, distichous, obovate to elliptic, fleshy, dark green, apiculate. Infl. to 7.5cm, cylindrical; fls purple tinged pink. Summer-autumn. Gdn origin. 'Blue Gem': fls red-violet, fil. violet. 'Variegata': lvs mottled and margined yellow, variegation tending to disappear in summer. Z7.

H. **'Gauntlettii'**. Lvs mid-green. Rac. large, pink. cf. *H. speciosa*.

H. gibbsii (T. Kirk) Ckn. & Allan. Shrub to 45cm, littlebranched. Lvs to 1.8cm, loosely overlapping, spreading or deflexed, elliptic to ovate, thick, glaucous, subacute, margins red, ciliate. Infl. to 1.5cm, simple, sometimes clustered; fls white. Summer. NZ.

H. glaucocaerulea (J.B. Armstr.) Ckn. = *H. pimeleoides* var. *glaucocaerulea*.

H. glaucophylla (Ckn.) Ckn. Shrub to 1m. St. smooth, grey. Lvs to 16×6mm, patent, decussate, lanceolate, short-stalked glaucous, acute, margin minutely pubesc. Rac. to 5cm, usually 2–4 near br. tips; fls white. Summer. NZ. 'Variegata': lvs greygreen, edged cream. Z7.

H. gracillima (T. Kirk) Ckn. & Allan. Shrub to 2m, ± erect, laxly branched. Branchlets minutely pubesc., yellow-green when young. Lvs to 6×4cm, spreading, narrow-lanceolate to oblong, with minute pubescence on midrib, margin and petiole. Rac. to 15cm, slender, lat.; fls white. Summer. NZ. Z9.

H. 'Great Orme'. Similar to *H.* 'Carnea' but more robust, internodes dark, lvs to 9cm, oblong-lanceolate, somewhat falcate. Lf bud sinus lacking.

H. haastii (Hook. f.) Ckn. & Allan. Sprawling shrub to 30cm. St. tortuous; branchlets light green. Lvs to 13×9mm, concealing st., loosely overlapping, ovate to obovate-spathulate, concave, coriaceous, subacute to obtuse. Infl. to 4cm, compact, oblong, comprising numerous crowded spikes; fls white. Summer. NZ.

H. × hagleyensis = *H.* 'Hagley Park'.

H. 'Hagley Park'. (*H. raoulii* × *H. hulkeana?*) To 40×60cm. Br. dark-pubesc. Lvs similar to but larger than in *H. raoulii*. Fls in term. pan. to 30cm, similar to *H. hulkeana* but a stronger lilac-pink.

H. hectoris (Hook. f.) Ckn. & Allan. Highly variable whipcord to 75cm. Br. crowded, or spreading to decumbent with age, somewhat rigid, yellow-green. Lvs to 0.4cm, scale-like, overlapping, closely adpressed, concealing st., ovate-triangular or variable, convex, glossy, yellow-green, obtuse, margins floccose. Infl. a congested term. head; fls white to pink. Summer. NZ. Z7.

H. hookeriana (Walp.) Allan = *Parahebe hookeriana*.

H. hulkeana (F. Muell.) Ckn. & Allan. NEW ZEALAND LILAC. Sprawling shrub to 1m, usually slender, habit loose. Internodes tinted purple-red. Lvs to 5×3cm, spreading, elliptic to suborbicular, subcoriaceous, glab. or faintly pubesc. on midrib, deep lustrous green above, pale beneath, obtuse to subacute, margin often flushed red, serrate. Pan. to 30cm, with br. to 15cm; fls lavender to white. NZ. 'Averil': lvs pale green, lacking red edge; infl. more compact. Z9.

H. 'James Platt'. Erect to 60cm. Internodes dark. Lvs to 1.25cm, oval-elliptic, somewhat concave, edged red. Fls lilac-blue in branching or simple rac.

H. 'Lady Ardilaun' = *H.* 'Amy'.

H. 'Lady Hagley' = *H.* 'Hagley Park'.

H. laevis (Benth.) Ckn. & Allan = *H. venustula*.

H. 'La Séduisante'. Young lvs lustrous, tinted purple. Fls red-purple in long showy rac., in late summer. cf *H. speciosa*.

H. lavaudiana (Raoul) Ckn. & Allan. Similar to *H. hulkeana* but smaller, fls white or mauve-tinged on more dense and compact infl. Br. decumbent. Lvs to 0.3×0.2cm, spreading, obovate to suborbicular, fleshy, glaucous, obtuse to subacute, margin minutely pubesc., crenate, red-tinged, underside often tinged mauve. Spikes to 5cm, term., simple; fls mauve-pink fading to white. Summer. NZ.

H. leiophylla Ckn. & Allan. Shrub to 1.2m. Lvs similar to those of *H. parviflora*, narrow. Rac. to 10cm. Summer. NZ. Z5.

H. linifolia (Hook. f.) Allan = *Parahebe linifolia*.

H. 'Loganioides'. Similar to *H.* 'Edinensis' but of neater habit and with smaller lvs which do not conceal the dark internodes. Fls white veined pink in short lat. rac. Z6.

H. loganioides (J.B.Armstr.) Wall = *H.* 'Loganioides'.

H. lyallii (Hook. f.) Allan = *Parahebe lyallii*.

H. lycopodioides (Hook. f.) Ckn. & Allan. Rigid and narrowly erect whipcord to 60cm. Resembles *H. hectoris* but br. tetragonal. Juvenile lvs linear-subulate; mature lvs to 3×2.5mm, scale-like, adpressed, cuneate, deltoid to semicircular, strongly keeled, ribbed or striped yellow, obtuse or subacute with cusp, margins yellow. Short term. spikes or heads to 12mm diam; fls white; anth. lilac-blue. Summer. NZ. Z7.

H. lycopodioides 'Aurea'. = *H. armstrongii*.

H. 'MacEwanii'. Erect, compact, to 60cm; br. red-brown pubesc. Lvs small, glaucous, lf bud sinus conspicuous. Fls pale blue, in branching infl.

H. macrantha (Hook. f.) Ckn. & Allan. Sprawling shrub to 60cm. Br. usually erect, sparse, leggy. Lvs 1–2.5cm×0.5–1.2cm, spreading, densely arranged, elliptic to obovate, coriaceous, pale to yellow-green, obtuse to subacute, dentate toward apex. Rac. profuse, to 2.5cm diam., short, dense; fls white. Spring. NZ. Z6.

H. macroura (Benth.) Ckn. & Allan = *H. stricta* var. *macroura*.

H. magellanica Gmel. = *H. elliptica*.

H. 'Margery Fish'. Compact, to 60cm. Internodes green. Lvs to 2.5cm, elliptic, acute, undulate, edged red at first. Fls lilac in rac. to 8cm.

H. 'Marjorie'. To 80cm×1m. Internodes tinted mauve, faintly pubesc. Lvs to 3.25cm, oblong-lanceolate, glossy green, margins and midrib puberulent. Fls pale blue in rac. to 10cm, often shorter.

H. matthewsii (Cheesem.) Ckn. Shrub, erect to 1.2m. Internodes often tinged purple with conspicuous pubescence. Lvs to 3.5×1.5cm, closely adpressed, oblong or elliptic, coriaceous, dull green, midrib distinct, obtuse, base rounded. Rac. to 10cm,

tapering; fls white. Summer. NZ.

H. 'Midsummer Beauty'. Robust, soon attaining 2m or more. Lvs deep green tinted purple-red below when young. Fls pale blue to lilac or magenta, often fading to pale rose, in long slender rac.

H. 'Mrs Winder'. Rounded, dense, to 1m. Internodes long, dark. Lvs to 3.25cm, narrow-obovate to lanceolate, green flushed red at base, faintly ciliate, margins and midrib colouring red-purple in cold weather. Fls blue.

H. obtusata (Cheesem.) Ckn. & Allan. Semi-prostrate, shrub to 60cm. Branchlets tinged red. Lvs to 5×2.5cm, obovate-oblong, subacute, subcoriaceous, finely pubesc. on midrib and margin beneath, dull green. Rac. to 6cm, numerous near tips of br.; fls mauve. Summer and autumn. NZ. Z9.

H. ochracea Ashwin. Whipcord to 60cm. Br. spreading, rigid, dark, bowed outwards; branchlets olive green to ochre, arising from upper side of br. Lvs to 1.5mm, ochre to olive, tightly adpressed, deltoid, keeled, subacute to obtuse. Fls small, white, in short spikes. Summer–autumn. NZ. Often confused with *H. armstrongii*, this sp. is the more commonly cultivated and can be distinguished by its ochre br. and strongly outspread to arching habit. 'Greensleeves': erect to 60cm; lvs rigid, green, erect to somewhat spreading, concealing internodes. 'James Stirling': v. compact. Z6.

H. odora (Hook. f.) Ckn. Shrub to 1.5m, habit variable. Internodes short, green. Lvs to 2.5×0.9cm, overlapping, distichous, elliptic to obovate, concave above, entire, glossy, subacute, margin cartilaginous, minutely crenulate or bevelled, spike solitary term. with 1–2 lat. br.; fls white. Summer. NZ. S Is. Often confused with *H. buxifolia*. *H. anomala* J.B. Armstr. is closely related, with branchlets yellow-green, tips tinged purple, lvs to 2×0.5cm, linear-oblong to oblong-lanceolate, coriaceous, glossy, dark green. Fls white in term. crowded pan.; anth. purple. Z6.

H. parviflora (Vahl) Ckn. & Allan. KOKOMURA TARANGA. Shrub to 6m. Lvs to 2.5cm, lanceolate, entire, rigid, acute, mucronate. Infl. to 3.5cm, lat., simple; fls white. NZ. var. *angustifolia* (Hook. f.) L.B. Moore. Shrub to 1.5m. St. brown, tinged purple. Lvs to 6×0.9cm, narrow-linear, acute. Infl. paired, to 12×2cm; fls white tinted lilac. Summer-autumn. var. *arborea* (Buch.) L.B. Moore. Laxly branching shrub or small tree attaining 7m in habitat. Lvs 2.5–6×0.4–0.6cm, linear-lanceolate, largely glab. Rac. to 7cm, slender; fls white, faintly suffused lilac. Z7.

H. parviflora hort. = *H.* 'Bowles Hybrid'.

H. pauciramosa (Ckn. & Allan) L.B. Moore. Little-branched shrub to 50cm. St. rigidly erect, leafy at tips. Lvs to 0.8×0.6cm, overlapping, later coriaceous, concave above, lustrous green, obtuse, base truncate, margin ciliate. Spikes to 2cm, borne near br. tips; fls white. Summer. NZ. Resembles *H. odora*, but smaller.

H. pimeleoides (Hook. f.) Ckn. & Allan. Densely branched low-growing shrub to 45cm; branchlets dark. Lvs 6–15mm, elliptic to broadly obovate, sometimes concave, spreading to recurved, glaucous, blue-grey, subacute, margins occas. red. Spikes lat., simple or branched; fls white flushed pale lilac to pale violet. Summer. NZ. 'Minor': minute, creeping; fls tinted lilac blue. 'Quicksilver': lvs esp. glaucous, small, recurved. var. *glaucocaerulea* (J.B. Armstr.) Ckn. & Allan. Erect to 35cm becoming decumbent. Br. dark. Lvs larger, broadly elliptic, concave, strongly glaucous, edged red (usually in summer). Fls violet-blue, in short spikes. 'County Park': to 20×50cm, decumbent; lvs grey-green edged red, red-purple in cold weather; fls violet, in short spikes. 'Wingletye': close to 'County Park' but lower-growing with strongly glaucous lvs that do not flush red in cold weather; fls lilac blue. var. *rupestris* Ckn. & Allan. Resembles var. *glaucocaerulea* but more spreading; branchlets dark brown; lf margins tinged yellow. Z7.

H. pinguifolia (Hook. f.) Ckn. & Allan. Procumbent or ascending to 1m, branchlets sea-green, softly pubesc. Lvs to 1.5×0.9cm, overlapping to spreading, obovate-elliptic, concave, thick, glaucous, blue-green, often edged red, obtuse to subacute. Spikes to 2.5cm, simple, compact, term.; fls white; anth. blue. Summer. NZ. Often confused with *H. carnosula*, which has broader lvs and glab. ovary and style. 'Godefroyana': lvs larger, somewhat greener. 'Pagei': to 15×60cm; lvs grey, oblong-obovate, scarcely concave; fls white in dense short spikes. 'Pageboy': close to 'Pagei', but lvs green. 'Sutherlandii': lvs a intense glaucous grey. Z6.

H. propinqua (Cheesem.) Ckn. & Allan. Whipcord to 1m, rarely more than 30cm in cult. Br. spreading, sometimes twisting, terete, nodes distinct. Lvs to 1.5mm, triangular, closely adpressed, bright green, obtuse. Spikes to 1cm, subterminal; fls white. Summer. NZ. 'Aurea': branchlets yellow-green, forming a dense cushion. 'Major': to 60cm; br. erect; branchlets short, sage green; possibly a hybrid between *H. cupressoides* and

H. propinqua. Z6.

H. 'Purple Queen' = *H.* 'Amy'.

H. **'Purple Picture'.** Erect to 1m. Internodes dark. Lvs flushed purple, paler beneath margins ciliate. Fls mauve in rac. to 8cm.

H. rakaiensis (J.B. Armstr.) Ckn. Shrub to 90cm. Branchlets slender, lf scars rough. Lvs to 2×0.6cm, spreading, obovate-oblong, entire, subcoriaceous, glossy, bright green, margin opaque, minutely ciliate. Rac. to 4cm, simple, lax, covering plant; fls white. Spring. NZ. Often labelled *H. subalpina* or *H. buxifolia* in gardens. Z6.

H. raoulii (Hook. f.) Ckn. & Allan. Sprawling shrub to 40cm. Branchlets dark. Lvs to 2.5×0.8cm, erecto-patent, obovate-spathulate, coriaceous, glab., mid-green, margins serrate, often red-tinged. Spikes to 6cm, term., often branched; fls white suffused lavender or lilac-pink. Late spring. NZ. var. *macgaskillii* Allan. Compact, erect to 20cm. Lvs to 1cm, spathulate, dark green, faintly edged red. Spikes short, term., seldom branching; fls white (pink in bud).

H. recurva Simps. & J. Thoms. Spreading shrub to 1m, much-branched. Lvs to 5×1cm, spreading, deflexed, narrow-lanceolate, glab., glaucous grey-green, midrib distinct, margin cartilaginous. Spikes to 6cm, simple; fls white (often pink in bud). Summer. NZ. Selections of *H. recurva* are available with variously larger, plain green lvs, particularly strong grey tones, and in some cases, fls mauve, fading to white. 'Aoira': to 60cm, compact, spreading; lvs to 2.75×0.4cm, lanceolate-falcate, deflexed, grey-green; rac. short; fls white.

H. salicifolia (Forst. f.) Pennell. Highly variable shrubs to 5m, usually shorter. Branchlets green. Lvs to 15×3cm, suberect to spreading, lanceolate-oblong, acuminate, entire or denticulate, glossy dark green except for fine hair on margin, midrib and petiole. Rac. to 20cm, simple, slender conical to cylindric; fls white, usually tinted pale lilac. Summer. NZ, Chile. Z7.

H. salicifolia var. *atkinsonii* (Ckn.) Ckn. & Allan = *H. stricta* var. *atkinsonii.*

H. salicifolia var. *communis* (Ckn.) Ckn. & Allan = *H. salicifolia.*

H. salicornioides (Hook. f.) Ckn. & Allan. Erect shrub to 1m. Branchlets whipcord, pale green, terete, nodal joint obscure. Lvs to 0.1cm, closely adpressed, fairly widely spaced, incurved, forming a sheathing collar, fleshy, obtuse or subacute. Rac. short, to 12-fld; fls white. Summer. NZ.

H. salicornioides hort. non (Hook. f.) Ckn. & Allan = *H. propinqua* 'Aurea'.

H. scott-thomsonii Allan = *H. rakaiensis.*

H. selaginoides hort. = *H.* 'Loganioides'.

H. **'Simon Delaux'.** Small rounded shrub. Fls deep crimson in large rac., cf. *H. speciosa.*

H. speciosa (A. Cunn.) Ckn. & Allan. Strong-growing shrub to 2m. Br. stout, somewhat angular. Lvs to 10×4cm, broadly elliptic to obovate, glossy, glab. except for minute pubescence on midrib and margin, obtuse, margin cartilaginous. Fls dark red to magenta, crowded in term. conic-cylindric rac. to 7cm. Summer–autumn. NZ. A highly variable sp. giving rise to many cvs and hybrids, many of which are far hardier. Z7.

H. **'Spender's Seedling'.** Dense, erect, to 60cm or more. Internodes green, pubesc. nodes dark. Lvs to 6cm, narrow-lanceolate, spreading or deflexed, mid- to dark green. Fls white in long rac., often misassigned to *H. salicifolia*, more probably derived from *H. recurva.*.

H. stricta (Banks & Sol. ex Benth.) L.B. Moore. To 3m, often procumbent. Br. diffuse. Lvs to 7.5×2.5cm, spreading, deflexed, lanceolate, dark green, not glossy, glab. except for minute pubescence on midrib and margin, acute or acuminate, sometimes faintly denticulate. Fls in lat. rac., white to pale blue. Summer. NZ. var. *atkinsonii* (Ckn.) L.B. Moore. Lvs to 10×1cm, elliptic to narrow-lanceolate, rarely acuminate. NZ. var. *macroura* (Benth.) L.B. Moore. Lvs to 8×3cm, ovate-oblong, thick. Rac. somewhat twisted; fls white. Z9.

H. subalpina (Ckn.) Ckn. & Allan. Densely branched, erect, to 2m. Branchlets green, nodes conspicuously tinted purple. Lvs to 4×1cm, outspread, lanceolate, glossy green, coriaceous. Rac. lat., simple, to 5cm; fls white. Spring. NZ. Plants labelled as *H. subalpina* are usually *H. rakaiensis.* Z7.

H. subsimilis (Colenso) Ashwin. Whipcord to 30cm. Br. erect, usually somewhat tetragonal, yellow-green nodes distinct. Lvs to 2mm, usually spreading incurved, deltoid to deltoid-oblong, concavo-convex, v. thick, weakly keeled beneath, subacute. Fls to 8 per infl., white. Late spring. NZ. var. *astonii* (Petrie) Ashwin. Br. more compact and yellow-green, obscurely tetragonal; lvs more strongly concavo-convex.

H. tetragona (Hook. f.) Ckn. & Allan. Erect whipcord to 1m, much-branched. Branchlets distinctly tetragonal, enclosed by lvs, yellow-green. Lvs to 3.5mm, decussate, adpressed, deltoid to subulate, v. thick, glab., glossy, apex keeled, acute. Fls to 12 per branchlet. Summer. NZ.

H. tetrasticha (Hook. f.) Ckn. & Allan. Dwarf whipcord, procumbent than ascending to 20×30cm. Br. slender, tetragonal, resembling *Cassiope*. Lvs to 2mm, closely imbricate, triangular. Fls white, 2–4 per term. spike. S Is., NZ. Z6.

H. 'Tom Marshall'. = *H. canterburiensis.*

H. topiaria L.B. Moore. To 1m, much-branched. Lvs to 1.2×0.6cm, erecto-patent, almost imbricate, elliptic to obovate, slightly fleshy, glaucous, subacute. Fls white, in short simple infl. Summer. NZ.

H. traversii (Hook. f.) Ckn. & Allan. To 2m in habitat, laxly branched. Lvs to 2.5×0.7cm, spreading, oblong, subcoriaceous, glab. except for upper margin, dull yellow-green. Rac. to 2.5cm; fls white. Summer. NZ. Closely allied to *H. glaucophylla*, from which it differs in the cor. tube, which greatly exceeds the cal. It is also confused with *H. brachysiphon*, whose lf buds have a large oblong sinus. Z7.

H. **'Tricolor'**. Lvs pale green, edged cream and tinged pink. Fls close to *H.* 'La Séduisante', cf *H. speciosa.*

H. venustula (Colenso) L.B. Moore. To 1.5cm, upright and rounded. Branchlets yellow-green with dark nodes. Lvs to 2×0.6cm, spreading, distichous, elliptic-oblong, acute, subcoriaceous, glab. except for margin, bright green, paler at margins. Rac. to 3.5cm; fls white, sky blue or powder blue. NZ. Z9.

H. vernicosa (Hook. f.) Ckn. & Allan. Seldom exceeding 30cm. Br. usually horizontal. Lvs 0.8–1.5cm, spreading, distichous, densely set, elliptic to obovate, concave below or with conspicuous midvein, subcoriaceous, glab., lustrous deep green, tip blunt and thickened. Rac. to 5cm, slender; fls white to lavender. Spring. NZ. Z7.

H. vernicosa var. *canterburiensis* (J.B. Armstr.) Ckn. & Allan = *H. canterburiensis.*

H. 'Waikiki' = *H.* 'Mrs Winder'.

H. 'Warleyensis' = *H.* 'Mrs Winder'.

H. **'Watson's Pink'**. Allied to *H. carnea* but with fls paler pink failing to open at rac. tips, giving a strong bicolour effect. Lvs to 4cm, more broadly oblong-lanceolate.

H. wilcoxii hort. = *H. buchananii.*

H. **'Youngii'**. (*H. elliptica* × *H. pimeleoides.*) To 15cm, procumbent, compact. Internodes dark pubesc. Lvs to 0.75cm, elliptic, dark green, faintly edged red at times. Fls deep violet fading to white, on short rac. Other clones of this cross include 'Gnome': close to 'Mini' but with upright br. and dark green lvs. 'Mini': v. compact; lvs to 0.5cm, narrow-elliptic, edged red in winter; fls violet. 'Morning Clouds': lvs to 0.5cm, obovate-elliptic, dark green bloomed grey above, glossy beneath; fls tinted blue; exhibiting influence of *H. pimeleoides* var. *glaucocaerulea.* 'Tiny Tot': lvs minute, concealing internodes; fls lilac. 'Winter Glow': lvs to 1cm, broadly elliptic, acute, concave, somewhat glaucous, tinted red in cold weather; fls blue in branching rac. Z8.

Hebeclinium DC. Compositae. 18 pubesc., perenn. herbs. Lvs opposite, cordate, dentate, petiolate. Cap. discoid, term., in many-fld crowded corymbs; phyllaries loosely imbricate, extended into pale appendices; flts usually white to pink. Trop. Amer. Z10.

H. macrophyllum (L.) DC. Erect, to 3m. Lvs to 20cm, broadly deltoid-ovate, acute to acuminate, crenate, finely pubesc. throughout, or slightly tomentose to velvety beneath. Cap. *c*7mm high, in leafy infl. to 40cm across; phyllaries sometimes tinged lilac. Spring.

Hebenstretia L. Scrophulariaceae. 25 ann. or perenn. herbs, subshrubs or shrubs. Fls in dense term. spikes; cal. spathe-like, cor. 4-lobed, tube often split. Trop. & S Afr. Z10.

H. aurea Andrews = *H. integrifolia.*

H. comosa Hochst. Perenn. with woody, angular, downy st. to 120cm. Lvs lanceolate or linear-lanceolate, toothed. Spikes to 15cm; fls fragrant at night, yellow or white with an orange-red blotch on limb. S Afr.

H. crassifolia Choisy = *H. robusta.*

H. dentata L. Ann. to 60cm. Lvs linear to linear-lanceolate, toothed. Spikes to 15cm; fls yellow or white blotched with orange on limb. S Afr.

H. integrifolia L. Perenn. or sometimes ann., 15–60cm high, shoots downy. Lvs filiform or linear-filiform, entire, glab. or scabrid. Spikes 7–15cm long; fls yellow, limb stained red. S Afr.

H. robusta E. Mey. Ann., 15–23cm, br. stout, spreading, downy. Lvs linear or oblong, rather fleshy, entire, glab. Spikes 2–10cm; fls white with an orange throat. S Afr.

H. scabra Thunb. = *H. integrifolia.*

H. tenuifolia Schräd. ex Rchb. = *H. integrifolia.*

H. watsonii Rolfe = *H. integrifolia.*

Hechtia Klotzsch. Bromeliaceae. 45 short-stemmed or stemless xerophytic herbs. Lvs in a rosette, stiff, recurved, tapering, spiny, dentate or entire. Infl. scapose, bracteate, paniculate, bipinnate or further divided, with long br.; fls green to yellow; pet. free or fused to fil. at centre. Mex., SW US. Z9.

H. argentea Bak. ex Hemsl. Lvs to 60cm, linear, densely covered in ash-grey scales, toothed with hooked brown spines to 7mm. Infl. loosely paniculate, simple, sparsely white-hairy; floral bracts brown, papery; sep. white-hairy; pet. white. C Mex.

H. capituligera Mez. Closely related to *H. glomerata* but smaller, with tripinnate infl; sep. covered in brown hairs. Mex.

H. desmetiana (Bak.) Mez. Lvs to 40cm, narrowly triangular, fleshy, brown-green, sparsely scaly above, densely scaly beneath, with stout spines to 7mm. Infl. glab., lax, pyramidal, bipinnate; floral bracts; leafy; sep. pink; pet. pink-orange. Mex.

H. epigyna Harms. Lvs to 40cm, linear-triangular, tapering to a short thread-like apex, densely scaly or glab. with age, spinose except near apex. Infl. glab., 2–3-pinnate, cylindric; floral bracts white; sep. pink. Mex.

H. ghiesbreghtii Lem. = *H. glomerata*.

H. glomerata Zucc. Lvs 25–40cm, linear-triangular, glossy above and white to pale brown and scaly beneath, often mark red near apex, with coarse hooked spines. Infl. compound, lax; br. capitate or cylindric, hairy and scaly; floral bracts yellow-brown; pet. white. S Tex., Mex., Guat.

H. marnier-lapostollei L.B. Sm. Lvs to 13cm, silvery, narrowly triangular, spines to 4mm. Infl. glab., 2-compound, loosely branching. Mex.

H. meziana L.B. Sm. Lvs thick, densely red-brown or grey scaly throughout, toothd, not spiny. Fl. bracts thin; sep. papery, pet. elliptic, obtuse. Mex.

H. montana Brandg. Lvs to 45cm, linear-triangular with ash-grey scales beneath, striped and glab. above, with sparse brown spines. Infl. loosely 2-compound, glab., slender and pyramidal; pet. pale yellow. Baja Calif.

H. pitcairniifolia hort. Berlin ex Verl. = *Fascicularia pitcairniifolia*.

H. podantha Mez. Infl. tripinnate (rarely bipinnate), with br. divided into 3 just above the base; pet white. C & NC Mex.

H. purpusii Brandg. = *H. tillandsioides*.

H. roezlii hort. ex Bak. = *H. rosea*.

H. rosea Morr. ex Bak. Lvs less fleshy than in *H. desmetiana*, densely scaly throughout, becoming red in strong light. Pet. pink. S Mex.

H. roseana L.B. Sm. Lvs rusty spinose, thick. Floral bracts triangular-ovate; pet. white. C Mex.

H. rubra hort. A name of no botanical standing.

H. scariosa L.B. Sm. Lvs narrowly triangular, glab. above with straight spines. Infl. loosely pyramidal, with minute scales; floral bracts dark pink with thin margins; sep. dark pink. SW Tex., N Mex.

H. schottii Bak. ex Hemsl. Lvs to 1m, narrowly triangular, glab. above, white-scaly, striate beneath, with straight spines to 5mm. Infl. 3–4-pinnate, to 1m diam.; floral bracts brown, thin; sep. brown with a pale margin; pet. white. CE & SE Mex.

H. stenopetala Klotzsch. To 2m. Lvs to 60cm, spine-tipped. Infl. 2–3 pinnate; pet. white. C Mex.

H. texensis S. Wats. Lvs to 80cm, linear-triangular, densely grey-scaly beneath, glab. above, laxly toothed with hooked spines to 8mm. Infl. lax. 2–3-pinnate, white-hairy when young; floral bracts transparent, dark-veined; sep. white, thin; pet. white. W Tex.

H. tillandsioides (André) L.B. Sm. Lvs graceful, resembling *Tillandsia*, sheaths slightly inflated; blades narrowly triangular, striped and channelled, finely toothed. Infl. 3-pinnate, glab.; pet. pale pink-white. C Mex.

→*Dyckia*.

Hedera L. IVY. Araliaceae. 11 everg., woody, climbing or creeping plants with distinct sterile juvenile and fertile arborescent stages. St. of juvenile stage climbing, supported by aerial rootlets; st. of arborescent stage without aerial rootlets. Lvs alt., simple, of juvenile stage conspicuously lobed or cordate, of arborescent stage more nearly entire, base cordate, obtuse or broadly cuneate, all lvs glab. and often waxy and shining above, stellate-hairy or scaly beneath. Fls perfect, in globose umbels which are solitary or in compound rac. or pan.; pedicels stellate-hairy or scaly; cal. 5-lobed, 1–3mm; yellow-green; sta. 5, alt. with pet. Fr. a subglobose drupe, 4–7mm, with black, sometimes orange, yellow or cream. Eur., Asia, N Afr.

H. algeriensis Hibb. ALGERIAN IVY. St. and undersides of young lvs red-hairy. Lvs to 13×3cm, glossy, of juvenile stage 3-lobed, 2 lat. lobes pointing sideways, yellow-green, of arborescent stage ovate to rounded, darker green. Medit. cost of Alg. and Tun. 'Gloire de Marengo': lvs light green, variegated yellow-white, more pronounced in young lvs and st. 'Goldleaf' ('Striata',

'Golden Leaf'): lvs deep green, glossy, with a yellow to pale green central splash. 'Margino-maculata': lvs dark green and pale green, margins mottled white or cream, otherwise similar to 'Gloire de Marengo', of which this is a clone. 'Montgomery': lvs small, deep green, matt. Z8.

H. amurensis Hibb. = *H. colchica*.

H. arborea Carr. = *H. helix*.

H. azorica Carr. Climbing. Young st., petioles and lf undersides white-pubesc. (not persistent above), hairs 3–8-rayed; internodes 3–4cm. Lvs 9–11×10–12cm, lobes to 7 bluntly acute, central longest, others reduced, matt green with pale venation. Azores. Z8.

H. canariensis 'Azorica' = *H. azorica*.

H. canariensis hort. non Willd. = *H. algeriensis*.

H. canariensis Willd. St. and undersides of young lvs covered with small, red, 15-rayed, stellate or scale-like hairs. Lvs of juvenile stage resemble those of *H. azorica* but the 2 lat. lobes shorter, pointing forward, thick and leather, matt; lvs of arborescent stage thinner, almost unlobed. Fr. 1cm, black. Z8.

H. canariensis 'Maderensis' = *H. maderensis*.

H. cavendishii Paul = *H. helix* 'Cavendishii'.

H. chrysocarpa Walsh = *H. helix* ssp. *poetarum*.

H. cinerea (Hibb.) Bean = *H. nepalensis*.

H. colchica (K. Koch) Hibb. PERSIAN IVY; COLCHIS IVY. Branchlets and petioles green, yellow-scaly. Lvs leathery with prominent venation beneath, smelling strongly of celery when crushed, lvs of juvenile stage 2–5cm, entire to 3-lobed, base cordate to cuneate, apex acuminate, red-hairy beneath at first, lvs of arborescent stage narrower than juvenile lvs. ovate to orbicular. Fls in umbels of 16–18 rays to 2cm across; pedicels scaly; cal. lobes triangular, conspicuous. Fr. 6–8mm, blue-black. Cauc., Turk. 'Dentata' (BULLOCKS HEART IVY): vigorous; st. purple-brown; petioles green-purple; lvs to 20×17cm, ovate, entire, pendent, basally cordate, deep pea-green, venation pale, minutely dentate, tips often incurved. 'Dentata-variegata': st. green-brown (juvenile stellate-pubesc.); internodes 8cm; petioles light green to purple-brown; lvs coriaceous, ovate, entire, or minutely dentate, light green mottled green-grey, margins ivory. 'Sulphur Heart': vigorous, light green, becoming purple-green; internodes 6cm; lvs entire, or regularly denticulate, 10–13×9–12cm, light green, blotched yellow or light green. Z6.

H. colchica var. **dentata** (Hibb.) Lawrence = *H. colchica* 'Dentata'.

H. communis S.F. Gray = *H. helix*.

H. cordifolia Hibb. = *H. colchica*.

H. coriaca Hibb. = *H. colchica*.

H. dentata hort. ex Carr. = *H. colchica* 'Dentata'.

H. grandiflora Hibb. = *H. canariensis*.

H. helix 'Deltoidea' = *H. hibernica* 'Deltoidea'.

H. helix L. COMMON IVY; ENGLISH IVY. Young st. and lvs long white-stellate pubesc., hair 4–10-rayed, standing out in different directions from lf surface. Lvs 2–15cm long, less than 5cm wide, leathery, those of juvenile stage entire with cordate base or 3–9-lobed, with pale venation, lvs of arborescent stage ovate or elliptic, entire, rounded or truncate. Fls with pedicels, peduncle and cal. white stellate-puubesc. Fr. to 9mm, yellow-orange to black. Eur., Scand., Russia. 'Angularis': st. and petioles green flushed purple; lvs 5×7cm, trilobed, central lobe acute, rarely obtuse, laterals obtuse, basal lobes vestigial, sinuses shallow, bright green. 'Atropurpurea': st. and petioles purple; lvs 4–6×5–7cm, 5-lobed, basal lobes vestigial, laterals bluntly acute, central acuminate, dull dark green becoming deep purple in winter. 'Baltica': as *H. helix* but exceptionally cold resistant. 'Cavendishii': st. light green; petioles darker; internodes 1–3cm; lvs basally truncate, trilobed, 6×7cm, medium green dappled grey-green, margin cream-yellow, flushed pink in autumn and winter, juvenile lvs lobes patent, acute, becoming obtuse or vestigial at maturity, sinuses shallow. 'Buttercup': lvs pale green to butter yellow. 'Chrysophylla' ('Spectabilis Aurea'; 'Aurea Spectabilis'): st. green, rarely tinted purple; internodes 2.5–4cm; lvs to 6×8cm, trilobed, lobes almost equal, basally truncate, mid to deep green, rarely tinted yellow, main veins raised above. 'Congesta' ('Minima'): st. creeping or erect, green-purple; petioles pale green, lvs 3–4×2–3cm, dark green, venation paler, entire to trilobed, sinuses shallow, lobes acute. 'Conglomerata': st. climbing, creeping or shrubby, green, often flattened; lvs 1–3×2–4cm, rich deep green, entire to trilobed, undulate, venation raised. 'Digitata': lvs 5-lobed, deeply divided, central lobes only slightly longer than laterals. 'Dealbata' ('Discolor'): st. slender, green-purple, internodes 3–3.5cm; petioles purple; lvs triangular, trilobed, 3–5×4–6cm, sinuses shallow, dark green mottled ivory. 'Erecta': st. green, creeping erect, rooting nodally; petioles pale green; lvs 4–6×4–6cm, trilobed or entire, acute, sinuses shallow, central lobe exceeding laterals, dark green, venation paler. 'Eva': lvs small with grey-green centre, splashed deep green, margined cream. 'Goldheart': st. climbing, pink-red, becoming brown; petioles pink, rarely light green or yellow; lvs 4–6×4–6cm, dark green, basally truncate, centrally marked yellow, trilobed, central lobe longest, acuminate, rarely with vestigial basal lobes. 'Glacier': lvs grey-green, striped silver. 'Glymii': lvs ovate-acuminate, glossy, becoming deep purple in winter. 'Gnome' ('Spetchley'): habit dwarf; st. creeping or climbing; lvs 0.5–2×0.5–1.5cm, slightly 3-lobed, deep grey-green. 'Green Ripple': habit climbing and bushy; lvs 5–10×5–7cm, 5-lobed, bright green with pale venation. 'Ivalace': lvs 5-lobed, finely undulate with crinkled margin, bright green with pale venation. 'Lobata Major': climbing; st. and lvs purple-green; lvs trilobed, 4–8×5–11cm, laterals at 90° to central lobe, basal lobes variable, dark green. 'Manda's Crested': lvs curled, 5-lobed, convolute, pale green with paler venation, tips downward-pointing. 'Maple Queen': st. deep red; lvs 3-lobed, medium deep green with paler venation. 'Marginata': margins pale yellow, blades tinted red in autumn. 'Minor Marmorata' (SALT AND PEPPER IVY): lvs 5-lobed, dark green, heavily spotted white. 'Ovata': lvs ovate, basally obtuse, usually entire, deep green. 'Palmata': st. and lvs green-purple; lvs 4–6×3.5–6cm, basally truncate, deep green, venation paler, prominent beneath, 3–5-lobed, 2 laterals and central lobe equal, acute, basal lobes smaller, sinuses narrow. 'Parsley Crested': habit branching and trailing; lvs unlobed, undulate with crinkled margin, bright green, prominently veined. 'Pedata' (BIRD'S FOOT IVY): climbing; st. and petioles green; lvs 4–5×5–6cm, dark green, appearing metallic grey-green, venation grey-white, 5-lobed, central lobe to 1cm wide, almost at 90° to alterals and exceeding them by ×1.5, basal lobes deflexed, apices acuminate. 'Professor H. Tobler': lvs deeply cut or with 3–5 lfts, bright green with paler venation. 'Sagittifolia': climbing; st. and lvs green-purple; lvs 3–5×4–6cm, sagittate, central lobe lanceolate, extended, laterals obtuse, often overlapping basally, basal lobes vestigial. 'Scutifolia': st. and petioles green to red; lvs trilobed, ovate, basally cordate, glossy deep green, venation paler. 'Shamrock': habit shortly trailing; lvs 3-lobed, lat. lobes occas. folded inwards, deep green, often flushed purple near base. 'Tricolor': climbing; st. dull brown to green-purple; petioles purple; lvs triangular, entire, rarely with vestigial basal lobes, grey-green edged ivory, edged pale pink extending in winter, venation pale grey-green to cream-yellow. ssp. **poetarum** Nyman. POET'S IVY; ITALIAN IVY. St. climbing, pale pink to green; internodes 4–5cm; petioles green-pink; lvs to 7×8cm, pale to yellow-green, lobes broadly acute, central slightly exceeding laterals, basal pair reduced. Fr. dull orange. Mediterranean. Medit. 'Emerald Gem': st. and petioles green to maroon; lvs deep green, venation paler, ovate, 3–5-lobed, central lobe wider than long. Z5.

H. helix 'Hibernica' = *H. hibernica*.

H. helix var. *canariensis* (Willd.) DC. = *H. canariensis*.

H. helix var. *rhombea* Miq. = *H. rhombea*.

H. hibernica (Kirchn.) Bean. ATLANTIC IVY. Young st. and underside of yong lvs long white-pubesc., the hairs lying parallel to lf surface, lvs of juvenile stage 5–9×8–14cm, with 5 triangular lobes, the term. lobe largest, apex acute, base cordate, with grey venation. Atlantic coast of GB, Ireland, W Fr., Spain, Port. 'Angularis Aurea': lvs bright green, veins yellow. 'Deltoidea' (SHIELD IVY; SWEETHEART IVORY): st. and petioles green, lvs 6–10×8–10cm, deltoid, basally cordate, shallowly trilobed or entire, dark green with purple autumn tints, venation paler. 'Digitata' ('Pensylvanica'; 'Taurica'): st. and petioles green-purple; lvs 7–9×7–10cm, basally truncate, dark green, lobes 5, digitate, acute, central exceed lobes, sinuses narrow. 'Gracilis': habit vining; st. purple; lvs 4×4cm, 3–5-lobed, lobes acute, slightly convolute, deep green with paler venation. 'Hamilton': lvs small, deeply lobed, pale green. 'Hibernica' (IRISH IVY): vigorous; st. green, climbing; petioles purple-green; lvs 5–9×8–4cm, basally cordate, acute, lobes 3–5, triangular, central lobe prominent, sinuses shallow, venation pale grey-green; a stabilized clone of *H. hibernica* intermediate between juvenile and mature types. 'Lobata Major': lvs 3-lobed, central lobe pointed; vigorous. 'Modern Times': st. purple-green; lvs 5×7cm, 5-lobed, dull green with pale green to white venation. 'Rona': lvs streaked yellow. 'Sulphurea': lvs irregularly 3–5-lobed, grey-green, edged and splashed sulphur yellow. Z7.

H. himalaica Tobler. = *H. nepalensis*.

H. japonica Paul = *H. rhombea*.

H. maderensis K. Koch. St. and lvs of juvenile stage beneath covered with fine, scale-like, red hairs. Lvs 5–8×7–10cm, mid-green, glossy. Lvs of juvenile stage 5-lobed. Madeira. Z9.

H. maroccana spec. nov. MOROCCAN IVY. St. and undersides of juvenile lvs covered with fine red hairs; st. and petioles red. Lvs 5-lobed, with prominent red veins above. Moroc., nat. S Spain and Canary Is. 'Spanish Canary': lvs v. large; hardy and fast-growing. Z8.

H. nepalensis K. Koch. NEPAL IVY. St. and young lvs of juvenile stage with small, red, 12–15-rayed hairs. Lvs of juvenile stage 5–12cm, 2–5-lobed or entire, base truncate, grey-green, lvs of arborescent stage oblong-ovate to lanceolate. Fls 8–20 per umbel. umbels gathered into rac. Fr. orange-yellow to red. Himal. var. *sinensis* (Tobler) Rehd. 'Marbled Dragon': lvs of juvenile stage entire to 3-lobed, lvs of arborescent stage ovate to lanceolate; fr. 1cm, yellow. 'Suzanne': lvs dark, particularly beneath, 5-lobed, term. lobe pointed, indumentum long. Z8.

H. pastuchovii Woron. St. and lvs of juvenile stage with fine red hairs. Lvs 4–6×3–4cm, ovate-rhombic, subacuminate, thick but less leathery than irregularly dentate, dark black-green, veins pale green, midrib red beneath, indumentum not so obviously stellate as *H. colchica*. Fr. black. Russia, Iran. Z7.

H. rhombea (Miq.) Bean. JAPANESE IVY. St. and undersides of juvenile lvs covered with fine red-brown hairs. Lvs of juvenile stage 2–4×4–5cm, triangular to ovate, slightly 3-lobed, base ± cordate, deep green with paler venation, lvs of arborescent stage 5–10, oblong-ovate, unlobed, leathery. Fr. black. Jap., Korea. 'Pierrot': st. wiry, creeping; lvs not variegated, smaller than sp. type, cordate, papery; possibly the juvenile stage of *H. rhombea* var. *formosana*. 'Variegata': lf margin white. Z7.

H. roegneriana Hibb. = *H. colchica*.

Hedge Bamboo *Bambusa multiplex*.
Hedge Bindweed *Calystegia sepium*.
Hedge Euphorbia *Euphorbia neriifolia*.
Hedge Gooseberry *Ribes alpestris*.
Hedgehog Aloe *Aloe humilis*.
Hedgehog Broom *Erinacea anthyllis*.
Hedgehog Fir *Abies pinsapo*.
Hedgehog Gourd *Cucumis dipsaceus*.
Hedgehog Holly *Ilex aquifolium* 'Ferox'.
Hedge Hyssop *Gratiola*.
Hedge Maple *Acer campestre*.
Hedge Nettle *Stachys*.
Hedge Thorn *Carissa bispinosa*.
Hedge Wattle *Acacia paradoxa*.
Hediondo *Lonchocarpus latifolius*.

Hedycarya Forst. & Forst. f. Monimiaceae. 12 trees and shrubs, everg., aromatic. Infl. a cyme or rac., axill., rarely term.; pedicel bracteolate; perianth seg. 5–10, inflexed, forming a broad cup, connate at base; sta. crowded. Fr. a drupe, few to several on single receptacle, stipitate; seed pendulous. Aus., NZ, S Pacific. Z10.

H. arborea Forst. & Forst. f. PIGEON WOOD Tree to 12m; bark dark brown. Lvs to 8–11cm, lanceolate to elliptic-obovate, coarsely serrate or entire, coriaceous, dark green above, pale beneath, midrib pubesc. Rac. often branching, fls inconspicuous. Drupes 12–14mm, 4–10, scarlet, somewhat crustaceous. NZ.

H. dentata Forst. = *H. arborea*.

H. scabra A. Cunn. = *H. arborea*.

Hedychium J.G. Koenig. GINGER LILY; GARLAND LILY. Zingiberaceae. 40 perenn. herbs with stout rhiz. and erect reed-like st. Lvs oblong-lanceolate, acuminate, in 2 ranks. Fls fragrant, in terminal dense spikes; bracts distant or imbricate; cor. tube slender, pet. 3; lip long with 2 lobes; lat. staminodes petaloid; fil. long and slender. Trop. Asia, Himal. and Madag.

H. acuminatum Roscoe = *H. spicatum* var. *acuminatum*.

H. angustifolium Roxb. = *H. coccineum* var. *angustifolium*.

H. aurantiacum Wallich ex Roscoe = *H. coccineum* var. *aurantiacum*.

H. carneum Roscoe = *H. coccineum* var. *aurantiacum*.

H. chrysoleucum Hook. f. To 1.5m. Lvs 40×8cm. Fls fragrant, 2–6 per bract; cor. white, tube 8cm; lip 3.5cm across, 2-lobed, white tinged orange-yellow or pink; lat. staminodes spreading, white, yellow at base; fil. equalling lip, deep orange. Summer. India. Z9.

H. coccineum Sm. RED GINGER LILY; SCARLET GINGER LILY. To 3m. Lvs 30–50×3.5cm. Fls 2–4 per bract; cor. pale to deep red or orange; lip 1–2cm wide, red and yellow to mauve; lateral staminodes to 2cm; fil. longer than lip. Autumn. Himal. 'Tara': bold spikes of orange fls. var. *angustifolium* Roxb. Lvs narrower. Fls brick-red or salmon pink. var. *aurantiacum* Roxb. Lvs narrower. Fls orange. Z9.

H. coronarium J.G. Koenig. BUTTERFLY LILY; GARLAND FLOWER; WHITE GINGER. To 3m. Lvs 60×11cm. Fls v. fragrant, 2–6 per bract; cor. tube to 7cm, white, lip obcordate, 2-lobed, 5cm across, white with yellow-green centre; fil. shorter than lip, white. Spring. India. 'F.W. Moore' (*H. coronarium* ×*H. coccineum*): spikes showy, fls fragrant, amber yellow, base of seg. blotched orange-yellow. var. *maximum* Roscoe. Lvs broader and fls larger; fil. tinged pink. var. *urophyllum* (Lodd.)

Bak. Lip entire. Z9.

H. coronarium var. *chrysoleucum* (Hook. f.) Bak. = *H. chrysoleucum.*

H. coronarium var. *flavescens* (Roscoe) Bak. = *H. flavescens.*

H. densiflorum Wallich. To 5m. Lvs 30–40×5–6cm. Fls vermilion, in dense, cylindric spikes; lip 0.7cm across; fil. longer than lip, red. Himal. 'Assam Orange': st. shorter (0.75m); fls vivid burnt orange, v. fragrant. 'Stephen': infl. larger, less narrowly cylindrical; fls dirty yellow or pale orange; fil. deep orange. Z8.

H. ellipticum Buch.-Ham. ex. Sm. To 2m. Lvs 30×13cm. Fls in dense 10cm spike; cor. 2-lobed, yellow-white; lip white; fil. purple. N India. Z10.

H. flavescens Roscoe. YELLOW GINGER. To 3m. Lvs 60×8cm. Fls in dense 20cm spike; cor pale yellow, lobes green, linear; lip red-yellow at base; staminodes yellow; fil. longer than lip, yellow. Bengal. Z10.

H. flavum Roxb. Lvs 30cm. Fls in dense 15cm spikes; cor. yellow or orange; lip broadly obovate, sometimes 2-lobed, yellow with orange patch at centre and base; fil. yellow. N India. Z9.

H. forrestii Diels. To 1.25m. Lvs 30–50×5cm. Fls in 20–25cm cylindric spike; cor. narrow-lobed, white or white flushed pink; lip, 3cm across, 2-lobed; fil. not longer than lip. SW China. Z9.

H. gardnerianum Ker-Gawl. KAHILI GINGER. To 2m+. Lvs 25–40×10–15cm. Fls white and yellow, in dense 25–35cm spike; cor. tube 5.6cm; lip cuneate, 1–2cm diam., 2-lobed, yellow; fil. bright red. Summer–autumn. N India, Himal. Z8.

H. glaucum Roscoe = *H. gracile.*

H. gracile Roxb. Lvs 12.5×3.25cm. Fls in 10cm spike; cor. tube 2.5cm; pet. 2cm, green-white; lip small; fil. red. India. Z9.

H. greenei W.W. Sm. To 2m. Lvs 20–25×5cm. Fls in 12cm spike; cor. red tube 2.5cm; lip 2-lobed, deep red; fil. longer than lip, bright red; may form bulbils. W Bhutan. Z10.

H. maximum Roscoe = *H. coronarium* var. *maximum.*

H. speciosum Wallich. To 2.5m. Lvs 30×9cm. Infl. 30cm; cor. yellow; lip 2.5×1.5cm, oblong, entire; staminodes linear, shorter than pet.; fil. longer than lip, red. Summer. Himal. Z9.

H. spicatum Sm. To 1m. Lvs 10–40×3–10cm. Infl. to 20cm, lax; lip 1.5–2cm diam., 2-lobed, yellow; lat. staminodes spathulate, white and pink; fil. shorter than lip, red-orange. Autumn. Himal. var. *acuminatum* (Roscoe) Wallich. Lvs distinctly petioled, not subsessile, downy beneath. Spike few-fld; staminodes and fil. purple. Z9.

H. thyrsiforme Buch.-Ham. To 2m. Lvs 35×10cm. Fls in dense 10cm spike; cor. white; lip 2-lobed, white; lat. staminodes white; fil. longer than lip, white. India. Z9.

H. urophyllum Lodd. = *H. coronarium* var. *urophyllum.*

H. yunnanense Gagnep. Lvs 40–8×10cm. Infl. bracts orange; cor. tube 5cm, slender; pet. 3cm, linear, twisted; lip deeply divided, obovate; fil. 4–5cm. Yunnan, Indochina.

Hedyotis L.

H. caerulea (L.) Hook. f. = *Houstonia caerulea.*

H. caerulea Fosb. = *Houstonia serpyllifolia.*

H. longifolia (Gaertn.) Hook. = *Houstonia longifolia.*

H. purpurea var. *longifolia* (Gaertn.) Fosb. = *Houstonia longifolia.*

H. purpurea (L.) Torr. & A. Gray = *Houstonia purpurea.*

H. serpyllifolia (Michx.) Torr. & A. Gray non Poir. = *Houstonia serpyllifolia.*

Hedysarum L. Leguminosae (Papilionoideae). 100 perenn. herbs, subshrubs or shrubs. Lvs imparipinnate. Fls pea-like in axill. rac. N temp. regions.

H. alpinum L. Perenn. 30–100cm. St. and lvs glab. or sparsely pubesc.; lfts 1.3×0.4–1cm, 15–17, lanceolate to oblong. Fls red-violet. N & E Russia. Z4.

H. boreale Nutt. non hort. SWEET VETCH. Perenn.; st. decumbent to erect, grooved, sparsely pubesc. to canescent, lfts 1.3×0.3–9cm, 5–15, elliptic, linear to obovate, canescent to glab. Fls pink to purple. N Amer. 'Rosea': fls rose-pink. ssp. *mackenzii* (Richardson) Löve & D. Löve. Decumbent perenn. Lfts long, pubesc. Fls large, violet-purple, in long rac. Colorado. Z3.

H. boreale hort. non Nutt. = *H. alpinum.*

H. coronarium L. FRENCH HONEYSUCKLE. Perenn., 30–100cm, sparsely adpressed-pubesc. Lfts 1.5–3.5×1.2–1.8cm, 7–15, elliptic to obovate-orbicular, glab. or subglab. above, pubesc. beneath. Fls intensely fragrant, bright red to purple. S Eur. 'Album': fls white. Z3.

H. elongatum Fisch. ex Lodd. = *H. alpinum.*

H. esculentum Ledeb. = *H. vicioides.*

H. exaltatum A. Kerner = *H. hedysaroides.*

H. grandiflorum Sessé & Moc. Lfts 1.5–4×0.8–3cm, 5–13, elliptic to ovate, glossy-hairy beneath. Fls yellow. SE Eur. to E Russia. Z6.

H. hedysaroides (L.) Schinz & Thell. Perenn., 10–40cm; glab. or sparsely pubesc. Lfts 1–2.5×0.5–1.2cm, 7–21, obtuse. Fls red-violet, occas. white. SC Eur., Arc. Russia, N & C Urals. Z4.

H. mackenzii Richardson = *H. boreale* ssp. *mackenzii.*

H. multijugum Maxim. Decid. shrub to 1.5m; br. grey-yellow, flexuous. Lfts 0.6–1.5cm, 15–29, ovate-oblong, obtuse or notched, densely silky-pubesc. beneath. Fls magenta. Mong. var. *apiculatum* Sprague. Lfts acuminate. Z4.

H. obscurum L. = *H. hedysaroides.*

H. occidentale Greene. Perenn. St. decumbent to erect, grooved, pubesc. Lfts 1–3.5×0.5–1.5cm, oblong, ovate or elliptic, round to obtuse, pubesc. Fls red-purple. N Amer. Z4.

H. pabulare A. Nels. = *H. boreale.*

H. sericeum Thunb. = *Lespedeza juncea.*

H. sibiricum Poir. = *H. vicioides.*

H. sikkimense Benth. Perenn. to 15cm; young st. pubesc. Lfts to 1.3cm, 21–27, obtuse, glab. above, obscurely pubesc. beneath with raised venation. Fls bright red. Himal. Z7.

H. vicioides Turcz. Perenn. to 80cm, aerial parts pubesc. Lfts 1.5–3×0.5–1cm. 10–25, narrow-ovate to broad-lanceolate, obscurely mucronate, subglab. above, pubesc., obscurely dotted with glands beneath. Fls pale yellow. N Korea to E Sib. Z3.

Hedyscepe Wendl. & Drude. UMBRELLA PALM. Palmae. 1 palm, to 10m. St. solitary, to 12cm diam., with prominent, white rings. Crownshaft silvery-blue and scaly. Lvs pinnate, curved, to 1.5m; pinnae subopposite, lanceolate, acute, single-fold, ± erect, glab. above, tomentose on margins beneath, midrib and 3 pairs of veins prominent above. Infl. infrafoliar, branched ×1–3; fls egg-yellow. Fr. ellipsoid, to 5×4cm, dull red. SW Pacific (Lord Howe Is.). Z9.

H. canterburyana (C. Moore & F. Muell.) Wendl. & Drude. →*Kentia.*

He Huckleberry *Lyonia ligustrina.*

Heimerliodendron Skottsb. = *Pisonia.*

Heimia Link. Lythraceae. 3 glab. subshrubs or perennials. Br. tetragonal. Fls solitary, axill. or in 3-forked pan.; cal. campanulate, lobes alternating with horn-like appendages; pet. 5–7; sta. 10–18. S US to Arg. Z8.

H. salicifolia (HBK) Link. Decid. shrub to 3m. Lvs linear-lanceolate. Fls 1.25cm diam., solitary; pet. to 1.7cm, yellow, ovate. S US, C & S Amer.

Helenium L. SNEEZEWEED. Compositae. c40 ann., bienn. or perenn. herbs. St. erect, simple or branched, terete to strongly winged. Cap. radiate or discoid, solitary or in a corymb, long-pedunculate; involucre globose to hemispheric; ray flts yellow, tinged red or red-brown to dark orange at the base; disc flts yellow to yellow-green, sometimes with brown, red-brown or purple lobes. Americas.

H. amarum (Raf.) H. Rock. BITTERWEED; BITTER SNEEZEWEED. Ann., to 70cm, slender, strongly smelling. Lvs to 4cm, lowest lvs oblanceolate, pinnatisect, upper lvs linear-filiform, clustered, sessile. Cap. to 2.5cm diam., many, shortly pedunculate, in a corymb; ray flts golden yellow, c8, spreading to reflexed. SE US.

H. autumnale L. SNEEZEWEED. Perenn., to 1.5m. Lvs to 15×4cm, linear-lanceolate to elliptic or ovate-lanceolate, usually serrate, decurrent, subglabrous, lower lvs often decid. Cap. to 5cm diam., clustered in a corymb; ray flts 10–20, yellow to bright yellow, soon reflexed. N Amer. 'Grandicephalum': to 150cm; ray flts yellow; heads large. 'Magnificum': to 60cm; pure yellow. 'Nanum Praecox': dwarf form; disc flts yellow. 'Peregrinum': mahogany with yellow borders. 'Praecox': yellow, brown and red; early. 'Pumilum': to 75cm; yellow. 'Pumilum Magnificum': to 90cm; pale yellow. 'Rubrum': dark red. 'Superbum': to 150cm bright yellow, borders wavy. See below for further cvs. Z3.

H. bigelovii A. Gray. Perenn., to 90cm. Basal lvs to 22×5cm, oblanceolate to linear-lanceolate, entire, petiolate, amplexicaul, glab. or sparsely pubesc.; upper lvs reduced, sessile, decurrent. Cap. 1 to few, long-pedunculate, to 6cm diam.; ray flts 13–30, yellow, reflexed. Summmer–autumn. Calif., Oreg. 'Aurantiacum': ray flts, gold. 'The Bishop' ('Superba'): clear yellow. Z7.

H. bolanderi A. Gray. Perenn., to 60cm. Basal lvs to 16×4cm, oblanceolate to obovate, petiolate, broadly amplexicaul, decurrent; st. lvs lanceolate, oblong or ovate, sessile. Cap. usually solitary, to 8cm diam.; ray flts 8–13, yellow or brown-purple, or 0. Summer–autumn. Calif., Oreg. Z8.

H. flexuosum Raf. Erect perenn., to 90cm. Basal lvs to 22×5cm, linear-lanceolate to oblanceolate, entire to pinnatifid, slightly dentate, densely pubesc. to glabrate, withering before anthesis, st. lvs linear-lanceolate to oblong, sessile, decurrent. Cap. to 5cm diam., few to several in a corymb; ray flts 8–13, yellow or brown-purple, or 0. Summer–autumn. E & C US. Z4.

H. grandicephalum hort. = *H. autumnale.*

H. hoopesii A. Gray. Perenn., to 1m. Lvs to 30×7cm, entire, basal lvs narrowly to broadly oblanceolate, base attenuate, broadly amplexicaul, st. lvs lanceolate. Cap. 3–8, in lax corymbs, to 8cm diam.; ray flts 13–21, orange, scarcely reflexed. Summer–autumn. SW–SC US. Z3.

H. nudiflorum Nutt. = *H. flexuosum.*

H. polyphyllum Small = *H. flexuosum.*

H. puberulum DC. ROSILLA. Ann. or short-lived perenn., to 1.5m. Lvs to 15×4cm, entire, minutely pubesc., decurrent, basal lvs petiolate, soon withering, st. lvs lanceolate-oblong to linear, sessile. Cap. to 1.5cm diam.; ray flts 5–10, inconspicuous, reflexed. Summer–autumn. SW US. Z8.

H. cvs. Height 60–150cm, with colours from yellow to red. Taller selections include the 150cm yellow 'Sonnenwunder', the gold, brown-centred 'Goldrausch', 'Zimbelstern' with wavy borders, and the brown-red 120cm 'Wonadonga' and 'Margot'; the 120cm 'Flammenrad' and 'Riverton Beauty' are yellow with red edges and eyes. Cvs of normal habit include the gold 'Butterpat', 'Waltraut', 'Bressingham Gold' and the bronze to crimson 'Moerheim Beauty', 'Goldlackzwerg', 'Baudirektor Linne', 'Bruno' and 'Wonadonga'. Smaller cvs include the yellow 'Aurantiacum', the gold and copper 'Wyndley', the red-brown 'Kupferzwerg' and the soft mahogany 'Crimson Beauty'. Z5.

H. pumilum Willd. = *H. autumnale.*

H. tenuifolium Nutt. = *H. amarum.*

→*Actinella* and *Gaillardia.*

Heliabravoa Backeb.

H. chende (Roland-Goss.) Backeb. = *Polaskia chende.*

Heliamphora Benth. SUN PITCHER. Sarraceniaceae. 6 carnivorous perenn. herbs. Lvs in basal rosette or ± cauline, pitcher-shaped, ventricose or tubular, green, often tinged red, expanded above, terminated by spoon-shaped cap with nectar-secreting glands on inner surface; paired narrow wings present to base of ventral side of pitcher. Rac. exceeding lvs, bracts green; sep. petaloid, white, 4 or 5–6, elliptic-lanceolate, nodding; cor. 0; sta. 10–20. Venez., Guyana. Z9.

H. heterodoxa Steyerm. Pitchers cauline, to 30cm, upper part of pitcher with uniform velvety indumentum or glab., cap large. Venez.

H. minor Gleason. Pitchers constricted above and below middle, usually not exceeding 7.5×1cm in cult., pubesc. in upper portion of interior, cap v. small, or 0. Venez.

H. nutans Benth. Pitchers basal, constricted above and below middle, to 20cm, green with red margins, pubesc. in upper portion of interior. Guyana.

Helianthella Torr. & A. Gray. Compositae. 8 perenn. herbs. St. leafy, simple or sparingly branched. Lvs oblong-lanceolate to ovate-lanceolate, entire, sessile. Cap. radiate, large, solitary or few, in flat-topped pan.; ray flts yellow, disc flts yellow or purple-tinged. W N Amer.

H. douglasii Torr. & A. Gray = *H. uniflora* var. *douglasii.*

H. parryi A. Gray. To 50cm. Lvs to 12cm, spathulate to lanceolate, upper lvs much reduced. Cap. solitary or few; ray flts to 2cm; disc flts yellow. Summer. SC US. Z8.

H. quinquenervis (Hook.) A. Gray. To 5m. Lvs to 50cm, ovate- to oblong-lanceolate, acuminate, tapering to a petiole-like base. Cap. term., solitary or few, axillary, nodding; ray flts to 4cm, disc flts yellow. Summer–autumn. C US, Mex. Z4.

H. uniflora (Nutt.) Torr. & A. Gray. To 1.2m. Lvs to 10cm, ovate- to elliptic-lanceolate, pubesc., sessile or short-petioled. Cap. scapose, upward-facing, usually solitary, occas. few in cymose clusters; disc flts pale yellow. Mont. to Colorado. Z3. var. *douglasii* (Torr. & A. Gray) A. Weber. Lvs sessile, glab. or sparsely hairy on veins beneath. Oreg. Z6.

→*Helianthus.*

Helianthemum Mill. ROCK ROSE; SUN ROSE. Cistaceae. 110 everg. or semi-everg. shrublets. Lvs opposite and decussate. Infl. a racemose cyme, often secund; fls short-lived; sep. 5, ovate to oblong; pet. 5, silky, obovate-orbicular; sta. many. Mid spring–late summer. Americas, Eur., Medit., N Afr., Asia Minor to C Asia. Z7 unless specified.

H. algarvense (Sims) Dunal = *Halimium ocymoides.*

H. alpestre (Jacq.) DC. = *H. oelandicum* ssp. *alpestre.*

H. alyssoides (Lam.) Vent. = *Halimium alyssoides.*

H. appeninum (L.) Mill. Soft subshrub to 50cm. St. grey to white-pubesc. Lvs 0.8–3cm, ellitpic-oblong to linear, grey to white-pubesc., often green above, revolute. Fls to 2.8cm diam;

pet. white, yellow at base. Late spring–mid summer. Eur., Asia Minor. var. *roseum* (Jacq.) Schneid. Lvs green, glab. above. Fls pink. Late spring–mid summer. NW It. Z6.

H. bicknellii Fern. Main st. simple, flowering st. branching. Lvs 2–3cm, linear-oblong to oblanceolate or elliptic. Fls 1.5–2cm diam.; pet. yellow, sometimes 0. Late spring–mid summer. N Amer.

H. canadense (L.) Michx. FROSTWEED. Perenn. to 50cm, br. sparsely, pubesc. Lvs to 2.5cm, linear-oblong to oblanceolate or elliptic, tomentose beneath. Fls to 2.5cm diam., yellow, sometimes 0. Late spring–mid summer. E US.

H. canum (L.) Baum. Variable procumbent shrub. St. 4–30cm. Lvs 3cm, ovate-lanceolate to elliptic, linear or lanceolate, green to grey-pubesc. above, grey-tomentose beneath. Fls to 2cm diam.; pet. yellow. Mid spring–late summer. S Eur., N Afr. Z6.

H. chamaecistus Mill. = *H. nummularium.*

H. cinereum (Cav.) Pers. Dwarf shrub, st. usually loosely tufted; br. erect. Lvs ovate to lanceolate, cordate or rounded at base, green, glab. to grey-tomentose throughout. Fls yellow. Mid spring–late summer. Medit.

H. corymbosum Michx. Grey-pubesc. subshrub to 30cm. Lvs to 2cm, oblong-lanceolate, grey-pubesc. or glab. above, slightly revolute. Fls yellow. Early spring–mid summer. SE US.

H. croceum (Desf.) Pers. Variable, compact shrub to 30cm; st. erect or procumbent. Lvs 0.5–2cm, suborbicular to linear-lanceolate, rather fleshy, stellate-pubesc. or with sparse simple hairs above, revolute. Fls to 2cm diam.; pet. white, yellow or apricot. Late spring–late summer. S Eur., N Afr.

H. glaucum Pers. = *H. croceum.*

H. globulariifolium (Lam.) Pers. = *Tuberaria globulariifolia.*

H. guttatum (L.) Mill. = *Tuberaria guttata.*

H. halimifolium (L.) Willd. = *Halimium halimifolium.*

H. hirsutum (Thuill.) Mérat = *H. nummularium* ssp. *obscurum.*

H. hirtum (L.) Mill. To 30cm; br. erect or sprawling. Lvs 0.3–2cm, elliptic to linear-lanceolate (those below usually more rounded), rather fleshy, deep green to grey above, hoary-tomentose beneath. Fls to 1.5cm diam.; pet. white or yellow. SW Eur. Z8.

H. italicum ssp. *alpestre* (Jacq.) Berger = *H. oelandicum* ssp. *alpestre.*

H. lasianthum (Lam.) Pers. = *Halimium lasianthum.*

H. libanotis Willd. in part. = *Halimium commutatum.*

H. lunulatum (All.) DC. Dwarf, tufted shrub to 20cm; br. ususally contorted, made prickly by petiole scars where bare. Lvs to 1cm, elliptic-lanceolate, obtuse, puberulent. Fls to 1.5cm diam.; pet. yellow with orange basal spot. Mid spring–late summer. S Eur.

H. majus Gray = *H. bicknellii.*

H. montanum sensu Willk. = *H. oelandicum.*

H. nitidum Clementi = *H. nummularium* ssp. *glabrum.*

H. nummularium (L.) Mill. Shrub, 5–50cm; br. procumbent or ascending. Lvs 0.5–5cm, oblong or lanceolate, ovate or orbicular, subglabrous to pubesc. above, grey-green to canescent beneath. Fls to 2.5cm diam., golden yellow, pale yellow, pink, white or orange, rarely cream. Late spring–late summer. Eur., Asia Minor. 'Amy Baring': dwarf, compact; lvs green; fls deep yellow. ssp. *glabrum* (Koch) Wilcz. Lvs subglabrous, midrib and margin sparsely pubesc.; pet. orange-yellow. C & SW Eur. ssp. *grandiflorum* (Scop.) Hayek. Lvs green, sparsely pubesc. beneath. Pet. 10–18mm, orange-yellow. C & SE Eur. ssp. *obscurum* (Čelak.) Holub. Lvs more pubesc. than in ssp. *grandiflorum.* Eur. Z5.

H. ocymoides (Lam.) Pers. = *Halimium ocymoides.*

H. oelandicum (L.) DC. Loosely tufted subshrub to 20cm. Lvs 0.6–1cm, oblong-lanceolate to lanceolate, mid to deep green, glab. or pubesc. Fls to 0.8cm diam.; pet. yellow. Late spring–mid summer. Eur. ssp. *alpestre* (Jacq.) Breistr. Compact, to 12cm. Lvs 0.6–1.8cm, lanceolate to oblanceolate, pubesc., revolute. Fls 1.5cm diam. Late spring–mid summer. C & S Eur. Z6.

H. ovatum ssp. *grandiflorum* (Scop.) Hayek = *H. nummularium* ssp. *grandiflorum.*

H. ovatum ssp. *hirsutum* Hayek = *H. nummularium* ssp. *obscurum.*

H. paniculatum Dunal = *H. cinereum.*

H. pilosum (L.) Pers. Freely branching, loosely tufted shrub to 30cm. Lvs 1–2cm, linear to linear-oblong, tomentose or thinly pubesc., green above, silvery beneath, revolute. Fls to 2.5cm diam.; pet. white with yellow basal spot. Late spring–mid summer. Medit.

H. polifolium Mill. = *H. appeninum.*

H. praecox hort. = *Tuberaria praecox.*

H. procumbens Dunal = *Fumana procumbens.*

H. pulverulentum auct. = *H. appeninum.*

H. rhodanthum Dunal = *H. appeninum* var. *roseum.*

H. rotundifolium Dunal = *H. cinereum.*

H. rubellum C. Presl. non Moench = *H. cinereum*.

H. scoparium Nutt. RUSH ROSE. Woody-based perenn. to 1m. Lvs to 2.5cm, linear, glab. to sparsely pubesc. Fls to 2.5cm diam., yellow. Early spring–mid summer. SE US.

H. × sulphureum Willd. (*H. appeninum* × *H. nummularium*). Low shrub. Lvs to 2.5cm, linear-lanceolate, green above, grey beneath, stellate-pubesc. Pet. pale yellow. Early spring-mid summer. Gdn origin.

H. tomentosum Sm. = *H. nummularium*.

H. tuberaria (L.) Mill. = *Tuberaria lignosa*.

H. umbellatum (L.) Mill. = *Halimium umbellatum*.

H. velutinum Jordan = *H. appeninum*.

H. vineale Pers. = *H. canum*.

H. violaceum Pers. = *H. pilosum*.

H. vulgare Gaertn. = *H. nummularium*.

H. vulgare var. *genuinum* Willk. in part. = *H. nummularium* ssp. *obscurum*.

H. cvs. The rock roses most frequently encountered in gardens tend to be hybrids with *H. apenninum*, *H. nummularium*, and *H. croceum* involved in their parentage. They range in fl. colour from white to dark red and have grey, green or silvery foliage. Examples are given below grouped by fl. colour. (*White*) 'Wisley White': lvs grey; fls single, pure white, with golden anth. (*Cream*) 'Snowball': lvs green; fls cream-white, with a pale yellow centre. 'The Bride': lvs silver-grey; fls cream-white, with a vivid yellow centre. (*Yellow*) 'Ben Fhada': lvs grey-green; fls golden yellow with an orange centre. 'Ben-Nevis': lvs green; fls deep buttercup-yellow, with a bronze crimson-centre. 'Golden Queen': lvs green; fls bright golden-yellow. 'Jubilee': lvs green; fls double, primrose yellow. 'Praecox': habit dense; lvs grey; fls lemon-yellow. 'Wisley Primrose': lvs pale grey-green; fls primrose-yellow, with a deep yellow centre. (*Orange*) 'Afflick': lvs green; fls deep orange-bronze, with a bronze centre. 'Ben Darg': lvs green; fls deep copper-orange, with a darker centre. 'Ben More': lvs dark green; fls vivid orange, with a darker centre. 'Fire Dragon': lvs grey-green; fls vivid orange-scarlet. 'Henfield Brilliant': lvs grey-green; fls bright orange. (*Pink*) 'Mrs Croft': lvs silver-grey; fls pink with orange flushes. 'Rhodanthe Carneum': lvs silver-grey; fls fleshy pink, with a orange centre. 'Rose of Leeswood': lvs green; fls double, rose-pink. 'Sudbury Gem': lvs grey-green; fls deep pink with a vivid red centre. 'Wisley Pink': lvs grey; fls pale pink. (*Rose to deep red*) 'Ben Hope': lvs pale grey-green; fls carmine, with deep orange centre. 'Ben Ledi': lvs dark green; fls deep, vivid rose. 'Cerise Queen': lvs green; fls double, scarlet. 'Coppernob': lvs grey-green; fls deep. shining copper, with a bronze-crimson centre. 'Jock Scott': lvs green; fls vivid, deep cherry-rose, with a darker centre. 'Mrs C.W. Earle': lvs dark green; fls double, scarlet, flushed yellow at base. 'Raspberry Ripple': lvs dark green; fls deep red-pink, tipped white. 'Red Dragon': lvs green; fls scarlet, with a yellow centre. 'Supreme' ('Red Orient'): lvs grey-green; fls crimson. 'Watergate Rose': lvs grey-green; fls rose-crimson, flushed orange in the centre. Z6.

→*Crocanthemum* and *Heteromeris*.

Helianthocereus Backeb.
H. grandiflorus (Britt. & Rose) Backeb. = *Echinopsis huascha*.

Helianthus L. SUNFLOWER. Compositae. 70 ann. to perenn. herbs. Cap. radiate, rarely discoid, terminal, solitary or clustered; ray flts yellow or red; disc flts yellow, brown, red or purple. N & S Amer.

H. altissimus L. = *H. giganteus*.

H. angustifolius L. SWAMP SUNFLOWER. Perenn. or bienn., to 2m. Lvs to 20cm, linear to narrowly lanceolate, sessile, revolute, roughly hairy above, pubesc. beneath. Cap. c5cm diam.; ray flts golden yellow; disc flts purple, rarely yellow. Early autumn. E US to Tex. Z6.

H. annuus L. COMMON SUNFLOWER. Stout, often giant ann., to 5m. Lvs to 40cm, broad-ovate to cordate, acute, coarsely toothed, petiolate, rough-hairy or bristly above, rough-hairy beneath, 3-nerved. Cap. to 30cm diam.; ray flts yellow, occas. tinged red or purple; disc flts red or purple. Mid summer–early autumn. US. 'Autumn Beauty': to 1m; fls sulphur with copper tint. 'Californicus': fls double. 'Citrinus': fls single, primrose yellow. Colour Fashion Hybrids: to 2m; fls single, yellow, bronze, red and purple; seed race. 'Flore Pleno': fls double. 'Italian White': to 1.5m; fls pale primrose-yellow. 'Mars': to 2m; fls yellow with dark brown disc. 'Nanus': dwarf; fls double. 'Purpureus': heads small, fls claret. 'Russian Giant': to 3.5m; heads v. large to 25cm diam.; fls single, yellow. 'Teddy Bear': sturdy dwarfs to 90cm; cap. large, to 13cm diam.; fls double, bright yellow. The so-called 'confectionery sunflowers' include 'Grey Stripe', 'Hopi Black Dye', 'Mammoth Russian' and 'Sundak'. Oil-seed sunflowers include 'Peredovik', 'Progress' and 'Rostov'.

H. argophyllus Torr. & A. Gray. Ann. to 3.5m. Lvs to 25cm, ovate to ovate-lanceolate, usually entire, tomentose, petiolate. Cap. to 3cm diam.; ray flts yellow; disc flts dark violet. Late summer–early autumn. Tex., Flor.

H. atrorubens L. DARK-EYE SUNFLOWER. Perenn. to 2m. Lvs crowded toward base, to 30cm, ovate to oblong-lanceolate, serrate to crenate, hairy, esp. on main veins beneath, winged-petiolate. Cap. to c9cm diam.; ray flts orange-yellow; disc flts maroon. Late summer–early autumn. SE US. 'Gullick's Variety': vigorous; fls small. 'Monarch': to 2m, heads large, to 15cm diam.; fls semi-double, gold. Z7.

H. bolanderi A. Gray. Ann., to 1.5m. Lvs to 15cm, linear-lanceolate to ovate, base attenuate, entire or dentate, petiolate, sparsely hairy. Cap. 1.5–2.5cm diam.; ray flts yellow; disc flts maroon or yellow. Mid summer–early autumn. Oreg., Calif. Z7.

H. californicus DC. Perenn., to 3m. Lvs to 20cm, lanceolate, entire or sparsely serrate, hispid. Cap. to 9cm diam.; ray flts yellow; disc flts yellow. Summer–early autumn. Calif. Z8.

H. ciliaris DC. BLUE WEED. Perenn., to 1m. Lvs to 8cm, lanceolate, entire, slightly toothed or shallowly lobed, often ciliate, glab. to sparsely hispid, mostly sessile. Cap. to c5cm diam.; ray flts inconspicuous, rarely 0; disc flts red. Summer–autumn. Tex. to Ariz., N Mex. Z8.

H. coloradensis Cockerell = *H. nuttallii* ssp. *nuttallii*.

H. cucumerifolius Torr. & A. Gray = *H. debilis* ssp. *cucumerifolius*.

H. debilis Nutt. Ann., to 2m. Lvs to 14cm, deltoid-ovate to lanceolate-ovate, entire to deeply serrate, glab. to hairy. Cap. to 6cm diam.; ray flts yellow; disc flts deep red-purple. Summer. Flor., Tex. 'Dazzler': cap. rich chestnut tipped orange. 'Excelsior': cap. zoned with chestnut-red and yellow. ssp. *cucumerifolius* (Torr. & A. Gray) Heiser. CUCUMBERLEAF SUNFLOWER. To 1m. St. mottled purple, coarsely hairy beneath. Lvs to 10cm, serrate, undulate. Cap. to 16cm diam. Spring–mid spring. SE Tex.

H. decapetalus L. THIN LEAF SUNFLOWER. Often bushy perenn., to 2m. Lvs to 20cm, lanceolate to broadly ovate, slightly rough-hairy, winged-petiolate. Cap. to 8cm diam.; ray flts light yellow; disc flts yellow. Summer–early autumn. C & SE US. 'Soleil d'Or': cap. semi-double, ray flts quilled. 'Flore-Pleno' ('Grand-iflorus', 'Maximus'): cap. large; ray flts pointed. Z5.

H. divaricatus L. Perenn., to 1.5m. Lvs to 15cm, lanceolate to ovate, base rounded, acuminate, slightly toothed, scabrous beneath, sessile or shortly petiolate. Cap. to c25cm diam.; ray flts yellow-orange; disc flts yellow. Summer–mid autumn. E US, Okl., Canada. Z4.

H. × doronicoides Lam. (*H. giganteus* × *H. mollis*.) Perenn., to 2m. Lvs to 15cm, ovate to oblong, entire or few-toothed, sessile. Cap. to c20cm diam.; ray flts yellow, disc flts yellow. Early autumn. E & NE US. Z4.

H. exilis A. Gray = *H. bolanderi*.

H. giganteus L. GIANT SUNFLOWER. Perenn., to 4m. Lvs to 20cm, lanceolate-ovate to lanceolate, shallowly toothed, slightly hairy, lower long-petiolate. Cap. to c8cm diam.; ray flts pale yellow; disc flts yellow. Summer–mid autumn. C & SE US to Canada. Z4.

H. giganteus Cav. = *Viguiera excelsa*.

H. gracilentus L. Perenn. to 2m, woody below. Lvs to 15cm, lanceolate to lanceolate-ovate, hispid, entire or few-toothed, sessile or shortly petiolate. Cap. to 7cm diam.; ray flts yellow or red; disc flts yellow. Late spring–mid autumn. Calif. Z8.

H. grosse-serratus Martens. Perenn., to 5m with a woody base. Lvs to 20cm, lanceolate, coarsely to shallowly toothed, base tapering to short petiolate, scabrous above, puberulent beneath. Cap. to c10cm diam.; ray flts, bright yellow; disc flts yellow. Autumn. New Engl. to S Dak. & Tex. Z4.

H. hirsutus Raf. Perenn., to 3m. Lvs to 20cm, narrowly lanceolate or ovate, acuminate, petiolate, rough above, hirsute beneath. Cap. to c7cm diam.; ray flts yellow; disc flts yellow. Summer–mid autumn. Penn. to Minn., Georgia, Mex. Z4.

H. × laetiflorus Pers. (*H. pauciflorus* × *H. tuberosus*.) Perenn., to 2m. Lvs to 30cm, lanceolate to narrowly ovate, tapered at both ends, occas. toothed, sessile to shortly petiolate. Cap. c10cm diam.; ray flts bright yellow; disc flts yellow. Autumn. C US. 'Miss Mellish': fls large, semi-double, clear yellow. 'Morning Sun': to 2m; semi-double, yellow. 'Semiplenum': semi-double, orange-yellow. Z4.

H. laevigatus Torr. & A. Gray. Perenn., to 2m. Lvs to 18cm, lanceolate, acuminate, narrowed to a short petiole, usually entire, often glab. Cap. c5.5cm diam.; ray flts yellow; disc flts yellow. Early autumn. Penn. to W Virg., to N Carol. Z5.

H. lenticularis Douglas = *H. annuus*.

H. macrophyllus Willd. = *H. strumosus*.

H. maximilianii Schräd. Perenn., to 3m. Lvs numerous, to 20cm, lanceolate, acuminate, occas. falcate, base tapered to a short winged petiole, or sessile, glaucous, scabrous, shallowly toothed or entire. Cap. *c*10cm diam.; ray flts golden-yellow; disc flts yellow. Autumn. Missouri & Tex. to S Canada. Z4.

H. microcephalus Torr. & A. Gray. Perenn., to 3m. Lvs to 15cm, lanceolate to ovate, acuminate, scabrous above, grey-pubesc. with resin dots beneath, denticulate, petiolate. Cap. to *c*4cm diam.; ray flts pale to golden yellow; disc flts yellow. Late summer–early autumn. NJ to S Mich. & SE US. Z4.

H. mollis Lam. ASHY SUNFLOWER. Rhizomatous perenn., to 2m. Lvs to 15cm, ovate to lanceolate or oblong, acute to acuminate, base sometimes cordate, sessile or sometimes clasping, slightly toothed, scabrous and densely hairy above, grey-pubesc. beneath. Cap. *c*10cm diam.; ray flts yellow; disc flts yellow. Late summer–early autumn. New Engl. to Georgia & Tex. Z4.

H. × multiflorus L. (*H. annuus × H. decapetalus*.) Perenn., to 2m, resembling *H. decapetalus* but cap. to 12cm diam., flts golden yellow, ray flts in 1 or 2 series, and disc flts occas. 0, replaced by ray flts. Only known in cult. 'Capenoch Star': to 1.5m; single, lemon-yellow. 'Flore Pleno': double, light gold. 'Loddon Gold': to 1.5m; double, vivid gold. 'Maximus': heads large; flts gold. 'Maximus Flore Pleno': heads large; double, gold. 'Meteor': to 150cm; semi-double, deep gold. 'Soleil d'or': vigorous to 180cm; semi-double, dark gold. 'Triomphe de Gand': to 1.5m; semi-double, gold. 'Triomphe von Gent': to 1.5m; double, gold. Z5.

H. nuttallii Torr. & A. Gray. Perenn., to 4m. Lvs to 20cm, lanceolate to nearly ovate, entire or toothed, smooth or rough above, densely hispid beneath. Cap. to *c*9cm diam.; ray flts orange-yellow; disc flts yellow. Rocky Mts. Z5. ssp. *nuttallii*. To 3m. St. glab. or rough. Lvs rough. Cap. few to numerous. Rocky Mts, Canada. Z5. ssp. *parishii* (A. Gray) Heiser. To 4m. St. glab. to densely hairy. Lvs occas. densely tomentose beneath, often hispid above, shallowly toothed, ± sessile. Cap. numerous. S Calif. Z8.

H. occidentalis Riddell. Perenn., to 2m. Lvs mostly toward base, to 20cm, oblong-lanceolate to ovate, sparsely toothed, rough to pilose, upper lvs much reduced. Cap. to *c*6cm diam.; ray flts, orange-yellow; disc flts yellow. Summer–early autumn. Minn. to Ohio, Flor. and Tex. Z4.

H. orygalis DC. = *H. salicifolius*.

H. parishii A. Gray = *H. nuttallii* ssp. *parishii*.

H. parviflorus Bernh. = *H. microcephalus*.

H. pauciflorus Nutt. Perenn., to 2m. Lvs to 25cm, lanceolate to narrowly ovate, entire or serrate, shortly hispid, subsessile or petiolate. Cap. to *c*9cm diam.; ray flts yellow; disc flts red-purple, rarely yellow. Summer. US. Z4.

H. petiolaris Nutt. PRAIRIE SUNFLOWER. Ann., to 2m. Lvs to 25cm, deltoid-ovate to lanceolate, entire or shallowly toothed, hispid, long-petiolate. Cap. to 8cm diam.; flts red-purple, rarely yellow. Summer–mid autumn. C to W US. Z4.

H. pumilis Nutt. Perenn., to 1.5m. Lvs to 15cm, ovate to lanceolate, entire or toothed, scabrous, ash-green, petiolate. Cap. to *c*8cm diam.; ray flts, pale yellow; disc flts yellow. Mid summer–early autumn. Rocky Mts, Colorado. Z3.

H. resinosus Small. Perenn., to 3m. Lvs to 20cm, lanceolate or rarely ovate, entire or toothed, scabrous, hispid, resin-dotted, ± sessile. Cap. *c*8.5cm diam.; ray flts light to golden yellow; disc flts yellow. Summer–early autumn. SE US. Z8.

H. rigidus (Cass.) Desf. = *H. pauciflorus*.

H. salicifolius A. Dietr. Perenn., to 3m. Lvs to 20cm, pendent, narrow-linear to lanceolate, slightly hairy, sessile. Cap. numerous, to *c*7.5cm diam.; ray flts golden yellow; disc flts purple, rarely yellow. Autumn. SC US. 'Lemon Queen': to 135cm; st. sturdy; several, single, gold. Z4.

H. scaberrimus Benth. non Elliott = *H. bolanderi*.

H. scaberrimus Elliott. non Benth. = *H. × laetiflorus*.

H. sparsifolius Elliott = *H. atrorubens*.

H. strumosus L. Rhizomatous perenn., to 2m. Lvs to 18cm, linear-lanceolate to ovate, acuminate, tapering to short petiole, dentate or entire, roughly hairy above, hispid to glab. beneath. Cap. to 11cm diam., many; ray flts deep yellow; disc flts yellow. Summer–early autumn. N Amer. Z4.

H. tomentosus Michx. non auctt. = *H. tuberosus*.

H. tomentosus sensu auctt. mult. = *H. resinosus*.

H. tuberosus L. JERUSALEM ARTICHOKE. Stout perenn., to 3m, with large irregular tubers. Lvs to 30cm, oblong-lanceolate to ovate, base occas. cordate, roughly hairy above, strigose beneath, toothed, winged-petiolate. Cap. to *c*10cm diam.; ray flt deep yellow; disc flts yellow. Autumn. Canada, SE US. Z4.

H. tubiformis Jacq. = *Tithonia tubiformis*.

H. uniflorus Nutt. = *Helianthella uniflora*.

Helichrysum Mill. EVERLASTING FLOWER. Compositae. *c*500 ann., bienn. and perenn. herbs, subshrubs and shrubs, often gland. Cap. radiate or discoid, solitary, or several often in a corymb; phyllaries in few to many, imbricate series, rigid, scarious, white or variously coloured; flts few to numerous, usually yellow. Warm OW, esp. S Afr. and Aus.

H. acuminatum DC. ORANGE EVERLASTING; ALPINE EVERLASTING. Perenn. herb to 30cm. Lvs 5–10cm, narrowly oblong to obovate, mucronate, base rounded, scabrous, gland., ciliate. Cap. to 5cmm diam., discoid, solitary, term.; phyllaries rigid, glossy deep gold to orange, often tinged brown or red. Spring–summer. SE Aus. Z9.

H. album N.E. Br. Perenn. herb to 20cm. Lvs in rosettes, to 6cm, obovate, lanate; st. lvs smaller, oblanceolate, tomentose. Cap. campanulate, to 4cm diam.; phyllaries in *c*11 series, loosely imbricate, white glossy, base crimson. Winter–spring. S Afr. (Natal, Les.). Z10.

H. alveolatum hort. = *H. splendidum*.

H. ambiguum (Pers.) C. Presl. Woody perenn. to 60cm; st. angular. Lvs to 6cm, oblong-spathulate to spathulate, white-tomentose, revolute. Cap. to 7cm diam., in a terminal corymb; phyllaries sometimes sparsely lanate at base, yellow, scarious. Spain (Balearic Is.). Z9.

H. anatolicum Boiss. = *H. plicatum*.

H. angustifolium (Lam.) DC. = *H. italicum*.

H. antennaria (DC.) F. Muell. ex Benth. = *Ozothamnus antennaria*.

H. anthemoides Sieb. ex Spreng. = *Helipterum anthemoides*.

H. apiculatum (Labill.) DC. YELLOW BUTTONS; COMMON EVERLASTING FLOWER. Perenn. to 60cm. Lvs to 4cm, oblanceolate, thick, grey-green- or silver-tomentose, apiculate. Cap. to 1.5cm diam., several to many, in term. clusters; phyllaries to 1cm, yellow or golden, outer scarious, partly enveloped in woolly-arachnoid hairs. Spring–summer. Aus. Z9.

H. arenarium (L.) Moench. YELLOW EVERLASTING FLOWER. Suffretescent perenn. to 30cm, grey-white lanate. Lvs to 7cm, broadly spathulate, to obovate-oblong, petiolate, white-tomentose. Cap. to 5cm diam. in loose corymbs; phyllaries yellow to red-orange. Summer. Eur. Z4.

H. argyrophyllum DC. Prostrate, mat-forming shrub, silver-white and rarely glossy tomentose. Lvs to 3cm, obovate or obovate-spathulate, obtuse, recurved, base attenuate, semi-amplexicaul. Cap. solitary or few in lax corymbs, to 20cm across; phyllaries lemon yellow, outer golden brown. Summer–autumn. S Afr. Z9.

H. argyrosphaerum DC. Prostrate or decumbent perenn. herb to 30cm; st. leafy, thinly tomentose. Lvs to 2.5cm, spathulate to oblanceolate, subacute, mucronate, thinly grey-tomentose. Cap. to 1cm diam., solitary or in corymbs, subglobose; phyllaries glossy-silver, increasingly pink-tinged inwards. Spring–summer. S Afr. Z9.

H. arwae J.R.I. Wood. Densely caespitose subshrub to 50cm; st. woody, prostrate, branched. Lvs to 1cm, linear-oblanceolate, white-sericeous-lanate. Cap. to 2cm diam., solitary; phyllaries in many series, white above, purple-red beneath. Spring. Yemen. Z9.

H. asperum (Thunb.) Hilliard & B.L. Burtt. Subshrub, to 40cm; st. tangled, grey-tomentose. Lvs to 1.5cm, linear, acute or obtuse, sessile, thinly white-tomentose or subglabrous, sometimes glandular-hispid, strongly revolute. Cap. to *c*5mm diam., solitary or 2–4 in small clusters, cylindric; phyllaries arachnoid, inner phyllaries light gold-brown, often tinged red beneath. Spring–summer. S Afr. Z9.

H. aureum (Houtt.) Merrill. Perenn. herb to 40cm. Lvs to 3cm, narrowly or broadly elliptic-spathulate, obtuse to subacute, amplexicaul, glandular-setose, sometimes tomentose. Cap. solitary or to 6 in corymbs, to *c*4cm diam.; phyllaries shiny, bright yellow, tinged pale brown, occas. white. Summer, autumn, winter. S Afr., Zimb., Angola. Z9.

H. aware hort. = *H. italicum*.

H. baccharoides F. Muell. = *Ozothamnus hookeri*.

H. baxteri Cunn. FRINGED EVERLASTING; WHITE EVERLASTING. Perenn. herb to 40cm. Lvs to 2cm, narrowly linear, revolute, white-tomentose, becoming dark green and glab. Cap. solitary, term., to 4cm diam.; phyllaries numerous, golden-brown, middle phyllaries white. Autumn–winter. Aus. Z9.

H. bellidioides (Forst. f.) Willd. Perenn. herb to 20cm; st. prostrate, rooting. Lvs to 6mm, orbicular, mucronate, cuneate, amplexicaul, arachnoid beneath. Cap. to 3cm diam., solitary; phyllaries linear, papery, white. Autumn–winter. NZ. Z7.

H. bellidioides hort. = *H. bellidioides*.

H. bracteatum (Vent.) Andrews. STRAWFLOWER; GOLDEN EVERLASTING; YELLOW PAPER DAISY. Ann. or perenn. herb to 1.5m. Lvs to 12cm, oblong-lanceolate, acuminate, flat, shortly petiolate, glab. or subglabrous. Cap. solitary, to 7cm diam.; phyllaries brown to deep golden. Spring–autumn. Aus., nat. Spain. Dwarf Hot Bikini: dwarf to 35cm; fls in many bright colours; seed race. Dwarf Spangle Mixed: dwarf to 30cm, wide colour range; improved selection of Bright Bikinis: fls in sulphur, orange, rose, bronze, red, purple, yellow and white; improved 'Swiss Giant' selection. Monstrosum Series: to 1m, hardy; heads to 7cm diam.; fls double, various bright colours.

'Silvery Rose': fls light pink suffused silver. Swiss Giants Mixture: to 90cm; st. sturdy; fls colours various; seed race. Tall Splendid Mix: to 1m; fls double, colour range of red, orange, yellow, violet, pink and white.

H. buddleioides DC. Shrub to 2m, white-grey- or brown-tomentose. Lvs to 12cm, elliptic-lanceolate, acuminate, with 3–9 parallel veins, densely tomentose. Cap. to 5cm diam., many, in globose clusters and corymbs to 20cm across; phyllaries yellow. India, Sri Lanka. var. **hookerianum** (Wight & Arn.) Hook. f. Lvs with 5–9 veins v. prominent beneath. Z10.

H. candolleanum Buek. Perenn. herb to 45cm, woody toward base; st. branched, prostrate or erect. Lvs to 3.5cm, lanceolate to oblong, base narrowed, semi-amplexicaul, grey-tomentose. Cap. to 5mm diam., many, in crowded, globose, term. clusters; phyllaries glossy silver-white, inner often tinged pink or crimson. Summer–autumn. S Afr. Z9.

H. chionophilum Boiss. & Bal. Tufted, suffrutescent perenn. densely white-tomentose herb to 20cm. Basal lvs to 2cm, oblanceolate-spathulate, st. lvs linear. Cap. c1cm diam., 1–5 in loose corymbs to 2.5cm across; phyllaries yellow. Summer–autumn. Turk., Iraq, Iran. Z8.

H. chionophyllum hort. = H. chionophilum.

H. cooperi Harv. Aromatic bienn. or rarely perenn. herb, to 1.5m. Lvs to 15cm, amplexicaul, gland. or v. sparingly tomentose, st. lvs oblong-lanceolate to lanceolate, apiculate, base cordate-amplexicaul, decurrent, winged, glandular-setose rarely thinly tomentose beneath, margins often white-woolly. Cap. many, in large spreading corymbs c2.5cm diam.; phyllaries glossy bright yellow. Winter–spring. S Afr. Z9.

H. coralloides Benth. & Hook. = Ozothamnus coralloides.

H. cordatum DC. HEART-LEAVED EVERLASTING. Woody perenn., herb to 1m; st. flexuous, white-tomentose. Lvs to 10cm, linear to lanceolate or oblong, cordate, green above, white-tomentose beneath. Cap. c5mm diam., in term. clusters; phyllaries yellow or tawny, sometimes red-tinged. Summer. W Aus. Z10.

H. cotula Benth. = Hyalosperma cotula.

H. dealbatum Labill. Caespitose perenn. herb to 30cm; st. slender. Lvs mostly crowded near the base, to 3cm, broadly or narrowly lanceolate to elliptic, obtuse or acuminate, glab. above, white or silvery beneath. Cap. c4cm diam., solitary; phyllaries tinged brown or red, middle white. SE Aus. Z9.

H. depressum (Hook. f.) Benth. = Ozothamnus depressus.

H. diosmifolium (Vent.) Sweet = Ozothamnus diosmifolius.

H. doefleri Rech. f. Densely tufted perenn. herb to 10cm; st. decumbent or ascending, white-tomentose. Lvs white-tomentose, 1–3cm, oblong-spathulate to oblanceolate-spathulate to linear. Cap. c1–2cm diam., 2–4, sometimes solitary; outer phyllaries becoming erose or apically lacerate. Crete. Z8.

H. elatum A. Cunn. ex DC. TALL WHITE EVERLASTING FLOWER; WHITE PAPER-DAISY. Perenn. herb or subshrub, to 2m; st. branched, woody, white-tomentose. Lvs to 12cm, narrowly elliptic to lanceolate or ovate, petiolate, dark green and becoming glab. above, white-tomentose beneath. Cap. c4cm diam., solitary or in loose, term. clusters; phyllaries silvery-white or pink. Spring. SE Aus. Z9.

H. ericeteum W.M. Curtis = Ozothamnus ericifolius.

H. ericifolium hort. = Ozothamnus ericifolius.

H. ericoides (Lam.) Pers. = Dolichothrix ericoides.

H. felinum Less. Suffrutescent perenn. herb, to 1m; st. branched above, erect, loosely grey-white-tomentose. Lvs to 10cm, lanceolate to elliptic, acute, mucronate, spreading or deflexed, arachnoid above, becoming scabrid, grey-tomentose beneath. Cap. c1cm diam., many, subglobose, in dense round corymbs to 4cm across; phyllaries white or tinged pink. Autumn–winter. S Afr. Z9.

H. filicaule Hook. f. Perenn. herb to 30cm; st. prostrate, rooting, branched, decumbent to erect, sparsely tomentose to glab. Lvs to 1.5cm, oblong to obovate, mucronate, semi-amplexicaul, arachnoid beneath. Cap. to 1cm diam., solitary, phyllaries densely tomentose beneath. Autumn–winter. NZ. Z8.

H. foetidum (L.) Cass. Bienn. herb, to 1m; st. simple or sparingly branched at base, thick. Lvs to 12cm, elliptic, obtuse to sub-acute, mucronate, auriculate-amplexicaul, sparsely pubesc. above, thinly white-tomentose beneath. Cap. many, in large leafy corymbs to 2.5cm across; phyllaries glossy, cream, straw-coloured or brown. Summer–autumn. S Afr. Z9.

H. frigidum (Labill.) Willd. Densely tufted, mat-forming sub-shrub, to 15cm; st. much-branched, leafy, grey-white or white-tomentose to glab. Lvs to 5mm, linear-oblong, obtuse, white-tomentose. Cap. solitary, term. to 1.5cm diam., phyllaries white. Spring–summer. Corsica, Sardinia. Z8.

H. fulgidum (L. f.) Willd. = H. aureum.

H. glomeratum Klatt. Rhizomatous perenn. to 50cm; st. 1–3, erect, usually simple, loosely grey-tomentose. Lvs to 3cm, lanceolate, lanate, rarely tomentose; st. lvs smaller, erect,

imbricate. Cap. to 0.5cm diam., in crowded, rounded corymbs to 5cm across; phyllaries tipped bright yellow. Spring. S Afr. Z9.

H. grandiceps (Hook. f.) T. Kirk = Leucogenes grandiceps.

H. grandiflorum (L.) D. Don. Subshrub to 45cm; st. several, decumbent. Lvs to 10cm, obovate, becoming oblong to oblong-lanceolate, obtuse to subacute, loosely tomentose. Cap. to c8mm diam., many, campanulate, in dense term. clusters; phyllaries pale cream. Winter–spring. S Afr. (Cape Prov.). Z9.

H. graveolens (Bieb.) Sweet. Resembles H. arenarium but aromatic, basal lvs villous-lanate and distinctly 3-veined, upper lvs often apiculate. Summer–autumn. Crimea. Z7.

H. guilelmii Engl. Perenn. herb to 50cm; st. leafy, tomentose. Lvs to 10cm, reflexed, lanceolate, acuminate, decurrent, lanate beneath, upper lvs erect. Cap. to c1cm, many, in a corymb; phyllaries tinged purple. S Afr. Z9.

H. gunnii (Hook. f.) Benth. = Ozothamnus gunnii.

H. hookeri (Sonder) Druce = Ozothamnus hookeri.

H. hookerianum Wight & Arn. = H. buddleioides var. hookerianum.

H. humboldtianum Gaudich. = Pteropogon humboldtianum.

H. humile (Andrews) Less. = Edmondia pinifolia.

H. italicum (Roth) G. Don. Suffrutescent aromatic, perenn. herb to 50m; st. angled, tomentose. Lvs to 3cm, narrowly linear, sparingly tomentose to glabrescent, revolute. Cap. 2–4mm diam. in a cluster to 8cm across; phyllaries usually tomentose. Summer–autumn. S Eur. ssp. **serotinum** (Boiss.) P. Fourn. CURRY PLANT. To 40cm, 'curry-scented'. Lvs to 4cm. Cap. c4mm diam. SW Eur. Z8.

H. lanatum DC. = H. thianschanicum.

H. ledifolium (DC.) Benth. = Ozothamnus ledifolius.

H. leontopodium Hook. f. = Leucogenes leontopodium.

H. leucopsideum DC. SATIN EVERLASTING. Perenn. herb or sub-shrub, to 60cm; st. erect, much-branched. Lvs to 4cm, narrowly linear or oblong, acute, margins sinuate, revolute, dark green, glab. above, white-tomentose beneath. Cap. c5cm diam., solitary, term.; phyllaries glossy, white or tinged pink, outer sometimes pale brown. Aus. Z10.

H. lindleyi H. Eichl. Ann. herb, to 50cm; st. erect, slender, branched, glandular-hairy. Lvs 5cm, linear. Cap. to 3cm diam., solitary; phyllaries brown to pink or white. Summer–autumn. SW W Aus.

H. marginatum hort. = H. milfordiae.

H. microcephalum Cambess. = H. italicum.

H. microphyllum hort. = Plectostachys serphyllifolia.

H. milfordiae Killick. Subshrub to 15cm, cushion-forming stoloniferous; st. prostrate, leafy. Lvs to 1.5cm, obovate to sub-spathulate, densely tomentose, bract-like above, apex scarious. Cap. 4cm diam., solitary, term.; phyllaries glossy white, usually crimson-tipped or brown-tipped. Spring. S Afr. Z7.

H. milliganii Hook. f. Perenn. herb or subshrub to 50m; st. simple or branched, tomentose. Lvs to 2.5cm, oblong-ovate or lanceolate-spathulate, acute, amplexicaul, flat, fleshy, sparingly lanate, with gland. hairs, ciliate. Cap. c4cm diam., solitary, term.; phyllaries glossy, scarious, white, stramineous or crimson. Tasm. Z9.

H. molle A. Cunn. ex DC. = Helipterum molle.

H. nanum Klatt. Perenn.; herb to 30cm, stoloniferous; st. decumbent, often tomentose. Lvs rosulate, to 3.5cm; linear, stiff, erect, obtuse, amplexicaul, sericeous, revolute. Cap. c5mm diam., forming dense term. clusters to 2cm across; phyllaries translucent, outer tinged brown, inner yellow, about equalling flts. Spring. S Afr. Z9.

H. niveum (L.) Less. Dwarf shrub to 20cm; st. erect, spreading or prostrate, leafy, white-tomentose. Lvs to 0.5cm, linear, obtuse, decurrent, grey-tomentose, glabrescent or glab., revolute. Cap. to 2cm diam. in term. clusters; phyllaries caducous, white, sometimes pink. Spring. S Afr. (Cape Prov.). Z9.

H. obcordatum (DC.) F. Muell. ex Benth. Shrub, to 1.5m. Lvs to 0.5cm, obovate to obcordate, mucronate, tip reflexed, narrowing to a short slender petiole at base, flat, green and glab. above, tomentose beneath. Cap. many, in dense term. corymbs to 5cm across; phyllaries golden. SE Aus. Z9.

H. obtusifolium F. Muell. & Sonder. BLUNT EVERLASTING. Perenn. herb or subshrub, to 40cmm, much branched, silver-tomentose. Lvs to 1.5cm, narrowly linear, obtuse, slightly succulent, revolute, subglabrous above, silver-tomentose beneath. Cap. to 3cm diam., solitary, term.; phyllaries brown to white, sometimes tinged brown or pink. Winter–spring. Aus. Z9.

H. odoratissimum (L.) Sweet. Subshrub or perenn. herb to 40cm; st. often decumbent, rooting. Lvs to 8cm, linear-oblong, lanceolate or spathulate, usually obtuse, mucronate, gland. and scabrid above, usually tomentose. Cap. to 8mm diam., many, matted together at base in term. cymose clusters; phyllaries pellucid, outer pale brown, inner pale or bright yellow. S Afr.,

Moz., Zimb., Malawi. Z10.

H. orientale (L.) Gaertn. Subshrub to 30cm; st. erect, densely lanate. Lvs to 6cm, oblong-spathulate, obtuse, petiolate, flat, white-lanate. Cap. 1cm diam. in term. corymbs to 8cm across. Summer. Greece, Aegean. Z7.

H. pachyrhizum Harv. = *H. candolleanum*.

H. petiolare Hilliard & B.L. Burtt. LIQUORICE PLANT. Climbing or spreading shrub to 1m; st. slender, branched, thinly grey-tomentose, leafy. Lvs to 3.5cm, subrotund to broadly ovate or rhomboid-elliptic, rounded at apex, truncate, subcordate or cuneate at base, grey-tomentose, petiole sometimes winged. Cap. *c*7mm diam., many, in loose term. corymbs; phyllaries grey-tomentose beneath, opaque white. Winter. S Afr. 'Dargan Hill Monarch': to 1m; fls large, gold; hardy. 'Limelight' ('Aurea'): lvs lime-green. 'Roundabout': dwarf and compact to 15cm; lvs variegated. 'Skynet': to 1m; fls large, cream washed with pink. 'Variegatum': lvs variegated grey and cream. Z10.

H. petiolatum hort. = *H. petiolare*.

H. plicatum DC. Perenn. herb to 40cm; st. erect or ascending, gland. Lvs to 4cm, oblong-spathulate to linear-lanceolate, viscid, gland., lanate on veins beneath, ciliate. Cap. to *c*8mm diam. in dense terminal corymbs 2–6cm across; phyllaries glossy yellow. Summer. SE Eur. Z7.

H. plicatum hort. = *H. stoechas* ssp. *barrelieri*.

H. plumeum Allan. Shrub to 60cm; st. stout, branched, leafy, tomentose. Lvs to *c*0.6cm, closely imbricate, adpressed, broadly triangular, obtuse, tawny-lanate. Cap. *c*6mm diam., solitary, term.; phyllaries scarious, glossy above. NZ. Z8. Similar to *Ozothamnus selago*.

H. praecurrens Hilliard. Densely caespitose, mat-forming, perenn. herb to 15cm. Lvs to 1cm, closely imbricate, linear to narrowly lanceolate, sericeous, silver-green. Cap. to 1.5cm diam., solitary, term.; phyllaries pellucid, v. pale brown to white or tinged pink, opaque. Autumn–winter. S Afr. (Natal), Les. Z10.

H. purpurascens (DC.) W.M. Curtis = *Ozothamnus purpurascens*.

H. retortum (L.) Willd. Suffrutescent perenn. herb to 50cm; st. prostrate. Lvs to 3cm, imbricate, oblong, oblanceolate or obovate, mucronate, often somewhat recurved, hooked, sericeous. Cap. to 4cm diam., solitary, terminal, phyllaries golden, sometimes tinged pink-red. Summer–early winter. S Afr. (Cape Prov.). Z9.

H. rosmarinifolium (Labill.) Steud. ex Benth. = *Ozothamnus rosmarinifolius*.

H. rosmarinifolium hort. non (Labill.) Steud. ex Benth. = *Ozothamnus thyrsoideus*.

H. rupestre (Raf.) DC. Subshrub or perenn., to 60cm; st. angular, tomentose. Lvs to 8cm, linear to lanceolate, or oblanceolate, white-tomentose, revolute. Cap. *c*8mm diam. in a dense term. cluster 3–7cm across; phyllaries scarious, yellow. W & C Medit. Z8.

H. rupicola DC. Perenn. herb or subshrub to 80cm; st. ± erect, branched, tomentose. Lvs 5cm, narrowly lanceolate, pale green above, densely tomentose beneath, sinuate, revolute. Cap. *c*2cm diam., solitary, term., yellow, about 2cm across. E Aus. Z9.

H. sandfordii Hook. f. = *Pteropogon humboldtianum*.

H. scorpioides (Poir.) Labill. BUTTON EVERLASTING. Suffrutescent perenn. herb to 40cm; st. ascending or erect, usually simple, lanate and minutely gland. Lvs to 6cm, oblanceolate to linear, apiculate, sessile, grey-green, scabrid above, woolly beneath, gland. Cap. to 2.5cm diam., solitary, terminal; outer phyllaries brown, tomentose, inner yellow, wrinkled, with a long green, woolly claw. Autumn. SE Aus., Tasm. Z9.

H. scutellifolium Benth. = *Ozothamnus scutellifolius*.

H. secundiflorum Wakef. = *Ozothamnus secundiflorus*.

H. selaginoides (Sonder & F. Muell.) F. Muell. ex Benth. = *Ozothamnus selaginoides*.

H. selago (Hook. f.) T. Kirk = *Ozothamnus selago*.

H. semipapposum (Labill.) DC. CLUSTERED EVERLASTING. Perenn. herb or subshrub to 1m. Lvs to 3.5cm, narrowly linear, aromatic, green, subglabrous above, white-tomentose beneath, revolute. Cap. 5mm diam. in dense term. corymbs 3–9cm across, and smaller term. clusters along st.; phyllaries golden. Spring–summer. Aus. Z9.

H. serotinum Boiss. = *H. italicum* ssp. *serotinum*.

H. sesamoides (L.) Willd. = *Edmondia sesamoides*.

H. sessile DC. Cushion-forming shrub, to 10cm; st. densely tufted, clothed with persistent lvs at base. Lvs closely imbricate, to 4cm, narrowly oblong or narrowly elliptic. Cap. to *c*8mm diam., solitary or to 12, terminal; phyllaries silvery, sometimes crimson above, tips opaque white, woolly at base. Winter. S Afr. Z9.

H. sibthorpii Rouy. Caespitose perenn. to 10cm; st. decumbent or ascending, white-tomentose. Lvs to 6cm, oblong-spathulate,

white-tomentose, upper lvs narrower. Cap. to 1.5cm diam., phyllaries white. NE Greece. Z7.

H. siculum (Spreng.) Boiss. = *H. stoechas* ssp. *barrelieri*.

H. splendidum (Thunb.) Less. Shrub to 1.5m; st. branched, leafy, thinly tomentose, glabrescent. Lvs to 6cm, linear, linear-oblong, or linear-lanceolate, semi-amplexicaul, tomentose beneath, glab. or subglabrous above, revolute. Cap. to 5mm diam., in crowded or loose, term. corymbs; phyllaries glossy, bright yellow, rarely orange. Autumn–winter. E & S Afr. Z7.

H. stoechas (L.) Moench. Perenn. herb or subshrub to 50cm; st. simple or branched, white-tomentose. Lvs to 3cm, linear to linear-spathulate, white-tomentose or lanate, sometimes aromatic, revolute. Cap. *c*7mm diam. in clusters to 3cm across; phyllaries scarious, white-glandular. Summer. S & W Eur. ssp. *barrelieri* (Ten.) Nyman Lvs usually less than 2cm, usually broadly linear to narrowly spathulate, scarcely aromatic. 'White Barn' ('Elmstead'): to 60cm; lvs felty-white; fls sulphur yellow. Z8.

H. subulifolium F. Muell. SHOWY EVERLASTING. Ann. to 50cm; st. usually simple, erect. Lvs to 12cm, subulate, glossy, glab. Cap. *c*4cm diam., solitary, term.; phyllaries brown. Spring–summer. W Aus.

H. swynnertonii S. Moore. Perenn. herb or subshrub to 20cm; st. many, branched below, ascending. Lvs to 8cm, erect, lanceolate-elliptic, acute, semi-amplexicaul, loosely grey-tomentose. Cap. *c*2cm diam., solitary, broadly campanulate; phyllaries glossy white, tinged yellow or brown. Autumn–winter. Zimb., S Afr. Z9.

H. thianschanicum Reg. Perenn. herb to 40cm, tomentose; st. erect, usually branched, leafy. Lvs to 10cm, lanceolate, st. lvs narrower. Cap. to 1cm diam., ovoid, in lat. and term. corymbs; phyllaries yellow, usually initially orange, lanate at base, hairy. Turkestan. 'Golden Baby' ('Goldkind', 'Fairy Gold'): to 30cm; lvs grey; fls gold. Z6.

H. thyrsoideum (DC.) Willis & Morris = *Ozothamnus thyrsoideus*.

H. trilineatum hort. = *H. splendidum*.

H. tumidum hort. = *Ozothamnus selago*.

H. virgineum (Sibth. & Sm.) Griseb., non DC. = *H. sibthorpii*.

H. virginicum hort. = *H. sibthorpii*.

H. viscosum Sieb. ex Spreng. Perenn. herb to 1m. Lvs to 9cm, linear to elliptical, viscid and minutely scabrous. Cap. solitary, term.; phyllaries yellow, straw-coloured or brown. SE Aus. Z9.

H. woodii N.E. Br. Shrub too 30cm; st. much branched, leafy, grey-white tomentose. Lvs to 5cm, elliptic to obovate, obtuse, tomentose. Cap. to 7mm diam. in dense, rounded, term. clusters 3–5cm across; phyllaries dull, pale straw-coloured. Summer. S Afr. (Natal). Z10.

H. woodii hort. = *H. arwae*.

H. cvs. 'Drakensberg Mountains': st. trailing; lvs tinted silver. 'Sulphur Light' ('Schwefellicht'): to 40cm; lvs tinted silver; infl. sulphur washed orange. 'Sussex Silver': to 1m; lvs small, silver. Z6.

Helicodiceros Schott ex K. Koch.
H. muscivorus (L. f.) Engl. = *Dracunculus muscivorus*.

Heliconia L. FALSE BIRD OF PARADISE; WILD PLANTAIN. Heliconiaceae. 100 large, everg. perenn. herbs, clump-forming. Habit musoid (banana-like), cannoid (canna-like), or zingiberoid (ginger-like). Pseudostems formed by overlapping sheathing lf bases. Lvs large; petiole ½ to ¾ length of blade; blade (measurement given below) usually oblong or spathulate, midrib thick. Infl. large, terminal, erect or pendulous, pedunculate, rachis straight or flexuous, often with colour of bracts; bracts 3–30 per infl., distichous or spiralling, usually large, carinate, waxy or leathery, brilliantly coloured, each enclosing few to many fls; perianth slender, cylindric, upcurved; sep. 3; pet. 3, small, ± connate. Fr. usually blue or violet, sometimes yellow, orange or red. C & S Amer., S Pacific Is. to Indon. Z10.

H. acuminata Rich. Musoid. St. 0.5–3m. Lvs 15–70cm, elliptic to narrowly elliptic or oblong, rarely sublinear. Infl. erect, 50–100cm; bracts distichous, alt. on flexuous rachis, 6–25cm, 4–6, red, orange or yellow, glab. to densely hairy; fls white, orange or yellow, usually with dark green 'eye-spots' toward apex, or olive-green with white or pale orange apices. Braz. to S Venez. and SE Peru. 'Cheri R': to 1.25m; bracts 4–6, bright orange to orange-red; fls. yellow-orange. 'Ruby': lvs and st. sometimes blotched purple-red, midrib red beneath; bracts 4–6, red to fuchsia pink; fls metallic blue or lime green tipped cream and dark blue-green. 'Taruma': bracts 5–6, deep crimson; fls. white tipped green-black and white. 'Yellow Waltz': bracts 5–6, slender, horizontal to slightly spiralled on straight rachis, yellow tinted green.

H. adeliana L. Emygdio & E. Santos = *H. bihai* 'Nappi'.

H. aemygdiana Burle-Marx. Musoid. To 4m. Lvs oblong, tough, often tattered. Infl. to half length of lvs, erect; rachis yellow-white; bracts 3–14, spiralling, remote, slender, spreading-reflexed, magenta; fls. green. Columbia, Boliv., SE Braz.

H. angusta Vell. Musoid. St. 1–3m. Lvs 0.25–1m, elliptic or oblong to sublinear, usually brown-woolly beneath. Infl. erect, to 70cm; bracts 6–22cm, 3–10, distant, distichous, alt., yellow or orange to vermilion or scarlet, lanceolate, usually glab.; fls white or yellow tipped green. SE Braz. 'Holiday': bracts 4–8, scarlet or vivid pink. 'Orange Christmas': petioles dark, silver-scurfy; bracts 7–11, brilliant orange becoming paler at tip. 'Yellow Christmas': bracts 5–9, rather closely ranked and somewhat ascending, chrome yellow. and green.

H. angustifolia Hook. = H. angusta.

H. aurantiaca Ghiesbr. ex Lem. Zingiberoid. St. to 2m, slender. Lvs 17–38cm, narrowly elliptic or oblong, glab. Infl. erect, distichous to loosely spiralled; peduncle 2–12cm with 1–2 leafy bracts; upper bracts 4–9cm, 2–5, broadly carinate, red to orange or yellow, sometimes tipped green or wholly green; fls pale yellow or cream to orange, often dark-tipped. S Mex. to C Costa Rica.

H. bicolor Benth. = H. angusta.

H. bihai (L.) L. WILD PLANTAIN; FIREBIRD; MACAW FLOWER; BALI-SIER. Musoid. St. 0.5–5m. Lvs 0.25–2m, oblong or oblong-oval, acuminate. Infl. erect, 45–110cm; bracts 3–15, distichous or alt. on a strongly flexuous rachis, sides red, keel yellow, margins green and/or yellow, ± glab., ovate-carinate to ovate-lanceolate; fls white, apex pale green. Summer. C & S Amer. Z9.

'Arawak': bracts 5–11, red at base, fading to yellow, tipped green. 'Aurea': rachis rather flexuous; bracts 6–12, scarlet at centre, edged gold, tipped glaucous green. 'Balisier': rachis straight, strongly erect, long; bracts 8–22, dull red edged green, rather swollen and short. 'Banana Split': rachis straight, short; bracts 6–9, slender-carinate, brown to dull red, edged yellow above. 'Chocolate Dancer': rachis short; bracts 6–9, chocolate-red edged gold above. 'Emerald Forest': to 4m; rachis short, straight; bracts slender, emerald green. 'Five A.M.': rachis straight; bracts 6–9, broadly carinate, blushing red at base fading to apricot, then orange, tipped green. 'Giant Lobster Claw': rachis straight; bracts 8–14, deep crimson to fiery red, yellow or orange at base and near edged, edged green. 'Hatchet': rachis slightly flexuous, short; bracts 4–7, sealing wax red. 'Jade Forest': rachis straight; bracts 3–10, jade green.

'Kamahameha': rachis slightly flexuous; bracts 6, fiery red edged golden yellow. 'Kuma Negro': rachis slightly flexuous; bracts 8–12, dull red, yellow at base, edged green. 'Lobster Claw One': rachis slightly flexuous; bracts ovate-carinate, deep red edged and tipped blue-green to yellow-green. 'Lobster Claw Two': rachis straight; bracts 7–13, broadly ovate-carinate, vermilion fading to orange then blue-green at edges. 'Nappi': rachis short, slightly flexuous; bracts 8–12, broadly carinate, red at base then golden, grading to lime green, edged blue-green; a taller plant with fewer, predominantly yellow bracts is also grown. 'Purple Throat': petioles maroon; rachis gently flexuous; bracts 7–10, deep red, edged green, apex and underside often rather darker and pruinose. 'Schaefer' ('Schaefer's Bihai'): rachis basically straight; bracts 6–10, deep to fiery red, edged tangerine to golden. 'Swish': lvs usually splitting into narrow seg.; rachis smoothly flexuous; bracts 5–7, deeply carinate, bright red edged yellow then (above) green, slender-tipped. 'Yellow Dancer': rachis v. straight; bracts 5–12, yellow tipped green. A hybrid between H. bihai and H. spathocircinata has been named 'Cinnamon Twist': rachis gently spiralling, erect; bracts 5–7, deep red, edged gold above and yellow within. See H. caribaea for further hybrids.

H. bourgaeana Petersen. Musoid. St. to 4.5m. Lvs to 2m, base densely glandular-hairy, midrib sometimes hairy beneath. Infl. 30–50cm, erect, straight; bracts '10–14cm, at least 12 per infl., distichous, red or pink; fls yellow tipped green. S Mex. to Hond.

H. brasiliensis Hook. = H. farinosa.

H. brevispatha Hook. = H. aurantiaca.

H. calatheaphylla Daniels & Stiles. Cannoid. To 3m. Lvs oblong-elliptic, with raised lat. veins above. Infl. erect; rachis short, slightly flexuous; bracts to 25cm, 3–4, distichous, slender-carinate, spreading, white to v. pale lilac or green-yellow; fls yellow-green. Costa Rica.

H. caribaea Lam. WILD PLANTAIN; BALISIER. Musoid. St. 2–5.5m. Lvs 60–130×40cm, oblong, abruptly acute. Infl. 20–40cm, sessile, erect; bracts to 25cm, 6–15 in 2 overlapping rows, broadly triangular, red or yellow, keels and apices sometimes green or yellow; fls white, apex green. Jam. and E Cuba to St Vincent.

'Barbados Flat': bracts 8–10, deeply carinate, closely overlapping, flattened, brick red edged pale red or yellow above. 'Black Magic': st., petioles thickly glaucous; bracts 10–40, deeply carinate, closely overlapping, garnet, pale at base, apex reflexed. 'Chartreuse': foliage waxy-pruinose beneath; bracts 11–12, sulphur yellow at base, deepening to lime green. 'Cream': lvs thickly waxy; bracts 10–22, amber spotted or flushing red; cf. 'Gold' with fewer, more graceful bracts and a stronger and more stable dark gold colouring. 'Flash': bracts 8–10, thick, deeply carinate, apex slender, outspread, base yellow, central area flushed red fading to yellow-green at edges. 'Purpurea': bracts 5–22, rigidly distichous and decreasing in size toward apex; infl. pyramidal, deep scarlet.

H. caribaea ×H. bihai: 'Carib Flame': bracts 7–9, red. 'Criswick': bracts 8–16, crimson shallowly edged green, close and diminishing toward summit of infl. 'Grand Etang': bracts 9–14, erect, narrow, closely overlapping, red fading to yellow, then green. 'Green Thumb': bracts 8–13, bright red with green at edge and beneath. 'Jacquinii': bracts 4–10, usually closely overlapping, fiery red deeply edged orange. 'Kawandri': bracts 5–7, red edged gold. 'Vermillion Lake': bracts 5–7, pale flame fading to orange, edged yellow. 'Yellow Dolly': bracts 7–11, deep, close and regular but scarcely overlapping, flushed scarlet in basal half, yellow above.

H. champneiana Griggs. Musoid. To 5.5m, st. covered with pale brown hairs. Lvs to 2m, base cordate, apex rounded, glab., midrib often red-flushed. Infl to 70cm, erect; rachis straight or slightly flexuous; bracts bright orange with red markings, to 14cm, about 9, distichous, alt., broadly ovate; fls green to yellow-white. Guat. 'Maya Blood' ('Firebird'): rachis v. straight; bracts 6–15, orange to brick-red. 'Maya Gold' ('Honduras', 'Cooper's Seed', 'Yellow Bourgaeana'): rachis straight or v. slightly flexuous; bracts outspread, gold, minutely dotted maroon, finely tipped green, not overlapping at base. 'Splash' ('Freckles', 'Lucita Wait'): rachis straight; bracts deep, pale gold flushed and mottled scarlet, slightly overlapping.

H. chartacea Lane ex Barreiros. Musoid. St. to 4m. Lvs oblong, often tattered. Infl. to 1m, pendent; rachis gently flexuous, fuschia pink; bracts to 40cm, 4–28, slender, loosely spiralling, carmine to blush pink edged lime green, somewhat glaucous; fls dark green. Guinas, Amaz. Basin. 'Sexy Pink' (sometimes listed under H. reticulata): infl. exceptionally graceful; rachis deep carmine; bracts glaucous, flamingo pink edged blue-green; superior in all respects to 'Sexy Scarlet'.

H. 'Choconiana' = H. psittacorum.

H. choconiana Wats. = H. aurantiaca.

H. collinsiana Griggs. Musoid. St. 4–6m. Lvs 1.1–2.5m. Infl. to 72cm, pendent; peduncle glab. to rusty-hairy; rachis red, flexuous; bracts 7–18 per infl., spirally arranged, yellow-pink to red and glab. inside, outside red to orange-red; fls yellow to orange, edged red. S Mex. to Nic.

H. curtispatha Petersen. Musoid. St. 6–7m. Lvs 1.9–2.3m red-hued on midrib and petiole, often waxy beneath. Infl. to 1.6m, pendent; rachis strikingly and sinuously flexuous, bracts 8.5–11cm. 20–40 per infl. in 2 rows or spirally arranged, deflexed (i.e. pointing upwards) cinnabar red, yellow-orange at base, yellow-orange to pink and rusty-pubesc. within; fls dark yellow. Nic., Costa Rica, E Panama, Colomb.

H. distans Griggs = H. latispatha.

H. farinosa Raddi. Musoid. St. 1–2.5m. Lvs 60–80cm, oval or elliptic, acute or acuminate, sometimes farinose. Infl. deltoid, erect, shortly hairy; bracts slender-carinate, distichous, alt., scarcely overlapping, red or scarlet, lanceolate; fls yellow or red. SE Braz. Closely related is H. velloziana L. Emygdio, with 7–14 vivid scarlet upcurved bracts and green sep.

H. 'Frosty' = H. metallica.

H. hirsuta L. f. Zingiberoid. St. 0.5–5m, slender. Lvs 15–50cm, ovate or oblong, hirsute beneath in upper lvs. Infl 20–70cm, erect, often hairy or cobwebby, compressed; bracts 3–9 slender, upcurved, loosely 2-ranked, sometimes rather thin, orange to red; fls yellow to orange or red, with dark green eye-spots near apex. Antilles and Belize to Boliv., N Parag. and E Braz. 'Alicia': to 2.5m; bracts 3–6 orange, short, thin; sep. orange banded green at tips. 'Costa Flores': to 2m; bracts 6–8, bright red, lobster-claw like; sep. orange banded black, tipped white. 'Halloween': to 2.75m; bracts 6–7, pale orange to deep peach, widely spaced; sep. orange banded black, tipped white. 'Pancoastal': to 2.5m; infl. sometimes arising on a distinct, non-leafy shoot; bracts 6–8, spreading, remote, sealing wax red; sep. bright yellow banded black. 'Roberto Burle Marx': to 2m; bracts 4–6, spreading, giving a triangular outline to infl., bright red to tangerine; sep. pale yellow, banded black, tipped white. 'Trinidad Red': to 2.5m; bracts 8–10, spreading to upcurved in a long-triangular configuration, tangerine at base deepening to fuschia pink; fls ascending, orange tipped dark blue-green. 'Twiggy': to 2m; bracts 3–4, thin-textured, spreading, orange deepening to scarlet; sep. large, orange, faintly tipped dark green. 'Yellow Panama': to 2.25m; bracts 5–10, yellow-green; sep. sulphur yellow tipped dark blue-green.

H. humilis hort. non Jacq. = H. stricta 'Dwarf Jamaican'.

H. humilis Jacq. = H. bihai.

H. indica Lam. Musoid. St. to 5m, stout. Lvs to 2.5m, thick paddle-shaped. Infl. to 1m, erect; bracts to 35cm, distichous, tough, carinate, spreading, often with leafy appendages, green; fls. green. Papua New Guinea. 'Spectabilis' ('Edwardus Rex', 'Illustris', 'Rubra', 'Rubricaulis'): lvs green above, purple-bronze beneath or purple-green throughout often with fine rose to white lat. striations (also on bracts). 'Striata' ('Aureo-Striata'): lvs green with green-yellow or white lat. striations (also on bracts).

H. latispatha Benth. Musoid. St. to over 3m. Lvs to 1.6×0.3m, broadly oblong-oval, sometimes edged red. Infl. 30–50cm, erect, held above lvs; bracts to 50cm, 3–20, slender carinate, spreading, remote, spiralling, not overlapping, dark red or orange to green-yellow; fls yellow, edged and tipped green. S Mex. to Colomb. and Venez. 'Red Yellow Gyro': to 6m; bracts 6–18, cinnabar red with a small zone of pale gold at base, obscurely spiralling. 'Orange Gyro': to 5m; bracts 7–17, dull orange, the lowest with a leafy appendage. The typical state has few bracts, of a fine pale cinnabar red spreading outwards from a pale gold rachis. It is sometimes named 'Distans'.

H. lennartiana Kress. Musoid. St. 2–3m. Lvs 3–4 per shoot, to 1.6m, midrib maroon above, blade green beneath, often faintly edged red. Infl. to 40cm erect; bracts to 14cm, 5–9, red with fine yellow and green marginal stripes, distichous, upturned, barely overlapping; fls white to green tipped dark green. Panama.

H. lingulata Ruiz & Pav. Musoid. St. to 3m. Lvs to 1m. Infl. 40–70cm, erect; bracts 8–32cm, 10–20 distichous, slender, spreading, glab. or almost so, yellow, purple-hued toward apex; fls pale yellow or pale green. C Peru to C Boliv. 'Fan' ('Candelabra', 'Yellow Fan'): to 5m; bracts 7–27, yellow or yellow-green deepening to amber or pale red at apex. 'Spiral Fan': to 3m; bracts to 20, yellow flushed orange, obscurely spiralling.

H. magnifica Kress. Similar to *H. pogonantha* and *H. ramonensis*, but with bracts woolly (less so than in *H. vellerigera*), more strongly decurved (i.e. upward-pointing) and distichous in groups of 6, the whole woolly. Panama.

H. mariae Hook. f. BEEFSTEAK HELICONIA. St. 4–7.5m. Lvs 1.7–2.5m. Infl. 100–150cm, pendulous, red to yellow-red, scurfy; bracts 4.5–6.5cm, 40–65, distichous and closely overlapping, broad, glossy, thick, crimson to blood red, tips usually deliquescing with age; fls pink to red. Belize and Guat. to N S Amer. 'Bushmaster' (*H. mariae* ×*H. pogonantha* var. *holerythra*): to 7m; infl. v. long, somewhat twisted; bracts dull red; fls pale yellow.

H. metallica Planch. & Lind. ex Hook. Cannoid. St. 0.5–4m. Lvs 0.25–1.4m, oblong-obovate, emerald-green above, midrib silver, metallic-purple beneath. Infl. 30–90cm, erect; bracts 5–14cm, 3–8, distichous, linear-lanceolate, green to red, cobwebby; fls rose pink to purple tipped white. Hond. to NW Colomb. and Boliv.

H. mutisiana Cuatrec. Musoid. robust. St. to 2–3m. Lvs to 1m, elliptic-oblong. Midrib hairy beneath. Infl. 100 to 130cm, pendent; peduncle silver-villous; rachis orange-red, villous, gently flexuous; bracts 10–26, distichous, alt., red-pink, broadly carinate, somewhat inflated, downy, viscid, decurved (i.e. pointing upwards); fls pale yellow. Colomb. Z9.

H. ×*nickeriensis* P. Maas & de Rooij. (*H. psittacorum* ×*H. marginata*.) Musoid. St. 1–4m, slender. Lvs 25–84cm. Infl. 20–80cm; peduncle orange, sometimes sparsely cobwebby; bracts 5–14cm, 3–7, red with a broad yellow to orange scarious margin; fls orange or yellow-orange. Guyana, Surinam.

H. nutans Woodson. Musoid. St. 1–2.5m. Lvs 50–100cm, midrib sometimes scurfy below. Infl. 60–100cm, pendent or nodding; peduncle red or red and green with golden hairs; bracts 7–11cm, 5–13 per infl., loosely spirally arranged or distichous, outside red to red-orange, glab. to puberulous; fls yellow. Costa Rica, Panama.

H. paka A.C. Sm. Musoid. St. 2–6m, stout. Lvs 2–3m, paddle-shaped. Infl. 60–70cm, erect; bracts 20–50cm, 12–16, green, loosely spiralling; fls green-white. Fiji. Z9.

H. pendula Wawra. Musoid. St. to 2m. Lvs 60–90×25–30cm undersides waxy-pruinose. Infl. pendent, waxy-farinose; bracts 30–45cm at infl. base, about 7.5cm at apex, spirally arranged, distant, not overlapping, 6–9, reflexed, pink-red; fls white. Guat. to Peru. Often grown as *H. collinsiana*. 'Bright Red': to 3m; bracts 4–9, bright red. 'Frosty': to 4m; bracts 8–10, crimson to scarlet fading to pale pink then white at apex. 'Red Waxy': to 6m; lvs v. waxy beneath; bracts 5–11, dull, glowing red.

H. peruviana hort. = *H. stricta* 'Ali'.

H. platystachys Bak. Musoid. St. 3–4m. Lvs 0.9–1.2m, oblong, waxy-pruinose beneath. Infl. 10–25cm, pendent, with a red, flexuous, brown-hairy rachis; bracts to 20cm, spirally arranged, 10–20 per infl., lanceolate, bases hairy, not overlapping, scarlet edged and tipped green or yellow; fls yellow to yellow-green. Costa Rica to N S Amer.

H. pogonantha Cuf. St. 4–7.5m. Lvs 1.2–3.3m. Infl. 120–200cm, pendent; peduncle red to yellow, slightly hairy to woolly; bracts 8–15cm, 20–55 per infl., distichous and loosely spiralling, not overlapping, red, sometimes yellow at base, stout, apex acute to acuminate; fls yellow, with golden hairs. Nic. to N S Amer. var. *holerythra* G. Daniels & Stiles. Bracts not yellow at base.

H. psittacorum L. f. PARROT'S FLOWER; PARAKEET FLOWER; PARROT'S PLANTAIN. Musoid. St. 0.5–2m, v. slender. Lvs 10–50cm, elliptic or oblong to linear; petioles often red. Infl. 12–70cm, erect; peduncle slender; bracts 4–16cm, 2–7, pink, orange or red sometimes edged yellow or green, upcurved, glab., waxy, not overlapping, slender; fls yellow-green, orange or red with a dark green apical band and tipped white. E Braz. to Lesser Antilles. 'Andromeda': bracts orange-red, waxy; sep. orange banded black. 'Black Cherry': bracts dark red to maroon; sep. green banded black. 'Choconiana': bracts olive to orange; sep. orange, banded black, tipped white. 'Fuchsia': bracts fuchsia pink; sep. sulphur yellow. 'Lady Di': bracts dark red; sep. pale yellow banded black. 'Lilian': somewhat paler than 'Lady Di'. 'Parakeet': bracts cream to pale pink; sep. yellow banded black. 'Peter Bacon': bracts green to rose pink; sep. orange banded black. 'St. Vincent Red': bracts orange-red; sep. orange. 'Sassy': bracts blue-green, glaucous tipped magenta; sep. orange banded black, tipped white. 'Shamrock': bracts emerald green at base deepening to blue-green, glaucous then violet; sep. orange banded black. 'Strawberries and cream': bracts cream-yellow to fuchsia pink; sep. pale yellow, banded black. This sp. has been crossed with *H. spathocircinata* to produce more robust plants with thicker bracts in shades of yellow, orange and fiery red. The cvs 'Alan Carter', 'Golden Torch' and 'Golden Torch Adrian' belong here.

H. ramonensis G. Daniels & Stiles. Musoid. St. 4–6m. Lvs 1–2m, sometimes maroon beneath. Infl. 100–150cm, pendent; peduncle pink to red, glab. to golden- or rusty-orange woolly; bracts 7–12cm, 20–40, distichous and spirally arranged, stout and somewhat inflated, decurved (i.e. pointing upwards), red to pink, glab. to woolly, acute to acuminate; fls white to pale pink, apex yellow and velvety. Costa Rica, Panama.

H. richardiana Miq. Musoid. St. 1–2m, slender. Lvs 25–90cm, elliptic to oblong, sometimes cobwebby on midrib beneath. Infl. 24–80cm, erect, orange or bright red, hairy; bracts 5–15cm, 4–7, spiralling, base red, otherwise yellow or yellow-green, ± glab.; fls bright yellow to green-yellow. E Braz. to Fr. Guiana, Surinam and Guyana.

H. rostrata Ruiz & Pav. Musoid. St. to 2m. Lvs 60–120cm. Infl. 30–60cm, pendent, rachis red, flexuous; bracts to 15cm, distichous, deeply carinate, like a thick bird's bill, not overlapping in fully developed infl., base red, apex yellow, margins green; fls yellow-green. Peru to Arg., widely cult. elsewhere.

H. schaeferiana Rodriguez = *H. bihai* 'Schaefer'.

H. schiedeana Klotzsch. Musoid. St. 1.5–3m, robust. Lvs to 1.5m, oblong, coarsely cobwebby on midrib beneath. Infl. 30–70cm, erect, red, sparsely to densely hairy, twisted at maturity; bracts 6–21cm, 5–14, slender reflexed, spiralling red or red-orange, occas. green or yellow-hued, hairy; fls yellow-green. S Mex.

H. spathocircinata Aristeg. Musoid. To 2m. Lvs to 80cm, oblong. Infl. erect, on stout peduncles, red; bracts 7–15cm, 8–10, loosely spiralling, sparsely hairy, red with yellow margins, apex rolled into a spiral; fls yellow. E Venez.

H. spissa Griggs. Musoid. St. 1–4m, robust. Lvs to 1.2m, often tattered, midrib sometimes hairy beneath; petioles to 70cm. Infl. 10–50cm, erect, densely hairy; peduncle with 1 leafy bract near infl.; bracts 4–14cm, 7–23, spiralling, spreading to reflexed, red with a green or yellow base or green or yellow with a red base, hairy, especially on keel; fls green-white, yellow or yellow-orange, woolly. S Mex. to N Nic. 'Guatemala Yellow': rachis red; bracts yellow. 'Mexico Red': rachis red; bracts dull red to green.

H. stricta Huber. Musoid. St. 0.5–4m. Lvs 40–150cm, oblong; petioles sometimes red. Infl. 20–30cm, erect; bracts 7.7–11.2cm, 3–10 per infl., distichous, overlapping, broadly carinate, slightly inflated, red or orange, keel and margins yellow, tipped green; fls. white or pale yellow at base and apex with a bright green band toward apex. S Venez. and Surinam to Boliv. and Ecuad. 'Ali' (*H. peruviana* hort.): to 50cm; lvs with red midribs; bracts 3–5, bright red edged green or yellow. 'Bucky': to 2m; bracts 3–6, bright red with narrowly edged green. 'Carli's Sharonii': to 1.75m; bracts 5–6, gold to green at base, red in centre, edged orange then green. 'Castanza': to 1m; bracts 3 to 5, pale pink or peach, yellow–orange on margins and keel. 'Dimples': to 1.75, bracts 3–5, bright red with pale yellow edges and keel. 'Dorado Gold': to 1.5m; bracts 5–6, yellow to apricot tinted pale red, edged green. 'Dwarf Jamaican' (*H. humilis* hort.): to 60cm; bracts 3–5, glowing peachy red, intensifying toward apex, edged dark green. 'Dwarf Wag': to 1m; bracts 6–8, green with red-yellow central patch. 'Fire Bird': to 1.5m; lvs with maroon midribs bracts 6–7, dark red edged green. 'Lee Moore': to 0.75m; bracts 3–5, upright, slender, fiery red edged yellow. 'Petite': to 50cm; bracts 3–4, orange-red edged green, the lowest with a leafy appendage. 'Tagami': to 3m; bracts 5–10, v. regularly disposed on a strongly erect rachis, yellow at base and on keel, otherwise red edged green.

H. subulata Ruiz & Pav. Cannoid. St. 1–3m. Lvs 28–85cm, oblong, midrib sometimes red beneath. Infl. 6–30cm, erect; peduncle sometimes partially concealed by sheaths; bracts 4–16cm, 4–11, red, sometimes green-hued, slender, spreading, distichous ± glab.; fls yellow with a green apex. N Ecuad. to N Parag. and C Braz.

H. triumphans hort. = *H. zebrina*.

H. vaginalis Benth. Cannoid. St. 1–3m. Lvs 20–100cm, elliptic, cobwebby beneath. Infl. 7–21 cm, erect, sessile or on peduncle to 45cm, hairy; bracts 6–26cm, 3–10, distichous, red, usually glab. or cobwebby, the lowest with a leaf-like appendage; fls yellow tipped green. S Mex. to NW Ecuad.

H. vellerigera Poepp. Similar to *H. pogonantha* but with bracts v. woolly with red to cinnamon hairs. Colomb., Ecuad., Peru.

H. velloziana L. Emygdio see *H. farinosa*.

H. wagneriana Petersen. Musoid. St. to 4m. Lvs 1.2–2m, undulate. Infl. 20–45cm, sessile, erect; bracts 13–14cm, 6–13 per infl., thick, distichous, overlapping, dark pink to crimson or orange, keel cream or yellow, edged green; fls white, apex dark green. Belize and Guat. to N Colomb.

H. xanthovillosa Kress. Close to *H. magnifica* but with bracts bright yellow with white woolly hairs. Panama.

H. zebrina Plowman, Kress & H. Kenn. Musoid. St. slender, 1–2m. Lvs to 75cm, dark green, often with transverse dark green or purple bands and blotches, purple beneath. Infl. 20–50cm, erect; peduncle red; bracts 6–21cm, 6–9 distichous, distant, narrow, spreading, red, ± glab.; fls pale yellow-green. CE Peru.

HELICONIACEAE Nak. See *Heliconia*.

Helicteres L. Sterculiaceae. 40 shrubs and trees. Cal. tubular, 2-lipped, 3–5-dentate, withering and surrounding androgynophore; pet. 5, red-glandular inside, clawed; androgynophore often long; staminal tube short, terminated by 6–10 sta. and 5 staminodes. Fr. 5 follicles, ± cylindrical, spirally twisted around one another. Trop. Amer. & Asia.

H. isora L. NUT-LEAVED SCREW-TREE. Shrub to 4m. Lvs 5–20cm, broadly obovate, serrate, apex ± lobed, base cordate. Fls 2–3 in cymes or clusters; cal. to 2cm, tubular; pet. 2.5–4cm, pale blue, turning bright red. Fr. 5–8cm. Malay Archipel.

Helictotrichon Besser ex Roem. & Schult. OATGRASS. Gramineae. 60 perenn. grasses. St. slender, forming tussocks. Lf blades flat, folded or revolute, ribbed. Fls in an erect or nodding, narrow pan. to 30cm; rachis flimsy, hairy; spikelets laterally flattened, glistening. Summer. Temp. N Hemis., S Afr.

H. planiculme (Schräd.) Pilger. to 1m. Lf blades flat or folded, 7.5–18cm, smooth; lower sheaths finely scabrous; ligules to 1cm. Fls in contracted, dense pan. to 27.5cm; spikelets 4–7-fld, linear to oblong, to 2.5cm, tinged purple. C & SE Eur., SW Asia. Z5.

H. sempervirens (Vill.) Pilger. To 1.2m. Lf blades tightly rolled or flat, to 22.5cm, rigid, glaucous; blue-green sheaths glab.; ligules minute. Fls in loose, open pan. to 17.5cm; spikelets to 3-fld, oblong, to 1.5cm, straw-coloured, marked purple. SW Eur. 'Pendula': infl. more nodding. 'Saphirsprundel': lvs tinted steel blue; wind-resistant. Z5.

→*Avena*.

Heliocauta Humphries. Compositae. 1 perenn. creeping herb, to 10cm. Lvs rosulate, to 8cm, oblong-oblanceolate, 3-pinnatisect, lobes linear, glab. to densely villous. Cap. discoid, to 1cm diam., solitary on axill. peduncles; phyllaries in 3 series, triangular to oblong-oblanceolate, margins scarious. N Afr. Z9.

H. atlantica (Litard. & Maire) Humphries.

→*Anacyclus*.

Heliocereus (A. Berger) Britt. & Rose. Cactaceae. 4 epiphytic or saxicolous shrubs; st. ascending, scrambling, or pendent, angled or ribbed, or flat; areoles with short or bristly spines. Fls solitary, funnelform. Fr. globose or ovoid, fleshy, spined.

H. amecamensis (Heese ex Rother) Britt. & Rose = *H. speciosus* var. *amecamensis*.

H. aurantiacus Kimnach. St. ascending, soon pendent; to 3m×1–2(–3)cm, 2–5-angled, margins serrate; rudimentary scale-leaves present; spines to 15mm, hair-like, nearly white. Fl 12.5–15.5×11cm; tep. mid-orange, often tinged magenta at base. Nic., Hond. Z9.

H. cinnabarinus (Eichlam) Britt. & Rose. St. ascending, later pendent, to 60×1–8cm, 5–6-angled below, usually 3–4 angled above, rarely flat, ± crenate; spines bristly, brown or white, or shorter and weaker. Fl. 12–16×8cm; tep. scarlet, often yellow towards base. S Mex., Guat., El Salvador. Z9.

H. coccineus (Salm-Dyck ex DC.) Britt. & Rose = *H. speciosus*.

H. elegantissimus Britt. & Rose = *H. schrankii*.

H. schrankii (Zucc.) Britt. & Rose. Resembling *H. speciosus*; st. thinner and less spiny. Fl. smaller; upper floral areoles nearly spineless; tep. narrow, acute, with no purple tinge. Mts of W Mex. Z9.

H. speciosus (Cav.) Britt. & Rose. St. erect or ascending, to 1m×2.5cm, with 3–5(–7) acute ribs; spines yellow at first, later brown. Fl. 11–17×8–13cm; tep. red, tinged purple. Summer. C Mex. var. *amecamensis* (Heese ex Rother) Weingart. Fl. white. C Mex. Z9.

H. superbus (Ehrenberg) A. Berger = *H. speciosus*.

Heliophila L. CAPE STOCK. Cruciferae. 71 ann. to perenn. herbs and subshrubs. St. erect, decumbent or climbing. Lvs entire, lobed or pinnately divided. Fls racemose, 4-merous; sep. sometimes saccate at base; pet. usually clawed, often with basal appendage; sta. 6, free. Summer. S Afr. Z9.

H. africana (L.) Marais. Erect or decumbent ann., to 1.5m. Lvs to 13×1cm, coarsely pubesc. or ± glab., pinnatifid in basal portion. Pet. 6.5–11mm, obovate to round, blue-purple.

H. amplexicaulis L. f. Ann., 15–45cm. Lvs to 6×1.6cm, entire, cordate, clasping. Pet. 3.5–8.5mm, white-purple, circular-obovate.

H. coronopifolia L. Erect, branching ann., 10–60cm. Lvs 6–15cm, simple or 1–2×pinnatifid, occas. hairy. Pet. 6.5–13mm, obovate to round, blue, base green-yellow.

H. crithmifolia Willd. Erect ann. Lvs 3–12cm, pinnately lobed. Pet. 4–10mm, obovate to broad-elliptic, violet, pink, purple or white.

H. filiformis L. f. = *H. coronopifolia*.

H. foeniculacea R. Br. = *H. crithmifolia*.

H. integrifolia L. = *H. africana*.

H. leptophylla Schltr. Erect ann., to 45cm. Lvs 2.5–5cm, blue-green, glab., filiform, erect. Pet. to 6mm diam., bright blue with yellow base, obovate, blunt.

H. linearifolia Burch. ex DC. Perenn. subshrub, to 90cm. St. erect or creeping. Lvs 2–12×1–1.7cm, bristle-tipped, entire or slightly lobed, sometimes clasping. Pet. 7–12mm, blue, base yellow, obovate to nearly round with a long appendage.

H. pilosa var. *integrifolia* (L.) DC. = *H. africana*.

H. scandens Harv. Perenn. woody climber, to 3m. Lvs 4–8cm, broad-elliptic to lanceolate, glab., fleshy. Pet. 8.5–14mm white, sometimes tinted rose, circular-obovate.

→*Cheiranthus*, *Ormiscus* and *Trentpohlia*.

Heliopsis Pers. OX-EYE. Compositae. 13 loosely branched, erect perenn. herbs. Cap. radiate; ray flts yellow, oblong, persistent in fr. N Amer.

H. helianthoides (L.) Sweet. To 1.5m. Lvs to 15cm, ovate to lanceolate, glab., occas. scabrous above. Cap. to 7.5cm diam., numerous, term.; peduncles to 25cm; ray flts pale to deep yellow, apex denticulate; disc flts yellow. Ont. to Flor. and Miss. Cvs mostly 1–1.5m high with 1- or many-ranked ray flts ranging in colour from light to dark gold; double-fld cvs include the 1m, fully double, bright gold 'Sonneschild', the 1.4m gold 'Goldgefieder', 'Incomparabilis', 'Vitellina', and the deep gold 'Zinniiflora'; semi-doubles include the 1.3m dark orange 'Hohlspiegel', the 1.4m dark gold 'Spitzentanzerin' and the 1.5m orange gold-tinted 'Lohfelden'; single-fld cvs include the small (to 1m) gold 'Ballerina' and 'Summer Sun', the massive orange-yellow 'Jupiter', and the 1.5m dark gold 'Mars'. ssp. *scabra* (Dunal) T.R. Fisher. Lvs coarsely hairy. Cap few or solitary. Mex. to NJ and Ark. Z4.

H. laevis Pers. = *H. helianthoides*.

Heliosperma (Rchb.) Rchb.

H. alpestre (Jacq.) Rchb. = *Silene alpestris*.

H. alpestre (Jacq.) Griseb. = *Silene alpestris*.

H. quadridentatum auct. hort. = *Silene alpestris*.

H. quadrifidum auct. hort. = *Silene alpestris*.

Heliotrope *Heliotropium* (*H. arborescens*).

Heliotropium L. HELIOTROPE; TURNSOLE. Boraginaceae. Some 250 ann. or perenn. herbs, shrubs or undershrubs. Lvs simple. Infl. of scorpioid spikes or rac., solitary, or in pairs or 3's; cal. 5-lobed; cor. tubular, cylindric or infundibular, 5-lobed, lacking faucal scales; sta. 5, included, fil. short. Trop. and temp. distrib. Z10 unless specified.

H. amplexicaule Vahl. Perenn., to 50cm, pubesc., gland. St. somewhat branched, ascending or decumbent. Lvs to 9cm, oblanceolate to oblong, rounded or acute. Cymes to 8cm, term. or axill., densely fld; cor. blue, purple or white, infundibular, limb to 8mm diam., tube to 5mm, exterior pubesc., interior plicate, densely short-villous. S Amer.

H. anchusifolium Poir. = *H. amplexicaule*.

H. arborescens L. HELIOTROPE; CHERRY PIE. Perenn. shrub to 2m, pubesc., branched. Lvs to 8cm, ovate or elliptic-oblong, acute. Infl. with short scorpoid br., strigose or villous; fls sweetly scented; cor. violet or purple to white, tube to 7mm, adpressed-strigose, limb to 5mm diam., lobes glabrescent, rounded. Peru. 'Chatsworth': fls purple, v. fragrant. 'Florence Nightingale': fls pale mauve. 'Grandiflorum': fls large. 'Iowa': habit bushy, dense and erect; lvs dark green, lightly tinted purple; fls dark purple, fragrant, in large clusters. 'Lemoine': to 60cm; fls deep purple, fragrant. 'Lord Roberts': habit small; fls soft violet. 'Princess Marina': fls deep violet. 'Marine': habit bushy and compact, to 45cm high; lvs dark green, wrinkled; fls deep violet, fragrant, in large clusters. 'Regal Dwarf': compact and dwarf; fls dark blue, fragrant, in large clusters – one of the Regal Hybrids. 'Spectabile' ('W.H. Lowther'): habit compact, to 1.2m high; fls pale violet, scented. 'White Lady': habit dwarf and shrubby; fls white, tinged pink in bud.

H. convolvulaceum (Nutt.) A. Gray. Ann., to 40cm, hispid. Br. ascending, elongate. Lvs to 4cm, ovate to lanceolate, acute, sometimes revolute. Fls solitary in lf-axils; cor. pure white with yellow throat, tube to 1mm, exterior strigose, limb to 22mm diam. N Mex., SW US.

H. corymbosum Ruiz & Pav. = *H. arborescens*.

H. curassavicum L. Ann. or perenn., halophytic, to 40cm, decumbent, succulent. Lvs to 5cm, fleshy, linear-lanceolate or oblanceolate, glab., pale green, apex rounded. Infl. to 10cm, a spike, usually term., solitary or paired; cor. white, becoming violet-purple, to 3mm, lobes to 1mm, ovate. Mostly Americas.

H. europaeum L. Ann., to 45cm, erect, densely pubesc., branched below. Lvs to 6cm, obovate to ovate-elliptic, apex obtuse or rounded, white-pubesc. Infl. to 8cm, mostly term., usually paired; cor. white or blue, to 3.5mm, tube cylindrical, exterior pubesc., lobes ovate to suborbicular, erect to spreading. Eur. to C Asia.

H. incanum Ruiz & Pav. shrub to 1m, sprawling or openly branched. Lvs to 6cm, brick-red becoming green, ovate or ovate-elliptic, ± hispid above, villous-tomentose beneath. Fls. white or purple, fragrant to 4mm diam. Peru.

H. indicum L. Ann., to 1m, hispid-setose, loosely branched. Lvs to 15cm, ovate to elliptic-lanceolate, distinctly stalked, acute, margin repand or undulate. Infl. a spike, to 30cm, usually solitary; cor. blue, violet or sometimes white, tube to 4.5mm, cylindrical, limb to 4mm diam. Trop. and Subtrop.

H. messerschmidoides Kuntze. Shrub to 3m. St. grey-green, sometimes pubesc. or setose. Lvs lanceolate or ovate-lanceolate, setose. Fls white, small. Canary Is. Z9.

H. peruvianum L. = *H. arborescens*.

H. tenellum (Nutt.) Torr. Ann., to 50cm, erect, slender-branched above, minutely strigose. Lvs to 5cm, linear, minutely strigose, revolute. Infl. a term. rac.; cor. white, lobes to 2mm, elliptic to obovate, tube to 3mm, interior glab. N Amer.

→*Euploca* and *Tournefortia*.

Helipterum DC. EVERLASTINGS; STRAWFLOWERS. Compositae. c50 ann. or perenn. herbs or shrubs. Lvs usually alt., entire, white-lanate. Cap. discoid; phyllaries conspicuous and persistent, functioning as ray flts. Aus., S Afr. Z9.

H. albicans (A. Cunn.) DC. HOARY SUNRAY. Perenn. herb to 40cm. Lvs to 12cm, linear to oblanceolate, white-lanate. Cap. solitary, to 3.5cm diam., on term. peduncles; inner phyllaries to 2cm with a linear or subulate claw and oval scarious blade, white or red-purple tipped, outer shorter, hyaline. SE & E Aus. var. *incanum* (Hook.) P.G. Wils. More densely white-lanate or -tomentose. Tasm. (Sieb.) DC.

H. anthemoides (Sieb. ex Spreng.) DC. Perenn. herb. to 30cm. Lvs to 12mm, linear, glab., often glandular-punctate. Cap. to 3cm diam., solitary; inner phyllaries to 1cm with broad claws and radiating blades, white, outer shorter, tinged brown. SE Aus., Tasm.

H. canescens (L.) DC. Subshrub, to 60cm. Lvs to 2.5cm, oblong or obovate, grey-lanate, uppermost lvs often bract-like. Cap. solitary, to 2.5cm diam.; phyllaries white, rose, deep red or mottled with red-brown and white, outer ovate, middle lanceolate-acuminate, inner short and truncate or bidentate. S Afr.

H. chlorocephalum (Turcz.) Benth. Glab. ann. to 30cm. Lvs to 1.5cm, linear to spathulate, upper lvs sparse and smaller. Cap. few term., to c2.5cm diam.; outer phyllaries short, scarious,

tinged brown, inner with claws and radiate laminae, yellow-green. S & W Aus.

H. corymbiflorum Schldl. GREY SUNRAY; SMALL WHITE PAPER DAISY. Erect ann., to 30cm, white-lanate. Lvs to 2cm, linear or lanceolate, obtuse. Cap. to 2cm diam. in loose, term. corymbs; phyllaries with linear or cuneate claws, radiating white blades. SE Aus.

H. cotula (Benth.) DC. = *Hyalosperma cotula*.

H. eximium (L.) DC. Small shrub to 40cm, lanate. Lvs to 8cm, ovate or elliptic, thick and soft. Cap. to 2cm diam., many, in a dense sessile or subsessile corymb; phyllaries ovate to elliptic-lanceolate, strongly concave, ruby-red, obtuse. S Afr.

H. floribundum DC. COMMON WHITE SUNRAY; LARGE WHITE PAPER DAISY. Perenn. herb, to 30cm, much-branched. Lvs to 3cm, linear, acute. Cap. solitary at br. apices, to 2cm diam.; phyllaries white and petal-like, outer short, sessile, inner to 5mm with scarious claws and radiatel lanceolate blades. Aus.

H. gnaphaloides (L.) DC. Subshrub, to 50cm, much-branched, white-tomentose. Lvs to 6cm, linear, obtuse. Cap. to 1.5cm diam., term., pedunculate; phyllaries densely imbricate, inner tapered at apex to a narrow, red-brown, reflexed appendage. S Afr.

H. humboldtianum (Gaudich.) DC. = *Pteropogon humboldtianum*.

H. incanum Hook. = *H. albicans* var. *incanum*.

H. manglesii (Lindl.) F. Muell. ex Benth. = *Rhodanthe manglesii*.

H. molle (A. Cunn. ex DC.) P.G. Wils. HOARY SUNRAY; SOFT SUNRAY; GOLDEN PAPER DAISY. Ann. or perenn. herb, to 40cm. Lvs to 10cm, broad-linear, grey-lanate, upper lvs scale-like. Cap. to 2.5cm diam., solitary, terminal on white-lanate peduncles; phyllaries imbricate, brown to yellow, acuminate. S & E Aus.

H. praecox F. Muell. = *Hyalosperma praecox*.

H. roseum (Hook.) Benth. = *Acroclinium roseum*.

H. speciosissimum (L.) DC. Subshrub or shrub to 60cm, branching at base, white-lanate. Lvs to 5cm, elliptic-oblong to ovate, acute, thick. Cap. to 3.5cm diam., solitary, pedunculate; phyllaries dull cream-white, outer ovate to lanceolate, inner elongate, stipitate, lanceolate-acuminate. S Afr.

H. splendidum Hemsl. SHOWY SUNRAY; SPLENDID EVERLASTING; SILKY-WHITE EVERLASTING. Ann. to 50cm; st. tufted. Lvs to 3cm, crowded at base, linear, grey-green, upper smaller. Cap. to 6cm diam., solitary, term.; phyllaries cream-white, often with a purple band. W Aus.

H. venustum S. Moore = *Hyalosperma glutinosum*.

→*Gnaphalium, Helichrysum, Schoenia, Staehelina* and *Xeranthemum*.

Hellebore *Helleborus*.

Helleborine Mill. = *Epipactis* (see also *Cephalanthera*).

Helleborus L. HELLEBORE. Ranunculaceae. 15 perenn. herbs with stout, ± buried rhiz. or exposed, simple st. Lvs basal or terminating st., pedate or palmate, long-stalked, usually coriaceous and glab. Fls solitary or in stalked cymes or pan., often with leafy apical bracts; outer perianth seg. 5, broadly ovate to elliptic, inner seg. tubular nectaries, usually green; sta. numerous, anth. yellow. Eur., esp. It. and Balk., Turk. to Caucasian Russia, W China.

H. abchasicus A. Braun = *H. orientalis* ssp. *abchasicus*.

H. angustifolius hort. = *H. multifidus*.

H. antiquorum A. Braun = *H. orientalis* ssp. *orientalis*.

H. argutifolius Viv. Everg. To 1m. St. erect or sprawling, soon becoming naked below. Lvs cauline, trifoliate, coriaceous, lfts 8–23cm, elliptic, lat. lfts rounded at base of outer side, glab., dull olive to grey-green, spiny-dentate. Infl. term., many-fld; fls pale green, cup- or bowl-shaped, to 5cm across. Winter–early spring. Corsica, Sardinia. Z7.

H. atropurpureus Schult. = *H. atrorubens*.

H. atrorubens Waldst. & Kit. To 35cm. Lvs basal decid., dark green flushed purple, pedate, glab., central lft, 10–21×2–2.5cm, lat. lfts divided into 3–5 lobes (to 7 seg. in all), coarsely serrate. Infl. to 30cm; fls produced before lvs, 2–3, violet suffused green within, pendent, flat or shallowly saucer-shaped, 4–5cm across. Winter–spring. NW Balk. *H. atrorubens* of gardens is usually either *H. orientalis* ssp. *abschasicus* or a bold, dark-fld selection of *H. orientalis*, now properly known as *H. orientalis* 'Early Purple'. f. *cupreus* (Host) Martinis. Fls tinted rusty brown or gold. f. *hircii* Martinis. Lvs with 11–15 seg. f. *incisis* Martinis. Lvs v. coarsely toothed. Z6.

H. bocconei Ten. = *H. multifidus* ssp. *bocconei*.

H. caucasicus A. Braun = *H. orientalis* ssp. *orientalis*.

H. chinensis Maxim. = *H. thibetanus*.

H. colchicus Reg. = *H. orientalis* ssp. *abchasicus*.

H. corsicus Willd. nom. nud. = *H. argutifolius*.

H. corsicus ssp. *lividus* (Ait.) Schiffn. = *H. lividus*.

H. cupreus Host = *H. atrorubens* f. *cupreus*.

H. cyclophyllus (A. Braun) Boiss. To 40cm. Lvs basal decid., coriaceous, pedate veins prominent, central leaflet sometimes divided, to 20×5cm, lat. lfts deeply divided into 5–7 lobes, densely hairy beneath. Infl. branched, equalled or exceeded by bracts; fls to 7, yellow-green, flat or shallowly saucer-shaped, 5–7cm diam. Winter–spring. Greece, S Balk., S Bulg., Albania. Z7.

H. dumetorum Waldst. & Kit. To 30cm. Lvs basal 2–3, decid., pedate, seg. 8–11, oblong-lanceolate to narrow-elliptic, 6–10×1–3cm, acute, glab. or papillose beneath, serrate. Infl. overtopped by leafy bracts with slender lobes; fls 2–4, pendent, green, cup-shaped, 2.5–3.5cm across. Spring. S Austria, N Balk., W Hung., SW & S & E Rom.

H. dumetorum ssp. *atrorubens* (Waldst. & Kit.) Merxm. & Podl. = *H. atrorubens*.

H. foetidus L. STINKING HELLEBORE; SETTERWORT; STINKWORT; BEAR'S FOOT. Perenn. to 80cm. St. erect, hard, terete, leafy, dying after fruiting. Lvs cauline, coriaceous, dark green or grey-green, pedate; seg. 7–10, narrow-lanceolate or narrow-elliptic, tapering, to 20×3cm, coarsely serrate or nearly entire. Infl. term., to 30cm, br. cymose, many-fld; fls pendent, green, usually flushed red-purple at apex, campanulate, to 2×2.5cm, sometimes fragrant. Winter–spring. W & C Eur. 'Italian Form': v. floriferous. 'Miss Jekyll's Scented Form': fls green without any red-purple colouring, scented. 'Wester Flisk': st., petioles and infl. br. tinted rhubarb red; fls yellow-green edged maroon. Z6.

H. guttatus A. Braun & Sauer = *H. orientalis* ssp. *guttatus*.

H. intermedius Hirc. non Host = *H. atrorubens* f. *hircii*.

H. istriacus (Schiffn.) Borb. = *H. multifidus* ssp. *istriacus*.

H. kochii Schiffn. = *H. orientalis* ssp. *orientalis*.

H. lividus Ait. To 45cm+. St. erect or sprawling, dying after fruiting. Lvs cauline, trifoliolate, coriaceous; lfts 10–20×5–10cm, central leaflet elliptic, laterals rounded at base, deep green with conspicuous pale reticulate veins above, suffused pink-purple beneath, serrate or entire. Infl. term.; fls to 10, creamy-green suffused pink-purple, flat to bowl-shaped, 3–5cm across; nectaries sometimes pink-purple. Winter–spring. Majorca. Z7.

H. lividus ssp. *corsicus* (Briq.) Tutin = *H. argutifolius*.

H. macranthus Freyn ex Schiff. = *H. niger* ssp. *macranthus*.

H. multifidus Vis. ssp. *multifidus*. Lvs basal, usually decid., coriaceous, green, pedate; lfts much-divided, seg. 20–45, linea-lanceolate, to 13×1.5cm, hairy beneath, occas. glab., coarsely serrate. Infl. exceeding lvs, branched; fls 3–8, conic to cup-shaped, nodding, green, to 4.5cm diam., scented. Winter–spring. C Balk. ssp. *bocconei* (Ten.) B. Mathew. Lfts divided to half-way or less, glab. or puberulent beneath, coarsely toothed. Fls to 6cm diam. C & S It., Sicily. ssp. *hercegovinus* (Martinis) B. Mathew. Young lvs green or dull brown, seg. 45–70, linear, to 6mm wide, hairy beneath. Fls 4–5cm diam. S Balk. ssp. *istriacus* (Schiffn.) Merxm. & Podl. Lvs less dissected, seg. 10–14, to 3.5cm wide, pubesc. beneath, finely serrate. Fls to 5.5cm diam. NW Balk., NE It. Z6.

H. multifidus ssp. *serbicus* (Adamovič) Merxm. & Podl. = *H. torquatus*.

H. niger L. CHRISTMAS ROSE. To 30cm. Lvs basal, overwintering, leathery, dark green, pedate, seg. 7–9, oblong or oblanceolate, to 20×7cm, acute or obtuse, toothed towards apex. Fls solitary or 2–3 on stout peduncle, white, tinged green at centre, becoming flushed pink or dull purple, to 8cm across. Winter–spring. C Eur. (Alps). 'Apple Blossom': white tinged rose, darker outside. 'De Graff's Variety': fls turn pale primrose with age. 'Flore Roseo': pink. 'Foliis Variegatis': young lvs variegated. 'Louis Cobbett': strong pink suffusion. 'Madame Fourcade': of dwarf habit; foliage light green; fls large, white. 'Potter's Wheel' ('Ladham's Variety'): fls large, white, rounded, with a distinct green eye. 'Riverston': fragrant; early-flowering. 'Rubra': rosy white, outside dark-red. 'St Brigid': foliage strong dark green, exceeding and hiding fls. 'Trotter's Form': fls large, white, apricot with age. 'Werdie Lodge': lvs narrow, mottled purple, stalk mottled purple; fls large, white, tinged pink. var. **angustifolius** Sweet. Lf seg. narrow. Fls small. var. **humilifolius** Hayne. Lvs obscurely toothed; st. unspotted; fls exceed lvs. var. **oblongifolius** Beck. Lvs with elongated central lft, narrowing abruptly at its base. var. **stenopetalus** Beck. Perianth seg. narrow. ssp. **macranthus** (Freyn) Schiffn. Lf seg. broadly lanceolate, blue-green or glaucescent, spinulose-serrate. Fls 8–11cm across. N It., N Balk. Z3.

H. niger ×H. lividus. Lvs pedate to trifoliate, deep green, venation cream. Fls large, flat, white suffused pink-brown or pink-purple, turning dull purple with age. 'December Dawn': fls 6–8cm diam.; bracts intermediate, the upper bracts undivided like *H. niger*, the lower bracts with small leaflike divisions at the apex like *H. lividus*. Z5.

H. niger ×H. ×sternii. V. variable. Lvs somewhat pedate with some of the faint venation of *H. lividus*. Fls large, white, tinged pink-brown or green outside, colouring more definitely with age. Z6.

H. ×nigercors J.T. Wall. (*H. niger ×H. argutifolius*.) St. short, leafy, with term. clusters of fls, but some lvs and solitary fls basal, axill. Lvs large, robust, grey-green, semi-rigid, trifoliate to pedate with 7 seg., dentate or spinulose. Fls large, saucer-shaped, white, tinged blue-green. Winter–spring. Gdn origin. 'Alabaster': lvs dark green; fls white, to 6cm across, waxy. 'Beatrix': a selected form. 'Hawkhurst': a selected form. Z7.

H. nigristern hort. = *H. niger ×H. ×sternii*.

H. occidentalis Reut. = *H. viridis* ssp. *occidentalis*.

H. odorus Waldst. & Kit. To 30cm. Lvs basal, overwintering, coriaceous, pedate, central leaflet undivided, laterals with 3–5 lobes, elliptic or oblanceolate, to 20×6.5cm, densely hairy beneath, coarsely serrate. Infl. branched, short at first; fls usually 3–5, saucer-shaped, facing outwards, to 6cm diam., green to yellow. Winter–spring. Balk., S Hung., S Rom. Z6.

H. odorus ssp. *laxus* (Host) Merxm. & Podl. = *H. multifidus* ssp. *istriacus*.

H. olympicus Lindl. = *H. orientalis* ssp. *orientalis*.

H. orientalis Lam. LENTEN ROSE. ssp. *orientalis*. To 45cm. Lvs basal, overwintering, coriaceous, deep green, pedate with central lft entire, laterals divided giving 7–9 elliptic or oblanceolate seg., to 25×11cm, coarsely serrate. Infl. to 35cm, branched; fls 1–4, nodding or facing outwards, saucer-shaped, 6–7cm across, white to cream or cream tinged green, flushed purple or pink particularly below and at centre, green or purple-green following fertilization. Winter–spring. NE Greece, N & NE Turk., Caucasian Russia. ssp. **abchasicus** (A. Braun) B. Mathew. Fls suffused red-purple, often finely spotted; nectaries purple or striped purple on green. Winter–spring. W Cauc., Russia. ssp. **guttatus** (A. Braun & Sauer) B. Mathew. Fls white or cream, spotted red-purple. C & E Cauc. Z6. Members of the *H. orientalis* complex will hybridise freely, producing plants with fls in shades of white, pale pink, rose, plum and deep purple, often flushed with another of these tones or spotted or streaked purple-red. Hybridization also occurs, often inadvertently, between *H. orientalis* and other spp. The influence of *H. purpurascens* will produce dark pruinose purple shades, e.g. 'Queen of the Night'. Crossing with *H. torquatus* introduces strong, glaucous, purple-black tones, e.g. 'Pluto': wine-purple outside, green and slaty purple inside, nectaries purple; 'Ballard's Black': fls dark purple-black. Hybrids involving *H. odorus*, *H. cyclophyllus* or *H. multifidus* exhibit shades of yellow and green, e.g. 'Citron': clear pale yellow; 'Orion': cream tinged green, purple stain in centre and purple nectaries; 'Yellow Button': fls small, deep yellow.

H. pallidus Host = *H. dumetorum*.

H. purpurascens Waldst. & Kit. To 20cm at flowering. Lvs basal, decid., coriaceous, palmate with 5 lfts, each divided into 2–6 lanceolate seg., to 20×4cm, hairy beneath, coarsely serrate. Infl. appearing before lvs, branched or simple; fls 2–4, nodding, cup-shaped, to 7cm across, externally purple-violet or red-purple to brown or green, glaucous, internally sometimes green; nectaries green or dull purple. Winter–spring. EC Eur. (Ukraine to Rom.). Z6.

H. serbicus Adamovič = *H. torquatus*.

H. siculus Schiffn. = *H. multifidus* ssp. *bocconei*.

H. ×sternii Turrill. (*H. argutifolius ×H. lividus*.) St. short to tall. Lvs dark grey-green, obscurely veined green-white or silver, suffused purple to pale green, entire or spiny. Infl. with fewer fls than *H. argutifolius*; fls lime green to green flushed pink or purple-brown. Gdn origin. 'Boughton Beaty': habit compact; fls and floral axis suffused rose; lvs marked and sometimes tinted rose-purple. 'Blackthorn Strain': compact growth; lvs leaden grey-green, conspicuously veined; fls slightly flushed with pink. Z7.

H. thibetanus Franch. To 45cm. Lvs pedately divided, pale to deep green, similar to *H. orientalis*, but bolder and more deeply and finely toothed; petioles often purple-tinged. Fls to 7cm diam., opening white flushed pink, becoming blush pink with darker veins, nodding and rather bell-shaped on a branched infl., subtended by leafy bracts. China. Z7.

H. torquatus Archer-Hind. To 40cm. Lvs basal, decid., emerging with or after fls, erect, coriaceous, pedate with 10–30 narrow seg., held horizontally to 17×3.5cm, tapered, dark green above, puberulent beneath, coarsely serrate. Infl. with apical leafy bracts; fls 1–10, nodding or facing outwards, saucer- to cup-shaped, to 5.5cm across, externally dark violet-purple, pruinose, internally same colour or blue-green. Winter–spring. Balk. 'Aeneas': double, predominantly green, exterior shaded maroon. 'Dido': double, interior lime green, exterior dark purple. *H. torquatus* is the parent of many dark-fld hybrids. 'Aerial': pale green, interior speckled crimson, exterior purple.

'Little Stripey': exterior dark violet, interior green striped violet. 'Miranda': exterior claret, interior paler and speckled. 'Neptune': slate purple. 'Zuleika': fls large, exterior red-purple, interior green-white flushed red. Z6.

H. vesicarius Aucher. To 60cm, becoming dormant in summer. Lvs basal, thin, bright green, to 8×15cm, pedate, with 3 primary divisions; lat. lfts bifid, deeply lobed, all lobes deeply toothed. Infl. loosely cymose with leafy bracts; fls erect, then pendent, campanulate, to 20×17mm, green stained brown toward apex. Fr. inflated, winged, to 7.5cm, pale yellow-green. Late winter--spring. S Turk., N Syr. Z7.

H. viridis L. To 40cm. Lvs usually 2, basal, decid., thin, glossy, pedate, seg. 7–13, oblong-lanceolate to narrow-elliptic, acute, to 10×3cm, pubesc. beneath, serrate. Infl. emerging with lvs, long-branched; fls 2–4, nodding, saucer-shaped or rather flat, to 5cm across, green. Spring. SE Fr. to Austria. ssp. *occidentalis* (Reut.) Schiffn. Lvs weakly pedate, glab. beneath, v. coarsely dentate-serrate; fls to 4cm across. Spring. W Eur. Z6.

H. viridis var. *cyclophyllus* A. Braun = *H. cyclophyllus*.
H. viridis var. *dumetorum* (Waldst. & Kit.) Sendt. = *H. dumetorum*.

Helmet Flower *Aconitum napellus*; *Scutellaria*.
Helmet Orchid *Coryanthes*.

Helminthostachys Kaulf. Ophioglossaceae. 1 terrestrial fern. Rhiz. creeping, thick. Stipes to 30cm; sterile frond blade tripartite, each division pinnatified; seg. 8–12×1–2.5cm, subdivided into 3–5 lfts, lanceolate, decurrent and confluent at base, entire or minutely dentate; fertile frond an offshoot of sterile frond; sporangia, globose, succulent in a stalked 'panicle' to 10cm. SE Asia, Australasia. Z10.
H. zeylanica (L.) Hook. FLOWERING FERN.

Helonias L. Liliaceae (Melanthiaceae). 1 everg. rhizomatous perenn. Lvs 15–45cm, oblong-lanceolate, glossy, forming basal rosettes. Scape 35–45cm, bracteate; fls 25–30, fragrant, stellate, 15mm wide, in dense, conical rac.; tep. 6, pink; anth. blue. Spring. N Amer. Z8.
H. bullata L. SWAMP PINK.
H. virginica Sims = *Melanthium virginicum*.

Heloniopsis A. Gray. Liliaceae (Melanthiaceae). 4 rhizomatous, perenn., everg. herbs. Lvs in a basal rosette, oblong or lanceolate. Fls scapose, nodding, solitary or few in a loose umbellate rac.; perianth seg. 6, spreading; anth. purple-blue. Jap., Korea, Taiwan.
H. breviscapa Maxim. = *H. orientalis* var. *breviscapa*.
H. japonica Maxim. = *H. orientalis*.
H. orientalis (Thunb.) Tan. Lvs 8–10×2.5cm, tinged brown toward apex. Scape to 20cm; fls nodding, racemose, 20–10; tep. 1–1.5cm, narrowly spathulate, pink or violet; anth. blue-violet. Spring. Jap., Korea, Sakhalin Is. var. *breviscapa* (Maxim.) Ohwi. Scape shorter; fls smaller, pale pink or white.

Helwingia Willd. Cornaceae. 3–5 decid. shrubs to 1.5m. Infl. borne on lf surface, fascicled; ♂ fls numerous, ♀ 1–3, pet. valvate, 3–5, green. Fr. a fleshy drupe. Himal., Jap., Taiwan. Z8.
H. chinensis Batal. Lvs 12×3.5cm, linear-lanceolate to subovate-lanceolate, serrulate above, subcoriaceous, green to olive. ♂ fls 8–20; pet. 2.5×1.5mm; ♀ fl. single. Fr. black. Trop. China.
H. japonica Dietr. Lvs 12×5.5cm, ovate-elliptic, acuminate, olive green above, paler beneath, serrulate. ♂ fls to 12; pet. 1.5×1.5mm; ♀ fl. single. Fr. black. China, S Jap.
H. rusciflora Hemsl. & Forbes non Willd. = *H. chinensis*.
H. rusciflora Willd. non Hemsl. & Forbes = *H. japonica*.

Helxine Req.
H. soleirolii Req. = *Soleirolia soleirolii*.

Hemerocallis L. DAY LILY. Liliaceae (Hemerocallidaceae). 15 rhizomatous, clump-forming, perenn. herbs. Lvs basal, linear, tapered, 2-ranked, curving, flat or folded. Fls ephemeral, bracteate, borne in a close rac. on a long smooth scape, sometimes branched; perianth funnelform to campanulate; tep. 6, free parts spreading, inner often wider; sta. 6, deflexed. E Asia, Jap., China.
H. altissima Stout. Lvs to 150×3cm. Scapes to 2m, branched toward apex, remontant; fls to 10×10cm, pale yellow, nocturnally fragrant; perianth tube to 3.7cm. Summer and autumn. China. Z6.
H. aurantiaca Bak. Lvs 60–80×1.5–2.5cm, glaucous, persisting. Scapes taller than foliage, forked; fls to 20, 10–13cm, widely

funnelform, orange and often flushed with purple; perianth tubes less than 3cm. China. Z6.
H. citrina Baroni. Scapes erect, branched above, taller than foliage; fls 20–65, 9–12cm, fragrant, pale lemon, tinged brown beneath, opening at night; perianth tube to 4cm; tep. narrow. China. Z4.
H. dumortieri E. Morr. Lvs 35×1.5cm. Scapes unbranched, shorter than or slightly exceeding lvs; fls 2–4, 5–7cm, flat-funnelform, tightly clustered, subtended by broad bracts; inner tep. less than 2cm wide; perianth tube to 1cm. Jap., E Russia, Korea. Z4.
H. flava L. = *H. lilio-asphodelus*.
H. forrestii Diels. Lvs 30×1.5cm. Scapes erect, slender, ascending, branched, mostly shorter than lvs; fls 4–8, to 7cm, not fragrant, yellow; bracts conspicuous; perianth tube to 1cm. China. Z5.
H. fulva L. Lvs 70×3cm. Scapes taller than foliage, forked; fls 10–20, 7–10cm, widely funnelform, rusty orange-red, usually with darker median zones and stripes; perianth tube 2.5cm. Origin uncertain, perhaps Jap. or China. Z4.
H. graminea Andrews = *H. minor*.
H. graminifolia Schldl. = *H. minor*.
H. lilio-asphodelus L. Lvs 50–65×1–1.5cm, falcate. Scapes closely branched above, weak, ascending, taller than foliage; fls 8–12, 7–8cm, fragrant, shortly funnelform, yellow; perianth tube to 2.5cm. Z4.
H. middendorffii Trautv. & Mey. Lvs 30×1–2.5cm. Scape erect, unbranched, slightly taller than foliage; fls 8–10cm, few, fragrant, yellow, tightly clustered, subtended by cup-shaped, bracts; perianth tube to 2cm. N China, Korea, Jap., E Russia. Z5.
H. minor Mill. Lvs 30–45cm×5–9mm. Scapes taller than foliage, forked or shortly branched above; fls 2–5, 5–7cm, shortly funnelform, lemon yellow, tinged brown outside; tep. narrow; perianth tube less than 2cm. Jap., China. Z4.
H. multiflora Stout. Lvs 60×1cm. Scapes erect, slender, much branched, glaucous above, taller than foliage; fls 75–100, 7–8cm, glistening chrome yellow within, tinged brown-red without; perianth tube to 2cm; tep. narrow. China. Z4.
H. thunbergii Bak. Lvs 30–60cm×5–8mm. Scapes erect, rigid, branched near apex; fls 3–15, 9–11cm, fragrant, shortly funnelform, yellow; perianth tube to 3cm; tep. narrow. China, Korea. Z4.
H. cvs.
Dwarf (below 30cm). 'Buffy's Doll': pink-buff with rose-wine eye-zone. 'Eenie Weenie': light yellow with fluted edges. 'Little Grapette': fls rounded, grape-purple.
Medium (30–60cm). 'American Revolution': medium-sized velvety black/red fls. 'Ava Michelle': rich yellow, green throat, ruffled edges. 'Becky Lynn': rose-pink, deeper shaded rose eye-zone, fragrant. 'Berlin Red': rich ruby red, gold throat; weatherproof. 'Bertie Ferris': small-fld persimmon self. 'Brocaded Gown': pale lemon-cream, v. ruffled. 'Burning Daylight': tall, deep orange which glows in the evening. 'Catherine Woodbery': pale lavender pink blooms, lime green throat, fragrant. 'Cherry Cheeks': deep cherry-red, white midrib, yellow throat contrasting with black-tipped sta. 'Chestnut Lane': light golden-brown with chestnut-brown eye-zone, golden throat. 'Chicago Apache': ruffled, deep scarlet self. 'Chicago Royal Robe': deep purple with contrasting green throat. Slightly fragrant. 'Christmas Island': low-growing; brilliant scarlet with strikingly contrasting green throat. 'Dancing Shiva': low-growing; shell pink with a blue cast, yellow-green throat. 'Double Pink Treasure': creamy-pink double. 'Fairy Tale Pink': delicate shell-pink of heavy substance with ruffled edges. 'Gentle Shepherd': low-growing, near white. 'Golden Chimes': small golden-yellow fls on well-branched scapes; the dark brown buds make a striking contrast. 'Golden Prize': large, bright glowing golden-yellow fls; slightly fragrant. 'Hope Diamond': wide creamy-yellow pet. with blush overlay; good texture and ruffled edges. 'Joan Senior': the nearest to pure white fl., with contrasting yellow-green throat; wide ribbed-textured pet. with ruffled edges. 'Kindly Light': citron-yellow with long, narrow recurved seg. 'Lusty Lealand': large blooms of rich, deep red with contrasting golden throat and reverse of pet. 'Luxury Lace': low-growing, producing a mass of creamy-lavender-pink fls with lime-green throat. 'Mauna Loa': flaming salmon-orange with contrasting green throat; rounded, ruffled and crimped fls. 'Real Wind': vivid pink-orange self, with wide, deep rose eye-zone. 'Ruffled Apricot': large ruffled apricot self. 'Siloam Baby Doll': apricot, rose eye-zone, green throat; small fl. 'Siloam Button Box': creamy yellow, maroon eye-zone, green throat, small fl. 'Stella d'Oro': low growing, remontant rounded canary-yellow fls with orange throat. 'Yellow Petticoats': clear yellow double.
Tall (over 1m). 'Elaine Strutt': fls trumpet-shaped, clear mid-pink. 'Marion Vaughan': pale lemon-yellow with green throat; fragrant; long-blooming. 'Mormon Spider': large-fld pale polychrome

blend of yellow, pink and lavender. 'Whichford': highly scented, narrow trumpet-shaped fls in palest green-yellow.

Hemieva Raf.
H. oregona (Wats.) Nels. & Macbr. = *Bolandra oregona*.

Hemigramma Christ. Dryopteridaceae. 6 terresttrial ferns. Rhiz. erect to ascending, sterile fronds subsessile to stipitate, rosette-forming, simple and entire to lobed at base or pinnatifid; fertile fronds simple to pinnate or pinnatifid, lobes or pinnae constricted; stipes clustered, scaly. Trop. E Asia. Z10.
H. decurrens (Hook.) Copel. Sterile fronds simple to pinnate or pinnatifid, term. lobe or pinna to 25×8cm, spathulate, lat. lobes or pinnae (when present) smaller, 1–2 pairs, decurrent; fertile fronds with term. lobe or pinna to 12×3cm; stipes to 50cm (sterile) or more (fertile). China, Taiwan, Vietnam.
H. latifolia (Meyen) Copel. Sterile fronds to 30×7cm, simple and entire or undulate to lobed or pinnatifid, lobes or pinnae few, base sometimes auriculate; fertile fronds simple to pinnate-pinnatifid, linear, lobes or pinnae few, linear; stipes to 4cm (sterile) or more (fertile). Java, Philipp.
→*Acrostichum, Gymnopteris, Hemionitis, Leptochilus* and *Poly-botrya*.

Hemigraphis Nees Acanthaceae. Some 90 ann. or perenn. herbs and subshrubs, usually low-growing, branching freely. Infl. a few-fld term. spike; fls small, subtended by conspicuous bracts; cor. tubular, slender, 5-lobed. Trop. Asia. Z10.
H. alternata (Burm. f.) Anderson. RED IVY; RED FLAME IVY. Everg. pubesc., perenn. herb. St. slender, prostrate, rooting. Lvs to 9cm, cordate-ovate, crenate, bullate, silver-grey above, flushed purple beneath. Fls to 1.25cm, white. India, Java.
H. colorata (Bl.) Hallier f. = *H. alternata*.
H. repanda (L.) Hallier f. Everg. perenn. herb. St. prostrate, slender, spreading and rooting, puberulous to glossy glab., strongly flushed red or maroon. Lvs to 5cm, linear-lanceolate, crenate, bluntly toothed or obscurely lobed, satiny leaden-grey deeply flushed red or purple. Fls to 1.5cm, white. Malaysia.

Hemionitis L. Adiantaceae. 7 ferns. Rhiz. short, suberect; stipes of sterile fronds short, of fertile fronds, long. Fronds crowded, rounded, cordate or palmately lobed. Trop. Amer. and Asia. Z10.
H. arifolia (Burm.) Moore. Stipes of sterile fronds 4–9cm. Fronds simple, sterile narrowly ovate to oblong, deeply cordate-hastate at base, coriaceous, hairy and scaly beneath, fertile oblong to triangular. India, Sri Lanka, Burm., Taiwan, Philipp.
H. esculenta Retz. = *Diplazium esculentum*.
H. latifolia (Meyen) Kurz. = *Hemigramma latifolia*.
H. palmata L. Stipes of sterile fronds to 10cm, of fertile to 25cm, black. Fronds 5–15cm, palmately 5-parted, cordate at base, brown pubesc. above; seg. ovate (lanceolate if fertile), obtusely serrate.
H. pozoi Lagasca. = *Stegnogramma pozoi*.
H. prolifera Retz. = *Ampelopteris prolifera*.

Hemiphragma Wallich. Scrophulariaceae. 1 perenn. herb. St. prostrate, pubesc., slender, to 60cm. Lvs to 1.2cm, pubesc., broadly ovate to cordate, becoming scale-like above. Fls sessile, axill.; sep. 5; cor. narrowly campanulate, 5-lobed, pale pink. Summer. W Himal., Assam. Z8.
H. heterophylla Wallich.

Hemiptelea Planch. Ulmaceae. 1 spiny, decid. tree or shrub to 15m; shoots pubesc. Lvs in 2 ranks, 2–6cm, elliptic to elliptic-oblong, serrate, base slightly cordate, apex acute, dark green with scattered hairs becoming glab., veins 8–12 pairs. Fls inconspicuous, axill.; sep. 5; cor. 0; sta. 4–5. Fr. a flat nutlet, to 6mm on a 2mm peduncle, wing narrow, membranous, 1-sided. Spring. N China, Korea. Z3.
H. davidii (Hance) Planch.
→*Planera* and *Zelkova*.

Hemitelia R. Br.
H. arborea (L.) Fée = *Cyathea arborea*.
H. costaricensis Klotzsch ex Kuhn = *Cyathea costaricensis*.
H. horrida R. Br. = *Cyathea horrida*.
H. moorei Bak. = *Cyathea howeana*.
H. smithii (Hook. f.) Hook. = *Cyathea smithii*.
H. walkerae (Hook.) Presl = *Cyathea walkerae*.

Hemithrinax Hook. f. = *Thrinax*.

Hemlock *Conium maculatum*; *Tsuga*.
Hemlock Spruce *Tsuga*.
Hemp *Cannabis*.

Hemp Agrimony *Eupatorium cannabinum*.
Hemp Bush *Gynatrix pulchella*.
Hemp Palm *Trachycarpus fortunei*.
Hemp Willow *Salix viminalis*.
Hen-and-chicken Fern *Asplenium bulbiferum*.
Henbane *Hyoscyamus niger*.
Henderson's Checker Mallow *Sidalcea hendersonii*.
Henna *Lawsonia*.

Henricia Cass.
H. sibbettii (L. Bol.) L. Bol. = *Neohenricia sibbettii*.

Hepatica Mill. Ranunculaceae. 10 small perenn. herbs. Lvs basal, 3–5-lobed, entire to crenate-dentate, long-petiolate, rather leathery. Fls solitary, appearing before new growth, scapose, involucre calyx-like, of 3 reduced lvs, closely addressed to fl.; sep. 5–12, petaloid; pet. 0. N temp.
H. acutiloba DC. Resembling *H. americana*, but plants to 25cm, lvs larger, deeply and acutely 3–5–7-lobed. Fls 12–25mm diam., pale pink-purple, or white. Spring. N US. Z4.
H. americana (DC.) Ker-Gawl. Lf lobes 3, rounded, obtuse, tinged purple beneath; petioles 5–15cm, hairy. Fls to 2cm diam., pale blue-purple, occas. white or pink; involucral bracts ovate, obtuse. Spring. SE Canada to SE US. Z4. Often confused with *H. nobilis*.
H. angulosa auct. non (Lam.) DC. = *H. transsilvanica*.
H. ×media Simonkai. (*H. transsilvanica* ×*H. nobilis*.) Intermediate between parents. 'Ballardii': fls deep blue, sep. many. 'Millstream Merlin': fls semi-double, deep blue. Z5.
H. nobilis Mill. Lf lobes 3, ovate, tinged purple and silky hairy to villous beneath; petioles 5–15cm. Fls 15–25mm diam., blue-purple to white or pink; involucral bracts ovate. Spring. Eur. 'Ada Scott': fls double, indigo. 'Alba': fls white (double forms occur). 'Barlowii': fls v. rounded, sky blue. 'Caerulea': fls blue. 'Little Abington': fls double, deep blue. 'Marmorata': lvs spotted white. 'Plena': fls double, blue. 'Rosea': fls pink. 'Rubra': fls red-pink (double forms occur). 'Rubra Plena': fls double, red. Z5.
H. transsilvanica Fuss. Similar to *H. nobilis*, but lf lobes crenate-dentate, fls 25–45mm diam. pale blue or opal-white, rarely tinted pink, involucral bracts with 2–4 teeth. Spring. Rom. 'Buis': robust; fls bright blue, free-flowering. Z5.
H. triloba auct. non Gilib. = *H. americana*.
H. triloba Gilib. = *H. nobilis*.
→*Anemone*.

Heptapleurum Gaertn.
H. arboricolum Hayata = *Schefflera arboricola*.

Heracleum L. Umbelliferae. 60 robust, irritant, bienn. or perenn. herbs; rootstock often thick. Lvs basal and reduced on st., simple, lobed, 1–2-pinnate or ternately cut, long-stalked. Umbels compound; involucre and involucel usually present. N temp., also Himal. and S India, and mts of Ethiop.
H. antasiaticum Mand. = *H. stevenii*.
H. flavescens Besser = *H. sphondylium* ssp. *sibiricum*.
H. giganteum auct. = *H. stevenii*.
H. laciniatum auct. = *H. stevenii*.
H. lanatum Michx. = *H. sphondylium* ssp. *montanum*.
H. lehmannianum Bunge. Bienn. or perenn. to 1.5m; st. hairy. Lvs pinnate, seg. 2–3 pairs, ovate, pinnatified with ovate lobes, glab. above to hairy beneath, toothed. Umbel with 45–50 pubesc. rays; involucre commonly 0; fls white or tinged pink. Summer. Turkestan.
H. mantegazzianum Somm. & Levier. GIANT HOGWEED; CARTWHEEL FLOWER. Giant bienn. or perenn. to 5.5m; st. ridged, hollow to 10cm diam., blotched purple. Lvs ternately or pinnately divided, seg. pinnately lobed, to 130cm, serrate, coarsely pubesc. Umbels massive with 50–150 rays, 15–50cm; fls white or tinged pink. Summer. SW Asia.
H. maximum Bartr. = *H. sphondylium* ssp. *montanum*.
H. minimum Lam. Rhizomatous, glab. perenn., 20–30cm; st. 1–2mm diam. Lvs 2-pinnatisect to -ternatisect, seg. with obovate to oblanceolate lobes to 1cm, glab. Umbels c6cm diam., with 3–6 unequal rays; involucre and involucel 0; fls white, occas. tinged pink. Summer. SE Fr.
H. montanum Schleich. ex Gaudin = *H. sphondylium* ssp. *montanum*.
H. persicum Desf. Perenn., 1–1.5m; st. stout, 1.5–2cm diam. hirsute. Lvs to 40cm, pinnate, seg. pinnatisect, lobes ovate, bright green, glab. above, serrate-dentate. Umbels with 20–50 rays; involucral bracts few; fls white. Summer. Iran.
H. platyaenium Boiss. Aromatic perenn. attaining 1.5m; st. c2cm diam. at base, hirsute to villous. Lower lvs trisect to pinnately lobed, c30cm, seg. stalked, grey-hairy beneath, palmately lobed

to crenate-dentate. Umbels to 30cm diam.; rays 25–80, unequal, fls white. Summer.

H. pubescens Bieb. Bienn. or perenn. to 80cm; st. ridged. Lvs pinnatisect, with 2–3 seg., lobes oblong-acuminate, serrate-dentage, pubesc. beneath. Umbels to 12cm diam.; rays 18–20; fls white. Summer. Russia. var. *wilhelmsii* Boiss. Umbels to 40cm diam. Summer. Cauc.

H. pyrenaicum Lam. = *H. sphondylium* ssp. *pyrenaicum*.

H. sibiricum L. = *H. sphondylium* ssp. *sibiricum*.

H. sphondylium L. HOGWEED. Bienn. or perenn. to 2.5m; st. sulcate, glab. to hispid. Lvs simple and palmately lobed to pinnate into *c*5 seg., crenate to serrate, pubesc. to hispid beneath. Umbels to 20cm diam.; rays 20–50; fls white to pale green-yellow, or tinged pink. Summer. Eur., Asia, N US. ssp. *montanum* (Schleich. ex Gaudin) Briq. MASTERWORT. Lower lvs ternate, seg. ovate, white-tomentose beneath. Umbels with 12–25 rays; fls white. C & S Eur., E Russia, US. ssp. *pyrenaicum* (Lam.) Bonnier & Layens. st. pubesc. Lvs simple, lobes 5–7, pubesc. to white-tomentose beneath. Umbels with 12–45 rays; fls white. Pyren., Alps, Balk. (mts). ssp. *sibiricum* (L.) Simonk-ai. Lower lvs pinnate, seg. 5–7, commonly pinnately lobed, pubesc. to hispid below. Fls green-white. NE to C Eur.

H. stevenii Mand. Bienn. or perenn. to 1m; st. hairy. Lvs rounded, lobes 5–7, obtuse or rounded, toothed, white-tomentose beneath. Umbels to 30cm diam.; rays numerous, scabrous; fls white. Summer. Cauc.

H. villosum auct. = *H. stevenii*.

Herald's Trumpet *Beaumontia grandiflora*.
Herb Bennet *Geum urbanum*.

Herbertia Sweet. Iridaceae. 6 perenn. cormous herbs. Lvs usually radical, sometimes sheathing st., lanceolate, plicate. Scape erect, simple or sparsely branched, fls short-lived, subtended by 2 spathes; perianth shortly tubular, the 3 outer broadly triangular-ovate, acute, spreading, inner 3 rounded, erect; sta. 3, united; style trifid. Temp. S Amer. Z9.

H. amatorum Wright. Lvs 15–22cm. Scapes 30–50cm; outer perianth seg. 3–3.5cm, violet, striped white toward base, with a yellow basal nectary, inner seg. violet, spotted brown at base. Spring. S S Amer.

H. amoena Griseb. Lvs 7.5–25cm. Scapes to 30cm; fls violet; outer perianth seg. to 2cm. Arg., Urug.

H. caerulea (Herb.) Herb. = *Alophia drummondii*.

H. drummondiana hort. = *Alophia drummondii*.

H. lahue (Molina) Goldbl. Lvs 5–10cm. Scape 8–15cm; outer perianth seg. 1–1.5cm, violet stained blue near base, inner perianth seg. violet. Spring. S Chile, Arg.

H. pulchella Sweet. Lvs 10cm. Scape 8–15cm; outer perianth seg. 2.5–2.8cm, blue to lilac or purple tinted pink, often with a central white stripe, claw white and bearded, flecked or flushed violet, inner seg. mauve. Spring. S S Amer. to S Braz.

H. watsonii Bak. = *Alophia drummondii*.

→*Alophia* and *Trifurcia*.

Herb Gerard *Aegopodium podagraria*.
Herb of Grace *Ruta graveolens*.
Herb Paris *Paris quadrifolia*.
Hercules' Club *Aralia spinosa*; *Lagenaria siceraria*; *Zanthoxylum clava-herculis*.

Hereroa Schwantes. Aizoaceae. 30+ short-stemmed, mat-forming succulent perennials. Lvs decussate, softly fleshy, ± united, semicylindric at the base, laterally compressed and expanded toward the tip. Fls several in a branched infl., or solitary. S Afr., Nam. Z9.

H. angustifolia L. Bol. = *H. puttkameriana*.

H. calycina L. Bol. Small shrub; br. dense. Lvs to 4cm, blue-green, one lf carinate beneath, expanded toward tip, the other laterally carinate, curved, ± falcate. Fls yellow to yellow-red. W Cape.

H. carinans (Haw.) L. Bol. Short-stemmed, mat-forming perenn. Lvs to 2.5cm, semicylindric at base, carinate and expanded above, tip somewhat incurved with obtuse angles, dull green with raised dots. Fls yellow. W Cape.

H. dolabriformis (L.) L. Bol. = *Rhombophyllum dolabriforme*.

H. dyeri L. Bol. Compact, to 10cm across with short st. covered by the old lf remains. Lvs with a blister-like swelling at the base, lf pairs unequal, one to 2.5cm, the other 2cm, carinate above, obtuse to truncate at the tip, margins and keel serrate, blue with raised dots. Fls golden yellow, fragrant. W Cape.

H. granulata (N.E. Br.) Dinter & Schwantes. Lvs to 4cm, spreading, often prostrate and slightly curved, semicylindric at base, carinate and expanded toward apex, mucronate, dark green with rough dots. Fls yellow. SE Cape.

H. herrei Schwantes. Closely resembles *H. granulata* except lvs not expanded. E Cape.

H. hesperanthera (Dinter) Dinter & Schwantes. Stiffly branched erect shrub to 30cm, leafy throughout. Lvs swollen, triquetrous, oblique to rounded, ± expanded at tip. Fls golden-yellow. Nam.: Great Namaqualand.

H. incurva L. Bol. Low, spreading perenn. Lvs to 3.5cm, acute to tapered, somewhat expanded at base, blue-green to flushed red with crowded dots. Fls golden yellow. W Cape.

H. muirii L. Bol. To 7cm. Lvs to 5cm, 4–6 per shoot, semicylindric, rounded-carinate below, granular. Fls yellow. SE Cape.

H. puttkameriana (Dinter & A. Berger) Dinter & Schwantes. Compact and densely leafy. Lvs to 6cm, bluntly triquetrous, semicylindric toward apex, slightly glossy, grey-green with raised dark dots, particularly along keel. Fls golden yellow to orange. Namaqualand.

H. uncipetala (N.E. Br.) L. Bol. Stemless, 5–7cm. Lvs 3cm, curved, long-tapered, rounded beneath at base, compressed-carinate toward tip with a keel, light grey-green with darker dots. Fls light yellow. W Cape.

→*Bergeranthus*, *Mesembryanthemum* and *Prepodesma*.

Heritiera Dryand. Sterculiaceae. 30 trees with large buttresses. Fls small, subterminal and axill. in much branched pan.; cal. campanulate or urceolate, 4–5-dentate; pet. 0; ♂ fls with a ring of 4–20 anth. near the apex of staminal column; ♀ fls with 3–5(–6) carpels, with sterile anth. at their base. SE Asia, Trop. Afr.

H. littoralis Dryand. Tree to 10m. Lvs 5–36cm, ovate-lanceolate, leathery, densely scaly, becoming glab. above and densely silvery beneath. Fls red. OW trop.

H. macrophylla Wallich ex Vogel. LOOKING GLASS TREE. Tree to 30m. Lvs to 35cm, oblong-lanceolate, acuminate, bright green above, opaque-silvery beneath. Fls small, green-yellow. India, Burm.

H. trifoliolata (F. Muell.) Kosterm. BOOYONG; HICKORY; CROW'S FOOT; ELM; STAVE WOOD; SILKY ELM; BROWN OAK. Tree to 40m. Lvs digitately 3–5-foliolate, lfts 8–18cm, lanceolate to elliptic, leathery, glossy above, densely silvery-scaly beneath. Fls white with green base. Celebes to New Guinea, trop. Queensld and NSW.

→*Argyrodendron* and *Tarrietia*.

Hermannia L. HONEYBELLS. Sterculiaceae. 100+ herbs and sub-shrubs, generally stellate-pubesc. at first, often with gland. hairs intermixed. Lvs with leafy stipules. Fls axill., solitary or several in cymes; cal. 5-lobed; tube campanulate to globose; pet. 5, obovate to oblong, spirally twisted; sta. 5, opposite the pet.; fil. expanded. Trop. & S Afr.

H. althaeifolia L. Ann. or short-lived perenn. herb, becoming woody at base. Lvs to 6cm, ovate, ovate-oblong or ovate-lanceolate, sinuate-crenate, sparsely stellate-pubesc. above, densely pubesc. beneath. Cymes 2-fld; pet. to 9mm, cadmium-yellow, not turning red with maturity, twisted. S Afr. (Cape).

H. candicans Ait. = *H. incana*.

H. conglomerata Ecklon & Zeyh. Perenn. herb to 60cm, base woody. Lvs to 2cm, suborbicular, crenate, stellate-pubesc. Cymes sessile, crowded at the ends of br., pet. to 3mm, strongly contorted and shortly exserted from the cal. tube. S Afr.

H. cristata Bol. Perenn. herb to 40cm, with a woody rootstock. Lvs to 6.5cm, elliptic-oblong or lanceolate, crenate-dentate, with simple bulbous-based hairs above, prominent veins and sparsely stellate-pubesc. beneath. Fls usually solitary on peduncles to 5cm; pet. 1–2cm, crimson, red-orange, orange or red, narrowing into a claw with infolded margins. S Afr.

H. denudata L. f. Shrub to 2m, glab. Lvs 1.3–6.5cm, lanceolate to almost oblong, coarsely dentate in upper half. Fls solitary or 2–3-fld in terminal cymes; pet. to 8mm, yellow to red and yellow, ovate-oblong, narrowed into a claw with infolded margins. S Afr. var. *erecta* (N.E. Br.) Davy & Green. Foliage rough with minute fringed scales and grouped hairs from a gland. base; fls red, yellow, or partly yellow and partly red. Transvaal and Swaz.

H. fasciculata Bak. = *H. linearifolia*.

H. flammea Jacq. NIGHT-SMELLING HERMANNIA. Perenn. herb to 80cm, with woody base. Lvs 0.5–2.5 cm, broadest at or near the apex, apex rounded to subtruncate, mucronate and toothed. Cymes term., racemose; pet. 8–9mm, red, yellow, or orange-red, stellate-pubesc. along edges of lower half. S Afr. (Cape).

H. incana Cav. Perenn. herb to 2m; st. erect, white grey-tomentose. Lvs 0.7–3.5cm, ovate oblong to oblong, base cuneate, softly stellate-tomentose, undulate-crenate, apex rounded to acuminate. Cymes leafy, paniculate; pet. 0.7–1cm, yellow, broadly rounded or truncate, narrowing into a claw, margins infolded, densely tomentose. S Afr. (Cape).

H. linearifolia Harv. Perenn. herb to 1m, woody at base, scaly, papillose and viscid at first. Lvs 1.2cm, narrowly obovate, plicate, with minute viscid papillae. Pseudoracemes at the ends of ultimate br.; pet. 1cm, deep wine red, red, brick-red, mauve or clear yellow, oblong-obovate attenuated into a claw with incurved margins, glab. S Afr.

H. linifolia Burm. f. Perenn. herb, woody at base; st. decumbent. Lvs 1.3–3cm, linear or acicular, acute or broad and lobed at apex, sparsely ciliate with long bulbous-based hairs. Cymes term., racemose; pet. to 9mm, yellow or orange-yellow, glab., oblong-orbicular, narrowed into a claw with infolded margins. S Afr. (Cape).

H. mollis Willd. = *H. incana*.

H. scoparia (Ecklon & Zeyh.) Harv. = *H. linifolia*.

H. verticillata (L.) Schum. HONEYBELLS. Perenn. herb, with woody base in the wild, herbaceous in cult. specimens; st. decumbent, to 30cm. Lvs to 4cm, pinnately dissected into linear seg. Fls solitary, or in pairs, slender, fragrant; pet. to 1.2cm, yellow. S Afr.

Hermanus Cliff Gladiolus *Gladiolus carmineus*.

Hermodactylus Mill. Iridaceae. 1 tuberous perenn., closely related to *Iris*. Lvs to 50cm, linear, tetragonal, grey-green. Flowering st. 15–40cm, covered in sheathing lvs; fls scented, 4–5cm diam., pale green, tube *c*5mm, falls 5cm, brown-black or dark blue, oblong, standards shorter, toothed. Late winter–early spring. S Eur.

H. tuberosus (L.) Mill. SNAKE'S HEAD IRIS; WIDOW IRIS. →*Iris*.

Hernandia L. Hernandiaceae. 20 everg. trees. Lvs entire, cordate, peltate, long-stalked. Fls yellow-green, in showy pan., subtended by 4-lobed involucre; ♀ fls with 8 perianth seg.; ♂ fls with 6 perianth seg., sta. 3. Fr. globose-ellipsoid, held within inflated involucel. Trop. Z10.

H. ovigera L. JACK IN THE BOX. To 10m. Lvs to 20cm, ovate. Fr. to 3.25cm, dark, surrounded by green-white, roughly globose involucel to 7cm. SE Asia.

H. peltata Meissn. = *H. ovigera*.

HERNANDIACEAE Bl. 4/68. *Hernandia*.

Herniaria L. RUPTURE-WORT. Caryophyllaceae. *c*15 low-growing annuals or perennials. Fls v. small, in dense axill. cymes, with 5 small sep. and 5 usually minute pet. on the rim of the bowl-shaped receptacle; sta. 5 or fewer. Eurasia and Afr., esp. Medit. area. Z5.

H. glabra L. Ann. to short-lived mossy perenn., ± glab., with a taproot and many prostrate shoots to 30cm. Lvs elliptic-obovate, acute. Fls inconspicuous; pet. minute, white. Widespread in much of Eur. and N Afr., extending into Asia.

Heron's Bill *Erodium*.

Herpestis Gaertn. f.

H. amplexicaulis (Michx.) Pursh = *Bacopa caroliniana*.

Herpolirion Hook. f. Liliaceae (Doryanthaceae). 1 perenn. slender-rhizomatous herb. Lvs 2–6cm, grass-like, 2-ranked, blue-green, keeled and sheathing. Fls solitary, on short scapes; perianth 1.1–1.5×0.5cm, seg. linear to narrowly obovate, pale blue to white, or cream, spreading. Summer. SE Aus., NZ. Z9.

H. novae-zealandiae Hook. f.

Herrea Schwantes. Aizoaceae. 26 perenn., decumbent, succulent herbs; caudex swollen, cylindric or irregular. St. 2.5×0.7cm, few, decid. Lvs semi-terete to terete, acute to obtuse at tip, fls opening in the afternoon; pet. numerous in 4–5 series. S Afr. (Cape Prov.). Z9.

H. elongata (Haw.) L. Bol. Caudex napiform. St. 30cm+, prostrate. Lvs 10–15cm, tapered, channelled above, rounded below, soft. Fls 8–12cm diam., glossy sulphur-yellow. Cape Prov.

→*Conicosia* and *Mesembryanthemum*.

Herreanthus Schwantes. Aizoaceae. 1 dense, mat-forming succulent perenn. Lvs 4×2×1.5cm, opposite and decussate, united below, triangular and tapered on the upper surface, flat, apiculate and slightly carinate beneath, firm-textured, blue-green, with slightly raised dots. Fls 2.5cm diam., fragrant, white. Late summer. S Afr. Z9.

H. meyeri Schwantes.

Hertia Less.

H. cheirifolia (Benth. & Hook. f.) Kuntze = *Othonna cheirifolia*.

Hesiodia Moench = *Sideritis*.

Hesperaloe Engelm. ex Wats. ex King. Agavaceae. 3 stemless everg. herbs, forming grass-like clumps. Lvs linear, soft, margins with thread-like appendages. Rac. or pan. sparsely branched; fls to 3cm, narrowly campanulate; perianth seg. 6, distinct; sta. 6. N Mex., SW US. Z7.

H. davyi Bak. = *H. funifera*.

H. engelmannii Krausk. = *H. parviflora* var. *engelmannii*.

H. engelmannii Bouillon non Krausk. = *H. funifera*.

H. funifera (K. Koch) Trel. Lvs to 1.8m, margins with coarse white fibres. Infl. to 2.5m, branched near top; fls green tinged purple. NE Mex.

H. nocturna Gent. Lvs to 1.5m, margins with few fine threads. Infl. to 2.5m, simple or 1–3 branched; fls green, tinged pink to lavender, white inside, opening at night. Summer. Mex.

H. parviflora (Torr.) J. Coult. Lvs 1.3m, leathery developing buds at base, spreading, margins with fine white threads. Infl. a slender pan. to 1.2m; fls dark to light red, golden yellow within, not opening fully. Summer. SW Tex. var. *engelmannii* (Krausk.) Trel. Fls more bell-shaped, 2.5cm. 'Rubra': fls bright red.

H. yuccifolia Engelm. = *H. parviflora*.

→*Aloe* and *Yucca*.

Hesperantha Ker-Gawl. Iridaceae. *c*55 cormous perenn. herbs. Lvs 3 to several, mostly basal, linear, smooth or ribbed. Scape erect, rarely subterranean; fls solitary or spicate, stellate or somewhat saucer-shaped, in most spp. opening in the evening, tube straight or curved, tep. 6, style br. 3, slender. Subsaharan Afr., with most sp. in S Afr. Z9.

H. baurii Bak. Scape to 20cm; spike laxly few-fld; fls 1–2cm diam., bright pink, tube 10–15mm, tep. spreading, to 10mm. Summer. S Afr., Les.

H. buhrii L. Bol. = *H. cucullata*.

H. cinnamomea (L. f.) Ker-Gawl. = *H. spicata*.

H. cucullata Klatt. Scape to 30cm, simple or branched, erect; spike 1–10-fld; fls scented, white with the outer tep. red outside, tube 6–9mm, tep. 15–20mm, ovate. Winter–spring. S Afr.

H. falcata (L. f.) Ker-Gawl. Scape 6–30cm, simple or with up to 3 br. near base; spike 1–8-fld; fls white, cream or pale to deep yellow, outer tep. flushed red, pink or brown on outside, white forms scented, yellow forms unscented and day-flowering, tube 4–9mm, tep. 12–18mm, ovate. Winter–early spring. S Afr.

H. kermesina Klatt = *Geissorhiza inflexa*.

H. longituba (Klatt) Bak. Scape to 30cm, usually unbranched, erect; spike 1–6-fld; fls scented, white, often tinged with pink or brown outside, tube 10–18mm, tep. 15–22mm, ovate. Winter–early spring. S Afr.

H. lutea Ecklon ex Bak. = *H. falcata*.

H. metelerkampiae L. Bol. = *H. vaginata* var. *metelerkampiae*.

H. muirii (L. Bol.) Lewis. Scape 10–20cm, erect, unbranched; spike 1–3-fld; fls cream or pale pink, rather irregular, tube 15–25mm, curved, tep. 15–25mm, elliptic. Spring. S Afr.

H. pilosa (L. f.) Ker-Gawl. Scape 10–32cm, erect, usually unbranched, glab. or sparsely hairy; spike 1–12-fld, fls white, magenta-pink, violet, blue or purple, tube 6–10mm, tep. 10–15mm, elliptic. Winter–spring. S Afr.

H. radiata (Jacq.) Ker-Gawl. Scape 10–60cm, erect, unbranched; spike (1-)6–15-fld, fls facing downwards white or green-white, often tinged with red-brown or purple on outside, tube 10–18mm, somewhat curved, tep. 7–15mm, slightly reflexed. Winter–spring or spring–summer. S Afr.

H. spicata (Burm. f.) N.E. Br. Scape 12–50cm, erect, unbranched; spike 4–20-fld, secund; fls white, the outer seg. purple-brown on outside, tube 4–6mm, tep. 4–9mm, narrowly ovate. Late winter–spring. S Afr.

H. stanfordiae L. Bol. = *H. vaginata* var. *stanfordiae*.

H. tysonii Bak. = *H. radiata*.

H. vaginata (Sweet) Goldbl. Scape 12–18cm, erect, simple or with 2–3 br. near base; spike 1–4-fld; fls about 6cm diam., bright yellow or yellow and brown, opening mid-afternoon, tube 5–8mm, tep. 30–35mm, lanceolate. Late winter–early spring. S Afr. var. *metelerkampiae* (L. Bol.) R. Fost. Fls bicoloured, yellow with dark brown in throat and on apical half of tep. var. *stanfordiae* (L. Bol.) R. Fost. Fls clear yellow.

Hesperis L. Cruciferae. 60 bienn. or perenn., erect herbs. Rac. lax; fls fragrant, esp. at evening; sep. 4, erect, rarely spreading, pet. 4, long-clawed; sta. 6, 4 long, 2 short. Spring–summer. Eur., N & W Asia. Z6.

H. acris Forssk. = *Diplotaxis acris*.

H. bicuspidata (Willd.) Poir. Perenn., 15–30cm, short stellate-forked pubesc. Lvs oblong-obovate to lanceolate, wavy to entire. Sep. 7–11mm; pet. violet. Asia Minor.

H. lutea Maxim. = *Sisymbrium luteum*.

H. matronalis L. DAMASK VIOLET; DAMES VIOLET; SWEET ROCKET. Bienn. or perenn., 60–100cm, simple, glandular-pubesc. Lvs ovate-lanceolate, tapering to a short petiole, wavy to entire. Sep 6–8mm; pet. 1–2cm, white-lilac. S Eur. to Sib. 'Alba': fls white. 'Alba Plena': fls white, double. 'Lilacina Flore Plena': fls double, lilac. 'Nana Candidissima': habit small; fls pure white. 'Purpurea': fls purple-red. 'Purpurea Plena': fls double, purple. Z3.

H. tristis L. Bienn. or perenn., 25–50cm, coarse-pubesc. St. branching above. Lvs ovate-lanceolate, petiolate, entire to finely toothed. Sep. 9–15mm; pet. 2–3cm, white or cream, rarely purple. C & S Eur.

H. violacea Boiss. = *H. bicuspidata*.

Hesperocallis A. Gray. Liliaceae (Agavaceae). 1 bulbous perenn. herb. St. to 30cm, leafy. Lvs to 30cm, linear, margins undulate-crispate, white. Rac. robust, term.; bracts scarious; fls fragrant, funnelform, to 7cm, lobes twice length of tube, white, outside broadly striped green. S Calif., W Ariz. Z9.

H. undulata A. Gray DESERT LILY.

Hesperochiron S. Wats. Hydrophyllaceae. 2 diminutive perenn. herbs. Lvs in a basal rosette, somewhat succulent. Fls solitary on long axill. stalks; cal. lobes 5; cor. funnelform or rotate, lobes 5. SW N Amer. Z7.

H. californicus (Benth.) S. Wats. Lvs to 5cm, oblong, grey-pubesc. Peduncles to 10cm; cor. to 1.85cm, white striped lavender, tube exceeding lobes. NW US to Baja Calif.

H. pumilus (Griseb.) Porter. Lvs to 6cm, linear-oblong to spathulate, somewhat downy beneath. Peduncles to 14cm; cor. white, pink or opalescent, faintly veined lavender and stained yellow at base, lobes exceeding tube. W US.

Hesperoscordum Lindl.

H. maritimum Torr. = *Muilla maritima*.

Hesperoyucca Bak. = *Yucca*.

Hesper Palm *Brahea*.

Heteranthemis Schott. Compositae. 1 gland., pubesc. ann. herb to 50cm. Lvs to 35cm, obovate to oblong, lower lvs toothed to pinnatifid, upper lvs toothed. Cap. radiate, pedunculate; involucre to 4cm diam.; ray flts yellow. SW Eur., N Afr.

H. viscidehirta Schott.

→*Chrysanthemum*.

Heteranthera Ruiz & Pav. MUD PLANTAIN. Pontederiaceae. 10 ann. or perenn. aquatic herbs. St. branched, submerged, rooting, floating or creeping on mud. Infl. spathaceous; fls solitary to many in a spike; perianth with long slender tube, seg. 6, linear to lanceolate; sta. 3. Amer., Trop. Afr., Aus.

H. callifolia Rchb. ex Kunth. Lvs broad-cordate, obtuse, 7cm; petioles to 20cm. Infl. to 10cm; fls several, white; perianth tube to 7.5mm, lobes spreading, oblong, obtuse, 5×2mm. Summer. Trop. Afr. Z10.

H. dubia (Jacq.) MacMill. WATER STAR GRASS. Lvs sessile, narrow-linear, obtuse, to 15cm. Fls solitary or paired, !ying on surface of water, pale yellow; perianth tube to 7mm, lobes spreading, linear or linear-lanceolate, 5×2mm. Summer. N Amer. Z8.

H. kotschyana Fenzl ex Schweinf. Lvs cordate, subacute, to 7.5cm; petiole to 20cm. Fls several, white; perianth tube to 6.5mm, lobes spreading, oblong, obtuse, to 5mm. Summer. Aus., E Afr. Z10.

H. limosa Willd. Lvs lanceolate to obovate, obtuse, 2–5cm; petioles to 20cm. Fls solitary, white or blue spotted white; perianth tube to 3.5mm, lobes linear-lanceolate. Summer. C US, C & S Amer., Carib. Z5.

H. peduncularis Benth. Lvs broad-cordate or rounded, 6×6cm; petioles to 20cm. Fls 3–16, blue; perianth tube to 8mm, limb spreading, to 15mm across. Summer. US (Kans. and Missouri), Mex. Z8.

H. reniformis Ruiz & Pav. Submerged lvs linear, floating lvs deeply cordate to reniform or nearly orbicular, 3×3.5cm; petiole to 20cm. Fls 2–8 in spike to 3cm, white or pale blue; perianth tube to 1cm, limb to 1cm across. Summer. C & S Amer. N to Neb. Z3.

H. zosterifolia Mart. Submerged lvs linear to oblong, 5×0.7cm, sessile, floating lvs elliptic to spathulate, 4cm; petioles to 8cm. Fls solitary or paired, pale blue; perianth to 1.5cm across. Braz., Boliv. Z10.

→*Zosterella*.

Heterocentron Hook. & Arn. Melastomataceae. 27 perenn.

herbs and low-growing shrubs. Fls solitary or in small pan.; pet. 4, spreading, ovate or obovate. C & S Amer. Z10.

H. elegans (Schldl.) Kuntze. SPANISH SHAWL. Carpet-forming subshrub. Lvs 1–2.5cm, ovate to oblong-vate, entire or crenate, bristly to downy. Fls solitary; pet. to 2.5cm, magenta to mauve. Mex., Guat., Hond.

Heteromeles M. Roem. TOYON; CHRISTMAS BERRY; TOLLON. Rosaceae. 1 everg., tree-like shrub to 9m. Lvs to 10cm, lanceolate to obovate, leathery, sharply toothed. Fls white in large, flattened, term., corymbose pan.; sep. and pet. 5; sta. 10. Fr. a berrylike, red pome. Calif. Z9.

H. arbutifolia (Ait.) M. Roem.

→*Photinia*.

Heteropappus Less. Compositae. 5 bienn. to perenn. erect herbs. Lvs alt., simple, entire to serrate or coarsely toothed. Cap. radiate, solitary and terminal, or in loose corymbose clusters; ray flts white to blue; disc flts yellow. Temp. E Asia. Z7.

H. altaicus (Willd.) Novop. To 35cm. Basal lvs to 10×3cm, lanceolate to oblong, withering at maturity, st. lvs 5×2cm, linear-lanceolate to spathulate. Ray flts purple to white. Iran to Himal.

H. decipiens Maxim. = *H. hispidus*.

H. hispidus (Thunb.) Less. To 1m. Basal lvs to 15×3cm, oblanceolate, st. lvs to 7.5×2cm, linear. Ray flts blue-purple to white. Jap., China, Taiwan.

→*Aster*.

Heterophragma DC.

H. adenophyllum Seem. ex Benth. and Hook. f. = *Fernandoa adenophylla*.

Heterorhachis Schultz-Bip. ex Walp. Compositae. 1 shrub, to 1m, much branched, white-tomentose. Lvs to 6cm, pinnatifid to pinnatisect, lobes to 25×3mm, strongly revolute. Cap. radiate, to 7cm diam., in term. rac.; phyllaries floccose; ray flts 3–4-toothed, yellow. S Afr. Z9.

H. aculeata (Burm. f.) Roessler.

→*Berkheya*.

Heterotheca Cass. Compositae. c20 erect, branched, ann. to perenn. herbs. Cap. radiate, few to many, often in corymbose clusters; flts yellow. S N Amer.

H. camporum (Greene) Shinn. Perenn., to 1m. Lvs lanceolate, to 12cm, erect, remotely toothed, pubesc., sessile. Cap. to over 1.5cm diam., in term. clusters; ray flts showy. C US. Z5.

H. falcata (Pursh) V.L. Harms = *Pityopsis falcata*.

H. graminifolia (Michx.) Shinn. = *Pityopsis graminifolia*.

H. inuloides Cass. Ann. to perenn. to 1.5m. Lvs to 8cm, ovate to lanceolate, entire or toothed. Cap. in a corymbose cluster. Mex. Z8.

H. nervosa (Willd.) Shinn. = *Pityopsis graminifolia* var. *latifolia*.

H. pinifolia (Elliott) Ahles = *Pityopsis pinifolia*.

H. rutteri (Rothr.) Shinn. Like *H. villosa* but silvery-silky throughout, cap. smaller and overlapped by leafy bracts. SE US. Z8.

H. subaxillaris (Lam.) Britt. & Rusby. CAMPHOR-WEED. Gland. ann. or bienn. to 1m. Lvs to 30cm, ovate to oblong, entire or toothed. Cap. to 2.5cm diam., in loose term. clusters. SE US, Mex. Z8.

H. villosa (Pursh) Shinn. HAIRY GOLDEN ASTER. Hairy perenn., to 1m. Lvs to 8cm, elliptic to oblanceolate, entire to minutely toothed. Cap. several, to 2.5cm diam. W & SC US. Z5.

→*Chrysopsis* and *Inula*.

Heuchera L. ALUM ROOT; CORAL BELLS. Saxifragaceae. 55 herbaceous, everg. perenn. herbs. Lvs usually basal, rounded, dentate; petiole slender. Infl. a slender, scapose rac. or pan.; fls small; sep. fused at base in a bell, 5-lobed above; pet. 5 or 0. Summer. N Amer.

H. acerifolia Raf. = *H. villosa*.

H. aceroides Rydb. = *H. longiflora*.

H. alba Rydb. = *H. pubescens*.

H. americana L. ROCK GERANIUM. Lvs 3.5–11cm, broadly ovate-cordate, lobes rounded to triangular, green mottled white, pubesc. above, glab. beneath. Infl. lax; cal. 3–7mm, lobes 1–2.5mm, rounded, erect; pet. 1–4×1mm. N Amer. 'Purpurea': lvs marbled purple-brown beneath. Z4.

H. barbarossa. Presl = *H. micrantha*.

H. bracteata (Torr.) Ser. To 28cm. Lvs 2–3cm wide, lobes rounded, often overlapping, setose-dentate, glandular-powdery sometimes glab., veins pilose beneath. Scape bearing 2–3 reduced lvs; sep. oblong, obtuse; pet. equal or exceeding sep. Rocky Mts, N Colorado, S Wyom. Z4.

H. brevistaminea Wiggins. To 25cm. Lvs suborbicular, cordate, 1.5–2.5cm wide, lobes often overlapping, dentate. Infl. bracts 1–2, small, purple; fls 4–5mm; sep. unequal; pet. pale red-purple. Z6.

H. ×brizoides hort. ex Lemoine. A range of hybrids with *H. sanguinea* as part of the parentage; the precise application of this name is obscure, but it is also likely to embrace hybrids involving *H. micrantha* and *H. americana*. 'Apple Blossom': tall; fls light pink. Bressingham Hybrids: infl. graceful, fls ranging in colour from pink through rose, carmine and red with some whites. 'Carmen': to 50cm, dark red. 'Coral Cloud': graceful sprays of coral-crimson fls. 'Feuerregen': to 50cm, fiery red. 'Firebird': spikes erect, fls deep red. 'Firefly': fls fragrant, orange-pink. 'Freedom': dwarf; fls pink. 'Gloriana': fls bright dark pink. 'Gracillima': fls pale pink. 'Green Ivory': infl. robust, fls green and white. 'Jubilee': to 50cm, pale pink, early summer. 'Lady Romney': to 60cm, attached to shell pink, pan. lax; summer. 'Mary Rose': fls deep pink. 'Pretty Polly': infl. to 30cm, fls v. large, clear pink. 'Red Spangles': fls scarlet. 'Scintillation': lvs marbled silver, fls tipped vivid pink. 'Shere Variety': infl. delicate, 45cm, fls brilliant scarlet. 'Silberregen': to 50cm, fls snow white. 'Snowflake': to 60cm, fls in lax pan., white. 'Sparkler': fls crimson and scarlet. 'Splendour': fls rich pink. 'Taff's Joy': lvs variegated cream and tinted pink. 'Weerlachs': to 70cm, fls salmon-pink in long-stalked pan. 'Widar': to 80cm, fls scarlet. Z4.

H. caulescens Pursh = *H. villosa*.

H. chlorantha Piper. To 1m. Lvs ovate-reniform, 4–8cm wide, twice dentate. Scape pilose, and glandular-pubesc. toward apex; sep. 7–9mm, bright green; pet. 0 or half sep. length. Sometimes confused in cult. with *H. cylindrica* 'Greenfinch'. NW N Amer. Z6.

H. ciliata Rydb. = *H. richardsonii*.

H. columbiana Rydb. = *H. cylindrica*.

H. crinita Rydb. = *H. villosa*.

H. cylindrica Douglas ex Hook. Similar to *H. chlorantha* except sep. cream, tinged green or red. 'Greenfinch': vigorous; fls sulphur-green. 'Hyperion': fls coral pink on 6cm spikes. 'Siskiyou Mountains.': dwarf; lvs scalloped; fls cream, in 10cm rac. Z4.

H. divaricata Fisch. ex Ser. = *H. glabra*.

H. diversifolia. Rydb. = *H. micrantha*.

H. flabellifolia Rydb. = *H. parvifolia*.

H. glabella Torr. A. Gray = *H. cylindrica*.

H. glaberrima Rydb. = *H. micrantha*.

H. glabra Willd. To 60cm. Lvs ovate-cordate, 3–9cm broad, near palmate, lobes incised, dentate, glab. above, sparsely gland. hairy beneath. Scape glandular-pubesc. toward apex, bearing 1–2 reduced lvs; cal. 2–3mm; pet. white, clawed, 2–4×sep. length. Alask. to Oreg. Z4.

H. gracilis Rydb. = *H. grossulariifolia*.

H. grossulariifolia Rydb. To 70cm. Lvs orbicular-reniform, cordate, 1–7cm broad, glab. or sparsely glandular-pubesc., margin dentate. Scape glandular-pubesc. sometimes glab. at base; cal. campanulate-tubular, 6.5mm; pet. white, clawed. Oreg., Washington. Z5.

H. hallii A. Gray. To 30cm. Lvs orbicular, 1–3cm diam., lobes deep, sometimes overlapping, setose-dentate. Scape with 1–3 occas. leafy bracts; sep. hairy; pet. to twice sep. length. Colorado (Rocky Mts). Z5.

H. hallii var. **grossulariifolia** (Rydb.) Rosend. = *H. grossulariifolia*.

H. lloydii Rydb. = *H. micrantha*.

H. longiflora Rydb. To 1m. Lvs cordate, 3–12cm, usually glab., often mottled milky white, denticulate. Scape glab. or minutely gland., pubesc.; sep. yellow, 6–13mm, incurved; pet. 1.5–9mm, white to pink-purple, ciliate. E US. Z5.

H. longipetala. Moc. ex Ser. = *H. micrantha*.

H. lucida Schlecht. = *H. americana*.

H. macrorhiza Small = *H. villosa*.

H. maxima Greene. To 60cm. Lvs orbicular, 6–18cm, crenate, glab. above, veins villous beneath. Pet. white, tinged pink, 3×sep. length, clawed. US, restricted to Santa Cruz, Santa Rosa. Z6.

H. micrantha Douglas ex Lindl. Similar to *H. glabra* but st. and petioles white-pilose at base, lvs shallowly lobed. BC to Sierra Nevada. 'Palace Purple': all parts deep glossy purple-bronze except for small white fls. Often assigned to *H. micrantha* var. *diversifolia* (Rydb.) Rossend., Butters & Lakela, it is more likely to be a hybrid. Z5.

H. missouriensis Rosend. = *H. parviflora*.

H. nuttallii Rydb. = *H. micrantha*.

H. ovalifolia Nutt. = *H. cylindrica*.

H. 'Palace Purple' see *H. micrantha*.

H. parviflora Bartling. To 45cm. Lvs orbicular-reniform, cordate, base cuneate, 3–13cm, lobed, pubesc., setose to denticulate.

Scape pubesc.; cal. 1–3mm, white, rarely pink, tips green; pet. 1.5–3mm, white, occas. pink. CE US. Z6.

H. parvifolia Nutt. ex Torr. & A. Gray. To 60cm, spreading. Lvs minutely glandular-pubesc., sometimes glab. beneath, 2–6cm wide, much shorter than broad, double-lobed, crenate. Scape naked; cal. green, 2–3mm, lobes spreading; pet. clawed, white, 1.5×length of sep. Rocky Mts to Mont. and C Idaho. Z5.

H. pilosissima Benth. To 55cm. Lvs rhombic, 4–9×3–9cm, setose-dentate, rusty-pubesc. throughout, hairs longer beneath. Scape naked or bearing 1–4 lvs; fls dull red, 2.5–4.5mm, broadly campanulate; sep. obtuse; pet. pink-white, to twice sep. length, clawed. Coastal Calif. Z6.

H. pubescens Pursh. To 1m. Lvs ovate, 3–9cm, lobes rounded, tips acute, sometimes setose. Scape bearing 2–5 lvs; cal. 5–13mm, lobes spreading; pet. 2.5–4.5mm, white to mauve, incurved, ciliate. Penn. to Virg. 'Alba': fls white. Z5.

H. pulchella Wooton & Standl. Lvs 1.3cm wide, deeply lobed, bright green, gland. beneath, with broad, bristle-tipped teeth. Scape naked, gland; infl. secund; cal. lobes blunt, 4mm, tinged purple; pet. filiform-linear, pale pink. S US, New Mex. Z9.

H. pulverulenta Raf. = *H. pubescens*.

H. racemosa S. Wats. = *Elmera racemosa*.

H. reniformis Raf. = *H. pubescens*.

H. ribifolia Fisch. & Avé-Lall. = *H. pubescens*.

H. richardsonii R. Br. To 70cm. Lvs 3–6cm wide, shallow-lobed, glab. above, canescent beneath. Scape naked, pubesc. at base, gland. at apex; cal. 6–9mm, green; pet. clawed, equal to or longer than sep. BC to Colorado, E to Wisc., Indiana. Z5.

H. rubescens Torr. To 36cm. Lvs orbicular-broadly ovate, 0.8–5cm wide, narrow-dentate. Scape with 2 to several bracts; fls 3–5mm, white to pink; sep. tips green, hoary-pilose; pet. white, 3–4mm. Calif., Nevada, Utah.

H. rugelii Shuttlew. ex Kunze = *H. parviflora*.

H. sanguinea Engelm. To 60cm. Lvs 2–5.5cm, broadly reniform to ovate, near pentagonal in outline, glandular-pulverulent, veins pubesc. beneath. Scape with 2–3 small lvs; bracts red; fls bright red, 6–12mm; sep. ovate-triangular; pet. 1.5–2mm. A parent of many cvs, particularly in the hybrid group *H. ×brizoides*. New Mex., Ari. Z6. 'Alba': fls white. 'Grandiflora': vigorous; fls large. 'Maxima': fls burgundy. 'Oxfordii': fls dark red. 'Splendens': fls rich red. 'Variegata': lvs variegated. 'Virginalis': fls white. Z3.

H. saxicola E.J. Nels. = *H. cylindrica*.

H. scabra. Rydb. = *H. longiflora*.

H. squamosa. Raf. = *H. villosa*.

H. suksdorfia Rydb. = *H. cylindrica*.

H. ×tiarelloides Lemoine = ✕ *Heucherella tiarelloides*.

H. utahensis Rydb. = *H. parvifolia*.

H. versicolor Greene. 15–20cm. Lvs suborbicular, base cordate, 3–4.5cm across, thin, usually 5–7-lobed, glab. above, slightly hairy beneath, margin lightly ciliate. Scape naked; infl. secund; cal. turbinate, pink becoming rose red; pet. 0 or much reduced; fil. sometimes petaloid. New Mex. Z9.

H. villosa Michx. Similar to *H. parviflora* except lf lobes triangular rather than rounded, pet. broadly lanceolate. Appalachians, Ark., Tenn., Kent. Z5.

→*Tiarella*.

✕ **Heucherella** Wehrh. (*Heuchera* ✕*Tiarella*.) Saxifragaceae. 2 perenn. herbs, to 45cm. Lvs to 13cm, orbicular, stalked, lobed, hispid, light green, mottled brown when young, tinted bronze in autumn. Scape to 40cm; infl. loose, slender; cal. fused into a pink cup; pet. 4mm, just exceeding sep. Late spring, summer. Gdn origin. Z5.

✕ **H. alba** (Lemoine) Stearn. (*Heuchera* ✕*brizoides* ✕*Tiarella wherryi*.) Close to ✕ H. tiarelloides, but lacking stolons and normally white-fld.

✕ **H. tiarelloides** (Lemoine) Wehrh., ex Stearn. (*Heuchera* ✕*brizoides* ✕*Tiarella cordifolia*.) Stoloniferous. Lvs cordate-suborbicular, coarsely toothed and lobed, crenate. Scapes tinted brown; fls pink. 'Bridget Bloom': fls shell pink, in dense spikes.

→*Heuchera*.

Hevea Aubl. Euphorbiaceae. 9 trees with copious latex. Lvs trifoliate. Infl. a panicled cyme, appearing before or with the new lvs; fls small, fragrant; cal. with a short tube and 5 sep.; pet. 0, sta. 10. Amaz. basin. Z10.

H. brasiliensis (A. Juss.) Muell. Arg. PARA RUBBER TREE; CAOUTCHOUC TREE. Decid. tree to 35m. Young lvs purple-bronze turning orange, brown or red, ultimately mid green; lfts 30–60cm, elliptic, thick and leathery; petioles to 30cm. Fls yellow-white. Amaz. & Orinoco Rivers.

→*Siphonia*.

Hexadesmia Brongn. Orchidaceae. Some 15 epiphytic orchids. Pbs clumped, slender fusiform, sometimes stalked. Infl. a term.

rac. or fascicle; fls small; sep. free, spreading, oblong to lanceolate; pet. similar to sep.; lip, reflexed or recurved. Trop. Amer. Z10.

H. brachyphylla Rchb. f. = *H. fusiformis*.

H. crurigera (Batem. ex Lindl.) Lindl. Pbs, to 14cm, bifoliate. Lvs to 20cm, narrowly linear. Rac. to 13cm, fractiflex; fls white; sep. to 7×3mm; pet. subequal to sep; lip to 10×5mm, oblong-cuneate or oblong-obovate, apex bilobed. Mex., Guat., El Salvador, Costa Rica.

H. fasciculata Brongn. Pbs to 30cm, bifoliate. Lvs to 25cm, linear-elliptic to lanceolate. Infl. a fascicle to 4cm; fls red-green or yellow-green; sep. to 11×3mm; pet. to 10×3mm; lip to 11×6mm, oblanceolate to narrowly obovate, acute or truncate, apiculate. Mex., Guat., Costa Rica, Panama.

H. fusiformis Griseb. Pbs to 6cm, unifoliate. Lvs to 13cm, linear to oblong. Infl. 1- or 2-fld; tep. white, pale yellow or pale cream-green, faintly veined pink, lip white; sep. to 10×3mm, pet. to 8×3mm; lip to 8×5mm, simple, obovate-pandurate or spathulate, truncate or obtuse. Costa Rica, Venez., Trin.

H. lindeniana A. Rich. & Gal. = *Scaphyglottis lindeniana*.

H. micrantha Lindl. Pbs to 6cm, usually bifoliate. Lvs to 12cm, linear. Rac. to 11cm, slender; fls white to green-violet; sep. to 2×1.5mm; pet. to 2×1mm; lip to 2×2.5mm, 3-lobed, midlobe obliquely subquadrate to suborbicular, apiculate. Guat., Panama, Br. Hond.

H. reedii Rchb. f. = *H. sessilis*.

H. sessilis Rchb. f. Pbs to 20cm, usually unifoliate. Lvs to 50cm, linear. Infl. a fascicle, to 8cm; fls pale green flushed brown; sep to 3.5×3mm; pet. to 4×3mm; lip to 7×5mm, pandurate-subquadrate. Mex., Venez., Colomb., Braz.

→*Scaphyglottis*.

Hexaneurocarpon Dop = *Fernandoa*.

Hexastylis Raf.
H. arifolia Michx. = *Asarum arifolium*.
H. shuttleworthii (Britt. & Baker) Small = *Asarum shuttleworthii*.
H. virginica (L.) Small = *Asarum virginicum*.

Hexisea Lindl. Orchidaceae. 5 diminutive, epiphytic orchids. Pbs slender, furrowed-cylindric, developing apically and laterally, producing chains of stem-length with leafy constrictions, overall appearance tufted, reed-like or shrubby. Lvs linear-lanceolate. Fls small, in short-stalked term. clusters, scarcely opening; sep. elliptic-lanceolate; pet. oblanceolate; lip similar to tep. Throughout the year. C & N S Amer. Z10.

H. bidentata Lindl. Aggregate pbs to 45cm. Lvs to 9cm, usually smaller. Fls to 6, to 1.5cm diam., vermilion, cinnabar red or scarlet. Throughout genus range.

Hiba *Thujopsis dolobrata*.

Hibanobambusa Maruyama & H. Okamura. Gramineae. 1 bamboo, possibly of hybrid origin, the parents being spp. in *Phyllostachys* and *Sasa*. Culms 2–5m×1–3cm, curved at the base; sheaths decid. with scattered hairs; br. 1 per node, rarely 2. Lvs 15–25×3.5–5cm, scaberulous, glab.; sheaths hairless, with auricles and bristles. Jap. Z8.

H. tranquillans (Koidz.) Maruyama & H. Okamura. INYOU-CHIKUZOKU. 'Shiroshima': culms, sheaths, lvs striped white and yellow.

→*Phyllostachys* and *Semiarundinaria*.

Hibbertia Andrews BUTTON FLOWER; GUINEA GOLD VINE. Dilleniaceae. Some 125 everg. shrubs, often climbing. Fls. term., solitary; pet. 5, spreading, alternating with 5, green, lanceolate, hairy sep.; sta. crowded in a ring. Madag., Australasia, Polyn. Z10.

H. bracteata (R. Br.) Benth. Erect, closely branched undershrub. Lvs 1–2cm, linear-oblong to lanceolate, minutely hairy beneath. Fls to 2cm diam.; pet. yellow, notched at apex. Aus. (NSW).

H. dentata R. Br. Shrub or subshrub. St. trailing or twining. Lvs to 5cm, ovate-oblong, sometimes prickle-toothed, base rounded. Fls to 5cm diam.; pet. deep yellow, obovate, mucronate. Aus. (NSW).

H. perfoliata Endl. Glab. shrub, erect or trailing. Lvs 2.5–7cm, ovate, perfoliate, entire or sparsely toothed. Fls to 3cm diam.; pet. obovate, primrose to golden yellow. W Aus.

H. scandens (Willd.) Dryand. ex Hoogl. SNAKE VINE; GOLD GUINEA PLANT. Shrub to 1.25m, procumbent or twining. Lvs 5–10cm, obovate to lanceolate, sericeous. Fls to 5cm diam., malodorous; pet. golden yellow, obovate-triangular, truncate-praemorse. Aus. (Queensld, NSW).

Hibiscus L. MALLOW; ROSE MALLOW; GIANT MALLOW. Malvaceae. c220 ann. or perenn. herbs, shrubs, subshrubs and trees. Lvs

petiolate, sometimes lobed or parted. Fls solitary, clustered or terminally aggregated; epical. seg. distinct or connate at base; cal. 5-lobed, symmetrical; pet. broadly obovate, usually spreading; staminal column 5-dentate at apex, anth. numerous; styles 5; stigmas capitate. Warm temp., subtrop. and trop. regions.

H. abelmoschus L. = *Abelmoschus moschatus*.
H. abutiloides Willd. = *H. tiliaceus*.
H. acerifolius (Link & Otto) DC., non Salisb. = *H. platanifolius*.
H. acerifolius Salisb. non (Link & Otto) DC. = *H. syriacus*.

H. acetosella Welw. ex Hiern. Ann. or woody-based perenn. herb to 1.5m, glabrate or rarely pubesc., tinted red. Lvs unlobed or 3- or 5-lobed or -parted. Fls solitary in lf axils; epical. seg. 9–10; pet. purple-red or yellow, deep purple at base. E & C Afr. 'Red Shield': lvs brilliant maroon. Z10.

H. africanus Mill. = *H. trionum*.

H. ×archeri Willd. Wats. (*H. rosa-sinensis* ×*H. schizopetalus*.) Similar to *H. rosa-sinensis* but branching more delicate, lvs more coarsely serrate, pet. red, laciniate or crenate. Gdn origin. 'Dainty La France': br. slender, erect; lvs mid-green, ovate; fls single, large, nodding, pet. lobed, frilled, vivid pink with darker veins. Z9.

H. arnottianus A. Gray. Shrub or small everg. tree to 8m, glabrate. Lvs to 25cm, dark green, ovate, entire or dentate. Fls weakly fragrant, solitary; epical. seg. 5–7; pet. 6–11cm, white, sometimes with pink veins; staminal column 8–18, exserted, fil. red. Hawaii. Z10.

H. brackenridgei A. Gray. Shrub to 3m, or small tree to 10m; st. sprawling to erect, sometimes spinescent; young br. glabrate to densely stellate-pubesc. Lf blades to 15cm, 3-, 5-, or 7-lobed, lobes ovate to obovate, serrate. Fls solitary or in short term. rac.; epical. seg. 7–10; cal. red to yellow; pet. 3.5–8cm, yellow, usually with a maroon spot at base, staminal column exserted. Hawaii. Z10.

H. californicus Kellogg = *H. lasiocarpos*.
H. calycinus Willd. = *H. calyphyllus*.

H. calyphyllus Cav. Perenn. herb or shrub to 3m; young st. stellate-tomentose. Lf blades to 12cm, unlobed or obscurely to distinctly 3- or less commonly 5-lobed, stellate-pubesc., serrate to crenate-dentate. Fls solitary; epical. seg. 5, connate at base; pet. 4–8cm, sulphur-yellow, basal part maroon; staminal column included. Trop. & S Afr., Madag., Masc. Is.; nat. Hawaii. Z10.

H. cameronii Knowles & Westc. PINK HIBISCUS. Shrub, subshrub or perenn. herb, to 2m; st. green, becoming dark grey. Lvs to 12cm, 3-, 5-, or 7-lobed, or unlobed, lobes serrate. Fls solitary or in leafy rac. or corymbs; epical. reduced to small teeth; pet. to 8cm, flushed pink, deep rose or red-purple at base; staminal column crimson, exserted, decurved. Madag., cult. in Hawaii as a hedge plant. Z10.

H. cannabinus L. KENAF; INDIAN HEMP; BIMLI; DECCAN HEMP. Ann. or short-lived woody-based perenn. to 3.5m, prickly glabrescent; st. shrubby, simple or branched. Upper lvs slightly lobed or unlobed and lanceolate; lower lvs deeply 3-, 5-, or 7-lobed, with a swollen gland on midrib beneath, lobes lanceolate to linear, serrate. Fls axill. or in rac.; epical. seg. 7–10, pet. 4–8cm, pale yellow or less commonly pale purple, with red-purple spot at the base; staminal column included. Exact origin unknown, probably E Indies. Z10.

H. chinensis Jacq. = *H. rosa-sinensis* or *H. syriacus*.

H. cisplatinus St.-Hil. Shrub to 3m; st. with stout yellow spines. Lvs to 15cm, upper lvs unlobed, ovate-triangular to lanceolate, lower lvs 3- or 5-lobed, toothed. Fls solitary; epical. seg. 10–12; pet. 5–8cm, rose above, darker to violet-purple at base. S Braz., Parag. to Arg.; cult. in Hawaii. Z10.

H. coccineus (Medik.) Walter. Tall, hemp-like, woody-based, perenn. herb to 3m, glaucous. Lvs palmately 3-, 5- or 7-parted, or compound, divisions linear-lanceolate, toothed. Fls solitary; epical. seg. 10–12; pet. to 8cm, deep red; staminal column exserted. SE US. Z7.

H. collinus Roxb. = *H. platanifolius*.

H. diversifolius Jacq. SWAMP HIBISCUS. Low shrub to 1m, often cultivated as ann., to 1m; st. stiff, stellate-pubesc., prickly. Lvs to 15cm, palmately 5-lobed, serrate, hispid. Fls solitary or in term. leafless rac.; epical. seg. about 8; pet. 4–6cm, yellow with maroon centre; staminal column 2cm, stigmas purple. Trop. Afr. and Asia, introd. into C & S Amer. Z10.

H. eetveldeanus De Wild. & T. Dur. = *H. acetosella*.

H. elatus Sw. CUBAN BAST; MAHOE. Tree to 25m, straight, sparingly branching in the upper part. Lvs variably hairy, sometimes glabrescent. Pet. 8–12cm, orange-yellow or orange-red, fading to deep crimson. Jam., Cuba. Distinguished from *H. tiliaceus* by the large cal., with epical. present in fr., and the large, not overlapping, pet. Z10.

H. esculentus L. = *Abelmoschus esculentus*.
H. farragei F. Muell. = *Radyera farragei*.
H. fulgens hort. = *H. rosa-sinensis*.

H. furcellatus Desr. Woody-based perenn. herb or subshrub;

young br. stellate-pubesc. Lvs 5–15cm, ovate to suborbicular, unlobed or shallowly to deeply 3-, 5- or 7-lobed, stellate-tomentose, serrate-dentate. Fls solitary or in rac.; epical. seg. 10–14; pet. 5–9cm, pale magenta to rose, darker at base; staminal column included, maroon. W Indies, Flor., Hawaii, C & S Amer. Z10.

H. fuscus Garcke. Shrub to 3m; st. densely stellate-hispid. Lvs to 7×5cm, narrowly ovate to suborbicular, sometimes lobed, brown stellate-tomentose, serrate. Fls forming leafy corymbose pan.; epical. seg. 10–12; pet. to 1.8cm, white or yellow, narrowly obovate; staminal tube 0.8–1.2cm, anth. orange. Ethiop. to S Afr. and westwards to Congo. Z10.

H. gossypinus Harv., non Thunb. = *H. fuscus*.

H. gossypinus Baill., non Thunb. = *H. platanifolius*.

H. grandiflorus Michx., non Torr. GREAT ROSE MALLOW. Often confused with forms and hybrids of *H. moscheutos*; distinguished by lvs 10–30cm, deeply 3-, or 5-lobed; pet. 12.5–15cm, white, pink or purple-rose, sometimes with a crimson spot at base. SE US. Z8.

H. hakeifolius Giord. = *Alogyne hakeifolia*.

H. hamabo Sieb. & Zucc. Shrub to 5m, differing from *H. tiliaceus* in having lvs to 7.5cm, transversely elliptic to ovate, mucronate, serrulate. Jap., Korea. Plants offered under this name are usually cvs of *H. syriacus*, with pink or pink-lavender single cor., with crimson spot at the base. Z10.

H. hastatus L. f. PURAU TERUERE. Shrub or small tree, differing from *H. tiliaceus* in having lvs commonly 3-lobed, with term. lobe about twice as long as the basal lat. lobes, and pet. generally lobed at apex. Society Is. Z10.

H. heterophyllus Vent. Everg. shrub or small tree to 6m; st. with few prickles. Lf blades 5–20cm, ovate, elliptic or narrowly obovate towards top of the plant, sometimes deeply 3-lobed, serrate, stellate-pubesc. beneath to almost glab. Fls solitary; epical. seg. about 10; pet. to 7cm, white with pink margin, pink or yellow, with thin stripe or purple-red basal spot. Aus. Z10.

H. huegelii Endl. = *Alyogyne huegelii*.

H. indicus (Burm. f.) Hochr. Differs from *H. mutabilis* in its 5–9 ovate, not linear, epical. seg. S China. Z10.

H. kokio Hillebrand ex Wawra. NATIVE RED HIBISCUS. Shrub or small tree to 7m; st. stiffly pubesc. Lvs 3–12cm, unlobed, elliptic to oblong-elliptic, ovate to obovate, glossy green, crenate to serrate, or entire. Fls solitary; epical. seg. 6–8; cal. pale yellow; pet. 4.5–7cm, red to orange-red or rarely yellow, sometimes with a basal red spot; staminal column conspicuously exserted, red to orange. Hawaii. Z10.

H. lampas Cav. = *Thespesia lampas*.

H. lasiocarpos Cav. Shrub to 2m; st. stellate-pubesc. or glabrate. Lvs 10–17cm, ovate to lanceolate, serrate-crenate to undulate or subentire, densely pubesc. Fls solitary; epical. seg. 10–12; pet. 7–8cm, white or pink, often with a small maroon spot at base; staminal column 2.5–4cm. US (Ill. to Flor & Calif.). Z6.

H. lavaterioides Moric. ex Ser. Shrub to 1.5m, stellate-pubesc. Lvs 3–8cm, cordate-ovate or slightly trilobed, crenate-dentate. Fls solitary; epical. seg. 9; cor. campanulate; pet. 2.5–4.5cm, lavender, pink, often with white veins; staminal column included; stigmas red. W Indies, C Amer. and Mex. Z10.

H. ludwigii Ecklon & Zeyh. Similar to *H. calyphyllus* but epical. seg. broadest at base, linear-lanceolate to ovate, usually exceeding cal. Ethiop. to S Afr. Z10.

H. macrophyllus Roxb. ex Hornem. LARGE-LEAVED HAU. Trees to 25m; young growth hispid, with spreading yellow-brown coarse-stellate hairs. Lvs 20–60cm, cordate-orbicular, upper lvs smaller and narrower, subentire. Fls solitary or few in open cymes; epical. seg. 8–14; pet. 6–7cm, yellow, with a purple-red basal spot; staminal column included. India throughout the Malay peninsula to Java, nat. in Hawaii. Z10.

H. manihot L. = *Abelmoschus manihot*.

H. militaris Cav. SOLDIER ROSE MALLOW; HALBERD-LEAVED MARSH MALLOW; HALBERD-LEAVED ROSE MALLOW. Tall, woody-based perenn. herb to 2m, glab. or glabrate. Lvs to 15cm, lower cordate-ovate, upper triangular and hastately 3- or 5-lobed. Fls solitary; epical. seg. 9–13; pet. 5–8cm, pale pink to almost white, base crimson; staminal column included. US. Z6.

H. moscheutos L. COMMON ROSE MALLOW; SWAMP ROSE MALLOW. Robust, woody-based perenn. herb to 2.5m; st. few to many, stellate-pubesc. Lvs 8–22cm, broadly ovate to lanceolate, unlobed or 3- or 5-lobed, white-pubesc. beneath, serrate to crenate. Fls solitary; epical. seg. 10–15; pet. 8–10cm, white, pink or rose, base sometimes crimson. S US. ssp. *moscheutos*. Lvs narrowly ovate to lanceolate, unlobed or 3-lobed below; pet. white, sometimes pink, always with a red band at base. Virg., Georgia, Flor., Alab., Tenn. and Kent. 'Blue River II': fls white. 'Cotton Candy': fls pink and white. 'Crimson Wonder': fls deep red. 'Fresno': fls pink. 'Lord's Pink': fls light pink. 'New Blood-red': lvs ovate, white-pubesc. beneath; fls to 20cm, scarlet. 'Poinsettia': fls strong red. 'Radiation': fls pink.

Satan': fls deep red. 'Super Rose': fls rose. 'Southern Belle': to 80cm; lvs serrate, white felted beneath; fls to 20cm, crimson, pet. edges sometimes rose. 'White Giant': fls white. ssp. *palustris* (L.) R.T. Clausen. MARSH MALLOW; SEA HOLLYHOCK. Lvs ovate to rounded, commonly 3-lobed. Pet. pink or rose, rarely white, without a red band at base. Mass. to N Carol. and westwards to N Indiana. Z5.

H. mutabilis L. COTTON ROSE; CONFEDERATE ROSE MALLOW. Shrubs to 3m or small trees to 5m; st. stellate-pubesc., with gland. hairs. Lvs 8–17cm, palmately 3-, 5- or 7-lobed, lobes shallow and triangular, serrate-crenate, stellate-puberulent beneath, glabrate above. Fls solitary or in clusters; epical. seg. 8–12; pet. 5–7cm, white or pink, with darker base; staminal column included. China. 'Raspberry Rose': vigorous; lvs large; fls single, large, raspberry. 'Ruber': lvs oval, coarsely toothed; fls single, large, scarlet. Z8.

H. oculiroseus Britt. = *H. moscheutos* ssp. *moscheutos*.

H. palustris L. = *H. moscheutos* ssp. *palustris*.

H. paramutabilis L.H. Bail. Shrub or small tree to 5m, similar to *H. mutabilis* but epical. seg. 4–6. E China. Z9.

H. pedunculatus L. f. Perenn. herb or subshrub to 2m; st. densely adpressed stellate-pillose. Lvs 2–8.5cm, 3-lobed, lobes mostly oblong, rounded with stiff hairs, bluntly dentate. Fls solitary; epical. seg 7–9; pet. 3–4.5cm, pale rose-purple or pale lilac, stellate-pubesc. outside; staminal column included. Moz. to S Afr. Z10.

H. platanifolius (Willd.) Sweet. Shrub or small tree to 5m. Lvs 3–6cm, mostly 3-lobed, lobes elliptic, acuminate, almost entire. Fls solitary; epical. seg. 6–9; pet. 4–6.5cm, white, base crimson; staminal column included. India. Z10.

H. radiatus Cav. Differs from *H. canabinus* in lvs lacking gland on midrib beneath, epical. seg. 10–12. S & SE Asia, often cult. as a vegetable or medicinal herb. Z10.

H. rosa-sinensis L. CHINESE HIBISCUS; HAWAIIAN HIBISCUS; ROSE-OF-CHINA; CHINA ROSE; SHOE BLACK. Shrub to 2.5m or tree to 5m, sparsely puberulent to glabrate. Lvs to 15cm, ovate to broadly lanceolate, serrate, glossy green. Fls solitary; epical. seg. 6–9; pet. 6–12cm, v. variable in colour, but commonly red to deep red, darker towards the base; staminal column slightly exserted, fil. 0.5–1cm, petaloid in double-fld forms. Probably native of Trop. Asia. Cvs with variegated lvs include 'Cooperi' (lvs narrowly lanceolate, olive green marbled red, pink and white; fls rose), 'Lateritia Variegata' (lvs pointed and irregularly lobed, heavily variegated off-white; fls gold), 'Snow Queen' (habit bushy; lvs broadly ovate, marbled white, and grey-green). Cvs selected for fl. colour and form include 'Aurora' (fls, pom-pon shape, blushing pink), 'Bridal Veil' (fls large, single, crêpe-textured, pure white), 'Crown of Bohemia' (fls fully double, gold with flaming orange throat), 'Fiesta' (fls large, single, crinkled edges, deep apricot orange with pink-red eye), 'Kissed' (pet. reflexed, vivid red), 'Percy Lancaster' (fls single, pet. narrow, palest pink washed apricot, eye russet), 'Ruby Brown' (fls single, large, brown tinted orange with dark red throat), 'Sunny Delight' (fls single, large, brilliant yellow, throat white). Z9.

H. sabdariffa L. ROSELLE; JAMAICA SORREL; RED SORREL; SORREL. Ann. or robust, woody-based perenn. herb or subshrub to 2.5m; st. sparsely prickly, glab. Lvs 8–15cm, glabrate, with a gland at the base of the midrib beneath, ovate, undivided, or palmately 3- or 5-divided, lobes to 15cm, elliptic to linear, serrulate. Fls solitary or in short leafy rac.; epical. seg. 7–10; cal. becoming red and fleshy; pet. 4–5cm, light yellow, purple-red at base; staminal column included. OW tropics, widely cult. Z10.

H. schizopetalus (Mast.) Hook. f. JAPANESE HIBISCUS; JAPANESE LANTERN. Shrub to 3m; st. slender. Lvs to 12cm, ovate, serrate. Fls on long slender pedicels; epical. minute; pet. to 7cm, deeply and irregularly laciniate, pink or red; staminal column long-exserted. Kenya, Tanz. and N Moz. Probably a selection of *H. rosa-sinensis*. Z10.

H. scottii Balf. f. Shrub or small tree, hispid. Lvs to 10cm, elliptic, ovate or suborbicular, entire or 3-lobed, crenate or toothed. Fls solitary or 2–3 together; epical. seg. 10–12; cor. to 6cm, bright golden-yellow, carmine at base, suborbicular; anth. pale yellow; stigma lobes globose, blood-red. Socotra. Z10.

H. sinensis Mill., non hort. = *H. mutabilis*.

H. sinensis hort., non Mill. = *H. rosa-sinensis*.

H. sinosyriacus L.H. Bail. Similar to *H. syriacus*, but lvs large epical. seg. longer and broader, to 2.5×1cm. C China. 'Autumn Surprise': fls white, base feathered cherry. 'Lilac Queen': fls white, lightly tinted mauve, base clear burgundy, profuse. 'Red Centre': st. with silver sheen when mature; fls white, centre red. 'Ruby Glow': fls white, base clear burgundy. Z8.

H. speciosus Sol. = *H. coccineus*.

H. syriacus L. Shrub or small tree to 3m; br. grey, ± glabrate. Lvs 3–7cm, 3-lobed, lobes narrow, coarsely toothed. Fls solitary or paired; epical. seg. 6–8, to 1.5×0.3cm; cor. single or double (by petaloidy of sta.); pet. 3.5–7cm, white, red-purple or blue-lavender, with crimson base; staminal column included. OW, widely cult. Cvs notable for foliage include 'Meehanii' (habit low; lvs edged yellow; fls single, lavender), 'Purpureus Variegatus' (lvs variegated white). Cvs notable for fls include 'Admiral Dewey' (fls double, wide, snow white, abundant), 'Ardens' (habit broad; fls densely double, purple tinted blue), 'Blue Bird' (habit erect; fls wide, v. large, sky blue with small red eye), 'Coelestis' (pale violet, rose at base, single), 'Diana' (habit upright; lvs trilobed, dark green; fls single, white, v. wide, crinkled edges, profuse), 'Duc de Brabant' (deep rosy purple, double), 'Hamabo' (fls single, light pink, crimson markings and eye), 'Hélène' (upright; fls single, large, white with dark red edge and surrounding veins, abundant), 'Jeanne d'Arc' (white, semi-double), 'Lady Stanley' ('Elegantissimus'): white suffused shell pink, maroon at base, semi-double. 'Lucy' (fls double, red), 'Monstrosus' (white with maroon eye, single), 'Snowdraft' ('Totus Albus') (white, large, single), 'Violet Clair Double' ('Violaceus Plenus', 'Puniceus Plenus'): vinous purple, red-purple at centre, double. 'William R. Smith' (pure white, single, v. large), 'Woodbridge' (fls single, large, rich pink to carmine at centre). Z5.

H. tiliaceus L. MAHOE. Everg. shrub or small tree to 8; br. spreading, glabrate. Lvs 7–16cm, broadly ovate to suborbicular, unlobed, leathery, puberulent beneath, entire or denticulate, with 1–5 glands at the base of veins beneath. Fls solitary; epical. seg. 7–12; pet. 4–7cm, yellow or white, red to brown-red at base; staminal column included. OW littoral tropics. Z10.

H. trionum L. FLOWER OF-AN-HOUR; BLADDER KETMIA. Erect or ascending hispid ann. or short-lived perenn. herbs to 1.2m; st. stellate-puberulent. Upper lvs to 7cm, deeply 3- or 5-lobed or -parted, lobes narrowly elliptic, pinnately incised, crenate-serrate, lower lvs entire. Fls solitary; epical. seg. 7–11; cal. with purple veins, becoming inflated; pet. to 4cm, white, cream or yellow, with red base. Arid OW Trop. Z10.

H. venustus Bl. = H. indicus.

H. vesicarius Cav. = H. trionum.

H. waimeae A.A. Heller. Tree to 10m; st. with grey bark, br. and foliage stellate-pubesc. Lvs 5–18cm, orbicular to broadly ovate-elliptic, grey velvet-tomentose beneath, crenate-serrate. Fls strongly fragrant, solitary; epical. seg. 7–8; pet. 8–13cm, opening white, fading to pink by noon; staminal column to 15cm, crimson-red at apex. Hawaii. Z10.

H. youngianus Gaudich. ex Hook. & Arn. = H. furcellatus.
→Althaea and Paritium.

Hiccough Nut Combretum bracteosum.
Hickory Carya; Heritiera trifoliolata.
Hickory Pine Pinus pungens.
Hickory Wattle Acacia implexa; A. penninervis.

Hicksbeachia F.J. Muell. Proteaceae. 2 small trees. Lvs rigid-coriaceous, pinnate or lobed, spiny-dentate. Infl. a rac.; perianth tube straight, lobes soon becoming reflexed. Fr. an indehiscent nut; seed solitary. Aus. Z10.

H. pinnatifolia F. Muell. RED BOPPLE NUT. To 12m. Lvs 70cm (-1m), pinnate, lobes to 25cm, serrate. Fls scented, purple-red, ageing cream, in 35cm pendent, cylindrical rac. Spring. E Aus.

Hicoria Raf.
H. alba Britt. = Carya tomentosa.
H. cordiformis Britt. = Carya cordiformis.
H. microcarpa (Nutt.) Britt. = Carya glabra.
H. ovata Britt. = Carya. ovata.
H. pallida Ashe = Carya pallida.
H. pecan Britt. = Carya illinoinensis.

Hidalgoa La Ll. & Lex. CLIMBING DAHLIA. Compositae. 5 sub-shrubby perenn. herbaceous lianes, climbing by means of petioles. Lvs pinnately divided. Cap. radiate, usually solitary. Mex., C Amer. Z10.

H. ternata La Ll. Perenn. to 50cm. Lvs to 10cm, ovate, 3-pinnate, seg. coarsely toothed, central leaflet to 7.5cm, lat. seg. smaller. Cap. to 5cm diam., solitary or few; ray flts 5, orange. Mex.

H. wercklei Hook. f. Subshrub to 1m+. Lvs to 6cm, ovate, 3-pinnate, toothed, teeth tipped red-brown. Cap. to 6cm diam., solitary; ray flts 10, scarlet above, yellow beneath. Costa Rica.
→Childsia.

Hidden Lily Curcuma roscoeana.

Hieracium L. HAWKWEED. Compositae. c10,000 perenn., ± hairy herbs, with milky sap. Basal lvs often in a rosette, usually petiolate, frequently withered by anthesis, or 0. Cap. ligulate, usually in ± paniculate infl.; receptacle ± flat; flts usually

yellow. Eur., to N & W Asia, NW Afr. and N Amer. Hieracium differs from Pilosella Hill in the absence of stolons, the ligules which lack a red dors. stripe, and the fact that the 'spp.' are nearly always apomictic.

H. albidum Vill. = H. intybaceus.

H. alpinum L. 5–35cm. Lvs with numerous long, white, simple hairs, few to many small marginal gland. hairs and occas. stellate hairs, basal lvs to 10×2cm, numerous, soft or somewhat rigid, outer oblong to elliptic or almost circular, obtuse, often pleated, inner lanceolate to spathulate, obtuse to acute, entire to pinnatifid, often undulate, base attenuate into a winged petiole. Cap. usually solitary, sometimes to 3; ligules deep yellow; styles and stigmas deep yellow. Summer. N & C Eur., N Asia and extreme E N Amer. Z3.

H. aurantiacum L. = Pilosella aurantiaca.

H. bombycinum Boiss. & Reut. = H. mixtum.

H. bornmuelleri Freyn. Lvs to 15×4cm, 6–25, ovate-elliptic to oblanceolate-oblong, usually acute, often folded, toothed, teeth sometimes remote, base attenuate, amplexicaul, lanate, with long plumose hairs. Cap. 1–20; ligules yellow; styles and stigmas yellow or discoloured. Summer. Turk. Z7.

H. brunneocroceum L. = Pilosella aurantiaca.

H. chaboissaei Arv.-Touv. 30–60cm. Lvs subplumose-hairy, basal lvs to 6.5×2cm, oblong or elliptic-lanceolate, obtuse to acute, ± entire to dentate, base attenuate. Cap. 2–12; ligules yellow; styles and stigmas discoloured. SW Alps. Z6.

H. conyzaefolium Gouan = Crepis conyzifolia.

H. faeroense Dahlst. = H. laevigatum.

H. glaucum All. 20–60cm. Basal lvs to 16×1.5cm, numerous, flat, glaucous, rarely spotted, ± rigid, narrowly elliptical, lanceolate or linear-lanceolate, usually acute, toothed, base attenuate into an often distinct petiole, with long simple hairs towards margin and dors. midrib, or glab. Cap. 2–15; ligules deep yellow; styles and stigmas yellow or frequently discoloured. Summer–early autumn. Alps, Apennines and N Balk. Z6.

H. gronovii L. 60–120cm. Lvs deep green, with soft or dense thick, curved hairs, and minute gland. hairs at margin and beneath, basal lvs frequently large, obovate, elliptic or oblong, rounded-obtuse or slightly acute, often furrowed, entire, base narrow, with long coarse stiff hairs. Cap. in racemose or corymbose infl.; ligules pale yellow; style discoloured. Summer–mid autumn. N Amer. Z4.

H. gymnocephalum Griseb. ex Pant. 15–65cm. Basal lvs 0, st. lvs to 20×4cm, to 15, sometimes crowded towards base forming a false rosette, broadly elliptic or oblong, often ligulate, rarely ± lanceolate, obtuse to ± acute, entire or barely denticulate, base long-attenuate, sessile, villous to lanate, with plumose hairs and other minute gland. hairs at margin of base. Cap. 1–30; ligules deep yellow; styles and stigmas deep yellow. Summer. W & S Balk. and Albania. Z6.

H. heldreichii Boiss. 20–100cm. Basal lvs 0, st. lvs to 7×4cm, 6–20 or numerous, soft or papery, bright yellow-green or olive, grey-green or white-green beneath, elliptic, oblong, oblong- or ovate-elliptic, acute to acuminate, cusped, denticulate to deeply dentate, rarely entire, base narrow or rounded, villous, with entangled plumose hairs, lower lvs often forming a false rosette. Cap. 1–10, lowest often aborted; ligules deep yellow; styles and stigmas yellow or discoloured. Summer. Balk. Penins. Z6.

H. humile Jacq. 10–30cm. Lvs sometimes yellow-green, with rigid coarse simple eglandular hairs and short gland. hairs, basal lvs in a rosette, to 11×4cm, obovate, elliptical or oblong to broadly lanceolate, rarely narrower, rounded-obtuse to acuminate, sometimes furrowed, usually deeply sinuate-dentate or incise-lobed, petiole violet, toothed. Cap. 1–12, ligules usually deep yellow; styles and stigmas deep yellow or discoloured. Summer. S & SC Eur. Z7.

H. intybaceus All. 5–30cm. Basal lvs 0, st. lvs to 16×2cm, numerous, deep yellow-green, soft, with dense yellow-green viscid hairs, lanceolate, ribbon-like or oblong to linear-lanceolate, acute or slightly obtuse, irregularly toothed, base attenuate into a short winged petiole or sessile or slightly amplexicaul, lower lvs often crowded towards base. Cap. 1–6; ligules white-yellow; styles and stigmas deep yellow or discoloured. Summer. Alps. Z6.

H. japonicum Franch. & Savat. 10–40cm. Lvs membranous, dirty green, toothed, with long spreading coarse brown hairs and gland. hairs, to 15×3cm, basal lvs broadly elliptical, oblong-spathulate or oblanceolate, rounded or obtuse, often pleated, base attenuate into a winged petiole, often withered at anthesis. Cap. 2–10, in lax racemose infl.; phyllaries black to green; ligules pale yellow; style and stigmas deep yellow. Summer–early autumn. Jap. Z8.

H. laevigatum Willd. 30–120cm. Lvs green to deep green, rarely ± purple-violet or red, with few to numerous bulbous based hairs, and sometimes stellate hairs esp. beneath, basal lvs usually 0 or withering early, st. lvs to 20×4cm, ovate- to linear- or oblong-lanceolate, apex acute, denticulate to dentate, base attenuate or contracted or rounded. Cap. few to many, in a branched, paniculate infl.; ligules golden-yellow; styles and stigmas deep yellow or discoloured. Late summer–early autumn. Eur., C & N Asia, N Amer. Z6.

H. lanatum Vill. 10–50cm. Lvs villous with dense, white, curled, slightly plumose hairs, sometimes with stellate hairs beneath; basal lvs few or 0, to 10×4cm, oblong, elliptical, lanceolate or ovate, obtuse or acute, entire or with few, occas. coarse teeth, base attenuate or broadly winged, petiolate. Cap. 2–12; ligules pale yellow; styles and stigmas deep yellow. Late spring––summer. SE Fr., W Switz., NW It. Z7.

H. maculatum Sm. 20–80cm. Lvs green or glaucous, spotted or blotched brown-purple, with simple eglandular hairs, usually sparsely so above, sometimes with stellate hairs beneath, basal lvs to 4.5cm, ovate, oblong, ovate- or narrowly-lanceolate, obtuse or acute, denticulate to dentate, base constricted or attenuate into a long petiole. Cap. 1 to numerous, often in a corymbose infl.; ligules pale or deep yellow; styles and stigmas yellow or discoloured. W & C Eur., sporadically elsewhere. Z6.

H. marmoreum Pančić & Vis.   To 30cm. Lvs 10–14, green, denticulate, granular and rough above, with numerous long, fine hairs throughout, lower oblong-obovate or ovate-oblong, large, moderately obtuse or slightly acute, base ± petiolate. Cap. 1–8; ligules yellow; style deep yellow. Summer. Balk., Bulg. Z6.

H. mixtum Froelich. 5–20cm. Lvs with numerous long, straight hairs on dors. midrib and petiole, basal lvs to 4×2.5cm, numerous, ovate, elliptical or ovate-lanceolate to obovate, mucronate-obtuse to slightly acute, entire to denticulate, ± undulate, base attenuate into a winged petiole. Cap. 1–4; globose or ovate; ligules deep yellow; styles and stigmas deep yellow. Summer. Pyren. and Cordillera Cantabrica. Z6.

H. murorum L. 10–80cm. Lvs green or grey-green, with simple eglandular hairs throughout or glab. above, sometimes with stellate hairs beneath, basal lvs to 25×7cm, green, oval, obovate, elliptic, oblong or lanceolate, obtuse to acute, entire to coarsely and deeply laciniate-dentate, base ± cordate, truncate, rounded or constricted, petiole long. Cap. 1–15 or numerous, often in paniculate or corymbose infl.; ligules yellow; styles and stigmas discoloured or rarely yellow. Spring–summer. Most of Eur., C & N Asia. Z6.

H. paludosum L. = Crepis paludosa.

H. pamphilii Arv.-Touv. = H. chaboissaei.

H. pannonicum Jacq. = Crepis pannonica.

H. pannosum Boiss. 10–60cm. Basal lvs 0, st. lvs to 20×5.5cm, rigid, sometimes forming a false rosette, oblanceolate-oblong, obovate, oblanceolate or elliptic, obtuse or acute, sometimes mucronate, entire to sparsely dentate or serrate, base attenuate, usually sessile, amplexicaul, lanate. Cap. 2–20 in a usually much-branched infl.; ligules yellow; styles and stigmas yellow or discoloured. Summer–early autumn. Balk. Penins., Aegean, Asia Minor. Z6.

H. pilosella L. = Pilosella officinarum.

H. praecox Schultz-Bip. = H. glaucum.

H. pyrenaicum L. = Crepis pyrenaica.

H. scouleri Hook. 30–60cm. Basal lvs often withering early, st. lvs to 18×2.5m, lanceolate, base attenuate into a long, broadly winged petiole, or sessile, lanate, with tufts of long weak hairs esp. towards base of the dors. midrib, entire or sparsely denticulate, with minute gland. hairs. Cap. few to numerous in loosely branched racemose infl.; ligules deep yellow; styles deep yellow. Mid summer–early autumn. Pacific N Amer. Z8.

H. staticifolium All. = Tolpis staticifolia.

H. tomentosum All. = H. lanatum.

H. umbellatum L. 10–150cm. Basal lvs 0, st. lvs 15 to numerous, crowded, linear to oblong or oblong-lanceolate, rarely lanceolate, acute to obtuse, acuminate, base attenuate or crenate, sometimes revolute, entire or remotely toothed, teeth sometimes long and cusped, with simple eglandular hairs, with stellate hairs beneath, often ± glab. above. Cap. 1 to many, in large, robust, condensed pan. or rac., the upper part sometimes umbellate; ligules golden yellow, rarely white-yellow; styles and stigmas deep yellow or slightly discoloured. Mid summer–mid autumn. Eur., C & N Asia, N Amer. Z6.

H. venosum L. 30–60cm. Basal lvs to 14×4cm, in a rosette, obovate or elongate lanceolate-ovate, obtuse, entire or denticulate, with fine hairs and few small gland. hairs, base with coarse stiff long hairs, attenuate into a short petiole, veins blood-red, often variegated. Cap. 2 to many, in a spreading corymbose infl.; ligules golden; style ± brown. Canada to SC US. Z3.

H. villosum Jacq. 15–40cm. Lvs ± glaucous, usually with numerous, long, simple eglandular hairs, basal lvs to 10×2.5cm, oblong or lanceolate, somewhat obtuse or acute, entire to short-ly dentate, often undulate, attenuate into a ± petiolate base. Cap. 1–4; ligules pale yellow; styles and stigmas yellow or dis-

coloured. Summer. Mts of Eur., from Jura and Carpath. to SW Alps, S Apennines and N Bulg. Z6.

H. waldsteinii Tausch 25–30cm. Basal lvs withering, st. lvs to 14×6cm, numerous, thickened, forming a false rosette, obovate or elliptic, obtuse or acute, base attenuate or petiolate. Cap. 2–25, usually in a ± laxly paniculate infl.; ligules yellow; styles and stigmas yellow. Summer. NW Balk. to NC Greece. Z6.

H. wilczekii Zahn.   To 45cm. Basal annd lower st. lvs sea-green, elliptical- to oblong-lanceolate, long-acute to acuminate, teeth often coarse and mucronate, base attenuate into a long, ± winged petiole, hairy above and at margin, hairy. Cap. 2–4, rarely more; ligules bright yellow; styles dark. Summer. Switz. Z6.

→Andryala.

Hieranthes Raf.
H. fragrans Raf. = Stereospermum chelonoides.

Hierba-de-vibora Ibervillea lindheimeri.

Hieronymusia Engl. = Suksdorfia.

Hierro de Costa Bourreria succulenta var. revoluta.
Higan Cherry Prunus subhirtella.
Highbush Blueberry Vaccinium corymbosum.
Highbush Cranberry Viburnum trilobum.
High Mallow Malva sylvestris.

Hilaria Kunth. Gramineae. 7 perenn. grasses to 1m. St. erect to spreading, rigid. Lf blades to 0.3cm wide, flat to inrolled, narrow. Pan. usually obtusely wedge-shaped; spikelets in clusters of 3. Summer. N Amer. Z7.

H. berlangeri (Steud.) Nash. CURLY MESQUITE.   To 30cm. St. flexuous, tufted, producing stolons. Lf blades rough, with soft, straight hairs, spikelets to 0.5cm; glumes convergent at base, stiff, rough, 2–3-ribbed, awned or mucronate. SW US.

H. jamesii (Torr.) Benth. GALLETA.   To 30cm. St. erect, tufted. Lf blades stiff, becoming inrolled. Spikelets to 1.5cm, hairy in lower part; glumes acuminate, awned. W US.

H. mutica (Buckley) Benth. TOBOSA GRASS.   To 60cm. St. tufted. Lf blades flat to inrolled. Spikelets to 0.5cm, densely hairy in lower part; glumes of staminate spikelets obtuse, downy at apex; glumes of hermaphrodite spikelet keeled, with numerous awns and narrow lobes at apex. SW US.

H. rigida (Thunb.) Benth. ex Scrib. BIG GALLETA.   To 1m. St. erect, softly downy with upright br. Lf blades ± inrolled, downy to glab. Spikelets to 0.5cm, villous at base; glumes unequal, 7-ribbed, 1–3 ribs extending to awns. SW US.

Hildegardia Schott. & Endl. Sterculiaceae. 11 trees; cal. tubular or divided into 4–5 seg.; pet. 0; ♂ fls with 8–10 anth. on an androgynophore; ♀ fls slightly larger than ♂, ovary spherical to ovoid, anth. few. Trop. Afr., Madag., India, Philipp., Indon., N Aus. and Cuba. Z10.

H. barteri (Mast.) Kosterm. Decid. To 30m, with buttresses. Lvs 10–25cm, broadly ovate, rarely obscurely 3-lobed, ± stellate-hairy beneath. Pan. slender, appearing before lvs; cal. scarlet, 2cm, constricted in the middle; ♂ fls with 8–10 anth. in a hemi-sperical exserted head. W trop. Afr.
→Erythropsis, Firmiana, Sterculia.

Hildewintera F. Ritter.
H. aureispina (F. Ritter) F. Ritter = Cleistocactus winteri.

Hill Cherry Prunus serrulata var. spontanea.
Hill Raspberry Rubus niveus.
Hilton Daisy Gerbera aurantiaca.

Himalayacalamus Keng f.
H. falconeri (Hook. ex Munro) Keng f. = Drepanostachyum falconeri.

Himalaya Honeysuckle Leycesteria formosa.
Himalayan Balsam Impatiens glandulifera.
Himalayan Birch Betula utilis.
Himalayan Bird Cherry Prunus cornuta.
Himalayan Box Buxus wallichiana.
Himalayan Cedar Cedrus deodara.
Himalayan Cherry Prunus rufa.
Himalayan Cypress Cupressus torulosa.
Himalayan Fir Abies spectabilis.
Himalayan Fleabane Erigeron multiradiatus.
Himalayan Hemlock Tsuga dumosa.
Himalayan Holly Ilex dipyrena.
Himalayan Knotweed Polygonum polystachyum.
Himalayan Lilac Syringa emodi.

Himalayan Manna Ash *Fraxinus floribunda.*
Himalayan Musk Rose *Rosa brunonii.*
Himalayan Pine *Pinus wallichiana.*
Himalayan Rhubarb *Rheum australe.*
Himalayan Spruce *Picea smithiana.*
Himalayan Yew *Taxus wallichiana.*

Himantoglossum Koch. Orchidaceae. 4 tuberous terrestrial orchids. Spike narrow-cylindric; sep. and pet. forming a hood; lip trilobed, central lobe strap-like, deeply cleft, divisions twisted. Late spring–mid summer. Eur., Medit. Z7.
H. **caprinum** (Bieb.) Spreng. To 100cm. Lvs ovate-lanceolate. Fls bright purple; hood green-purple; pet. 2-veined; lip with dark purple basal hairs, central lobe to 15mm. E Eur.
H. **hircinum** (L.) Spreng. LIZARD ORCHID. 20–90cm. Lvs elliptic-oblong. Fls malodorous, green or grey-green, striped and spotted red; lip spotted purple at base, central lobe 25–45mm, spiral. S Eur., Medit.
H. **longibracteatum** (Bernh.) Schltr. = *Barlia robertiana.*

Hime-iaw-giboshi *Hosta gracillima.*
Hinoki Cypress *Chamaecyparis obtusa.*

Hippeastrum Herb. AMARYLLIS; KNIGHT'S STAR LILY. Amaryllidaceae. *c*80 perenn. bulbous herbs. Lvs basal, linear or strap-shaped. Scapes stout, hollow; fls 2 to several held horizontally or drooping in an umbel subtended by 2 large spathes; perianth tubular, throat often closed or with scales or a corona, lobes 6, erect, spreading, inner 3 sometimes narrower; fil. and style often declinate and exserted. Americas.
H. ×**ackermannii** Lem. = *H.* ×*acramannii.*
H. ×**acramannii** hort. (*H. aulicum* ×*H. psittacinum.*) Intermediate between parents. Fls 15cm, lobes acute, margin somewhat undulate, green in throat, white at centre, remainder bright scarlet with white margins. Cult.
H. **advenum** (Ker-Gawl.) Herb. = *Rhodophiala advena.*
H. **aglaiae** (Cast.) Fls 2–3, green-yellow below, butter-yellow above; perianth tube 5mm, with short scales at throat, outer lobes 70×25mm, spathulate, acute, inner lobes to 22mm broad, lowermost to 14mm broad. Arg. & Boliv.
H. **alberti** Lem. = *H. reginae.*
H. **ambiguum** Herb. AMBIGUOUS KNIGHT'S STAR LILY. Fls 4–5; perianth tube to 7.8cm, white, lobes each with 2 stripes of Tyrian rose, throat with many long hairs. Arg., Peru, Braz., Ecuad., Costa Rica.
H. **andicola** (Poepp.) Bak. = *Rhodophiala andicola.*
H. **andreanum** Bak. Fls 4–6, 10cm long; perianth tube v. short, corona 0, perianth lobes oblanceolate-acute, to 2cm broad, pale red with steaks of darker red. Colomb.
H. **araucanum** Philippi = *Rhodophiala araucana.*
H. **argentinum** (Pax) Hunz. Fls to 15×8cm. 2, trumpet-shaped, fragrant; perianth tube green, to 55mm, lobes oblanceolate, green at the base, otherwise white, undulate, outer lobes to 92mm, apiculate, inner lat. pair to 87mm, lower inner pair narrower. Arg., Boliv.
H. **aulicum** (Ker-Gawl.) Herb. LILY OF THE PALACE. Fls usually 2, crimson, to 15cm, throat green, lobes obovate, pointed, the 2 upper inner ones much broader than the others, corona in the throat green. Braz., Parag. var. *platypetalum* Lindl. More vigorous, with broader perianth lobes.
H. **bagnoldii** (Herb.) Bak. = *Rhodophiala bagnoldii.*
H. **barbatum** Herb. = *H. puniceum.*
H. **bifidum** (Herb.) Bak. = *Rhodophiala bifida.*
H. **blossfeldiae** (Traub & Doran). Fls 4–5; perianth tube to 5cm, green or yellow, lobes to 8cm, light nasturtium red. Braz.
H. **blumenavium** (K. Koch & Bouché ex Carr.) Sealy. Fls 4 or 5, drooping, to 8cm; perianth lobes spreading, to 8cm diam., white, with longitudinal lines and bands of red-purple, undulate. SE Braz.
H. **brachyandrum** Bak. = *Habranthus brachyandrus.*
H. **breviflorum** Herb. Fls 5–6; perianth limb to 3.75cm, funnel-form, tube shorter, seg. oblanceolate-oblong, acute, white with a red keel, outer ones to 2cm broad, the inner to 1.25cm. Arg.
H. **bukasovii** (Vargas). Fls 2, 10×12–14cm; perianth tube 1cm, perianth scales minute, throat with large green-white star, lobes obovate, unequal, acute, to 3.8cm wide, all dark red with conspicuous yellow-green tip to 3cm.
H. **calyptratum** (Ker-Gawl.) Herb. Fls to 2 or 3, green; perianth tube to 2.5cm, conical, the 3 outer lobes claw-like, curving inwards, with a prominent midrib, the inner lobes rolled outwards. Braz.
H. **candidum** Stapf. Fls 6, fragrant, funnel-shaped, to 20cm long; perianth tube to 10×0.5cm, green, outer lobes oblanceolate, 9–12×2cm, apex recurved, crisped, pure white, inner lobes narrower. Arg.
H. **chilense** (L'Hérit.) Bak. = *Rhodophiala chilensis.*

H. **correiense** (Bury) Worsley = *H. organense.*
H. **crocatum** Herb. = *H. reginae.*
H. **cybister** (Herb.) Benth. & Hook. f. Fls 4–6, 7.5–10cm long; perianth tube v. short, with incurved corona, lobes tapering upwards, bright crimson, tinged green at apex and externally, upper 3 twisted upwards, lower 3 close together. Boliv. (Andes).
H. **doraniae** (Traub). Fls 2–4, trumpet-shaped, 12×9.5cm, borne horizontally, becoming declinate; perianth tube green, lobes lanceolate, somewhat undulate, green in lower third, carmine-rose above, paler at apex. Venez.
H. **elegans** (Spreng.) H.E. Moore. Lvs to 2.5cm broad. Flowering st. to 60cm; fls 2–4, pale green, to 25cm; tube to 12.5cm; stigma capitate. S Amer.
H. **elegans** 'Longiflorum' = *H. ambiguum.*
H. **elwesii** C.M. Wright. = *Rhodophiala elwesii.*
H. **equestre** Herb. = *H. puniceum.*
H. **evansiae** (Traub & Nels.) H.E. Moore. Fls 2 or 3, held horizontally; perianth tube to 7cm, throat green, corona 0, sometimes undulate, chartreuse green or straw yellow, outer 3 to 9.3×3.7cm, broadly or narrowly elliptic, inner 3 to 9.4×1.8cm, narrowly elliptic. Boliv.
H. **forgetii** Worsley. Resembling *H. pardinum* but fls only partially striped, unspotted, lobes dull crimson, to 15cm across, keeled in lower half, base green; sta. included. Peru.
H. **fulgidum** Herb. = *H. reginae.*
H. **ignescens** Reg. = *H. puniceum.*
H. **immaculatum** (Traub & Mold.). = *H. candidum.*
H. ×**johnsonii** hort. (*H. reginae* ×*H. vittatum.*) Intermediate between parents. Fls 4, funnel-shaped, to 12.5×10cm, bright scarlet with narrow white streaks, green at base within and externally. Gdn origin.
H. **lapacense** (Cardenas). Fls 2; perianth tube 3mm, outer lobes to 10×3.7cm, inner to 9.5×3.5cm, lanceolate, white, with green bases and keels, streaked crimson and hairy inside. Boliv.
H. **leopoldii** Dombrain. Fls usually 2, large, regular, to 18cm; lobes obovate, to 5cm across, dull crimson below, green-white at the tip, bright red between with a forked white mark at the base and a green-white throat. Boliv.
H. **machupijchense** (Vargas) D.R. Hunt. Fls 1–2, 18×16cm, tubular-campanulate; perianth tube 4–6mm, pale green, lobes narrow-elliptic or obovate, to 10×3cm, acute, pale green externally with margin red, dark red within, with pale green throat and longitudinal streaks. Peru.
H. **maracasum** (Traub) H.E. Moore. Fls 2; perianth tube to 14×11cm, brick red with darker reticulation and a green star in the throat, with white bristles above the sta., 2 lowest lobes to 11×3.2cm, sickle-shaped, the uppermost to 12×6cm, the other 3 narrower. Braz.
H. **morelianum** Lem. = *H. aulicum.*
H. **oconequense** (Traub) H.E. Moore. Fls 4, to 10.5×5cm, red inside, the outside red above, red-brown below. SE Peru.
H. **organense** (Hook. ex Herb.) Fls 2 to 15cm; perianth tube 1.3cm, with incurved green corona at throat, lobes oblong, acute, crimson, with green keel in lower portion, outer lobes to 4.4cm broad, inner lobes narrower. Braz.
H. **papilio** (Ravenna). Fls 2, to 9×13.5cm, laterally compressed, pale green streaked and stained dark red; perianth seg. oblanceolate, in outer whorl to 14×2.7cm inner whorl 9.5×4.4cm, somewhat undulate, acuminate. S Braz.
H. **pardinum** (Hook. f.) Dombrain. Fls usually 2, to 18cm; perianth tube less than 2.5cm, throat constricted or closed, lobes to 13cm, oblong, acute, cream or yellow-green, dotted crimson, the lowest inner lobe the narrowest. Peru.
H. **petiolatum** Pax. Fls to 7cm, 1–2, scarlet; perianth short, the throat with small scales between bases of fil., lobes oblong, acute, to 1.5cm broad. Arg.
H. **phycelloides** (Herb.) Bak. = *Phycella phycelloides.*
H. **pratense** (Poepp.) Bak. = *Rhodophiala pratensis.*
H. **procerum** (Duchartre) Lem. = *Worsleya rayneri.*
H. **psittacinum** (Ker-Gawl.) Herb. Fls 2–4; perianth tube short, throat constricted, lobes to 13cm, oblong, acute, with undulate crimson margins, main part green-white striped crimson, the lower middle lobes narrower than the others. S Braz.
H. **pulverulentum** Herb. = *H. reginae.*
H. **puniceum** (Lam.) Urban. BARBADOS LILY. Fls to 13cm long and 10cm diam., bright red, scarlet or pink with green-yellow throat. Mex. to Chile, Boliv., Braz. to W Indies. 'Semiplenum': fls semi-double to double, bright red.
H. **pyrrochroum** Lem. = *H. puniceum.*
H. **reginae** (L.) Herb. MEXICAN LILY. Fls 2–4, drooping, red; perianth tube to 2.5cm, lobes to 13cm, obovate, acute, the lowest innermost one narrower than the others, all bright red with a large green-white star in the throat. Mex. to Peru and Braz., W Indies and W Afr.
H. **reticulatum** (L'Hérit.) Herb. Fls 3–6; perianth tube to 2.5cm,

throat not constricted, lobes to 10cm, obovate, mauve or red-purple with crimson stripes and cross lines. S Braz.

H. rhodolirion (Philippi) Bak. = *Rhodophiala rhodolirion*.

H. robustum A. Dietr. = *H. aulicum*.

H. roseum (Sweet) Bak. = *Rhodophiala rosea*.

H. rutilum (Ker-Gawl.) Herb. = *H. striatum*.

H. solandrifolium (Lindl.) Herb. = *H. elegans*.

H. spathaceum Sims = *H. puniceum*.

H. stenopetalum A. Dietr. ex Koch = *H. reginae*.

H. striatum (Lam.) H.E. Moore. Fls 2–4, to 10cm, crimson, keeled green to halfway up the lobes. Braz.

H. stylosum Herb. LONG-STYLED KNIGHT'S STAR LILY. Fls 3–8, light red or pink, to 10cm diam.; perianth tube to 12mm, green, throat not constricted, lobes oblanceolate-acute, pink-brown, veined and speckled a deeper colour. Guyana, Braz.

H. subbarbatum Herb. = *H. reginae*.

H. texanum Bak. = *Habranthus tubispathum*.

H. traubii (Mold.) H.E. Moore. Fls 4, variable in size; perianth tube triquetrous, to 2.3cm, brown-green, lobes lanceolate, acute, white-green in lower third, rose above, to 7.4×3.2cm. Peru.

H. vittatum (L'Hérit.) Herb. Fls 3–6, to 12cm diam.; perianth tube to 2.5cm, lobes obovate-oblong, to 4cm across, keel white, margins irregular and white, striped red in between. Peruvian Andes.

H. cvs. 'Appleblossom': fls white flecked soft pink. 'Beautiful Lady': fls pale mandarin red. 'Best Seller': scape short; fls cerise. 'Bouquet': fls salmon. 'Byjou': fls soft burnt apricot. 'Cantate': fls milky deep red. 'Christmas Gift': fls white. 'Dazzler': fls pure white. 'Dutch Belle': fls opal rose. 'Ludwig's Goliath': fls large, bright scarlet. 'Lydia': fls pale salmon. 'Oskar': fls rich deep red. 'Orange Sovereign': fls pure orange. 'Picotte': fls white rimmed red. 'Red Lion': fls dark red. 'Royal Velvet': fls deep velvety red. 'Star of Holland': fls scarlet with white star at throat. 'Susan': fls large, soft pink. 'United Nations': fls white striped vermillion. 'Valentine': fls white with pink veins, heavier towards edges. 'White Dazzler': fls pure white.

→*Amaryllis*.

HIPPOCASTANACEAE DC. 2/15. *Aesculus*.

Hippocrepis L. HORSESHOE VETCH. Leguminosae (Papilionoideae). Some 21 ann. or perenn. herbs or small shrubs. Lvs imparipinnate. Fls in capitate rac., pea-like, yellow. Fr. flat, curved, breaking into horseshoe-like seg. Eur., W Asia, Medit. Z8.

H. comosa L. HORSESHOE VETCH. Woody-based perenn., to 40cm. Lfts to 1.5×04.cm, linear to obovate. Cap. to 12-fld; peduncles exceeding lvs; cor. to 1cm+. Fr. red-brown-papillose. Spring–summer. C & S Eur., N Afr. 'E.R. Janes': compact.

H. multisiliquosa L. Slender ann., to 60cm. Lfts to 1.5×0.5cm, oblong-obovate. Cap. 2–6-fld; peduncle equalling lvs; cor. to 8mm. Fr. glab. W Medit., S Port., Greece.

Hippolytia Polj. Compositae. *c*17 hairy perenn. herbs. Lvs usually basally arranged, occas. dissected. Cap. discoid, in term., dense or loose rac.; flts yellow. C Asia to N China.

H. herderi (Reg. & Schmalh.) Polj. Grey-hairy perenn., to 30cm. Lvs in compact rosettes. Cap. in corymbose rac.; flts bright yellow. Turkestan. Z7.

→*Tanacetum*.

Hippophaë L. SEA BUCKTHORN. Elaeagnaceae. 3 decid. thorny trees or shrubs, initially scaly-pubesc. Lvs generally lanceolate to linear, thinly downy. Fls small, precocious; ♂ in short spikes to 4–8, with 2 tep., ovate, 4 sta.; ♀ fls in short rac. Fr. globose, drupe-like. Himal., China.

H. rhamnoides L. Thorny shrub, 1–9m. Twigs rigid, metallic-scaly then grey, thorny. Lvs 1–6×0.3–1cm, silver to bronze-scaly. Fr. 6–8mm, orange, clothing bare branchlets in winter. Spring. Eur., Asia. var. *procera* Rehd. Shrub or tree to 18m, with sparse, stout thorns. Lvs 3–6×0.6–1cm, green above, white beneath. Fr. yellow to dark red. W China. Z3.

H. salicifolia D. Don. Shrub or tree to 11m, with drooping br., less spiny than in *H. rhamnoides*. Young shoots downy. Lvs 4.5–8.5cm, narrow-oblong, covered in stellate hairs. Fr. yellow. S Himal. Z8.

H. tibetana Schldl. Shrub to 80cm. St. twisted, shoots erect, terminating in a thorn. Lvs 0.8–3×0.2–0.3cm, whorled, green to silver above, with silver or rusty hairs beneath. Himal. Z8.

Hiptage Gaertn. Malpighiaceae. 20–30 erect or climbing shrubs. Lvs simple, coriaceous. Rac. terminal or axill.; pet. 5, clawed, 4 white, one discoloured; sta. 10. Trop. Asia to Fiji. Z10.

H. benghalensis (L.) Kurz. Large shrub or tall climber, white- or yellow-sericeous. Lvs to 20cm, lanceolate to ovate-lanceolate. Fls 10–30 in rac., pink or white, marked yellow, v. fragrant. Sri Lanka, SE Asia to Philipp. and Taiwan.

H. madablota Gaertn. Tall climber, glab. except infl. Lvs 10–15cm, oblong or ovate-lanceolate; acuminate. Fls to 2.5cm diam., v. fragrant; pet fimbriate, the fifth marked yellow at base. Sri Lanka and India to Burm. and Malaysia.

H. obtusifolia DC. Large shrub to 6m, close to *H. madablota* but smaller. Lvs oblong, obtuse. Fls fragrant; fifth pet. flushed pink, with yellow base. S China.

Hispaniolan Palmetto *Sabal blackburniana*.
Hispaniolan Royal Palm *Roystonea hispaniolana*.

Histiopteris (Agardh) J. Sm. Dennstaedtiaceae. 1 terrestrial fern. Rhiz. long-creeping. Fronds to 3×2m, stipitate, erect to ascending; stipes remote, lustrous, straw-coloured to chestnut; blade 2–4 pinnate, ovate or deltoid to lanceolate, often glaucous, pinnae to 40×20cm+, ovate to lanceolate, base with abbreviated, stipulate or pinnule-like processes, pinnules to 7×2cm, linear to oblong, seg. ovate to lanceolate or deltoid, subentire to notched or lobed. Cosmop. Z9.

H. brunoniana Endl. = *H. incisa*.

H. incisa (Thunb.) J. Sm.

H. montana Colenso = *H. incisa*.

→*Pteris*.

Hoary Alison *Berteroa incana*.
Hoary Cherry *Prunus canescens*.
Hoary Cinquefoil *Potentilla argentea*.
Hoary Goldenbush *Hazardia*.
Hoary Leaf Ceanothus *Ceanothus crassifolius*.
Hoary Manzanita *Arctostaphylos canescens*.
Hoary Pea *Tephrosia*.
Hoary Plantain *Plantago media*.
Hoary Sunray *Helipterum albicans; H. molle*.
Hoary Vervain *Verbena stricta*.
Hoary Willow *Salix candida; S. elaeagnos*.
Hobble Bush *Viburnum lantanoides*.

Hodgsonia Hook. f. & Thoms. Cucurbitaceae. 1 climber to 30m. Lvs palmate, glab., lobes 3–5, 14–18cm. ♂ fls in rac., ♀ solitary, cal. tube to 9cm; pet. to 5cm, 5 obovate, truncate with curling apical fil. to 9cm, off-white tinted yellow with rusty hairs. Fr. globose, grooved red-brown, tomentose, 5–11cm. Indomalesia. Z10.

H. heteroclita Hook. f. & Thoms. = *H. macrocarpa*.

H. macrocarpa (Bl.) Cogn.

Hoffmannia Sw. Rubiaceae. 45+ herbs or shrubs. St. terete or 4-angled. Fls small, yellow to red, in sessile to pedunculate, axill. cymes; cor. subcylindric to funnelform, tube glab. at throat, lobes 4 or 5. Fr. a berry, 2-celled. Trop. Amer. Z10.

H. bullata L.O. Williams. TAFFETA PLANT; QUILT PLANT. St. to 1m, terete, erect, purple, downy. Lvs 8–12cm, narrowly obovate, thickly textured, appearing quilted, dull metallic green above, often tinted purple-red, purple-red beneath. Mex. to C Amer. 'Vittata': lvs conspicuously veined and edged silver-grey above.

H. discolor (Lem.) Hemsl. Herb or subshrub, to 2m. St. terete, pubesc. Lvs to 14×7cm, ovate to obovate, lustrous and somewhat leathery, silky green above, red-brown, glab., sparsely pubesc. beneath. Mex.

H. ghiesbreghtii (Lem.) Hemsl. Herb or shrub, to 1m. St. strongly 4-angled, ± glab., usually tinted purple. Lvs to 30×9cm, elliptic to obovate or oblanceolate, soft-textured with veins deeply impressed above, appearing quilted, upper surface satiny, olive to metallic green tinted purple, undersurface minutely pubesc., flushed deep purple-red. 'Fantasia': vigorous; lvs obovate, deep olive tinted bronze, red tinted below. 'Variegata' ('Strawberry Splash'): lvs tapered, pale coppery green splashed pink and white, pale pink beneath.

H. jamaicensis Spreng. = *H. pedunculata*.

H. pedunculata Sw. Shrub, to 2m. St. terete, initially pubesc. Lvs to 19×6cm, opposite, obovate or oblanceolate to elliptic, soft, glab. above to rusty-pubesc, beneath, esp. on veins. Jam.

H. refulgens (Hook.) Hemsl. = *H. bullata*.

H. regalis (Lind.) Hemsl. Subshrub, to 30cm. St. terete or obscurely 4-angled, fleshy, glab. Lvs ovate to suborbicular, rugose, leathery, lustrous dark green above, red-brown beneath. Mex. 'Roezlii': st. to 7.5cm, glab., 4-angled. Lvs 7.5–16cm, rounded-ovate, bullate, dark green tinted purple, satiny above, purple-red beneath. Fls dark red.

H. roezlii hort. ex Gentil = *H. regalis* 'Roezlii'.

→*Campylobotrys*.

Hog Cranberry *Arctostaphylos uva-ursi.*
Hog Millet *Panicum miliaceum.*
Hog Peanut *Amphicarpaea.*
Hog Plum *Poupartia borbonica*; *Prunus americana*; *Spondias mombin.*
Hogweed *Heracleum sphondylium.*

Hohenbergia Schult. f. Bromeliaceae. 40 perenn., stemless herbs, terrestrial or epiphytic. Lvs in many rows forming a rosette; sheaths large, dark brown; blades ligulate or subtriangular, pale-scaly, toothed and spinose. Infl. 1–4-pinnate, term., scapose, consisting of dense, cone-shaped spikes. W Indies, SE Braz. Z9.
H. blanchetii (Bak.) E. Morr. To 70cm in fl. Lvs linear, margins conspicuously spined. Scape stout, cutaneous, white; infl. compound, elongated to 30cm, spikes 30, 1–2cm, cone-shaped; pet. lavender tipped white. Braz.
H. erythrostachys Brongn. = *H. stellata.*
H. rosea L.B. Sm. & Read. To over 50cm in fl. Lvs ligulate, apex dark, stoutly cuspidate, densely toothed. Infl. laxly cylindric; bracts shorter than spikes, narrowly triangular; spikes in bundles of 3 at br. tips, to 8cm, subcylindric; floral bracts pink, woolly; pet. blue or pale violet. Braz.
H. stellata Schult. f. To 1.2m in fl. Lvs ligulate, abruptly acute, laxly toothed. Infl. tripinnate, simple at apex; bracts red or yellow, papery; spikes 2–8, term. spike sessile, subglobose, 3–7cm; floral bracts purple or bright red, sep. white flushed red, apex blue; pet. purple or bright blue. Trin. and Tob., Venez., NE Braz.

Hoheria A. Cunn. LACEBARK. Malvaceae. 5 everg. or decid. shrubs and small trees. Fls solitary or in abbreviated cymes; epical. 0; cal. campanulate, 5-fid; pet. 5, white, cream or ivory; clawed; staminal column split toward the apex into 5 bundles or fil. NZ. Z8.
H. angustifolia Raoul. Everg. tree to 10m with slender flexible br. Juvenile lvs 4–8×4–7mm, broadly obovate to suborbicular, dentate near apex; mature lvs 2–5×0.5–1cm, narrowly obovate, oblanceolate to oblong-lanceolate, coarsely spinulose, dentate to serrate. Fls to 2cm diam.; pet. snow white, obliquely narrow-oblong, notched.
H. glabrata Sprague & Summerh. Decid. tree to 10m. Juvenile lvs 1–3×1–3cm, ovate to cordate, deeply lobed, crenate-dentate; mature lvs 4×2–10cm, glabrate, broadly ovate to ovate-lanceolate, acuminate, crenate-dentate. Fls to 4cm diam.; pet. white to cream, obovate; anth. purple.
H. 'Glory of Amlwich'. (*H. glabrata* ×*H. sexstylosa.*) Small tree. Lvs to 9cm, ovate and slender-pointed, serrate, pale green. Fls to 4cm diam., snow white, profuse.
H. lyallii Hook. f. LACEBARK. Decid. tree to 6m. Juvenile lvs 2–7×2–6cm, thin, ovate to suborbicular, 2–5-lobed, crenate; mature lvs 5–10×2–5cm, cordate-ovate, acuminate, grey-green, felty white-pubesc. Fls 2–3cm diam., snow white; pet. obovate; anth. purple.
H. populnea A. Cunn. LACEBARK. Everg. tree to 10m; branchlets slender, bark pale often exfoliating in fine ash-grey strips. Juvenile lvs 1–3cm, broadly ovate, deltoid or suborbicular, serrate; mature lvs 7–14×4–6cm, broadly ovate or ovate-lanceolate to elliptic, acuminate, serrate-dentate. Fls 2.5–3cm diam., pure white. 'Alba Variegata': lvs broadly edged white. 'Osbornei': lvs flushed rose or maroon beneath; sta. opalescent blue. 'Purpurea': lvs flushed and veined maroon beneath. 'Variegata': lvs pale yellow-green edged dark green.
H. populnea var. **angustifolia** (Raoul) Hook. f. = *H. angustifolia.*
H. populnea var. **lanceolata** Hook. f. = *H. sexstylosa.*
H. sexstylosa Col. RIBBON-WOOD. Everg. tree to 6m; bark glossy red-brown, overlaid with grey exfoliating strips. Juvenile lvs 1–3×1–2.5cm, broadly ovate to suborbicular, 3–5-lobed, dentate; mature lvs 5–15×1–5cm, lanceolate to ovate-lanceolate, acuminate, glossy. Fls 2–2.5cm diam., pure white, fragrant; pet. oblong, notched; anth. white. 'Crataegifolia': lvs small, coarsely toothed; juvenile form.
→*Gaya* and *Plagianthus.*

Hoho *Pseudopanax chathamicus.*

Holacantha A. Gray = *Castela.*

Holarrhena R. Br. Apocynaceae. 4 decid. trees and shrubs; branchlets usually pendulous. Fls white, fragrant, in dense corymbose cymes; cal. 5-lobed; cor. funnelform, tube constricted slightly at middle, mouth glab., limb 5-lobed, flared. Fr. a pair of cylindric, slender follicles. Trop. Afr. and Asia. Z10.
H. antidysenterica (L.) Wallich ex A. DC. = *H. pubescens.*
H. antidysenterica var. **pubescens** (Buch.-Ham.) Steward &

Brandis = *H. pubescens.*
H. febrifuga Klotzsch = *H. pubescens.*
H. floribunda (G. Don) Dur. & Schinz. Medium-sized tree. Lvs to 12.4cm, oval to oblong. Fls in cymes to 6cm across; cor. tube 6.5–9mm. W Trop. Afr.
H. pubescens (Buch.-Ham.) Wallich ex G. Don. EASTER TREE; CONESSI; KURCHI; JASMINE TREE; IVORY TREE. Shrub or tree 0.6–18m. Lvs to 30cm, oval to ovate. Fls in cymes 7.5–15cm across; cor. tube 9–19mm. Trop. Afr. and Asia.
H. wulfsbergii Stapf = *H. floribunda.*

Holboellia Wallich. Lardizabalaceae. 5 everg., twining shrubs. Lvs composed of palmately arranged, stalked lfts. Corymbs or rac. axill.; fls unisexual; pet. reduced to nectaries, sep. petaloid, 6, fleshy. Fr. a fleshy berry, oblong-ovoid. N India to China.
H. coriacea Diels. To 7m. Lvs trifoliolate, central lft 5–15cm, ovate to obovate or lanceolate, lat. lfts ovate, entire, coriaceous. Fls white or white-green delicately flushed purple. Fr. 5cm, purple. Summer. C China. Z9.
H. fargesii Reaub. V. close to *H. coriacea*, from which it can be distinguished by its 5–9 lfts (blue-green beneath). Summer. C China. Z9.
H. hexaphylla hort. = *Stauntonia hexaphylla.*
H. latifolia Wallich. To 5m. Lfts 4–12cm, 3–7, ovate-oblong, entire, glab., central lft longer. ♂ fls green-white, ♀ fls purple. Fr. 5–10cm, red to purple. Spring. Himal. var. **angustifolia** (Wallich) Hook. f. & Thoms. Lfts 7–9, narrower. Z9.

Holcoglossum Schltr. Orchidaceae. 4 monopodial, epiphytic orchids. Lvs terete, tapering. Infl. axill., slender, pendent; fls spurred; dors. sep. oblong to oblong-ovate, lat. sep. oblong; pet. spathulate; lip trilobed. SE Asia. Z10.
H. amesianum (Rchb. f.) Christenson. 30–50cm. Fls to 4cm diam., fragrant, white, streaked or suffused pink. SE Asia.
H. kimballianum (Rchb. f.) Garay. To 30cm. Fls to 5cm diam.; dors. sep. and pet. white, often tinted violet, lat. sep. white; lip midlobe with two shallow lobes and toothed margins, violet-red with darker veins, lateral lobes spotted yellow-red. Burm., China (Yunnan), Thail.
→*Vanda.*

Holcus L. Gramineae. 8 ann. or perenn. grasses. St. erect, tufted. Lf blades linear, flat or folded. Fls in spicate pan.; spikelets stalked, laterally flattened, 2-fld. Summer. Eur., temp. Asia, N & S Afr. Z5.
H. bicolor L. = *Sorghum bicolor.*
H. halapensis (L.) Brot. = *Sorghum halapense.*
H. lanatus L. YORKSHIRE FOG. Perenn. to 1m. Rhiz. creeping; st. downy, joints glab. Lvs to 5mm wide, grey-green, downy. Fls in a soft, contracted, dense pan. to 15cm; spikelets to 3mm, light green to pink-purple. Eur.
H. mollis L. CREEPING SOFT GRASS. Perenn. to 45cm. Rhiz. creeping; st. joints hairy. Lvs to 1cm wide, grey-green, glab. to slightly hairy. Fls in narrowly oblong to ovate, dense to loosely branched pan. to 12cm; spikelets to 5mm. Eur. 'Albovariegatus' ('Variegatus'): lvs broadly edged white with a narrow green central stripe.
H. sorbus L. = *Sorghum bicolor.*

Holland Rose *Rosa* ×*centifolia.*
Holly *Ilex.*
Holly Fern *Polystichum.*
Holly Flame Pea *Chorizema ilicifolia.*
Holly Grape *Mahonia.*
Hollyhock *Alcea rosea*; *Althaea.*
Holly-leaf Begonia *Begonia gracilis*; *B. cubensis.*
Holly-leaf Begonia *Begonia acutifolia.*
Holly-leaf Ceanothus *Ceanothus purpureus.*
Holly-leaved Banksia *Banksia ilicifolia.*
Holly-leaved Cherry *Prunus ilicifolia.*
Holly-leaved Hovea *Hovea chorizemifolia.*
Holly-leaved Oak *Quercus ilex.*
Holly Olive *Osmanthus heterophyllus.*
Holm Oak *Quercus ilex.*

Holmskioldia Retz. Verbenaceae. 10 scandent shrubs. Infl. a short term. pan. or axillary rac.; cal. usually red, rotate-campanulate, membranous; cor. tubular, bilabiate; sta. 4, exserted. Trop. Afr., Asia.
H. sanguinea Retz. CUP AND SAUCER PLANT; MANDARIN'S-HAT; CHINESE-HAT PLANT. Lvs to 7.5cm, ovate or ovate-elliptic, base rounded, slightly serrate, minutely pubesc. beneath when young. Pedicels filiform; cal. to 2.5cm diam., brick-red to orange, net-veined, glab.; cor. scarlet. Himal.
H. tettensis Vatke. Lvs to 3.5cm, obovate, base cuneate, sparsely pubesc. above, densely pubesc. beneath, entire or with few

teeth. Pedicels elongate, puberulent; cal. to 2.5cm diam., pubesc. Trop. Afr., Asia.

Holodiscus (K. Koch) Maxim. Rosaceae. 8 decid. shrubs. Fls cream-white (sometimes pink in bud), small, v. numerous, in large, usually pendulous pan.; cal. deeply 5-lobed; pet. 5, rounded; sta. 20. W N Amer. to Colomb.

H. ariifolius (Sm.) Greene = *H. discolor.*

H. boursieri (Carr.) Rehd. To 1m. Lvs to 3cm, broad-obovate to orbicular, cuneate at base, pubesc. above, grey or white and villous to tomentose beneath, often gland., usually 6–8-dentate, teeth rounded. Fls in villous pan. to 8cm. Calif., Nevada. Z5.

H. discolor (Pursh) Maxim. CREAMBUSH; OCEAN-SPRAY. To 5m. Lvs to 9cm, ovate, obtuse, truncate or broad-cuneate at base, shallowly 4–8-lobed, lobes crenate, rugose above, white-tomentose beneath. Fls in 30cm plume-like pan. Summer. W N Amer. Z5.

H. discolor var. *dumosus* (Nutt.) Coult. = *H. dumosus.*

H. dumosus (Nutt.) Heller. ROCK SPIRAEA. To 5m. Lvs to 4cm, obovate, cuneate at base, grey-green and soft-pubesc. above, lanate beneath, 6–12-dentate. Fls in erect pan. to 20cm. Summer. Utah to New Mex. Z4.

H. microphyllus Rydb. To 2m. Lvs 2cm, obovate to spathulate, rounded, glabrescent above, with many gland. droplets, 4–6-dentate only on apical half of the blade, teeth small, rounded. Fls in narrow and compact, rarely compound, downy pan. to 10cm long. Mts from Oreg. and Calif. to Utah. Z4.
→*Spiraea.*

Holoptelea Planch. Ulmaceae. 2 large decid. trees. Infl. a fascicle or corymb of inconspicuous ♂ and hermaphrodite fls; cal. seg. 5; cor. 0; anth. 5–8. Fr. a samara, wing orbicular or obovate-reticular. India and Trop. Afr. Z9.

H. integrifolia (Roxb.) Planch. Young shoots pubesc.; bark in long flakes, pale grey. Lvs 7–15cm, elliptic or obovate-oblong, entire, coriaceous, apex acuminate, subcordate at base, occas. pubesc. beneath. Fr. 2–3cm, suborbicular. S Himal. to Sri Lanka.
→*Ulmus.*

Holoschoenus Link.
H. australis (Murr) Rchb. = *Scirpoides holoschoenus.*
H. vulgaris Link = *Scirpoides holoschoenus.*

Holostigma Spach = *Camissonia.*

Holy Basil *Ocimum tenuiflorum.*
Holy Clover *Onobrychis* (*O. viciifolia*).
Holy Rose *Rosa* ×*richardii.*
Holy Thistle *Silybum marianum.*

Homalanthus A. Juss. Euphorbiaceae. 35 everg. shrubs and trees. Fls inconspicuous, without pet., in term. rac., ♀ at base. Asia to Aus. and the Pacific. Z10.

H. polyandrus (Muell. Arg.) Cheesem. Differs from *H. populifolius* in having broad-ovate lvs with a ± obtuse apex and ♂ fls with 30–35 sta. Kermadec Is.

H. populifolius Graham. BLEEDING HEART TREE; QUEENSLAND POPLAR. Everg. spreading shrub to 5m. Lvs smooth, heart-shaped, 15cm wide, the older lvs turning rich red. Fls yellow, in catkins; sta. 4–10. Indomal. to Pacific.

Homalocephala Britt. & Rose.
H. texensis (Hopffer) Britt. & Rose = *Echinocactus texensis.*

Homalocladium (F. Muell.) L.H. Bail. Polygonaceae. 1 erect shrub, to 3m. St. flat and ribbon-like, 1–2cm wide, jointed, green. Lvs lanceolate, 1.5–6cm, usually 0 at flowering. Fls in small clusters at joints or along edges of br., white-green. Fr. enclosed by fleshy, red to purple perianth. Spring. Solomon Is.

H. platycladum (F. Muell.) L.H. Bail.
→*Muehlenbeckia.*

Homalomena Schott. Araceae. 140 everg. perenn. herbs; st. short. Lvs entire, ovate, triangular or lanceolate, cordate; petiole sheathing. Infl. several from one axil, spathes with margins unrolling above at anthesis; spadix included, cylindric. Fr. a berry. Trop. S Asia, SW Pacific, S Amer. Z10.

H. lindenii (Rodigas) Lindl. St. to 25cm. Lvs triangular-ovate, deeply cordate, dark green above, veins impressed, white to yellow-green petiole longer than lamina. Spathe to 7cm, pale green. New Guinea.

H. wallisii Reg. St. short. Lvs elliptic- or ovate-oblong, base rounded or cordate, smooth, dark green with irregular yellow markings and white above, rough, glaucous, tinged red beneath; petiole shorter than lamina. Spathe to 8cm, pale red-purple.

Colomb. 'Mauro': dense; lvs thick, shiny deep green, marbled dove grey to pale chartreuse green.
→*Alocasia.*

Homeria Vent. Iridaceae. 31 cormous, herbaceous perennials. Lvs linear-ensiform. Flowering st. leafy, erect, branched; fls subtended by 2 bracts, produced in succession, radially symmetric; perianth seg. 6, forming a cup, inner seg. slightly smaller than outer. Summer. S Afr. Z9.

H. breyniana (L.) Lewis = *H. collina.*

H. breyniana var. *aurantiaca* (Zucc.) Lewis = *H. flaccida.*

H. collina (Thunb.) Salisb. Flowering st. 16–38cm, simple or sparsely branched; fls pale golden yellow to peach or pink, scented, outer seg. to 3.5cm, inner seg. with deep golden, green-edged nectaries.

H. collina var. *aurantiaca* (Zucc.) Bak. = *H. flaccida.*

H. collina var. *ochroleuca* (Salisb.) Bak. = *H. ochroleuca.*

H. elegans (Jacq.) Sweet. Similar to *H. collina*, from which it differs in outer perianth seg. to 1cm, yellow with large blue-green, orange-tipped blotch toward their apices and the anth.

H. flaccida Sweet. Flowering st. 40–60cm, sparsely branched; fls yellow to peach with distinct golden or sulphur-yellow nectaries, outer perianth seg. to 4cm.

H. lineata Sweet = *H. miniata.*

H. miniata (Andrews) Sweet. Differs from *H. ochroleuca*, in having fls tawny red, apricot to pink, golden or white; outer perianth seg. 1.5–2.25cm, nectaries spotted green.

H. ochroleuca Salisb. Flowering st. 40–80cm, with 1 or several br. Fls pale yellow, occas. stained orange at centre, muskily scented; outer perianth seg. to 4cm.

Homoglossum Salisb.
H. abbreviatum (Andrews) Goldbl. = *Gladiolus abbreviatus.*
H. aureum (Bak.) Oberm. = *Gladiolus aureus.*
H. huttonii N.E. Br. = *Gladiolus huttonii.*
H. merianellum (Thunb.) Bak. = *Gladiolus bonaespei.*
H. priorii (N.E. Br.) N.E. Br. = *Gladiolus priorii.*
H. quadrangulare (Burm. f.) N.E. Br. = *Gladiolus quadrangularis.*
H. schweinfurthii (Bak.) Cuf. = *Gladiolus schweinfurthii.*
H. watsonium (Thunb.) N.E. Br. = *Gladiolus watsonius.*

Homogyne Cass. Compositae. 3 low, perenn. herbs. Lvs basal, mostly broadly cordate, rounded, dentate. Cap. disciform, solitary to several; flts white to purple or red. Eur. (mts). Z7.

H. alpina (L.) Cass. ALPINE COLTSFOOT. To 15cm. Basal lvs 2–4cm, reniform, leathery, glab., petiole to 10cm, hairy. Cap. solitary, on scape too 40cm, base hairy; involucre 8–10mm; phyllaries purple; flts purple-red. Eur. (mts).

H. discolor (Jacq.) Cass. Like *H. alpina* but basal lvs 1–3cm, smooth above, white and pubesc. beneath, scape to 25cm, purple, often with 2 clasping scale lvs and flts bright purple. E Alps.

H. sylvestris Cass. Like *H. alpina* but basal lvs 3–7cm, shallowly 5–9-lobed, sparsely hairy beneath; scapes often branched, hairy and gland. above, involucre 10–12mm. SE Alps, Balk.
→*Tussilago.*

Homoranthus Cunn. ex Schauer. Myrtaceae. 7 shrubs. Lvs opposite, linear, gland., strongly aromatic. Floral tube cylindrical or urn-shaped, with 5 longitudinal ribs, usually smooth; cal. lobes 5; pet. 5; sta. 10; style exserted. Aus. Z9.

H. darwinioides (Maid. & Betche) Cheel Dwarf to small shrub. Br. erect to slightly spreading. Lvs 2–4×1mm, terete, green to grey-green, gland., aromatic. Fls cream to red-flushed, paired, pendent, on slender red axill. stalk, floral tube *c*7mm, cream and green, purple with age; cal. lobes fringed; style to 12mm, cream to red.

H. flavescens Cunn. ex Schauer. Dwarf, spreading, flat-topped shrub. Br. horizontal or slightly ascending. Lvs 6–13×1mm, flattened to semi-terete, grey-green to green, tinged red during winter, gland. Fls pale yellow-green, clustered at ends of short branchlets; floral tube *c*4mm; cal. lobes awned; style to *c*8mm, cream.

H. papillatus Byrnes MOUSE PLANT; MOUSE AND HONEY PLANT. Dwarf to small, spreading shrub. Br. horizontal to slightly ascending. Lvs 6–12×1mm, trigonous, incurved, grey-green covered in minute hairs. Fls pale green-yellow, clustered at ends of short branchlets, strongly scented; floral tube to *c*4mm; cal. lobes awned; style to *c*12mm, cream.

H. virgatus Cunn. ex Schauer. Dwarf shrub. Br. erect, twiggy. Lvs 7–10×1mm, ± terete, grey-green, glandular-dotted, glab. Fls pale green-yellow, clustered near ends of br.; floral tube to 5mm; cal. lobes awned; style exceeding pet. by less than 3mm, cream.

Honduran Pine *Pinus caribaea* var. *hondurensis*.
Honesty *Lunaria annua*.
Honewort *Cryptotaenia canadensis*.
Honey Bells *Cephalanthus occidentalis*; *Freylinia lanceolata*; *Hermannia* (*H. verticillata*).
Honey Berry *Melicoccus bijugatus*.
Honey Bush *Hakea lissocarpha*.
Honey Flower *Melianthus major*.
Honey Locust *Gleditsia* (*G. triacanthos*).
Honey Mesquite *Prosopis glandulosa*.
Honey Myrtle *Melaleuca* (*M. huegelii*).
Honey Palm *Jubaea*.
Honeysuckle *Aquilegia canadensis*; *Lonicera* (*L. periclymenum*).
Honey Tree *Tecomella*.
Hongkong Wild Kumquat *Fortunella hindsii*.
Hooded Pitcher Plant *Sarracenia minor*.
Hooded Smokebush *Conospermum glumaceum*.

Hoodia Sweet ex Decne. Asclepiadaceae. Some 17 succulent, perenn., leafless herbs. St. grey-green with teeth and conical, often spiny tubercles on angles. Fls large, solitary to clustered near st. apex, in furrows between angles; cor. flat or cup-shaped, lobes reduced to 5 small points; corona in 2 whorls, each 5-lobed, outer whorl cup-shaped. S Afr., Nam. Z9.
H. albispina N.E. Br. St. 15-angled, tubercles tipped with a white spine. Cor. 7.5–9cm diam.; lobes broad, rough papillose in the centre. W Cape.
H. bainii Dyer. St. to 15-angled, tubercles compressed, spiralled, spines pale brown. Cor. 2–7cm diam., deeply cup-shaped to flat, pale yellow to buff, veins darker; corona v. dark red-brown. Summer. Cape Prov.
H. barklyi Dyer. St. many-angled, tubercles with stout spines. Cor. 5–6cm diam., sinuate, lobes obtuse, yellow spotted red around centre. Karroo.
H. burkei N.E. Br. St. to 14-angled, spines to 8mm, slender. Cor. to 10cm diam. smooth, glab., dark brown, flat; lobes 6mm, acute, slightly crenate. Cape Prov.
H. currori (Hook.) Decne. St. many-angled, spines acute, sharp. Cor. to 12cm diam., green to ivory or pink, later yellow-pink, densely violet-hairy, cup-shaped, tube red-yellow to orange. SW Angola, NW Nam.
H. dregei N.E. Br. 20–24 angled, with acute, conical bristly tubercles. Cor. to 3.5cm diam., subcampanulate, pale brown, exterior glab., interior densely white-hairy, lobes broad, apices subulate, to 3mm. S Afr.
H. gibbosa Nel. St. 14-angled, tubercles with stiff spines. Cor. 8cm diam., slightly concave, round, margins slightly triangular, exterior glossy grey-green, interior purple to claret, covered with purple hairs, mouth of tube orange. Nam.
H. gordonii (Masson) Sweet. St. to 14-angled, to 5cm diam., tubercles with brown, woody, spines to 1cm. Cor 8–10cm diam., saucer-shaped, flesh-pink to maroon, lobes small, interior roughly papillose with furrow. Summer. W Cape, S Nam.
H. husabensis Nel. St. 16–20angled bristles 7mm. Cor. 7cm diam., almost circular, lobes rounded with a 1mm point, pink-violet to grey-violet, striped with a tuft of black-purple hairs in the centre. Nam.
H. longii Oberm. & Letty. St. 14-angled, tubercles 4–8mm. Cor. 5cm diam., cup-shaped, pink-brown, lobes rounded with a 3mm tip, interior covered with hairs. W Cape, Bots.
H. lugardii N.E. Br. St. 16-angled with small spiny tubercles. Cor. campanulate-rotate, slightly 5-lobed, lobes narrowing to a 7–10mm tip, interior brick-red, sparsely hairy. Cape Prov., Bots., Nam.
H. macrantha Dinter. St. to 24-angled. Cor. to 20cm diam., flat, pale purple veined yellow, covered in 2–3 purple hairs, tube orange-yellow, crateriform, lobes to 4cm. Summer. Nam.
H. montana Nel. St. 20–24-angled, tubercles with stiff bristles. Cor. 9cm diam., slightly concave, tip of lobes 5–7mm, light yellow with purple hairs, orange band 2–3mm wide around mouth, long purple-hairy. Nam.
H. pillansii N.E. Br. St. with 15–18 tuberculate angles. Cor. 6–6.5cm diam., margins 5-angled, lobe tips 3–4mm, base and middle minutely rough-papillose, salmon pink, peach in centre. W Cape.
H. rosea Oberm. & Letty. St. with 14 spiny-tuberculate angles. Cor. 7cm diam. cup-shaped, 5-angled, lobes light pink, interior sparsely hirsute. Cape Prov., Bots.
H. ruschii Dinter. St. with spine-tipped angles, spines 6mm. Cor. broadly campanulate, 4cm diam., lobes incised to 6mm, interior red-brown, yellow in centre, with minute papillate hairs. Nam.
H. senilis Jacobsen = *Tavaresia barklyi*.
H. triebneri Schuldt. 10–20cm; st. 12-angled, tubercles spinose. Cor. 4cm diam., green-pink, almost flat, glab., lobes broadly attenuate. Nam.

Hoodiopsis Lückh. Asclepiadaceae. 1 succulent perenn. herb to 30cm. St. ridges, toothed, striped purple. Lvs scale-like, short-lived. Fls solitary, midway on st.; cor. 5-lobed, flat with short tube, 10cm diam., claret inside, papillose, ridged, margins recurved; corona black-purple. Possibly a hybrid between *Hoodia* and *Caralluma*. Z10.
H. triebneri Lückh.

Hooked-spur Violet *Viola adunca*.

Hookera Salisb.
H. coronaria Salisb. = *Brodiaea coronaria*.

Hooker's Banksia *Banksia hookeriana*.
Hooker's Evening Primrose *Oenothera elata*.
Hoop Petticoat Daffodil *Narcissus bulbocodium*.
Hoop Pine *Araucaria cunninghamii*.

Hoorebekia Steud.
H. chiloensis Cornelisson = *Grindelia chiloensis*.

Hop *Humulus*.
Hop Bitter Pea *Daviesia horrida*.
Hop Clover *Medicago lupulina*.
Hop-headed Barleria *Barleria lupulina*.
Hop Hornbeam *Ostrya carpinifolia*.
Hop Marjoram *Origanum dictamnus*.
Hop-tree *Ptelea* (*P. trifoliata*).

Hordeum L. BARLEY. Gramineae. Some 20 ann. or perenn. grasses. Lvs linear, flat or rolled; sheaths auricled; ligules short, membranous. Fls in dense, narrow, cylindric, or flattened, spike-like pan.; spikelets in groups of 3 at each joint of rachis in 2 ranks, 1- (2-) flowered. Summer. Temp. N hemis. and S Amer.
H. hystrix Roth. MEDITERRANEAN BARLEY. Ann. to 37.5cm. St. solitary or geniculate. Lvs to 7.5×0.5cm, downy. Fls in ovate to oblong-ovate, grey-green to purple-tinged spikes to 6×2cm. Medit., C Asia. Z7.
H. jubatum L. SQUIRRELTAIL BARLEY; FOX-TAIL BARLEY. Ann. or perenn. to 60cm. St. smooth. Lf to 15×0.5cm, scabrous. Fls in dense, finely bristly, silky, nodding, pale green to purple-tinged spikes to 12.5×8cm. N Amer., NE Asia. Z5.

Horehound *Marrubium*.

Horkelia Cham. & Schldl. Rosaceae. Some 17 woody-based perenn. herbs. Lvs pinnate. Fls 5-merous, in dense cymes; cal. tube shallowly cylindrical; pet. round to spathulate, short-clawed; sta. 10. W N Amer. Z8.
H. frondosa (Greene) Rydb. To 80cm, gland., pilose. Lvs to 35cm; lfts 3–5 pairs, to 6cm, ovate to oblong, serrate to parted. Fls to 1cm diam., white, in clusters in forked cymes; sta. lanceolate and linear in 2 ranks. Spring–autumn. Calif.
H. gordonii Hook. = *Ivesia gordonii*.
H. truncata Rydb. To 50cm, thinly glandular-pubesc. Lvs to 12cm; lfts 3–7, to 4cm, oblong, rounded to truncate and toothed at apex. Fls to 1.5cm diam., white. Fls mostly solitary, in forked cymes; sta. essentially in 1 row, fil. dilated, those opposite sep. deltoid. Spring–summr. Calif.
→*Potentilla*.

Hormathophylla Cullen & T. Dudley.
H. lapeyrousiana (Jordan) Kupffer = *Alyssum lapeyrousianum*.
H. spinosa (L.) Kupffer = *Alyssum spinosum*.
H. pyrenaica (Lapeyr.) Cullen & T. Dudley = *Alyssum pyrenaicum*.

Horminum L. PYRENEAN DEAD-NETTLE; DRAGON MOUTH. Labiatae. 1 perenn. rhizomatous herb to 45cm. St. erect, tetragonal. Lvs to 7×5cm, ovate, base cordate, crenate-serrate. Fls to 6 per axill. whorl; cal. tubular-campanulate, bilabiate; cor. violet, lower lip 3-lobed, midlobe notched. Summer. Pyren., Alps. Z7.
H. pyrenaicum L. 'Album': fls white. 'Grandiflorum': fls large. 'Roseum': fls pink flushed purple.

Hornbeam *Carpinus*.
Hornbeam Maple *Acer carpinifolium*.
Horned Holly *Ilex cornuta*.
Horned Maple *Acer diabolicum*.
Horned Pondweed *Zannichellia palustris*.
Horned Poppy *Glaucium*.
Horned Rampion *Phyteuma*.
Horned Violet *Viola cornuta*.
Horn-leaved Bossiaea *Bossiaea biloba*.
Horn of Plenty *Datura metel*.

Horoeka *Pseudopanax crassifolius.*

Horridocactus Backeb. = *Neoporteria.*

Horse Balm *Collinsonia.*
Horse Cassia *Cassia grandis.*
Horse Chestnut *Aesculus hippocastanum.*
Horsefly Weed *Baptisia tinctoria.*
Horse Gentian *Triosteum.*
Horse Gram *Macrotyloma uniflorum*; *Vigna unguiculata.*
Horsehead Philodendron *Philodendron bipennifolium.*
Horsemint *Mentha longifolia*; *Monarda.*
Horse Nettle *Solanum carolinense.*
Horse Parsley *Smyrnium olusatrum.*
Horseradish *Armoracia rusticana.*
Horseradish Tree *Moringa oleifera.*
Horseshoe Vetch *Hippocrepis* (*H. comosa*).
Horsetail *Equisetum.*
Horsetail Tree *Casuarina equisetifolia.*
Horseweed *Conyza canadensis.*
Hortensia *Hydrangea macrophylla.*

Hosta Tratt. PLANTAIN LILY. Liliaceae (Funkiaceae, Hostaceae). 40 clump-forming herbaceous perennials. Rhiz. short, sometimes stoloniferous; roots fleshy. Lvs in a basal mound, large, entire, glab.; petiole usually long, sulcate, terete. Infl. a scapose rac., the scape bearing large leafy and small floral bracts; fls campanulate-tubular or funnelform with 6 ± spreading lobes; sta. 6, declinate. Jap., China, Korea.

H. albomarginata (Hook.) Ohwi = *H. sieboldii.*

H. atropurpurea Nak. KUROBANA-GIBOSHI. Lvs 18×5cm, lanceolate or oblong-lanceolate, pruinose throughout with veins in 5–9 pairs. Scapes to 60cm; fl. bracts broadly ovate, glaucous purple; fls dark purple, glaucous. Jap. f. *albiflora* Tatew. Fls white; sometimes confused with *H. rectifolia* var. *chionea* f. *albiflora.*

H. bella Wehrh. = *H. fortunei* var. *obscura.*

H. caerulea var. *capitata* Koidz. = *H. capitata.*

H. capitata (Koidz.) Nak. IYA-GIBOSHI. Lvs to 13×8cm, cordate-ovate, apex abruptly acuminate, thinly undulate, deep olive green above, glossy beneath, veins in 7–9 pairs, sunken above, papillose beneath. Scape to 40cm, with 3 leafy bracts below infl.; fls deep purple. Midsummer (well-established plants remontant in favoured sites). Korea, Jap.

H. cathayana Nak. ex Maek. AKIKAZE-GIBOSHI. Close to *H. tardiva* but with lvs smaller, more lustrous; scape to 75cm; fl. bracts bright green; fls lavender. Late summer. Jap., China.

H. chibai auct. = *H. tibai.*

H. clausa Nak. TSUBOMI-GIBOSHI. Lvs 15–20cm, lanceolate, acuminate, flat, olive green above, paler and lustrous beneath with veins in 4–5 pairs. Scape to 40cm; fls purple-rose, deepening to strong purple-rose. Mid- to late summer. Korea. var. *normalis* Maek. Fls lilac to mauve, funnelform, open.

H. crassifolia Araki. ATSUBA-GIBOSHI. Differs from *H. montana* is lvs ovate-oblong, heavy-textured, bright green above. Jap.

H. crispula Maek. SAZANAMI-GIBOSHI. Lvs 18–25×10–15cm, ovate-lanceolate, undulate, apex acuminate, often twisted and decurved, base cordate or rounded, usually inrolled over petiole, strongly undulate, dull olive green, deeply and irregularly edged white above, lustrous beneath, veins impressed in 7–9 pairs. Scape to 90cm, bracts leafy small, green-white to pale green; fls pale mauve. Gdn origin (Jap.). Sometimes confused with *H.* 'Thomas Hogg' and *H. fortunei* 'Albomarginata'. It can be distinguished from both by its slender, deeply grooved petioles. It is likely that L.H. Bailey's name *H. fortunei* var. *marginato-alba* refers to *H. crispula*; it has certainly come to do so through gdn usage. 'Lutescens': lvs spotted or blotched yellow, usually reverting in summer. f. *viridis* C. Brickell. Lvs plain green.

H. crispula f. *lutescens* (Sieb.) Sieb.). = *H. crispula* 'Lutescens'.

H. cucullata Koidz. = *H. montana.*

H. decorata L.H. Bail. OTAFUKU-GIBOSHI. Lvs 16×12cm, ovate to suborbicular, apex short-acuminate or blunt, base rounded, contracted, margin flat, white, dull dark green and leathery above, lustrous beneath with veins in 4–6 pairs, smooth. Scape 50cm, with white-margined, olive green, clasping bracts; fls deep violet or white. Midsummer. Jap. var. *normalis* Stearn. Lvs plain green, slightly rugose, apex acute. *H. decorata* is often confused with other hostas with white-edged lvs, particularly *H. undulata* var. *albomarginata* (the true 'Thomas Hogg'), *H. crispula* and *H. fortunei* 'Albomarginata': it may be easily identified by its stoloniferous habit.

H. decorata var. *marginata* Stearn = *H. decorata.*

H. elata Hylander = *H. montana.*

H. fluctuans Maek. KURONAMI-GIBOSHI. Lvs to 25×10cm, tapering, twisting and undulating, dull, deep olive green above,

glaucous grey beneath, veins in 9–10 pairs. Scape to 1m, glaucous; fl. bracts slender; fls pale violet. Jap. An ivory-edged variant has been introduced, currently known by the Japanese name Sagae-giboshi. 'Parviflora': fls smaller. 'Variegated': lvs large, with wide creamy gold edge.

H. fortunei (Bak.) L.H. Bail. RENGE-GIBOSHI. Lvs to 30×20cm, cordate to cordate-ovate or lanceolate-ovate, apex acute or acuminate, margins undulate or flat, heavy-textured, matt mid to dark green, sometimes glaucous and rugose above, glaucous beneath with veins in 8–10 pairs. Scape to 90cm, often glaucous, usually with 1 or more leafy bracts; fl. bracts lanceolate, in a cone-like head before anthesis, often tinted violet; fls mauve to pale violet. Late summer. Gdn origin (Eur.). 'Albomarginata': v. large; lvs to 30×17cm, oblong-ovate, acute, irregularly and deeply edged pale ivory to white, dull mid- to deep green above, faintly glaucescent beneath with veins in 7–8 distant pairs. (The name *H. fortunei* var. *marginato-alba* L.H. Bail. is often thought to be a synonym of *H. crispula*; this name is poorly defined and might equally be applied to any other large, white-edged hosta.) 'Aoki': lvs tinted grey. 'Aurea': lvs vivid soft yellow slowly turning green. 'Gloriosa': lvs narrow, cupped, dark green with thin white edge. 'Gold Haze': form of 'Aurea' with longer lasting colouring. 'Spinners' ('Aureo-alba'): robust; lvs sage green boldly edged creamy yellow which ages to white, edges undulate. var. *albopicta* (Miq.) Hylander. Lvs large, rather thin-textured with veins in 8–9 pairs, unfurling creamy yellow, unevenly edged mid- to dark green, ultimately green with a trace of variegation. f. *aurea* Wehrh. Lvs smaller than in var. *albopicta*, somewhat rugose above, glaucous beneath, lacking green margins, turning pale matt green in summer. f. *viridis* Hylander.

Lvs green. var. *hyacinthina* Hylander. Lvs glaucous, green-green above, blue-grey beneath, slightly coriaceous, margins v. shallowly undulate, hyaline. Variegated clones of this var. tend to lose their colouring after midsummer. var. *obscura* Hylander. Lvs to 23×16cm, broadly cordate-ovate, shortly acuminate, somewhat rugose, dully deep green above, slightly glaucous beneath. Scape far exceeding lvs. 'Aureomarginata' ('Yellow Edge'): lvs edged gold. var. *rugosa* Hylander. Similar to var. *hyacinthina* and var. *stenantha* but lvs smaller and more glaucous than in var. *stenantha* and deeply rugose between the veins, matt and glaucous above, less so than in var. *hyacinthina* with veins in 8–9 pairs. var. *stenantha* Hylander. Lvs mid- to dark green, lustrous above, slightly glaucous beneath, shallowly undulate, veins 9–10 pairs. Sometimes confused with *H. ventricosa.*

H. fortunei 'Aureomaculata' = *H. fortunei* var. *albopicta.*

H. fortunei Maek. non (Bak.) L.H. Bail. = *H. montana.*

H. fortunei 'Robusta' = *H. montana.*

H. fortunei var. *gigantea* L.H. Bail. = *H. montana.*

H. fortunei var. *obscura-marginata* Maek. = *H. fortunei* var. *obscura* 'Aureomarginata' ('Yellow Edge').

H. glauca auct. non (Sieb.) Stearn = *H. fortunei* var. *hyacinthina.*

H. glauca (Sieb.) Stearn = *H. sieboldiana.*

H. glauca Sieb. ex Miq. = *H. sieboldiana* var. *hypophylla.*

H. gracillima Maek. HIME-IAW-GIBOSHI. Lvs 32–6×1–2cm, spreading, lanceolate, apex acuminate, base blunt, lustrous or matt above, slightly glossy beneath with veins in 3 pairs, undulate. Scape to 25cm; fl. bracts linear; fls violet-rose. Autumn. Jap. 'Variegated': lvs finely edged ivory.

H. helenioides Maek. HAKAMA-GIBOSHI. Lvs to 20×2.5cm, linear-elliptic, apex rounded, margin flat or undulate, matt olive green above, glossy beneath, thin-textured, veins in 3–4 pairs. Scapes to 60cm, with navicular leafy bracts; fl. bracts oblong-lanceolate; fls mauve streaked purple. Jap. f. *albopicta* Maek. Lvs edged ivory.

H. hypoleuca Murata. URAJIRO-GIBOSHI. Lvs to 45×30cm, broadly ovate, base cordate, slightly undulate, softly subcoriaceous, glossy or glaucous above, mealy-white beneath with veins in 8 distant pairs. Scape to 35cm, sometimes with a few large leafy bracts toward summit; fl. bracts ovate to oblong, pale; fls pale lavender to chalky white. Summer. Jap.

H. ibukiensis Araki. IBUKI-GIBOSHI. Differs from *H. sieboldii* in lvs deep green, fls funnelform, not campanulate. Jap.

H. japonica var. *fortis* L.H. Bail. = *H. undulata* var. *erromena.*

H. japonica var. *japonica* hort. = *H. plantaginea* var. *grandiflora.*

H. jonesii Chung. TADOHAE-BIBICH'U. Lvs 6–13×3–5cm, erect, arranged in a loose spiral, lanceolate or elliptic, apex obtuse or acuminate, matt deep green, somewhat rigid, margins narrowly outlined in white, veins in 5–7 pairs. Scapes 35–60cm, with 2 leafy bracts below infl.; fl. bracts navicular, green; fls pale mauve. Korea.

H. kikutii Maek. HYUGA-GIBOSHI. Lvs ovate-lanceolate, arching, apex acuminate, base narrow-cordate, dull or glossy mid-green above, lustrous beneath, veins in 7–10 pairs, deeply sunken. Scapes with leafy bracts and lowermost fl. bracts large, tightly enclosing infl., with a curving slender tip, upper fl. bracts navicular, purple-tinted; fls white or ivory, sometimes v. faintly flushed purple. Jap. 'Green Fountain': lvs to 25×9cm, wavy; scapes v. bent. var. *caput-avis* Maek. Scapes deflexed near base, growing close to the ground; infl. particularly beak-like. var. *polyneuron* Fujita. Habit smaller, lvs broader; gold-lvd forms occur. var. *pruinosa* Maek. Habit erect. Lvs pruinose beneath. var. *yakusimensis* (Masam.) Maek. Lvs dark green, lying close to ground.

H. laevigata Schmidt = *H. jonesii*.

H. lancifolia (Thunb.) Engl. Lvs 10–17×1.75–2.75cm, lanceolate or oblong-lanceolate, apex narrowly acuminate, thin-textured, lustrous deep olive green above, glossy beneath with veins in 5–6 pairs. Scape to 45cm, with several large leafy bracts; fl. bracts glossy green, navicular; fls deep mauve. Gdn origin. 'Aurea': lvs pale gold turning green by late summer, or, persistently gold. The name 'Subcrocea' applied to these plants refers strictly to a golden-lvd variant of *H. sieboldii*.

H. lancifolia 'Viride-marginata' = *H. sieboldii* var. *alba* f. *kabitan*.

H. lancifolia var. *albomarginata* (Hook.) Stearn = *H. sieboldii*.

H. lancifolia var. *aureomaculata* Wehrh. = *H. fortunei* var. *albo-picta*.

H. lancifolia var. *tardiflora* (W. Irv.) L.H. Bail. = *H. tardiflora*.

H. lancifolia var. *thunbergii* Stearn = *H. lancifolia*.

H. latifolia var. *albomarginata* Wehrh. = *H. crispula*.

H. longipes (Franch. & Savat.) Matsum. Lvs to 14×8–10cm, cordate-ovate or elliptic-vovate, sometimes orbicular, apex acuminate, slightly undulate, matt mid to deep green above, glossy beneath, with glaucous veins and purple spotting on either side of base of midrib. Scape short; fl. bract pale green-white tinted purple; fls pale purple to chalky white or ivory. Late summer–autumn. Jap. Hybridizes freely with *H. kikutii*. f. *hypoglauca* Maek. Lvs pruinose, blue above, white beneath. Fls white. f. *viridipes* Maek. Lvs lanceolate. Scape dotted purple; fls off-white. var. *caduca* Honda Autumn-flowering. var. *latifolia* Maek. Lvs broad, flushed purpled at base. Golden-lvd forms occur.

H. longipes hort. = *H. rectifolia*.

H. longissima (Honda) Honda. MIZU-GIBOSHI; NAGABA-GIBOSHI. Lvs to 17×2cm, erect to arching, linear-oblong, apex long-acuminate, base blunt, decurrent, subcoriaceous, dull mid- to dark green above, rather glossy beneath with veins in 3–4 pairs. Scape to 55cm; fl. bracts glossy green, navicular; fls pale rosy mauve veined purple. Late summer. Jap. Forms occur with v. narrow, white-edged, white or golden-streaked and cloudy variegated lvs.

H. minor (Bak.) Nak. KIRIN-GIBOSHI. Lvs to 8.5×5.5cm, broadly ovate or cordate, apex acuminate, base truncate, decurrent, undulate, lustrous, mid to dark green, veins in 5–6 pairs. Scapes to 60cm; bracts spreading, green and purple; fls mauve. Summer (sometimes remontant). Korea. f. *alba* Maek. Fls white. *H. minor* is sometimes mistakenly thought to be a dwarf form of *H. ventricosa*. Several diminutive *Hosta* spp. and cvs are misnamed 'Minor'. The name *H. minor* 'Alba' is misapplied to *H. sieboldii* 'Alba', a plant sometimes confused with the rare *H. minor* f. *alba*. Young plants of *H. minor* are frequently mistaken for *H. venusta*.

H. montana Maek. OBA-GIBOSHI. Lvs to 30×18cm, broadly ovate, ovate-oblong or ovate-cordate, apex acuminate to cuspidate, base cordate to subtruncate, sometimes undulate, dull or shiny mid to deep green or glaucous above, pale green beneath, veins in 9–13 pairs, deeply impressed. Scape tall with leafy bracts in the apical half; fl. bracts spreading, lanceolate; fls grey-mauve to white. Jap. Included as a synonym here is *H. elata*, sometimes treated as a hybrid complex developing in European gardens since the 1860s. It encompasses many forms; some have strongly undulate lvs suggesting affinity with *H. crispula*; others show the influence of *H. sieboldiana* and *H. fortunei*. 'Emma Foster': lvs gold. 'Fuji no Setsuki': lvs sharply acute, twisted, with central white variegation, striped and speckled at base. f. *aureomarginata* Maek. Lvs narrower, broadly and irregularly edged gold, margins undulate. var. *praeflorens* Maek. Lvs more rigid; fls opening earlier. var. *liliiflora* Maek. Infl. to 30cm, becoming lax after flowering.

H. nakaiana (Maek.) Maek. KANZASHI-GIBOSHI. Lvs to 6×3.5cm, cordate-ovate, apex sharply recurved, base cordate-truncate, undulate, thinly subcoriaceous, pale and lustrous beneath, veins prominent in 5–7 pairs. Scape to 38cm, slender with a single, green, leafy bract; fl bracts navicular, tinted mauve; fls lilac, campanulate. Summer. Korea, Jap. The parent of several fine hybrids including 'Birchwood Parky's Gold' ('Golden') with gold lvs. 'Candy Hearts': lvs cordate, uniformly green.

H. nigrescens (Mak.) Maek. KURO-GIBOSHI. Lvs to 28×18cm, broadly ovate to elliptic, base cordate, inrolled and decurrent on petiole, dark green, initially ashy pruinose, somewhat concave with 8–13 pairs of slightly sunken veins above. Scape 1–2m, with 2–4 spreading, leafy bracts; fl. bracts green-white, edged

purple; fls milky white (pale mauve in bud). Late summer. Jap. f. *elatior*: larger and epruinose.

H. opipara Maek. NISHIKI-GIBOSHI. Closely resembles *H. rectifolia*. Lvs spreading, 14–20×7.5–13cm, ovate-elliptic, apex acuminate, margin undulate, cream, leathery, green, with veins in 9 pairs. Scape to 60cm; fls lilac. Jap.

H. plantaginea (Lam.) Asch. AUGUST LILY; MARUBA; YUSAN; TAMANO-GIBOSHI-KANZASHI. Lvs 20–28×15–24cm, apex shortly acuminate, base cordate, decurrent, shallowly undulate, glossy, yellow-green above, glossy beneath, veins conspicuous, raised, in 6–9 pairs. Scape to 65cm; leafy bracts sparse, fl. bracts green-white; fls white, fragrant. Late summer–autumn. China. Sometimes mistakenly labelled *H.* 'Thomas Hogg'. 'Aphrodite': fls with petaloid sta. f. *stenantha* Maek. Fls shorter, narrower. var. *grandiflora* Lem. Habit open, lax. Lvs narrower. Fls larger, longer. 'Chelsea Ore': lvs golden with a shallow green margin.

H. pulchella Fujita. UBATAKE-GIBOSHI. Lvs to 5×1.5cm, semi-erect, ovate to cordate, apex gently tapering, glossy above with to 4 pairs of raised, glaucous veins beneath. Scape far exceeding lf. mound with lanceolate leafy bracts; fl. bracts green, navicular; fls pale mauve or lavender, often fragrant. Late summer. Jap. Forms with glaucous and yellow-edged lvs are grown.

H. pycnophylla Maek. NOSHI SETOUCHI-GIBOSHI. Lvs to 20×10cm, ovate-lanceolate, gently acuminate, strongly undulate, dull sage green above, thickly pruinose beneath, thin-textured with veins in 6–8 remote pairs. Scape exceeding lvs with a single, small, leafy bract; fl. bracts navicular; fls pale mauve to dark purple. Late summer–autumn. Jap.

H. rectifolia Nak. TACHI-GIBOSHI. Lvs 15–23×5cm, ovate-elliptic, erect, slightly involute, apex shortly acuminate, base tapering, margin flat, dull mid-green on both surfaces, with veins in 6–9 pairs. Scape 60–75cm, with several leafy bracts in upper half; fl bracts navicular, green striped purple; fls violet. Late summer. Jap. 'Tall Boy': lvs large, green; fls lavender, on tall scapes. f. *pruinosa* Maek. Lvs, scapes and bracts intensely pruinose. var. *chionea* Maek. Lvs lanceolate, white-edged, long-petioled. var. *chionea* f. *albiflora* Tatew. Fls white; sometimes mistaken for *H. atropurpurea* f. *albiflora*. Round-leaved and yellow-margined forms have been recorded.

H. rohdeifolia Maek. OMOTO-GIBOSHI. Lvs to 18×6cm, erect, lanceolate to oblong-lanceolate, apex acuminate, base narrow, margins slightly involute, shining dark olive green above, usually edged pale yellow, with veins in 5–6 pairs. Scape to 1m, with several cream-edged leafy bracts; fl. bracts navicular, edged ivory; fls pale mauve striped purple. Summer. Gdn origin. f. *viridis* Maek. Lvs wholly green. W Jap.

H. rupifraga Nak. HACHIJO-GIBOSHI. Lvs to 12×7cm, broadly ovate-cordate, funnel-shaped at base, somewhat concave, coriaceous, heavy-textured, smooth, glossy dark olive green above with 6–8 pairs of impressed veins, paler beneath. Scape to 40cm; fl. bracts pale purple; fls light mauve. Autumn. Jap. A tetraploid form is offered.

H. sieboldiana (Hook.) Engl. & Prantl Lvs to 50×30cm, ovate-cordate to suborbicular, apex acute or acuminate, base cordate, flat, heavily textured, puckered, matt, glaucous grey-blue to blue-green or olive above, paler beneath, distinctly pruinose throughout, with veins in 14–18 pairs. Scape to 60cm, with elongated leafy bracts; fl. bracts scarious, concave; fls pale lilac-grey, fading to white tinted lilac or wholly white. Jap. 'Aurea' ('Golden Sunburst'): lvs golden. var. *amplissima* Maek. Lvs v. large, elliptic-ovate, apex abruptly acute, base cordate, margins undulate. Scape arching with fls pendent. var. *elegans* Hylander. Lvs v. thickly glaucous, heavily and deeply puckered. Fls pale nacreous lilac. (*H. sieboldiana* × *H. tokudama*?). var. *hypophylla* Maek. Lvs rounded, usually equalling or concealing scapes. var. *mira* Maek. Exceptionally vigorous and robust. Lvs markedly acute, petioles long, stout, arching, distinctly glaucous, flushed purple. Scape far exceeding lf mound. 'Semperaurea': lvs golden. For further cvs of *H. sieboldiana*, see general listing below.

H. sieboldiana (Mak.) Engl. non (Hook.) Engl. & Prantl = *H. montana*.

H. sieboldiana auct. non (Hook.) Engl. = *H. sieboldii*.

H. sieboldiana var. *glauca* Mak. & Matsum. = *H. tokudama*.

H. sieboldiana var. *longipes* (Franch. & Savat.) Matsum. = *H. longipes*.

H. sieboldiana var. *nigrescens* Mak. = *H. nigrescens*.

H. sieboldiana f. *fortunei* Voss = *H. tokudama*.

H. sieboldii (Paxt.) J. Ingram. KOBA-GIBOSHI. Lvs to 15×6cm, lanceolate-elliptic, apex broadly acuminate, base tapering, flat or undulate, somewhat rugose, matt mid-green above edged pure white, rather lustrous beneath, veins in 3–4 pairs. Scape to 50cm, with 1–2 leafy bracts; fl. bracts small, green tinted violet; fls pale mauve striped violet and lined white. Late summer–early autumn. Jap., Sakhalin. f. *kabitan* Maek. Lvs to

8.3cm, lanceolate to oblong-lanceolate, ruffled and undulate, acuminate, thin-textured, golden-edged dark green. Fls deep purple. 'Emerald Isle': lvs edged white; fls white. 'Sentinel': lvs v. narrow, glossy; fls deep purple. 'Shiro-kabilan': lvs twisted, white-edged. 'Shirobana-kika': fls white with irregular number of pet.; anth. exserted prior to anthesis. 'Subcrocea': lvs ruffled, gold. 'Yakushima-mizu': dwarf. var. *alba* (W. Irv.) Hylander. Lvs green; fls white, sometimes called *H. minor* 'Alba'.

H. ×tardiana hort. (*H. sieboldiana* var. *elegans* ×*H. tardiflora*.) 'Blue Diamond' (mound to 30cm high; lvs pointed, blue), 'Bright Glow' (lvs heavy, creamy gold), 'Devon Blue' (vigorous; lvs to 18×10cm, ovate-cordate, pointed, glaucous, flushed blue-grey, veins widely spaced), 'Happiness' (lvs narrow, tinted grey), 'Nicola' (lvs to 15×6.5cm, dull dark green; fls pink, scapes tall).

H. tardiflora (W. Irv.) Stearn. Lvs to 15×6.5cm, erect, lanceolate to narrow-elliptic, apex acuminate, base narrowed, not decurrent, margin flat or shallowly undulate, semi-rigid, thick-textured, glossy deep olive green above, matt beneath with 5 pairs of prominent veins. Scape to 35cm, held at 45 degrees; fl. bracts white to pale purple; fls clear mauve. Autumn. Not known in the wild.

H. tardiva Nak. NANKAI-GIBOSHI. Lvs to 12.5×5cm, erect to spreading, ovate or ovate-oblong, apex acuminate, base tapering or blunt, ± undulate, glossy deep green above, paler beneath with veins in 8 pairs. Scape to 37cm; fls bright purple at first. Early autumn. Jap. Sometimes confused with *H. lancifolia*, from which it may be distinguished by its broader lvs and later flowering period. A pale-striped form exists.

H. 'Thomas Hogg'. = *H. undulata* var. *albomarginata*.

H. tibai Maek. NAGASAKI-GIBOSHI. Lvs to 15×10cm, erect to spreading, ovate to ovate-elliptic, apex tapering sharply, base cordate, glossy above with veins in 4–7 pairs. Scape to 50cm, branching; fl. bracts green, navicular; fls pale mauve. Autumn. Jap.

H. tokudama Maek. TOKUDAMA-GIBOSHI. Lvs cordate to orbicular, apex tapering, semi-rigid, flat, heavily textured, rugose, vividly glaucous blue above, with to 13 prominent vein pairs. Scape to 30cm; fl. bracts oblong-lanceolate, suffused purple; fls pale grey-mauve to off-white. Summer–late summer. Gdn origin (Jap.). Possibly a hybrid involving *H. sieboldiana*. 'Buckshaw Blue': lvs deep blue, heavily dished; fls grey-lavender, scape short. f. *flavocircinalis* Maek. Lvs larger, more ovate and less finely tapered, edged bright yellow; origin of gold-lvd clones grouped as 'Gold Bullion'. f. *aureonebulosa* Maek. Lvs clouded yellow at centre, edged glaucous blue; a variable form encompassing such selections as 'Blue Shadows'. f. *flavoplanata* Maek. Lvs deep yellow at centre, narrowly edged glaucous blue.

H. tortifrons Maek. KOGARASHI-GIBOSHI. Close to *H. tardiflora*, from which it differs in lvs contorted and twisted; thick-textured, subcoriaceous. Gdn origin, Jap.

H. tsushimensis Fujita. TSUSHIMA-GIBOSHI. Lvs to 22×11cm, ovate, apex broadly acuminate, base cordate, mid-green and somewhat glossy above, with veins prominent in 5–9 pairs beneath. Scape to 75cm, with ascending, purple-spotted leafy bracts; fl. bracts green, navicular; fls green-white, sometimes strongly flushed rose-purple at base or purple. Late summer-autumn. Jap.

H. undulata (Otto & Dietr.) L.H. Bail. SUJI-GIBOSHI. A varied assemblage of gdn clones characterized by their twisted lvs. Lvs 11–15×4–6cm, ovate-oblong to lanceolate-elliptic, strongly undulate, apex acuminate, often twisted, thin but leathery, centre cream, margin olive green, irregular, glossy with veins in 7–9 pairs beneath. Scape to 30cm, with leafy bracts, white-green variegated; fl. bracts white with green margins, fls pale purple. Gdn origin (Jap.). var. *albomarginata* Maek. Lvs ovate-elliptic, flat, margin slightly undulate, apex more rounded, veins in 9 or more pairs, centre olive-green, margin cream-white, irregular. var. *erromena* (Stearn) Maek. Lvs to 23cm, broadly ovate, wholly dull mid-green. var. *univittata* (Miq.) Hylander. Lvs larger, ovate, twisted, margin less undulate, central cream zone 2cm wide, more distinct.

H. ventricosa Stearn. MURASAKI-GIBOSHI. Lvs to 24×18cm, broadly ovate to cordate, apex sharply acuminate, base blunt, decurrent, slightly undulate, rather rigid, thin, lustrous dark green above, glossy mid to dark green beneath, veins in 7–9 pairs. Scape to 1m, with a single leafy bract at midpoint; fl. bracts pale green; fls deep lilac mauve. China. var. *aureomaculata* Henson. Smaller, lvs bright yellow in centre, irregularly edged dark-green; variegation fades during summer. 'Variegata' ('Aureomarginata'): irregularly edged, creamy white. *H. ventricosa* is sometimes mistaken for *H. undulata* var. *erromena* and *H. fortunei* var. *stenantha*; it can be distinguished from both by its darker lvs with more remotely spaced veins.

H. venusta Maek. OTOME-GIBOSHI. Lvs 3×1.7cm, ovate, cordate,

apex acuminate, base rounded, contracted downwards, decurrent, undulate or flat, margin slightly coarse, dull mid to dark olive green, glossy beneath, veins in 3–4 pairs. Scape to 35cm, fl. bracts small, green; fls pale violet. Late summer–mid-autumn. Korea, Jap. 'Variegata': lvs splashed cream.

H. yingeri S. Jones. Differs from the related *H. jonesii* in its low, almost flattened habit, short-stalked lvs, delicate rac. of fls disposed around the floral axis. Korea.

H. cvs. The cvs listed below are valued for their lf colour and form, and classed according to size, texture and colour. Spp. giving rise to these cvs are listed at the beginning of each category; their botanical variants and direct selections can be found under each sp. description.

LEAVES VERY LARGE. Clump to 100cm across; lvs to 45cm; *H. elata, H. fluctuans, H. montana, H. nigrescens, H. sieboldiana*.

Lvs glaucous blue: 'Big Daddy' (lvs round, puckered, deep glaucous-blue, heavy; fls near-white; pest-resistant). 'Big Mama' (lvs more pointed, cupped, puckered, strong deep glaucous-blue, deeply puckered, petiole short, widly grooved and deeply angled; fls lavender; scape with one or more narrow leafy bracts, tinted purple). 'Blue Piecrust' (lvs ovate-cordate, somewhat rugose, deep glaucous-blue, margins ruffled, deeply cupped). 'Blue Umbrellas' (lvs broad, green-blue, glaucous, thick, veins widely spaced). 'Bressingham Blue' (lvs wide, cup-shaped, rugose, heavy, deep blue-green, glaucous; fls pearly white).

Lvs grey-blue: 'Blue Angel' (lvs heart-shaped, slightly undulate, glaucous grey-blue; fls near-white; slow to mature). 'Krossa Regal' (lvs graceful, glaucous grey, deeply ribbed; st. tall and arching; fls pale lilac in tall wavy spikes).

Lvs green: 'Green Acres' (lvs deeply ribbed, pale green; fls near-white. 'Green sheen' (lvs pale green, v. shiny; fls pale lavender, in tall scapes). 'Ruffles' (lvs pointed, deeply ruffled).

Lvs gold: 'Golden Sculpture' (lvs cordate, heavy, bright pale gold, sun-tolerant; fls white on tall scape). 'Sum and Substance' (lvs smooth, pale chartreuse yellow, v. heavy; fls pale lavender; sun-tolerant; pest-resistant). 'Zounds' (lvs v. puckered, heavy, gold with metallic sheen; fls pale lavender).

Variegated: 'Francis Williams' (lvs cordate, cupped, deeply corrugated, glaucous blue with wide creamy margin; fls pale lavender). 'Frosted Jade' (lvs frosted green with white margin; fls pale lavender). 'Northern Halo' (lvs rounded, cupped and puckered, glaucous blue with creamy white margin; fls pale lavender).

LEAVES NARROW. Lvs to 4cm wide: *H. gracillima, H. helenioides, H. lancifolia, H. longissima, H. rohdeifolia, H. sieboldii, H. tortifrons*.

Lvs blue: 'Hadspen Heron' (small; lvs lanceolate, undulate, margin shallowly rippled, thick, glaucous blue to green; scape low-spreading; fls lavender in dense rac.).

Lvs gold: 'Anne Arret' (habit open; blade decurrent, pale yellow, darker later, with ruffled white edge; petiole deeply grooved, ruffled and white margined). 'Chartreuse Wiggles' (lvs v. undulate, pale chartreuse yellow, lying nearly flat; fls purple). 'Wogon Gold' (stoloniferous; lvs rich gold; fls purple, on tall scapes).

Variegated: 'Bold Ribbons' (medium; lvs arching, matt dark green widely margined creamy white). 'Elfin Power' (lvs with white margin, glossy beneath; fls lavender, on tall upright scapes). 'Ginko Craig' (small; lvs dark green margined clear white; fls violet in tall spikes). 'Kabitan' (lvs lance-shaped, chartreuse yellow with narrow, dark green margin, ruffled; fls deep violet, in tall spikes; needs shade). 'Louisa' (lvs lanceolate, blunt-tipped, to 11×3cm, margined white, petioles to 20cm; fls white). 'Shirokabitan' ('White Kabitan': lvs with white centre and dark green margin). 'Vera Verde' (small; lvs decurrent, somewhat rugose, matt olive with thin creamy margin, petiole to 13cm, white edged; scape to 15cm; fls light mauve).

LEAVES LARGE. Clump to 75cm across; lvs to 25cm; *H. crispula, H. undulata* var. *erromena, H. fortunei, H. hypoleuca, H. plantaginea, H. rectifolia, H. ventricosa*.

Lvs blue: 'Blue Seer' (lvs puckered, intense blue, heavy; fls off-white), 'Blue Wedgwood' (open; lvs triangular, margin rippled, smooth, glaucous blue-green; fls pale lavender). 'Silver Bowl' (lvs round, cupped, heavy, some puckering, blue-grey, silver beneath; fls white).

Lvs green: 'Green Fountain' (lvs glossy mid-green, arching; fls pale lavender). 'Honeybells' (lvs as *H. plantaginea* var. *grandiflora*: fls white streaked violet; growth rapid). 'Royal Standard' (lvs ovate, somewhat stiff, bright green; fls white, in tall rac.). 'Sea Lotus Leaf' (lvs round, cupped, glossy dark green; fls pale lavender).

Lvs gold: 'Aspen Gold' (lvs v. rugose, heavy, cupped, gold, colour lasting; fls near-white, low; slow-growing). 'August Moon' (lvs pale golden yellow, faintly glaucous, corrugated; fls near white; sun tolerant; vigorous). 'Gold Standard' (lvs chartreuse green to light yellow, narrowly and irregularly margined dark green; fls lavender; needs shade). 'Piedmont Gold' (lvs smooth, bright gold, ruffled margin; fls lavender). 'Sun Power' (lvs pointed, wavy margined, pale chartreuse to bright gold; fls pale lavender).

Variegated; 'Antioch' (lvs arching, ovate and pointed, matt green centre with green marbling and margins splashed creamy white, veins prominent; fls lavender). 'Christmas Tree' (lvs wide, crinkled, heavy, deep green with creamy white margin). 'France' (lvs dark green margined clear white, in elegant mount; fls lavender; growth rapid). 'Great Expectations' (lvs puckered, centre chartreuse becoming cream white, with wide blue-green margin; fls white, on tall scapes). 'Ground Master' (slightly stoloniferous; lvs lanceolate-ovate, margin wavy, matt dark green with wide white margin; fls lavender). 'Leola Fraim' (lvs cupped, puckered between veins, deep green with white margin usually wider at tip; fls lavender). 'Moon Glow' (lvs pale golden-yellow, margined white; fls pale lavender). 'Moonlight' (lvs ovate, cupped and ruogse, gold with white margin when unfurled). 'Northern Lights' (lvs elongate, incurving, somewhat undulate, irregularly coloured cream centre with green margin and chartreuse overlap). 'Shade Fanfare' (lvs heart-shaped pale green with cream margin; fls lavender). 'Snow Cap' (lvs heavy, blue with creamy white margin; fls large, white, fragrant, vigorous). 'Sugar and Cream' (sport of 'Honeybells': lvs deep green with white wavy margin; fls pale lavender in tall rac.). 'Wide Brim' (lvs heavily puckered, dark green with wide, irregular cream margin; fls lavender).

LEAVES MEDIUM. Lvs to 15cm: *H. capitata*, *H. nakaiana*, *H. tokudama*, *H. undulata*.

Lvs blue: 'Blue Dimples' (lvs cordate, tapering to fine tip, margins undulate and lf dimpled when mature). 'Dorset Blue' (lvs cordate-orbicular, v. rugose, heavy, glaucous, dark turquoise blue; fls pale grey-lavender, on low, stout scapes). 'Hadspen Blue' (lvs cordate, smooth, closely veined, gflaucous deep blue; fls lavender on low scapes). 'Halcyon' (lvs heart-shaped, glaucous-blue; fls lavender-grey, in dense rac.). 'Love Pat' (lvs rounded, cupped and puckered, glaucous-blue).

Lvs grey: 'Pastures New' (lvs cordate, margins shallowly undulate, thin, glaucous grey-green; fls lavender on slender scape). 'Pearl Lake' (lvs cordate, glaucous grey; fls lavender-pearl, in dense rac., on tall rac., sometimes remontant).

Lvs green: 'Claudia' (lvs spathulate, shiny green; fls deep purple). 'Invincible' (lvs lanceolate, hevy, glossy green; fls pale lavender, fragrant; pest resistant). 'Leather Sheen' (lvs lanceolate, heavy, v. dark glossy green). 'Minnie Klopping' (lvs heart-shaped, glaucous-green; fls pale lavender, in tall rac.). 'The Twister' (ground-hugging; lvs lanceolate, twisted through centre and margins, dark green).

Lvs gold: 'Gold Bullion' (lvs cupped and undulate, pale yellow flushed green). 'Golden Prayers' (upright; lvs puckered and cupped, bright gold, heavy; fls pale lavender).

Variegated: 'Brim Cup' (lvs cupped, some puckering between veins, wide margin is white and later cream yellow; fls white, lavender in bud). 'Golden Tiara' (neat clump; lvs heart-shaped, green margined brilliant gold; fls lavender in tall rac., sometimes remontant; growth rapid). 'Neat Splash' (stoloniferous; lvs lanceolate, streaked and splashed yellow, variegation unstable and may revert to the yellow-margined 'Neat Splash Rim').

LEAVES SMALL AND DWARF. Lvs to 10cm; *H. kikutii* (some forms): *H. minor*; *H. pulchella*; *H. tsushimensis*; *H. venusta*.

Lvs blue: 'Blue Moon' (lvs heart-shaped, glaucous-blue, good substance; fls mauve-grey, in dense spikes; slow growing). 'Po Po' (lvs dwarf, to 5cm long, heart-shaped, blue-grey).

Lvs green: 'Emerald Skies' (lvs thicky shiny dark green; fls mauve; slow-growing). 'Saishu Jima' (lvs narrow, undulate, dark green; fls violet, on tall spike, v. floriferous). 'Shining Tot' (lvs dwarf, to 5cm long, deep green, thick; fls lilac). 'Tiny Tears' (dense mound; lvs dwarf, narrow, dark green; fls violet on tall scapes).

Lvs gold: 'Gold Edger' (lvs pale gold; fls light mauve), 'Hydon Sunset' (lvs cordate to ovate, vivid gold fading to dull green; fls deep purple on tall petioles). 'Lemon Lime' (neat clump; lvs undulating, yellow-green; fls violet, on tall rac., re-blooming; rapid increaser). 'Little Aurora' (lvs rugose, somewhat cupped, heavy, bright gold; scape and rac. large, fls near-white). 'Vanilla Cream' (flat-growing clump; lvs heart-shaped, cupped and puckered, cream to pale yellow; fls lavender; pest resistant).

Variegated: 'Butter Rim' (lvs matt dark green with creamy yellow margin; fls white). 'Duchess' (dense mound; lvs dark green edged white; fls purple). 'Geisha' (habit upright; lvs twisted, dark green with chartreuse to gold centre; fls light purple).
→*Funkia*.

Hot-dog Cactus *Senecio articulatus*.
Hotei-chiku *Phyllostachys aurea*.
Hot Pepper *Capsicum frutescens*.
Hot-rock Penstemon *Penstemon deustus*.
Ho-tsutsuji *Tripetaleia paniculata*.

Hottentot Bean *Schotia afra*.
Hottentot Bread *Dioscorea elephantipes*.
Hottentot Fig *Carpobrotus edulis*.

Hottonia L. Primulaceae. 2 aquatic, perenn. herbs, rooting or floating. Lvs whorled on st., pinnately dissected. Peduncles emergent; fls racemose, verticillate; cal. lobes 5, linear; cor. salverform, 5-lobed. Z6.
H. inflata Elliott. AMERICAN FEATHERFOIL. Lvs 1–5cm, ovate or oblong, lobes narrow-linear. Fls 0.5–0.8cm, white. E US.
H. palustris L. WATER VIOLET. Lvs 2–13cm, lobes linear, sometimes further divided. Fls to 2.5cm diam., violet, throat yellow. Eur., W Asia.

Hot Water Plant *Achimenes*.

Houlletia Brongn. Orchidaceae. 10 epiphytic orchids. Pbs ovoid, fleshy, unifoliate. Lvs terminal, elliptic to lanceolate, plicate, petiolate. Rac. lat., fls large; sep. spreading, free; pet. similar, narrower; lip fleshy, hypochile narrow, with 2 horns, epichile articulated, sometimes separated from basal portion by mesochile, simple or obscurely lobed. Trop. S Amer. Z10.
H. boliviana Schltr. = *H. odoratissima*.
H. brocklehurstiana Lindl. Infl. to 45cm, erect; fls to 7.5cm diam., fragrant; tep. dark red-brown marked deep purple or yellow, oblong, concave; lip yellow or yellow-white spotted and flushed purple-brown, shorter than pet. Braz.
H. landsbergii Lind. & Rchb. f. = *H. tigrina*.
H. odoratissima Lind. ex Lindl. & Paxt. Infl. to 85cm, erect; fls to 7.5cm diam., fragrant; sep. chocolate-brown or deep maroon, edged pale brown, ovate to elliptic-oblong, obtuse; pet. linear-spathulate; lip to 2.5cm, white marked and striped red. Autumn. Colomb., Venez., Peru, Boliv., Braz.
H. picta Lind. & Rchb. f. = *H. odoratissima*.
H. sanderi Rolfe. Infl. to 30cm, erect; fls to 8cm diam., white-cream to bright yellow; sep. round-ovate, apiculate, concave; pet. shorter, broadly obovate, acute; lip to 3cm. Peru, Boliv.
H. tigrina Lind. ex Lindl. Infl. to 35cm, arching or pendent; fls. to 9cm diam.; sep. pale yellow-brown to red-orange, spotted red-brown, ovate-elliptic, concave; pet. yellow marked pale red, ovate-lanceolate to spathulate; lip to 4.5cm, hypochile white banded red, epichile white to white-yellow, spotted red. Guat., Costa Rica, Panama, Venez., Colomb., Nic.
H. vittata Lindl. = *Polycycnis vittata*.

Houmspara *Pseudopanax lessonii*.
Hound's Tongue *Cynoglossum* (*C. virginiaticum*).
Hound's Tongue Fern *Microsorium diversifolium*.
Houpara *Pseudopanax lessonii*.
House Leek *Sempervivum*.
House-of-plenty *Fedia cornucopiae*.
House Pine *Araucaria heterophylla*.

Houstonia L. Rubiaceae. 50 perenn. herbs or shrubs. Fls in axill. cymes; frequently dimorphous; cor. funnel- or salver-shaped, lobes 4, valvate. N Amer., Mex. Z6.
H. caerulea L. BLUETS; INNOCENCE; QUAKER-LADIES. Perenn., to 20cm; rhiz. thread-like, mat-forming. Lvs ovate or obovate to elliptic, obtuse to attenuate at base, rounded to acute at apex, to 1.5cm, glab. or slightly bristly. Fls few, solitary on filiform peduncles to 6cm; cor. salver-shaped, to 1cm, pale blue to lilac or violet, or white, and yellow-eyed, interior glab.; anth. included. Spring–summer. N Amer. 'Alba': tightly mat-forming; fls white. 'Fred Millard' ('Millard's Variety'): mat-forming; fls deep blue.
H. longiflora (Cav.) Gray = *Bouvardia longiflora*.
H. longifolia Gaertn. LONGLEAF BLUETS. Erect perenn., to 3m; st. simple or sparsely-branched. Lvs elliptic to linear-oblanceolate, obtuse to attentuate at apex and base, to 5cm, occas. ciliate. Fls numerous in cymes; cor. white or purple, funnel-shaped, to 8mm, interior pubesc., anth. exserted. Summer. E US.
H. purpurea L. MOUNTAIN HOUSTONIA. Erect perenn., to 50cm. St. solitary or numerous. Lvs oval or ovate or lanceolate or elliptic, to 5cm, glab. or sparsely pubesc. Fls in dense cymes or clusters; cor. pale purple, lilac or white, funnel-shaped, to 8mm; anth. exserted. Summer. C & S US.
H. serpyllifolia Michx. Perenn., to 8cm, st. prostrate; flowering st. ascending. Lvs suborbicular, occas. ovate or oval, rounded or obtuse, to 0.5cm, usually minutely ciliate. Fls on erect or ascending elongate peduncles, to 4cm; cor. violet-blue or white, salver-shaped, to 1cm, interior pubesc.; anth. included. Spring–summer. SE US.
→*Hedyotis*.

Houttuynia Thunb. Saururaceae. 1 aromatic perenn. herb of damp places, clump-forming or spreading by buried st. St. mostly erect, to 60cm, leafy. Lvs 3.5–9cm, ovate-cordate, leaden-green above, paler beneath, glandular-punctate, usually with red-tinted margins. Fls small, crowded in term. spikes, subtended by 4–6 petal-like green-white, obovate bracts. E Asia.

H. cordata Thunb. 'Chameleon' ('Tricolor', 'Variegata'): lvs brilliantly painted red, cream and dark green. 'Plena': involucral bracts numerous and showy, resembling a minute white water-lily. Z5.

Hovea R. Br. ex Ait. f. PURPLE PEA. Leguminosae (Papilionoideae). 20 everg. shrubs. St. usually hairy. Lvs tough, prominently veined. Fls pea-like in axill. clusters or v. short rac. Aus., Tasm. Z9.

H. acutifolia Cunn. Erect, bushy shrub, to 1.5m; br. densely tomentose. Lvs 8cm, elliptic-oblong, loosely tomentose-villous beneath. Fls purple, in clusters of 2 or 3. Aus. (NSW, Queensld)

H. celsii Bonpl. = *H. elliptica*.

H. chorizemifolia DC. HOLLY-LEAVED HOVEA. To 80cm, with sparse, rusty coloured br. Lvs 7cm, ovate, sharp-acuminate, prickly-serrate. Fls 2–3 per cluster, bright blue, standard white-patched at base. W Aus.

H. elliptica DC. KARRI BLUE BUSH. To 2m. St. slender, erect. Lvs 7.5cm, elliptic, entire, long-petioled, prominently veined. Fls downy, in short clusters, deep blue, standard white-patched at base. Spring. W Aus.

H. lanceolata Sims = *H. longifolia*.

H. longifolia R. Br. RUSTY PODS. To 3m. St. erect, tomentose. Lvs 7cm, narrow, ovate-elliptic, obtuse, glossy, leathery. Fls solitary or 2–3, in clusters, standard blue, dark-veined, with a central blotch. Summer. Aus. (NSW, Tasm., Vict., Queensld).

H. pungens Benth. To 1.5m. St. erect, stiff; br. tomentulose. Lvs 2.5cm, narrow-lanceolate, leathery. Fls 1–3, in a short stalk blue to purple, white- to yellow-patched. Summer. W Aus.

H. purpurea Sweet = *H. longifolia*.

H. stricta Meissn. To 50cm, st. erect, rigid, loosely tomentose. Lvs to 2.5cm, lanceolate or linear, rigid, basally rounded or cordate. Fls 2 or 3 per cluster. W Aus.

H. trisperma Benth. To 1m. St. prostrate. Lvs 7.5cm broad, blunt. Fls 2–3-clustered, lavender. Summer. W Aus.

Hovenia Thunb. Rhamnaceae. 2 decid. shrubs or trees. Infl. cymose, usually twice-branched; cal. 5-lobed, pet. 5, v. small, concave, enclosing sta. Fr. berry-like. Summer. E & S Asia, so widely cult. that its native range is blurred. Z6.

H. dulcis Thunb. RAISIN TREE; CHINESE/JAPANESE RAISIN TREE. Tree to 20m, young twigs downy. Lvs 10–20cm broadly ovate, apex acuminate, base cordate, coarsely toothed, downy beneath. Infl. 5–7cm across; fls 6mm diam., green-yellow. Pedicels fleshy becoming red and edible after frost, fr. partially enclosed by pedicel. E Asia. var. *glabra* Mak. Lvs smaller, glab. Jap., N China. var. *koreana* Nak. 3–5m, often shrubby in habit. Jap. var. *latifolia* Nak. Tree, 15–20m. Lvs 11–14×8.5–11cm, elliptic-ovate or cordate. Jap.

Howea Becc. Palmae. 2 palms. St. solitary, erect, bare, base sometimes swollen. Lvs to 3m, pinnate, sheath fibrous; pinnae crowded, single-fold, glab. scaly or floccose along midrib beneath. Spikes interfoliar, to 2m becoming pendent. Fr. to 3cm, ellipsoid, hard, olive to red. Lord Howe Is. Z10.

H. belmoreana (C. Moore & F. Muell.) Becc. BELMORE SENTRY PALM; CURLY PALM. To 7m. Trunk markedly ringed, usually swollen at base. Pinnae to 2.5cm diam.

H. forsteriana (C. Moore & F. Muell.) Becc. SENTRY PALM; FORSTER SENTRY PALM; KENTIA PALM; THATCH LEAF PALM. To 18m but grown as a stemless juvenile. Trunk obliquely ringed, straight. Pinnae c3–4cm diam.

→*Denea*, *Grisebachia* and *Kentia*.

Howellia A. Gray.
H. ovata (Eastw.) Rothm. = *Antirrhinum ovatum*.

Howittia F. Muell. Malvaceae. 1 rusty-pubesc. shrub to 1m or more. Lvs to 10cm, ovate to lanceolate, pale green to white beneath, entire, undulate or serrate. Fls cup-shaped, slender-stalked, solitary or 2–3 per cluster; epical. 0; cal. 5-lobed, to 7mm; pet. 12–25mm, pale violet; sta. united in a tubular column. S Aus., New S Wales. Z9.

H. trilocularis F. Muell.

Hoya R. Br. PORCELAIN FLOWER; WAX FLOWER. Asclepiadaceae. 200–230 perenn., everg., branching climbers and epiphytes, some more shrubby or succulent. Lvs opposite, often leathery

or fleshy, mostly glab. Infl. axill., pendent, nectariferous umbels or cymes bearing successive clusters of fls; fls 5-merous fragrant, waxy; cal. small, cor. lobes thick, spreading; corona often highly coloured. Asia, Polyn., Aus. Z10.

H. acuta Haw. Lvs 10cm, ovate-lanceolate, base cuneate, apex acute, pale green. Cor. 1.5cm diam., white, hairy within; corona dark pink above, white below. Summer. India to Malaysia and Indon.

H. archboldiana Norman. Robust vine. Lvs 20–30cm, shiny, oblong, base cordate, apex acute. Cor. 3.5cm diam., lobes triangular, reflexed, red-pink tipped white; corona yellow-brown to black when dry. New Guinea. Z10.

H. australis R. Br. ex Traill. Succulent climber to 5m. Lvs to 12cm, obovate or suborbicular, acute, thick. Fls honeysuckle-scented; cor. lobes broad, white, waxy, flat and glab. with papillose margins; corona red-purple. Summer. Aus.

H. bandaensis hort. = *H. australis*.

H. bella Hook. = *H. lanceolata* ssp. *bella*.

H. carnosa (L. f.) R. Br. WAX PLANT. Succulent, climber to 6m or more. Lvs to 8cm, lanceolate-ovate, base cordate, apex blunt, dark green, sometimes flecked white. Cor. 1.5cm diam., lobes recurved, white to flesh-pink, papillose above; corona waxy white with a red centre. Summer. India, Burm., S China. 'Alba': fls pure white. 'Exotica': lvs variegated yellow and pink, margins green. 'Picta': lf margins creamy white. Further lf colour variants occur, including some with only sparse and faint silver mottlings or yellow zones. Forms with contorted lvs are also grown. Z9.

H. carnosa var. *compacta* hort. = *H. compacta*.

H. carnosa var. *picta* (Sieb.) Bl. = *H. carnosa* 'Picta'.

H. compacta C.M. Burton. Pendulous shrub. Lvs folded. Fls almond-scented, similar to those of *H. carnosa* but lobes broader and shorter. Origin unknown.

H. coriacea Bl. Vigorous climber. Lvs to 12cm, ovate or ovate-elliptic, dark green, leathery, slightly fleshy. Cor. 1.5cm diam. lobes ivory, buff yellow or v. pale brown; corona white with crimson or maroon centre. India and Burm. to Indon.

H. coronaria Bl. Climber to 3m, thick-stemmed, pubesc. Lvs to 10cm, oval, mucronate, almost glab. above, revolute. Cor. to 2cm diam., strongly scented at night, lobes pale green-white to creamy yellow, forming a shallow bell shape; corona with 5 crimson spots. Summer. S Indon., Malaysia, Thail., Philipp., New Guinea.

H. cumingiana Decne. Erect, shrubby climber. Lvs to 7cm, cordate, flat, closely set together, slightly downy beneath. Cor. lobes glossy, yellow-green, reflexed; corona yellow with dark maroon or red centre. Spring–early summer. Malaysia.

H. dalrympleana Muell. = *H. australis*.

H. darwinii hort. = *H. australis*.

H. fraterna Bl. Robust, sprawling, thick-stemmed. Lvs to 30cm, broadly elliptic, base subcordate, thick, leathery, apex acute, revolute. Fls to 2.5cm diam.; cor. red-pink; corona bright yellow to buff, shiny. Indon.

H. fusca Wallich. Large vine. Lvs to 22cm, oblong, flat, thick and leathery, base obtuse, apex mucronate. Cor. to 2cm diam., lobes bright yellow, lanceolate, margins reflexed; corona truncate, dark brown. Summer. Nepal to S China and Thail.

H. fuscomarginata N.E. Br. = *H. pottsii*.

H. globulosa Hook. f. Climber with downy st. Lvs to 15cm, oblong, puberulent, leathery, base rounded, apex slender-acute. Cor. lobes cream-yellow or straw-yellow; corona with a pink base, apex cream. Spring, summer. N India, Nepal, Tibet.

H. griffithii Hook. f. Climber, st. twining. Lvs 10–25cm, oblanceolate to elliptic. Cor. 2.5–4cm diam.; lobes dark rose-red, with 2 faint pink stripes; corona waxy-white. Summer. NE India to S China.

H. 'Hindu-rope' = *H. compacta*.

H. imperialis Lindl. Robust climber to over 6m, st. covered by a thick down. Lvs 15–22cm, elliptic to narrow oblong, thick, leathery, base cordate, apex mucronate, margins wavy. Cor. 7cm diam., lobes spreading, dark rusty-brown or magenta and finely hairy above, waxy; corona creamy white. Summer. Indon., Malaysia.

H. kerrii Craib. Climber to 3m, st. smooth, pale. Lvs to 10cm or longer, broadly obovate to orbicular-cordate, dark green, paler and downy beneath, leathery, emarginate. Cor. 1.2cm diam., densely hairy inside, creamy white; corona rose-purple. Summer. Thail., Laos.

H. keysii Bail. = *H. australis*.

H. lacunosa Bl. St. and br. thin. Lvs fleshy, either to 3cm, thick, ovate or to 7cm, oblanceolate, with ridged margins. Cor. lobes to 8mm, white-green, with dense, tiny, soft hairs, apices reflexed; corona yellow. Spring, early summer. Thail., Malaysia, Indon.

H. lanceolata Wallich ex D. Don ssp *lanceolata*. Shrub-like, to 1m, st. pendulous, short-hairy. Lvs to 2.5cm, usually lanceolate, base rounded, fleshy, green, fls sweetly scented; cor. snow white, lobes to 6mm, flat or slightly reflexed, hairy; corona rose-red to amethyst-violet, translucent. Summer. Himal. ssp. *bella* (Hook.) D.H. Kent. MINIATURE WAX PLANT. To 45cm, st. arching, densely downy. Lvs to 3cm, ovate-lanceolate, fleshy, convex, apex acute, base rounded. Fls 1.5cm diam., v. sweetly scented; cor. lobes to 7mm, waxy-white, margins slightly incurved; corona amethyst-violet. Summer. Himal. to N Burm. Z9.

H. lasiantha (Bl.) Korth. Climber. Lvs to 16cm, elliptic, short-acute, papery. Cor. lobes about 1.5cm, yellow to pale orange, strongly reflexed, bases with dense, long hairs; corona orange. Summer. S Thail., Malaysia, Indon.

H. latifolia G. Don. Lvs to 25cm, ovate to oblong-ovate, thick, leathery, copper-coloured when young. Cor. pink. S Thail., Malaysia, Indon.

H. linearis Wallich ex D. Don. St. woody with slender, pendent br. Lvs 2.5–5cm, v. narrow, subcylindric, deeply grooved below, revolute, dark green above. Fls slightly fragrant, 1cm diam.; cor. ivory-white; corona yellow, tinged pink. Summer-autumn. Himal. var. *sikkimensis* Hook. f. St. weaker, more flaccid. Cor. 1.3cm diam., glab. within, lobes recurved. Summer-autumn. Himal. to N Burm. Z9.

H. longifolia Wallich. STRING BEAN PLANT. St. slender. Lvs 6–15cm, linear-lanceolate, acuminate, dark green, fleshy almost pendent. Fls delicate, 1–4cm diam., fragrant; cor. white, sometimes flushed pink; corona rose-pink or red. Early summer. Himal. to S Thail. and Malaysia.

H. macgillivrayi Bail. Lvs to 20cm, broad-ovate or ovate, base cordate, apex cuspidate, glab., dark green, copper when young. Fls 8cm diam., cup-shaped; cor. lobes dark red, bases sometimes white, acute, with recurved margins; corona dark red, occas. white-centred. Aus. (Queensld).

H. macrophylla Bl. Shrub-like, scrambling climber. Lvs to 25cm, ovate-lanceolate or elliptic-lanceolate, fleshy, base rounded, apex acute, with 3 longitudinal yellow veins. Fls about 1.2cm diam.; cor. lobes white, fleshy, papillose at base inside; corona creamy white. Indon.

H. motoskei Teijsm. & Binnend. Vigorous climber. Lvs to 6cm, with irregular silver flecks, broadly elliptic or orbicular, leathery, waxy. Fls strongly scented, long-lasting; cor. white to pale creamy pink; corona maroon. Jap., Okinawa.

H. multiflora Bl. Robust climber, often loosely shrubby. Lvs to 10cm, linear to elliptic, bright green, often blotched white, leathery, fls strongly scented; cor. lobes about 2.5cm, creamy white to straw-yellow with orange tips, reflexed; corona white. Late summer. SE Asia.

H. obscurinerva Merrill = *H. pottsii*.

H. ovalifolia Wight & Arn. ex Wight. Lvs to 4–10cm, elliptic to rhomboid, narrow, dark green, fleshy, revolute. Cor. bright yellow, corona red. Summer. India to Malaysia.

H. parasitica (Roxb.) Wallich ex Wight = *H. acuta*.

H. paxtonii hort. ex Williams = *H. lanceolata* Bl. *bella*.

H. polyneura Hook. f. FISHTAIL HOYA. Epiphytic shrub. Lvs to 10cm, broadly rhomboid-ovate, acute, dark green with paler venation. 1.2cm diam. or more, white to cream; corona red to purple. Himal. to S China.

H. pottsii Traill. Climber to 3m. Lvs to 7cm, cordate or oblong, apex narrow acute, rusty-red above, white-green beneath. Fls fragrant; cor. pale yellow, slightly hairy; corona purple-centred. N India to China.

H. pubicalyx Merrill. RED BUTTONS. Scrambling shrub. Lvs 10–14cm, oblong to oblong-ovate, fleshy, leathery, apex acuminate, base obtuse. Fls fragrant, 1.8cm diam.; cor. lobes broadly triangular, spreading, apices recurved, densely papillose inside; corona red-brown. Philipp.

H. purpureofusca Hook. Robust climber to over 5m. Lvs 8–13cm, ovate, fleshy, dark green mottled silver-pink, acute. Cor. lobes red-brown to ash-grey, densely white-hairy above; corona pink to purple. Summer. Indon.

H. rubida Schltr. Epiphyte. Lvs to 6cm, ovate, fleshy, dark glossy green above, paler beneath. Cor. 1.2cm diam., glossy, bright maroon; corona red. New Guinea.

H. sana Bail. = *H. australis*.

H. serpens Hook. f. Pendent shrub. Lvs to 5cm, ovate to broadly elliptic, papillose, hairy. Cor. to 1.2cm diam., white to pink, hairy inside; corona red. Himal. to Burm.

H. shepherdii Short ex Hook. Climber, st. hairy. Lvs 5–15cm, channelled and dark green above, paler beneath, linear-lanceolate, pendent. Cor. 1cm, white to pink, margins hairy; corona white, red or pink-centred. Summer. India. Z9.

H. sikkimensis hort. = *H. lanceolata*.

H. trinervis Traill = *H. pottsii*.

H. variegata Sieb. ex Morr. = *H. carnosa* 'Picta'.

Huamuchil *Pithecellobium dulce*.

Huannco *Cinchona micrantha*.

Huckleberry *Gaylusaccia*.

Huckleberry Oak *Quercus vacciniifolia*.

Hudsonia L. BEACH HEATHER. Cistaceae. 3 small, decumbent everg. subshrubs. Lvs scale-like or subulate, grey-green. Fls term., solitary; sep. 3; pet. 5, yellow; sta. 10–30. Early spring--early summer. N Amer. Z6.

H. ericoides L. GOLDEN HEATHER; FALSE HEATHER. 20cm. Lvs to 14mm, imbricate, subulate. Fls to 8mm diam.; pedicel to 1.4cm.

H. montana Nutt. To 18cm. Lvs to 12mm, subulate. Fls to 1cm diam.; pedicel longer than fl.

H. tomentosa Nutt. POVERTY GRASS; BEACH HEATHER. To 20cm. Lvs scale-like, smaller than in *H. ericoides*, addpressed, tomentose.

Huernia R. Br. DRAGON FLOWER. Asclepiadaceae. Some 70 succulent, perenn. herbs. St. basally branched, cylindrical, glab., fleshy, usually angled. Lvs rudimentary, caducous. Fls in a small cluster or solitary, sessile or on a short peduncle, borne between base and midpoint of st., often malodorous; cor. fleshy, campanulate to rotate; tube short, lobes 5, with 5 smaller teeth in the sinuses; corona ring-shaped, 2-whorled. S Afr. to Ethiop. and Arabia, 1 sp. W Afr. Z10.

H. andreana (Rauh) Leach. St. to 1m, grey-green spotted white, ribbed ×4–5. Cor. 25–27mm diam., pale wine-red, lobes triangular, exterior pale ochre, interior with black-violet hairs. Kenya.

H. appendiculata A. Berger = *H. hystrix* var. *appendiculata*.

H. arabica N.E. Br. = *H. macrocarpa* var. *arabica*.

H. aspera N.E. Br. St. to 15cm, bluntly 5–6-angled, teeth short, brown. Cor. 2–2.5cm diam., red-brown below, interior deep maroon, roughly papillose and spotted white. Tanz.

H. barbata (Masson) Haw. St. 2–6cm, glaucous sinuately 4–5-angled, teeth long. Cor. c5cm diam., blood-red, interior densely covered by long, purple hairs or papillae, lobes triangular-attenuate, pale sulphur-yellow to buff, spotted blood-red, with long, blood-red hairs. S Afr. var. *griquensis* N.E. Br. Cor. lobes v. pointed, hairs more scattered.

H. blackbeardae R.A. Dyer = *H. zebrina* var. *magniflora*.

H. boleana M. Gilbert. St. to 8×1.5cm, 5-angled, teeth soft, to 6mm, grey-green to green mottled purple. Cor. 17mm diam., lobes deltoid acuminate, inner surface blood-red, covered with large yellow papillae. Ethiop.

H. brevirostris N.E. Br. Variable. St. to 5cm, spotted brown, 4–5-angled, ridges toothed and sinuate. Cor. 2.5–4cm diam., waxy, papillose, interior pink with base crimson, lobes triangular-attenuate, exterior light green, pink-green spotted crimson within. Cape Prov. var. *ecornuta* (N.E. Br.) White & B.L. Sloane. Cor. 33–37cm diam., pale canary-yellow spotted light red, roughly papillose. var. *histronica* White & B.L. Sloane. Cor. sulphur-yellow with large purple blotches. var. *immaculata* (N.E. Br.) White & B.L. Sloane. Cor. 37–43mm diam., primrose-yellow, unspotted. var. *intermedia* N.E. Br. Cor. wrinkled, primrose-yellow with purple-tipped papillae, tube paler, base purple. var. *longituba* (N.E. Br.) White & B.L. Sloane. Cor. 25–31mm diam., lobes 9–10mm, yellow with small furrows, rough. var. *pallida* (N.E. Br.) White & B.L. Sloane. Cor. 32–40mm diam., tube broader, lobes v. pointed, canary-yellow inside, spotted light red, tube base purple-red. var. *parvipuncta* White & B.L. Sloane. Spots inside cor. smaller. var. *scabra* (N.E. Br.) White & B.L. Sloane. Cor. 32–40mm diam., tube 10mm diam. with annular thickening, lobes pointed, pale fresh-coloured to canary-yellow within, minutely papillose with light red spots, annulus with larger papillae.

H. campanulata (Masson) R. Br. St. 5–10×2cm, green spotted red, 4–5-angled, angles sinuate-dentate. Cor. lobes broad triangular pointed, exterior off-white, interior sulphur-yellow with large black-purple blotches, tube with long purple hairs and black-red bands. Cape Prov.

H. clavigera (Jacq.) Haw. St. to 8cm, spotted red, 4–5-angled toothed. Cor. 3–4cm diam., exterior brown-green, interior ochre to green-yellow with purple cilia and crimson spots, merging in base of striate tube, lobes broadly triangular, papillose. Cape Prov.

H. concinna N.E. Br. = *H. macrocarpa* ssp. *concinna*.

H. confusa E. Phillips. St. to about 6cm, 4–5-angled, teeth acute. Cor. 3cm diam., yellow to crimson, smooth, with a white-spotted annulus at mouth, lobes v. pale green, irregularly spotted red, with tiny papillae. Transvaal.

H. distincta N.E. Br. St. 4–6cm, bluntly 8–9-angled. Cor. dull yellow with complex crimson markings, about 2.5cm diam., lobes acute, spreading, papillae with short, apical crimson hairs. Cape Prov.

H. erectiloba Leach & Lavranos. St. 4–20cm, 4-angled, teeth to 5mm. Cor. to 3cm diam., exterior cream with red spots and pronounced veins, interior deep blood-red below, papillose above with blood-red convergent lines, tube hirsute in mid region, cream spotted blood-red, lobes erect, deep blood-red, tuberculate. Moz.

H. erinacea Bally. St. 20–60. Cor. 16–17mm diam., fleshy, lobes pointed-triangular, upper surface with long papillae, yellow blotched dark purple. Kenya.

H. flava N.E. Br. = *H. primulina* var. *rugosa*.

H. flavicorona hort. = *H. macrocarpa*.

H. guttata (Masson) N.E. Br. St. 6–8cm, 4–5-angled, ridges sinuate, teeth projecting. Cor. to 4cm diam., tube with minute, pointed papillae, lobes broadly triangular, attentuate, sulphur-yellow with tiny, blood-red markings. Cape Prov.

H. hadramautica Lavranos. St. 4–6cm, 5-angled, teeth truncate. Cor. to 2.5cm diam., exterior cream and densely papillose, interior dark purple-red, papillose, tube pink below, lobes triangular, pink. S Arabia.

H. hallii E. Lamb & B. Lamb = *H. namaquensis* ssp. *hallii*.

H. hislopii Turrill. St. 5cm, 5–7-angled, teeth 3mm. Cor. about 2.5cm diam., blood-red, base swollen, with short hairs on white, red-tipped papillae towards mouth, lobes triangular attenuate, cream with blood-red spots. Zimb. ssp. *robusta* Leach & Plowes. Cor. obscurely concentrically lined in tube. W Zimb.

H. hystrix (Hook. f.) N.E. Br. St. 5–12cm, 5-angled, ridges blunt, stoutly toothed, pale green or tinged purple. Cor. 3–4cm diam., lobes triangular-attenuate, ochre with crimson spots and lines, densely covered in red, fleshy papillae, margins revolute. N S Afr., Zimb., SW Moz. var. *appendiculata* (A. Berger) White & B.L. Sloane. St. more creeping, teeth sharper. Cor. lobes sulphur-yellow below, markings and papillae more conspicuous.

H. immaculata N.E. Br. = *H. brevirostris* var. *immaculata*.

H. ingeae Lavranos. St. 2–4cm, 4-angled, pale green mottled purple. Cor. fleshy, 14mm wide at mouth, prominently veined, cream, interior glab. at base of tube, red-brown, then cream and densely covered with stiff, clavate, red-brown hairs and spots, lobes papillose, erect, deltoid. Cape Prov.

H. insigniflora Maass. St. 5–10cm, 4-angled, teeth 5–6mm, pointed. Cor. 4–4.5cm diam., margin dark purple-brown, lobes 10–12mm with a raised central rib, exterior minutely papillose, interior glab. with pale pink markings. S Afr.

H. keniensis R.E. Fries. KENYAN DRAGON FLOWER. St. 5–12cm, 5-angled to semiterete. Cor. to 3cm diam., interior dark purple, papillose, exterior red-purple and covered in rough calli, lobes, broad. C Kenya. var. *grandiflora* Bally. Cor. 5cm diam., exterior off-white, ± glab. with few veins, interior v. dark black-purple, covered with minute flat papillae. var. *molonyae* White & B.L. Sloane. Cor. 3.5cm diam., exterior less tuberculate, interior deep dark purple or almost dark blue, slightly papillose, lobes 4.5×1.5mm. var. *nairobiensis* White & B.L. Sloane. Cor. 3.5cm diam., exterior red-purple with prominent yellow markings, rough, interior deep red-purple, minutely papillose, lobes 5×16mm.

H. kennedyana Lavranos. St. almost spherical, 2×2cm, reticulate-tuberculate, dark purple-green. Cor. 2.2cm diam., lobes pointed, exterior pink to cream with scattered purple blotches and 5 prominent veins, interior cream with red-brown blotches and bands, glab. below, elsewhere covered with white papillae. S Afr. (Cape Prov.).

H. kirkii N.E. Br. St. 2.5–4cm, acutely 4–5-angled, teeth acute, 2–2.5mm. Cor. to 5cm diam., tube dark purple, swollen and constricted at mouth, papillae red-tipped, pointed, fleshy, lobes broad, sulphur-yellow spotted maroon. Transvaal, S Zimb., Moz.

H. laevis Wood. St. 4–6cm, angles 4–5, sinuate-dentate, teeth 7–8mm. Cor. broadly campanulate, 3cm diam., interior cream irregularly spotted and lined purple-brown, surface smooth. Yemen.

H. leachii Lavranos. St. to 1.5m, indistinctly 4-angled. Cor. to 2cm diam., lobes triangular-tapering, exterior cream, with small purple-brown spots and densely white-papillose, interior with dark purple-brown bands and bristly dark brown papillae. Moz.

H. levyi Oberm. St. 7cm, deeply furrowed, teeth 1cm long. Cor. 3.5cm diam., exterior rough and red-purple-spotted, tube dark maroon, cylindrical, lobes triangular-attenuate, spreading, cream-yellow spotted red, papillose. N Zimb., Zam.

H. loadarensis Lavranos. St. 5–7cm, compressed, grey-green blotched purple, 5-angled, teeth pointed. Cor. to 3.5cm diam., exterior cream, minutely tuberculate, interior cream with a narrow purple border and purple-brown spots, papillose, lobes with 5 prominent veins. S Yemen.

H. loesneriana Schltr. St. to 4cm, acutely 4-angled, often tinged purple, teeth to 3mm. Cor. 2.5cm diam., red-brown, lobes triangular, exterior rough and red-brown, interior dark yellow with red-brown spots and narrow bands, bluntly papillose toward apex. Transvaal.

H. longii Pill. St. 3–5cm, 6–8-angled, toothed. Cor. 1.8–2cm

diam., ivory blotched crimson, tube, papillose toward mouth, lobes deltoid-acuminate, covered with hair-tipped papillae. Cape Prov.

H. longituba N.E. Br. St. 2–5cm, acutely 4–6-angled. Cor. to 3.5cm diam., exterior glab., prominently 20-veined, interior ivory spotted dark red, covered in small calli, tube maroon, lobes triangular. S Afr. ssp. *cashalensis* Leach & Plowes. St. 5–6-angled. Tube interior long-hairy.

H. macrocarpa (A. Rich.) Spreng. St. to 9cm, 4–7-angled, thick, ridges sinuate, teeth to 8mm. Cor. 11–20mm diam., papillose to smooth, exterior yellow green, interior pale yellow with concentric maroon bands or wholly purple to crimson, lobes broadly triangular, attenuate. Eritrea, SW Saudi Arabia, S Yemen. var. *arabica* (N.E. Br.) White & B.L. Sloane. St. slender, 4-angled. Cor. 11mm diam., interior rough-papillose. S Yemen. var. *cerasina* White & B.L. Sloane. Cor. chestnut-brown and light yellow inside. var. *penzigii* (N.E. Br.) White & B.L. Sloane. Cor. 2cm diam., interior deep black-red, papillose-tuberculate. Ethiop. var. *schweinfurthii* (A. Berger) White & B.L. Sloane. Cor. interior dark red-brown. ssp. *concinna* (N.E. Br.) M. Gilbert. Cor. over 2cm diam., pale and smooth outside, interior yellow, minutely dotted red, papillae yellow.

H. macrocarpa A. Berger non Tauberg = *H. macrocarpa* var. *penzigii*.

H. macrocarpa Tauberg non A. Berger = *H. macrocarpa* ssp. *concinna*.

H. marnierana Lavranos. St. 4–6cm, 5-angled, spotted brown, with compressed teeth. Cor. 33mm diam., fleshy, 5-veined, exterior cream, tube pink edged red or wholly red, covered in small calli, lobes tipped brown. SW Arabia.

H. namaquensis Pill. St. 1.5–6cm, sometimes flecked purple, 4–5-angled, teeth to 4mm. Cor. to 26mm diam., exterior pale yellow, interior ivory to pale pink, sparsely spotted purple, setose papillae at mouth, lobes triangular-attenuate, apex cream-yellow, more densely spotted, papillose. Namaqualand. ssp. *hallii* (E. & B. Lamb) P.V. Bruyns. Papillae inside cor. sparse, under 0.25mm. Nam.

H. nouhuysii Verdoorn. St. 8–20cm, with 4–6 spirally contorted, dentate angles. Cor. campanulate, 2cm diam., lobes triangular, interior green-white, spotted and lined red with small red-tipped conical protuberances up to the lobe tips. S Afr.

H. occulta Leach & Plowes. St. to 32cm, deeply furrowed, 5 rounded angles, teeth 1–3mm, distant. Cor. 2.5cm diam., interior of tube shiny dark purple-black, limb and lobes cream with tawny red spots, lobes papillose, triangular, erect, 5-veined outside. Zimb.

H. ocellata (Jacq.) Schult. St. 5–10cm, 4–5 sinuate-dentate angles with small projecting teeth. Cor. 3cm diam., tube hirsute toward mouth with a large, broad, smooth annulus, lobes broad-triangular-pointed, exterior glab., pale, interior yellow with small blood-red spots, densely papillose. S Afr.

H. oculata Hook. f. St. 8–12cm, angles 4–5, laterally compressed, sinuate, teeth large, soft. Cor 2.5cm diam., campanulate, dark red-brown with white throat, exterior green, minutely papillose, lobes deltoid-attenuate. Nam.

H. pendula E.A. Bruce. St. 45–150cm. Slightly 4-angled to cylindrical, with paired tubercles. Cor 15mm diam., dark maroon-brown, interior densely covered in tiny calli, longitudinally ribbed, lobes 4mm. Cape Prov.

H. penzigii N.E. Br. = *H. macrocarpa* var. *penzigii*.

H. penzigii var. *arabica* A. Berger = *H. macrocarpa* var. *arabica*.

H. penzigii var. *schweinfurthii* A. Berger = *H. macrocarpa* var. *schweinfurthii*.

H. pillansii N.E. Br. COCKLEBUR. St. to 4cm, subglobose when young, with conical tubercles in many rows, apices softly setose. Cor. to 4mm diam., cream to pink with red spots, lobes recurved, attenuate, interior pale yellow with crimson spots, densely red-papillose. Cape Prov.

H. praestans N.E. Br. St. to 5cm, 4-angled, spotted red, teeth projecting. Cor. 4cm diam., tube cream spotted red, base red, glossy, lobes triangular-acute, cream to pink, with red veins and ribs, shortly papillose, with 5 triangles of short, dark red hairs and cream papillae on limb adjacent to the lobes. Cape Prov.

H. primulina N.E. Br. St. to 8cm, sometimes spotted red, ridges sinuate, with dark, hooked teeth. Cor. 2.5cm diam., pale to sulphur-yellow, smooth, fleshy and waxy, sometimes tinged red, lobes triangular-attenuate. Cape Prov. var. *rugosa* N.E. Br. Cor. limb tuberculate.

H. procumbens (R.A. Dyer) Leach. St. 10–15cm, with a purple sheen and markings, bluntly 5-angled. Cor. 2.5–3cm diam., annulus chestnut-brown, lobes narrow-lanceolate, parchment-white covered with short dark purple-red hairs, margins terracotta. S Afr.

H. quinta (E. Phillips) A. White & B.L. Sloane. St. 7cm, stout, acutely 4-angled, teeth horned. Cor. 27mm diam., yellow, tube banded dark red with setae and papillae at mouth, lobes ovate, papillose. Transvaal.

H. recondita M. Gilbert. St. to 50cm, bluntly 4–7-angled, tubercles obscure. Cor. to 18mm diam., tube banded red and yellow, lobes deltate-acute, pale yellow, blotched red, papillae banded red and yellow, longer and denser on limb. S Ethiop.

H. repens Lavranos = *H. volkartii* var. *repens*.

H. reticulata (Masson) Haw. St. 5–10cm, sharply and sinuately 5-angled, spotted red, teeth large. Cor. 5cm diam., annulus glossy red-black, tube glossy blood-red, densely covered in purple hairs, lobes broadly triangular, yellow, with purple spots giving a reticulate appearance. Cape Prov.

H. saudi-arabica D.V. Field. St. 4–8cm, mottled dark purple, 5-angled, teeth to 6mm. Cor. 4cm diam., lobes deltoid-acuminate, exterior pale purple with pale cream veins, interior purple-red with pale yellow papillae, base of tube deep purple. Saudi Arabia.

H. scabra N.E. Br. = *H. brevirostris* var. *scabra*.

H. scabra var. *ecornuta* N.E. Br. = *H. brevirostris* var. *ecornuta*.

H. scabra var. *longituba* N.E. Br. = *H. brevirostris* var. *longituba*.

H. scabra var. *pallida* N.E. Br. = *H. brevirostris* var. *pallida*.

H. schneideriana A. Berger. RED DRAGON FLOWER. St. to 20cm, slender, 5–7-angled, teeth minute. Cor. about 3cm diam., tube black-purple, exterior brown, interior black-hairy, lobes red to flesh-pink, border red-brown, papillose, recurved. Malawi, Moz.

H. somalica N.E. Br. St. 4–5cm, bluntly 5-angled, spotted brown, teeth large. Cor. 2.5–4cm diam. dull purple, lobes broadly triangular, recurved, pink-brown, with minute, spiny tubercles. N Somalia, SE Ethiop.

H. stapelioides Schltr. St. about 4cm, sharply 4-angled, teeth spreading, sharp. Cor. 3cm diam., broad-campanulate, yellow, banded maroon, lobes triangular, densely papillose. Transvaal.

H. striata Oberm. St. 5–8cm, bluntly 4–6-angled, teeth 2–4mm. Cor. 3cm diam., light yellow banded dark red, tube finely striped, exterior pale green or maroon, lobes triangular. Nam.

H. tanganyikensis (Bruce & Bally) Leach. St. 15–20cm with 5 rounded angles. Cor. 2.5–2.7cm diam., annulus deep dark red, lobes tapered-triangular, salmon-pink, glab., slightly replicate. Tanz.

H. tavaresii Welw. = *Tavaresia angolensis*.

H. thuretii Cels. St. 3–5cm, glaucous, acutely 4–5-angled, teeth sharp. Cor. about 2.5cm diam., annulus and base blood-red, lobes ochre, broadly triangular, spotted and banded blood-red, not papillose. Cape Prov.

H. transmutata A. White & B.L. Sloane. St. 5cm, 4–5-angled, teeth short, sharp. Cor. 3cm diam., tube maroon spotted cream, lobes attenuate, dark maroon with pale yellow basal blotches, apex papillose, with transverse yellow lines. Known only in cult.

H. transvaalensis Stent. St. 4–6cm, 4–5-angled, teeth 4–7mm, acute. Cor. 4–5cm diam., exterior flushed purple, smooth, tube purple-black flecked yellow, densely purple-hairy, red-papillose, annulus shiny, dark purple, convex, lobes maroon with yellow bands and spots, attenuate, inner whorl purple. Transvaal.

H. verekeri Stent. St. to 10cm, 5–7-angled, sharply furrowed, teeth deltoid, spreading. Cor. 3.5cm diam., white suffused red, annulus 5-angled, lobes attenuate, yellow-green, red-hairy. Transvaal, Swaz. var. *pauciflora* Leach. St. longer creeping, angles rounded, teeth smaller.

H. volkartii Werderm. & Peitscher. St. 7cm, 4–5-angled, to 7mm diam. Cor. 2cm diam., tube inside cream with pink spots or transverse lines, smooth or with a papillose throat, exterior densely covered in small calli, lobes spreading, cream-papillose. Angola, Moz., Zimb., Nigeria. var. *repens* (Lavranos) Lavranos. Usually prostrate, 5-angled. Cor. 2.2cm diam.

H. whitesloaneana Nel. St. to 5cm, angles 4–5, ± spirally contorted, teeth sharp. Cor. to 1.4cm diam., campanulate, exterior ribbed and blotched purple, tube blood-red, mouth papillose with 5 maroon rings in centre, lobes acute, yellow, spotted purple, with large papillae. Transvaal.

H. zebrina N.E. Br. OWL-EYES; LITTLE OWL. St. to 8cm, 5-angled, teeth 4–5mm, conical. Cor. 3.5–4cm diam., annulus convex, fleshy, yellow blotched red-brown, lobes triangular, lime or sulphur-yellow, interior downy, banded red-brown. N Transvaal, Bots., Nam. var. *magniflora* Phillips. Cor. 6.5–7cm diam., yellow-white, banded light purple or crimson.

→*Duvalia* and *Stapelia*.

Huerniopsis N.E. Br. Asclepiadaceae. 2 dwarf, succulent, perenn. herbs. St. angled, decumbent to prostrate, dentate, club-shaped. Fls malodorous, in clusters along st.; cor. tube bell-shaped, lobes spreading to recurved, lacking small teeth between the lobes; corona lobes erect, thick, fleshy, outer corona 0 or reduced. S, SW Afr., Nam. Z10.

H. atrosanguinea (N.E. Br.) A. White & B.L. Sloane. St. to 8cm, 4-angled, ridges sharply toothed. Cor. 4cm diam., dull crimson, lobes ovate-attenuate.

H. decipiens N.E. Br. St. 3–7cm, 4–5-angled, teeth spiny. Cor. 2.5cm diam., dull crimson or red-brown with a few yellow spots within, lobes triangular, recurved.

H. gibbosa Nel = *H. atrosanguinea*.

H. papillata Nel = *H. atrosanguinea*.

→*Caralluma*.

Hugueninia Rchb. Cruciferae. 1 perenn., stellate-pubesc. herb, 30–70cm. Lvs to 30cm, pinnately divided, seg. lanceolate to broadly linear, serrate. Fls 4-merous, yellow. Spring. S Eur. (mts). Z7.

H. tanacetifolia (L.) Rchb. TANSY-LEAVED ROCKET.

→*Sisymbrium*.

Huigen *Schinus polygamus*.

Hulsea Torr. & A. Gray Compositae. 7 ann. or perenn., balsam-scented herbs. Basal lvs in 1 or more rosettes, st. lvs much reduced, entire, glandular-pubescent. Cap. 1–3cm, radiate, solitary or in rac. or cymose infl. NW US. Z7.

H. algida A. Gray. Caespitose perenn. to 40cm. Basal lvs 5–10×0.5–2cm, lanceolate to oblanceolate, undulate to irregularly lobed, with small, deltoid, obtuse divisions, petiole broad. Cap. solitary, scapose; ligules and disc flts yellow. Summer. SW Mont. to Calif.

H. nana A. Gray. Caespitose perenn. to 20cm. Basal lvs 2–6×1cm, spathulate, deeply lobed with numerous oblong, obtuse divisions, gland., densely villous. Cap. solitary; ligules and disc flts yellow. W Washington to N Calif.

Humata Cav. Davalliaceae. 50 scaly epiphytic or lithophytic ferns. Rhiz. long-creeping. Fronds stipitate, uniform or dimorphous (fertile fronds more finely cut than sterile), simple or to several times pinnate or pinnatifid, usually glab., leathery. Trop. OW. Z10.

H. angustata (Wallich) J. Sm. Fronds slightly dimorphous (fertile narrower than sterile), simple, lanceolate, shallowly lobed and dentate, dark green to chestnut, to 20×2cm; stipes to 6cm. Malaysia.

H. dryopteridifrons Hayata = *Leucostegia immersa*.

H. gaimardiana (Gaud.) J. Sm. = *H. pectinata*.

H. griffithiana (Hook.) C. Chr. Fronds to 30×20cm, 3-pinnatifid, pentagonal to deltoid, primary pinnae narrowly acute, pinnules lanceolate to oblong, obtuse, seg. obtuse; stipes to 12cm. India, China, Taiwan.

H. heterophylla (Sm.) Desv. Fronds somewhat dimorphous, simple deltoid, narrowly acute at apex, obtuse to cuneate at base, entire or shallowly lobed (fertile more deeply so), to 12×3cm, lobes obtuse, notched, to 5mm wide; stipes to 5cm. Indon. to Aus., Polyn.

H. ophioglossa (Cav.). = *H. heterophylla*.

H. parallela (Wallich) Brackenr. = *H. pectinata*.

H. parvula (Wallich) Mett. Fronds to 25×25mm, deeply pinnatifid, lobes filiform, toothed at apex (fertile); stipes to 3cm. Malaysia, Indon.

H. pectinata (Sm.) Desv. Fronds to 16×7cm, deeply pinnatifid, lobes linear to oblong, obtuse, entire or dentate (sterile), or sinuate (fertile), to 6mm wide; stipes to 14cm. Taiwan, Malaysia, to New Guinea, Philipp.

H. pedata (Sm.) J. Sm. = *H. repens*.

H. pyxidata (Cav.) Desv. = *Davallia pyxidata*.

H. repens (L. f.) Diels. Fronds somewhat dimorphous, to 10×6cm (fertile often 3×2cm), deeply pinnatifid, lobes subfalcate, oblong to lanceolate, entire (upper), or lobed (lower), final lobes obtuse and (in fertile) toothed at apex; stipes to 12cm. Indochina to Taiwan, Jap., and Malaysia to Aus.

H. tyermannii T. Moore. BEAR'S FOOT FERN. Fronds to 15×10cm, 3–4-pinnate or -pinnatifid, primary pinnae to 8cm, lanceolate to deltoid, narrowly acute, pinnules to 6×2cm, lanceolate to ovate or oblong, deltoid to oblong, entire or sinuate; stipes to 8cm. Indochina.

→*Davallia*.

Humble Bush Cherry *Prunus humilis*.

Humble Plant *Mimosa pudica*.

Humboldtia Vahl.

H. misera (Lindl.) Kuntze = *Platystele misera*.

H. stenostachya (Rchb. f.) Kuntze = *Platystele stenostachya*.

Humea Sm.

H. elegans Vent. = *Calomeria amaranthoides*.

Hummingbird Bush *Grevillea thelemanniana.*
Hummingbird Flower *Epilobium canum.*
Hummingbird's Trumpet *Epilobium canum.*
Humped Fig *Ficus tinctoria.*

Humulus L. HOP. Cannabidaceae. 2 tall, twining, herbaceous perennials. Lvs opposite, ovate-cordate, 3–7-lobed. ♂ infl. a loose axill. pan., ♀ infl. a short bracteate spike, cone-like at maturity; bracts inflated, overlapping, each enclosing 2 fls. Temp. Eur., N Amer., C & E Asia. Z5.
H. americanus Nutt. = *H. lupulus.*
H. japonicus Sieb. & Zucc. JAPANESE HOP. St. v. rough. Lvs 5–7-lobed, strongly serrate, petioles longer than blades. ♀ infl. an ovoid spike, bracts ovate-orbicular, green. Fr. to 2cm, dull green, tinged purple. Temp. E Asia. 'Lutescens': foliage pale gold to lime green. 'Variegatus': foliage blotched and streaked white.
H. lupulus L. COMMON HOP; EUROPEAN HOP; BINE. St. rough. Lvs 3–5-lobed, coarsely toothed; petioles usually shorter than blades. ♀ infl. a round spike; bracts papery, orbicular, to 2cm. Fr. 3–5cm, straw-coloured. N temp. regions, widely nat. 'Aureus': lvs golden yellow.

Hunangamoho Grass *Chionochloa conspicua.*
Hungarian Clover *Trifolium pannonicum.*
Hungarian Hawthorn *Crataegus nigra.*
Hungarian Lilac *Syringa josikaea.*
Hungarian Oak *Quercus frainetto.*

Hunnemannia Sweet. MEXICAN TULIP POPPY; GOLDEN CUP. Papaveraceae. 1 perenn., glab., glaucous herb to 1m. St. woody at base, with flimsy br. Lvs finely dissected, to 10cm. Fls solitary, to 8cm diam., pet. 4, yellow, spreading, obovate to orbicular, concave, undulate; sta. numerous. Summer. Mex. Z8.
H. fumariifolia Sweet. 'Sunlite' to 60cm; lvs feathery, green tinged blue; fls large, yellow.

Hunter's-robe *Epipremnum aureum.*
Huntingdon Elm *Ulmus* 'Vegetata'.

Huntleya Batem. ex Lindl. Orchidaceae. 10 epiphytic orchids. Pbs 0. Lvs strap-like, 2-ranked, arranged in a fan, pale green, obscurely ribbed. Infl. axill., shorter than lvs; fls solitary, large, fleshy, waxy; sep. spreading, lanceolate, or rhombic; pet. similar to sep.; lip dilated above, basal callus long-fimbriate or lacerate. C & S Amer. Z10.
H. burtii (Endress & Rchb. f.) Rolfe = *H. meleagris.*
H. cerina Lindl. = *Pescatorea cerina.*
H. heteroclita (Poepp. & Endl.) Garay. Lvs to 44×6.5cm. Infl. to 15cm; fls to 8cm diam.; tep. dull yellow shaded purple-brown, lip violet, midlobe recurved, ovate-rhombic, acuminate, callus white. Peru.
H. lucida (Rolfe) Rolfe. Lvs to 25×6cm. Infl. to 18cm; fls to 8cm diam.; tep. purple-chestnut, white at base, with a green central band; lip dark red, base and apex white, simple or obscurely 3-lobed, ovate-lanceolate, callus lined brown. Venez.
H. meleagris Lindl. Lvs to 40×5cm. Infl. to 17cm; fls to 12cm diam.; sep. cream to pale yellow, faintly diamond-patterned and deepening to glossy chestnut-brown toward apex; pet. similar sometimes bearing a lustrous, purple-brown blotch toward base (*H. burtii*); lip deep red-brown, base yellow to white, sometimes streaked purple, ovate, trilobulate, callus with maroon hairs. Summer–autumn. Costa Rica, Panama, Colomb., Braz., Ecuad., Guyana.
H. wallisii (Rchb. f.) Rolfe = *H. meleagris.*
→*Batemannia.*

Huntsman's Cup *Sarracenia purpurea.*
Huon Pine *Lagarostrobus franklinii.*
Hupeh Crab *Malus hupehensis.*
Hupeh Rowan *Sorbus hupehensis.*

Hura L. Euphorbiaceae. 2 trees. Lvs alt., long-petiolate. Infl. subterminal to axillary, fls unisexual (♂ spicate, ♀ solitary), subsessile; cal. cupulate, dentate; pet. 0; sta. 8 to several; ovary 5–20-locular. Fr. small, pumpkin-like, explosive. Trop. Amer. Z10.
H. crepitans L. HURU; SANDBOX TREE. To 20m+. Crown spreading; bark pale grey, spiny. Lvs ovate to rounded, to 15cm, entire, papery. Infl. to 15cm; ♂ section conic to cylindric, dull red. Fr. to 8×4cm, lobed, smooth.
H. senegalensis Baill. = *H. crepitans.*

Huru *Hura crepitans.*
Husk Tomato *Physalis* (*P. pubescens*).

Hutchinsia R. Br. = *Pritzelago.*

Hyacinth *Hyacinthus*
Hyacinth Bean *Lablab purpureus.*

Hyacinthella Schur. Liliaceae (Hyacinthaceae). Some 20 small, bulbous, perenn. herbs. Lvs mostly 2 slender, basal. Fls to 1.5cm, ± campanulate, in term. scapose rac.; perianth 6-partite; sta. 6. E Eur. to W Asia and Isr. Z8.
H. azurea (Fenzl) Chouard = *Muscari azureum.*
H. dalmatica (Bak.) Chouard = *H. pallens.*
H. glabrescens (Boiss.) Persson & Wendelbo. Lvs to 2cm wide, glab. Fls to 6mm, tubular to campanulate, deep violet-blue, on distinct pedicels. CS Turk.
H. heldreichii (Boiss.) Chouard. Close to *H. glabrescens*, but differing in its slightly wavy lvs and almost sessile fls. SW to CS Turk.
H. hispida (Gay) Chouard. Lvs to 1.2cm wide, white-pubesc. Fls 5–6mm, ± campanulate, dark blue-violet. CS Turk.
H. lineata (Steud.) Chouard Lvs to 1.5cm wide, with long hairs beneath, ciliate. Fls to 6mm, almost campanulate, light blue to deep violet-blue, on distinct pedicels. W Turk.
H. nervosa (Bertol.) Chouard. L*Dolichos lablab*; lvs to 2cm wide, glab. minutely ciliate. Fls 1cm, tubular to narrow-campanulate, sessile, pale blue. SE Turk., through Syr., Jord. and Iraq, to Isr.
H. pallens Schur. Lvs to 0.6cm wide, glab. with rough margins. Fls to 0.5cm, narrow-campanulate, pale to medium blue. Balk.
→*Hyacinthus.*

Hyacinthoides Heister ex Fabr. Liliaceae (Hyacinthaceae). 4 perenn. bulbous herbs. Lvs linear-lanceolate. Rac. term., scapose; bracts 2 per fl., linear-lanceolate, tinged blue; tep. 6, free, oblong-lanceolate. W Eur., N Afr. Z5.
H. hispanica (Mill.) Roth. Close to *H. non-scripta*. Lvs to 2.5cm wide. Fls 6–8, unscented, widely campanulate, borne in a rather loose, not 1-sided rac.; tep. spreading, not curved at tips; anth. blue. SW Eur., N Afr. Plants cultivated as *H. hispanica* are often hybrids between this sp. and *H. non-scripta*. 'Alba': fls white. 'Danube' ('Donau'): fls dark blue, abundant. 'Excelsior': tall; fls large, blue violet, with marine blue stripe. 'La Grandesse': fls pure white. 'Mount Everest': fls white, in a broad spike. 'Myosotis': fls porcelain blue, with sky blue stripe; broad spike. 'Queen of the Pinks': fls deep pink. 'Rosabella': fls soft pink. 'Rose': fls violet pink, in a large spike. 'White City': fls white.
H. italica (L.) Chouard ex Rothm. Scape 10–40cm. Lvs 10–25cm×3–12mm. Fls 6–30, borne in dense, conical, erect, not 1-sided rac.; tep. 5–7mm, spreading widely, blue-violet, occas. white; anth. blue. SE Fr., NW It., Spain, Port.
H. non-scripta (L.) Rothm. BLUEBELL. Scape 20–50cm. Lvs 20–45cm×7–15mm. Fls 6–12, fragrant, tubular with tep. curved at tips in loose, 1-sided, drooping rac.; tep. 1.5–2cm, oblong-lanceolate, violet-blue, occas. pink or white; anth. cream. W Eur. 'Alba': fls white. 'Rosea': fls pink.
→*Endymion* and *Scilla.*

Hyacinthus L. Liliaceae (Hyacinthaceae). 3 bulbous perenn. herbs. Lvs 2 or more per bulb, linear to broadly linear-lanceolate. Rac. shortly scapose, many-fld, cylindrical; bracts small; perianth tubular-campanulate, lobes 6, spreading to recurved. W & C Asia.
H. amethystinus L. = *Brimeura amethystina.*
H. candicans Bak. = *Galtonia candicans.*
H. ciliatus Cyr. = *Bellevalia ciliata.*
H. corymbosus L. = *Polyxena corymbosa.*
H. dubius Guss. = *Bellevalia dubia.*
H. kopetdaghi Czerniak = *H. transcaspicus.*
H. lineatus Steud. = *Hyacinthella lineata.*
H. litwinowii Czerniak. 10–25cm. Lvs 15–17×1.5–5cm, 3–4, ovate-lanceolate to ovate, glaucous above. Fls 3–13, not fragrant; perianth 1.8–2.5cm, green-blue, tube constricted above ovary, lobes longer than tube, spreading and recurved above; fil. longer than anth. C Asia, E Iran.
H. orientalis L. COMMON HYACINTH. About 30cm. Lvs 15–35×0.5–4cm, 4–6, linear-lanceolate, bright green; fls 2–40, waxy, heavily scented; perianth 2–3.5cm, pale blue to deep violet, pink, white or cream, tube as long as or exceeding lobes, constricted above ovary, lobes spreading or recurved; anth. longer than fil. C & S Turk., NW Syr., Leb. 'Amethyst': fls lilac. 'Anna Marie': fls light pink. 'Appleblossom': miniature; fls shell pink. 'Ben Nevis': fls double, large, ivory white, compact. 'Blue Jacket': fls navy, striped purple. 'Carnegie': fls white, compact, late-flowering. 'City of Haarlem': primrose, late-flowering. 'Delft Blue': fls soft blue. 'Distinction': fls deep burgundy to purple. 'Gipsy Queen': fls pale salmon orange. 'Hollyhock': double, crimson, compact. 'Jan Bos': fls cerise. 'Lord Balfour':

miniature; fls claret tinted violet. 'Multiflora White': multiple st., to 4; fls sparse, white. 'Myosotis': fls palest blue. 'Ostara': large, purple-blue. 'Pink Pearl': fls deep pink, paler edges. 'Sunflower': miniature; fls bright yellow. ssp. *orientalis.* Lvs rarely to 1.1cm wide. Fls 2–12; perianth 2–3cm, pale violet-blue at base shading to white above, lobes to four-fifths length of tube. Plants naturalized in S Europe have broader lvs and bear to 18 fls per st. ssp. *chionophilus* Wendelbo. Lvs 1.2–1.5cm wide, rarely to 3.6cm wide; perianth lobes equalling tube, otherwise like ssp. *orientalis.* C Turk.

H. princeps Bak. = *Galtonia princeps.*
H. revolutus L. f. = *Ledebouria revoluta.*
H. romanus L. = *Bellevalia romana.*
H. saviczii (Voron.) Vved. = *Bellevalia saviczii.*
H. spicatus Sibth. & Sm. non Moench = *Bellevalia hyacinthoides.*
H. transcaspicus Litv. Lvs 7–16×0.4–1.5cm, 2–3, linear to lanceolate. Fls 1.3–1.5cm, 4–10, violet-blue; perianth tube cylindric, lobes shorter than tube, divergent or spreading; fil. exceeding anth. Turkmenistan, NE Iran.

Hyalolepis Kunze = *Belvisia.*

Hyalosperma Steetz. Compositae. 9 ann. herbs. St. narrow, simple or branched. Lvs narrow. Cap. discoid, solitary; phyllaries glossy, glab. or sparsely lanate, margin scarious, inner petal-like, or 0; flts usually pale yellow. Temp. Aus.
H. cotula (Benth.) P.G. Wils. Erect, to 25cm. St. lanate above, sparsely cottony below. Lvs 5–15mm, terete, cottony, apex tapered, blunt or acute, red-brown and resinous. Cap. to 2cm diam., phyllaries scarious, pale brown, base lanate, inner white or yellow; flts pale yellow. W Aus.
H. glutinosum Steetz. Erect, 10–20cm. St. ± flexuous, glab. or sparsely lanate. Lvs 5–40mm, thread-like, glab. to sparsely lanate, apex ± rounded, with short scarious appendages. Cap. to 1cm diam.; phyllaries glossy, brown, ± glab.; flts yellow. S & W Aus.
H. praecox (F. Muell.) P.G. Wils. Erect, 10–20cm. St. sparsely cottony. Lvs 10–15mm, ± glab., uppermost sometimes with a scarious appendage, apex acuminate. Cap. to 2.5cm diam.; phyllaries white, sometimes yellow, lanate; flts yellow. NSW, Vict.
→*Helichrysum* and *Helipterum.*

Hybanthus Jacq. Violaceae. 80 herbs, subshrubs and shrubs. Fls solitary or clustered, sep. 5, free, ± equal; pet. 5, the lowest the largest with broad dilated concavity or claw in the base; sta. 5, free or almost connate at base; style cylindrical to claviform, generally curved. Trop. and subtrop. regions. Z10.
H. calceolaria Ging. Hirsute shrub to 60cm. Lvs 3.7×1.5cm, ovate, acute. Fls white, solitary, axill. Venez., Guyana, Braz.
H. capensis (Thunb.) Engl. LADY'S SLIPPER. Subshrub to 150cm; st. puberulent. Lvs obovate, revolute. Fls solitary, white or lilac. S Afr.
H. ipecacuanha (L.) Baill. = *H. calceolaria.*
H. parviflorus (Mutis) Baill. Ann. or perenn. herb to 40cm; st. generally glandular-pubesc. Lvs to 3cm, ovate to elliptic-lanceolate. Fls to 4mm, grouped at br. apices; pet. white with violet tints. Spring. Chile, Arg.
→*Ionidium* and *Viola.*

Hybophrynium Schum.
H. braunianum Schum. = *Trachyphrynium braunianum.*

Hybrid Larch *Larix* ×*marschlinsii.*

Hydnocarpus Gaertn. Flacourtiaceae. 10–40 trees. Lvs leathery. Fls solitary or in fascicles or rac., unisexual; sep. 4–5 or more, imbricate; pet. 4–5 or more, with a basal scale; sta. many. Fr. a round berry with a hard rind. Indo-Malaysia. Z9.
H. alpina auct. = *H. anthelmintica.*
H. anthelmintica Pierre ex Lanessan. To 30m. Lvs to 30cm, ovate-lanceolate or ovate-oblong, yellow-brown above, yellow-green beneath entire. ♂ fls in axill. subcymes; pet. 5, purple to 1.4cm; ♀ fls 1–2 in the axils. Fr. to 12cm diam., brown or chest-nut. Indochina, Thail.
H. kurzii (King) Warb. To 20m. Lvs to 22cm, lanceolate to oblong, acuminate, entire. ♂ fls 5–7 in axill. cymes; pet. 8, 4mm ciliate. ♀ fls 10cm diam. Burm., Assam.
H. laurifolia (Dennst.) Sleumer. To 16m. Lvs to 25cm, oblong, pubesc. beneath, serrate or entire. ♂ fls in axill. subcymes with dense rusty hair; pet. 5, to 2mm, fleshy, pale green, densely white-fimbriate. ♀ fls solitary. Fr. to 10cm diam., with dense brown hairs. W India.
H. wightiana Bl. = *H. laurifolia.*
→*Taraktagenos.*

Hydnophytum Jack. Rubiaceae. 60 epiphytic glab. shrubs with grossly swollen lower st. with internal chambers sometimes inhabited by ants. Br. erect, slender. Lvs elliptic, obtuse, coriaceous. Fls solitary or clustered, axill., sessile; cal. ovoid-cylindric; cor. salver-shaped, with 4 lobes, white. Fr. a berry. Aus., Polyn. to Malaysia.
H. formicarium Jack. Swollen st. to 20cm diam., irregularly lobed, fleshy. Lvs 5–6.5cm, dark green. Fls to 7mm, clustered. Fr. orange-red. Malaysia, Indon.

Hydrangea L. Hydrangeaceae. 23 decid. or everg. shrubs, small trees or climbers. Bark often flaking when mature. Fertile fls small, radially symmetric, in pan. or corymbs; sep. 4 or 5, inconspicuous; pet. 4 or 5, white; sta. 8+. Many sp. bear larger, sterile fls with a petaloid, enlarged cal. on the peripheries of the infl. China, Jap., the Himal., Philipp., Indon., N & S Amer.
H. altissima Wallich = *H. anomala.*
H. anomala D. Don. Decid. climber to 12m. Shoots becoming rough and peeling. Lvs 7.5–13cm, ovate, apex shortly acuminate, cordate at base, coarsely toothed, downy tufts in the vein axils beneath. Corymbs fairly flat 15–20cm across, with few, white, peripheral sterile fls each 1.5–3.7cm across, and numerous, small cream fertile fls. Early summer. Himal., China. Z5.
H. anomala ssp. *petiolaris* (Sieb. & Zucc.) E. McClintock = *H. petiolaris.*
H. arborescens L. Loose, open, decid. shrub, 1–3.5m. Shoots downy at first. Lvs 7.5–17.5cm, broadly ovate, acuminate, with coarse, teeth, shiny, dark green above, paler and downy beneath on veins. Corymbs fairly flat, much-branched, 5–15cm across, with 0–8 long-stalked, creamy white sterile fls each 1–1.8cm across; fertile fls numerous, small, dull white. E US. ssp. *discolor* Ser. Lvs with tiny warts, downy hairs beneath. Usually seen as the cv. Sterilis, in which most of the fls are sterile. ssp. *radiata* (Walter) E. McClintock. Lvs darker green with an indumentum of thick, downy, white hairs beneath. Z3.
H. aspera D. Don. Spreading decid. shrub or small tree, to 4m. Shoots at first with spreading hairs, later hairless and peeling. Lvs 9–25cm, lanceolate to narrowly ovate, acute or acuminate, rounded or tapered to the base, serrate, densely downy beneath, sparsely hairy above. Corymbs fairly flattened, to 25cm across, with few to many white to pale pink or purple, darker-veined, sterile fls with 4 rounded sep., each to 2.5cm across; fertile fls small, numerous, white-purple or pink. Summer. Himal., W & C China, Taiwan, Java, Sumatra. ssp. *strigosa* (Rehd.) E. McClintock. Lvs bear short, stiff hairs beneath. Summer–autumn. China. Z7.
H. aspera ssp. *robusta* misapplied = *H. longipes.*
H. aspera ssp. *robusta* (Hook. & Thoms.) E. McClintock = *H. robusta.*
H. aspera ssp. *sargentiana* (Rehd.) E. McClintock = *H. sargentiana.*
H. aspera var. *macrophylla* Hemsl. = *H. aspera* ssp. *strigosa.*
H. chinensis Maxim. = *H. scandens* ssp. *chinensis.*
H. cinerea Small = *H. arborescens* ssp. *discolor.*
H. davidii Franch. = *H. scandens* ssp. *chinensis.*
H. dumicola W.W. Sm. = *H. heteromalla.*
H. fulvescens Rehd. = *H. aspera.*
H. heteromalla D. Don. Decid. shrub to 3m. Shoots hairy at first later glab. Lvs 8.75–20cm, narrowly ovate, rounded, cuneate or sometimes cordate at base, toothed and bristly at the margins, pubesc. beneath. Corymbs flattened, 15cm across, with few white or ivory sterile fls, each 2.5–5cm across; fertile fls numerous, small, white. Summer. Himal., W & N China. 'Bretschneideri': bark peeling; lvs white beneath; fls white (lace-cap). Z6.
H. hirta Sieb. V. similar to *H. scandens* but lvs hairy throughout and sterile fls usually 0. Summer. Jap. Z7.
H. hortensis Sieb. = *H. macrophylla.*
H. hypoglauca Rehd. = *H. heteromalla.*
H. integerrima (Hook. & Arn.) Engl. = *H. serratifolia.*
H. involucrata Sieb. Fairly open, decid. shrub to 2m. Shoots at first bristly. Lvs 7.5–15cm, broadly ovate-oblong, acuminate, finely toothed, bristly. Corymbs irregular, 7.5–12.5cm across, enclosed by c6 broadly ovate bracts covered with flattened, white hairs; sterile fls few, long-stalked, pale blue or faintly pink, 1.8–2.5cm across; fertile fls numerous, small, blue. Late summer. Jap., Taiwan. 'Hortensis': fls more numerous, double, pink-white, sterile. Z7.
H. japonica Sieb., in part = *H. serrata.*
H. kawakamii Hayata = *H. aspera.*
H. khasiana Hook. & Thoms. = *H. heteromalla.*
H. longipes Franch. Loose, spreading, decid. shrub, 2–2.5m. Shoots at first loosely downy. Lvs 7.5–17cm, rounded-ovate, apex abruptly acuminate, rounded-cordate at base, sharply toothed, bristly. Corymbs fairly flat, 10–15cm across; sterile fls

8–9, white or faintly purple, 1.9–2.4cm across; fertile fls small, white, numerous. Late summer–autumn. C & W China. Z7.

H. macrophylla (Thunb.) Ser. Spreading decid. shrub to 3m. Shoots ± glab. Lvs 10–20cm, broadly ovate, acute or acuminate, coarsely toothed, glab. Corymbs flattened, much-branched, with few pink lilac or blue sterile fls 3–5cm across and numerous small blue or pink fertile fls. Summer. Jap. Z5.

The wild type, sometimes called *H. macrophylla* var. *normalis* Wils. (*H. maritima* Haworth-Booth) is a maritime plant with a corymb of the 'Lacecap' type; it is thought to be the ancestor of v. many 'Hortensia' cvs of both 'lacecap' and 'mophead' types. In most cvs the colour of the corymbs is influenced by the presence of aluminium in the soil. Some 'lacecap' cvs, such as 'Bluebird' are often associated with *H. macrophylla*; they belong, however, to *H. serrata*, which some authorities treat as a ssp. of *H. macrophylla*.

MOPHEADS (*Hortensias*). Sterile fls single to double, freely or occas. produced; infl. compact to loose, usually rounded. 'Ami Pasquier': semi-dwarf; fls crimson to plum, non-fading. 'Ayesha' ('Silver Slipper'): lvs glossy green; fls cupped, lilac-like, in flattened heads, misty lilac to pink. 'Générale Vicomtesse de Vibraye': tall, fls light aqua blue in dense heads. 'Hamburg': large; fls deep vivid pink to purple, long-lasting; sep. deeply serrated. 'Heinrich Seidel': growth stiff; fls cherry red to purple in dense heads. 'Holstein': fls pink to sky blue, abundant; sep. serrate. 'Joseph Banks' ('Hortensis'): 2.25m; fls opening green, ageing pink to blue; the original introduction from China. 'Madame Emile Mouillère' ('Sedgwick's White'): st. unspotted; fls white with a pink to blue eye. 'Mathilde Gutges': fls intense blue to purple; compact growth, late. 'Niedersachen': fls v. pale blue or pink; tall, reliable. 'Nigra': st. almost black; fls rose to blue. 'Nikko Blue': fls pink to bright blue. 'Otaksa': lvs rounded; fls pink to blue; an early 'Hortensia' from Japan. 'Pia': v. dwarf, to 30cm; fls pink to red in irregular infl. 'Preziosa': hybrid with *H. serrata*, tinged purple-red throughout; fls rose to purple red. 'Vulcain': dwarf; fls deep pink-purple or orange and green. 'West-falen': fls red to purple, nearest to crimson on alkaline soils.

LACECAPS. Sterile fls largely peripheral with pedicel to 5cm; infl. flattened. 'Geoffrey Chadbund': fls red to purple. 'Lanarth White': compact; fertile fls pink to blue, ray fls white. 'Lilacina': pink through lilac to blue, fls serrate; strong growing. 'Mariesii': fls pale pink, reluctantly blue; infl. includes large and small ray flts. 'Blue Wave': fls blue, edged by blue to pink single ray flts. 'Quadricolor': lvs mottled cream, yellow, pale and dark green. 'Sea Foam': fls blue, edged by white ray fls; arose as a branch-sport on a plant of 'Joseph Banks', and is closest to the type. 'Tricolor': lvs mottled cream, yellow, pale and dark green. 'Veitchii': lvs dark green; fls white ageing pink. 'White Wave': fertile fls pink to blue, surrounded by ray fls of pearly white.

H. macrophylla ssp. *serrata* (Thunb.) Mak. = *H. serrata*.

H. macrophylla var. *acuminata* (Sieb. & Zucc.) Mak. = *H. serrata*.

H. mandarinorum Diels = *H. heteromalla*.

H. opuloides (Lam.) anon. = *H. macrophylla*.

H. paniculata Sieb. Large decid. shrub or small tree to 4m. Shoots at first pubesc. Lvs 7.5–15cm, ovate, acuminate, toothed, sparsely bristly. Pan. conical or pyramidal, 15–20cm, with few white-pink sterile fls, each 1.75–3cm across; fertile fls numerous, yellow-white. Summer–autumn. E & S China, Jap., Sakhalin. 'Everest': lvs dark green; fls all sterile, white to pink in large heads. 'Floribunda': infl. long, narrow; fls largely sterile, packed. 'Grandiflora': fls small, sterile, white turning pink-red, in v. large pan. 'Greenspire': sterile fls green, becoming red-tinged. 'Kyushu': erect; lvs dark, shining, tapering; sterile fls mauve. 'Pink Diamond': sterile fls becoming pink in large pan. 'Praecox': early-flowering with toothed sterile fls in small pan. 'Tardiva': late-flowering. 'Unique': infl. v. large with many white sterile fls. Z3.

H. pekinensis hort. = *H. heteromalla* 'Bretschneideri'.

H. petiolaris Sieb. & Zucc. Decid. climber to 20m. Shoots later rough and peeling. Lvs 3.5–11cm, ovate-rounded, shortly acuminate, ± cordate at base, finely toothed, sometimes pubesc. beneath. Corymbs flat, 15–25cm across, with to 12 white, peripheral sterile fls, each 2.5–4.5cm across; fertile fls small, numerous, off-white. Summer. Jap., Sakhalin, Korea, Taiwan. Z5.

H. platanifolia hort. = *H. quercifolia*.

H. quercifolia Bartr. Loose, rounded, decid. shrub, 1–2.5m. Shoots thick, red-downy, then hairless and flaky. Lvs 7.5–20cm, ovate-rounded and deeply 5–7-lobed (rather like those of *Quercus rubra*), minutely toothed, bristly, turning red-bronze in winter. Pan. conical-pyramidal, 10–25cm, with numerous long-stalked, white sterile fls each 2.5–3.5cm across; fertile fls numerous, small, white. Summer. SE US. 'Snow Flake': sterile flts predominant, double, green turning white as they mature. Z5.

H. radiata Walter = *H. arborescens* ssp. *radiata*.

H. rehderiana Schneid. = *H. aspera*.

H. robusta Hook. & Thoms. Differs from *H. longipes* in larger, thicker lvs with dense bristles beneath; corymbs to 30cm across, with 20 or more large white sterile fls and blue fertile fls. Summer–autumn. China. Z6.

H. rosthornii Diels = *H. robusta*.

H. sargentiana Rehd. Loose, spreading, decid. shrub to 3m. Shoots with small, erect hairs and translucent bristles. Lvs 10–25cm, broadly ovate, rounded at the base, velvety above, densely bristly beneath. Corymb fairly flattened, 12.5–22.5cm across, with a few, pink-white peripheral sterile fls to 3cm across; fertile fls numerous, small, pale purple. Summer. China. Z7.

H. scandens (L. f.) Ser. Spreading or almost pendulous shrub to 1m. Shoots glab. or v. finely pubesc. Lvs 5–9cm, lanceolate or oblong-ovate, shortly toothed, finely pubesc. on the veins beneath. Corymbs fairly flattened, to 7.5cm across, with few white-blue sterile fls, 1.75–3.75cm across; fertile fls numerous, white, with small, clawed pet. Summer. S Jap., E Asia. ssp. *chinensis* (Maxim.) E. McClintock. Larger plant with tough, woody twigs and more leathery lvs. The name *H. chinensis* covers a number of different variants, including *H. lobbii* Maxim, from the Philippines with large, white sterile fls and f. *macrosepala* Hayata from Japan. Z9.

H. scandens Maxim. non L. f. (Ser.) = *H. petiolaris*.

H. seemanii Riley. Everg. climber or creeper with dark green, leathery, elliptic-acuminate lvs and white fls. Differs from *H. serratifolia* in infl. a single term. corymb (not many) and presence of large, sterile fls. Mexico. Z9.

H. serrata (Thunb.) Ser. Spreading decid. shrub to 2m. Shoots at first finely pubesc. Lvs 5–15cm, lanceolate, acuminate, glab. above, veins beneath with short hairs. Corymbs flattened, 5–10cm across, with to 12 pink or blue sterile fls, 1–1.5cm across; fertile fls numerous, small, pink or blue. Summer. Jap. and Korea (Quelpaert Is.). Lace-cap cvs derived from *H. serrata* include 'Bluebird', 'Blue Deckle', 'Diadem' and 'Miranda', blue, compact, tending to be hardier than those of *H. macrophylla* origin and some of the best for general gdn use. A smaller, compact variant, known as var. *thunbergii* Sieb. is occas. seen, differing in its v. dark st. and lvs toothed only toward the apex, slightly hairy above. Z6.

H. serrata f. *acuminata* (Sieb. & Zucc.) Wils. = *H. serrata*.

H. serratifolia (Hook. & Arn.) Philippi. Everg. climber, to 30m in favourable situations. Shoots at first finely pubesc. Lvs 5–15cm, elliptic, acuminate, base often cordate, usually entire, leathery. Infl. to 15×9cm, composed of numerous small corymbs arranged one above the other, each at first enclosed by 4 papery bracts; fls small, fertile, white, some variants exist with 1 or few white sterile fls. Summer. Chile, Arg. Z9.

H. strigosa Rehd. = *H. aspera* ssp. *strigosa*.

H. strigosa var. *macrophylla* (Hemsl.) Rehd. = *H. aspera* ssp. *strigosa*.

H. umbellata Rehd. = *H. scandens* ssp. *chinensis*.

H. vestita Wallich = *H. heteromalla*.

H. villosa Rehd. = *H. aspera*.

H. virens (Thunb.) Ser. = *H. scandens*.

H. xanthoneura Diels = *H. heteromalla*.

HYDRANGEACEAE Dumort. 17/170. *Carpenteria, Decumaria, Deinanthe, Deutzia, Fendlera, Hydrangea, Jamesia, Kirengeshoma, Philadelphus, Pileostegia, Platycrater, Schizophragma.*

Hydrastis Ellis ex L. GOLDEN SEAL. Ranunculaceae. 2 rhizomatous perenn. herbs St. simple, hairy. Lvs palmately lobed, cauline and basal. Fls solitary, small; cal. composed of 3 petaloid sep., caducous; cor. 0; sta. numerous. Fr. a globose cluster of dark red berries. NE US, Jap.

H. canadensis L. GOLDEN SEAL; YELLOW ROOT; TURMERIC ROOT. Perenn., 20–50cm, from thick, yellow rhiz. Basal lf 12–20cm, rounded, 5–9-palmately lobed, biserrate, dark green, petiolate, st. lvs 2, near top of st. Fls to 15mm diam., green-white sometimes tinged pink. Fr. c15mm. Spring–summer. NE US. Z3.

Hydriastele H.A. Wendl. & Drude. Palmae. 8–9 palms. St. usually clustered, erect, bare, ringed. Crownshaft well defined. Lvs pinnate, neatly abcising; pinnae mostly single-fold, regularly spaced, apices praemorse, with few ramenta on midrib beneath. Infl. infrafoliar, branched×1–2. Fr. to 1cm diam., subglobose, bright red to purple. New Guinea, N Aus. Z10.

H. microspadix (Becc.) Burret. St. to 3m. Lvs 1.5–2m; pinnae irregularly clustered, sharply truncate. N Guinea.

H. wendlandiana (F. Muell.) H.A. Wendl. & Drude. St. to 12m. Lvs to 3m; pinnae, irregularly arranged, truncate and dentate. NE Aus.

→*Adelonenga* and *Kentia*.

Hydrilla Rich. Hydrocharitaceae. 1 submerged aquatic, ann. or perenn. herb; st. to 2m, creeping and stoloniferous or erect, slender. Lvs to 2×0.4cm, paired or in whorls, linear to lanceolate, pungent, serrulate to denticulate. Infl. spathaceous, axill.; fls solitary or paired; ♂ fl. floating to surface in bud then opening, minute; ♀ ruptures spathe on maturing. Cosmop. Z5.
H. muscoides (Harv.) Planch. = Lagarosiphon muscoides.
H. verticillata (L. f.) Royle.
→Elodea and Vallisneria.

Hydrocharis L. FROGBIT. Hydrocharitaceae. 2 freshwater perenn. aquatic herbs. St. slender, stolon-like, usually floating and rooting. Lvs petiolate, rosulate. Fls 3-merous, on stalks subtended by 2-valved spathe, ♂ 1–4, ♀ solitary. Eur., W Asia, N Afr.
H. morsus-ranae L. FROGBIT. Lvs peltate, circular or reniform, basally cordate. Pet. 10mm, broadly ovate, white with basal yellow spot. Eur., W Asia. Z4.
H. spongia Bosc = Limnobium spongia.

HYDROCHARITACEAE Juss. 16/90. Egeria, Elodea, Hydrilla, Lagarosiphon, Limnobium, Ottelia, Stratiotes, Vallisneria.

Hydrocleys Rich. Limnocharitaceae. 9 stoloniferous ann. or perenn. aquatic herbs, free-floating or rooted in shallow water. Lvs basal or along st. Fls solitary, in axill. clusters or term. umbels; sep. 3, persistent, green; pet. 3, fugacious, yellow; sta. 6 to many. S Amer. Z10.
H. commersonii Rich. = H. nymphoides.
H. humboldtii Endl. = H. nymphoides.
H. nymphoides (Willd.) Buchenau. WATER POPPY. Perenn., prostrate and rooting at nodes. Lvs 5–8cm wide, floating, broad-ovate, cordate at base, thick, petiole long. Fls emergent, solitary 5–7cm diam.; pet. rounded, yellow; sta. numerous, purple; staminodes many, purple. Summer. Trop. S Amer.
→Limnocharis and Stratiotes.

Hydrocotyle L. PENNYWORT; NAVELWORT. Umbelliferae. 75 low creeping perennials of damp places; st. rooting at nodes. Lvs simple or palmatifid, sometimes peltate, petiolate. Fls green-white, whorled or in small, simple umbels; involucral bracts small or 0. Cosmop.
H. americana L. Lvs 1–5cm diam., orbicular to ovate, crenate, shallowly 6–10-lobed, glab., glossy. Umbels sessile to subsessile; fls 3–5 per umbel. Americas, NZ. Z8.
H. dissecta Hook. f. Lvs 1–1.5cm, pilose to hispid, deeply toothed or cut, seg. obovate-cuneate, acute. Umbels 15–20-fld, to 5mm diam., slender-stalked. Summer. NZ. Z8.
H. microphylla A. Cunn. Lvs 3–9mm diam., orbicular, with a narrow sinus, 5–7-lobed, crenate. Fls 2–5 per umbel, subsessile. Summer. NZ. Z8.
H. moschata Forst. f. Lvs to 2cm diam., orbicular, with a deep sinus and 5–7 toothed lobes, hispid. Umbels with 10–20 subsessile fls. Summer. NZ, nat. SW Ireland. Z8.
H. novae-zelandiae DC. Lvs to 3cm diam., reniform with open sinus, obscurely 5–7-lobed, lobes crenate, thin to subcoriaceous. Umbels to 7mm diam., 5–10-fld. Summer. NZ. Z8.
H. peduncularis R. Br. ex A. Rich. = H. sibthorpioides.
H. ranunculoides L. f. Lvs to 8cm diam., reniform to suborbicular, with deep basal sinus, lobes 5–6, crenate or lobed. Umbels 5–10-fld. Spring–summer. Americas, Eur. Z6.
H. rotundifolia Roxb. = H. sibthorpioides.
H. sibthorpioides Lam. Lvs to 1cm diam., suborbicular to cordate or reniform, glab. to sparsely hairy, lobes 7, crenate. Umbels on slender peduncles to 2cm, with 3–10 fls. Asia, widely nat. Z6.
H. umbellata L. WATER PENNYWORT. Lvs to 7.5cm, peltate, orbicular, crenate to crenately lobed. Umbels simple, with many fls on pedicels 2–25mm. Summer. N US to S Amer., Bermuda and W Indies. Z5.
H. verticillata Thunb. Lvs 0.5–6cm diam., orbicular, peltate, with 8–14 shallow crenate lobes. Fls whorled in forked or interrupted spikes to 15cm. Spring–summer. Americas, Aus. Z9.
H. vulgaris L. Lvs 0.8–3.5cm diam., orbicular, peltate, crenate, glab. Fls 3–6 per simple umbel or in whorls, tinted pink. Summer. Eur. Z6.

Hydrodea N.E. Br.
H. boissiana Dinter = Mesembryanthemum cryptanthum.
H. cryptantha (Hook. f.) N.E. Br. = Mesembryanthemum cryptanthum.
H. hampdenii N.E. Br. = Mesembryanthemum cryptanthum.
H. sarcocalycantha (Dinter & Berger) Dinter = Mesembryanthemum cryptanthum.

Hydromystria G. Mey.

H. laevigata (Humb. & Bonpl. ex Willd.) Diaz-Miranda & Philcox = Limnobium laevigatum.

HYDROPHYLLACEAE R. Br. 22/275. Emmenanthe, Eriodictyon, Hesperochiron, Hydrophyllum, Nemophila, Phacelia, Pholistoma, Romanzoffia, Wigandia.

Hydrophyllum L. WATERLEAF. Hydrophyllaceae. 8 bienn. and perenn. herbs; those described below perenn. with spreading rhiz., ascending st., and pinnately lobed or divided lvs. Fls in lax or compact term. cymes; cal. lobes 5; cor. usually campanulate, lobes 5; sta. 5, exserted. N Amer.
H. capitatum Douglas ex Benth. CAT'S BREECHES. 20–35cm. Ashy-puberulent. Lvs to 12cm, pinnatifid, seg. usually divided ×2–3. Fls in capitate cymes, indigo to white. W N Amer. Z5.
H. virginianum L. VIRGINIA WATERLEAF; SHAWNEE SALAD; INDIAN SALAD; JOHN'S CABBAGE. To 1m. Lvs to 30cm, pinnatifid, seg. toothed ×5–7. Fls in loose cymes, white to violet or mauve. E N Amer. var. **atranthum** (Alexander) Constance. Lvs divided ×7–9. Fls amethyst. W Virg. to N Carol. Z4.

Hygrophila R. Br. Acanthaceae. 100 perenn. herbs of watery places. Lvs polymorphic according to degree of submergence. Infl. racemose or paniculate, composed of pseudowhorls; bracts inconspicuous; cal. lobes 5, linear; cor. bilabiate, tube dilated. Trop.; often weeds of paddyfields and waterways. Z10.
H. difformis (L. f.) Bl. WATER WISTERIA. Everg. St. to 60cm, slender, soft, rooting. Immersed lvs to 10cm, pinnatifid, translucent, brittle, emersed lvs smaller, thicker, lanceolate to ovate, crenate. Cor. to 2cm, lilac or violet marked purple on lower lip. SE Asia.
H. polysperma (Roxb.) Anderson. Decid. St. to 50cm, submerged, rather woody. Lvs to 3.25cm, narrow-oblong to lanceolate, pale green. Cor. to 0.8cm, white to sky blue or pale lilac, downy. India, Bhutan.
→Synnema.

Hylocereus (A. Berger) Britt. & Rose. Cactaceae. 16 epiphytic, climbing or scrambling cacti; st. usually 3-winged or angled, segmented, often producing aerial roots; with short spines or spineless. Fls large, funnelform, nocturnal; pericarpel and tube stout; sta. numerous; style thick. C Amer., the W Indies, Colomb. and Venez. Z10.
H. antiguensis Britt. & Rose = H. trigonus.
H. calcaratus (Weber) Britt. & Rose. St. 4–7cm diam., rather soft, green; ribs 3, thin, prominently lobed; spines 2–4, small, bristly, white. Fl. 35–37×20–30cm, white, fragrant. Costa Rica.
H. costaricensis (Weber) Britt. & Rose. St. 5–10cm diam., glaucous; margins straight or undulate; spines 2–4, short, stout, brown, accompanied by 2 hair-like bristles. Flower-buds purple; fl. c30cm, fragrant; outer tep. narrow, tinged red, inner pure white. Costa Rica, Nic.
H. escuintlensis Kimnach. St. to 5m; seg. 10–30×3–4cm, shallowly lobed, dark green, margins horny; spines 1–2, 1–1.5mm, subulate. Fl. 28–31×24–36cm; outer tep. green-yellow, sometimes maroon-tinged, inner tep. creamy white. Sometimes mislabelled H. guatemalensis. Guat.
H. extensus (Salm-Dyck ex DC.) Britt. & Rose. St. slender, 1.5cm diam.; ribs low, obtuse; spines 2–4, 1–2mm, dark brown, accompanied by fine bristles. Fl. large; tube green; outer tep. green-yellow, inner tep. white, tinged pink. Trin.
H. guatemalensis (Eichlam) Britt. & Rose. St. 2–7cm broad, glaucous; ribs 3, low-undulate, margins horny; spines 2–4, to 3mm, conic. Fl. 30cm; outer tep. pink, inner white. Guat. Z9.
H. lemairei (Hook.) Britt. & Rose. St. 2–3cm diam., grey-green; ribs low, slightly elevated at areoles; spines usually 2, v. short, conic. Fl. 27cm; tep. white, tinged pink near base. Trin., Surinam.
H. minutiflorus Britt. & Rose. St. 1.5–3.5cm wide, deep green; ribs 3, low, acute, crenate; margins not horny; spines usually 1–3, minute, brown. Fl 3–3×8–9cm, v. fragrant; tube 1cm or less, purple or green at base; outer tep. with red midvein and tip, inner v. narrow, white. September. S Mex. to Hond.
H. monacanthus (Lem.) Britt. & Rose. Spines 1–2, minute. Fl. 28–17cm; outer tep. tinged green, inner tep. white. Colomb., Panama.
H. napoleonis (Graham) Britt. & Rose = H. trigonus.
H. ocamponis (Salm-Dyck) Britt. & Rose. St. glaucous; ribs 3–4, acute, deeply undulate; margins horny; spines 3–8, 5–12mm. Fls 25–32×20–25cm; pericarpel scales purple-margined; outer tep. green or purple, inner white. Mex.
H. polyrhizus (Weber) Britt. & Rose. St. slender, 3–4cm diam., white and later green; ribs 3, low; margins nearly straight. Spines 2–4, 2–4mm, brown, with 2 decid. hair-spines. Flower-buds purple; fl. 25–30cm, fragrant; pericarpel scales red- or purple margined; outer tep. red, inner nearly white. Panama to

Ecuad.

H. purpusii (Weingart) Britt. & Rose = *H. ocamponis*.

H. stenopterus (Weber) Britt. & Rose. St. 4cm broad, soft, light green; ribs 3, low, thin; spines 1–3, small, yellow. Fl. 9–12×13–15cm; tube short; scale margins purple, tep. purple-red. Costa Rica.

H. triangularis (L.) Britt. & Rose. Closely related to *H. undatus*, but a more slender-stemmed plant with the stem-wings not horny. Fl. c20cm. Cuba, Hispan., Jam. Z9.

H. trigonus (Haw.) Safford. St. elongate, 2–4cm diam., 3-angled, green, margins shallowly crenate; spines 2, 4 or 8, 4–7mm dark brown. Fl. 14–25×c21cm; tep. white. Puerto Rico to Grenada.

H. undatus (Haw.) Britt. & Rose. Epiphytic or climbing to 5m or more; st. usually segmented, 3-winged, 4–7.5cm diam., margins crenate, horny; spines 0–3, 3–6mm, conical, grey-brown. Fl 25–30×15–25cm; tep. white. Fr. to 15cm diam., globose, edible. Summer. Trop. Amer.

→*Wilmattea*.

Hylomecon Maxim. Papaveraceae. 1 herbaceous perenn. herb, to 30cm. Lvs to 25cm, mostly basal, pinnate, lanceolate-oblong, lfts in 2–3 pairs, to 7.5×3cm, lanceolate-oblong, serrate; petioles to 20cm; st. lvs to 2cm, subsessile. Fls to 5cm diam., yellow-orange; peduncles to 10cm, solitary, erect; pet. 4; sta. many, yellow. Summer. Jap., Korea, E China. Z7.

H. japonicum (Thunb.) Prantl & Kündig.

Hylotelephium H. Ohba. Crassulaceae. 28 glab. perenn. herbs from low hummocks to more bushy, erect, plants. Lvs cauline, succulent, not forming rosettes, flat, broad, usually sessile. Flowering st. ann., usually with scattered lvs; infl. term., compound, corymbose, paniculate to umbel-like; pet. 5, occas. 4; sta. 10, occas. 8. Eur., N Amer. through Cauc., Sib. and E Asia.

H. anacampseros (L.) H. Ohba. LOVE-RESTORER. Low robust plant to 10cm high; st. decumbent, sparsely branched, stout. Lvs to 2cm, clustered toward tips of st., apex rounded with shallow notch, bending downwards. Infl. dense, cymose; fls to 6mm diam.; pet. 5, pale mauve-purple; anth. yellow-green. Summer. N Spain, Tyrol, Alps. Z6.

H. caucasicum (Grossh.) H. Ohba. To 40cm. Lvs to 5×7.5cm, deep green, broadly ovate, mainly opposite, concave, irregularly short-dentate or crenate, base clasping. Flowering st. erect, spreading; infl. dense, paniculate-corymbose, forked br. in threes; fls 6–9mm diam.; sep. red-tipped, pet. 5, green-white; anth. purple-yellow. Late summer. C & W Eur., Asia minor, E Sib. A variable sp., intergrading with *H. telephium*. Z6.

H. cauticolum (Praeger) H. Ohba. To 10–15cm, ± erect. Lvs 10–25×7–20mm, mainly opposite, ovate to circular or elliptic, glaucous, somewhat toothed. Infl. dense; pet. 5–7mm, pink-purple; anth. red-purple. Early autumn. Jap. 'Lidakense': lvs grey; fls purple. 'Robusta': larger; fls carmine red.

H. cyaneum (Rudolph) H. Ohba. Low compact plant with creeping, decumbent and upright st. to 10cm long, branching below. Lvs to 15mm, alt., glaucous, narrowing at base, apex rounded to slightly pointed. Infl. a compact cyme; fls to 9mm wide; pet. 5, lilac-purple, ovate; anth. brown. Late summer. E Sib. 'Rosenteppich': more deeply coloured.

H. erythrostictum (Miq.) H. Ohba. Robust; st. 30–60cm. Lvs 5–10×2.5–5cm, usually opposite, ovate or broader toward apex, toothed. Infl. a dense corymb to 15cm across; fls 9–12mm diam.; pet. 5, white. Autumn. China, Jap.

H. ewersii (Ledeb.) H. Ohba. 11–30cm, branching below. Lvs 6–25mm, broader toward base, closely opposite, broadly ovate, ± glaucous, apex obtuse, base cordate, entire or slighty toothed. Infl. a dense cyme; fls 7–8mm diam.; sep. marked red; pet. 5, pale pink-mauve, darker markings below; anth. dark purple. Late summer. Himal., C. Asia, Mong. 'Turkestanicum': identical to type. Similar to *H. sieboldii* and *H. cauticolum* but with non-petiolate paired lvs.

H. pallescens (Freyn) H. Ohba. As for *H. telephium* but with thinner roots; lvs cuneate at base; fls pink. E Sib.

H. pluricaule (Kudô) H. Ohba. Low hummock-forming plant; st. creeping. Lvs 10–25×4–6mm, opposite, larger and more clustered toward tips of st., oblong to somewhat orbicular. Infl. a dense cyme; fls to 9mm diam.; sep. marked red; pet. 5, pale purple to pink-purple anth. purple. Summer. E Sib.

H. populifolium (Pall.) H. Ohba. to 25cm, much-branched. Lvs petiolate, to 25mm, pale green, alt., larger and more clustered towards tips of st., irregularly toothed, grooved above. Infl. dense, corymbose; fls to 12mm diam.; sep. tipped red; pet. 5, white, pink-tipped, anth. deep red. Summer. C & W Sib. Z2.

H. sieboldii (Sweet ex Hook.) H. Ohba. Low-growing perenn. to 10cm; st. 15–30cm. Lvs 10–15×13–20mm, fleshy, glaucous to purple or more green, margin irregularly toothed towards apex, stems bright red, st. somewhat pendulous at top. Infl. a

dense cyme; fls 6–9mm diam.; pet. 5, pale pink; anth. red-purple to purple. Autumn. Jap. 'Mediovariegatum': lvs yellow white at centre. 'Variegatum': lvs glaucous blue, marbled cream. Similar to *H. ewersii* and *H. cauticolum*; somewhat more vivid in appearance than either of these.

H. sordidum (Maxim.) H. Ohba. To 40cm. Lvs alt. or opposite, petiolate, 20–40×15–30mm, obtuse, green to purple or brown-purple, somewhat red beneath, slightly toothed. Infl. a cyme of 30–120 fls; pet. 4mm, white, but overall fl. tone yellow-green; anth. brown-purple. Summer–early autumn. C Jap.

H. spectabile (Boreau) H. Ohba. ICE PLANT. Glaucous perenn. to 70cm; st. thick, erect. Lvs opposite or in whorls, 4–10×2–5cm, scattered, broadly ovate-elliptic, slightly crenate. Infl. a 3-forked dense cyme; fls to 10mm across, clustered in flat pale-pink to dull red heads; pet. 5, anth. purple. Summer–early autumn. China, Korea. 'Album': fls white. 'Brilliant': deep pink-fld. 'Carmen': fls carmine. 'Humile': lower; lvs pale green; fls large, pink. 'Iceberg': fls white, occas. pink. 'Indian Chief': fls deep pink-red. 'Meteor': fls deep carmine-red. 'Snowqueen': fls white. 'Stardust': lvs v. pale green; fls white-green. 'Variegatum': lvs variegated; fls deep pink.

H. tatorinowii H. Ohba. Low growing plant to 12.5cm; st. arching or erect, 10–20cm, remaining as hummock. Lvs alt., 12–25mm, lanceolate, oblanceolate, obtuse, coarsely dentate. Infl. corymbose, overall white tinged pink, pet. to 6mm, white. Summer. N China, Mong., Shansi.

H. telephioides (Michx.) H. Ohba. To 20cm; st. erect. Lvs to 35mm, alt., bending out and downwards at tip, irregularly toothed towards acute apex. Infl. dense, cymose, term., many-fld heads; fls to 9mm diam.; sep., red-tipped; pet. 5, white; anth. red. Late summer–early autumn. E US (Appalachians).

H. telephium (L.) H. Ohba. ORPINE; LIVE-FOREVER. St. to 60cm, erect. Lvs alt., 25–75×12–35mm, oblong or ovate, slightly toothed. Infl. term.; fls to 9mm diam.; pet. 5, usually red-purple. Late summer. E Eur. to Jap. V. variable, intergrading with *H. caucasicum*. 'Atropurpureum': lvs burgundy; fls rose-red. 'Munstead Red': lvs bronze-purple; fls deep red.

H. ussuriense (Komar.) H. Ohba. St. to 38cm, becoming prostrate, unbranched, trailing. Lvs to 3cm, almost as wide, opposite, concave, cordate base clasping st., slightly crenate. Infl. a dense cyme; fls to 6mm diam.; pet. 5, pale pink-purple, anth. red-purple. Late–summer. E Sib., Ussuri.

H. verticillatum (L.) H. Ohba. To 60cm; st. erect. Lvs 3–13×1–3cm, ovate, oblong or broadly lanceolate, dentate, spotted brown whorled, petiolate. Infl. compact, green-yellow, many-fld; pet. to 4mm, anth. dark purple. Late summer–early autumn. E Sib., N China, Korea, Jap.

Hybrids. 'Autumn Joy' ('Herbstfreude') (*H. telephium* ×*H. spectabile*): fls bright salmon pink, becoming bronze. 'Bertram Anderson': lvs blue-purple; fls red. 'Moonglow': lvs silver-green. 'Ruby Glow' (*H. cauticolum* ×*H. telephium*): lvs purple-grey; fls rich ruby-red. 'Sunset Cloud' (*H. telephium* ssp. *maximum* 'Atropurpureum' ×*H.* 'Ruby Glow'): lvs dark glaucous; fls deep burgundy. 'Vera Jameson' (*H. telephium* ssp. *maximum* 'Atropurpureum' ×*H.* 'Ruby Glow'): lvs deep purple; fls pale pink.

→*Anacampseros* and *Sedum*.

Hymenanthera R. Br. Violaceae. 7 dioecious everg. shrubs. Lvs alt. or clustered. Fls minute, solitary or in fascicles, axill. or on thorny twigs below lvs. Fr. a globose berry to 0.7cm diam. Early summer. E Aus., NZ, Norfolk Is. Z9.

H. alpina (T. Kirk) W. Oliv. To 60cm. Br. rigid, spiny. Lvs narrow-obovate to linear, to 1.5cm, coriaceous. Fr. white flecked purple. NZ.

H. angustifolia R. Br. ex DC. Slender shrub or tree, to 3m. Br. graceful, flexuous. Lvs linear to oblong, 3cm, entire or sinuate. Fr. white stained purple. Winter. NZ.

H. chathamica (F. Muell.) T. Kirk. Erect shrub, to 3m. Lvs lanceolate, to 12cm, usually bluntly serate. Fr. white. NZ. Sometimes labelled incorrectly as *H. novae-zelandiae*.

H. crassifolia Hook. f. Spreading to erect shrub, to 2m. Br. divaricate, pubesc., apex spiny. Lvs spathulate to obovate, thickly leathery, to 2cm, blunt to retuse, revolute. Fr. purple. NZ.

H. dentata R. Br. Shrub to 6m. Br. apices usually spiny. Lvs oblong, sparsely dentate, to 4cm. Fr. purple. S Aus., Tasm., NZ.

H. dentata var. *alpina* T. Kirk = *H. alpina*.
H. dentata var. *angustifolia* (R. Br.) Benth. = *H. angustifolia*.
H. latifolia T. Kirk = *H. novae-zelandiae*.
H. latifolia var. *tasmanica* T. Kirk = *H. novae-zelandiae*.
H. novae-zelandiae (Cunn.) Hemsl. Shrub, to 3m. Lvs obovate to elliptic, to 6cm, apex obtuse, revolute, often sinuate to dentate. Fr. purple. NZ.

H. obovata T. Kirk.   Spreading to erect shrub, to 3m. Lvs obovate, entire or somewhat dentate, 4cm, margin revolute. Fr. purple. NZ.

Hymenlobium Benth. = *Platymiscium*.

Hymenocallis Salisb. SPIDER LILY. Amaryllidaceae.   30–40 bulbous perenn. herbs. Lvs basal, sessile and lorate, or petiolate and ovate to oblong. Scapes topped with an umbel of fragrant white or ivory fls; perianth straight or funnelform, lobes 6, narrow, spreading; sta. 6, fused below into a conspicuous serrate cup or corona inserted into the top of the perianth tube. Americas.

H. adnata Herb. = *H. caribaea*.

H. amancaes (Ruiz & Pav.) Nichols.   Lvs lorate, dark green, bases forming a thick false st., free parts to 45×5cm. Scape to 30cm; fls 2–5; perianth tube narrow, to 7cm, tinged green, lobes to 5cm, linear, bright yellow; staminal cup to 6×9cm, funnelform to campanulate, green-striped, dentate, free parts of fil. to 2cm, pointing inwards. Peru. Z9.

H. americana (Mill.) Roem. = *H. littoralis*.

H. amoena (Salisb. sec. Ker-Gawl.) Herb. = *H. ovata*.

H. andreana (Bak.) Nichols. = *Lepidochiton quitoensis*.

H. borskiana De Vries = *H. tubiflora*.

H. calathina (Ker-Gawl.) Nichols. = *H. narcissiflora*.

H. caribaea (L. emend. Ker-Gawl.) Herb.   Lvs to 60×7.5cm, broad-ensiform or suboblong. Scape to 60cm, fls 8–10; perianth tube to 6.5cm, lobes to 11cm; staminal cup to 3cm, funnelform, with erect margins, fil. to 5cm. W Indies. Z10.

H. caroliniana (L.) Herb.   Lvs to 45×1.7cm, lorate. Scape 70cm; fls 5–10 perianth tube to 5.5cm, lobes to 8cm; staminal cup funnelform, margins erect and dentate, to 4.5cm, fil. to 1.4cm, anth. to 1.7cm. SE US. Z7.

H. caymanensis Herb. = *H. latifolia*.

H. choretis Hemsl. = *H. glauca*.

H. concinna Bak.   Lvs to 30×4.6cm, oblong-elliptic to ensiform, with a petiole-like base. Scape to 30cm; fls 2–8; perianth tube to 5cm, lobes to 67×5mm, spreading-recurved; staminal cup funnelform, to 2×2cm, fil. to 3cm. Mex. Z10.

H. cordifolia Micheli.   Lvs ovate, cordate at base, to 36×14.8cm, petiole to 14cm. Scape to 42cm; fls 12; perianth tube to 11cm, green at base, white above, lobes to 80×6mm, spreading, decurved; staminal cup to 2×2cm, funnelform, toothed, white, fil. to 4cm, green, anth. 1.5cm, orange. Mex. Z10.

H. crassifolia Herb.   Lvs 6–8, lorate, 60×5cm, thick. Scape 60cm; fls 4; perianth seg. linear, 8cm. SE US. Z7.

H. crassifolia Herb. = *H. latifolia*.

H. deflexa (Herb.) Bak.   Lvs ensiform, 30×5cm. Scape, fls 3–4; perianth tube curved, 3.5–5cm, seg. linear, 7.5–10cm; corona funnel-shaped, to 7.5cm long, with recurved processes to 2.5cm. Peru. Z9.

H. dillennii Roem. = *H. concinna*.

H. eucharidifolia Bak.   Lvs to 30×9cm, oblong-elliptic, acuminate, narrowing to a petiole. Scape to 30cm; fls 4–5, perianth tube to 10cm, lobes to 2.5cm; staminal cup to 3×2.5cm, funnelform, with erect, minutely dentate margins, fil to 3cm. Origin unknown. Z10.

H. expansa (Herb.) Herb.   Lvs to 77×7.5cm, broad oblong-ensiform or oblong-lanceolate, tapering. Scape to 80cm; fls 10–20, perianth tube to 10.6cm, lobes to 14.5cm; staminal cup narrow-funnelform, to 3.5cm deep, mouth to 2.4cm diam., with erect, fluted, dentate margins, fil. to 6cm. W Indies. Z10.

H. ×festalis hort. ex Schmarse. (*H. longipetala* × *H. narcissiflora*.)   Lvs to 90×6.5cm, base sheathing. Scape 10cm, fls pure white; perianth tube curved, 4cm, lobes to 11.5×1.3cm, curved; staminal cup to 5×6.5cm, with reflexed teeth, free ends of fil. to 4cm; style far exserted. Gdn origin. Z9.

H. fragrans (Salisb.) Salisb.   Lvs to 33×8cm, elliptic; petioles to 7cm. Scape to 45cm; fls 12; perianth tube to 8cm, lobes to 10cm; staminal cup funnelform, to 3cm high, with erect, entire margins, fil to 4.5cm. W Indies. Z10.

H. glauca (Herb.) Bak.   Lvs to 45×8cm, elliptic or elliptic-lorate, glaucous. Scape to 35cm; fls 2–4; perianth tube to 15cm or longer, lobes to 90×7mm. Mex. Z10.

H. guianensis (Ker-Gawl.) Herb. = *H. tubiflora*.

H. harrisiana Herb.   Lvs to 27×5.1cm, oblanceolate to oblong, tapering to a petiole-like base. Scape to 23cm; fls to 6; perianth tube to 13cm, green-tinged, lobes to 7.5cm, white; staminal cup funnelform, to 1.5×1.8cm, margins spreading, fil to 3.5cm. Mex. Z10.

H. horsmannii Bak. = *H. glauca*.

H. humilis S. Wats. = *H. palmeri*.

H. keyensis Small = *H. latifolia*.

H. lacera Salisb. = *H. rotata*.

H. latifolia (Mill.) Roem. CAYMAN ISLANDS SPIDER-LILY; CHRYSOLITE LILY.   Lvs to 80×8cm, fleshy, sessile, linear or linear-oblong. Scape, equalling lvs; fls 6–12, perianth tube to 16cm, lobes to 10cm, linear, arching. perianth. Flor., Cuba, Haiti, Cayman Is. Z10.

H. liriosome (Raf.) Shinn.   Lvs linear, 60×2–4. Scape sharply 2-edged; fls to 20cm across, snowy-white, tinged yellow in throat; perianth tube 6–8cm, green or yellow. SE US. Z7.

H. littoralis (Jacq.) Salisb.   Lvs to 120×3.8cm, lorate, tapering at either end. Scape 60cm, fls 5–11; perianth tube to 17cm, green-tinged, lobes to 12.5cm, linear; staminal cup funnelform with spreading margins, to 3.5cm, fil. to 6cm. Colomb., Surinam, Mex. 'Variegata': lvs to 50cm, bright green striped and edged cream. Z10.

H. longipetala (Lindl.) Macbr.   Lvs to 90×3.5cm, linear. Scape exceeding lvs; fls 5–10; perianth tube funnelform, to 9mm, lobes to 10cm, linear, narrow, acuminate, with undulate margins, semi-transparent, white; staminal cup funnel-shaped, to 3.5cm, white, membranous, with a reflexed dentate margin; sta., declinate, free parts of fil. to 6cm. Peru. Z9.

H. ×macrostephana Bak.   (probably   *H. narcissiflora* × *H. speciosa*.)   Lvs oblanceolate, 50–90×6–8cm, obtuse. Scape 30–45cm; perianth tube to 8.5cm, green below, white above, seg. linear-lanceolate, 9–11cm, white to pale green-yellow, outer whorl with thickened green apices; corona funnel-shaped, to 6×7.5cm, bluntly toothed, white; free part of fil. 2.5cm, style far exserted. Late winter. Gdn origin. Z9.

H. mexicana Herb. = *H. harrisiana*.

H. moritziana Kunth = *H. tubiflora*.

H. narcissiflora (Jacq.) Macbr. BASKET FLOWER; PERUVIAN DAFFODIL.   Lvs sheathing to form a false st., free parts to 60×5cm. Scape equalling lvs; perianth tube funnelform above, to 10cm, spreading, green, lobes to 10×1.2cm, lanceolate; staminal cup striped green, to 5cm long and more than 5cm diam., striped green, with rounded spreading toothed processes, fil. to 12mm, pointing inwards; style exceeding limb. Boliv. Andes. 'Minor': lvs and peduncle shorter. 'Sulphurea': fls deep ivory to pale yellow. Z9.

H. occidentalis (Le Conte) Kunth = *H. caroliniana* or *H. rotata*.

H. ovata (Mill.) Sweet.   Lvs to 28×11cm, broadly elliptic. Scape to 45cm; perianth tube to 5cm, green, stout, lobes to 10×0.7cm, white, spreading-recurved; staminal cup funnelform, to 2.5×2cm, toothed or entire, white, fil. green, to 4cm; anth. orange, to 1.5cm. W Indies. Z10.

H. palmeri S. Wats. ALLIGATOR LILY.   Lvs to 30×0.6cm, linear. Scape to 25cm; perianth tube 8cm, yellow-green, lobes to 10cm, filiform, linear, spreading from base; staminal cup funnelform, with erect dentate margins, to 3.5cm, fil. 4cm. Flor. Z9.

H. pedalis Herb.   Lvs to 45×7cm, oblong-oblanceolate, tapering at base. Scape to 45cm; fls to 15cm; perianth tube to 18cm, green and glaucous, lobes to 10cm, linear-lanceolate, spreading; staminal cup funnelform, fil. to 7cm, white at the base, apex green; style green, exceeding sta. E S Amer. Z9.

H. quitoensis Herb. = *Lepidochiton quitoensis*.

H. rotata (Ker-Gawl.) Herb.   Lvs to 68×3.6cm, lorate to ensiform, narrowing in basal part, glaucous. Scape 60cm; fls 2 or 3; perianth tube to 9.5cm, lobes to 9.5cm, spreading; staminal cup to 5cm, base and green and tubular, expanding to funnelform to wide cupular or rotate, white, fil. 2–3cm. Flor., W Indies. Z10.

H. schizostephana Worsley.   Lvs to 31×8.7cm, 6–8, oblong-elliptic, acute, cuneate at the base; petioles to 10cm. Scape to 30cm; fls 10–20; perianth tube to 5.5cm, lobes 7cm; staminal cup to 1.5cm, vase-shaped, cut between fil., fil. to 4cm. Braz. Z10.

H. senegambica Kunth & Bouché = *H. littoralis* or *H. pedalis*.

H. speciosa (Salisb.) Salisb.   Lvs to 65.5×15.5cm, broad-elliptic; petioles to 17cm. Scape to 40cm; fls 7–12, green-tinged; perianth tube to 9cm, lobes to 15cm; staminal cup funnelform, to 5cm, dentate between fil., fil. nearly erect, to 5cm. W Indies. Z10.

H. tenuiflora Herb.   Lvs to 68×6.4cm, broadly lorate in upper half, acute narrowing below, arching. Scape to 55cm; fls 9–16; perianth tube to 14cm, slender, green-tinged, lobes to 11cm, v. narrow; staminal cup funnelform, to 2cm with erect margins, to 2cm high, fil. to 5.5cm. Guat., Ecuad. Z10.

H. tenuifolia (Bak.) Nichols. = *Lepidochiton quitoensis*.

H. tubiflora Salisb.   Lvs to 38×15cm, elliptic or lanceolate-elliptic to ovate; petioles to 30cm. Scape to 60cm; fls to 20; perianth tube to 20cm, lobes to 13.5cm; staminal cup funnelform, margins erect or only slightly spreading, to 2cm, fil. to 6.5cm. NE S Amer. Z10.

H. undulatum (HBK) Herb. = *H. tubiflora*.

H. virescens (Lindl.) Nichols.   Lvs to 10×2cm, striate. Scape exceeding lvs; fls pale green; perianth tube to 4cm, slightly drooping, cylindric, lobes to 4cm, concave, acute; staminal cup with lobes 1cm, shorter than limb, ovate-cuneate, fil. equalling lobes, anth. yellow. Peru. Z9.

H. cvs.   'Sulphur Queen': fls primrose, throat yellow, striped green. 'Zwanenburg': to 60cm; lvs bright green; fls white flushed green, trumpet-shaped, outer seg. reflexed. outer seg. reflexed.

→*Elisena, Ismene* and *Pancratium.*

Hymenocyclus Dinter & Schwantes.
H. croceus (Jacq.) Schwantes = *Malephora crocea.*
H. englerianus (Dinter & A. Berger) Dinter & Schwantes = *Malephora engleriana.*
H. herrei Schwantes = *Malephora herrei.*
H. luteus L. Bol. = *Malephora lutea.*
H. purpureocroceus (Haw.) Schwantes = *Malephora crocea* var. *purpureocrocea.*
H. smithii L. Bol. = *Malephora herrei.*
H. thunbergii (Haw.) L. Bol. = *Malephora thunbergii.*

Hymenolepis Cass. Compositae. 7 shrubs, with stellate hairs. Cap. discoid, in dense corymbs. Cape Prov. Z9.
H. parviflora (L.) DC. Robust, densely leafy, often to over 1m. St. corymbosely branched. Lvs 3–9cm, deeply and pinnately 5–9-lobed in the upper half, lobes narrowly linear, woolly at first. Cap. *c*2×4mm, in much-branched, spreading corymbs; flts 3–4 per head, sulphur-yellow. Mts of SW Cape.
→*Athanasia.*

Hymenopappus L'Hérit. Compositae. 10 ann., bienn. or perenn. herbs. Lvs mostly radical, pinnatisect to entire. Cap. discoid or radiate, few to many in loose paniculate clusters; inner phyllaries petaloid, white or yellow at apex; flts white or yellow. S N Amer. Z5.
H. caroliniensis (Lam.) Porter = *H. scabiosaeus.*
H. corymbosus Torr. & A. Gray = *H. scabiosaeus* var. *corymbosus.*
H. douglasii Hook. = *Chaenactis douglasii.*
H. scabiosaeus L'Hérit. Bienn., to 1m. St. branching, tomentose below, villous above. Lvs to 25cm, 1–2-pinnatifid, white-tomentose beneath, glab. and green above. Cap. discoid, to 12mm diam., several to many in loose clusters; phyllaries broadly ovate or obovate, with white tips; flts white. Mid–spring. SC & SE US. var. *corymbosus* (Torr. & A. Gray) B. Turner. Phyllaries oblong to oblong-ovate. C & SC US.

HYMENOPHYLLACEAE Link. 10 genera. *Hymenophyllum*; *Trichomanes.*

Hymenophyllum L. FILMY FERN. Hymenophyllaceae. 300 terrestrial or epiphytic ferns; rhiz. long-creeping, mat-forming, often filiform. Stipes winged or entire; fronds erect or pendent, lamina v. thin, filmy, often pellucid, simple or divided. Cosmop.
H. australe Willd. Stipes winged to base. Fronds to 15cm, semi-erect, pinnate to tripinnate, dark green. N India to Malaysia, Aus., NZ, Antarc. Is. Z9.
H. bivalve (Forst. f.) Sw. Stipes unwinged. Fronds to 35cm, erect, broadly triangular, tripinnatifid, deeply dissected, minutely dentate. Aus., NZ. Z9.
H. demissum (Forst.) Sw. Stipes v. narrowly winged for part of their length. Fronds erect; 10–30cm, deltoid-ovate to lanceolate, 3–4 pinnatifid, acuminate, pinnae triangular-rhomboid. NZ, Philipp., Malaysia. Z9.
H. dilatatum (Forst.) Sw. Stipes narrowly winged almost to base, 5–15cm. Fronds to 75cm, erect or pendulous, tripinnate, v. finely divided, bright pellucid green, membranous. NZ. Z9.
H. flabellatum Labill. SHINY FILMY FERN. Stipes unwinged. Fronds to 20cm, pendulous, broadly tripinnatifid, pale green. Australasia, Polyn. Z10.
H. hirsutum (L.) Sw. Stipes broadly winged above middle. Fronds 3–9cm, ovate to oblong-lanceolate, pinnae 6–12 each side, deeply pinnatifid. Trop. Amer., W Indies. Z10.
H. javanicum Spreng. Stipes winged to base. Fronds to 25cm, stiffly erect, pinnate to bipinnatifid, v. dark green; seg. sparse. Aus. Z10.
H. peltatum (Poir.) Desv. ALPINE FILMY FERN. Stipes unwinged. Fronds 8cm or occas. to 16cm, semi-erect, branched on upper side only, pinnae to bipinnatifid, dark green. S Afr., Polyn., Australasia. Z9.
H. polyanthos (Sw.) Sw. Stipes occas. narrowly winged above. Fronds 2.5–6cm broad, linear-oblong to deltoid-ovate, deeply 3–4 pinnatifid, ultimate seg. linear to linear-oblong, 1mm broad, dark brown. Pantrop. Z10.
H. sanguinolentum (Forst. f.) Sw. Stipes rather stout, narrowly winged. Fronds 5–15cm, broadly ovate to oblong, tripinnatifid to subpinnate, dull olive green, strongly scented, term. seg. crowded, oblong to narrowly oval. NZ. Z9.
H. tunbrigense (L.) Sm. TUNBRIDGE WELLS FILMY FERN. Stipes terete, filiform, short v. narrowly winged. Fronds 4×1cm, erect or ascending, oblong to ovate-oblong, pinnae 4–8 each side, subflabellately divided into several simple or forked seg., minutely dentate. Sporadic over Temp. & Trop. regions. Z7.

H. wilsonii Hook. Resembles *H. tunbrigense* except fronds deflexed, linear-oblong to narrowly ovate-oblong. NW Eur., Azores. Z6.
→*Mecodium.*

Hymenopyramis Wallich ex Griff. Verbenaceae. 6 scandent shrubs. Infl. a term. or axill. pan., bracteate; cal. 4-toothed, enlarging in fr.; cor. infundibular, limb 4-lobed; sta. exserted. India, SE Asia. Z10.
H. bracteata Wallich. Lvs to 12.5cm, chartaceous, ovate-oblong to ovate-lanceolate, acuminate, grey-velutinous beneath. Infl. puberulent; fls white. India, SE Asia.

Hymenosporum R. Br. ex F. Muell. Pittosporaceae. 1 everg. tree or large shrub; crown narrow. Lvs 7–15cm, oval-oblong to obovate, glossy above. Pan. lax, term., 10–20 diam.; fls *c*2.5cm diam., fragrant, cream-white, later golden-yellow; pet. fused into a 3mm tube, limb with 5, spreading lobes. Early spring. Aus. Z9.
H. flavum (Hook.) F. Muell.
→*Pittosporum.*

Hymenoxys Cass. Compositae. *c*30 ann. to perenn. herbs and subshrubs. Lvs mostly basal, aromatic, gland. dotted. Cap. radiate, solitary or many in corymbs; ray flts yellow, becoming white and reflexed. W N Amer. to Arg.
H. acaulis (Pursh) K. Parker = *Tetraneuris acaulis.*
H. californica Hook. = *Lasthenia coronaria.*
H. cooperi (A. Gray) Cockerell. Short-lived perenn. to 80cm. Lvs to 10cm, pinnatisect, pubesc. Cap. to about 4cm diam., clustered, pedunculate; ray flts to 1cm. Late spring–early autumn. SW US. Z5.
H. grandiflora (Torr. & A. Gray) K. Parker = *Tetraneuris grandiflora.*
H. linearifolia Hook. = *Tetraneuris linearifolia.*
H. scaposa (DC.) K. Parker = *Tetraneuris scaposa.*

Hyophorbe Gaertn. BOTTLE PALM; PIGNUT PALM. Palmae. 5 palms, to 8m. St. often strongly swollen at base or middle, then tapering to a slender neck, grey, ringed. Crownshaft conspicuous, pale green. Lvs pinnate, arched. Masc. Is. Z10.
H. amaricaulis sensu Lem. = *H. lagenicaulis.*
H. commersoniana Mart. = *H. indica.*
H. indica Gaertn. Trunk to 8m×15cm, tapering narrowly at crown, grey, with adventitious roots at base. Petiole to 30cm; rachis 1.3–1.8m; pinnae to 40 each side of rachis, 11–76×3cm+, of different lengths lf, midrib and 1 pair of lat. veins prominent above and beneath. Réunion Is.
H. lagenicaulis (L.H. Bail.) H.E. Moore. BOTTLE PALM. Trunk to 6m, closely ringed, grey, with vertical cracks, flask-shaped, expanded base to 70cm diam. Petiole to 18cm; rachis 1.24–1.65m; pinnae to 70 each side of rachis, 17–60cm, 2 pairs of lat. veins prominent above and beneath. Round Is.
H. verschaffeltii H.A. Wendl. SPINDLE PALM. Trunk to 5m, grey, markedly ringed to 25cm diam., straight becoming tapered. Petiole to 9cm; rachis to 1.5m; pinnae to 80 each side of rachis, glossy green above, dull green beneath, midrib prominent above, no veins prominent beneath. Rodrigues Is.
→*Areca* and *Mascarena.*

Hyoscyamus L. Solanaceae. 15 ann., bienn. to perenn., pubesc., sticky and foetid herbs. Infl. racemose or spicate, leafy; cal. tubular to campanulate, 5-lobed, expanding after flowering; cor. funnel-shaped to campanulate, 5-lobed. Fr. a circumscissile capsule, enveloped by cal. W Eur., N Afr. to C & SW Asia.
H. albus L. Ann. or bienn., to 90cm. Lvs orbicular to ovate, to 10×8cm, dentate. Infl. compact, unilateral; fls sessile; cor. to 3cm, tubular to campanulate, tube white tinged green or yellow. S Eur. Z7.
H. aureus L. Bienn. to perenn., to 50cm. Lvs orbicular to ovate, to 6×5cm, dentate. Infl. racemose; fls stipitate; cor. funneliform, to 4.5×2.5cm, golden yellow, tube tinged purple. Zone 8.
H. bohemicus F.W. Schmidt = *Hyoscyamus niger.*
H. niger L. HENBANE; BLACK HENBANE; STINKING NIGHTSHADE. Ann. or bienn., to 80cm. Lvs ovate to lanceolate-ovate, dentate to incised. Infl. spicate; fls subsessile; cor. to 3cm diam., olive green to dull yellow, purple-veined. Fr. to 13mm, black. Summer–autumn. Eur. Z5.
H. orientalis Bieb. = *Physochlaina orientalis.*
H. scopolia Jacq. = *Scopolia carniolica.*

Hyparrhenia Anderss. ex Fourn. Gramineae. 53 ann. or perenn. grasses. St. tufted, erect. Lf blades linear, flat. Fls in compound infl. composed of paired, spike-like rac.; rac. stalked, with a spathe-like bract at base; spikelets in pairs, one sessile, the other stalked. Afr., Madag., Trop. Amer., Trop. Asia. Z9.

H. cymbaria (L.) Stapf. Trop. & S Afr. Perenn. to 6m. Lf blades to 45×1cm. Fls in a much-branched infl. to 60cm; bracts at rac. bases ovate, red or maroon. Late summer–autumn.

H. rufa (Nees) Stapf. Perenn., 1–3m. Lf blades to 75×1.5cm. Fls in a loose or contracted compound infl. to 60cm; bracts at rac. bases narrowly lanceolate, green. Summer. Trop. Afr.

Hypecoum Benth. & Hook. Fumariaceae. 15 dwarf ann. herbs. Lvs glaucous, mostly forming a basal rosette, bipinnatisect. Fls in scapose cymes; pet. 4, outer pair usually 3-lobed, inner 3-fid; sta. 4 with winged fil. enclosed by middle lobes of inner pet. Medit. to C Asia and N China. Z8.

H. imperbe Sibth. & Sm. To 25cm. Lvs seg. narrow-linear. Fls orange, 1.5cm diam. Summer. Medit.

H. procumbens L. To 30cm. Lvs pinnate, lobes 2-pinnatifid. Fls bright yellow, 1.5cm diam. Spring–summer. S Eur.

Hypericum L. Guttiferae. Over 400 small trees, shrubs or herbs, everg. or decid., with pale or dark glands, glab. or with simple hairs. St. usually 2–4(6)-ridged at first, eventually terete. Lvs paired or whorled, sessile or shortly stalked, entire or rarely gland-fringed. Fls solitary and term. or in term. and sometimes axill. cymes, sep. 5 (rarely 4), free or partly united, entire or glandular-ciliate or glandular-toothed; pet. 5 (rarely 4), usually yellow, bud often tinged red; sta. numerous, in bundles or free in a showy boss, fil. long, anth. small. Fr. a 3–5 (rarely 2)-celled capsule, sometimes fleshy. Cosmop. except for trop. lowlands, arctic, high altitude and desert regions.

H. acmosepalum N. Robson. Shrub to 0.6–2m, br. erect, gradually outcurving. Lvs 1.8–6 oblong or elliptic oblong, obtuse to rounded, paler or glaucous beneath, thinly coriaceous to thickly papery. Fls 3–5cm, diam., 1–3(–6), term., star-shaped; pet. 1.6–2.5cm, deep yellow, sometimes red-tinged, obovate. Summer. S China. Z7.

H. acutum Moench invalid. = **H. tetrapterum**.

H. addingtonii N. Robson. Shrub 1.5–2m tall, arching to spreading. Lvs 2–8.5cm, elliptic-oblong to oblong-oblanceolate, apiculate-obtuse to rounded, paler beneath, not glaucous, thickly papery. Fls 3–6.5cm diam., 1–5, term., shallowly cupped; pet. 2–3.2cm, golden yellow, not red-tinged, broadly obovate to subcircular. Summer. SW China. Many plants grown as **H. leschenaultii** belong to this sp.

H. adenotrichum Spach. Perenn. herb, 7–32cm, erect to decumbent, forming loose cushions. Lvs 7–26mm, oblong or oblanceolate to linear, apex rounded, margins black glandular-fimbriate, paler beneath, not glaucous, thickly papery. Fls 1.5–2.5cm diam., star-shaped, 2–c17 in a corymbiform to shortly cylindric infl.; pet. 9–15mm, golden yellow, tinged red, oblong-oblanceolate, superficial black dots toward apex. Summer. Turk. (W & C Anatolia).

H. aegypticum L. Low shrub, seldom exceeding 0.5m, erect to decumbent. Lvs 3–16mm, narrowly oblong to elliptic, acute, glaucous, coriaceous. Fls 0.7–0.9cm diam., solitary, term. and crowded on short br. in a cylindrical pseudo-raceme, ± tubular below; pet.8–14mm, pale yellow, sometimes red-tinged in bud, oblanceolate. Spring–summer. S Moroc., Malta, Sardinia, Libya, Greece.

H. alpestre Steven = **H. linarioides**.

H. alpinum Waldst. & Kit. = **H. richeri** ssp. **grisebachii**.

H. ambiguum Elliott = **H. galioides**.

H. amoenum Pursh = **H. frondosum**.

H. anagalloides Cham. & Schldl. Perenn. or ann. herb, 3–15cm, decumbent to ascending, rooting. Lvs 3–15mm, ovate or orbicular to elliptic or oblong or oblanceolate, apex rounded, membranous. Fls 0.3–0.8cm diam., star-shaped, 1–c14 at term. node, pet. 1.7–5mm, (sometimes 4) golden yellow to salmon-orange, oblanceolate. Summer. SW Canada (S BC) to S Baja Calif.

H. androsaemum L. TUTSAN. Decid. shrub, 0.3–0.7m, bushy, erect. Lvs 4–15cm, sometimes amplexicaul, oblong-ovate to broadly ovate, rounded, paler beneath, thin-textured, sometimes tinted red. Fls 1.5–2cm diam., star-shaped or cupped, 1–11, from 1–2 nodes; infl. br. ascending; pet. 0.6–1.2cm, golden, obovate. Fr. persistent, black or rusty brown. Summer. W & SW Eur., NE Alg., N Tun., SE Bulg. to Transcauc. and NE Iran, S Turk. 'Albury Purple': young parts suffused dull purple. 'Aureum': lvs golden-yellow lined. f. **variegatum** D. McClintock & C. Nels. Lvs variegated pink and white. Z6.

H. anglicum Bertol. = **H. ×inodorum**.

H. annulatum Moris. Perenn. herb to 65cm, erect, sometimes decumbent at base, shortly canescent. Lvs 15–55mm, ovate to elliptic, apex rounded, somewhat paler beneath, thin-textured, with pale down. Bracts with densely gland. auricles. Fls 1.5–2cm diam., star-shaped, 9 to many from 2–4 nodes, infl. pyramidal to subcorymbiform; pet. 9–12mm, bright yellow. Summer. Sardinia, N Balk. Penins., SE Saudi Arabia, NE & E Afr. Z8.

H. apigenum Kit. = **H. richeri** ssp. **grisebachii**.

H. apollinis Boiss. & Heldr. = **H. rumeliacum** ssp. **apollinis**.

H. ×arnoldianum Rehd. (**H. lobocarpum** ×**H. galioides**.) Low-growing shrub to 0.5m, dense, rounded. Lvs 2.5–3cm. Infl. corymbiform; fls c2cm diam. Gdn origin. Plants grown under this name are more likely to be the result of **H. lobocarpum** ×**H. densiflorum**. Z6.

H. ascyron L. Perenn. herb, 50–150cm, usually erect. St. 4-lined. Lvs 4–9.7cm, narrowly oblong-lanceolate to lanceolate or ovate, apex acute to obtuse, amplexicaul, paler beneath, thickly papery. Fls 3–8cm diam., star-shaped, in a subcorymbiform to narrowly pyramidal infl., floral whorls in fives; pet. 15–41mm, golden or pale yellow. Summer. China, Taiwan, Jap., Korea, Russia (Altai Mts to S. Kamchatka), NE US and adjacent Canada. Z3.

H. aspalathoides Willd. = **H. fasciculatum**.

H. assamicum S.N. Biswas = **H. sampsonii**.

H. athoum Boiss. & Orph. Similar to **H. delphicum**, but smaller and more sparsely and softly hairy. St. c10–20cm, many, slender. Lvs 8–17mm, broadly elliptic to ovate, thinly pubesc. Fls 0.8–1cm, 1–7, at terminal nodes; pet. 6–7mm, pale yellow, veined red. NE Greece (Mt Athos, Pangeoin), N Aegean Is.

H. atomarium Boiss. Differs from **H. annulatum** in the infl. more nearly cylindric, not corymbiform, and bracts without auricles; pet. sometimes with sparse superficial black glands. Summer. S Greece, W Turk.

H. atomarium hort. non Boiss. = **H. annulatum**.

H. atomarium ssp. **degenii** (Bornm.) Hayek = **H. annulatum**.

H. augustinii N. Robson. Shrub 70–130cm, bushy, erect or arching. Lvs 3–7.5 broadly ovate to oblong-lanceolate, acute to rounded-apiculate, glaucous, leathery. Fls (1)3–13 from 1–2 nodes, forming sub-corymbiform infl., 4–6.6cm, stellate to shallowly cupped; pet. 2–3.6cm, pale to bright golden yellow, obovate. Late summer–autumn. SW China. Z8.

H. aureum Bartr. = **H. frondosum**.

H. axillare Lam. = **H. galioides**.

H. bacciferum Lam. = **H. androsaemum**.

H. balearicum L. Everg. shrub or tree, 0.6–2m, spreading. St. and lvs glandular-verruculose. Lvs 0.6–1.5cm, ovate to oblong, rounded, somewhat undulate. Fls 1.5–4cm diam., solitary, star-shaped; pet. 5, 1–2cm, golden, exterior faintly red-tinged, narrowly obovate to oblanceolate. Summer. Balearic Is. Z7.

H. barbatum Jacq. Perenn. herb, 10–45cm, erect or decumbent, glaucescent. Lvs 6–40mm, lanceolate to linear-oblong or elliptic-oblong, apex subacute, margin sometimes revolute, slightly paler beneath, glaucous, thickly papery. Fls 1.5–2.5cm, star-shaped; pet. 10–15mm, golden, sometimes veined red, broadly oblanceolate, with black dots. Summer. E Austria to N Greece, S It. Z6.

H. beanii 'Gold Cup'. = **H. ×cyathiflorum**.

H. beanii N. Robson. Shrub 0.6–2m, bushy, robust, erect or arching. Lvs 2.5–6.5cm, narrowly elliptic or oblong-lanceolate to lanceolate or ovate-lanceolate, acute to rounded, paler or glaucous below, thickly papery to thinly coriaceous. Fls 3–4.5cm diam., 1–14, term., star-shaped to cupped; pet. 1.5–3.3cm, golden yellow, oblong-obovate to subcircular. Summer. China. Z7.

H. beanii 'Eastleigh Gold' = **H.** 'Eastleigh Gold'.

H. bellum H.L. Li. Shrub 0.3–1.5m, erect to arching. Lvs 1.5–7.8cm, oblong-lanceolate to ovate or subcircular, obtuse to rounded or indented, often apiculate, paler or glaucous beneath, thickly papery. Fls 2.5–6cm diam., 1–7, term., cupped; pet. 1.5–3cm, golden to butter-yellow or pale yellow. Summer. W China, N Burm., N India. ssp. **bellum**. To c1cm. Lvs often undulate. Fls 2.5–3.5cm, diam., golden or pale yellow. SW China, N India. ssp. **latisepalum** N. Robson. To c1.5m. Lvs not undulate. Fls mostly 4–6cm diam. always golden yellow. SW China, N Burm. Z6.

H. bracteatum Kellogg non Wallich = **H. concinnum**.

H. bracteatum Wallich = **H. cordifolium**.

H. bryophytum Elmer = **H. anagalloides**.

H. buckleii M.A. Curtis. Dwarf shrub, forming low compact mats. St. ascending. Lvs ascending 4.5mm, oblong or elliptic to oblanceolate or obovate, apex rounded, paler beneath, thin-textured. Fls 2–2.5cm, 1(3–5), from term. node; pet. 5, 6–10.5mm, golden yellow, oblanceolate. Summer. E US. Z5.

H. buckleyi invalid. = **H. buckleii**.

H. bupleuroides Griseb. Perenn. herb, 45–75cm, erect. Lvs 7–12cm, paired-perfoliate, ovate or elliptic-ovate, apex rounded-apiculate, paler beneath, thinly papery. Fls 2.7–4cm, star-shaped, usually in a broadly pyramidal infl.; pet. 15–20mm, golden yellow, narrowly oblanceolate. Summer. NE Turk., SE Georgia. Z6.

H. burseri (DC.) Spach = **H. richeri** ssp. **burseri**.

H. calycinum L. Robson. Shrub 0.2–0.6m tall, everg., with creeping branching stolons and erect st. Lvs 4.5–10.4cm, oblong to elliptic or narrowly ovate, obtuse or apiculate paler beneath, leathery. Fls 1 (rarely 2–3), star-shaped, pet. 2.5–4cm, bright yellow, obovate to oblanceolate. Summer. SE Bulg., NW and NE Turk. Z6.

H. cambessedesii Barceló = *H. hircinum* ssp. *cambessedesii*.

H. canadense var. *majus* A. Gray = *H. majus*.

H. canariense L. Shrub or small tree, 1–4m tall, erect to spreading. Lvs 20–65mm, narrowly elliptic to narrowly oblong-elliptic, apex acute to subacute, thin-textured, paler beneath. Fls 2–3cm diam., star-shaped, many forming a broadly to narrowly pyramidal infl.; pet. 12–17mm, bright yellow, narrowly oblanceolate. Summer. Canary Is., Madeira. Z9.

H. canariense var. *floribundum* (L.) Bornm. = *H. canariense*.

H. capitatum Choisy. Perenn. herb, 15–50cm, erect or decumbent at base, sometimes with small amber glands. Lvs 8–28, narrowly oblong to linear, apex subapiculate or rounded sometimes revolute ± glab. Fls 0.8–1.2cm diam., star-shaped, numerous, in a pyramidal to corymbiform infl. 3–10cm long; pet. 5–7mm, orange or blood-red to crimson, obovate-oblanceolate, clawed, black-glandular-ciliate. Summer. S Turk. var. *luteum* N. Robson. Fls yellow. Z8.

H. cerastoides (Spach) N. Robson. Perenn. herb, 7–27cm, often shrubby at base, decumbent or ascending. Lvs 8–30mm, oblong to elliptic or ovate, apex rounded, downy, slightly paler beneath, thickly papery. Fls 2–4.5cm diam., star-shaped, 1–5; pet. 9–12mm, bright yellow, obovate to obovate oblong, with black glands on margins. S Bulg., NE Greece, NW Turk. Z6.

H. cernuum D. Don = *H. oblongifolium*.

H. chinense L. non Osbeck = *H. monogynum*.

H. chinense var. *salicifolium* (Sieb. & Zucc.) Choisy = *H. monogynum*.

H. choisianum N. Robson. Shrub 1–2m, bushy; br. erect to arching. Lvs 2.5–8.8cm, triangular-lanceolate to ovate, acute or acuminate to obtuse or rounded, paler beneath, thickly papery. Fls 4–7cm diam., 1–7, terminal, cupped; pet. 1.6–3cm, deep golden yellow, sometimes red-tinged, broadly obovate to obovate-circular. Summer. SW China, N Burm., Bhutan to Pak. Z7.

H. ciliatum Lam. = *H. perfoliatum*.

H. cistifolium Lam. Shrub 0.3–1m, erect, sometimes sparsely branched toward summit. Lvs 15–40mm, narrowly lanceolate to linear-elliptic or narrowly-oblong to oblanceolate, apex obtuse to rounded, revolute, paler beneath, sometimes glaucous, thinly coriaceous. Fls 0.9–1.2cm diam., forming rounded, corymbiform cymes; pet. 5, golden yellow, 5–6.5mm, obovate-oblanceolate. Summer. SE US. Z8.

H. concinnum Benth. Perenn. herb, 15–33cm. St. wiry, erect or ascending, 4–2-lined; br. straight, slender, forming small bushes. Lvs 13–32mm, narrowly elliptic or narrowly oblong to linear, acute to subacute, grey green, thinly coriaceous, with black glands. Fls 2–3.5cm diam., sometimes more, star-shaped, infl. crowded, subcorymbiform to cylindric; pet. 10–15mm, bright yellow, oblong-obovate to obovate with marginal black glands. Summer. N Calif. Z8.

H. confertum Choisy. Perenn. herb, 10–35cm, erect or ascending, glab. to pubesc. Lvs 0.7–2cm, lanceolate to oblong-linear, apex acute to apiculate-obtuse, somewhat revolute, paler beneath, pruinose or minutely downy. Fls 1.7–2.5cm diam., star-shaped, in a narrowly pyramidal to cylindric or interrupted-spicate infl.; pet. 7–16mm, golden yellow, tinged or veined red, obovate to elliptic-obovate, with elongate translucent glands. Summer. W & SW Turk., NW Syr., Leb., Cyprus. ssp. *confertum*. St. usually downy to pruinose. W Turk. ssp. *stenobotrys* (Boiss.) Holmb. St. glab. S Turk., Syr., Leb., Cyprus. Z8.

H. cordifolium Choisy. Shrub 1–1.3m, erect or arching or pendent. Lvs 1.8–6.2cm, elliptic-oblong to oblong, apiculate or shortly acuminate, ± glaucous, thinly leathery. Infl. round-pyramidal to cylindric; fls. 3–5cm, stellate; pet. bright yellow, sometimes tinged red, 1.5–2.2cm, narrowly obovate to oblanceolate. Summer. Nepal. Z7.

H. coris L. Dwarf subshrub or perenn. herb, 10–45cm. Erect or ascending tufted, woody at base. Lvs 4–18mm, in whorls, linear, apex shortly apiculate to rounded revolute, glaucous beneath, coriaceous. Fls 1.5–2cm diam., star-shaped, 1-c20, in a broadly pyramidal to shortly cylindric infl.; pet. 9–12mm, golden yellow, sometimes veined-red, oblanceolate. Summer. SE Fr., Switz., N & C It. Z7.

H. corymbosum Muhlenb. = *H. punctatum*.

H. crenulatum Boiss. Perenn. herb, 5–30cm, ascending or procumbent, often straggling, woody at base. Lvs 0.3–1.2cm, elliptic to oblanceolate or suborbicular, apex rounded, strongly undulate, glaucous, thickly papery. Fls 1.5cm diam., star-shaped, in a corymbiform infl.; pet. 5–9mm, golden yellow, tinged red, oblong-elliptic, with elongate, translucent glands. Summer. S Turk. (C Taurus Mts) Z7.

H. crux-andreae (L.) Crantz. Shrub to 1m, erect, simple or with few br. Lvs 1.2–3.6cm, elliptic-oblong to obovate, obtuse to

acute, glaucescent beneath, coriaceous. Fls 2–3cm diam. 1–3, from term. node, with 1–3-fld br. from 1–3 lower nodes; pet. 11–18mm, 4, golden to apricot yellow, obovate. Summer. SE US. Z6.

H. cuneatum Poir. = *H. pallens*.

H. curvisepalum N. Robson. Shrub 0.3–1.2m, spreading to pendulous, young growth flushed purple red. Lvs 2–4cm, triangular-lanceolate to triangular-ovate, acute to rounded, rather glaucous beneath, thickly papery. Fls 2–4cm diam., 1(3), term., deeply cupped; pet. deep yellow, 1.2–2.2cm, broadly ovate to subcircular. Summer. SW China. Z7.

H. × cyathiflorum N. Robson. (probably *H. addingtonii* × *H. hookerianum*.) Shrub to c1.5m, widely spreading. Lvs 3–7.5cm, lanceolate, acute to apiculate, paler beneath, thickly papery. Fls 4–5cm diam., forming subcorymbiform infl., cupped; pet. 2–3cm, golden yellow, broadly oblong-obovate. Summer. Known only in cult. Introduced as *H. patulum* 'Gold Cup'. Z7.

H. × dawsonianum Rehd. (*H. lobocarpum* × *H. prolificum*.) As *H. prolificum* but fls smaller, more numerous. Gdn origin. Z4.

H. decipiens H. Wats. = *H. undulatum*.

H. decussatum Kunze = *H. orientale*.

H. degenii Bornm. = *H. annulatum*.

H. delphicum Boiss. & Heldr. Perenn. herb, 11–45cm. St. ascending, branching and rooting, hispidulous below infl. Lvs 12–35mm, ovate to oblong-ovate, apex rounded, amplexicaul, slighly paler beneath, thin-textured, hispidulous. Fls c1.2–2cm diam., star-shaped, c5–40, from 1–4 nodes, infl. dense, short-cylindric to corymbiform; pet. 8–10mm, bright yellow, oblanceolate. Summer. Greece (Euboea, Andros). Z9.

H. densiflorum Pursh. Shrub 0.6–3m, erect, densely bushy. Lvs 2–4.5cm, v. narrowly elliptic-oblong or oblanceolate to linear, apex rounded-apiculate to subacute, paler beneath, often glaucous, thin-textured. Fls 1–1.7cm diam., in a broadly pyramidal to broadly cylindric-obpyramidal infl.; pet. 6–9mm, 5 golden yellow, obovate-oblanceolate. Mid- to late summer. E US. *H. nothum* described by Rehder as *H. kalmianum* × *densiflorum*, has been shown to apply to pure *H. densiflorum*. Some plants labelled *H. × nothum* do, however, exhibit characters intermediate between the parents of Rehder's putative cross. Moreover, intermediates between *H. densiflorum* and *H. prolificum* are in cult. and may well be hybrids. Z5.

H. densiflorum var. *lobocarpum* (Gatt.) Svenson = *H. lobocarpum*.

H. dubium Leers = *H. maculatum* ssp. *obtusiusculum*.

H. × dummeri N. Robson. (*H. forrestii* × *H. calycinum*.) Shrub to c0.7m, erect, base creeping to ascending. Lvs 3.5–4.8cm, oblong-ovate, apex subapiculate to rounded, paler or somewhat glaucous beneath, thinly coriaceous. Fls c5.5cm diam., 1–4, term., shallowly cupped; pet. c3cm diam., deep golden yellow, sometimes tinged red, narrowly obovate. Summer. Gdn origin. Lvs sometimes variegated, particularly in the first flushes of growth. 'Peter Dummer': pet. tinged red. Z7.

H. dyeri Rehd. Shrub 0.6–1.2m; br. widely spreading. Lvs 1–6cm, oblong-lanceolate or lanceolate to ovate, acute to rounded, markedly glaucous beneath, thickly to thinly papery. Fls 1.5–3.5cm diam., terminal, star-shaped, the overall infl. subcorymbiform to broadly pyramidal; pet. 1–1.8cm, bright yellow, oblanceolate. Late summer. Nepal to Pak. Frequently confused with *H. stellatum*. Z8.

H. dyeri misapplied = *H. stellatum*.

H. 'Eastleigh Gold'. Shrub to c1m; br. lax, spreading or drooping. Lvs 2.5–5.1cm, elliptic-oblong-lanceolate, obtuse to rounded, paler or glaucous beneath, thickly papery. Fls 5–6.5cm diam., 1–4, terminal, v. shallowly cupped; pet. 3–3.5cm, golden, yellow, oblong-obovate. Summer. Gdn origin (Hillier). A hybrid possibly involving *H. kouytchense*. Z6.

H. elatum auct. non Ait. = *H. grandifolium*.

H. elatum Ait. = *H. × inodorum*.

H. electrocarpum Maxim. = *H. sampsonii*.

H. elegans Willd. Perenn. herb, 15–55cm, erect or decumbent, 2-lined. Lvs 10–30mm, lanceolate or oblong to linear-oblong, apex acute to acuminate, amplexicaul, paler beneath, with translucent gland. dots. Fls 1.5–2cm, star-shaped, in a broadly pyramidal to cylindric infl.; pet. 10–13mm, bright-yellow, oblanceolate, with black dots on margins. Summer. C Eur. to Sib. Z5.

H. ellipticum Hook. Perenn. herb. 0.15–0.4m, arising from a slender creeping rhiz. Lvs 12–30mm, oblong to elliptic or oblanceolate, apex rounded, paler beneath, thin-textured. Fls 1–1.5cm, in a lax, flat, corymbiform cyme; pet. 6–9mm, (4–)5, golden yellow, obovate to oblong-oblanceolate. Summer. SE Canada, NE US, Newfoundland. Z3.

H. elodeoides Choisy. Perenn. herb, 15–73cm, erect or creeping. Lvs 10–36mm, ovate-lanceolate or oblong-lanceolate to linear, acute to subacute, base amplexicaul, paler beneath, upper lvs with glandular-ciliate auricles. Fls 1–1.7cm diam., star-shaped, overall infl. cylindric to subcorymbiform; pet. 7–12mm, pale yellow, ± broadly oblanceolate. Summer. Himal. from Pak. to Yunnan. Z7.

H. elodes L. Marsh or aquatic perenn. herb, 10–30cm. St. thickly white-pubesc. unless immersed. Lvs 5–30mm, broadly ovate to orbicular, apex rounded, base amplexicaul, thin-textured, hoary. Fls 1–1.5cm, pseudotubular, 3–10, from nodes of a slender, apparently lat. stalk; pet. 7–11mm, bright yellow, oblanceolate, with ligule. Summer. W Eur., Azores. Z8.

H. elongatum Ledeb. Perenn. herb, (10–)15–70cm, erect, sometimes with amber glands. Lvs 8–32mm, narrowly oblong or narrowly elliptic to narrowly lanceolate or linear, acute to apiculate or rounded, usually revolute, sometimes glaucous, papery. Fls 1.5–2cm diam., star-shaped, in a narrowly cylindric to narrowly pyramidal infl.; pet. 0.7–1.8cm, golden sometimes tinged or veined red, oblanceolate, clawed, with black-glandular cilia. Summer. Moroc. and S Spain to W Sib. (Altai Mts). Z3.

H. empetrifolium Willd. Shrublet to 60cm erect, tufted and narrowly branched, or cushion-like, sometimes procumbent, rooting at nodes. Lvs 2–12mm, in whorls, linear or narrowly elliptic, revolute, paler beneath, coriaceous. Fls 1–2cm diam., star-shaped, 1–40 in cylindric to slender pyramidal infl.; pet. 5–10mm, golden yellow, oblong-elliptic. Summer. N Albania, Greece, Crete, extreme SW Turk., Cyprus, Libya (Cyrenaica). ssp. *empetrifolium.* Low-growing subshrub. St. erect. Lvs 7–11mm. Fls 8–10. Distrib. as above, but only lowland in Crete. ssp. *oliganthum* (Rech. f.) Hagemann. Cushion-forming dwarf shrub. St. decumbent diffuse. Lvs 4.5–6mm. Fls 4–7; pet. 4–6. Crete. ssp. *tortuosum* (Rech. f.) Hagemann. Dwarf prostrate shrub. Br. spreading horizontally. Lvs 2–3mm. Fls 1, rarely 2–4. Crete. Z9.

H. empetrifolium var. *prostratum* invalid = *H. empetrifolium* ssp. *oliganthum.*

H. erectum Thunb. Perenn. herb. 15–70cm. St. solitary or few, erect usually simple. Lvs 20–55mm, triangular-lanceolate to elliptic-oblong, apex obtuse to rounded, thickly papery, gland. dots black. Fls *c*1–1.5cm diam., star-shaped, numerous, in corymbiform to pyramidal infl.; pet 7–9mm, bright yellow, obovate to oblong-obovate, with marginal black glands and black dots and streaks or lines. Summer. S Sakhalin, Jap., N Kuriles, Taiwan, China. Z6.

H. ericoides L. Dwarf shrub or subshrub, 2–25cm, erect to decumbent. Lvs 1.5–3.5mm, in whorls, linear-lanceolate, apex obtuse to mucronulate, revolute, glaucous, densely papillose, coriaceous. Fls *c*0.8cm diam., star-shaped, in a broadly pyramidal or corymbiform infl.; pet. 5–6mm, golden yellow, oblong-elliptic. E & SE Spain, Tun., Moroc. Z8.

H. ericoides ssp. *maroccanum* Maire & Wilcz. = *H. ericoides.*

H. ericoides ssp. *robertii* (Battand.) Maire & Wilcz. = *H. ericoides.*

H. eudistichum invalid = *H. henryi* ssp. *uraloides.*

H. fallax Grimm = *H. maculatum* ssp. *maculatum.*

H. fasciculatum Lam. Shrub 1–1.5m, erect densely bushy, bark spongy. Lvs 10–18mm, often clustered, linear-subulate, mucronate, strongly revolute, glaucous beneath, coriaceous. Fls 1.5–1.8cm diam., in a rounded corymbiform infl.; pet. 5, golden yellow, 7–9mm, obovate-oblanceolate. Summer. SE US. Differs from *H. nitidum* Lam. in its spongy bark and more crowded infl. Z8.

H. fimbriatum Lam. = *H. richeri* ssp. *richeri.*

H. fimbriatum var. *burseri* DC. = *H. richeri* ssp. *burseri.*

H. floribundum Ait. = *H. canariense.*

H. foliosum Ait. Decid. shrub, 0.5–1m, bushy, erect or spreading. Lvs 3.5–6cm, crowded, narrowly ovate to triangular-lanceolate, apex obtuse to rounded, base rounded to cordate, thin-textured. Fls 2.3–5cm diam., star-shaped, 1–9, from 2–3 nodes, on narrowly ascending branchlets; pet. 1–1.8cm, golden, oblanceolate. Summer. Azores. Z9.

H. formosum Kunth. Perenn. herb, to *c*93cm, erect. Lvs 25–50mm, broadly ovate to oblong, apex rounded, base amplexicaul, thinly papery with dense black gland dots. Fls *c*1.5–2cm diam., star-shaped, in a corymbose to pyramidal infl.; pet. 1–1.2cm, golden yellow, tinged red, oblanceolate, gland. dots black. Summer. WC Mex. Z9.

H. formosum misapplied = *H. scouleri.*

H. formosum ssp. *scouleri* (Hook.) Hitchc. = *H. scouleri.*

H. formosum var. *scouleri* (Hook.) Coult. = *H. scouleri.*

H. forrestii (Chitt.) N. Robson. Shrub, 0.3–1.5m, bushy ± erect. Lvs 2–6cm, lanceolate or triangular-ovate to broadly ovate, obtuse to rounded, paler beneath, thickly papery. Fls 2.5–6cm diam., 1–20, term. usually deeply cupular; pet. 1.8–3cm, golden, broadly obovate. Summer. SW China, NE Burm. Z5.

H. fragile Boiss. Perenn. herb. 4–16cm. St. suberect to straggling, glaucous, jointed. Lvs 2–7mm, ovate to oblong or suborbicular, apex rounded, glaucous, coriaceous. Fls 1–1.5cm diam., star-

shaped, term., in a sub-corymbiform infl.; pet. 8–9mm, oblanceolate, bright yellow, tinged red, with elongate translucent glands. Summer. E Greece. Plants grown under this name are usually *H. olympicum.* Z8.

H. frondosum Michx. Shrub 0.6–1.3m, erect, forming a rounded bush. Lvs 25–65 oblong or elliptic to oblong-lanceolate or oblanceolate, apex apiculate-obtuse to rounded, blue- or yellow-green, somewhat glaucous beneath, thickly papery. Fls 2.5–4.5cm diam., 1–3(–7) from terminal node, rarely with br. infl. at node below or single fl.; pet. 12–25mm, 5(4), golden, obovate to oblanceolate. Mid to late summer. SE US. 'Sunburst': fls large. Z5.

H. galioides Lam. Shrub 0.5–1.5m, erect, broad, rounded. Lvs 0.5–3.7cm, v. narrowly oblong-elliptic or oblanceolate to linear, apex rounded to acute, revolute, thin-textured. Fls 0.9–1.4cm diam., in a narrowly cylindric infl.; pet. 5–9mm, 5, golden, obovate-oblanceolate. SE US. Z8.

H. galioides var. *ambiguum* (Elliott) Chapm. = *H. galioides.*

H. galioides var. *aspalathoides* (Willd.) Torr. & A. Gray = *H. fasciculatum.*

H. galioides var. *fasciculatum* (Lam.) Svenson = *H. fasciculatum.*

H. gebleri Ledeb. = *H. ascyron.*

H. gentianoides (L.) Britt., Sterns & Pogg. ORANGE GRASS. Ann. wiry herb, 0.7–6cm. St. erect freely branched, narrowly angled. Lvs 1.4mm, narrowly triangular-subulate to linear-subulate, margin incurved, thickly papery. Fls 0.3–0.5cm diam., star-shaped, overall infl. pyramidal; pet 2–4mm, orange-yellow to bright yellow, tinged red, oblong. Summer. S Ont., E US. Z3.

H. glandulosum Ait. Shrub or subshrub, 0.25–3m, spreading; br. ascending. Lvs 23–55mm, elliptic to oblanceolate, paler beneath, thin-textured. Fls *c*1.5–2cm diam., shallowly funnel-shaped, whole infl. broad, rounded-subcorymbiform, pet. 9.11mm, pale yellow, tinged red, narrowly oblanceolate. Summer. Canary Is., Madeira. Z9.

H. glomeratum Small = *H. densiflorum.*

H. gracile Boiss. = *H. lanuginosum.*

H. gramineum Forst. f. Perenn. or ann. herb, 2.5–72cm, erect or decumbent. Lvs 4–25mm, lanceolate or ovate-lanceolate to oblong or linear, apex obtuse to rounded, base amplexicaul, paler and rather glaucous beneath, thin-textured. Fls 0.5–1.2(–1.5)cm diam., star-shaped, overall infl. obconic to narrowly ellipsoid; pet. 5–10mm, pale yellow to orange, obovate to oblanceolate. Summer. Bhutan to Taiwan and S to Aus. and NZ. Z9.

H. grandifolium Choisy. Decid. shrub 0.5–*c*2m, bushy, br. ascending to erect. Lvs (3–)4–9cm, stem-clasping, broadly triangular-ovate to oblong-ovate, apex obtuse to rounded, thin-textured. Fls 2.5–4.5cm diam., 1–13, star-shaped, infl. br. divergent; pet. 1.6–3cm, golden, faintly tinged red, narrowly oblong-lanceolate. Summer–autumn. Canary Is., Madeira. Z9.

H. graveolens Buckley. Erect, branching perenn. herb, 30–65cm. Lvs 2.5–6.5cm, apex acute to rounded, base cuneate to cordate, amplexicaul, thickly papery, gland. dots translucent and sometimes black. Fls 2–3cm diam., star-shaped, 5–22, in a corymbiform infl.; pet. 11.5–18mm, bright yellow, obovate to elliptic, glands black, marginal. Summer. SE US. Hybrids of *H. graveolens* and *H. punctatum* (*H.* × *mitchellianum* Rydb.) have arisen in nature and may do so in cult. Z7.

H. grisebachii Boiss. = *H. richeri* ssp. *grisebachii.*

H. henryi A. Lév. & Vaniot. Shrub 0.5–3m, bushy, erect to arching. Lvs 1–4cm, narrowly elliptic or lanceolate to ovate, densely glaucous beneath, thickly papery. Fls 1.5–5.2cm diam., forming subcorymbiform infl., shallowly to deeply cupped; pet 0.8–2.5cm, golden to pale yellow, sometimes red-tinged, narrowly to broadly. Summer, early autumn. SW China, N Vietnam, E Burm., N Thail., Indon. ssp. *henryi.* St. slender, erect to arching or spreading, not or weakly frondose, internodes persistently 4-lined. Lvs usually ovate-lanceolate to broadly ovate. SW China. ssp. *hancockii* N. Robson. St. erect, not frondose, internodes sometimes becoming 2-lined. Lvs narrowly elliptic or lanceolate to ovate-oblong. S China to N Sumatra. ssp. *uraloides* (Rehd.) N. Robson. St. erect to arching, sometimes frondose above internodes persistently 4-lined. Lvs narrowly elliptic or narrowly lanceolate to ovate lanceolate. SW China, E Burm. Plants grown as ssp. *hancockii* usually represent a form intermediate between it and ssp. *henryi.* Z7.

H. henryi hort. = *H. acmosepalum.*

H. henryi auct. = *H. pseudohenryi.*

H. '**Hidcote**'. (probably *H. cyathiflorum* 'Gold Cup' × *H. calycinum.*) Shrub to 1.75m, bushy; br. arching to spreading. Lvs 3–6cm, triangular-lanceolate, acute to obtuse or slightly mucronate, thickly papery. Fls 3.5–6.5cm diam., produced over a long time, forming subcorymbiform infl., cupped; pet. 1.5–3.5cm, golden yellow, obovate. Summer. Z7.

H. 'Hidcote Gold' = *H.* 'Hidcote'.

H. hircinum L. Decid. shrub 0.5–1.5m, bushy, smelling of goats. Lvs 2–7.5cm, broadly ovate to triangular-lanceolate sometimes glaucous, thinly to thickly papery. Fls 2–4cm diam., star-shaped (1-)3-c20, from 1–4 nodes, infl. br. narrowly ascending; pet. 1.1–2.1cm, bright to golden yellow, oblanceolate to narrowly obovate. Summer. W Fr. and NW Spain to the Levant, S Spain and Moroc., SW Saudi Arabia. ssp. *hircinum*. St. to c1m. Lvs 2.5–4.5cm, usually broadly ovate. Pet. 1.5–1.8cm. Corsica & Sardinia. ssp. *albimontanum* (Greuter) N. Robson. St. 0.5–1m. Lvs 3–4.5cm, broadly ovate to ovate-lanceolate, undulate. Pet. 1.8–2cm, deeper yellow. S Greece, Crete, Andros, Cyprus. ssp. *cambessedesii* (Barceló) Sauvage. St. 0.2–1m. Lvs 2.2–4.8cm, lanceolate to triangular-lanceolate. Pet. 1–1.5cm. Balearic Is. ssp. *majus* (Ait.) N. Robson. St. 0.5–1.5m. Lvs 3–7.5cm, narrowly ovate to triangular-lanceolate. Pet. 1.3–2.1cm. W Eur. Z7.

H. hircinum ssp. *obtusifolium* (Choisy) Sauvage = *H. hircinum* ssp. *hircinum*.

H. hircinum var. *albimontanum* Greuter = *H. hircinum* ssp. *albimontanum*.

H. hircinum var. *cambessedesii* (Barceló) Ramos = *H. hircinum* ssp. *cambessedesii*.

H. hircinum var. *majus* Ait. = *H. hircinum* ssp. *majus*.

H. hircinum var. *minus* Ait. in part. = *H. hircinum* ssp. *cambessedesii*.

H. hircinum var. *minus* Ait. in part. = *H. hircinum* ssp. *hircinum*.

H. hircinum var. *obtusifolium* Choisy = *H. hircinum* ssp. *hircinum*.

H. hircinum var. *pumilum* Wats. = *H. hircinum* ssp. *hircinum*.

H. hirsutum L. Perenn. herb, 35–100cm. St. erect, decumbent, pubesc. Lvs 2–6cm, oblong to elliptic or lanceolate, apex rounded, paler beneath, thickly papery, stiffly hairy. Fls c1cm diam., star-shaped, in a loose cylindric to narrowly pyramidal infl.; pet. 8–10mm, pale yellow sometimes veined red, narrowly elliptic, with elongate translucent glands. Summer. Br. Isles, Fr., Spain and Alg. to C Sib. and China, Cauc., NW Iran. Z4.

H. hookerianum Wight & Arn. Shrub 0.3–2.1m, bushy, round-topped erect to spreading. Lvs (1.7-)2.5–8cm, narrowly lanceolate to oblong-lanceolate, acute to rounded, paler or glaucous beneath, thickly papery. Fls 3–6cm diam., 1–5, term., deeply cupped; pet. 1.5–3cm, deep to pale yellow, broadly obovate to subcircular. Summer. S India; NW Thail. to Bangladesh and E India; SW China to C Nepal. three forms are in cult.: (1) from C Burma and E India with persistently 4-angled st., oblong-ovate to broadly ovate rounded lvs, fls 4–6cm with ribbed sep. (*H. hookerianum* 'Charles Rogers', also known as 'Rogersii' and var. *rogersii*); (2) similar to form 1, but with st. soon terete and sep. not ribbed (from Nepal); (3) with slender arching, terete br., narrowly lanceolate lvs, smaller and sometimes paler fls, and unribbed, sep. (from Assam, NW Burma and Yunnan). Z7.

H. hookerianum 'Gold Cup' = *H.* ×*cyathiflorum*.

H. hookerianum 'Hidcote' = *H.* 'Hidcote'.

H. hookerianum 'Rowallane' = *H.* 'Rowallane'.

H. hookerianum 'Buttercup' = *H. uralum*.

H. hookerianum in part, misapplied = *H. lobbii*.

H. hookerianum var. *leschenaultii* misapplied = *H. choisianum*.

H. humifusum L. Short-lived perenn. or ann. herb, 3–30cm, decumbent to prostrate and rooting, 2-ridged. Lvs 0.3–2cm, oblong to obovate to oblanceolate, thin-textured, usually with translucent glands. Fls 0.8–1.2cm diam., star-shaped, in a loose infl.; pet. 4–6mm, (4-)5, golden or bright yellow, usually tinged red, elliptic, rarely with black dot. Summer. W & C Eur., Madeira, Azores. Z6.

H. hypericoides (L.) Krantz. Shrub (0.3-)5–1.2(–1.5)mm, erect to diffuse, branched at base. Lvs 0.5–3.4cm, linear to oblanceolate, margin slightly recurved, thickly papery. Fls c1.5–2.5cm diam., overall infl. narrowly cylindric. Summer. SE US, E Mex. to Hond. Rep., Carib. ssp. *hypericoides*. St. erect. Lvs broadest near middle. ssp. *multicaule* (Michx.) N. Robson. St. decumbent to prostrate. Lvs broadest above middle. Z6.

H. hypericoides var. *multicaule* (Michx.) Fosberg = *H. hypericoides* ssp. *multicaule*.

H. hyssopifolium Vill. Erect perenn. herb, 20–60cm. Lvs 15–27 narrowly elliptic-oblong to linear, apex rounded, often revolute, papery, underside paler. Fls 1–1.5cm diam., numerous, star-shaped, in a ± narrowly cylindric infl. 5–19cm long; pet. golden yellow, tinged red, 7–10mm, obovate, with short black-glandular cilia. Summer. Mts of E Spain, SE Fr., NW It., SE Balk., Bulg. Z6.

H. hyssopifolium ssp. *elongatum* (Ledeb.) Woron. = *H. elongatum*.

H. hyssopifolium var. *elongatum* (Ledeb.) Ledeb. = *H. elongatum*.

H. ×**inodorum** Mill. (*H. androsaemum* ×*H. hircinum*.) Decid. shrub 0.6–2m, bushy, erect branching from base. Lvs 3.5–11cm, oblong-lanceolate to broadly ovate, subacute to rounded, somewhat paler beneath papery. Fls 1.5–3cm diam., star-shaped or cupped, infl. br. usually narrowly ascending; pet. 0.8–1.5cm, golden yellow, oblanceolate to narrowly obovate. Summer. NW Spain to NW It., Corsica; widely nat. Yellow-leaved and variously variegated cvs include 'Summergold', 'Ysella', 'Goudelsje', 'Hysan' and 'Beattie's Variety', 'Elstead' (*H.* ×*persistens* 'Elstead') is a selection (or back-cross to *H. androsaemum*) with large fr. that flush rosy-red, not the usual cerise, during ripening. Z8.

H. inodorum Willd. non Mill. = *H. xylosteifolium*.

H. involutum (Labill.) Choisy = *H. gramineum*.

H. japonicum Murray. Ann. herb, 2–50cm. St. 4-angled, erect to decumbent or sometimes prostrate and rooting. Lvs 2–18mm, broadly ovate or suborbicular to oblanceolate, paler or glaucous beneath, membranous. Fls 0.4–0.8cm diam., star-shaped, overall infl. diffuse; pet. 1.7–5mm, pale yellow to orange, obovate to oblong or elliptic. Summer. Jap. and Korea to Nepal, S India, SE Aus., NZ. The most commonly cult form ('*H. pusillum*') is from New Zealand with diffuse prostrate st., elliptic to oblanceolate lvs rounded at apex, and apparently axill. fls.

H. jaubertii Spach = *H. orientale*.

H. kalmianum L. Shrub to 60cm, erect, forming a narrow, domed flat-topped bush. Lvs 1.5–4.5 narrowly oblong to oblanceolate or linear, apex rounded to subapiculate-obtuse, ± revolute, rather glaucous beneath, thin-textured. Fls 2–3.5cm, 1–7, from term. node, sometimes with 3-fld paired br. below; pet. 8–15mm, (4-)5, golden yellow, obovate to oblong. Mid to late summer. US and Canada (Great Lakes region). Z2.

H. kelleri Baldacci. Ann. or perenn. herb, 1–10cm. St. glaucous, prostrate, mat-forming and rooting. Lvs 2–8mm, oblong or elliptic, glaucous throughout, thin-textured, surfaces undulate papillose or almost smooth. Fls solitary, star-shaped; pet. 6–7mm, usually 4, golden yellow, tinged red, elliptic, with few scattered black dots. Summer. W Crete. Differs from *H. trichocaulon* in its mat-forming habit, undulate-papillose lvs and smaller, usually 4-merous fls. Z8.

H. keniense Schweinf. = *H. revolutum* ssp. *keniense*.

H. kiusianum var. *yakusimense* (Koidz.) T. Kato = *H. yakusimense*.

H. kohlianum Spreng. = *H. elegans*.

H. kotschyanum Boiss. Perenn. herb, 10–25(–30)cm, erect or ascending, shortly grey-hairy. Lvs 5–15mm, narrowly oblong to linear-lanceolate, apex rounded, paler beneath, revolute, thickly papery, cinereous-pubesc. Fls 1.4–2.2cm diam., star-shaped, in a narrowly cylindric to pyramidal infl.; pet. 7–11mm, golden, often veined red, oblanceolate with elongate, translucent glands. Summer. Mts of S Turk. Z7.

H. kouytchense A. Lév. Shrub 1–1.8m, bushy; br. arching or pendulous. Lvs 2–5.8cm, elliptic to ovate or lanceolate, acute to obtuse or rounded-apiculate, paler beneath, thickly papery. Fls 4–6.5cm diam., 1–7(11), from 1–2 nodes, star-shaped; pet. 2.4–4cm, bright golden yellow, not red-tinged, obovate-oblong to obovate, often recurving. Summer. China. Z6.

H. kouytchense auct. = *H. acmosepalum* or *H. wilsonii*.

H. laeve Boiss. & Hausskn. = *H. capitatum* var. *luteum*.

H. laeve var. *rubrum* (Hochst.) Boiss. = *H. capitatum*.

H. lagarocladum N. Robson. Shrub 0.5–1.5m, diffuse; br. arching or spreading, slender. Lvs 1.8–4.5cm, narrowly elliptic to broadly oblong-elliptic, acute to rounded, paler beneath, thickly papery. Fls 3–4.5cm diam., 1–3 (sometimes more), term., star-shaped to shallowly cupped; pet. 1.8–2.3cm, golden yellow, not red-tinged, obovate. Summer. S China. Z7.

H. lancasteri N. Robson. shrub 0.3–1m, suberect to spreading, young growth flushed purple-red. Lvs 3–6cm, oblong-lanceolate or lanceolate to triangular-lanceolate, acute to rounded, paler or glaucous beneath, thickly papery. Fls 3–5.5cm diam., 1–11, from 1–3 nodes, forming lax infl., star-shaped to slightly cupped; pet. 1.7–2.8cm, golden yellow, oblong-ovate. Summer. SW China. Close to *H. stellatum*, with a stouter infl. Z7.

H. lanceolatum misapplied = *H. revolutum* ssp. *revolutum*.

H. lanuginosum Lam. Differs from the closely related *H. annulatum* in having bracts lacking auricles; pet. rarely veined red. Summer. S Turk. to N Isr., Cyprus. Plants grown as *H. lanuginosum* are often *H. annulatum*.

H. lanuginosum var. *gracile* (Boiss.) Boiss. = *H. lanuginosum*.

H. 'Lawrence Johnston' = *H.* ×*cyathiflorum*.

H. laxum (Bl.) Koidz. = *H. japonicum*.

H. leschenaultii Choisy. Shrub 0.5–2.5m, everg., ± spreading. Lvs 2.5–8cm, triangular-lanceolate to ovate, acute to rounded-apiculate glaucous beneath, thinly coriaceous. Fls 3.5–7cm diam., forming subcorymbiform infl., shallowly cupped; pet. 2–4.5cm, deep golden yellow. Summer. Sumatra to Lombok and SW Sulawesi. *H. leschenaultii* is much confused in gardens. The true sp. is rare in cult. (cf. *H. addingtonii*). Z9.

H. leschenaultii auct. = *H. addingtonii* or *H. augustinii*.

H. leucoptychodes A. Rich. = *H. revolutum* ssp. *revolutum*.

H. linariifolium Vahl.   Perenn. herb, 20–50cm, erect to decumbent and rooting. Lvs 0.5–3.5cm, narrowly oblong to narrowly lanceolate or linear, apex obtuse to rounded, paler beneath, revolute, thickly papery, pruinose. Fls *c*1.5cm diam., star-shaped, in a corymbiform to broadly pyramidal infl.; pet. 8–12mm, golden yellow, oblanceolate. Summer. N Wales to NW Spain and Port., Madeira. Z7.

H. linarioides Bosse.   Perenn. herb, 5–33cm, erect or ascending, rooting and branching at base. Lvs 0.5–3cm, narrowly oblong or narrowly elliptic to linear, apex obtuse, often revolute, glaucous, thickly papery. Fls 1.2–2.2cm diam., star-shaped, in a narrowly cylindric to subspicate infl. to 14cm long; pet. 5–12mm, golden often tinged or veined red, broadly elliptic. Summer. S Balk. Penins., Crimea, Cauc., Turk. (N Anatolia) NW Iran. Z6.

H. lobbii N. Robson.   Shrub 1.2–2m, erect. Lvs 2–4.5cm, ovate-lanceolate to triangular-ovate, obtuse to rounded, apiculate, somewhat glaucous beneath, thinly coriaceous. Fls 3–5cm diam., 1–*c*24, shallowly cupped; sep. glandular-denticulate; pet. 2–2.6cm, golden yellow, broadly obovate. Late summer. India (Khasi Hills). Z9.

H. lobocarpum Gatt.   Shrub 0.9–1.5 (–2)m, erect, forming broad clumps. Lvs 35–50 narrowly oblong to lanceolate or lienar, apex rounded-apiculate to obtuse, revolute, paler or glaucous beneath, thin-textured. Fls 1–1.5cm diam., in a globose-cylindric to broadly pyramidal infl.; pet. 6–8mm, 5, golden, obovate-oblanceolate. Late summer. SE US. Z6.

H. lysimachioides Dyer = *H. dyeri*.

H. lysimachioides auct. = *H. stellatum*.

H. maclarenii N. Robson.   Shrub 0.75–1m, erect to spreading. Lvs 2.5–4cm, narrowly lanceolate, acute to subacute, glaucous beneath, thickly papery. Fls 4–5cm diam., 1–6, term., star-shaped; pet. 2–2.5cm, golden yellow, sometimes red-tinged, obovate-oblanceolate. Summer. China. Z7.

H. maculatum Crantz.   Perenn. herb. 15–100cm. St. erect, rooting at base; br. 2–4-lined. Lvs 10–50mm, elliptic or oblong to ovate, apex rounded, paler beneath, thickly papery. Fls 2–3cm diam., star-shaped, in a broadly to narrowly pyramidal infl.; pet. 0.9–1.2cm, bright yellow, not red-tinged, oblong-oblanceolate, with superficial black gland. streaks and/or dots. Summer. Ireland, Fr. and Pyren. to W Sib. ssp. **maculatum**. Lvs lacking translucent glands. Infl. narrowly branched; pet. covered with black dots or short streaks. Scotland, Ardennes, Massif Central, Pyren. and from Scand., Germ. and the Alps eastward. ssp. **obtusiusculum** (Tourlet) Hayek. Lvs with some translucent glands. Infl. broadly branched; pet. with black streaks and lines. NW Eur., Lower Alps. Z6.

H. maculatum Walter non Crantz = *H. punctatum*.

H. majus (A. Gray) Britt.   Perenn. herb of marshy places, 5–70cm. St. 4-angled, erect, ± simple. Lvs 10–45mm, lanceolate to narrowly oblong-elliptic, apex acute to rounded, base amplexicaul, thin-textured. Fls 0.6–0.8cm diam., star-shaped, 3–*c*30 at term. node, and on flowering br. at up to 5 nodes below, infl. compactly cylindric to corymbiform; sep. 3.5–6.5mm, lanceolate to narrowly elliptic, acute, entire; pet. 3.5–6mm, golden, sometimes veined-red, oblanceolate. Summer. S Canada, N US. Z3.

H. maritimum Sieb. = *H. aegypticum*.

H. minus invalid = *H. hircinum* ssp. *cambessedesii*.

H. monogynum L.   Shrub 0.5–1.3m, semi-evergreen, bushy or with br. lax and spreading. Lvs 2–11.2cm, oblanceolate or elliptic to oblong, acute to rounded, paler beneath, thinly coriaceous. Fls 3–6.5cm diam., forming a lax subcorymbiform usually term.; pet. 2–3.4cm, golden to lemon yellow, triangular-obovate. Summer. SE China, Taiwan. A variable sp. The first introduction was of the more tender, lowland form with oblong to lanceolate, obtuse to rounded lvs and dense infl. Some later introductions were from Japan, where the hardier upland form ('var. *salicifolium*') with narrowly elliptic to oblanceolate lvs had been in cult. for some time. Z9.

H. montanum L.   Perenn. herb, 20–80cm, erect, glab. Lvs 2–7cm, sessile, ovate to lanceolate or oblong-elliptic, apex rounded, base amplexicaul, somewhat paler beneath and rough, thinly papery. Fls 1.5–2.5cm diam., star-shaped, overall infl. congested, shortly cylindric to corymbiform; bract auricles glandular-ciliate; pet. 8–12mm, pale yellow, elliptic. W & C Eur., C Russia, Transcauc., NW Afr. Z5.

H. montbretii Spach.   Perenn. herb, 15–60cm, erect or decumbent, often glaucous. Lvs 15–55mm, broadly ovate to oblong or triangular-lanceolate, apex obtuse to rounded, base amplexicaul, sometimes glandular-ciliate in upper lvs, glaucous beneath, papery. Fls 1.5–2.5cm diam., star-shaped, in a corymbiform infl.; pet. 8–14mm, golden yellow, oblanceolate, sometimes dotted black toward apex. Summer. SE Balk.

Penins., W Turk. Z6.

H. × moserianum André (*H. patulum* ×*H. calycinum.*)   Shrub 00.3–0.5(0.7)m, semi-evergreen, spreading or arching. Lvs 2.2–6cm, oblong-lanceolate to oblong-ovate or ovate, acute to rounded-apiculate, paler beneath, thinly leathery. Fls 4.5–6cm diam., 1–8, forming subcorymbiform infl. star-shaped or slightly cupped; pet. 2.1–3cm, bright yellow, obovate. Gdn origin. 'Tricolor': lvs variegated cream, pink and green; st. strongly flushed red; fls smaller than in unvariegated form. Z7.

H. 'Mrs Gladys Brabazon' = *H. androsaemum* f. *variegatum*.

H. multiflorum invalid = *H. × inodorum*.

H. mutilum L.   Perenn. or ann. herb of wet places, 15–60cm. St. 4-angled, erect or decumbent. Lvs 5–27mm, ovate or ovate-deltoid to elliptic-oblong, apex obtuse to rounded, paler beneath, membranous. Fls 0.3–0.5cm diam., star-shaped, overall infl. cylindric; pet. 1.75–3.5mm, golden oblong. Summer. E Canada, E US. Z3.

H. nanum Poir.   Dwarf shrub, 0.05–0.5m. Habit erect, domed, branching dense, pseudo-dichotomous. Lvs 0.8–2cm, ovate to broadly elliptic, apex obtuse to rounded, glaucous, thickly papery. Fls 1.5–2cm diam., star-shaped, 3–9, term.; pet. 7–11mm, yellow, oblanceolate. Summer. Syr., Leb. Z9.

H. napaulense Choisy = *H. elodeoides*.

H. nitidum hort. non Lam. = *H. fasciculatum*.

H. nortoniae (M.E. Jones) J.M. Gillett = *H. scouleri* ssp. *nortoniae*.

H. nothum Rehd. = *H. densiflorum*.

H. nudicaule Walter = *H. gentianoides*.

H. nudiflorum Michx.   Slender shrub 1–2m, erect, fragile, intricately branched at base. Lvs 22–70mm, lanceolate or elliptic to oblong, apex obtuse to rounded, thin-textured. Fls 1.2–1.5cm diam., forming flat corymbiform infl.; pet. 6.5–8mm, 5, pale yellow becoming deflexed. Summer. SE US. Z7.

H. nummularium L.   Perenn. herb, 8–30cm, erect to decumbent, spreading and rooting. Lvs 5–18mm, broadly ovate to orbicular, apex subobtuse to rounded, glaucous beneath, thinly coriaceous. Fls 1.5–3cm diam., star-shaped, in a subcorymbose infl.; pet. 8–14mm, bright yellow, sometimes veined red, obovate to elliptic, with translucent glands. Summer. Pyren. & N Spain, SW Alps (Fr., It.). Z6.

H. oblongifolium Choisy.   Shrub 0.45–2.4m; br. spreading or drooping. Lvs 3–9.3cm, elliptic to oblong or ovate-oblong, obtuse or apiculate to rounded, sometimes glaucous, thickly papery. Fls 3.5–7.5cm diam., star-shaped, 1–8, forming cylindric-ellipsoid infl.; pet. 2–3cm, bright yellow to yellow-orange, obovate to oblanceolate. Summer. W Himal. (Pak. to Nepal). Z9.

H. oblongifolium misapplied = *H. hookerianum* or *H. lobbii*.

H. oblongifolium hort. = *H. acmosepalum*.

H. obtusum Moench invalid = *H. maculatum* ssp. *maculatum*.

H. ocymoides Lodd. invalid = *H. ascyron*.

H. officinarum Krantz = *H. perforatum*.

H. olympicum L.   Dwarf shrub, 10–55cm. St. erect to creeping; br. ascending. Lvs 5–38mm, oblong to elliptic or ovate to linear, apex acute to obtuse, thinly glaucous, thinly coriaceous. Fls 2–6cm diam., star-shaped, 1–5; pet. 14–30mm, golden to lemon yellow, sometimes tinged red, oblanceolate to oblong-oblanceolate. Summer. Greece, S Balk., S Bulg., NW & S Turk. f. **olympicum**. St. usually erect. Lvs 2–3.8cm, elliptic or elliptic-oblong to lanceolate. Pet. 1.7–3cm, golden yellow. N Greece, NE Turk. f. **uniflorum** D. Jordanov & Kozuh. St. erect to spreading. Lvs 0.8–2.3cm, broadly elliptic to obovate. Pet. 2–2.5cm, golden or lemon yellow. N & C Greece, S Bulg. 'Sunburst': robust; fls large. 'Citrinum': fls lemon yellow. f. **minus** Hausskn. St. decumbent to straggling. Lvs 0.6–1.5cm, narrowly elliptic to narrowly oblong. Pet. 1.4–1.8cm, golden or lemon. S Greece. Broad lvd. plants under the name *H. polyphyllum* usually belong to f. *uniflorum*. Plants with lemon-yellow fls and narrow lvs (*H. polyphyllum citrinum* invalid; *H. repens citrinum* invalid) are properly f. *minus* 'Sulphureum'. Decumbent to prostrate clones are usually named *H. fragile* or *H. repens*: the true *H. polyphyllum* of Boissier and Balansa is v. rare at present. Z6.

H. olympicum citrinum invalid = *H. olympicum* f. *uniflorum* 'Citrinum'.

H. opacum Torr. & A. Gray = *H. cistifolium*.

H. orientale L.   Perenn. herb. 7–45cm, erect or decumbent. Lvs 1–4cm, narrowly oblong or elliptic-oblong to oblanceolate or linear, apex rounded to subacute, with golden gland-tipped teeth or glandular-ciliate, thickly papery. Fls 1.5–3cm diam., star-shaped, in a corymbiform to shortly cylindric infl. Summer. W & N Anatolia, E Georgia, W Azerbaijan. *H.* 'Jaubertii': st. erect; lvs broad; fls large. *H.* 'Ptarmicifolium': st. decumbent; lvs narrow; fls small. Z7.

H. orientale var. *ptarmicifolium* (Spach) Boiss. = *H. orientale* 'Ptarmicifolium'.

H. origanifolium Willd. Perenn. herb, 5–37cm. St. suberect to ascending, pale grey- to dirty white-pubesc. Lvs 5–30mm, elliptic oblong to ovate or obovate, apex acute to obtuse, pubesc., thickly papery. Fls 1.5–2.5cm diam., star-shaped, in a corymbiform to broadly pyramidal infl; pet. 9–15mm, golden yellow, veined red, obovate to oblanceolate, with superficial glands black or amber. Summer. Turk. (NW Anatolia). Z7.

H. pallens Banks & Sol. Dwarf shrublet. St. 0.05–0.25m, straggling. Lvs 3–25mm, oblong or elliptic to oblanceolate or obovate, apex obtuse to rounded, glaucous beneath, thinly papery. Fls 1.4–1.8(–2.5)cm diam., 1(2–3), term., star-shaped, tipped red in bud; pet. 6–12mm pale yellow, red-tinged, oblong, usually sparsely dotted with glands. Summer. S Turk., W Syr. Z8.

H. parviflorum Willd. = *H. mutilum*.

H. patulum Thunb. Shrub 0.3–1.5m, bushy, arching to spreading, sometimes weakly frondose. Lvs 1.5–6cm, lanceolate or oblong-lanceolate to oblong-ovate, obtuse to rounded, apiculate glaucous beneath, thickly papery. Fls 2.5–4cm diam., forming subcorymbiform infl., cupped; pet. 1.2–2.8cm, golden yellow, oblong-obovate to broadly obovate. Summer, early autumn. China, introd. Taiwan and Jap. Distinguished from *H. henryi* by the 2-lined stem-internodes, apiculate lvs and toothed or ciliolate sep. Z6.

H. patulum 'Gold Cup' = *H. ×cyathiflorum*.
H. patulum 'Rothschilds Form' = *H. forrestii*.
H. patulum auct. = *H. henryi*.
H. patulum misapplied = *H. henryi* ssp. *henryi*.
H. patulum 'Hidcote Variety' = *H.* 'Hidcote'.
H. patulum 'Hidcote' = *H.* 'Hidcote'.
H. patulum 'Sungold' = *H. kouytchense*.
H. patulum 'Laplace' = *H. kouytchense*.
H. patulum 'Summergold' = *H. kouytchense*.
H. patulum auct. = *H. uralum*.
H. patulum var. *forrestii* Chitt. = *H. forrestii*.
H. patulum var. *grandiflorum* invalid = *H. kouytchense*.
H. patulum var. *henryi* hort. = *H. acmosepalum*.
H. patulum var. *henryi* Bean = *H. beanii*.
H. patulum var. *henryi* auct. = *H. pseudohenryi*.
H. patulum var. *oblongifolium* hort. = *H. acmosepalum*.
H. patulum var. *oblongifolium* misapplied = *H. hookerianum*.
H. patulum var. *uralum* (D. Don) Koehne = *H. uralum*.
H. patulum f. *forrestii* (Chitt.) Rehd. = *H. forrestii*.
H. penduliflorum invalid = *H. kouytchense*.

H. perfoliatum L. Perenn. herb, 15–75cm. St. ascending, usually glaucous. Lvs 13–60mm, broadly ovate to triangular-lanceolate or linear-lanceolate, apex usually rounded, base amplexicaul, sometimes black glandular-ciliate, glaucous, thickly papery. Fls 1.2–2.5cm diam., star-shaped, numerous, in a suborymbiform to broadly pyramidal infl.; pet. 9–14mm, golden yellow, oblanceolate, sometimes with black dots or streaks toward tip. Summer. Medit. (except SE), Canary Is., Madeira. Z9.

H. perforatum L. Perenn. herb, 10–110cm. St. erect or decumbent, rooting at base, 2-lined; br. ascending. Lvs 8–30mm, narrowly ovate or lanceolate to linear, apex obtuse to rounded, paler beneath, thickly papery, with trnslucent glands. Fls 1.5–3.5cm diam., star-shaped, in a subcorymbose to pyramidal infl.; pet. 8–18mm, bright yellow, oblanceolate, sometimes with black streaks. Summer. Eur. to C China, N Afr., W Himal.; introd. N Amer. and S temp. regions. var. *angustifolium* DC. Fls small; lvs narrow. var. *latifolium* Koch. Fls large; lvs broad. var. *microphyllum* DC. Fls small; lvs small *H. perforatum* hybridizes with *H. maculatum*, producing *H. ×desentangsii* Lamotte. Hybrids with *H. maculatum* ssp. *obtusiusculum* have pointed and finely toothed sep apices. Z3.

H. ×persistens I.F. Schneid. = *H. ×inodorum*.
H. ×persistens 'Elatum' = *H. ×inodorum*.
H. pilosum Walter = *H. setosum*.
H. polygonifolium Rupr. = *H. linarioides*.
H. ×polyphyllum hort. non Boiss. & Bal. = *H. olympicum* f. *uniflorum, minus*.

H. prolificum L. Shrub 0.2–2m, erect to ascending, habit rounded or loosely bushy. Lvs 30–70mm, narrowly oblong to narrowly elliptic or oblanceolate, apex rounded-apiculate to acute, underside paler or glaucous, thickly papery. Fls 1.5–3cm diam., in a cylindric infl.; pet. 7–15mm, 5, golden yellow, obovate to oblanceolate-spathulate. Summer. C & E US, S Ont. Readily distinguished from *H. frondosum* by the cylindrical infl. and narrower lvs. Plants intermediate between these spp. have been named *H. ×vanfleetii* Rehd. Z4.

H. prolificum var. *densiflorum* (Pursh) A. Gray = *H. densiflorum*.

H. pseudohenryi N. Robson. Shrub 0.7–1.7m, bushy; br. erect or somewhat arching. Lvs 2–6.6(–8)cm, ovate or ovate-oblong to lanceolate or lanceolate-oblong, apiculate-obtuse or usually rounded, pale or somewhat glaucous beneath, thickly papery. Fls 3–5.5cm diam., 1–7(–25), term., star-shaped or slightly cupped; pet. 1.6–3cm, golden yellow, obovate. Summer. SW China. Z6.

H. pseudohenryi auct. = *H. beanii*.
H. pseudopetiolatum var. *yakusimense* (Koidz.) Y. Kimura = *H. yakusimense*.
H. ptarmicifolium Spach = *H. orientale*.

H. pulchrum L. Perenn. herb, (3–)10–90cm, erect or ascending. Lvs 0.6–2cm, broadly ovate to oblong, apex obtuse, base amplexicaul, paler, beneath, coriaceous. Fls *c*1.5cm diam., star-shaped, in a loose cylindric to narrowly pyramidal infl. some 17cm long; pet. 7–9mm, golden or rarely pale yellow, tinged red, elliptic, with translucent glands, anth. orange to pink-red. NW Eur., with scattered localities further E and S. f. *procumbens* Rostrup. Habit dwarf. Fls sparse. var. *pallidum* Rouy & Fouc. Pet. pale yellow, contrasting with red anth. Z5.

H. punctatum Lam. Perenn. herb, 14–105cm, erect, slightly 2-lined or terete, black glandular-punctate. Lvs 2–6cm, triangular-lanceolate to oblong-elliptic or oblanceolate, apex abruptly apiculate to rounded, base amplexicaul, paler beneath, thinly papery, gland dots sometimes black. Fls 0.8–1.4cm diam., star-shaped, massed in corymbiform to pyramidal infl.; pet. 3–7mm, deep to golden yellow, elliptic, with dense black glands, dots and streaks. Summer. E US, SE Canada. Z3.

H. pusillum Choisy = *H. japonicum*.
H. pyramidatum Ait. = *H. ascyron*.
H. quadrangulum auct. non L. = *H. maculatum*.
H. quadrangulum L. nom. confus. = *H. tetrapterum*.
H. quadrangulum ssp. *obtusiusculum* Tourlet = *H. maculatum* ssp. *obtusiusculum*.
H. quinquenervium Walter = *H. mutilum*.
H. ramosissimum Ledeb. = *H. xylosteifolium*.

H. reflexum L. f. Shrub to *c*1m. Habit spreading; br. ascending, densely white-tomentose. Lvs 9–25mm, closely 4-ranked, narrowly oblong to triangular-lanceolate or elliptic, apex acute, base amplexicaul, thinly coriaceous. Fls *c*1.5–2cm diam., somewhat star-shaped, overall infl. subcorymbiform to hemispherical; pet. 8–10mm, yellow, sometimes tinged red, oblanceolate. Summer. Canary Is. Z9.

H. repens misapplied = *H. linarioides* and *H. trichocaulon*.

H. reptans Dyer. Shrublet, prostrate or ascending to 0.3m, forming clumps or mats, with br. pinnatiform, rooting. Lvs 0.7–2.2, elliptic to obovate, obtuse to rounded, paler beneath, leathery. Fls 2–3cm diam., solitary, ± deeply cupped; pet. 1.1–1.8cm, deep golden yellow, sometimes tinged red, broadly obovate. Mid-late summer. E Himal. Z7.

H. revolutum Vahl. Everg. shrub or small tree to 12m. Lvs 1.5–4.5cm, narrow-elliptic to narrow-oblong or oblanceolate. Fls 3.5–8cm diam., solitary, star-shaped; pet. 1.5–4.3cm, 5, orange-yellow to golden yellow, tinged red to orange, obovate-oblanceolate. Summer. SW Saudi Arabia to S Afr. (E Cape), Cameroun, Fernando Pó. ssp. *revolutum*. Pet. tinged orange outside. ssp. *keniense* (Schweinf.) N. Robson. Pet. tinged red outside. E & C Afr. Z10.

H. rhodoppeum Friv. = *H. cerastoides* ssp. *meuselianum*.

H. richeri Vill. Perenn. herb, 10–50cm. St. usually glaucous, creeping and rooting at base. Lvs 10–55mm, ovate to triangular-ovate or elliptic, apex subacute to obtuse, base amplexicaul, undersurface, glaucous, thinly papery. Fls 2–4.5cm diam., star-shaped, in a dense subcorymbiform infl.; pet. 10–25mm, golden, tinged red, oblanceolate, clawed, with black dots. Summer. Mts of S & SC Eur. ssp. *richeri*. Lvs usually subacute, base subamplexicaul, rounded. Pet. 1–1.7cm. SW & C Alps, Jura, Apennines. ssp. *burseri* (DC.) Nyman. Lvs usually obtuse, base amplexicaul. Pet. 1–2.5cm. Pyren., Cantab. Mts. ssp. *grisebachii* (Boiss.) Nyman. Lvs usually obtuse, base rounded to cuneate. Pet. 1–1.8cm. SE Alps, Balk. Penins., Carpath. Z6.

H. richeri ssp. *alpigenum* (Kit.) E. Schmid = *H. richeri* ssp. *grisebachii*.
H. robertii Battand. = *H. ericoides*.

H. 'Rowallane'. (Probably *H. leschenaultii* ×*H. hookerianum* 'Charles Rogers'.) Shrub to 3m; br. erect, gradually outcurving. Lvs 2.7–6.7cm, ovate to oblong-ovate or oblong-lanceolate, apiculate-obtuse, paler or glaucous beneath, thinly coriaceous to thickly papery. Fls 5–7.5cm diam., 1–3, term., shallowly cupped; pet. 3–4cm, golden, obovate to subcircular. Late summer to autumn. Gdn origin. Z8.

H. rubrum Hochst. = *H. capitatum*.

H. rumeliacum Boiss. Perenn. herb, 5–40cm. St. erect to procumbent, sometimes rooting, usually glaucous. Lvs 6–35mm, linear-oblong to broadly ovate, apex subacute to rounded, sometimes black-glandular-ciliate, thickly papery, glaucous. Fls 2–3.5cm diam., star-shaped, term.; pet. *c*12–18mm, deep yellow, sometimes tinged red, oblanceolate to elliptic, with scattered black dots. Summer. S Balk. Penins., N Greece. ssp. *rumeliacum*. St. suberect to ascending. Lvs narrowly oblong to broadly oblong-lanceolate. Fls 2–3cm diam., pet. without red tinge. S Rom. to Eur. Turk., W to Albania and NE Greece. ssp. *apollinis* (Boiss. & Heldr.) N. Robson & Strid. St. ascending to procumbent. Lvs ovate-elliptic. Fls 2.5–3.5cm diam.; pet. usually tinged red. C & NW Greece, S Albania. Z7.

H. salicifolium Sieb. & Zucc. = *H. monogynum*.

H. sampsonii Hance. Perenn. herb, 20–80mm. St. solitary, few or erect, terete; br. erect. Lvs 30–80mm, paired-perfoliate, rounded, pale or glaucous beneath, thickly papery. Fls 0.6–1.5cm diam., star-shaped, in an open corymbiform to cylindric infl.; pet. 0.4–0.8(–1.3)cm, bright-yellow, elliptic-oblong, with marginal black glands and sometimes black dots and streaks. Summer. S Jap. to C Burm., NE India. Z9.

H. sarothra Michx. = *H. gentianoides*.

H. saturejifolium Jaub. & Spach = *H. confertum* ssp. *confertum*.

H. scouleri Hook. Perenn. herb, 5–60cm. St. erect or spreading and rooting; br. erect. Lvs 10–28mm, elliptic-oblong to ovate or elliptic, apex rounded, base amplexicaul, thickly papery. Fls 1–1.5(–2)cm diam., star-shaped, in a broadly to narrowly pyramidal infl.; pet. 7–12mm, golden yellow, often tinged red, obovate to oblong-oblanceolate, glands black, marginal. Summer. SW Canada, W US, C Mex. ssp. *scouleri*. St. tall, branched; lvs clustered; fls numerous. ssp. *nortoniae* (M.E. Jones) J.M. Gillett. St. shorter, spreading and rooting; lvs not clustered; fls solitary or in simple cymes. Z4.

H. seleri R. Keller = *H. concinnum*.

H. setosum L. Perenn. or ann. herb, 20–80cm. St. erect, usually simple pubesc. Lvs 4–15mm, narrowly ovate or lanceolate to narrowly oblong-elliptic, apex acute to obtuse, margin recurved, subcoriaceous, pubesc. Fls 0.5–1.1cm diam., star-shaped, overall infl. cylindric to subcorymbiform; pet. 4–7mm, deep yellow. Summer. SE US. Z6.

H. spathulatum (Spach) Steud. = *H. prolificum*.

H. spruneri Boiss.. Perenn. herb, 30–60cm. St. erect or decumbent, usually glaucous. Lvs 20–60mm, deltoid-lanceolate to narrowly elliptic or linear-oblong, apex obtuse to rounded, base amplexicaul, usually glaucous, thickly papery. Fls 1.5–2.5cm diam., star-shaped, in a corymbiform to broadly pyramidal infl.; pet. 11–14mm, golden, sometimes tinged red, oblanceolate, dotted black. Summer. SE It., NE Greece, Albania, W & NW Balk. Z6.

H. stans (Michx.) Adams & N. Robson = *H. crux-andreae*.

H. stellatum N. Robson. Shrub *c*1–2.5m, br. spreading to sub-pendulous. Lvs 2–5.5cm, oblong-lanceolate or lanceolate to narrowly ovate, acute to rounded-apiculate, glaucous beneath, thickly papery, venation not reticulate. Fls 2.5–4cm diam., 1–14, term., forming lax infl., stellate; pet. star-like, red; pet. 1.2–2cm, golden, sometimes red-tinged, obovate. Summer. China. Z6.

H. stenobotrys Boiss. = *H. confertum* ssp. *stenobotrys*.

H. stragulum P. Adams & N. Robson = *H. hypericoides* ssp. *multicaule*.

H. subsessile N. Robson Shrub 1–1.5m, everg., bushy, erect to arching. Lvs 3.5–6.5cm, narrowly elliptic to oblanceolate, acute to rounded-apiculate, paler to glaucous beneath, thinly leathery. Fls 3.5–4.5cm diam., 1–8, term., star-shaped to shallowly cupped; pet. 1.7–2cm, bright yellow, sometimes red-tinged, oblanceolate-obovate. Fr. large, purple-red. Summer. SW China Z7.

H. tapetoides A. Nels. = *H. anagalloides*.

H. tenuicaule Dyer. Shrub *c*1.5m, with br. arching to ascending. Lvs 1.5–5.8cm, lanceolate to elliptic, acute to rounded, somewhat glaucous beneath, leathery. Fls 1.5–3cm diam., 1–7, deeply cupped; pet. 1–1.3cm, bright yellow, sometimes tinged red, obovate to subcircular. Summer. E Nepal to W Bhutan. Differs from *H. uralum* in the divaricate, not frondose, branching and terete st. internodes. Z8.

H. tetrapterum Fries. Perenn. herb, 10–100cm. St. erect from a creeping base, or decumbent, 4-winged. Lvs 10–40mm, ovate or elliptic-oblong to circular, rounded, base amplexicaul, thinly papery, with numerous translucent glands. Fls 1–1.5cm diam., star-shaped, in a dense corymbiform to cylindric infl.; pet. 5–8mm, bright-yellow, oblanceolate. Summer. Z5.

H. tomentosum L. Perenn. herb, 10–90cm. St. decumbent, rooting, tomentose. Lvs 5–22mm, ovate to oblong, apex obtuse to rounded, base amplexicaul, papery, thickly hoary-pubesc. Fls *c*0.8–1.6cm diam., star-shaped, overall infl. subcorymbiform or with br. from all nodes then cylindric; pet. 6–11mm, bright yellow, oblanceolate. Summer. Moroc., W Medit. *H. pubescens* differs in sep. with apex eglandular and marginal glands sessile. Z8.

H. tournefortii Spach = *H. orientale*.

H. trichocaulon Boiss. & Heldr. Perenn. herb, 5–25cm, rarely to 45cm. St. procumbent or ascending or pendulous, rather glaucous. Lvs 5–14mm, ovate-oblong to elliptic or linear, apex obtuse, pale, somewhat glaucous. Fls 2–2.5cm diam., solitary or 2–3, star-shaped, red-tipped in bud; pet. 1–1.2cm, golden yellow, red-tinged, obovate, with black dots toward apex. Summer. W & C Crete. Z8.

H. triflorum Bl. = *H. leschenaultii*.

H. undulatum Willd. Perenn. herb, 15–100cm; st. ascending, 4-winged. Lvs 7–40mm, narrowly ovate to elliptic or narrowly oblong, rounded, base amplexicaul, undulate, papery, with many translucent glands. Fls 1.2–1.7cm diam., star-shaped, in a lax subcorymbiform to cylindric infl.; pet. 7.5–10mm, bright yellow, tinged-red, elliptic. Summer. Wales and SW Engl. to Moroc., Madeira, Azores. Z8.

H. uraloides Rehd. = *H. henryi* ssp. *uraloides*.

H. uralum D. Don. Shrub 0.3–2m, bushy; br. often frondose. Lvs 1–4cm, with short flat petiole, lanceolate to ovate, acute to rounded-apiculate, glaucous beneath, thickly papery. Fls 1.5–3cm diam., forming subcorymbiform infl., ± deeply cupped; pet. 0.9–1.2cm, golden to deep yellow, broadly obovate to subcircular. Summer. SW China, NW Burm., India to Pak. Distinguished from *H. henryi* ssp. *uraloides* by the entire sep., frond-like br. and smaller fls. Z8.

H. × *urberuagae* P. & S. Dupont = *H.* × *inodorum*.

H. vacciniifolium Hayek & Siehe. Dwarf erect to decumbent shrub, 0.08–0.2m. Habit rounded; br. many, erect. Lvs 9–18mm, broadly elliptic or elliptic-oblong to oblanceolate, apex rounded, glaucous beneath, thickly papery. Fls star-shaped 1(22–3), term. and on axill. shoots; pet. 10–12mm, yellow, oblong-oblanceolate. Summer. S Turk. Z8.

H. vanfleetii Rehd. = *H. prolificum*.

H. villosum (L.) Krantz = *H. setosum*.

H. vulgare Gaertn. = *H. androsaemum*.

H. vulgare Lam. = *H. perforatum*.

H. webbii Spach = *H. aegypticum*.

H. wilsonii N. Robson. Shrub 0.5–1m, spreading; br. pendulous to prostrate. Lvs 2.3–6cm, elliptic to lanceolate or ovate-lanceolate, subacute to rounded, glaucous beneath, thickly papery. Fls 4–6cm diam., usually terminal only, star-shaped; pet. 2–2.5cm, golden yellow, obovate. Summer. C China. Z6.

H. xylosteifolium (Spach) N. Robson. Decid. shrub to 1.5m. Br. spreading, forming thickets. Lvs 1.5–7.3cm, oblong to elliptic to lanceolate or oblong-ovate, apex obtuse to rounded, paler beneath, thickly papery. Fls 1.5–3cm diam., star-shaped, infl. pyramidal to corymbiform; pet. 0.8–1.5cm, golden, narrowly oblanceolate to narrowly obovate. Summer. NW Turk., E Georgia. Z5.

H. yakusimanum invalid = *H. yakusimense*.

H. yakusimense Koidz. Perenn. or ann. herb, 3–8cm, tuft-forming, prostrate to ascending. Lvs 3–8mm, narrowly oblong to oblanceolate or obovate, rounded, thickly membranous, gland dots translucent or black. Fls 6–7mm diam., star-shaped, 1–3, term.; 6–7mm, bright yellow, tinged red, narrowly oblong, glands black or translucent. Summer. Jap. f. *yakusimense*. Lvs and pet. with superficial black glands. f. *lucidum* Y. Kimura. Lvs and pet. lacking superficial black glands. Z8.

Hyphaene Gaertn. Palmae. 10 stemless or shrubby or arborescent palms. St. dichotomously branched in larger sp., clothed with old lf bases, becoming bare. Lvs costapalmate. Infl. interfoliar. Fr. orange to brown, smooth, irregularly ovoid or obpyriform. Afr., Madag., Arabia, India, Sri Lanka. Z10.

H. coriacea Gaertn. DOUM PALM. St. to 5m, solitary or suckering, dichotomously branching in one plane. Lvs to 0.9m diam., grey-green to glaucous, waxy and sparsely black-scaly; petioles coarsely spiky. Fr. 3–2.5–6×4cm, brown, fibrous. Somalia to Moz., S Afr., Madag.

H. crinita Gaertn. ILALA; MLALA. St. to 10m, suckering or clumped. Lvs to 1.2m diam., grey-green margins of seg. white-hairy, sinuses with fil.; petioles armed with black, ascending spines. Fr. to 6.3cm diam., hard, brown. S Afr.

H. natalensis Kuntze = *H. coriacea*.

H. thebaica (L.) Mart. GINGERBREAD PALM. St. branching, frequently clothed with persistent lf bases above. Lvs erect, and rigid, grey-green; petioles coarsely spiny. Fr. orange-brown, orange, tasting of gingerbread. N Afr.

Hypocalymma Endl. Myrtaceae. 13 shrubs. Fls axill., paired or in clusters; cal. 5-lobed; pet. 5, broadly obovate or orbicular, spreading; sta. numerous, not exceeding pet. W Aus. Z9.

H. angustifolium Endl. WHITE MYRTLE. Dwarf to small shrub. Br. many, glab. 4-sided, somewhat red when young. Lvs 1–4cm, narrow-linear, semi-terete or 3-angled, channelled above, glab., pointed. Fls to 0.8cm diam., white maturing to deep pink or always white or cream, in axill. pairs. var. *densiflorum* Benth. Habit compact. Lvs small. Fl. heads crowded, almost spike-like.

H. boroniaceum F. Muell. ex Benth. = *H. speciosum*.

H. cordifolium (Lehm.) Schauer. Dwarf to small shrub. Young st. 4-sided, tinged red. Lvs 0.4–1.3cm, broadly to narrowly orbicular-cordate, or nearly triangular, glab., margins revolute, wavy, ciliate, apex pointed. Fls 0.4–1cm diam., white, axill., solitary or 2–3. 'Golden Veil': lvs variegated cream.

H. hypericifolium Benth. = *H. myrtifolium.*

H. myrtifolium Turcz. Small shrub. Young st. tinged red, somewhat 4-angled, glab. Lvs 2–3cm, elliptic to ovate, glab., margins revolute and faintly toothed or fringed, axpex ± blunt. Fls *c*1.5cm diam., white to cream, axill., clustered, with a strong spicy fragrance.

H. puniceum C. Gardn. LARGE MYRTLE. Small shrub. Young st. pale lime green, glab. Lvs 1–2.5cm, linear, erect, 3-sided, usually channelled with small hooked point. Fls to *c*2cm diam., deep pink, solitary, axill., spicily fragrant.

H. robustum Endl. SWAN RIVER MYRTLE. Dwarf to small shrub. Br. ascending, twiggy, glab. Lvs 1–2.5cm, linear, ascending 3-sided, usually channelled above, grey-green, glab., gland., with small hooked point. Fls to *c*2cm diam., deep pink, solitary, axill., spicily fragrant.

H. speciosum Turcz. Dwarf shrub. Young st. tinged red. Br. 4-sided, glab. Lvs to 1.5cm, orbicular-cordate, often tinged red in winter, glab., blunt. Fls *c*1cm diam., deep pink, axill., clustered on pendent stalks, spicily fragrant.

H. strictum Schauer. Dwarf shrub. Br. upright, twiggy, glab. Lvs 0.7–1.5cm, linear, 3-angled, erect, glab., pointed or blunt. Fls *c*6mm diam., pale to mid-pink, axill., paired, with slight spicy fragrance. var. *pedunculata* Benth. Br., lvs and fl. stalks more slender.

H. xanthopetalum F. Muell. Dwarf to small shrub. Young growth densely hairy. Br. ascending to arching. Lvs 1–2cm, narrow-oblong to almost obovate, margins fringed, apex pointed to slighly blunt. Fls *c*12mm diam., yellow, axill., paired, fragrant. Sometimes offered as *H. tetrapterum*, which has glab. br. and lvs.

Hypocalyptus Thunb. Leguminosae (Papilionoideae). 3 everg. shrubs or trees. Br. dark red-brown, smooth, grooved, 3-foliolate. Fls pea-like in term. rac. S Afr. (Cape). Z9.

H. obcordatus Thunb. = *H. sophoroides.*

H. sophoroides (Bergius) Druce Shrub or small tree to 4m. Br. downy at tips. Lfts 9–30×6.5–18mm, apex blunt or broadly refuse, apiculus to 1.5mm, sharp to awl-shaped, base narrowly cuneate. Rac. spicate and bluntly pyramidal, becoming ovoid; cor. purple, standard with yellow basal spot, circular, 11–13.5×11–15mm. Cape Prov.

Hypochoeris L. CAT'S EAR. Compositae. *c*50 ann. and perenn. herbs, with milky sap. Lvs in basal rosettes, occas. cauline. Cap. scapose, solitary or several; flts pink, yellow or white, outer sometimes with a green or red dors. stripe. Eur., N Afr., S Amer., nat. N US.

H. lanata Dusén. Perenn. to 12cm. Lvs *c*8cm, linear-lanceolate, pinnatifid, lanate. Cap. solitary or few, to 2.5cm diam.; phyllaries linear-lanceolate, sometimes tomentose below; flts pink or white. Patagonia.

H. maculata L. Perenn. to 35cm. Lvs to 22cm, occas. cauline, elliptic to ovate or obovate, entire to dentate, often streaked dark purple, glab. to hispid. Cap. to 4.5cm diam.; phyllaries setose-hispid; flts pale yellow. Eur.

H. meyeniana (Walp.) Griseb. Perenn. to 1m. Lvs oblanceolate to spathulate, lobed or coarsely dentate, glabrate or slightly hirsute, sessile, ciliate. Cap. solitary; phyllaries ovate or oblong-lanceolate, glab. or with stiff hairs below; flts yellow. Andes of Peru, Arg.

H. radicata L. SPOTTED CAT'S EAR. Perenn. to 60cm. Lvs to 25cm, oblong to elliptic or oblanceolate, hispid, dentate to pinnatifid. Cap. to 3cm diam.; phyllaries glab. or setose on midvein; flts bright yellow. Eurasia, N Afr., widely nat.

H. uniflora Vill. Perenn. to 45cm. Lvs to 22cm, oblong-lanceolate to oblanceolate, pubesc., ciliate, toothed. Cap. solitary, to 6cm diam.; outer phyllaries densely tomentose to hispid; flts golden-yellow. C Eur. to Russia (mts).

Hypocyrta Mart.

H. nummularia Hanst. = *Nematanthus gregarius.*

Hypodematium Kunze. Dryopteridaceae ·(Athyriaceae). 3 rupestral ferns. Rhiz. short-creeping. Fronds 3–4-pinnate to -pinnatifid, thin-textured and herbaceous, occas. gland., pubesc. to bristly on veins. Trop. Afr., Asia. Z10.

H. crenatum (Forssk.) Kuhn. Stipes to 30cm. Fronds to 33×30cm, 4-pinnate to -pinnatifid, arched, ovate to deltoid, densely bristly, pinnae to 22cm, ovate or deltoid to oblong, pinnules to 2×1cm, seg. oblong, obtuse, notched. Trop. Afr., Asia (China to Malaysia).

Hypoderris R. Br. Dryopteridaceae. 1 terrestrial or epilithic fern. Rhiz. long-creeping. Stipes to 40cm. Fronds to 45×20cm, suberect, simple, lanceolate to oblong, apex narrowly acute, subcordate to hastately lobed at base, thin-textured, scaly. Tropica Amer. Z10.

H. brownii Hook.

→*Woodsia.*

Hypoestes Sol. ex R. Br. Acanthaceae. 40 perenn. herbs and everg. shrubs. Fls solitary or clustered in upper axils; cal. lobes 5; cor. bilabiate, tube slender, exceeding cal., upper lip erect, 3-lobed, lower lip entire. S Afr., Madag., SE Asia. Z9.

H. aristata R. Br. RIBBON BUSH. Everg. shrubby perenn., erect to 1m. Lvs to 8cm, ovate, downy. Fls to 2.5cm, deep pink to rosy purple, sometimes lined or spotted mauve or white within. S Afr.

H. phyllostachya Bak. POLKA DOT PLANT; MEASLES PLANT; FLAMINGO PLANT; FRECKLE FACE; PINK DOT. Everg. subshrub to 1m. St. slender, dark green, downy. Lvs to 5cm, ovate, softly downy, dark green spotted pink to purple-red. Fls to 1cm, magenta to lilac. 'Splash': lf. spots pink, larger showier. 'Carmina': lvs bright red. 'Purpuriana': lvs plum. 'Wit': lvs marbled white.

H. sanguinolenta hort. non (Van Houtte) Hook. f. = *H. phyllostachya.*

Hypolepis Bernh. Dennstaedtiaceae. 40–45 terrestrial ferns. Rhiz. long-creeping. Stipes distant, erect. Fronds 2–4-pinnate or -pinnatifid. Trop. and subtrop. Z10.

H. anthriscifolia (Schldl.) Presl = *H. sparsisora.*

H. aspera (Kaulf.) Presl = *H. sparsisora.*

H. distans Hook. Fronds to 40×20cm, 2–3-pinnate or -pinnatifid, ovate or deltoid to lanceolate, leathery, pinnae to 12×3cm, distant, ovate to lanceolate, narrowly acute, pinnules to 15×5mm, distant, lanceolate to oblong, seg. to 2mm, ovate or deltoid to oblong, toothed; rachis glab. or sparsely pubesc.; stipes to 20cm, red-brown. NZ.

H. mexicana Liebm. = *H. repens.*

H. millefolium Hook. Fronds to 45×25cm, 3–4-pinnate, ovate to deltoid, membranous, pinnae to 25×10cm, petiolate, distant, ovate to oblong, narrowly acute, secondary pinnae to 6×2cm, approximate to imbricate, ovate to oblong, attenuate, pinnules to 10×4mm, ovate to oblong, seg. 5mm, deeply toothed; rachis sparsely pubesc.; stipes to 25cm, brown. NZ.

H. petrieana Carse = *H. punctata.*

H. punctata (Thunb.) Mett. Fronds to 40×25cm (occas. to 2m), 2–3-pinnate, ovate to deltoid, leathery, densely pubesc., pinnae to 15×8cm, distant ovate to oblong, narrowly acute, pinnules to 4×1cm, ovate to oblong, subacute to obtuse, seg. to 5×2mm, oblong, obtuse, entire or toothed to undulate; rachis pubesc.; stipes to 15cm, straw-coloured to brown. NZ.

H. repens (L.) Presl. Fronds sprawling, to 4×1m, 3-pinnate or -pinnatifid, deltoid to oblong, attenuate, sparsely pubesc., pinnae to 75×35cm, ovate or deltoid to oblong, narrowly acute, pinnules to 15×6cm, lanceolate to oblong, narrowly acute, seg. notched to lobed; rachis sometimes spiny; stipes to 1m, straw-coloured to brown. Trop. Amer.

H. rugulosum (Labill.) J. Sm. Fronds to 80×50cm, erect, 2–3-pinnate, ovate to lanceolate, leathery, ± pubesc., pinnae to 15×4cm or more, distant, ovate or deltoid to lanceolate, narrowly acute, pinnules to 5×2cm, ovate to lanceolate to oblong, seg. to 4mm, deltoid to oblong, entire to toothed, occas., ciliate; rachis tuberculate; stipes to 15cm, brown. Trop. Amer., Trop. Asia, Afr., Aus. and NZ.

H. sparsisora (Schräd.) Kuhn. Fronds to 2m, erect, 3–4-pinnate or -pinnatifid, glab. to sparsely pubesc. on veins, pinnae to 1m, ovate to deltoid, pinnules distant, lanceolate, seg. to 1cm, oblong, notched to lobed; rachis glab.; stipes to 1m, straw-coloured. Trop. Afr. (Zaire, Kenya, to S Afr.), Madag.

H. tenuifolia (Forst. f.) Bernh. Fronds to 90×60cm, 3–4-pinnate or -pinnatifid, deltoid, leathery to membranous, pinnae to 50×25cm, ovate or lanceolate to oblong, acute, secondary pinnae to 10×5cm, ovate or lanceolate to oblong, acute, pinnules to 10×5mm, oblong, obtuse, seg. to 2mm, oblong, obtuse, entire or toothed; rachis pubesc.; stipes to 50cm, straw-coloured to brown. Aus., NZ, Polyn.

→*Cheilanthes, Dicksonia* and *Lonchitis.*

Hypoxis L. STAR GRASS. Hypoxidaceae. 150 cormous perenn. herbs. Lvs basal, sheathing, conduplicate, midrib pronounced. Fls. racemose or solitary, scapose; tep. 6, outer 3 wider than inner, outside hairy. N Amer., Afr., Aus., Trop. Asia. Z9 unless specified.

H. angustifolia Lam. Lvs 6–12, 10–15×3.75–5cm, grass-like, sparsely pilose to glab. Peduncles 5–15cm, 2-fld. S Afr.

H. baurii Bak. = *Rhodohypoxis baurii*.

H. biflora Bak. = *H. angustifolia*.

H. capensis (L.) Druce. WHITE STAR GRASS. Glab. Lvs 10–30×1cm. Fls solitary on 5–25cm st.; tep. 1–3cm, white or yellow with purple basal spots. Spring–summer. S Afr.

H. colchicifolia Bak. Lvs 30–60×3–5cm, leathery, ribbed, hairless. Infl. 10–12 fls, in lf axils; tep. to 1cm diam., densely hairy outside, yellow. Spring–summer. S Afr. (Natal, Transvaal).

H. decumbens L. Lvs 7.5–30×0.2–1.3cm, sparsely pilose to glab. Peduncles 1–4 fld, 5–15cm, tep. to 1cm, lanceolate, acute, yellow, green and pilose dorsally. Americas.

H. elata Schult. = *H. capensis*.

H. elata sensu Hook. f., non Schult. = *H. hemerocallidea*.

H. erecta L. = *H. hirsuta*.

H. goetzei Harms. Lvs 6–12×2–3.5cm, ovate to lanceolate, glab. above, fringed on margin and main vein beneath. Fls 5–12 per rac.; tep. to 1.5cm, pale yellow lanceolate, hirsute outside.

H. hemerocallidea Fisch., Mey. & Avé-Lall. Lvs 45–60×3–5cm, ribbed, leathery, veins and margins hairy. Infl. 6–12 fld, racemose; tep. to 1.6cm, yellow; outer 3 hairy outside. Spring–summer. S Afr.

H. hirsuta (L.) Cov. Lvs to 30cm×1cm, ribbed, hairy. Scape densely hairy; 3–7fld; tep. to 1cm, outer 3 hairy outside, yellow. Spring–summer. E N Amer. Z5.

H. hygrometrica Labill. GOLDEN WEATHER GRASS; GOLDEN STAR. Lvs 6–15cm, filiform, sparsely hairy outside. Infl. solitary or a 2–3-fld corymbose rac.; tep. to 1.5cm, yellow, glab. or slightly hairy. Spring–summer. SE Aus.

H. latifolia Hook. non Wight = *H. colchicifolia*.

H. leptocarpa (Engelm. and A. Gray) Small. Closely resembles *H. hirsuta*. Lvs to 8×1.5cm, almost glab., thin, flaccid. Scape pubesc., 1–3-fld; inner 3 tep. linear-lanceolate, to 0.8cm. Spring–summer. SE US.

H. mexicana Roem. & Schult. = *H. decumbens*.

H. micrantha Pollard. Resembles *H. hirsuta*, differs in lvs 2–6mm wide; infl. 1–2-fld. SE N Amer.

H. multiceps Buchinger. Lvs 15–30×1.9–2.5cm, rigid, leathery, striate, white-setose. Peduncles 7.5–15cm, 2–4-fld, hispid; to 1.9cm, yellow, densely villous outside. S Afr.

H. neocanaliculata (Garside) Geer. Resembles *H. capensis*, differs in lvs rounded in section, midrib 0; perianth orange, basal spot not iridescent. Spring–summer. S Afr. (Cape).

H. nitida Verdoorn. Lvs 18–23×1–2cm, in 3 vertical ranks, erect, becoming arcuate, then twisted, shiny, white ciliate. Peduncle to 15cm, grey pubesc. to 12-fld; tep. to 2×1.2cm, oblong-ovate, outer 3 green and hairy outside, inner 3 chrome-yellow with green keel. S Afr.

lets sessile, 1–4 clustered per joint, 1–4-fld. N Amer., N India, China, NZ.

H. patula Moench. St. flimsy. Lf blades to 1.5cm wide. Pan. arching to 15cm; spikelets usually paired, to 1.5cm; awns to 4cm. Summer. N Amer. Z4.

Hyuga-giboshi *Hosta kikutii*.

H. platypetala Bak. = *Rhodohypoxis baurii* var. *platypetala*.

H. rooperi T. Moore. Lvs 12–18, 30–45cm, lanceolate, leathery, white-pilose above. Infl. a corymbose rac.; pet. to 2cm, oblong or lanceolate, dorsally villous. S Afr.

H. stellata (Thunb.) L. f. = *H. capensis*.

→*Spiloxene*.

Hypsela C. Presl. Campanulaceae. 4 small, prostrate perenn. herbs. Cor. tubular, exceeding cal. lobes, lobes 5, acuminate, forming a slightly bilabiate limb. S Amer., NZ, Aus. Z8.

H. longiflora (Hook. f.) Benth. & Hook. f. = *H. reniformis*.

H. reniformis (Kunth) C. Presl. St. to 5cm, creeping, forming mats. Lvs to 1cm, crowded, elliptic to reniform, entire. Fls small, solitary, pedicellate, white suffused pink, veined carmine, yellow punctate at base. S Amer. 'Greencourt White': lvs bright green; fls white.

Hyssop *Hyssopus officinalis*.

Hyssopus L. Labiatae. 10 aromatic perenn. herbs or dwarf shrubs. Infl. a sparsely flowered, secund spike; cal. tubular, 15-veined, teeth 5, equal; cor. bilabiate, upper lip erect, lower lip 3-lobed with middle lobe largest and notched. S Eur. to C Asia.

H. aristatus Godron = *H. officinalis* ssp. *aristatus*.

H. officinalis L. HYSSOP. St. erect to 60cm. Lvs to 5×1cm, aromatic, mid-green, linear-lanceolate, slightly revolute, glab. Spike slender; bracts linear; cor. to 12mm, violet or blue, occas. white. Late summer. S & E Eur., widely nat. Eur. and US. ssp. *aristatus* (Godron) Briq. Bracts awned. France, Spain, Balk. 'Albus': fls white. 'Grandiflorus': fls large. 'Purpurascens' ('Ruber'): fls deep red. 'Roseus': fls rose pink. 'Sissinghurst': habit dwarf and compact. Z3.

H. officinalis ssp. *pilifer* (Griseb. ex Pantl.) Murb. = *H. officinalis* ssp. *aristatus*.

Hystrix Moench. BOTTLE-BRUSH GRASS. Gramineae. 6 perenn. grasses. Lf blades flat, arching, linear, flimsy; ligules papery, translucent. Fls in a narrow, spike-like, loose, bristly rac.; spike-

I

Iberis L. CANDYTUFT. Cruciferae. 30 ann. or perenn. herbs and subshrubs. Lvs linear or obovate, entire or pinnatisect. Fls 4-merous, sometimes fragrant, in corymbs or (rarely) rac.; outer 2 pet. larger than inner, white or purple. S Eur., W Asia. Z7 unless specified.

I. acutiloba Bertol. = *I. odorata.*

I. amara L. Ann., 15–40cm. St. erect, branching. Lvs lanceolate, entire or toothed. Fls white or purple-white. Summer. A variable sp., much cultivated. W Eur.

I. bernardiana Gren. & Godron. Ann. or bienn., about 15cm. Lvs spathulate or linear-oblong, lobed, in compact rosettes. Fls pink-violet. Pyren.

I. cappadocica DC. = *Bornmuellera cappadocica.*

I. carnosa Willd. Similar to *I. pruitii* except st. somewhat tortuous. Fls purple-white in domed clusters 5cm diam. Early summer. Pyren. to Sicily.

I. contracta Pers. Prostrate subshrub, to 15cm. Lvs linear, toothed. Fls white. Late spring. Spain.

I. crenata Lam. Erect ann., to 30cm, br. straight and bare. Lvs spathulate to linear, finely toothed. Corymb convex; fls white. Summer. C & S Spain.

I. gibraltarica L. Evergr. tufted subshrub, to 30cm. Lvs wedge-shaped, in rosettes, toothed near apex. Fls white often tinged pink or red. Summer. Gibraltar.

I. jordanii Boiss. = *I. pruitii.*

I. lagascana DC. = *I. pruitii.*

I. linifolia Loefl. Laxly tufted perenn. to 30cm. Lvs linear, fleshy, entire, or toothed. Fls pink-purple or white. Summer. Spain, Port., N Afr.

I. odorata L. Ann., 15–30cm. Lvs linear-spathulate, pinnatifid. Corymb flat, short-stalked; fls white. Greece to Syr.

I. oppositifolia Pers. = *Aethionema oppositifolium.*

I. pectinata Boiss. = *I. crenata.*

I. petraea Jordan = *I. carnosa.*

I. pinnata L. Ann. or bienn., 15–30cm. Br. long, bare. Lvs oblong-linear, pinnatisect. Fls fragrant, white-lilac. C & S Eur., Asia Minor.

I. pruitii Tineo. Perenn. or ann., subshrub, 3–15cm. Lvs in a rosette, obovate-spathulate, ± fleshy, entire to toothed. Fls white-lilac. Summer. Medit.

I. raynevallii Boiss. = *I. contracta.*

I. saxatilis L. Evergr. subshrub, 7–15cm. Lvs linear, almost cylindrical, fleshy, ciliate. Fls white, often tinged purple with age. Summer. Pyren. to Sicily. 'Pygmaea': habit shrub-like, compact; lvs needle-shaped; st. tall; fls white. Z6.

I. semperflorens L. Evergr. subshrub, to 80cm. Lvs narrow-obovate, somewhat fleshy. Fls fragrant, white. Winter. Sicily, It.

I. sempervirens L. Evergr., spreading subshrub, 20–30cm. Lvs oblong-spathulate. Fls white; corymb 4–5cm diam. Spring–summer. S Eur. 'Autumn Beauty': to 25cm; fls white, spring and autumn. 'Autumn Snow': fls white, spring and autumn. 'Climax': to 20cm; lvs deep green, spathulate. 'Compacta': habit v. dense. 'Finden': fls large, white. 'Little Gem' ('Weisser Zwerg'): mound-forming, compact, to 15cm; lvs linear; fls small, white; spring-flowering. 'Nana': habit erect, to 15cm; lvs narrow, lanceolate, dark green; fls pure white. 'Perfection': habit rounded, compact; fls abundant, long-lasting; vigorous. 'Purity': mound-forming, to 20cm. 'Snowflake' ('Schneeflocke'): mound-forming, low; lvs deep green; fls sparkling white, in spring. 'Snowmantle': fls pure white, abundant, long-lasting. 'Zwergeschneeflocke': mound-forming, low; lvs deep green; fls sparkling white, spring. Z4.

I. stylosa Ten. = *Thlaspi stylosum.*

I. taurica DC. Ann. or bienn., to 20cm. St. canescent. Lvs linear-spathulate. Fls in loose rac., white-lilac. Asia Minor.

I. tenoreana DC. = *I. carnosa.*

I. umbellata L. Ann. Lvs linear-lanceolate, toothed or entire. Fls in term. umbels, usually purple. Spring–summer. S Eur. Widely cultivated, available in a number of fl. colours.

Ibervillea Greene ex Small. Cucurbitaceae. 4 perenn. vines. St. often swollen at base. Tendrils simple. Lvs reniform to broadly ovate, deeply 3–5-lobed. ♂ fls yellow in rac., clusters, or solitary; ♀ fls solitary. Fr. ovoid to globose, brightly coloured. SW US and N Mex. Z10.

I. lindheimeri (A. Gray) Greene. WILD BALSAM; HIERBA-DE-VIBORA. St. slender, 2–4m. Lvs to 12cm, seg. 3–5, cuneate to

rhombic-ovate, toothed to lobed. Fr. globose, 25–35mm diam., orange-red. Summer. SW US and N Mex.

I. sonorae (S. Wats.) Greene. Differs from *I. lindheimeri*, in v. swollen caudex, lvs more deeply dissected, seg. coarsely sinuate-toothed. Summer. N Mex.

→*Sicydium.*

Ibicella Eselt. UNICORN PLANT; DEVIL'S-CLAW; ELEPHANT-TUSK; PROBOSCIS FLOWER. Pedaliaceae. 2 ann. herbs, aromatic, gland. Infl. term., racemose; cal. 5-parted to base; cor. tube short, funnelform-campanulate, 5-lobed; sta. 4. Capsule 2-valved with curved horns at apex, crested above. S Amer.

I. lutea (Lindl.) Eselt. YELLOW DEVIL'S CLAW. St. spreading, 30–60cm. Lvs 10cm, suborbicular. Fls few, 2.5cm, bright yellow, sometimes tinged orange or green, often red-spotted within, gland. without. Fr. oblong-ovoid, ribbed, 5cm, horns to 10cm. Summer. N Arg., S Braz., Parag., Urug.; nat. Calif., Aus. and S Afr.

→*Proboscidea.*

Ibo Coffee *Coffea zanguebariae.*

Iboza N.E. Br.

I. multiflorum (Benth.) E.A. Bruce = *Tetradenia riparia.*

I. riparium (Hochst.) N.E. Br. = *Tetradenia riparia.*

I. urticifolium (Bak.) E.A. Bruce = *Tetradenia riparia.*

Ibuki-giboshi *Hosta ibukiensis.*

ICACINACEAE Miers. 60/320. *Citronella.*

Icaco Cimarron *Cordia leucosebestena.*

Ice-cream Bean *Inga edulis.*

Icelandic Poppy *Papaver nudicaule.*

Ice Plant *Delosperma; Hylotelephinum spectabile.*

Ichant Papeda *Citrus ichangensis.*

Ichthyomethia P. Browne.

I. piscipula (L.) A. Hitchc. ex Sarg. = *Piscidia piscipula.*

Idesia Maxim. Flacourtiaceae. 1 decid. tree to 12m, habit tiered, spreading. Lvs to 20cm, ovate-cordate, acuminate, dark green, equalling red petiole. Fls green-yellow, apetalous, fragrant, ♂ 1.6cm diam. 2 × length ♀, in pendulous pan. to 30cm. Berries small, red, in clusters after lf fall. S Jap., Taiwan, C & W China, Korea.

I. polycarpa Maxim. var. **vestita** Diels. Young lvs tomentose beneath. Fr. dull rusty-red. Sichuan. Z5.

→*Polycarpa.*

Idria Kellogg.

I. columnaris Kellogg = *Fouquieria columnaris.*

Ifafa Lily *Cyrtanthus mackenii.*

Ilala *Hyphaene crinita.*

Ilama *Annona diversifolia.*

Ilang-ilang *Cananga odorata.*

Ilex L. HOLLY. Aquifoliaceae. 400 everg. and decid. trees, shrubs and climbers. Lvs simple, spiny, serrate or entire; stipules present. Fls regular, rarely ♂, small, solitary or in fascicles or cymes; sep. 4–8; pet. 3–8; sta. 4–8, adnate to pet.; ovary superior. Fr. a berry usually globose, with 2–20 pyrenes. Cosmop.

I. aestivalis Lam. = *I. decidua.*

I. × altaclarensis (hort. ex Loud.) Dallim. (*I. aquifolium × I. perado.*) Large everg. shrubs and trees to 20m, differing from *I. aquifolium* in more vigorous growth, often broader and larger lvs, fls and fr., and smaller spines, spination varies even on same plant. Gdn origin. Cvs: (*green-leaved*) 'Atkinsonii': st. purple-green; lvs to 10×5cm, broadly ovate, glossy dark green, spiny, corrugated; ♂. 'Balearica': st. green; lvs broadly ovate, to 9cm; free-fruiting, ♀, vigorous. 'Camelliifolia': st. tinged purple; lvs elliptic-oblong, dark glossy green, to 13cm, usually spineless; fr. scarlet. 'Hendersonii': vigorous; st. green; lvs oblong-ovate, dull green, to 11.5cm; fr. long-lasting, brown-red. 'Hodginsii' ('Shepherdii', 'Nobilis'): st. purple; lvs broadly ovate, glossy black-green, to 10cm; usually

♂; extremely robust. 'James G. Esson': st. purple; lvs ovate, to 9cm; free-fruiting. 'Jermyns': st. brown-green; lvs to 10cm, glossy green, ♂. 'Maderensis': st. green; lvs broadly ovate, dark glossy green, to 11cm; ♂, vigorous. 'Mundyi': st. green; lvs ovate-oblong, concave, dull green, to 10.5cm; ♂. 'Nigrescens': columnar; st. olive-green; lvs broadly ovate, often concave, to 9.8cm, not v. spiny; ♂. 'Purple Shaft': a sport from 'Balearica'; columnar; st. green-purple; lvs to 9cm, dark glossy green. 'Wilsonii': st. purple-green, lvs broadly ovate, glossy green, to 10.5cm, spiny; free-fruiting, vigorous. 'W.J. Bean': st. green, lvs ovate to oblong-ovate, undulate, spiny; ♀. (*golden-variegated*) 'Belgica Aurea' ('Silver Sentinel'): upright st. green with yellow streaks; lvs to 11cm, elliptic-lanceolate, flat, dark green, mottled, grey-green in centre, yellow irregular margin, few-spined; ♀. 'Cameliifolia Variegata': lvs 11.5cm, glossy, dark green stippled with light green, edged gold, some entirely gold. 'Golden King' ('King Edward VII'): lvs dark green in centre with broad bright golden margin, to 10.5cm; ♀. 'Lawsoniana': st. green streaked with yellow; lvs dark green splashed irregularly with gold and lighter green in centre, to 11cm; ♀. (*silver-variegated*) 'Howick': st. green; lvs dark green splashed with grey-green in centre, margin recurved, creamy-white, to 9cm; ♀. Z6.

I. ambigua (Michx.) Chapm. CAROLINA HOLLY; SAND HOLLY. Decid. shrub or small tree to 7m. Lvs 2–5cm, elliptic or obovate, acute, serrate. Fls solitary or in cymes, 4–5-merous, white. Fr. 4–7mm diam., red. US (coastal plains). Z7.

I. amelanchier M.A. Curtis. SARVIS HOLLY; SWAMP HOLLY. Decid. shrub to 2.5m. Lvs 5–9cm, oblong to ovate-lanceolate, entire or serrulate, tomentose. Fls solitary or in cymes, 4-merous, white. Fr. 8–10mm diam., dull velvety red. US (coastal plains). Z8.

I. aquifolium L. COMMON HOLLY; ENGLISH HOLLY. Everg. shrub or tree to 25m. Bark grey. Lvs 5.5–9.5cm, elliptic or ovate, dark glossy green, undulate, entire or spinose. Fls 4-merous, white or tinged pink. Fr. 6–11mm diam., red. S & W Eur., N Afr., W Asia. Cvs: (*green-leaved*) 'Alaska': hardy, compact; lvs spiny; ♀; berries plentiful, red. 'Amber': st. green; lvs elliptic, 6.5–7.5cm, often entire; ♀; fr. bronze-yellow. 'Angustifolia' ('Petit', 'Petite', 'Pernettiifolia'): st. green or purple; lvs lanceolate or lanceolate-ovate, 2–4.2cm, black-green, apex prolonged, weakly spined; ♂ or ♀; fr. red. 'Atlas': hardy; st. green; lvs oval, 6–7.3cm, spiny; ♂. 'Ciliata Major': open- and upright, st. green; lvs 6–6.5cm, ovate, dark green; marginal spines, long curved; ♀. 'Crassifolia' (LEATHERLEAF; SAW-LEAVED HOLLY): st. purple; lvs oblong, 4.2–5cm black-green, spines thickened; ♀; fr. red. 'Crispa' ('Contorta'): st. purple; lvs elliptic, 4–5.5cm, thickened and contorted, some spines; ♂. 'Ferox' (HEDGEHOG HOLLY): st. purple; lvs oval, 4–6cm, spiny, ♂. 'Fructu Luteo' (YELLOW-BERRIED HOLLY): fr. yellow. 'Bacciflava': is similar. 'Green Pillar': habit columnar, ♀. 'J.C. van Tol' ('Polycarpa'): v. hardy; st. dark purple; lvs elliptic, 6.2–7.5cm, bullate, black-green; ♀, parthenocarpic; fr. bright red. 'Pyramidalis': st. yellow-green; lvs 6–6.5cm; fertile. 'Pyramidalis Fructu Luteo': st. green; lvs mainly spineless; berries bright yellow. 'Pyramidalis': habit pendulous, ♀; fr. red. (*golden-leaved*) 'Aureamarginata': st. purple; lvs elliptic, 5–7cm, dark glossy green, margin narrow golden, spiny; ♀; fr. red. 'Aurifodina' ('Muricata'): st. tinged purple; lvs elliptic, 4.5–6cm, olive green with golden-yellow spiny margins, tawny in winter; ♀; fr. deep scarlet. 'Ferox Aurea' (GOLDEN HEDGEHOG HOLLY): lvs splashed gold. 'Flavescens' (MOONLIGHT HOLLY): st. purple-red; lvs 7–8.7cm, flushed yellow; ♀; fr. red. 'Gold Flash' ('Bosgold'): sport from 'J.C. van Tol' but lvs centrally blotched with gold, ♀. 'Golden Milkboy': st. tinged purple; lvs elliptic, 6–8.2cm centre heavily blotched yellow, spiny; ♂; tends to revert. 'Golden Queen' ('Aurea Regina'): st. green streaked cream; lvs broadly ovate, 6.5–8cm, margin broad, golden, spiny; ♂. 'Madame Briot': st. tinged purple; lvs broadly ovate, 8–9.5cm, margin bright golden, spiny; ♀; fr. scarlet. 'Myrtifolia Aureomaculata': dense and compact; st. purple-green; lvs 5–5.5cm, ovate, dark green with central golden splash, spines regular; ♂. 'Ovata Aurea': st. purple; lvs 4.5–6.5cm, ovate, thick, with gold margins and short spines. 'Watereriana' (WATERER'S GOLD): compact dense bush; st. green streaked with yellow; lvs elliptic, 4.5–6cm, grey-green central mottling with a broad yellow margin, spiny to non-spiny; ♂. (*silver-leaved*) 'Argentea Marginata' (SILVER MARGINED HOLLY): st. green streaked cream; lvs broadly ovate, 5.5–7.5cm, margins broad, cream, spiny, young lvs pink; ♀; berries red. 'Argentea Marginata Pendula' ('Perry's Weeping Silver'): pendulous; st. purple, lvs elliptic, 5.5–8cm, margin broad creamy, spiny, young lvs pink; ♀; fr. red. 'Ferox Argentea' (SILVER HEDGEHOG HOLLY): as 'Ferox', but margins cream; ♂. 'Handsworth New Silver': st. purple; lvs oblong-elliptic, 7–9.5cm, margin broad and creamy, spiny; ♀; fr. bright red.

'Silver Milkmaid' ('Argentea Media Picta'): st. green streaked yellow; lvs elliptic, 5–6cm, spiny with a large central silver splash; ♀; fr. scarlet. Tends to revert. 'Silver Queen' ('Argentea Regina'): small dense bush; st. purple; lvs elliptic, 4.5–6.5cm, broad creamy margin, spiny, young lvs pink; ♂. Z6.

I. aquifolium var. *altaclerensis* hort. ex Loud. = *I.* × *altaclerensis*.

I. aquifolium var. *caspia* Loes. = *I. colchica*.

I. aquifolium var. *caspia* f. *spinigera* Loes. = *I. spinigera*.

I. aquifolium var. *chinensis* Loes. = *I. centrochinensis*.

I. aquifolium var. *heterophylla* Ait. = *I. aquifolium*.

I. × *aquipernyi* Gable. (*I. aquifolium* × *I. pernyi*.) Everg. shrub or small tree to 6m. Lvs nearer *I. pernyi*, to 3.5cm apex prolonged, spines undulate. Fr. red. Gdn origin. Z7. 'Aquipern': lvs green, 5–7-spined; ♂. 'San José': lvs green, 5–9-spined; ♀; fr. red. Z6.

I. asiatica Spreng. = *I. integra*.

I. × *attenuata* Ashe. (*I. cassine* × *I. opaca*.) TOPAL HOLLY. Lvs 5–10cm, obovate-lanceolate, flat, light green, toothed near apex. Fr. red. S US. Z7. 'East Palatka': lvs obovate, few-spined; ♀; fr. red. 'Savannagh': to 2m; lvs nearly spineless; ♀; fr. bright red. 'Sunny Foster': slow-growing; lvs narrow, golden yellow; ♀; fr. bright red.

I. azorica Gand. = *I. perado* ssp. *azorica*.

I. balearica Desf. = *I. aquifolium*.

I. × *beanii* Rehd. (*I. dipyrena* × *I. aquifolium*.) Variable shrub or tree, to 7m. Lvs close to *I. dipyrena*, but shorter and broader. Gdn origin. Z7.

I. bessoni hort. = *I. integra*.

I. bioritsensis Hayata. Everg. shrub to 5m. Lvs ovate to rhomboid, 3–6.2cm, apex prolonged, sporadically spined. Fls 4-merous, creamy-white. Fr. 6–9cm diam., red. Burm., SW China, Taiwan. Z7. Name sometimes misapplied to *I. pernyi* var. *veitchii*. Sometimes mislabelled *I. ficoidea*.

I. bioritsensis var. *ciliospinosa* (Loes.) Comber = *I. ciliospinosa*.

I. buergeri Miq. Everg. tree, to 50m in the wild. Lvs ovate to lanceolate, 5–6.5×1.5–2.5cm, caudate-acuminate or acute with obtuse tip, serrate. Fls 4-merous, white. Fr. 4.5–6mm diam., red. Jap., E China. Z7.

I. californica Brandg. = *I. tolucana*.

I. canadensis Michx. non Weston = *Nemopanthus mucronatus*.

I. caroliniana (Walter) Trel. = *I. ambigua*.

I. caroliniana Mill. = *I. cassine*.

I. cassine L. non Walter. DAHOON. Everg. tree to 13m. Lvs oblong or oblanceolate, 5.6–15cm, acute or rounded, dark glossy green, midrib often pubesc., entire or few teeth near apex. Fls 4-merous, yellow-white. Fr. 5–6mm diam., red. SE US, Cuba. Z6. 'Loweii': fr. yellow. var. *angustifolia* Ait. Lvs smaller and narrower.

I. cassine Walter non L. = *I. vomitoria*.

I. cassine var. *myrtifolia* (Walter) Sarg. = *I. myrtifolia*.

I. castaneifolia hort. = *I.* × *koehneana* 'Chestnut Leaf'.

I. centrochinensis hort. non S.Y. Hu = *I. corallina*.

I. ciliospinosa Loes. Everg. shrub to 6m. Lvs elliptic-ovate, 4–5.5cm, acute, weakly spined, dull dark green. Fls 4-merous, white. Fr. 0.5–0.7 diam., red. W China. Z5.

I. colchica Pojark. Shrub-like, to 6m. Lvs elliptic-lanceolate or oblong-elliptic, 5–8cm, acute, often flat, glossy green, black in death, strongly spined. Fls 4-merous, white. Fr. 8–10mm diam., red. Bulg., Cauc., Turk. Z6.

I. collina Alexander. Decid. small tree to 4m. Lvs elliptic to obovate or broadly obovate, 3–7cm, acuminate, serrate. Fls 6-merous, white. Fr. 7–8mm diam., bright red. Virg. Z6.

I. corallina Franch. Variable. Tree to 12m. Lvs ovate-lanceolate or elliptic, 5–10.5cm, acuminate, serrate or weakly spined, v. spiny when young, glossy green. Fls 4-merous, white. Fr. 2–4mm diam., red. W & SW China. Z6.

I. coriacea (Pursh) Chapm. LARGE GALLBERRY. Everg. shrub to 3m. Lvs elliptic to obovate, 3.5–7cm, acute to shortly acuminate, crenate-serrate or entire. Fls 6–10-merous, white, Fr. 6–10mm diam., black. US. Z7.

I. cornuta Lindl. & Paxt. CHINESE HOLLY; HORNED HOLLY. Everg. shrub to 4m, habit dense, rounded. Lvs rectangular, 5–8cm, dull green, spines variable. Fls 4-merous, white. Fr. 8–10mm diam., red. China, Korea. 'Burfordii': round, to 4m; lvs with term. spine only; ♀; fr. red. 'Carissa': lvs v. glossy; ♀. 'Dazzler': compact and upright; fr. bright crimson; ♀. 'Dwarf Burford' ('Burfordii Nana'): dense compact habit to 2.5m; ♀; fr. dark red. 'O' Spring': upright growth, lvs grey-green blotched yellow and striped throughout, spiny; ♀; fr. red. 'Rotunda': compact spreading habit to 2m; ♀; fr. red. 'Willowleaf': habit dense and broad; lvs slightly twisted; ♀; fr. blood red. var. *fortunei* (Lindl.) S.Y. Hu. Fr. pedicels longer. Z6.

I. crassifolia Meerb. = *I. perado* ssp. *perado*.

I. crenata Thunb. BOX-LEAVED HOLLY; JAPANESE HOLLY. Everg. shrub or small tree, to 5m. Lvs ovate or elliptic, 1.5–3cm, acute, crenate, dark green, punctate beneath. Fls 4-merous, white. Fr.

about 5mm diam., glossy black. Sakhalin Is., Jap., Korea. 'Bad Zwischenahn': lvs grey-green, v. hardy. 'Bruns': compact growth; lvs grey-green; ♀; hardy. 'Chesapeake': habit pyramidal; lvs deep green, glossy, convex. 'Compacta': habit dwarf and compact, similar to 'Helleri' but slightly faster growing. 'Convexa' ('Bullata'): to 2.5m; st. purple-green; lvs puckered, glossy black-green, spines few; ♀; berries black. 'Glory': a compact globe; lvs small, deep green. 'Green Island': slow-growing and low-spreading; lvs deep green. 'Green Lustre': compact; lvs dark green. 'Helleri': low spreading shrub to 1.5m; st. green; lvs elliptic with few spines; ♀; fr. black. 'Hetzii': horizontal habit; lvs 1.3–2cm; ♀; fr. black. 'Ivory Hall': ♀; fr. yellow. 'Latifolia': shrub to small tree, to 6m; lvs oval, minutely toothed; ♀; fr. black. 'Mariesii': slow-growing, erect to 1.5m; lvs orbicular, crenate at apex; ♀; fr. black. 'Schwoebel's Compact': low-spreading dwarf to 1m; v. hardy. 'Stokes': dwarf; rounded dense habit; lvs tiny. (*variegated-leaved*) 'Golden Gem': compact growth; lvs suffused yellow; ♀ but rarely fls, best in full sun. 'Shiro-Fukurin': upright growth; lvs grey-green and cream; ♀; fr. black. 'Variegata' ('Aureovariegata', 'Luteovariegata'): to 4m; lvs spotted or blotched yellow; tends to revert. var. *paludosa* (Nak.) Hara. As type but prostrate. Z6.
I. crenata var. *nummularioides* (Lancaster) Lancaster = *I. crenata*. 'Mariesii'.
I. crenata f. *latifolia* (Goldr.) Rehd. = *I. crenata*. 'Latifolia'.
I. cyrtura Merrill. Everg. tree to 16m. Lvs oblong or elliptic-oblanceolate, 9–15cm, acuminate or falcate, serrate. Fls 4-merous, yellow-green, in downy pan. or subfascicles. Fr. 4–5mm diam., scarlet. Upper Burm., Bhutan, Yunnan. Z7.
I. dahoon Walter = *I. cassine*.
I. decidua Walter. POSSUM HAW; WINTERBERRY. Decid. shrub to 3.5m, rarely to 10m. Lvs oval or narrowly obovate, 2.5–8cm, blunt, crenate, often crowded on short spurs. Fls 4-merous, white. Fr. 4–9mm diam., orange. SE & C US. Z6.
I. decidua var. *longipes* (Chapm. ex Trel.) Ahles = *I. longipes*.
I. dimorphophylla Koidz. Everg. shrub to 1.5m. Lvs 1.3–2cm, ovate, entire with apical spine, juvenile foliage v. spiny. Fls 4-merous, white. Fr. 3mm diam., red. Liukiu Is. Z7.
I. dipyrena Wallich. HIMALAYAN HOLLY. Everg. tree to 15m. Lvs 5.6–11cm, oblong or elliptic, acute or shortly acuminate, entire or (juveniles) spinose, dull mid-green. Fls 4-merous, green white, occas. tinged purple. Fr. globose or elliptic, 6–7.5mm diam., red. E Himal., W China. Z7.
I. dubia var. *macropoda* (Miq.) Loes. = *I. macropoda*.
I. elliptica (Dallim.) Bean non HBK = *I. ×beanii*.
I. fargesii Franch. Everg. shrub to small tree, to 12m. Lvs coriaceous dull dark green. Fls 4-merous, white-green; ♂ in 3-fld branchlets, ♀ fasciculate, solitary. Fr. 4–7mm diam., scarlet. China. ssp. *fargesii* var. *fargesii*. Lvs 6.2–12.2cm, oblanceolate to oblong-elliptic, acuminate, rarely caudate or falcate, entire below or serrate throughout. Sichuan, Hubei, Yunnan. ssp. *fargesii* var. *brevifolia* S. Andrews. Shrub to 4m. Lvs 6–7.3cm, elliptic to elliptic-lanceolate, acuminate, spiny throughout or entire below. Hubei. ssp. *melanotricha* (Merrill) S. Andrews. Lvs 8.7–12×2.9–4cm, oblanceolate to oblong-elliptic, acuminate, finely serrate throughout. Burm., Yunnan, Tibet. Z7.
I. fortunei Lindl. = *I. cornuta* var. *fortunei*.
I. franchetiana Loes. = *I. fargesii* ssp. *fargesii* var. *fargesii*.
I. franchetiana sensu Comber pro parte = *I. fargesii* ssp. *melanotricha*.
I. fujisanensis Sakata = *I. pedunculosa*.
I. furcata Lindl. = *I. cornua*.
I. geniculata Maxim. Decid. shrub to 2.5m. Lvs 4–10cm, ovate to ovate-lanceolate, acuminate, serrate. Fls 5–6-merous, white. Fr. 4mm diam., brown-red on jointed pedicels. C Jap. Z6.
I. georgei Comber. Wide-spreading, dense shrub to 5m. Lvs 3–5cm, lanceolate or ovate, acuminate, weakly spined, coriaceous, dark glossy green. Fls 4-merous, green-yellow. Fr. elliptic-globose, 3–3.5mm diam., red. Upper Burm., Yunnan. Z8.
I. glabra (L.) A. Gray. GALLBERRY; INKBERRY. Everg., erect shrub to 3m. Lvs 2–5cm, narrowly obovate to oblanceolate, entire or a few teeth near apex, glossy green, punctate beneath. Fls 5–7 merous, white. Fr. 4–8mm diam., black. E N Amer. 'Compacta': v. hardy, slow-growing and compact; ♀; fr. black. 'Nigra': lvs dark claret in winter. 'Nana': dwarf. 'Nordic': v. hardy, dense and compact, to 120cm; lvs v. glossy. f. *leucocarpa* F.W. Woods. Fr. white. 'Ivory Queen': improved white-berried form. Z3.
I. goshiensis Hayata. Everg. small tree. Lvs 3–6cm, elliptic, acute or obtuse, entire. Fls 4-merous, green-white. Fr. 3.5mm diam., red. Jap., Liukiu Is. Z8.
I. hyrcana Pojark. = *I. spinigera*.
I. insignis Hook. f. non Heer = *I. kingiana*.
I. integra Thunb. Everg. shrub to 7m. Lvs 5–8cm, obovate or elliptic, obtuse, entire, dark glossy green. Fls 4-merous, creamy

yellow. Fr. 1cm diam., dark red. Jap., Liukiu Is., Korea, Taiwan. Z7.
I. integra var. *leucoclada* Maxim. = *I. leucoclada*.
I. intricata Hook. f. f. *intricata*. Prostrate everg. shrub to 1m. Twigs warty. Lvs 0.8–1.5cm, obovate-elliptic, serrate, glossy dark green. Fls 4-merous, crimson to pale chocolate. Fr. 3–5mm diam., bright red. Nepal, Bhutan, Sikkim, Burm., Yunnan. Z5.
I. intricata var. *oblata* W.E. Evans = *I. nothofagifolia*.
I. latifolia hort. non Thunb. = *I. ×koelieana*.
I. kingiana Cockerell. Everg. tree to 5.5m. Lvs 11–22cm, oblong, long-acuminate, slightly serrate or entire (juveniles v. spiny), coriaceous, glossy green. Fls 4-merous, green-yellow. Fr. 1cm diam., bright red in large clusters. E Himal., Yunnan. Z8.
I. ×koehneana Loes. (*I. aquifolium* ×*I. latifolia*.) Everg. tree to 7m. Lvs 8–14.5cm, oblong to elliptic, acute, glossy mid-green. Fls 4-merous, white. Fr. 6–6.5cm diam., bright red. Gdn origin. 'Chestnut Leaf': lvs yellow-green; ♂ and ♀. 'Chieftain': lvs light green; ♂. 'Jade': lvs black-green; ♂. 'Lassie': ♀. 'Ruby': lvs glossy, deep dark green with wavy margins; ♀. 'Wirt L. Winn': lvs dark green; ♀; fr. plentiful, bright red. Z7.
I. kusanoi Hayata. Decid. shrub or small tree. Lvs 4–6.5cm, ovate, obtuse or shortly acuminate, serrulate-serrate. Fls 4–6-merous, white. Fr. red. Liukiu Is., Taiwan. Z8.
I. laevigata (Pursh) A. Gray. SMOOTH WINTERBERRY. Differs from *I. verticillata* in its glab. lvs and longer fruiting pedicels. Fr. 5–8mm diam., orange-red. E US. f. *herveyi* Robinson. Fr. yellow. Z4.
I. latifolia Thunb. TARAJO. Everg. upright shrub to 7m. Lvs 8–18cm, oblong or ovate-oblong, obtuse or shortly acuminate, serrate, leathery, dark glossy green. Fls 4-merous, yellow-green. Fr. 7mm diam., orange-red. Jap., China. Z7.
I. laxiflora Lam. = *I. opaca* f. *xanthocarpa*.
I. leucoclada (Maxim.) Mak. Everg. shrub. Lvs 8–15cm, oblong or obovate-oblong, narrowly obtuse, entire or serrate in upper half. Fls 4-merous, creamy-white. Fr. 8–10mm diam., red. Jap. Z7.
I. longipes Chapm. ex Trel. Decid. shrub to small tree, to 7m. Lvs 4–6cm, elliptic to obovate, serrulate. Fls 4-merous, white. Fr. subglobose, 5–8mm diam., red. S Appalachians. f. *vantrompii* Brooks. Fr. yellow. Z6.
I. macrocarpa Oliv. Decid. tree to 17m. Branchlets spur-like. Lvs 7–11cm, elliptic or ovate-elliptic, acuminate, denticulate. Fls 5–8-merous, white. Fr. depressed globose 18cm diam., black. S & SW China. Z7.
I. macropoda Miq. Decid. tree to 13m. Branchlets spur-like. Lvs 4–7cm, ovate, acuminate, serrate. Fls 4–5-merous, green-white. Fr. 7mm diam., red. Jap., Korea, China. Z7.
I. maderensis Lam. = *I. perado* ssp. *perado*.
I. ×makino Hara. (*I. leucoclada* ×*I. rugosa*.) Differs from *I. rugosa* in its larger parts. Lvs 5–7cm, narrowly oblong, acute. Jap. Z7.
I. mariesii Veitch ex Dallim. = *I. crenata* 'Mariesii'.
I. melanotricha Merrill = *I. fargesii* ssp. *melanotricha*.
I. ×meserveae S.Y. Hu. (*I. aquifolium* ×*I. rugosa*.) Everg. shrub to 2m. Lvs often blue-green, spiny, resembling small-leaved *I. aquifolium*. Fls white to pink-white. Fr. red. Gdn origin. 'Blue Angel' ((*I. aquifolium* ×*I. rugosa*) ×*I. aquifolium*): slow-growing, compact; st. dark purple; lvs 4.3–4.7cm, elliptic, dark glossy green-blue; fls pink-white; ♀. 'Blue Boy': as 'Blue Girl' but ♂, sometimes sold as 'Blue Eagle'. 'Blue Girl': st. purple-green; lvs 3.8–4.6cm, ovate, dark glossy green-blue; fls white. 'Blue Maid': improved dense shrub to 5m. 'Blue Prince': improved form of 'Blue Boy'; st. tinged purple; lvs 4.5–6.2cm, ovate to oblong-elliptic, bright glossy green, slightly undulate or bullate; fls tinged-pink; ♂. 'Blue Princess' (*I. rugosa* ×*I. aquifolium*): improved form of 'Blue Girl' with larger, glossier foliage and a better fr. set. 'Blue Stallion': improved form of 'Blue Prince' with better branching. 'Goliath': st. green; lvs elliptic-lanceolate, 5.1–6.8cm, entire or finely spiny, matt green; fls ♀, white. Z6.
I. mollis A. Gray = *I. montana* var. *mollis*.
I. montana Torr. & A. Gray. MOUNTAIN HOLLY. Decid. shrub or tree to 12m. Lvs 6–10cm, ovate or oblong-lanceolate, acuminate, sharply serrate. Fls 4-merous, white. Fr. 8–12mm diam., orange-red. E US. var. *mollis* (A. Gray) Britt. Lvs pubesc. beneath. Z5.
I. montana var. *macropoda* (Miq.) Fern. = *I. macropoda*.
I. monticola A. Gray = *I. montana*.
I. myrtifolia Walter. MYRTLE HOLLY; MYRTLE DAHOON. Differs from *I. cassine* in its smaller, narrower lvs, 2–5×0.5–1.2cm and solitary fr. SE US. Z7.
I. nobilis Gumbl. = *I. kingiana*.
I. nothofagifolia Kingdon-Ward ('*nothofagacifolia*'). Everg. tree to 9m, br. horizontal. Lvs 1–2cm broadly ovate or orbicular, cuspidate, serrate or aristate, glossy dark green. Fls 4-merous, white. Fr. globose, 1.5–2cm diam., scarlet. NE Upper Burm.,

Assam, Yunnan. Z7.

I. oldhamii Miq. = *I. purpurea*.

I. opaca Ait. AMERICAN HOLLY. Everg. tree to 15m. Lvs 5–12cm, oblong to elliptic, with apical spine, spiny or entire, leathery matt green above. Fls 4-merous, creamy-white. Fr. 5–13mm diam., crimson. E & C US. Many cvs: of the ♀, some of the hardier cvs include the dense and compact 'Hedgeholly', 'Johnson' (selected for hardiness in colder climates) the slow-growing 'Old Faithful' and 'Waltemyer', and the large-berried 'Yule'. Males most noted for hardiness include the free-flowering 'Santa Claus' and 'Cobalt', one of v. few selections to survive −32°C in the winter of 1934. Notable dwarf females include the 120cm 'Cardinal Hedge' ('Cardinal Improved'), the red-berried 'Dupré', the low-spreading, yellow-berried 'Maryland Dwarf' and the slow-growing 'Salem Compact'. Fast-growing, vigorous selections include the ♀ 'Christmas Spray', 'Howard', 'Mentantico', 'Pride Berry', and the orchard tree 'St Ann' ('Saint Ann'). Fast-growing males include the profuse 'Silica King' and 'Dr T.B. Symons'. Several ♀ selections are noted for the profusion and colour of fr. 'Arden', a heavy-bearer, has berries turning from yellow to crimson. 'Boyle Thompson Xanthocarpa', 'Canary', 'Goldie', 'Marion', 'Morgan Gold' and 'Mrs Davies' are all noted for the profusion of their yellow fr. Profuse red fruiters include the intense red of 'Big Red', the dark-lvd. 'Delia Bradley', 'Jersey Princess' and 'Mamie Eisenhower', the orchard tree 'Elizabeth', 'Emily' (berries to 1.5cm diam.), and the crimson of 'Katz', 'Norfolk' and 'Perfection'. Noted for their lvs are 'Golden Fleece' (lvs flushed yellow in sun), 'Maxwell Point' (lvs unusually large), 'Victory' (lvs keeled, curved and dark green), 'Natalie Webster' and 'Jersey Knight' (lvs deep green). 'Mrs Santa' is a compact hedge holly and 'St Mary' ('Saint Mary') has become popular as a potplant at Christmas: it is an early fruiter, compact, with well-displayed berries. f. *xanthocarpa* Rehd. Fr. yellow. Z5.

I. paraguariensis A. St.-Hil. MATÉ; YERBA MATÁ; PARAGUAY TEA. Everg. tree, to 15m in the wild. Lvs 7.5–11cm, obovate to obovate-oblong, obtuse, serrate. Fls 4-merous, green-white. Fr. 4–5.5mm diam., red. S Amer. Z10.

I. pedunculosa Miq. Everg. tree to 10m. Lvs 4–8cm, ovate, acuminate, entire, dark glossy green. Fls 4–5-merous, white. Fr. 7–8mm diam., bright red, long-stalked. Jap., China, Taiwan. Z5.

I. pedunculosa f. *continentalis* Loes. = *I. pedunculosa*.

I. perado Ait. Everg. shrub or tree to 15m. Petioles often winged. Fls 4-merous, white or pink-white. Fr. red. ssp. *perado*. Lvs to 8cm, ovate or obovate, spathulate in cult., often spineless. Madeira. ssp. *azorica* (Loes.) Tutin. Shrub to 5m. Lvs to 6.6cm, orbicular or ovate, often spineless. Azores. ssp. *platyphylla* (Webb & Benth.) Tutin var. *platyphylla*. Lvs to 13cm, broadly ovate or oblong, somewhat spiny, hardier. Tenerife, Gomera. Z7.

I. perado 'Aurea' = *I.* ×*altaclerensis* 'Belgica Aurea' ('Silver Sentinel').

I. pernyi Franch. Everg. shrub to small tree, to 8.5m. Lvs 1.2–3.4cm, triangular, acuminate, 5-spined, squared at the base, dark glossy green. Fls 4-merous, tinged yellow. Fr. 4–7mm diam., red. C & W China. 'Accent': vigorous and conical, to 2m after 10 years; lvs thorny; ♂. 'Jermyns Dwarf': low arching growth; fr. red; ♀. var. *veitchii* Bean. Lvs larger and broader, 3.5–6cm, 3–5 spines per side. W China. Z5.

I. platyphylla Webb & Benth. = *I. perado* ssp. *platyphylla* var. *platyphylla*.

I. poneantha Koidz. = *I. kusanoi*.

I. pringlei Standl. Everg. shrub or tree. Lvs 4–6cm, ovate or elliptic, acuminate or abruptly acute, entire or sparsely spiny. Fls 6–7-merous, white. Fr. 6mm diam., red. Mex. Z8.

I. prinoides Ait. = *I. decidua*.

I. pubescens Hook. & Arn. Everg. pubesc. shrub to 3.5m. Lvs 2–5.5cm, elliptic or obovate-elliptic, upper half serrate. Fls 6–8-merous, purple-red to pink. Fr. 4mm diam., scarlet. S China, Taiwan. Z8.

I. purpurea Hassk. Everg. tree to 12m. Lvs 7–12cm, oblong-elliptic, acuminate, crenate, thin-textured. Fls 4–5-merous, lavender or red. Fr. ellipsoid, 6–8mm diam., glossy scarlet. Jap., China. Z8.

I. quercifolia Meerb. = *I. opaca*.

I. radicans Nak. = *I. crenata*. var. *paludosa*.

I. radicans var. *paludosa* Nak. = *I. crenata*. var. *paludosa*.

I. rosmarinifolia Lam. = *I. myrtifolia*.

I. rotunda Thunb. Everg. tree, to 23m in the wild. Lvs 5–8cm, elliptic to ovate, entire, thin. Fls 4–6-merous, white. Fr. ellipsoid, 6–8mm diam., red. Ryuku Is., Korea, China, Taiwan. Z7. 'Lord': habit conical; ♀. 'Romal': habit spreading, ♂. var. *microcarpa* (Lindl. ex Pax) S.Y. Hu. Fr. globose, 5mm diam.

I. rugosa F. Schmidt. Everg. prostrate shrub. Lvs 2–3.5cm, broadly lanceolate, entire, lustrous dark green. Fls 4-merous,

white. Fr. 5mm diam., red. Sakhalin Is., Kurile Is., Jap. 'Goliath Male': ♂, low-growing. Z3.

I. serrata Thunb. JAPANESE WINTERBERRY. Decid. shrub to 4m. Lvs 4–8cm, elliptic, acute to long-acuminate, serrulate, puberulous. Fls 4–6-merous, pink. Fr. 5mm diam., red. Jap., China. 'Koshobai': to 1m; fr. tiny, red. 'Leucocarpa': fr. white. 'Xanthocarpa': fr. yellow. var. *argutidens* (Miq.) Rehd. Branchlets and lvs glab. Z5.

I. sieboldii Miq. = *I. serrata*.

I. sikkimensis Kurz var. *coccinea* Comber. Everg. tree to 15m. Term. buds with large pubesc. bracts. Lvs 11–14cm, broadly oblong to oblong-lanceolate, acute to shortly acuminate, serrate. Fls 4-merous, white. Fr. 4mm diam., scarlet. N India, Bhutan, Sikkim, Yunnan. Z7.

I. spinigera (Loes.) Loes. Differs from *I. colchica* mainly in its pubesc. br., smaller undulate lvs and contorted spines. Iran and neighbouring C Asia. Z7.

I. stenocarpa Pojark. = *I. colchica*.

I. subtilis Miq. = *I. serrata*.

I. sugerokii Maxim. Differs from *I. yunnanensis* mainly in its entire lvs on lower half and glab. branchlets. var. *longipedunculata* (Maxim.) Mak. Everg. shrub to 5m. Lvs 2–4cm, ovate-elliptic, acute to acuminate, serrate above only, glossy green. Fls 4–6-merous, white. Fr. 5–6mm diam., red, stalks to 3.5cm. Jap. var. *brevipedunculata* (Maxim.) S.Y. Hu. Fr. stalks to 2cm. Jap., Taiwan. Z7.

I. tolucana Hemsl. Everg. tree, to 15m in the wild. Lvs 5–7cm, lanceolate to oblanceolate, serrulate, lustrous green. Fls 4-merous, white. Fr. 4–6mm diam., red. Mex., El Salvador, Hond. Z9.

I. verticillata (L.) A. Gray. BLACK ALDER; WINTERBERRY. Decid., suckering shrub to 2m. Lvs 4–10cm, obovate or lanceolate, acuminate, serrate, bright green, pubesc. beneath. Fls 4–7 merous, white. Fr. 4–5mm diam., red. E N Amer. 'Red Sprite': dwarf fruits large red. 'Oosterwijk': fr. red, 8–9mm diam., fruiting br. sold for cut-flower trade. 'Winter Red': to 3m; lvs darker green than type, bronze in autumn; fr. red, long-lasting. 'Xmas Cheer': upright growth; fr. red. f. *aurantiaca* (Mold.) Rehd. Fr. orange. f. *chrysocarpa* Robinson. Fr. yellow. Z3.

I. vomitoria Ait. YAUPON. Everg. shrub to small tree, to 6m. Lvs 1–4.5cm, ovate or elliptic, obtuse, crenate, dark glossy green. Fls 4-merous, white. Fr. 5–6mm diam., scarlet. SE US, Mex., nat. Bermuda. 'Nana': dwarf to 90cm; lvs glossy, fr. red. 'Otis Miley': lvs small; fr. yellow. 'Pendula': br. pendulous; fr. translucent red. 'Pyramidalis': pyramidal and compact in growth. 'Stoke's Dwarf': dense, spreading, mound-forming dwarf; lvs v. rich green. 'Straughan's Dwarf': shrubby dwarf; lvs dark green. 'Tricolour': lvs dark green with broad cream margins. 'Virginia Dare': fr. orange. 'Wiggin's Yellow': lvs light gold. f. *pendula* Foret & Solymosy. Growth pendulous. Z7.

I. ×*wandoensis* T. Dudley. (*I. integra* ×*I. cornuta*.) Natural hybrid, more like *I. cornuta* but foliage variable. Korea. Z7.

I. wilsonii Loes. Everg. tree, to 10m in the wild. Lvs 3–6.5cm, ovate or obovate-oblong, acuminate to caudate, blunt-tipped, glossy green. Fls 4-merous, white, entire. Fr. 4mm diam., red. C, W & E China, Taiwan. Z8.

I. yunnanensis Franch. Everg. shrub to 4m. Branchlets puberulous. Lvs 2–3.5cm, ovate or ovate-lanceolate, crenate to serrulate, glossy dark green. Fls 4-merous, white, rarely red or pink. Fr. 5–6mm diam., red. Upper Burm., W China. Z6.

Further hybrids. 'Apollo' (*I. serrata* ×*I. verticillata*): decid., ♂. 'Autumn Glow' (*I. serrata* ×*I. verticillata*): decid., ♀, berries large, dark red. 'Brighter Shines' (*I. cornuta* ×*I. pernyi*): everg., ♀, berries red. 'Brilliant' (*I. aquifolium* ×*I. ciliospinosa*): lvs to 4.5×2cm, dull green, sharp-thorned; fr. red. 'China Boy' (*I. rugosa* ×*I. cornuta*): fast-growing and compact, to 2×2.5m after 10 years; ♂, heavy pollinator; hardy to −30°C. 'China Girl' (*I. rugosa* ×*I. cornuta*): similar to *I.* 'China Boy' in habit and hardiness; ♀; fr. bright red, profuse. 'Clusterberry' (*I.* 'Nellie R. Stevens' ×*I. leucoclada*): everg., ♀, berries red. 'Drace' (*I. cornuta* ×*I. pernyi*): everg., ♀, berries red. 'Dragon Lady' (*I. pernyi* ×*I. aquifolium*): upright and spreading in growth; lvs glossy and spiny; ♀; fr. red. 'Dr Kassab' (*I. cornuta* ×*I. pernyi*): everg., ♀, berries red. 'Edward Nosal' (*I. pernyi* ×*I. aquipernyi*): everg., ♂. 'Elegance' (*I. integra* ×*I. pernyi*): narrow and conical, to 2×0.6m after 10 years; ♀; fr. red. 'Foster No. 2' (*I. cassine* var. *angustifolia* ×*I. opaca*): pyramidal, to 7m; ♀; fr. red. 'Foster No. 4': ♂ pollinator for ♀ Foster hollies. 'Good Taste' (*I. cornuta* ×*I. pernyi*): everg., ♀, berries red. 'Harry Gunning' (*I. cornuta* ×*I. ciliospinosa*): everg., ♂. 'Howard Dorsett' (*I. cornuta* ×*I. ciliospinosa*): everg., ♀. 'Indian Chief' (*I. cornuta* ×*I. pernyi*): everg., ♀, berries red. 'John T. Morris' (*I. cornuta* ×*I. pernyi*): everg., ♂. 'Lydia Morris' (*I. cornuta* ×*I. pernyi*): everg., ♀, berries red. 'Oriole' (*I. myrtifolia* ×*I. opaca*): everg., ♀; fr. red. 'Nellie R. Stevens'

(*I. aquifolium* ×*I. cornuta*): everg. ♀, berries orange-red. 'Rock Garden' (*I.* ×*aquipernyi* ×*I.* 'Accent'): everg., ♀, berries bright red. 'September Gem' (*I. ciliospinosa* ×*I.* ×*aquipernyi*): everg., ♀, berries red. 'Shin Nier' (*I. opaca* ×*I. cornuta*): everg., ♀, 'Sparkeberry' (*I. serrata* ×*I. verticillata*): decid., ♀, berries scarlet. 'Tanager' (*I. myrtifolia* ×*I. opaca* F2): everg., ♀, berries red. 'Virgo' (*I. cornuta* ×*I. pernyi*): everg., ♀, berries red. 'Washington' (*I. cornuta* ×*I. pernyi*): everg., ♀, berries dark red. 'William Cowgill' (*I. cornuta* ×*I. ciliospinosa*): everg., ♀, berries dark red.
→*Cassine, Nemopanthus, Othera* and *Prinos.*

Iliamna Greene. WILD HOLLYHOCK. Malvaceae. 7 perenn. herbs or subshrubs. Lvs palmately lobed. Fls solitary or in interrupted spikes or rac.; epical. seg. 3; pet. 5, clawed; staminal column, tubular, hirsute. N Amer.
I. acerifolia Nutt. ex Torr. & A. Gray = *I. rivularis.*
I. remota Greene. Herb to 1.8m, hairy. Lvs 5–20cm, lobes 3–5–7. Fls to 2.5cm diam., pale rose-mauve. Ill. Z5.
I. rivularis (Douglas) Greene. MOUNTAIN HOLLYHOCK. Herb to 1.8m, glab. or glabrate. Lvs 5–15cm, lobes 3–7. Fls 2.5–5cm diam., white or pink. BC, Oreg., Calif., Mont., Colorado. Z3.
→*Shaeralcea.*

Illawara Cypress-pine *Callitris muelleri.*
Illawarra Flame Tree *Brachychiton acerifolius.*
Illawarra Palm *Archontophoenix cunninghamiana.*

Illecebrum L. CORAL NECKLACE. Caryophyllaceae. 1 glab. ann. Taproot slender. Br. to 20cm, thin, decumbent. Lvs obovate. Fls in axill. clusters, with silvery bracts, forming shining white whorls; pet. white, shorter than sep. Summer. Macaronesia and W Eur., esp. W Medit. and Atlantic coastal areas.
I. verticillatum L.

Illicium L. ANISE TREE. Illiciaceae. *c*40 anise-scented glab. everg. shrubs and small trees. Lvs alt. or in pseudowhorls, entire, thick, glossy. Fls axillary, solitary, or clustered, cauliflorous; seg. to 30, petaloid, unequal; sta. 5–20, thick. Fr. star-shaped, carpels woody, 1-seeded. SE Asia, SE US, W Indies.
I. anisatum L. STAR ANISE. Shrub or small tree to 8m, highly aromatic. Lvs 4–12cm, narrowly oval to lanceolate, blunt. Fls to 2.75cm diam.; seg. to 30, yellow-green to white. Jap., Taiwan. Z7.
I. floridanum Ellis. PURPLE ANISE. Shrub or small tree to 3m. Lvs 5–15cm, narrowly oval to lanceolate, acuminate. Fls to 5cm diam., on nodding slender pedicels; seg. 20–30, dark red, purple or maroon. SE US. Z7.
I. henryi Diels. Shrub or small tree to 7m. Lvs 6–15cm, lanceolate to obovate, abruptly acuminate. Fls to 2cm diam., cupped; seg. 10–14, copper to dark red. C & W China. Z8.
I. religiosum Sieb. & Zucc. = *I. anisatum.*
I. verum Hook. CHINESE ANISE. Small tree, ultimately to 18m. Lvs 5–16cm, oblanceolate to narrow-elliptic, abruptly tapered. Fls 1.5cm diam., strongly cupped; seg. 10, ciliolate, yellow, sometimes flushing pink to red. China, Vietnam. Z8.

Illyarrie *Eucalyptus erythrocorys.*

Imitaria N.E. Br.
I. muirii N.E. Br. = *Gibbaeum nebrownii.*

Immortelle *Helichrysum bracteatum; Xeranthemum.*
Imo-no-ki *Gamblea innovans.*
Impala Lily *Adenium.*

Impatiens L. PATIENCE PLANT; BALSAM; BUSY LIZZIE; SULTANA. Balsaminaceae. 850 ann. or perenn. herbs or subshrubs. St. ± succulent. Lvs simple, usually toothed. Fls solitary or in clusters or rac., sometimes laterally compressed, sep. 3 or 5, the lowest extended into a sac or spur, lat. sep. small. Pet. 5, the upper one (standard) free, the lower 4 fused into 2 lobed pairs (wing pet.), lower wing pet. usually hiding the spur; sta. 5; style short, ovary superior, 5-celled. Capsule explosive, rolling suddenly inwards when touched. Cosmop. except S Amer., Aus. and NZ. Z10 unless specified.
I. arguta Hook. f. & Thoms. Perenn., 30–60cm; st. procumbent. Lvs 3–12cm, elliptic to ovate-elliptic, serrulate. Fls to 3.5cm, purple, pink-purple or violet, throat dull white or yellow, spur short, incurved. Himal. to S China. Z9.
I. asymmetrica Hook. f. = *I. textanha.*
I. auricoma Baill. Perenn. 50–80cm. Lvs 8–15cm, obovate to broadly elliptic, crenate, bristled, midrib red. Fls to 3cm, orange or yellow, long-stalked, spur short, recurved, yellow with red streaks. Comoro Is.

I. balfourii Hook. f. Ann. to 50cm. Lvs 2–13cm, ovate to ovate-elliptic, minutely crenate. Fls in loose rac. to 3.5cm, white flushed pink, wings with lower lobe pale yellow, upper lobe bright rose, spur cylindrical. W Himal.
I. balsamina L. GARDEN BALSAM; ROSE BALSAM. Erect ann., 20–75cm. Lvs 2.5–9cm, lanceolate to narrow-elliptic or oblanceolate, deeply toothed, petioles gland. Fls 2.5–5cm diam. solitary or clustered, white, cream-yellow, pink to lilac, bright red, crimson, some bicoloured, spur incurved. SE Asia (widely nat. in the Trop.), India. Camellia Flowered Mixed: to 70cm; fls large, double, mixture of colours including pink, red mottled white. 'Double Blackberry Ice': to 70cm; fls double, purple splashed white, abundant. 'Double Strawberry Ice': as 'Double Blackberry Ice', fls red splashed white. 'Tom Thumb': v. dwarf; fls large, double.
I. bicornuta Wallich. Ann., to 150cm; st. branched. Lvs alt., 7–22.5cm, elliptic to elliptic-ovate, acuminate, crenate. Fls in rac. to 4cm, pink or purple with throat yellow, spotted purple, lower lat. pet. forming elongate lip; spur slender to 0.8cm. Himal. (W Nepal to Bhutan).
I. biflora Walter = *I. capensis.*
I. campanulata Wight. Glaucous perenn., 29–100cm. Lvs 8–16cm, ovate to ovate-elliptic, toothed. Fls to 2cm, 2–5 on a long stalk, white spotted red in throat and on lower pet., spur short, incurved. India.
I. capensis Meerb. JEWELWEED; LADY'S EARRINGS; ORANGE BALSAM. Glab. ann. to 1.5m. Lvs to 9cm, ovate to elliptic, coarsely toothed. Fls few drooping in rac., mostly orange-yellow with red-brown spots; lower sep. to 2.5cm, spur incurved. N US, nat. GB and Eur. Z2.
I. chinensis L. Ann. to 60cm. Lvs lanceolate, bristly-toothed. Fls solitary or in pairs in lf axils, red; spur long, v. slender. Summer. S China, SE Asia.
I. cristata Wallich. Ann., 40–70cm. Lvs 1.5–8cm, ovate to elliptic, serrate. Fls 2.5–4cm, 2–3 in a short rac., or solitary, deeply pouched, yellow or cream, spotted brown in throat; upper pet. crested; spur short. W & C Himal.
I. edgeworthii Hook. f. Ann. to 70cm. Lvs to 18cm, elliptic glandular-toothed. Fls branched clusters, light yellow and white or pale pink and white, throat orange; spur curved slender, upper pet. orange crested. Summer. Pak. to Kashmir.
I. elegantissima Gilg. = *I. tinctoria* ssp. *elegantissima.*
I. epiphytica G.M. Schulze = *I. keilii.*
I. flaccida Arn. Perenn. 20–70cm. Lvs 5–13cm, ovate, serrate. Fls 5cm, solitary or 2–3 in clusters, rose-purple; sep. boat-shaped; spur slender, curved. India, Sri Lanka. 'Alba': fls white.
I. flanaganae Hemsl. Tuberous perenn., 1–2m; st. succulent, often red-tinged. Lvs spirally arranged, 10–24cm, oblong to ovate-elliptic, crenate-dentate to almost serrate. Fls 6–12 in stout rac., to 2.5cm diam., pink with throat pale yellow, upper pet. hooded, spur long slender, curved. S Afr. Z9.
I. gigantea Edgew. = *I. sulcata.*
I. glandulifera Royle. POLICEMAN'S HELMET; HIMALAYAN BALSAM. Stout ann., 1–2m. St. thick, red-tinged. Lower lvs 15–23cm, whorled, lanceolate to elliptic, serrate. Fls fragrant, to 4cm, deeply saccate, in long-stalked rac., pink to rose-purple to lavender or white with yellow-spotted interior. Summer. Himal., nat. N US and GB. 'Candida': to 2m; fls large, pure white. New T&M Hybrids: to 1.5m; fls large, open, mixture of cream, rose, pink, red, burgundy and bicolours.
I. gordonii Horne ex Bak. Glab. perenn. to 1m; st. erect, branched, tinged pink. Lvs spirally arranged, 8–15cm, ovate-lanceolate to lanceolate-elliptic, fleshy, crenate-serrate. Fls to 4.5cm across, flattened, white with anth. and spur pink. Seych.
I. grandis Heyne. Glab. perenn. to 150cm, much-branched. Lvs alt., broadly elliptic to oval, large, crenate. Fls to 5.5cm, white with red or purple markings on lower pet. Autumn–winter. Sri Lanka.
I. hawkeri Bull. Branched perenn. herb to 11cm. St. red, stout. Lvs 4–24cm, opposite or whorled, ovate to lanceolate or elliptic, tinged bronze or purple, toothed. Fls 6–8cm diam., red, crimson, pink, purple or white; spur 8cm; seg. claws white with blue patches. Summer–autumn. New Guinea to Solomon Is. New Guinea Hybrids: lvs green, bronze, red or variegated; fls single or double, white through pinks, lavender to red and bicoloured with blotches or star, occas. frilled. Singles include 'Big Top' (fls white), 'Headliner' (fls vivid coral), 'Showboat' (fls raspberry), 'Star Dancer' (lvs striped; fls lavender), Spectra Mixed (compact; lvs bronzed or variegated; fls pink, lilac or orange), 'Tango' (vigorous; lvs bronze; fls v. large, bright orange). Doubles include 'Apple Blossom' (fls semi-double, pink, abundant), 'Damask Rose' (lvs claret; fls deep red), 'Double Salmon' (fls large, deep salmon, frilled, abundant).
I. herzogii Schum. = *I. hawkeri.*
I. holstii Engl. & Warb. = *I. walleriana.*
I. hookeriana Arn. = *I. grandis.*

I. javensis (Bl.) Steud. Ann. St. creeping, branched. Lvs to 4×3.5cm, opposite, ovate, crenate-serrulate. Fls to 3.5cm diam., red-purple, pink or rarely white, centre red, spur curved. Java (mts).

I. jerdoniae Wight. Dwarf perenn. to 23cm. Lvs in upper parts of thickened st. Fls large, green, red and yellow. Summer. E Indies.

I. keilii Gilg. Creeping glab. perenn. Lvs alt., 3.5–15.5cm, ovate to lanceolate, crenate. Fls to 3cm, red and yellow, spur short. Burundi, Tanz.

I. leveillei Hook. f. = *I. arguta*.

I. linearifolia Warb. = *I. hawkeri*.

I. marianae Rchb. f. ex Hook. f. Creeping or erect perenn., pubesc. Lvs to 50cm, alt., oblong-ovate, variegated grey-cream between veins, serrate. Fls 2–3cm long, pale purple; standard pet. with hairy ridge; spur long. Summer. Assam.

I. mirabilis Hook. f. Stout trunk to 120cm, branching at top. Lvs to 30cm, in term. tufts, fleshy, ovate to elliptic, crenate. Fls 4cm, lilac or yellow dotted darker pink, throat blotched yellow. Summer. Malaysia: Langkawi Is.

I. niamniamensis Gilg. Perenn. herb to 90cm, st. simple. Lvs 5.5–22cm, alt., ovate to elliptic, crenate. Fls large, waxy, laterally compressed, saccate, sep. red, standard green-yellow; spur strongly curved. E Trop. Afr. 'Congo Cockatoo': fls large bright red and yellow.

I. noli-tangere L. TOUCH ME NOT. Ann. to 20–120cm; st. sparsely branched. Lvs to 13cm, alt., elliptic to ovate toothed. Fls to 4cm, yellow, interior spotted red. Summer. Eur. and Asia.

I. oliveri C.H. Wright & Will. Wats. = *I. sodenii*.

I. oppositifolia L. Upright, loosely branched, ann. Lvs opposite, lanceolate, slightly serrate. Fls 2.5cm diam., purple, rosy-red or pink. India, Sri Lanka.

I. parviflora DC. Ann. weed to 70cm; st. simple or branched. Lvs alt., 4–20cm, ovate-elliptic, serrate. Fls insignificant, pale yellow, spur white. C Asia, widely nat. Eur.

I. petersiana Gilg. ex Grignan = *I. walleriana*.

I. platypetala Lindl. Ann. to 45cm. St. stout, branched, succulent, red-purple. Lvs to 15cm, whorled or opposite, oblong-lanceolate, toothed. Fls 4cm diam., pink, salmon-pink, or purple-red with deep spot at centre, or white. Summer. Java. 'Tangerine': fls salmon orange with dark crimson centre.

I. pseudoviola Gilg. Much-branched, semi-trailing perenn. Lvs to 2cm, alt., ovate, toothed. Fls white suffused rosy-pink, pet. striped violet rose. E Afr.

I. repens Moon. Creeping perenn. St. branched. Lvs to 2.5cm, alt., reniform, crenate. Fls to 4cm, yellow, downy. Sri Lanka, India.

I. roylei Walp. = *I. glandulifera*.

I. scabrida DC. Ann. to 90cm. St. branched, hairy, purple, ± angled. Lvs 5–15cm, lanceolate, glandular-toothed. Fls to 4cm, yellow, dotted brown-purple. Kashmir to Bhutan.

I. scabrida hort. = *I. cristata*.

I. schlechteri Warb. = *I. hawkeri*.

I. sodenii Engl. & Warb. ex Engl. Shrubby perenn. to 3m. Lvs to 20cm, whorled, oblanceolate, serrate. Fls to 6cm diam., long-stalked, light lilac or rose-pink or pure white. Summer. E Trop. Afr.

I. stenantha Hook. f. Ascending perenn., 20–70cm. Lvs alt., 2.5–9cm, elliptic-oblanceolate, crenulate. Fls to 3.3cm, yellow with red spur. E Nepal, Sikkim.

I. sulcata Wallich. Closely resembling *I. glandulifera* but to 1.5m. Lvs ovate to broad-lanceolate, crenate. Fls pink, purple or crimson, lower sep. dark-spotted. Himal.

I. sultani Hook. f. = *I. walleriana*.

I. thomassetii Hook. f. apud Hemsl. = *I. gordonii*.

I. tinctoria A. Rich. Tuberous perenn.; st. 1–2m. Lvs spirally arranged, 7.5–23cm, oblong to lanceolate, crenate or serrate. Fls to 6.5cm diam., fragrant, white with pink or magenta markings in throat. Ethiop., S Sudan, E Zaire, W Uganda. ssp. *elegantissima* (Gilg) Grey-Wilson. Fls smaller. S & C Kenya, E Uganda.

I. usambarensis Grey-Wilson. Close to *I. walleriana*, but to 2m. Lvs narrow-ovate or oblong-elliptic, serrulate. Fls 4–5.5cm, deep pink to deep red or vermilion. NE Tanz.

I. verticillata Wight. Glab. perenn. to 70cm; st. branched. Lvs whorled, narrow-elliptic to lanceolate, crenate-serrate. Fls somewhat flattened, to 2.5cm diam., bright scarlet. SW India.

I. walleriana Hook. f. BUSY LIZZIE; PATIENCE PLANT; SULTANA. Perenn. treated as an ann., 15–60cm. St. branching, succulent. Lvs 2.5–13cm, alt., or opposite, ovate to elliptic, crenate, sometimes red-tinged. Fls 2.5–5cm diam., flat, bright red, crimson, orange, pink, white or multicoloured; spur slender. Summer. Tanz. to Moz. Hybrids include Accent Series (compact; fls large, coral, red and violet with coloured eye or central stripe on each pet.), Blitz Series (fls extra large, to 6.5cm diam.), Cinderella Variegated Mixed (fls bright coloured with white

stripe), Princess Series (dwarf; fls large, bright coloured; suitable for baskets), Starbright Mixed (fls large, bicolours of rose, red, orange or violet), Tempo Pastel Mixed (compact; fls large, in soft shades, early-flowering; suitable for baskets) and Confection Series (fls mainly double).

Imperata Cyr. Gramineae. 1 perenn., herbaceous grass. To 80cm, slender, lvs to 50cm, flat, linear to linear-lanceolate, semi-erect. Pan. to 20cm, spike-like, silver-white; spikelets to 4.5cm, lanceolate. Jap.

I. cylindrica (L.) Beauv. CHIGAYA; FUSHIGE-CHIGAYA. Jap. 'Red Baron' ('Rubra') (JAPANESE BLOOD GRASS): lvs and shoots strongly tinted wine-red, becoming scarlet in fall. Z8.

Imperial Japanese Morning Glory *Ipomoea ×imperialis*.
Imperial Taro *Colocasia esculenta*.
Inaja *Maximiliana*.

Incarvillea Juss. Bignoniaceae. 14 ann. or perenn. herbs. Lvs radical or cauline, odd-pinnate or pinnatifid, entire or toothed. Rac. or pan. term., 1- to many-fld; cal. tubular; cor. tube campanulate, lobes 5. Summer. C & E Asia, Himal.

I. arguta (Royle) Royle. Erect perenn. to 1.5m, woody-based. Lvs 5–20cm, seg. in 2–6 opposite pairs, lanceolate or elliptic. Rac. 5–20-fld; cor. white or pink, tube to 3.8cm, lobes rounded, to 1.4×1cm. Assam, Punjab to W China. Z8.

I. bonvalotii Bur. & Franch. = *I. compacta*.

I. brevipes (Sprague) hort. = *I. mairei*.

I. chinensis Poir. = *I. sinensis*.

I. compacta Maxim. Perenn., stemless, to 30cm. Lvs 3–20cm, ovate-cordate, term. seg. to 4cm, rounded. Rac. 1–10-fld; cor. lobes to 3.9cm, orbicular, pale purple outside, gold-yellow inside with purple lines, rarely white. Tibet, China. Z6.

I. compacta var. *brevipes* (Sprague) Wehrh. = *I. mairei*.

I. compacta var. *grandiflora* (Bur. & Franch.) Wehrh. = *I. mairei* var. *grandiflora*.

I. delavayi Bur. & Franch. Stemless perenn. Lvs lyrate-pinnatifid, 8–25cm, seg. 6–11 pairs, lanceolate, crenate, term. seg. obovate. Rac. 2–10-fld; cor. tube to 6cm, purple and yellow outside, yellow lined purple inside, lobes to 3cm, purple, orbicular. China. 'Bee's Pink': fls pale pink. Z6.

I. diffusa Royle = *I. arguta*.

I. emodi (Lindl.) Chatterj. Perenn. to 50cm. St. to 5cm. Lvs to 25cm, thick, seg. 4–5 pairs, to 4cm, ovate. Rac. to 18-fld; cor. pale purple with golden-yellow throat, tube to 5.8cm, glandular-pubesc. inside, lobes to 1.5cm, rounded. Spring. Afghan., Pak., Kashmir, India. Z8.

I. emodi Wallich = *I. emodi*.

I. farreri hort. = *I. sinensis*.

I. grandiflora Bur. & Franch. = *I. mairei* var. *grandiflora*.

I. grandiflora var. *brevipes* Sprague = *I. mairei*.

I. koopmannii Lauche = *I. olgae*.

I. longiracemosa Sprague = *I. lutea* ssp. *longiracemosa*.

I. lutea Bur. & Franch. Perenn., erect to 1m. Lvs 10–40cm, seg. 6–10 pairs, 1.5–8cm, ovate or elliptic. Rac. 6–12-fld; cor. pale yellow tinged green, spotted brown or crimson, or tinted red, tube to 5.5cm, lobes to 3cm. ssp. *longiracemosa* (Sprague) Grierson. Lvs basally clustered, seg. in 3–5 pairs, sparsely puberulent. Tibet. Z6.

I. mairei (Lév.) Grierson. Stemless perenn. Lvs 4–35cm, seg. 4–7 pairs, to 7cm, ovate to oblong. Cor. tube 3.3–6.5cm, deep pink-red outside, white to grey or yellow inside, lobes 1.1–2.8cm, crimson, orbicular. SW China. var. *grandiflora* (Bur. & Franch.) Grierson. Lvs with 1–2 pairs seg. Fls large, usually solitary, rich carmine with yellow throat. 'Frank Ludlow': miniature form; fls v. large, crimson tinted pink. 'Nyoto Sama': to 15cm high; fls v. large, shocking pink. Z4.

I. olgae Reg. Erect, perenn. to 1m. Lvs to 15cm, seg. 3–4 pairs, to 6cm, elliptic. Rac. 3–10-fld, paniculate; cor. rose-pink or white, tube to 3.5cm, glandular-pubesc. within, lobes to 0.9cm, rounded. Turkestan, Bokhara, Afghan. Z7.

I. principis Bur. & Franch. = *I. lutea*.

I. sinensis Lam. Puberulent ann. or perenn., 15–85cm. Lvs 4–16.5cm, bi- or tripinnatisect, pinnae 5–8.5cm, seg. linear or linear-lanceolate. Rac. 4–18-fld; cor. red tinted purple, tube 1.9–3.9cm, glandular-pubesc. within, lobes to 1.3cm, rounded. ssp. *variabilis* (Batal.) Grierson. Perenn. Cor. rose. China, Tibet. f. *przewalskii* (Batal.) Grierson. Fls yellow. Z4.

I. variabilis Batal. = *I. sinensis* ssp. *variabilis*.

I. variabilis var. *farreri* W.W. Sm. = *I. sinensis*.

I. younghusbandii Sprague. Stemless perenn. Lvs pinnate, bullate, to 5.5cm in fr., seg. 3–7 pairs, 0.6–0.9cm, ovate or oblong. Fls solitary; cor. rose-purple, throat lined white, tube to 5cm, lobes to 2×2.5cm, orbicular. Summer. Tibet, Nepal. Z7.
→*Amphicome*.

Incense Cedar *Calocedrus* (*C. decurrens*).
Incense Plant *Calomeria amaranthoides*.
Incense Rose *Rosa primula*.
Incienso *Encelia farinosa*.
Indaya do Campo *Syagrus petraea*.
Indaya Rasteiro *Syagrus petraea*.
Inderab *Cordia africana*.
India Date *Phoenix sylvestris*.
India Date Palm *Phoenix rupicola*.
Indian Almond *Sterculia foetida*; *Terminalia catappa*.
Indian Apple *Datura innoxia*.
Indian Arrowroot *Curcuma angustifolia*; *Tacca leontopetaloides*.
Indian Banyan *Ficus benghalensis*.
Indian Basket Grass *Xerophyllum tenax*.
Indian Bean *Catalpa bignonioides*; *Lablab purpureus*.
Indian Beech *Pongamia pinnata*.
Indian Blackwood *Dalbergia latifolia*.
Indian Blanket *Gaillardia pulchella*.
Indian Breadroot *Psoralea esculenta*.
Indian Broomrape *Aeginetia indica*.
Indian Cherry *Cordia nitida*.
Indian Chocolate *Geum rivale*.
Indian Cigar *Catalpa bignonioides*; *C. speciosa*.
Indian Corn *Zea*.
Indian Cress *Tropaeolum majus*.
Indian Crocus *Pleione*.
Indian Cucumber Root *Medeola virginiana*.
Indian Currant *Symphoricarpos orbiculatus*.
Indian Date *Tamarindus indica*.
Indian Fig *Opuntia ficus-indica*.
Indian Ginger *Alpinia calcarata*.
Indian Grass *Sorghastrum nutans*.
Indian Hawthorn *Rhaphiolepis indica*.
Indian Hemp *Hibiscus cannabinus*.
Indian Horse Chestnut *Aesculus indica*.
Indian Jujube *Ziziphus mauritanica*.
Indian Laburnum *Cassia fistula*.
Indian Laurel *Calophyllum inophyllum*; *Ficus microcarpa*.
Indian Lettuce *Lactuca indica*.
Indian Madder *Oldenlandia umbellata*; *Rubia cordifolia*.
Indian Mallow *Abutilon*.
Indian Millet *Oryzopsis hymenoides*.
Indian Mint *Plectranthus amboinicus*.
Indian Mulberry *Morinda citrifolia*.
Indian Mustard *Brassica juncea*.
Indian Oak *Barringtonia acutangula*; *Tectona grandis*.
Indian Paint *Chenopodium capitatum*.
Indian Paintbrush *Asclepias tuberosa*; *Castilleja*.
Indian Pea *Lathyrus sativus*.
Indian Physic *Gillenia trifoliata*.
Indian Pink *Ipomoea quamoclit*; *Lobelia cardinalis*; *Spigelia marilandica*.
Indian Poke *Phytolacca acinosa*.
Indian Potato *Apios americana*.
Indian Red Waterlily *Nuphar rubra*.
Indian Rhododendron *Melastoma malabathricum*.
Indian Rhubarb *Darmera peltata*.
Indian Root *Asclepias curassavica*.
Indian Rosewood *Dalbergia latifolia*.
Indian Salad *Hydrophyllum virginianum*.
Indian Sandalwood *Santalum album*.
Indian Shot *Canna indica*.
Indian Spinach *Basella alba*.
Indian Strawberry *Duchesnea*.
Indian Tobacco *Lobelia inflata*.
Indian Turnip *Arisaema triphyllum*.
Indian Warrior *Pedicularis densiflora*.
Indian Wood Apple *Limonia acidissima*.
India Rubber Fig, India Rubber Tree *Ficus elastica*.
Indigo Bush *Dalea*.

Indigofera L. Leguminosae (Papilionoideae). Some 700 small trees, shrubs or herbs. Lvs imparipinnate, trifoliolate, or simple. Fls usually small, pea-like, in rac. or spikes, rarely solitary. Widespread trop. and subtrop. regions.
I. amblyantha Craib. Shrub 1.5–2m. Lvs 10–15cm; lfts 13–32mm, 7–11, narrow-ovate, pale-pubesc. Rac. to 11cm, packed, erect; fls to 6mm, pale rose-pink to scarlet. China. Z5.
I. atropurpurea Buch.-Ham. ex Roxb. Shrub c1.5m. Lvs 15–23cm; lfts 25–38mm, 11–17, oval, initially hirsute. Rac. to 20cm, slender; fls to 9mm, deep crimson. Summer. SE Asia. Z9.
I. australis Willd. Shrub, 0.5–1.75m. Lfts 5–25mm, 9–21, oblong to linear, glab. above, hairy beneath. Rac. shorter than or equalling lvs; fls to 8mm, red. Summer–autumn. Temp. Aus. Z9.

I. cassioides DC. Shrub, 1.22–1.83m. Lvs 7.6–15.2cm, lfts 20–25mm in 5 pairs, obovate-elliptic, generally notched, sparsely grey-hirsute. Rac. 25–76mm long; fls to 12mm, scarlet. Himal. and Indian hill ranges. Z9.
I. cylindrica DC. TREE INDIGOFERA. Shrub or small tree to 4.5m. Lvs 5–10cm; lfts 8–25mm, in 4–7 pairs, ovate, glab., apex usually notched. Rac. dense; fls to 6mm, white, rosy-purple or pink. Cf. *I. frutescens*. Summer. S Afr. Z9.
I. decora Lindl. Shrub, 30–80cm. Lvs 7–20cm, lfts 25–40mm, 7–13, narrow-oblong, ± glab. above, puberulous beneath. Rac. axillary 10–20cm, erect; fls to 19mm, white, suffused pale crimson at base; wings pink. Spring–summer. Jap., C China. Z5.
I. dielsiana Craib. Shrub, 90–150cm. Lvs 6.4–12.7cm, lfts 8–22mm, 7–11 pairs, elliptic-oblong to obovate, densely short-pubesc. Rac. to 15cm, delicate, erect; fls c13mm, pale red-pink, downy. Summer–autumn. SW China. Z6.
I. dosua Buch.-Ham. ex D. Don. Shrub to 50cm. Lvs 2.5–8cm, lfts 6–13mm, 10–15 pairs, oval, rusty-pubesc. Rac. 25–76mm, long-stalked; fls to 13mm, scarlet. Summer. India. Z10.
I. frutescens L. f. Shrub or small tree to 5m. Lfts to 2.25cm, in 2–4 pairs, remote, obovate, glaucous. Fls similar to those of *I. cylindrica* but larger, in loose rac. S Afr. Z9.
I. gerardiana Graham = *I. heterantha*.
I. hebepetala Benth. ex Bak. Shrub to 1.2m. Lvs 15–23cm, lfts 25–64mm, 5–11, ovate-oblong, hirsute beneath. Rac. 7–23cm long; 12–16mm, vivid crimson and rosy pink. Summer–autumn. NW Himal. Z8.
I. heterantha Wallich ex Brandis. Shrub to 2.5m. Lvs 5–10cm, lfts 10–16mm, 13–21, obovate or oval, grey-downy. Rac. packed, erect 7–15cm; fls 13mm, pale pink, rosy purple or crimson. Summer–early autumn. NW Himal. Z7.
I. incarnata (Willd.) Nak. = *I. decora*.
I. kirilowii Maxim. ex Palib. Shrub, 60–80cm. Lvs 8–15cm; lfts 10–30mm, 7–13, ovate to elliptic, sparsely pubesc. Rac. packed, erect, 12.5cm; fls 12–20mm, rosy pink. Spring–summer. Korea, N China, S Jap. Z5.
I. pendula Franch. Shrub, 2.5–3m. Lvs 20–25cm, lfts 19–32mm, 19–27, oblong to oval, pale-hirsute beneath. Rac. delicate, drooping, 25–45cm long; fls 8–13mm, rosy-purple. Late summer–early autumn. SW China. Z9.
I. potaninii Craib. Shrub, 1–1.5m. Lvs 5–8cm, lfts 5–9, elliptic-oblong, densely pubesc. above, less so beneath. Rac. 5–12.5cm, erect, axill.; fls 10mm, pale pink-violet. Summer–early autumn. Cf. *I. amblyantha*. SW China. Z5.
I. pseudotinctoria Matsum. Subshrub, 30–90cm. Lvs 4–8cm, lfts 8–25mm, 7–9(–11), oblong, downy. Rac. packed, 4–10cm; fls 4mm, light red to pale pink or white tinted rose. Summer–autumn. Taiwan, Jap., C China. Z6.
I. pulchella auct. = *I. cassioides*.
I. sumatrana Gaertn. = *I. tinctoria*.
I. tinctoria L. Subshrub, 1.5–2m. Lfts to 3cm in 4–7 pairs, obovate, hairy beneath. Rac. slender, ascending, shorter than lvs; standard pale red to rose, wings and keel of a somewhat deeper blue. SE Asia. Z10.
I. violacea Buch.-Ham. ex Roxb. = *I. cassioides*.

Indigo Squill *Camassia scilloides*.

Indocalamus Nak. Gramineae. 25 running bamboos with large dull green thick ovate-lanceolate lvs. China, Jap., Malaysia.
I. latifolius (Keng) McClure. Culms 0.5–1m×0.5cm, pubesc. Lvs 10–40×1.5–8cm, slightly hairy beneath. E China. Z8.
I. tessellatus (Munro) Keng. Culms 1–2.5m×0.5–1.5cm, sub-glabrous. Lvs to 60×10cm, glab. C China, Jap. Z8.
→*Arundinaria*, *Sasa* and *Sasamorpha*.

Indoor Clover *Alternanthera dentata*.

Inga Mill. ICE-CREAM BEAN. Leguminosae (Mimosoideae). 350 trop. trees or shrubs. Lvs paripinnate; lfts large, few; rachis with stalked glands. Fls in mimosiform heads or spikes. Fr. cylindric or flat, seeds in white pulp. Trop. & subtrop. Amer. Z10.
I. dulcis (Roxb.) Willd. = *Pithecellobium dulce*.
I. edulis Mart. ICE-CREAM BEAN. Tree to 17m. Lfts 6–8, elliptic, woolly beneath. Fls in masses, 5cm diam., white. Range as for the genus.
I. fagifolia (L.) Willd. ex Benth. = *I. laurina*.
I. guadalupensis (Pers.) Desv. = *Pithecellobium keyense*.
I. inga (L.) Britt. = *I. vera*.
I. laurina (Sw.) Willd. ex L. SPANISH OAK; SWEET PEA; GUAMA. Tree to 9m. Lfts 1–3, glab. Fls in spikes some 10cm long, white. C Amer., W Indies, Puerto Rico.
I. pulcherrima Cerv. ex Sweet = *Calliandra tweedii*.
I. vera Willd. ex L. GUABA. Tree to 15m+. Lfts 4–6, oblong to elliptic, pubesc. to subglabrous. Fls in dense, rusty spikes,

white. Mex. to N S Amer., Greater Antilles, Puerto Rico.
→*Mimosa*.

Inkberry *Ilex glabra*.
Innocence *Collinsia bicolor*; *Houstonia caerulea*.
Inside-out Flower *Vancouveria*.
Interior Live Oak *Quercus wislizeni*.
Intermediate Wheatgrass *Elymus hispidus*.
Interrupted Fern *Osmunda claytonia*.

Inula L. Compositae. *c*90 mostly perenn. herbs or subshrubs. St.
erect or ascending, usually branching. Lvs simple, entire to
serrate, lower stalked, upper usually sessile, often clasping.
Cap. solitary or few in a pan. or corymb, radiate or discoid; outer flts ligulate to tubular, yellow or orange; disc flts tubular,
yellow. Temp. and warm OW.
I. acaulis Schott & Kotschy ex Boiss. Rhizomatous perenn. herb
or subshrub to 20cm; st. simple, often tinged purple, villous. Lvs
3–6cm, oblanceolate or spathulate, acute, entire, minutely
gland., ciliate. Cap. radiate, solitary, rarely few; involucre to
2.5cm diam., ray flts to 15mm. Summer. Asia Minor. Z6.
I. barbata Wallich. Perenn. herb or subshrub to 50cm; st. erect,
simple or sparingly branched, pilose above. Lvs to 9cm,
narrowly oblong-lanceolate, acute, serrulate, glab. or scabrous,
often ciliate with tawny hairs. Cap. solitary, radiate; involucre
to 2cm diam., ray flts to 9mm. Summer, autumn. W Himal. Z7.
I. britannica L. Perenn. herb to 75cm; st. erect, branched, pubesc. Lvs to 15cm, elliptic or ovate-elliptic, entire or serrulate,
villous, rarely silky. Cap. radiate, usually in corymbs, rarely
solitary; involucre to 1.5cm diam.; ray flts to 2.5cm. Summer,
autumn. Eurasia. Z7.
I. candida (L.) Cass. Perenn. herb or subshrub to 30cm, st.
slender, simple or shortly branched above. Lvs to 9cm,
lanceolate, obtuse, entire, white-tomentose or lanate. Cap.
radiate, solitary; involucre to 1cm diam.; ray flts to 7mm.
Greece, Crete. Z7.
I. conyza DC. = *I. conyzae*.
I. conyzae (Griess.) Meikle. Erect bienn. or short-lived perenn.
to 1.5m; st. branched above, pubesc. or thinly tomentose. Lvs
to 12cm, ovate-oblong, acute or obtuse, irregularly dentate,
tapered to a flattened petiole, pubesc. Capital discoid in dense
corymbs; ♀ flts with lobes to 0.3mm. W, C & S Eur., Turk.,
Cauc., N Iran, Alg. Z6.
I. dysenterica L. = *Pulicaria dysenterica*.
I. ensifolia L. Erect perenn. herb to 60cm; st. simple, glab. or
tomentose. Lvs to 9cm, linear-lanceolate or lanceolate, entire,
glab., ciliate, sessile. Cap. radiate, solitary or few; involucre
1–2cm diam.; ray flts to 22mm. Summer. E & EC Eur.
'Compacta': small, to 15cm; fls gold. 'Gold Star': to 30cm; fls
gold. 'Mediterranean Sun': to 20cm; lvs narrow; fls yellow,
borne late in season. Z5.
I. glandulosa Willd. = *I. orientalis*.
I. grandiflora Willd. = *I. orientalis*.
I. helenium L. ELECAMPNE. Robust perenn. herb to 3m, with
thick aromatic rhiz.; st. stout, erect, branched above, pubesc.
Lvs dentate, somewhat undulate, subglabrous to adpressed-
pilose above, pubesc. or tomentose beneath, to 70cm, ovate-
elliptic, acute. Cap. radiate, in lax corymbs or narrow rac.; involucre to 2.5cm diam., ray flts to 3cm. Summer. Eurasia. Z5.
I. hirta L. Perenn. herb, to 50cm; st. branched, erect, hairy. Lvs
to 8cm, obovate-oblong or oblanceolate-oblong, entire or
denticulate, with prominent reticulate venation, hairy. Cap.
solitary, or few in corymbs; involucre to 1.3cm diam.; ray flts to
3cm. Summer. Eur. to Sib. Z4.
I. hookeri C.B. Clarke. Perenn. herb or subshrub to 60cm; st.
simple or sparingly branched, pilose above. Lvs to 13cm,
oblong-lanceolate, acute, minutely toothed, hairy. Cap. radiate,
solitary or 2–3; involucre to 4cm diam.; ray flts *c*2.5cm.
Summer, autumn. Himal. Z6.
I. limonifolia (Sibth. & Sm.) Boiss. ex Raulin. = *I. candida*.
I. macrocephala Boiss. & Kotschy ex Boiss. Perenn. herb, to
60cm; st. erect, simple, hairy. Lvs to 25cm, elliptic-lanceolate,
acute, denticulate, minutely gland. Cap. radiate, solitary, rarely
2; involucre 3.5–5cm diam.; ray flts *c*12mm. Summer. Cauc. Z6.
I. macrocephala hort. = *I. royleana*.
I. magnifica Lipsky. Perenn. herb or subshrub to 2m; st. robust,
striate, villous, black-purple. Lvs to 25cm, elliptic-ovate to
ovate, dentate, dark green, glab. above, villous beneath. Cap.
radiate, in a corymb; involucre to 3cm diam.; ray flts to 2cm. E
Cauc. Z6.
I. montana L. Perenn. herb to 40cm; st. erect, branched, villous
or arachnoid, silky. Lvs to 12cm, oblong-oblanceolate, entire or
denticulate, silky-villous. Cap. radiate, solitary; involucre to
1.5cm diam.; ray flts to 2.5cm. Summer. W Medit. Z7.
I. oculus-christi L. Rhizomatous perenn. herb to 50cm; st. erect,
silky or arachnoid. Lvs to 14cm, oblong-lanceolate to oblong-

elliptic, entire or denticulate. Cap. radiate, usually 3–5, in a
corymb; involucre to 2.6cm diamm.; ray flts to 2cm. Summer. E
Eur., Turk., Cauc., N Iraq, Iran. Z6.
I. orientalis Lam. Perenn. herb or subshrub to 60cm; st. erect,
leafy, simple, with sparse yellow or brown hairs, minutely
gland. Lvs to 12cm, ovate-elliptic or oblanceolate, acute, base
subcordate, denticulate or weakly serrate, densely and minutely
gland., pilose, yellow-hairy. Cap. radiate, solitary; involucre to
3cm diam.; ray flts *c*2.5cm. Summer. Cauc. Z6.
I. racemosa Hook. f. Robust perenn. herb to 2m; st. branched,
rough, grooved. Lvs to 30cm, obtusely dentate, scabrid above,
tomentose beneath, elliptic-lanceolate to lanceolate, base
deeply lobed. Cap. radiate, shortly pedunculate or almost
sessile, in a rac.; involucre to 3cm diam.; ray flts *c*1.5cm.
Summer. W Himal. Z7.
I. rhizocephala Schrenk. Perenn. herb to over 1m; st. branched,
erect, hairy. Lvs radical prostrate, to 8cm, oblong or oblong-
lanceolate, obtuse, broadly petiolate, ciliate. Cap. radiate,
densely clustered at the centre of the rosette; involucre to 1.5cm
diam.; ray flts to *c*1cm. Summer. Iran, Afghan., Pak., C Asia.
Z6.
I. rhizocephaloides C.B. Clarke = *I. rhizocephala*.
I. royleana DC. Robust perenn. herb to 60cm; st. often
branched, grooved, pubesc. or villous and gland. Lvs to 25cm,
ovate or oblong, obtuse, denticulate, subglabrous, pubesc. or
villous above, sometimes tomentose beneath, petiole long,
winged. Cap. radiate, solitary; involucre to 5cm diam.; ray flts
to 5cm. Summer, autumn. W Himal. Z6.
I. salicifolia hort. = *I. salicina*.
I. salicina L. Perenn. herb to 75cm with slender white stolons; st.
erect, stiff, v. leafy. Lvs to 6cm, oblanceolate, acute, entire or
remotely denticulate, prominently reticulately veined above,
stiffly ciliate, glab. or sparsely hairy on veins beneath. Cap.
radiate, in a few-fld corymb or solitary; involucre *c*12mm diam.;
ray flts to 2cm. Summer. Eur., Asia. Z6.
I. spiraeifolia L. Perenn. herb to 60cm; st. erect, pubesc. below.
Lvs to 8cm, lanceolate to ovate, denticulat eor serrulate,
prominently reticulately veined above, sparsely hairy. Cap.
radiate, in a corymb, or solitary; involucre to 1.5cm diam.; ray
flts to 17mm. Summer. S & E Eur. Z6.
I. squarrosa L. = *I. spiraeifolia*.
I. subaxillaris Lam. = *Heterotheca subaxillaris*.
I. thapsoides (Bieb. ex Willd.) Spreng. Rhizomatous perenn.
herb to 90cm, densely villous; st. erect, leafy. Lvs to 18cm,
ovate, acute, serrate, veins sometimes prominent beneath. Cap.
radiate, few or many, in rather dense corymbs; involucre to
1.5cm diam.; ray flts to 5mm. Summer. Crimea, Cauc., Iran.
Z6.
I. verbascifolia (Willd.) Hausskn. Perenn. herb to 50cm; st.
simple or sparingly branched above. Lvs to 9cm, ovate-
lanceolate, often acute, cuneate at base, entire to crenate-
serrate, prominently veined beneath, sparsely lanate. Cap.
radiate, solitary or few in a cluster; involucre to 1.5cm diam.;
ray flts 6–15mm. Summer. Balk., SE It. Z6.
I. viscosa (L.) Ait. Bushy, gland. perenn. herb or subshrub to
1.5m, with woody rootstock; st. much-branched, erect. Lvs to
9cmm, lanceolate, acute or acuminate, serrate or serrulate,
sessile or semi-amplexicaul. Cap. radiate, in a loose pyramidal
pan.; involucre to 1.2cm diam.; ray flts 6–7mm. Summer,
autumn. Medit. Z7.
→*Aster*.

Inu-medo-hagi *Lespedeza juncea*.
Inushoma *Cimicifuga biternata*.
Inyou-chikuzoku *Hibanobambusa tranquillans*.

Iochroma Benth. Solanaceae. 20 shrubs and small trees. Lvs entire. Fls clustered or paired, 5-merous, cor. long-tubular to
trumpet-shaped, 5-lobed. Trop. Amer. Z9.
I. coccinea Scheidw. Shrub to 3m. Lvs to 13cm, undulate; fls scarlet, throat pale yellow, limb to 1.8cm diam. C Amer.
I. cyanea (Lindl.) Green. Shrub, to 3m; lvs to 20cm, lanceolate,
grey-green, pubesc. Fls to 20 per cluster, to 3.5cm, purple-blue.
NW S Amer.
I. fuchsioides Miers. Shrub to 3m. Lvs to 10cm, glab.; fls orange-
scarlet, to bright red, throat yellow, limb to 1.3cm diam. Andes.
I. grandiflora Benth. Shrub to 1.2m. Lvs to 13cm, ovate-cordate,
soft-pubesc. Fls 6–8 per cluster, 3.5cm, rich purple. Ecuad.
I. lanceolata (Miers) Miers = *I. cyanea*.
I. tubulosa Benth. = *I. cyanea*.

Ione Manzanita *Arctostaphylos myrtifolia*.

Ionidium Vent.
I. capense Roem. & Schult. = *Hybanthus capense*.
I. ipecacuanha Vent. = *Hybanthus calceolaria*.

Ionopsidium Rchb. Cruciferae. 5 glab., ann. herbs. Lvs in rosettes. Fls small, 4-merous, solitary. Medit. Z9.

I. acaule (Desf.) Rchb. VIOLET CRESS. To 8cm. Lvs rounded-ovate, entire to 3-lobed. Fls long-stalked, lilac, or white tinged violet. Summer–winter. Port.

Ionopsis HBK. Orchidaceae. 10 epiphytic or terrestrial orchids, compact, tufted. Pbs small or 0. Lvs narrow, rigid, distichous. Infl. a rac. or delicate pan.; fls showy; sep. subequal, erect or spreading, lat. sep. forming a short sac below lip; lip large, simple, exceeding tep. Trop. and subtrop. Americas. Z10.

I. paniculata Lindl. = *I. utricularioides*.
I. satyrioides (Sw.) Rchb. f. Lvs to 14cm, semi-terete, subulate. Infl. to 15cm, exceeding lvs; fls cream-white, often veined lilac; lip to 8×3mm, obovate, undulate. Spring–autumn. W Indies, Colomb., Venez., Trin., Demerara.
I. tenera Lindl. = *I. utricularioides*.
I. teres Lindl. = *I. satyrioides*.
I. testiculata Lindl. = *I. satyrioides*.
I. utricularioides (Sw.) Lindl. Lvs to 17cm, linear or lanceolate, carinate. Infl. to 75cm; fls white to rose-purple or magenta; lip to 16×8mm, flabellate-obcordate, cleft, undulate or crenulate. Winter–spring. Flor., W Indies, Mex. to Braz., Peru.

Ipheion Raf. Liliaceae (Alliaceae). 10 tufted, bulbous perennials, smelling of garlic. Lvs basal, linear-strap-shaped. Fls 1–2 per scape, perianth salverform, lobes spreading; sta. 6 in 2 series. S Amer.

I. uniflorum (Graham) Raf. SPRING STARFLOWER. Lvs to 25cm, glaucescent, narrowly strap-shaped. Scapes to 20cm, slender, numerous; fls 4cm diam., solitary, tep. shortly united, white tinged blue to violet-blue. Spring. Urug., temp. Arg., nat. GB and Fr. 'Album': fls large, pure white. 'Froyle Mill': fls dark violet. 'Rolf Fiedler': fls clear blue, regular in form, on stout scapes. 'Wisley Blue': tep. pale blue, darker toward tips. Z6.
→*Milla* and *Triteleia*.

Ipomoea L. MORNING GLORY. Convolvulaceae. 450–500 ann. to perenn. herbs, shrubs or small trees, often climbing. Lvs entire to compound. Fls solitary or in cymes or pan.; sep. herbaceous to coriaceous; cor. subentire to lobed, funnel-shaped, campanulate, or tubular. Widely distrib. in Trop. and Subtrop. regions.

I. acuminata (Vahl) Roem. & Schult. = *I. indica*.
I. alba L. MOONFLOWER; BELLE DE NUIT. Perenn. climber, woody at base, 5–30m, with fleshy st. protruberances. Lvs 5–15cm, entire or 3-lobed, apex caudate, base cordate. Fls nocturnally fragrant; 9–15cm long, 8–11cm diam., hypocrateriform, white tinted green outside. Summer. Pantrop. 'Giant White': fls v. large, white. Z9.
I. batatas (L.) Poir. SWEET POTATO. Perenn. climber with tuberous rootstock. Lvs 5–10cm, cordate to ovate, entire or 3-lobed. Fls often 0, massive or 4–7cm lavender to pale purple, darker inside, sometimes white. Pantrop. 'Boniato': tubers dry-fleshed, medium sweet. 'Bush Porto Rico': compact plant, tubers sweet, red-orange flesh. 'Centennial': tubers sweet, deep orange flesh, early-maturing. 'Jewel': tubers deep orange, rich-flavoured, soft-textured flesh; most widely grown tuber cv. 'Vardaman': tubers rich-flavoured, deep orange flesh, compact, climate-adaptable plant. Z9.
I. biloba Forssk. = *I. pes-caprae*.
I. bona-nox L. = *I. alba*.
I. brasiliensis (L.) Sweet = *I. pes-caprae*.
I. cairica (L.) Sweet. Climbing or prostrate tuberous-rooted perenn. Lvs 3–10cm, palmate, lobes 5, to 4cm, elliptic-ovate. Fls 3–6cm, funnel-shaped, red, purple or white with tube purple inside, sometimes wholly white. Trop. and subtrop. Afr. and Asia, widely introd. elsewhere. Z8.
I. carnea Jacq. Shrubs or climbers to 2.5m, base woody. Lvs 10–25cm, ovate-cordate to suborbicular. Fls 5–8cm long, 8–12cm diam., pink to pink-purple, tube dark below lip; base funnel-shaped. Flor. to Parag. ssp. *fistulosa* (Mart. ex Choisy) D. Austin. Habit erect and shrubby. Lvs lanceolate-elongate. Summer. Pantrop. by introduction. Frequently cult. Z9.
I. cavanillesii Roem. & Schult. = *I. cairica*.
I. coccinea L. RED MORNING GLORY; STAR IPOMOEA. Ann. herb climbing 2–4m. Lvs 2–14cm, ovate-cordate, entire or coarsely toothed. Fls 1.5–2.5cm, limb 1.7–2cm diam., scarlet, buff-yellow inside. Summer. US. Z7.
I. coccinea var. *hederifolia* (L.) A. Gray = *I. hederifolia*.
I. congesta R. Br. = *I. indica*.
I. crassicaulis Benth. = *I. carnea*.
I. digitata Auct. non L. = *I. mauritiana*.
I. dissecta Pursh = *Merremia dissecta*.
I. fistulosa Mart. ex Choisy = *I. carnea* ssp. *fistulosa*.

I. hederacea (L.) Jacq. Ann. hairy climber to 3m. Lvs 3–12cm, ovate-cordate to suborbicular, usually 3-lobed. Fls 2–4cm, limb 2–3cm diam., funnel-shaped, usually blue, sometimes purple, tube white, occas. wholly white. Summer. S US to Arg. 'Roman Candy': lvs green and white; fls cerise and white. Z8.
I. hederifolia L. Ann. to 1.6m. Lvs 2–15cm, cordate, 3- or 5- (rarely 7-) lobed, coarsely toothed. Fls 2.5–4.5cm, limb 1.8–2.5cm diam., subhypocrateriform, red or orange, buff-yellow inside. Summer. Pantrop., introd. in Afr. and Asia. Z8.
I. horsfalliae Hook. Woody climber to 8m. Lvs 5–20cm palmate lobes 3–5, ovate-lanceolate to linear-lanceolate. Fls about 4cm, limb *c*4–5cm diam., hypocrateriform, red to maroon, with 5 rounded lobes. W Indies, sometimes introd. in other trop. regions. 'Briggsii': floriferous, cor. magenta to crimson. Z9.
I. ×imperialis hort. IMPERIAL JAPANESE MORNING GLORY. Differs from *I. nil* in larger, double fls, often with fringed or fluted limbs. Summer. Gdn origin. Z9.
I. indica (Burm.) Merrill. BLUE DAWN FLOWER. Herbaceous climber to 6m. Lvs 5–17cm ovate-cordate to ovate, entire or 3-lobed. Fls 5–7cm, limb 6–8cm diam., funnel-shaped, blue or purple, rarely white. Pantrop. Z9.
I. learii Paxt. = *I. indica*.
I. lobata (Cerv.) Thell. SPANISH FLAG. Weakly climbing ann. or short-lived perenn. to 5m. Lvs 3–16cm, ovate-cordate, entire or palmately 3-lobed, coarsely sinuately toothed. Fls on erect secund rac., 1.8–2.2cm, narrow-tubular-urceolate, slightly curved, scarlet fading to yellow then white, all three colours often present, limb v. small. Mex. Z8.
I. mauritiana Jacq. Woody-based climber to 5m, roots tuberous. Lvs 5–8cm, orbicular in outline, lobes 3–9, ovate-acuminate. Fls 4–6cm, funnel-shaped, pink to pale maroon, tube dark at base. Pantrop. Long confused with *I. digitata*, a rare endemic of Hispaniola. Z9.
I. ×multifida (Raf.) Shinn. (*I. coccinea* ×*I. quamoclit*.) CARDINAL CLIMBER. Ann. climber to 1m. Lvs 2–4.5cm, deeply and narrowly 3–7-lobed, lobes sometimes themselves lobed. Fls 2.5–5cm, salverform, scarlet or crimson, limb 2–2.5cm diam. with a white eye. Summer. Gdn origin. Z8.
I. nil (L.) Roth. Ann. herb to 5m, climbing, hairy. Lvs 4–14cm, ovate to orbicular, entire or 3-lobed. Fls 3–6cm, limb 4–5cm diam., funnel-shaped, blue, rarely purple or red, tube white. Summer. Pantrop. 'Chocolate': fls pale chocolate-brown. 'Early Call': fls large, limb to 7cm diam., scarlet with a white tube. 'Flying Saucers': large round fls, marbled sky-blue and white. 'Limbata': fls violet-purple with a white margin. Platycodon Flowered White: fls white. Platycodon Mixed: fls single and semi-double, red, purple edged white or white, abundant. 'Scarlett O'Hara': fls red. 'Scarlet Star': fls cerise with white star, abundant. Spice Island Mix: non-climbing; lvs variegated fls white; colour variable. Z9.
I. palmata Forssk. = *I. cairica*.
I. pandurata (L.) G. Mey. WILD SWEET POTATO VINE; WILD POTATO VINE; MAN OF THE EARTH. Climbing perenn. to 10m, roots tuberous. Lvs to 15cm, ovate or panduriform, sometimes 3-lobed. Fls to 10cm diam., broadly funnel-shaped, white, purple at base. Summer. US (Conn. to Flor. and Tex.). Z7.
I. pes-caprae (L.) R. Br. BEACH MORNING GLORY; RAILROAD VINE. Prostrate perenn. to 40m, semisucculent. Lvs 3–10cm, fleshy, ovate, elliptic or to reniform, emarginate. Fls 3–5cm, funnel-shaped, pink to pale purple, darker purple at tube base. Pantrop. Z9.
I. pes-caprae ssp. *brasiliensis* (L.) Ooststr. = *I. pes-caprae*.
I. purpurea (L.) Roth. COMMON MORNING GLORY. Ann. climber to 2.5m, usually hairy. Lvs 2–10cm, ovate or orbicular, entire or 3-lobed. Fls to 3.5cm, funnel-shaped, blue, purple, pink, red, white, or with stripes of these colours on a white background. Summer. Origin probably Mex., now pantrop. by introduction. var. *diversifolia* (Lindl.) O'Don. Lvs entire or 3(–5)-lobed on same plant. 'Alba': fls white. 'Huberi': lvs marked silver; fls pink to purple, edged white. 'Violacea': fls deep violet, double. Z7.
I. quamoclit L. CYPRESS VINE; STAR-GLORY; INDIAN PINK. Slender ann. climber to 3m. Lvs 1–9cm, deeply pinnatisect with 9–19 pairs of linear lobes. Fls 2–3cm, hypocrateriform, limb 1.8–2cm diam., distinctly and stellately 5-lobed, scarlet, crimson or white. Summer. Trop. Amer., nat. elsewhere. Platycodon Flowered Red Picotee: cor. with a white margin, often semi-double. Relli-Valley Strain: lvs fern-like; fls plum, pink or white. Z8.
I. rubro-caerulea Hook. = *I. tricolor*.
I. ×sloteri (House ex L.H. Bail.) Van Ooststr. = *I. ×multifida*.
I. tricolor Cav. MORNING GLORY. Ann. or perenn. climbing herb to 4m. Lvs 3.5–7cm ovate-cordate, long-acuminate. Fls 4–6cm, funnel-shaped, bright sky-blue, tube white, golden-yellow at base inside. Summer. Mex. and C Amer., widely introd. elsewhere. 'Blue Star': fls sky-blue striped dark blue. 'Crimson

Rambler': fls crimson, throats white. 'Heavenly Blue': intense sky-blue. 'Heavenly Blue Improved': fls large, bright blue with paler centre. 'Flying Saucers': fls marbled blue and white. 'Pearly Gates': fls marbled white and blue. 'Rainbow Flash': dwarf; fls rose, carmine, white and deep blue. 'Summer Skies': fls light sky-blue. 'Wedding Bells': fls rose-lavender. Z8.

I. tuberosa L. = *Merremia tuberosa*.

I. versicolor Meissn. = *I. lobata*.

I. violacea auct. non L. = *I. tricolor*.

→*Calonyction, Convolvulus, Mina, Pharbitis* and *Quamoclit*.

Ipomopsis Michx. Polemoniaceae. 24 ann. and perenn. herbs. Lvs basal, rosulate or cauline alt., entire to pinnatifid, often villous, sometimes gland. Pan. term.; cor. tubular or hypocrateriform. Spring–summer. US, S Arg.

I. aggregata (Pursh) V. Grant. SCARLET GILIA; SKYROCKET. Erect, hairy or gland. bienn. 30–80cm. Lvs 3–5cm, pinnate, seg. linear. Pan. thyrsoid; cor. 2–4.5cm, pink to magenta or bright red mottled with yellow, rarely wholly white or yellow; sta. exserted. Summer. BC to New Mex. Z7. ssp. *aggregata*. Cor. tube stout, expanded at throat. ssp. *attenuata* (A. Gray) A.D. & V. Grant. Cor. tube slender, barely expanded at throat. Z7.

I. longiflora (Torr.) V. Grant. Erect glab. or gland. ann., 15–30cm. Lvs to 4cm, lower pinnatifid seg. linear, sometimes entire and linear. Pan. corymbose; cor. 3–5cm, white to pink or blue-hued; sta. included. Summer. Neb. and Utah to Tex. and Ariz., N Mex. Z7.

I. rubra (L.) Wherry. STANDING CYPRESS. Erect, glabrate unbranched perenn. or bienn. to 2m. Lvs to 2.5cm, pinnate, seg. filiform. Pan. thyrse-like, narrow; cor. 2–2.5cm, scarlet, yellow and red-spotted inside. Summer–autumn. S Carol. and Flor. to Tex. Z8.

I. spicata (Nutt.) V. Grant. Villous bienn. herb, 15–35cm. Lvs linear, pinnate to entire, seg. linear. Pan. dense; bracts long; cor. 1–1.2cm, white, cream or purple-hued, tube longer than lobes; sta. included. W US. ssp. *capitata* (A. Gray) V. Grant. Infl. globose. Late spring–early summer. Z8.

→*Gilia*.

Iresine P. Browne. BLOODLEAF. Amaranthaceae. 80 ann. or perenn. herbs or subshrubs. Lvs simple, entire, often brilliantly marked. Fls white or green, insignificant, in term. or axill. bracteate spikes. Americas, Aus. Z9.

I. herbstii Hook. BEEF PLANT; BEEFSTEAK PLANT; CHICKEN GIZZARD. Ann., erect, to 1.5m. Br. green, purple or red, somewhat succulent. Lvs ovate, variegated, green with yellow veins to purple with pink veins, waxy, 2–6cm. Braz. 'Aureoreticulata': lvs green-red with yellow veins. 'Brilliantissima': lvs rich crimson. 'Wallisii': dwarf; lvs purple-black.

I. lindenii Van Houtte. Perenn., erect, branching, to 1m. Lvs narrow, ovate-acuminate or lanceolate, glossy deep blood-red, veins prominent, deep or light red. Ecuad. 'Formosa': lvs yellow, veins crimson.

I. reticulata hort. = *I. herbstii*.

Iriartea Ruiz & Pav.

I. andicola (Humb. & Bonpl.) Spreng. = *Ceroxylon alpinum*.

IRIDACEAE Juss. 92/1800. *Alophia, Anothemaca, Aristea, Babiana, Belamcanda, Bobartia, Calydorea, Chasmanthe, Cipura, Crocosmia, Crocus, Cypella, Dierama, Dietes, Diplarrhena, Eleutherine, Ferraria, Freesia, Galaxia, Geissorhiza, Gelasine, Gladiolus, Gynandiris, Herbertia, Hermodactylus, Hesperantha, Homeria, Iris, Ixia, Klattia, Lapeirousia, Libertia, Melasphaerula, Micranthus, Moraea, Nemastylis, Neomarica, Nivenia, Olsynium, Orthrosanthus, Pardanthopsis, Patersonia, Rigidella, Romulea, Schizostylis, Sisyrinchium, Solenomelus, Sparaxis, Synnotia, Syringodea, Tigridia, Trimezia, Tritonia, Tritoniopsis, Watsonia, Witsenia*.

Iris L. FLAG; FLEUR-DE-LIS; SWORD LILY. Iridaceae. 300 rhizomatous or bulbous perenn. herbs. Flowering st. branched or unbranched. Lvs linear to ensiform, channelled, flat or tetragonal (ultimate length given below), basal lvs in fans or from growth point of bulb; cauline lvs sheathing st. or in apical tuft or fan. Fls 1 to several in bracteate heads; perianth tubular, seg. 6, free, the outer 3 (falls) narrowed basally into a haft, spreading to deflexed above, sometimes with a beard, coloured hairs or crest, often with patch of colour (signal), inner 3 (standards) clawed, sometimes reduced, bristle-like, sta. 3, style br. 3, petaloid, usually arching over falls. N temp. zones.

There follows a classification of *Iris*. Species descriptions should be read with reference to the relevant subgenus or section, indicated by number.

Subgenus IRIS. Plants with well developed rhiz., sometimes slender and stolon-like; roots not swollen and tuber-like. Falls with a distinct beard of long hairs.

1. Section *Iris* (The Bearded or Pogon irises). Rhiz. stout, giving rise to fans of lvs. Flowering st. simple or branched, 2- to several-fld; falls and standards well-developed, beard multicellular.

2. Section *Psammiris* (Spach) J. Tayl. Rhiz. usually stoloniferous. Flowering st. simple; fls to 5cm diam., yellow or sometimes purple-lavender, 1–3 per st.; beard hairs unicellular.

3. Section *Oncocyclus* (Siemssen) Bak. Rhizomatous. Flowering st. simple; fls to 5cm diam. or more, solitary, variously coloured, rarely yellow; beard hairs unicellular.

4. Section *Regelia* Lynch. Flowering st. simple, normally with 2 fls produced from 2 bracts.

5. Section *Hexapogon* (Bunge) Bak. Flowering st. simple, with 3 or more fls produced from 3 or 4 bracts.

6. Section *Pseudoregelia* Dykes. Plants usually dwarf. Rhiz. compact, non-stoloniferous. Flowering st. simple. Falls bearded, lilac or purple prominently blotched dark lilac or purple, hairs unicellular.

Subgenus LIMNIRIS (Tausch) Spach (The Beardless irises). Rhiz. well developed, sometimes slender and stolon-like; roots not swollen and tuber-like. Falls without beard but sometimes with cockscomb-like crests.

7. Section *Lophiris* (Tausch) Tausch (The Evansia irises). Plants creeping. Rhiz. widely spreading, often ascending as cane-like st. Lvs persistent in an apical fan, soft-textured, green. Falls with 1 or more ridges or crests, usually dissected.

8. Section *Limniris* Series *Chinensis* (Diels) Lawrence. Rhiz. thin, wiry, often wide-creeping. Lvs prominently ribbed.

9. Series *Vernae* (Diels) Lawrence. Plants small. Fls blue.

10. Series *Ruthenicae* (Diels) Lawrence. Plant low, compact, clump-forming.

11. Series *Tripetalae* (Diels) Lawrence. Standards muchreduced, often bristle-like.

12. Series *Sibiricae* (Diels) Lawrence (The Siberian irises). Lvs narrow. Flowering st. hollow, stigma triangular.

13. Series *Californicae* (Diels) Lawrence (The Pacific Coast irises). Lvs tough. Stigma triangular.

14. Series *Longipetalae* (Diels) Lawrence. St. persisting for a year or more after flowering. Stigma bidentate.

15. Series *Laevigatae* (Diels) Lawrence. Robust, moistureloving. Stigma bilobed.

16. Series *Hexagonae* (Diels) Lawrence (The Louisiana irises). Robust plants from marsh and swampland. St. with leaf-like spathes and large fls.

17. Series *Prismaticae* (Diels) Lawrence. Plants from wet grassy habitats. Rhiz. thin, wide-creeping. St. tall, bracts brown.

18. Series *Spuriae* (Diels) Lawrence. Stigma bidentate.

19. Series *Foetidissimae* (Diels) Lawrence. Plants everg. Lvs wide. Seeds scarlet, remaining attached to capsule.

20. Series *Tenuifoliae* (Diels) Lawrence. Rhiz. with shiny brown lf bases at apex. Perianth tube to 14cm; stigma bilobed.

21. Series *Ensatae* (Diels) Lawrence. Plants from salt marshes. Perianth tube to 3mm; ovary 6-grooved, beaked.

22. Series *Syriacae* (Diels) Lawrence. Rhiz. almost vertical, covered with spiny fibres.

23. Series *Unguiculares* (Diels) Lawrence. Plants low. Lvs narrow. Perianth tube to 16cm; style branched, with golden marginal glands.

24. Subgenus NEPALENSIS (Dykes) Lawrence. Rootstock with small growing point to which the plant dies back during winter with some storage roots attached. Lvs prominently veined. Fls fugacious; falls with a linear crest or uncrested.

25. Subgenus XIPHIUM (Mill.) Spach (The Spanish irises). Bulbous. Bulb tunics papery to tough and coriaceous, not netted. Roots thin, fibrous. Lvs channelled. St. to 90cm, simple, 1–3-fld; falls unbearded; standards upright, not greatly reduced.

26. Subgenus SCORPIRIS Spach (The Juno irises). Bulbs with papery tunics, not netted-fibrous, usually with thickened fleshy roots when dormant. Lvs channelled. Standards much reduced, sometimes bristle-like, often horizontal or deflexed; falls beardless, with a central, raised ridge.

27. Subgenus HERMODACTYLOIDES Spach (The Reticulata irises). Dwarf, bulbous plants. Bulb tunics fibrous and netted. Lvs quadrangular to subterete in cross section.

I. acutiloba Mey. [3.] 25cm. Lvs sickle-shaped, 2–6mm wide. Fls 1, 5–7cm diam., white-yellow, strongly veined and lined brown-grey; falls with 2 spots-one central and one rust-black, beard hairs purple-brown. Spring–early summer. Transcauc. ssp. *lineolata* (Trautv.) B. Mathew & Wendelbo. Falls with only one spot.

I. aequiloba Ledeb. = *I. pumila*.

I. afghanica Wendelbo. [4.] 15–35cm. Lvs curved. Fls 1, 8–9cm diam., cream-white, veins dense, purple-brown; falls bearded, signal patch purple, beard hairs dark, standards yellow, beard tinged green. Spring. Pak., E Afghan.

I. alata Poir. = *I. planifolia*.

I. alberti Reg. [1.] 30–70cm. Lvs broad, grey-green. Fls 1–3, 6–8cm diam., lilac to violet-purple, fall haft veined red-brown, beard white to pale blue, tips yellow. Late spring. Kazakstan.

I. albicans Lange. [1.] 30–60cm. Lvs in fans, broadly lanceolate, grey-green. Fls 1–3, 8–9cm diam., scented, perianth white or blue, fall haft green-yellow, beard white, tips green, standard haft green-yellow. Saudi Arabia, Yemen. *I. germanica* 'Florentina' is distinguished by its brown papery bracts. 'Madonna': fls blue.

I. albomarginata R. Fost. [26.] To 30cm. Lvs channelled, to 3cm wide, grey-green with white margins. Fls 2–5; perianth blue, fall blade with white ridge surrounded by yellow. Spring–early summer. Russia.

I. alexeenkoi Grossh. [1.] To 30cm. Similar to *I. pumila* but lvs larger, fls 7–8cm diam., purple-blue, beard yellow.

I.×altobarbata Murray. Name sometimes applied to the tall bearded irises.

I. amoena DC. Name applied to a group of bearded irises with white standards and coloured falls, probably derived from *I. variegata*.

I. antilibanotica Dinsm. [3.] To 40cm. Lvs to 10cm, falcate. Fls 1, large; falls rich purple with central blue blotch, veins purple, beard yellow, standards violet. Spring–early summer. Syr.

I. aphylla L. [1.] To 30cm. Lvs decid., in fans, 0.5–2cm wide. Fls 1–5, 6–7cm diam., pale to deep purple to blue-violet, beard hairs blue-white, tips yellow. Spring. C & E Eur. to W Russia and N Cauc.

Aril Irises (Regeliocyclus Hybrids). 'Ancilla': fls white veined purple, falls flaked and netted purple. 'Chione': standards white veined lilac blue, falls veined grey, blotched black-brown. 'Clotho': standards deep violet with black beard, falls brown, veins and blotch black. 'Dardanus': standards tinged lilac, falls cream blotched matt purple. 'Theseus': standards violet with darker veins, falls ivory marked deep violet. 'Thor': fls grey veined purple, blotch bright purple. 'Vera': fls chocolate-brown tinged purple with blue beard. **Aril-Median Irises:** (Aril ×Miniature Tall Bearded irises). 'Canasta': to 28cm; standards pale violet, falls rich beige with deep red signal and veining, the latter paling at edges, beard brown-bronze. 'Little Orchid Annie': to 30cm; standards pale amethyst veined and shaded green-gold, ruffled, midrib green, falls orchid edged yellow-green, signal and veining red, beard dark yellow. **Arilbred Irises** (Aril ×Tall Bearded irises). 'Lady Mohr': to 75cm; standards light mauve-blue, falls yellow and green with deep red markings, beard brown. 'Loudmouth': to 25cm; fls deep red, falls with black signal. 'Nineveh': standards purple shaded pink, falls violet-red, beard dark brown. 'Saffron Charm': fls in blend of deep yellow, grey and lavender.

I. arctica Eastw. = *I. setosa* var. *arctica*.

I. assadiana Chaudhary, Kirkwood & Weymouth. [3.] To 15cm. Lvs 5–10cm, strongly curved. Fls 1, to 7.5cm diam., dark maroon, veins deeper; signal patch velvety, beard hairs short, purple, and long, white or yellow, style br. light orange-red streaked purple. Syr.

I. atrofusca Bak. [3.] Lvs erect, *c*1cm wide. Fls 1, 8–9cm diam.; falls purple-brown, signal patch black, beard hair dense yellow; standards paler, claret. Spring. Isr.

I. atropurpurea Bak. [3.] 15–25cm. Lvs *c*15cm, falcate. Fls 1, 8cm diam.; v. deep black-purple, standards paler than falls, signal patch yellow, beard hairs yellow. Isr. var. *eggeri* Dinsm. Fls purple-brown. var. *gileadensis* Dinsm. Fls brown, veined and dotted red.

I. atropurpurea Dinsm. non Bak. = *I. bostrensis*.

I. attica (Boiss. & Heldr.) Hayek. [1.] 5–10cm high. Lvs in fans, 4–7cm, falcate. Fls 1, 4.5cm diam., yellow or purple or bicoloured. Spring. Greece, S Balk., W Turk.

I. aucheri (Bak.) Sealy. [26.] To 40cm. Lvs 25cm. Fls 3–6, blue, rarely almost white, fall blade with central yellow ridge, standards 2–3.5cm, horizontal to deflexed. Late winter–spring. SE Turk., N Iraq, N Syr., Jord., NW Iran.

I. aurantiaca Dinsm. [3.] To 50cm. Fls 1, 12–15cm diam., yellow spotted brown, appearing bronze, signal patch maroon, beard hair yellow tipped purple. Late spring. Syr. var. *unicolor* Mout. Signal patch and spotting 0.

I. bakeriana Fost. [27.] To 15cm. Fls 1, white tipped violet on falls with a cream ridge surrounded by violet spots and veins, haft spotted and veined violet, standards and style br. lilac. SE Turk., N Iraq, W Iran.

I. baldschuanica B. Fedtsch. [26.] To 15cm. Fls 1–3, cream; tube to 10cm; fall blade with central yellow ridge, standards horizontal to slightly deflexed; style br. pink-brown. Spring. C Asia, NW Afghan.

I. balkana Janka = *I. reichenbachii*.

I. barnumae Bak. & Fost. [3.] 10–30cm. Lvs curved, grey-green. Fls 1, 7–8cm diam., deep purple-violet, sparsely veined, beard narrow, hairs yellow, sometimes tipped purple, cream or white, signal patch obscure. Late spring. E Turk., NE Iraq, Iran. f. *urmiensis* (Hoog) B. Mathew & Wendelbo. Fls yellow, without spots or veins. f. *protonyma* (Stapf) B. Mathew & Wendelbo. Falls brown-purple, beard hairs purple-black, thick, broad, standards purple-violet. ssp. *demavendica* (Bornm.) B. Mathew & Wendelbo. Fls larger, blue-violet, beard narrow, white-cream. Iran.

I. basaltica Dinsm. [3.] To 70cm. Lvs erect to subfalcate, to 2cm wide. Fls 1, 15cm diam., falls green-white heavily veined and dotted black-purple, signal patch rounded, beard brown-purple, tips yellow, standards white or light green, markings faint. Spring. Syr.

Bearded (Pogon) Irises. (1) *Border Bearded* (st. to 70cm; fls large): 'Brown Lasso': standards butterscotch, falls pale violet and brown. 'Carnival Glass': fls red-brown, occas. tinged blue or red. 'Impelling': fls bright pink and yellow with an orange beard. 'Impetuous': fls sky-blue, ruffled, beard white. 'Marmalade Skies': fls apricot-orange. 'Whoop Em Up': fls vivid golden-yellow, falls clear chestnut-red, rimmed with bright yellow. (2) *Intermediate Bearded* (st. to 70cm; fls abundant). 'Annikins': fls deep violet blue. 'Black Watch': fls v. dark velvety black-purple. 'Golden Muffin': standards ruffled, yellow, falls amber-brown edged yellow. 'Indeed': standards clear lemon-yellow, falls translucent white edged bright yellow with a white beard. 'Silent Strings': fls clear blue. 'Why Not': fls bright apricot-orange with darker beard. (3) *Miniature Dwarf Bearded* (st. to 20cm, to 2 fls per st.). 'April Ballet': standards light blue with a violet-blue spot. 'Egret Snow': standards pure white, falls occas. flecked blue. 'Jasper Gem': rust-red bicolor. 'Orchid Flare': fls pink with white beard. (4) *Miniature Tall Bearded* (st. to 70cm; fls 8 or more). 'Carolyn Rose': fls cream-white lined rose-pink. 'Dappled Pony': standards dark blue, falls white heavily flecked violet. 'Smarty Pants': fls yellow with red stripes on falls. 'Surprise Blue': fls lavender blue with white hafts. (5) *Standard Dwarf Bearded* (to 40cm; fls 3 or 4 per st.). 'Austrian Sky': fls blue with darker markings on falls. 'Blue Denim': fls blue, flaring with a violet-blue spot. 'Gingerbread Man': fls deep ginger-brown with a bright blue beard. 'Green Halo': fls pale olive-green with a darker 'halo'. 'Melon Honey': fls melon-orange with a white beard. 'Toots': fls velvet burgundy with a yellow beard. (6) *Tall Bearded* (over 70cm high; fls large, usually ruffled). 'Broadway': standards golden-yellow, beard orange, falls white. 'Going My Way': fls white striped violet-purple. 'Jane Phillips': fls large, pale blue. 'Love's Allure': standards grey-lilac flecked purple, falls edged sandy gold. 'Red Lion': fls deep brown-burgundy. 'Vanity': fls light pink flashed white with a pink-red beard.

I. battandieri Fost. = *I. xiphium* 'Battandieri'.

I. belouinii Boiss. & Cornault. [1.] Similar to *I. germanica* but lvs decid. Moroc.

I. biggeri Dinsm. [1.] To 50cm. Lvs almost straight. Fls 1, large, falls with merging red-violet dots, signal patch deeper, beard hairs white tipped purple, standards paler, veins fine, purple. Spring. Isr.

I. biliotii Fost. [1.] To 80cm. Fls fragrant; falls red-purple, haft white veined brown-purple, beard white tipped yellow; standards blue-purple. Late spring. Turk.

I. bismarckiana Reg. [3.] Lvs short, in a fan. Fls 1, 10–12cm diam., cream yellow, spotted and veined red brown or purple; signal patch black-purple, beard deep purple; standards white spotted and veined purple-blue. NE Isr., S Syr.

I. bloudowii Bunge. Similar to *I. humilis*, 15–35cm high. Lvs larger; fls 2–3, 5cm diam., yellow stained purple-brown at base; beard yellow. Spring. C & E Russia, China.

I. boissieri Henriq. [25.] 30–40cm. Lvs narrow. Fls solitary, deep purple, perianth tube to 5cm, beard a narrow band of yellow hairs. Summer. N Port., NW Spain.

I. bosniaca Beck = *I. reichenbachii*.

I. bostrensis Mout. [3.] 10–15cm. Lvs to 5mm wide. Fls 1, 6–8cm diam., yellow-green or light brown, spotted and veined dark purple-brown, signal patch dark maroon, velvety, beard hairs dense, yellow tipped purple. Spring. S Syr.

I. bracteata Wats. [13.] 20–30cm. Lvs v. thick, becoming bract-like and red-tinged on st. Fls 2 per st., 6–7.25cm diam.; falls spreading, cream to yellow veined brown or red-purple, central zone deep yellow. Early summer. W US.

I. brandzae Prodan = *I. sintenisii* ssp. *brandzae*.

I. brevicaulis Raf. [16.] To 50cm. Lvs 3–6, to 45cm. Flowering st. flexuous; to 11cm diam., pale blue to blue-violet, falls large, broad-ovate, reflexed, banded yellow in centre, haft veined white-green, standards smaller, spreading. Summer. C US. 'Brevipes': falls ovate, pale mauve-pink, veined lilac, standards pale violet to pale blue-violet. 'Flexicaulis': falls obovate, dark violet, standards narrow-spathulate, violet. 'Mississippiensis': falls suborbicular, pale violet, veined green-brown, standards pale violet with white base.

I. brevipes Alexander = *I. brevicaulis* 'Brevipes'.

I. bucharica Fost. [26.] To 40cm. Lvs to 20cm, shiny green, margins white. Fls 2–6; perianth tube to 4.5cm, golden yellow to white, fall with central ridge yellow suffused green to dull purple, standards spreading, trilobed or lanceolate. Spring. C Asia, NE Afghan.

I. bulleyana Dykes. [12.] To 45cm. Lvs 45cm, linear. Fls 1–2, 6–8cm diam., falls obovate, dotted streaked and veined bright blue-purple on cream ground, haft green-yellow, standards shorter than falls, lilac. Summer. W China, N Burm.

I. caespitosa Pall. & Link. [10.] Lvs to 15cm, grasslike. Fls solitary, aromatic, dark violet. Spring. E Eur. Possibly a dwarf variant of *I. ruthenica*.

I. camillae Grossh. [3.] 20–40cm. Lvs falcate. Fls 1, to 8cm diam., light yellow to blue-violet, falls smaller than standards, light yellow to blue-violet, sometimes bearded yellow and with a violet signal patch. Transcauc. 'Caerulea': fls light blue. 'Lutea': fls light yellow. 'Pallida': falls intensely veined, standards white. 'Speciosissima': falls bronze, veins dark, signal patch almost black, beard yellow, standards blue. 'Spectabilis': falls cream, veins thick deep brown, signal patch black-brown, standards white. 'Sulphurea': falls golden yellow, signal patch red-purple, standards blue.

I. caucasica Hoffm. [26.] To 15cm. Lvs falcate, 10–12cm, margins white. Fls 1–4, green to yellow, tube to 4cm; falls obovate, central ridge yellow; standards horizontal. Late winter–spring. C & NE Turk., NE Iraq, NW Iran, Russia. var. *multiflora* Grossh. Fls to 10. S Transcauc.

I. chamaeris = *I. lutescens*.

I. cedretii Dinsm. ex Chaudhary. [3.] To 40cm. Lvs straight to curved, 1–2cm wide. Fls 1, 8–11cm diam., white, thickly covered with fine red-brown veins and spots, falls with rounded signal patch, deep red-brown, beard brown-purple, hairs long. Spring. Leb.

I. chrysographes Dykes. [12.] To 50cm. Lvs 50cm. Fls 1–4, fragrant, 5–10cm diam., dark red-purple streaked gold on deflexed falls; standards spreading. Late spring–summer. W China, NE Burm. 'Black Night': fls indigo-violet. 'Inshriach': fls almost black. 'Margot Holmes': fls purple-crimson lined yellow at throat. 'Rubella': fls burgundy.

I. chrysophylla Howell. [13.] To *c*20cm. Lvs 3–5mm wide. Fls 6–7cm diam., paired, cream to palest yellow veined darker yellow; tube 4.5–12cm; sep. narrow, acute. Late spring–summer. W US. 'Alba': fls white. 'Caerulea': fls blue.

I. citrina anon. = *I. tenuissima*.

I. clarkei Bak. [12.] To 60cm. Lvs to 2cm wide, fls paired, 5–10cm diam., blue-violet to red-purple; falls with large, white, central signal patch, veined violet; haft ± yellow. Late spring–early summer. E Himal.

I. colchica Kem.-Nat. = *I. graminea*.

I. collettii Hook. [24.] To 5cm. Fls subsessile, 1–2 per br., to 3cm diam., fragrant, light blue, with yellow-orange crest; tube to 10cm. Spring–summer. SW China, N Burm.

I. confusa Sealy. [7.] To 1.5m. St. cane-like, branching, with an apical fan of sword-shaped lvs. Infl. to 90cm, branched; fls to 5cm diam., short-lived, white spotted yellow or mauve; falls 2.5×5cm, crest yellow, signal patch yellow. Spring. W China.

I. cretensis Janka = *I. unguicularis* ssp. *cretensis*.

I. cretica Bak. = *I. unguicularis* ssp. *cretensis*.

I. cristata Sol. [7.] Lvs to 15×1–3cm, linear. Fls 1–2 per spathe, 3–4cm diam., pale lilac to purple; falls to 10cm; falls obovate, reflexed, central patch white, crest yellow, 3-ridged; standards erect, shorter than falls. Early summer. NE US. 'Alba': fls white. 'Caerulea': fls blue.

I. crocea Jacq. [18.] Lvs to 75cm, sword-shaped. Infl. to 1.5m, branched; fls 12–18cm diam., dark golden yellow; fall margins crisped; standards erect, slightly crisped. Kashmir.

I. cycloglossa Wendelbo. [26.] To 50cm. Lvs to 30×1.5cm. Fls 1–3, 8–10cm diam., lilac, aromatic, tube to 4.5cm, falls 7cm, orbicular, centre white, blotched yellow, without ridge; standards obovate, becoming horizontal with age. Spring. NW Afghan.

I. cypriana Bak. & Fost. Similar to *I. germanica* but fls to 15cm diam., scarcely scented. Cyprus.

I. damascena Mout. [3.] To 15–30cm. Lvs curved, to 1cm wide. Fls 1, 7–9cm diam., white, thickly veined and spotted purple-brown; signal patch deep purple, beard hairs sparse, purple; standards veined purple. Spring. Syr.

I. danfordiae (Bak.) Boiss. [27.] To 15cm. Lvs 1–15cm, quadrangular. Fls 1, to 5cm diam., yellow; tube to 7.5cm; falls lightly spotted green in centre and lower part; standards bristle-like. Early spring. Turk.

I. darwasica Reg. [4.] To 40cm. Lvs linear, to 30cm, glaucous. Fls 2, 5–6cm diam., lilac veined purple; falls elliptic-lanceolate, 6×1cm, beard blue-purple; standards to 6cm, claw sometimes bearded. Spring. Russia.

I. decora Wallich. [24.] To 30cm. Lvs erect, linear, ribbed, 2–5mm wide. Fls 1–3, scented, 4–5cm diam., pale lilac to deep red-purple; tube 3.5–5cm; crest wavy, orange-yellow, apex white or purple, haft white or yellow; standards spreading, shorter than falls. Summer. Himal.

I. delavayi Micheli. [12.] To 1.5m. Lvs to 90cm, grey-green, fls 7–9cm diam., light to deep purple-violet; fall blade rounded, notched, signal patch white; standards inclined, lanceolate, small. Summer. W China. Hybrids with *I. wilsonii* have purple fls, falls yellow veined blue-purple.

I. demavendica (Bornm.) Dykes = *I. barnumae* ssp. *demavendica*.

I. diversifolia Merino = *I. boissieri*.

I. doabensis B. Mathew. [26.] 10–15cm. Lvs 20cm, shiny green. Fls 1–5, scented, bright deep yellow; tube 7–8cm; fall crest darker, haft margins down-turned; standards ovate to 1cm. Spring. NE Afghan.

I. douglasiana Herb. [13.] Lvs to 100cm, base stained red, ribbed. Infl. 15–70cm; fls 2–3, 7–10cm diam., lavender to purple, veins darker; tube to 3cm; falls yellow in centre. Summer. W US. 'Alba': fls white. 'Southcombe Velvet': fls deep violet.

I. dragalz Horvat = *I. variegata*.

I. drepanophylla Aitch. & Bak. [26.] 10–30cm. Lvs to 20×2.5cm, curving, ciliate. Fls 2–8, 4–5cm diam., yellow to green; tube 3.5–4cm; fall crest darker; standards reduced, bristle-like. Spring. C Asia, NE Iran, N & W Afghan. ssp. *chlorotica* B. Mathew & Wendelbo. Fls silvery green; fall crest white to pale yellow-green. NE Afghan.

Dutch Irises see *I. hollandica*, *I. xiphium*.

I. dykesii Stapf. Similar to *I. chrysographes* but larger; fls bright dark violet-purple, veins in fall centre white and yellow. Summer. China.

English Iris see *I. latifolia*.

I. elizabethae Siehe = *I. sprengeri*.

I. ensata Thunb. JAPANESE WATER IRIS. [15.] Aquatic or marginal. Lvs 20–60×0.4–1.2cm, leathery midrib prominent. Flowering st. 60–90cm; fls 3 or 4 per br., 8–15cm diam., purple to red-purple; tube 1–2cm; fall haft yellow, blade suffused yellow. Summer. Jap., N China, E Russia. Large number of cvs, many from Japan, with a few (such as some of the Higo Hybrids) just beginning to enter western gardens; fls to 20cm in shades of white, pink, blue and violet often mottled or flecked; single to double; often with spreading standards. 'Alba': fls pure white. 'Blauer Berg' ('Blue Mountain'): fls bright sky blue, abundant; middle to late season. 'Gei Sho Ne': habit unusually short; fls violet; middle to late season. 'Good Omen': growth strong; fls double, violet tinged red, abundant; early season. 'Major': habit tall to 46cm; fls darker. 'Moonlight Waves': fls white with lime-green centre. 'Peacock Dance': falls white, veins red-violet, signal patch yellow; standards dark red-purple; style br. purple. 'Prairie Love Song': fls white, signal patch yellow. 'Raspberry Rimmed': fls white, margins red-pink, signal patch yellow. 'Returning Tide': fls pale blue, signal yellow. 'Sorcerer's Triumph': fls double, white, veins red-purple, signal orange. 'Stranger in Paradise': fls white, margins pink, signal patch yellow. 'Summer Storm': fls to 18cm diam., violet tinged red, veined blue; late flowering. 'The Great Mohgul': fls black-purple. 'Unschuld' ('Innocence'): fls clear white, perianth seg. undulate; early flowering. 'Variegata': lvs striped white; fls purple. 'Aichi-no-Kagayaki' (*I. ensata* ×*I. pseudacorus*): fls large, bright yellow, veins brown. 'Chance Beauty' (*I. ensata* ×*I. pseudacorus*): fls large, bright yellow, veins red-brown.

I. eulefeldii Reg. = *I. scariosa*.

I. extremorientalis Koidz. = *I. sanguinea*.

I. falcifolia Bunge. [1.] 10–20cm. Lvs grey-green, curved, 2–4mm wide. Fls 2–5 per br., 3–4cm diam., lavender, veins darker; beard white. Spring. C Asia.

I. fernaldii R. Fost. [13.] 20–45cm. Lvs grey-green, 7–9mm wide, base purple. Fls 2.7–8cm diam., light primrose with darker yellow line, sometimes faintly tinged or veined purple, tube 3–6cm. Summer. W US.

I. filifolia Boiss. [25.] 25–45cm. Lvs almost thread-like, channelled. Fls 1–2, rich red-violet; tube 2.5cm; fall striped yellow in centre. Summer. S Spain, NW Afr.

I. fimbriata hort. = *I. japonica* or *I. tectorum*.

I. flexicaulis Small = *I. brevicaulis* 'Flexicaulis'.

I. foetidissima L. ROAST BEEF PLANT; GLADWYN; GLADDON IRIS; STINKING GLADWYN. [19.] Lvs everg., sword-shaped, in a basal fan, deep green. Flowering st. 30–90cm, 2–3-branched; fls to 5 per br., 5–7cm diam., malodorous; falls obovate, blade lilac to topaz or yellow, veins purple, haft bronze to brown. Seeds scarlet, persisting in capsule. Summer. S & W Eur., N Afr., Atlantic Is. 'Fructoalba': seed white. 'Variegata': lvs striped cream. var. *citrina* Syme. Fls pale yellow veined mauve. var. *lutescens* Maire. Fls pure yellow.

I. foliosa Mackenzie & Bush = *I. brevicaulis*.

I. fontanesii Godron = *I. tingitana* var. *fontanesii*.

I. fontanesii var. *mellori* C. Ingram. = *I. tingitana* var. *mellori*.

I. formosana Ohwi. [7.] Similar to *I. japonica* but spreading by slender stolons, st. erect, to 10cm; infl. branching, fls larger, somewhat compressed, lilac-blue, fall crest yellow. Taiwan.

I. forrestii Dykes. [12.] Lvs narrow-linear, shiny above. Flowering st. 35–40cm, unbranched; fls 2, scented, 5–6cm diam., yellow lined purple-brown on fall haft; falls oblong-ovate, blade 5cm. Summer. W China, N Burm.

I. fosteriana Aitch. & Bak. [26.] 10–15cm. Lvs to 17×0.4–0.8cm, lanceolate, silver-edged. Fls 1–2; tube to 4cm; fall and blade orbicular, to 5cm, pale yellow, crest sometimes deeper, patch brown-veined; standards obovate, purple. NE Iran, Turkmenistan, NW Afghan.

I. fulva Ker-Gawl. [16.] To 90cm. Lvs 1.5–2.5cm wide, ensiform. Fls to 6.5cm diam., bright red to rust, orange or rarely deep yellow; tube to 2.5cm, falls oblanceolate, to 2.5cm wide, standards notched, to 5×2cm. Summer. C US.

I. ×fulvala Dykes. (*I. fulva* ×*I. brevicaulis*.) Fls purple-red.

I. galatica Siehe. [26.] 5–12cm. Lvs 3–4, channelled, expanding to 12×1.2cm. Fls 1–2.5–10cm diam., red-purple or silver-purple or yellow-green with purple falls; tube to 6cm; fall crest conspicuous, orange or yellow; standards to 2cm. Spring. N Turk.

I. gatesii Fost. [3.] 40–60cm. Lvs linear 0.5–1cm wide. Fls 1, 13–20cm diam., cream, opal blue or, more usually, pearl grey, heavily overlaid with maroon or dark-mauve veins and stippling, beard yellow or maroon, signal patch 0 or small and dark. Summer. N Iraq, SE Turk.

I. germanica L. [1.] Lvs equitant, 30–40×2.5–4.5cm, grey-green. Flowering st. 60–120cm; fls 9–10cm diam., in shades of blue, violet, white, beard yellow, standards sometimes paler than falls; bracts broad, apex purple-brown, base purple or green. Late spring. Widely nat.; either a Medit. native or an ancient fertile hybrid. 'Amas': falls deep blue-purple, standards paler blue, prominent blue-white beard tipped orange. 'Askabadensis': tall, flowering later; falls red-purple, veins on hafts yellow-brown, beard tipped yellow, standards paler blue. 'Karput': lvs edged red-purple; falls narrow, black-purple, standards paler red-purple. 'Nepalensis': falls and standards both dark purple-red tipped orange; beard blue-white grading to white. Katmandu. 'Sivias': fls more blue; beard white, hairs scarcely tipped yellow. var. *florentina* (L.) Dykes. Smaller than type. Fls scented, palest blue-white; veins on haft of falls yellow, beard yellow.

I. giganticaerulea Small. [16.] St. 70–180cm. Fls to 15cm diam., light blue to dark indigo, some white, fall signal ridge yellow, blades ± deflexed, 9×4cm, standards erect. Spring. S US. 'Miraculosa': fls white.

I. glaucescens Bunge = *I. scariosa*.

I. glockiana Schwarz = *I. suaveolens*.

I. goniocarpa Bak. [6.] 10–30cm. Lvs grassy, 2–3mm wide. Fls 1, flat, to 3cm diam., lilac to blue-purple with darker blotching or mottling; tube v. short; beard hair tips orange. China, Himal.

I. gormanii Piper = *I. tenax*.

I. gracilipes A. Gray. [7.] 10–15cm; clump-forming. St. slender. Lvs grassy, to 30×0.5–1cm. Fls 3–4cm diam., pink to blue-lilac veined violet; tube 1.5cm, falls notched, centre white, crest yellow and white. Early summer. China, Jap. 'Alba': fls white.

I. graebneriana Sealy. [26.] To 40cm. Lvs distichous, margins white. Fls 4–6, 7cm + diam., blue sometimes tinged violet; tube to 6cm, fall blade deeper blue, centre ridge white on veined white ground. Spring. Russia.

I. graminea L. [18.] St. 20–40cm, flattened or 2 winged. Fls 1–2, fruit-scented, 7–8cm diam.; falls rounded, 12mm wide, violet, blade white at centre veined violet, haft occas. tinged green or yellow; standards purple. Summer. NE Spain to W Russia, N & W Cauc. var. *achteroffii* Prodan. Fls yellow-white. var. *pseudocyperus* (Schur) Beck. Larger. Fls unscented. Rom. & Czech.

I. grant-duffii Bak. [22.] 25–30cm. St. unbranched. Lvs 35×0.5–1cm, grey-green, margins white. Fls 1, to 6cm diam., slightly scented; tube 5mm; falls 6–7cm, sulphur-yellow with signal patch orange, sometimes streaked black, haft veins often purple, standards to 7cm, similar colour to falls. Late spring. Isr., Syr.

I. grossheimii Woron. [3.] 13cm. Fls 1, 7–8cm diam., claret to deep brown, veins brown-purple; signal patch large, black-brown, standards larger than falls. Cauc.

I. halophila Pall. = *I. spuria* ssp. *halophilia*.

I. hartwegii Bak. [13.] 10–30cm. Lvs 2–6mm wide. Fls 6–8cm diam., cream-yellow to lavender, veins darker; tube short, 5–10cm; seg. narrow. Summer. W US. ssp. *australis* (Parish) Lenz. To 40cm. Fls violet and purple. S Calif. ssp. *columbiana* Lenz. Fls pale yellow with darker yellow veins. C Calif. ssp. *pinetorum* (Eastw.) Lenz. Fls cream veined yellow.

I. haynei (Bak.) Mallet. [3.] To 40cm. Fls 1, 10–12cm diam., fragrant, with dark brown veins and dots on a pale ground giving overall grey-lilac colour, standards purple, signal patch black-brown. Spring. N Isr.

I. heldreichii Siehe = *I. stenophylla*.

I. heweri Grey-Wilson & B. Mathew. [4.] 10–15cm. Lvs curved, to 5mm wide. Fls 1–2, 5cm diam., falls dark purple-blue, haft off-white, veined purple, beard lilac; standards purple, beard paler. Late spring. NE Afghan.

I. hexagona Walter. [16.] 30–90cm. St. lvs long, c2.5cm wide. Fls 10–12cm diam., lilac; tube to 2.5cm; falls to 11×5cm, deflexed, signal patch yellow, haft marked white-yellow and green. Summer. SE US.

I. hippolyti Vved. [26.] 10cm. Lvs 1–1.5cm wide, distichous, channelled. Fls 1, pale violet; tube c4cm; fall blade centre yellow, crest white, standards 1.5cm. Kyzyl Kum Desert.

I. hispanica Steud. = *I. xiphium*.

I. histrio Rchb. f. [27.] Lvs 30–60cm, 4-angled. Fls 6–8cm diam., falls lilac, streaked and spotted, ridge yellow surrounded by pale blue-spotted area, standards lilac. Winter–early spring. S Turk., Syr., Leb. var. *aintabensis* (G.P. Bak.) B. Mathew. Smaller, fls pale blue. S Turk.

I. histrioides (G.F. Wils.) S. Arn. [27.] Lvs 4-angled, to 50cm. Fls 6–7cm diam., blue, fall blade pale spotted blue with a yellow ridge. Early spring. N Turk. 'Major': fls showy purple-blue, spotted white on falls. A plant with much larger, dark violet blue fls with almost horizontal falls has also been offered as *I. histrioides* 'Major'. var. *sophenensis* (Fost.) Dykes. Fls seg. narrower, dark violet-blue, lightly spotted; fall ridge yellow.

I. ×hollandica hort. The Dutch Irises, *I. xiphium* ×*I. tingitana*, possibly with the influence of *I. latifolia*. See *I. xiphium*.

I. hoogiana Dykes. [4.] 40–60cm. Lvs erect, tinged purple, to 50×1.5cm. Fls 2–3 per bract, 7–10cm diam., scented, plain grey-blue; tube to 2.5cm; falls and standards bearded yellow. Late spring. Russia. 'Alba': fls white, with a faint overlay of pale lavender-blue. 'Bronze Beauty': fls grey-violet, falls deep rich violet, edged cinnamon-brown. 'Noblesse': fls blue-violet, crest golden yellow. 'Purpurea': fls deep purple.

I. hookeri G. Don = *I. setosa* ssp. *canadensis*.

I. hookeriana Fost. [6.] Similar to *I. kamaonensis* but with flowering st. to 12cm and fls scented like lily of the valley, lilac to indigo with darker markings, white in some forms. Late spring. W Himal.

I. humboldtiana anon. = *I. tenuissima*.

I. humilis Georgi. [2.] 5–25cm. Lvs erect, 2–7mm wide, tips curved inwards. Fls 1–2, 3–4cm diam., flattened; falls yellow, veined purple, beard orange, spreading horizontally; standards yellow or purple; veined purple. Spring. E Eur., Russia.

I. humilis M. Bieb. = *I. pontica*.

I. hymenospatha B. Mathew & Wendelbo. [26.] To 12cm. Lvs 3–4, 4–9mm wide, channelled, dark green above, margin white, veins prominent silver. Fls 1–3, ± stemless, almost white, veins violet; tube to 7cm, crest faint yellow on blue-violet, standards to 2×0.5cm. Spring. S Iran.

I. hyrcana Woron. ex Grossh. Similar to *I. reticulata* but fls light blue with few markings, crest bright yellow, narrow.

I. iberica Hoffm. [3.] To 20cm. Lvs 2–6mm diam., grey-green, linear-falcate. Fls 1, to 6.5cm, falls white densely veined brown and spotted, signal patch black-brown, velvety, beard hair purple-brown, standards to 8.5cm, white to pale lilac, obscurely veined. Late spring. SW Asia. ssp. *elegantissima* (Sosn.) Fed. & Takht. Falls cream to ivory spotted and veined maroon, standards white, sometimes veined brown at base. Spring. NE Turk., NW Iran, Russia. ssp. *lycotis* (Woron.) Takht. Fls densely veined purple on pale ground, falls curving out at an angle, signal patch velvety, brown. Spring. NE Iraq, SE Turk., NW & W Iran, Russia.

I. imbricata Lindl. [1.] Similar to *I. taochia* but fls larger, 7–9cm diam., always yellow with yellow beard. Spring–summer. Iran to E Transcauc.

I. innominata Henderson. [13.] To 25cm. Lvs 2–4mm wide. Fls 1–2 per st., 6.5–7.5cm diam., cream-yellow to orange or pink-lilac to dark purple, veins darker; falls to 6.5mm, margins frilly, standards shorter. Summer. W US. 'Lilacina': fls lavender. 'Lutea': fls yellow. 'Spinners': fls soft brown-yellow, veined and marked rich brown.

Japanese Irises see *I. ensata*, *I. laevigata*.

I. japonica Thunb. [7.] 45–80cm. St. erect, branched. Lvs to 45cm, in fans dark green, ensiform. Fls 3–4 per br., 4–5cm diam., spreading, margins fringed, white to light blue-lilac; falls 2cm wide, blade with orange frilly crest on purple blotched area; standards lilac. Spring. C China, Japan. 'Ledger's Variety': fls frilled, white, marked purple, crest orange. 'Rudolph Spring': fls pale purple-blue marked orange. 'Variegata' ('Aphrodite'): lvs conspicuously striped white and marked purple.

I. jordana Dinsm. [3.] To 45cm. Lvs erect, concealing st. Fls 12–15cm diam., 1, white densely streaked and dotted purple, maroon or rosy pink, signal patch velvety purple-black, beard hairs cream-yellow. Spring. Isr.

I. juncea Poir. [25.] To 40cm. Lvs to 60cm×0.5–3mm. Fls usually 2, scented, bright yellow; tube 3.5–5cm, fall blade orbicular, 2.5cm wide; standards oblanceolate, shorter than falls. Summer. N Afr., S Spain & Sicily. var. *mermieri* Lynch. Fls sulphur-yellow. var. *numidica* anon. Fls lemon-yellow. var. *pallida* Lynch. Fls large, soft yellow.

I. junonia Schott & Kotschy. [1.] 50–65cm. Lvs grey-green, 30–35×4–5cm. Fls smaller than in *I. germanica*, white or cream to dark yellow, pale blue to lavender, beard yellow, haft white, often veined brown-purple. Early summer. Cilicia.

I. kaempferi Sieb. = *I. ensata*.

I. kamaonensis Wallich ex D. Don. [6.] To 45cm. Lvs to 45×1cm, ± linear. Fls fragrant, 4–5cm diam., tube 5–7.5cm, purple-striped; falls lilac mottled darker, beard dense, hairs white, tips yellow; standards paler. Late spring. Himal.

I. kashmiriana Bak. [1.] To 125cm. Lvs to 60×2–3cm, glaucous, ribbed. Fls 2–3 per br., 10–12cm diam., fragrant, white to pale lilac-blue; tube 2.5cm; falls to 9.5cm, beard white, tipped yellow; standards to 9cm, bearded below. Spring. Kashmir, Afghan. 'Kashmir White' ('Alba'): fls white.

I. kerneriana Bak. [1.] Lvs linear, to 5mm wide. Fls 2–4 per br., 7–10cm diam., cream to pale yellow; fall blade elliptic, to 2cm wide, with deep yellow central blotch, strongly recurved; standards erect, wavy, notched. Summer. N & C Turk.

I. kirkwoodii Chaudhary. [3.] To 75cm. Lvs curved, 1–1.5cm wide. Fls 8–12cm diam., white to pale green, dotted and veined dark purple, falls to 8cm, ovate, signal patch dark purple, beard hairs long, purple to maroon; standards pale blue, veins and speckling darker. Late spring. N Syr., N Turk. var. *macrotepala* Chaudhary. Falls larger, beard purple and/or gold. ssp. *calcarea* Dinsm. ex Chaudhary. Fls 8cm diam.; signal patch velvety, maroon, beard hairs sparse, long, maroon, standards light blue, veined darker purple.

I. klattii Kem.-Nat. = *I. spuria* ssp. *musulmanica*.

I. ×kochii Kerner ex Stapf. Similar to *I. germanica* but to 45cm; falls and standards deep blue-purple; fall haft veined brown-purple. N It.

I. kolpakowskiana Reg. [27.] To 25cm. Lvs 3–4, channelled to 25cm. Fls on short st., usually pale lilac-blue to palest purple; tube to 7cm; tall blade dark red-purple, ridge yellow-orange, haft white. Late winter. Russia.

I. kopetdagensis (Vved.) B. Mathew & Wendelbo. [26.] Similar to *I. drepanophylla* but with lf margins ± glab. and fall haft narrower. NE Iran and adjacent Russia, NW & C Afghan.

I. koreana Nak. [8.] Similar to *I. minutiflora*. Lvs to 35×1.3cm. Flowering st. shorter than lvs; fls 2, tube long, falls obovate, to 4cm wide, yellow, standards elliptic, nearly erect, notched, yellow, haft suffused brown. Spring. Korea.

I. korolkowii Reg. [4.] 40–60cm. Lvs linear, 0.5–1cm wide. Fls 2–3 per spathe, 6–8cm diam., cream-white lightly veined deep maroon, falls oblong, to 4×2.5cm, signal patch dark green to black-brown, beards inconspicuous. Early summer. C Asia, NE Afghan. 'Concolor': fls bright blue-purple. 'Violacea': fls cream

veined red-violet.

I. kuschakewiczii B. Fedtsch. [26.] 10–15cm. Lvs 4–5, dark green, channelled, 1–1.5cm wide, margin white. Fls 1–4, 6.5–8cm diam., palest violet; tube 3.5–4.5cm; fall crest white, dark violet markings to sides, standards 3-lobed. Spring. C Asia.

I. kuschkensis Grey-Wilson & B. Mathew. [26.] 30–50cm. Lvs 6–8mm wide, erect. Fls 2, 6cm diam., purple-bronze, veins of a deeper colour, falls and standards bearded pale purple, falls rounded, to 5cm. Spring. NW Afghan.

I. lactea Pall. [21.] 6–40cm. Lvs to 40×0.3cm, ribbed. Fls 2–3, fragrant, 4–6cm diam., blue to purple, tube 2–3mm, falls oblanceolate, to 2cm wide, white-yellow veined darker, standards shorter. Early summer. S Russia, China, Mong., Himal.

I. lacustris Nutt. [7.] Similar to *I. cristata* but smaller; lvs to 1cm wide. Fls sky blue; to 2cm, crest frilly, gold, falls white-blotched. Late spring–summer. N Amer.

I. laevigata Fisch. [15.] Aquatic or marginal, to 45cm. Lvs 1.5–4cm wide without prominent midvein. Fls 2–4, 8–10cm diam., blue-violet, tube to 2cm; fall haft pale yellow. Summer–autumn. E Asia. Some 30 cvs; fls in a range of colours from white through yellow and pink to blue. 'Alba': fls white, style br. mauve. 'Albopurpurea': falls purple, mottled white around edges, standards white. 'Atropurpurea': fls red-purple. 'Colcherensis': fls white, fall centre dark blue. 'Lilacina': fls light blue. 'Midnight': fls v. deep blue, pet. lined white. 'Montrosa': fls v. large, deep blue centred white. 'Mottled Beauty': fls white, falls spotted pale blue. 'Regal': fls red-purple. 'Rose Queen': fls soft old rose; falls broad, drooping. 'Snowdrift': fls double, white, style br. light violet. 'Variegata': lvs striped green and white; fls pale blue.

I. lamancei hort. ex Lynch = *I. brevicaulis*.

I. latifolia Mill. ENGLISH IRIS. [26.] To 80cm. Lvs to 65×0.8cm, channelled, grey-white. Fls 1–2 per spathe, 8–10cm diam., violet-blue, falls with central yellow blotch, broad, ovate-oblong, to 7.5cm, standards to 6cm. Late spring–summer. Spain and Pyren. 'Almona': fls light blue-lavender. 'Blue Giant': standards blue-purple, speckled darker, falls deep blue. 'Isabella': fls pink-mauve. 'La Nuit': fls dark purple-red. 'Mansfield': fls magenta-purple. 'Mont Blanc': fls white. 'Queen of the Blues': fls rich purple-blue.

I. lazica Albov. [23.] To 25cm. Lvs in fans, to 1.5cm wide. Fls sessile, tube 7–10cm, falls purple-blue, blade orbicular, spotted lavender with central yellow stripe, haft white, dotted and veined lavender; standards lavender. Autumn–spring. NE Turk., Georgia.

I. leichtlinii Reg. = *I. stolonifera*.

I. lepida Heuff. = *I. variegata*.

I. leucographa Kerner = *I. variegata*.

I. lineata Fost. ex Reg. [4.] 15–35cm. Lvs erect, 3–6mm wide. Fls green-yellow, veins brown-purple, beard tinted blue, falls and standards to 5cm, narrow, pointed. Tadjikstan, NE Afghan.

I. linifolia (Reg.) O. Fedtsch. [26.] St. 5–10cm. Lvs curved, linear, 4–7mm wide, channelled. Fls 1–2, pale yellow; tube 4cm; fall blade darker, crest white, standards much reduced, to 1cm. Spring. Russia.

I. loczyi Kanitz. [20.] To 30cm. Lvs 10–30×0.2–0.4cm. Fls 4–6cm diam., tube 10–14cm; falls pale cream, veins violet, centre tinged yellow, standards light blue to purple. NE Iran to Russian C Asia.

I. longipetala Herb. [14.] 30–60cm. Lvs dark green, 6–9mm wide, ensiform. Fls 3–8 in a term. head, 6–7cm diam., white veined violet, tube 5–13mm funnel-shaped, falls drooping, to 3cm wide, sometimes with a bright yellow signal area, standards erect, to 7.5×2cm. Late spring–summer. W US.

I. longiscapa Ledeb. [5.] Similar to *I. falcifolia* but lvs narrower, 0.5–1.5mm wide. Fls 4cm diam. C Asia.

I. lorea Jank. [18.] Similar to *I. sintenisii* but lvs paler green; bracts green (papery in *I. sintenisii*). It.

I. lortetii Barbey. [3.] To 50cm. Lvs linear, to 1.5cm wide. Fls 1, 8–9cm diam.; falls 7.5cm wide, pale grey-lilac, spotted and striped red-brown, signal patch deep crimson, beard hairs sparse, red, standards to 10cm wide, pale-grey, finely veined and dotted red-brown, wavy. Late spring. S Leb.

Lousiana Hybrids. Hybrids of the Series *Hexagonae* (including *I. fulva*): fls in shades of yellow, pink, red, brown, purple and blue. 'Black Gamecock': habit vigorous; fls blue-black with lime signal. 'Mme. Dorothea K. Williamson' (*I. fulva* ×*I. brevicaulis*): hardy, vigorous; st. horizontal; fls v. large, plum-purple. 'Gold Reserve': fls golden-orange veined red. 'May Roy': standards pale pink, falls pink tinged purple. 'Roll Call': to 90cm; fls violet with green styles. 'Sea Wasp': to 110cm; fls blue with yellow line signal.

I. lupina Fost. = *I. sari*.

I. ×lurida Ait. = *I. ×sambucina*.

I. lusitanica Ker-Gawl. = *I. xiphium* 'Lusitanica'.

I. lutescens Lam. [1.] To 30cm. Lvs 30×0.5–2.5cm, equitant. Fls 1–2, 6–8cm diam., yellow, violet, purple, white or bicoloured, tube to 3.5cm, falls oblong-spathulate, to 7.5×2cm, beard yellow, standards oblong, to 7.5×2.5cm, crisped. Early to mid-spring. NE Spain, S Fr. and It. 'Campbellii': habit v. dwarf, to 15cm; fls bright violet-blue, falls darker. 'Jackanapes': fls blue and white. 'Nancy Lindsay': habit dwarf; fls pale yellow.

I. macrosiphon Torr. [13.] To 15–25cm. Lvs linear, to 30cm. Fls fragrant, 3.5–8.5cm, 2 per st., 5–6cm diam., scented, white to yellow or light lavender to dark violet, veins fine, tube 3–9cm, falls obovate, 2cm wide, signal patch white. Early summer. W US.

I. magnifica Vved. [26.] 30–60cm. Lvs 3–5cm wide, channelled, lustrous. Fls 3–7, to 8cm diam., pink-lilac, tube 4–4.5cm, falls yellow at centre, crest white, fall haft widely-winged, standards obovate, to 3cm. Late spring. Russia.

I. mangaliae Prodan = *I. variegata*.

I. mariae Barbey. [3.] 15–25cm. Lvs 3–6mm wide, curved. Fls 8–10cm diam., lilac to pink, fall haft, beard and signal patch dark purple, standards larger than falls, veins dark. Spring. Isr.

I. marschalliana anon. = *I. pontica*.

I. marsica I. Ricci & Colasante. [1.] To 80cm. Lvs equitant, to 5cm wide. Flowering st. branched; fls 8–9cm diam., pale to dark violet with veining on fall haft, tube to 3.5cm, beard yellow or white. Late spring–early summer. C Appennines.

I. masiae Stapf ex Fost. [22.] 25–70cm. Lvs 6–8, 60×0.3–0.5cm. Fl. falls and standards to 6cm, blue-violet, veins conspicuous, fall centre and haft white. Mid-late spring. SE Turk., N & C Syr. and adjacent Iraq.

I. meda Stapf. [1.] To 25cm. Lvs to 4mm wide, glaucous. Fls 5–7cm diam., wavy, cream to lilac, heavily veined golden brown; signal patch large, deep brown, beard dense, yellow, standards longer than falls. Spring. W Iran.

I. melanosticta Bornm. Similar to *I. masiae* but fls yellow, fall blade thickly lined with black. Spring. S Syr.

I. mellita Janka = *I. suaveolens*.

I. mesopotamica Dykes. [1.] To 120cm. Lvs dark green, tinged grey, 5cm wide. Fls pale blue, centre tinged red, falls obovate, beard white to orange, standards obovate, paler than falls.

I. microglossa Wendelbo. [26.] Lvs to 25×1.5–2.5cm, grey-green, margins white, downy. Fls 1–4, c4.5–5.5cm diam., light blue-lavender to white, crest white to light yellow, tube 3–4.5cm, standards horizontal, to 2cm. Spring. NE Afghan.

I. milesii Fost. [7.] Flowering st. 30–75cm. Lvs in fans, 30–60×4–7cm, pale green. Fls 6–8cm diam., pink-lilac, falls mottled darker purple, spreading, margins often wavy, fringed, yellow or orange. Summer. Himal.

I. minutiflora Mak. [8.] To 10cm. Lvs linear, to 40cm×0.3cm. Fls 1, to 2.5cm diam., tube 2.5cm, falls spathulate, yellow, sometimes spotted brown-purple, standards smaller, lighter yellow, haft suffused brown. Spring. Korea, China, Jap.

I. mississippiensis Alexander = *I. brevicaulis* 'Mississippiensis'.

I. missouriensis Nutt. [14.] To 75cm. Lvs to 7mm wide. Fls 2–3 per spathe, 5–8cm diam., long-stalked, white, lilac, lavender or blue; falls obovate, veined, signal patch yellow; standards upright. Late spring–summer. W US. 'Alba': fls white.

I. ×monnieri DC. (Possibly *I. orientalis* ×*I. xanthospuria*.) To 120cm. Lvs to 60cm, lanceolate. Fls lemon-yellow, fragrant; fall blade rounded, 4.5cm wide, notched; standards oblanceolate-spathulate, 7.5×2.5cm. Summer. Turk., Crete.

I. munzii R. Fost. [13.] To 75cm. Lvs 1.5–2cm wide, grey-green. Fls 2–4, 6–7.5cm diam., light blue to dark red-purple, veins often darker; tube 7–10mm; seg. margins often crisped. Summer. W US.

I. musulmanica Fomin = *I. spuria* ssp. *musulmanica*.

I. narbutii O. Fedtsch. [26.] To 15cm. Lvs 4–6, curved, channelled. Fls 1–2.5cm diam., tube 4–5cm, falls pale yellow to light violet, blotched deep velvety violet, crest white on yellow area, haft to 7mm wide, standards obovate, to 3.5cm, bright violet. C Asia.

I. nectarifera Güner. [3.] To 40cm. Lvs to 1cm wide, curved. Fls 8–9cm diam., ivory to pale yellow, veined bronze or chestnut, signal patch maroon, beard slender, dense, yellow. Spring. Syr., Iraq.

I. ×neglecta Hornem. = *I. ×sambucina*.

I. ×nelsonii Randolph. (*I. fulva* ×*I. giganticaerulea*.) ABBEVILLE IRIS. To 110cm. Lvs 50–75×1–3cm. Fls to 12cm diam., red to purple or yellow, falls 6–8cm, reflexed, with or without signal patch, standards reflexed.

I. nertschinskia anon. = *I. sanguinea*.

I. nicolai Vved. [26.] To 15cm. Lvs to 25×5–6cm. Fls 1–3.5–6cm diam., slate-blue to white, tube to 1cm, fall tip blotched dark purple, crest golden with dark violet vein either side, standards obovate to 2.5cm, flushed purple. Spring. C Asia, NE Afghan.

I. nigricans Dinsm. [3.] To 30cm. Lvs narrow, strongly recurved. Fls 1, 8–10cm diam., white heavily veined brown-purple, falls

obovate, signal patch black, beard dark purple, on pale ground, standards white, heavily veined deep purple. Spring. Jord.

I. odontostyla B. Mathew & Wendelbo. [26.] To 13cm. Lvs to 18×1.5cm, channelled, margins white. Fls 1, 5–5.5cm diam., grey-violet; tube 4cm; fall blade rounded, hafts winged, crest yellow-orange on white ground. Afghan.

I. orchioides Carr. [26.] Lvs 18×1–3cm, pale green, channelled. Fls 3–4, 5cm diam., light yellow suffused mauve, tube 3–6cm, crest deep yellow, toothed, on dark yellow ground veined green or mauve, standards to 15mm. Tien Shan mts.

I. orchioides hort. non Carr. = *I. bucharica*.

I. orientalis Mill. [18.] To 90cm. Lvs to 90×1–2cm. Fls 2–3 per spathe, 10cm diam., white; fall blade rounded, signal area yellow, haft narrow, slightly pubesc., standards to 8.5cm, erect. Summer. NE Greece, W Turk.

I. orientalis Thunb. non Mill. = *I. sanguinea*.

Pacific Coast or Californian Irises. (*I. douglasiana* ×*I. innominata* etc.) 'Arnold Sunrise': fls white flushed blue, fall marked with orange. 'Banbury Fair': standards off-white, falls pale lavender flecked lavender at centre. 'Blue Ballerina': fls white, falls marked with purple. 'Broadleigh Rose': fls marked with shades of pink. 'Lavender Royal': fls lavender with darker flushes.

I. trientalis Thunb. non Mill. = *I. sanguinea*.

I. palaestina (Bak.) Boiss. [26.] Similar to *I. planifolia* but fls usually somewhat transparent, green-white or blue-tinted, stigma not bilobed. Winter. E Medit.; coastal Isr., Leb.

I. pallida Lam. DALMATIAN IRIS. [1.] To 120cm. Lvs glaucous, 20–60×1–4cm. Fls 2–6, fragrant, 8–12cm diam., soft lilac-blue; beard yellow. Late spring–early summer. W Balk. 'Argentea Variegata': Lvs striped blue-green and white. 'Aurea Variegata' ('Aurea', 'Variegata'): lvs striped yellow. ssp. *cengialtii* (Ambr.) Fost. Lvs usually decid.; fls deep blue-purple, beard hairs white, tipped orange or yellow. NE It.

I. pamphylica Hedge. [27.] To 10–20cm. Lvs to 55cm. Fl. seg. narrow; falls deep brown-purple to green, mottled purple or olive green, blotched bright yellow in blade centre, haft green, veined purple, standards light blue to green, base dappled purple-brown, style br. arched. Late winter–spring. SW Turk.

I. panormitana Tod. = *I. pseudopumila*.

I. paradoxa Steven. [3.] 10–25cm. Lvs linear, falcate, 2–4mm wide. Fls showy, tube to 2cm, falls to 4cm, oblong, horizontal, smaller than standards, pale purple, beard v. dense, velvety, black-purple, veins black-purple, standards to 10cm, rounded, erect, white densely dotted deep blue-violet. E Turk., N Iran, C Asia. f. *atrata* Grossh. Falls and standards violet-black. f. *paradoxa* Falls purple-black, standards dark violet. f. *choschab* (Hoog.) B. Mathew & Wendelbo. Falls narrow, black-purple-maroon, banded pale violet; standards palest mauve heavily veined purple. f. *mirabilis* Gawrilenko. Falls golden yellow, beard dark, yellow as orange; standards pale yellow and/or pale blue.

I. persica L. [26.] Lvs 3–4 in tufts, to 10×0.5–1.5cm, linear. Fls 1–4 on v. short st., 5–6cm diam., violet-scented, green-blue, silver, yellow or brown, tube 6–8cm, falls oblong-spathulate, 1cm wide, crest yellow, blade dark purple-brown. Winter–spring. S & SE Turk., N Syr., NE Iraq.

I. petrana Dinsm. [3.] Similar to *I. nigricans* but fls smaller, to 8cm diam., dark lilac, veins sparse, signal patch v. dark black-purple, beard dense, hairs tipped purple; style br. brown-lilac. Jord.

I. planifolia (Mill.) Fiori & Paol. [26.] 10–15cm. Lvs many, lanceolate to 30×1–3cm. Fls 1–3, 6–7cm diam., lilac purple, tube 8–15cm, falls oblong, to 5×2.5cm, with darker veins around yellow crest, haft winged; standard oblanceolate, to 2.5cm, usually toothed. Winter. Spain and Port., Sardinia, Sicily, Crete, N Afr. 'Alba': fls white. 'Marginata': fls deep blue, fall margins white.

I. polysticta Diels. [18.] To 30cm. Lvs 2–4mm wide, stiff, grooved. Fls 6cm diam., blue-mauve, tube wide, falls spreading, narrow, to 1cm wide, pale, veined, haft centre spotted, standards v. narrow. Summer. China.

I. pontica Zapal. [18.] Lvs 20–40×0.25cm, grassy. Flowering st. 4–10cm; fls 1, 5–6cm diam., violet, veined darker, fall blade orbicular, haft winged, centre pale green-yellow veined violet. C & NE Rom., W Ukraine, Cauc.

I. porphyrochrysa Wendelbo. [26.] To 10cm. Lvs 3–5, 10–15×0.5–1cm, grey-green. Fls 1–3, to 5.5cm diam., bronze; tube to 4cm; fall blade dark yellow, crest orange, haft narrow, standards bronze, bristle-like. Afghan.

I. prismatica Pursh ex Ker-Gawl. [17.] To 80cm. Lvs grassy, to 70×0.2–0.7cm, glaucous. Fls 2–3 per cluster to 7cm diam., pale violet veined blue; tube to 3mm, falls spreading, blade ovate, haft green-violet veined violet, standards oblanceolate, sub-erect. Summer. E US.

I. pseudacorus L. YELLOW FLAG. [15.] Aquatic or marginal to 2m. Lvs to 90×3cm, grey-green, midrib prominent. Fls 4–12,

5–12cm diam., bright yellow veined brown or violet; tube to 1.5cm, falls rounded, to 4cm wide, blotched deeper yellow; standards oblanceolate to 3cm. Early–midsummer. Eur. to W Sib., Cauc., Turk., Iran, N Afr. 'Alba': fls creamy white, with brown veins near tips. 'Gigantea': st. to 2.5m; fls large, golden yellow. 'Golden Fleece': fls deep yellow without darker veins. 'Mandschurica': fls matt yellow. 'Variegata': lvs striped yellow at first. var. *bastardii* (Boreau) Lynch. Fls pale yellow; fall blade not blotched.

I. pseudacorus var. *acoriformis* (Boreau) Lynch = *I. pseudacorus*.

I. pseudocaucasica Grossh. [26.] To 13cm. Similar to *I. aucheri* but lvs grey-green beneath. Fls to 4.5–6cm diam., pale blue or green yellow, fall crest yellow, haft wide-winged. Early summer. SE Turk., NE Iraq, N & NW Iran, C Asia.

I. pseudopumila Tineo. [1.] To 25cm. Lvs grey-green, persisting, to 1.5cm wide, curved or straight. Flowering st. to 3cm; fls 1, 6–8cm diam., purple, yellow or white, sometimes bicoloured, tube to 7.5cm. Spring. Sicily, Malta, Gozo, SE It., Balk.

I. pumila L. [1.] To 15cm. Lvs grey-green, to 15×1.5cm. Flowering st. v. short; fls 1(–3), mostly purple-violet, some white, yellow or blue; tube 5–10cm, beard blue or yellow. Spring. SE & EC Eur. to Urals. var. *elongata* anon. A parent of the dwarf bearded cvs. Flowering st. to 12cm.

I. purdyi Eastw. [13.] To 35cm. Lvs glossy, base suffused pink. Fls 2, 8cm diam., appearing flat due to spreading seg., cream, sometimes tinged mauve, tube 3–5cm, falls veined and spotted purple or pink. N Calif.

I. reginae Horvat = *I. variegata*.

I. regis-uzziae Feinbrun. [26.] To 10cm. Lvs 5–7, to 4cm wide, curved. Fls 1–2, 5–6cm diam., light blue, blue-mauve or somewhat transparent yellow-green; tube 4cm; falls with central yellow ridge, haft wing wide; standards to 2.5cm, spathulate. Winter–early spring. Isr., S Jord.

I. reichenbachii Heuff. [1.] Similar to *I. suaveolens* but to 30cm; lvs to 1.5cm wide; fls 6cm diam., yellow or purple-brown, veins often darker, tube shorter, to 2.5cm; beard white, tipped blue, purple or yellow. Spring–early summer. Balk.

I. reticulata Bieb. [27.] Lvs 4-angled, to 30×0.2cm. Fls 1, sessile, dark violet blue to paler blue to red-purple; tube 4–7cm; falls 5cm, often yellow-ridged, haft 2.5cm; standards erect, 6cm. Early spring. N & S Turk., NE Iraq, N & W Iran, Russia.

Reticulata Hybrids (derived from *I. histrioides* and *I. reticulata*) 'Alba': fls white. 'Cantab': fls v. pale Cambridge blue, crested yellow. 'Clairette': standards sky-blue, falls deep blue marked white. 'Edward': fls dark blue marked orange. 'Gordon': fls light blue with orange blotch on white ground lightly striped blue. 'Harmony': standards blue, falls royal blue blotched yellow and white. 'Ida': standards light blue, falls paler, blotch pale yellow on white ground slightly spotted blue. 'Jeannine': fls violet, falls blotched orange with white-and-violet striped patches; fragrant. 'Joyce': standard lavender-blue, falls deep sky-blue with yellow markings and grey-brown stripes. 'J.S. Dijt': fls dark red-purple; fragrant. 'Natascha': fls white tinged blue, falls veined green with golden-yellow blotch. 'Pauline': fls purple-violet with dark purple falls blotched blue and white. 'Purple Gem': fls violet, falls black-purple blotched purple and white. 'Royal Blue': standard deep velvet blue, falls blotched yellow. 'Spring Time': standards pale blue, falls dark blue tipped white, with purple spots and yellow midrib. 'Violet Beauty': standards velvet-purple, falls deep violet with orange crest.

I. ×robusta E. Anderson. (*I. versicolor ×I. virginica*.) Intermediate between parents. 'Gerard Darby': lvs rich purple at base; fls blue on purple st.

I. ×rosaliae Prodan. (*I. variegata ×I. pallida*.) Used extensively in early breeding programmes but probably no longer in cult.

I. rosenbachiana Reg. [26.] Similar to *I. nicolai* but fls light purple; falls blotched deep purple, crest orange. Winter–early spring. C Asia. var. *baldschuanica* Smaller, fls pale primrose veined and blotched brown-purple.

I. rossii Bak. [8.] To 15cm. Lvs to 30×0.3cm, linear, ribbed, glaucous. Fls 1, 3–4cm diam., tube to 7cm, falls obovate, spreading, purple, haft short, white, veins and spots violet, centre suffused yellow, standards obovate, purple. Spring. N China, Korea, Jap.

I. rubromarginata Bak. = *I. suaveolens*.

I. rudskyi Horvat = *I. variegata*.

I. ruthenica Ker-Gawl. [10.] To 20cm. Lvs grassy, to 30×0.2cm. Fls 1–2, fragrant, short-stemmed, to 5cm diam.; falls ovate, white marked violet, 1cm wide; standards erect, lanceolate, 6mm wide. Late spring. E Eur. through C Asia to China and Korea.

I. samariae Dinsm. [3.] Similar to *I. lortetii* but fls to 10cm diam. on st. to 30cm; falls cream, veined and spotted purple, beard brown-yellow to purple; standards purple-pink. Late spring.

NW Jord.

I. ×sambucina L. (*I. variegata ×I. pallida*.) To 60cm. Fls many, falls red or violet-brown, haft strongly veined, beard orange or yellow, standards violet-brown, often tinged yellow. Summer. N It., NW Balk.

I. sanguinea Hornem. ex Donn. [12.] Similar to *I. sibirica* but lvs as tall as or taller than unbranched flowering st. to 75cm. Fls 2, blue-purple marked white. Early summer. SE Russia, Korea, Jap. 'Alba': fls white. 'Kobana': fls usually narrow, white. 'Snow Queen': fls ivory.

I. sari Schott ex Bak. [3.] To 30cm. Lvs 9×0.6–1.2cm. Fls 1, 7–10cm; tube 4cm; falls lanceolate, 8×4cm, yellow or green, sometimes blue, veins brown-red, signal patch red-brown, wavy, beard yellow; standards wider and longer, suffused red-brown, wavy. Late spring. C & S Turk.

I. scariosa Willd. ex Link. [1.] To 20cm. Lvs glaucous. Fls 2, 4–5cm diam., red-purple, lilac or pale yellow, tube 3cm, purple-brown, fall veined deep red-purple or yellow, beard white on blade, yellow on haft. Spring. Russia.

I. schachtii Markgr. [1.] To 30cm. Lvs glaucous. Fls 1, to 6cm diam., green-yellow, beard yellow or blue, bracts green suffused purple, margins translucent, tube to 2cm, fall haft veined green, brown or purple. Spring. C Turk.

I. schelkownikowii Fomin. [1.] Similar to *I. acutiloba* but fls fragrant, larger, lilac or fawn, veins darker, fine, signal patch purple, beard yellow, standards darker and larger than falls. Azerbaijan.

I. scorpioides Desf. = *I. planifolia*.

I. serotina Willk. [25.] 40–60cm. Lvs narrow, channeled. Fls 1–2 violet-blue, tube to 1cm, fall centre yellow, standard 1cm, extremely narrow. Late summer. SE Spain.

I. setosa Pall. ex Link. [11.] 15–90cm. Lvs to 50×2.5cm, base suffused red. Fls to 15, 5–9cm diam., tube to 10mm, falls orbicular, 2.5cm diam., light blue-purple to purple, haft narrow, palest yellow, veins blue-purple, standards greatly reduced, bristle-like. Late spring–early summer. NE N Amer., E Russia, N Korea, Jap., Aleutian, Sakhalin & Kurile Is. to Alask. 'Kosho-en': fls white. 'Nana': fls purple. f. *alpina* Komar. St. short. Sib. f. *platyrhyncha* Hult. Fls solitary, standards larger. Alask. f. *serotina* Komar. Fls 1, sessile. Sib. var. *arctica* (Eastw.) Dykes. Dwarf; fls purple, white-variegated. Alask. var. *nasuensis* Hara. St. to 1m; lvs wider; fls larger. Jap. ssp. *canadensis* (Fost.) Hult. Dwarf, to 15cm. Lvs few. Fls usually 1, lavender-blue. E N Amer. ssp. *hondoensis* Honda. St. to 75cm; fls large, rich-purple. ssp. *interior* (Anderson) Hult. Lvs narrow. Bracts violet, papery. Alask.

I. shrevei Small = *I. virginica* var. *shrevei*.

I. sibirica L. [12.] 50–120cm. Lvs narrow, grassy. Fls to 5, to 7cm diam. on long st.; falls blue-purple, veined and marked white and gold, haft paler but darker-veined. Late spring–summer. C & E Eur., NE Turk., Russia. 'Alba': fls white.

Siberian Hybrids (*I. sibirica ×I. sanguinea*). Fls range in colour from white and yellow through pink and red to violet. 'Ann Dasch': fls dark blue, falls marked yellow. 'Anniversary': fls white with yellow hafts. 'Butter and Sugar': fls white and yellow. 'Caesar's Brother': fls dark pansy purple. 'Ego': fls rich blue. 'Ewen': fls burgundy, large. 'Helen Astor': fls dark plum tinged rosy red, conspicuous white veins near throat. 'Mrs Rowe': fls small, grey-pink. 'Papillon': fls pale blue. 'Ruffled Velvet': fls red-purple marked yellow. 'Sparkling Rose': fls rose-mauve, falls flecked blue. 'Tropic Night': fls blue-violet. 'Wisley White': fls white.

Siberian Iris see *I. sibirica*.

I. 'Sindpur'. (*I. aucheri ×I. galactica*.) To 25cm. Fls green-blue.

I. ×sindpers Hoog. = *I. 'Sindpur'.*

I. sintenisii Janka. [18.] To 35cm. Lvs linear, acuminate, 45×0.2–0.5cm. Fls 1–2, fragrant, to 6cm diam., fall blade elliptic, to 12mm wide, white, veins purple, standards blue-purple, erect, oblanceolate. Summer. SE Eur., N Turk., SW Russia. ssp. *brandzae* (Prodan) D.A. Webb & Chater. Lvs 1.5–3.5mm wide. Fls less densely veined. Rom.

I. sisyrinchium L. = *Gynandriris sisyrinchium*.

I. skorpilii Velen. = *I. reichenbachii*.

I. sofarana Fost. [3.] 30–40cm. Lvs to 2.5cm wide. Fls to 13cm diam., cream, veined and spotted purple, signal patch black-purple, beard not dense, deep purple, standards paler than falls. Late spring. Leb. f. *franjieh* Chaudhary. Fls white, veined and spotted yellow. ssp. *kasruwana* (Dinsm.) Chaudhary. Standards veined ± as densely as falls, signal patch pear-shaped.

I. speculatrix Hance. [7.] 20–35cm. Lvs 100cm+, grassy, cross-veined, base white. Fls 2, short-lived, to 5cm diam., tube 1cm, falls obovate, 1.5cm wide, mauve-lilac, ridge yellow, surrounded by white mottled purple, with purple border, standard obovate, 1.5cm wide, mauve-lilac. Spring–summer. SE China, Hong Kong.

I. sprengeri Siehe. [3.] To 20cm. Lvs 3–5mm wide. Fls to 6cm diam., yellow, veins purple-brown, tube to 1.5cm, signal patch red-purple, beard yellow; standards white, veins red-purple and black; style br. yellow, veined and spotted red-brown. Late spring. C Turk.

I. spuria L. [18.] To 80cm. Lvs 30×1.2cm. Fls 6–8cm diam., lilac or blue-violet, veined violet; falls to 6cm, rounded, striped yellow, standards oblanceolate. Summer. Eur., Asia, Alg. ssp. *carthaliniae* (Fomin) B. Mathew. To 95cm. Fls 4–5, sky blue or white, veined deeper blue. Russia. ssp. *halophila* (Pall.) B. Mathew & Wendelbo. 40–85cm. Fls 4–8, 6–7cm diam., white, dull light yellow to bright yellow, veined deeper. S Rom., Russia. ssp. *maritima* (Lam.) Fourn. 30–50cm. Fls to 4, falls to 4.5cm diam., veins dense, purple, blade deep purple, haft longer than blade, centrally striped green. SW Eur. ssp. *musulmanica* (Fomin) Takht. 40–90cm. Fls light violet to dark lavender-violet, veins darker, falls to 8cm, blade striped yellow, base tinged yellow. E Turk., N & NW Iran, C Asia. ssp. *notha* (Bieb.) Asch. & Gräbn. 70–90cm. Fls 3–5, violet-blue, fall haft striped yellow. Russia.

Spuria group. Fls white and yellow through orange, red and brown to blue; includes – 'Connoisseur': fls lavender blue. 'Elixir': fls saffron. 'Imperial Bronze': fls deep yellow veined brown. 'Protégé': standards blue, falls white veined blue. 'Red Oak': fls brown-purple. 'Shelford Hybrid': fls blue.

I. ×squalens L. = *I. ×sambucina*.

I. stenophylla Hausskn. ex Siehe & Bak. [26.] 6–12cm. Lvs 4–5, to 20×1cm, curved, sometimes glaucous beneath. Fls 1–2, fragrant, to 5cm diam., violet, tube to 9cm, blade deep blue-violet, crest yellow surrounded by white spotted violet, haft wide-winged, standards to 2.5cm. Early spring. S Turk. ssp. *allisonii* B. Mathew. Lvs broader wavy; fls bluer.

I. stocksii (Bak.) Baker. [26.] To 30cm. Lvs to 15×1.5cm, lanceolate. Fls 1–4, 5.5cm diam., pale blue-violet, veins dark mauve; tube 3–5cm; falls obovate, crest yellow, haft winged; standards obovate. Spring. C & S Afghan., W Pak.

I. stolonifera Maxim. [4.] 30–60cm. Lvs blue-green, to 60×0.5–1.5cm, prominently veined. Fls 2–3, to 8cm diam., light to deep brown-purple; falls and standard blades marked pale to dark blue, beard hairs yellow or blue. Late spring. Russia. 'Compacta': fls brown. 'Zwanenburg Bronze': fls bronze-purple with frilled margins.

I. stylosa Desf. = *I. unguicularis*.

I. suaveolens Boiss. & Reut. [1.] 8–15cm. Lvs in fans. Fls 1–2 on short st., 5cm diam., yellow, purple, maroon or yellow and brown, bract keeled, tube to 4.5cm, beard yellow, blue in purple forms. Spring–early summer. SE Eur., NW Turk.

I. subbiflora Brot. [1.] 25–40cm. Lvs to 2.5cm wide. Fls 1–2, 7–8cm diam., deep violet or blue; tube to 5cm; falls obovate, to 4×2.5cm, beard blue or white, or yellow on haft; standards erect, 5×2.5cm. Spring–summer. Port., SW Spain. var. *lisbonensis* (Dykes) Dykes. St. lvs 0; bracts green, not tinged purple.

I. susiana L. MOURNING IRIS. [3.] Similar to *I. sofarana* and *I. basaltica* but with lvs almost straight; fls to 12cm diam., pale lilac-grey heavily veined deep purple, falls and standards similarly marked, to 8cm wide, signal patch velvety purple-black, beard deep brown-purple. Late spring. Origin unknown, possibly Leb.

I. susiana f. *sofarana* (Fost.) Sealy = *I. sofarana*.

I. susiana f. *westii* (Dinsm.) Sealy = *I. westii*.

I. taitii Fost. = *I. xiphium* 'Taitii'.

I. taochia Woron. ex Grossh. [1.] To 30cm. Lvs to 2.5cm wide. Fls 2–5, 5–6cm diam., light to bright yellow, dull purple to violet, bracts inflated, green, papery, beard white, sometimes tipped yellow, fall haft white or yellow, veins brown-purple. NE Turk.

I. tauri Siehe ex Mallet = *I. stenophylla*.

I. taurica Lodd. = *I. pumila*.

I. tectorum Maxim. ROOF IRIS. [7.] St. sometimes branched, to 40cm. Lvs ribbed, glossy dark green, to 30×2–2.5cm. Fls 2–3 per spathe, to 10cm diam., somewhat flat, blue-lilac, veined and patched darker, falls 2.5cm wide, crest frilly, white, spotted darker; standards and falls wavy. Early summer. C & SW China, possibly Burm., nat. Jap. 'Alba': fls white, sparsely veined yellow. 'Variegata': lvs boldly striped and streaked cream.

I. tenax Douglas ex Lindl. [13.] To 30cm. Lvs green, tinged pink at base. Fls 1–2, 7–9cm diam., pale yellow to lavender or red-purple; tube short, to 1cm, falls lanceolate, 2.5cm wide, reflexed, with a white or yellow central patch of purple, standards lanceolate, 6mm wide. Early summer. NW US. ssp. *klamathensis* Lenz. Fl. tube 1–2cm; fls straw to light pink-orange, veined red-purple or brown. SW Calif.

I. tenuifolia Pall. [20.] 10–30cm. Lvs to 40×0.3cm, glaucous. Fls 1–2, 4–6cm diam.; tube to 8cm, fall blade narrow, 1.5cm wide, pointed, heavily veined violet, centrally striped pale yellow,

standards narrow, 1.5cm wide, pointed, blue-violet. Late spring. SE Russia through C Asia to Mong. and W China.

I. tenuis S. Wats. [7.] To 35cm. Flowering st. branched. Lvs 30×1–1.5cm. Fls 1 per br., 3–4cm diam., falls 3cm, white with some yellow marks, veins blue-purple, ridge yellow, undivided, standards erect, blue-white. Late spring. W US.

I. tenuissima Dykes. [13.] To 30cm. Lvs grey-green, 4–6mm wide. Fls 2, 6–8cm diam., cream, tube to 6cm, apex dilated; falls spreading, to 8cm diam., veined brown-purple; style lobes narrow, pointed, reflexed. Early summer. W US. ssp. *purdyiformis* (R. Fost.) Lenz. Fls cream to light yellow, lightly veined. N Sierra Nevada.

I. tigrida Bunge ex Ledeb. To 15cm. Lvs erect, to 10×10cm. Fls 1–2 per st., to 5cm diam., lilac to dark blue, mottled purple, fall centre white streaked purple, beard white, tips sometimes yellow. SE Russia, Mong., NW China.

I. tingitana Boiss. & Reut. [25.] To 60cm. Lvs to 45cm, silver-green. Fls blue; tube to 3cm; falls obovate, pointed, to 7.5cm, ridge orange-yellow; standards to 10cm. Late winter–spring. NW Afr. A parent of Dutch Irises. var. *fontanesii* (Godron) Maire. Flowering later; fls deeper violet-blue. var. *mellori* anon. To 90cm. Fls purple, falls rounded.

I. timofejewii Woron. [1.] 10–25cm. Lvs to 5cm wide, falcate, grey-green. Fls 1–2, to 5cm diam., deep violet-red, tube 4–5cm; beard white, tips purple. E Cauc.

I. tridentata Pursh. [11.] To 70cm. Fls 1–2, fragrant, to 10cm diam., tube 2.5cm, fall blade rounded, 3.5cm diam., violet with darker veins, signal patch white with central yellow patch, haft white, veins reticulate; standards oblanceolate, 1.5cm, violet. E US.

I. tripetala Walt. = *I. tridentata*.

I. trojana Kerner ex Stapf. [1.] Similar to *I. germanica* but with long-branched st. 70cm+; fls 10cm diam., fragrant, falls obovate, reflexed, purple, beard white, tips yellow, haft lightly veined; standards obovate, lighter blue. Early summer. W Turk.

I. tubergeniana Fost. [26.] To 15cm. Lvs 4–6, to 2.5cm wide, edged white, curved. Fls 1–3, to 6cm diam., yellow; tube to 5cm; fall crest fringed, surrounded by veins and dots of green-violet, haft narrow-winged, standards 1.5cm, trilobed, deflexed. Spring. C Asia.

I. tuberosa L. = *Hermodactylus tuberosus*.

I. 'Turkey Yellow'. [18.] 50–100cm. Lvs 1–1.8cm across, shorter than or equalling fls. Fls 9–11cm diam., pure deep yellow. C & S Turk.

I. unguicularis Poir. ALGERIAN IRIS. [23.] Lvs tufted, grassy, to 60×1cm. Fls solitary, short-stemmed, fragrant, tube to 20cm, falls obovate, reflexed, 2cm wide, white veined lavender, central band yellow, haft linear, veins dark, standards of similar size and shape to falls, erect, lilac; style br. yellow-glandular above. Winter–spring. Alg., Tun., W Syr., S & W Turk. ssp. *carica* f. *angustifolia* (Boiss. & Heldr.) A.P. Davis & Jury. ('Angustifolia') Lvs narrower; fls small, lilac-blue, falls with white centre, margins blue-lilac, standard white at base. ssp. *cretensis* (Janka) A.P. Davis & Jury. Dwarf. Lvs grassy, to 3mm wide. Fl. seg. to 5.5cm, purple-blue, fall blade and haft white veined violet, blade striped orange in centre. S Greece, Crete. 'Alba': fls white, falls with central green-yellow line. 'Ellis's Variety': lvs narrow; fls bright violet-blue. 'Marginata': fls lilac, margins white. 'Mary Barnard': fls violet-blue. 'Oxford Dwarf': fls deep blue, falls white veined purple, with central orange line, tips lavender. 'Speciosa': lvs short, narrow; fls fragrant, deep violet, central yellow stripe. 'Starker's Pink': dwarf; lvs shorter, narrower; fls pink-lavender. 'Variegata': fls mottled and streaked purple on lavender ground. 'Walter Butt': fls large, robust, fragrant, pale silver-lilac; late autumn–winter.

I. urmiensis Hoog = *I. barnumae* f. *urmiensis*.

I. vaga Fost. = *I. stolonifera*.

I. variegata L. [1.] 20–50cm. Lvs sword-shaped, ribbed, to 30×3cm. Fls 3–6, 5–8cm diam., bract swollen, tinged green-purple, tube to 2.5cm, falls obovate, 2cm wide, reflexed, white to light yellow or brown-red, veined red-brown, beard bright yellow, standards oblong, erect, bright yellow; style br. yellow. Spring–summer. C & SE Eur.

I. vartanii Fost. [27.] To 3cm. Lvs 4–angular in section, to 20cm. Fls almond-scented, slate blue, fall blade veined darker, crest yellow, hafts v. narrow; style br. long and narrow. Autumn–winter. Isr., possibly Syr. 'Alba': fls white.

I. verna L. [9.] To 6cm at flowering. Lvs equitant, to 15×1cm, glaucous. Fls to 5cm diam., bright blue-lilac, tube 2–5cm, falls obovate, 4×1cm, centre striped orange with brown spots, standard obovate, erect. Spring. SE US.

I. versicolor L. BLUE FLAG. [15.] 20–80cm. Lvs 35–60×1–2cm. Fls several per br., 6–8cm diam., violet to red-purple, falls wide-spreading, blade oval, 8–2.5cm, blotched green-yellow, surrounded by white veined purple, haft white, purple-veined, standards oblanceolate, smaller, 4cm, paler, erect. Summer. E

US. 'Gerald Derby' (*I. versicolor* × *I. virginica*): taller; fls large, purple-blue. 'Kermesina': fls red-purple. 'Rosea': fls pink.

I. vicaria Vved. [26.] 20–50cm. Lvs 5–7, 15×1.5–3cm. Fls 2–5, 4–5cm diam., light blue-violet, crest wavy, white or yellow on yellow patch, haft unwinged, dark-lined, standards to 2.5cm, dark veined. Spring. C Asia.

I. violacea Klatt = *I. spuria* ssp. *musulmanica*.

I. virescens Delarb. = *I. variegata*.

I. virginica L. SOUTHERN BLUE FLAG. [15.] Similar to *I. versicolor* but flowering st. usually unbranched, often curved. Lvs 1–3cm wide, soft. Fls 1–4, blue, fall centre yellow-hairy (not bearded). Summer. E US. 'Alba': lvs wide, fls white. 'Giant Blue': fls large, blue. 'Wide Blue': lvs blue-green; fls blue. var. *shrevei* (Small) E. Anderson. Flowering st. branched.

I. warleyensis Fost. [26.] 20–45cm. Lvs 6–7, channelled, to 20×3cm. Fls to 5, 5–7cm diam., pale to dark violet to blue-purple, tube 5cm, falls orbicular, margins white, crest white to yellow, on yellow ground, dissected, haft unwinged, standard deflexed, linear to trilobed, to 2cm. Spring. Russia. 'Warlsind' (*I. warleyensis* × *I. aucheri*): to 25cm; falls yellow, blade blotched purple-blue, ridge yellow, standards and styles white.

I. wattii Bak. [7.] 1–2m, similar to *I. confusa* but st. much-branched. Fls 2–3 per br., large, 6cm diam., falls reflexed, 5×3.5cm, lavender-lilac, centre white spotted deep yellow and dark lilac, crest orange, or white spotted yellow, standards horizontal, 4×2cm. Spring–summer. India, W China.

I. wendelboi Grey-Wilson & B. Mathew. [26.] To 10cm. Lvs to 20×1cm, glaucous, arching. Fls 1–2, to 5.5cm diam., deep violet, tube 3cm; falls not winged, crest bright golden yellow, frilly, standards much reduced, to 5mm. Spring. SW Afghan.

I. westii Dinsm. [3.] To 30cm. Lvs to 1cm wide. Fls 1, 12–15cm diam., falls pale yellow, veined and blotched purple, signal patch dark brown, beard hairs sparse, long, purple, standards pale lilac veined and spotted deeper blue-lilac. Late spring. Leb.

I. willmottiana Fost. [26.] To 20cm. Lvs glossy green. Fls 4–6, to 7cm diam., deep lavender to bright blue or white, tube 5cm, fall blade blotched white and deeper lavender, haft winged, crest white, slightly wrinkled, standards 1.5cm. Spring. Russia.

I. wilsonii C.H. Wright. [12.] To 75cm. Lvs glaucous. Fls 2 per br., fragrant, 6–8cm diam., pale yellow, falls obovate, veined and spotted brown-purple, standards oblique, undulate. Summer. W China.

I. winogradowii Fomin. [27.] To 15cm. Differs from *I. histrioides* in pale primrose fls spotted green on the fall haft and centre of blade. Early spring. Russia. (*I. winogradowii* × *I. histrioides*): 'Frank Elder': fls pale blue shaded yellow. 'Katherine Hodgkin': fls yellow veined blue, tinged slate-blue.

I. xiphioides = *I. latifolia*.

I. xiphium L. SPANISH IRIS. [25.] 40–60cm. Lvs 20–70×0.3–0.5cm, channelled. Fls 1–2, usually blue or violet, sometimes white, yellow or mauve, tube 1–3mm, fall blade centre usually orange, or yellow, haft unwinged. Spring–early summer. Spain, Port., SW Fr., S It., Corsica, Moroc., Alg., Tun. Hybridized with *I. tingitana* to produce Dutch irises. 'Battandieri': fls white, ridge on fall blades orange-yellow. 'Blue Angel': fls bright blue, central falls marked yellow. 'Bronze Queen': fls golden brown, suffused purple and bronze. 'Cajanus': fls yellow. 'King of the Blues': fls blue. 'Lusitanica': fls yellow. 'Praecox': flowering earlier; fls large blue. 'Professor Blaauw': fls bright violet-blue. 'Queen Wilhelmina': fls white. 'Taitii': fls pale blue. 'Thunderbolt': falls bronze-brown, blotched yellow, standards purple-brown.

I. xiphium var. *praecox* Dykes = *I. xiphium* 'Praecox'.

I. yebrudii Dinsm. ex Chaudhary. [3.] To 20cm. Lvs short, rigid, glaucous. Fls 9cm diam., falls pale yellow veined and spotted brown-purple, signal patch small, deep purple, beard hairs long, purple, standards pale yellow, veins open, purple. Syr. ssp. *edgecombei* Chaudhary. Fls 10–12cm diam., falls marked red-purple, signal patch deep red-purple, beard hairs pale, tipped yellow, standards white, densely veined maroon.

I. zaprjagajewii N. Abramov. [26.] To 15cm. Lvs to 4cm wide, glaucous. Fls 1–3 on st. to 4cm, 5.5cm diam., white, tube to 9cm, tube and seg. base sometimes tinged blue, fall margins decurved, crest yellow, standards slightly reflexed, reduced to 1cm. Spring. C Asia.

Irish Gorse *Ulex europaeus.*
Irish Heath *Erica erigena.*
Irish Ivy *Hedera hibernica.*
Irish Lace *Tagetes filifolia.*
Irish Marsh Orchid *Dactylorhiza traunsteineri.*
Irish Moss *Selaginella involens*; *Soleirolia soleirolii.*
Irish Potato *Solanum tuberosum.*
Irish Rose *Rosa* × *hibernica.*
Irish Spurge *Euphorbia hyberna.*
Irish Yew *Taxus baccata.*

Ironbark *Eucalyptus.*
Iron-cross Begonia *Begonia masoniana.*
Iron Fern *Rumohra adiantiformis.*
Irontree *Parrotia.*
Ironweed *Vernonia.*
Ironwood *Backhousia sciadophora*; *Cliftonia monophylla*; *Eugenia confusa*; *Mesua ferrea*; *Ostrya virginiana*; *Parrotia.*

Isabelia Barb.-Rodr. Orchidaceae. 1 epiphytic orchid. Pbs to 1cm, ovoid, clustered. Lvs to 6cm, needle-like. Infl. short; fls 1–2, to 1.2cm, waxy; sep. white tinted rose-violet, obovate-oblong; pet. snow-white, narrow-oblong; lip white, broadly ovate. Braz. Z10.

I. virginalis Barb.-Rodr.

Isatis L. WOAD. Cruciferae. 30 ann. and perenn. herbs. Lvs entire. Fls 4-merous, in loose rac. Summer. Eur., Medit. to C Asia. Z7.

I. boissieriana Rchb. f. Ann., erect to 30cm. Lvs oblong, glab., pet. to 7mm, twice sep. length, obovate, white. C Asia.

I. glauca Boiss. Perenn. to 130cm. Lvs oblong, glab. Pan. large, pet. to 5mm yellow. Asia Minor, Iran.

I. heterocarpa Reg. et Schmalh. = *I. boissieriana.*

I. tinctoria L. DYER'S WOAD. Bienn. to 1m. Lvs oblong-lanceolate. Pet. 2.5–4mm, yellow. Eur.

Ischnosiphon Körn. Marantaceae. *c*30 perenn. herbs. St. often branched, erect or sprawling. Lvs basal and/or cauline, distichous ovate to elliptic. Infl. term. or lat., branched, bracteate; fls paired, slender-tubular. Nic. to S Braz. Z10.

I. leucophaeus (Poepp. & Endl.) Körn. To 1m. Lvs to 20cm, basal, ovate-oblong. Rac. with bracts to 2.5cm, fls white to rose. Panama, Braz.

I. smaragdinum (Lind.) Eichl. = *Monotagma smaragdinum.*
→*Calathea.*

Isertia Schreb. Rubiaceae. 20+, shrubs or trees. Lvs opposite or in whorls of 3, leathery, ± downy beneath. Fls in term. cymose pan. to 20cm; cal. 4–6-toothed; cor. funnel- or salver-shaped, ribbed, lobes 4–6. W Indies, Trop. Amer. Z10.

I. coccinea (Aubl.) J. Gmel. Shrub or tree, to 4m. Lvs to 34cm, oval or oblong-oval. Cor. to 8cm, exterior velvet-haired, scarlet. Summer. Guyana, Braz.

I. haenkeana DC. Shrub, to 3m. Lvs to 45cm, obovate to oval-obovate. Cor. to 3.5cm, exterior glabrate, yellow or orange-red. Mex. to Colomb., Cuba.

I. parviflora Vahl. Shrub or tree, to 10m. Lvs to 25cm, oblong. Cor. to 2cm, glab., pale pink or white. W Indies, trop. Amer. S to Braz.
→*Guettarda.*

Island Bush-snapdragon *Galvezia speciosa.*
Islay *Prunus ilicifolia.*

Islaya Backeb. = *Neoporteria.*

Ismene Salisb ex Herb.
I. amancaes (Ruiz. & Pav.) Herb. = *Hymenocallis amancaes.*
I. calathina (Ker-Gawl.) Nichols. = *Hymenocallis narcissiflora.*
I. deflexa Herb. = *Hymenocallis deflexa.*
I. × *festalis* hort. = *Hymenocallis* × *festalis.*
I. harrisiana hort. = *Hymenocallis harrisiana.*
I. longipetala (Lindl.) Meerow = *Hymenocallis longipetala.*
I. narcissiflora M. Roem. = *Hymenocallis narcissiflora.*
I. virescens Lindl. = *Hymenocallis virescens.*

Isochilus R. Br. Orchidaceae. 2 epiphytic or terrestrial orchids. St. slender, erect. Lvs distichous, linear-lanceolate to oblong. Fls small, in term. rac.; tep. free, equal; lip 3-lobed. Flowering throughout the year. C Amer., N S Amer., W Indies. Z10.

I. linearis (Jacq.) R. Br. Lvs to 65×3mm, linear. Infl. to 60cm; tep. to 0.8cm white, orange-yellow to bright rose-purple; lip usually deep rose-purple. Mex. to Braz., W Indies.

I. livida Lindl. = *Scaphyglottis livida.*

I. major Cham. & Schltr. Fls more numerous and crowded than in above. Mex. to Panama, Jam.

I. proliferum R. Br. = *Scaphyglottis prolifera.*

ISOETACEAE Rchb. 2/77. *Isoetes.*

Isoetes L. QUILLWORT. Isoetaceae. 75 everg. aquatic or marginal perenn. herbs. Lvs quill-like, clumped; sporangia sunken in swollen lf bases. Worldwide, except Polyn.

I. engelmannii A. Braun. Lvs 10–30cm, terete, usually only the bases submerged. NE N Amer. Z3.

I. lacustris L. Lvs 5–15cm, obscurely 4-angled, usually semi-submerged. N Eur. to Sib. Z3.

Isolepis R. Br. Cyperaceae. 40 ann. or perenn. herbs. St. leafy, upright or prostrate. Lvs grasslike, narrow. Infl. a term. spikelet or umbel of spikelets subtended by a leaflike bract; fls minute, hermaphrodite. Widespread temp. regions and trop. mts. Z8.
I. cernua (Vahl) Roem. & Schult. Similar to *I. setacea* except bract often shorter than infl., spikelets solitary. W & S Eur., N Afr.
I. prolifera R. Br. Creeping perenn. St. tufted, bearing bladeless lf sheath. Bract short, concealed by infl; spikelets in dense clusters; glumes blunt. S Afr., Aus.
I. setacea (L.) R. Br. BRISTLE SCIRPUS. Tufted ann., 3–30cm. St. v. thin. Lvs 1–6cm. Bract longer than infl.; spikelets 2–3; glumes bristle-tipped. Eur. to S Afr. and W Asia.
→*Scirpus*.

Isoloma Decne.
I. amabile (Planch. & Lind.) hort. ex Bellair & St.-Léger = *Kohleria amabilis*.
I. ceciliae (André) hort. ex Bellair & St.-Léger = *Kohleria amabilis*.
I. erianthum (Benth.) Benth. ex Decne. = *Kohleria eriantha*.
I. hirsutum hort. = *Kohleria eriantha*.
I. pictum hort. = *Kohleria bogotensis*.

Isometrum Craib. Gesneriaceae. 2 perenn. herbs. Rhiz. fleshy. Lvs rosulate, crenate-serrate or lobulate, pilose. Rac. bracteate, cymose; cor. cylindric, gibbous at base, 5-lobed, 2-lipped. China. Z10.
I. farreri Craib. Lvs to 3.7×2cm, obovate-oblanceolate or ovate. Fls 5–7 per cyme, bright pink, glandular-pubesc. China.

Isoplexis (Lindl.) Loud. Scrophulariaceae. 3 subshrubs. Lvs c2cm, alt., dentate. Rac. erect, term.; cal. 5-partite; cor. incurved, limb 5-lobed, 2-lipped. Summer. Canary Is., Madeira. Z9.
I. canariensis (L.) Lindl. ex G. Don. To 1.2m. Lvs lanceolate to ovate-lanceolate. Rac. to 30cm; fls to 3cm, orange-yellow to yellow-brown. Canary Is.
I. sceptrum Loud. To 1.8m. Lvs ovate to ovate-oblong. Rac. to 13cm; fls smaller than in above sp., yellow, with tawny veins. Madeira.
→*Digitalis*.

Isopogon R. Br. Proteaceae. 30 shrubs. Lvs rigid, coriaceous. Spike dense cone-like, involucrate; fls in scale axils; perianth tube slender, lobes 4, linear or oblong. Aus. Z9.
I. anemonifolius (Salisb.) Knight. BROAD-LEAF DRUMSTICKS. To 2m high, spreading. Lvs to 10cm, bipinnate, lobes linear. Fls yellow; heads 18cm diam. Spring–early summer. E Aus.
I. anethifolius (Salisb.) Knight. NARROW-LEAF DRUMSTICKS. To 2m high, spreading. Lvs to 16cm, pinnatisect, seg. terete, erect. Fls yellow; heads 4.5cm diam. Spring–early summer. E Aus.
I. baxteri R. Br. STIRLING RANGE; CONE-FLOWER. Shrub to 1.5m, erect. Lvs to 5cm, wedge-shaped, prickly-lobed. Fls pink, hairy. Late winter–spring. W Aus.
I. buxifolius R. Br. Shrub to 1.3m, erect. Lvs to 2.5cm, ovate-tip recurved. Fls woolly-white, cone enclosed in floral lvs. Late winter–spring. W Aus.
I. cuneatus R. Br. Many-branched shrub, 1–2.5m. Lvs to 10cm, obovate to elliptic-oblong. Fls pink-purple, glab. with tufts of hairs at tips; cone scales villous. Spring. W Aus.
I. divergens R. Br. SPREADING CONEFLOWER. Spreading or erect shrub, to 1.5m. Lvs to 10cm, pinnately divided, seg. 3–6cm, terete, divaricate. Fls to 2.5cm, pink to purple; cone scales hairy. Late winter–spring. W Aus.
I. dubius (R. Br.) Druce. ROSE CONEFLOWER. Shrub, to 1.5m spreading. Lvs to 7cm, linear, ternately divided, prickly. Fls pink to purple; heads to 2cm diam. Late winter–spring. W Aus.
I. formosus R. Br. Erect shrub to 1.5m. Lvs 5cm, 1–3× ternately divided into short, narrow seg. Fls rose-pink, glab.; heads 4–5cm diam. Spring. W Aus.
I. latifolius R. Br. Erect shrub, 1–3m. Lvs to 10cm, obovate to elliptic-oblong. Fls pink to purple, slender, glab. Spring. W Aus.
I. longifolius R. Br. Erect shrub to 3m. Lvs to 20cm, linear to oblanceolate, entire or deeply, lobed. Fls yellow, silky, heads 2cm diam. Mid-spring–early summer. W Aus.
I. sphaerocephalus Lindl. Erect, hairy shrub, to 1.5m. Lvs to 10cm, linear to linear-lanceolate. Fls yellow, hairy-tipped, in heads 3–4cm diam. Late winter–spring.
I. trilobus R. Br. Erect shrub to 1m. Lvs 7cm, wedge-shaped, thick, with 3–5(9) teeth. Fls cream-yellow silky in cones 2.5cm diam. Spring. W Aus.

Isopyrum L. Ranunculaceae. FALSE RUE ANEMONE. 30 rhizomatous or tuberous perenn. herbs. Lvs fern-like 1–3-ternate. Fls cupped, nodding, solitary or in pan.; sep. 5, petaloid; pet. small or 0, fil. clavellate. N Hemis.
I. adiantifolium Hook. f. & Thoms. Basal lvs ternate; lfts 5–7, obtuse, crenate. Fls to 1.3cm diam., solitary, white. Spring–summer. N India. Z9.
I. adoxoides DC. = *Semiaquilegia adoxoides*.
I. biternatum (Raf.) Torr. & A. Gray. Basal lvs 2–3-ternate, lfts obovate, rounded, 1–2.5cm. Fls 1–2cm diam. white. Spring. N Amer. Z3.
I. hallii A. Gray. Basal lvs 2–3-ternate, lfts 1.5–4cm, cuneate, incised and toothed. Fls 1–2cm diam., in subumbellate clusters, tinged pink. Summer. NW US. Z6.
I. thalictroides L. Basal lvs ternate, lfts ovate, 3-lobed. Fls 1–2cm diam., white. Eur. Z6.

Isotrema Raf. = *Aristolochia*.

Isu Tree *Distylium racemosum*.
Italian Alder *Alnus cordata*.
Italian Bellflower *Campanula isophylla*.
Italian Buckthorn *Rhamnus alaternus*.
Italian Clover *Trifolium incarnatum*.
Italian Corn Salad *Valerianella eriocarpa*.
Italian Cress *Eruca*.
Italian Cypress *Cupressus sempervirens*.
Italian Honeysuckle *Lonicera caprifolium*.
Italian Ivy *Hedera helix*.
Italian Jasmine *Solanum seaforthianum*.
Italian Maple *Acer opalus*.
Italian Millet *Setaria italica*.
Italian Parsley *Petroselinum crispum* var. *neapolitanum*.
Italian Poplar *Populus nigra* var. *betulifolia*.
Italian Woodbine *Lonicera caprifolium*.
Italian Yellow Jasmine *Jasminum humile*.

Itea L. Grossulariaceae (Iteaceae). 10 everg. and decid. shrubs and trees. Lvs dentate. Fls small, in catkin-like many-fld rac. and pan., 5-partite. NE Asia, E N Amer.
I. ilicifolia Oliv. Erect everg. shrub to 5m, shoots glab. Lvs 5–12cm, elliptic, spiny-toothed, olive to dark green, lustrous above. Rac. slender, pendulous to 35cm, pet. cream to gold. Summer. W China. Z7.
I. virginica L. SWEETSPIRE; VIRGINIA WILLOW; TASSEL-WHITE. Arching decid. shrub to 3m, shoots felted at first. Lvs 3–10cm, narrow elliptic to oblong, finely serrate, rich red before falling. Rac. erect 5–15cm; pet. cream. Summer. E US. 'Beppu': upright to 1.3m, lvs colouring beautifully in autumn. Z5.
I. yunnanensis Franch. Differs from *I. ilicifolia* in lvs 5–10cm, narrower, almost entire to dentate; infl. shorter; pet. white. Summer. Yunnan. Z7.

ITEACEAE R. Agardh. See *Itea*.

Ithuriel's Spear *Triteleia laxa*.

Ithycaulon Copel.
I. inaequale (Kunze) Copel. = *Saccoloma inaequale*.

Ivesia Torr. & A. Gray. Rosaceae. 23 perenn. herbs; rootstocks thick. Lvs pinnate, mostly basal; lfts usually with numerous, narrow, imbricate, silky lobes. Fls usually 5-merous, in crowded cymes; sta. 5–20. W N Amer.
I. gordonii (Hook.) Torr. & A. Gray. To 20cm, often sticky. Lvs to 18cm; lfts 10–25 pairs, to 8mm. Cymes dense, capitate; pet. yellow, spathulate to oblanceolate, to 2mm. Summer. NW US. Z4.
→*Horkelia* and *Potentilla*.

Ivory Curl Flower *Buckinghamia celsissima*.
Ivory Fig *Ficus septica*.
Ivory Tree *Holarrhena pubescens*.
Ivy *Hedera*.
Ivy Flat-pea *Platylobium triangulare*.
Ivy Geranium *Pelargonium peltatum*.
Ivy Gourd *Coccinia grandis*.
Ivy-leaf Pepper *Peperomia griseoargentea*.
Ivy-leaved Bellflower *Wahlenbergia hederacea*.
Ivy-leaved Toad Flax *Cymbalaria muralis*.
Ivy-leaved Violet *Viola hederacea*.
Ivy of Uruguay *Cissus striata*.
Ivy Tree *Schefflera* (*S. heptaphylla*).
Iwa-hige *Cassiope lycopodioides*.

Ixia L. Iridaceae. 50 perenn. cormous herbs. St. erect, slender. Lvs distichous, basal and cauline. Spike term.; fls almost always regular; perianth tube straight, lobes ± equal, oblong-obovate, usually joined at base; style br. 3. S Afr. Z9.

I. aristata Thunb. non Ker-Gawl. = *I. campanulata*.

I. aristata Ker-Gawl. non Thunb. = *I. longituba*.

I. aulica Ait. = *I. latifolia*.

I. aurantiaca Klatt = *I. polystachya* var. *lutea*.

I. campanulata Houtt. 10–35cm. Lvs 15–20cm, linear or awl-shaped. Spike dense; fls white, sometimes flushed red, or crimson. Spring–early summer.

I. capillaris L. f. 20–45cm. Lvs 6–18cm, linear or filiform, often spirally twisted. Spike lax; fls white, pale blue or mauve, sometimes pale green in throat. Winter–spring.

I. cochlearis Lewis. 15–45cm. Lvs 10–30cm, linear. Spike rather lax, usually flexuous; fls salmon-pink or rose-pink with dark median veins. Early summer.

I. columellaris Ker-Gawl. = *I. monadelpha*.

I. conferta Fost. 15–35cm. Lvs 7–24cm, lanceolate or sword-shaped. Spike capitate; fls purple or red with purple-black blotch in middle. Late winter–early spring. var. *ochroleuca* (Ker-Gawl.) Lewis. Fls white to yellow with brown or purple-black stain in middle. Spring.

I. crateroides Ker-Gawl. = *I. campanulata*.

I. curta Andrews. 15–40cm. Lvs 8–25cm, narrowly lanceolate, sometimes twisted. Spike short; fls orange with brown or green-brown blotch often edged with red in middle, outer lobes often red-tinged outside. Spring.

I. dubia Vent. 20–75cm. Lvs 10–50cm, linear. Spike capitate; fls orange or golden-yellow, usually dark brown or purple in centre, outer lobes flushed with red. Spring–summer.

I. flexuosa L. 36–65cm. Lvs 5–35cm, linear or awl-shaped, usually spirally twisted. Spike dense flexuous; fls slightly scented, white, pale pink or mauve, sometimes yellow in centre, and with purple veins. Winter–spring.

I. framesii L. Bol. 15–38cm. Lvs 12–40cm, linear. Spike dense; fls salmon-pink or red-pink with a darker circle in middle. Spring.

I. grandiflora Delaroche = *Sparaxis fragrans*.

I. incarnata Jacq. = *I. latifolia*.

I. latifolia Delaroche 40–60cm. Lvs 8–28cm, linear or lanceolate. Spike lax or dense; fls pale to deep pink, mauve, violet, purple or magenta. Spring–summer.

I. leipoldtii Lewis. 11–25cm. Lvs 7–20cm, narrowly lanceolate. Spike dense; fls white, base of lobes maroon-red, tube yellow. Spring.

I. leucantha Jacq. = *I. polystachya*.

I. longifolia Berg = *I. paniculata*.

I. longituba N.E. Br. 35–75cm. Lvs 10–30cm, lanceolate or sword-shaped, often spirally twisted. Spike lax; fls pale to deep pink, occas. white. Spring–summer.

I. maculata L. 18–50cm. Lvs 10–35cm, linear, lanceolate or awl-shaped, usually spirally twisted. Spike capitate; fls orange or yellow-orange with dark brown, black or purple mark in centre, usually with yellow or orange star in middle. Spring. var. *nigroalbida* (Klatt) Bak. Fls white, with black central mark. var. *ornata* Bak. Fls white, tinged purple, with deep crimson central mark.

I. micrandra Bak. 20–60cm. Lvs 12–30cm, *c*1mm or less wide, filiform. Spike short; fls white, pale to deep pink or mauve. Winter–spring.

I. monadelpha Delaroche 15–40cm. Lvs 8–28cm, lanceolate or sword-shaped, spirally twisted. Spike dense; fls white, pale pink, mauve, violet, pale to deep blue, purple, with a green, brown or red-brown circular mark in middle, edged with a band of another colour. var. *columnaris* (Andrew) Bak. Fls claret without central mark. var. *grandiflora* (Pers.) Bak. Fls lilac, with blue throat. var. *latifolia* (Klatt) Bak. Lvs broad, not twisted. Fls lilac, with green-brown throat. var. *purpurea* (Klatt) Bak. Fls claret.

I. monadelpha var. *curta* Ker-Gawl. = *I. curta*.

I. odorata Ker-Gawl. 20–55cm. Lvs 12–18cm, linear or lanceolate, often spirally twisted. Spike dense; fls yellow, the outer lobes sometimes tinged with red on outside. Spring–summer.

I. paniculata Delaroche 30–100cm. Lvs 15–60cm, linear or lanceolate. Spike lax or dense; fls cream or pale yellow, the outer lobes often tinged pink or red outside. Spring–summer.

I. patens Ait. 18–50cm. Lvs 10–35cm, lanceolate. Spike rather lax; fls pink, rose-purple or crimson, rarely white, sometimes with a small round white or green mark in centre. Spring.

I. polystachya L. 30–100cm. Lvs distichous, more than half as long as st., grass-like. Spike lax or dense; fls slightly scented, white, pale to deep mauve, golden or orange-yellow, sometimes with yellow, blue, mauve, green or purple mark in centre. Spring–summer. var. *polystachya*. Fls white to mauve, with or

without a central stain, often green- or blue-tinged on outside. var. *lutea* (Ker-Gawl.) Lewis. Fls golden yellow or orange-yellow, rarely with dark mark in centre, sometimes red- or purple-tinged outside.

I. rapunculoides Delaroche. 25–75cm. Lvs 10–30cm linear, lanceolate or sword-shaped. Spike lax or dense; fls white, mauve-pink, pale blue or purple, the tube often yellow or green. Winter–spring.

I. scariosa Thunb. = *I. latifolia*.

I. scillaris L. 20–50cm. Lvs 7–25cm lanceolate or sword-shaped. Spike lax; fls scented, white, mauve, pale to deep pink or magenta, usually with a small, green mark in centre. Winter–spring.

I. speciosa Andrews = *I. campanulata*.

I. spectabilis Salisb. = *I. viridiflora*.

I. splendida Lewis. 30–60cm. Lvs 18–45cm, linear. Spike capitate; fls pale pink. Spring.

I. vanzijliae L. Bol. 18–40cm. Lvs 4–16cm, lanceolate, spirally twisted, undulate. Spike dense; fls pink or mauve-pink with darker mark in centre. Winter–spring.

I. viridiflora Lam. 50–100cm. Lvs 40–55cm, linear. Spike lax; fls sea-green with purple, purple-black or red blotch in centre. Spring.

I. cvs. 'After Glow': outer pet. delft red, inner pet. green with black-red centre. 'Blue Bird': inner pet. white, outer pet. with broad violet streak tipped dark purple, centre black shaded purple, dark purple. 'Bridesmaid': fls white centred red, abundant. 'Castor': fls violet purple splashed yellow. 'Giant': fls ivory tipped purple with dark centre. 'Hogarth': fls cream centred purple. 'Hubert': fls orange centred magenta. 'Mabel': fls large, outside cyclamen purple, outer pet. shaded brown-red. 'Marquette': fls rich yellow tipped purple, centre dark purple. 'Rose Emperor': fls pale pink, outer pet. darker pink, centre deep carmine. 'Rose Queen': fls entirely pale pink. 'Uranus': fls dark lemon-yellow centred red. 'Venus': fls magenta with dark centre. 'Vulcan': fls carmine red and orange.

Ixiolirion (Fisch.) Herb. Amaryllidaceae. 4 bulbous perenn. herbs. Lvs basal, in a rosette. Infl. an umbel or loose rac.; perianth seg. 6, free or united in a tube; sta. 6, included. SW & C Asia.

I. kolpakowskianum Reg. Similar to *I. tataricum* but lvs linear, fls usually solely in an umbel, perianth 2–2.5cm, white to violet. Spring–summer. C Asia. Z7.

I. montanum (Labill.) Herb. = *I. tataricum*.

I. ledebourii Fisch. & Mey. = *I. tataricum* Ledebourii group.

I. pallasii Fisch. & Mey. = *I. tataricum*.

I. tataricum (Pall.) Herb. Lvs linear-lanceolate. Scape to 40cm; umbel sometimes with to 4 fls below it; perianth 2–5cm, blue or violet-blue, tep. with 3 darker central lines. SW & C Asia, Kashmir. Ledebourii group: fls bright violet. var. *macranthum* hort. Fls large, deep blue tinted purple. 'Sintensii': fls pale blue.

→*Kolpakowskia*.

Ixodia R. Br. IXODIA; FIREWEED. Compositae. 2 viscid, aromatic everg. shrubs. Lvs alt., simple, entire. Cap. discoid, in term. corymbs; inner phyllaries with a large, petal-like lamina; receptacle conic, with a large scale subtending each flt; flts tubular. Aus. Z9.

I. achilleoides R. Br. MOUNTAIN DAISY. Shrub to 2m. Lvs decurrent, glab., dark green above, paler beneath. Involucre 2–8mm diam.; phyllaries glab. to woolly; flts cream, often tinged red or green. S Aus.

Ixora L. Rubiaceae. 400 everg. shrubs or trees. Fls 4-merous, hermaphrodite in paniculate or corymbose cymes; cal. often red, tooted or lobed; cor. salver-shaped, tube narrowly cylindrical; anth. exserted. Fr. a drupe, red ripening black. Trop. (Old and New World). Z10.

I. acuminata Roxb. Shrub, to 2m. Lvs 20cm, elliptic or oblong-elliptic. Fls white, fragrant, in dense, corymbose or subcapitate cymes; cor. tube 2–3.5cm. Trop. Asia (India).

I. acuminata Thwaites, non Roxb. = *I. thwaitesii*.

I. alba J.W. Parham, non L. = *I. finlaysonia*.

I. alba L., non J.W. Parham = *I. chinensis* 'Alba'.

I. amboinica (Bl.) DC. = *I. longifolia*.

I. amoena Wallich ex G. Don = *I. javanica*.

I. arborea Sm. = *I. pavetta*.

I. bandhuca Roxb. = *I. coccinea* var. *bandhuca*.

I. barbata Roxb. ex Sm. Shrub, to 2m. Lvs 15–20cm, elliptic. Fls white; infl. lax; spreading; cor. tube 2.3–3.2cm. Trop. Asia (Andaman and Nicobar Is.).

I. brachypoda DC. Shrub or tree. Lvs 12–34cm, oblong, elliptic-oblong or lanceolate-oblong. Fls white with pink or red flecks in compact or subcapitate cymes; cor. tube 4.7–6.5cm.

I. casei Hance. Shrub to 3m. Lvs 27–30cm, elliptic-oblong to oblong. Fls red in corymbose cymes; cor. tube 3–3.5cm. Trop. Pacific (Caroline Is.).

I. chinensis Lam. Shrub to at least 2m. Lvs 6cm, obovate to elliptic or ovate. Fls pink, orange, red or white; infl. densely corymbose; cor. tube to 3.5cm. 'Alba': fls white. 'Dixiana': fls deep orange. Rosea': fls pale pink, darker later.

I. coccinea L. JUNGLE GERANIUM; FLAME OF THE WOODS; JUNGLE FLAME; BURNING LOVE; RED IXORA. Shrub, to 2.5m. Lvs to 10cm, elliptic to oblong or obovate. Fls red, orange, pink or yellow in lax corymbose cymes; cor. tube 2.5–3.5cm. Trop. Asia (India & Sri Lanka). 'Fraseri': fls vivid salmon pink. 'Morsei': fls brilliant orange tinted red. 'Orange King': compact; fls vivid orange. f. *coccinea*. Cor. red, lobes broadly lanceolate to narrowly ovate, acute. S India. f. *lutea* (Hutch.) Fosb. & Sachet. Cor. yellow, lobes broadly ovate or broadly elliptic, acute at apex. Gdn origin. var. *aureo-rosea* Corner. Cor. lobes yellow becoming pink-streaked. var. *bandhuca* (Roxb.) Corner. Fls in compressed corymbs; cor. scarlet, lobes rhombic. India. var. *decolorans* Corner. Cor. lobes fading from yellow to pale pink-white. var. *intermedia* Fosb. & Sachet. Cor. red, lobes ovate or elliptic, acute. var. *rosea* Corner. Cor. pink, lvs hairy. 'Dwarf coccinea': lvs 1–1.5cm wide, cordate at base (thus differing from 'Sunkist').

I. concinna R. Br. ex Hook. f. TROGON IXORA. Tree, to 8m. Lvs 5–12cm, elliptic or oblanceolate to oblong. Fls fragrant, yellow or pink, turning red in lax, corymbose cymes; cor. tube 0.8–1cm. Trop. Asia (Malay Penins., Sumatra).

I. congesta Roxb. Shrub, to 1m. Lvs 15cm, elliptic, elliptic-oblong or lanceolate. Fls yellow, orange or red in dense corymbose cymes; cor. tube 3–3.5cm. Trop. Asia (Burm. and Malay Penins.).

I. decipiens DC. = *I. pavetta*.

I. dixiana hort. ex Gentil = *I. chinensis*.

I. duffii T. Moore = *I. casei*.

I. ferrea (Jacq.) Benth. Shrub or tree 3–5m. Lvs 7–12cm, lanceolate-elliptic, or oblong-elliptic. Fls white, flesh-coloured or with tube white and lobes pink; infl. pseudoaxillary, few-fld; cor. tube 0.8–1cm. W Indies and Cuba, central to N S Amer.

I. findlayana auct. = *I. finlaysonia*.

I. finlaysonia Wallich ex G. Don. SIAMESE WHITE IXORA. Shrub or tree, to 6m. Lvs 9–17cm, elliptic, obovate or oblanceolate. Fls white or cream, in corymbose cymes; cor. tube 2.3–3cm. Burm., Thail.

I. fraseri hort. ex Gentil = *I. coccinea* 'Fraseri'.

I. fulgens Roxb. ex Hook. Shrub to 1m. Lvs 10–23cm, narrowly elliptic or oblong-elliptic. Fls scarlet to orange-red in many-fld, corymbose cymes; cor. tube 3.8–4.5cm. Burm., Malay Penins.

I. glaucina (Teysm. & Binnend.) Kurz = *I. fulgens*.

I. griffithii Hook. = *I. congesta*.

I. hookeri (Oudem.) Bremek. Shrub or small tree. Lvs 11–15.5cm, oblong-elliptic. Fls white tinged pink or red in many-fld, lax, corymbose cyme; cor. tube 6–8cm. Madag.

I. incarnata Wallich = *I. chinensis*.

I. javanica (Bl.) DC. COMMON RED IXORA; JAVANESE IXORA. Shrub or tree 1–4m. Lvs 8.5–16cm, elliptic or oblong-elliptic. Fls red or less often pink or orange in lax, densely-fld, corymbose cymes; cor. tube 2.5–3.6cm. Java, Malay Penins.

I. lanceolaria Colebr. ex Roxb. = *I. malabarica*.

I. laxiflora Sm. Shrub or tree. Lvs 10–13cm, lanceolate-oblong. Fls white flushed pink or red in lax, often pendent, corymbose cymes; cor. tube 2–2.3cm. W Afr.

I. lobbii Loud. GLOSSY IXORA. Shrub or treelet. Lvs glossy, 14–22cm, oblong-elliptic or oblong-ovate. Fls orange to red in lax, many-branched corymbose cymes; cor. tube 2.5–3.2cm.

I. longifolia Sm. Shrub 1.5–3m. Lvs 22–30cm, lanceolate to lanceolate-oblong. Fls red in lax, corymbose cyme; cor. tube 2.5–3cm. Moluccas.

I. macrothyrsa (Teysm. & Binnend.) T. Moore = *I. longifolia*.

I. malabarica (Dennst.) Mabb. Shrub. Lvs 9–14cm, lanceolate to linear-lanceolate. Fls white in loose corymbose cymes; cor. tube 1.3–2cm. India.

I. multibracteata Pearson ex King & Gamble = *I. umbellata* var. *multibracteata*.

I. nigricans R. Br. ex Wight & Arn. WHITE NEEDLES. Shrub to 5m. Lvs 7–12.5cm, obovate or oblong. Fls fragrant, white, in lax corymbose cymes; cor. tube 1.2cm. India, Burm., Malay Penins.

I. odorata Hook., non Spreng. nec Boerl. = *I. hookeri*.

I. parviflora Vahl, non Lam. = *I. pavetta*.

I. pavetta Andrews TORCH TREE. Branched small tree. Lvs 7–15cm, elliptic or oblong-elliptic. Fls white, crowded; cor. tube to 8mm. India, Bangladesh, Pak., Sri Lanka.

I. plumea Ridl. = *I. nigricans*.

I. polyantha Wight. Small shrub. Lvs 10–30cm. Fls white in large, dense, corymbose cymes; cor. tube 1.5–3cm. India.

I. radiata Hiern = *I. brachypoda*.

I. rosea Wallich = *I. chinensis*.

I. salicifolia (Bl.) DC. Shrub 1–1.5m. Lvs 15–22cm, narrowly oblong to linear-oblong. Fls orange to red in compact, many-fld cymes; cor. tube 3.5–5cm. Java.

I. siamensis Wallich ex G. Don. Shrub to 3m. Lvs to 5–10.5cm, elliptic to oblong-elliptic. Fls pink in compact cymes; cor. tube 1.6–2.5cm. Thail. cf. *I. coccinea*.

I. spectabilis Wallich ex G. Don. Tree. Lvs 13–26.5cm, elliptic or oblong-elliptic. Fls white packed in open-branched cymes; cor. tube 0.6–1cm. India, Burm.

I. stricta Roxb. = *I. chinensis*.

I. 'Sunkist'. Dwarf bush to 1m. Lvs 1.7–8cm, lanceolate-elliptic to lanceolate-obovate. Fls pinky apricot-yellow turning brick-red in compact corymbose cyme; cor. tube 2.2–3.3cm. Gdn origin (Singapore).

I. thwaitesii WHITE IXORA. Shrub or tree, to 6m. Lvs 6–15.5cm, oblanceolate, elliptic or narrowly oblong. Fls white to cream; in dense, corymbose cymes; cor. tube 0.3–0.5cm. Sri Lanka; in widespread cult.

I. umbellata Koord. & Val. MALAYAN WHITE IXORA. Shrub or tree to 7m. Lvs 18–25cm, oblong or lanceolate-elliptic. Fls white in lax, rounded cymes; cor. tube 3–3.7cm. Java, Sumatra, Malay Penins. var. *multibracteata* (Pearson ex King & Gamble) Corner Infl. bracts numerous.

I. undulata Roxb. Shrub or small tree. Lvs to 8–22cm, elliptic or lanceolate-elliptic. Fls fragrant, white in paniculate or corymbose cymes; cor. tube 0.6–9cm. India.

I. williamsii Sandw. Shrub or tree. Lvs 11.5–17.5cm, elliptic to broadly elliptic. Fls red or pink, in lax, corymbose cymes; cor. tube 3cm. Gdn origin (Trin.).

→*Pavetta*.

Iya-giboshi *Hosta capitata*.

J

Jaboncillo *Clethra mexicana; Sapindus saponaria.*

Jaborosa Juss. Solanaceae. 20 perenn. herbs. Lvs basal. Fls solitary or in few-fld cymes; cal. tubular to campanulate; cor. tubular or campanulate, limb spreading, 5-lobed. Fr. a berry or drupe. S Amer. Z8.
J. integrifolia Lam. Lvs to 16cm, oval to elliptic, entire. Fls green to white, solitary, to 6cm diam., lobes narrow. S Braz., Urug., Arg.

Jaboticaba *Myrciaria cauliflora.*

Jacaranda Juss. Bignoniaceae. 45 trees. Lvs usually bipinnate. Fls in pan.; cal. campanulate or cupular, 5-lobed or truncate; cor. tubular-campanulate. Trop. Amer. Z9.
J. acutifolia hort. non HBK = *J. mimosifolia.*
J. amazonensis Vatt. = *J. copaia* ssp. *spectabilis.*
J. arborea Urban. To 8m. Lvs bipinnate; pinnules 1–2cm, 1–5 pairs, obovate. Fls to 3cm, purple or rose, downy. Cuba.
J. bahamensis R. Br. = *J. caerulea.*
J. caerulea (L.) St.-Hil. To 20m. Lvs bipinnate; pinnules 1–2cm, 4–13 pairs, rhombic to lanceolate-elliptic. Fls 3.5–4cm, blue, purple or white. W Indies.
J. caroba (Vell.) DC. To 5m. Lvs bipinnate; pinnules 1.2–7cm, 1–8 pairs, elliptic to obovate or rhomboid. Fls to 7cm, pale to dark violet. Braz.
J. caroliniana Pers. = *J. caerulea.*
J. chelonia Griseb. = *J. mimosifolia.*
J. clausseniana Casar. = *J. caroba.*
J. coerulea Griseb. = *J. caerulea.*
J. copaia (Aubl.) D. Don. To 30m. Lvs bipinnate; pinnules 1.5–8cm, elliptic to obovate. Fls pale to dark blue. ssp. *copaia.* Pinnules elliptic to oblong-elliptic, petiolate. Braz. to Venez. ssp. *spectabilis* (Mart. ex DC.) A. Gentry. Pinnules rhomboid to elliptic, sessile.
J. curialis Vell. = *J. jasminoides.*
J. cuspidifolia Mart. ex DC. To 12m. Lvs bipinnate; pinnules 10–45mm, 9–20 pairs, ovate to elliptic. Fls blue to violet, 3.5–6.2cm. Arg., Parag., Braz., Boliv.
J. filicifolia D. Don = *J. obtusifolia* ssp. *rhombifolia.*
J. intermedia Sonder = *J. micrantha.*
J. jasminoides (Thunb.) Sandw. To 4m. Lvs 12–25cm, entire or pinnate; pinnae 1.8–6cm, 1–5 pairs, ovate to elliptic. Fls dark purple, lobes hairy, 3.5–5cm. Braz., Mex.
J. lasiogyne Bur. & Schum. = *J. obtusifolia.*
J. micrantha Cham. To 25m. Lvs bipinnate, 40–90cm; pinnules 1.3–10cm, 2–11 pairs, obovate to elliptic. Fls 3.5–5cm, pale violet, pubesc. outside. Braz., Arg.
J. mimosifolia D. Don. To 15m. Lvs bipinnate; pinnules 0.3–1.2cm, narrowly elliptic. Fls 2.4–5.2cm, blue-purple, throat white. Arg., Boliv. Often mislabelled as *J. acutifolia.* 'Alba': fls white.
J. obtusifolia Humb. & Bonpl. To 10m. Lvs bipinnate; pinnules to 1.2cm, rhomboid. Braz., Boliv., Peru, Colomb., Arg. ssp. *rhombifolia* (G. Mey.) A. Gentry. Lvs v. ferny. Braz. to Venez.
J. ovalifolia R. Br. = *J. mimosifolia.*
J. procera (Willd.) R. Br. = *J. copaia.*
J. pubescens Guill. ex DC. = *J. jasminoides.*
J. rhombifolia G. Mey. = *J. obtusifolia* ssp. *rhombifolia.*
J. sagraeana Griseb. non DC. = *J. arborea.*
J. sagraeana DC. non Griseb. = *J. caerulea.*
J. spectabilis Mart. ex DC. = *J. copaia* ssp. *spectabilis.*
J. subvelutina Mart. ex DC. = *J. jasminoides.*
J. superba Pittier = *J. copaia* ssp. *spectabilis.*
J. tomentosa R. Br. = *J. jasminoides.*
→*Kordelestris* and *Rafinesquia.*

Jackal's Food *Euphorbia mauritanica.*
Jack Bean *Canavalia ensiformis.*
Jackfruit *Artocarpus heterophyllus.*
Jack-In-The-Box *Hernandia ovigera.*
Jack-in-the-pulpit *Arisaema triphyllum; Arum maculatum.*
Jack Pine *Pinus banksiana.*

Jacksonia R. Br. Leguminosae (Papilionoideae). 50 shrubs; lf-less except when juvenile. St. and br. striate, often flattened. Rac. term., bracteate; fls pea-like. Aus.

J. scoparia R. Br. Broom-like shrub or small tree, erect to 3m. Lvs entire, soon abscising. Fls to 9mm, vivid yellow. Queensld, NSW. Z9.

Jacobea Thunb.
J. elegans (L.) Moench = *Senecio elegans.*

Jacobean Lily *Sprekelia formosissima.*

Jacobinia Nees ex Moric.
J. carnea (Lindl.) Nichols. = *Justicia carnea.*
J. coccinea (Aubl.) Hiern = *Pachystachys coccinea.*
J. incana (Nees) Hemsl. = *Justicia leonardii.*
J. magnifica (Nees) Lindau = *Justicia carnea.*
J. mohintli (Nees) Hemsl. = *Justicia spicigera.*
J. obbisior (Nees) L.H. Bail. = *Justicia carnea.*
J. pauciflora (Nees) Lindau = *Justicia rizzinii.*
J. pohliana (Nees) Lindau = *Justicia carnea.*
J. spicigera (Schldl.) L.H. Bail. = *Justicia spicigera.*
J. velutina (Nees) Voss non Lindau = *Justicia carnea.*

Jacobite Rose *Rosa* ×*alba.*
Jacob's Coat *Acalypha wilkesiana.*

Jacobsenia L. Bol. & Schwantes. Aizoaceae. 2 shrublets; st. bushy. Lvs paired, ± cylindric and unequal. Fls pedicellate. S Afr. (Cape Prov.). Z9.
J. hallii L. Bol. To 15cm. Lvs 4–7×1×1cm, flat above, lower surface and sides convex, bluntly carinate toward the tip. Fls to 8.8cm diam., white to lemon yellow. W Cape.
J. kolbei (L. Bol.) L. Bol. & Schwantes To 24cm. Lvs 2–3.5×0.8–0.9×0.8–0.9cm, cylindric to flat above, obtuse or acute, minutely papillose. Fls to 1.5cm diam., white. W Cape.
→*Drosanthemum.*

Jacob's Ladder *Pedilanthus tithymaloides; Polemonium caeruleum.*
Jacob's Rod *Asphodeline.*
Jacob's Staff *Fouquieria splendens.*

Jacquemontia Choisy. Convolvulaceae. 120 largely herbaceous twiners, differing from *Ipomoea* in smaller fls in denser clusters and 2, flattened stigmas. Trop. Z10.
J. pentantha (Jacq.) G. Don Fast-growing everg. twiner. Lvs to 5cm, cordate-ovate. Fls to 2.5cm diam., funnelform, violet-blue to blue in long-stalked cymes. Trop. Amer.

Jacquinia L. Theophrastaceae. 30 everg. trees and shrubs. Lvs entire or spiny-toothed. Fls 5-merous, staminodes petaloid, alternating with cor. lobes. Fr. a small leathery berry. C Amer., W Indies. Z10.
J. aculeata (L.) Mez. Shrub or tree to 4m. Lvs to 2.5cm, lanceolate, spiny, rigid, pungent. Fls red, solitary or in drooping umbels. Fr. red. Cuba.
J. armillaris Jacq. = *J. barbasco.*
J. barbasco (Loefl.) Mez. BARBASCO; BRACELET WOOD. Shrub or tree to 15m. Lvs to 10cm, spathulate or obovate-oblong, obtuse, retuse or mucronate, rather fleshy. Fls white, fragrant, in rac. or corymbs. Fr. yellow-red. W Indies.
J. pungens A. Gray. Shrub to 4m. Lvs to 7cm, narrow-lanceolate to elliptic-oblong, sharply pungent. Fls yellow-red in contracted rac. Fr. yellow to apricot. Mex.
J. ruscifolia Jacq. = *J. aculeata.*

Jacquinia-leaved Fig *Ficus americana.*

Jacquiniella Schltr. Orchidaceae. 4 epiphytic orchids. St. tufted, slender. Lvs fleshy, distichous, narrow. Infl. apical, one- to several-fld; tep. free, fleshy, linear-oblong to elliptic-lanceolate; lip simple or trilobed. Spring–summer. Trop. Amer. Z10.
J. globosa (Jacq.) Schltr. To 15cm. Lvs linear. Fls usually solitary, green-yellow; sep. to 3×1.5mm, elliptic; lip to 3×1.5mm. Mex. to Braz., W Indies.
J. teretifolia (Sw.) Britt. & Wils. To 60cm. Lvs subterete. Fls usually solitary, yellow-green, fleshy; sep. to 12×2mm, lanceolate; lip to 9×3mm. W Indies, Mex. to Panama, Venez., Colomb.
→*Epidendrum.*

Jade Plant *Crassula ovata.*
Jade Tree *Crassula ovata.*
Jade Vine *Strongylodon macrobotrys.*
Jaggery Palm *Caryota urens.*
Jagua *Genipa americana.*
Jamaica Caper Tree *Capparis cynophallophora.*
Jamaica Cherry *Ficus citrifolia.*
Jamaica Dogwood *Piscidia (P. piscipula).*
Jamaica Flower *Hibiscus sabdariffa.*
Jamaica Gold Fern *Pityrogramma sulphurea.*
Jamaica Honeysuckle *Passiflora laurifolia.*
Jamaican Cherry *Muntingia calabura.*
Jamaican Kino *Coccoloba uvifera.*
Jamaican Oak *Catalpa longissima.*
Jamaican Palmetto *Sabal jamaicensis.*
Jamaican Thatch *Thrinax radiata.*
Jamaica Nutmeg *Monodora myristica.*
Jamaica Sorrel *Hibiscus sabdariffa.*
Jamaica Vervain *Stachytarpheta jamaicensis.*
Jamberry *Physalis ixocarpa; P. philadelphica.*
Jambhiri Orange *Citrus jambhiri.*
Jambolan *Syzygium cumini.*

Jambosa Adans. = *Syzygium.*

Jambu Mawar *Syzygium jambos.*

Jamesia Torr. and A. Gray. CLIFFBUSH; WAXFLOWER. Hydrangeaceae. 1 spreading decid. shrub to 1.5m. St. downy, bark then papery. Lvs 3–7cm, ovate, toothed, velvety. Fls 1cm diam. in term. pan. to 6cm; pet. 5, white. Early summer.
J. americana Torr. and A. Gray. 'Rosea': fls pink. var. *californica* (Small) Jeps. Smaller in most respects. Z6.
→*Edwinia.*

Jamesonia Hook. & Grev. Adiantaceae. 17 ferns. Rhiz. creeping, long. Stipes bent then ascending, tomentose or gland. Fronds generally linear, pinnate or pinnatisect, tomentose or gland.; pinnae mostly overlapping in 2 series. S Amer. Z10.
J. canescens Kunze. Stipes 2–10cm. Fronds 10–50cm pinnate; pinnae 2–4×1–5mm, reniform to orbicular, dentate, tomentose above, rusty beneath. Venez.
J. imbricata (Sw.) Hook. & Grev. Stipes 1–15cm. Fronds 7–80cm, pinnate; pinnae 1–6×1–4mm, orbicular to ovate, gland. above, white to rusty beneath. Colomb., Ecuad., Peru.
J. nivea Karst. = *J. canescens.*
J. tolimensis (Hieron.) C. Chr. = *J. verticalis.*
J. verticalis Kunze. Stipes 3–45cm. Fronds 8–40cm, pinnatisect or pinnate; pinnae 8–22×2–10mm, ovate to orbicular, gland. above, hairy beneath. Colomb., Ecuad.
→*Gymnogramma.*

Jamestown Weed *Datura stramonium.*

Jancaea see *Jankaea.*

Jankaea Boiss. Gesneriaceae. 1 perenn. herb. Lvs radical, rosulate 2–4cm, obovate, entire, white-pubesc. Fls 1–2 per scape; cal. 5-lobed; cor. pale lilac, broadly campanulate, 4(–5)-lobed. C Greece (Mt Olympus). Z8.
J. heldreichii Boiss.

Japanese Alder *Alnus japonica.*
Japanese Alpine Cherry *Prunus nipponica.*
Japanese Anemone *Anemone hupehensis.*
Japanese Angelica Tree *Aralia elata.*
Japanese Apricot *Prunus mume.*
Japanese Aralia *Fatsia japonica.*
Japanese Arrowhead *Sagittaria sagittifolia.*
Japanese Arrowroot *Pueraria lobata.*
Japanese Artichoke *Stachys affinis.*
Japanese Aspen *Populus sieboldii.*
Japanese Banana *Musa basjoo.*
Japanese Beech *Fagus crenata.*
Japanese Big-leaf Magnolia *Magnolia hypoleuca.*
Japanese Bird Cherry *Prunus grayana; P. ssiori.*
Japanese Bitter Orange *Poncirus trifoliata.*
Japanese Black Pine *Pinus thunbergii.*
Japanese Blood Grass *Imperata cylindrica.*
Japanese Blue Beech *Fagus japonica.*
Japanese Bunching Onion *Allium fistulosum.*
Japanese Carpet Grass *Zoysia matrella.*
Japanese Cedar *Cryptomeria.*
Japanese Cherry Birch *Betula grossa.*
Japanese Chestnut *Castanea crenata.*

Japanese Climbing Fern *Lygodium japonicum.*
Japanese Cornel *Cornus officinalis.*
Japanese Cornelian Cherry *Cornus officinalis.*
Japanese Creeper *Parthenocissus tricuspidata.*
Japanese Dead Nettle *Meehania.*
Japanese Douglas Fir *Pseudotsuga japonica.*
Japanese Emperor Oak *Quercus dentata.*
Japanese Evergreen Oak *Quercus acuta.*
Japanese Fatsia *Fatsia japonica.*
Japanese Felt Fern *Pyrrosia lingua.*
Japanese Fir *Abies firma.*
Japanese Flag *Iris ensata.*
Japanese Flowering Apricot *Prunus mume.*
Japanese Flowering Plum *Prunus mume.*
Japanese Ginger *Zingiber mioga.*
Japanese Hackberry *Celtis sinensis.*
Japanese Hazel *Corylus sieboldiana.*
Japanese Hemlock *Tsuga diversifolia; T. sieboldii*
Japanese Hibiscus *Hibiscus schizopetalus.*
Japanese Holly *Ilex crenata.*
Japanese Holly Fern *Cyrtomium falcatum; Dryopteris varia.*
Japanese Honeysuckle *Lonicera japonica.*
Japanese Hop *Humulus japonicus.*
Japanese Hornbeam *Carpinus japonica.*
Japanese Horse Chestnut *Aesculus turbinata.*
Japanese Horseradish *Wasabia.*
Japanese Hydrangea Vine *Schizophragma hydrangeoides.*
Japanese Iris *Iris ensata; I. laevigata.*
Japanese Ivy *Hedera rhombea; Parthenocissus tricuspidata.*
Japanese Knotweed *Polygonum japonicum.*
Japanese Lace Fern *Polystichum polyblepharum.*
Japanese Lacquer Tree *Toxicodendron vernicifluum.*
Japanese Lady Fern *Deparia petersenii.*
Japanese Lantern *Hibiscus schizopetalus.*
Japanese Larch *Larix kaempferi.*
Japanese Lawn Grass *Zoysia japonica.*
Japanese Leek *Allium fistulosum.*
Japanese Lime *Tilia japonica.*
Japanese Loquat *Eriobotrya japonica.*
Japanese Maple *Acer japonicum; A. palmatum.*
Japanese Medlar *Eriobotrya japonica.*
Japanese Millet *Setaria italica.*
Japanese Mountain Ash *Sorbus matsumurana.*
Japanese Mountain Cherry *Prunus serrulata var. spontanea.*
Japanese Nutmeg-yew *Torreya nucifera.*
Japanese Pagoda Tree *Sophora japonica.*
Japanese Pepper *Piper kadzura.*
Japanese Persimmon *Diospyros kaki.*
Japanese Photinia *Photinia glabra.*
Japanese Pittosporum *Pittosporum tobira.*
Japanese Plum *Prunus salicina.*
Japanese Plum Yew *Cephalotaxus harringtonia.*
Japanese Poinsettia *Euphorbia heterophylla.*
Japanese Poplar *Populus maximowiczii.*
Japanese Privet *Ligustrum japonicum.*
Japanese Quince *Chaenomeles.*
Japanese Red Pine *Pinus densiflora.*
Japanese Roof Iris *Iris tectorum.*
Japanese Rose *Kerria; Rosa multiflora; R. rugosa.*
Japanese Sago Palm *Cycas revoluta.*
Japanese Shield Fern *Dryopteris erythrosora.*
Japanese Snowball Tree *Viburnum plicatum.*
Japanese Spikenard *Aralia cordata.*
Japanese Spindle *Euonymus japonicus.*
Japanese Spiraea *Spiraea japonica.*
Japanese Spurge *Pachysandra.*
Japanese Stewartia *Stewartia pseudocamellia.*
Japanese Thuja *Thuja standishii.*
Japanese Tree Lilac *Syringa reticulata.*
Japanese Umbrella Pine *Sciadopitys.*
Japanese Varnish Tree *Firmiana simplex.*
Japanese Walnut *Juglans ailanthifolia.*
Japanese Water Iris *Iris ensata.*
Japanese White Birch *Betula mandschurica var. japonica.*
Japanese White Pine *Pinus parviflora.*
Japanese Winterberry *Ilex serrata.*
Japanese Wisteria *Wisteria floribunda.*
Japanese Witch-hazel *Hamamelis japonica.*
Japanese Yellow-wood *Cladrastis platycarpa.*
Japanese Yew *Taxus cuspidata.*
Japanese Zelkova *Zelkova serrata.*
Japan Pepper *Zanthoxylum piperitum.*
Japonica *Chaenomeles.*
Jarrah *Eucalyptus marginata.*
Jarrilla *Larrea divaricata.*

Jasione L. SHEEP'S BIT. Campanulaceae. 20 ann., bienn. or perenn. herbs. Lvs simple, lanceolate. Fls small, 5-merous, in term. heads or compact pan. with involucral bracts; pet. lanceolate. Temp. Eur., Medit.

J. amethystina (Lagasca & Rodr.) Tutin. Tufted perenn., to 10cm. Lvs rosulate, oblong to oblanceolate, dentate. Bracts ovate, occas. denticulate, tinged purple; fls blue suffused purple. Summer. S Spain. Z7.

J. bulgarica Stoj. & Stef. Perenn. to 20cm. Lower lvs rosulate, obovate-spathulate, usually entire. Bracts elliptic to lanceolate; fls tinged pale blue to lilac. Bulg. Z5.

J. crispa (Pourr.) Samp. Pubesc. perenn. to 5cm. Lvs thick, linear-oblanceolate to lanceolate, usually entire, ciliate. Bracts narrowly ovate, serrate; fls blue. SW Eur. Z6.

J. heldreichii Boiss. & Orph. Glab. to villous perenn. or bienn. to 10cm. Lvs linear-lanceolate, sometimes sparsely ciliate, bracts lanceolate to linear-lanceolate, dentate; fls blue. W & C Eur. Z6.

J. humilis Lois. Perenn. to 25cm. Lvs to 1cm, oblong-oblanceolate. Bracts broadly ovate; fls blue. Pyren. Z5.

J. jankae Neilr. = *J. montana*.

J. laevis Lam. SHEPHERD'S SCABIOUS; SHEEP'S BIT. Densely tufted perenn. to 15cm. Lvs narrow-obovate to oblanceolate, sub-entire. Bracts ovate to deltoid, dentate; fls blue. S & W Eur. 'Blaulicht' ('Blue Light'): fls vivid blue. Z5.

J. montana L. SHEEP'S BIT. Ann. or bienn., to 50cm, pubesc. Lvs linear to narrowly ovate, undulate. Bracts ovate to deltoid, crenate to serrate; fls blue occas. tinged red or white. Summer. Eur. Z6.

J. perennis Lam. = *J. laevis*.

J. pyrenaica Sennen = *J. laevis*.

Jasionella Stoj. & Stef. = *Jasione*.

Jasmin *Gardenia augusta*.
Jasmine *Jasminum*.
Jasmine Tobacco *Nicotiana alata*.
Jasmine Tree *Holarrhena pubescens*.

Jasminocereus Britt. & Rose Cactaceae. 1 arborescent cactus to 8m. Br. segmented, green or grey-green; ribs 11–22; areoles 5–25mm apart; central spines usually 2–4, to 7.5cm, radial spines shorter. Fls salverform, 5–9×2–6cm, nocturnal, creamy white. Galapagos Is. Z9.

J. thouarsii (Weber) Backeb.

Jasminum L. JASMINE; JESSAMINE. Oleaceae. 200 shrubs and woody climbers. Lvs trifoliolate, imparipinnate or with only one leaflet. Fls in term. or axill. cymes; cor. tubular, 5-lobed. Fr. a 2-valved berry. Trop. and temp. Old World, 1 sp. in Amer.

J. affine Carr. = *J. officinale* 'Affine'.

J. angulare Vahl. Everg. climbing shrub, lfts 3, rarely 5, ovate to lanceolate. Fls unscented, in threes, to 3cm diam., white. S Africa. Z9.

J. azoricum L. Everg. twining shrub. Lfts 3, ovate, undulate. Fls fragrant, in term. pan.; white. Late summer. Azores. Z9.

J. beesianum Forr. & Diels. Decid., sprawling to twining shrub. Lvs simple, ovate-lanceolate, slightly downy. Fls in threes, fragrant, pale pink to deep rose, 1cm diam. Fr. black, glossy. Early summer. China. Z7.

J. blinii Lév. = *J. polyanthum*.

J. dispermum Wall. Climber. Lvs trifoliolate to pinnate. Fls white flushed pink, fragrant in axill. and term. cymes. Summer. Himal.; W China. Z9.

J. diversifolium Kobuski = *J. subhumile*.

J. farreri Gilmour = *J. humile* f. *farreri*.

J. floridum Bunge. Erect to semi-pendent, semi-everg. shrub. Lfts 3–5, oval to ovate, acuminate, glab. Fls in cymes, profuse, yellow. Late summer. China. Z9.

J. fluminense hort. = *J. azoricum*.

J. fruticans L. Dense everg. or semi-everg. shrub to 1.25m. Lfts 3, tough, narrow-oblong, obtuse, minutely ciliate. Fls to 5 per term. cyme, yellow. Summer. Medit., Asia Minor. Z8.

J. giraldii hort. = *J. humile* f. *farreri*.

J. grandiflorum L. = *J. officinale* f. *grandiflorum*.

J. heterophyllum Roxb. = *J. subhumile*.

J. humile L. ITALIAN YELLOW JASMINE. Everg. or semi-everg. shrub to 6m, erect. Lfts to 7, ovate-lanceolate. Fls in near-umbellate clusters, yellow, poorly scented, 1cm wide. Middle East, Burm., China. 'Revolutum' Semi-everg. Lfts 3–7. Fls 2.5cm wide, yellow, fragrant. Summer. f. *farreri* (Gilmour) P. Green. Everg. shrub to 1.5m; lfts 3, oval-lanceolate, acuminate. Fls yellow. Summer. Upper Burm. f. *wallichianum* (Lindl.) P. Green. Shoots v. angular. Lfts 7–13, ovate-lanceolate. Fls to 3 per pendent cyme. Nepal. Z8.

J. humile var. *glabrum* (DC.) Kob. = *J. humile* f. *wallichianum*.

J. humile var. *revolutum* (Sims) Stokes = *J. humile* 'Revolutum'.

J. mesnyi Hance. PRIMROSE JASMINE. Everg. rambling shrub to 2m. Lfts 3, subsessile, lanceolate, glossy. Fls 3–5cm wide, usually semi-double, bright yellow. Summer. W China. Z8.

J. nudiflorum Lindl. WINTER JASMINE. Decid., slender, arching to scandent shrub, to 3m. Lfts 3, oval-oblong, dark green, glab., ciliate. Fls solitary to 3cm wide, yellow. Winter–early spring. N China. 'Aureum': lvs yellow, liable to revert to green. 'Nanum': dwarf, slow-growing, compact. Z6.

J. officinale L. COMMON JASMINE; TRUE JASMINE; JESSAMINE. Decid. scandent to twining shrub to 10m. Lfts 5–9, elliptic, acuminate, margins minutely downy. Fls to 5 per cyme, highly fragrant, white, 2cm wide. Summer–early autumn. Asia Minor, Himal., China. 'Affine': fls larger, exterior pink. 'Argenteovariegatum': lvs grey green edged creamy white. 'Aureum': lvs blotched golden yellow. f. *grandiflorum* (L.) Kob. More robust; lfts 5–7. Fls to 4cm diam., white flushed pink at base. Summer. Himal. Z7.

J. parkeri Dunn. Everg. dwarf shrub, to 30cm. Lfts 3–5, ovate, acuminate, entire, sessile. Fls solitary or paired, yellow, 1.5cm wide. Summer. NW India. Z7.

J. polyanthum Franch. Semi-evergreen climber. Lfts 5–7, lanceolate, narrow-acuminate, coriaceous. Fls in axill. pan., highly fragrant, white, exterior pink. Summer. SW China. Z8.

J. primulinum Hemsl. = *J. mesnyi*.

J. pubigerum var. *glabrum* DC. = *J. humile* f. *wallichianum*.

J. reevesii hort. = *J. humile* 'Revolutum'.

J. revolutum Sims. = *J. humile* 'Revolutum'.

J. rex S.T. Dunn. Everg. climber. Lft large, 1, broadly ovate. Fls 2–3 per axill. cyme, unscented, white, tube to 2.5cm. Summer. Thail. Z8.

J. sambac (L.) Ait. ARABIAN JASMINE. Everg. climber. Lvs to 7cm, simple, shiny broad-ovate. Fls in clusters 3–12, highly fragrant, waxy white, pink with age, tube 12mm. Fls continuously. Widespread through cult.; may originate in India. 'Grand Duke of Tuscany': fls double. Z9.

J. sieboldianum Bl. = *J. nudiflorum*.

J. ×stephanense Lemoine. (*J. beesianum* ×*J. officinale*.) Vigorous twiner to 5m. Lvs simple or 3–5-parted, flushed cream on emergence. Fls pale pink, small, in sparse cymes. Mid-summer. Gdn origin, also said to occur wild in W China. Z7.

J. suavissimum Lindl. Tall twiner. Lvs 2.5–6cm, linear. Fls white, fragrant, in lax pan. Late summer. Aus. Z10.

J. subhumile W.W. Sm. Scandent shrub. Shoots purple-tinted. Lvs usually simple, occas. with 1–2 narrow secondary lfts, dark green, glossy, tough. Fls small, yellow, starry in narrow cymes. Late spring. E Himal., W China. Z8.

J. triumphans hort. = *J. humile* 'Revolutum'.

J. wallichianum Lindl. = *J. humile* f. *wallichianum*.

Jata de Guanbacoa *Copernicia macroglossa*.
Jata-uba *Syagrus cocoides*.

Jatropha L. TARTOGO; GOUT PLANT; BARBADOS NUT; PHYSIC NUT; CORAL PLANT; PEREGRINA; JICAMILLA. Euphorbiaceae. 170 tall perenn. herbs and shrubs, or trees with milky or watery sap. Lvs simple or palmately lobed or cut. Fls small, 5-merous in term., flat-topped, many-branched cymes, peduncle stout, often coloured. Trop. and warm temp., mainly S Amer. Z10.

J. curcas L. PHYSIC NUT; PURGING NUT; PULZA; BARBADOS NUT. Shrub or small tree, 2.5–6m, decid. Lvs to 15cm diam. ovate to 3–5-palmately lobed. Fls green-yellow to yellow-white. Trop. Amer.

J. hastata Jacq. = *J. integerrima*.

J. integerrima Jacq. PEREGRINA; SPICY JATROPHA. Everg. tree to 6m. Lvs dark green, pandurately 3-lobed, green-brown beneath. Fls bright rose-red. Cuba, W Indies.

J. multifida L. CORAL PLANT; PHYSIC NUT. Shrub or tree, to 7m. Lvs to 30cm diam., palmately 7–11 lobed, lobes finely dissected. Fls scarlet. Trop. Amer.

J. pandurifolia Andrew = *J. integerrima*.

J. podagrica Hook. GOUT PLANT; TARTOGO. St. to 2.5m, gouty, with a central swelling. Lvs orbicular-ovate, to 30cm wide, 3–5-lobed, blue-green. Fls coral red. Guat. and Panama.

J. texana Muell. Arg. = *Cnidoscolus texanus*.

J. urens L. = *Cnidoscolus urens*.

J. urens var. *inermis* Calvino = *Cnidoscolus chayamansa*.

Java Apple *Syzygium samarangense*.
Java Dacryberry *Dacrycarpus imbricatus*.
Java Glory Bean *Clerodendrum ×speciosum*.
Javanese Ixora *Ixora javanica*.
Javan Grape *Tetrastigma*.
Java Olives *Sterculia foetida*.
Java Staghorn Fern *Platycerium willinckii*.

Java Tree *Ficus benjamina.*
Java Willow *Ficus virens.*
Jazmin Del Monte *Brunfelsia lactea.*

Jeffersonia Barton. TWIN LEAF. Berberidaceae. 2 perenn. herbs. Lvs round to reniform, radical, 2-lobed, peltate, angled to toothed, long-petioled. Fls solitary, on slender scapes; pet. 5–8, flat, oblong, sta. 8. N Amer., E Asia. Z5.
J. diphylla (L.) Pers. RHEUMATISM ROOT. Lvs to 15cm across, glaucous beneath. Scapes exceeding petioles; fls white, 2.5cm across. Spring. Ont. to Tenn.
J. dubia (Maxim.) Benth. and Hook. f. ex Bak. & Moore. Lvs to 10cm across, glaucous, tinged mauve. Scapes shorter than petioles; fls lavender to pale blue, 3cm. across. Spring–summer. NE Asia.

Jeffrey's Pine *Pinus jeffreyi.*

Jehlia Rose = *Lopezia.*

Jelly Palm *Butia* (*B. yatay*).
Jenneb *Cordia africana.*

Jensenobotrya Herre. Aizoaceae. 1 dwarf shrub. St. woody, with withered lf remains. Lvs to 1.5cm diam., spherical, v. succulent, red-flushed. Fls solitary or paired, 2–2.5cm diam., pale magenta. Nam. Z9.
J. lossowiana Herre.

Jepsonia Small. Saxifragaceae. 3 rhizomatous, perenn. herbs. Rhiz. tuber-like. Lvs basal, orbicular-cordate, palmatifid to serrate; petiole long. Fls small, 5-merous in scapose cymes. S Calif. Z7.
J. parryi (Torr.) Small. Lvs 5cm diam. Scape to 30cm, fls 4; cal. tube to 1cm, olive striped purple; pet. to 1cm, white marked purple. Autumn. *J. heterandra* Eastw. and *J. malvifolia* (Green) Small are closely related spp. sometimes included in *J. parryi.* Both differ from this sp. in having branching rhiz. and ± 10 fls per scape.
→*Saxifraga.*

Jeriva *Syagrus comosa.*
Jersey Elm *Ulmus* 'Sarniensis'.
Jersey Lily *Amaryllis belladonna.*
Jerusalem Artichoke *Helianthus tuberosus.*
Jerusalem Cherry *Solanum pseudocapsicum.*
Jerusalem Cross *Lychnis chalcedonica.*
Jerusalem Oak *Chenopodium botrys.*
Jerusalem Pea *Vigna unguiculata.*
Jerusalem Sage *Phlomis fruticosa*; *Pulmonaria officinalis*; *Pulmonaria saccharata.*
Jerusalem Thorn *Parkinsonia aculeata.*
Jessamine *Jasminum* (*J. officinale*).
Jesuit's Bark *Cinchona.*
Jesuits' Nut *Trapa natans.*
Jew Bush *Pedilanthus.*
Jewel-leaf Plant *Graptopetalum amethystinum.*
Jewelled Aloe *Aloe distans.*
Jewel Mint of Corsica *Mentha requienii.*
Jewel Orchid *Anoectochilus.*
Jewels of Opar *Talinum paniculatum.*
Jewelweed *Impatiens capensis.*
Jew's Apple *Solanum melongena.*
Jew's Mallow *Kerria.*
Jew's Myrtle *Ruscus aculeatus.*
Jicama *Pachyrhizus.*
Jicamilla *Jatropha.*
Jicara *Crescentia alata.*
Jim Brush *Ceanothus sorediatus.*
Jim Sage *Salvia clevelandii.*
Jimson Weed *Datura stramonium.*
Jobo *Spondias mombin.*
Job's Tears *Coix lacryma-jobi.*
Jocote *Spondias purpurea.*
Joe Pye Weed *Eupatorium maculatum*; *E. purpureum.*
Johnny-go-to-bed-at-noon *Tragopogon pratensis.*
Johnny-jump-up *Viola pedunculata*; *V. tricolor.*
John's Cabbage *Hydrophyllum virginianum.*
Johnson Grass *Sorghum halapense.*
Johnstone River Hardwood *Backhousia bancroftii.*
Johnston River Fern *Asplenium laserpitiifolium.*
Jointed Rush *Juncus articulatus.*
Joint Fir *Ephedra.*
Jojoba *Simmondsia chinensis.*
Jonquil *Narcissus jonquilla.*

Jordaaniella Hartmann. Aizoaceae. 4 succulent mat-forming perennials. Lvs paired, subcylindrical, spindle-shaped, glaucous. Fls solitary, large, on long pedicels. S Afr. (W Cape), Nam. Z9.
J. clavifolia (L. Bol.) Hartmann. Lvs to 3×0.5cm, clavate, obtuse to short-tapered toward tip, apiculate, lower surface rounded. Fls 5cm diam., yellow or coppery red.
J. cuprea (L. Bol.) Hartmann. Lvs to 6.5×1.3cm, acute or short-tapered, clavate with an indistinct keel. Fls to 8cm diam., coppery-red, yellow toward centre, outside pink.
J. dubia (Haw.) Hartmann. Lvs to 5×0.8cm, cylindric or semicylindric, short-tapered. Fls 3.5–7.5cm diam., yellow, sometimes with salmon pink, white or violet.
J. uniflora (L. Bol.) Hartmann. Lvs to 6×0.7cm, clavate, tapered. Fls to 7cm diam., golden yellow.
→*Cephalophyllum* and *Mesembryanthemum.*

Josephine's Lily *Brunsvigia josephinae.*
Joseph's Coat *Alternanthera.*
Joshua Tree *Yucca brevifolia.*

Jossinia Comm. ex DC. = *Eugenia.*

Jounama Snow Gum *Eucalyptus pauciflora.*

Jovellana Ruiz & Pav. Scrophulariaceae. 6 tender herbs and shrubs with fls in cymose pan., resembling *Calceolaria*, but differing in having 2 near equal, pouched cor. lobes. Summer. Chile, NZ. Z9.
J. punctata Ruiz & Pav. Shrub to 120cm, puberulent. Lvs to 10cm oblong to oblong-ovate, acute, doubly serrate. Fls to 2cm diam., pale violet, spotted purple. Summer. S Chile.
J. sinclairii (Hook.) Kränzl. Subshrub to 50cm, glandular-pubesc. Lvs to 1cm, ovate-oblong, obtuse, doubly serrate or lobed. Fls pale lilac to white, spotted red, to 0.8cm diam. Summer. NZ.
J. violacea (Cav.) G. Don. Puberulent shrub to 2m. Lvs to 2cm, ovate, coarsely dentate or lobed, deep green, above. Fls violet spotted purple, throat blotched yellow, to 1.5cm diam. Summer. Chile.
→*Calceolaria.*

Jovibarba Opiz. Crassulaceae. 5 stoloniferous perenn. herbs with monocarpic fleshy lf rosettes. Infl. erect, leafy, cymose; fls campanulate, usually 6-merous. Eur.
J. allionii (Jordan & Fourr.) = *J. hirta* ssp. *allionii.*
J. arenaria (Koch) Opiz = *J. hirta* ssp. *arenaria.*
J. heuffelii (Schott) Löve and D. Löve. Rosettes 5–7cm across. Lvs green or glaucous, sometimes tipped brown, finely hairy. Infl. dense, flat, 5cm across; sep. glandular-hairy; pet. pale yellow or yellow-white. E Carpath., Balk. Penins. Some 100 named cvs. 'Bronze Ingot': lvs dark purple-red, edged bronze. 'Chocoleta': lvs dark chocolate brown. 'Greenstone': lvs bright green, tipped dark brown. 'Inferno': habit large, spreading; lvs red-brown. 'Miller's Violet': lvs dark violet-brown, with paler margins and tips. 'Sun Dancer': lvs pale yellow-green, tinged pink and red. 'Tan': lvs dark red-brown in summer. 'Giuseppi Spiny', 'Bermuda', 'Cameo' and 'Beacon Hill' are also offered. Z6.
J. hirta (L.) Opiz. Rosettes 2–5cm across. Lvs glab., ciliate, green, tipped brown or red-brown, lanceolate to obovate-oblanceolate. Infl. 5–8cm across; sep. hairy; pet. pale yellow-brown. Summer. C & SE Eur. 'Borealis': rosettes large, pale. 'Emerald Spring': lvs vivid red and green in summer. 'Pressinana': lvs tinged pink-red. ssp. *allionii* (Jordan and Fourr.) Soó. Rosettes only 1.5–2.5cm across. Lvs tipped red, finely glandular-hairy above. SW Alps. ssp. *arenaria* (Koch) Parnell. Rosettes 0.5–2cm across. Lvs widest at or below middle, tip occas. red, glandular-ciliate. E Alps. Z7.
J. sobolifera (Sims) Opiz. Rosettes 2–4cm across. Lvs obovate to oblong, bright green, glab., margin ciliate, red-tipped with age. Infl. 5–7cm across; sep. glandular-hairy, red tipped; pet. yellow to yellow-green. Summer. C & SE Eur. 'Green Globe': lvs bright yellow-green. Z5.
J. velenovskyi (Cesm.) Holub. Rosettes 5–10cm across. Lvs oblong or broadly ovate, with a white bristle tip, glaucous, later suffused red. Infl. 3-branched; sep. tinged red; pet. yellow to white. Bulg. Z6.
→*Diopogon* and *Sempervivum.*

Joyweed *Alternanthera* (*A. ficoidea* var. *amoena*).

Juanulloa Ruiz & Pav. Solanaceae. 10 epiphytic, climbing or sprawling shrubs. Lvs simple, entire, coriaceous. Infl. a cluster, short rac. or pan.; cal. large, campanulate, fleshy, deeply ridged; cor. tubular, lobes 5. C & S Amer. Z9.

J. aurantiaca Otto & Dietr. = *J. mexicana.*

J. eximia Hook. = *Dyssochroma eximia.*

J. mexicana (Schldl.) Miers. Lvs oblong, to 20cm, tomentose. Fls pendent; cal. to 1.5cm diam., waxy, pale orange; cor. to 4cm, waxy, brilliant orange. Peru, Colomb., C Amer. Z8.

J. parasitica Ruiz & Pav. = *J. mexicana.*

Jubaea Kunth. CHILEAN WINE PALM; HONEY PALM; SYRUP PALM; COQUITO PALM; LITTLE COKERNUT. Palmae. 1 unarmed palm to 25m. St. to 1.3m diam. at base, becoming bare, with scars and cracks. Lvs to 5m, pinnate; sheaths fibrous; pinnae single-fold, crowded in same plane, linear, rigid. Fr. to 5cm, ovoid, egg-yellow. Chile. Z8.

J. chilensis (Molina) Baill.

J. spectabilis HBK = *J. chilensis.*

Jubaeopsis Becc. Palmae. 1 unarmed palm to 6m. Lvs 4m, arched, pinnate; petioles to 1m; pinnae numerous, slender, pale green, 2-dentate or divided. Fr. subglobose, yellow. S Afr. Z9.

J. caffra Becc. PONDOLAND PALM.

Judas Tree *Cercis siliquastrum.*

JUGLANDACEAE A.Rich. ex Kunth. 7/59. *Carya, Cyclocarya, Engelhardia, Juglans, Platycarya, Pterocarya.*

Juglans L. WALNUT. Juglandaceae. 15 decid., monoecious trees, rarely shrubs. Bark furrowed. Lvs alt., pinnate; lfts serrate to entire. ♂ fls in axill. catkins; ♀ fls in term. spikes. Fr. a 2-4-celled drupe, indehiscent; pericarp thick, furrowed; seed 2-4-lobed. Late spring. N & S Amer., SE Eur., Asia.

J. ailanthifolia Carr. JAPANESE WALNUT; HEARTNUT. To 15m, young br. gland.-pubesc. Lvs to 50cm; lfts 11–17, to 15×5cm, oblong to elliptic, acuminate, serrate, grey-tomentose to glab. above, gland.-pubesc. beneath. Fr. globose to ovoid, glutinose-pubesc. Jap. var. *cordiformis* (Maxim.) Rehd. Lfts narrower. Hybrids between *J. ailanthifolia* and *J. cinerea* (sometimes called *J.* ×*bixbyi*) combine the best qualities of the two: 'Fioka', heavy and ann. cropper; 'Mitchell', v. hardy. Z4.

J. alata Schelle = *J.* ×*quadrangulata.*

J. andina Triana ex Pérez Arb. = *J. neotropica.*

J. arizonica Dode = *J. major.*

J. californica S. Wats. CALIFORNIA WALNUT. Similar to *J. hindsii* but shrub or small tree to 9m; lfts 9–15, to 13cm, ovate; fr. small, to 1.5cm. W US. Z8.

J. californica var. *hindsii* Jeps. = *J. hindsii.*

J. cathayensis Dode. CHINESE WALNUT; CHINESE BUTTERNUT. Shrub or tree to 23m. Young br. viscid. Lvs to 80cm, viscid; lfts 11–19, to 15×8cm, oblong-lanceolate, finely dentate, pubesc. above, stellate-pubesc. beneath. Fr. ovoid to 4.5cm, in clusters of 6–10. C & W China, Taiwan. Z5.

J. cinerea L. BUTTER NUT; WHITE WALNUT. To 30m. Young br. gland.-glutinose. Lvs 25–50cm; rachis gland.; lfts 11–19, 6–12cm, oblong-lanceolate, acuminate, adpressed irregular-serrate, pubesc., gland. beneath. Fr. in clusters of 2–5, to 10cm, gland.-glutinose. NE US. Z4.

J. cinerea Bello non L. = *J. jamaicensis.*

J. colombiensis Dode = *J. neotropica.*

J. cordiformis Maxim. = *J. ailanthifolia* var. *cordiformis.*

J. cordiformis var. *ailanthifolia* (Carr.) Rehd. = *J. ailanthifolia.*

J. domingensis Dode = *J. jamaicensis.*

J. draconis Dode = *J. cathayensis.*

J. duclouxiana Dode = *J. regia* ssp. *fallax.*

J. equatoriensis Lind. = *J. neotropica.*

J. fallax Dode = *J. regia* ssp. *fallax.*

J. fraxinifolia Descourt. non Lam. = *J. jamaicensis.*

J. granatensis Lind. = *J. neotropica.*

J. hindsii (Jeps.) Rehd. 10–15m. Young br. densely pubesc. Lvs 25–30cm; petiole villous; lfts 15–19, to 10×2.5cm, ovate-lanceolate to lanceolate, acuminate, coarsely serrate. Fr. globose, pubesc. N & C Calif. Z8.

J. honorei Dode = *J. neotropica.*

J. illinoinensis Wangenh. = *Carya illinoinensis.*

J. ×**intermedia** Carr. (*J. nigra* ×*J. regia.*) Similar to *J. regia* but lfts 11, ovate to elliptic, remotely denticulate, dark green and glab. above, axill. tufts of hair beneath. var. *pyriformis* Carr. Lfts 9–13, finely dentate. Fr. obovoid. var. *vilmoreana* (Carr.) Schneid. Fr. globose. Z5.

J. ×*intermedia* var. *quadrangulata* Carr. = *J.* ×*quadrangulata.*

J. jamaicensis C. DC. WEST INDIAN WALNUT; NOGAL; PALO DE NEUZ. To 45m. Twigs red-gland.-pubesc. Lvs to 55×25cm; lfts 16–20, to 11×4.5cm, oblong to ovate-lanceolate. Fr. dark brown, subglobose to short-ovoid, glab. to minutely pubesc. Puerto Rico, Dominican Rep., Haiti, Cuba. Z10.

J. major (Torr. ex Sitsgr.) Heller. To 15m. Young br. pubesc. Lfts 9–13, 7–10cm, oblong-lanceolate to ovate, acuminate, coarsely serrate, glab., occas. pubesc. beneath. Fr. globose to ovoid, to 3cm wide, rust-brown-pubesc. W Tex., Ariz., Mex. Z9.

J. mandshurica Maxim. MANCHURIAN WALNUT. To 20m. Br. gland. pubesc., green, yellow in second year; shoots suckering. Lvs 45–50cm; petiole and midrib gland.-pubesc.; lfts 9–17, 6–13cm, oblong, becoming glab. above, gland.-pubesc. beneath. NE China, Korea. Z5.

J. microcarpa Berl. Similar to *J. major* but shrub or small tree, to 7m; young shoots grey-brown to grey; lfts 15–23, finely serrate. Tex., New Mex., NW Mex. Z6.

J. nana Engelm. = *J. microcarpa.*

J. neotropica Diels. To 30m. Young br. pubesc. becoming red-gland.-pubesc., lenticulate. Lvs 34×30cm; lfts 12–19, about 11×5cm, ovate to ovate-oblong, rugose, coarsely serrate, mid-rib and main veins red gland.-pubesc. above. Fr. subglobose, about 4×3.5cm, black. Venez., Colomb., Ecuad., Peru. Z10.

J. nigra L. BLACK WALNUT. To 45m. Lfts 15–23, to 11cm, ovate-oblong, pubesc. beneath. Fr. globose, about 4cm diam., pubesc. E US, nat. C Eur. 'Laciniata': lfts laciniate. Z4.

J. ×**notha** Rehd. (*J. ailanthifolia* ×*J. regia.*) Lfts 7–9, elliptic to elliptic-oblong, glab. above, glab. to pubesc. beneath, margins finely and sparsely denticulate. Fr. globose to ovoid, sticky-pubesc. Z5.

J. orientis Dode = *J. regia* ssp. *turcomanica* var. *orientis.*

J. ovata Mill. = *Carya ovata.*

J. portoricensis Dode = *J. jamaicensis.*

J. pterococca Roxb. pro parte = *Engelhardia spicata.*

J. pterococca Roxb. pro parte = *Engelhardia roxburghiana.*

J. ×**quadrangulata** (Carr.) Rehd. (*J. cinerea* ×*J. regia.*) Lfts usually 9, elliptic to oblong, sparsely serrate, pubesc. beneath. Fr. subglobose, about 5cm. France, nat. US. Z5.

J. regia L. ENGLISH WALNUT; PERSIAN WALNUT; MADEIRA WALNUT. To 30m. Br. glab. Lfts 5–9, rarely more, 6–12cm, elliptic to obovate, entire or serrate on younger lvs, axill. tufts beneath. Fr. subglobose, glab., green, 4–5cm across. SE Eur. to Himal. and China, C Russia, nat. US. ssp. *fallax* (Dode) Popov. Lfts shorter, elliptic-ovate, acuminate. S China, Himal. ssp. *turcomanica* Popov. Lfts oblong-lanceolate to ovate-lanceolate. Origin unknown. var. *orientis* (Dode) Kitam. Lvs glab.; lfts 3–9, obtuse. Nut thin-shelled. 'Adspersa': lfts speckled or striped white. 'Bartheriana': nut almond-shaped. Carpathian group (v. cold hardy): 'Ashworth', 'Buccaneer', 'Cascade', 'Hansen'. 'Corcyrensis': large-lvd form, 3 apical lfts to 20×12cm, others smaller, pale green and glossy above, dull green beneath. 'Franquette': late-flowering, nuts of good flavour. 'Heterophylla': lfts long, narrow, lobes irregular. 'Laciniata': arching shrub or tree; lfts incised. 'Maxima': nuts large. 'Monophylla': lvs reduced to a large term. lft, sometimes with a smaller lateral pair of lfts. 'Pendula': br. and twigs pendulous. 'Purpurea': lvs dull red. 'Racemosa': infl. in groups of 10–15, racemose. 'Rubra': nut blood-red (sometimes only speckled), flesh dull pink-red. Z5.

J. rupestris Engelm. = *J. microcarpa.*

J. rupestris var *major* Torr. = *J. major.*

J. sieboldiana Maxim. = *J. ailanthifolia.*

J. sieboldiana var. *cordiformis* (Maxim.) Mak. = *J. ailanthifolia* var. *cordiformis.*

J. tomentosa Poir. = *Carya tomentosa.*

J. torreyi Dode = *J. major.*

J. vilmoriniana Meuniss. = *J.* ×*intermedia* var. *vilmoreana.*

Jumbie Bead *Ormosia coarctata.*

Jumellea Schltr. Orchidaceae. 60 epiphytic orchids. Pbs 0. St. leafy. Lvs usually distichous and strap-shaped. Fls solitary, white or green-white turning apricot with age; dors. sep. reflexed, lat. sep. fused below spur, directed downwards; lip entire, spurred. Madag., Masc. Is., Comoros Is., Afr. Z10.

J. comorensis (Rchb. f.) Schltr. St. to 30cm, pendent, branched. Lvs 3–7cm. Infl. short; tep. to 2.2cm; lip to 2cm; spur 9–11cm, tinged green toward apex. Comoros Is.

J. densefoliata Sengh. St. to 8cm clumped. Lvs 4–7cm. Infl. 1.5–2.5cm; tep. to 1.5cm, lip to 1cm; spur 11–12cm. Madag.

J. filicornoides (De Wildeman) Schltr. St. 20–30cm, forming clumps. Lvs 4.5–11cm. Fls v. fragrant; tep. 2.2cm; lip 2.5cm; spur 2.5–3cm. Tanz. to Moz. and S Afr.

J. fragrans (Thouars) Schltr. St. erect, flattened. Lvs 4.5–15cm, thin-textured. Infl. 1.5cm; tep. to 2cm; lip 2cm; spur 3–3.5cm. Masc. Is.

J. gracilipes Schltr. St. 5–7cm. Lvs 8–40cm, in fan at top of st. Infl. 2.5–5.5cm; tep. to 2.5cm; lip 2.3cm; spur 11–15cm. Madag.

J. major Schltr. St. 40–60cm long, pendent. Lvs to 45cm. Infl. 6–7cm; tep 4.5cm; lip 3cm; spur 6.5–7cm. Madag.

J. maxillarioides (Ridl.) Schltr. St. 8–20cm, forming large clumps. Lvs 20–25cm. Infl. short; tep. 3.5cm, spur 4cm. Madag.

J. sagittata H. Perrier. Short-stemmed. Lvs 25–30cm. Infl. pendent, 2–3 arising below lvs; tep. 3–4cm; lip 4cm, spur 5–6cm. Madag.

J. spathulata Schltr. St. stout, to 30cm. Lvs to 3cm, thick-textured. Infl. short; pet. lanceolate-spathulate; lip ovate-spathulate; spur 2.5cm. Madag.

J. teretifolia Schltr. St. short. Lvs 10–20cm, cylindric. Infl. wiry, longer than lvs; tep. 3.5cm; lip 3cm; spur about 13cm. Madag. →*Angraecum*.

Jumping Orchid *Catasetum macrocarpum*.
Jumrool *Syzygium samarangense*.

JUNCACEAE Juss. 10/325. *Juncus, Luzula*.

JUNCAGINACEAE Rich. 4/18. *Triglochin*.

Junction Root *Anthurium grandifolium*.

Juncus L. RUSH. Juncaceae. 225 rhizomatous perenn. grassy plants. St. terete, slender, tufted. Lvs basal and stem-like or cauline and reduced, often subtending infl. Infl. a term. or apparently lat. cyme; fls green or brown, small; perianth seg. rigid, chaffy in 2 whorls of 3. Cosmop., but rare in the tropics.

J. arcticus ssp. *balticus* (Willd.) Hylander = *J. balticus*.

J. articulatus L. JOINTED RUSH. St. to 60cm, or to 100cm when growing in water, erect or ascending. Infl. with 5–20 heads each of to 15 fls; perianth seg. to 3.5mm, ovate or lanceolate. Boreal regions, Aus. Z8.

J. balticus Willd. BALTIC RUSH. St. to 100cm, glaucous. Infl. lat., with 60 fls; perianth seg. to 5mm, subequal, ovate. Boreal regions. Z3.

J. bufonius L. TOAD RUSH. St. to 50cm, often much shorter, weak. Infl. loose, apical; perianth seg. to 8mm, unequal, narrow-ovate. Temp. regions. Z5.

J. bulbosus L. St. to 30cm, or to 100cm in water, with a basal bulbous swelling. Infl. of 3–20 heads, each with 2–15 fls; perianth seg. to 3mm. Temp. regions. Z5.

J. castaneus Sm. CHESTNUT RUSH. St. solitary, to 32cm. Infl. of 1–3 heads, each with to 10 fls; perianth seg. to 5.5mm, dark brown, ovate. Boreal and arctic regions. Z3.

J. chamissonis Kunth. Densely tufted; st. to 40cm. Infl. compact, with to 25 fls; perianth outer seg. ovate, inner seg. lanceolate. Temp. S Amer. Z8.

J. communis hort. = *J. effusus*.

J. compressus Jacq. ROUND-FRUITED RUSH. Loosely tufted or with a creeping rhiz.; st. to 40cm. Infl. loose; fls to 60; perianth seg. to 3mm. Temp. regions. Z5.

J. effusus L. COMMON RUSH; SOFT RUSH. St. to 150cm, soft, densely tufted. Infl. a diffuse cyme, to 5cm; perianth seg. to 3mm, pale brown or yellow-green. Eurasia, N Amer., Aus., NZ. 'Aureus Striatus': st. banded ivory to lime. 'Spiralis': spiralling strongly. 'Vittatus': narrowly banded ivory. 'Zebrinus': deeply banded green-white. Z4.

J. ensifolius Wikstr. To 80cm, loosely tufted or with a creeping rhiz. Infl. of 1–6 globose, many-fld heads; perianth seg. to 4mm. W N Amer. Z3.

J. glaucus Sibth. = *J. inflexus*.

J. imbricatus Laharpe = *J. chamissonis*.

J. inflexus L. HARD RUSH. To 120cm, glaucous. Infl. lat., lax, with straight br.; fls many; perianth seg. to 4mm, ovate. 'Afro': to 60cm, compact; lvs blue-green, in spirals; fls brown. Z4.

J. kochii F.W. Schultz = *J. bulbosus*.

J. lampocarpus Ehrh. ex Hoffm. = *J. articulatus*.

J. leseurii Bolander. SALT RUSH. St. to 90cm, thick, smooth. Fls in 3–4 branched cymes to 3.5cm; perianth seg. deep brown edged purple-maroon. N Amer., Pacific Coast. Z6.

J. longicornis Bast. = *J. inflexus*.

J. nodosus Weber = *J. subnodulosus*.

J. obtusifolius Ehrh. ex Hoffm. = *J. subnodulosus*.

J. subnodulosus Schrank. BLUNT-FLOWERED RUSH. St. to 130cm, with 3–4 basal sheaths. Lvs to 10cm, sword-shaped. Infl. of 50 hemispherical heads each with to 30 fls; perianth seg. to 2.5mm, elliptical. Eur.; boreal Asia. Z6.

J. supinus Moench = *J. bulbosus*.

Juneberry *Amelanchier*.
June Grass *Poa pratensis*.

Junellia Mold.

J. scabrido-glandulosa (Turrill) Mold. = *Verbena scabrido-glandulosa*.

J. tridens (Lagasca) Mold. = *Verbena teucroides*.

Jungle Brake *Pteris umbrosa*.

Jungle Flame *Ixora coccinea*.
Jungle Geranium *Ixora coccinea*.
Juniper *Juniperus*.
Juniper Bush *Retama raetam*.
Juniper Myrtle *Agonis juniperina*.

Juniperus L. JUNIPER. Cupressaceae. 45–60 everg., mostly dioecious, aromatic, coniferous trees or shrubs. Bark exfoliating in strips or scales. Juvenile lvs 0.6–2.5cm needle-like or subulate; adult lvs 0.3–0.6cm scale-like, addressed or spreading, imbricate. ♂ cones ovoid, yellow, to 0.5cm, ♀ cones, (described below) globose, ovoid or irregular, scales 3–9, indistinct in decussate whorls of 2–3, dry to pulpy, often fibrous, mostly resinous. N Hemis. from Arc. to C Amer., Himal., Taiwan, E Afr.

J. ashei Buchholz ASHE JUNIPER. To 6m. Trunk divided near base. Crown irregular or spherical. Bark ash-grey; br. ascending, red-grey. Lvs scale-like in whorls of 2–3, triangular-ovate, grey-green, sometimes with a red-brown resin gland. Cones 6–8mm diam.; pulp soft, blue, bloom waxy. US, Mex. Z7.

J. barbadensis L. To 15m. Crown conic. Br. slender. Lvs ovate, acute or obtuse, bright green. Cones to 5mm, grey-blue. W Indies. Z10.

J. bermudiana L. BERMUDA JUNIPER. To 15m. Bark maroon-brown. Br. tetragonal. Lvs 4-ranked ovate, obtuse, incurved, blue-green. Cones to 5mm diam., globose, glaucous-violet. Bermuda. Z9.

J. blancoi Martinez. To 15m, close to *J. scopulorum* except bark not exfoliating, fissured. Shoots slender often pendulous. Lvs 1.5–2mm, adult and juvenile lvs mixed, yellow to bright green. Cones irregular, to 7×8mm. NW Mex. Z8.

J. brevifolia (Seub.) Antoine. Small tree or shrub. Br. dense. Lvs needle-like, in whorls of 3, bright green, with 2 blue-white stripes. Cones to 1cm diam., maroon. Azores. Z9.

J. californica Carr. CALIFORNIA JUNIPER. Tree or shrub to 12m. Bark grey-brown, ridged. Crown conic. Lvs in threes, scale-like, ovate, yellow-green, denticulate. Cones 1–2cm diam., red-brown bloomed, dry. Calif., Baja Calif. Z8.

J. cedrus Webb & Berth. To 30m, usually shrubby, shorter. Branchlets pendulous; shoots glaucous. Lvs in whorls of 3, needle-like, strongly forward-pointed, glaucous green above, 2 white bands below. Cones red-brown, 6–15mm diam. Canary Is. Z9.

J. chinensis L. CHINESE JUNIPER. Tree or shrub, to 20m. Bark brown, exfoliating in strips. Crown conic. Foliage pungently scented. Juvenile lvs subulate, in whorls of 3 or decussate, dark green above with 2 stomatal bands beneath, sharply acuminate; adult lvs rhombic, addressed, obtuse, 4-ranked, imbricate. Cones 5–9mm, violet to brown, bloomed. China, Mong., Jap. Numerous dwarf, bushy and tree-sized cvs, some bearing only juvenile, or mixed juvenile and adult lvs, ranging from blue-green to yellow or variegated white. 'Aurea': to 20m, ovoid-columnar; foliage dull yellow; ♂ clone. 'Columnaris Glauca' ('Blue Column' in US): columnar, foliage all juvenile, bright blue-green, dense. 'Glauca': grey-blue foliage all adult; ♂ clone with dense yellow ♂ cones in spring. 'Keteleerii': narrow conic; dark grey-green, all foliage adult; ♀ clone, numerous 7mm cones. See *J. × media* for other cvs of hybrid origin. Z4.

J. communis L. COMMON JUNIPER. Densely branching shrub or tree to 10m. Bark smooth red-brown, peeling in plates, becoming grey, fissured. Lvs always needle-like, in whorls of 3, deep green on outer surface, inner face with one white band. Cones 4–8mm, ripening dark blue. Eurasia (British Is S to Spain & E to Japan), zones 2–7 depending on origin. Numerous cvs available, columnar, compact, spreading, prostrate, dwarf; lvs blue-green, yellow to golden. 'Suecica' (var. *suecica* (Mill.) Ait.): narrow-columnar, br. erect, tips nodding, lvs 8–12mm, blue-green. 'Hibernica' ('Stricta'): similar, but tips erect. 'Oblonga Pendula': br. level, open, shoots pendulous, lvs long, to 2cm, sparse. ssp. *alpina* (Suter) Čelak. MOUNTAIN JUNIPER. Shrub, procumbent or prostrate, to 30cm. Lvs incurved, short, dark green with a broad band. Eurasia, N Amer. Z6. ssp. *depressa* (Pursh) Franco. Procumbent to ascending, lvs narrowly banded. N Amer., Greenland. ssp. *hemispherica* (Presl & C. Presl) Nyman. Shrub to 2.5m. Densely branched. Lvs shorter and broader. Medit.

J. communis ssp. *nana* Syme = *J. communis* ssp. *alpina*.

J. conferta Parl. SHORE JUNIPER. Shrub, procumbent then ascending. Bark red-brown. Needles in groups of 3, inner surface glaucous, grooved, with 1 stomatal band, outer surface lustrous green. Cones 8–10mm diam., shiny dark purple. Jap., Sakhalin. 'Blue Pacific': procumbent; lvs blue-green. 'Emerald Sea': dense, procumbent; lvs emerald green, grey-green above, yellow-green in winter. Z5.

J. convallium Rehd. & Wils. Tree or shrub to 20m. Most lvs scale-like, decussate, pale grey-green, blunt or acute, denticulate. Cones 6–8mm, shining brown. China. Z7.

J. coxii Jackson = *J. recurva* var. *coxii*.

J. davurica Pall. Semi-prostrate shrub. Bark grey, flaking. Juvenile lvs acicular, spreading; adult lvs scale-like, adpressed, diamond-shaped, acuminate. Cones 4–6mm diam., purple-brown. E Mong., China, SE Sib. 'Expansa': to 1×3m+; br. almost horizontal; lvs mixed juvenile and adult, sage green. 'Expansa Aureospicata': sprays and branchlet tips spotted golden yellow. 'Expansa Aureovariegata': variegated golden yellow. Z3.

J. deppeana Steud. ALLIGATOR JUNIPER. Tree to 20m. Bark thick, cross-ridged, grey, marked brown. Adult lvs 4-ranked, diamond-shaped, adpressed, grey-green; juvenile lvs in whorls of 2–3, acicular. Cones 12–16mm diam. flesh fibrous, red-brown with violet bloom. SW US, Mex. Z8. 'Silver Spire': narrowly columnar, silver-grey.

J. distans Florin = *J. tibetica*.

J. drupacea Labill. SYRIAN JUNIPER. Tree to 15m wild. Bark exfoliating in vertical strips, red-brown. Lvs to 2.5cm, in decussate whorls, needle-like, hard, sharp acuminate, shiny green. Cones 20–25mm diam., red-brown heavily bloomed violet. S Greece (rare), S Turk. to NW Syr. Z7.

J. durangensis Martinez. DURANGO JUNIPER. Shrub or tree to 5m; bark thin ashy-brown, fibrous. Adult lvs in pairs, thick, raised and bead-like, grey-green, obtuse. Cones 6–7mm, orange-red bloomed pale blue, soft. NW Mex. Z8.

J. erythrocarpa Cory. To 8m; as for *J. pinchotii*, except bark ash-grey, flaking in long strips; lvs with glaucous band on inner surface. Cones orange or red, glaucous therefore pink. SW US, N Mex. Z7.

J. excelsa Bieb. GREEK JUNIPER. Tree to 20m or erect shrub; crown broad ovoid, br. curving up; bark stringy, pink-grey to red-brown. Juvenile lvs acicular; semi-juvenile lvs 1–2mm, slightly spreading; adult lvs scale-like, grey-green, in pairs. Cones 7–12mm, irregular, dark grey-purple, bloomed. Greece, Turk., Crimea, Leb., SE Arabia. Z6.

J. fargesii (Rehd. & Wils.) Komar. = *J. morrisonicola*.

J. flaccida Schldl. DROOPING JUNIPER; MEXICAN JUNIPER. To 12m. Bark red-brown, split in narrow plates. Branchlets drooping. Juvenile lvs acicular, in whorls of 3, inner surface with 2 bands; adult lvs scale-like, opposite, apex slightly spreading, inner face with oil gland. Cones 8–20mm, orange- to red-brown, bloomed. US (W Tex.), Mex. (mts). Z8.

J. flaccida hort. non Schldl. = *J. blancoi*.

J. foetidissima Willd. Tree to 26m, much smaller in cult. Crown rounded; bark stringy, pale grey-brown. Lvs scale-like, bright green. Cones 7–10mm, ripening purple bloomed blue. SE Eur., Turk., Crimea, Cauc.

J. formosana Hayata. TAIWAN JUNIPER. To 10m, crown columnar. Bark brown, fibrous, branchlets drooping. Needles in whorls of 3, sharply acuminate, outer surface glossy, inner with 2 narrow bands. Cones 1cm diam., red to red-brown. S China, Taiwan. Z8.

J. glaucescens Florin = *J. komarovii*.

J. 'Grey Owl'. (Probable hybrid between *J. virginiana* 'Glauca' and *J. ×media* 'Pfitzeriana'.) Shrub 2×3m, br. spreading, lvs grey-blue. 'Hetzii': similar, to 4m, grey-green; ♀ cv. with abundant cones. 'Sulphur Spray': sport of 'Hetzii' with sulphur-yellow young foliage, greener with age. Z6.

J. horizontalis Moench. CREEPING JUNIPER. Low to prostrate shrub. Lvs ± acicular, in whorls of 3 or 2, grey-green; some lvs scale-like, elliptic, acuminate. Cones 6–8mm, dark blue. N Amer. Cvs numerous, variable, usually dwarf or prostrate shrubs, br. mostly procumbent; lvs glaucous, green to grey-green or blue, becoming bronze or maroon-tinted in winter. 'Bar Harbour': foliage steel-blue, v. salt resistant. 'Douglasii': glaucous, bronzed purple in winter. 'Wiltonii': v. low, persistently glaucous. Z4.

J. indica Bertol. Probably syn. of *J. pseudosabina* but may refer to *J. wallichiana*, in which case this name has priority.

J. komarovii Florin. To 10m, similar to *J. tibetica*. Crown dense; br. ascending. Lvs scale-like, mostly in whorls of 3; juvenile lvs acicular, in whorls of 3. Cones 6–11mm, brown to blue-black. China. Z6.

J. lemeeana Lév. & Blin. = *J. morrisonicola*.

J. macropoda Boiss. PERSIAN JUNIPER. Similar to *J. excelsa*, but shoots less dense. To 12m. Bole 70cm across. Lvs more rigid and pointed. Cones 7–11mm, blue-black, bloomed pale grey. Iran, Afghan., Baluchistan, W Himal. Z7.

J. ×media Van Melle. (Probably *J. sabina* × *J. chinensis*.) Spreading shrub to 2m, similar to *J. sabina* but with thicker shoots; crown spiky with long horizontal tips; bark scaly, red-brown. Adult lvs in pairs, or 3's, yellow- to grey-green, glaucous; juvenile lvs acicular. Cones similar to *J. sabina*, 4–6mm, dark purple bloomed pale blue. Origin uncertain but may occur wild in Inner Mong. Cvs bushy to prostrate: 'Golden Saucer': best

golden-lvd cv, low-growing, compact. 'Hetzii': see under *J.* 'Grey Owl'. 'Mathot': all-juvenile lvd sport of 'Pfitzeriana', acicular lvs to 7mm. 'Pfitzeriana': ♂ clone, to 3m×5m wide, dull grey-green. 'Pfitzeriana Aurea': dull yellow version of same. 'Pfitzeriana Compacta': low-growing to 0.5m×2m, grey-green. 'Pfitzeriana Glauca': ♂, blue-green. 'Plumosa': ♂, dark green. Z3.

J. monosperma (Engelm.) Sarg. ONE-SEED JUNIPER. Tree or shrub to 10m. Bark peeling in long shreds, grey. Crown spreading, open. Shoots tetragonal. Lvs scale-like, ovate, dark green. Cones 5–8mm, copper bloomed pink. SW US. var. *gracilis* Martinez. Shoots more slender, and spreading; cones oval, not globose. NE Mex. Z4.

J. monticola Martinez. Prostrate shrub, rarely tree to 10m; bark thick, grey-brown, fibrous. Adult lvs mostly in pairs, thick, raised centre with prominent gland, rounded or obtuse. Cones 5–9mm. Mex. Z7.

J. morrisonicola Hayata. Prostrate shrub or, more often, a tree to 12m. Bark grey-brown, furrowed. Branchlets drooping at tips. Lvs all juvenile, subulate, ovate-lanceolate, glossy green on outer face, inner face with a blue-grey band. Cones 5–8mm, black. Taiwan & W China, mts. 'Prostrata': as 'Wilsonii' but prostrate. 'Wilsonii' (*J. squamata* f. *wilsonii* Rehd.; *J. pingii* var. *wilsonii* (Rehd.) Silba): dense erect shrub to 2m, shoots nodding at tips; lvs crowded, tinged purple in winter. Z7.

J. nipponica Maxim. = *J. rigida* ssp. *nipponica*.

J. occidentalis Hook. f. WESTERN JUNIPER. Shrub or small tree to 12m; bark rust-brown, grooved. Crown horizontal to drooping. Lvs scale-like, in pairs or 3's, rhombic, acute, glaucous green. Cones to 1cm diam., dark blue with a pale bloom. NW US. var. *australis* (Vasek) A.H. & N.H. Holmgren. SIERRA JUNIPER. Tree to 20m, v. long lived. Sierra Nevada, Calif. Z5.

J. osteosperma (Torr.) Little. UTAH JUNIPER. Shrub or small tree to 10m, differs from *J. californica* in adult lvs mostly in pairs, yellow-green; cones 6–18mm, red-brown pale-bloomed, dry. W US. Z5.

J. oxycedrus L. PRICKLY JUNIPER. Shrub or small tree to 15m. Bark red-grey. Lvs to 2cm, acicular, acute, green, 2 white bands on inner surface. Cones orange- or red-brown. Medit. S to Iran. ssp. *macrocarpa* (Sm.) Ball. Lvs to 2.5cm, flexible. Cones to 1.5cm diam., brown, then dull black. Medit. (Moroc. to Greece, coastal). Z7.

J. pachyphlaea Torr. = *J. deppeana*.

J. phoenicea L. PHOENICIAN JUNIPER. Shrub or small tree to 8m; bark brown. Crown conic or procumbent. Juvenile lvs acicular, in whorls of 3; adult lvs scale-like, in pairs, ovate to rhombic, acute, light green to blue-green. Cones to 1cm diam., maroon-brown, dry. Medit., Canary Is. Z9.

J. pinchotii Sudw. PINCHOT JUNIPER. Shrub or small tree to 6m; bark light grey-brown. Crown irregular. Juvenile lvs subulate, in whorls of 3; adult lvs scale-like, deltoid in pairs or 3's, dull yellow-green. Cones 6–8mm, bronze to rusty-brown, soft. US (Tex.), Mex. Z7.

J. pingii Cheng ex de Ferré = *J. morrisonicola*.

J. potaninii Komar. = *J. tibetica*.

J. procera Hochst. & Endl. AFRICAN JUNIPER. Tree to 30m. Bark brown, peeling in strips. Juvenile lvs in whorls of 3; adult lvs in pairs or 3's, ovate-lanceolate, acute. Cones 5–8mm, dark red-brown to blue-black, v. pruinose. E Afr., SE Arabia. Z9.

J. procumbens (Endl.) Miq. to 0.75m, procumbent. Bark maroon-brown, smooth. Lvs in whorls of 3, mostly linear, sharply acuminate, light green, inner face with 2 grey-green bands. Cones 6–9mm, dark brown. S Jap. 'Bonin Isles': procumbent, dense. 'Golden': lvs tipped golden yellow. 'Nana': compact, br. shorter. 'Santa Rosa': dwarf, compact form. Z8.

J. przewalskii Komar. To 12m; br. often erect. Lvs scale-like, adpressed or outspread, acute, grey-green. Cones 8–13mm, maroon. W China. Z6.

J. pseudosabina Fisch. & Mey. DWARF BLACK JUNIPER. Prostrate or low shrub to 4m. V. close to *J. wallichiana*, distinguished by autumn (not spring) flowering and smaller, black cones (6–10mm). N China to Himal. Z4.

J. recurva Buch.-Ham. ex D. Don. Tree to 20m, or shrub. Bark red-brown, peeling in strips. Crown conic. Br. tips recurved-weeping. Lvs growing forward along st., subulate-lanceolate, grey-green, light grey on inner face with indistinct midrib, texture dry. Cones 6–11mm, dark green-brown to black. SW China, E Himal. 'Castlewellan': taller, branchlets pendent; lvs thread-like. 'Densa': low-growing, spreading, br. tips ascending. 'Nana': dwarf, spreading; br. decurved; lvs grey-green. var. *coxii* (Jackson) Melville. COFFIN JUNIPER. Bark rusty-brown. Crown spreading; br. more pendulous. Lvs more widely spaced, bright green. N Burm. Z7.

J. rigida Sieb. & Zucc. TEMPLE JUNIPER. Tree to 15m or shrub, crown open; br. pendulous. Bark brown to yellow-brown, peeling. Lvs in whorls of 3, acicular, v. sharply pointed, bright green, dors. face with single blue-grey band. Cones 7–11mm diam. dark maroon to purple. Jap., Korea, N China. ssp. *nipponica* (Maxim.) Franco. Prostrate shrub. Lvs densely arranged, dors. surface deeply grooved. Jap. (mts). Z5.

J. sabina L. SAVIN. Shrub spreading or tree to 4m. Bark rust-brown, flaking. Lvs strongly aromatic: juveniles paired, sub-ulate, grey-green to blue-green; adult lvs scale-like, dark green to grey-green opposite, adpressed, ovate, obtuse. Cones 3–7mm, v. dark blue, bloomed white. C & S Eur., Cauc., to mts of C Asia & NW China. Cvs variable, spreading, semi-prostrate or procumbent, dwarf, slow-growing or vigorous; lvs juvenile or adult, dark green to grey-green or grey-blue. 'Aureovariegata': br. tips yellow, adult foliage. 'Blue Danube': grey-blue, all adult foliage. 'Cupressifolia': low, compact; adult foliage blue green; ♀; cones abundant. 'Tamariscifolia': low, spreading; lvs mostly juvenile, in pairs or 3's; bright green. Z3.

J. sabinioides Griseb. = *J. foetidissima*.

J. sabinioides (HBK) Nees, non Griseb. = *J. monticola*.

J. saltillensis M.T. Hall. SALTILLO JUNIPER. Small tree or shrub to 7m; bark thick, pale grey, furrowed. Adult lvs in pairs, adpressed, obtuse light grey-green. Cones 4.5–8mm, dark blue heavily bloomed pale blue, soft. NE Mex. Z8.

J. saltuaria Rehd. & Wils. SICHUAN JUNIPER. Tree or shrub to 15m, allied to *J. wallichiana*. Adult lvs in pairs, adpressed, dark mid-green, blunt. Cones 5–8mm, glossy black. China. Z8.

J. sargentii (Henry) Tak. Prostrate shrub, to 80cm. Lvs scale-like in pairs, dark blue-green; juvenile lvs in whorls of 3, acicular, smelling of camphor. Cones 5–7mm, blue-black. Jap., NE China. 'Compacta': dense; lvs pale green, margin dark, juvenile lvs dark green above, glaucous beneath. 'Glauca': br. ascending; lvs blue-green. 'Viridis': lvs light green. Z4.

J. scopulorum Sarg. ROCKY MOUNTAIN JUNIPER. Shrub or tree to 15m. Bark red-brown, fissured. Crown open. Lvs opposite, scale-like, ovate, sharply pointed, yellow to dark green. Cones 5–8mm, blue-black, light blue pruinose. Rocky Mts. Numerous cvs ranging from dwarf or medium shrubs to small, narrow-columnar or conical trees, habit lax or dense; adult and juvenile lvs on same tree, lvs grey-blue to grey or blue-green, sometimes tinged purple in winter. 'Blue Heaven': conic, v. bright blue-green; abundant cones. 'Repens': procumbent; lvs juvenile, blue-green. 'Silver King': procumbent, silver-blue. 'Skyrocket': v. slender columnar tree, bright grey-green. 'Springbank': narrow conic with pendulous shoot tips; intense silver-blue. Z3.

J. semiglobosa Reg. RUSSIAN JUNIPER. Tree or shrub to 12m; crown slender, open, shoots drooping. Adult lvs mostly in pairs, tightly adpressed, dark glossy green, acute. Cones 5–8mm, dark brown slightly bloomed pale. C Asia. Z4.

J. silicicola (Small) Bail. SOUTHERN REDCEDAR. As for *J. virginiana*, except branchlets more pendulous and slender; cones to 5mm, v. glaucous. SE US. Z8.

J. squamata Buch.-Ham. ex D. Don FLAKY JUNIPER. Prostrate to erect shrub to 8m; br. tips somewhat drooping; bark rusty brown, flaky. Lvs all juvenile, in whorls of 3, subulate, dark grey-green to silvery blue-green with bright blue-white band. Cones 6–9mm, glossy black. NE Afghan., Himal., W & C China, mts. Cvs range from dwarf and prostrate to columnar or bushy, mostly with bright silver-blue lvs, some tinged lilac in winter. 'Blue Carpet': sport of 'Meyeri', procumbent, to 40cm×3m. 'Blue Star': compact dwarf to 40cm. 'Chinese Silver': large bush, bright blue-green with vivid silver stomata. 'Meyeri': broad spiky blue-green shrub to 8m, dead twigs persistent, rusty. Z5.

J. squamata var. *fargesii* Rehd. & Wils. = *J. morrisonicola*.

J. squamata var. *morrisonicola* (Hayata) Li & Keng = *J. morrisonicola*.

J. squamata f. *wilsonii* Rehd. = *J. morrisonicola* 'Wilsonii'.

J. standleyi Steyerm. Tree to 15m, or prostrate shrub. Adult lvs in pairs or 3's, ovate with rounded or obtuse adpressed tips, yellow to dark green, longer and tinged brown on strong shoots. Cones 7–9mm, dark blue, pruinose, soft. Mex., Guat. Z8.

J. suecica Mill. = *J. communis* 'Suecica'.

J. taxifolia Hook. & Arn. LUCHU JUNIPER. To 12m, or procumbent shrub. Br. horizontal; shoots drooping. Lvs in loose whorls of 3, obtuse, bright green to 2cm; dors. face with 2 grey bands. Cones maroon, glossy, 6–10mm. S Jap. Z9.

J. thurifera L. SPANISH JUNIPER. Tree or shrub to 20m. Bark brown, peeling. Crown conic, becoming rounded. Br. upswept. Juvenile lvs acicular, opposite, spreading, light green on inner face, with 2 white bands; adult lvs scale-like, in opposite pairs. Cones 6–10mm, dark purple, pruinose. Spain, SE Fr., NW Afr. (Atlas Mts). Z8.

J. tibetica Komar. Tree to 30m, or shrub. Bark light brown, flaking. Crown elliptic, densely branched. Juvenile lvs in pairs or whorls of 3, acicular, light green, dors. face with 2 white bands; mature lvs scale-like, opposite, incurved, dark green, 1.5–3mm. Cones 9–16mm, dark brown to grey- or red-brown. Tibet, W

China. Z6.

J. utahensis (Engelm.) Lemmon = *J. osteosperma*.

J. virginiana L. PENCIL CEDAR; EASTERN RED CEDAR. To 20m, rarely 30m. Bark rust-brown, peeling in shreds. Crown conic to columnar, br. spreading. Juvenile lvs acicular, in pairs, rarely 3's, sharply pointed, dors. face grey-green, marked white, green beneath; adult lvs scale-like, paired, rhombic, acute. Cones to 5mm, purple, glaucous. E N Amer. Cvs ranging from dwarf, spreading or prostrate shrubs to small trees; br. often ascending; lvs pale to bright or dark green, some turning purple in winter; often similar to cvs of *J. chinensis* and *J.* ×*media*, from which told by weaker soapy or paint-like scent of crushed lvs. 'Burkii': conic-columnar to 3m, br. erect; most lvs juvenile, bronzed or purple in winter. 'Canaertii': vigorous conic-columnar, almost all lvs adult, bright green; ♀ cv, cones abundant. 'Filifera': shoots sparse, long, slender. 'Glauca': narrow columnar, blue-green; cones abundant. 'Hillii': as 'Burkii' but less erect. 'Schottii': as 'Canaertii' but yellow-green lvs. 'Silver Spreader': procumbent, grey-green lvs. 'Skyrocket': see *J. scopulorum*. 'Grey Owl': see *J.* 'Grey Owl'. Z4.

J. wallichiana Hook. f. ex Brandis. BLACK JUNIPER. Tree to 20m, possibly conspecific with *J. pseudosabina*. Crown conic to irregular; bark orange to red-brown, falling in strips. Juvenile lvs predominating in cult. mostly in whorls of 3, acicular, outer face bright green, inner with glaucous band. Adult lvs scale-like in pairs, grey to dark green, mucronate, with a musty soapy scent when crushed. Cones 8–12mm, glossy black, epruinose. Himal. (Pak. to Yunnan). Z6.

J. zaidamensis Komar. = *J. przewalskii*.

→*Arceuthos*.

Juniper Wattle *Acacia ulicifolia*.
Jupiter's Beard *Anthyllis barba-jovis*; *Centranthus ruber*.
Jupiter's Distaff *Salvia glutinosa*.

Jurinea Cass. Compositae. *c*250 bienn. and perennials herbs and subshrubs. Lvs in a basal rosette or alt. on st., entire or pinnatifid, white-hairy beneath and occas. above. Cap. solitary, or few to several in a corymb, discoid; flts pink, red, lilac or purple tinged. C & S Eur., SW & C Asia. Z6.

J. alata (Desf.) Cass. Bienn. or perenn. herb, to 1m. Basal lvs to 15cm, oblong, lyrate-pinnatifid, subglabrous above, hairy beneath. Cap. many, to 2.5cm diam., in a globose pan.; phyllaries narrowly linear, outer reflexed, inner tinged red; flts purple-blue. Summer. Cauc.

J. anatolica Boiss. = *J. mollis* ssp. *anatolica*.

J. arachnoidea Bunge = *J. consanguinea* ssp. *arachnoidea*.

J. ceratocarpa Benth. & Hook. f. = *Saussurea ceratocarpa*.

J. consanguinea DC. Perenn. herb, to 50cm. Basal lvs to 20cm, usually pinnatifid, seg. 7–12, narrowly linear to lanceolate, green above, tomentose beneath, revolute. Cap. solitary, to 7cm diam.; phyllaries wispy-hairy; flts lilac-purple or dark red. Spring–summer. SE Europe, W Turkey. ssp. *arachnoidea* (Bunge) Kozuh. Lf seg. with only slightly revolute margins. Cap. to 4cm diam.

J. cyanoides (L.) Rchb. f. Perenn. herb, to *c*60cm. Basal lvs to 15cm, 1–2-pinnatifid, seg. 1–2mm wide, linear, or entire and linear, revolute, glab. above, white-tomentose beneath. Cap. 1 to several, to 3cm diam.; phyllaries lax, erect or slightly in-curved, green, outer wispy-hairy; flts pale purple to pink. Summer. C Eur. to C Asia.

J. depressa (Steven) C.A. Mey. = *Jurinella moschus*.

J. dolomiaea Boiss. = *Dolomiaea macrocephala*.

J. glycacantha (Sibth. & Sm.) DC. Perenn. herb, to 70cm. Basal lvs to 20cm, shallowly pinnatifid, seg. oblong to oblong-lanceolate, undulate, arachnoid-tomentose above, tomentose beneath. Cap. solitary to 7.5cm diam.; phyllaries linear to linear-lanceolate, outer strongly recurved, slightly hooked, tomentose; flts purple. Balk., EC Eur. to Turk.

J. humilis (Desf.) DC. Stemless perenn. herb, to 4cm. Lvs to 4cm, entire and oblong-obovate or pinnatifid, seg. linear-lanceolate or oblong, wispy-hairy, revolute. Cap. solitary, to 2.5cm diam.; phyllaries straight or recurved, green, subglabrous to wispy-hairy. Summer. SW Eur., Sicily.

J. macrocalathia K. Koch = *J. glycacantha*.

J. macrocephala DC. Perenn. herb, to 50cm. Lvs to 7cm, entire, oblong-lanceolate, acute, spreading or deflexed, glandular-floccose. Cap. solitary, to 7cm diam.; phyllaries lanceolate, out-er lax, to 4cm, tapered to spine, floccose; flts lilac-pink. Summer–autumn. Turk., Iran.

J. mollis (L.) Rchb. Perenn. herb, to 70cm. Basal lvs to 15cm, pinnatifid, seg. lanceolate, oblong-lanceolate or ovate, green, wispy-hairy above, white-tomentose beneath, revolute or un-dulate. Cap. solitary, to 4.5cm diam.; outer phyllaries acicular, inner erect, lanceolate, scarious; flts rose-purple. Spring–summer. SE Eur. ssp. *anatolica* (Boiss.) Stoj. & Stef. Lvs grey-tomentose. Cap. to 3cm diam.; phyllaries wispy-hairy. Bulg., Aegean, W Turk.

J. moschus (Hab.) Bobrov = *Jurinella moschus*.

J. spectabilis Fisch. & C.A. Mey. Bienn. or perenn. herb, to c15cm. Lvs to 20cm, pinnatisect with seg. oblong and obtuse, or lyrate with term. seg. ovate-orbicular, glab. above, canescent beneath. Cap. solitary, to 5cm diam.; phyllaries few, lanceolate, spreading or recurved, mucronate, arachnoid. Early summer. Cauc.

→*Carduus* and *Serratula*.

Jurinella Jaub. & Spach. Compositae. 2 low, alpine, perenn. herbs. Lvs radical, simple, tomentose, at least beneath. Cap. discoid, solitary. SW Asia.

J. moschus (Hab.) Bobrov. Lvs lyrate or pinnatifid, subglabrous, eglandular or sparsely hairy and densely pitted above, densely wispy-hairy beneath. Cap. to 4cm diam., subglobose; phyllaries wispy-hairy; flts lilac-pink, fragrant. Cauc., NW Iran. Z6.

→*Jurinea*.

Jurua *Syagrus macrocarpa*.

Jussiaea L.

J. grandiflora Michx. = *Ludwigia grandiflora*.
J. helminthorrhiza Mart. = *Ludwigia helminthorrhiza*.
J. hexapetala Hook. & Arn. = *Ludwigia hexapetala*.
J. longifolia DC. = *Ludwigia longifolia*.
J. peploides Kunth = *Ludwigia peploides*.
J. repens var. *peploides* (HBK.) Griseb. = *Ludwigia peploides*.
J. uruguayensis Cambess. = *Ludwigia grandiflora*.

Justicia L. WATER WILLOW. Acanthaceae. 420 perenn. herbs, subshrubs or shrubs. Lvs oblong-ovate to ovate, usually entire. Fls in spikes, cymes or pan., subtended by bracts; sep. 5; cor. tubular-campanulate, tube short, straight or curved, limb bilabiate. Trop. and subtrop., temp. N Amer.

J. adhatoda L. Everg. shrub, 2–3m. Lvs to 2cm, ovate-elliptic. Fls in spikes; cor. 3cm, white, lower lip veined red or purple-pink. Summer. India, Sri Lanka.

J. brandegeana Wassh. and L.B. Sm. SHRIMP PLANT; MEXICAN SHRIMP PLANT; SHRIMP BUSH; FALSE HOP. Everg., downy shrub to 1m. Lvs to 7.5cm, ovate or elliptic. Fls in compact arching to pendent spikes to 8cm; bracts cordate, yellow to brown to brick red to rose, densely overlapping; cor. white, lower lip marked with purple or red. Mex. 'Yellow Queen': bracts bright yellow or lime.

J. californica (Benth.) D. Gibson CHUPAROSA HONEYSUCKLE. Subshrub to 1.5m. Br. green-white hairy, arching. Lvs 0, or to 7.5cm, ovate, pubesc. Fls in short rac.; bracts inconspicuous; cor. red. Deserts of S N Amer.

J. carnea Lindl. BRAZILIAN PLUME; PLUME FLOWER; PLUME PLANT; FLAMINGO PLANT; PARADISE PLANT; KING'S CROWN. Everg. shrub to 2m. Lvs to 25cm, ovate-acuminate, velutinous. Spikes to 10cm, dense, erect, plume-shaped; bracts to 2cm, green; cor. 5cm, flesh-pink to purple-red. N S Amer.

J. coccinea Aubl. = *Pachystachys coccinea*.
J. floribunda hort. = *J. rizzinii*.
J. ghiesbreghtiana hort. = *J. spicigera*.

J. leonardii Wassh. Densely pubesc. shrub to 1m. Lvs 15cm, narrowly ovate, glab. above. Fls in cymes; cor. 3.25cm, red. Mex.

J. pauciflora (Nees) Griseb. non Vahl = *J. rizzinii*.

J. rizzinii Wassh. Small, rounded, pubesc., shrub. Lvs 2cm, oblong-elliptic to obovate. Fls in nodding clusters; cor. 2cm, scarlet with yellow tips. Winter. Braz.

J. spicigera Schldl. MOHINTLI. Shrub to 1.8m. Lvs to 17.5cm, oblong-lanceolate to ovate. Fls few in a secund rac.; cor. to 4cm, orange or red. Mex. to Colomb.

J. suberecta André = *Dicliptera suberecta*.

→*Adhatoda, Belperone, Cyrtanthera, Drejerella, Jacobinia, Libonia* and *Sericographis*.

Juttadinteria Schwantes. Aizoaceae. 12 highly succulent subshrubs, caespitose or clump-forming. Lvs paired, decussate, thick semi-ovoid to broadly navicular, triquetrous toward the tip. Fls subsessile. Late summer. S Afr., Nam. Z9.

J. albata L. Bol. St. short and erect. Lvs 2–2.5cm expanded, then tapered toward apex, carinate, white-green to grey-green with scattered spots, keel and margins tinged red. Fls 3–5cm diam., white. W Cape.

J. cinerea (Marloth) Schwantes = *Namibia cinerea*.
J. dealbata (N.E. Br.) L. Bol. = *Dracophilus dealbatus*.

J. decumbens Schick & Tisch. Mat-forming. Lvs 1.5–3cm, united for one-third of their length, broadly carinate toward the acute tip, smooth, white-green. Fls 2.5–3cm diam., white. W Cape.

J. delaetiana (Dinter) Dinter & Schwantes = *Dracophilus delaetianus*.

J. deserticola (Marloth) Schwantes. St. short, erect. Lvs suborbicular to tapered, with a faint keel, smooth, grey-green with scattered dots. Fls 1.8cm diam., white. Nam.

J. kovismontana (Dinter) Schwantes. Cushion-forming to 20cm diam. Lvs 1.5–2.2cm, tip triquetrous, with flat tubercles along margin, densely granulate. Fls 2.2cm diam., white. Nam.

J. longipetala L. Bol. Clump-forming; st. dense, short. Lvs 4cm, crowded, keel rounded, blue-green to pink. Fls 4–7cm diam., pale pink. Nam.

J. montis-draconis (Dinter) Dinter & Schwantes = *Dracophilus montis-draconis*.

J. pomonae (Dinter) Schwantes = *Namibia pomonae*.
J. proxima L. Bol. = *Dracophilus proximus*.
J. rheolens L. Bol. = *Dracophilus dealbatus*.

J. simpsonii (Dinter) Schwantes. St. ascending, forming cushions. Lvs 2.5–3.5cm, tip keeled, tubercles along both keel and margins, with red teeth, surface slightly rough, light blue-green with faint dots. Fls 3–5cm diam., white. Nam.

J. suavissima (Dinter) Schwantes. St. prostrate or ascending to 30cm. Lvs 20–40cm, obtusely triquetrous, tip recurved with several blunt teeth, light grey-green with indistinct dots. Fls strongly scented, 4–5cm diam., white. Nam.

→*Mesembryanthemum* and *Namibia*.

K

Kadsura Juss. Schisandraceae. 22 twining, everg. shrubs. Lvs entire or toothed. Fls solitary; sep. and pet. similar, 9–15; sta. 20–80, fil. fused forming a fleshy head. E & SE Asia.
K. japonica (L.) Dunal. Glab. climber to 4m. Lvs 4–11cm, elliptic to ovate-lanceolate, remotely toothed. Fls to 1.5cm diam., ivory. Berries scarlet. Jap., Korea. 'Variegata': lvs edged yellow to cream. Z7.

Kaempferia L. Zingiberaceae. 50 rhizomatous aromatic perenn. herbs. Lvs basal or in 2 ranks on short st. Fls term. in spikes on leafy st. or scaly, terminal scapes; fls 1 per bract; cal. tubular; pet. 3, narrow; lip large, deeply 2-lobed; lat. staminodes large, petaloid. Trop. Asia. Z9.
K. aethiopica (Schweinf.) Ridl. = *Siphonochilus aethiopicus.*
K. angustifolia Roscoe. Lvs 15cm, lanceolate, bright green. Fls fragrant; cor. white; lip lilac; staminodes white. E Himal.
K. atrovirens N.E. Br. PEACOCK PLANT. Lvs 15cm, basal, ovate, bronze, iridescent above. Fls few; cor. tube 5cm, white; lip lavender, pink or violet, spotted yellow at base. Borneo.
K. brachystemon Schum. = *Siphonochilus brachystemon.*
K. decora Van Druten = *Siphonochilus decorus.*
K. elegans (Wallich) Bak. Lvs 12.5–15cm, oblong, sometimes spotted silver-grey. Cor. tube 5cm; pet. 2.5cm, lanceolate, green; lip and lat. staminodes lilac. S Asia. Closely related to *K. pulchra.*
K. ethelae J.M. Wood = *Siphonochilus aethiopicus.*
K. galanga L. Lvs 15cm, 2 or 3, spreading, suborbicular, sometimes with red margin. Fls fragrant; cor. tube 2cm, white; lip white, mottled lilac at base. Summer. India.
K. gilbertii Bull. VARIEGATED GINGER LILY. Lvs 10×4cm, oblong, pale green with wide silver-white border. Cor. tube to 2cm, white; lip striped violet. India.
K. kirkii (Hook. f.) Wittm. & Perring = *Siphonochilus kirkii.*
K. lancifolia Schum. = *Scaphochlamys malaccana.*
K. macrosiphon Bak. = *Siphonochilus brachystemon.*
K. malaccana Schum. = *Scaphochlamys malaccana.*
K. masonii hort. = *K. pulchra.*
K. ornata N.E. Br. = *Boesenbergia ornata.*
K. ovalifolia Roxb. = *K. parishii.*
K. pandurata Roxb. = *Boesenbergia rotunda.*
K. parishii Hook. f. Lvs 15–20cm, oblong-lanceolate. Fls few; cor. tube 2.5cm, white; lip bright purple, yellow in throat, staminodes white. Burm.
K. parvula King ex Bak. = *Camptandra parvula.*
K. pulchra Ridl. Lvs to 14cm, elliptic, pale green suffused and feathered with dark purple-green or bronze-green feathered silver-green. Cor. lilac; lip deeply cleft. Thail., Malaysia.
K. roscoeana Wallich. PEACOCK LILY; DWARF GINGER LILY. Lvs usually 2, 10cm diam., suborbicular, deep green, marked paler green above, flushed red beneath. Cor. white. Burm.
K. rosea Bak. = *Siphonochilus kirkii.*
K. rotunda L. RESURRECTION LILY. Lvs to 20cm, 2, oblong-acuminate, green marked silver above, tinted purple beneath. Infl. bracts tinged purple, cor. 5cm across, white; lip lilac. SE Asia, widely cult., origin obscure.
K. vittata N.E. Br. = *Boesenbergia vittata.*

Kaffir Bread *Encephalartos caffer.*
Kaffir Corn *Sorghum bicolor.*
Kaffir Fig *Carpobrotus edulis.*
Kaffir Lily *Clivia; Schizostylis.*
Kaffir Orange *Strychnos spinosa.*
Kaffir Plum *Harpephyllum caffrum.*

Kageneckia Ruiz & Pav. Rosaceae. 5 everg. shrubs or small trees. Lvs simple. Staminate fls in pan., pistillate fls solitary or in loose pan.; cal. tube campanulate or turbinate, lobes 5; pet. 5, alternating with cal. lobes; sta. 15–20. Fr. star-shaped. Chile, Peru. Z9.
K. oblonga Ruiz & Pav. To 4m. Lvs to 6cm, oblong to ovate, coriaceous, glandular-serrate. Pet. white broadly oblong, to 8mm. Summer. Chile.

Kahikatea *Dacrycarpus dacrydioides.*
Kahili Ginger *Hedychium gardnerianum.*
Kaitha *Limonia acidissima.*
Kai Tsoi *Brassica juncea.*

Kaki *Diospyros kaki.*

Kalanchoe Adans. Crassulaceae. 125 perenn., ann. or bienn. succulent shrubs, herbs and climbers. St. fleshy, woody at base. Lvs sometimes viviparous, simple to twice pinnatisect, fleshy, flattened. Infl., a pan. with cymose br.; fls showy, cal. 4, fleshy; cor. 4, exceeding sep., tube often swollen at middle or base; sta. 8, in 2 whorls of 4. Summer–winter. Trop., esp. OW.
K. antonasyana Drake = *K. orygalis.*
K. beauverdii Hamet. Climber to 6mm. St. thin woody. Lvs 2–10cm, linear-lanceolate to ovate, base cordate or tapered, plantlets formed near apex, lower lvs terete. Pan. lax; fls pendent; cor. green-purple, tube 11–15mm, lobes 12–17mm rounded. Madag.
K. beharensis Drake. Felty shrub to 6m. St. slender. Lvs to 35cm, spear-shaped to triangular, toothed, brown, concave above, silvery beneath. Fls ± erect, green-yellow, tube urceolate, lobes obovate, violet inside. Madag.
K. bentii C. H. Wright ex Hook. f. Perenn. to 1.5m. St. little branched, becoming corky. Lvs 7.5–10cm, terete, grooved above, glaucous. Pan. flat-topped; fls scented; cor. white, tube 3–4cm, somewhat swollen at base, lobes 7–16mm, recurved. Somalia.
K. blossfeldiana Poelln. FLAMING KATY. Compact perenn. to 40cm. Lvs 2–7.5cm, oblong-ovate, glossy green, base rounded, crenate. Fls small, erect in crowded bunches; cor. red, orange, pink or yellow, tube to 10mm, lobes to 6mm, elliptic. Madag. A common house and window box plant. Plants grown under this name are often of hybrids with *K. flammea* and *K. pumila* in their parentage. Variegated forms are available.
K. brasiliensis Cambess. = *K. crenata.*
K. brevicaulis Bak. = *K. pumila.*
K. coccinea Britten = *K. crenata.*
K. constantinii Hamet = *K. beauverdii.*
K. crenata (Andrews) Haw. Perenn. to 2m. Lvs 4–25cm, spathulate to ovate, glab., green, crenate. Pan. lax; fls erect; cor. yellow to red, tube 8–16mm, lobes to 10mm, elliptic. Arabia to Natal and S Amer.
K. daigremontiana Hamet & Perrier. DEVIL'S BACKBONE. Robust erect perenn. to 1m. Lvs 15–20cm, lanceolate, fleshy, marbled brown-purple beneath, margins toothed, bearing plantlets. Fls pendent, violet-grey. Madag.
K. delagonensis Ecklon & Zeyh. Perenn. shrublet to 2m. Lvs 2–12cm, grey-green, narrow, terete, opp. or whorled, apex toothed and bearing plantlets. Infl. large, dense; fls pendent; cor. deep magenta to pale orange, tube 20–25mm, lobes 8–12mm, spreading. Madag., S Afr.
K. eriophylla Hilsenb. & Bojer. Canescent perenn. to 20cm. St. slender. Lvs 1.6–3cm, oblong, v. thick. Infl. dense, few-fld; fls erect; cor. violet-blue, to 14mm. Madag.
K. farinacea Balf. Perenn. to 30cm, erect. Lvs 2–7cm, crowded at br. tips, obovate, thick, waxy, pale green, entire, tinged pink. Infl. crowded, rounded; fls erect; cor. red, tinged yellow at base, tube 8–12mm, lobes 4–6mm, ovate. Socotra.
K. fedtschenkoi Hamet & Perrier. Dense shrublet to 50cm, decumbent at first. Lvs crowded at st. bases, 1.2–6cm, oblong to ovate, glaucous blue, toothed near apex. Infl. small, loose; fls pendent; cor. purple-red, tube 15×20mm, campanulate, lobes to 7mm, obovate. Madag. 'Variegata': lvs marked cream.
K. flammea Stapf. Similar to *K. glaucescens* except lvs subentire. Cor. never yellow. Somalia.
K. gastonis-bonnieri Hamet & Perrier. Perenn. to 1m. Lvs forming rosettes, 9–17cm, lanceolate, tinged white, purple-blotched, mealy, crenate. Infl. corymbose; fls pendent; cor. pale red-yellow, tube to 30mm, lobes to 12mm, recurved. Madag.
K. glaucescens Britten. Perenn. to 1.5m. St. decumbent to erect. Lvs 3–10cm, spathulate to ovate, glaucous, crenate, sometimes tinged red, particularly beneath. Infl. dense, corymbose; fls pendent; cor. pink or yellow to red, tube to 15mm, lobes spreading, v. short. E Afr.
K. gracilipes (Bak.) Baill. Similar to *K. manginii* except lvs glab., crenate-serrate; cor. pink-brown. Madag.
K. gracilipes ×K. manginii. Similar to *K. manginii* except lvs all oblong-ovate, toothed; infl. not viviparous, fls paler. Gdn origin. 'Tessa': fls pale peach.
K. grandiflora Wight & Arn. Perenn. to 1m. St. erect, glab. Lvs violet-blue, waxy, 4–10cm, obovate to ovate, dentate-crenate.

Infl. compact, cymose; fls erect; cor. bright yellow, tube to 14mm, lobes to 17mm, obovate. S India.

K. guillaminii Hamet = *K. rotundifolia*.

K. hildbrandtii Baill. Arborescent shrub to 5m. Lvs 1.5–4cm, obovate to round, with silver stellate hairs, entire. Fls erect, crowded in pan.; cor. sparsely hairy, white, sometimes tinged green, tube to 5mm, lobes to 4mm.

K. jongmansii Hamet & Perrier Perenn. to 30cm. St. sprawling, hairy. Lvs 7–45mm, linear-elliptic, fleshy, entire. Fls ± erect in axils and br. tips; cor. golden yellow, tube to 25mm, lobes to 9mm, ovate. Madag.

K. ×kewensis Dyer. (*K. flammea* ×*K. bentii*.) Similar to *K. bentii* except st. sometimes decumbent, lvs to only 30cm, basal lvs often flat; infl. sometimes corymbose; cor. lobes not spreading. Gdn origin.

K. laciniata (L.) DC. CHRISTMAS TREE KALANCHOE; FIR TREE KALANCHOE. Perenn. to 1.2m, sometimes monocarpic. St. erect. Lvs usually pinnately cut, seg. 3–5, entire to crenate. Pan. dense; fls erect; cor. pale orange to green-white, tube to 16mm, lobes to 7mm, ovate, spreading. E Afr., S India, Thail.

K. lateritia Engl. Perenn. to 1.5m. St. erect, hairy. Lvs 4.5–16cm, obovate-ovate, densely hairy, crenate. Infl. dense; fls erect; cor. pink to red or pale yellow, tube 8–11mm, lobes to 8mm, spreading, ovate. Zimb. to Kenya.

K. laxiflora Bak. Similar to *K. fedtschenkoi* except lvs evenly spread on st., pale green, round to oblong, base auriculate not tapered. Madag.

K. longiflora Schldl. Perenn. to 60cm. St. decumbent, glaucous, 4 angled. Lvs 4–8cm, obovate, toothed towards tip. Cor. orange to green yellow, tube to 17mm, lobes to 5mm, spreading. S Afr. (Natal). Z8.

K. macranther Bak. = *K. marmorata*.

K. manginii Hamet & Perrier. Creeping perenn. to 30cm. St. thin, branching, hairy. Lvs 12–30mm, obovate to ovate-spathulate, glandular-hairy, entire or notched. Infl. lax, pendulous, often viviparous; cor. red, tube long-urceolate, 20–30mm, lobes to 7mm, ovate. Madag.

K. marmorata Bak. PENWIPER. Perenn. to 1.3m, erect or decumbent. Lvs 6–20cm, obovate, glaucous, often with purple markings, serrate. Pan. erect; cor. white sometimes tinged pink or yellow, tube 40–120mm, lobes to 25mm, lanceolate. E Afr.

K. millottii Hamet & Perrier Perenn. shrublet to 35cm, much branched from base, hairy. Lvs 3–6cm, ovate, with dense, white hair, crenate. Corymbs dense; fls small; cor. tube campanulate, green yellow, to 11mm, lobes to 4mm, tinged red. Madag.

K. miniata Hilsenb. & Bojer. Perenn. to 80cm, erect or decumbent. Lvs 2–13cm, simple, occas. 3-lobed, glab., crenulate or entire, base auriculate. Infl. gland.-hairy; fls pendent; fls sometimes replaced by plantlets; cor. red-pink or yellow, tube to 30mm, lobes to 6mm, recurved, ovate, occas. tinged purple. Madag.

K. nyikae Cuf. Perenn. to 2m, erect or decumbent, glaucous. Lvs 6.5–18cm, ovate to ± peltate. Fls erect; cor. cream-yellow or pink, tube to 20mm, lobes to 11mm, lanceolate-ovate, spreading. E Afr.

K. orygalis Bak. Perenn. shrublet to 1.5m. Lvs 7.5–12cm, ovate-spathulate, rusty-pubesc., entire. Infl. elongate; fls erect; cor. yellow, tube to 10mm urceolate; lobes to 7mm, ovate. Madag.

K. peltata (Bak.) Baill. Perenn. subshrub to 2m, decumbent at first. Lvs 3–12.5cm, ovate to ± peltate, often red spotted, crenulate. Fls pendent, corymbose; cor. rose to red, tube campanulate-cylindric, to 27mm, lobes to 6mm, ovate, spreading. C Madag.

K. petitiana A. Rich. Perenn. to 1.5m, decumbent. Lvs 4–16cm, ovate, glab. or gland.-hairy. Pan. lax; fls erect; cor. pink, tube to 24mm, lobes to 7mm, oblong. Ethiop. Name often misapplied to *K. longiflora*.

K. pinnata (Lam.) Pers. Perenn. to 2m, erect. Lower lvs simple, upper lvs pinnate with 3–5 lfts, crenate, glab. Fls pendent, paniculate; Cal. green tinged red, inflated; cor. tinged red, gland.-hairy, tube to 4cm, lobes ovate, somewhat recurved. Widespread, Trop.

K. porphyrocalyx (Bak.) Baill. Perenn. shrublet to 30cm. St. thick, fleshy. Lvs 2–5.5cm, oblong-ovate, crenate. Infl. simple; fls few, pendent; cor. rose to red, orange to yellow at tip, tube urceolate to 31mm, lobes ovate to 6mm. Madag.

K. prolifera (Bowie) Hamet. Perenn. to 1.5m, erect, often suckering at base. Lvs to 45cm, pinnately divided; lfts 7–15cm, oblong-lanceolate, crenate. Infl. often forming plantlets; fls long-stalked, pendent; cor. yellow-green, pink at tips, tube to 24mm, lobes to 4mm, recurved, ovate. Madag.

K. pumila Bak. Sprawling shrublet to 30cm. Lvs 2–3.5cm, chalky, ovate, toothed towards apex. Fls erect, densely clustered; cor. pink with purple lines, tube to 9mm, campanulate, lobes to 10mm, obovate. Madag.

K. quartiniana A. Rich. Perenn. shrub to 1m, erect. Lvs 10–20cm, oblong-ovate, blunt, crenate. Fls erect; cor. white tube to 50mm; lobes to 20mm, spreading, obovate. Malawi to Ethiop.

K. rhombopilosa Mannoni & Boit. Small slow-growing shrub to 50cm, erect, few-branched. Lvs 2–3cm, obovate, grey-green with red markings, with grey scale like hairs, irregularly crenate. Pan. small, loose; fls erect; cor. green-yellow, red lined, tube to 4mm, urceolate, lobes to 3mm, ovate. Madag.

K. rotundifolia Haw. Perenn., erect or decumbent, slender. Lvs 1–8.5cm, ovate-spathulate to circular, usually glaucous, entire to crenulate, or 3-lobed. Infl. loose; fls erect; cor. pink to red or orange, tube to 10mm, lobes to 5mm, elliptic, spreading. Socotra to S Afr.

K. schizophylla (Bak.) Baill. Woody climber to 8m. Lvs to 13cm, ovate, toothed, to pinnately divided; lfts in 6–8 pairs with hooked lobes. Infl. large, loose; proliferous; fls pendulous; cor. violet, tube 13–17mm, campanulate, lobes to 4mm, ovate. Madag.

K. schweinfurthii Penzig = *K. laciniata*.

K. somaliensis Bak. = *K. marmorata*.

K. synsepala Bak. To 30cm, short, stoloniferous. Lvs 15cm, lanceolate to ovate-spathulate, toothed to pinnately divided. Fls erect on slender erect lat. infl.; cor. hairy, tube to 12mm, campanulate, lobes to 7mm, elliptic. Madag.

K. thyrsiflora Harv. Perenn. to 1m, increasing by offsets. St. square in cross section. Lvs 6–14cm, oblanceolate, pairs united at base in loose basal rosettes. Pan. elongate; fls erect to spreading, fragrant; cor. yellow, tube 11–20mm, lobes 2–5mm, recurved. S Afr.

K. tomentosa Bak. PANDA PLANT. To 1m, erect. Lvs 2–9cm, oblong, grooved above, with furry silver hairs, thick, entire or toothed and stained red-brown towards tip. Fls yellow-green, with red gland. hairs, tube to 12mm, lobes to 4mm, tinged purple. Madag.

K. tubiflora (Harv.) Hamet = *K. delagonensis*.

K. uniflora (Stapf) Hamet. Prostrate perenn., st. slender, creeping, rooting. Lvs 4–35mm, oblong-orbicular, convex, sparsely crenate. Infl. few-fld; fls pendent; cor. red-purple, tube to 2cm, lobes to 5mm, ovate. Madag.

K. 'Wendy' (*K. miniata* ×*K. porphyrocalyx*.) Similar to *K. porphyrocalyx* except lvs to 7cm, cor. tube tinged purple. Gdn origin.

K. vantieghemi Hamet = *K. beharensis*.

K. zimbabwensis Rendle = *K. lateritia*.

→*Bryophyllum, Cotyledon* and *Kitchingia*.

Kalgan *Boronia heterophylla.*

Kalimeris Cass. Compositae. 10 perenn. herbs. Lvs alt., linear-ovate to elliptic, dentate to pinnatifid. Cap. radiate, subglobose, few to many, clustered in pan.; ray flts white, purple-tinged or violet, spreading; disc flts yellow. E Asia.

K. incisa (Fisch.) DC. To 1.5m. Basal lvs to 10cm, oblong-lanceolate to lanceolate, acuminate, dentate to serrate, glab., margins ciliate, sessile. Cap. 3–3.5cm diam.; ray flts purple to white. NE Asia. Z4.

K. mongolica (Franch.) Kit. To 90cm. Basal lvs to 15cm, deeply pinnatifid, oblong, subobtuse, scabrid, ciliate, petiolate. Cap. to 7cm diam.; ray flts tinged purple. Summer. Mong. Z6.

K. pinnatifida (Maxim.) Kit. To 1.5m. Basal lvs to 8cm, oblong to ovate-oblong, pinnatifid, linear, seg. in 3–4 pairs, obtuse, mucronate, pubesc. Cap. 2.5cm diam., in loose corymbs; ray flts pink or tinted blue. Summer–autumn. Jap. Z6.

→*Aster* and *Boltonia*.

Kalmia L. Ericaceae. 7 everg. shrubs. Lvs leathery. Fls in small corymbs, umbels or fascicles; pedicels slender; cal. lobes 5; cor. campanulate, 5-lobed, pleated with 10 anth. pockets; sta. included. US, Cuba.

K. angustifolia L. SHEEP LAUREL; PIG LAUREL; LAMBKILL. To 1.5m. Lvs 2–6cm, opposite or in whorls, oblong to elliptic, red-brown beneath when young. Fls in axill. corymbs, 7–12mm diam., scarlet-pink. Summer. E US, nat. Germ. and NW GB. 'Candida': fls white. 'Nana': dwarf to 40cm. 'Rosea': fls pink-red. 'Rubra' ('Pumila'?): fls dark purple. var. *ovata* Pursh. Lvs broader, ovate to obovate or elliptic. Z2.

K. angustifolia var. *carolina* (Small) Fern. = *K. carolina*.

K. carolina Small. Like *K. angustifolia* but lvs finely grey-velvety-downy beneath; fls rose-purple, lobes recurved. Summer. SE US. Z6.

K. cuneata Michx. WHITE WICKY. To 1.2m. Young shoots gland.-hirsute, red-tinted. Lvs 1.5–5cm, alt., oblong to obovate, sparsely gland.-hirsute beneath. Fls in axill. fascicles, 12–16mm diam., white or pink, with red ring at base. Summer. SE US. Z7.

K. glauca var. **microphylla** Hook. = K. polifolia var. microphylla.

K. hirsuta Walter. To 60cm. Young shoots downy. Lvs 0.6–1.5cm, alt., lanceolate, downy at first. Fls solitary or 2–3 per axil, 8–20mm diam., pink. Summer. SE US. Z8.

K. latifolia L. MOUNTAIN LAUREL; CALICO BUSH; IVY. 3–10m. Young shoots downy. Lvs 5–12cm, alt., elliptic-lanceolate, glab. Fls in large, term. corymbs, 20–25mm diam., white to deep rose. Late spring–summer. E US. 'Angustata': lvs narrow. 'Bettina': fls to 100 in densely packed infl.; cor. campanulate to urceolate, rose-purple. 'Bullseye': lvs tinged red; fls white with prominent red-purple band. 'Clementine Churchill': fls mauve-pink on outside, dark pink inside. 'Elf': habit small, compact; fls light pink. 'Freckles': fls spotted with purple band. 'Fuscata': cor. white, inner limb with a purple-brown band. 'Heart of Fire': buds red, fls large, pink with darker edges. 'Myrtifolia': dwarf shrub; lvs 2–5cm, dark green. 'Olympic Fire': lvs wavy, fls bright red, flat, rounded. 'Ostbo Red': buds red, fls deep pink. 'Pink Charm': fls pink from pink buds. 'Polypetala': cor. distinctly 5-parted. 'Rubra': cor. deep crimson-pink. 'Tiddlywinks': miniature, fls pink. 'Yankee Doodle': buds red, fls rose-white with maroon-red band. Z4.

K. microphylla (Hook.) Heller = K. polifolia var. microphylla.

K. polifolia Wangenh. BOG KALMIA; SWAMP LAUREL; BOG LAUREL. 10–50cm. Shoots initially downy. Lvs 0.6–4cm, opposite or in whorls, elliptic to oblong, glaucous beneath. Fls 1–12 in term. corymbs, 10–20mm, vivid pink or purple-rose. Late spring–early autumn. N US, Canada, SE Alask. 'Leucantha': fls white. var. **microphylla** (Hook.) Rehd. Dwarf, 15–20cm. Lvs 1–2cm, ovate. Fls in racemose clusters, c12mm diam., pink-lilac. N Amer. Z2.

Kalmiopsis Rehd. Ericaceae. 1 erect everg. shrub to 30cm. Young shoots downy. Lvs to 3cm, oval or obovate, bright green, flecked with glands beneath. Fls in rac. grouped in erect umbels 2.5–5cm; cal. red, lobes 5; cor. 14–20mm diam., rotate to campanulate, lobes 5, rose-purple; sta. 10. Spring. US (Oreg.).

K. leachiana (Henderson) Rehd. 'Umpqua Valley Form': exceptionally strong habit, compact. Z7.

Kalopanax Miq. Araliaceae. 1 sparingly branched tree to 31m; br. and trunk prickly. Lvs to 35cm across, long-stalked, glabrescent, palmate, lobes 5–7, ± ovate, toothed. Umbels in broad term. pan.; fls 4–5-merous, white. Fr. blue-black, 4mm wide. Summer–late summer. China, Korea, Sakhalin, S Kuriles, Ryukyu Is. Z5.

K. innovans (Sieb. & Zucc.) Miq. = Gamblea innovans.

K. pictus (Thunb.) Nak. = K. septemlobus.

K. ricinifolius (Sieb. & Zucc.) Miq. = K. septemlobus.

K. septemlobus (Thunb. ex A. Murray) Koidz. HARAGIRI; SEN-NO-KI; TREE ARALIA. Lvs glabrescent. var. **magnificus** (Zab.) Hand.-Mazz. Lvs densely pubesc. beneath, lobes shallow, ovate. Br. ± unarmed. var. **maximowiczii** (Van Houtte) Hand.-Mazz. Lvs densely pubesc. beneath, lobes deep. (Probably juvenile stage.) Z5.
→Aralia.

Kamahi Weinmannia racemosa.
Kamchatka Bilberry Vaccinium praestans.
Kampong Oroxylum.
Kamuro-zasa Pleioblastus auricoma.
Kan-chiku Chimonobambusa marmorea.
Kangaroo Apple Solanum aviculare; S. laciniatum.
Kangaroo Fern Microsorium diversifolium.
Kangaroo Paw Anigozanthos.
Kangaroo Thorn Acacia paradoxa.
Kangaroo Treebine Cissus antarctica.
Kangaroo Vine Cissus antarctica.
Kanniedood Aloe Aloe variegata.
Kansas Gay Feather Liatris pycnostachya.
Kanzashi-giboshi Hosta nakaiana.
Kapok Ceiba (C. pentandra).
Kapok Bush Eriocephalus.
Kara-medo-hagi Lespedeza juncea.
Karanja Pongamia pinnata.
Karapincha Murraya koenigii.
Karashina Brassica juncea.

Karatas Mill. = Bromelia.

Karee Rhus lancea.

Karimbolea Descoings. Asclepiadaceae. 1 subshrub, around 15cm; br. prostrate then erect, tuberculate. Lvs 1–1.5mm, caducous. Fls 3–6 per infl., pale pink to violet, lobes to 1cm, thick. Madag. Z10.

K. verrucosa Descoings.

Karo Pittosporum crassifolium.
Karoo Boerboon Schotia afra.
Karoo Cycad Encephalartos lehmannii.
Karri Eucalyptus diversicolor.
Karri Blue Bush Hovea elliptica.
Karum Tree Pongamia pinnata.
Kashgar Tree Tamarix hispida.
Kashmir Cypress Cupressus himalaica var. darjeelingensis.
Kassod Tree Senna siamea.
Katsura Tree Cercidiphyllum japonicum.

Kaulfussia Nees.
K. aesculifolia Bl. = Christensenia aesculifolia.
K. amelloides hort. = Amellus strigosus.

Kauri Agathis australis.
Kauri Blanc Agathis moorei.
Kauri Pine Agathis (A. australis).
Kava Piper methysticum.
Kava-kava Piper methysticum.
Kawaka Libocedrus plumosa.
Kawa-kawa Macropiper excelsum.
Kazanlik Rose Rosa × damascena var. semperflorens.
Keck Anthriscus sylvestris.

Kedrostis Medik. Cucurbitaceae. 23 prostrate or climbing herbs, with caudiciform bases. Lvs entire or lobed; tendrils usually simple. Fls small, white to yellow-green: ♂ fls in a rac. or a corymb; cal. campanulate, lobes 5; cor. rotate, lobes 5, sta. 3 or 5. ♀ fls solitary or clustered; staminodes 3 or 0. Berry ovoid or subglobose, rostrate, ripening red. Afr. to trop. Asia. Z10.

K. africana (L.) Cogn. Base v. swollen; climbing st. to 6m, slender. Lvs to 10cm diam., usually glab., deeply pinnately or palmately lobed. Fr. to 15mm diam., glab. Afr.

K. boehmii Song. = Corallocarpus boehmii.

K. foetidissima (Jacq.) Cogn. Climbing st. to 2m, often branched. Lvs to 9cm diam., simple or slightly 3–5-lobed, pubesc. Fr. to 22mm, long-pubesc. Trop. Afr. to trop. Asia.
→Trichosanthes.

Keeled Garlic Allium carinatum.
Keeled Heath Epacris rigida.

Keerlia DC.
K. skirrhobasis DC. = Aphanostephus skirrhobasis.

Kefersteinia Rchb. f. Orchidaceae. 15 epiphytic orchids. Pbs 0. Lvs equitant, linear-lanceolate to oblanceolate. Infl. 1- to few-fld; fls thin-textured; tep. spreading, slightly concave, oblong-lanceolate to elliptic-ovate; lip entire to trilobed, base often saccate, apex finely dentate to fimbriate, callus basal, fleshy. Costa Rica and Nic. to Braz. and Peru. Z10.

K. costaricensis Schltr. Lvs 12–18cm, lanceolate, plicate. Fls to 2cm diam. white or cream, often spotted maroon. Costa Rica, Panama.

K. graminea (Lindl.) Rchb. f. Lvs 18–36cm, linear-lanceolate, carinate beneath. Fls to 4cm diam., pale green or yellow-green, spotted and marked maroon or red. Venez., Colomb., Ecuad.

K. lactea (Rchb. f.) B.D. Jackson. Lvs 8–12cm, oblong to elliptic-lanceolate, obscurely plicate. Fls to 2cm diam., white, slightly spotted and streaked brown. Panama, Costa Rica.

K. lojae Schltr. Lvs 15–20cm, oblanceolate. Fls to 2.1cm diam., white, densely spotted red at centre. Peru, Ecuad.

K. sanguinolenta Rchb. f. Lvs 15–20cm, oblanceolate to linear-oblanceolate. Fls to 2cm diam., pale yellow to green, spotted purple or dark red. Venez., Ecuad.

K. tolimensis Schltr. Lvs 18–25cm, broadly lanceolate. Fls to 4.8cm diam. cream to yellow, spotted dark brown-maroon or violet. Venez., Colomb., Ecuad.
→Chondrorhyncha and Zygopetalum.

Kegeliella Mansf. Orchidaceae. 3 epiphytic orchids. Pbs ovoid, 1–3-leaved at apex. Lvs ovate to elliptic-lanceolate, plicate. Rac. basal, pendent; sep. spreading, with gland. hairs; pet. smaller; lip trilobed, callus erect, fleshy. Costa Rica, Panama, Jam., Trin., Surinam, Venez. Z10.

K. houtteana (Rchb. f.) L.O. Williams. Pbs to 3.5cm. Lvs to 18×5cm, maroon beneath. Infl. to 10cm; axis gland.-pubesc.; fls to 3cm diam., pale green or pale yellow, with red gland. hairs. Jam., Panama, Trin., Venez., Surinam.

Kei Apple Dovyalis caffra.
Kei Cycad Encephalartos princeps.

Kelseya (S. Wats.) Rydb. Rosaceae. 1 everg., cushioned subshrub to 8cm. Lvs simple, entire, overlapping, silky. Fls solitary,

to 8.5mm diam.; cal. lobes 5, to 1.5mm; pet. 5, overlapping white, occas. flushed pink, spathulate; sta. 10. W US. Z3.
K. uniflora (S. Wats.) Rydb.
→*Eriogynia*.

Kembang *Clerodendrum buchananii*.
Kenaf *Hibiscus cannabinus*.
Kenilworth Ivy *Cymbalaria muralis*.

Kennedia Vent. CORAL PEA. Leguminosae (Papilionoideae). 16 woody or herbaceous perenn. climbers, sometimes twining, usually pubesc. Lvs alt.; lfts 3, v. rarely 1 or 5. Fls pea-like in axill. umbels or rac. Aus., Tasm., New Guinea. Z10.
K. beckxiana F. Muell. Woody, twining, to 3m. Lfts to 5cm, 3, lanceolate-ovate. Fls 1–5 in a loose umbel; standard narrow-obovate, red, yellow-patched at base. Summer. W Aus.
K. coccinea Vent. CORAL VINE. Prostrate or twining, often woody, to 2m. Lfts to 1.5cm, usually 3, linear to cuneate. Fls 4–20 in umbels; standard orbicular, red spotted-yellow edged purple at base. Spring. Aus., Tasm.
K. dilatata A. Cunn. ex Lindl. = *K. coccinea*.
K. eximia Lindl. Prostrate, sometimes twining to 1m. Lfts to 2.5cm, 3, ovate, to lanceolate. Fls 1–6 in umbel or short rac.; standard broadly obovate, rarely orbicular, scarlet. Spring–summer. W Aus.
K. glabrata (Benth.) Lindl. Twining, to 50cm, glabrate. Lfts to 2.5cm, 3, obovate or cuneate. Fls in umbels; standard scarlet, suborbicular, emarginate. Spring–summer. W. Aus.
K. macrophylla (Meissn.) Benth. Twining, to 3m. Lfts to 6cm, 3, obovate-orbicular. Infl. racemose, standard red, orbicular. Spring. Aus.
K. marryattae Lindl. = *K. prostrata*.
K. nigricans Lindl. BLACK CORAL PEA; BLACK BEAN. Woody climber to 6m, glabrescent. Lfts to 12.5cm, 1 or 3, ovate. Fls in rac., violet-purple or black blotched yellow. Spring–summer. W Aus.
K. procurrens Benth. St. prostrate. Lfts to 5cm, 3, ovate to elliptic. Fls in rac. Aus. (Queensld).
K. prostrata R. Br. RUNNING POSTMAN; SCARLET RUNNER. Prostrate or trailing, densely pubesc. Lfts to 13cm, 3, rarely 1 or 2, ovate-obovate. Fls 1–2, standard narrow, obovate, bright scarlet-pink, yellow at base. Autumn. W Aus.
K. rubicunda (Schneev.) Vent. DUSKY CORAL PEA. Twining or mat-forming to 3m. Lfts 15cm, 3, ovate. Fls in slender umbels. Standard abruptly reflexed, dark red with a pale blotch at base. Spring. Aus. (NSW, Vict.).
K. splendens Meissn. = *Camptosema rubicundum*.
K. stirlingii Lindl. Prostrate or twining, to 2m. Lfts to 6cm, 3, obovate-lanceolate. Fls 1–3; standard brick red, orbicular, keel with yellow patch. Spring. W Aus.

Kensitia Fedde. Aizoaceae. 1 succulent perenn. 30–60cm. St. erect to prostrate, tinged red. Lvs opposite, 2.8–3.3cm, acutely triquetrous, slightly incurved, blue-green. Fls 3–5cm diam., solitary, purple-pink. S Afr. Z9.
K. pillansii (Kensit) Fedde.
→*Mesembryanthemum* and *Piquetia*.

Kentan *Lilium lancifolium*.

Kentia Bl.
K. acuminata H.A. Wendl. & Drude = *Carpentaria acuminata*.
K. baueri Seem. = *Rhopalostylis baueri*.
K. canterburyana C. Moore & F. Muell. = *Hedyscepe canterburyana*.
K. fipan hort. = *Veitchia joannis*.
K. forsteriana C. Moore & F. Muell. = *Howea forsteriana*.
K. joannis (Wendl.) F. Muell. = *Veitchia joannis*.
K. microspadix Warb. = *Hydriastele microspadix*.

Kentia Palm *Howea forsteriana*.

Kentiopsis Brongn.
K. macrocarpa Brongn. = *Chambeyronia macrocarpa*.

Kentish Red Cherry *Prunus cerasus* var. *caproniana*.

Kentranthus Necker.
K. ruber L. = *Centranthus ruber*.

Kentucky Blue Grass *Poa pratensis*.
Kentucky Coffee Tree *Gymnocladus dioica*.
Kentucky Wisteria *Wisteria macrostachys*.
Kentucky Yellow-wood *Cladrastis lutea*.
Kenya Ivy *Senecio macroglossus*.
Kenyan Dragon Flower *Huernia keniensis*.

Ke-oroshima-chiku *Pleioblastus pygmaeus*.
Kermadec Nikau Palm *Rhopalostylis cheesemanii*.
Kermadec Pohutukawa *Metrosideros kermadecensis*.
Kermes Oak *Quercus coccifera*.

Kernera Medik. Cruciferae. 2 perenn. herbs. St. many. Lvs simple. Fls white, 4-merous in long rac. C & S Eur.
K. alpina (Tausch) Prantl = *Rhizobotrya alpina*.
K. boissieri Reut. Similar to *K. saxatilis*, except lvs spathulate, obtuse. SE Spain. Z8.
K. saxatilis (L.) Rchb. 10–30cm. Lvs obovate-lanceolate, occas. spathulate, acute, hairy, entire to toothed. Pet. 2–4mm. Spring. C & S Eur. Z7.
→*Cochlearia*.

Kerosene Weed *Ozothamnus ledifolius*.

Kerria DC. JEW'S MALLOW; JAPANESE ROSE. Rosaceae. 1 decid. shrub to 2.25m, st. green, rod-like, branching in second season, suckering. Lvs to 7×3.5cm, oval, acuminate, serrate. Fls to 5cm diam., solitary; pet. typically 5, yellow. China, Jap. Z4.
K. japonica (L.) DC. 'Golden Guinea': fls v. large, single, golden yellow. 'Pleniflora' ('Flora Pleno'): fls double. 'Simplex': the typical plant. 'Variegata' ('Picta'): lvs edged white.
K. tetrapetala Sieb. = *Rhodotypos scandens*.

Keteleeria Carr. Pinaceae. 3 everg., coniferous trees to 50m, resembling *Abies*. Crown conic, then domed. Br. in whorls. Lvs scattered, flat, acicular (lanceolate on young trees), leathery, shiny bright green. ♂ cones in umbels. ♀ cones lat., on peduncles not abscising cleanly as in *Abies*. C & S China, Taiwan, Laos, Vietnam.
K. calcarea Cheng & L.K. Fu = *K. davidiana*.
K. chienpeii Flous = *K. davidiana*.
K. cyclolepis Flous = *K. fortunei*.
K. davidiana (Bertr.) Beissn. To 45m. Shoots rusty brown, densely hairy. Lvs to 5×0.4cm, straight to falcate, subulate, sharply acute on young plants, obtuse, faintly emarginate on older plants. Cones 8–20×3–4.5cm; scales obovate, apex rounded and recurved. China. var. *formosana* (Hayata) Hayata. To 35m. Shoots short-pubesc. or glab. Lvs to 4cm. Cones cylindric, 5–13×3–4cm; scales obtuse. Taiwan. Z7.
K. evelyniana Mast. To 40m. Shoots rusty brown, glab. or slightly hairy. Lvs linear with pale stomatal bands beneath, mucronate in older plants. Cones 6–20×3–5cm; scales truncated triangular, apex recurved. SW China, Laos, Vietnam. Z8.
K. formosana Hayata = *K. davidiana* var. *formosana*.
K. fortunei (Murray) Carr. To 30m. Shoots grey-brown, glabrescent. Lvs 2.5–4cm, linear; pungent, obtuse and shorter on older shoots. Cones 6–20cm, scales broader than other spp., not reflexed at apex. SE China, Hong Kong. Z9.
K. hainanensis Chun & Tsiang = *K. evelyniana*.
K. oblonga Cheng & L.K. Fu = *K. fortunei*.
K. roulletii Flous = *K. evelyniana*.
K. sacra (Franch.) Beissn. = *K. davidiana*.
K. xerophila Hsueh & Hao = *K. davidiana*.

Keurboom *Virgilia divaricata*.
Key Palm *Thrinax* (*T. morrisii*).
Khair *Acacia catechu*.
Khanyu *Ficus semicordata*.
Khas Khas *Vetiveria zizanoides*.
Khat *Catha edulis*.
Khesari *Lathyrus sativus*.
Khingan Fir *Abies nephrolepis*.
Khira *Cucumis sativus*.
Khus Khus Grass *Vetiveria zizanoides*.
Kiaat *Pterocarpus angolensis*.

Kickxia Dumort. Scrophulariaceae. 46 gland.-pubesc. subshrubs, perenn. or ann. herbs. St. prostrate, erect or scandent. Lvs linear to suborbicular, entire or toothed. Fls solitary in axils, or in leafy rac.; cal. lobes 5; cor. tubular, 2-lipped. Summer. Medit., Afr., SC & SW Asia. Z9.
K. elatine (L.) Dumort. Ann., prostrate to ascending to 1m. Lvs oblong-lanceolate to orbicular, often dentate. Cor. yellow with blue hue, upper lip violet, palate sometimes spotted violet, spur straight. Medit.
K. spuria (L.) Dumort. Ann., decumbent or prostrate, to 50cm. Lvs ovate-lanceolate, ovate to suborbicular, entire or denticulate. Cor. yellow, upper lip dark purple, spur curved. Eur., Asia (nat. US, Aus.).
→*Linaria*.

Kidney Bean *Phaseolus vulgaris*.
Kidney Begonia *Begonia dichotoma*; *B.* ×*erythrophylla*.

Kidney Fern *Trichomanes.*
Kidney-leaved White Violet *Viola renifolia.*
Kidney Saxifrage *Saxifraga hirsuta.*
Kidney Vetch *Anthyllis vulneraria.*
Kiepersol *Cussonia.*

Kigelia DC. SAUSAGE TREE. Bignoniaceae. 1 tree to 20m. Lvs to 50cm, pinnate. Fls in pendent pan. to 2m, nocturnally scented; cor. to 10cm, tubular-campanulate, interior velvety red. Fr. to 1m, an oblong-cylindric pendulous berry, rind woody. Trop. Afr. Z10.
K. africana (Lam.) Benth.
K. pinnata (Jacq.) DC. = *K. africana.*
→*Crescentia* and *Tecoma.*

Kigelianthe Baill. = *Fernandoa.*

Kiggelaria L. Flacourtiaceae. 3 or 4 shrubs or small trees. Lvs sparse, simple. Fls 5-merous; ♂ in axill. cymes; ♀ solitary; sta. 8–10. Fr. a leathery, 5-valved capsule. S Afr. Z9.
K. africana L. WILD PEACH. Erect shrub, to 5m. Lvs to 7.5cm, ovate to lanceolate, serrulate. Fr. 12mm diam.; seeds with a scarlet, fleshy coating. S Afr.

Ki-hagi *Lespedeza buergeri.*
Kikkouchiku *Phyllostachys edulis* f. *heterocycla.*
Killarney Fern *Trichomanes speciosum.*
Kilmarnock Willow *Salix caprea* 'Kilmarnock'.

Kinepetalum Schltr. Asclepiadaceae. 1 caudiciform perenn. herb. St. erect, to 1m, forked, minutely hairy, grey to violet. Lvs 4–6cm, linear. Fls solitary or paired; cor. campanulate, interior long-hairy, white spotted green, lobes to 3cm, filiform, grey-green. Namaqualand. Z9.
K. schultzei Schltr.
→*Kinepetalum.*

King Anthurium *Anthurium veitchii.*
King Begonia *Begonia rex.*
Kingcup *Caltha palustris.*
King Dryandra *Dryandra proteoides.*
King Fern *Angiopteris; Marattia fraxinea; Todea barbara.*
Kingfisher Daisy *Felicia* (*F. bergeriana*).

Kingidium P. Hunt. Orchidaceae. 4 epiphytic, monopodial orchids. Fls many in pan. or rac. India to W Malaya. Z10.
K. delicosum (Rchb. f.) Sweet. Lvs to 20cm, oblong lanceolate. Fls 1.5–2cm diam., yellow, lip marked pink-purple. SE Asia.
K. taeniale (Lindl.) P. Hunt. Lvs to 10cm, oblong-elliptic, narrow. Fls to 2cm diam., pink-mauve. India, Burm.
→*Doritis* and *Phalaenopsis.*

King Mandarin *Citrus nobilis.*
King Monkey Cup *Nepenthes rajah.*
King-of-Siam *Citrus nobilis.*
King Orange *Citrus nobilis.*
King Palm *Archontophoenix.*
King Protea *Protea cynaroides.*
King's Crown *Justicia carnea.*
King's Gentian *Gentiana sceptrum.*
King's Mantle *Thunbergia erecta.*
King's Spear *Asphodeline lutea.*
King William Pine *Athrotaxis selaginoides.*
Kinnikinick *Arctostaphylos uva-ursi.*

Kinugasa Tatew. & Sûto. Liliaceae (Trilliaceae). 1 perenn. herb. Rhiz. short. St. 30–80cm. Lvs 20–30×3–8cm, obovate to elliptic, acuminate, whorled. Fls term., solitary; pedicel 3–8cm; sep. 3–5cm, lanceolate-ovate, 8–10, white, petaloid; pet. white, minute or 0. Fr. fleshy, dark purple. Jap. Z8.
K. japonica (Franch. & Savat.) Tatew. & Sûto.
→*Paris, Trillidium* and *Trillium.*

Kirin-giboshi *Hosta minor.*

Kirengeshoma Yatabe. Hydrangeaceae. 1 graceful perenn. herb to 120cm, erect to arching. Lvs 10–17cm, broadly ovate, palmatifid to unevenly incised, pale green. Fls slender-stalked in upper lf axils, to 3cm diam., campanulate, pet. 5, pale yellow to apricot, overlapping. Jap., Korea. Z5.
K. palmata Yatabe. As for the genus.

Kirkia Oliv. Simaroubaceae. 5 decid. trees or shrubs. Lvs imparipinnate. Infl. an axillary thyrse; fls small, 4-merous, green-cream. Fr. tetragonal. Trop. & S Afr. Z10.

K. acuminata Oliv. Tree to 20m; crown spreading. Lvs to 40cm, lfts to 7.5cm, lanceolate to ovate-lanceolate. Infl. less than half as long as lvs; pet. valvate. Trop. Afr.
K. wilmsii Engl. PEPPER TREE. Tree to 8m; crown round. Lvs to 22cm, lfts to 2cm, lanceolate. Infl. as long or longer than lvs; pet. imbricate. S Afr.

Kiss-me-over-the-garden-gate *Polygonum orientale.*

Kissodendron Seem. = *Polyscias.*

Kitaibela Willd. Malvaceae. 1 erect, hoary perenn. herb to 2.5m. Lvs to 18cm, rhombic to suborbicular-cordate, 5–7-lobed, coarsely toothed. Fls solitary or in axill. cymes; epical. seg. to 2cm, 6–9, exceeding sep.; pet. 2–2.5cm, 5, white or rose; sta. united in a tubular column. Balk. Z6.
K. vitifolia Willd.

Kitaibelia auct. = *Kitaibela.*

Kitchen-garden Purslane *Portulaca oleracea* var. *sativa.*

Kitchingia Bak.
K. gracilipes Bak. = *Kalanchoe gracilipes.*
K. peltata Bak. = *Kalanchoe peltata.*
K. schizophylla Bak. = *Kalanchoe schizophylla.*

Kitembilla *Dovyalis hebecarpa.*
Kite Tree *Nuxia floribunda.*
Ki Tong Tokang *Oroxylum.*
Kitten-tails *Besseya.*
Kitul Tree *Caryota urens.*
Kiwi Fruit *Actinidia deliciosa.*

Klattia Bak. Iridaceae. 2 shrubby herbs; st. leafy. Fls in dense, spathaceous term. clusters; perianth tube short, lobes 6, narrow; style unbranched. S Afr. Z9.
K. partita Bak. To 60cm. Lvs 10–18cm, linear. Perianth tube yellow-green, to 0.8cm, seg. dark blue, to 6cm. Cape Prov.

Kleberg Grass *Dichanthium annulatum.*

Kleinhovia L. Sterculiaceae. 1 everg. tree to 20m. Lvs 5–25cm, ovate-cordate, acuminate, entire or serrate, subglabrous beneath. Pan. to 50cm; cal. 0.6–1cm, red, lobes 5; pet. 6–7mm, 4, red; androgynophore 4–7mm. Fr. a capsule to 2.5cm, pyriform, inflated, 5-lobed. Trop. Asia to Aus. Z10.
K. hospita L.

Kleinia Mill. Compositae. c40 perenn. succulents. St. angled or terete, usually succulent. Lvs subulate, flat or terete, often succulent, usually entire and glab. Cap. usually discoid. Mostly trop. and S African also NW Afr., Canary Is., Madag., SW Arabia, S India and Sri Lanka. Z10 unless specified.
K. abyssinica (A. Rich.) A. Berger. Erect herb, to 2.7m. St. to 2.5cm diam., fleshy, terete, usually unbranched, stained purple, with distinct cuneate lf scars. Lvs to 26cm, spreading, fleshy, milky green, sometimes with purple markings, flat, elliptic to obovate, acute, usually entire, midrib prominent beneath. Cap. to 2cm diam., 1–10, nodding, becoming erect later, in term. branched corymbs; flts yellow in bud, pink to red on opening. C & E Afr. var. *hildebrandtii* (Vatke) C. Jeffrey. Erect herb, to 60cm. St. pale green-grey, stained purple. Lvs to 21cm, pale to dark green, midrib impressed, rarely prominent, tinged pink. Cap. to 1.5cm diam., solitary, or 2–9 in lax branched cymes, peduncle purple; flts red.
K. acaulis (L. f.) DC. = *Senecio acaulis.*
K. amaniensis (Engl.) A. Berger. Erect, woody, robust, glab. herb, to 1.4m. St. 2cm diam., branched or simple, somewhat fleshy, pale green with white mottling, shallowly furrowed. Lvs to 12.5cm, somewhat flattened, fleshy, obovate to oblanceolate, rounded, mucronate or notched, base decurrent, entire, purple, midrib impressed above, prominent beneath. Cap. to 3cm diam., nodding, 12–18, in a ± horizontally branched infl. peduncles purple, swollen beneath head; flts orange. Tanz.
K. anteuphorbium (L.) Haw. Erect, glab., shrubby, to 2.5m. St. to 2cm diam., with lax, elongated br., fleshy, terete, smooth, pale green or glaucous, with 3 dark lines running down st. from each lf base. Lvs to 4cm, flat, narrowly oblong to lanceolate, medially grooved, mucronate, entire. Cap. c2cm diam., solitary; peduncles to 6cm; flts green-white, fading to yellow-white or pink-white, smelling of marzipan. Moroc. Z9.
K. articulata (L. f.) Haw. = *Senecio articulatus.*
K. ficoides (L.) Haw. = *Senecio ficoides.*
K. fulgens Hook. f. Erect, subshrub, to 90cm, with adventitious roots. St. to 1cm diam., fleshy, glab., glaucous, often swollen

towards base, green with prominent lf scars when mature. Lvs to 15cm, often in a false rosette, flat, fleshy, lanceolate to oblong, often expanded towards apex, glaucous, often tinged purple beneath, grooved above, irregularly toothed or ± pinnatifid. Cap. to 3cm diam., solitary, in a few-headed cymose infl., peduncles long; flts bright red, crimson later. Trop. & S Afr.

K. galpinii Hook. f. Erect, subshrub, to 30cm. St. to 1cm diam., fleshy, terete, white-glaucous. Radical lvs to 8.4cm, fleshy, oblanceolate, flat, keeled beneath, acute, acuminate, st. lvs smaller, narrowly ovate. Cap. to 4cm diam., in a much-branched leafy infl.; flts light to dark orange, smelling of apricots. Transvaal. Z9.

K. gomphophylla Dinter = *Senecio herrianus*.

K. grandiflora (Wallich ex DC.) N. Rani. Erect herb or subshrub, to 30cm, rarely to 2.5m. St. to 2cm diam., simple or branched, pallid, fleshy, terete, swollen beneath, prominent lf bases. Lvs to 18cm, fleshy, flat, lanceolate-obovate to lanceolate, keeled beneath. Cap. to 2.5cm diam., in a 1–7-headed corymbose infl., peduncle to 15cm; flts creamy-white. India, Nepal, Sri Lanka.

K. grantii (Oliv. & Hiern) Hook. f. Erect or decumbent herb, to c40cm. St. 7–10mm diam., fleshy, terete, stained purple, smooth. Lvs rosulate at first, later crowded toward st. base, flat, fleshy, white-blue-green with a heavy bloom, purple-stained, to 15cm, spreading to reflexed, narrowly obovate, acute, mucronate, midrib impressed above. Cap. to 5cm diam., erect, in a ± scapose infl., peduncles purple-white-glaucous; flts red. Late spring–early summer. Trop. E Afr.

K. gregorii (S. Moore) C. Jeffrey. PEPPERMINT STICK. Erect or decumbent, fleshy, glab. herb, to 50cm. St. 7–13mm diam., simple or branched, terete, shallowly grooved, with about 3 dark lines running down from each lf base. Lvs to 6mm, fleshy. Cap. to 2.6cm diam., solitary, peduncle to 19cm, green-purple; flts red. Kenya, Tanz.

K. implexa (Bally) C. Jeffrey. Creeping succulent herb, to c8cm. St. prostrate, to 70cm long ×6mm diam., sparsely branched, pubesc. Lvs to 6.2cm, oblanceolate, to 4mm thick, v. succulent, minutely pubesc., acute, mucronate, entire, base attenuate into a petiole. Cap. to 3.3cm diam., solitary; peduncles to 30cm, erect, flts scarlet. Kenya, Tanz.

K. kleiniiformis (Süsseng.) Boom = *Senecio kleiniiformis*.

K. leptophylla C. Jeffrey. Erect or decumbent, fleshy, glab. herb, to c15cm. St. 1–1.5cm diam., simple or branched, ± segmented, seg. 1–15cm, green, terete, young st. with dark green lines descending from lf bases, older st. peeling. Lvs to 6cm, erect, occas. reflexed, fleshy, glossy green, decid., semi-terete, sometimes lanceolate-elliptic, often reflexed. Cap. to 2cm diam., solitary, peduncle to 29cm; flts crimson in bud, on opening tube white to pink, lobes magenta. Kenya, Ethiop., Saudi Arabia.

K. longiflora DC. Erect, fleshy, glab. shrub, to 1.8m. St. to 1cm diam., green-grey, often mottled purple, terete, becoming angular and segmented, seg. to 30cm, with dark lines descending from lf bases. Lvs to 8cm, erect, flat, fleshy, elliptic-oblong, midrib impressed above. Cap. to 2.7cm diam., in a 1–8-headed infl., peduncle to 2cm; flts yellow or white. S trop. and S Afr.

K. madagascarensis (Humbert) P. Halliday. Erect, ± spreading herb, to over 75cm, much-branched. St. to 2cm diam., green-grey, fleshy, spreading at an oblique angle, 11–22cm or more, with dark ribs from bases of lf scars. Lvs to 2cm, shiny green, flat, fleshy, lanceolate to oblong, acute, mucronate, revolute. Cap. to 2cm diam., solitary, peduncles usually 1, sometimes to 5 from the same st. apex; flts white-green. Madag.

K. mandraliscae Tineo = *Senecio mandraliscae*.

K. mweroensis (Bak.) C. Jeffrey. Erect or prostrate, fleshy, glab. herb, to 12cm, spreading to 90cm across. St. c2cm diam., segmented, irregularly terete, with prominent lf scars from which descend 5–7 dark lines. Lvs to 3.5cm, flat, fleshy, dark green, ovate-lanceolate to elliptic, acute, acuminate, entire, midrib prominent beneath; petiole persistent. Cap. to 3.5cm diam., in a 1–2-headed infl., peduncle to 25cm; flts red-orange. Tanz. and Zam.

K. neriifolia Haw. Erect, branched treelet, to 3m. St. to 3cm diam., fleshy, later producing ± woody transverse plates, terete, with 1–3 deep green lines extending down st. from circular lf scars. Lvs to 22cm, crowded at st. apex, flat, fleshy, glaucous, green, purple-stained beneath, linear to narrowly lanceolate, midrib keeled beneath. Cap. to 3cm diam., solitary, in paniculate corymbs, peduncle short; flts white, smelling acidic or of hyacinths. Canary Is. Z9.

K. odora (Forssk.) DC. Erect, much-branched, glab., shrub to 1m. St. to 1cm diam., blue-green at first, becoming green-white, purple above, lterete, segmented, with dark lines descending from lf bases. Lvs to 3.5cm, fleshy, glossy, obovate, obtuse, entire with 2, often red, veins. Cap. to 3cm diam., in a 5–7-headed corymbose infl., peduncles ± winged; flts white, yellowing later, sweet smelling. E & NE trop. Afr., Arabia.

K. pendula (Forssk.) DC. Prostrate or decumbent herb, to c20cm, forming tangled mats. St. rising, then descending to root on touching the ground forming jointed seg., often growing underground, seg. about 12×1–1.5cm, fleshy, terete or laterally compressed, grey-green or brown, spotted white, with 3–7 dark green or brown lines extending from lf scars. Lvs 9mm, cylindrical, linear, fleshy, ciliate. Cap. to 2cm diam., solitary, peduncles to 9cm, green with dark veins; flts bright red. NE trop. Afr., Yemen.

K. petraea (R.E. Fries) C. Jeffrey. Prostrate, glab. herb, spreading by stolons. St. to 8mm diam., fleshy, green to grey with purple mottling, branched, rooting at nodes, to 50cm. Lvs to 7cm, erect, fleshy, flat, obovate, keeled beneath, stained, purple, mucronate. Cap. to 2.5cm diam., nodding, in a 1–4-headed corymbose infl., peduncle to 30cm; flts bright orange-red. Trop. E Afr.

K. picticaulis C. Jeffrey. Erect, glab., rhizomatous herb, to 35cm. St. thickening upwards, to c2cm diam., shiny, green, stained red, usually unbranched, angular, lf scars obvious, 3–5 long straight lines decurrent from each. Lvs to 12cm, shiny, green, narrow, terete with a shallow depression. Cap. to 2.5cm diam., in 1–4-headed infl.; peduncle to 20cm; flts red. Kenya, Tanz., Sudan, Ethiop.

K. polytoma Chiov. Much-branched condensed shrub, to over 1m. St. to 1cm diam., fragile, fleshy, terete, almost fastigiate, covered with thick white wax, later green-blue, ± angular and spotted white, repeatedly 2–5-branched, segmented, seg. usually with 3 dark lines descending down st. from lf bases. Lvs to 2cm, fleshy, flattened, glab., usually narrowly oblanceolate, revolute. Cap. to 1.7cm, in a 4–15-headed, umbel-like infl., peduncle to 15mm, flts purple, red, yellow or white. Somalia.

K. pteroneura DC. = *K. anteuphorbium*.

K. radicans (L. f.) Haw. = *Senecio radicans*.

K. repens Haw. = *Senecio serpens*.

K. saginata P. Halliday. Glab. herb, to 20cm. St. to 4cm diam., green, marked white, segmented, spherical, lengthening later to 6cm, lf scars on low protuberances with 5–8 diverging dark lines. Lvs to 3cm, fleshy, narrowly lanceolate to oblanceolate, acute. Cap. to 2.6cm diam., solitary erect, peduncle to 30cm, lined purple, flts red. Oman.

K. scottii (Balf. f.) P. Halliday. Erect, fleshy, rigid, glab. herb, to 60cm or more. St. to 1.5cm diam., green-white, terete, br. ± umbellate, seg. to 6.2cm. Lvs to 5.3cm, flat, fleshy, white-green, narrowly lanceolate. Cap. to 1.8cm diam., erect, in a 1–4-headed infl., peduncle to 30cm; flts white-yellow or white-green. Socotra, Abd al Kuri.

K. spiculosa Sheph. = *Senecio spiculosus*.

K. squarrosa Cuf. Shrub, to c1m. Br. c5mm diam., woody inside, moderately succulent outside, in dry state bark shiny, contracted, longitudinally sulcate, remains of lvs persistent, somewhat cone-shaped, truncate, perpendicularly spreading. Lvs to 3cm, moderately thick, lanceolate or narrowly spathulate, glab. Cap. to 2.5cm diam., 1–3, congested at br. apices, peduncle c10mm, slender; flts pale violet-purple. E & NE trop. Afr.

K. stapeliiformis (E. Phillips) Stapf. Erect herb, 35cm. St. to 2cm diam., fleshy, glaucous, green with purple staining, simple or branching basally, young shoots at first growing underground, 20cm or more, obtuse or ± acutely angular, angles notched producing leaf-tipped teeth linked by several dark green lines running down from each lf base. Lvs c5mm, fastigiate, thread-like, green to purple, fleshy becoming thorny. Cap. to 4cm diam., solitary, peduncles to 8.5cm; flts red or red-orange. Transvaal. Z9.

K. subulifolia (Chiov.) P. Halliday. Erect to prostrately arching, fleshy herb, to 30cm, rooting at nodes. St. to 5mm diam., segmented, white-green at first, glossy green later, terete, sometimes compressed, with 6–7 dark lines radiating from lf bases. Lvs to 1.8cm, erect, spiny, lf scars circular. Cap. to 5cm diam., solitary, peduncle to 37cm, with dark green lines; flts red-orange. Somalia.

K. tomentosa (Haw.) Haw. = *Senecio haworthii*.

→*Cacalia, Crassocephalum, Gynura, Notonia, Notoniopsis* and *Senecio*.

Kleinkoraalboom *Erythrina humeana*.

Klopstockia Karst.
K. quindiuensis Karst. = *Ceroxylon quindiuense*.

Knapweed *Centaurea*.

Knautia L. Dipsacaceae. 60 herbs. Lvs paired, simple to pinnatifid. Fls in long-stalked, flat-topped heads subtended by leafy bracts; receptacle bristly; epical. cup-shaped, toothed; cal. cup-shaped, with 8–16 bristles or teeth; cor. lobes 4–5, (peripheral fls larger). Eur., Cauc., Sib., Medit. Z6.

K. arvensis (L.) Coult. BLUE BUTTONS. Perenn. to 1.5m. Lvs hirsute, entire to lyrate, pinnatifid higher up st. Fls pale purple-blue. Eur., Cauc., Medit., nat. E N Amer.

K. macedonica Griseb. Perenn. to 80cm. Lvs pubesc., lyrate at base of plant, entire or pinnatifid higher up st. Fls deep purple. C Eur.
→*Scabiosa*.

Knawel *Scleranthus*.
Knesheneka *Rubus arcticus*.
Knife-leaf Wattle *Acacia cultriformis*.

Knightia R. Br. Proteaceae. 3 trees or shrubs. Lvs leathery, entire or toothed. Rac. dense; perianth cylindrical, lobes spirally recurved; sta. 4; style long-exserted. New Caledonia, NZ.

K. excelsa R. Br. REWA REWA; NEW ZEALAND HONEYSUCKLE. Erect slender tree to 30m. Shoots angled downy. Lvs to 15cm, narrow, oblong, toothed, stiff. Fls to 3.5cm, red, in a bottlebrush-like rac. to 10cm. NZ. Z9.

Knight's Star Lily *Hippeastrum*.

Kniphofia Moench. Liliaceae (Aloeaceae). 68 perenn. herbs. Rhiz. short thick, forming clumps. Lvs strap-like. Fls tubular-cylindric in a spike-like, scapose rac. S Afr. unless stated. Z8.

K. aloöides Moench. = *K. uvaria*.

K. angustifolia (Bak.) Codd. Lvs grasslike. Infl. graceful, lax; fls 20–30mm, white to yellow, orange and coral. *K. rufa* Bak. may be a hybrid derived from this sp.

K. breviflora Bak. Dwarf. Lvs grasslike. Fls 7–11mm, yellow or white.

K. bruceae Codd. Robust. Infl. dense, cylindric; fls orange-red, 25–30mm.

K. burchellii (Herb. ex Lindl.) Kunth = *K. uvaria*.

K. carinata C.H. Wright = *K. pumila*.

K. caulescens Bak. ex Hook. f. Robust, forming short st. Lvs thick, glaucous, keeled. Infl. dense, oblong-cylindric; buds tinged red; fls creamy white, tinted peach, 22–24mm. Z7.

K. citrina Bak. Related to *K. uvaria* but smaller; infl. globose; fls ivory to yellow-green, 22–27mm.

K. composa Hochst. = *K. pumila*.

K. elegans Engl. = *K. schimperi*.

K. ensifolia Bak. Robust, to 2m. Infl. dense, cylindric; buds red to red-green; fls white, 15–20mm.

K. foliosa Hochst. Medium-sized. Infl. dense, cylindric; fls yellow, orange or red, 20–30mm. Ethiop.

K. galpinii Bak. Medium-sized. Lvs almost grasslike. Infl. small, dense, red at the apex shading to orange-yellow; fls 27–35mm. Distinguished from *K. triangularis* by the bicoloured infl., and fls with perianth lobes not flared. Z7.

K. galpinii hort. non Bak. = *K. triangularis*.

K. gracilis Harv. ex Bak. Medium-sized. Lvs narrow. Infl. fairly dense to v. lax; fls yellow to ivory, 12–18mm.

K. insignis Rendle. Medium-sized. Infl. fairly dense, with pink buds grading down to pink to white; fls 30–40mm. Ethiop. Z9.

K. isoetifolia Hochst. Medium-sized. Infl. fairly dense, globose; opening from the top downwards; fls 30–40mm, creamy white, yellow, pale salmon-orange or red. Ethiop. Z9.

K. kirkii Bak. Robust. Infl. dense, oblong; fls orange-pink, coral or red-orange, 35–42mm. Tanz. Z9.

K. laxiflora Kunth. Medium-sized. Infl. lax to medium-lax; fls 25–35mm, pale yellow or yellow-green to orange, salmon-pink, coral-red or orange-red.

K. leichtlinii Bak. = *K. pumila*.

K. linearifolia Bak. Robust; allied to *K. uvaria* but infl. larger, ovoid; fls 28–35mm, bright to dull red in bud, opening orange-yellow or green-yellow.

K. longicollis Bak. = *K. rooperi*.

K. macowanii Bak. = *K. triangularis*.

· **K. multiflora** J.M. Wood & M. Evans. Robust, to 2m in fl. Infl. elongated; buds often tinged red; fls 8–12mm, white to pale yellow.

K. natalensis Bak. = *K. laxiflora*.

K. nelsonii Mast. = *K. triangularis*.

K. northiae Bak. Robust, often forming a st. Lvs broad. Infl. dense, oblong; buds tinged red; fls creamy white to pale yellow, 22–30mm.

K. pallidiflora Bak. Small. Lvs narrow. Infl. small, lax; fls white, 9–12mm. Madag. Z9.

K. pauciflora Bak. Small. Lvs grasslike. Infl. small, lax; fls pale yellow, 14–18mm.

K. ×praecox Bak. (*K. uvaria* or *K. linearifolia* × *K. bruceae*.) RED-HOT POKER. Hybrids, typically with narrow midgreen lvs and tall spikes of crowded nodding fls in shades of flame red, orange and cream; progeny of *K. linearifolia* has oblong, rounded infl.

bracts; that of *K. bruceae* narrow, acuminate bracts. See **cvs** below. Summer–winter. Z7.

K. primulina Bak. Probably a yellow-cream-fld form of *K. ×praecox*.

K. pumila (Ait.) Kunth. Small to medium-sized. Infl. dense, oblong to cylindric; fls opening from the top downwards, somewhat funnel-shaped, yellow to orange, 12–18mm; sta. far-exserted.

K. quartiniana A. Rich. = *K. foliosa*.

K. rooperi (T. Moore) Lem. Robust; allied to *K. uvaria* but infl. large, globose; fls bright red to green-yellow, 35–42mm.

K. rufa Bak. See *K. angustifolia*.

K. sarmentosa (Andrews) Kunth. Medium-sized. Lvs glaucous. Infl. fairly dense, oblong; fls pink-red, 25–35mm.

K. schimpferi Bak. Medium-sized. Infl. lax, oblong; fls yellow, orange or red, 15–30mm. Ethiop. Z10.

K. sparsa N.E. Br. = *K. gracilis*.

K. splendida E.A. Bruce. Robust. Infl. cylindric; fls yellow-orange, 20–25mm.

K. triangularis Kunth. Small to medium-sized. Lvs narrow to grasslike. Infl. small, dense; fls coral-orange, 25–35mm; perianth lobes spreading. This sp. has probably contributed the coral colours found in some cultivated *Kniphofia* hybrids.

K. tuckii Bak. Closely resembles *K. ensifolia* but shorter, to 120cm, with red buds.

K. tysonii Bak. Robust, differs from *K. uvaria* in infl. cylindric; fls shorter (20–28mm); sta. well-exserted.

K. uvaria (L.) Oken. Medium-sized. Infl. oblong to ovoid, dense; fls brilliant red to green-yellow, 30–40mm. Z5.

K. woodii Wats. = *K. gracilis*.

K. cvs. Dwarf (50–90cm) or tall (100–180cm), fls white to yellow, orange and red, or bicoloured. 'Ada': dwarf; fls primrose. 'Alcazar': tall; fls bright orange-red. 'Amberlight': fls golden amber; spikes compact. 'Apple Court': fls cream tipped with coral pink; spikes large. 'Apricot': to 75cm; fls buff yellow; spikes slender. 'Atlanta': tall; fls sunset yellow, profuse, early. 'August Gold': fls golden yellow; spikes large. 'Bee's Orange': fls rich orange-yellow; spikes dense. 'Bee's Sunset': to 90cm; lvs narrow; fls soft orange. 'Bee's Yellow': fls chrome yellow; later flowering. 'Bressingham Comet': dwarf, to 50cm; fls orange tipped red. 'Bressingham Dwarf': fls deep flame orange. 'Bressingham Flame': to 75cm; fls deep orange. 'Bressingham Glow': to 50cm; fls v. bright orange; late flowering. 'Bressingham Torch': fls flame orange; flowering intermittently throughout season. 'Brimstone': dwarf; fls yellow from green bud; late flowering. 'Broncoleuter': to 60cm; fls clear bronze. 'Burnt Orange': to 75cm; brown tinge in bud opening to deep orange fls; spikes slender. 'Buttercup': fls clear yellow; early flowering. 'Canary Bird': dwarf; fls yellow. 'Candlelight': to 50cm; lvs long and narrow; fls clear yellow; spikes slender. 'Cardinal': to 80cm; fls red. 'Comet': fls cream turning soft orange-red at apex. 'Cool Lemon': dwarf, to 60cm. 'Corallina': to 65cm; fls orange-brown. 'Dr E.M. Mills': to 120cm; fls red. 'Earliest of All': fls coral red; spikes long. 'Early Buttercup': fls bright yellow; spikes large; early flowering. 'Erecta': fls bright coral red; spike inverted. 'Enchantress': dwarf; fls coral and red, bicoloured. 'Evered': to 70cm; fls red; v. long-flowering. 'Express': fls dull green-yellow tipped red; spikes triangular. 'Fiery Fred': to 120cm; fls orange-red. 'Fireflame': dwarf; fls burning red. 'Firefly': fls orange-red. 'Fireking': fls orange-red; late-flowering. 'Fyrwerkeri': to 80cm; fls orange-red. 'Green Jade': to 120cm, hardy; fls bright green; late flowering. 'Gold Else': to 75cm; fls yellow; spikes slender; early flowering. 'Goldfinch': to 90cm; fls amber-yellow. 'Ice Queen': fls cream tinged green; spikes tall. 'Indian': fls dull brown-red. 'Jenny Brown': to 90cm; fls peach and cream blotched pink. 'John Benary': to 150cm; spikes loose, fls deep scarlet. 'Lemon Ice': to 90cm; buds lemon opening to near white. 'Little Elf': to 75cm; lvs long and narrow; fls flame orange. 'Little Maid': dwarf; spikes ivory tipped soft yellow. 'Lye End': spikes long, fls light pink-scarlet. 'Maid of Orleans': dwarf; fls pastel ivory, abundant. 'Modesta': dwarf, to 60cm; fls cream and coral. 'Nobilis': tall; fls deep orange. 'Percy's Pride': to 90cm; fls green-yellow. 'Pfitzeri': fls scarlet tinged carmine; spikes large. 'Prince Igor': tall; fls bright cherry. 'Redstart': to 90cm; fls clear orange; flowering throughout season. 'Royal Standard': fls bright yellow and vermilion. 'Safrangvogel': fls salmon pink. 'Samuel's Sensation': to 150cm; fls carmine shading to yellow at base; spikes v. long; somewhat later flowering. 'Scarlet Cap': to 90cm; fls scarlet and yellow. 'Shining Sceptre': to 120cm; fls bright yellow to off-white. 'Slim Coral Red': to 75cm; buds shaded darker; spikes compact, narrow. 'Snow Maiden': dwarf: fls flushed rose. 'Spanish Gold': tall; fls rich mustard. 'Springtime': to 100cm, robust; fls buff yellow and coral red. Stark's Hybrids: fls red and yellow. 'Sunningdale Yellow': dwarf; fls yellow, long-lasting. 'Torchbearer': dwarf; fls cream-primrose. 'Tubergeniana': dwarf; fls soft primrose.

'White Fairy': dwarf; fls white, abundant. 'Wrexham Butter-cup': tall; fls clear lemon. Z7.

Knobby Hibiscus *Radyera farragei.*
Knobcone Pine *Pinus attenuata.*
Knobkerry *Lagenaria siceraria.*
Knotroot *Stachys affinis.*
Knotted Geranium *Pelargonium gibbosum.*
Knotted Marjoram *Origanum majorana.*
Knotweed *Polygonum.*
Koa *Acacia koa.*
Koba-giboshi *Hosta sieboldii.*
Kochang Lily *Lilium distichum.*

Kochia Roth.
K. scoparia (L.) Schräd. = *Bassia scoparia.*

Kodo Wood *Ehretia acuminata.*

Koeleria L. Gramineae. 25 ann. and perenn. grasses. St. flimsy, erect. Lf blades narrow. Pan. cylindric, v. dense, spike-like, to 10cm; spikelets compressed, 2–8-fld. Temp. regions, Trop. Afr.
K. argentea Griseb. Perenn. Lf sheaths scarious, shiny, silvery. Spikelets 5mm; awns to 2mm. Himal. Z6.
K. brevis Steven = *K. lobata.*
K. cristata (L.) Pers. = *K. macrantha* or *K. pyramidata.*
K. degenii Domin = *K. lobata.*
K. generensis Domin = *K. pyramidata.*
K. glauca Coleman ex Willk. & Lange. Perenn. to 60cm. St. thickened at base. Lf blades v. glaucous. Pan. to 10cm, spikelets to 5mm. Summer. C Eur., Sib. Z4.
K. gracilis Pers. = *K. macrantha.*
K. lobata (Bieb.) Roem. & Schult. Perenn. To 35cm, forming compact tufts. St. enlarged at base. Lvs to 5cm, glaucous. Pan. dense, to 2.5cm; spikelets to 7mm. SE Eur. Z5.
K. macrantha (Ledeb.) Schult. CRESTED HAIR GRASS. Perenn. 10–50cm. St. in compact clumps. Lf blades to 20cm, grey-green. Pan. to 10×2cm, narrow-oblong, interrupted, tinged grey or purple; spikelets to 5mm. Summer. Eur., Asia, N Amer. Z2.
K. phleoides (Vill.) Pers. = *Rostraria cristata.*
K. pyramidata (Lam.) Beauv. Perenn. to 90cm, loosely tufted. Lvs to 23cm, green or glaucescent, glab. or white-pubesc. at margins. Pan. pyramidal to 22×3cm, spikelets to 8mm. EC Eur. Z2.
K. vallesiana (Honck.) Bertol. Perenn., densely tufted. St. stiff, erect. W Eur.

Koellensteinia Rchb. f. Orchidaceae. 10 terrestrial or epiphytic orchids. St. short, usually pseudobulbous, 1–3-lvd. Lvs linear to elliptic-oblong, plicate. Rac. or a pan., lat.; fls small; tep. free, oblong to ovate; lip trilobed. S Amer. Z10.
K. brachystalix (Rchb. f.) Schltr. = *Otostylis brachystalix.*
K. graminea (Lindl.) Rchb. f. Pbs ± 0. Lvs to 26cm, linear to linear-lanceolate. Infl. to 25cm; fls 1–several, to 2cm diam., white, cream or pale yellow, veined magenta, sometimes tinged green. Spring. Colomb., Venez., Braz., Guianas, Trin.
K. hyacinthoides Schltr. Pbs to 10cm, cylindrical. Lvs to 35cm, lanceolate to oblong-lanceolate. Infl. to 30cm; fls many, to 3cm diam., light yellow or yellow-green. Venez., Braz.
K. ionoptera Lind. & Rchb. f. Pbs to 5cm, narrowly ovoid. Lvs to 25cm, elliptic-lanceolate. Fls to 2.5cm diam., several, yellow-white, marked or suffused violet; lip white to yellow streaked red-violet. Peru, Ecuad.
K. kellneriana Rchb. f. Pbs to 3cm, subterete. Lvs to 70cm, linear-lanceolate. Infl. to 45cm; fls few to many, to 2cm diam., fragrant, pale green, lip white marked maroon-pink. Mostly spring–early summer. Panama, Colomb., Venez., Braz., Guyana.
K. tricolor (Lindl.) Rchb. f. Differs from *K. kellneriana* in smaller lvs. Fls to 1.5cm diam., green-white, lip white banded pale purple. Spring. Braz., Guianas.
→*Aganisia* and *Zygopetalum.*

Koellikeria Reg. Gesneriaceae. 3 perenn. herbs. Rhiz. scaly. Lvs soft, downy. Infl. racemose; fls small; cal. lobes 5, narrow; cor. tubular, 5-lobed, bilabiate, lower lip dentate or fimbriate. Costa Rica to Boliv. Z10.
K. argyrostigma (Hook.) Reg. St. to 30cm. Lvs to 6.5cm, clustered at st. apex, obovate to elliptic, crenate, velvety green with white spots, pilose. Cor. 0.5cm, white or cream with red spots and purple throat. Costa Rica to Peru.
K. erinoides (DC.) Mansf. Low-growing. Lvs to 10cm, rosulate, ovate to obovate, dentate, velvety green with white spots, flushed red, hairy. Cor. 1cm, tube red above, white below, upper lip garnet, lower lip cream, ciliate, throat spotted yellow. Venez.

×**Koellikohleria** Wiehler (*Koellikeria* ×*Kohleria.*) Gesneria-ceae. 1 pilose herb to 30cm. Rhiz. scaly. Lvs 10cm, ovate to obovate, crenate, unspotted, often tinted red beneath. Infl. slender, 11cm; cal. tube pale green, lobes 4mm, bronzy green; cor. 14mm, tube red and white with purple hairs, white within, limb magenta, lower lip striped white. Z10.
×*K. rosea* Wiehler (*Koellikeria erinoides* × *Kohleria spicata.*)

Koelreuteria Laxm. GOLDEN RAIN TREE; SHRIMP TREE; CHINESE RAIN TREE. Sapindaceae. 3 spreading, decid. shrubs or trees. Lvs 1–2×pinnate, pinnae serrate. Pan. large, term.; cal. 5-lobed; pet. 4–5; sta. 5–8; style trifid. Capsule bladder-like, in-flated. China, Taiwan.
K. bipinnata Franch. Tree to 5m. Lvs to 50cm, bipinnate, pinnae 7–12, lfts 5–7cm, oval-oblong, finely serrate to entire. Fls yellow, with a red spot at base of pet. Fr. to 5cm, ellipsoid, ripening red, splitting into 3 ovate seg. Summer. SW China. Z8.
K. chinensis Hoffsgg. = *K. bipinnata.*
K. elegans (Seem.) A.C. Sm. FLAMEGOLD; CHINESE RAIN TREE. Tree to 18m. Lvs to 45cm, bipinnate, pinnae 9–16, lfts to 11cm, narrowly ovate, entire to serrate. Fls yellow. Fr. 3cm, splitting into 3 rose-coloured, ovate, papery seg. Summer–autumn. Taiwan, Fiji. Z9.
K. formosana Hayata = *K. elegans.*
K. henryi Dümmer = *K. elegans.*
K. integrifolia Merrill = *K. bipinnata.*
K. paniculata Laxm. PRIDE OF INDIA; VARNISH TREE; GOLDEN RAIN TREE. Tree to 15m. Lvs to 35cm, 1(–2)×pinnate, pinnae 7–15, 3–8cm, ovate-oblong, crenate-serrate, emerging pink-red, fall-ing bright yellow. Fls yellow. Fr. to 5cm, oblong-ovoid, splitting into 3 brown, papery seg. Summer. N China, Korea. 'Fastigiata': columnar in habit; 'September Gold': fls in late summer. var. *apiculata* (Rehd. & Wils.) Rehd. Lvs bipinnate. Fls light yellow. Z6.
K. paullinoides L'Hérit. = *K. bipinnata.*
K. vitiensis A.C. Sm. = *K. elegans.*

Kogarashi-giboshi *Hosta tortifrons.*
Koghis Kauri *Agathis lanceolata.*

Kohleria Reg. Gesneriaceae. 50 hirsute herbs and shrubs. Lvs serrate or crenate, thick, hirsute or velvety. Fls with sep. erect, thick, pubesc.; cor. tubular, ventricose, usually scarlet, red-hirsute, limb narrow. Trop. Amer. Z10.
K. allenii Standl. & L.O. Williams. To 1.5m; st. ascending, woody. Lvs 7cm, lanceolate to ovate, minutely serrate, pilose. Infl. many-fld; cor. tube gibbous, 27mm, lobes pale yellow, with dark red blotches. Costa Rica.
K. amabilis (Planch. & Lind.) Fritsch. 30–60cm erect, white-hairy. Lvs to 10cm, ovate, crenate, sometimes with silver mark-ings, often flushed red. Fls pendulous; cor. tube to 2.5cm, deep rose with brick-red bars and stripes, lobes rose with maroon bars and spots. Colomb.
K. bella C. Morton. St. to 40cm, pale red-hairy. Lvs to 9cm, ovate to ovate-elliptic, crenate-serrate. Infl. umbellate; cor. tube 4cm, tinged yellow below, red elsewhere, lobes 3mm, yellow with purple spots. Costa Rica.
K. bogotensis (Nichols.) Fritsch. Erect, to 60cm; st. somewhat hirsute. Lvs to 7.5cm, ovate, dentate with pale green or white markings above, densely hairy. Fls solitary or in pairs; cor. tube 2.5cm, red fading to yellow at base, yellow with red spots below, lower lobes 6mm, yellow with red spots, upper lobes smaller, red. Autumn to early winter. Colomb.
K. digitaliflora (Lind. & André) Fritsch. Erect, st. white-hairy. Lvs to 20cm, elliptic-lanceolate to ovate, crenate. Fls few to several; cor. tube to 3cm, white flushed deep rose above, densely lanate, lobes 6mm, green with purple spots. Colomb.
K. eriantha (Benth.) Hanst. Shrub to 120cm; st. densely hairy. Lvs to 12cm, ovate to ovate-lanceolate, crenate, margins red-hairy. Fls solitary or 3–4; cor. tube to 5cm, orange-scarlet to cinnabar-red, lobes 6mm, lower 3 with yellow spots. Colomb.
K. ×gigantea (Planch.) Fritsch. (*K. bogotensis* ×*K. warscewiczii.*) To 1m. Lvs to 7.5cm, ovate, dentate, dark green with pale or white markings. Fls 9–12; cor. tube 3cm, red fading to yellow at base, yellow with red spots below, lower lobes 6mm, yellow with red spots, upper lobes smaller, red.
K. hirsuta (HBK) Reg. Suffruticose, to 1m, densely hairy. Lvs to 15cm, ovate-oblong, dentate. Fls solitary or several; cor. tube 3cm, orange-scarlet without, orange-yellow within, pilose, lobes 3mm, yellow with central red crescent. Trin., Guyana to Colomb.
K. hirsuta hort. non (HBK) Reg. = *K. eriantha.*
K. ocellata (Hook.) Fritsch. Suffruticose, to 60cm, purple-pubesc. Lvs to 12cm, elliptic-ovate, dentate, flushed purple beneath, rugose. Fls 1 or few, pendulous; cor. tube 2cm, bright red, lobes spreading, upper 2 smaller, red with black spots, lower 3 red

marked purple-black and white or pale yellow. Panama to Colomb.

K. picta hort. non (Hook.) Hemsl. = *K. bogotensis*.

K. seemannii (Hook.) Hanst. To 60cm, villous; st. usually simple, rather stout. Lvs broadly ovate, serrate. Infl. racemose; cor. tube cylindric, orange at base, then bright brick-red, villous, lobes brick-red with deep red spots, gland.-hairy. Autumn. Panama.

K. spicata (HBK) Ørst. To 1.5m; st. simple, red-hirsute. Lvs to 15cm, elliptic or elliptic-lanceolate, crenate-serrate, red-tomentose beneath. Fls solitary or in pseudo-rac.; cor. tube 2cm, orange-scarlet, upper 2 lobes evenly coloured, lower 3 orange-scarlet with paler spots. Mex. to N S Amer.

K. warscewiczii Hanst. To 1m, villous. Lvs ovate, crenate. Infl. umbellate; cor. tube yellow at base, scarlet above, hirsute, lobes yellow to green, with red or brown spots. Colomb.

→*Gesneria* and *Isoloma*.

Kohlrabi *Brassica oleracea* Gongylodes group.

Kohlrauschia Knuth.
K. saxifraga (L.) Dandy = *Petrorhagia saxifraga*.

Kohuhu *Pittosporum tenuifolium*.

Kokia Lewton. Malvaceae. 4 decid. trees to 10m. Lvs palmately 5-, 7- or 9-lobed, glabrate above, pubesc. beneath. Fls showy, solitary, axill., near ends of br.; pedicels with bract at joint; epical. exceeding cal., seg. 3–5, foliaceous; cal. lobes 2–5, caducous; pet. yellow-pubesc., twisted at base; staminal column exserted, 5-toothed at top. Hawaii. Z10.

K. cookei Deg. Tree to lvs 5–13cm, 5- or 7-lobed. Pedicels 3–8cm; epical. seg. 2.5–3.5cm, broadly ovate; pet. to 8cm, orange-red; staminal column 6.5cm.

K. drynarioides (Seem.) Lewton. KOKIO. Tree to 8m. Lvs 8–20cm, 7- or 9-lobed. Pedicels 5–10cm; epical. seg. 4–7cm, broadly ovate to suborbicular; pet. to 11cm, scarlet-red; staminal column to 11cm.

K. rockii Lewton = *K. drynarioides*.

Kokio *Kokia drynarioides*.
Kokomura Taranga *Hebe parviflora*.

Kolkwitzia Gräbn. BEAUTY BUSH. Caprifoliaceae. 1 decid. shrub to 3.5m, bark ultimately exfoliating; young branchlets pubesc. Lvs 3–7.5cm, broad-ovate, sparsely pubesc. above. Fls paired, in term. corymbs; cal. persistent, seg. 5–6, slender, densely villous to setose; cor. to 1.6cm, tubular-campanulate, 5-lobed, white stained rose-pink outside, throat marked deep yellow to orange. Spring–summer. C China. Z4.

K. amabilis Gräbn. 'Pink Cloud': fls clear pink, numerous. 'Rosea': fls strongly flushed damask pink.

Kolpakowskia Reg.
K. ixiolirioides Reg. = *Ixiolirion kolpakowskianum*.

Komarov's Bugbane *Cimicifuga heracleifolia*.
Komeba-tsugazakura *Arcterica nana*.
Kooboo Berry *Cassine sphaerophylla*.

Kopsia Bl. Apocynaceae. 25 trees and shrubs with milky sap. Lvs oval-lanceolate, entire. Fls in short cymes; cor. salverform, tube long, slender, throat hairy, limb 5-lobed, flaring. SE Asia. Z10.

K. arborea Bl. Tree to 10m. Lvs to 18cm, yellow-green above. Fls to 3cm diam., white, sweetly scented. Indon.

K. flavida Bl. SHRUB VINCA; PENANG SLOE. Shrub or tree to 12m. Lvs to 9–22cm, glossy white, colouring deep red. Fls to 5cm diam. white, yellow in throat. New Guinea.

K. fruticosa (Ker-Gawl.) A. DC. SHRUB VINCA. Shrub to 6m. Lvs 10–20cm, glossy above. Fls to 5cm diam., palest pink with a crimson throat. Late spring. Malay Penins.

Koraalboom *Erythrina caffra*.
Korean Fir *Abies koreana*.
Korean Forsythia *Forsythia ovata*.
Korean Grass *Zoysia japonica*.
Korean Hornbeam *Carpinus eximia*.
Korean Lawn Grass *Zoysia japonica*.
Korean Maple *Acer pseudosieboldianum*.
Korean Mountain Ash *Sorbus alnifolia*.
Korean Pine *Pinus koraiensis*.
Korean Thuja *Thuja koraiensis*.
Korean Velvet Grass *Zoysia tenuifolia*.

Korolkowia Reg.
K. sewerzovii (Reg.) Reg. = *Fritillaria sewerzowii*.

Kosteletzkya Presl. SEASHORE MALLOW; FEN ROSE. Malvaceae. 30 perenn. herbs and subshrubs. Lvs simple or palmately lobed, often hastate. Fls solitary or in term. rac. or pan.; epical. seg. 5–12; cal. seg. 5; pet. 5; staminal column entire or 5-toothed. N Amer., Mex., Trop. & S Afr., Madag. Z10.

K. hastata Presl = *K. pentasperma*.

K. pentacarpos (L.) Ledeb. Perenn. herb to 2m. Lvs triangular-ovate to cordate, simple or 3- or 5-lobed. Fls solitary or in cymes; pet. 2–2.5cm, lilac-pink. E Spain, Balearic Is., It., SE Russia.

K. pentasperma (Bertero ex DC.) Griseb. Perenn. herb or subshrub to 3m. Lower lvs 3-, 5- or 7-lobed, upper lvs often hastate. Fls in pan.; pet. 1.2–1.8cm, white, yellow or purple. W Indies, Mex., N S Amer.

K. virginica (L.) Presl ex A. Gray. SALT MARSH MALLOW. Perenn. herb or subshrub to 1.2m. Lvs 5–15cm, 3- or 5-lobed, dentate or crenate-serrate, upper lvs triangular-hastate. Fls solitary or in pan.; pet. 3–4cm, spreading, pink, villous-hirsute. E US.

Kou-chiku *Phyllostachys sulphurea* var. *viridis*.
Kousa *Cornus kousa*.
Kowhai *Sophora tetraptera*.

Kraenzlinella Kuntze = *Pleurothallis*.

Krainzia Backeb.
K. guelzowiana (Werderm.) Backeb. = *Mammillaria guelzowiana*.
K. longiflora (Britt. & Rose) Backeb. = *Mammillaria longiflora*.

Krigia Schreb. DWARF DANDELION. Compositae. 7 ann. or perenn. herbs with milky sap. Lvs in a basal rosette, or cauline and alt. or nearly opposite. Cap. solitary, ligulate, pedunculate; flts yellow or orange. N Amer.

K. biflora (Walter) S.F. Blake. Perenn., to 60cm. St. branched. Lvs mostly basal, to 26cm, lanceolate to elliptic or oblanceolate, entire, dentate or runcinnately or lyrately pinnatifid, subsessile. Flts orange, to 15mm. Spring–summer. S & E US. Z4.

K. bulbosa hort. = *K. dandelion*.

K. dandelion (L.) Nutt. Perenn., to 50cm. St. simple. Lvs basal early lvs to 6×2cm, elliptic to oblanceolate, obtuse, entire or denticulate, subsessile or with petiole to 6cm, later lvs longer, narrower, acute, entire to remotely laciniately pinnatifid, with a winged petiole. Flts pale beneath to yellow-orange, sometimes tinged purple, to 17mm. Spring. C & SE US. Z5.

K. montana (Michx.) Nutt. Perenn., to 40cm. St., branched, becoming bushy. Lvs mostly basal, to 16cm, oblong-lanceolate to linear-lanceolate, entire, denticulate to irregularly runcinately pinnatifid, base clasping. Flts yellow, to 18mm. Spring–autumn. SE US. Z5.

K. virginica (L.) Willd. Ann. Lvs in a basal rosette, to 7cm, cuneate-oblong, spathulate, oblong or oblanceolate, broadly acute, remotely denticulate to pinnatifid, petiole to 3cm. Flts yellow, to 7mm. Spring–autumn. E & SE US.

Krishna Fig *Ficus benghalensis* 'Krishnae'.
Krishna's Cup *Ficus benghalensis* 'Krishnae'.
Kris Plant *Alocasia sanderiana*.
Ku-chiku *Phyllostachys bambusoides*.
Kudu Lily *Adenium*.
Kudzu Vine *Pueraria lobata*.
Kukumakranka *Gethyllis*.
Kuma Zasa *Sasa veitchii*.
Kumquat *Fortunella*.

Kunzea Rchb. f. Myrtaceae. 25 everg. shrubs, and small trees. Lvs small, entire. Fls sessile, in term. heads; cal. lobes 5; pet. 5, small, orbicular; sta. many, exceeding pet. Aus. Z9.

K. affinis S. Moore. Slender shrub, to 2×1m. Lvs small and heath-like. Fls fluffy and pink. W Aus.

K. ambigua (Sm.) Druce. Shrub to 2.5×1.5m. Lvs fine and heath-like. Fls white, fluffy. NSW, Vict., Tasm.

K. baxteri (Klotz) Schauer. Erect shrub, to 3×3m. Lvs *c*2cm, narrow, radiating from the st. Fls scarlet-red, resembling a bottle-brush. W Aus.

K. capitata Rchb. f. Erect, rounded shrub, to 1.5×1.5m. Lvs *c*5mm, narrowly obovate. Fls deep pink, in small, knobby heads. NSW, Queensld.

K. ericifolia Rchb. f. Prostrate shrub, to 0.3×1.5m. Lvs grey-green and heath-like. Fls brush-like and yellow. W Aus.

K. micrantha Schauer. Shrub to 3.5m. Lvs to 1cm, rigid, linear or linear-cuneate. Fls blue or purple, in dense globular heads. W Aus.

K. *parvifolia* Schauer. Mat-forming shrub, to 0.3×3m. Lvs c0.4cm, broad, recurved. Fls pink-mauve, in small term. heads. NSW, Vict.

K. *peduncularis* F. Muell. Shrub or tree, 5–7m. Lvs 1–1.5cm, linear to oblanceolate. Fls white or pink, solitary or in twos or threes, forming leafy cylindrical spikes. Vict.

K. *pomifera* F. Muell. MUNTRIES. Mat-forming shrub to 0.3×2m. Lvs 0.5cm, oval or orbicular, stiff and smooth. Fls 0.5cm, white and feathery, in dense heads. Fr. purple, edible. Vict.

K. *recurva* Schauer. Erect shrub to 2.5×1.5m. Lvs bright green, recurved, c6mm. Fls bright yellow, in globular heads. W Aus.

K. *sericea* (Labill.) Turcz. Erect shrub to 2.5×1.5m. Lvs c1cm, grey-green, with rounded ends. Fls red, in short, bottlebrush-like heads. W Aus.

Kurakkan *Eleusine coracana.*
Kurchi *Holarrhena pubescens.*
Kurile Cherry *Prunus nipponica* var. *kurilensis.*
Kurile Larch *Larix gmelinii* var. *japonica.*

Kurobana-giboshi *Hosta atropurpurea.*
Kuro-chiku *Phyllostachys nigra.*
Kuro-giboshi *Hosta nigrescens.*
Kuronami-giboshi *Hosta fluctuans.*
Kurrajong *Brachychiton populneus.*
Kurrat *Allium ampeloprasum.*
Kusamaki *Podocarpus macrophyllus.*
Kweek *Cynodon dactylon.*
Kybean Gum *Eucalyptus parvifolia.*

Kydia Roxb. Malvaceae (Bombacaceae). 1 everg. shrub or tree to 15m. Lvs to 15cm, suborbicular to cordate, shallowly lobed. Fls unisexual in pan., or solitary; epical. with 4–6 seg.; pet. 1–1.2cm, white or pink, fringed; ♂ fls with short staminal column; ♀ fls with 3-branched style, exceeding sterile staminal column. Sikkim to SE Asia. Z9.

K. *calycina* Roxb.

Kyo-chiku *Dendrocalamus giganteus.*

L

LABIATAE Juss. 221/5600. *Acinos, Adenandra, Agastache, Ajuga, Amethysteya, Ballota, Calamintha, Cedronella, Clinopodium, Colebrookea, Collinsonia, Colquhounia, Conradina, Cunila, Dracocephalum, Elsholtzia, Eremostachys, Galeopsis, Glechoma, Horminum, Hyssopus, Lallemantia, Lamium, Lavandula, Leonotis, Leonurus, Lepechinia, Lycopus, Macbridea, Marrubium, Meehania, Melissa, Melittis, Mentha, Micromeria, Moluccella, Monarda, Monardella, Nepeta, Ocimum, Origanum, Perilla, Perovskia, Phlomis, Physostegia, Plectranthus, Prostanthera, Prunella, Pycnanthemum, Pycnostachys, Rosmarinus, Salazaria, Salvia, Satureja, Scutellaria, Sideritis, Solenostemon, Stachys, Tetradenia, Teucrium, Thymbra, Thymus, Tinnea, Trichostema, Westringia.*

Lablab Adans. Leguminosae (Papilionoideae). 1 twining perenn. herb, to 6m. Lvs trifoliolate, lfts to 15cm, ovate to rhombic. Infl. to 40cm, axill., erect; fls fragrant, in clusters of 5, white or purple; standard to 15mmm, reflexed, notched, wings obovate; sta. 10. Fr. to 15×5cm, oblique-oblong, maroon. Trop. Afr., widely cult. in India, SE Asia, Egypt, Sudan. Z9.

L. niger hort. = *L. purpureus.*

L. purpureus (L.) Sweet. DOLICHOS BEAN; HYACINTH BEAN; BONAVIST; LUBIA BEAN; SEIM BEAN; INDIAN BEAN; EGYPTIAN BEAN. 'Giganteus': fls large, white.
→*Dolichos.*

Labrador Tea *Ledum groenlandicum.*
Labrador Violet *Viola labradorica.*

+Laburnocytisus C. Schneid. Leguminosae (Papilionoideae). A graft hybrid between *Laburnum anagyroides* and *Chamaecytisus purpureus*. Tree to 7.5m. As for *L. anagyroides* in overall habit, rac. smaller, fls smaller, yellow tinged purple, appearing fleshy pink or pale bronze; sporadic outgrowths of either parent occur where chimaera breaks down. Spring. Gdn origin. Z5.
+L. adamii (Poit.) C. Schneid.
→*Cytisus* and *Laburnum.*

Laburnum Medik. BEAN TREE. Leguminosae (Papilionoideae). 2 decid. shrubs or trees to 7m, bark smooth, green to grey. Lvs trifoliolate; lfts to 8cm, elliptic-obovate. Rac. pendent, simple; cal. campanulate, 5-toothed; standard rounded to obovate, keel convex, wings obovate. SC & SE Eur., W Asia.

L. adamii Kirchn. = +*Laburnocytisus adamii.*

L. alpinum (Mill.) Bercht. & Presl. SCOTCH LABURNUM; ALPINE GOLDEN CHAIN. Twigs glab., green. Lfts pale green beneath. Infl. to 35cm+, denser than in *L. anagyroides*; pedicels equalling fls; cor. 1.5cm+, bright yellow. Early summer. SC Eur. 'Pendulum': slow-growing, crown low-domed, br. weeping. 'Pyramidale': br. erect. Z5.

L. alschingeri K. Koch = *L. anagyroides.*

L. anagyroides Medik. COMMON LABURNUM; GOLDEN CHAIN. Twigs grey-green, weakly pubesc. Lfts short-pubesc. beneath when young. Infl. to 20cm, pubesc.; pedicels shorter than fls; cor. 2cm, lemon to golden yellow. Late spring. C & S Eur. 'Pendulum': br. pendent. 'Aureum': lvs pale yellow to lime green. 'Autumnale' ('Semperflorens'): second flush of fls produced in autumn. 'Erect': br. stiffly erect. 'Quercifolium': lfts deeply lobed. Z5.

L. anagyroides var. *pendulum* (Bosse) Rehd. = *L. anagyroides* 'Pendulum'.

L. caramanicum Benth. & Hook. f. = *Podocytisus caramanicus.*

L. purpurascens hort. ex Vilm. = +*Laburnocytisus adamii.*

L. × vossii hort. = *L. × watereri* 'Vossii'.

L. vulgare Presl = *L. anagyroides.*

L. × watereri (Kirchn.) Dipp. (*L. alpinum × L. anagyroides.*) Closer to *L. anagyroides*, but only shoot apices pubesc. Lfts pubesc. on veins beneath. Rac. to 50cm, fragrant. Tyrol, S Switz. 'Parkesii': habit as for *L. alpinum*; shoots glab.; lfts sparsely pubesc. beneath; rac. to 30cm; standard with brown lines at base. 'Alford's Weeping': crown widely spreading, weeping. 'Vossii': exceptionally floriferous with long rac. Z6.

Laccopetalum Ulbr. Ranunculaceae. 1 large perenn. herb. Lvs to 0.75m, fleshy, dark green or silvered, obovate, toothed or lobed, long-stalked, rosulate. Scape to 1.75m; infl. loosely

paniculate; fls to 10cm diam.; sep. fleshy, petaloid, grey-green; staminodes petaloid, yellow-orange. Peru. Z8.

L. giganteum (Wedd.) Ulbr. GIANT BUTTERCUP.

Laccospadix Drude & H.A. Wendl. ATHERTON PALM. Palmae. 1 unarmed palm to 6m. St. solitary or clustered, ringed. Lvs pinnate, arching to 2m; petiole to 1m, sparsely scaly; pinnae single-fold. Fls in sunken triads on simple spikes exceeding 1m. Fr. to 1.5cm, yellow, red when ripe. NE Queensld. Z10.

L. australasica H.A. Wendl. & Drude.

Lace Aloe *Aloe aristata.*
Lace Aralia *Polyscias guilfoylei.*
Lacebark *Hoheria*; *Ulmus parvifolia.*
Lacebark Pine *Pinus bungeana.*
Lace Cactus *Mammillaria elongata.*
Lace Fern *Paesia scaberula.*
Lace-flower Vine *Alsobia dianthiflora.*
Lace Leaf *Aponogeton madagascariensis.*
Lacepod *Thysanocarpus.*

Lachenalia Jacq. f. ex Murray. Liliaceae (Hyacinthaceae). 90 bulbous perenn. herbs. Lvs basal, highly varied in shape number and colour. Fls zygomorphic, tubular or campanulate in a scapose spike or rac.; perianth seg. free, 6, in 2 whorls, outer whorl forming a fleshy tube or cup, often with swollen tips, inner whorl protruding, usually broader and more showy; sta. 6; ovary superior. S Afr., Nam.; all spp. described are from the SE Cape unless otherwise specified. Z9.

L. aloides (L.f.) Engl. Lvs 2, lorate-lanceolate, glossy or glaucous, blotched green or purple above. Rac. to 28cm, scape often mottled and tinted red-brown; fls pendulous, tubular to funnelform, outer seg. fleshy, lemon yellow to apricot or white, sometimes flushed orange, scarlet or blue-green from the base, apical swellings bright green, inner seg. 2–3.5cm, tipped cinnabar red, magenta, scarlet or green. Winter–early summer. 'Pearsonii': Lvs spotted red-brown above. Scape to 18cm, mottled red-brown; outer seg. to 1.5cm, apricot, apical swelling lime green, inner seg. to 3cm, apricot to gold, tips stained red to maroon. A popular gdn plant developed in New Zealand and possibly of hybrid origin. The true *L. pearsonii* is a narrow-lvd plant with small, campanulate white fls tipped brown or opal; it hails from the Great Karasberg and is not cultivated. var. *aurea* (Lindl.) Engl. Lvs sometimes blotched or spotted maroon. Fls golden yellow, apical swelling on outer seg. lemon yellow to lime green. 'Nelsonii': lvs spotted purple. Fls bright yellow tipped green. var. *luteola* (Jacq.). Lvs glaucous, marked purple-brown. Outer perianth seg. pale yellow shading to green with green apical swellings, inner perianth seg. yellow-green, uppermost fls unopened and red. var. *quadricolor* (Jacq.) Engl. Lvs glaucous, blotched maroon. Fl. buds scarlet; outer perianth seg. scarlet or orange-red at base, fading to yellow or apricot with large lime green apical swellings, inner perianth seg. yellow tipped magenta or crimson. var. *vanzyliae* W. Barker. Fls grey-blue to white, with grey-green apical swellings.

L. arbuthnotiae W. Barker. Lvs 1–2, lanceolate, green or maroon, sometimes spotted. Infl. 18–40cm, spicate; fls yellow fading to red, tipped pale green. Late winter–spring.

L. bachmanii Bak. Resembles *L. contaminata* but lvs 2, linear, unmarked, inner perianth seg. slightly protruding with dark red tip.

L. bulbifera (Cyr.) Engl. Lvs 1–2, narrowly ovate, lorate, heavily spotted above, sometimes producing bulbils on margins. Infl. 8–30cm, racemose; fls pendulous, orange to red, apical swelling on outer seg. dark red or brown, inner seg. tips green, edged purple. Winter–spring.

L. carnosa Bak. Robust. Lvs 2, ovate-lanceolate, conspicuously veined and pustular above. Infl. 8–25cm, spicate; fls urceolate-oblong, white, swelling on outer seg. green or maroon, inner seg. tips white or magenta. Spring.

L. contaminata Ait. WILD HYACINTH. Lvs numerous, grass-like. Scape mottled; infl. 6–25cm, subspicate; fls campanulate, white, apical swelling on outer seg. maroon, inner seg. striped maroon near tips. Spring.

L. elegans W. Barker. Lvs 1–2, lanceolate, sometimes spotted. Infl. 18–24cm, spicate; fls oblong-urceolate, outer seg. bright blue at base shading to rose, apical swelling brown, inner seg.

protruding, white with pink spot near tips. var. *flava* W. Barker. Fls bright yellow tipped maroon, apical swelling on outer seg. pale green, margin of inner seg. narrow, white, membranous. Winter. var. *membranacea* W. Barker. Inner seg. pale green stained brown near tips, margin broad, white. Early spring. var. *suaveolens* W. Barker. Fls fragrant, outer seg. pale blue or green at base shading to pink to dark maroon, apical swelling dark maroon, inner seg. tipped dark maroon. Early spring.

L. glaucina Jacq. = *L. orchioides* var. *glaucina*.

L. glaucina var. *pallida* Lindl. = *L. orchioides*.

L. juncifolia Bak. Lvs 2, filiform to linear, ± terete, banded maroon at base. Infl. 7–23cm, racemose; fls oblong-campanulate, outer seg., white tinged pink, apical swelling purple, deep pink or green, inner seg. with pink keels. Late winter–spring. var. *campanulata* W. Barker. Fls white, campanulate, apical swelling on outer seg. deep rose, inner seg. with deep rose keels.

L. liliiflora Jacq. Lvs 2, lanceolate, tuberculate above. Infl. 10–20cm, subspicate to racemose; fls oblong-campanulate, white, apical swelling on outer seg. brown, inner seg. tipped dark magenta. Spring.

L. massonii Bak. = *L. trichophylla*.

L. mathewsii W. Barker. Lvs 2, glaucous, narrow-lanceolate. Infl. 10–20cm, subspicate; fls yellow, oblong-campanulate, apical swelling on outer seg. bright green, inner seg. spotted green near tip. Spring.

L. mediana Jacq. Lvs 2, lanceolate. Infl. 20–40cm, subspicate; fls oblong or oblong-campanulate; outer seg. pale blue to dull white, swelling green or purple, inner seg. dull white, marked green or purple near tip. Spring. var. *rogersii* (Bak.) W. Barker. Lf solitary, undulate to crispate, banded maroon. Fls blue to pink.

L. mutabilis Sweet. Lf solitary, sometimes glaucous, occas. spotted or banded maroon, often crispate. Infl. 10–45cm, spicate; outer seg. pale blue to white, apical swelling dark brown, inner seg. dark yellow with brown markings near tip. Winter.

L. namaquensis Schltr. ex W. Barker. Lvs 1–2, linear-lanceolate, plicate. Infl. 8–23cm, spicate; fls urceolate-oblong, outer seg. pale blue at base, shading to magenta, apical swellings green-purple or maroon, upper pair of inner seg. white tipped magenta, lower pair magenta. Winter–spring. Namaqualand.

L. orchioides (L.) Ait. Lvs 1–2, lanceolate or lorate, sometimes spotted above. Infl. 8–40cm, spicate; fls fragrant, oblong-cylindrical, outer seg. pale blue at base shading to green-yellow or cream, apical swellings green. Winter–spring. var. *glaucina* (Jacq.) W. Barker. Outer seg. blue at base, shading to purple, with apical swelling dark purple, sometimes entirely blue with dark blue swelling.

L. orthopetala Jacq. Lvs 4–5, grass-like, channelled above, sometimes spotted. Infl. 9–27cm, subspicate; fls oblong-campanulate, erect, white, sometimes with a pale maroon central stripe, outer seg. with dark maroon apical swelling, inner tipped dark maroon. Spring.

L. ovatifolia L. Guthrie = *L. carnosa*.

L. pallida Ait. Lvs 1–2, sometimes tuberculate. Infl. 12–30cm, subspicate; fls oblong-campanulate, cream to yellow, outer seg. with brown or green apical swelling. Late winter–spring.

L. pearsonii hort. non (Glover) W. Barker = *L. aloides* 'Pearsonii'.

L. peersii Marloth ex W. Barker. Lvs 1–2, lorate. Infl. 15–30cm, racemose; fls white fading to dull pink, swelling on outer seg. green-brown. Early summer.

L. pendula Ait. = *L. bulbifera*.

L. purpureocaerula Jacq. Lvs 2, lanceolate or lorate, tuberculate above. Infl. 10–28cm, subspicate; fls campanulate, fragrant, outer seg. blue to white shading to magenta or purple, apical swelling green-brown, inner seg. magenta. Early summer.

L. pustulata Jacq. Lvs 1–2, lanceolate or lorate, pustular above. Infl. 15–35cm, racemose; fls oblong-campanulate, cream or straw-yellow, apical swelling on outer seg. green, inner seg. tipped dark pink or pale green. Later winter–early summer.

L. reflexa Thunb. Lvs 1–2, bright green, glaucous, lanceolate to lorate, sometimes spotted above, undulate. Infl. to 20cm, subspicate; fls cylindrical, erect, green-yellow fading to dull red, outer seg. with green or yellow-green apical swelling. Winter.

L. roodeae Phillips = *L. splendida*.

L. rosea Andrews. Lf solitary, sometimes marked maroon. Infl. 8–30cm, racemose; fls oblong-campanulate, outer seg. blue to rose pink, apical swelling brown or deep pink, inner seg. rose pink. Winter–midsummer.

L. rubida Jacq. Lvs 1–2, lanceolate or lorate, often spotted. Infl. 6–25cm, subspicate; fls pendulous, cylindrical, outer seg. bright pink to ruby red, or pale yellow spotted red, apical swelling yellow-green or pink-red, inner seg. tipped purple, marked white. Autumn–winter.

L. salteri W. Barker. Lvs 2, lanceolate, sometimes blotched brown. Infl. 15–35cm, subspicate; fls oblong-campanulate, cream or red-purple, outer seg. often pale blue at base, apical swelling brown-purple, inner seg. pink. Early summer.

L. splendida Diels. Lvs 2, lanceolate. Infl. 6–25cm, spicate; fls oblong-campanulate; outer perianth seg. pale blue shading to white or pale lilac, apical swelling green-brown, inner seg. lilac striped purple stripe. Winter.

L. trichophylla Bak. Lf solitary, cordate, stellate-hairy. Infl. 8–20cm, spicate; fls oblong-cylindric, pale yellow, sometimes flushed pink, apical swellings green. Spring.

L. tricolor Jacq. f. = *L. aloides*.

L. tricolor var. *luteola* Jacq. = *L. aloides* var. *luteola*.

L. unicolor Jacq. Lvs 2, lanceolate, or lorate, usually tuberculate. Infl. 8–30cm, racemose; fls oblong-campanulate, cream with green apical swelling on outer seg. to pink, lilac, magenta, blue or purple with darker swellings. Spring.

L. unifolia Jacq. Lf solitary, linear, base banded maroon. Infl. 10–35cm, racemose; fls oblong-campanulate, outer seg. blue at base, shading to white, pale yellow or pink, apical swellings brown or pink, inner seg. white. Winter–early summer.

L. unifolia var. *rogersii* Bak. = *L. mediana* var. *rogersii*.

L. violacea Jacq. Lvs 1–2, lanceolate, sometimes spotted maroon, undulate to crispate. Infl. 10–35cm, racemose; fls campanulate, outer seg. pale blue-green to magenta or purple, swellings brown, inner seg. purple to violet. Winter–spring. var. *glauca* W. Barker. Lf solitary, lanceolate, undulate. Fls coconut-scented, outer seg. grey-blue to pale magenta, inner seg. pale magenta.

L. viridiflora W. Barker. Lvs 2, lanceolate, sometimes spotted or tuberculate. Infl. 8–20cm, subspicate; fls cylindrical-ventricose, outer seg. viridian to turquoise, inner seg. tipped white, striped green. Winter.

Lachnosiphonium Hochst.

L. niloticum (Stapf) Dandy = *Catunaregam nilotica*.

L. obovatum Hochst. = *Catunaregam spinosa*.

Laciniaria Hill.

L. ligustylis A. Nels. = *Liatris ligustylis*.

L. scariosa var. *novae-angliae* Lunell = *Liatris novae-angliae*.

Lacquered Pepper *Piper magnificum*.
Lacquered Wine-cup *Aechmea* 'Foster's Favorite'.
Lac Tree *Schleichera oleosa*.

Lactuca L. LETTUCE. Compositae. c100 ann. or perenn. herbs with milky sap. St. usually solitary, erect, branched. Lvs alt., sometimes rosulate, entire to pinnatifid, often prickly. Cap. few to many, ligulate; involucre cylindrical; ligules yellow or blue, rarely almost white. Cosmop., esp. N Temp.

L. albana C.A. Mey. = *Cicerbita racemosa*.

L. alpina (L.) A. Gray = *Cicerbita alpina*.

L. macrantha C.B. Clarke = *Cicerbita macrantha*.

L. macrophylla (Willd.) A. Gray = *Cicerbita macrophylla*.

L. macrorhiza (Royle) Hook. = *Cephalorrhynchus macrorhizus*.

L. perennis L. BLUE LETTUCE. Perenn. to 80cm, glab., branched above. Lvs deeply dissected, grey-green, seg. lanceolate, entire or dentate. Cap. few, 3–4cm diam. in a loose corymbose pan.; ligules blue to lilac. Spring–summer. C & S Eur. Z6.

L. plumieri (L.) Gren. & Godron = *Cicerbita plumieri*.

L. racemosa Willd. = *Cicerbita racemosa*.

L. sativa L. GARDEN LETTUCE; COMMON LETTUCE. Ann. or bienn., to 1m, glab. Rosulate lvs to 25cm, undivided or runcinate-pinnatifid, shortly petiolate; st. lvs ovate to orbicular, simple, sessile, cordate, clasping. Cap. many, to 1.5cm diam., in a dense, corymbose pan.; ligules pale yellow, frequently streaked with violet. Summer. Probably originated in Near E, Medit. or Sib. from *L. serriola*. For cvs see **Lettuce** in *New RHS Dictionary*. Z6.

L. scariola L. = *L. serriola*.

L. serriola L. PRICKLY LETTUCE. Ann. or bienn., to 1.8m. St. glab. or setose. Lvs stiff, grey-green, dors. midrib spinulose; basal lvs to 20cm, narrowly obovate-oblong, usually pinnatifid, petiolate, st. lvs less divided, erect. Cap. many, c12mm diam., in a much-branched pyramidal or spike-like pan.; ligules pale yellow. Spring–summer. Eurasia and N Afr. Z7.

L. tenerrima Pourr. Perenn., to 50cm. St. setose below, Lvs deeply pinnatisect, glab. or spinulose, esp. on veins, seg. narrow, linear, lower lvs shortly petiolate, middle and upper lvs clasping. Cap. usually solitary; ligules pale yellow. Summer. SW Eur., Moroc. Z8.

L. virosa L. Ann. or bienn., to 2m; roots foetid. St. glab. or setose below. Lvs obovate-oblong, dentate or shallowly pinnatifid, spinulose on midrib below, st. lvs horizontal. Cap.

1cm diam., many, in a long, pyramidal pan.; ligules pale yellow. Summer. S, W & C Eur. Z6.

Ladanum *Cistus ladanifer.*
Ladder Fern *Nephrolepis* (*N. cordifolia*).
Ladies'-Delight *Viola* ×*wittrockiana.*
Ladies' Tobacco *Antennaria* (*A. plantaginifolia*).
Lad's Love *Artemisia absinthium.*
Ladybells *Adenophora.*
Lady Fern *Athyrium filix-femina.*
Lady Hair *Malpighia cubensis.*
Lady Nipples *Solanum mammosum.*
Lady of the Night *Brassavola nodosa*; *Brunfelsia americana*; *Cestrum nocturnum.*
Lady Orchid *Orchis purpurea.*
Lady Palm *Rhapis* (*R. excelsa*).
Lady's Eardrops *Fuchsia.*
Lady's Earrings *Impatiens capensis.*
Lady's Finger *Abelmoschus esculentus.*
Lady's Hand *Cyanella hyacinthoides.*
Lady's Leek *Allium cernuum.*
Lady's Mantle *Alchemilla.*
Lady's Slipper *Hybanthus capense.*
Lady's Slipper Orchid *Cypripedium*; *Paphiopedilum; Phragmipedium.*
Lady's Smock *Cardamine pratensis.*
Lady's Tresses *Spiranthes spiralis.*
Lady Tulip *Tulipa clusiana.*

Laelia Lindl. Orchidaceae. 70 epiphytic or lithophytic orchids. Rhiz. creeping; pbs subglobose to cylindrical. Lvs 1 to several, at apex of pb., leathery, ovate or linear-lanceolate. Infl. term., sheathed, solitary or racemose; fls showy; tep. free, spreading, pet. elliptic-ovate usually wider than sep.; lip trilobed, lat. lobes enveloping column, midlobe often crested, undulate. C & S Amer., from W Indies S to Braz. Z10.

L. acuminata Lindl. = *L. rubescens.*
L. albida Lindl. Pbs *c*5cm, ovoid, 2-lvd. Lvs *c*15cm, linear to ligulate. Fls 3–8, scented, *c*5cm diam., white tinged pink, lip lined yellow. Winter. Mex.
L. anceps Lindl. Pbs 5–7cm, ovoid, obscurely 4-angled or compressed, 1–2-lvd. Lvs to 15cm, elliptic-lanceolate. Fls 3–6, fragrant, 8–10cm diam., rose-lilac or magenta, lip deep purple tinged with pink and yellow in the throat, sometimes wholly white. Winter. Mex., Hond. 'Alba': fls wholly white.
L. angereri Pabst. Pbs *c*20cm, cylindrical, 1-lvd. Lvs *c*18cm, lanceolate. Fls *c*10, 5cm diam., brick-red. Braz.
L. autumnalis Lindl. Pbs 6–15cm, flask- or pear-shaped, 2–3-lvd. Lvs 10–15cm, lanceolate. Fls 3–6, scented, to 10cm diam., rose-purple, lip rose-white with purple apex and yellow in centre. Autumn. Mex. *L. gouldiana*: stouter plants with broader, solid magenta blooms; possibly a cross between *L. anceps* and *L. autumnalis.*
L. autumnalis var. *furfuracea* (Lindl.) Rolfe = *L. furfuracea.*
L. bahiensis Schltr. Pbs 4–7cm, cylindrical, 1-lvd. Lvs 6–9cm, narrowly oblong. Fls 4–8, 4cm diam., golden-yellow. Braz.
L. boothiana Rchb. f. = *L. lobata.*
L. bradei Pabst. Pbs 4cm, cylindrical. Lvs 3cm, elliptic. Fls few, to 3.5cm diam., pale yellow. Braz.
L. briegeri Blum. Pbs to 4cm, pyriform. Lvs ovate-elliptic. Fls to 5.5cm diam., yellow, on long-stalked rac. Braz.
L. cinnabarina Lindl. Pb. 10–20cm, cylindrical, 1- rarely 2-lvd. Lvs 15–25cm, linear-lanceolate. Fls 5–15, *c*5cm diam., deep orange-red, slender. Spring–early summer. Braz.
L. crispa (Lindl.) Rchb. f. Pbs remote, to 25cm, ovate-ellipsoid, somewhat stalked. Lvs to 30cm, 1–2 per bulb, oblong. Fls 4–7, 12cm diam., white, lip usually mainly purple with some yellow marks. Autumn. Braz.
L. crispata (Thunb.) Garay. Pbs 4–10cm, oblong-cylindrical, 1-lvd. Lvs to 16cm, narrowly oblong. Fls 2–10, to 4.5cm diam., pale pink, lip white in throat, midlobe purple. Braz.
L. discolor A. Rich. = *L. albida.*
L. endsfeldzii Pabst. Pbs 12×1.5cm, conical, 1-lvd. Lvs oblong-lanceolate. Fls several, 3.5cm diam., pale yellow. Braz.
L. esalqueana Blum. Pbs pyriform. Lvs oblong-elliptic. Fls few, 2.8cm diam., yellow to orange. Braz.
L. ×*esperito-santensis* Pabst. (*L. pumila* ×*L. xanthina.*) Fls to 8.5cm diam., golden and mauve. Braz.
L. fidelensis Pabst. Pbs *c*4cm, ovoid, compressed, 1-lvd. Lvs 10–12cm, oblong. Fls 2, to 10cm diam., rose-pink, disc usually pale yellow or white. Braz.
L. ×*finckeniana* O'Brien. (*L. anceps* var. *sanderiana* ×*L. albida.*) Fls white, the lip striped purple towards base, with a purple crescent-shaped mark on the midlobe and 3 yellow ridges at junction of lobes.

L. flava Lindl. Pbs 3–4cm, narrowly ovoid, 1-lvd. Lvs 7–8cm, elliptic. Fls 3–10, canary yellow, *c*6cm diam. Late spring. Braz.
L. fulva Lindl. = *L. flava.*
L. furfuracea Lindl. V. similar to *L. autumnalis.* Pbs to 4cm, ovoid, 1-lvd. Lvs to 10cm, lanceolate. Fls 1–3, to 12cm diam., tep. light purple, lip deep purple; ovary mealy-glandular. Mex.
L. ghillanyi Pabst. Pbs about 3cm, narrowly ovoid, 1–2-lvd. Lvs 4cm, elliptic. Fls 3, to 4cm diam., pale to deep rose-violet or violet and white. Braz.
L. gloedeniana Hoehne. Pbs 7–10cm, almost cylindrical, 1-lvd. Lvs 7–10cm, elliptic. Fls *c*8, 4.5cm diam., yellow, lip veined red. Braz.
L. gloriosa (Rchb. f.) L.O. Williams = *Schomburgkia gloriosa.*
L. gouldiana Rchb. f. see *L. autumnalis.*
L. grandiflora Lindl. = *L. speciosa.*
L. grandis Lindl. & Paxt. Pbs to 30cm, conical, 1–2-lvd. Lvs to 25cm, oblong. Fls 2–5, 10–18cm diam., tep. yellow-brown, lip white or off-white veined rose-purple. Late spring–summer. Braz.
L. harpophylla Rchb. f. Pbs 15–30cm, slender, 1–2-lvd. Lvs 15–20cm, linear-lanceolate. Fls 3–7, 5–8cm diam., vermilion, lip with a paler margin and yellow in centre. Winter–spring. Braz.
L. humboldtii (Rchb. f.) L.O. Williams = *Schomburgkia humboldtii.*
L. itambana Pabst. Pbs 2.5–3.5cm, cylindrical. Lvs 4.5cm, ovate. Fls 5cm diam., 2, deep yellow. Braz.
L. jongheana Rchb. f. Pbs 5cm, oblong, 1-lvd. Lvs erect, 10–15cm, elliptic. Fls 12cm diam. 1–2, rose-purple, sometimes pure white, lip yellow and white in throat. Spring. Braz.
L. liliputana Pabst. Pbs 0.8–1.5cm, globose or oblong. Lvs 10–15mm, ovate. Fls solitary, 3cm diam., rose pink. Braz.
L. lobata (Lindl.) Veitch. Pbs to 10cm, conical or fusiform, 1-lvd. Lvs to 20cm, lanceolate. Fls *c*13cm diam., 2–5, rose-purple with darker veins, rarely pure white, lip with carmine-red markings. Spring. Braz.
L. longipes Rchb. f. Pbs 6–8cm, narrowly oblong or conical, 1-lvd. Lvs 7–15cm, elliptic-oblong. Fls to 5cm diam., 2–4, tep. pale mauve-purple, rarely pure white, lip golden yellow or white with yellow throat. Braz.
L. lucasiana Rolfe. Pbs squat, pyriform. Fls few, 4cm diam., lilac to purple. Braz.
L. lundii Rchb. f. & Warm. Pbs 3–4cm, oblong. Lvs 8–9cm, fls 2, 4.5cm diam., white with rose-purple veins on lip. Braz.
L. lyonsii (Lindl.) L.O. Williams = *Schomburgkia lyonsii.*
L. majalis Lindl. = *L. speciosa.*
L. milleri Bl. Pbs to 4cm, flask-shaped. Lvs to 6×3cm, rarely 2 per bulb, ovate-oblong. Fls 6cm diam., few, orange-red, tinged with yellow in throat. Summer. Braz.
L. monophylla (Griseb.) Hook. f. = *Neocogniauxia monophylla.*
L. ostermayeri Hoehne = *L. lucasiana.*
L. peduncularis Lindl. = *L. rubescens.*
L. perrinii Batem. Pbs 15–25cm, ovoid, compressed, 1-lvd. Lvs 15–25cm. Rac. 2–6-fld; fls showy, 12–14cm diam., flat, rose-pink or pure white, lip magenta with a yellow botch in the throat. Winter. Braz.
L. pfisteri Pabst & Sengh. Pbs 5–6cm, pyriform 1-lvd. Lvs *c*7cm, narrowly elliptic. Fls 3–5, 3.5cm diam., purple, lip white in centre, edged dark purple. Braz.
L. pumila (Hook.) Rchb. f. Pbs 3–10cm, 1-lvd, slender. Lvs 4–10cm, oblong. Fls solitary, to 10cm diam., flat, slightly drooping, rose-purple, rarely white, lip deep purple with yellow throat, sometimes edged and veined amethyst (*L. dayana* Rchb. f.). Spring or autumn. Braz.
L. purpurata Lindl. Pbs to 50cm, compressed ellipsoid, 1-lvd. Lvs 30–40cm, narrowly elliptic. Fls 15–20cm diam., 3–7, tep. white tinged with pink, sometimes pure white, lip white at apex, purple towards base, yellow with purple veins in throat, rarely deep violet. Spring–summer. Braz.
L. reguellii Barb. Rodr. = *L. lundii.*
L. rubescens Lindl. Pbs 3–6.5cm, orbicular to oblong, compressed, glossy, 1–2-lvd. Lvs 5–20cm, oblong-elliptic. Fls to 8cm diam., few to several, scented, v. pale mauve to rose-purple, rarely white, lip with central purple or carmine blotch. Mex. to Panama.
L. rupestris Lindl. = *L. crispata.*
L. sincorana Schltr. Pbs 2–2.5cm, subglobose, 1-lvd. Lvs 3.5–4.5cm, ovate or elliptic. Fls to 9cm diam., 1–2, purple. Braz.
L. speciosa (HBK) Schltr. Pbs to 6cm, ovoid-turbinate, 1-lvd. Lvs to 6–15cm, oblong. Fls 12–18cm diam., 1–2, tep. rose-lilac, rarely white, lip white spotted with deep lilac, margin pale lilac. Mex.
L. superbiens Lindl. = *Schomburgkia superbiens.*
L. tenebrosa Rolfe. Pbs conical to fusiform, to 30cm, 1-lvd. Lvs 20–30cm, oblong. Fls *c*16cm diam., 4; tep. copper-bronze, lip purple, darker in throat. Summer. Braz.

L. tereticaulis Hoehne = *L. crispata*.

L. thomsoniana (Rchb. f.) L.O. Williams. Pbs 15–20cm, fusiform, yellow-green. Fls to 7cm diam., many in a large pan., creamy-white to yellow, lip dark purple. Spring. Cuba, Cayman Is.

L. undulata (Lindl.) L.O. Williams = *Schomburgkia undulata*.

L. virens Lindl. = *L. xanthina*.

L. weberbaueriana (Kränzl.) Schweinf. = *Schomburgkia weberbaueriana*.

L. xanthina Lindl. Pbs to 25×3cm, club-shaped, 1-lvd. Lvs to 30cm, ligulate. Fls to 8cm diam., 2–6, tep. rich yellow, lip white, yellow in throat, streaked crimson-purple. Spring–summer. Braz.

L. grexes and cvs. There are many cvs and grexes of *Laelia*, either slender or stout in habit with large or small fls in shades of pink, mauve, yellow, orange, red and white.

✗ Laeliocattleya. (*Laelia* × *Cattleya*.) Orchidaceae. Gdn hybrids intermediate between or following either of the parents in size and habit with fls in a wide range of shades of white, green, yellow, orange, red, purple, mauve and pink, often banded red, white or yellow on lip.

Laeliopsis Lindl. Orchidaceae. 2 epiphytic orchids. Pbs clustered, ovoid to fusiform, 1–3-lvd. Infl. term., racemose; fls showy; tep. spreading; pet. broad; lip entire or obscurely trilobed, tubular. W Indies. Z10.

L. domingensis (Lindl.) Lindl. Pbs to 6cm. Lvs to 18cm, oblong, tough. Infl. to 1m, erect, usually a pan.; fls to 6cm diam., pink to lavender veined purple, lip yellow within, banded purple, fringed. Mostly spring–summer. Hispan.

→*Broughtonia*.

Lagarosiphon Harv. CURLY WATER THYME. Hydrocharitaceae. 9 perenn., aquatic herbs. St. terete, branched. Lvs dark green, usually spiralling, linear-lanceolate. ♂ infl. axill., with many 3-merous, free-floating fls. ♀ infl. sessile in lf axil; perianth tube 6-segmented, staminodes 3. Afr., introd. to Eur. and NZ. Z4.

L. dregeana Presl = *L. muscoides*.

L. major (Ridl.) Moss. St. to 3mm diam. Lvs 6.5–25×2–4.5mm, thick, opaque. S Afr., introd. to Eur. and NZ.

L. muscoides Harv. St. 0.5–1.5 diam. Lvs 5–20×0.5–1.5mm, thin, transparent. C & S Afr.

L. muscoides var. *major* Ridl. = *L. major*.

L. schweinfurthii Caspary = *L. muscoides*.

→*Hydrilla*.

Lagarostrobus Quinn. Podocarpaceae. 2 everg. conifers. Juvenile lvs narrow-linear, spiral, but twisted into an apparently distichous arrangement, adult lvs scale-like, appressed. ♂ cones solitary, term., sessile. ♀ cones to 2cm, term., lax; scales to 10, spreading, concave. NZ, Tasm.

L. colensoi (Hook.) Quinn. WESTLAND PINE. Tree to 12m, smaller in cult. Crown conic; bark exfoliating in large plates. Lvs 1.5–2.5mm. NZ. Z8.

L. franklinii (Hook. f.) Quinn. HUON PINE. Tree to 30m. Crown conic to spreading; bark smooth, silver-grey to brown; br. arching. Lvs to 1mm. W Tasm. 'Pendulum': br. slender, weeping. Z8.

→*Dacrydium*.

Lagenandra Dalz. Araceae. 12 rhizomatous aquatic everg. perennials. Lvs simple, narrow-elliptic to ovate; petioles sheathing, long. Spathe tubular below, spreading or hooded above, purple-green; spadix shorter than spathe; fls unisexual. Sri Lanka, India. Z10.

L. insignis Trimen = *L. ovata*.

L. koenigii (Schott) Thwaites. Lvs to 60cm, narrowly linear-lanceolate, spotted white beneath. Peduncle to 20cm; spathe to 9cm, limb much longer than tube, smooth within, subulate. Sri Lanka.

L. lancifolia (Schott) Thwaites. Lvs to 10cm, elliptic to lanceolate, spotted white beneath. Spathe to 5cm, oblong, acuminate, rugose within. Sri Lanka.

L. ovata (L.) Thwaites. Lvs to 45cm, ovate-lanceolate to elliptic, spotted beneath. Spathe to 30cm, limb to 15cm across, caudate, undulate, verrucose. Sri Lanka, S. India.

L. ovata misapplied. = *L. praetermissa*.

L. praetermissa De Wit. Close to *L. ovata*. Lvs to 50cm, narrow-ovate. Spathe to 12cm+, rough. Sri Lanka.

L. thwaitesii Engl. Lvs to 20cm, oblong- to linear-lanceolate, margin undulate, silver-white. Peduncle to 2.5cm; spathe to 5cm, slender, finely wrinkled. Sri Lanka.

→*Cryptocoryne*.

Lagenaria Ser. WHITE-FLOWERED GOURD; CALABASH GOURD; BOTTLE GOURD. Cucurbitaceae. 6 ann. or perenn. climbing or scandent herbs. Tendrils simple or bifid. Lvs simple or 3–5-lobed; petiole with paired glands. ♂ fls solitary or in rac.; pet. 5, white, free, obovate; sta. 3; ♀ fls solitary, campanulate, white; staminodes 3; ovary pubesc. Fr. to 1m, hard, shaped like a club or a crooknecked flask. Pantrop., widely nat. Z10.

L. leucantha Duchesne = *L. siceraria*.

L. longissima hort. = *L. siceraria*.

L. siceraria (Molina) Standl. Ann. to 10m, viscid-pubesc. Lvs to 20cm, ovate-cordate, sinuate-toothed; petiole 3–13cm. Fls solitary; ♂ peduncle to 12cm, ♀ shorter; pet. obovate, 3–4.5cm, ♂ larger than ♀. Fr. smooth, green-yellow, sub-globose to lageniform. Pantrop., domesticated separately in the Old and New Worlds. The many cultivated variants of *L. siceraria* are named according to their appearance and the use to which they are put, e.g. SUGAR TROUGH GOURD; HERCULES' CLUB; BOTTLE GOURD; DIPPER; KNOBKERRY; TRUMPET GOURD.

L. vulgaris Ser. = *L. siceraria*.

→*Cucurbita*.

Lagenophora Cass. Compositae. 15 perenn. herbs, to 40cm. Lvs mostly basal, dentate or lobed, petiolate. Cap. radiate, usually solitary; involucre campanulate to hemispherical. Australasia, C & S Amer.

L. pinnatifida Hook. f. Lvs to 6×3cm, obovate-spathulate, obtuse, cuneate, usually deeply crenate to pinnatifid, lobes in 4–6 pairs, apiculate, soft, densely long-hairy. Cap. 10–15mm diam.; ray flts white to purple. Summer. NZ. Z7.

L. pumila (Forst. f.) Cheesem. Lvs to 2cm, suborbicular to ovate-oblong or broadly elliptic, obtuse, cuneate, crenate-dentate to v. shallowly lobed or subentire, thinly coriaceous, roughly hairy. Cap. 10–12mm diam.; ray flts white to pink. Spring–autumn. NZ. Z7.

L. stipitata (Labill.) Druce. Lvs to 5×1.5cm, oblanceolate to elliptic, serrate to crenate or sublobate, densely hairy. Cap. 4–10mm diam.; ray flts white, pink or tinged blue. Spring–summer. E & S Aus., Tasm., Papua New Guinea. Z9.

→*Lagenifera*.

Lagerstroemia L. Lythraceae. 53 shrubs or trees. Lvs simple, usually entire, undulate. Pan. axillary and term., erect, pyramidal to cylindric; cal. lobes 6 or 7–9, ovate; pet. 6 or more, clawed, crumpled, crispate; sta. many, fil. slender, exserted. Trop. Asia to Aus.

L. elegans Wallich ex Paxt. = *L. indica*.

L. flos-reginae Retz. = *L. speciosa*.

L. indica L. CRAPE MYRTLE; CREPE FLOWER. Decid. tree or shrub to 6m. Bark red-brown, exfoliating. Lvs obovate to oblong, to 10×4cm, glossy. Pan. subpyramidal to 20cm; pet. suborbicular, to 1×1.5cm, pink, purple or white; sta. 36–42. Spring–autumn. China, Indochina, Himal., Jap. *Tall growing shrubs or trees*: 'Basham's Party Pink' (to 10.5m, spreading; lvs pale green, yellow to orange-red in autumn; fls lavender in large clusters), 'Country Red' (upright; fls blood red; late-flowering) 'Natchez' (vigorous, fast growth, v. tolerant; bark dark brown; fls white), 'Tuskegee' (hardy, broad habit; bark mottled, exfoliating; lvs orange-red in autumn; fls dark pink), 'Wichita' (upright, vase-shaped; bark russet; fls lavender, recurrent), 'Wonderful White' (fls white). *Medium growing shrubs or trees*: 'Catawba' (lvs bright orange-red; fls purple), 'Comanche' (habit upright, spreading; bark pale; lvs orange to purple red in autumn; fls dark pink), 'Near East' (habit semi-weeping; fls pink in large clusters), 'Sioux' (to 2.5m, densely upright; fls v. large, pink), 'William Toovey' (to 3.5m, broad, spreading habit; fls pale red). *Small shrubs or trees*: 'Acoma' (habit spreading; lvs red in autumn; fls white, pendulous), 'Hopi' (v. tolerant of cold, compact, spreading habit; lvs orange-red in autumn; fls clear pink), 'Okmulgee' (fls dark red), 'Zuni' (habit globose; lvs orange-red in autumn; fls lavender). *Dwarf shrubs*: 'Lavender Dwarf' (low, spreading habit; fls lavender), 'Pink Ruffles' (to 150cm; fls pink), 'Victor' (compact; fls bright red, abundant), 'White Dwarf' (rounded habit; fls white, abundant). Z7.

L. speciosa (L.) Pers. QUEEN'S CRAPE MYRTLE; PRIDE OF INDIA; PYINMA. Tree to 24m. Lvs oblong or elliptic-oblong, to 19.5×8.5cm, leathery. Pan. erect, to 40cm; pet. suborbicular, to 3×2cm, purple or white; sta. 130–200. Spring–autumn. Trop. Asia. var. *intermedia* (Koehne). Fl. buds smaller, to 9×2mm. Z9.

Lagos Rubber Tree *Ficus lutea*.

Lagotis Gaertn. Scrophulariaceae. 20 glab. perenn. herbs. Lvs mostly basal, simple. Rac. dense, term., spike-like, bracteate; cal. spathe-like, 2-lobed; cor. tube cylindrical, sharply curved, limb bilabiate; lower lip 2 or 3-lobed; sta. slightly exserted. N &

C Asia to Cauc., Himal., W China.

L. armena Boiss. = *L. stolonifera.*

L. stolonifera (K. Koch) Maxim. Stoloniferous. Lvs 1.5–13cm, narrow, oblong-elliptic, entire or subcrenate, glab. Spike dense, oblong-ovoid, bracts enclosing cal.; cor. 8–12mm, blue or purple to mauve-pink. C Asia. Z6.

→*Gymnandra.*

Lagunaria G. Don. Malvaceae. 1 pyramidal everg. tree to 15m; young growth scurfy. Lvs 5–10cm, ovate to broadly lanceolate, entire, white-scurfy beneath. Fls 4–6cm diam., solitary; epical. 3–5-parted; cal. shallowly 5-lobed; pet. pale pink to magenta; staminal column included. Australasia (Queensld, Norfolk Is., Lord Howe Is.). Z9.

L. patersonii (Anderss.) G. Don. NORFOLK ISLAND HIBISCUS; QUEENSLAND PYRAMID TREE; COW ITCH TREE.

Lagurus L. HARE'S TAIL. Gramineae. 1 ann. grass to 60cm. St. tufted, erect, hairy. Lf blades to 20×1cm, arching, linear-lanceolate, downy. Pan. spicate, ovoid to oblong-cylindric, dense, softly hairy, light green or tinged mauve, to 6×2cm; spikelets overlapping. Summer. Medit. Z9.

L. ovatus L. 'Nanus': v. dwarf, to 15cm.

Lake Crinum *Crinum submersum.*

La-kwa *Momordica charantia.*

Lallemantia Fisch. & Mey. Labiatae. 5 ann. or short-lived perenn., grey-puberulous herbs to 50cm. St. tetragonal. Lvs petiolate, or sessile higher on plant. Fls 6 per whorl in a spike; cal. tubular, 15-veined, teeth 5; cor. tube slender, upper lip erect, 2-lobed, folded, lower lip 3-lobed. SW Asia, C Asia, Himal. Z7.

L. canescens (L.) Fisch. & Mey. To 50cm. Lower lvs to 1.5cm, obovate to lanceolate. Cor. blue or lavender, rarely white. Late summer. Iran, Anatolia, Transcauc.

L. iberica (Bieb.) Fisch. & Mey. To 40cm. Lower lvs to 2cm, generally ovate, crenate. Cor. blue. Late spring. Cauc., nat. elsewhere.

L. peltata (L.) Fisch. & Mey. To 50cm. Lower lvs to 4.5cm, long-stalked. Cor. violet rarely white. Anatolia, Iraq, Iran, C Asia.

L. royleana (Benth. in Wallich) Benth. To 20cm. Lower lvs 3×2cm, obovate, crenate, glandular-pubesc., blue. Iran, Afghan., S Russian, S China.

→*Dracocephalum* and *Nepeta.*

Lamarckia Moench. GOLDEN TOP. Gramineae. 1 ann. grass to 30cm. St. tufted, smooth. Lf blades flat, linear, to 12.5×1cm. Pan. oblong, secund, dense, plumose, golden-yellow, often tinged purple, to 7.5×2.5cm; spikelets in groups of 5, 1 fertile. Summer. Medit. Z7.

L. aurea (L.) Moench.

Lambertia Sm. Proteaceae. 10 shrubs. Lvs usually in whorls of 3. Fls solitary or in terminal clusters subtended by coloured bracts; perianth tube elongate, incurved, lobes 4, spirally revolute. Aus. Z9.

L. ericifolia R. Br. Shrub to 3m. Lvs 1–1.5cm, linear to lanceolate. Fls cream, orange or pink in clusters of 7. Throughout the year. W Aus.

L. formosa Sm. MOUNTAIN DEVIL. Shrub to 2m. Lvs 5cm, linear. Fls red in clusters of 7. Throughout the year. E Aus.

L. multiflora Lindl. MANY-FLOWERED HONEYSUCKLE. Shrub to 1.5m. Lvs to 5cm, broad-linear. Fls yellow in clusters of 7. Late winter–early summer. W Aus.

Lambkill *Kalmia angustifolia.*
Lamb's Ears *Stachys byzantina.*
Lamb's Lettuce *Valerianella locusta.*
Lamb's Tail Cactus *Echinocereus schmollii.*
Lamb's Tails *Stachys byzantina.*
Lamb's Tongue *Stachys byzantina.*

LAMIACEAE Lindl. See Labiatae.

Lamiastrum Heist. ex Fabr.

L. galeobdolon (L.) Ehrend. & Polats. = *Lamium galeobdolon.*

Lamium L. DEAD NETTLE. Labiatae. 50 creeping and stoloniferous perenn. or ann. herbs. Lvs opposite, ovate to kidney-shaped, base usually cordate. Fls in verticillasters; bracts leafy; cal. tubular to bell-shaped, teeth 5; cor. 2-lipped, upper lip hooded, lower lip spreading, 3-lobed. Medit.

L. album L. WHITE DEAD NETTLE. Perenn. to 1m. St. erect to ascending, stoloniferous, 4-angled, pubesc. Lvs to 6cm, ovate to oblong, toothed to notched, gland., glab. to pubesc.

Verticillasters 8–10-fld, distant; cor. white, tube to 16mm, interior pubesc. Eur. to W Asia. 'Friday': lvs two shades of green, with central area gold. 'Goldflake': lvs striped gold. 'Pale Peril': shoots tinted gold when young. Z4.

L. brachyodon (Bordz.) Kuprian. = *L. album.*

L. galeobdolon (L.) L. YELLOW ARCHANGEL. Vigorous perenn. to 60cm. St. erect to creeping, occas. stoloniferous, 4-angled, white-pubesc. Lvs to 5.5cm, ovate to orbicular, toothed to notched. Verticillasters 2–10-fld, approximate; cor. to 2cm, yellow, flecked brown. Summer. Eur. to W Asia. 'Florentinum': tall; lvs large, splashed silver, and, in winter, purple; st. upright. 'Hermann's Pride': mat-forming; lvs narrow, toothed, streaked and spotted silver. 'Silberteppich' ('Silver Carpet'): slow growing, clump-forming; lvs silver. 'Silver Angel': prostrate, fast-growing; lvs marked silver; st. upright. 'Silver Spangled': spreading; lvs jagged-edged, hairy, heavily spotted silver. 'Variegatum': lvs smaller, oval, mid green marked silver. 'Type Ronsdorf': similar to 'Variegatum'. Z6.

L. garganicum L. Perenn. to 45cm. St. ascending or mat-forming. Lvs to 7×5cm, ovate or deltoid to reniform, notched. Verticillasters 2–12-fld, approximate or distant; cor. pink or red to purple or, rarely, white, tube to 3cm, interior glab. Eur. and N Afr. to W Asia. 'Golden Carpet': to 45cm high; lvs variegated gold; fls pink and white striped.

L. luteum (Huds.) Krocker = *L. galeobdolon.*

L. maculatum L. Perenn. to 80cm. St. ascending to trailing, stoloniferous, pubesc. Lvs to 9×7cm, ovate or deltoid to sub-orbicular, margin notched, pubesc., white-mottled or -striped. Verticillasters 4–8-fld, distant; cor. red to purple, rarely white, tube to 2cm, curved, interior pubesc. Summer. Eur. and N Afr. to W Asia. 'Album': lvs blotched silver; fls white. 'Aureum': lvs gold with white centre; fls pink. 'Beacon's Silver': habit low; lvs silver, thin green edge; fls pink. 'Cannon's Gold': lvs gold; fls purple. 'Chequers': lvs broad, thin silver stripe. 'Immaculate': lvs green; fls purple. 'Pink Pewter': lvs tinted silver; fls rich pink. 'Red Nancy': lvs silver, thin green edge; fls red. 'Shell Pink': lvs blotched white; fls large, pink, abundant. 'Sterling Silver': lvs pure silver; fls purple. 'White Nancy': lvs silver, thin green edge; fls white. Z4.

L. orvala L. Perenn. to 1m. St. to 15cm, ovate to deltoid, toothed. Cor. red to purple, occas. white, tube to 2cm, pubesc., lips to 2cm, toothed, lat. lobes of lower lip deltoid. Summer. SC Eur. 'Album': lvs large, glab.; fls large, off-white. Z6.

L. vulgatum var. *album* (L.) Benth. = *L. album.*

→*Galeobdolon, Galeopsis, Lamiastrum* and *Leonurus.*

Lampangit *Schefflera longifolia.*

Lampranthus N.E. Br. Aizoaceae. 200 succulent subshrubs to 50cm. St. erect then procumbent. Lvs terete or 3-angled. Fls 1 to several, term. or axill. Summer. S Afr. (Cape Prov.). Z9.

L. aurantiacus (DC.) Schwantes. Lvs 2–3cm, tapered, apiculate, grey-pruinose, minutely rough, spotted. Fls 4–5cm diam., orange. S Cape.

L. aureus (L.) N.E. Br. Lvs 5cm+, mucronate, fresh green, slightly grey-pruinose, minutely spotted. Fls 6cm diam., golden orange. S Cape.

L. bicolor (L.) N.E. Br. Lvs 1.2–2.5cm, semicylindric, tapered, triquetrous above, green with translucent spots. Fls 3.5cm diam., yellow, deep red below. S Cape.

L. bicolorus (L.) Jacobsen = *L. bicolor.*

L. blandus (Haw.) Schwantes. Lvs 3–4cm, triquetrous, short-tapered, light grey-green with minute translucent spots. Fls 6cm diam., pale pink-red. W Cape.

L. comptonii (L. Bol.) N.E. Br. Lvs to 4cm, falcate, swollen, triquetrous, red-apiculate. Fls 2.7cm diam., white, tinged pink below. W Cape.

L. conspicuus (Haw.) N.E. Br. Lvs 6–7cm, inward-curving, tapered, semicylindric, green edged red, often spotted. Fls 5cm diam., purple-red. W Cape.

L. copiosus (L. Bol.) L. Bol. Lvs 1.5–2cm, laterally compressed, ± falcate. Fls 2.6cm diam., pink, opening day and night. Cape Prov.

L. deltoides (L.) Glen. Lvs 1–2cm, triquetrous, short, expanded toward apex with a short point, entire or with margins denticulate, grey-green. Fls 1.2–1.8cm diam., pink to red, sometimes fragrant. W Cape.

L. emarginatus (L.) N.E. Br. Lvs semicylindric, 1.2–1.6cm, mucronate, curved, grey-green, rough with raised dots. Fls 3cm diam., violet to pink. W Cape.

L. falcatus (L.) N.E. Br. Lvs to 0.6cm, triquetrous, compressed, falcate, grey-green, spotted. Fls 1.2–1.6cm diam., pink, fragrant. Cape. var. *galpinii* (L. Bol.) L. Bol. More erect, to 25cm, rarely mat-forming. Lvs 0.5–0.7cm. Fls 17mm diam., pink. W Cape.

L. glaucoides (Haw.) N.E. Br. = *L. aurantiacus.*

L. haworthii (Donn) N.E. Br. Lvs 2.4–4cm, semicylindric, tapered, light green, densely light grey-pruinose. Fls to 7cm diam., light purple. Cape.

L. multiradiatus (Jacq.) N.E. Br. Creeping. Lvs 2.5–3cm, compressed triquetrous, apiculate, decussate, green to grey-green, ± glaucous with translucent dots. Fls to 4cm diam., pale pink to rose-red. S Cape.

L. primavernus (L. Bol.) L. Bol. Lvs 2.4cm, falcate, laterally compressed, tip short-tapered. Fls many together 1.8cm diam., pink to salmon pink. W Cape.

L. promontorii (L. Bol.) N.E. Br. Lvs 1–3cm, compressed triquetrous, apiculate, falcate. Fls 1.4–2.3cm diam., yellow. SW Cape.

L. roseus (Willd.) Schwantes = *L. multiradiatus*.

L. spectabilis (Haw.) N.E. Br. Lvs 5–8cm, upcurved, triquetrous, carinate, awn reddened. Fls 5–7cm, diam., purple-red. Cape. 'Tresco Apricot': fls apricot. 'Tresco Brilliant': fls magenta. 'Tresco Red': fls fiery red.

L. vereculatus (L.) L. Bol. = *Scopelogena vereculata*.

→*Erepsia, Mesembryanthemum, Mesembryanthus* and *Oscularia.*

Lampshade Poppy *Meconopsis integrifolia.*
Lampwick Plant *Phlomis lychnitis.*
Lanceolate Spleenwort *Asplenium billotii.*
Lance Water Fern *Blechnum camfieldii.*
Lancewood *Acacia doratoxylon; Pseudopanax (P. crassifolius).*

Lancisia Fabr. = *Cotula.*

Land Cress *Barbarea verna.*
Langkap *Arenga westerhoutii.*

Langloisia E. Greene Polemoniaceae. 5 sparsely branching, ann. herbs. Lvs narrow, pinnate. Infl. capitate; bracts leafy, spine-tipped; cal. lobes 5, spine-tipped; cor. actinomorphic to 2-lipped, tubular-funnelform; sta. 5. SW US. Z9.

L. punctata (Cov.) Goodd. LILAC-SUNBONNET. 3–5cm, sub-glabrous. Lvs 2.5–3cm, linear, bristly-toothed. Cor. 1.5–2cm, subactinomorphic, lilac, lobes purple-spotted, entire; sta. exserted. Spring–early summer.

→*Gilia.*

Languas J.G. Koenig = *Alpinia.*

Lanium (Lindl.) Benth. Orchidaceae. 6 rhizomatous epiphytic orchids. Secondary st. pseudobulbous or cane-like. Lvs rigid to fleshy, oblong to elliptic-ovate. Infl. a term. rac. or a pan.; fls small; sep. linear-lanceolate to ovate-lanceolate; pet. shorter; lip short-tubular, blade simple, concave. Colomb., Venez., Guianas, Braz., Peru. Z10.

L. avicula (Lindl.) Benth. St. to 3cm, pseudobulbous. Lvs to 3cm, term., broadly elliptic to suborbicular. Rac. to 16cm; peduncle densely tomentose; fls cream to yellow-brown or yellow-green, sometimes spotted red; sep. to 7mm, tomentose. Braz., Peru.

L. microphyllum (Lindl.) Benth. St. to 4cm, slender. Lvs to 3cm, distichous, linear-oblong. Rac. to 7cm; peduncle pilose; fls yellow-brown flushed pink; sep. to 8mm, pilose. Venez., Colomb., Ecuad., Peru, Surinam, Guianas.

→*Epidendrum.*

Lankesteria Lindl. Acanthaceae. 7 shrubby herbs and small shrubs. Lvs entire. Fls in dense bracteate term. spikes, clusters or pan.; cal. lobes 5, narrow; cor. tube slender, limb spreading, lobes 5, usually obovate. Trop. Afr., Madag. Z10.

L. barteri Hook. f. Lvs to 20cm, ovate-oblong. Infl. a spike; bracts closely overlapping; cor. primrose yellow, limb with a vivid orange central blotch extending into throat. Trop. W Afr.

L. elegans (P. Beauv.) Anderson. Lvs to 22cm, elliptic. Infl. a spike; bracts loosely overlapping; cor. pale orange darkening with age. Trop. N Afr.

→*Eranthemum.*

Lanolin Bush *Franklandia fucifolia.*

Lantana L. SHRUB VERBENA. Verbenaceae. 150 shrubs or perenn. herbs. Lvs often rugose, dentate. Fls in spreading heads or spikes, sessile; cal. small, membranous; cor. salver-form, limb 4 or 5-lobed; sta. 4, included. Fr. a drupe. Trop. Americas and Afr., a widespread weed elsewhere in the tropics and sub-trop. Z10.

L. camara L. Shrub to 2m, puberulent to subglabrous. Lvs to 12cm, ovate to ovate-oblong, pubesc., scabrous above, some-what crenate-dentate. Fls in hemispherical heads; cor. yellow to orange or red often with a brighter 'eye', tube to 12mm, curved, exterior puberulent, limb to 9mm diam. Trop. Amer. Over 20

cvs: habit dwarf to standard; fls mostly bicolours, shades ranging from white through yellow and salmon to red, including dwarf forms such as 'Arlequin': fls dark pink and yellow; 'Brazier': fls bright red; 'Fabiola': fls salmon pink and yellow; 'Hybrida': low-growing; fls orange. 'Mr. Bessieres': strong growth; fls pink and yellow; 'Miss Tibbs': fls yellow turning pink; 'Naide': white, with yellow eye; 'Professor Raoux': fls scarlet and orange; 'Schloss Ortenburg': fls brick red and salmon yellow; 'Varia': fls yellow, exterior turning purple, interior orange.

L. camara var. *aculeata* (L.) Mold. = *L. camara.*

L. delicatissima hort. = *L. montevidensis.*

L. hispida HBK = *L. camara.*

L. horrida HBK = *L. camara.*

L. montevidensis (Spreng.) Briq. Herb or shrub to 1m, trailing or scandent, strigose or hirsute. Lvs to 3.5cm, ovate to oblong or lanceolate, coarsely dentate, pubesc. Fls in heads; cor. rose-lilac to violet, tube to 10mm, pubesc., limb to 6mm diam. S Amer.

L. rugulosa HBK. Shrub. Lvs to 6cm, ovate, scabrous above, pubesc. beneath. Heads hemispherical, cor. lilac. Ecuad.

L. sellowiana Link & Otto = *L. montevidensis.*

L. tiliifolia Cham. Shrub to 1.5m, hirsute. Lvs to 10×7cm, broad-ly ovate to elliptic or suborbicular, crenate-dentate. Heads to 5cm diam., hemispherical; cor. to 10mm, yellow or orange becoming brick red with age, tube white-pubesc. S Amer.

L. trifolia L. Erect shrub to 2m, villous. Lvs to 12×6cm, usually whorled, oblong-lanceolate to elliptic-lanceolate, villous, crenate-serrate. Infl. a dense spike; cor. pink, lavender or vio-let, sometimes white, tube to 7mm, interior glab., limb to 6mm diam. W Indies, Mex., C & S Amer.

L. urticifolia Mill. = *L. camara.*

→*Lippia.*

Lantern Tree *Crinodendron hookerianum.*

Lapageria Ruiz & Pav. CHILEAN BELLFLOWER; CHILE BELLS; COPIHUE. Liliaceae (Philesiaceae). 1 everg. perenn. St. twin-ing, wiry, woody at base with sharp bracts. Lvs 6–12cm, ovate-lanceolate to subcordate, glossy, leathery, with prominent parallel veins. Fls campanulate, pendulous, short-stalked, solitary or clustered in axils; tep. 6.5–9.5cm, 6 in 2 whorls, outer tep. flesh pink to magenta, crimson or white, inner tep. narrower, brighter, often faintly spotted or streaked; sta. 6. Summer–winter. Chile. Z9.

L. rosea Ruiz & Pav. 'Beatrice Anderson': fls deep red. 'Flesh Pink': fls flesh coloured. 'Nash Court Pink': fls pink, marbled darker. 'Nash Court Red': fls red. 'Penheale': fls dark red. 'Superba': fls brilliant crimson. var. *albiflora* Hook. Fls white.

Lapeirousia Pourr. Iridaceae. 38 perenn. cormous herbs. Lvs 1 to several, linear-lanceolate, ribbed, winged, usually branched. Infl. a spike or pan; fls regular or zygomorphic; perianth short-tubular, tep. 6; sta. 3; style with 3 br. Trop. & S Afr. Z9.

L. anceps (L. f.) Ker-Gawl. Spike about 6-fld, distichous; fls irregular, white or pink, the lower 3 seg. marked red; tube 25–80mm, v. slender; tep. 10–30mm, narrowly lanceolate. Late winter–spring. S Afr.

L. compressa Pourr. = *L. fabricii.*

L. corymbosa (L. f.) Ker-Gawl. Pan. several-fld, each br. 2-fld; fls regular or slightly irregular, white, yellow, blue or violet, the seg. often with a dark mark at base; tube 4–15mm, tep. usually also 4–15mm. Late spring–summer. S Afr. ssp. *alta* Goldbl. Tep. shorter than perianth tube. ssp. *corymbosa*. Fls blue, marked with white in throat, rarely cream, less than 20cm; tep. 7–10mm, tube 4–10mm. ssp. *fastigiata* (Lam.) Goldbl. Fls over 20mm, violet not marked with white, or cream or yellow with purple marks.

L. denticulata (Lam.) Lawrence = *L. fabricii.*

L. divaricata Bak. Spike 5–12-fld. Fls irregular, somewhat 2-lipped, white or cream, often pink-tinged; perianth tube to 15mm long; tep. to 16mm. Late winter–spring. S Afr.

L. erythrantha (Klotzsch ex Klatt) Bak. Infl. paniculate, many-fld; fls slighty irregular, violet-blue with white, arrow-shaped mark outlined in purple on lower tep., or crimson; tube 6–14mm, slender; tep. 6–11mm. Summer. S trop. Afr.

L. fabricii (Delaroche) Ker-Gawl. Spike to 8-fld; fls large, irregular, cream or yellow with red marks, often pink-tinged on outside; tube 30–50mm, slender; tep. 13–20mm. Spring–early summer. S Afr.

L. fissifolia (Jacq.) Ker-Gawl. = *L. pyramidalis.*

L. jacquinii N.E. Br. Infl. to 10-fld, lax; fls irregular, violet with cream marks, the tube paler; tube 30–40mm, erect; tep. sub-equal. Late winter–spring. S Afr.

L. laxa (Thunb.) N.E. Br. = *Anomatheca laxa.*

L. purpureolutea (Klatt) Bak. = *L. corymbosa* ssp. *fastigiata.*

L. pyramidalis (Lam.) Goldbl. Infl. many-fld, at first distichous, later spirally arranged; fls white, pale to deep blue or carmine red, the lower seg. marked with white or cream; tube 20–40mm. Winter–spring. S Afr.

L. rhodesiana N.E. Br. = *L. erythrantha*.

L. sandersonii Bak. = *L. erythrantha*.

L. silenoides (Jacq.) Ker-Gawl. Spike fairly densely several- to many-fld; fls irregular, magenta or cerise with cream-yellow markings on lower seg.; tube 30–50mm, slender; tep. subequal, lower 3 forming a lip, each with red spot in centre. Winter. S Afr.

Lapidaria (Dinter & Schwantes) Schwantes ex N.E. Br. Aizoaceae. 1 succulent perenn. forming open mats. Lvs united below, divaricate, much thickened, to 1.5×1cm, upper surface flat, lower surface convex and carinate, triquetrous toward tip, smooth, white, margins reddened. Pedicels 5–6cm, broadly compressed; fls 3–5cm diam., golden-yellow. Nam. Z9.

L. margaretae (Schwantes) Schwantes ex N.E. Br.
→*Argyroderma*, *Dinteranthus* and *Mesembryanthemum*.

Lapiedra Lagasca. Amaryllidaceae. 2 bulbous perenn. herbs. Lvs few, basal. Fls 4–9, erect in a scapose umbel; tep. 6, spreading. W Medit. Z8.

L. martinezii Lagasca. Lvs to 25×1cm, with a pale band above. Tep. 8–12mm, white, striped green beneath. Late summer. S Spain, N Afr.

Lapland Willow *Salix lapponum*.

Lappula Gilib.

L. micrantha Eastw. = *Hackelia micrantha*.

Lapsana L.

L. capillaris L. = *Crepis capillaris*.

L. zacintha L. = *Crepis zacintha*.

Larch *Larix*.

Lardizabala Ruiz & Pav. Lardizabalaceae. 2 everg. climbers. Lvs compound. Fls small, unisexual, sep. 6, petaloid, nectaries 6, petaloid: ♂ racemose with 6 united sta.; ♀ solitary, with 6 staminodes. Fr. a many-seeded berry. Chile.

L. biternata Ruiz & Pav. Twining to 4m. Lvs ternate to biternate, dark green above, coriaceous, lfts 5–10cm, ovate, entire or sparsely toothed below. ♂ infl. 7.5–10cm; fls green edged dark brown-purple. Fr. 6cm, ovoid-oblong, dark purple. Winter. Chile. Z9.

LARDIZABALACEAE Decne. 8/21. *Akebia, Decaisnea, Holboellia, Lardizabala, Sinofranchetia, Stauntonia*.

Large Beard-tongue *Penstemon grandiflorus*.
Large Brown Afrikaner *Gladiolus liliaceus*.
Large-cluster Blueberry *Vaccinium amoenum*.
Large Cranberry *Vaccinium macrocarpon*.
Large-flowered Calamint *Calamintha grandiflora*.
Large-flowered Evening Primrose *Oenothera glazioviana*.
Large-flowered Magnolia *Magnolia grandiflora*.
Large Gallberry *Ilex coriacea*.
Large Kangaroo Apple *Solanum laciniatum*.
Large-leaf Pea Bush *Pultenaea daphnoides*.
Large-leaved Cucumber Tree *Magnolia macrophylla*.
Large-leaved Hau *Hibiscus macrophyllus*.
Large-leaved Lime *Tilia platyphyllos*.
Large-leaved White Violet *Viola incognita*.
Large-leaved Wild Coffee *Coffea zanguebariae*.
Large Myrtle *Hypocalymma puniceum*.
Larger Mountain Monkey Flower *Mimulus tilingii*.
Large Self-heal *Prunella grandiflora*.
Large White Paper Daisy *Helipterum floribundum*.
Large White Petunia *Petunia axillaris*.
Large Woodsia *Woodsia obtusa*.
Large Yellow Foxglove *Digitalis grandiflora*.
Large Yellow Gourd *Cucurbita maxima*.
Large Yellow Restharrow *Ononis natrix*.

Larix Mill. LARCH. Pinaceae. c14 decid., coniferous trees. Bark furrowed, exfoliating. Crown conic becoming irregular; br. horizontal or drooping; shoots long and short. Lvs acicular, in loose spirals on long shoots and in pseudowhorls on short shoots. Cones term. on short shoots; ♂ cones spherical to ovoid, pink or yellow; ♀ cones erect, cylindric or ovoid to spherical, green, red or purple, then brown. N Hemis.

L. americana Michx. = *L. laricina*.

L. chinensis Beissn. = *L. potaninii*.

L. dahurica Turcz. ex Trautv. = *L. gmelinii*.

L. decidua Mill. EUROPEAN LARCH. To 50m. Bark grey-brown, fissured, flaking. Crown slender, conic; br. horizontal, branchlets drooping. Lvs 2–4(-6.5)cm, soft, flat or slightly keeled beneath pale green. Cones 1.5 to 6cm, conic to cylindric, brown; scales 40–50, straight or incurved, sometimes short-hairy on outer surface. Alps, Carpath. About 20 cvs described, nearly all varying in habit, from dwarf ('Compacta', 'Corley', 'Repens'), erect ('Fastigiata'), pendulous ('Pendula', 'Viminalis') to twisted ('Cervicornis', 'Tortuosa') and sparsely branched ('Virgata'). In 'Alba', the immature cones are pale green, almost white. ssp. *polonica* (Racib.) Domin. POLISH LARCH. To 30m, crown v. slender. Branchlets drooping. Cones smaller, 1–2.8cm, blunter, scales concave. W Poland, Ukraine. Z4.

L. ×eurolepis Henry. = *L. ×marschlinsii* Coaz non hort.

L. europaea DC. = *L. decidua*.

L. gmelinii (Rupr.) Rupr. ex Kuzn. DAHURIAN LARCH. To 35m or shrubby. Bark rust-brown. Crown broad conic, open; br. and branchlets horizontal. Lvs to 3cm, obtuse, light green, with two stomatal bands beneath and a diffuse band above. Cones 1.5–3, rarely 4×1–2cm, ovoid, lustrous pale brown; scales truncate, undulate. E Asia. var. *japonica* (Reg.) Pilger. KURILE LARCH. Shoots rust-brown to purple, pruinose. Lvs to 2.5cm, outspread, rigid, subulate. Cones ovoid, 1–2cm, rarely to 3cm; scales more pointed. Russia (Sakhalin, Kurile Is.) var. *olgensis* (Henry) Ostenf. & Larsen. OLGA BAY LARCH. Shoots beige, densely brown-pubesc. Lvs subulate, to 2.5cm. Cone scales truncate to obtuse, faintly emarginate. E Sib. Z1.

L. gmelinii var. *principis-rupprechtii* (Mayr) Pilger = *L. principis-ruprechtii*.

L. griffithiana (Lindl. & Gordon) Carr. SIKKIM LARCH. To 40m, to 20m in cult. Bark grey-brown, grooved in rough ridges. Crown conic; shoots buff, short-hairy. Lvs obtuse, 25–50×2mm, light green, keeled with stomata in 2 bands beneath and scattered above. Cones narrow conic-cylindric, 4–8×1.5cm closed, opening to 3cm wide near base, 2cm wide near apex, purple-brown; scales to 1.5cm broad, base pubesc. Himal. Z7.

L. griffithiana var. *speciosa* (Cheng & Law). = *L. speciosa*.

L. griffithii Hook. f. = *L. griffithiana*.

L. himalaica Cheng & L.K. Fu. To 40m; crown similar to *L. potaninii*. Shoots pendulous on level br. Lvs 10–25×1.5–2mm, pale green with two indistinct stomatal bands beneath. Cones 4–6.5×2cm, pale buff; scales slightly truncate rounded. SC Tibet, C Nepal. Z7.

L. kaempferi (Lamb.) Carr. JAPANESE LARCH. To 45m. Bark rust-brown to greyer, fissured and scaly. Crown broad conic; br. and shoots horizontal or slightly ascending. Lvs 2–3.5cm, slightly keeled beneath, grey-green, with stomatal bands throughout. Cones 2–3, rarely 4cm; ovoid; scales truncate to emarginate, apex reflexed. Jap. About 20 cvs described, mainly varying in habit, and mostly dwarf ('Blue Dwarf', 'Nana', 'Varley', 'Wehlen') or with pendulous branchlets ('Georgengarten', 'Inversa', 'Pendula'), or both ('Hanan'). In 'Blue Haze' the lvs are v. bright glaucous, as also in the semifastigiate 'Pyramidalis Argentea'. Z4.

L. laricina (Du Roi) K. Koch. TAMARACK; AMERICAN LARCH. To 20(–30)m. Bark grey, becoming brown and scaly. Crown conic; br. horizontal, branclets drooping. Lvs 2–3cm, keeled, pale green with 2 stomatal bands beneath. Cones ovoid, 12–24mm, green or purple, becoming straw-brown; scales 15–20, nearly circular, margins slightly incurved. N N Amer. 'Arethusa Bog': dwarf; shoots short, narrow, br. over-arching. 'Aurea': young lvs gold, later light green. 'Glauca': lvs metallic blue. var. *alaskensis* (Wight) Raup. Cones 1–1.5cm with paler, more spreading scales. C Alask. Z2.

L. leptolepis (Sieb. & Zucc.) Gordon = *L. kaempferi*.

L. lyallii Parl. SUBALPINE LARCH. Closely related to *L. occidentalis*, but shoots initially densely pubesc.; to 25m, bark thin, flaking, grey-brown. Lvs 2–4cm, slender, quadrangular, glaucous above, two pale stomatal bands beneath. Cones 2.5–4.5cm, pubesc. at first, maturing glab., buff, with broad, long exserted purple bracts, scales to 1cm. N Amer. (Rocky Mts). Zone 3.

L. ×marschlinsii Coaz. (*L. decidua* ×*L. kaempferi*.) DUNKELD LARCH; HYBRID LARCH. Vigorous. Similar to *L. decidua* but shoots and lvs faintly glaucous. Cones conic, scale tips slightly reflexed. Gdn origin.

L. ×marschlinsii hort. non Coaz. (*L. kaempferi* ×*L. russica*.) Cultivated hybrid intermediate between the two spp. It has no currently valid name.

L. mastersiana Rehd. & Wils. To 25m. Bark dull brown, furrowed. Br. horizontal; long shoots drooping. Lvs 1–3.5cm, keeled, acuminate, light green, with 2 stomatal bands beneath. Cones 3–4cm, subsessile, cylindric, finely downy; seed scales reniform to broadly rounded. W China. Z7.

L. occidentalis Nutt. WESTERN LARCH. To 50m. Bole to 1.8m diam. Bark grey-brown, flaking in thin scales, becoming maroon-brown and deeply furrowed. Br. horizontal. Lvs 2.5–5cm, keeled beneath, slightly convex above, acute, blue-green to grey-green, with 2 stomatal bands beneath. Cones 2.5–4.5×1cm ovoid, scales rounded, to 12mm broad, reflexed on opening, to 2.5cm broad. W N Amer. Z4.

L. olgensis Henry = *L. gmelinii* var. *olgensis*.

L. ×*pendula* (Sol.) Salisb. (*L. decidua* ×*L. laricina*.) WEEPING LARCH. To 30m. Branchlets pendent. Lvs similar to *L. decidua*, apex blunter. Cones 2–3.2cm, ovoid; scales 20–30, exterior base downy. Origin obscure, possibly Newfoundland but not found in the wild. 'Contorta': young shoots twisted. 'Repens': br. creeping horizontally. Z4.

L. potaninii Batal. CHINESE LARCH. To 40m, to 20m in cult. Bark becoming deeply grooved, brown. Crown columnar. Lvs 1.5–3cm, keeled, acute, light green (glaucous on some plants). Cones 3–5cm, oblong-ovate, purple becoming brown; scales rounded, often emarginate. W China. var. *macrocarpa* Law. Shoots lustrous red-brown. Cones stout, cylindric-conic, 5–8.5×2cm; scales long, broad-based, erect. SW China. Z5.

L. principis-rupprechtii Mayr. PRINCE RUPPRECHT LARCH. To 40m, crown broad conic, br. level. Lvs similar to *L. gmelinii*, but to 35mm. Cones 2.5–4×2cm; scales numerous, shorter than in *L. gmelinii*, smoothly rounded and scarcely wavy or emarginate at apex. N China. Z4.

L. russica (Endl.) Sab. ex Trautv. SIBERIAN LARCH. To 30m. Bark rust-brown, scaly, becoming deeply grooved. Crown narrowly conic; br. horizontal to upswept. Lvs 2.5–4cm, clustered, v. narrow, soft, bright green above, with 2 stomatal bands beneath and scattered stomata above. Cones 2.5–3.5cm, rarely 4cm, seed scales thick, pubesc, margins incurved. Russia. 'Fastigiata': columnar and compact. 'Glauca': needles glaucous. 'Longifolia': needles longer. 'Pendula': br. weeping. 'Robusta': more vigorous. Z1.

L. sibirica Ledeb. = *L. russica*.

L. speciosa Cheng & Law. To 30m; crown as *L. potaninii*. Lvs 25–55×1.5–2mm, green with 2 white-green stomatal bands beneath. Cones with reflexed bracts as in *L. griffithiana*, but cylindric and stouter, 7–9×2–3cm opening to ×4cm. SW China, NE Burm. Z8.

L. thibetica Franch. = *L. potaninii*.

L. wulingschanensis Liou & Wang = *L. principis-rupprechtii*.

Larkspur *Consolida; Delphinium.*
Larkspur Violet *Viola pedatifida.*

Larrea Cav. CREOSOTE BUSH. Zygophyllaceae. 5 xerophytic resinous, everg. shrubs. St. jointed, suckering. Lvs compound, lfts to 1.5cm. Fls solitary, ♂; sep. 5, unequal; pet. to 1cm, yellow, 5, oblong-spathulate, clawed; sta. 10 on a lobed disc; ovary 5-loculate, superior. S Amer. to W US.

L. divaricata Cav. JARRILLA. 1–4m, much-branched; shoots angular, grooved. Lfts 3–5, ovate-oblong, acuminate, olive green. Arg. Z9.

L. nitida Cav. 1–3m; shoots angular, downy. Lfts 11–15, linear-oblong, obtuse. Chile, Arg. Z9.

L. tridentata (DC.) Cov. CREOSOTE BUSH; COVILLE. To 4m, aromatic; bark dark grey to black. Lfts 2–3, oblong-lanceolate, mucronate, dark to yellow-green. SW US to N Mex. Z8.

Lasiagrostis Link.
L. calamagrostis (L.) Link. = *Stipa calamagrostis*.
L. splendens (Trin.) Kunth. = *Stipa splendens*.

Lasianthaea DC. Compositae. 12 perenn. herbs or shrubs. Cap. radiate, solitary, or terminal, few in umbelliform clusters; involucre campanulate or hemispheric. Ariz. to Venez. Z9.

L. aurea (D. Don) K. Becker. Perenn. herb, to 60cm, st. simple or sparingly branched. Lvs 7×2cm, lanceolate or elliptic, acute or obtuse, base subauriculate, sessile, margins serrulate or denticulate, often revolute. Cap. 2–2.5cm diam., solitary or few in clusters; ray floorets to 10×5mm, 8–11, bright yellow; disc flts yellow. Summer–autumn. Mex.

L. helianthoides DC. Shrub or subshrub to 4m; st. branched. Lvs to 12×6cm, ovate or lanceolate, apex acute or shortly acuminate, base rounded or subcordate, margin crenate-denticulate or serrate, somewhat revolute. Cap. 2–4cm diam., 3–12, in dense clusters; ray flts to 15×7mm, 9–21, bright yellow or orange, disc flts yellow or orange. Summer–autumn. Mex.

→*Tithonia* and *Wedelia*.

Lasiostelma Benth.
L. sandersonii Oliv. = *Brachystelma sandersonii*.

Lasthenia Cass. Compositae. 16 ann. to perenn. herbs. Lvs opposite, simple, entire oor pinnatifid. Cap. radiate, term., often showy, pedunculate; receptacle conical. Pacific N Amer.,

C Chile.

L. californica Lindl. = *L. glabrata*.

L. chrysostoma (Fisch. & Mey.) Greene. Erect to decumbent, white-pubesc. ann., to 40cm. Lvs linear, occas. shortly dentate, hirsute or strigose. Ray flts to 1cm, bright yellow, apex sometimes lighter. Oreg. to NW Mex. and Ariz.

L. coronaria (Nutt.) Ornd. Erect, pubesc. ann., to 40cm. Lvs to 6cm, linear and entire, or pinnate, or laciniate with seg. to 3cm. Ray flts to 1cm, yellow. SW Calif. to NW Mex.

L. glabrata Lindl. Erect, glab. or pubesc. ann., to 60cm. Lvs to 15cm, linear or subulate, entire or obscurely dentate, fleshy, glab., connate at base. Ray flts to 14mm, golden- or lemon-yellow. CW Calif.

L. gracilis (DC.) Greene = *L. chrysostoma*.

L. hirsutula Greene = *L. chrysostoma*.

L. macrantha (A. Gray) Greene. Erect or decumbent, ± caespitose, short-lived perenn., rarely ann. or bienn., pubesc. Lvs to 21cm, linear to oblong, entire or few-dentate, glab. to densely hirsute, margins ciliate. Ray flts to 16mm, bright yellow. SW Oreg. to CW Calif. Z8.

→*Baeria, Burrielia, Hymenoxys* and *Ptilomeris*.

Lastrea Bory.
L. acuminata Houlst. = *Lastreopsis acuminata*.
L. articulata Brackenr. = *Arthropteris articulata*.
L. decomposita (R. Br.) J. Sm. = *Lastreopsis decomposita*.
L. gracilescens Bedd. = *Parathelypteris beddomei*.
L. hispida (Sw.) Moore & Houlst. = *Lastreopsis hispida*.
L. maximowiczii (Bak.) Moore = *Arachniodes maximowiczii*.
L. microsora (Endl.) Presl = *Lastreopsis microsora*.
L. oreopteris (Ehrh.) Bory = *Oreopteris limbosperma*.
L. quinquangulare (Kunze) J. Sm. = *Lastreopsis microsora*.
L. standishii Moore = *Arachniodes standishii*.
L. thelypteris (L.) Bory = *Thelypteris palustris*.

Lastreopsis Ching. Dryopteridaceae. 30–35 terrestrial or epiphytic ferns. Rhiz. short- to long-creeping, tufted, or erect. Fronds 2–5-pinnate or -pinnatifid, ± deltoid, glandular-pubesc., seg. decurrent; stipes often ridged and glandular-pubesc. Trop. Z10.

L. acuminata (Houlst.) Morton. SHINY SHIELD FERN. Rhiz. tufted. Fronds to 90cm, 2-pinnate-pinnatifid, deltoid, apex narrowly acute, lustrous, seg. oblong, toothed; rachis pubesc.; stipes to 80cm. Aus.

L. calantha (Endl.) Tind. Fronds to 80cm, 3–4-pinnate, glaucous; stipes approximate and clustered. Norfolk Is.

L. decomposita (R. Br.) Tind. Rhiz. short-creeping. Fronds to 50×40cm, 2–4-pinnate, ovate to deltoid or pentagonal, leathery to membranous, initially pubesc., pinnae to 35×25cm, stalked, ovate to deltoid, acute, secondary pinnae ± sessile, distant, ovate to lanceolate, pinnules alt., lanceolate to oblong, seg. ovate to lanceolate, margin entire or notched; stipes to 50cm, rough and scaly at base, pale brown. Aus.

L. effusa (Sw.) Tind. Rhiz. short-creeping. Fronds to 1×1m, 2–5-pinnate or -pinnatifid, deltoid, lustrous above, glab. to glandular-pubesc. beneath, pinnae to 45×30cm, stalked, deltoid, pinnules stalked, approximate, lanceolate, seg. ovate to lanceolate to oblong, notched to lobed; stipes to 1m, scaly at base, straw-coloured. Trop. Amer.

L. glabella (A. Cunn.) Tind. SMOOTH SHIELD FERN. Rhiz. short-creeping or erect. Fronds to 35×25cm, 2–3-pinnate, ovate to deltoid, membranous, pinnae to 12×8cm, ovate to deltoid, pinnules lanceolate, oblong, seg. approximate or distant, ovate to deltoid, margin toothed and spiny; stipes to 30cm, glab. or sparsely pubesc. at base. Aus., NZ, Polyn.

L. grayi D. Jones. Rhiz. tufted. Fronds to 90cm, 2-pinnate or -pinnatifid, deltoid, lustrous, seg. distant; stipes flexible, sparsely scaly, brown. Aus.

L. hispida (Sw.) Tind. BRISTLY SHIELD FERN. Rhiz. long-creeping. Fronds to 40×25cm, 3–4-pinnate or -pinnatifid, deltoid, leathery to membranous, pinnae to 13×10cm, stalked, ovate or lanceolate to deltoid, secondary pinnae stalked, ovate or lanceolate to rhomboid, pinnules opposite, seg. falcate, ovate or lanceolate to deltoid, or oblong, toothed; stipes to 50cm, grooved, scaly at base, pubesc. to bristly, lustrous, grey to brown. Aus., NZ.

L. marginans (F. Muell.) D.A. Sm. & Tind. Rhiz. short-creeping. Fronds to 70×60cm, 3–4-pinnate, pentagonal, leathery and lustrous, pinnae to 12×8cm, 13–18 pairs, sessile to stalked, often falcate, ovate, pinnules 14–20 pairs, sessile to short-stalked, lanceolate to rhomboid or oblong, seg. sessile, ovate to deltoid, entire or toothed; stipes to 50cm, scaly at base and sparsely pubesc., red-brown. Aus.

L. microsora (Endl.) Tind. CREEPING SHIELD FERN. Rhiz. long-creeping. Fronds to 50×45cm, 3–4-pinnate or -pinnatifid, deltoid to pentagonal, glab. or pubesc. beneath, pinnae to 40×20cm, stalked, approximate to overlapping, ovate to lanceolate, secondary pinnae ovate or lanceolate to oblong, pinnules stalked, alt., ovate or lanceolate to oblong, seg. sessile, toothed; stipes to 50cm, rough, brown. Aus., NZ.

L. munita (Mett.) Tind. Rhiz. long-creeping. Fronds to 50×45cm, 2–3-pinnate, pentagonal, leathery, lustrous above, pinnae to 25×19cm, stalked, ovate to lanceolate, pinnules sessile or stalked, alt., lanceolate or elliptic to oblong, truncate or obtuse, seg. sessile, alt., elliptic to oblong, truncate, toothed; stipes to 50cm, rough, scaly at base, pubesc., brown. Aus.

L. nephrodioides (Bak.) Tind. Rhiz. long-creeping. Fronds to 90cm, 2–3-pinnate, deltoid, firm-textured, lustrous, pinnae to 10cm, pinnules to 25mm, uppermost reduced, approximate to imbricate, margin toothed to lobed. Aus.

L. rufescens (Bl.) Ching. Rhiz. short-creeping. Fronds to 45×30cm, 2–3-pinnate or -pinnatifid, deltoid, lustrous, glab., initially dark green to purple, pinnae to 20×10cm, deltoid, pinnules lanceolate, toothed to lobed; rachis sparsely pubesc.; stipes to 45cm, glab. or sparsely pubesc. Trop. Asia; Aus.

L. shepherdii (Kunze ex Mett.) Tind. = *L. acuminata*.

L. smithiana Tind. Rhiz. tufted to erect. Fronds to 45×45cm, 2–4-pinnate or -pinnatifid, deltoid, stiff, ± lustrous, pinnae to 28×22cm, 10–25 pairs, stalked, distant, falcate, ovate to lanceolate, secondary pinnae 12–15 pairs, distant, seg. alt., falcate, rhomboid to oblong, obtuse, toothed and spiny; stipes to 55cm, scaly at base, pubesc. above, lustrous above. Aus.

L. velutina (A. Rich.) Tind. Rhiz. erect. Fronds to 45×40cm, 2–4-pinnate, deltoid, membranous, pubesc., pinnae to 25×15cm, ovate to deltoid, secondary pinnae, lanceolate, pinnules oblong, seg. deltoid to oblong; stipes to 50cm, scaly at base, pubesc. above, brown. NZ.

→*Aspidium, Ctenitis, Deparia, Dryopteris, Lastrea, Phegopteris, Polystichum* and *Rumohra*.

Latace Philippi. Liliaceae (Alliaceae). 1 perenn. bulbous herb. Lvs 2, basal, narrow. Scape to 25cm; fls small, in a term. umbel; perianth seg. 6, white, lower half united into a tube, sta. 3, staminodes 3; style included. Summer. Chile. Z9.

L. volckmannii Philippi.

Latania Comm. Palmae. 3 palms to 16m. St. solitary, erect, scarred, sometimes swollen at base. Crown dense; lvs costapalmate; sheath angled, base split; petiole to 1m, channelled above near base, convex and floccose beneath, sometimes armed; blade divided to halfway, seg. single-fold, rigid, floccose or waxy beneath. ♂ infl. interfoliar, shorter than lvs, branched at apex into radiating rachillae. Fr. oblong or obovoid, 3-seeded, smooth. Masc. Is.; almost extinct in the wild. Z10.

L. aurea Duncan = *L. verschaffeltii*.

L. borbonica Lam. = *L. lontaroides*.

L. commersonii J.F. Gmel. = *L. lontaroides*.

L. loddigesii Mart. BLUE LATAN. Lf blades to 1.5m, blue-green. Maur. Is.

L. lontaroides (Gaertn.) H.E. Moore. RED LATAN. Lf blades to 1.5m, grey-green; petiole and base of blade ringed red-purple. Réunion.

L. rubra Jacq. = *L. lontaroides*.

L. verschaffeltii Lem. YELLOW LATAN. Lf blades to 1.35m, tinged pale green and edged yellow. Rodrigues Is.

Latanier Balai *Coccothrinax argentea*.
Latanier Caye *Copernicia berteroana*.
Latanier Latte *Verschaffeltia*.
Latanier Palm *Phoenicophorium*.
Late Dutch Honeysuckle *Lonicera periclymenum* 'Serotina'.
Late Poplar *Populus* ×*canadensis*.
Late Spider Orchid *Ophrys holoserica*.
Late Sweet Blueberry *Vaccinium angustifolium*.

Lathraea L. Scrophulariaceae. 7 root parasites, lacking chlorophyll. Lvs fleshy, scale-like, decussate on largely subterranean rhiz. Rac. emergent; cal. erect, campanulate, 4-lobed; cor. tubular, 2-lipped, upper lip hooded, lower lip entire or 3-lobed; sta. 4, concealed or protruding. Summer. Temp. Eur., Asia. Z6.

L. clandestina L. St. stout, clumped, subterranean, ivory with rounded yellow scale lvs. Infl. congested, scarcely emergent; cal. to 2cm, lilac; cor. to 5cm, violet. SW Eur., nat. in GB.

L. squamaria L. TOOTHWORT. St. narrow, ivory with acute scale lvs, becoming buff above ground. Infl. elongate, secund, clearly emergent; cal to 1cm, flesh pink; cor. to 2cm, white tinted lilac or rose. Eur.

Lathyrus L. VETCHLING; WILD PEA. Leguminosae (Papilionoideae). 110 ann. or perenn. herbs, often climbing by lf tendrils. St. usually winged. Lvs usually paripinnate; stipules often leaf-like. Fls papilionaceous in axill. rac., or solitary. Fr. a narrow-

oblong, flat legume. Eurasia, N Amer., mts of E Afr. and temp. S Amer.

L. acutifolius Vogel = *L. pubescens*.

L. affinis Guss. = *L. aphaca*.

L. americanus (Mill.) Kupicha = *L. nervosus*.

L. andicolus Gand. = *L. pubescens*.

L. angustifolius Martrin-Donos = *L. latifolius*.

L. angustifolius Medik. = *L. sylvestris*.

L. aphaca L. YELLOW VETCHLING. Ann. to 1m; st. angled. Mature lvs terminate in tendril; lfts 1 pair on juvenile lvs, 0 on mature lvs. Fls usually stipular; cor. yellow, to 1.8cm. Late spring–summer. W & C Eur.

L. armitageanus Westc. ex Loud. = *L. nervosus*.

L. asiaticus (Zalk.) Kudrj. = *L. sativus*.

L. aureus (Steven) Brândza. Ann. Sparsely pubesc. Lfts 2.5–5cm across, in 3–6 pairs, oval to ovate, with brown glands beneath. Fls in rac.; cor. 1.7–2.2cm, brown to yellow-orange. Balk. Z6.

L. aureus hort. non (Steven) Brândza = *L. gmelinii*.

L. azureus hort. = *L. sativus*.

L. californicus Douglas = *L. japonicus* ssp. *maritimus*.

L. cyaneus (Steven) K. Koch. Perenn., to 30cm. St. angular. Lfts to 8cm, in 1–3 pairs, linear-lanceolate. Rac. 1–15-fld; cor. to 2.5cm, blue-lilac, white at base. Summer. Cauc. Z6.

L. davidii Hance. Perenn. to 120cm, glab. Lvs terminate in a branched tendril; lfts to 8cm, 3–4 pairs, rhomboid-oval, or oval-oblong. Rac. many-fld; cor. yellow-white, later ochre. Summer. Manch., N China, Korea, Jap. Z6.

L. drummondii hort. = *L. rotundifolius*.

L. dumetorum Philippi = *L. pubescens*.

L. ewaldii (Meinsh.) Meinsh. = *L. laevigatus*.

L. gmelinii (Fisch. ex DC.) Fritsch. To 1.5m; st. glab. or pubesc. Lfts to 10cm, 3–6 pairs, broad-lanceolate, slightly glaucous beneath. Rac. 4–15-fld; cor. to 3cm, light- to orange-yellow, brown-striped. Summer. C & S Urals, mts of C Asia. Z4.

L. gmelinii auct. non (Fisch. ex DC.) Fritsch = *L. laevigatus*.

L. gramineus A. Gray = *L. nissolia*.

L. grandiflorus Sibth. & Sm. TWO-FLOWERED PEA; EVERLASTING PEA. Perenn. to 2m; st. angled, scabrous to pubesc. Lvs terminating in a 3-branched tendril; lfts to 5cm, 1 pair (rarely 3 pairs), ovate. Rac. 1–4-fld; cor. to 3cm, standard violet, keel pink, wings mauve. Summer. S It., Sicily, S Balk. Z6.

L. heterophyllus L. Resembles *L. latifolius*, but with 2–3 pairs of lfts, and fls smaller. Summer. C & W Eur. Z6.

L. hirsutus L. SINGLETARY PEA; CALEY PEA; ROUGH PEA; WINTER PEA; AUSTRIAN PEA. Perenn. to 50cm; st. angular. Lvs not terminating in a tendril; lfts to 4cm, 1 pair, lanceolate to suborbicular, acute. Rac. 2–6-fld; cor. to 2cm, blue-violet. SE Eur. Z7.

L. incurvus Rchb. = *L. palustris*.

L. inermis Rochel ex Friv. = *L. laxiflorus*.

L. japonicus Willd. CIRCUMPOLAR PEA; BEACH PEA; SEA PEA. Perenn. to 90cm; st. angled; lfts to 4cm, 2–5 pairs, elliptic. Rac. 2–7-fld; cor. to 2.5cm, purple, becoming blue. Summer. Coasts of W & N Eur., China, N Amer. ssp. *maritimus* (L.) P.W. Ball. Rac. 5–12-fld; cor. to 18mm. Coasts of W Eur. & Baltic, N Amer. Z3.

L. japonicus var. *glaber* (Ser.) Fern. = *L. japonicus* ssp. *maritimus*.

L. laetiflorus Greene. Perenn. to 2m. Lvs terminate in a tendril; lfts to 5cm, 4–6 pairs, narrow-linear to ovate. Rac. 5–12-fld; cor. to 2.5cm, white or pink-flushed, to blue or crimson. Summer. W US. Z8.

L. laevigatus (Waldst. & Kit.) Gren. To 70cm. St. angular, glab. or soft-hairy. Lfts to 7cm, 2–6 pairs, elliptic to ovate, blue-green beneath. Rac. 3–17-fld; cor. 2.5cm, yellow. Summer. C Eur. to N Spain, N Balk. and N Ukraine. Z5.

L. latifolius L. PERENNIAL PEA; BROAD-LEAVED EVERLASTING PEA. Perenn. to 3m; st. winged, pubesc. or glab. Lvs terminate in a 3-branched tendril; lfts to 15cm, 1 pair, linear to elliptic, somewhat blue-green. Rac. 5–15-fld; cor. to 3cm diam., magenta-purple, pink, or white. Summer. C & S Eur., nat. N Amer. 'Albus' ('Snow Queen'): fls white. 'Blushing Bride': fls white flushed pink. 'Pink Beauty': fls dark-purple and red. 'Red Pearl': fls carmine red. 'Rosa Perle' ('Pink Pearl'): vigorous; fls pink, long-lasting. 'Splendens': fls deep-pink. Z5.

L. laxiflorus (Desf.) Kuntze. Glab. or pubesc. perenn. to 50cm. Lfts 1 pair, 2–4cm, lanceolate to suborbicular. Rac. 2–6-fld; cor. 1.5–2cm, violet. SE Eur. Z7.

L. linifolius (Reichard) Bässler. var. *montanus* (Bernh.) Bässler. St. to 50cm, winged. Lfts 1–5cm, in 1–4 pairs, oval or linear. Rac. 2–6-fld; cor. 1–1.6cm, deep pink to blue. W & C Eur. Z6.

L. luteus (L.) Peterm. non Moench = *L. gmelinii*.

L. luteus hort. non (L.) Peterm. = *L. aureus*.

L. magellanicus Lam. = *L. nervosus*.

L. megalanthus Steud. = *L. latifolius*.

L. membranaceus C. Presl = *L. latifolius*.

L. montanus Bernh. = *L. linifolius* var. *montanus*.

L. myrtifolius Muhlenb. = *L. palustris*.

L. nervosus Lam. LORD ANSON'S BLUE PEA. Perenn. to 60cm. Lvs terminate in a 3-branched tendril; lfts to 4cm, 1 pair, ovate to ovate-oblong. Rac. long-stalked, 3–7-fld; cor. to 2.2cm, indigo. Summer. S Amer. Z9.

L. neurolobus Boiss. & Heldr. Perenn. to 50cm. Lower lvs with compound tendrils, upper lvs with simple tendril; lfts to 12cm, 1 pair, oblong. Rac. 1–2-fld; cor. to 1cm, blue. Crete. Z8.

L. niger (L.) Bernh. BLACK PEA. Perenn. to 80cm. St. angular. Lfts to 3.5cm, 3–6 pairs, elliptic or oblong-oval, mucronate. Rac. 3–6-fld; cor. to 1.5cm, lilac-violet. Summer. Eur., Cauc., Syr., N Afr. Z6.

L. nissolia L. GRASS VETCHLING. Ann. to 90cm, glab. Lvs simple, reduced to a blade-like midrib, without a tendril. Rac. 1–2-fld; cor. to 18mm, crimson. Late spring–early summer. Eur.

L. occidentalis Nutt. ex Torr. & A. Gray = *L. palustris*.

L. odoratus L. SWEETPEA. Ann. to 2m; st. somewhat downy. Lfts to 6cm, 1 pair, oval to ovate-oblong. Rac. 1–3-fld; cor. to 3.5cm, typically purple, now highly developed resulting in a vast range of cvs with fls clustered or on long racs, large or small, sometimes ruffled or 'double', sweetly to heavily scented, in shades of red, rose, mauve, purple, purple-black, white, opal, blue, lilac, peach, cream, pale yellow and variously mottled or veined. Summer. Crete, It., Sicily. var. *nanellus* L.H. Bail. Plants compact, not climbing.

L. ornatus Nutt. ex Torr. & A. Gray. Erect perenn. to 30cm or more. Lfts in 4–7 pairs, linear. Rac. 3–5-fld; cor. 2.5cm, purple. US. Z3.

L. palustris L. MARSH PEA. Perenn. to 120cm; st. narrow-winged. Lvs terminate in branched tendrils; lfts to 8cm, in 2–5 pairs, linear to lanceolate. Rac. long-stalked, 2–8-fld; cor. to 2.2cm, purple-blue. Summer. Eur. to E Asia, Jap. and E N Amer. Z5.

L. petiolaris Vogel = *L. pubescens*.

L. pilosus Cham. = *L. palustris*.

L. polyanthus Boiss. & Bl. = *L. aphaca*.

L. pratensis L. COMMON VETCHLING; MEADOW VETCHLING; YELLOW VETCHLING. Perenn. to 120cm. Lvs terminate in a tendril; lfts 4cm, 1 pair, linear-lanceolate to elliptic. Rac. long-stalked, 2–12-fld; cor. to 1.6cm, yellow. Late spring–summer. Eur., N Afr. to Asia, Sib. and Himal. Z4.

L. pseudoaphaca Boiss. = *L. aphaca*.

L. pubescens Hook. & Arn. Perenn. to 3m; st. pubesc., gland. Lvs terminate in a 3-branched tendril; lfts to 7.5cm, 1–2 pairs, elliptic-lanceolate. Rac. 6–16-fld; cor. 2.5cm diam., lilac or indigo. Summer. Chile, Arg. Z9.

L. roseus Steven. Perenn. to 1.5m; st. angular, glab. Lvs not usually terminating in a tendril; lfts to 5cm, 1 pair, ovate-orbicular. Rac. 1–5-fld; cor. to 2cm, rose-pink. Summer. Turk., Cauc. Z6.

L. rotundifolius Willd. PERSIAN EVERLASTING PEA. Perenn. to 1m; st. angular, glab. Lvs terminate in a 3-branched tendril; lfts to 6cm, 1 pair, ovate-orbicular. Rac. 3–8-fld; cor. to 2cm, deep-pink. Summer. E Eur., W Asia. Z6.

L. sativus L. INDIAN PEA; RIGA PEA; DOGTOOTH PEA; KHESARI. Ann. to 1m; st. angular. Stipules to 2.5×0.5cm, lanceolate, semi-sagittate; lfts to 15×1cm, 1–2 pairs, linear to lanceolate, acuminate. Fls solitary on stalks to 3cm long; cal. short-campanulate; cor. to 2.5cm, white, pink or blue. Eur.

L. splendens Kellogg. PRIDE OF CALIFORNIA. Shrubby perenn. to 3m; st. angled. Lvs terminate in a branched tendril; lfts o 7cm, 3–5 pairs, narrow-linear to ovate-oblong. Rac. 4–12-fld; cor. to 4cm, rose, violet, or magenta-red. Calif., Baja Calif. Z8.

L. strictus Torr. & A. Gray = *L. laetiflorus*.

L. sylvestris L. FLAT PEA; NARROW-LEAVED EVERLASTING PEA. Perenn. to 2m; st. angular, winged. Lvs with a branched tendril; lfts to 15cm, 1 pair, linear to lanceolate. Rac. long-stalked, 3–12-fld; cor. to 2cm, purple-pink mottled purple and green. Summer. Eur. 'Wagneri': fls deep red. Z6.

L. tingitanus L. TANGIER PEA. Ann. to 120cm; st. winged, glab. Lfts to 8cm, 1 pair, linear-lanceolate to ovate. Rac. 1–3-fld; cor. to 3cm, rose-pink. S & E Iberian Penins., Sardinia, Azores.

L. tuberosus L. EARTH CHESTNUT; TUBEROUS PEA; FYFIELD PEA; EARTH-NUT PEA; DUTCH-MICE; TUBEROUS VETCH. Perenn. to 120cm; st. 4-angled, glab., from a rootstock which produces small tubers. Lvs terminate in a 3-branched tendril; lfts to 4.5cm, 1 pair, oblong-ovate. Rac. long-stalked, 2–7-fld; cor. to 2cm, rose-pink. Summer. Eur. (except N and extreme S). Z6.

L. variegatus (Ten.) Gren. & Godron = *L. venetus*.

L. venetus (Mill.) Wohlf. Resembles *L. vernus*, but lfts ovate-orbicular, acute, v. short-acuminate; fls more numerous, 6–30 on rac., cor. smaller, to 1.5cm. SE & EC Eur. Z6.

L. venosus Muhlenb. ex Willd. Perenn. to 1m; st. stout, erect or climbing, strongly 4-angled, pubesc. Lvs terminate in a well-developed, usually simple tendril; lfts to 6cm, 4–7 pairs, oblong-ovate. Rac. 5–25-fld; cor. to 2cm, purple. Late summer. N Amer. Z4.

L. vernus (L.) Bernh. SPRING VETCH. Bushy herbaceous perenn. to 60cm; st. angular. Lvs terminate in a point, not a tendril; lfts to 10cm, 2–4, oval to lanceolate. Rac. 3–15-fld, to 25.5cm; cor. to 2cm, red-violet, becoming green-blue. Winter–spring. Eur. (except extreme N). 'Albiflorus': fls blue-white. 'Alboroseus': fls rose-white. 'Roseus': fls rose-blue. Z4.

L. vestitus Nutt. ex Torr. & A. Gray. Perenn. to 40cm. Lfts 3.5cm, in 5 pairs. Fls white veined pink or purple, pink to violet blue or purple-red, fading to yellow. US (Oreg., Calif.). ssp. *puberulus* (Wight ex Greene) Hitchc. Taller, usually twining, pubesc. Fls pink to pale purple. Calif. Z8.

L. violaceus auct. = *L. laetiflorus* and *L. vestitus*.

→*Orobus* and *Pisum*.

Lattice Leaf *Aponogeton madagascariensis*.

LAURACEAE Juss. 45/2200. *Cinnamomum, Cryptocarya, Laurus, Lindera, Neolitsea, Persea, Phoebe, Sassafras, Umbellularia*.

Laurel *Laurus nobilis; Prunus laurocerasus*.
Laurel Cherry *Prunus caroliniana; P. laurocerasus*.

Laurelia Juss. Monimaceae. 2 aromatic everg. trees. Lvs opposite, coriaceous, usually glab. Infl. a pan. or rac., axill., bracteate; fls inconspicuous: ♂ with perianth 5–12-parted in 2–3 series, sta. 6–12, staminodes sometimes present; ♀ or hermaphrodite fls with perianth elongating in fr., staminodes always present, ovary superior. Fr. a pilose achene. NZ, Chile, Peru. Z9.

L. aromatica Juss. = *L. sempervirens*.

L. novae-zealandiae (Hook. f.) A. Cunn. PUKATEA. To 30m; trunk becoming buttressed. Lvs 3–7cm, elliptic oblong to obovate, entire or serrate, glaucescent above. Rac. to 2.5cm; perianth silky-pubesc., 5–6-parted. NZ.

L. philippiana Looser = *Laureliopsis philippiana*.

L. sempervirens (Ruiz & Pav.) Tul. CHILEAN LAUREL. To 30m. Lvs 6–9cm, elliptic to ovate, entire below, otherwise serrate, glossy green. Infl. a pan. 5–17 fld, peduncle 1–3cm; perianth 8- or more times parted, ciliate. Chile, Peru.

L. serrata Bertero non Philippi = *L. sempervirens*.

L. serrata Philippi non Bertero = *Laureliopsis philippiana*.

→*Atherosperma*.

Laureliopsis Schodde. Monimaceae. 1 aromatic tree. Lvs to 4.5cm, elliptic to obovate, serrate above. Infl. a thyrse, bracteate; fls 3–11; perianth seg. 8, in 2 whorls, oblong, pubesc.; sta. and staminodes in 2–3 tetramerous whorls, more numerous in ♂fls. Fr. cylindrical, 8-ribbed. S Chile, Patagonia. Z9.

L. philippiana (Looser) Schodde.

→*Laurelia*.

Laurel Negro *Cordia gerascanthus*.
Laurel Oak *Quercus laurifolia*.
Laurel Poplar *Populus laurifolia*.
Laurel Willow *Salix pentandra*.
Laurelwood *Calophyllum inophyllum*.

Laurocerasus Duhamel.

L. caroliniana (Mill.) M. Roem. = *Prunus caroliniana*.
L. lusitanica (L.) Roem. = *Prunus lusitanica*.
L. maackii Schneid. = *Prunus maackii*.
L. officinalis Roem. = *Prunus laurocerasus*.

Laurus L. Lauraceae. 2 everg. trees or shrubs. Lvs simple, semi-rigid, aromatic. Fls to 1cm diam., green-yellow, unisexual; perianth 4-parted, ♂ fls with at least 12 sta.; ♀ fls with 2–4 staminodes. Berry to 1.5cm diam., subglobose, black. S Eur., Canary Is., Azores.

L. azorica (Seub.) Franco. CANARY LAUREL. Tree to 10m. Young branchlets soft-pubesc. Lvs 5–12×3–8cm, broadly lanceolate-elliptic to suborbicular, dark green, dark green, glab. above, paler and pubesc., esp. on midrib beneath; petiole to 1.2cm. Canary Is., Azores. Z9.

L. benzoin L. = *Lindera benzoin*.
L. camphora L. = *Cinnamomum camphora*.
L. canariensis Webb & Berth. = *L. azorica*.
L. glandulifera Wall. = *Cinnamomum glanduliferum*.
L. nobilis L. TRUE LAUREL; BAY LAUREL; SWEET BAY; BAY TREE. Small tree or shrub 3–15m. Young branchlets glab. Lvs 5–10×2–4cm, narrowly elliptic to oblong-ovate, entire, dark green, glab. above, glab. beneath; petiole to 0.8cm. Medit. 'Aurea': lvs tinged yellow. 'Angustifolia' ('Salicifolia'): lvs narrowly oblong-elliptic. 'Crispa' ('Undulata'): lf margin conspicuously undulate. Z8.

Laurustinus *Viburnum tinus.*
Lau Takka *Schefflera littorea.*
Lava Cactus *Brachycereus nesioticus.*

Lavandula L. LAVENDER. Labiatae. 28 intensely aromatic shrubs and subshrubs, erect or spreading. Lvs linear-oblong, simple and entire or dentate to pinnate. Infl. a term., long-stalked, bracteate, verticillate spike; cal. cylindrical or urceolate, 5-toothed; cor. 2-lipped, upper lip 2-lobed, lower lip 3-lobed. Atlantic Is., Medit., N Trop. Afr., W Asia, Arabia, India.

L. abrotanoides Lam. = *L. canariensis.*

L. angustifolia Mill. ENGLISH LAVENDER. Shrub, 1–2m. St. tomentose. Lvs 2–6cm, entire, lanceolate, oblong or linear, revolute, tomentose, grey when young, green with age. Spike 2–8cm; cal. 4–7mm, 13-veined, teeth often purple, lanuginose; cor. 10–12mm, dark purple or blue, lobes large. Medit. ssp. *angustifolia*. Lvs narrow. 'Alba': fls white. 'Rosea': fls pink. 'Atropurpurea': fls v. dark purple. 'Dutch White': tall; lvs to 7cm long; fls white, in small heads, profuse. 'Folgate': compact, to 75cm; lvs narrow, grey-green, fls lavender blue. 'Grappenhall': tall, robust, broad-lvd; fls lavender blue. 'Hidcote': to 30cm, dense; lvs lanceolate, grey; fls lilac, cal. deep lilac, spikes dense. 'Hidcote Giant': v. tall; fls deep purple. 'Hidcote Pink': as 'Hidcote' but lvs linear; cal. grey, in loose spikes, fls pale lilac-pink. 'Imperial Gem': similar to 'Hidcote', but prolific; lvs grey; fls dark purple. 'Jean Davis': lvs grey-green; fls pale pink, in compact heads. 'Loddon Pink': to 45cm; fls soft pink. 'Munstead' ('Compacta Nana'): to 45cm; lvs small; fls large, blue-lilac, spikes loose, cal. purple. 'Nana Alba' ('Alba Nana'): dwarf and compact, to 15cm; lvs linear, silver-grey; fls white. 'Old English': large, to 50cm; lvs to 7cm; flowering spikes branching, to 115cm; fls pale lavender to violet, spikes dense, cal. lilac. 'Royal Purple': fls lavender, in long heads. 'Seal': tall; st. strong; fls pale lavender. 'Twickel Purple': broad, bushy and compact; lvs sometimes flushed purple in winter; fls purple, spikes long, dense. 'Vera' (DUTCH LAVENDER): tall, robust, with rather broad grey lvs and lavender fls. var. *delphinensis* Rouy & Foucaud. Revolute. Lvs lanceolate to oblong, scarcely revolute. Spikes tall, more interrupted. Switz., Fr., It. ssp. *pyrenaica* (DC.) Guinea. Infl. bracts larger, exceeding cal. Pyrennees, N Spain. Z5.

L. canariensis Mill. Shrub to 1.5m. St. glab. Lvs to 3cm, bipinnatisect, green, pubesc. Spikes to 10cm, branched at base; bracts tinged blue towards apex; cal. 15-nerved; cor. 10–12mm, pubesc. Canary Is. Z9.

L. dentata L. Shrub to 1m. St. grey-tomentose. Lvs 1.5–3.5cm, oblong, linear or lanceolate, crenate-dentate to pinnatifid, grey-tomentose beneath. Spikes 2.5–5cm; bracts usually tinged purple, apical bracts sometimes in coma; cal. 5–6mm, 13-veined; cor. 8mm, powder-blue to dark purple. Spain, N Afr. var. *balearica* Ging. Lvs smaller, more revolute, sparsely tomentose. Spikes shorter, coma often prominent. Balearic Is. var. *candicans* Battand. Most parts white-tomentose; lvs larger. N Afr., Madeira, Cape Verde Is. 'Silver Form': lvs soft, silver; fls large, blue. Z9.

L. × intermedia Lois. (*L. angustifolia* × *L. latifolia*). Many wild variants differing in size, bract shape, density of pubescence, length of peduncle, etc.; also cultivated hybrids which might collectively come under this name. Some previously called *L. spica* L. are of hybrid origin. Z5.

L. lanata Boiss. Shrub to 1m, white-lanate throughout. Lvs 3–5cm, linear, spathulate or oblong-lanceolate, scarcely revolute. Spike 4–10cm; cal. 8-veined; cor. 8–10mm, lilac. S Spain (mts). 'Richard Gray': habit upright, to 60cm; st. short; lvs grey tinted silver; fls large, rich purple. Z8.

L. latifolia Medik. Shrub, 1–2m. St. grey-tomentose. Lvs 6cm, elliptic, spathulate, to oblong-lanceolate, entire, grey-tomentose, gland. beneath. Spikes branching, to 20cm; cal. 13-nerved, grey-tomentose, sometimes tinged purple; cor. dark purple, 8–10mm. Medit. Z7.

L. multifida L. Subshrub to 1m. St. grey-tomentose, often with large straight hairs. Lvs to 3.5cm, green, puberulent, bipinnatisect. Spike 2–7cm, branching at base; cal. 15-veined, white-tomentose; cor. 12mm, blue-violet, lobes large. S, C & SW Eur., N Afr. 'French Lace': lvs lacy green-grey. Z7.

L. officinalis Chaix = *L. angustifolia.*

L. pedunculata Mill. = *L. stoechas* ssp. *pedunculata.*

L. pinnata L. f. Shrub to 1m, canescent throughout. Lvs to 8.5cm, pinnate, lobes broad. Spikes to 9cm, branched at base; bracts tinged blue-purple; cal. 15-nerved, sometimes tinged purple; cor. 10mm. Canary Is. var. *buchii* Benth. Lvs smaller, lf seg. narrower. Confused with *L. canariensis* Mill. Z9.

L. spica L. = *L. angustifolia.*

L. stoechas L. FRENCH LAVENDER. Shrub, 30–100cm. Lvs 1–4cm, linear to oblong-lanceolate, entire, usually grey-tomentose. Spike 2–3cm; fertile bracts small, sterile bracts 10–50mm, oblong-obovate, erect, petal-like, red-purple, rarely white; cal. 13-veined; cor. 6–8mm, purple, white or pale pink. Medit. region. var. *leucantha* Lassaraz. Fls and bracts white. 'Alba': fls white. ssp. *pedunculata* (Mill.) Rozeira. Peduncle 20–30cm; sterile bracts tinged red, forming a coma, rarely white. 'James Compton': habit upright, to 1m; lvs tinted grey, fragrant; fls deep purple, bracts large, pale purple. 'Papillon': sterile bracts v. long, narrow, bright purple. Z8.

L. vera DC. = *L. angustifolia.*

L. viridis L'Hérit. Shrub to 1m. St. and lvs shortly hirsute, usually gland. Peduncle equal to or longer than spike; cor. to 8mm green-white or white. Spain, Port., Madeira. Z9.

Lavatera L. TREE MALLOW. Malvaceae. 25 ann. bienn. and perenn. herbs or soft-wooded shrubs, usually stellate-pubesc. Lvs long-petiolate, palmately angled or lobed. Fls axill. or in term. clusters or rac.; epical. seg. 3–9, connate at the base; pet. 5, obovate, ± clawed, emarginate; styles filiform. Macaronesia, Medit. to NW Himal., C Asia, E Sib., Aus., Calif. and Baja Calif.

L. alba Medik. = *L. trimestris.*

L. arborea L. TREE MALLOW. Tree-like bienn. or perenn. to 3m, young parts stellate-tomentose. Lvs 8–18cm, orbicular-cordate, 5-, 7- or 9-lobed, stellate-pilose, crenate. Fls in clusters of 2–7; epical. seg. 3, 0.8–1cm, elliptic to suborbicular; cal. lobes 3.5–4.5mm, triangular, white-pilose; pet. 1.5–2.5cm, lilac or purple-red, with darker veins at the base. Eur., Medit., Macaronesia; nat. Calif. and Baja Calif. 'Ile d'Hyéres': to 3.5m; lvs large, palmate; fls small, magenta, in lf axils, early summer. 'Variegata': habit vigorous; lvs large, marbled white. Z8.

L. assurgentiflora Kellogg. MALVA ROSA. Decid. shrub to 6m; trunk grey, twisted; br. sparsely stellate-pubesc. Lvs 8–15cm, 5- or 7-lobed, lobes triangular, coarsely toothed, white-pubesc. beneath. Fls solitary or in clusters of 2–4; epical. seg. 3, 5mm, ovate; cal. 1cm, campanulate, deeply 5–7-toothed, pubesc.; pet. 4cm, red-purple, with darker veins, obovate, emarginate. SW US, nat. Calif. and Baja Calif. Z9.

L. bicolor Rouy = *L. maritima.*

L. cachemiriana Cambess. Ann. or short-lived perenn. herb to 2.5m, soft-pubesc. Lvs downy beneath, cordate-orbicular, crenate, 3- or 5-lobed. Fls solitary long-stalked; epical. seg. 3, ovate; cal. longer than epical.; pet. to 4cm, pink, deeply bifid. Kashmir. Z8.

L. cretica L. Ann. or bienn. herb to 2m, stellate-pubesc. Lvs to 20cm, 5- or 7-lobed, denticulate. Fls 2–8 per cluster; epical. seg. 3, to 6mm, ovate; cal. to 8mm, triangular-ovate; pet. 1–2cm, lilac to purple. S Eur.

L. davaei Cout. = *L. mauritanica* ssp. *davaei.*

L. insularis S. Wats. = *L. occidentalis.*

L. maritima Gouan. Shrub to 1.2m, new growth grey, stellate-pubesc. Lvs to 6cm, suborbicular, lobes 5–7, broadly triangular, crenate-serrate. Fls 1–2; epical. seg. 3, 0.8–1.3cm, elliptic-ovate; cal. 1.3–1.5cm, campanulate, lobes ovate, apiculate; pet. 1.8–3cm, white, rose or pink, with long purple veins at the base, cordate, clawed. W Medit. Z9.

L. mauritanica Durieu. Ann. herb to 80cm, stellate-tomentose. Lvs suborbicular to cordate, lobes 5–7, dentate. Fls in clusters; epical. seg. 6–7mm, ovate to oblong; sep. 8–9mm, triangular-ovate; pet. 0.8–1.5cm, purple. Alg., Moroc. ssp. *davaei* (Cout.) Cout. Differs in its smaller fr. and more accrescent sep. Port. and Spain. Z9.

L. occidentalis S. Wats. Shrub to 1.2m. Lvs grey-green, puberulous, lobes 5–7, dentate. Fls solitary; cal. stellate-puberulent, 3–4cm; pet. 4–6cm, spreading, cream or pale green with purple veins, narrowly spathulate. Guadelupe and Coronado Is., off Baja Calif. Z9.

L. olbia L. TREE LAVATERA. Shrub to 2m; st. hispid, young parts stellate-tomentose. Lvs tomentose, to 15cm, 3- or 5-lobed, mid-lobe longest, ± trilobulate. Fls solitary, or in elongate rac.; epical. seg. 3, 0.7–1.3cm, ovate-acuminate; pet. 1.5–3cm, red-purple. W Medit. The true *L. olbia* is scarcely cultivated; the plant widely grown under that name is *L. thuringiaca.*

L. olbia hort. non L. = *L. thuringiaca.*

L. rosea Medik. = *L. trimestris.*

L. thuringiaca L. TREE LAVATERA. Perenn. herb to 1.8m, all parts grey-tomentose. Lvs to 9cm, cordate-orbicular, 3- or 5-lobed. Fls solitary or in loose rac.; epical. seg. 3, to 1cm; cal. to 1.2cm, sep. triangular; pet. 1.5–4.5cm, purple-pink. C & SE Eur. 'Barnsley': shrub, to 2m; lvs lobed; fls opening white with red eye, fading to pink. 'Barnsley Perry's Dwarf': habit low, to 1.2m; st. slender; from a cutting of 'Barnsley'. 'Bredon Springs': shrub, to 2m; lvs softly pubesc.; fls dusky pink flushed mauve, packed on spikes to 90cm long. 'Bressingham Pink': to 1.8m; fls pale pink. 'Burgundy Wine': habit sprawling, to 1.2m high; fls vivid light peony-purple. 'Candy Floss': lvs softly tinted grey; fls bright pink, sta. white. 'Ice Cool' ('Peppermint Ice'): to 1.8m;

lvs pale green; fls pure white, occas. fading to pink. 'Kew Rose': habit robust, to 4m; fls dark pink. 'Rosea': to 2m; lvs downy, tinted grey; fls pinky mauve, in lf axil, free-flowering, long-lasting. 'Shorty': habit semi-prostrate, to 1m high; a sport of 'Rosea'. 'Wembdon Variegated' ('Variegata'): to 2m; lvs marbled yellow and white; fls dark pink. Z8.

L. trimestris L. Ann. herb to 1.2m, sparsely hairy. Lvs 3–6cm, suborbicular to cordate, slightly 3-, 5- or 7-lobed. Fls solitary; epical. seg. 3, broadly ovate; sep. 1–1.4cm; pet. 2.5–4.5cm, white, rose, pink or red. Medit. 'Loveliness': to 1.2m; fls large, trumpet-shaped, striking deep rose. 'Mont Blanc': habit dwarf and compact, to 50cm; lvs dark green; fls pure white. 'Pink Beauty': habit dwarf and bushy, to 60cm; fls large, delicate pale pink with violet veins and eye area. 'Silver Cup': habit dwarf and bushy, to 60cm; fls large, to 12cm diam., glowing pink. 'Splendens': fls large, white or red.

Lavauxia Spach = Oenothera.
L. taraxacoides Wooton & Standl. = Oenothera flava ssp. taraxacoides.

Lavender Lavandula.
Lavender Cotton Santolina chamaecyparissus.
Lavender Globe Lily Allium tanguticum.
Lavender Mist Thalictrum.

Lawsonia L. HENNA; MIGNONETTE TREE. Lythraceae. 1 shrub to 6m. Lvs decussate, narrowly obovate to broadly lanceolate, entire, mucronate. Infl. a pyramidal term. pan. to 40cm; fls 4-merous, to 0.5cm across, fragrant; cal. turbinate; lobes ovate-triangular; pet. small, clawed, reniform, crumpled, white, pink or scarlet; sta. 8. N Afr., SW Asia, Aus., nat. trop. Amer. Z9.
L. inerma L.

Lawson's Cypress Chamaecyparis lawsoniana.
Lawyer Cane Calamus australis.

Laxmannia R. Br. Liliaceae (Asphodelaceae). 8 fibrous-rooted perenn. herbs. St. short, tufted or long, diffuse. Lvs narrow-linear or subulate, trigonous or channelled, sheaths sometimes awned. Infl. axill., several- to many-fld heads, subtended by bracts divided into woolly hairs; tep. 6 in 2 whorls, outer 3 free, inner 3 fused below. Aus. Z10.
L. gracilis R. Br. St. to 30cm+, in loose tufts. Lvs 1.25–2.5cm, crowded at base and ends of br., sheaths woolly-hairy. Fls pink. W Aus.
L. grandiflora Lindl. St. to 4cm, in a compact tuft. Lvs 2.5–5cm, crowded in dense terminal tufts, sheaths armed. Fls white. W Aus.

Layia Hook. & Arn. Compositae. 15 ann. herbs. Lvs narrow, subentire or dentate to pinnatifid. Cap. usually radiate, solitary, term.; disc flts yellow. W US.
L. calliglossa A. Gray = L. chrysanthemoides.
L. chrysanthemoides (DC.) A. Gray. St. erect, branched, to 40cm. Lower lvs pinnate, seg. linear or oblong, obtuse, glab., scabrous. Ray flts yellow with white lobes. Spring. Calif.
L. douglasii Hook. & Arn. = L. glandulosa.
L. elegans Torr. & A. Gray = L. platyglossa.
L. emarginata Hook. & Arn. = Ormosia emarginata.
L. glandulosa (Hook.) Hook. & Arn. St. usually branched, to 40cm, hispid, often red. Lower lvs dentate or lobed, hispid, often densely strigose above. Ray flts white, becoming rose-purple, anth. yellow. Spring–summer. Washington to New Mex.
L. platyglossa (Fisch. & G. Mey.) A. Gray. TIDY TIPS. St. decumbent to erect, stout, gland., hirsute, to 30cm. Lower lvs linear to narrow oblong, dentate to pinnatifid, seg. rounded, shortly hirsute or pilose. Ray flts yellow with white tips, anth. black. Spring–summer. Calif.

Lazy Daisy Aphanostephus.
Lazy Man's Grass Eremochloa ophiuroides.
Lead Plant Amorpha canescens.
Lead Tree Leucaena leucocephala.
Leadwort Plumbago.
Leafy Jacob's Ladder Polemonium foliosissimum.
Leafy Rose Rosa foliolosa.
Leafy Spurge Euphorbia esula.
Least Bur Reed Sparganium natans.
Least Snowbell Soldanella minima.
Least Willow Salix herbacea.
Leather Fern Acrostichum aureum; Rumohra adiantiformis.
Leather Flower Clematis; C. versicolor; C. viorna; C. virginiana.
Leatherleaf Chamaedaphne; Ilex aquifolium 'Crassifolia'.
Leatherleaf Fern Rumohra adiantiformis.
Leatherleaf Sedge Carex buchananii.

Leather Oak Quercus durata.
Leather Pepper Peperomia crassifolia.
Leatherwood Cyrilla racemiflora; Dirca (D. palustris); Eucryphia lucida.
Leathery Grape Fern Botrychium multifidum.
Leathery Polypody Polypodium scouleri.
Lebanon Oak Quercus libani.
Lebombo Cycad Encephalartos lebomboensis.

Lecanopteris (Reinw.) Bl. Polypodiaceae. Some 15 epiphytic ferns. Rhiz. slender to swollen, interior hollow, in habitat often ant-inhabited. Fronds simple or pinnate, glab., somewhat fleshy; stipes joined to swollen phyllopodia. SE Asia to New Guinea. Z10.
L. crustacea Copel. Rhiz. to 5cm across, gouty, crustaceous. Fronds to 35×15cm, oblong, deeply pinnately lobed, leathery, sterile lobes to 17 pairs, to 8×2cm, oblong, fertile lobes to 30 pairs, to 10×0.5cm, linear, obtuse at apex; stipes to 20cm. Malaysia to Indon.
L. sinuosa (Wallich) Copel. Rhiz. to 2cm across, long-creeping, fleshy to woody. Fronds simple, leathery; sterile fronds to 20×3cm, elliptic to oblong, entire; fertile fronds to 40×2cm, linear to oblong, sinuous; stipes to 7cm. Malaysia to Solomon Is.
→Onychium and Phymatodes.

Le Conte Pear Pyrus ×lecontei.

LECYTHIDACEAE Poit. 20/280. Barringtonia, Bertholletia, Couroupita, Grias, Gustavia, Lecythis, Napoleonaea.

Lecythis Loefl. Lecythidaceae. 26 decid. or everg. trees. Lvs alt., simple, usually glab., leathery, dentate or entire. Infl. a rac., spike or corymb; fls 6-merous, zygomorphic; androecium extended into a flat hood, appendages sometimes bearing anth.; staminal ring with 70–100 sta. Fr. a large woody capsule, a 'monkey pot' with lid and inverted rim, containing large nuts. Nic. to S Braz. Z9.
L. elliptica HBK = L. minor.
L. lurida (Miers) Mori. To 35m. Lvs to 18cm, ovate, elliptic or oblong, glab., chartaceous to coriaceous, crenate to nearly entire. Rac. to 10cm; fls to 4cm diam.; sep. green, sometimes with red markings; pet. red or pink outside, white inside; androecial hood yellow, with inwardly curved antherless appendages. Fr. depressed-globose, to 9×11cm; seeds to 6×5cm. E coastal Braz. and E Amazonia.
L. minor Jacq. To 25m. Lvs to 24.5cm, ovate to oblong, glab., leathery, crenulate to serrate. Rac. to 35cm; fls to 7cm diam.; sep. green; pet. white; androecial hood with inwardly curving antherless appendages, white or pale yellow. Fr. globose or turbinate, to 7×9cm; seeds to 3×2cm. Venez., Colomb., Panama, Cuba.
L. pisonis Cambess. PARADISE NUT; CREAM NUT; BRAZILIAN MONKEY POT. To 50m. Lvs flushed before flowering, to 15cm, ovate to elliptic, glab., leathery, crenate. Rac. to 15cm; fls 3–7cm diam.; sep. purple; pet. purple or white; androecial hood flat, purple or white, appendages bearing anth. Fr. globose, to 15×30cm; seeds to 6×3cm. Carib., Peru, Braz.
L. tuyrana Pittier. PANAMA MONKEY POT. To 60m. Lvs to 37cm, oblong, glab., leathery, entire to crenulate. Spike with rusty pubescence when young; fls to 6cm diam.; sep. green; pet. sulphur yellow; androecial hood yellow, with vestigial anth. or none. Fr. to 14.5×17.5cm, subglobose; seeds to 7×3cm. Panama, Ecuad., Colomb.
L. urnigera Mart. ex Berg. = L. pisonis.
L. usitata Miers = L. pisonis.
L. zabucaya Aubl. SAPUCAIA NUT; PARADISE NUT; MONKEY NUT. To 55m. Lvs to 11.5cm, elliptic, glab., papery, crenate. Rac. to 10.5cm; fls to 5cm diam.; sep. green; pet. yellow or white, often with purple margins; androecial hood flat, yellow or white. Fr. to 16.5×17.5cm, globose to turbinate; seeds to 4×1.5cm. Guianas, E Venez., Amazonia.

Ledebouria Roth. Liliaceae (Hyacinthaceae). 16 bulbous, perenn. herbs. Lvs basal, often marked blue. Rac. axillary, simple; fls small or minute, green or purple; perianth seg. recurved; ovary superior. S Afr. Z9.
L. apertiflora (Bak.) Jessop. Lvs 4–7, to 35×2.5cm, sublinear. Rac. crowded, erect or flexuous; perianth seg. green, grey or marked pink.
L. concolor (Bak.) Jessop. Lvs 2–6, to 15×5cm, oblong-lanceolate to ovate, often undulate. Rac. dense suberect; perianth seg. green, grey or marked pink.
L. cooperi (Hook. f.) Jessop. Lvs 1–3, to 25×2cm, somewhat fleshy, oblong to ovate-oblong or linear, sometimes striped

brown. Rac. suberect; perianth seg. pale purple or with a green keel.

L. floribunda (Bak.) Jessop. Lvs 4 or 5, to 35×15cm, lanceolate to oblong-linear. Rac. dense, suberect; perianth seg. grey or green with pink.

L. hypoxidioides (Schönl.) Jessop. Lvs 2–4, to 15×3.5cm, oblong-lanceolate to oblong-ovate, sericeous. Infl. suberect, 75–50-fld; perianth seg. green, grey or marked pink.

L. inquinata (C.A. Sm.) Jessop. Lvs to 15×3.5cm, ovate-lanceolate, glaucous, mostly without spots. Infl. suberect to flexuous, 50–150-fld; perianth seg. green, grey or marked pink.

L. luteola Jessop. Lvs 4–10, to 8cm, linear-lanceolate, spotted or with indistinct bands. Infl. suberect, 30–60-fld; perianth seg. yellow-green, grey or marked pink.

L. marginata (Bak.) Jessop. Lvs 4–10, to 16×3cm, with prominent venation. Infl. mostly flexuous, 50–150-fld; perianth seg. green, grey or marked pink.

L. ovalifolia (Schräd.) Jessop. Lvs 3–5, to 3.5×1cm, oval. Infl. to 9cm, to 20-fld; perianth seg. striped pink.

L. ovatifolia (Bak.) Jessop. Lvs 2–5, to 25cm, ovate. Infl. mostly flexuous, 50–150-fld; perianth seg. green, grey or marked pink.

L. revoluta (L. f.) Jessop. Lvs 4–8, to 15×3cm, lanceolate to narrowly ovate, often with dark spots above. Infl. suberect, to 100-fld; perianth seg. green.

L. socialis (Bak.) Jessop. Lvs to 10×2cm, slightly fleshy, lanceolate, nacreous with some dark green blotches above, green or deep pink-purple beneath. Infl. suberect, to 25-fld; perianth seg. pale purple with green keels.

L. undulata (Jacq.) Jessop. Lvs to 15×2cm, lanceolate or linear-lanceolate. Infl. erect, lax; perianth seg. green, sometimes striped pink.

L. viscosa Jessop. Lvs 1 to 3, to 23×3cm, erect, spathulate-oblanceolate, viscid. Infl. erect, 20–30-fld; perianth seg. grey, green, sometimes striped pink.

→*Drimia, Hyacinthus* and *Scilla*.

Ledger Bark *Cinchona officinalis.*

Ledum L. Ericaceae. 4 everg. shrubs, erect to decumbent. Lvs scented, entire, linear or oblong, coriaceous. Fls small, in term., umbellate corymbs; pedicels slender; cal. small, lobes 5; cor. rotate, white, pet. 5; sta. 5–10, fil. slender. N Temp.

L. buxifolium Berg. = *Leiophyllum buxifolium.*

L. glandulosum Nutt. TRAPPER'S TEA; GLANDULAR LABRADOR TEA. 50–150cm. Branchlets gland., downy. Lvs 1.5–6cm, oblong to broadly elliptic-oval, sometimes revolute, dark green above, glaucous and glandular-scaly beneath. Fls in term. clusters to 5cm diam.; pet. 5–8mm, oblong; sta. 10. Summer. W N Amer. var. *columbianum* (Piper) C. Hitchc. Lvs 3–5×1cm, strongly revolute.

L. groenlandicum Oeder. LABRADOR TEA. 50–200cm. Branchlets ferruginous-lanate. Lvs 2–6cm, linear-oblong, revolute, dark green and somewhat hirsute above, thickly ferruginous-lanate beneath. Fls in corymbs, grouped in terminal clusters to 5cm diam.; pet. 5–8mm, oblong; sta. 5–10. Late spring–summer. N Amer., Greenland. 'Compactum': habit dwarf.

L. hypoleucum Komar. = *L. palustre.*

L. latifolium Jacq. = *L. groenlandicum.*

L. nipponicum (Nak.) Tolm. = *L. palustre.*

L. palustre L. CRYSTAL TEA; WILD ROSEMARY. 30–120cm. Branchlets ferruginous-lanate. Lvs 1.2–5cm, linear to elliptic-oblong, revolute, dark green above, ferruginous-hirsute beneath. Fls many in densely packed, term. clusters; pet. 4–8mm, obovate, sta. 7–10. Late spring–summer. N & C Eur., N US. Z2.

Ledum Boronia *Boronia ledifolia.*

Leea Royen ex L. Leeaceae. 34 shrubs and small trees. St. glab., glossy, sometimes lenticellate. Lvs simple or 1–3-pinnate, usually outspread, often flushed bronze or red; petiole slender. Infl. a crowded axillary corymb or term. cyme; fls small; fil. united at base into a tube arising from perianth, anth. introrse. Fr. a berry. OW tropics. Z10.

L. amabilis hort. Shrub to 2m. St. slender, erect, sparsely branched, glossy. Lvs 1–3-pinnate, lfts to 6cm, lanceolate, sparsely toothed, lustrous bronze above with a broad white central stripe, claret beneath with a translucent, central, green stripe. Borneo. 'Splendens': whole plant flushed dark bronze-red.

L. coccinea Planch. non Bojer. WEST INDIAN HOLLY. Shrub to 2.25m. Lvs 2–3 pinnate, lfts 5–10cm, elliptic to obovate, revolute, sometimes toothed. Fls pink. Burm.

L. coccinea Bojer non Planch. = *L. guineensis.*

L. guineensis G. Don. Shrub, 2.2–7.5m. Lvs 1–2-pinnate, lfts 10–20cm, elliptic, obscurely serrate towards apex, glab. Fls yellow-orange. Trop. Afr.

L. manillensis Walp. Shrub or tree to 6m. Lvs 3–4 pinnate, lfts 3–22cm, elliptic to ovate-oblong, serrulate. Fls yellow-pink. Philipp.

L. sambucina (L.) Willd. Shrub to 4m. Lvs 1–3 pinnate, lfts 1–1.75cm, broadly elliptic, crenately toothed, flushed bronze, veins sometimes tinted rosy-purple. Fls green-white. Trop. Asia, Polyn., New Guinea, N Aus.

L. sambucina Blanco non (L.) Willd. = *L. manillensis.*

LEEACEAE Dumort. 1/34. *Leea.*

Leech Lime *Citrus hystrix.*

Leek *Allium porrum.*

Legousia Durande. Campanulaceae. 15 small ann. herbs. Lvs ovate to lanceolate, lower ones shortly petiolate. Fls 5-merous in pan., compact corymbs or solitary near end of br.; cor. rotate to campanulate. Medit.

L. hybrida (L.) Delarb. VENUS' LOOKING GLASS. To 35cm, shortly hispid or subglabrous. Lvs oblanceolate to oblong, sinuate. Fls in small term. clusters; cor. broadly campanulate, maroon to lilac. Eur., N Afr.

L. pentagonia (L.) Druce. To 30cm, often hispid, occas. glab. Lvs to obovate to oblong. Fls solitary or in pan.; cor. campanulate, white at base, blue to violet further up. E Medit., Balk.

L. speculum-veneris (L.) Chaix. VENUS' LOOKING GLASS. St. to 30cm, glab. or hispidulous. Lvs oblanceolate to oblong, sinuate. Fls solitary or in pan.; cor. rotate, violet, rarely white or mauve. C & S Eur. 'Alba': fls white. 'Grandiflora': fls larger.

→*Campanula* and *Specularia.*

LEGUMINOSAE Juss. 657/16,400. *Acacia, Acrocarpus, Adenanthera, Adenocarpus, Afzelia, Albizia, Amicia, Amorpha, Amphicarpaea, Anadenanthera, Anagyris, Andira, Anthyllis, Apios, Argyrocytisus, Aspalathus, Astragalus, Baphia, Baptisia, Bauhinia, Bolusanthus, Bossiaea, Brachysema, Brachystegia, Brownea, Burtonia, Butea, Caesalpinia, Cajanus, Calicotome, Calliandra, Calophaca, Calpurnia, Camoensia, Camptosema, Campylotropis, Canavalia, Caragana, Carmichaelia, ×Carmispartium, Cassia, Castanospermum, Centrosema, Ceratonia, Cercis, Chamaecrista, Chamaecytisus, Chesneya, Chordospartium, Chorizema, Christia, Cicer, Cladrastis, Clianthus, Clitoria, Codariocalyx, Colutea, Colvillea, Corallospartium, Coronilla, Crotalaria, Cyamopsis, Cytisophyllum, Cytisus, Dalbergia, Dalea, Daviesia, Delonix, Derris, Desmanthus, Desmodium, Dichrostachys, Dillwynia, Dipogon, Dorycnium, Ebenus, Enterolobium, Erinacea, Erythrina, Eutaxia, Galega, Gastrolobium, Genista, Geoffroea, Gleditsia, Gliricidia, Glycine, Glycyrrhiza, Gymnocladus, Haematoxylum, Halimodendron, Hardenbergia, Hedysarum, Hippocrepis, Hovea, Hypocalyptus, Indigofera, Inga, Jacksonia, Kennedia, Lablab, +Laburnocytisus, Laburnum, Lathyrus, Lens, Lespedeza, Leucaena, Lonchocarpus, Lotus, Lupinus, Lysidice, Lysiloma, Maackia, Macrotyloma, Medicago, Millettia, Mimosa, Mucuna, Mundulea, Myroxylon, Neptunia, Notospartium, Onobrychis, Ononis, Ormocarpum, Ormosia, Oxylobium, Oxytropis, Pachyrhizus, Paramacrolobium, Parkia, Parkinsonia, Parochetus, Peltophorum, Petteria, Phaseolus, Phyllocarpus, Phyllota, Pickeringia, Piptanthus, Piscidia, Pisum, Pithecellobium, Platylobium, Platymiscium, Podalyria, Podocytisus, Pongamia, Prosopis, Psophocarpus, Psoralea, Psorothamnus, Pterocarpus, Pterolobium, Pueraria, Pultenaea, Retama, Robinia, Sabinea, Saraca, Schizolobium, Schotia, Senna, Sesbania, Sophora, Spartium, Strongylodon, Sutherlandia, Swainsona, Tamarindus, Templetonia, Tephrosia, Thermopsis, Tipuana, Trifolium, Trigonella, Ulex, Vicia, Vigna, Viminaria, Virgilia, Wagatea, Wiborgia, Willardia, Wisteria.*

Lehua *Metrosideros polymorphus.*

Leibnitzia Cass. Compositae. 4 scapose perenn. herbs, with spring and autumn flowering forms. Lvs in a basal rosette, pinnatifid-lyrate or sinuate, petiolate. Cap. solitary, dimorphic, radiate. Spring state: lvs often few or 0, arachnoid to tomentose; cap. small; flts all fertile, ray flts 12. Autumn state: lvs large; cap. large, ray flts inconspicuous. Himal., S & E Asia.

L. anandria (L.) Turcz. Spring state: lvs to 13cm, lanceolate, sinuate, subglabrous above, arachnoid to tomentose beneath, petiole to 7.5cm. Cap. to 2cm diam.; peduncles to 26cm; ray florets white above and rose-pink beneath or white-pink to rose above and beneath. Autumn state: lvs to 23cm, elliptic-oblong, ovate, lyrate or pinnatifid-lyrate or sinuate, apical seg. usually large, rounded, cordate or ± triangular, base margin crenate various. Cap. to 2×4cm; ray flts white. Spring–autumn. S Sib. to Nepal and Jap. Z3.

L. kunzeana (R. Br. & Asch.) Pobed. = *L. nepalensis.*

L. nepalensis (Kunze) Kitam. Spring state: lvs to 8cm, tomentose beneath, petiole to 4cm. Cap. 1cm diam.; peduncles to 5cm; ray flts like *L. anandria*. Autumn state: lvs to 21cm, lyrate with a cordate terminal apical seg. and rounded lat. seg., or sinuate, slightly undulate and remotely crenate, petiole to 13cm. Cap. to 2×2cm; ray flts red, or white with red tips. Spring–autumn. Himal. Z8.
→*Gerbera*.

Leiophyllum (Pers.) Hedw. f. Ericaceae. 1 everg. shrub, erect or prostrate, 5–30cm. Lvs 6–12mm, simple, entire, oblong, ovate or obovate, glossy, coriaceous. Fls c6mm diam., in dense, term., umbellate corymbs 18–25mm diam.; pedicels gland.; cal. lobes 5, narrowly lanceolate; pet. 5, white to pale pink, oval; sta. 10, fil. narrow. Late spring–early summer. E US.
L. buxifolium (Berg) Elliott. SAND MYRTLE. 'Nanum': habit dwarf; br. abundant; fls pink. var. *hugeri* (Small) Schneid. Shrub to 20cm, habit more cushion-like. Lvs longer. Fls pink. var. *prostratum* (Loud.) A. Gray. ALLEGHENY SAND MYRTLE. Lvs 7–12×4–6mm, orbicular to elliptic, downy. Z5.
L. lyonii (Sweet) Sweet = *L. buxifolium* var. *prostratum*.

Leiostemon Raf.
L. thurberi Greene = *Penstemon thurberi*.

Leipoldtia L. Bol. Aizoaceae. 21 erect or prostrate succulent shrublets to 50cm. Lvs laterally compressed, obtuse to truncate, glab., smooth. Fls on bracteate pedicels; sep. 5; stigmas to 10. Capsule with winged valves. S Afr. (Cape Prov.), Nam. Z9.
L. amplexicaulis (L. Bol.) L. Bol. Prostrate. Lvs 1.2–3cm, sabre-shaped, swollen, rounded triquetrous, tip rounded. Fls 2.5–3cm diam., purple-pink. W Cape.
L. frutescens (L. Bol.) Hartmann. Erect or prostrate. Lvs 5–8cm, cylindric, apiculate. Fls 6cm diam., yellow. W Cape.
L. weigangiana (Dinter) Dinter & Schwantes. Erect. Lvs to 1.5cm, navicular, triquetrous, blue-green, densely spotted. Fls 2cm diam., violet-pink. Nam.: Great Namaqualand.
→*Mesembryanthemum* and *Rhopalocyclus*.

Leitneria Chapm. Leitneriaceae. 1 decid. tree or suckering shrub to 5m. Br. downy at first, later grey and thick-barked with v. light wood. Lvs 6.5–16cm, ovate-lanceolate or elliptic, entire, downy then grey-sericeous beneath only. Catkins grey-green, erect, axill. borne before lvs, ♂ to 3.5cm, longer and stouter than ♀; perianth 0; sta. 8–12. Fr. a brown drupe. E US. Z5.
L. floridana Chapm. CORKWOOD.

LEITNERIACEAE Benth. See *Leitneria*.

Leleba Nak.
L. multiplex (Lour.) Nak. = *Bambusa multiplex*.
L. oldhamii (Munro) Nak. = *Bambusa oldhamii*.
L. vulgaris (Schräd. ex Wendl.) Nak. = *Bambusa vulgaris*.

Lemaireocereus Britt.
L. beneckei (Ehrenb.) Britt. & Rose = *Stenocereus beneckei*.
L. cartwrightianus Britt. & Rose = *Armatocereus cartwrightianus*.
L. chende (Roland-Goss.) Britt. & Rose = *Polaskia chende*.
L. chichipe (Roland-Goss.) Britt. & Rose = *Polaskia chichipe*.
L. deficiens Otto & A. Dietr. = *Stenocereus griseus*.
L. dumortieri (Scheidw.) Britt. & Rose = *Stenocereus dumortieri*.
L. eruca (Brandg.) Britt. & Rose = *Stenocereus eruca*.
L. euphorbioides (Haw.) Werderm. = *Neobuxbaumia euphorbioides*.
L. gladiger (Lem.) Backeb. = *Stenocereus griseus*.
L. godingianus Britt. & Rose = *Armatocereus godingianus*.
L. griseus (Haw.) Britt. & Rose = *Stenocereus griseus*.
L. gummosus (Engelm. ex Brandg.) Britt. & Rose = *Stenocereus gummosus*.
L. hollianus (F.A.C. Weber ex J. Coult.) Britt. & Rose = *Pachycereus hollianus*.
L. laetus (Kunth) Britt. & Rose = *Armatocereus laetus*.
L. littoralis (Brandg.) Gates = *Stenocereus thurberi*.
L. marginatus (DC.) A. Berger = *Pachycereus marginatus*.
L. martinezii Gonz. Ortega = *Stenocereus martinezii*.
L. pruinosus (Pfeiff.) Britt. & Rose = *Stenocereus pruinosus*.
L. queretaroensis (F.A.C. Weber) Safford = *Stenocereus queretaroensis*.
L. stellatus (Pfeiff.) Britt. & Rose = *Stenocereus stellatus*.
L. thurberi (Engelm.) Britt. & Rose = *Stenocereus thurberi*.
L. treleasei Britt. & Rose = *Stenocereus treleasei*.
L. weberi (J. Coult.) Britt. & Rose = *Pachycereus weberi*.

Lemandarin *Citrus* ×*limonia*.

Lemboglossum Halbinger. Orchidaceae. 14 epiphytic orchids. Rhiz. short. Pbs clustered, rounded-ovoid, laterally compressed. Lvs apical and sheathing. Rac. or pan. basal; pet. subequal to sep. or wider; lip short-clawed, callus fleshy. C Amer., Mex. Z10.
L. bictoniense (Batem.) Halbinger. Pbs to 18cm. Lvs to 45cm, elliptic-oblong to lanceolate or linear. Rac. or pan. erect to 80cm; fls often fragrant; tep. usually pale green or yellow-green banded or spotted red-brown, sep. to 2.5×1cm, elliptic-lanceolate to elliptic-oblanceolate, pet. smaller; lip to 2×2.5cm, subcordate, crisped or crenulate, white to rose or magenta-tinted. Mex., Guat., El Salvador. White, golden and lime-green self-coloured forms occur.
L. cervantesii (La Ll. & Lex.) Halbinger. Pbs to 6cm. Lvs to 15×3cm, ovate-lanceolate to elliptic-oblong. Rac. to 32cm; fls fragrant; tep. white to rose irregularly banded brown-red in basal half, sep. to 3.5×1cm, narrowly ovate-oblong; pet. broader; lip white to rose, striped purple at base, to 2.5×3cm, 3-lobed, lat. lobes erect, midlobe broadly cordate, irregularly dentate, callus yellow, 2-lobed; column white, to 1cm. Mex., Guat.
L. cordatum (Lindl.) Halbinger. Pbs to 7.5cm. Lvs to 30×5cm, elliptic to lanceolate or oblong-ligulate. Rac. or pan. to 60cm; tep. yellow blotched and barred deep red-brown, sep. to 5×1cm, elliptic-lanceolate, pet. shorter; lip to 2.5×2cm, usually white spotted red-brown, cordate, margins involute at apex, slightly erose. Mex., Guat., Hond., Costa Rica, Venez.
L. maculatum (La Ll. & Lex.) Halbinger. Pbs to 9.5cm. Lvs to 32×5.5cm, elliptic-lanceolate to elliptic-ligulate. Infl. to 40cm, pendent, sometimes branched; sep. chestnut-brown or pale yellow marked red-brown, sometimes barred green at base, to 4×1cm, lanceolate; pet. yellow heavily spotted red-brown at base, elliptic-lanceolate; lip similar in colour to sep., to 2×2.5cm, cordate-reniform or triangular, crisped, callus yellow marked red, fleshy. Mex., Guat.
L. majale (Rchb. f.) Halbinger. Pbs to 7cm. Lvs to 30×3cm, linear-ligulate. Rac. to 14cm, 2–4-fld; tep. purple or rose, sep. to 3×1cm, narrowly oblong to lanceolate, pet. smaller; lip rose blotched deep purple or carmine, to 3×3cm, ovate-subquadrate. Guat.
L. rossii (Lindl.) Halbinger. Pbs to 6cm. Lvs to 14×2.75cm, elliptic to elliptic-lanceolate. Rac. to 20cm, 1–4-fld; tep. white, pale yellow or pale pink, the sep. and lower portions of pet. mottled and spotted chocolate to rust, sep. to 4.5×1cm, oblong-elliptic to linear-lanceolate, broader, crisped to undulate; lip to 3×3cm, broadly orbicular-subcordate, undulate, callus deep yellow spotted red-brown. Mex., Guat., Hond., Nic.
L. stellatum (Lindl.) Halbinger. Pbs to 6cm. Lvs to 15×2.5cm, narrowly elliptic to oblanceolate or linear-ligulate. Rac. to 8.5cm, 1–2-fld; tep. yellow-bronze barred brown, to 30×5mm, linear-lanceolate, pet. sometimes yellow-white; lip white or pink marked mauve, to 2×2cm, ovate-triangular to suborbicular, lacerate-dentate. Mex., Guat., El Salvador.
L. uro-skinneri (Lindl.) Halbinger. Resembles *L. bictoniense* except tep. deep red to green, barred and mottled brown, to 3×1.5cm, lip to 3×3.5cm, pink, veined or spotted white. Guat., Hond.
→*Odontoglossum*.

Lembrotropis L.
L. nigricans (L.) Griseb. = *Cytisus nigricans*.

Lemmaphyllum Presl. Polypodiaceae. 4 epiphytic ferns. Rhiz. creeping, filiform. Stipes remote where present; frond blades short-stipitate or sessile, usually dimorphous: sterile fronds simple, ovate to obovate or elliptic, entire, fleshy; fertile fronds simple, linear to oblanceolate. India, China, Jap., to Malaysia, Indon., Polyn. Z10.
L. accedens (Bl.) Donk. Sterile fronds to 3×2cm, elliptic to ovate, apex obtuse or acute, entire, membranous to glab.; fertile fronds elliptic to ovate, apex narrowed, base broadly cuneate, occas. entirely fertile and narrowed to 15×1cm, entire, leathery; stipes to 5mm. Malaysia, New Guinea, Polyn.
L. carnosum Presl. Sterile fronds to 7cm, elliptic-lanceolate to heart-shaped, entire, fleshy, leathery; fertile fronds to 6cm, spathulate to linear, stipes short, remote. India to China.
L. microphyllum Presl. Sterile fronds to 5×1.5cm, often sessile, rounded to obovate, or spathulate, apex obtuse, base cuneate, entire, leathery, glab.; fertile fronds to 3×0.5cm, stipitate, simple, narrowly linear to oblanceolate. China, Taiwan, Korea, Jap.
→*Drymoglossum*, *Pleopeltis* and *Polypodium*.

Lemna L. DUCKWEED; DUCKMEAT; FROG'S BUTTONS. Lemnaceae. 13 minute floating aquatic herbs. Plant body leaf-like. Root solitary, vertical. Fls v. small, sunken in margins. Cosmop.

L. aequinoctialis Welw. Fronds 1–6.5×0.8–4.5mm, entire, 3-veined, usually with one papule above the node. Root to 3.5cm, root sheath wing 1–2.5 ×longer than wide, rootcap pointed. Widely distrib. in tropics and subtrop. Z10.

L. gibba L. Fronds 1–8×0.8–6mm, rather shiny and sometimes spotted red above, usually without distinct papules, 4–5-veined (rarely 7-), rootcap usually rounded, 0.6–1.8mm. Temp. regions, esp. in Amer., Eur., Afr., SW Asia. Z4.

L. miniscula Herter. Fronds 0.8–4.0×0.5–2.5mm, usually pale green, often with a pale line above, veins 0 or 1; root to 1.5cm, rootcap often rounded to rather pointed. Amer., Eur., E Asia. Z4.

L. minor L. COMMON DUCKWEED; LESSER DUCKWEED. Fronds 1–8×0.6–5.0mm, to 1mm thick, shiny and occas. tinged red above, papules indistinct, 3-veined (rarely 4–5); rootcap usually rounded. Temp. regions with mild winters, except E Asia, Aus. Z4.

L. paucicostata Hegelm. = *L. aequinoctialis*.

L. perpusilla Torr. Fronds 1–4×0.8–3.0mm, 3-veined, often with 2–3 papules above the node; root sheath wing 2–3 longer than wide, rootcap jointed. N Amer. Z5.

L. trisulca L. STAR DUCKWEED. Fronds 3–15×1–5mm, cohering and often forming branched chains, toothed at the base, 3-veined; root to 2.5cm (sometimes not developed), rootcap pointed. Cosmop. in temp. climates, except N Amer.

LEMNACEAE Gray. 6/30. *Lemna, Spirodela, Wolffia, Wolffiella*.

Lemon *Citrus limon*.
Lemonade Berry *Rhus integrifolia*.
Lemonade Sumac *Rhus integrifolia*.
Lemon Balm *Melissa officinalis*.
Lemon Bottlebrush *Callistemon pallidus*.
Lemon-fld Gum *Eucalyptus woodwardii*.
Lemon Geranium *Pelargonium crispum*.
Lemon Grass *Cymbopogon citratus*.
Lemon Ironwood *Backhousia citrodora*.
Lemon Lily *Lilium parryi*.
Lemon Mint *Mentha ×piperita*.
Lemon-scented Boronia *Boronia citriodora*.
Lemon-scented Gum *Eucalyptus citriodora*.
Lemon-scented Ironbark *Eucalyptus staigeriana*.
Lemon-scented Myrtle *Backhousia citrodora; Darwinia citriodora*.
Lemon Sumac *Rhus aromatica*.
Lemon Verbena *Aloysia triphylla*.
Lemon Vine *Pereskia aculeata*.
Lemonwood *Pittosporum eugenioides*.
Lenga *Nothofagus pumilio*.

Lenophyllum Rose. Crassulaceae. 6 succulent perenn. herbs. St. branching. Lvs thick, concave above. Fls solitary or in a branched rac.; sep. 5, fused below; pet. 5, erect, tips spreading, just exceeding sep.; sta. 10, 5 fused to pet., 5 free. SW US, New Mex. Z9.

L. acutifolium Rose. Similar to *L. pusillum* except infl. a spike or rac.; pet. green-yellow. Mex.

L. guttatum Rose. To 30cm. St. much-branched near base. Lvs 20–30mm, ovate-elliptic, blunt, grey-green, spotted dark purple. Infl. 3–4-branched; pet. 5mm, yellow turning red. Autumn. Mex.

L. pusillum Rose. To 7cm. Lvs 8–16mm, pointed, concave above. Flowering st. 4–5cm with numerous, small, thick lvs; fls term., solitary; pet. 6–7mm, lemon yellow. Tex., Mex.

L. texanum (J.G. Sm.) Rose. 10–20cm. Lvs 15–30mm, lanceolate to ovate, pointed. Infl. a spike or thryse; fls subsessile; pet. 4–5mm, suffused red. Late summer–autumn. Tex.

L. weinbergii Britt. Lvs 15×10–15mm, obovate-ovate, grooved above, blunt. Infl. few-fld; pet. 4–5mm yellow. Mex.

→*Sedum* and *Villadia*.

Lens Mill. Leguminosae (Papilionoideae). 6 ann. herbs, resembling *Vicia* but with cal. teeth equal, to twice length of cal. tube. Fr. flattened; seeds flat, orbicular. Medit., W Asia, Afr. Z8.

L. culinaris Medik. LENTIL; MASUR; SPLIT PEA. Erect to 45cm. Lvs pinnate, bearing a term. tendril; lfts to 2×0.8cm, in 4–7 pairs, narrowly oblong-lanceolate. Fls cleistogamous, blue, solitary or few in rac. Fr. to 16mm, 1- or 2-seeded; seeds lens-shaped. SW Asia, occas. nat. Eur.

L. esculenta Moench = *L. culinaris*.

→*Ervum*.

Lenten Rose *Helleborus orientalis*.

LENTIBULARIACEAE Rich. 4/245. *Genlisea, Pinguicula, Utricularia*.

Lentil *Lens culinaris*.
Lentisco *Pistacia lentiscus; P. texana; Rhus virens*.
Lent Lily *Narcissus pseudonarcissus*.

Leocereus Britt. & Rose Cactaceae. 1 shrubby cactus. St. to 3m×2.5cm, slender, erect or clambering, ribs 10–20, rounded, spines yellow or brown, central spines erect, to 2cm, radial spines adpressed, to 0.5cm. Fl. 4–7×2–3cm, tubular, subapical, nocturnal, outer tep. green to brown, inner tep. white. E Braz. Z9.

L. bahiensis Britt. & Rose. Z9.

L. melanurus (Schum.) Britt. & Rose = *Arthrocereus melanurus*.

Leochilus Knowles & Westc. Orchidaceae. 15 epiphytic orchids. Rhiz. short. Pbs clustered, ovoid to ellipsoid, laterally compressed. Lvs ligulate to elliptic-lanceolate, sheathing and apical. Infl. a rac. or pan., basal; fls small; sep. subequal, spreading; pet. slightly wider; lip spreading, simple or obscurely trilobed, disc fleshy. Mex. to Arg., W Indies. Z10.

L. carinatus (Lindl.) Knowles & Westc. Pbs to 2.5×2cm. Lvs to 12×1.5cm. Infl. to 15cm, erect to pendent; fls fragrant; sep. to 12×6mm, free, yellow-green flushed brown; pet. cream-yellow striped chestnut-brown; lip cream-yellow spotted brown near callus. Mostly summer. Mex.

L. labiatus (Sw.) Kuntze. Pbs to 1.5×1.5cm. Lvs to 6.5×2cm. Infl. to 23cm, erect to arching; fls fragrant; tep. to 8×5mm, yellow-green marked dark red-brown, elliptic-oblong; lip yellow streaked red-brown. Mostly spring–summer. W Indies, Guat., Hond., Panama, Trin., Costa Rica, Venez.

L. lieboldii Rchb. f. = *Papperitzia lieboldii*.

L. major Schltr. = *L. scriptus*.

L. mattogrossensis Cogn. = *Solenidium lunatum*.

L. oncidioides Knowles & Westc. Pbs to 5×2.5cm. Lvs to 17×3cm. Infl. to 16cm, arching to pendent; fls fragrant; tep. to 11×5mm, grey-green spotted and tinged dull red; lip grey-green with large red central blotch, pilose to shortly pubesc. Autumn–winter. Mex. to Guat., Hond.

L. pulchellus (Reg.) Cogn. = *Oncidium waluewa*.

L. scriptus (Scheidw.) Rchb. f. Pbs to 5×2.5cm. Lvs to 15×3cm. Infl. to 25cm, erect to arching; fls fragrant; tep. to 12×6mm, pale yellow-green, marked or striped red-brown, elliptic to lanceolate; lip similar in colour, callus cup-shaped, pilose to shortly pubesc. Mostly autumn–winter. Mex., Braz., Guat. to Panama, Cuba.

→*Oncidium, Rodriguezia* and *Cryptosaccus*.

Leonotis (Pers.) R. Br. LION'S EAR. Labiatae. 30 aromatic, ann. or perenn. herbs and subshrubs. St. tetragonal. Lvs opposite, toothed, simple. Infl. whorled; cal. tubular, 10-veined, 8–10-toothed; cor. tubular, bilabiate, upper lip much longer than lower, fringed; sta. 4. 1 sp. pantrop., the others S Afr.

L. leonurus (L.) R. Br. Pubesc. shrub to 2m. Lvs lanceolate to oblanceolate, to 11cm, entire or crenate. Cor. to 6cm, orange-red to scarlet. Late autumn. S Afr. 'Harrismith White': fls white. Z9.

L. nepetifolia (L.) R. Br. Pubesc. ann. to 120cm. Lvs ovate, to 13cm, serrate. Cor. to 4cm, orange, with 3 distinct rings of hairs inside tube. Winter. India, pantrop., nat. US. Z8.

L. ocymifolia (Burm. f.) Iwarsson. Subshrub to 70cm. St. hirsute. Lvs ovate-cordate, to 8cm, dentate, villous beneath. Cor. to 4cm, orange, hairy. S Afr. var. *ocymifolia*. Lvs grey-green, densely pubesc. beneath, crenate. var. *raineriana* (Vis.) Iwarsson. Lvs silver-pubesc. to yellow-pubesc. beneath. Cor. hairs rarely cream. S Afr. Z9. 'E.M. Rix': fls white marked red-brown.

→*Phlomis*.

Leontice L. Berberidaceae. 5 perenn. herbs. Rhiz. tuberous. Lvs mostly radical, 2–3 pinnately divided or cut. Fls yellow in scapose rac. or pan.; sep. 6–9, petaloid; pet. 6, smaller than sep.; sta. 6. Fr. a dry, inflated capsule. SE Eur. to E Asia.

L. alberti Reg. = *Gymnospermium alberti*.

L. altaica Pall. = *Gymnospermium altaicum*.

L. chrysogonum L. = *Bongardia chrysogonum*.

L. leontopetalum L. 20–80cm. Rhiz. large, knobbly. Lvs to 20cm wide, 2–3× ternately divided, somewhat fleshy, seg. ovate-obovate. Infl. many-fld; sep. to 0.8cm, round to obovate; pet. one-third length of sep. Spring. E Medit., Aegean. Z6.

Leontodon L. HAWKBIT. Compositae. 40 scapose, ann. to perenn. herbs, with milky sap. Lvs in basal rosettes, entire to pinnatifid. Cap. 1 to many, ligulate. Temp. Eurasia to Medit. and Iran. Z6.

L. apenninum Ten. = *Taraxacum apenninum*.
L. aureum L. = *Crepis aurea*.
L. glaucanthum Ledeb. = *Taraxacum glaucanthum*.
L. hispidus L. ROUGH HAWKBIT. Perenn. to 70cm. Lvs to 35×4cm, oblanceolate, sinuate-dentate to runcinately pinnatifid, narrowed to winged petiole, usually hispid. Cap. usually solitary, to 2.5–4cm; flts bright yellow, outermost orange or tinged red, rarely grey-violet beneath. Summer. Eur. to N Iran.
L. megalorhizon Forssk. = *Taraxacum megalorhizon*.
L. terglouensis Jacq. = *Crepis terglouensis*.

Leontopodium R. Br. ex Cass. EDELWEISS. Compositae. 35 perenn. herbs. St. erect or ascending. Lvs mostly crowded at base, simple and entire. Cap. discoid, small, often woolly, in compact term. cymes, surrounded by a star-shaped arrangement of conspicuous, ray-like, lanceolate, usually white-woolly hairy lvs. Eurasia esp. mts, possibly also Andes.
L. aloysiodorum hort. = *L. haplophylloides*.
L. alpinum Cass. EDELWEISS. To 20cm. St. erect, simple. Basal lvs spathulate; st. lvs to 4cm, linear-lanceolate, green above; infl. lvs linear-oblong, densely white-woolly, star to 10cm diam. Mts of Eur. Z4. 'Mignon' ('Silberstern'): compact, to 10cm; flts white. ssp. *nivale* (Ten.) Tutin. To 5cm. Lvs spathulate, white-woolly, infl. lvs spathulate, only equalling cap. Mts of SE & SC Eur. Z5.
L. alpinum var. *campestre* Beauv. non Ledeb. = *L. leontopodioides*.
L. alpinum var. *sibiricum* (Cass.) O. Fedtsch. = *L. sibiricum*.
L. alpinum var. *stracheyi* Hook. f. = *L. stracheyi*.
L. calocephalum (Franch.) Beauverd. To 50cm. St. erect. Lower lvs to 17cm, lanceolate to linear-lanceolate, acute, upper lvs shorter, ovate-lanceolate, glab. to grey-hairy above, white- or grey-hairy beneath, infl. lvs triangular, acute, white-hairy above, green beneath, star to 11cm diam. Himal. of W China and Tibet. Z5.
L. campestre (Ledeb.) Hand.-Mazz. = *L. ochroleucum* var. *campestre*.
L. crasense hort. = *L. alpinum* ssp. *nivale*.
L. discolor Beauverd. To 25cm. Lvs to 6cm, lanceolate or linear-lanceolate, arachnoid or glab. above, white-downy beneath, infl. lvs densely white-downy above, more sparsely so beneath, star to 7cm diam. Jap., SE China to Korea. Z6.
L. fauriei (Beauverd) Hand.-Mazz. To 20cm. Lvs to 7cm, spathulate-lanceolate, acute, grey-downy above, silver-downy beneath; basal lvs long-petiolate, upper st. lvs sessile, infl. lvs many, crowded, densely silvery grey-villous, star to 5cm diam. Jap. Z6.
L. haplophylloides Hand.-Mazz. To 36cm. St. erect. Lvs to *c*40m, narrowly linear-lanceolate, hairy, strongly lemon-scented, revolute, infl. lvs many, white-hairy, star to 5cm diam. S China. Z6.
L. hayachinense (Tak.) Hara & Kitam. To 20cm. Lvs to 8cm, lanceolate, green, woolly above, grey-woolly beneath, amplexicaul, infl. lvs 5–15, narrowly lanceolate, acute, star to 7cm diam. Jap. Z6.
L. himalayanum DC. To 25cm. St. erect. Lvs to 5cm, lanceolate, acute, silver-hairy, infl. lvs silver-woolly, star to 7cm diam. Himal. of China, Tibet and Kashmir. Z5.
L. jacotianum Beauverd. To 27cm. St. erect, Lvs to 3cm, lanceolate or linear-lanceolate, acute, white-hairy, esp. beneath, upper largest, infl. lvs many, larger than st. lvs, white-hairy, star to 6cm diam. N India, SW China, Burm. Z7.
L. japonicum Miq. To 50cm. St. erect. Lvs to 7cm, narrowly or ovate-lanceolate, acute; infl. lvs many, ovate or oblong, pale grey-hairy, star to 4cm, or in several irregular stars forming a corymb to 10cm diam. E China, Korea, Jap. Z5.
L. kamtschaticum Komar. = *L. kurilense*.
L. kurilense Tak. To 20cm. St. erect. Lvs to 5cm, obovate-lanceolate or spathulate, obtuse, grey-downy, infl. lvs many, woolly, star to 4cm. E Sib. Z4.
L. leontopodinum (DC.) Hand.-Mazz. = *L. ochroleucum*.
L. leontopodioides (Willd.) Beauverd. To 46cm. St. simple or branched above. Lvs to 5cm, linear to linear-lanceolate, acute, grey-villous, infl. lvs few, oblong or linear, to 2.5× length of infl., not forming a conspicuous star. S Sib., Mong., NE China. Z5.
L. monocephalum Edgew. To 12cm. St. purple, white-woolly. Lvs to 1.5cm, spathulate, obtuse, densely white- or sulphur yellow-woolly, infl. lvs to 5mm wide, yellow-woolly, star to 3.5cm diam. Himal. Z6.
L. nivale (Ten.) Huet ex Hand.-Mazz. = *L. alpinum* ssp. *nivale*.
L. ochroleucum Beauverd. To 30cm. St. tufted. Lvs to 5.5cm, spathulate or linear-lanceolate, infl. lvs pale yellow-hairy star to 3.5cm diam., regular. C Tibet and Sikkim Himal. to Altai Mts. var. *campestre* (Ledeb.) Grubov. To 17cm. Infl. lvs, pale yellow

or white, star to 2.5cm, irregular. Z4.
L. palibinianum auctt. = *L. ochroleucum* var. *campestre*.
L. shinanense Kitam. To 7cm. St. woolly. Lvs to 2cm, oblanceolate or spathulate, grey-woolly, infl. lvs to 14mm, 6–9, lanceolate. Jap. Z6.
L. sibiricum Cass. = *L. leontopodioides*.
L. souliei Beauverd. To 25cm. St. often geniculate at base. Lvs to 4cm, long-linear or lingulate-linear, acute, silvery silky-hairy, margins reflexed, infl. lvs many, silver-hairy, star to 5cm diam., compact. S China. Z5.
L. stoechas Hand.-Mazz. To 70cm. St. much-branched. Lvs to 3.5cm, narrow-oblong, obtuse, undulate, sparsely downy above, white- or glaucous-hairy beneath, infl. lvs few, star to 4cm diam. China. Z6.
L. stracheyi (Hook. f.) C.B. Clarke. To 50cm. St. erect. Lvs to 4.5cm, ovate-lanceolate to linear, acute, sometimes undulate, sparsley grey-hairy above, pale grey-downy beneath, infl. lvs many, grey-hairy, or green and gland. at tips and beneath, star to 6.5cm diam., or rarely 2 small stars. Himal. Z5.
L. tataricum Komar. = *L. discolor*.
L. wilsonii Beauverd. To 25cm. St. erect or ascending, simple. Lvs to 6cm, narrow-lanceolate, acute, pale green above, brown-downy beneath, margins narrowly reflexed, infl. lvs many, compact, white-hairy above, brown-downy beneath, star, to 2cm diam. China, Tibet. Z6.
→*Antennaria* and *Gnaphalium*.

Leonurus L. Labiatae. 9 perenn. herbs. Lvs lobed or toothed, sometimes palmately so. Infl. remotely whorled; cal. campanulate, teeth 5 spine-tipped; cor. tube shorter than cal., 2-lipped. Eur., temp. Asia, tropics.
L. cardiaca L. MOTHERWORT. 60–200cm; st. branched, usually pubesc. Lower lvs palmate, 5–7-lobed, dentate, upper lvs shallowly trilobed. Fls *c*1.2cm, white or pale pink, usually with purple dots. Eur. from Scand. to N Spain, It. and Greece, nat. S Britain. Z3.
L. galeobdolon (L.) Scop. = *Lamium galeobdolon*.

Leopard Begonia *Begonia manicata*.
Leopard Lily *Belamcanda chinensis*; *Lilium catesbaei*; *L. pardalinum*.
Leopard Orchid *Ansellia africana*.
Leopard Plant *Ligularia*.
Leopard's Bane *Doronicum*.

Leopoldia Parl.
L. tenuiflora Heldr. = *Muscari tenuiflorum*.

Lepachys Raf..
L. columnaris (Sims) Torr. & A. Gray = *Ratibida columnifera*.
L. pinnata (Vent.) Torr. & A. Gray = *Ratibida pinnata*.

Lepanthes Sw. Orchidaceae. 60 dwarf epiphytic orchids. Rhiz. short. St. tufted, slender, bearing a single term. lf. Lvs coriaceous, sometimes papillose, ovate to suborbicular. Fls small, solitary, clustered or racemose. Trop. Amer., W Indies. Z10.
L. calodictyon Hook. Lvs 2.5–5.25cm, sessile, lime to emerald-green, densely veined or patterned chocolate-brown to rusty red. Fls v. small; tep. yellow and red, ciliate; lip red, spathulate. Peru.
L. chiriquensis Schltr. = *L. lindleyana*.
L. lindleyana Ørst. & Rchb. f. Lvs 2.5–4.5cm, ovate to linear-lanceolate, acuminate. Fls to 1.5cm diam.; sep. yellow to tan, veins red-brown, minutely ciliate; pet. orange-yellow and scarlet, ciliate; lip maroon or dull red, papillate, transversely oblong-bilobed. Costa Rica, Panama, Colomb., Venez., Nic.
L. micrantha Ames = *L. lindleyana*.
L. pulchella (Sw.) Sw. Lvs 0.8–1.5cm, ovate, acute. Fls to 1.6cm diam.; sep. yellow with a median crimson line, ciliate; pet. crimson, margins yellow, lobed, ciliate; lip crimson, obscurely lobed, ciliate. Jam.
L. rotundifolia L.O. Williams. Lvs 1.6–2.5cm, suborbicular to ovate-suborbicular. Fls to 0.6cm diam., yellow and red; lip and pet. bilobed. Panama.
L. secunda Barb.Rodr. = *Lepanthopsis floripectin*.

Lepanthopsis Ames. Orchidaceae. 6 diminutive epiphytic orchids. Rhiz. minute, creeping. St. tufted, slender, bearing a single term. lf. Lvs suborbicular to elliptic-oblong. Fls axill., solitary, clustered or racemose, minute lat. sep. connate; pet. thin, elliptic-oblong to orbicular; lip simple. Trop. Americas. Z10.
L. astrophora (Rchb. f. ex Kränzl.) Garay. Lvs to 2.5×1cm, coriaceous, elliptic to oblong-elliptic, obtuse. Infl. to 12cm, many-fld; fls bright rose-purple, papillose. Venez.

L. floripectin (Rchb. f.) Ames. Lvs to 3.5×1.2cm, fleshy, suborbicular to elliptic-oblong, rounded. Infl. to 10cm, 1 to many-fld; fls thin-textured, white to yellow-green, slightly tinged pink. Spring. Hond., Costa Rica, Colomb., Venez., Braz., Panama, Peru.

L. vinacea Schweinf. Lvs to 2×1cm, fleshy, ovate to elliptic-oblong, obtuse. Infl. to 5cm, few to many-fld; fls bright purple, smooth-glandular. Venez.
→*Pleurothallis* and *Lepanthes.*

Lepechinia Willd. Labiatae. 35 shrubs or perenn. herbs. Infl. spicate, paniculate or racemose, fls in cymes, verticils, glomerules or solitary in lf axils; cal. 5-toothed, 2-lipped to nearly regular; cor. weakly bilabiate, upper lip bilobed, lower lip trilobed, tube interior with ring of hairs. Americas. Z8.

L. calycina (Benth.) Epling. PITCHER SAGE. Shrub, 1–3m, much-branched. Lvs 4–11cm, ovate, bullate to smooth, dentate to nearly entire. Infl. racemose, fls solitary; cal. 1.5–3cm, scarcely bilabiate, villous, inflated at base; cor. 2.5–3.8cm, lavender or pink, rarely white, broadly campanulate. Calif.

L. chamaedryoides (Balb.) Epling. Shrub to 3m. Lvs 1–4.5cm, linear-oblong to linear, bullate. Infl. spicate, paniculate or racemose; fls solitary; cal. to 2cm, weakly 2-lipped; cor. 1.5–2cm, blue, broadly campanulate. Chile.

L. salviae (Lindl.) Epling. Shrub to 2m. Lvs 5–8cm, ovate to deltoid, bullate and tomentose. Infl. spike-like; fls 1–3 in whorled cymes; cal. to 2.5cm, weakly 2-lipped, campanulate; cor. 2–3cm, red, slender, somewhat decurved. Chile.

L. subhastata (Benth.) Epling = *L. salviae.*
→*Dracocephalum* and *Sphacele.*

Lepechiniella Popov.
L. microcarpa (Boiss.) Riedl = *Paracaryum microcarpum.*

Leper Lily *Fritillaria meleagris.*

Lepidium L. Cruciferae. 150 ann., bienn. and perenn. herbs. Lvs pinnatifid to simple. Infl. small, racemose; sep. 4; pet. 4 (or 0); sta. 6, 4 or 2. Fr. a silicle; seeds 2. Cosmop.

L. alpina L. = *Pritzelago alpina.*
L. oppositifolium Labill. = *Aethionema oppositifolium.*
L. sativum L. COMMON GARDEN CRESS; PEPPER GRASS; PEPPERWORT. Ann., 20–60cm. St. branching. Basal lvs 1–3× pinnatifid; st. lvs bipinnate to entire. Pet. 2–3mm, white-lilac. Fr. 6×5mm, broadly elliptic-ovate or nearly round, bluntly winged. Most N temp. regions.

Lepidochiton Sealy. Amaryllidaceae. 2–3 bulbous perenn. herbs. Lvs synanthous, linear, keeled. Fl. solitary, large, scapose, somewhat declinate, fragrant; perianth crateriform, tube long, seg. lanceolate, recurved; staminal cup large, free fil. short, incurved; style exceeding sta. S Amer.

L. andreana (Bak.) Nichols. = *L. quitoensis.*
L. quitoensis (Herb.) Sealy. Lvs 30–60×1.5–3cm, glossy above, dull beneath. Scape 8–35cm; perianth 15–20×13–20cm, tube erect, curved, green, seg. white; staminal cup 4.5–6.5×7–9cm, 2-lobed or bifid between fil., laciniate to coarsely dentate, striped green, throat yellow. Ecuad.
→*Hymenocallis.*

Lepidothamnus Philippi. Podocarpaceae. 3 coniferous everg., shrubs or trees. Lvs dimorphic, narrow-linear, subulate or adpressed. Cones solitary, term., sessile; ♀ with 5 bracts, 2 fertile; seeds on a fleshy receptacle. S Chile, NZ.

L. fonkii Philippi. CHILEAN RIMU. Prostrate shrub with short erect branchlets. Juvenile lvs narrow triangular, grading into adult scale lvs, 1–1.5mm. Fr. similar to *L. laxifolius.* S Chile. Z7.

L. intermedius (T. Kirk) Quinn. YELLOW SILVER PINE. Shrub or small tree, to 10m+. Juvenile lvs linear-spathulate, 10–15mm; adult lvs 1.5–3mm, scale-shaped, triangular, densely imbricate. Receptacle orange. NZ. Z8.

L. laxifolius (Hook. f.) Quinn. MOUNTAIN RIMU. Low-growing to prostrate. St. spreading, branchlets erect. Lvs subulate, spreading, to 12mm on young plants, later linear-oblong, to 2mm. Receptacle crimson. NZ. Z7.
→*Dacrydium.*

Lepidozamia Reg. Zamiaceae. 2 cycads. Trunks columnar, to 20m. Lvs pinnate, to 3m, borne at crown in whorls, arching; pinnae to 35×3cm, to 200, opposite, somewhat reflexed, entire, lanceolate, recurved to falcate, light green above, conspicuously veined beneath. ♀ strobilus ovoid, to 60×25cm. ♂ strobilus oblong-cylindric, to 80×15cm. Seeds to 6×3cm with fleshy, scarlet outer coat. Aus. Z10.

L. hopei Reg. (Described above.) NE Queensld.

L. peroffskyana Reg. Differs from *L. hopei* in pinnae to 35×1.2cm, linear-lanceolate, dark green, with green-yellow, waxy gland at base. Subtropical Queensld & N coast NSW.

Lepisanthes Bl. Sapindaceae. 24 trees or shrubs, sometimes climbing. Lvs pinnate. Infl. term., axill. or cauliflorous; fls unisexual; sep. 4–5, free; pet. 4–5, clawed; disc crescent-shaped, lobed; sta. 8; ovary 2–3-chambered. Fr. with smooth or slightly warty skin, seeds black to brown, shining. OW Trop., W Afr., New Guinea. Z9.

L. rubiginosa (Roxb.) Leenh. Shrub or tree to 9m. Lvs to 60cm, pinnae 4–16, to 18cm, oblong-lanceolate to elliptic. Infl. 10–35cm. Fr. red becoming black, 1–3-lobed. Trop. Asia to N Aus.

L. senegalensis (Poir.) Leenh. Small tree. Lvs to 60cm, pinnae 6–12, to 25cm, ovate-lanceolate to elliptic. Infl. to 50cm, fls red. Fr. red to dark purple, 2-lobed with edible aril. Himal.
→*Aphania, Erioglossum, Euphoria, Nephelium, Sapindus, Scytala.*

Lepismium Pfeiff. Cactaceae. 14 cacti, epiphytic or saxicolous; st. cylindric or flat, usually segmented; rudimentary scale-leaves and spines present or 0. Fls mostly small, rotate, campanulate or tubular-campanulate. Fr. berry-like, spiny or naked. Braz., Boliv. and Arg.

L. commune Pfeiff. = *L. cruciforme.*
L. cruciforme (Vell. Conc.) Miq. St. to 50cm, 3–5-angled or winged, or flat, margins crenate; areoles white-hairy, bristly. Fl. 10–13mm, almost white; outermost tep. tinged red or brown. Fr. c6mm diam., subglobose, purple-red. Summer–autumn. SE Braz. to N Arg. Z9.
L. dissimile G.A. Lindb. = *Rhipsalis dissimilis.*
L. floccosum (Salm-Dyck) Backeb. = *Rhipsalis floccosa.*
L. gibberulum (F.A.C. Weber) Backeb. = *Rhipsalis floccosa.*
L. grandiflorum (Haw.) Backeb. = *Rhipsalis hadrosoma.*
L. houlletianum (Lem.) Barthlott. St. 1–2m, slender and terete below, 2–4mm diam., flat above 10–20×1–5cm, margins serrate, areoles without bristles or hairs. Fl. 1.5–2cm, tep. almost white. Fr. 5–6mm diam., globose, red. Autumn–winter. E Braz. Z9.
L. ianthothele (Monv.) Barthlott. St. to 60cm, spreading or pendent, st. seg. 8–12×1–2cm; ribs 3–5, crenate-tuberculate; areoles spiny. Fl. 15mm; pericarpel tinged purple; tep. pale yellow. Fr. 12–16mm, globose, red, spiny. Spring. NW Arg. Z9.
L. lumbricoides (Lem.) Barthlott. St. slender, to 3–4m×6mm, terete or slighty angled, creeping or clinging with aerial roots; areoles of mature growth spineless. Fl. c2×2.5(–3.5)cm, scented. Fr. globose, ripening deep purple, with purple pulp. Spring. Urug., N Arg. Z9.
L. megalanthum (Loefgr.) Backeb. = *Rhipsalis megalantha.*
L. micranthum (Vaupel) Barthlott. St. to 1m×1.5–2cm, erect then sprawling, flat or 3-winged, crenate; areoles spiny. Fl. 27×24mm; tep. suberect, purple-red. Fr. 1cm, globose to short-cylindric, slightly angled, areoles with wool. SE Peru. Z9.
L. monacantha (Griseb.) Barthlott. St. to 45×2–3cm, erect then pendent, flattened or 3-angled, crenate-serrate; areoles white-felted with spines. Fl. c15×12mm pericarpel 5-angled; tep. bright waxy orange. Fr. to 12mm diam., globose, orange-red, fading to pale pink. Spring–summer. NW Arg. Z9.
L. paradoxum Salm-Dyck ex Pfeiff. = *Rhipsalis paradoxa.*
L. pulvinigerum (G.A. Lindb.) Backeb. = *Rhipsalis pulvinigera.*
L. puniceo-discus (G.A. Lindb.) Backeb. = *Rhipsalis puniceodiscus.*
L. trigonum (Pfeiff.) Backeb. = *Rhipsalis trigona.*
L. warmingianum (Schum.) Barthlott. St. slender, 3–4-angled or flat, margins crenate, areoles glab. Fl. c2cm, white, scented. Fr. 5–6mm diam., globose, dark purple or nearly black. E Braz. Z9.
→*Acanthorhipsalis, Pfeiffera* and *Rhipsalis.*

Lepisorus J. Sm. Ching. Polypodiaceae. 25 epiphytic ferns. Rhiz. creeping. Fronds in 2 rows, uniform, short-stipitate, simple, linear to lanceolate or elliptic, entire, fleshy or leathery. Asia.

L. clathratus (Clarke) Ching. Fronds to 15×1.8cm, lanceolate to elliptic; stipes to 4cm. N India, Nepal and Afghan. N to Sib., E to China, Taiwan and Jap. Z6.

L. thunbergianus (Kaulf.) Ching. Fronds 25×1cm, narrowly linear to elliptic; stipes to 3cm. China, Taiwan, Korea, Jap., Philipp. Z9.

Leptarrhena R. Br. Saxifragaceae. 1 rhizomatous perenn. herb, to 40cm. Lvs mostly basal, 3–15cm, ovate to obovate, glab., crenate, ± short-stalked. Infl. cymose, crowded; sep. 5, 1mm; pet. 5, 2mm, white, spathulate; sta. 10, 1.5× pet. length. Fr. a red, many-seeded follicle, 5–6mm. Summer. NW US. Z5.

L. amplexifolia (Sternb.) R. Br. = *L. pyrolifolia.*

L. pyrolifolia (D. Don) R. Br. ex Ser.
→*Saxifraga*.

Leptasea Haw.
L. flagellaris (Willd.) Small = *Saxifraga flagellaris*.

Leptinella Cass. Compositae. 30 tufted or ann. to perenn. creeping herbs, usually aromatic. Cap. discoid, stalked; involucre hemispherical. Australasia, temp. S Amer. Z8 unless specified.

L. albida (D. Lloyd) D. Lloyd & C. Webb. Creeping perenn., forming compact mats, to 1m diam., densely silver-hairy. Lvs to 10×3mm, pinnatifid, lobes in 4–8 pairs, entire, leathery, dark green, densely hairy. Cap. to 1cm diam., flts pale yellow or yellow-red. NZ.

L. atrata (Hook. f.) D. Lloyd & C. Webb. Tufted perenn. to 40cm. Lvs to 8×1.3cm, broadly elliptic, 2-pinnatifid, lobes in 5–15 pairs, grey-green, leathery, fringed red. Cap. to 1.3cm diam.; flts pale yellow or dark red, almost black. NZ. ssp. *luteola* (D. Lloyd) D. Lloyd & C. Webb. Lvs less divided, lobes 5–10. Cap. conic, not convex; flts yellow, with a red-brown apex.

L. dendyi (Ckn.) D. Lloyd & C. Webb. Tufted perenn., to 40cm. Lvs to 5×0.8cm, 2-pinnatifid, grey-green, tinged red, lobes in 8–10 pairs, leathery. Cap. to 2cm diam.; flts yellow, apex brown. NZ.

L. dioica Hook. f. Creeping, fleshy perenn., to 15cm. Lvs to 12×1.5cm, obovate or elliptic, entire to pinnatifid, often dentate, lobes or teeth in 4–12 pairs, green, glab. Cap. to 7mm diam.; flts yellow-green. NZ. Z5.

L. dioica var. *rotundata* Cheesem. = *L. rotundata*.

L. goyenii (Petrie) D. Lloyd & C. Webb. Creeping perenn., forming compact mats to 1m diam., long silver-hairy. Lvs to 10×3mm, pinnatifid, lobes in 4–8 pairs, entire, leathery, dark green, densely tomentose. Cap. to 1cm diam.; flts pale yellow or yellow-red, sometimes with 1–2 dark stripes. NZ.

L. lanata Hook. f. Diffuse, creeping perenn., to 20cm, lanate becoming glab. Lvs to 2.5×1cm, elliptic, pinnatifid, lobes in 3–5 pairs, toothed, light green, thick. Cap. to 1cm diam.; flts yellow-green. NZ.

L. pectinata (Hook. f.) D. Lloyd & C. Webb. Tufted or creeping perenn. to 15cm. Lvs to 4×1cm, pinnatifid, occas. entire, lobes in 1–10 pairs, sometimes toothed, villous or glab. Cap. to 8mm diam., flts white or pale yellow-red, often with 1–2 dark stripes. NZ.

L. plumosa Hook. f. Creeping perenn., to 20cm. Lvs to 20×6cm, elliptic, 1–2-pinnatifid, lobes in 5–20 pairs, green, glab. or villous. Cap. to 1cm diam.; flts yellow-green. NZ.

L. potentillina F. Muell. Creeping perenn., to 20cm. Lvs to 12×2.5cm, pinnate, lobes in 6–15 pairs, toothed, yellow-green, glab. Cap. to 8mm diam.; flts yellow-green. NZ.

L. pyrethrifolia (Hook. f.) D. Lloyd & C. Webb. Creeping perenn., spreading in patches, to 1m diam. Lvs to 4×1cm, elliptic to ovate, pinnatifid, occas. entire and narrow, lobes in 1–5 pairs, fleshy, dark green, glab. Cap. to 1.5cm diam.; flts white. NZ.

L. reptans (Benth.) D. Lloyd & C. Webb. Creeping perenn., to 25cm, glab. or pubesc. Lvs to 10×2.5cm, ovate, pinnatifid, lobes ovate, toothed or divided, into short linear segs. Cap. to 5mm diam., ♀ flts, many, yellow. S & SE Aus., Tasm.

L. rotundata (Cheesem.) D. Lloyd & C. Webb. Creeping perenn., to 10cm, forming a loose tuft. Lvs elliptic to oblong, to 5×1.5cm, toothed in distal half, obtuse, yellow-green, with scattered long hairs. Cap. to 7mm diam., convex; flts yellow-green. NZ.

L. scariosa Cass. Creeping perenn., to 15cm. Lvs to 5×1cm, elliptic or obovate, 1-pinnatifid, lobes in 6–12 pairs, toothed, leathery, green. Cap. to 6mm diam.; flts yellow-green. Temp. S Amer.

L. squalida Hook. f. Creeping perenn., to 15cm. Lvs to 10×2cm, elliptic or obovate, pinnatifid, lobes in 6–20 pairs, bright green, glab. to pilose. Cap. to 5mm diam.; flts yellow-green. NZ. Z5.

L. traillii (T. Kirk) D. Lloyd & C. Webb. Creeping perenn., forming a loosely matted turf. Lvs to 5×1cm, obovate, pinnatifid, lobes in 4–10 pairs, toothed, dark green, leathery. Cap. to 5mm diam.; flts yellow-green. NZ.
→*Cotula*.

Leptocereus (Berger) Britt. & Rose. Cactaceae. 12 succulent trees and shrubs, sometimes prostrate or scandent; st. usually segmented, ribbed, areoles spiny. Fls tubular-campanulate, clustered or solitary, epignial tube short; perianth-limb short, spreading or rotate. Fr. globose to oblong, fleshy, spiny to nearly naked. Cuba, Hispan. and Puerto Rico.

L. weingartianus (Hartmann ex Dams) Britt. & Rose. Decumbent or climbing shrub to 10m, eventually with a woody

trunk; br. 1–2cm thick; ribs 4–7; central spines 6, to 1.5cm, radial spines 10–12, shorter. Fl. c4cm, white to pale green. Summer. Hispan. Z9.
→*Neoabbottia*.

Leptochilus Kaulf. Polypodiaceae. 12 epiphytic ferns. Rhiz. creeping or climbing. Fronds dimorphous: sterile fronds subsessile or short-stipitate, simple and entire or lobed, broadly lanceolate to ovate; fertile fronds long-stipitate, narrowly linear. Trop. Asia. Z10.

L. cladorrhizans (Spreng.) Maxon = *Bolbitis portoricensis*.
L. cuspidatus C. Chr. = *Bolbitis quoyana*.

L. decurrens Bl. Sterile fronds to 35×10cm, ovate, acute, base cuneate, long-decurrent, entire or pinnatifid, membranous; fertile fronds to 25×1cm; stipes to 30cm. Trop. Asia to Polyn.

L. harlandii (Hook.) C. Chr. = *Hemigramma decurrens*.
L. kanashirai Hayata = *Hemigramma decurrens*.
L. nicotianifolius (Sw.) C. Chr. = *Bolbitis nicotianifolia*.
L. zeylanicus C. Chr. = *Quercifilix zeylanica*.
→*Acrostichum* and *Gymnopteris*.

Leptodactylon Hook. & Arn. Polemoniaceae. 12 perenn. shrubs, subshrubs or herbs. Lvs gland., subpinnately to palmately divided. Fls in dense cymes, glomerules or solitary; cal. lobes entire, linked by membrane; cor. hypocrateriform or narrowly funnelform; sta. and style included. W N Amer. Z8.

L. californicum Hook. & Arn. PRICKLY PHLOX. Shrub, to 1m; hairy but not gland. Lvs palmately 5–9-lobed, lobes 3–12mm, linear, sharp. Infl. bracteate; cor. 2–2.5cm, hypocrateriform, lavender-pink to bright rose-pink, lobes 1–1.5cm, rounded to elliptic-ovate. Late winter–summer. Calif.

L. pungens (Torr.) Rydb. GRANITE GILIA. Shrub to 1m, glandular-villous. Lvs palmately 3–7-lobed, central lobe 8–15mm, sharp. Infl. a glomerule; cor. 1.5–2.5cm, narrowly funnelform, white to cream-yellow or pink-purple-hued, tube narrow, lobes 7–10mm, narrowly obovate. Late spring–summer. BC to Calif. and Baja Calif.
→*Gilia*.

Leptodermis Wallich. Rubiaceae. 30 decid. shrubs. Fls subsessile, in bracteate clusters or pan.; bracteoles united, tubular; cal. lobes 5, leathery; cor. funnelform to tubular, often hairy, lobes 5; sta. 5; ovary 5-celled, style filiform, 5-armed. Fr. a 5-valved capsule. India and China (Himal.), Jap.

L. kumaonensis Parker. To 1.5m; branchlets glab. Lvs to 8cm, ovate-lanceolate to narrow-elliptic, downy. Fls 3–5 in axill. clusters; cor. to 1cm, white, pink or purple. Summer. C to NW Himal. Z8.

L. lanceolata Wallich. To 2m; branchlets scabrous, bristly or glab. Lvs to 10cm, lanceolate to ovate- or elliptic-lanceolate, pubesc., esp. beneath. Fls in loose term. pan.; cor. to 1cm, white to purple. Summer–autumn. N India. Z9.

L. oblonga Bunge. To 1m; branchlets purple, minutely pubesc. Lvs to 1.8cm ovate to oblong, scabrous above, sparsely pubesc. beneath. Fls few, clustered in axill; cor. to 18mm, violet-purple. Summer–autumn. N China. Z6.

L. pilosa Diels. To 3m; branchlets pubesc. Lvs to 2.5cm, ovate, glaucous, pilose. Fls in dense term. and axill. clusters; cor. to 1cm, lilac. Summer–autumn. C to SW China. Z8.

L. purdomii Hutch. To 3m; branchlets at first minutely pubesc. Lvs to 1cm, linear-oblanceolate, glab. Fls in sessile, axill. clusters; cor. to 1cm, pink, tubular, lobes erect. Summer–autumn. N China. Z6.
→*Hamiltonia*.

Leptolepia Mett. Dennstaedtiaceae. 1 terrestrial fern. Rhiz. slender, creeping. Fronds to 60×3cm, deltoid, 3-pinnatifid to 3-pinnate, glab., pale green; primary pinnae ovate to lanceolate-oblong, to 15×5cm, secondary pinnae oblong to ovate, to 6×1cm, tertiary pinnules lanceolate to ovate, pinnatifid to pinnatisect, to 1cm, seg. oblanceolate to deltoid. NZ. Z9.

L. novae-zelandiae (Colenso) Kuhn.
→*Davallia*.

Leptomeria R. Br. Santalaceae. 17 small decid. shrubs. Br. terminating in pseudospines. Lvs scale-like, caducous. Infl. racemose; fls small; sep. 5; sta. 5. Fr. drupaceous. Aus. Z10.

L. billardieri R. Br. Fls white. Fr. red. NSW, Queensld.

Leptopteris Presl. Osmundaceae. 6 or 7 terrestrial fans. Rhiz. erect, trunk-like. Fronds arching, tripinnate to tripinnatifid. Polyn., Australasia, New Guinea. Z10.

L. fraseri (Hook. & Grev.) Presl. CREPE FERN. Stipes 15–22cm. Frond blades 30–60×20–30cm, bipinnate to tripinnatifid, light or dark green, filmy, pinnae 10–15×2–2.5cm, close-set, lanceolate, seg. linear-oblong, sharply dentate, 12×3–6mm. Aus.

L. hymenophylloides (A. Rich.) Presl. Stipes 15–30cm. Frond blades 30–60×20–30cm, tripinnatifid; pinnae 10–15×2–3cm, close-set, lanceolate; pinnules 12–20×6mm, close-set, linear-oblong, linear, simple or forked. NZ.

L. ×*intermedia* hort. (*L. hymenophylloides* ×*L. superba*.) Stipes 15–30cm, lanate. Frond blades 30–60×20–30cm, tripinnatifid; pinnae 10–15×2–3cm, close-set, lanceolate; pinnules 12–20×6mm, close-set, linear-oblong, seg. linear, simple or forked. Gdn origin.

L. moorei (Bak.) Christ. Fronds to 45×60×30cm including stipes, broadly oblong, thicker and more substantial than in other spp.; pinnae overlapping, 4–5cm wide, lanceolate: pinnules close-set, lanceolate, seg. ligulate, obtuse, dentate. Lord Howe Is.

L. superba (Colenso) Presl. PRINCE-OF-WALES'S FERN; PRINCE-OF-WALES'S PLUME. Stipes 5–7.5cm. Frond blades 60–120×15–25cm, tripinnatifid; pinnae 10–12×1.5cm, close-set, narrowly lanceolate; pinnules close-set, 6–20mm, linear-oblong, seg. linear, simple or forked. NZ.

→*Todea.*

Leptospermum Forst. & Forst. f. TI-TREE; TEA TREE. Myrtaceae. 79 shrubs or trees; young st. often silky. Lvs alt., elongate-subelliptic to rhombic, often firm, aromatic. Fls 1–2 on ends of modified lat. branchlets; sep. 5, imbricate; pet. 5, spreading; sta. usually shorter than pet. Fr. a rigid or woody capsule with valves opening at the top. Australasia, SE Asia. Z9 unless specified.

L. arachnoides Gaertn. Shrub, prostrate or attaining 2m. Bark rough and peeling in flaky layers. Lvs 10–20mm, elliptical to lanceolate or oblanceolate. Fls white, c10mm diam. SE Queensld to NSW.

L. attenuatum Sm. = *L. trinervium.*

L. baccatum Sm. = *L. arachnoides.*

L. bullatum hort. ex Loud. = *L. scoparium.*

L. citratum Chall. = *L. petersonii.*

L. citriodorum auct. = *L. liversidgei.*

L. cunninghamii hort. non S. Schauer = *L. lanigerum* 'Silver Sheen'.

L. cunninghamii S. Schauer = *L. myrtifolium.*

L. epacridoideum Cheel. Erect rather rigid shrub, to 2m+. Bark close, firm, corrugated towards base. Lvs 2–3mm, somewhat aromatic, dense, elliptic to orbicular, incurved, thick. Fls white or pink, c10mm diam. NSW.

L. flavescens Sm. = *L. polygalifolium.*

L. floribundum Jungh. non Salisb. = *L. javanicum.*

L. floribundum Salisb. = *L. scoparium.*

L. grandiflorum Lodd. Shrub 1.5 to 5m or more. Bark rough and close. Lvs 10–15mm, narrowly to broadly ovate or elliptic, thick, grey-green, often pubesc. Fls white or pink, c20mm diam. Tasm.

L. humifusum Cunn. ex Schauer, nom. nud. = *L. rupestre.*

L. javanicum Bl. Shrub or tree, often gnarled, to 8m+. Bark persistent and rather flaky. Lvs usually 15–35mm, broadly oblanceolate to obovate. Fls white, rarely flushed pink, c10–12mm diam. Burm. and S Thail. to Philipp.

L. juniperinum Sm. Erect, compact, shrub, 2–3m. Bark close. Lvs c5–15mm, dense, the youngest silvery sericeous, narrowly elliptic or lanceolate, subterete. Fls white, 6–10mm diam. Queensld to NSW.

L. laevigatum (Gaertn.) F. Muell. Shrub or small tree, to 4m. Bark shed in strips from the older trunks. Lvs 15–30mm, narrowly obovate, thin-textured. Fls white, usually 15–20mm diam. S Aus., Vict., NSW, Tasm. 'Compactum': habit neat, to 1m.

L. lanigerum (Sol. ex Ait.) Sm. Shrub or tree to 5mm+. Bark close, firm. Lvs 2–15mm, oblong to narrowly oblanceolate, usually grey-pubesc. Fls white, c15mm diam. Tasm., S Aus., NSW, Vict. 'Silver Sheen' (*L. cunninghamii* of gardens): lvs silver-grey on red-tinted st.; fls produced later than in *L. lanigerum* (i.e. summer, not spring); v. cold-hardy. Z8.

L. liversidgei R. Bak. & H.G. Sm. Compact shrub to 4m, often less. Bark close. Lvs usually 5–7mm, lemon-scented, dense, narrowly obovate, thick. Fls white or pink, c10–12mm diam. NSW, Queensld. Z8.

L. minutifolium C.T. White. Shrub to 2m+. Bark close or smooth flaking. Lvs usually 2–4mm, usually dense, obovate, thick, concave, glossy. Fls white, usually c8mm diam. Queensld, NSW.

L. myrtifolium Sieber ex DC. Slender shrub 1–2(–3)m. Bark close forming flaky layers. Lvs 5–10mm, broadly obovate to oblanceolate or elliptic, silky, grey-green, thick. Fls white, 7–11mm diam. NSW, Vict. Z8.

L. nitidum Hook. f. Compact shrub to 2m. Bark scaly, layered.

Lvs usually 8–20mm, aromatic, dense, elliptic, usually glossy, ciliate. Fls white, usually c15mm diam. Tasm.

L. obovatum Sweet. Dense erect shrub, 2m or more. Bark close and firm. Lvs 5–20mm, aromatic, narrowly oblanceolate to broadly obovate. Fls white, 8–12mm diam. NSW, Vict.

L. parviflorum Val. Multi-stemmed shrub or small tree to 6m. Bark exfoliating in strips to expose a shining, purple-red surface below. Lvs diverging, 20–70mm, linear-lanceolate, rather thin. Fls white or cream, 2–7mm diam. New Guinea, W Aus., N Territ., Queensld.

L. persiciflorum Rchb. f. = *L. squarrosum.*

L. petersonii Bail. Dense shrub or small tree to 5m+. Bark rather flaky, persistent fibrous. Lvs usually 20–40mm, lemon-scented, elliptic to narrowly lanceolate. Fls white, 10–15mm diam. Queensld, NSW.

L. polygalifolium Salisb. Shrub, from 0.5 to 3m, or tree to 7m. Bark usually close and firm later sometimes soft, thick and flaky. Lvs sometimes aromatic, 5–20mm, oblanceolate-elliptic to narrowly linear-elliptic. Fls white, often green or creamy-white, occas. pink, usually 10–15mm diam. E Aus., Lord Howe Is. Z8.

L. pubescens Lam. = *L. lanigerum.*

L. rodwayanum Summerh. & Comber = *L. grandiflorum.*

L. roei Benth. Spreading slender shrub to 2m. Bark close but shedding fibres. Lvs usually 7–13mm, elongate-obovate to narrowly cuneate, often sericeous. Fls white or pink, usually 10–13mm diam. W Aus.

L. rotundifolium (Maid. & Betche) F. Rodway ex Cheel. Shrub to 2m+. Bark close and ultimately gnarled. Lvs mostly 4–7mm, generally orbicular, thick. Fls white to purple-pink, to 3cm diam.+. NSW.

L. rupestre Hook. f. Shrub, usually low-growing. Bark flaky. Lvs 2–7mm, aromatic, obovate to elliptic, rather glossy, thick. Fls white, 7–10mm diam. Tasm.

L. scoparium Forst. & Forst. f. MANUKA; TEA TREE. Shrub 2(–4)m. Bark usually close and firm, rarely layered. Lvs 7–20mm, elliptic, or broadly lanceolate or oblanceolate, often silvery pubesc. at first. Fls white, or rarely, pink or red, usually 8–12mm diam. NSW, Vict., Tasm., NZ. 'Album Flore Pleno': habit compact, erect; fls white, double. 'Boscawenii': compact; fls to 2.5cm diam, white with a rose centre. 'Burgundy Queen': fls deep red. 'Chapmanii': lvs maroon to red-green; fls cerise. 'Cherry Brandy': lvs deep red-bronze; fls cerise. 'Decumbens': semi-prostrate; fls pale rose. 'Gaiety Girl': fls double, salmon pink. 'Jubilee': habit densely bushy. 'Keatleyi': young growth red-tinted, silky; fls large, waxy, pink. 'Kiwi': dwarf; foliage bronze; fls deep pink. 'Nanum': dwarf form to 30cm; fls rose, profuse. 'Nanum Tui': dwarf; lvs bronze. 'Nichollsii': lvs purple-red to bronze; fls carmine. 'Pink Cascade': habit weeping. 'Red Damask': fls double, deep red, long-lasting. 'Roseum Multipetalum': fls double, rose pink, profuse. 'Ruby Glow': fls semi-double, crimson with a darker centre. Z8.

L. scoparium var. *prostratum* Hook. non Hook. f. = *L. rupestre.*

L. sericeum Labill. Medium-sized. Lvs small, bright green, pointed. Young st. tinted red. Fls white. Tas.

L. sphaerocarpum Cheel. Shrub to 2m, usually erect. Bark close and firm. Lvs mostly 5–20mm, elliptic, rather thick. Fls green-white or pink, 15–20mm diam. NSW.

L. spinescens Endl. Spinescent shrub, to 1.5m. Bark corrugated, corky. Lvs 5–15mm, obovate, elliptic, thick. Fls white or green-cream, 10–15mm diam. W Aus.

L. squarrosum Gaertn. Rather open shrub to more than 4m. Bark close, firm. Lvs 5–15mm, broadly elliptic to broadly ovate-lanceolate, occas. narrower. Fls white or pink, to 10–20mm diam. NSW.

L. stellatum Cav. = *L. trinervium.*

L. trinervium (Sm.) J. Thomps. WEEPING TI-TREE. Shrub or small tree 2–5m. Bark in many thin layers. Lvs 10–20mm, broadly ovate to v. narrowly elliptic and somewhat falcate. Fls white, 7–15mm diam. Queensld, Vict., NSW.

→*Melaleuca.*

Leptosyne DC.

L. bigelovii A. Gray = *Coreopsis bigelovii.*

L. californica Nutt. = *Coreopsis californica.*

L. douglasii DC. = *Coreopsis douglasii.*

L. gigantea Kellogg = *Coreopsis gigantea.*

L. stillmanii A. Gray = *Coreopsis stillmanii.*

Leptotes Lindl. Orchidaceae. 4 diminutive epiphytic orchids. Rhiz. short-creeping. Pbs cylindrical, apically unifoliate. Lvs fleshy, terete or subterete. Infl. a short, term. rac.; sep. and pet. subequal, free; lip trilobed. Braz., Parag., Arg. Z10.

L. bicolor Lindl. Pbs to 3cm. Lvs to 10cm, usually shorter, terete, grooved above. Fls to 5cm diam., fragrant, tep. linear-oblong, sparkling white, the lip with a rose to purple, white-tipped mid-lobe. E Braz., Parag.

L. tenuis Rchb. f. Resembles *L. unicolor* except tep. yellow, lip white with a central violet blotch. Braz.

L. unicolor Barb. Rodr. Pbs to 1.5cm. Lvs to 5.5cm, subterete, grooved above. Fls to 6cm diam., nodding, fragrant, white-pink to pale rose-lilac; sep. linear-ligulate; pet. linear-subspathulate, somewhat darker than sep. Winter. Braz.
→*Tetramicra*.

Lerp Mallee *Eucalyptus incrassata*.

Leschenaultia R. Br. Goodeniaceae. 24 heath-like herbs, subshrubs or shrubs. Lvs usually linear. Fls solitary and term. or several in term., leafy corymbs; cal. tube adnate to ovary, lobes narrow; cor. tube split to base, interior lanate, lobes 5, erect or spreading. Aus. Z9.

L. acutiloba Benth. Shrubby erect ann. to 30cm. Lvs to 3mm, acute or obtuse. Fls solitary; cor. to 12mm, cream, lobes short, erect to spreading, acute or acuminate. W Aus.

L. arcuata Vriese = *L. linarioides*.

L. biloba Lindl. Everg. shrub to 60cm, erect or straggling. Lvs to 10mm. Fls in corymbs; cor. bright blue, sometimes white, lobes to 1.25cm wide, winged, 2-lobed, mucronate. W Aus.

L. drummondii Vriese = *L. biloba*.

L. expansa R. Br. Shrubby diffuse ann. to 60cm. Lvs to 10mm. Fls in dense corymbs; cor. to 8mm, blue, mauve or white, lobes narrowly winged, wings undulate, white-ciliate. W Aus.

L. floribunda Benth. Shrubby erect, ann. to 1m. Lvs to 8mm, narrowly oblong to linear. Fls in loose corymbs; cor. to 16mm, blue or white, lobes narrowly winged, mucronate, wings flat or undulate, slightly ciliate. W Aus.

L. formosa R. Br. Short-lived shrub to 60cm. St. much-branched, suckering. Lvs to 12mm. Fls solitary; cor. to·2cm diam., red, scarlet or orange, lobes large, spreading, erect, rounded. W Aus.

L. grandiflora DC. = *L. biloba*.

L. hirsuta F. Muell. Short-lived erect or decumbent subshrub to 60cm. Lvs to 3cm. Fls solitary; cor. to 3cm, bright scarlet, exterior slightly glandular-pubesc., lobes shorter than tube. W Aus.

L. laricina Lindl. Short-lived erect shrub to 60cm. Lvs to 12mm. Fls in upper lf axils; cor. usually vivid red (white and lilac forms reported), tube to 13mm, lobes broadly winged, 2-lobed at apex with a mucro in the sinus. W Aus.

L. linarioides DC. Short-lived shrub to 10cm. St. erect or procumbent, br. sometimes sprawling. Lvs to 20mm. Fls solitary; cor. tube to 10mm, limb to 3.25cm diam., 2-lipped, upper 3 lobes broadly winged, deep yellow, lower 2 lobes vivid red. W Aus.

L. longiloba F. Muell. Prostrate shrub to 15cm. Lvs small. Fls in upper lv axils; cor. to 2.5cm, cream and red, lobes spreading, equalling tube, acuminate-mucronate. W Aus.

L. multiflora Lodd. = *L. formosa*.

L. splendens Hook. = *L. laricina*.

L. superba F. Muell. Virgate ann. shrub to 60cm. Lvs to 2.5cm. Fls in term. clusters; cor. to 2.5cm, yellow, orange or red, tube cylindric, lobes short, broadly winged. W Aus.

L. tubiflora R. Br. Shrub to 15cm. St. prostrate, br. divaricate or virgate. Fls solitary, at tips of short br.; cor. cream, orange, pink or red, tube cylindric, lobes shorter than tube, wings short. W Aus.

Lespedeza Michx. BUSH CLOVER. Leguminosae (Papilionoideae). 40 perenn. or ann. shrubs or herbs. Lvs trifoliolate, petiolate; stipules small. Fls small, rarely solitary, usually arranged in rac., fascicles or pan., showy, pea-like or cleistogamous, far smaller, and located in separate rac. Fr. rounded or elliptic, compressed. E US, E & Trop. Asia, Aus.

L. bicolor Turcz. EZO-YAMA-HAGI. Bush to 3m; woody-based, somewhat scandent. Lfts 1–7.5cm, ovate or elliptic, thinly downy above while young, pilose to glab. beneath. Fls loosely packed in axill. rac., or in term., paniculate clusters; cor. 1–1.2cm, purple-rose or rose-violet. Late summer. E Asia, nat. SE US. 'Summer Beauty': habit spreading, to 1.6m tall; fls long-lasting. 'Yakushima': habit dwarf, to 30cm tall; lvs and fls small. Z5.

L. buergeri Miq. KI-HAGI. Shrub to 1m, spreading, downy. Lfts 2–4cm, elliptic-ovate, sharp-tipped, usually glab. above, adpressed-downy beneath. Fls in ascending rac.; cor. 1–1.2cm white or purple. Late summer. Jap., China. Z6.

L. capitata Michx. Perenn., 50cm–1.5m. Lfts 1.5–4.5cm, oblong to narrowly elliptic, glab. to adpressed-sericeous above, velutinous to sericeous beneath. Fls overlapping in densely packed axill. rac.; cor. to 1cm, yellow-white or plain white, standard blotched purple at base. Late summer–early autumn. US. Z4.

L. cyrtobotrya Miq. MARABU-HAGI; MIYAMA-HAGI. Scandent or erect woody-based herb to 1.2m. Lfts 2–4.4cm, obovate or elliptic, rounded, blunt or notched, glab. above, downy beneath. Fls crowded in axill. clusters or rac.; cor. to 1.5cm, rose-purple. Late summer–early autumn. Jap., China, Korea. Z6.

L. juncea (L. f.) Pers. KARA-MEDO-HAGI; INU-MEDO-HAGI. Erect, rather woody perenn., 60cm–1.2m. Lfts 0.8–2cm, narrowly obovate to oblanceolate, canescent beneath, glab. above. Fls 2–6 in axill., umbellate rac.; cor. to 0.8cm, yellow-white, standard blotched purple. Autumn. Jap., E Asia, E Sib., Aus. (SE Queensld). Z5.

L. kiusiana Nak. Small shrub; foliage soft green; fls pale rosy purple in large pan. Jap., Korea.

L. macrocarpa Bunge = *Campylotropis macrocarpa*.

L. maximowiczii C. Schneid. CHOSEN-KI-HAGI. Spreading shrub to 4m. Lfts 2.5–5cm, oval-elliptic to ovate, sharp-tipped, sericeous beneath. Fls in ascending rac.; cor. 1cm, purple. Summer. Jap., Korea. Z5.

L. thunbergii (DC.) Nak. MIYAGINO-HAGI. Perenn. herb or subshrub, 1–2m. Lfts 3–5cm, narrowly oblong, ovate or elliptic, sharp-tipped, glab. above, adpressed grey-hirsute beneath. Fls in numerous pendulous rac. to 15cm, these grouped in term. 60–80cm pan.; cor. 1.5–1.8cm, rose-purple. Late summer. Jap., China. 'Alba': fls white. Z6.
→*Hedysarum*.

Lesquerella S. Wats. BLADDER POD. Cruciferae. 40 ann. or perenn. herbs, densely hairy. Basal lvs linear-oblanceolate, usually borne in rosettes, flowering st. lvs usually sessile, smaller. Infl. a rac.; fls small, 4-merous; sep. erect to spreading; pet. broad-obovate to narrow-spathulate; sta. 6. Fr. a silicle, usually globose, sometimes compressed. N Amer., Greenland. Z5.

L. alpina (Nutt.) S. Wats. Perenn. to 25cm. Base woody, branched. St. erect, simple. Lvs to 7cm, oblanceolate-spathulate to linear. Pet. 4–10mm, yellow, oblong-elliptic. Fr. 2.5–8mm. Rocky Mts. Z5.

L. arctica (Wormsk. ex Hornem.) S. Wats. Perenn., 30cm. Base woody. St. few. Lvs to 15cm, oblanceolate or linear-spathulate, silver-hairy. Pet. obovate, yellow. Fr. 4–9mm. Summer. N N Amer., Greenland. Z3.

L. globosa (Desv.) S. Wats. Perenn., to 50cm. Base woody. Lvs to 5cm, white-pubesc., oblanceolate to obovate, entire to sinuate, sometimes pinnatifid. Pet. 3.5–7mm, bright yellow. Fr. to 3mm. Indiana to Tenn. Z6.

L. gracilis (Hook.) S. Wats. Ann. or bienn., to 70cm. St. numerous, scabrid, thin. Lvs 1–11cm, oblanceolate to lyrate, subglabrous, mostly entire. Pet. 6–11mm, ovate, yellow-orange. Fr. 3–10mm. Summer. Tex., Okl., Kans.

L. grandiflora (Hook.) S. Wats. Ann., to 75cm. St. densely hairy, branched. Lvs hairy, oblong, pinnatifid. Pet. 8–12mm, broadovate to nearly round, yellow. Fr. 4–6mm. Summer. Tex.

L. ludoviciana (Nutt.) S. Wats. Perenn. to 50cm. St. few, lvs rosulate, outermost 2–9cm, oblanceolate and obtuse, innermost linear-elliptic, erect. Pet. 5–11mm, oblanceolate, yellow. Fr. to 10mm. Spring–summer. Colorado to Mont. and Minn. Z3.

L. montana (Gray) S. Wats. Perenn., to 35cm. Base woody. St. erect or prostrate. Lvs 2–7cm, nearly round to obovate-elliptic, entire or sinuate. Pet. 7–12mm, yellow-orange fading to purple. Fr. 7–12mm. New Mex., Colorado, Wyom. Z3.

L. spatulata Rydb. = *L. alpina*.
→*Alyssum* and *Vesicaria*.

Lesser Bladderwort *Utricularia minor*.
Lesser Bottlebrush *Callistemon phoeniceus*.
Lesser Bullrush *Typha angustifolia*.
Lesser Burdock *Arctium minus*.
Lesser Butterfly Orchid *Platanthera bifolia*.
Lesser Calamint *Calamintha nepeta*.
Lesser Celandine *Ranunculus ficaria*.
Lesser Duckweed *Lemna minor*.
Lesser Galangal *Alpinia officinarum*.
Lesser Knapweed *Centaurea nigra*.
Lesser Knotweed *Polygonum campanulatum*.
Lesser Periwinkle *Vinca minor*.
Lesser Quaking Grass *Briza minor*.
Lesser Spearwort *Ranunculus flammula*.
Lesser Twayblade *Listera cordata*.
Lesser Wintergreen *Pyrola minor*.
Lesser Yellow Trefoil *Trifolium dubium*.

Lessingia Cham. Compositae. 7 gland., white-woolly or glab. annuals; st. simple or branched. Cap. discoid; involucre cylindric to campanulate; outermost flts enlarged, reflexed. W US.

L. hololeuca Greene. To 30cm, erect or ascending, branching from base. Basal lvs to 12cm, obovate to oblanceolate, entire or toothed, sessile or attenuate at base. Cap. solitary, term.; flts 13–18, pink or mauve.

L. leptoclada A. Gray. To 80cm, glabrescent, erect, branching above. Basal lvs to 5cm, oblanceolate or spathulate, attenuate at base, entire or toothed. Cap. term., solitary; flts to 22, mauve to purple.

Lesueur Hakea *Hakea megalosperma.*
Lettuce *Lactuca sativa.*
Lettuce-leaf Begonia *Begonia ×erythrophylla.*

Leucadendron R. Br. Proteaceae. 80 shrubs or trees. Lvs entire, toughened, downy when young. Infl. term., solitary, surrounded by large, coloured involucral lvs; ♂ fls with 4 sessile anth., stigma abortive; ♀ fls with 4 sessile staminodes. Fr. a nut or samara concealed in the bracts of a thick, woody cone. S Afr. Z9.

L. argenteum Meissn. SILVER TREE. Tree to 10m. Branchlets pilose. Lvs to 15cm, lanceolate, mucronate at apex, with adpressed brilliant silvery hairs. ♂ infl. villous, with oblong, obtuse, villous involucral lvs to 7mm; ♀ infl. to 4cm diam., spheric, involucral lvs v. broadly ovate to suborbicular, minutely velvety-tomentose without, glab. and slightly shining within. Summer. S Afr. (Cape Penins.).

L. ascendens R. Br. = *L. salignum.*

L. daphnoides Meissn. in DC. Branchlets softly downy. Lvs to 5.5cm, lanceolate, mucronate at apex, coriaceous, softly tomentose or subglabrous, lat. veins distinct. ♂ infl. 4cm diam., depressed-globose, involucral lvs 12mm, imbricate, oblanceolate-spathulate, tawny villous without; ♀ infl. 2.5–3cm diam., subglobose, involucral lvs to 1.5cm, ovate, coloured, pilose beneath. S Afr. (Cape Prov.).

L. discolor Buek. Branchlets, purple, glab. Lvs 2.5–4cm, oblanceolate, coriaceous, margins cartilaginous, minutely tomentose. ♀ infl. to 3cm diam., subglobose to ellipsoid-globose; involucral bracts oblong, rounded, 8–10mm, hirsute-tomentose on upper part without, otherwise glab. S Afr. (Cape Prov.).

L. gandogeri Schinz ex Gand. Robust shrub to 160cm. Lvs 8cm+, elliptic, softly hairy when young, shiny when mature, young lvs turning red in late summer or autumn. Involucral lvs, bright yellow, flushed orange and red. S Afr.

L. laureolum (Lam.) Fourc. Shrub to 2m, ♂ plants bushy, ♀ plants smaller and sparser. Lvs to 9.5cm, oblong, obtuse, recurved at apex, green, tinged red at tip, glabrescent. ♂ infl. spherical, to 2cm diam., surrounded by yellow involucral lvs; ♀ infl. elongated, to 1.4cm diam., concealed by lime-green involucral lvs. Summer. S Afr. (Cape Prov.).

L. 'Safari Sunset'. (*L. salignum × L. laureolum.*) Vigorous, to 2.5m. Lvs 9×1.5cm, deep green, flushed red particularly towards br. apices. Involucre 10–20cm diam.; bracts light red becoming wine red fading to golden yellow. Autumn–winter. Gdn origin.

L. salignum Bergius. Shrub to about 1m, with lignotuber. Lvs linear-lanceolate, acute, to 6cm, glab. ♂ infl. spherical, to 1.5cm diam., surrounded by yellow involucral lvs; ♀ infl. to 1.2cm diam., by ivory involucral lvs. Summer. S Afr. (Cape Prov.).

L. tinctum Williams. Shrub to 130cm at most, low and bushy. Lvs oblong, rounded. Involucral lvs large, yellow during flowering season. Fr. with spicy aroma. S Afr. (Cape Prov.).

Leucaena Benth. Leguminosae (Mimosoideae). 40 everg. shrubs or trees. Lvs bipinnate. Infl. mimosoid, solitary or fascicled; cal. small, tubular to campanulate, 5-lobed; sta. 10, free, eglandular. Subtrop. Amer., Polyn. Z9.

L. glauca auct. = *L. leucocephala.*

L. latisiliqua (L.) Gillis = *L. leucocephala.*

L. leucocephala (Lam.) De Wit. LEAD TREE; WHITE POPINAC. Pinnae 8–16; lfts to 1.4cm, 26–42. Fl. heads 2cm diam., white tinged yellow. S Flor., S Tex., S Calif.

L. pulverulenta (Schldl.) Benth. Pinnae 8–30; lfts to 0.5cm, 40 or more. Fl. heads to 2cm diam. Mex.

L. retusa Benth. Pinnae 4–8; lfts 8–16. Fl. heads to 2.5cm diam., golden yellow. US (Tex.), N Mex.

→*Caudoleucaena.*

Leucanthemella Tzvelev. Compositae. 2 perenn. herbs. St. pilose, usually branched. Lvs simple, lanceolate to broadly elliptic, gland. punctate. Cap. radiate, solitary or few in a loose corymb; receptacle strongly convex; ray disc flts tubular or tubular-campanulate, yellow. SE Eur., E Asia. Z7.

L. serotina (L.) Tzvelev. To 1.5m. St. branched above. Lvs to 12cm, lanceolate to oblong, base 2–4-lobed, sessile middle st. lvs, with forward pointing teeth. Ray flts white or red. SE Eur.

'Herbstern': fls clear white, centres tinted yellow.
→*Chrysanthemum* and *Pyrethrum.*

Leucanthemopsis (Giroux) Heyw. Compositae. 6 dwarf, tufted perennials. Lvs pinnately lobed or dissected, glab. or hairy. Cap. radiate, solitary; receptacle convex; ray flts yellow or white; disc flts tubular-campanulate, usually yellow. Eur. mts and N Afr.

L. alpina (L.) Heyw. Tufted or matting to 15cm. Lvs to 4cm, ovate to spathulate, crenate to pinnatifid or palmatifid, grey-hairy or glab. Cap. to 4cm diam.; ray flts white, sometimes becoming pink; disc flts orange-yellow. Eur. mts. ssp. **tomentosa** (Lois.) Heyw. Extreme dwarf. Lvs ovate, palmatifid, with 5–7, closely proximate lobes. Z6.

L. hosmariense hort. = *Chrysanthemopsis hosmariensis.*

L. pallida (Mill.) Heyw. Ascending, white-pubesc., to 20cm, un-branched. Lower lvs spathulate, dissected. Cap. to 5cm diam.; ray flts yellow, or white with a yellow or purple base. Mts of C & E Spain. ssp. **spathulifolia** (Gay) Heyw. Lvs cuneate- to orbicular-spathulate, incised-toothed; ray flts yellow. SE Spain. Z8.

L. radicans (Cav.) Heyw. Ascending, densely tufted, with stolons. Lvs pinnate, lobes oblong, 5–9. Cap. to 2cm diam.; ray flts yellow, becoming orange-red. Fr. 3–6-ribbed. S Spain. Z8.

→*Chrysanthemum* and *Pyrethrum.*

Leucanthemum Mill. Compositae. 25 ann. or perenn. herbs. Cap. usually radiate, term., solitary or in small clusters; receptacle usually convex, naked; ray flts white or tinged pink; disc flts tubular-campanulate, usually yellow. Eur., N Asia.

L. atlanticum (Ball) Maire = *Chrysanthemopsis atlantica.*

L. atratum (Jacq.) DC. Perenn. St. 10–50cm, simple or branched, sometimes hairy. Basal lvs spathulate, crenate or lobed, apex often 3–5-toothed, petioles long, st. lvs oblong to linear, deeply toothed to pinnatifid. Cap. 2–5cm diam., solitary; ray flts white. Summer. SE Eur. mts. ssp. **ceratophylloides** (All.) Horvatić. St. usually 20–30cm. Basal lvs spathulate-cuneate; mid-stem lvs pinnatifid to bipinnatifid. Alps, Apennines. ssp. **coronopifolium** (Vill.) Horvatić. St. usually 20–30cm. Basal lvs spathulate-cuneate, incised-dentate. Alps. Z6.

L. burnatii Briq. & Cavillier. Perenn. St. erect or ascending. Basal lvs linear-oblong, cuneiform, entire, apex sometimes 2–3-toothed; st. lvs linear to filiform, entire to remotely toothed, amplexicaul base persistent, white and scarious. Cap. 2–4cm diam., solitary. SE Fr. Z7.

L. catananche (Ball) Maire = *Chrysanthemopsis catananche.*

L. depressum (Ball) Maire = *Chrysanthemopsis depressa.*

L. gayanum (Coss. & Dur.) Maire = *Chrysanthemopsis gayana.*

L. graminifolium (L.) Lam. Perenn. St. 15–30cm, simple, often woody, red-tinted and pubesc. below. Basal lvs oblong-lanceolate or obovate-spathulate, apex with 3–5 teeth, on long, red-hairy petioles, st. lvs oblong to linear, lower lvs bristly toothed at base, other lvs sparsely toothed to entire. Cap. 3–3.5cm diam., solitary. Fr. Z7.

L. hosmariense (Ball) Font Quer = *Chrysanthemopsis hosmariensis.*

L. lacustre (Brot.) Samp. Differs from *L. vulgare* in basal lvs toothed; cap. 4.5–6cm diam. Summer. W Port. Z8.

L. maresii (Coss.) Maire = *Chrysanthemopsis maresii.*

L. mawii hort. = *Chrysanthemopsis gayana.*

L. maximum (Ramond) DC. Differs from *L. vulgare* in basal lvs entire to toothed and cap. to 9cm diam. Pyren. Z6.

L. maximum (hort.) non (Ramond) DC. = *L. × superbum.*

L. nipponicum Franch. ex Maxim. = *Nipponanthemum nipponicum.*

L. pallens (Gay) DC. Similar to *L. vulgare* but basal lvs crenate-dentate; petioles with basal wings; cap. 1.5–5cm diam. S Eur. mts (Spain to Albania). Z7.

L. paludosum (Poir.) Bonnet & Barratte. Glab. ann. St. to 15cm, branched. Lvs toothed to pinnatifid, basal lvs obovate-spathulate, lower lvs oblong-cuneate, petiole basally auriculate, upper lvs oblong to lanceolate. Cap. 2–3cm diam.; ray flts pale yellow or white tinged yellow near base; disc flts ± zygomorphic. S Spain, S Port., Balearic Is.

L. × superbum (J. Ingram) Bergmans ex Kent. (*L. maximum × L. lacustre.*) SHASTA DAISY. Perenn., erect, glab. to 1m+. Lvs dentate, lower lvs to 30cm, oblanceolate, petiolate, upper lvs lanceolate, sessile. Cap. to 10cm diam., solitary; ray flts pure white; disc flts yellow. Gdn origin. Over 50 cvs, mostly white, some clones, others (such as the Princess group) seed raised; the original single fls now mostly superseded by fringed, semi-double and double cvs: notable single-fld cvs include the old 'Phyllis Smith' and the feathery 'Bishopstone': notable semi-doubles include 'Aglaia' and the 90cm 'Esther Read': anemone-centred doubles include 'Wirral Supreme' and 'T.E. Killin': fully double fls include 'Cobham Gold' with yellow central flts and the tall (to 100cm) 'Fiona Coghill' and 'Starburst'; dwarf cvs include 'Powis Castle' and the 45cm 'Little Silver Princess'. Z5.

L. vulgare Lam. OX-EYE DAISY; MOON DAISY; MARGUERITE. Perenn. herb. To 1m, simple or branched. Basal lvs 1.5–10cm, obovate-spathulate to oblong, crenate, on long petioles; stem lvs oblong to lanceolate, entire to pinnatifid, green or glaucous, uppermost sessile. Capitula 2.5–9cm diam., solitary or clustered; ray florets white, occasionally short or absent. Summer. Temp. Eurasia. 'Hofenkröne': erect to 60cm; fls fully double, white. 'Hullavington': st. and lvs blotched yellow. 'Maikönigin' ('May Queen'): to 70cm; fls white; early. 'Maistern': to 60cm; fls profuse, white. 'Rheinblick': to 60cm; fls single, profuse. Z3.

L. waldsteinii (Schultz-Bip.) Pouzar. Perenn. 20–70cm, simple or sparingly branched, densely leafy. Basal and lower stem lvs broadly ovate to suborbicular, cordate, crenate-toothed upper petiolate lvs cuneiform to ovate-oblong. Capitula 4–6cm diam., solitary or clustered in a loose corymb. Carpath. Z6.

→*Chrysanthemum*.

Leuchtenbergia Hook. Cactaceae. 1 cactus, rarely to 70cm high, simple or clustering; st. globose to short-cylindric; tubercles to 10cm, glaucous, narrowly triangular, almost resembling a crown of ripped *Agave* lvs; areoles apical; spines to 15cm, papery, flattened. Fls to 8×5–6cm, yellow.

L. principis Hook.

Leucocarpus D. Don Scrophulariaceae. 1 perenn. herb, to 80cm. St. 4-angled, winged. Lvs to 25cm, lanceolate, basally cordate, clasping, serrate. Fls in axill. long-stalked cymes; cal. 5-lobed; cor. yellow, to 2cm, 2-lipped with pubesc. calli. Fr. a white berry. Summer. Mex. Z9.

L. perfoliatus (Kunth) Benth.

Leucocoryne Lindl. Liliaceae (Alliaceae). 12 herbaceous, bulbous, garlic-scented perenn. Lvs linear, often channelled. Fls funnel-shaped, in scapose umbels with 2 spathes; perianth seg. 6; sta. 6, 3 joined to perianth within tube, staminodes 3, club-shaped, joined to perianth at mouth of tube. Chile. Z9.

L. alliacea Lindl. 15–30cm. Lvs to 20cm, grass-like. Tep. 1.8cm narrow, acute, white, tinged green. Spring.

L. ixioides (Hook.) Lindl. GLORY OF THE SUN. To 45cm. Lvs to 45cm, grass-like. Fls fragrant; tep. to 1.5cm, free portions white or deeply edged lilac to violet-blue, tube white; sta. and staminodes yellow-white. Spring.

L. ixioides var. *purpurea* (Gay) Bak. = *L. purpurea*.

L. odorata Lindl. Differs from *L. ixioides* in tep. smaller, pale blue.

L. purpurea Gay. To 50cm. Lvs to 30cm, grass-like. Tep. to 3cm, obovate, white tinted purple, ageing mauve-indigo; staminodes yellow tipped purple. Spring.

→*Brodiaea*.

Leucocrinum Nutt. ex A. Gray. SAND LILY; STAR LILY; MOUNTAIN LILY. Liliaceae (Funkiaceae). 1 perenn., rhizomatous, fleshy-rooted herb. Lvs 10–20×0.2–0.6cm, narrowly linear, radical. Fls fragrant, clustered on ± subterranean st.; perianth white, salverform, tube 2.5–12cm, lobes 6, to 2cm; anth. yellow. W US.

F. montanum Nutt. ex A. Gray.

Leucogenes Beauv. Compositae. 2–3 tomentose, perenn. herbs, woody at base. Lvs dense, imbricate. Cap. discoid, in a dense cluster, subtended by a collar of leaves. Summer. NZ. Z8.

L. grandiceps (Hook. f.) Beauv. SOUTH ISLAND EDELWEISS. Lvs to 10×4cm, obovate-cuneate, apex obtuse, tomentose. Cap. 5–15, subtended by a collar of some 15 tomentose lvs. S Is.

L. leontopodium (Hook. f.) Beauv. NORTH ISLAND EDELWEISS. Lvs to 2×0.5cm, linear to lanceolate-oblong, apex acute to sub-acute, silver-white- to yellow-tomentose. Cap. to 2.5cm diam., subtended by a conspicuous collar of some 20 white lvs.

→*Helichrysum* and *Raoulia*.

Leucohyle Klotzsch. Orchidaceae. 4 epiphytic orchids. Rhiz. short. Pbs small or minute, apically unifoliate. Lvs fleshy to sub-coriaceous, linear or narrow-lanceolate. Rac. basal; tep. spreading, sometimes twisted; lip simple to trilobed, concave, callus 2-ridged. Trop. Amer. from Panama to Peru. Z10.

L. subulata (Sw.) Schltr. Pbs to 3cm, cylindrical. Lvs to 25×1cm. Infl. to 15cm, pendent; fls to 4cm diam., slightly fragrant; tep. white to pale yellow, lanceolate, slightly twisted; lip white spotted rose-purple, obscurely trilobed, erose-lacerate. Panama, Trin., Peru, Venez., Colomb.

→*Trichopilia*.

Leucojum L. SNOWFLAKE. Amaryllidaceae. 10 bulbous perenn. Lvs filiform to linear or broadly ligulate. Scape slender and solid or stout and hollow, spathaceous; pedicels pendulous; perianth seg. free, equal, oblanceolate or oblanceolate-oblong, acute or apiculate, white, sometimes spotted green or yellow at apex. W Eur. to Middle E, N Afr.

L. aestivum L. SUMMER SNOWFLAKE; LODDON LILY. Lvs to 50cm, ligulate. Scape stout, hollow, somewhat flattened with 2 wings, to 60cm; spathe 1; fls 2–7, faintly chocolate-scented; seg. broad-oblong, to 2cm, white, marked green just below apiculate apex. Spring. Eur. inc. GB to Iran. 'Gravetye' ('Gravetye Giant'): robust, vigorous, to 75cm; fls 5–7; seg. to 2.5cm (GB, early 20th century). var. *pulchellum* (Salisb.) Fiori. Smaller. Scape lacking transparent wing; fls 2–4; seg. to 14mm. Flowering earlier. Balearic Is., Sardinia. Z4.

L. autumnale L. Lvs filiform, to 16cm, pale green, appearing after fls. Scape slender, green- to red-brown, usually about 15cm; spathe 1; fls 1–4; seg. oblong, apiculate or toothed, 1cm, crystalline white flushed pink at base. Summer–autumn. W Eur. (Port., Spain, Sardinia, Sicily, Crete), N Afr. 'Cobb's Variety': to 20cm; fls white flushed pink. var. *oporanthum* (Jordan & Fourr.) Maire. Scape to 25cm; seg. 3-toothed. Moroc. var. *pulchellum* (Jordan & Fourr.) Dur. & Schinz. Lvs present at flowering. Outer seg. 3-toothed; inner seg. entire, acute. Moroc., Gibraltar. Z5.

L. hernandezii Cambess. = *L. aestivum* var. *pulchellum*.

L. hiemale DC. = *L. nicaeense*.

L. longifolium (M. Roem.) Gren. & Godron. Lvs slender, to 25cm. Scape slender, to 20cm; spathes 2, linear, 2.5cm; fls 1–3; seg. oblanceolate, 9mm, white. Spring. Corsica. Z7.

L. nicaeense Ardoino. Lvs narrow-linear, to 30cm, often curled. Scape to 15cm, usually less; spathes 2; fls 1–3; seg. oblanceolate, 3 outer seg. apiculate, to 12mm, white, spreading. Spring. S Fr., Monaco. Z7.

L. roseum Martin. Lvs narrow-linear, to 10cm, often appearing after fls. Scape to 15cm; spathes 2; fl. 1; seg. oblanceolate, to 9mm, pale pink, deepest along median line. Summer–autumn. Corsica, Sardinia. Z7.

L. trichophyllum Schousb. Lvs filiform, to 20cm often withered before flowering. Scape slender, to 25cm; spathes 2; fls 2–4; seg. oblanceolate-oblong, 3 outer seg. apiculate, to 2.5cm, white or flushed pink to purple. Winter–spring. S Port., SW Spain, Moroc. Z7.

L. valentinum Pau. Lvs narrow-linear, to 25cm, grey-green, appearing after fls. Scape to 15cm; spathes 2; fls 1–3; seg. broad-obovate, apiculate, to 1.5cm, milk-white. Autumn. C Spain, Greece. Z7.

L. vernum L. SPRING SNOWFLAKE. Lvs stout, ligulate, to 20cm. Scape stout, hollow, to 20cm, deep green; spathe 1; fls 1(–2); seg. broad-oblong, acute, 2×1cm, white, marked green or yellow just below apex. Winter. Fr. to EC Eur., nat. GB. var. *vagneri* Stapf. Robust. Scape to 25cm; fls paired. Hung. ssp. *carpathicum* (Loud.) E. Murray. Fls solitary; seg. marked yellow at tips. Poland, Rom. Yellow markings usually constant in ssp. *carpathicum*, but sometimes occur in other vars., esp. in newly opened fls. Z5.

Leucophyllum Humb. & Bonpl. Scrophulariaceae. 12 low everg. spreading shrubs. Lvs simple, entire, tomentose to glab. Fls axill., solitary; cal. and cor. 5-lobed; cor. campanulate to funnel-shaped, 2-lipped; sta. 4. Summer. SW US. Z9.

L. frutescens (Berl.) I.M. Johnst. BAROMETER BUSH; ASH PLANT. White-tomentose shrub, to 2m. Lvs to 2.5cm, woolly-grey, elliptic to obovate. Cor. pink to mauve, campanulate, to 25mm diam. Spring–summer. Tex., Mex. 'Compactum': compact shrub, loosely branched; lvs silver-grey; fls pink, bell-like. 'Green Cloud': small shrub, compactly branched; lvs dark green; fls purple-violet.

L. minus A. Gray. Woolly shrub, to 1m. Lvs to 1.3cm, spathulate-obovate, tapering basally. Cor. purple, funnel-shaped, slender. Spring–summer. SW US.

L. texanum Benth. = *L. frutescens*.

Leucopogon R. Br. Epacridaceae. 150 everg. shrubs or small trees. Lvs aristate or with a callused tip, glab. or ciliolate, entire. Fls subtended by a pair of bracteoles and bracts, solitary or clustered in spikes; cal. 5-lobed; cor. tubular, lobes 5, spreading, bearded. Fr. a drupe. Aus., NZ, Malaysia, New Caledonia, Pacific Is. Z9.

L. amplexicaulis R. Br.. Small shrub to 1m; branchlets pubesc. Lvs to 2.5cm, cordate, ciliolate. Fls white, 6–10 in axill. rac.; cor. lobes recurved, pubesc. Summer. Aus.

L. australis R. Br. Erect glab. shrub to 2.5m. Lvs to 5cm, lanceolate to narrowly elliptic, convex above, veins conspicuous. Fls white, in dense spikes 3.25–5cm; cor. to 5mm, densely bearded. Autumn. Aus., Tasm.

L. colensoi Hook. f. = *Cyathodes colensoi*.

L. collinus (Labill.) R. Br. Low-growing shrub to 70cm; glab. or downy. Lvs 0.5–1cm, linear to obovate, often ciliate. Fls white, usually crowded in term. spikelets; cor. to 5mm, lobes villous within. Summer. Aus., Tasm.

L. ericoides (Sm.) R. Br. Heath-like shrub to 90cm; br. pubesc. Lvs to 0.5cm, oblong to linear, shortly aristate, glab. Fls white, crowded in v. short axill. spikes or clusters, giving the impression of a long pan.; cor. 2–4mm, interior minutely tomentose. Summer. S & W Aus., Tasm.

L. ericoides Schldl. non (Sm.) R. Br. = *Brachyloma ericoides*.

L. forsteri A. Rich. = *Cyathodes juniperina*.

L. fraseri A. Cunn. Dwarf shrublet. Branchlets decumbent. Lvs densely overlapping, glossy green. Fls small, white to lilac. Fr. orange. Summer. NZ.

L. interruptus R. Br. Small glab. shrub to 70cm. Lvs to 3cm, ovate to oblong. Fls small, white, borne in short interrupted spikes; cor. tube to 0.5cm, lobes bearded at tips. Summer. W Aus.

L. lanceolatus (Sm.) R. Br. Upright, glabrescent shrub to 3m. Lvs 2–5cm, elliptic to narrow-lanceolate, entire to serrulate, glaucous. Fls white in terminal and axill. spikes 2.5–5cm; cor. tube to 2mm, interior densely pubesc. Spring. S Aus., Tasm.

L. parviflorus Andrews = *Cyathodes parviflora*.

L. richei (Labill.) R. Br. = *Cyathodes parviflora*.

L. verticillatus R. Br. Erect shrub to 2m; branchlets glab., bronze-brown. Lvs 5–10cm, whorled, elliptic to lanceolate. Fls in slender whorled spikes to 3.25cm, rose to crimson; cor. to 5mm, lobes bearded at base only. Autumn. Aus.

L. virgatus (Labill.) R. Br. Decumbent diffuse shrub to 60cm; branchlets wiry, glab. Lvs to 1.5cm, linear-lanceolate to ovate, margin with minute hooked hairs. Fls in congested ± flattened clusters; cor. tube 2–4mm, white, densely long-pubesc. Summer. S Aus., Tasm.

→*Styphelia*.

Leucospermum R. Br. Proteaceae. 46 small trees or subshrubs. Lvs tough. Infl. cone-like, with overlapping or spreading ovate-elliptic involucral bracts; perianth tubular in bud, bilaterally symmetric in fl.; pistils v. long, curving upwards and inwards, far-exserted, highly coloured. S Afr., Zimb. Z9.

L. attenuatum R. Br. = *L. cuneiforme*.

L. catherinae Compton. CATHERINE'S PINCUSHION; CATHERINE-WHEEL LEUCOSPERMUM. Shrub to 2.5m. Lvs 10–12cm, oblong, 3–4 dentate at apex, green tinged grey or yellow, often flushed red at teeth and along margins, glab. Infl. to 15cm diam.; fls pale orange, deepening to red-gold. Late spring–early summer. S Afr.

L. conocarpodendron L. Shrub or small tree, 2–2.5m. Lvs 5–10cm, obovate to oblanceolate, 4–9-dentate at apex, margins and base hirsute, otherwise glabrescent. Infl. 5–7cm; fls golden yellow. S Afr. (Cape Prov.).

L. conocarpum R. Br. = *L. conocarpodendron*.

L. cordifolium (Knight) Fourc. Shrub to 2m. Lvs 2–8cm, ovate, entire or apically 3–6-dentate, cordate at base, glabrescent. Infl. spherical, to 12cm diam.; fls yellow, orange or crimson. Summer. S Afr. (Cape Prov.).

L. cuneiforme (Burm.) Rourke. Shrub to 3m, with lignotuber. Lvs 4.5–11cm, linear to lanceolate, apically 3–11-dentate, glab. Infl. ovoid, 9cm diam.; fls yellow, becoming orange with age. Summer. S Afr. (Cape Prov.).

L. ellipticum (Thunb.) R. Br. = *L. cuneiforme*.

L. lineare R. Br. Slender bush decumbent or erect. Lvs linear, subobtuse, 6–8mm broad, glab. Infl. 4–5cm diam.; fls orange-yellow. S Afr. (Cape Prov.).

L. nutans R. Br. = *L. cordifolium*.

L. reflexum Buek ex Meissn. in DC. Small erect shrub to 2m. Lvs 2–4cm, oblong to oblanceolate, obtuse, entire or 3-dentate, grey-tomentose. Infl. 4.5–6cm diam.; fls crimson. S Afr.

L. tottum R. Br. Slender shrub. Lvs 2.5–4cm, oblong, obtuse to subacute, callous-pointed, occas. 3-dentate, ± hairy. Infl. 4–5cm diam., brick red to pale rose. S Afr. (Cape Prov.).

L. vestitum (Lam.) Rourke. Erect bush to 2.5m. Lvs oblong, entire or distinctly notched or dentate at apex, deep green, slightly pubesc. when young. Flowerheads globose, to 9cm diam.; fls purple or dark red. Winter–summer. S Afr.

Leucostegia Presl. Davalliaceae. 2 epiphytic or terrestrial ferns. Rhiz. creeping, fleshy, scaly. Fronds stipitate, 3 or 4× finely pinnate, deltoid, pinnae deltoid; stipes remote, jointed with phyllopodia. Trop. Asia to Polyn. Z10.

L. falcinella (Presl) J. Sm. = *Trogostolon falcinellus*.

L. hirsuta J. Sm., nom. nud. = *Davallodes hirsutum*.

L. immersa (Wallich) Presl. Rhiz. scales russet. Fronds 60×40cm or more, 3–4-pinnate, pinnae to 8×3cm, final seg. rhomboid,

acute or obtuse at apex, truncate at base, dentate, veins prominent, pinnate; stipes to 25cm, red. SE Asia.

L. membranulosa Wallich = *Davallodes membranulosum*.

L. pallida (Mett.) Copel. Rhiz. scales pale brown. Fronds to 60×60cm, 4-pinnate, pinnae to 7×4cm, alt., final seg. rhomboid to obovate, obtuse at apex, cuneate at base, notched, veins indistinct, forked; stipes to 40cm, light green to straw-coloured. Malaysia and Indon. to Polyn.

→*Davallia* and *Humata*.

Leucothoë D. Don. Ericaceae. 44 decid. and everg. shrubs. Lvs leathery, deep green, usually dentate, leathery. Fls in rac. or pan.; bracts and bracteoles small; cal. lobes 5, overlapping; cor. ovoid, tubular or urceolate, lobes 5, small. US, S Amer., Himal., E Asia, Madag.

L. acuminata (Ait.) G. Don = *L. populifolia*.

L. axillaris (Lam.) D. Don. Everg. shrub c1.5m. Shoots finely downy when young. Lvs 5–11cm, ovate to ovate-oblong, abruptly acute, dentate in apical half, lustrous green, glab. above, paler and sparsely hirsute beneath. Rac. axill. 2–7cm; cor. 6–8mm, white, urceolate or cylindric. Spring–early summer. SE US. 'Compacta': habit compact. Z6.

L. catesbaei (Walter) A. Gray. Everg. shrub to 1.8m. Br. diffuse, somewhat procumbent; young shoots red, downy. Lvs 7.5–15cm, lanceolate or ovate, acute, setose-dentate, sparsely setose beneath. Rac. term., crowded; cor. c6mm, white, cylindric. Spring. SE US. Z5.

L. davisiae Torr. SIERRA LAUREL. Everg. shrub, 30–180cm. Br. erect, glab. Lvs 2–7cm, ovate-oblong, acute or obtuse, glossy green above, sparsely toothed. Rac. erect, ± bristly, term., 5–15cm; cor. c6mm, white, pitcher-shaped. Summer. Calif. Z5.

L. editorum Fern. & Schubert = *L. fontanesiana*.

L. fontanesiana (Steud.) Sleumer. DOG-HOBBLE; DROOPING LAUREL; SWITCH IVY. Everg. shrub to 2m. Br. diffuse, arching, tinged red, downy when young. Lvs 6–16cm, oblong-lanceolate to ovate-lanceolate, tapering to a long point at apex, glab., ciliate, dentate, dark green, lustrous above. Rac. axill., 4–6cm; cor. c8mm, white, almost cylindric. Spring. SE US. 'Lovita': vigorous, compact, mound-forming; lvs deep-bronze in winter. 'Nana': compact, low-growing. 'Rainbow' ('Girard's Rainbow'): young growth crimson; lf variegation pink and cream, later white and green. 'Rollissonii': lvs small, narrow. 'Scarletta': lvs rich scarlet turning green shaded burgundy in winter. 'Trivar': strong grower; lvs red with cream and green variegation. Z5.

L. grayana Maxim. Decid. or almost everg. shrub, 50–120cm. Shoots tinged red, bright and glossy in winter, glab. Lvs 3.8–8.8cm, oval, oblong or obovate, acute, setose and conspicuously veined beneath, margins setose, bronze-yellow tinted purple in fall. Rac. 7–10cm, terminal, drooping; cor. 4–6mm, pure white to somewhat pink, campanulate. Late spring–early autumn. Jap. Z6. var. *oblongifolia* (Miq.) Ohwi. Smaller, more stiffly upright; br. dark, glossy plum to red in winter. Lvs smaller, oblong, yellow with fiery tints in fall. Jap.

L. griffithiana Clarke. Everg. shrub, c1m. Twigs pendulous. Lvs 7–12cm, lanceolate, apex a tail-like appendage, base tapered to almost round, margins finely crenate to subentire. Rac. elongate axill.; cor. white. Summer. Bhutan, W China. Z8.

L. keiskei Miq. Everg. shrub. Br. erect or prostrate, slender. Young shoots red, glab. Lvs 3.8–8.8cm, narrow-ovate to broadly lanceolate, apex long and slender, margins shallowly dentate, sparsely setose beneath. Rac. 3–5cm drooping, sparse; cor. 12–20mm, white, cylindric. Summer. Jap. Z5.

L. populifolia (Lam.) Dipp. Everg. shrub to 1m. St. glab., arching. Lvs 3–10cm, lanceolate to ovate-lanceolate, tapering slenderly, margins entire or inconspicuously serrate. Rac. axill., cor. c15mm, white cylindric. Spring–summer. SE US. Z8.

L. racemosa (L.) A. Gray. FETTER BUSH; SWEET BELLS. Decid. shrub, 1–2.5m. Young shoots finely pubesc. Lvs 2.5–6.2cm, oblong to ovate or elliptic, acute, shallowly round-dentate and finely serrate. Rac. 2.5–10cm, curved, secund; cor. c8mm, white, cylindric to long-ovoid. Spring–late summer. E US. var. *elongata* (Small) Fern. Shoots soft-hirsute. Z5.

L. recurva (Buckl.) A. Gray. RED TWIG. Diffuse, decid., shrub, 90cm–3.6m. Shoots tinted red when young and in winter, somewhat pubesc. or glab. Lvs 3.8–10cm, elliptic-lanceolate to obovate, tip sharp, margins serrate. Rac. 2–10cm, secund, decurved; cor. c6mm, white, cylindric. Spring. SE US. Z6.

→*Andromeda* and *Lyonia*.

Leuzea DC. Compositae. 3 bienn. or perenn. herbs. St. simple or sparingly branched. Lvs entire to lyrate or pinnatifid. Cap. discoid, solitary, ovoid-globose, terete. Medit.

L. centauroides (L.) Holub. Perenn. to 1m; st. arachnoid-tomentose, to 100cm. Basal lvs to 30×20cm, petiolate, pinnatisect, seg. lanceolate, white-tomentose beneath, serrate-dentate, st. lvs smaller, sessile. Involucre 5cm diam., globose; flts purple. Pyren.

L. conifera (L.) DC. Perenn. to 30cm; st. white-lanate. Lower lvs ovate-lanceolate, entire or lyrate-pinnatifid, petiolate, white-tomentose beneath. Involucre to 4cm diam., ovoid-globose; flts purple to white. Summer. W Medit., Port. Z8.

L. rhapontica (L.) Holub. Perenn.; st. white-lanate. Lvs glab. above, tomentose beneath, basal lvs 60×15cm, base, sub-cordate, petiolate, st. lvs entire to lyrate, sessile. Involucre to 11cm diam., globose; flts red or purple. Late summer–autumn. Alps. Z6.

→*Centaurea* and *Cnicus*.

Levant Cotton *Gossypium herbaceum.*
Levant Garlic *Allium ampeloprasum.*
Levant Madder *Rubia peregrina.*

Levisticum Hill. Umbelliferae. 1 glab. perenn. herb to 2m, strongly scented of celery; st. hollow, striate. Lvs to 70cm, out-line triangular-rhombic, 2–3-pinnate, seg. rhombic, toothed and lobed. Umbels 12–20-rayed, involucrate; fls green-yellow. Summer. E Medit., nat. Eur. and US. Z4.

L. officinale Koch. LOVAGE.

Levya Bur. ex Baill.
L. nicaraguensis Bur. ex Baill. = *Cydista aequinoctialis* var. *hirtella.*

Lewisia Pursh. Portulacaceae. 19 glab., low-growing, perenn. herbs. Lvs mostly basal, rosulate, succulent. Fls solitary, cymose or paniculate; sep. 2, small, or 2–9, petaloid; pet. (4–)5–19, thin-textured; sta. 5–50. W N Amer.

L. brachycalyx Engelm. ex A. Gray. Decid., to 10cm in fl. Basal lvs 3–8cm, tufted, oblanceolate, slightly glaucous. Scape 1-fld, 1–6cm long; fls sessile, 3–6cm diam.; pet. 5–9, 12–26mm, obovate, white or occas. veined with pink, or wholly white-pink. S Calif., Ariz., possibly also S Utah and New Mex. 'Phyllellia' (*L. brachycalyx* × *L. cotyledon*): fls pale pink striped rose, on low stalks. Z5.

L. cantelovii J.T. Howell. Perenn. to 30cm in fl. Basal lvs 2–5.5cm, spathulate, thick and fleshy. Pan. many-fld, 15–30(–40)cm long; fls 1–1.5cm diam.; pet. 5 or 6, 6–9mm, elliptic-ovate or elliptic obovate, white or pale pink veined darker pink. NE Calif. Z7.

L. columbiana (Howell ex A. Gray) Robinson. Everg., to 30cm in fl. Basal lvs many, 2–10cm, narrowly oblanceolate or linear, fleshy, flat or slightly channelled above. Pan. many-fld, 10–12cm long; fls 1–2.5cm diam.; pet. 4–9(–11), 5–13mm, oblong or obovate, off-white veined pink to pink or deep pink-magenta. W N Amer. A widespread and variable sp. 'Rosea': st. long; lvs narrow; fls brilliant magenta. ssp. *rupicola* (English) Ferris. Pet. 10–13mm, mid- to deep purple magenta or rose. ssp. *wallowensis* (Hitchc.) J.E. Hohn ex B. Mathew. 5–15cm in fl. Lvs to 4cm. Pet. 5–11mm, white veined pink. Z5.

L. congdonii (Rydb.) S. Clay. Decid. to 60cm in fl. Basal lvs 5–20cm, tufted, oblanceolate, pale green, fleshy, flaccid, flat. Pan. lax, 20–60cm long; fls 1.5–2cm diam.; pet. 6–7, 7.5–10mm, obovate, pale pink, veined darker purple-red with a yellow-green base. Calif. Z7.

L. cotyledon (S. Wats.) Robinson. Everg., to 30cm in fl. Basal lvs 3–14cm, spathulate, oblanceolate or obovate, slightly glaucous, sometimes tinged pink, fleshy. Pan. compact, 10–30cm long; fls 2–4cm diam.; pet. 7–10, 10–20mm, oblanceolate, obovate or spathulate, pink-purple with pale and dark stripes, sometimes white, cream with pink-orange stripes, apricot or yellow. var. *cotyledon.* Lf margins smooth. Pet. (8–)12–14mm. NW Calif., SW Oreg. var. *heckneri* (C. Morton) Munz. Lf margins with fleshy teeth. Pet. 16–20mm. N Calif. var. *howellii* (S. Wats.) Jeps. Lf margins strongly crisped-undulate. Pet. 12–15mm. NW Calif., SW Oreg. Ashwood Strain: lvs usually darker veined; fls pink, red, apricot, yellows, seed race. 'Carroll Watson': fls pure yellow. 'John's Special': lvs sinuate; fls rose-purple. 'Kathy Kline': fls white. 'Pinkie': dwarf; lvs narrow, fleshy; fls in shade of pink, abundant. 'Rose Splendour': fls pale pink. Sunset Strain: lvs sinuate; fls in range of oranges; seed race. 'Trevosia' (*L. cotyledon* var. *howelli* × *L. columbiana*): lvs fleshy, dark green; fls salmon pink. Z6.

L. disepala Rydb. Decid., to 5cm in fl. Basal lvs 8–20mm, tufted, fleshy, terete, linear or slightly clavate, dying away at flowering. Scapes 1-fld, 5–30mm long; fls 2.5–3(–3.5)cm diam.; pet. 5–7, 13–18mm, oblanceolate or obovate, pale rose pink. Calif. Z5.

L. eastwoodiana Purdy = *L. leana.*
L. finchiae Purdy = *L. cotyledon* var. *cotyledon.*
L. heckneri (C. Morton) Gabr. = *L. cotyledon* var. *heckneri.*
L. howellii (S. Wats.) Robinson = *L. cotyledon* var. *howellii.*
L. kelloggii K. Brandg. Decid., to 3cm in fl. Basal lvs many, 1–6.5cm, spathulate, fleshy. Scapes 1-fld, 0.5–5cm long; fls

2–3cm diam.; pet. 5–12, 10–15mm, obovate or oblanceolate, white. Calif., C Idaho. Z5.

L. leana (T. Porter) Robinson. Everg., 10–20cm in fl. Basal lvs many, 1.5–6cm, tufted, linear and somewhat terete, glaucous. Pan. many-fld, 8–20cm long; fls 1–1.4cm diam.; pet. 5–8, 5–7mm, obovate, magenta, pale purple-pink, white with magenta veining or occas. white. Calif., Oreg. Z6.

L. longifolia S. Clay = *L. cotyledon* var. *cotyledon.*
L. millardii S. Clay = *L. cotyledon* var. *heckneri.*
L. minima (A. Nels.) A. Nels. = *L. pygmaea.*
L. nevadensis (A. Gray) Robinson. Decid., to 15cm in fl. Basal lvs 4–15cm, tufted, narrowly linear or linear-oblanceolate, fleshy. Scapes 1-fld; fls 2–3.5cm diam.; pet. 5–10, 10–15mm, elliptic or oblanceolate, white or rarely pink-white. Washington to New Mex., W Colorado; possibly also in Idaho, Wyom., Utah, and Ariz. Z4.

L. oppositifolia (S. Wats.) Robinson. Decid., to 20cm in fl. Basal lvs opposite, few, 4–10cm, shiny, linear-spathulate or linear-oblanceolate. Corymbs or subumbels 1–6-fld; fls 2–3cm diam.; pet. 8–11, 9–15mm, oblanceolate or obovate, pink in bud, open-ing to white or sometimes faintly pink. SW Oreg., NW Calif. Z6.

L. purdyi (Jeps.) Gabr. = *L. cotyledon* var. *cotyledon.*
L. pygmaea (A. Gray) Robinson. Decid., to 10cm in fl. Basal lvs 3–9cm, tufted, dark green, linear or linear-oblanceolate. Scapes 1–7-fld; fls 1.5–2cm diam.; pet. 5–9, 6–10mm, narrowly oblong, elliptic or oblanceolate, white or pink to magenta-purple, some-times green at base. Alask. S to New Mex., E to Wyom. Z3.

L. rediviva Pursh. BITTERROOT. Decid., to 5cm in fl. Lvs many, 1.5–5cm, linear or clavate, subterete, tufted, withered at flower-ing. Scapes 1-fld; fls 5–6(–7.5)cm diam.; pet. 12–19, 15–35mm, elliptic, oblong or oblanceolate, rose-pink, purple-pink or white. N Amer. Z4. ssp. *minor* (Rydb.) A. H. Holmgren. Smaller in all respects. Utah, Nevada, S. Calif.

L. rupicola English = *L. columbiana* ssp. *rupicola.*
L. triphylla (S. Wats.) Robinson. Decid., 2–25cm in fl. Basal lvs to 5cm, narrowly linear, withered at flowering. Infl. sub-umbellate or paniculate, to 25-fld; fls 8–14mm diam.; pet. 5–9, 4–7mm, elliptic, elliptic-obovate or elliptic-ovate, white or pink, with darker veins. N Amer. Z5.

L. tweedyi (A. Gray) Robinson. Everg., 10–20cm in fl. Basal lvs 4–8cm, loosely tufted, green, often with purple suffusion, broadly oblanceolate or obovate. Scapes 1–8-fld; fls 4–5.5(–7)cm diam.; pet. (7–)8–9(–12), 2.5–4cm, obovate, pink-peach to yellow or rarely white. Washington State, Canada. 'Alba': fls white. 'Elliot's Variety': fls tinged pink, abundant. Z5.

L. × whiteae Purdy. A natural hybrid between *L. cotyledon* and *L. leana.* Lvs narrow. Fls salmon-rose. Z6.

L. cvs. 'Ben Chace': fls large, pink. 'George Henley': fls brick red, abundant. 'Joyce Halley': fls pink to red. 'Karen': fls salmon-pink, red-veined. 'L.W. Browne': fls mauve, flushed salmon-pink. 'Paula': fls pale purple. Z5.

Leycesteria Wallich. Caprifoliaceae. 6 decid. or semi-everg. suckering shrubs. St. cane-like. Lvs opposite, petioled. Rac. pendent, conspicuously bracteate; sep. 5, small; cor. funnel-form, gibbous, usually 5-lobed; sta. 5. Fr. a many-seeded berry. W Himal. to SW China.

L. crocothyrsos Airy Shaw. To 2.5m. Lvs 5–16cm, ovate, acuminate, rounded at base, sparsely serrate, somewhat glaucous, lanuginose beneath. Fls rich yellow in whorls of 6 on arching, term. rac. to 10cm. Fr. globose, translucent, yellow-green. Himal. (Assam), N Burm. Z9.

L. formosa Wallich. HIMALAYA HONEYSUCKLE. To 1.5m. Lvs 7–18cm, ovate-acuminate, cordate at base, entire or serrulate, deep green above, downy beneath when young. Fls purple, in whorls on pendulous rac. to 10cm; bracts wine red, ovate. Fr. bead-like, sea-green becoming maroon then purple-black, ripening at different speeds giving a multicoloured effect. Summer–autumn. Himal., W China, E Tibet. 'Rosea': fls pink. Z7.

Leyland Cypress × *Cupressocyparis leylandii.*

Leymus Hochst. Gramineae. 40 rhizomatous, perenn. grasses. Lvs stiff, flat or rolled, glaucous, scabrous. Infl. racemose, lin-ear; spikelets solitary or paired. N Temp., 1 sp. Arg.

L. angustus (Trin.) Pilger. St. to 1m. Lvs to 1cm diam., inrolled, scabrous above. Spike to 25cm; spikelets paired, 2–3-fld. Russia. Z3.

L. arenarius (L.) Hochst. LYME GRASS; SEA LYME GRASS; EUROPEAN DUNE GRASS. St. to 1.5m. Lvs flat, to 60×1.5cm, margins convolute. Spikes to 25×25cm; spikelets paired, oblong to deltoid, to 3.5cm, 4-fld. Summer–autumn. N & W Eur., Eur-asia. Z6.

L. chinensis (Trin.) Tzvelev. St. to 45cm; spike to 20cm. China.

L. condensatus Presl & C. Presl. GIANT WILD RYE. St. to 2.7m. Lvs to 75×2cm, ribs conspicuous above, scabrous. Spikes upright, compact, to 30cm; spikelets in fascicles to 5, to 4-fld, to 2cm. Calif. Z7.

L. mollis (Trin.) Hara. St. to 1.3m. Lvs to 1.5cm, broad, with in-rolled margins, rigid, smooth beneath, scabrous above. Spikes to 26cm, dense, 3–5-fld. Russia. Z4.

L. multicaulis (Karel. & Kir.) Tzvelev. ARAL WILD RYE. Close to *L. arenarius*, but differing in its shorter rhiz. and more erect lvs. Russia. Z4.

L. racemosus (Lam.) Tzvelev. St. to 1.2m. Lvs to 30×1.5cm, glab. below, scabrous above. Spikes to 35×2cm; apex attenuate; spikelets flattened, in clusters to 6, to 6-fld. Summer–autumn. Eurasia. 'Glaucus': upright to arching, to 75cm; lvs clear light blue. Z5.

L. secalinus (Georgi) Tzvelev. St. to 1.2m. Lvs narrow, to 20×1.5cm, convolute, scabrous. Infl. graceful; spikelets to 6-fld. US. Z5.

→*Elymus* and *Agropyron*.

Liabum Adans.
L. maronii (André) Nichols. = *Munnozia maronii*.
L. ovatum (Wedd.) J. Ball. = *Paranephelius ovatus*.
L. uniflorum (Poepp. & Endl.) Schultz-Bip. = *Paranephelius uniflorus*.

Liatris Gaertn. ex Schreb. BUTTON SNAKE ROOT; GAY FEATHER; BLAZING STAR; SNAKE ROOT. Compositae. 35 perenn. herbs arising from corms or much-flattened rootstocks. Lvs alt., linear to ovate-lanceolate, simple, glandular-punctate, radical lvs elongate, st. lvs numerous, reduced above. Cap. discoid, clustered in erect, cylindrical corymbose spikes or rac.; flts tubular, purple to rose-purple, rarely white. E N Amer.

L. acidota Engelm. & A. Gray. To 80cm. Lvs to 40×0.5cm, linear-lanceolate, shorter above. Cap. numerous, loosely clustered in a spike, sessile; flts red-purple. Coastal Louisiana and Tex. Z9.

L. aspera Michx. To 1.1m. Lvs to 15×2cm, rhombic-lanceolate to linear-lanceolate or almost linear, esp. above, long-petiolate, glab. and often rough, upper becoming sessile. Cap. at least 20, in a long open spike, sessile or pedunculate; flts usually purple, rarely white. Z5.

L. callilepis hort. = *L. spicata*.

L.* × *creditonensis Gaiser. (*L. ligulistylis* × *L. squarrosa*.) To c50cm. Lvs to 20×1cm, linear-lanceolate, glab., uppermost grading into the phyllaries. Cap. few to many in a racemose infl.; flts pale purple. Gdn origin. Z4.

L. cylindracea Michx. To 60cm. Lvs to 20×0.5cm, linear, rigid, glandular-punctate, mostly glossy, glab., mostly radical. Cap. few to several in a lax corymbose infl., often only the term. developing; flts purple or rarely white. Late summer–early autumn. Ont. to Missouri. Z4.

L. elegans (Walter) Michx. To 1.2m. Lvs to 10×0.5cm, linear to linear-lanceolate, glab., reduced upwards, upper soon deflexed. Cap. few to many, subsessile, in cylindrical or pyramidal racemose infl.; inner phyllaries red-pink, elongated and petaloid; flts white or purple. Autumn. S & SE US. Z7.

L. glabrata Rydb. = *L. squarrosa*.

L. gracilis Pursh. St. slender to stiff, often thick, usually purple. Autumn. CE & SE US. Z6.

L. helleri Porter. To 20cm. Lvs to 30×1cm, radical, linear-lanceolate, attenuate to long, winged petioles, st. lvs gradually reducing upwards. Cap. few to many, in dense clusters to 7cm; flts purple. N Carol. Z7.

L. ligulistylis (Nels.) C.B. Lehm. To 60cm. Lvs to 15×1.5cm, lanceolate-oblong or oblanceolate, usually long-petiolate, glab. to sparingly hispidulous on midvein beneath, or densely pubesc. on both surfaces, ciliate, reduced abruptly upwards. Cap. few, in a racemose cluster, shortly pedunculate; flts purple. Autumn. S Manit. and Wisc. to N New Mex. Z3.

L. montana hort. = *L. spicata*.

L. novae-angliae (Lunell) Shinn. To 60cm. Lvs to 15×1cm, numerous, often twisted, glab. or sparsely hairy along lower midrib, or hairy beneath and margin ciliate, lower amplexicaul, upper linear-lanceolate, sessile, gradually reduced. Cap. few to many in a simple rac.; flts purple, rarely white. SW Maine to Penn. Z4.

L. pumila Lodd. = *L. spicata*.

L. punctata Hook. SNAKEROOT. To 80cm. Lvs to 15×0.6cm, numerous, glab., rigid, linear, glandular-punctate, gradually reduced above. Cap. numerous, crowded in a usually dense spike, to 30×3cm; flts purple, rarely white. Autumn. E Canada to SE US and New Mex. Z3.

L. pycnostachya Michx. BUTTON SNAKEROOT. to 1.5m. Lvs to 10×0.5cm, linear, hirsute or glab., gradually reduced up st.

Cap. crowded in v. dense spikes to 30×3cm, sessile; flts red-purple, sometimes white. Autumn. SE US. Z3.

L. scariosa (L.) Willd. To 80cm. Lvs few to many, to 15×5cm, broadly oblanceolate, oblong to ovoid, base attenuate, amplexicaul, gradually reduced up st. Cap. few to many, in spicate infl.; phyllaries sometimes coloured; flts purple. SE US. 'Alba': flts white. 'Gracious': to 1.5m; flts snow-white. 'Magnifica' ('Alba Magnifica'): fl. heads v. large, white. 'September Glory': to 125cm; fls deep purple. 'White Spire': fls in long white spikes. Z3.

L. spicata (L.) Willd. BUTTON SNAKEWORT. To 1.5m. Lvs to 40×2cm, linear-lanceolate or linear. Cap. clustered in a dense spike, to 70cm; phyllaries purple-tinged; flts red-purple. Late summer. E US. 'Alba': flts white. 'Blue Bird': fls vivid blue. 'Floristan': to 90cm; fls white ('Floristan Weiss') and deep violet ('Floristan Violet'); seed race. 'Kobold' ('Goblin'): dwarf to 40cm; flts bright violet. 'Picador': fls ranging from white to violet; seed race. 'Snow Queen': to 75cm; fls snow-white. T & M Border Mixed: to 1.5m, fls from white to dark purple-blue. Z3.

L. squarrosa (L.) Michx. To 60cm. Lvs to 25×0.7mm, linear, rigid, glandular-punctate, glab. or hirsute, gradually reduced upwards. Cap. 1 to few in a rac., or many in a branched pan.; phyllaries squarrose; flts red-purple. Summer–early autumn. CE & SE US. Z4.

L.* × *weaveri Shinn. (*L. aspera* × *L. punctata*.) To 50cm. Lvs to 15×1cm, linear to narrowly linear-lanceolate, glandular-punctate, reduced gradually upwards. Cap. numerous, in a dense spike-like infl., to 30cm long; flts purple. Ont. Z2.

→*Anonymos*, *Laciniaria*, *Serratula* and *Staehelina*.

Libanothamnus Ernst. Compositae. 1 shrub, to 4m. St. stout, white-lanate. Lvs in congested whorls, 10–20cm, lanceolate, entire, sessile, leathery, glab. above, densely white-lanate with black gland-like marginal spots beneath. Cap. radiate, 15–22mm diam., shortly pedunculate, in a terminal branched corymb; receptacle convex, scaly; ray flts 15–18, white, elliptic; disc flts 40–50, green-yellow. Venez. Z10.
L. neriifolius (Bonpl. ex Humb.) Ernst.
→*Espeletia* and *Trixis*.

Liberian Coffee *Coffea liberica*.

Libertia Spreng. Iridaceae. 20 rhizomatous perenn. herbs. Lvs tufted, basal, or few on st., equitant, flattened, linear. Flowering st. equalling or exceeding lvs, erect; fls radially symmetric, emerging from sheathing bracts in term. clusters or pan.; perianth seg. free, spreading, inner seg. usually exceeding outer; style br. 3, entire, slender. Aus., temp. S Amer. Z8.

L. caerulescens Kunth. Basal lvs 30–45cm, rigid, green. Flowering st. to 60cm; fls crowded in umbels; outer seg. bronze-green, inner seg. to 0.6cm, sky blue. Spring. Chile.

L. chilensis Klotzsch = *L. formosa*.

L. formosa Graham. Basal lvs 12–40cm, linear-ensiform. Infl. composed of crowded umbels; outer perianth seg. olive to bronze, inner seg. longer, 1.2–1.8cm, obovate to cuneate, white or pale yellow. Spring. Chile.

L. grandiflora (R. Br.) Sweet. Differs from *L. ixioides* in its lvs 30–70cm, 3–6-fld umbels, outer perianth seg. with an olive to bronze keel, inner seg. to 1.5cm. Summer. NZ.

L. ixioides (Forst.) Spreng. Basal lvs 20–40cm, linear, rigid. Infl. a broad pan. composed of umbellate 2–10-fld clusters; outer perianth seg. white tinted brown or green, inner seg. 0.6–0.9cm, white. Summer. NZ, Chatham Is.

L. ixioides Klatt = *L. formosa*.

L. paniculata (R. Br.) Spreng. Basal lvs 25–60cm, linear. Flowering st. branched; infl. composed of many-fld umbels; outer seg. white green-tinged externally, inner white, 0.8–1.2cm. Aus. (Queensld, NSW, Vict.).

L. peregrinans Ckn. & Allan. Basal lvs to 70cm, with conspicuous veins. Fls to 2cm, on a branched st.; inner seg. twice size outer seg. NZ.

L. pulchella Spreng. Basal lvs 5–15cm, linear, pliable. Fls 3–8 in umbellate clusters; outer perianth seg. white, inner seg. 0.4–0.6cm, white.

L. cvs. 'Gold Leaf': lvs golden orange; fls white.

Libidibia Schltr.
L. coriaria (Jacq.) Schltr. = *Caesalpinia coriaria*.
L. punctata (Willd.) Britt. = *Caesalpinia punctata*.

Libocedrus Endl. Cupressaceae. 6 coniferous, everg. trees. Crown ovoid to conic, bark brown, exfoliating in strips. Branchlets in 2 flattened planes. Juvenile lvs flat, linear, in decussate whorls. Immature lvs in decussate pairs on fan-like sprays; facial lvs scale-like, 1–4mm; side lvs larger, falcate. Adult lvs ± decussate, scale-like. ♂ cones small, oblong, apical. ♀ cones apical, ovoid, with 2 pairs of enlarged bract-like lvs at base and 4, rarely 6 valvate scales, each scale with a bract. SW of S Amer., NZ, New Caledonia.

L. arfakensis Gibbs = *Papuacedrus arfakensis.*

L. austrocaledonica Brongn. & Griseb. Tree to 8m. Immature shoots flattened; lvs broad-triangular, to 8×6mm at sides, facial lvs 3×2mm, green with white stomatal patches beneath. Adult lvs scale like, falcate-subulate at sides to 7mm, facial lvs 2mm. Cones 8–10mm, bracts 1cm long, straight. New Caledonia. Z10.

L. bidwillii Hook. f. PAHAUTEA. Tree to 20m. Immature shoots flattened, with 3mm lat. lvs and 1mm facial lvs; adult shoots tetragonal, all lvs equal, 2mm. Cones 8–10mm; bracts 3–4mm, outcurved or S-shaped. NZ. Z8.

L. chevalieri Buchholz. To 5m, similar to *L. austrocaledonica* but adult shoots narrower, lat. and facial lvs, to 3–4mm and 2–4mm respectively. Cone larger, 15mm; bracts curved, 6mm. New Caledonia. Z10.

L. chilensis (D. Don Endl. = *Austrocedrus chilensis.*

L. decurrens Torr. = *Calocedrus decurrens.*

L. doniana (Hook.) Endl. = *L. plumosa.*

L. formosana Florin = *Calocedrus formosana.*

L. macrolepis (Kurz.) Benth. & Hook = *Calocedrus macrolepis.*

L. papuana F. Muell. = *Papuacedrus papuana.*

L. plumosa (D. Don) Sarg. KAWAKA. Tree to 25m. Immature shoots v. flattened, with 5mm falcate lat. lvs and 1–2mm facial lvs; adult shoots slightly flattened with many shoots in one plane, lat. lvs 2–3mm, facial lvs 1.5–2mm. Cones 14–16mm; bracts 4–6mm, s-shaped or spreading. NZ. Z8.

L. tetragona (Hook.) Endl. = *L. uvifera.*

L. torricellensis Schltr. ex Laut. = *Papuacedrus papuana.*

L. uvifera (D. Don) Pilger. Tree to 20m. Immature shoots scarcely flattened, largely in two planes, with all lvs 3–4mm, outcurved-falcate; adult shoots tetragonal, all lvs scale-like, equal, 2mm. Cones 7–8mm; bracts 3–4mm, adpressed to scales and incurved at tips. S Chile and SW Arg., to Tierra del Fuego. Z7.

L. yateensis Guillaum. To 8m, similar, to *L. austrocaledonica* but adult shoots narrower, and less difference between lat. and facial lvs, to 3–4mm and 2–3mm respectively. Cone 10mm; bracts straight, 9mm. New Caledonia. Z9.

→*Pilgerodendron.*

Libonia K. Koch.

L. floribunda K. Koch = *Justicia rizzinii.*

Licania Aubl. Chrysobalanaceae. 171 trees or shrubs. Lvs simple, stipulate. Infl. a simple or branched rac. of hermaphrodite fls; receptacle tube 1–6mm, variable in shape, hairy within; sep. 5, subequal; pet. 5, or 0; sta. 3–40; style filiform, 3-lobed. Fr. a dry or fleshy drupe. Americas, Afr., Asia.

L. michauxii Prance. Shrub or small tree. St. spreading to 30m, mostly subterranean. Lvs lanceolate to oblong-lanceolate, 4–11cm, serrulate, leathery, sometimes pubesc. beneath. Pan. lax, ± term.; fls 3mm; receptacle tube campanulate; pet. 5, pubesc.; sta. 14–17. Fr. ovoid, to 3cm, smooth. Spring. SE US.

→*Chrysobalanus* and *Geobalanus.*

Licorice *Glycyrrhiza glabra.*
Licorice Fern *Polypodium glycyrrhiza.*

Licuala Thunb. PALAS. Palmae. 108 stemless or shrubby palms. Lvs palmate, marcescent, fibrous; petiole to 1.5m, channelled above, usually armed with spines; blade entire or divided to base into multiple-fold, cuneate seg. Fls in simple or 1–3-branched spikes amid sheathing bracts; cor. exceeding cal. with 3 valvate lobes. Fr. globose to ovoid, red. SE Asia to Aus. Z10.

L. elegans Bl. = *L. pumila.*

L. gracilis Bl. = *L. pumila.*

L. grandis H.A. Wendl. St. solitary, to 3m, fibrous. Lf blades orbicular, usually entire, sometimes divided into 3 broadly cuneate to rounded, undulate seg. to 90cm across. New Hebrides.

L. horrida Bl. = *L. spinosa.*

L. muelleri H.A. Wendl. & Drude = *L. ramsayi.*

L. pumila Bl. St. to 1.5m. Lf blades to 45cm across, divided into 7–8 several-folded seg. or 20–24 2-folded seg. Java, Sumatra.

L. ramsayi Domin. St. to 12m, fibrous. Lf blades to 1m across, divided, seg. cuneate, sometimes of varying width or fused at apex, juvenile blades entire. NE Queensld.

L. spinosa Thunb. St. clustered, to 5m, fibrous. Lf blades to 1m across, divided into many seg., seg. cuneate, apices truncate, praemorse. W Indon., Philipp., Malay Penins., Thail.

→*Dammera* and *Pericycla.*

Licuri *Syagrus coronata.*
Licuryseiro *Syagrus coronata.*

Lifelong Saxifrage *Saxifraga paniculata.*
Life-of-man *Aralia racemosa.*
Lightwood Wattle *Acacia implexa.*
Lignum Vitae *Guaiacum officinale.*

Ligularia Cass. LEOPARD PLANT. Compositae. 180 perenn. herbs. Basal lvs broad, ovate-oblong to reniform, usually cordate, long-stalked, st. lvs bract-like. Cap. usually radiate, few to many, in corymbs or rac.; involucre cylindrical or campanulate; ray flts yellow to orange; disc flts yellow. Temp. Eurasia.

L. achyrotricha (Diels) Ling. Erect, to c1m. St. minutely fulvous-pubesc. Basal lvs to 33×41cm, broadly orbicular, base strongly cordate, undulate, dentate, glab. above, minutely fulvous-pubesc. beneath, palmately veined. Cap. discoid, to 1cm diam., in a pan.; flts to 1.5cm. NW China. Z5.

L. altaica DC. Erect, to 1m. Basal lvs elliptic, obtuse, cuneate, ± entire. Cap. in a dense, bracteate rac.; ray flts 3–5, yellow. Altai Mts. Z5.

L. clivorum (Maxim.) Maxim. = *L. dentata.*

L. dentata (A. Gray) Hara. To 1m, glab. to hairy above. Basal lvs to 30×40cm, reniform-orbicular, deeply cordate, dentate, thinly chartaceous, pubesc. beneath and on veins above. Cap. to 12cm diam., few to many, in lax corymbs; ray flts c10, to 5cm, orange. China, Jap. 'Dark Beauty': lvs v. dark; fls vivid light orange. 'Desdemona': to 120cm; lvs purple; fls deep orange. 'Dunkellaubig': to 100cm; fls bright orange. 'Golden Queen': fls bright gold. 'Gregynog Gold' (*L. dentata* × *L. veitchiana*): to 120cm; lvs green; rounded, saw-edged; fls orange, in pyramidal spikes. 'Moorblut' ('Moor's Blood'): lvs v. dark purple; fls orange. 'Orange Princess': to 120cm; lvs green; fls light orange. 'Orange Queen': lvs green; heads large, fls deep orange. 'Othello': to 120cm; lvs rounded, long-stemmed, dark purple; fls deep orange. 'Sommergold': fls rich gold. Z4.

L. fischeri (Ledeb.) Turcz. To 2m. St. arachnoid below, pubesc. above. Basal lvs to 32×40cm, reniform-cordate, dentate, chartaceous, glab. except at margins. Cap. to 5cm diam., many, in a rac. to 75cm; ray flts to 25×4mm, 5–9. E Sib., China, Korea, Jap.

L. ×hessei (Hesse) Bergmans. (Probably *L. dentata* ×*L. wilsoniana.*) Intermediate between parents. To 2m. Lvs cordate-reniform. Cap. to 9cm diam., in a pan.; flts orange-yellow. Gdn origin. Z5.

L. hodgsonii Hook. To 80cm. St. succulent, striate, tinged purple below, green and pubesc. above. Basal lvs to 13×27cm, cordate to suborbicular, serrate-dentate, chartaceous, glab., petiole v. long. Cap. to 5cm diam., in capitate corymbs; ray flts to 27×8mm, orange or bright yellow. Jap. Z5.

L. intermedia Nak. To 1m. Lvs to 23×33cm, reniform or broadly cordate, coarsely dentate, glab., palmaticaul. Cap. to 4cm diam., in cylindrical rac. to 35×7cm; ray flts 1–5, spreading, bright yellow, 8–20mm; disc flts few. N China, Jap.

L. japonica (Thunb.) DC. to 1m. St. glab., purple-spotted. Basal lvs to 30×30cm, cordate-orbicular, palmately-parted, seg. coarsely lobed and incised, revolute, densely pubesc. beneath at first, chartaceous, petiole winged. Cap. 2–8, c10cm diam., in a corymb; ray flts c10, orange-yellow, to 6.5×1cm. China, Korea, Jap. Z5.

L. kaempferi Sieb. & Zucc. = *Farfugium japonicum.*

L. macrophylla (Ledeb.) DC. To 1.8m. Basal lvs to 60×30cm, elliptic to ovate-oblong, dentate, petiole winged, decurrent, glaucous. Cap. 2.5–5cm diam., in dense pan. to 30cm; ray flts 3–5, bright yellow; disc flts few. Altai Mts. Z4.

L. ×palmatiloba hort. (*L. dentata* ×*japonica.*) Intermediate between parents. To 1m. Lvs orbicular, cordate, palmately lobed, serrate. Cap. several, in a corymb; flts yellow. Gdn origin. Z5.

L. przewalskii (Maxim.) Diels. To 2m. St. dark purple. Basal lvs deeply palmately lobed, seg. lobed or toothed. Cap. many, small, in a long, narrow rac.; ray flts c2, yellow; disc flts c3. N China. Z4.

L. sibirica (L.) Cass. To 1.5m, often purple-tinged. St. glab. or hairy. Basal lvs to 25×20cm, triangular-reniform to subsagittate, dentate, subglabrous to densely hairy beneath. Cap. numerous, c3cm diam., in lax rac.; ray flts 7–11, yellow, to 20×5mm; disc flts many. Temp. Eurasia. Z3.

L. smithii hort. = *Senecio smithii.*

L. stenocephala (Maxim.) Matsum. & Koidz. To 1.5m. St. dark purple. Basal lvs to 35×30cm, spreading or ascending, hastate-cordate to triangular, acuminate, basal seg. acute, dentate, thinly chartaceous, shortly pilose on veins beneath. Cap. radiate or discoid, to 3cm diam., many, in long slender rac.; ray flts 1–3, to 25×4mm or 0; disc flts 6–12. China, Jap., Taiwan. 'The Rocket': to 180cm; st. black; fls in long yellow rac. 'Weihenstephan': to 180cm; fls large, gold. Z5.

L. tangutica (Maxim.) Bergmans = *Sinacalia tangutica.*

L. tussilaginea (Burm. f.) Mak. = *Farfugium japonicum.*

L. veitchiana (Hemsl.) Greenman To 1.8m, subglabrous. Basal lvs to 30×35cm, triangular-cordate, dentate, bright green, petioles semiterete, solid. Cap. to c6.5cm diam., many; ray flts 8–12, to 2.5cm, bright yellow; disc flts many. China. Z5.

L. wilsoniana (Hemsl.) Greenman GIANT GROUNDSEL. To 2m. Basal lvs to 50×25cm, reniform-cordate, sharply dentate, deep green, petiole hollow. Cap. c2.5cm diam., many, in an elongated rac.; ray flts 6–8, yellow. China. Z5.

→*Arnica, Cineraria* and *Senecio*.

Ligusticum L. ALPINE LOVAGE. Umbelliferae. 25 perenn. herbs. Lvs 2–5-pinnate or ternate. Fls in umbels; lateral umbels sterile or ♂, smaller bracts decid.; cal. teeth small or 0; fls white to green, occas. tinged purple. Circumboreal.

L. acutilobum Sieb. & Zucc. = *Angelica acutiloba*.
L. aromaticum Hook. f. = *Anisotome aromatica*.
L. capillifolium Cheesem. = *Anisotome capillifolia*.
L. haastii F. Muell. ex Hook. f. = *Anisotome haastii*.
L. imbricatum Hook. f. = *Anisotome imbricata*.
L. latifolium Hook. f. = *Anisotome latifolia*.
L. lucidum Mill. To 1.5m. Lvs c30cm, 3–5-pinnate, seg. linear, to 1.5cm. Umbels 20–50-rayed; involucre often 0. Summer. Mts S Eur. Z6.
L. mutellina (L.) Crantz. ALPINE LOVAGE. To 50cm. Lvs to 10cm, 2–3-pinnate, seg. linear-lanceolate, c5mm. Umbels 7–15-rayed; involucral bracts few or 0; fls tinged red or purple. Summer. C & SE Eur. Z6.
L. mutellinoides (Crantz) Vill. SMALL ALPINE LOVAGE. To 30cm. Lvs to 10cm, 2–3-pinnate, seg. linear-lanceolate, 2–5mm. Umbels with 8–20 rays; involucral bracts 5–20, often 2–3 parted; fls white to pink. Summer. Mts C Eur. Z3.
L. piliferum Hook. f. = *Anisotome pilifera*.
L. pyrenaeum Gouan = *L. lucidum*.
L. scoticum L. SCOTS LOVAGE. To 90cm, celery-scented. Lvs 8–25cm, 2-ternate, seg. ovate-cuneate, 2–5cm, dentate to lobed. Umbels 8–20-rayed; involucral bracts 3–6, linear; fls green-white or tinged pink. Summer. N Eur., Greenland and E N US. Z4.
L. seguieri Vill. = *L. lucidum*.

Ligustrum L. PRIVET. Oleaceae. 50 shrubs and small trees, decid. or everg. New growth usually downy. Lvs opposite, entire, glab., oblong or ovate. Fls usually white, small, in term. pan.; cor. tubular, 4-lobed; sta. 2. Fr. a small black drupe. Eur., N Afr., E & SE Asia, Aus.

L. acuminatum Koehne = *L. tschonoskii*.
L. acutissimum Koehne Decid. shrub to 3m., v. similar to *L. obtusifolium*. Lvs finely acuminate, not acute nor obtuse. China.
L. amurense Carr. Decid., erect to 3m; twigs pubesc. Lvs 3–6cm, elliptic-oblong, dull green, ciliate. Pan. 4–5cm, lax, floccose-pubesc. Fr. black, ± pruinose. N China. Z3.
L. angustifolium hort. = *L. massalongianum*.
L. brachystachyum Decne. = *L. quihoui*.
L. californicum hort. = *L. ovalifolium*.
L. chenaultii Hickel. Differs from *L. compactum* in acute dormant buds and lvs to 25cm. SW China. Z8.
L. ciliatum Rehd. non Sieb. ex Bl. = *L. tschonoskii*.
L. ciliatum Sieb. ex Bl. = *L. ibota*.
L. compactum (Wallich ex G. Don) Hook. f. & Thom. ex Brandis. Small tree to 8m. Lvs to 17cm, lanceolate, acuminate, glab. dark green. Fls off-white, malodorous in term. pan. to 15×15cm at base; anth. pink. Fr. purple-black, pruinose. Summer. NW Himal., SW China. Z8.
L. confusum Decne. Medium-sized, semi-everg. or decid. tree. Lvs to 9cm, lanceolate, pale green, glossy, glab. Fls to 4mm wide, in pubesc. pan.; anth. pink, fil. white. Fr. blue-black. Summer. E Nepal, Bhutan, India. Z8.
L. coriaceum Carr. = *L. japonicum* 'Rotundifolium'.
L. delavayanum Hariot. Everg. shrub, to 2m, divaricate. Lvs to 3cm, elliptic to ovate, glossy above, paler beneath, midrib pubesc. Fls in pan. to 5cm; cor. tube to 5mm, twice as long as lobes; anth. mauve. Fr. black. Late spring. W China, Burm. Z7. Z8.
L. formosanum Rehd. = *L. pricei*.
L. gracile Rehd. Decid. shrub to 3m, br. arching. Lvs to 4cm, glab. Fls in pan. to 7×7cm; cor. tube as long as lobes. Late spring. China Z8.
L. henryi Hemsl. Everg. shrub to 3m. Lvs to 3cm, oval, acuminate, dark green above. Fls in term. pan. to 15cm, fragrant; cor. 6mm. Fr. oblong, black. Summer. C China. Z7.
L. ×ibolium Coe (*L. obtusifolium × L. ovalifolium*.) Semi-everg., close to *L. ovalifoium* except young br., infl. axis and lf undersides pubesc. Gdn origin. 'Variegatum': fast-growing, erect and tightly branched; lvs edged with soft cream. Z4.
L. ibota Sieb. & Zucc. Decid. shrub to 2m. Shorter growths pubesc. Lvs to 5cm, ovate or lozenge-shaped, minutely ciliate, olive green above, paler beneath with downy midrib. Fls white, to

8mm, in heads to 1.5cm. Summer. Jap. Z5.
L. ibota Sieb. (1830) non Sieb. & Zucc. (1846). = *L. obtusifolium*.
L. indicum (Lour.) Merrill. Everg. shrub to 8m. Lvs to 8cm, oblong, acuminate, glossy green above, yellow to pale green beneath. Fls fragrant, small, off-white, in pan. to 18cm. Early summer. Himal., Indochina. Z8.
L. ionandrum Diels = *L. delavayanum*.
L. japonicum Thunb. Related to *L. lucidum*, differs in having darker, often smaller, lvs with prominent rather than sunken veins beneath and cor. tube twice length of cal., as are lobes. Everg. shrub to 4m. Lvs to 10cm, glab., dark green, broadly ovate, often with red-green margins and midrib. Fls scented, in pyramidal pan. to 15cm. Late summer. Jap., Korea. 'Revolutum': narrow, erect, to 1m; lvs small to 3cm, narrow. 'Rotundifolium': rigidly erect everg. shrub to 2m; lvs crowded, to 4cm, round or broadly ovate. 'Silver Star': slow-growing, compact, erect; lvs dark green edged with cream, tinged silver. 'Texanum': vigorous; lvs large, to 5cm, thick and lustrous, paler when young, later v. dark green. 'Variegatum': lvs stippled and edged white. Z7.
L. longifolium Carr. non hort. = *L. compactum*.
L. longifolium hort. non Carr. = *L. massalongianum*.
L. lucidum Ait. f. CHINESE PRIVET; WHITE WAX TREE. Resembles *L. japonicum*. Everg. shrub or small tree to 10m. Lvs to 10cm, ovate-elliptic, long-acuminate, glab. Fls in pan. 10–20cm. Fr. blue-black. Late summer. China, Korea, Jap. 'Alivonii': young lvs yellow-variegated, otherwise dull green. 'Aureovariegatum': lvs yellow-variegated, tough. 'Ciliatum': lvs small. 'Compactum': dense in growth; lvs waxy, dark green. 'Excelsum Superbum': vigorous, lvs deep yellow, flecked and edged off-white. 'Gracile' and 'Nobile': upright, br. fastigiate. 'Latifolium': lvs v. large, glossy dark green. 'Macrophylum': lvs large. 'Microphyllum' lvs small. 'Pyramidale': narrow and conic in growth. 'Recurvifolium': lf margins recurved. 'Repandum': lvs narrow, curling upwards. 'Tricolor': vigorous, lvs smaller, marked white and yellow, flushed pink when young. Z7.
L. magnoliifolium hort. = *L. lucidum*.
L. massalongianum Vis. Everg. shrub, erect to 1m. Lvs 4–8cm, linear-oblong, narrow-acuminate, glab., falling in cold conditions. Fls crowded in branching pan. to 8cm. Fr. blue. Summer. Himal. Z8.
L. medium Franch. & Savat. non hort. = *L. ovalifolium*.
L. medium hort. non Franch. & Savat. = *L. tschonoskii*.
L. nepalense Wallich = *L. indicum*.
L. obtusifolium Sieb. & Zucc. Broad, decid. shrub to 3m. Lvs 2–9cm, oblong to obovate, dark green above, often becoming purple in autumn, paler beneath, midrib pubesc. Fls in semipendent pan. to 5cm, cor. to 10mm. Fr. dark grey. Summer. Jap. var. *regelianum* (Koehne) Rehd. To 2m. Growth spreading. Lvs in 2 ranks, obovate, 5–7cm, pubesc. beneath, purple-red in autumn. Summer. Jap. Z3.
L. ovalifolium Hassk. CALIFORNIA PRIVET. Semi-everg. shrub to 4m, upright. Lvs 3–7cm, elliptic-ovate, blunt to acute, glossy, dark above, yellow-green beneath. Fls off-white, malodorous, many, in pan. to 10cm. Jap. This is the Oval-Leaved Privet, one of our most frequently used hedging plants. 'Albomarginatum': lvs edged white. 'Argenteum': lvs margined silver. 'Aureum': lvs yellow, margins broad and golden. 'Compactum': dense and slow-growing. 'Globosum' and 'Nanum': dwarf, dense and slow-growing. 'Lemon and Lime': similar to 'Aureum' with lvs variegated pale green and yellow. 'Multiflorum': particularly floriferous. 'Tricolor': new growth flushed pink, lvs ultimately variegated yellow-white. 'Variegatum': lvs stippled pale yellow. Z5.
L. prattii Koehne = *L. delavayanum*.
L. pricei Hayata. Everg. shrub to 3m. New growth purple-green. Lvs 3cm, oval, acuminate, dark green, glab.; petiole purple-green. Fls insignificant, in term. pan. to 5cm, slightly pubesc., loose, nodding. Summer. Taiwan. Z8.
L. quihoui Carr. Decid. shrub to 2m. Shorter br. bearing spinelike reduced shoots, rusty-pubesc. Lvs to 5cm, oblong-lanceolate, glossy, glab. above; petiole downy. Fls fragrant, in lax, cylindric pan. to 20cm. Late summer. China. Z6.
L. rosmarinifolium hort. = *L. massalongianum*.
L. sempervirens (Franch.) Lingl. Everg. shrub to 2m. Lvs to 4cm, ovate, glab., tough, shiny, punctate beneath. Fls many, in pan. to 10cm; cor. to 1cm, tube twice length of lobes. Summer. W China. Z7.
L. simonii Carr. = *L. compactum*.
L. sinense Lour. Decid. shrub to 4m, erect. Lvs to 7cm, elliptic-oblong, olive green above, paler beneath, midrib downy. Fls off-white, fragrant, in pan. to 10cm. Fr. claret-coloured. Summer. China. 'Multiflorum': particularly floriferous, anth. tinted red. 'Pendulum': br. pendulous. 'Variegatum': lvs variegated soft grey-green and white. 'Wimbei': dwarf to 50cm after 5 years, upright and columnar in growth; lvs small, to

6mm, v. dark green. var. *stauntonii* (DC.) Rehd. Shorter and more spreading, to 3×2m. Smaller br. flushed purple. Lvs to 4cm, ovate, obtuse, deep green above, paler, sparsely pubesc. beneath. Late summer. C China. Z7.

L. spicatum Hamilt. = *L. indicum*.

L. stauntonii (A. DC.) = *L. sinense* var. *stauntonii*.

L. strongylophyllum Hemsl. Everg., erect shrub. Br. slender, grey pubesc. Lvs to 2.5cm, broadly ovate, coriaceous, glossy, deep green above, paler beneath. Fls to 7mm, white, borne loosely in pyramidal pan. to 10cm. Summer. C China. Z9.

L. **'Suwannee River'**. Slow-growing and compact. Br. ascending. Lvs lustrous, dark green, dense and adpressed to st.

L. tschonoskii Decne. Decid. shrub, erect, to 2m. Br. arising. Lvs to 8cm, rhombic or ovate, acuminate, ciliate. Fls in short-stalked pan., 4–6cm, densely pubesc. Summer. Jap. Z6.

L. × *vicaryi* Rehd. (*L. ovalifolium* × *L. vulgare*.) Decid., spreading. Br. densely divaricate. Lvs golden. Gdn origin. Z5.

L. villosum May = *L. sinense*.

L. vulgare L. COMMON PRIVET. Decid. shrub to 5m, upright, dense. Lvs oblong-ovate to lanceolate, glab., dark green. Fls off-white in dense, erect pan. to 5cm, malodorous. Fr. black, glossy. Summer. N Eur., Medit., N Afr., Asia Minor; distrib. enlarged and confused by cult. Numerous cvs include: 'Argenteovariegatum': lvs speckled white. 'Aureovariegatum': lvs marked golden yellow. 'Aureum': lvs golden. 'Buxifolium': lvs persistent, small, ovate. 'Chlorocarpum': fls green-yellow. 'Glaucum': lvs appearing grey-green due to thick cuticle. 'Laurifolium': vigorous, erect, dense habit; lvs ovate, tough, dark green, suffused purple in winter. 'Leucocarpum': fr. white-green. 'Lodense': semi-prostrate, matted habit; lvs narrow-elliptic, dark green, to 5cm, bronze, persistent in winter. 'Pyramidale': fastigiate; side shoots dense, appearing whorled. 'Xanthocarpum': fr. bright yellow. Z4. var. *italicum* (Mill.) Vahl. ('Sempervirens'): lvs everg.

L. yunnanense L. Henry = *L. compactum*.

→*Parasyringa*.

Lijiang Spruce *Picea likiangensis*.
Likiang Lily *Lilium papilliferum*.
Lilac *Syringa*.
Lilac Hibiscus *Alyogyne huegeli*.
Lilac Sunbonnet *Langloisia punctata*.

LILIACEAE Juss. 240/4640. *Agapanthus, Agrostocrinum, Albuca, Alectorurus, Aletris, Allium, Aloe, Alstroemeria,* × *Alworthia, Amianthum, Androcymbium, Androstephium, Anemarrhena, Anthericum, Aphyllanthes, Arthropodium, Asparagus, Asphodeline, Asphodelus, Aspidistra, Astelia, Astroloba,* × *Astroworthia, Baeometra, Behnia, Bellevalia, Bessera, Blandfordia, Bloomeria, Bomarea, Bowiea, Brimeura, Brodiaea, Bulbine, Bulbinella, Bulbinopsis, Bulbocodium, Burchardia, Calochortus, Caloscordum, Camassia, Camptorrhiza, Cardiocrinum, Chamaelirion, Chionodoxa, Chionographis,* × *Chionoscilla, Chlorogalum, Chlorophytum, Clintonia, Colchicum, Conanthera, Convallaria, Daiswa, Danaë, Daubenya, Dianella, Dichelostemma, Dipcadi, Disporum, Drimia, Drimiopsis, Eremurus, Erythronium, Eucomis, Fritillaria, Gagea, Galtonia,* × *Gasteraloe,* × *Gasterhaworthia, Gasteria,* × *Gastroloba, Gilliesia, Gloriosa, Haworthia, Helonias, Heloniopsis, Hemerocallis, Herpolirion, Hesperocallis, Hosta, Hyacinthella, Hyacinthoides, Hyacinthus, Ipheion, Kinugasa, Kniphofia, Lachenalia, Lapageria, Latace, Laxmannia, Ledebouria, Leucocoryne, Leucocrinum, Lilium, Liriope, Littonia, Lloydia, Lomatophyllum, Luzuriaga, Maianthemum, Massonia, Medeola, Melanthium, Merendera, Milla, Milligania, Muilla, Muscari, Narthecium, Nectaroscordum, Nomocharis, Notholirion, Nothoscordum, Ophiopogon, Ornithogalum, Paradisea, Paris, Pasithea, Peliosanthes, Periboea, Petronymphe,* × *Philageria, Philesia, Poellnitzia, Polygonatum, Polyxena, Pseudogaltonia, Puschkinia, Reineckea, Ripogonum, Rohdea, Ruscus, Sandersonia, Scilla, Scoliopus, Semele, Simethis, Smilacina, Smilax, Sowerbaea, Speirantha, Stenanthium, Streptopus, Stypandra, Tecophilaea, Theropogon, Thysanotus, Tofieldia, Trichopetalum, Tricyrtis, Trillium, Tristagma, Triteleia, Tulbaghia, Tulipa, Urginea, Uvularia, Veltheimia, Veratrum, Whiteheadia, Wurmbea, Xanthorrhoea, Xeronema, Xerophyllum, Zigadenus*.

Lilium L. LILY. Liliaceae (Liliaceae). 100 bulbous perenn. herbs. Bulbs with white or yellow fleshy scales, sometimes purple when exposed to light. St. simple, leafy, sometimes rooting at base and/or developing bulbils in lf axils. Lvs linear to elliptic, whorled, scattered or alt., usually sessile. Fls in a term. rac. or umbel, occas. solitary, erect (cup-shaped), horizontal (funnel-shaped or bowl-shaped), pendulous (bell-shaped or 'turk's-cap' – with recurved tep.); tep. 6, free, nectary and fil. of sta. at base of each tep.; anth. versatile; stigma 3-lobed, style 1, ovary superior. Temp. N hemis.

L. albanicum Griseb. = *L. pyrenaicum* ssp. *carniolicum* var. *albanicum*.

L. alexandrae (Wallace) Coutts. UKE-YURI. St. to 1m. Lvs 20cm, lanceolate to ovate, petiolate. Fls 1–5, fragrant, bowl-shaped, horizontal or erect; tep. to 18×3–4cm, white with green bases and tips, exterior occas. striped pink; anth. and pollen brown. Summer. Jap., Ryukyu Is. Z5.

L. amabile Palib. St. to 90cm, pubesc. Lvs to 9cm, scattered, lanceolate. Fls 1–5, turk's-cap, in a rac., malodorous; tep. 5.5cm, red with dark purple spots, 2–3 fleshy papillae on upper surface; anth. dark brown; pollen red. Summer. Korea. var. *luteum* anon. Fls yellow. Z5.

L. artvinense Misch. = *L. pyrenaicum* ssp. *ponticum* var. *artvinense*.

L. atrosanguineum anon. = *L. maculatum*.

L. auratum Lindl. GOLDED-RAYED LILY OF JAPAN; MOUNTAIN LILY; YAMA-YURI. St. 60–150cm. Lvs to 22cm, scattered, lanceolate, dark green, petiolate. Fls 6–30, bowl-shaped, horizontal or slightly pendulous, in a rac., v. fragrant; tep. 12–18×4–5cm, white with yellow or crimson central streaks and crimson-spotted, fleshy papillae on basal part, tips recurved; pollen chocolate to red. Summer–autumn. Jap. 'Apollo': central band and spots ruby-red. 'Crimson Beauty': cherry red, margin white. 'Praecox': heavily spotted; early flowering. 'Rubrum': tep. band crimson. 'Tom Thumb': dwarf. Crossed with *L. speciosum*, *L. japonicum* and *L. rubellum* to give rise to a wide range of cvs. var. *platyphyllum* Bak. St. to 2.3m. Lvs broadly lanceolate. Fls larger, fewer spots on tep. var. *rubrovittatum* Duchartre. Band on tep. yellow at base, deep crimson at apex. var. *virginale* Duchartre. St. to 2m. Albino form, tep. white, streaked yellow, spotted pale yellow or pink. 'Album': fls white. Z6.

L. × *aurelianense* Debras. (*L. henryi* × *L. sargentiae*.) St. to 2.5m. Lvs 12cm, lanceolate, bulbils in axils. Fls to 12, scented, 12.5cm wide, horizontal or slightly pendulous. Autumn. Gdn origin. Many cvs, white to apricot and pink fls.

L. australe Stapf = *L. brownii*.

L. avenaceum Fisch. = *L. medeloides*.

L. bakerianum Collett & Hemsl. St. 60–90cm, usually hairy. Lvs 10cm, scattered, linear to lanceolate. Fls 1–6, bell-shaped, pendulous; tep. white, interior spotted red-brown, exterior tinged green, 7×1.5cm, margins wavy, tips recurved; anth. orange. Summer. N Burm., SW China. Z8.

L. batemanniae Wallace = *L. maculatum*.

L. biondii Baroni = *L. davidii* var. *unicolor*.

L. bloomerianum Kellogg = *L. humboldtii*.

L. bolanderi S. Wats. St. to 140cm, glaucous, marked brown. Lvs to 5cm, in whorls, sessile, oblanceolate. Fls 1–18, funnel-shaped, pendulous; tep. 3–4.5×1cm, maroon, interior spotted dark red or purple, exterior green at base, tube yellow, spotted chocolate; anth. purple; pollen deep yellow. Summer. W US. Z5.

L. brownii Miellez. St. to 1m, green tinged dark brown. Lvs to 25cm, scattered, lanceolate. Fls fragrant, 1–4, funnel-shaped; tep. 12–15×2.5–6.5cm, interior white, exterior purple, tinged green; anth. brown; pollen red-brown. Summer. China, Burm. var. *australe* (Stapf) Stearn. St. to 3m. Interior of tep. white, exterior flushed green. SE China, Hong Kong. var. *viridulum* Bak. St. green. Fls strongly scented, exterior of tep. tinged yellow-green and pale purple, tube interior yellow, fading to white. China. Z6.

L. bulbiferum L. FIRE LILY. St. 40–150cm, ribbed, occas. spotted purple, woolly above, with axill. bulbils. Lvs 10cm, lanceolate, scattered. Fls usually to 5, occas. to 50, erect, cup-shaped, tep. 6–8.5×2–3cm, bright orange, bases and tips deeper in colour, interior spotted maroon; anth. brown; pollen orange. Summer. S Eur. var. *croceum* (Chaix) Pers. Tep. orange, bulbils 0. Z7.

L. × *burbankii* anon. (*L. pardalinum* × *L. parryi*.) St. 1–2m. Lvs in whorls. Fls horizontal, fragrant; tep. reflexed, 8cm, yellow, spotted chocolate-brown, tips red. Summer. Gdn origin. Z5.

L. callosum Sieb. & Zucc. SLIMSTEM LILY. St. to 90cm. Lvs 8–13cm, scattered, linear, tips thickened. Fls to 10, pendulous turk's-cap, in a rac.; tep. 3–4cm, orange-red, spotted black toward base; pollen orange. Late summer. China, Jap., Korea, Taiwan, E Russia. Z6.

L. canadense L. MEADOW LILY; WILD MEADOW LILY. St. to 1.5m. Lvs 15cm, lanceolate to oblanceolate mostly in whorls. Fls 10–12, bell-shaped, pendulous, in an umbel; tep. 5–7.5×1–2.5cm, yellow, basally spotted maroon, apices recurved; pollen yellow to red-brown. Summer. E N Amer. 'Chocolate Chips': tep. exterior and tips crimson, fading to orange then yellow toward the interior base, spots large. 'Fire Engine': tep. slightly recurved, exterior and interior tips crimson, fading to orange then yellow near the base; pollen burnt-orange. 'Melted Spots': lvs whorled; fls yellow-orange, spots dense on the basal two-thirds. 'Peaches and Pepper': fls

L. candidum L. MADONNA LILY; WHITE LILY. St. 1–2m, dark
maroon. Basal lvs to 22×5cm, produced in autumn, st. lvs
scattered, 7.5cm, lanceolate. Fls 5–20, funnel-shaped, fragrant,
in a rac.; tep. 5–8×1–4cm, white, interior base yellow, tips
recurved; pollen bright yellow. Summer. Balk., E Medit. var.
plenum West. Fls double. var. *salonikae* Stoker. St. dark
green. Tep. widely spreading; pollen pale yelow. W Greece.
Z6.

peach-orange; tep. recurved, finely spotted. var. *coccineum*
Pursh. Fls red, throat yellow. var. *editorum* Fern. Lvs broader.
Fls red, tep. 8–13mm wide. Appalachian Mts. Z5.

L. carniolicum Koch = *L. pyrenaicum* ssp. *carniolicum*.

L. carniolicum ssp. *ponticum* P.H. Davis & D.M.
Henderson = *L. pyrenaicum* ssp. *ponticum* var. *ponticum*.

L. catesbaei Walter. LEOPARD LILY; PINE LILY; TIGER LILY. St.
30–60cm. Lvs to 10cm, alt., lanceolate. Fls 1–2, erect, cup-
shaped; tep. 5–12×1–2.5cm, clawed, interior deep yellow, tips
recurved, scarlet, exterior pale yellow to green; pollen orange-
red; stigma dark red. Late summer. SE US. Z5.

L. cathayanum Wils. = *Cardiocrinum cathayanum*.

L. centifolium Stapf = *L. leucanthum* var. *centifolium*.

L. cernuum Komar. NODDING LILY. St. to 60cm, sometimes
spotted brown, ribbed. Lvs 8–15cm, scattered, crowded around
middle of st., sessile. Fls 1–14, turk's-cap, 3.5cm wide, fragrant,
in a pendent rac.; tep. lilac, purple, pink or occas. white,
spotted purple; pollen lilac. Summer. Korea, NE Manch.,
Russia. Z3.

L. chaixii Maw = *L. bulbiferum*.

L. chalcedonicum L. SCARLET TURK'S-CAP LILY; RED MARTAGON OF
CONSTANTINOPLE. St. 45–150cm. Lvs to 11.5cm, linear-
lanceolate, edged silver, spirally arranged, sessile. Fls to 12,
pendulous, turk's-cap, 7.5cm wide, slightly scented; tep. scarlet,
recurved, without spots; pollen scarlet. Summer. Greece, S
Albania. 'Maculatum': scarlet, spotted black. *L. chalcedonicum*
×*L. ×testaceum* has produced a number of cvs including
'Apollo', 'Hephaistos' and 'Zeus'. Z5.

L. chinense Baroni = *L. davidii* var. *willmottiae*.

L. ciliatum P.H. Davis. St. 60–150cm, white-hairy above. Lvs
7–12.5cm, spirally arranged, glab., margins hairy. Fls 5–8,
sometimes to 21, turk's-cap, 5cm wide, scented; tep. ivory,
cream or pale yellow, interior purple-brown toward base, upper
portion finely spotted; pollen orange-red. Summer. NE Turk.
Z5.

L. colchicum Steven = *L. monadelphum*.

L. columbianum Bak. COLUMBIA TIGER LILY; OREGON LILY. St. to
2.5m. Lvs 5–14cm, oblanceolate, upper lvs scattered, lower lvs
in whorls. Fls 6–10, occas. to 40, pendulous, turk's-cap, in a
long-stalked rac.; tep. 3.5–6.5×0.8–1.2cm, recurved, yellow to
orange-red, base spotted maroon; pollen deep yellow to brown.
Summer. W N Amer. 'Ingramii': fls large, many, deep orange.
Z5.

L. concolor Salisb. MORNING STAR LILY. St. 30–90cm, flushed
purple, lightly pubesc. Lvs 8.5cm, scattered, linear or linear-
lanceolate, ciliate. Fls 1–10, erect, star-shaped; pedicels erect,
5cm; tep. 3–4×1cm, recurved, scarlet, glossy, unspotted; pollen
red. Summer. China. 'Racemosum': taller; more vigorous. var.
partheneion (Sieb. & De Vries) Bak. Fls red, streaked green
and yellow, black spots few. var. *pulchellum* (Fisch.) Reg. St.
green, glab. Fls spotted, buds woolly. Summer. NE Asia. Z4.

L. cordatum (Thunb.) Koidz. = *Cardiocrinum cordatum*.

L. ×creelmannii hort. = *L. ×imperiale*.

L. croceum Chaix = *L. bulbiferum* var. *croceum*.

L. dahuricum Elwes = *L. dauricum*.

L. ×dalhansonii Baden-Powell. (*L. hansonii* ×*L. martagon* var.
cattaniae.) St. 1.5–2m. Fls turk's-cap, 3cm, malodorous; tep.
recurved, dark maroon, to pink, white or yellow, spotted darker; style purple. Summer. 'Backhouse hybrids': fls cream,
yellow, pink to maroon with darker spots. 'Damson': fls plum-
purple. 'Destiny': fls yellow, spotted brown; tep. tips reflexed.
'Discovery': fls turk's-cap, rose-lilac, base white, tinged pink,
spotted deep crimson, tips darker, exterior pink with a silvery
sheen.

L. dauricum Ker-Gawl. St. to 75cm, ribbed, spotted red-brown,
woolly. Lvs 5–15cm, scattered, linear to lanceolate, ciliate. Fls
1–6, erect, cup-shaped, in an umbel; pedicels hairy, to 9cm; tep.
5–10×1.5–3.5cm, recurved, oblanceolate, vermilion to scarlet,
spotted brown-red, base yellow, narrow; pollen red. Summer.
NE Asia. Z5.

L. davidii Elwes. St. 1–1.4m, spotted brown. Lvs 6–10cm, linear,
finely toothed and inrolled, basally white-hairy. Fls 5–20,
turk's-cap, pendulous, long-stalked in a rac., buds hairy; tep. to
8cm, vermilion spotted purple; pollen orange or scarlet.
Summer. W China. var. *unicolor* (Hoog) Cotton. St. shorter, to
1m. Lvs more numerous and longer, v. crowded. Fls paler, spots
red, mauve or 0. Summer. N China. var. *willmottiae* (Wils.)
Raffill. St. to 2m, arching. Lvs to 6mm wide. Fls to 40.

Summer. China. Z5.

L. davimottiae. Name given to the hybrid between *L. davidii* var.
davidii and *L. davidii* var. *willmottiae*.

L. davuricum Wils. = *L. dauricum*.

L. distichum Nak. in Kamib. KOCHANG LILY. Resembles
L. tsingtauense but tep. recurved and bulb scales jointed. St.
60–120cm, ribbed below. Lvs 8–15cm, obovate-elliptic, in 1–2
whorls in middle of st., none below, sparsely scattered above.
Fls 3–8, turk's-cap, horizontal or slightly pendulous, in a rac.;
pedicels 6–8cm; tep. 3.5–4.5×0.6–1.3cm, recurved, pale orange
usually with darker spots. Summer. E Russia, N Korea, NE
China. Z5.

L. duchartrei Franch. MARBLE MARTAGON. St. 60–100cm, flushed
brown, ribbed, white-hairy in lf axils. Lvs 10.5cm, pale beneath,
lanceolate, scattered, sessile, margin rough. Fls to 12, turk's-
cap, pendulous, fragrant, in an umbel; pedicels 7–15cm; tep.
recurved, interior white, spotted deep purple, tube green at
base, exterior white flushed purple, ageing red; pollen orange.
Summer. W China. Z5.

L. elegans Thunb. = *L. maculatum*.

L. excelsum Endl. & Hartinger = *L. ×testaceum*.

L. farreri Turrill = *L. duchartrei*.

L. fauriei Lév. & Vaniot = *L. amabile*.

L. formosanum Wallace. St. 30–150cm, purple-brown below. Lvs
7.5–20cm, scattered, dark, oblong-lanceolate, crowded near
base. Fls 1–2, sometimes to 10, in umbels, fragrant, funnel-
shaped; pedicels 5–15cm, erect; tep. 12–20×2.5–5cm, interior
white, exterior white flushed purple, recurved, nectary furrows
green; anth. yellow to purple; pollen brown or yellow.
Summer-autumn. Taiwan. var. *pricei* Stoker. St. 30–60cm. Fls
1–2, more deeply coloured. Summer. Taiwan. Z5.

L. formosum Lem. = *L. dauricum*.

L. forrestii W.W. Sm. = *L. lankongense*.

L. fortunei Lindl. = *L. maculatum*.

L. giganteum Wallich non hort. = *Cardiocrinum giganteum*.

L. glehnii F. Schmidt = *Cardiocrinum cordatum*.

L. grayi S. Wats. St. to 1.75m. Lvs to 5–12cm, lanceolate or
oblong-lanceolate, sessile, in whorls. Fls 1–8, unscented, bell-
shaped; pedicels to 20cm; tep. 6.25×0.5cm, interior light red
with yellow base, spotted purple, exterior crimson, darker
towards base, upper part spreading, lower part forming a tube;
anth. yellow, pollen orange-brown. Summer. E US (Allegheny
Mts). 'Gulliver's Thimble': fls bright crimson. Z5.

L. hansonii Moore. St. to 120cm. Lvs 18cm, dark green,
oblanceolate to elliptic. Fls 3–12, turk's-cap, fragrant,
pendulous; tep. 3–4×1.5cm, thick, recurved, oblanceolate, deep
orange-yellow, spotted purple-brown toward base; anth. purple;
pollen yellow. Summer. E Russia, Korea, Jap. Z5.

L. harrisii Carr. = *L. longiflorum* var. *eximium*.

L. heldreichii Freyn = *L. chalcedonicum*.

L. henrici Franch. St. to 90cm, flushed brown. Lvs 10–12cm,
numerous, lanceolate, margins rough. Fls 1–7, in a rac., bell-
shaped; pedulous; tep. 3.5–5×1–2cm, recurved with a short
basal tube, white suffused purple, tube dark purple within,
anth. and pollen yellow. Summer. SW China. Z5.

L. henryi Bak. St. 1–3m, marked purple. Lvs 8–15cm, shiny,
scattered, upper lvs ovate, sessile, basal lvs lanceolate,
petiolate, some axils bulbiliferous. Fls 4–20, turk's-cap,
pendulous, in a rac.; pedicels 5–9cm; tep. 6–8×1–2cm, orange,
spotted black, lanceolate, recurved; anth. deep red. Summer.
China. 'Citrinum': fls pale lemon-yellow, spotted brown. Z5.

L. ×hollandicum Bergmans. (*L. maculatum* ×*L. bulbiferum*.)
UMBEL LILY. St. 70–130cm. Lvs crowded, veins 3. Fls erect,
cup-shaped, to 7.5cm wide, in umbels; tep. yellow, orange or
red. Summer. Gdn origin. Z5.

L. howellii I.M. Johnst. = *L. bolanderi*.

L. humboldtii Ducharte. St. to 2.25m, flushed purple. Lvs to
12.5cm, oblanceolate, in whorls. Fls 10–15, ocasionally 80,
pendulous, turk's-cap, in a rac.; tep. 6.5–10×1.5–2.5cm,
recurved, yellow to orange, spotted maroon and purple; pollen
brown. Summer. US (Calif.). var. *ocellatum* (Kellogg) Elwes.
Tep. tinged red, the spots ringed red, eye-like. Z5.

L. ×imperiale Wils. (*L. regale* ×*L. sargentiae*.) SARGALE LILY.
St. to 120cm, grey-green. Lvs alt., linear, axils of upper lvs
bulbiliferous. Fls bowl-shaped; tep. recurved, interior white,
basal tube yellow, exterior purple; anth. orange-brown.
Summer. Z5.

L. iridollae M.G. Henry. POT-OF-GOLD LILY. St. to 175cm. Lvs to
10cm, usually whorled, obovate, basal rosettes of lvs persisting
through winter. Fls 1–8, pendulous, turk's-cap; tep. 10×2.5cm,
yellow, spotted brown, apex speckled red; anth. red-brown.
Late summer. SE US. Z4.

L. isabellinum Kunze = *L. ×testaceum*.

L. jankae Kerner = *L. pyrenaicum* ssp. *carniolicum* var. *jankae*.

L. japonicum Houtt. BAMBOO LILY; SASA-YURI. St. 40–90cm. Lvs
15cm, scattered, lanceolate, margins rough, petiolate. Fls 1–5,

fragrant, funnel-shaped, horizontal; tep. 10–15×2–3.5cm, oblanceolate to oblong, white, pink or white; anth. brown; pollen red or brown. Summer. Jap. 'Albomarginatum': lf margins white. 'Album': fls white. var. *platyfolium* anon. Lvs broader. Z5.

L. **kelleyanum** Lemmon. St. to 1m. Lvs 5–15cm, lanceolate to elliptic, scattered, sometimes in 2 whorls. Fls pendulous, turk's-cap, fragrant; tep. 2.5–5×1cm, yellow or orange, maroon or basally spotted brown, apex sometimes red; anth. brown. Summer. W US. Z5.

L. **kelloggii** Purdy. St. 30–125cm. Lvs to 10cm, in whorls of 12 or more, sessile, lanceolate or oblanceolate. Fls to 20, pendulous, turk's-cap, fragrant, in a rac.; tep. 5.5×1cm, reflexed, mauve-pink or white with dark purple spots and central yellow stripe toward base; anth. and pollen orange. Summer. W US. Z5.

L. **kesselringianum** Misch. St. to 1m. Lvs lanceolate, 9–13cm. Fls 1–3, 9–14cm wide, bell-shaped; tep. 9cm, recurved, pale cream to yellow, spotted purple; anth. brown; pollen orange. Summer. S Russia (Georgia), NE Turk. Z5.

L. **krameri** Hook. f. = *L. japonicum*.

L. **lancifolium** Thunb. DEVIL LILY; KENTAN; TIGER LILY. St. 60–150cm, dark purple with white hairs with black bulbils in axils. Lvs 12–20cm, lanceolate, scattered, margins rough. Fls to 40, in a rac., pendulous, turk's-cap, to 12.5cm wide, unscented; pedicels to 10cm; tep. 7–10×1–2.5cm, lanceolate, gradually spreading, interior orange, spotted deep purple; anth. orange-red to purple; pollen brown. Summer–early autumn. E China, Jap., Korea. 'Flore Pleno': fls double; tep. many, narrow; sta. 0. 'Yellow Tiger': fls lemon-yellow, spotted dark purple. var. *flaviflorum* Mak. Fls yellow. Jap. var. *fortunei* (Standish) V. Matthews. St. to 2m, densely woolly. Fls 30–50, tep. orange-red. Korea, China. var. *splendens* (Van Houtte) V. Matthews. St. black with shiny bulbils. Fls to 25, larger, bright orange-red, spotted black. Jap. Z4.

L. **lankongense** Franch. St. to 120cm, rough, ribbed. Lvs 10cm, sessile, scattered, crowded near base, oblong-lanceolate, margins rough. Fls to 15, 5cm wide, in a rac., pendulous, turk's-cap, fragrant; pedicels recurved, 12.5cm; tep. 4–6.5×1–2.5cm, rose-pink, spotted purple; green central stripe, recurved; anth. purple; pollen brown. Summer. W China. Z5.

L. **ledebourii** (Bak.) Boiss. St. slender to 1.25m. Lvs scattered, spirally arranged, lower 12–12cm, upper narrower. Fls 1–5, fragrant, turk's-cap; tep. 6–7×1.3cm, creamy white to yellow, centrally spotted dark purple or red; anth. and pollen red. Summer. NW Iran, Azerbaijan. Z5.

L. **leichtlinii** Hook. f. St. to 120cm, with a few white hairs in lf axils. Lvs to 15cm, scattered, linear-lanceolate, margins rough. Fls 1–6, in a rac., unscented, pendulous, turk's-cap, buds white-hairy; tep. to 8×2cm, lemon yellow spotted maroon, lanceolate, tips recurved; anth. and pollen red-brown. Summer. Jap. var. *maximowiczii* (Reg.) Bak. St. to 2.5cm. Lvs numerous, linear-lanceolate. Fls 1–12; tep. bright orange-red, spotted purple-brown; anth. and pollen red. Jap., C Korea. Z5.

L. **leucanthum** (Bak.) Bak. var. *centifolium* (Stapf) Stearn. St. 2–3m, glaucous. Lvs 15–20cm, ascending, recurved, scattered, linear to lanceolate. Fls to 18, scented, funnel-shaped, horizontal or slightly pendulous; pedicels horizontal, 6–12cm; tep. 14–18×3–6cm, interior white with yellow basal tube, exterior flushed purple-red, green toward base, recurved; anth. red-brown; pollen brown. Summer. W China. Z5.

L. **linifolium** Hornem. = *L. pumilum*.

L. **longiflorum** Thunb. EASTER LILY. St. to 1m. Lvs to 18cm, scattered, lanceolate or oblong-lanceolate. Fls to 6, funnel-shaped, scented, in an umbel; pedicels horizontal, to 12cm; tep. to 18cm, white, forming a basal tube, tips slightly recurved; pollen yellow. Summer. S Jap., Taiwan. 'Albomarginatum': lvs blue-green, margins white. 'Gelria': fls white; tep. slightly recurved at apex; pollen yellow. 'Holland's Glory': fls white, to 20cm. 'White America': fls white, tips and nectary green, pollen deep yellow. 'White Europe' (Georgia', 'Avai No. 5'): fls white; tep. strongly recurved, throat veined green, exterior green-white below, veined cream above, pollen lemon-yellow. var. *eximium* (Courtois) Bak. Tep. more recurved, basal tube narrower. Jap. 'Howardii' ('Romanii'): fls pure white, firm-textured. var. *takeshima* Duchartre. St. taller, purple-brown. Fls flushed purple outside; pollen orange. Jap. 'Erabu No Hikari' ('Erabu'): taller, more floriferous. Z5.

L. **lowii** anon. = *L. bakerianum*.

L. **mackliniae** Sealy. St. to 40cm, sometimes tinged purple. Lvs 3–6cm, spiral, linear-lanceolate or elliptic-lanceolate. Fls 1–6, in a rac., pendulous, bell-shaped; tep. 5×2cm, interior rose-pink, exterior purple-pink; anth. purple; pollen yellow-orange or brown. Late spring–summer. NE India. Z5.

L. **maculatum** Thunb. (*L. dauricum* × *L. concolor*?). St. to 60cm, ribbed. Lvs 5–15cm, lanceolate to elliptic, scattered. Fls cup-shaped, erect; tep. 8–10cm, yellow, orange or red, variably spotted. Summer. Jap. 'Alutaceum': fls deep apricot, spotted

purple-black. 'Aureum': fls orange-yellow, spotted black. 'Bicolor': fls brilliant orange, margins bright red, spots few, faint. 'Biligulatum': fls deep chestnut-red. 'Sanguineum': st. to 40cm; fls solitary, orange-red. 'Wallacei': fls apricot with raised maroon spots. Many selections have been made. Z4.

L. **makinoi** Koidz. = *L. japonicum*.

L. **× marhan** Bak. (*L. hansonii* × *L. martagon* var. *album*.) St. to 1.5m. Fls pendulous, turk's-cap, 5–6cm wide; tep. thick, orange-yellow, spotted red-brown. Summer. Gdn origin. Z5.

L. **maritimum** Kellogg. COAST LILY. St. 30–70cm, occas. 2m. Lvs 12.5cm, linear to oblanceolate, scattered, with a central whorl. Fls 1–12, pendulous, wide bell-shaped, in a rac.; pedicels arching; tep. 4.5cm, apically recurved, deep crimson or orange, spotted maroon inside; pollen brown. Summer. W US. Z4.

L. **martagon** L. MARTAGON; TURK'S-CAP. St. to 2m, purple-green. Lvs to 16cm, oblanceolate, 7–9-veined, in whorls of 8–14. Fls to 50, in rac., pendulous, recurved, turk's-cap, fragrant; pedicels short; tep. 3–4.5×0.6–1cm, dull pink, spotted maroon; pollen yellow; stigma purple. Summer. NW Eur., NW Asia. var. *albiflorum* Vukot. Fls white, pink spotting, rare in cult. Balk. var. *album* Weston. St. green. Fls white, not spotted. var. *cattaniae* Vis. St. and buds hairy. Fls maroon, unspotted. Balk. var. *caucasicum* Misch. St. to 2.5m. Fls lilac-pink. var. *hirsutum* Weston. St. hairy, purple. Lvs downy beneath. Fls purple-pink, spotted. var. *pilosiusculum* Freyn. St. purple, hairy. Lvs narrow, margins hairy. Fls deep red, sparsely spotted; bracts and buds hairy. Mong., Sib. var. *sanguineopurpureum* G. Beck. Fls dark maroon, spotted. Balk. Z4.

L. **martagon** var. *dalmaticum* Elwes = *L. martagon* var. *cattaniae*.

L. **maximowiczii** Reg. = *L. leichtlinii* var. *maximowiczii*.

L. **medeoloides** A. Gray. WHEEL LILY. St. to 75cm. Lvs to 12cm, lanceolate, sessile or short-petioled, 1–2-whorled, a few scattered. Fls 1–10, turk's-cap, unscented, in a rac. or umbel; pedicels erect, arched; tep. lanceolate, 4.5×1cm, recurved, apricot to orange-red, usually with darker spots; anth. purple; pollen orange-red. Summer. China, Jap., S Korea, Russia. Z5.

L. **michauxii** Poir. CAROLINA LILY. St. to 1m, sometimes spotted. Lvs to 11.5cm, fleshy, glaucous, oblanceolate to obovate, in whorls of 3–7. Fls 1–5, pendulous, turk's-cap, scented; tep. to 10cm, lanceolate, recurved, orange-red to pale crimson, yellow toward base, inner surface spotted purple or black; anth. brown; pollen red. Early autumn. SE US. Z6.

L. **michiganense** Farw. St. to 1.5m. Lvs 9–12cm, lanceolate or elliptic-lanceolate, in up to 4 whorls of 4–8. Fls 3–6, occas. to 25, pendulous turk's-cap; pedicels to 24cm; curved; tep. 7×2cm, recurved, orange-red, spotted deep crimson, basal tube green; pollen orange-brown. Summer. Central N Amer. Z4.

L. **monadelphum** Bieb. CAUCASIAN LILY. St. 100–150cm. Lvs 12.5cm, lanceolate or oblanceolate, spirally arranged. Fls 1–5, occas. to 30, fragrant, pendulous, turk's-cap; tep. 6–10×1–2cm, recurved, yellow, interior spotted purple or maroon, exterior flushed purple-brown; pollen orange-yellow. Summer. NE Turk., Cauc. var. *armenum* (Misch.) P.H. Davis & D.M. Henderson. Inner tep. acute, 1–1.6cm wide. NE Turk., Armenia. Z5.

L. **montanum** Nels. = *L. philadelphicum*.

L. **myriophyllum** Franch. = *L. sulphureum*.

L. **nanum** Klotzsch. St. 6–45cm. Lvs to 12cm, linear, scattered. Fls solitary, pendulous, bell-shaped, scented; tep. to 1–4×0.3–1.6cm, pale pink to purple wth fine dark purple or brown mottling; anth. yellow-brown. Summer. Himal., W China. var. *flavidum* (Rendle) Sealy. Fls pale yellow. Z5.

L. **neilgherrense** Wight = *L. wallichianum* var. *neilgherrense*.

L. **nepalense** D. Don. St. to 1m. Lvs to 14cm, oblong-lanceolate. Fls 1–3, slightly pendulous, funnel-shaped, with a musky nocturnal scent; pedicels ascending, to 10cm; tep. to 15cm, recurved, ribbed, green-white to green-yellow, base red-purple; anth. purple; pollen orange-brown. Summer. Bhutan, Nepal, N India. var. *concolor* Cotton. Fls green-yellow, throat not red. Bhutan. Z5.

L. **nevadense** Eastw. = *L. kelleyanum*.

L. **nitidum** Bull = *L. columbianum*.

L. **nobilissimum** (Mak.) Mak. St. purple-green, to 1.7m. Lvs to 12cm, scattered, short-petioled, axils bulbiliferous. Fls 1–3, vertical, 15×13cm, funnel-shaped, fragrant; tep. white; anth. green; pollen yellow-brown. Summer. S Jap. Z6.

L. **occidentale** Purdy. EUREKA LILY. St. 70–200cm, tinged purple. Lvs to 13cm, in whorls, linear-lanceolate to lanceolate. Fls 1–5, occas. 20, in a rac., turk's-cap; pedicels arching, to 15cm; tep. 3.5–6×1.5cm, reflexed, crimson with green-yellow throat, or vermilion with orange throat and brown spots; anth. purple; pollen orange-red. Summer. W US. Z5.

L. **oxypetalum** (Royle) Bak. St. to 25cm. Lvs to 7.5cm, scattered, sessile, elliptic, whorled below infl. Fls 1–2, cup-shaped, pendulous; pedicels v. short; tep. to 5.5cm, ovate, lemon-yellow, often spotted purple; pollen orange. Summer. NW

Himal. var. *insigne* Sealy. Fls purple. Z4.

L. papilliferum Franch. LIKIANG LILY. St. to 90cm, mottled purple. Lvs to 10cm, scattered, linear or linear-oblong. Fls 1–3, in a rac., fragrant, pendulous, turk's-cap; tep. 4×1.5cm, reflexed, deep purple or maroon with lighter central stripe, exterior green; anth. brown; pollen orange-yellow. Late spring–late summer. SW China. Z5.

L. ×pardaboldtii Woodcock & Coutts. (*L. humboldtii* ×*L. pardalinum*.) St. to 150cm. Lvs whorled. Fls pendulous, turk's-cap; tep. orange-red, spotted dark crimson. Summer. Includes orange-fld Bellingham Hybrids.

L. pardalinum Kellogg. LEOPARD LILY; PANTHER LILY. St. 2–3m. Lvs to 18cm, in whorls of to 16, elliptic or oblanceolate. Fls to 10 in a rac., unscented, turk's-cap; pedicels arching; tep. to 9cm, reflexed, lanceolate, acute, orange-red to crimson, spotted deep maroon toward base, some spots outlined yellow; anth. red-brown; pollen orange. Summer. W US. 'Californicum': fls deep orange, spotted maroon, tips scarlet. 'Johnsonii': st. tall; fls finely spotted. var. *angustifolium* Kellogg. Lvs narrow. US (Calif.). var. *giganteum* Woodcock & Coutts. St. to 2.5m. Fls to 30; tep. crimson and yellow, densely spotted. *L. pardalinum* 'Red Sunset' is a synonym of *L. pardalinum* var. *giganteum*. Z5.

L. ×parkmanii T. Moore. (*L. auratum* ×*L. speciosum*.) Lvs broad. Fls fragrant, bowl-shaped, to 20cm wide; tep. recurved. Summer. 'Allegra': fls white with sparse pink papillae. Casablanca': fls large, pure white with papillae at base of tep. 'Empress of China': fls white, spotted pink. 'Empress of India': fls deep red, margin white. 'Empress of Japan': fls white with a golden band, spotted deep maroon. 'Excelsior': fls china-rose, pet. tips and narrow margins white. 'Imperial Crimson': fls deep crimson, margin white. 'Imperial Silver': fls white with small maroon spots. 'Jillian Wallace': fls rose, margin white, interior spotted deep crimson few. 'Pink Glory': fls shell-pink to salmon-pink, golden spots few.

L. parryi S. Wats. LEMON LILY. St. to 2m. Lvs to 15cm, oblanceolate, margins slightly rough. Fls to 15, occas. many more, fragrant, horizontal, funnel-shaped; pedicels long, sharply angled; tep. to 7×10×0.8–1.2cm, oblanceolate, apically recurved, lemon-yellow, base sparsely spotted maroon; anth. orange-brown; pollen red. Fr. to 5cm. Summer. S Calif., S Ariz. Z5.

L. parviflorum Hook. = *L. columbianum*.

L. parvum Kellogg. SIERRA LILY. St. to 2m. Lvs 12.5cm, mostly in whorls, lanceolate or linear. Fls to 30, bell-shaped, borne horizontally in a rac.; tep. to 4cm, oblanceolate, recurved, red, interior spotted deep maroon. Summer. W US. f. *crocatum* Stearn. Fls yellow or orange. Z4.

L. pennsylvanicum Ker-Gawl. = *L. dauricum*.

L. philadelphicum L. WOOD LILY. St. to 1.25m. Lvs 5–10cm, mostly in whorls of 6–8, oblanceolate, margins sometimes rough. Fls 1–5, cup-shaped, erect, in an umbel; tep. to 7.5cm, oblanceolate, orange to vivid orange-red, spotted purple, revolute; pollen deep red. Summer. E N Amer. var. *andinum* (Nutt.) Ker-Gawl. Lvs to 5mm wide, scattered. US and S Canada (Rocky Mts). Z4.

L. philippinense Bak. St. 30–40cm, occas. to 1m, purple below. Lvs to 15cm, scattered, linear. Fls 1–6, scented, to 25cm, funnel-shaped; tep. oblanceolate to spathulate, apices spreading, interior white, exterior flushed green and purple; anth. yellow; pollen yellow. Summer. Philippine Is. Z9.

L. pitkinense Beane & Vollmer. St. to 1.2m. Lvs scattered and in 2–3 whorls, linear or lanceolate. Fls 1–3, occas. to 8 in cult., unscented, in an umbel or rac.; pedicels long, arched; tep. scarlet, yellow toward base, spotted dark purple; anth. purple; pollen brown. Summer. W US. Z5.

L. polyphyllum D. Don. St. 1–2m. Lvs to 12cm, scattered, linear to oblong-lanceolate. Fls 1–6, sometimes to 30, fragrant, turk's-cap, 11cm wide, in an umbel or rac.; tep. recurved, white or pink, sometimes spotted red, base yellow-green; pollen orange. Summer. Afghan., W Himal. Z7.

L. pomponium L. St. to 1m, base spotted purple. Lvs to 12.5cm, crowded, linear, silver-ciliate. Fls to 6, pendulous, turk's-cap, 5cm wide, in a rac., malodorous; pedicels long; tep. recurved, bright scarlet, base spotted black inside, outside purple-green toward base; pollen orange-red. Summer. Eur. (Maritime Alps). Z4.

L. ponticum K. Koch = *L. pyrenaicum* ssp. *ponticum*.

L. ponticum var. *artvinense* P.H. Davis & D.M. Henderson. = *L. pyrenaicum* ssp. *ponticum* var. *artvinense*.

L. primulinum Bak. OCHRE LILY. St. to 2.4m, spotted brown, or wholly brown. Lvs to 15cm, scattered, lanceolate. Fls 2–8, occas. 18, fragrant, pendulous; pedicels to 15cm, decurved; tep. 6–15×1–5cm, oblong-lanceolate, recurved, yellow, sometimes with purple-red markings; pollen brown. Summer–autumn. W China, N Burm., Thail. var. *primulinum*. Tep. entirely yellow, upper half recurved. N Burm. var.

burmanicum (W.W. Sm.) Stearn. St. 120–240cm. Tep. 6.5–15cm, upper third recurved, base purple-red. N Burm., Thail. var. *ochraceum* (Franch.) Stearn. St. to 120cm. Lvs narrower. Tep. 6cm, red-purple toward base, upper two-thirds recurved. Z4.

L. ×princeps Wils. = *L. ×imperiale*.

L. pseudotigrinum Carr. = *L. leichtlinii* var. *maximowiczii*.

L. pulchellum Fisch. = *L. concolor* var. *pulchellum*.

L. pumilum DC. CORAL LILY. St. 15–45(–90)cm. Lvs to 10cm, scattered, sessile, linear. Fls to 7–20, scented, pendulous, turk's-cap, in a rac.; buds woolly; tep. 5×5cm, oblong-lanceolate, reflexed, scarlet, base sometimes dotted black; pollen scarlet. Summer. N China, N Korea, Mong., Sib. 'Golden Gleam': fls apricot yellow. Z5.

L. pyrenaicum Gouan. St. 15–135cm, sometimes spotted purple. Lvs to 12.5cm, linear-lanceolate, margins sometimes silver or ciliate. Fls to 12, pendulous, turk's-cap, 5cm wide, in a rac.; pedicels to 12.5cm; tep. recurved, green-yellow, streaked and spotted dark maroon; pollen orange-red. Summer. Eur. (SE Alps, Pyren., Balk., NE Turk.), Georgia. 'Aureum': fls deep yellow. ssp. *pyrenaicum*. St. 30–135cm, sparsely spotted purple. Lvs 7–15cm. Fls to 12; tep. 4–6.5cm, yellow, interior lined and spotted dark purple. SW Fr., N Spain. ssp.f. *rubrum* Stoker. Fls orange-red. ssp. *carniolicum* (Koch) V. Matthews. St. to 120cm. Lvs 3–11cm, pubesc. beneath. Fls 6–12; tep. 3–7cm, yellow, orange or red, sometimes spotted purple. SE Eur. var. *albanicum* (Griseb.) V. Matthews. St. to 40cm. Lf veins not pubesc. Fls yellow. Albania, NW Greece, SW Balk. var. *jankae* (Kerner) Matthews. St. to 80cm. Lf veins pubesc. beneath. Fls yellow. W Bulg., NW It., C Rom., NW Balk. ssp. *ponticum* (K. Koch) V. Matthews. St. 15–90cm. Lvs 3–8cm, pubesc. beneath. Fls 5–12, tep. 7–10mm wide, deep yellow or deep orange, interior red-brown, spotted purple toward base. NE Turk., Georgia. var. *artvinense* (Misch.) V. Matthews. Fls deep orange; tep. 5–6mm wide. NE Turk., Georgia. Z3.

L. regale Wils. St. 50–200cm, grey-green flushed purple. Lvs 5–13cm, scattered, sessile, linear. Fls 1–25, fragrant, horizontal, funnel-shaped, in an umbel; pedicels 2–12cm; tep. 12–15×2–4cm, recurved, white, interior of basal tube yellow, exterior tinted purple; anth. and pollen golden. Summer. W China. 'Album': fls almost pure white; anth. orange. 'Royal Gold': fls yellow. Z5.

L. rhodopaeum Delip. St. to 80–100cm. Lvs alt., linear, hairy on margins and veins beneath. Fls 1–5, funnel-shaped, pendulous, strongly scented; tep. 8–12cm, lemon yellow, recurved; anth. and pollen scarlet. Summer. Bulg., Greece. Z6.

L. roezlii Reg. non Purdy = *L. pardalinum* var. *angustifolium*.

L. roezlii Purdy non Reg. = *L. vollmeri*.

L. rubellum Bak. St. 30–80cm. Lvs 10cm, scattered, petiolate, ovate-lanceolate to oblong-elliptic. Fls 1–9, v. fragrant, horizontal, funnel-shaped; tep. 7.5cm, oblanceolate to oblong, recurved, rose-pink, base sometimes spotted maroon; pollen orange-yellow. Summer. Jap. Z6.

L. rubescens S. Wats. CHAPARRAL LILY. St. to 3m, flushed purple. Lvs to 12cm, lanceolate to oblanceolate, scattered and in 1–4 whorls. Fls 1–30, occas. 100 or more, fragrant, broadly funnel-shaped, in an umbellate rac.; tep. 3.5–6.5cm, apically recurved, white, finely spotted purple, ageing to purple, pollen yellow. Summer. W US. Z6.

L. ×sargale Crow = *L. ×imperiale*.

L. sargentiae Wils. St. to 1.5m, purple. Lvs 10–20cm, fleshy, scattered, sessile, linear-oblong to oblong-lanceolate, axils bulbiliferous. Fls 2–5, fragrant, funnel-shaped, horizontal or pendulous, in a corymb or umbel; pedicels horizontal or ascending, 3–10cm; tep. 12–15cm, interior white with yellow basal tube, exterior suffused green or purple; anth. purple; pollen brown. Summer. W China. Z6.

L. shastense Eastw. = *L. kelleyanum*.

L. sherriffiae Stearn. St. 35–90cm, flushed purple. Lvs 3–13cm, scattered, linear-lanceolate or linear. Fls 1–2, narrow funnel-shaped; tep. recurved, acute, dark purple outside, inside tessellated golden yellow-green toward apex; pollen yellow. Summer. Bhutan, Nepal. Z6.

L. speciosum Thunb. St. 120–170cm, tinged purple. Lvs to 18cm, scattered, lanceolate, petiolate. Fls to 12, fragrant, pendulous, in a rac.; pedicels to 10cm; tep. to 10×4.5cm, white, base papillate, flushed carmine, spotted pink or crimson, recurved, lanceolate or ovate-lanceolate, margins wavy; pollen dark red. Late summer. China, Jap., Taiwan. 'Grand Commander': fls deep pink tinted lilac, edged white, spotted red. 'Krätzeri': fls white, exterior with central green stripe. 'Melpomene': fls deep carmine, seg. edged white. 'Uchida': fls brilliant crimson, spotted green, tips white. var. *album* Mast. ex Bak. St. purple-brown. Fls white. var. *gloriosoides* Bak. Tep. spotted scarlet. China, Taiwan. var. *magnificum* Wallace. Fls rose, spotted deep crimson, margins paler; pollen red. var. *roseum* Mast. ex

Bak. Fls rose. var. *rubrum* Mast. ex Bak. St. purple-brown. Fls carmine. Z8.

L. **sulphureum** Bak. St. 150–200cm, ribbed, mottled with purple. Lvs to 20cm, scattered, linear-lanceolate, with brown axill. bulbils. Fls 1–15, fragrant, pendulous or horizontal, funnel-shaped; tep. to 25×6cm, apically recurved, interior surface creamy white with yellow basal tube, exterior flushed pink; anth. brown; pollen orange-brown. Late summer. Burm., W China. *L.* sulphureum ×*L.* regale is known as *L.* ×*sulphurgale*. Z6.

L. **superbum** L. TURK'S-CAP LILY. St. 1.5–3m high, green, mottled purple. Lvs 3.5–11cm, lanceolate or elliptic, in whorls of 4–20 and scattered. Fls to 40, pendulous, turk's-cap in a rac.; pedicels ascending, bracteolate; tep. recurved, orange flushed red, spotted maroon toward green base; anth. red, 1.6–2cm; pollen orange-brown. Summer. E US. Z3.

L. **sutchuenense** Franch. = *L.* davidii var. willmottiae.

L. **szovitsianum** Fisch. & Avé-Lall. = *L.* monadelphum.

L. **taliense** Franch. St. to 140cm, dark purple or green, mottled purple. Lvs to 12.7cm, scattered, sessile, linear-lanceolate. Fls to 12, scented, pendulous turk's-cap, in a rac.; pedicels horizontal, tep. to 6×1.5cm, recurved, lanceolate, white, interior spotted purple; anth. mauve-white; pollen yellow. Summer. W China. Z5.

L. **tenuifolium** Schrank = *L.* pumilum.

L. ×**testaceum** Lindl. NANKEEN LILY. (*L.* candidum ×*L.* chalcedonicum.) St. to 100–150cm, purple with grey bloom. Lvs 5–10cm, scattered, linear, ciliate, veins pubesc. beneath. Fls 6–12, scented, pendulous, turk's-cap; tep. to 8cm, yellow to pale orange, interior spotted red; anth. red; pollen orange. Summer. Gdn origin. Z6.

L. **thayerae** Wils. = *L.* davidii.

L. **thunbergianum** Schult. & Schult. f. = *L.* maculatum.

L. **tigrinum** Ker-Gawl. = *L.* lancifolium.

L. **tigrinum** var. *fortunei* Standish = *L.* lancifolium var. fortunei.

L. **tigrinum** var. *flaviflorum* Mak. = *L.* lancifolium var. flaviflorum.

L. **tigrinum** var. *splendens* Van Houtte = *L.* lancifolium var. splendens.

L. **tsingtauense** Gilg. St. to 120cm. Lvs to 15×4cm, glab., oblanceolate, petiolate, often in 2 whorls. Fls 2–7, in a rac., unscented, erect, bowl-shaped; pedicels to 8.5cm, tep. to 5×1.5cm, orange or vermilion with purple spotting; anth. and pollen orange. Summer. NE China, Korea. var. *carneum* Nak. Fls red, unspotted. var. *flavum* Wils. Fls yellow, spotted red. Z6.

L. **umbellatum** hort. = *L.* ×hollandicum.

L. **vollmeri** Eastw. St. to 1m. Lvs to 15cm, scattered or in 1–2 whorls, elliptic-linear. Fls 1–10, turk's-cap, in a rac.; pedicels long, arching; tep. to 8×1cm, reflexed, red-orange with dark margins, dark purple or black spots ringed with yellow on inner surface; pollen orange-red. Summer. W US. Z5.

L. **wallichianum** Schult. & Schult. f. St. to 2m, tinged purple. Lvs 25cm, scattered, linear or lanceolate. Fls 1–4, scented, horizontal, funnel-shaped, 20cm wide with basal tube to 10cm; tep. 15–30cm, apically recurved, interior creamy white, exterior tinged green; pollen yellow. Summer–autumn. Himal. var. *neilgherrense* (Wight) Hara. St. to 90cm. Lvs to 12×3cm, lanceolate. S India. Z7.

L. **wardii** F. Stern. St. to 1.5m, flushed purple. Lvs 3–8cm, scattered, sessile, glab., oblong to linear-lanceolate. Fls to 35, fragrant, pendulous, turk's-cap, in a rac.; pedicels stiff, horizontal; tep. 5–6.5×1.5cm, pink with purple basal median line and spotting, recurved; anth. mauve; pollen yellow. Summer. W China. Z5.

L. **washingtonianum** Kellogg. St. 2.5cm. Lvs to 15cm, in whorls, oblanceolate, margins wavy. Fls to 20, scented, bowl-shaped, horizontal, in a rac.; pedicels erect; tep. 8×2.5cm, oblanceolate, white, spotted purple at base, apex acute, recurved; pollen yellow. Summer. W US. var. *purpurascens* Stearn. Fls opening white, becoming pink then purple. Z4.

L. **washingtonianum** var. *purpureum* hort. = *L.* rubescens.

L. **washingtonianum** var. *rubescens* S. Wats. = *L.* rubescens.

L. **wigginsii** Beane & Vollmer. St. to 90cm. Lvs to 22cm, linear-lanceolate. Fls solitary or in a rac., pendulous, turk's-cap; pedicels arching; tep. to 7cm, reflexed, yellow with variable purple spotting; pollen yellow. Summer. W US. Z4.

L. **wilsonii** Leichtlin. St. to 1m. Lvs 10cm, lanceolate. Fls cup-shaped, erect, 12.5cm wide, tep. recurved, to 10cm, orange-red with basal central yellow stripe, dark spotting. Summer. Jap. Z5.

L. **Hybrids and cvs** (classified in accordance with the *International Lily Register*).

Division 1: Hybrids derived from such spp. or hybrid groups as *Ll. cernuum*, *davidii*, *lancifolium*, *leichtlinii*, *maculatum*, ×*hollandicum*, *amabile*, *pumilum*, *concolor* and *bulbiferum*.

1(a): Early-flowering with upright fls, single or an umbel. 'Apeldoorn': 80cm; fls bright orange-red. 'Connecticut King': to 1m; fls golden-yellow. 'Connecticut Star': fls yellow, with yellow-orange throat, sparsely flecked purple. 'Cote d'Azur': fls deep pink with paler centre. 'Enchantment': 75cm; fls bright nasturtium red, to 15 per st. 'Joan Evans': fls orange, with basal spots inside pet. 'Marilyn Monroe': to 1.2m; fls yellow. 'Ming Yellow': to 1.2m; lvs glossy; fls broad, somewhat recurved, bright golden yellow. 'Mont Blanc': fls broad, open, cream-white, spotted brown. 'Peach Blush': to 90cm; fls rose-pink, darker at the base, sparsely spotted maroon. 'Sterling Star': to 1.2m; fls white with a cream tinge and brown spots.

1(b): Fls outward-facing. 'Brandywine': to 1m; fls deep orange with red spots. 'Corsage': to 1.2m; fls pale pink with an ivory-white centre, spotted burgundy, tinged yellow and cream outside. 'Fireking': to 90cm; fls bright orange-red with purple spots. 'Prosperity': fls lemon-yellow. 'Tamara': fls red with yellow-orange centre and grey-purple flecks.

1(c): Fls pendent. 'Black Butterfly': 90cm; fls deep burgundy-red. 'Citronella': to 1.5m; lemon-yellow, with small, feint, black spots, to 30 per st. 'Connecticut Yankee': st. 1.2m; fls vivid orange-red, unspotted. Fiesta hybrids: fls golden-yellow to bright red. Harlequin Hybrids: to 1.5m; fls salmon-pink, with shades of cream, lilac, rose, and purple. 'Lady Bowes Lyon': fls rich red with black spots. Tiger Hybrids: fls dark red.

Division 2: Hybrids of Martagon type of which one parent has been a form of *L.* martagon or *L.* hansonii. Backhouse hybrids: fls ivory, yellow, cream, pink, and burgundy, occas. flecked pink. 'Marham': to 1.3m, fls orange with red-tinged spots, or bright yellow with dark purple-brown spots.

Division 3: Hybrids derived from *L.* candidum, *L.* chalcedonicum, and other related European spp. (but excluding *L.* martagon). 'Apollo': to 75cm; fls dwarf, pure white. 'Ares': fls bright orange-red. 'Artemis': fls pale pink to rich yellow-orange. 'Prelude': fls orange-red, darker red at tips.

Division 4: Hybrids of American spp. Bellingham Hybrids: fls bicoloured orange-yellow and red, with deep brown spots. 'Bellmaid Hybrids': fls golden-yellow, tinged orange, eventually turning red, with median spots.

Division 5: Hybrids derived from *L.* longiflorum and *L.* formosanum. 'Formobel': fls v. large, white, flushed green on the throat. 'Formolongi': fls snow-white.

Division 6: Hybrid Trumpet Lilies and Aurelian Hybrids derived from Asiatic spp. including *L.* henryi, but excluding those derived from *Ll.* auratum, speciosum, japonicum, and rubellum.

6(a): Fls trumpet-shaped. 'African Queen': 1.5m; fls large, rich apricot orange. 'Black Dragon': fls white inside, v. dark rich purple-red outside. 'Black Magic': fls snow-white inside, purple-black outside. 'Golden Clarion': fls golden-yellow. 'Golden Splendour': fls deep golden-yellow; pet. with one dark burgundy stripe outside. 'Green Dragon': fls snow-white inside with yellow flush at base, striped brown and green outside. 'Limelight': fls lime-yellow. Olympic Hybrids: fl. white outside, shade cream or fuchsia-pink inside, occas. tinged green. 'Pink Perfection': 1.5m; fls v. large, deep purple-pink, fragrant.

6(b): Fls bowl-shaped. 'First Love': fls golden-yellow, edged pink, with pale-green throat. 'Heart's Desire': fls flushed yellow through cream to white, occas. with orange throat. 'New Era': fls large, white, tinged green.

6(c): Fls flat, or only tep. tips recurved. 'Christmas Day': fls cream, with bright orange and clear green centre. 'Golden Showers': fls golden-yellow inside, brown outside. 'Summer Song': fls yellow.

6(d): Fls with tep. distinctly recurved 'Bright Star': fls ivory-white, with light orange star in centre. 'Golden Sunburst': fls vivid golden-yellow, veined green outside. 'Magic Fire': fls deep apricot. 'Mimosa Star': fls yellow, fragrant. 'T.A. Havemeyer': fls deep orange with dark ivory tips and green throat. 'White Henryi': fls white, flushed deep orange on throat.

Division 7: Hybrids of Far Eastern spp., such as *Ll.* auratum, speciosum, japonicum and rubellum, including any of their hybrids with *L.* henryi. 'Dominique': fls red-purple, with red spotted throat and somewhat crinkled pet. 'Empress of Mars': fls blood-red, tipped white. 'Omega': fls white, with a medium band of salmon-pink on each pet. 'Suzanne Sumerville': fls white, blotched pale pink and lavender.

7(a): Fls trumpet-shaped.

7(b): Fls bowl-shaped. 'Bonfire': fls carmine inside with a silver edge, silver-white outside with a v. pale pink flush. 'Casablanca': fls v. large, pure white, v. fragrant. 'Empress of China': fls pure white, with heavy dark red or burgundy spots inside. 'Empress of India': fls carmine, edged white. 'Empress of Japan': fls pure white, banded gold, spotted deep burgundy. 'Imperial Jewel': fls white with red throat.

7(c): Fls flat. 'Imperial Red Band': fls v. large, with a deep red stripe on each pet. 'Imperial Pink': fls large, pink. 'Imperial

Salmon': fls large, salmon-pink. 'Imperial Silver'; fls large, pure white, spotted burgundy. 'Spectre': fls pale to deep pink. 'Stargazer': fls v. wide, rich carmine, spotted crimson. 'Troubador': fls v. large, heavily spotted, rich carmine at centre, edged pink and white.

7(d): Fls with tep. recurved. 'Jamboree': fls carmine with darker spots, edged white. 'Journey's End': fls v. large, carmine, tipped and margined white, spotted red. 'Pink Solace': fls off-white, turning red, with yellow-green throat. Rangotito hybrids: fls white through pink to deep rich red, occas. with burgundy spots or white margin.
→Nomocharis.

Lilly Pilly Acmena smithii.
Lily Lilium.
Lily Leek Allium moly.
Lily of the Incas Alstroemeria.
Lily of the Nile Agapanthus africanus.
Lily of the Palace Hippeastrum aulicum.
Lily-of-the-valley Convallaria.
Lily-of-the-valley Bush Pieris japonica.
Lily-of-the-valley Orchid Osmoglossum pulchellum.
Lily-of-the-valley Shrub Pieris japonica.
Lily-of-the-valley Tree Clethra arborea.
Lily-pad Begonia Begonia nelumbiifolia, B. peltata.
Lily Thorn Catesbaea spinosa.
Lily Tree Magnolia denudata.
Lily Turf Liriope.
Lima Bean Phaseolus lunatus.
Limber Pine Pinus flexilis.
Lime Citrus aurantifolia; Tilia
Limeberry Triphasia (T. trifolia).
Lime Loosejacket Citrus jambhiri.
Limequat ×Citrofortunella floridana; ×C. swinglei.
Limestone Buckler Fern Dryopteris submontana.
Limestone Fern Gymnocarpium robertianum.
Limestone Saxifrage Saxifraga callosa.
Lime Wood Backhousia hughesii.

LIMNANTHACEAE R. Br. 2/8. Limnanthes.

Limnanthemum S.G. Gmel.
L. aquaticum (Walter) Britt. = Nymphoides aquatica.
L. indicum Thwaites = Nymphoides indica.
L. nymphoides (L.) Hoffsgg. & Link = Nymphoides peltata.
L. peltatum S.G. Gmel. = Nymphoides peltata.

Limnanthes R. Br. MEADOW FOAM. Limnanthaceae. 7 ann. herbs. Lvs pinnately divided. Sep. and pet. 5, pet. obovate, ± emarginate with a U-shaped band of hairs on the claw. W US. Z8.
L. douglasii R. Br. POACHED EGG FLOWER. To 30cm. Lvs 2-pinnatifid, ± succulent, lfts dentate. Fls fragrant, to 2.5cm diam., pet. yellow with white tips, or entirely white. Calif., S Oreg. var. sulphurea C. Mason. Pet. yellow. Calif.

Limnobium Rich. Hydrocharitaceae. 2 perenn. aquatic herbs, forming floating mats. Lvs rosulate on runner-like st., stalked, sometimes aerenchymatous. Fls unisexual, cymose, 3-merous; ♂ sessile or stalked, held above water, 1–25, sta. 2–5; ♀ sessile or subsessile, pet. white, sometimes 0, staminodes 2–6. Americas.
L. laevigatum (Humb. & Bonpl. ex Willd.) Heine. Lvs 2-5×1–4cm, spathulate, elliptic, rarely obovate, apex rounded, rarely acute. Sta. in 2–3 whorls; ♀ pet. poorly developed or 0. C & S Amer. Z10.
L. spongia (Bosc) Steud. AMERICAN FROGBIT. Lvs 1–10×1–8cm, ovate to depressed-ovate or cordate, acute. Sta. in 5–6 whorls; ♀ pet. well developed. US. Z5.
→Hydrocharis and Hydromystria.

Limnocharis Humb. & Bonpl. Limnocharitaceae. 2 ann. or perenn. aquatic herbs without stolons. Lvs in rosettes, stalked, lanceolate to ovate. Peduncle erect, triangular; fls yellow, 3-merous, umbellate, hermaphrodite; pet. fugacious; sta. numerous surrounded by staminodes. SE Asia, Malesia.
L. commersonii Spreng. = Hydrocleys nymphoides.
L. emarginata Humb. & Bonpl. = L. flava.
L. flava (L.) Buchenau. Perenn. Lvs 20cm, ovate, base cordate; petiole long. Fls 2–12 per umbel, 2.5cm diam. Summer. W Indies, trop. Amer. 'Minor': dwarf. Z10.
L. humboldtii Rich. = Hydrocleys nymphoides.
L. nymphoides Michx. = Hydrocleys nymphoides.
L. plumieri Rich. = L. flava.

LIMNOCHARITACEAE Tacht. ex Cronq. 3/12. Hydrocleys, Limnocharis.

Limnophila R. Br. Scrophulariaceae. 36 ann. or perenn. aquatic or marsh herbs. St. creeping, or erect, rooting; aerial lvs entire to serrate; aquatic lvs pinnatifid to pinnate. Fls in spikes or rac. or solitary; cal. 5-lobed; cor. c1cm, white, pink, mauve or yellow, campanulate, bilabiate, 5-lobed. Summer. OW Trop. Z9.
L. heterophylla Benth. Perenn. to 60cm. Aquatic lvs whorled, 6–12, filiform. Aerial lvs whorled, crenate to entire. Summer. Indon., Malaya.
L. indica (L.) Druce. Aromatic perenn. to 90cm. Upper lvs whorled, dissected, gland.; aquatic lvs finely dissected, to 3cm, whorled. Summer. Trop. Afr., Asia, N Aus.
L. sessiliflora Bl. Perenn. to 20cm. Aquatic lvs whorled, pinnatisect; aerial lvs lanceolate to pinnatifid, entire or dentate. Summer. Indon., Jap.

Limonetto Aloysia triphylla.

Limonia L. Rutaceae. 1 spiny tree to 9m, ± everg. in warm climates. Lvs 7.5–10cm, imparipinnate, ultimately glab., with aniseed scent; lfts 2.5–4cm, 2–3 pairs, ovate to obovate, entire to crenulate; petiole winged. Fls numerous in small axill. pan.; cal. 5-dentate, v. small; pet. usually 5, ovate, white to green stained purple; sta. 10–12, anth. dark red. Fr. 5–6cm, globose, exterior woody, rough, grey; pulp gum-like, bitter-sweet. India, Sri Lanka. Z10.
L. acidissima L. WOOD APPLE; INDIAN WOOD APPLE; KAITHA; ELEPHANT APPLE.
→Feronia.

Limoniastrum Heist. ex Fabr. Plumbaginaceae. 10 small, everg. shrubs and subshrubs. Lvs in rosettes, simple, entire or pinnatifid. Fls in spicate corymbose pan.; cal. tubular, often coloured; cor. tubular, lobes 5, equalling tube; sta. 5. Medit.
L. monopetalum (L.) Boiss. To 1.2m, much-branched. Lvs to 5×2cm, oblanceolate to spathulate, somewhat fleshy, glaucous. Pan. large, loose spikes 5–10cm; fls 1–2cm diam., pink to purple. S Port. and N Medit. Z8.
→Statice.

Limonium Mill. SEA LAVENDER; MARSH ROSEMARY; STATICE. Plumbaginaceae. 150 perenn. herbs or shrubs, rarely annuals. Lvs simple, entire or pinnatifid, in basal rosettes or clustered at axils. Infl. a corymbose pan. of term. spikelets; cal. tubular; cor. 5-lobed, slightly exceeding cal., connate only at base or short-tubular; sta. 5. Cosmop.
L. angustatum (A. Gray) Small. Perenn. herb, slender. Lvs 5–9×0.5–2cm, linear to lanceolate. Flowering st. to 30cm, erect; pan. 12–24cm diam., loose; spikelets 1-fld. S & E US. Z6.
L. arborescens (Brouss.) Kuntze. Shrub, 0.5–2m. Lvs 15–30×5–10cm, oblong-obovate, mucronate, coriaceous. Pan. large, br. winged; spikelets 2-fld; cal. blue; cor. about 6mm wide, white. Late spring. Tenerife. Z9.
L. aureum (L.) Hill ex Kuntze. Perenn. herb to 30cm. Lvs 1–5×0.2–1cm, oblong-spathulate to lanceolate, grey-green. Pan. to 20cm, verruculose; spikelets 3–5-fld; cal. about 5mm, partially pubesc., limb bright yellow; cor. orange-yellow. Sib., Mong. 'Sahin's Gold': to 75cm; fls yellow, profuse. 'Supernova': to 1m; fls vibrant yellow, papery. Z3.
L. auriculaeursifolium (Pourr.) Druce. To 40cm, glab. Lvs 2.5–10×1–2cm, spathulate-oblanceolate, mucronate, glab. Infl. pyramidal; spikelets 2–3-fld; cal. to 5.5mm; cor. to 8mm, blue-violet. Fr., Iberian peninsula, Balearic Is. Z8.
L. australe (Spreng.) Kuntze. Perenn. herb, about 30cm, glab. Lvs 3–7cm, oblong-obovate to oblong-spathulate, entire. Pan. to 50cm, forking, corymbose; spikelets 4–5-fld; cal. white to pale pink; cor. yellow. Spring. Aus. Z9.
L. bellidifolium (Gouan) Dumort. Perenn. herb, 10–30cm, woody at base. Lvs 2–5×1.5–2cm, obtuse to broadly rounded or spathulate. Flowering st. branching from base, tuberculate; spikelets 1–4-fld; cal. pilose; cor. about 5mm, blue-violet. Medit. and Black Sea to E Engl. 'Filigree': fls purple-blue. 'Spangle': to 1m; fls small, pale blue, in loose sprays. Z8.
L. binervosum (G.E. Sm.) Salmon. Perenn. herb to 30cm; rhiz. woody. Lvs c5×1cm, in many rosettes, obovate to spathulate. Infl. to 30cm, pyramidal; spikelets 1–3-fld; cal. about 5mm, pubesc. beneath; cor. about 8mm, blue-violet. W Eur.
L. bourgaei (Webb) Kuntze. Perenn. herb to 40cm, woody-based. Lvs broadly ovate-rhombic, often sinuately lobed at base. Flowering st. and br. pubesc.; cal. deep violet, funnel-shaped; cor. white. Lanzarote. Z7.
L. brasiliense (A. Gray non Boiss.) Small = L. carolinianum.

L. brassicifolium (Webb & Berth.) Kuntze. Perenn. herb 20–40cm; rhiz. woody, thick; st. winged. Lvs 10–30cm, broadly ovate, lobed. Infl. paniculate; spikelets single-fld; cal. purple; cor. white. Canary Is., nat. Iberia. Z9.

L. caesium (Girard) Kuntze. Perenn. herb branching from base. Lvs to 3cm, obovate, spathulate. Pan. to 60cm with white sterile br.; spikelets single-fld; cal. to 5mm; cor. c8mm, deep pink. Spain.

L. californicum A. Gray = *L. commune* var. *californicum*.

L. callicomum (C.A. Mey.) Kuntze = *Goniolimon callicomum*.

L. carolinianum (Walter) Britt. Perenn. herb. Lvs to 15cm, spathulate to elliptic or obovate-elliptic. Pan. to 60cm; cal. to 6mm; cor. lilac. E US. Z5.

L. caspium (Willd.) Gams. = *L. bellidifolium*.

L. commune var. ***californicum*** (A. Gray) Greene. To 45cm. Lvs to 23cm, obovate to oblong spathulate, obtuse or retuse. Cor. violet-purple. Calif. Z8.

L. confusum (Gren. & Godron) Fourr. Perenn. glab. herb 10–50cm. Lvs rosulate, obovate-spathulate, mucronate. Spikelets 2–3-fld, remote; cal. tube pilose; cor. violet. S Fr., Iberia, Sardinia. Z8.

L. cordatum (L.) Mill. Herb to 30cm, grey-pubesc. Lvs 1.5–3×0.2–0.6cm, linear-spathulate. Pan. br. corymbose, some sterile spikelets 1-fld; cal. c5mm; cor. violet. It., SE Fr. Z8.

L. cosyrense (Guss.) Kuntze. Perenn. glab., woody-based herb 15–50cm. Lvs 2–2.5×2.5–3cm, linear-spathulate, in basal rosettes. Pan. 15cm, slender, dichotomously branching; spikelets 1-fld; cal. c4mm; cor. c8mm. SE Eur., Malta. Z9.

L. delicatulum (Girard) Kuntze. Perenn. herb, 40–70cm, glab. Lvs 3.5–5×2–3cm, oblanceolate to spathulate. Infl. a corymb, dichotomously branching; spikelets 2–3 fld; cal. about 4mm, tubular; cor. about 6mm, pale pink. Medit. Spain, Balearic Is. ssp. ***tournefortii*** Pign. Lvs spathulate, rounded, truncate or emarginate; spikelets 2–3-fld. E Spain, Balearic Is. ssp. ***valentinum*** Pign. Lvs oblanceolate-spathulate. Spikelets 2-fld. E Spain. Z8.

L. dregeanum (Presl) Kuntze. Perenn. herb, tufted, becoming woody. Lvs to 4cm, linear-spathulate, scabrid, pitted. Spikelets 3–9-fld; cal. 3mm, tubular, partially pubesc.; cor. pink. S Afr. (Natal). Z9.

L. dubium Gamaun. = *L. tomentellum*.

L. echioides (L.) Mill. Ann. herb, 15–25cm. Lvs 2–3.5×0.5–1.2cm, obovate or spathulate. Infl. branched at base; spikelets 1- or 2-fld; cal. c5mm, hirtellous; cor. pink or pale violet. Medit. Z8.

L. elatum Fisch. & Spreng. = *Goniolimon elatum*.

L. emarginatum (Willd.) Kuntze. To 50cm, glab. Lvs 4–6×1–1.5cm, linear, somewhat spathulate, truncate or emarginate. Infl. cylindric; spikelets 1–2-fld; cal. c7mm; cor. to 12mm, purple. S Spain. Z8.

L. eximium (Schrenk) Kuntze = *Goniolimon eximium*.

L. ferulaceum (L.) Kuntze. St. to 40cm, flexuous. Lvs ovate, short-lived. Spikes borne towards apex of flowering st.; spikelets 1-fld; cal. c3mm; cor. c6mm, pink. Iberia to C Medit. Z7.

L. fruticans (Webb) Kuntze. Shrub; st. short glab. Lvs 4–5cm, ovate, mucronate. Pan. to 15cm, br. downy, winged; cal. bright blue, glab.; cor. yellow. Tenerife. Z9.

L. globulariifolium (Desf.) Kuntze. = *L. ramosissimum*.

L. globulariifolium ssp. *provinciale* Pign. = *L. ramosissimum* ssp. *provinciale*.

L. globulariifolium ssp. *tommasinii* Pign. = *L. ramosissimum* ssp. *tommasinii*.

L. gmelinii (Willd.) Kuntze. Perenn. herb to 60cm. Lvs 10–30×2–8cm, broadly elliptic to obovate-ovate, in basal rosettes. Flowering st. to 70cm, paniculate; spikelets 2–3-fld; cal. 3–5mm, pubesc.; cor. blue. E Eur., Sib. Z4.

L. gmelinii var. *tomentellum* ((Boiss.) Trautv. = *L. tomentellum*.

L. gougetianum (Girard) Kuntze. Perenn. to 20cm. Lvs 1.5–3×0.3–1cm, in basal rosettes, obovate to spathulate. Pan. to 25cm; spikelets 2–3-fld; cal. tubular, red below, white above; cor. lavender. Alg., Balearic Is. Z9.

L. halfordii hort. = *L. macrophyllum*.

L. hirsuticalyx Pign. = *L. gmelinii*.

L. imbricatum (Webb ex Girard) Hubb. Perenn. herb. Lvs caespitose, pinnatifid, lobes broadly lanceolate to ovate, pubesc. Flowering st. and br. winged; cal. mauve, funnelform; cor. white. Tenerife. Z9.

L. insigne (Coss.) Kuntze. Perenn. herb to 60cm. Lvs 4–5×1–1.5cm, obovate, emarginate. Pan. dichotomously branching; sterile br. many; spikelets usually 1–2-fld; cor. to 1.5cm, dark rose. SE Spain. ssp. ***carthaginense*** Pign. Pan. br. white. Spikelets usually 1-fld. Z8.

L. japonicum (Sieb. & Zucc.) Kuntze = *L. tetragonum*.

L. latifolium (Sm.) Kuntze. Stellate-pubesc., woody-based perenn. to 80cm. Lvs 20–60×8–15cm, basal, spathulate to elliptic, sparsely pubesc. Pan. to 60cm, subspherical; spikelets 1–2

fld; cal. about 3mm, white; cor. about 6mm, pale violet. SE & C Eur. 'Violetta': fls violet blue. Z5.

L. lychnidifolium (Girard) Kuntze = *L. auriculaeursifolium*.

L. macrophyllum (Brouss.) Kuntze. Subshrub to 70cm. Lvs obovate-spathulate, obtuse, sinuate. Pan. much-branched, to 70cm; upper br. 3-winged; spikelets 2-fld; cal. blue, minutely pubesc.; cor. yellow to yellow-white. Late spring. Tenerife. Z9.

L. macropterum (Webb & Berth.) Kuntze. Perenn. herb. Lvs to 35×12cm, obovate, lobed. Pan. to 30cm, branching towards apex; spikelets 2–4 fld; cal. 1cm diam.; cor. deep blue to purple. Canary Is. Z9.

L. minutum (L.) Fourr. 1–15cm, br. short, woody. Lvs c1×0.3cm, in tight cushion-like rosettes, spathulate, revolute. Infl. 2–12cm; spikelets 1–4-fld; cal. c0.5cm; cor. purple. SE Fr. Z8.

L. mouretii (Pitard) Maire. Woody-based perenn. Lvs 7–15×1–3cm, basal, oblanceolate, mucronate, glab., lobes irregular. Flg st. to 80cm, thinly branched, br. slightly winged; cal. lobes purple-tinged; cor. bright white. Summer–early autumn. Moroc. Z9.

L. nashii Small. Perenn. Lvs 4–10cm, basal, oblong or elliptic to narrowly obovate, apex rounded or notched. Pan. to 30cm, spreading; cal. 6–7mm, sparsely pubesc. at base; cor. deep blue. SE US. Z6.

L. oleifolium Pign. non Mill. = *L. virgatum*.

L. ornatum (Ball) Kuntze. To 1m; st. numerous. Lvs radical, lanceolate-spathulate, glab. Pan. lax, with pink-red bracts; cal. 4–5mm; cor. about 1cm, rose-purple. Moroc. Z9.

L. otolepis (Schrenk) Kuntze. Perenn., 40–80cm. Basal lvs to 7cm, obovate-spathulate; st. lvs 1–3cm, rounded-reniform to suborbicular. Pan. dense; spikelets 1–2-fld; cal. about 3mm, white; sparsely pubesc.; cor. blue. Summer. Asia Minor, C Asia. Z6.

L. pectinatum (Ait.) Kuntze. Subshrub, glab. Lvs to 4×1cm, obovate-spathulate, emarginate, in basal rosettes. Flowering st. to 70cm; br. winged; spikelets 3-fld; cal. lavender or pale violet; cor. pale pink to rose. Late summer. Canaries. Z9.

L. peregrinum (Bergius) R.A. Dyer. Shrub to 1m. Lvs to 10cm, obovate, scabrid-glandular. Flowering st. scabrid, dichotomously branching; spikelets 1-fld; cal. to 2cm, bright pink; cor. bright pink. S Afr. Z9.

L. perezii (Stapf) Hubb. Subshrub to 70cm; st. woody. Lvs 12–15×6–10cm, triangular-ovate, glab., truncate. Pan. pubesc.; cal. purple to blue, downy; cor. yellow. Canary Is. Z9.

L. perfoliatum (Karel.) Kuntze = *L. reniforme*.

L. preauxii (Webb) Kuntze. To 70cm, somewhat woody. Lvs to 20cm, orbicular-triangular. Pan. br. flattened; cal. lavender; cor. white. Canary Is. Z9.

L. ×profusum Hubb. (*L. macrophyllum* × *L. puberulum*.) Subshrub, 30–70cm. Lvs 15–20×4–5cm, oblong-obovate, dark, ciliate, sparsely downy. Pan. br. winged; cal. blue-purple; cor. white, shorter than cal. Autumn. Gdn origin. Z9.

L. puberulum (Webb) Kuntze. Small shrub or subshrub, puberulous to white-pilose. Lvs to 3cm, basal, obovate, stellate-pubesc. Pan. to 25cm, spikelets 2-fld; cal. purple; cor. white. Canary Is. Z9.

L. ramosissimum (Poir.) Maire. To 50cm. Lvs 3–10×1–2cm, oblanceolate-spathulate. Infl. 20–50cm; spikelets 2–5-fld; cal. c5mm; cor. c6mm, pale pink or violet. Medit. ssp. ***confusum*** (Gren. & Godron) Pign. Lvs to 5×1cm, oblanceolate-spathulate, rounded. W Medit. ssp. ***doerfleri*** (Hal.) Pign. Lvs to 5×1.5cm, obovate-spathulate to spathulate. Cyclades. ssp. ***provinciale*** (Pign.) Pign. Lvs to 10×2cm, obtuse or acute spikes to 4cm. SE Fr., Sardinia and Corsica. ssp. ***siculum*** Pign. Lvs to 6×1.5cm. Infl. with numerous sterile br. at base. Sicily. ssp. ***tommasinii*** (Pign.) Pign. Lvs to 4×1.2cm. Sterile br. few. NE It. Z8.

L. reniforme (Girard) Lincz. Perenn., 60–80cm occas. taller. Basal lvs 3–8×1–2cm, obovate-spathulate, glaucescent; st. lvs 4–6×3cm, ovate or oblong-elliptic. Flowering st. few, erect, paniculate; cal. 3–4mm, limb white, lobes tinged red; cor. red-violet. Late spring–early autumn. Iran. Z8.

L. reticulatum Mill. = *L. bellidifolium*.

L. roseum (Sm.) Kuntze = *L. peregrinum*.

L. sieberi (Boiss.) Kuntze. Suffruticose perenn. Lvs 2–5×0.5–1cm, obovate-spathulate. Flowering st. branching from base; sterile br. many; spikelets 1–2-fld; cal. to 7mm, adpressed-pilose; cor. pale violet. S Greece, N Syr. Z8.

L. sinense (Girard) Kuntze = *L. tetragonum*.

L. sinuatum (L.) Mill. Perenn. to 40cm, densely pubesc. Lvs 3–10×1–3cm, oblong-lanceolate, pinnatifid or pinnatisect, sinuate. Flowering st. winged; infl. dense; spikelets compact; cal. pubesc., white or pale violet; cor. papery, white or pink, becoming purple. Medit. *L. bonduellii* (Lestib.) Kuntze is probably conspecific with this plant. Art Shades: fls in range of pastel colours including cream, rose, lilac and gold, uniform flowering time. California series: fls in range of colours including 'American Beauty' (deep rose), 'Apricot' (salmon), 'Blue Bonnet' (sky blue), 'Gold Coast' (fls deep yellow), 'Iceberg' (white), 'Midnight' (deep violet), 'Pacific Twilight' (clear pink), 'Purple Monarch' (deep purple) and 'Roselight' (carmine rose). Fortress Hybrids: fls white, yellow, apricot, rose, dark blue, sky blue, purple. Soirée Hybrids: to 80cm, st. strong; fls richly coloured, from yellow, through to deep blue. Sunburst Mixed: fls large, uniform colour, in white, yellow, rose, light blue, dark blue. Z9.

L. spathulatum (Desf.) Kuntze. Perenn. Lvs to 4cm, basal, spathulate, glaucous. Pan. to 25cm, dichotomously branching; cal. to 1cm, white; cor. purple. Medit. Z7.

L. speciosum (L.) Kuntze = Goniolimon incanum.

L. spicatum (Willd.) Kuntze = Psylliostachys spicata.

L. suworowii (Reg.) Kuntze = Psylliostachys suworowii.

L. tataricum (L.) Mill. = Goniolimon tataricum.

L. tetragonum (Thunb.) Bullock. Bienn., glab. Lvs 8–15×1.5–3cm, oblong-spathulate, radical, muricate. Flowering st. 20–50cm, few, erect; cal. 5–6mm, pink, white-pilose; cor. yellow. Autumn. Jap., Korea, China, New Caledonia. Z6.

L. tetragonum hort. = L. dregeanum.

L. thouinii (Viv.) Kuntze. Ann. to 20cm, glaucous. Lvs 3–6×1–2cm, basal, oblong-lanceolate, coarsely pinnatifid. Pan. compact, br. winged; spikelets 23-fld; cal. to 1cm, exceeding cor., pale blue or white; cor. yellow. Medit.

L. tomentellum (Boiss.) Kuntze. Perenn., 30–80cm. Lvs 5–15×3–7cm, radical, ovate to broadly elliptic, round-tipped or mucronate, glaucescent, pubesc. Flowering st. few, terete, forming a pan.; spikelets 2–3-fld; cal. 3–5mm, pale violet; cor. blue-violet. Summer. Russia, Crimea. Z6.

L. transwallianum (Pugsley) Pugsley = L. binervosum.

L. virgatum (Willd.) Fourr. Subshrub. Lvs to 3cm, oblong to lanceolate-spathulate, rounded or acute. Pan. 30cm, dichotomously branching; sterile br. many; spikelets 3–4-fld; cal. tubular, pilose; cor. pale violet. Medit. & W Eur. Z7.

L. vulgare Mill. Perenn., 15–70cm, glab. Lvs 10–15×1–4cm, in basal rosettes, oblong-lanceolate, mucronate. Flowering st. to 30cm, branching above; sterile br. few or 0; spikelets usually 2-fld; cal. 3–6mm, pale purple, pubesc.; cor. 6–8mm deep blue. NW Eur. to N Afr. ssp. **serotinum** (Rchb.) Gams. To 70cm. Flowering st. often branching below middle; cal. 3–5mm. S Eur., N Afr. Z6.

→Statice.

LINACEAE Gray. 15/300. *Linum, Reinwardtia.*

Linanthus Benth. Polemoniaceae. 35 ann. or perenn. herbs. Lvs simple or subpinnately or palmately lobed. Fls long-stalked in lax cymes or dense heads; cal. deeply lobed; cor. hypocrateriform or campanulate to funnelform; sta. 5, stigma 3–4-lobed. W US, Chile. Z7.

L. androsaceus (Benth.) Greene. Pubesc. ann., 5–30cm, usually erect. Lvs 1–3cm, lobes 5–9, ciliate, oblanceolate or narrowly so. Infl. term., a dense, head; cor. 0.9–2.4(–3.6)cm, hypocrateriform, white or cream to pink or lilac, usually yellow at apex, lobes 5–8mm, obovate; sta. subexserted. Spring–early summer. S Calif. ssp. **luteus** (Benth.) H.L. Mason. Cor. yellow to lilac. Spring. ssp. **micranthus** (Steud.) H.L. Mason. Cor. lilac or pink to yellow, style long-exserted. Spring.

L. aureus (Nutt.) E. Greene. Slender ann., 5–16cm, erect or ascending hairy or gland. to subglabrous. Lf lobes 3–6mm, 3–7, linear-oblong. Infl. a lax cyme; cor. 6–13mm, funnelform, dark to pale yellow, throat brown-purple to orange. Spring–early summer. Nevada to Baja Calif.

L. dianthiflorus (Benth.) E. Greene. GROUND-PINK. V. slender, erect, puberulent ann., 5–12cm. Lvs 1–2cm, entire, filiform. Infl. a few-fld, leafy cyme or fls solitary; cor. 1–2.5cm, short-funnelform, white or pink to lilac, dark-spotted at base, throat yellow, lobes long, toothed. Spring–summer. S Calif. to Baja Calif.

L. dichotomus Benth. EVENING SNOW. Slender, erect ann., 5–20cm, usually glab. Lf lobes 3–7, 1–2.2cm, linear-filiform. Infl. a cyme; fls opening in the evening; cor. 1.5–3cm, funnelform, wholly white or with some purple markings in throat; lobes broadly obovate. Spring–summer. Calif., Nevada, Ariz.

L. grandiflorus (Benth.) E. Greene. Erect ann., puberulent to subglabrous, 10–50cm. Lf lobes 5–11, 1–3cm, linear. Infl. a dense head; cor. 1.5–3cm, funnelform, pale lilac to white. Spring–summer. S Calif.

L. liniflorus (Benth.) E. Greene. Erect ann., 10–50cm, glab. to puberulent. Lf lobes 3–9, 1–3cm. Infl. a cymose pan.; cor. 1–3cm, white, blue or pink to lilac, lobes obovate. Spring–summer. Calif.

L. nuttallii (A. Gray) E. Greene ex Milliken. Bushy, villous-hispid perenn., 10–20cm, base woody. Lf lobes 3–9, 1–1.5cm.

Infl. cymose or subcapitate; cor. 1.2–1.5cm, subhypocrateriform to funnelform, yellow, lobes oblanceolate, white. Calif. to Washington. ssp. **nuttallii.** 10–20cm. Lvs clustered in axils, lf lobes 5–9, linear-oblanceolate. Infl. subcapitate. Spring–summer. ssp. **floribundus** (A. Gray) Munz. 10–40cm. Lf lobes 3–5, subfiliform. Infl. lax, cymose. Late spring–summer. Colorado to Baja Calif.

→Gilia.

Linaria Mill. TOADFLAX; SPURRED SNAPDRAGON. Scrophulariaceae. 100 ann. to perenn. herbs. Lvs whorled to alt., simple, entire, usually narrow. Fls snapdragon-like, solitary or in term. rac. or spikes; cal. 5-lobed; cor. tube cylindric, spurred, upper lip 2-lobed, erect, lower 3-lobed, palate ± bearded and prominent, closing tube mouth or depressed and leaving tube open; sta. 4, included. N temp. regions, esp. Eur.

L. aequitriloba (Viv.) A. Spreng. = Cymbalaria aequitriloba.

L. aeruginea (Gouan) Cav. Perenn., or ann., glaucous, glab. or minutely glandular-pubesc.; st. 3–40cm, decumbent to ascending, simple. Lvs 4–18×0.5–1.5mm, linear. Infl. racemose, dense, 2–35-fld; cor. 15–27mm, yellow tinged purple-brown, rarely completely purple-brown, violet, yellow or creamy white, lobes of lower lip v. short, spur 5–11mm. Port., S & E Spain, Balearic Is. var. **nevadensis** (Boiss.) Valdés. Smaller in all parts; cor. always yellow. Spain & Port., in mts. Z6.

L. alpina (L.) Mill. Ann., bienn. or perenn., glaucous, generally glab.; st. 5–25cm, decumbent or ascending; simple or branched. Lvs linear-lanceolate to oblong-lanceolate. Infl. racemose, 3–15-fld, dense; cor. 13–22mm, violet with yellow palate, rarely wholly yellow, white or pink, spur 8–10mm. Summer–autumn. C & S Eur. (mts). 'Alba': fls white. 'Rosea': fls rose-pink, palate orange-yellow. Z4.

L. amethystea (Lam.) Hoffm. & Link. Ann., glab. to minutely glandular-pubesc.; st. 5–35cm ascending, usually simple. Lvs 4–20×0.5–2.5mm, linear to oblanceolate. Infl. racemose, interrupted, 2–5-fld, lax, violet-pubesc.; cor. 10–22mm, blue-violet, rarely white or yellow, with purple spots, spur 4–11mm, violet. Spain and Port. ssp. **multipunctata** (Brot.) Chater & D.A. Webb. Cor. 19–27mm, yellow, spotted, spur 10–15mm, often violet. C Port., SW Spain.

L. angustifolia Rchb. = L. angustissima.

L. angustissima (Lois.) Borb. Similar to L. vulgaris but glab.; lvs 1–2mm wide; cor. 15–20mm, pale yellow, spur 7–10mm. Summer. S & EC Eur., 0 from much of Medit. region. Z6.

L. anticaria Boiss. & Reut. Perenn., glaucous, glab. below infl.; st. to 45cm, procumbent to ascending, much-branched. Lvs 10–30×2–10mm, elliptic-lanceolate to linear. Infl. racemose, dense; cor. 2cm, white with blue stripes, or yellow, palate purple tinged blue, sometimes with yellow spot, spur about half total length of cor., lilac. Spring. S Spain. Z8.

L. antirrhinifolia hort. = L. cavanillesii.

L. antirrhioides Coss. ex Boiss. = L. cavanillesii.

L. aparinoides Dietr. = L. heterophylla.

L. bipartita (Vent.) Willd. CLOVEN-LIP TOADFLAX. Ann., glab.; st. to 40cm, slender. Lvs 40–50×2–5mm, linear. Infl. racemose, lax; cor. 20–24mm, violet, lips widely diverging, palate orange, spur 10–12mm. Summer–early autumn. NW Afr., Port. 'Alba': fls white. 'Queen of Roses': fls pink. 'Splendida': fls deep purple.

L. blanca Pau = L. repens.

L. broussonetii (Poir.) Chav. = L. amethystea.

L. caesia (Pers.) DC. ex Chav. Ann., bienn. or perenn., glaucous, glab. below; st. 10–40cm, procumbent to erect, simple. Lvs 5–30×0.5–2mm, linear-subulate to linear-oblong. Infl. racemose, glandular-pubesc.; cor. 19–25mm, yellow with red-brown stripes, spur 9–12mm. Port., W Spain. Z9.

L. canadensis (L.) Dum.-Cours. OLD-FIELD TOADFLAX. Ann. or bienn., glab., glaucous; st. 25–80cm, erect, simple. Lvs 15–30×1–2.5mm, linear to linear-oblanceolate. Infl. racemose, dense; cor. 10–15mm, lilac to off-white, palate rudimentary, lower lip v. large, spur 4–6mm. Americas; nat. C Russia. Z4.

L. cavanillesii Chav. Perenn., glandular-pubesc.; st. 15–40cm, decumbent or ascending, simple or branched. Lvs 1.5–2×1–1.5cm, ovate to ovate-elliptic. Infl. racemose, dense; cor. 25–30mm, yellow, spur 10–12mm. S & E Spain. Z7.

L. cymbalaria (L.) Mill. = Cymbalaria muralis.

L. dalmatica (L.) Mill. = L. genistifolia ssp. dalmatica.

L. delphinioides Gay ex Knowles & Westc. = L. elegans.

L. ×dominii Druce. 'Yuppie Surprise': to 1m; lvs glaucous; fls pink-lilac.

L. elatine (L.) Mill. = Kickxia elatine.

L. elegans Cav. Ann., glandular-pubesc. above; st. 20–70cm, erect. Lvs 7–35×0.5–4mm, filiform to linear-lanceolate. Infl. racemose, long; cor. 17–25mm, violet to lilac, palate pale to white, mouth of tube ± open, spur 10–14mm. N & C Spain, N Port. Z7.

L. faucicola Leresche & Levier. Ann. or short-lived perenn., glab.; st. 10–25cm, ascending, branched. Lvs 7–20×1.5–5mm, linear-oblong to oblanceolate. Infl. racemose, lax; cor. 22–27mm, violet, throat paler, palate blue-violet, densely hairy, spur 10–13mm. Summer. NW Spain. Z7.

L. filicaulis Boiss. ex Leresche & Levier. V. similar to *L. alpina*, except infl. lax, few-fld. Spring. NW Spain. Z7.

L. fragrans Porta & Rigo = *L. nigricans*.

L. geminiflora F. Schmidt = *L. japonica*.

L. genistifolia (L.) Mill. Perenn., glab.; st. 30–100cm, erect, branched above. Lvs to 1.5cm wide; linear to ovate, ± amplexicaul, rigid. Infl. racemose, lax to dense; cor. 13–22mm, lemon-yellow to orange, palate orange-bearded, spur 0.5–2.5cm. SE & C Eur. (It. to Russia), Asia Minor. ssp. *dalmatica* (L.) Maire & Petitmengin. Lvs suberect, ovate to lanceolate, to 4cm wide, rigid; cor. 2–5cm. Summer. Balk. Penins., Rom., S It.; nat. locally in C Eur. 'Nymph': fls cream. Z5.

L. glacialis Boiss. Ann. to perenn., glaucous, mostly glab.; st. ascending, simple, 5–15cm. Lvs 10–15×2–6mm, elliptic to linear-oblanceolate. Infl. capitate, glandular-pubesc.; cor. 20–27mm, violet tinged yellow, spur 8–15mm, yellow with violet veining. Spring. S Spain (Sierra Nevada). Z6.

L. hepaticifolia (Poir.) Steud. = *Cymbalaria hepaticifolia*.

L. heterophylla Desf. Ann.; st. 15–60cm, erect, sometimes hairy near base. Lvs 7–40×0.5–1mm, linear, glab. Infl. racemose, short, glandular-pubesc.; cor. 18–30mm, bright yellow or v. occas. violet, lips approximately closed, spur 9–18mm. Summer. It. & Sicily, NW Afr. 'Aureopurpurea': fls purple and orange. 'Purpurea': fls purple. Splendens': fls crimson, palate conspicuous, golden.

L. hirta (L.) Moench. Ann., glandular-pubesc.; st. 15–80cm, erect, simple, ± stout. Lvs 2.5–5×0.5–1.5cm, oblong-lanceolate. Infl. racemose, dense; cor. 2–3cm, yellow, spur 10–16mm. Spring–early autumn. Spain & Port.

L. italica Trev. = *L. angustissima*.

L. japonica Miq. Perenn., glaucous and glab.; st. 15–40cm, erect, branched. Lvs 1.5–3×0.5–1.5cm, elliptic to elliptic-lanceolate. Infl. racemose, short; cor. 15–18mm, pale yellow, spur 5–10mm. Summer. Jap. Z8.

L. japonica var. *geminiflora* (F. Schmidt) Nak. = *L. japonica*.

L. jattae Palanza = *L. genistifolia* ssp. *dalmatica*.

L. macedonia Griseb. = *L. genistifolia* ssp. *dalmatica*.

L. maroccana Hook. f. Ann., glab. below, viscid-pubesc. above; st. to 45cm, erect, branched. Lvs to 4cm, linear. Infl. racemose, term.; cor. 1.5cm, brilliant violet-purple, palate orange to yellow with smaller paler patch, spur 1–2cm. Summer. Moroc.; nat. NE US. var. *hybrida* hort. Fls red to rose, lilac and violet. 'Carminea': fls bright rosy carmine. 'Diadem': fls v. large, rich violet with white eye. Excelsior hybrids: fls in many shades, from white to yellow and beige, to salmon, rose-carmine and crimson, to purple and blue. 'Fairy Bouquet': fls large, copiously produced, colour range similar to Excelsior hybrids. 'Fairy Bride': fls white. 'Fairy Bridesmaid': fls rich lemon yellow. 'Ruby King': fls deep blood red. 'White Pearl': fls large, glistening white. 'Yellow Prince': fls pure yellow.

L. melantha Boiss. & Reut. = *L. aeruginea*.

L. minor (L.) Desf. = *Chaenorrhinum minus*.

L. monspessulana (L.) Mill. = *L. repens*.

L. multipunctata (Brot.) Hoffm. & Link = *L. amethystea* ssp. *multipunctata*.

L. nevadensis (Boiss.) Boiss. & Reut. = *L. aeruginea* var. *nevadensis*.

L. nigricans Lange in Willk. & Lange. Ann., glab. or minutely glandular-pubesc.; st. to 17cm, simple or branched. Lvs 5–12×1–2mm, linear-oblong to broadly elliptic. Infl. racemose, lax; cor. 16–20mm, lilac or violet, spur straight, 9–12mm. SE Spain.

L. origanifolia (L.) Cav. = *Chaenorrhinum origanifolium.*.

L. petraea Jordan = *L. alpina*.

L. petraea Steven non Jordan = *L. genistifolia*.

L. pilosa (Jacq.) Lam. & DC. = *Cymbalaria pilosa*.

L. purpurea (L.) Mill. Perenn. glab. and glaucous; st. 20–60cm, ascending to erect, often branched above. Lvs 20–60×1–4mm, linear. Infl. racemose, slender; cor. 9–12mm, violet tinged purple, spur curved, 5mm. Summer. C It. to Sicily, nat. elsewhere including GB. 'Canon J. Went': tall; fls tiny, pale pink. 'Springside White': lvs grey-green; fls white. Z6.

L. repens (L.) Mill. STRIPED TOADFLAX. Perenn., glab.; base decumbent, rootstock creeping; st. 30–120cm, erect, branched above. Lvs 15–40×1–2.5cm, linear to linear-oblanceolate. Infl. racemose, long; cor. 8–15mm, white to pale lilac with violet veining, palate orange, spur 3–5mm. W Eur. (N It. & N Spain to NW Germ., Britain); nat. C Eur. 'Alba': to 30cm; fls white. Z6.

L. reticulata (Sm.) Desf. PURPLE-NET TOADFLAX. Ann., glaucous;

st. 60–120cm. Lvs linear. Infl. racemose, short, downy; cor. deep purple, reticulate-veined, palate coppery orange or yellow with purple striations, spur less than half length of cor. Late spring to summer. Port., N Afr. 'Aureopurpurea': fls deep rich purple with orange or yellow palate. 'Crown Jewels': clouds of small bright fls, bicolour, in maroon, red, gold and orange.

L. sagittata Poir. Perenn., glab. throughout; st. 2–3m, ascending, twining. Lvs 2.5–4cm, lanceolate-oblong, hastate at base, entire. Fls solitary, axillary; cor. to 4cm, broad, yellow. Summer. N Afr. Z9.

L. sapphirina Hoffm. = *L. nigricans*.

L. saxatilis (L.) Chaz. Perenn., rarely ann., subglabrous to glandular-pubesc.; st. 7–50cm, ascending. Lvs 4–20×1–5mm, linear to oblong-elliptic. Infl. racemose, to 10-fld; cor. 9–17mm, yellow with pair of brown marks on palate, spur slender, 5–8mm. Summer. N & C Spain, Port. Z8.

L. spartea (L.) Willd. Ann.; st. erect, branched, 15–60cm, non-flowering st. hairy. Lvs 7–40×0.5–1mm, linear. Infl. glandular-pubesc.; cor. 18–30mm, bright yellow or violet, lips ± closed, spur 9–18mm. Summer–autumn. SW Eur. Z7.

L. spuria (L.) Mill. = *Kickxia spuria*.

L. striata L. = *L. repens*.

L. stricta (Sibth. & Sm.) Guss. = *L. heterophylla*.

L. supina (L.) Chaz. Ann., bienn. or perenn., glaucous, glab. below; st. 5–30cm, procumbent to erect. Lvs 5–20×0.5–1mm, linear to linear-oblanceolate. Infl. racemose, lax or dense, glandular-pubesc.; cor. 13–20mm, pale yellow sometimes tinged violet, spur 5–15mm. Spring–autumn. SW Eur.

L. supina ssp. *nevadensis* (Boiss.) Nyman = *L. aeruginea* var. *nevadensis*.

L. triornithophora (L.) Willd. THREE-BIRDS-FLYING. Perenn., glab. and somewhat glaucous; st. 50–130cm, erect or diffuse. Lvs 2.5–7.5×0.5–3cm, lanceolate to ovate-lanceolate. Infl. lax. Fls 3(–4) per whorl; cor. 3.5–5.5cm, pale lavender striped purple in tube with yellow palate, tube inflated, spur 16–25mm. Summer. W Spain, N & C Port. 'Rosea': fls pink. Z7.

L. triphylla (L.) Mill. Ann. or perenn., glab., glaucous; st. 10–45cm, single, erect, stout. Lvs 1.5–3.5×1–2.5cm, elliptic to obovate, rather fleshy. Infl. racemose, dense; cor. 2–3cm, white, occas. faintly tinged violet or yellow, palate orange or yellow, spur 8–11mm. Spring–summer. Medit. Eur. Z8.

L. tristis (L.) Mill. DULL-COLOURED LINARIA; SAD-COLOURED LINARIA. Perenn., glaucous, glab. or glandular-pubesc. below; st. 10–90cm, decumbent to ascending, simple. Lvs 0.5–4.5cm, linear to oblong-lanceolate. Infl. racemose, 2–15-fld, glandular-pubesc.; cor. 21–28mm, yellow tinged purple-brown, spur stout, striped, 11–13mm. Summer. S Spain & S Port., NW Afr., Canary Is. Z9.

L. ventricosa Coss. & Bal. Perenn., glaucous and glab.; st. to 1m, erect. Lvs to 5cm, lanceolate. Infl. racemose, dense; cor. 3cm, pale yellow with yellow-brown or red veining, palate hairy, spur 1cm. Summer. SW Moroc. Z9.

L. verticillata Boiss. Perenn., glandular-pubesc. below; st. to 30cm, ascending to erect, usually simple. Lvs oblong to elliptic. Infl. racemose, dense; cor. 15–35mm, yellow, sometimes with violet or green tinged stripes, palate orange, striate, spur 9–17mm. Spring–early summer. S Spain. Z8.

L. viscida Moench. Ann., glandular-pubesc.; st. erect, branched, 8–25cm. Lvs oblong to linear-lanceolate. Infl. short, conic; cor. 8–10mm, pale violet, throat yellow, spur conic. Summer–autumn. Medit. Eur. Z8.

L. vulgaris Mill. COMMON TOADFLAX; BUTTER-AND-EGGS; WILD SNAPDRAGON. Perenn.; st. 15–90cm, erect, simple or branched, glandular-pubesc. above. Lvs 20–60×1–5mm, linear to linear-oblanceolate. Infl. racemose, dense; cor. 25–33mm, pale to bright yellow, palate coppery, spur 10–13mm. Spring–autumn. Eur. inc. GB, except extreme N and much of Medit. region. The peloric form has cor. regular, 5-spurred. Z4.

→*Antirrhinum*.

Lindelofia Lehm. Boraginaceae. 12 hairy perenn. herbs. Basal lvs petiolate; cauline lvs sessile or short-stalked, ovate to linear-lanceolate. Infl. terminal or axill.; cal. deeply lobed; cor. infundibular to cylindrical or cylindrical-campanulate, lobes spreading; faucal appendages mostly conspicuous; sta. 5, fil. short. C Asia to Himal.

L. anchusoides (Lindl.) Lehm. St. to 100cm, erect or sometimes decumbent, fistulose, simple or branched above. Basal lvs to 25×7cm, lanceolate, acute, bristly above. Infl. few-fld, long-stalked; cor. to 10mm, blue, pink or purple, campanulate, lobes suborbicular, faucal appendages puberulent. Afghan. to W Himal. Z7.

L. longiflora (Benth.) Baill. St. to 60cm, simple, covered with white bristle-hairs. Basal lvs to 18×8cm, lanceolate, acute, bristly throughout. Infl. ultimately to 15cm; cor. to 15mm, dark blue, infundibular, lobes to 6mm, ovate, faucal appendages ciliate. W Himal. Z7.

L. spectabilis Lehm. = *L. longiflora.*

→*Cynoglossum.*

Linden *Tilia.*

Lindenbergia Lehm. Scrophulariaceae. 15 ann. or perenn. herbs and subshrubs. St. decumbent or erect. Lvs simple. Fls in axils, spikes or rac.; cal. 5-lobed; cor. 2-lipped, upper lip bilobed or notched, lower lip trilobed, throat with 2 pouches; sta. 4. Summer. OW Trop. Z9.

L. grandiflora Benth. Villous clambering perenn. to 60cm. Lvs 5–20cm, ovate, dentate. Rac. lax, foliose; cor. to 2.5cm, yellow, throat and palate spotted red.

Lindenia Benth. Rubiaceae. 4 shrubs; br. terete. Lvs short-petiolate, entire, opposite, stipulate. Fls term., solitary to few in clusters; cal. turbinate, 5-ribbed or -angled, lobes 5; cor. salverform, pubesc., lobes 5; sta. 5, inserted at top of cor. C Amer., SW Pacific Is. Z10.

L. acutiflora Hook. = *L. rivalis.*

L. rivalis Benth. Shrub, everg., to 1m; br. red-brown. Lvs to 15×2cm, clustered, lanceolate to narrow-elliptic, glab. above. Fls in clusters, or solitary; cor. to 15cm, white, pubesc., lobes 3cm; anth. 1cm, yellow. Spring–summer. Mex. to Guat.

Linden-leaved Maple *Acer distylum.*

Lindera Thunb. Lauraceae. 80 aromatic, everg. or decid. shrubs or trees. Lvs alt., entire or 3-lobed. Fls small, apetalous, yellow-green, in clusters or involucrate pseudoumbels. Fr. a 1-seeded drupe. Temp. and trop. E Asia, N Amer.

L. benzoin (L.) Bl. SPICE BUSH; BENJAMIN BUSH. Decid., rounded, highly aromatic shrub to 4×3m. Br. glab. or initially puberulent. Lvs 6–15cm, obovate, thin, glab. above, entire, ciliate. Fls clustered. Fr. to 0.75cm, ellipsoid bright red. E US. 'Xanthocarpa': fr. yellow. Z5.

L. megaphylla Hemsl. Everg. shrub or tree to 20m. Br. initially dark purple-brown, with pale lenticels. Lvs 10–20cm, lanceolate-elliptic, coriaceous, lustrous above, glaucous beneath. Fls in umbels. Fr. 1.5cm, black. Spring. China. Z8.

L. obtusiloba Bl. Decid. shrub or small tree to 10m. Br. grey-yellow sometimes purple, lenticellate. Lvs 6–12cm, ovate, apex often bluntly 3-lobed, glaucous beneath, pale gold in autumn. Fls to precocious, in crowded clusters. Fr. to 0.75cm diam., black. Korea, China, Jap. Z6.

L. praecox (Sieb. & Zucc.) Bl. Decid. shrub or small tree to 7m. Young br. glossy brown, with prominent lenticels. Lvs 2.5–8.75cm, ovate, oval or orbicular, thin, glab., deep green above, paler, glaucous beneath. Fls in short-stalked clusters. Fr. to 2cm diam., olive to red-brown, spotted. Jap., Korea. Z8.

L. strychnifolia (Sieb. & Zucc.) Vilm. Everg. tree or shrub to 10m. Br. brown, initially downy. Lvs to 6cm, ovate to ovate-oblong, coriaceous. Fls clustered. Fr. pubesc. China, Taiwan, Philipp., SE Asia. Z9.

L. umbellata Thunb. Decid. shrub to 4m. Br. deep red-brown, lacking lenticels. Lvs 0.6–1.25cm, obovate-elliptic. Fls in clusters. Fr. to 1cm diam., black. Jap. Z8.

→*Benzoin, Laurus* and *Parabenzoin.*

Lindheimera A. Gray & Engelm. Compositae. 1 ann. herb to 65cm. Lower lvs alt., oblanceolate, coarsely pinnatifid, petiolate, upper lvs opposite, ovate-lanceolate, entire, bract-like. Cap. radiate, to 4cm diam., clustered in a corymb; ray florpets white; disc flts yellow. Late spring. S US.

L. texana A. Gray. TEXAS STAR.

Lindsaea Dryand. Dennstaedtiaceae. 200 terrestrial or epiphytic ferns. Rhiz. creeping, caespitose or scandent, finely scaly. Fronds stipitate, 1–3-pinnate to -pinnatifid; rachis 4-angled, stipes 2-ranked, usually sulcate, occas. 4-angled. Trop. and subtrop. Z10.

L. adiantoides J. Sm. Rhiz. short-creeping. Fronds to 15×3cm, tufted, pinnate, lanceolate, pinnae upwardly overlapping, semiovate, entire at lower margin, curved and lobed at upper margin, to 12×6mm, lobes erose, membranous; stipes to 5cm, lustrous black. Malaysia to Philipp., Polyn.

L. clavata (L.) Mett. = *Sphenomeris clavata.*

L. concinna J. Sm. Rhiz. short-creeping. Fronds to 30×2cm, tufted, pinnate, herbaceous, pinnae crowded toward apex, remote at base, flabellate, somewhat notched at upper margin, to 8×4mm, membranous; stripes wiry, to 8cm. Malaysia.

L. cultrata (Willd.) Sw. Rhiz. short-creeping. Fronds to 30×3cm, pinnate, lanceolate to linear, acute glab., pinnae to 18×7mm, short-stalked, horizontal, crescent- or kidney-shaped, entire at lower margin, usually lobed at upper margin, lobes to 4, obtuse

or truncate; stipes to 15cm, wiry, lustrous green-brown to black. Madag., Trop. Asia, Aus. (Queensld)

L. cuneata (Forst. f.) C. Chr. = *L. trichomanoides.*

L. davallioides Bl. Rhiz. short-creeping. Fronds 1–2-pinnatifid, deltoid to ovate, pinnae sessile, falcate, lanceolate, acute upcurved at lower margin, lobed at upper margin, to 12×4mm, thin-textured, lobes 4–6, close, oblique, obtuse; stipes crowded, 10cm+. Malaysia to Philipp.

L. decomposita Willd. Rhiz. short-creeping. Fronds to 20×4cm, 1–2-pinnatifid, pinnae 13, to 20×8mm, subsessile, lanceolate, falcate at lower margin, lobed at upper margin, lobes 3–4; stipes to 20cm, pale purple to brown. Sri Lanka, Malaysia, to Polyn.

L. dubia Spreng. Rhiz. short-creeping. Fronds to 20×5cm, pinnate, oblong to ovate, pinnae to 25×3mm, lanceolate to linear, acute, cuneate and oblique at lower margin, notched at upper margin; stipes to 15cm, wiry, dark brown. Trop. Amer.

L. guianensis Dryand. Rhiz. short-creeping. Fronds to 60cm, 2-pinnatifid, pinnae 13, to 12×6mm, falcate, strap-shaped to linear, narrowly acute, pinnules close or overlapping, obtuse, entire at lower margin, rounded at upper margin; stipesto 30cm, terete, erect, rigid. Trop. Amer.

L. lancea (L.) Bedd. Rhiz. short- to -long-creeping. Fronds to 50cm, 1–2-pinnatifid, pinnae to 30cm, pinnules to 33×11mm, falcate, trapeziform, entire and plane or curved at lower margin, rounded at upper margin; stipes to 30cm, purple or brown. Trop. Amer.

L. linearis Sw. Rhiz. creeping, to 1mm wide. Fronds to 20×1cm, pinnate, linear, membranous, pinnae to 6×4mm, sessile or subsessile, flabellate to deltoid, oblong, or crescent-shaped, entire at lower margin, shallowly to deeply lobed or toothed at upper margin; stipes wiry, to 30cm, russet to black. Aus., NZ.

L. lobata Poir. = *L. decomposita.*

L. media R. Br. Rhiz. long-creeping. Fronds to 30×17cm, 2-pinnate, oblong or deltoid, papery or grass-like in texture, pinnae *c*50×6mm, subopposite, rhomboid to ovate or flabellate, lobed or notched and plane at lower margin, entire and rounded at upper margin, leathery, seg. flabellate or trapezoid, to 10×6mm; stipes wiry, to 30cm, straw-coloured to brown. Aus.

L. microphylla Sw. Rhiz. short-creeping. Fronds to 45×10cm, 2–3-pinnate or -pinnatifid, lanceolate to oblong, pinnae to 5cm, sterile pinnules lanceolate to ovate, lobed or toothed, fertile pinnules obovate, wedge-shaped or flabellate, entire or with deltoid lobes; stipes wiry, to 15cm, lustrous brown. Aus., NZ.

L. odorata Roxb. Rhiz. short- to long-creeping. Fronds to 30×3cm, erect, pinnate, oblong to lanceolate or elliptic, grass-like in texture, pinnae to 20×8mm, stalked, alt., rhomboid or elliptic, acute or obtuse, convex and entire at lower margin, plane at upper margin, lobes to 6; stipes to 20cm, straw-coloured to brown. Trop. Afr., Madag., to Trop. Asia.

L. orbiculata (Lam.) Mett. ex Kuhn. Rhiz. short-creeping. Fronds to 20×3cm, 1–2-pinnate or pinnatifid, deltoid or lanceolate to linear, pinnae flabellate, dentate or incised, pinnules stalked, ovate, elliptic or flabellate, dentate or lobed, rounded at upper margin, to 12×6mm; stipes to 20cm, lustrous red-brown. China, Taiwan, Jap.

L. parvula Fée. Rhiz. creeping. Fronds to 35cm, 2-pinnate, papery to leathery, pinnae 9 lat. and 1 term., sessile or stalked, subopposite, linear, attenuate, to 12×1cm, pinnules to 6×4mm, alt. or subopposite, ovate; stipes to 60cm, straw-coloured to red-brown. W Indies, S Amer.

L. pectinata Bl. Rhiz. scandent to creeping. Fronds to 40×4cm, pinnate, membranous, pinnae to 16×8mm, ± sessile, oblong, obtuse, subentire to notched or lobed at upper margin; stipes to 3cm. Malaysia to Philipp.

L. recurvata Wallich = *L. decomposita.*

L. rigida Hook. Rhiz. long-creeping. Fronds to 35cm, rigid, bipinnatifid, oblong, pinnae 9–13, alt., linear, to 25×2cm, pinnules, flabellate to rhomboid, oblong, or ovate, convex at upper margin, notched or dentate in sterile fronds, with 3–4 lobes in fertile fronds; stipes to 30cm, prickly at base, purple to brown. Malaysia to Polyn.

L. stricta (Sw.) Dryand. Rhiz. short-creeping. Fronds 60cm+, erect, 1–2-pinnatifid, rigid, pinnae to 8×4mm, opposite, linear, pinnules trapezoid to flabellate, lunate or cuneate, upper margin subentire to notched; stipes straw-coloured to brown. W Indies, C to S Amer.

L. stricta var. *parvula* (Fée) Kramer = *L. parvula.*

L. taiwaniana Ching = *L. orbiculata.*

L. trapezoidea Copel. = *L. decomposita.*

L. trichomanoides Dryand. Rhiz. creeping. Fronds to 25×10cm, 2–3-pinnate or -pinnatifid, lanceolate to ovate or oblong, leathery, pinnae to 8cm, deeply incised, pinnules obovate or oblong to cuneate, upper margin entire to dentate or lobed; stipes wiry, to 15cm, lustrous dark brown. Aus., NZ.

L. trilobata Colenso = *L. linearis.*

→*Odontoloma.*

Ling *Calluna*; *Trapa bicornis.*
Lingberry *Vaccinium vitis-idaea* var. *minus.*
Lingen, Lingenberry, Lingonberry *Vaccinium vitis-idaea* var. *minus.*

Linnaea Gronov. TWIN-FLOWER. Caprifoliaceae. 1 creeping, dwarf, everg. shrub. Br. slender, trailing. Lvs 0.25–1×0.25–0.75cm, oval, rounded, entire or toothed above, glossy dark green and sparsely pubesc. above, downy beneath. Fls fragrant, paired and nodding atop a slender stalk to 8cm; cor. to 1.5cm, campanulate, pale pink with deeper markings, lobes 5, rounded. Summer. Circumpolar regions. Z2.
L. americana Forbes = *L. borealis* var. *americana.*
L. borealis L. As above. var. *americana* (Forbes) Rehd. Lvs glab., ciliate only at base. Cor. deep rose. N Amer.

Linoma Cook.
L. alba (Bory) Cook = *Dictyosperma album.*

Linospadix H.A. Wendl. Palmae. 11 unarmed monoecious palms. St. solitary or clustered, conspicuously ringed. Crown-shaft not well developed. Lvs pinnately divided or simple and deeply emarginate; sheaths scaly, with fibrous margins; petiole channelled above; pinnae 1- to several-fold. Fls in triads (2 ♂, 1 ♀) on simple, erect spikes to *c*1m. Fr. *c*1cm, ellipsoid, smooth, scarlet. New Guinea, Aus. Z10.
L. monostachya (Mart.) H.A. Wendl. WALKING STICK PALM. St. solitary, slender, to *c*3m. Lvs to 1m, pinnate. Aus.
→*Bacularia.*

Linum L. FLAX. Linaceae. 200 ann., bienn. or perenn. herbs or shrubs. Lvs simple, entire. Fls 5-merous, ephemeral, in rac., clusters or spike-like heads; cor. rotate, pet. rounded, clawed; sta. 5, sometimes with a whorl of staminodes; styles 5. Temp. N hemis.
L. africanum L. Shrubby perenn. to 90cm. Lvs to 1.5cm, narrow-lanceolate, sessile. Fls in forked corymbs, yellow. S Afr. Z9.
L. album Kotschy ex Boiss. Glab., glaucous perenn. herb to 30cm. Lvs to 2cm, elliptic-oblanceolate, sessile. Fls in lax cymes, white. Iran. Z9.
L. alpinum Jacq. = *L. perenne* ssp. *alpinum.*
L. alpinum ssp. *julicum* (Hayek) Hayek = *L. perenne* ssp. *alpinum.*
L. altaicum Ledeb. ex Juz. Glab., caespitose perenn. to 60cm. Lvs to 3cm, oblong to linear-lanceolate. Fls violet blue. C Asia. Z7.
L. angustifolium Huds. = *L. bienne.*
L. arboreum L. Glab. shrub to 1m. Lvs to 2cm, spathulate, thick, often crowded in rosettes. Fls yellow, in a compact, few-fld cyme. S Aegean. Z8.
L. austriacum L. Glab., erect perenn. to 60cm. Lvs to 1.5cm, linear, with many pellucid dots. Fls blue in a many-fld cyme. S Eur. 'Loreyi': semi-prostrate; fls lilac with darker lines. ssp. *collinum* Nyman. Smaller; lvs shorter. Z5.
L. bienne Mill. PALE FLAX. Glab. ann. or perenn. to 60cm, with several st. from base. Lvs to 2.5cm, linear. Fls pale blue, in loose cymes. W Eur., Medit. Z7.
L. bulgaricum Podp. = *L. tauricum.*
L. campanulatum L. Glab. perenn. to 30cm, base woody. Lower lvs spathulate, upper lvs lanceolate, margins hyaline, minutely gland. at base. Fls yellow, veined orange, in 3–5-fld corymbs. S Eur. Z7.
L. capitatum Kit. ex Schult. Robust perenn. to 45cm. Lvs obovate-lanceolate to lanceolate with glands toward base. Fls yellow in a subcapitate cyme. S Eur. In cult., often confused with *L. flavum*, which has fls in a looser head. Z7.
L. collinum Guss. = *L. austriacum* ssp. *collinum.*
L. compactum A. Nels. Pubesc. perenn. to 10cm. Lvs to 1cm, linear. Fls yellow. C US. Possibly not distinct from *L. rigidum.* Z3.
L. dolomiticum Borb. Tufted perenn., 15–20cm. Basal lvs to 4.5cm, linear-oblanceolate, st. lvs to 1.25cm, oblong-lanceolate. Fls yellow. Hung. Z6.
L. elegans Sprun. ex Boiss. Perenn. to 15cm, tufted from a woody base. Basal lvs in rosettes, obovate to spathulate, st. lvs linear. Fls yellow with distinct veins in 2–7-fld cymes. Balk. Penins. Z6.
L. flavum L. GOLDEN FLAX. Erect, glab. perenn., 30–40cm, base woody. Lvs 2–3.5cm, lower lvs spathulate, upper lvs narrow-lanceolate, with marginal glands at base. Fls golden yellow, in dense, much-branched cymes. C & S Eur. 'Compactum': dwarf form; fls cool yellow. Z5.
L. 'Gemmels Hybrid' (*L. campanulatum* × *L. elegans.*) To 15cm. Lvs tinted grey. Fls rich yellow. Z6.
L. grandiflorum Desf. FLOWERING FLAX. Erect glab. ann. to 75cm, branched at base. Lvs to 3cm, linear-lanceolate, sparsely

hairy. Fls rose with a dark centre in loose pan. N Afr. 'Bright Eyes': to 45cm; fls ivory with deep brown centre. 'Caeruleum': fls blue-purple. 'Coccineum': fls scarlet. 'Roseum': fls rose pink. 'Rubrum': fls bright red.
L. hirsutum L. Erect perenn. to 45cm, ± downy. Lvs to 1.5cm, broad-lanceolate. Fls lavender with white or pale yellow eye. C Eur., Medit. Z6.
L. hologynum Rchb. Glab. perenn., to 60cm. Lvs linear to lanceolate. Fls blue. C Eur. (mts). Z6.
L. julicum Hayek = *L. perenne* ssp. *alpinum.*
L. lewisii Pursh = *L. perenne* ssp. *lewisii.*
L. maritimum L. Perenn., to 60cm. Lvs oblanceolate or elliptic to linear-lanceolate. Fls yellow, in loose pan. Sardinia. Z8.
L. monogynum Forst. f. Glab. perenn., to 60cm; st. shrubby, erect. Lvs to 2.5cm, linear to lanceolate. Fls white in corymbs. NZ. Z8.
L. muelleri Moris = *L. maritimum.*
L. narbonense L. Glab., glaucous perenn. to 60cm. Lvs to 2cm, linear-lanceolate. Fls azure with white eye, in few-fld cymes. Medit. Close to *L. perenne*, distinguished by more robust habit and scarious-margined infl. bracts. 'Heavenly Blue': fls clear vivid blue. 'Six Hills': fls bright blue. Z5.
L. nervosum Waldst. & Kit. Perenn., 30–40cm; st. hairy at base. Lvs lanceolate. Fls blue, in loose pan. E Eur. Z6.
L. perenne L. PERENNIAL FLAX. Glab., erect perenn., to 60cm. Lvs to 2.5cm, linear to lanceolate. Fls pale blue, in much-branched pan. Eur. 'Album': fls white. 'Caeruleum': fls sky blue. ssp. *alpinum* (Jacq.) Ockend. To 30cm. Lvs to 2cm, linear-lanceolate, usually close together on lower st. Fls smaller. ssp. *lewisii* (Pursh) Hult. PRAIRIE FLAX. Stouter with lvs longer (to 3cm). W N Amer. Z7.
L. rhodopeum Velen. Close to *L. flavum*, differs in its fewer st. and smaller pet. S Bulg., N Greece. Z7.
L. rigidum Pursh. Glab. perenn. to 50cm; br. rigid, angled. Lvs few, linear, with stipular glands. Fls yellow. N Amer.
L. salsoloides Lam. = *L. suffruticosum* ssp. *salsoloides.*
L. sibiricum DC. = *L. perenne.*
L. strictum L. Ann., to 40cm. Lvs to 2.5cm, linear-lanceolate, strongly revolute. Fls yellow, small, in tight clusters. C Eur. and Medit. to Iran and Afghan. Z6.
L. suffruticosum L. Perenn., 25–40cm, base woody, flowering st. procumbent. Lvs linear, involute. Fls white, veined purple with a violet or pink centre. Spain. ssp. *salsoloides* (Lam.) Rouy. St. to 25cm, less woody at base. Lvs narrower. Fls pearly-white. Spain to N It. 'Nanum': prostrate, forming clumps 8–10cm high and to 45cm across. Z5.
L. sulcatum Riddell. Erect ann. to 75cm; st. angled. Lvs to 2.5cm, linear, with minute glands at base. Fls yellow. E US. Z3.
L. tauricum Willd. Perenn. to 40cm with sterile lf rosettes. Basal and lower st. lvs narrow-spathulate, upper lvs narrower. Fls pale yellow. SE Eur. Z6.
L. tenuifolium L. Glab., shrubby perenn. to 40cm. Lvs to 2.5cm, linear, sometimes revolute. Fls lilac to pale pink, with purple veins or centre. C Eur., Medit. Z6.
L. trigynum Roxb. non L. = *Reinwardtia indica.*
L. usitatissimum L. FLAX. Erect ann., to 120cm. Lvs linear to lanceolate, to 3mm wide. Fls blue in term., leafy, corymbose pan. Eur. An ancient cultigen, probably originating in Asia, an escape in N America. Cvs have been selected for their fibre content (linen) and the oil content of their seeds (linseed). Z4.
L. viscosum L. Glandular-hairy perenn. to 60cm. Lvs to 1.5cm, oblong-lanceolate, glandular-ciliate. Fls lilac-rose or rarely blue, with violet lines in erect term. corymbs. S Eur. Z6.
→*Cathartolinum.*

Lion's-beard *Geum triflorum.*
Lion's Ear *Leonotis.*
Lion's Foot *Nabalus serpentarius.*
Lion's Spoor *Euphorbia clavarioides.*
Lion's Tail *Leonotis.*

Liparis Rich. Orchidaceae. 250 terrestrial and epiphytic orchids, usually pseudobulbous. Lvs thin and plicate, or stiff and leathery. Rac. term., few- to many-fld; fls fairly small; tep. spreading or reflexed; pet. often linear; lip entire or bilobed. Pantrop. and also temp., with 1 sp. in GB. Z10 unless specified.
L. atropurpurea Lindl. Terrestrial; pbs obscure. Lvs 3–4, 7.5–10cm, ovate-orbicular; petiole 2–2.5cm. Rac. 10–20cm, laxly several-fld; fls dull purple. Sri Lanka, S India.
L. bituberculata (Hook.) Lindl. = *L. nervosa.*
L. bowkeri Harv. Terrestrial or epiphytic; pbs to 7cm, conic. Lvs 2–5, 6–12×3–6cm, lanceolate or ovate, plicate, light green. Rac. to 15cm, several-fld; fls yellow or yellow-green, turning buff-orange. Throughout much of trop. Afr.; S Afr. Z9.
L. caespitosa (Thouars) Lindl. Epiphytic, with ovoid pbs 1–2cm set close together on a creeping rhiz. Lf 1, erect, coriaceous,

light green, $c10\times1$cm, oblanceolate. Rac. to 15cm, many-fld; fls yellow or yellow-green, v. small. EC Afr., Indian Ocean Is., Sri Lanka and from NE India to Philipp. and Pacific Is.

L. condylobulbon Rchb. f. Epiphytic, forming dense clumps; pbs to 24×2cm, pyriform-cylindrical. Lvs 2, to 20×2.5cm, narrowly lanceolate, thin-textured. Rac. to 22cm, 15–35-fld; fls scented, cream to pale green. SE Asia, Polyn., New Guinea, Aus.

L. cordifolia Hook. f. Terrestrial; pbs to 4cm, ovoid, compressed, clustered. Lf 1, to 13×10cm, broadly ovate, cordate. Infl. of similar length to lf; fls green. Sikkim. Z9.

L. elata Lindl. = L. nervosa.

L. elegans Lindl. Terrestrial, with slender, creeping rhiz.; pbs set 1–2.5cm apart, 2–3cm long, ovoid, 2-lvd. Lvs 12–25×2–3cm, oblanceolate, petiole 2–6cm. Rac. erect, 25–35cm, many-fld; fls yellow-green with an orange to salmon lip. Sumatra to Philipp. (not Java), Malaysia.

L. guineensis Lindl. = L. nervosa.

L. lacerata Ridl. Pbs 2–3cm, ovoid, 1-lvd. Lf to 18×4cm, lanceolate, petiole 4cm. Rac. c20cm, many-fld; fls white with an orange lip. Malaysia, Borneo, Sumatra.

L. latifolia (Bl.) Lindl. Pbs c8cm, conical, with large red-brown sheaths at base, flattened, 1-lvd. Lf to 33×7.5cm, lanceolate. Rac. erect, of similar length to lf, many-fld; fls yellow with orange-brown lip. Malaysia, Sumatra, Borneo, Java.

L. liliifolia (L.) Rich. ex Lindl. Terrestrial, to 25cm; pbs 2cm, ovoid, covered with dry sheaths, 2-lvd. Lvs to 18×6cm, ovoid or elliptic, glossy green, keeled below. Rac. several- to many-fld; fls purple with a translucent mauve lip veined purple. Late spring–summer. N Amer., Sweden. Z4.

L. loeselii (L.) Rich. FEN ORCHID. Terrestrial (epiphyte on sphagnum) to 25cm; pbs 1cm, ovoid, sheathed, 2-lvd. Lvs to 20×6cm, oblong or elliptic, acute or obtuse, keeled below, glossy green. Rac. laxly few- to several-fld; fls dull yellow-green. Summer. N Eur.; N Amer. Z4.

L. longipes Lindl. = L. viridiflora.

L. macrantha Rolfe = L. nigra.

L. neglecta Schltr. = L. bowkeri.

L. nervosa (Thunb.) Lindl. Terrestrial or lithophytic; pbs conical, to 4cm. Lvs 2–3, to 35×6cm, lanceolate, plicate, light green. Rac. densely many-fld; fls green or yellow-green, often with a maroon-purple lip. Trop. Afr., trop. Amer., India to Jap. and Philipp.

L. nigra Seidenf. Terrestrial, usually about 35cm but occas. reaching 1m; pbs about 20×1cm, cylindrical. Lvs c5, to 15×6cm, ovate, plicate. Rac. 25–35cm, fairly densely many-fld; scape winged, dark red-purple; fls deep red-purple. Taiwan.

L. nutans Ames. Terrestrial; pbs to 3cm, pyriform, sheathed, 1-lvd. Lf 18–30×1.5–3cm, narrowly oblong-lanceolate. Infl. shorter than lf; peduncle winged; rac. nodding, covered with distichous bracts, to 5cm, densely many-fld; fls brick red. Philipp.

L. torta Hook. f. Terrestrial; pbs about 2cm, conical, 1-lvd. Lf 14–15×2.5–3.5cm, lanceolate, coriaceous. Rac. of similar length to lf, few- to many-fld; fls cadmium yellow. India.

L. tricallosa Rchb. f. Pbs conical, c12cm, 1-lvd. Lf to 18×5.4cm, ovate. Rac. to 45cm, scape and rachis purple; sep. pale green, pet. purple, green towards base, lip pale green with purple-pink veins, becoming pink-tinged. Sumatra to Philipp.

L. viridiflora (Bl.) Lindl. Epiphytic; pbs clustered, 1–9cm, ovoid or conical, 2–3-lvd. Lvs to 25×2.5cm, narrowly oblanceolate. Rac. pendent, 17–18cm, densely many-fld; fls green, v. small. Sri Lanka, India, Burm., Malaysia, China, Jap., Sumatra, Borneo, Philipp. and Fiji.

Lip Fern Cheilanthes.

Lippia L. Verbenaceae. 200 herbs, shrubs or small trees, often aromatic. Lvs entire, dentate or crenate. Infl. an axill. spike, usually with conspicuous bracts; cal. small, usually campanulate, membranous; cor. tube cylindrical, erect or curved, limb 4-lobed; sta. 4; ovary bilocular, style term., stigma obscurely bilobed. Trop. Afr., Americas.

L. canescens HBK = Phyla canescens.

L. citriodora (Lam.) HBK = Aloysia triphylla.

L. dulcis Trev. MEXICAN LIPPIA; YERBA DULCE. Perenn. herb or subshrub to 60cm, erect or decumbent, glab. or strigulose. Lvs to 5cm, ovate to rhombic, aromatic, strigulose and obscurely gland. beneath, crenate-serrate. Infl. with a solitary peduncle, to 5cm; cor. to 1.5mm, white. Mex., Guat. to Panama.

L. graveolens HBK. MEXICAN OREGANO. Aromatic shrub to 2m, br. shortly pilose. Lvs to 6cm, elliptic to oblong or ovate-oblong, usually obtuse, pilose above, gland. and tomentose or pilose beneath, finely crenate. Infl. with 2–6 peduncles, to 12mm; cor. white, tube strigulose, to 3mm. S US Mex., Guat., Nic., Hond.

L. micromera Schauer. SPANISH THYME. Aromatic shrub to 2m, pilose-hirsute. Lvs to 1.5cm, chartaceous, narrowly obovate,

acute to obtuse, gland., sparingly strigose-hirsute above, hirsute beneath, entire or crenate. Infl. with a solitary peduncle, to 4mm; cor. white, exterior gland. tube to 5mm, distally pubesc. W Indies, Trin., Venez., Guyana.

L. montevidensis Spreng. = Lantana montevidensis.

L. nodiflora (L.) Michx. = Phyla nodiflora.

L. repens hort = Phyla nodiflora var. rosea.

L. wrightii A. Gray = Aloysia wrightii.

→Phyla.

Lipstick Palm Cyrtostachys lakka.
Lipstick Plant Aeschynanthus radicans.
Lipstick Tree Bixa orellana.

Liquidambar L. SWEET GUM. Hamamelidaceae. 4 large decid. trees with fine autumn colour. Lvs palmately lobed, similar to Acer but alt., not opposite. Fls inconspicuous; ♂ fls in catkin-like rac., 5–7cm, made up of sta. only; ♀ flowerheads made up of fused cal. and carpels only. Fr. a globose head of dehiscent capsules. N Amer., Eurasia, China.

L. formosana Hance. FORMOSAN GUM. Straight-trunked tree to 40m, young shoots often corky. Lvs to 15cm diam., 3-lobed, sometimes with subsidiary lobes at base, base cordate to truncate, margins finely serrate, glab. above, usually downy beneath; petioles to 6cm. S China, Taiwan. Z7. Monticola group: plants originally introduced from China by E.H. Wilson, characterized by their large, glab., 3-lobed lvs colouring beautifully in autumn and cold-hardiness.

L. formosana var. **monticola** Rehd. & Wils. = L. formosana Monticola group.

L. imberbe Ait. = L. orientalis.

L. orientalis Mill. ORIENTAL SWEET GUM. Slow-growing, bushy-headed, small tree to 30m in the wild; young shoots glab. Lvs usually 5-lobed, 5–7cm diam., lobes oblong, deep, glab., coarsely toothed and gland.; petioles 2.5–5cm. Spring. Asia Minor. Z8.

L. styraciflua L. SWEET GUM; AMERICAN SWEET GUM; RED GUM. Tall, narrowly pyramidal tree, to 45m in the wild; young shoots smooth, often corky later. Lvs 5- or 7-lobed, 15cm diam., lobes triangular, shining and glab. above, hairy in vein axils beneath. Spring. E US. 'Aurea': lvs mottled and striped yellow. 'Burgundy': autumn colour deep red, turning later and persisting longer than other forms. 'Festival': erect habit; autumn shades of yellow, peach, pink. 'Golden Treasure': lf margins golden yellow. 'Lane Roberts': autumn colour deep black crimson-red. 'Moonbeam': lvs variegated cream; autumn colour vivid. 'Palo Alto': autumn colour orange-red. 'Pendula': upright, columnar; shoots pendent. 'Rotundiloba': lf lobes rounded. 'Variegata': lvs mottled yellow. 'Worplesdon': pyramidal; autumn tints red. Z5.

Liquorice Glycyrrhiza glabra.
Liquorice Fern Polypodium glycyrrhiza.
Liquorice Plant Helichrysum petiolare.
Liquorice Tree Cassia grandis.

Liriodendron L. Magnoliaceae. 2 decid. trees, to 60m. Bark grey, fissured. Lvs oblong in outline, apex wide-emarginate, truncate or retuse, base broadly 1–2-lobed on each side, golden-yellow in fall; stipules free, caducous. Fls term., solitary; tep. 9, outer 3 sepaloid, reflexed, inner petaloid, in 2 whorls of 3; sta. spirally arranged; gynoecia sessile, styles elongate. Fr. cone-like, fusiform. E N Amer., China, Indochina. Z5.

L. chinense (Hemsl.) Sarg. CHINESE TULIP TREE. As for L. tulipifera but to 16m. Lvs more deeply lobed. Fls smaller, inner tep. to 4cm, green, veined yellow; gynoecia protruding. Fr. to 9cm. C China, Indochina. Z8.

L. figo Lour. = Michelia figo.

L. tulipifera L. TULIP TREE; YELLOW POPLAR; TULIP POPLAR; CANARY WHITEWOOD. Tree to 50m+. Lvs to 12cm, bright green, paler beneath. Fls pale yellow-green, banded orange near base; inner tep. 6×3cm; gynoecia included. Fr. to 7cm. E N Amer. 'Aureomarginatum': lf margins yellow or green yellow. 'Contortum': lvs contorted. 'Fastigiatum' ('Pyramidale'): habit narrow-pyramidal; br. fastigiate. 'Integrifolium': lvs oblong, side lobes 0. Z4.

L. tulipifera var. **sinense** Diels = L. chinense.

Liriope Lour. LILY TURF. Liliaceae (Convallariaceae). 5 perenn., everg., tufted or rhizomatous herbs. Lvs grass-like. Fls grape-like, clustered in a scapose spike or rac.; tep. 6; ovary superior, not semi-inferior as in Ophiopogon. Fr. black, berry-like. Jap., China, Vietnam.

L. exiliflora (L.H. Bail.) H. Hume. To 45cm, rhizomatous. Lvs to 45cm, ligulate. Fls mauve, in a lax rac., with a violet rachis and violet-brown scape. Jap., China. 'Silvery Sunproof' ('Ariake Janshige';): lvs striped white to gold. Z7.

L. graminifolia (L.) Bak. To 20cm, rhizomatous. Lvs to 30cm, v. grassy, linear-lanceolate. Fls deep violet-purple to white, clustered in an open, spike-like rac. 15–30cm long, on a black-purple scape. Jap., China. Plants grown under this name are often *L. muscari*. Z8.

L. graminifolia hort. non (L.) Bak. = *L. muscari*.

L. graminifolia var. *densiflora* Bak. = *L. muscari*.

L. japonica hort. = *Ophiopogon japonicus*.

L. minor (Maxim.) Mak. Close to *L. muscari* but smaller and with fewer fls. Z6.

L. muscari (Decne.) L.H. Bail. To 45cm, tufted, with thick, dark tubers. Lvs to 60cm, linear-ligulate, glossy dark green. Fls dark mauve, densely clustered. on a spike-like rac. China, Taiwan, Jap. Over 30cvs; height 18–60cm, dwarf to sturdy; lvs deep green, occas. variegated white or yellow; spikes with variable density; fls white to lilac, violet or dark mauve; cvs notable for habit include 'Grandiflora' (to 60cm; lvs narrow, arching; fls lavender); 'Christmas Tree' (to 20cm; fls large); for lvs: 'Variegata' (lvs boldly striped yellow at margin); 'Gold-banded' (compact; lvs wide, dark green edged gold, arching); 'John Burch' (lvs wide, yellow-green central stripe fls large, spike tall); 'Silvery Midget' (to 18cm; lvs variegated white); for fls: 'Monroe White' (fls large, pure white, abundant); 'Big Blue' (fls lavender, in dense spikes); 'Lilac Beauty' (st. stiff, tall; fls dark lilac, abundant); 'Curly Twist' (fls lilac flushed burgundy; lvs twisting); 'Majestic' (tall; fls rich violet); 'Ingwersen' (fls deep violet); 'Royal Purple' (fls dark purple, profuse). Z6.

L. muscari var. *densiflora* hort. = *L. muscari*.

L. muscari var. *exiliflora* L.H. Bail. = *L. exiliflora*.

L. platyphylla F.T. Wang & Tang. = *L. muscari*.

L. spicata Lour. To 25cm, rhizomatous. Lvs to 35cm, grass-like, minutely serrate. Fls pale mauve to nearly white, more distinctly tubular than in *L. muscari*, rachis mauve, scape mauve-brown. China, Vietnam. 'Alba': to 22cm, spreading; lvs narrow, dark green; fls white. 'Silver Dragon': to 20cm, compact; lvs narrow, striped silvery white; fls pale purple; fr. white-green marked green. Z4.

Lisianthius P. Browne. Gentianaceae. 27 glab. herbs and shrubs. Lvs opposite, sometimes amplexicaul, entire. Fls large, 5-merous, in cymes, corymbs or umbels; cor. tube long, lobes spreading; anth. included in tube. C & S Amer., Carib. Z9.

L. exaltatus (L.) Lam. = *Eustoma exaltatum*.

L. nigrescens Cham. & Schltr. FLOR DE MUERTO. Shrub to 2m. Lvs oblong-lanceolate, acuminate, nearly united at base. Infl. to 1m, diffuse; fls to 5cm, blue-black, nodding. Summer. S Mex., C Amer.

L. russellianus Hook. = *Eustoma russellianum* and *E. grandi-florum*.

L. zelanicus Spreng. = *Exacum trinervium*.

Lissochilus R. Br.

L. giganteus Welw. = *Eulophia horsfallii*.

L. horsfallii Batem. = *Eulophia horsfallii*.

L. krebsii Rchb. f. = *Eulophia streptopetala*.

L. speciosus R. Br. ex Lindl. = *Eulophia speciosa*.

Listera R. Br. Orchidaceae. 25 herbaceous, terrestrial orchids. Rhiz. short. St. erect. Lvs 2, sessile, almost opposite, sited just below st. centre. Rac. spike-like, slender; tep. subequal, narrow-elliptic, incurved; lip deeply divided from apex, sometimes with 2 basal lobes. Late spring–summer. Temp. Asia, N Amer., Eur. Z6.

L. cordata (L.) R. Br. LESSER TWAYBLADE. To 20cm. Lvs 1–3cm, ovate-deltate or triangular-cordate. Rac. to 6cm; fls olive-green to rust; lip to 0.8cm, green flushed mauve, linear with 2 small lat. lobes at base and apex broadly cleft. Eur., Asia, N Amer., Greenland.

L. ovata (L.) R. Br. TWAYBLADE. To 60cm. Lvs 20–60cm, ovate to broadly elliptic. Rac. 7–25cm; fls green, rarely tinged red-brown; lip 7–15mm, ligulate, apically cleft, lat. lobes 0 or greatly reduced. Eur. to C Asia.

Listrostachys Rchb. f. Orchidaceae. 1 monopodial epiphytic orchid. St. to 8cm. Lvs 8–35cm, ligulate or linear-oblong, 2-ranked. Rac. erect or spreading, 10–25cm, many-fld; fls small, distichous, white, sometimes spotted red toward base, sep. 2–3mm, ovate, pet. shorter and narrower; lip entire, 2–3mm, obovate or ± quadrate; spur 3.5–5mm, red. W Afr. to Zaire. Z10.

L. monteiroae Rchb. f. = *Cyrtorchis monteiroae*.

L. pertusa (Lindl.) Rchb. f.

L. sedenii Rchb. f. Schltr. = *Cyrtorchis arcuata*.

→*Angraecum*.

Litchee *Litchi chinensis*.

Litchi Sonn. Sapindaceae. 1 tree, 12–20m. Lvs to 25cm, pinnate, pinnae 2–8, to 20cm, entire, coriaceous, elliptic-oblong to lanceolate. Pan. term., to 30cm; fls unisexual, white tinged green or yellow, in 5–12-fld cymes; cal. shallowly 4- or 5-lobed; pet. 0, sta. usually 8, fil. hairy; ovary 2-branched; ovary bilobed, style 2-branched; ovary bilobed, bilocular. Fr. a drupe, c3.5×3cm, shell thin but tough, apricot to bright red to purple when ripe, smooth to corrugated with dense, pointed blisters; seeds single, large, with a white fleshy edible aril. S China. Z9.

L. chinensis Sonn. LYCHEE; LITCHEE. So long improved in cult. that wild forms are thought to be unknown. ssp. *chinensis* Sonn. Twigs slender, diam. to 3.5mm. ssp. *philippinensis* (Radlk.) Leenh. Lvs with pinnae in 1–2, rarely 3 pairs. ssp. *javensis* Leenh. Twigs thick, to 7mm diam. Fls in sessile clusters. →*Nephelium*.

Lithi *Lithrea caustica*.

Lithocarpus Bl. TANBARK OAK. Fagaceae. 300 everg. trees. Lvs leathery, mostly entire, rarely dentate. ♂ fls in erect spikes, sta. 10–12; ♀ fls at the base of ♂ spikes or in stout, stiff spikes; cal. 4–6-lobed; pet. 0; styles 3. Fr. a v. hard-shelled, acorn-like nut in a cal. cupule. SE Asia and Indon., 2 in Jap. and 1 in W N Amer.

L. cleistocarpus (Seemen) Rehd. & Wils. Tree to 20m+; young shoots glab. Lvs 10–20cm, lanceolate or narrowly elliptic, long-acuminate, entire, grey-green, glab. Fr. 2–2.5cm thick, in dense clusters on stiff, 5–7cm-long spikes. C China. Z7.

L. cordifolius (L. f.) L. Bol. = *Aptenia cordifolia*.

L. densiflorus (Hook. & Arn.) Rehd. TANBARK OAK. Tree to 30m, rarely 45m, bark red-brown. Young shoots white-woolly. Lvs 5–13cm, elliptic to oblong, acute, stiff and leathery, toothed, initially stellate-pubesc. above, white tomentose beneath. Fr. 2–2.5cm, grouped 1–3. N Amer. var. *echinoides* (R. Br.) Abrams. Shrub to 3m. Lvs only 3–6cm, obtuse. Z7.

L. edulis (Mak.) Nak. Small tree to 10m+, often a shrub in cult.; young shoots glab. Lvs 7–15cm, narrowly elliptic to oblanceolate, entire, leathery, acuminate, glossy yellow-green above, grey-green beneath. Fr. 2.5×0.8cm, grouped 2–3 together on an axill. spike. Jap. Z7.

L. glaber (Thunb.) Nak. Tree to 7m, or shrub; young shoots tomentose. Lvs 7–14cm, elliptic-oblong to lanceolate, leathery, tough, acuminate, entire or with teeth at apex, glossy above, white-tomentose beneath. Fr. 1.5–2cm, sessile and pubesc. on term., 5–12cm spikes. Jap., E China. Z7.

L. henryi (Seemen) Rehd. & Wils. Tree to 20m+ with a rounded crown; young shoots grey-brown, soft-pubesc. with white lenticels. Lvs 10–25cm, elliptic-oblong, long-acuminate, entire, glossy above, paler beneath. Fr. 2cm, many, on stiff, 15cm, erect spikes. C China. Z7.

L. pachyphyllus (Kurz) Rehd. Tree to c35m with spreading br. Young shoots soft-pubesc. Lvs 10–23cm, elliptic-lanceolate, acuminate, entire, leathery, tough, glossy dark green above, silvery-green stellate pubesc. beneath. Fr. in 3's on thick spikes to 15cm with 6 or 9 acorn cups fused into a mass 3–4cm thick. E Himal. Z9.

Lithodora Griseb. Boraginaceae. 7 shrublets and subshrubs. Lvs linear to elliptic to obovate, often setose. Cymes small, term., leafy; cal. lobes 5, narrow; cor. infundibular or hypocrateri-form, throat without appendages, lobes ovate to suborbicular; sta. usually included; style filiform, simple or branched above. SW Eur. to Asia Minor.

L. diffusa (Lagasca) Johnst. St. to 60cm, procumbent or strag-gling, setaceous. Lvs to 3.8cm, elliptic or oblong to linear, margin sometimes inflexed, setose. Cor. to 21mm, blue, sometimes purple, exterior pubesc., throat with a dense ring of long white hairs. NW Fr. to SW Eur. 'Alba': fls white. 'Cambridge Blue': to 8cm high; fls light blue. 'Grace Ward': habit low and trailing, to 15cm high; lvs narrow, dark green; fls azure blue, long-lasting. 'Heavenly Blue': habit v. low, to 8cm high; fls small, azure blue, profuse. Z7.

L. fruticosa (L.) Griseb. St. to 60cm, tufted, erect, white-setose when young, dark grey with age. Lvs to 2.5cm, linear or oblong-linear, white-setulose, margins tuberculate-hispid, revolute. Cor. to 15mm, blue or purple, lobes setulose. Spain, S Fr. Z8.

L. oleifolia (Lapeyr.) Griseb. St. to 45cm, slender, diffuse, ascending. Lvs to 4cm, obovate or oblong-obovate, slightly hispid above, white-sericeous beneath. Cor. pink becoming blue, exterior sericeous, interior glab., tube to 12mm, lobes to 3mm, rounded. E Pyren. 'Barker's Form': habit spreading, to 12cm high, v. vigorous; fls pale sky blue. Z7.

L. prostrata (Lois.) Griseb. = *L. diffusa*.

L. rosmarinifolia (Ten.) Johnst. St. to 60cm, tufted; br. erect or pendent, grey-pubesc. above. Lvs to 6cm, narrowly lanceolate to linear, dark green, glab. or setulose above, densely grey-setose beneath, margin revolute. Cor. tube to 12mm, lilac, blue or white, exterior setulose, throat slightly gland., limb to 17mm diam., lobes oblong, rounded. S It., Sicily, NE Alg. Z8.

L. zahnii (Heldr. ex Hal.) Johnst. St. to 60cm, tufted, much-branched; br. erect or ascending, sericeous, becoming black and leafless with age. Lvs to 4cm, coriaceous, linear or linear-oblong, grey-green and hispid above, densely grey-setose beneath, revolute. Cor. white or blue, glab., tube to 10mm, limb to 15mm diam., lobes ovate, obtuse. S Greece. Z8.

→*Lithospermum*.

Lithophragma (Nutt.) Torr. & A. Gray. WOODLAND STAR. Saxifragaceae. 9 fibrous-rooted and bulbiliferous perenn. herbs. Lvs basal, rosulate, petiolate, reniform to orbicular, 3-lobed or trifoliate. Flowering st. simple or branching, leafy; infl. racemose; fl. small, often replaced by bulbils; sep. 5, triangular; pet. 5, clawed, longer than sep.; sta. 10. W N Amer. Z8.

L. affine A. Gray. Lvs pubesc., orbicular to reniform, 3–5-lobed, petiole to 22cm. Flowering st. to 55cm, simple; pet. white 6–13mm, usually 3-lobed.

L. anemonoides Green = *L. parviflorum*.

L. austromontanum Heller = *L. parviflorum*.

L. bolanderi A. Gray. Lvs orbicular, pubesc., 3–5 lobed; petiole to 25cm. Flowering st. to 85cm, 2–3-branched; fls fragrant; pet. white, 4–7mm, usually entire.

L. brevilobum Rydb. = *L. tenellum*.

L. bulbiferum Rydb. = *L. glabrum*.

L. glabrum Nutt. Lvs sparsely pubesc., orbicular to trifoliate, often tinged red; petiole 1–4cm. Flowering st. to 35cm, sometimes branched; fls often replaced by bulbils; pet. pink, rarely white, 5–7mm, 5-lobed.

L. heterophyllum (Hook. & Arn.) Torr. & A. Gray. Similar to *L. affine* except petiole to 8cm, flowering st. often many-branched.

L. parviflorum (Hook.) Nutt. ex Torr. & A. Gray. Lvs 3-lobed to trifoliate, nearly glab. to densely pubesc.; petiole less than 6cm. Flowering st. to 50cm, unbranched; pet. white-pink 7–16mm, 3-cleft.

L. rupicola Greene = *L. tenellum*.

L. tenellum Nutt. Lvs 3–5 irregularly lobed or digitate, sparsely pubesc.; petiole less than 8cm. Flowering st. to 30cm, simple; pet. pink or white, 3–7mm, 5-lobed.

L. tenellum var. *florida* Suksd. = *L. glabrum*.

L. thompsonii Hoover = *L. tenellum*.

L. trilobum Rydb. = *L. heterophyllum*.

→*Tellima*.

Lithops N.E. Br. LIVING STONES; FLOWERING STONES; PEBBLE PLANTS. Aizoaceae. 35. Succulent, tufted, stemless perennials. Plant body composed of 2 lobes, united for most of their length with a marked central fissure, the face or upper surface of each elliptic to reniform, concave, flat or convex, with a range of stone-like characters and often a central panel differing in colour from body. Fls solitary, emerging from the fissure. Mid-summer–early winter. S Afr., Nam. Z9.

L. alpina Dinter = *L. pseudotruncatella*.

L. annae Boer = *L. gesineae* var. *annae*.

L. archerae Boer = *L. pseudotruncatella* ssp. *archerae*.

L. aucampiae L. Bol. Body 20–32mm, face elliptic-reniform, brick to sandy brown or ochre with sienna to green-brown dots, often joined by slender fissures, sometimes forming a semi-lucent green-brown panel with blotches and a broken margin. Fls 3–5.2cm diam., yellow. Early autumn. NW Cape. 'Betty's Beryl': upper surface yellow-green, largely covered with an olive panel with many blotches and irregular margins; fls white. 'Storm's Snowcap': face pale ginger to sandy brown, marked darker brown; fls white. var. *koelemanii* (Boer) Cole. Face pale rust to grey-brown, covered with fine, broken lines resembling hieroglyphs or cerebral folds. Fls 3–5.5cm, yellow. ssp. *euniceae* (Boer) Cole. Face dove-grey to pale brown, central panel brown, minute and sparse or large and congested blotches spreading to margins as fringe of crazed veins. var. *fluminalis* Cole. Face pale grey, sometimes tinged pink, panel translucent grey, irregular, often with blotches spreading outwards by dendritic fissures. Fls 2.5–4.5cm diam., yellow.

L. aurantiaca L. Bol. = *L. hookeri*.

L. bella N.E. Br. = *L. karasmontana* ssp. *bella*.

L. bella var. *lericheana* (Dinter & Schwantes) Boer = *L. karasmontana* var. *lericheana*.

L. brevis L. Bol. = *L. dinteri* var. *brevis*.

L. bromfieldii L. Bol. Body 15–32mm, lobes equal, face elliptic-reniform, buff to grey with rugae sunken, irregular, dark red edged grey-green, brain-like. Fls 2.5–4.5cm diam., yellow. NW

Cape. var. *glaudinae* (Boer) Cole. Face dove-grey or dull olive, flat, glaucous with many translucent olive or dark brown spots and figures, some appearing polished, resembling a pitted, ore-bearing stone. var. *insularis* (L. Bol.) Fearn. Face ± concave with large pitted dots merging to form a loose network of crazed bronze-green markings. 'Sulphurea': upper surface dull mustard-yellow marked grey-green, otherwise as for var. *insularis*. var. *mennellii* (L. Bol.) Fearn. Face dull dove-grey, often with a brown or pink tint, with deep, broken, chocolate to dark green fissures.

L. bromfieldii var. *insularis* f. *sulphurea* Y. Shimada) = *L. bromfieldii* var. *insularis* 'Sulphurea'.

L. christinae Boer = *L. schwantesii* var. *urikosensis*.

L. chrysocephala Nel = *L. julii*.

L. commoda Dinter = *L. karasmontana*.

L. comptonii L. Bol. Body 25–30mm, face elliptic-reniform, rounded-convex, smooth, sublustrous, blue-grey to lilac-grey, panel slate-grey with blotches and crazed to fissured edges. Fls 2–3cm diam., yellow with white centre. W Cape. var. *weberi* (Nel) Cole. Body sides dove-grey, faces buff (as are numerous raised, scattered blotches) ± covered by a slate-grey panel with fissured edges.

L. comptonii var. *viridis* H. Lück.) Fearn. = *L. viridis*.

L. dabneri L. Bol. = *L. hookeri* var. *dabneri*.

L. dendritica Nel = *L. pseudotruncatella* ssp. *dendritica*.

L. dinteri Schwantes. Body 20–30cm, face elliptic-reniform, flat to convex, buff, panel grey-green with an irregular or broadly lobed edge, a scattering of small milky blotches and blood-red dots or dashes. Fls 2–3, 2cm diam., yellow. Nam. 'Dintergreen': markings rather clouded, grey-green, red spots obscure. var. *brevis* (L. Bol.) Fearn. Body 15–20mm, face buff to grey, panel leaden grey with a relatively unbroken edge, no blotches and few or no red dashes. NW Cape. ssp. *frederici* (Cole) Cole. Body 15–20mm, face rounded, buff to pale grey, panel so thickly crowded by blotches, lobes and dots as to be reduced to scattered, misshapen dark grey figures with embedded red flecks. ssp. *multipunctata* (Boer) Cole. Body 20–30mm, face mushroom-grey to pale buff, slightly darker toward centre, panel occluded appearing as irregular distinct hieroglyphs or blood-red spots.

L. dinteri var. *marthae* (Loesch & Tisch.) Fearn. = *L. schwantesii* var. *marthae*.

L. dinteri var. *multipunctata* Boer = *L. dinteri* ssp. *multipunctata*.

L. divergens L. Bol. Body 15–20mm, face oblong-reniform, dove-grey, sometimes suffused tan or rose, panel glossy, dark grey-green, filled with small dots and figures. Fls 1.5–2.7cm diam., yellow with a white centre. NW Cape. var. *amethystina* Boer. Body 20–25mm, fissure and margins of upper surface strongly tinted lilac-mauve.

L. dorotheae Nel. Body 20–30mm, convex, rounded, dark biege or buff, panel translucent grey-green or olive with jagged to lobed edges and large blotches (sometimes reducing it to a pattern of hieroglyphs), with red dots. Fls 2.5–4.2cm diam., yellow. NW Cape.

L. eberlanzii (Dinter & Schwantes) Boer & Boom = *L. karasmontana* ssp. *eberlanzii*.

L. edithae N.E. Br. = *L. pseudotruncatella* var. *riehmerae*.

L. edithiae L. Bol. = *L. karasmontana* ssp. *eberlanzii*.

L. eksteeniae L. Bol. = *L. dorotheae*.

L. elevata L. Bol. = *L. optica*.

L. elisabethiae Dinter = *L. pseudotruncatella* var. *elisabethiae*.

L. elisae Boer = *L. marmorata* var. *elisae*.

L. erniana Tisch. & Jacobsen = *L. karasmontana* ssp. *eberlanzii*.

L. farinosa Dinter = *L. pseudotruncatella* var. *dendritica*.

L. fossulifera Tisch. nom. nud. = *L. karasmontana* var. *tischeri*.

L. framesii L. Bol. = *L. marmorata*.

L. francisci (Dinter & Schwantes) N.E. Br. Body 25–30mm, face elliptic-reniform, flat to convex, dove-grey, panel remaining as obscure darker grey fissures, whole surface dotted dark grey-green, dots sometimes coalescing. Fls 1.5–2cm, diam., yellow. Nam.

L. frederici Cole = *L. dinteri* ssp. *frederici*.

L. friedrichiae (Dinter) N.E. Br. = *Conophytum friedrichiae*.

L. fulleri N.E. Br. = *L. julii* ssp. *fulleri*.

L. fulleri var. *chrysedha* (Nel) Boer = *L. julii*.

L. fulleri var. *kennedyi* Boer = *L. verruculosa* ssp. *kennedyi*.

L. fulleri var. *ochracea* Boer = *L. hallii* var. *ochracea*.

L. fulleri var. *tapscottii* L. Bol. = *L. julii* ssp. *fulleri*.

L. fulviceps (N.E. Br.) N.E. Br. Body 25–30mm, face oblong, reniform, flat, tawny, buff or grey tinted rose, covered with polished, raised, grey-green spots sometimes linked by blood-red sunken dots. Fls 2.5–3.5cm diam., yellow. Nam. to NW Cape. var. *lactinea* Cole. Body blue-grey, face lilac-lined, spots many, blue-green, linked by sunken, blood-red rugae.

L. gesineae Boer. Body 18–22mm, face flat to domed, dull tan to grey, panel translucent olive, occluded by jigsaw-like blotches, appearing as a pattern of mossy green speckles or narrow dark fissures. Fls 2.5–4cm diam., yellow. Nam. var. *annae* (Boer) Cole. Larger with darker markings forming a denser pattern.

L. geyeri Nel. Body 20–25mm, face elliptic, flat or slightly convex, pale buff, panel translucent, olive to mahogany, virtually entire and unblotched in a smooth half moon or occluded, forming a blurred, crazed pattern. Fls 2.5–4cm diam., yellow, often with white centre. NW Cape.

L. glaudinae Boer = *L. bromfieldii* var. *glaudinae*.

L. gracilidelineata Dinter. Body to 35mm, face flat, rugose, reniform, pale grey overlaying a broken pattern of fine, sunken, black or cinnamon lines; in some forms, the vein colour tints much of the surface pale fleshy brown. Fls 2.5–4.5cm diam., yellow. Nam. 'Fritz's White Lady': fls white. var. *waldroniae* Boer. Somewhat smaller. Face pearly grey impressed with fine, intricately branching blood-red lines. Fls 1–2cm diam., yellow. ssp. *brandbergensis* (Boer) Cole. Body to 36mm, face beige, darker toward centre, with obscure spots and chestnut dendritic lines.

L. gulielmi L. Bol. = *L. schwantesii*.

L. hallii Boer. Body 17–20mm, face flat, grey-buff or pale brown, panel translucent dark olive to brown, often with bright red dots in marginal sinuses, with many raised blotches. Fls 2.5–4.5cm diam., white. NW Cape. var. *ochracea* (Boer) Cole. Smaller with lobes and tinted ginger, panel pale brick-red, unblotched with indented edges, each sinus containing a red spot or blotched and reticulate. Fls 2.5–4.7cm, diam., white. NW Cape. 'Green Soapstone': face lime-green, panel jade to olive.

L. helmutii L. Bol. Body 20–25mm, face elliptic-reniform, v. convex, battleship grey marbled or speckled glossy grey-green. Fls yellow with white centre. NW Cape.

L. herrei L. Bol. Body 20–25mm, face flat, dull grey, pale or grey tinted lilac, panel grey-green translucent, with scattered blotches and deeply lobed edges or ± occluded and only a broken pattern of fine crazed lines. Fls 1.5–2.3cm diam., yellow or bronze-yellow with a white centre. NW Cape, S Nam.

L. herrei var. *geyeri* (Nel) Boer & Boom = *L. geyeri*.

L. herrei f. *albiflora* Jacobsen = *L. marmorata*.

L. hookeri (Berg) Schwantes. Body 20–23mm, face flat, reniform-elliptic, buff to pale glaucous brown, panel rich brown, filled by interlocking fleshy figures with deep dark grooves, forming a vermiculate pattern. Fls 2.5–4.5cm diam., yellow. NW Cape. var. *dabneri* (L. Bol.) Cole. Face pale grey, vermiculate patterning v. close, dark grey or grey-green. var. *elephina* (Cole) Cole. Face buff to tan with panel olive-green, fewer, broader blotches and a more open pattern resembling wrinkled hide. var. *lutea* (Boer) Cole. Differs in more open network of deep-sunken, rusty-red grooves over a pale buff surface. var. *marginata* (Cole) Cole. Face dull pink to ochre, minutely and intricately vermiculate, pattern dark grey-green to dull red. var. *subfenestrata* (Boer) Cole. Dull tan with panel olive to grey-green, somewhat lustrous and occluded by heavy-textured, vermiculate blotches. var. *susannae* (Cole) Cole. Body 15–20mm, face pale grey, sometimes with an obscure, darker panel, markings dark, sunken, forming a broken network.

L. inae Nel = *L. verruculosa*.

L. inornata L. Bol. = *L. schwantesii* var. *marthae*.

L. insularis L. Bol. = *L. bromfieldii* var. *insularis*.

L. jacobseniana Schwantes = *L. karasmontana*.

L. julii (Dinter & Schwantes) N.E. Br. Body 20–30mm, face reniform, flat to slightly concave, dove- to dark grey, panel dark brown to olive with red dots, eroded edges and broad blotches, leaving a pattern of loose reticulation, often with a brown stain on the inner lip of each lobe. Fls 2.5–4.5cm diam., white. Nam. A pallid form exists with a bold lip stain but patterning obscured by the grey ground colour. 'Peppermint Crème': is a milky blue-green form with a pale grey panel and olive lip stains. ssp. *fulleri* (N.E. Br.) Fearn. Body 12–14mm, face buff to dull grey, panel translucent grey, sometimes with pale blotches, edges eroded and lobed, with dark brown or red spots or dashes in sinuses. 'Fullergreen': body and markings pale grey-green, panel dull sap-green, eroded-reticulate. var. *brunnea* (Boer) Cole. Body 12–14mm, face slightly convex, buff, panel olive to chocolate-brown with few, minute or many, distinct markings, edges shallowly to deeply eroded with red-brown flecks in sinuses. var. *rouxii* (Boer) Cole. Body 15–20mm, face flat, reniform, pale grey or beige, sometimes tinted pink, panel paler still, slightly translucent, with obscure markings, edges only slightly eroded, outlined yellow or ochre with etched red dashes resembling stitches.

L. julii var. *brunnea* Boer = *L. julii* ssp. *fulleri* var. *brunnea*.

L. julii var. *littlewoodii* Boer = *L. julii*.

L. julii var. *pallida* Tisch. = *L. julii*.

L. karasmontana (Dinter & Schwantes) N.E. Br. Highly variable. Body 30–40mm, face elliptic-reniform, flat, concave or convex, rugose, dull grey or beige, panel dark brown, with an

impressed pattern of faint dendritic lines, or, in some variants, pale beige with face rugose and entirely suffused pale brick-red. Fls 2.5–4.5cm diam., white. Nam. var. *lericheana* (Dinter & Schwantes) Cole. Body 15–20mm, lobes near equal, buff, face rounded, rugose, pink-tinted, pale olive to dull jade-green, markings few, large, edges eroded with lobes irregular. var. *tischeri* Cole. Body 20–25mm, face broadly reniform, flat, rugose, capped pale ginger, panel dark olive to chocolate, so obscured by markings and irregular marginal incursions as to be an open pattern of dull, impressed 'veins'. ssp. *bella* (N.E. Br.) Cole. Body 25–30mm, face convex, grey to buff, panel dull olive reduced to an open, jagged-edged network by broad markings and marginal incursions. ssp. *eberlanzii* (Dinter & Schwantes) Cole. Body 25–30mm, close to ssp. *bella*, but with panel paler, markings larger, thus with a closer and more obscure network, often with red dots and dashes. 'Avocado Cream': pale grey capped buff tinted lime, network close, broken, dark olive.

L. kuibisensis Dinter & Jacobsen = *L. schwantesii*.

L. kuibisensis Dinter = *L. schwantesii* var. *urikosensis*.

L. latenitia Dinter = *L. karasmontana*.

L. lericheana (Dinter & Schwantes) N.E. Br. = *L. karasmontana* var. *lericheana*.

L. lesliei (N.E. Br.) N.E. Br. Body 20–45mm, face elliptic-reniform, flat to convex, grey-green to buff to pale terracotta, sometimes capped pale gold, panel pale to dark olive, with eroded edges and dense, dotted, irregular markings forming a fine, mossy, dendritic pattern. Fls 3–5.5cm diam., yellow. N Cape, OFS, Transvaal. 'Albiflora': upper surface of lobes buff marked olive; fls white. 'Albinica': face pale gold, panel dull olive, finely marked; fls white. 'Storm's Albinigold': close to 'Albinica' but with fls yellow. var. *hornii* Boer. Body 20–30mm, lobes grey-buff, face beige to brick, capped pale ginger, pale olive-grey crowded by fine, irregular markings, edges with minute branching channels. var. *mariae* Cole. Body 20–30mm, lobes grey-buff, face sandy gold, panel olive, finely and densely marked appearing minutely green-gold-speckled. var. *minor* Boer. 15–18mm, face terracotta, panel dark green with minutely eroded margins and many, irregular, perforated markings. var. *rubrobrunnea* Boer. Close to var. *minor* but larger, face terracotta to dusty pink, more closely marked over olive panel. Fls yellow, to 3.5cm diam. var. *venteri* (Nel) Boer & Boom. Body pale grey, panel dark grey to grey-green, unmarked with minutely eroded edges or with fine and dense markings leaving a mossy, dark, dendritic pattern. ssp. *burchellii* Cole. Body pale grey or buff, panel charcoal-grey with many fine markings creating an intricate, spreading network, or virtually unmarked, characterized by radiating marginal lines with expanded tips.

L. lesliei var. *applanata* Boer nom. nud. = *L. lesliei*.

L. lesliei var. *luteoviridis* Boer = *L. lesliei*.

L. lesliei f. *albiflora* Cole). = *L. lesliei* 'Albiflora'.

L. lesliei f. *albinica* Cole) = *L. lesliei* 'Albinica'.

L. lineata Nel = *L. ruschiorum* var. *lineata*.

L. localis (N.E. Br.) Schwantes = *L. schwantesii* ssp. *terricolor*.

L. lydiae L. Bol. = *L. fulviceps*.

L. marginata Nel = *L. hookeri* var. *marginata*.

L. marmorata (N.E. Br.) N.E. Br. Body 28–30mm, face narrow-reniform, flat to convex, pale grey or beige sometimes tinted green or lilac, panel translucent, dark grey or grey-green, spreading outward from an arc on inner lip, closely and deeply marked with jagged edges, resembling a grey fissured stone. Fls 2.5–4.5cm diam., white. NW Cape. var. *elisae* (Boer) Cole. Body 15–25mm, usually buff or beige, panel so crowded with a few large markings as to appear a pale, loose pattern of crazed and impressed veins.

L. marthae Loesch & Tisch. = *L. schwantesii* var. *marthae*.

L. maughanii N.E. Br. = *L. julii* ssp. *fulleri*.

L. mennellii L. Bol. = *L. bromfieldii* var. *mennellii*.

L. meyeri L. Bol. Body 20–30mm, face elongate-elliptic to reniform, flat and smooth or slightly concave and wrinkled, pale lilac-grey capped dove-grey, with a slightly darker, semi-translucent, unmarked panel. Fls 2.5–4cm diam., yellow with a white centre. NW Cape. 'Hammeruby': body lobes dull garnet.

L. mickbergensis Dinter = *L. karasmontana*.

L. naureeniae Cole. Body 20–25mm, face reniform, slightly convex, grey to buff, panel olive, unmarked with a finely fringed edged or scattered with jigsaw-piece markings, edges deeply eroded and lobed. Fls 2.5–3.5cm diam., yellow with a white centre. NW Cape.

L. nelii Schwantes = *L. ruschiorum*.

L. olivacea L. Bol. Body to 20mm, face flat, reniform with a straight inner margin, pale grey or beige, panel translucent, olive, edge slightly eroded, clear or with a few, scattered, raised markings. Fls 2.5–4cm diam., yellow with white centre. SW Cape.

L. opalina Dinter = *L. karasmontana*.

L. optica (Marloth) N.E. Br. Body 20–30mm, face reniform to broadly elliptic, convex, grey-green to dove-grey with a blue-green panel, unmarked with edges slightly eroded or marked, resembling a broad bean. Fls 1.2–2cm diam., white, often pink-tipped. Nam. 'Rubra': body lobes dull ruby-red, panel darker, unmarked.

L. orpenii L. Bol. nom. nud. = *L. lesliei*.

L. otzeniana Nel. Body 25–30mm, face reniform-elliptic, convex, buff, panel dull olive-brown, semi-translucent with edges deeply eroded and a few broad, intramarginal markings. Fls 2.3–5cm diam., yellow with white centre. NW Cape. 'Aquamarine': body and markings grey-green, panel dark blue-green.

L. peersii L. Bol. = *L. schwantesii L. terricolor*.

L. pilarsii L. Bol. = *L. ruschiorum*.

L. pseudotruncatella (A. Berger) N.E. Br. Body 25–30mm, face broadly reniform, flat to slightly concave, grey to buff, panel olive-brown, obscured and appearing as a fine network of dots and mossy 'veins', terminating in dull red dashes, sometimes staining edges pale copper. Fls 2.5–5cm diam., yellow. Nam. var. *elisabethiae* (Dinter) Boer & Boom. Slightly smaller, body grey tinted lilac-blue or pink, markings dark grey, marginal dashes bright red. var. *riehmerae* Cole Slightly smaller, body milky grey with a fine, moss-like, pale olive pattern. ssp. *archerae* (Boer) Cole. Face reniform, pale grey with a slightly darker central zone, faint, delicate radial fissures, obscure spotting and, sometimes, marginal red dots and dashes. ssp. *dendritica* (Nel) Cole. Face grey with a regular network of fine, dark hieroglyph-like markings, radiating from a distinct, straight line of colour at inner margin. ssp. *groendrayensis* (Jacobsen) Cole. Body 20–40mm, face elliptic-reniform, flat, slightly rugose, pale grey with the faintest blue-grey central zone, sometimes fissured, sometimes with a scattering of minute red dots. ssp. *volkii* (Schwantes ex Boer & Boom) Cole. Body 30–40mm, lobes unequal, upper surface rounded-reniform, pale milky grey with faint marbling or dots.

L. pseudotruncatella var. *alta* Tisch. = *L. pseudotruncatella*.

L. pseudotruncatella var. *edithae* (N.E. Br.) Boer & Boom = *L. pseudotruncatella* var. *riehmerae*.

L. rugosa Dinter = *L. schwantesii* var. *rugosa*.

L. ruschiorum (Dinter & Schwantes) N.E. Br. Body 20–45mm, face convex, pale grey or cream, glaucous, plain or with faint impressed dots or a broken network of crazed lines inlaid with dark rust dashes. Fls 1.5–3cm diam., yellow. Nam. var. *lineata* (Nel) Cole. Lobes buff to beige with a network of brown to red capillary-like lines.

L. salicola L. Bol. Body 20–25mm, face reniform-elliptic, slightly convex, grey, panel translucent sap-green with eroded and red-dotted edges and embedded markings or with many small, scattered golden markings. 'Malachite': body grey-green, panel olive edged ochre, ragged-edged, markings ochre or lime-green, some clouded.

L. salicola var. *reticulata* Boer = *L. hallii*.

L. schwantesii Dinter. Body 30–40mm, face oblong-reniform, rugose, grey or buff capped pale plum, panel olive-grey with a network of cinnamon lines. Fls 2.5–3.6cm diam., yellow. Nam. var. *marthae* (Loesch & Tisch.) Cole. Body 20–30mm, fawn to grey, panel grey edged ochre, markings few, vein-like, brick-red. var. *rugosa* (Dinter) Boer & Boom. Body 15–20mm, grey-buff to pale lilac, panel fleshy pink or sandy brown with a close network of impressed brown lines and figures, appearing rugose, darkly dotted. var. *urikosensis* (Dinter) Boer & Boom. Body 12–30mm, fissure deep, fawn capped pale ochre, closely netted burn sienna, the lines broken and sunken, often appearing dotted. ssp. *gesneri* (Boer) Cole. Body 20–25mm, lobes apex, grey-tan, capped pale brown with a network of red-brown lines. ssp.*steineckeana* Tisch. Body 15mm, face semicircular, convex, grey-white suffused dirty cream, usually with a few grey-green dots, panel small, opaque, seldom present. Fls 2–3.2cm diam. Possibly a gdn hybrid. ssp. *terricolor* N.E. Br. Body 20–25mm, face oblong-reniform; slightly convex, buff to tan, closely spotted olive or mid-green. Fls 1.5–3.5cm diam., yellow, occas. with a white centre. 'Silver Spurs': golden, spotted olive; fls pure white. 'Speckled Gold': lobes grey-green, capped dull gold, spotted olive.

L. schwantesii var. *begseri* Boer = *L. schwantesii* ssp. *gesneri*.

L. schwantesii var. *nutupsdriftensis* Boer = *L. schwantesii* var. *urikosensis*.

L. triebneri L. Bol. = *L. schwantesii*.

L. turbiniformis (Haw.) N.E. Br. = *L. hookeri*.

L. turbiniformis var. *brunneo-violacea* Boer = *L. hookeri* var. *subfenestrata*.

L. turbiniformis var. *dabneri* (L. Bol.) Cole = *L. hookeri* var. *dabneri*.

L. turbiniformis var. *elephina* Cole = *L. hookeri* var. *elephina*.

L. turbiniformis var. *lutea* Boer = *L. hookeri* var. *lutea*.

L. turbiniformis var. *subfenestrata* Boer = *L. hookeri* var. *subfenestrata*.

L. urikosensis Dinter = *L. schwantesii* var. *urikosensis*.

L. ursulae nom. nud. = *L. karasmontana*.

L. vallis-mariae (Dinter & Schwantes) N.E. Br. Body 20–40mm, face flat, broadly reniform-elliptic, dove-grey with a network of obscure, translucent grey lines, sometimes appearing as scattered dots. Fls 2–3cm diam., straw-yellow, rarely orange-yellow, sometimes tinged pink or bronze. Nam.

L. vallis-mariae var. *margarethae* Boer = *L. vallis-mariae*.

L. vanzylii L. Bol. = *Dinteranthus vanzylii*.

L. verruculosa Nel. Body 20–30mm, face reniform-oblong to rounded-triangular, grey capped tan, sometimes with a darker grey translucent panel and small tan markings, finely fissured, covered with raised red-brown dots. Fls 2–3.5cm diam., yellow to orange rose or white, frequently with a contrasting centre. NW Cape. var. *glabra* Boer. Body 20–25mm, grey edged buff panel dark grey, edge eroded, with fewer red dots. Fls 2–3cm diam., white. ssp. *deboeri* (Schwantes) Cole. Has many more markings, occluding the panel with a deeply fissured network. ssp. *kennedyi* (Boer) Cole. Lobes dove-grey capped pale ginger, panel dull olive with scattered ginger markings.

L. viridis H. Lück. Body 17–20mm, face reniform to semicircular, convex, dull grey, panel translucent grey-green, usually clear and covering most of upper surface, edge slightly eroded. Fls 2.5–3.5cm diam., yellow with white centre. NW Cape.

L. volkii Schwantes ex Boer & Boom = *L. pseudotruncatella* ssp. *volkii*.

L. weberi Nel = *L. comptonii* var. *weberi*.

L. werneri Schwantes & Jacobsen Body 10–15mm, face oblong-reniform, flat to convex, pale grey, panel dark olive, obscured by many dark dots fused to form a dendritic pattern branching toward outer margin. Fls 1.5–2.8cm diam., yellow. Nam.

→*Mesembryanthemum*.

Lithospermum L. GROMWELL'S PUCCOON. Boraginaceae. 60 ann. or perenn. herbs. St. erect or decumbent, herbaceous or shrubby, hispid, strigose or villous. Lvs alt. Fls bracteate, stalked, in term. rac. or solitary in lf axils; cal. usually 5-lobed, cor. infundibular to hypocrateriform, exterior pubesc., plicate or gibbous at throat, often with appendages, lobes equal; sta. 5, included; ovary 5-lobed, style usually filiform. Cosmop. (except Aus.).

L. angustifolium Michx. = *L. incisum*.

L. benthamii (Wallich ex G. Don) Johnst. = *Arnebia benthamii*.

L. brevifolium Engelm. & Gray = *L. incisum*.

L. calycinum Morris = *Amsinckia calycina*.

L. canescens (Michx.) Lehm. PUCCOON; INDIAN PAINT. Perenn., canescent. St. to 40cm, adpressed-pubesc. Lvs to 4cm, linear-oblong to ovate-oblong, cor. yellow to orange-yellow, limb to 15mm diam., tube to 8mm, interior glab., with gland. appendages in throat. N Amer. Z3.

L. caroliniense (Walter) MacMill. Perenn., hispid. St. to 100cm, minutely adpressed-pubesc. Lvs to 4cm, lanceolate or linear-lanceolate, hispid; cor. orange-yellow, exterior villous-hispid, lobes to 10mm, ovate to suborbicular, tube to 13mm, throat appendages puberulent. E N Amer. Z6.

L. decumbens Vent. = *Arnebia decumbens*.

L. densiflorum Ledeb. ex Nordm. = *Arnebia densiflora*.

L. diffusum Lagasca = *Lithodora diffusa*.

L. distichum (G. Don) Ortega. Perenn. St. to 20cm, ascending, often branched at base, sericeous. Lvs strigose; basal lvs to 8.5cm, oblong-lanceolate to spathulate, cauline lvs to 3cm, lanceolate to oblong. Cor. white, tube to 6mm, lobes to 4mm, rounded. Mex., Guat. Z9.

L. doerfleri hort. = *Moltkia doerfleri*.

L. echioides Benth. = *Mertensia echioides*.

L. elongatum Decne. = *Mertensia elongata*.

L. ×froebelii Sünderm. = *Moltkia ×intermedia* 'Froebelii'.

L. fruticosum L. = *Lithodora fruticosa*.

L. gastonii Benth. = *Buglossoides gastonii*.

L. gmelinii Michx. = *L. caroliniense*.

L. graminifolium Viv. = *Moltkia suffruticosa*.

L. griffithii (Boiss.) Johnst. = *Arnebia griffithii*.

L. hirtum (Muhlenb.) Lehm. = *L. caroliniense*.

L. incisum Lehm. St. to 50cm, solitary to numerous, erect, usually strigose, becoming branched. Basal lvs to 12cm, oblanceolate; cauline lvs to 6cm, linear to linear-lanceolate, hispidulous. Cor. to 35mm, yellow, exterior slightly strigose, lobes to 7mm, ovate, erose-fimbriate, throat appendages slightly glanduliferous, truncate. Central N Amer. Z3.

L. ×intermedium Froebel = *Moltkia ×intermedia*.

L. linarifolium Goldie = *L. incisum*.

L. mandanense Spreng. = *L. incisum*.

L. multiflorum Torr. Perenn., grey-pubesc. St. to 50cm, few to numerous, erect, sometimes branched above. Lvs to 7cm, linear-lanceolate to lanceolate. Cor. yellow-orange, exterior somewhat villous, tube to 10mm, lobes to 3.5mm, broadly ovate, obtuse or rounded, usually entire, throat appendages glanduliferous. W N Amer. Z3.

L. officinale L. St. to 100cm, solitary or numerous, erect, branched, hairy. Lvs to 8cm, lanceolate, revolute, adpressed-bristly. Cor. green, yellow or yellow-white, tube to 4mm, limb to 4mm diam., lobes to 1.5mm, spreading, throat appendages trapeziform, glanduliferous. Eur., Asia. Z6.

L. oleifolium Lapeyr. = Lithodora oleifolia.

L. petraeum (Tratt.) DC. = Moltkia petraea.

L. prostratum Lois. non Buckley = Lithodora diffusa.

L. purpurascens Gueldenst. = Buglossoides purpureocaeruleum.

L. purpureocaeruleum L. = Buglossoides purpureocaeruleum.

L. rosmarinifolium Ten. = Lithodora rosmarinifolia.

L. ruderale Douglas ex Lehm. Perenn. St. to 60cm, usually numerous, erect or decumbent, green-grey pubesc. Lvs to 10cm, linear-lanceolate to lanceolate, clustered. Cor. pale yellow to yellow green, tube to 7mm, limb to 13mm diam., lobes entire, ascending. W N Amer. Z4.

L. tinctorium L. = Alkanna tinctoria.

L. zahnii Heldr. ex Hal. = Lithodora zahnii.

L. zollingeri A. DC. = Buglossoides zollingeri.

→Batschia.

Lithrea Miers ex Hook. & Arn. Anacardiaceae. 3 trees. Lvs simple or compound; lfts 5; rachis alate. Fls small, yellow in axill. or term. pan.; bracts deltoid, caducous; cal. 5-lobed; pet. 5, lanceolate; sta. 10; disc 10-lobed, style 1, stigmas 3, ovary unilocular. Fr. a drupe. S Amer. Z9.

L. aroeirinha Marchand ex Warm. = L. molleoides.

L. caustica (Molina) Hook. & Arn. LITRE; LITHI. Shrub or small tree to 4m, everg. Lvs to 3×5cm, simple, coriaceous, glab., lanceolate to ovate, veins white. Pan. 1–5, sparsely pilose. Fr. to 1.2cm, epicarp creamy yellow. C Chile.

L. laurina Walp. = Malosma laurina.

L. molle Gay = Schinus latifolius.

L. molleoides (Vell.) Engl. AROEIRA BRANCA; AROEIRA BRAVA. To 5m, densely puberulent at first. Lvs ternately compound, rarely 5-foliate; lfts to 5×2cm, thinly coriaceous, ovate to ovate-lanceolate. Pan. erect, shortly branched, 5–6cm. Fr. 5cm, epicarp cream. Braz., Arg.

L. veneosa Miers = L. caustica.

→Duvana, Mauria, Persea, Rhus and Schinus.

Litre Lithrea caustica.

Litsea Lam.

L. glauca Sieb. = Neolitsea sericea.

Little Club Moss Selaginella.

Little Cokernut Jubaea.

Little Ebony Spleenwort Asplenium resiliens.

Little Fantasy Pepper Peperomia caperata.

Little Kangaroo Paw Anigozanthos bicolor.

Little Lemmon's California Poppy Eschscholzia hypecoides.

Little Leaf Fig Ficus rubiginosa.

Little Linden Tilia cordata.

Little Luina Luina hypoleuca.

Little Owl Huernia zebrina.

Little Pickles Othonna capensis.

Little Prince's Pine Chimaphila menziesii.

Little Shellbark Hickory Carya ovata.

Little Sur Manzanita Arctostaphylos edmundsii.

Little Walnut Juglans microcarpa.

Littonia Hook. Liliaceae (Colchicaceae). 8 perenn., tuberous, climbing herbs. Lvs cauline, lanceolate, tendrilous at apex. Fls campanulate, nodding, solitary in lf axils, tep. 6, with basal, nectar-bearing scale; sta. 6; style simple. S Afr., Arabia. Z9.

L. modesta Hook. St. to 1.2m, simple, slender, often prostrate or runner-like. Lvs linear to ovate-lanceolate, alt. to whorled, glab. Tep. to 5cm, orange-yellow, lanceolate. S Afr. var. *keitii* Leichtlin. St. branched, fls abundant.

Live-and-die Mimosa pudica.

Live-forever Hylotelephium telephium.

Live Oak Quercus chrysolepis; Q. virginiana.

Liver Balsam Erinus alpinus.

Liver Berry Streptopus amplexifolius.

Living Baseball Euphorbia obesa.

Living Granite Pleiospilos.

Living Rock Pleiospilos.

Living Rock Cactus Pleiospilos bolusii.

Livingstone Daisy Dorotheanthus bellidiformis.

Living Stones Lithops.

Livistona R. Br. Palmae. 28 shrubby or arborescent palms. St. solitary, erect, clothed with lf sheaths, becoming bare and ringed. Lvs palmate or costapalamate; petioles sometimes armed; blade to 2m, divided into mostly single-fold seg., waxy beneath. Infl. interfoliar, branched ×5, amid tubular bracts. Fr. globose to ovoid or pyriform. Asia, Australasia. Z10.

L. altissima Zoll. = L. rotundifolia.

L. australis (R. Br.) Mart. GIPPSLAND PALM; CABBAGE PALM; AUSTRALIAN PALM; AUSTRALIAN FAN PALM. St. to 25m×30cm, spiny fibrous at first, becoming bare, blades to 1.75cm, glossy, seg. to 70, with drooping, cleft tips. Fr. to 2cm, spherical, red-brown to black, waxy. E coastal Aus.

L. chinensis (Jacq.) R. Br. ex Mart. CHINESE FAN PALM. St. to 12m×30cm, swollen at base. Blades dull, seg. deeply cut to base. Fr. to 2.5cm, ovoid to spherical, deep blue-green to grey-pink, glassy. S Jap., Ryuku, Bonin Is., S Taiwan.

L. cochinchinensis (Bl.) Mart. = L. saribus.

L. decipiens Becc. Resembles L. australis but shorter. Lvs to 2m, cut to halfway, seg. hanging like a curtain. Fr. glossy, not waxy. Queensld.

L. hoogendorpii Teijsm. & Binnend. ex Miq. = L. saribus.

L. humilis R. Br. To 6m. Lvs divided to halfway into 30–35 seg., seg. deeply emarginate, rigid, to 45cm. Fr. c1.5cm, obovoid-ellipsoid, black. N Aus.

L. jenkinsiana Griff. To 9m. Lvs to 1.8m diam., pale beneath, divided into large, entire central portion and many deeply cleft seg. Fr. deep blue, globose, c2.5cm. Himal. foothills.

L. mariae F. Muell. CENTRAL AUSTRALIAN FAN PALM. St. to 30m×30cm, swollen at base, with persistent lf bases. Lvs bronze-red to blue-green; blades to 2m, prominently ribbed, coated with wax beneath, cut to halfway, seg. deeply cleft with drooping tips. Fr. glossy, black, spherical to 2cm. Aus.

L. merrillii Becc. To 18m. Lvs to 1.35m, pale beneath, seg. deeply emarginate, drooping at tips. Fr. globose, c2.5cm diam. Philippine Is.

L. muelleri Bail. To 6m. Lvs green, rigid, divided to two-thirds depth into 50 seg., seg. shallowly emarginate. Fr. black, globose to ovoid. N Aus.

L. oliviformis (Hassk.) Mart. = L. chinensis.

L. robinsoniana Becc. Lf blades deep glossy green, thin; seg. shallowly cleft, pendent, apices truncate. Fr. to 1.5cm, orange. Philipp.

L. rotundifolia (Lam.) Mart. St. to 24m×20cm. Lvs erect to pendent; petioles spiny below; blades shorter than petioles, glossy deep green, seg. rigid, shallowly emarginate. Fr. to 2cm, spherical, scarlet to black. Philipp., Sabah, Sulawesi, Moluccas.

L. saribus (Lour.) Merrill ex A. Chev. To 22.5m. Lvs to 1.5m, unevenly divided into several-fold seg., seg. further shallowly divided into deeply emarginate seg.; petiole coarsely and sharply toothed below. Fr. to 1.25cm, globose, blue. SE Asia, Indon., Philippine Is.

→Corypha and Latania.

Lizard Orchid Himantoglossum hircinum.

Lizard Plant Tetrastigma voinierianum.

Lizard's Tail Saururus.

Llavea Lagasca. Adiantaceae. 1 calcicole fern. Rhiz. thick, scaly, short. Fronds to 60×30cm, lime to olive green, glaucous beneath, lower pinnae to 5cm, ovate, sterile, upper pinnae to 8cm, linear, revolute, fertile, stipes yellow, scaly. Mex. to Guat. Z9.

L. cordifolia Lagasca.

Lloydia Salisb. ex Rchb. Liliaceae (Liliaceae). 12 bulbous, low-growing perenn. Lvs basal and cauline, narrow-linear. Fls 1–2, term.; perianth seg. 6, free, ovate-lanceolate with a gland at base; sta. inserted at perianth base. Temp. N Hemis. Z5.

L. longiscapa Hook. Similar to L. serotina but fls larger, drooping, marked purple or red at base. Summer. Himal., W China.

L. serotina (L.) Salisb. ex Rchb. SNOWDON LILY To 15cm. Basal lvs 2–3, st. lvs 2–5, to 20cm. Fls erect to 1.5cm, white, pale yellow at base, veined red-purple. Spring–summer. Temp. N Hemis.

Llume Palm Gaussia attenuata.

Loasa Adans. Loasaceae. 105 ann., bienn. or perenn. herbs or subshrubs covered in stinging bristly hairs, bushy, decumbent or twining. Lvs entire, lobed or decompound. Fls on decurved pedicels, solitary or in short rac. or pan.; pet. 5, spreading, deeply concave above, appearing inflated, each with a basal nectar-scale. Mex. to S Amer. Z10.

L. acanthifolia Desr. ex Lam. Ann. or short-lived perenn. to 1.5m. Lvs to 10cm, cordate-ovate, sinuately palmatifid to pinnatifid and irregularly toothed. Fls to 2cm diam., yellow, solitary.

L. aurantiaca hort. = *Caiophora lateritia.*

L. canarinoides Britt. Ann. or short-lived perenn. to 1.75cm. Lvs to 10cm, cordate-oblong to lyrate, deeply pinnatifid, toothed. Fls to 4cm diam., dull orange to cinnabar-red. C Amer.

L. lateritia (Klotzsch) Gillies ex Arn. = *Caiophora lateritia.*

L. triphylla Juss. Ann. to 40cm, sometimes loosely twining. Lvs to 6cm, trifoliolate or simple, lobes deeply toothed or serrate. Fls to 1.8cm diam.; pet. white, nectar-scales yellow concentrically barred red and white. S Amer. var. *papaverifolia* (HBK) Urban & Gilg. Lower lvs with 2–4 slender, irregularly toothed, pinnate lobes each side. Fls to 2.5cm diam. var. *volcanica* (André) Urban & Gilg Lvs more shallowly lobed. Fls to 5cm diam.

L. volcanica André = *L. triphylla* var. *volcanica.*

LOASACEAE Dumort. 15/260. *Blumenbachia, Caiophora, Eucnide, Loasa, Mentzelia*

Lobed Spleenwort *Asplenium pinnatifidum.*

Lobelia L. Campanulaceae. 365 ann. or perenn. herbs, shrubs and treelets. Lvs alt., simple, often sessile. Fls in rac. or solitary; cal. tube sometimes gibbous; cor. slit to the base on the upper side, bilabiate, lower 3 lobes large and spreading, upper 2 lobes small, recurved. Trop. to temp. climates, particularly Amer.

L. aberdarica R.E. Fries & T.C.E. Fries. Narrowly columnar tree to 2.7m. Lvs to 35cm, linear to linear-ovate. Fls in erect, term., pyramidal pan. to 1.8m; cor. to 4cm, blue to white. E Afr. Z10.

L. amoena Michx. Perenn., to 1.2m. Lvs to 20cm, linear-lanceolate, dentate, glab. Fls in secund, many-fld rac., pale blue. Summer. N Amer.

L. anceps L. Perenn., st. prostrate. Lvs oblanceolate-obovate, narrower above. Fls blue, throat stained white or yellow. Summer. S Afr. Z9.

L. angulata Forst. f. = *Pratia angulata.*

L. aquatica Cham. Aquatic herb; st. to 60cm, rooting at nodes or floating. Lvs to 2.5cm, lanceolate to oblong. Fls solitary; cor. to 0.5cm, blue marked with white. W Indies, S Amer. Z10.

L. campanulata Lam. = *Monopsis campanulata.*

L. cardinalis L. CARDINAL FLOWER; INDIAN PINK. Short-lived perenn. herb, to 90cm, strongly tinged purple-bronze. Lvs to 10cm, glossy, often purple-red, basal and rosulate or cauline and alt., narrow-ovate to oblong-lanceolate, toothed. Fls in bracteate spikes; cor. to 5cm, bright scarlet. Summer. N Amer. 'Alba': fls white. 'Rosea': fls pink. Z3.

L. comosa L. Glab. perenn. herb to 60cm. Lvs to 5cm, linear to oblanceolate. Fls in lax spikes; cor. to 1cm, dark blue, throat dilated, tinged with yellow. S Afr. Z9.

L. coronopifolia L. Decumbent perenn. herb. Lvs narrow-ovate, irregularly, dentate. Fls few, long pedicellate, clear blue. Summer. S Afr. Z9.

L. davidii Franch. Small, erect shrub to 90cm. Lvs to 10cm, linear-elliptic to narrow-ovate, serrate. Fls in long-racemes; bracts foliaceous; cor. lobes to 2.5cm, linear-lanceolate, purple to violet. China, Burm.

L. dortmanna L. WATER LOBELIA. Aquatic, glab., perenn. herb to 60cm; st. almost leafless. Basal lvs rosulate, oblong. Fls few, pendulous, in emergent rac.; cor. to 2cm, pale mauve. Summer. N Amer., W Eur. Z4.

L. erinus L. EDGING LOBELIA; TRAILING LOBELIA. Small perenn. herb; br. slender, sprawling then ascending or cascading. Lvs dark green, glab., ovate to linear-obovate, toothed. Fls in lax spikes; cor. to 2cm, throat yellow to white, tube blue to violet. Summer. S Afr. 'Alba': fls white. 'Blue Cascade': trailing; fls pale blue. 'Blue Moon': fls dark violet-blue. 'Blue Stone': fls intense sky-blue. Cascade Mixed: habit trailing; fls violet through blue to pink and white. 'Compacta': habit low, dense. 'Crystal Palace': habit v. dwarf, densely branched; lvs obovate, minute; fls numerous, deep blue. 'Emperor William': fls globose, vivid blue. 'Erecta': habit erect, compact. 'Gracilis': st. slender. 'Kathleen Mallard': fls double, blue. 'Mrs Clibran Improved': fls deep blue with a white centre. 'Pendula': st. drooping. 'Pink Flamingo': habit erect, branching; fls bright pink. 'Pumila': habit dwarf. 'Rosamund': fls deep cherry-red with a white centre. 'Rosea': fls pink-violet. Royal Hybrids: habit compact, prostrate; fls blue or white. 'Sapphire': habit trailing; fls glossy deep blue with a white centre. 'Snowball': fls snow-white, occas. pale blue. 'Speciosa': fls large, blue. 'Waverly Blue': habit compact; fls large, sky-blue. 'White Cascade': habit trailing; fls pure white.

L. fenestralis Cav. Upright ann. or perenn. herb, to 60cm. Lvs to 7cm, linear, serrate. Fls in spikes; cor. to 1cm, pubesc., blue, violet or white. SW US to Mex. Z9.

L. fulgens Willd. Close to *L. cardinalis* but slightly hairy, slender in habit; lvs to 15cm, linear-lanceolate; infl. ± secund; fls scarlet, exterior ± downy. Tex., Mex. 'Illumination': lvs dark green; fls scarlet in large spikes. Z8.

L. fulgens Hemsl. = *L. splendens.*

L. × gerardii Chabanne ex Nicholas. (*L. cardinalis × L. siphilitica.*) Robust perenn., to 1.5m. Lvs ovate to elliptic in a basal rosette. Fls in dense, large rac.; cor. violet tinged with pink, to purple, lower lip with 2 deltoid white marks. Summer. Gdn origin. 'Rosenkavalier': fls pure pink. 'Vedrariensis': lvs dark green, tinged red, fls dark violet. Z7.

L. glandulosa Walter. Perenn., to 1.3m. Lvs narrow-ovate to linear, with gland. or cartilaginous teeth, glab., bright green. Fls blue in a lax rac., sometimes secund. Autumn. S US. Z9.

L. gracilis Andrews. Ann., to 60cm, glab. Lvs to 2cm, linear-ovate to oblong. Fls in lax, secund rac.; cor. to 1cm, upper lip densely pubesc., deep blue, throat yellow. Summer. S Aus.

L. heterophylla Labill. non Lindl. Erect ann. to 40cm. Lvs linear to filiform, entire, dentate, or pinnatisect. Fls in a secund rac.; cor. blue, often yellow in throat. Autumn and winter. Aus.

L. heterophylla Lindl. non Labill. = *L. tenuior.*

L. holstii Engl. Perenn., ascending to 30cm. Lvs to 4cm, crowded near base, narrowly ovate, bluntly dentate. Fls in lax rac. Autumn. Trop. E Afr. Z10.

L. ilicifolia Ker-Gawl. Prostrate perenn. to 15cm. Lvs narrow-ovate, remotely and deeply dentate, glab. Fls solitary, axill.; cor. pink, inverted. Summer. S Afr. Z9.

L. inflata L. INDIAN TOBACCO. Spreading pubesc. ann., to 90cm. Lvs to 6cm, oblong, crenate to serrate. Fls in loose rac.; cal. inflated after anthesis; cor. to 1cm, blue, purple or tinged with pink. Summer–autumn. N Amer.

L. kalmii L. Prostrate or creeping to upright perenn., to 30cm. Lower lvs obovate to spathulate, upper lvs linear to filiform. Fls in loose spikes; cor. to 1cm, white or blue with prominent white eye. Summer. N Amer. Z4.

L. laxiflora HBK. Perenn. herb or shrub to 90cm, branching, finely pubesc. Lvs to 8cm, lanceolate to elliptic, acuminate, serrate. Fls slender-stalked, pendulous; cor. red and/or yellow. Summer. Ariz., Mex., Colomb. Z9.

L. linnaeoides (Hook. f.) Petrie. Glab., perenn. herb; st. prostrate, slender. Lvs 0.8cm, orbicular, serrate-sinuate in upper half, thick. Fls on slender-pedicels; cor. elongated, white to pale blue, tinged purple. NZ. Z8.

L. perpusilla Hook. f. = *Pratia perpusilla.*

L. physaloides (A. Cunn.) Hook. f. = *Pratia physaloides.*

L. pinifolia L. Shrub, to 60cm. Lvs to 2.5cm, filiform. Fls in narrow spikes; cor. blue-violet or pale pink. S Afr. Z9.

L. plumieri L. = *Scaevola plumieri.*

L. pratiana Gaudich. = *Pratia repens.*

L. ramosa Benth. = *L. tenuior.*

L. repens Thunb. = *Pratia repens.*

L. sessilifolia Lamb. Glab. perenn. to 60cm; st. slender, simple, erect. Lower lvs lanceolate, shallowly dentate. Fls in dense term. spikes; cor. violet. Summer. Taiwan, Korea, Manch., Jap. Z5.

L. siphilitica L. GREAT LOBELIA; BLUE CARDINAL FLOWER. Perenn. herb to 60cm; st. erect, v. leafy. Lvs to 10cm, ovate-lanceolate, somewhat pubesc., dentate. Fls in dense spikes; cor. to 2.5cm, blue. Summer–autumn. E US. 'Alba': fls white. 'Nana': habit rather smaller; fls blue. 'Nana Alba': compact; fls white. Z5.

L. × speciosa Sweet. (*L. cardinalis × L. fulgens × L. siphilitica.*) Hispid perenn. Lvs oblong-obovate, acuminate, sessile. Cor. to 3cm, red or mauve tinged with purple or violet. Gdn origin. 'Bees Flame': lvs bronze-red; fls scarlet. 'Brightness': fls brilliant red. 'Dark Crusader': lvs green to dark bronze; fls blood-red. 'Jack McMasters': fls mauve. 'Queen Victoria': lvs beetroot-red; fls vivid red. 'Russian Princess': lvs tinged red; fls bright purple. 'Will Scarlet': lvs tinged red; fls bright scarlet. Z3.

L. spicata Lam. PALE SPIKE. Perenn. or bienn., simple or branched, to 1.2m. Like *L. inflata*, but st. finely pubesc. at base; cal. partially dilated. N Amer. Z4.

L. splendens Hemsl. = *L. fulgens.*

L. subnuda Benth. Ann. Lvs rosulate, cordate-lanceolate, pinnatifid, tinged purple beneath, veins prominent, green. Fls pale blue in lax rac. Mex. Z9.

L. tenuior R. Br. Diffuse ann. or perenn. herb to 60cm. Lower lvs small, oblong-obovate, dentate, upper lvs narrower, pinnatifid to entire. Fls in loose rac. or pan.; cor. bright blue, throat with a white or yellow eye. Autumn. W Aus. 'Blue Wings': fls v. numerous, cobalt-blue. Z9.

L. tomentosa L. f. Perenn. shrublet, to 50cm. Lvs pinnatifid, lobes bifurcate, tomentose, involute. Fls blue to purple; cor. throat usually purple, hispidulous. Autumn. S Afr. Z9.

L. triquetra L. = *L. comosa.*

L. tupa L. Perenn. to 2m; st. upright, robust, simple. Lvs to

30cm, lanceolate, decurrent, white to pale green velutinous. Fls in term. spikes, large, brick red. Autumn. Chile. Z8.
→*Pratia*.

Lobel's Maple *Acer cappadocicum* ssp. *lobelii*.

Lobivia Britt. & Rose.
L. allegraiana Backeb. = *Echinopsis hertrichiana*.
L. andalgalensis (F.A. Weber ex Schum.) Britt. & Rose = *Echinopsis huascha*.
L. arachnacantha Buining & Ritter = *Echinopsis arachnacantha*.
L. backebergii (Werderm. ex Backeb.) Backeb. = *Echinopsis backebergii*.
L. binghamiana Backeb. = *Echinopsis hertrichiana*.
L. boliviensis Britt. & Rose = *Echinopsis pentlandii*.
L. breviflora Backeb. = *Echinopsis sanguiniflora*.
L. bruchii Britt. & Rose = *Echinopsis bruchii*.
L. caespitosa Purpus = *Echinopsis maximiliana*.
L. chlorogona Wessner = *Rebutia famatinensis*.
L. chorrillosensis Rausch. = *Echinopsis haematantha*.
L. chrysantha (Werderm.) Backeb. = *Echinopsis chrysantha*.
L. chrysochete (Werderm.) Wessner = *Echinopsis chrysochete*.
L. cinnabarina (Hook.) Britt. & Rose = *Echinopsis cinnabarina*.
L. corbula Britt. & Rose = *Echinopsis maximiliana*.
L. cylindrica Backeb. = *Echinopsis aurea*.
L. densispina (Werderm.) Wessner = *Echinopsis kuehnrichii*.
L. drijveriana Backeb. = *Echinopsis kuehnrichii*.
L. ducis-pauli misapplied. = *Echinopsis longispina*.
L. elongata Backeb. = *Echinopsis haematantha*.
L. famatimensis (Speg.) Britt. & Rose = *Rebutia famatinensis*.
L. ferox Britt. & Rose = *Echinopsis ferox*.
L. formosa (Pfeiff.) Dodds = *Echinopsis formosa*.
L. glauca Rausch. = *Echinopsis marsoneri*.
L. grandiflora Britt. & Rose = *Echinopsis huascha*.
L. grandis Britt. & Rose = *Echinopsis bruchii*.
L. grandis (Britt. & Rose) Backeb. = *Echinopsis bruchii*.
L. haematantha (Speg.) Britt. & Rose = *Echinopsis haematantha*.
L. hermanniana Backeb. = *Echinopsis maximiliana*.
L. higginsiana Backeb. = *Echinopsis pentlandii*.
L. hualfinensis Rausch. = *Echinopsis haematantha*.
L. huascha (F.A. Weber) W.T. Marshall = *Echinopsis huascha*.
L. incaiaca Backeb. = *Echinopsis hertrichiana*.
L. jajoiana Backeb. = *Echinopsis marsoneri*.
L. janseniana Backeb. = *Echinopsis chrysantha*.
L. johnsoniana Backeb. = *Echinopsis pentlandii*.
L. kieslingii Rausch. = *Echinopsis formosa*.
L. kuehnrichii Fric = *Echinopsis kuehnrichii*.
L. kupperiana Backeb. = *Echinopsis lateritia*.
L. larae Cárdenas = *Echinopsis pentlandii*.
L. lateritia (Gürke) Britt. & Rose = *Echinopsis lateritia*.
L. longispina Britt. & Rose = *Echinopsis longispina*.
L. maximiliana (Heyder ex A. Dietr.) Backeb. = *Echinopsis maximiliana*.
L. muhriae Backeb. = *Echinopsis marsoneri*.
L. nealeana Backeb. = *Echinopsis saltensis*.
L. neohaageana Backeb. = *Rebutia pygmaea*.
L. orurensis Backeb. = *Rebutia pygmaea*.
L. pampana Britt. & Rose = *Echinopsis pampana*.
L. peclardiana Krainz = *Echinopsis tiegeliana*.
L. pectinata Backeb. = *Rebutia pygmaea*.
L. pentlandii (Hook.) Britt. & Rose = *Echinopsis pentlandii*.
L. polycephala Backeb. = *Echinopsis sanguiniflora*.
L. pseudocachensis Backeb. = *Echinopsis saltensis*.
L. pugionacantha (Rose & Boed.) Backeb. = *Echinopsis pugionacantha*.
L. pygmaea (R.E. Fries) Backeb. = *Rebutia pygmaea*.
L. raphidacantha Backeb. = *Echinopsis pentlandii*.
L. rebutioides Backeb. = *Echinopsis haematantha*.
L. rossii (Boed.) Backeb. & F. Knuth = *Echinopsis pugionacantha*.
L. saltensis (Speg.) Britt. & Rose = *Echinopsis saltensis*.
L. sanguiniflora Backeb. = *Echinopsis sanguiniflora*.
L. schieliana Backeb. = *Echinopsis schieliana*.
L. schreiteri Cast. = *Echinopsis schreiteri*.
L. silvestrii (Speg.) G. Rowley = *Echinopsis chamaecereus*.
L. steinmannii (Solms-Laubach) Backeb. = *Rebutia steinmannii*.
L. sublimiflora Backeb. ex Wessner = *Echinopsis haematantha*.
L. tegeleriana Backeb. = *Echinopsis tegeleriana*.
L. tiegeliana Wessner = *Echinopsis tiegeliana*.
L. varians Backeb. = *Echinopsis pentlandii*.
L. vatteri Krainz = *Echinopsis marsoneri*.
L. walteri Kiesling = *Echinopsis walteri*.
L. walterspielii Boed. = *Echinopsis cinnabarina*.
L. wegheiana Backeb. = *Echinopsis pentlandii*.
L. westii Hutchison = *Echinopsis maximiliana*.

Loblolly Bay *Gordonia lasianthus*.
Loblolly Pine *Pinus taeda*.
Lobster Cactus *Schlumbergera truncata*.
Lobster Claw *Clianthus puniceus*.
Lobster Claws *Vriesea carinata*.
Lobster Plant *Euphorbia pulcherrima*.
Lobster-pot Pitcher Plant *Sarracenia psittacina*.

Lobularia Desv. Cruciferae. 5 ann. or perenn. hairy herbs. Lvs narrow, simple, entire. Fls 4-merous, white, scented in compact term. rac.; sta. 6, free. N temp. regions.
L. maritima (L.) Desv. SWEET ALISON; SWEET ALYSSUM. Ann. or perenn., 10–55cm. St. much-branched. Lvs 8–35mm, linear-ligulate, somewhat silvery. Rac. capitate, elongating in fr., to 18cm; fls fragrant; sep. 1–5mm, hairy; pet. to 3.5mm, blade rounded. S Eur., widely nat. Z7. 'Carpet of Snow': ground-hugging, to 10cm, to 15cm diam.; fls white. 'Little Dorrit': to 10cm; fls white. 'Navy Blue': to 10cm; fls deep purple. 'New Carpet of Snow': compact, to 10cm; fls pure white, free-flowering. 'Oriental Nights': spreading, to 10cm; fls rich purple, fragrant; early-flowering. 'Rosie O'Day': to 10cm, wide-spreading to 25cm diam.; fls rose-pink, later pink, long-lasting, fragrant. 'Royal Carpet': to 10cm; fls deep purple, fragrant. 'Snow Crystals': mound-forming, to 25cm diam.; fls bright white, v. large. 'Sweet White': to 10cm; fls white, honey-scented. 'Wonderland Rose': compact, low-spreading; fls bold purple; early-flowering. 'Wonderland White': compact, low spreading; fls white; early-flowering.
→*Alyssum* and *Clypeola*.

Lock Elm *Ulmus plottii*.

Lockhartia Hook. Orchidaceae. 30 epiphytic orchids. St. to 40cm, simple, elongate. Lvs cauline, numerous, distichous, often folded with bases overlapping. Infl. a short rac. or a pan., lat. or term., few- to many-fld; fls small; tep. free, spreading, elliptic-oblong, pet. usually longer than sep.; lip entire to 3(–5)-lobed. Trop. Amer. Z10.
L. acuta (Lindl.) Rchb. f. Lvs to 3cm, ovate-triangular. Infl. to 9cm, many-fld; fls to 1cm diam., tep. white or pale yellow, sometimes marked pale brown; lip to 6×4mm, yellow marked pale brown, lat. lobes linear, obtuse, midlobe subquadrate, obtuse, emarginate; callus 2-ridged, pilose. Panama, Trin., Venez., Colomb.
L. amoena Endress & Rchb. f. Lvs to 3.5cm, ovate-triangular. Infl. to 3cm, few-fld; fls to 2cm diam; tep. bright yellow; lip to 10×8mm, bright yellow, slightly marked red-brown at base, lat. lobes linear-ligulate, incurved, midlobe subquadrate, truncate, undulate, 4-lobulate, callus slightly papillose. Costa Rica, Panama.
L. elegans Hook. Lvs to 2cm, obliquely triangular. Infl. 1- to many-fld; tep. pale yellow, to 5×3mm; lip to 6×5mm, yellow slightly marked purple-maroon, lat. lobes triangular, midlobe large, oblong-ligulate, undulate, callus tuberculate. Colomb., Venez., Trin., Braz.
L. lunifera (Lindl.) Rchb. f. Lvs to 2cm, narrowly triangular-ligulate. Infl. 1- to few-fld; tep. golden yellow, to 6×5mm; lip to 8×4mm, golden yellow finely spotted purple, lat. lobes linear, midlobe obscurely 4-lobulate, verrucose. Braz.
L. micrantha Rchb. f. Lvs to 2cm, narrowly triangular. Infl. 1- to few-fld; tep. yellow to 4×3mm; lip to 5×5mm, lat. lobes linear-oblong, midlobe subrhombic to obovate, deeply retuse. Nic. to Surinam, Braz.
L. oerstedii Rchb. f. Lvs to 4cm, triangular. Infl. 1- to several-fld; tep. bright yellow to 8×5mm; lip to 14×14mm, bright yellow spotted and barred dark red below, 5-lobed, apical lobe bilobulate, undulate, callus light brown, pilose, with papillose keels. Mex. to Panama.
L. pallida Rchb. f. = *L. acuta*.
L. pittieri Schltr. Lvs to 3.5cm, narrowly triangular to linear-lanceolate. Infl. 1-fld; tep. to 5×2mm, yellow to yellow-orange; lip to 8×6mm, oblong-subquadrate, deeply emarginate, entire to obscurely 3-lobed, disc with an ovate-oblong callus, orange, slightly papillose. Costa Rica, Panama, Br. Hond.
L. robusta (Batem.) Schltr. = *L. oerstedii*.
→*Fernandezia*.

Locoweed *Oxytropis* (*O. lambertii*).
Locust *Ceratonia*.
Loddon Lily *Leucojum aestivum*.
Loddon Pondweed *Potamogeton nodosus*.
Lodgepole Pine *Pinus contorta*.

Lodoicea Comm. ex DC. SEYCHELLES NUT; COCO DE MER; DOUBLE COCONUT. Palmae. 1 dioecious solitary-stemmed palm, to 30m. Trunk slightly swollen at base, faintly ringed. Lvs to

7m, costapalmate, rigid; petiole 4m, grooved above, tomentose; seg. single-fold, shallowly emarginate, apices pendent, shiny above, dull and tomentose along ridges beneath. Infl. interfoliar, pendent, enclosed in 2 bracts. Fr. to 50cm, ovoid-cordate, bilobed, resembling a giant wooden heart. Seych. Z10.

L. maldivica (Gmel.) Pers.

L. sechellarum Labill. = *L. maldivica*.

→*Coco*.

Lofty Fig *Ficus altissima.*
Loganberry *Rubus ursinus* cv.

Logania R. Br. Loganiaceae. 20 herbs, subshrubs, or spreading, tufted shrubs. Lvs opposite, entire. Fls small, fragrant, 4–5-merous, solitary or in a term. or axill. cyme or head; cor. campanulate or salverform, tube cylindrical. NZ, Aus., New Caledonia. Z9.

L. albidiflora (Andrews) Druce. To 1m. Lvs lanceolate. Pan. axill. shorter than lvs; fls white. Early summer. Aus.

L. floribunda R. Br. = *L. albidiflora*.

L. latifolia R. Br. = *L. populifolia*.

L. longifolia R. Br. = *L. populifolia*.

L. populifolia (Lam.) Leeuwenb. To 2m+. Lvs elliptic, obovate or lanceolate. Pan. leafy, cymose, long-stalked; fls white. Aus.

L. vaginalis (Labill.) F.J. Muell = *L. populifolia*.

LOGANIACEAE C. Mart. 29/600. *Anthocleista, Buddleja, Desfontainia, Fagraea, Gelsemium, Geniostoma, Logania, Nuxia, Spigelia, Strychnos.*

Log Fern *Dryopteris celsa.*
Logwood *Haematoxylum campechianum.*

Loiseleuria Desv. Ericaceae. 1 small everg. shrub, 7.5–20cm. St. prostrate. Lvs 0.4–1.2cm, crowded, oval to oblong, entire, strongly revolute, leathery, glossy above, midvein impressed, glaucescent or tomentose beneath. Fls solitary or 2–5 in small, term. clusters; cal. campanulate, purple-tinted, deeply 5-lobed, half cor. length; cor. 4×6mm, rose-pink or white tinted rose, broadly campanulate to cupped, lobes 4–5, spreading, equalling tube; sta. 5, alt. with cor. lobes. Spring–early summer. N Amer., Eur., Asia, in high alpine and subarc. regions. Z2.

L. procumbens (L.) Desv. ALPINE AZALEA; MOUNTAIN AZALEA; MINEZUO.

Lollipop plant *Pachystachys lutea*

Lomagramma J. Sm. Lomariopsidaceae. 18 large ferns. Rhiz. scandent. Fronds pinnate or bipinnate, membranous, dimorphic; sterile pinnae numerous, lanceolate, serrate or entire, covered in peltate scales; fertile fronds with pinnae reduced. SE Asia. Z10.

L. sorbifolia (Willd.) Ching. Rhiz. wide-creeping or long-trailing. Sterile fronds to 1.8m; pinnae 15–20×4cm, ligulate, cut almost to rachis into close, entire, obtuse lobes; fertile pinnae narrower. China, Solomon Is.

Lomaria Willd.

L. alpina Spreng. = *Blechnum penna-marina*.

L. attenuata Willd. = *Blechnum attenuatum*.

L. gibba Labill. = *Blechnum gibbum*.

L. colensoi Hook. f. = *Blechnum colensoi*.

L. elongata Bl. = *Blechnum colensoi*.

L. falcata Spreng. = *Blechnum discolor*.

L. magellanica Desv. = *Blechnum magellanicum*.

L. nipponica Kunze = *Blechnum nipponicum*.

L. rigida J. Sm. = *Blechnum durum*.

L. rotundifolia Colenso = *Blechnum fluviatile*.

L. speciosa Bl. = *Photinopteris speciosa*.

LOMARIOPSIDACEAE Alston. 7 genera. *Bolbitis, Elaphoglossum, Lomagramma, Peltapteris.*

Lomatia R. Br. Proteaceae. 12 divaricately branching woody evergreens to 12m. Foliage emerging silky or rusty-downy; lvs entire, toothed, pinnatifid or pinnately compound. Fls paired in lax rac. or pan.; perianth obliquely tubular, the limb splitting as 4 narrow twisted lobes. Spring–summer. Australasia, S Amer.

L. dentata R. Br. To 4m. Lvs to 8cm, holly-like, elliptic, strongly toothed, dark glossy green above, pale or grey-green below. Fls green-white. Chile. Z8.

L. ferruginea R. Br. To 7m. Lvs to 20cm, narrowly triangular in outline; pinnae to 17, leathery, olive green above, tomentose beneath, coarsely pinnatifid, initially rusty-tomentose. Fls scarlet fading at tips and centre to olive green. Chile, Patagonia. Z8.

L. hirsuta (Lam.) Diels. To 12m. Lvs to 10cm, emerging golden or rusty-pubesc., hardening glab., dark green, broadly ovate, obtuse or abruptly acute, crenate. Fls olive green to ivory. Chile, Peru. Z8.

L. longifolia R Br. = *L. myricoides*.

L. myricoides (Gaertn. f.) Domin. To 2.5m. Lvs to 12.5cm, narrow-linear to lanceolate, glab., tough, subentire to coarsely and remotely dentate in apical half, emerging brown-puberulent brown. Fls ivory to yellow-green, fragrant. SE Aus. Z8.

L. obliqua (Ruiz & Pav.) R. Br. = *L. hirsuta*.

L. silaifolia (Sm.) R. Br. To 1m. Lvs to 20cm, pinnate, bipinnate or tripinnate; seg. lanceolate, acute initially silky, then coriaceous, glab., dark green, somewhat revolute. Fls ivory. E Aus. Z8.

L. tinctoria (Labill.) R. Br. To 75cm. Lvs to 8cm, pinnate or bipinnate; seg. linear-lanceolate, dark green, finer than in *L. silaifolia*. Fls ivory to topaz, sweetly scented. Tasm. Z8.

Lomatophyllum Willd. Liliaceae (Aloeaceae). 12 perenn. succulents, closely resembling *Aloe* but differing in fr. fleshy not dry. St. thick, unbranched. Lvs in term. rosettes, ligulate, long-acuminate, spiny-serrate. Fls tubular, in pan. Indian Ocean Is. Z10.

L. borbonicum Willd. = *L. purpureum*.

L. occidentale Perrier. To 1m. Lvs 80–100×10–12cm, stiff, recurved, deeply channelled, sparsely spinose. Fls deep pink. W Madag.

L. purpureum (Lam.) Dur. & Schinz. To 2m. Lvs 80×10cm, channelled, margins thickened, red, spiny. Fls yellow to red. Maur.

Lombardy Poplar *Populus nigra* var. *betulifolia*.

Lonas Adans. AFRICAN DAISY; YELLOW AGERATUM. Compositae. 1 ann. herb to 30cm. Lvs alt., lower lvs tripartite, petiolate, lobes dentate, upper lvs pinnatifid, sessile or short-petiolate. Cap. discoid, 2–10 in a dense, term. corymb; receptacle elongate-conical, scaly; flts yellow. SW Medit.

L. annua (L.) Vines & Druce.

L. inodora (L.) Gaertn. = *L. annua*.

Lonchitis L. Dennstaedtiaceae. 2 terrestrial or epilithic ferns. Rhiz. short-creeping, fleshy, scaly. Fronds stipitate, 2–3-pinnate or -pinnatifid, ovate to lanceolate, membranous, fleshy, ± pubesc., esp. below. Trop. Amer., Afr. and Madag. Z10.

L. currori (Hook.) Kuhn = *Blotiella currori*.

L. hirsuta L. Fronds to 2×1m, pubesc., ascending, deltoid to oblong, pinnules to 12×3cm, deltoid to oblong, seg. to 9mm wide, subfalcate, oblong, subentire to lobed; stipes to 1m, pubesc., straw-coloured. Trop. Amer.

L. lindeniana Hook. = *Blotiella lindeniana*.

L. natalensis Hook. = *Blotiella natalensis*.

L. repens L. = *Hypolepis repens*.

L. tenuifolia Forst. f. = *Hypolepis tenuifolia*.

→*Antiosorus*.

Lonchocarpus Kunth BITTER WOOD; TURTLE BONE; CABBAGE BARK; WATERWOOD. Leguminosae (Papilionoideae). 150 everg. trees or shrubs. Lvs imparipinnate. Fls pea-like in simple or paniculate rac. Trop. Amer., Afr. and Aus. Z10.

L. domingensis (Pers.) DC. GENOGENO; CAPASSA. Tree to 15m. Branchlets initially pubesc. Lfts to 12cm, 7–13, oblong to elliptic-oval, glab. to pubesc. Fls pink to purple, standard 15mm, suborbicular, white at base, silky. Trop. Amer. and Afr., Carib.

L. griftonianus (Baill.) Dunn = *Millettia griftoniana*.

L. latifolius HBK. FORTEVENTURA; HEDIONDO; PALO HEDIONDO; PALO SECO. Tree to 16m. Branchlets tomentose to glab. Lfts to 24cm, 5–9, ovate to elliptic-oblong, glab. above, pubesc. beneath. Fls purple, pink or yellow, standard 8mm, silky. Trop. Amer., Carib.

L. maculatus (Kunth) DC. = *Gliricidia sepium*.

L. punctatus Kunth. Close to *L. violaceus*, distinguished by lfts to 5cm, in 2–4 pairs, ovate-oblong and densely spotted fls. Trin., NE Venez.

L. violaceus Benth. Small, glab. tree. Lfts to 9cm, in 3–5 pairs, ovate, translucent-dotted. Fls white outside, pale purple or pink inside. W Indies.

L. violaceus hort. non Benth. = *L. punctatus*.

→*Dalbergia*.

London Plane *Platanus ×acerifolia.*
London Pride *Saxifraga ×urbium.*
Longan *Dimocarpus longan.*
Long Beech Fern *Phegopteris connectilis.*
Long-flowered Marlock *Eucalyptus macrandra.*

Long-head Coneflower *Ratibida columnifera.*
Long Jack *Triplaris weigeltiana.*
Long John *Triplaris.*
Longleaf Bluets *Houstonia longifolia.*
Longleaf Pine *Pinus palustris.*
Longleaf Smokebush *Conospermum longifolium.*
Long-leaved Indian Pine *Pinus roxburghii.*
Long-spine Thorn Apple *Datura ferox.*
Long-spurred Violet *Viola rostrata.*
Long-styled Knight's Star Lily *Hippeastrum stylosum.*
Long-tubed Painted Lady *Gladiolus angustus.*

Lonicera L. HONEYSUCKLE. Caprifoliaceae. 180 decid. or everg., bushy, scandent, twining or creeping shrubs. Lvs opposite, usually simple, entire, sometimes pinnately lobed, upper lf pairs sometimes fused, forming a disc. Fls paired and axill. or in whorls in term. spikes, clusters or pan., bracteate; sep. 5; cor. tubular to campanulate, tube bilabiate with upper lip 4-lobed, or with regular 5-lobed limb; sta. 5; ovary inferior. Fr. a berry. N Hemis.

L. acuminata Wallich. Scandent or creeping shrub. Branchlets pubesc. Lvs 10×4.5cm, oblong, acuminate, scattered-pubesc. or glabrescent. Fls in term. cap., also paired, axill.; cal. tube glab., sep. glab. or ciliate; cor. to 2cm, yellow to red, tube funnelform, setose-pubesc., lobes pubesc. or glab. Fr. black. Summer. Himal. (Nepal to Sikkim). Z5.

L. affinis Hook. & Arn. Scandent, semi-evergreen shrub to 7m. Br. gland., white-puberulent when young. Lvs to 9×5cm, ovate or oblong-elliptic, glab. above, glandular-pubesc. beneath. Fls paired, term.; cal. glab., sep. narrow-deltoid; cor. white to yellow, bilabiate, narrow, to 6cm, glab. outside. Fr. 7mm diam., blue-black pruinose. Spring–summer. Jap., China. Z6.

L. alberti Reg. Low decid. shrub to 120cm. Young branchlets glab. or gland. Lvs to 3×0.3cm, linear-oblong, often few-toothed, blue-green, glab. above, white beneath. Fls fragrant, paired, axill.; cor. rose-lilac, tube cylindric, to 12.5mm, slender, pubesc. inside, glab. outside, lobes patent, oblong. Fr. 8.5mm diam., maroon to white, pruinose. Turkestan, Tibet. Z6.

L. albiflora Torr. & A. Gray. WHITE HONEYSUCKLE. Bushy, to 2.5m, somewhat scandent. Lvs to 3cm, rarely to 6.5cm, rigid, suborbicular to oval or obovate, rounded at base, somewhat glaucous, uppermost pair connate at base. Cor. 1.5–3cm, white or yellow-white, glab. or pilose outside, bilabiate. Fr. orange. Spring. S N Amer. Z6.

L. alpigena L. Decid. shrub, 1m, of narrow habit. Branchlets sparsely gland. and pubesc. Lvs to 10cm, elliptic to oblong, acuminate, dark green above, paler and pubesc. beneath, margins ciliate. Fls long-stalked, paired; cor. to 1.5cm, yellow-green tinged red, bilabiate, pubesc. inside. Fr. to 13mm, shiny dark red. Spring. C & S Eur. 'Macrophylla': lvs large, glab. f. *nana* (Carr.) Nichols. Dwarf shrub. Lvs scattered-pubesc. beneath. Fls deep red. Z6.

L. alpigena var. *glehnii* (F. Schmidt) Nak. = *L. glehnii.*

L. alseuosmoides Gräbn. Scandent everg. shrub. Young branchlets slender, glab. Lvs to 6×0.85cm, narrow-oblong, acuminate, glab., margins adpressed-pubesc. Fls in short broad pan.; cor. 12.5mm, inside purple and pubesc., outside yellow and glab. Fr. to 6.5mm diam., black, purple-pruinose. Summer–autumn. W China. Z6.

L. altaica Pall. = *L. caerulea* var. *altaica.*

L. altmannii Reg. & Schmalh. Decid. shrub to 2.5m. Young branchlets purple-pubesc. Lvs to 5×3.5cm, ovate to elliptic, mostly acute, ciliate; apex usually pubesc. Fls paired; cor. 1.2cm, white-yellow, tube slender, gibbous, pubesc. Fr. 8mm, orange-red. Spring. Turkestan. var. *hirtipes* Rehd. Lvs to 5cm, broad-ovate, hispid. Shoots densely setose-pubesc. Alatau Mts. var. *pilosiuscula* Rehd. Lvs ovate, to 4cm, sparsely pubesc. above, glab. or with veins pubesc. beneath. Branchlets fine-pubesc. and sparsely setose. Alatau Mts. var. *saravshanica* Rehd. Lvs to 2.5cm, densely grey-tomentose beneath, apex subobtuse. Saravshan, W Bukhara. Z5.

L. ×*americana* (Mill.) K. Koch. (*L. caprifolium* ×*L. etrusca.*) Resembles *L. caprifolium* in growth and foliage, but lower lvs more acute. Young st. purple, glab. Fls fragrant, yellow tinted maroon, in crowded whorls from axils of connate lvs and small bracts. Summer. S & SE Eur., NW Balk. 'Atrosanguinea': fls deep red outside. 'Quercifolia': lvs broadly cleft, sometimes with yellow margin and red striped. 'Rubella': fls light purple outside, buds more deeply coloured. Z6.

L. amherstii Dipp. = *L. strophiophora.*

L. ×*amoena* Zab. (*L. korolkowii* ×*L. tatarica.*) Vigorous decid. shrub to 3m. Lvs to 4×2.5cm, ovate, slightly cordate at base, grey-green. Fls 18mm diam., light pink or white, paired, crowded at shoot tips. Summer. 'Alba': habit shrub-like, rounded; shoots more pubesc.; fls white, later tinted yellow, fragrant, abundant. 'Arnoldiana': habit open; shoots pendulous;

lvs oblanceolate, grey-green; fls white, tinted pink on opening, prolific. 'Rosea': fls pink, later yellowing, fragrant. Z5.

L. angustifolia Wallich. Decid. shrub to 2.5m, rounded. Outer br. pendent. Lvs to 5×1.25cm, elliptic-lanceolate, glab. above, paler and lightly pubesc. beneath. Fls paired; cor. 8mm, pale pink, tubular. Fr. red, joined in pairs, edible. Spring–summer. Himal., Kashmir. Z5.

L. arborea Boiss. Erect decid. shrub to 2m, or small tree. Shoots 4-angled, white-pubesc. Lvs to 3.5cm, ovate to elliptic, rounded to slightly emarginate, grey-pubesc., becoming glab. Cor. 1.5cm, red, soft-pubesc., somewhat gibbous. Fr. orange-yellow. S Spain, N Afr. Z7.

L. arborea var. *persica* (Jaub. & Spach) Rehd. = *L. nummularifolia.*

L. arizonica Rehd. Erect decid. shrub. Lvs to 7cm, ovate to oval, apex rounded, ciliate, deep green and glab. above, often white-pubesc. beneath. Fls in whorls or subcapitate spikes; cor. to 4.5cm, orange inside, muddy red tinged outside, glab. Fr. red. Spring–summer. SW US. Z6.

L. balearica (DC.) DC. Like *L. implexa*, but lvs fewer, oval or obovate to oblong, lower lvs truncate to cordate at base. Medit. Z8.

L. ×*bella* Zab. (*L. morrowii* ×*L. tatarica.*) Erect decid. shrub. Lvs to 5cm, ovate, soon glab. Fls more red-coloured than parents, later yellow, paired. Fr. red. Summer. 'Atrorosea': fls deep pink to red; fr. dark red. 'Candida' ('Albida'): fls white. 'Chrysantha': fls yellow. 'Dropmore': habit pendulous, to 2m high; fls white, later yellow, abundant. 'Incarnata': fls red. 'Polyantha': fls pink-red, prolific. 'Rosea': fls pale pink, turning white, eventually yellow. Z4.

L. biflora Desf. Decid. shrub. Branchlets white-velutinous. Lvs to 6×4.5cm, ovate to ovate-elliptic, dark green, soon glab. above, grey-green and densely pubesc. beneath. Fls fragrant, axill., paired; cor. to 4cm, yellow, grey-puberulent. Fr. globose, black. SE Spain, Sicily, N Afr. Z9.

L. brachypoda DC. = *L. japonica* var. *repens.*

L. bracteolaris Boiss. & Buhse. Erect decid. shrub. Lvs to 5cm, ovate to elliptic, blunt, blue-green above, paler beneath, glab. or slightly ciliate. Fls paired, subtended by bracteoles; cor. 12mm, white to pale gold, glab., gibbous. Fr. 8mm diam., orange-red. Spring. Transcauc. Z5.

L. brandtii Franch. & Savat. = *L. tschonoskii.*

L. breweri A. Gray = *L. conjugialis.*

L. ×*brownii* (Reg.) Carr. (*L. sempervirens* ×*L. hirsuta.*) SCARLET TRUMPET HONEYSUCKLE. Resembles *L. sempervirens.* Scandent decid. shrub to 3m. Lvs elliptic, blue-green and somewhat pubesc. beneath, uppermost lf pairs connate. Fls in cap. resembles those of *L. hirsuta.* Spring–summer. 'Dropmore Scarlet': vigorous; fls long trumpet-shaped, bright scarlet, midsummer-early autumn, long lasting. 'Fuchsioides': fls orange-scarlet, bilabiate. 'Plantierensis': fls large, coral-red, lobes orange. 'Punicea': fls orange-red outside; slow-growing. 'Youngii': fls deep crimson. Z5.

L. bungeana Ledeb. = *L. microphylla.*

L. caerulea L. Erect decid. shrub to 2m, much-branched. Branchlets glab. or sparse-pubesc. Lvs to 8×3cm, elliptic, sometimes obovate, ovate or oblong, glab. or pubesc. beneath. Fls paired; cor. to 15mm, yellow-white, gibbous, pubesc. Fr. dark blue, pruinose. Spring. NE Eur., Pyren. to Bulg. and SW Czech. 'Globosa': fr. almost globose. 'Sphaerocarpa': fr. oval to globose. 'Viridifolia': habit shrub-like, erect; shoots red; lvs to 3cm, elliptic to obovate, strong green, paler beneath, pubesc.; cor. tube long, thick. var. *altaica* (Pall.) Sweet. Branchlets setose. Lvs to 7cm, pubesc. above and beneath; cor. pubesc. outside; sta. included. Z2.

L. caerulea var. *reticulata* Zab. = *L. venulosa.*

L. calcarata Hemsl. Tall scandent shrub. Lvs to 14cm, ovate to elliptic-lanceolate, acuminate. Fls axill., paired; cor. 3cm, red-yellow, with a 1.5cm spur. China. Z6.

L. canadensis Bartr. FLY HONEYSUCKLE. Erect, decid. shrub to 1.5m, broad. Branchlets rufous, glab. Lvs to 8cm, ovate to elliptic, pale green, ciliate. Fls yellow-white, tinged red, paired; cor. to 2cm, tubular to funnelform, glab. outside. Fr. pale orange-red. Spring. N Amer. Z3.

L. canescens Schousb. = *L. biflora.*

L. caprifolium L. ITALIAN WOODBINE; ITALIAN HONEYSUCKLE. Scandent decid. shrub to 6m. Branchlets subglabrous. Lvs to 10×5cm, obovate or oval, apex rounded, glab., glaucous, term. pair connate. Fls fragrant, in 4–10-fld, sessile whorls from axils of terminal 3 pairs of lvs; cor yellow-white tinged pink, bilabiate, upper lip erect to reflexed, 4-lobed, to 5cm, tube slender. Fr. orange-red. Spring–summer. Eur., W Asia. 'Pauciflora': cor. tube to 3cm, purple or rose outside, off-white inside. 'Praecox': lvs greygreen; fls cream, often tinted light red, later turning yellow, early-flowering. Z5.

L. caprifolium var. *major* Carr. = *L.* ×*americana.*

L. caucasica Pall. Erect decid. shrub to 2m. Young br. glab. Lvs to 10×3cm, elliptic to ovate, acute or acuminate, base rounded. Fls paired, axill., fragrant; cor. bilabiate, to 12mm, pink, glab. or pubesc.; tube expanded one side. Fr. to 1cm diam., black. Spring–summer. Cauc. Z6.

L. cerasina Maxim. Decid. small shrub. Young br. light green, glab. Lvs to 12×4cm, elliptic-lanceolate, oblong-lanceolate or obovate-oblong, apex obtuse, base broad-cuneate, glab. or sparse-pubesc. above, glab. beneath, ciliate. Cor. 1cm, yellow-white, bilabiate, gibbous. Fr. to 8mm diam., red. Spring–summer. Jap. Z7.

L. chaetocarpa (Batal. ex Rehd.) Rehd. Erect decid. shrub to 2m. Branchlets setose, gland. Lvs to 8cm, ovate to oblong, occas. oval, truncate to acute, grey-green beneath, setose. Fls solitary or paired subtended by large leafy pale bracts; cor. tubular, 3cm, yellow to cream, 5-lobed, lobes rounded, pubesc. and gland. outside. Fr. bright red cupped by red-tinted leafy bracts. Summer. W China. Z5.

L. chamissoi Bunge. Erect decid. shrub to 1m, densely branched. Young br. glab., subglaucous. Lvs chartaceous to membranous, sessile, broad-ovate to elliptic, to 5×2.5cm, obtuse or rounded. Fls paired; cor. 1cm, deep red-violet, glab. outside, pubesc. Fr. 8mm, scarlet. Summer. Jap., Kuriles, Sakhalin, Kamchatka, Amur. Z5.

L. chinensis Wats. = *L. japonica* var. *repens*.

L. chrysantha Turcz. Decid. small tree to 4m. Young br. long-patent-pubesc. and glandular-punctate. Lvs to 12×6cm, obovate, ovate-elliptic or oblong-ovate, pubesc. esp. on veins beneath. Fls paired; cor. bilabiate, to 1.5cm, pale yellow, gibbous, upper lip divided to centre. Fr. globose, dark red. Spring–summer. NE Asia to C Jap. Z3.

L. ciliosa (Pursh) Poir. Twining everg. shrub. Lvs to 10cm, ovate or oval, ciliate, blue-green and glaucous beneath, term. pair connate. Fls in terminal, 1–3-whorled spikes; cor. to 4cm, yellow to scarlet, pubesc., more bilabiate than in *L. sempervirens*, swollen at base. Fr. 5mm diam., red. Summer. N Amer. Z5. var. **occidentalis** (Hook.) Nichols. Fls slightly larger; cor. tube glab., dark orange outside. Z5.

L. coerulea hort. non Hook. = *L. caerulea* var. *altaica*.

L. coerulea Hook. non hort. = *L. villosa*.

L. coerulea var. *villosa* (Michx.) Torr. & A. Gray = *L. villosa*.

L. coerulescens Dipp. = *L.* × *xylosteoides*.

L. confusa (Sweet) DC. Twining decid. to semi-everg. shrub. Branchlets short-pubesc. Lvs elliptic to oblong, to 7cm, pubesc. and ciliate, becoming glab., grey-green beneath. Fls fragrant, in short, dense pan.; cor. 4cm, white later yellow, slender, glandular-pubesc. Fr. black. Summer–autumn. E China. Z8.

L. conjugialis Kellogg. Straggling decid. shrub to 1.5m, much-branched. Branchlets strigulose. Lvs to 4cm, oblong-ovate to oblong-obovate, pale green and subglabrous above, lighter and pubesc. beneath. Fls paired, axill.; cor. to 8mm, dull purple, bilabiate, white-pubesc. Fr. to 6mm, bright red. Summer. W US. Z8.

L. deflexicalyx Batal. Decid. shrub to 1.5m, spreading. Branchlets purple, pubesc. Lvs to 8×2.3cm, narrow-ovate, dull green and pubesc. above, grey and pubesc. beneath. Fls paired, axill.; cor. to 1.5cm, yellow, outside pubesc., base gibbous, Fr. pink-red. Spring–summer. China, Tibet. var. **xerocalyx** (Diels) Rehd. Lvs to 10cm, narrower, slightly glaucous beneath. Ovaries enveloped by a cupule composed of connate bracteoles. SW China. Z5.

L. delavayi Franch. = *L. similis* var. *delavayi*.

L. demissa Rehd. Decid. shrub to 4m, much-branched. Young br. dark purple, short-pilose. Lvs to 3.5×1.25cm, broad-oblanceolate to narrow-obovate, occas. narrow-oblong, pubesc. beneath. Fls paired; cor. bilabiate, to 12mm, pale yellow, short-pubesc. outside, gibbous. Fr. to 6×8mm, dark red, shiny. Spring–summer. Jap. Z6.

L. depressa Royle = *L. myrtillus* var. *depressa*.

L. dioica L. Patent or twining decid. shrub to 1.5m, branchlets glab. Lvs to 9×5cm, oval or oblong, glab. intensely glaucous beneath, upper pairs connate into disc. Fls in term. clusters; cor. to 1.5cm, yellow-green tinged purple, bilabiate, gibbous, glab. outside. Fr. red. Spring–summer. NE Amer. Z5.

L. discolor Lindl. Erect decid. shrub to 2m. Young shoots rufous. Lvs to 8cm, oblong to elliptic, deep green above, pale blue-green beneath, glab. Fls on middle and upper part of br., paired; cor. to 3cm, yellow-white, often tinted red outside, tube short, gibbous, pubesc. inside. Fr. to 1cm diam., black. Spring–summer. Kashmir to Afghan. Z6.

L. diversifolia Wallich = *L. quinquelocularis*.

L. douglasii Koehne, non DC. = *L. glaucescens*.

L. dumetorum Lam. = *L. xylosteum*.

L. ebractulata Rydb. = *L. utahensis*.

L. edulis Turcz. = *L. caerulea*.

L. emphyllocalyx Maxim. = *L. caerulea*.

L. etrusca Santi. Scandent semi-evergreen shrub to 4m. Young shoots maroon, glab. Lvs to 8×5cm, oval or obovate, apex rounded, glaucous, usually pubesc. beneath, upper lvs connate. Fls packed in whorls in term. spikes, often 3 together; cor. yellow tinted red becoming deep yellow, bilabiate, 5cm, occas. glab. or gland.; sta. much exserted. Fr. 6mm diam., red. Summer. Medit. region. 'Donald Waterer': fls red and white, yellowing with age, fragrant. 'Michael Rosse': fls cream and pale yellow, later darkening, slightly fragrant. 'Superba': shoots flushed red; fls cream, later orange, in large term. pan.; strong-growing. Z7.

L. etrusca var. *brownii* Reg. = *L.* × *brownii*.

L. ferdinandi Franch. Spreading decid. shrub to 3m. Shoots gland. and setose when young. Lvs 5×4.5cm, ovate, acuminate, cordate at base, dull green, setose, stipules connate, surrounding st. Fls axill., paired; cor. bilabiate, to 2cm, yellow, tube saccate, gland. Fr. bright red. Summer. Mong., N China. var. *leycesterioides* (Gräbn.) Zab. Branchlets often subglabrous. Lvs to 7cm, ovate-oblong to lanceolate. Cor. eglandular. Mong. Z6.

L. flava Sims. YELLOW HONEYSUCKLE. Somewhat scandent decid. shrub to 2.5m, often bushy. Branchlets glab., pruinose. Lvs to 8cm, elliptic, acute, blue-green and pruinose beneath, uppermost pair connate into a disc. Fls grouped in 1–3 superimposed and spreading whorls, fragrant; cor. bilabiate, yellow then orange, 3cm. Fr. 6.5mm diam., red. Spring–summer. SE US. Z5.

L. flavescens Dipp. = *L. involucrata* var. *flavescens*.

L. flexuosa Thunb. = *L. japonica* var. *repens*.

L. floribunda Boiss. & Buhse. Low decid. shrub, densely branched. Shoots fine-tomentose. Lvs to 3cm, broad-ovate to elliptic, somewhat pubesc. above, grey-green and soft-pubesc. beneath. Cor. red, broad-saccate. Fr. yellow-red. Iran. Z8.

L. fragrantissima Lindl. & Paxt. Everg. to decid. shrub to 2m, spreading. Young shoots glab., longer than in *L. standishii*, pruinose. Lvs to 7×3.5cm, oval, cuneate apex and base, setose on margins when young, dull green above, blue-green beneath. Fls fragrant, paired, axill.; cor. bilabiate, cream, 12.5mm, tube short, glab. Fr. dull red. Winter–spring. China. Z5.

L. gibbiflora Maxim. non Dipp. = *L. chrysantha*.

L. giraldii Rehd. Scandent everg. to 2m. Br. twining, yellow-pubesc. when young. Lvs to 7×2.5cm, narrow-oblong, acuminate, cordate at base, dense-pubesc. Fls in capitate term. clusters; cor. 2cm, yellow-pubesc., tube slender. Fr. purple-black, pruinose. Summer. W China. Z6.

L. glabrata Wall. Vigorous everg. climber. St. hairy. Lvs lanceolate, base cordate, hairy, glossy dark green. Fls in term. clusters and axill. pairs, somewhat fragrant; cor. bilabiate, yellow tinged red, later white tinged pink. Fr. black. Summer and autumn. Himal. Z7.

L. glauca Hill = *L. dioica*.

L. glaucescens (Rydb.) Rydb. Closely resembles *L. dioica*. Twining decid. shrub. Shoots glab. Lvs to 8cm, elliptic to oblong, blue-green and pubesc. beneath, uppermost pair fused. Cor. yellow, red, 2cm. Fr. pale red. Spring–summer. NE N Amer. Z3.

L. glehnii F. Schmidt. Closely resembles *L. alpigena*. Decid. shrub. Shoots glandular-pubesc. Lvs obovate, ovate or oblong-elliptic with cordate base, pubesc. beneath. Fls green-yellow. Jap. Z6.

L. gracilipes Miq. Shrub to 180cm. Br. pubesc. Lvs to 6×5cm, broad-lanceolate to ovate to rhombic, pubesc., blue-green beneath. Fls solitary, rarely paired, nodding; cal. cup-like; cor. pink to carmine, narrow-funnelform, to 2cm, short-lobed. Fr. ellipsoid, 1cm, scarlet. Spring. Jap. 'Alba': fls white. Z6.

L. gracilipes var. *glandulosa* Maxim. = *L. tenuipes*.

L. grata Ait. = *L.* × *americana*.

L. griffithii Hook. f. & Thoms. Decid. twining shrub to 5m. Young shoots glab. Lvs to 5×2.5cm, broad-ovate, oblong or rounded, glaucous, often lobed. Fls in term. clusters of 2–3 whorls; cor. rose to white, bilabiate, 2.5cm, fine-glandular-pubesc. Spring. Afghan. Z9.

L. gynochlamydea Hemsl. Erect decid. shrub to 3m. Young shoots purple, glab. Lvs to 10×4cm, lanceolate, long-acuminate, midrib lanate above. Fls erect, paired; cor. white tinged pink, bilabiate, to 12mm, tube short, broader at base, pubesc. Fr. white or purple-white, translucent. Spring. China. Z6.

L. × heckrottii Rehd. (? *L. sempervirens* × *L.* × *americana*.) Scarcely scandent decid. shrub, spreading. Lvs to 6cm, oblong or elliptic, glaucous beneath, uppermost pairs connate at base. Fls abundant, 4cm, exterior pink, interior yellow, pubesc., in whorls on term. spikes; cor. bilabiate, tube slender. Fr. red. Summer. 'Goldflame': lvs dark green; fls yellow inside, flushed strong purple (a dark selection of the cross). Z5.

L. henryi Hemsl. Scandent everg. or semi-decid. shrub. Shoots slender, strigose. Lvs to 9×4cm, oblong-lanceolate to oblong-ovate, acuminate, deep green above, glossy, ciliate. Fls usually paired, crowded in pan., spikes, or heads; cor. to 2cm, maroon or yellow, bilabiate. Fr. purple-black. Summer. W China. Z4.

L. heteroloba Batal. Resembles *L. tatsiensis*, but lvs smaller, more densely pubesc., esp. on midrib. NW China.

L. heterophylla Decne. Resembles *L. webbiana*, but branchlets glab., lvs to 9cm, elliptic to oblong-lanceolate, sometimes lobed, glab. Fls yellow, becoming tinted red, glandular-pubesc. Himal. var. *karelinii* (Bunge) Rehd. Lvs to 8cm, thick, not lobed, glandular-pubesc. on veins. Cor. yellow-white, tinted red, 1.5cm gland. Fr. red. C Asia. Z5.

L. hildebrandiana Collett & Hemsl. GIANT BURMESE HONEYSUCKLE; GIANT HONEYSUCKLE. Vigorous scandent everg., sometimes semi-decid., to 25m. Lvs to 12×10cm, broad-ovate, or oval, deep green, gland. beneath. Fls fragrant, paired or grouped in large infl.; cor. to 16×10cm, white to cream turning amber, bilabiate. Summer. China, SE Asia. Z9.

L. hirsuta Eaton. HAIRY HONEYSUCKLE. Twining decid. shrub. Young shoots slender, glandular-pubesc. Lvs to 10×5cm, oval, dull green above, grey beneath, pubesc., ciliate, upper lvs fused. Fls whorled in term. or axill. spikes; cor.-tube bilabiate, to 3cm, yellow-orange glandular-pubesc. outside, base saccate. Fr. yellow-red. Summer. NE Amer. Z3.

L. hispanica Boiss. & Reut. = *L. periclymenum* var. *glauco-hirta*.

L. hispida Roem. & Schult. Decid. shrub to 1.5m. Young shoots hispid. Lvs to 8×3.5cm, ovate-oblong, setose, esp. on margins and veins beneath, grey-green beneath. Fls paired, axill., pendent; cor. to 3cm, yellow-white, funnelform, with 2, ovate, persistent white bracts. Fr. 1.5cm, bright red. Spring–summer. Turkestan. Z6.

L. hispida var. *chaetocarpa* Batal. ex Rehd. = *L. chaetocarpa*.

L. hispidula Douglas ex Torr. & A. Gray. Procumbent or scandent decid. shrub. Branchlets usually hispid. Lvs to 6cm, oval-oblong, pubesc. to glab. above, soft-pubesc. beneath, ciliate, uppermost lf pair fused. Fls closely whorled in spikes; cor. white becoming red, bilabiate, tube 1.5cm, glab. or pubesc. Fr. red. Summer. BC to Calif. Z6.

L. humilis Karel. & Kir. Erect dwarf shrub. Lvs 0.8–2cm, ovate or oval, coriaceous, ciliate, adpressed-pilose. Fls appearing with or before lvs; cor. tubular-campanulate, pilose, white to yellow-white, bilabiate. Turkestan. Z6.

L. iberica Bieb. Robust, erect decid. shrub to 2m. Young shoots pubesc. Lvs to 5×2.5cm, ovate, or rounded, dull green above, grey beneath, pubesc. Fls paired; cor. to 1.5cm, pubesc., pale yellow or white, bilabiate, tube strongly gibbous. Fr. to 8mm diam., bright red, puberulent. Summer. Cauc., Persia, N Iran. 'Erecta': habit narrowly fastigiate. 'Microphylla': prostrate; twigs drooping; lvs to 2cm, tinted blue. Z6.

L. ibotiformis Nak. = *L. demissa*.

L. implexa Sol. MINORCA HONEYSUCKLE. Scandent everg. 2.5m+. Young shoots slender, purple, glab. or setose. Lvs to 7×2.5cm, elliptic to oblong, glab., strongly glaucous beneath, lf pairs on flowering shoots connate. Fls in the axils of the 3 uppermost lf pairs; cor. to 4.5cm, yellow, suffused pink outside, tube pubesc. inside. Summer. Medit. Z9.

L. implexa f. *balearica* DC. = *L. balearica*.

L. interrupta Benth. CHAPARRAL HONEYSUCKLE. Twining everg. shrub. Branchlets glab., glaucous. Lvs to 4cm, orbicular to elliptic, entire, glab. or somewhat pubesc., glaucous beneath, uppermost lf pairs connate. Fls in interrupted spikes to 16cm; cor. to 2cm, yellow, funnelform, gibbous, glab. outside. Fr. 5mm diam., red. Summer. SW US. Z8.

L. involucrata (Richardson) Spreng. TWINBERRY. To 90cm. Resembles *L. ledebourii*, but smaller. Lvs to 12.5cm, narrower, ovate to oblong-lanceolate, less pubesc. Fls paired, involucrate; cor. to 1.25cm, yellow or red, tubular. Fr. 8mm diam., purple-black, subtended by spreading purple-red bracts. Spring. Mex., W N Amer., S Canada. var. *flavescens* (Dipp.) Rehd. Lvs to 12cm, oblong-lanceolate, glab. Cor. yellow. NW US. Z4.

L. involucrata var. *ledebourii* (Eschsch.) Zab. = *L. ledebourii*.
L. italica Schmidt = *L. ×americana*.

L. japonica Thunb. JAPANESE HONEYSUCKLE; GOLD-AND-SILVER FLOWER. Scandent everg. or semi-evergreen shrub. Br. gland., patent-pubesc. when young. Lvs to 8×3cm, oblong to ovate-elliptic, entire, often incised-sinuate, light green, pubesc. or glab., ciliate. Fls paired, intensely fragrant; cor. to 4cm, white, becoming pink later yellow, bilabiate, soft-pubesc. outside. Fr. to 7mm diam., blue-black. Spring–summer. E Asia; nat. SE US. var. *repens* (Sieb.) Rehd. St. sometimes maroon. Lvs soon glab., often deeply lobed markedly purple-tinged on veins beneath. 'Aureoreticulata' ('Reticulata'): lvs small, bright green, netted gold, sometimes lobed. 'Dart's World': habit spreading and bushy, to 25m high, to 1.2m wide; st. dark maroon; lvs to 7×3cm, ovate, dark green, tinted blue and pubesc. with red venation beneath; fls often flushed rosy red, later yellow and strong red, in pairs. 'Halliana': lvs pubesc. when young, rich

green; fls v. fragrant, white, later yellow. 'Hall's Prolific': lvs ovate; fls white, later cream to yellow, strongly scented, profuse. 'Purpurea': lvs tinted purple; fls maroon outside, white inside. 'Variegata': lvs variegated yellow. Z4.

L. japonica var. *chinensis* (Wats.) Bak. = *L. japonica* var. *repens*.
L. japonica var. *flexuosa* (Thunb.) Nichols. = *L. japonica* var. *repens*.
L. kaiensis Nak. = *L. praeflorens*.
L. karelinii Bunge = *L. heterophylla* var. *karelinii*.

L. kesselringii Reg. Closely resembles *L. caucasica*, but lvs to 6×2cm, oblong or elliptic-lanceolate; fls pink, in pairs, smaller, and cor.-tube less swollen. Kamchatka. Z6.

L. koehneana Rehd. Vigorous erect shrub to 3.5m. Lvs to 10cm, ovate or rhombic-ovate to obovate, subglabrous above, hairy and glaucescent beneath. Fls paired; cor. 2cm, yellow, bilabiate, pubesc. Fr. dark red or yellow. China. Z6.

L. korolkowii Stapf. Decid. shrub to 3m, spreading. Young shoots pubesc. Lvs to 3×2cm, ovate or oval, acuminate, glaucous blue-green beneath, pubesc. Fls paired, axill.; cor. 1.5cm, pale rose, bilabiate, tube narrow, pubesc. Fr. bright red. Summer. Mts of C Asia, Afghan., Pak. 'Aurora': to 2.5m high; twigs pendulous; lvs narrowly ovate, small, velvety beneath; fls small, to 8mm, shocking pink; fr. dark orange. 'Floribunda': lvs broadly ovate, obtuse, velvety; cor. to 15mm, tube somewhat swollen, white. Z5.

L. korolkowii var. *zabelii* (Rehd.) Rehd. = *L. tatarica* 'Zabelii'.

L. ledebourii Eschsch. Sturdy erect decid. shrub to 2m. Young shoots rarely pubesc. Lvs to 12×2.5cm, ovate-oblong, lanate beneath, margins pubesc. Fls subtended by 2–4 purple-tinged and gland. cordate bracts; cor. deep orange-yellow, to 2cm, funnelform, glutinous-pubesc. Fr. black, with persistent, red bracts. Summer. W US. Z6.

L. leycesterioides Gräbn. = *L. ferdinandi* var. *leycesterioides*.
L. ligustrina Wallich = *L. nitida*.
L. ligustrina var. *yunnanensis* Franch. = *L. nitida* 'Fertilis'.

L. maackii (Rupr.) Maxim. Erect decid. shrub to 5m. Young br. purple, white-pubesc. Lvs 8×4cm, narrow-obovate to broad-lanceolate, long-acuminate, dark green and minutely pubesc. above, lighter beneath; petioles purple. Fls fragrant, axill., paired; cor. 2cm, white then yellow, bilabiate, glab. or lightly pubesc. Fr. to 4mm diam., dark red or black. Spring–summer. E Asia. 'Erubescens': fls suffused pink; otherwise as f. *podocarpa*. 'Rem Red': habit upright and rounded, to 5m high; lvs dark green; fls white, later yellow; fr. 5mm diam., bright red. f. *podocarpa* Rehd. Shrub to 3m, wide-spreading. Fls white to yellow. Fr. red. Z2.

L. maximowiczii (Rupr.) Maxim. Erect decid. shrub to 3m. Young shoots tinted purple, glab. or setose. Lvs to 11.5×5.5cm, oval, dark green and glab. above, lightly pubesc. beneath. Fls paired; cor. purple-red, 1cm, glab., bilabiate, tube enlarged at base. Fr. red, fused. Spring–summer. Manch., Korea, China. var. *sachalinensis* F. Schmidt. Lvs broad, markedly blue-green beneath. Fls dark purple, to 18mm. Fr. dark red. Sachalin, Jap. Z4.

L. microphylla Roem. & Schult. Sturdy decid. shrub to 90cm. Branchlets short, glab., rigid. Lvs to 2.5×1.25cm, oval or obovate, glaucous, finely pubesc., above, fine-lanuginose beneath. Fls paired; cor. pale yellow, 1cm, glab. to fine-pubesc. Fr. bright red. NW Himal., Tibet, Sib. Z3.

L. ×minutiflora Zab. (*L. morrowii* × *L. xylosteoides*.) Erect decid. shrub. Branchlets spreading, fine-pubesc. Lvs to 3cm, oval-oblong to oblong, fine-pubesc. beneath. Cor. white bilabiate. Fr. red. Spring–summer. Z6.

L. morrowii A. Gray Decid. shrub to 2m. Young br. 4-angled, short-pubesc. Lvs to 5×2.5cm, oblong or ovate to elliptic, green and pubesc. beneath. Fls paired, axill.; cor. 13mm, white, later yellow, pubesc. Fr. dark red, shiny. Spring–summer. Jap. 'Xanthocarpa': fr. yellow. Z3.

L. ×muendeniensis Rehd. (*L. ×bella* × *L. ruprechtiana*.) Erect, decid. shrub. Lvs to 7cm, ovate to lanceolate, acuminate, pubesc. beneath. Fls white to yellow-white, sometimes tinted red. Fr. red. Spring. Z5.

L. ×muscaviensis Rehd. (*L. morrowii* × *L. ruprechtiana*.) Erect decid. shrub. Young shoots pubesc. Lvs to 5cm, ovate to oval-oblong, acuminate, sparse-pubesc. above, dense-pubesc. beneath. Fls white. Fr. bright red. Spring–summer. Z5.

L. myrtilloides Purpus. Decid., finely branched shrub, to 1.5m. Young shoots glandular-pubesc. Lvs to 3cm, oblong to elliptic, pubesc. at least on midrib. Fls fragrant, nodding; cor. white, red at base, pubesc. Fr. red. Spring–summer. Himal. Z6.

L. myrtillus Hook. f. & Thoms. Decid. shrub to 1m, compact young shoots pubesc. Lvs to 2.5cm×6.5mm, oval or ovate, glab., dark green above, paler and glaucous beneath. Fls in pairs, fragrant; cor. yellow-white, to 8mm, glab. Fr. orange-red. Spring–summer. Himal., Afghan. var. *depressa* (Royle) Rehd.

Peduncles longer than in type, i.e. equalling lvs; bracts oval, not narrow-oblong, broader. Himal. (Nepal, Sikkim). Z6.

L. nepalensis Kirchn. = *L.* ×*xylosteoides*.

L. nervosa Maxim. Decid. shrub, erect, to 3m. Young shoots glab., tinged purple. Lvs to 6×2.5cm, oval to oblong, glab., red at first, later bright green above, except veins. Fls paired; cor. 1cm, pale pink with cupular bracts. Fr. black. Spring–summer. China. Z6.

L. nigra L. Decid. shrub to 1.5m, rounded. Br. rigid. Lvs to 5cm, oval, glab. or pubesc. on midrib beneath. Fls in axill. pairs; cor. pink, bilabiate. Fr. blue-black. Spring–summer. Mts of C & S Eur. Z6.

L. nitida Wils. Densely branched everg. shrub to 3.5m. Young shoots erect, purple, setose. Lvs 0.5–1.2cm, dark green, ovate to rounded, blunt, shiny above, lighter beneath, usually glab. Fls paired; cor. to 1cm, cream to white. Fr. 6.5mm diam., shiny blue-purple, transparent. Spring. SW China. Commonly used for hedging. 'Aurea': habit erect; lvs gold. 'Baggesen's Gold': habit low, dense; br. nodding; lvs small, gold, later sulphur green; fls cream; fr. purple tinted blue. 'Elegant': habit shrub-like, to 1m high; twigs loose, spreading, sometimes almost horizontally; lvs small, to 1.5cm, mainly distichous, suborbicular to narrowly ovate, dull green; fls white, freely produced; fr. purple. 'Ernest Wilson': habit spreading; br. arching to drooping; lvs tiny, ovate, glossy green. 'Fertilis': habit erect, to 2.5m; st. upright or arching; lvs large, broadly ovate to elliptic; fls and fr. prolific. 'Graciosa': habit low and mat-forming, densely branched; shoots arching; lvs small; fls and fr. rare; a seedling of 'Elegant'. 'Hohenheimer Findling': habit shrub-like, to 1.25m wide; twigs nodding; lvs to 1.8cm, narrowly oval, strong green. 'Maygreen' ('Maigrün'): habit squat, compact, to 80cm high, to 80cm wide; lvs shiny, long-lasting. 'Yunnan': habit erect, wide, similar to 'Ernest Wilson'; shoots erect; lvs large, not usually distichous; fls abundant. Sometimes misnamed *L. yunnanensis*. Z7.

L. ×*notha* Zab. (*L. ruprechtiana* ×*L. tatarica*.) Vigorous erect decid. shrub. Young shoots subglabrous. Lvs to 6cm, ovate to lanceolate-elliptic, lightly pubesc. to subglab. beneath. Fls paired; cor. 18mm white, yellow or pink, bilabiate. Fr. red. Spring–summer. 'Alba': fls white. 'Carneorosea': fls crimson. 'Gilva': fls pale yellow, edged pink. 'Grandiflora': fls large, white tinted yellow, later tinted pink; fr. maroon. 'Ochroleuca': fls flushed yellow; fr. orange. Z4.

L. nummularifolia Jaub. & Spach Erect shrub to 9m. Young br. puberulent or glandular-villous. Lvs to 5×3.5cm, ovate-lanceolate to suborbicular, obtuse, villous, sometimes glandular-pubesc. Fls paired, axill.; cor. to 2cm, pubesc., cream to yellow. Fr. yellow. Turkestan, S Greece, Crete. Z6.

L. oblongifolia (Goldie) Hook. SWAMP FLY HONEYSUCKLE. Erect decid. shrub to 1.5m. Branchlets fine soft-pubesc. Lvs to 8cm, subsessile, oblong to oblanceolate, obtuse, fine-pubesc., blue-green above, grey-green beneath. Fls paired; cor. to 1.5cm, yellow, tubular, deeply bilabiate. Fr. red. Spring. NE N Amer. Z3.

L. obovata Royle. Erect decid. shrub to 2m, bushy. Branchlets glab. Lvs to 1.2cm, obovate, subglabrous, white beneath. Fls paired; cor. 1cm, yellow-white, glab. outside, base saccate. Fr. blue-black. Spring. Himal. to Afghan. Z5.

L. occidentalis Hook. = *L. ciliosa* var. *occidentalis*.

L. ochroleuca St.-Lager = *L. xylosteum*.

L. odoratissima hort. ex Dipp. = *L. fragrantissima*.

L. orientalis Lam. Erect decid. shrub to 3m. Branchlets glab. Lvs to 10cm, ovate to lanceolate, dark green above, grey-green beneath, glab. except veins. Fls paired; cor. to 1.2cm, pink to violet, bilabiate, tubular. Fr. blue-black. Spring–summer. Asia Minor. Z4.

L. orientalis var. *caucasica* (Pall.) Rehd. = *L. caucasica*.

L. orientalis var. *discolor* Clarke = *L. discolor*.

L. orientalis var. *longifolia* Dipp. = *L. kesselringii*.

L. parvifolia Edgew. non Hayne = *L. obovata*.

L. periclymenum L. WOODBINE; HONEYSUCKLE. Twining shrub to 4m. Young shoots hollow. Lvs to 6.5×4cm, ovate, oval or obovate, lightly pubesc. becoming glab., glaucous and blue-green beneath, uppermost pair separate. Fls fragrant, in 3–5-whorled term. spikes; cor. to 5cm, red and yellow-white, glandular-glutinous, bilabiate. Fr. bright red. Summer. Eur., Asia Minor, Cauc., W Asia. var. *glaucohirta* Kunze. Lvs pubesc., glaucous blue beneath. Spain, Moroc. 'Aurea': lvs variegated yellow. 'Belgica': habit bushy, to 3×3m; lvs glab., thick, elliptic-oblong; fls white, flushed purple outside, later yellow, scented, in large clusters; fr. large, red, abundant. 'Belgica Select': a fast-growing selection of 'Belgica'. 'Berries Jubilee': lvs tinted blue, glaucous grey beneath; fls yellow; fr. bright red; vigorous grower. 'Graham Thomas': fls large, white, later yellow tinted copper, long-lasting. 'Quercina': lvs 'oak-like', sinuate, sometimes variegated white. 'Serotina': lvs

narrower, glab., longer-stalked; fls dark purple outside, later fading, yellow inside, profuse; fr. red. 'Serotina Florida': habit compact; fls dark red outside, yellow and white inside, crimson in bud; fr. translucent red; slow-growing. 'Serpentine': twigs deep maroon when young; lvs narrow, pale blue beneath; fls to 7cm, interior cream, exterior light mauve with white edge, later yellow. Z4.

L. periclymenum f. *serotina* Ait. = *L. periclymenum* 'Serotina'.

L. persica Jaub. & Spach = *L. nummularifolia*.

L. phylomelae Carr. = *L. gracilipes*.

L. pileata Oliv. Low, often prostrate, everg. or semi-decid. shrub. Young shoots purple, pubesc. Lvs to 3×1.25cm, distichous, oblong-lanceolate, dark green or lozenge-shaped, subglabrous, shiny. Fls in sessile pairs; cal. produces collar covering cupule margin; cor. to 8mm, yellow-white, funnelform, pubesc. Fr. amethyst, translucent. Spring. China. 'Moss Green': habit low-spreading, compact; lvs bright green; not vigorous. 'Royal Carpet': habit prostrate, to 45cm high, to 1.5m wide; br. straight, spreading; lvs glossy green; fr. purple. Z5.

L. pileata f. *yunnanensis* (Franch.) Rehd. = *L. nitida* 'Fertilis'.

L. pilosa Maxim. = *L. strophiophora*.

L. praeflorens Batal. Decid. shrub to 2m. Branchlets sometimes puberulent. Lvs to 6.5×4cm, broad-ovate, pubesc., eesp. beneath, subglaucous. Fls precocious; cor. to 1.5cm, white tinted yellow, funnelform, glab. Fr. red. Spring. Jap., Korea, Manch., Ussuri. Z5.

L. prolifera (Kirchn.) Rehd. GRAPE HONEYSUCKLE. Rarely scandent, decid. shrub to 180cm; branchlets lax, blue-pruinose. Lvs to 10×6.5cm, thick, oval, obovate or oblong, glaucous, upper lvs connate, forming disc. Fls usually in 4 superimposed whorls; cor.-tube 3cm, yellow, pubesc. inside. Fr. scarlet. Summer. C N Amer. (Ohio to Tenn. & Mo.) Z5.

L. ×*propinqua* Zab. (*L. alpigena* ×*L. ledebourii*.) Decid. shrub. Two forms, one resembling *L. alpigena*, the other *L. ledebourii*. Cor. tawny, bilabiate, expanded; bracts densely gland. Z6.

L. prostrata Rehd. Procumbent decid. shrub. Br. thin, hollow; young shoots pubesc., purple. Lvs to 3×1.25cm, oval or ovate, pubesc. above, later glab., veins pubesc. beneath. Fls axill., paired; cor. pale yellow, bilabiate, 1.5cm. Fr. red. Summer. W China. Z5.

L. ×*pseudochrysantha* Barua. (*L. chrysantha* ×*L. xylosteum*.) Similar to *L. chrysantha* but with broader bracts. Z3.

L. pubescens Stokes non Sweet = *L. xylosteum*.

L. pubescens Sweet non Stokes = *L. hirsuta*.

L. purpurascens Walp. Decid. sturdy bush to 3m. Young shoots purple, fine-pubesc. Lvs to 4×2.5cm, oblong or obovate, pubesc. esp. beneath, dull green above, grey beneath; petiole purple. Cor. purple, tubular-funnelform, 1.5cm, pubesc. Fr. blue-black. Spring. Himal., Kashmir, Afghan. Z6.

L. ×*purpusii* Rehd. (*L. fragrantissima* ×*L. standishii*.) Erect semi-evergreen shrub to 3m. Branchlets arching, glab. or setose. Lvs to 10cm, ovate-elliptic, dark above, paler beneath, glab., pubesc. on veins beneath, margin setose. Fls fragrant, axill., 2–4-clustered; cor. cream-white, glab. Fr. red. Winter–spring. 'Winter Beauty': fls creamy white, v. fragrant, winter-flowering. Z6.

L. pyrenaica L. Erect decid. shrub to 2m. Lvs to 4×1cm, sessile, obovate to oblanceolate, glaucous. Fls nodding, paired; cor. 2cm, cream, rose-tinted, funnelform-campanulate. Fr. red. Spring–summer. E Pyren., Balearic Is. Z5.

L. pyrenaica Kit. non L. = *L. xylosteum*.

L. quinquelocularis Hardw. Decid. shrub, sometimes a small tree, to 4m. Young shoots somewhat purple, pubesc. Lvs to 5×4cm, oval, obovate or orbicular, initially pubesc. above, grey and more pubesc. beneath. Fls axill., paired; cor. cream white, later yellow, bilabiate, to 2cm, pubesc. outside, tube slender, slightly expanded. Fr. translucent white. Summer. Himal., China. f. *translucens* (Carr.) Zab. Lvs longer, base cordate. Cor. tube gibbous. Z5.

L. reticulata Champ. Twining everg., rarely decid., shrub. Br. short-pubesc. or glab. Lvs to 7cm, oblong-ovate, glab. above, tomentose and strongly reticulate beneath. Fls in axill. pairs, usually in terminal pan. or rac.; cor. to 6cm. Fr. usually black. Hong Kong. Z10.

L. reticulata Maxim. non Champ. = *L. venulosa*.

L. rubra Gilib. = *L. xylosteum*.

L. rupicola Hook. f. & Thoms. Decid. dense bush to 2.5m. Br. interlacing; branchlets lightly pubesc. or glab. when young. Lvs to 2.5×1.25cm, oblong or ovate, dull green and glab. above, lighter and ± pubesc. beneath. Fls fragrant, axill., paired; cor., pale pink to lilac, lobes ovate, tube pubesc. outside. Fr. red. Spring–summer. Himal., Tibet. Z8.

L. rupicola var. *thibetica* (Bur. & Franch.) Zab. = *L. thibetica*.

L. ruprechtiana Reg. Decid. bushy shrub to 3m, sometimes to 6m. Young shoots pubesc. Lvs to 10×4cm, ovate to oblong, often slender-acuminate, dark green above, lighter, pubesc. beneath. Fls axill., paired; cor. 2cm, white, later yellow, bilabiate, glab. outside. Fr. bright red, translucent. Spring–summer. NE Asia, Manch., China. 'Xanthocarpa': lvs densely pubesc.; fls small; fr. yellow. Z6.

L. saccata Rehd. Shrub to 1.5m, of slender-branched habit. Lvs to 5cm, oblong, obtuse to acute, pubesc. beneath. Fls paired; cor. tubular-campanulate, 12mm, white or yellow-white, saccate at base. Fr. orange-red or scarlet. Spring. China. Z6.

L. sachalinensis (F. Schmidt) Nak. = *L. maximowiczii* var. *sachalinensis*.

L. sempervirens L. TRUMPET HONEYSUCKLE; CORAL HONEYSUCKLE. Vigorous scandent everg. shrub. Young shoots glab. Lvs to 8×5cm, oval or slightly obovate, glab. above, glaucous and often pubesc. beneath, 1–2 uppermost pairs of lvs connate. Fls in 3–4 superimposed whorls; cor. to 5cm, rich scarlet-orange outside, more yellow inside. Fr. bright red. Spring–autumn. E & S US (Conn. to Flor. & Tex.). var. *minor* Ait. Semi-evergreen. Lvs elliptic to oblong-lanceolate. Fls more abundant, orange-red to scarlet, smaller, narrower. 'Magnifica': fls red outside, interior yellow; semi-evergreen. 'Sulphurea' ('Flava') to 10m; fls bright yellow, long- and late-flowering. 'Superba' ('Red Coral', 'Red Trumpet', 'Rubra', 'Dreer's Everlasting'): lvs ovate-elliptic, glab. above; fls bright scarlet; decid. Z3.

L. sempervirens var. *brownii* (Reg.) Lav. = *L. ×brownii*.

L. sericea Royle = *L. purpurascens*.

L. serotina (Ait.) Gand. = *L. periclymenum* 'Serotina'.

L. setifera Franch. Medium-sized shrub. Shoots setose-pubesc. Lvs to 7.5cm, oblong-lanceolate, soft-pubesc., usually coarse-dentate. Fls precocious, fragrant, setose in clusters; cor. yellow to pink, to 8mm. Fr. red, setose. Winter–spring. Himal., Assam, China. Z8.

L. shikokiana Mak. = *L. cerasina*.

L. similis Hemsl. Scandent semi-evergreen shrub. C & W China, India, Burm. var. *delavayi* (Franch.) Rehd. Scandent, everg., glab. shrub. Lvs to 6cm, lanceolate, white-lanate beneath. Infl. racemose; fls in axill. pairs; cor. to 8cm, yellow-white, bilabiate; sta. and style strongly exserted. Fr. black. SW China. Z9.

L. sororia Piper = *L. conjugalis*.

L. spinosa (Decne.) Walp. Decid., almost leafless, shrub to 120cm. Br. armed. Lvs to 3cm, narrow-oblong, glab., occas. 2-toothed. Fls paired; cor. 2cm, lilac-pink, tubular-funnelform, tube slender, glab. outside. Fr. white or purple, pruinose. NW Himal., Tibet, E Turkestan. Z6.

L. spinosa var. *alberti* (Reg.) Rehd. = *L. alberti*.

L. splendida Boiss. Vigorous scandent everg. Lvs to 5cm, oval to oblong, glab., rarely pilose, glaucous, upper pair connate. Fls in term., sessile clusters of densely compound whorls; cor. to 5cm, yellow-white then maroon, bilabiate, fine-pubesc. outside. Summer. Spain. Z9.

L. standishii Jacq. Decid. or semi-evergreen bush to 2.5m. Bark exfoliating; young shoots tuberculate, setose. Lvs to 10×5cm, oblong-lanceolate, slender-acuminate, pubesc., setose on margins and midrib. Fls fragrant axillary, paired, usually pubesc., outside; cream-white sometimes tinted palest pink, bilabiate. Fr. obcordate, red. Winter–spring. China. var. *lancifolia* Rehd. Lvs v. narrow. Z6.

L. strophiophora Franch. Decid. shrub to 2.5m. Bark grey; young br. often dark purple-brown, glab. or scattered glandular-pubesc. Lvs to 8cm, broad-ovate to ovate-oblong, coarse-pilose, esp. on midrib beneath. Fls paired, nodding; cor. to 2cm, pale yellow, narrow-funnelform, glab. Fr. red, pilose. Spring–summer. Jap. Z6.

L. subaequalis Rehd. Scandent decid. shrub. Br. glab. Lvs to 10cm, oval to oblong-obovate, glab., uppermost pair connate. Fls in sessile whorls; cor. to 3cm, funnelform, gland. outside. W China. Z6.

L. subspicata Hook. & Arn. Scandent everg. shrub to 2.5m. Branchlets puberulent. Lvs to 4×1cm, linear-oblong to oblong, coriaceous, grey-pubesc., uppermost pairs connate. Fls whorled in short, leafy spikes to 12cm; cor. bilabiate, yellow-cream, to 1cm, glandular-pubesc., tube gibbous. Fr. yellow or red. Summer. W US. Z8.

L. sullivantii A. Gray = *L. prolifera*.

L. syringantha Maxim. Decid. shrub to 3m, graceful. Young shoots glab. Lvs to 2.5cm, oblong or ovate, somewhat glaucous. Fls paired, fragrant; cor. to 1cm, lilac, campanulate, pubesc. inside. Fr. red. Spring–summer. China, Tibet. 'Grandiflora': fls large. Z4.

L. szechuanica Batal. Closely resembles *L. tangutica*, but lvs to 2.5cm, cuneate-obovate, obtuse, glab., glaucous and blue-green beneath, cor. 12mm, slender. W China. Z6.

L. tangutica Maxim. Low decid. shrub. Shoots slender, glab. Lvs to 3cm, obovate to oblong, acute, ciliate, sparsely pilose above and on the veins beneath, otherwise glab. Fls paired, pendulous, slender-stalked, to 1.4cm, narrow, base slightly swollen, white-yellow, becoming pink. Spring–summer. China.

Z6.

L. tatarica L. Erect, decid. shrub to 4m. Shoots grey, glab. Lvs to 6cm, ovate to lanceolate, usually glab., glaucous beneath. Fls paired, axillary; cor. to 2.5cm, pink, tube straight or base slightly swollen. Fr. scarlet to yellow-orange. Spring–summer. S Russia to C Asia. Habit ranges from 'Grandiflora' (tall, vigorous; fls v. large, pure white) to 'Nana' (dwarf; fls small, pink) and 'Louis Leroy' (low, rounded; lvs tinted blue; fls large, cor. lobes dusky pink, bordered white; fr. orange). 'Fenzlii' has lvs striped and speckled yellow. Cvs notable for fl. colour include 'Alba' (fls white), 'Virginalis' (fls v. large, white; fr. bright red), 'Discolor' (cor. pale pink inside, margin and dors. side deep red; fr. orange), 'Latifolia' (syn 'Grandiflora Rosea'; shoots thick; lvs large; fls pale pink with dark stripes), 'Rosea' (fls large, pale pink; fr. deep red). 'Sibirica' (syn 'Rubra'; f. *sibirica* (Pers.) Rehd.) cor. lobes deep red, wide white border), 'Hack's Red' (fls dark pink-red), 'Arnold's Red' (habit dense and woody; br. arching; lvs tinged blue; fls darkest red, fragrant; fr. bright red); 'Zabelii' (fls bright pink. Those notable for fr. include 'Lutea' (fr. yellow), 'Morden Orange' (fls light pink; fr. orange). Z3.

L. tatsienensis Franch. Erect, decid. shrub, to 2m. Branchlets glab. Lvs to 4cm, ovate to oblong-ovate, acuminate, pilose, esp. beneath; margin rarely lobed. Fls paired, axill.; cor. to 1.2cm, bilabiate, deep purple, pilose at base. Spring–summer. Tibet. Z6.

L. ×tellmanniana hort. (*L. sempervirens* × *L. tragophylla*.) Vigorous, decid., scandent shrub. Branchlets glab. Lvs to 10cm, ovate to oblong, deep green above, white-pruinose beneath, upper pair fused. Infl. term. whorls; cor. tube to 4.5cm, rich orange. Summer. Gdn origin. Z5.

L. tenuiflora Reg. & Winkl. = *L. altmannii*.

L. tenuipes Nak. Erect, decid. shrub, to 3m. Shoots yellow to rufous, pubesc., then glab. Lvs to 6cm, obovate to oblong-ovate, pubesc. above, brown-lanate beneath. Fls solitary; cor. to 1.8cm, red, pubesc. outside, base gibbous. Fr. red. Spring. Jap. Z6.

L. thibetica Bur. & Franch. Decid. shrub to 1.5m, erect to procumbent, tomentose. Lvs to 3cm, oblong-lanceolate, deep green, shining above, white-tomentose beneath. Fls paired, axill.; cor. 1.5cm, pale purple, erect, tubular-campanulate, often pubesc. outside. Fr. red. Summer. Tibet, W China. Z4.

L. tomentella Hook. f. & Thoms. Decid., spreading shrub, 1.5–3m. Branchlets rigid, tomentose. Lvs 1.5–4cm, paired and opposite, oblong, acute, pubesc. to glab. above, villous beneath. Fls paired, axill., cernuous; cor. 1.6cm, tubular-campanulate, lobes spreading, white tinted pink, tube straight, pubesc. outside. Fr. blue-black. Summer. Himal., Sikkim. Z5.

L. tragophylla Hemsl. Decid., vigorous, scandent shrub. Branchlets hollow. Lvs to 14cm, oblong, glaucous, midrib pubesc. beneath, uppermost 1–3 pairs fused. Fls 1–2 whorls in a term. head; cor. 7–8cm, lightly hairy inside, orange to yellow, often tinted red above. Fr. red. Summer. China. Z6.

L. trichosantha Bur. & Franch. Decid., erect, spreading shrub, to 1.5m. Br. slender, nearly glab. Lvs 2.5–4cm, broadly ovate, mucronate, pilose on veins beneath. Fls paired, axill.; cor. 1.8–2cm, bilabiate, pubesc. yellow or white becoming yellow, tube short, base gibbous. Fr. bright red. Summer. Tibet, W China. Z6.

L. tschonoskii Maxim. Erect shrub. Br. slender, glab. Lvs 6–9cm, elliptic-oblong. Fls on upper half of br.; bracteoles fused forming a cupule; cor. to 1cm, bilabiate, yellow-white, to pink or violet. Fr. black. Summer. Jap. Z6.

L. uniflora Bl. = *L. gracilipes*.

L. utahensis S. Wats. Closely related to *L. canadensis*. Low shrub to 1.5m. Lvs to 6cm, ovate to oblong, obtuse, glab. or puberulous beneath. Fls in axils of lower lvs; cor. to 2cm, tubular-campanulate, yellow-white tinted red, base saccate. Fr. orange-red. Spring. BC to Oreg., Utah, Wyom., Mont. Z4.

L. velutina DC. = *L. villosa*.

L. venulosa Maxim. Closely related to *L. caerulea*. Lvs oval, glab., occas. lightly puberulent beneath at first. Cor. bilabiate, glab., tube longer than limb, venation reticulate, esp. below. Fr. blue. Jap. Z6.

L. vesicaria Komar. Related to *L. ferdinandi*. Robust shrub. Br. bristly. Lvs 5–10cm, ovate to ovate-oblong, midrib ciliate beneath, lvs bract-like toward apex of br. Fls in axils of upper lvs; cor. bilabiate, yellow, hairy. Korea. Z5.

L. villosa (Michx.) Roem. & Schult. Closely related to *L. caerulea*. Decid. shrub, young shoots tomentose. Lvs villous. Cor. funnelform, pilose outside. Fr. blue, edible. N Amer. var. *solonis* (Eaton) Fern. To 75cm. Lvs to 4cm, pubesc. to glab. above, long-pubesc. beneath. Cor. white tinted yellow, sometimes glab. outside, long-pubesc. inside. Fr. blue-black. Spring–summer. Minn. to Newfoundland. Z2.

L. ×vilmorinii Rehd. (*L. deflexicalyx* ×*L. quinquelocularis*.)

Resembles *L. quinquelocularis*, except lvs wider, shorter, apex more obtuse. Infl. shorter. Fr. yellow, tinted pink, spotted red. Gdn origin. Z6.

L. vulgaris Borkh = *L. xylosteum*.

L. webbiana Wallich. Erect, decid. shrub, to 3m. Lvs 6–10cm, ovate to oblong-obovate, acuminate, pubesc., often gland. Fls on lower half of branchlets; cor. c1cm, bilabiate, tube gibbous, villous inside, white tinted yellow-green. Fr. scarlet. Spring. SE Eur., Afghan., Himal. Z6.

L. xerocalyx Diels = *L. deflexicalyx* var. *xerocalyx*.

L. ×xylosteoides Tausch. (*L. tatarica* ×*L. xylosteum*.) Erect, much branched, decid. shrub, to 2m; br. rigid-pubesc. Lvs to 6cm, broadly elliptic, ovate or obovate, ciliate and pubesc., blue-green. Fls light red, pubesc., base swollen. Fr. yellow to red. 'Clavey's Dwarf' ('Claveyi'): habit rounded, to 1.5m high; lvs tinted blue-grey; fls white; fr. red; slow-growing. 'Compacta' ('Emerald Mound', 'Nana'): habit dense, mound-forming to hemispherical, to 1.2m high, to 1.8m wide; lvs tinted blue-grey; fls off-white; fr. dark red. 'Miniglobe': habit dwarf, compact; lvs strong green. Spring–summer. Gdn. orig. Z6.

L. xylosteum L. FLY HONEYSUCKLE. Erect, decid. shrub to 3m. Lvs 3–7cm, ovate to honeysuckle or oblong, pubesc. Fls in middle or lower half of br.; cor. 1cm, yellow-white, often tinted red, bilabiate. Fr. red, rarely yellow. Summer. Eur., Cauc., Sib., China. 'Mollis': lvs more pubesc. Z3.

L. yunnanensis Franch. Everg., scandent shrub, to 4m; shoots glab. Lvs 3–12cm, oblong to ovate-lanceolate, almost glab. above, blue-white beneath, uppermost pair fused. Fls in whorls, gathered into spikes, or solitary; cor. to 2.5cm, yellow, tube swollen, interior pubesc. SW China. The epithet *yunnanensis* was also applied by Franchet to the plant we now call *L. nitida* 'Fertilis' – this and *L. nitida* 'Yunnan' are both sometimes styled *L. yunnanensis* or *L. nitida/pileata* var. *yunnanensis*. var. *tenuis* Rehd. Smaller. Lvs to 3cm, lightly pubesc. beneath. Fls in single whorls; cor. to 2cm, white to yellow. SW China. Z7.

L. cvs. 'Freedom': to 3m high, vigorous; lvs tinted blue; fls white flushed pale pink; fr. red; resistant to honeysuckle witches. 'Hedge King': habit upright, rounded, to 1.5m high, to 1m wide; lvs tinted grey; fls white to yellow; fr. red; resistant to aphid. 'Hidcote': lvs tinted pale grey, decid.; fls dark orange to red. Z6.

Lontar Palm *Borassus flabellifer*.
Loofah *Luffa cylindrica*.
Looking-glass Plant *Coprosma repens*.
Looking-glass Tree *Heritiera macrophylla*.
Loose Silky Bent *Apera spica-venti*.
Loosestrife *Lysimachia*; *Lythrum*.

Lopezia Cav. Onagraceae. 21 ann. or perenn. herbs, sometimes woody, swollen. Lvs stipulate, in spirals or opposite. Fls zygomorphic in bracteate terminal rac.; sep. 4, lanceolate; pet. 4, clawed, often unequal, upper 2 free or partly fused with upper 3 sep.; sta. 2, one usually sterile, staminode petaloid, sometimes enveloping fertile sta. and releasing it explosively. C Amer. Z10.

L. albiflora Schldl. = *L. racemosa*.
L. angustifolia Robinson = *L. racemosa*.
L. axillaris Thunb. ex Schweig. = *L. racemosa*.
L. cordata Hornem. = *L. racemosa*.
L. corymbosa Sprague & Riley = *L. racemosa*.
L. elegans Rose = *L. racemosa*.
L. foliosa Brandg. = *L. racemosa*.
L. glandulosa Rose = *L. racemosa*.
L. haematodes Kunze = *L. racemosa*.
L. hirsuta Jacq. = *L. racemosa*.
L. integrifolia DC. = *L. racemosa*.
L. lineata Zucc. = *L. racemosa*.
L. mexicana Jacq. = *L. racemosa*.
L. minima Lagasca ex Schrank = *L. racemosa*.
L. minuta Lagasca = *L. racemosa*.
L. oppositifolia Lagasca = *L. racemosa*.
L. parvula Rose = *L. racemosa*.
L. pringlei Rose = *L. racemosa*.

L. racemosa Cav. Variable ann. or perenn. to 1.5m, glab. or hairy. Lower lvs 1–8cm, ovate to lanceolate, ± serrate, upper lvs 0.5–5cm, ovate to narrow-lanceolate, serrate to entire. Sep. 3.5–7.5mm, hairy, sometimes gland.; pet. white to white tinted lilac, or purple, pink to red or vermilion, lower pet. 3.5–10mm, obovate to suborbicular, upper pet. 4–8.5mm, linear to oblong-lanceolate; fertile anth. grey-green to blue-green; staminode white, tinted pink. Mex., El Salvador. ssp. *racemosa*. MOSQUITO FLOWER. Perenn., hairy, strigulose, glandular-hairy or subglabrous. Lvs 0.5–8cm, pubesc. to subglabrous, ovate to lanceolate, serrate or with few teeth.
→*Riesenbachia*.

Lophanthera A. Juss. Malpighiaceae. 4 shrubs or small trees with white latex. Lvs opposite, entire, elliptic to obovate, stipulate. Infl. a term. thyrse, with many br.; fls v. numerous, bracts and bracteoles persistent; cal. 5-lobed, with 10 basal glands; pet. 5, decid., posterior pet. differentiated; sta. 10. N S Amer. Z10.

L. lactescens Ducke. Tree to 15m. Lvs 15–24cm, obovate, obtuse or apiculate, gland. beneath; stipules 8–12mm, triangular. Infl. 30–40cm, pendulous, pubesc.; fls 300–500; pet. 5–7mm, yellow. Braz.

Lophocereus (A. Berger) Britt. & Rose.
L. australis (K. Brandg.) Britt. & Rose = *Pachycereus schottii*.
L. mieckleyanus (Weingart) Borg = *Pachycereus schottii*.
L. sargentianus (Orcutt) Britt. & Rose = *Pachycereus schottii*.
L. schottii (Engelm.) Britt. & Rose = *Pachycereus schottii*.

Lophochloa Rchb.
L. cristata (L.) Hylander = *Rostraria cristata*.
L. phleoides (Vill.) Rchb. = *Rostraria cristata*.

Lophomyrtus Burret. Myrtaceae. 2 shrubs or small trees. Lvs simple, leathery, punctate. Fls solitary, axill., 4-merous, white; sta. numerous; ovary inferior, 2-celled. Fr. a many seeded berry, purple-black to red. NZ. Z9.

L. bullata (Sol. ex A. Cunn.) Burret. RAMA RAMA. To 5.4m. Lvs to 5cm, broadly ovate to suborbicular, strongly bullate, glossy often tinged purple-red. Fls c1.25cm diam. Fr. 1cm diam.

L. obcordata (Raoul) Burret. ROHUTU. To 4.5m. Lvs to 1.25cm, obcordate, cuneate, emarginate. Fls to 6.5mm diam. Fr. 6.5mm diam.

L. ×ralphii (Hook. f.) Burret. (*L. bullata* ×*L. obcordata*.) Intermediate between parents; lvs puckered; fls white-pink. 'Purpurea': lvs deep purple-red.
→*Myrtus*.

Lophophora J. Coult. Cactaceae. 2 cacti; rootstock napiform; st. depressed-globose, usually clustering, weakly tuberculate-ribbed, spineless. Fls to 2.4×2.2cm, at woolly st. apex, campanulate; pericarpel and tube naked; sta. touch-sensitive. Fr. cylindric to clavate, pink or red, naked. E & N Mex. and S Tex.

L. diffusa (Croizat) H. Bravo. St. simple, 2–7×5–12cm, yellow-green; ribs v. poorly defined; areoles irregularly and widely spaced. Inner tep. 2–2.5mm wide, white, pale yellow or v. pale pink. Summer. E Mex. Z9.
L. echinata Croizat = *L. williamsii*.
L. lewinii (J. Coult.) Rusby = *L. williamsii*.
L. lutea (Rouhier) Backeb. = *L. diffusa*.
L. williamsii (Lem. ex Salm-Dyck) J. Coult. MESCAL; PEYOTE. St. 3–6×4–11cm, blue-green; ribs 4–14, ± tuberculate; areoles woolly, regularly spaced. Inner tep. 2.5–4mm wide, pink with pale to white margins. Spring–autumn. N & NE Mex., S Tex. Z9.
L. ziegleri Werderm. ex Borg = *L. diffusa*.
→*Echinocactus*.

Lophosoria Presl. Dicksoniaceae. 1 terrestrial fern. Rhiz. erect to 1m and trunk-like or creeping, covered in dense hairs and roots. Fronds to 4m, 2-, 3- or 4-pinnate to -pinnatifid, deltoid to ovate, glaucous beneath, pinnae, to 45cm, lanceolate to oblong or ovate, pinnules to 10×3cm, oblong, acute, incised, seg. to 1.2cm, lanceolate-acute, notched; stipes straw-coloured to brown. Trop. to temp. C & S Amer. Z9.
L. pruinata (Sw.) Presl. = *L. quadripinnata*.
L. quadripinnata (Gmel.) C. Chr.

Lophospermum D. Don.
L. scandens D. Don = *Asarina lophospermum*.

Lophostemon Schott. Myrtaceae. 6 lacticiferous trees or tall shrubs. Lvs crowded at the ends of the branchlets. Infl. a dichasium; sep. persistent; pet. 5, white to cream; sta. in more than one whorl, united into fascicles opposite the pet. N & E Aus., S New Guinea. Z10.
L. confertus (R. Br.) P.G. Wils. & J.T. Waterhouse. BRUSH BOX. 35–40m. Bark pink-brown, decid. on the upper br. Lvs to 15cm, lanceolate, acute; pseudoverticils of 4 or 5 lvs. Cymes 3–7-fld, pet. 6–9mm; staminal fascicles 10–15mm, sta. exceeding 70 per fascicle. E Aus. (Queensld, NSW).
L. lactifluus (F. Muell.) P.G. Wils. & J.T. Waterhouse. Bark red-brown, fibrous-papery, persistent. Lvs to 15cm, elliptic to ovate-lanceolate; pseudoverticils of 2 or 3 lvs. Cymes many-fld, pet. 2–3mm; staminal fascicles 2–3mm, sta. 12–25 per fascicle. Aus. (N Territ.).

L. suaveolens (Sol. ex Gaertn.) P.G. Wils. & J.T. Waterhouse. To 15m. Bark red-brown, fibrous-papery. Lvs to 10cm, ovate to lanceolate, obtuse or acuminate; pseudoverticils of 3–4 lvs. Cymes 7–15-fld, pet. 4–5mm; staminal fascicles 3–5mm, sta. 30–50(–58) per fascicle. New Guinea and E Aus. (NSW).
→*Melaleuca* and *Tristania*.

Lophotocarpus T. Dur.
L. guyanensis (HBK) J.G. Sm. = *Sagittaria guyanensis*.

Loquat *Eriobotrya japonica*.
Loquat-leaved Fig *Ficus saussureana*.

LORANTHACEAE Juss. 70/940. *Loranthus, Nuytsia*.

Loranthus Jacq. Loranthaceae. 1 semi-parasitic dioecious shrub to 1m, found on Fagaceae. St. dull brown, jointed. Lvs 1–5cm, opposite, decid., obovate-oblong, obtuse, dark green, coriaceous. Infl. a terminal rac. or spike to 4cm; fls small; sep. 4; pet. 4–6, green-yellow. Fr. a viscid berry, 1cm, yellow. C & SE Eur.
L. europaeus Jacq.

Lord Anson's Blue Pea *Lathyrus nervosus*.
Lords-and-ladies *Arum maculatum*.

Loropetalum R. Br. ex Rchb. Hamamelidaceae. 2 everg. stellate-hairy shrubs or small trees, to 3m. Lvs alt., entire, ovate. Fls in clusters of 6–8, in term. heads; cal. 4-lobed; pet. 4, long and narrow; sta. 4. Fr. a woody 2-horned capsule. Himal., China, Jap. Z8.
L. chinense (R. Br.) Oliv. Twiggy shrub, to 3m in the wild. Lvs to 4cm, dark green, bristly-white, stellate-pubesc. Pet. 2cm, white, undulate-ligulate, giving a feathery appearance. Late winter–early spring. India, China, Jap. 'Roseum': fls pink.
L. indicum Oliv. = *L. chinense*.

Lorraine Begonia *Begonia ×cheimantha*.
Lote Tree *Celtis australis*.
Lotus *Nelumbo; Nymphaea lotus*.

Lotus L. Leguminosae (Papilionoideae). 100 ann. or perenn. herbs. Lvs simple, ternate or pinnate. Infl. an umbellate rac.; fls pea-like. Medit. Eur., S to Sahara Desert, W to Asia; W US; Aus.; S Afr.
L. alpinus (DC.) Schleich. ex Raym. = *L. tenuis*.
L. angustissimus L. SLENDER BIRD'S FOOT TREFOIL. Procumbent ann., 5–50cm. Lfts 3, 8–12×2.5–4mm, obovate to oblong. Infl. 1–3-fld, on peduncles 3mm–2cm long; cor. 5–8mm, yellow, becoming pale red, standard ± equal to keel. Summer. Eur., nat. US. Z6.
L. argophyllus (Gray) Greene. Perenn., 10–60cm tall, spreading or sprawling. Lfts 6–12mm, 3–7, silver-pubesc., lanceolate-elliptic to obovate. Infl. 4+-fld on 1–3mm peduncles; cor. yellow, becoming red or amber; keel ridged. Spring–summer. Eur., nat. US. Z8.
L. berthelotii Lowe ex Masf. CORAL GEM; PARROT'S BEAK; PELICAN'S BEAK. Cascading perenn. subshrub, to 1m. Br. slender, ash-grey. Lvs v. short-stalked, costapalmate, thus appearing simple and clustered; lfts 1–1.8cm, linear to filiform, 3–5, spreading, soft silver-grey. Infl. bunched on short peduncles; cor. 2–4cm, orange-red to scarlet or purple, keel long, slender, beak- or claw-like. Spring–summer. Canary Is., Cape Verde Is., Tenerife; nat. US. 'Kew Form': lvs silver; fls red, summer-flowering, remontant.
L. corniculatus L. BIRD'S FOOT TREFOIL. Perenn., 5–40cm, ascending or prostrate. Lfts 5–15mm, 3, obovate, oblanceolate to oblong. Infl. 4–8-fld, on long peduncles; cor. 10–14mm, yellow, darkening to red flecked orange, ascending, keel crescent-shaped. Spring–summer. Eur., Asia, nat. US. 'Plenus' ('Flore Pleno', 'Pleniflorus'): habit mat-forming, vigorous; fls double, yellow, orange in bud. Z5.
L. creticus L. Perenn., 30–60cm, woody-based, pubesc., erect or prostrate. Lfts 7–18mm, 3, thick, upper lfts obovate, sericeous. Rac. 3–6-fld, on thick peduncles; cor. 12–18mm, vivid yellow, standard entire, keel with a long, purple-tipped beak. Port., Medit. region. Z8.
L. formosissimus Greene. Perenn., 10–40cm, glab., decumbent to ascending. Lfts 6–20mm, 5–7, obovate. Infl. pedunculate; cor. 10–16mm, standard yellow, wings fading becoming white, keel purple-tipped. Spring–summer. Eur., US. Z6.
L. jacobaeus L. Erect perenn., 30–90cm, grey-hirsute. Lfts and stipules elongated or elongate to broad-ended, mucronate. Fls in clusters; cor. dark maroon to velvety brown, standard yellow. Cape Verde Is. Z9.
L. maritimus L. Perenn., 10–40cm, prostrate or ascending, glab. or pubesc. Lfts to 30mm, ciliate. Fls 2.5–3cm, usually solitary,

cor. pale yellow, standard exceeding wings. W, C & S Eur., Ukraine, N Afr. Z6.
L. mascaensis hort. non Burchard. = *L. sessilifolius*.
L. ornithopoides L. Ann., 15–50cm, prostrate, pubesc. Upper lfts 3, 8–18mm, obovate to rhombic, lower lfts 2, slightly smaller, ovate. Infl. 7–10mm, 2–5-fld, on delicate peduncles; cor. 7–10mm, yellow, standard equalling wings, keel shorter, curved. Spring. S Eur.
L. palustris Willd. Perenn., to 1m, villous or pubesc., prostrate or ascending. Lfts 14–20mm, lanceolate-ovate to obovate. Infl. 2–4-fld, long-stalked; cor. 6–10mm, yellow, keel generally equal to standard and wings. Spring–summer. S & E Medit. regions. Z8.
L. pedunculatus Cav. = *L. uliginosus*.
L. peliorhynchus Hook. f. = *L. berthelotii*.
L. pinnatus Hook. Perenn., 20–40cm, glab.; st. slender, ascending. Lfts to 19mm, 5–9, obovate. Rac. 3–7-fld; exceeding lvs; cor. 12–15mm, standard and keel yellow; wings white, obovate. Spring–summer. Eur., US. Z8.
L. scoparius (Nutt.) Ottley. WILD BROOM; DEER CLOVER. Perenn., to 2m, erect or prostrate, glabrate or hispidulous; st. green, grouped, furrowed. Lvs 1–2cm, caducous; lfts 6–15mm, 3–6, oblong, oblanceolate. Infl. subsessile; fls 2–7; cor. 7–11mm, yellow, becoming amber or red. Spring–summer. Eur., US. Z6.
L. sessilifolius DC. Shrub, ashy-grey, sericeous, low-growing. Lvs palmate, sessile; lfts 5–10mm, 5, oblong-lanceolate. Fls 14–15cm, 3–5, vivid yellow. Spring. Canary Is. Z9.
L. tenuis Waldst. & Kit. ex Willd. NARROWLEAF TREFOIL. Perenn. herb, 20–90cm, glab. or pubescous. Br. delicate, usually twining. Lfts linear, 5–15mm. Infl. 1–6-fld, long-stalked; cor. 6–12mm, yellow, wings obovate to elongate, keel long-beaked. Summer. Eur., nat. US. Z4.
L. tetragonolobus L. WINGED PEA; ASPARAGUS PEA. Ann. to 40cm; st. sprawling or creeping. Lfts to 2.5cm, 3, obovate to broadly elliptic. Fls to 19mm, crimson to maroon, on 1–2-fld peduncles exceeded by, or equal to lvs. Fr. to 76mm, tetragonal and conspicuously 4-winged. S Eur.
L. uliginosus Schkuhr GREATER BIRD'S FOOT TREFOIL. Perenn., 10–80cm, ascending or erect, glab. to villous; st. tubular. Lfts 8–25mm, 3, ovate-elliptic to elliptic, glaucous beneath. Infl. 8–12-fld, on 3–10cm peduncles; cor. 10–18mm, rich yellow, frequently dappled red, becoming darker. Spring–summer. Eur., N Afr. Z6.
→*Tetragonolobus*.

Loulu Palms *Pritchardia*.

Lourea Necker. = *Christia*.

Lousewort *Pedicularis*.
Lovage *Levisticum officinale*.
Love Apple *Lycopersicon esculentum*.
Love Charm *Clytostoma callistigioides*.
Love Grass *Eragrostis*.
Love-in-a-mist *Nigella* (*N. damascena*); *Passiflora foetida*.
Love-in-idleness *Viola tricolor*.
Love-lies-bleeding *Amaranthus caudatus*.
Lovely Penstemon *Penstemon venustus*.
Love-nest Sundew *Drosera intermedia*.
Love Restorer *Hylotelephium anacampseros*.
Love Tree *Cercis siliquastrum*.
Low Bilberry *Vaccinium vaccillans*.
Low Blueberry *Vaccinium vaccillans*.
Low-bush Blueberry *Vaccinium angustifolium*.
Low Hop Clover *Trifolium dubium*.
Lowland Fragile Fern *Cystopteris protrusa*.
Low's Fir *Abies concolor*.
Low Sweet Blueberry *Vaccinium angustifolium*; *V. vaccillans*.

Loxsoma R. Br. Loxsomataceae. 1 terrestrial fern. Rhiz. stout, somewhat tortuous, densely hairy. Fronds 15–60cm, deltoid-triangular, tripinnate, dark above, glaucous beneath, coriaceous; primary pinnae to 20cm, secondary pinnae to 10cm; pinnules oblong, notched, to 5cm; stipes stout, 20–60cm, erect, brown, glab. except for bristles at base. NZ. Z10.
L. cunninghamii R. Br.

LOXSOMATACEAE C. Presl. *Loxsoma*.

Loxoscaphe T. Moore.
L. brachycarpa (Mett.) Kuhn = *Asplenium brachycarpum*.

Loxostigma C.B. Clarke. Gesneriaceae. 3 perenn. herbs. Lvs in unequal pairs. Fls axill., several on pendent peduncles; cor. tubular, inflated toward base, shallowly 2-lipped. India (E Himal.). Z10.

L. griffithii (Wight) C.B. Clarke. Lvs to 17.5×8cm, ovate, short-pubesc. Cor. to 3.5cm, pale yellow marked brown.
L. kurzii (C.B. Clarke) B.L. Burtt. Lvs to 20×10cm, elliptic, dentate. Cor. to 3cm, yellow, spotted rusty-red in throat.
→*Briggsia* and *Chirita*.

Lubia Bean *Lablab purpureus.*
Lucerne *Medicago sativa.*
Luchu Juniper *Juniperus taxifolia.*
Lucifershout *Schefflera morototonii.*

Lucilia Cass. Compositae. *c*22 rhizomatous, perenn. herbs. St. lanate. Lvs simple, entire, densely lanate. Cap. radiate, rarely discoid, sessile, clustered or solitary; ray flts white, thread-like; disc flts 2–23, white. Andes, S Braz. to NW Arg. Z9.
L. chilensis Hook. & Arn. Caespitose herb to 5cm, forming silvery-white cushions. Arg., Chile.
→*Gnaphalium.*

Lucky Bean Tree *Erythrina caffra; E. lysistemon.*
Lucky Clover *Oxalis tetraphylla.*
Lucombe Oak *Quercus ×hispanica* 'Lucombeana'

Luculia Sweet. Rubiaceae. 5 shrubs or small trees. Lvs opposite, stipulate. Fls in terminal, many-fld corymbs or pan., fragrant; cal. lobes 5, linear or oblong to subulate; cor. salver-shaped, lobes 5; sta. 5, inserted at mouth of cor. tube. E Asia.
L. grandifolia Ghose. To 6m. Lvs to 35×25cm, ovate to elliptic, margin and veins red. Fls in cymes to 20cm wide, white; cor. tube to 4cm, lobes to 2cm. Bhutan. Z9.
L. gratissima (Wallich) Sweet. To 5m. St. lenticellate, red-pubesc. Lvs to 20×10cm, ovate or lanceolate to elliptic or oblong, leathery to membranous, pubesc. beneath. Fls in pubesc. corymbs to 20cm wide, pink; cor. tube to 3cm, lobes to 1.5cm. Autumn–winter. Himal. Z10.
L. gratissima Wallich, non Sweet = *L. pinceana.*
L. intermedia Hutch. To 7m. St. verrucose. Lvs to 15×7cm, lanceolate to oblong. Fls in cymes to 18cm wide, red; cor. tube to 3.5cm, lobes appendaged. Winter. Yunnan. Z9.
L. pinceana Hook. To 3m. St. pubesc. Lvs to 15×5cm, ovate or lanceolate to elliptic, leathery, sparsely pubesc. beneath. Fls in glab. corymbs to 20cm wide, white and pink-flushed; cor. tube to 5cm, lobes to 5cm wide, 2-appendaged. Summer–autumn. Nepal to Yunnan. Z9.
→*Cinchona* and *Mussaenda.*

Lucuma auct. non Molina.
L. campechiana HBK = *Pouteria campechiana.*
L. mammosa auct. non (L.) Gaertn. f. = *Pouteria sapota.*
L. nervosa A. DC. = *Pouteria campechiana.*
L. salicifolia HBK = *Pouteria campechiana.*

Ludisia A. Rich. Orchidaceae. 1 terrestrial or lithophytic orchid. St. succulent, prostrate to ascending, segmented, rooting. Lvs subcordate to broad-elliptic, to 7.5cm, velvety-papillose, red-bronze to black with 5 longitudinal copper-red veins and broken venation between. Rac. term., bracteate to 15cm; fls small, numerous, sparkling white, column yellow. SE Asia, China, Indon. Z9.
L. discolor (Ker-Gawl.) A. Rich. A single variable sp. that includes *L. dawsoniana*, a large plant (lvs to 12cm) of particular vigour, and *L. otletae* with finely patterned narrow-lanceolate lvs.
→*Goodyera* and *Haemaria.*

Ludvigia L. = *Ludwigia.*

Ludwigia L. Onagraceae. 75 herbaceous or woody aquatic or marginal perennials. Lvs simple. Fls actinomorphic, solitary and axill. or in term. clusters; sep. 4–5; pet. 0 or 4–5; sta. 4, or 10 in 2 whorls; ovary inferior, 4- or 5-locular. Cosmop., esp. in warmer regions.
L. alternifolia L. RATTLE BOX; SEED BOX. St. erect, branched, 45cm–1m. Lvs 3.5–10cm, linear to linear-lanceolate. Fls 4-merous, solitary; pet. 0 or 4–5; sta. 4, or 10 in. Z4.
L. grandiflora (Michx.) Zardini, Gu & Raven. Like a larger *L. hexapetala*. SE US, S Amer. Z9.
L. helminthorrhiza (Mart.) Hara. Floating herb rooting at nodes, with pneumatophores. Lvs 1–5cm, rounded. Fls solitary, mostly 5-merous; pet. to 1.3cm, broad, white with a basal yellow spot. S Mex. to S Amer. Z9.
L. hexapetala (Hook. & Arn.) Zardini, Gu & Raven. Semi-submerged long-hairy perenn. herb with rooting and erect br. to 1.5m tall, with pneumatophores. Lvs 3–13cm, spathulate to oblanceolate. Fls solitary, 5–6-merous; pet. 12–30mm, bright

golden-yellow with a darker spot at base, obovate. SE US to Arg.; introd. Eur. Z6.
L. longifolia (DC.) Hara. Erect perenn. to 2m. St. winged, glab. Lvs 10–20cm, lanceolate. Fls solitary 4-merous; pet. to 2.5cm, pale yellow. Braz. to Arg.
L. natans Elliot. Aquatic herb rooting at nodes. Lvs elliptic to obcordate, tinged purple beneath. Fls axill.; cap. 2–4mm, 4-triangular; pet. yellow, quickly shed. N Amer. and W Indies. Z9.
L. octovalis (Jacq.) Raven. Robust herb, sometimes woody at base or shrubby, to 4m. Lvs 0.7–14.5cm, linear to subovate. Fls axill.; sep. 4, 3–15mm, ovate or lanceolate; pet. 3–17mm, yellow, obovate or cuneate. Trop. Z10.
L. palustris (L.) Elliot. WATER PURSLANE. St. weak, floating in water or creeping in mud, forming mats. Lvs 0.7–4.5cm, lanceolate to elliptic-ovate, red or red-purple beneath. Fls axill. and paired; sep. 4, 1.4–2mm; pet. 0; sta. 4, green. Americas, Eur. and Asia. Z3.
L. peploides (Kunth) Raven. Herb with st. sprawling and rooting at nodes or floating, ascending when flowering. Lvs 1–9.5cm, elliptic. Fls solitary; sep. 5, 4–12mm; pet. bright golden-yellow with a darker spot at the base, obovate, 7–17mm. N & S Amer.; nat. SW Fr. Z7.
L. peruviana (L.) Hara. Shrub 0.5–3m tall, villous, with long inflated pneumatophores arising from submerged roots. Lvs 4–12cm, lanceolate. Fls solitary; sep. 10–18mm, 4 or 5, lanceolate, serrulate, villous; pet. bright yellow, suborbicular, 15–24mm, clawed. SE US to S Amer.; introd. in the OW. Z9.
L. uruguayensis (Cambess.) Hara = *L. grandiflora.*
→*Jussiaea.*

Ludwigiantha (Torr. & A. Gray) Small = *Ludwigia.*

Lueddemannia Lind. & Rchb. f. Orchidaceae. 2 epiphytic orchids. Pbs clustered, ovoid to ovoid-oblong. Lvs 2, apical, lanceolate to elliptic, plicate. Rac. lat., pendent, many-fld; fls large, fleshy; sep. free, ovate-elliptic to oblong-elliptic; pet. smaller, oblanceolate to spathulate-elliptic; lip clawed, apex trilobed, lat. lobes erect, midlobe triangular, callus, crested or tuberculate. Venez., Peru, Ecuad., Colomb. Z10.
L. pescatorei (Lindl.) Lind. & Rchb. f. Pbs to 13cm. Lvs to 40cm. Infl. to 50cm; sep. to 27×14mm, light red-brown spotted purple, interior red-maroon with pale brown margins; pet. to 23×9mm, bright golden-yellow, edged red; lip to 26mm, golden-yellow, fleshy, midlobe minutely papillose, callus warty. Venez., Colomb., Ecuad., Peru.
L. triloba Rolfe = *L. pescatorei.*
→*Cycnoches.*

Luetkea Bong. Rosaceae. 1 tufted, procumbent, everg. subshrub. Lvs to 1.5cm, rigid, bright green, divided ×2–3, lobes linear. Fls small, in narrow rac. to 5cm; cal. lobes 2mm, ovate; pet. to 3.5mm, 5, white, round-obovate; sta. 20, fil. basally connate. Summer. Mts of NW Amer. Z3.
L. caespitosa Kuntze = *Petrophytum caespitosum.*
L. pectinata (Pursh) Kuntze.
→*Saxifraga* and *Spiraea.*

Luffa Mill. LOOFAH; DISHCLOTH GOURD; RAG GOURD; STRAINER VINE. Cucurbitaceae. 6 ann. herbs trailing or climbing by tendrils. Lvs simple, palmately angled or lobed. Fls large; cal. tube campanulate, lobed; pet. 5, free; ♂ fls in rac., sta. 3–5; ♀ fls solitary, sta. 0; stigmas 3. Fr. elongate, cylindric, fleshy becoming dry and skeletal-spongy, dehiscent through term. operculum. Pantrop., probably introd. to Americas. Z9.
L. acutangula (L.) Roxb. ANGLED LOOFAH; SING-KWA. Climber. St. 4–5-angled. Tendrils 4–7-fid. Lvs palmate, glab., *c*17×11cm; lobes 5–7. ♂ rac. to 15cm; cor. yellow, to 5cm diam. Fr. deeply 10-angled, to 30cm+, *c*10cm diam. Pak., widely cult. throughout Trop. var. *amara* (Roxb.) Clark. Lvs smaller, villous. Fr. to 8cm. India, Pak., Yemen.
L. aegyptiaca Mill. = *L. cylindrica.*
L. amara Roxb. = *L. acutangula* var. *amara.*
L. cylindrica (L.) M. Roem. LOOFAH; VEGETABLE SPONGE. Climber or trailer to 15m. St. finely pubesc. Tendrils 3 to 6-fid. Lvs palmate, ovate-cordate, 6–18×6–20cm, lobes 3–5, ovate, sometimes lobulate, serrate or entire. ♂ rac. 12–35cm; cor. to 9cm diam., yellow. Fr. ellipsoid to cylindric, glab., to 50cm, obscurely 10-ribbed. Trop. Asia and Afr.
L. gigantea hort. = *L. cylindrica.*
L. macrocarpa hort. = *L. cylindrica.*
L. marylandica hort. = *L. cylindrica.*
L. operculata (L.) Cogn. St. climbing or trailing, striate. Tendrils bifid. Lvs palmate, subreniform, scabrous, to 15cm, lobes 3–5, entire or slightly denticulate. ♂ rac. to 20cm; cor. to 2.5cm diam., yellow. Fr. about 6cm, ellipsoid to fusiform, slightly

ribbed, spinose. Mex. to Colomb. and Peru.
→*Cucumis* and *Momordica*.

Luina Benth. Compositae. 3 perenn. herbs, with many erect, simple st. from a woody base. Lvs alt. Cap. discoid, in term. corymbs; flts tubular, usually yellow. W N Amer.

L. *hypoleuca* Benth. LITTLE-LEAF LUINA. St. 15–40cm, white-tomentose, leafy. Lvs 2–6cm, broadly elliptic or ovate, sub-entire, sessile, green and thinly tomentose to glab. above, white-tomentose beneath. Involucre 5–8mm high, thinly tomentose or becoming glab.; receptacle to 1cm diam.; flts 10–17, dull yellow or cream. Summer to early autumn. BC to Calif.

L. *nardosmia* (A. Gray) Cronq. = *Cacaliopsis nardosmia*.

Luisia Gaudich. Orchidaceae. 30 epiphytic, monopodial orchids. St. slender, terete, branching near base. Lvs alt., fleshy, terete. Fls small, clustered in v. short axill. heads; sep. and pet. obovate; lip lobed. Trop. Asia to Polyn. Z9.

L. *alpina* Lindl. = *Trudelia alpina*.

L. *psyche* Rchb. f. Lvs blunt, erect, to 15cm. Fls to 3cm diam., pale yellow-green, lip violet-brown, chequered white or yellow. Burm., Laos.

L. *teretifolia* Gaudich. Lvs tapering to a point, curving upwards, to 20cm. Fls to 2.5cm diam., yellow, green, or pale pink, lip base green and purple or yellow. India, SE Asia to New Caledonia.

Lulo *Solanum quitoense*.

Luma A. Gray. Myrtaceae. 4 everg. shrubs or small trees to *c*10m, gland., puberulent to villous. Lvs subcoriaceous. Fls white, 4-merous, solitary or in 3's. Fr. a fleshy, somewhat spongy berry. Arg., Chile. Z9.

L. *apiculata* (DC.) Burret. ARRAYÁN; PALO COLORADO; TEMU; COLLIMAMOL. Shrub or small tree to *c*10m. Bark cinnamon, peeling to expose ash-grey wood. Lvs 1–4.5cm, elliptic to sub-orbicular, less often ovate, apiculate, veins beneath and margins hairy. Pet. suborbicular, 3–5mm, ciliate; sta. 170–300, *c*5–7mm. Fr. to 1cm diam., dark purple. Arg., Chile. 'Glanleam Gold': lvs deeply edged creamy yellow, tinged pink at first. 'Penwith': lvs blue and grey-green edged cream-white tinted red-ink in winter.

L. *chequen* (Molina) A. Gray. CHEQUÉN; ARRAYÁN BLANCO. Shrub or small tree up to *c*9m. Bark grey-brown. Lvs 0.5–2.5cm, elliptic, ovate or lanceolate, rarely suborbicular, acute, glab. or pubesc. along midvein and margins beneath. Pet. suborbicular, *c*4–7mm; sta. *c*90–230, 3–7mm. Fr. 0.6–1cm diam., dark purple. Chile.

→*Eugenia*, *Myrceugenella*, *Myrceugenia* and *Myrtus*.

Luma *Amomyrtus luma*.

Lunaria L. Cruciferae. 3 bienn. or perenn. herbs. St. erect, branching. Lvs cordate, toothed. Fls 4-merous, in term. rac.; pet. 4, long-clawed. Fr. a silique, v. compressed, oblong-elliptic to nearly round, septum pearly white, papery. Spring–summer. C & S Eur. Z8.

L. *annua* L. HONESTY; SILVER DOLLAR; PENNY FLOWER. Bienn. to 1m. Lvs ovate-lanceolate, cordate, coarsely toothed. Fls un-scented; pet. 15–25mm, purple to white, sometimes white freaked or flecked purple. Fr. 20–70×15–35mm, oblong-round, blunt, apiculate. 'Alba': to 85cm; fls white. 'Alba Variegata': to 100cm; lvs suffused white; fls pure white. 'Haslemere': to 85cm; lvs green variegated off-white; fls purple, freely produced. 'Variegata': lvs green, variegated and edged cream. 'Violet': fls bright purple.

L. *biennis* Moench = *L. annua*.

L. *rediviva* L. PERENNIAL HONESTY. Similar to *L. annua* except perenn., lvs finely toothed, not sessile higher up st. Fls fragrant. Fr. tapering at base and apex.

Lungen *Dimocarpus longan*.
Lungwort *Pulmonaria*.
Lupin *Lupinus*.

Lupinus L. LUPIN. Leguminosae (Papilionoideae). 200 ann. or perenn. herbs or shrubs. Lvs palmate, long-stalked; stipules slender. Fls pea-like, often whorled in erect, terminal rac. or spikes. Fr. an oblong, laterally compressed legume, usually hairy. W N Amer., Medit., S Amer., S Eur., N Afr.

L. *affinis* J. Agardh. Ann., erect to 60cm. St. strigose or short-villous. Lfts to 4cm, 6–8, oblanceolate. Fls deep blue, in rac. to 22cm of somewhat remote whorls. Spring. W US.

L. *albifrons* Benth. Shrub to 1.5m, habit rounded. St. adpressed-sericeous. Lfts to 3cm, 7–10, oblanceolate to spathulate, silver-

sericeous. Fls blue to maroon or lavender, mostly whorled in rac. to 30cm. Spring–summer. W US. var. *emineus* (Greene) C.P. Sm. Fls slightly larger. Z8.

L. *albus* L. WHITE LUPINE; FIELD LUPINE; WOLF BEAN; EGYPTIAN LUPIN. Ann. to 120cm. St. short-pubesc. Lfts to 5cm, obovate or obovate-cuneate, mucronulate, villous beneath. Fls white or tinted pale blue, alt., in sessile rac. to 10cm. S Balk., Aegean.

L. *andersonii* var. *grayi* Wats. = *L. grayi*.

L. *angustifolius* L. Ann. to 50cm. St. slender, hairy. Lfts *c*3cm, 5–9 linear, obtuse, sericeous beneath. Fls blue. Summer. Medit.

L. *arboreus* Sims. TREE LUPIN. Everg. shrub to 3m. Branchlets rather woody, sericeous-pubesc. Lfts to 5cm, 7–9, oblanceolate, acute or mucronate, lanuginose beneath, grey-green. Fls sulphur-yellow, sometimes blue or lavender, in erect, lax, term. rac. to 25.5cm. Spring–summer. W US. 'Golden Spire': fls gold. 'Mauve Queen': fls lilac. 'Snow Queen': fls white. 'Yellow Boy': fls bright yellow. Z8.

L. *arcticus* S. Wats. V. similar to *L. perennis*; but with longer petioles and acute lfts. N Amer. Z4.

L. *argenteus* Pursh. Erect perenn. to 60cm. Br. short-strigose. Lfts to 4.5cm, 5–9, linear-oblanceolate, strigose beneath. Fls blue, lilac or lavender, less commonly white or rose, sub-verticillate, in lax rac. to 12cm. Summer–autumn. Calif., New Mex. var. *depressus* (Rydb.) C. Hitchc. To 25cm. Fls crowded. Z4.

L. *benthamii* Heller. Erect ann. to 60cm. St. villous. Lfts to 5cm, 7–10, linear, villous. Fls blue with a yellow-spotted standard, in rac. to 20cm. Spring. W US.

L. *bicolor* Lindl. Erect ann. to 40cm. St. villous. Lfts to 3cm, 5–7, oblanceolate to cuneate, villous. Fls blue (standard with a purple-dotted white flash or suffused purple), 1–3-verticillate, in rac. to 7cm. Spring–summer. Calif. to BC.

L. *breweri* A. Gray. Perenn. St. tufted, decumbent or prostrate, silver-sericeous. Lfts to 2cm, 7–10, oblanceolate to spathulate. Fls violet (standard with white-yellow patch), dense-fld rac. to 5cm. Summer. W US. Z5.

L. *brittonii* Abrams = *L. albifrons* var. *eminens*.

L. *burkei* S. Wats. = *L. polyphyllus* var. *burkei*.

L. *chamissonis* Eschsch. Somewhat shrubby perenn., erect to 90cm. Young shoots sericeous-pubesc. Lfts to 3cm, 5–7, lanceolate, abruptly acuminate, silver adpressed-pubesc. Fls blue or lilac, standard blotched yellow, subverticillate, in erect rac. to 15cm. Summer–autumn. W US. Z8.

L. *chamissonis* var. *longifolius* S. Wats. = *L. longifolius*.

L. *confertus* Kellogg. Thick-rooted, robust perenn. to 35cm. St. several, white-sericeous. Lfts to 4cm, usually 7, elliptic-oblanceolate, grey-sericeous. Fls violet-purple, in dense rac. to 30cm. Summer. SW US. Z5.

L. *cruckshanksii* Hook. = *L. mutabilis* var. *cruckshanksii*.

L. *cytisoides* J. Agardh = *L. latifolius*.

L. *densiflorus* Benth. Ann. to 40cm. St. simple or branched, adpressed-pubesc. Lfts to 2cm, 7–9, oblanceolate, obtuse to mucronate, glab. above. Fls white, violet- or rose-tinted or -veined, 5–12-whorled in rac. to 20cm. Spring–summer. W US. var. *aureus* (Kellogg) Munz. Fls pale yellow, sometimes bordered red. var. *glareosus* (Elmer) C.P. Sm. Fls pale blue, standard with white spot. var. *lacteus* (Kellogg) C.P. Sm. St. and pedicels long-pubesc. Fls white, pale pink or lavender. 'Ed Gedling': fls gold.

L. *depressus* Benth. = *L. argenteus* var. *depressus*.

L. *diffusus* Nutt. Much-branched perenn. to 40cm+. St. diffuse to spreading, rusty-pubesc. Lfts to 12cm, solitary, oblong, ellip-tic, obovate or oblanceolate, mucronate, short-adpressed-pubesc. Fls blue, standard blotched cream, subverticillate, in many-fld rac. to 30cm. SE US. Z7.

L. *excubitus* Jones. Erect, freely branching, sericeous shrub to 1.5m. Lfts to 3cm, 5–8, oblong-lanceolate to spathulate. Fls to 12.5mm, blue, lilac or violet, standard marked yellow, in verticillate rac. to 25cm. Spring–summer. W US. var. *hallii* (Abrams) C.P. Sm. Lvs less downy. Z8.

L. *formosus* Greene. Perenn. to 80cm. St. decumbent or ascend-ing, adpressed-sericeous. Lfts to 7cm, 7–9, oblanceolate, seric-eous. Fls to 1.5cm, violet to blue, lilac, or white, in somewhat verticillate dense rac. to 25cm. Spring–autumn. W US. Z8.

L. *grayi* (S. Wats.) S. Wats. To 35cm. St. ascending to decumbent, grey-tomentose and villous. Lfts to 3.5cm, 5–11, oblanceolate, tomentose. Fls to 1.5cm, deep violet to lilac, standard yellow at centre, in subverticillate rac. to 15cm. Spring–summer. W US. Z8.

L. *hartwegii* Lindl. Ann. to 90cm. St. tufted, much-branched, v. densely pale-villous. Lfts to 4.5cm, 7–9, oblong to oblanceolate, apiculate, densely pubesc. Fls 1.5cm, in crowded elongate rac. to 20cm; standard green-white above when young, later lilac tinged, wings blue, keel white, tipped green. Summer–autumn. Mex.

L. *hirsutissimus* Benth. Robust ann. to 1m. St. sparsely

branched, densely tawny-hirsute. Lfts to 5cm, 5–8 cuneate-obovate, pubesc. Fls red-violet to magenta, standard blotched yellow, in rac. to 25cm. Spring. Calif., Baja Calif.

L. hirsutus sensu L. 1763 non L. 1753. = *L. micranthus.*

L. latifolius Lindl. ex J. Agardh. Perenn. to 120cm. St. erect, leafy, subglabrous to minutely strigose. Lfts to 10cm, 7–9, broad-lanceolate, ± glab. above. Fls blue to purple, rarely somewhat yellow, verticillate or scattered, in lax rac. to 45cm. Spring–summer. W US. var. *subalpinus* (Piper & Robinson) C.P. Sm. Dwarf, 10–25cm, with long, soft red to white hairs. Z7.

L. laxiflorus Douglas ex Lindl. Perenn. to 60cm. Lfts to 5cm, 7–11, pubesc. or glab. above, pubesc. beneath. Fls white, occas. blue or purple-tinged, in short-stalked, lax rac. W US. Z8.

L. lepidus Douglas ex Lindl. Perenn. to 30.5cm. St. tufted, grey to rusty-pubesc. Lfts 5–9 densely pubesc. Fls violet-blue, in dense rac. to 15cm. N Amer. Z3.

L. leucophyllus Douglas ex Lindl. Erect perenn. to 90cm. St. stout, simple or branched, v. leafy, grey lanate-villous. Lfts to 6.5cm, 7–9, oblanceolate, acute, sericeous-velutinous. Fls white, pink or blue-flushed, or purple, subverticillate, crowded. Spring–summer. W US. Z4.

L. littoralis Douglas. Perenn. to 80cm. Roots bright yellow. St. decumbent or prostrate, slender, branched, patent-villous. Lfts to 3.5cm, 5–9, oblanceolate, strigose. Fls blue or lilac, in few-verticillate rac. to 15cm. Spring–summer. Calif. to BC. Z7.

L. longifolius (S. Wats.) Abrams. Subshrub to 1.5m. St. erect, adpressed-grey-pubesc. Lfts to 6cm, 6–9, elliptic- or oblong-oblanceolate, obtuse, subsericeous. Fls deep blue to violet standard blotched yellow, scattered or subverticillate, in rac. to 40cm. Spring–summer. Calif., Baja Calif. Z9.

L. luteus L. YELLOW LUPINE. Ann. to 80cm. St. densely pilose. Lfts to 6cm, 7–11, obovate-oblong, mucronate, sparsely villous. Fls bright yellow, verticillate. Summer. Iberian Penins., It., W Medit. Is. Z6.

L. lyallii Gray. Tufted, semi-prostrate perenn. to 12cm; st. silky, from a woody base. Lfts to 1.2cm, 5–6, oblanceolate, adpressed-sericeous. Fls blue, standard sometimes with a pale spot, in capitate rac. to 3cm. Summer–autumn. W US. Z8.

L. menziesii Agardh = *L. densiflorus* var. *aureus.*

L. micranthus Guss. Ann. to 40cm. St. brown-hirsute. Lfts to 7cm, 5–7, obovate-cuneate to obovate-oblong, mucronate, sparsely hirsute. Fls deep blue, standard with a purple-spotted white flash, keel dark violet, alt. or irregular-verticillate in rac. to 12cm. C & S Port., Medit., W N Amer. Z8.

L. mutabilis Sweet. Erect subshrub to 1.5m. St. branched, glab. Lfts 6×1.5cm, 7–9, oblanceolate, glab. above, pubesc. and somewhat glaucous beneath. Fls 2cm; standard retuse, white and blue, becoming blue and with a large yellow blotch at centre, sometimes violet-tinged, wings and keel white. Summer. S Amer. (Andes). var. *cruckshanksii* (Hook.) L.H. Bail. Fls large; standard shaded purple, wings deep blue. Peru. Z9.

L. nanus Douglas. Erect ann. to 50cm, usually smaller. St., simple or branched at base, villous and minute-pubesc. or strigulose. Lfts to 3cm, 5–7, linear to spathulate, acute. Fls rich blue, standard with purple-dotted white or yellow spot, verticillate, in rac. to 24cm. Spring–summer. W US. 'Pixie Delight': to 45cm; fls softly coloured.

L. nootkatensis Donn ex Sims. Closely resembles *L. perennis*, but st. usually stouter and villous or hirsute, lvs 6–8-foliolate, lfts to 6cm. NW N Amer., NE Asia. Z4.

L. ornatus Douglas ex Lindl. Herbaceous perenn. to 75cm; st. and lvs sericeous. Lfts 4–7, rarely more. Rac. 15–30cm; standard pink with pale centre, wings blue. Early summer–autumn. Z7.

L. perennis L. SUNDIAL LUPINE; WILD LUPINE. Stout perenn. to 70cm. Lfts to 5cm, 7–11, oblanceolate, obtuse, glab. above, sparse-pubesc. beneath. Fls violet, pink, white or multi-coloured, alt. or verticillate, in lax rac. to 30cm. Spring. E US (Maine to Flor.). Z4.

L. plattensis S. Wats. Perenn. to 60cm. St. pubesc. Lfts to 4cm, 7–9, thick, pubesc., slightly glaucous. Fls light blue, standard dark-spotted. Summer. W US. Z4.

L. polyphyllus Lindl. Stout perenn. to 1.5m, usually unbranched. St. minutely pubesc. Lfts to 15cm, 9–17, obovoate-lanceolate, glab. above, sparsely sericeous beneath. Fls blue, purple, pink or white, verticillate, in somewhat dense rac. to 60cm. Summer. Calif. to BC. 'Moerheimii': fls white and rose. var. *burkei* (S. Wats.) C. Hitchc. To 60cm. St., petioles and lfts glab. or white pubesc. Z3.

L. pubescens Benth. Ann. to 90cm. St. soft-pubesc. Lfts 7–9. Fls violet-blue, white at centre, verticillate, in long rac. Mex., Guat.

L. rivularis Douglas ex Lindl. Closely resembles *L. latifolius*, but st. villous, and lfts to 4cm, strigulose esp. beneath. Fls to 16mm, keel ciliate. Spring–summer. Calif. to BC. Z8.

L. **Russell Hybrids** see *L.* **cvs.**

L. saxatilis Ulbr. Branched subshrub to 40cm. St. densely hairy at first. Lfts 1.25–3cm, 7, narrowly oblanceolate, silky-hairy beneath. Fls bright purple-blue, in 4-fld whorls or rac. to 12.5cm. Peruvian Andes. Z9.

L. sericatus Kellogg. Erect to decumbent perenn. to 50cm. St. usually unbranched, minutely downy. Lfts to 4cm, 6–7, spathulate-obovate, obtuse or retuse, minutely sericeous. Fls violet to lavender, scattered or subverticillate, in somewhat dense rac. to 30cm. Spring–summer. W US. Z8.

L. sparsiflorus Benth. Erect, branched ann. to 40cm. St. slender, strigose and villous. Lfts to 3cm, 5–9, linear to oblanceolate, strigose and villous. Fls pale blue to lilac, standard with yellow spot, in rac. to 20cm. Spring. W US, Baja Calif. Z9.

L. stiversii Kellogg. Freely branching ann. to 45cm. St. minutely pubesc. Lfts to 4cm, 6–8, cuneate to obovate, strigose. Fls bright yellow, in rac. to 3cm long; wings rose-pink or purple, keel rather paler or white. Spring–summer. W US.

L. subalpinus Piper and Robinson = *L. latifolius* var. *subalpinus.*

L. subcarnosus Hook. TEXAS BLUEBONNET. Decumbent ann. to 40cm, branched at base. St. downy. Lfts to 2.5cm, 5–7, oblanceolate, rounded, sometimes truncate, subglabrous above, sericeous beneath. Fls bright blue, standard white at centre, turning purple, crowded, in several-fld rac. to 12cm long; wings somewhat inflated. Spring. SW US.

L. succulentus Douglas ex K. Koch. Stout ann. to 1m; st. succulent or fistulose. Lfts to 7cm, 7–9, cuneate to cuneate-obovate, deep green, glab. above, strigulose beneath. Fls deep violet, standard yellow at centre, verticillate, in rac. to 30cm. Winter–spring. Calif., Baja Calif.

L. sulphureus Douglas ex Hook. Perenn. to 1m, hairy. Lfts to 5cm, 9–11, oblanceolate, glab. or pubesc. above, pubesc. beneath. Fls small, yellow to blue-violet. BC to Calif. Z8.

L. texensis Hook. TEXAS BLUEBONNET. Closely resembles *L. subcarnosus*, but lfts usually acute, cor. wings deep blue and not inflated, pubesc. SW US.

L. tidestromii Greene. To 30cm, branched. Roots yellow; st. slender, adpressed-sericeous. Lfts to 2cm, 3–5, oblanceolate, silver-sericeous. Fls blue, standard paler at centre, fading to violet, verticillate, in rac. to 10cm. Spring–summer. W US. Z8.

L. tomentosus DC. Perenn. to 1.5m. Base woody, st. much branched, sericeous. Lfts 8–10, sericeous. Rac. to 20cm; fls straw-yellow striped light blue at first, darkening with age becoming blue-purple, variable. Summer. Peru. Z9.

L. truncatus Nutt. ex Hook. & Arn. Branched ann. to 70cm. St. deep green, subglabrous to sparsely strigulose. Lfts to 4cm, 5–7, linear, truncate to emarginate or dentate, subglabrous to sparse-strigulose. Fls violet, deepening to red with age, in rac. to 15cm. Spring. W US. Z9.

L. vallicola A.A. Heller. Erect ann. to 35cm. St. usually villous and minute-pubesc. or strigulose. Lfts to 2.5cm, 6–8, linear. Fls bright blue, verticillate, in rac. to 10cm long. Spring–summer. W US. Z8.

L. villosus Willd. Decumbent, much-branched perenn. to 90cm. St. many, villous. Lfts to 15cm, solitary, oblong or elliptic, piculate, densely villous. Fls lilac to purple, subverticillate, crowded in erect rac. to 30cm. N Amer. Z8.

L. volcanicus Greene = *L. latifolius* var. *subalpinus.*

L. **cvs.** The most commonly cultivated cvs are derived mainly from *L. polyphyllus* and its crosses with *L. arboreus* and probably some of the ann. spp. Some of the finest of these are the Russell Lupins, raised by George Russell of York over a period of 25 years and introduced in 1937. Named selections are chosen for colour and height, from dwarf races such as Garden Gnome, Minarette and Dwarf Gallery, which seldom exceed 45–60cm/18–24in., to the well-proportioned heights of *L.* Band of Nobles, which may achieve 150cm/5ft. Colour ranges from cream and white shades through yellows in *L.* Chandelier, orange reds in *L.* Flaming June, carmine in *L.* The Pages to rich, deep violets in *L.* Thundercloud and includes strong primary colours and bicolours, as in *L.* The Châtelaine and *L.* The Governor. More subtle shades are found in *L.* Blushing Bride, ivory white, *L.* George Russell, creamy pink, *L.* Wheatsheaf, golden-yellow flushed pink.

Luronium Raf. Alismataceae. 1 perenn., aquatic herb. St. elongate, rising in water or creeping and rooting. Submerged lvs basal, linear, floating, emergent lvs elliptic to ovate, to 5cm, apex obtuse. Fls axillary, long-pedunculate; pet. 7–10mm, white, with a yellow spot at the base; sta. 6. Summer. W & C Eur. Z8.

L. natans (L.) Raf.
→*Alisma.*

Luteola (Tourn.) Webb & Berth.
L. complicata (Bory) Webb = *Reseda complicata.*

Lutzia Gand. Cruciferae. 1 shrubby, everg., perenn. herb, to 30cm. Lvs silver-hairy, oblanceolate to obovate. Fls in a rac.; pet. 4, golden, oblong, 12–20mm. Crete, Greece Carpath. Mts. Z8.

L. cretica (L.) Greuter & Burdet.

L. fruticosa Gand. = *L. cretica*.

→*Alyssoides* and *Alyssum*.

Luzula DC. WOOD-RUSH. Juncaceae. 80 perenn. or ann. herbs. Lvs mostly basal, grass-like. Fls inconspicuous, bracteolate, in umbel-like, paniculate, corymbose or congested infl. Cosmop., esp. temp. Eurasia. Z6.

L. albida (Hoffm.) DC. = *L. luzuloides*.

L. campestris (L.) DC. FIELD WOOD-RUSH. To 30cm, loosely tufted. Basal lvs to 4mm wide, sparsely ciliate, soft and flat. Infl. with 1 sessile and a few pedunculate clusters of 5–12 brown fls. Eur. as far N as Norway.

L. campestris ssp. *multiflora* (Retz.) Buchenau = *L. multiflora*.

L. campestris ssp. *occidentalis* V. Krecz. = *L. multiflora*.

L. cuprina Rochel & Steud. = *L. luzuloides*.

L. lutea (All.) DC. To 30cm, loosely tufted. Basal lvs short, linear-lanceolate, to 6mm wide, glab. Infl. erect, condensed into pedunculate clusters of straw-coloured fls. S Eur.

L. luzuloides (Lam.) Dandy & Willmott. To 65cm, loosely tufted. Basal lvs to 6mm wide, flat, with long hairs. Infl. corymbose, loose or condensed into clusters of 2–10 dirty-white to pink fls. S & C Eur.

L. maxima (Rich.) DC. To 80cm, loosely tufted, in large tussocks. Basal lvs to 2cm wide, channelled, with a few or many silky hairs. Infl. spreading, with many brown fls in groups of 2–5. S, W & C Eur. 'Aurea': lvs broad, golden-yellow. 'Marginata' ('Aureomarginata'): habit dense; lvs deep green edged white; spikelets gold and brown, hanging. 'Tauernpass': lvs v. broad.

L. multiflora (Retz.) Lej. MANY-FLOWERED WOOD-RUSH. To 30cm, densely tufted, erect. Basal lvs to 4mm wide, sparsely hairy. Infl. umbel-like, with to 10 clusters of 18 brown fls each. Eur., Amer., Aus.

L. nemorosa (Pollich) E. Mey. = *L. luzuloides*.

L. nivea (L.) DC. SNOW RUSH. To 60cm, loosely tufted. Basal lvs linear, to 4mm wide, flat; st. lvs to 20cm. Pan. loose with to 20 clusters of off-white fls. Alps, C Eur.

L. pilosa (L.) Willd. HAIRY WOOD-RUSH. To 35cm, tufted. Basal lvs to 10mm wide, flat, sparsely to densely hairy. Infl. with unequal spreading br., deflexed in fr.; fls brown. Eur.

L. subpilosa (Gilib.) V. Krecz. = *L. campestris*.

L. sylvatica (Huds.) Gaudin = *L. maxima*.

L. cvs. 'Botany Bay': young lvs off-white, broad. 'Mount Dobson': hardy; dark brown cymes. 'N.Z. Ohau': large, hardy.

Luzuriaga Ruiz & Pav. Liliaceae (Luzuriagaceae). 4 perenn. herbs. St. trailing or climbing, rather shrubby. Lvs jointed to st.; petiole twisted. Fls showy, solitary or a few together, axill., pedicels equalling perianth; tep. 6; sta. 6. Peru, Chile, Falkland Is., NZ. Z9.

L. erecta Kunth = *L. polyphylla*.

L. polyphylla Hook. f. Shrub-like, scrambling or twining. Lvs 1.25–2.5cm, elliptic to oblong. Fls to 2cm diam., white, sometimes spotted red-brown, broadly campanulate. Summer. Chile.

L. radicans Ruiz & Pav. St. vining, sparsely branched. Lvs 1–3.5cm, linear-oblong to elliptic-ovate or ovate-lanceolate. Fls to 3.25cm diam., pure white, fragrant, star-shaped. Summer. Chile, Peru.

Lycaste Lindl. Orchidaceae. 35 epiphytic, terrestrial or lithophytic orchids. Pbs usually ovoid, clustered. Lvs at apex of pb. and sheathing base, lasting 1–2 seasons, plicate, lanceolate. Fls large, waxy, solitary on basal stalks; sep. erect to spreading, lanceolate to elliptic-lanceolate; pet. shorter, enclosing column; lip trilobed, lat. lobes erect, disc often pubesc., callused. Mex., C Amer., W Indies, S Amer. Z10.

L. aromatica (Graham ex Hook.) Lindl. Pbs to 10cm. Lvs to 50cm. Fls sweetly scented; sep. to 4×2cm, green-yellow; pet. to 3.5×2cm, deep yellow, lip to 3cm, golden yellow, dotted orange. Spring. Mex., Hond., Guat.

L. barringtoniae (Sm.) Lindl. Pbs to 9cm. Lvs to 50cm. Fls pendent; tep. olive-green, to 4.5×1.5cm; lip light buff-brown, to 4.5cm, fimbriate. Spring–summer. Cuba, Jam.

L. bradeorum Schltr. = *L. tricolor*.

L. brevispatha (Klotzsch) Lindl. Pbs to 6.5cm. Lvs to 50cm. Sep. to 3×1.5cm, pale green, dotted pale rose; pet. to 2.5×1.5cm, white to rose; lip to 3cm, white, spotted rose to purple. Costa Rica, Nic., Panama, Guat.

L. candida Rchb. = *L. brevispatha*.

L. ciliata (Ruiz & Pav.) Rchb. Pbs to 7cm. Lvs to 25cm. Fls to

10cm diam., not opening fully, waxy, fragrant, ivory tinted green, lip fimbriate, sometimes yellow, callus orange to yellow. Spring. Peru.

L. cochleata Lindl. & Paxt. Similar to *L. aromatica*. Fls to 5cm diam.; sep. green-yellow; pet. deep orange; lip fimbriate. Spring. Guat., Hond.

L. consobrina Rchb. f. = *L. aromatica*.

L. costata (Lindl.) Lindl. = *L. ciliata*.

L. crinita Lindl. Resembles *L. aromatica* except disc of lip pubesc.; pbs and lvs more robust; scapes longer. Spring–summer. Mex., Guat.

L. crocea Lindl. = *L. fulvescens*.

L. cruenta (Lindl.) Lindl. Pbs to 10cm. Lvs to 45cm. Fls spicily scented; sep. to 5×2.5cm, yellow-green; pet. to 4×2.5cm, bright yellow to yellow-orange; lip yellow, dotted maroon, spotted crimson at base, saccate, midlobe pubesc. Spring. Mex., Guat., Costa Rica, El Salvador.

L. denningiana Rchb. f. Pbs to 10cm. Lvs to 70cm. Sep. fleshy, to 11×2.5cm, light yellow-green; pet. to 5×2cm, green to cream; lip bright orange, to 5×2.5cm, rigid, crispate. Winter. Venez., Colomb., Ecuad.

L. deppei (Lodd.) Lindl. Pbs and lvs similar to *L. aromatica* except more robust. Sep. to 6×2.5cm, pale green flecked or faintly lined oxblood to red; pet. to 4.5×2cm, white, flecked red at base; lip bright yellow with red dots, base striped red, strongly veined, crenate. Spring–autumn. Mex., Guat.

L. dowiana Endl. & Rchb. f. = *L. macrophylla*.

L. fimbriata (Poepp. & Endl.) Cogn. = *L. ciliata*.

L. fulvescens Hook. Allied to *L. longipetala*. Pbs to 10cm. Lvs to 80cm, fls nodding; tep. yellow-green tinted bronze, to 5.5×1.5cm; lip to 2.5×1.5cm, lat. lobes orange-red, midlobe with yellow, fimbriate margins. Summer. Venez., Colomb.

L. gigantea Lindl. = *L. longipetala*.

L. lasioglossa Rchb. f. Pbs to 10cm. Lvs to 55cm. Sep. to 7×2cm, red-brown; pet. to 4×2cm, bright yellow; lip to 4×2cm, yellow flecked and striped purple, midlobe pubesc. Spring–winter. Guat., Hond.

L. leucantha (Klotzsch) Lindl. Pbs to 7.5cm. Lvs to 65cm. Sep. brown-green to apple green, to 4.5×2cm; pet. yellow-white, to 4×2cm; lip to 3×2cm, lat. lobes yellow, midlobe cream-white, pubesc. Costa Rica, Panama.

L. leuco-flavescens hort. = *L. leucantha*.

L. locusta Rchb. f. Similar to *L. longipetala*. Fls to 9cm; tep. sea-green; lip dull green, margin white, midlobe large, fimbriate. Spring. Peru.

L. longipetala (Ruiz & Pav.) Garay. Pbs to 15cm. Lvs to 80cm, tep. yellow-green, tinged brown. Sep. to 8.5×3cm, pet. smaller; lip red-brown to violet-purple, denticulate or fimbriate. Summer. Ecuad., Peru, Colomb., Venez.

L. macrobulbon (Hook.) Lindl. Resembles *L. longipetala* except more robust. Fls to 6cm diam.; sep. green-yellow; pet. white-yellow; lip yellow, spotted brown at base. Spring–summer. Colomb.

L. macrophylla (Poepp. & Endl.) Lindl. Pbs to 7cm. Lvs to 50cm. Sep. olive-green, edged pink-brown, to 4×2cm; pet. white, spotted rose-pink, to 3.5×2cm; lip white, margins dotted rose, midlobe spreading, ciliate. Spring–summer. Costa Rica, Panama, Colomb., Venez., Braz., Peru, Boliv.

L. powellii Schltr. Pbs to 7cm. Lvs to 45cm. Fls to 10cm diam.; sep. pale green marked brown or red, margins yellow; pet. cream-yellow to white, dotted pink or red; lip white, dotted red. Summer–autumn. Panama.

L. schilleriana Rchb. f. Habit similar to *L. longipetala*. Fls to 12cm; sep. pale olive green; pet. white, dotted brown; lip yellow-white, midlobe white, flecked rose-pink, fringed. Spring. Columbia.

L. skinneri (Lindl.) Lindl. Pbs to 10cm. Lvs to 75cm. Sep. white to pink to violet-rose, to 8×3.5cm; pet. pink to red-violet, often marked crimson, to 7.5×4cm; lip white to pale rose, flecked red-violet, to 5cm, lat. lobes pubesc., disc pubesc. fleshy. Autumn–spring. Guat., Mex., Hond., El Salvador.

L. tricolor (Klotzsch) Rchb. f. Pbs to 8cm. Lvs to 35cm. Sep. to 4×1cm, pale green, tinged rose-pink; pet. white to pink, dotted rose; lip white dotted pink, midlobe denticulate. Guat., Costa Rica, Panama.

L. virginalis (Scheidw.) Lindl. = *L. skinneri*.

L. xytriophora Lind. & Rchb. f. Similar to *L. longipetala*, lvs shorter. Sep. green-brown, to 4×2cm; pet. yellow-green, tips white, to 3×2cm; lip white tinted rose-pink on interior surface, to 3×1.5cm, midlobe undulate, callus yellow, dotted red. Spring–summer. Costa Rica, Ecuad.

L. grexes and cvs (see also under ×*Angulocaste*).

There are many grexes of *Lycaste*, usually producing large, waxy, long-stemmed fls in shades of rose, red, orange, yellow, cream, white and green, sometimes marked red or bronze.

Lychee *Litchi chinensis.*

Lychnis L. CATCHFLY. Caryophyllaceae. 20 mostly perenn. herbs, differing from *Silene* in having 5, not 3, styles and a capsule opening with 5, not 6, teeth. Widespread in the N Temp. zone.

L. alba Mill. = *Silene latifolia.*

L. alpina L. Glab., tufted perenn. to 15cm. Lvs in rosettes, linear-spathulate. Infl. dense, ± capitate, of 6–20 fls; pet. usually pale purple, deeply bifid. Summer. Subarc. regions and N Hemis. mts. 'Alba': fls white. 'Rosea': fls rose pink. Z5.

L. chalcedonica L. MALTESE CROSS. Erect, hispid perenn. with simple st. to 50cm. Basal lvs ovate, acute; cauline lvs amplexicaul. Infl. capitate, 10–50-fld; pet. limb c15mm, bifid, bright scarlet. Summer. Eur. Russia; widely cult. 'Alba': fls pale off-white. 'Flore Plena': fls double, red. 'Grandiflora': fls large, brilliant red. 'Red Tiger': fls bright scarlet. 'Rosea': fls rose. 'Salmonea': fls salmon pink. Z4.

L. coeli-rosa (L.) Desr. = *Silene coeli-rosa.*

L. coronaria (L.) Desr. DUSTY MILLER; ROSE CAMPION. Stout, grey-white hairy, erect bienn. or short-lived perenn. to 80cm. Lvs ovate-lanceolate. Infl. few-fld; fls long-stalked; pet. limb c12mm, entire or shallowly 2-toothed, purple-red. Summer. SE Eur., but locally nat. elsewhere from widespread cult. 'Alba': fls white. 'Angel Blush': fls large, white flushed pink. 'Atrosanguinea': lvs pale grey; fls deep carmine pink. 'Blood Red': fls red; early flowering. Dancing Ladies Mixed: fls white, carmine, often with dark eye. 'Flore Pleno': fls double. 'Oculata': fls white with cherry pink eye. Z4.

L. coronata Thunb. Nearly glab. perenn. to 60cm. Lvs ovate-elliptic, sessile. Infl. a few-fld cyme; pet. claw exceeding cal. limb c20mm, orange-red, toothed. Summer. E China; cult. in Jap. var. *sieboldii* (Van Houtte) Bail. See *L. sieboldii.* Z6.

L. dioica L. = *Silene dioica.*

L. flos-cuculi L. RAGGED ROBIN. Sparsely hairy perenn. with erect flowering st. to 75cm. Basal lvs oblanceolate to spathulate, stalked; cauline lvs linear-lanceolate, connate at base. Infl. a loose, few-fld cyme; fls on slender pedicels; pet. limb 12–15mm, pale purple, deeply 4-fld with narrow seg. Summer. Eur.; also Cauc. and Sib. A dwarf variant not exceeding 15cm is sometimes grown in rock gardens. 'Alba': fls white. 'Alba Plena': fls double, white. 'Rosea Plena': fls double, pink. Z6.

L. flos-jovis (L.) Desr. White-tomentose perenn. with erect, usually unbranched st. to 80cm. Lvs lanceolate-spathulate. Infl. ± capitate 4–10-fld; pet. limb c8mm, scarlet, bifid with broad, often cut lobes. Summer. Native in Eur. Alps, but long cult. and locally nat. elsewhere. 'Alba': fls white. 'Hort's Variety': dense; fls rose pink. 'Nana' ('Minor'): habit dwarf, to 25cm; fls red. Z5.

L. fulgens Sims. Sparsely white-hairy perenn. to 60cm. Lvs narrowly ovate, sessile. Infl. a few-fld cyme; pet. limb deep red, deeply bifid; lobes shallowly toothed. Summer. E Russia, Manch., Korea, Jap. Z6.

L. grandiflora Jacq. = *L. coronata.*

L. × haageana Lemoine. Short-lived perenn. to 60cm clothed with downwardly pointing hairs. Lvs lanceolate, glandular-hairy. Infl. few-fld, glandular-hairy; pet. limb c20mm, broadly obovate, bifid, with a narrow tooth on each side and variably toothed on margins, scarlet or rich orange-red. Name applied to a group of gdn hybrids of uncertain parentage but clearly involving Far Eastern spp., esp. *L. fulgens* and *L. sieboldii.* Selections from crosses between these hybrids and *L. chalcedonica,* known as *L. × arkwrightii* hort. include cv Vesuvius with dark foliage and v. large orange-scarlet fls. These hybrids are best treated as summer annuals. 'Grandiflora': fls large, red. 'Hybrida': fls red. 'Salmonea': fls salmon pink. Z6.

L. lagascae Hook. f. = *Petrocoptis glaucifolia.*

L. miqueliana Rohrb. ex Franch. & Savat. Sparsely hairy perenn.; flowering st. to 60cm. Lvs ovate or oblong, acute. Infl. few-fld; fls large; pet. limb 25–30mm, cuneate-obovate, nearly entire, vermilion. Summer. Jap. Z6.

L. nivalis Kit. Dwarf, caespitose, glab. perenn. with simple flowering st. to 20cm. Basal lvs crowded, oblong-lanceolate to spathulate; cauline lvs 1 or 2 pairs, usually linear. Fls 1–3 on short pedicels; pet. limb bilobed, pale purple or white. Summer. Romanian Carpath. Z5.

L. oculata Backh. = *Silene coeli-rosa.*

L. pyrenaica Bergeret = *Petrocoptis pyrenaica.*

L. sieboldii Van Houtte. Like *L. coronata,* but hairy, with a rather dense infl. and deep red, broadly cuneate pet., shallowly lobed with toothed lobes. Summer. Jap. Z6.

L. vespertina Sm. = *Silene latifolia.*

L. viscaria L. Glab. or sparsely hairy perenn. with stiff st. to 60cm, simple or slightly branched above, sticky below upper nodes. Lvs elliptic- to oblong-lanceolate. Infl. a narrow, interrupted, spike-like pan.; pet.-limb 8–10mm, entire or shallowly bifid, usually purple-red. Summer. Widespread in Eur. and W

Asia. 'Alba': fls white. 'Albiflora': fls double, white. 'Fontaine': vigorous; fls large, double, pale red. 'Kugelblitz': fls carmine pink. 'Nana': dwarf. 'Rosea': fls pink. 'Splendens Snow': fls white. 'Splendens Dwarf Fireball': to 30cm; fls red. 'Splendens Fire': fls bright red. 'Splendens Plena' (Flore Pleno): lvs dark; fls double, bright magenta pink. 'Thurnau': fls brilliant red. 'Zulu': to 60cm; fls rich red. ssp. *atropurpurea* (Griseb.) Chater. Fls deep purple. Balk. Penins. Z4.

L. × walkeri hort. (*L. coronaria* × *L. flos-jovis.*) Gdn hybrid. 'Abbotswood Rose': neat grey-tomentose perenn., st. to 40cm, lvs ovate. Fls numerous, bright pink, in more compact infl. than in *L. coronaria.* Z6.

L. wilfordii Reg. ex Maxim. Sparsely hairy perenn.; flowering st. to 60cm. Lvs narrowly ovate, clasping at base. Infl. few-fld; pet. limb c20mm, deep red, deeply and finely laciniate. Summer. E Russia, Manch., Korea, Jap. Z6.

L. yunnanensis Bak. f. Small, hairy perenn.; flowering st. slender to 20cm. Lvs linear or linear-lanceolate. Fls solitary or few in a loose corymb; pet. limb, bifid, white. Summer. SW China. Related to *L. flos-cuculi.* Z7.

→*Agrostemma* and *Viscaria.*

Lycianthes Hassl. Solanaceae. 200 shrubs or vines. Lvs simple, entire. Fls solitary or fascicled in axils; cal. campanulate-truncate, with 10 toothed ribs; cor. rotate, 5-lobed, plicate at base; sta. 5. Fr. a berry. Trop. Amer., E Asia. Z10.

L. rantonnetii Carr. BLUE POTATO BUSH. Shrub to 180cm. Lvs to 10cm, ovate to lanceolate, undulate. Infl. 2–5-fld; cor. 10–25mm diam., dark blue or violet, paler blue or tinged yellow in centre. Fr. to 2.5cm, red. Arg. to Parag. 'Royal Robe': fls violet blue with yellow centres, fragrant, long-flowering.

Lycium L. BOXTHORN; MATRIMONY VINE. Solanaceae. 100 decid. and everg. shrubs, often spiny; st. slender. Lvs alt., small; entire. Fls solitary or clustered, small, cal. 3–5-toothed, bell-shaped; cor. funnelshaped, lobes 5, to ⅓ length of tube; sta. 5, exserted. Fr. an ovoid-globose berry. Cosmop.; temp. and subtrop. regions.

L. afrum L. Erect to 2m, decid. with stout thorns. Lvs to 2cm, linear-spathulate, dark green, glab. Fls solitary, to 22mm, purple-brown. Fr. to 8mm, red, becoming dark purple. N & S Afr. Z9.

L. barbarum L. COMMON MATRIMONY VINE; DUKE OF ARGYLL'S TEA TREE. Decid., erect or spreading, to 3.5m, usually spiny. Lvs to 5cm, narrowly oblong-lanceolate, grey-green. Fls in clusters of 1–4; to 9mm, dull lilac. Fr. to 2cm, orange-red or yellow. A widespread and variable shrub probably including *L. chinense* and *L. europaeum.* SE Eur. to China. Z6.

L. carnosum hort., non Poir. = *L. chinense.*

L. carolinianum Walter. CHRISTMAS BERRY. To 1.5m, everg., spiny, glab. Lvs to 2cm, spathulate-clavate, fleshy. Fls to 6mm, blue, mauve or white. Fr. to 12mm diam., red. S Carol. to Flor. and Tex. Z8.

L. chilense Bertero To 2m, decid.; br. often procumbent, mostly unarmed. Lvs to 2cm, oblong, sometimes glandular-pubesc. Fls usually solitary, to 8mm, yellow, pubesc. outside, lobes purple within. Fr. to 8mm diam., orange-red. Chile. Z9.

L. chinense Mill. CHINESE MATRIMONY VINE. To 4m, decid., arching or procumbent, usually unarmed. Lvs to 8cm, rhombic-ovate to ovate-lanceolate, bright green, glab. Fls 1–4, purple, to 15mm. Fr. to 2.5cm, scarlet. China. Z6.

L. depressum Stocks. Erect to 3m, decid., thorny. Lvs to 7cm, lanceolate, thick, grey-green above, glab. Fls in clusters of 2–4, nodding, to 10mm, pink. Fr. small, red. W & C Asia. Z5.

L. europaeum L. To 4m, decid., with stout thorns. Lvs to 5cm, oblanceolate, grey-green, seldom hairy. Fls solitary or in clusters, 11–13mm, pink or white. Fr. to 8mm, red. Medit., Port. Z9.

L. flaccidum Koch = *L. barbarum.*

L. glaucum Miers = *L. ruthenicum.*

L. gracile Meyen = *L. chilense.*

L. grevilleanum Miers = *L. chilense.*

L. halimiifolium Mill. = *L. barbarum.*

L. horridum HBK = *L. tetrandrum.*

L. intricatum Boiss. = *L. europaeum.*

L. mediterraneum Dunal = *L. europaeum.*

L. ovatum Lois. = *L. chinense.*

L. pallidum Miers. Erect to 2m, decid.; br. spreading, spiny. Lvs to 3cm, oblanceolate, thick, fleshy. Fls solitary or in pairs, to 2cm, pale yellow-green, pink at the base. Fr. to 1cm diam., scarlet. Ariz. and Utah to Mex. Z6.

L. rhombifolium Dipp. = *L. chinense.*

L. ruthenicum Murray. Decid., to 2m; twigs with narrow thorns. Lvs to 3cm, narrow-lanceolate, pale grey-green, smooth fleshy. Fls to 10mm, pale violet with darker veins. Fr. black. C & SE Asia. Z6.

L. tetrandrum Thunb. Small, much-branched, thorny with lat. twigs leafy at the base, spine-tipped. Lvs to 4cm, obovate, dark green, shiny. Fls solitary, violet. Fr. red, enclosed within the cal. Peru, Andes. Z9.

L. turcomanicum Turcz. = *L. depressum*.

L. vulgare Dunal = *L. barbarum*.

Lycopersicon Mill. Solanaceae. 7 glandular-hairy, aromatic herbs. Lvs pinnate or pinnatifid, toothed. Infl. term., appearing lat.; fls in monochasial cymes; cal. 5-lobed; cor. rotate, yellow, limb to 5-, to 6-lobed. Fr. a mucilaginous berry, to 3- or more chambered. W S Amer., Galapagos Is. Z9.

L. esculentum Mill. TOMATO; LOVE APPLE. Coarse perenn. herb, grown as an ann., to 2m. St. erect to scrambling. Lvs to 20×25cm; pinnae to 9, to 8cm, dentate. Fls to 12 per cyme; cor. 6-lobed, lobes acuminate, to 1cm, yellow. Fr. globose to cylindric or ovoid, to 15cm diam., fleshy, to 9-chambered, usually red, sometimes orange or yellow. var. *cerasiforme* (Dunal) A. Gray. CHERRY TOMATO. Fr. small, to 2.5cm diam., 2-chambered. var. *pimpinellifolium* (Jusl.) Mill. CURRANT TOMATO. Fr. to 1cm diam., 2-chambered. var. *pyriforme* (Dunal) Alef. Fr. pear-shaped, to 5cm.

L. lycopersicum L. = *L. esculentum*.

L. peruvianum (L.) Mill. Resembles *L. esculentum* but fls in paired rac. or solitary. Fr. long, villous. Andes.

LYCOPODIACEAE Mirb. in Lam. & Mirb. 1/450. *Lycopodium*.

Lycopodium L. CLUB MOSS. Lycopodiaceae. 450 everg. terrestrial or epiphytic moss-like herbs. St. erect or prostrate, branched. Lvs rigid, fir- or cypress-like, imbricate or sub-verticillate, typically yellow- to olive-green. Sporangia in lf axils or on sporophylls, often organized in strobili.

L. alpinum L. St. trailing; br. ascending, lower flabellulate-compound; branchlets tetragonal, to 2mm diam. Lvs adpressed, ovate-lanceolate. Strobili term., cylindric, to 2.5cm. Arc. zones and mts of the temp. zone in both hemispheres. Z2.

L. annotinum L. St. trailing, long; br. ascending, lower compound. Lvs to 6mm, spreading or reflexed, lanceolate, mucronate, minutely dentate. Strobili term., cylindric, to 3.6cm. Arc. zones and mts of the temp. zone of both hemispheres. Z2.

L. australe Willd. = *L. phlegmaria*.

L. boryanum A. Rich. = *L. cernuum*.

L. capillaceum Willd. = *L. cernuum*.

L. carinatum Desv. St. to 30cm, pendulous, dichotomously branched. Lvs to 8mm, close, ascending, lanceolate, entire. Strobili square. SE Asia. Z10.

L. cernuum L. St. to 120cm, stiffly erect, branched above, branchlets ascending or pendulous, compound, divaricate. Lvs 3mm, crowded, linear, subulate. Strobili term., many per br., cylindric to 18mm. Trop. of both hemispheres, extending to Jap., the Azores, Cape Prov., NZ. Z10.

L. clavatum L. GROUND PINE; RUNNING PINE. St. trailing, v. long; lower br. compound, to 12cm. Lvs to 4mm, crowded, ascending, lanceolate, often minutely dentate. Strobili 1–3 on a long common peduncle. Arc. and alpine zones of both hemispheres, mts of trop. Asia, Afr., Amer., Masc. Is. and Polyn. Z10.

L. complanatum L. GROUND PINE; GROUND CEDAR. Main st. trailing, long; br. ascending, compound. Lvs dimorphic, free, lanceolate erect or adpressed, linear. Strobili several to a common peduncle, cylindric, 25–50mm. N temp. zones of both hemispheres. Z10. var. *digitatum* (A. Br.) A. Br. Br. in a fan-like arrangement. N Amer. Z3.

L. dalhousieanum Spring. St. 60cm, pendulous, little-branched, stramineous. Lvs to 25mm, crowded, lanceolate, entire, glaucous. Strobili to 25cm, flexuous. Borneo and Malay Penins. (mts). Z9.

L. dendroideum Klotzsch non Michx. St. trailing; lower br. compound, to 60cm; branchlets divaricate. Lvs to 4mm, crowded, ascending, lanceolate, mucronate. Strobili to 7.5cm, several to each main br., or 2–3 on a short peduncle. Ecuad. Z8.

L. dendroideum Michx. non Klotzsch = *L. obscurum*.

L. epiceaefolium Desv. = *L. squarrosum*.

L. ericaefolium Presl = *L. phlegmaria*.

L. flagellaria Bory = *L. carinatum*.

L. juniperfolium Lam. = *L. annotinum*.

L. laxum Presl = *L. carinatum*.

L. lucidulum Michx. SHINING CLUB MOSS. St. 15–30cm, suberect, 1–3 dichotomously forked. Lvs to 8mm, crowded, lanceolate, entire, unequal, upper lvs spreading, lower reflexed. Sporangia in lf axils. N Amer., Jap., China. Z5.

L. obscurum L. GROUND PINE; PRINCESS PINE. St. erect, simple at base, branched above, to 45cm, br. ascending. Lvs 3mm, lax, lanceolate, mucronate, green or tinged red. Strobili to 3.6cm,

1–6, term. on the upper branchlets, cylindric. N Amer., Jap., Kamshatka, Sib. Z3.

L. phlegmaria L. St. to 60cm, thick, pendulous, dichotomously branched, stamineous. Lvs to 2cm, close, spreading or ascending, subulate or ovate-lanceolate. Strobili to 15cm, copious, usually forked, flaccid. Trop. OW to E Himal., Aus. (Queensld), NZ. Z10.

L. phlegmarioides Gaudich. St. to 45cm, pendulous, dichotomously branched. Lvs 6–8mm, ovate, obtuse or subacute, entire. Strobili to 10cm, forked, v. slender. Malay and Polyn. Is. Z10.

L. polytrichoides Kaulf. St. 30cm, v. pendulous, dichotomously branched. Lvs to 3mm, dense, linear-subulate, entire. Sporophylls ovate, green. Sandwich Is. Z10.

L. reflexum Sw. = *L. lucidulum*.

L. rubellum Presl = *L. obscurum*.

L. selago L. St. to 23cm, erect, dichotomously branched; branchlets erect, 6mm diam. Lvs to 6mm, crowded, ascending, lanceolate, entire or minutely dentate. Sporangia axill. Arc. and N temp. zones of both hemispheres. Z2.

L. spurium Willd. = *L. dendroideum*.

L. squarrosum Forst. St. to 60cm; pendulous, dichtomously branched; br. and branchlets long. Lvs to 18mm, crowded, spreading or ascending, lanceolate, entire. Strobili simple, long. E Himal., Malesia. Z10.

L. taxifolium Sw. St. to 60cm, pendulous, dichotomously branched. Lvs dense, lanceolate or linear, entire. Sporangia axill. Trop. Amer. Z10.

L. tristachyum Pursh. Main st. creeping, erect st. repeatedly branched, to 30cm. Lvs lanceolate-subulate, sharply attenuate, tinged blue, those of the facial rank adpressed, small, those of the 2 lat. ranks, incurved, larger. Strobili 3–4, borne on elongate peduncles, 1.5–2.5cm, linear-cylindric. N Amer. Z3.

L. ulicifolium Vent. = *L. squarrosum*.

Lycopsis L.

L. echioides L. = *Arnebia pulchra*.

L. pulchra Willd. ex Roem. & Schult. = *Arnebia pulchra*.

Lycopus L. Labiatae. 14 perenn. rhizomatous herbs. Fls packed in remote whorls; cal. campanulate, with 5 equal teeth; cor. tube shorter than cal., lobes 4, upper two spreading; sta. 2, exserted. Eur., N Amer., 1 sp. in Aus.

L. americanus Muhlenb. ex W. Barton WATER HOREHOUND. St. to 80cm, simple or branching, hairy at nodes. Lvs 3–8cm, ovate-lanceolate, incised-dentate or subpinnatisect. Cal. 1–3mm, cor. 2–3mm, white or pink. N Amer. Z4.

L. europaeus L. GYPSYWORT. St. 20–120cm, sparsely to densely hairy. Lvs 3–10cm, ovate-lanceolate or elliptical, pinnatifid or pinnatisect at base, lobed or toothed at apex. Cal. 3.5–4.5mm; cor. 3–4mm, white, with a few small purple dots. Eur. to NW Asia. Z5.

L. virginicus L. BUGLEWEED. Tuber-bearing. St. 20–80cm, erect, puberulent, often tinged purple. Lvs 2–14cm, ovate, oblong-ovate to elliptic, coarsely dentate. Cal. 1–2mm; cor. 1–2mm, white. E US. Z5.

Lycoris Herb. Amaryllidaceae. 12 bulbous perenn. herbs. Lvs basal, linear or lorate. Fls in scapose umbels; perianth bilaterally or radially symmetric, lobes 6, united into a short tube at base, spreading; sta. 6, erect or ascending. China, Jap.

L. africana (Lam.) M. Roem. = *L. aurea*.

L. albiflora Koidz. V. similar to *L. radiata*. Lvs to 1.25cm across; fls white. Z7.

L. aurea (L'Hérit.) Herb. GOLDEN HURRICANE LILY; GOLDEN SPIDER LILY. Lvs to 60×1.2–1.8cm, lorate, fleshy, glaucous. Scape to 60cm; fls 5–6, erect; perianth 9.5–10cm, golden-yellow, funnelform, tube 1.5–2cm, lobes recurved, wavy. Spring–summer. China, Jap. Z7.

L. incarnata Comes ex Spreng. Habit as *L. aurea* but scape to 45cm, fls fragrant, pale flesh-pink or rose, perianth lobes neither reflexed nor wavy. China. Z7.

L. radiata (L'Hérit.) Herb. SPIDER LILY; RED SPIDER LILY. Lvs 30–60×0.6–0.8cm, linear-lorate. Scape to 50cm; fls 4–6, nodding; perianth 4–5cm, rose-red to deep red, tube 6–8mm, lobes strongly reflexed, wavy. Summer–autumn. Jap. 'Variegata': fls crimson, edged white as they fade. 'Alba': fls white, perianth lobes tinged yellow at base. Z3.

L. sanguinea Maxim. Lvs c1cm wide, linear. Scape to 50cm; fls 4–6, erect; perianth 5–6cm, dull red, funnelform, tube 12–15mm, lobes slightly recurved, margins not crisped. Summer. China, Jap. Z6.

L. sprengeri Bak. Resembles *L. squamigera* but shorter, scape to 30cm; fls many, erect, perianth tube v. short, margins of lobes not wavy. Jap. Z6.

L. squamigera Maxim. MAGIC LILY; RESURRECTION LILY. Lvs 30×1.8–2.5cm, lorate. Scape to 70cm; fls 6–8, slightly nodding, fragrant; perianth 9–10cm, pale rose-pink flushed or veined lilac or purple, funnelform, tube 2.5cm, lobes recurved, slightly wavy. Summer. Jap. Z5.

Lydenburg Cycad *Encephalartos inopinus.*

Lygodium Sw. CLIMBING FERN. Schizaeaceae. *c*40 climbing ferns. Rhiz. subterranean. Stipes to 8m, twining, wiry, pinnae borne in distant pairs on short stalks, 1–2×pinnate or palmately lobed, pinnules entire or serrate. Trop. Z10 unless specified.
L. articulatum A. Rich. Sterile fronds bipinnatifid, seg. 5–7.5×1–1.5cm, 4, ligulate-oblong, obtuse at apex, distinctly auriculate at base, shortly petiolate, fertile fronds multi-dichotomous. NZ.
L. circinatum (Burm. f.) Sw. Pinnules deeply digitate, into 5–6 lobes, or 1–2-forked sterile pinnules with ultimate division 10–30×1–2cm. Trop. Asia and Australasia.
L. dichotomum Sw. = *L. circinatum.*
L. flexuosum (L.) Sw. Pinnules linear-lanceolate, subacute at apex, articulate at base, shortly stalked, term. seg. 8–15×1–2cm, ligulate-oblong, with 3–4 similar seg. each side, occas. hastate or pinnate below, fertile fronds smaller than sterile. Trop. Asia and Australasia.
L. forsteri Lowe = *L. reticulatum.*
L. hastatum (Willd.) Desv. = *L. volubile.*
L. japonicum (Thunb.) Sw. Pinnae broadly pinnatisect; pinnules 10–20×8–18cm, deltoid, terminal seg. pinnatifid or hastate, lat. seg. 2–3 per side, v. unequal, stalked pinnate in lower part, entire, serrate or minutely crenate. Jap. to Aus.
L. microphyllum (Cav.) R. Br. CLIMBING MAIDENHAIR FERN; SNAKE FERN. Pinnules 3–6 each side, stalked, glab., sterile pinnules lanceolate-ovate, cordate at base, fertile pinnules ovate to deltate. Trop., widespread in OW, nat. Jam. and Flor. Z6.
L. palmatum (Bernh.) Sw. Sterile pinnae 2–4×3–6cm, on stalk to 2cm, deeply palmately lobed, cordate at base, glab., lobes to 25×12mm, to 6, entire, rounded at apex, fertile pinnae apical, dichotomously branched, terminal seg. numerous, 3–5×1.5mm. E US.
L. pedatum Sw. = *L. circinatum.*
L. pinnatifidum Sw. = *L. flexuosum.*
L. reticulatum Schkuhr. Pinnules 15–22×10–15cm, with term. seg. and 6 subequal seg. each side, ligulate-oblong or cordate-haste, rounded or cordate at base, articulate at base, 5–7.5×1–2cm, lowest shortly stalked. Aus., Polyn.
L. scandens Sw. = *L. microphyllum.*
L. volubile Sw. Sterile pinnules 4–10×0.5–1.5cm, alt., 2–4 per side, oblong-lanceolate, cuneate or truncate at base, acute to acuminate at apex, margins minutely crenate-serrate, fertile pinnules usually shorter than sterile. C Amer., W Indies, N S Amer.

Lygos Adans.
L. sphaerocarpa (L.) Heyw. = *Retama sphaerocarpa.*

Lyme Grass *Elymus*; *Leymus arenarius.*

Lyonia Nutt. Ericaceae. 35 everg. or decid. shrubs or small trees. Br. angled. Lvs rusty-lepidote, petiolate. Fls densely packed in axill. fascicles or, short rac.; cal. lobes, 4–8-persistent, valvate; cor. ovoid, campanulate, urceolate or cylindric, lobes small, 4–7; sta. 8–16, fil. often hirsute, sometimes appendaged. US, E Asia, Himal., Antilles.
L. arborea (L.) D. Don = *Oxydendrum arboreum.*
L. ferruginea (Walter) Nutt. RUSTY LYONIA. Everg., diffuse shrub or small tree to 5m, often lepidote. Lvs 1–9cm, elliptic to ovate or obovate, entire, usually revolute, leathery, densely lepidote beneath. Fls 1–10 in axill., pendulous fascicles; cor. 2–4×2–4mm, white, urceolate. Late winter–spring. SE US. Z9.
L. ferruginea var. *arborescens* (Michx.) Rehd. = *L. ferruginea.*
L. fruticosa (Michx.) Torr. ex Robinson. STAGGER BUSH. Erect, everg. shrub, 1.5–3m. Twigs somewhat angled, sparsely lepidote. Lvs 0.5–6cm, obovate or elliptic, lepidote beneath. Fls 1–10 in fascicles or short rac.; cor. 2.5–5×2.5–4mm, urceolate, white or tinged pink. US Coastal Plain. Z8.
L. ligustrina (L.) DC. MALE BERRY; HE HUCKLEBERRY; MALE BLUEBERRY; BIG BOY. Decid. shrub to 4m. Young twigs glab. or lightly downy. Lvs 3–7cm, oblong, elliptic, lanceolate or obovate, entire or finely serrate. Fls densely packed in downy, term. pan. 8–15cm long; cor. *c*4mm, oval-urceolate to sub-spherical, off-white, downy. Late spring–early summer. E US. Z3.
L. ligustrina var. *foliosiflora* (Michx.) Fern. = *L. ligustrina.*
L. lucida (Lam.) K. Koch. FETTER BUSH; SHINY LYONIA. Erect, glab., everg. shrub to 2m. Br. 3-angled. Lvs to 7.5cm, elliptic to oblong-ovate, entire, lustrous above, punctate beneath. Fls in axill., umbel-like clusters; cor. 3–9mm, oval-urceolate, white

sometimes tinged pink. Spring–summer. SE US. 'Rubra': fls dark pink. Z5.
L. macrocalyx (Anthony) Airy Shaw. Shrub, everg. Young shoots glab., grey-brown. Lvs 5–10cm, ovate to oblong or oval-lanceolate, entire, apex tapering to a slender point, glaucous beneath, finely brown setose-hirsute. Fls in drooping, axillary rac. 7–10cm long; cor. 10mm, urceolate, yellow-white. Summer. SW China, SE Tibet. Z8.
L. mariana (L.) D. Don. STAGGER BUSH. Decid. shrub to 1.5m. Twigs glab., cylindric. Lvs 3–6cm, oblong, elliptic or obovate, entire, red in autumn, brown glandular-punctate beneath. Fls in pendulous, axill. clusters; cor. 7–9mm, ovate-cylindric, white to pale pink. Late spring–late summer. E US. Z5.
L. ovalifolia (Wallich) Drude. Decid. or small tree to 12m. Br. terete. Lvs 6–10cm, ovate-elliptic, ovate or ovate-oblong, sharp-tipped, finely downy, somewhat setose beneath. Fls in downy rac. 3–6cm; cor. 8–10mm, ± white, tubular-urceolate, downy. Late spring–late summer. China, Jap., Taiwan, Himal. var. *lanceolata* (Sieb. & Zucc.) Hand.-Mazz. Lvs elliptic-oblong to lanceolate. Himal., W China. var. *elliptica* (Sieb. & Zucc.) Hand.-Mazz. Lvs elliptic. Fls in short rac. Z6.
L. racemosa D. Don = *Leucothoe racemosa.*
→*Andromeda* and *Pieris.*

Lyonothamnus A. Gray. CATALINA IRONWOOD. Rosaceae. 1 everg. tree to 15m; crown narrow; bark red-grey, exfoliating in narrow strips. Lvs to 16cm, simple to pinnate, lanceolate-oblong, thick, glossy above, pubesc. beneath, entire to crenate-serrate or lobed toward base. Fls in term. pan. to 20cm diam.; cal. tube campanulate, lobes 5; pet. 5, white, rounded, to 5mm; sta. 15, inserted on a lanate disc. Spring–summer. Calif. Z9.
L. asplenifolius E. Greene = *L. floribundus* ssp. *asplenifolius.*
L. floribundus A. Gray. ssp. *asplenifolius* (E. Greene) Raven. Lvs broad-ovate, bipinnatifid, pinnae 2–7, to 11.5×1.5cm, seg. to 13mm.

Lyperanthus R. Br. Orchidaceae. 8 terrestrial herbaceous orchids. Lf usually solitary, basal. Rac. erect, term.; dors. sep. incurved or erect; lat. sep. and pet. lanceolate, spreading or erect; lip entire or trilobed, papillose. Summer–autumn. Aus., NZ, New Caledonia. Z9.
L. forrestii F. Muell. To 23cm. Lvs 3, ovate-lanceolate. Fls to 4; tep. white tinted pink spotted and striped crimson, to 2.5cm, dors. sep. hooded. W Aus.
L. nigricans R. Br. RED BEAK. To 20cm. Lf 1, ovate-cordate. Fls 2–8; tep. white lined crimson tipped red-brown, to 3.5cm, dors. sep. incurved; lip crimson-veined tipped purple. SW Aus.
L. suaveolens R. Br. BROWN BEAKS. To 45cm. Lf 1, linear-lanceolate. Fls 2–8, sometimes fragrant, dark red to brown; tep. to 2.5cm, dors. sep. hooded; lip gland. SE Aus., Tasm.

Lysichiton Schott. SKUNK CABBAGE. Araceae. 2 robust, clump-forming, herbaceous perenn. Rhiz. thick. Lvs basal, ovate-oblong, base cordate-truncate, ± undulate, glab., soft-textured, musky. Spathe large, ovate-lanceolate, base sheathing, arising before or with lvs; spadix cylindric, long-stalked. NE Asia, W N Amer. Z6.
L. americanus Hult. & H. St. John. Lvs 50–125×30–80cm. Spathe to 40cm, bright yellow. W N Amer.
L. camtschatcensis (L.) Schott. Close to *L. americanus*, but more compact in all parts, spathe white, not yellow. NE Asia.

Lysidice Hance. Leguminosae (Caesalpinioideae). 1 shrub or tree, to 7.5m. Lvs to 15cm, pinnate, leathery, glab.; lfts 4–8, ovate to lanceolate. Infl. paniculate, bracts to 2cm, white to pink; pet. to 1.2cm, pink to purple, 5, 3 clawed, spoon-shaped, 2 inconspicuous; sta. 6, protruding. Spring. S China, Vietnam. Z8.
L. rhodostegia Hance.

Lysiloma Benth. Leguminosae (Mimosoideae). 30 shrubs and trees. Lvs alt., gland. between or below lowest pinnae. Fls in axill. fascicles, heads or spicate rac.; cor. short, funnel-shaped, lobes shorter than tube; sta. many, 12–30, exserted. Fr. linear-oblong, flat. Trop. and subtrop. Amer. Z9.
L. bahamensis auct. = *L. latisiliqua.*
L. latisiliqua (L.) Benth. WILD TAMARIND. Tree, to 10m+. Pinnae 4–8-paired; lfts to 1.5cm, 20–30, elliptic-oblong, paired. Infl. white, to 2cm diam., borne to 3 in lf axils or in small rac. Fr. to 10×4cm. Antilles, S Flor., Mex. Z9.
L. microphylla Benth. var. *thornberi* (Britt. & Rose) Isely. Shrub or small tree. Pinnae 8–14-paired; lfts to 0.6cm, 30–40, oblong, paired. Infl. white, to 1cm diam. Fr. to 12×1cm. Summer. S Ariz. Z9.
L. sabicu Benth. SABICU. Shrub or small tree. Pinnae 4–8-paired; lfts to 2.5cm, 8–12, paired, elliptic to obovate. Infl. white, to

2.5cm diam. Fr. to 12×4cm. Spring. W Indies. Z10.

L. thornberi Britt. & Rose = *L. microphylla* var. *thornberi*.

L. watsonii ssp. *thornberi* (Britt. & Rose) Felger & Lowe = *L. microphylla* var. *thornberi*.

Lysimachia L. LOOSESTRIFE. Primulaceae. 150 erect or procumbent herbs, rarely dwarf shrubs. Lvs entire or crenate. Fls 5-merous, subtended by slender bracts, axill., solitary or clustered, or in term. pan. or rac.; cor. rotate. N Amer., Eurasia, S Afr.

L. atropurpurea L. Puberulent; st. 20–65cm, erect; br. few near base. Lvs to 8×1cm, rarely to 10×2cm, alt., petiolate, linear or lanceolate to spathulate, crenate and undulate, glaucous. Infl. a terminal spike; cor. to 5mm diam., dark purple, lobes oblong, spathulate. Balk. Penins. Z6.

L. azorica Hook. = *L. nemorum*.

L. barystachys Bunge. Puberulent; st. to 60cm, erect, simple or branched above. Lvs to 8×1.5cm, alt., rarely opposite, linear-oblong to lanceolate, entire, pubesc., ciliate. Infl. a term. spike, reclinate then erect; cor. white, lobes oblong or lanceolate, obtuse. Russia, China, Jap., Korea. Z5.

L. bulbifera Curtis = *L. terrestris*.

L. ciliata L. St. to 102cm, erect, glab. Lvs to 14×6cm, opposite or in whorls of 4, ovate to lanceolate, glab. except for ciliate margin. Fls solitary or paired, in axils of upper lvs; cor. to 1cm diam., lobes obovate, yellow with red basal blotches. N Amer., nat. Eur. Z4.

L. clethroides Duby. GOOSENECK LOOSESTRIFE. St. to 1m, erect, simple. Lvs to 13×5cm, alt., narrow-ovate to lanceolate-acute, sparsely pubesc., glandular-punctate. Fls in slender, nodding, dense term. rac.; cor. to 1cm diam., white, lobes ovate-lanceolate to spathulate, obtuse; cal. dark. China, Jap. Z4.

L. davurica Ledeb. = *L. vulgaris*.

L. decurrens Forst. f. Glab.; st. to 45cm, erect, simple or slightly branched. Lvs opposite or alt., to 4cm, lanceolate or oblong-lanceolate. Fls racemose, fragrant; cor. pink or white, lobes obovate-spathulate, obtuse. Himal. to Macronesia. Z6.

L. delavayi Franch. Glab.; st. simple or weakly branched to 45cm. Lvs to 8×1cm, alt., rarely opposite, narrow-lanceolate, glaucous beneath, raised dots above. Infl. a long rac., loosely fld at base; cor. white, often tinged purple, to 1cm diam., lobes oblong, undulate. C China, Yunnan. Z6.

L. ephemerum L. Glab.; st. to 1m, simple, erect. Lvs to 15×3cm, opposite, linear or lanceolate to spathulate, amplexicaul, glab., glaucous grey-green. Infl. a narrow terminal rac., rarely with smaller axill. rac. at base; cor. to 1cm diam., white, lobes lanceolate to spathulate, obtuse; cal. purple-tinted. SW Eur. Z7.

L. fortunei Maxim. Similar to *L. clethroides*. St. to 50cm, erect, sometimes branched above, red-brown, glab. or slightly glandular-pubesc. toward infl. Lvs to 6×1.5cm, alt., narrowly or broadly lanceolate, obtuse, entire, glab., minutely punctate. Infl. a loose, many-fld rac.; cor. to 5mm diam., white to rose-pink, lobes broad-obovate, rounded. China, Jap. Z7.

L. henryi Hemsl. St. trailing, tips ascending, to 30cm high, upper part pubesc. Lvs thick, almost all opposite, some alt., to 6×3cm, ovate-lanceolate; petiole 1–2cm. Infl. term.; cor. yellow, lobes oblong-ovate, obtuse. Yunnan, Sichuan. Z7.

L. hillebrandii Hook. f. ex Gray. Shrub to 2.5m, sometimes prostrate, young shoots, rusty-tomentose. Lvs alt., or sub-opposite, size v. variable, lanceolate, ovate or linear, coriaceous. Infl. 4–8-fld clusters, in axils of upper lvs; cal. campanulate, red-purple, lobes obovate, obtuse. Hawaii. Z10.

L. japonica Thunb. St. to 25cm, puberulent, simple or slightly branched, obscurely 4-angled, prostrate or erect. Lvs to 2.5×2cm, opposite, round-ovate or ovate, entire, pubesc., ciliate. Fls 1–3 in axils; cor. yellow, lobes lanceolate-ovate or ovate, crenate. Eurasia. Z6.

L. lanceolata Walter. St. erect, glab., 4-angled, to 45cm. Lvs to 10cm, opposite, lower lvs spathulate, upper lvs lanceolate to linear. Fls axill., solitary or in pan.; cor. pale yellow, lobes erose and cuspidate-pointed. E US. Z5.

L. leschenaultii Duby. Erect, simple or slightly branched, glab. Lvs 0.4–1cm, opposite or alt., lanceolate, ± sinuate. Infl. racemose; cor. lilac, purple or red-purple, lobes obovate, obtuse. SW Asia. Z9.

L. lichiangensis Forr. Erect, glab., to 45cm; st. slightly branched from base. Lvs alt., to 5cm, lanceolate, often clasping st., dotted and striped. Fls in term. spikes; cor. pink, veined rose-pink, wide-campanulate, tube densely gland., lobes entire. Yunnan. Z8.

L. lobelioides Wallich. Glab.; st. to 25cm, branched from base. Lvs usually opposite, to 5cm, ovate or round, entire. Fls in loose slender rac.; cor. white, campanulate, lobes oblanceolate-spathulate. N India, W China. Z8.

L. longifolia Pursh. Erect, glab., to 60cm. Lvs ± erect, opposite, to 4cm, linear, revolute. Fls axill.; cor. large, golden yellow, lobes broadly ovate, acuminate, sparsely toothed. N US. Z5.

L. mauritiana Lam. Glab. herb or subshrub; st. simple or branching basally, erect to 40cm. Lvs usually opposite, spathulate, lower lvs with short winged petiole, revolute. Infl. a rac., or pan.; cor. white, tube deep yellow, lobes obovate, denticulate, erose. SE Asia, S Pacific. Z10.

L. nemorum L. YELLOW PIMPERNEL. Everg., glab.; st. to 45cm, procumbent. Lvs to 3×2cm, opposite, ovate to ovate-lanceolate, acute. Fls solitary slender-stalked in axils of middle lvs; cor. to 1cm diam., yellow. W & C Eur. Z6.

L. nummularia L. CREEPING JENNY; MONEYWORT. Everg., glab.; st. to 50cm, prostrate, fast creeping, expansive and rooting at nodes. Lvs to 2×2.5cm, opposite, closely spaced, broad-ovate to suborbicular, obtuse, base rounded or cordate, dotted with glands. Fls solitary, rarely in pairs, in axils of middle lvs; cor. 1–2cm diam., yellow, lobes obovate, minutely glandular-pubesc. Eur., nat. E N Amer. 'Aurea': lvs golden yellow. Z4.

L. nutans Nees. Erect, sparsely branched, to 60cm. Lvs opposite, to 8cm, lanceolate, glab., base contracted to winged petiole. Fls in term. rac.; cor. purple, tube to 3cm, lobes obovate. S Afr. Z9.

L. paridiformis Franch. Erect, glab., st. sometimes grooved, to 30cm. Lvs to 1.3cm, 4 whorled at st. apex, ovate, attenuate, margins cartilaginous. Infl. dense, capitate; cor. large, bright yellow, lobes lanceolate, acute. W China. Z7.

L. phyllocephala Franch. Tufted, to 60cm, puberulent. Lvs to 5cm, ovate or elliptic, crowded below infl. Infl. close term. clusters; cor. bright yellow, to 2cm diam., shortly funnel-shaped, lobes obovate, with scale-like glands. S & W China. Z8.

L. pseudo-henryi Pamp. Similar to *L. henryi*, but puberulent. Lvs elliptic or ovate-elliptic. China. Z8.

L. punctata L. Puberulent; st. to 90cm, erect. Lvs to 7.5×3.5cm, opposite or in whorls of 3–4, lanceolate to elliptic, apex acute, base rounded, ciliate, puberulent, dotted with glands beneath. Fls whorled; cor. to 15mm diam., yellow, lobes ovate to lanceolate, glandular-pubesc. C Eur., Asia Minor, nat. N Amer. Z5.

L. ramosa Wallich ex Duby. Glab.; st. erect, simple or slightly branched, 60–120cm. Lvs alt., linear-lanceolate or oblong, acuminate, dotted with round glands. Fls axill.; cor. yellow, lobes obovate, acute or obtuse. SE Asia. Z10.

L. repens Stokes = *L. nummularia*.

L. terrestris (L.) Britt., Sterns & Pogg. Glab. herb, erect, to 80cm. Lvs to 9×1.5cm, opposite, lanceolate, dotted with black glands, subsessile; usually with bulbils in axils. Infl. a term. rac.; cor. 5–10mm diam., yellow, lobes streaked and dotted with red or black. N Amer. Z5.

L. thyrsiflora L. Usually glab., but pubesc. under dry conditions; st. to 70cm, erect. Lvs to 9.5×2cm, sessile, lanceolate, with numerous black glands. Infl. in dense stalked axill. rac.; fls 7-merous; cor. to 5mm diam., yellow, lobes linear-lanceolate; sta. longer than cor. Eur. Z6.

L. verticillata Spreng. Resembling *L. punctata* except lvs ovate-oblong, apex blunt, softly pubesc. beneath. Infl. whorls many-fld. W Asia. Z8.

L. vulgaris L. YELLOW LOOSESTRIFE. Pubesc., stoloniferous; st. 50–160cm, erect. Lvs to 9×3.5cm, opposite or in whorls of 3–4, ovate to lanceolate, acuminate. Pan. term. erect; cor. to 10mm diam., bright yellow sometimes dotted orange or black; cal. dark-edged. Eur., Asia. Z5.

Lysionotus G. Don. Gesneriaceae. 20 everg. subshrubs and herbs, often epiphytic. Lvs coriaceous, entire or toothed. Fls in axill. and term. cymes, or solitary; cal. 5-partite, seg. narrow; cor. tube elongate, limb bilabiate, upper lip 2-lobed, lower lip 3-lobed; sta. 2, included. E Asia, Himal.

L. carnosa Hemsl. Dwarf shrub, glab.; st. branched, green. Lvs to 5cm in whorls of 3, fleshy, ovate, sparsely dentate. Fls to 3cm, borne in pairs, white, tinged with lilac. Autumn. E Asia. Z9.

L. pauciflora Maxim. Epiphytic, glab. shrub to 20cm; st. usually unbranched, pale grey-brown. Lvs to 6cm, oblong-lanceolate, mucronate-dentate. Fls to 3cm, solitary, pale pink-mauve. E Asia. Z8.

L. serrata D. Don. Terrestrial herb; st. erect, to 60cm, glab. Lvs to 25cm, ovate-lanceolate, serrate. Fls 5–10 per peduncle, pale lilac or blue with purple veins. Himal. Z10.

LYTHRACEAE St-Hil. 26/580. *Cuphea, Heimia, Lagerstroemia, Lawsonia, Lythrum, Rotala, Woodfordia.*

Lythrum L. LOOSESTRIFE. Lythraceae. 38 perenn. or ann. herbs or small shrubs. St. 4-angled. Lvs opposite, alt. or whorled, usually glab., ovate to linear. Fls 6-merous, regular, in erect, leafy term., spike-like racs; cal. tube cylindric, lobes alt. with appendages; pet. 4–8; sta. 6 or 12. N Amer., Eur., OW. Z5.

L. alatum Pursh. Erect perenn., to 1m, st. much-branched. Lvs to 8cm, oblong-ovate to linear-lanceolate, dark green above, grey-green beneath. Fls 1 per axil; cal. tube green to 7mm, appendages 2× length of lobes; pet. to 6.5mm, purple. Summer. E & C US. var. *alatum* Pursh. St. slender, to 80cm. Lvs ovate to oblong, base subcordate to rounded. var. *lanceolatum* (Elliott) Torr. & Gray ex Rothr. Robust, to 1m. Lvs lanceolate, tapering at base. Z3.

L. cordifolium Nieuwl. = *L. alatum* var. *alatum*.

L. dacotanum Nieuwl. = *L. alatum* var. *alatum*.

L. fruticosum L. = *Woodfordia fruticosa*.

L. lanceolatum Elliott = *L. alatum* var. *lanceolatum*.

L. petiolatum L. = *Cuphea viscosissima*.

L. salicaria L. PURPLE LOOSESTRIFE; SPIKED LOOSESTRIFE. Erect, pubesc. perenn. to 120cm. Lvs to 10cm, lanceolate. Fls in whorled clusters; cal. tube to 6mm with appendages 2–3× lobe length; pet. to 9mm, pink-purple. Summer. OW, nat. NE US. 'Atropurpureum': fls dark purple. 'Roseum Superbum': fls larger, rose-pink. var. *tomentosum* (Mill.) DC. Cal. and bracts white-tomentose. 'Brightness': to 90cm; fls deep rose-pink. 'Feuerkerze' ('Firecandle'): to 90cm; spikes slender, rose-pink. 'Happy': dwarf to 60cm; lvs small; fls red. 'Lady Sackville': to 100cm; spikes deep pink. 'Pink Spires': spikes tall, bright pink. 'Purple Dwarf': dwarf; fls purple, abundant. 'Purple Spires': vigorous; fls rosy-purple, abundant. 'Red Gem': to 100cm; spikes long, red. 'Robert': to 90cm; habit neat; spikes bright pink. Z3.

L. virgatum L. Similar to *L. salicaria* but lvs narrower, glab., base acute not cordate. Fls paired or clustered; appendages equal or shorter than cal. lobes. Summer. Eur. and Asia, nat. New Engl. 'Dropmore Purple': fls purple. 'Morden Gleam': to 140cm, fls rose-pink. 'Morden Pink' fls magenta; hybridization of this mutant with *L. alatum* has produced. 'Morden Rose': compact, fls rose-red. 'Rose Queen': to 90cm; fls pink from purple buds. 'The Rocket': to 75cm; fls vivid rose-pink.

L. cvs. 'Croftway': to 1m; fls in spikes, large, bright red. 'Stichflamme' ('Flash Fire'): fls bright pink. 'Zigeunerblut' (Gypsy Blood'). Z4.

M

Maackia Rupr. & Maxim. Leguminosae (Papilionoideae). 8 decid. shrubs or trees. Lvs imparipinnate. Fls pea-like in dense branching rac. Fr. semi-elliptic to oblong, flat. E Asia.
M. amurensis Rupr. & Maxim. Tree to 20m, often a shrub in cool climates. Lvs to 20cm; lfts to 8cm, 7–11, ovate, acute, glab. Infl. term.; fls to 1.2cm; cor. white or cream to yellow, then brown, standard notched. Fr. to 5cm, winged. Summer. E Asia. var. *buergeri* (Maxim.) Schneid. Lfts pubesc. beneath. Z4.
M. chinensis Tak. As for *M. amurensis*, but lfts to 2cm, 11–13, downy; fr. to 7cm, oblong to elliptic. Summer–autumn. China. Z5.
M. faurei (Lév.) Tak. As for *M. amurensis*, but to 8m; lfts to 5cm, 9–13, ovate, obtuse, glabrescent. Fr. to 4cm, semi-elliptic to short-rectangular, lower margin winged. Summer. Korea, C China. Z5.
M. honanensis Bail. = *M. tenuifolia*.
M. hupehensis Tak. = *M. chinensis*.
M. tenuifolia (Hemsl.) Hand.-Mazz. Shrub. Lvs to 10cm; lfts to 8cm, 3–7, elliptic to ovate, ciliate, glabrescent. Infl. axill.; fls to 2cm; cor. yellow or white, standard entire. Fr. to 5cm, oblong not winged. China. Z6.
→*Cladrastis*.

Macadamia F. Muell. Proteaceae. 10 trees or shrubs. Lvs whorled, entire or serrate. Infl. a cylindrical rac.; fls to 1.5cm, in pairs; perianth usually regular; nectary glands sometimes united around ovary; fil. short. Fr. a hard drupe; seeds 1 or 2. Madag. to Aus. Z10.
M. integrifolia Maid. & Betche. MACADAMIA NUT. Tree to 20m. Lvs to 14cm, in whorls of 3, oblong to obovate, young foliage serrate. Fls white in pendent rac. to 30cm. Fr. spherical, to 3.5cm diam. Winter–spring. E Aus.
M. ternifolia F. Muell. MAROOCHIE NUT. Tree to 6m. Lvs 16cm, in whorls of 3, obovate to elliptic, toothed. Fls pink in 4–20cm rac. Late winter–spring. E Aus.
M. tetraphylla L. Johnson QUEENSLAND NUT. Tree to 18m. Lvs to 20cm, oblong-obovate, usually in whorls of 4. Fls creamy pink to purple, in pendulous rac. to 45cm. Fr. globose, to 3.5cm diam. Winter–spring. E Aus.

Macadamia Nut *Macadamia integrifolia*.
Macamba *Acrocomia aculeata*.
Macartny Rose *Rosa bracteata*.
Macaw Fat *Elaeis guineensis*.
Macaw Flower *Heliconia bihai*.
Macaw Palm *Aiphanes erosa*.

Macbridea Elliott ex Nutt. Labiatae. 2 perenn. herbs. St. rarely branched. Lvs opposite, puberulent. Fls in axill. cymes forming pseudowhorls and sometimes pan.; cal. campanulate, 3-lobed; cor. tube inflated, 2-lipped, upper lip arching, concave, entire or incised, lower lip 3-lobed. SE US. Z9.
M. alba Chapm. Like *M. pulchra*, but with fls white.
M. pulchra Elliott. St. 30–60cm. Lvs 4–8cm, elliptic, oblong or linear-elliptic, undulate or repand-serrate. Cymes 4-fld forming axill. whorls; cor. 3–3.5cm, rose-purple striped white and purple, upper lip 1cm across, entire. Late summer.

Macdougal's Vervain *Verbena macdougalii*.
Macedonian Pine *Pinus peuce*.
Mace *Myristica fragrans*.
Mace Sedge *Carex grayi*.

Macfadyena A. DC. Bignoniaceae. 4 shrubby vines. Lvs bifoliolate with term., trifid, claw-like tendril. Fls in axill. cymes or thyrses; cal. variable; cor. tubular-campanulate. Fr. a linear capsule. Mex., W Indies to Urug.
M. unguis-cati (L.) A. Gentry. ANIKAB; BEJUCO EDMURCIELAGO; MANO DE LAGARIJA. Lfts 5–16cm, ovate, lepidote, glab. or puberulent esp. on veins, gland. beneath. Infl. 1–3(–15)-fld; cor. yellow striped orange in throat, tube 3.3–6.9cm, lobes 1.2–3.1cm. Mex. and W Indies to Arg. Z8.
→*Bignonia, Doxantha* and *Microbignonia*.

Machaeranthera Nees. Compositae. 26 ann. to perenn. herbs, with branched st. Lvs alt., entire to pinnatisect of spiny-toothed.

Cap. usually radiate, solitary to numerous in pan. or cymes. W N Amer.
M. bigelovii (A. Gray) Greene. Bienn. or perenn. to 35cm. Lvs to 8cm, linear-oblong to oblanceolate, entire or toothed, glab. Cap. few to many in a cyme; ray flts violet or pink or purple. W US. Z8.
M. blephariphylla (A. Gray) Shinn. Erect subshrubby perenn. to 30cm. Lvs to 2.5cm, oblong-spathulate to linear-lanceolate, toothed, scabrous and puberulent. Cap. solitary; ray flts white, tinged pink and violet. Late summer. W Tex., New Mex. Z9.
M. canescens (Pursh) A. Gray. Bienn. to perenn. with branched st. to 70cm. Basal lvs to 9cm, linear-oblanceolate, st. lvs smaller, linear or bract-like, grey-puberulent and spinulose, often gland. Cap. numerous; ray flts pale indigo. Summer–early autumn. BC to Ariz. Z8.
M. tanacetifolia (Kunth) Nees. TANSY LEAF ASTER. Glab. to villous ann., to 50cm. Lvs to 14cm, 1–2 pinnatifid or pinnatisect, lobes setaceous. Cap. solitary or many in a cyme; ray flts pink-purple to blue-purple. W US. Z8.
M. tortifolia (Torr. & A. Gray) Cronq. & Keck. MOJAVE ASTER. Subshrubby perenn. with numerous branched st., to 70cm. Lvs to 6cm, linear to lanceolate, spiny-toothed, often tomentose. Cap. solitary; ray flts blue-violet to lavender. Spring–autumn. Utah to Ariz. Z5.
→*Aster, Haplopappus* and *Xylorhiza*.

Machaerocarpus Small.
M. californicus (Torr. ex Benth.) Small = *Damasonium californicum*.

Machaerocereus Britt. & Rose.
M. eruca (Brandg.) Britt. & Rose = *Stenocereus eruca*.
M. gummosus (Engelm. ex Brandg.) Britt. & Rose = *Stenocereus gummosus*.

Machairophyllum Schwantes. Aizoaceae. 10 compact, cushion-forming, succulent, glaucous perennials. Lvs 2.5–10cm, linear-lanceolate, rarely oblong or rhombic, obliquely truncate in profile. Fls 1–3, 4.5–5cm diam., opening in the afternoon or at night. S Afr. (Cape Prov.). Z9.
M. acuminatum L. Bol. Lvs 40–45×8–11mm, pale green, triquetrous, long-tapered. Fls solitary, golden yellow. W Cape.
M. albidum (L.) Schwantes. Lvs 7–100×20mm, incurved, carinate-triquetrous toward tip, off-white. Fls in threes, inside yellow, outside flushed red. SW Cape.
M. cookii (L. Bol.) Schwantes. Lvs 35–80×9mm, crowded, spreading, triquetrous, tapered, blue-green. Fls 4.5cm diam., yellow. W Cape.
→*Bergeranthus, Carruanthus* and *Mesembryanthemum*.

Mackaya Harv. Acanthaceae. 1 everg., spreading shrub to 1.5m. Lvs opposite, 7.5cm, elliptic, lustrous, sinuate-dentate. Fls in term., loose spikes; cal. deeply 5-lobed; cor. 5cm, tubular-campanulate, pale violet, lobes 5, large, flared, with darker veins. Spring–autumn (winter). S Afr. Z9.
M. bella Harv.
→*Asystasia*.

Mackay's Heath *Erica mackaiana*.

Macleania Hook. Ericaceae. 40 everg. shrubs. St. often swollen below; br. slender, often pendulous. Lvs simple, coriaceous, often tinged red when young; petioles short. Fls in fascicles or rac.; cal. usually 5-toothed; cor. tubular, limb 5-lobed; sta. 10. Fr. a globose drupe. Trop. C & S Amer. Z10.
M. angulata Hook. To 1m. Lvs 3–7cm, elliptic-ovate. Fls 3 or more in axill. fascicles; cor. *c*20mm, urceolate, angular, scarlet, lobes small, yellow. Summer. Peru.
M. cordifolia Benth. 1.2–2.4m. Lvs 3–10cm, oblong-ovate. Fls 3–10 in short rac.; cor. 19–25mm, scarlet or crimson, cylindric, lobes white or ivory, thickly white-hirsute inside mouth. Spring. Peru, Ecuad.
M. insignis M. Martens & Gal. To 1.8m. Lvs 4–10cm, elliptic. Fls 1–4 in axill. fascicles; cor. 22–37mm, angled, orange to orange-scarlet at base, lobes deltoid, finely hirsute inside mouth. Summer. S Mex., Hond., Guat.
M. longiflora Lindl. To 1.5m. Lvs 5–7.5cm, ovate-oblong or

ovate-lanceolate. Fls 1–3 or several in lf axils; cor. 22–26mm, dark and dull red, cylindric. Spring. Peru.

M. ovata Klotzsch. To 1.5m. Lvs 3–6cm, narrowly elliptic-oblong to broadly ovate. Fls in fascicles; cor. 18–26mm, angled, orange to orange-pink, mouth finely hirsute inside. Costa Rica, Panama.

M. pulchra Hook. f. To 1.5m. Lvs 5–12.5cm, oval to oblong. Fls axill., drooping, cal. scarlet; cor. *c*30mm, tubular, scarlet, lobes yellow-white, deltoid. Spring. New Grenada.

M. punctata Hook. Low shrub. Lvs 3.5–6cm, oval to cordate. Fls in large, term. clusters; cor. 30mm, cylindric to urceolate, angular, dark rose, lobes ivory. Ecuad.

Macleaya R. Br. Papaveraceae. 3 perenn. herbs to 2.5m. Rhiz. creeping, sometimes invasive. St. erect, glaucous; latex yellow. Lvs shallow-palmatifid, serrate. Fls apetalous, numerous, small, in term., plume-like, branched, spreading rac. Fr. a papery capsule. Late spring–summer. E Asia.

M. cordata (Willd.) R. Br. PLUME POPPY; TREE CELANDINE. To 2.5m. Lvs to 20cm across, rounded-cordate, obtusely toothed and lobed, grey to olive-green above, downy white beneath. Fls beige to cream-white, in plumed rac. to 1m; sta. 25–30. Fr. oblanceolate, seeds 4–0. China, Jap. 'Alba': fls white. 'Flamingo': st. grey-green; fls small, buff pink. var. *thunbergii* (Miq.) Miq. Lvs glaucous beneath. Z3.

M. × kewensis Turrill. (*M. cordata × M. microcarpa.*) To 2.5m. Lvs ovate, 5–9-lobed, base subcordate. Fls cream to buff. Gdn origin. Z4.

M. microcarpa (Maxim.) Fedde. As for *M. cordata* exceppt fls beige, flushed pink below; sta. 8–12. Fr. circular; seeds solitary. C China. 'Coral Plume': fls pinker than type. 'Kelway's Coral Plume': fls deep coral. Z5.

→*Bocconia*.

✕**Maclellanara**. (*Brassia × Odontoglossum × Oncidium.*) Orchidaceae. Gdn hybrids with tall spikes of large fls usually in shades of cream or yellow-green with brown spots.

✕**Macludrania** André. Moraceae. (*Cudrania × Maclura.*)
✕*M. hybrida* André. (*Cudrania tricuspidata × Maclura pomifera.*) Small to medium-sized decid. tree. Bark tinged yellow, furrowed; twigs spiny. Lvs to 15cm, ovate, glab., tinted violet beneath. Gdn origin. Z6.

Maclura Nutt. OSAGE ORANGE; BOW WOOD. Moraceae. 12 spiny dioecious shrubs, treelets or climbers. Infl. axillary, ♀ globose-capitate, with yellow dye-containing glands in tep. and bracts; tep. 4; sta. 4, pistillode present in staminate fl.; stigmas 1 or 2, filiform. Fr. large, fleshy. Amer., Asia, Afr.

M. aurantiaca Nutt. = *M. pomifera*.

M. excelsa (Welw.) Bur. = *Milicia excelsa*.

M. pomifera (Raf.) Schneid. Tree, to 18m, decid., with rounded, irregular head; bark orange-brown, branchlets green, thorns to 2.5cm+. Lvs 5–15cm, ovate-acuminate, lustrous above, tomentose beneath; yellow in autumn. Fls inconspicuous, green, ♂ in short rac., ♀ in dense heads. Fr. *c*8.5–12.5cm diam., globose, with a deeply rugose and polished surface, initially green, orange when ripe, inedible. Early summer. US (Ark. to Tex.) 'Inermis': thornless. 'Pulverulenta': lvs white, powdery. 'Fan d'Arc': hardy; lvs large, dark. Z5.

M. tinctoria D. Don ex Steud. = *Chlorophora tinctoria*.

M. tricuspidata Carr. = *Cudrania tricuspidata*.

Macodes (Bl.) Lindl. Orchidaceae. 10 everg., terrestrial orchids with fleshy creeping rhiz., velvety-papillose lvs and small fls in erect spikes. Summer. Malesia to Papuasia.

M. petola (Bl.) Lindl. Lvs to 9×6cm, elliptic to ovate, bottle green with 5 longitudinal veins and many finer reticulate golden veins in obscure transverse bands above, purple-green beneath. Fls white, lip rusty brown. Sumatra to Philipp. var. *javanica* (Hook. f.) A.D. Hawkes. Lvs to 10cm, veins silver-green. Java.

M. sanderiana Rolfe. Lvs to 7×4.5cm, broadly ovate to orbicular, emerald green with 5 golden, longitudinal veins and finer reticulation above, purple-green beneath. Fls brown-white, lip white. Papua New Guinea.

→*Anoectochilus*.

Macquarie Lily *Crinum flaccidum*.

Macradenia R. Br. Orchidaceae. 12 epiphytic orchids. Pbs cylindrical. Lvs oblong-lanceolate, fleshy to coriaceous. Rac. lat., erect to pendent; fls small; sep. equal, slightly spreading; pet. similar to sep.; lip erect, 3-lobed, midlobe narrow, lat. lobes round, erect. Flor., W Indies, Mex., S Amer. Z10.

M. brassavolae Rchb. f. Pbs to 4.5×1cm. Lvs to 18×3cm. Infl. to 25cm, pendent, few- to many-fld; peduncle dark maroon-red; fls

maroon sometimes striped white, margins yellow-green; tep. to 20×5mm, lanceolate to linear-lanceolate; lip to 19×8mm. Mex., C Amer., Colomb., Venez.

M. lutescens R. Br. Pbs to 5×1cm. Lvs to 16×3cm. Infl. to 17cm, pendent, few-fld; fls white-yellow or dull yellow marked brown-purple; tep. to 12×4mm, elliptic-oblong; lip to 10×7mm. Winter. Flor., W Indies, Venez., Colomb., Guyana, Surinam.

Macrobia (Webb & Berth.) Kunkel = *Aichryson*.

Macropiper Miq. Piperaceae. 9 shrubs or small trees. Br. swollen at nodes. Lvs entire. Fls minute, crowded in unisexual spikes. Fr. a small drupe. S Pacific. Z10.

M. excelsum (Forst. f.) Miq. PEPPER TREE; KAWA-KAWA. Shrub or tree to 6m, glab. throughout, aromatic; br. flexuous. Lvs 7.5×9cm, broadly ovate to suborbicular, cordate at base, dark green, subcoriaceous. Spikes solitary or in pairs, 2–8cm. Fr. obovoid, angular, 2–3mm diam., yellow to orange. NZ. Variegated forms are available.

Macroplectrum Pfitz
M. sesquipedale (Thonars) Pfitz = *Angraecum sesquipedale*.

Macropodium R. Br.
M. laciniatum Hook. = *Thelypodium iaciniatum*.

Macrosiphonia Muell. Apocynaceae. 10 herbs and subshrubs close to *Mandevilla*, differing in their non-climbing habit and solitary fls that open at dusk, with v. long slender cor. tube. Americas. Z9.

M. macrosiphon (Torr.) A.A. Heller. Erect subshrub to 40cm. Lvs to 5cm, ovate-elliptic to rounded, tomentose. Fls term.; cal. lobes leafy, tomentellous; cor. to 10cm, funnelform, white, limb to 5cm diam., exterior ± downy. Tex. to Mex.

Macrothelypteris (H. Itô) Ching. Thelypteridaceae. 9 terrestrial ferns. Rhiz. suberect to creeping, scaly. Frond blades 2–3-pinnate to -pinnatifid, gland., or pubesc., pinnules adnate; rachis scaly; stipes approximate and clustered, pubesc., scaly at base. Masc. Is., Trop. Asia to Polyn., NE Aus.; nat. Americas. Z10.

M. polypodioides (Hook.) Holtt. Stipes to 1m. Frond blades to 80cm, deltoid, pinnae to 60×35cm, subsessile, apex narrowly acute, pinnules narrowly acute at apex, lobed, to 7×2cm; rachis scaly, costa pubesc. Taiwan, Thail., Philipp., New Guinea, Queensld, Polyn.

M. setigera (Bl.) Ching. Stipes to 80cm. Frond blades to 1m, deltoid, pinnae to 30×15cm, pinnules lanceolate, deeply lobed, to 10×3cm; rachis densely scaly, costa white-pubesc. Malay Is.

M. torresiana (Gaudich.) Ching. Stipes to 50cm. Frond blades to 70×50cm, lanceolate, deeply tripinnatifid, pinnae to 30×10cm, deltoid, pinnules deeply lobed to 8×3cm, lobes oblique, dentate, notched or lobed, to 12×5mm, rachis and costa pubesc. below. Masc. Is., Trop. Asia, Jap. to Queensld and Polyn.

→*Alsophila*, *Dryopteris* and *Thelypteris*.

Macrotomia DC = *Arnebia*.

Macrotyloma (Wight & Arn.) Verdc. Leguminosae (Papilionoideae). 24 ann. or perenn. herbs, some woody at base. Lvs 3-foliolate, rarely 1-foliolate, stipulate. Fls pea-like, few in axill. clusters or pseudoracemes. Fr. oblong, straight or falcate, laterally compressed, seeds compressed. E Afr., S Afr., India, Malaysia, W Indies, Aus. Z10.

M. uniflorum (Lam.) Verdc. HORSE GRAM; POOR MAN'S PULSE. Ann.; st. climbing, hairy. Lfts 3, oblong, term. leaflet 1.8–2.5cm. Fls yellow or green-yellow, 1–3 on short pedicels. Fr. 2.5–5.5cm, linear-oblong; seeds 6–8.

→*Dolichos*.

Macrozamia Miq. Zamiaceae. 12 cycads, palm-like in appearance. St. subterranean, short and swollen or tall, columnar, usually simple. Lvs in apical whorls, pinnate, glossy, coriaceous; pinnae numerous, opposite, sometimes with a callus at insertion on rachis. ♀ strobili axillary (apparently term.) among lvs; sporophylls peltate, bearing 2 ovules on inward-facing margins. ♂ strobilus narrower; sporophylls spine-tipped. Seeds large, ovoid, with a fleshy coating. Aus. Z9.

M. communis L. Johnson. BURRAWONG. To 3m. St. largely subterranean. Lvs to 2m, many, pinnae to 130, to 25×1cm, rigid, widely spaced, linear, pungent, pale beneath. NSW.

M. corallipes Hook. f. = *M. spiralis*.

M. denisonii C. Moore & F. Muell. var. *hopei* (W. Hill) Schust. = *Lepidozamia hopei*.

M. diplomera (F. Muell.) L. Johnson. To 2m. St. subterranean. Lvs to 120cm, many, pinnae to 120, to 20×1cm, dichotomously divided, seg. pungent, basal portion narrowed to waxy yellow callosity. NSW.

M. douglasii W. Hill = *M. miquelii.*

M. dyeri F. Muell. = *M. riedlei.*

M. fawcettii C. Moore. To 1.5m. St. ovoid, subterranean. Lvs to 1.2m, few, woolly then glab.; pinnae to 25×1.5cm linear-lanceolate, spirally twisted with a few teeth at tip, basal callosity red-green, rachis terete, twisted spirally. NSW.

M. fraseri Miq. = *M. riedlei.*

M. heteromera C. Moore. Related to *M. stenomera,* from which it differs in having stomata above. To 1m. Pinnae lobed, rigid, dull green, glaucous above, less so beneath; rachis slightly twisted. NSW.

M. heteromera var. *tenuifolia* Schust. = *M. stenomera.*

M. hopei W. Hill ex Bail. = *Lepidozamia hopei.*

M. lucida L. Johnson. Related to *M. spiralis* from which it differs in its long, slender, untwisted rachis; pinnae 35×1.5cm, falcate, v. glossy, basal zone white, callosity 0. S Queensld.

M. miquelii (F. Muell.) A. DC. To 2.5m. St. massive, mostly sub-terranean, ovoid. Lvs to 2m, many, downy then glab.; pinnae to 50 pairs, linear, falcate, pungent, 30×1cm, somewhat glaucous, basal callosity white to red. Queensld, NSW.

M. moorei F. Muell. To 9m. St. columnar, exposed, to 7m tall. Lvs to 3m, many, smooth, semi-erect; pinnae to 50 pairs, linear-lanceolate to 30×1cm, pungent, somewhat glaucous. Queensld, NSW.

M. oldfieldii (Miq.) A. DC. = *M. riedlei.*

M. pauli-guilielmi W. Hill & F. Muell. St. swollen, ovoid, often subterranean. Lvs to 1m, few, woolly then smooth, grey-green, spiralling, pinnae to 120, erect, narrow-linear to filiform, to 20×0.5cm; rachis flattened, v. twisted, woolly at base. Queensld.

M. plumosa hort. = *M. pauli-guilielmi.*

M. preisii Lehm. = *M. riedlei.*

M. riedlei (Fisch. ex Gaudich.) Gardn. To 6m. St. to 4m, exposed. Lvs to 2m, many, erect then arching, pinnae to 150, densely set, rigid, linear to 35×1cm, pungent, basal callosity red-green; rachis woolly at base. W Aus.

M. secunda C. Moore Differs from *M. spiralis* in its rigid, narrow, glaucous pinnae, held semi-erect. NSW.

M. spiralis (Salisb.) Miq. St. subterranean. Lvs to 2m, few to many, slightly twisted; pinnae to 25×1cm, crowded, dark green, linear-falcate, basal callosity pink-orange. NSW.

M. spiralis (Salisb.) Miq. = *M. heteromera.*

M. spiralis var. *cylindrica* Reg. = *M. communis.*

M. stenomera L. Johnson. St. subterranean. Lvs to 1m; pinnae with stomata beneath, lobed ×2–3, lax, dark green. NSW.

M. tridentata (Willd.) Reg. = *M. spiralis.*

M. tridentata ssp. *mountperryensis* (Bail.) Schust. = *M. miquelii.*

Macuililllo Mano de Leon *Oreopanax xalapensis.*

Madagascar Dragon Tree *Dracaena cincta.*

Madagascar Jasmine *Stephanotis floribunda.*

Madagascar Palm *Pachypodium.*

Madagascar Pepper *Piper nigrum.*

Madagascar Periwinkle *Catharanthus roseus.*

Madagascar Plum *Flacourtia indica.*

Madake *Phyllostachys bambusoides.*

Mad Apple *Solanum melongena.*

Madden Cherry *Maddenia hypoleuca.*

Maddenia Hook. f. & Thoms. Rosaceae. 4 decid. shrubs or trees. Fls inconspicuous, unisexual, in terminal rac.; sep. 10, v. small; pet. 0; sta. 25–40. Fr. a 1-seeded drupe. Himal., China.

M. hypoleuca Koehne. MADDEN CHERRY. Shrub or small tree to 6m. Lvs emerging bronze, to 12cm, ovate-oblong, long-acuminate, biserrate, glab. above, blue-white beneath. Rac. dense, to 5cm; fls tinted red; sta. yellow. Fr. ellipsoid, 8mm, black. Winter–spring. C & W China. Z5.

M. hypoxantha Koehne. Resembles *M. hypoleuca,* but lvs yellow beneath, slightly pubesc. on veins. W China. Z7.

M. wilsonii Koehne. Differs from *M. hypoleuca* in lvs emerging green, downy beneath; fls green. Z7. W Sichuan.

Madder *Rubia tinctoria.*

Madeiran Orchid *Dactylorhiza foliosa.*

Madeiran Whortleberry *Vaccinium padifolium.*

Madeira Vine *Anredera cordifolia.*

Madeira Walnut *Juglans regia.*

Madeira Winter Cherry *Solanum pseudocapsicum.*

Maden *Weinmannia trichosperma.*

Madia Molina. Compositae. 18 erect ann. to perenn. herbs. St. gland. Lvs aromatic. Cap. radiate, solitary or few to many in clustered in loose pan.; ray flts yellow; disc flts often yellow. Fls open in the morning or evening, closing in bright sunlight. W N Amer. and Chile.

M. elegans D. Don ex Lindl. COMMON MADIA; COMMON TARWEED. Ann. to 1.5m. Lvs to 14×1.5cm, linear or lanceolate, usually entire. Cap. in corymbs, long-pedunculate; ray flts 8–16, 1–2cm, sometimes with a red-brown spot near base; disc flts yellow or maroon. Summer. WN Amer. (Washington to Baja Calif.).

M. madioides (Nutt.) Greene. Perenn. to 80cm. Lvs to 13×1.5cm, basal lvs rosulate, linear to linear-oblong, entire to toothed. Cap. in a rac. or cyme, usually shortly pedunculate; ray flts 8–15. Summer. WN Amer. (Vancouver Is. to Calif.). Z8.

M. nuttallii A. Gray = *M. madioides.*

M. sativa Molina. CHILE TARWEED; COAST TARWEED; MADIA OIL PLANT. Ann. to 1.3m. Lvs to 20×1.5cm, lanceolate to linear, broad at base, tar-scented. Cap. in rac., pan. or glomerules, short-pedunculate; ray flts 5–12, to 6mm. Summer. W N Amer., Chile.

M. viscosa Cav. = *M. sativa.*

Madia Oil Plant *Madia sativa.*

Madonna Lily *Lilium candidum.*

Madras Thorn *Pithecellobium dulce.*

Madre de Cacao *Gliricidia sepium.*

Madroña, Madrone *Arbutus (A. menziesii).*

Madwort *Alyssum.*

Maesa Forssk. Myrsinaceae. 100 everg., erect or scandent shrubs and small trees. Lvs coriaceous, simple, often gland-dotted. Fls small, white in axill. rac. or pan.; cal. 5-lobed; cor. ± campanulate, sta. 5. Fr. a fleshy drupe. Trop. and subtrop. areas, excluding Americas. Z10.

M. indica (Roxb.) Wallich. Shrub or small tree, to 10m. Lvs to 18cm, elliptic-oblong to elliptic, toothed. Infl. a many-fld rac., fls fragrant. Fr. creamy-white, edible. Early winter. India.

M. japonica (Thunb.) Moritzi. Shrub or small tree, 1–5m. Lvs to 15cm, obovate to elliptic-lanceolate, entire to serrate. Infl. a short pan. E Asia.

Magic Flower, Magic Flower of the Incas *Cantua buxifolia.*

Magic Lily *Lycoris squamigera.*

Magnolia L. Magnoliaceae. 125 everg. or decid. shrubs or trees. Buds enveloped by silver to grey-pubesc. stipular scales. Lvs alt. or clustered, entire, petiolate. Fls stellar or cupulate, term., solitary, often fragrant; perianth seg. in whorls of 3 or more, outer whorl often sepal-like, others petaloid; sta. arranged spirally; gynoecium sessile or short-stipitate, cylindric to sub-globose; carpels many, spirally arranged, each with 2 ovules. Fruiting cones subglobose to cylindric; seeds colourful, suspended from follicles. Jap., Himal., W Malesia (to Java), E N Amer. to Trop. Amer.

M. acuminata (L.) L. CUCUMBER TREE. Decid. tree to 30m; habit conical, later candelabriform. Lvs to 24cm, ovate to elliptic or oblong-ovate, apex acute, base often unequal, cuneate, dark green above, downy or glaucescent beneath. Fls cupulate, erect; seg. 9, grey-green tinged green to yellow-green, sometimes flushed maroon, oblanceolate to oblong-spathulate, to 9×3cm. Spring–summer. E N Amer. 'Variegata': lvs stippled bright gold. f. *aurea* (Ashe) Hardin. Inner seg. golden yellow. var. *subcordata* (Spach) Dandy. YELLOW CUCUMBER TREE. Habit more shrubby, to 7.5m. Twigs sericeous. Lvs to 15cm, obovate-oblong, base subcordate, pubesc. beneath. Fls faintly scented; seg. to 7cm, lime-green to clear yellow. 'Butterflies': fls strong yellow, finely shaped. 'Golden Glow': fls yellow. 'Elizabeth' (*M. acuminata* × *M. denudata*): fls precocious, yellow fading to cream. 'Golden Star' (*M. acuminata* var. *subcordata* 'Miss Honeybee' × *M. stellata* 'Rubra'): densely branching shrub bearing yellow gardenia-like fls on bare twigs, even on young plants; fr. vivid red. 'Yellow Bird' (*M. acuminata* × *M. ×brooklynensis*): fls yellow. 'Yellow Lantern' (*M. acuminata* × *M. ×soulangiana* 'Alexandrina'): habit upright, large; fls lemon yellow. Z4.

M. acuminata var. *cordata* Sarg. = *M. acuminata* var. *subcordata.*

M. amoena Cheng. Tree, 8–12m. Lvs 10–15×3.5–5cm. Fls 6cm diam., cupular, appearing before lvs, fragrant; seg. 9, oblanceolate or nearly spathulate, pale to mid-pink; fil. purple-red. E China. Z8.

M. ashei Weatherby. As for *M. macrophylla* but smaller, to 10m. Twigs glaucous and downy at first. Lvs to 60cm, in pseudo-whorls, broadly oblanceolate, basally cordate to auriculate, glossy above, grey-green beneath, undulate. Fls smaller than *M. macrophylla,* to 13.5×6cm. US (NW Flor.). Z7.

M. aulacosperma Rehd. & Wils. = *M. biondii.*

M. auriculata Bartr. = *M. fraseri.*

M. biondii Pamp. Closely related to *M. salicifolia* but lvs green beneath, vegetative buds and pedicels sericeous. Fls 9–10cm diam., lemon-scented; seg. 6, white flushed pink at base. C China. Z8.

M. ×*brooklynensis* Kalmb. (*M. acuminata* ×*M. liliiflora.*) Habit as for *M. acuminata*, but bark smooth, grey. fl. buds rose to purple, shaded yellow and green; fls campanulate, to 9cm across, erect; seg. 6. Spring–summer. Gdn origin. 'Evamaria': fls purple washed with ochre. 'Woodsman': outer seg. green, otherwise purple and, at centre, soft pink fading to white. Z5.

M. *campbellii* Hook. & Thoms. ssp. *campbellii*. Robust decid. tree to 30m. Lvs to 23cm, elliptic-ovate to oblong-lanceolate, acute, base rounded, unequal, coriaceous, dark sea green above, paler, sometimes sericeous beneath. Fls precocious, erect; seg. to 14×6cm, to 16, broad, fleshy, concave, white or crimson to rose-pink, paler above, inner whorls erect, outer whorls often reflexed. Early spring. Himal. to China. Z9. 'Betty Jessel': fls bright red-pink, almost crimson. 'Darjeeling': fls v. dark pink to claret. 'Ethel Hillier': vigorous and fast-growing; fls large, white, faintly flushed pink at base. 'Late Pink': fls late, pink. 'Sidbury': fls earlier. 'Trewithen Dark Form': seg. light carmine beneath, dark pink above. 'Trewithen Light Form': seg. dark pink beneath, pink washed white above. var. *alba* Griff. Fls white; the form most often found in the wild. 'Maharaja': fls large, white, purple at base. 'Maharanee': fls white. 'Strybing White': fls large, white. ssp. *mollicomata* (W.W. Sm.) Johnstone. Twigs and pedicels thickly bronze-downy. Hardier and flowering while still young. Fls produced earlier, usually bright pink beneath, white above. 'Lanarth': habit fastigiate; lvs broad, thick; fls opening deep red. 'Mark Jury' (*M.* 'Lanarth' ×*M. sprengeri* var. *robusta*): fls to 25cm diam., purple. 'Iolanthe' (*M.* 'Mark Jury' ×*M.* ×*soulangiana* 'Lennei'): fls soft violet, paler within, borne on young plants. *M.* ×*raffillii* hort. (*M. campbellii* ssp. *campbellii* ×*M. campbellii* ssp. *mollicomata.*) 'Charles Raffill': fl. buds stained claret; seg. purple-pink beneath, white stained pink at margin above. 'Kew's Surprise': fls darker pink than in 'Charles Raffill'. 'Wakehurst': fls darker than in 'Charles Raffill'. Z8.

M. '*Charles Coates*'. (*M. sieboldii* ×*M. tripetala.*) Small tree to 6m. Lvs 26cm, in whorls at br. apices, ovate, acute, base cuneate. Fls 10cm diam., fragrant, ivory-white with a boss of red sta. Z6.

M. ×*coatesii* hort. = *M.* 'Charles Coates'.

M. *coco* (Lour.) DC. Everg. shrub to 120cm. Lvs to 26cm, elliptic, glossy dark green, coriaceous. Fls nocturnally v. fragrant; larger seg. 6–9, cupped, creamy white, often tipped pale rose. S China, Java. Z9.

M. *compressa* Maxim. = *Michelia compressa*.

M. *conspicua* Salisb. = *M. denudata*.

M. *conspicua* var. *soulangiana* hort. ex Pamp. = *M.* ×*soulangiana*.

M. *cordata* Michx. = *M. acuminata* var. *subcordata*.

M. *cylindrica* Wils. Decid. tree to 9m. Twigs rusty sericeous when young. Lvs to 15cm, obovate-elliptic, glab., dark green above, paler beneath with adpressed pubescence on major veins. Fls precocious, cupular, resembling *M. denudata*; seg. to 10×4cm, creamy-white tinged pink at base, usually 9, spathulate to obovate. Spring. E China. Similar to *M. salicifolia* and *M. kobus* but cones cylindric. 'Albatross' (*M. cylindrica* ×*M.* ×*veitchii*): fast-growing, erect tree; fls large, pure white, borne profusely in early spring. Z6.

M. *dawsoniana* Rehd. & Wils. Decid. tree or shrub to 12m. Branching open; twigs glab. or sericeous. Lvs 13.5cm, obovate, or elliptic, occas. emarginate, burnished dark green above, puberulent, pale green beneath. Fls fragrant, precocious, held horizontally or nodding; seg. 11×5cm, usually 9, recurving, ultimately drooping, oblanceolate to oblong-spathulate, white to pale rose, pale pink above; sta. scarlet. Spring. China. 'Chyverton': hardier and possibly a hybrid between *M. dawsoniana* and *M. sprengeri*, seg. crimson below, white above. 'Diva': frost-tolerant, bright crimson, colouring more deeply in cold weather. 'Clark's Variety': fls deep pink, produced on young plants. Z9.

M. *dealbata* Zucc. Differs from *M. ashei* and *M. macrophylla* in fr. follicles beaked; perianth seg. never marked purple below. Summer. Mex. Z9.

M. *delavayi* Franch. Bold everg. tree, to 10m, often cut back by hard winters. Twigs glab. blue-green, terminating in a glab., conical bud. Lvs to 50×20cm, ovate to oblong, sinuate, base round to cordate, coriaceous, glab., deep sea-green above, grey-green, glaucescent beneath. Fls to 20cm across, slightly fragrant, inner seg. 6–7, to 10×5cm in 2 whorls, fleshy, ivory to topaz, cupped. Late summer. SW China. Z9.

M. *denudata* Desr. YULAN; LILY TREE. Decid. tree to 15m. Habit broadly pyramidal; young twigs pubesc. Lvs to 15cm, obovate to ovate, softly pubesc. beneath. Fls to 15cm diam. citrus-scented, precocious, goblet-shaped, erect; seg. to 7.5cm, 9, white to ivory. E & S China. 'Purple Eye': habit broadly spreading; fls highly fragrant, inner seg. snow-white, flushed purple at base. Z6.

M. *denudata* var. *purpurascens* (Maxim.) Rehd. & Wils. = *M. sprengeri*.

M. De Vos and **Kosar Hybrids**. (*M. liliiflora* 'Nigra' ×*M. stellata* 'Rosea'.) 'Anne': early flowering (mid April); fls erect, 6.5×10cm, seg. 6–8, dark claret. 'Betty': early flowering (mid April) and vigorous; fls v. large, to 20cm diam., seg. to 19, dark claret beneath, cream above. 'Judy': fls small, to 7.5cm diam., seg. 10, red-purple beneath, cream above. 'Randy': erect and columnar, profusely flowering in late April, fls to 12.5cm diam., claret beneath, white above. 'Ricky': vigorous, erect, columnar; fls to 15cm diam., red-purple, late April. 'Susan': compact in habit; fls fragrant, seg. claret, slightly twisted, late April. (*M. liliiflora* ×*M. stellata* 'Waterlily'.) 'George Henry Kern': fls produced over a long period (spring to mid-summer), seg. 8–10, strap-shaped, heavy-textured, rose-pink in bud, opening pale pink. In N America, colour is often deeper still. 'Jane': strong and vigorous, late flowering with small fls to 10cm diam., fragrant, red purple beneath, snow white above. 'Lilenny': probably also belongs here. 'Pinkie': late-flowering, habit more spreading, fls to 18cm diam., seg. 12, pale, mauve beneath, white above, claret outside, white inside. Z5.

M. *discolor* Vent. = *M. liliiflora*.

M. *foetida* Sarg. = *M. grandiflora*.

M. *fraseri* Walter. EAR-LEAVED UMBRELLA TREE. Erect decid. tree to 16m. Bark grey or brown; shoots glab. Lvs to 27×18cm, in false whorls at br. tips, obovate, base deeply cordate or auriculate, glab. light green, sometimes glaucous beneath. Fls fragrant, tulip-shaped, expanding to 20cm diam.; seg. 9, to 12×5cm, white tinted yellow at first, later ivory, spathulate to obovate. Spring. SE US (mts). Z6.

M. *fraseri* var. *pyramidata* (Bartr.) Pamp. = *M. pyramidata*.

M. Freeman Hybrids. (*M. grandiflora* ×*M. virginiana.*) Hardier than *M. grandiflora*; fls and lvs are also somewhat smaller and tighter than in *M. grandiflora*, the fls being virginal white, the lvs a strong glossy green. *M. grandiflora* 'Exmouth' is likely to belong here. 'Freeman': hardy, early flowering; fls larger than in *M. virginiana*. 'Maryland': fls similar to 'Freeman' but larger, lemon-scented. 'Timeless Beauty': dense, upright habit, long-flowering; fls white to ivory, cupped, spicily fragrant. Z5.

M. *fuscata* Andrews = *Michelia figo*.

M. *glauca* L. = *M. virginiana*.

M. *glauca* var. *major* Sims = *M.* ×*thompsoniana*.

M. *glauca* var. *thompsoniana* Loud. = *M.* ×*thompsoniana*.

M. *globosa* Hook. & Thoms. Decid. shrub or tree to 7m. Br. spreading, twigs rusty-red pubesc. at first. Lvs 21cm, elliptic to obovate, grey-green and rusty- or golden-pubesc. at first, later dark glossy above, glaucous and finely pubesc. beneath. Fls to 12cm diam., pendent, opening after lvs, subglobose or cupulate; seg. 9–12, ivory, inner seg. 7×3cm, spathulate to obovate or elliptic; fil. purple tinged red. Summer. Sikkim, E Nepal, Bhutan, NE Assam to SE Tibet, Burm., W China. Z9.

M. *globosa* var. *sinensis* Rehd. & Wils. = *M. sieboldii* ssp. *sinensis*.

M. *gracilis* Salisb. = *M. liliiflora*.

M. *grandiflora* L. LARGE-FLOWERED MAGNOLIA; BULL BAY; SOUTHERN MAGNOLIA. Everg. tree, to 30m. Young shoots and buds rusty-tomentose. Lvs to 20cm, elliptic to ovate, stiffly coriaceous, glossy dark green above, rust-red pubesc. beneath. Fls to 25cm diam. fragrant, erect; seg. 9–12 to 12×9cm, creamy white, obovate or spathulate, fleshy, cupped; fil. purple. Summer–autumn. SE US. 'Angustifolia': lvs to 20×5cm, narrowly obovate-elliptic. 'Cairo': early and long-flowering, lvs pliable and glossy. 'Charles Dickens': lvs broad and blunt, fls large, fr. red. 'Edith Bogue': notable for hardiness. 'Exmouth' ('Exoniensis', 'Lanceolata', 'Stricta'): habit conic; lvs narrow, acuminate, finely pubesc. beneath, margins recurved; fls to 25cm diam. 'Ferruginea': erect and compact, lvs rust-brown tomentose beneath, glossy dark green above. 'Galissonière': v. hardy, regular in habit, lvs russet beneath. 'Gloriosa': habit compact; fls to 35cm diam. 'Goliath': habit bushy; lvs short, broad, obtuse, blistered, glab. beneath. 'Little Gem': dwarf and slow growing (to 4m in 15 years); fls profuse, white, cup-shaped. 'Nantensis': fls profuse, double. 'Praecox': early and long-flowering. 'Praecox Fastigiata': early and long-flowering, narrow and erect in habit. 'Russet': early blooming, compact, upright and pyramidal growth, lvs long, dark green above, rusty and suede-like beneath, fls cream, fragrant, to 25×30cm. 'Saint George': an American selection with a large number of seg. 'Saint Mary': free-flowering from early age, lvs long to 30cm, dark, rusty-tomentose beneath. 'Samuel Sommer': hardy, lvs russet-tomentose beneath, glossy green above, fls to 40cm across. 'Victoria': hardy, lvs rust beneath, fls small. See also Freeman hybrids. Z6.

M. Gresham Hybrids. Strong, ascending, medium trees with scented fls composed of 12 seg., 8 reflexed at maturity, the inner 4 remaining erect. (i) Svelte Brunettes (*M. liliiflora* 'Nigra'

×M. ×veitchii). 'Dark Raiment': fls to 12cm deep, red-violet. 'Heaven Scent': hardy, free-flowering, vigorous and spreading; fls to 12cm deep, flushed dark pink, honey-scented. 'Peppermint Stick': fls white, violet at base, heavily flushed deep pink, with a median longitudinal stripe of violet on the exterior. 'Raspberry Ice': fls lavender-pink, paler toward tips. 'Royal Crown': small tree; fls large, seg. 12 purple-pink below fading to white, white above. (ii) Buxom Nordic Blondes (M. ×veitchii M. ×soulangiana 'Lennei Alba'). 'Manchu Fan': fls large, goblet-shaped, seg. 9, broad, creamy white, innermost flushed purple-pink below. 'Rouged Alabaster': fls white flushed clear pink. 'Sayonara': fls to 20cm diam., rounded, white flushed pink. 'Sulphur Cockatoo': fls large, fragrant, white, the inner seg. stained violet-pink at base. 'Tina Durio': vigorous fast-growing tree; fls v. large, borne profusely, heavy-textured, white. (iii) M. ×veitchii ×M. ×soulangiana 'Rustica Rubra': 'Todd Gresham', 'Darrell Dean', 'Joe McDaniel', 'Peter Smithers' – large, fast-growing trees with large cup- or bowl-shaped fls to 30cm diam., colours ranging from deep pink to rose-purple to claret. (iv) M. ×veitchii 'Peter Veitch' ×M. ×soulangiana 'Lennei Alba'. 'Mary Nell': habit close to M. ×soulangiana; fls to 25cm diam., produced relatively late in season, heavy-textured, white, stained claret at base. Z6.

M. halleana Parsons = *M. stellata.*

M. heptapeta (Buc'hoz) Dandy = *M. denudata.*

M. ×highdownensis Dandy = *M. wilsonii.*

M. hypoleuca Sieb. & Zucc. Decid., to 30m, crown pyramidal; twigs smooth, tinted purple-red. Lvs to 40cm, obovate, grey-green, in spreading pseudowhorls. Fls to 20cm diam., fragrant, cup-shaped or spreading; seg. to 12, ivory flushed yellow-pink with age, fleshy; sta. crimson to blood-red. Cones red, showy. Summer. Jap. Z6.

M. 'Kewensis'. (*M. kobus* ×*M. salicifolia.*) Broadly spreading small to medium tree. Lvs to 12.5cm, oblong-lanceolate to elliptic, resembling *M. salicifolia* but not anise-scented. Fls to 12.5cm diam., precocious, fragrant; seg. 6, snow white. Z6.

M. kobus DC. Decid. shrub or tree to 30m, spreading, conical or domed; twigs congested (in types described as var. *borealis*) or straight, slender (var. *kobus*). Lvs to 19cm, oblong-elliptic, pubesc. beneath. Fls to 10cm diam. precocious, erect; seg. 7×3.5cm, usually 6, creamy white, often stained wine-red or pink, spathulate to obovate. Winter–spring. Jap. 'Wada's Memory': see *M. salicifolia.* Z5.

M. kobus var. *borealis* Sarg. = *M. kobus.*

M. kobus var. *loebneri* (Kache) Spongb. = *M. ×loebneri.*

M. kobus var. *stellata* (Sieb. & Zucc.) Blackburn = *M. stellata.*

M. liliiflora Desr. MU-LAN; WOODY ORCHID. Decid. shrub to 4m. Lvs to 20cm, elliptic to obovate, acute, sparsely pubesc., sap.-green above, paler beneath. Fls erect, goblet-shaped; seg. 9, inner 6 to 7.5cm, obovate-oblong, obtuse, concave at top, thick, white often flushed pink to claret. Spring. China. 'Gracilis': habit and lvs slender and small. Fls deep purple. 'Holland Red': exceptionally dark. 'Nigra' ('Nigricans'; *M. ×soulangiana* 'Nigra'): seg. numerous, claret to amethyst above, paler below. 'O'Neill': vigorous; fls large, dark purple. *M. liliiflora* 'Nigra' has been crossed with *M. campbellii* to produce *M.* 'Star Wars': vigorous; fls large, spreading, purple-pink. Z6.

M. ×loebneri Kache. (*M. kobus* ×*M. stellata.*) Shrub or small tree, habit as for *M. stellata* but twigs velutinous, lvs 15cm, narrow-obovate, larger, fls larger with 12 spathulate seg. to 8×3cm, white, occas. tinged pink. Gdn origin. 'Ballerina': slow-growing, late-flowering; fls fragrant, white flushed pink at base, seg. to 30. 'Leonard Messel' (*M. kobus* ×*M. stellata* 'Rosea'): hardy; fls to 13cm diam., lilac-pink. 'Merrill': vigorous; fls larger than *M. stellata*, semi-double, seg. 15. 'Neil McEacharn': attaining 4.5m after 15 years; fls borne in profusion, with many white and pink-flushed seg. 'Snowdrift': lvs and fls somewhat larger than typical *M. ×loebneri.* 'Spring Snow': seg. broad, white, tinted green at base. Z5.

M. macrophylla Michx. LARGE-LEAVED CUCUMBER TREE; GREAT-LEAVED MACROPHYLLA; UMBRELLA TREE. Large decid. shrub or tree to 20m. Lvs to 95cm, in dense false whorls, elliptic, oblanceolate to oblong-ovate, base cordate to auriculate, pale green, glab. above, downy white beneath. Fls fragrant, to 30cm+ diam.; seg. 6–9, 20×14cm, thick, matt ivory or cream, inner 3 spotted or tinged purple toward base, outer seg. narrow-spathulate, tinged green. Cones rose pink; seeds red. SE US. Distinguished from the closely related *M. ashei* by its ovoid-globose (not ovoid-cylindric) cones. Z6.

M. macrophylla ssp. *ashei* (Weatherby) Spongb. = *M. ashei.*

M. major C. Schneid. = *M. ×thompsoniana.*

M. 'Michael Rosse'. (*M. campbellii* var. *alba* ×*M. sargentiana* var. *robusta.*) Fls large, pale purple. Z9.

M. mollicomata W.W. Sm. = *M. campbellii* ssp. *mollicomata.*

M. nicholsoniana hort. non Rehd. & Wils. = *M. sieboldii* ssp. *sinensis.*

M. nicholsoniana Rehd. & Wils. non hort. = *M. wilsonii.*

M. nitida W.W. Sm. Everg. tree or shrub to 10m. Young growth glab. lustrous. Lvs 6–15cm, elliptic to obovate, leathery, dark glossy green above, paler beneath. Fls fragrant, 6–8cm diam., seg. 9, narrowly obovate, creamy white. Late spring–early summer. SW China, SE Tibet. Z9.

M. obovata Thunb. = *M. hypoleuca.*

M. officinalis Rehd. & Wils. Decid. tree to 20m. Bark ash-grey; twigs initially sericeous. Lvs to 40cm, oblong-lanceolate, rounded, undulate, light green above, glaucescent, downy beneath. Fls to 20cm diam., strongly fragrant; seg. cupped, 9–12, fleshy, thick, inner 10×5cm, creamy white; sta. red. W & C China. var. *biloba* Rehd. & Wils. Lvs emarginate. Z8.

M. oyama hort. = *M. sieboldii.*

M. parviflora Sieb. & Zucc. non Bl. = *M. sieboldii.*

M. parviflora var. *wilsonii* Finet & Gagnep. = *M. wilsonii.*

M. praecocissima Koidz. = *M. kobus.*

M. 'Princess Margaret'. (*M. campbellii* var. *alba* ×*M. sargentiana* var. *robusta.*) Fls to 25cm diam., dark claret beneath, cream tinged purple above. Z9.

M. ×proctoriana Rehd. (*M. salicifolia* ×*M. stellata.*) Spreading, small tree to 7.5m. Lvs resembling *M. salicifolia* but paler beneath and less aromatic. Fls to 10cm diam., precocious, white tinted pink at base, somewhat fragrant. 'Slavin's Snowy': fls fragrant, to 15cm diam., seg. 6–9, white, distinctively blotched pink at base. Z5.

M. pumila Andrews = *M. coco.*

M. purpurea Curtis = *M. liliiflora.*

M. pyramidata Bartr. ex Pursh. Resembles *M. fraseri* but smaller with lvs rhombic to pandurate. SE US. Z8.

M. quinquepeta (Buc'hoz) Dandy = *M. liliiflora.*

M. ×raffillii hort. see *M. campbellii* cvs.

M. rostrata W.W. Sm. Medium-sized rather skeletal decid. tree. Lvs to 0.5m, broadly obovate, prominently veined, covered at first in tawny-velvet-like hair. Fls fleshy, cream to pink. Fr. cone long, pink, showy. Summer. China, Burma. Z9.

M. salicifolia (Sieb. & Zucc.) Maxim. ANISE MAGNOLIA; WILLOW-LEAF MAGNOLIA. Tree or shrub to 12m. Twigs scented of lemon or anise, smooth at first. Lvs to 12cm, narrow-oval to lanceolate, glab., dull green above, paler beneath, sometimes downy. Fls precocious, inner 6 seg. to 9×4cm, lanceolate to spathulate, white, occas. tinged green or flushed pink at base. Jap. 'Else Frye': fls to 9cm diam., dark carmine at base fading to white at apex; fil. pink. 'Fasciata': shoots narrowly upright. 'Jermyns': slow-growing and late-flowering; lvs wider, fls larger than in type. 'Wada's Memory' (*M. kobus* ×*M. salicifolia* ?): small tree, habit upright, compact; lvs elliptic, flushed red-brown at emergence; fls to 17cm diam., fragrant, white, seg. 6, at first borne horizontally, then drooping and fluttering. Z6.

M. salicifolia var. *fasciata* Millais = *M. salicifolia* 'Fasciata'.

M. sargentiana Rehd. & Wils. Decid. tree to 25m. Twigs glab. Lvs to 18cm, elliptic to obovate, occas. oblong or suborbicular, deep glossy green above, paler, grey-pubesc. beneath. Fls fragrant, precocious, pendent; seg. 10–14, to 9×3.5cm, spathulate or oblong-oblanceolate, white to pale purple-pink above, purple-pink below. Spring. W China. 'Treve Holman': one of the many offspring arising from the union of *M. sargentiana* and *M. campbellii.* var. *robusta* Rehd. & Wils. Habit bushy. Lvs oblanceolate, to 21cm, emarginate. Fls to 30cm+ diam., initially rose-purple. 'Caerhays Belle' (*M. s.* var. *robusta* ×*M. sprengeri* 'Diva'): seg. 12, broad, large, pale carmine to salmon pink. Z9.

M. sieboldii K. Koch. Decid. shrub or tree to 10m. Lvs 12cm, oblong to ovate-elliptic, deep green, subglabrous above, glaucescent, pubesc. beneath. Fls to 10cm, fragrant, cupulate, later dish-shaped, held horizontally, not nodding as in *M. wilsonii* and *M. sieboldii* ssp. *sinensis;* seg. to 12, white, obovate to spathulate, to 6×4.5cm; sta. crimson. Spring–summer. E Asia. 'Semiplena': fls semi-double. ssp. *sinensis* (Rehd. & Wils.) Spongb. CHINESE MAGNOLIA. Differs from *M. wilsonii* in lvs broader, fls larger, more strongly scented of lemon. Broadly branching shrub or tree to 6m. Young shoots initially sericeous. Lvs 7.5–21cm, oval to oblong, obovate or suborbicular, glab. above, glaucescent and, at first, velutinous beneath. Fls to 13cm diam.; nodding; seg. *c*9, 2.5–5cm across, white obovate, to oblong-spathulate; sta. bright crimson. Z7.

M. sinensis (Rehd. & Wils.) = *M. sieboldii* ssp. *sinensis.*

M. ×soulangiana Soul.-Bod. SAUCER MAGNOLIA; CHINESE MAGNOLIA. (*M. denudata* ×*M. liliiflora.*) Decid. shrub or tree to 10m; habit of *M. denudata* but more slender. Lvs to 16.5cm, broadly elliptic to suborbicular, shiny green above, often puberulent beneath. Fls precocious, erect; seg. 9, cupped, oblong-obovate, concave at tip, white, marked rose-pink to violet-purple beneath to 11×7cm+. Spring. Gdn origin. The most widely cultivated magnolia, its many cvs are differentiated by colour, ranging from white to claret, and whether early or late flowering. Of the white cvs, notable early fls include the 5m

'Alba Superba', the slow-growing 'Amabilis' and the cream 'Sundew'; late-flowerers include 'Lennei Alba'. Of those with fls that are carmine at base, the vigorous 'Alexandrina', streaked with dark purple and with white above, is notable as an early flowerer; among the later-flowerers are the fast-growing 'Brozzonii', the fragrant 'Speciosa', 'Verbanica', and the warm pink of 'E. Soulange Bodin'. Of the darker-fld cvs, ranging from deep carmine to dark claret, the large-fld 'San Jose' and the flushed 'Just Jean' are notable early-floweners. The inappropriately named 'Burgundy' has fls lavender-pink. Among the late cvs in this range are the fast-growing 'Lennei', the long-flowering 'Lombardy Rose', the free-flowering 'Norbertii' like a smaller 'Alexandrina', the small-fld 'Rustica Rubra', the v. dark burgundy of 'Vanhouttei' and 'Dark Splendour'. 'Variegata' has fls stippled with yellow. 'Picture' was used by Pickard's Magnolia Gardens to produce a wide range of fragrant large-fld hybrids, prominent among which are the carmine 'Pickard's Charm', the purple-claret 'Pickard's Ruby' and the deep burgundy 'Pickard's Garnet'. Z5.

M. speciosa Geel = *M.* ×*soulangiana*.

M. sprengeri Pamp. Decid. tree to 20m. Young shoots yellow-green, glab. Lvs to 13.5cm, obovate to lanceolate-elliptic, glab., above, pale, glab. to villous beneath. Fls precocious, fragrant, dish-shaped; seg. 12×5.5cm, 12–14, spathulate to oblong-ovate, white, occas. tinged red to pale pink. Spring. China. 'Burncoose': seg. rose-purple. 'Claret Cup': seg. claret beneath, fading to white above. 'Diva': seg. rosy red. 'Lanhydrock': seg. red-purple. var. *elongata* (Rehd. & Wils.) Stapf. Lvs twice as long or longer than wide. Seg. white. Z9.

M. stellata (Sieb. & Zucc.) Maxim. STAR MAGNOLIA. As for *M. kobus* but smaller, to 7.5m. Twigs silky-pubesc., bark muskily scented at first. Lvs 13.5cm, narrow-oblong to ovate. Fl. seg. 12–33, spreading, star-like, 6.5×1.5cm, snow white, faintly flushed pink with age. Spring–summer. Jap., possibly of gdn origin. 'Centennial': hardy, vigorous to 1.5m, fls white. 'Crysanthemiflora' ('Crysanthemumiflora' (sic)): fls fully double, pale pink fading white. 'Dawn': seg. pale pink, up to 45 per fl. on a mature plant. 'George Henry Kern': small-fld and attractive, seg. mauve beneath, white above. 'Norman Gould': v. slow-grower (5m after 35 years); fls to 15cm diam., white, precocious, borne profusely from an early age, seg. few. 'Rosea': fls tinged rose-pink fading to white. 'Rose King' ('King Rosea'): dense and twiggy in growth, buds soft rose-pink opening to white fls tinged pink at base. 'Rosea Massey': an American selection; fls pale pink fading white. 'Royal Star': fast-growing; fls open some 10 days later than sp. type, seg. to 30, snow white. 'Rubra': vigorous, to 2m, br. profuse; seg. stained purple-pink. 'Waterlily': seg. long and slender, pink in bud. Z4.

M. taliensis W.W. Sm. = *M. wilsonii*.

M. ×*thompsoniana* (Loud.) Vos. (*M. virginiana* ×*M. tripetala*.) Semi-decid. large rangy shrub. Lvs to 18cm, obovate to elliptic, glossy above, glaucous beneath. Fls to 15cm diam., cream to primrose, fragrant, vase-shaped. Summer. Gdn origin. 'Urbana': fully hardy. Z5.

M. thuberi Parsons = *M. kobus*.

M. tomentosa Thunb. = *M. stellata*.

M. tripetala L. UMBRELLA TREE; ELKWOOD; UMBRELLA MAGNOLIA. Decid. tree, to 12m. Crown broadly divaricate. Bark grey, shiny. Lvs 50×26cm+, in pseudowhorls at ends of br., oblanceolate, conspicuously veined; pale pubesc. beneath at first. Fls creamy-white, erect, vase-shaped, muskily scented; seg. 9–12, oblong-spathulate, fleshy. Cones to 10cm, red-pink; seeds red. Spring–summer. E N Amer. 'Bloomfield': lvs to 70×30cm; fls v. large. 'Silver Parasol' (*M. tripetala* ×*M. hypoleuca*): narrowly pyramidal; bark grey; lvs large, in showy, umbrella-like pseudowhorls, silver beneath; fls like *M. hypoleuca*. 'Woodlawn': cones to 12.5cm, bright red. Z5.

M. tsarongensis W.W. Sm. & Forr. = *M. globosa*.

M. umbrella Desr. = *M. tripetala*.

M. ×*veitchii* Bean. (*M. denudata* ×*M. campbellii*.) Decid. tree, to 30m. Twigs at first tinted purple, adpressed-pubesc. Lvs 22cm, oblong to obovate, dark green with veins pubesc. above, often tinted purple at first. Fls precocious, vase-shaped, erect; seg. 7–10, obovate to spathulate, 12.5×6cm, white tinged violet to pink beneath, pale pink above. Gdn origin. 'Isca': fls borne early in season, off-white turning pale pink. 'Peter Veitch': fully hardy; fls white flushed pale garnet. 'Rubra': close to 'Peter Veitch' but hardier, with fls wine red in bud, borne even on young plants. Z7.

M. verecunda Koidz. = *M. sieboldii*.

M. virginiana L. SWEET BAY; SWAMP BAY; SWAMP LAUREL. Everg. or semi-decid. shrub or tree, to 30m+ often multi-stemmed and straggling. Lvs 11cm, narrow-oblong to suborbicular, shiny green above, glaucous to silver-velvety pubesc. beneath. Fls globose to cupulate, 6cm diam., white to ivory, highly fragrant;

seg. 6–15, 5×2cm, obovate or suborbicular. Summer–autumn. E US. 'Havener': fls large with many seg. 'Mayer': habit shrubby. See also Freeman hybrids. var. *australis* Sarg. A southern variant with a more arborescent habit and densely sericeous young st. Carolinas, Flor. Z5.

M. ×*watsonii* Hook. f. = *M.* ×*wiesneri*.

M. ×*wiesneri* Carr. (*M. hypoleuca* ×*M. sieboldii*.) Distinguished from *M. sieboldii* by its larger fls and broader, tougher lvs. Tree or shrub to 7m+. Twigs pubesc. at first. Lvs appearing whorled, obovate, undulate, veins pubesc. above, green, glaucous beneath with velvety midvein. Fls spicily fragrant, cupulate, erect; seg. 9, 6×3.5cm, obovate, creamy white; sta. crimson. Gdn origin. Z6.

M. wilsonii (Finet & Gagnep.) Rehd. Closely related to *M. sieboldii*. Decid. shrub or tree to 8m+. Twigs purple-red, velvety-pubesc. at first. Lvs 16cm, lanceolate to oblong-ovate, matt green above, velvet-pubesc. beneath. Fls fragrant, nodding, cupulate, becoming saucer-shaped; seg. 9–12, inner seg. 6.5×4.5cm, white, spathulate to narrow-lanceolate, incurved; sta. rose-purple. W China. Z7.

M. yulan Desf. = *M. denudata*.

M. zenii Cheng. Spreading decid. tree to 7m. Branchlets flushing purple. Lvs 7–16cm, oblong to oblong-obovate, pale green and glab. above, paler beneath. Fls 12cm diam., precocious, cupular, fragrant; seg. 9, to 7.8×3.8cm, near spathulate, white shaded and lined purple. E China. Z9.

→*Talauma*.

MAGNOLIACEAE Juss. 7/200. *Liriodendron, Magnolia, Manglietia, Michelia*.

Maguey *Agave*.
Mahala Mats *Ceanothus prostratus*.
Maharajah Palm *Cyrtostachys lakka*.

✕**Mahoberberis** Schneid. Berberidaceae. (*Mahonia* ✕*Berberis*.) 4 everg. shrubs to 2m with polymorphic foliage, resembling *Mahonia aquifolium* in fl. and unarmed st., *Berberis* in bearing some or all simple lvs. Gdn origin. Z6.

✕*M. aquicandidula* Krüssm. (*M. aquifolium* ✕*B. candidula*.) To 1m, low-growing, rather weak. Lvs ovate, acuminate, to 4cm with to 4 prominent teeth per side, glossy above, white pruinose beneath. Late winter.

✕*M. aquisargentii* Krüssm. (*M. aquifolium* ✕*B. sargentiana*.) To 2m; upright, robust. Lvs variable, tinted red-brown in winter; those on unbranched, erect growth tripartite, coarse, ovate, to 7cm, glossy with to 6 spiny teeth per side, lat. pinnae reduced, spiny, those on older growth simple or greatly reduced-tripartite, serrulate. Late winter.

✕*M. miethkeana* Meland. & Eade. (*B. julianae* ✕*M. aquifolium*.) Robust, erect, to 2m. Lvs variable, as in ✕*M. aquisargentii*, elliptic-lanceolate, dentate with large spines, glossy dark green above, paler beneath, turning copper-red in autumn. Late winter.

✕*M. neubertii* (Lem.) Schneid. (*M. aquifolium* ✕*B. vulgaris*.) To 1m with expansive habit, erect. Lvs simple, ovate to 7.5cm, serrulate, or rigid, ovate-acute, tripartite, serrate. 'Latifolia': spreading; lvs obovate, dull-green, somewhat glaucous.

Mahoe *Hibiscus elatus, H. tiliaceus*.

Mahonia Nutt. OREGON GRAPE; HOLLY GRAPE. Berberidaceae. 70 everg. shrubs. St. erect or sprawling, simple or sparsely branched. Lvs alt. or in whorls atop st., imparipinnate or trifoliolate; lfts spiny-serrate, semi-rigid, basal pair sometimes stipule-like. Fls yellow unless stated, sometimes sweetly scented, in radiating fascicles of short rac., umbellate clusters or pan. Fr. berry-like, globose-ellipsoid, pruinose blue-black unless stated. Asia, N & C Amer. The reunion of *Berberis* and *Mahonia* has been proposed, in which case, the following together with ✕*Mahoberberis* would be transferred to *Berberis*.

M. acanthifolia G. Don. Robust erect shrub to 5m. Lvs to 60cm; lfts 17–27, 5–10cm, oblong-ovate to oblong-lanceolate, apex acute to acuminate, base truncate, thinly leathery, dull to slightly glossy above with veins impressed, sinuately toothed, teeth 3–7 on lower margin, 2–5 on upper margin. Rac. to 30cm, spreading, 3–4 per fascicle, rather thick and crowded; fls deep yellow. Late autumn–early winter. Himal. Z8. Differs from *M. napaulensis* in longer lvs with more numerous, dull-textured lfts and fls produced earlier. 'Maharajah': fine form with deep yellow fls.

M. alexandri Schneid. = *M. lomariifolia*.

M. aquifolium (Pursh) Nutt. OREGON GRAPE. Shrub to 2m, sparingly branched, suckering freely; st. thin. Lfts 5–13, to 8×4cm, ovate, with to 12 spiny teeth per side, glossy, dark green turning purple-red in winter. Fls golden, on erect rac. to 8cm, 3–4-

fascicled. Late winter. NW Amer. 'Apollo': low-growing, expansive, to 60cm; lvs larger, dull, good winter colour. 'Atropurpurea': lvs red-purple in winter; fls in short rac. 'Donewell': broad and arching to 1m; lvs long-thorned, tinted blue below; rachis red, fls yellow. 'Forescate': to 1m; lvs tinted blue beneath, spring, winter and young lvs tinted red. 'Orange Flame': low-growing, to 60cm; lvs robust, becoming bronze, tinted with orange-red after first season, dark red in winter; fls golden; susceptible to rust and mildew. 'Smaragd': spreading; winter colour red-bronze; fls profuse. Z5.

M. arguta Hutch. Shrub to 2m. Lfts 9–23, to 9×2cm, lanceolate, base cuneate, serrate with to 3 spiny teeth per side, lustrous, reticulate. Fls pale yellow, to 60 in arching pan. to 40cm. Late spring. C Amer. Z9.

M. bealei (Fort.) Carr. Erect, scarcely branching shrub to 2m. Lvs to 50cm; lfts to 10×6cm, (term. lft. larger and broader), 9–15, widely spaced, obliquely and broadly ovate acuminate, coarsely and sinuately spiny-toothed (3–4 teeth per side), bases sometimes overlapping, rigid, olive green. Fls scented, pale yellow in short, crowded erect racs, 6–9-fascicled. Often confused with *M. japonica* and sometimes treated as a var. or cv of that plant. The true *M. bealei* is rare in gardens; plants usually offered as 'Bealei' are vigorous selections of *M. japonica* with broad lfts. Late winter. W China (Hubei). A hybrid between this sp. and *M. napaulensis* has been offered under the name *M. japonica* 'Trifurca', an upright shrub with bold ruffs of outspread lvs, the lfts broad and v. sharply and coarsely toothed, the fls pale yellow in short, erect, clustered rac. A hybrid between *M. bealei* and *M. lomariifolia* has been recorded: *M.* 'Arthur Menzies' has an upright, compact habit, lvs to 45cm, lfts to 19, deep blue-green, 3–4 spines per side, and lemon-yellow fls in erect rac. Z6.

M. confusa Sprague. Small shrub resembling *M. fortunei*. Lfts to 20, more crowded than in *M. fortunei*, narrow-lanceolate, spinose, sea-green to leaden grey above, silvery beneath; rachis purple-tinted. Fls pale yellow in erect, slender rac. Autumn to winter. China. Z8.

M. dictyota (Jeps.) Fedde. Shrub to 1m. Lfts to 4×2.5cm, ovate, in 3 overlapping pairs, serrate with to 4 spiny teeth per side, glossy, reticulate above, dull beneath. Fls in rac. to 7cm. Late spring. SW US. Z8.

M. eutriphylla Fedde. To 1.5m. Lvs to 11cm; lfts 3, 2 opposite, oblong-ovate, to 4×2cm with to 5 teeth per side, term. leaflet petiolate, to 1cm, glossy, reticulate above, grey-green beneath. Fls in rac. to 2cm. Fr. blue-black, glossy. Late spring. Mex. Z9.

M. eutriphylla hort. non Fedde = *M. trifolia*.

M. fascicularis DC. = *M. pinnata*.

M. fortunei (Lindl.) Fedde. To 2m. St. erect, unbranched. Lvs to 25cm; lfts to 10×2.5cm, 7–13, elliptic-lanceolate, long-acuminate, flexible with 10 teeth per side, dark green above, pale beneath. Rac. slender to 5cm, 4–8-fascicled; fls bright yellow. Late autumn. China. Z7.

M. fremontii (Torr.) Fedde To 4m. Lvs to 10cm; lfts 3–7, to 6×1.5cm, oblong-lanceolate, sinuately spiny serrate, bright glaucous blue. Fls in a subumbellate cluster, pale yellow. Fr. yellow to red. Summer. SW US. Z8.

M. glumacea DC. = *M. nervosa*.

M. gracilipes (Oliv.) Fedde. Suckering, to 1.5m. Lvs to 65cm; lfts 5–7, widely spaced, to 12×5cm, semi-rigid, spiny-serrate and cusped above, dull green above, glaucous beneath, term. leaflet petiolate, to 15cm. Rac. to 50cm, 3-fascicled; sep. maroon; pet. white. W Sichuan. Z7.

M. gracilis (Hartw.) Fedde. Lfts 5–13, to 5×3cm, often overlapping, ovate, spiny-serrate, shiny, light green above, paler beneath. Otherwise resembling *M. aquifolium* except style persistent in fr. Late winter. Mex. Z8.

M. haematocarpa (Wooton) Fedde. St. slender, erect, usually simple, to 4m. Lfts to 4×1cm, 7, tough, oblong-lanceolate, with to 4 spiny teeth per side, apex cusped, blue-grey. Fls pale yellow, to 6 in narrow, subumbellate rac. Fr. dark red. Late spring. W US. Z8.

M. herveyi Ahrendt = *M. repens* 'Rotundifolia'.

M. 'Heterophylla'. To 1.5m. St. red at first. Lvs to 30cm, polymorphic; lfts to 7, lanceolate, to 9cm×1.5cm, entire or with to 10 teeth per side, variable, often reflexed or twisted, glossy green. Fls seldom produced. Gdn origin. Z7.

M. japonica (Thunb.) DC. To 3m. Lvs 30–40cm; lfts 7–19, 5–11cm, obliquely ovate-lanceolate to oblong-lanceolate, apex acuminate, base rounded with 4–6 sinuate, spiny teeth per side, v. leathery, dull dark green to sea green. Rac. 10–20cm, slender, spreading to ascending or pendulous; fls sulphur yellow, scented of lily of the valley. Often confused with *M. bealei* esp. in forms with broader lfts. Late winter–early spring. Jap., in cult. only; possibly China, Taiwan. 'Hiemalis': lvs to 50cm, lfts narrow red-tinted, rac. to 35cm, flowering profusely in mid-winter. Z6.

M. japonica 'Trifurca' see *M. bealei*.

M. leschenaultiana (Wall.) Tak. Similar to *M. siamensis*. Differs in more crowded, overlapping glossy lfts and deep orange-yellow fls. S. India. Z9.

M. × lindsayae P.F. Yeo. (*M. japonica* × *M. siamensis*.) 'Cantab': medium-sized shrub, spreading. Lvs long, arching; lfts to 15, remote, with to 6 spines per side; petiole tinted red in cold weather. Fls lemon yellow, large, fragrant on spreading or drooping rac. Winter. Z7.

M. lomariifolia Tak. St. erect to 4m, to 10m in habitat, seldom branching above base. Lvs to 60cm, outspread; lfts to 7×1cm, 18–41, crowded, overlapping toward apex, oblong-ovate to oblong-lanceolate, with to 7 spines per side, sharply acuminate, subfalcate, dark green. Fls pale yellow, crowded on erect spikes to 15cm, to 17-fascicled. Flowering time varies. Burm., W China. Z7.

M. × media C. Brickell. (*M. japonica* × *M. lomariifolia*.) Tall vigorous hybrids with spreading rufts of rigid dark green lvs and long ± erect rac. of yellow fls. Z7. 'Buckland': infl. to 65cm diam., rac. to 14, fls fragrant, pale yellow. 'Charity': erect to 5m; lfts 21, ovate-lanceolate, long-acuminate, to 3 teeth on upper margin, to 4 on lower; fls deep yellow in erect rac. to 35cm, to 20-fascicled; winter. 'Faith': similar to *M. lomariifolia*, lfts broader; fls paler. 'Hope': fls densely, bright pale yellow. 'Lionel Fortescue': fragrant, erect infl. 'Underway': habit branching, bushy; fls autumn. 'Winter Sun': rac. horizontal; fls topaz-yellow, first opening in autumn.

M. napaulensis DC. Differs from *M. acanthifolia* in shorter lvs with fewer, rather narrower lfts, usually more closely toothed and glossy. Fls faintly scented, produced in later winter, early spring. Nepal, Sikkim, Assam. Z8.

M. nervosa (Pursh) Nutt. To 1m, suckering. Lvs to 60cm; lfts 11–23, thick, to 7cm, decreasing toward apex, changing upwards from ovate to oblong-lanceolate, serrate, grey-green above, yellow-green beneath. Rac. to 20cm, to 4-fascicled. Late winter. NW Amer. Z6.

M. nevinii (Gray) Fedde. Erect to 2.25m. Lfts to 3cm, 3–7, narrow-lanceolate, with to 6 spiny teeth per side, grey blue-glaucous. Fls in loose subumbellate rac. Spring. Calif. Z8.

M. pinnata (Lagasca) Fedde. Distinguished from *M. aquifolium* by its more erect, rigid habit, and more finely serrate lfts. To 2.5m. Lfts 5–9, to 6×1.5cm, ovate-lanceolate, ± sinuate with to 13 slender, forward-pointing spines per side, dull sea green above, tinted red in winter, pruinose beneath. Rac. to 6cm, to 5-fascicled; fls primrose yellow. Spring. Calif. Z7. Plants grown under this name are often *M. × wagneri*, particularly the clone 'Pinnacle'.

M. pinnata var. *wagneri* Jouin = *M. × wagneri*.

M. pumila (Greene) Fedde. Suckering, to 0.5m. Lvs to 14cm; lfts 5–7, to 3×3cm, base broadly cuneate, apex acuminate, to 8 spiny teeth per side, grey-green, sparsely papillose. Fls glaucescent in rac. to 4cm, to 5-fascicled. Spring. W US. Z7.

M. repens G. Don. Suckering, semi-prostrate shrub to 0.5m. Lvs to 25cm; lfts usually 5, ovate, dull green above, papillose beneath, glaucous at first, with 9–18 spiny teeth per side. Fls deep yellow, in rac. to 8cm, to 6-fascicled. Late spring. NW Amer. 'Rotundifolia': robust; lvs ovate, entire or serrulate. Z6.

M. schiedeana (Schldl.) Fedde = *M. trifolia*.

M. siamensis Tak. To 4m, bark becoming corky, fissured. Lvs to 70cm; lfts 11–17, obliquely lanceolate to ovate, 14–17cm; sinuately toothed, dull green, v. leathery with veins impressed. Rac. 12–25cm, 6–10-fascicled, ascending to erect; fls deep yellow, v. fragrant. Late winter. N. Thailand to Burma, China. Z9.

M. swaseyi (Buckley) Fedde. Differs from *M. nevinii* in attaining 2.5m, thick, reticulate lvs and narrower rac. to 6cm. Fr. white-yellow, flushed red. Spring. Texas. Z8.

M. toluacensis Bean = *M.* 'Heterophylla'.

M. trifolia Cham. & Schltr. Prostrate or erect to 5m. Lfts to 3×2.5cm, 3–5(–7) ovate, undulate with to 3 spines per side, dark to grey-green above, paler beneath turning purple-red in cold weather. Fls golden on short rac. to 2cm, to 3-fascicled. Spring. Mex. Z8.

M. trifoliolata (Moric.) Fedde. var. *glauca* I.M. Johnst. Erect to 2.25m. Lfts 3, to 6.8cm, narrowly lanceolate, rigid, undulate with 1–4 fine-like marginal spines per side, blue-green, glaucous. Fls in short corymbs. Fr. red-plum. Spring. Mex. Z7.

M. × wagneri (Jouin) Rehd. (*M. pinnata* × *M. aquifolium*.) Late spring. Gdn origin. 'Aldenhamensis': vigorous and erect to 1.5m; lvs large, sea-green, tinted blue beneath, young lvs bronze; fls yellow. 'Fireflame': to 1.25m; lfts 7, dull green or glaucous blue above, grey-green beneath, blood red to bronze in winter. 'Hastings Elegant': dense, compact and upright; lvs everg.; fls in large heads, profuse, yellow 'King's Ransom': narrowly upright to 1.6m; young lvs pruinose, tinted dark blue; fls pale yellow; fr. pruinose, v. dark blue. 'Moseri': erect to 80cm; young lvs tinged bronze-red, later dark green; fls yellow;

fr. pruinose, blue-black. 'Pinnacle' ('Pinnata'): erect to 1.5m, vigorous; young and winter lvs tinted copper otherwise bright green; fls yellow. 'Undulata': erect to 1.5m, vigorous; lvs v. glossy, margins undulate, young and winter lvs tinted red-bronze; fls in dense rac., pale yellow. 'Vicaryi': broadly erect to 1m; lvs small, some autumn lvs tinted red; fls in small dense rac.; yellow; fr. pruinose, v. dark blue. Z7.

Maianthemum Wigg. Liliaceae (Convallariaceae). 3 small perenn., rhizomatous herbs. St. erect. Lvs cauline, 2 or 3. Fls in term. rac.; stalks slender; tep. 4, free; sta. 4; ovary superior, 2-celled. Fr. a berry. N temp. regions.
M. bifolium (L.) Schmidt. FALSE LILY OF THE VALLEY. St. 5–20cm. Lvs 3–8cm, broadly cordate-ovate, thinly-textured, short-stalked with a deep open sinus. Fls 8–20 per rac., tep. 1–3mm, white. Fr. 5–6mm, red. W Eur. to Jap. Z3.
M. canadense Desf. TWO-LEAVED SOLOMON'S SEAL. St. 5–20cm. Lvs 5–10cm, broadly ovate-cordate, ± sessile with a narrow sinus. Fls 8–22 per rac., white fragrant. Fr. pale red. N. Amer. Z3.

Maiden Grass *Miscanthus.*
Maidenhair Berry *Gaultheria hispidula.*
Maidenhair Fern *Adiantum.*
Maidenhair Spleenwort *Asplenium trichomanes.*
Maidenhair Tree *Ginkgo biloba.*
Maidenhair Vine *Muehlenbeckia complexa.*
Maiden Pink *Dianthus deltoides.*
Maiden's Blush *Rosa ×alba.*
Maiden's Gum *Eucalyptus globulus.*
Maiden's Wattle *Acacia maidenii.*
Maiden's Wreath *Francoa.*

Maihuenia (Philippi ex F.A. Weber) Schum. Cactaceae. 2 low, caespitose shrubs; st. succulent with small seg. Lvs small, terete; spines usually 3. Fls term., solitary; perianth spreading. Arg., Chile.
M. patagonica (Philippi) Britt. & Rose. Resembling *M. poeppigii*; stem-seg. cylindric, 2–8cm. Lvs 2–4mm; central spine 2–5cm. Fl. 4.5–5.5×3–4.5cm, white or pink. Summer. S Arg. Z5.
M. poeppigii (Otto ex Pfeiff.) Schum. Dwarf shrub, forming low mounds; stem-seg. short-cylindric, 1.2–3cm. Lvs 4–6mm; central spine 1–1.5cm. Fl. 3–4.5×3cm, yellow. Summer. S Arg., S Chile. Z5.

Maihueniopsis Speg. = *Opuntia.*

Maikoa *Brugmansia arborea.*

Mairia DC. Compositae. 14 perenn. herbs or subshrubs. Lvs alt., often radical. Cap. radiate, solitary or few clustered in a corymb; ray flts purple or white; disc flts yellow. S Afr. Z7.
M. crenata (Thunb.) Nees. Perenn. herb. Lvs 8×2cm, obovate-oblong, bluntly toothed, arachnoid. Cap. solitary, 2.5cm diam., on peduncle to 25cm. S & SW Cape.
→*Arnica* and *Aster.*

Maize *Zea mays.*
Majorcan Peony *Paeonia cambessedii.*
Makola *Afzelia quanzensis.*
Malabar Cardamom *Elettaria cardamomum.*
Malabar Gourd, Malabar Melon *Cucurbita ficifolia.*
Malabar Nightshade *Basella.*
Malabar Rosewood *Dalbergia latifolia.*
Malabar Spinach *Basella alba.*

Malachodendron Cav.
M. pentagynum (L'Hérit.) Small = *Stewartia ovata.*

Malachra L. Malvaceae. 6 hispid herbs or subshrubs. Lvs un-lobed to palmately lobed. Fls small, in head-like clusters; bracts conspicuous leaf-like; epical. somettines present; cal. of 5 sep., campanulate; pet. 5; staminal tube short; styles 10. Trop. & sub-trop. Z10.
M. fasciata Jacq. Ann. to 1.2m, villous. Lvs to 15cm, 3–5-lobed, serrate; stipules 1.5–3cm. Fls in axill., 5-fld heads; cor. 8–10mm, white turning pink. Mainly C Amer., also Pacific Is.
M. radiata (L.) L. Herb or subshrub to 2.5m, yellow-hispid. Lvs to 12cm, deeply 3–5-lobed; stipules to 1cm. Fls in term. heads; cor. 1–1.2cm, pink. C & S Amer., Trop. Afr.
→*Sida.*

Malacocarpus Salm-Dyck non Fisch. & C.A. Mey. = *Parodia.*

Malacothamnus Greene. CHAPARRAL MALLOW. Malvaceae. 20 subshrubs shrubs or small trees. St. densely stellate-tomentose.

Lvs rounded to cordate in outline, palmately lobed. Fls in clusters, forming term. heads, spikes, rac. or pan.; epical. seg. 3, filiform to ovate; sep. 5, united at base; pet. 5; sta. united in a tubular column. Calif., Baja Calif. Z9.
M. davidsonii (Robinson) Greene. Shrub to 4m. Lvs 2.5–10cm diam., thick, 3-, 5- or 7-lobed. Fls in short rac. forming pan., often many abortive; pet. 12–15mm, pink or rose.
M. fasciculatus (Nutt. ex Torr. & A. Gray) Greene. Shrub to 2m. Lvs 2–4cm diam., unlobed or 3-, 5- or 7-lobed, subcoriac-eous. Fls in interrupted spikes or open pan.; pet. 12–18mm, pale to deep mauve.
→*Malvastrum* and *Sphaeralcea.*

Malanga *Xanthosoma.*

Malaxis Sol. ex Sw. Orchidaceae. c300 largely decid. orchids. Rhiz. tuberous, creeping. Lvs 1 to several, thin-textured, plicate. Rac. term., many-fld; fls usually small; sep. and pet. free, spreading; lip larger than tep., entire or lobed, often denticulate. Cosmop., mainly trop. Asia. Z10.
M. calophylla (Rchb. f.) Kuntze. Terrestrial, st. erect, usually 3-lvd. Lvs 7–12cm, ovate, yellow-green with bronze central patch and transverse lines, often undulate. Rac. to 20cm, many-fld; fls to 8mm diam; tep. slender, pale pink or creamy yellow. Mal-aysia, Thail. In addition to this sp., *M. discolor* (Lindl.) Kuntze with green-edged purple-bronze lvs, *M. metallica* (Rchb.f) Kuntze with metallic purple-red lvs and *M. scottii* (Hook.f.) Kuntze with lime-edged copper lvs are sometimes grown.
M. ophioglossoides Muhlenb. ex Willd. = *M. unifolia.*

Malayan White Ixora *Ixora umbellata.*
Malay Apple *Syzygium malaccense.*
Malay Banyan *Ficus microcarpa.*
Malay Ginger *Costus speciosus.*
Malay Jewel Vine *Derris scandens.*
Malaysian Sickle Pine *Falcatifolium falciforme.*

Malcolmia R. Br. MALCOLM STOCK. Cruciferae. 35 ann. or perenn. herbs. Lvs alt., entire or pinnately lobed. Fls in loose rac.; sep. 4, erect; pet. 4, linear or awl-shaped. Fr. a silique. Medit. to Afghan.
M. bicolor Boiss. & Heldr. = *M. graeca* ssp. *bicolor.*
M. chia (L.) DC. Ann., to 30cm. St. erect, rarely reclining, branched above. Lvs obovate to ovate, rarely lyrate, toothed. Rac. few-fld; pet. 6–10mm, pink to violet, claw long, white or green. Fr. 25–70×1mm. E Medit., Greece, Turk. Z9.
M. flexuosa (Sibth. & Sm.) Sibth. & Sm. Similar to *M. maritima* except little-branched, br. short. Fr. to 3mm diam. Aegean coast, Crete, Cyprus. Z9.
M. graeca Boiss. & Sprun. Ann., 5–20cm. St. branched from base. Lvs in rosettes, lanceolate-obovate, toothed, lyrate or pinnatifid. Fls scented; pet. 8–17mm, purple-violet. Fr. 10–50mm. Greece. ssp. *bicolor* (Boiss. & Heldr.) Stork. Pet. violet-pink, base yellow. S Albania, Greece. Z9.
M. littorea (L.) R. Br. Perenn., 10–40cm. Lvs linear-lanceolate, hairy, wavy-toothed. Pet. 14–22mm, bright purple-pink. Fr. 30–65×1.5mm. Summer. SW Eur. Z7.
M. maritima (L.) R. Br. VIRGINIA STOCK. Ann., to 35cm. St. diffusely branched. Lvs round to obovate-elliptic, hairy, toothed or entire. Rac. many-fld, straight; fls fragrant; pet. 12–25mm, red-purple, rarely violet, notched, long-clawed. Fr. 35–80×1–2mm. Spring-autumn. Medit., widespread. Compacta Mixed: compact, to 40cm; fls small, pink, white and red, fra-grant. Z8.
→*Cheiranthus.*

Malcolm Stock *Malcolmia.*
Male Berry, Male Blueberry *Lyonia ligustrina.*
Male Fern *Dryopteris*, (*D. filix-mas*).

Malephora N.E. Br. Aizoaceae. 15 erect or creeping shrubby perennials. Lvs united at the base, triquetrous-prismatic, semicylindric, soft-fleshy, blue-pruinose. Fls axill. or term., 1 or few, short-pedicellate. Late summer–winter. S Afr.; Nam. Z9.
M. crocea (Jacq.) Schwantes. St. stout, gnarled. Lvs 2.5–4.5cm, indistinctly triquetrous, pruinose. Fls 3cm diam., golden yellow inside, reddened outside. W Cape. var. *purpureocrocea* (Haw.) Jacobsen & Schwantes. Fls brilliant red. W Cape.
M. engleriana (Dinter & A. Berger) Schwantes. Dense, soft, spreading shrub. Lvs 2–4cm, obtuse-triquetrous, curved, slightly waxy, v. soft. Fls 2cm across, orange-yellow inside, orange-red outside. Nam.: Great Namaqualand.
M. herrei (Schwantes) Schwantes. St. prostrate. Lvs to 5cm, triquetrous, rounded-carinate. Fls 5cm diam., golden yellow, orange beneath. S Afr.

M. lutea (Haw.) Schwantes. Erect shrub. Lvs spreading, 2.5–4cm, compressed-triquetrous, white-pruinose. Fls 3–4cm diam., yellow. W Cape.

M. thunbergii (Haw.) Schwantes. St. prostrate, rigid. Lvs crowded, 5cm+, semicylindric, bluntly triquetrous above, fresh green, spotted. Fls 3.5–4cm diam., yellow. SW Cape.

→*Crocanthus, Hymenocyclus* and *Mesembryanthemum.*

Mallotus Lour. Euphorbiaceae. 140 decid. trees and shrubs. Lvs wide, simple, stipulate. Fls unisexual, apetalous, small, in spikes or pan.; sta. numerous. Fr. a capsule. OW Subtrop. & Trop.

M. japonicus (Thunb.) Muell. Arg. Decid. tree or shrub, 3–4m. Shoots thick, pithy, red-hairy then grey. Lvs 10–20×6–15cm, broadly ovate, long-acuminate, entire, with yellow translucent glands beneath and 2 glands at base; petiole long. Fls inconspicuous, in 8–15cm long pyramidal pan., white-pubesc. Jap., China, Korea.

Mallow *Hibiscus, Malva.*

Malope L. Malvaceae. 4 ann. and perenn. herbs. Lvs simple or palmately lobed. Fls axill., solitary, on long pedicels; epical. seg. 3, broader than the sep.; pet. 5. Medit. to W Asia.

M. grandiflora Dietr. = *M. trifida.*

M. malacoides L. Ann. or perenn. herb to 50cm; st. ascending, hispid. Lvs 2–5cm, oblong-lanceolate to ovate, crenate, upper lvs often 3-lobed. Epical. seg. to 1.2cm, cordate-orbicular; sep. acuminate, longer and narrower than epical. seg.; pet. 2–4cm, deep pink or purple. Medit. to W Russia. Z8.

M. stipulacea Cav. = *M. malacoides.*

M. trifida Cav. Ann. glabrescent herb to 1.2m; st. erect. Lvs to 10cm, suborbicular, crenate-dentate, upper lvs with 3–5 triangular lobes. Epical. seg. 1.5cm, orbicular-cordate; sep. lanceolate-ovate; pet. 4–6cm, purple-red. W Medit. 'Alba': fls white. 'Grandiflora': fls large, dark rose. 'Rosea': fls rose red. 'Vulcan': fls large, bright red.

Malortiea H.A. Wendl.

M. gracilis H.A. Wendl. = *Reinhardtia gracilis.*

M. simplex H.A. Wendl. = *Reinhardtia simplex.*

Malosma (Nutt.) Engl. Anacardiaceae. 1 small everg. tree or shrub, to 4m. Br. slender, glaucescent. Lvs ovate or elliptic, coriaceous, entire, tinged red above, paler beneath, margins white. Fr. a white drupe. Calif. Z9.

M. laurina (Nutt.) Nutt. ex Engl.

→*Lithrea, Rhus* and *Toxicodendron.*

Malpighia L. BARBADOS CHERRY; ACEROLA. Malpighiaceae. 45 erect shrubs or small trees. Lvs opposite, ovate to lanceolate, entire or dentate, often with irritant hairs. Fls in umbellate clusters or corymbs, or solitary; sep. 5, gland.; pet. 5, clawed, fimbriate or ciliate; sta. 10. Fr. a drupe with 3 stones. Carib., trop. Amer. Z10.

M. angustifolia Hitchc. non L. = *M. cubensis.*

M. aquifolia L. Shrub to 2m, br. smooth. Lvs lanceolate, spinydentate, with irritant bristles beneath. Fls pale pink. S Amer.

M. coccigera L. MINIATURE HOLLY; SINGAPORE HOLLY. Shrub to 1m, often prostrate. Lvs 0.6–2.5cm, orbicular or broad-elliptic to obovate, sinuate, with lobes aristate-dentate, coriaceous. Fls pink or lilac. Fr. red, 0.5–1.5cm diam. W Indies.

M. cubensis Kunth in HBK. LADY HAIR. Shrub to 2m. Lvs 1.5–2.5cm, narrow-oblong, covered by yellow irritant hairs. Fls white or pale pink. Cuba, W Indies.

M. emarginata Sessé & Moc. ex DC. BARBADOS CHERRY. Shrub or small tree 2–6m. Lvs 2.5–10cm, ovate or elliptic or obovate, entire. Fls pink or purple. Fr. red, to 1cm diam. W Indies, Mex. S to Venez. and Peru.

M. glabra L. BARBADOS CHERRY. Shrub to 3m. Lvs to 10cm, ovate-lanceolate or elliptic-lanceolate, entire, glossy. Fls red or rose. Fr. globose, red, to 1cm diam. Tex. to N S Amer., W Indies. 'Fairchild': habit weeping; lvs small, fls pink.

M. mexicana A. Juss. Lvs ovate to obovate-lanceolate, glab. to hairy. Fls purple, to 2cm across. Fr. globose, red. Mex.

M. punicifolia auct., non L. = *M. emarginata.*

M. punicifolia L. = *M. glabra.*

M. suberosa Small. Lvs to 10cm, oblong to oblong-ovate, crenulate, bright green. Fls white or pink. Fr. yellow-red. Cuba.

M. urens L. COWHAGE; COW ITCH CHERRY. Erect or scrambling shrub to 3m. Lvs oblong-ovate, glab. above, bristly beneath. Fls pink or pale purple. W Indies.

MALPIGHIACEAE Juss. 68/1100. *Acridocarpus, Bunchosia, Hiptage, Lophanthera, Malpighia, Sphedamnocarpus, Stigmaphyllon.*

Maltese Cross *Lychnis chalcedonica.*

Malu Creeper *Bauhinia vahlii.*

Malus Mill. APPLE. Rosaceae. 35 trees and shrubs. Lvs serrate, occas. lobed. Fls in corymbs; cor. rotate, pet. 5, obovateorbicular; sta. (15–)20; carpels (3–4–)5. Fr. a pome, locules with 2 ovaries producing 1–2 seeds. Eur., Asia, US.

M. acerba Mérat = *M. sylvestris.*

M. ×adstringens Zab. (*M. baccata* ×*M. pumila.*) Lvs softly downy beneath. Fls pink, cal. and pedicel shortly hairy. Fr. 4–5cm, subglobose, short-stalked, cal. occas. persistent, red, yelow, or green. 'Almey': habit rounded, upright, to 4m; lvs tinted purple when young, later bronzed; buds chestnut; fls profuse, deep purple, pet. lighter at base; fr. globose, to 2cm diam., orange with a red cheek, to completely red. 'American Beauty': habit upright, vigorous; lvs bronzed red when young, later bronzed green; fls double, clear red; fr. sparse. 'Crimson Brilliant': habit shrub-like, slow-growing; lvs bronzed purple; fls single to semi-double, carmine with a white star; fr. to 2cm diam., dark purple. 'Helen': habit shrub-like; twigs spreading; lvs light red; fls single, purple; fr. purple stained red. 'Hopa': habit broad, loosely upright, to 4m; lvs oval-elliptic, bronzed red; fls profuse, red washed lilac; fr. clear orange to bright red, edible. 'Irene': lvs finely serrate, tinted red; fls profuse, single, purple; fr. to 2cm diam., maroon. 'Nipissing': habit shrub-like; fls carmine, later darker, soon fading; fr. orange to dark red, bronzed green on shaded side. 'Osman': habit large, shrub-like; fls single, pink washed white; fr. to 4cm diam., orange to red. 'Patricia': habit upright, to 5m; crown rounded; lvs bronzed; fls single, dark red, early; fr. to 2.5cm diam., dark red; seedling of 'Hopa'. 'Pink Beauty': fls single, dark carmine; fr. bright red. 'Pink Giant': fls simple, pink, later light pink washed lilac; fr. to 2cm diam., dark orange. 'Purple Wave': habit spreading, to 4m; lvs tinted red when young, later darker; fls single, purple; fr. purple. 'Radiant': habit dense, upright; lvs tinted red when young, later dark green; buds deep rd, fls profuse, single, dark pink; fr. small, to 13mm, light blackcurrant; seedling of 'Hopa'. 'Red Silver': lvs silver pubesc. when young, later chestnut to bronzed red; fls single, dark pink, later fading; fr. maroon; from 'Niedzwetzkyana'. 'Red Splendor': fls dark pink, later lighter; fr. to 1.5cm diam., red; from 'Red Silver'. 'Robin': fls dark pink, soon fading; fr. to 4cm diam, sunset orange, edible. 'Simcoe': fls single, dark pink, soon fading; fr. to 2.5cm diam., dark orange; from 'Niedzwetzkyana'. 'Sissipuk': fls single, rich dark red, fading to light pink, late; fr. to 2.5cm diam., purple. 'Timiskaming': lvs red in autumn; fls single, rich purple; fr., to 2cm diam., maroon. 'Transcendent': habit broad, shrub-like; buds pink, fls white; fr. striped dark yellow and red, sour, edible. 'Vanguard': habit narrow and upright, later spreading; lvs tinted red when young, later dark green; fls profuse, single, light pink; fr. to 2cm diam., vivid red. 'Wabiskaw': habit columnar to narrow upright, vigorous; lvs tinted red when young, later bronzed; fls single to semi-double, dark red stained purple, anth. gold; fr. to 3cm diam., dark pink. Z3.

M. angustifolia (Ait.) Michx. Shrub or small tree, 5–7m. Shoots soon glab. Lvs 3–7cm, lanceolate-oblong to oval, almost entire or serrate, smooth or felted beneath. Fls 2.5cm diam., whitepink, aromatic, in sparse corymbs; late flowering. Fr. 1.5–2.5cm, yellow-green, aromatic. S US. 'Prince Georges' (*M. angustifolia* × *M. ioensis* 'Plena'): shrub-like; lvs persistent; fls fragrant, pink, v. late; sterile. Z6.

M. ×arnoldiana (Rehd.) Sarg. (*M. baccata* ×*M. floribunda.*) Shrub to 2m, resembling *M. floribunda.* Shoots arching, soon glab. Lvs 5–8cm, elliptic to ovate, long-tapered, biserrate, ultimately glab. except for veins beneath. Fls 4–6 in cymes, carmine-red in bud, later pink becoming white. Fr. 15mm, globose, yellow-green. Gdn origin. 'Linda': fls single, carmine, later light pink; fr. to 3cm diam., carmine. Z4.

M. asiatica Nak. = *M. prunifolia* var. *rinki.*

M. ×astracanica Dum.-Cours. (*M. prunifolia* ×*M. pumila.*) Resembles *M. pumila,* differing in rougher, more deeply serrate lvs; fls bright red; fr. pruinose. Thought to have arisen in Asia. Z3.

M. ×atrosanguinea (Späth) Schneid. (*M. haliana* ×*M. sieboldii.*) Habit spreading, shoots slightly pendulous. Lvs ovate, serrate, basally lobed on strong shoots, waxy. Fls simple, deep carmine. Fr. 1cm, globose, red or yellow flushed red. Gdn origin. Z4.

M. baccata (L.) Borkh. Tree or shrub to 5m, often confused with *M. robusta,* shoots slender, glab. Lvs 3–8cm, ovate, longtapered, serrate, glab. Fls 3–3.5cm diam., in small clusters, white. Fr. 1cm, globose, yellow and red. NE Asia to N China. 'Columnaris': habit narrow upright, to 8×2m; fls snow white; fr. yellow with red cheek. 'Dolgo': habit shrub-like, upright; fls single, white, early; fr. to 3cm diam., bright red. 'Gracilis': habit shrub-like, slow-growing; br. slender, dense; lvs small, narrow; buds pink, fls white, stellate; fr. small red. 'Lady Northcliffe':

buds light pink, fls profuse, white; fr. to 1.5cm diam., dark orange. 'Macrocarpa': fr. large, to 3cm diam., glossy yellow stained red. 'Orange': habit large, shrub-like; buds light pink, fls white; fr. large, to 4cm diam.; red washed orange. 'Red River' ('Dolgo' ×'Delicious'): habit upright; fls single, pink; fr. large, to 5cm, bright red, edible. 'Rudolf': buds carmine, fls single, pink, later fading; fr. dark orange to red. 'Spring Snow': habit upright; fls large, white; fruitless; seedling of 'Dolgo'. var. *himalaica* (Maxim.) Schneid. Lvs wide, elliptic, roughly serrate, glab., veins on lower lf surfaces downy. Fls 3cm diam., pink in bud. Fr. 1–1.5cm, yellow flushed red. W Himal., SW China. var. *jackii* Rehd. Crown broader, br. stout. Lvs broadly elliptic. Fls 3cm diam., white. Fr. 1cm, red, waxy. Korea. var. *mandschurica* (Maxim.) Schneid. Lvs broadly elliptic, margins with few serrations, lower surfaces downy at first. Fls to 4cm diam., white, scented. Fr. 12mm, ellipsoid, bright red, ripening early. C Jap., C China. Z2.

M. bracteata Rehd. Resembles *M. ioensis*, differing in less deeply incised serrations and smaller lobes, often recurved. Small tree to 7m, shoots becoming glab. Lvs oval to ovate-elliptic, serrate, soon glab. Fls 3–5 in clusters, pink. Fr. 3cm, yellow. S US. Z6.

M. brevipes (Rehd.) Rehd. Crown stiff, compact. Lvs resemble those of *M. floribunda*, 5–7cm, finely serrate. Fls many, white-pale cream. Fr. subglobose, on rigid, red stalks, scarlet, slightly ribbed. Z5.

M. cerasifera Spach = *M. baccata* var. *mandschurica*.

M. communis Poir. = *M. pumila*.

M. coronaria (L.) Mill. Small tree to 7m wide, spreading, shoots with numerous short-thorned laterals, becoming glab. Lvs 5–10cm, ovate-oblong, pointed, serrate, slightly lobed, becoming glab. and scarlet-orange. Fls 4–6 in clusters, to 4cm diam., pink. Fr. 4cm, depressed globose, green, base slightly ribbed. NE US. 'Charlottae' ('Charlotta'): lvs red stained orange in autumn; fls double, soft pink, fragrant. 'Kola': habit conic, later spreading; crown rounded; lvs tinted silver; fls pink, fragrant; fr. large, waxy, yellow and stained green. 'Nieuwlandiana': habit shrub-like, to 3×3m; fls in large hanging clusters, vivid pink, v. fragrant; fr. blue pruinose. var. *dasycalyx* Rehd. Lvs paler green beneath. Fls smaller, 3.5cm diam., pink, highly aromatic. Fr. 4cm, yellow-green. N Amer. var. *elongata* (Rehd.) Rehd. Lvs larger, oval-narrow triangular or lanceolate, lobes reduced. Fls 3.5cm diam., pink. Fr. 3cm, green. US. Z4.

M. crataegifolia Koehne = *M. florentina*.

M. dasyphylla Borkh. = *M. pumila*.

M. ×dawsoniana Rehd. (*M. fusca* ×*M. pumila*.) Resembles *M. fusca*, differs in wider habit. Lvs 6–8cm, pointed, margins serrate, rarely lobed. Fls simple, 2.5–3.5cm diam., pale pink becoming white. Fr. 4×2.5cm, ellipsoid, yellow. Late flowering. Gdn origin. Z5.

M. ×denboerii Krüssm. (*M. ioensis* ×*M. ×purpurea*.) Resembles *M. ioensis*, but growth vigorous, more upright. Lvs on strong shoots resemble *M. ioensis*, others elliptic, unlobed, bronze-purple. Fls 2.5cm diam., deep pink. Fr. 2.5cm, globose, red, with red flesh. Gdn origin. 'Evelyn': upright, vigorous; lvs bronzed, tinted red in autumn; fls profuse, single, dark salmon; fr. to 3cm, tinted red. 'Lisa': less vigorous than 'Evelyn'; fls dark pink, later fading, fragrant; fr. small to 2.5cm diam., carmine, sometimes stained orange. Z4.

M. diversifolia Roem. = *M. fusca*.

M. domestica Poir. non Borkh. = *M. pumila*.

M. domestica Borkh. non Poir. = *M. sylvestris* var.*domestica*.

M. florentina (Zucc.) Schneid. Shrub at first, becoming a spreading tree to 8m, shoots downy. Lvs 5–7cm, hawthorn-like, broadly ovate, serrate, lobes incised, felted beneath, scarlet in fall. Fls white in downy clusters of 2–6. Fr. 1cm, ellipsoid, red. N It. Z6. Thought to be a hybrid between *Malus sylvestris* and *Sorbus torminalis* (×*Malosorbus florentina*).

M. floribunda Van Houtte. JAPANESE CRAB. Shrub to 4m, or tree to 10m, crown dense, shoot tips slightly pendulous, downy. Lvs 4–8cm, long-tapered, deeply serrate, sometimes slightly lobed. Fls 2.5–3cm diam., along br., deep pink in bud fading to pale pink, white inside. Fr. 0.5cm, yellow. Jap. 'Peachblow': habit upright; buds dark pink, fls white; fr. to 3cm, red. Z4.

M. floribunda var. *arnoldiana* Rehd. = *M. ×arnoldiana*.

M. floribunda var. *brevipes* Rehd. = *M. brevipes*.

M. formosana (Kawak. & Koidz.) Kawak. & Koidz. Tree or shrub to 12m, shoots downy, usually thorny. Lvs 8–15cm, ovate-oblong, pointed, unevenly serrate, soon glab. Fls 2.5cm diam., in small downy clusters. Fr. 4–5cm, ovoid. China, Taiwan. Z8.

M. fusca (Raf.) Schneid. Shrub to 7m or tree to 10m, shoots downy at first. Lvs 3–10cm, long-oval to oblong-elliptic, long-tapered, serrate, usually 3-lobed, becoming glab. Fls in clusters of 6–12, pink-white, soon fading. Fr. 1cm, yellow or red. W US. Z6.

M. glabrata Rehd. Differs from *M. glaucescens* in lvs plain green

beneath. Lvs fine, smooth, distinctly lobed. Fls 3cm diam., pink. Fr. 3cm, depressed-globose, yellow-green, base ribbed. SE US. Z6.

M. glaucescens Rehd. Shrub or small tree, spreading, br. sometimes thorny. Lvs 5–8cm, oval-triangular, pointed, shallowly triangular lobed, becoming glab., blue-green beneath. Fls 3.5cm diam., in clusters of 5–7, white-pink. Fr. 3–4cm, depressed-globose, yellow, shiny, aromatic. E US. Z5.

M. ×gloriosa Lemoine. (*M. pumila* 'Niedzwetzkyana' ×*M. ×schiedeckeri.*) Differs from *M. schiedeckeri* in bronze red young lvs, purple crimson fls to 4cm diam. Fr. to 3cm. Gdn origin. 'Oekonomierat Echtermeyer': habit widely pendulous; lvs tinted red when young, later bronzed green; fls single, carmine; fr. to 2.5cm diam., brown tinted red. Z4.

M. halliana Koehne. Shrub 2–4cm, crown irregular. Lvs 4–8cm, oval-oblong, pointed, margins with shallow rounded notches, red-green at first, glab. Fls 3–4cm diam., in small, often pendulous bunches of 4–7, red in bud opening deep pink, often semi-double. Fr. 6–8mm, obovoid, red-brown ripening late. China. 'Parkmanii': shrub-like; fls in hanging clusters, soft pink; fr. to 1.5cm diam., red. var. *spontanea* (Mak.) Koidz. Short, wide-spreading shrub. Lvs 3–4cm, elliptic to obovate. Fls to 3cm diam., smaller. Fr. 1cm, yellow-green. Jap. Z5.

M. ×hartwigii Koehne. (*M. baccata* ×*M. halliana.*) Br. ascending, shoots dark brown. Lvs 6–8cm, ovate, pointed, entire. Fls 4cm, semi-double, deep pink in bud fading white. Fr. 1cm, globose to pyriform, yellow-green. Gdn origin. 'Katherine': habit upright, slightly spreading; lvs acuminate; fls fully double, pink, later white; fr. to 1cm diam., yellow, sometimes tinted red. Z4.

M. 'Henrietta Crosby'. (*M. ×arnoldiana* ×*M. pumila* 'Niedzwetzkyana'.) Vigorous. Fls single, pink. Fr. to 2.5cm diam., vivid red. Z4.

M. 'Henry F Dupont'. (*M. ×arnoldiana* ×*M. ×purpurea* 'Eleyi'.) Habit spreading. Buds purple, fls single to semi-double, pink. Fr. to 12mm diam., red tinted brown, persistent. Z4.

M. ×heterophylla Spach. Resembles *M. ×soulardii* but lvs smaller, wider, with downy petioles; fls 4cm, pink in bud becoming white; fr. to 6cm, green. 'Red Tip': vigorous; lvs with red tips when young, orange in autumn; fls solitary, dark salmon; fr. large, to 4cm diam., yellow stained green. Z4.

M. honanensis Rehd. Shrub closely resembling *M. kansuensis*, less vigorous, more slender. Lvs 6–8cm, rounded-ovate, downy, margins with 2–5 pairs of serrated lobes, autumn colour scarlet. Fls 2cm diam., in clusters of about 10, white. Fr. 1cm, pitted, yellow-green. NE China. Z6.

M. hupehensis (Pamp.) Rehd. Tree or shrub, 5–7m; shoots spreading, soon glab. Lvs 5–10cm, ovate to oblong, long-tapered, deeply incised, slightly downy beneath. Fls 4cm diam., in clusters of 3–7, pink fading to white. Fr. 1cm, rounded, yellow-green, flushed red. India (Assam). 'Rosea': fls profuse, cherry blossom pink; fr. yellow, sometimes tinted red. Z4.

M. hybrida var. *gloriosa* Lemoine = *M. ×gloriosa*.

M. ioensis (Wood) Britt. PRAIRIE CRAB. Small tree, br. well-spaced, becoming glab., red-brown. Lvs 5–10cm, oblong-ovate, pointed, serrate, yellow-green felted beneath. Fls 4cm diam., white tinged pink, scented. Fr. 3cm, ellipsoid, shiny green. C US. 'Fimbriata': lvs narrower; fls double, pink, fimbriate. 'Klehm's': vigorous; lvs large; fls double, pink, fragrant; fr. sparse, green. 'Nova': fls dark pink, sterile; mutation of 'Plena'. 'Plena': (BECHTEL'S CRAB): fls profuse, v. large, double, soft pink; fr. to 3cm diam., green. 'Prairiefire': bark glossy dark red; lvs persistent; fls vivid red; fr. conic, maroon; disease and scab-resistant. var. *creniserrata* Rehd. Habit columnar, twigs downy at first, never thorny. Lvs elliptic-ovate to oval-oblong, scalloped or entire, almost biserrate. var. *palmeri* Rehd. Small tree, differing in smaller, finer, downy, more oblong lvs, scalloped only on flowering br. var. *spinosa* Rehd. Small shrub 1.5–2.5m, shoots slender, thorny. Lvs small, serrate, only lobed on strong shoots. Fls 3.5cm diam., pink. Fr. 3cm, green. var. *texana* Rehd. Shrub to 4m, shoots dense, first year wood felted. Lvs smaller but broader, lobes reduced or 0, felty. Z2.

*M. 'John Downie': see cvs at end.

M. kaido hort. ex K. Koch = *M. ×micromalus*.

M. kansuensis (Batal.) Schneid. Shrub or small tree to 5m, shoots, becoming glab., red-brown. Lvs 5–8, ovate with 3 or 5 lobes, serrate, paler beneath, downy on veins. Fls 1.5cm diam., in bunches of 4–10, white. Fr. 1cm, ellipsoid, yellow to purple, lightly pitted. NW China. f. *calva* Rehd. Lvs, cal. petiole and new growth always glab.; fr. deeper yellow. NW China. Z5.

M. lancifolia Rehd. Shrub or small tree to 6m, crown spreading, shoots thorny. Lvs 3–7cm, oval-lanceolate, sometimes rounded, pointed, biserrate, rarely lobed. Fls 3cm diam., in corymbs of 3–6, pet. rosy pink. Fr. 3cm in pendulous bunches, green, waxy. E US. Z5.

M. ×magdeburgensis Hartwig. (*M. pumila* ×*M. spectabilis*.)

Shrub or small tree, resembling *M. spectabilis*. Crown globose. Lvs 6–8cm, elliptic, acuminate, downy beneath. Fls 4.5cm diam., bright red in bud, opening deep pink. Fr. 3cm, rounded, green-yellow flushed red. Gdn origin. Z4.

M. 'Mary Potter'. (*M.* ×*atrosanguinea* × *M. sargentii* 'Rosea'.) Habit low, broad, vigorous. Buds pink, fls white. Fr. to 1cm diam., bright red.

M. ×*micromalus* Mak. (*M. baccata* × *M. spectabilis*.) Shrub or small erect tree, 4×3m; shoots soon glab., dark brown. Lvs 5–10cm, elliptic-oblong, long-tapered, coriaceous, serrulate, becoming glab., wavy. Fls 4.5cm diam., in clusters of 3–5, always pink. Fr. 1.5cm, slightly pointed, yellow, basal eye depressed. Jap. Z4.

M. ×*moerlandsii* Doorenbos. (*M.* ×*purpurea* 'Lemoinei' × *M. sieboldii*.) Tall shrub. Lvs green brown, slightly lobed, shiny. Fls red-pink, numerous. Fr. 1–1.5cm, rounded, purple. Gdn origin. 'Liset': habit shrub-like, upright; lvs maroon, later glossy dark green; fls profuse, single, vivid purple-red; fr. to 15mm diam., dark brown. 'Nicoline': habit shrub-like, tall; lvs purple stained green; fls in clusters, small, dark maroon. 'Profusion': upright, to 4m; lvs tinted red, later bronzed green; fls single, light maroon with pink centre; fr. small, to 1.5cm diam., oxblood-red, pruinose. Z5.

M. ×*platycarpa* Rehd. (*M. coronaria* × *M. pumila*.) Tree to 6m, crown spreading, shoots without thorns, felted only at first. Lvs 5–8cm, ovate to elliptic, apex rounded, roughly biserrate, occas. lobed on strong shoots, veins beneath downy. Fls 3.5cm diam., pink in bud opening white. Fr. 4–5cm, depressed-globose, yellow-green, rarely red, apex and base hollowed. SE US 'Hoopesii': lvs ± unlobed; fls pink washed white; fr. to 5cm diam., green. Z6.

M. prattii (Hemsl.) Schneid. Erect shrub or small tree to 7m, shoots downy at first. Lvs 6–15cm, elliptic-oblong, long-tapered, finely biserrate, veins downy beneath. Fls 2cm diam., in clusters of 7–10. Fr. 1–1.5cm, rounded-ovate, red or yellow, pitted. W China. Z6.

M. prunifolia (Willd.) Borkh. Small tree to 10m, shoots downy at first. Lvs 5–10cm, elliptic or ovate, sinuate, downy beneath. Fls 3cm diam., in clusters of 6–10, pink in bud opening white. Fr. 2cm, ovoid-conical, yellow-green to red. NE Asia. 'Cheal's Crimson': habit upright to broad, to 5m; buds pink, fls single, white; fr. prolific, to 2.5cm diam., light orange with scarlet cheek. 'Cheal's Golden Gem': fls single, white; fr. rounded, gold. 'Fastigiata': habit narrow upright, later spreading; fls white; fr. yellow and red. 'Hyslop': habit upright to spreading; crown broad; fr. globose, to 4cm diam., yellow stippled and blotched light red, edible. 'Pendula': br. weeping. var. *rinki* (Koidz.) Rehd. Lvs downy beneath. Fls 5cm diam., pink. Fr. 1.5–3cm, yellow-green, edible but bitter. Z3.

M. pumila Mill. Tree, 5–15m; crown rounded; shoots felted, thornless. Lvs 4–10cm, elliptic-ovate, sinuate, soon glab. Fls to 3cm diam., white, becoming pink. Fr. 2–6cm, rounded green, indented at both ends. Eur., Asia Minor (Cauc., Turkestan). The name *M. pumila* is also misapplied to *M. sylvestris* and its var. *domestica*. var. *paradisiaca* Schneid. PARADISE APPLE. Commonly used as a rootstock. Over 30 cvs, several descended from 'Niedzwetzkyana' (small tree; young growth red; fls purple-red; fr. large, conical, dark red, pruinose) known as the Rosybloom group. 'Aldenham Purple': fls lilac; fr. purple; 'Cowichan': fls white; 'Redford': fls and fr. red; 'Rosseau': lvs red; fls purple; fr. dark red; 'Scugog': fls pink; 'Sundog': fls pink; 'Thunderchild': fls pink; fr. purple. Other cvs notable for fl colour include: 'Dartmouth': fls white. 'Elise Rathke': weeping habit; fr. large, to 7cm diam., apple-shaped. 'Garry': fls purple; fr. carmine. 'Kingsmere': fls purple; fr. carmine. 'Montreal Beauty': fls white. 'Redfield': fls and fr. red. 'Trial': fls white. 'Translucent': fls white. 'Veitch's Scarlet': fls white; fr. bright scarlet. Z3.

M. ×*purpurea* (Barbier) Rehd. (*M. astrosanguinea* × *M. pumila* 'Niedzwetzkyana'.) Large shrub or small tree, bark red-black. Lvs 8–9cm, ovate, scalloped, occas. lobed, brown-red at first, shiny. Fls 3–4cm diam., purple-red, soon fading. Fr. 1.5–2.5cm, rounded, purple-red. Gdn origin. 'Aldenhamensis': habit shrub-like, low-growing to 3.5m; lvs bronze red; buds deep red, fls profuse, maroon; fr. red tinted brown. 'Amisk': buds carmine, fls simple, pink; fr. conic, to 3cm diam., red and yellow. 'Chilko': fls single, light maroon, later darker; fr. scarlet. 'Eleyi': habit shrub-like, slightly spreading; lvs darker; fls single, maroon; fr. ovate, purple. 'Eleyi Compacta': habit compact, shrub-like; br. short; lvs, fls and fr. purple. 'Hoser': buds dark purple; fls pink; fr. pruinose purple. 'Jadwiga': habit pendulous; crown broad; buds maroon, fls pink; fr. conic, to 5cm diam., blackcurrant purple. 'Jay Darling': fls maroon; fr., to 2.5cm diam., purple. 'Kobendza': fls purple washed brown outside, pink inside; fr. globose, to 1.5cm diam., purple. 'Lemoinei': habit shrub-like, upright, vigorous; lvs dark purple,

later bronzed or dark green; fls single to semi-double, maroon; fr. to 1.5cm diam., dark purple. 'Neville Copeman': fr. dark orange to vivid carmine; seedling of 'Eleyi'. 'Sophia': buds dark purple, fls fading to pink; fr. small, globose, pruinose purple. 'Szafer': buds violet, fls fading to lilac washed light pink; fr. small, to 12mm, globose, purple. 'Wierdak': buds oblong, rich purple, fls lilac washed pink; fr. to 1.5cm diam., glossy maroon. Z4.

M. ringo Sieb. ex Dipp. = *M. prunifolia* var. *rinki*.
M. ringo var. *sublobata* Dipp. = *M. sublobata*.
M. rivularis M. Roem. = *M. fusca*.
M. ×*robusta* (Carr.) Rehd. (*M. baccata* × *M. prunifolia*.) Vigorous, conical shrub or small tree. Lvs 8–11cm, elliptic, margins scalloped, bright green. Fls 3–4cm diam., in corymbs of 3–8, white occas. pink. Fr. 1–3cm, ellipsoid to rounded, yellow or red, long-stalked, sometimes pruinose. Gdn origin. 'Alexis': buds light pink, fls single, white; fr. to 3cm diam., vivid pink-red, pruinose. 'Beauty': habit narrowly upright; fls single, white; fr. to 3cm diam., scarlet. 'Erecta': habit narrowly upright when young, later spreading; fls single to semi-double, white stained light pink; fr. small, to 2cm diam., yellow with red cheeks, pruinose. 'Fairy': habit upright, vigorous; fls single, white; fr. large, to 4cm diam., scarlet. 'Joan': fls single, white, early; fr. large, to 35mm, scarlet, persistent. 'Red Sentinel': fls single, white, early; fr. glossy scarlet, persistent. 'Red Siberian': fr. bright red. 'Yellow Siberian': fr. yellow. var. *persicifolia* Rehd. Large shrub, br. slender. Lvs 5–10cm, oval-lanceolate, finely scalloped. Fls 4cm diam., numerous, pink in bud opening white. Fr. 2cm, abundant, rounded or oblong, red. N China. Z3.

M. rockii Rehd. Resembles *M. baccata*, young shoots densely downy, tufted. Lvs to 12cm, elliptic to ovate, shallowly serrate, downy beneath. Fls 2.5cm diam., red-pink in bud, opening white. Fr. ovoid to globose, sometimes tapered, yellow flushed red. W China. Z5.

M. sargentii Rehd. Shrub to 2m, spreading, thorny. Lvs 5–8cm, ovate, serrate with 3 lobes, orange in fall. Fls 2.5cm diam., along whole length of shoot, buds pale pink, opening white. Fr. 1cm, globose, dark red. 'Rosea': buds dark pink, fls fading to white. Z4.

M. ×*schiedeckeri* Späth ex Zab. (*M. floribunda* × *M. prunifolia*.) Shrub to 3m, shoots erect, downy at first. Lvs ovate, serrate, usually with a large tooth, downy beneath. Fls 4–5cm diam., semi-double, pale pink, deeper in bud. Fr. 1cm, yellow-orange, pedicel long. Gdn origin. 'Barbara Ann': lvs tinted red; fls semi-double, maroon fading to pink; fr. to 12mm diam., purple. 'Dorothea': low and slow-growing; fls semi-double to double, carmine to pink; fr. to 13mm diam., yellow. 'Exzellenz Thiel': br. strongly pendulous; buds pink, fls white; fr. to 2cm diam., yellow and red. 'Hillieri': shrub-like, vigorous; fls semi-double, light pink; fr. globose, to 2cm diam., yellow and orange. 'Red Jade': twigs slender, pseudulous; buds pink, fls white; fr. to 1.5cm, scarlet; probably a seedling of 'Exzellenz Thiel'. Z4.

M. 'Selkirk'. (*M. baccata* × *M. pumila*.) Vigorous; crown rounded. Fls in clusters, clear pink. Fr. bright scarlet. Z4.

M. sempervirens Desf. = *M. angustifolia*.
M. sibirica Borkh. = *M. baccata*.
M. sieboldii (Reg.) Rehd. Shrub to 4m, shoots arched, black-brown. Lvs 3–6cm, ovate-elliptic, dentate and 3–5-lobed, downy, red or yellow in fall. Fls 2cm diam., deep pink in bud, eventually white. Fr. small, globose, red to yellow-brown, persistent. Jap. 'Fuji': habit low, spreading; fls anemone-centred, white stained green or purple; fr. small, to 12mm, orange. 'Gorgeous': habit shrub-like, upright; fls soft pink, fading to white; fr. prolific, large, to 2.5cm diam., dark orange to light red. 'Henry Kohankie': pendulous; fr. in clusters, to 4, large, to 3.5×3cm, scarlet. 'Seafoam': ± pendulous; fls solitary, dark carmine, fading to white flushed with pink. 'White Angel': upright, later nodding; fls in clusters, to 6, snow-white; fr. prolific, small, scarlet. 'Winterglod': shrub-like, upright to spreading; lvs irregularly serrate; buds pink, fls fading white; fr. gold, persistent. var. *arborescens* Rehd. Tree to 10m. Lvs large, less conspicuously lobed. Fls 3cm diam., white. Fr. 1cm, yellow-red. Korea. Z5.

M. sieboldii var. *calocarpa* Rehd. = *M.* ×*zumi* var. *calocarpa*.
M. sikkimensis (Wenz.) Koehne. Tree, 5–7m, resembles *M. baccata*; shoots felted. Lvs 5–7cm, oval-oblong, long-tapered, deeply serrate, felted beneath. Fls 2.5cm diam., in clusters of 4–9, white, sometimes pale pink. Fr. 1.5cm, pyriform, yellow-red, pitted. N India. Z6.

M. sinensis Dum.-Cours. = *Pseudocydonia sinensis*.
M. ×*soulardii* (Bail.) Britt. (*M. ioensis* × *M. pumila*.) Tall shrub. Lvs 5–8cm, broad-elliptic, scalloped, slightly lobed, coriaceous, downy beneath. Fls 3.5cm diam., pink, soon fading. Fr. to 5cm, yellow-green flushed red. US. 'Red Flesh': lvs bronzed red; fls single, carmine to light maroon; fr. scarlet. 'Wynema': habit low, open, spreading, to 4m; fls single, salmon pink, later dark-

er, late; fr. large, to 5cm diam., scarlet, sometimes with red cheeks, edible. Z4.

M. **spectabilis** (Ait.) Borkh. ASIATIC APPLE. Large shrub or small tree to 8m, pyramidal at first, later spreading; shoots becoming red-brown. Lvs 5–8cm, elliptic-oblong, short-tapered, dentate, downy beneath. Fls 4–5cm diam., single or semi-double, dark pink in bud, opening pale pink. Fr. 2–3cm, rounded, yellow. China. 'Blanche Amis': habit shrub-like, upright; buds carmine, fls semi-double, white inside, dark carmine outside; fr. globose, small, to 8mm diam., yellow. 'Dorothy Rowe': fls single to semi-double, light cream, anth. yellow; fr. scarlet. 'Plena' ('Frau Luise Dittman'): fls profuse, double, pink, soon fading; fr. globose, to 2cm diam., yellow. 'Riversii': fls double, pink; fr. large, to 3.5cm diam., yellow. Z4.

M. spectabilis 'Kaido'. = *M.* ×*micromalus*.

M. **sublobata** (Dipp.) Rehd. (*M. prunifolia* ×*M. sieboldii*.) Tree; crown conical, shoots downy. Lvs 4–8cm, narrow-elliptic, sometimes with 1–2 lobes, felted at first. Fls to 4cm diam., pale pink. Fr. 1.5cm, subglobose, yellow. Jap. Z6.

M. **sylvestris** (L.) Mill. EUROPEAN APPLE; WILD CRAB. Tree or shrub to 7m, slightly thorny. Lvs 4–8cm, oval to rounded, scalloped or incised, subglabrous. Fls to 4cm diam., pink-white outside, pinker within. Fr. 2–4cm, rounded, yellow-green flushed red. C Eur. 'Plena': fls double, soft pink, fading to snow white; fr. scarlet, sometimes blotched yellow; often listed as *M. spectabilis alba plena*. var. **domestica** (Borkh.) Mansf. ORCHARD APPLE. The form giving rise to cultivated apples.

M. theifera Rehd. = *M. hupehensis*.

M. toringo Sieb. = *M. sieboldii*.

M. **toringoides** (Rehd.) Hughes. Shrub or small tree to 8m, soon glab. Lvs 3–8cm, ovate and crenately lobed or simple, veins downy beneath. Fls 2cm diam., in bunches of 3–6, white. Fr. 1.5cm, globose to pyriform, yellow flushed red, persistent. W China. Z5.

M. **transitoria** (Batal.) Schneid. Closely resembles *M. toringoides*, smaller, narrower; shoots felted when young; lvs 2–3cm, broadly ovate, deeply narrow-lobed, downy; fls to 2cm diam.; white; fr. 1.5cm, red. NW China. Z5.

M. transitoria var. *toringoides* Rehd. = *M. toringoides*.

M. **trilobata** (Labill.) Schneid. Erect shrub or small tree. Lvs 5–8cm, 3-lobed, shiny, soon glab., intense red in fall. Fls 3.5cm diam., in clusters of 6–8, white. Fr. 2cm, ellipsoid, red. W Asia. Z6.

M. **tschonoskii** (Maxim.) Schneid. Tree to 12m, pyramidal then spreading; shoots felted. Lvs 7–12cm, ovate-elliptic, serrate to slightly lobed, white felted at first, orange-red in fall. Fls 3cm diam., in clusters of 2–5, white. Fr. 2–3cm, rounded, yellow-green flushed red. Jap. Z6.

M. **'Van Eseltine'**. (*M.* ×*arnoldiana* ×*M. spectabilis*.) Habit upright to columnar. Fls vivid pink. Fr. to 2cm diam., yellow with red cheek or completely yellow. Z4.

M. yezoensis Koidz. = *M. prunifolia* var. *rinki*.

M. **yunnanensis** (Franch.) Schneid. Compact, erect tree to 10m, shoots felted at first. Lvs 6–12cm, broadly ovate, roughly biserrate, occas. with 3–5 pairs of broad lobes, felted beneath, red-orange in fall. Fls 1.5cm diam., usually in crowded corymbs to 5cm, white. Fr. 1–1.5cm, red, pitted. W China. var. *veitchii* Rehd.. Lvs ovate, base strongly cordate, margins slightly lobed, soon glab. Fls smooth, to 1.2cm diam. Fr. to 1.3cm, red with white pits. C China. Z6.

M. ×*zumi* (Matsum.) Rehd. (*M. baccata* var. *mandshurica* ×*M. sieboldii*.) Small pyramidal tree, shoots ± downy. Lvs 5–9cm, ovate, long tapered, scalloped to lobed, downy beneath at first. Fls 3cm diam., pink bud, fading to white. Fr. 1cm, rounded, red. Jap. var. *calocarpa* Rehd. More spreading; lvs smaller, always entire on fruiting wood, distinctly lobed on strong shoots; fls smaller, white. Fr. 1–1.3cm, prolific in crowded bunches, scarlet. 'Bob White': buds soft pink, fls single, fading to white; fr. small, to 1.5cm diam., muddy yellow, persistent throughout winter. 'Golden Hornet': fls white; fr. to 3cm diam., gold. 'Professor Sprenger': fr. to 1cm diam., orange, persistent. Z5.

M. **cvs**. 'Adams': disease-resistant. 'Brandywine': rose-form pink fls and silver winter bark. 'Centurion': fls bright red. 'Coralburst': dwarf. 'Gibbs Golden Gage': late flowering, fr. prolific, waxy translucent yellow, winter-persistent. 'Indian Magic': fr. prolific, scarlet. 'John Downie': fls large, white; fr. large, conical bright red and orange, edible. V. popular. 'Red Baron': fls and fr. dark red. 'Ormiston Roy': late flowering, winter persistent. 'Pink Spire': narrowly upright. 'Snowdrift': fls large, white. 'Strawberry Parfait': fls single, pink, fragrant. 'Sugar Tyme': disease-resistant.

→*Eriolobus* and *Pyrus*.

Malva L. Malvaceae. MALLOW. 30 ann. or perenn. herbs and subshrubs. Lvs orbicular, suborbicular, cordate or reniform, en-

tire to lobed. Fls axill., solitary or in clusters; epical. 1–3-parted; cal. 5-lobed; pet. 5, free obcordate; styles linear-filiform. Fr. a discoid schizocarp, mericarps 1-seeded. Eur., Asia, Trop. & S Afr., Indomal.; widely introd.

M. **alcea** L. Perenn. herb to 80cm; st. pilose. Lower lvs suborbicular, crenate, upper lvs palmatisect. Pet. 2.5–4cm, pale red. Mericarps rugose, with a dors. crest. S Eur., nat. US. 'Fastigiata': to 1m, habit narrowly upright; fls deep pink. Z4.

M. crispa (L.) L. = *M. verticillata*.

M. involucrata Torr. & A. Gray = *Callirhoë involucrata*.

M. mauritiana L. = *M. sylvestris*.

M. **moschata** L. MUSK MALLOW. Perenn. erect to 1m; st. hirsute. Basal lvs shallowly 3-lobed, upper lvs deeply divided, 3-, 5- or 7-lobed, lobes pinnatifid or bipinnatifid. Pet. 2–3cm, white or pink. Mericarps hispid, white-pubesc. Eur., NW Afr., nat. US. 'Alba': to 60cm; lvs deeply cut; fls silky white. 'Rosea': fls rose tinted purple. Z3.

M. **neglecta** Wallr. COMMON MALLOW. Ann. to 50cm; st. prostrate to ascending, pilose. Lvs suborbicular, shallowly lobed, crenate, pilose. Pet. 0.8–1.2cm, hairy at base, pink or white. Mericarps pilose, smooth. Eur., NW Afr., SW Asia, nat. US.

M. **nicaeensis** All. Ann. or short-lived perenn. to 50cm; st. ascending, sparsely pilose. Lvs suborbicular or with lobes 3, 5 or 7, shallow, crenate-dentate. Pet. 0.8–1.2cm, pink-lilac, hairy at base. Mericarps reticulate, glab. or hairy. Medit., Arabia to Iran, S Russia; nat. US. Z7.

M. setosa Moench = *M. nicaeensis*.

M. **sylvestris** L. TALL MALLOW; HIGH MALLOW; CHEESES. Perenn. to 1m; st. erect or ascending, pilose. Lvs broadly cordate or suborbicular, to 10cm diam., 3-, 5- or 7-lobed. Pet. 1.5–2cm, mauve, paler and hairy at base, notched at apex. Mericarps glab. or pubesc. rugose-reticulate on dors. side. Eur., N Afr., SW Asia; introd. US as gdn escape. 'Alba': to 75cm; fls pure white, along st. 'Brave Heart': habit upright, to 90cm; lvs large; fls large, pale purple with dark eye. 'Cottenham Blue': to 75cm; fls pale blue, veins darker, early flowering. 'Primley Blue': habit prostrate, to 20cm; fls soft violet, veins darker. Z5.

M. **verticillata** L. Ann. or bienn. to 1.8m; st. erect. Lvs suborbicular, 5- or 7-lobed. Pet. 1–1.2cm, white or purple. Mericarps glab., transverse-ridged. Eur., Asia, nat. US. 'Crispa': 2m; lvs wavy-edged; fls small, pale lavender, grouped in axils; ann. or bienn. Z6.

MALVACEAE Juss. 116/1550. *Abelmoschus, Abutilon, Alcea, Alogyne, Althaea, Anisodontea, Anoda, Asterotrichion, Bakeridesia, Callirhoë, Eremalche, Goethea, Gossypium, Gynatrix, Hibiscus, Hoheria, Howittia, Iliamna, Kitaibela, Kokia, Kosteletzkya, Kydia, Lagunaria, Lavatera, Malachra, Malacothamnus, Malope, Malva, Malvaviscus, Napaea, Pavonia, Phymosia, Plagianthus, Radyera, Robinsonella, Sida, Sidalcea, Sphaeralcea, Thespesia, Wercklea.*

Malva Rosa *Lavatera assurgentiflora.*

Malvastrum A. Gray.
M. **fasciculatum** var. *laxiflorum* (A. Gray) Munz & I.M. Johnst. = *Malacothamnus fasciculatus*.

M. hypomandarum Sprague = *Anisodontea* × *hypomandarum*.

M. rotundifolium A. Gray = *Eremalche rotundifolia*.

M. virgatum (Murray) A. Gray & Harv. = *Anisodontea capensis*.

Malvaviscus Adans. Malvaceae. 3 shrubs, sometimes vine-like. Lvs unlobed or palmately lobed. Fls solitary in axils or in term. few-fld rac. or cymes; epical. seg. 6–16; cor. funnelform; column, exceeding pet.; ovary 5-celled. Fr. a berry; seeds with red fleshy coat. C & S Amer. Z9.

M. **arboreus** Cav. WAX MALLOW. To 4m. Lvs 0–3-lobed, velvety, 6–12cm, ovate or cordate to suborbicular, toothed, downy. Fls long-stalked; pet. 2.5–5cm, rich red. Mex. to Peru and Braz. var. *drummondii* (Torr. & A. Gray) Schery. Lvs almost as long as broad, lobed with simple hairs above; pet. 2.5–3cm. Flor., Tex., Mex. var. *mexicanus* Schldl. TURK'S CAP. Almost glabrate; lvs lanceolate to ovate, ± unlobed. Pet. 2.5–5cm. Mex. to Colomb.

M. **candidus** Moc. & Sessé ex DC. Differs from *M. arboreus* in 5-lobed lvs, to 18cm, hairy throughout; pet. to 8cm, to ⅔ length staminal column. Mex.

M. conzatti Greenman. = *M. arboreus* var. *mexicanus*.

M. drummondii Torr. & A. Gray = *M. arboreus* var. *drummondii*.

M. grandiflorus Moc. & Sessé ex DC. = *M. arboreus* var. *mexicanus*.

M. mollis Ait. DC. = *M. arboreus*.

Mamaku *Cyathea medullaris.*

Mamane *Sophora chrysophylla.*

Mamillopsis (Morr.) Britt. & Rose.
M. senilis (Salm-Dyck) Britt. & Rose = *Mammillaria senilis.*

Mammea L. Guttiferae. 50 everg. trees or shrubs with white or yellow latex. Lvs entire, leathery to papery with glands or secretory channels. Fls solitary or in short cymes, sometimes cauliflorous; cal. bilobed; pet. 4 (–5–6), caducous; sta. (in ♂ fls) numerous, fused at base, fewer or staminodal in ♀ fls; ovary 2–4-locular. Fr. a berry or drupe. Trop. Amer. (1), Afr. (1), Madag., Indomalesia, Pacific. Z10.

M. africana Sab. Tree, 30–45m. Lvs 9–35cm, oblong to elliptic, acuminate, glossy. Fls solitary, white to 4cm across; ♂ fls smaller. Fr. 10–18cm diam., orange, spotted brown, subglobose to pyriform, pericarp thick, aril yellow. Trop. Afr.

M. americana L. MAMMEE; MAMMEE APPLE; SOUTH AMERICAN APRICOT. Tree to 18m. Lvs to 25cm, obovate, obtuse, glossy, translucent-spotted. Fls solitary, axill., fragrant, white, 2.5cm across. Fr. to 15cm diam., globose, pericarp russet, leathery, aril yellow, sweet and fragrant. Carib., S Amer.

M. siamensis (Miq.) Anderson. Tree to 10m. Lvs 15–20cm, linear-oblong to oblong-lanceolate, obtuse. Fls axill., solitary, paired, white, to 1.6cm across or clustered, fragrant. Fr. ovoid, mucronate, 3cm diam., glab. Thail.

Mammee, Mammee Apple *Mammea americana.*
Mammee Sapote *Pouteria sapota.*

Mammillaria Haw. Cactaceae. 150 low-growing cacti, simple or clustering; st. globose to cylindric, tuberculate; dors. portion of areoles at tubercle-apex, spiny; ventral portion 'axillary', naked, felted, or bristly. Fls at 'axillary' areoles solitary, campanulate to funnelform; tube short. Fr. berry-like. SW US, Mex., C Amer., Carib. region, Colomb., Venez. Z10.

M. aggregata Engelm. = *Echinocereus triglochidiatus* var. *melanacanthus.*

M. alamensis Craig = *M. sheldonii.*

M. albescens Tiegel. Intermediate between *M. decipiens* and *M. camptotricha*; central spines 0, radial spines shorter and straighter than in *M. captotricha*, white. Autumn. EC Mex.

M. albicans (Britt. & Rose) A. Berger. Clustering; st. to 15cm or more ×4cm, cylindric; axils woolly and bristly; central spines mostly 4–8, 7–10mm, straight, radial spines 14–21, 5–8mm. Fl. pink or nearly white with purple stigmas. Summer. NW Mex.

M. albicoma Boed. Clustering; st. to 5×3cm; axils with hair-like bristles; central spines 0 or 3–4, 4–5mm, straight, white, tipped darker, radial spines 30–40, 8–10mm, hair-like, white. Fl. creamy. Summer. NE Central Mex.

M. albilanata Backeb. Simple or offsetting; st. to 15×8cm, shortly cylindric; tubercles conic; axils hoary; central spines 2 or 4, v. short or up to 7mm, white at first, brown tipped, radial spines 18–22, 2–6mm, white, brown at base. Fl. dark carmine red. Spring. SW Mex.

M. angularis Link & Otto ex Pfeiff. = *M. compressa.*

M. anniana Glass & Fost. Clustering; st. to 3cm diam., tubercles 4–7mm, axils with 4–5 hair-like bristles to 13mm; central spines 5–9, 9–12mm, one often hooked, yellow, radial spines 13–14, 6–11mm, stiff, pale. Fl. pale yellow. Spring. NE Mex.

M. applanata Engelm. ex Salm-Dyck = *M. heyderi.*

M. arida Rose ex Quehl. Resembling *M. baxteriana*. Simple; central spines 4–7, 12–16mm, dark brown, finely acicular, radial spines c15, pale. Summer. NW Mex.

M. arizonica Engelm. = *Escobaria vivipara.*

M. armillata K. Brandg. Simple or clustering, narrowly columnar, to 30×4.5cm; tubercles somewhat ascending; axils sparsely woolly, with bristles; central spines 1–4, 10–20mm, one or more hooked, yellow-brown, radial spines 9–15, 7–12mm. Fl. pale yellow or flesh-coloured, stigmas tinged pink. Summer. Baja Calif.

M. aureilanata Backeb. St. simple, base tuberous; tubercles cylindric; axils naked; central spines 0, radial spines 25–30, setaceous to wool-like, transparent then pale yellow. Fl. white to v. pale pink. Spring. NE Mex.

M. aurihamata Boed. Clustering; st. to globose to ovoid; axils with about 8 white bristles; central spines 4, lowermost hooked, 1.5–2.5cm, radial spines 15–20, to 8mm. Fl. pale yellow. Spring. NC Mex.

M. backebergiana Buchenau. Usually simple; st. 4–6cm diam., cylindric, tubercles ± pyramidal, 5mm; axils naked or rarely with 1–3 bristles; central spines 1–3, 7–8mm, yellow to brown, radial spines 10–12, 8–10mm, brown-tipped. Fl. purple-red, stigmas green. Spring. C Mex.

M. barbata Engelm. Simple or clustering; st. depressed-globose; tubercles 8×3mm; axils naked; central spines several, 1–2 hooked, erect, dark, radial spines seriate, outermost to 40,

hair-like, inner 10–15, stronger. Fl. exterior green, interior rose to gold or pale green; stigmas green-yellow. Spring. N Mex.

M. baumii Boed. Densely clustering; st. to 6–7×5–6cm, subglobose to ovoid; tubercles cylindric; areoles white wool at first; axils soon naked; central spines 5–6(–8–11), to 18mm, acicular, pale yellow, radial spines 30–35(–50), up to 15mm, v. thin. Fl. exterior green-brown, interior yellow. Spring. NE Mex.

M. baxteriana (Gates) Backeb. & F. Knuth. Simple or clustering; st. to 10cm diam., depressed-globose; tubercles conic; axils with white wool; central spines usually 1, 15–20mm, white with brown tip, radial spines 8–10, the lower to 15mm, white. Fl. yellow with light red markings on outer tep. Summer. NW Mex.

M. bella Backeb. Usually simple; st. to 15×9cm; tubercles conic; axils bristly; central spines 4–6, c20mm lowermost to 30mm, sometimes hooked, tipped red, radial spines to 20, to 8mm glassy white. Fl. carmine; stigmas green. Summer. SW Mex.

M. beneckei Ehrenb. Simple or clustering; st. to c10×7cm, globose to short-cylindric; tubercles soft; central spines 2–6, 8–12mm, 1 or 2 longer, hooked, dark, radial spines 8–15, 6–8mm, pale. Fl. orange-yellow. Summer. W Mex.

M. blossfeldiana Boed. Simple or clustering; st. globose to short-cylindric; axils sparsely woolly, without bristles; central spines 4, the upper like the radials, the lower hooked, 10(–12)mm, dark, radial spines 13–20, 5–7(–10)mm, pale yellow, dark-tipped. Fl. nearly white with rose stripes. Summer. C Baja Calif.

M. bocasana Poselger. Freely clustering; st. ± globose, almost hidden by spines; axils naked or with fine hairs or bristles; central spines 1(–5), 5–10mm, 1–2 hooked, red or brown, radial spines 25–50, 8–10(–20)mm, hair like, white. Fl. creamy white; outer tep. with pale pink stripe. Spring. C Mex.

M. bocensis Craig. Simple or clustering; st. depressed-globose to short cylindrical; axils usually without bristles; central spines 1, 8–12mm, red-brown, radial spines 6–8, 5–14mm, chalky white to red, dark-tipped. Fl. pale pink or green with brown stripes. Summer. NW Mex.

M. bogotensis Werderm. = *M. columbiana.*

M. bombycina Quehl. Clustering, st. to 20×7–8cm, short cylindric, tubercular axils white-woolly; central spines 4, lowest longest, 20mm, hooked, yellow- or red-brown, radial spines 30–40, up to 10mm, white. Fl. carmine red. Spring. WC Mex.

M. boolii Lindsay. Simple or rarely clustering; st. to 5cm diam., globose; axils naked; central spines 1, 15–20mm, hooked, horn-coloured, radial spines about 20, 15mm, white. Fl. pink or lavender pink; stigmas pale green. Summer. NW Mex.

M. brandegeei (J. Coult.) K. Brandg. Simple; st. globose to cylindric; axils woolly in youth; central spines (1–)3–4, 10–12mm, red-brown, black-tipped, radial spines about 10, 7–10mm, rigid white. Fl. pale yellow, tinged green or brown. Summer. NW Mex.

M. brauneana Boed. Simple; st. globose; axils with wool and bristles; central spines 2–4, 7–9mm, red-brown or horn-coloured, radial spines 25–30, up to 5mm. Fl. red-violet. Spring. NE Mex.

M. bravoae Craig. Resembling *M. hahniana*. Simple or later clustering; st. globose; axils with wool and bristles; central spines 2, 6–8mm, brown, tinged pink, black tipped, radial spines 28–30, 4–7mm, white. Fl. deep pink; stigmas pink-brown. Spring–summer. EC Mex.

M. bucareliensis Craig = *M. magnimamma.*

M. bullardiana (Gates) Backeb. & F. Knuth = *M. hutchisoniana.*

M. bumamma Ehrenb. = *Coryphantha bumamma.*

M. caerulea Craig = *M. chionocephala.*

M. calacantha Tiegel. Resembling *M. rhodantha*, but with strongly curved and ± adpressed central spines. Simple; st. globose to short cylindric; axils with wool at first and sparse bristles; central spines 2 or 4, up to 15mm, acicular, at first red-brown, becoming paler, radial spines usually 25, 5–6mm, pale yellow. Fl. carmine. Summer. C Mex.

M. camptotricha Dams. Clustering; st. c4–7cm diam., globose; tubercles elongate; areoles woolly at first; axils sparsely hairy with few bristles; central spines 0, radial spines (2–4)4–5(–8), up to 3cm, straight to curved or tortuous, white to golden brown. Fls white, scented. Autumn. EC Mex.

M. candida Scheidw. Simple or clustering; individual st. to c14cm diam., globose to stoutly cylindric; tubercles cylindric; areoles with scant wool; axils with fine white bristles; central spines 8–12, to 1cm, white or tipped pink or brown, radial spines numerous, to 1.5cm, white. Fl. rose pink, stigmas purple-red. Spring. NE Mex.

M. canelensis Craig. Simple; st. globose; axils woolly and bristly, central spines 2–4, to 3cm, straight to curved, yellow to orange-brown, radial spines 22–25, 5–15mm, fine, white. Fls red or yellow. Summer. NW Mex.

M. capensis (Gates) Craig. Clustering; st. to 25×3–5cm, cylindric; axils naked or with 1–3 bristles; central spines, 1, 15–20mm long, hooked or straight, white to red-brown tipped black, radial spines 13, 8–15mm. Fl. pale pink; stigmas green-yellow. Summer. Baja Calif.

M. caput-medusae Link & Otto ex Pfeiff. = *M. sempervivi.*

M. carmenae Castañeda. Clustering; st. globose to ovoid; central spines 0, radial spines more than 100, up to 5mm long, pale, ± ascending. Fl. white, tinged pink or cream; stigmas yellow. Spring. EC Mex.

M. carnea Zucc. Simple or more often clustering; st. to 85mm diam., globose to clavate-cylindric; tubercles 4-angled, often red-brown towards tip; axils with wool but no bristles; spines usually 4, all 6–15mm, or uppermost to 20mm, or lowermost to 50mm, pink-brown, tipped black. Fl. flesh pink. Spring. S Mex.

M. carretii Rebut ex Schum. Simple or clustering; st. depressed-globose, tubercles 7–10×7mm; central spine 1, 14–18mm, hooked, brown, radial spines 12–14, to 13mm, pale yellow. Fl. creamy white; inner tep. with pink stripe. Spring. NE Mex.

M. celsiana Lem., misapplied. = *M. muehlenpfordtii.*

M. centricirrha Lem. = *M. magnimamma.*

M. cephalophora Quehl, non Salm-Dyck = *M. aureilanata.*

M. ceratites Quehl = *Neolloydia conoidea.*

M. chapinensis Eichlam & Quehl = *M. voburnensis.*

M. chionocephala Purpus. Simple or clustering; st. subglobose to shortly cylindric; axils with wool and bristles up to 2cm; central spines 2–4 rarely 5–6, 4–6mm white or dark tipped, radial spines 22–24 up to 8mm, white. Fl. nearly white or flesh with red stripe. Spring. NE Mex.

M. chlorantha Engelm. = *Escobaria vivipara.*

M. cirrifera Mart. = *M. compressa.*

M. clava Pfeiff. = *Coryphantha octacantha.*

M. coahuilensis (Boed.) Moran. Simple; st. to 5cm diam., globose; tubercles trigonous; axils sparsely woolly; central spines 1, 6mm, straight, brown-tipped, radial spines *c*16(–25), weaker, grey-white, the lower to 6mm, all spines finely pubesc. Fl. with outer tep. rose with pale brown mid-stripe, inner white with rose mid-stripe; stigmas yellow-green. Spring. N Mex.

M. collina Purpus = *M. haageana.*

M. collinsii (Britt. & Rose) Orcutt = Fl. *voburnensis.*

M. columbiana Salm-Dyck. Simple or clustering; st. cylindric; axils woolly; central spines 3–7, 6-8mm, pale yellow to brown, radial spines 18–20(–30), 4–6mm, white. Fl. pink. Spring. SE Mex., Guat., Jam., N & S Amer.

M. compacta Engelm. = *Coryphantha compacta.*

M. compressa DC. Series *Mammillaria.* Clustering; individual st. 5–8cm diam., clavate-cylindric; tubercles gibbous, angled; axils with wool and, usually, bristles; spines 4–6, unequal, lowermost to 15–70mm, white to pale red with darker tip. Fl. deep purple-pink. Spring. C Mex.

M. confusa (Britt. & Rose) Orcutt = *M. karwinskiana.*

M. conoidea DC. = *Neolloydia conoidea.*

M. conspicua Purpus = *M. haageana.*

M. cornifera DC. = *Coryphantha cornifera.*

M. cowperae Shurly = *M. moelleriana.*

M. craigii Lindsay. Simple; st. depressed globose; axils woolly; central spine 1, up to 3cm, golden with brown tip, radial spines 8, up to 2.5cm. Fl. deep purple-pink; stigmas green-yellow. Summer. NW Mex.

M. crocidata Lem. = *M. polythele.*

M. crucigera Mart. Simple or branching; st. cylindric or obovate; axils with white wool; central spines 4(–5), 2mm, rigid, waxy yellow or brown, radial spines 24 or more, 2mm, white. Fl. purple; stigmas purple. Summer. S Mex.

M. dasyacantha Engelm. = *Escobaria dasyacantha.*

M. dawsonii (Houghton) Craig = *M. baxteriana.*

M. dealbata A. Dietr. = *M. haageana.*

M. decipiens Scheidw. Clustering; st. to 10×4–7cm, globose to clavate; tubercles cylindric-terete, with axill. bristles; central spines 1–2, rarely none, to 18–27mm, brown, radial spines 5–11, 7–15mm, pale yellow or white. Fl. white, slightly scented. Autumn. EC Mex.

M. deherdtiana Farwig. Simple; st. 2.5×4.5cm, depressed-globose; tubercles conic; axils slightly woolly or naked; central spines 0–6, 3–7mm long, red-brown or yellow, radial spines (25–)33–36, 3–6mm, somewhat curved, yellow to white, sometimes tipped red-brown. Fl. large, bright rose-violet; stigmas white. Summer. SW Mex.

M. densispina (J. Coult.) Orcutt. Usually simple; st. to 12×6(–10)cm, globose to short-cylindric; central spines 5–6, 10–12(–15)mm, straight, black-tipped, radial spines about 25, unequal, 8–10mm, yellow. Fl. pale yellow. Spring. C Mex.

M. denudata (Engelm.) A. Berger = *M. lasiacantha.*

M. deserti Engelm. = *Escobaria vivipara.*

M. dietrichiae Tiegel = *M. parkinsonii.*

M. dioica K. Brandg. Simple or clustering, st. to 10–15×8cm, cylindric to columnar; axils with bristles, as long as the tubercles; central spines 3–4, to 15mm, hooked, dark brown, radial spines 11–22, bristly, off-white. Fl. creamy yellow,

stigmas pale yellow or brown, tinged green. Summer. Baja Calif., SW Calif.

M. discolor Haw. Simple, depressed-globose to short-columnar, to 15×10cm or larger; tubercles cyindric-terete; axils sometimes with scant wool; central spines 4–8, lowest to 22mm, amber sometimes with scant wool; central spines 4–8, lowest to 22mm, amber to brown, radial spines 16–28, to 8–9mm, glassy white sometimes tinged yellow. Fl. cream yellow to pale pink, tinged brown or bright pink. Spring. C Mex.

M. dixanthocentron Backeb. ex Mottram. Simple; st. to 30×7–8cm, stout-cylindric; tubercles *c*6mm; axils woolly; central spines 2, divaricate, the upper *c*5mm, lower to 15mm, pale yellow or brown; radial spines *c*19–20, 2–4mm, white. Fl. pale red. Spring. S Mex.

M. dodsonii Bravo. Simple or clustering; st. up to 3×4cm, depressed-globose; tubercles conic, 5×4mm; axils naked; central spines 3–5, 1–2cm, red-brown, straight or slightly curved, radial spines 20–21, the lowest to 18mm, white. Fl. large, purple; fil. cream, anth. yellow. Summer. SW Mex.

M. dolichocentra Lem. = *M. polythele.*

M. dumetorum Purpus. Clustering; individual st. depressed-globose to cylindric-globose; tubercles conic; axils with a few curly hairs; central spines 0, radial spines numerous, 4–6mm, bristly. Fls white, tinged green. Spring or autumn. EC Mex.

M. duoformis Craig & Dawson. Resembling *M. nunezii*, but st. to 9×3–4cm, slender, elongate-cylindric; central spines 4, 10–12mm, lowermost longest, stout, hooked or straight, pink-brown below, almost black above, radial spines 18–20, 5–7mm, slender, orange-tan at v. base, pale above. Fl. crimson. Spring. SC Mex.

M. durispina Boed. = *M. kewensis.*

M. echinaria DC. = *M. elongata.*

M. echinus Engelm. = *Coryphantha echinus.*

M. eichlamii Quehl. Clustering; st. cylindric to sub-clavate; axils with pale yellow wool at first and white bristles; central spine 1, 1cm, yellow at base, red-brown above, radial spines 6, 5–7mm, pale yellow with darker tip. Fl. 2cm, yellow. Summer. Hond.

M. elegans DC. misapplied. = *M. haageana.*

M. elephantidens Lem. = *Coryphantha elephantidens.*

M. elongata DC. Clustering; st. 1–3cm diam., cyindric, elongate; tubercles short; central spines 0–3, to 15mm, pale yellow to brown, radial spines 14–25, 4–9mm, yellow. Fl. pale yellow or tinged pink. Spring. C Mex.

M. emskoetteriana Quehl = *Escobaria emskoetteriana.*

M. erecta Lem. ex Pfeiff. = *Coryphantha erecta.*

M. erectohamata Boed. = *M. aurihamata.*

M. eriacantha Pfeiff. Simple, sometimes clustering later; st. to 30(–50)×5cm, slender cylindric; tubercles 7×6mm; axils often woolly in flowering zone; central spines 2, 8–10mm, yellow, minutely hairy, radial spines 20–24, 4–6mm. Fl. small, yellow, tinged green. Spring. E Mex.

M. erythrosperma Boed. St. to 5×4cm, freely clustering; axils with hair-like bristles; central spines 1–3, rarely 4, up to 10mm, lowest hooked, pale yellow below, red-brown above; radial spines 15–20, 8–10mm, v. thin white. Fl. dark red. Spring. EC Mex. A white-fld form is also grown.

M. exsudans Zucc. = *Coryphantha ottonis.*

M. fasciculata Engelm. ex B.D. Jackson = *Echinocereus fendleri* var. *fasciculatus.*

M. fera-rubra Craig. Usually simple; st. 10×9cm, globose to short cylindric; tubercles 9×7mm; axils with short wool; central spines 6(–7), 12mm, orange brown, radial spines 15–18, 3–7mm, upper shorter. Spring–summer. WC Mex.

M. floribunda Hook. = *Neoporteria subgibbosa.*

M. formosa Scheidw. Usually simple; st. to 15cm diam., depressed-globose to short-cylindric; tubercles obscurely 4-angled; axils white-woolly, without bristles; central spines usually 6, to 8mm, pink-brown, darker tipped, later grey brown, radial spines 20–25, 3–6mm, white. Fl. pale pink or nearly white. Spring. NE Central Mex.

M. fragilis Salm-Dyck ex K. Brandg. = *M. gracilis.*

M. fraileana (Britt. & Rose) Boed. St. to 15×3cm+ cylindric; axils naked or with a single bristle; central spines 3–4, 10mm, one hooked, dark brown, radial spines 11–12, 8–10mm. Fl. pale pink, large; stigmas long, purple. Summer. NW Mex.

M. fuauxiana Backeb. = *M. albilanata.*

M. gabbii Engelm. ex J. Coult. = *M. brandegeei.*

M. galeottii Scheidw. ex C.F. Först. = *M. polythele.*

M. gasseriana Boed. = *M. stella-de-tacubaya.*

M. gaumeri (Britt. & Rose) Orcutt. Clustering; st. to 15cm, globose to short cylindric; tubercles nearly terete; axils naked; central spines 1, usually brown, radial spines 10–12(–20), white and brown. Fl. creamy white. Spring. SE Mex.

M. geminispina Haw. Soon clustering and forming mounds; individual st. 6–8cm diam., becoming cylindric; axils with wool and short bristles; central spines 2 or 4, uppermost 15–40mm, white, dark-tipped, radial spines 16–20, 5–7mm, chalky white. Fl. deep pink. Summer–autumn. C Mex.

M. gigantea Schum. Simple; st. to 30cm diam., depressed-globose to globose; tubercles to 10mm or more; axils woolly; central spines 4–6, robust, lowermost to 2cm or more, yellow, brown or almost black, radial spines up to 12, less than 5mm, white. Fl. pale yellow, tinged green. Spring. C Mex.

M. glareosa Boed. = *M. baxteriana.*

M. glassii R.A. Foster. Clustering; to 3×3cm, st. globose, to cylindric, to 10cm; tubercles terete, to 7mm; axils with 20–30 bristly to hairy; central spines 1, 4–5mm, hooked or straight, golden, 6–8, radial spines 50–60, 10–15mm, hair-like, interlacing. Fl. light pink. Spring. NE Mex. Several larger-fld. varieties have been described.

M. globosa Link = *M. longimamma.*

M. goldii Glass & Fost. Resembling *M. saboae*, but less inclined to cluster, and with more spines; st. to 35mm diam., subglobose; tubercles terete, 5–7mm; central spines 0, radial spines 35–45, 2–3mm, thin, subpectinate, interlacing, white. Fl. dark lavender pink within, anth. orange yellow. Summer. NW Mex.

M. goodridgei Scheer ex Salm-Dyck. Clustering; st. to 10×4cm, erect, cylindric; central spines 4, brown above, lowermost hooked, radial spines 12, interlacing. Fl. cream-coloured; stigmas olive green. Summer. NW Mex.

M. gracilis Pfeiff. Offsetting v. freely; st. to 13×1–3cm, cylindric; tubercles short, obtusely conic; central spines 0–2(–5), up to 10–12mm, white or dark brown, radial spines 11–17, 3–8mm, bristly, white. Fl. pale yellow with pink or brown midline. Spring. EC Mex.

M. graessneriana Boed. = *M. columbiana.*

M. grahamii Engelm. Simple or branched at base, 7.5–10×7.5–11cm, globose to ovoid, grey-green; tubercles ovoid-cylindric; central spines 1–3, longest hooked, to 18(–25)mm, dark brown, radial spines 20–35, 6–12mm, white. Fl. pink; outer tep. erose; stigmas pale green. Summer. SW US.

M. grusonii Runge. Mostly simple, globose to cylindric, to 50×25cm; tubercles four-angled; central spines 2–3, 4–6mm, red-brown at first, later white, radial spines 12–14, 6–8mm. Fl. yellow. Spring. N Mex.

M. guelzowiana Werderm. Simple to clustering; st. to 7cm or more diam., flattened-globose; tubercles conic-cylindric, flabby; central spine 1(–3), 8–10mm, hooked, red or yellow, radial spines 60–80, 15–20mm, hair-like, tortuous, white. Fl. large, purple-pink; stigmas green. Summer. NW Mex.

M. guerreronis (Bravo) Backeb. & F. Knuth. Clustering; st. to 60×6cm, cylindric; tubercles cylindric; axils woody and bristly; central spines usually 4(2–5), upper straight, to 15mm, lowermost often hooked, to 25mm, brown at first, radial spines 20–30, 5–10mm, bristly, white. Fl. small, red. Summer. SW Mex.

M. guirocobensis Backeb. = *M. sheldonii.*

M. gummifera Engelm. Simple 7–10×7.5–12.5cm, hemispheric; tubercles pyramidal; axils woolly at first; central spines 1–2, 4mm, dark, radial spines 10–12, upper 4–6mm, bristly, pale, lower, stronger, dark. Fl. pink tep. with darker midstripe. Summer. N Mex.

M. haageana Pfeiff. Usually simple (clustering in var. *schmollii* (Craig) D. Hunt), reaching 15×5–10cm in larger variants; tubercles small, crowded; axils often woolly and sometimes with bristles; central spines usually 2, sometimes 1 or 4, to 15mm, brown, radial spines 15–25, 3–6mm, white. Fl. small, deep purple-pink. Spring. SE C Mex.

M. hahniana Werderm. Simple or clustering; individual st. to 20×12cm; tubercles v. numerous, triangular-conic, small; axils with long white bristles; central spines 1(–4), up to 4mm, white tipped brown, radial spines 20–30, 5–15mm, hairlike, white. Fl. deep purple-pink. Spring. C Mex.

M. halei Brandg. Clustering; st. cylindric, 30–50×5–7.5cm; tubercles short, rounded; axils woolly; central spines 3–4, 25mm, straight, radial spines 10–21, 12mm. Fl. scarlet. Summer. NW Mex.

M. hamata Lehm. ex Pfeiff. Clustering; st. cylindric, to 60×10cm or more; central spines 3–4, lowest longest, usually hooked, to 3cm, brown, radial spines 15–20, white. Spring. SC Mex.

M. hamiltonhoytea (Bravo) Werderm. = *M. gigantea.*

M. haudeana Lau & Wagner = *M. saboae.*

M. heeseana McDowell = *M. petterssonii.*

M. heidiae Krainz. Simple or clustering; st. *c*3×5.5cm; tubercles cylindric; axils with 1–5 fine bristles to 10mm; central spines 0–2, *c*12mm, hooked, red-brown, or only 1–2mm, straight, radial spines 16–24, to 11mm, bristly. Fl. yellow, tinged green; stigmas emerald green. Summer. S Mex.

M. hemisphaerica Engelm. = *M. heyderi.*

M. herrerae Werderm. Simple or clustering; st. usually 2–3cm in diameter, globose to cylindric, tubercles numerous, small; central spines 0, radial spines 60–100 or more, unequal, *c*1–5mm, bristly, almost white. Fl. lavender pink to white;

stigmas green. Spring. EC Mex.

M. heyderi Muehlenpf. St. 7.5–15cm diam., usually simple, depressed to subglobose; tubercles conic, elongate; axils naked or woolly; central spines 0–2, 3–10mm, brown, radial spines 9–22, 4–14mm, brown or white. Fl. white, pale yellow or pale pink. Spring. SW US, N Mex.

M. hidalgensis Purpus = *M. polythele.*

M. hoffmanniana (Tiegel) Bravo = *M. polythele.*

M. humboldtii Ehrenb. Simple or clustering; st. to *c*7cm diam., depressed-globose or globose; tubercles cylindric; axils with wool and white bristles; central spines 0, radial spines 80 or more, 4–6mm, purple-pink, stigmas green. Spring. EC Mex.

M. hutchisoniana (Gates) Boed. Soon clustering; rootstock fibrous; st. to 15×4–6cm, cylindric; tubercles short, conic; central spines 4, 7–10mm, light tan with purple tip, at least the lowermost hooked, radial spines 10–20, purple-tipped. Fl. pale pink or creamy white; outer tep. striped dull maroon or brown; stigmas green or olive green. Summer. Baja Calif. *M. goodridgei* Salm-Dyck (Cedros Island) may belong here.

M. inaiae Craig = *M. swinglei.*

M. insularis Gates. Simple or clustering; individual st. to 6×5cm, depressed-globose; tubercles conic, blue-green; axils sometimes slightly woolly; central spines 1, 1cm, hooked, black-tipped, radial spines 20–30, 5mm, acicular, white. Fl. 15–25mm, funnelform; outer tep. light green, inner light pink with white midstripe. Fr. 1cm, clavate, orange red, tending to be hollow. Summer. NW Mex.

M. jaliscana (Britt. & Rose) Boed. Clustering; st. 5cm diam., globose; tubercles 4–5mm; central spines 4–6, one hooked, red-brown, radial spines 30 or more. Fl. pale pink or tinged purple, fragrant; stigmas white. Spring. WC Mex.

M. johnstonii (Britt. & Rose) Orcutt. Usually simple; st. eventually 15–20×10cm, globose to short-cylindric; tubercles 4-angled; central spines usually 2, sometimes 4 or 6, 10–25mm, purple-brown to black, radial spines 10–18, 6–9mm, white, tipped brown. Fl. white. Summer. NW Mex.

M. karwinskiana Mart. Simple at first, later dividing apically and/or offsetting; st. to 15×10cm, depressed-globose to short cylindric; tubercles pyramidal-conic, obscurely angled; axils with bristles; spines 4–7, subequal 5–12–25mm, red-brown at first. Fl. v. pale yellow, often striped red on outer tep. Spring or autumn. S Mex.

M. kelleriana Craig = *M. kewensis.*

M. kewensis Salm-Dyck St. simple, subglobose to columnar; tubercles conic; axils woolly at first; spines (4–)6–8, somewhat recurved or adpressed, the lateral 6–7mm, the upper and/or lower sometimes longer, grey-white or dark. Fl. purple-pink. Summer. C Mex.

M. klissingiana Boed. Simple at first, eventually clustering; individual st. 16×9cm, globose to clavate; tubercles 5×2mm; axils with white bristles; central spines 2–4, 2mm, almost white, darker towards tip, radial spines 30–35, to 5mm, almost white. Fl. rose pink, stigmas yellow. Spring. NE Mex.

M. knebeliana Boed. = *M. pygmaea.*

M. kraehenbuehlii (Krainz) Krainz. Densely clustering; individual st. 3–12×3.5cm, cylindric, softly fleshy; tubercles attenuate to conic; central spines 0–1, thicker and longer than radials, brown-tipped, radial spines 18–24, *c*3–8mm, mostly curving and interlacing, white, brown-tipped. Fl. lilac-carmine; stigmas yellow-white. Spring. S Mex.

M. kunthii Ehrenb. = *M. haageana.*

M. lanata (Britt. & Rose) Orcutt = *M. supertexta.*

M. lasiacantha Engelm. Usually simple; st. small, globose or globose-ovoid; tubercles cylindric; central spines 0, radial spines 40–80 in series, 3–5mm, white, pubesc. or glab. Fl. white, tep. striped red, stigmas yellow-green.Spring. SW US, N Mex.

M. laui D. Hunt. Clustering; individual st. to 6×4.5cm, depressed-globose to globose or shortly oblong; tubercles terete, hidden by spines; axils sometimes sparsely woolly; central spines 0-numerous, intergrading with radial spines 35–60+, in several series, *c*6–9mm, setaceous to hair-like, white. Fl. purple-pink, stigmas white. Spring. EC Mex. f. *laui*, with up to 12 white central spines 7–10mm long intergrading with the radials; f. *subducta* D. Hunt, with up to 12 stronger pale yellow brown centrals 7–10mm; f. *dasyacantha* D. Hunt, with v. slender white centrals, scarcely or not distinguishable from the radials.

M. lehmannii Link & Otto ex Pfeiff. = *Coryphantha octacantha.*

M. lenta K. Brandg. Branching dichotomously; individual st. 3–5cm diam., forming flat-topped clusters; tubercles slender conic, *c*1cm; axils with short wool and an occasional bristle; central spines 0, radial spines 30–40, 3–7mm, soft and fragile, pale. Fl. white, tep. with pink or pale mid-stripe; stigmas olive-green. Summer. N Mex.

M. leona Poselger = *M. pottsii.*

M. leucantha Boed. Simple or rarely clustering; st. up to 3.5cm diam., globose or somewhat elongate-globose; tubercles $c7\times2$mm; axils sparsely woolly with fine bristles; central spines 3–4, up to 5–6mm, amber-yellow, mostly hooked, radial spines $c18$, up to 5mm, thinner, white, upper tipped brown-yellow. Fl. white. Spring. NE Mex.

M. leucocentra Berg. Resembling *M. geminispina*. Simple or clustering, globose to short-columnar, to $c12\times11$cm; tubercles terete-conic, $c8\times9$mm, glaucous green; axils with white bristles; central spines 4–6, to 12mm, white with dark tip, radial spines 30–35, $c6$mm, chalky white. Fl. deep pink. C Mex.

M. leucotricha Scheidw. = *M. mystax*.

M. lloydii (Britt. & Rose) Orcutt. Usually simple. St. sometimes 10×6–7cm, depressed-globose to short-cylindric; tubercles 4-angled; axils slightly woolly; central spines 0, radial spines 3–4, uppermost red or dark brown, others white, 2–5mm. Fl. 15×15mm; outer tep. dark red, interior white, with a tinge of red and red mid-stripe. Spring. NC Mex.

M. longicoma (Britt. & Rose) A. Berger. Clustering; st. 3–4cm diam.; tubercles conic; axils with long white hairs; central spines 4, 10–12mm, 1–2 hooked, brown above, radial spines 25+ hair-like, interlacing. Fl. white, outer tep. pink with darker mid-stripe. Spring. C Mex.

M. longiflora (Britt. & Rose) A. Berger. Usually simple; st. 3–9cm diam., globose; tubercles $c1$cm, plump; central spines 4, the upper 3 straight, lowermost hooked, 11–25mm, dark brown to yellow or white, radial spines 25–30, 10–13mm, bristly, white. Fl. pink or purple-pink with distinct tube. Spring. NW Mex.

M. longimamma DC. Simple or clustering; st. to 10–12cm diam.; tubercles oblong-terete, v. large (to 5cm), remote; central spines 0–3, usually 1, bristly, to 25mm, radial spines 6–10, 12–18mm, all spines pale brown, yellow or white. Fl. large, bright yellow. Summer. EC Mex.

M. longiseta Muehlenpf. = *M. compressa*.

M. macdougalii Rose = *M. heyderi*.

M. macracantha DC. = *M. magnimamma*.

M. macromeris Engelm. = *Coryphantha macromeris*.

M. magallanii Schmoll ex Craig. Simple; st. $c6\times4$–5cm, cylindric-clavate; tubercles 6×4mm; axils with scant wool; central spines 0–1, 1–3mm, straight, curved or hooked, tan at base, brown at tip, radial spines 70–75, 2–5mm, horizontal and interlacing, becoming chalky white, brown at tip. Fl. cream tep. with brown or pink mid-stripe. Spring. N Mex.

M. magnifica Buchenau. Clustering; individual st. to 40×5–9cm, cylindric; tubercles rounded pyramidal or conic; axils with bristles; central spines 4–5 or more, the lowest 15–55mm, hooked, remainder shorter, clear yellow-brown, radial spines 17–24, 3–8mm, white or yellow. Fl. pink-red. Spring. SC Mex. Z9.

M. magnimamma Haw. Variable; usually clustering and forming mounds 50cm or more diam.; individual heads to 10–12cm diam.; tubercles pyramidal-conic, $c10\times10$mm; axils woolly in flowering zone; spines 3–6, usually 1 longer and stronger than the others and ± curved. Fl. pale yellow to deep purple-pink. Spring. C Mex.

M. mainiae K. Brandg. Simple or clustering; st. to 10–12×6–7cm, globose; tubercles terete, axils often red; central spines 1, $c15$mm, hooked and ± twisted, brown or pale yellow with dark tip, radial spines 8–15, 6–12mm, upper somewhat shorter, pale yellow to white and dark-tipped. Fl. pale pink with darker mid-stripe; stigmas long, purple. Summer. SW US, N Mex.

M. mammillaris (L.) Karst. Simple or clustering; st. to 6×7cm+ globose to short-cylindric; tubercles terete-conic, axils slightly woolly; central spines 3–5, 7–10mm, red-brown, darker tipped, radial spines 10–16, 5–8mm, tinged red-brown. Fl. small, pale yellow. Summer. Dutch W Indies, Grenadines, Venez.

M. maritima (Lindsay) D. Hunt. Clustering and forming clumps to 1m diam.; st. 3–7cm diam., erect or decumbent, cylindric, blue-green; tubercles subconic, somewhat flattened; fl. axils woolly; central spines 4, red-brown, upper 3 ascending, 1–2cm, lowermost 2–5cm, hooked, radial spines 10–15, $c1$cm, red-brown. Fl. trumpet-shaped, scarlet. Summer. Baja Calif.

M. marksiana Krainz. Simple at first, later clustering; st. 6–15×5–12cm, globose, apex woolly; tubercles gibbous-pyramidal; flowering axils woolly; spines $(4$–9–$11(-21)$, 8–11mm, more numerous on offsets, golden yellow or sometimes brown. Fl. yellow. Summer. NW Mex.

M. martinezii Backeb. = *M. supertexta*.

M. matudae H. Bravo. Simple or clustering. st. to 20cm or more $\times3$–5cm, elongate-cylindric; tubercles conic; central spines 1, 4–5mm, pink-brown, later dirty white, radial spines 18–20, 2–3mm, translucent white. Fl. light purple-red. Spring. C Mex.

M. mazatlanensis Schum. ex Gürke. Clustering; st. slender-cylindric, to 15×2–4cm; tubercles shortly conic; axils naked or with 1–2 short bristles; central spines 3–4, to 15mm, hooked in some plants, red-brown above, paler below, radial spines 13–15, 5–10mm, white. Fl. carmine red; stigmas green. Summer. NW

Mex.

M. meiacantha Engelm. Simple; st. depressed-globose; tubercles compressed, quadrangular-pyramidal; central spines 0–1, 3–7mm, ascending, radial spines 5–9, 6–10mm, all spines white to dirty yellow, brown-tipped. Fl. with tep. pink to white with pink mid-stripe. Summer. SW US, N Mex.

M. melaleuca Karw. ex Salm-Dyck. Simple or sometimes clustering; st. globose, tubercles ovoid-terete. Central spine (0–)1, brown, radial spines 8–9, 12–14mm, recurved, the upper 4 longer, brown, lower white. Fl. yellow. Summer. NE Mex.

M. melanocentra Poselger. Simple; st. to 15cm diam., depressed-globose, glaucous; tubercles pyramidal, large, axils woolly at first; central spines 1, to 3cm, stout, black, radial spines 7–9, unequal, 6–22mm, the lowest longest, black when young. Fl. deep pink. Spring. N Mex.

M. mendeliana (Bravo) Werderm. Resembling *M. hahniana*; axill. bristle-hairs 15–25mm; central spines (2–)4, lowermost to 2cm, radial spines poorly developed or lacking. Spring. C Mex.

M. mercadensis Patoni. Simple or clustering, st. 5–6cm diam., ± globose; axils naked; central spines 4 or more, usually one hooked, 15–25mm, pale yellow to red-brown, radial spines 25–30, bristly, white to yellow. Fl. pale pink; stigmas cream. Spring. Mex.

M. mexicensis Craig = *M. grusonii*.

M. meyranii Bravo. Clustering; st. to 55×4–5cm, cylindric; tubercles conic, axils with sparse wool at first; central spines 2, divergent, to 1cm, orange yellow with chestnut brown tip, later dirty white, radial spines 17–19, 3–6mm, white with yellow base. Fl. purple; stigmas green. Spring. Mex.

M. microcarpa Engelm. provisional name. = *M. milleri*.

M. microhelia Werderm. Simple or clustering; st. to 25×3.5–6cm, cylindric; tubercles shortly conic; axils soon naked; central spines 0–4(–8), to 11mm, dark red-brown, radial spines (30–)50, 4–6mm, yellow, often slightly recurved. Fl. creamy white to red or purple. Spring. C Mex.

M. microheliopsis Werderm. = *M. microhelia*.

M. micromeris Engelm. = *Epithelantha micromeris*.

M. microthele Muehlenpf. = *M. formosa*.

M. mieheana Tiegel. Clustering; st. to 15×5cm, cylindric; tubercles shortly ovoid; upper axils somewhat white-woolly; central spines 3–6, to 15mm, almost straight, honey-yellow or brown, radial spines 18–20, similar, white to pale yellow. Fl. yellow. Spring. C Mex.

M. milleri (Britt. & Rose) Boed. Simple at first, later clustering; st. up to $c15\times4$–8cm, cylindric, green; tubercles $c10\times10$mm; central spines 1(–2)(–4), the principal one 12–15mm, hooked, black-purple, second, shorter, paler, radial spines 18–28, 6–12mm, light brown to red. Fl. lavender-pink with light green or pale brown stigmas. Summer. SW US, N Mex.

M. missouriensis Sweet = *Escobaria missouriensis*.

M. moelleriana Boed. Simple; st. to 11×10cm, globose to short cylindric; tubercles ovoid; axils naked; central spines 8–10, the (2–)4 lowermost hooked, to 20(–30)mm, the upper shorter, straight, honey yellow to dark red-brown; radial spines $c30$–40(–50), 7–9mm, white, faintly yellow at base. Fl. pale pink with darker stripes. Spring. WC Mex.

M. mollendorffiana Shurly. Simple; st. to 35×6–12cm or taller, globose to cylindric; tubercles subcylindric; axils woolly, ultimately with 4–5 bristles; central spines 4–6mm, 14mm light yellow brown with darker tip, radial spines 18–28, 3–5mm, white. Fl. purple. Summer. C Mex.

M. mollihamata Shurly = *M. pygmaea*.

M. morganiana Tiegel. Simple at first, later dividing apically; individual heads depressed-globose, to 8cm diam.; tubercles pyramidal; axils with fine hairs to 2cm; central spines 4–6, 10mm, white, tipped brown, radial spines, hair-like, white. Fl. pink tep. with darker mid-stripe. Spring. C Mex.

M. muehlenpfordtii C.F. Först. Simple at first, often dividing apically later; individual heads depressed-globose, 10–15cm diam.; tubercles conic; axils with fine bristles; young areoles with pale yellow wool; central spines 4(–7), lowermost 5–35mm, often curved, remainder 4–14mm, pale to dark yellow, often tipped brown, radial spines 40–50, 2–8mm, glassy white. Fl. deep purple-pink. Summer. C Mex.

M. multiceps Salm-Dyck = *M. prolifera*.

M. multidigitata Radley ex Lindsay. Freely clustering; individual st. 5–8(–20)$\times2$–5cm, cylindric; tubercles obtuse; axils slightly woolly; central spines usually 4, $c8$mm, white with brown tip, radial spines 15–25, 6–8mm, white. Fl. white, stigmas green. Summer. NW Mex.

M. multiformis (Britt. & Rose) Backeb. = *M. erythrosperma*.

M. mazatlanensis Ehrenb. = *M. karwinskiana*.

M. multiseta Ehrenb. = *M. karwinskiana*.

M. mundtii Schum. Simple; 6–7cm diam., st. depressed-globose; tubercles conic; central spines 2–4, red-brown, radial spines 10–12, to 5mm, white. Fl. carmine red. Summer. C Mex.

M. mutabilis Scheidw. = *M. mystax*.

M. mystax Mart. Simple; st. to 15×7–10cm, globose to cylindric, eventually dividing, tubercles pyramidal; axils bristly; central spines 3–4, 15–20mm often one to 7cm, tortuous, purple-brown at first, tipped darker, later grey, radial spines 3–10, 4–8mm, white, brown-tipped. Fl. deep purple-pink. Spring. S Mex.

M. napina Purpus. Simple; st. to c5cm diam., globose; tubercles conic; axils sometimes woolly. Spines about 12, usually radial, 8–9mm, somewhat curved, white or yellow at base. Fl. pale pink, tep. with deeper mid-stripe. Summer. SW Mex.

M. nealeana Craig, invalid. = *M. muehlenpfordtii*.

M. nejapensis Craig & Dawson. Clustering; st. to 15×5–7.5cm, ovoid to cylindric-clavate; tubercles 5–8×6–8mm, axils with tortuous white bristles; spines 3–5, upper 2–5mm, lowermost to 25(–50)mm, white with red-brown tip. Fl. pale cream tep. with brown red to scarlet mid-stripe. Spring or autumn. SW Mex.

M. neopalmeri Craig. Usually clustering; st. to 5×5cm, cylindric; tubercles cylindric, glaucous; axils with dense wool and bristles; central spines 2–5, 6–8mm, straight or hooked, pale brown with darker tip, radial spines 15–20, 3–5mm, white. Fl. small, ± white. Summer. NW Mex.

M. neopotosina Craig = *M. muehlenpfordtii*.

M. neumanniana Mart. = *M. magnimamma*.

M. nickelsiae Brandg. = *Coryphantha nickelsiae*.

M. nigra Ehrenb. = *M. polythele*.

M. nivosa Link ex Pfeiff. Simple or clustering; st. globose to short-cylindric; tubercles obtusely conic, sometimes bronze; axils woolly, without bristles; spines 7–14, longest to 2cm, bright yellow to dark brown. Fl. yellow. Summer. W Indies.

M. nunezii (Britt. & Rose) Orcutt Simple or clustering; st. to 15×8cm, globose to cylindric; tubercles terete; axils bristly; central spines 2–6, 10–12mm, straight, or lowermost hooked, brown, or white with brown tip, radial spines 10–30, 5–8mm, bristly, white. Fl. purple-pink. Spring. SW C Mex.

M. obconella Scheidw. = *M. polythele*.

M. occidentalis (Britt. & Rose) Boed. = *M. mazatlanensis*.

M. ochoterenae (Bravo) Werderm. = *M. discolor*.

M. ocotillensis Craig = *M. gigantea*.

M. octacantha DC. = *Coryphantha octacantha*.

M. oliviae Orcutt = *M. grahamii*.

M. ortizrubiana (Bravo) Werderm. = *M. candida*.

M. ottonis Pfeiff. = *Coryphantha ottonis*.

M. pacifica (Gates) Backeb. & F. Knuth = *M. baxteriana*.

M. painteri Rose ex Quehl. Simple at first, later clustering; st. 2cm diam., globose; tubercles terete; central spines 4–5, to 1cm, 1 hooked, dark brown, puberulent, radial spines c20, to 5mm, bristly, white, puberulent. Fl. ± white with outer tep. tinged brown; stigmas cream. EC Mex.

M. parkinsonii Ehrenb. Simple at first, later dividing apically; individual st. 7–15cm diam.; tubercles pyramidal; axils with wool and bristles; central spines 2–4(–5), upper 6–8mm, lowermost to 3.5cm, often curved, white or red-brown, tipped dark brown, radial spines 30–35, white. Fl. creamy yellow, tinged brown or pink. Spring. C Mex.

M. pectinata Engelm. = *Coryphantha echinus*.

M. pectinifera F.A. Weber. Simple; st. to 3–5cm diam., globose to short-cylindric; tubercles small; areoles elongate, spines 20–40, 1.5–2mm, bristly, pectinate, adpressed, white. Fl. to creamy yellow or pale pink, tep. with pale brown mid-stripe. Spring. SE C Mex.

M. peninsularis (Britt. & Rose) Orcutt. Simple or clustering; st. depressed-globose, grey-green; tubercles erect, 4-angled; axils woolly at first; spines 4–8, nearly erect, short and pale with brown tips. Fl. with outer tep. narrow, tinged red, inner narrow, acuminate, green or light yellow, erose. Summer. Baja Calif.

M. pennispinosa Krainz. Usually simple; st. c3×3.5cm, depressed-globose, tubercles cylindric; axils woolly at first; central spines 1(–3), 1 hooked, 10–12mm, yellow at base, brown-red above, pubesc., others similar to radials, radial spines 16–20, 5–8mm, slender, feathery-pubesc., grey-white. Fl. white tep. with pale pink mid-stripe; stigmas yellow. Spring. N Mex.

M. perbella Hildm. ex Schum. Clustering and forming low mounds by apical division; individual st. c5cm diam., depressed-globose; tubercles small; axils with short bristly hairs; central spines usually 2, sometimes 1 or 0, 1–4mm, brown or white with red-black tip, radial spines 12–22, 1.5–4mm. Fl. purple-pink. Spring. C Mex.

M. petrophila K. Brandg. Simple; st. to 15×15cm; tubercles short; axils woolly; central spines 1–2, nearly 2cm, dark chestnut brown, radial spines c10, c1m. Fl. yellow, tinged green. Summer. NW Mex.

M. petterssonii Hildm. Simple; st. to 30cm diam., subglobose; tubercles angled; axils woolly; central spines 5–7, one to 45mm, the others shorter, brown at first, tipped darker, radial spines c10, 2–10mm, uppermost shorter and weaker, white. Fl. purple-pink. Spring. C Mex.

M. phellosperma Engelm. = *M. tetrancistra*.

M. phitauiana (Baxter) Werderm. Clustering; st. to 15–25cm, cylindric; tubercles conic; axils bristly; central spines 4, 4–6mm, all straight or, 1 hooked, brown above, radial spines 4–12mm, lower longest, white. Fl. white, outer tep. with red midrib. Summer. NW Mex.

M. picta Meinsh. Usually simple; st. often c5×5cm; globose or ovoid, becoming tuberous at base; tubercles cylindric-terete; axils with fine bristles; spines 15–20, 10–12mm, pubesc.; central spines darker than the radials; lower radials slender, white. Fl. white tinged pale green. Spring. NE C Mex.

M. pilcayensis Bravo (as 'pitcayensis', orth. error). Resembling *M. spinosissima*. Simple or clustering; st. to 50×4–5cm, slender-cylindric; tubercles 5×2–3mm; axils woolly and with 8–10 slender bristles; central and radial spines about 30, 5–6mm, bristly, pale yellow. Fl. purple-red. Spring. SW C Mex.

M. pilispina Purpus. Clustering; st. 4cm diam., subglobose; tubercles cylindric; axils with wool and few hair-like bristles; central spines 5–8, 6–10mm, brown above, white or yellow below, radial spines c40, 7–10mm, hair-like, pubesc., white, in a ring. Fl. creamy white. Spring. EC Mex.

M. plumosa F.A. Weber. Clustering to form mounds to 40cm or more diam.; st. to 6–7cm diam., globose, hidden by spines; tubercles cylindric; axils woolly; spines up to 40, 3–7mm, feathery, white. Fl. small, creamy white or tinged brown-pink. Winter. NE Mex.

M. polyedra Mart. Simple at first, later clustering; st. to 30×10–12cm, subglobose; tubercles flattened-pyramidal, 6–7-sided; axils with wool and bristles; spines 4–6, 6–25mm, the uppermost longest and strongest, horn-coloured, tipped dark purple. Fl. pink. Spring. S Mex.

M. polythele Mart. Simple; st. to 30–80×8–12(–17)cm, cylindric; tubercles pyramidal-conic, dark blue-green; axils woolly; central spines 2–4, 8–17(–25)mm, dark or yellow-brown, radial spines 0 or rudimentary. Fl. purple-pink. Summer. C Mex.

M. pondii Greene. Simple or few-branched; st. to 30cm, cylindric; axils with bristles; central spines more than 25mm, rigid, strongly hooked, dark brown above, radial spines 20–30, white, slender. Fl. large, bright scarlet. Summer. NW Mex.

M. poselgeri Hildm. Branching from the base; st. to 0.3–2m×4–7cm, cylindric, elongate; tubercles, conic-pyramidal, upswept; axils woolly and rarely setose; central spines 1, 15–25mm, hooked, radial spines 7–9, 9–12mm, all spines white, brown tipped. Fl. 3cm or more; tube curved; tep. bright scarlet. Summer. NW Mex.

M. potosina hort, non *M. potosiana* Jacobi = *M. muehlenpfordtii*.

M. pottsii Scheer ex Salm-Dyck. Clustering; st. to 20×3cm, slender cylindric; central spines c7, 7–12mm, uppermost longest, tipped dark brown, radial spines 40–45, about 6mm, bristly, chalky white. Fl. deep red. Spring. N Mex., SW Tex.

M. pringlei (J. Coult.) K. Brandg. Resembling *M. rhodantha* but yellow- or golden-spined. Simple or branching dichotomously; st. to 15×12cm, depressed-globose to globose; tubercles rounded-conic; axils with fine hairs to 1cm; central spines 6–8, 2–3cm, stout, ± flexuous, upper usually longest and recurved, radial spines 18–22, 7–9mm, fine. Fl. rose-purple with rose-purple or pale yellow stigmas. Summer. C Mex.

M. prolifera (Mill.) Haw. Forming dense clumps; st. to c9×4.5cm, globose to cylindric-clavate; tubercles terete; axils naked or with fine white hairs; central spines 5–12, 4–9mm, straight, puberulent, white to red-brown, sometimes dark-tipped, radial spines intergrading with the centrals, 25–40, 3–12mm, fine, straight to tortuous, white. Fl. creamy yellow, or tinged pink, outer tep. brown-striped. Spring. NE Mex., SW US, Cuba, Hispan.

M. pseudocrucigera Craig = *M. sempervivi*.

M. pseudomammillaris Salm-Dyck = *M. discolor*.

M. pseudoperbella Quehl. Simple, or perhaps branching dichotomously; individual heads globose, later cylindric, 7–10×5–8cm, apex sunken and woolly; tubercles cylindric, losing spines; flowering axils with wool and bristles, eventually naked; central spines 2(–4), c3–5mm, thick, brown with black tip, the lower shorter, paler, radial spines 20–30, 2–3mm, pure white. Fl. with pink-striped inner tep. Summer. C Mex.

M. pubispina Boed. Simple; st. to 4cm diam., globose; tubercles cylindric; axils pale-green or white with fine tortuous bristles; central spines (3–)4, pubesc., lowermost hooked, c9mm, pale below, dark-tipped, the upper 10mm straight, pale or white, radial spines c15, c8–12mm, hair-like, ± crooked, pubesc., white. Fl. with dirty pink, white-edged outer tep., inner tep. pure white or cream striped pale pink. Spring. C Mex.

M. purpusii Schum. = *Pediocactus simpsonii*.

M. pycnacantha Mart. = *Coryphantha pycnacantha*.

M. pygmaea (Britt. & Rose) A. Berger. Simple or clustering, individual st. depressed-globose to ovoid-cylindric, to 6×5.5cm; tubercles cylindric; axils with bristly hairs; central spines 4, upper 3 straight, erect, 5–7mm, tinged pink at first, later yellow to brown, lowermost hooked, 5–6mm, pubesc., radial spines 22–28, to 6mm, v. fine, white, pubesc. Fl. with outer tep. apiculate, red tinged, inner creamy white. Spring. EC Mex.

M. radians DC. = *Coryphantha radians*.

M. radiosa Engelm. = *Escobaria vivipara*.

M. raphidacantha Lem. = *Coryphantha clavata*.

M. recurvata Engelm. = *Coryphantha recurvata*.

M. rekoi (Britt. & Rose) Vaupel. Simple; st. to 12×5–6cm, globose to short-cylindric; tubercles terete; axils with wool and 1–8 long white bristles; central spines 4, 10–15mm, brown, the lower one sometimes hooked, radial spines *c*20, 4–6mm, white. Fl. deep purple; stigmas pale green. Spring. S Mex.

M. rettigiana Boed. Simple; st. depressed or elongate-globose; tubercles cylindric; axils naked or with a little wool; central spines 3–4, red-brown, the 2–3 upper straight, 12mm, the lowermost hooked, to 15mm, radial spines 18–20, to 10mm, thin. Fl. pale pink; stigmas almost white. Spring. C Mex.

M. rhodantha Link & Otto. Usually simple, occas. offsetting or branching; st. to 40×12cm, cylindric; tubercles obtuse-conic to cylindric, axils woolly at first and with a few bristles; central spines 4–9, to 18(–25)mm, usually recurved, typically red-brown, radial spines typically 17–24, 4–9mm, glassy white to pale yellow. Fl purple-red; stigmas purple. Summer. C Mex.

M. ritteriana Boed. = *M. chionocephala*.

M. robustispina Schott ex Engelm. = *Coryphantha scheeri* var. *robustispina*.

M. roseoalba Boed. Simple; st. depressed-globose; tubercles angled; axils densely woolly; spines 4–5(–6), to 8mm, somewhat unequal, spreading regularly and recurved, almost white, pink-brown towards base. Fl. with outer tep. pink, tinged brown, inner nearly white. Spring–summer. NE Mex.

M. roseocentra Boed. & Ritter = *M. magallanii*.

M. rubida Schwarz ex Backeb. Simple, st. to 9×13cm, depressed-globose, blue-green at first, later dull red; tubercles pyramidal; axils woolly; central spines 1, to 2cm, radial spines 8, to 1.5cm, all spines red-brown. Fl. with outer tep. striped dull red, inner almost white, tinged green. Summer. W Mex.

M. ruestii Quehl = *M. columbiana*.

M. saboae Glass. Clustering; st. 1–2×1–2cm, ovoid; tubercles small, rounded; central spines 0, rarely 1, 2mm, straight, radial spines 17–25, 2mm, slender, glassy white, slightly curved, yellow at the base. Fl. long, funnelform, pink; anth. pale yellow. Spring. Mts of NW Mex.

M. saffordii (Britt. & Rose) Bravo = *M. carretii*.

M. sartorii Purpus. Clustering; st. often 10×8–9cm, tall, globose to somewhat cylindric-globose, flat-topped, dark glaucous green; tubercles pyramidal; axils with dense white or pale yellow wool and bristles; central spines 2–10, only 1–2mm or rarely to 8cm, 2–8 spreading, 2–8mm, off-white or pale brown with brown tip, radial spines 0–12, rudimentary, 1–2mm, bristle-like. Fl. pale carmine, tep. with darker mid-stripe; stigmas pale yellow or red-tinged. Summer. SE Mex.

M. scheeri Muehlenpf. 1845, not Muehlenpf. 1847. = *Neolloydia conoidea*.

M. schiedeana Ehrenb. Clustering; st. to 10×6cm, depressed-globose; tubercles tapering, cylindric-terete; axils with long white woolly hairs; central spines 0, radial spines v. numerous, *c*80, 2–5mm, adpressed, minutely pubesc., white, pale yellow towards base, golden yellow at the base, the tip usually hair-like, creamy white. Autumn.

M. schmollii (Bravo) Werderm. = *M. discolor*.

M. schumannii Hildm. Clustering; st. to 6–8×3–4cm, ovoid to short-cylindric; tubercles short, grey green; axils soon naked; central spine usually 1, 1–1.5cm, hooked, dark brown to white with dark tip, radial spines 9–15, 6–12mm. Fl. lavender pink; stigmas tinged green or pale yellow. Summer. NW Mex. Z9.

M. scrippsiana (Britt. & Rose) Orcutt. Simple at first, later clustering; individual st. to 8cm diam., globose to short cylindric; tubercles blue-green; axils woolly; central spines 2, 8–10mm, red-brown, radial spines 8–10, 6–8mm, off-white. Fl. pink, tep. with paler margins; stigmas yellow. Spring. WC Mex.

M. sempervivi DC. Simple at first, sometimes later dividing apically or offsetting; st. to 10cm diam., depressed-globose; tubercles angled-conic, dark blue-green; axils woolly; central spines usually 2, sometimes 4, to 4mm, brown or black, later grey, radial spines rudimentary, on juvenile st. only. Fl. nearly white or pale pink. Spring. EC Mex.

M. senilis Salm-Dyck. Clustering; st. to 15×10cm, globular to cylindric; tubercles conic, obtuse; axils with bristles; central spines 4–6, white, at least the upper and lower hooked, radial spines 30–40, 2cm, white. Fl. long-tubular, tep. minutely toothed, scarlet. Spring. NW Mex.

M. setispina (J. Coult.) K. Brandg. Clustering; st. to 30×3–6cm; tubercles short and broadly conic; axils woolly; central spines 1–4, 2–5cm, upper straight, lowest one longest, hooked, radial

spines 10–12, v. unequal, 10–34mm, slender, flexuous, white with black tips. Fl. *c*5cm. Summer. Baja Calif.

M. sheldonii (Britt. & Rose) Boed. Clustering; st. *c*8cm, slender-cylindric; axils without bristles; central spine 1, hooked, radial spines 12–24, with dark tips, the 3 or 4 upper ones darker, a little stouter and 1 or 2 of them subcentral. Fls pale purple tep. with paler margins; fil. and style light purple. Summer. NW Mex.

M. shurliana (Gates) Gates = *M. blossfeldiana*.

M. similis Engelm. = *Escobaria missouriensis*.

M. simplex Haw. = *M. mammillaris*.

M. simpsonii (Engelm.) M.E. Jones = *Pediocactus simpsonii*.

M. sinistrohamata Boed. Simple; st. to 4.5cm diam., globose; tubercles short-cylindric; axils naked; central spines 4, lowest hooked, to 14mm, others straight, equalling the radials, pale yellow, radial spines *c*20, 8–10mm, glab., white. Fl. nearly white, tinged green, tep. with pale green or red mid-stripe. Spring. NC Mex.

M. solisii (Britt. & Rose) Boed. = *M. nunezii*.

M. sonorensis Craig. Simple and later clustering; st. depressed-globose to stout cylindric; tubercles globose-quadrangular; axils with wool, typically without bristles; spines variable; central spines 1–4, 5–20(–45)mm, red-brown, radial spines 8–10(–15), 1–20mm, upper shortest, slender acicular to acicular, off-white to cream, tipped red-brown. Fl. usually deep pink; style and stigmas olive-green. Spring. NW Mex.

M. sphacelata Mart. Clustering and sometimes forming mounds 50cm or more diam; st. 20cm or more ×15–30mm, cylindric, erect or decumbent; tubercles conic; axils slightly woolly or naked; central spines (1–)3–4, 4–8mm, straight, ivory or chalky white, tipped or speckled red or black, radial spines (10–)11–14(–15), 5–8mm, similar to the centrals. Fl. purple-red; stigmas pale yellow-green. Spring. S Mex.

M. sphaerica A. Dietr. Clustering and forming low clumps to 50cm wide, st. subglobose, 5cm diam.; tubercles conic-cylindric, flabby; axils slightly woolly; central spines 1, 3–6mm, yellow, radial spines 12–14, 6–9mm, off-white to pale yellow. Fl. large, yellow. Summer. NE Mex., US (SE Tex.).

M. spinosissima Lem. Simple at first, later often clustering; st. cylindric, to 30×8cm; tubercles ovate-conic; axils slightly woolly but without bristles; central spines 4–9 or more, 10–15mm, bristly, red-brown or pale yellow, radial spines 14–26, 4–10mm, bristly, nearly white. Fl. purple-pink. Spring. C Mex.

M. standleyi (Britt. & Rose) Orcutt. Simple or sometimes clustering; st. to 9×12cm, depressed-globose, pale blue-green; tubercles obtuse; axis with wool and bristles. Central spines 4–5, 5–9mm, white, tipped red-brown, radial spines 13–19, 4–8mm, white. Fl. purple-pink. Spring. NW Mex.

M. stella-aurata Mart. ex Zucc. = *M. elongata*.

M. stella-de-tacubaya Heese. Simple, 4–5×3–4cm, bright green, covered with white spines; tubercles cylindric; areoles elliptic, with white wool; axils sparsely woolly; central spines 1, 5–6mm, hooked, black, radial spines 35–40, 3–5mm, interlacing, white. Fl. with outer tep. striped dark salmon-pink, inner nearly white. Spring. N Mex.

M. sulcolanata Lem. = *Coryphantha sulcolanata*.

M. supertexta Mart. ex Pfeiff. Simple; st. to 15×7cm, subglobose to cylindric or oblong; tubercles small, crowded, conic; axils woolly; central spines 0–2, 3mm, white, sometimes tipped black, radial spines 16–18, to 5mm, white. Fl. small, deep red or pink. Spring. S Mex.

M. surculosa Boed. Freely clustering; rootstock tuberous; st. *c*3×2cm; tubercles cylindric. Central spine 1, to 2cm, slender, hooked, amber yellow, darker tipped, radial spines *c*15, 8–10mm, bristly, pale yellow. Fl. funnelform, sulphur yellow. Spring. NE Mex.

M. swinglei (Britt. & Rose) Boed. St. 10–20×3–5cm, cylindric; tubercles *c*7×7mm; axils with bristles 4–5mm; central spines 4, ascending, dark brown or black, the lowest 10–17mm, hooked or straight, radial spines 11–18, 5–8mm, dull white with dark tips. Fl. outer tep. tinged green or pink, inner tep. nearly white with brown mid-stripe; stigmas green. Summer. NW Mex.

M. tesopacensis Craig. Simple; st. to 18×13cm, globose to cylindric; tubercles pyramidal-conic; axils naked or with scant wool; central spines 1(–2), 10–12mm, red-brown at first, black-tipped, later ashy brown, radial spines 10–15, 4–7mm. Fl. with inner tep. cream striped pink or deep purple-pink; stigmas pale green or yellow-green. Summer. NW Mex.

M. tetracantha Pfeiff. = *M. polythele*.

M. tetrancistra Engelm. Simple or clustering; st. to 25×3.5–7.5cm, cylindric or ovoid-cylindric; tubercles cylindric; axils with bristles; central spines 3–4, the upper 2–3 to 14mm, straight or one or more hooked, 18–25mm, radial spines 30–60 in two series, the outer setaceous, *c*6–10mm, white, the inner stouter, longer and dark tipped or tinged purple. Fl. lavender, tep. edged white; stigmas white. Summer. SW US, NW Mex.

M. theresae Cutak. Simple or sparingly clustering, subglobose to cylindric, to c4cm×10–25mm, from stout taproots; tubercles cylindric, sometimes tinged purple; axils sparsely woolly; central spines 0, radial spines 22–30, 2mm, plumose, translucent white. Fl. narrowly funnelform; outer tep. green-brown, inner violet-purple; anth. deep yellow. Spring. Mts of NW Mex.

M. thornberi Orcutt. Clustering by suckers and offsets; st. usually 5–10×1.5–2.5cm, slender-cylindric, tapered at base; tubercles 5–9×5–9mm; central spines 1, 9–18mm, hooked, pale to dark red-brown, radial spines 13–20, 5–9mm, white or pale yellow, tipped red-brown. Fl. purple-pink; stigmas red. Summer. SW US, N Mex.

M. tolimensis Craig = *M. compressa.*

M. tuberculosa Engelm. = *Escobaria tuberculosa.*

M. turbinata Hook. = *Strombocactus disciformis.*

M. uncinata Zucc. ex Pfeiff. Usually simple; st. usually 6–10×8–10cm, depressed-globose; tubercles obtuse-conic, somewhat angled; axils woolly at first; central spines 1(–2), 7–10mm, hooked, red-brown, tipped darker, radial spines 3–7, to 5–6mm, rigid, subequal, the upper shorter, pink-tinged or off-white, darker-tipped. Tep. white with brown-red mid-stripe. Spring. C Mex.

M. vaupelii Tiegel = *M. haageana.*

M. vetula Mart. Clustering; st. to 4cm diam., globose to short-cylindric; tubercles obtuse-conic; axils slightly woolly or naked; central spines 1–7, c1cm, red-brown, radial spines 18–45, 4–12mm, white. Fl. pale yellow; stigmas white. Autumn. EC Mex.

M. viereckii Boed. = *M. picta.*

M. villifera Otto ex Pfeiff. = *M. polyedra.*

M. viperiana Purpus. Clustering, with elongate, decumbent, cylindric st. usually 1.5–2cm diam.; tubercles short cylindric or globose; axils slightly woolly and sometimes with fine white bristles; spines numerous, to 5mm, fine, white to black-brown. Fl. red. Summer. S Mex.

M. viridiflora (Britt. & Rose) Boed. St. 5–10×5–7.5cm, simple or clustering, globose to short-oblong, obscured by spines; tubercles terete; central spines 1(–4), 1.5–3cm, 1+ hooked, red-brown, radial spines 20–30, 10–12mm, bristle-like, with brown tip. Fl. tinged green or pink. Spring. SW US, N Mex.

M. vivipara (Nutt.) Haw. = *Escobaria vivipara.*

M. voburnensis Scheer. Clustering by offsets; st. 5–12×3–8cm, cylindric; tubercles pyramidal, red towards apex; axils with wool and bristles; central spines 1–3, 12mm, rigid, straight, subulate, brown at first, radial spines 6–9, 5–9mm, nearly white. Tep. pale yellow, the outer with red stripe. Autumn. S Mex., Guat.

M. waltheri Boed. = *M. heyderi.*

M. wiesingeri Boed. Simple; rootstock stout; st. to 4×8cm or larger, depressed-globose; tubercles c10×3–4mm, slender-pyramidal; axils naked or with bristles; central spines 4(–6), 5–6mm, red-brown, radial spines c20, 5–6mm, glassy white. Fl. carmine red; stigmas white. Summer. EC Mex.

M. wilcoxii Toumey ex Schum. = *M. wrightii* var. *wilcoxii.*

M. wildii A. Dietr. Clustering; st. to about 12×5cm, globose to cylindric; tubercles terete, obtuse; axils bristly; central spines 4, 8–10mm, lowermost hooked, yellow to brown, radial spines 8–10, 6–8mm, bristly, pale yellow to white. Fl. with outer tep. nearly white with brown-red mid-stripe, inner transparent white; stigmas yellow-green. Spring. C Mex.

M. winterae Boed. Simple; st. to 20–30cm diam., depressed-globose; tubercles quadrangular; axils naked at first, later rather densely white-woolly; spines 4, the upper and lower to 30mm, the lat. to 15mm, all stout; straight or curved, pale grey or faintly red, tipped brown. Fl. with outer tep. pale yellow with brown-red mid-stripe, inner nearly white with pale sulphur-yellow mid-stripe. Summer. NE Mex.

M. woburnensis auct. = *M. voburnensis.*

M. woodsii Craig. Simple; st. 5×8cm, flattened-globose to clavate; tubercles angled and keeled below to rounded at apex; axils with dense wool in flowering zone and white hair-like bristles to 25mm; central spines 2 (or 4), lowermost to 16mm, upper 4–5mm, purple-pink with black tip, radial spines 25–30, 4–8mm, hair-like, tortuous, white. Fl. pink. Spring–summer. C Mex.

M. wrightii Engelm. & Bigelow. Usually simple; st. to 6cm diam., flattened-globose to short cylindric, tubercles terete; central spines 1-several, 1 or more hooked, 5–21mm, brown, radial spines bristle-like, 8–20 (averaging 13), white. Fl. to 5cm, purple, pink or rarely white. Spring. SW US, N Mex. var. **wilcoxii** (Toumey ex Schum.) W.T. Marshall. Central spines usually 1–2; radials 12–30 (averaging 20). Fl. somewhat smaller. SW US, N Mex.

M. yaquensis Craig. Clustering freely, joints easily detached, to 7×1.5cm; tubercles short conic; axils faintly woolly; central spines 7mm, hooked, red-brown, radial spines 18, 5–6mm, smooth, cream, tipped light brown. Fl. with inner tep. pale pink

with deeper mid-stripe; stigmas purple-red. Summer. NW Mex.

M. yucatanensis (Britt. & Rose) Orcutt = *M. columbiana.*

M. zahniana Boed. Simple, to 6×10cm, depressed-globose; tubercles pyramidal, tetragonal; axils with sparse wool; spines 4, straight, subulate, tipped black, the lowest 15mm, the upper 8mm. Fl. with outer tep. pale yellow, tinged green, with white margins and red mid-stripe, inner sulphur to dark yellow with pale margins. Summer. NE Mex.

M. zeilmanniana Boed. Freely clustering; st. to 6×4.5cm; tubercles subcylindric; central spines 4, the upper 3 straight, the lowest hooked, slightly longer, all red-brown, radial spines c15–18, finely bristly, pubesc., white. Fl. violet-pink or purple, rarely white; stigmas pale yellow. Spring. C Mex.

M. zephyranthoides Scheidw. Simple; rootstock stout; st. to 8×10–15cm, flattened-globose; tubercles slender, flabby; central spines 1–2, to 14mm, hooked, red-brown or paler, radial spines 12–18, 8–10mm, hair-like, white. Fl. white with pink mid-stripe; stigmas green. Summer. C Mex.

M. zeyeriana Haage f. ex Schum. Simple; st. to 20×20cm, globose to shortly cylindric; tubercles conic, lightly angled and obliquely truncate; central spines 4, curved, red-brown, uppermost 2cm or more, lower shorter, radial spines c10, to 10mm, from upper part of areole, spreading, straight, white. Fl. white or pale yellow, tinged pink-brown. Spring. N Mex.

M. zuccariniana Mart. = *M. magnimamma.*

→*Bartschella, Cochemiea, Dolichothele, Krainzia, Mamillopsis, Pelecyphora, Phellosperma* and *Solisia.*

Mamoncillo *Melicoccus bijugatus.*

Manac *Brunfelsia uniflora.*

Manaco *Euterpe.*

Mana Grass *Cymbopogon nardus.*

Manchester Poplar *Populus nigra* var. *betulifolia.*

Manchurian Alder *Alnus hirsuta.*

Manchurian Ash *Fraxinus mandshurica.*

Manchurian Birch *Betula mandschurica.*

Manchurian Cherry *Prunus maackii.*

Manchurian Fir *Abies holophylla.*

Manchurian Fir *Abies nephrolepis.*

Manchurian Linden *Tilia mandshurica.*

Manchurian Maple *Acer mandschuricum.*

Manchurian Spikenard *Aralia continentalis.*

Manchurian Walnut *Juglans mandshurica.*

Manchurian Wild Rice *Zizania latifolia.*

Mandarin Lime *Citrus ×limonia.*

Mandarin Orange *Citrus reticulata.*

Mandarin's-hat *Holmskioldia sanguinea.*

Manda's Woolly Bear Begonia *Begonia subvillosa* var. *leptotricha.*

Mandevilla Lindl. Apocynaceae. 120 tuberous, perenn. herbs, subshrubs and twining lianes with milky sap. Infl. a lat. rac.; cal. 5-parted; cor. funnelform, tube cylindric to ovoid, throat campanulate to oblong, lobes 5. C & S Amer. Z10 unless specified.

M. ×amabilis (hort. Buckl.) Dress. (*M. splendens* ×?.) Climber to 4m. Lvs 10–20cm oblong-acute, rugose. Fls 9–12.5cm diam., rose pink, rosy crimson at centre, throat yellow, lobes rounded, short-acuminate. Gdn origin.

M. ×amoena hort. (*M. ×amabilis* × *M. splendens.*) A backcross with more abundantly produced, darker fls to 10cm diam. Includes *M.* 'Alice du Pont' and *M.* 'Splendens Hybrid'.

M. boliviensis (Hook. f.) Woodson. WHITE DIPLADENIA. Slender climber to 4m. Lvs to 10cm, glossy, elliptic to obovate-elliptic, caudate-acuminate. Fls 3–7 per rac.; cor. to 5cm, white, throat golden yellow, lobes to 4cm, acuminate. Boliv., Ecuad.

M. laxa (Ruiz & Pav.) Woodson. CHILEAN JASMINE. Climber to 4m. St. verruculose. Lvs 5–7cm, cordate-oblong, acuminate, glossy above, purple or grey-green beneath with pubesc. axils. Fls highly fragrant; cor. to 5cm diam., white to ivory, tube downy within. Arg. Z9.

M. sanderi (Hemsl.) Woodson. Climber to 5m. Lvs to 6m, broadly oblong-elliptic, briefly acuminate, coriaceous. Rac. 3–5-fld; cor. rose-pink, throat to 4.5cm, lobes to 3.5cm, acuminate. Braz. 'Rosea' (BRAZILIAN JASMINE): lvs to 5cm, ovate, lustrous above, bronze-green beneath; fls to 8cm, salmon pink, throat and tube yellow within.

M. splendens (Hook. f.) Woodson. Climber to 6m. Lvs to 20cm, broadly elliptic, acuminate, thin v. finely downy. Rac. 3–5-fld; cor. 7.5–10cm diam., rose pink, tube to 4cm, lobes to 3.25cm, briefly acuminate. SE Braz. 'Rosacea': fls rose-pink, flushed and bordered deeper rose, tube yellow within, ringed bright rose at throat.

M. suaveolens Lindl. = *M. laxa.*

M. tweediana Gadeceau & Stapf = *M. laxa.*

→*Dipladenia.*

Mandioca *Manihot esculenta.*
Mandioqueira *Schefflera morototonii.*

Mandragora L. Solanaceae. 6 acaulescent or v. short-stemmed perenn. herbs. Taproots stout, often forked, said to resemble the human form. Lvs simple, basal, in a dense rosette. Fls short-stalked axill., solitary, actinomorphic; cal. bell-shaped, 5-lobed; cor. bell-shaped, 5-lobed; sta. 5, slightly protruding. Fr. fleshy, short-stalked, toxic. Medit. to Himal.
M. acaulis Gaertn. = *M. officinarum.*
M. autumnalis Bertol. Resembles *M. officinarum*, but lvs oblong-lanceolate, ovate, to 25cm. Cor. to 3cm, violet or white. Fr. ellipsoid, orange to yellow. Winter–spring. E Medit.
M. officinarum L. MANDRAKE; DEVIL'S APPLES. Lvs to 30cm, ovate to lanceolate, entire, bullate-undulate. Cor. to 2.5cm, blue to purple, lobes triangular. Fr. to 3cm diam., globose, yellow. Spring. N It., W Balk.
M. vernalis Bertol. = *M. officinarum.*

Mandrake *Mandragora officinarum.*

Manettia Mutis Rubiaceae. 80 everg. herbs or subshrubs, usually twining. Fls axill. and solitary, or in few-fld pan. or cymes; cal. tube turbinate or obovoid to campanulate, lobes usually 4, often with intervening teeth; cor. tubular to funnelform, terete to 4-angled, lobes usually 4. Trop. Amer. Z10.
M. asperula Benth. = *M. cordifolia.*
M. bicolor Hook. f. non Paxt. = *M. luteorubra.*
M. coccinea (Aubl.) Willd. Climbing herb to 2m. St. 4-angled, glab. to short-pubesc. Lvs to 10cm, ovate or lanceolate or oblong, acute, thin-textured, lustrous, rough above, glab. to short-pubesc. beneath. Cor. salverform, pink to scarlet spotted, red, tube to 2.5cm, exterior and throat yellow-pubesc. Summer. W Indies and Cuba to N S Amer.
M. cordifolia Mart. FIRECRACKER VINE. Climbing herb, to 4m. St. terete. Lvs to 8cm, variable, ovate to ovate-lanceolate, apex acute, thin-textured, lustrous above, glab. or pubesc. beneath. Cor. to 5cm, vivid red or dark orange fading to yellow at lobes, tube distended above, interior pubesc. Winter–summer. S Amer. (Boliv. to Arg., Peru).
M. costaricensis Wernham = *M. coccinea.*
M. discolor hort. = *M. luteorubra.*
M. glabra Cham. & Schldl. = *M. cordifolia.*
M. grandiflora Vell. = *M. cordifolia.*
M. inflata Sprague = *M. luteorubra.*
M. luteorubra Benth. BRAZILIAN FIRE CRACKER; TWINING FIRE CRACKER; FIRECRACKER VINE. Climbing perenn. herb or shrub to 4m. St. strongly twining, somewhat 4-angled, coarsely pubesc., somewhat viscid. Lvs 2.5–10cm, ovate-rhombic to ovate-lanceolate, acute, subcoriaceous. Cor. to 5cm, tube cylindric, bright red, hispidulous, lobes yellow. Parag., Urug.
M. micans Poepp. & Endl. = *M. cordifolia.*
M. reclinata L. Climbing herb to 1m. St. terete, glab. Lvs to 7cm, ovate to elliptic, narrowly acute, thin-textured, occas. sparsely pubesc. Cor. red, tube to 2cm, exterior minutely pubesc., interior with winged hairs. W Indies and Cuba, Mex. to N S Amer.

Man Fern *Cibotium splendens.*

Manfreda Salisb. Agavaceae. 18 ± stemless perenn. herbs, with succulent roots, fleshy subterranean st. or bulbous root-stocks. Lvs rosulate, basal, narrow, flexible. Infl. spike-like; fls radially symmetric; perianth seg. 6, united below to form tube; sta. 6, anth. long-exserted. SE US to Mex.
M. longiflora (Rose) Verh.-Will. Lvs 10–25×2cm, linear, minutely serrate, spotted dark green or brown. Flowering st. 30–100cm; fls 4cm; perianth white tinged green at first, brick red in age, seg. spreading, oblong. Spring–summer. S Tex., N Mex.
M. maculosa (Hook.) Rose. Lvs 15–30×1–2cm, linear-lanceolate, recurved, concave, minutely dentate, margins hyaline, glaucous with brown or green markings, fleshy. Flowering st. 90–120cm; fls 4–5cm, fragrant; perianth lobes oblong, white tinged green, flushed pink. Spring–summer. Tex., Mex.
M. variegata (Jacobi) Rose. Lvs 20–45×2–4cm, lanceolate, slightly tapered to base, margins incurved, glaucous with brown markings, deeply grooved. Flowering st. 90–130cm; fls 4cm, fragrant; perianth lobes green tinged brown. Spring. Tex., Mex.
M. virginica (L.) Salisb. Lvs 60×2.5–5cm, oblong-spathulate, gradually tapered to base, sinuate, dark green with red stripes, thick, flaccid somewhat grooved. Flowering st. 80–180cm; fls 2.5–5cm, fragrant; perianth seg. linear-oblong, yellow tinged green or brown. Summer. S US.
→*Agave, Polianthes* and *Runyonia.*

Mangelwurzel *Beta vulgaris.*

Mangifera L. MANGO. Anacardiaceae. 35 andromonoecious trees. Lvs simple. Pan. term. or axill.; fls numerous, small; cal. 4–5-lobed; pet. 4–5, overlapping, sometimes with gland. ridges; sta. 1–12, usually 5, sometimes with staminodes. Fr. a fleshy, resinous drupe, ovoid to ellipsoid; endocarp fibrous; seed 1. India to S China and Solomon Is., nat. N Aus. Z10.
M. caesia Jack. Tree to 35m. Trunk occas. buttressed, bark grey-brown, fissured. Lvs coriaceous, elliptic, ovate, ovate-oblong or lanceolate. Pan. pyramidal, 15–75cm, puberulent; fls yellow-red. Fr. rough, brown to yellow-brown or pale green, to 19×10cm. Sumatra, Malay Penins., nat. elsewhere in Malaysia.
M. foetida Lour. Tree to 40m. Bark green or red-brown, rough, fissured or scaly. Lvs 14–35cm, stiff-sericeous, oblanceolate to elliptic, obtuse, sometimes emarginate. Pan. pyramidal, glab., 10–40cm; fls pink to dark red. Fr. yellow or grey-green. Spring. Indochina, Malaysia.
M. foetida Bl. non Lour. = *M. caesia.*
M. foetida var. *odorata* Griff. = *M. ×odorata.*
M. horsfieldii Miq. = *M. foetida.*
M. indica L. MANGO. Tree to 30m. Bark grey, fissured. Lvs to 30cm, subcoriaceous or papery, oblong-elliptic or oblong-lanceolate. Pan. tomentose; fls yellow-white to brown-red. Fr. 4–25×1–10cm, yellow, green or red, flesh yellow-apricot. Burm., widely nat. trop. Asia. Large numbers of cvs exist.
M. indica Bl. non L. = *M. foetida.*
M. kemanga Bl. = *M. caesia.*
M. leschenaultii Marchand = *M. foetida.*
M. oblongifolia Hook. f. = *M. ×odorata.*
M. ×odorata Griff. (*M. indica* ×*M. foetida.*) Tree to 35m. Bark grey, smooth or fissured. Lvs to 35×10cm, coriaceous, elliptic-lanceolate or lanceolate. Pan. 15–50cm, pyramidal, ± puberulous; fls yellow to red. Fr. dark green, to 13×10cm, flesh yellow. Origin unknown, nat. Malaysia.
M. pinnata L. f. = *Spondias pinnata.*
M. verticillata C. Robinson = *M. caesia.*

Mangle Bobo *Bontia daphnoides.*

Manglietia Bl. Magnoliaceae. 25 shrubs and trees close to *Magnolia*, differing in fls with 9 tep. in 2 whorls and 6 (not 2) ovules per carpel. Malesia to S China, E Himal. Z9.
M. insignis (Wallich) Bl. Tree, to 12m; young shoots grey-pubesc. Lvs to 20cm, oblong to elliptic, glossy above, glaucous beneath, coriaceous. Fls solitary, erect, to 7.5cm diam., tep. sepaloid, inner tep. obovate, white tinged pink or carmine. Spring. W China, Himal., Burm.

Mango *Mangifera indica.*
Mango Ginger *Curcuma amada.*
Mangold *Beta vulgaris.*
Mangosteen *Garcinia* (*G. mangostana*).
Mangrove Fern *Acrostichum speciosum.*
Mangrove Palm *Nypa.*

Manihot Mill. CASSAVA; MANIOC; YUCA; TAPIOCA PLANT. Euphorbiaceae. 98 trees, shrubs and herbs, with milky latex. Lvs usually digitately 3- to 7-lobed or parted, stalked. Fls usually rather large, in rac. or pan., females below males; cal. campanulate, 5-lobed, usually green-white to yellow, sometimes tinged purple; sta. 10. Fr. a capsule. Trop. and warm temp. Amer. Z10.
M. dulcis (J.F. Gmel.) Pax SWEET CASSAVA. Differs from *M. esculenta* in smaller roots. S Amer.
M. esculenta Crantz. BITTER CASSAVA; MANIOC; MANDIOCA; TAPIOCA; GARI. Shrubby tree to 3m, with long tuberous edible roots, and soft, brittle st. Lf lobes 3–7, spathulate or linear-lanceolate, soft mid-green. Braz. 'Variegata': lvs bright green, variegated yellow along veins.
M. glaziovii Muell. Arg. Tree to 10m. Lf lobes 15–20cm, numerous, ribs white. Braz.
M. manihot (L.) Cockerell = *M. esculenta.*
M. utilissima Pohl = *M. esculenta.*

Manila Bean *Psophocarpus tetragonolobus.*
Manila Grass *Zoysia matrella.*
Manila Hemp *Musa* (*M. textilis*).
Manila Palm *Veitchia* (*V. merrillii*).
Manila Tamarind *Pithecellobium dulce.*

Manilkara Adans. Sapotaceae. 70. Everg. trees with milky latex. Fls axill., solitary or in clusters; sep. (4–)6(–8), in 2 whorls; cor. 6(–9) lobed, tube usually shorter than lobes; sta. 6(–12), usually alternating with (0–)6(–9) staminodes. Fr. a fleshy berry. Pantrop. Z10.
M. bidentata (A. DC.) A. Chev. BALATA. Tree to at least 30m. Lvs 6–21cm, narrowly elliptic or oblong, coriaceous to chartac-

eous, glab. Infl. (2–)5–20-fld; cor. 3–6.5mm, lobes 6. Fr. 1–3(–4)cm, ellipsoid to globose, smooth, seeds 1–2. W Indies (Windward Is), Panama, Colomb., Venez., Peru, Braz.

M.zapota (L.) Royen. SAPODILLA; NISPERO; CHICLE. Tree to at least 30m. Lvs 6.6–14cm, elliptic to oblong-elliptic or elliptic-lanceolate, subglabrous, chartaceous. Fls solitary, cor. 8–11mm, lobes 6(–7). Fr. 3.5–8×6cm, broadly ovoid or ellipsoid, rough, pulp sweet, somewhat granular, pale yellow-brown; seeds 2–10. Mex. to Costa Rica.
→*Achras*.

Manioc *Manihot* (*M. esculenta*).
Manipur Lily *Lilium mackliniae*.
Manna Ash *Fraxinus ornus*.
Manna Grass *Glyceria*.
Manna Gum *Eucalyptus viminalis*.
Manna Plant *Tamarix gallica*.
Manna Wattle *Acacia microbotrya*.
Mano de Lagarija *Macfadyena unguis-cati*.
Mano de Leon *Oreopanax peltatus*.
Man of the Earth *Ipomoea pandurata*.
Man Orchid *Aceras anthropophorum*.
Manroot *Marah*.

Mansoa DC. Bignoniaceae. 15 lianes. Lvs trifoliolate, term. leaflet often replaced by simple tendril. Rac. or pan. axill. or term.; cal. cupular to tubular-campanulate, truncate or 5-toothed; cor. tubular, 5-lobed. Mex. to Braz. Z10.

M.alliacea (Lam.) A. Gentry. BEJUCO DE AJO. Vegetation smells strongly of onions. Lfts 5–10cm, ovate-elliptic. Fls in groups of 6–25; cor. 4–6cm, dark to pale purple. Americas.

M.difficilis (Cham.) Bur. & Schum. Lfts 5–11cm, oblong-ovate. Cor. 5.5–9cm, violet, purple or vermilion, limb 6.5cm diam., puberulent. Braz.

M.hymenaea (DC.) A. Gentry. Plant smells strongly of onions. Lfts 4.8–9.4cm, ovate to narrow-ovate. Infl. puberulent; cor. pale lilac to purple, pink or white, tube glab., 3–3.6cm, lobes 0.6–1.3cm, puberulent. Winter. Mex. to Braz.
→*Adenocalymma, Anemopaegma, Cydista, Pachyptera, Petastoma* and *Pseudocalymma*.

Mañío *Podocarpus salignus*.
Man Tree Fern *Cibotium splendens*.
Manuka *Leptospermum scoparium*.

Manulea L. Scrophulariaceae. 60 ann. or perenn. herbs or sub-shrubs. Lvs radical, rosulate and cauline. Infl. term., racemose, spicate or paniculate; cal. deeply 5-cleft, rarely bilabiate; cor. tubular-subcampanulate, limb spreading, lobes 5; sta. didynamous. S Afr. Z10.

M.rubra L. Ann. or perenn. to 60cm. St. decid., ascending, canescent. Lvs to 6cm, oblanceolate, toothed. Fls subsessile in an interrupted rac., with thyrsoid br. near base; cor. ruddy, orange or golden yellow, exterior pubesc. above. Summer.

M.tomentosa L. Hoary subshrub to 75cm; br. decumbent or ascending. Lvs 2–4cm, grey, glandular-hairy, toothed. Fls sessile or nearly so in clusters, in dense, term. rac. to 8cm; cor. orange or yellow, exterior glandular-tomentose. Spring–autumn.

Many-flowered Honeysuckle *Lambertia multiflora*.
Many-flowered Wood-rush *Luzula multiflora*.
Many-headed Dryandra *Dryandra polycephala*.
Manzanita *Arbutus*; *Arctostaphylos* (*A. manzanita*).
Maple *Acer*.
Maple-leaf Begonia *Begonia dregei*; *B. ×weltoniensis*.
Maple-leaved Bayur *Pterospermum acerifolium*.
Marabu-hagi *Lespedeza cyrtobotrya*.

Marah Kellogg. BIGROOT; MANROOT. Cucurbitaceae. 7 monoecious, herbaceous vines. Tubers v. large, globose to cylindric. Tendrils simple to 3-fid. Lvs suborbicular, cordate, palmately 5–7-lobed. ♂ infl. a rac. or peduncle; cor. green-white to 1×2cm, campanulate to rotate, gland., seg. usually 5; anth. 3; ♀ fls solitary, co-axillary with ♂; cal. and cor. larger. Fr. a capsule, globose to fusiform, pendulous, often spinose. W N Amer. Z8.

M.fabaceus (Naudin) Greene. St. to 7m, sparsely pubesc. Lvs 5–10cm, diam., glab. to scabrous. Fr. globose, densely spinose, 4–5cm. Calif.

M.macrocarpus (Greene) Greene. CHILICOTHE. St. 1–7m, deeply striated. Lvs scabrous above, hispid beneath. Fr. cylindric, 8–12cm, spines dense. Calif., Baja Calif.

M.oreganus (Torr. & A. Gray) Howell. St. 1–7m, often sparsely pubesc. Lvs glab. to pubesc., 8–35cm diam. Fr. striped, sparsely spinose. SW US to S Canada.
→*Echinocystis* and *Sicyos*.

Maranon *Anacardium occidentale*.

Maranta L. Marantaceae. 32 perenn. herbs. Rhiz. sometimes swollen. Lvs obovate to elliptic, exhibiting 'sleep' movements; petioles slender, pulvinate. Infl. 2 to several per shoot, simple or sparsely branched with 2–6 pedicellate cymules; bracts persistent, papery; fls usually zygomorphic; sep. thin; cor. tube green; staminodes petaloid. Trop. C & S Amer. Z10.

M. allouia Aubl. = *Calathea allouia*.
M. argyraea hort. = *Calathea argyraea*.
M.arundinacea L. ARROWROOT; OBEDIENCE PLANT. St. slender, erect, branching, to 2m. Lvs to 25cm, oblong-lanceolate, acuminate, ± pubesc. Infl. sparingly branched; fls white. Throughout genus range. 'Aurea': lvs golden, intermittently marked light green. 'Variegata': lvs dark green variegated lime green and sulphur yellow. Has been misnamed *Phrynium variegatum*, properly a synonym of *Calathea variegata*.
M. asymmetrica hort. = *Calathea taeniosa*.
M. bachemiana hort. = *Calathea bachemiana*.
M. baraquinii Lem. = *Calathea baraquinii*.
M. bella Bull = *Calathea bella*.
M.bicolor Ker-Gawl. To 35cm. Shoots prostrate. Lvs to 15cm, glaucous, oblong-elliptic to ovate, pale green spotted brown along paler central zone, purple beneath. Infl. a solitary spike; fls white with purple-maroon lines. NE S Amer.
M. compressa A. Dietr. = *Ctenanthe compressa*.
M. cuspidata Roscoe = *Marantochloa cuspidata*.
M. cylindrica A. Dietr. = *Calathea cylindrica*.
M. eximia Mathieu = *Calathea exima*.
M. fasciata Lind. = *Calathea fasciata*.
M. glabra Körn. = *Ctenanthe glabra*.
M. indica Tussac = *M. arundinacea*.
M. insignis H.W. Ward = *Calathea lancifolia*.
M. jacquinii Roem. & Schult. = *Stromanthe jacquinii*.
M. kegeliana hort. = *Calathea bachemiana*.
M. kegeljanii E. Morr. = *Calathea bella*.
M. kummerana E. Morr. = *Ctenanthe kummerana*.
M. legrelliana Lind. = *Calathea legrelliana*.
M. leopardina Bull = *Calathea leopardina*.
M.leuconeura E. Morr. PRAYER PLANT; TEN COMMANDMENTS. Low-growing, rhiz. spreading. Lvs to 12cm, elliptic, lustrous dark green, zoned grey or maroon, veined silver, red or purple above, grey-green or maroon beneath. Infl. a slender, solitary spike; fls white or violet or spotted violet. Braz. 'Erythroneura' ('Erythrophylla') HERRINGBONE PLANT: Lvs velvety black-green with prominent sealing wax red veins and a lime green zone along midvein. 'Massangeana': lvs tinted blue, dull rusty-brown toward centre, jagged silver band along midrib and silver lines along lat. veins. var. *leuconeura*. Lvs broad-elliptic, dark green above with a pale, comb-like central zone and pinnate silver veins. var. *kerchoviana* E. Morr. RABBIT'S FOOT. Lvs grey-green with a row of purple-brown to dark olive blotches on each side of midrib.
M. lietzei hort. = *Calathea lietzei*.
M. lubbersiana auct. = *Ctenanthe lubbersiana*.
M. lushnathiana Reg. & Körn. = *Ctenanthe compressa* var. *lushnathiana*.
M. lutea Aubl. = *Calathea lutea*.
M. maculata Pav. = *Calathea pavonii*.
M. makoyana E. Morr. = *Calathea makoyana*.
M. massangeana E. Morr. = *M. leuconeura*.
M. mazellii hort. = *Calathea virginalis*.
M. mediopicta E. Morr. = *Calathea mediopicta*.
M. micans Mathieu = *Calathea micans*.
M. oppenheimiana hort. = *Ctenanthe oppenheimiana*.
M. oppenheimiana var. *tricolor* hort. = *Ctenanthe oppenheimiana* 'Tricolor'.
M. orbifolia (Lind.) H. Kenn. = *Calathea orbifolia*.
M. ornata Lind. = *Calathea majestica*.
M. pilosa Schauer = *Ctenanthe pilosa*.
M. pinnato-picta hort. = *Calathea applicata*.
M. porteana (Gris) Körn. = *Stromanthe porteana*.
M. protracta Miq. = *M. arundinacea*.
M. pruinosa Reg. = *Pleiostachya pruinosa*.
M. pulchella E. Morr. non Lind. = *Calathea pulchella*.
M. pulchella Lind. non E. Morr. = *Calathea zebrina* 'Humilior'.
M. ramosissima Wallich = *M. arundinacea*.
M. roseopicta Lind. = *Calathea roseopicta*.
M.ruiziana Körn. Low, scandent. Lvs to 7.5cm, pubesc., ash-green, densely villous on midrib. Fls small. C & N S Amer.
M. sanderiana hort. = *Calathea* 'Sanderiana'.
M. sanguinea hort. = *Stromanthe sanguinea*.
M. setosa (Roscoe) A. Dietr. = *Ctenanthe setosa*.
M. silvatica Roscoe = *M. arundinacea*.
M. smaragdina Lind. = *Monotagma smaragdinum*.
M. splendida Lem. = *Calathea splendida*.

M. tonckat Aubl. = *Stromanthe tonckat*.
M. truncata Link = *Calathea truncata*.
M. veitchiana Van Houtte = *Calathea veitchiana*.
M. wallisii Lind. = *Calathea wallisii*.
M. warscewiczii Mathieu = *Calathea warscewiczii*.
M. wiotii E. Morr. = *Calathea wiotii*.
M. zebrina Sims = *Calathea zebrina*.

MARANTACEAE Petersen. 31/550. *Ataenidia, Calathea, Ctenanthe, Donax, Ischnosiphon, Maranta, Marantochloa, Megaphrynium, Monotagma, Phrynium, Pleiostachya, Stachyphrynium, Stromanthe, Thalia, Thaumatococcus, Trachyphrynium*.

Marantochloa Brongn. & Gris. Marantaceae. 3 perenn. herbs. St. and rhiz. somewhat hardened, branching or simple. Lvs alt., asymmetric, 1 side curved, the other straight, midrib ridged above; petiole slender, sheathing at base. Infl. simple or branching; fls in bracteate cymules; sep. free, often chaffy, linear; cor. tubular, long, lobes acute; outer staminodes 2, petaloid. Trop. Afr. Z10.
M. cuspidata (Roscoe) Milne-Redh.　St. erect, to 60cm. Lvs to 40cm, triangular-lanceolate, acuminate, subtruncate at base, glab. above, pubesc. beneath. Infl. racemose, slender; bracts persistent; cor. *c*2cm, yellow. Senegal to Ivory Coast.
M. flexuosa (Benth.) Hutch. = *M. cuspidata* and *M. purpurea*.
M. purpurea (Ridl.) Milne-Redh. St. branching, erect or climbing to 1m. Lvs to 45cm, ovate to ovate-oblong, narrowly acuminate, rounded at base, glab. above, pruinose beneath. Infl. branched; bracts caducous, red; cal. and cor. rose-pink to light brown; outer staminodes white, inner staminodes yellow. W & C Afr. to Angola.
→*Clinogyne, Donax, Maranta* and *Phrynium*.

Maraschino Cherry *Prunus cerasus* var. *marasca*.

Marattia Sw. Marattiaceae. 60 large everg. ferns. Rhiz. large, succulent. Stipes thick, succulent with adnate stipules at base; frond blades 2–3-pinnate; pinnules oblong, glossy. Trop.
M. alata Sw.　Stipes 30–60cm, paleate; blades 90–120cm, tripinnatifid, chaffy below; pinnae, lower pinnae largest, seg. oblong, serrate or crenate. Trop. Amer., W Indies.
M. alata Hook. & Arn. non Sw. = *M. douglasii*.
M. attenuata Labill. Stipes 90–120cm, smooth; blades 90–120cm, 3-pinnate, glab.; pinnae 45–60cm on stalk to 15cm; pinnules 2–3 each side; seg. 10–15×2.5–3.5cm, serrate at apex. Aus.
M. cicutifolia Kaulf. Stipes 30–60cm, smooth; blades 150–180cm, bipinnate, glab.; lower pinnae 30–45×30cm; pinnules 10–15× 2.5cm, oblong-lanceolate, entire or minutely serrate. Braz.
M. douglasii (Presl) Bak.　DOUGLAS MULESFOOT FERN; PALA. Rhiz. surrounded by succulent black auricles; stipes subterete, to 1.5m, pale green or foxy below, blackened at base, smooth, rather succulent; blades to 120cm, tripinnate, brittle and fleshy; pinnae oblong-lanceolate; pinnules 10–25×6–8mm, linear, rachis winged, seg. ovate to oblong, bluntly serrate. Hawaii.
M. fraxinea (Poir.) Sm. KING FERN; PARA FERN.　Stipes swollen below, 30–60cm, smooth, paleate; blades 2–5m, bipinnate or occas. tripinnate; pinnae 30–60cm; pinnules 10–15×1.5–4cm, oblong-lanceolate, entire or minutely serrate. Asia, Afr., Trop. Amer., NZ.
M. fraxinea Luerssen non (Poir.) Sm. = *M. smithii*.
M. laevis Sm. = *M. alata*.
M. salicina J. Sm. POTATO FERN.　Rhiz. short-creeping, stout with swollen roots; stipes dark and swollen at base, tuberculate, stipules ear-like; blades arching, pinnate or bipinnate; pinnules alt.; rachis tuberculate. Trop. Asia, Australasia.
M. smithii Mett. ex Kuhn. Stipes 1.5m, stout; blades to 3×1.5m, bipinnate; pinnae to 1m; pinnules 12–15×1.5cm, linear-oblong, shallowly serrate. Polyn.
M. sorbifolia Brackenr. non Sw. = *M. smithii*.

MARATTIACEAE Bercht. & J. Presl. *Angiopteris, Christensenia, Marattia*.

Marble Leaf *Peristrophe hyssopifolia*.
Marble Martagon *Lilium duchartrei*.
Marble Pea *Vigna unguiculata*.
Marble Plant *Neoregelia marmorata*.

Marcetella Svent.
M. moquiniana (Webb & Berth.) Svent. = *Bencomia moquiniana*.

Mareer *Cordia subcordata*.
Mareer Docol *Cordia monoica*.
Marer *Cordia monoica; C. subcordata*.

Marer Deylab *Cordia monoica*.

Margaritaria L. Euphorbiaceae. 14 dioecious shrubs or trees, usually decid. Lvs distichous, entire. Fls in axill. clusters; sep. 4, sta. 4. Old and New World Trop. Z10.
M. discoidea (Baill.) Webster. Shrub or tree to 30m. Lvs 3–15cm, ovate-elliptic to obovate-oblanceolate, thin, glab. except on midribs. ♂ fls in many-fld clusters, ♀ fls in lf-axils. Fr. to 1cm diam., subglobose to oblate, 3-lobed. W to E & SE Afr.
→*Phyllanthus*.

Marginaria Bory.
M. augustifolia (Sw.) Presl = *Campyloneurum augustifolium*.
Marcgravia L. see Marcgraviaceae.

MARCGRAVIACEAE Choisy. 5/108. Trop. American family of epiphytic shrubs and climbers, often attached by clinging roots and with leathery lvs in 2 states – overlapping and shingle-like and lax and longer-stalked. Fls inconspicuous in term. spikes or umbels but with showy bracts modified into waxy, pitcher like nectaries. *Marcgravia rectiflora* an ivy or philodendron-like shrub is sometimes cult., as is the spectacular *Norantea guianensis* (RED HOT POKER), a climber from the W Indies with leathery, elliptic lvs and erect spikes of brilliant orange-red bladder-like bracts.

Marguerite *Argyranthemum; Leucanthemum vulgare*.
Marguerite Jaune *Rudbeckia hirta*.

Margyricarpus Ruiz & Pav. Rosaceae. 1 everg. subshrub to 60cm; branchlets densely leafy. Lvs to 2cm, imparipinnate, rachis thorny; petioles to 2mm; lfts usually 9, linear, to 10mm, glabrescent, margins wooly. Fls small, 1–3 per axil or in sparse cymes; pet. 0; sta. 1–3, anth. purple. Fr. globose, to 7mm diam., white with purple tints. Spring–summer. S Amer. (Andes). Z9.
M. pinnatus (Lam.) Kuntze. PEARL FRUIT.
M. setosus Ruiz & Pav. = *M. pinnatus*.
→*Empetrum*.

Maria *Calophyllum brasiliense*.

Marianthus Hueg. ex Endl. Pittosporaceae. 15 perenn., everg. shrubs usually slender-stemmed, often climbing. Fls in term. or axill. clusters, 5-merous; pet. connivent at base and appearing fused. Fr. a capsule, compressed, membranaceous. Aus. Z8.
M. erubescens Putterl. Climber to 5m. Lvs leathery, broad. Fls many, 2.5cm, brilliant red. Late spring. W Aus.
M. ringens (J.L. Drumm. & Harv.) F.J. Muell. Climber to 3m. Lvs broad, leathery. Fls many, *c*2.5cm. Spring. W Aus.

Maria Rosa *Syagrus macrocarpa*.
Marigold *Calendula; Tagetes*.
Marijuana *Cannabis*.
Marine Ivy *Cissus trifoliata*.
Marine Vine *Cissus trifoliata*.
Maripa *Maximiliana*.
Mariposa Lily *Calochortus*.
Mariposa Tulip *Calochortus*.

Mariscus Vahl.
M. cyperoides (L.) Urban = *Cyperus cyperoides*.
M. sieberianus Nees. = *Cyperus cyperoides*.

Maritime Ceanothus *Ceanothus maritimus*.
Maritime Pine *Pinus pinaster*.
Marjoram *Origanum*.

Markea Rich. = *Dyssochroma*.

Markhamia Seem. ex Schum. Bignoniaceae. 12 trees. Lvs imparipinnate. Fls in term. rac. or pan.; cal. spathaceous, usually narrow; cor. 4–9cm, tubular-campanulate. Afr., Asia. Z10.
M. hildebrandtii (Bak.) Sprague = *M. lutea*.
M. lutea (Benth.) Schum. 5–10m. Lfts 4.5–21cm, 7–13, oblong to ovate, rarely dentate. Cor. yellow lined red in throat, lobes scaly outside. Ghana to Cameroun, Zaire, Burundi.
M. obtusifolia (Bak.) Sprague.　To 10m. Lfts to 15cm, 5–11, oblong-ovate to lanceolate. Cor. yellow striped brown in throat, lobes gland. Afr.
M. platycalyx Bak. = *M. lutea*.
M. stipulata (Wallich) Seem. Lfts to 30cm, oblong-elliptic. Cor. yellow, purple-red in mouth, lobes crenulate. SE Asia.
→*Dolichandrone, Muenteria* and *Spathodea*.

Marking Nut Tree *Semecarpus anacardium*.
Markweed *Toxicodendron radicans*.

Marlberry *Ardisia escallonioides*; *A. japonica*.
Marmalade Bush *Streptosolen jamesonii*.
Marmalade Orange *Citrus aurantium*.
Marmalade Plum *Pouteria sapota*.
Marn Elm *Ulmus villosa*.

Marniera Backeb.
M. chrysocardium (Alexander) Backeb. = *Epiphyllum chryso-cardium*.

Maroochie Nut *Macadamia ternifolia*.
Maroonhood *Pterostylis pedunculata*.
Marram Grass *Ammophila*.
Marri *Eucalyptus calophylla*.
Marrow *Cucurbita pepo*.

Marrubium L. HOREHOUND. Labiatae. 40 perenn. aromatic herbs. St. tetragonal. Lvs opposite, rugose. Fls in verticillate spikes; cal. campanulate, usually enclosing cor., teeth 5–10, spiny; cor. bilabiate, upper lip bilobed, lower lip trilobed, sta. within tube. Temp. Eurasia, 1 sp. adventive in N Amer. Z8.
M. astracanicum Jacq. = *M. kotschyi*.
M. brachyodon Boiss. = *M. kotschyi*.
M. candidissimun auct., non L. = *M. incanum*.
M. cylleneum Boiss. & Heldr. To 50cm; st. lanate. Lvs obovate, crenate, tomentose. Fls yellow. Greece, Albania. Z7.
M. goktschaicum N. Popov = *M. kotschyi*.
M. incanum Desr. To 50cm; st. white-tomentose, branched. Lvs ovate, crenate to dentate, tomentose. Fls white. It., Balk. Z7.
M. kotschyi Boiss. & Hohen. To 40cm. Lvs elliptic, crenate. Fls red or purple, rarely white. Summer. Iraq, Kurdistan. Z8.
M. leonuroides Desr. To 45cm; st. tomentose. Lvs reniform, dentate, grey-pubesc. beneath. Fls pink or lilac. Crimea, Cauc. Z6.
M. libanoticum Boiss. St. lanate, exceeding cal. ascending green-yellow. Lvs round or ovate, crenulate. Fls pink. Summer–early autumn. Leb. Z8.
M. purpureum Bunge = *M. kotschyi*.
M. supinum L. To 45cm; st. simple, lanate below, tomentose above. Lvs reniform, cordate at base, crenate. Fls pink to lilac. C & S Spain. Z7.
M. velutinum Sibth. & Sm. To 45cm; st. white-lanate. Lvs round, crenate, near glab. above, tomentose beneath. Fls yellow. Summer. N & C Greece. Z8.
M. vulgare L. COMMON HOREHOUND; WHITE HOREHOUND. To 45cm, thyme-scented; st. usually white-pubesc. Lvs round to ovate, crenate, tomentose beneath, downy to glab. above. Fls white. Summer. Eur., N Afr., Canary Is., Asia. Z3.
→*Thymus*.

Marsdenia R. Br.
M. erecta (L.) R. Br. = *Cionura erecta*.

Marsh Afrikaner *Gladiolus tristis*.

Marshallia Schreb. Compositae. 10 erect perenn. herbs. Lvs alt., simple, entire, sessile to amplexicaul. Cap. discoid, numerous; flts tubular. N Amer.
M. caespitosa Nutt. ex DC. St. v. short. Lvs to 15×1cm, mostly basal, linear-lanceolate, glab. Peduncle to 30cm; involucre 15–25×6–12mm; flts 10–12mm, white or cream, occas. pale lavender; anth. white or cream, rarely tinged blue. Spring. US. Z6.
M. grandiflora Beadle & F.E. Boynt. St. to 50cm. Lvs 8–25×2–3cm, oblanceolate, elliptic or ovate-lanceolate, lower lvs with sheathing petioles. Peduncle to 15cm; involucre 25×13mm diam.; flts 10–15mm, purple; anth. purple. Summer. CE US. Z5.
M. obovata (Walter) Beadle & F.E. Boynt. St. to 50cm. Lvs 5–12×0.5–2cm, oblanceolate to elliptic. Peduncles to 35cm, involucre to 25×12mm; flts 10–12mm, pale lavender to purple, cream, occas. white; anth. tinged blue, rarely cream or white. Spring–early summer. SE US. Z7.
M. trinervia (Walter) Trel. ex Branner & Cov. St. to 1m, often purple-tinged. Lvs to 9×3mm, oblong to ovate-lanceolate. Peduncles 10–20cm; involucre to 20×10mm; flts 10–15mm, lilac-purple; anth. purple. Summer. SE US. Z7.

Marsh Andromeda *Andromeda polifolia*.
Marsh Bellflower *Campanula aparinoides*.
Marsh Blue Violet *Viola obliqua*.
Marsh Buckler Fern *Thelypteris palustris*.
Marsh Clematis *Clematis crispa*.
Marsh Felwort *Swertia perennis*.
Marsh Fern *Thelypteris palustris*.
Marsh Gentian *Gentiana pneumonanthe*.

Marsh Grass *Spartina*.
Marsh Grindelia *Grindelia humilis*.
Marsh Helleborine *Epipactis palustris*.
Marsh Mallow *Althaea officinalis*; *Hibiscus moscheutos*.
Marsh Marigold *Caltha palustris*.
Marsh Pea *Lathyrus palustris*.
Marsh Rosemary *Limonium*.
Marsh Speedwell *Veronica scutellata*.
Marsh Trefoil *Menyanthes*.
Marsh Violet *Viola palustris*.

Marsilea L. PEPPERWORT; WATER CLOVER; NARDOO. Marsileaceae. 65 aquatic or marshy ferns. Rhiz. long, slender, creeping. Fronds erect, emergent or ± submerged, consisting of 2 pairs of lfts arranged like a 4-lvd clover on a slender stipe. Trop. and temp. regions.
M. drummondii A. Br. COMMON NARDOO. Lfts broadly obovate-cuneate or fan-shaped, rather crenate, short-lobed, entire, glab. on floating plants, sericeous on terrestrial plants; stipes to 30cm. Aus. Z9.
M. fimbriata Schum. Fronds large, lfts crenate. Ghana. Z10.
M. hirsuta R. Br. Lfts narrowly oblong or obovate to cuneate, ± hirsute beneath; stipes to 15cm. Aus. Z9.
M. mutica Mett. Lfts broad, rounded at apex, inner and outer zone 2 different shades of glossy green, separated by a brown or light green band, glab.; stipes to 90cm. Aus. Z9.
M. quadrifolia L. Lfts deltoid, rounded, entire, glab.; stipes 8–15cm. Warm temp. Eur., N Asia, E US. Z5.

MARSILEACEAE Mirb. 3 genera. *Marsilea, Pilularia, Regnellidium*.

Martagon *Lilium martagon*.
Martinez Pinyon *Pinus maximartinezii*.
Martin Gil *Tabebuia nodosa*.

Martynia L. UNICORN PLANT; DEVIL'S-CLAW; ELEPHANT-TUSK; PROBOSCIS FLOWER. Pedaliaceae. 1 ann. or perenn. herb, 1–2m, viscid-pubesc. Lvs to 25cm, ovate to deltoid, 5–7-lobed or simple, irregularly dentate; petioles to 25cm. Infl. racemose, 7–20-fld; sep. 5, lanceolate, to 1.5cm; cor. 5–5cm, cream to maroon, tube usually yellow-, orange- or red-spotted within, lobes blotched deep purple. Fr. an elongate-ovoid capsule to 5cm, with 2 fierce apical horns. C Amer. & W Indies; nat. India and New Caledonia.
M. angulosa Lam. = *M. annua*.
M. annua L.
M. arenaria Engelm. = *Proboscidea arenaria*.
M. diandra Gloxin = *M. annua*.
M. fragrans Lindl. = *Proboscidea fragrans*.

Maruba *Hosta plantaginea*.
Marula *Sclerocarya birrea*.
Marumi Kumquat *Fortunella japonica*.
Marvel Dewberry *Rubus mirus*.
Marvel of Peru *Mirabilis jalapa*.
Maryland Pinkroot *Spigelia marilandica*.

Mascarena L.H. Bail.
M. lagenicaulis L.H. Bail. = *Hyophorbe lagenicaulis*.
M. revaughanii L.H. Bail. = *Hyophorbe lagenicaulis*.
M. verschaffeltii (H.A. Wendl.) L.H. Bail. = *Hyophorbe verschaffeltii*.

Mascarene Grass *Zoysia tenuifolia*.

Masdevallia Ruiz & Pav. Orchidaceae. 300 tufted, everg., epiphytic or lithophytic orchids; rhiz. short-creeping. Secondary st. short, erect, apically unifoliate, thinly sheathed. Lvs glab., coriaceous, dorsally carinate, erect or suberect, narrowed, to sulcate petiole. Infl. a term. rac.; fls solitary or several in succession; inner margins of lat. sep. ± fused, in a triangular tubular or spreading synsepalum and distinct from dors. sep., distal portions spreading, terminating in tails; pet. much smaller, narrow; lip insignificant. Mex. to Braz. and Boliv. Z10.
M. abbreviata Rchb. f. Lvs to 15cm, spathulate to oblong-oblanceolate. Infl. to 18cm, several-fld; sepaline tube white spotted crimson, to 6mm, campanulate, dors. sep. suborbicular-ovate or triangular-ovate, dentate, tail to 1.5cm, yellow, lat. sep. similar to dors. sep., obliquely ovate. Peru, Ecuad.
M. acrochordonia Rchb. f. = *M. trochilus*.
M. amabilis Rchb. f. Lvs to 18cm, oblong to oblanceolate. Infl. to 30cm, 1-fld; sepaline tube to 2.5cm, yellow-orange with crimson venation, narrowly campanulate-cylindrical, dors. sep. free portion ovate to triangular, orange-yellow or rose, with red vena-

tion, tail to 5cm, dull red, lateral sep. connate for half of length, ovate-triangular, orange-red tinged crimson, tails to 3.5cm. Peru.

M. amethystina Rchb. f. = *Porroglossum amethystinum.*

M. anchorifera Rchb. f. = *Scaphosepalum anchoriferum.*

M. attenuata Rchb. f. Lvs to 13cm, linear-oblanceolate. Infl. 1-fld, usually shorter than lvs; fls somewhat campanulate, green-white, to 2.5cm; sepaline tube sometimes streaked red, interior pubesc., tails to 1.5cm, orange-yellow, lat. sep. connate for basal third. Costa Rica, Panama.

M. aureopurpurea Rchb. f. & Warsc. Lvs to 12.5cm, oblong-oblanceolate. Infl. subequal to lvs, 1–3-fld; sepaline tube yellow tinged brown, to 1.5cm, dors. sep. connate with lateral sep. deeply connate, free portion ovate-triangular, tail to 2.5cm, bright yellow. Peru, Ecuad., Colomb., Boliv.

M. barlaeana Rchb. f. Lvs to 12.5cm, elliptic-oblanceolate or oblong. Infl. to 25cm, 1-fld; sepaline tube narrow, scarlet, campanulate-cylindric, slightly decurved, dors. sep. to 4cm, red-orange with red lines, ovate-triangular to subquadrate, lat. sep. connate for two-thirds, bright carmine shaded scarlet, with scarlet lines, tails to 14mm, sometimes crossing. Peru.

M. bella Rchb. f. = *Dracula bella.*

M. biflora Reg. = *M. caloptera.*

M. bonplandii Rchb. f. Lvs to 8×2cm, oblong-spathulate. Infl. to 20cm, 1-fld; fls yellow-green, sepaline tube spotted brown-purple, to 2cm, sep. triangular to oblong-ligulate, acute, 2-keeled. Peru, Ecuad.

M. brevis Rchb. f. = *Scaphosepalum breve.*

M. bruchmuelleri hort. = *M. coriacea.*

M. caloptera Rchb. f. Lvs to 8cm, ovate-oblong to lanceolate. Infl. to 15cm, 2–5-fld; fls small; sep. white streaked and spotted rust to crimson, tails yellow-orange, dors. sep. round-triangular, hooded, minutely dentate, tail slender, erect, to 1cm, lat. sep. ovate-oblong, recurved, tails to 1cm, decurved. Ecuad., Colomb., Peru.

M. calura Rchb. f. Lvs to 10cm, broadly oblanceolate. Infl. to 10cm, 1-fld; fls to 10.5cm across, deep burgundy with a black hue; sep. apices yellow, sepaline tube to 1.5cm, cylindrical, curved, dors. sep. triangular, tails to 5cm, filiform, lat. sep. connate for 2cm, ovate-oblong, reflexed, slightly papillose above, tails filiform, parallel. Costa Rica.

M. calyptrata Kränzl. = *M. corniculata.*

M. candida Klotzsch & Karst. = *M. tovarensis.*

M. caudata Lindl. Lvs to 8cm, obovate-spathulate. Infl. subequalling lvs, 1-fld, fls slightly fragrant, to 15cm across, usually smaller; sepaline tube short, cup-like, dors. sep. lime to buff, spotted and lined lilac, free portion to 2.5cm, obovate, concave, tails to 6.5cm, slender, yellow, lat. sep. buff flushed or spotted lilac or rose, free portion to 1.5cm, ovate, tails to 5cm, pale green, deflexed. Colomb., Venez., Ecuad.

M. chestertonii Rchb. f. = *Dracula chestertonii.*

M. chimaera Rchb. f. = *Dracula chimaera.*

M. civilis Rchb. f. & Warsc. Lvs to 25cm, linear or linear-oblong. Infl. to 8cm, 1-fld; fls glossy, scented; sepaline tube to 2.5cm, cylindrical, gibbous below, yellow-green spotted purple, interior papillose, free portions, yellow-green, purple at base, to 4cm, ovate-triangular, tails short, yellow, recurved. Peru.

M. coccinea Lind. ex Lindl. Lvs to 23cm, narrow-oblong to obovate-lanceolate. Infl to 40cm, 1-fld; fls waxy, variable in colour, sep. deep magenta, crimson, scarlet, pale yellow or cream-white, sepaline tube to 2cm, campanulate-cylindric, slightly compressed, curved, dors. sep. to 8cm, triangular or linear, tail slender, erect or recurved, lat. sep. ovate-triangular, large, fused and flattened-decurved to falcate with ridges and short tails. Colomb., Peru.

M. colibri hort. = *M. trochilus.*

M. coriacea Lindl. Lvs to 20cm, linear-oblanceolate. Infl. to 20cm, 1-fld; sepaline tube to 1.5cm, pale yellow spotted purple along veins, cylindrical, dors. sep. to 4cm, ovate-triangular, with short, broad tail, lat. sep. to 3.5cm, yellow, oblong, acuminate. Colomb.

M. corniculata Rchb. f. Lvs to 25cm, oblong-lanceolate. Infl. to 10cm, 1-fld; fls to 8cm across, pale yellow marked or suffused red-brown; sepaline tube broadly cylindrical, curved, gibbous below, to 2cm, dors. sep. free portion triangular, tail to 5cm, lat. sep. connate for 3cm, oblong, reflexed, tails shorter, recurved. Colomb.

M. cyathogastra Schltr. = *M. nidifica.*

M. davisii Rchb. f. Lvs to 20cm, oblong-oblanceolate. Infl. to 25cm, 1-fld; fls fragrant, bright orange-yellow; sepaline tube narrowly campanulate-cylindric, to 1.7cm, dors. sep. ovate-triangular, tail slender, to 2.5cm, lat. sep. exceeding dors. sep., connate for half length, obliquely ovate-oblong, tails to 7mm. Peru.

M. dayana Rchb. f. = *Zootrophion dayanum.*

M. echnida Rchb. f. = *Porroglossum echnidum.*

M. edwallii Cogn. = *Dryadella edwallii.*

M. elephanticeps Rchb. f. = *M. mooreana.*

M. ephippium Rchb. f. = *M. trochilus.*

M. erythrochaete Rchb. f. = *Dracula erythrochaete.*

M. estradae Rchb. f. = *M. ludibunda.*

M. Falcata Tall plant, to 35cm; fls brilliant orange with red in the centre and with red tails.

M. floribunda Lindl. Lvs to 12cm, oblong-oblanceolate. Infl. exceeding lvs, 1-fld; fls to 4cm across; sep. pale yellow or buff spotted brown-crimson, sepaline tube to 1.5cm, cylindrical, dors. sep. free portion to 1cm, ovate-triangular, tail to 12mm, lat. sep. free portion rotund to ovate, to 1.5cm, tails to 6mm, recurved. Mex., Guat., Hond., Costa Rica.

M. fragrans Woolw. = *M. civilis.*

M. fulvescens Rolfe = *M. schroederiana.*

M. galeottiana A. Rich. & Gal. = *M. floribunda.*

M. gibberosa Rchb. f. = *Scaphosepalum gibberosum.*

M. harryana Rchb. f. = *M. coccinea.*

M. herzogii Schltr. = *M. auropurpurea.*

M. ignea Rchb. f. Lvs to 23cm, elliptic-lanceolate or oblong-lanceolate. Infl. to 40cm, 1-fld; fls to 8cm across; sep. scarlet to orange, often tinged crimson, sepaline tube to 2cm, cylindrical, hooded, curved, dors. sep. free portion to 1cm, triangular, tail to 4cm, strongly deflexed, lateral sep. connate for 2.5cm, broadly falcate-ovate, tails short. Colomb.

M. inflata Rchb. f. = *M. corniculata.*

M. infracta Lindl. Lvs to 14cm, lanceolate to oblong. Infl. to 25cm, 1–5-fld; fls yellow-white to ochre, white at base of tube, flushing orange to blood-red, campanulate, pendent; sepaline tube to 13mm, cupped, curved, dors. sep. free portion to 5cm, ovate to triangular, tail to 4cm, lat. sep. free portion to 5cm, rotund-oblong, connate for 2cm, tails to 4cm, strongly divergent. Braz., Peru.

M. ionocharis Rchb. f. Lvs to 12cm, narrowly elliptic-lanceolate. Infl. to 10cm, 1-fld; fls to 1.5cm diam., excluding sep. tails; sepaline tube campanulate, to 13mm, yellow-white, sep. free portion green-white blotched rose-purple, triangular-ovate, tails to 2cm, slender, yellow. Peru.

M. Kimballiana Vigorous plants to 15cm; fls tubular at base, then opening widely, orange or yellow with self-coloured tails.

M. klabochorum Rchb. f. = *M. caudata.*

M. laucheana Bonhof. Lvs to 12.5cm, obovate-oblanceolate. Infl. shorter than lvs, 1-fld; fls to 1.8cm diam., excluding sep. tails; sepaline tube campanulate, white flushed rose to mauve at base, free portions white to buff, ovate-triangular, tails to 2cm, rigid, incurved. Costa Rica.

M. laucheana Kränzl. ex Woolw. non Bonhof. = *M. attenuata.*

M. lindenii André = *M. coccinea.*

M. longicaudata Lem. = *M. infracta.*

M. ludibunda Rchb. f. Lvs to 7.5cm, elliptic-spathulate. Infl. exceeding lvs, 1-fld; fls to 7.5cm across, spreading; sepaline tube to 8mm, campanulate, dors. sep. bright magenta with yellow base and margins, free portion obovate, concave, to 1.5cm, tails yellow, to 2.5cm, lat. sep. oblong, obtuse, white above, base magenta, tails yellow, to 4cm. Colomb.

M. macrura Rchb. f. Lvs to 37cm, elliptic-oblong. Infl. usually equalling lvs, 1-fld; fls to 25cm across; sep. red to dull brown-yellow, with maroon warts, sepaline tube to 1.5cm, cylindrical or flattened, ribbed, dors. sep. free portion to 15cm, lanceolate to triangular, tail long, yellow-green, lat. sep. to 12.5cm, ovate to oblong, connate for basal 4cm, tail long, strongly decurved. Colomb., Ecuad.

M. maculata Klotzsch & Karst. Lvs to 18cm, linear-lanceolate. Infl. to 25cm, several-fld; sep. yellow or yellow-green, spotted and tinged red, sepaline tube to 16mm, flattened-cylindrical, orange-yellow above, red below, dors. sep. free portion ovate-cylindrical, orange-yellow above, red below, dors. sep. free portion ovate-triangular, tail to 7cm, lat. sep. connate to middle, ovate-oblong, tails tapering, pale yellow, parallel or divergent. Venez., Peru, Colomb.

M. Measuresiana Robust plant to 15cm with long slender infl. bearing 1–2 white or pale pink fls.

M. mejiana Garay. Lvs to 12cm, oblong-lanceolate. Infl. to 10cm, 1–2-fld; fls to 7cm across, white flecked pink, tails yellow-orange; sepaline tube campanulate, free portions spreading, broadly ovate, or wholly fused, tails fleshy, divergent. Colomb.

M. melanopus Rchb. f. Lvs to 12.5cm, oblong-spathulate or oblanceolate. Infl. to 25cm, 3–8-fld; fls to 2.5cm across, white minutely spotted and flecked purple; sepaline tube shortly campanulate, to 6mm, gibbous below, sep. free portion triangular or suborbicular, concave, tails to 13mm, bright yellow. Colomb., Ecuad., Peru.

M. militaris Rchb. f. = *M. ignea.*

M. mooreana Rchb. f. Lvs to 20cm, linear-oblong. Infl. to 10cm, 1-fld; fls to 9cm across; sepaline tube broadly cylindrical, slightly ventricose below, sep. long, tapering, forward-pointing, dors.

sep. yellow-white streaked purple at base, triangular, tail yellow, to 5cm, lat. sep. crimson to purple, interior with black-purple papillae, triangular, tail yellow toward apex. Colomb., Venez.

M. mordax Rchb. f. = *Porroglossum mordax*.

M. muscosa Rchb. f. = *Porroglossum muscosum*.

M. myriostigma Morr. = *M. floribunda*.

M. nidifica Rchb. f. St. short. Lvs to 5cm, spathulate or oblanceolate. Infl. almost equalling lvs, 1-fld; fls small; sep. white, green-white or pale yellow, spotted and striped crimson, maroon to olive below, sepaline tube to 7mm, slightly inflated, pubesc. within, dors. sep. rotund to ovate-triangular, concave, pubesc. within, tails to 3cm, crimson, lateral sep. ovate, tails similar to dors. sep., yellow. Costa Rica, Peru, Ecuad., Colomb.

M. normanii hort. = *M. reichenbachiana*.

M. pachyantha Rchb. f. Lvs to 20cm, oblanceolate. Infl. exceeding lvs, 1-fld; fls to 12cm including tails; sepaline tube pale orange-yellow, cylindrical, slightly curved, dors. sep. pale yellow-green veined brown-purple, triangular, tail to 2.5cm, erect, lat. sep. connate almost to middle, ovate-oblong, pale yellow-green heavily spotted rose-purple, tail bright yellow, shorter than dors. tail. Colomb.

M. pandurilabia Schweinf. Lvs to 12cm, obovate, oblanceolate or elliptic. Infl. to 20cm, 1-fld; fls small, yellow-brown; sepaline tube to 5mm, interior pubesc., dors. sep. suborbicular-ovate, tail to 3.5cm, lat. sep. obliquely semiorbicular-ovate; tails similar to dors. sep. Peru.

M. peristeria Rchb. f. Lvs to 15cm, linear-lanceolate or oblong. Infl. to 7cm, 1-fld; fls to 12.5cm diam., fleshy, spreading; sepaline tube to 2cm, broadly cylindric, gibbous below, ribbed, sep. yellow or yellow-green spotted crimson, ovate-triangular, tails fleshy, to 3.5cm, tips triquetrous. Spring–summer. Colomb.

M. polysticta Rchb. f. non Hook. f. Lvs to 15cm, subspathulate or oblanceolate. Infl. to 25cm, 3–9-fld; fls to 5cm diam., white or pale lilac spotted dark red or purple; sepaline tube short, interior papillose, dors. sep. free portion broadly ovate, cucullate, tail to 2.5cm, lat. sep. narrowly oblong-lanceolate, with a yellow central line, slightly ciliate, tail to 2.5cm. Ecuad., Peru.

M. pulvinaris Rchb. f. = *Scaphosepalum pulvinare*.

M. pumila Poepp. & Endl. Lvs to 9cm, linear-oblanceolate or linear-spathulate. Infl. to 3.5cm, 1-fld; fls small, pure white; sepaline tube to 5mm, cylindrical, dors. sep. small, triangular-lanceolate, to 3cm including fleshy tail, lat. sep. large. Peru, Venez.

M. punctata Rolfe = *Scaphosepalum anchoriferum*.

M. racemosa Lindl. Lvs to 12.5cm, elliptic-oblong. Infl. to 35cm, 4–15-fld; fls to 6cm across, bright orange-scarlet shaded crimson, sometimes yellow; sepaline tube to 1.5cm, cylindrical, narrow, dors. sep. smaller than lateral sep., free portion ovate-triangular, reflexed, tail to 6mm, suberect, lat. sep. connate for basal 2.5cm, broadly obcordate, spreading, apiculate, with dark longitudinal veins. Colomb.

M. reichenbachiana Endress. Lvs to 15cm, oblanceolate-spathulate. Infl. exceeding lvs, 1–3-fld; fls to 6cm across; sepaline tube white-yellow below, red-scarlet above, to 2.5cm, curved, funnel-shaped, hooded or almost closed at apex by depressed dors. sep., dors. sep. red to pale yellow-white, lined red within, free portion to 12mm, triangular, tail to 5cm, recurved, yellow, lat. sep. yellow-white, connate for half of length, ovate-triangular, decurved, tails to 3.5cm, slender, yellow. Spring–autumn. Costa Rica.

M. rolfeana Kränzl. Resembles *M. reichenbachiana* except smaller. Infl. shorter than lvs; fls to 5cm long, chocolate-brown to dark purple; sepaline tube cupped, yellow at base, to 12mm; lip red. Spring–summer. Costa Rica.

M. rosea Lindl. Lvs to 20cm, elliptic-lanceolate to obovate. Infl. slightly exceeding lvs, 1-fld; sepaline tube to 2.5cm, scarlet and vermilion, dors. sep. to 5cm, slender, tail-like, red above, yellow below, arching over broader, carmine, short, red-tailed lat. sep. Spring–summer. Colomb., Ecuad.

M. schlimii Lind. ex Lindl. Lvs to 20cm, obovate to elliptic. Infl. to 35cm, to 8-fld; fls nodding; sepaline tube short-cylindrical, ochre or golden below, maroon within, dors. sep. narrow-triangular, long-tailed, golden-green, decurved over larger lat. sep., tail horizontal, to 4.8cm, lat. sep. to 3cm, decurved, oblong-ovate, fused, forming a heart-shaped shield with maroon papillae, tails to 4cm, yellow, divergent. Spring. Colomb., Venez.

M. schroederiana hort. Sander ex Gdn. Lvs to 15cm, oblanceolate. Infl. to 21cm, 1-fld; fls to 8cm across; sepaline tube short-campanulate, white, ribbed, expanding as a flattened oblong platform formed by a fusion of lat. sep., pearly white flushed ruby red in upper portions and at dors. sep., tails long, yellow, lat. tails held horizontally, dors. tail erect. Winter–summer. Peru.

M. shuttleworthii Rchb. f. = *M. caudata*.

M. simula Rchb. f. = *Dryadella simula*.

M. swertiifolia Rchb. f. = *Scaphosepalum swertiifolium*.

M. tenuicauda Schltr. = *M. nidifica*.

M. tovarensis Rchb. f. Lvs to 14cm, obovate to oblanceolate. Infl. to 18cm, 1–4-fld; fls to 3.5cm across, pure white, tailed cream or jade; sepaline tube cylindrical, to 6mm, dors. sep. free portion to 4×0.6cm, filiform, erect, lat. sep. to 4×1cm, shaped like a lyre, connate for half of length, ribbed, tails short, often crossing. Venez.

M. triangularis Lindl. Lvs to 15cm, obovate or elliptic-oblong. Infl. to 15cm, 1-fld; fls to 12cm including tails; sepaline tube broadly campanulate, sep. yellow-green spotted purple-brown, free portion to 2cm, ovate-triangular, concave, tails to 4cm, purple slender. Colomb., Venez.

M. triaristella Rchb. f. Dwarf to 8cm. Fls 1–2, buff stained chocolate-maroon; lat. sep. fused in a carinate blade with 2.5cm green divergent tails, dors. sep. hooded, long-tailed. Costa Rica.

M. triglochin Rchb. f. = *Trisetella triglochin*.

M. trochilus Lind. & André. Lvs to 18cm, elliptic-lanceolate. Infl. to 30cm, 1–3-fld; fls to 20cm; sepaline tube yellow, short, cylindrical, dors. sep. interior tawny yellow, exterior yellow stained chestnut-brown, concave, suborbicular, tail yellow, to 8cm, reflexed, lat. sep. forming a chestnut-brown hemispherical cup, ribbed, tails similar to dors. sep. Colomb., Ecuad.

M. tubulosa Lindl. Lvs to 11cm, oblanceolate. Fls 1 per infl., 6–12cm, white to ivory; sep. narrow, forward-pointing, tubular. Colomb., Venez.

M. uniflora HBK = *M. bonplandii*.

M. vampira Luer = *Dracula vampira*.

M. veitchiana Rchb. f. Lvs to 25cm, oblong to narrowly oblanceolate. Infl. to 45cm, 1-fld; fls to 8cm across, sep. interior shining vermilion covered with many iridescent purple papillae, sepaline tube to 3cm, campanulate-cylindrical, dors. sep. free portion to 3cm, triangular-ovate, tail, to 3.5cm, lat. sep. larger than dors. sep., broadly ovate or triangular, acuminate, curving downwards, connate for 3cm, tails short, often forward-pointing or overlapping. Peru.

M. velifera Rchb. f. Lvs to 20cm, lanceolate or linear-elliptic. Infl. to 10cm, 1-fld; fls to 7.5cm, malodorous; sepaline tube to 2cm, broadly cylindrical, gibbous below, dors. sep. yellow-brown spotted red-brown, triangular, concave, tail to 5cm, stout, lat. sep. connate for 5cm, sometimes shiny red-brown, oblanceolate-oblong, tail yellow, stout. Colomb.

M. verrucosa Rchb. f. = *Scaphosepalum verrucosum*.

M. wageneriana Lindl. Lvs to 5cm, elliptic to spathulate. Infl. 1-fld to 5cm, slender; fls to 6cm light green-yellow or cream, orange-yellow toward base, spotted and streaked violet, sepaline tube short, dors. sep. free portion broadly ovate-oblong, to 1cm, concave, tail slender, to 5cm, sharply recurved, lat. sep. similar to dors. sep., connate for more than half of length. Venez.

M. xanthina Rchb. f. Lvs to 7.5cm, obovate-oblong. Infl. to 8cm, 1-fld; sepaline tube obscure, sep. bright yellow or cream with dark yellow venation, dors. sep. obovate-oblong, cuculate, tail orange-yellow, erect, to 3.5cm, lateral sep. with purple spot at base, lanceolate, tails to 33mm, orange-yellow, slender. Colomb., Ecuad.

M. xipheres Rchb. f. = *Porroglossum muscosum*.

M. zebrina Porsch = *Dryadella zebrina*.

Mask Flower *Alonsoa* (*A. warscewiczii*).

Massonia Thunb. ex L. f. Liliaceae (Hyacinthaceae). 8 bulbous perenn. herbs. Lvs 2, usually opposite, fleshy, lying close to or directly upon soil surface. Scape barely emerging from lf cleavage; fls fragrant, in an umbel-like head, subtended by large spathes; perianth tube cylindric, lobes 6; fil. conspicuous. Late autumn–early winter. S Afr. Z9.

M. amygdalina Bak. = *M. echinata*.

M. angustifolia L. f. = *Polyxena angustifolia*.

M. bolusiae Barker = *M. echinata*.

M. bowkeri Bak. = *M. jasminiflora*.

M. brachypus Bak. = *M. depressa*.

M. depressa Houtt. Lvs 7–15cm, orbicular to oblong, glab. or sparsely ciliate. Fls 20–30, green, yellow, white, cream or pink to red or brown, occas. flecked purple. Cape Prov.

M. echinata L. f. Lvs 2–8cm, ovate to oblong, usually hairy. Fls 5–20, yellow, white or pink. Cape Prov.

M. ensifolia Ker-Gawl. = *Polyxena pygmaea*.

M. jasminiflora Bak. Lvs 3–6cm, ovate to broadly oblong, glab. occas. ciliate, rarely papillose. Fls to 15 (usually fewer), fragrant, white or pink. S Afr., Les.

M. latifolia L. f. = *M. depressa*.

M. longifolia var. *candida* Ker-Gawl. = *M. echinata*.
M. odorata Hook. f. = *Polyxena odorata*.
M. pustulata Jacq. Lvs 3–10cm, ovate-orbicular to oblong, pustulate-papillose above. Fls 15–25, pink, white, yellow or tinged green. Cape Prov.
M. sanguinea Jacq. = *M. depressa*.
M. scabra Thunb. = *M. echinata*.
M. violacea Andrews = *Polyxena pygmaea*.

Masterwort *Angelica atropurpurea*; *Astrantia*; *Heracleum sphondylium*; *Peucedanum ostruthium*.
Mastic *Mastichodendron foetidissimum*; *Pistacia lentiscus*.

Mastichodendron (Engl.) H.J. Lam. Sapotaceae. 6 everg. trees with milky latex. Lvs entire. Fls clustered in axils; sep. 5; cor. 5-lobed; sta. and staminodes 5; ovary superior, locules 5. Fr. 1–3-seeded. W Indies, C Amer., Mex., US (Flor.). Z10.
M. foetidissimum (Jacq.) H.J. Lam. MASTIC. Tree to 25m, with hard, orange wood. Lvs to 20cm, oblong-ovate to broadly elliptic, glab.; petioles to 7cm. Fls to 4mm, green-yellow. Fr. 1–2.5cm, yellow, later black, ovoid to pyriform. Flor. and W Indies to Belize and Mex.
→*Sideroxylon*.

Mast Wood *Catalpa longissima*.
Masur *Lens culinaris*.
Mata Ajam *Clerodendrum buchananii*.
Matai *Prumnopitys taxifolia*.
Matal *Asclepias curassavica*.
Matasano *Casimiroa tetrameria*.
Match-stick Banksia *Banksia cuneata*.
Matchweed *Gutierrezia*.
Maté *Ilex paraguariensis*.
Mathers *Vaccinium ovalifolium*.
Matilija Poppy *Romneya*.

Matricaria L. Compositae. 5 ann. herbs. St. erect or ascending, usually branched, leafy. Lvs finely 2–3-pinnatisect, seg. narrowly-linear. Cap. discoid or radiate, solitary or in corymbs; ray flts white; disc flts tubular, yellow. Eurasia.
M. africana P. Bergius = *Oncosiphon africanum*.
M. asteroides L. = *Boltonia asteroides*.
M. aurea (L.) Schultz-Bip. Ann. herb, 4–25cm. St. slender, decumbent or ascending, often flexuous. Lvs 0.5–2.5cm; seg. with a sharp point. Cap. 1 to numerous, discoid, 4–7mm diam. Spring. W Medit., SW Asia to W Himal.
M. capensis L. = *Oncosiphon africanum*.
M. capensis hort. non L. = *Tanacetum parthenium*.
M. caucasica (Willd.) Poir. = *Tripleurospermum caucasicum*.
M. chamomilla L. = *M. recutita*.
M. coreanum Lév. & Vaniot = *Dendranthema coreanum*.
M. globifera (Thunb.) Fenzl ex Harv. = *Oncosiphon piluliferum*.
M. grandiflora hort. = *Tripleurospermum inodorum*.
M. grandiflora (Thunb.) Fenzl ex Harv. = *Oncosiphon grandiflorum*.
M. inodorum L. = *Tripleurospermum inodorum*.
M. maritima L. = *Tripleurospermum maritimum*.
M. matricarioides (Less.) Porter PINEAPPLE WEED. Ann. herb, 5–45cm, strongly aromatic. St. erect or ascending. Lvs 2–6; seg. flattened, acute, bristle-pointed. Cap. discoid, 1–40, occas. to 1cm diam. receptacle conical; flts green-yellow. Summer. NE Asia, introd. elsewhere.
M. oreades Boiss. = *Tripleurospermum oreades*.
M. parthenium L. = *Tanacetum parthenium*.
M. perforata Mérat = *Tripleurospermum inodorum*.
M. recutita L. SWEET FALSE CHAMOMILE; WILD CHAMOMILE; GERMAN CHAMOMILE. Ann. herb, sweetly scented, 15–60cm. St. erect or ascending. Lvs 4–7cm; seg. acute. Cap. radiate, 1 to 120, 1–2.5cm diam.; receptacle conical; ray flts white. Summer. Eur., W Asia to India.
M. suffruticosa Fenzl ex Harv. = *Oncosiphon suffructicosum*.
M. tchihatchewii (Boiss.) Voss = *Tripleurospermum oreades* var. *tchihatchewii*.
→*Chamomilla* and *Cotula*.

Matrimony Vine *Lycium*.
Mat Spike Moss *Selaginella kraussiana*.

Matteuccia Tod. OSTRICH FERN. Woodsiaceae. 4 terrestrial ferns. Base short, trunk-like. Fronds tufted, glab., fertile fronds smaller, more erect, darker and longer-petioled than the sterile. Temp. N Amer., Eur., E Asia.
M. orientalis (Hook.) Trev. Sterile fronds to 60cm, arched; blade triangular, to 15cm wide, bright green, pinnae pinnatifid, crenately lobed, coriaceous, stipe to 20cm; fertile fronds to

30cm, dull green becoming dark brown, pinnae distant, linear. India (Sikkim), W China, Jap.
M. struthiopteris (L.) Tod. OSTRICH FERN; SHUTTLECOCK FERN. Spreading by buried runners. Sterile fronds to 170×35cm, in a semi-erect shuttlecock-like rosette; stipe v. short with scales at base; blade to 120×40cm, broadly lanceolate, soft, bright green, pinnae 30–70, narrowly lanceolate, pinnatifid; fertile fronds to 60×6cm, erect, dark brown, pinnae to 6cm, linear, strongly inrolled. Eur., E Asia, E N Amer. Z2.
→*Onoclea* and *Struthiopteris*.

Matthiola R. Br. STOCK; GILLYFLOWER. Cruciferae. 55 ann. or perenn. herbs or subshrubs. Lvs simple or pinnatifid, entire or toothed. Rac. term.; fls often nocturnally fragrant; sep. 4, erect, saccate at base; pet. 4, long-clawed; sta. 6. Fr. a silique, often with horn-like projections on either side of stigma. W Eur., C Asia, S Afr. Z6.
M. annua Sweet = *M. incana*.
M. bicornis hort. = *M. longipetala*.
M. fenestralis R. Br. = *M. incana*.
M. fruticulosa (L.) Maire. Perenn. Base woody. Lvs oblanceolate-linear, white-hairy, entire to wavy-toothed. Pet. 12–28mm, yellow-purple. Fr. 25–12mm; cylindrical; stigma usually horned. S Eur.
M. incana (L.) R. Br. BROMPTON STOCK. Bienn. Base woody, 30–80cm. Lvs lanceolate, grey-green, hairy, rarely wavy-toothed. Pet. 2–3cm, purple, sometimes pink or white. Fr. 4.5–16cm, somewhat compressed. Summer–autumn. S & W Eur. 'Annua': the fast-growing TEN WEEKS STOCK, grown as an ann.
M. longipetala (Vent.) DC. NIGHT-SCENTED STOCK. Ann., 8–50cm. Lvs oblong-linear, simple or pinnatisect, entire or toothed. Pet. 1.5–2.5cm, yellow, green-white or pink. Fr. 4.5–15cm, narrow-linear, slightly compressed, hairy, horned. Greece to SW Asia, S Ukraine.
M. odoratissima (Bieb.) R. Br. Woody-based short-lived perenn., 30–60cm. Lvs white downy, toothed or pinnatifid. Pet. buff becoming mauve-bronze. Fr. 8.5–18mm, compressed, not horned. Summer. Bulg., Cauc., Iran.
M. scabra L. = *Guettarda scabra*.
M. tricuspidata (L.) R. Br. Ann., 7–35cm. Lvs oblong, obtuse, wavy-toothed to pinnatifid. Pet. 15–22mm, bright lilac, paler near base. Fr. 2.5–10cm, cylindrical, 3-horned. Summer. Medit.
M. tristis R. Br. = *M. fruticulosa*.
→*Cheiranthus*.
M. cvs. Modern selections of gdn stocks, largely derived from *M. incana* and *M. sinuata*, are available in an enormous range of size, from the 20cm/8in. dwarf Stockpots, to the Column types approaching a metre in height, and in colours from soft pastel pinks to deep blues and carmines, and in shades of yellow, copper and gold. They are classified horticulturally into a number of groups.
The annuals are by far the largest group, and include the Tenweek (flowering ten weeks from sowing) and, the dwarf, bushy Trisomic seven-week races.
Annuals are classified into a number of strains of different form, habit, and gdn use, thus: (a) Ten-week Dwarf Large-flowering: compact, free flowering, to 30cm/12in., excellent for bedding purposes. (b) Ten-week Excelsior (Column): of upright habit, to 80cm, producing the single columnar densely flowered spike valued by florists; for cult. in the glasshouse or outdoors and excellent for cutting. The Pacific strain is also of this columnar type, and better suited to outdoor cult. (c) Ten-week Giant Imperial: of bushy and branching habit, to 60cm/24in., with long well-shaped spikes; for cutting and bedding. (d) Ten-week Giant Perfection: of erect and bushy habit, to 70cm/28in., with long spikes of large fls. For bedding and cutting and exhibition. (e) Ten-week Mammoth or Beauty: erect, bushy and compact, to 45cm/18in., producing several spikes of large fls; for bedding, cutting and for glasshouse cult. for winter bloom. (f) Perpetual-flowering, or All the Year Round: dwarf, vigorous plants, with large spikes of pure white fls, excellent for cutting, and pot culture. The other major divisions comprise the Brompton stocks, erect and bushy biennials, to 45cm/18in., used for bedding. The Intermediate, or East Lothian stocks which, when treated as annuals, flower to follow on from the Ten-week stocks, are also grown as biennials for flowering in spring and early summer. The Virginia Stock is *Malcolmia maritima*.

Mattiastrum (Boiss.) Brand.
M. himalayense (Klotzsch) Brand = *Paracaryum himalayense*.
M. lithospermifolium (Lam.) Brand = *Paracaryum lithospermifolium*.
M. racemosum (Schreb.) Brand = *Paracaryum racemosum*.

Mattress Vine *Muehlenbeckia complexa*.

Matucana Britt. & Rose Cactaceae. 9 low, simple or clustering cacti; st. globose to short-cylindric; ribs broad, low, ± tuberculate, spiny or not. Fl. subapical, funnelform to narrowly tubular-funnelform; limb usually ± zygomorphic; staminodal hairs sometimes also present. Fr. hollow, somewhat fleshy at first. Peru.

M. aurantiaca (Vaupel) F. Buxb. Variable. Simple or clustering; st. to 15×15cm, flattened-globose to globose or short-cylindric; ribs usually about 16, somewhat spiralled, tuberculate; areoles elliptic, spines red-brown below and yellow-brown at first; central spines 3–7, up to 4.5cm, radial spines c16–18, 0.5–2.5cm. Fl. 7–9cm, orange-red. N Peru. Z9.

M. aureiflora Ritter. Simple; st. to 13cm diam., flattened-globose; ribs 11–27, tuberculate; areoles oval; spines c10–12, 7–18mm, subpectinate, yellow-brown above, darker below, central spines on old plants only, to 2.5cm. Fl. 3–4.5cm, regular funnelform, bright golden yellow. Peru. Z7.

M. haynei (Otto ex Salm-Dyck) Britt. & Rose. Usually simple, sometimes clustering; st. to 60×10cm, globose to cylindric; ribs 25–30, tuberculate; areoles small, woolly at first; central spines usually 3, 3.5–5cm, dark-tipped, radial spines c30, to 2cm, bristly, white to yellow-brown. Fl. 6–7cm, nearly regular, scarlet to purple-crimson. N Peru. Z9.

M. icosagona (Kunth) F. Buxb. = *Cleistocactus icosagonus.*

M. madisoniorum (Hutch.) G. Rowley. Simple; st. to 10(–30)×8–15cm, globose to columnar, papillose, viscid; ribs 7–12, obscure; areoles 2–2.5cm apart; spines 0 or 1–3 on mature plants, 5–6cm, curved or twisted, dark brown to black. Fl. 8–10cm, almost regular, orange-red. N Peru. Z9.

M. myriacantha (Vaupel) F. Buxb. Usually simple; st. to 30×7–12cm, globose to short-cylindric, green; ribs 30–40, straight, tuberculate; areoles round to oval; spines 25–50, 1–3cm, white to red-brown. Fl 5–7cm, tube deep pink; floral areoles naked or with numerous red-brown hairs; tep. from deep pink to almost white. Peru. Z9.

M. oreodoxa (Ritter) Slaba. Usually simple; st. to 8cm diam., globose; ribs 7–12, 3–6mm deep, with low tubercles; round to oval; spines pale brown, straight or curved; central spines 0–2, 1.5–4cm, radial spines 4–10, 1–3cm. Fl. 4–6cm, regular, orange-yellow. Peru. Z9.

M. paucicostata Ritter. Clustering from the base; st. 7–15cm, globose to ovoid; ribs 7–11, broad, straight, with conic tubercles; areoles round or oval; spines red-brown at first, curved; central spines 0–1, to 3cm, radial spines 4–8, 0.5–3cm. Fl. 6cm, red; pericarpel with white hairs. Peru. Z9.

M. ritteri Buining. Resembling *M. aurantiaca*; to 3–5×5–10cm, depressed-globose, taller in cult.; ribs 12–22, broad; areoles oval; spines black-brown at first; central spines 1–2(–5), 2–4cm, radial spines 7–10(–14). Fl. 7–9cm; tep. carmine-red, edged violet. Peru. Z9.

M. weberbaueri (Vaupel) Backeb. Resembling *M. aurantiaca*; usually simple; st. to 20×12cm, depressed-globose to short-cylindric; ribs 18–30, somewhat spiralled, tuberculate; areoles round to elliptic; spines 25–30, 1–5cm, yellow to brown. Fl. 6cm, yellow or orange-red. NE Peru. Z9.
→*Borzicactus.*

Maughaniella L. Bol.
M. luckhoffii (L. Bol.) L. Bol. = *Diplosoma luckhoffii.*

Maule's Quince *Chaenomeles japonica.*
Maul Oak *Quercus chrysolepis.*

Maurandya Ortega.
M. barclaiana Lindl. = *Asarina barclaiana.*
M. erubescens (D. Don) A. Gray = *Asarina erubescens.*
M. lophospermum L.H. Bail. = *Asarina lophospermum.*
M. purpurea hort. = *Asarina purpusii.*
M. scandens (D. Don) A. Gray non (Cav.) Pers. = *Asarina lophospermum.*
M. scandens (Cav.) Pers. = *Asarina scandens.*

Mauria Kunth.
M. schickendantzii Hieron. ex Engl. = *Schinus latifolius.*
M. simplicifolia Humb. & Kunth ex Hook. & Arn. = *Lithrea caustica.*

Mauritania Vine Reed *Ampelodesmos.*
Mauritius Hemp *Furcraea foetida.*
Mauritius Papeda *Citrus hystrix.*
Mauritius Raspberry *Rubus rosifolius.*
Mauritius Spleenwort *Asplenium daucifolium.*

Maxillaria Ruiz & Pav. Orchidaceae. 300+ epiphytic, lithophytic, or terrestrial orchids. Rhiz. long or short, horizontal or ascending. Pbs large, small or almost 0, usually 1-leafed at apex

and enclosed in leafy sheaths. Fls solitary on slender stalks from base of pbs or lf axils in non-pseudobulbous spp.; sep. subequal, lat. sep. joined to column foot forming a mentum with it; pet. usually smaller; lip concave, entire or trilobed. Trop. Amer. from W Indies and Mex. to Braz., with 1 sp. in Flor. Z10.

M. abelei Schltr. = *M. rufescens.*

M. acicularis Herb. Pbs 1.5–2cm, clustered. Lvs to 7cm, filiform. Fls borne low down, wine red, lip dark purple; sep. and pet. elongate; lip obscurely trilobed. Braz.

M. acutifolia Lindl. = *M. rufescens.*

M. alba Lindl. Rhiz. ascending; pbs 4–5cm, ellipsoid. Lvs to 30cm, ligulate; fls white; sep. 20mm, oblong-ligulate, acuminate; pet. 16–18mm, oblong-elliptical, acute; lip 11–12mm, fleshy, obscurely trilobed with callus running from base to middle. Throughout most of trop. Amer.

M. amparoana Schltr. = *M. ringens.*

M. angustifolia Hook. = *M. variabilis.*

M. arachnites Rchb. f. Pbs small. Lvs 15–25cm, lanceolate. Fls fragrant, flushed maroon; sep. yellow-green 55–57mm, lanceolate; pet. white 45mm, lanceolate; lip 17mm, golden, trilobed, denticulate. Venez., Colomb., Ecuad.

M. arbuscula Rchb. f. Rhiz. slender, branched, with or without pbs. Lvs 2cm, linear-ligulate. Fls somewhat globose, 1cm diam.; tep. ligulate, white sometimes spotted red, lip deep red, ligulate with apex enlarged. Peru, Ecuad.

M. articulata Klotzsch = *M. rufescens.*

M. aurea hort. ex Rchb. f. Rhiz. creeping or ascending; pbs ovoid. Lvs 15–25cm, linear-elliptic. Fls yellow, lip with brown marks; sep. 10–15mm, lanceolate-elliptic; pet. slightly smaller. Colomb.

M. boothii Lindl. = *Nidema boothii.*

M. bractescens Lindl. = *Xylobium bractescens.*

M. brevipedunculata Ames & Schweinf. = *M. nasuta.*

M. callichroma Rchb. f. Pbs clustered, to 5cm, ovoid, dark brown. Lvs 30–45cm, fls yellow and white flushed with dark red; dors. sep. to 55mm, lanceolate, lat. sep. slighty shorter; pet. to 52mm, lanceolate; lip to 24×14mm, trilobed, callus pubesc. Venez., Colomb.

M. camaridii Rchb. f. Rhiz. to 150cm, branched, pendent; pbs to 8cm, ovoid, fls white, the lip yellow on midlobe, sometimes with streaks of red-brown; dors. sep. 26mm, oblong or oblanceolate, lat. sep. shorter and wider; pet. 24mm, oblong; lip 13mm, trilobed, with toothed, hairy callus. C Amer., W Indies, Venez., Colomb., Braz., Peru.

M. cobanensis Schltr. Rhiz. short; pbs 1.5–2cm, densely packed, cylindrical. Lvs 3.5–6cm, elliptic-ligulate. Fls dull pink-tan, veined red-brown; sep. to 14mm, ligulate, apiculate, lat. sep. oblique; pet. slightly shorter, ligulate-spathulate; lip 10mm, concave, obovate, obscurely trilobed. Summer. Mex. to Costa Rica.

M. coccinea (Jacq.) L.O. Williams ex Hodge. To 50cm; pbs to 4cm, ovoid. Lvs to 35cm, linear-oblong. Fls bright rose-pink, carmine or vermilion; sep. to 12mm, fleshy, ovate-lanceolate; pet. to 8mm, ovate or ovate-lanceolate; lip to 8mm, fleshy, trilobed. Greater & Lesser Antilles.

M. concava Lindl. = *Xylobium foveatum.*

M. consanguinea Klotzsch. Rhiz. creeping; pbs elongated, ribbed. Lvs oblong-lanceolate. Sep. about 25mm, yellow edged red, lanceolate, acute, spreading; pet. pale yellow, shorter and narrower, acuminate; lip yellow-white with purple spots 25mm, trilobed with a tongue-shaped callus. Braz.

M. coriacea Barb. Rodr. = *M. desvauxiana.*

M. crassifolia (Lindl.) Rchb. f. Rhiz. short; pbs 1.5–3cm, oblong. Lvs to 45cm, fleshy, linear to linear-oblong. Fls campanulate, fleshy, yellow to orange, usually with purple marks; sep. 14–18mm, lanceolate; pet. 12–15mm, linear-oblanceolate, lip 13–15mm, elliptic, obscurely trilobed with longitudinal, hairy callus, entire or denticulate. US (Flor.), C Amer., W Indies, Venez., Braz.

M. crassipes Kränzl. Rhiz. creeping; pbs to 25mm, conical. Lvs to 9cm, lanceolate, fleshy-coriaceous. Fls yellow edged red, apex of lip purple; sep. 25mm, ovate-lanceolate; pet. 18mm, ligulate-lanceolate; lip 15mm, trilobed above, undulate. Braz.

M. cucullata Lindl. Pbs 4–5cm, ellipsoid. Lvs to 20cm, ligulate, obtuse. Fls dingy dark brown; tep. 25–28mm, lanceolate; lip 23mm, dark purple-red, trilobed. Mex.

M. curtipes Hook. Pbs clustered, 3.5–4cm. Lvs about 15cm, linear-lanceolate. Fls buff-yellow sometimes mottled or flushed red, underside of lip speckled with red; tep. 13–16mm, oblong; lip oblong, obscurely trilobed with a shiny, purple-brown callus. Mex.

M. cyanea (Lindl.) Beer = *Warreella cyanea.*

M. decolor Lindl. = *Xylobium palmifolium.*

M. densa Lindl. Rhiz. ascending; pbs to 8cm, oblong. Lvs to 40cm, linear to oblong-lanceolate. Fls green-white, yellow-green, white tinged with purple, dark maroon or red-brown;

sep. about 10mm, linear-lanceolate; pet. slightly smaller; lip obscurely trilobed, oblong, concave. Mex., Guat., Hond., Belize.

M. densa Lindl. = *Ornithidium densum.*

M. desvauxiana Rchb. f. Rhiz. stout, creeping. Pbs close, 4cm, ovoid. Lvs to 45cm, elliptic. Fls fleshy; sep. to 35mm, ovate, apiculate, dull apricot tipped maroon; pet. to 30mm, obovate, rounded, maroon with paler margins; lip to 25mm, pink, maroon at centre, edge white, 3-lobed, undulate, verrucose. Guyana, Fr. Guiana, Surinam, Venez., Braz.

M. dichroma Rolfe = *M. elegantula.*

M. discolor (Lodd.) Rchb. f. Pbs clustered, to 7cm, ovoid. Lvs to 35cm, ligulate. Fls waxy, apricot spotted maroon, lip orange with deep maroon spots; sep. 22mm, lanceolate, pet. 18mm, oblanceolate; lip 13mm, trilobed, fleshy, with glandular-hairy callus. Guyana, Fr. Guiana, Venez.

M. echinochila Kränzl. Pbs clustered, 30–35mm, long-ovoid. Lvs to 10cm, linear. Fls brown; sep. 20mm, oblong, lat. sep. somewhat curved; pet. slightly narrower; lip 15mm, entire, obovate, undulate. Braz.

M. elegantula Rolfe. Rhiz. stout, creeping; pbs to 6cm, narrowly ellipsoid. Lvs to 30cm, oblong-elliptic. Fls large, white tinged with purple-brown; sep. 25–45mm, oblong, lat. sep. slightly longer, pet. slightly shorter and narrower, obliquely lanceolate; lip 17mm, oval, obscurely trilobed. Peru, Ecuad.

M. elongata Lindl. & Paxt. = *Xylobium elongatum.*

M. equitans (Schltr.) Garay. St. almost erect, clustered, to 30cm, leafy. Pbs obsolete. Lvs to 10cm, fleshy, conduplicate, base sheathing. Sep. 14–15mm, cream tinted pink, oblong, rather fleshy; pet. 13mm; cream narrowly lanceolate; lip 14mm, violet edged white, fleshy, obscurely trilobed. Venez., Guyana, Braz., Colomb., Peru.

M. ferdinandiana Barb. Rodr. Rhiz. 10–25cm, creeping, branched; pbs ovoid. Lvs 6–9cm, linear-lanceolate; tep. greenwhite spotted purple. About 10mm, oblong; lip 10mm, white with purple spots, broadly ovate, obscurely trilobed. Braz.

M. fletcheriana Rolfe. Pbs clustered, 3–5cm, oblong-ovoid. Lvs to 24cm, oblong or elliptic. Fls white or yellow with purple lines; sep. to 45mm, ovate; pet. shorter and narrower. Lip to 50mm, obovate with oblong, fleshy callus above middle, obscurely trilobed, midlobe undulate, trilobulate. Peru.

M. foveata Lindl. = *Xylobium foveatum.*

M. friedrichsthalii Rchb. f. Rhiz. erect or pendulous; pbs clustered, to 5cm, elliptic-oblong. Lvs 3–18cm, ligulate; fls variable in colour and size, yellow-green to green-mauve; sep. to 30mm, linear-lanceolate; pet. slightly smaller; lip entire, narrowly oblanceolate, thickened at apex. Mostly summer. Mex. and C Amer.

M. fuscata Klotzsch = *M. picta.*

M. gracilis Lodd. Pbs clustered, 20–25mm, ovoid. Lvs 10–20cm, linear-ligulate. Fls scented, yellow, tep. flushed with purple on outer edge, lip with purple marks; sep. 17–22mm, fleshy, narrowly lanceolate; pet. 12–20mm, linear-lanceolate; lip 12–15mm, deeply trilobed, midlobe oblong, undulate-denticulate. Braz.

M. grandiflora (HBK) Lindl. Pbs to 6cm, oblong-ovoid. Lvs 11–28cm, elliptic to ligulate. Fls nodding, milk-white, scented, fleshy; dors. sep. 35–45mm, ovate-oblong, concave, lat. sep. slightly longer and wider; pet. shorter and narrower; lip 25×15mm, ovate, obscurely trilobed, apex fleshy; disc with 3 calli. Summer. Ecuad., Peru, Colomb., Venez., Guyana.

M. heuchmannii Hook. = *M. variabilis.*

M. hirtilabia Lindl. = *M. parkeri.*

M. iridifolia Rchb. f. = *M. valenzuelana.*

M. juergensii Schltr. Rhiz. with short, erect br.; pbs 1cm, ribbed. Lvs needle-like, 3–4cm. Fls 12mm diam., v. dark red, almost black, lip tongue-like, with wet-looking surface. Autumnwinter. Braz.

M. jugosa Lindl. = *Pabstia jugosa.*

M. kautskyi Pabst. Slender, tufted; pbs 15mm, globose, 4-angled. Lvs 17–25mm, linear. Fls yellow, lip spotted dark purple towards apex; sep. 13–15mm, narrowly oblong; pet. linear; lip 12mm, broadly trilobed, midlobe 3×4mm, oblong. Braz.

M. kegelii Rchb. f. = *M. parkeri.*

M. kreysigii Hoffsgg. = *M. picta.*

M. lactea Schltr. = *M. ringens.*

M. leontoglossa Rchb. f. = *Xylobium leontoglossum.*

M. lepidota Lindl. Pbs clustered, to 5cm, ovoid. Lvs linear-ligulate, to 35cm. Tep. yellow, marked red at base, lip creamy yellow with maroon marks; sep. to 60mm, lanceolate; pet. to 45mm, curved-lanceolate; lip 20mm, fleshy, callus bordered with hairs, midlobe covered with yellow-green farina. Venez., Colomb., Ecuad.

M. leucochila Hoffsgg. = *M. picta.*

M. lindeniana A. Rich. = *M. meleagris.*

M. linearis C. Schweinf. Rhiz. erect, with short br. Lvs 13.5–40cm, narrowly linear. Dors. sep. 26mm, linear, lat. sep. slightly wider and curved; pet. smaller; lip 10mm, with callus in basal two-thirds, trilobed near apex, midlobe about 2mm, fleshy, narrowly triangular. Peru.

M. longifolia (Barb. Rodr.) Cogn. = *M. tarumaensis.*

M. loretoensis Schweinf. = *M. parkeri.*

M. lorifolia Rchb. f. = *M. parkeri.*

M. luteoalba Lindl. Pbs clustered, ovoid, dark brown. Lvs to 50cm, linear-ligullate. Fls white and yellow, side lobes of lip with purple-brown veining; sep. 52mm, lanceolate; pet. 46mm, lanceolate-falcate; lip 25mm, with pubesc. callus, thick-textured, midlobe broadly ovate. Costa Rica, Panama, Venez., Colomb., Ecuad.

M. lutescens Scheidw. = *M. camaridii.*

M. macleei Batem. ex Lindl. = *M. uncata.*

M. macrura Rchb. f. Pbs compressed, spherical, forming row on rhiz. Lvs ligulate. Fls pink-tan, lip with red longitudinal streaks, to 12cm diam.; tep. linear-lanceolate, caudate; lip trilobed, oblong in outline, with an oblong callus. Mex.

M. marginata Fenzl. V. similar to *M. picta,* differing mainly in rather smaller fls; sep. dull yellow with brown margin; lip short, white, edged and spotted with brown, slightly undulate, lat. lobes short. Braz.

M. mattogrossensis Brade = *M. equitans.*

M. meleagris Lindl. V. similar to *M. tenuifolia* but with broader lvs and more clearly marked tep. Pbs clustered, 2.5–5cm, ellipsoid or ovoid. Lvs 15–40cm, linear. Fls scented of coconut, buff-orange, buff-olive or flesh-coloured, marked with dark red, lip dark blood red; sep. 12–30mm, elliptic; pet. shorter; lip 7–16mm, trilobed, recurved, midlobe fleshy, tongue-like. Mex., Guat., Panama.

M. monoceras Klotzsch = *M. picta.*

M. mosenii Kränzl. Rhiz. stout; pbs 4–4.5cm, 4- or 8-angled, glossy green-black. Lvs 10–15cm, linear-lanceolate. Fls yellow-brown, spotted dull lilac; dors. sep. 20mm, lanceolate, concave, lat. sep. 20mm, oblong-lanceolate; pet. 15mm, obovate-oblong; lip 17mm, almost entire. Braz.

M. nana Hook. = *M. uncata.*

M. nasalis Rchb. f. = *M. nasuta.*

M. nasuta Rchb. f. Pbs to 9×4cm, compressed, clustered. Lvs to 60cm, linear. Fls yellow-green flushed maroon, lip maroon or red, with yellow apex; sep. 32–37mm, lanceolate, rather fleshy; pet. 25mm, oblanceolate; lip 18mm, with a sticky callus, obscurely trilobed. Guat., Costa Rica, Venez., Colomb., Braz.

M. nigrescens Lindl. Pbs long-ovoid, compressed. Lvs to 35cm, linear, rigid. Tep. maroon-red, orange-maroon at apex, grading to yellow at base of sep., lip maroon-black; sep. 45–60mm, lanceolate; pet. 40–55mm, falcate-lanceolate; lip to 17mm with callus at base, trilobed, fleshy. Venez., Colomb.

M. ochroleuca Lindl. Pbs clustered, to 8×4cm, ovoid, v. compressed, ribbed. Lvs to 45cm, linear. Fls strongly scented, tep. white to yellow in apical half, lip white with orange midlobe; sep. 32mm, narrowly lanceolate; pet. slightly smaller; lip 11mm, trilobed, sparsely hairy, midlobe fleshy, rough-textured. var. *longipes* Sander. Fls larger, lip marked ochre. Venez., Braz.

M. oxysepala Schltr. = *M. nasuta.*

M. pachyacron Schltr. = *M. reichenheimiana.*

M. pachyphylla Schltr. Rhiz. pendent; pbs close, 25–35mm, cylindrical to conical, ribbed. Lvs 10–15cm, oblanceolate, thick. Fls pale yellow, lip yellow streaked rose-pink near margin; sep. 18mm, ovate-oblong; lip 17mm, with linear callus, trilobed. Braz. var. *brunneofusca* Hoehne. Fls deep yellow-brown.

M. pallidiflora Hook. = *Xylobium pallidiflorum.*

M. palmifolia (Sw.) Lindl. = *Xylobium palmifolium.*

M. parkeri Hook. Pbs clustered, 3.5cm, ovoid to subglobose, somewhat compressed. Lvs to 45cm, linear-ligulate. Sep. yellow, pet. white with maroon veining towards base, lip orange-yellow, lat. lobes maroon-veined, midlobe margin white; sep. 32–33mm, ovate, fleshy; pet. 28mm, lanceolate; lip 23mm with hairy callus, trilobed, midlobe oblong-ovate, fleshy. Guyana, Venez., Peru.

M. pendens Pabst. Rhiz. to 2m, sometimes branched; pbs remote to 6cm, ovoid. Lvs to 25cm, lanceolate. Fls cream flushed with pink, sep. yellow at apex; sep. 16–21mm, lanceolate; pet. 13–16mm, oblong; lip 12mm, with basal callus with keeled veins, trilobed, midlobe cleft, erose. Guyana, Venez., Colomb., Braz.

M. pertusa Lindl. = *M. lepidota.*

M. petiolaris A. Rich. ex Rchb. f. = *M. desvauxiana.*

M. picta Hook. Pbs usually clustered, to 6cm, ovoid, ribbed. Lvs to 30cm, ligulate. Fls large, golden yellow inside, cream-yellow outside, banded and flecked purple-brown, lip yellow-white or cream spotted red; sep. *c*30mm, oblong; pet. slightly shorter and narrower; midlobe tongue-shaped. Winter. Braz.

M.plebeja Rchb. f. Rhiz. ascending; pbs oblong, compressed. Lvs ligulate. Fls pale yellow, lip darker, tep. sparsely spotted dark purple; sep. ovate; pet. ligulate; lip oblong, obscurely trilobed, with an oblong, waxy callus. Braz.

M.porphyrostele Rchb. f. Pbs clustered, to 4.5cm, broadly ellipsoid. Lvs to 20cm, linear-ligulate. Fls yellow, about 4cm diam.; sep. c20mm, lanceolate, the tips incurved; pet. shorter. Winter–spring. Braz.

M.pubilabia Schltr. = *M.ringens*.

M.punctata Lodd. = *M.gracilis*.

M.punctostriata Rchb. f. = *M.meleagris*.

M.punktulata Klotzsch = *M.marginata*.

M.reichenheimiana Rchb. f. Pbs clustered, to 1.5cm, sub-globose, compressed. Lvs to 4cm, elliptic, fleshy, blue-green mottled grey. Sep. to 35mm, lanceolate, orange, tinged maroon, pet. to 25mm, yellow-orange, lip 15mm, with scattered gland. hairs, trilobed, midlobe yellow, fleshy, ovate, undulate, lat. lobes dark maroon. Trin., Costa Rica, Venez.

M.revoluta Klotzsch = *M.variabilis*.

M.ringens Rchb. f. Pbs close to 4cm, ellipsoid or ovoid, compressed. Lvs to 54cm, elliptic-oblong. Tep. yellow-cream, tinged orange-pink at apex, lip cream, apex dark maroon; sep. 18–40mm, oblong; pet. to 26mm, narrowly lanceolate; lip 13–17mm, with scattered white hairs, trilobed, midlobe fleshy, truncate, undulate. Mex. to Panama; Venez. to Peru.

M.rollissonii Lindl. = *Promenaea rollissonii*.

M.rousseauae Schltr. = *M.ringens*.

M.rubrofusca Klotzsch = *M.nigrescens*.

M.rufescens Lindl. Rhiz. creeping; pbs clustered, 1.5–6cm, small, subglobose, compressed to long-ovoid and 4-angled. Lvs 4–30cm, elliptic, oblong or ligulate. Fls green-brown and cream to dull yellow or orange flushed with maroon, or maroon and white; dors. sep. 9–24mm, oblong, concave, lat. sep. wider; pet. slightly shorter, oblong or lanceolate; lip 8–20mm with long-itudinal callus, trilobed, midlobe truncate. Widespread in Trop. Amer.

M.rugosa Scheidw. = *M.rufescens*.

M.sanderiana Rchb. f. Rhiz. short or long; pbs clustered, to 5cm, subglobose to ovoid, compressed. Lvs to 40cm, narrowly oblong, leathery. Fls large, fleshy, tep. white flecked violet-purple, lip dull yellow with red markings, dark purple on outer surface; dors. sep. 60–75mm, oblong-lanceolate, lat. sep. wider and longer; pet. somewhat shorter; lip 30–35mm, ovate, obscurely trilobed, midlobe ovate to suborbicular, margin crisped. Peru, Ecuad.

M.sanguinea Rolfe. Rhiz. creeping; pbs 1–2.5cm, ellipsoid, compressed. Lvs 25–40cm, linear. Sep. red-brown, apices yellow, pet. pale yellow with red-brown spots, lip carmine-red or crimson-purple with black-purple callus; sep. 12–16mm, oblong; pet. linear-oblong; lip 12–14mm, almost entire, oblong, with a shiny callus. C Amer.

M.saxicola Schltr. = *M.lepidota*.

M.seidelii Pabst. To 5cm; rhiz. ascending; pbs minute, linear-oblong. Lvs 2.5–3cm, awl-shaped. Fls white, erect; sep. 8–8.5mm, ligulate; pet. 7mm, ligulate; lip 7mm, narrow, fleshy at base, lat. lobes obscure, densely puberulous. Braz.

M.serotina Hoehne = *M.consanguinea*.

M.setigera var. *angustifolia* Klinge = *M.callichroma*.

M.sophronites (Rchb. f.) Garay. Rhiz. long, creeping; pbs 1–1.5cm, subglobose later compressed. Lvs to 2cm, elliptic, fleshy. Tep. orange-red, lip midlobe yellow with cream edge, lateral lobes cream; sep. 11–13mm, ovate, apiculate; similar, shorter; lip 7mm, trilobed toward base, lat. lobes erose, mid-lobe ovate, glandular-tubercular, erose. Venez.

M.squalens (Lindl.) Hook. = *Xylobium variegatum*.

M.squamata Barb. Rodr. = *M.uncata*.

M.stapelioides Lindl. = *Promenaea stapelioides*.

M.stenobulbon Klotzsch = *Xylobium pallidiflorum*.

M.stenostele Schltr. = *M.uncata*.

M.striata Rolfe. Pbs clustered, 4.5–8cm, oblong to ovoid. Lvs to 24cm, oblong to elliptical, leathery. Fls large, green-yellow with purple-red stripes, lip white, lat. lobes veined with red-purple; dors. sep. 45–70mm, oblong-lanceolate, concave, lat. sep. much wider at base and acuminate; pet. shorter and narrower than dors. sep.; lip 35–40mm, with linear callus in basal half, obscurely trilobed near apex, midlobe ovate-lanceolate, recurved, undulate. Peru.

M.superba La Ll. & Lex. = *Govenia superba*.

M.tarumaensis Hoehne. Pbs to 3cm, compressed. Lvs to 50cm, ligulate. Tep. yellow-brown, lip purple-red with longitudinal green stripe; sep. 14mm, oblong-elliptic; pet. narrower; lip 13mm, obscurely trilobed, elliptic, with raised, sticky callus. Braz., Venez.

M.tenuifolia Lindl. Rhiz. ascending; pbs about 2.5cm, ovoid. Lvs 20–35cm, narrowly linear. Fls with a strong coconut scent, deep red mottled with yellow towards base of tep., lip yellow, marked

dark blood red; sep. spreading, 20–25mm, lanceolate or ovate; pet. shorter, projecting forwards; lip about 16mm, obscurely trilobed, midlobe tongue-shaped, fleshy. Spring–summer. Mex. to Hond. and Nic.

M.tricolor Lindl. = *M.marginata*.

M.triloris E. Morr. Pbs clustered, to 6cm, ovoid, compressed. Lvs to 40cm, linear-ligulate. Fls fragrant, tep. yellow, white at base, with maroon patch on reverse, lip lat. lobes white with maroon veins, midlobe yellow with white margin; sep. 65–70mm, lanceolate or oblanceolate; pet. 60mm, lanceolate; lip 28mm, stiff, with hairy longitudinal callus, trilobed, midlobe oblong, thickened, sparsely pubesc., undulate. Venez.

M.tuerckheimii Schltr. = *M.ringens*.

M.uncata Lindl. Rhiz. to 80cm, pendent, pbs obscure, to 5mm. Lvs to 8cm, stiff, linear. Fls green-cream, sometimes tinged light maroon; sep. 11–14mm, ovate, apiculate, pet. to 9mm, obliquely ovate, apiculate; lip to 13mm, with smooth callus, obscurely trilobed, midlobe slightly smooth callus, obscurely trilobed, midlobe slightly emarginate. Mex. to Braz. and Peru. \

M.valenzuelana (A. Rich.) Nash. Pendulous, lacking pbs. Lvs to 18×1.5cm, fleshy, equitant, conduplicate. Fls about 2.5cm diam., tep. yellow-green, lip light brown with purple spots; 11–14mm, ovate, acute or apiculate, light brown with purple spots; sep. 11–14mm, ovate, acute or apiculate, fleshy; pet. 9mm, oblong-lanceolate; lip 10mm, callus white glandular-hairy, obscurely trilobed, fleshy. C Amer., W Indies, Venez., Colomb., Ecuad., Braz.

M.vandiformis (Schltr.) C. Schweinf. = *M.equitans*.

M.vanillodora A. Rich. ex Rchb. f. = *M.rufescens*.

M.variabilis Lindl. Rhiz. creeping or ascending; pbs 2–4cm, cylindrical, flattened. Lvs 15–25cm, oblong-linear, leathery. Fls small, pale yellow to dark red; sep. spreading, elliptic-lanceolate; pet. similar but forward projecting; lip slightly short-er, tongue-shaped, with dark red central callus. Throughout the year. Mex. to Panama.

M.variegata Ruiz & Pav. = *Xylobium variegatum*.

M.venusta Lindl. Pbs 4–5cm ovoid, somewhat flattened. Lvs to 30cm, ligulate. Fls nodding, tep. milk-white, lip yellow with 2 red spots, margins of lateral lobes red; sep. to 75mm, lanceolate, dorsall sep. concave, lateral sep. curved; pet. slightly shorter; lip fleshy, trilobed, midlobe triangular; recurved. Winter–spring. Colomb.

M.villosa (Barb. Rodr.) Cogn. Pbs clustered, to 8cm, cylindrical to oblong-ovoid. Lvs to 44cm, ligulate to oblong, leathery. Fls small, bell-shaped, yellow, yellow-brown or orange, lip some-times white; sep. 15–20mm, ovate-oblong, concave; pet. shorter and narrower; lip 13–15mm, oblong-ovate, obscurely trilobed, lat. lobes erect. Peru, Braz., Guyana.

M.vittariifolia L.O. Williams. Pbs clustered, 5–6mm diam., sub-globose. Lvs about 9cm, narrowly ligulate. Fls 10cm diam., milk-white, lip with yellow lat. lobes and red midlobe. Summer–autumn. Costa Rica, Panama, Colomb.

M.xanthina Lindl. = *Promenaea xanthina*.

Maximiliana Mart. MARIPA; INAJA; CURCURITA PALM. Palmae. 1 monoecious palm. St. solitary, to 18m tall, to 50cm diam., becoming bare and ringed. Lvs pinnate, to 6m; pinnae emerging scurfy, later glab., lanceolate, to 1m×5cm, semi-rigid, in whorls of up to 5 held at differing planes along rachis, longest near base. Fls on ♂spikes, branching ×350, amid 3 bracts, ♂ at base of branchlets, ♀ near apex. Fr. ovoid, 3-seeded. N S Amer., W Indies. Z10.

M.caribaea Griseb. & H.A. Wendl. = *M.maripa*.

M.maripa (Corr.) Drude.

M.martiana Karst. = *M.maripa*.

M.regia Mart. = *M.maripa*.

→*Englerophoenix*.

May *Crataegus laevigata*.

May Apple *Passiflora incarnata*; *Podophyllum peltatum*.

May-blob *Caltha palustris*.

Maybush, Mayday Tree *Prunus padus*.

Mayes Dewberry *Rubus almus*.

Mayflower *Epigaea repens*.

Mayfly Orchid *Acianthus caudatus*.

May Lily *Maianthemum*.

May Poplar *Populus* ×*canadensis*.

May Pops *Passiflora incarnata*.

May Rose *Rosa majalis*.

Mayten *Maytenus boaria*.

Maytenus Molina. Celastraceae. 255 shrubs or small trees, some-times spinose. Lvs alt., often distichous, entire or dentate. Fls clustered in cymes, thyrses, rac. or fascicles, 4–5-merous; pet. spreading; disc conspicuous. Fr. a capsule, 2–5-valved; seeds with a fleshy red or white aril. Trop. and subtrop. regions.

M. boaria Molina. MAYTEN. Everg. shrub or tree to 24m, glab. throughout; branchlets drooping. Lvs 2.5–5cm, lanceolate to narrowly elliptic, finely serrate. Fls clustered 2–5, inconspicuous, white tinged green. Fr. yellow; seeds 2, aril scarlet. Spring. Chile. Z8.

M. chilensis DC. = *M. boaria*.

M. chubutensis (Speg.) Lourteig, O'Donnell & Sleumer. Dwarf everg. shrub to 60cm. Lvs 1cm, broad-elliptic to broad-ovate, stiffly pubesc. above. Fls solitary or in clusters, small, pale red. Arg. Z9.

M. ilicifolia Reisseck ex Mart. Shrub or tree to 5m. Lvs holly-like, 2–15cm, elliptic or oblong, spiny-dentate. Fls in crowded fascicles, yellow, small. Fr. 2-valved, tinged red; seed 1–4, aril red. S Amer. (Boliv., Parag., S Braz., E to Arg.). Z10.

M. magellanica (Lam.) Hook. f. Tree or shrub to 7m. Lvs 1.5–9.5cm, ovate to lanceolate, serrate and thickened, glab. Fls in fascicles, red with white margins. Fr. to 6mm, seeds 2, with fleshy aril. Autumn. S Chile, S Arg., Tierra del Fuego. Z9.

M. phyllanthoides Benth. Low shrub or tree to 3m. Lvs to 3cm, oblong-ovate, obscurely crenate, glab. Fls to 3mm diam., solitary or in sparse clusters. Fr. to 8mm, seed 1–3, arils red. US (Flor., Mex.). Z9.

M. serratus (Hochst. ex A. Rich.) R. Wilcz. Everg. shrub to 2m+, sometimes spiny. Lvs to 7.5cm, elliptic to ovate to oblanceolate, serrate. Fls in branching clusters, pale white. Fr. 3-valved. Ethiop. Z10.

→*Gymnosporia*.

Mayweed *Anthemis cotula*.

Mazus Lour. Scrophulariaceae. 30 low-growing, ann. or perenn. herbs. Fls in a term. rac. or solitary; cal. campanulate, 5-lobed; cor. tube short, 2-lipped, upper lip erect, 2-lobed, lower lip larger, spreading, 3-lobed, with 2 distinct blisters in the throat; sta. 4. SE Asia, China, Taiwan, Malay Archipel., Australasia.

M. pumilio R. Br. Perenn., rhizomatous, almost prostrate. Lvs 2–5cm, narrowly obovate-spathulate, entire or sinuately toothed, glab. or almost so. Rac. 1–6-fld; cor. white or blue, throat yellow, lobes 6–12mm diam.; broad, obtuse. Summer. Australasia. Z7. 'Albus': fls white.

M. radicans (Hook. f.) Cheesem. Perenn., creeping, st. sometimes subterranean. Lvs linear-obovate, almost entire, usually pilose. Rac. 1–3-fld; cor. 12–18mm, white, throat yellow, lips sometimes blotched purple. Summer. NZ. Z6.

M. reptans N.E. Br. Perenn., prostrate. Lvs to 1cm, lanceolate to elliptic, coarsely toothed. Rac. 2–5-fld; cor. purple-blue, lower lip blotched white, yellow and red-purple. Summer. Himal. 'Albus': fls white. Z3.

→*Mimulus*.

Mazzard *Prunus avium*.
Mbocaya Tota *Acrocomia aculeata*.
Meadow Beauty *Rhexia*.
Meadow Bright *Caltha palustris*.
Meadow Buttercup *Ranunculus acris*.
Meadow Cat's Tail *Phleum pratense*.
Meadow Clary *Salvia pratensis*.
Meadow Cranesbill *Geranium pratense*.
Meadow Cress *Cardamine pratensis*.
Meadow Fern *Myrica gale*; *Thelypteris palustris* var. *pubescens*.
Meadow Fescue *Festuca elatior*.
Meadow Foam *Limnanthes* (*L. douglasii*).
Meadow Foxtail *Alopecurus pratensis*.
Meadowgrass *Poa*.
Meadow Hyacinth *Camassia scilloides*.
Meadow Leek *Allium canadense*.
Meadow Lily *Lilium canadense*.
Meadow Milkvetch *Oxytropis campestris*.
Meadow Phlox *Phlox maculata*.
Meadow Rue *Thalictrum*.
Meadow Saffron *Colchicum autumnale*.
Meadow Saxifrage *Saxifraga granulata*.
Meadow Sidalcea *Sidalcea campestris*.
Meadow Spike Moss *Selaginella apoda*.
Meadowsweet *Filipendula*, *F. ulmaria*; *Spiraea alba*, *S. latifolia*.
Meadow Vetchling *Lathyrus pratensis*.
Mealberry *Arctostaphylos uva-ursi*.
Mealie *Zea mays*.
Mealy Sage *Salvia farinacea*.
Mealy Stringybark *Eucalyptus cephalocarpa*.
Mealy Wattle *Acacia farinosa*.
Means Grass *Sorghum halapense*.
Measles Plant *Hypoestes phyllostachya*.

Mecodium C. Presl. ex Copel.

M. australe (Willd.) Copel. = *Hymenophyllum australe*.
M. flabellatum (Labill.) Copel. = *Hymenophyllum flabellatum*.

Meconella Nutt. Papaveraceae. 3–4 ann. herbs. St. erect, dichotomously branching, somewhat glaucous. Lvs mostly basal, spathulate. Fls solitary, on axillary peduncles; sep. 3, hairy; pet. 6, rarely 5; sta. 6–12. Fr. a linear capsule, valves 3, spiralling once open. Summer. W N Amer. Z6.

M. linearis (Benth.) Nels. & Macbr. Similar to *M. oregana*, except to 25cm. Lvs to 7cm, basal, linear. Fls cream.

M. oregana Nutt. ex Torr. & A. Gray. To 10cm. St. filiform. Basal lvs spathulate, to 1.5cm, st. lvs to 1cm, oblong-lanceolate. Fls to 0.5cm diam.; pet. oblong-cuneiform, cream with an ivory patch at base.

Meconopsis Vig. ASIATIC POPPY. Papaveraceae. 43 ann., bienn. or perenn. herbs, often monocarpic. Sap yellow. Lvs mostly basal, rosulate. Flowering st. scapose and simple or branched and leafy; fls solitary or in rac.; sep. 2, caducous; pet. silken, 4, rarely 5–9; sta. 20+. Himal. to W China, W Eur.

M. aculeata Royle. Monocarpic perenn., to 60cm. Basal lvs and lower lvs petiolate, to 27.5×5cm, irregularly pinnatifid or pinnatisect, with yellow-brown bristly spines; lobes oblong, obtuse to rounded, or deltoid, acute. Fls solitary on axill. stalks to 22.5cm, with bract-like lvs near apex; pet. 4, rarely 6, to 3×3cm, sky blue, rarely mauve or red. Summer. W Himal. Z7.

M. baileyi Prain = *M. betonicifolia*.

M. ×*beamishii* Prain (*M. grandis* ×*M. integrifolia*.) To 1.2m. Basal lvs to 25cm, oblanceolate. Base often blotched, pet. 6–8, yellow, base sometimes blotched purple, obovate, to 7.5×6.5cm. Gdn origin.

M. bella Prain. Perenn., to 15cm. Basal lvs pinnate or pinnatifid, to 17.5×2.5cm, glab. to sparsely setose; lobes obovate to oblong, obtuse, ultimate lobes trifid. Fls solitary on flimsy setose scapes; pet. 4, rarely 5–6, obovate to suborbicular, to 3×3cm, pink, pale blue or purple. Summer. Himal. Z8.

M. betonicifolia Franch. BLUE POPPY. Short-lived perenn., to 2m. Basal and lower st. lvs to 35×7.5cm, petiolate, oblong to ovate, obtuse at apex, serrate, sparsely setose. Fls 5 to 6, in somewhat drooping cymes on axill. scapes to 25cm; pet. 4, obovate to suborbicular, obtuse, to 5×5cm, mauve-pink to bright sky blue. Summer. China. 'Alba': to 110cm; fls white. Harlow Carr Strain: perenn.; fls blue. Z7.

M. cambrica (L.) Vig. WELSH POPPY. Perenn. to 60cm. Basal lvs pinnatisect toward base, pinnatifid toward apex, to 20cm, glab. to hairy above, seg. pinnatifid or irregularly lobed. Fls solitary, in axils of upper st. lvs; pedicels to 25cm; pet. 4, or double in cvs, obovate to suborbicular, to 3×3cm, yellow. Summer. W Eur. var. *aurantiaca* hort. ex Wehrh. Fls orange. 'Frances Perry': fls scarlet. 'Flore-Pleno': fls semi-double, yellow or orange. Z6.

M. cathcartii hort. = *M. villosa*.

M. chelidoniifolia Bur. & Franch. Perenn., to 1m. Basal lvs pinnatisect; seg. distant, pinnatisect to pinnatifid, bristly, glaucous beneath. Fls on flimsy, axill. pedicels; pet. 4, obovate or suborbicular, to 2.5×2.5cm, yellow. Summer. China. Z8.

M. ×*cookei* G. Tayl. (*M. punicea* ×*M. quintuplinervia*.) Lvs basal, elliptic to oblanceolate, entire, to 15×2cm. Scape to 40cm; fls pendent, ruby-red; pet. 4, ovate, to 5×4cm. Gdn origin. Z7.

M. delavayi (Franch.) Franch. ex Prain. Perenn. to 27.5cm. Lvs all basal, ovate to narrowly oblanceolate, entire, to 15×3cm, sparsely setose throughout, glaucous beneath. Fls solitary, on flimsy term. scapes; pet. usually 4, occas. 6 or 8, ovate or orbicular, to 3×2.5cm, deep purple, rarely deep pink. Summer. SW China. Z8.

M. dhwojii G. Tayl. ex Hay. Monocarpic perenn., to 60cm. Basal lvs petiolate, pinnatisect toward base, pinnatifid toward apex, to 32.5cm, seg. lobed, sparsely setose, bristles dark purple at base. Fls in branching rac., lower br. to 5-fld; pet. 4, obovate to orbicular, to 3×3cm, yellow. Summer. Nepal. Z8.

M. ×*finlayorum* G. Tayl. (*M. integrifolia* ×*M. quintuplinervia*.) Lvs basal, elliptic to broadly lanceolate, 6.5–8×2–3.5cm, petiole winged. Peduncles to 36cm; bristly; pet. white, 4–6, ovate, 3–3.5×2–2.5cm. Gdn origin. Z7.

M. gracilipes G. Tayl. Monocarpic perenn, to 60cm. Basal lvs to 25cm, rosulate, bristly, deeply cut throughout. Fls on flimsy stalks to 35cm; lower br. 3-fld; pet. 4, yellow, obovate or orbicular, to 3×2.5cm. Summer. Nepal. Z8.

M. grandis Prain. Perenn., to 120cm. Basal and lower st. lvs to 30cm, narrowly oblanceolate to elliptic-oblong, irregularly serrate, broadly crenate, rusty-setose throughout. Fls 3+, on pedicels to 45cm; pet. 4–9, suborbicular or broadly ovate, to 6×5.5cm, purple or deep blue. Summer. 'Miss Dickson' ('Puritan'): fls white. Z5.

M. horridula Hook. f. & Thoms. Short-lived perenn., to 80cm. Lvs elliptic to narrowly obovate, entire or sinuate, to 25×3cm, grey-green with purple or yellow spiny bristles. Fls 1–2, nodding, on axill. pedicels to 22.5cm, covered with spiny bristles; pet. 4–8, ovate to suborbicular, minutely toothed at apex, 4–3cm, cobalt blue to violet or white. Summer. Himal. to W China. Z6.

M. integrifolia (Maxim.) Franch. Short-lived perenn., to 90cm, covered with downy, orange-red hairs. Basal lvs entire, oblanceolate to obovate or linear, to 37.5×5cm, densely hairy throughout. Fls 4–5, solitary on axill. pedicels or scapes; pet. 6–8, suborbicular to obovate, to 3×3cm, yellow or white. Summer. Tibet, Upper Burm., W China. Z7.

M. latifolia (Prain) Prain. Short-lived perenn., to 120cm. Basal lvs oblong to ovate or broadly lanceolate, to 20×3cm, with yellow-brown, crenate or deeply serrate. Fls many, solitary on spiny pedicels to 2.5cm; pet. 4, obovate or suborbicular, to 3×2.5cm, pale blue, rarely white. Spring–summer. N Kashmir. Z7.

M. × musgravei G. Tayl. (*M. betonicifolia* × *M. superba*.) To 62cm. Basal lvs oblong, pubesc., margins densely serrate, to 7.5cm. Pet. white, ovate to suborbicular, to 5×5cm. Gdn origin. Z7.

M. napaulensis DC. SATIN POPPY. Perenn., to 2.6m. Basal lvs pinnatisect, to 50×10cm; seg. pinnately lobed, yellow-brown-setose, lobes acute to rounded. Fls drooping, to 17 per branched cyme; pedicels setose, to 7.5cm; pet. 4, obovate to suborbicular, to 4×3cm, red or purple or blue, rarely white. Spring–summer. C Nepal to SW China. 'Alba': fls white. Z8.

M. paniculata (D. Don) Prain. Short-lived perenn., to 2m. Basal lvs pinnatisect, villous and setose throughout, seg. lanceolate, oblong or deltoid, lobed or entire. Fls solitary on axill. pedicels and in 2–6-fld rac.; pet. 4, ovate to suborbicular, to 5×5cm, yellow. Spring–summer. E Nepal to NE Assam. Z8.

M. punicea Maxim. Perenn., to 75cm. Lvs to 38×3cm, oblanceolate. Fls solitary, drooping, on bristly scapes; pet. 4, occas. 6, rhombic-elliptic, to 10×5cm, deep red. Spring–summer. NE Tibet, W China. Z7.

M. quintuplinervia Reg. Perenn., to 30cm. Lvs to 25×3cm, golden to rusty-setose, obovate to narrowly oblanceolate. Fls solitary, pendent on hispid scapes; pet. 4, occas. 6, obovate or orbicular, to 3×3cm, pale mauve-blue or light violet, rarely white. Spring–summer. NE Tibet, China. Z8.

M. regia G. Tayl. Perenn., to 60cm, with soft, white or pale yellow hairs. Basal lvs to 40×9cm, narrowly elliptic, deeply serrate, covered with dense silver-grey or golden silky hairs. Fls many, borne on axill. br. from upper lvs; pet. 4, rarely 6, suborbicular, to 6×5cm, yellow. Spring–summer. C Nepal. Z8.

M. × sarsonii Sarsons. (*M. betonicifolia* × *M. integrifolia*.) Close to *M. betonicifolia* in habit, to *M. integrifolia* in fl. shape and colour. Gdn origin.

M. × sheldonii G. Tayl. (*M. betonicifolia* × *M. grandis*.) Lvs oblong-lanceolate, bristly throughout, serrate. Fls solitary on axill. pedicels from upper st. lvs; pet. 4, obovate to suborbicular, to 3cm, blue. Gdn origin. 'Branklyn' lvs coarsely toothed; fls to 20cm diam. Crewdson Hybrids: fls blue-green. 'Ormswell': to 80cm; fls deep blue. 'Slieve Donard': to 1m; fls blue-green. Z6.

M. simplicifolia (D. Don) Walp. Perenn., to 80cm. Lvs to 37×5cm, oblanceolate to ovate, with flimsy bristles throughout, entire or serrate to lobed. Fls solitary; pedicels 1–5, to 70cm, setose; pet. 5–8, obovate, to 5×4cm, purple to light blue. Spring–summer. C Nepal to SE Tibet. Z7.

M. sinuata Prain. Ann., to 75m. Basal lvs to 17.5×3cm, obovate to oblanceolate, sharply setose, deeply lobed. Fls 4–8, solitary on axill. pedicels to 22.5cm; pet. 4, obovate, emarginate, to 3×2cm, blue, purple or mauve. Spring–summer. Nepal to Bhutan. Z8.

M. superba King ex Prain. As for *M. regia* except lvs more roughly hairy. Fls solitary on main axis, white. Summer. Tibet, W Bhutan. Z7.

M. villosa (Hook. f.) G. Tayl. Perenn., to 60cm. Basal lvs to 12.5×12cm, ovate to suborbicular, 3–5-lobed, sparsely setose, glaucous beneath, lobes subacute to rounded; petioles to 20cm, setose, st. lvs widespread on st., to 10×10cm. Fls 1–5, solitary; pedicels axill., setose, to 14cm; pet. 4, suborbicular to ovate, obtuse, to 2.5×3cm, yellow. E Nepal to Bhutan. 'White Swan': to 90cm; fls white. Z7.

M. wallichii Hook. = *M. napaulensis*.

Medake *Pleioblastus simonii*.

Medeola L. Liliaceae (Trilliaceae). 2 perenn. herbs. Rhiz. horizontal, thick. St. slender. Lvs in 2 whorls. Fls few in a term. umbel; fil. slender. Fr. a few-seeded berry. NE Amer.

M. asparagoides L. = *Asparagus asparagoides*.

M. virginiana (L.) Merrill. INDIAN CUCUMBER ROOT. St. 30–70cm. Lvs of lower whorl 6–12cm, 5–11, oblong-lanceolate, lvs of upper whorl 3–6cm, usually 3, ovate. Infl. 3–9-fld; tep. green-yellow, to 8mm. Fr. dark purple. Summer. E Canada, E US. Z3.

Medicago L. MEDIC; MEDICK. Leguminosae (Papilionoideae). 56 ann. or perenn. herbs or small shrubs. Lvs 3-foliate. Rac. short, axill.; fls pea-like. Fr. curved or spirally twisted, sometimes falcate, reniform or straight, often spiny. Eur., Medit., Ethiop., S Afr., Asia.

M. arborea L. MOON TREFOIL. Shrub 1–2m, finely grey-pubesc. Lfts 6–18mm, obovate, finely toothed. Rac. 4–8-fld; fls 12–15mm, yellow. Fr. in spiral of 1–1.5 turns. Late spring–early autumn. S Eur. Z8.

M. cretacea Bieb. Shrub to 25cm, adpressed-pubesc. Lfts to 8mm, broad-ovate, mucronate, ± entire, pubesc. Rac. many-fld; fls to 7mm, yellow. Fr. falcate, compressed, glabrescent. Summer. SE Eur. to Crimea. Z9.

M. denticulata Willd. = *M. polymorpha*.

M. echinus Lam. = *M. intertexta*.

M. falcata (L.) Arcang. SICKLE MEDICK. Herbaceous perenn.; st. prostrate, 60cm–1.2m. Lfts oblong, toothed at apex. Rac. dense; fls 5–8mm, pale yellow, sometimes violet and green. Fr. almost straight to falcate. Summer. Eur., N Asia, India. Z7.

M. hispida Gaertn. = *M. polymorpha*.

M. intertexta (L.) Mill. CALVARY CLOVER. Nearly glab. procumbent or ascending ann. to 50cm. Lfts obovate, denticulate, sometimes with a dark spot. Rac. 1–7- or 10-fld; fls 6–9mm, yellow. Fr. in a spiral of 3 or 6–10 turns, ovoid, cylindric or discoid, spiny. Medit., Port.

M. lupulina L. BLACK MEDICK; HOP CLOVER; NONSUCH; YELLOW TREFOIL. ± pubesc. ann. or short-lived perenn., 5–60cm. Lfts orbicular, obovate, or rhombic-, apiculate. Rac. 10–50-fld; fls 2–3mm, yellow. Fr. reniform, reticulate. Eur. (except extreme N), nat. N Amer. Z5.

M. marina L. Procumbent, white-tomentose, perenn., 20–50cm. Lfts obovate, denticulate at apex. Rac. 5–12-fld; fls 6–8mm, pale yellow. Fr. in a spiral of 2–3 turns, cylindric, white-tomentose, with 2 rows of spines. Eur. Medit., Black Sea and Atlantic coasts. Z8.

M. orbicularis (L.) Bartal. Glab. or sparsely pubesc. procumbent ann., 20–90cm. Lfts obovate-cuneate, dentate at apex. Rac. 1–5-fld; fls 2–5mm, yellow. Fr. in a spiral of 4–6 turns, lenticular, glab. or glandular-pubesc. S Eur., W Asia.

M. polymorpha L. Glab. or pubesc. ann. to 40cm. Lfts obovate to obcordate, dentate near apex. Rac. 1–5-fld; fls 3–4.5mm, yellow. Fr. in a lax spiral, usually glab. and spiny. Eur., Asia.

M. sativa L. ALFALFA; LUCERNE. ± pubesc. perenn. to 80cm. Lfts obovate to linear, dentate at apex. Rac. 5–40-fld; fls 6–11mm, blue to purple. Fr. nearly straight, falcate, or in a spiral of 1–3 twists.

M. scutellata (L.) Mill. Glandular-pubesc. ann., 20–60cm. Lfts obovate to eliptic, dentate in upper part. Rac. 1–3-fld; fls 6–7mm, yellow. Fr. in spiral of 4–8 overlapping turns, glandular-pubesc. S Eur.

Medic, Medick *Medicago*.

Medinilla Gaudich. Melastomataceae. *c*150. Everg. shrubs, some climbing or epiphytic. Lvs simple, entire, leathery or fleshy, conspicuously 3–9-nerved. Fls appearing whorled amid conspicuous bracts in pendulous cymes or pan.; cal. entire or 4- or 6-toothed; pet. 4–5 or 6, ovate. Trop. Afr., SE Asia, Pacific. Z10.

M. magnifica Lindl. Robust epiphytic shrub to 3m. Br. stout, tetragonal to winged, jointed. Lvs 20–30cm, broadly ovate, deep glossy green. Pan. to 40cm, strongly pendulous; bracts v. large, pink, paired, concave; fls to 2.5cm diam., pink to coral-red. Philipp.

Mediocactus Britt. & Rose in part.

M. coccineus Britt. & Rose, not. = *Selenicereus setaceus*.

M. megalanthus (Schum. ex Vaupel) Britt. & Rose = *Selenicereus megalanthus*.

Mediolobivia Backeb. = *Rebutia*.

Mediterranean Fan Palm *Chamaerops*.
Mediterranean Barley *Hordeum hystrix*.
Mediterranean Cypress *Cupressus sempervirens*.
Mediterranean Hackberry *Celtis australis*.
Medlar *Mespilus; Mimusops elengi*.
Medusa's Head *Euphorbia caput-medusae*.

Meehania Britt. JAPANESE DEAD NETTLE. Labiatae. 6 creeping perenn. herbs. Fls in sparse, remote verticils amid lf-like bracts or spikes; cal. campanulate, 15-nerved, 2-lipped; cor. tube gradually expanding, limb 2-lipped, upper lip 2-lobed, concave, lower lip 3-lobed. Asia, N Amer.

M. cordata (Nutt.) Britt. MEEHAN'S MINT; CREEPING MINT. Finely pubesc. St. 10–20cm, scattered with rough hairs. Lvs 2.5–6cm, broadly cordate, crenate. Fls 3–6 per verticil; cor. 2.5–3.5cm, broadly expanding, lavender or lilac blue, hairy in the throat. E US. Z4.

M. fargesii (A. Lév.) C.Y. Wu. Finely pubesc. St. 15–40cm, scattered with gland. hairs. Lvs 2.5–6.5cm, deltoid-subcordate, irregularly serrate. Fls 2–6 per verticil; cor. 2.8–4.5cm, long, blue, streaked purple, lobes white. W China. Z7.

M. urticifolia (Miq.) Mak. Pubesc. St. 15–30cm. Lvs 2–5cm, deltoid-ovate to ovate-cordate, coarsely obtuse-serrate. Fls 3–12 in term. one-sided spikes; cor. 4–5cm, blue-purple, lower lip, spotted dark purple. Jap., NE China, Korea. Z5.

→*Dracocephalum* and *Glechoma*.

Meehan's Mint *Meehania cordata*.
Meeting Houses *Aquilegia canadensis*.

Megacarpaea DC. Cruciferae. 7 large, perenn. herbs. Roots v. thick. Lvs pinnately cut. Infl. paniculate; fls large; sep. 4, broadly elliptic; pet. 4, obovate; sta. 6–16. Eur. to C Asia and China. Z7.

M. bifida Benth. Similar to *M. polyandra* except lf seg. entire, fls yellow, 5mm across; sta. 7–11. Early summer. Himal.

M. laciniata DC. = *M. megalocarpa*.

M. megalocarpa (Fisch.) Schischkin. 20–40cm. Lvs 15–16cm, white-hairy, lobes irregular. Fls small, lowermost lacking perianth and sta., uppermost with undeveloped ovaries, linear, white-yellow pet. and 6 sta. Mong.

M. polyandra Benth. 1–2m. Lvs 15–30cm, lobes toothed. Rac. dense, 20cm; fls 1cm across; pet. yellow-white; sta. 8–16. Spring-summer. Himal.

→*Biscutella*.

Megacodon (Hemsl.) H. Sm. Gentianaceae. 1 perenn. herb. St. simple, robust, erect, to 2m. Basal lvs 30cm, elliptic, 5-veined, cauline lvs 10–15cm, paired. Fls often paired, nodding in upper axils; cal. tube 1.5cm, funnel-shaped, lobes 2cm ovate; cor. 6–8cm, broadly campanulate, pale yellow, netted green within, lobes broadly ovate. Summer. C Nepal to SW China. Z7.

M. stylophorus (C.B. Clarke) H. Sm.

→*Gentiana*.

Megalopanax Ekman = *Aralia*.

Megaphrynium Milne-Redh. Marantaceae. 5 tall perenn. herbs. Lvs basal. Fls in cymules in the nodes of a bracteate pan.; sep. free; cor. tube v. short, lobes oblong, outer staminodes linear-lanceolate, subulate, sometimes 1 0. W Afr. Z10.

M. macrostachyum (Benth.) Milne-Redh. To 2m. Lvs to 50cm, elliptic to ovate-oblong; petiole sheathing. Pan. to 20cm; cor. tube yellow, violet at base, lobes to 1cm. Togo, Guinea.

→*Phrynium*.

Megasea Haw. = *Bergenia*.

Megaskepasma Lindau. Acanthaceae. 1 everg. shrub to 3m. St. downy at first, obscurely 4-angled. Lvs 12–30cm, ovate-elliptic to oblong-elliptic, midrib and petiole tinted rose. Spike term. to 30cm; bracts to 3.25cm, crimson; cal. lobes 5; cor. to 7.5cm, white or shell pink, tube slender, limb 2-lipped. Venez. Z10.

M. erythrochlamys Lindau. BRAZILIAN RED CLOAK; RED JUSTICIA.

Mei *Prunus mume*.

Meiracyllium Rchb. f. Orchidaceae. 2 epiphytic orchids. Rhiz. creeping. St. short or 0, single-leaved. Lf coriaceous. Fls 1–several, term., disproportionately large; sep. oblong-elliptic, spreading, pet. broader; lip saccate or gibbous. C Amer. Z9.

M. trinasutum Rchb. f. St. obscure. Lvs to 5cm, orbicular to elliptic. Fls several, red-purple; lip ovate-cordate. Mex., Guat.

M. wendlandii Rchb. f. St. curved, to 1cm. Lvs to 5cm, obovate, or oblong. Fls solitary, purple, base yellow; concave; lip obovate or flabellate. Mex., Guat.

M. wettsteinii Porsch = *Neolauchea pulchella*.

Meissner's Banksia *Banksia meissneri*.
Meiwa Kumquat *Fortunella crassifolia*.
Melagueta Pepper *Aframomum melegueta*.

Melaleuca L. HONEY MYRTLE; BOTTLEBRUSH; PAPERBARK. Myrtaceae. 150 everg. trees and shrubs. Bark usually papery, many-layered. Lvs usually subsessile, entire, flat or

semicylindrical, usually small and crowded, firm, with oil glands. Fls sessile, in axill. heads or cylindrical spikes, the axis usually growing beyond into a leafy shoot; cal. tube 4-lobed; pet. 5, concave; sta. conspicuous, numerous, much longer than pet., in 5 bundles opposite pet. Fr. a woody capsule, often embedded in thickened axis. Mainly Austral.; also New Caledonia, New Guinea and Malesia. Z9.

M. abietina Sm. = *M. cuticularis*.

M. acuminata F. Muell. To 4m. Lvs 5–10×2–4mm, decussate, flate or concave, ovate, often pungent. Infl. 1- or few-fld; sta. white. NSW, Vict., S & W Aus.

M. alba hort. ex Steud. = *M. armillaris*.

M. armillaris (Sol. ex Gaertn.) Sm. BRACELET. To 8m. Lvs 14–28×0.7–1.3mm, spirally arranged, linear or narrowly elliptic to compressed or semiterete. Infl. 25–70-fld; sta. white to mauve. NSW, Vict., S Aus.

M. biconvexa Byrnes. To 10m. Lvs 7–18×2–4mm, opposite, channelled above, keeled beneath, ovate, sometimes apiculate, villous, soon glab. Infl. a few-fld, dense, term. head or short spike; sta. white or pale yellow. NSW, Aus.

M. cajuputi Powell. To 25m. Lvs 45–120×8–20mm, scattered, ovate or obovate, acute. Infl. a many-fld term. or upper-axill. spike; fls in triads; sta. white. Aus. to Malesia.

M. callistemonea Lindl. = *M. lateritia*.

M. chlorantha Bonpl. = *M. diosmifolia*.

M. coccinea A.S. George. To 2.7m. Lvs 5.6–20×0.9–4.4mm, decussate, narrowly triangular or ovate to broadly ovate, usually reflexed. Infl. 22–38-fld; sta. red. W Aus.

M. cordata Turcz. To 3m. Lvs to 12mm, alt., ovate-cordate, somewhat clasping. Infl. in term., dense, globose heads; sta. red-purple. W Aus.

M. coronata Andrews = *M. thymifolia*.

M. corrugata J.M. Black ex Eardley = *M. fulgens*.

M. crassifolia Benth. = *M. laxiflora*.

M. curvifolia Schldl. = *M. lanceolata*.

M. cuticularis Labill. SALT-WATER PAPERBARK. 1.5–3m. Lvs 6–10–2–3mm, linear-oblong or narrow-lanceolate. Fls 1–3, in small term. clusters; sta. cream-white. W & S Aus.

M. decora (Salisb.) Britt. To 12m. Lvs 15–16×1–2mm, scattered, flat or concave above, linear, oblong or narrowly elliptic, with prominent midrib. Infl. a many-fld, open spike; sta. white. Queensld, NSW.

M. decussata R. Br. ex Ait. f. To 4m. Lvs 4–15×3mm, decussate, narrowly obovate to linear, usually obtuse. Infl. a many-fld usually dense, axill. spike; sta. purple. Vict., S Aus.

M. densa R. Br. To 2m. Lvs to 3mm, opposite, overlapping, ovate. Infl. short spikes. W Aus.

M. diffusa Forst. f. = *Metrosideros diffusa*.

M. diosmifolia Andrews. To 3m. Lvs 9–13×3–5mm, spiralling elliptic. Infl a 20–30-fld spike; sta. green. W Aus.

M. elliptica Labill. To 3m. Lvs to 5–6mm, opposite, ovate to suborbicular, close, leathery. Infl. in oblong or cylindrical spikes; sta. red. W Aus.

M. ericifolia Sm. SWAMP PAPERBARK. To 8m. Lvs scattered, or paired 7–15(–18)×c1mm, linear. Infl. a dense, rarely open, term. spike; sta. white. NSW, Vict., Tasm.

M. erubescens Otto = *M. diosmifolia*.

M. foliosa Dum.-Cours. = *M. diosmifolia*.

M. fulgens R. Br. 0.4–2.6m. Lvs 8.3–35×1–4.3mm, decussate, narrowly elliptic or slightly obovate. Infl. a spike of 6–20 fls; sta. scarlet or deep pink (rarely white). W & C Aus. ssp. *steedmanii* (C. Gardn.) Cowley. Lvs flat, obovate.

M. genistifolia Sm. = *M. decora*.

M. gibbosa Labill. To 3m. Lvs 2–6×1–4mm, decussate, keeled beneath, broadly ovate to obovate. Infl. a few- or many-fld axill. spike or cluster; sta. purple to pink. S Aus. and Tasm.

M. glaberrima F. Muell. 0.5–2m. Lvs 5–10×0.5–1mm, spirally arranged, sometimes subfalcate, semiterete. Infl. 10–40-fld; sta. mauve, pink or purple. W Aus.

M. huegelii Endl. HONEY MYRTLE. To 3m. Lvs to 6mm, spirally arranged, overlapping, ovate-acuminate, striate. Infl. a dense narrow spike; sta. white, pink in bud. W Aus.

M. hypericifolia Sm. To 6m. Lvs 10–40×4–10mm, opposite, biconvex or flat, elliptic to obovate. Infl. a many-fld, dense axill. spike; sta. crimson-red. NSW.

M. incana R. Br. To 3m. Lvs to 12mm, alt. or subopposite, spreading, linear or linear-lanceolate. Infl. a term., dense, ovoid to oblong spike; sta. off-white. W Aus.

M. juniperina Sieb. ex Rchb. f. = *M. nodosa*.

M. lanceolata Otto. MOONAH. To 8(–12)m. Lvs 3.8–18× 0.7–1.9mm, spirally arranged, linear to elliptic. Infl. a dense leafy spike; sta. white or cream. S Aus.

M. lateritia A. Dietr. ROBIN-REDBREAST BUSH. 1–3m. Lvs 13–20mm, scattered, linear. Infl. in showy cylindrical or oblong spikes; sta. scarlet-red, c15mm. W Aus.

M. laurina Sm. = *Tristaniopsis laurina*.

M. laxiflora Turcz.   0.5–1(–2)m. Lvs 15–20×2–4mm, spirally arranged, narrowly obovate, flat. Infl. 6–20-fld; sta. pink to mauve. W Aus.

M. leucadendra (L.) L. RIVER TEATREE; WEEPING TEATREE; BROAD-LEAVED PAPERBARK; PAPERBARK; BROAD-LEAVED TEATREE.   Tree to 30m. Lvs scattered, 8–23×0.9–4cm, narrowly ovate to elliptic, thinly leathery. Infl. a many-fld, open spike; sta. white. N Aus., W Aus., Queensld, also in Malesia and New Caledonia.

M. linariifolia Sm.   To 10m. Lvs 10–30×1–3mm, mostly opposite, rigid, linear or narrowly elliptic. Infl. a many-fld, usually open spike; sta. white. N & E Aus.

M. longicoma Benth. = *M. macronychia*.

M. macronychia Turcz.   To 3m. Lvs 8.7–27×4.5–12.6mm, spiral, broadly elliptic to obovate. Spike 30–65-fld; sta. red. W Aus.

M. magnifica Specht = *Asteromyrtus magnifica*.

M. microphylla Sm.   Shrub. Lvs alt., scattered, spreading or recurved, to 10mm, linear. Spikes short; sta. off-white. W Aus.

M. nesophila F. Muell. WESTERN TEA MYRTLE.   To 7m+. Lvs to 23mm, alt., obovate-oblong to oblong-cuneate. Infl. in term. dense heads; sta. lavender or rose-pink. W Aus.

M. nodosa (Gaertn.) Sm.   To 7m. Lvs alt., 15–40×1–3mm, terete or linear-ovate, acute, cuspidate. Fls in axill. and term. heads; sta. yellow. Queensld, NSW.

M. nummularia Turcz. = *M. elliptica*.

M. parviflora Lindl. non Rchb. f. = *M. laxiflora*.

M. pauciflora auct. non Turcz. = *M. biconvexa*.

M. preissiana Schauer PREISS'S PAPERBARK.   9–13m, br. flexuous. Lvs with nearly parallel sides and blunt ± callose tip. W Aus.

M. pubescens Schauer = *M. lanceolata*.

M. quinquenervia (Cav.) S.T. Blake = *M. viridiflora* var. *rubriflora*.

M. radula Lindl.   0.3–2.4m. Lvs 13–41.5×0.8–1.3mm, decussate, narrowly elliptic, with margins strongly revolute. Infl. a spike of 2–8(–10) fls; sta. purple, mauve, lilac, pink or white. W Aus.

M. seorsiflora F. Muell. = *M. lanceolata*.

M. spathulata Schauer.   To 1m. Lvs to 7mm, alt., obovate, narrowed at base. Infl. in terminal globose clusters; sta. pink or red. W Aus.

M. squamea Labill.   To 3m, rarely taller. Lvs scattered, flat or concave above, 4–10×1–3mm, lanceolate. Infl. a few-fld term. head or short spike; sta. purple, pink or white. NSW, Vict., Tasm.

M. squarrosa Sm.   To 15m. Lvs 5–15×4–7mm, decussate, ovate, almost pungent. Infl. a dense term. spike; sta. white or pale yellow. S & SE Aus.

M. steedmanii C. Gardn. = *M. fulgens* ssp. *steedmannii*.

M. styphelioides Sm.   To 20m, usually less. Lvs 4–25×2–6mm, scattered, flat, often ± twisted, ovate, tapering to a rigid point. Infl. a few- to many-fld spike; sta. white. E Aus.

M. suaveolens Sol. ex Gaertn. = *Lophostemon suaveolens*.

M. symphyocarpa F. Muell. = *Asteromyrtus symphyocarpa*.

M. tenella Benth.   Shrub to 5m. Lvs to 5mm, alt., linear. Infl. a term. globose or short-cylindrical spike; sta. white. W Aus.

M. teretifolia Endl.   Tall shrub. Lvs to 5cm, alt., linear-subulate, cylindrical. Fls in heads, white. W Aus.

M. thymifolia Sm.   Usually 1m, rarely to 6m. Lvs 5–15×1–3mm, opposite, stiff, narrowly elliptic. Infl. usually a dense spike; sta. pink to purple. Queensld, NSW.

M. trinervia Sm. = *Leptospermum trinervium*.

M. viridiflora Sol. ex Gaertn.   To 25m. Lvs 5–22×0.6–7cm, scattered, obovate, elliptic or broadly ovate. Infl. a many-fld spike, often 2–4 together; sta. white, yellow, green, pink or red. New Guinea, New Caledonia, Aus. var. *rubriflora* Brongn. & Gris. Lvs thinner, shorter, sta. shorter red.

M. wilsonii F. Muell.   To 1.5m. Lvs 8–15×1–2mm, decussate, flat or concave above, ovate, cuspidate, glabrescent. Infl. a 1- or few-fld axill. (sometimes term.) cluster; sta. pink. Vict., S Aus.

Melampodium L. Compositae. 37 ann. to perenn. herbs and subshrubs. Lvs linear to ovate, pinnatisect to dentate or entire. Cap. radiate; involucre cup-shaped; ray flts white to pale yellow; disc flts yellow. Trop. and warm Amer.

M. cinereum DC.   Subshrub to 20cm, strigose. Lvs to 5×1cm, linear-oblong, entire to pinnately 10-lobed. Cap. to 2cm diam.; ray flts to 6×2mm, cream. Spring–autumn. Tex., N Mex. Z9.

M. leucanthum Torr. & A. Gray.   Subshrub to 60cm, strigose. Lvs to 4×1cm, linear-oblong, entire to pinnately 6-lobed. Cap. to 3.5cm diam.; ray flts to 12×6mm, cream. Spring–autumn. Mex. to Colorado. Z4.

Melandrium Röhling.
M. album (Mill.) Garcke = *Silene latifolia*.
M. californicum (Dur.) Rohrb. = *Silene californica*.
M. dioicum (L.) Casson & Germaine = *Silene dioica*.
M. elisabethae (Jan) Rohrb. = *Silene elisabethae*.

M. keiskii (Miq.) Ohwi = *Silene keiskii*.
M. rubrum (Weigel) Garcke = *Silene dioica*.
M. virginicum (L.) A. Braun = *Silene virginica*.
M. zawadskii (Herbich) A. Braun = *Silene zawadskii*.

Melanoselinum Hoffm. Umbelliferae. 7 monocarpic, shrubby herbs. Lvs pinnatisect to pinnate. Involucral bracts laciniate; pet. notched, white or tinged purple. Madeira and Azores. Z9.

M. decipiens (Schräd. & Wendl.) Hoffm. BLACK PARSLEY.   Bienn. or monocarpic perenn. to 2.5m; st. erect, slightly woody, simple. Lvs *c*40cm, in term. rosette, 2–3-pinnate, seg. ovate to lanceolate, serrate, 2–12cm; petiole inflated. Umbels in crowded, pubesc. infl. to 90cm; rays *c*30, to 5cm; involucral bracts 10–12, irregularly cut to pinnatifid, to 3cm; fls fragrant. Spring–summer. Madeira.

Melanthium L. Liliaceae (Melanthiaceae). 5 rhizomatous perenn. herbs. Lvs linear to oblanceolate, basal and cauline. Infl. a large, open, term. pan., roughly hairy; fls small; perianth seg. 6, free with 2 dark spots at base; sta. 6. Summer. N Amer.

M. hybridum Walter.   To 150cm. Lvs to 7.5cm wide, oblanceolate. Fls green; perianth seg. 0.6cm, suborbicular, undulate, claw as long as blade. E US. Z6.

M. latifolium Desr. = *M. hybridum*.

M. massoniifolium Andrews = *Whiteheadia bifolia*.

M. virginicum L. BUNCHFLOWER.   To 170cm. Lvs to 30×3cm, linear, conduplicate, grassy. Fls cream at first, later green-yellow, darkening to brown with age; perianth seg. 0.8cm, broadly oblong-cordate to ovate, margins flat, 2–3× longer than claw. E US. Z5.

→*Helonias*.

Melasphaerula Ker-Gawl. Iridaceae. 1 cormous perenn. herb. St. 20–50cm, straggling, branched. Lvs 5–25×1cm, 6–7 lanceolate, grass-like. Spikes flexuous, laxly 3–7-fld; fls small, irregular, white or cream, usually purple-veined; perianth seg. 6, 10–15mm. S Afr. Z9.

M. graminea Ker-Gawl. = *M. ramosa*.

M. ramosa (L.) N.E. Br.

Melastoma L. Melastomataceae. 70 everg. shrubs. Lvs oblong or lanceolate, entire, leathery, 3–7-veined. Infl. cymose, term.; fls subtended by 2 bracts; cal. stiffly hairy, lobes alternating with bristle-tipped appendages; pet. usually 5; sta. 10, rarely 14, dimorphic. Fr. a leathery or fleshy berry. SE Asia. Z10.

M. banksii A. Cunn. ex Triana = *M. malabathricum*.

M. candidum D. Don.   1.2–2.5m; br. hoary, bluntly 4-angled. Lvs 5–15cm, ovate, 7-veined, bristly above, hairy beneath. Fls fragrant, 3–7cm; pet. 3–4cm; pink or white. Taiwan and Ryuku Is. to SE Asia and Philipp.

M. decemfidum Roxb. = *M. sanguineum*.

M. malabathricum L. INDIAN RHODODENDRON.   To 1.8–2.5m; br. subterete, densely covered with adpressed scales. Lvs 7.5–10cm, ovate to broadly lanceolate, 3–5-veined, strigose. Fls 1–5 in a corymb; pet. to 1.5cm, purple. India, SE Asia.

M. sanguineum Sims.   2–6m; br. covered with long red hairs. Lvs to 20cm, oval-oblong, slender-pointed, 5-veined, bristly above, pale beneath. Fls few, 5–8cm diam.; pet. purple. Malaysia to Java.

M. septemnervium Lour. non Jacq. = *M. candidum*.

M. villosum Aubl. & Sims.   90–120cm; br. terete, hairy. Lvs ovate, acute, 5-veined, hairy. Fls in few-fld clusters; pet. rose-pink, obovate. Spring. S Amer.

→*Tibouchina*.

MELASTOMATACEAE Juss. 215/4750. *Bertolonia, Centradenia, Dissotis, Heterocentron, Medinilla, Melastoma, Memecylon, Monolena, Osbeckia, Rhexia, Sonerila, Tibouchina*.

Mel Grass *Ammophila*.

Melia L. Meliaceae. 5 decid. or semi-evergreen trees or shrubs. Lvs alt., pinnate or 2-pinnate. Fls in axill. pan.; cal. 5–6-lobed, small, pet. 5–6, free; sta. united in a cylindrical, erect tube, with 10–12 lobes at apex and bearing 10–12 anth. between lobes. Fr. drupaceous. OW Trop., Aus.

M. azadirachta A. Juss.   Tree to 16m. Lvs to 50cm; lfts to 2.75cm, ovate-lanceolate, slender-pointed, toothed or lobed. Fls white, in pan. 15–22.5cm long. Fr. 1–7cm, purple. Late spring–early summer. E Indies. Z10.

M. azedarach L. CHINABERRY; PERSIAN LILAC; PRIDE OF INDIA; BEAD TREE.   Decid. tree to 15m. Lvs to 80cm, lfts to 5cm, ovate to elliptic, serrate or lobed. Fls 2cm diam., lilac, in pan. 10–20cm long; staminal tube violet. Fr. 1–5cm diam., yellow. Summer. N India, China. 'Floribunda': bushy, v. floriferous. 'Umbraculiformis' (TEXAN UMBRELLA TREE): br. radiating in a spreading head.

M. composita Willd. = *M. dubia*.

M. dubia Cav. Large tree. Lvs 23–60cm, bipinnate lfts 3.5–5cm, ovate to oval-lanceolate, slender-pointed, entire or toothed. Fls green-white, in crowded downy pan. 12–20cm long. E Indies. Z10.

M. japonica G. Don = *M. azederach*.

M. sempervirens Sw. = *M. azederach*.

MELIACEAE Juss. 51/575. *Aphanamixis, Melia, Toona, Turraea.*

MELIANTHACEAE Link. 2/8. *Melianthus.*

Melianthus L. Melianthaceae. 6 foetid, everg. shrubs with robust, sparsely branched st., often semi-herbaceous in colder locations. Lvs imparipinnate with conspicuous stipules, lfts toothed. Fls in erect rac., profusely nectariferous, irregular; sep. and pet. 5, the uppermost hooded, the lowermost forming a short spur; sta. 4, exserted. S Afr.; *M. major* nat. in India. Z9.

M. major L. HONEY FLOWER. To 2.25m. St. thick, sea-green and thickly glaucous at first. Lvs to 50cm, glaucous blue; lfts 5–13cm, 9–11, ovate-oblong, coarsely serrate; petiole strongly winged, amplexicaul; stipules to 10cm. Rac. to 80cm; fls brown-red.

M. minor L. To 2m, less robust in all parts than *M. major*, downy, not glaucous. Lvs to 20cm; lfts 4–5.25cm, 9–13, oblong-lanceolate, serrate, grey-green and rather coarsely pubesc. above; petiole winged. Rac. to 38cm; fls brick-red.

Melic *Melica*.

Melica L. MELIC. Gramineae. 70 perenn. grasses to 150cm. Rhiz. creeping; st. clumped, often bulbous at base. Lf blades linear, arching; sheaths clasping. Pan. open or contracted; spikelets 2-to several-fld, somewhat laterally compressed. Summer. Temp. regions (except Aus.).

M. altissima L. SIBERIAN MELIC. To 150cm. Rhiz. creeping. Lf blades to 22.5cm, scabrous; ligules to 5mm. Pan. erect, secund, dense, interrupted at base, to 25×2.5cm; spikelets oblong, to 1cm; fertile fits 2. C & E Eur. 'Alba': spikelets v. pale green. 'Atropurpurea': spikelets deep mauve, sweeping downwards and overlapping. Z5.

M. ciliata L. SILKY-SPIKE MELIC. To 75cm. St. densely tufted. Lf blades involute and filiform or flat and broader, acute, to 17.5cm, grooved, ligules to 2mm. Pan. spike-like, nodding, cylindric, 15×1cm, silky, pale green or tinged purple; spikelets elliptic-oblong, to 0.5cm; fits silky. Eur., N Afr., SW Asia. Z6. 'Alba': flts white.

M. nutans L. MOUNTAIN MELIC; NODDING MELLIC. To 60cm. St. clumped or solitary, tetragonal in section. Lf blades to 20cm, green, pubesc. above; ligules to 0.1cm. Pan. secund, loose, nodding to 15cm; spikelets to 1cm, elliptic-oblong, obtuse, purple or maroon; fertile flts 2–3. Eur., N & SW Asia. Z6.

M. transsilvanica Schur. As for *M. ciliata* except to 1m; lvs flat, to 0.6cm wide; fls in a shorter pan. Eurasia. Z6.

M. uniflora Retz. WOOD MELIC. To 60cm. St. tufted. Lf blades to 20cm, pubesc. above, fresh green. Pan. lax, sparsely branched, to 20cm; spikelets obovate, to 0.8cm, purple or tinged brown; fertile flt solitary. Eur., SW Asia. 'Alba': v. pale green form with white fls. 'Aurea': lvs tinted gold. 'Variegata': v. small; lvs striped cream and green. Z7.

Melicocca L.

M. bijuga L. = *Melicoccus bijugatus*.

Melicoccus P. Browne. Sapindaceae. 2 glab. trees. Lvs alt., pinnate, pinnae sessile, almost opposite. Rac. or pan. many-fld; fls regular; pet. 4 or 5; sta. 8. Fr. a 1-seeded drupe. Trop. Amer., W Indies. Z10.

M. bijugatus Jacq. SPANISH LIME; HONEY BERRY; MAMONCILLO; GENIPE. Slow-growing tree to 18m. Lvs to 15cm, pinnae 4–6, to 10cm, elliptic-lanceolate, glab. Fls fragrant, white tinged yellow. Fr. to 3cm diam., globose, green, pulp juicy, tinged yellow.
→*Melicocca*.

Melicope Forst. & Forst. f. Rutaceae. 150 trees or shrubs. Lvs, simple or trifoliolate, gland-dotted. Fls in cymes or pan., or solitary, small; sep. minute; sta. 8. Fr. of 4, 1-seeded cocci. Trop. Asia to Aus. Z10.

M. ternata Forst. & Forst. f. Shrub or small tree to 6m, spreading. Lvs to 10×4cm, lfts 3, ovate or obovate-oblong to elliptic, entire. Fls in axill. cymes; sep. to 1.5mm, ovate-oblong, gland-dotted; pet. to 5mm, green or green-white, gland-dotted. NZ.

Melicytus Forst. & Forst. f. Violaceae. 4 dioecious shrubs or trees. Lvs obovate to lanceolate. Fls small, solitary or clustered; cal. 5-lobed; pet. 5; anth. 5. Fr. a berry. Spring. NZ, Norfolk Is., Fiji, Solomon Is. Z9.

M. lanceolatus Hook. f. To 5m+. Bark grey-brown. Lvs to 16×3cm, serrulate. Fls 3–5mm diam., purple-tinged, to 6 per cluster. Fr. stained dark purple. NZ.

M. ramiflorus Forst. & Forst. f. WHITEY WOOD. Tree, to 10m+. Bark grey-white. Lvs to 15×5cm, coarsely serrate. Fls to 4mm diam., yellow-green, to 10 per cluster. Fr. lavender to violet, dark blue or purple. Distrib. as for the genus.

Meliosma Bl. Sabiaceae. 20–25 decid. or everg. trees or shrubs to 25m. Lvs simple or pinnate. Infl. a large, pyramidal pan.; fls small, fragrant; sep. (4–)5; pet. 5, outer 3 concave, orbicular, inner 2 smaller, bifid or scale-like; sta. 5, outermost sterile, reduced to cupular staminodes, inner whorl fertile. Fr. a 1-seeded drupe. Trop. Amer., trop. and temp. Asia.

M. alba (Schldl.) Walp. Decid. tree to 25m. Lvs to 30cm, pinnate, lfts 2.5–15cm (smaller below), 5–13, usually 9, ovate to elliptic or oblong, fine-toothed or entire, shining above, dull beneath where pubesc. in vein-axils. Pan. axill., to 20×10cm; fls to 6mm across, cream-white. Fr. 6mm, black. Late spring. Mex., W China. Z8.

M. beaniana Rehd. & Wils. = *M. alba*.

M. cuneifolia Franch. = *M. dilleniifolia* ssp. *cuneifolia*.

M. dilatata Diels = *M. parviflora*.

M. dilleniifolia (Wight & Arn.) Walp. Decid. shrub or tree to 10–15m. Lvs 3–24cm, obovate to elliptic or oblong, aristate-serrulate, scabrous above, subglab. to pubesc. beneath. Pan. term., erect or deflexed 10–50cm; fls white. Fr. 4–5mm, globose. Himal. to China and Jap. ssp. *dilleniifolia*. Lvs 7–30cm, pubesc., finely dentate. Pan. erect, to 28cm. S Himal. ssp. *cuneifolia* (Franch.) Beus. Lvs 3–24cm, subglab. to pubesc., dentate. Pan. erect, to 50cm; fls to 4mm, yellow-white, becoming pure white, v. fragrant. Fr. 6mm, black. Summer. W China. ssp. *flexuosa* (Pamp.) Beus. Shrub to 5m; young shoots purple-hairy. Lvs 4–16cm, subglab. to sparsely pubesc. beneath, dentate. Pan. term., erect or deflexed, 7–22cm; fls 4mm, white. Summer. EC China. ssp. *tenuis* (Maxim.) Beus. Decid. shrub or small tree; young shoots purple-pubesc. Lvs 3–16cm, subglab., hairy in vein-axils beneath, coarsely dentate. Pan. erect to deflexed, to 15cm; fls 4mm, yellow-white. Summer. Jap. Z9.

M. flexuosa Pamp. = *M. dilleniifolia* ssp. *flexuosa*.

M. meliantha auct. = *M. myriantha*.

M. myriantha Sieb. & Zucc. Decid. shrub or small tree, 6.5–15m. Lvs 5–25cm, apex short-acuminate, base broad-cuneate or rounded, dentate, midrib red-hairy (serrate above and more closely downy in ssp. *pilosa* (Lecomte) Beus.). Pan. term., 15–20cm; fls 3mm, yellow-white, v. fragrant. Fr. small, dark red. Summer. Jap., Korea. Z9.

M. oldhamii Maxim. = *M. pinnata*.

M. parviflora Lecomte. Decid. tree to 8m. Lvs 6.5–8cm, obovate, toothed, glab. except on veins beneath. Pan. term., 20–30cm, axes red-pubesc.; fls v. small, white. Fr. 3mm, red. Summer. W & C China. Z9.

M. parvifolia hort. = *M. parviflora*.

M. pendens Rehd. & Wils. = *M. dilleniifolia* ssp. *flexuosa*.

M. pinnata (Roxb.) Walp. Decid. tree, 20–40m. Lvs 17.5–35cm, pinnate, lfts 5–13, lowermost 2.5×2cm, orbicular to ovate, term. leaflet 7.5–14cm, dentate, pubesc. above when young. Pan. term., 15–30cm; fls to 6mm, pure white. Fr. to 6mm. Summer. Korea, China. Z9.

M. pungens (Wallich ex Wight & Arn.) Walp. = *M. simplicifolia* ssp. *pungens*.

M. rhoifolia Maxim. = *M. pinnata*.

M. simplicifolia (Roxb.) Walp. Everg. shrub or tree to 20m. Lvs 3–50cm, elliptic or obovate to lanceolate, somewhat coriaceous, glab. to pubesc. beneath, esp. in vein axils, entire or spiny-toothed. Pan. term., erect, 10–60cm; fls small. Fr. 4–10mm. S & SE Asia (Sri Lanka to Indon.). ssp. *pungens* (Walp.) Beus. Small tree; shoots red-pubesc. Lvs 5–20cm, oblong or lanceolate, coriaceous, coarsely dentate. Pan. 10–55cm; fls large. Fr. 8mm. Sri Lanka, India. Z10.

M. sinensis Nak. = *M. pinnata*.

M. stewardii Merrill = *M. myriantha*.

M. tenuis Maxim. = *M. dilleniifolia* ssp. *tenuis*.

M. veitchiorum Hemsl. Decid. tree to 50m. Lvs 45–75cm, pinnate, lfts 8.5–17.5cm, 7–9, ovate or oblong, entire or sparsely toothed, midrib pubesc. beneath. Pan. term., to 45cm; fls to 6mm, cream-white. Fr. 6–8mm, violet to black. Late spring. W China. Z8.

Melissa L. Labiatae. 3 perenn. decid. herbs. Lvs ovate. Infl. whorled; cal. campanulate, bilabiate with 13 veins, upper lip 3-toothed, lower lip 2-toothed; cor. bilabiate. Medit. Eur., gdn escapee in N Eur. and N Amer.

M. grandiflora L. = *Calamintha grandiflora*.

M. officinalis L. BEE BALM; LEMON BALM. Lvs crenate, lemon-scented, rugose. Fls 4–12 per whorl; cal. glandular-pubesc.; cor. to 15mm, yellow-white. Late summer. S Eur. 'All Gold': lvs golden yellow; fls palest lilac. 'Aurea': lvs golden. Z4.

M. umbrosa Bieb. = *Clinopodium umbrosum*.

Melittis L. BASTARD BALM. Labiatae. 1 herbaceous perenn. to 50cm. St. erect, hairy. Lvs oval, to 8cm, crenate, hispid, honey-scented. Fls to 6 per whorl; cal. bilabiate, upper lip with 2–3 small teeth, lower lip bilobed; cor. to 40mm, white, pink or purple or with large purple blotch on lower lip. Summer. WC & S Eur. to Ukraine. Z6.

M. melissophyllum L. As above. ssp. *albida* (Guss.) P.W. Ball. St. densely covered with stalked glands. ssp. *carpatica* (Klokov) P.W. Ball. Lvs to 15cm with to 32 large teeth on each side.

Melkbos *Euphorbia mauritanica*.

Melo Mill. = *Cucumis*.

Melocactus Link & Otto. Cactaceae. 30 cacti seldom exceeding 1m. St. only branching if damaged, globose to cylindric, strongly ribbed, spiny. Flowering zone an apical cephalium; fl. small, tubular. Fr. a berry, usually clavate. Trop. Amer., esp. E Braz. and Amazonia, Peru, Venez., Central Amer. and the Carib. Z10.

M. ×*albicephalus* Buining & Brederoo. E Braz. (A natural hybrid of *M. ernestii* and *M. glaucescens*.) Resembling *M. ernestii* but ribs more acute and spines much shorter. Cephalium with white wool; bristles v. short and hidden.

M. amoenus Hoffsgg. = *M. intortus*.

M. amoenus hort. non Hoffsgg. = *M. curvispinus*.

M. amstutziae Rauh & Backeb. = *M. peruvianus*.

M. antonii (Britt.) F. Knuth = *M. intortus*.

M. azureus Buining & Brederoo. St. to 13–45×14–19cm, grey-green or glaucous; ribs 9–10, acute; areoles 2.8–3.5cm apart; central spines 1–4, 2–5.3cm, radial spines 7–11, to 5.3cm. Fl. 19–23mm, magenta. Fr. to 17mm, white to pale pink. E Braz.

M. bahiensis (Britt. & Rose) Lützelb. St. 9.5–21×11–21cm, depressed-globose to conic; ribs 8–14, acute to rounded; areoles to 2.4cm apart; central spines 1–4, 1.7–5cm, radial spines 7–12, 2–6cm. Fl. 20–23mm, pink. Fr. to 25mm, red to crimson. E Braz.

M. brederooianus Buining = *M. bahiensis*.

M. broadwayi (Britt. & Rose) A. Berger. St. 10–20cm tall, ovoid, yellow-green; ribs 14–18, rounded; areoles 1cm+ apart; central spines 1–3, radial spines 8–10, 1.0–1.5cm, incurved. Fl. purple. Fr. to 2.5cm, magenta. Tob., Grenadines, St Vincent.

M. caesius Wendl. = *M. curvispinus*.

M. communis (Ait.) Link & Otto = *M. intortus*.

M. concinnus Buining & Brederoo. Intermediate between *M. violaceus* and *M. zehntneri*. St. 8–12×11–16cm, depressed-globose to globose; ribs 8–12, acute; areoles 1.3–2cm apart; central spine 1, 1.0–1.9cm, curved, radial spines 6–8, to 1.5–2.6cm. Fl. 20–23mm, pink. Fr. 13–18mm, pink. E Braz.

M. conoideus Buining & Brederoo. St. to 10–17cm, strongly depressed to hemispheric; ribs 11–14; areoles to c15mm apart; central spine 1, 2.0–2.2cm, radial spines 8–11, lowermost 2–3.5cm, recurved. Fl. c22mm, magenta-pink. Fr. c18mm, lilac-magenta. E Braz.

M. curvicornis Buining & Brederoo = *M. zehntneri*.

M. curvispinus Pfeiff. V. variable; St. 6–30×8–27cm, depressed-globose, globose or ovoid; ribs 10–16, ± acute; central spines 1–4(–5), to 5.2cm, radial spines 7–11(–15), 1.6–4.2cm, curved, rarely straight. Fl. 20–43mm. Fr. 20–60mm, bright red. C & S Amer. (SW & E Mex. to Colomb. and Venez.), Cuba.

M. depressus Hook. = *M. violaceus*.

M. ernestii Vaupel. St. 9–45×7–22(–35)cm, subglobose to short-cylindric; ribs 9–13, ± rounded; areoles to 2.8cm apart; central spines 4–8, to 3.2–9cm, radial spines 7–13, lowermost 4.5–15cm, flexible, slender. Fl. 20–29mm. Fr. 14–45mm. E Braz.

M. glaucescens Buining & Brederoo. St. to 13–18×14–24cm, globose to slightly pyramidal, grey-green to grey-blue; ribs 8–15, acute; areoles 1–2cm apart; central spines 1–2, ascending, to 2cm, radial spines 5–8, lowermost to 2cm. Fl. 25mm, lilac-magenta. Fr. 9.5–16mm. E Braz.

M. harlowii (Britt. & Rose) Vaupel. St. to 25(–30)×6–16cm, ellipsoid to cylindric, light green, ribs 10–13; areoles closely set; central spines (1–)3–4, to 5cm, radial spines c12, 1–2(–3)cm. Fl. to 20mm. Fr. 12–22mm, pink to white. SE Cuba.

M. intortus (Mill.) Urban. St. to 60(–90)×30cm, globose to tapered-cylindric; ribs (9–)14–27, rounded, thick; central spines 1–3, radial spines 10–14, 2–7cm, stout, ± straight. Cephalium growing tall; fl. 15–20mm, pink. Fr. 10–25mm, pink to red. W

Indies (Turks & Caicos southwards to Martinique).

M. jansenianus Backeb. = *M. peruvianus*.

M. levitestatus Buining & Brederoo. St. 15–60×14–30cm, globose to cylindric; ribs 9–15, to 8cm broad at base; areoles 3–4.2cm apart; spines to 3.3cm, brown-red; central spines 1–4, radial spines 7–10. Fl. to 20–27mm, red. Fr. 12–20mm. E Braz.

M. macracanthos (Salm-Dyck) Link & Otto. V. variable; st. 9–30cm diam., usually depressed-globose, green; ribs 11–23, rounded-tuberculate; central spines 1–4(–6), to 7cm, red, brown or yellow, radial spines much shorter, 9–17, v. fine-acicular. Fl. c20mm. Fr. 15–20mm. Netherlands Antilles.

M. matanzanus León. Resembling *M. violaceus* and *M. neryi*, but ribs 8–9. Cephalium with dense orange-red bristles. N Cuba.

M. maxonii (Rose) Gürke = *M. curvispinus*.

M. melocactoides Hoffsgg. = *M. violaceus*.

M. neryi Schum. Resembling *M. violaceus*, but st. dark blue-green; spines curved, sometimes longer. Venez. to N Braz.

M. oaxacensis (Britt. & Rose) Backeb. = *M. curvispinus*.

M. obtusipetalus Lem. = *M. curvispinus*.

M. oreas Miq. St. 8–15(–35)×10–18cm, depressed-conic to elongate; ribs 10–16, rounded to obtuse; areoles 1–1.8cm apart; central spines 1–4, 2–4.5cm, radial spines mostly 8–11, lowermost to 4.8cm. Fl. 17–22mm. Fr. to 28mm, bright red or crimson-red. E Braz.

M. peruvianus Vaupel. St. to 20(–40)×20cm, globose to pyramidal or cylindric; ribs 8–16, ± acute, low; central spines 0 or 1–4 to 6cm, radial spines (4–)6–10(–14), to 6cm, straight to strongly curved. Fl. to 23mm, purple-red. Fr. 10–25mm, red. Peru, SW Ecuad.

M. salvadorensis Werderm. St. 12–20×12–25cm, depressed-globose, grey-green or glaucous; ribs 8–14, acute; areoles 2–3cm apart; central spines 1–4, 1.5–3cm, radial spines 7–10, lowermost 2–4.6cm. Fl. to 25mm, pink. Fr. c17mm, lilac-magenta. E Braz.

M. trujiloensis Rauh & Backeb. = *M. peruvianus*.

M. violaceus Pfeiff. St. 5–18×6–17m, depressed-globose to sub-pyramidal; ribs 8–15, acute; areoles 0.6–1.8cm apart; central spine 0–1, ascending, shorter than radials, radials 5–9(–11), to 1–2.4cm, straight. Fl. 15–25mm, deep pink. Fr. 12.5–19mm, pink or white. E Braz.

M. zehntneri (Britt. & Rose) Lützelb. St. 11–48×9–25cm, depressed-globose to short-cylindric; ribs 10–16(–22), acute; areoles 2–4cm apart; central spines (0–)1–2(–4), 1.5–4cm, ascending, radial spines 7–11, 1.9–3.9cm, rather stout. Fl. to 25mm, pink. Fr. 12–20mm, pink. NE Braz.

→*Cactus*.

Melon *Cucumis melo*.

Melon Cactus *Melocactus intortus*.

Melon-leaf Nightshade *Solanum citrullifolium*.

Melon-loco *Apodanthera undulata*.

Melon Pear *Solanum muricatum*.

Melon Shrub *Solanum muricatum*.

Melon Spurge *Euphorbia meloformis*.

Melon Tree *Carica*.

Melothria L. Cucurbitaceae. 10 herbaceous ann. or perenn. climbers or trailers. Tendrils simple. Lvs entire or palmately lobed. ♂ infl. a rac. or corymb; sta. 3; pistillode globose; ♀ fls solitary or clustered, similar to ♂ except staminodes 3, ovary globose to fusiform. Fr. a berry, long-stalked. Subtrop. and trop. Americas. Z10.

M. indica (L.) Lour. = *Zehneria indica*.

M. japonica (Thunb.) Maxim. = *Zehneria indica*.

M. maderspatana (L.) Cogn. = *Mukia maderaspatana*.

M. pendula L. St. slender, often rooting. Lvs ovate-cordate to triangular, angulate, entire or lobulate, acuminate, scabrous above, paler and pubesc. beneath. Fls yellow. Fr. subglobose to ovoid, to 2cm, purple dappled green. S US to S Amer.

M. punctata Cogn. = *Zehneria scabra*.

M. scabra (L. f.) Naudin. = *Zehneria scabra*.

Memecylon L. Melastomataceae. 150 shrubs or trees. Fls 4-merous in cymose pan.; sta. 8; ovary inferior, 1-celled. Fr. a berry to 1.5cm diam., usually purple to black. Trop. Afr., Asia, Malay Archipel.

M. caeruleum Jack = *M. floribundum*.

M. floribundum Bl. Shrub to 3m. Lvs to 18cm, ovate-elliptic, obtuse, coriaceous. Pet. 5–6mm, exterior tinged red, interior purple-blue. Java.

M. umbellatum Burm. f. Small tree to 7.5m. Lvs to 15cm, oblong-ovate, acuminate, coriaceous. Pet. deep blue to purple. India, SE Asia, N Aus.

Memorial Rose *Rosa wichuraiana*.

Mendocino Ceanothus *Ceanothus* ×*mendocinensis*.

Mendocino Cypress *Cupressus goveniana* var. *pygmaea*.
Mendocino Shore Pine *Pinus contorta*.

Mendoncella A.D. Hawkes. Orchidaceae. 4 epiphytic orchids. Rhiz. short. Pbs short, often clustered, enveloped by bracts and lf sheaths, apex 1–2-leaved. Lvs lanceolate, plicate. Rac. basal; fls often large; sep. subsimilar, free or connate at base, spreading, ovate-lanceolate; pet. wider; lip trilobed, lat. lobes often fimbriate, midlobe large, entire to fimbriate, disc with fleshy toothed callus. Mex. to Guyana, Braz., Peru. Z10.

M. burkei (Rchb. f.) Garay. Pbs to 12cm, oblong-cylindrical. Lvs 45×2cm. Infl. to 60cm, loosely few-fld; fls to 5cm diam., fragrant, waxy; tep. pale brown, marked chestnut-brown, often edged green, the lip white marked violet on callus, interior densely pubesc. Venez., Guianas, Braz., Surinam.

M. grandiflora (A. Rich.) A.D. Hawkes. Pbs to 8cm, ovoid. Lvs to 50×7cm. Infl. to 20cm, 2- to several-fld; fls to 8cm diam., waxy, fragrant, green or yellow-green, broadly striped red-brown, the lip fimbriate, white streaked red. Mex., C Amer.

M. jorisiana (Rolfe) A.D. Hawkes. Pbs to 10cm, ovoid-oblong. Lvs to 27×6cm. Infl. to 27cm, few-fld. Fls to 7cm diam., pale green marked dark green or purple-green, the lip white, darkening to pale yellow at midlobes and marked purple on callus, fimbriate. Venez., Braz.

M. marginata (Rchb. f.) Garay = *Cochleanthes marginata*.
→*Batemannia, Galeottia* and *Zygopetalum*.

Men in a Boat *Tradescantia spathacea*.

Meniscium Schreb. Thelypteridaceae. 20 terrestrial ferns. Rhiz. creeping, sparsely scaly. Fronds stipitate, pinnate or simple; pinnae entire to serrate or notched. Trop. Amer. Z10.

M. angustifolium Willd. Rhiz. short-creeping. Lamina to 50×30cm, erect, slightly dimorphous (sterile pinnae smaller than fertile), oblong; pinnae to 16×2cm, stalked, linear to lanceolate, ± entire; stipes to 45cm, minutely pubesc. W Indies, Central Amer. S to Boliv.

M. reticulatum (L.) Sw. Rhiz. short-creeping. Lamina to 120×60cm, erect, slightly dimorphous (sterile pinnae shorter-stalked than fertile), lanceolate or oblong to deltoid; pinnae to 30×10cm, narrowly lanceolate or deltoid to strap-shaped, entire to notched or undulate; stipes to 1m, minutely pubesc. Flor., W Indies, Central Amer. S to Peru.

M. triphyllum Sw. = *Pronephrium triphyllum*.
→*Dryopteris* and *Thelypteris*.

MENISPERMACEAE Juss. 78/520. *Cocculus, Menispermum*.

Menispermum. L. Menispermaceae. 2 woody-based twiners. St. slender, tangled, pale green and decid. or persistent becoming woody. Lvs obscurely 5–7-lobed, peltate, petiole long. Fls inconspicuous, yellow-green in axill. rac. or pan.; sep. 4–10, exceeding pet.; pet. 6–9; sta. in ♂ fls 9–24, in ♀, 6, sterile. Fr. to 1cm diam., subglobose, hanging in grape-like bunches; seeds crescent-shaped. E N Amer., E Asia.

M. canadense L. YELLOW PARILLA. St. to 6m, usually persistent. Lvs 5–20cm, ovate-cordate to suborbicular, entire or obscurely 5–7-lobed, dark green above, paler, initially downy beneath. Rac. long. Fr. pruinose purple-red to blue-black. E N Amer. Z5.

M. dauricum auct. = *M. davuricum*.

M. davuricum DC. Distinguished from *M. canadense* by its largely ann. st., its shorter, more crowded and frequently paired rac., lvs to 10cm, distinctly peltate, sharply lobed; fr. larger, black. E Asia. Z4.

Mentha L. MINT. Labiatae. 25 aromatic herbaceous perenn. or ann. herbs. Rhiz. fleshy and creeping. St. erect, branching. Fls in axill. verticils forming an interrupted spike; cal. regular or weakly 2-lipped, 10–13-veined; cor. weakly 2-lipped with 4 subequal lobes, tube shorter than cal. Eurasia, Afr.

M. aquatica L. WATERMINT. Subglabrous to tomentose perenn. St. 15–90cm, often red-purple. Lvs 2–6cm, ovate to ovate-lanceolate, serrate. Infl. a term. head comprising 2–3 verticillasters, cal. 3–4mm, tubular, veins distinct, teeth subulate; cor. lilac. Eurasia. Z6.

M. arvensis L. CORN MINT. Variable perenn. 10–60cm. St. hairy. Lvs 2–6.5cm, elliptic-lanceoalte to ovate, shallowly crenate or serrate, hairy. Fls in remote verticillasters; cal. 1.5–2.5mm, campanulate, hairy deltate; cor. lilac, pink or rarely white, hairy. GB, Eur., N Asia, Himal., Jap. var. *piperascens* Malinv. Lvs ovate, gland-dotted, distinctly petioled. Cal. teeth long-acuminate. Jap., Korea, Sakhalin. var. *villosa* (Benth.) Stewart. Lvs lanceolate, cuneate at base, pubesc., angles of st. pubesc. Cor. white or pink. N Amer. Z4.

M. canadensis L. = *M. arvensis* var. *villosa*.
M. cardiaca (S.F. Gray) Bak. = *M. ×gracilis*.

M. cervina L. Subglab. perenn., 10–40cm, with scent of pennyroyal. St. procumbent and rooting below. Lvs 1–2.5cm, linear-oblanceolate, glab., entire or obscurely dentate, sessile. Verticillasters many-fld; cal. tubular, teeth 4, deltoid with white awns, hairy within; cor. lilac or white. SW Eur. Z7.

M. crispa L. = *M. spicata*.
M. ×gentilis L. = *M. ×gracilis*.

M. ×gracilis Sole. (*M. arvensis* ×*M. spicata*.) GINGERMINT; REDMINT. Variable perenn., 30–90cm. St. erect, usually glab., often tinged red. Lvs 3–7cm, ovate-lanceolate, oblong or elliptic, entire or remotely serrate, glab. or sparsely pubesc. Fls in distant verticillasters; cal. 2–3.5mm, campanulate, glab. below, teeth subulate, ciliate; cor. lilac, sta. included. N Eur. inc. GB, widely cult. 'Aurea': to 30cm; spreading; lvs gold, strongly fragrant. 'Variegata': vigorous; lvs flecked gold, scent fruity, flavour ginger. Z6.

M. hirsuta Huds. = *M. aquatica*.
M. incana Willd. = *M. longifolia*.
M. insularis Req. = *M. suaveolens*.

M. longifolia (L.) Huds. HORSEMINT. Creeping perenn., 40–120cm, strongly scented. St. tomentose, or subglabrous. Lvs usually sessile, linear-lanceolate to oblong-elliptic, sharply serrate, slightly rugose above, grey-tomentose beneath. Verticillasters congested, forming a tapering often much-branched spike; cal. 1–3mm, narrowly campanulate, hairy; cor. white, lilac or mauve. Eur., W Asia, C Russia, Ethiop., S Afr. 'Variegata': lvs grey splashed with yellow, hairy. ssp. *capensis* (Thunb.) Briq. Lvs 5–10cm, linear-lanceolate, densely pubesc. S Afr., Les., Zimb. ssp. *noeana* (Boiss. ex Briq.) Briq. Lvs with distinct petioles. Iraq, NW Iran, SE Turk. ssp. *polyadena* (Briq.) Briq. Lvs 3–8cm, oblong-lanceolate, glab. or sparsely hairy. S Afr. ssp. *typhoides* (Briq.) Harley. Lvs less than 5×2cm, concolorous on both surfaces. Infl. slender, lateral br. pedunculate. SE Eur., SW Asia. ssp. *wissii* (Lanert) Codd. Lvs linear, less than 5mm wide. Nam. Z6.

M. macrostachya Ten. = *M. suaveolens*.
M. nigricans Mill. = *M. ×piperita*.
M. odorata Sole = *M. ×piperita* 'Citrata'.

M. ×piperita L. (*M. aquatica* ×*M. spicata*.) PEPPERMINT. Perenn., 30–90cm, usually glab., often tinged red-purple. Lvs 4–9cm, ovate-lanceolate to lanceolate, petiolate, serrate, apex acute, usually glab. or thinly hairy. Verticillasters congested forming a term. oblong spike; cal. 3–4mm, tubular, tube usually glab., teeth ciliate; cor. lilac-pink. Eur. 'Candymint': st. tinted red; lvs sweetly fragrant. 'Citrata' (LEMON MINT; EAU DE COLOGNE MINT): 'Crispa': to 50cm; lvs crinkled. 'Lime Mint': lvs scented of lime. 'Variegata': lvs deep green mottled cream, peppermint flavour. Z3.

M. pulegium L. PENNYROYAL. Subglab. to tomentose perenn., 10–40cm. St. procumbent or upright. Lvs 5–30mm, narrowly elliptical to oval entire or toothed, usually glab. above, pubesc. beneath. Verticillasters distant; cal. 2–3mm, teeth ciliate, lower teeth subulate, upper teeth shorter; cor. 4–6mm, lilac. SW & C Eur. to GB. 'Cunningham Mint' ('Dwarf Pennyroyal'): low; lvs oval, light green. Z7.

M. requienii Benth. CORSICAN MINT. Glab. or sparsely hairy procumbent perenn. St. 3–10cm, thread-like, creeping, forming cushions or mats. Lvs 2–7mm, ovate orbicular, entire or sinuate. Cal. 1–2mm, teeth deltoid, subulate; cor. scarcely exserted, lilac. Corsica, It., Sardinia. Z6.

M. rotundifolia 'Variegata', = *M. ×villosa* 'Variegata'.
M. rubra Sm. non Mill. = *M. ×smithiana*.

M. ×smithiana R.A. Graham. (*M. aquatica* ×*M. arvensis* ×*M. spicata*.) Robust perenn., 50–150cm, subglabrous and red-tinged, sweetly scented. Lvs 3–9cm, ovate, subglabrous. Verticillasters remote, sometimes crowded at st. apex; cal. 5-lobed, tubular, glab. or sparsely hairy, teeth to 1.5mm, ciliate. N & C Eur. Z6.

M. spicata L. SPEARMINT. Perenn., 30–100cm. Lvs 5–9cm, lanceolate or lanceolate-ovate, smooth or rugose, serrate, glab. to hairy. Infl. a cylindrical spike, 3–6cm; cal. 1–3mm, campanulate, glab. or hairy, teeth subequal; cor. lilac, pink or white. S & C Eur. 'Chewing Gum': lvs deep mahogany, bubble gum scented. 'Crispa': lvs strongly curled. 'Kentucky Colonel': lvs large, ruffled, richly scented. Z3.

M. suaveolens Ehrh. APPLEMINT. Perenn., 40–100cm. St. white-tomentose, apple-scented. Lvs 3–4.5cm, rugose, pubesc., serrate. Verticillasters usually congested, forming a term. spike 4–9cm, often interrupted and branched; cal. 1–2mm, campanulate, hairy; cor. white or pink. S & W Eur. Often found under the name of *M. rotundifolia*. 'Variegata' (PINEAPPLE MINT): lvs streaked white, with a fruity aroma. Z6.

M. sylvestris L. = *M. longifolia*.
M. ×villosa Huds. (*M. spicata* ×*M. suaveolens*.) A variable

hybrid. var. *alopecuroides* (Hull) Briq. Middle cauline lvs 4–8cm, broadly ovate or orbicular, softly hairy, serrate. Infl. robust; cal. 2mm, cor. pink. Gdn origin. Also much cult. is another sterile hybrid *M.* ×*villosonervata* Opiz, (*M. spicata* × *M. longifolia*); this plant has narrower lvs with widely spreading teeth and v. sparse indumentum. Z5.

M. viridis (L.) L. = *M. spicata*.

Mentocalyx N.E. Br.

M. muirii N.E. Br. = *Gibbaeum schwantesii*.

M. velutinus (L. Bol.) Schwantes = *Gibbaeum velutinum*.

Mentzelia L. Loasaceae. 60 ann., bienn. or perenn. herbs or shrubs, lacking stinging hairs. Lvs coarsely toothed or pinnatifid. Fls solitary or in short rac. or cymes, nocturnal or opening in bright sunlight; pet. usually 5, free, ovate-elliptic; sta. free. Americas.

M. aurea hort. non Nutt. = *M. lindleyi*.

M. laevicaulis (Douglas) Torr. BLAZING STAR. Bienn., to 1.25m. St. bright white. Lvs sinuately toothed. Fls 5–10cm diam., pale yellow, opening in early morning. SW US.

→*Bartonia* and *Nuttallia*.

M. lindleyi Torr. & A. Gray. Ann. to 0.6m. Lvs pinnatisect to pinnatifid. Fls to 5cm diam., golden, stained orange-red at base, fragrant, nocturnal. Calif.

MENYANTHACEAE Dumort. 5/40. *Menyanthes, Nephrophyllidium, Nymphoides, Villarsia.*

Menyanthes L. BOG BEAN; BUCK BEAN; MARSH TREFOIL. Menyanthaceae. 1 perenn. aquatic and marginal herb. Rhiz. creeping, then ascending, thick, rooting. Lvs trifoliolate, glab.; lfts 3–6cm, elliptic to obovate, entire, petioles 7–20cm, sheathing. Fls to 2.5cm, 10–20 in an erect rac. exceeding lvs, white flushed pink, short-lived, pet. 5, heavily fringed and bearded. Circumboreal. Z3.

M. crista-galli Menz. ex Hook. = *Nephrophyllidium crista-galli*.

M. trifoliata L.

Menziesia Sm. Ericaceae. 7 decid. shrubs. Fls 2–8, drooping in term. umbels; pedicels long, usually 2–8, hirsute; cal. short, usually gland. hirsute, lobes 4 or 5; cor. campanulate, urceolate or cylindric, pubesc. within, lobes 4 to 5; sta. 5–10, not exserted; style filiform. Fr. a capsule, coriaceous, 4–5-valved. US, E Asia.

M. azorica hort. = *Daboecia cantabrica*.

M. bryantha Sw. = *Bryanthus gmelinii*.

M. ciliicalyx (Miq.) Maxim. Erect shrub, 30cm–1m. Young branchlets glab. or sparsely downy. Lvs 2.5–5cm, obovate or ovate-oblong, hirsute, glaucous with hirsute midrib beneath. Cal. lobes 0; cor. 13–17mm, yellow or green-white, purple-tipped, tubular to urceolate, white downy inside, lobes 4 or 5, small; sta. 8 or 10, pubesc. Late spring–early summer. Jap. Z6. var. *bicolor* Mak. Cal. lobes short, rounded to elliptic. Late spring–summer. Jap. var. *multiflora* (Maxim.) Mak. Cal. lobes lanceolate to linear-lanceolate, ciliate; cor. usually purple-tinted, subcampanulate. Jap. var. *purpurea* Mak. Lvs coarsely long- and soft-hirsute above; cal. lobes short; cor. purple. Summer. Jap.

M. ferruginea Sm. RUSTY LEAF; FOOL'S HUCKLEBERRY. Suberect shrub, 50cm×2m. Young br. finely downy and glandular-hirsute. Lvs 2–6cm, elliptic-ovate to elliptic-obovate, serrate, ferruginous downy above and on midrib beneath. Cal. downy to glandular-ciliate, lobes tapering; cor. 6–8mm, yellow-rose, cylindric, lobes 4, diffuse; sta. 8, fil. glab. or hirsute at base. Late spring–summer. W US. var. *glabella* (Gray) Beck. Usually to 1m, rarely more. Lvs 2.5–6cm, obovate, ciliate and finely serrate, downy to subglab. Cal. lobes ciliate; cor. 7–9mm, cream-coloured, ovoid-campanulate. Late spring. N Amer. Z6.

M. globularis Salisb. = *M. pilosa*.

M. lasiophylla Nak. = *M. ciliicalyx* var. *multiflora*.

M. multiflora Maxim. = *M. ciliicalyx* var. *multiflora*.

M. pentandra Maxim. Soft-hirsute shrub, 70cm–1.2m. Lvs 2.5–5cm, narrowly elliptic, green above, paler beneath, coarsely hirsute above and on midrib beneath. Cal. gland.-ciliate; cor. 5–7mm, yellow-white, obliquely urceolate, downy inside tip and on lobes; sta. 5, hairless. Late spring–early summer. Jap., Sakhalin. Z6.

M. pilosa (Michx.) Juss. MINNIE BUSH. Erect shrub, 1–2m; twigs somewhat downy. Lvs 2–5cm, elliptic to obovate, adpressed downy above and on margins. Cal. lobes small, ciliate, sharp-tipped; cor. c6mm, campanulate, ivory to orange-pink; sta. 8, hairless. Late spring–early summer. E US. Z4.

M. polifolia Juss. = *Daboecia cantabrica*.

M. purpurea Maxim. Shrub, 70cm–2.4m; shoots glab. Lvs 2.5–4cm, oval-elliptic to oblong-obovate, sparsely setose above and on midrib beneath. Cal. lobes ovate-oblong, gland.-ciliate;

cor. 12–16mm, tubular-campanulate, red to purple, lobes 4 or 5, ciliate; sta. 4–10, densely hirsute. Late spring–early summer. Jap. Z6.

Mercury *Chenopodium bonus-henricus.*

Merendera Ramond. Liliaceae (Colchicaceae). 10 perenn., cormous herbs. Lvs basal, linear to linear-lanceolate, partially developed at flowering. Fls solitary or grouped, emerging from spathes; tep. 6, valvate, later spreading; sta. borne near base of tep., anth. versatile or basifixed, styles 3; free to base. Medit., N Afr., W Asia, outliers in Middle E and NE Afr.

M. aitchisonii Hook. = *M. robusta*.

M. androcymbioides Valdes. Close to *M. attica* but with anth. yellow and lvs slightly broader. Balk. Penins., Turk. Z8.

M. attica (Tomm.) Boiss. & Sprun. Lvs to 18×0.3–0.8cm, 2–6, linear to linear-lanceolate. Fls 2–6, white to lilac; tep. 15–27×2.5mm, linear to narrow-elliptic, usually with basal teeth; anth. black, deep purple-black or green-white, versatile. Autumn. Balk. Penins., Turk. Z8.

M. brandegiana Markgr. = *M. attica*.

M. bulbocodium Ramond = *M. montana*.

M. caucasica Bieb. = *M. trigyna*.

M. eichleri Boiss. = *M. trigyna*.

M. filifolia Cambess. Lvs 15×0.1–0.3cm, 5–15, linear. Fls solitary, rose to red-purple; tep. 20–40×2–8mm, narrow-elliptic to narrow oblong-elliptic; anth. yellow, basifixed. Spring. SW Eur., W Medit., N Afr. Z8.

M. hissarica Reg. Close to *M. robusta*, from which it differs in its solitary white fls and 2 lvs per corm. Z8.

M. kurdica Bornm. To 17cm, 3, lanceolate to narrow-lanceolate. Fls 1–2, pale to deep purple; tep. 3–3.5×0.5–1cm with basal auricles; anth. yellow. Spring. SE Turk., NE Iraq. Z8.

M. linifolia Munby = *M. filifolia*.

M. manissadjiania Aznav. = *M. trigyna*.

M. montana Lange. Lvs to 44×0.4–1cm, 3 or 4, linear, channelled, subfalcate. Fls 1–2, pale magenta to rosy purple; tep. 26×3–11mm, narrow-elliptic to narrow oblong-oblanceolate; anth. yellow, basifixed. Autumn. Iberian Penins., C Pyren. Z6.

M. navis-noae Markgr. = *M. trigyna*.

M. persica Boiss. & Kotschy = *M. robusta*.

M. pyrenaica (Pourr.) Fourn. = *M. montana*.

M. raddeana Reg. = *M. trigyna*.

M. rhodopea Velen. = *M. attica*.

M. robusta Bunge. Lvs to 25cm, 3–6, linear-lanceolate, concave above. Fls 1–4, deep pink to pale lilac or white, flask-shaped, fragrant; tep. 18–40×2–9mm, oblong-elliptic to linear-elliptic; anth. green-yellow, basifixed. Spring. C Iran, S Russia, N India. Z8.

M. sobolifera Mey. Corm v. small, terminating an underground shoot. Lvs linear, 3, to 10–21×0.3–1.3cm. Fls 1, occas. 2, rosy-lilac; tep. to 2.5cm, linear-elliptic; anth. black-violet, versatile. Spring. E Eur., Iran, C Asia. Z6.

M. trigyna (Adams) Stapf. Lvs to 17×0.3–1.8cm, 3, narrow lanceolate, blunt-tipped. Fls 1–3, rose to white; tep. 20–30×4–9mm, oblong or narrow-elliptic, usually toothed at base; anth. brown to yellow, versatile. Spring. E Turk., Iran, Cauc. Z7.

→*Bulbocodium* and *Colchicum*.

Merinthosorus Copel. Polypodiaceae. 11 epiphytic fern. Rhiz. thick, scaly, short-creeping, fleshy. Fronds to 120×30cm+, broadly lanceolate, short-stipitate, basal lobes dilated, collecting plant-litter, papery to thinly leathery; central lobes sterile, to 20×3cm, oblong, acute; uppermost part fertile, pinnate, pinnae to 30×3cm, sessile, narrowly elongate-linear, entire, thinly leathery. Malaysia to Polyn. Z10.

M. drynarioides (Hook.) Copel.

→*Acrostichum*.

Mermaid Weed *Proserpinaca.*

Merremia Dennst. Convolvulaceae. 60–80 perenn., herbaceous or woody climbers, erect to procumbent. Lvs entire or compound. Infl. axill., 1- to few-fld, with narrow bracts; sep. usually subequal; cor. campanulate or funnel-shaped, entire or lobed. Pantrop. Z9.

M. aurea (Kellogg) O'Donnell. Slender, tuberous climber to 2.5m. Lv lobes 5, 2–4cm, entire. Fls solitary, on glab. pedicel; cor. 5–10cm diam., 3–8cm long, funnel-shaped, golden-yellow, midpetaline areas darker. Baja Calif.

M. dissecta (Jacq.) Hallier f. Herbaceous climber to at least 8m. Lf lobes to 10cm, 7–9, lanceolate, glab. or sparsely hairy, coarsely and sinuately toothed. Infl. 1–4-fld, on a 5–7cm peduncle; cor. 3–4.5cm long, broadly funnel-shaped, white with a purple or magenta tube. S US to Trop. S Amer.

M. tuberosa (L.) Rendle. WOOD ROSE; YELLOW MORNING GLORY; SPANISH WOODBINE. Woody tuberous climber to 20m. Lvs 8–15cm, lobes 7, glab., elliptic to lanceolate, entire, acuminate. Infl. 1- to several-fld; peduncles 10–20cm; cor. 5–6cm, campanulate, bright yellow. Mex. to Trop. S Amer., introd. in many other trop. regions.

→*Ipomoea*.

Merry-bells *Uvularia*.
Merryhearts *Zigadenus nuttallii*.

Mertensia Roth. Boraginaceae. 50 perenn. herbs. St. solitary to numerous, erect to decumbent. Basal lvs long-petiolate, cauline lvs shorter, often sessile. Cymes usually term., scorpioid, often paniculate; cal. deeply 5-lobed; cor. tubular, campanulate, cylindrical or infundibular, usually with 5 scales in the throat; sta. included or slightly exserted. N Temp.

M. alpina (Torr.) G. Don. St. to 30cm, erect or ascending, glab. Lvs strigose above, glab. beneath, to 7×3cm, linear-lanceolate to oblong. Infl. becoming slightly paniculate; cor. dark blue, tube to 6mm, interior glab., limb to 6mm; scales conspicuous. N Amer.

M. bakeri Greene. St. to 40cm, erect or ascending, pubesc. Lvs hoary-pubesc., to 11×3.5cm, ovate-elliptic to linear-lanceolate. Infl. a pan., loosely to densely-fld; cor. blue, tube to 9mm, with basal ring of hairs, limb to 6mm, scales usually conspicuous. N Amer.

M. ciliata (James) G. Don. St. to 120cm, erect or ascending. Lvs ciliate, often papillose above, to 15×10cm, ovate or lanceolate to oblong. Infl. axill., elongate with age; cor. bright blue, to 8mm, interior glab. or crisped-pubesc., scales conspicuous. N Amer. Z4.

M. echioides (Benth.) Benth. & Hook. f. St. to 30cm, erect or decumbent, pubesc. Lvs to 9×2.5cm, lanceolate or ovate to elliptic-lanceolate. Infl. to 13cm, scorpioid, elongate, many-fld; cor. deep blue to blue-purple, to 7mm, infundibular to sub-cylindrical, lobes erect, scales inconspicuous or 0. Pak., Kashmir, Tibet. Z6.

M. elongata (Decne.) Benth. & Hook. f. St. to 25cm, simple, erect, green-white, adpressed-pubesc. Lvs with adpressed, tuberculate-based bristle hairs throughout to 60×12mm, oblong to oblong-lanceolate or elliptic-lanceolate, ciliate. Infl. elongating with age, many-fld; cor. blue to deep purple-blue to 9mm, campanulate to cylindric-campanulate, lobes to 3.5×3mm, sub-rotund, spreading, scales usually inconspicuous. Pak., Kashmir. Z6.

M. lanceolata (Pursh) A. DC. St. to 45cm, erect or ascending. Lvs to 14×4cm, elliptic-oblong to ovate-lanceolate, glab. to short-strigose or pustulate above, glab. beneath. Infl. scorpioid, paniculate with age; cor. blue, tube to 6.5mm, interior with a basal ring of hairs, limb to 9mm, usually campanulate, scales conspicuous. N Amer. Z4.

M. longiflora Greene. St. to 35cm, erect. Lvs glab. to hirsute above, glab. beneath, to 8×4.5cm, spathulate to ovate-elliptic. Infl. short, dense; cor. bright blue, tube to 15mm, interior glab. or basally puberulent, limb to 7mm, scales prominent. N Amer. Z3.

M. maritima (L.) S.F. Gray. OYSTER PLANT. St. to 100cm, decumbent or spreading. Lvs to 10×5cm, fleshy, spathulate to oblong-ovate, glaucous sea green papillose above. Cor. pink becoming blue, tube to 5mm, limb to 4mm, scales inconspicuous or 0. Alask. to Mass., Greenland, Eurasia. Z3.

M. oblongifolia (Nutt.) G. Don. St. to 30cm, erect or ascending. Lvs strigose above, glab. beneath, to 8×2cm, elliptic-oblong or spathulate to linear. Infl. dense, ultimately branching; cor. blue, tube to 12mm, interior glab., limb to 7mm, scales conspicuous. N Amer. Z4.

M. paniculata (Ait.) G. Don. St. to 75cm, erect. Lvs scabrous and adpressed-pubesc. above, spreading-pubesc. beneath, to 20×14cm, ovate-subcordate to elliptic-lanceolate, (basal lvs long-stalked). Infl. scorpioid; cor. pink when young, blue with age, sometimes white, tube to 7mm, interior glab. or pubesc., limb to 9mm, scales prominent. Canada, N US. Z4.

M. platyphylla Heller. St. to 90cm, erect. Lvs minutely strigose above, somewhat hirsute beneath, to 14×7cm, ovate-subcordate to lanceolate. Infl. scorpioid; cor. blue, sometimes white, tube to 6mm, interior glab. or puberulent, limb to 9mm, scales prominent. N Amer. Z4.

M. primuloides (Decne.) Clarke. St. to 15cm, strigose. Lvs to 7×1cm, lanceolate to oblong or linear-lanceolate. Infl. few-fld; cor. deep blue to white or yellow, to 15mm, hypocrateriform, tube cylindrical, limb to 10mm diam., scales conspicuous. Afghan., Pak., Tibet. Z5.

M. pterocarpa (Turcz.) Tatew. & Ohwi = *M. sibirica*.
M. pulchella Piper = *M. longiflora*.
M. sibirica (L.) G. Don St. to 45cm, erect, unbranched. Lvs sub-orbicular to broadly elliptic or cordate. Fls blue-purple on twinned rac. with 1 fl. in fork. Eurasia. 'Alba': fls white. Z3.
M. tibetica (Decne.) Clarke = *M. primuloides*.
M. tweedyi Rydb. = *M. alpina*.
M. umbratilis Greenman. St. to 60cm, erect or ascending. Lvs glab. or strigose above, glab. beneath to 11×6cm, ovate to ovate-oblong, ± ciliate. Infl. axill., scorpioid; cor. blue, tube to 14mm, interior glab., limb to 9mm, scales conspicuous. N US (Washington to Oreg.). Z6.
M. virginica (L.) Pers. ex Link. BLUEBELLS; VIRGINIA BLUEBELLS; VIRGINIA COWSLIP; ROANOKE BELLS. St. to 70cm, erect, lvs to 20×12cm, elliptic to ovate, glab. to slightly papillose above. Infl. axill., scorpioid; cor. blue, sometimes pink or white, tube to 21mm, interior with a dense basal ring of hairs, limb to 13mm, campanulate, scales inconspicuous. N Amer. 'Alba': fls white. 'Rubra': fls pink. Z3.
M. viridis (A. Nels.) A. Nels. Perenn. to 30cm. Lvs to 10×3cm, elliptic to oblanceolate, glab. or shortly pubesc. or linear. Fls erect to pendent; cor. deep to light blue or white, tube to 9mm, interior densely pubesc., limb to 9mm, glab. or pubesc. Mont., Colorado, Utah. Z3.

→*Eritrichium, Lithospermum, Pseudomertensia* and *Pulmonaria*.

Meryta Forst. & Forst. f. Araliaceae. 25–30 small to medium everg., pachycaulous, dioecious trees. Lvs simple, spirally arranged, ± tufted, large, coriaceous. Infl. term., to 3× compound; fls in heads or umbels. Pacific Is. Z10.

M. denhamii Seem. Tree to 10m, crown dense. Juvenile lvs linear-elliptic, dark green, to 30×1.3cm; adult lvs elliptic, to 125×22cm, with coarse, rounded teeth. Infl. small, stout, with few fl. heads. New Caledonia.

M. sinclairii (Hook. f.) Seem. PUKA. Round-headed tree to 8m, without distinct juvenile foliage. Lvs oblong-obovate, to 50cm, entire. Infl. to 45cm; fls green-white, in dense umbels. Fr. black, fleshy, to 13mm. NZ.

M. latifolia (Endl.) Seem. from Norfolk Island and *M. sonchifolia* Lind. & André, from New Caledonia with v. large pinnatifid lvs, are sometimes cultivated.

→*Aralia* and *Oreopanax*.

Mescal Bean *Sophora secundiflora*.
Mescal Button *Lophophora williamsii*.

Mesembryanthemum L. emend. L. Bol. Aizoaceae. 40–50 succulent annuals or biennials, glossy-papillose throughout. St. usually thick, fleshy, with a basal rosette of lvs; br. often prostrate. Lvs shortly united, cylindrical or flat. Fls solitary or numerous. S Afr., Nam. Z9.

M. aduncum Jacq. = *Ruschia schollii*.
M. aitonis Jacq. Lvs obovate-spathulate, 5×2.5cm, somewhat obtuse. Fls red. E Cape.
M. alkalifugum Dinter nom. nud. = *M. barklyi*.
M. altile N.E. Br. = *Conophytum ficiforme*.
M. angulatum Thunb. = *M. aitonis*.
M. aquosum L. Bol. = *M. hypertrophicum*.
M. arenarum (N.E. Br.) L. Bol. = *M. inachabense*.
M. astridae Dinter = *Titanopsis hugo-schlechteri*.
M. aureum L. = *Lampranthus aureus*.
M. barklyi N.E. Br. To 60cm, blue-green, tinged purple; st. 4-angled. Lvs expanded-spathulate, to 28×18cm, with undulating margins. Fls 3.6cm diam., white. W Cape, Nam.
M. bellum (N.E. Br.) Dinter = *Lithops karasmontana* ssp. *bella*.
M. bergerianum Dinter = *Hereroa hesperanthera*.
M. bicolor Curtis = *Lampranthus coccineus*.
M. bicolorum (L.) Rothm. = *Lampranthus bicolor*.
M. bidentatum Haw. = *Glottiphyllum semicylindricum*.
M. bigibberatum Haw. = *Glottiphyllum semicylindricum*.
M. brachyphyllum Pax = *Drosanthemum paxianum*.
M. caducum Auct. non Ait. = *M. inachabense*.
M. calycinum Ecklon & Zeyh. = *Sphalmanthus canaliculatus*.
M. canaliculatum Salm-Dyck = *Sphalmanthus salmoneus*.
M. candidissimum (Haw.) N.E. Br. = *Cheiridopsis denticulata*.
M. canum (Haw.) Berger = *Aloinopsis peersii*.
M. carinatum Vent. = *Semnanthe lacera*.
M. caulescens Mill. = *Lampranthus deltoides*.
M. clavatum Haw. = *Dorotheanthus gramineus*.
M. claviforme DC. = *Dorotheanthus gramineus*.
M. copticum L. = *M. nodiflorum*.
M. corallinum Haw. = *Lampranthus coralliflorus*.
M. cryptanthum Hook. f. Prostrate; st. thick. Lvs 3–4×0.6–0.8cm, lower lvs flat, thick and fleshy, lvs on flowering st. ± cylindrical, clavate, green or red, sometimes waxy yellow.

Fls 1–2cm diam., white to deep pink or yellow. Nam., Red Sea coast.

M.crystallinum L. St. spreading, papillose. Lvs ovate or ovate-spathulate, thick-fleshy, v. papillose, undulate. Fls 2–3cm diam., white. Nam., W Cape, introd. Medit., Canary Is., Calif.

M. crystallinum Auct. non L. = *M. guerichianum*.

M. crystallophanes Ecklon & Zeyh. = *M. aitonis*.

M. cultratum Salm-Dyck = *Glottiphyllum latum* var. *cultratum*.

M. cupreum L. Bol. = *Cephalophyllum caespitosum*.

M. dactylindum Welw. ex Oliv. = *M. cryptanthum*.

M. damarum N.E. Br. = *Lithops karasmontana*.

M. demissum Willd. = *Disphyma australe*.

M. densum Haw. = *Trichodiadema densum*.

M. dentatum Kerner = *Semnanthe lacera*.

M. depressum Haw. = *Glottiphyllum depressum*.

M. didymaotum Marloth = *Didymaotus lapidiformis*.

M. digitiforme Thunb. = *Dactylopsis digitata*.

M. dinterae Dinter = *Chasmatophyllum musculinum*.

M. divergens Kensit = *Gibbaeum fissoides*.

M. diversifolium Haw. = *Cephalophyllum diversiphyllum*.

M. dubium L. Bol. = *Cephalophyllum decipiens*.

M. eberlanzii Dinter & Schwantes = *Lithops karasmontana* ssp. *eberlanzii*.

M. echinatum Ait. = *Delosperma pruinosum*.

M. educale var. *virescens* Haw. Moss = *Carpobrotus virescens*.

M. emarcidum Thunb. = *Sceletium emarcidum*.

M. evolutum N.E. Br. = *Ruschia evoluta*.

M. exacutum N.E. Br. = *Ruschia acuminata*.

M. exile hort. ex Haw. = *Carpobrotus aequilaterus*.

M. expansum L. = *Sceletium expansum*.

M. falcatum Thunb. = *Semnanthe lacera*.

M. falcatum var. *galpinii* L. Bol. = *Lampranthus falcatus* var. *galpinii*.

M. fenchelii Schinz = *M. guerichianum*.

M. ferrugineum Schwantes = *Lithops lesliei*.

M. fibulaeforme Haw. = *Conophytum fibuliforme*.

M. filamentosum DC. = *Erepsia mutabilis*.

M. fimbriatum Sonder = *Ruschia pygmaea*.

M. flanaganii Kensit = *Delosperma tradescantioides*.

M. flexile Haw. = *Lampranthus emarginatus*.

M. forficatum Jacq. = *Erepsia mutabilis*.

M. forskahlii Hochst. = *M. cryptanthum*.

M. francisci Dinter & Schwantes = *Lithops francisci*.

M. fulleri (L. Bol.) L. Bol. = *M. inachabense*.

M. fulviceps N.E. Br. = *Lithops fulviceps*.

M. garicusianum Dinter = *M. guerichianum*.

M. gibbosum Haw. = *Gibbaeum gibbosum*.

M. glaciale Haw. = *M. crystallinum*.

M. gladiatum Jacq. = *Semnanthe lacera*.

M. glaucinum Haw. = *Erepsia mutabilis*.

M. grandifolium auct. non Schinz = *M. barklyi*.

M. grandifolium Schinz ex Range = *M. guerichianum*.

M. gratum N.E. Br. = *Conophytum gratum*.

M.guerichianum Pasc. Highly succulent; st. thick, cylindrical. Basal and lower cauline lvs decussate 15×8cm, ovate to rhombic, narrowed below, upper lvs smaller. Fls 2.5–4cm diam., white or green to yellow-white and pink to light red. Cape Prov., Nam.

M. heathii N.E. Br. = *Gibbaeum heathii*.

M. hispidum var. *pallidum* Haw. = *Drosanthemum floribundum*.

M. hookeri Berg = *Lithops hookeri*.

M.hypertrophicum Dinter. Forming flat cushions; st. spreading, prostrate. Lvs 1–1.3cm thick, cylindrical to hemispherical, soft, v. fleshy. Fls 4–6cm diam., white or red. Nam., Little Namaqualand.

M. imbricans Haw. = *Lampranthus emarginatus*.

M. imbricatum var. *rubrum* Haw. = *Ruschia tumidula*.

M.inachabense Engl. Soft-fleshy, prostrate, erect or curved ascending, basally branching. Basal and lower cauline lvs 2–5×1–2cm, oblong-spathulate to obovate. Fls 1–1.5cm diam., fragrant, yellow or white; stigmas red. W Cape.

M. incurvum var. *roseum* DC. = *Lampranthus roseus*.

M. insititium Willd. = *Malephora crocea*.

M.intransparens L. Bol. Robust; main st. erect to 50cm, flowering st. elongated, prostrate, to 1m, hexagonal. Lvs 11×9cm, ovate, undulate. Fls 4cm diam., white. W Cape.

M. julii Dinter & Schwantes = *Lithops julii*.

M. karasbergens (L. Bol.) Friedrich = *Hereroa hesperanthera*.

M. karasmontanum Dinter & Schwantes = *Lithops karasmontana*.

M. laeve Thunb. = *Malephora thunbergii*.

M. lanceolatum sensu lato Haw. = *M. aitonis*.

M. lepidum Haw. = *Lampranthus productus* var. *lepidum*.

M. lericheanum Dinter & Schwantes = *Lithops karasmontana* var. *lericheana*.

M. lesliei N.E. Br. = *Lithops lesliei*.

M. leve N.E. Br. = *Ruschia mollis*.

M. linguiforme var. *latum* Salm-Dyck = *Glottiphyllum latum*.

M. locale N.E. Br. = *Lithops schwantesii*.

M. longispinulum Sonder = *Sphalmanthus canaliculatus*.

M.macrophyllum L. Bol. Covered with short papillate hairs, velvety; st. to 70cm, prostrate, 4-angled. Lvs 40×23×0.5cm, rosulate, oblong-ovate, undulate, hirsute beneath. Infl. 50×50cm; fls 4–5cm diam., mauve-pink. W Cape.

M. magnipunctatum Haw. = *Pleiospilos compactus* ssp. *canus*.

M. marmoratum N.E. Br. = *Lithops marmorata*.

M. micans Thunb. non L. = *Delosperma expersum*.

M. minusculum N.E. Br. = *Conophytum minusculum*.

M. minutum Haw. = *Conophytum minutum*.

M. multipunctatum Salm-Dyck = *Cheiridopsis rostrata*.

M. muricatum Haw. = *Lampranthus deltoides*.

M. nigrescens Haw. = *Carpobrotus aequilaterus*.

M. nobile Haw. = *Pleiospilos compactus* ssp. *canus*.

M.nodiflorum L. To 20cm, grey-green with large papillae. Lvs 1–2.5×0.1–0.2cm, linear, ciliate beneath. Fls white. W Cape, introd. S Eur., Middle East, Calif., Baja Calif.

M. obtusum Haw. = *Gibbaeum fissoides*.

M. opticum Marloth = *Lithops optica*.

M. paxii Engl. = *Drosanthemum paxianum*.

M. perviride Haw. = *Gibbaeum gibbosum*.

M. pinque L. Bol. = *M. barklyi*.

M. polyphyllum Haw. = *Lampranthus emarginatus*.

M. ponderosum Dinter = *Juttadinteria longipetala*.

M. pseudotruncatellum A. Berger = *Lithops pseudotruncatella*.

M. pugioniforme L. = *Conicosia pugioniformis*.

M. pugioniforme L. Bol. = *Herrea robusta*.

M. pyropaeum Haw. = *Dorotheanthus gramineus*.

M. ramulosum Haw. = *Cheiridopsis rostrata*.

M. recumbens N.E. Br. = *Chasmatophyllum musculinum*.

M. recurvum Haw. = *Ruschia schollii*.

M. reflexum Willd. = *Sphalmanthus canaliculatus*.

M. ringens var. *caninum* L. = *Carruanthus ringens*.

M. roseum Haw. = *Drosanthemum striatum*.

M. rostellatum DC. = *Ruschia rostella*.

M. rubrocinctum Ecklon & Zeyh. = *Carpobrotus acinaciformis*.

M. ruschii Dinter & Schwantes = *Lithops ruschiorum*.

M. ruschiorum Dinter & Schwantes = *Lithops ruschiorum*.

M. salmoneum Haw. = *Sphalmanthus salmoneus*.

M. sarcocalycanthum Dinter & Berger = *M. cryptanthum*.

M. saxetanum N.E. Br. = *Conophytum saxetanum*.

M. scalpratum Haw. = *Glottiphyllum linguiforme*.

M. sexipartitum N.E. Br. = *Delosperma lehmannii*.

M. spathulatum L. Bol. = *Drosanthemum uniflorum*.

M. spathulifolium Willd. = *Dorotheanthus bellidiformis*.

M. squamulosum (Dinter) Dinter = *M. barklyi*.

M. steingroeveri Pax ex Engl. = *Ruschia odontocalyx*.

M. stellatum hort. = *Erepsia gracilis*.

M. stenophyllum L. Bol. = *Ruschia stenophylla*.

M. stramineum Willd. = *Cephalophyllum tricolorum*.

M. suavissimum Dinter = *Juttadinteria suavissimum*.

M. subrostratum Willd. = *Cephalophyllum subulatoides*.

M. torquatum Haw. = *Drosanthemum floribundum*.

M. tortuosum DC. non L. = *Sceletium expansum*.

M. tortuosum L. = *Sceletium tortuosum*.

M. tricolor Jacq. = *Erepsia mutabilis*.

M. tricolorum Haw. = *Cephalophyllum tricolorum*.

M. trigonum N.E. Br. = *Cerochlamys pachyphylla*.

M. truncatellum Hook. f. = *Lithops hookeri*.

M. truncatellum Dinter = *Lithops pseudotruncatella*.

M. turbiniformis Haw. = *Lithops hookeri*.

M. vallis-mariae Dinter & Schwantes = *Lithops vallis-mariae*.

M. varians Haw. = *Sceletium tortuosum*.

M. vernae Dinter & A. Berger = *Malephora engleriana*.

M. vescum N.E. Br. = *Cheiridopsis cigarettifera*.

M. violaceum DC. = *Lampranthus emarginatus*.

M. volckameri Haw. = *M. aitonis*.

→*Amoebophyllum, Cryophytum, Halenbergia, Hydrodea, Opophytum* and *Platythyra*.

Mesospinidium Rchb.

M. cochliodum Rchb. f. = *Symphyglossum sanguineum*.

Mespilus L. MEDLAR. Rosaceae. 1 decid. tree or shrub, to 5m. Bark grey-brown, fissured. Br. arching, divaricate; branchlets brown-tomentose at first, usually thornless in cult. Lvs to 12cm, oblong-lanceolate, subsessile, dull green above, tomentose beneath, serrate, golden in fall. Fls white to pale rose, to 5cm wide, usually solitary; hypanthium tomentose, cal., lobes 5, lanceolate-acute; pet. 5, obovate; sta. usually 25–40. Fr. turbinate, to 2.5cm, brown when ripe, crowned with the 5 cal. lobes, apex domed to flat, showing ends of carpel vessels. Spring–summer. Eur., Asia Minor.

M. *acuminata* Lodd. = *Cotoneaster acuminatus*.
M. *amelanchier* L. = *Amelanchier rotundifolia*.
M. *arborea* Michx. f. = *Amelanchier arborea*.
M. *arbutifolia* L. = *Aronia arbutifolia*.
M. *arbutifolia* var. *melanocarpa* Michx. = *Aronia melanocarpa*.
M. *canadensis* L. = *Amelanchier canadensis*.
M. *crenulata* D. Don = *Pyracantha crenulata*.
M. *flabellata* Spach = *Crataegus flabellata*.
M. *fontanesiana* Spach = *Crataegus fontanesiana*.
M. **germanica** L.
M. *grandiflora* Sm. = × *Crataemespilus grandiflora*.
M. *japonica* Thunb. = *Eriobotrya japonica*.
M. *oliveriana* Dum.-Cours. = *Crataegus oliveriana*.
M. *pruinosa* Wendl. = *Crataegus pruinosa*.
M. *prunifolia* Marshall = *Aronia prunifolia*.
M. *pyracantha* L. = *Pyracantha coccinea*.
M. *racemiflora* Desf. = *Cotoneaster racemiflorus*.
M. *sorbifolia* Poir. = × *Sorbaronia sorbifolia*.
M. *tanacetifolia* Lam. = *Crataegus tanacetifolia*.

Mesquite *Prosopis*.
Mesquitilla *Calliandra eriophylla*.
Messmate *Eucalyptus obliqua*.
Messmate Stringybark *Eucalyptus obliqua*.

Mestoklema N.E. Br. Aizoaceae. 7 shrublets, usually with a tuberous caudex; young st. papillose. Lvs united at the base, triquetrous or cylindrical, lf bases persisting as a thorn. Fls in small branched term. infl., small. S Afr. (Cape Prov.) Nam., Réunion Is. Z9.
M. *arboriforme* (Burchell) N.E. Br. Tree-like, 30–45cm, freely branching above. Lvs 12×2×2mm, minutely hirsute. Fls 5mm diam., yellow to orange. W Cape, Nam.
M. *macrorhizum* (DC.) Schwantes. Caudex tuberous; st. 2.5–7.5cm. Lvs crowded, obtusely triquetrous. Fls 1–3 together, small, white. Réunion Is.
M. *tuberosum* (L.) N.E. Br. Much-branched shrub, 50–70cm, caudex large. Lvs 10–15×2–3mm, triquetrous, minutely papillose, light green. Fls 7–8mm diam., red-yellow. S Afr., Nam.
→*Delosperma* and *Mesembryanthemum*.

Mesua L. Guttiferae. 3 everg. trees or shrubs. Lvs opposite, crowded, narrow, leathery, distinctly veined and pellucid-dotted. Fls solitary or paired, axill., large; sep. and pet. 4; sta. v. numerous. Fr. with woody rind, 1-celled, 4-valvate. In-domalesia. Z10.
M. *ferrea* L. IRONWOOD; NA. Tree to 13m, erect. Lvs linear-lanceolate to oblong-lanceolate, to 15cm, red becoming glossy dark green, glaucous beneath. Fls white, to 7.5cm across, fragrant; sta. yellow. Fr. subglobose, to 5cm. Summer. India to Malaysia.

Metake *Pseudosasa japonica*.
Metallic-leaf Begonia *Begonia metallica*.

Metapanax Frodin. Araliaceae. Everg. shrubs or trees of bushy habit. Lvs simple or palmately lobed, lobes toothed to almost entire. Infl. term., paniculate, 1–2× compound, pyramidal to conical; fls in small umbels at ends of main axis; cal. subentire to minutely 5-toothed; pet. 5, abutting one another, free; sta. 5. Fr. drupaceous. China, N Vietnam.
M. *davidii* (Franch.) Frodin. Shrub or tree to 12m. Lvs to 15×6cm, broadly toothed, simple, entire or trilobed or trifid, to 2–3-foliolate; petioles to 20cm. Infl. to 18cm; umbels about 18mm across; fls green-yellow. Fr. black, to 6mm across. Summer. W & C China, N Vietnam. Z7.
M. *delavayi* (Franch.) Frodin. Shrub to 5m. Lvs usually 3–5-foliolate, occas. 2-foliolate or simple; lfts oblong-lanceolate, to 12×2.5cm, broadly toothed or subentire; petiole to 12cm. Infl. to 15cm; umbels as in M. *davidii* but slightly larger. Summer. SW China, N Vietnam. Z9.
→*Nothopanax*, *Panax* and *Pseudopanax*.

Metasequoia Miki ex Hu & Cheng. Cupressaceae. 1 decid. conifer to 45m+. Bole to 2m diam., deeply ridged and buttressed. Bark furrowed, fibrous, rust-coloured. Crown conic to columnar. Br. ascending or level. Lvs distichous, linear, flexible, bright green above, lighter with 2 stomatal bands beneath, 2–2.5cm, turning gold to red-brown in fall. Cones on 2–4cm stalks, globose to ovoid and acute at apex, dark brown 1.5–3×1.5–2cm. W China. Z5.
M. *glyptostroboides* Hu & Cheng. DAWN REDWOOD. 'Emerald Feathers': lvs v. bright green, luxuriant; vigorous. 'National': crown narrowly conic.

Methysticodendron R.E. Schult. = *Brugmansia*.

Metrosideros Banks ex Gaertn. Myrtaceae. 50 aromatic shrubs, trees or woody climbers. Lvs opposite, simple, gland-dotted. Fls in axill. or term. cymes sometimes reduced to a single fl., often aggregated; sep. 5; pet. 5; sta. numerous, 2 or more × as long as pet. Fr. a leathery capsule. S Afr., Malesia, Australasia, Pacific Is. Z9.
M. *aurea* hort. = M. *fulgens*.
M. *carminea* Oliv. Liane to 15m+. Lvs 15–35mm, elliptic to ovate-oblong to broad-ovate, coriaceous. Infl. in term. compound cymes; fls bright carmine; sep. broad-oblong, 2mm; pet. suborbicular, shortly clawed usually toothed; sta. 10–15mm. NZ.
M. *colensoi* Hook. f. Slender liane to 6m+. Lvs to 15–20mm, ovate-lanceolate, densely pubesc. when young. Infl. of few-fld cymes; sep. narrow-triangular, acute; pet. pink to white, orbicular; sta. c10cm. NZ.
M. *collina* (Forst. & Forst. f.) A. Gray. Tree or shrub, 1–20m. Lvs 4–8.5cm, elliptic-lanceolate to oblong or obovate-elliptic, coriaceous, copiously glandular-punctate. Fls aggregated; pet. obovate to orbicular, to 4×4mm; sta. 12–20mm. Samoa and SE Polyn.
M. *collina* ssp. *polymorpha* (Gaud.) Rock = M. *polymorpha*.
M. *diffusus* Forst. f. SMALL RATA VINE. Slender liane to 6m+. Lvs 7–8mm, oblong to ovate-lanceolate to ovate-oblong, somewhat pubesc. when young. Infl. of few-fld lat. cymes, usually below lvs; sep. ovate-triangular; pet. suborbicular, white to pink; sta. slender, 7–9mm, white to pink. NZ.
M. *excelsa* Sol. ex Gaertn. CHRISTMAS TREE; POHUTUKAWA. Tree to 20m. Lvs 5–10cm, elliptic to oblong, coriaceous, thick, white-tomentose beneath. Infl. of broad, compound cymes; sep. deltoid; pet. crimson, oblong; sta. crimson, 30–40mm. NZ.
M. *florida* Sm. = M. *fulgens*.
M. *fulgens* Sol. ex Gaertn. Liane to 10m+. Lvs 35–60mm, elliptic-oblong, glab. Infl. of terminal cymes; sep. oblong, obtuse; pet. suborbicular, orange-red; sta. scarlet, 20–25mm. NZ.
M. *kermadecensis* Oliv. KERMADEC POHUTUKAWA. Tree to 30m. Lvs 2–5cm, broadly ovate to elliptic-ovate, coriaceous, densely white-tomentose beneath. Infl. term. compound cymes; sep. deltoid to triangular, gland-tipped; pet. oblong, pubesc.; crimson; sta. crimson, 12–20mm. NZ (Kermadec Is.). Has been confused in cult. with M. *excelsa* but the lvs are of a different shape. 'Variegata': lvs marked grey-green and cream.
M. *lucida* (Forst. f.) A. Rich. = M. *umbellata*.
M. *parkinsonii* Buch. Straggling shrub or tree to c7m. Lvs 35–50mm, ovate-lanceolate, coriaceous. Infl. in compound cymes, usually below lvs; fls many, bright crimson; sep. ovate-triangular; pet. oblong, somewhat toothed; sta. 20–25mm. NZ.
M. *perforata* (Forst. & Forst. f.) A. Rich. FLOWERY RATA VINE. Liane to 15m+. Lvs 6–12mm, broad-ovate to broad-oblong to suborbicular, glab., pale beneath and ± setose. Infl. of axillary few-fld cymes; sep. broad, obtuse; pet. suborbicular, white or pink; sta. 8–10mm, white to pink. NZ.
M. *polymorpha* Gaud. LEHUA. Small erect to prostrate shrub to tall tree. Lvs 1–8cm, obovate to orbicular, sometimes elliptic or ovate, rounded to acute, lower surface glab. or woolly or pub-esc. Fls red, in panicle. of 2–5-pairs of cymules; sep. rounded to triangular; pet. obovate to orbicular; sta. 10–30mm. Hawaii.
M. *robusta* A. Cunn. RATA; NORTHERN RATA. Tree to 25m+. Lvs 25–50mm, elliptic to ovate-oblong, glab., coriaceous. Infl. a many-fld term. cyme; sep. broad-triangular; pet. oblong; sta. red, c30mm. NZ.
M. *scandens* (Forst. & Forst. f.) Druce = M. *fulgens*.
M. *speciosa* sensu Colenso = M. *fulgens*.
M. *tomentosa* A. Rich. = M. *excelsa*.
M. *umbellata* Cav. SOUTHERN RATA. Tree to 15m+. Lvs 30–50mm, glab., coriaceous. Infl. of terminal cymes; sep. oblong-triangular to ovate; pet. light red, suborbicular; sta. light red, c20mm. NZ.
→*Melaleuca*.

Metroxylon Rottb. Palmae. 6 erect, monocarpic palms. St. ringed, dead. Crownshaft 0. Lvs pinnate, densely clustered; petioles smooth; pinnae opposite, linear-lanceolate. Fls paired, 1 ♂ and 1 ♀. Fr. ellipsoid or subglobose, 1-seeded. Malaysia to Fiji. Z10.
M. *sagu* Rottb. SAGO PALM. St. to 10m. Lvs to 7m, arching; petioles long, robust, clasping at base; pinnae long, tapering at the apex, margins occas. prickly. Infl. to 7m. Fr. yellow-brown. Malaya.

Meu *Meum athamanticum*.

Meum Mill. Umbelliferae. 1 glab., aromatic perenn. to 60cm. St. striate. Lvs mostly basal, 3–4-pinnate, seg. crowded, filiform, to 5mm. Umbels compound, rays 3–15, to 5cm; fls white or white tinged purple. Summer. Eur. Z7.
M. athamanticum Jacq. BALDMONEY; MEU; SPIGNEL.

Mexican Apple *Casimiroa edulis.*
Mexican Bamboo *Polygonum japonicum.*
Mexican Basswood *Tilia mexicana.*
Mexican Bird Cherry *Prunus salicifolia.*
Mexican Blood Flower *Distictis buccinatoria.*
Mexican Blue Fan Palm *Brahea armata.*
Mexican Blue Oak *Quercus oblongifolia.*
Mexican Buck-eye *Ungnadia speciosa.*
Mexican Bush Sage *Salvia leucantha.*
Mexican Clover *Richardia scabra.*
Mexican Creeper *Antigonon leptopus.*
Mexican Cypress *Cupressus lusitanica.*
Mexican Daisy *Erigeron karvinskianus.*
Mexican Douglas Fir *Pseudotsuga guinieri.*
Mexican Firecracker *Echevaria setosa.*
Mexican Fire Plant *Euphorbia cyathophora.*
Mexican Flameleaf *Calliandra tweedii; Euphorbia pulcherrima.*
Mexican Flamevine *Pseudogynoxys chenopodioides.*
Mexican Foxglove *Tetranema roseum.*
Mexican Gem *Echeveria elegans.*
Mexican Gold *Eschscholzia mexicana.*
Mexican Hat *Ratibida.*
Mexican Husk Tomato *Physalis ixocarpa.*
Mexican Hyssop *Agastache.*
Mexican Ivy *Cobaea scandens.*
Mexican Juniper *Juniperus flaccida.*
Mexican Lily *Hippeastrum reginae.*
Mexican Lippia *Lippia dulcis.*
Mexican Love Grass *Eragrostis mexicana.*
Mexican Mint *Plectranthus amboinicus.*
Mexican Nut Pine *Pinus cembroides.*
Mexican Orange *Choisya ternata.*
Mexican Oregano *Lippia graveolens.*
Mexican Palo Verde *Parkinsonia aculeata.*
Mexican Petunia *Strobilanthes atropurpureus.*
Mexican Poppy *Argemone mexicana.*
Mexican Rubber *Castilla.*
Mexican Shell Flower *Tigridia.*
Mexican Shrimp Plant *Justicia brandegeana.*
Mexican Snow Ball *Echeveria elegans.*
Mexican Stone Pine *Pinus cembroides.*
Mexican Sunflower *Tithonia.*
Mexican Swamp Cypress *Taxodium mucronatum.*
Mexican Tarragon *Tagetes lucida.*
Mexican Tea *Chenopodium ambrosioides.*
Mexican Tree Fern *Cibotium schiedei.*
Mexican Tulip Poppy *Hunnemannia.*
Mexican Violet *Tetranema roseum.*
Mexican Washingtonia *Washingtonia robusta.*
Mexican Weeping Pine *Pinus patula.*
Mexican White Pine *Pinus ayacahuite.*
Mexican Yew *Taxus globosa.*

Mexicoa Garay. Orchidaceae. 1 orchid. Pbs to 4×2cm, ovoid to pyriform, 1–2-lvd at apex. Lvs to 15×1.5cm, equitant, coriaceous, linear-lanceolate, arcuate. Fls to 3cm diam., in basal rac. seldom exceeding lvs; tep. elliptic to oblanceolate, white or yellow-tinged, veined rose; lip 3-lobed, yellow, callus orange-yellow. Mex. Z10.
M. ghiesbreghtiana (A. Rich. & Gal.) Garay.
→*Oncidium.*

Meyer Lemon *Citrus meyeri.*

Meyerophytum Schwantes. Aizoaceae. 4 succulent perennials, slender, freely branched, papillose. Lvs paired, united, lf pairs dimorphic. Fls solitary. S Afr. Z9.
M. meyeri (Schwantes) Schwantes. Highly succulent, forming dense mounds. Lvs 10–4mm, united to form round, scarcely cleft bodies, becoming red-tinged. Fls to 3.5cm diam., flame-coloured. W Cape.
→*Mitrophyllum.*

Mezereon *Daphne mezereum.*

Meziothamnus Harms = *Abromeitiella.*

Miami Mist *Phacelia purshii.*

Mibora Adans. EARLY SAND-GRASS; SAND BENT. Gramineae. 1 ann. grass to 3cm, rarely to 15cm. Lvs tufted, arching, grey-green; blades to 2.5cm, v. narrow; ligules obtuse, translucent. Rac. spike-like, secund, erect to drooping, to 2cm, tinged red or purple; spikelets distichous, overlapping, laterally compressed, oblong, 1-fld to 3mm. Late winter–spring. Medit., coastal W Eur. Z7.
M. minima (L.) Desv.
M. verna P. Beauv. = *M. minima.*

Michaelmas Daisy *Aster novi-belgii.*

Michauxia L'Hérit. Campanulaceae. 7 short-lived robust perenn. herbs. Lvs irregularly dentate, pinnately lobed or lyrate. Fls in dense spikes, rac. or pan., 8–10-merous; cal. with reflexed appendages between lobes; cor. lobes narrow, recurved; sta. free; style thick, projecting. E Medit., SW Asia. Z7.
M. campanuloides L'Hérit. ex Ait. St. stout, to 1.75m, hispid, branched near top. Lvs lyrate or pinnatifid, lower lvs with long winged petiole. Fls pendulous, on st. and br.; cal. lobes to 1cm, ciliate; cor. lobes suffused purple. Summer. Syr., E Medit.
M. laevigata Vent. Stout, to 2m, usually glab. Lower lvs oblong lanceolate, biserrate, pubesc., long-petiolate. Fls in lax rac.; cal. lobes to 0.6cm, ciliate; cor. lobes white. Summer. N Iran.
M. tchihatchewii Fisch. & C.A. Mey. Stout, to 2m. Lvs pubesc., long-petiolate, oblong. Fls pendulous, in a dense spike; cal. lobes to 12mm; cor. white, initially campanulate. Summer. E Medit.
→*Mindium.*

Michelia L. Magnoliaceae. 45 everg. or decid. shrubs or trees, as for *Magnolia* but fls axill., tep. 6–21, subequal in 2 or more whorls. SE Asia, India, Ceylon. Z9.
M. champaca L. CHAMPACA. Everg. tree, to 25m. Lvs to 28×11cm, lanceolate, ovate, pubesc. beneath. Fls highly fragrant, orange to white; tep. to 20, to 3×0.5cm. India, China, Himal.
M. compressa (Maxim.) Sarg. Erect, everg., tree-like shrub, to 12m. Lvs to 10×4cm, oblong or oblong-ovate, shiny above, pale beneath, coriaceous. Fls fragrant, to 3cm diam., occas. more; tep. 12, oblanceolate, white, exterior purple at base, frequently tinged pale yellow. Jap.
M. doltsopa Buch.-Ham. ex DC. Tree, to 12m. Lvs to 18×8cm, oblong-lanceolate, glossy above, grey-sericeous beneath. Fls to 5×4cm, ovoid to globose, fragrant, tep. oblong-lanceolate, white. SW China, E Himal., E Tibet.
M. excelsa (Wallich) Bl. ex Wallich = *M. doltsopa.*
M. figo (Lour.) Spreng. BANANA SHRUB. Everg. shrub to 4.5m, densely branched. Lvs 10×5cm, elliptic-oblong, dark green. Fls to 3cm diam., cupulate, scented of banana; tep usually ± erect, ivory tinged yellow, base and margins tinged rose to purple. China.
M. fuscata (Andrews) Wallich = *M. figo.*
M. glauca Wight = *M. nilagirica.*
M. lanuginosa Wallich = *M. velutina.*
M. nilagirica Zenk. Shrub or medium-sized tree. Lvs to 15cm, elliptic, hard, shiny, glab., or pubesc. only on veins beneath. Fls white or creamy, to 10cm across, tep. 9–12, obovate, short-lived. S India.
M. ovalifolia Wight = *M. nilagirica.*
M. pulneyensis Wight = *M. nilagirica.*
M. sinensis Hemsl. & Wils. Tree to 15m. Bark dary grey. Lvs to 14×5cm, ovate-oblong or oblanceolate, glossy above, glaucous beneath, coriaceous. Fls ivory-white, tep. to 14. W China.
M. velutina DC. As for *M. doltsopa*, but lvs narrower, to 25×6cm, grey-pubesc. beneath. Fls to 5cm across, tep. oblanceolate. India (Bhutan, Sikkim).
M. wilsonii Finet & Gagnep. = *M. sinensis.*
→*Liriodendron, Liriopsis* and *Magnolia.*

Michoacan Pine *Pinus devoniana.*
Mickey-mouse Plant *Ochna serrulata.*

Micranthemum Michx. Scrophulariaceae. 3 short-lived aquatic herbs. Lvs opposite, sessile. Fls solitary, small, axill.; cal. 4-partite; cor. 1–2-lipped; sta. 2, from throat. Summer. Americas. Z9.
M. micranthemoides (Nutt.) Wettst. St. to 20cm, sprawling or floating, then ascending. Lvs 0.5cm, elliptic, entire. Fls white. E US.
M. umbrosum (J.F. Gmel.) S.F. Blake. St. sprawling, to 30cm. Lvs to 1cm, elliptic or orbicular. Fls white. SE US, C & S Amer.

Micranthocereus Backeb. Cactaceae. 9 subshrubby to tall columnar cacti; st. cylindric, ribbed; areoles close-set, with spines and sometimes wool. Fls from cephalium, tubular; pericarpel and tube naked; tep. short, erect or spreading. Fr. red. CE Braz.

M. polyanthus (Werderm.) Backeb. Shrub to 1.2m, branching from base; st. 3.5–5cm diam.; ribs c15–20; areoles woolly; central spines c3–7, to 3cm, yellow, brown or red-brown, radial spines c20–30, 5–12mm, white to golden. Fls numerous, 16–18mm; tube pink-red; tep. erect, 2–3mm, outer pink, inner creamy white. E Braz. Z9.
→*Arrojadoa.*

Micranthus (Pers.) Ecklon. Iridaceae. 3 perenn. cormous herbs. Lvs linear, partly sheathing. Spikes distichous, fls irregular; tube slightly curved, lobes ± equal, spreading; sta. inserted near top of tube, usually arched; style br. 6, short. S Afr. Z9.

M. junceus (Bak.) N.E. Br. St. 20–70cm, usually unbranched. Lvs 3–4, the 2 lowest long, terete, with axill. bulbils. Spike to 25cm, often with bulbils in lower bracts; fls slightly scented, pale to deep blue; tube 4–5mm, lobes 5–6mm, oblong. Summer.

M. plantagineus (Pers.) Ecklon. St. 25–40cm, sometimes branched. Lvs 3, the 2 lowest often with bulbils at base. Spike to 20cm; fls slightly scented, pale to deep blue, outer lobes sometimes tipped red; tube 4–5mm, lobes 5–6mm, oblong. Summer.

M. tubulosus (Burm.) N.E. Br. St. 20–35cm, unbranched. Lvs 3–5, the lowest 2–3 with tubular, inflated blades. Spike 7–17cm, often with bulbils in lower bracts; fls scented, blue to white; tube 5–6mm, lobes 5–6mm, oblong. Summer.

Microbiota Komar. Cupressaceae. 1 prostrate everg. conifer to 70cm high, to 2m or more across. Foliage aromatic, resinous, in flat sprays, curving downwards, bright green turning bronze in cold conditions, lvs to 3×1mm, facial lvs triangular or needle-like, lat. lvs convex. Cones globose, to 2×6mm; scales to 4, coriaceous to woody. One seed per cone, 2mm, smooth ovoid, unwinged. SE Sib. Z3.
M. decussata Komar.

Microcachrys Hook. f. ex Hook. Podocarpaceae. 1 everg. spreading conifer to 1m. Branchlets procumbent, whip-like, tetragonal. Lvs decussate, overlapping, scale-shaped, 1.5–3mm. Fertile cones ovoid to globose, 5–8×5mm, scales spirally arranged, 15–30, fleshy, triangular, 2mm, red when mature, translucent. W Tasm. Z8.
M. tetragona Hook. f.

Microcitrus Swingle. Rutaceae. 5 or 6 shrubs or small trees, armed or unarmed. Juvenile lvs small cataphylls, intermediate lvs small, linear-elliptic, adult lvs described below. Fls small, 4–5-merous, white to cream, fragrant; sta. numerous, free; ovary 4–8-locular. Fr. rounded ovoid to cylindric, full of acid pulp. Aus., New Guinea. Z10.

M. australasica (F. Muell.) Swingle. FINGER LIME. Tall shrub or small tree; spines to 1cm. Lvs to 2.5×1.5cm, lozenge-shaped, obscurely dentately above, truncate at base, truncate or emarginate at apex. Fr. 7–10×2cm, cylindric-fusiform, often slightly curved, yellow tinged green, peel rough. Aus. (S Queensld & N NSW).

M. australis (Planch.) Swingle. AUSTRALIAN ROUND LIME; NATIVE ORANGE. Tree, 9–18m, spines to 1cm. Lvs 3–4×2–3cm, entire, obovate or obcordate, cuneate at base. Fr. 2.5–5cm, strongly aromatic, globose, grass-green. NE Aus.

M. papuana H.F. Winters. Shrub to 2.5m, spiny, foliage slightly lime-scented when crushed. Lvs 15–25×2–6mm, linear to elliptic or obovate, minutely crenate, emarginate at apex, tapered to base, black glandular-punctate beneath. Fr. 5–8×1cm, cylindric, beaked at apex, green maturing to yellow, peel thin and granular, with oil glands. New Guinea.

M. warburgiana (Bail.) Tan. Twigs v. slender; spines 4mm. Lvs 4–6×1–2cm, rhombic-lanceolate to elliptic, minutely crenate, rounded or emarginate at apex, cuneate at base. Fr. 2cm diam., globose, peel thin, with numerous oil glands. SE New Guinea.

Microcycas (Miq.) A. DC. Zamiaceae. 1 everg., arborescent cycad to 20m. St. columnar, simple. Lvs to 2m, pinnate in dense term. crowns, downy at first; pinnae to 80 pairs, to 20cm, lanceolate, glossy, reflexed. ♀ strobilus to 70×15cm with many hexagonal russet, felty sporophylls. Cuba. Z10.
M. calocoma (Miq.) A. DC. PALMA CORCHO.

Microglossa DC.
M. albescens (DC.) Benth. ex C.B. Clarke. = *Aster albescens.*

Microgramma Presl. Polypodiaceae. 20 epiphytic ferns. Rhiz. creeping, covered with roots and scales. Fronds entire, leathery; sterile fronds ovate, fertile narrower; stipes distant. Trop.

Amer., Afr. Z10.
M. bifrons (Hook.) Lell. = *Solanopteris bifrons.*

M. ciliata (Willd.) Alston. Allied to *M. piloselloides*, distinguished by narrowly linear fronds. Trop. Amer.

M. heterophyllum (L.) Wherry. Epiphytic or epilithic fern. St. climbing or wide-creeping, 1mm wide. Sterile fronds to 10×2cm, oval or elliptic to broadly lanceolate or linear-lanceolate, entire to undulate, notched or pinnatifid; fertile fronds to 16cm, narrower; stipes to 2cm, glab. Flor., W Indies.

M. lycopodioides (L.) Copel. Epiphytic or epilithic fern. Rhiz. wide-creeping, much-branched. Sterile fronds to 15×2.5cm, strap-shaped to linear-lanceolate, entire or somewhat undulate; fertile fronds to 20×1.5cm, linear to oblong or elliptic; stipes to 1.5cm. Trop. Amer., Afr.

M. nitida (J. Sm.) A.R. Sm. Epiphytic fern. Rhiz. long-creeping, much-branched, to 7mm wide; sterile fronds to 15×4cm, lanceolate or elliptic, entire and somewhat cartilaginous, lustrous; fertile fronds, linear to oblong; stipes 1cm. C Amer., W Indies.

M. owariensis (Desv.) Alston. Related to *P. lycopodioides*, but with sterile fronds oval or ovate, smaller, wider. Trop. Afr.

M. piloselloides (L.) Copel. SNAKE POLYPODY. Epiphytic fern. Rhiz. wide-creeping or climbing, 1mm wide. Sterile fronds to 5×2cm, ovate or obovate or lanceolate or elliptic; fertile fronds to 9×1cm, linear to lanceolate, occas. dentate; stipes to 2cm. Trop. Amer.

M. piloselloides (L.) Copel. = *Drymoglossum piloselloides.*

M. squamulosa (Kaulf.) Sota. Epiphytic fern. Rhiz. creeping. Fronds to 8cm, stipitate, virtually uniform, erect, linear-lanceolate to oblong-elliptic. Trop. Amer.

M. vacciniifolia (Langsd. & Fisch.) Copel. Epiphytic fern. Rhiz. wide-creeping or climbing, much-branched. Sterile fronds to 5×1cm, rounded or ovate to elliptic, obtuse; fertile fronds to 10×0.7cm, linear to strap-shaped, acute or truncate, entire and often revolute. W Indies, Trop. S Amer.
→*Phlebodium* and *Polypodium.*

Microlepia Presl. Dennstaedtiaceae. 45–50 terrestrial or epilithic ferns. Rhiz. creeping, subterranean, covered with bristles and massed roots. Fronds stipitate, uniform, 1–4-pinnate or -pinnatifid, thin-textured, pubesc., seg. notched to lobed. Trop. & subtrop. Z10.

M. firma Mett. Rhiz. erect. Fronds to 80cm, 2–3-pinnate or -pinnatifid, deltoid, sparsely pubesc., firm-textured, pinnae to 20×10cm, ovate to deltoid, pinnules notched to lobed; stipes to 40cm, brown. Trop. Asia (Indochina).

M. galeottii Fée = *Saccoloma inaequale.*

M. grandissima Hayata = *M. platyphylla.*

M. hirsuta Presl. = *Davallodes hirsutum.*

M. hirta Presl. Rhiz. creeping. Fronds to 1.8m×60cm, 3–4-pinnate or -pinnatifid, ovate to deltoid, densely pubesc., pinnae to 30×10cm, ovate or deltoid to lanceolate, pinnules lanceolate, seg. oblong, toothed to lobed; stipes to 80cm, pubesc. Trop. Asia (India, Sri Lanka).

M. hirta sensu auct., non Presl = *M. pyramidata.*

M. inaequalis (Kunze) Presl = *Saccoloma inaequale.*

M. jamaicensis (Hook.) Fée = *M. speluncae.*

M. marginata (Panz.) C. Chr. Rhiz. long-creeping. Fronds to 55×40cm, 1–2-pinnate or -pinnatifid, ovate to lanceolate, pubesc., pinnae to 20×3cm, linear, notched to lobed or pinnatifid, seg. oblong; stipes to 50cm, pubesc. Trop. Asia.

M. platyphylla (D. Don) J. Sm. Rhiz. creeping. Fronds to 1.4m, 2–3-pinnate or -pinnatifid, ovate to deltoid, leathery, glab., pinnae to 40×20cm, lanceolate, pinnules to 12cm, distant, linear to lanceolate, seg. obtuse, toothed; stipes to 1m, glab. Trop. Asia.

M. pyramidata (Wallich) Lacaita. Rhiz. creeping. Fronds to 1.8m×60cm, 3–4-pinnate or -pinnatifid, deltoid, pubesc. on veins beneath, pinnae to 30×10cm, ovate to lanceolate, pinnules lanceolate, seg. oblong, margin toothed; stipes to 60cm. Trop. Asia (China).

M. speluncae (L.) Moore. Rhiz. to 1cm wide. Fronds to 1.5×1m, 3–4-pinnate or -pinnatifid, deltoid, papery, pinnae to 50×20cm, deltoid or lanceolate to oblong, pinnules to 80×25mm, lanceolate to deltoid, seg. oblong, toothed or notched to lobed; stipes to 50cm, rough, sparsely short-pubesc. Trop.

M. strigosa (Thunb.) Presl. Rhiz. to 5mm wide, creeping. Fronds to 80×30cm, 2–3-pinnate or -pinnatifid, ovate to lanceolate, short-pubesc. on veins, pinnae to 20×4cm, to 5cm, linear to lanceolate, pinnules to 25×10mm, rhomboid to oblong, notched at apex, toothed or lobed; stipes to 35cm, rough, pubesc. Trop. Asia (India to Jap., Sri Lanka to Polyn.).
→*Acrophorus, Aspidium, Davallia, Scypholepis* and *Trichomanes.*

Micromeles Decne.
M. keissleri Schneid. = *Sorbus keissleri*.
M. rhamnoides Decne. = *Sorbus rhamnoides*.

Micromeria Benth. Labiatae. 70 aromatic perenn. or ann., herbs or dwarf shrubs. St. tetragonal, erect. Infl. a whorled spike; cal. 13–15-veined, teeth 5; cor. bilabiate, upper lip erect, lower lip 3-lobed, tube straight; sta. 4. Medit., Cauc., SW China. Z7 unless specified.
M. alternipilosa K. Koch = *Satureja spicigera*.
M. chamissonis (Benth.) Greene. YERBA BUENA. Perenn. with st. trailing and rooting, to 70cm. Lvs to 3.5cm, ovate, obtuse, crenate, glab., petiolate. Fls solitary, axill; cor. to 1cm, white or purple. Spring and autumn. W US.
M. corsica (Benth.) Lév. = *Acinos corsicus*.
M. croatica (Pers.) Schott. Densely pubesc. tufted shrub to 20cm. Lvs to 1×0.8cm, ovate, acute, entire. Whorls to 12-fld; cor. to 15mm, violet. Balk.
M. dalmatica Benth. Perenn. herb, pubesc., to 50cm. St. erect, simple or branched. Lvs to 2×1.5cm, ovate, obtuse, obscurely dentate, punctate beneath. Whorls to 60-fld; cor. to 6mm, white or pale lilac. Balk. Z6.
M. douglasii (Benth.) Benth. = *M. chamissonis*.
M. ericifolia (Roth) Bornm. = *M. varia*.
M. graeca (L.) Benth. Dwarf shrub to 50cm. St. many, erect, simple. Lvs to 1.2×0.7cm, ovate, revolute. Infl. loose; fls to 18 per whorl; cor. to 13mm, purple. Medit. ssp. *graeca*. Wider middle and upper lvs. ssp. *consentina* (Ten.) Guinea. Autumn-flowering. ssp. *fructicosola* (Bertol.) Guinea. Lvs fascicled. ssp. *garganica* (Briq.) Chater. Upper lvs linear. ssp. *imperica* Chater. Linear middle and upper lvs. ssp. *longiflora* (C. Presl) Nyman. Peduncles rigid. ssp. *tenuifolia* (Ten.) Nyman. Whorls to 4-fld.
M. juliana (L.) Benth. SAVORY. Dwarf pubesc. shrub, to 40cm. St. numerous, erect, mostly simple. Lvs to 1.3cm, ovate to linear-lanceolate, revolute, sessile. Whorls to 20-fld, sessile; cor. to 4mm, purple. Medit.
M. marginata (Sm.) Chater. Dwarf shrub to 20cm. St. puberulent, ascending, mostly simple. Lvs to 1.2×0.5cm, ovate, entire, puberulent or glab. beneath. Whorls lax, to 12-fld; cor. to 16mm, purple or violet. Maritime Alps.
M. piperella (Bertol.) Benth. = *M. marginata*.
M. rupestris (Wulf. ex Jacq.) Benth. = *M. thymifolia*.
M. thymifolia (Scop.) Fritsch. Perenn. to 50cm. St. woody at base, glab. or puberulent. Lvs to 2×1.2cm, ovate to oblong, petiolate, punctate beneath. Whorls to 30-fld, with short pedicels; cor. to 9mm, white or violet. Balk., S It., Hung. Z6.
M. varia Benth. Procumbent perenn. to 30cm. St. woody at base. Lvs ovate to lanceolate, revolute. Whorls to 10-fld; fls small; cor. slightly larger than cal., purple. Summer. Madeira. 'Aurea': lvs golden.
→*Satureja* and *Thymus*.

Micropterum Schwantes.
M. cuneifolium (Jacq.) Schwantes = *Dorotheanthus bellidiformis*.
M. limpidum (Ait.) Schwantes = *Dorotheanthus bellidiformis*.

Microsorium Link. Polypodiaceae. (*Microsorum*). 40 largely epiphytic ferns. Rhiz. creeping or climbing, smooth or curved in scales and roots. Fronds stipitate, simple, pinnatifid or pinnate. Trop. Afr. to Asia, Australasia, Polyn. Z10.
M. alternifolium (Willd.) Copel. = *M. nigrescens*.
M. diversifolium (Willd.) Copel. KANGAROO FERN; HOUND'S TONGUE FERN. Epiphytic or epilithic. Rhiz. long-creeping, to 8mm wide, fleshy, glaucous. Fronds leathery, glab., bright green; simple fronds to 25×5cm, linear to oblong, entire or undulate; irregularly pinnatifid fronds to 30×15cm, seg. to 10×3cm, broadly lanceolate to oblong; regularly and deeply pinnatifid fronds to 45×22cm, seg. to 15×2.5cm, linear to oblong; stipes to 20cm, glab., grooved, pale brown. Aus., Tasm., NZ.
M. ensatosessilifrons (Hayata) H. Itô = *Colysis hemionitidea*.
M. fortunei (Moore) Ching. Rhiz. to 4mm wide. Fronds to 60×5cm, simple, somewhat undulate; stipes to 25cm, mostly glab. China, Taiwan.
M. linguaeforme (Mett.) Copel. Epiphytic fern. Rhiz. creeping. Fronds to 50×9cm, sessile or short-stipitate, erect, simple, base enlarged, scarious, collecting plant-litter, entire or undulate, thin-textured, brown at base. Philipp., Borneo, to New Guinea, Fiji.
M. membranaceum (D. Don) Ching. Rhiz. creeping, to 1cm wide. Fronds to 1m×15cm, simple or pinnatifid, elliptic to lanceolate, entire or undulate, membranous; seg. narrowed; stipes to 12cm, winged. India, Sri Lanka, to China, Taiwan, Philipp.

M. musifolium (Bl.) Ching. Epiphytic or epilithic fern. Rhiz. short-creeping. Fronds to 1m×12cm, sessile, erect, simple, ovate to oblong or strap-shaped, entire, papery to leathery. Malaysia, Indon., Philipp. to New Guinea, Polyn.
M. nigrescens (Bl.) Copel. PIMPLE FERN. Epiphytic or epilithic fern. Rhiz. creeping, fleshy. Fronds to 80×45cm or more, deeply pinnatifid, oblong, membranous, dark blue-green, seg. to 30×4cm, lanceolate, to oblong or linear, entire or undulate; stipes to 50cm, lustrous brown. S India, Sri Lanka, Malaysia, to Aus. (Queensld), Polyn.
M. normale (D. Don) Ching. Epiphytic fern. Rhiz. long-creeping or climbing, to 5mm wide. Fronds to 60×5cm, lanceolate to strap-shaped, entire or undulate, thin-textured; stipes to 5cm, straw-coloured. N India to S China, Malaysia and New Guinea, Aus.
M. novae-zelandiae (Bak.) Copel. Epiphytic fern. Rhiz. long-creeping or climbing, to 1cm wide, woody. Fronds to 120×35cm, deeply pinnatifid, lanceolate to oblong, firmly leathery, dark green, seg. to 20cm×15mm, lanceolate to linear or oblong, entire to somewhat undulate at base; stipes to 30cm, lustrous, light brown. NZ.
M. pappei (Mett. ex Kuhn) Tard. Epiphytic or epilithic fern. Rhiz. creeping, to 3mm wide. Fronds to 70×8cm, simple, elliptic, entire to undulate, leathery to membranous; stipes to 15cm, light green. Trop. Afr., Madag.
M. parksii (Copel.) Copel. Epiphytic or terrestrial fern. Rhiz. creeping, to 5mm wide. Fronds to 45×30cm, deeply pinnatifid to pinnate, erect, papery, seg. to 20cm×15mm, somewhat undulate; stipes to 60cm, glab., straw-coloured. Fiji.
M. pteropus (Bl.) Copel. Epilithic, amphibious fern. Rhiz. creeping, to 3mm wide, fleshy, green. Fronds membranous; simple fronds to 20×4cm, lanceolate to obovate; trilobate fronds to 40×5cm; stipes to 20cm, scaly. India, Malaysia, to S China, Taiwan, Philipp.
M. punctatum (L.) Copel. CLIMBING BIRD'S-NEST FERN. Epiphytic fern. Rhiz. medium-creeping, to 12mm wide, woody to fleshy. Fronds to 120×8cm, simple, lanceolate, entire, leathery and fleshy, glab.; stipes to 1cm. Trop. Afr., Asia, Australasia, Polyn. 'Cristatum': fronds erect, tipped with a crest, pale green. 'Grandiceps': fronds pendent, crested, spreading and branched at apex, leathery.
M. rubidum (Kunze) Copel. Epiphytic fern. Rhiz. wide-creeping, to 1cm wide, fleshy. Fronds 1m×30cm, pinnatifid almost to rachis, narrowly oblong, leathery, seg. to 25×1.5cm, narrowly oblong, entire to undulate; stipes to 50cm. N India, Malaysia to Polyn.
M. scandens (Forst. f.) Tind. FRAGRANT FERN. Epiphytic fern. Rhiz. long-creeping and climbing, to 7mm wide, much-branched. Fronds to 35×1cm, thin-textured, musk-scented, dull dark green, simple and narrowly lanceolate or elliptic to linear, entire to deeply and irregularly pinnatifid, to 50×15cm, seg. to 10×1.5cm, linear to lanceolate, or oblong, or ovate. Stipes to 10cm, grooved, ± glab. Aus., NZ.
M. scolopendrium (Burm. f.) Copel. WART FERN. Rhiz. long-creeping, to 1cm wide, fleshy. Fronds to 40×30cm, deeply pinnatifid, oblong to ovate, or simple, lanceolate, lustrous, light green, seg. to 15×3cm, lanceolate to linear; stipes to 30cm. Trop. Afr., Asia, Australasia, Polyn.
M. steerei (Harrington) Ching. Rhiz. to 12mm wide. Fronds to 40×8cm, elliptic to lanceolate to oblong, entire, membranous. China, Taiwan, SE Asia.
M. superficiale (Bl.) Ching. Epiphytic fern. Rhiz. long-creeping or climbing, woody. Fronds to 30×5cm, simple, lanceolate to oblong or linear, entire, membranous; stipes to 15cm, glab. N India, Indon., Jap., to Aus.
→*Acrostichum, Drynaria, Phymatodes, Phymatosorus, Pleopeltis* and *Polypodium*.

Microstrobos J. Gdn & L. Johnson. Podocarpaceae. 2 dioecious shrubs to 2m, spreading. Lvs spirally arranged, imbricate, scale-like. ♂ cones ovoid or subglobose, erect, to 3mm; 10–15 scales. Seed cones term., to 3mm, with 4–8 scales; scales 1–1.5mm, thick-based with acuminate tip, containing 1 seed, green-brown, dry. SE Aus., Tasm. Z8.
M. fitzgeraldii (F. Muell.) J. Gdn & L. Johnson. BLUE MOUNTAIN PINE. Semiprostrate shrub, to 60cm×1m. Twigs to 5mm diam., pendent. Lvs to 3mm, loosely overlapping, olive green; stomatal bands white below. NSW. Z8.
M. niphophilus Gdn & Johnson. TASMAN DWARF PINE. Shrub to 2m. Br. short, stiff. Lvs 1.5–2×1.5mm, densely arranged, green. Tasm. Z8.
→*Pherosphaera*.

Microterangis Schltr. ex Sengh. Orchidaceae. 4 epiphytic monopodial orchids. Lvs to 15×4cm, ligulate to obovate-oblong, 2-ranked on short st. Rac. many-fld; fls small, sep. and pet. free, similar; lip entire or dentate at apex, spurred; spur about same length as lip. Madag., Masc. Is., Comoros Is. Z9.

M. boutonii (Rchb. f.) Sengh. Rac. to 17cm, many-fld, fls yellow; tep. ovate-triangular, pet. slightly shorter than sep.; lip tridentate at apex; spur filiform. Comoros Is.

M. hariotiana (Kränzl.) Sengh. Rac. numerous, pendent, sometimes 2–3 arising together; 10–20cm, many-fld; fls red-brown; 1–2mm, ovate, obtuse; lip 2mm, entire, subcordate at base, similar to tep. but slightly wider; spur apex swollen. Comoros Is.

M. hildebrandtii (Rchb. f.) Sengh. Rac. laxly many-fld; fls yellow-orange; tep. 2–3mm, ligulate, apex rounded; lip 2–3mm, oblong, acute; spur filiform but swollen at apex. Comoros Is.

→*Angraecopsis, Angraecum* and *Chamaeangis*.

Microtis R. Br. Orchidaceae. 12 herbaceous terrestrial orchids. Lf solitary. Fls in dense spike; dors. sep. incurved, erect, lat. sep. oblong or lanceolate; pet. narrower, incurved; lip sessile, disc callose. E Asia, Aus., NZ. Z9.

M. unifolia (Forst. f.) Rchb. f. To 50cm. Lf terete, elongate. Fls v. small, golden to pale green. Late autumn–winter.

Midnight Horror *Oroxylum*.
Mignonette *Reseda odorata*.
Mignonette Tree *Lawsonia*.
Mignonette Vine *Anredera cordifolia*.

Mikania Willd. Compositae. *c*300 everg., perenn., woody or herbaceous lianes. Lvs usually opposite, entire to dentate. Cap. discoid, small, clustered in spikes, rac. or pan.; involucre cylindric to ovoid. Trop., esp. New World.

M. amara Willd. = *M. parviflora*.
M. apiifolia DC. = *M. dentata*.
M. dentata Spreng. Woody, clothed in purple hairs. Lvs palmately lobed, 5–7, oblong-rhombic to oblanceolate-rhombic, entire to pinnatifid or 3-lobed, dark green above, purple beneath. Cap. clustered in lax corymbs; flts white tinged yellow. C & S Braz. Z10.

M. hemisphaerica Schultz-Bip. ex Bak. Herbaceous, glab. Lvs to 10cm, ovate, cordate at base, acuminate, serrate-dentate. Cap. in a corymbose pan.; flts white flushed with pink. Braz. Z10.

M. parviflora (Aubl.) Karst. Herbaceous to woody. Lvs large, ovate, entire to remotely dentate, apex acuminate, base acute or decurrent, glab. or nearly so. Cap. in cymes; flts pale lime green or pale blue. C & Trop. S Amer. Z10.

M. scandens (L.) Willd. WILD CLIMBING HEMP-WEED; CLIMBING HEMP-VINE. Herbaceous, subglabrous. Lvs to 10cm, triangular to hastate, base deeply cordate, entire or remotely repand-dentate, glab. to slightly scabrous or pubesc. Cap. in dense corymbs, strongly vanilla-scented; flts white, tinged yellow, or lilac to purple. Summer. Trop. Amer. Z4.

M. ternata (Vell.) Robinson = *M. dentata*.

Mila Britt. & Rose. Cactaceae. 1 low, clustering cactus; st. 30×(1–)1.5–2.5(–4)cm, short-cylindric; ribs 10–13; areoles 2–5mm apart, felted at first; spines usually more than 20, central 1–8, 1–3cm, radial spines 10–40, 5–20mm. Fl. 2–3.5×2–3cm, subapical, funnelform-campanulate, yellow. Fr. to 12–15mm, globose, red-tinged, woolly. C Peru. Z9.

M. caespitosa Britt. & Rose.
M. kubeana Werderm. & Backeb. = *M. caespitosa*.
M. nealeana Backeb. = *M. caespitosa*.

Mile-a-minute Vine *Polygonum baldschuanicum*.
Mile Tree *Casuarina equisetifolia*.
Milfoil *Achillea; Myriophyllum*.

Milicia (Sim) C. Berg. Moraceae. 2 trees. Lvs distichous, stipulate. Infl. axill., spicate, bracteate; ♂ fls with tep. 4, basally connate; sta. 4, inflexed in bud, pistillode present; ♀ fls with tep. 4, basally connate; stigmas 2, filiform, unequal. Fruiting perianth enlarged, fleshy, green; fr. drupaceous. Trop. Afr. Z10.

M. africana Sim = *M. excelsa*.
M. excelsa (Welw.) C. Berg. Tree, to 30(–50)m. Lvs 6–20×3.5–10cm, coriaceous, elliptic to oblong, acuminate, base cordate, repand to subentire, puberulent to pubesc. on main veins only, esp. beneath. ♂ infl. a spike, 8–20×0.5cm; ♀ infl. a spike, 2–3×0.5cm. Fr. 2.5–3mm, ellipsoid. Trop. Afr.

→*Chlorophora, Maclura* and *Morus*.

Military Orchid *Orchis militaris*.

Milium L. Gramineae. 6 grasses to 2m. St. in loose tussocks. Lf blades flat; ligules papery, translucent. Pan. loose or contracted; spikelets single-fld. Summer. Eurasia, N Amer. Z5.

M. effusum L. WOOD MILLET. Perenn. to 180cm. Lf blades 30×1.5cm, glab., undulate. Pan. to 30×20cm, lax, lanceolate to ovate or oblong, nodding, light green or tinged purple; br. whorled, flexuous; spikelets to 5mm. 'Aureum' ('Bowles' Golden Grass'): lvs and spikelets pale golden yellow to lime green. 'Variegatum': lvs bright green striped white; weak growing. Z6.

M. multiflorum Cav. = *Oryzopsis miliacea*.

Milk-and-wine Lily *Crinum zeylanicum*.
Milk Barrel *Euphorbia cereiformis; E. heptagona*.
Milk Bush *Euphorbia tirucalli*.
Milkmaids *Burchardia*.
Milk Parsley *Peucedanum palustre*.
Milk Thistle *Sonchus*.
Milk Tree *Brosimum*.
Milk Vetch *Astragalus*.
Milkweed *Asclepias*.
Milkwort *Polygala* (*P. vulgaris*).
Milkwort Boronia *Boronia polygalifolia*.

Milla Cav. Liliaceae (Alliaceae). 6 cormous perenn. herbs. St. erect. Lvs 2–7, linear, flat to terete. Fls 2–4 per scapose umbel, rarely solitary, with long pedicels; tep. united forming a long tube, lobes 6; sta. 6, protruding beyond cor.; ovary 3-celled. S US, C Amer. Some spp. formerly in *Milla* are now found under *Brodiaea* and *Leucocoryne*.

M. biflora Cav. To 30cm. Lvs 2–7, 10–50cm, narrow-linear, channelled above, subterete, blue-green. Fls 1–6, occas. 8; perianth campanulate-funnelform, seg. 1.5–3.5cm, overlapping, white sometimes tinted lilac, usually striped or veined green beneath.

M. uniflora Graham = *Ipheion uniflorum*.

Millet *Panicum miliaceum; Sorghum*.

Millettia Wight & Arn. Leguminosae (Papilionoideae). 90 usually everg. lianes, shrubs or trees. Lvs imparipinnate. Fls pea-like usually in pan. or rac. Fr. linear or oblong, swollen or flat, ligneous or coriaceous. E Asia, India, Afr., Madag. Z10 unless specified.

M. dura Dunn. Small tree or shrub to 13m. Lvs initially rusty-pubesc.; petiole 3–5cm; lfts 8–9×2–3cm, 15–19, lanceolate-oblong, glab. above except on midrib and margins, downy beneath. Fls mauve in rusty-pubesc., drooping pan. 10–20cm long. E Afr.

M. grandis (E. Mey) Skeels. Tree to 12m. Lvs *c*15cm×10–13cm; petioles velvety, red; lfts *c*7×1.9cm, in 5 or 6 or 7 pairs, oblong or broadly lanceolate, thinly sericeous beneath. Fls purple. Spring. S Afr.

M. griffoniana Baill. Tree to 17m. Lfts to 10cm, in 3–4 pairs, oval, apex acuminate. Fls in erect rac. to 15cm, deep purple. Trop. W Afr.

M. nitida Benth. Tall liane. Lfts 0.5–7.5cm, usually 5, ovate or elliptic-oblong, leathery, glab. Fls large, purple, densely packed in downy pan. S China, Hong Kong, Taiwan. Z8.

M. ovalifolia Kurz. Glab. tree of medium height. Lvs to 45cm; lfts in 3 pairs, ovate-elliptic, apex tapering, somewhat glaucous beneath. Fls blue in solitary or grouped delicate rac. to 7.5cm long. Burm.

M. reticulata Benth. Tall ascending shrub. Lfts 3–9×1.5–5.5cm, 5–9, lanceolate to elliptic, apex blunt, base cordate, glab., subcoriaceous. Fls large, fragrant, rose to blue, densely packed in erect, term., glab. or downy pan. 15–20cm. S China, Taiwan. Z9.

M. stuhlmannii Taub. Tree to 20m. Lfts to 13×1cm, 7–9, elliptic-obovate, rounded or notched, subglabrous above, sparsely downy beneath. Fls lilac-white in grey-velutinous, drooping pan. to 25cm long. Malawi, Moz.

Milligania Hook. f. Liliaceae (Asphodelaceae). 4–5 perenn. herbs. St. simple or branched, pilose. Basal lvs tufted, linear-lanceolate, coriaceous, usually woolly, sheathing below; st. lvs few, diminishing. Fls small, campanulate in a term. pan.; perianth seg. 6, spreading. Tasm. Z9.

M. densiflora Hook. f. Lvs 20–25cm, with white silky hairs. St. stout, woolly, many-branched. Perianth seg. 0.6cm, white, sometimes flushed mauve. Midsummer.

M. johnstonii Muell. Dwarf. Lvs to 10cm, white-woolly. Corymbs just exceeding lvs; perianth seg. 0.7cm, white, narrowly oblong, obtuse. Midsummer.

M. longifolia Hook. f. St. 30–60cm, to 5cm diam., villous, br. ascending. Lvs to 60cm, grass-like, sparsely villous beneath. Pan. large, many-fld; bracts large, villous; pedicels arched, silky; perianth seg. white, oblong, obtuse, 0.6cm; anth. yellow. Summer.

Millingtonia L. Bignoniaceae. 1 everg. or decid. tree to 25m. Trunk to 30cm diam., bark corky. Lvs to 1m, 2–3-pinnate, lfts to 6×3cm, lanceolate-elliptic, entire, undulate or crenate. Fls nocturnally fragrant in term., erect, 10–40cm thryses; cal. to 4mm, campanulate, 5-lobed; cor. white ageing ivory, 5-lobed, tube to 8cm, widening to 5cm diam., lobes ovate, acute, 1.5cm; sta. 4, slightly exserted. SE Asia and E Java through Lesser Sunda Is. and S Celebes. Z10.

M. dubiosa Span. = *M. hortensis.*

M. hortensis L.

M. pinnata Blanco = *Radermachera pinnata.*

M. quadripinnata Blanco = *Radermachera pinnata.*

Miltomate *Physalis philadelphica.*

Miltonia Lindl. PANSY ORCHID Orchidaceae. 20 epiphytic orchids. Rhiz. creeping or short. Pbs oblong-ovoid, laterally compressed with 1 or 2 apical strap-shaped lvs, enveloped below by leafy sheaths. Infl. axill., a rac. or rarely a pan., erect or arching; fls widely spreading; pet. similar to sep. or wider; lip broadly spreading from column base, simple or pandurate. Costa Rica to Ecuad. and Braz. Z10.

M. **Bluntii** Lvs and pbs. yellow-green. Fls lilac pink, lip darker. Gdn. orig.

M. **candida** Lindl. Resembles *M. clowesii* except tep. oblong-obtuse; lip shorter than other seg., clasping column at base. Autumn. Braz.

M. **clowesii** Lindl. Infl. to 45cm; tep. yellow, heavily blotched and barred chestnut-brown; sep. to 4×1cm, lanceolate, acuminate, undulate; pet. to 3.5×1cm; lip white at tip, deep purple at base, to 4×2cm, subpandurate, caudate; callus white or yellow, 5–7-keeled. Autumn. Braz.

M. **cuneata** Lindl. Similar to *M. clowesii.* Tep. chocolate-brown tipped and barred yellow-green; lip obovate, slightly undulate, white-cream; callus basal, 2-keeled, spotted rose-purple. Winter–spring. Braz.

M. endresii (Rchb. f.) Nichols. = *Miltoniopsis warscewiczii.*

M. **flavescens** Lindl. Infl. to 10-fld; fls fragrant, straw-yellow; tep. to 50×5mm, linear-oblong to linear-lanceolate; lip to 2.5cm, yellow, spotted blood-red, ovate-oblong, acute, undulate, base pubesc., transversed by 4–6 radiating lines. Summer–autumn. Braz.

M. **Gattonense** Fls white, lip marked yellow. Gdn. orig.

M. moreliana Warn. = *M. spectabilis* var. *moreliana.*

M. phalaenopsis (Lind. & Rchb. f.) Nichols. = *Miltoniopsis phalaenopsis.*

M. **regnellii** Rchb. f. Infl. to 40cm; tep. cream suffused rose to lilac or pale amethyst; sep. to 3×1cm, oblong-lanceolate, recurved; pet. wider; lip to 3.5×3.5cm, pale rose streaked lilac or amethyst, margins white, rotund to obovate, obscurely trilobed; callus of several radiating yellow lines. Early autumn. Braz.

M. roezlii (Rchb. f.) Nichols. = *Miltoniopsis roezlii.*

M. **russelliana** Lindl. Infl. to 30cm; tep. to 3cm, ovate-oblong, red-brown, margins green-yellow; lip oblong, concave, rose-lilac, apex white or pale yellow; disc purple, with 3 ridges. Winter–spring. Braz.

M. **schroederiana** (Rchb. f.) Veitch. Infl. to 50cm; fls fragrant; tep. chestnut brown, marked and tipped pale yellow; sep. to 3×0.5cm, linear-lanceolate, revolute; pet. similar to sep., to 2.5×5cm; lip rose-purple at base, white above to 2.5×1.5cm, subpandurate; callus of 3 protuberances. C Amer.

M. **spectabilis** Lindl. Infl. to 25cm; fls solitary; sep. to 4×1.5cm, white, often tinged rose at base, lanceolate-oblong; pet. similar with white patch at base; lip rose-violet, margins white or pale rose, to 5×4.5cm, obovate-orbicular; callus yellow with pink lines. Autumn. Braz. var. *bicolor* hort. Fls larger; lip with large blotch of violet on upper half. var. *moreliana* (Warn.) Henfr. Fls deep plum-purple; lip streaked and shaded rose, deeply veined.

M. superba Schltr. = *Miltoniopsis warscewiczii.*

M. vexillaria (Rchb. f.) Nichols. = *Miltoniopsis vexillaria.*

M. **warscewiczii** Rchb. f. Infl. to 54cm; tep. cinnamon, white or yellow at apex, to 2.5×1.5cm, oblong-spathulate, undulate; lip to 3×2.5cm, rose-purple, tinged yellow and red-brown, margins white, ovate-suborbicular or suborbicular-obovate, deeply bilobed at apex; disc with 2 small yellow teeth. Peru, Colomb., Costa Rica.

M. **grexes and cvs**
There are many cvs and grexes in *Miltonia*, with pale green foliage and fls in shades of white, pink, red and lilac, among them the classic pansy orchids with broad blooms in deep velvety red.

✕**Miltonidium**. (*Miltonia* ✕*Oncidium*.) Orchidaceae. Gdn hybrids with tall branching sprays of medium-sized fls usually yellow marked brown.

Miltonioides Brieger & Luckel.

M. warscewiczii (Rchb. f.) Brieger & Luckel = *Miltonia warscewiczii.*

Miltoniopsis Godef.-Leb. Orchidaceae. 5 epiphytic or lithophytic orchids closely allied to and resembling *Miltonia.* Z10.

M. **phalaenopsis** (Lind. & Rchb. f.) Garay & Dunsterv. Rac. to 20cm, 3–5-fld; tep. pure white; sep. to 2×1cm, elliptic-oblong, acute; pet. wider, elliptic, obtuse; lip to 2.5×3cm, white blotched and streaked purple-crimson or pale purple, 4-lobed; callus teeth 3, small, blunt with yellow spot on either side. Late spring. Colomb.

M. roezlii (Rchb. f.) Godef.-Leb. Rac. to 30cm, 2–5-fld; sep. to 5×2cm, white, ovate-oblong, acuminate; pet. to 5×2.5cm, white blotched wine-purple at base; lip to 5×5.5cm, white, orange-yellow at base, widely obcordate, callus 3-ridged, 2-toothed. Colomb.

M. vexillaria (Rchb. f.) Godef.-Leb. Rac. to 30cm, 4–6-fld; tep. rose-pink or white flushed rose-pink; sep. to 3×1.5cm, obovate-oblong, recurved above; pet. slightly wider, margins white; lip much larger than sep., white or pale rose, deep rose on disc, subpandurate, cleft; callus yellow, small, 3-toothed. Colomb., Ecuad.

M. warscewiczii (Rchb. f.) Garay & Dunsterv. Rac. to 30cm, 3–6-fld; fls cream-white, each seg. with a rose-purple blotch at base, 3×1.5cm, ovate-elliptic, acute; lip to 3.5×3.5cm, widely pandurate, basal lobes 2 small, rounded, midlobe emarginate; callus yellow, with 3 short ridges. Winter. Costa Rica.

→*Miltonia* and *Odontoglossum.*

Mimetes Salisb. Proteaceae. 12 undershrubs. St. simple, tomentose or villous. Lvs entire or toothed at apex, silky-tomentose or villous. Cap. sessile, solitary in upper lf-axils, 3–12-fld; involucral bracts usually shorter than fls, frequently coloured, often hairy; perianth tube v. short or 0, seg. 4, filiform, often villous; sta. 4. Fr. ovoid, glabrescent, slightly hardened. S Afr. Z9.

M. **cucullata** R. Br. St. 120–150cm, sometimes decumbent, tomentose or villous. Lvs 3–7.5cm, oblong or oblong-lanceolate, 3–5-fid at apex, or entire, glabrescent. Cap. sessile, 5cm, 4–10-fld; bracts linear or lanceolate, minutely pubesc. to subglab.; perianth tube 4mm, seg. filiform, 3mm, pilose, limb 5–6mm, linear, villous; style 5cm. Cape Prov.

M. lyrigera Knight = *M. cucullata.*

Mimicry Plant *Pleiospilos.*

Mimosa *Acacia* (*A. dealbata*).

Mimosa L. Leguminosae (Mimosoideae). 400 thorny and prickly herbs, shrubs or small trees. Lvs bipinnate; pinnae digitately to pinnately arranged, often exhibiting sleep movements and sensitive to touch; lfts paired, opposite; petioles long, pulvinate. Fls sessile, 4–5-merous, in stalked, rounded heads or, less frequently, spikes or rac.; cal. tubular to campanulate, lobes 4–6, narrow; pet. 4 or 5; sta. to 10, fil. long, showy. Fr. oblong, compressed, straight to curved or twisted, flat to moniliform, often prickly. C & S Amer., S US, Asia, Trop. & E Afr. Z9.

M. **argentea** hort ex L.H. Bail. Climber. Young shoots flushed pink. Lvs with 2–3 pairs of pinnae; lfts 40, tipped pink, silvery grey flushed pink beneath. Fl. heads red. Summer. Braz.

M. contorti-siliqua Vell. = *Enterolobium contortisiliqua.*

M. cyclocarpa Jacq. = *Enterolobium cyclocarpa.*

M. fagifolia L. = *Inga laurina.*

M. illinoensis Michx. = *Desmanthus illinoensis.*

M. inga L. = *Inga vera.*

M. juliiflora Sw. = *Prosopis juliiflora.*

M. laurina Sw. = *Inga laurina.*

M. **marginata** Lindl. non Lam. Prostrate shrub with long, slender shoots. Lfts ciliate. Fl. heads purple, long-stalked. Subtrop. S Amer.

M. natans L. f. = *Neptunia oleracea.*

M. nemu Poir. = *Albizia julibrissin.*

M. **pigra** L. Prickly, thicket-forming, pubesc. shrub, 1–4m. Pinnae 4–6 pairs; lfts 3–4mm, crowded, oblong. Fl. heads to 1cm diam., fragrant, bright lilac pink fading to white, ovoid to capitate. S Tex., tropics and warm regions of both hemispheres.

M. plena L. = *Neptunia plena.*

M. **polycarpa** Kunth. Much-branched shrub or subshrub, to 3m rather like a taller, coarser and more prickly *M. pudica.* Lvs sensitive; pinnae 1 pair, lfts to 1.6cm. Fls pink to lilac in globose heads to 2.5cm diam. S Amer. var. *spegazzinii* (Pirotta) Burkart. Lfts 1.25cm, minutely downy.

M. **pudica** L. SENSITIVE PLANT; TOUCH-ME-NOT; SHAME PLANT; LIVE-AND-DIE; HUMBLE PLANT; ACTION PLANT. Prostrate or semi-erect herb to shrub, 0.3–0.8m, often forming compact bush. Lvs v. sensitive; pinnae (1–)2 pairs; lfts 10–25 pairs, grey-green, soft-textured, oblong. Fls pale pink to lilac, in stalked heads to 2cm diam. Summer. S Mex. to C Amer., W Indies, Hawaii, Fiji, Aus. Z9.

M. sensitiva L. SENSITIVE PLANT. Semi-climbing shrub to 2m. Lvs sensitive but less so than in the similar but less woody *M. pudica*; pinnae 1 pair per lf; lfts ovate, acute, glab. above, adpressed-hairy beneath. Fl. heads purple. Trop. Amer.

M. spegazzinii Pirotta = *M. polycarpa* var. *spegazzinii*.

M. ynga Vell. = *Inga edulis*.

Mimosa Bush *Acacia farnesiana*.
Mimose de Quatre Saisons *Acacia retinodes*.

Mimulus L. MONKEY FLOWER; MUSK. Scrophulariaceae. 150 ann. or perenn. herbs or shrubs. Lvs opposite, entire to dentate. Fls axill. or on spike-like rac.; cal. tube usually inflated, angled, unequally 5-toothed or -lobed; cor. 2-lipped, depressed-funnelform, ventrally ridged and downy; sta. 4. Mostly Amer., also S Afr. & Asia.

M. alsinoides Douglas ex Benth. CHICKWEED MONKEY FLOWER. Ann. herb, somewhat glandular-pubesc. to glabrescent. St. 5–25cm, ascending or decumbent, v. slender, often much-branched. Lvs 1–2.5cm, ovate to oblong, minutely dentate. Lvs 1–2.5cm, ovate to oblong, minutely dentate. Pedicels 1–3cm; cor. 10–12mm, yellow, throat narrowly campanulate, faintly 2-ridged, glab., upper lobes ascending, lower lip longer with large dark purple or crimson spot at base of central lobe. Spring–early summer. Amer., Vancouver Is. to Calif.

M. aridus (Abrams) A.L. Grant. Shrub similar to *M. aurantiacus*. Lvs to 4cm, oblanceolate to oblong, crowded. Fls to 5cm, pale flesh-white to yellow. S Calif.

M. aurantiacus Curtis. BUSH MONKEY FLOWER; ORANGE BUSH MONKEY FLOWER. Shrub, 60–120cm, much-branched, finely glandular-pubesc. Lvs 3–7cm, oblong or lanceolate-oblong, serrate, finely pilose beneath. Pedicels 7–15mm, glandular-pubesc.; cor. 3.5–4.5cm, orange or deep yellow, glutinous without, campanulate-funnelform, throat with 2 pubesc. ridges, lobes rounded or erose. Spring–summer. S Oreg. to Calif. Z8.

M. ×bartonianus Rivoire. (*M. cardinalis* ×*M. lewisii*.) Fls rose-red, yellow in throat, spotted red-brown. Gdn. orig.

M. bifidus Penn. Close to *M. longiflorus*. Cor. to 6.5cm, pale yellow, lobes cleft. Calif.

M. brevipes Benth. WIDE-THROATED YELLOW MONKEY FLOWER. Ann. herb, ± minutely glandular-pubesc. St. erect, 40–100cm. Lvs to 10cm, broadly oblong to linear-lanceolate, minutely dentate to entire. Pedicels 0.5–1cm; cor. 2.5–4cm, funnelform, clear yellow with maroon spots within, pubesc. within on 2 ventral ridges, lobes rounded. Spring–summer. Calif. & Baja Calif.

M. ×burnetii hort. (*M. cupreus* ×*M. luteus*.) Perenn. herb. St. tufted, to 30cm. Lvs ovate to oblong, palmately veined. Fls copper-yellow; cor. throat yellow, palate spotted. Gdn origin. Z7.

M. caespitosus Greene = *M. tilingii* var. *caespitosus*.

M. cardinalis Douglas. SCARLET MONKEY FLOWER. Perenn. herb. St. 40–120cm, erect, freely branched, hirsute. Lvs 7–11cm, ovate to oblong-elliptic, minutely sharply sinuate-dentate, glandular-pubesc. Pedicels 5–8cm; cor. 4.5–5cm, strongly bilabiate, lobes scarlet, throat narrow, tinged yellow, with 2 ventral yellow hairy ridges. Summer. Oreg. to Calif. and Nevada, Baja Calif. 'Aurantiacus' ('Orange Perfection'): fls fiery orange-red. 'Grandiflorus': fls dark red. 'Roseus': fls v. large, pink with dark spots. 'Roseus Superbus': fls large, dark pink-red. Z7.

M. cupreus Dombrain. Ann. herb, ± dwarf, glab. or minutely pubesc. St. 10–30cm, branched from base. Lvs 15–30×8–15mm, elliptic to subrhombic-ovate, serrate; cor. 2.5–3.5cm, tube yellow, throat dilated, lower side of lower lip spotted red, lobes spreading, golden yellow aging copper. Summer. S Chile. Cvs listed under this name are referred to *M. ×hybridus*.

M. flemingii Munz. Viscid shrub to 1m. Lvs to 7cm, ovate-oblong to obovate, entire or toothed. Cor. to 4cm, red. S Calif (Channel Is.).

M. fremontii (Benth.) A. Gray. Ann. herb, glandular-pubesc. St. 5–20cm, erect. Lvs to 2.5cm, spathulate to oblanceolate or oblong-lanceolate, dentate to entire. Pedicels 2–4mm; cor. 2–2.5mm, broadly funnelform, crimson or deep pink tinged purple, pubesc. without, ventral ridges 2, yellow, pubesc.; throat deep purple, with yellow with purple spots, lobes rounded-truncate, slightly retuse. Spring–summer. Calif. to N Baja Calif.

M. glutinosus Wendl. = *M. aurantiacus*.
M. glutinosus var. *brachypus* A. Gray = *M. longiflorus*.
M. glutinosus var. *puniceus* A. Gray = *M. puniceus*.
M. grandiflorus T.J. Howell = *M. guttatus*.

M. guttatus Fisch. ex DC. COMMON LARGE MONKEY FLOWER. Ann. or bienn. herb, glab. except infl. St. 40–100cm, erect or decumbent, branched, sometimes stoloniferous. Lvs 1.5–15cm, obovate to subrotund, minutely sinuate-dentate or pinnatifid-dentate towards base. Infl. finely glandular-pubesc.; pedicels 2–6cm; cor. 3–4.5cm, bright yellow, throat with pair of red to purple-brown-spotted hairy ridges, lower lip longer, lobes deflexed-spreading. Spring–summer. Alask. to Mex. 'A.T. Johnson': to 15cm; fls yellow spotted red. Z6.

M. hirsutus Bl. = *Torenia flava*.

M. ×hybridus hort. ex Siebert & Voss. (*M. luteus* ×*M. guttatus*.) Fls large, colour variable. 'Andean Nymph': fls pink with cream-tipped pet. 'Bee's Dazzler': brilliant crimson-red. 'Brilliant': fls deep purple-crimson. Calypso Hybrids: fls large, burgundy, scarlet and gold. 'Duplex': cal. enlarged, colourful. 'Fireflame': bright flame red. 'Highland Pink': fls rich pink. 'Highland Red': fls deep red. 'Highland Yellow': fls yellow. 'Hose in Hose': fls soft tan, one sitting inside the other. 'Inschriach Crimson': dwarf, carpet-forming; fls crimson. 'Leopard': yellow, spotted rust. 'Malibu': to 25cm, growth strong; fls orange. 'Mandarin': fls bright orange, abundant. 'Nanus': habit dwarf; lvs glossy; fls bright orange to gold, with red throat. 'Old Rose': to 15cm; fls bright red. 'Queen's Prize': dwarf; fls large, in bright colours, many spotted and blotched. 'Royal Velvet': to 20cm; fls large velvety, mahogany red with gold throats speckled mahogany. 'Roter Kaiser' ('Red Emperor'): to 20cm high, fls crimson to scarlet. 'Shep': fls large, yellow splashed brown. 'Whitecroft Scarlet': fls vermilion. 'Wisley Red': to 15cm; fls velvety blood red. Z6.

M. langsdorfii Donn ex Greene = *M. guttatus*.

M. lewisii Pursh GREAT PURPLE MONKEY FLOWER. Perenn. herb, glandular-pubesc. St. erect, 30–90cm. Lvs 3–7cm, oblong-elliptic, minutely dentate. Pedicels stout, 3–10cm; cor. 2–5cm, campanulate lobes scarcely differentiated, magenta or white, throat with 2 yellow hairy ridges and maroon spots. Summer. Alask. to Calif. 'Albus': fls white. Z5.

M. longiflorus (Nutt.) Grant. SALMON BUSH MONKEY FLOWER. Glutinous shrub. St. 30–90cm or more, much-branched, pubesc. Lvs 4–8cm, lanceolate or oblanceolate, minutely serrate to entire, glutinous-pubesc. Pedicels 2–7mm, glutinous-pubesc.; cor. 5–6cm, campanulate-funnelform cream to yellow tinged salmon, gland. or glutinous without, throat with 2 low orange ridges, lobes rounded. Spring–summer. var. *linearis* (Benth.) A.L. Grant. Lvs linear-lanceolate. Fls pale yellow. var. *rutilus* A.L. Grant. Fls dark red. ssp. *calycinus* (Eastw.) Munz. Cal. tube expanded; cor. lemon yellow. S Calif. to N Baja Calif. Z9.

M. luteus L. MONKEY MUSK; YELLOW MONKEY FLOWER. Perenn. herb, glab. St. 10–30cm, decumbent to ascending, hollow. Lvs 2–3cm, broadly ovate to oblong, dentate. Cor. 2–5cm, yellow, with deep red or purple spots. Summer. Chile; nat. elsewhere. Z7.

M. luteus var. *cupreus* Hook. in Curtis = *M. cupreus*.
M. luteus var. *variegatus* Hook. = *M. variegatus*.

M. moschatus Douglas. MUSK FLOWER; MUSK PLANT. Perenn. herb, glandular-pilose, sometimes aromatic. St. 10–40cm, decumbent. Lvs to 2.5cm, lanceolate-ovate to oblong-ovate, entire to sinuate-dentate, thin. Pedicels filiform, 1–4cm; cor. 18–25mm, pale yellow, throat tubular, finely brown-spotted and streaked with black, with 2 pilose ridges, lobes similar, spreading. Summer. BC to Newfoundland, S to W Virg. and Calif. Once valued for its heady fragrance, musk; in this century it has been grown in predominantly unscented clones. 'Harisonii': fls larger, 3.5–4cm diam. Z7.

M. nepalensis Benth. ± glab. perenn. herb. St. slender, sprawling, rooting. Lvs to 3.5cm, ovate to ovate-oblong, toothed. Cor. to 2cm, yellow, throat dotted red, palate densely bearded. Himal., China, Jap. Z8.

M. primuloides Benth. Perenn. herb, rhizomatous, rosulate or short-stemmed, downy. St. to 10cm. Lvs to 1–4.5cm, oblanceolate to elliptic-obovate, entire to dentate; cor. 15–20mm, yellow, throat narrowly campanulate, palate deeper yellow and densely hairy, brown-spotted, lobes notched and spreading. Summer. Washington to Calif., E to Idaho, Utah and Ariz. Z4.

M. puniceus (Nutt.) Steud. RED BUSH MONKEY FLOWER. Glutinous shrub. St. 60–150cm, erect, much-branched, minutely pubesc. Lvs 3–10cm, lanceolate, entire or undulate-serrate, minutely pubesc. Pedicels 10–25mm, finely pubesc.; cor. 3.5–4.5cm, narrowly campanulate, scarlet to carmine or salmon-orange, minutely pubesc. and somewhat glutinous without, throat with 2 narrow orange to flame-scarlet ridges, lobes truncate, emarginate or lobed. Spring–summer. Calif. to N Baja Calif. Z9.

M. radicans Hook. f. = *Mazus radicans*.

M. ringens L. ALLEGHENY MONKEY FLOWER. Perenn. herb, glab. St. to 1m, 4-angled or narrowly winged. Lvs 5–10cm, lanceolate to narrowly oblong or oblanceolate, obscurely crenate. Pedicels erect, 2–4cm; cor. 25–30mm, violet-blue, rarely pink or white, throat v. narrow. Summer. N Amer. Z3.

M. roseus Douglas ex Lindl. = *M. lewisii.*

M. tigrinus hort. = *M. ×hybridus.*

M. tilingii Reg. LARGER MOUNTAIN MONKEY FLOWER. Perenn. herb, forming dense mats, glab. St. 5–30cm, decumbent. Lvs 1–3cm, ovate to oval, sinuate-dentate. Pedicels 2.5–5cm; cor. to 4cm, yellow, throat darker with 2 red to brown-spotted hairy ridges, upper lip with ascending-erect lobes, lower lip longer. Summer. W US var. *caespitosus* Grant. Smaller, finely pubesc. St. 3–10cm, crowded. Lvs 5–12mm, narrowly elliptic to ovate, entire to minutely dentate. Cor. 2–3cm. Washington to BC. Z7.

M. variegatus Lodd. Similar to *M. luteus*, but habit more compact. Fls larger; cor. with 2 yellow ventral ridges with brown spots, throat yellow, lobes crimson purple, violet on back. Chile. Z8.

→*Diplacus.*

Mimusops L. Sapotaceae. 57 everg. shrubs and trees. Lvs leathery. Fls in axill. clusters; sep. 6–8, in 2 whorls; cor. 6–8-lobed, each lobe with 2 appendages, sta. and staminodes 8, ovary superior, 8-locular. Fr. a berry. Trop. Afr., 1 sp. India to Malaysia, Burm. and Pacific Is. Z10.

M. elengi L. SPANISH CHERRY; MEDLAR; TANJONG TREE. Tree to at least 20m, with a spreading crown. Lvs 5–16cm, elliptic or ovate to oblong-elliptic, undulate. Fls 1–1.5cm diam., white, then brown, v. fragrant. Fr. 2.5–3.5cm, ovoid or oblong, smooth, orange-red, pulp yellow, edible; seed 1, large. India to Burm., Malaysia and Pacific Is.

Mina La Ll. & Lex.

M. lobata Cerv. = *Ipomoea lobata.*

Mindanao Gum *Eucalyptus deglupta.*
Mind-your-own Business *Soleirolia soleirolii.*
Miner's Lettuce *Montia* (*M. perfoliata*).
Minezuo *Loiseleuria procumbens.*
Min Fir *Abies recurvata.*
Ming Aralia *Polyscias fruticosa.*
Miniature Date Palm *Phoenix roebelinii.*
Miniature Fan Palm *Rhapis excelsa.*
Miniature Grape Ivy *Cissus striata.*
Miniature Holly *Malpighia coccigera.*
Miniature Japanese Ivy *Parthenocissus tricuspidata.*
Miniature Pine Tree *Crassula tetragona.*
Miniature Tree Fern *Blechnum gibbum.*
Miniature Wax Plant *Hoya lanceolata.*
Minnie Bush *Menziesia pilosa.*
Minorca Honeysuckle *Lonicera implexa.*
Mint *Mentha.*
Mint Bush *Prostanthera rotundifolia.*
Mint Geranium *Tanacetum balsamita.*
Mint-leaved Bergamot *Monarda menthifolia.*

Minuartia L. SANDWORT. Caryophyllaceae. 100 perenn. or ann. herbs. Habit mat-forming. Lvs usually linear. Fls usually 5-merous. Capsule with same no. of teeth as styles (usually 3). Widely distrib. in temp. and arctic N hemis. Z5 unless specified.

M. aretioides (Sommerauer) Schinz & Thell. = *M. cherlerioides.*

M. cherlerioides (Hoppe) Bech. Dense cushion-plant with oblong-elliptic, fleshy lvs to 3mm. Fls solitary on v. short stalks; sep. 3-veined; pet. 4, 2–4mm, lanceolate. Summer. C & E Eur. Alps.

M. graminifolia (Ard.) Jáv. Cushion-plant with linear-lanceolate, rigid lvs to 4cm, usually glandular-hairy and flowering st. to 14cm. Infl. a 2–7-fld cyme; sep. 5–7-veined; pet. 8–10mm, white, narrowly obovate. Summer. S Eur. (mts).

M. laricifolia (L.) Schinz & Thell. Loosely tufted, with a woody stock and glab. flowering st. to 30cm. Lvs linear, rigid, often falcate, to 10mm. Infl. a few-fld cyme, somewhat hairy; sep. 3-veined; pet. 6–10mm, white, obovate. Summer. Mts of S & C Eur.

M. obtusiloba (Rydb.) House. Mat-forming. Fls usually solitary on st. to 4cm; sep. ovate, v. obtuse, purple-tipped; pet. narrowly oblanceolate pet. Summer. Alask. to Oreg. Z3.

M. recurva (All.) Schinz & Thell. Densely tufted with woody stock and flowering st. to 15cm. Lvs falcate, glandular-hairy, to 10mm. Infl. (1)–2–8-fld; sep. 5–7-veined; pet. 4–8mm, white, ovate. Summer. Mts of S & C Eur.

M. sedoides (L.) Hiern. Glab. cushion-plant with densely packed, somewhat fleshy, linear-lanceoalte lvs to 15mm, and solitary, subsessile fls. Sep. 3-veined; pet. (if present) small, not longer than sep., tinged yellow. Summer. Eur. mts from Pyren. to Carpath.; also Scotland.

M. verna (L.) Hiern. Loosely-tufted perenn., usually glandular-hairy, with flowering st. to 15cm and linear-subulate lvs to 2cm. Infl. a loose cyme; sep. 3-veined; pet. 4–6mm, white, obovate. Summer. Widespread in Eur. ssp. *grandiflora* (Presl) Hayek. Pet. larger. Z2.

M. verna 'Aurea' = *Sagina subulata* 'Aurea'.

→*Alsine, Alsinopsis* and *Arenaria.*

Mioga Ginger *Zingiber mioga.*

Mirabilis L. UMBRELLAWORT; MARVEL OF PERU. Nyctaginaceae. 50 ann. or perenn. herbs. Roots tuberous, elongate. St. dichotomously branched, glab. to gland.-pubesc., sometimes viscid. Lvs opposite, ovate. Infl. an axill. corymb; fls 1–several, subtended by a 5-lobed involucre; perianth tubular to campanulate, 5-lobed; sta. 5–6, exserted. Summer. SW US, S Amer. Z8.

M. californica A. Gray = *M. laevis.*

M. dichotoma L. To 60cm. Lvs ovate, acute, rounded at base. Fls yellow. Mex.

M. froebelii Greene = *M. multiflora* var. *pubescens.*

M. ×hybrida hort. (*M. jalapa* ×*M. longiflora.*) To 1m. Lvs ovate-cordate, sometimes basally truncate, sinuate. Infl. dense, fls white, sometimes marked or tinted crimson or yellow, perianth tube glab. or pubesc., lobes spreading. Gdn origin.

M. jalapa L. MARVEL OF PERU; FOUR-O'-CLOCK; FALSE JALAP. Erect perenn., to 1m. Lvs 5–10cm, ovate, entire, cordate at base. Fls fragrant, opening in the late afternoon, 1 per involucre; perianth 3–5cm, purple, crimson, apricot, yellow or white, several shades often present on one plant, often striped or mottled, limb 2.5cm diam. Peru, gdn escape in N Amer.

M. laevis Curran. To 1m, st. often decumbent, viscid-pubesc. Lvs 1–3.5cm, ovate to linear-ovate, subglabrous to pubesc. Fls 1–3 per involucre; perianth 1–1.5cm, rose to purple-red, lobes sub-ovate. Calif.

M. linearis (Pursh) Heimerl. To 60cm+. St. glab. or pubesc. below, viscid above. Lvs to 10cm, linear to linear-lanceolate. Fls 2 per involucre, pale pink to maroon. S Dak. to Mex.

M. longiflora L. To 1m. St. glandular-pubesc., viscid. Lvs ovate-cordate to ovate-lanceolate, slender-acuminate. Fls 3 or more per involucre; perianth tube to 15cm, white, sometimes tinged or marked pink or violet, viscid-pubesc., nocturnally fragrant. W Tex., Ariz., Mex. var. *wrightiana* (A. Gray) Kearney & Peebles. To 120cm. St. puberulent. Lvs distinctly petioled.

M. multiflora (Torr.) A. Gray. Much-branched to 1m. Lvs ovate to ovate-linear, grey-green, glaucous. Fls 6–8 per involucre; bracts maroon, perianth tube to 5cm, pink to purple. Utah, Colorado to Tex. var. *pubescens* Zipp. ex Span. in L. Glandular-pubesc.

M. nyctaginea Michx. To 1m+. St. subglabrous. Lvs to 10cm, deltoid to linear-ovate. Fls 3 per involucre, white to pale pink. Wisc. to Mex.

M. uniflora Schrank = *M. jalapa.*

M. viscosa Cav. To 1m, viscid-pubesc. Lvs to 10cm, ovate, usually cordate at base. Fls usually 1 per involucre; perianth 1.5cm, funnel-shaped, purple, red, pink or white. Mex., Colomb., Ecuad., Peru.

M. wrightiana A. Gray = *M. longiflora* var. *wrightiana.*

→*Allionia, Hesperonia* and *Oxybaphus.*

Miraculous Berry *Synsepalum dulcificum.*
Mirbeck's Oak *Quercus canariensis.*
Miro *Prumnopitys ferruginea.*
Mirror Plant *Coprosma repens.*

Miscanthus Anderss. Gramineae. 17 rhizomatous perenn. grasses. Culms reed-like, clumped. Lf blades narrow, somewhat folded, arching. Pan. term., with arching, spike-like, pubesc. rac.; spikelets in pairs. OW Trop., S Afr., E Asia.

M. floridulus (Labill.) Warb. To 2.5m, glab. Lvs to 3cm diam., light glaucous green, scabrous at margins, pubesc. above towards base. Infl. to 50cm, white, puberulent-scaberulous; rac. to 20cm, slender, branched at base, subsessile; spikelets lanceolate, to 5mm, acute, tufted-pubesc. Summer. Ryukyus, Taiwan, Pacific Is. Z6.

M. formosanus A. Camus = *M. floridulus.*

M. japonicus Anderss. = *M. floridulus.*

M. sacchariflorus (Maxim.) Hackel. AMUR SILVER GRASS. To 3m. Lvs to 90×3cm, linear, acute, flat, stiff, smooth, margins rough, midrib pale. Infl. to 40×13cm, v. pale green, tinged red or purple; rac. to 30cm, flimsy; spikelets narrow, to 5mm, beige, with long silky hairs. Late summer–autumn. Asia; escaped in US. 'Aureus': to 1.5m; lvs striped gold. 'Robustus': vigorous, to 2.2m 'Variegatus': lvs narrowly striped white. Z8.

M. sieboldii Honda = *M. tinctorius.*

M. sinensis Anderss. EULALIA. To 4m. Lvs to 120×1cm, linear, flat, glab. to puberulous above, blue green. Infl. to 40×15cm, obpyramidal, pale grey tinted brown or mauve; rac. to 20cm; spikelets to 0.5cm, lanceolate, with long silky hairs in ring at base. E Asia. Many cvs: habit ranges from erect to gently arching or fountain-like; height of foliage from 0.85–2.00m; height of infl. 1.2–2.7m; lvs narrow to wide, green, or finely or boldly variegated in white or yellow, striped or banded, autumn colour inconspicuous to deep red tinted bronze; fls early to late, plumes silver to flushed pink, red or bronze. *Habit* 'Goliath': large, to 2m. 'Gracillimus': all parts more slender than type; lvs with a white midrib. 'Grosse Fontaine': fountain-like; early-flowering. 'Strictus': as for 'Zebrinus', but smaller, v. erect; lvs banded yellow. 'Yaku Jima': v. dwarf, to 85cm; lvs narrow, arching. *Lvs striped* 'Cabaret': lvs wide, broad central creamy white band and dark green edge, flushed pink in autumn; pan. copper. 'Goldfeder': lvs edged and striped yellow. 'Morning Light': lvs narrow, arching, neatly edged white; pan. red-bronze. 'Sarabande': lvs with wide central silver stripe. 'Variegatus': lvs with white or cream-white stripes. *Lvs banded* 'Tiger Tail': lvs banded cream. 'Zebrinus' ZEBRA GRASS: lvs with bands of white and yellow. 'Graziella': lvs narrow, somewhat arching, burgundy and orange with bronze tints in autumn; pan. large, white, nodding. 'Purpureus' ('Purpurascens'): small; lvs with pink-tinted central vein, browns and orange-reds in autumn; pan. oatmeal flushed pink. *Fls* 'Flamingo': pan. tinted flamingo pink. 'Kleine Fontaine': small; lvs graceful, arching; fls early. 'Malepartus': robust; lvs burgundy in autumn; pan. large, copper to silver tinted mauve. 'Rotsilber': pan. tinted red. 'Silberfeder': upright; lvs narrow; st. slender; pan. loose, silver occas. flushed pink. Z4.

M. tinctorius (Steud.) Hackel. Tufted perenn. to 1m. Lvs flat, broad-linear, to 40cm×12mm, margins scabrous, mostly glab., pilose towards base. Infl. erect, with a v. short axis; rac. 2–12 to 15cm; spikelets to 6mm, acute, tufted-pubesc. at base, awn 0. Autumn. Jap. 'Variegatus': dwarf, to 20cm; lvs streaked cream. Z6.

M. transmorrisonensis Hayata. Similar to *M. floridulus* but with graceful, golden, sparsely branched pan. Taiwan.

M. zebrinus (Beal) Nak. ex Matsum. = *M. sinensis* 'Zebrinus'.

Misopates Raf. WEASEL'S SNOUT. Scrophulariaceae. 6 ann. herbs similar to *Antirrhinum*. Lvs entire, subsessile or sessile. Fls 3–4 in spike-like rac.; cal. lobes unequal, longer than cor.; cor. tubular. Summer. Medit., W Atlantic Is., SW & C Asia. Z6.

M. orontium (L.) Raf. St. erect, simple, to 50cm, glab. to pubesc. Lvs 2–5cm, elliptic, linear or lanceolate. Rac. term., lax; cor. to 1.5cm, pink or white, shorter or equal to cal. Summer. SW & C Eur., nat. in temp. zones.
→*Antirrhinum*.

Mission Bells *Fritillaria biflora*.
Mission Manzanita *Arctostaphylos bicolor*.
Missouri Currant *Ribes aureum*.
Missouri Currant *Ribes odoratum*.
Missouri Flag *Iris missouriensis*.
Missouri Gooseberry *Ribes missouriense; R. setosum*.
Missouri Gourd *Cucurbita foetidissima*.
Missouri Violet *Viola missouriensis*.
Miss Willmott's Ghost *Eryngium giganteum*.
Mistflower *Conoclinium coelestinum*.
Mistletoe *Viscum album*.
Mistletoe Cactus *Rhipsalls*.
Mistletoe Fig *Ficus deltoidea*.
Mistletoe Rubber Plant *Ficus deltoidea*.

Mitchella L. PARTRIDGE BERRY. Rubiaceae. 2 everg. trailing herbs. Lvs opposite, petiolate, ovate-lanceolate, glossy, dark green. Fls in pairs, term., fragrant; cal. 4-toothed; cor. funnel-form, lobes 4, spreading, interior pubesc.; sta. 4. Fr. to 1cm diam., a 2-eyed, berry-like drupe, scarlet or white. N Amer., Jap.

M. repens L. PARTRIDGE BERRY; TWO-EYED BERRY; RUNNING BOX. Lvs to 2cm, apex obtuse, base subcordate, often veined white. Cor. to 1.2cm, white (rarely tinged purple), lobes ovate. N Amer. f. *leucocarpa* Bissell. Fr. white. Z3.

M. repens var. *undulata* (Sieb. & Zucc.) Mak. = *M. undulata*.

M. undulata Sieb. & Zucc. Lvs to 2.5cm, apex acute, margins undulate. Cor. to 1.5cm, pink, lobes fringed white. Jap., S Korea. Z6.

Mitella L. BISHOP'S-CAP; MITREWORT. Saxifragaceae. 20 perenn., minutely pubesc. herbs. Rhiz. short. Lvs ovate, cordate at base, lobed, crenate; petiole slender. Flowering st. with to 3 sessile lvs; rac. slender, usually second; fls small; sep. 5, fused at base;

pet. 5, fringed or lobed; sta. 5(–10). Late spring–summer. N Amer., NE Asia.

M. breweri Gray To 10cm. Lvs 4–10cm broad, glab. to coarsely hairy, shallowly 5–11-lobed and 1–2×toothed. Flowering st. leafless. Fls 20–60, green-yellow; pet. 1–2mm, divided into 5–9 seg. BC to Calif. and Idaho. Z5.

M. caulescens Nutt. Flowering st. 1–3 leaved. Fls to 25; pet. yellow, purple at base. W N Amer. Z5.

M. diphylla L. Flowering st. to 40cm with a single pair of lvs. Rac. to 20cm; fls to 6mm diam.; pet. white, deeply fringed. N Amer. f. *oppositifolia* (Rydb.) Rosend. Lvs on flowering st. distinctly stalked. Z3.

M. diversifolia Green Lvs 3–6cm broad, 5-lobed, entire to crenate. Fls 8–35; pet. 2mm, white suffused pink or purple, long-clawed, tip 3–5-lobed. Cascade Mts. Z5.

M. grandiflora Pursh = *Tellima grandiflora*.

M. hallii Howell = *M. ovalis*.

M. micrantha Piper = *M. trifida*.

M. nuda L. To 20cm. Usually stoloniferous. Lvs 1–3cm, double crenate. Flowering st. leafless, or with a single sessile lf at base. Fls 3–12; pet. green-yellow, 4mm, pinnately divided in to 8 seg. N N Amer., E Asia. Z4.

M. oppositifolia Rydb. = *M. diphylla* f. *oppositifolia*.

M. ovalis Green. To 30cm. Lvs 2–4×3–6cm, 5–9-lobed, finely toothed. Flowering st. leafless. Fls 20–60, green-yellow, 1cm across; pet. pinnately divided into 4–7 seg. BC to Calif. Z7.

M. pentandra Hook. To 40cm. Lvs 2–5cm broad, 5–9-lobed, bicrenate. Flowering st. naked or with small scales. Fls 6–25; pet. green, 2–3mm, pinnately divided into 8 seg. Alask. to Calif. Z3.

M. stauropetala Piper. To 50cm. Lvs 2–8cm wide, 5–7-lobed, often suffused purple, crenate. Flowering st. leafless; fls 10–35; pet. white or purple, 2–4mm, 3-lobed or entire. Mont. to Colorado, Oreg. Z4.

M. stenopetala Piper = *M. stauropetala*.

M. trifida Graham. To 40cm. Lvs 2–6cm broad, obscurely 5–7-lobed, crenate. Fls to 20; pet. white to purple, 1.5–2.5mm, 3-lobed or entire. BC to Calif., Rocky Mts. Z6.

M. violacea Rydb. = *M. trifida*.

Mithridate Mustard *Thlaspi arvense*.

Mitragyna Korth. Rubiaceae. 12 trees or shrubs. Lvs opposite, petiolate, stipulate. Fls in dense heads; bracts 2, leaflike; bracteoles many; cal. turbinate or truncate, limb tubular, abbreviated or 0; cor. tube cylindric to funnelform, lobes 5; sta. 5, anth. often exserted. Trop. Afr. and Asia. Z10.

M. africana Korth. = *M. inermis*.

M. inermis (Willd.) Kuntze. Lvs to 12×8cm, elliptic or obovate, narrowly acute at apex. Fls in dense globose heads 3cm wide, white or cream to yellow, fragrant. Summer–winter. Afr. (Mauritania to Sudan).

M. parvifolia (Roxb.) Korth. Lvs to 11×7cm, elliptic, oval, obovate or orbicular, obtuse to narrowly acute. Fls in heads 2.5cm wide, pale yellow. Summer–autumn. N India, Sri Lanka.
→*Nauclea*.

Mitraria Cav. Gesneriaceae. 1 straggling, everg. perenn. sub-shrub; st. villous becoming woody at base, tangled. Lvs to 2cm, opposite, ovate, dentate, coriaceous, hairy. Fls solitary on arching axill. stalks; floral bract 1, bilobed; cal. lobes 4–5, to 1.2cm, lanceolate; cor. to 3cm, tubular, scarlet or orange-red, inflated about halfway up, narrowing to mouth, pilose, lobes to 0.7cm, rounded, reflexed. Summer–autumn. Chile. Z10.

M. coccinea Cav.

Mitrewort *Mitella*.

Mitriostigma Hochst. Rubiaceae. 5 shrubs and small trees. Lvs simple, opposite, stipulate. Fls in axill. or lat. cymes; cal. tube ovoid or obconical, 5-lobed; cor. cylindric to bell- or funnel-shaped, lobes 5; sta. 5. Subsaharan Afr.

M. axillare Hochst. Everg. shrub or small tree, 3–4m. Lvs to 15×5cm, lanceolate, elliptic-lanceolate, or ovate, entire, dark green, glab. Fls in secund axill. cymes, white, occas. pink-flushed, to yellow. Spring. S Afr. (Natal, Transvaal).
→*Gardenia*.

Mitrophyllum Schwantes. Aizoaceae. 6 succulent shrublets. St. branching. Lvs trimorphic: partly fused and paired in a cone, wholly fused and paired in a sheath or paired and remote on flowering shoots. Fls short-pedicellate. Growing season v. short, late summer–early autumn. S Afr. (Cape Prov.). Z9.

M. chrysoleucum (Schltr.) Schwantes = *Monilaria chrysoleuca*.

M. meyeri Schwantes = *Meyerophytum meyeri*.

M. mitratum (Marloth) Schwantes. Forming mats of thick st., becoming woody. Cone lvs 7–8cm long, 2cm thick, the free parts 10–12mm long, bluntly triquetrous, light green, glossy-papillose. Fls 2.5–3cm diam., white tipped red. W Cape.

M. pisiforme (Haw.) Schwantes = *Monilaria pisiformis*.
→*Conophyllum* and *Mesembryanthemum*.

Mitsuba *Cryptotaenia canadensis*.
Miyagino-hagi *Lespedeza thunbergii*.
Miyako-zasa *Sasa nipponica*.
Miyama Cherry *Prunus maximowiczii*.
Miyama-hagi *Lespedeza cyrtobotrya*.
Miyama-ho-tsutsuji *Tripetaleia bracteata*.
Mizu-giboshi *Hosta longissima*.
Mlala *Hyphaene crinita*.
Mlanji Cedar *Widdringtonia nodiflora*.
Moccasin Flower *Cypripedium*.
Mock Azalea *Adenium*.
Mock Cucumber *Echinocystis lobata*.
Mockernut *Carya tomentosa*.
Mock Heather *Ericameria ericoides*.
Mock Mesquite *Calliandra eriophylla*.
Mock Orange *Bumelia lycioides*; *Philadelphus*; *Pittosporum tobira*; *Prunus caroliniana*.
Mock Privet *Phillyrea*.
Mock Strawberry *Duchesnea*.

Modecca Lam. = *Adenia*.

Modjadji Cycad *Encephalartos transvenosus*.
Modoc Cypress *Cupressus bakeri*.

Moehringia L. SANDWORT. Caryophyllaceae. 20 herbs, distinguished from *Arenaria* in having 4- (not 5-) petalled fls. Temp. and arctic N Hemis. Z5.
M. muscosa L. St. thin, intertwining, matted, glab. Lvs to 4cm, linear. Fls cymose, slender-stalked, pet. 4, white, 4–5mm, ovate-lanceolate. Summer. Mts of C & S Eur.

Mohavea A. Gray. Scrophulariaceae. 2 branching viscid annuals. Lvs simple, entire. Rac. densely leafy; cal. 5-lobed; cor lips fan-shaped. Summer. SW US. Z7.
M. confertiflora Jeps. St. to 60cm. Lvs linear-lanceolate to ovate-lanceolate, fleshy. Cor. yellow spotted brown, palate darker.

Mohintli *Justicia spicigera*.

Mohria Sw. Schizaeaceae. 4 terrestrial ferns. Rhiz. prostrate, scaly. Fronds erect, bipinnate. Afr.
M. caffrorum (L.) Desv. SCENTED FERN. Sweetly aromatic. Rhiz. to 10mm diam. Fronds tufted; blade 20–58×5–11cm, narrowly oblong to elliptic, pinnae pinnatifid to bipinnate, crenate. Trop. & Subtrop. Afr. and adjacent islands.

Mojave Aster *Machaeranthera tortifolia*.
Mojave Penstemon *Penstemon incertus*.
Mojave Sand Verbena *Abronia pogonantha*.

✕**Mokara.** (*Arachnis* ✕*Ascocentrum* ✕*Vanda*.) Orchidaceae. Gdn hybrids with strap-shaped, 2-ranked lvs and tall erect spikes of fls in shades of yellow, orange, brick red, purple, cerise, mauve and white, sometimes marked mauve or red.

Mole Plant *Euphorbia heterophylla*; *E. lathyris*.

Molineria Colla.
M. capitulata (Lour.) Herb. = *Curculigo capitulata*.
M. latifolia (Dryand.) Herb. = *Curculigo latifolia*.
M. plicata Colla = *Curculigo capitulata*.
M. recurvata (Dryand. in Ait.) Herb. = *Curculigo capitulata*.

Molinia Schrank. Gramineae. 2–3 perenn. grasses. St. tufted; basal internode bulbous. Lvs flat; ligule a row of hairs. Pan. narrow-lanceolate, loose; spikelets laterally compressed, 1–4-fld. Eurasia. Z5.
M. altissima Link = *M. caerulea* ssp. *arundinacea*.
M. arundinacea Schrank = *M. caerulea* ssp. *arundinacea*.
M. caerulea (L.) Moench. PURPLE MOOR-GRASS. To 120cm. Lf blades to 45×1cm. Pan. dense, to 40×10cm, purple to olive-green; spikelets to 1cm. Summer–autumn. 'Dauerstrahl' ('Ramsey'): st. tall, tinted yellow. 'Edith Buksaus': to 1m; st. strong; pan. dark, long-lasting. 'Heidebraut' ('Heatherbride'): st. soft straw yellow, to 1.5m; spikelets tinted yellow, forming a glistening cloud. 'Moorhexe' ('Bog Witch'): narrowly upright; st. slender, to 50cm; fls dark. 'Moorflamme': to 70cm; lvs

coloured well in autumn; infl. dark. 'Nana Variegata': dwarf form of 'Dauerstrahl', to 80cm. 'Overdam': to 60cm; st. strong; lvs fine. 'Strahleonguelle' ('Fountain Spray'): st. curving. 'Variegata': tufted, compact; st. slender and upright, bright ochre, to 60cm; lvs striped dark green and cream-white; pan. oatmeal, spikelets tinted purple; slow-growing. ssp. *arundinacea* (Schrank) H. Paul. To 2.5m. Lvs to 12mm diam. Pan. with long, spreading br. W Eur. 'Altissima': to 1m; lvs golden-yellow in autumn. 'Bergfreund' ('Mountain's Friend'): lvs strong yellow in autumn; pan. brown. 'Fontäne' ('Fountain'): st. inclining, forming a fountain. 'Karl Foerster': tall, lvs to 80cm. 'Skyracer': tall, lvs to 1m, clear gold in autumn. 'Transparent': spikelets sparse, giving the whole infl. a light, spacious, transparent quality. 'Winspiel' ('Windplay'): st. slender, swaying; plumes gold-brown, dense.
M. litoralis Host = *M. caerulea* ssp. *arundinacea*.

Molle *Schinus latifolius*; *S. lentiscifolius*; *S. molle*; *S. polygamus* var. *parviflorus*.

Molle (Tourn.) Adans. = *Schinus*.

Moltkia Lehm. Boraginaceae. 6 perennials. St. herbaceous or shrubby, strigose. Cymes short, term., solitary or crowded, cal. lobes 5, narrow; cor. infundibular, tube cylindrical, glab., lobes erect, overlapping rounded, lacking throat scales; sta. exserted; style exserted, slender. N It. to N Greece, SW Asia.
M. caerulea (Willd.) Lehm. Hairy perenn. St. to 20cm, simple. Lvs to 8cm, oblanceolate. Cymes 2 or 3; cor. to 19mm, blue, lobes to 2mm, sparsely adpressed-pubesc. above. W Asia.
M. doerfleri Wettst. St. to 50cm, simple, adpressed-setulose. Lvs lanceolate, acute, adpressed-setulose. Cor. to 22mm, deep purple, lobes to 2.5mm. Albania.
M. graminifolia (Viv.) Nyman = *M. suffruticosa*.
M.✕*intermedia* (Froebel) J. Ingram. (*M. petraea* ✕*M. suffruticosa*.) Closely resembles *M. suffruticosa* except larger and more shrubby. Lvs broader. Fls deep bright blue, in spreading heads. Eur. to Asia. 'Froebelii': fls azure-blue. Z6.
M. petraea (Tratt.) Griseb. White-bristly slender shrublet to 40cm. Lvs to 5cm, oblanceolate or oblong-lanceolate to linear, revolute. Cymes compact; cor. to 8mm, blue or violet-blue, lobes to 1.5mm. Balk. to C Greece. Z6.
M. suffruticosa (L.) Brand. Loosely branched, bristly tufted shrublet to 25cm. Lvs to 15cm, linear, sometimes revolute. Cymes short, dense, clustered; cor. to 17mm, blue, lobes to 3.5mm. N It. Z8.
→*Echium, Lithospermum, Onosma* and *Pulmonaria*.

Moluccella L. Labiatae. 4 tall, glab., ann. or short-lived perenn. herbs. St. tetragonal. Lvs opposite, crenate, petiolate. Infl. a terminal spike composed of axill. whorls; cal. tube large, campanulate with 5–10 spiny teeth, expanding to become papery, disc-like and conspicuously reticulate; cor. small, tubular, bilabiate. Medit. to NW India. Z7.
M. laevis L. BELLS OF IRELAND. Ann., erect to 60cm. Lvs to 6cm, deeply crenate. Cal. light green, white-reticulate, campanulate or saucer-shaped, spiny; cor. white to pale lilac. Late summer. W Asia.
M. spinosa L. Ann., erect to 1m. Lvs to 6cm, ovate to cordate, deeply serrate or lobed. Cal. 2-lipped, upper lip erect with strong spine, lower lip 7–10-spined; cor. white, velvety. Late summer. Medit.

Mombin *Spondias mombin*.
Momi Fir *Abies firma*.

Momordica L. Cucurbitaceae. 45 ann. or perenn. scramblers and climbers to 7m. Tendrils simple or bifid. Lvs palmate or pedate, dentate or undulate. Fls unisexual: ♀ usually solitary; ♂ solitary or in clusters or rac., the stalks conspicuously bracteate; cal. tubular; cor. showy, rotate or campanulate, deeply lobed; sta. 3. Fr. pendulous, yellow orange, bursting and expanding in a starlike configuration, oblong, tuberculate or ridged; seed often glossy red, suspended in white to orange pulp. Afr., Indomalesia, nat. Americas. Z9.
M. balsamina L. BALSAM APPLE. Lvs ovate to reniform, cordate, pubesc., deeply palmately lobed, 90–120mm, sharply dentate. Fls solitary; pet. to 1.5cm, yellow with green veins. Fr. to 7cm, ovoid or ellipsoid, covered with ridged, irregular protuberances, green ripening orange and bursting. E Indies, widely nat.
M. brachybotrys Poepp. & Endl. = *Cyclanthera brachybotrys*.
M. cardiospermoides Klotz. Lvs biternately 9–15-foliolate, lfts ovate-oblong, 5–30×4–20mm, acute, apiculate. Fls solitary; pet. yellow, 2–2.5cm. Fr. ellipsoid, irregularly tubercled. S Afr.
M. charantia L. BALSAM PEAR; BITTER GOURD; BITTER CUCUMBER; LA-KWA. Lvs deeply 3–7-lobed, pubesc. on nerves, lobes

obovate to rhombic, acute and apiculate. Fls solitary, vanilla-scented; pet. to 2.2cm, pale yellow to orange. Fr. oblong or ovoid, orange yellow, strongly rugose-tuberculate, dehiscent, 7–25cm. Trop., introd. to Americas.

M. cochinchinensis (Lour.) Spreng. SPINY BITTER CUCUMBER. Lvs orbicular, 3–10cm, across, cordate, glab., lobes 5–9, deeply divided, apiculate, sometimes obscurely pinnatifid. Fls showy, solitary; pet. to 2cm, yellow. Fr. oblong or oval, tapering, ribbed and warty to subspinose, to 20cm. India to Jap. and New Guinea.

M. cylindrica L. = *Luffa cylindrica.*

M. elateria L. = *Ecballium elaterium.*

M. foetida Schumacher. Lvs ovate-cordate, simple, apiculate, subentire to dentate, 1–16cm. ♂ fls 1–9 per fascicle; pet. white to pale yellow. Fr. ellipsoid, softly spiny, to 1.5cm. Trop. Afr. and Amer.

M. involucrata E. Mey. Lvs palmate, glab., lobes 5, to 2.5cm, crenate, mucronate. Fls solitary; pet. at least 1cm. Fr. globose-ovoid, attenuate, rugose, orange, *c*3cm diam. S Afr. (Natal).

M. lanata Thunb. = *Citrullus lanatus.*

M. operculata L. = *Luffa operculata.*

M. rostrata Zimm. Lvs pedately biternate; lfts usually 9, elliptic to suborbicular, serrate or dentate, to 5×3cm. ♂ infl. sub-umbellate; ♀ fls solitary; pet. orange-yellow. Fr. ovoid, beaked, slightly ridged. E Afr.

Monachosorum Hance.

M. maximowiczii (Bak.) Hayata = *Ptilopteris maximowiczii.*

Monadenium Pax. Euphorbiaceae. 50 herbaceous perennials to st. succulents to large shrubs, resembling *Euphorbia*, but cyathia zygomorphic, involucre, bracteate, cupulate; involucral gland horseshoe-shaped, with a wide rim; bracts persistent behind rim. C, SW, mainly trop. E Afr. Z10.

M. cannellii Leach. As for *M. spinescens*, but smaller, to 1.5m. Spines solitary, not in 3's. Infl. stalks ridged. Angola.

M. coccineum Pax. Perenn., to 1m+. St. unarmed, erect or creeping, simple or branched, 5-sided. Lvs oblanceolate to obovate, 8.5cm, fleshy, serrate. Cymes forked, forming heads to 4cm diam.; peduncles scarlet above, to 7cm; bract cup scarlet. Tanz. Z9.

M. echinulatum Stapf. Somewhat prickly succulent, to 70cm. St. simple, to 1cm diam. Lvs elliptic to elliptic-lanceolate, to 12cm, cymes to 5× dichotomous; bract cup to 21mm diam., green, occas. flushed pale pink. Trop. W Afr., Tanz.

M. elegans S. Carter. Small tree or shrub, to 3.5m; br. pendulous; spines in groups of 3. Lvs spathulate, to 4cm, glab. peduncle ridged spiny; bract cup rim white, bordered red, segmented. Tanz.

M. invenustum N.E. Br. Perenn. herb, to 80cm. St. erect, un-armed, glaucous. Lvs fleshy orbicular ovate, to 4cm, dark green above, slightly pubesc. below, occas. crenulate. Cymes short-stalked, bract cup to 6mm, dark green, banded paler green. Kenya. var. *angustum* Bally. Lvs oblanceolate.

M. laeve Stapf. Perenn. herb. St. 1 to several, erect to procumbent, to 1m. Lvs elliptic-ovate to oblanceolate, to 17cm. Cymes long-stalked, 2–4× dichotomous; bract cup pendent, un-dulate. Tanz., N Malawi.

M. lugardae N.E. Br. Perenn. herb, to 60cm. St. to 3cm diam., hexagonal to pentagonal. Lvs obovate, to 9cm, acute, crenate to serrate. Cymes solitary; bract cup to 7mm, apex notched; in-volucre pendent, exterior pale green, interior yellow or orange brown. Bots., Natal, S Zimb.

M. magnificum E.A. Bruce. Shrub, to 1.5m. St. 1 to several, to 4cm diam; br. with spiny angles. Lvs elliptic to obovate, to 15cm, fleshy, dark green, later tinged red. Infl. stalks to 14cm, with red small spines; involucral bracts fleshy, pale green, fringed, rhombic. Tanz.

M. montanum var. *rubellum* Bally = *M. rubellum.*

M. rhizophorum Bally. Succulent rhizomatous glab. herb, to 10cm. St. to 7cm diam. Lvs to 3.5cm, obovate to spathulate, mucronate. Cymes forming bracteate heads; peduncle green-white, striped dark brown; bract cup oblique, to 7×5mm; green tinged yellow, rim gland., yellow. Kenya.

M. rhizophorum var. *stoloniferum* Bally = *M. stoloniferum.*

M. ritchiei Bally. Succulent perenn. herb, to 40cm. St. to 3cm diam., with spiny warts. Lvs to 3cm, ovate to subcircular, apiculate. Infl. cymes few; bract cup oblique, to 8mm; involucre to 6×5mm, fleshy, gland. rim scarlet. Kenya. ssp. *marsabitense* S. Carter. St. decumbent, to 2cm diam.; warts spirally arranged. Lvs puberulous. Bract cup grey-green, occas. flushed pink. ssp. *nyambense* S. Carter. Lvs glab. Bract cup vivid pink.

M. rubellum (Bally) S. Carter. Glab. perenn. herb. St. fleshy, erect, decumbent, to 25cm, to 5mm diam., ridged, striped green-purple. Lvs lanceolate, to 4.5cm, tinged purple. Infl. stalk 17mm, forked; bract cup to 6×4mm, pink tinged rose. Kenya.

M. schubei (Pax) N.E. Br. Succulent perenn. herb, to 45cm. St. erect, to 4cm diam., with large, spiny warts. Lvs oblanceolate, to 6.5cm. Infl. 1–2× dichotomous; bract cup to 6×5mm green, margin white, occas. tinged pink, veins dark green. Tanz., S Zimb.

M. spectabile S. Carter. Succulent shrub, to 3m. St. ± simple to 5cm diam., somewhat 5-sided, waxy, spiny. Lvs obovate, to 33cm, fleshy. Infl. bright red, spiny; bract cup to 6×8mm. Tanz.

M. spinescens (Pax) Bally. Tree, to 6m. Br. to 2.5cm diam., warty; spines in 3's below lf scars. Lvs oblanceolate to obovate, to 9cm. Cymes crowded, 7× dichotomous or more, forming heads to 7cm diam.; involucral bracts to 10×7mm, pale green tinged pink; involucre lobes bearing threadlike processes; styles to 3mm. Tanz.

M. stapelioides Pax. Cushion-forming perenn., to 15cm. St. glab., warts spirally arranged. Lvs borne on warts, obovate to rhombic or spathulate, to 3cm. Cymes solitary; peduncles pale green flushed pink; involucre to 7×5cm. Kenya, N Tanz.

M. stoloniferum (Bally) S. Carter. Glab. perenn. herb. St. to 15cm, procumbent. Lvs ovate, to 5cm, entire, green tinged purple. Peduncle to 15mm, forked; bract cup to 6×4cm, dark green, midrib white. Kenya.

M. subulifolium Chiov. = *Kleinia subulifolia.*

M. succulentum Schweick. = *M. stapelioides.*

M. torrei Leach. As for *M. spinescens*, but smaller, to 3m; young br. more warty; spines borne on wart apices, solitary. N Moz., Tanz.

Monanthes Haw. Crassulaceae. 12 herbs or shrubby annuals and perennials. Lvs succulent, entire, in dense term. rosettes. Infl. branched; fls small; sep. 6–8, usually joined at base; pet. 6–8, linear, free; sta. twice as numerous as pet. Summer. Canary Is. and N Afr. Z8.

M. agriostaphys Christ. = *M. laxiflora.*

M. anagensis Praeger. Similar to *M. laxifolia* except lvs 2.5cm, opposite although appearing alt., linear-lanceolate, thin, green, often tinged red; sep. narrow. Tenerife.

M. brachycaulon (Webb & Berth.) Lowe. Erect, stolon-forming perenn. St. simple, bulb-like. Lvs 1.4–2cm, papillose, oblanceolate, blunt, green, mottled purple towards base. Infl. 5–7-fld; fls green-purple, to 10mm across. Spring. Tenerife and Salvage Is.

M. laxiflora (DC.) Bolle. Perenn. woody-based herb, hanging or diffuse, irregularly branching. Lvs 1.2–1.6cm, v. thick, oval, fleshy, dark or silvery. Infl. 6–10-fld; fls purple to yellow, spotted red. Spring. Canary Is.

M. muralis (Webb & Bolle) Christ. Erect tree-like subshrub, to 8cm. Lvs to 0.6cm, obovate, v. thick, mottled purple. Infl. 3–7-fld; fls white, spotted and veined red. Spring. Canary Is.

M. pallens (Webb & Christ) Christ. St. short, thick, bulbous. Lvs 3–5cm diam., ovate-round, densely papillose. Infl. many-fld, leafy; fls small, yellow to white, lined red. Spring. Canary Is.

M. polyphylla Haw. Minute, mat-forming perenn. Lvs 1–2cm across, terete, papillose at apex. Fls 1–4, red, covered in white hairs. Spring. Canary Is.

M. subcrassicaulis (Kuntze) Praeger. Similar to *M. polyphylla* ex-cept lvs not dense rosettes but rather long elongate rosettes. Flowering st. hairy. Canary Is.

→*Sempervivum.*

Monarch Birch *Betula maximowicziana.*
Monarch of the East *Sauromatum venosum.*

Monarda L. WILD BERGAMOT; HORSEMINT; BEEBALM. Labiatae. 16 aromatic ann. or perenn. herbs. St. erect, simple or sparsely branched. Lvs simple, usually serrate. Fls in dense glomerules, term. and solitary or in an interrupted spike, subtended by leafy bracts; cal. tubular, 13–15-veined, teeth 5; cor. narrowly tubular, strongly 2-lipped, upper lip erect or hooded, lower lip spreading, 3-lobed; sta. 2. N Amer.

M. allophylla Michx. = *M. clinopodia.*

M. aristata Nutt. = *M. citriodora.*

M. citriodora Cerv. ex Lagasca. Ann., 30–60cm. St. pubesc. Lvs 3–6cm, lanceolate or oblong, puberulent, remotely serrate or ciliate. Glomerules 1.5–3.5cm across, inner bracts oblong, or lanceolate, 5–9mm broad, tapering to a spinose bristle, inner surfaces canescent often purple; cor. white or pink, dotted with purple, tube 7–19mm long. C & S US, N Mex.

M. clinopodia L. Perenn. to 1.25m. St. glab. or thinly pubesc. Lvs ovate to deltoid 5–13cm, hirsute, serrate. Glomerules 1.5–3cm, across, outer bracts green with purple midveins; cor. white with purple spots, 1.4–3cm, glab. or short-pubesc. N Amer. Z5.

M. coccinea Michx. = *M. didyma.*

M. cornata Rydb. = *M. menthifolia.*

M. didyma L. BEE BALM; BERGAMOT; OSWEGO TEA. Perenn. herb, 70–120cm. St. glab. or thinly pilose. Lvs 6–14cm, ovate, deltoid to ovate-lanceolate, serrate, hirsute. Glomerules 2–4cm across, outer bracts tinged red; cal. usually red; cor. bright crimson, 3–4.5cm. Canada, US. 'Adam': to 1m; fls cerise. 'Alba': fls white. 'Cambridge Scarlet': fls red. 'Croftway Pink': fls rose-pink. 'Salmonea': fls salmon pink. 'Burgundy': fls dark purple-red. Z4.

M. dispersa Small = *M. citriodora*.

M. fistulosa L. Differs from *M. didyma* in st. bluntly 4-angled; glomerules usually 1 only (not 2 superimposed); fls fewer; bracts tinted purple-pink; cal. throat densely, not sparsely hairy. Perenn. herb, 35–120cm. St. pubesc. above. Lvs 4–10cm, ovate or lanceolate, serrate to nearly entire, pubesc. or rarely glab. Glomerules 1.5–3cm across, outer bracts frequently pink tinted; cor. lavender, lilac or pink, 2–3cm, pubesc., upper lip comose. Canada, US, Mex. Z4.

M. kalmiana Pursh = *M. didyma*.

M. lasiodonta Small = *M. punctata* ssp. *villicaulis*.

M. lutea Michx. = *M. punctata* ssp. *punctata*.

M. menthifolia Graham. MINT-LEAVED BERGAMOT. Perenn. herb, 30–75cm. St. glab. or pubesc. above. Lvs 3.5–9cm, ovate or lanceolate, serrate or subentire, glab. or hirtellus above, pubesc. beneath. Glomerules 1.5–2.5cm across, outer bracts frequently tinted pink; cor. lavender or rose-purple, 2.5–3.5cm, pubesc., upper lip comose. Canada, US. Z3.

M. mollis L. = *M. fistulosa*.

M. nuttallii A. Nels. = *M. pectinata*.

M. oswegoensis Barton = *M. didyma*.

M. pectinata Nutt. PLAINS LEMON MONARDA. Ann., 15–30cm. St. pubesc., branched. Lvs 2–5cm, oblong-lanceolate or oblong, glab. to puberulent, serrate to subentire. Glomerules 1.5–2.5cm across, outer bracts foliar, inner bracts oblong, 2–7mm wide, acuminate to a spinose bristle, margins ciliate, glab.; cor. pink or nearly white, tube 8–14mm, lips equal, shorter than tube. S US.

M. penicillata Gray = *M. pectinata*.

M. punctata L. Perenn., bienn. or ann. 0.3–1m. St. pubesc. Lvs 1.5–9.5cm, lanceolate to oblong, serrate to subentire. Glomerules 1.5–2.5cm across; bracts green-white or tinged purple; cor. yellow or pink, usually dotted purple. US. ssp. *punctata*. Perenn. or bienn., 25–85cm. St. pubesc. Lvs 3–7cm, sparsely puberulent; cor. yellow or white with purple spots; tube 6–8mm. E US, along seaboard. ssp. *arkansana* Epling. Perenn. herb, 50–115cm. St. pubesc., with bristles. Lvs 4–10cm, sparingly pubesc. above, more densely so beneath; cor. yellow with purple spots, tube 4–6mm. Ark. ssp. *coryi* Epling. Perenn. herb, 40–60cm. St. pubesc.; cor. pink without purple dots, tube 5–8mm. Tex. ssp. *intermedia* Epling. Perenn. herb, 40–60cm tall. St. pubesc. Lvs 5–7cm, pubesc.; cor. yellow with purple dots, tube 5–8mm. Tex. ssp. *occidentalis* Epling. Ann., 30–40cm. St. pubesc. Lvs 2.5–5cm, pubesc.; cor. white or pink, sometimes dotted purple, tube 4–7mm. US, Mex. ssp. *stanfieldii* (Small) Epling. Perenn. herb, 35–75cm. St. canescent. Lvs 6–9cm, puberulent. Cor. yellow with purple dots, tube 8–11mm. Tex. ssp. *villicaulis* Pennell. Perenn. herb, 20–70cm. St. densely hairy. Lvs 3.5–8cm, tomentose, silvery beneath; cor. yellow with purple dots, tube 5–7mm. E US. Z6.

M. punctata var. *humilis* Torr. = *M. pectinata*.

M. punctata var. *lasiodonta* Gray = *M. punctata*.

M. punctata var. *occidentalis* Palmer & Steyerm. = *M. punctata* ssp. *occidentalis*.

M. ramaleyi A. Nels. = *M. menthifolia*.

M. scabra Beck = *M. fistulosa*.

M. stanfieldii Small = *M. punctata* ssp. *stanfieldii*.

M. stricta Wooton = *M. menthifolia*.

M. tenuiaristata Gray = *M. citriodora*.

M. cvs. (selections or hybrids of *M. didyma* and *M. fistulosa*); 'Beauty of Cobham': tall; fls lilac-pink. 'Blue Stocking' ('Blaustrumpf'): tall; fls brilliant deep violet. 'Capricorn': fls purple. 'Croftway Pink': fls clear rose pink. 'Kardinal': tall; fls red tinted purple. 'Loddon Crown': fls maroon. 'Mahogany': tall; fls deep wine red. 'Morning Red' ('Morgenröte'): fls dark salmon. 'Pisces': fls strong pink, cal. green. 'Prairie Night' ('Prärienacht'): fls rich violet. 'Snow Queen': low; fls creamy white. Z4.

Monardella Benth. Labiatae. 19 often creeping, aromatic ann. or perenn. herbs. Lvs small. Glomerules term., bracteate; cal. narrow, 10–15-nerved, teeth 5; cor. small, upper lip 2-lobed, lower lip 3-lobed; sta. 4. W N Amer.

M. acuta Greene = *M. lanceolata*.

M. australis Abrams = *M. odoratissima* ssp. *australis*.

M. discolor Greene = *M. odoratissima* ssp. *discolor*.

M. glabra Nutt. = *M. odoratissima* ssp. *euodoratissima*.

M. glauca Greene = *M. odoratissima* ssp. *glauca*.

M. ingrata Greene = *M. odoratissima* ssp. *glauca*.

M. lanceolata A. Gray. Erect ann. to 50cm. St. puberulent. Lvs 3–4cm, lanceolate, entire, puberulent. Glomerules 1.5–3cm diam.; bracts ovate-lanceolate, reticulate-veined; cor. rose-purple, 12–15mm. Calif., Nevada, Ariz. var. *microcephala* A. Gray. More densely branched. Glomerules to 1cm across. Calif., Baja Calif.

M. linioides A. Gray. Shrubby perenn. St. decumbent, 30–50cm, silvery. Lvs 1–4cm, narrowly oblong to narrowly lanceolate, entire, silvery. Glomerules 2–3cm diam., bracts ovate to lanceolate, white-puberulent or tinged rose to purple; cor. 12–15mm rose to purple. Calif., Nevada, Ariz., Baja Calif. ssp. *eulinoides* Epling. Bracts ovate to rotund, off-white. Calif., Baja Calif. ssp. *stricta* (Parish) Epling). Bracts lanceolate, purple-coloured. Calif., Baja Calif., Nevada, Ariz.

M. macrantha A. Gray. Decumbent subshrubby perenn. St. 10–30cm, pubesc. or villous. Lvs 0.5–3cm, subcoriaceous, variable. Glomerules 2–4cm diam.; bracts oblong-eliptical, membranous, sparsely villous; cor. scarlet to yellow, puberulent, long-tubular, limb to 1cm. Calif., Baja Calif. ssp. *eumacrantha* Epling. Lvs 1–3cm, glabrate above, pubesc. beneath. Glomerules 3–4cm diam.; bracts purple; cor. 3.5–4.5cm. Calif., Baja Calif. ssp. *nana* (A. Gray) Epling. Lvs 0.5–1.5cm, ovate. Glomerules 2–3.5cm diam., bracts usually tinged white; cor. 2.5–3cm. Calif., Baja Calif. Z9.

M. modocensis Greene = *M. odoratissima* ssp. *glauca*.

M. muriculata Greene = *M. odoratissima* ssp. *parvifolia*.

M. nana A. Gray = *M. macrantha* ssp. *nana*.

M. nervosa Greene = *M. odoratissima* ssp. *discolor*.

M. odoratissima Benth. Woody-based decumbent silvery perenn. Lvs 1–3cm, ovate-lanceolate to oblong-lanceolate, entire or serrate. Glomerules 1–5cm diam.; bracts membranous, ovate or rotund, purple, villous or tomentose; cor. 1–2cm, rose-purple to pallid, puberulent. W US. ssp. *australis* (Abrams) Epling. Lvs 1–2.5cm, lanceolate or oblong, green or cinereous. Bracts lanceolate, slightly hairy; cor. 1.5cm. ssp. *discolor* (Greene) Epling. Lvs 2cm, ovate, hoary-pubesc. Bracts ovate; cor. c1.3cm. ssp. *euodoratissima* Epling. Lvs 2cm, nearly glab. Bracts ovate to rotund, pubesc.; cor. 1.5cm. ssp. *glauca* (Greene) Epling. Lvs 1.5–4cm, ovate-lanceolate, elliptical or oblong, appearing glaucous. Bracts ovate to orbicular, purple; cor. 1–2cm. ssp. *pallida* (Heller) Epling. Lvs 2–3cm, lanceolate-oblong, cinereous. Cor. 1–1.5cm, pallid. ssp. *parvifolia* (Greene) Epling. Lvs 1–2cm, lanceolate or oblong, cinereous. Glomerules small; bracts inconspicuous; cor. usually less than 1cm. ssp. *pinetorum* (Heller) Epling. Lvs softly pubesc., ovate to lanceolate, 1.5–2.5cm. Bracts inconspicuous, tinged purple. Cor. rose-coloured, 1–1.5cm. Z8.

M. odoratissima Howell non Benth. = *M. odoratissima* ssp. *euodoratissima*.

M. ovata Greene = *M. odoratissima* ssp. *glauca*.

M. pallida Heller = *M. odoratissima* ssp. *pallida*.

M. parvifolia Greene = *M. odoratissima* ssp. *parvifolia*.

M. peninsularis Greene = *M. lanceolata* var. *microcephala*.

M. pinetorum Heller = *M. odoratissima* ssp. *pinetorum*.

M. purpurea Howell = *M. odoratissima* ssp. *glauca*.

M. rubella Greene = *M. odoratissima* ssp. *glauca*.

M. sanguinea Greene = *M. lanceolata*.

M. villosa Benth. Subglab. or hairy woody-based decumbent perenn. Lvs 1–3cm, ovate to lanceolate or rotund, entire, crenate-serrate or dentate, usually villous. Glomerules compact, 2–4cm across, bracts leaflike; cor. 10–18mm, pale rose to rose-purple, lobes v. narrow. Calif., Oreg. 'Sheltonii': to 60cm, well-branched; fls small, light purple. ssp. *neglecta* (Greene) Epling. St. tinted purple. Lvs to 1.5cm, ovate, serrate. Inner bracts purple, ciliate; cor. 12–14mm, rose-purple. Calif. Z8.

Monastery Bells *Cobaea scandens*.
Mondurup Bell *Darwinia macrostegia*.

Moneses Salisb. WOOD NYMPH; ONE-FLOWERED WINTERGREEN. Pyrolaceae. 1 perenn., everg., stoloniferous herb to 10cm. Lvs opposite or whorled, ovate to obovate, to 3cm, minutely toothed, dark green, glab. Fls term., solitary, nodding; sep. 5, fringed; pet. 5, to 1cm, orbicular, entire or fringed, spreading, waxy white to shell pink; sta. 10. N temp. Z2.

M. uniflora (L.) A. Gray.
→*Pyrola*.

Money Tree *Crassula ovata*.
Moneywort *Lysimachia nummularia*.
Mongolian Lime *Tilia mongolica*.

Monilaria Schwantes. Aizoaceae. 5 low-growing, clump-forming succulents; st. short, often jointed like a string of beads. Lf pairs alternating, of 2 types: one semicylindric, papillose, united at base, the other wholly united into subglobose bodies. Fls long-stalked. S Afr. (Cape Prov.). Z9.

M. chrysoleuca (Schltr.) Schwantes.   St. fleshy, 6–10cm. Cylindrical lvs 30–50×5mm. Fls 3cm diam., snow-white or pink-purple. W Cape.

M. luckhoffii (L. Bol.). = *Diplosoma luckhoffii.*

M. moniliformis (Haw.) Schwantes.   St. and br. 7.5–10cm. Cylindrical lvs 10–15cm×4–5mm. Fls 3cm diam., white. W Cape.

M. peersii L. Bol. = *M. moniliformis.*

M. pisiformis (Haw.) Schwantes.   Freely branched; short st. 2–3cm. Cylindrical lvs 5–6cm×3–4mm. Fls 3cm diam., yellow or flushed red with a white border. W Cape.

→*Conophyllum,   Mesembryanthemum,   Mitrophyllum*   and *Schwantesia.*

MONIMIACEAE Juss. 35/450. *Atherosperma, Hedycarya.*

Monizia Lowe. Umbelliferae. 1 woody-based, thickly taprooted herb to 1m. Lvs to 30cm, mostly basal, triangular in outline, 3–4-pinnatisect, seg. narrow, bright green, incised-serrate. Umbels compound, compact, with 20–25 rays; involucral bracts 6–10, linear-lanceolate; fls dull white. Spring. Madeira. Z9.

M. edulis Lowe. CARROT TREE; DESERTA CARROT.
→*Melanoselinum.*

Monkey-bread Tree *Adansonia.*
Monkey Cup *Nepenthes mirabilis.*
Monkey Flower *Mimulus.*
Monkey Jack *Artocarpus lakoocha.*
Monkey Musk *Mimulus luteus.*
Monkey Nut *Arachis hypogaea; Lecythis zabucaya.*
Monkey Orchid *Orchis simia.*
Monkey Plant *Ruellia makoyana.*
Monkey Pod *Albizia saman.*
Monkey Puzzle *Araucaria araucana.*
Monk's-hood *Aconitum.*
Monk's Rhubarb *Rumex alpinus.*
Monoao *Halocarpus kirkii.*

Monochoria C. Presl. Pontederiaceae. 5 ann. or perenn. aquatic herbs. Rhiz. short or 0; st. erect or creeping. Lvs emergent on long sheathing petioles, basal or cauline. Rac. elongate, scapose with a sheathing lf; perianth seg. 6, oblong, free; sta. 6. Afr., Asia to Aus. Z10.

M. vaginalis (Burm. f.) Kunth. Rhiz. short. St. creeping; rooting. Lvs linear to ovate-cordate, to 10cm. Infl. erect, to 60cm, sub-spicate; fls to 15mm across, upper fls opening first; perianth seg. unequal, blue, spotted red. Summer. S & SE Asia.

Monodora Dunal. Annonaceae. 20 everg. trees and shrubs. Lvs alt., entire, petiolate. Fls pendulous, solitary or paired, long-stalked; sep. swollen; pet. 6, in 2 unequal whorls, undulate to crisped, inner pet. converging at apex; sta. short, crowded; pistils numerous. Carpels fusing to form a globose syncarp. Trop. Afr., Madag. Z10.

M. myristica (Gaertn.) Dunal CALABASH NUTMEG; JAMAICA NUTMEG. To 8m. Lvs to 35cm, obovate-oblong, glossy, emerging purple. Fls fragrant on pedicels to 20cm; outer pet. 6–10cm, elliptic, undulate, incurved, yellow marked purple-brown, inner pet. shorter, ovate-cordate, off-white beneath. Fr. to 15cm diam., furrowed, pulp nutmeg-scented. Trop. W Afr. S to Angola.

Monolena Triana. Melastomataceae. 8 everg. and decid. fleshy herbs. Aerial st. virtually 0, arising from a large, misshapen, succulent rhiz. Lvs fleshy, entire or shallow-toothed, petiolate. Fls subsesile in slender scorpioid cymes; cal. tube fleshy, turbinate; pet. 5, rounded-obovate to spathulate. Trop. S Amer.

M. primuliflora Hook. f. Rhiz. to 13×8cm, exposed, golden-brown. Lvs to 18cm, semi-deciduous, ovate-elliptic, thinly fleshy, finely toothed, ciliate, lustrous light green, above, pink-tinted beneath; petioles to 10cm, flushed pink. Cymes to 15cm; fls to 2.5cm diam., candy-pink. Colomb.
→*Bertolonia.*

Monolopia DC. Compositae. 4 erect, ann. herbs, floccose. Lvs simple, entire or toothed sessile. Cap. radiate, rather large, term., pedunculate; receptacle conic; phyllaries usually with black hairs at apex; ray flts yellow, disc flts yellow. Calif.

M. lanceolata Nutt.   St. to 60cm, simple to diffusely much-branched, lanate. Lvs to 10cm, broadly lanceolate to linear, entire to undulate-dentate. Peduncles to 12cm; involucre to 1cm; phyllaries free; ray flts to 2cm. Spring. Calif.

M. major DC.   Similar to *M. lanceolata* but st. to 1m, sparingly branched, involucre to over 1cm, phyllaries connate in lower half. Spring. Calif.

M. major var. *lanceolata* A. Gray = *M. lanceolata.*

Monopanax Reg.
M. ghiesbreghtii (Versch. ex E. Morr.) Reg. = *Oreopanax xalapensis.*

Monopsis Salisb. Campanulaceae. 18 small ann. or perenn. herbs. Fls small on slender stalks, solitary, axill.; cal. tube oblique, lobes spreading; cor. bilabiate, tube longer than the short lobes, slit above. Trop. S Afr.

M. campanulata (Lam.) Sonder. Prostrate ann. St. to 25cm. Lvs to 1.5cm, obovate-lanceolate, entire to irregularly denticulate, linear-lanceolate above. Fls deep blue. S Afr.

M. debilis (L. f.) C. Presl. Slender erect ann. herb to 20cm. Lvs to 4cm, linear, dentate. Fls dark blue. Autumn. S Afr., nat. W Aus.

M. unidentata (Ait. f.) F. Wimm. Prostrate perenn. Lvs to 2cm, oblong-orbicular, to linear, irregularly dentate. Fls violet to blue. S Afr.
→*Dobrowskya* and *Lobelia.*

Monopyle Moritz ex Benth. & Hook. f. Gesneriaceae. 8 sparsely branched perenn. herbs. Lvs paired, opposite, the smaller lf often reduced. Fls in rac. or pan.; cal. lobes 5; cor. open-campanulate, minutely strigillose, limb with 5 spreading lobes; sta. 4. S Amer. Z10.

M. racemosa Benth. Softly pubesc.; st. brown-purple. Lvs ovate-lanceolate, acuminate, serrulate; petiole to 1cm, maroon-red with a purple-spotted green blotch at base. Fls in a many-fld rac.; cor. to 2.5×2cm, white, interior faintly spotted pink, lower 3 lobes deeply toothed. Colomb.

Monostiche Horan.
M. colorata (Hook.) Körn. = *Calathea colorata.*
M. daniellii Horan. = *Thaumatococcus daniellii.*

Monotagma Schum. Marantaceae. 20 rhizomatous perenn. herbs. Lvs rosulate, long-stalked. Pan. term., usually densely branched; bracts rolled, green or brightly coloured, diverging from rachis to give a comb-like appearance; sep. linear, thin; cor. tube longer with slightly hooded lobes; outer staminode petaloid, coloured. Trop. Amer. Z10.

M. smaragdinum (Lind.) Schum. Erect, to 40cm. Lvs basal, lanceolate to oblong-lanceolate, emerald-green with dark pubescence along midrib above. Infl. spicate, to 13cm; bracts to 3cm, papery; fls 4–8; cor. lobes lanceolate; outer staminode obovate. Ecuad.
→*Calathea, Ischnosiphon* and *Maranta.*

Monox *Empetrum nigrum.*

Monsonia L. Geraniaceae. 25 herbs or subshrubs, similar to *Sarcocaulon*, but st. not so woody, lacking spines. Fls solitary or in umbels, 5-merous; sep. free or fused; pet. free; sta. 15, in groups of 3 or rarely 5, fused at base. Afr., Madag., SW Asia. Z10.

M. lobata Montin = *M. speciosa.*

M. speciosa L. Everg., perenn. subshrub to 30cm. Br. to 16cm, glab. or pubesc. Lvs to 60×60cm, palmately divided, lobes 5–7-pinnatifid or simple, toothed to crenulate, glandular-hairy beneath, densely pubesc. above. Fls solitary, long-stalked; pet. to 6.5×4cm, rose, crimson, purple, base and veins darker, with black lines at base, 5-toothed. Spring. S Afr.

Monstera Adans. SWISS-CHEESE PLANT; WINDOWLEAF. Araceae. 22 robust, everg., epiphytic lianes. St. thick, long, sprawling, leafy, clinging by aerial roots. Lvs dark green, glossy, in 2 ranks; juvenile foliage often entire, overlapping and held close to plant in a shingle-like arrangement; adult lvs entire or pinnatifid, often perforated, coriaceous with long petioles. Peduncle short; spathe large, cymbiform, usually white or cream; spadix covered by hermaphrodite fls, shorter than spathe. Fr. a packed aggregate of polygonal white berries, aromatic, sometimes edible. Trop. Amer. Z10.

M. acuminata K. Koch. SHINGLE PLANT. Lvs to 28×13cm, ovate, base v. unequal, cordate, entire or pinnatifid with 1–2 seg. to 5cm wide. Spathe to 7.5cm, spadix 5cm, oblong-ovate. C Amer.

M. adansonii Schott. Lvs to 90×25cm, ovate to oblong-ovate or -elliptic, v. unequal, perforations irregular, large, elliptic-oblong, in single series on one or both sides, seldom breaking margin. Spathe to 20cm, white, spadix to 10cm, slender. N S Amer. var. *laniata* (Schott) Madison. Lvs 22–55cm, ovate, with many performations. Spadix to 13×2cm, yellow. Costa Rica to Braz.

M. deliciosa Liebm. CERIMAN; SWISS-CHEESE PLANT. Lvs 25–90×25–75cm, orbicular-ovate, cordate, regularly pinnatifid in adults, seg. curved, oblong, usually perforate with elliptic to oblong holes between marginal perforation and midrib. Spathe to 30cm; spadix to 25×3cm, swelling in fr., cream coloured, tasting of banana and pineapple when mature. Mex. to Panama. 'Albovariegata': lvs large, partly rich deep green with other sections a contrasting creamy-white. 'Variegata': lvs and st. irregularly variegated cream or yellow.

M. dubia (HBK) Engl. & K. Krause. Adult lvs to 130×60cm, oblong, regularly pinnatisect, seg. 12–20; linear in juvenile forms and silver-variegated. Spathe large, white; spadix to 42.5cm. C Amer.

M. epipremnoides Engl. Lvs to 90×55cm, ovate- to oblong-elliptic, pinnatifid, seg. to 3.5cm across, perforate with 2–3 ranks of oblong holes, outermost holes breaking margin. Spathe to 40cm, spadix to 19cm. Costa Rica.

M. falcifolia Engl. = M. obliqua.

M. guttifera hort. = M. standleyana.

M. karwinskyi Schott. Lvs 55–85×33–55cm, entire, ovate to oblong-elliptic, with 1 narrow-oblong hole between main lat. veins. Spathe green externally, white within; spadix to 14cm, cream. Trop. Mex.

M. latiloba K. Krause = M. subpinnata.

M. leichtlinii hort. = M. epipremnoides.

M. nechodomii hort. = Epipremnum pinnatum.

M. obliqua (Miq.) Walp. St. slender. Lvs to 20×7cm, elliptic to oblong-lanceolate, much-perforated, with holes covering more area than laminal tissue, or entire. Spathe short, spadix to 3.5cm. N S Amer.

M. pertusa (L.) De Vriese, non Schott = M. adansonii.

M. punctulata Schott. Resembling M. deliciosa but lvs 120×60cm, ovate- to oblong-elliptic, petioles spotted white. Spathe to 14cm, pink-buff externally, white within. Trop. Mex.

M. standleyana Bunting. Lvs to 60×33cm, entire, oblong-ovate, not perforate; spathe 28cm; spadix 15cm. Costa Rica.

M. subpinnata (Schott) Engl. Lvs to 33cm, orbicular-ovate, pinnatifid with 3–4 remote pairs of narrowly oblanceolate seg., each 15×2.5cm. Spathe to 15cm, spadix to 10cm. Peru.

M. uleana Engl. = M. subpinnata.

→Philodendron and Raphidophora.

Montanoa La Ll. & Lex. Compositae. 20 vines or pachycaul treelets and trees. St. terete to tetragonal, herbaceous parts green to purple or brown, woody parts with resinous sap. Lvs opposite, entire to serrate or pinnatifid, rarely pinnatisect, petiolate. Cap. usually radiate, in corymbs or pan.; ray flts white or cream to rose or purple; disc flts yellow to grey-green or black. Trop. Amer. Z10.

M. bipinnatifida (Kunth) K. Koch. Shrub or tree to 10m. Lvs to 30×40cm, broadly ovate to ovate-lanceolate, serrate to deeply 1–2-pinnatifid, entire above, seg. acute to acuminate, dark green, hairy; petioles to 20cm. Cap. pendulous, 2–4cm diam., in term. clusters of over 20 heads; ray flts white; dic flts yellow. Late autumn–winter. S Mex.

M. hibiscifolia Benth. Shrub to 6m; st. terete, light brown. Lvs to 40×30cm, ovate to pentagonal, deeply 3–5-lobed, occas. subentire to serrate, pubesc. beneath; petioles to 6cm, usually auriculate. Cap. pendulous, 1–2cm diam., numerous, in compound corymbs; ray flts white; disc flts yellow. Autumn–winter. S Mex. to Guat. and Costa Rica.

M. mollissima Brongn. & Groenl. Shrub to 2m, downy at first. Lvs to 17×10cm, lanceolate to triangular, entire to irregularly dentate to 3-lobed, base cordate, subglabrous above, softly downy beneath, sessile or petioles to 6cm, usually winged and auriculate. Cap. erect, 1–2cm diam., in compound corymbs; ray flts white; disc flts yellow. Autumn. Mex.

M. tomentosa Cerv. ZOAPATLE. Shrub to 3m, densely branched, downy. Lvs to 20×15cm, triangular-ovate, entire to serrate, irregularly dentate or lobed, base cordate to cuneate, downy beneath; petiole to 4cm. Cap. erect, 3–8mm diam., numerous, in a broad, pan. to 40cm diam.; ray flts cream to white or 0; disc flts yellow. Autumn. Mex.

Montbretia Crocosmia.

Montbretia hort.

M. crocosmiiflora Lemoine = Crocosmia ×crocosmiiflora.

M. pottsii (Bak.) Bak. = Crocosmia pottsii.

Monterey Ceanothus Ceanothus rigidus.

Monterey Cypress Cupressus macrocarpa.

Monterey Manzanita Arctostaphylos hookeri.

Monterey Pine Pinus radiata.

Montezuma Moc. & Sessé ex DC. Bombacaceae. 1 everg. tree to 16m; br. spreading. Lvs 5–20cm, cordate, ovate to orbicular, acute to acuminate, coriaceous; petioles to 12.5cm. Fls axill., solitary; pedicels to 14cm; cal. truncate, to 2.5cm; pet. 5, 6–11×4–7.5cm, pink to crimson above, tan to orange beneath, stellate-pubesc.; sta. united into column to 7cm, fil. white. Fr. ovoid, indehiscent, dry when mature, somewhat succulent when young. Puerto Rico (originally thought to occur in Mex.). Z10.

M. speciosissima Moc. & Sessé ex DC.

→Thespesia.

Montezuma Pine Pinus montezumae.

Monthly Rose Rosa ×damascena var. semperflorens.

Montia L. MINER'S LETTUCE; WINTER PURSLANE. Portulacaceae. 15 small, soft, often glaucous ann. or perenn. herbs. Lvs rather fleshy, basal and stalked or cauline and sessile. Fls small, in simple to compound, axill. or term. rac.; sep. 2; pet. 2–5 (rarely 6); sta. as many as pet. N temp. regions, S Amer., trop. Afr. and Asia.

M. chamissoi (Ledeb. ex Spreng.) T. Dur. & B.D. Jacks. Floating or creeping perenn., rooting at nodes. Lvs to 5cm, spathulate to oblanceolate. Fls to 5mm, pale rose, 1–9 in a rac. Alask. to New Mex. Z3.

M. flagellaris (Bong.) Robinson = Claytonia parvifolia var. flagellaris.

M. parviflora (Douglas) J.T. Howell = M. perfoliata f. parviflora.

M. parvifolia (Moc. ex DC.) Greene = Claytonia parvifolia.

M. parvifolia ssp. flagellaris (Bong.) Ferris = Claytonia parvifolia var. flagellaris.

M. perfoliata (Donn) J.T. Howell. MINER'S LETTUCE; WINTER PURSLANE; CUBAN SPINACH. Ann., 10–30cm or more. Lvs basal, rhombic-ovate to lanceolate, long-petioled. Fls white subtended by a perfoliate leafy disc-like organ. N Amer., nat. GB. f. parviflora (Douglas ex Hook.) J.T. Howell. Basal lvs linear to oblanceolate. Infl. elongate; fls with sep. only c3mm.

M. sibirica (L.) J.T. Howell. SIBERIAN PURSLANE. Usually an ann., to 40cm. Rhombic-ovate to lanceolate, long-stalked, sometimes with bulbils in axils. Fls white to pink, in many-fld term. rac. to 30cm. N Amer. Z3.

→Claytonia.

Montpelier Rock Rose Cistus monspeliensis.

Montpellier Maple Acer monspessulanum.

Monvillea Britt. & Rose.

M. campinensis (Backeb. & Voll) Backeb. = Cereus campinensis.

M. cavendishii sensu Britt. & Rose = Cereus saxicola.

M. diffusa Britt. & Rose = Cereus diffusus.

M. haageana Backeb. = Cereus haageana.

M. insularis (Hemsl.) Britt. & Rose = Cereus insularis.

M. lindenzweigiana (Gürke) Backeb. = Cereus spegazzinii.

M. marmorata (Zeissold) Frič & Kreutz. = Cereus spegazzinii.

M. phatnosperma (Schum.) Britt. & Rose = Cereus spegazzinii.

M. rhodoleucantha (Schum.) A. Berger = Cereus saxicola.

M. smithiana (Britt. & Rose) Backeb. = Cereus smithianus.

M. spegazzinii (F.A. Weber) Britt. & Rose = Cereus spegazzinii.

Moonah Melaleuca lanceolata.

Moon Carrot Seseli.

Moon Daisy Leucanthemum vulgare.

Moonflower Ipomoea alba.

Moonlight Holly Ilex aquifolium 'Flavescens'.

Moonseed Menispermum.

Moonstones Pachyphytum oviferum.

Moon Trefoil Medicago arborea.

Moonwort Botrychium.

Moorberry Vaccinium uliginosum.

Moosewood Acer pensylvanicum.

MORACEAE Link. 48/1200. Antiaris, Artocarpus, Brosimum, Broussonetia, Castilla, Chlorophora, Cudrania, Dorstenia, Ficus, ×Macludrania, Maclura, Milicia, Morus.

Moraea Mill. Iridaceae. 120 cormous perenn. herbs. Lvs basal or borne on st. St. simple or branched; fls in term. clusters enclosed by paired spathes; tep. 6, free, outer 3 usually with a ± erect claw with nectary at base and spreading or reflexed blade often with nectar guides, inner 3 similar but smaller, or tricuspidate, much reduced or 0; sta. 3, opposite outer tep., fil. usually forming column surrounding style; style with 3 br., usually flat, crested and petaloid. Subsaharan Afr. from Ethiop. to S Afr. Z9 unless specified.

M. alpina Goldbl. To 12cm, sometimes branched. Lf 1 terete, less than 1mm diam. Fls violet to deep blue with orange-yellow nectar guides; outer tep. 12–18mm; inner tep. 11–13mm, lanceolate, usually reflexed. Spring–summer. S Afr., Les. Z8.

M. angusta (Thunb.) Ker-Gawl. 20–40cm, unbranched. Lf 1, stiff, terete. Fls pale yellow, usually brown- or grey-tinged, or grey-blue; outer tep. with yellow nectar guides 30–50mm; inner tep. 25–35mm, later reflexed. Late winter–summer. S Afr.

M. arenaria Bak. = *M. serpentina.*

M. aristata (Delaroche) Asch. & Gräbn. 25–35cm, sometimes with 1 br. Lf 1, to 5mm wide, linear. Fls white, outer tep. with concentric crescents of green, blue-violet or black at base; outer tep. 30–35mm, inner tep. 15–20mm, tricuspidate. Spring. S Afr.

M. bellendenii (Sweet) N.E. Br. 50–100cm, usually branched. Lf 1, to 10mm wide, linear. Fls yellow speckled brown-purple in centre; outer tep. 22–33mm, inner tep. tricuspidate, 8–10mm, coiled inwards. Spring. S Afr.

M. bicolor Steud. = *Dietes bicolor.*

M. caeca Barnard ex Goldbl. 20–40cm, occas. 1-branched. Lf 1, to 3mm wide, linear, channelled. Fls lilac-purple, the outer tep. with yellow claws and yellow or black nectar guides at base, 23–28mm, inner tep. tricuspidate to 18mm. Spring. S Afr.

M. calcicola Goldbl. 30–40cm, sometimes with 1 br. Lf 1, usually trailing, 3–5mm wide, linear, channelled, hairy. Fls slightly scented, blue-violet, outer tep. with blue-black nectar guides, 25–35mm, inner tep. 14–22mm, tricuspidate, the central cusp spreading. Spring. S Afr.

M. catenulata Lindl. = *Dietes iridioides.*

M. ciliata (L. f.) Ker-Gawl. 2.5–20cm, unbranched, st. subterranean. Lvs 3–4, 3–35mm wide, usually pubesc., often undulate or crisped. Fls scented, white, yellow, pale brown or blue with yellow nectar guides; outer tep. 20–35mm, inner tep. 16–30mm, erect or spreading, linear or lanceolate. Winter––spring. S Afr. (Cape Prov.).

M. edulis (L. f.) Ker-Gawl. = *M. fugax.*

M. filicaulis Bak. = *M. fugax* ssp. *filicaulis.*

M. fugax (Delaroche) Jacq. 12–50cm, branched. Lvs 1 or 2, trailing, linear or filiform, channelled. Fls scented, white, yellow or blue; outer tep. 20–40mm, blade horizontal or reflexed; inner tep. 20–35×5–8mm, spreading or erect. Late winter–spring, occas. to summer. S Afr. ssp. *fugax.* Lvs 1 or 2, linear, channelled. Fls yellow, white or deep blue; outer tep. 27–40mm. ssp. *filicaulis* (Bak.) Goldbl.. Lvs 2, filiform. Fls white or cream sometimes tinged pink or violet, or deep violet; outer tep. 20–26(–35)mm.

M. gawleri Spreng. To 45cm, usually with 3–5 br. Lvs 1–3, 1–6mm wide, linear, erect or coiled, sometimes wavy or crisped. Fls cream, yellow or brick-red, often with darker veins; outer tep. 12–28mm; inner tep. 10–20mm long, reflexed. Winter––spring. S Afr.

M. gigandra L. Bol. 20–40cm, occas. with 1 br. Lf 1, linear, glab. or somewhat pubesc. Fls blue-purple (rarely orange or white) with bright blue nectar guides bordered white; outer tep. 30–45mm; inner tep. 9–15mm, tricuspidate. Spring. S Afr.

M. glaucopis (DC.) Drapiez = *M. aristata.*

M. gracilenta Goldbl. 30–80cm, with many br. Lf 1, linear, channelled. Fls scented, shortlived, mauve-blue; outer tep. 20–30mm, inner tep. 18–28mm, blade spreading. Spring––summer. S Afr.

M. huttonii (Bak.) Oberm. To 1m, occas. with 1–2 short br. Lf 1, 0.5–2.5cm wide, linear. Fls scented, yellow with darker yellow marks; style crests with brown or purple blotch; outer tep. to 55mm, inner tep. to 45mm, lanceolate, erect. Spring–early summer. S Afr., Les.

M. insolens Goldbl. To 35cm, usually branched. Lf 1, 2–4mm wide, linear, channelled. Fls bright orange-red or cream, claws and nectar guides dark brown; outer tep. to 30mm; inner tep. to 25mm. Spring. S Afr.

M. iridioides L. = *Dietes iridioides.*

M. loubseri Goldbl. 15–20cm, usually with 1 br. Lf 1, 2–3mm wide, linear, channelled, pubesc. Fls violet-blue, black and bearded in centre, with dark blue nectar guides; outer tep. 20–24mm, inner tep. 15–20mm, tricuspidate. Late winter––spring. S Afr.

M. moggii N.E. Br. To 70cm, unbranched. Lf 1, to 1.5cm wide, linear, flat or channelled above, channelled beneath. Fls white, cream or yellow, the outer tep. 40–75mm with bright yellow nectar guides bordered with purple veins; inner tep. to 60mm, erect. Summer–autumn. S Afr., Swaz.

M. natalensis Bak. 15–45cm, branched. Lf 1, narrowly linear to subterete. Fls lilac to violet-blue, outer tep. 14–20mm, with yellow nectar guides bordered purple, inner tep. to 15mm, linear-lanceolate, reflexed. Summer. S Afr., Zimb., Zam., Malawi, Moz., Zaire.

M. neopavonia R. Fost. 30–60cm, sometimes with 1 br. Lf 1, 3–5mm wide, linear, channelled, pubesc. Fls orange, rarely

orange-red, the outer tep. 22–40mm with deep blue nectar guides, sometimes speckled, the claws speckled with deep blue, inner tep. entire or tricuspidate. Spring. S Afr.

M. papilionacea (L. f.) Ker-Gawl. 10–15cm, usually branched. Lvs 2–4, to 7mm wide, linear, usually hairy, ciliate. Fls scented, pale yellow or salmon-pink, the outer sep. 22–28mm, with yellow nectar guides edged with yellow, green or red, inner tep. 20–22mm, reflexed. Late winter–spring. S Afr.

M. pavonia (L. f.) Ker-Gawl. = *M. neopavonia.*

M. polyanthos L. f. 10–45cm, usually branched above. Lvs 2–3, basal, longer than st., 3–6mm wide, linear, channelled. Fls scented, white, lilac or pale to deep purple-blue, all tep. with yellow nectar guides; claws forming cup, outer tep. 23–40mm, inner tep. 18–55mm, spreading. Winter–spring. S Afr.

M. polystachya (Thunb.) Ker-Gawl. To 80cm, branched. Lvs 3–5, usually trailing, 6–20mm wide, linear, flat or channelled. Fls pale blue or violet, outer tep. 36–55mm with yellow or orange nectar guides; inner tep. 30–45mm, erect or reflexed. Autumn–winter. S Afr., Nam., Bots.

M. ramosa (Thunb.) Ker-Gawl. = *M. ramosissima.*

M. ramosissima (L. f.) Druce. 50–120cm, branched. Lvs numerous, 1.5–3cm wide, somewhat channelled. Fls bright yellow, outer tep. 30–40mm, with darker yellow nectar guides, reflexed, inner tep. to 35mm, also reflexed; style to 20–25mm, crests prominent. Spring–summer. S Afr.

M. robinsoniana (F. Muell.) Benth. & F. Muell. = *Dietes robinsoniana.*

M. schimperi (Hochst.) Pichi-Serm. 20–50cm, unbranched. Lf 1, 9–15mm wide, linear, channelled below. Fls purple-blue, outer tep. 40–65mm, with yellow nectar guides; inner tep. 35–45mm, lanceolate, erect. Spring–early autumn. Trop. Afr.

M. serpentina Bak. 4–20cm, br. several. Lvs 1–5, linear, sometimes pubesc., wavy or coiled. Fls white to yellow, inner tep. sometimes flushed with violet or mauve-pink, outer tep. 24–30mm, with large, deep yellow nectar guides, inner tep. 20–30mm, erect, oblanceolate. Spring. S Afr.

M. spathacea (Thunb.) Ker-Gawl. = *M. spathulata.*

M. spathulata (L. f.) Klatt. 50–90cm, usually unbranched. Lf 1, to 1.5cm wide, linear, flat or channelled. Fls yellow, outer tep. 35–50mm with darker yellow nectar guides, inner tep. erect, 30–40mm. Flowering time variable. S Afr., Les., Swaz., Zimb., Moz. Z8.

M. speciosa (L. Bol.) Goldbl. 40–75cm, branching toward apex. Lvs several, to 4cm wide, channelled, undulate. Fls erect or drooping, pale blue-mauve, all tep. with yellow nectar guide, outer tep. 30–45mm, inner tep. narrower. Winter–spring. S Afr.

M. stricta Bak. 15–25cm, usually with 3–6 br. Lf 1, 1.5mm wide, terete. Fls lilac or violet-blue, outer tep. to 24mm, with yellow or orange nectar guides; inner tep. 15–18mm, erect, linear or lanceolate. Winter–spring. E Ethiop. to E Cape. Z8.

M. thomsonii Bak. 15–30cm, usually with 3–6 br. Lf 1, 1.5mm wide, terete. Fls pale blue-violet, all tep. with yellow nectar guide; outer tep. 20–24mm, lanceolate or obovate, inner tep. 16–18mm, lanceolate, spreading. Winter–spring or early summer. Tanz., Malawi, S Afr. (E Transvaal).

M. tricolor Andrews. 5–15cm, unbranched. Lvs usually 3, glab. or pubesc., ciliate. Fls yellow, pink, red or pale purple, outer tep. 20–25mm, with yellow nectar guides sometimes bordered with maroon; inner tep. narrower. Winter–spring. S Afr.

M. tripetala (L. f.) Ker-Gawl. 10–50cm, sometimes branched. Lf 1(–2), trailing, linear or lanceolate, sometimes pubesc. Fls pale to deep blue or purple, sometimes yellow pale pink, outer tep. 20–35mm, with white or yellow nectar guide; inner tep. v. small, usually filiform. Late winter–summer. S Afr.

M. trita N.E. Br. = *M. stricta.*

M. vegeta L. 10–30cm, usually branched. Lvs several, linear, glaucous. Fls small, dull-coloured, yellow, brown, pink or blue, outer tep. 20–25mm, with yellow nectar guide lanceolate, inner tep. smaller. Spring. S Afr.

M. villosa (Ker-Gawl.) Ker-Gawl. 15–40cm, branched or unbranched. Lf 1, linear, channelled, pubesc. Fls white, cream, pink, lilac, orange or purple, outer tep. 28–40mm, with yellow nectar guides edged with 1 or 2 broad outer bands of darker colour; inner tep. 16–30mm, tricuspidate. Late winter–early spring. S Afr. ssp. *villosa.* St. usually branched. Fls pink, blue or purple (rarely cream or green); outer tep. 30–40mm, blades ± horizontal. ssp. *elandsmontana* Goldbl. St. usually unbranched. Fls orange, nectar guides edged dark blue (rarely white with brown nectar guides), rather cup-shaped.

Morangaya G. Rowley.

M. pensilis (K. Brandg.) G. Rowley = *Echinocereus pensilis.*

Morass Royal *Roystonea princeps.*

Morawetzia Backeb.
M. doelziana Backeb. = *Oreocereus doelzianus*.

Morello Cherry *Prunus cerasus* var. *austera*.
Moreton Bay Chestnut *Castanospermum*.
Moreton Bay Fig *Ficus macrophylla*.
Moreton Bay Pine *Araucaria cunninghamii*.

Moricandia DC. VIOLET CABBAGE. Cruciferae. 8 often woody-based, branching ann. or perenn. herbs. Lvs dense, simple, sessile, fleshy, glab., becoming broader and clasping higher up st. Rac. loose; sep. 4, inner sep. saccate at base; pet. 4, large; sta. 6. Fr. a silique. Medit.
M. arvensis (L.) DC. To 60cm. Lvs glaucous, entire, obovate. Fls 10–20; pet. 2cm, violet. Fr. to 8cm, angled in section. W Medit. Z8.
M. hesperidiflora DC. = *Diplotaxis acris*.
M. moricandioides (Boiss.) Heyw. Similar to *M. arvensis* except lvs sometimes toothed. Fls more numerous. Fr. terete. SC & E Spain. Z8.
M. ramburii Webb = *M. moricandioides*.
→*Brassica*.

Morina L. Morinaceae. 4 perenn. herbs. Lvs tough, glossy mostly basal, tufted, undulate and spiny-toothed, diminishing to spiny leafy bracts subtending fls in marked verticillasters on a term. spike. Cal. 2-lipped, enclosed within bristle-tipped involucel; cor. tubular, 5-lobed, limb ± bilabiate. E Eur. to Asia. Z6.
M. coulteriana Royle. To 80cm. Lvs narrowly oblong-lanceolate, margins spiny. Cor. to 1.75cm, pale yellow. W Himal.
M. longifolia Wallich ex DC. WHORLFLOWER. To 1.3m. Lvs to 30cm, narrowly oblong, undulate to pinnatifid, spiny-toothed. Cor. to 2.5cm, white, flushing shell pink, then bright crimson, particularly the limb. Himal.
M. persica L. 30–90cm. Lvs 15–20cm, linear to elliptic, dentate to pinnatifid. Cor. 3cm, villous, yellow with pink lips flushing dark pink after fertilization. Balk. Penins. Z6.

MORINACEAE J. Agardh. 3/13. *Morina*.

Morinda L. Rubiaceae. 80 shrubs, climbers or trees. Lvs opposite or in whorls of 3, stipulate. Fls in dense, often paniculate or umbellate clusters, often united by cal.; cal. tube obovoid or urn-shaped, limb truncate or minutely toothed; cor. tube funnel- or salver-shaped, lobes 4–7, usually 5; sta. 4–7. Fr. a syncarp, fleshy. Trop.
M. citrifolia L. INDIAN MULBERRY; AWL TREE; PAINKILLER. To 6m+; br. 4-angled, glab. Lvs to 25×10cm, oblong to elliptic, sublustrous and dark above, pale beneath. Fls sessile, few to several in heads; cor. tube 1cm, pubesc. at throat, white or green. Fr. ovoid, to 4×3cm, pale yellow or green to white. Spring. Trop. Asia, Aus. and Polyn.; widely nat. in Trop. Amer., W Indies. 'Potteri': to 4m; lvs mottled white. 'Variegata': lvs marbled white. var. *bracteata* Roxb. Infl. occas. bracteate; cal. with spathulate or lanceolate, leaflike, white-lobed, to 8cm. India, Sri Lanka.
M. citrifolia Bedd. non L. = *M. tinctoria*.
M. citrifolia var. *potteri* Deg. = *M. citrifolia* 'Potteri'.
M. exserta Roxb. = *M. tinctoria*.
M. jasminoides Cunn. Shrub, to 6m, glab. Lvs to 8cm, ovate to oblong-lanceolate or elliptic. Fls cream to buff, sweetly fragrant, to 12 or more in heads. Fr. globose, 1cm wide. Spring. Aus.
M. quadrangularis hort. = *M. citrifolia*.
M. royoc hort. = *M. umbellata*.
M. tinctoria Roxb. Tree; br. pubesc. Lvs to 25cm, oblong to elliptic-obovate or lanceolate, glab. or, rarely, pubesc. beneath. Infl. solitary or paniculate; fls white; cor. tube to 2cm, hairy. Fr. to 2.5cm wide, green. India, SE Asia.
M. umbellata L. Shrub, erect or climbing, to 6m. Br. glab. or pubesc. Lvs to 10×5cm, oblong to elliptic, glab. or pubesc. beneath. Fls white in umbellate heads; cor. rotate, to 6mm, hairy at throat. Fr. to 1.25cm wide, orange-red. Trop. Asia, Aus.

Morinda Spruce *Picea smithiana*.

Moringa Adans. Moringaceae. 14 decid., somewhat succulent trees; trunk thick, bark resinous. Lvs large, 2–3-pinnate. Fls in axill. rac. or pan., zygomorphic; sep. and pet. 5, free; sta. 10. Fr. a pod-like capsule; seeds oily. Afr., Madag., India, Arabia. Z10.
M. longituba Engl. Small bush with large rootstock. Lvs bipinnate. Fls precocious, coral red, tubular, to 8mm. W Somalia, Kenya.
M. oleifera Lam. HORSERADISH TREE; BEN; OIL OF BEN TREE. Tree, to 8m. Lvs to 60cm, 2–3-pinnate. Fls cream, 2.5cm diam.,

fragrant, in loose pan. to 15cm. Fr. to 50×1.5cm, 9-ribbed, light brown. Arabia and India; nat. W Indies, S Asia and Afr.
M. ovalifolia Dinter & A. Berger. AFRICAN MORINGO. Tree to 7m; trunk squat, succulent. Lvs to 60cm, bipinnate. Fls white, to 3mm diam., many, in pan. Fr. to 40cm, 3-sided, flattened. Nam.
M. pterygosperma Gaertn. = *M. oleifera*.

Moringaceae Dumort. 1/14. *Moringa*.

Morisia Gay. Cruciferae. 1 hairy perenn. herb. Lvs basal, 5–8cm, densely rosulate, oblong-lanceolate, pinnatisect, glossy above, veins pubesc. beneath. Fls 8–16, solitary on erect pedicels, 4-merous, golden-yellow, to 2cm across. Spring–early summer. Corsica, Sardinia. Z7.
M. hypogaea J. Gay = *M. monanthos*.
M. monanthos (Viv.) Asch. 'Fred Hemingway': fls larger.

Mormodes Lindl. Orchidaceae. 20 epiphytic orchids. Rhiz. short. Pbs 10–20cm, fleshy, cylindrical to fusiform. Lvs c40cm, narrowly elliptic to linear-lanceolate; distichous, sheathing pb. and apical, plicate, usually thin-textured. Rac. lat.; fls fleshy; tep. free, spreading or reflexed, often narrow; lip v. fleshy, simple to 3-lobed. C & S Amer. Z9.
M. aromatica Lindl. Infl. to 32cm, ascending, many-fld; fls to 4cm diam., green-brown to purple-brown spotted dark purple, spicily fragrant; sep. fleshy, ovate-elliptic, acute; pet. darker than sep., elliptic-ovate, acute, finely dentate; lip lat. lobes apiculate, midlobe triangular, long-apiculate. Mex., El Salvador, Hond.
M. atropurpurea Hook. = *M. hookeri*.
M. buccinator Lindl. Infl. to 50cm, erect to arching, few to many-fld; fls to 6.5cm diam., colour variable; green flushed pink with an ivory lip, bright lime green to pale yellow, wholly deep yellow-orange (var. *aurantiaca* Rolfe), maroon with a paler lip, bronze with a rose-pink lip or wholly white; tep. linear to oblong-lanceolate, reflexed; lip strongly curved over column, slender-clawed, obovate or ovate-elliptic, apiculate, reflexed, apex truncate. Mostly late winter. Mex., Guat., Panama, Colomb., Venez., Guyana.
M. colossus Rchb. f. Infl. to 60cm, arching many-fld; fls to 12cm diam., fragrant, usually spreading, olive green to yellow tinted rose at base, lip bronze to bright yellow with red spots at base; sep. to linear-lanceolate; pet. lanceolate; lip to short-clawed, simple, ovate-rhombic to ovate-elliptic, acute or acuminate, lat. margins strongly recurved. Spring. Costa Rica, Panama.
M. histrio Lind. & Rchb. f. = *M. warscewiczii*.
M. hookeri Lem. Infl. short, erect, few-fld; fls to 4cm diam., fragrant, red to deep red-brown; sep. lanceolate, reflexed; pet. somewhat shorter; lip obovate, truncate, apiculate, obscurely 3-lobed; lat. lobes pubesc. Winter. Costa Rica, Panama.
M. ignea Lindl. & Paxt. Infl. to 60cm, arching, few to many-fld; fls to 5cm diam., fragrant, variable in colour – yellow, olive-green or tan to red, often spotted red-brown, lip white, yellow, olive, tan or brick red; sep. lanceolate, reflexed; pet. elliptic-lanceolate, reflexed; lip v. fleshy, clawed, subrotund, shortly apiculate. Spring. Costa Rica, Panama, Colomb.
M. macrantha Lindl. & Paxt. = *M. colossus*.
M. maculata (Klotzsch) L.O. Williams. Pbs to 15cm. Infl. to 40cm, arching to horizontal, many-fld; fld to 4cm, fragrant, pale tawny-yellow spotted red-chocolate; tep. upcurved, ovate, acuminate; lip lat. lobes acuminate, midlobe large, acuminate. Autumn-early winter. Mex. var. *unicolor* (Hook.) L.O. Williams. Fls clear pale yellow.
M. pardina Batem. = *M. maculata*.
M. pardina var. *unicolor* Hook. = *M. maculata* var. *unicolor*.
M. rolfeana Lind. Infl. to 15cm, erect, few-fld; fls to 10cm, pale green to golden-yellow marked red, lip sometimes heavily stained dark red-brown within; sep. ovate to lanceolate; pet. elliptic-oblong to obovate, obtuse or apiculate; lip simple, obovate-oblong to elliptic, apex recurved. Peru.
M. vernixium Rchb. f. = *M. buccinator*.
M. warscewiczii Klotzsch. Infl. to 50cm, several-fld; fls 8cm diam., v. fleshy, variable in colour – maroon, olive or yellow-green mottled maroon or striped and spotted rusty red, the lip maroon, green-white or yellow sparsely spotted purple or red-brown; sep. lanceolate to oblong-lanceolate, reflexed; pet. elliptic-lanceolate, reflexed, undulate; lip pubesc., lateral lobes linear-oblanceolate, twisted, midlobe linear to subtriangular, truncate or rounded. Mex., Guat., Hond.
M. wendlandii Rchb. f. = *M. colossus*.
→*Catasetum*.

Mormolyca Fenzl. Orchidaceae. 6 epiphytic orchids. Rhiz. short, sometimes creeping. Pbs subglobose to ellipsoid-cylindrical, apically unifoliate. Lvs erect, elliptic-oblong to ligulate. Fls fleshy, solitary on long stalks, borne basally; sep. similar, spreading; pet. smaller; lip 3-lobed, lat. lobes erect, small, mid-lobe large, decurved, disc callose. C Amer., N S Amer. Z10.

M. gracilipes (Schltr.) Garay & Wirth. Infl. to 23cm, usually exceeding lvs; fls to 6cm diam; tep. yellow-brown; sep. lanceolate to ovate-lanceolate, margins involute, long-acuminate; pet. obliquely linear or linear-lanceolate, acute, base twisted; lip yellow-brown finely marked dark purple-brown, obovate or obovate-rhombic, abruptly acute, lat. lobes indented. Venez., Colomb., Ecuad., Peru.

M. lineolata Fenzl = *M. ringens*.

M. peruviana Schweinf. Infl. to 12cm, several, slender, erect; fls to 3cm diam., yellow; sep. oblong-lanceolate, mucronate; pet. linear-oblong, acute or apiculate; lip ovate-subquadrate, lat. lobes porrect, triangular-lanceolate, acuminate, midlobe sub-orbicular, truncate or rounded. Peru.

M. ringens (Lindl.) Schltr. Infl. to 35cm, usually equalling lvs; fls to 3cm diam., fleshy, yellow to lavender; sep. lined purple, elliptic-oblong, obtuse; pet. elliptic-oblong, obtuse or rounded, convex; lip pilose, ciliolate, lavender to maroon, lat. lobes minute, acute to obtuse, midlobe suborbicular, decurved. Mex. to Costa Rica.
→*Trigonidium*.

Morning Glory *Ipomoea* (*I. tricolor*).
Morning-noon-and-night *Brunfelsia australis*.
Morning Star Lily *Lilium concolor*.
Morning Widow *Geranium phaeum*.
Moroccan Broom *Argyrocytisus battandieri*.
Moroccan Cypress *Cupressus sempervirens* var. *atlantica*.
Moroccan Fir *Abies pinsapo* var. *marocana*.
Moroccan Ivy *Hedera maroccana*.
Morrison Feather Flower *Verticordia nitens*.
Morro *Crescentia alata*.
Mortitia *Vaccinium mortinia*.

Morus L. MULBERRY. Moraceae. 12 decid., monoecious or dioecious trees and shrubs to 20m. Crown rounded, br. often rugged; bark rough, often burred. Shoots exuding latex when cut. Lvs mostly ovate-cordate and serrate, simple or 2–5-lobed; petiole short. Fls inconspicuous in green, axill., bracteate, unisexual catkins. Fr. superficially resembling a raspberry, 20–100 per catkin, closely packed but separate, drupaceous, forming a syncarp. W N Amer. and S Eur. E to Jap., S to lowland tropics in C Afr.

M. acidosa Griff. = *M. australis*.

M. alba L. WHITE MULBERRY. Tree to 16m. Young shoots downy at first. Lvs 8–20×6–12cm, broad ovate-cordate, dentate, apex rounded to acute, often bi- or tri-lobed; glossy above, glab. beneath except veins. Fr. 1–2.5cm, green-white ripening pink to dark red. China. Z5. 'Aurea': lvs and bark yellow. 'Chaparral': vigorous growth; br. slender, drooping; lvs bright green; no fr. 'Constantinopolitana': compact, thickly branched tree; lvs ovate, to 15cm long, leathery, coarsely serrate, dark green and glossy above, lighter beneath. 'Fegyvernekiana': dwarf, to 80cm. 'Fruitless': sterile, fast-growing, to 18m, crown rounded; lvs oblong-ovate, glossy. 'Kingan': sterile; suitable where fr. drop a nuisance. 'Laciniata' ('Skeletoniana'): lvs deeply lobed and toothed. 'Macrophylla': lvs mostly large, 20×15cm. 'Multicaulis': suckering shrub; lvs to 35cm; fr nearly black when ripe. Probably more than one clone involved. 'Nana': habit dwarf, shrubby, rounded; lvs regularly lobed. 'Nigrobacca': fr ripen dark purple. 'Pendula': shoots hanging; crown weeping if trained or grafted high on st. of type. 'Pyramidalis': conic. 'Striblingii': ♂ fls falling early; no fr. 'Venosa': lvs slender-tapered, with conspicuous pale downy veins. var. *tartarica* (Pall.) Ser. V. hardy, small, bushy. Lvs and fr. smaller.

M. alba var. *latifolia* Burret = *M. alba* 'Multicaulis'.
M. alba var. *multicaulis* (Perrott.) Loud. = *M. alba* 'Multicaulis'.
M. alba var. *stylosa* (Ser.) Bur. = *M. australis*.

M. australis Poir. Tree or shrub to 8m; young shoots glab. Lvs 5–15×3–10cm, mostly cordate-ovate, serrate, often deeply 3–5-lobed, scabrous green above, thinly pubesc. beneath at first, soon glab. Fr. 1.5cm, deep red, sweet. E Asia. Z6.

M. bombycis Koidz. = *M. alba*.

M. cathayana Hemsl. Tree to 15m; young shoots downy. Lvs 7–15×5–12cm, cordate, blunt-serrate, cuspidate, simple,to 3-lobed, scabrous above, pubesc. beneath. Fr. 2.5cm, ripening red to dark purple. C China. Z6.

M. celtidifolia Sarg. = *M. microphylla*.
M. excelsa Welw. = *Milicia excelsa*.
M. indica Roxb. non L. = *M. australis*.
M. japonica Bail. = *M. alba*.
M. kagayamae Koidz. = *M. alba*.
M. laevigata Wallich ex Brandis = *M. macroura*.
M. macroura Miq. Tree to 10m. Lvs 7–20cm, cordate or rounded at base, sparsely pubesc. Himal., Burm., S China. Z8.

M. microphylla Buckl. TEXAS MULBERRY. Tree or shrub to 6m; shoots nearly glab. Lvs 3–7cm, commonly 2–5-lobed or simple, glossy above, glabrate beneath. Fr. 1–1.5cm, dark purple. Ariz. to W Tex. and N Mex. Z6.

M. mongolica (Bur.) Schneid. = *M. alba*.

M. nigra L. BLACK MULBERRY. Tree to 15m; young shoots tomentose. Lvs 8–12×6–8cm, simple broad ovate-cordate, coarsely, often double-serrate, scabrous above, paler and pub-esc. beneath. Fr. 2–2.5cm, green ripening through orange and red to deep purple. Probably SW Asia, but extensive early cult. has obscured range. Z5.

M. rubra L. RED MULBERRY. Tree to 15m, rarely 20m. Shoots thinly pubesc. Lvs 8–12×6–8cm, simple suborbicular to slightly cordate (not strongly as in *M. nigra*) at base, larger and 2–3-lobed on strong shoots, serrate, scabrous above, paler and pub-esc. beneath. Fr. 2.5–3cm, green ripening through orange and red to purple. E US, extreme SE Canada. Z5. 'Nana': dwarf, slow-growing; lvs smaller, 3–5-lobed.

M. stylosa Ser. = *M. australis*.

Mosaic Fig *Ficus aspera*.
Mosaic Plant *Fittonia verschaffeltii*.

Moscharia Ruiz & Pav. Compositae. 2 pubesc. ann. herbs. St. erect, branched above. Lower lvs elliptic, pinnate, upper lvs entire or lobed, amplexicaul. Cap. discoid, term., sessile, in a many-branched, flat-topped cyme of many smaller heads surrounding a central, solitary, larger head. Chile. Z10.

M. pinnatifida Ruiz & Pav. To 70cm. Basal lvs to 18×3cm, seg. dentate, st. lvs lanceolate. Infl. hemispherical, to 8×10cm; flts white to pale rose. Spring. C Chile.

Moschatel *Adoxa moschatellina*.
Moses in his Cradle, Moses in the Bulrushes, Moses on a Raft *Tradescantia spathacea*.
Moso Bamboo *Phyllostachys edulis*.
Mosquito-bills *Dodecatheon hendersonii*.
Mosquito Fern *Azolla* (*A. caroliniana*).
Mosquito Flower *Lopezia racemosa*.
Mosquito Grass *Bouteloua gracilis*.
Mosquito Orchid *Acianthus exsertus*.
Moss Campion *Silene acaulis*.
Moss Cypress *Crassula muscosa*.
Moss Fern *Selaginella pallescens*.
Moss Locust *Robinia hispida*.
Moss Phlox *Phlox subulata*.
Moss Pink *Phlox subulata*.
Moss Rose *Portulaca*.
Moss Verbena *Verbena tenuisecta*.
Mossy Cup Oak *Quercus macrocarpa*.
Mossy Saxifrage *Saxifraga bryoides*; *S. hypnoides*.
Moth Bean *Vigna aconitifolia*.
Mother-in-law's Seat *Echinocactus grusonii*.
Mother-in-law's Tongue *Dieffenbachia*; *Sansevieria* (*S. trifasciata*).
Mother of Pearl Plant *Graptopetalum paraguayense*.
Mother of Thousands *Saxifraga stolonifera*.
Mother of Thyme *Acinos arvensis*.
Mother Shield Fern *Polystichum proliferum*.
Mother Spleenwort *Asplenium bulbiferum*.
Motherwort *Leonurus cardiaca*.
Moth Mullein *Verbascum blattaria*.
Moth Orchid *Phalaenopsis*.
Mottlecah *Eucalyptus macrocarpa*.
Mottled Gum *Eucalyptus mannifera*.
Mottled Spurge *Euphorbia lactea*.
Mountain Alder *Alnus tenuifolia*.
Mountain Ash *Eucalyptus regnans*; *Sorbus aucuparia*.
Mountain Asphodel *Xerophyllum asphodeloides*.
Mountain Avens *Dryas* (*D. octopetala*).
Mountain Azalea *Loiseleuria procumbens*.
Mountain Banksia *Banksia canei*.
Mountain Beech *Nothofagus solanderi* var. *cliffortioides*.
Mountain Bladder Fern *Cystopteris montana*.
Mountain Blueberry *Vaccinium membranaceum*.
Mountain Box *Arctostaphylos uva-ursi*.
Mountain Buckler Fern *Oreopteris limbosperma*.
Mountain Camellia *Stewartia ovata*.
Mountain Correa *Correa lawrenciana*.
Mountain Cranberry *Vaccinium vitis-idaea*.
Mountain Currant *Ribes alpinum*.
Mountain Daisy *Celmisia achilleoides*.
Mountain Dandelion *Agoseris*; *Oenothera flava*.
Mountain Devil *Lambertia formosa*.
Mountain Dogwood *Cornus nuttallii*.
Mountain Ebony *Bauhinia* (*B. variegata*).

Mountain Fern *Oreopteris limbosperma.*
Mountain Fetter Bust *Pieris floribunda.*
Mountain Flax *Phormium colensoi.*
Mountain Fringe *Adlumia fungosa.*
Mountain Guava *Psidium montanum.*
Mountain Gum *Eucalyptus dalrympleana.*
Mountain Heath Myrtle *Baeckea gunniana.*
Mountain Hemlock *Tsuga mertensiana.*
Mountain Hickory *Acacia penninervis.*
Mountain Holly *Ilex montana; Nemopanthus.*
Mountain Hollyhock *Iliamna rivularis.*
Mountain Houstonia *Houstonia purpurea.*
Mountain Immortelle *Erythrina poeppigiana.*
Mountain Ivy-tree *Pseudopanax colensoi.*
Mountain Juniper *Juniperus communis.*
Mountain Laurel *Kalmia latifolia.*
Mountain Lily *Leucocrinum; Lilium auratum; Ranunculus lyallii.*
Mountain Long Pepper *Piper sylvaticum.*
Mountain Lover *Paxistima canbyi; P. myrtifolia.*
Mountain Mahogany *Cercocarpus.*
Mountain Male Fern *Dryopteris oreades.*
Mountain Maple *Acer spicatum.*
Mountain Melic *Melica nutans.*
Mountain Misery *Chamaebatia.*
Mountain Ninebark *Physocarpus monogynus.*
Mountain Panax *Pseudopanax simplex* var. *sinclairii.*
Mountain Pansy *Viola lutea.*
Mountain Parsley Fern *Cryptogramma crispa.*
Mountain Pawpaw *Carica pubescens.*
Mountain Pennycress *Thlaspi montanum.*
Mountain Pepper *Drimys lanceolata.*
Mountain Phlox *Phlox ovata, P. subulata.*
Mountain Pine *Halocarpus bidwilli; Pinus mugo.*
Mountain Pitcher Plant *Sarracenia rubra.*
Mountain Pride *Penstemon newberryi.*
Mountain Rhubarb *Rumex alpinus.*
Mountain Rimu *Lepidothamnus laxifolius.*
Mountain Rocket *Bellendena montana.*
Mountain Rose *Protea nana.*
Mountain Sedge *Carex montana.*
Mountain Sorrel *Oxyria digyna.*
Mountain Sow Thistle *Cicerbita alpina.*
Mountain Spleenwort *Asplenium montanum.*
Mountain Spotted Gum *Eucalyptus mannifera.*
Mountain Spray *Holodiscus dumosus.*
Mountain Spruce *Picea engelmannii.*
Mountain Sumac *Rhus copallina.*
Mountain Swamp Gum *Eucalyptus camphora.*
Mountain-sweet *Ceanothus americanus.*
Mountain Tassel *Soldanella montana.*
Mountain Tea *Gaultheria procumbens.*
Mountain Thistle *Acanthus montanus.*
Mountain Trumpet *Schefflera morototonii.*
Mountain Willow *Salix arbuscula.*
Mountain Wood Fern *Oreopteris limbosperma.*
Mount Atlas Mastic *Pistacia atlantica.*
Mount Cook Lily *Ranunculus lyallii.*
Mount Etna Broom *Genista aetnensis.*
Mount Morgan Wattle *Acacia podalyriifolia.*
Mount St Helena Ceanothus *Ceanothus divergens.*
Mount Tranquillon Ceanothus *Ceanothus papillosus* var. *roweanus.*
Mount Vision Ceanothus *Ceanothus gloriosus* var. *porrectus.*
Mournful Widow *Scabiosa atropurpurea.*
Mourning Bride *Scabiosa atropurpurea.*
Mourning Iris *Iris susiana.*
Mourning Widow *Geranium phaeum.*
Mouse And Honey Plant *Homoranthus papillatus.*
Mouse-ear Chickweed *Cerastium.*
Mouse Garlic *Allium angulosum.*
Mouse Plant *Arisarum proboscideum; Homoranthus papillatus.*
Mousou-chiku *Phyllostachys edulis.*
Moutan *Paeonia suffruticosa.*
Mowbulan Whitewood *Polyscias elegans.*
Moxie Plum *Gaultheria hispidula.*
Msasa *Brachystegia spiciformis.*
Mucaja *Acrocomia aculeata.*

Mucuna Adans. Leguminosae (Papilionoideae). 100 lianes, climbing herbs and erect shrubs. Lvs trifoliolate. Fls pea-like in axill. clusters or rac., often pendulous. Fr. oblong to linear, often toulose, thickly amber or dark-brown velutinous and/or bristly. Tropics and subtrop. Z10.
M. aterrima (Piper & Tracy) Holland = *M. pruriens* var. *utilis.*
M. bennettii F. Muell. NEW GUINEA CREEPER. Woody climber to 20m. Lfts 11–13.5cm, elliptic, glab. Fls to 8.5cm, vivid scarlet or flame-coloured, in short infl. New Guinea.
M. cochinchinensis (Lour.) A. Chev. = *M. pruriens.*
M. deeringiana (Bort) Merrill = *M. pruriens* var. *utilis.*
M. kraetkei Warb. = *M. novoguineensis.*
M. nivea DC. = *M. pruriens.*
M. novoguineensis R. Scheff. Woody climber to 30m. Lfts 10–19cm, elliptic, glab. or pubesc. throughout. Fls 5–8cm, flame-coloured to scarlet, in pendulous, conical infl., 7–60cm long. New Guinea.
M. pruriens (L.) DC. VELVET BEAN. Ann. or perenn. semi-woody, climbing herb to 4m. Lfts 5–19cm, ovate, obovate, rhomboid or elliptic, grey-hirsute. Rac. to 30cm; fls 3–4cm, dark damson coloured to pale purple or white. Asia; nat. elsewhere. var. *utilis* (Wallich ex Wight) Bak. ex Burck. VELVET BEAN; FLORIDA BEAN; BENGHAL BEAN. Rac. to 30cm, pendulous; standard purple flushed green, wings dirty red.
M. sempervirens Hemsl. Perenn. everg. climber to 12m. Lfts prominently reticulate-veined, to 12cm. Rac. short, nodding; fls waxy, bruised purple-black, malodorous. Spring. China.

Mudgee *Acacia spectabilis.*
Mud Midget *Wolffiella gladiata.*
Mud Plantain *Heteranthera.*

Muehlenbeckia Meissn. Polygonaceae. 15 climbing or procumbent subshrubs and shrubs. St. initially robust, erect or stoloniferous, later densely branched with dark, wiry interlacing branchlets. Lvs small, usually dark, glossy green. Fls green-white, minute; perianth deeply 5-lobed; sta. 8; styles 3. Fr. a 3-angled black achene usually surrounded by white, fleshy peri-anth cup. S Amer., NZ, Aus., New Guinea.
M. adpressa (Labill.) Meissn. Spreading or climbing shrub, often twining to 2m. Lvs 1–6cm, orbicular to ovate or lanceolate, cordate at base, minutely crisped. Aus. Z9.
M. adpressa var. *hastata* Meissn. = *M. gunnii.*
M. australis (Forst. f.) Meissn. Stout vine to 10m, branchlets slender. Lvs ovate to nearly orbicular, 2–8cm. Summer–early autumn. NZ. Z8.
M. axillaris (Hook. f.) Walp. Small prostrate or straggling shrub, forming clumps to 1m across. Lvs 5–10mm, oblong to orbicular, glab., dark green above, grey beneath. Summer–early autumn. Aus., Tasm., NZ. Z8.
M. complexa (Cunn.) Meissn. MAIDENHAIR VINE; WIRE VINE; MATTRESS VINE; NECKLACE VINE. Semi-decid. liane, creeping or climbing to 5m forming dense tangles. Lvs 5–20mm, purple or silver beneath, oblong to circular or pandurate, rounded or cordate at base. Summer. NZ. 'Nana': dwarf; lvs pandurate. var. *microphylla* (Colenso) Ckn. Dense shrub to 60cm. Lvs few, rounded, v. small. var. *triloba* (Colenso) Cheesem. Lvs pandurate, deeply lobed. Z8.
M. ephedroides Hook. f. Prostrate to sprawling shrub; st. to 1m, rush-like, deeply grooved. Lvs 8–25mm, linear to sagittate, often 0, dark to grey-green. Summer. NZ. var. *muriculata* (Colenso) Cheesem. Small shrub. St. v. slender, almost thread-like. Lvs, 3–12mm. Z8.
M. gunnii (Hook. f.) Walp. Climbing shrub, resembling *M. adpressa* but st. to 10m; lvs 3–8cm, broadly lanceolate-hastate. Aus. Z9.
M. muriculata Colenso = *M. ephedroides* var. *muriculata.*
M. nana Thurst. = *M. axillaris.*
M. platyclada (F. Muell.) Meissn. = *Homalocladium platycladum.*
M. sagittifolia (Ortega) Meissn. Liane or climbing shrub. Lvs 4–9cm, sagittate or lanceolate, upper lvs linear. Summer. Braz., Parag., Urug. Z9.
M. triloba Colenso = *M. complexa* var. *triloba.*
M. varians Meissn. = *M. complexa* var. *triloba.*

Muenteria Seem.
M. lutea (Benth.) Seem. = *Markhamia lutea.*
M. platycalyx (Bak.) Sprague = *Markhamia lutea.*

Mugga *Eucalyptus sideroxylon.*
Mugwort *Artemisia (A. vulgaris).*

Muilla S. Wats. Liliaceae (Alliaceae). 5 herbaceous cormous perenn. to 60cm, resembling *Allium* but lacking characteristic odour. Lvs nearly terete. Fls in scapose spathaceous umbels; tep. 6, bases united, forming tube. SW US, Mex. Z9.
M. maritima S. Wats. To 50cm. Lvs to 60cm. Fls 4–70; spathes 3–6; pedicels 1–5cm; tep. 3–6mm, white, tinged green, midrib brown; anth. purple. Spring–summer. Calif., Mex. Z9.
M. serotina Green = *M. maritima.*
→*Allium, Bloomeria, Hesperoscordum* and *Nothoscordum.*

Muiria N.E. Br. Aizoaceae. 1 clump-forming lf succulent, for-ming a large body with a pair of lvs united completely except for

a tiny apical slit; body ± compressed, ovoid to spherical, sometimes angular, soft-fleshy, light green, covered with velvety hairs. Fls solitary, pink-white, 8–20mm diam., rupturing apex of body. Summer–early autumn. S Afr. Z9.
M. hortenseae N.E. Br.

Mukdenia Koidz. Saxifragaceae. 2 herbaceous perenn. to 60cm. Rhiz. short, creeping. Lvs peltate, round to reniform, cordate at base, palmately, 5–9-lobed, bronze-green, dentate; petioles long. Fls numerous, small, white, campanulate, 5-merous, in scapose paniculate rac. Spring. N China, Manch., Korea. Z7.
M. rossii (Oliv.) Koidz.
→*Aceriphyllum* and *Saxifraga*.

Mukia Arn. Cucurbitaceae. 4 climbers. St. hispid, becoming woody at base. Tendrils simple. Infl. a sessile cluster; fls small, unisexual, yellow; cal. campanulate, lobed; pet. joined at base; ♂ fls with 3 sta. inserted on cal.; ♀ fls often solitary; staminodes sometimes present. Fr. a berry. OW Trop. Z9.
M. maderaspatana (L.) Roem. Climbing perenn., to 3m. Lvs 1.5–11cm, ovate-cordate to hastate or sagittate, sometimes toothed or lobed, hairy. Afr., India to China and Malaysia, Aus.
→*Cucumis* and *Melothria*.

Mukumariauhi *Cordia africana*.
Mulan *Magnolia liliiflora*.
Mulberry *Morus*.
Mulberry Fig *Ficus sycomorus*.
Mule Fat *Baccharis viminea*.
Mule's Fern *Asplenium sagittatum*.
Mule Tail *Conyza canadensis*.
Mulga *Acacia aneura*.

Mulgedium Cass.
M. bourgaei Boiss. = *Cicerbita bourgaei*.
M. macrorhizum Royle = *Cephalorrhynchus macrorhizus*.
M. uralense Rouy = *Cicerbita macrophylla* ssp. *uralensis*.

Mullein *Verbascum*.
Mullein Pink *Lychnis coronaria*.

Mundulea (DC.) Benth. Leguminosae (Papilionoideae). 15 small trees or shrubs. Lvs imparipinnate. Fls pea-like in term. pseudoracemes. Fr. a many-seeded, densely pubesc. pod. Madag. and OW Trop. Z10.
M. sericea (Willd.) A. Chev. Shrub or small tree, 2–7m. Lvs to 10cm; lfts to 4cm, in c6 pairs, oblong ovate, elliptic or lanceolate, minutely pubesc. Fls paired, purple-blue; standard 2.1×1.5cm. Fr. to 8cm, yellow-brown, softly pubesc., torulose. OW Trop.

Mung Bean *Vigna radiata*.
Munich Verbena *Verbena monacensis*.
Muninga *Pterocarpus angolensis*.
Munj *Saccharum bengalense*.
Munjeet *Rubia cordifolia*.

Munnozia Ruiz & Pav. Compositae. c40 ann. to perenn. herbs and subshrubs, with milky sap. Cap. radiate, pedunculate, in a term., corymbose pan.; ray flts yellow, white or lavender, disc flts yellow. Trop. S Amer., particularly Andes. Z10.
M. maronii (André) H. Robinson. Perenn. herb to 60cm, mostly white-hairy. Lvs to 12cm, triangular-hastate to triangular-cordate, remotely dentate, densely lanate. Cap. in long-pedunculate corymbs. Braz.
→*Liabum*.

Muntingia L. Elaeocarpaceae. 1 everg. tree to 12m. Lvs to 12.5cm, oblong-lanceolate, serrate, tomentulose beneath. Fls to 2.5cm diam., ephemeral, axillary, solitary or in clusters; sep. ovate-lanceolate to subulate, green, downy; pet. white, 5, spreading, obovate, clawed, crepe-like; sta. numerous in a central boss. Fr. a white berry 1.5cm diam. Trop. Amer. Z10.
M. calabura L. CALABURA; JAMAICAN CHERRY.

Muntries *Kunzea pomifera*.
Murasaki-giboshi *Hosta ventricosa*.
Murchison Claw-flower *Calothamnus homalophyllus*.

Murdannia Royle. Commelinaceae. 40–45 ann. or perenn. herbs. Cincinni borne in pan. or verticils or solitary; fls zygomorphic or nearly actinomorphic; sep. 3, equal; pet. 3, subequal; sta. 2–6, some staminodal, some with bearded fil. OW tropics. Z10.

M. nudiflora (L.) Brenan. Weak, prostrate ann. herb, st. rooting. Lvs 3–6cm, lanceolate or linear, sparsely hairy or glab. Cincinnus usually solitary with c5–8 fls, stalk 2–5cm or more; fls c4mm diam., white, blue or purple-pink. Asia, widely nat. in trop. Amer. Z9.
M. simplex (Vahl) Brenan. Fleshy-rooted perenn. Lvs to 30cm, forming a loose rosette, linear-lanceolate, channelled, glab. or ciliate towards base. Flowering st. to 1m, infl. a lax pan., cincinni notched with abscission scars; fls 1–1.5cm diam., pale to dark blue or purple. Spring–summer. Trop. Asia, Afr. Z9.
→*Aneilema*.

Murebu *Cordia crenata*.
Muriel Bamboo *Thamnocalamus spathaceus*.

Murraya Koenig ex L. Rutaceae. 5 aromatic trees. Lvs imparipinnate; lfts alt. Fls 5-merous, in cymes or pan.; sep. lanceolate; pet. lanceolate or linear; sta. 10, free. Fr. a small berry. India and China S to Aus. Z10.
M. alata Drake. Shrub to 1m. Lvs to 10cm, 5–7-foliolate, glab., lfts 3–4cm, oblong or rhombic, entire or crenate, coriaceous; rachis winged. Infl. cymose, few-fld, 2–3cm; pet. erect, obovate, 1–1.5cm. Fr. ovoid, red, fleshy 1–2. N Vietnam, Hainan Is.
M. exotica L. = *M. paniculata*.
M. koenigii (L.) Spreng. CURRY LEAF; KARAPINCHA. Everg. tree, 4.5–6m. Lvs pungently aromatic, lfts 2.5–4cm, 5–10 each side, oblong-lanceolate to ovate, minutely serrate, membranous. Infl. term., corymbose; pet. 4–6mm, oblong-lanceolate, white or tinged yellow. Fr. ellipsoid, dark blue tinged black. Asia.
M. ovatifoliolata (Engl.) Domin. V. similar to *M. paniculata*, but habit more straggling; twigs hirsute; lvs 3–9-foliolate, lfts broadly ovate; cal., pet. and ovary hirsute. Aus. (Queensld).
M. paniculata (L.) Jack. ORANGE JESSAMINE; SATIN-WOOD; COSMETIC BARK TREE; CHINESE BOX. Tree or shrub, 4.5–7.5m, everg. Lvs pinnate or 3-foliolate, glab. and glossy, lfts 2.5–4cm, dark green, cuneate-obovate to rhombic. Infl. term., corymbose, small, dense, fragrant; pet. 12–18mm, recurved, white. Fr. oblong-ovoid, orange to red. Fls several times per year. China and India S to Aus.
M. paniculata var. *ovatifoliolata* Engl. = *M. ovatifoliolata*.
M. stenocarpa (Drake) Swingle. Small tree, to 1m. Lvs to 4–12cm, 1-foliolate, elliptic or oblanceolate, serrate, glossy, subcoriaceous, oil glands distinct. Infl. axill., cymose, few-fld; fls small; pet. oblong. Fr. oblong, red. Distrib. as for the genus.

Murray Lily *Crinum flaccidum*.
Murray Red Gum *Eucalyptus camaldulensis*.

Musa L. BANANA; PLANTAIN; MANILA HEMP. Musaceae. 40 large, rhizomatous or suckering herbs. Lvs oblong or elliptic, entire often tearing, pinnately veined, midrib with deep rounded groove above; sheaths forming pseudostem. Infl. a term. spike; fls in ranks subtended by fleshy coloured bracts, ♀ or hermaphrodite at base, ♂ toward apex; tep. cream, 2; sta. 5, rarely 6; ovary inferior. Fr. a many-seeded berry, seeds black. Trop. Afr., Indian subcontinent, SE Asia, N Queensld.
M. acuminata Colla. BANANA; PLANTAIN. Pseudostems to 7m or more, green blotched brown, sometimes dark-flecked above, green or purple beneath. Infl. pendulous; peduncle brown-pubesc.; bracts acute, grooved, bright red to purple or yellow; ♀ fls in 2 rows in each lower bract. Fr. to 12×2.5cm, glab. bright yellow, pulp white to yellow. Flowering irregular. SE Asia, N Queensld. Possibly includes the BLOOD BANANA, *M. sumatrana* with lvs blotched wine red above, stained red beneath – colouring strong and persistent in 'Rubra'. Z10.
M. arnoldiana De Wildeman = *Ensete ventricosum*.
M. aurantiaca G. Mann. Pseudostems many, closely grouped, to 3m. Infl. erect; bracts red or yellow; fls bright yellow. Fr. green. Assam. Z10.
M. balbisiana Colla. Pseudostems clustered, to 7m and 28cm diam., green or yellow-green. Lvs to 3m, glaucous beneath. Infl. pendulous; peduncle glab.; ♀ fls clustered; bracts obtuse, grooved, exterior purple, crimson inside; ♂ fls to 20 per bract. Fr. to 10×3cm, pale yellow, pulp cream. Indian subcontinent, S China, Philipp., New Guinea. Z10.
M. basjoo Sieb. & Zucc. JAPANESE BANANA. To 3m, stoloniferous; pseudostem green, waxless. Lvs 2×0.7m, oblong-lanceolate, bright green. Infl. horizontal to pendulous; peduncle downy; bracts grooved, downy, outside yellow-green or tinged purple-brown, inside pale yellow-green; ♂ fls about 20 per bract. Fr. to 6×2.5cm, yellow-green with white pulp. Jap., Ryuku Is. 'Variegata': lvs banded or flecked lime green, cream and white. Z9.
M. cavendishii Lamb. ex Paxt. = *M. acuminata*.
M. chinensis Sweet = *M. acuminata*.

M. coccinea Andrews = *M. uranoscopus.*

M. ensete J. Gmel. = *Ensete ventricosum.*

M. fehi Bertero ex Vieill. = *M. troglodytarum.*

M. japonica Thiéb. & Ketel. = *M. basjoo.*

M. mannii H. Wendl. To 1.5m, stoloniferous, pseudostem slender, about 70cm, tinged or blotched black. Lvs 0.8×0.2m, oblong, midrib red. Infl. erect, to 14cm; bracts crimson to red-purple, slightly grooved; ♀ fls in clusters of 3. Fr. green, small. Spring. NE India. Z9.

M. nana auct. non Lour. = *M. acuminata.*

M. ornata Roxb. FLOWERING BANANA. St. slender, 2–3m, glaucous, sometimes flushed purple-red beneath. Lvs to 2×0.4m, slightly glaucous. Infl. erect; fls orange-yellow, in single row; bracts pale purple, grooved. Fr. about 6×2cm, yellow. Flowering irregular. Bangladesh, Burm. Z10.

M. ×paradisiaca L. EDIBLE BANANA; FRENCH PLANTAIN. (*M. acuminata* ×*M. balbisiana.*) To 8m. Lvs to 2.5×0.7m, oblong, green. Infl. pendulous, to 1.5m; bracts purple-red. Fr. usually seedless, often yellow, pulp white. Trop. Z9. There may be as many as 300 cvs of edible banana worldwide. The leading commercial cv. was for a century 'Gros Michel' ('Bluefields') now being phased out owing to susceptibility to destructive Panama disease. It has largely been replaced by Cavendish cvs bred from *M. acuminata.* 'Koae': lvs striped laterally white and pale green on dark green, young fr. variegated, later yellow. 'Vittata': lvs variegated pale green and white, midrib white, edged red.

M. paradisiaca var. *sanguinea* (Hook.) Welw. = *M. sanguinea.*

M. religiosa Dyb. = *Ensete gilletii.*

M. rosacea hort. non Jacq. = *M. ornata.*

M. sanguinea Hook. Similar to *M. uranoscopus* except pseudostem to 1.5m, slender; lvs to 90×15cm; infl. and rachis red. NE India. Z9.

M. sapientum L. = *M. ×paradisiaca.*

M. sumatrana Becc. See *M. acuminata.*

M. superba Roxb. = *Ensete superbum.*

M. textilis Née. MANILA HEMP; ABACA. Pseudostems to 6m, green to purple-green. Lvs to 2m, oblong, bright green, often spotted brown above, glaucous beneath. Infl. horizontal to pendulous; fls biseriate; bracts polished, revolute, outside red to purple, inside paler. Fr. indehiscent, glab., to 7cm. Philipp. Z9.

M. troglodytarum L. FE'I BANANA. A range of seedless and seeded cultigens grown throughout Polynesia and Melanesia, notably cvs Aiuri, Borabora, Rureva and Soaga. Pseudostems to 7m, clumped, dark green, becoming maroon or violet-blue at base or wherever cut. Lvs to 4×3m. Infl. erect; ♀ fls to 12 per cluster; bracts green. Fr. to 14cm, orange-brown, pulp sour unless cooked. Distrib. described originally as Sumatra for *M. troglodytarum* and Tahiti for *M. fehi.* Z10.

M. uranoscopus Lour. Pseudostem to 1m, glossy red-green. Lvs to 75×30cm, oval to elliptic, glossy above, somewhat waxy beneath, midrib green to rose-pink. Infl. to 0.75m, erect; bracts magenta to scarlet, fleshy, often tipped yellow-green, shiny; fls 2 per bract. Fr. oblong to cylindric, to 5×2.5cm, red-purple to pink-green, reportedly ripening orange-yellow. Indochina. Z10.

M. velutina Wendl. & Drude. Pseudostems to 1.5m, yellow-green to purple-green. Lvs to 1m, dark green above, paler with red midrib beneath. Infl. erect; peduncle pubesc.; fls in monoseriate clusters; bracts magenta to plum, purple-haired, not grooved. Fr. to 9×3cm, pink, pubesc., pulp white. NE India. Z9.

M. zebrina Van Houtte ex Planch. See *M. acuminata* 'Sumatrana'.

Musanga R. Br. UMBRELLA TREE. Cecropiaceae. 2 everg. trees. Lvs palmately compound in term. rosettes; seg. entire, narrow. ♀ infl. solitary or in pairs, small round heads, perianth obovoid-tubular; ♂ infl. in pairs, fls minute; perianth tubular, narrow. Fr. succulent, perianth persistent. W & C Trop. Afr. Z10.

M. cecropioides R. Br. UMBRELLA TREE; CORK WOOD; PARASOLIER. Stilt-rooting, slender-stemmed tree to 20m. Bark with prominent lenticels. Lf seg. to 45cm, grey-hairy; petiole to 70cm; stipules to 20cm, red, hairy. Fr. yellow. W Afr. to Angola and Uganda.

Muscadine Grape *Vitis rotundifolia.*

Muscadinia (Planch.) Small.
M. rotundifolia (Michx.) Small = *Vitis rotundifolia.*

Muscari Mill. GRAPE HYACINTH. Liliaceae (Hyacinthaceae). 30 bulbous perenn. herbs. Lvs basal, linear, rather fleshy. Rac. dense, scapose, uppermost fls often sterile, forming a tuft (coma); perianth campanulate, tubular or urceolate, lobes 6, small, reflexed; sta. 6. Spring. Medit., SW Asia

M. armeniacum Bak. Lvs to 30×6cm, 3–7, linear to linear-oblanceolate. Rac. 2.5–7.5cm, fls crowded, fertile fls 3.5–5.5mm, obovoid to urceolate, azure, sometimes flushed purple, rarely white, lobes paler or white, sterile fls few, smaller and paler. SE Eur. to Cauc. 'Album': fls white. 'Argaei': fls bright blue. 'Argaei Album': fls white; spike small; late-flowering. 'Blue Spike': to 15cm, vigorous; infl. branched, fls large, fully double, profuse, soft blue. 'Cantab': strong-growing; stalks short; fls pale Cambridge blue. 'Dark Eyes': fls bright blue, rimmed white. 'Heavenly Blue': fls vivid blue. 'Saphir': fls dark blue, rim white, long-lasting, sterile. 'Sky Blue': fls pale turquoise, rim white, compact. Z4.

M. atlanticum Boiss. & Reut. = *M. neglectum.*

M. aucheri (Boiss.) Bak. Lvs 5–20×0.2–1.5cm, usually 2, falcate to narrowly spathulate. Rac. dense, ovoid or cylindric; fertile fls 3–5mm, subspherical or ovoid, bright azure, rarely white, lobes paler or white, sterile fls paler. Turk. Z6.

M. azureum Fenzl. Lvs 6–20×0.3–1.5cm, 2–3, narrowly oblanceolate. Rac. 1.5–3cm, dense; fertile fls 4–5mm, campanulate, bright blue with a darker stripe on the lobes, sterile fls smaller and paler. E Turk. 'Album': fls pure white. 'Amphibolis': fls pale blue, larger, earlier. Z8.

M. botryoides (L.) Bak. Lvs 5–20×0.5–1.3cm, 2–4, spathulate, often ribbed above. Rac. dense then loose and cylindric; fertile fls 2.5–5mm, subspherical, scented, azure or white, lobes white. C & SE Eur. 'Album': fls pure white. 'Caeruleum': fls bright blue. 'Carneum': fls flesh pink. Z3.

M. comosum (L.) Mill. TASSEL HYACINTH. Lvs 3–7, linear, channelled. Rac. loose; fertile fls 5–9mm, oblong-urceolate, brown-olive, lobes yellow-brown, sterile fls subspherical or obovoid, rarely tubular, bright violet, on violet, ascending pedicels. S & C Eur., N Afr., SW Asia; nat. Eur. 'Plumosum' ('Monstrosum'): infl. sterile, mauve-blue, massively branched. Z4.

M. cyaneoviolaceum Turrill = *M. armeniacum.*

M. latifolium T. Kirk. Lvs 7–30×1–3cm, 1, rarely 2 broadly oblanceolate. Rac. dense then loose; fertile fls 5–6mm, oblong-urceolate, tube strongly constricted, deep violet; sterile fls blue. S & W Asia. Z4.

M. luteum Tod. = *M. macrocarpum.*

M. macrocarpum Sweet. Lvs to 30cm. Rac. loose; fertile fls 8–12mm, oblong-urceolate, blue-violet then yellow, expanded to form brown or yellow corona, sterile fls tinged purple, few or 0. Aegean Is., W Turk. Z7.

M. massayanum Grunert. Lvs to 25×1–2.5cm, linear, falcate or sinuous, glaucous. Flowering st. stout; rac. dense, cylindric; fertile fls to 1.1cm, pink to violet at first, later pale green- or yellow-brown, lobes dark brown, sterile fls pink or violet on ascending pedicels, forming a dense tuft. E Turk. Z7.

M. moschatum Willd. = *M. muscarimi.*

M. muscarimi Medik. Lvs 10–20×0.5–1.5cm, grey-green. Fls muskily scented, fertile fls 8–14mm, narrowly urceolate, purple then pale green to ivory, strongly contracted then expanded to form a brown corona, sterile fls purple-tinged, rarely present. SW Turk. Z6.

M. neglectum Guss. ex Ten. COMMON GRAPE HYACINTH. Lvs 6–40×0.2–0.8cm, channelled to subterete. Rac. dense in fl.; fertile fls 1.5–3.5mm, ovoid to oblong-urceolate, strongly constricted, deep blue-black, lobes white, sterile fls smaller and paler blue. Eur., N Afr., SW Asia. Z4.

M. pallens Bieb. Lvs to 20cm+, linear. Rac. long-stalked, short, oblong, dense; fertile fls nodding, ovoid, white or blue tinged violet, teeth reflexed; sterile fls small. Cauc.

M. paradoxum misapplied. = *Bellevalia pycnantha.*

M. pinardii Boiss. = *M. comosum.*

M. racemosum Lam. & DC. = *M. neglectum.*

M. szovitsianum Bak. = *M. armeniacum.*

M. tenuiflorum Tausch. Like *M. comosum* but with 3–7 narrower lvs; fls fewer, pale grey-brown, lobes pale cream, sterile fls bright violet. C Eur. Z5.

M. tubergenianum Turrill = *M. aucheri.*

→*Bellevalia, Botryanthus, Hyacinthella* and *Leopoldia.*

Mushugushugu *Dyschoriste thunbergiiflora.*

Musk *Mimulus.*

Musk Bush *Ceanothus jepsonii.*

Musk Clover *Erodium moschatum.*

Musk Flower *Mimulus moschatus.*

Musk Mallow *Abelmoschus moschatus; Malva moschata.*

Musk Melon *Cucumis melo* Reticulatus group.

Musk Plant *Mimulus moschatus.*

Musk Root *Adoxa moschatellina.*

Musk Rose *Rosa moschata.*

Musk Thistle *Carduus nutans.*

Musk Willow *Salix aegyptiaca.*

Muskwood *Olearia argophylla.*

Mussaenda L. Rubiaceae. 100 shrubs, subshrubs and herbs, sometimes twining. Lvs simple, opposite or 3-whorled, membranous. Fls few- to many-fld pan. or cymes; cal. tube turbinate to ovoid, lobes 5, linear to lanceolate, one often developed into an enlarged, leaf-like, colourful limb; cor. tubular to funnelform, lobes 5, spreading; sta. 5. Fr. a berry. Trop. OW. Z10.

M. abyssinica Chiov. = *M. arcuata.*

M. albiflora Hayata, non Merrill = *M. pubescens.*

M. arcuata Poir. Shrub, to 7m. St. erect or climbing, viscid, glab. or short-pubesc. Lvs to 20cm, obovate or elliptic to suborbicular, lustrous and leathery glab. above. Fls yellow, fragrant in few-fld pan. or cymes; cal. tube to 4mm, limb decid., lobes to 15×3mm, linear or spathulate, toothed; cor. tube to 25mm, red-pubesc. Trop. Afr., Madag.

M. coccinea Poir. = *Warszewiczia coccinea.*

M. erythrophylla Schumach. & Thonn. Shrub, to 8m. St. erect or climbing, red-pubesc. Lvs to 18cm, ovate or elliptic to suborbicular, pubesc. Fls in dense, pan. or cymes, pink to red and white to yellow; cal. tube to 5mm, pubesc., limb decid., lobes to 2×3mm, lanceolate, enlarged lobe to 10cm, oval, scarlet; cor. tube to 3mm, pubesc. Trop. Afr. 'Queen Sirikit': br. drooping; lvs broad, wavy, head of enlarged deep pink to ivory cal. lobes.

M. formosa Jacq. = *Randia formosa.*

M. frondosa L. Shrub, to 3m. St. erect, glab. or pubesc. to tomentose. Lvs to 15cm, ovate, lanceolate or elliptic, tomentose beneath. Fls yellow in dense, term. corymbs; cal. to 2cm, enlarged lobe to 5cm, white; cor. tube to 25mm, pubesc. Summer–autumn. Trop. Asia (Indochina to Malaysia). 'Aurorae': lvs to 15cm long, wavy, softly haired; infl. gold.

M. glabra Vahl. COMMON MUSSAENDA. Shrub, to 3m. St. ascending to diffuse, ± glab. Lvs to 15cm, oblong to lanceolate or elliptic, leathery, sparsely pubesc. beneath. Fls in many-fld cymes, orange to red; cal. to 6mm, tube campanulate, limb decid., lobes lanceolate, enlarged lobe to 10cm, white; cor. tube to 25mm. India to Malaysia.

M. incana Wallich. Shrub, to 1m. St. erect, pubesc. Lvs to 15cm, ovate or elliptic to oblong. Fls in subsessile corymbs, chrome yellow; cal. lobes filiform, enlarged lobe to 7cm, pubesc., white to cream or yellow; cor. to 2cm. India to Malaysia.

M. kotoensis Hayata = *M. macrophylla.*

M. luculia Buch.-Ham. ex D. Don = *Luculia gratissima.*

M. macrophylla Wallich. Shrub, to 2m. St. climbing, simple, sparsely pubesc. Lvs to 25cm, ovate to oblong. Fls orange in dense cymes; cal. tube to 2mm, limb decid., lobes lanceolate, enlarged lobe to 12cm, rhomboid, white to yellow; cor. to 3cm, pubesc. Summer. India to Taiwan, Malaysia, Philipp.

M. parviflora Kanehira, non Miq. = *M. pubescens.*

M. pubescens Ait. f. Shrub to 2m. St. erect to climbing, pubesc. Lvs to 8cm, ovate or elliptic to oblong, papery, pubesc. Fls yellow in dense cymes or corymbs; cal. tube to 3mm, pubesc., lobes linear, pubesc., enlarged lobe to 9×5cm, ovate to elliptic, white; cor. tube to 3cm. China, Taiwan.

M. roxburghii Hook. f. Shrub to 4m. St. erect, pubesc. Lvs to 30cm, lanceolate or elliptic to oblong, membranous, glab. to pubesc. beneath. Fls in dense cymes or corymbs; cal. limb persistent, lobes filiform, pubesc., enlarged lobe to 7cm, glab., white; cor. tube to 2cm, silky. Himal.

M. sanderiana Ridl. Shrub, to 2m. St. erect to creeping. Lvs lanceolate, sericeous. Fls in term. cymes, yellow; enlarged lobe to 8cm, white, sericeous. Indochina.

Mustang Grape *Vitis mustangensis.*
Mustard Cabbage *Brassica juncea.*
Mustard Tree *Capparis cynophallophora; Nicotiana glauca; Salvadora persica.*
Muster-john-henry *Tagetes minuta.*

Mutisia L. f. Compositae. 60 shrubs or lianes. Lvs alt., simple or pinnate, often terminating in a tendril. Cap. radiate, term., solitary, pedunculate; receptacle flat to convex; disc flts usually yellow. S Amer. Z9 unless specified.

M. acuminata Ruiz & Pav. Much-branched shrub to 1m; br. flexuous. Lvs 8–10cm, pinnatisect, terminating in a trifid tendril; lfts to 4×1cm in 9–14 pairs, elliptic-lanceolate; base decurrent. Cap. on peduncles to 12cm; ray flts 5–8, bright red or scarlet. Andes (Peru to Boliv.).

M. arachnoidea Mart. ex D. Don = *M. speciosa.*

M. breviflora Philippi = *M. ilicifolia.*

M. clematis L. f. Liane to 10m. Lvs 5–10cm, pinnate; with a long, trifid, term. tendril, lfts to 7×3cm, in 4–5 pairs, elliptic, tomentose beneath. Cap. to 6cm diam., pendulous, shortly pedunculate; ray flts 9–10, bright orange to scarlet or maroon. Summer–autumn. N Andes.

M. decurrens Cav. Much-branched, rhizomatous subshrub to 2m. Lvs to 10×2cm, lanceolate, with long, bifid, term. tendril, decurrent at base, entire or sharp-toothed. Cap. to 12cm diam., on peduncles to 10cm; ray flts 10–15, brilliant orange. Summer. S Andes (Chile, Arg.). Z8.

M. ilicifolia Cav. Branched shrub to 3m. Lvs to 6×4cm, ovate to ovate-elliptic, sessile, with a long, simple, term. tendril, base cordate and semi-amplexicaul, margin spinose-dentate, subcoriaceous, tomentose or glabrescent beneath. Cap. 2–3cm diam., on peduncles to 4cm; ray flts c8, pale pink. Chile.

M. latifolia D. Don. Shrub to 1.5m; br. 2–3-winged, ascending or sprawling. Lvs to 5.5×3.5cm, ovate or elliptic, sessile, apex truncate, base cordate and semi-amplexicaul, spinose-dentate, midrib prolonged into a terminal tendril, subcoriaceous, tomentose or subglabrous. Cap. to 7.5cm diam., on peduncles to 4cm; ray flts 10–15, lilac or deep rose. Autumn. C Chile.

M. linearifolia Cav. Dwarf creeping shrub to 30cm. Lvs to 3×0.5cm, linear, sessile and decurrent, acute and shortly mucronate, entire, strongly revolute, glab. Cap. to 6cm diam., shortly pedunculate; ray flts 8–10, red. S Andes (N Arg., C Chile).

M. oligodon Poepp. & Endl. Straggling shrub or liane to 1m. Lvs to 3.5×1.5cm, oblong to elliptic, acute or obtuse, sessile, base cordate, 1–2 dentate near apex, upper lvs few, terminating in a tendril, tomentose beneath. Cap. to 7cm diam. on peduncle to 5cm; ray flts c10, bright red. S Chile, S Arg.

M. pulchella Speg. = *M. spinosa* var. *pulchella.*

M. retusa Rémy = *M. spinosa* var. *pulchella.*

M. sinuata Cav. Low shrub to 30cm, often creeping; br. flexuous, winged. Lvs to 3×0.6cm, lanceolate, sessile, acute, base attenuate and decurrent, margins revolute, with 6–8 triangular teeth, glab., upper lvs terminating in a simple tendril. Cap. to 5cm diam., shortly pedunculate; ray flts 8–10, to 2cm, white to light yellow above, pink or grey below. S Andes (C Chile and Arg.).

M. speciosa Ait. Shrub to 6m; br. ribbed to winged. Lvs 4–12cm, pinnate, terminating in a trifid tendril, lfts in 4–7 pairs, lanceolate, base cuneate. Cap. to 8cm diam., usually on peduncles to 1.5cm; ray flts 13–20, pink to red. Andes of Ecuad., S Braz.

M. spinosa Ruiz & Pav. Liane to 6m. Young br. spinose-winged. Lvs to 6×3.5cm, elliptic to ovate-elliptic, base cordate and semi-amplexicaul, entire or with 1–2 pairs of spinose teeth near apex, terminating in a long simple tendril, sparsely lanate or glab. beneath. Cap. to 6cm diam., on peduncles to 8cm; ray flts 8–10, pale pink. S Arg., Chile. var. *pulchella* (Speg.) Cabr. Lvs persistently white-tomentose beneath.

M. subulata Ruiz & Pav. Low, often creeping shrub to 50cm, st. undulate. Lvs to 7×0.1cm, linear-subulate, with apical spine or tendril, sessile, revolute, entire. Cap. to 7.5cm diam., shortly pedunculate; ray flts c10, brilliant red to scarlet. S Andes (C Chile).

M. versicolor Philippi = *M. subulata.*

M. viciaefolia Cav. = *M. acuminata.*

Mutter Pea *Pisum sativum* var. *arvense.*
Myallwood *Acacia omalophylla.*

MYOPORACEAE R. Br. 5/220. *Bontia, Eremophila, Myoporum.*

Myoporum Banks & Sol. ex Forst. f. Myoporaceae. 30 gland., perenn., everg. trees and shrubs, sometimes heath-like in habit. Fls in axill. cymes, pairs or solitary; cal. 5-lobed; cor. campanulate-hypocrateriform with a short tube, lobes 5; sta. 4. Fr. a drupe. Aus. and NZ to E Asia and Maur.

M. acuminatum R. Br. = *M. tenuifolium.*

M. debile (Andrews) R. Br. Low, spreading shrub, twigs tinged red. Lvs 4–8cm, linear-lanceolate, minutely toothed above and below. Infl. 1–2-fld; cor. 6–8mm, pink to purple, shorter than tube, villous inside; sta. 4. Fr. white below, maroon above. Aus., NZ. Z9.

M. insulare R. Br. BOOBYALLA. Tree or large shrub to 10m. Lvs to 7.5cm, obovate to lanceolate, thick, entire or with few teeth. Infl. 2–4-fld; cor. to 6mm, white with pink spots. Fr. blue-purple. Aus. Z9.

M. laetum Forst. f. Tree to 10m, twig apices and buds sticky. Lvs 4–10cm, lanceolate to obovate, somewhat fleshy, crenate to sinuate. Infl. 2–6-fld; cor. c1cm diam., campanulate, white with purple spots. lobes villous above. Fr. pale to dark maroon. NZ. Z9.

M. parvifolium R. Br. Low, spreading, glab. shrub to 50cm. Lvs 1–2.5cm, linear. Infl. 1–3-fld, honey-scented; cor. to 1cm wide, white, deeply 5-lobed. Summer. Aus. Z9.

M. sandwiciense (A. DC.) A. Gray BASTARD SANDALWOOD; NGAIO; NAIO. Tree to 20cm, wood smelling of sandalwood. Lvs to 15cm, ovate-lanceolate. Cor. to 8mm diam., white or pink lobes 5–6(–7). Hawaii. Z9.

M. serratum R. Br. = *M. tetrandrum*.

M. tenuifolium Forst. f. Round-crowned to 8m. Lvs 4.5–10cm, lanceolate, entire, glossy. Infl. (1–)5–9-fld; cor. tube 4–5mm, limb 10–12mm diam., white with purple spots. Fr. dark purple. Early summer. Aus., introd. in SW Eur. Z9.

M. tetrandrum (Labill.) Domin Erect shrub or small tree. Lvs 2.5–5cm, elliptic-oblong to lanceolate, mucronate or obtuse, toothed to entire. Infl. 2–6-fld; cor. to 9mm diam., white with pink. Aus., introd. Port. Z9.

Myosotidium Hook. Boraginaceae. 1 perenn. or bienn. herb. St. succulent, stout. Basal lvs to 30cm, fleshy, reniform to broadly ovate-cordate, lustrous bright green, veins deeply impressed; petioles long. Fls in a dense corymbose cyme, to 15cm; cal. deeply 5-lobed; cor. dark or pale blue, tube short, throat with 5 protuberances, lobes 5, rounded. NZ. Z8.

M. hortensia (Decne.) Baill. CHATHAM ISLANDS FORGET-ME-NOT.

M. nobile Hook. = *M. hortensia*.

→*Myosotis*.

Myosotis L. FORGET-ME-NOT; SCORPION GRASS. Boraginaceae. 50 ann., bienn. or perenn. herbs. Fls usually in paired cymes, usually with a conspicuous 'eye'; cal. 5-lobed; cor. rotate or salverform, lobes 5, obtuse, spreading, faucal scales 5, distinct. Temp. distrib., mainly Eur., NZ.

M. alpestris F.W. Schmidt. Tufted perenn. to 30cm. Basal lvs to 8×1.5cm, oblong, ovate-oblong or lanceolate, petiolate pubesc. Cor. bright or deep blue to 9mm diam., lobes rounded, spreading. Eur., Asia, N Amer. Z4.

M. alpina Lapeyr. Perenn. St. to 12cm, densely tufted. Basal lvs lingulate, sessile, glab. beneath. Cor. bright or deep blue to 8mm diam. Eur. Z6.

M. arvensis (L.) Hill. Ann. or bienn. to 50cm. Basal lvs to 8×1.5cm, oblanceolate, short-petiolate to subsessile, pubesc. Cor. bright blue to dark purple to 3mm diam., campanulate, limb ascending or spreading. Eur., NE Afr., Asia; nat. N Amer. Z6.

M. australis R. Br. Perenn. br. to 30cm. Basal lvs to 6cm, elliptic or spathulate, with spreading hairs above and short retrorse hairs beneath; petiolate. Cor. white or yellow, lobes rounded, concave. Aus., Tasm., NZ. Z8.

M. azorica H. Wats. Perenn. to 60cm, with white, retrorse hairs below. Basal lvs to 10×2cm, narrowly obovate or oblanceolate, densely pubesc. Cor. blue with a white eye to 6mm diam. Azores, Canary Is., Alg. Z9.

M. caespitosa Schultz. Perenn. to 60cm, sparingly covered with white hairs. Basal lvs to 4×1cm, ovate-oblong, subobtuse or rounded, sparsely adpressed-pubesc. above, often glab. beneath. Cor. blue to 3mm, limb to 4mm diam., lobes ovate-spreading. Eur., Asia, N Afr., N Amer. Z6.

M. colensoi (T. Kirk) Macbr. Perenn. decumbent. Basal lvs to 3×1cm, lanceolate, subacute, adpressed-pubesc., sometimes glab. beneath, short-petiolate. Cor. white to 8mm diam., tube to 5mm, cylindrical, lobes rounded. NZ. Z8.

M. decora T. Kirk ex Cheesem. = *M. colensoi*.

M. dissitiflora Bak. Closely resembles *M. sylvatica* except lower in habit, pubesc. Fls deep sky blue. Switz. Z6.

M. explanata Cheesem. Perenn. to 30cm, white-pubesc. Basal lvs to 7×1.5cm, obovate to linear or spathulate, rounded, pubesc.; petiole to 6.5cm. Cor. to 10mm diam., tube to 10mm, white, lobes rounded. NZ. Z8.

M. hortensia Decne. = *Myosotidium hortensia*.

M. laxa Lehm. Ann. to perenn. St. to 50cm, decumbent, adpressed-pubesc. Lvs to 8×1.5cm, lanceolate to spathulate. Cor. bright blue with a yellow eye to 5mm diam. Eur., N Amer. Z6.

M. lithospermifolia (Willd.) Hornem. Perenn., densely pubesc. to 40cm, grey-green. Basal lvs to 6×1cm, narrowly elliptic or obovate, obtuse, petiolate. Cor. to 6mm diam., bright blue, rotate. W Asia. Z6.

M. lyallii Hook. f. Decumbent perenn. Basal lvs to 3.5×1cm, ovate-spathulate to elliptic, obtuse, pubesc., sometimes glab. beneath; petiole to 3.5cm. Cor. to 8mm diam., white, tube cylindrical, lobes to 3mm, oblong. NZ. Z8.

M. macrantha (Hook. f.) Benth. ex Hook. f. Perenn. to 30cm, erect to ascending. Basal lvs to 12×2cm, spathulate, lanceolate to obovate, with adpressed or spreading hairs above and sparse retrorse hairs beneath; petiole to 11cm. Cor. to 8mm diam., yellow to brown-orange, infundibular, tube to 10mm, lobes rounded. NZ. Z8.

M. macrophylla Adams = *Brunnera macrophylla*.

M. oblongata Link = *M. sylvatica*.

M. palustris (L.) Nath. Closely resembles *M. caespitosa* except cor. to 8mm diam. Eur., Asia, N Amer. 'Alba': fls white. 'Mer-

maid': st. thick; lvs dark green; fls deep blue, eye yellow.

M. pyrenaica Pourr. = *M. alpina*.

M. rehsteineri Wartm. Resembles *M. scorpioides* except smaller, caespitose. St. to 10cm, adpressed-pubesc. Lvs to 2.5×1cm. Cor. to 10mm, pink to bright blue. Eur. Z6.

M. scorpioides L. FORGET-ME-NOT. Perenn. Rhiz. creeping. St. to 50cm, angled, mostly glab. Lvs to 10×2cm, oblong-lanceolate to oblanceolate, usually adpressed-pubesc., sometimes glabrescent. Cor. bright blue, with white, yellow or pink eye, to 8mm diam., limb flat. Eur. 'Sapphire': fls bright sapphire blue. 'Semperflorens': habit dwarf, to 20cm; fls in summer. 'Thuringen': fls sky blue. Z5.

M. scorpioides ssp. *caespititia* (DC.) Baumann = *M. rehsteineri*.

M. scorpioides var. *arvensis* L. = *M. arvensis*.

M. scorpioides var. *lithospermifolia* Willd. = *M. lithospermifolia*.

M. scorpioides var. *palustris* L. = *M. palustris*.

M. stricta Link ex Roem. & Schult. Ann. to 40cm, with white hairs at base. Basal lvs to 4×1cm, oblong to oblong-spathulate or lanceolate, obtuse to rounded, hairy. Cor. pale to bright blue, to 2mm diam., tubular-campanulate. N Afr., Eur., W Asia. Z6.

M. sylvatica Ehrh. ex Hoffm. GARDEN FORGET-ME-NOT. Bienn. to perenn. St. to 50cm, hairy. Basal lvs to 11×3cm, elliptic-oblong to oblong-lanceolate, obtuse to rounded, petiolate. Cor. bright blue, purple or white-blue varying to pink with a yellow eye to 8mm diam., lobes rounded, spreading. N Afr., Eur., W Asia. 'Blue Ball': small and compact; fls rich indigo. 'Blue Basket': compact; fls indigo. 'Blue Bird': tall; fls deep blue. 'Carmine King': erect; fls rosy carmine. 'Compacta': dense and low. 'Fischeri': dwarf; fls blue fls bright pink, long-lasting. 'Royal Blue': tall; fls indigo, early-flowering, abundant. 'Robusta Grandiflora': vigorous; fls large. 'Rosea': tall; fls soft pink. 'Stricta': br. erect and straight. 'Tall Blue': to 45cm; fls light blue, early. Victoria Mixed: fls blue, pink, rose, white; seed race. 'White Ball': small and compact; fls large, white. Z5.

M. sylvatica ssp. *alpestris* (F.W. Schmidt) Gams = *M. alpestris*.

M. traversii Hook. Perenn. st. branched to 15cm, erect or ascending. Basal lvs to 7×1cm, spathulate, pubesc. Cor. white to lemon-yellow, to 4mm diam., tube to 5mm, cylindric, lobes rounded. NZ. Z8.

M. uniflora Hook. Perenn., tufted. Lvs to 5×1.5mm, overlapping, thin, triangular to subulate, adpressed-pubesc. Cor. yellow, to 5mm diam., tube to 5mm, cylindric, lobes orbicular. NZ. Z8.

M. welwitschii Boiss. & Reut. Ann. to bienn. to 60cm, with deflexed hairs at base. Lvs to 7×1.5cm, elliptic or ovate-lanceolate, pubesc. Cor. bright blue with a yellow-white eye, to 10mm diam. Spain, Port., Moroc. Z9.

→*Exarrhena*.

Myrceugenella Kausel.

M. chequen (Molina) Kausel = *Luma chequen*.

M. gayana (Barnéoud) Kausel = *Luma chequen*.

Myrceugenia Berg. Myrtaceae. 38 everg. trees and shrubs. Fls white to cream, solitary, axill. or in dichasia. Fr. a red-black 1–5-seeded berry. SE Braz. to Chile and Arg. Z9.

M. apiculata (DC.) Niedenzu = *Luma apiculata*.

M. exsucca (DC.) Berg = *Amomyrtus luma*.

M. ferruginea (Hook. f. & Arn.) Reiche = *M. rufa*.

M. planipes (Hook. f. & Arn.) Berg. Small tree to c8m. Lvs 2.2–8cm, elliptic, acuminate. Infl. 1–4-fld; cal. lobes broadly ovate, concave, 1.8–3×2.5–4mm; pet. suborbicular, 3–6mm diam.; sta. 120–220, 7–12mm. Chile, Arg.

M. rufa (Colla) Skottsb. Shrub, 1–2m. Lvs 0.5–1.8cm, elliptic, ovate or oblong, blue-green to yellow-green, puberulent and lustrous above, red-brown to white-yellow and pubesc. beneath. Fls solitary; cal. lobes ovate to suborbicular, 1.2–2.6mm; pet. ± orbicular, 2–3mm diam., sta. 60–100, 3–6mm. Chile.

Myrcia DC. ex Guillem.

M. lechleriana Miq. = *Amomyrtus luma*.

Myrciaria O. Berg. Myrtaceae. 40 everg. trees or shrubs. Fls white, clustered in axils or on st.; cal. tubular, 4-lobed; pet. 4, small; sta. many. Fr. a globose berry. Americas. Z10.

M. cauliflora (DC.) O. Berg. JABOTICABA. Cauliflorous tree to 13m. Lvs to 10cm, lanceolate or somewhat broader, acuminate. Fr. globose, 1.5–3.5cm diam., white to purple, edible. S Braz.

M. edulis (Vell.) Skeels. Tree to 7m. Br. pendent. Lvs 5–7.5cm, willow-like, rusty-pubesc. when young. Fls in axill. or term. clusters. Fr. pear-shaped, c5cm, orange-yellow, downy, foetid. Braz.

M. floribunda (West ex Willd.) O. Berg. Tree to 10m. Lvs to c7cm, lanceolate to ovate-lanceolate. Fls in lateral clusters. Fr.

globose, to 13mm across, red or yellow, edible. W Indies, S Mex. to C Amer., Guyana and Braz.

M. myriophylla (Casar.) O. Berg. Much-branched shrub. Lvs to 4cm, v. narrow and crowded. Fls solitary. Braz.

→*Eugenia.*

Myriad Leaf *Myriophyllum verticillatum.*

Myrica L. Myricaceae. 35 decid. or everg. shrubs or small trees. Lvs simple, subsessile or short-petiolate. Fls unisexual; ♂ infl. a catkin; perianth 0, sta. 2–8, ♀ infl. ovoid and sessile, ovary unilocular, with bracteoles. Fr. an ovoid or spherical drupe. Widespread.

M. californica Cham. CALIFORNIA WAX MYRTLE; CALIFORNIA BAY-BERRY. Everg. shrub or small tree to 10m. Lvs 6–10cm, narrow-elliptic to oblanceolate, toothed. ♂ infl. to 2cm. Fr. to 6mm diam., deep purple, waxy. Coastal W US. Z7.

M. caroliniensis auct. non Mill. = *M. pensylvanica.*

M. caroliniensis Mill. = *M. cerifera.*

M. cerifera L. Everg. shrub or tree to 12m. Lvs 3–9cm, oblanceolate, entire or serrate above. ♂ infl. to 2cm. Fr. to 3mm diam., grey-white, pruinose. E & SE US. Z6.

M. faya Ait. CANDLEBERRY MYRTLE. Everg. shrub or small tree to 8.25m. Lvs to 10.8cm, oblanceolate. ♂ infl. 2cm, often branched. Fr. to 5mm diam., red to black, waxy. Canary Is., Madeira, S Port. Z9.

M. gale L. SWEET GALE; BOG MYRTLE; MEADOW FERN. Decid. shrub to 2m, usually shorter. Lvs 2–6cm, oblanceolate, apex obtuse or acute, toothed. ♂ infl. to 1.5cm. Fr. to 3mm diam., yellow-brown, dotted with resin. N Amer., Eur. to Jap. Z1.

M. heterophylla Raf. Similar to *M. pensylvanica* and *M. cerifera* but decid., lvs 5–12cm, oblanceolate. Fr. 2–4mm diam., grey-white, pruinose. E US. Z6.

M. pensylvanica Lois. BAYBERRY; CANDLEBERRY; SWAMP CANDLE-BERRY. Decid. or semi-evergreen shrub to 2.75m. Lvs 2–8cm, broadly oblanceolate, apex obtuse or abruptly acute, entire or sparsely toothed. ♂ infl. to 1.5cm. Fr. to 4mm diam., globose, grey-white, waxy. E N Amer. Z2.

M. rubra Sieb. & Zucc. Small everg. tree. Lvs 6–12cm, oblanceolate to obovate, apex usually obtuse, entire or toothed. Fr. 1.5–2.5cm diam., dark purple-red. E Asia. Z10.

MYRICACEAE Bl. 3/50. *Comptonia, Myrica.*

Myricaria Desv. FALSE TAMARISK. Tamaricaceae. 10 decid. shrubs and subshrubs differing from Tamarix in sta. 10, united, not 4–8, free. S Eur., Asia, China, Sib.

M. davurica (Willd.) Ehrenb. Simliar to *M. germanica*; rac. usu-ally axill.; sta. often only one-third connate. Russia. Z5.

M. germanica (L.) Desv. Shrub, narrowly upright, 1–2m, young shoots blue-green. Lvs scale-like, blue-green. Fls bright red, in 10–15cm, spike-like rac., mostly term.; sta. connate to midway. C & S Eur. Z6.

→*Tamarix.*

Myriocarpa Benth. Urticaceae. 15 small trees or shrubs. Lvs toothed, stipulate. Fls unisexual in slender axill. rac. or spikes; ♂ with 4–5-lobed perianth, ♀ lacking perianth. C & S Amer. Z10.

M. stipitata Benth. Shrub or small tree to 12m. Lvs 10–30cm, ovate or obovate-elliptic, densely pubesc. when young, often silver. Fls green-white, in long rac. Summer. S Amer.

→*Boehmeria.*

Myriophyllum L. MILFOIL. Haloragidaceae. 45 aquatic or terrestrial herbs, perenn. or sometimes ann. St. slender, rooting then ascending, often floating, emergent lvs whorled or alt., en-tire or slightly dentate; submerged lvs usually whorled, finely pinnatifid. Fls usually in red-green terminal spikes, sessile or subsessile, minute; sep. 4 or 0, erect; pet. 2 to 4 or 0; sta. 4 or 8. Cosmop.

M. alterniflorum DC. St. to 120cm. Lvs to 2.5cm, in whorls of 3–5; submerged lvs pinnatifid, seg. 6–18. NE Amer., Eur. Z6.

M. aquaticum (Vell.) Verdc. PARROT FEATHER; DIAMOND MILFOIL. St. to 2m. Lvs subsimilar, in whorls of 4 or 5, to 4cm, pinnatifid, seg. short, bright yellow-green or blue-green. S Amer., Aus., NZ, Java. Z10.

M. brasiliense Cambess. = *M. aquaticum.*

M. elatinoides Gaudich. St. to 120cm. Lvs in whorls of 3–5, emergent lvs to 8×5mm, ovate-oblong, obtuse, subentire to en-tire, submerged lvs to 2cm, finely pinnatifid. Mex., S Amer., NZ, Aus. Z10.

M. heterophyllum Michx. St. to 1m. Emergent lvs lanceolate to oblong or linear, sharply dentate, submerged lvs to 5cm, crowded. NE Amer. Z6.

M. hippuroides Nutt. ex Torr. & A. Gray. WESTERN MILFOIL. St. to 60cm. Lvs in whorls of 4 or 5, pale green, emergent lvs linear to lanceolate, entire to serrate, submerged lvs to 2cm. SW US. Z7.

M. pinnatum (Walter) BSP. St. to 60cm. Lvs in whorls of 4 or 5, emergent lvs linear, pectinate or serrate, submerged lvs to 2cm, seg. 6 to 10. N Amer. Z6.

M. proserpinacoides Gillies ex Hook. & Arn. = *M. aquaticum.*

M. scabratum Michx. = *M. pinnatum.*

M. spicatum L. St. to 3m. Lvs to whorls of 4–5, emergent lvs to 10×2mm, ovate to obovate, obtuse, usually entire, submerged lvs to 2.5×2cm, with 7–11 pairs of filform seg. N Amer., Eur., Asia, N Afr. Z6.

M. verticillatum L. MYRIAD LEAF. St. to 1m. Emergent lvs to 1cm, petinate-pinnatifid, submerged lvs to 4×4cm, in whorls of 4–6, with 8–16 pairs of opposite seg. N Amer., Eur., Asia. Z3.

Myristica Gronov. Myristicaceae. 100 everg., dioecious trees. Fls in axill. rac. or clusters, the males subtended by a bracteole; cal. teeth 3–5; sta. 6+, fil. united, anth. large, united. Fr. large, succulent, arillate. Asia, Australasia. Z10.

M. fragrans Houtt. NUTMEG; MACE. To 10m. Lvs to 12cm, alt., oblong, entire, initially silver-scaly, aromatic. Fls to 1cm, pale yellow; cor. 0. Fr. to 5cm; albumen (nutmeg) brown, tough, mottled, enclosed by a thin, pink-scarlet splitting perisperm (mace). Indon.

MYRISTICACEAE R. Br. 19/440. *Myristica.*

Myrobalan *Prunus cerasifera.*

Myrobalanus Gaertn.

M. bellirica Gaertn. = *Terminalia bellirica.*

M. chebula (Retz.) Gaertn. = *Terminalia chebula.*

Myroxylon L. f. Leguminosae (Papilionoideae). 3 everg. trees. Lvs imparipinnate. Rac. term. or axill.; cal. campanulate, lobes subequal; standard wide, clawed, keel and wings similar; sta. 10; free. Fr. flat, 2-winged; seed solitary. Trop. N S Amer., nat. OW. Z10.

M. balsamum (L.) Harms. TOLU BALSAM TREE. To 12m, balsamiferous, citrus-scented. Rachis to 15cm; lfts to 1.2×0.3cm, 5–13, elliptic-oblong or ovate, shiny.Infl. congested; cor. to 1cm+ white. Mex. to N S Amer., Venez. to Peru. var. *pereirae* (Royle) Harms. BALSAM OF PERU. Lfts smaller. Z8.

M. pereirae Royle = *M. balsamum* var. *pereirae.*

M. peruiferum auct. = *M. balsamum.*

M. senticosum (Hance) Warb. = *Xylosma congestum.*

M. toluiferum A. Rich. = *M. balsamum.*

Myrrhis Mill. Umbelliferae. 1 sweetly aromatic, perenn. herb to 2m; st. puberulent. Lvs 2–3-pinnate, seg. 1–3cm, oblong-lanceolate, pinnatifid or deeply toothed, often blotched white. Umbels compound with 4–20 pubesc. rays 1.5–3cm; involucre usually 0; bracteoles *c*5, narrow. Early summer. Eur. Z5.

M. odorata (L.) Scop. SWEET CICELY; GARDEN MYRRH.

MYRSINACEAE R. Br. 37/1250. *Ardisia, Maesa, Myrsine.*

Myrsine L. Myrsinaceae. 5 aromatic everg. trees and shrubs, to 6m. Lvs leathery, usually entire. Fls small in umbels or clusters, 4–5 merous; cor. lobes imbricate in bud, sta. 4–5. Fr. a small drupe, 1-seeded. Azores to China and NZ.

M. africana L. CAPE MYRTLE; AFRICAN BOXWOOD. Shrub, 0.5–1.5m, young shoots softly hairy. Lvs 0.6–2cm, narrowly obovate to elliptic, apex rounded or truncate, sparsely toothed toward apex. Fls pale brown, 3–6 per cluster. Fr. 6mm diam., blue-lilac. Late spring. Azores, mts of E & S Afr., Himal., China. Z9.

M. australis (A.Rich) Allan. MAPAU. Small shrub. Young br. slender, orange-red. Lvs oblong-elliptic, undulate. NZ. Z9.

M. chathamica F. Muell. Tree to *c*6m, twigs covered in stiff hairs. Lvs 2–7.5cm, obovate or elliptic or broadly elliptic, blunt or emarginate. Fls in a group of clusters or solitary, fimbriate. Fr. (5–)6–9mm diam., purple. NZ. Z8.

M. nummularia Hook. f. Prostrate to scandent shrub to 30cm, twigs red-brown. Lvs 0.4–1cm, obovate to suborbicular or obovate oblong, minutely apiculate or retuse. Fls minute, ciliolate, solitary or in small clusters. Fr. 5–6.5mm diam., blue-purple. NZ. Z7.

M. retusa Ait. = *M. africana.*

M. semiserrata Wall. Large shrub to small tree. Lvs to 12cm, elliptic-ovate, acuminate, serrate. Fls clustered, red-white. Fr. red-purple. Himal. Z9.

→*Rapanea* and *Suttonia.*

MYRTACEAE Juss. 120/3850. *Acca, Acmena, Actinodium, Agonis, Amomyrtus, Angophora, Asteromyrtus, Backhousia,
Baeckea, Beaufortia, Callistemon, Calothamnus, Calytrix, Chamelaucium, Darwinia, Eucalyptus, Eugenia, Homoranthus, Hypocalymma, Kunzea, Leptospermum, Lophomyrtus, Lophostemon, Luma, Melaleuca, Metrosideros, Myrceugenia, Myrciaria,
Myrteola, Myrtus, Pileanthus Psidium, Regelia, Rhodomyrtus,
Syzygium, Tristania, Tristaniopsis, Ugni, Verticordia.*

Myrteola O. Berg. Myrtaceae. 12 shrubs sometimes included in
Myrtus, usually represented in cult. by the diminutive creeping
M. nummularia with minute, rounded, 2-ranked lvs, white .fls
and pink fr. S Argentina, S Chile, Falkland Is. Z6.

Myrtillocactus Console. Cactaceae. 4 arborescent or shrubby
cacti; br. ascending, few-ribbed, spiny. Fls small, up to 9 per
areole; floral areoles slightly woolly; tube v. short; perianth
rotate. Fr. small, berry-like. Mex., Guat.
M. cochal (Orcutt) Britt. & Rose. Resembling *M. geometrizans*,
but st. green, spines fewer; tree to 3m; ribs 6–8; spines nearly
black at first; central spine 0–1, 2cm, radial spines 3–5, short. Fl.
2.5×2.5cm pale yellow, tinged green. Fr. 12–18mm diam., dark
red. Baja Calif. Z9.
M. geometrizans (Mart. ex Pfeiff.) Console. Tree 4–5m, with
short trunk; br. numerous, upcurving, 6–10cm diam., blue-
green; ribs 5–6; areoles 1.5–3cm apart; central spine 1, 1–7cm,
dagger-like, almost black, radial spines 5–9, 2–10mm, red-
brown then grey. Fl. *c*2×2.5cm, creamy white. Fr. 1–2cm diam.,
dark red or purple. C & S Mex. Z9.
M. pugionifer (Lem.) A. Berger = *M. geometrizans*.
M. schenckii (Purpus) Britt. & Rose. Resembling
M. geometrizans, but st. dark green, ribs 7–8, areoles 5mm
apart, black-felted; central spine 1, 2(–5)cm, radial spines 6–8,
5–12mm. S Mex. Z9.
→*Cereus.*

Myrtle *Cyrilla racemiflora; Myrtus communis; Umbellularia cali-
fornica.*
Myrtle Beech *Nothofagus cunninghamii.*
Myrtle Dahoon *Ilex myrtifolia.*
Myrtle Flag *Acorus calamus.*
Myrtle Holly *Ilex myrtifolia.*
Myrtle Lime *Triphasia trifolia.*
Myrtle Oak *Quercus myrtifolia.*
Myrtle Spurge *Euphorbia lathyris.*
Myrtle Wattle *Acacia myrtifolia.*
Myrtle Willow *Salix myrsinites.*

Myrtus L. Myrtaceae. 2 everg. shrubs. Lvs entire, with aromatic
oil glands. Fls solitary in axils; cal. (4–)5-lobed; pet. 4, spread-
ing; sta. numerous, longer than the pet. Fr. a berry. Medit., N
Afr. Z8.
M. apiculata (DC) = *Luma apiculata.*
M. boetica Mill. = *M. communis.*
M. bullata (Sol.) A. Cunn. = *Lophomyrtus bullata.*
M. buxifolia Raf. = *M. communis* 'Buxifolia'.
M. chequen (Molina) Spreng. = *Luma chequen.*
M. communis L. MYRTLE. Much-branched erect shrub to 5m. Lvs
to 5×1.5cm, ovate-lanceolate, coriaceous, lustrous green,
transparently dotted, aromatic. Fls white or pink-white, to 3cm
diam., fragrant; pet. suborbicular, white. Fr. subglobose,
7–10mm, blue- or red-black. Medit. and SW Eur.; widely cult.

since ancient times, native range uncertain. 'Albocarpa': fr.
white. 'Buxifolia': lvs broadly elliptic. 'Compacta': habit dwarf,
dense. 'Flore Pleno': fls double, white. 'Leucocarpa': fr. white.
'Microphylla': habit dwarf, densely leafy; twigs brown; lvs less
than 2.5cm, linear-lanceolate, overlapping, glossy. 'Microphylla
Variegata': lvs striped white. 'Minima': dwarf habit, lvs small.
'Variegata': habit small; lvs with white margins or stripes,
pointed, leathery. var. *acutifolia* L. Habit erect. Shoots tinged
red. Lvs lanceolate, long-acuminate, with cuneate base. var.
italica L. Narrowly upright. Lvs 3×1cm, oval-lanceolate. var.
latifolia Tinb. & Lagasca. Lvs 2–3×1–1.5cm, oval-oblong to
oblong-lanceolate, acuminate. var. *romana* Mill. Lvs
3–4.5×1–1.5cm, broadly ovate, strongly acuminate, light green,
in whorls of 3–4. ssp. *tarentina* (L.) Nyman. Compact, rounded
habit with small, narrow, dark lvs and pink-tinted cream fls; fr.
white.
M. gayana (Barnéoud) Berg = *Luma chequen.*
M. italica Mill. = *M. communis.*
M. latifolia (Berg) Badillo = *M. communis.*
M. lechleriana (Miq) Sealy = *Amomyrtus luma.*
M. luma auct. = *Luma appiculata.*
M. luma Molina = *Amomyrtus luma.*
M. minima Mill. = *M. communis* 'Minima'.
M. obcordata (Raoul) Hook. f. = *Lophomyrtus obcordata.*
M. romana Hoffsgg. = *M. communis.*
M. samarangensis Bl. = *Syzygium samarangense.*
M. tomentosa Ait. = *Rhodomyrtus tomentosa.*
M. ugni Molina = *Ugni molinae.*

Mysore Fig *Ficus drupacea* var. *pubescens.*
Mysore Raspberry *Rubus niveus.*
Mysore Thorn *Caesalpinia decapetala.*

Mystacidium Lindl. Orchidaceae. 11 monopodial epiphytic
orchids. St. short. Lvs distichous, usually ligulate. Rac. axill. or
arising from st. below lvs; fls white, green or yellow-green; sep.
and pet. free, similar; lip entire or lobed, spurred. Trop. & S
Afr. Z10.
M. brayboniae Summerh. Lvs 3–4, 2–5×1cm, elliptic. Rac. 5–8-
fld; fls white, *c*2cm diam., slightly cup-shaped; lip trilobed, midlobe ovate, obtuse; spur 2cm, tapering from a wide mouth. S
Afr.
M. capense (L. f.) Schltr. Lvs 4–10, 8.5–13×1–1.5cm, ligulate.
Rac. 6–12-fld; fls white, 1.5–2.5cm diam., lip trilobed,
lanceolate, acute; spur 4–6cm, straight, slender, tapering. S
Afr., Swaz.
M. filicorne Lindl. = *M. capense.*
M. millari Bol. Lvs 2–6, to 12×1.5cm, ligulate, net-veined. Rac.
pendent, 7–10-fld; fls white with green anther-cap, 0.8–1.5cm
diam., lip oblong-obovate, recurved at tip; spur 2cm, funnel-
shaped in basal quarter, narrowing abruptly. S Afr. (Natal, E
Cape).
M. tanganyikense Summerh. Lvs 3–4, to 5×1cm, oblanceolate,
net-veined. Rac. several-fld; fls pale green or creamy white; lip
lanceolate, entire; spur 1–2cm, tapering, slender, straight or
slightly incurved. Tanz., Malawi, Zam., Zimb.
M. venosum Harv. ex Rolfe. Lvs 3–4, to 6×1cm, ligulate, sometimes net-veined. Rac. 4–7-fld; fls white, 1.7–2cm diam.; lip
lanceolate, with 2 small, rounded lobes at base; spur 3–4.5cm,
slender, tapering. S Afr., Swaz.
→*Angraecum.*

N

Na *Mesua ferrea.*

Nabalus Cass. RATTLESNAKE ROOT; DROP-FLOWER. Compositae. 15 perenn. herbs. St. usually simple, sometimes purple. Lvs dentate or pinnatifid, mostly petiolate below, auriculate and amplexicaul above. Cap. ligulate, small, numerous, in open or spike-like term. pan. and drooping axill. corymbose clusters. N Amer., temp. E Asia.

N. albus (L.) Hook. WHITE LETTUCE. To 1.5m, usually glab. and glaucous. Lvs to 20cm, triangular-hastate, sinuate-dentate or pinnatifid, usually petiolate, uppermost lanceolate and entire. Cap. *c*6mm diam., pendulous, in paniculate or thyrsoid, often axill., clusters; flts white, tinged, green or yellow, fragrant. Summer. NE N Amer. Z5.

N. asper (Michx.) Torr. & A. Gray. To 1.5m, scabrous or pubesc. Lvs to 8cm, ovate to oblong or oblanceolate, base attenuate, winged-petiolate, commonly obtuse, st. lvs acute, dentate, uppermost entire. Cap. 6–8mm diam., erect, spreading or slightly drooping, in a long narrow thyrse; flts pale yellow to cream. Late summer–early autumn. EC SE US. Z6.

N. autumnalis (Walter) C. Jeffrey To 1m, glab., somewhat glaucous. Lvs to 25cm, lanceolate to oblanceolate, sinuate-pinnate or pinnatisect, lobes entire or dentate, distant, petiolate, reduced upwards, upper lvs entire, sessile. Cap. to *c*4mm diam., pendulous, in a term., narrow, simple or branched, often unilateral thyrse; flts white or pale pink. Autumn. E US. Z5.

N. serpentarius (Pursh) Hook. LION'S FOOT; GALL-OF-THE-EARTH. To 1.5m, glab. or sparsely pubesc. Lvs to 20cm, pinnatifid or pinnately to palmately divided, dentate or entire, thick, rigid. Cap. *c*6mm diam., pendulous, in paniculate axill. clusters; flts white, cream or pink, rarely yellow. Autumn. E US. Z5.
→*Prenanthes.*

Naboom *Euphorbia grandidens*; *E. ingens*; *E. tetragona.*
Nagaba-giboshi *Hosta longissima.*
Nagami Kumquat *Fortunella margarita.*
Nagasaki-giboshi *Hosta tibai.*

Nageia Gaertn. Podocarpaceae. 5 everg. conifers. Crown columnar. Lvs decussate, broad-lanceolate, apex acuminate, base cuneate, lacking midrib, rigid. ♂ cones solitary or in groups, ovoid-cylindric, subtended by sterile scales. ♀ cones solitary or paired; seed with a thinly fleshy, pruinose, blue-black coating. S Jap., NE India, SE China, Taiwan to Malaysia, Philipp., Moluccas, New Guinea. Easily told from all other genera in *Podocarpaceae* by the absence of lf midrib, but superficially similar to *Agathis.*

N. fleuryi (Hickel) Laub. Tree to 10m+. Lvs 10–18×3.5–5cm. ♂ cones to 3.5cm. Seeds to 2cm diam. China to Vietnam & Kampuchea. Z9.

N. formosensis (Dümmer) Page = *N. nagi.*
N. mannii (Hook. f.) Laub. = *Afrocarpus mannii.*
N. nagi (Thunb.) Kuntze. NAGI. Tree to 25m. Lvs 4–8×1.5–3cm, glaucous beneath. ♂ cones to 2cm, seeds 1–1.5cm diam. S China to Taiwan & S Jap. Z8.

N. wallichiana (Presl) Kuntze. Tree to 40m. Lvs 10–15×3–5cm, to 22×7cm on vigorous trees. ♂ cones to 2cm. Seeds to 2cm diam. Assam & Burm. to New Guinea. Z9.
→*Decussocarpus* and *Podocarpus.*

Nageliella L.O. Williams. Orchidaceae. 2 epiphytic or terrestrial orchids. Pbs semiterete, clavate, striate, unifoliate. Lvs term., semi-erect, fleshy, thickly coriaceous, rugulose, tongue-like in appearance, sometimes with midrib obscurely impressed above. Rac. term, slender; fls small; sep. erect, connivent; pet. linear to lanceolate; lip swollen or saccate, simple to obscurely 3-lobed. C Amer. Z10.

N. angustifolia (Booth ex Lindl.) Ames & Correll. Lvs to 10×2cm, linear-lanceolate to oblong-lanceolate, marked dark red-brown. Infl. to 30cm; peduncle terete, filiform; fls bright magenta, to 1.3cm diam. Guat.

N. purpurea (Lindl.) L.O. Williams. Lvs to 12×3cm, lanceolate to ovate-lanceolate, often spotted brown-purple. Infl. to 50cm; peduncle semi-terete to compressed; fls red-purple, to 1.8cm diam. Mex., Guat., Hond.
→*Hartwegia.*

Nagi *Nageia nagi.*
Nagoonberry *Rubus arcticus.*
Naiad *Najas.*
Nailrod *Typha latifolia.*
Naio *Myoporum sandwiciense.*

Najadaceae Fuss. See *Najas.*

Najas L. NAIAD; WATER NYMPH. Najadaceae. 35 submerged aquatic herbs, inhabiting fresh or brackish water. St. 60cm+, filiform, much branched. Lvs opposite, alt. or whorled, linear to narrowly oblong, entire or toothed, sheathed at base. Fls small, solitary or fascicled in sheath-axils, minute. Cosmop.

N. falciculata A. Braun = *N. indica.*
N. flexilis (Willd.) Rostk. & W.L.E. Schmidt. Lvs to 2.5×0.1cm, in whorls of 3, linear, minutely denticulate, sheath not auriculate. E N Amer., N & C Eur. Z5.

N. graminea Delile. Lvs to 4×0.1cm, whorled, linear or subulate, acuminate, minutely denticulate, sheaths with long-triangular auricles. S Eur., Asia, Australasia, N & E Afr. Z8.

N. guadalupensis (Spreng.) Morong. Lvs 2.5×0.1cm, linear, acute to acuminate, minutely denticulate, sheath not auriculate. Calif. to S Amer., inc. Galapagos. Z9.

N. indica (Willd.) Cham. Lvs to 4.5cm, linear, minutely spinulose, sheath with overlapping edges, sometimes auriculate. India, Malaysia to Philipp. and Jap. Z10.

N. kingii Rendle = *N. indica.*
N. microdon A. Braun = *N. guadalupensis.*
N. minor All. Lvs to 3×0.1cm, linear, minutely spinulose, sheath with rounded-truncate auricles. Eur., Asia, N & C Afr. Z6.

Naked Coral Tree *Erythrina americana.*
Naked Ladies *Colchicum.*
Naked Lady Lily ×*Amarygia parkeri.*

Namibia Schwantes. Aizoaceae. 2 succulent perennials forming dense hemispherical clumps. Shoots with 1–2 pairs of highly succulent, thick, soft, finely rough lvs. Fls sessile or short-stalked. Nam. Z9.

N. cinerea (Marloth) Dinter & Schwantes. Lvs 13×10–12×12mm, rounded-triangular on upper surface, ± recured at tip, lower surface navicular and rounded-carinate, grey-greenn, rough with white dots. Fls 3cm diam., violet.

N. pomonae (Dinter) Dinter & Schwantes. Lvs 30×15–18×14mm, united for 10–12mm, broadly navicular, angles distinct, keel obtuse, apiculate, white-grey or light grey. Fls 3cm diam., white.

N. ponderosa (Dinter) Dinter & Schwantes = *Juttadinteria longipetala.*
→*Juttadinteria.*

Nana *Clethra alnifolia.*

Nananthus N.E. Br. Aizoaceae. 10 dwarf, tufted, glab. succulents. St. caudiciform, tuberous. Lvs 4–6 per st., opposite, widest in the middle, lower surface obtusely keeled, often white-punctate. Fls solitary. S Afr. Bots. Z9.

N. albipunctus (Haw.) N.E. Br., also (Haw.) Schwantes = *Rabiea albipuncta.*

N. aloides (Haw.) Schwantes. Lvs 5cm, obliquely lanceolate or narrowly rhombic, carinate-triquetrous above, dark green with numerous white, tuberculate dots and rough angles. Fls 2.5–3.5cm diam., pet. yellow, sometimes with a darker yellow stripe. W Cape, Bots.

N. cradockensis L. Bol. = *Aloinopsis jamesii.*
N. crassipes (Marloth). L. Bol. = *Aloinopsis spathulata.*
N. dyeri L. Bol. = *Aloinopsis rubrolineata.*
N. jamesii (L. Bol.) L. Bol. = *Aloinopsis jamesii.*
N. lodewykii (L. Bol.) L. Bol. = *Aloinopsis lodewykii.*
N. luckhoffii (L. Bol.) L. Bol. = *Aloinopsis luckhoffii.*
N. malherbei L. Bol. = *Aloinopsis malherbei.*
N. orpenii (N.E. Br.) L. Bol. = *Aloinopsis orpenii.*
N. peersii L. Bol. = *Aloinopsis peersii.*
N. rubrolineatus (N.E. Br.) N.E. Br. = *Aloinopsis rubrolineata.*
N. schooneesii (L. Bol.) L. Bol. = *Aloinopsis schooneesii.*
N. soehlemannii F.A. Haage = *Aloinopsis peersii.*

N. transvaalensis (Rolfe) L. Bol. Similar to *N. vittatus* but lvs 2–3cm, with large tubercles crowded toward lf margins. Fls 2–3cm diam., pet. light yellow. Transvaal.

N. villetii L. Bol. = *Aloinopsis villetii.*

N. vittatus (N.E. Br.) Schwantes. Lvs 2–3cm long, unequal, obliquely lanceolate, acute, shortly apiculate, semicylindric, expanded above, dull green with tuberculate dots. Fls 2–2.5cm diam., pet. light yellow with a thin red median strip. OFS.

N. wilmaniae (L. Bol.) L. Bol. Lvs to 2.5cm, base oblong, broadening midway, ovate at tip, acute, lower surface carinate, with pallid dots, olive green. Fls 2cm diam., pet. yellow with red longitudinal stripes. W Cape.
→*Aloinopsis* and *Mesembryanthemum.*

Nandina Thunb. HEAVENLY BAMBOO. Berberidaceae. 1 everg. or semi-deciduous shrub to 2m. St. erect, clumped, ± simple, cane-like. Lvs clustered toward summit, bi- to tripinnate, to 90cm, triangular in outline, semi-erect or horizontal; lfts to 7cm, elliptic, lanceolate or narrow-rhombic, glab., subcoriaceous, emerging slightly glaucous, tinted rose, hardening sap-green, red to purple in autumn; petioles slender, glossy. Pan. term., to 40cm; fls white, to 7.5mm diam. Fr. a bright red berry, to 1cm diam. Summer. India to Jap. Z7.

N. domestica Thunb. 'Firepower': dwarf, strong autumn colours, crimson and green. 'Flora': fr. golden yellow. 'Harbour Dwarf': small; lvs somewhat puckered, tinted brilliant red. 'Little Princess': strong colour in spring and autumn; fls white. 'Longifolia': pinnae narrow-oblong, to 10cm. 'Nana Purpurea' ('Purpurea'): to 1.25m; lvs shorter, sparsely bipinnate; pinnae broader, fewer, softer, retaining purple-red flush throughout season and colouring brilliantly in autumn. 'Richmond': vigorous; fr. scarlet in winter. 'Variegata': lvs, petioles and young st. variegated white, cream and candy pink. 'Woods Dwarf': vigorous, low-growing; lvs light gold, tinted red in winter. var. *leucocarpa* Mak. Fr. dull white. Jap.

Nankai-giboshi *Hosta tardiva.*
Nankeen Lily *Lilium* ×*testaceum.*
Nanking Cherry *Prunus tomentosa.*

Nannoglottis Maxim. Compositae. 8 erect, perenn. herbs, to 1m. Lvs elliptic to oblong or oblanceolate, entire or toothed, membranous, lower petiolate, upper winged, decurrent. Cap. radiate, solitary, or few in a lax corymb; flts yellow, numerous; ray flts reflexed, oblong; disc flts campanulate. W China, Himal. Z8.

N. hookeri (C.B. Clarke ex Hook. f.) Kit. Robust herb, to 80cm. Lvs to 15cm, elliptic to oblanceolate, obtuse or acute, entire or irregularly toothed, basal lvs 0 or soon withering. Cap. few, 3–4.5cm diam., long-pedunculate; ray flts to 13mm. W China to Nepal.

Nanodes Rchb. Orchidaceae. 3 diminutive epiphytic orchids. St. tufted, cane-like, clothed in overlapping lf sheaths. Lvs 2-ranked, rather fleshy. Fls solitary or paired, small, waxy, translucent with a simple lip. C & S Amer. Z10.

N. discolor Lindl. St. to 10cm, densely clustered. Lvs 1.75–3cm, elliptic to linear-oblong. Fls usually paired, translucent yellow-green or green-brown to pale pink-purple, lip 0.7–0.9×0.9–1.1cm, reniform to ovate-suborbicular, apiculate, erose-ciliate. C & S Amer.

N. mathewsii Rolfe. St. to 10cm. Lvs 1.5–2cm, oblong. Fls solitary, light purple-green; lip 0.75–1×1–1.8cm, transversely oblong, decurved. Mex. to Panama, Venez. to Peru.

N. medusae Rchb. f. St. to 25cm, somewhat pendulous. Lvs 4–7cm, narrowly ovate-oblong. Fls usually solitary; tep. yellow-green tinged red-brown, lip 3–4.5×4–5.5cm, deep maroon, transversely oblong, v. deeply lacerate-fimbriate. Ecuad.
→*Epidendrum* and *Neolehmannia.*

Napaea L. GLADE MALLOW. Malvaceae. 1 coarse perenn. herb, erect to 2.5m. Lvs to 60cm, palmately 5–11-lobed, lobes serrate to pinnatifid. Pan. cymose; epical. 0; cal. to 6mm; pet. white, ♂ to 1.2cm, slightly longer than ♀; anth. 15–20, at tip of staminal column; ♀ fls with sterile anth.; styles 10. E & C US (Ohio to Ill. and Minn.). Z4.

N. dioica L. GLADE MALLOW.
→*Sida.*

Naples Garlic *Allium neapolitanum.*

Napoleonaea P. Beauv. Lecythidaceae. 10 everg. trees or shrubs. Lvs glab., usually entire. Fls solitary or in pan., axill. or cauliflorous, subsessile or short-pedicellate; cal. 5-lobed; pet. 0; sta. many, in 4 whorls on a gland. disc, outer 3 whorls sterile and united to form a wheel-shaped pseudocorolla and corona.

Fr. a berry, sometimes lobed. W & C Afr. Z10.

N. cuspidata Miers = *N. imperialis.*

N. imperialis P. Beauv. Shrub to 7m. Lvs to 22×9cm, elliptic to obovate, acuminate. Fls subsessile, solitary or clustered; pseudocorolla to 5cm diam., outermost whorl ochre above, brown below, 2nd whorl yellow, innermost 2 whorls incurved, pink-white. Fr. to 5cm diam., globose, obscurely lobed. Nigeria, Equat. Guinea.

N. miersii Hook. f. = *N. imperialis.*

Nara *Acanthosicyos horridus.*
Naranjilla *Solanum quitoense.*
Naranjuelo *Capparis odoratissima.*

Naravelia DC. Ranunculaceae. 5 woody climbers. Lvs pinnate with tendrils at end of rachis. Fls in term. pan.; sep. petaloid, 4; staminodes 9–14, linear to clavate; sta. numerous. Fr. narrow achenes with plumose style. India to Malaya. Z10.

N. zeylanica DC. Lvs trifoliolate, lower 2 lfts ovate, entire or 1–2-toothed, central lft transformed to tendril, 3-fld at apex. Fls yellow. Autumn–winter. Trop. India, Malaya, Sri Lanka.
→*Atragene.*

Narcissus L. DAFFODIL. Amaryllidaceae. *c*50 perenn. bulbous herbs. Lvs 1 to several, erect to prostrate, linear to strap-shaped. Fls scapose, solitary or in an umbel of 2–20, subtended by a one-valved, membranous spathe; perianth tubular at the base with 6 seg., with a conspicuous corona in the form of a trumpet or a smaller ring or cup; sta. 6. S Eur. and Medit.; also N Afr., W Asia, China and Jap.

N. abscissus (Haw.) Schult. & Schult. f. = *N. bicolor.*

N. albescens Pugsley = *N. pseudonarcissus* ssp. *moschatus.*

N. alpestris Pugsley = *N. pseudonarcissus* ssp. *moschatus.*

N. assoanus Dufour. RUSH-LEAVED JONQUIL. Lvs to 20×0.2cm, cylindric, slightly striate, green. Scape 7–25cm; fls 2–3, to 2.2cm diam., horizontal or slightly ascending, yellow, fragrant; perianth tube 1.2–1.8cm, straight; seg. obovate, 0.7–1×0.7cm patent, incurved, imbricate at base; corona cup-shaped conic, 0.5×1.1–1.7cm, crenate, deeper yellow than seg. S Fr., S & E Spain. Z7.

N. asturiensis (Jordan) Pugsley. Lvs 8×0.6cm, glaucous-green, spreading, channelled. Scape 7–14cm, not erect, striate; fl. solitary, to 3.5cm across, usually drooping, soft yellow; perianth tube to 8mm, green-yellow; seg. to 1.4×0.4cm, usually twisted, deflexed; corona 1.7cm, widened below, constricted at middle, mouth spreading, fimbriate. N Port., NW & NC Spain. 'Giant': larger in all parts. Z4.

N. aureus L. = *N. tazetta* ssp. *aureus.*

N. barlae L. = *N. papyraceus* ssp. *panizzianus.*

N. bertolonii Parl. = *N. tazetta* ssp. *aureus.*

N. bicolor L. Lvs 30–35×1.1–1.6cm, green or glaucous, erect, flat. Scape 35cm; fl. solitary, horizontal or ascending; perianth tube 1cm, green-to orange-yellow, broad; seg. 3.5–4cm, cream or pale sulphur-yellow, almost parallel, 1.5–2cm diam., mouth with little or no flange, lobed or dentate. Pyren. and Corbières. Z6.

N. ×*biflorus* Curtis = *N.* ×*medioluteus.*

N. broussonetii Lagasca. Lvs 4, 28×0.9cm, glaucous, erect, lightly striate. Scape to 40cm; fls 1–8, ascending, white, to 3.5cm diam., fragrant; perianth tube to 2.8cm, funnel-shaped, white; seg. 1.6×1.2cm, patent or incurving, slightly imbricate; corona rudimentary; sta. exserted, bright yellow. Autumn. Moroc. Z8.

N. bulbocodium L. HOOP PETTICOAT DAFFODIL; PETTICOAT DAFFODIL. ssp. *bulbocodium.* Lvs 10–30(–40)cm×1–5mm, semi-cylindric, dark green. Scape 2.5–20cm; fl. solitary, horizontal, to 4.5cm diam.; perianth tube 6–25mm, yellow, often tinged green, esp. below; seg. narrow, much shorter than corona, 0.6–2cm×0.5–5mm, often tinged green; corona funnel-shaped, 0.9–3.2×0.7–3.4cm, yellow, margin of mouth spreading or incurved, entire to dentate or crenate; anth. included or slightly exserted, style sometimes long-exserted. W Fr., Spain, Port., N Afr. var. *bulbocodium* including *N. bulbocodium* 'Tenuifolius'. Plants usually dwarf. Lvs prostrate or spreading. Fls golden-yellow; perianth to 3cm long. var. *conspicuus* (Haw.) Bak. Plant robust. Lvs erect. Fls dark yellow to citron, 3–3.5cm long, corona 2cm diam. Includes var. *citrinus* hort., loosely applied to large-fld pale yellow plants, but not var. *citrinus* Bak. ssp. *obesus* (Salisb.) Maire. Lvs to 30×0.2cm, ± prostrate, sinuous, channelled, lightly striate. Scape 10cm; fl. to 3.5cm diam., horizontal or ascending, bright yellow; perianth tube to 2.5cm, conic, yellow; seg. 1.4×0.5cm, patent, twisted; corona to 1.8×2cm, mouth crenate or slightly incurved, deeper yellow than seg. WC Port. Z6.

N. bulbocodium ssp. *romieuxii* (Braun-Blanquet & Maire) Emberger & Maire = *N. romieuxii.*

N. calathinus L. = *N.* ×*odorus.*

N. campernellii hort. ex Haw. = *N. ×odorus*.

N. canaliculatus hort. = *N. tazetta* 'Canaliculatus'.

N. cantabricus DC. WHITE HOOP PETTICOAT DAFFODIL. ssp. **cantabricus.** Lvs 2, or 4–5 in var. *foliosus* (Maire) Fernandes, ascending or spreading, to 15cm×1mm, semicylindrical, slightly channelled ± striate. Scape 5–10cm; fl. solitary, ascending, to 4cm diam., fragrant; perianth tube to 2.4×1.2cm, funnel-shaped, white, green below; seg. 1.2×0.5cm, white, nearly patent; corona to 1.5×4cm, entire or crenate or undulate. S Spain, N Afr. var. *petunioides* Fernandes. Scape 6cm; fls pure white, horizontal; corona nearly flat, 3–4cm diam., deeply crenate, margin recurved. Alg. ssp. *monophyllus* (Dur.) Fernandes. Lf solitary, 27cm×1mm; fl. horizontal or ascending, to 4.5cm diam. S Spain, N Afr. Z8.

N. cavanillesii A. Barra & G. Lopez. = *N. humilis*.

N. clusii Dunal = *N. cantabricus* ssp. *cantabricus*.

N. confusus Pugsley = *N. pseudonarcissus* ssp. *major*.

N. corcyrensis (Herb.) Nyman = *N. tazetta* ssp. *corcyrensis*.

N. cupularis (Salisb.) Schult. = *N. tazetta* ssp. *aureus*.

N. cyclamineus DC. Lvs 12(–30)cm×4–6mm, bright green, spreading, keeled. Scape to 20cm; fl. solitary, drooping or pendent, deep yellow; perianth tube 2–3mm, green; seg. sharply reflexed, 2×0.4cm, twisted or not twisted; corona 2cm, slightly constricted just below flared margin, 12-lobed or fimbriate. NW Port., NW Spain. Z6.

N. dubius Gouan. Lvs 50cm×7mm spreading, dark green, inner face flat, outer striate. Scape 15–25cm; fls 2–6, ascending, 16mm diam., white; perianth tube 1.6×0.2cm, green, white at distal end; seg. 7×6mm, apiculate, patent; corona 4×7mm, cup-shaped, crenate. S Fr., SE Spain. Z7.

N. elegans (Haw.) Spach. Lvs 12–25cm×3–3mm, erect, glaucous, striate on outer surface, apex hooded. Scape 20cm; fls 2–7, horizontal, 2.5–3.5cm diam., fragrant; perianth tube 1.6×0.2cm, green; seg. 1.5×0.3–0.7cm, white, patent, becoming twisted; corona 1×2mm, green, becoming dull orange. Autumn. W & S It., Sicily, Corsica, Sardinia, N Afr. Z8.

N. fernandesii Pedro. Lvs 33cm×3mm, green, erect to prostrate, finely striate, channelled at base. Scape 17cm; fls 1–5, ascending, 2.8cm diam., yellow; tube 2×0.3cm, sometimes slightly curved, green except for distal end; seg. 1.2×0.7cm, apiculate, patent but reflexed at base; corona 6×8mm, slightly deeper yellow than seg. C Port., SW Spain. Z8.

N. gaditanus Boiss. & Reut. Lvs 20cm×2mm, ascending or prostrate, dark green, tip rounded, channelled below, outer surface striate. Scape 9–14cm; fls 1–3, ascending, 1.4–1.6cm, diam.; perianth tube 1.5×0.3cm, green or yellow, straight or slightly curved; seg. 5×4mm, apiculate, yellow, reflexed; corona 3–5× 6–7mm, yellow, cup-shaped, entire. S Port., S Spain. Z8.

N. ×gracilis Sab. = *N. ×tenuior*.

N. hedraeanthus (Webb & Heldr.) Colmeiro. Lvs to 6×0.1–0.15cm, erect to spreading, dark green. Scape shorter than lvs, curved or ascending; fl. solitary, horizontal or ascending, pale yellow, base green; seg. 1.2×0.2cm, patent or spreading; corona 0.7×1cm, margin crenate; anth. and style exserted. S Spain. Z8.

N. hispanicus Gouan = *N. pseudonarcissus* ssp. *major*.

N. humilis (Cav.) Traub. Lvs to 20×0.1cm, solitary or occas. 2, erect, channelled at base. Scape 7–20cm; fl. solitary 2.5cm diam., ascending, yellow; perianth tube 0; seg. 1–1.8×0.2–0.3cm; corona 0. Autumn. S Spain, Alg., Moroc. Z8.

N. ×incomparabilis Mill. (*N. poeticus* ×*N. pseudonarcissus*.) Lvs to 35×1.2cm, glaucous, linear, flat. Scape to 45cm; fl. solitary, to 8cm diam.; perianth tube to 2.5cm, narrowly obconic, widening to throat; seg. narrow-obovate, 2.5–3×1.2–1.6cm, patent, pale yellow; corona to 2.2×2cm, deep orange-yellow, margin undulate, lobulate. Wild in S & SC Fr., also of gdn origin and widely nat. Z4.

N. ×intermedius Lois. (*N. jonquilla* ×*N. tazetta*.) Lvs 4, sub-cylindric, to 45×0.8cm, deeply channelled, brigh green. Scape to 40cm; fls 3–6, to 3.5cm diam., fragrant; perianth tube to 2cm, tinged green; seg. ovate, to 1.4cm, imbricate, bright lemon-yellow; corona 4mm high, orange yellow. W Medit. Z8.

N. italicus Ker-Gawl. = *N. tazetta* ssp. *italicus*.

N. italicus ssp. *lacticolor* (Haw.) Bak. = *Narcissus tazetta* ssp. *italicus*.

N. jonquilla L. JONQUIL. Lvs 2–4, erect to spreading, to 40–45×0.8cm, channelled at base, cylindric above, striate, green. Scape to 40cm; fls 1–6, to 3cm diam., ascending; perianth tube to 3cm, slightly curved, pale green, seg. elliptic to 1.3cm, apiculate, patent, yellow; corona cup-shaped, 7–10×2–4mm, yellow, margin shallowly lobed or somewhat crenate. S & C Spain, S & E Port., nat. elsewhere. var. *henriquesii* Fernandes. Lvs to 25×0.3cm. Scape to 21cm fls 1–2, to 3.8cm diam.; horizontal; perianth tube to 1.8cm, straight; seg. to 1.7cm, margins curving inwards; corona cup-shaped, to 0.6×1cm, 6-

lobed. C Port. Z4.

N. jonquilloides Willk., non Willk. ex Schult. f. = *N. willkommii*.

N. juncifolius auct. = *N. assoanus*.

N. juncifolius ssp. *rupicola* Dufour = *N. rupicola*.

N. ×leedsii hort. = *N. ×incomparabilis*.

N. lobularis hort. = *N. minor*.

N. longispathus Pugsley. Lvs 20–40(–60)×1cm, erect, striate, glaucous. Scape 10–45(–175)cm spathe to 10cm, green; fls 1–3, 4–9cm diam., ascending; perianth tube 1.5cm, green; seg. 2–3cm, patent, sometimes twisted, yellow; corona subcylindric, margin expanded, crenate, yellow. SE Spain. Z8.

N. major Curtis = *N. pseudonarcissus* ssp. *major*.

N. maximus hort. = *N. pseudonarcissus* ssp. *major*.

N. ×medioluteus Mill. (*N. poeticus* ×*N. tazetta*.) PRIMROSE PEERLESS. Lvs to 70×1cm, glaucous, flat. Scape to 60cm; fls 2, occas. 1 or 3, 3–5cm diam., fragrant; perianth tube to 2.5cm, cylindric, broader at throat; seg. broad-obovate to 2.2cm, white; corona to 5×12mm, bright yellow, margin crenate, white-scarious. S Fr. Z7.

N. minimus hort. = *N. asturiensis*.

N. minor L. Lvs 3–4, erect, 8–15×0.4–1cm, sage-green or glaucous, flat or channelled. Scape 14–20cm, terete; fl. solitary, to 3.7cm diam., horizontal or ascending; perianth tube 1–1.8cm, yellow or green-yellow; seg. ovate-lanceolate, 1.5–2.2cm, somewhat twisted, drooping, yellow; corona 1.7×2.5cm, plicate, dilated at mouth, frilled. Pyren., N Spain. Z4.

N. minutiflorus Willk. = *N. gaditanus*.

N. moschatus L. = *N. pseudonarcissus* ssp. *moschatus*.

N. nanus Spach = *N. minor*.

N. ×nelsonii hort. ex Bak. = *N. ×incomparabilis*.

N. nevadensis Pugsley = *N. pseudonarcissus* ssp. *nevadensis*.

N. nobilis Haw. = *N. pseudonarcissus* ssp. *nobilis*.

N. obesus Salisb. = *N. bulbocodium* ssp. *obesus*.

N. obvallaris Salisb. = *N. pseudonarcissus* ssp. *obvallaris*.

N. ×odorus L. CAMPERNELLE JONQUIL. (*N. jonquilla* ×*N. pseudo-narcissus*.) Lvs to 50×0.8cm, strongly keeled, bright green. Scape to 40cm; fls 1–4, ascending, bright yellow, v. fragrant, perianth tube to 2cm; seg. to 2.5×1.3cm; corona to 1.8×2cm, regularly lobed to subentire. Gdn origin; nat. S Eur. 'Rugulosus': larger. 'Plenus': fls double. Z6.

N. ornatus Haw. = *N. poeticus*.

N. pachybolbus Durieu. Lvs 7, to 50×3.8cm, flat or slightly twisted, finely striate, pale green. Scapes to 7 per bulb, 30(–50)cm; fls 3–17, to 1.8cm diam., white; perianth tube 1.4cm; seg. ovate-oblong, 7mm, obtuse, imbricate; corona 2–3mm deep, entire. Moroc., Alg. Z9.

N. pallens Freyn ex Willk. = *N. assoanus*.

N. pallidiflorus Pugsley = *N. pseudonarcissus* ssp. *pallidiflorus*.

N. panizzianus Parl. = *N. papyraceus* ssp. *panizzianus*.

N. papyraceus Ker-Gawl. PAPER-WHITE NARCISSUS. Lvs to 30×1.7cm, erect, keeled, glaucous. Scape to 40cm+; fls 2–20, 2.5–4cm, diam., ascending, fragrant; perianth tube 15×3mm, green below, white above, seg. white, to 1.8cm, ovate, apiculate, imbricate; corona cup-shaped, 3–6×8–11mm, entire or slightly notched, white. Winter-spring. ssp. *polyanthus* (Lois.) Asch. & Gräbn. Lvs green, to 25×1.5–2cm. Fls 3–12(–20), 2.5–4cm diam., horizontal; corona entire, pale sulphur-yellow becoming white. W Medit. ssp. *panizzianus* (Parl.) Arcang. Scape to 28cm; fls 2–8, 2–2.5cm diam. SE Fr., SW Spain, Port. Z8.

N. ×poetaz hort. ex L.H. Bail. = *N. ×medioluteus*.

N. poeticus L. POET'S NARCISSUS; PHEASANT'S-EYE NARCISSUS. Lvs 4, to 45×0.6–1cm, erect, channelled, green or somewhat glaucous. Scape 35–50; fl. solitary, 4.5–7cm diam., horizontal to ascending, fragrant; perianth tube cylindric, 2.5×0.4cm, green; seg. suborbicular to cuneate, to 3×2.2cm, ± patent, white, yellow at base externally; corona flat and discoid, to 2.5×14mm, yellow with red frilled margin; upper 3 anth. exserted. Late spring. Fr. to Greece. var. *recurvus* (Haw.) Fernandes PHEASANT'S EYE NARCISSUS. Perianth seg. strongly reflexed, pure white; corona with throat green, margin red. Late spring. var. *hellenicus* (Pugsley) Fernandes. Scape to 50cm; fl. 4.5cm diam., somewhat ascending; seg. rounded, becoming reflexed; corona 3mm high, yellow, throat green, margin scarlet. Greece. ssp. *radiflorus* (Salisb.) Bak. Perianth seg. to 3cm, narrow, green-white, unguiculate; corona to 2.5×10mm, shortly cylindric, sometimes wholly red (var. *poetarum* Burb. & Bak.); anth. all exserted. S & C Eur., W Balk. Z4.

N. poeticus ssp. *angustifolius* (Haw.) Hegi = *N. poeticus* ssp. *ra-diiflorus*.

N. polyanthus Lois. = *N. papyraceus* ssp. *polyanthus*.

N. portensis Pugsley = *N. pseudonarcissus* ssp. *portensis*.

N. provincialis Pugsley = *N. minor*.

N. pseudonarcissus L. WILD DAFFODIL; LENT LILY; TRUMPET NARCISSUS. Lvs 8–50×0.5–1.5cm, erect, ligulate, usually glaucous. Scape 12–50(–90)cm; fl. usually solitary, occas. 2–4, horizontal to drooping, sometimes ascending, fragrant; perianth tube 1.5–2.5cm; seg. 1.8–4cm, patent to erect-patent, sometimes twisted, white to deep yellow; corona 1.5–4.5cm, white to deep yellow; margin subentire to 6-lobed. W Eur. to N Engl. ssp. *pseudonarcissus*. Lvs 12–35×0.6–1.2cm, erect, glaucous. Scape 20–35cm; fl. solitary, horizontal or drooping, to 6.5cm diam.; perianth tube 1.5–2.2cm, white, usually tinged green; seg. 2–3.5cm, twisted, deflexed, white to sulphur yellow, usually darker than seg. W Eur. except Port. & S Spain. ssp. *major* (Curtis) Bak. Lvs 20–50×0.5–1.5cm, erect, twisted, glaucous blue. Scape to 50cm; fl. solitary to 9.5cm diam., deep yellow; perianth tube 1.8cm, green-yellow; seg. 1.8–4cm, twisted, inner deflexed, outer reflexed; corona 2–4cm, margin expanded. Spain, Port., S Fr., nat. elsewhere. ssp. *moschatus* (L.) Bak. Lvs 10–40×0.5–1.2cm, erect, glaucous. Scape 15–35cm; fl. solitary, 5–6cm diam., horizontal or drooping, usually uniform sulphur-white; perianth tube 8–15mm, green; seg. 2–3.5cm twisted; corona 3–4cm, slightly flanged. Pyren. ssp. *nevadensis* (Pugsley) Fernandes. Lvs 12–30×0.5–1cm, erect, glaucous. Scape to 30cm; fls 1–4, 5cm diam., ascending; perianth tube 1.5cm, green-yellow; seg. white with a yellow central streak; corona 1.5–2.5cm, subcylindric, margin slightly expanded, yellow. S Spain (Sierra Nevada). ssp. *nobilis* (Haw.) Fernandes. Lvs 15–50×0.8–1.5cm, glaucous. Scape 15–30cm; fl. solitary, horizontal or ascending, 8–12cm diam.; perianth tube to 2.5cm, bright yellow; seg. 3–4cm, ± patent, twisted, white with yellow mark at base on reverse; corona 3–4cm, margin expanded, deeply dentate. N Port., NW & NC Spain. ssp. *obvallaris* (Salisb.) Fernandes. TENBY DAFFODIL. Lvs 30×0.6cm, erect, glaucous. Scape 20cm; fl. solitary, 4cm diam., horizontal; perianth tube 1cm, yellow with green stripes; seg. to 3cm, nearly patent, slightly twisted, yellow; corona to 3.5cm, margin dilated, 6-lobed, sometimes reflexed. S Wales but true origin unknown; similar plants recorded from C Spain. ssp. *pallidiflorus* (Pugsley) Fernandes. Lvs 15–40×0.5–1.2cm, erect, slightly glaucous. Scape 30cm; fl. solitary, horizontal or drooping, 7.5cm diam.; perianth tube 2.5cm, green, with yellow streaks; seg. 3–4cm, twisted, pale yellow with darker median streaks; corona 3–4cm, margin expanded, recurved, pale yellow, slightly deeper than seg. Pyren., Cordillera Cantabrica. ssp. *portensis* (Pugsley) Fernandes. Lvs 8–12×0.5–0.7cm, suberect, nearly flat, glaucous. Scape 12–20cm; fl. solitary, drooping, horizontal or ascending, deep yellow; perianth tube to 2.2cm, green; seg. 2–3cm, narrow, deflexed, median veins green; corona obconic, 2.5–3.5cm, margin 6-lobed or crenulate, but not expanded. N Port., NW & C Spain. Z4.

N. pumilus Salisb. = *N. minor*.

N. radiiflorus Salisb. = *N. poeticus* ssp. *radiiflorus*.

N. requienii Roem. = *N. assoanus*.

N. romieuxii Braun-Blanquet & Maire. ssp. *romieuxii*. Lvs to 20×0.1cm, erect or spreading, dark green, weakly striate. Scape 10–20cm; fl. solitary, 2.5–4cm diam., horizontal or ascending, pale to medium yellow; perianth tube to 2.5cm, green at base, yellow above; seg. 1.3×0.4cm, nearly patent; corona 1.5×3cm, margin 6-lobed and crenate, anth. exserted. N Afr. var. *mesatlanticus* Maire. Fls pale yellow. 'Julia Jane': Selected form with wide corona, resembling *N. cantabricus* ssp. *cantabricus* var. *petunioides*, but fl. pale yellow. ssp. *albidus* (Emberger & Maire) Fernandes. Lvs to 22cm, subterete with shallow channel, erect, green. Scape to 9cm; fl. solitary, to 3cm diam., ascending; perianth tube 1.7cm, green at base, white above; seg. 9×3mm, patent, white; corona 0.9×2cm, margin crenate, white. Alg. Z7.

N. rupicola Dufour. ssp. *rupicola*. Lvs 18×0.3cm, erect, 2-keeled, glaucous. Scape 14–23cm; fl. solitary, to 3cm diam., ascending; perianth tube 2.2cm, green or green-yellow; seg. to 1.5×1.1cm, patent, imbricate, apiculate, yellow; corona 3–5×6–18mm, conic or reflexed, deeply 6-lobed to crenate or subentire, yellow. Spain, Port. ssp. *watieri* (Maire) Maire & Weiller. Fls white. Moroc. Z8.

N. scaberulus Henriq. Lvs 7–30×0.2cm, erect or prostrate and sinuous, often scabrid, glaucous. Scape 5–25cm; fls 1–5, 1.8cm diam., ascending; perianth tube to 1.4cm, green; seg. to 7×5mm, apiculate, patent or slightly reflexed, slightly imbricate, deep orange-yellow; corona cup-shaped, 5×7mm, margin often incurved, crenulate or entire, deep yellow. NC Port. Z8.

N. serotinus L. Lvs 1–2, 10–20×0.1–0.5cm, erect or spreading, dark green, sometimes with longitudinal white stripes. Scape 13–30cm; fls solitary or 2–3, to 3.4cm diam., ascending, fragrant; perianth tube to 2cm, dark green; seg. oblong-lanceolate, to 1.6×0.7cm, patent or sometimes recurved, twisted, white; corona to 1.5×4mm, 6-lobed, dark yellow to orange. Autumn. Medit. Z8.

N. tazetta L. BUNCH-FLOWERED NARCISSI; POLYANTHUS NARCISSI. Extremely variable. ssp. *tazetta*. Lvs 20–50×0.5–2.5cm, erect,

twisted, keeled, glaucous. Scape 20–45cm; fls 1–15, 4cm diam., horizontal, fragrant; perianth tube cylindric, 2cm, pale green; seg. broad-ovate, 0.8–2.2cm, patent, incurving, white; corona cup-shaped, 0.5×1cm, bright to deep yellow. S Port., Medit., E to Iran, probably introd. further E, nat. in Kashmir, China and Jap. ssp. *aureus* (Lois.) Bak. Perianth seg. deep yellow to golden yellow; corona deep yellow to orange. SE Fr., It., Sardinia, Alg., nat. elsewhere. ssp. *corcyrensis* (Herb.) Bak. Perianth seg. narrow, sometimes reflexed, pale yellow; corona yellow. Corfu. ssp. *italicus* (Ker-Gawl.) Bak. Perianth seg. cream or v. pale yellow; corona deeper yellow. NE Medit., N Afr. 'Canaliculatus': to 20cm; lvs narrow, erect, glaucous, striate; fls small; seg. white, corona ochre yellow, origin unknown. Z8.

N. tazetta ssp. *papyraceus* (Ker-Gawl.) Bak. = *N. papyraceus*.

N. tenuifolius Salisb. = *N. bulbocodium* var. *bulbocodium*.

N. × tenuior Curtis. (*N. jonquilla* × *N. poeticus*.) To 30cm. Lvs linear, flat. Fls 2–3, to 5cm diam.; corona flat, to 5mm, deeper yellow than perianth seg. Probably gdn origin. Z4.

N. tortuosa Haw. = *N. pseudonarcissus* ssp. *moschatus*.

N. triandrus L. ANGEL'S TEARS. Lvs 15–30×1.5–5mm, keeled or striate, flat or channelled, erect or decumbent, sometimes curled at tip, green, or slightly glaucous. Scape 20–30cm; fls 1–6, pendulous, white to bright yellow, usually concolorous; perianth tube 1.5cm, green below, yellow above; seg. sharply reflexed, lanceolate to linear-oblong, 1–3cm, often with deeper median streak; corona cup-shaped, 0.5–1.5(–2.5)×0.7–2.5cm, entire, somewhat undulate; 3 anth. exserted. Spain & Port., NW Fr. Many variants described, based on fl. colour, number of fls and size of floral parts. var. *albus* (Haw.) Bak. is typical of wild populations. var. *concolor* (Haw.) Bak. fls deep yellow and lvs 2mm wide; the name is loosely applied in horticulture to any yellow-fld plant. Z4.

N. viridiflorus Schousb. Lvs 30–60×0.4cm, cylindric, hollow, striate, glaucous dark green. Scape 9–25(–40)cm; fls 1–5, ascending, 2.5cm diam., dull green, malodorous; perianth tube 1.5cm; seg. linear-oblong, 1–1.6×0.2cm, patent or reflexed; corona 1×4mm, 6-lobed. SW Spain, Moroc. Z8.

N. watieri Maire = *N. rupicola* ssp. *watieri*.

N. willkommii (Samp.) Fernandes. Lvs to 37×0.3cm, erect, flattened at base, rounded above, glaucous dark green. Scape to 18cm; fls usually solitary, 3cm diam., horizontal; perianth tube to 1.6cm, straight, green-yellow; seg. broad-elliptic, 0.6–1.3×0.7cm, apiculate, patent, or reflexed and curving inwards, yellow; corona cup-shaped, 0.6×1cm, deeply 6-lobed,yellow. S Port., SW Spain. Z8.

N. cvs. For a full classification of Daffodils together with examples see *Narcissus* in *New RHS Dictionary*, vol. III. The RHS system of classification is summarized as follows.

Under the current (1989) system daffodils fall into 12 divisions.

Division 1. *Trumpet daffodils of gdn origin*. One fl. to a st.; corona ('trumpet') as long as, or longer than the perianth seg.

Division 2. *Large-cupped daffodils of gdn origin*. One fl. to a st.; corona ('cup') more than one-third, but less than equal to the length of the perianth seg. ('petals').

Division 3. *Small-cupped daffodils of gdn origin*. One fl. to a st.; corona ('cup') not more than one-third the length of the perianth seg. ('petals').

Division 4. *Double daffodils of gdn origin*. One or more fls to a st., with doubling of the perianth seg. or the corona or both.

Division 5. *Triandus daffodils of gdn origin*. Characteristics of *N. triandrus* clearly evident: usually two or more pendent fls to a st.; perianth seg. reflexed.

Division 6. *Cyclamineus daffodils of gdn origin*. Characteristics of *N. cyclamineus* clearly evident: usually one fl. to a st.; perianth seg. reflexed; fl. at an acute angle to the st., with a v. short pedicel ('neck').

Division 7. *Jonquilla daffodils of gdn origin*. Characteristics of the *N. jonquilla* group clearly evident: usually 1–3 fls to a rounded st.; lvs narrow, dark green; perianth seg. spreading not reflexed, fls fragrant.

Division 8. *Tazetta daffodils of gdn origin*. Characteristics of the *N. tazetta* group clearly evident: usually 3–20 fls to a stout st.; lvs broad; perianth seg. spreading not reflexed; fls fragrant.

Division 9. *Poeticus daffodils of gdn origin*. Characteristics of the *N. poeticus* group without admixture of any other; usually one fl. to a st.; perianth seg. pure white; corona usually disc-shaped, with a green or yellow centre and a red rim; fls fragrant.

Division 10. *Species, wild variants and wild hybrids*. All spp. and wild or reputedly wild variants and hybrids, including those with double fls. Spp. and natural varieties.

Division 11. *Split-corona daffodils of gdn origin*. Corona split rather than lobed and usually for more than half its length.

Division 12. *Miscellaneous daffodils*. All daffodils not falling into any one of the above divisions.

→*Braxireon, Carregnoa* and *Tapeinanthus*.

Nardoo *Marsilea*.

Nardostachys DC. Valerianaceae. 2 perenn. herbs. Root thick, fibrous aromatic. Lvs entire, mostly basal. Fls in term., capitate cymes; cal. 5-lobed, enlarging in fr.; cor. 5-lobed, sta. 4. India, Himal., China.
N. grandiflora DC. SPIKENARD. St. to 25cm. Lvs to 10cm, elliptic-lanceolate or spathulate, acute. Fls pale rose-purple, in v. dense cymose pan. Himal.

Narihira Bamboo *Semiarundinaria fastuosa*.
Narihiradake *Semiarundinaria fastuosa*.
Narras *Acanthosicyos horridus*.
Narrow Beech Fern *Phegopteris connectilis*.
Narrow Buckler Fern *Dryopteris carthusiana*.
Narrow Cottonwood *Populus angustifolia*.
Narrow-leaf Drumsticks *Isopogon anethifolius*.
Narrow-leaf Fig *Ficus binnendykii*.
Narrow-leaf Trefoil *Lotus tenuis*.
Narrow-leaved Apple *Angophora bakeri*.
Narrow-leaved Ash *Fraxinus angustifolia*.
Narrow-leaved Bottlebrush *Callistemon linearis*.
Narrow-leaved Bottletree *Brachychiton rupestris*.
Narrow-leaved Bower Wattle *Acacia cognata*.
Narrow-leaved Coffee *Coffea stenophylla*.
Narrow-leaved Everlasting Pea *Lathyrus sylvestris*.
Narrow-leaved Ironbark *Eucalyptus crebra*.
Narrow-leaved Peppermint *Eucalyptus nicholii*; *E. radiata*.
Narrow-leaved Pittosporum *Pittosporum phillyreoides*.
Narrow-leaved Plantain *Plantago lanceolata*.
Narrow-leaved Reedmace *Typha angustifolia*.
Narrow-leaved Spleenwort *Athyrium pycnocarpon*.
Narrow-leaved Strap Fern *Campyloneurum augustifolium*.
Narrow-leaved Vervain *Verbena simplex*.
Narrow-leaved Wattle *Acacia longissima*.

Narthecium Moehr. BOG ASPHODEL. Liliaceae (Melanthiaceae). 8 herbaceous, rhizomatous plants of marshy places. Lvs equitant, basal and clothing st., linear, striate, rush-like. Rac. scapose; bracts as long as pedicels; perianth seg. 6, equal, yellow; sta. 6, fil. woolly. summer. N temp. regions.
N. americanum Ker-Gawl. YELLOW ASPHODEL. To 45cm. Lvs to 20×6cm. Perianth seg. 0.4cm, linear; anth. yellow. E US. Z6.
N. asiaticum Maxim. To 60cm. Lvs to 25×1cm, linear. Perianth seg. 0.5cm, linear; anth. pale yellow. Jap. Z7.
N. californicum Bak. To 50cm. Lvs to 30×0.6cm. Perianth seg. 0.5cm, linear-lanceolate; anth. red. W US. Z7.
N. ossifragum (L.) Huds. BOG ASPHODEL. To 40cm; st. deep orange after flowering. Lvs to 30×5cm. Perianth seg. 0.6–0.8cm, linear-lanceolate, deep orange after flowering; anth. orange. W Eur. (Scand. to N Spain and Port.). Z6.

Narwan *Ulmus androssowii*.

Nassauvia Comm. ex Juss. Compositae. 40 perenn. herbs, often woody at base, or dwarf shrubs. Lvs small, usually rigid and spinulose. Cap. discoid, usually sessile, solitary or grouped in dense, globose to ovoid infl. S S Amer. Z8.
N. lagascae (D. Don) F. Meigen. Perenn. herb to 8cm, procumbent to ascending, sparingly branched. Lvs to 13×4mm, densely imbricate, oblong, recurved, apex 5–9-dentate, lanate beneath. Cap. numerous, scented in a dense, globose spike to 4cm; flts white or mauve. Summer. W Arg., E Chile.
N. revoluta D. Don. Dwarf shrub to 20cm, ascending, branched, densely leafy. Lvs to 10×6mm, imbricate, ovate to ovate-lanceolate, recurved above, mucronate-dentate. Cap. in dense glomerules to 2.5cm diam.; flts white. Patagonia.

Nasturtium *Tropaeolum* (*T. majus*).

Nasturtium R. Br. WATERCRESS. Cruciferae. 6 perenn., rhizomatous, often semi-aquatic herbs. Lvs pinnate. Fls small, 4-merous, racemose. Fr. a silique. Eur. to C Asia, N Afr. and N Amer. Z6.
N. amphibium (L.) R. Br. = *Rorippa amphibia*.
N. armoracia (L.) Fries = *Armoracia rusticana*.
N. fontanum (Lam.) Asch. = *N. officinale*.
N. microphyllum (Boenn.) Rchb. Similar to *N. officinale* except fls larger; pedicel to 15mm. Fr. 16–24mm, seeds in one row. W Eur.
N. officinale R. Br. COMMON WATERCRESS. St. creeping, often floating. Lvs deep glossy green; lat. lfts in 3–5 pairs, wavy to entire, term. leaflet much larger. Pet. 4–6mm, white; pedicel 6–12mm. Fr. 11–18mm; seeds in 2 rows per locule. Spring–early summer. Eur. to SW Asia, introd. N Amer. and elsewhere.
→*Cardamine, Rorippa* and *Sisymbrium*.

Natal Bottlebrush *Greyia*.
Natal Bride's Bush *Pavetta natalensis*.
Natal Creeper *Carissa macrocarpa*.
Natal Cycad *Encephalartos natalensis*.
Natal Fig *Ficus natalensis*.
Natal Gardenia *Gardenia cornuta*.
Natal Grass *Rhynchelytrum repens*.
Natal Ivy *Senecio macroglossus*.
Natal Laburnum *Calpurnia aurea*.
Natal Orange *Strychnos spinosa*.
Natal Plum *Carissa macrocarpa*.
Native Australian Frangipani *Hymenosporum flavum*.
Native Cranberry *Astroloma humifusum*.
Native Currant *Coprosma billardieri*.
Native Fig *Ficus obliqua*.
Native Holly *Platylobium obtusangulum*.
Native Hops *Dodonaea viscosa*.
Native Orange *Capparis mitchellii*; *Microcitrus australis*.
Native Pomegranate *Capparis arborea*.
Native Red Hibiscus *Hibiscus kokio*.
Native Willow *Acacia salicina*.

Nauclea L. Rubiaceae. Some 10 shrubs or trees. Lvs petiolate, opposite, stipulate. Fls term. or lat. and solitary, or in globose heads; bracts present; cal. glab. or pubesc., lobes 4–5; cor. funnelform, lobes 4–5, sta. 4–5. Fr. a berry. Trop. Afr., Asia to Polyn. Z10.
N. cordata Roxb. = *N. orientalis*.
N. diderrichii (De Wildeman) Merrill. Tree, to 40m. Lvs to 40×20cm, elliptic, apex obtuse or narrowly acute, base obtuse or cuneate. Fls in term. heads to 3cm wide, cor. funnel-shaped, white or yellow or green, tube to 8mm, lobes to 3×1mm. Fr. to 4cm, ribbed, white or grey to pale brown. Trop. Afr.
N. esculenta (Sab.) Merrill = *Sarcocephalus latifolius*.
N. latifolia Sm. = *Sarcocephalus latifolius*.
N. officinalis (Pierre ex Pitard) Merrill ex Chun. Tree, to 30m. Lvs to 25×14cm, obovate to elliptic, apex acute, base acute or obtuse, leathery to papery. Fls in term. heads; cor. tube to 4mm, glab., lobes to 1mm. Trop. Asia.
N. orientalis (L.) L. Tree, to 12m. Lvs to 25×15cm, ovate, acute, base obtuse, undulate. Fls yellow in dense, globular heads; cor. tube to 8mm. Trop. Asia to Aus., Polyn.
N. parvifolia Roxb. = *Mitragyna parvifolia*.
N. undulata Roxb. = *N. orientalis*.
→*Cephalanthus* and *Sarcocephalus*.

Naupaka *Scaevola taccada*.

Nauplius (Cass.) Cass. Compositae. 8 subshrubs or annuals, erect to ascending, branched, gland. Lvs alt., sessile, often succulent. Cap. radiate, solitary, term.; involucre to campanulate; outer phyllaries often toothed, foliaceous, with a ± yellow base; ray flts oblong, yellow to white, sometimes tinged purple beneath; disc flts yellow. Medit. and Macronesia. Z9.
N. aquaticus (L.) Cass. Ann. to 50cm, fragrant. St. often purple-tinged. Lvs to 8×2cm, oblong to ovate-oblong, base auriculate, folded along pale midrib, pubesc., densely gland. Cap. to 2cm diam.; receptacle flat; ray flts to 30, yellow, to 7mm. Spring–summer. W Medit., Canary Is.
N. sericeus (L. f.) Cass. Subshrub to 1m, fragrant. St. gland., grey-tinged. Lvs to 6×2cm, spathulate, silver grey-pilose. Cap. to 5cm diam.; receptacle convex; ray flts 30+, yellow, to 20mm. Canary Is.
→*Asteriscus, Buphthalmum* and *Odontospermum*.

Nautilocalyx Lind. ex Hanst., emend. Wiehler. Gesneriaceae. 38 perenn. herbs and subshrubs. St. erect, or creeping, succulent. Lvs thinly ± fleshy, usually opposite in pairs. Fls bracteate, axill., solitary or in cymes; sep. unequal, rarely connate; cor. tubular with basal spur, limb 5-lobed. Trop. Amer. Z10.
N. adenosiphon (Leeuwenb.) Wiehler. St. to 20cm, creeping or ascending, tomentose at apex. Lvs ovate, crenate-serrate, adpressed-pubesc. above, minutely pilose beneath. Fls solitary; cor. to 3.5×0.5cm, white, pilose. Venez.
N. bicolor (Hook.) Wiehler. St. short, hairy, creeping and procumbent. Lvs ovate to cordate, serrate, pubesc. Fls in clusters; cor. tube white, spotted purple inside, limb white with a broad purple border. Colomb.
N. bracteatus (Planch.) Sprague. St. simple, pubesc. Lvs ovate, irregularly serrate. Fls solitary; bracts flushed purple; cor. to 3.5cm, white. Colomb.
N. bullatus (Lem.) Sprague. St. to 670cm, erect. Lvs elliptic, bullate, purple beneath. Fls in axill. cymes; cor. to 3.2cm, densely pilose, pale yellow. Peru.

N. forgetii (Sprague) Sprague. As for *N. lynchii* except lvs marked with red on veins, markedly undulate; sep. often tinged red. Peru.

N. glandulifer Wiehler. St. to 20cm, erect or ascending, with long maroon hairs. Lvs oblanceolate, crenate-undulate, flushed maroon above, wine-red beneath. Fls in axill. cymes; cor. to 4.2cm, cream-white, sericeous, upper lobes speckled maroon, striped maroon inside. Ecuad.

N. hirsutus (Sprague) Sprague. St. to 50cm, erect, villous. Lvs oblanceolate, somewhat bullate, villous on veins beneath. Fls in axill. cymes; cor. to 3cm, pale yellow, glandular-pilose. Peru.

N. lucianii (Fourn.) Wiehler. St. stout at base. Lvs ovate, succulent, dark green with pale veins above, flushed red beneath. Fls in axill. clusters; cor. rose-red, outside red-pilose. Colomb.

N. lynchii Hook. f. Bushy, to 60cm, erect. Lvs elliptic-lanceolate, dentate, flushed dark purple or red-brown, glossy above, puberulent beneath. Fls in axill. cymes; sep. flushed with maroon; cor. to 3cm, pale yellow, outside red-pilose, inside marked with purple flecks. Colomb.

N. melittifolius (L.) Wiehler. St. trailing, rooting at nodes. Lvs ovate, crenate, sparsely adpressed-hairy above, puberulent beneath. Fls in a loose axill. cyme; cor. to 2cm, pilose, cherry-red. Lesser Antilles.

N. pallidus (Sprague) Sprague St. to 50cm, usually erect, pilose. Lvs ovate-lanceolate, glab. except for pubesc. veins, crenate-serrate, sparsely ciliate. Fls in axill. cymes; cor. to 5cm, cream-white, glandular-pilose, inside spotted and lined purple. Peru.

N. panamensis (Seem.) Seem. St. to 20cm, tetragonal, villous. Lvs ovate-acuminate, sparsely pilose above, almost glab. beneath, crenate-serrate. Fls in axillary fascicles; cor. to 3cm, cylindric, pale yellow. Mex., Panama, Colomb.

N. picturatus (L.) Skog. St. to 20cm, erect, densely branched from base. Lvs elliptic, denticulate, rugose, marked maroon and pubesc. beneath. Fls in axillary clusters; cor. to 3cm, white, purple-striped, hairy outside. Peru.

N. pictus (Hook.) Sprague. St. to 30cm, purple or green, creeping or ascending, glabrescent. Lvs often bullate, oblong-elliptic or oblong-lanceolate, crenate-serrate. Fls solitary or in axill. cymes; cor. to 4.5cm, outside pilose, cream or pale yellow. N Braz., Guyana.

N. speciosus Wiehler. St. erect, to 25cm, rose-pink, sericeous. Lvs oblanceolate, serrate, sometimes marked with pink and sericeous beneath. Fls in axill. cymes; floral bracts pink; cor. to 5cm, spurred, white, sericeous, lobes marked purple on veins. Panama.

N. villosus (HBK) Sprague. St. erect or ascending, purple or green, glabrescent. Lvs elliptic or oblong-elliptic, coarsely serrate or crenate-serrate. Fls 1–several; cor. to 5.5cm, white, outside pilose, inside marked purple. Venez., Guyana.
→*Alloplectus* and *Episcia*.

Navarretia Ruiz & Pav. Polemoniaceae. 30 ann. herbs. Lvs usually pinnate or bipinnate, spine-tipped or acerose towards apex. Infl. a densely bracteate, spiny head; fls 4- or 5-merous; cal. divided to base, lobes linked by membrane; cor. hypocrateriform to funnelform. W N Amer., Chile and Arg. Z7.

N. mellita E. Greene. Erect, branching, glandular-pubesc., to 20cm tall, with a honey-like scent. Lvs irregularly and pinnately or bipinnately lobed, lobes lanceolate, rigid. Fls clustered or solitary; cor. 6–7mm, tube c1.5mm, pale blue, throat with purple veins. Spring–summer. Calif.

N. squarrosa (Eschsch.) Hook. & Arn. Erect, branching, to 50cm, glandular-pubesc., with a skunk-like smell. Lvs irregularly and pinnately or bipinnately lobed, lobes lanceolate, rigid. Fls clustered or solitary; cor. 1–1.2cm, blue to purple, lobes 2–3mm. Summer. Calif. to BC.
→*Gilia*.

Navarro Ceanothus *Ceanothus gloriosus* var. *exaltatus*.
Navelseed *Omphalodes*.
Navelwort *Hydrocotyle*; *Omphalodes*; *Umbilicus rupestris*.

Navia Mart. ex Schult. f. Bromeliaceae. 74 much-branched to cushion-forming perenn. herbs. Lvs in a rosette, or in a dense spiral along st., blades narrow, entire or toothed. Infl. term., usually stemless, a compound head; pet. fused to form a slender tube. SE Colomb., N Braz., E Venez. and Guyana. Z10.

N. acaulis Mart. ex Schult. f. Short-stemmed, sometimes branched. Lvs to 12cm, glab., densely toothed. Infl. globose, stemless; floral bracts 5mm lanceolate. S. Colomb.

N. arida L.B. Sm. & Steyerm. ± stemless. Lvs to 38cm long, linear, caudate-attenuate, white-scaly below, laxly toothed. Infl. stemless, simple, densely capitate; outer bracts tinged red; floral bracts about 2.5cm, v. narrowly triangular, red; pet. yellow, tips

pink. S Colomb.
→*Dyckia*.

Nealie *Acacia rigens*.

Neanthe P. Browne.
N. bella Cook = *Chamaedorea elegans*.

Nebraska Fern *Conium maculatum*.
Necklace Poplar *Populus deltoides*.
Necklace Tree *Ormosia* (*O. monosperma*).
Necklace Vine *Crassula rupestris*; *Muehlenbeckia complexa*.

Nectaroscordum Lindl. Liliaceae (Alliaceae). 3 onion-scented, bulbous perennials, resembling *Allium* but outer tep. with 3–7 veins; pedicel apices swollen beneath fls. Lvs linear, sheathing base of st. Umbel scapose; perianth seg. free; sta. 6. S Eur., W Asia, Iran. Z7.

N. bulgaricum Janka = *N. siculum* ssp. *bulgaricum*.

N. dioscoridis = *N.siculum* ssp. *bulgaricum*.

N. siculum (Ucria) Lindl. SICILIAN HONEY GARLIC. Lvs 30–40×1–2cm. Scapes to 120cm; fls 10–30, bell-shaped, pendulous; tep. to 15×9mm, nearly white, flushed flesh-pink and dark red, green toward base below. Spring-summer. Fr., It. ssp. *bulgaricum* (Janka) Stearn. Tep. white to yellow, flushed pale pink and green above, edged white, flushed green below. E Rom., Bulg., Turk., Crimea. Z6.
→*Allium*.

Needle Bush *Hakea lissosperma*.
Needle-bush Wattle *Acacia rigens*.
Needle Furze *Genista anglica*.
Needle Grass *Stipa*.
Needle Palm *Rhapidophyllum* (*R. hystrix*); *Yucca filamentosa*.
Needle Spike Rush *Eleocharis acicularis*.
Needlewood *Hakea leucoptera*.
Negro Pepper *Xylopia aethiopica*.

Neillia D. Don. Rosaceae. 10 shrubs. Branching flexuous. Lvs alt., usually 3-lobed, serrate, stipulate. Fls small in rac. or pan.; cal. tube cylindric to campanulate, lobes 5; pet. 5, short-clawed; sta. 10–30. E Himal. to China and W Malaysia.

N. affinis Hemsl. Shrub to 2m; branchlets glab. Lvs to 9cm, ovate to oval-oblong, long-acuminate, cordate at base, small-lobed, slightly pubesc. on veins beneath. Fls pink, in elongate, 10+-fld rac. to 8cm. Spring-summer. W China. var. *pauciflora* (Rehd.) J.E. Vidal. Rac. contracted, to 4cm, 5–10-fld; fls fascicled at the end of the axis. SW China. Z6.

N. amurensis (Maxim.) Bean = *Physocarpus amurensis*.
N. bracteata (Rydb.) Bean = *Physocarpus bracteatus*.
N. capitata (Pursh) Greene = *Physocarpus capitatus*.
N. longiracemosa Hemsl. = *N. thibetica*.
N. malvacea Greene = *Physocarpus malvaceus*.
N. millsii Dunn = *N. uekii*.
N. monogyna (Torr.) Greene = *Physocarpus monogynus*.
N. monogyna var. *alternans* Jones = *Physocarpus alternans*.
N. opulifolia (L.) Brewer & S. Wats. = *Physocarpus opulifolius*.
N. pauciflora Rehd. = *N. affinis* var. *pauciflora*.
N. ribesioides Rehd. = *N. sinensis* var. *ribesioides*.

N. sinensis Oliv. Shrub to 3m; branchlets glab. Lvs to 8cm, oval-oblong, long-acuminate, incised-serrate and lobed, teeth sharp. pubesc. on veins beneath, later glab., light green. Fls white to pink in cernuous, 12–20-fld, rac. to 6cm. Spring–summer. C China. var. *ribesioides* (Rehd.) J.E. Vidal. Cal. tube less than 6.5mm. Summr–autumn. Z6.

N. tanakae Franch. & Savat. = *Stephanandra tanakae*.

N. thibetica Bur. & Franch. Shrub to 2m; branchlets fine-pubesc. Lvs to 8cm, ovate, long-acuminate, subcordate at base, biserrate and lobulate, later glab. above, finely and densely pubesc. beneath. Fls pink to white, in dense, 8–15cm rac. Summer. W China. Z6.

N. thyrisflora D. Don. Shrub to 3m. Lvs to 12cm, ovate, acuminate, rounded or shallow-cordate at base, irregularly serrate, usually shallowly trilobed. Fls white in large, term. pan. Himal. to W China, Burm., S to Indon. Z8.

N. torreyi of Bot. Mag. t. 7758, non S. Wats. = *Physocarpus malvaceus*.

N. torreyi S. Wats. = *Physocarpus monogynus*.

N. uekii Nak. Shrub to 3m. Branchlets briefly stellate-pubesc. Lvs 5-lobed, glab. above, sparsely pubesc. beneath. Fls. pink. Korea. Z9.

Nekbudu *Ficus lutea*.

Neltuma Raf.
N. constricta (Sarg.) Britt. & Rose = *Prosopis constricta*.

N. glandulosa Torr. Britt. & Rose = *Prosopis glandulosa*.
N. neomexicana Britt. = *Prosopis neomexicana*.

Nelumbium Juss.
N. luteum Willd. = *Nelumbo lutea*.
N. speciosum Willd. = *Nelumbo nucifera*.

Nelumbo Adans. LOTUS. Nelumbonaceae. 2 perenn. aquatic herbs. Rhiz. cylindrical, swollen. Lvs long-petiolate, usually emergent, blades peltate, concave-orbicular. Peduncle radical, slender, equalling or exceeding lvs; fls solitary, large and showy; sep. 4–5; pet. numerous, spirally arranged; sta. 200–400; ovaries in distinct whorls, sunken within swollen fleshy receptacle. Fr. of hard-walled nuts, pitted on the dors. surface of a turbinate receptacle. E N Amer., warm Asia to Aus.
N. lutea (Willd.) Pers. WATER CHINQUAPIN; AMERICAN LOTUS; YANQUAPIN. Lvs to 2m above water surface, lamina 50cm across, glaucous. Infl. equalling petioles; fl. 10–25cm across, pale yellow. Summer. E N Amer. 'Flavescens': lvs splashed red in centre; fls small. Z6.
N. nucifera Gaertn. SACRED LOTUS. Lvs to 2m above water surface, lamina to 80cm across, glaucous. Infl. exceeding lvs; fls pink or white, sometimes double in selected cvs, v. fragrant, to 30cm diam. Summer. Asia from Iran to Jap., S to Aus. 'Alba': lvs large, pea-green; fls large, white, fragrant. 'Alba Grandiflora': lvs deep green; fls white. 'Alba Plena': fls large, double, cream tinged green, later pure white, scented. 'Alba Striata': sep. white edged pale pink. 'Charles Thomas': fls deep pink tinged lavender. 'Chawan Basu': habit semi-dwarf; fls white edged pink, abundant. 'Empress': pet. white fringed crimson. 'Lotus Blossom': fls white heavily tipped pink. 'Maggie Belle Slocum': fls large, pink, held above lvs, fragrant. 'Momo Botan': lvs medium-sized. 'Mrs. Perry D. Slocum': fls large, deep pink turning cream-yellow. 'Pekinensis Rubra': fls carmine-pink. 'Pekinensis Rubra Plena': fls double, large, carmine-pink. 'Red Lotus': fls deep red, pet. large. 'Rosea Plena': fls double to 30cm across, rose-pink, fragrant. 'Shiroman': fls double, large, cream acquiring green centre, later pure white. 'Speciosa': fls single, light pink. 'Shirokunshi': to 45cm; fls tulip-shaped. 'Tulip': habit dwarf; fls pure white, tulip-shaped. Z8.
N. pentapetala (Walter) Fern. = *N. lutea*.
N. speciosa auct. = *N. nucifera*.
→*Nelumbium*.

Nelumbonaceae See *Nelumbo*.

Nemastylis Nutt. Iridaceae. 7 bulbous perenn. herbs. Lvs long, linear, plicate. Fls short-lived, in few-fld spathaceous clusters; tep. 6, similar; sta. 3; style with 6 long, divided br. N & Trop. Amer. Z9.
N. acuta (Bartr.) Herb. PRAIRIE IRIS. 15–60cm, sometimes branched. Lvs to 30cm. Fls 4–6cm diam., blue-violet. Spring. S US.
N. floridana Small. To 1.5m, often less, sometimes branched. Lvs to 45cm. Fls to 5cm diam., violet, white in centre. Late autumn. SE US.
N. geminiflora Nutt. = *N. acuta*.
N. tenuis ssp. *pringlei* (Wats.) Goldbl. St. unbranched. Fls scented, pale blue. Mex.

Nematanthus Schräd. Gesneriaceae. Some 30 epiphytic climbing or trailing subshrubs. Infl. cymose, bracteate; pedicel usually filiform; cal. lobes linear to ovate, enclosing cor. tube; cor. cylindric or tubular, often curved and pouched, lobes 5, sta. 4, coherent. S Amer. Z10.
N. chloronema Mart. = *N. crassifolius*.
N. corticola Schräd. To 1.2m. Lvs to 15cm, variable, elliptic-ovate, pale green, entire, veins purple beneath. Fls solitary, stalks to 20cm; cal. to 1.5cm, purple at base; cor. to 5cm, pink except at white base, inner surface tinged yellow. N S Amer.
N. crassifolius (Schott) Wiehler. St. climbing or pendent, to 1.5m. Lvs to 15cm, variable, ovate-elliptic, apex cuspidate, succulent, pale green, rarely purple-tinged, margin entire, ciliate. Fls 1–2 per cyme; stalks to 20cm; cal. to 3.5cm, purple toward apex; cor. to 5cm, bright red, marked with white within. E S Amer.
N. dichrus (Spreng.) Wiehler = *N. hirtellus*.
N. fissus (Vell. Conc.) Skog. St. trailing to ascending, to 0.6m, densely pubesc. toward tips. Lvs to 9cm, obovate, acute to cuspidate, succulent, hairy above, densely pubesc. beneath, somewhat serrate. Fls 2–4 per cyme; cal. to 1.8cm, green, often tinged red; cor. to 3.5cm, saccate, then constricted, bright red, occas. marked yellow, densely pubesc. E S Amer.
N. fluminensis (Vell. Conc.) Fritsch. St. erect or pendent, woody at base, to 1.5m, glab. Lvs 5–17cm, ovate or obovate, cuspidate,

succulent, green above, spotted purple beneath, entire. Fls 1–2 per axil, stalks to 4cm, purple; cal. to 2.5cm, often tinged purple; cor. 4–5cm, yellow, densely pubesc. Spring–autumn. S Amer.
N. fornix (Vell. Conc.) Charteris. St. climbing, shrubby at base, to 70cm. Lvs to 6cm, elliptic, acute, fleshy, sparsely hairy above. Fls solitary; stalk to 2cm; cal. to 2cm, marked with red; cor. to 3cm, bright red. E S Amer.
N. fritschii Hoehne. St. pendent, to 1.5m, densely pubesc. Lvs to 13cm, ovate-elliptic, slightly cuspidate, succulent, bright green above with a large dark patch beneath. Fls solitary; stalk to 10cm; cal. to 3cm, tinged purple; cor. to 4.5cm, pouched, outer surface pink, inner surface white and mauve. E S Amer.
N. gregarius Denh. CLOG PLANT. St. climbing or pendent, to 80cm. Lvs to 3cm, elliptic to ovate, subobtuse, fleshy, glab. Fls 1–3 per cyme short stalked; cal. to 1.5cm, marked orange at apex; cor. to 2.5cm, pouched, bright orange with a purple-brown stripe leading to each lobe. E S Amer. 'Variegatus': lvs spreading, glossy, green with yellow centre; fls orange.
N. hirtellus (Schott) Wiehler. St. woody at base, to 80cm, glab. Lvs to 16cm, ovate, slightly cuspidate, somewhat fleshy, sparsely pubesc. above, with red pubesc. veins beneath, entire. Fls 1–4 per cyme, short-stalked; cal. to 2cm, orange-green tinged purple, cor. to 3.5cm, yellow striped purple throughout, densely pubesc. E S Amer.
N. ionema Mart. = *N. corticola*.
N. lanceolatus (Poir.) Charteris. St. woody at base, to 1.5m. Lvs to 12cm, obovate-elliptic, slightly cuspidate, succulent, red-veined, finely pubesc. Fls 1–6 per cyme; to 1cm, tinged red; cor. to 3cm, red-orange, densely pubesc., lobes yellow. E S Amer.
N. longipes DC. = *N. crassifolius*.
N. nervosus (Fritsch) H.E. Moore = *N. fornix*.
N. perianthomegus (Vell. Conc.) H.E. Moore = *N. hirtellus*.
N. radicans C. Presl = *N. strigilosus*.
N. radicans (Klotzsch & Hanst. ex Hanst.) H.E. Moore non C. Presl = *N. gregarius*.
N. selloanus (Klotzsch & Hanst.) H.E. Moore = *N. fissus*.
N. strigilosus (Mart.) H.E. Moore. St. climbing, woody at base, to 1.5m. Lvs to 3.5cm, obovate, obtuse, sparsely pubesc. above, densely pubesc. on veins beneath, entire. Fls solitary short-stalked; cal. to 1cm, green to red-brown; cor. to 2cm, tube orange, limb yellow. E S Amer.
N. wettsteinii (Fritsch) H.E. Moore. St. usually pendent, to 50cm, becoming glabrescent. Lvs to 2.5cm, elliptic-ovate, subotuse, fleshy, glab. above, marked red beneath, entire. Fls 1–2 in axils, short-stalked; cal. to 0.7cm, sparsely pubesc., lobes linear-lanceolate; cor. to 2.4cm, orange, lobes yellow. E S Amer.
N. cvs. 'Bijou': lvs dull red beneath; fls pendent, pink. 'Black Gold': fls copper-orange, cal. dark orange. 'Black Magic': lvs small, dark, glossy, dark green; fls orange with yellow tip. 'Candy Corn': lvs small, thick, glossy, dark green; fls orange with yellow tip. 'Freckles': lvs dark green; fls yellow, flecked with red. 'Jungle Lights': habit compact and trailing; lvs small, glossy, tinged dark-purple; fls orange and pink. 'Tropicana': habit erect, freely branching; lvs dark green, glossy; cal. bright red, cor. yellow with maroon stripes.
→*Alloplectus, Columnea* and *Hypocyrta*.

Nemesia Vent. Scrophulariaceae. *c*65 ann. or perenn. herbs or subshrubs. Fls axill. or in short term. rac.; cal. 5-lobed; cor. bilabiate, tube v. short, produced into spur or pouch at front, upper lip 4-lobed, lower entire or bilabiate, with palate almost closing throat. S Afr. Z9.
N. azurea Diels. Ann. herb, glandular-pilose 10–20cm. Lvs ovate to linear-oblong, minutely dentate to entire, subglabrous. Infl. racemose; cor. purple to violet without, azure-blue within, palate yellow, lobes of upper lip 5–6mm, lip 6–7mm, emarginate. Summer. S Afr.
N. barbata (Thunb.) Benth. Ann. herb to 50cm, glab. or nearly so. Lvs 1–3cm, ovate to lanceolate, dentate to subentire. Infl. racemose; cor. 1.5cm, blue, upper lip pale blue within with white margin and purple lines, white without, with short obtuse lobes, lower lip longer than upper, entire or nearly so, deep blue, lower part white striped purple. S Afr.
N. chamaedrifolia Vent. Perenn. herb, to 50cm. Lvs ovate, dentate, acute, glab. or pubesc. Fls in upper lf axils; cor. white or flushed pale pink, lower lip simple, obtuse, approximately same length as upper, spur about as long as lips. S Afr.
N. compacta hort. ex Vilm. = *N. versicolor* f. *compacta*.
N. cynanchifolia Benth. in Hook. Ann. herb, 15–60cm, pubesc. to glab. Lvs 1.2–3cm, ovate-lanceolate to lanceolate, sinuate-dentate. Infl. subcorymbose; cor. lilac-blue to purple, upper lip 6–9mm, lower lip emarginate, 6–8mm, palate hairy, spur 6–8mm, cylindric. Summer. S Afr.
N. floribunda Lehm. Ann. herb, erect, somewhat pilose above, 15–40cm. Lvs 1–4cm, ovate or lanceolate, subentire to dentate.

Infl. subcorymbose, fls fragrant; cor. white or v. pale, upper lip 3–4mm, lower lip 5–6mm, bilobed, palate shortly hirsute, spur 5mm, conic. S Afr.

N. foetens Vent. Perenn. herb to 60cm, somewhat shrubby, glab. or almost so. Lvs to 4cm, linear to lanceolate, entire or dentate. Infl. racemose, cor. to 1.5cm, lips and spur ± equal, pale blue, pink, lavender or white, with spur, crest and throat yellow. S Afr.

N. grandiflora Diels. Erect herb, subglabrous, 30–50cm. Basal lvs 2cm, oblong, dentate. Infl. gland., cor. lobes oblong, upper 5–6mm, lower scarcely emarginate, 9–12mm, throat bearded, palate hirsute, spur to 4mm, conic, short. S Afr.

N. lilacina N.E. Br. Minutely glandular-pubesc. perenn. to 35cm. Lvs to 3.5cm, narrowly lanceolate, dentate. Infl. racemose, to 30cm; cor. small lilac, upper lip to 4mm, with purple stripes, lower lip to 4mm, palate with yellow markings, spur short, white. S Afr.

N. linearis Vent. Perenn. herb; st. to 60cm, br. ascending. Lvs linear-lanceolate, entire or remotely dentate. Cor. purple, upper and lower lips approx. same length, spur straight, shorter than lips. Spring–early autumn. S Afr.

N. macrocarpa (Ait.) Druce = *N. chamaedrifolia*.

N. macroceras Schldl. Ann. herb, erect, slender to 30cm, sub-glabrous. Lvs to 7cm, lanceolate to linear, ± dentate. Infl. lax.; fls slightly fragrant; cor. with upper lip white, lobes 6–7×2mm, lower lip 6mm, emarginate, yellow, spur deflexed, cylindric, 8mm. S Afr.

N. pageae L. Bol. Plant 22–30cm, bushy, st. branched. Fls small; cor. bright cherry red, lower lip rich yellow. Summer. S Afr.

N. strumosa Benth. in Hook. Ann. herb, 15–60cm, erect, some-what glandular-pilose above. Lvs to 7.5cm, oblanceolate-spathulate, entire to dentate. Infl. subcorymbose; cor. yellow or purple to white, often veined purple without, throat yellow with darker markings, lower lip 2–3cm broad, notched at apex, bearded within. S Afr.

N. versicolor E. Mey. ex Benth. Ann. herb, to 50cm, glab. or subglabrous. Lvs to 5cm, ovate to broadly linear, somewhat sinuate or dentate. Infl. racemose; cor. to 12mm, blue, mauve, yellow or white, lips often different colours, lower lip broad, obtuse, shortly bilobed, palate broad, scarcely lobed, spur approximately same length as lower lip. S Afr. f. *compacta* Voss Plants more compact, 20–30cm; fls profuse, white, rose, violet and blue.

N. cvs and hybrids. Mostly derived from *N. strumosa* and *N. versicolor*, these are the nemesias popular for summer bedding. 'Blue Gem': habit bushy, to 20cm; cloud of sky-blue fls. Carnival Hybrids: compact bushes to 30cm; v. floriferous. 'Funfair': to 25cm; fls brilliant colours; seed race. 'Grandiflora': fls large. 'Mello Red and White': fls raspberry red and white. 'Mello White': fls white. 'Nana Compacta': habit dwarf. 'Suttonii': to 50cm; fls irregularly shaded, with broad lip in front and pouch at base, from carmine, through yellow and pink to white. 'Tapestry': to 25cm, habit upright; fls richly coloured.

Nemopanthus Raf. MOUNTAIN HOLLY. Aquifoliaceae. 1 decid., stoloniferous shrub to 3.5m. Lvs alt., oblong-ovate, to 6cm, en-tire or slightly serrate. Fls small, 4–5-merous, green-yellow. Fr. spherical, red; pyrenes 3–5. E N Amer. Z5.

N. collinus (Alexander) Clark = *Ilex collina*.

N. mucronatus (L.) Trel.

N. mucronatus hort. non (L.) Trel. = *Ilex collina*.

→*Ilex*.

Nemophila Nutt. Hydrophyllaceae. 11 ann. herbs. St. branched and spreading, somewhat succulent. Lvs usually pinnatifid. Fls usually solitary, stalked; cal. deeply 5-lobed, sinuses appendaged; cor. campanulate, cylindrical or rotate, pet. 5. W N Amer.

N. aurita Lindl. = *Pholistoma auritum*.

N. insignis Douglas & Benth. = *N. menziesii*.

N. maculata Benth. ex Lindl. FIVE SPOT. To 30cm, glab. to hispidulous, erect to spreading. Lvs 4–7-lobed. Fls to 4.5cm diam., solitary, long-stalked, axill.; pet. white, each with a deep violet blotch near or at the apex, sometimes faintly veined or tinted mauve-blue. C Calif.

N. menziesii Hook. & Arn. BABY-BLUE-EYES. To 12cm, hirsute, spreading-procumbent. Lvs 9–11-lobed, rarely entire. Fls to 4cm diam., solitary, long-stalked, axill.; pet. white to sky-blue, often with a white or yellow-stained centre, or spotted or stained darker blue or purple black. Calif. 'Alba': fls white with a black centre. 'Crambeoides': fls pale blue veined purple, unspotted. 'Coelestis': fls white edged sky-blue. 'Grandiflora': fls pale blue with a white centre. 'Insignis': fls pure blue. 'Marginata': fls blue edged white. 'Occulata': fls pale blue with a purple-black centre. 'Pennie Black': pet. deep purple-black edged bright white. 'Purpurea Rosea': fls purple-pink. var. *atromaria* (Fisch. & C.A.

Mey.) Chandl. Fls white spotted black-purple. var. *discoidalis* (Lem.) Voss. Fls bronze-purple edged white.

Neoabbottia Britt. & Rose = *Leptocereus*.

Neoalsomitra Hutch. Cucurbitaceae. 12 climbers. Tendrils simple or bifid. Lvs simple or 3–5-foliolate. ♂ fls in pan. or loose rac.; cal. cup-shaped, lobes 5; cor. rotate, deeply 5-lobed; sta. 5; ♀ fls in rac.; ovary 1–3-locular, styles 3–4. Fr. clavate to cylindric, terete to bluntly triangular. Indomal. to Aus. and W Pacific. Z10.

N. podagrica Steenis St. to 30m, glab., base thickened, with hard, green spines below. Lfts obovate, blunt, stalked, middle lft 6–11cm, lateral lfts 5–10cm, outermost lfts smaller. ♂ fls green-yellow, in pan. to 40cm. Fr. tubular to cup-shaped, 1.5–2cm. S Malaysia.

Neobakeria Schltr.

N. angustifolia Schltr. = *Polyxena angustifolia*.

N. namaquensis Schltr. = *Polyxena angustifolia*.

Neobathiea Schltr. Orchidaceae. 6 monopodial epiphytic orchids. St. usually short. Lvs ligulate, elliptic or oblanceolate. Rac. 1- to few-fld; fls white; tep. free; lip trilobed, spurred. Madag. Z9.

N. filicornu Schltr. St. to 6cm. Lvs 4–5cm, narrowly elliptic. Fls solitary; peduncle 2–2.5cm; sep. 1.3cm, narrowly oblanceolate; pet. slightly shorter and narrower; lip 2×1cm; spur pendent, 14cm.

N. perrieri (Schltr.) Schltr. Almost stemless. Lvs 3.5–7cm, oblong-spathulate, undulate. Fls 1–2; peduncle 6–12cm; sep. 2cm, narrowly oblanceolate, acute; pet. slightly smaller; lip trilobed at about halfway , 2×2cm; spur 7–10cm, curving for-wards, then pendent.

Neobenthamia Rolfe. Orchidaceae. 1 terrestrial or lithophytic orchid. St. slender, clustered, branched,leafy, to 2m. Lvs linear-lanceolate, grass-like, distichous, to 28cm. Infl. term., many-fld; fls to 2.5cm diam., white, the lip with a pubesc. yellow centre edged with pink dots, undulate. Tanz. Z10.

N. gracilis Rolfe.

Neobesseya Britt. & Rose.

N. asperispina (Boed.) Boed. = *Escobaria missouriensis*.

N. missouriensis (Sweet) Britt. & Rose = *Escobaria missouri-ensis*.

N. notesteinii (Britt.) Britt. & Rose = *Escobaria missouriensis*.

N. rosiflora Lahman ex G. Turner = *Escobaria missouriensis*.

N. similis (Engelm.) Britt. & Rose = *Escobaria missouriensis*.

N. wissmannii (Hildm. ex Schum.) Britt. & Rose = *Escobaria missouriensis*.

N. zilziana (Boed.) Boed. = *Escobaria zilziana*.

Neobuxbaumia Backeb. Cactaceae. 8 massive columnar or tree-like cacti; st. cylindric, ribbed. Fertile zone unmodified, or with larger areoles with wool and bristles and bristly spines; fl. apical in branched spp., lat. in unbranched spp., tubular-campanulate or tubular-funnelform, nocturnal.

N. euphorbioides (Haw.) F. Buxb. Columnar, 3–5; st. un-branched, 10–15cm diam., dark green or blue-green, sometimes tinged red; ribs usually 8–10; spines dark grey. Fl. 6–8cm, funnelform, pale to deep red-pink; tube and outer tep. wine-red; throat cream. E Mex. Z9.

N. macrocephala (F.A. Weber ex Schum.) Dawson. Tree with main axis to 7–15m and trunk 30–60cm diam.; lat. br. few to several, 30–40cm diam.; ribs 17–26; spines pink or red at first, becoming nearly black. Fl. 4–5cm, narrowly campanulate-funnelform; outer tep. purple-red, reflexed at anthesis, inner white, with red tip and pale red mid-stripe. S Mex. Z9.

N. mezcalaensis (Bravo) Backeb. Columnar; st. unbranched, to 5–10m; ribs 13–25; spines white or pale yellow, tinged red or brown. Fl. 5.5cm, tubular-funnelform; outer tep. tinged red, green or yellow, inner white, sometimes tinged green or pink. SW Mex. Z9.

N. polylopha (DC.) Backeb. Columnar, to 15m×50cm, normally unbranched; ribs 22–36 or more; spines bristly, yellow. Fl. 5–8cm, shortly campanulate-funnelform; pericarpel dull purple-brown; inner tep. pink. C Mex. Z9.

N. tetetzo (F.A. Weber ex Schum.) Backeb. Columnar, to 15m tall, usually unbranched; trunk to 60cm diam.; ribs 13–17; spines dark brown to black. Fl. 5.5cm, tubular-funnelform; in-ner tep. white, tinged green. S Mex. Z9.

→*Carnegiea, Cephalocereus, Cereus, Lemaireocereus* and *Pachy-cereus*.

Neocabreria R. King & H. Robinson. Compositae. 3 erect sub-shrubs, sparingly branched, pubesc. Lvs rather crowded. Cap.

discoid, in a corymbose pan., shortly pedunculate; receptacle flat to convex; flts white to rose-purple. Trop. S Amer. Z10.

N. serrulata (DC.) R. King & H. Robinson. Lvs to 6×1.5cm, lanceolate, toothed, pubesc. above. Cap. numerous; involucre ovoid. Braz.
→*Eupatorium*.

Neocallitropsis Florin. Cupressaceae. 1 everg. conifer to 10m. Bark grey-brown, resinous. Crown conic; br. spreading. Lvs dimorphic, 8-ranked in decussate whorls of 4, densely arranged: juveniles acicular, to 1.5cm; adult lvs 6mm, incurved, acute, minutely denticulate, keeled. ♂ cones term., on long branchlets. ♀ cones term., on short branchlets; scales 8, with a long reflexed acuminate spine. New Caledonia. Z10.

N. araucarioides (Compton) Florin. = *N. pancheri*.
N. pancheri (Carr.) Laub.

Neocardenasia Backeb.
N. herzogiana Backeb. = *Neoraimondia herzogiana*.

Neochilenia Backeb. ex Dölz = *Neoporteria*.

Neocogniauxia Schltr. Orchidaceae. 2 epiphytic orchids. Rhiz. creeping. Secondary st. short, slender, terete, enveloped by 1–3 tubular sheaths, apically unifoliate. Lvs coriaceous. Infl. term., slender, surpassing lvs; fls solitary; tep. subequal, free; lip small, simple to obscurely triblobed, often papillose. Jam., Cuba, Haiti, Dominican Rep. Z10.

N. monophylla (Griseb.) Schltr. Secondary st. to 9cm. Lvs to 25×1cm. Infl. to 30cm; bracts spotted purple; fls to 5cm diam., bright orange-scarlet; lip to 1cm, apiculate, midlobe cordate-semicircular, papillose, with a sac-like growth on central keel. Autumn–winter. Jam.
→*Laelia* and *Trigonidium*.

Neocussonia Hutch.
N. umbellifera (Sonder) Hutch. = *Schefflera umbellifera*.

Neodawsonia Backeb.
N. apicicephalium (Dawson) Backeb. = *Cephalocereus apicicephalium*.

Neodonnellia Rose = *Tripogandra*.

Neoevansia W.T. Marsh.
N. striata (Brandg.) Sanchez-Mej. = *Peniocereus striatus*.

Neofinetia Hu. Orchidaceae. 1 epiphytic monopodial orchid, to 15cm. St. branching basally, appearing tufted. Lvs to 10cm, in two ranks, basally overlapping, narrow-ligulate, falcate to recurved, fleshy, conduplicate. Rac. axill.; fls white; tep. to 1cm, spreading, linear-oblong to linear-lanceolate; lip 1cm, recurved, midlobe ligulate, spur v. slender. China, Jap., Korea. Z9.

N. falcata (Thunb.) Hu. Variegated forms are also grown.

Neogaerrhinum Rothm.
N. filipes (A. Gray) Rothm. = *Antirrhinum filipes*.

Neogardneria Schltr. ex Garay. Orchidaceae. 3 epiphytic orchids. Pbs ovoid. Lvs lanceolate, plicate. Infl. lax; sep. and pet. similar; lip triloded, midlobe narrow, abruptly deflexed, callus fan-shaped, crested. NE Trop. Amer. Z10.

N. murrayana (Gardn.) Garay. Pbs to 7.5cm. Lvs lanceolate. Scapes shorter than lvs; tep. ovate-lanceolate, pale yellow-green, lip white, lat. lobes streaked dark-purple. Braz.
→*Zygopetalum*.

Neoglaziovia Mez. Bromeliaceae. 2 short-stemmed, rhizomatous, perenn., terrestrial herbs. Lvs in a bundle-like rosette, linear. Infl. loosely racemose, erect, term., bracteate; lower floral bracts linear, upper triangular, shorter. NE Braz. Z10.

N. concolor C.H. Wright. Lvs to 60cm, densely white-scaly, serrate. Infl. 30cm; scape canescent; lower floral bracts longer than fls; sep. red; pet. 2cm, bright purple.

N. variegata (Arruda) Mez. Lvs to 150cm, with broad white bands beneath, pungent, margins incurved. Infl. to 25cm, lower floral bracts equal fls.

Neogomesia Castañeda.
N. agavoides Castañeda = *Ariocarpus agavoides*.

Neohenricia L. Bol. Aizoaceae. 1 v. small leaf-succulent. St. freely branched, creeping, densely mat-forming. Lvs to 1×0.5cm, 4 together on a shoot, convex above, with many white

tubercles. Fls to 1.4cm diam., white, nocturnal, fragrant. S Afr. Z9.

N. sibbettii (L. Bol.) L. Bol.
→*Henricia*.

Neolauchea Kränzl. Orchidaceae. 1 epiphytic orchid. Rhiz. creeping. Pbs 1.8–2.5cm, narrowly ovoid. Lvs solitary, 4–6cm, coriaceous, subterete. Infl. to 5cm, slender; fls solitary, small, rose-red or lilac; dors. sep. broadly ovate, apiculate, concave, lateral sep. shortly connate, forming a sac-shaped mentum; pet. larger than sep., ovate-oblong; lip broadly ovate-oblong, concave. S Braz. Z10.

N. pulchella Kränzl.
→*Mieracyllium*.

Neolehmannia Kränzl.
N. porpax (Rchb. f.) Garay & Dunsterville = *Nanodes mathewsii*.

Neolitsea (Benth.) Merrill. Lauraceae. Some 60 everg. trees and shrubs. Lvs entire, leathery. Infl. umbellate. Fr. a red or black berry. E & SE Asia, Indomal.

N. glauca (Sieb.) Koidz. = *N. sericea*.
N. latifolia Koidz. non S. Moore = *N. sericea*.
N. sericea (Bl.) Koidz. Tree to 6m. Lvs to 18×7cm, oblong or ovate-oblong, oblong, obtuse, 3-veined from the base, densely yellow-pubesc. above at first, dark green above, glaucous and white beneath, aromatic when crushed. Fls yellow. Fr. to 1.5cm, red. Temp. E Asia. Z9.

N. sieboldii (Kuntze) Nak. = *N. sericea*.
→*Litsea*.

Neolloydia Britt. & Rose. Cactaceae. 14 low-growing or dwarf cacti, simple or clustering; st. depressed-globose to short cylindric, tuberculate; spines never hooked. Fls mostly small, short funnelform. Fr. globose to turbinate, dry or slightly fleshy. E & NE Mex. and SW Tex.

N. beguinii Britt. & Rose, nom illegit. = *N. smithii*.
N. ceratites (Quehl) Britt. & Rose = *N. conoidea*.
N. clavata (Scheidw.) Britt. & Rose = *Coryphantha clavata*.
N. conoidea (DC.) Britt. & Rose. St. simple or clustering, 5–24×3–6cm, globose-ovoid to shortly cylindric, grey to slightly yellow-green. Fl. 2–3cm, magenta. Summer. E & NE Mex., SW US (SW Tex.). Z9.

N. durangensis (Runge) L. Bens. = *Sclerocactus unguispinus*.
N. erectocentra (J. Coult.) L. Bens. = *Sclerocactus erectocentrus*.
N. gielsdorfiana (Werderm.) F. Knuth. St. simple, rarely clustering, to 5–7×4.5–5cm, globose to ovoid or short cylindric, light blue- to grey-green or yellow-green. Fl. 1.3–2.4×1.5–2cm, tep. pale yellow with faint red-brown mid-stripe. NE Mex. Z9.

N. grandiflora (Pfeiff.) F. Knuth = *N. conoidea*.
N. horripila (Lem.) Britt. & Rose. St. simple or clustering, 7–10(–18)×4–9cm, globose or elongate, yellow- to olive- or blue-green. Fl 2.2–4×2.5–4cm; tep. magenta, paler near base. Spring. E Mex. Z9.

N. intertexta (Engelm.) L. Bens. = *Sclerocactus intertextus*.
N. johnsonii (Engelm.) L. Bens. = *Sclerocactus johnsonii*.
N. knuthiana (Boed.) F. Knuth. St. usually simple, 3–6×3.5–7cm, slightly depressed-globose, blue-green. Fl. 2.3–3×1.8–2–5cm; tep. pale pink with darker mid-stripe. E Mex. Z9.

N. laui (Glass & Fost.) E.F. Anderson. St. simple, 0.5–1.5×1.2–3.5cm, depressed-globose, yellow-green. Fl. to 3.5cm diam.; tep. pale pink with darker mid-stripe. Summer. E Mex. Z9.

N. lophophoroides (Werderm.) E.F. Anderson. St. simple, depressed-globose to ovoid. Fl. to 3.5cm diam.; tep., silvery-white to pale pink. Summer. E Mex. Z9.

N. macdowellii (Quehl) H.E. Moore = *Thelocactus macdowellii*.
N. mandragora (Fric ex A. Berger) E.F. Anderson. St. simple, 3–7×3–6cm, globose to ovoid, green to grey-green. Fl. 2–3×1.5–3.5cm; tep., white, mid-stripe tinged green, brown or magenta. Spring. NE Mex. Z9.

N. matehualensis Backeb. = *N. conoidea*.
N. odorata (Boed.) Backeb. = *Coryphantha odorata*.
N. pseudomacrochele (Backeb.) E.F. Anderson. Simple, rarely clustering; st. 2–4×2.5–3.5cm, globose to short-cylindric, dark blue-green. Fl. 2.5–3.2×3–3.5cm; tep. creamy white or pink with darker mid-stripe. Summer. EC Mex. Z9.

N. pseudopectinata (Backeb.) E.F. Anderson. Simple; st. 2–3×2–3.5cm, depressed-globose, covered by spines. Fl. like those of *N. valdeziana* or slightly larger. NE Mex. Z9.

N. saueri (Boed.) F. Knuth. Simple; st. 3–5×4–7.5cm, depressed-globose, grey- to blue-green. Fl. 1.5–2.3×2–2.5cm; tep. white with pale pink mid-stripe. NE Mex. Z9.

N. schmiedickeana (Boed.) E.F. Anderson. Simple or clustering in cult.; st. 1–3×1.5–5cm, depressed-globose to globose or short-cylindric, dark blue to grey-green. Fl. 1.5–2.6×1–3.2cm; tep. white, yellow or pink to magenta. Spring. NE Mex. var. *schmiedickeana*. St. dull dark green. Fl. 2–2.7×1.8–2.8cm; tep. white to pink with magenta mid-stripe. NE Mex. var. *dickinsoniae* (Glass & Fost.) E.F. Anderson. St. dark green. Fl. 2×1.7cm; tep. white with pale red-brown mid-stripe. NE Mex. var. *flaviflora* (G. Frank & Lau) E.F. Anderson. St. grey-green. Fl. 1.5×1–1.5cm; tep. pale yellow. E Mex. var. *gracilis* (Glass & Fost.) E.F. Anderson. St. grey-green. Fl. 2×1.5cm; tep. white, sometimes with faint pink mid-stripe. NE Mex. var. *klinkeriana* (Backeb. & Jacobsen) E.F. Anderson. St. blue-green to grey-green or tinged brown. Fl. 1.5–2.3×1–2.7cm; tep. white with magenta mid-stripe. E Mex. var. *macrochele* (Werderm.) E.F. Anderson. St. grey-green to yellow-green. Fl. 2–2.6×2.3–3.2cm; tep. white with faint brown to pink mid-stripe. E Mex. var. *schwarzii* (Shurly) E.F. Anderson. St. grey-green. Fl. 2–2.5×2.5–3.2cm; tep. white with faint pink mid-stripe. E Mex. Z9.

N. smithii (Muehlenpf.) Klad. & Fittkau. St. simple, mostly 7–12×4–9cm, globose to short-cylindric, grey- or blue-green. Fl. 1.8–3.5×1.2–4cm; tep. magenta with paler margins. Spring. NE Mex. Z9.

N. subterranea (Backeb.) H.E. Moore = *N. mandragora*.

N. texensis Britt. & Rose = *N. conoidea*.

N. unguispina (Engelm.) L. Bens. = *Sclerocactus unguispinus*.

N. valdeziana (H. Möller) E.F. Anderson. Simple; st. 1–2.5×1.5–2.5cm, depressed-globose to ovoid, bright green but hidden by the spines. Fl. 2–2.5×2.2–2.5cm; tep. white with pale pink mid-stripe, or magenta with paler margins. Spring. NE Mex. Z9.

N. viereckii (Werderm.) F. Knuth. Simple or clustering; st. 2–7×3–6.5cm, globose to globose-cylindric, blue green. Fl. 1.5–3.5cm diam.; tep. white or magenta and white near base. NE Mex. Z9.

→*Gymnocactus, Mammillaria, Pelecyphora, Strombocactus, Thelocactus, Tourneya* and *Turbinicarpus*.

Neomacfadya Baill. = *Arrabidaea*.

Neomarica Sprague. Iridaceae. 15 rhizomatous, herbaceous perennials. Lvs tough, ensiform, equitant. Flowering st. erect, somewhat compressed, bearing a single terminal lf and 1–4 long-stalked axill., sometimes viviparous bracts; fls clustered, short-lived; perianth radiially symmetric, outer seg. 3, lanceolate-ovate, broadly clawed, erecto-patent, inner seg. 3, far smaller, erect then reflexed; fil. free; style br. cleft or trifid. Trop. Amer., W Afr. Z10.

N. brachypus (Bak. f.) Sprague. Lvs to 50×4cm. Fls to 8cm diam., yellow banded chestnut at base. Summer. W Indies.

N. caerulea (Ker-Gawl.) Sprague. Lvs to 160cm. Flowering st. to 60cm; fls 8–10cm diam., outer perianth seg. pale blue to lilac, inner seg. deep blue, the claws and blade bases of all yellow-white banded brown and orange-yellow. Summer. Braz.

N. gracilis (Hook.) Sprague. Differs from *N. northiana*, in its flowering st. seldom exceeding 60cm, fls to 5.75cm diam., style br. with 3 (not 2) erect teeth. Summer. S Mex. to N Braz.

N. longifolia (Link & Otto) Sprague. Closely related to *N. brachypus*. Lvs to 30×2.5cm. Flowering st. 30–90cm; fls to 5cm diam., yellow banded brown. Summer. Braz.

N. northiana (Schneev.) Sprague. Lvs to 60×5cm. Flowering st. to 90cm, viviparous; fls 6–8cm diam., scented; outer perianth seg. white to yellow mottled crimson or maroon at base, inner seg. barred or stained violet to blue at apex, veined red at base. Spring–summer. Braz.

Neomirandea R. King & H. Robinson. Compositae. 24 large perenn. herbs, shrubs or small trees, often epiphytic; st. somewhat branched, often hollow. Lvs usually opposite. Cap. discoid, in a broad, corymbose pan.; involucre cylindric; flts white, lavender, pink or maroon. Mex. to Ecuad. Z10.

N. araliifolia (Less.) R. King & H. Robinson. Epiphytic shrub to 4m. Lvs to 16×7cm, ovate-elliptic, base cuneate, somewhat fleshy, glab.; petiole to 6cm. Cap. to 1cm high; flts white. Panama to Mex.

→*Eupatorium*.

Neomoorea Rolfe. Orchidaceae. 2 epiphytic orchids. Pbs ovoid, stout. Lvs 2, borne at apex of pbs, elliptic-lanceolate, plicate. Infl. basal; fls waxy, fragrant; tep. spreading; lip deeply triloded, mobile, midlobe lanceolate, concave, acuminate. Columbia, Panama. Z10.

N. irrorata (Rolfe) Rolfe. Pbs 4–11cm. Lvs 45–75cm. Infl. 15–45cm; tep. 2–2.8cm, red-brown, base white, lip pale yellow, banded and marked brown-purple, midlobe yellow, spotted red.

Neomortonia Wiehler. Gesneriaceae. 1 perenn. epiphytic herb. St. to 60cm, slender, pendent or climbing, pilose, often purple flushed. Lvs opposite, to 3×1.5cm, ovate, broadly elliptic or obovate, toothed, often flushed purple. Fls solitary, axill., pilose; cal. to 1cm, dentate, flushed purple, pilose; cor. to 3cm, spurred, white, tube funnel-shaped, inflated at base, flushed pink, throat marked with orange-brown, limb 5-lobed. Colomb., Panama, Costa Rica. Z10.

N. rosea Wiehler.

Neopanax Allan.

N. arboreus (Murray) Allan = *Pseudopanax arboreus*.

N. colensoi (Hook. f.) Allan = *Pseudopanax colensoi*.

N. kermadecensis (Oliv.) Allan = *Pseudopanax arboreus*.

N. laetus (T. Kirk) Allan = *Pseudopanax laetus*.

N. simplex (Hook. f.) Allan = *Pseudopanax simplex*.

Neoporteria Britt. & Rose. Cactaceae. 25 cacti, mostly small, simple, rarely clustering; st. globose to short-cylindric; ribs usually divided into tubercles; areoles oval, depressed, felted; spines central and radial. Fl. arising at apex or crown, funnelform or campanulate. Fr. globose to ovoid, sometimes balloon-like (*N. islayensis*). Chile, S Peru and W Arg.

N. acutissima (Otto & Dietr.) Borg = *N. subgibbosa*.

N. aricensis (Ritter) Donald & G. Rowley. Simple; st. to 55×10cm; globose at first, eventually cylindric and decumbent; ribs 13–21; spines yellow-brown or rarely black-brown, becoming grey. Fl. c2×2cm pale yellow. Chile. Z9.

N. atrispinosa (Backeb.) Backeb. = *N. villosa*.

N. bicolor (Akers & Buining) Donald & G. Rowley = *N. islayensis*.

N. bulbocalyx (Werderm.) Donald & G. Rowley. Simple; st. eventually 50×12cm, globose to short-cylindric, dull grey-green; ribs 12–17, spines pale yellow or dark brown to grey. Fl. 4–4.5cm, yellow with red throat. N Arg. Z9.

N. castaneoides (Cels ex Salm-Dyck) Werderm. = *N. subgibbosa*.

N. cephalophora (Backeb.) Backeb. = *N. villosa*.

N. chilensis (Hildm. ex Schum.) Britt. & Rose. Simple or clustering from the base; st. globose to short-columnar, woolly at apex; ribs 20–21; spines glassy white. Fl. 5cm diam., pink or pale yellow. Chile. Z9.

N. clavata (Söhr.) Werderm. St. to 60×8–12cm, globose to elongate-cylindric, glaucous green; ribs 9–18; spines almost black, or grey. Fl 2–7cm; tep. purple pink, paler below. Chile. Z9.

N. confinis (Ritter) Donald & G. Rowley. St. 6–12cm diam., semi-globose to cylindric, green, apex naked to spiny; ribs 13–21; spines pale yellow to grey-brown or almost black. Fl. 3–4.5cm diam., tube olive-green; outer tep. red with pale margins, inner tep. white with pale red mid-stripe. Chile. Z9.

N. curvispina (Bertero) Donald & G. Rowley Variable; simple; st. to 15–30cm diam., globose, grey-green; ribs 13–16 or more; spines stout, upcurved. Fl. to 5.5×4–6cm; tep. pale yellow with narrow to broad red mid-stripe. Chile. Z9.

N. froehlichianus (Schum.) Backeb. = *N. horrida*.

N. gerocephala Y. Ito = *N. nidus*.

N. heteracantha (Backeb.) W.T. Marshall = *N. subgibbosa*.

N. horrida (Rémy & Gay) D. Hunt. Simple or sometimes clustering; st. to 10cm diam. or more, short-cylindric, dark green to blue-green; ribs 14–20, spines strong, subulate, black or brown and yellow below. Fl. 4.5–5×3.5–4cm; outer tep. with red-brown mid-stripe, inner white or dingy yellow. Chile. Z9.

N. islayensis (C.F. Först.) Donald & G. Rowley. V. variable; simple; st. usually 10–15(–75)×10cm, globose to short-cylindric, apex densely woolly; ribs 12–21; spines numerous, variable. Fl. 1.5–2.5×1.5–2cm; yellow. S Peru, N Chile. Z9.

N. jussieui (Monv. ex Salm-Dyck) Britt. & Rose. Simple; st. globose or short-cylindric, dark or grey green to almost black; ribs 12–17, spines dark brown. Fl. 3–3.5cm; pale pink or yellow. Chile. Z9.

N. krainziana (Ritter) Donald & G. Rowley = *N. islayensis*.

N. kunzei sensu Ritter, non (C.F. Först.) Backeb. = *N. confinis*.

N. kunzei (C.F. Först.) Backeb. = *N. curvispina*.

N. litoralis Ritter = *N. subgibbosa*.

N. napina (Philippi) Backeb. Variable; simple; st. to 10×5cm, globose to ovoid, grey-green or tinged red; ribs c14; spines almost black. Fl. 3–3.5cm; perianth pale yellow or the outer tep. tinged pink. Chile. Z9.

N. nidus (Söhr.) Britt. & Rose. Simple; st. to 30×5–9cm, globose to short-cylindric; ribs 16–18; spines weak and tortuous, interlaced, brown, yellow or almost white. Fl. 4–6×2.5cm, pink. Chile. Z9.

N. nigricans (Linke) Ritter = *N. horrida*.

N. nigricans (Linke) Britt. & Rose = *N. horrida*.

N. nigrihorrida (Backeb.) Backeb. = *N. clavata*.

N. occulta (Philippi) Britt. & Rose. Usually simple; st. 3–8cm diam., depressed-globose to globose, dark grey-green or tinged maroon; ribs 12–14 or more, spines usually lacking, or 4–8, adpressed, dark. Fl. 2.3–4cm; tep. nearly white with pale red mid-stripe. Chile. Z9.

N. odieri (Lem. ex Salm-Dyck) Backeb. Simple or clustering, depressed, globose, to 6cm diam., dark red-brown or nearly black; ribs 8–13, spines thin, almost black or red-brown. Fl. 2.5–5cm, white, yellow or pale pink. Chile. Z9.

N. paucicostata (Ritter) Donald & G. Rowley. Simple; st. c15–30×6–8cm, hemispheric at first, later cylindric, pale grey-green; ribs 8–13; grey-brown, tipped black or off-white. Fl. 3–5×3–5cm; outer tep. pink-tinged, inner white. Chile. Z9.

N. pilispina Ritter = *N. taltalensis*.

N. polyrhaphis (Pfeiff. ex Salm-Dyck) Backeb. = *N. villosa*.

N. reichei (Schum.) Backeb. Simple; depressed-globose, grey-green; ribs resolved into spirally arranged tubercles; spines hyaline or white at first, later grey. Fl. 2.5–3.3×4cm; tep. yellow. Chile. Z9.

N. senilis (Philippi) Backeb. = *N. nidus*.

N. strausiana (Schum.) Donald & G. Rowley. Simple; st. to 20×8–15cm, globose to elongate, black-green, apex without wool; ribs 12–14; spines almost black, tinged purple, upcurved. Fl. 4×5cm, tep. pale yellow or tinged red. W Arg. Z9.

N. subcylindrica (Backeb.) Backeb. = *N. subgibbosa*.

N. subgibbosa (Haw.) Britt. & Rose. Variable; simple; st. eventually to 1m×10cm, globose to short cylindric at first, green to grey-green; ribs 16–20; spines yellow, brown or nearly black at first or amber-yellow. Fl. 3–6cm, pink, paler towards the throat. Chile. Z9.

N. taltalensis (Werderm.) Hutchison. Simple; st. to 8cm diam., globose, dull dark green; ribs 10–16; spines dark grey-brown to almost black, radial spines, curving to tortuous, brown, fading to white. Fl. 3×2.5cm or larger, fuchsia-purple, yellow or white. Chile. The names *N. fobeana* (Mieckley) Backeb., *N. fusca* (Muehlenpf.) Britton & Rose and *N. hankeana* (C.F. Först.) Donald & Rowley may be referable here. Z9.

N. tuberisulcata (Jacobi) Donald & G. Rowley = *N. horrida*.

N. tuberisulcatus (Jacobi) A. Berger = *N. horrida*.

N. umadeave (Fric ex Kreutz.) Donald & G. Rowley. Simple; st. to 40×10–20cm, globose to slightly elongate, dark green; ribs c18–21 or more; spines, ± upcurved, white or tinged violet. Fl. 3–3.5cm; tep. pale yellow. NW Arg. Z9.

N. villosa (Monv.) A. Berger. Simple; st. to 15×8cm, short-cylindric, grey-green, becoming tinged purple-black; ribs 13–15, spines bristly, dark, and hair-like, pale brown or off-white. Fl. c2cm, pink with white throat. Chile. Z9.

N. wagenknechtii Ritter. Simple; st. to 30×11cm, globose to cylindric, grey-green; ribs 11–17; spines almost black at first, later grey-brown, or dark grey. Fl. 2.2cm, purple. Chile. Z9.

→*Mammillaria*, *Neochilenia* and *Pyrrhocactus*.

Neoraimondia Britt. & Rose. Cactaceae. 2 shrubby or arborescent cacti, much branched from the base or with a definite trunk; st. erect, few ribbed; non-flowering areoles large, brown-felted, usually spiny; flowering areoles nearly spineless. Fls 1–2 per areole, small. Peru, N Chile, Boliv.

N. arequipensis (Meyen) Backeb. Robust shrub, branching from the base; st. columnar, to 10m×20–40cm; ribs 4–10; spines to 25cm. Fl. 2.5–4×2–4cm, pink, purple-red or white with green tinge. Coastal belt of Peru, N Chile. Z9.

N. gigantea Backeb. = *N. arequipensis*.

N. herzogiana (Backeb.) F. Buxb. Eventually a tree 7–10m, with a distinct trunk 1–2m×50cm; st. 15–20cm diam.; ribs 5–7; spines as in *N. arequipensis*. Fl. 7–7.5×5–6cm, purple with paler or white margins. Boliv. Z9.

N. macrostibas (Schum.) Backeb. = *N. arequipensis*.

N. roseiflora (Werderm. & Backeb.) Backeb. = *N. arequipensis*.

→*Neocardenasia*.

Neoregelia L.B. Sm. Bromeliaceae. 71 mostly terrestrial, perenn. herbs. Lvs in a dense, funnel-shaped or tubular rosette toothed and spinose. Infl. bracteate, hidden in rosette centre, usually simple, dense, capitiform, corymbose or umbellate, on a short, enclosed scape. S Amer. Z10.

N. carolinae (Beer) L.B. Sm. BLUSHING BROMELIAD. Lvs 40–60cm, innermost with scarlet bases when in fl., ligulate, sparsely scaly beneath, closely toothed. Infl. bracts bright red, papery; pet. to 3cm, lavender blue. Braz. f. *tricolor* (M.B. Fost.) M.B. Fost. ex L.B. Sm. Lvs with longitudinal yellow, white and green stripes. Gdn origin.

N. chlorosticta (Bak.) L.B. Sm. Lvs 20–30cm, outer green, inner dark purple blotched pale green, sometimes banded silver beneath, linear, spiny-denticulate. Infl. red-purple; pet. blue-violet. Braz.

N. compacta (Mez) L.B. Sm. Lvs to 26cm, erect, in a dense rosette, ligulate, green, the innermost red when in fl., margins red or denticulate; pet. red. Braz.

N. concentrica (Vell.) L.B. Sm. Lvs to 40cm, broadly, strap-shaped, mid green often with obscure, darker spots, spiny teeth black, inner lvs flushing purple-pink at base when in fl. Infl. bracts yellow-white flushed violet or purple; pet. white or blue. Braz. 'Plutonis': bracts flushed red.

N. cruenta (Graham) L.B. Sm. Lvs 30–90cm, rigid, inner red in fl., green banded mahogany beneath with a large blood-red spot at apex, abruptly acute, spines bright red; sheaths flushed purple. Infl. bracts green or white; pet. blue or purple with a pale line. Braz.

N. fosteriana L.B. Sm. Lvs to 30cm, copper-red with a few green spots, pale grey-scaly, apex dark red, margins laxly toothed. Infl. compound, red; pet. red. Braz.

N. kautskyi Pereira. Lvs to 30cm, papery, sparsely scaly, inner lvs green, outer chartreuse-green, with dense red-brown blotches, laxly denticulate. Infl. corymbiform; pet. white, tipped violet. Braz.

N. macwilliamsii L.B. Sm. Lvs 30cm or more, entire, pale-scaly, base red with green spots, apex green. Infl. dark red. Braz.

N. marmorata (Bak.) L.B. Sm. MARBLE PLANT. Lvs to 60cm, laxly toothed; sheaths purple spotted pale green; blades ligulate, darkly mottled or spotted, particularly at base, apex sometimes with a bright red spot; pet. white tinged pink. Braz.

N. melanodonta L.B. Sm. Lvs 15–20cm, scurfy throughout, sheaths broadly elliptic, yellow-green, blotched purple; blades broadly ligulate, blotched magenta, apex spiny, retuse, with a magenta spot, margins with black teeth. Infl. few-fld, narrowly ellipsoid, on a v. short scape; pet. light blue. Braz.

N. pineliana (Lem.) L.B. Sm. St. short, erect. Lvs to 50cm, densely scaly; sheaths broadly ovate, purple; blades linear, green and less scaly above, copper-green beneath, denticulate. Infl. surrounded by reduced, carmine inner lvs, occas. bright red bracts; pet. violet, apex dark blue. Braz.

N. princeps (Bak.) L.B. Sm. Stemless. Lvs 20–50cm laxly toothed; sheaths orbicular, large, green, densely scaly; blades ligulate, green, grey-scaly beneath, inner bright red in fl.; pet. white tipped dark blue. S Braz.

N. spectabilis (Moore) L.B. Sm. PAINTED FINGERNAIL; FINGERNAIL PLANT. Lvs 40–45cm, grey-scaly and banded white beneath, ligulate, outer green with a bright red apical spot, inner sometimes wholly red, often edged purple, subentire or denticulate. Infl. bracts red or purple; pet. violet-blue. Braz.

N. tristis L.B. Sm. Lvs 20–60cm, in a slender, funnel-shaped rosette; sheaths large, dark brown with pale spots; blades ligulate, green and glab. above, banded red-brown and pale-scaly beneath, toothed. Infl. bracts brown-purple to dark purple; pet. lavender tipped blue. CE Braz.

N. cvs. 'Amazing Grace': lvs dark green striped red and pale green. 'Cathryn Wilson': lvs broad, vivid maroon mottled green; fls tinted blue. 'Marcon' (*N. marmorata* ×*N. spectabilis*): 'Marconfos' (*N. marmorata* ×*N. concentrica*): edged with brown spines; infl. low, fls lilac. 'Vulcan' (*N. concentrica* ×*N. johannis*): compact; lvs wide, thick, blotched, tinted purple in centre.

→*Nidularium*.

Neotchihatchewia Rausch. Cruciferae. 1 erect perenn. herb to 25cm. Lvs 2.5–7cm, narrow-elliptic, hairy, toothed. Fls vanilla-scented, in rounded corymbs 10cm across; sep. 4, 6–8mm; pet. 4, clawed, red-purple. Spring. Armenia, W Turk. Z7.

N. isatidea (Boiss.) Rausch.

→*Tchihatchewia*.

Neottopteris J. Sm.

N. antiqua (Mak.) Masam. = *Asplenium antiquum*.

N. australasica J. Sm. = *Asplenium australasicum*.

Neowerdermannia Backeb. Cactaceae. 2 small, tap-rooted cacti; st. globose; ribs indistinct, spiralling, divided into triangular tubercles. Fl. funnelform. N Arg., S Boliv., Peru, N Chile.

N. chilensis Backeb. Resembling *N. vorwerkii*, but fl. creamy white. N Chile to border with Arg. Z9.

N. vorwerkii Fric. St. broadly flattened-globose; spines to 10, lowest almost hooked, to 4cm, nearly black at first, remainder to 1.5cm, off-white. Fl. c2cm diam.; tep. white with light lilac-pink mid-stripe, or pale lilac. N Arg., S Boliv., Peru, N Chile. Z9.

Nepal Alder *Alnus nepalensis*.

Nepalese White Thorn *Pyracantha crenulata*.

Nepal Ivy *Hedera nepalensis*.

Nepal Trumpet Flower *Beaumontia grandiflora*.

Nepenthaceae Dumort. See *Nepenthes*.

Nepenthes L. PITCHER PLANT; TROPICAL PITCHER PLANT. Nepenthaceae. 70 climbing or scrambling, carnivorous shrubs or semi-woody herbs to 5m. Lvs ligulate to lanceolate, entire, coriaceous, with midrib prolonged into tendril; pitchers often dimorphic – those at base of plant, squatter – all held upright at end of pendulous tendrils, hollow and containing water, cylindric to rounded, lip of pitcher thickened, ribbed and often colourful; apex a fixed 'lid' projecting over pitcher-mouth, with nectar-secreting glands; outward face of pitcher with 2 toothed, longitudinal wings, usually reduced to toothless ridges in upper pitchers. Madag., Seych., Trop. Asia to N Queensld. Z10.

N. alata Blanco. Pitchers weakly dimorphic; lower 6.5–13cm, cylindric above, constricted at centre, inflated at base, light green with red flecks, or heavily suffused red, lip green or occas. red, lid elliptic with gland. crest at base; wings prominent, fimbriate; upper pitchers elongate. Philipp., Malaysia, Borneo, Sumatra.

N. albomarginata Lobb. Pitchers to 12.5cm, cylindric, narrowed to base where it becomes upcurved, green sometimes spotted red, or pink, with conspicuous white band immediately below the finely ribbed, narrow lip, lid oblong, rounded, green, spotted red, wings narrow, sparsely toothed. Malaysia, Sumatra, Borneo.

N. ampullaria Jack. Pitchers to 5cm, rounded, squat, produced low on plant, green spotted and blotched deep red, or entirely green or deep red, lip with narrow rim, lid to 3.5cm, narrow, wings broad, widely spreading, strongly toothed. Malaysia, Borneo, Sumatra to New Guinea.

N. bicalcarata Hook. f. Pitchers dimorphic; lower to 10cm, rounded, green, sometimes suffused rust-red or entirely rust-red, green, lid well raised above pitcher, reniform, with ends of lip forming 2 decurved spurs, wings broad, toothed; upper pitchers to 13cm, campanulate to funnel-shaped. Borneo.

N. burbidgeae Burb. Pitchers dimorphic; lower to 18cm, ovate, pale green to white with red blotches, lip broad, yellow-white with red bands, lid orbiculate, undulate, wings narrow, toothed; upper pitcher to 13cm, funnel-shaped, contracted just below mouth. Borneo.

N. × chelsonii hort. Veitch ex Mast. (*N. × dominii × N. × hookeriana.*) Intermediate between parents. Pitchers broadly ovoid, yellow-green spotted purple-red, mouth oblique, oval, lip dark purple, wings broad, toothed. Gdn origin.

N. × coccinea hort. (*N. × dominii × N. mirabilis.*) Pitchers to 15cm, yellow-green heavily marked purple-red, inflated below, cylindric above, lip with red and black ridges, lid ovate-oblong, green with red markings, wings broad, toothed. Gdn origin.

N. curtisii Mast. = *N. maxima.*

N. × dominiana Nichols. = *N. × dominii.*

N. × dominii Veitch. (*N. rafflesiana × N. gracilis.*) Pitchers to 15cm, light green, heavily marked dark red, cylindric but tapering upwards, mouth oblique, oval, lip narrow, pale green, lid green, suffused red, wings broad, spreading, toothed. Gdn origin.

N. × dormanniana hort. (*N. mirabilis × N. × sedenii Veitch (N. gracilis × N. khasiana).*) Pitchers 15cm, green with many red spots and blotches, flask-shaped, somewhat inflated below middle, lip broad, green, finely ridged, lid broadly ovate, wings broad, undulate, toothed. Gdn origin.

N. gracilis Korth. Pitchers dimorphic: lower to 7.5cm, shortly flask-shaped, rounded below, light green with dark red spots, or suffused pink, or dark maroon to almost black, lip narrow, green; lid orbicular, dark red, wings narrow, shortly toothed; upper pitchers to 15cm, constricted at middle and somewhat inflated at base, dark mahogany-red or red-brown, lip green to red-brown, interior white or pink-white. Indon. (Borneo to Sulawesi), Philipp.

N. × henryana Nichols. (*N. hookeriana × N. × sedenii.*) Pitchers to 15cm, irregularly flask-shaped, inflated below with long cylindric neck, predominantly red-purple with few green flecks, mouth oblique, oval, lip broad, crimson shaded violet, interior green with violet spots, wings narrow, toothed. Gdn origin.

N. × hookeriana Lindl. (*N. rafflesiana × N. ampullaria.*) Natural hybrid. Pitchers dimorphic; lower to 11cm, ovoid, pale green with dark red spots, or sometimes heavily blotched red, lip broad, descending into pitcher, green, lid flat, obovate, wings broad, fimbriate; upper pitchers to 12.5cm, funnel-shaped. Malaysia, Sumatra, Borneo.

N. × intermedia hort. Veitch. (*N. gracilis × N. rafflesiana.*) Pitchers to 15cm, green heavily blotched red, subcylindric, tapering gradually above; lip dark red, lid with distinct column, ovate, obtuse, wings broad, long-toothed. Gdn origin.

N. khasiana Hook. f. Pitchers dimorphic; lower 7.5–17.5cm, inflated below, tapering above, green, tinged pink, upper pitchers to 20cm, cylindric, slightly inflated at base, green with red markings, lip pale red, lid oval, green externally, red within. Assam.

N. madagascariensis Poir. Pitchers dimorphic; lower to 13cm,

squat-cylindric, red or green, spotted red, lip ribbed, red, lid curved over pitcher mouth, orbiculate to reniform; upper pitchers to 17cm, funnel-shaped, bright yellow-green, sometimes suffused red. Madag.

N. × mastersiana hort. Veitch ex Mast. (*N. sanguinea × N. khasiana.*) Pitchers 11cm, cylindric with slight constriction at middle, deep claret-red with deeper purple spots, thinly hairy, lip red, interior pink-cream, spotted red, lid rounded, wings narrow, sparsely toothed in lower pitchers. Gdn origin.

N. maxima Reinw. ex Nees. Pitchers dimorphic; lower to 20cm, cylindric, pale green, streaked red, lip wide, dark red, lid somewhat cordate, green, mottled purple, wings narrow, toothed; upper pitchers to 30cm, trumpet-shaped. Indon. (Borneo, Sulawesi) to New Guinea.

N. mirabilis (Lour.) Druce. MONKEY CUP. Pitchers cylindric or slightly inflated at base, to 18cm, pale green with red spots, or wholly red, lip broad, flattened, striped red, lid orbicular to ovate, wings present in lower pitchers, toothed. S China, SE Asia to New Guinea and Queensld.

N. × mixta Mast. (*N. northiana × N. maxima.*) Pitchers weakly dimorphic, 10–35cm; lower cylindric, pale green, spotted purple-red, lip broad, strongly ribbed, glossy ruby red, lid finely spotted red, wings narrow, toothed; upper pitchers funnel-shaped. Gdn origin.

N. northiana Hook. f. Pitchers to 30cm, cylindric, pale green, heavily spotted purple, lip v. broad, outer margin undulate, yellow, striped purple, lid ovate-oblong, glossy, spotted black on lower surface, wings narrow, toothed. Borneo.

N. phyllamphora Willd. = *N. mirabilis.*

N. rafflesiana Jack. Pitchers dimorphic; lower to 12.5cm, ventricose, rounded at base, green, heavily spotted red, lip broad, crimson, ribbed, narrowing upwards to form elongate process to lid, spiny above, lid oblong-orbicular, wings to 2.5cm broad, teeth incurved; upper pitchers to 23cm, funnel-shaped. Malaysia, Sumatra, Borneo.

N. rajah Hook. f. KING MONKEY CUP. Pitchers dimorphic; lower to 35×15cm, rounded, green lightly spotted red, or entirely red to purple externally, spotted red and purple-black within, lip broad, outer margin projecting, undulate, ribbed, crimson with darker bands, lid large, wings narrow, toothed; upper pitchers funnel-shaped. Borneo.

N. reinwardtiana Miq. Pitchers to 20cm, cylindric, somewhat inflated at base with slight constriction at middle, green externally, glaucous blue-green within, lip v. narrow, green, lid elliptic; wings untoothed. Borneo.

N. stenophylla Mast. Pitchers dimorphic; lower to 15cm, narrow-cylindric, pale yellow-green, longitudinally flecked purple, lip narrow, banded red, lid rounded, with narrow connective neck, wings v. narrow, sparsely toothed; upper pitchers to 28cm. Borneo.

N. tentaculata Hook. f. Pitchers dimorphic; lower to 7cm, squat flask-shaped, inflated below, cylindric above, pale green to white, marked red-purple, lip narrow, red, lid with distinct upright bristles on upper surface, wings narrow, toothed; upper pitchers to 15cm, purple-green to dark-red. Borneo.

N. veitchii Hook. f. Pitchers to 20cm, cylindric, pale green, mouth oblique, ovate, lip strongly ribbed, canary-yellow, lid small, oblong, wings broad, toothed. Borneo.

N. ventricosa Blanco. Pitchers numerous, to 18cm, inflated at base with middle constricted, pale to white-green, sometimes flecked red; mouth shallowly oblique, ovate, lip broad, strongly ribbed, red, or green with red bands; lid ovate; wings 0. Philipp.

N. cvs. Many of the hybrids and selections popular in the last century are lost to cult.; among those still grown are 'Courtii': pitchers marbled wine-red towards apex, wings fringed. 'Dir. G.T. Moore': pitchers purple-red marbled green, wings prominent, lip lined purple. 'Henry Shaw': pitchers large, solid, pale green spotted wine-red. 'Lieut. R.B. Pring': pitchers pear-shaped, red-purple acquiring green marbling with age, wings prominent with purple hairs. 'St. Louis': pitchers pear-shaped, dark red becoming paler with age, slightly marbled green, wings mottled. 'Superba': vigorous; pitchers variable from urn-shaped to funnel-shaped, green tinged yellow and splashed maroon, rim ribbed in maroon and crimson, lid striped red, fringe with red hairs.

Nepeta L. Labiatae. *c*250 perenn. herbs, often aromatic. Fls in verticillasters, frequently forming dense spikes or heads, rarely in rac. or pan.; cal. 15-nerved, teeth 5, subequal; cor. tubular-campanulate or funnel-shaped, bilabiate, tube long, slender at base, upper lip 2-lobed, lower lip 3-lobed. Summer. Eurasia, N Afr., mts of trop. Afr.

N. amethystina Poir. = *N. nepetella.*
N. aragonensis Lam. = *N. nepetella.*
N. boissieri Willk. = *N. nepetella.*

N. camphorata Boiss. & Heldr. St. to 45cm, lanate, viscid. Lvs to 2cm, ovate, cordate at base, crenate, lanate, viscid, smelling of camphor when crushed. Fls in distant verticillasters; cor. to 12mm, white spotted purple. S Greece. Z8.

N. cataria L. CATNIP; CATMINT. St. to 1m, branched, erect, grey-pubesc. to tomentose. Lvs 3.5–8cm, ovate, cordate at base, serrate, grey-tomentose beneath. Infl. spike-like, lower verticillasters distant; cor. 6–10mm, white spotted blue-violet. Eur. (widely nat.), SW & C Asia. 'Citriodora': lemon-scented. Z3.

N. erodifolia Boiss. = *Lallemantia royleana.*

N. ×faassenii Bergmans ex Stearn. (*N. racemosa* × *N. nepetella.)* To 60cm, short-pubesc. St. branching at base. Lvs to 3cm, narrow-lanceolate to oblong-ovate, truncate at base, crenate, silver-grey. Fls in elongate or remote rac.; cor. to 12mm, pale lavender with darker spots. 'Blue Wonder': compact, to 35cm high; fls blue, long-lasting. 'Dropmore': upright, fls deep lavender, in tall spikes. 'Little Titch': dwarf, to 15cm high. 'Porzellan': lvs narrow, grey; fls soft porcelain blue. 'Six Hills Giant': taller and tougher than type; fls in large sprays, lavender-blue. 'Snowflake': low and spreading; lvs tinted grey; fls snow white. 'Souvenir d'André Chaudron' ('Blue Beauty'): roots invasive; lvs grey-green; fls large, tubular, rich lavender-blue. 'Superba': spreading; lvs tinted grey; fls dark blue, abundant. 'Walker's Low': to 75cm; st. arching. Z3.

N. glechoma Benth. = *Glechoma hederacea.*

N. govaniana Benth. St. erect, branching, somewhat pubesc. Lvs large, ovate-oblong or oblong-elliptic, rounded at base, crenate. Rac. elongated, lax, verticillasters remote; cor. yellow. W Himal. Z5.

N. grandiflora Bieb. St. erect to 40–80cm, branched, glab. or minutely pubesc. Lvs to 10cm, ovate, cordate at base, crenulate, glab. Spikes elongated interrupted; cor. 14–17mm, blue. Cauc., E and EC Eur. (locally nat.). Z3.

N. hederacea (L.) Trev. = *Glechoma hederacea.*

N. incana Thunb. = *Caryopteris incana.*

N. laevigata (D. Don) Hand.-Mazz. St. to 90cm, br. often spreading. Lvs to 10cm, ovate or triangular-cordate, serrate, petiolate. Fls pale blue in oblong or cylindric spike. W Himal. Z5.

N. macrantha Fisch. ex Benth. = *N. sibirica.*

N. marifolia Boiss. & Huet = *N. racemosa.*

N. melissifolia Lam. St. 20–40cm, ascending, pubesc. to villous. Lvs 1.5–3.5cm, ovate, cordate at base, coarsely crenate, pubesc. Infl. elongate, racemose; cor. 12–15mm, blue spotted red. S Aegean.

N. murcica Guirão ex Willk. = *N. nepetella.*

N. mussinii hort. non Spreng. = *N. ×faassenii.*

N. mussinii Spreng. in Henck. = *N. racemosa.*

N. nepetella L. St. to 80cm, branched, minutely pubesc. Lvs to 4cm, lanceolate to oblong-lanceolate, truncate at base, crenate to dentate, pubesc. to lanate, green to glaucous. Infl. usually branched, whorled; cal. often tinged pink or blue; cor. 10–12mm, pink or white. SW Eur. to S It. ssp. **amethystina** (Poir.) Briq. Cor. blue-violet. N Afr., Iberian Penins. Z8.

N. nervosa Royle ex Benth. To 60cm, subglabrous. Lvs to 10cm, linear-lanceolate, entire or somewhat dentate, strongly veined. Rac. dense, cylindric; cor. to 12mm, blue or yellow. Kashmir. Z5.

N. nuda L. St. to 1.2m, glab. to minutely pubesc. Lvs 1.5–7cm, ovate to ovate-oblong, base cordate. Infl. whorled, many-fld, paniculate; cor. 6–10mm, white or violet-blue. S Eur., Asia. ssp. **nuda**. Infl. lax, cor. pale violet. Eur. to C Russia. ssp. **albiflora** Gams. Infl. compact; cor. white. Greece, Balk., SW Asia. Z6.

N. pannonica L. = *N. nuda* ssp. *nuda.*

N. phyllochlamys P.H. Davis. St. to 25cm, many, decumbent, densely tomentose or villous. Lvs 0.7–1.4cm, triangular-ovate, truncate or subcordate at base, crenulate, grey-white, felty. Infl. simple, verticillasters distant; cor. 10mm, lilac-pink. E Medit. Z8.

N. prattii Lév. St. erect to 90cm. Lvs to 40–50cm, ovate-lanceolate, crenate. Infl. dense verticillasters; cor. to 25mm, blue-violet. W China. Z6.

N. pseudomussinii Floto = *N. ×faassenii.*

N. racemosa Lam. Aromatic. St. to 30cm, many, decumbent, ascending or erect, densely tomentose. Lvs 1–3cm, ovate, cordate at base, veins prominent. Fls in distant, many-fld verticillasters; cal. densely violet-tomentose; cor. 10–18mm, deep violet to lilac-blue. Cauc., N & NW Iran. Plants in cult. under this name are usually *N. ×faassenii*. Z4.

N. raphanorhiza Benth. St. to 45cm, somewhat glab. Lvs to 1.2cm, ovate to ovate-cordate. Fls in dense ovoid rac.; cor. to 6mm, purple-blue. W Himal. Z5.

N. sibirica L. To 1m, glab. to subglabrous. Lvs 5–9cm, oblong-lanceolate, cuneate or cordate at base, dentate, dark green and minutely pubesc. above, glandular-punctate beneath, short-stalked. Infl. to 12 many-fld remote verticillasters in rac. to 25cm; cor. 25–30mm, straight, blue or lavender. Sib. Z3.

N. spicata Benth. = *N. laevigata.*

N. stewartiana Diels Differs from related *N. sibirica* in its smaller fls and curved not straight cor. tube. China. Z6.

N. tuberosa L. Rhiz. tuberous. St. to 80cm, simple, pubesc. to lanate. Lvs to 8cm, ovate-lanceolate to oblong, cordate at base, subglabrous to villous; bracts tinged pink or red-purple. Fls in a simple spike; cor. 9–12mm, violet or purple. Spain, Port., Sicily. Z8.

N. ucranica L. St. to 50cm, erect, branched, subglabrous. Lvs to 4cm, oblong-lanceolate, crenate-serrate, glab. Fls in numerous, lax 3–5-fld cymes; cal. often tinged blue; cor. 7–9mm, blue-violet. SE Eur., Asia. Z9.

N. veitchii Duthie. Close to *N. sibirica*. Lvs ± toothed to entire, sessile. Fls with cor. straight, in closely arranged, not remote, whorls. W China. Z6.

N. wilsonii Duthie. Resembles *N. sibirica*. Lvs oblong, obtuse, regularly crenate. Fls in close whorls; cor. tube to 25mm, much curved. W China. Z6.

→*Dracocephalum.*

Nephelaphyllum Bl. Orchidaceae. 17 terrestrial orchids. Rhiz. creeping. Pbs 1-leaved. Lvs ribbed, fleshy. Rac. erect; sep. and pet. similar; lip trilobed or entire; spur short. Indon., Philipp., Hong Kong, India, China. Z10.

N. pulchrum Bl. Pbs subterete, dull purple, to 2.5cm. Lvs ovate-cordate, 6–10cm, olive green mottled grey to bronze above, often flushed red-purple beneath. Fls to 3cm diam., fragrant; tep. pale green, veined purple, lip white, base pale green and purple with yellow ridges; spur inflated. Java.

Nephelium L.

N. litchi Cambess. = *Litchi chinensis.*

N. longana Lour. = *Dimocarpus longan.*

N. rubrum G. Don = *Lepisanthes senegalensis.*

Nephrodium Michx.

N. banksiifolium Presl = *Osmunda banksiifolia.*

N. beddomei Bak. = *Parathelypteris beddomei.*

N. calanthum Endl. = *Lastreopsis calantha.*

N. canum Bak. = *Pseudocyclosorus canus.*

N. chinense Bak. = *Dryopteris chinensis.*

N. cicutarium (L.) Bak. = *Tectaria cicutaria.*

N. decompositum R. Br. = *Lastreopsis decomposita.*

N. glabellum Cunn. = *Lastreopsis glabella.*

N. gymnosorum Mak. = *Dryopteris gymnosora.*

N. lancilobum Bak. = *Lastreopsis decomposita.*

N. microsorium Endl. = *Lastreopsis microsora.*

N. pennigerum Hook., nom. nud. = *Sphaerostephanos penniger.*

N. pentangularum Colenso = *Lastreopsis microsora.*

N. sherringiae Jenman = *Tectaria trifoliata.*

N. sparsum Hamilt. ex D. Don = *Dryopteris sparsa.*

N. velutinum (A. Rich.) Hook. f. = *Lastreopsis velutina.*

Nephrolepis Schott. LADDER FERN; SWORD FERN; BOSTON FERN. Oleandraceae. 30 epiphytic or terrestrial ferns. Rhiz. usually with spreading, wiry stolons. Fronds erect to pendent, pinnate, pinnae numerous, often basally auricled on one side. Pantrop. Z10.

N. acuminata (Houtt.) Kuhn = *N. davallioides.*

N. acutifolia (Desv.) Christ. Rhiz. v. long-creeping, stolons short, branched. Stipes to 15cm, deciduously scaly, pale brown; frond-blade to 100cm or more ×*c*12cm, suberect, narrowly elliptic, pinnae to 6×1.5cm (sterile) or 7×1cm (fertile), to 65 pairs, short-stalked, oblong, apex acuminate, base obtuse or truncate, slightly auricled, entire or dentate, sparsely pubesc. Trop. Afr., SE Asia to Polyn.

N. barbata Copel. = *N. falcata.*

N. biserrata (Sw.) Schott. BROAD SWORD FERN. Rhiz. erect. Stipes 12–60cm, with pale brown linear scales; frond-blade to 3×0.3m, pendent, linear-oblong or broadly linear; pinnae numerous 7–15×1.2–2.5cm, short-stalked, linear-oblong, apex acute to acuminate, base unequal and truncate to cuneate and sometimes subauriculate finely dentate-serrulate to crenate, crenations often minutely toothed, sparsely to densely hairy beneath. Pantrop.

N. bostoniensis hort. = *N. exaltata* 'Bostoniensis'.

N. cordifolia (L.) Presl. ERECT SWORD FERN; LADDER FERN. Rhiz. to 12mm wide, erect or suberect, with stolons, occas. bearing scaly tubers. Stipes 4–20cm, deciduously scaly; frond-blade to 60×5cm, erect, arching or pendent, lanceolate to linear, acute or acuminate, pinnae to 20×9mm (sterile) or 30×5mm (fertile), to 70 pairs, short-stalked, oblong to linear, apex toothed, base unequal and cordate to obtuse, entire or dentate. Pantrop. 'Duffii' (DUFF'S SWORD FERN): rachis usually forked, pinnae orbicular, crowded, attached in more than one plane. 'Plumosa': pinnae lobed.

N. davallioides (Sw.) Kunze. Rhiz. short and erect. Stipe 15–30cm, the base densely covered with scales. Frond blade to 2×0.3m, arching to pendent, linear to lanceolate, attenuate to narrowly acute, pinnae to 12×2cm (sterile pinnae) or 12–20×1.5cm (fertile pinnae), linear to lanceolate, acute at apex, truncate to cuneate to obtuse at base, crenate or lobed. Malay Penins. & Philipp. to New Guinea.

N. duffii Moore = **N. cordifolia** 'Duffii'.

N. exaltata (L.) Schott. BOSTON FERN. Rhiz. short, suberect, with slender stolons. Fronds erect, often in false rosettes; stipes 6–20cm, deciduously scaly; blades linear, 50–250×6–15cm, pinnae numerous, 2–8×0.7–1.3cm, apex acute or subacute, base subcordate with auricle overlapping rachis, bluntly serrulate to crenate. Pantrop. 'Bostoniensis': fronds erect to pendent; the 'original' Boston Fern, which has produced, among others the following sports: 'Childsii': fronds approximate and overlapping, to 4-pinnate, deltoid. 'Elegantissima': fronds 2-pinnate. 'Fluffy Ruffles': fronds dense, to 3-pinnate, deltoid. 'Hillii': fronds 2-pinnate or -pinnatifid, to 1m, pinnae lobed and undulate at margin. 'Rooseveltii': fronds pinnate, pinnae unequal and auriculate at base, undulate. 'Smithii': fronds finely 3-pinnate, lace-like. 'Teddy Junior': fronds dense, pinnae undulate. 'Verona': fronds dense, pendent, to 4-pinnate. 'Whitmannii': fronds to 3-pinnate.

N. falcata (Cav.) C. Chr. Rhiz. short and erect. Stipes 10–20cm, scaly, purple to brown; frond-blade to 2m×10cm, arching to pendent, pinnae close, falcate, apex acute or obtuse, base slightly auricled, minutely crenate, c5.5×1.3cm. Ceylon, Maldives, Burm., Indochina to Philipp. & New Guinea. f. *furcans* Moore (FISHTAIL FERN): pinnae forking at apex.

N. hirsutula (Forst.) Presl. Rhiz. short and erect with slender stolons. Stipes to 25cm or more, erect, scaly near base. Frond black to 100×16cm, arching, pinnae to 8×2cm (sterile) or 8×1cm (fertile), overlapping, apex attenuate to acute, base truncate and auricled, crenate, pubesc. Trop. Asia to Polyn.

N. multiflora (Roxb.) Jarrett ex Morton. ASIAN SWORD FERN. Rhiz. erect, with wiry stolons. Stipes stout; frond-blade 30–100×7–20cm, linear-lanceolate, narrowed towards the base, pinnae 3.5–10×0.5–1.3cm, linear-oblong, acute to long-acuminate, slightly unequal at base, one side rounded, truncate or short-auriculate, the other with a narrow auricle, crenate to sharply serrate. India & trop. Asia, widely nat. Flor., W Indies, C & S Amer.

N. pectinata (Willd.) Schott. BASKET FERN; TOOTHED SWORD FERN. Rhiz. erect, abundantly stoloniferous. Stipes 10–20cm; frond-blades to 30–45×2.5–4cm, elliptic or linear, thin-textured, pinnae 40–50 pairs per frond, apex obtuse, base auriculate, margin shallowly crenate; rachis glab. S Mex. to Peru & Braz., W Indies.

N. pendula (Raddi) J. Sm. Rhiz. suberect to short-creeping, bearing numerous stolons. Stipe 10–35cm; frond-blade 30–150×3.5–7cm, pendent, glab., pinnae sessile or subsessile, apex obtuse, base with rounded auricle, margin entire or slightly crenate. S Mex. to Boliv. & Braz.

→*Aspidium, Davallia, Polypodium* and *Tectaria*.

Nephrophyllidium Gilg. Menyanthaceae. 1 aquatic or marginal rhizomatous perenn. herb. Lvs basal, bluntly toothed, reniform, 5–10cm diam., long-stalked. Fls to 1.25cm diam., in erect stalked term. cymes; pet. white, 5, lanceolate, crested and crisped. Jap. to NW N Amer. Z3.

N. crista-galli (Menz. ex Hook.) Gilg. DEER CABBAGE.

→*Fauria, Menyanthes* and *Villarsia*.

Nephrosperma Balf. f. Palmae. 1 palm to 10m. St. slender, erect, simple, bare and ringed. Lvs pinnate, to 2m, tinged red when young, neatly abcising; sheaths tomentose, covered at first with black spines; pinnae 25–40, to 1m, 1–3-fold, glab. above, scaly beneath. Infl. interfoliar, to 4m, branched once. Fr. to 1cm across, spherical, red. Seych.

N. vanhoutteanum (H.A. Wendl. ex Van Houtte) Balf. f.

→*Oncosperma*.

Nephthytis Schott. Araceae. 7 rhizomatous perenn. herbs. Lvs sagittate or hastate, long-stalked. Peduncle subequal to or much shorter than petiole; spathe expanded, erect, hooded; spadix sessile or shortly stipitate. Fr. an orange berry, in clusters. Trop. W Afr.

N. afzelii Schott. Lvs 35×25cm, sagittate, lobes acute; petiole to 50cm. Peduncle to 45cm; spathe to 7×1cm, green; spadix subsessile, to 6cm.

N. gravenreuthii Engl. = **N. poissonii**.

N. poissonii N.E. Br. Close to **N. afzelii**, but lf. lobes narrow-

acuminate; spathe finely spotted; spadix shortly stipitate.

N. triphylla hort. = *Syngonium podophyllum*.

Neptunia Lour. Leguminosae (Mimosoideae). 12 spreading, occas. floating (marginal) perenn. herbs and shrubs. St. sometimes armed, angled when young, forming massive ribbons of aerenchyma in semi-aquatic spp. Lvs bipinnate, with 'sleep movents' (cf *Mimosa pudica*). Spike crowded, capitate to subspicate; fls usually yellow in globose heads. Cosmop. Z7.

N. lutea (Leavenw.) Benth. Pubesc., perenn. herb. St. to 2m+, often hairy. Lvs with 3–11 pairs of pinnae; lfts to 8×3mm, some 20 pairs per pinna, short-oblong, obtuse or broadly acute. Infl. bright yellow. Late spring–early summer. SC US. Z7.

N. natans (L.) Druce = **N. oleracea**.

N. oleracea Lour. Perenn. herb or subshrub, floating or prostrate near water's edge. St. to 1.5m, developing dense white spongy tissue. Pinnae to 4 per lf; lfts to 18×3.5mm, to 20 pairs per pinna, oblong, obtuse to broadly acute. Infl. yellow-green. Pantrop. Z7.

N. plena (L.) Benth. Similar to **N. oleracea**, distinguished by lvs with 5 pairs pinnae; lfts slightly smaller, to 38 pairs per pinna. Infl. bright yellow. Summer. C Amer., now widespread throughout trop. and subtrop. Z10.

N. tenuis Benth. = **N. lutea**.

→*Acacia* and *Mimosa*.

Nerine Herb. Amaryllidaceae. c30 bulbous perennials. Lvs appearing with or soon after the fls. Infl. umbellate, scapose; perianth funnel-shaped, usually zygomorphic, lobes 6, narrowly lanceolate, free; sta. 6 inserted at the base of the perianth lobes, suberect or declinate, 2 lengths; style filiform, straight or declinate, stigma simple or trifid. S Afr., Les., Bots., Swaz. Z9 unless specified.

N. bowdenii Will. Wats. Lvs to 30×3cm, strap-shaped. Scape to 45cm; fls muskily scented; tep. to 7cm, candy pink to deep rose, rarely white, darker at midrib, undulate; fil. shorter than tep. S Afr. 'Alba': fls white with a blush of pink. 'Hera' (**N. bowdenii** ×**N. sarniensis**): fls rich pink. 'Mark Fenwick' ('Fenwick's Variety'): vigorous; fls soft cyclamen pink, early-flowering. 'Pink Triumph': fls deep pink. 'Wellsii': fls dark pink, tep. crinkled. Z8.

N. curvifolia Herb. = **N. fothergillii**.

N. duparquetiana Bak. Lvs usually prostrate, slender. Scape to 25cm; tep. to 4.5cm, white, suffused or ribbed red-pink and sometimes tinted yellow, strongly recurved and twisted; fil. exceeding tep. S Afr.

N. filamentosa Barker. Lvs to 10cm, v. slender, sometimes sprawling and curling. Scape to 20cm, usually shorter; tep. to 2cm, bright rose, strongly recurved and rolled at tips; fil. far exceeding perianth. S Afr.

N. filifolia Bak. Lvs to 20cm, v. slender, suberect. Scape to 30cm, somewhat glandular-pubesc.; tep. to 2.5cm, white, rose pink, magenta or bright crimson, clawed, crisped; fil. shorter than tep. S Afr.

N. flexuosa Herb. Lvs to 2cm wide, linear-lorate, arching, sometimes rough and pustular. Scape to 1m, flexuous; pale pink or white to 3cm, crisped; fil. shorter than tep. 'Alba': fls white, edges somewhat ruffled. S Afr.

N. fothergillii M. Roem. Lvs 6–8, falcate. Scape to 60cm; tep. scarlet, 2cm, subundulate, strongly recurved, somewhat spiralling; fil. slightly exceeding tep. S Afr.

N. humilis Herb. Lvs to 30×1.5cm, linear, suberect. Scape to 35cm; tep. bright pale pink to deep rose, to 3cm, crisped; fil. equalling tep. S Afr.

N. masonorum Bol. Lvs to 20cm, threadlike. Scape to 30cm, downy; tep. to 1.5cm, pale to deep rose-pink, recurved, undulate, with a deep pink longitudinal stripe. S Afr. (Cape Prov.).

N. sarniensis Herb. GUERNSEY LILY. Lvs to 30×2cm, suberect. Scape to 45cm; tep. to 3.5cm, pale rose-red to scarlet, pink, rarely white, strongly recurved at tips, slightly crisped; fil. 1.2cm longer than tep. Coastal S Afr. 'Kirstenbosch White': fls pure white.

N. undulata Herb. Lvs to 45×1.2cm, linear. Scape to 45cm; tep to 2cm, pale candy pink or rose, strongly crisped; fil. equalling lobes. S Afr.

N. veitchii hort. = **N. bowdenii**.

N. cvs. V. short. 'Hero': to 34cm; flowerheads 16cm diam.; fls 12, 7cm wide, red-violet. 'Hotspur': to 34cm; flowerheads 10cm wide; fls 13, 6cm wide, deep magenta. 'Ixanthia': to 30cm; flowerheads 5.5cm wide; fls 11, 5cm wide, pink-carmine. 'Kate Cicely': to 30cm; fls 8, 8cm wide, flame. 'Latu': to 36cm; flowerheads 14cm wide; fls 14, 6cm wide, white, red-ribbed. 'Patina': to 38cm; flowerheads 11cm wide; fls 11, 5cm wide, pale pink. 'Phoebe': to 30cm; flowerheads 13cm wide; fls 6, 5.5cm wide, blue-violet. 'Priscilla': to 37cm; flowerheads 13cm wide; fls 13,

6cm wide, pink. 'Pym': to 36cm; flowerheads 12cm wide; fls 7, 6.5cm wide, pink.

V. early (July-August). 'Anna Fletcher': to 51cm; flowerheads 12.5cm wide; fls 11, 6cm wide, apricot. 'Catherine': to 51cm; flowerheads 17cm wide; fls 14, 5cm wide, light red. 'Diana Wharton': to 42cm; flowerheads 13cm wide; fls 8, 6.5cm wide, mid-red. 'Fothergillii Major': to 51cm; fls 12, 14cm wide, fls 12, 6cm wide, deep orange-red. 'Glensavage Gem': to 78cm; flowerheads 21cm wide; fls 13, crimson. 'Hera': to 90cm; flowerheads 21cm wide; fls 16, 8cm wide, rose-carmine. 'Miss Eva Godman': to 42cm; flowerheads 16cm wide; fls 8, 6cm wide, light red. 'Mrs Bromely': to 60cm; flowerheads 12cm wide; fls 11, 6cm wide, red-orange. 'Paula Knight': to 60cm; fls 12, 7cm wide, china rose. 'Plymouth': to 60cm; flowerheads 16cm wide; fls 12, 7cm wide, mid-red.

V. tall. 'Blush Beauty': to 120cm; flowerheads to 16cm wide; fls 14, 7cm wide, v. pale pink. 'Guy Fawkes': to 72cm; flowerheads 15cm wide; fls 14, 6½cm wide; light cerise. 'Kilwa': to 84cm; flowerheads 17cm wide; fls 14, 7cm wide; magenta. 'Kingship': to 75cm; flowerheads 15cm wide; fls 17, 5cm wide; cerise-purple. 'Mansellii': to 72cm; flowerheads 16cm wide; fls 18, 6cm wide; mid-cerise. 'Mischief': to 75cm; flowerheads 14cm wide; fls 14, 7cm wide; cerise-mauve. 'Namba': to 120cm; flowerheads 19cm wide; fls 17, 4cm wide; mid-pink. 'Parbet II': to 123cm; flowerheads 19cm wide; fls 10, 7½cm wide; pink, deep pink. 'Rushmere Star': to 72cm; flowerheads 16cm wide; fls 10, 7cm wide; bright magenta. 'Supremo': to 108cm; flowerheads 24cm wide; fls 15, 7cm wide; white/pale pink.

V. late (late October and November). 'Ancilla': to 66cm; flowerheads 12cm wide; fls 15, 6cm wide; purple-red. 'Bennet Poe': to 54cm; flowerheads 13cm wide; fls 13, 6½cm wide; mid-cerise. 'Cranfield': to 75cm; flowerheads 15cm wide; fls 16, 6cm wide; cerise. 'Konak': to 75cm; flowerheads 14cm wide; fls 12, 5cm wide; white/purple. 'Koriba': to 66cm; flowerheads 12cm wide; fls 12, 7cm wide; cerise. 'Kymina': to 75cm; flowerheads 14cm wide; fls 14, 7cm wide; pale pink. 'Mansellii': to 72cm; flowerheads 16cm wide; fls 18, 6cm wide; mid-cerise. 'Namba': to 120cm; flowerheads 19cm wide; fls 17, 4cm wide; mid-pink. 'Pink Triumph': to 60cm: flowerheads 15cm wide; fls 15, 6cm wide; fuchsia pink. 'Wombe': to 57cm; flowerheads 16.5cm wide; fls 14, 6cm wide; orange-red. 'Zeal Giant': fls vivid deep pink, in large heads.

Nerium L. OLEANDER; ROSE BAY. Apocynaceae. 1 toxic glab. evergr. shrub, 2–6m. Br. spreading to erect. Lvs 10–22cm, lanceolate, sharp-tipped, coriaceous, dark green, midrib prominent above; petiole short. Cymes compound, terminal; fls showy, often fragrant; cal. lobes 5, to one quarter length of cor.; cor. funnelform, white to deep pink or pale yellow, tube slender-cylindric, throat dilated, limb 2.5–5cm diam., spreading, deeply 5-lobed, encircling a crown of 5 ragged seg. at throat; sta. attached below throat, included. Medit. to W China, widely nat. Z9

N. indicum Mill. = *N. oleander*.

N. odorum Sol. = *N. oleander*.

N. oleander L. Over 400 cvs have been recorded. For a checklist, see F.JJ. Pagen, *Agricultural University Wageningen Papers*, 87–2 (1987). These are variously scented or unscented, conform to one of three cor. types – single, superposed (hose-in-hose) and fully double, and range in colour from white to cream, pink, red, carmine, purple, yellow, salmon, apricot, flesh and copper. Several have variegated lvs.

Nero's Crown *Tabernaemontana divaricata*.

Nertera Banks & Sol. ex Gaertn. Rubiaceae. 15 mossy diminutive, creeping perenn. herbs. St. threadlike. Lvs bright green, minute, opposite. Fls solitary, inconspicuous. Fr. a drupe, sometimes colourful. S China and SE Asia to Aus., NZ, Polyn., Antarc. and Hawaii to C & S Amer., Tristan da Cunha. Z9.

N. balfouriana Ckn. Forming mats to 25cm wide. Lvs to 5×4mm, usually broad-ovate or -oblong, or obovate, obtuse at apex and base. Fr. to 1cm, squat-pyriform, yellow-orange. NZ.

N. ciliata T. Kirk. Forming mats to 20cm wide, sometimes pilose. Lvs to 5×5mm, ovate, apex acute or obtuse, base cuneate and obtuse, ciliate. Fr. 4mm diam., globose minutely pubesc., orange. NZ.

N. cunninghamii Hook. f. Forming mats to 20cm wide. Lvs to 8×3mm, narrowly ovate, apex narrowed and acute, base narrowed and obtuse. Fr. to 4mm diam., globose, red. NZ.

N. depressa Banks & Sol. ex Gaertn. = *N. granadensis*.

N. granadensis (Mutis) Druce. BEAD PLANT; CORAL MOSS; ENGLISH BABYTEARS. Forming patches to 40cm wide or more. Lvs to 8×5mm, usually smaller ovate to orbicular, apex obtuse or acute, base narrowed and obtuse or subcordate. Fr. 5mm wide, globose or ovoid, orange to dark red. S Amer., Taiwan and SE

Asia, Aus. and Tasm., NZ. cf. *Soleirolia soleirolii* (*Helxine soleirolii*), for which this plant is sometimes mistaken when not in fr.

Nerve Plant *Fittonia verschaffeltii* var. *argyroneura*.

Nervilia Comm. ex Gaudich. Orchidaceae. 80 terrestrial tuberous orchids. Lf broad, usually cordate, often pleated and lustrous, solitary, erect or prostrate, appearing after flowering. Rac. 1- to many-fld, scapose, tep. narrowly lanceolate, projecting forwards; lip semi-tubular, entire or trilobed. Arabia, mainland Afr., Madag., Masc. Is., India, SE Asia to Jap., Pacific Is. and Aus. Z10.

N. bicarinata (Bl.) Schltr. To 75cm. Lf to 17×22cm, reniform, apiculate, cordate at base, dark green, pleated, petiole 18–20cm. Fls scape, lip creamy white, veined purple; tep 20–30mm, lip 28–30×20–24mm, with 2 fleshy ridges running from base to junction of lobes, midlobe ovate, acute. Widespread in trop. Afr.; Arabia.

N. kotschyi (Rchb. f.) Schltr. 10–28cm. Lf 3–12×4–13cm, broadly cordate or ovate, acute, ribbed, veins jagged above. Fls veined green-brown, lip white or pale yellow, marked purple; tep. 14–20mm; lip 14–18×9–12mm, midlobe ovate, undulate, pubesc. between 2 longitudinal, fleshy ridges. Trop. Afr. (widespread). Z10.

N. purpurata (Rchb. f. & Sonder) Schltr. To 22cm. Lf to 10×4cm, ovate or elliptic, green above, purple beneath with prominent veins, petiole to 15cm. Fls green or yellow-green, lip veined purple; tep. to 28mm; lip 18×13mm, pubesc. between 2 longitudinal fleshy ridges, midlobe triangular-ovate, obtuse. Zaire, Zam., Tanz., Angola, S Afr.

N. umbrosa (Rchb. f.) Schltr. = *N. bicarinata*.

Net Bush *Calothamnus*.

Netleaf Oak *Quercus reticulata*.

Netted Brake *Pteris comans*.

Nettle-leaved Bellflower *Campanula trachelium*.

Nettle-leaved Mullein *Verbascum chaixii*.

Nettle-leaved Vervain *Verbena urticifolia* var. *leiocarpa*.

Nettle Tree *Celtis*.

Net-veined Willow *Salix reticulata*.

Never-never Plant *Ctenanthe oppenheimiana*.

Neviusia A. Gray. SNOW WREATH. Rosaceae. 1 erect, decid., extremely stoloniferous shrub to 1.5m. Shoots slender, lanuginose at first. Lvs to 7cm, subdistichous, oval or oblong, downy later glab., doubly serrate above. Fls to 2.5cm diam. in short, open cymes; pet. 0; sta. conspicuous to 8.5mm, fil. white, anth. yellow. Summer. SE US. Z5.

N. alabamensis A. Gray.

Newbouldia Seem. Bignoniaceae. 1 tree, 3–10m. Lvs imparipinnate; lfts 5–28cm, 7–11, elliptic to narrow-obovate, entire to dentate, scaly beneath. Cor. pale purple-red or pink with darker streaks, tube 3–4cm, lobes 1–2cm. Fr. 1.6–32× 0.3–1.6cm, linear. Senegal to Cameroun and Gabon. Z10.

N. laevis (P. Beauv.) Seem. ex Bur.

N. pentandra (Hook.) Seem. = *N. laevis*.

→*Spathodea*.

New Caledonian Yew *Austrotaxus*.

New Caledonia Pine *Araucaria columnaris*.

New England Ash *Eucalyptus andrewsii*.

New England Blackbutt *Eucalyptus andrewsii*.

Newfoundland Dwarf Birch *Betula michauxii*.

New Guinea Creeper *Mucuna bennettii*.

New Jersey Tea *Ceanothus americanus*.

New Mexican Privet *Forestiera neomexicana*.

New Mexico Prairie Mallow *Sidalcea neomexicana*.

New Year Lily *Gladiolus cardinalis*.

New York Fern *Parathelypteris novae-boracensis*.

New Zealand *Halocarpus bidwilli*.

New Zealand Bluebell *Wahlenbergia albomarginata*.

New Zealand Blueberry *Dianella nigra*.

New Zealand Brass Buttons *Cotula perpusilla*.

New Zealand Bur *Acaena*.

New Zealand Cabbage Palm *Cordyline australis*.

New Zealand Christmas Tree *Metrosideros excelsus*.

New Zealand Dacryberry *Dacrycarpus dacryidioides*.

New Zealand Edelweiss *Leucogenes*.

New Zealand Flax *Phormium tenax*.

New Zealand Hemp *Phormium tenax*.

New Zealand Honeysuckle *Knightia excelsa*.

New Zealand Laurel *Corynocarpus*.

New Zealand Lilac *Hebe hulkeana*.

New Zealand Privet *Geniostoma*.

New Zealand Satin Flower *Libertia grandiflora.*
New Zealand Tea Tree *Leptospermum scoparium.*
New Zealand Wind Grass *Stipa arundinacea.*
New Zealand Wine Berry *Aristotelia serrata.*

Neyraudia Hook. f. Gramineae. 6 perenn. grasses to 3m, resembling *Phragmites* in general appearance. Lvs linear. Infl. an open many-fld pan.; spikelets 4–8-fld. OW Trop. Z9.
N. reynaudiana (Kunth) Keng ex A. Hitchc. BURMA REED. St. to 3m. Lvs flat, to 1m×4cm. Pan. pendent, to 80cm; spikelets to 9mm. S Asia.
→*Arundo.*

Ngaio *Myoporum sandwiciense.*
Nibung Palm *Oncosperma tigilarum.*

Nicandra Adans. Solanaceae. 1 glab. ann. herb to 130cm. St. erect, branching. Lvs to 10cm or more, elliptic-lanceolate to rhombic-ovate, wavy-toothed to slightly lobed. Fls to 3.5cm, solitary, ephemeral; cal. 5-lobed, accrescent, purple, later scarious, to 3cm; cor. broadly campanulate, to 4cm diam., cor. tube white, limb lilac-purple to blue and white. Fr. a 3–5-chambered subglobose berry, to 15mm diam., brown, enclosed by cal. Summer–autumn. Peru. Z8.
N. physaloides (L.) Gaertn. SHOO FLY; APPLE OF PERU. 'Violacea': upper section of cor. indigo, lower white.

Nicarago Britt. & Rose.
N. vesicaria (L.) Britt. & Rose = *Caesalpinia vesicaria.*

Nicaraguan Cocao-shade *Gliricidia sepium.*
Nichol's Willow-leafed Peppermint *Eucalyptus nicholii.*

Nicodemia Ten.
N. diversifolia (Vahl) Ten. = *Buddleja indica.*

Nicolaia Horan.
N. elatior (Jack) Horan = *Etlingera elatior.*
N. speciosa (Bl.) Horan = *Etlingera elatior.*

Nicotiana L. TOBACCO. Solanaceae. Some 67 mostly clammy aromatic, ann. or perenn. herbs and shrubs. Lvs simple. Infl. term., paniculate; fls actinomorphic to zygomorphic, nocturnally scented; cal. tubular to subglobose, or campanulate, pentamerous; cor. tubular to funnelform, 5-lobed; sta. 5, included to slightly exserted. Trop. Amer., Aus., Nam.
N. acuminata (Graham) Hook. Ann., to 2m. St. viscid, branched. Lvs broad-ovate to lanceolate or triangular-lanceolate, to 25cm, acuminate, petiolate, undulate. Cor. white tinged green, lined dark green or violet-red; tube to 8cm, limb to 2cm diam. Summer. Chile, Arg. var. *acuminata.* Cor. 5–9cm. var. *multiflora* (Philippi) Reiche. Lvs stalked. Cor. 2.5–4cm. var. *compacta* Goodsp. Lvs sessile. Cor. 2.5–4cm.
N. affinis hort. ex T. Moore = *N. alata.*
N. alata Link & Otto. JASMINE TOBACCO; FLOWERING TOBACCO. Perenn., to 1.5m. St. viscid, sparsely branched. Lvs spathulate-ovate, to 25cm, apex obtuse, base decurrent or clasping, petiole winged. Cor. green-white, interior white, to 10cm, pubesc., limb to 2.5cm diam. For cvs see *N. × sanderae.* Summer. NE Arg. to S Braz. Z7.
N. attenuata Torr. ex S. Wats. Ann. to 140cm. St. simple or branched, sticky pubesc. Lvs elliptic, to 10cm, viscid, upper lvs narrower, smaller. Cor. white tinged rose, tube to 3cm, interior white, limb to 1cm diam. SW US, Mex. Z8.
N. axillaris Lam. = *Petunia axillaris.*
N. bigelovii (Torr.) S. Wats. Ann., to 2m. St. clammy-pubesc., br. ascending. Lvs oblong-lanceolate, to 20cm, upper lvs smaller, to 8cm, apex obtuse. Cor. to 5cm, white tinged green, limb to 3cm+ diam. Summer. W US. Z6.
N. forgetiana hort. Sander ex Hemsl. Ann. or short-lived perenn., to 90cm. St. pubesc., branched below. Lvs oblong, pubesc., to 30cm, papery, apex obtuse, lower lvs winged below, upper lvs decurrent. Cor. narrow, to 3cm, tube interior pale green, exterior purple-red, limb scarlet. Braz. Z8.
N. fragrans Hook. Perenn., to 2m. St. soft-pubesc., occas. viscid. Lvs in apical clusters, narrow-linear to oblanceolate, to 20cm. Cor. tube to 10cm, white, tinged green, limb to 1.2cm diam., white. S Pacific, Polyn. Z10.
N. glauca Graham. TREE TOBACCO; MUSTARD TREE. Shrub, to 6m+. St. erect, soft-woody, glab., glaucous. Lvs to 30cm, elliptic to lanceolate or cordate-ovate, glaucous, weakly sinuate. Cor. cream yellow-green, exterior pubesc., tube to 4.5cm, limb to 0.4cm, terete to 5-ridged, lobes short, throat slightly inflated. Autumn. S Boliv. to N Arg., nat. US. Z8.
N. langsdorffii J.A. Weinm. Ann., to 1.5m+. St. erect, branched, viscid-pubesc. Lvs ovate, undulate, apex blunt, base

attenuate, upper lvs decurrent. Cor. lime green, tube to 2.5cm, viscid, limb small, pleated. Summer. Braz. Z9.
N. longiflora Cav. Ann., to 1.5m. St. slender, sparsely stiffly pubesc. Lvs lanceolate to spathulate, undulate, apex slender. Cor. violet, exterior green or pearly violet; tube to 12cm, pubesc., limb to 4cm diam. Autumn. Tex. to Chile, Arg. Z8.
N. noctiflora Hook. Perenn., to 90cm+. St. slender, erect to procumbent, pubesc., branched. Lvs oblong-lanceolate, undulate, apex acute. Cor. interior white, exterior green tinged purple, limb to 1.5cm diam. Autumn. Chile. Z8.
N. persica Lindl. = *N. alata.*
N. ruralis Vell. = *N. langsdorffii.*
N. rustica L. TOBACCO; WILD TOBACCO. Ann., viscid-pubesc., to 1.5m. Lvs ovate to ovate-obtuse or elliptic, to 30cm+; cor. to 2cm, yellow tinged green, limb to 0.6cm+ diam. Summer-autumn. S Amer. (Andes, Ecuad. to Boliv.), Mex. Z8.
N. × sanderae hort. Sander ex Will. Wats. (*N. alata × N. forgetiana.*) Shrubby, viscid-pubesc. ann. to 60cm+. Lvs spathulate, undulate, upper lvs oblong-lanceolate. Cor. tube green-yellow at base, limb to 4cm+ diam., red, occas. white or green to rose or purple. Gdn origin. 'Breakthrough': dwarf, compact, fls fragrant in a range of colours; early flowering. 'Crimson King': fls deep crimson. 'Daylight Sensation': fls day-blooming in shades of lavender, purple, white and rose. 'Dwarf White Bedder': habit low, bushy; fls pure white, fragrant. 'Fragrant Cloud': fls pure white, large, fragrant at night. 'Grandiflora': fls large, cor. throat large, widely dilated. 'Lime Green': fls bright yellow tinged green, abundant. 'Nana': habit dwarf. Nikki Hybrids: habit bushy, hardy; fls in range of colours including white, shades of pink, red and yellow. 'Rubella': fls rose-red. Sensation Hybrids: fls in range of colours including pink, red and white, fragrant. 'Sutton's Scarlet': cor. dark red. 'White': fls heavily scented. Z7.
N. suaveolens Lehm. Ann., to 1.5m. St. numerous, densely pubesc. below. Lvs oblanceolate to ovate-lanceolate, to 25cm; petiole winged. Cor. green-purple, interior white; tube slender, to 45mm, limb to 35mm diam. Summer. SE Aus. Z8.
N. sylvestris Speg. & Comes. Ann., to 1.5m. St. robust, branched, base woody. Lvs to 35cm, sessile, elliptic to elliptic-ovate, blue-grey, wrinkled, pinnatifid, term. lobe enlarged to 30cm+. Fls white, fragrant; cor. tube spindle-shaped, to 8.5cm, swollen above, exterior pubesc., limb to 3cm diam. Summer. Arg. Z8.
N. tabacum L. TOBACCO; COMMON TOBACCO. Ann. or bienn., viscid-pubesc., to 120cm. St. often becoming woody at base. Lvs ovate to elliptic or lanceolate, to 25cm. Cor. green-white to rose, tube inflated, to 5.5cm, exterior soft pubesc., limb to 1.5cm. Summer. NE Arg., Boliv. var. *macrophylla* Schrank. Lvs to 40cm, undulate, ovate or cordate. Fls rose to carmine red. Z8. 'Variegata' ('Connecticut Shade'): lvs to 30cm, variegated cream with green; fls white tinged pink.
N. tomentosa Ruiz & Pav. Shrub to 7m. St. to 3, branched. Lvs ovate to lanceolate, to 11cm, viscid; petiole winged. Cor. exterior glandular-pubesc., to 3.5cm, pale green-yellow, limb pink to red or white. S & C Peru, WC Boliv. Z9.
N. torreyana Nels. & Macbr. = *N. attenuata.*
N. undulata Vent. = *N. suavolens.*
N. wigandioides Koch & Fintelm. Perenn. shrub, sticky-pubesc., to 3m. St. white-pubesc. Lvs ovate, to 50cm, undulate, pubesc. above, acute or acuminate; petiole to 12cm. Cor. white, tinged yellow or green, salverform, to 1.5cm, limb to 1.3cm diam. Summer. Boliv. Z9.

Nicury *Syagrus coronata.*

Nidema Britt. & Millsp. Orchidaceae. 2 epiphytic orchids. Rhiz. elongate. Pbs fusiform to cylindrical, stalked, apically unifoliate. Lvs coriaceous, ligulate to linear-lanceolate. Rac. term.; bracts lanceolate; fls small; sep. free, linear to lanceolate; pet. smaller, broader; lip simple, acute or acuminate, sometimes papillose, disc with a grooved callus. Trop. Amer. Z10.
N. boothii (Lindl.) Schltr. Pbs to 6cm. Lvs to 25×1.5cm. Infl. to 15cm; fls white-green or ivory, fragrant; sep. to 20mm, linear lanceolate; lip to 11×4mm, oblong-oblanceolate to linear-spathulate, subacute to rounded, serrulate, calli yellow. Mex. to Panama, W Indies, N S Amer.
N. ottonis (Rchb. f.) Britt. & Millsp. Pbs to 4cm. Lvs to 19×1cm. Infl. to 11cm; fls white or cream, sometimes tinged yellow or green; sep. to 11mm, lanceolate or oblong-lanceolate; lip to 7×2mm, linear-oblong, apiculate, incurved, canaliculate. W Indies, Panama, Colomb., Peru, Braz., Nic., Venez.
→*Epidendrum* and *Maxillaria.*

Nidularium Lem. Bromeliaceae. 23 stemless, perenn., terrestrial or epiphytic herbs. Lvs in a flat rosette, innermost reduced, brilliantly coloured in fl.; leaf-sheaths large, forming funnel-shaped tanks, blades ligulate. Infl. term., compound; fls in flat fascicles, surrounded by showy bracts; scape short, bracteate; pet. fleshy, erect, fused into a tube. E & SE Braz. Z10.

N. billbergioides (Schult. f.) L.B. Sm. Lvs 30–70cm, green, laxly toothed, spines 0.5mm. Infl. c8cm; scape slender, erect; bracts green to orange and red-brown at infl. apex; pet. white. var. *citrinum* (Burchell ex Bak.) Reitz. Infl. bracts bright yellow.

N. burchellii (Bak.) Mez. Lvs to 50cm, dark green above, flushed purple and slightly scaly beneath, spiny-denticulate. Infl. orange, crowded, subglobose, red-tomentose; scape short, red-brown, scurfy; pet. white.

N. carolinae Lem. ex Bak. = *Neoregelia carolinae*.

N. ×chantrieri André. (*N. innocentii ×N. fulgens*.) Lvs dark green, mottled maroon, with maroon margins and spines. Infl. bracts bright cerise; pet. white. Gdn origin.

N. fulgens Lem. Lvs to 40cm, pale green with darker mottling, pungent, slightly scaly beneath, laxly toothed. Infl. crowded, domed, on a v. or 0 short scape; bracts bright cerise, coarsely toothed; sep. red; pet. white, tipped dark blue, with white margins.

N. innocentii Lem. Lvs 20–60cm, purple- to blood-red beneath or throughout, shiny, toothed. Scape short; infl. bracts red tipped green, large, toothed; floral bracts papery; sep. white or pink; pet. white with green bases. var. *lineatum* (Mez) L.B. Sm. Lvs pale green with many fine, longitudinal white lines. Infl. bracts green, apices brick-red. Known only in cult. var. *paxianum* (Mez) L.B. Sm. Lvs green, with a single, large, median white stripe. Infl. bracts green, tipped red. var. *striatum* Wittm. Lvs green, with longitudinal white stripes. Infl. bracts carmine. Known only in cult.

N. lindenii Reg. = *Canistrum lindenii*.

N. lineatum Mez = *N. innocentii* var. *lineatum*.

N. makoyanum E. Morr. ex Mez = *N. innocentii* var. *striatum*.

N. marechalii hort. (Makoy) ex Bak. = *Neoregelia princeps*.

N. microps E. Morr. ex Mez. Lvs to 25cm, channelled, toothed. Infl. subsessile, crowded, capitate, rusty-tomentose; infl. bracts purple, large, with tiny teeth; sep. dark red; pet. white.

N. mooreanum hort. (Haage & Schmidt) = *Neoregelia pineliana*.

N. paxianum Mez = *N. innocentii* var. *paxianum*.

N. pictum hort. ex Bak. = *N. fulgens*.

N. princeps E. Morr. ex Bak. = *Neoregelia princeps*.

N. procerum Lindm. Rosette large, robust, erect. Lvs 0.4–1m, broadly acuminate, tough, finely toothed, pale waxy green tinted copper. Infl. bracts tinted red to strong red (var. *kermesianum*); fls vermilion tipped blue. Brazil.

N. seidelii L.B. Sm. & Reitz. Lvs to 80cm, slightly scaly. Infl. to 15cm, subcylindric; scape to 30cm, erect, rusty-tomentose; infl. bracts to 6cm, yellow to purple, concealing fls; sep. brown-tomentose at base; pet. white.

N. 'Souvenir de Casmir Morobe'. (*N. rutilans ×Neoregelia princeps*.) Large. Lvs broad, lush green with light marbling, inner rosette brilliant red.

N. spectabile hort. ex Bak. = *Neoregelia princeps*.

→*Aechmea*.

Nierembergia Ruiz & Pav. CUPFLOWER. Solanaceae. 23 ann. or perenn. herbs or subshrubs. St. slender, creeping, spreading or erect. Fls solitary, term. or in cymes; cal. tubular to campanulate, lobes spreading; cor. tubular, limb spreading, 5-lobed. S Amer. Z8 unless specified.

N. angustifolia HBK = *N. scoparia*.

N. caerulea Sealy = *N. hippomanica* var. *violacea*.

N. calycina Hook. Procumbent shrublet. St. glandular-pubesc. Lvs to 2cm, obovate to spathulate, obtuse; petiole to 3mm. Cor. tube to 6cm yellow, limb white. Autumn. Urug., Arg.

N. filicaulis Lindl. = *N. linariifolia*.

N. frutescens Durieu. Shrublet to 80cm, profusely branched. Lvs to 5cm, sessile, linear to narrow-spathulate. Cor. to 2.5cm diam., tube yellow, limb pale blue, fading to white at margin. Summer–autumn. Chile. 'Albiflora': fls white. 'Atroviolacea': compact; fls deep purple. 'Grandiflora': fls large to 3cm wide. 'Purple Robe': mat-forming, dense to 15cm; fls rich violet-blue, cup-shaped.

N. gracilis Hook. Perenn. herb. St. softly pubesc., to 45. Lvs to 3cm, lanceolate, obtuse, pubesc. to glab.; petiole to 1cm. Cor. white streaked purple, centre yellow, tube to 1.5cm, limb to 4cm diam. Summer. Parag., Arg. Z7.

N. hippomanica Miers. Herb to 30cm+. St. erect, densely branched, stiffly white-pubesc. Lvs to 0.8cm, spathulate, pubesc., acute. Cor. blue tinged violet, tube to 9mm, to 18mm diam., slender, yellow. Summer–autumn. Arg. var. *violacea* Millán. Fls violet blue. 'Purple Robe': rounded habit; lvs narrow; fls purple-blue.

N. hippomanica hort. non Miers = *N. calycina*.

N. linariifolia Graham. Herb to 30cm. St. slender, erect, glandular-pubesc. Lvs linear-lanceolate. Cor. lilac, throat

yellow, exterior glandular-pubesc., interior glab., tube purple. Spring. Arg.

N. repens Ruiz & Pav. WHITECUP. Spreading procumbent perenn. herb. St. slender, glab. to pubesc. Lvs spathulate, obtuse. Cor. tube cylindric, to 6cm×1mm, white, tinged yellow or rose pink at base. Summer. Andes, warm temp. S Amer. 'Violet Queen': fls rich purple-blue. Z7.

N. rivularis Miers = *N. repens*.

N. scoparia Sendt. TALL CUPFLOWER. To 50cm. St. densely branched, subglabrous, glaucous. Lvs to 2cm, spathulate, obtuse. Cor. violet, pilose, tube to 1.5cm, limb to 3cm diam. Braz., Urug., Arg. var. *glaberrima* Millán. Glab., fls smaller.

N. veitchii Hook. Prostrate herb. St. slender, branching, glab. to sparsely pubesc. Lvs to 3.5cm, ovate to oblong. Cor. pale lilac to violet, tube slender, campanulate, to 3.5cm, pubesc. S Amer.

Nigella L. FENNEL FLOWER; WILD FENNEL; LOVE-IN-A-MIST; DEVIL-IN-A-BUSH. Ranunculaceae. Some 14 ann. herbs. St. erect, usually simple. Lvs finely 1–3-pinnatisect, seg. linear to v. slender. Fls solitary, terminal and axill., often subtended by an involucre of conspicuously veined lvs terminating in hair-like divisions; sep. 5, petaloid; pet. 5–10, smaller than sep., sta. numerous. Fr. composed of united follicles forming a capsule, ultimately inflated with persistent horn-like styles. Eurasia.

N. aristata Sibth. & Sm. = *N. arvensis* ssp. *aristata*.

N. arvensis L. WILD FENNEL. To 50cm. Lvs pinnatisect, 3-parted or entire, seg. filiform. Fls 2–3cm diam., pale blue, lacking an involucre. Fr. follicles united for two-thirds of length, 3-veined, with long-beak-like style. Summer. Eur. ssp. *aristata* (Sibth. & Sm.) Nyman. Lvs glaucescent, rigid, seg. narrower; uppermost lvs forming an involucre. Greece (Cyclades).

N. ciliaris DC. Resembling *N. orientalis*. All parts sparsely villous. Fls yellow-white. Fr. follicles flattened, connate for one-third their length, prominently 3-veined. Syr.

N. damascena L. LOVE-IN-A-MIST. To 50cm. Lf seg. filiform. Involucral lvs finely divided; fls white, rose pink, pale or purple-blue, 3.5–4.5cm diam. Fr. a subglobose inflated capsule, 10-locular, follicles wholly fused. S Eur., N Afr. 'Blue Midget': to 25cm; fls blue. 'Cambridge Blue': st. long; fls double, large, blue. 'Dwarf Moody Blue': dwarf, neat; fls semi-double, violet turning sky-blue. Miss Jekyll Hybrids: tall; fls semi-double in variety of colours including white, pink and blue. 'Mulberry Rose': fls double, large, pale pink. 'Oxford Blue': fls double, large, dark blue. Persian Jewels: fls white, pink, red and purple. 'Red Jewel': fls deep rose.

N. diversifolia Franch. = *N. integrifolia*.

N. hispanica L. FENNEL FLOWER. To 20–40cm, branching. Lf seg. slender but not filiform. Fls 4–5cm diam., solitary or paired, lacking involucre, bright blue; sta. red. Follicles ribbed, almost entirely fused, gland., styles spreading. Summer. Spain, S Fr. 'Alba': fls white. 'Atropurpurea': fls purple. 'Curiosity': fls deep blue, centre black, sta. maroon.

N. integrifolia Reg. St. to 25cm, pubesc., simple or much branched. Lower lvs linear-lanceolate to oblong-lanceolate, entire, 2–3cm; st. lvs palmatiparite, seg. linear, sessile. Fls 1–1.6cm diam., pale blue, in cymes; involucre exceeding fl. Fr. follicles 3, connate most of length, capsule 8–12mm, with short beak, hairy. Summer. Turkestan.

N. nigellastrum (L.) Willk. St. 20–40cm, slightly branched. Lvs v. finely divided into long, linear seg. Fls 10mm diam., white-green tinged red. Fr. follicles 2–3, connate at base. Summer. Medit. to SW Asia.

N. orientalis L. St. 10–90cm. Lf seg. linear, somewhat glaucous. Fls to 3cm diam., yellow-white, spotted red, involucre 0. Fr. of 2–14 follicles, united to middle, divergent above, beak erect, shorter than follicle. Spring–summer. SW Asia.

N. sativa L. BLACK CUMIN; NUTMEG FLOWER; ROMAN CORIANDER. St. to 30cm, erect, branched, pubesc. Lvs 2–3cm, seg. linear to oblong-lanceolate, short. Fls 3.5–4.5cm diam., white tinged blue, without involucre. Fr. inflated, follicles 3–7, fused to base of outspread styles. Summer. SW Asia, cult. Eur. and N Afr.

Night-blooming Cereus *Hylocereus undatus*.
Night Jessamine *Cestrum nocturnum*.
Night Phlox *Zaluzianskya capensis*.
Night-scented Stock *Matthiola longipetala*.
Nightshade *Solanum*.
Night-smelling Hermannia *Hermannia flammea*.

Nigritella Rich. Orchidaceae. 1 tuberous terrestrial orchid. St. 5–30cm, slender. Lvs linear-lanceolate. Spike term., 10–25cm, dense, conical-ovoid; fls back-crimson, vanilla-scented; tep. lanceolate to triangular; lip subtriangular or ovate-lanceolate, entire or trilobed, spur short. Summer. Scand. to Greece. Z7.

N. nigra (L.) Rchb. f. BLACK VANILLA ORCHID.

Nikau Palm *Rhopalostylis* (*R. sapida*).
Nikko Fir *Abies homolepis*.
Nikko Maple *Acer maximowiczianum*.
Ninebark *Physocarpus opulifolius*.
Nin-sin *Panax ginseng*.
Niobe Willow *Salix* ×*pendulina*.

Niphaea Lindl. Gesneriaceae. 5 perenn. herbs. Lvs often crowded near st. apex, thin, petiolate. Fls small, white, 2+ per axil; pedicels usually drooping, hairy; cal. turbinate-campanulate, 5-lobed; cor. subrotate, tube v. short, lobes 5, broad. C & S Amer. Z10.
N. oblonga Lindl. Small herb; st. rusty-hairy. Lvs ovate, obtuse or acute at apex, coarsely serrate, hirsute. Winter. Guat.
N. roezlii Reg. Dwarf herb, white- to rusty-hairy throughout. Lvs ovate, obtuse at apex, crenate, 5cm, dark green, rugose.
→*Phinaea*.

Niphidium J. Sm. Polypodiaceae. 10 epiphytic, lithophytic or terrestrial ferns. Rhiz. creeping, covered with roots as well as scales. Fronds stipitate, simple, entire, leathery, glaucous. Trop. Amer. Z10.
N. americanum (Hook. J. Sm. = *N. longifolium*.
N. crassifolium (L.) Lellinger. Fronds to 90×13cm, ovate or lanceolate to elliptic, narrowly acute at apex; costa sparsely scaly; stipes to 30cm. C to S Amer.
N. longifolium (Cav.) C. Morton & Lellinger. Fronds to 60×2cm, linear, apex narrowly acute, glab. and lustrous above, stellate-pubesc. beneath; stipes to 10cm. S. Amer.

Nipomo Ceanothus *Ceanothus impressus* var. *nipomensis*.
Nipple Fruit *Solanum mammosum*.

Nippocalamus Nak.
N. argenteostriatus (Reg.) Nak. = *Pleioblastus argenteostriatus*.
N. argenteostriatus var. *distichus* (Mitford) Nak. = *Pleioblastus pygmaeus* var. *distichus*.
N. chino var. *akebono* (Mak.) Mak. = *Pleioblastus akebono*.
N. chino (Franch. & Savat.) Nak. = *Pleioblastus chino*.
N. fortunei (Van Houtte) Nak. = *Pleioblastus variegatus*.
N. humilis (Mitford) Nak. = *Pleioblastus humilis*.
N. pygmaeus (Miq.) Nak. = *Pleioblastus pygmaeus*.
N. simonii (Carr.) Nak. = *Pleioblastus simonii*.

Nipponanthemum Kitam. Compositae. 1 perenn. herb or subshrub to 1m. Lvs to 9cm, alt., spathulate, crenate-dentate, minutely pubesc., lustrous, sessile. Cap. radiate, to 6cm diam., solitary, long-pedunculate; ray flts to 3cm, white; disc flts yellow. Jap. Z8.
N. nipponicum (Franch. ex Maxim.) Kitam.
→*Chrysanthemum* and *Leucanthemum*.

Nippon Bells *Shortia uniflora*.
Nipponese Cherry *Prunus nipponica*.
Nire *Nothofagus antarctica*.
Nirrhe *Eucryphia glutinosa*.
Nishiki-giboshi *Hosta opipara*.
Nispero *Eriobotrya japonica*; *Manilkara zapota*.

Nitella Agardh. STONEWORT. Characeae. 100 sp. of submerged aquatic plants with fragile erect st. and whorled, filiform br.; branchlets leaf-like. Cosmop. Z6.
N. flexilis (L.) Agardh. Br. in whorls of 6–8, straight or slightly incurved, 1.5–2 times longer than internodes. N Amer., Eurasia.
N. gracilis (Sm.) Agardh. Br. in whorls of 5–8, straight, sometimes condensed into heads, mostly shorter than internodes. Cosmop.

Nivenia Vent. Iridaceae. 9 everg., shrubby, perennials, related to *Aristea*. Lvs stiff, arranged in a fan, linear or swordshaped. Fls solitary or in corymbs; perianth tube slender, tep. 6, spreading; fil. short, anth. small. S Afr. Z9.
N. corymbosa Bak. Branched subshrub, 0.5–2m. Fls 2cm diam., dark blue in flattened corymbs. Summer–autumn.
N. fruticosa (L. f.) Bak. Dwarf subshrub 9–20cm tall; fls pale blue. Summer.
N. stokoei N.E. Br. Dwarf subshrub, 40–60cm. Fls 3cm diam., dark blue. Summer-autumn.
→*Aristea* and *Witsenia*.

No-azami *Cirsium japonicum*.
Noble Cypress × *Cupressocyparis notabilis*.
Noble Fir *Abies procera*.

Noccaea Rchb.
N. alpina (L.) Rchb. = *Pritzelago alpina*.

Nodding Banksia *Banksia nutans*.
Nodding Catchfly *Silene pendula*.
Nodding Lily *Lilium cernuum*.
Nodding Mellic *Melica nutans*.
Nodding Onion *Allium cernuum*.
Nogal *Juglans jamaicensis*.

Nolana L. f. Nolanaceae. 18 gland. ann. or perenn. herbs or subshrubs. Lvs basal and cauline (narrower, sessile). Fls solitary or clustered, axill.; cal. tubular-campanulate, lobes 5, imbricate; cor. campanulate, 5-lobed, sometimes bilabiate to ½ wider than deep; sta. 5, inserted on corolla-tube alt. with cor. lobes, fil. slender, often hairy. Chile to Peru, Galapagos. Z10.
N. acuminata (Miers) Miers ex Dunal = *N. paradoxa* ssp. *atriplicifolia*.
N. atriplicifolia D. Don ex Sweet = *N. paradoxa* ssp. *atriplicifolia*.
N. grandiflora Lehm. ex G. Don = *N. paradoxa* ssp. *atriplicifolia*.
N. humifusa (Gouan) Johnst. Ann. or perenn. to 15cm, often decumbent, viscid glandular-pubesc. Basal lvs to 2.5×1cm, elliptic or spathulate to oblanceolate. Cor. to 1.7cm, funnel-shaped, lilac with throat while, streaked violet or purple. Summer. Peru. 'Shooting Star': highly floriferous, st. trailing; fls lilac to lavender, streaked dark purple.
N. lanceolata (Miers) Miers ex Dunal = *N. paradoxa* ssp. *atriplicifolia*.
N. paradoxa Lindl. ssp. *paradoxa*. Ann. or perenn. to 25cm, usually decumbent, puberulent to gland. Basal lvs 5.5×2cm, ovate to elliptic, obtuse, somewhat succulent. Cor. to 3.5cm, funnel-shaped, bright dark blue, throat yellow or white. Summer. Chile. 'Blue Bird': fls deep sky-blue with white throats, trumpet-shaped, abundant. 'Cliff Hanger': habit trailing; lvs bright green; fls cornflower blue, pale yellow throats. ssp. *atriplicifolia* (D. Don) Mesa. St. to 10cm. Lvs spathulate to linear. Cor. to 3×4cm, blue, violet or white, tube yellow or white. Summer. Peru, Chile.
N. prostrata L. f. = *N. humifusa*.
N. rupicola Gaudich. = *N. paradoxa* ssp. *atriplicifolia*.
N. ×*tenella* Lindl. (*N. humifusa* ×*paradoxa*.) Cor. pale purple-blue, throat white, veined purple. Summer. Gdn hybrid.

Nolanaceae Dumort. See *Nolana*.

Nolina Michx. Agavaceae. c24 xeromorphic, everg. perennials. Stemless or, more usually with caudex, swollen and conical. Bark corky. Lvs linear, tough and fibrous. Fls small, crowded in long pseudo-term. pan.; tep. 6, cream-white flushed mauve. S US, Mex. to Guat. Z10.
N. bigelowii (Torr.) Wats. St. 1–3m, base expanded. Lvs in term. rosettes, to 12×3.5cm, rigid, persisting brown and deflexed around the trunk, margins smooth, splitting into fibres. Ariz. to Baja Calif.
N. erumpens (Torr.) Wats. St. 60–150cm. Lvs to 9×1cm, thick, straight, rigid, channelled, apex brushlike. W Tex., N Mex.
N. georgiana Michx. St. straight, cylindric. Lvs narrow strapshaped, serrulate, from a large bulb-like rosette. Georgia.
N. gracilis (Lem.) Cif. & Giac. Similar to *N. stricta* but lvs glaucous with roughter margins.
N. guatemalensis (Rose) Cif. & Giac. Tree to 6m or more. Trunk tapered, branching. Lvs in dense rosettes, to 1m×2.5cm, recurving, base broad, edges smooth. Guat.
N. hartwegiana Hemsl. Trunk to 6m, base greatly enlarged. Lvs tufted, to 60×0.4cm, linear, entire, rough. Mex.
N. hookeri (Trel.) G. Rowley. Caudex irregular, swollen to 1m wide; br. short or 0. Lvs to 90cm, wiry, glaucous, grass-like in tufts on caudex. EC Mex.
N. lindheimerana (Schelle) Wats. St. 0 or v. short. Lvs 60–90×0.5cm, grasslike, wiry, flat, in rosettes of 15–20, apex entire. Tex.
N. longifolia (Schult.) Hemsl. Trunk to 2m or more, base swollen, tapering above with short br. Lvs to 1m×2.5cm, thin, dark green with rough margins, recurved and hanging in dense rosettes, apex twisting. Mex.
N. microcarpa S. Wats. BEARGRASS; SACAHUISTA. Lvs 60–120×0.6–1.2cm, grasslike, densely tufted, arching, serrulate, apex brushlike. SW US, Mex.
N. parryi S. Wats. Similar to *N. bigelowii* but lf margins serrulate, not fibrous. SW US.
N. recurvata (Lem.) Hemsl. BOTTLE PALM; ELEPHANT FOOT TREE; PONY TAIL. Trunk flask-shaped, to 8m, swollen to 2m diam. at base, sparingly branched. Lvs in term. rosettes, to 1.8×2cm, linear, channelled, recurved, dark green, serrulate. SE Mex.
N. stricta (Lem.) Cif. & Giac. St. stout, to 6m or more, flask-shaped somewhat branched. Lvs to 1m×1.4cm, channelled,

rigid, straight, glaucous, coarse, pale green with yellow-green margins. Mex.
N. tuberculata hort. = *N. recurvata.*
→*Beaucarnea, Calibanus, Dasylirion* and *Yucca.*

Noltea Rchb. Rhamnaceae. 2 everg. glab. shrubs, to 4m. In florescence axill. or terminal, corymbose, few-fld; cal. lobes 5, alternating with 5 orbicular, hollow pet.; sta. 5, as long as pet. Fr. a drupe-like berry. Late spring. S Afr. Z9.
N. africana (L.) Rchb. Lvs 4–6cm, with auriculate stipules with gland., red margins, elliptic to oblong-lanceolate, toothed glossy. Infl. 1–1.5cm wide, fls white. S Afr.

Nomocharis Franch. Liliaceae (Liliaceae). 7 bulbous perenn. herbs. Lvs in whorls on upper half of st. or scattered along st. in pairs or triads toward apex, linear to lanceolate or oblong-ovate. Fls in uppermost lf axils, flat to bowl-shaped; perianth seg. 6, broadly ovate to elliptic, free; inner seg. with basal nectary; sta. 6. Summer. W China, SE Tibet, Burm., N India. Z7.
N. aperta (Franch.) Wils. To 80cm. Lvs scattered, 6.5–10cm, elliptic to lanceolate. Fls flattened, 5–10cm diam.; outer seg. entire, pink to deep pink, spotted red in lower half, usually blotched maroon at base and pale green near tip; inner seg. blotched with fleshy nectaries. Summer. W China.
N. farreri (W.E. Evans) R. Harrow. To 1m. Lvs whorled, 3.5cm, linear to lanceolate. Fls 5–11cm diam., saucer-shaped, drooping, later upright or horizontal; outer seg. elliptic to ovate, entire, blotched dark maroon at base with finer spots toward centre; inner seg. ovate entire or subserrate, maroon at base with a pale green patch toward centre and a few finer blotches. NE Burm.
N. ×*finlayorum* Synge. (*N. farreri* ×*N. pardanthina.*) To 70cm. Lvs whorled. Fls 2–7, white to pink; usually red-maroon spotted only in lower half, entire to subserrate.
N. mairei Lév. = *N. pardanthina.*
N. meleagrina Franch. To 85cm. Lvs whorled, lanceolate, acuminate, to 13cm. Fls 6–12cm diam. nodding, flattened, white, occas. flecked pink below, blotched purple above; outer seg. blotched purple at base; inner seg. entire to fimbriate, purple at base. W China.
N. nana Wils. = *Lilium nanum.*
N. ×*notabilis* Sealy. (*N. saluenensis* ×*N. farreri.*) To 42cm. Lvs scattered. Fls nodding, saucer-shaped, to 6cm diam., pink to mauve, spotted maroon, usually in lower half; outer seg. with a deep crimson basal blotch and smaller markings above this; nectaries with black markings.
N. oxypetala Royle = *Lilium oxypetalum.*
N. pardanthina Franch. To 90cm. Lvs whorled, elliptic to lanceolate, 2.5–10.5cm. Fls 5–9cm diam. nodding to erect, flattened; outer seg. entire, white to pink, blotched purple, dark maroon at base; inner seg. more densely blotched, apex fimbriate. W China. f. *punctulata* Sealy. Perianth seg. spotted only at base, shallow-fimbriate to subserrate. W China.
N. saluenensis Balf. f. To 85cm. Lvs scattered, elliptic to elliptic-oblong, 2–4cm. Fls horizontal or drooping, saucer-shaped, 6–9cm diam.; outer seg. rose pink, paler in lower part, dark maroon patch at base with small spots over lower half; inner seg. entire. W China, NE Burm.
N. synaptica Sealy. Similar to *N. saluenensis.* Fls white, tinted purple, spotted dark maroon throughout; perianth seg. with a dark purple, yellow-fringed, basal blotch. India (Assam).

Nonko *Ficus saussureana.*
Nonsuch *Medicago lupulina.*
Noors *Euphorbia caerulescens.*
Nootka Cypress *Chamaecyparis nootkatensis.*
Nootka Rose *Rosa nutkana.*

Nopalea Salm-Dyck.
N. auberi (Pfeiff.) Salm-Dyck = *Opuntia auberi.*
N. cochenillifera (L.) Salm-Dyck = *Opuntia cochenillifera.*
N. dejecta (Salm-Dyck) Salm-Dyck = *Opuntia dejecta.*

Nopalxochia Britt. & Rose Cactaceae. 4 epiphytic cacti; st. branching, terete at base, flattened above, crenate, spineless except on young growth. Fl. solitary, funnelform or campanulate-funnelform; tube shorter than or equalling the limb. S Mex. Z10.
N. ackermannii (Haw.) F. Knuth. St. to 20–70×5–7cm, obscurely 3-ribbed. Fl. 12–14×10–14cm, curved-funnelform, pericarpel and tube pale yellow-green; floral areoles mostly with short wool and bristly spines; tep. orange-red. Spring. S Mex. Z9.
N. conzattiana MacDougall. Resembling *N. ackermannii*, and perhaps only a var. of it. Fl. smaller, 11–12×5–6cm. S Mex. Z9.
N. macdougallii (Alexander) W.T. Marshall. St. 15–45×2–5cm,

linear 2-winged. Fls 7–8×c6.5cm, tubular-funnelform; pericarpel and tube brown-green; floral areoles almost naked; tep. purple-pink. Spring. SE Mex. Z9.
N. phyllanthoides (DC.) Britt. & Rose. St. to 40×0.6cm. Fl 8–10×7–9cm, campanulate-funnelform; tube pale green; floral areoles naked; tep. pink. Spring. S Mex. Z9.
→*Epiphyllum.*

Norantea Aubl. See Marcgraviaceae.

Nordic Currant *Ribes spicatum.*
Norfolk Island Hibiscus *Lagunaria patersonii.*
Norfolk Island Pine *Araucaria heterophylla.*
Norfolk Island Tree Fern *Cyathea brownii.*
Norfolk Palm *Rhopalostylis baueri.*
Norka *Acacia colletioides.*

Normanbya F. Muell. ex Becc. BLACK PALM. Palmae. 1 unarmed palm to 20m. St. solitary, erect, ringed, grey, swollen at base. Crownshaft conspicuous, pale grey. Lvs to 2.5m, pinnate; petiole short, curved; pinnae cuneate, dark green above, glaucous and scaly beneath, singlefold, divided into 7–9 linear, lax seg., hanging in several planes. N Queensld. Z10.
N. merrillii Becc. = *Veitchia merrillii.*
N. normanbyi (W. Hill) L.H. Bail.

North American Sea Oats *Uniola paniculata.*
North America Wild Oats *Chasmanthium latifolium.*
Northern Bangalow Palm *Archontophoenix alexandrae.*
Northern Bedstraw *Galium boreale.*
Northern Beech Fern *Phegopteris connectilis.*
Northern Black Currant *Ribes hudsonianum.*
Northern Blue Violet *Viola septentrionalis.*
Northern Bog Violet *Viola nephrophylla.*
Northern Catalpa *Catalpa speciosa.*
Northern Dewberry *Rubus flagellaris.*
Northern Downy Violet *Viola fimbriatula.*
Northern Elkhorn Fern *Platycerium hillii.*
Northern Grey Ironbark *Eucalyptus siderophloia.*
Northern Holly Fern *Polystichum lonchitis.*
Northern Jacob's Ladder *Polemonium boreale.*
Northern Japanese Hemlock *Tsuga diversifolia.*
Northern Kentia Palm *Gronophyllum ramsayi.*
Northern Lady Fern *Athyrium filix-femina.*
Northern Maidenhair Fern *Adiantum pedatum.*
Northern Marsh Orchid *Dactylorhiza purpurella.*
Northern Oak Fern *Gymnocarpium robertianum.*
Northern Pin Oak *Quercus ellipsoidalis.*
Northern Pitch Pine *Pinus rigida.*
Northern Rata *Metrosideros robusta.*
Northern Red Oak *Quercus rubra.*
Northern Sloe *Prunus alleghaniensis.*
Northern Washingtonia *Washingtonia filifera.*
Northern White Violet *Viola renifolia.*
Northern Woodsia *Woodsia alpina.*
North Island Edelweiss *Leucogenes leontopodium.*
North Japanese Hemlock *Tsuga diversifolia.*
Norway Maple *Acer platanoides.*
Norway Spruce *Picea abies.*
Nosegay *Plumeria.*
Noshi Setouchi-giboshi *Hosta pycnophylla.*

Notechidnopsis Lavranos & Bleck. Asclepiadaceae. 2 dwarf, succulent, leafless herbs. St. prostrate to ascending, angled, glab., with tubercles and teeth. Fls in clusters above; sep. 5, small, fleshy; cor., tube shallow, lobes 5, outer corona whorl 10-lobed, inner whorl 5-lobed. S Afr. (Cape Prov.). Z10.
N. columnaris (Nel) Lavranos & Bleck. St. 15–18×2–2.5cm, 8-angled, teeth curving downward. Cor. 4–8mm diam., exterior blotched red, interior white-hairy, yellow-green with red spots. S Afr. (Cape Prov.).
N. tessellata (Pill.) Lavranos & Bleck. St. to 12×1.3cm, 6–10-angled, tubercles giving tessellated appearance, teeth soft. Cor. to 9mm diam., mauve, interior densely bristly, corona sulphur-yellow, sometimes ringed white.
→*Echidnopsis* and *Trichocaulon.*

Nothofagus Bl. SOUTHERN BEECH. Fagaceae. About 40 everg. and decid. trees and shrubs. Bark smooth with distinct lenticels, becoming thick and scaly to furrowed on old trees. Branchlets slender in a distinctive herring-bone pattern. Lvs alt., ovoid to oblong or trullate, entire, waved or toothed, short-stalked. ♂ fls axill., in groups of 1–3, sta. 3–90; ♀ fls axill., solitary, rarely in 3-grouped, with 3(–7) styles. Fr. solitary; a 1 to many-seeded ovoid involucre, 5–25mm, covered with entire or branched, often sticky lamellae; nuts 3–20mm, ovoid-acute. Temp. S S

Amer., NZ, E Aus., and trop. high altitude New Caledonia and New Guinea.

N. alessandrii Espin. RUIL. Decid. tree to 30m. Lvs 6–14cm, ovate to subcordate, 11–13 pairs of veins, finely serrate; bright green above, paler blue-green beneath, thinly glandular-pubesc. C Chile. Z9.

N. ×alpina (Poepp. & Endl.) Krasser. (*N. procera* ×*N. pumilio*.) Similar to *N. procera* but lvs v. small, 2–3cm. Possibly a mountain form of *N. procera*; if synonymous with *N. procera*, name *N. alpina* has priority. C Chile. Z7.

N. antarctica (Forst.) Ørst. NIRE. Decid. tree or shrub to 17m. Lvs 1.5–4cm, oblong, finely but irregularly toothed, with 4 pairs of veins, glossy rich green above, paler beneath, often sweetly aromatic, glab. except a few hairs on veins. Tierra del Fuego to Chile. var. **uliginosa** A. DC. Lvs more pubesc. 'Benmore' ('Prostrata'): low-spreading form with interlacing br. in a dense mound. Z7.

N. ×apiculata (Colenso) Krasser. (*N. solanderi* ×*N. truncata*.) Natural hybrid intermediate between parents. NZ. Z8.

N. betuloides (Mirb.) Bl. COIGUE DE MAGELLANES; GUINDO BEECH. Everg. tree to 25m, or shrub in exposed sites. Lvs 1–3cm, ovate, crenate, apex blunt acute, glossy dark green, slightly sticky, finely freckled with white glands beneath, veins often pink. Chile, W Arg. Z7.

N. ×blairii (T. Kirk) Ckn. (*N. fusca* ×*N. solanderi* var. *cliffortioides*.) Natural hybrid intermediate between parents. NZ. Z8.

N. cliffortioides (Hook. f.) Ørst. = *N. solanderi* var. *cliffortioides*.

N. cunninghamii (Hook. f.) Ørst. MYRTLE BEECH. Everg. tree to 55m, related to *N. menziesii*. Shoots slender, brown, pubesc. Lvs 0.6–1cm, deltoid or trullate to nearly orbicular, irregularly blunt-toothed, apex blunt-acute, glossy green, without pits beneath. Tasm. Z9.

N. dombeyi (Mirb.) Bl. COIGUE. Everg. tree to 50m. Lvs 2–4cm, ovoid-acute to lanceolate, irregular-serrate, glossy dark green above, matt and pale beneath, minutely freckled black. Chile, Arg. Z8.

N. fusca (Hook. f.) Ørst. RED BEECH. Everg. tree to 35m. Lvs 3–5cm, broad-ovate, with 4–8 large, acute teeth on each side, papery, veins 3–5 pairs, matt yellow-green to dark green above, shiny beneath with minute pits at base, turning bright red before falling. NZ. var. **colensoi** (Hook. f.) Ørst. Lvs thicker and stronger, margin with finer, blunter teeth. Z9.

N. glauca (Philippi) Krasser. Decid. tree to 30m. Lvs 5–8cm, broad-oblong, base cordate, 10 pairs of veins, undulate, crenulate, glaucous above, pale glaucous beneath with hair tufts in vein axils. C Chile. Z9.

N. gunnii (Hook. f.) Ørst. TANGLEFOOT BEECH. Low to prostrate decid. shrub to 3m, rarely a small tree. Lvs 1–4cm, crinkled, nearly orbicular, 5–7 pairs of veins, similar to *N. pumilio*, but lobes between the veins not notched. Tasm. (mts). Z8.

N. ×leonii Espin. (*N. glauca* ×*N. obliqua* var. *macrocarpa*.) Decid. tree. Lvs to 10cm, ovate, obtuse, margin doubly serrate, denticulate, base cuneate to truncate. Chile Z7.

N. menziesii (Hook. f.) Ørst. SILVER BEECH. Everg. tree to 30m. Lvs 1–1.5cm, orbicular to broadly ovoid-acute, apex obtuse or acute, margin double-crenate, silvery grey on young trees, glossy dark green on older trees, coriaceous, glab. except for hair-rilled vein axils at base of blade. NZ. Z9.

N. moorei (F. Muell.) Krasser. AUSTRALIAN BEECH. Everg. tree to 35m. Lvs 3–8cm, rarely 11.5cm, ovate-lanceolate, glab., glossy dark green above, paler beneath, apex acuminate, margin finely sharp-serrate, 9–16 pairs of veins. Aus. (NE NSW, SE Queensld). Z9.

N. nervosa (Philippi) Dimitri & Milano = *N. procera*.

N. nitida (Philippi) Krasser. COIGUE DE CHILOE. Everg. tree to 40m. Lvs 2.5–4cm, trullate, coarsely serrate, apex acute, coriaceous, dark glossy green tinged brown above, paler beneath. W Chile. Z7.

N. obliqua (Mirb.) Bl. ROBLE BEECH. Decid. tree to 40m. Lvs 3–8cm, ovoid-oblong, mid-green above, paler beneath, glab., base slightly oblique, apex acute, margin double toothed; veins 7–12 pairs, impressed above each ending in a large lobe-like tooth, itself 1–3-toothed each side. Chile, W Arg. The hybrids *N. obliqua* ×*N. procera* and *N. obliqua* ×*N. menziesii* have occurred in Britain; they are as yet unnamed. var. **macrocarpa** A. DC. Fr. larger cupule to 12mm, not 7–9mm; nuts 10mm. Z8.

N. procera (Poepp. & Endl.) Ørst. RAULI BEECH. Decid. tree to 40m. Lvs 4–15cm, to 20cm on vigorous young trees, ovoid-lanceolate to trullate, matt green and thinly pubesc., apex blunt-acute, margin slightly scalloped, finely crenate-serrate; veins 15–22 pairs, impressed above, vein ending in a slight sinus with 4 to 5 unequal intervening teeth. Chilean Andes. Z7.

N. pumilio (Poepp. & Endl.) Krasser. LENGA. Decid. tree to 40m. Lvs 2–4cm, broad-oval to ovoid, glossy green above, paler beneath with scattered adpressed long hairs on veins, apex

rounded, margin ciliate, lobed; veins 5–7 pairs, prominent beneath, each ending in a sinus with a single, notched lobed between. Tierra del Fuego to Chilean Andes. Z7.

N. solanderi (Hook. f.) Ørst. BLACK BEECH. Tree to 30m. Lvs 0.7–1.3cm, v. regular ovate, entire, flat, coriaceous, apex mostly obtuse, glossy dark green above with scattered hairs at first, soon glab., thinly pale green-tomentose beneath. NZ. var. **cliffortioides** (Hook. f.) Poole. MOUNTAIN BEECH. Tree to 30m or shrub at high altitude. Lvs twisted and buckled with margins bent down and acute tip bent up. Intermediates with type common. NZ. Z8.

N. solandri hort. = *N. solanderi*.

N. truncata (Colenso) Ckn. HARD BEECH. Everg. tree allied to *N. fusca*, but lvs more coriaceous with 5–6 pairs of veins, margin with 8–12 shallow blunt teeth, blade without pits. NZ. Z8.

Notholaena R. Br.
N. bonariensis (Willd.) C. Chr. = *Cheilanthes bonariensis*.
N. candida (Mart. & Gal.) Hook. = *Cheilanthes candida*.
N. canescens Kunze = *Cheilanthes lasiophylla*.
N. distans R. Br. = *Cheilanthes distans*.
N. laevis Mart. & Gal. = *Cheilanthes sinuata*.
N. newberryi D.C. Eaton = *Cheilanthes newberryi*.
N. parryi D.C. Eaton = *Cheilanthes parryi*.
N. pruinosa Fée = *Cheilanthes sinuata*.
N. sinuata (Lagasca ex Sw.) Domin = *Cheilanthes sinuata*.
N. trichomanoides (L.) R. Br. = *Cheilanthes trichomanoides*.
N. vellea R. Br. = *Cheilanthes vellea*.

Notholirion Wallich ex Boiss. Liliaceae (Liliaceae). 4 bulbous perennials to 1.5m. Lvs basal and cauline, linear-lanceolate, to 45cm. Rac. subtended by a short, linear bract; fls trumpet-shaped to spreading; perianth seg. 6, free, recurved; sta. 6, anth. versatile; stigma distinctly trifid. Summer. Afghan. to W China. Z7.

N. bulbuliferum (Lingl.) Stearn. To 1.5m. Fls horizontal, trumpet-shaped, to 4cm, pale lilac, tipped green. Nepal to W China.

N. campanulatum Cotton & Stearn. to 80cm. Fls to 20, pendulous, to 5cm, crimson to maroon tipped green. N Burm., W China.

N. hyacinthinum (Wils.) Stapf = *N. bulbuliferum*.

N. macrophyllum (D. Don) Boiss. To 40cm. Fls 1–7, horizontal to nodding, trumpet-shaped to 5cm, pale pink to light mauve throughout. Himal.

N. thomsonianum (Royle) Stapf. To 1m. Fls 10–30, horizontal to ascending, trumpet-shaped, to 6.5cm, pale mauve. W Himal., Afghan.

Nothopanax Miq.
N. arboreus (Murray) Seem. = *Pseudopanax arboreus*.
N. cochleatus (Lam.) Miq. = *Polyscias scutellaria* 'Cochleata'.
N. colensoi (Hook. f.) Seem. = *Pseudopanax colensoi*.
N. crispatus (Bull) Merrill. = *Polyscias* 'Crispata'.
N. davidii (Franch.) Harms ex Diels = *Metapanax davidii*.
N. delavayi (Franch.) Harms ex Diels = *Metapanax delavayi*.
N. elegans (C. Moore ex Muell.) Seem. = *Polyscias elegans*.
N. fruticosus (L.) Miq. = *Polyscias fruticosa*.
N. fruticosus var. *plumatus* (Bull) Merrill = *Polyscias* 'Plumata'.
N. guilfoylei (Bull) Merrill = *Polyscias guilfoylei*.
N. laetus (T. Kirk) Cheesem. = *Pseudopanax laetus*.
N. linearis (Hook. f.) Harms. = *Pseudopanax linearis*.
N. ornatus (Bull) Merrill. = *Polyscias filicifolia* 'Ornata'.
N. pinnatus (Lam.) Miq. = *Polyscias cumingiana*.
N. sambucifolius (Sieb.) K. Koch = *Polyscias sambucifolia*.
N. simplex (Hook. f.) Seem. = *Pseudopanax simplex*.
N. sinclairii (Hook. f.) Seem. = *Pseudopanax simplex* var. *sinclairii*.
N. tricochleatus Miq. = *Polyscias scutellaria* 'Tricochleata'.

Nothoscordum Kunth FALSE GARLIC; GRACE GARLIC. Liliaceae (Alliaceae). 20 bulbous perennials, resembling *Allium* but lacking characteristic odour. Lvs linear, basal. Fls in loose scapose umbels; spathe 1, 2-lobed; tep. 6, united at base. Americas.

N. bivalve (L.) Britt. To 20cm. Lvs 3–4, to 4mm wide. Fls 4–8, almost stellate; tep. white to yellow, midrib green. Spring. S US. Z5.

N. fragrans (Vent.) Kunth = *N. gracile*.

N. gracile (Ait.) Stearn. Lvs 6–8, to 8mm wide. Fls 8–15, fragrant, funnel-shaped; tep. white to lilac, streaked brown and pink below, midrib pink or mauve. Spring–summer. S Amer., Mex. Z7.

N. maritimum Hook. f. = *Muilla maritima*.
N. neriniflorum (Herb.) Traub = *Caloscordum neriniflorum*.
N. striatum (Jacq.) Kunth = *N. bivalve*.
→*Allium*.

Nothotaxus Florin.
N. chienii (Cheng) Florin = *Pseudotaxus chienii*.

Nothotsuga Hu ex Page. Pinaceae. 1 coniferous, everg. tree, to 35m. Shoots slender, pendulous at tips. Lvs narrowly linear-elliptic, 1–2.5cm×1–2mm, dark green above, paler beneath, midrib conspicuous, base pulvinate. ♂ cones clustered, term. ♀ cones erect, solitary, oblong-ovoid, 3–6cm; scales thinly woody, rhombic to ovate. S China. Z8.
N. longibracteata (Cheng) Hu.
→*Tsuga*.

Notobuxus Oliv. Buxaceae. 7 box-like shrubs or small trees. Lvs opposite, entire, papery or leathery. Fls green, fascicled or cymose: ♂ with sep. 4, sta. 6; ♀ with sep. 4, styles 3. Trop. and S Afr.; Madag. Z10.
N. macowanii (Oliv.) Phillips. CAPE BOXWOOD. Shrub or small tree to 9m, slow-growing. Lvs 1.5–2.5cm, glab., dark green, elliptic, apex obtuse, base narrowly-cuneate. Winter. S Afr.

Notocactus (Schum.) Frič.
N. alacriportanus (Backeb. & Voll) F. Buxb. = *Parodia alacriportana*.
N. apricus (Arech.) A. Berger = *Parodia concinna*.
N. arachnites Ritter = *Parodia crassigibba*.
N. arechavaletae (Speg.) Herter = *Parodia ottonis*.
N. concinnus (Monv.) A. Berger = *Parodia concinna*.
N. corynodes (Otto ex Pfeiff.) Krainz = *Parodia erinacea*.
N. crassigibbus Ritter = *Parodia crassigibba*.
N. erinaceus (Haw.) Krainz = *Parodia erinacea*.
N. floricomus (Arech.) A. Berger = *Parodia mammulosa*.
N. fricii (Arech.) Krainz = *Parodia erinacea*.
N. graessneri (Schum.) A. Berger = *Parodia graessneri*.
N. grossei (Schum.) Frič = *Parodia schumanniana*.
N. haselbergii (Ruempl.) A. Berger = *Parodia haselbergii*.
N. herteri (Werderm.) Buining & Kreuzinger = *Parodia herteri*.
N. leninghausii (Schum.) A. Berger = *Parodia leninghausii*.
N. mammulosus (Lem.) A. Berger = *Parodia mammulosa*.
N. minimus Frič & Kreuzinger = *Parodia caespitosa*.
N. mueller-melchersii Backeb. = *Parodia mueller-melchersii*.
N. muricatus (Pfeiff.) A. Berger, misapplied? = *Parodia concinna*.
N. ottonis (Lehm.) A. Berger = *Parodia ottonis*.
N. pauciareolatus (Arech.) Krainz = *Parodia erinacea*.
N. rutilans Daeniker & Krainz = *Parodia rutilans*.
N. schumannianus (Nicolai) Frič = *Parodia schumanniana*.
N. scopa (Spreng.) A. Berger = *Parodia scopa*.
N. submammulosus (Lem.) Backeb. = *Parodia mammulosa*.
N. tabularis (Ruempl.) A. Berger = *Parodia concinna*.
N. uebelmannianus Buining = *Parodia crassigibba*.
N. velenovskyi (Frič) Frič = *Parodia mammulosa*.
N. vorwerkianus (Werderm.) Krainz = *Parodia erinacea*.
N. werdermannianus Herter = *Parodia werdermannii*.

Notonia DC.
N. abyssinica A. Rich. = *Kleinia abyssinica*.
N. amaniensis Engl. = *Kleinia amaniensis*.
N. grandiflora DC. = *Kleinia grandiflora*.
N. grantii Oliv. & Hiern = *Kleinia grantii*.
N. gregorii S. Moore = *Kleinia gregorii*.
N. hildebrandtii Vatke = *Kleinia abyssinica* var. *hildebrandtii*.
N. madagascarensis Humbert = *Kleinia madagascarensis*.
N. petraea R.E. Fries = *Kleinia petraea*.

Notospartium Hook. f. PINK BROOM; SOUTHERN BROOM. Leguminosae (Papilionoideae). 3 shrubs and trees. Mostly leafless with slender, weeping, branchlets. Fls pea-like in pendulous lat. rac. NZ. Z8.
N. carmichaeliae Hook. f. Shrub to 5m. Branchlets rushlike, slightly flattened or subcylindrical, grooved, glab., to 5mm wide. Rac. to 5cm, 12–20-fld, sericeous, crowded; fls to 1cm, light purple to pink. Summer.
N. exsul F. Muell. = *N. carmichaeliae*.
N. glabrescens Petrie. Round-headed tree to 9m. Br. weeping, flattened to terete, slightly grooved, glab. Rac. to 5cm, 15–25-fld, glabrescent; fls to 1cm, magenta with standard paler stained dark purple-red. Late spring–early summer.
N. torulosum T. Kirk. Resembles *N. carmichaeliae* but of weaker, more slender habit, fls deeper purple, sparse.

Notothlaspi Hook. f. PENWIPER PLANT. Cruciferae. 2 fleshy, taprooted alpine herbs. Lvs spathulate, petiolate, basal. Rac. corymbose; fls large, fragrant, 4-merous. Summer. NZ. Z8.
N. rosulatum Hook. f. Erect, pyramidal herb, 7–25cm. Lvs numerous, overlapping, fleshy, white-hairy at first, toothed. Fls white, crowded, in pyramidal rac.

Notylia Lindl. Orchidaceae. Some 40 epiphytic orchids. Pbs small or 0. Lvs sheathing and term., fleshy or coriaceous, distichous, imbricate or equitant. Rac. or pan. lat.; fls small usually stalked and slender, ± arching; sep. narrow, erect or spreading; pet. smaller; lip entire or obscurely lobed. Trop. C & S Amer. Z10.
N. albida Klotzsch = *N. barkeri*.
N. barkeri Lindl. Pbs to 3cm, oblong to ellipsoid. Lvs to 20×4cm, elliptic to ligulate. Rac. to 30cm, narrowly cylindric, arching to pendent; fls white to green-white, sometimes spotted yellow, faintly scented; sep. to 7×3mm; lip to 6×2mm, ovate to narrowly triangular, subobtuse to acuminate. Mex. to Panama.
N. bicolor Lindl. Pbs to 1cm, ovoid. Lvs to 5×1cm, linear-lanceolate to elliptic-lanceolate. Rac. to 10cm, oblong, erect to pendent; sep. to 15×2mm, white; pet. white to purple-lavender spotted dull purple; lip to 9×2mm, white to purple-lavender, apex dilated, erose, disc spotted dark purple. Summer. Mex., Guat., Costa Rica.
N. bipartita Rchb. f. = *N. barkeri*.
N. bungerothii Rchb. f. Pbs to 3cm, oblong. Lvs to 20×7cm, oblong. Rac. to 45cm, pendent; fls pale green to green-yellow; sep. to 8×2mm; pet. white marked yellow; lip 6×2mm, white, ovate. Venez.
N. carnosiflora Schweinf. Pbs to 1cm, subcylindrical. Lvs to 6.5×2cm, oblong-elliptic. Rac. arching; fls fleshy; sep. to 7×3mm; lip to 4×2mm, ovate-triangular. Peru.
N. mirabilis Schweinf. Pbs reduced to 0. Lvs to 1.4×0.3cm, equitant, linear-oblong to linear-elliptic. Pan. to 3.5cm; fls membranous, spreading, pale lilac and dark violet; sep. to 4×2mm; lip to 4×2mm, ovate or obovate, apiculate. Venez., Peru.
N. multiflora Lindl. = *N. sagittifera*.
N. pentachne Rchb. f. Pbs to 3cm, oblong to ovate-oblong. Lvs to 20×5cm, ligulate to oblong-lanceolate or elliptic. Rac. to 35cm, pendent; sep. and pet. pale green to yellow, to 10×3mm, lat. sep. forming a synsepalum, pet. sometimes with a few orange spots, lip to 6×3mm, white, dilated, to trulliform, acuminate. Panama, Colomb., Venez.
N. rhombilabia Schweinf. Pbs to 2cm, narrowly cylindrical. Lvs to 14–2cm, linear to linear-oblong. Rac. to 25cm, arching; fls pale yellow-green, fleshy; sep. to 8×3mm, lat. sep. forming a synsepalum; lip to 7×5mm, white, waxy, rhombic or ovate-rhombic. Peru, Venez.
N. sagittifera (HBK) Link & Klotzsch. Pbs to 1.5cm oblong. Lvs to 18×5cm, oblong or oblong-elliptic. Rac. to 30cm, arching; fls clear green; the pet. with 2 round yellow spots; sep. to 7×3mm, membranous lat. sep. forming a synsepalum; lip white, to 5×2mm, fleshy, ovate-triangular, acute to acuminate. S Amer. to Peru.
N. tridachne Lindl. & Paxt. = *N. barkeri*.
N. wullschlaegeliana Focke. Pbs to 0.5cm. Lvs to 3×0.5cm, equitant, oblong-lanceolate. Rac. to 5cm, subumbellate; fls pale yellow-green or white marked purple, translucent; sep. to 7×2mm; lip to 6×1mm, oblong-linear toothed. S Amer. to Peru.
N. yauaperyensis Barb. Rodr. Pbs to 6×3mm, obliquely oblong. Lvs to 15×2cm, oblong to linear-oblong. Rac. to 12cm, arching to pendent; fls white; sep. to 5×2mm; lip to 4×2mm, fleshy, pubesc., ovate, cordate at base.

Nouletia Endl.
N. pterocarpa (Cham.) Pichon = *Cuspidaria pterocarpa*.

Nuphar Sm. COW LILY; SPATTERDOCK; YELLOW POND LILY; WATER COLLARD. Nymphaeaceae. Some 25 perenn., aquatic herbs. Rhiz. stout. Lvs large, with a basal sinus; floating lvs coriaceous; submerged lvs membranous. Fls emergent, subspherical, solitary; sep. 4 to 6 (to 9), coriaceous, broadly ovate to orbicular; pet. numerous, yellow, oblong or linear; sta. numerous, in several rows. Fr. berry-like, ovoid to flask-shaped. Temperature regions of N Hemis.
N. advena (Ait.) Ait. Lvs to 33×25cm, erect, usually emergent, sometimes floating, ovate to oblong, broadly rounded, sinus to 10cm. Fls to 4cm diam.; sep. usually 6, to 35mm, broadly ovate to suborbicular pet. to 8×5mm, yellow tinged red. E & C US, Mex., W Indies. Z3.
N. japonica DC. Floating lvs to 40×12cm, narrowly ovate to oblong, basally sagittate; submerged lvs narrow, undulate. Fls to 5cm diam.; yellow; sep. 5, to 2.5cm; pet. to 8mm, spathulate or oblong. Jap. 'Rubrotincta': fls tinted red. Z6.
N. kalmiana Ait. Floating lvs to 10×7.5cm, broadly oblong to suborbicular, broadly rounded; sinus to 3.5cm; submerged lvs orbicular. Fls to 18mm diam.; sep. 5, to 10mm, yellow, elliptic or obovate; pet. to 6×3mm, orange, margins yellow, spathulate. E US. Z5.
N. lutea (L.) Sm. YELLOW WATER LILY; BRANDY BOTTLE. Floating lvs to 40×30cm, ovate-oblong to suborbicular; sinus to 20cm;

submerged lvs broadly ovate to orbicular. Fls to 6cm diam.; sep. 5, to 3cm, interior bright yellow, broadly ovate; pet. to 10mm, spathulate. E US, W Indies, N Afr., Eurasia. Z4.

N. microphylla (Pers.) Fern. = *N. kalmiana*.

N. polysepala Engelm. Lvs usually floating, to 40×25cm, ovate to oblong, broadly rounded; sinus to 10cm. Fls to 7cm diam; sep. usually 9, to 5.5cm, oblong to orbicular, outer sep. green, interior tinged purple-brown. N Amer. Z4.

N. pumila (Timm) DC. Resembles *N. lutea*, except floating lvs to 14×13cm, broadly ovate to suborbicular. Fls to 3cm diam.; sep. 4 to 5, orbicular; pet. rounded. Eur., Russia, Jap. Z4.

N. sagittifolia (Walter) Pursh. Floating lvs to 28×10cm, narrowly oblong to oblong-lanceolate; sinus to 3.5cm, V-shaped; submerged lvs to 36×7cm, undulate. Fls to 3cm diam.; sep. 6 to 2.5cm, oblong to orbicular, canary yellow tipped green; pet. and sta. pale yellow. SE US. Z8.

N. variegata Engelm. Floating lvs to 28×22cm, ovate or oblong; sinus to 7.5cm, submerged lvs similar. Fls to 4.5cm diam.; outer sep. green, inner sep. lemon yellow, tinged red toward base; pet. subspathulate, clear yellow or sometimes bright green. N Amer. Z4.

Nutgall *Rhus chinensis*.
Nut-leaved Screw-tree *Helicteres isora*.
Nutmeg *Myristica fragrans*.
Nutmeg Flower *Nigella sativa*.
Nutmeg Hickory *Carya myristicaeformis*.
Nutmeg Yew *Torreya*.

Nuttallia Raf.
N. cerasiformis Torr. & A. Gray = *Oemleria cerasiformis*.

Nuttall's Cyperus *Pycreus filicinus*.
Nuttall's Oak *Quercus nuttallii*.

Nuxia Comm. ex Lam. Loganiaceae. 15 trees and shrubs with fibrous bark. Lvs leathery, abscising with conspicuous scars. Fls numerous, small, 4-parted in term., round-topped pan.; cor. tube cylindrical, usually shorter than cal., lobes recurved; sta. protruding. Arabia to Trop. Afr., Masc. Is., S Afr.

N. floribunda Benth. KITE TREE. Tree or shrub 2–25m. Lvs 4–16cm, oblong-elliptic, entire, crenate or toothed; petioles 0.3–5cm. Fls white, fragrant. Trop. & S Afr. Z9.

Nux-vomica Tree *Strychnos nux-vomica*.

Nuytsia R. Br. ex G. Don f. FIRE-TREE; FLAME-TREE; CHRISTMAS TREE. Loranthaceae. 1 root-parasitic glab. everg. shrub or small tree to 7m. Lvs 2.5–10cm, lanceolate, apex acute to rounded, narrowing to base, sessile. Infl. to 25cm, term., clustered; pet. 6–8, to 1.5cm, linear, erect, free, brilliant orange-yellow. W Aus. Z9.

N. floribunda (Labill.) R. Br. ex G. Don f.

NYCTAGINACEAE Juss. 34/350. *Abronia, Bougainvillea, Mirabilis, Nyctaginia, Pisonia*.

Nyctaginia Choisy. Nyctaginaceae. 1 viscid, tuberous, perenn. herb, erect or decumbent, to 40cm. Lvs to 9cm, ovate to triangular, usually sessile. Cymes long-peduncled, capitate, subtended by bracts; cal. funnel-shaped, 5-lobed; perianth to 4cm, deep red, sta. 5–8. SW US, N Mex. Z9.

N. capitata Choisy. SCARLET MUSK FLOWER.

Nycteranthus Necker.
N. canaliculatus (Haw.) Schwantes = *Sphalmanthus canaliculatus*.
N. salmoneus (Haw.) Schwantes = *Sphalmanthus salmoneus*.
N. splendens (L.) Schwantes = *Sphalmanthus splendens*.

Nycterinia D. Don.
N. capensis (Walp.) Benth. = *Zaluzianskya capensis*.
N. lychnidea D. Don = *Zaluzianskya lychnidea*.
N. maritima Benth. = *Zaluzianskya maritima*.
N. villosa (F.W. Schmidt) Benth. = *Zaluzianskya villosa*.

Nyctocalos Teijsm. & Binnend. Bignoniaceae. 3 climbers. Lvs 2-foliolate or pinnate. Fls fragrant, opening at night; cal. cupular, truncate, 5-toothed; cor. tube long, narrow, swollen at throat, lobes 5, overlapping. SE Asia. Z10.

N. assamica Hook. f. = *N. cuspidata*.
N. brunfelsiiflorus Miq. = *N. cuspidata*.
N. cuspidata Miq. Lfs 6–18cm, ovate or obovate or oblong, apex acuminate to cuspidate, bse rounded. Fls cream; cor. tube 15–19cm, lobes rounded, to 2cm. Assam, Philipp., Celebes.
N. macrosiphon Teijsm. & Binnend. = *N. cuspidata*.

N. thomsonii Hook. = *N. cuspidata*.
→*Tecoma*.

Nyctocereus (A. Berger) Britt. & Rose.
N. serpentinus (Lagasca & Rodriguez) Britt. & Rose = *Peniocereus serpentinus*.

Nymphaea L. WATER LILY. Nymphaeaceae. Some 50 aquatic, perenn. herbs. Rhiz. submerged, sometimes tuberous or stoloniferous. Lvs usually floating, usually simple, subcoriaceous, base deeply cleft with plantlets sometimes formed in sinus, subpeltate; petioles elongate. Fls solitary, floating or emergent, usually fragrant, opening diurnally or nocturnally; sep. usually 4, free; pet. many, spreading, free; sta. numerous. Cosmop.

N. alba L. EUROPEAN WHITE LILY. Lvs to 30cm diam., broadly ovate to suborbicular, entire, dark green above, red-green to yellow beneath. Fls to 20cm, diam., white, opening diurnally, floating, faintly fragrant; sta. yellow to orange. Eurasia, N Afr. Z5.

N. amazonium Mart. & Zucc. Lvs to 32cm, broadly ovate to elliptic, entire or subentire, green spotted purple-brown above, purple-brown beneath. Fls to 12cm diam., floating, cream-white or pale yellow; sta. pale yellow. C Amer., Trop. S Amer. Z10.

N. ampla (Salisb.) DC. Lvs to 40cm diam., suborbicular, subentire, green spotted purple-black above, red-purple spotted black beneath. Fls to 13cm diam., white; outer pet. tinged yellow-green; sta. yellow. Trop. & subtrop. Amer. Z10.

N. blanda G. Mey. Lvs to 21cm, broadly elliptic to suborbicular, entire, glossy green above, paler beneath. Fls to 10cm diam., floating, cream-white to pale yellow; sta. cream-white or yellow. C Amer., N S Amer. Z10.

N. caerulea Savigny. BLUE LOTUS. Lvs to 40cm diam., orbicular or suborbicular, entire or undulate, green above, spotted purple beneath. Fls to 15cm diam., pale blue, emergent, opening diurnally; sta. yellow. N & trop. Afr. Z10.

N. calliantha Conard. Lvs to 28cm, ovate to suborbicular, entire, green above, margin purple beneath. Fls to 15cm diam., light blue, pink or violet; sta. yellow. C & SW Afr.

N. candida Presl & C. Presl. Closely resembles *N. alba* except all parts smaller. Fls to 7.5cm diam., unscented. N Eurasia. Z4.

N. capensis Thunb. CAPE BLUE WATER LILY. Lvs to 40cm diam., orbicular or ovate-orbicular, dentate-undulate, green, spotted purple beneath when young. Fls to 20cm diam., bright blue, opening diurnally, sweetly fragrant, emergent; sta. golden. S & E Afr., Madag. 'Eastoniensis': lvs serrate; fls steel blue. var. *zanzibariensis* (Casp.) Conard. Lvs smaller, tinged purple beneath; fls to 30cm diam., deeper blue. 'Azurea': fls light blue. 'Jupiter': fls large, dark violet blue, scented, sep. purple interior. 'Rosea': lvs tinted red beneath; fls pale pink flushed red. Z10.

N. ×*chrysantha* Marliac. (*N. rubra* ×*N. mexicana*.) Lvs green mottled brown above. Fls yellow to yellow-vermilion; sta. bright orange. Gdn origin.

N. citrina Peter. Closely resembles *N. mexicana* except fls to 15cm diam., fragrant.Lvs to 25cm diam., suborbicular, green above and beneath, lobes rounded, not acute. E Afr. Z10.

N. colorata Peter. Lvs to 12.5cm diam., suborbicular, dark green with pale green venation above, green-brown beneath, dentate-sinuate towards base. Fls to 10cm diam., light blue; anth. violet. cf *N. stellata*. Tanz. Z10.

N. ×*daubenyana* hort. (*N. caerulea* ×*N. micrantha*.) Lvs viviparous. Fls 5–18cm diam., emergent, azure blue, opening in the morning.

N. elegans Hook. Lvs to 18cm diam., suborbicular or broadly ovate, entire or slightly undulate, dark green above marked purple-black when young, bright red-purple beneath spotted purple. Fls to 13cm diam., pale violet, opening diurnally, fragrant; sta. yellow, apices blue. Tex. and N Mex. to Guat. Z9.

N. fennica Mela. Lvs to 12cm, elliptic-cordate. Fls to 7cm diam., white to rose-pink, cupular. Finland. Z4.

N. flava Leitn. = *N. mexicana*.

N. flavovirens Lehm. Vigorous. Lvs to 45cm diam., suborbicular to ovate, subentire to deeply sinuate, sometimes red beneath. Fls to 20cm diam., white, strongly fragrant, opening diurnally, emergent; sta. deep yellow. Mex., S Amer. Over 20 cvs and hybrids. 'Astraea' (*N. astraea*): fls star-shaped, blue shading to white centre, sta. yellow. 'Mrs C.W. Ward' ('Red Star'): fls rosy red, sta. golden yellow tipped pink. 'Purpurea' ('Blue Star'): fls vivid purple, sta. gold. 'Stella Gurney' ('Pink Star'): fls large, pale pink. 'William Stone': fls large, dark blue, violet at centre, sta. gold tipped blue. Z10.

N. gardneriana Planch. Lvs to 21cm, suborbicular to elliptic, entire, mottled rusty brown beneath. Fls to 15cm diam., cream-white, floating; pet. distinctly whorled; sta. cream-white. S Amer. Z10.

N. gigantea Hook. AUSTRALIAN WATER LILY. Lvs to 60cm diam., ovate to orbicular, undulate, dentate, tinged pink to purple beneath, finely dentate. Fls to 30cm diam., sky blue to blue-purple, opening diurnally, emergent; sta. bright yellow. Trop. Aus., New Guinea. Z10.

N. ×helvola hort. (*N. tetragona ×N. mexicana.*) Lvs to 6cm, red blotched brown; fls to 5cm diam., canary-yellow; sta. orange. Gdn origin. Z6.

N. heudelotii Planch. Lvs to 11cm, ovate to orbicular, entire or subentire, red-purple flecked black beneath. Fls to 5cm diam., blue-white. Angola. Z10.

N. jamesoniana Planch. Lvs to 24cm, broadly elliptic, entire, sometimes flecked black. Fls cream-white, floating; sta. cream-white. Trop. & subtrop. Americas. Z10.

N. Laydekeri Hybrids (*N. ×Laydekeri* Marliac.) Involving *N. alba* var. *rubra*, *N. tetragona* and others. Hardy gdn hybrids lacking the vigour of the Marliacea Hybrids, usually with brown-mottled or -tinted lvs and fls 6–8cm diam. Includes 'Fulgens' (lvs mottled brown; fls to 9cm diam., crimson-magenta, sta. red); 'Lilacea' (fls lilac-pink, fragrant, sta. orange-red) and 'Purpurata' (lvs green; fls crimson, sta. orange-red).

N. lotus L. EGYPTIAN WATER LILY; LOTUS; WHITE LILY. Lvs to 50cm diam., suborbicular, undulate-serrate, dark green above, green or brown and usually pubesc. beneath. Fls to 25cm diam., white, sometimes tinged pink, opening diurnally or nocturnally, slightly fragrant, emergent. Egypt to trop. & SE Afr. var. *dentata* (Schum. & Thonn.) Nichols. Lvs glab.; fls white; fil. with an apical purple spot. C Afr. Z10.

N. Marliacea Hybrids (*N. ×Marliacea* Marliac.) Involving *N. alba*, *N. odorata* var. *rosea*, *N. mexicana* and others. Hardy, robust gdn hybrids with large fls held above the water. Includes 'Albida' (fls fragrant, white, exterior tinted pink below; sta. yellow); 'Carnea' (fls fragrant, flesh-pink to deep rose); 'Chromatella' (lvs mottled purple-bronze, fls chrome yellow, semi-double, 15–20cm diam.) and 'Rosea' (lvs flushed purple at first; fls rosy red).

N. mexicana Zucc. YELLOW WATER LILY. Lvs to 18cm diam., floating or emergent, ovate or orbicular, subentire to dentate-undulate, green blotched brown above, green-purple to deep purple beneath. Fls to 13cm diam., pale to bright yellow, slightly fragrant, floating or emergent. Flor., Tex. and Mex. Z9.

N. micrantha Guill. & Perrott. Lvs to 7cm, round-cordate, entire, pale green above, red dotted violet-black beneath. Fls 8–13cm diam., white to bright blue; sta. white. W Afr. Z10.

N. odorata Ait. FRAGRANT WATER LILY; POND LILY. Lvs to 25cm diam., orbicular, entire, dull dark green above, usually purple and rough beneath. Fls to 15cm diam., white, usually floating, sweetly fragrant, opening diurnally; sta. gold. E US. 'Eugene de Land': fls pale orange-pink, scented, held above water. 'Exquisita': fls small, star-shaped, rose. 'Helen Fowler': fls large, deep pink, v. fragrant, held above water. 'Roswitha' ('Buggele'): fls rich rose red. 'Sulphurea Grandiflora' (*N. odorata ×N. mexicana*): lvs dark green, marbled; fls v. large, stellate, bright rich yellow. 'William B. Shaw': fls large, flat, creamy pink, internal zone of dark red fine pet. var. *rosea* Pursh. Fls to 10cm diam., deep pink, strongly scented. E US. 'Prolifera': fls abundant. Z3.

N. pubescens Willd. Lvs to 25cm, ovate or broadly oblong, floating, dark green above, dull purple-green and pubesc. beneath, undulate. Fls to 20cm diam., white, nocturnal. India to Philippine Is, S to Java and Aus. Z10.

N. pygmaea Ait. = *N. tetragona*.

N. 'Pygmy Yellow' = *N. ×helvola*.

N. rubra Roxb. INDIAN RED WATER LILY. Closely resembles *N. lotus* except lvs to 45cm diam., dark bronze-red, pubesc. beneath; fls to 25cm diam., deep red-purple. India. 'Rosea': fls soft red, abundant. Z10.

N. rudgeana G. Mey. Lvs to 36cm diam., suborbicular, irregularly dentate, sometimes purple above, green or purple-brown beneath. Fls cream-white to light yellow, sometimes tinged pink, emergent or floating; sta. white-cream to light yellow. N and E S Amer. Z10.

N. stellata Willd. Lvs to 15cm diam., suborbicular to elliptic, irregularly dentate-sinuate, sometimes blotched brown above, pink to purple beneath. Fls to 12cm diam., pale blue to pink or white, emergent, opening diurnally; sta. pale yellow with blue apices. S & SE Asia. 'Berlin': fls large, sky blue. Z10.

N. stuhlmannii (Schweinf.) Gilg. Lvs to 25cm, ovate to orbicular, entire. Fls to 15cm diam., bright yellow, sweetly fragrant; sta. orange-yellow. Afr. Z10.

N. sulfurea Gilg. Lvs to 55cm, broadly ovate to suborbicular, entire, red-green above, dark red beneath. Fls to 7cm diam., deep sulphur-yellow, fragrant, opening diurnally; sta. bright yellow. Angola. Z10. Often confused with the hardy hybrid, *N.* 'Sulfurea'.

N. tetragona Georgi. PYGMY WATER LILY. Hardy. Lvs to 10cm,

ovate, entire, blotched brown when young above, dull red beneath. Fls to 5cm diam., white, sometimes faintly lined purple, floating, slightly fragrant; anth. golden yellow. NE Eur., N Asia to Jap., N Amer. 'Alba': lvs small, oval, purple beneath; fls to 2.5cm diam., white. 'Hyperion': fls dark amaranth. 'Johann Pring': fls to 5cm diam., rich pink, inner ring sta. light orange, outer ring dark pink. 'Rubis': fls deep red, lacking white dots on outer pet. 'Rubra': lvs tinted purple, red beneath; fls dark red, sta. orange. Z2.

N. tuberosa Paine. Lvs to 38cm diam., orbicular, entire, green above and beneath. Fls to 23cm diam., pure white, floating or emergent, sometimes faintly scented, opening diurnally. NE US. Z3.

N. cvs. TROPICAL DAY-BLOOMING HYBRIDS. (white) 'Alice Tricker' (improved form of 'Mrs George H. Pring'): vigorous; fls large, pet. broad, white. 'Mrs George H. Pring' ('White Star') ('Mrs Edward Whitaker' ×*N. ovalifolia*): lvs large, blotched rich brown; fls to 25cm diam., star-shaped, white with a hint of cream, sta. yellow tipped white, scented. 'Trailblazer': lvs bright green, tinted purple below; fls star-shaped, deep yellow. 'Yellow Dazzler': lvs v. large, fls large, flat, star-shaped, lemon yellow, held high, abundant. (pink): 'Afterglow': fls combine pink, orange and yellow. 'Enchantment': lvs oval, dotted; fls rich salmon pink, scented. 'General Pershing' ('Mrs Edwards Whitaker' ×'Castaliiflora'): lvs pink, large, tinted purple fls large, deep pink, fragrant, held to 30cm above water. 'Pink Pearl': fls vivid silvery pink, sta. yellow tipped pink, held above water. 'Pink Platter': lvs bright green marbled rich brown; fls open, soft pink; viviparous. (red): 'American Beauty' (*N. flavovirens* 'Williams' ×*N. colorata*): Lvs large, orbicular, edges waved, veined; fls large, soft magenta, centre yellow. 'Jack Wood': lvs dotted brown; fls raspberry red, centre gold, scented. (purple): 'Mrs Martin E. Randig': lvs bronze beneath; fls dark purple, sep. pink, scented; viviparous. 'Panama Pacific': lvs bronze, veins marked red; fls deep plum, sta. gold, anth. purple. (blue): 'August Koch' ('Mrs Woodrow Wilson' ×'Blue Beauty'): lvs dark green, flushed pink beneath; fls to 25cm diam., blue, sta. orange, fls held above water. 'Blue Beauty' ('Pennsylvania', 'Pulcherrima') (*N. caerulea ×N. capensis* var. *zanzibariensis*): lvs v. large, long-lobed, edges waved, dark green spotted brown; fls deep blue with central gold disc, sta. yellow, anth. violet, scented, sep. marked black. 'Henry Shaw' (form of 'Castaliiflora'): lvs soft green, spotted brown above, tinted pink beneath; fls soft blue, scented, sta. yellow tipped blue. 'Leopardess': lvs dark green, splotched deep brown; fls cobalt blue, scented. 'Margaret Randig': vigorous; lvs dark green spotted bronze; fls large, pet. wide, rich deep blue, scented. 'Mrs Edwards Whitaker' ('Castaliiflora' ×*N. ovalifolia*): lvs orbicular, margins waved; fls large, to 30cm diam., lavender blue, fading to silver, sta. yellow.

TROPICAL NIGHT-BLOOMING HYBRIDS. (white): 'Missouri' ('Mrs George C. Hitchcock' ×'Sturtevantii'): lvs marbled purple, edges indented; fls v. large, to 40cm diam., pet. wide, snow white, held above water. 'Sir Galahad': vigorous; lvs large, waxy; fls star-shaped, cool white, sta. yellow. 'Wood's White Knight' ('Sir Galahad' ×'Missouri'): fls light cream; sta. deep yellow. (pink) 'Mrs George Hitchcock' ('Omarana' ×'Omarana'): lvs tinted copper, edges wavy; fls large, clear pink, sta. orange. 'Rosa de Noche': lvs large, tinted red; fls pink shading to apple blossom toward yellow centre. 'Sturtevantii' (*N. lotus* ×'Devoniensis'): lvs tinted red to copper, undulating; fls large, pearl pink, scented, held above water. 'Emily Grant Hutchings': lvs small, edges wavy, flushed bronze; fls large, to 30cm diam., cupped, rich pink-red, sta. purple. 'Mrs John A. Wood': lvs tinted deep red; fls star-shaped, burgundy. 'Red Flare': lvs rich mahogany; fls star-shaped, vivid red, scented.

HARDY HYBRIDS. (white): 'Gladstoniana' ('Gladstone') (seedling of *N. tuberosa* ×*N. alba*): lvs round, dark red; fls v. large, snow white, pet. thick, incurving, sta. gold. 'Hermine' ('Hermione') (selection of *N. alba*): lvs ovate, dark green; pet. long, sep. bright green. 'Gonnere' ('Crystal White', 'Snowball') (*N. tuberosa* 'Richardsonii' ×?): lvs large; fls large, round, pure white, sep. green. 'Gloire de Temple-sur-Lot': large; fls v. double, blush pink ageing to white, pet. incurving, sta. yellow. 'Virginalis': lvs tinted purple; fls semi-double, pure white, sta. yellow, sep. tinted pink. (yellow): 'Charlene Strawn': fls yellow, held above water, scented. 'Solfatare': lvs dark green marbled dark red; fls star-shaped, soft yellow with red hues. 'Sunrise': lvs elliptic, sometimes marked brown, tinted red beneath; fls to 20cm diam., bright yellow, scented. (sunset): 'Comanche': lvs purple when young; fls small, rich orange turning copper, held above water. 'Graziella': lvs dull green marked purple and brown; fls v. small, orange-red, sta. orange. 'Sioux': lvs bronze, marbled brown; fls buff yellow turning peach then deep orange-red. (pink): 'Amabilis' ('Pink Marvel'): lvs large, rich green; fls large, to 25cm diam., star-shaped, flesh pink, darkening later, sta. gold, later orange. 'Fire Crest': fls deep pink, sta. red, pet. pointed, v. profuse, fragrant.

'Lustrous': lvs copper when young; fls silky pale pink, sta. yellow, sep. pink inside, profuse. 'Pink Opal': lvs tinted bronze; fls double, cupped, soft pink to coral red, held above water, buds globose. 'Pink Sensation': lvs rounded; fls to 20cm diam., pet. oval, stellate, rich pink, held above water. 'Ray Davis': fls v. double, delicate, stellate, shell pink. 'Rene Gerard': fls open, rose pink with crimson marks near centre. 'Rose Arey': lvs tinted red; fls large, star-shaped, rose pink, sta. yellow, anise scented. (red): 'Attraction': lvs large; fls large, to 25cm diam., vivid red dotted white, sta. deep red-brown with gold top, sep. tinted pink. 'Charles de Meurville': strong-growing; lvs olive green; fls large, deep claret, striped white from tip. 'Ellisiana': fls small, claret, sta. orange, profuse, early-flowering. 'Gloriosa' ('Glory'): large; lvs tinted bronze; fls large, to 15cm diam., deep red. 'James Brydon' ('Brydonia Elegans'): large; lvs tinted purple, sometimes spotted dark red; fls large, double, cupped, bright red with metallic sheen, sta. deep orange tipped yellow, scented. 'Splendida' ('Splendide'): lvs dull green; fls ruby red, darkening with age, sta. orange. 'William Falconer': lvs purple when young, green with red venation; fls erect, blood red, sta. yellow.
N. venusta Hentze = *N. alba*.
N. zanzibariensis Casp. = *N. capensis* var. *zanzibariensis*.

NYMPHAEACEAE Salisb. 6/60. *Euryale, Nuphar, Nymphaea, Victoria.*

Nymphoides Hill. FLOATING HEART. Menyanthaceae. 20 aquatic creeping, rhizomatous perenn. herbs. Lvs floating, long-stalked. Fls yellow or white, axill., 1 to many on slender stalks, flowering nodes sometimes with clusters of tuberous spur roots; cor. subrotate, lobes 5, entire or fringed. Cosmop.
N. aquatica (Walter) Kuntze. BANANA PLANT; FAIRY WATER LILY. Lvs 3.5–15cm diam., suborbicular to reniform, pitted beneath. Flowering nodes with clusters of short spur roots. Fls 1.2–1.75cm diam., white; pet. unfringed. E N Amer. Z6.
N. cordata (Elliott) Fern. Lvs 2–2.5cm diam., ovate, deeply cordate at base, obscurely pitted beneath. Flowering nodes with clusters of slender spur roots. Fls to 1.2cm diam., cream or white; pet. unfringed. E N Amer. Z5.
N. indica (Thwaites) Kuntze. WATER SNOWFLAKE. Lvs to 15cm diam., usually far smaller, orbicular. Fls to 2cm diam., white

stained deep yellow at centre; pet. covered in white gland. hairs or densely papillose, fringed. Trop. Z10.
N. lacunosa (Vent.) Kuntze = *N. aquatica*.
N. nymphaeoides Britt. = *N. peltata*.
N. peltata (S.G. Gmel.) Kuntze. YELLOW FLOATING HEART; WATER FRINGE. Freely stoloniferous. Lvs 5–10cm diam., ovate-orbicular, repand, mottled. Fls to 2.5cm diam., sometimes more, bright gold-yellow; pet. short-fringed. Eur., Asia; nat. US. Z6.
→*Limnanthemum* and *Villarsia*.

Nypa Steck. MANGROVE PALM. Palmae. 1 unarmed palm of coasts and waterways. St. subterranean, immersed or prostrate, branched. Lvs pinnate, erect, to 7m; pinnae single-fold, re-duplicate, coriaceous, to 90cm, regularly spaced, midrib prominent, chestnut brown, with papery scales beneath. Infl. interfoliar, erect, 5–6×branched; yellow. Fruits smooth, angled in a term. head. Malay Archipel. to Bay of Bengal, Solomon and Ryuku Is., trop. Aus. Z10.
N. fruticans Wurmb.

Nyssa L. TUPELO. Nyssaceae. 5 decid. trees, to 30m. Fls in stalked unisexual or ♂ heads at base of new growth; cal. minutely lobed; pet. 5, small, green; sta. 10. Fr. a drupe. Early summer. E N Amer., E Asia.
N. sinensis Oliv. CHINESE TUPELO. Similar to *N. sylvatica* but 10–15m and more spreading. Lvs to 20cm, oblong-lanceolate, apex acuminate, base broad-cuneate to rounded, sparsely pub-esc. and tinged red when young. Autumn colour usually surpassing that of *N. sylvatica*. C China. Z7.
N. sylvatica Marshall. BLACK GUM; PEPPERIDGE; SOUR GUM. Broadly columnar to conical, 20–30m. Lvs to 15cm, ovate to elliptic or obovate, apex abruptly acuminate, base cuneate, entire, downy on the veins beneath, flame-coloured in fall. Fr. ovoid, 1cm, blue-black. E N Amer. 'Jermyns Flame' and 'Sheffield Park' selected for autumn colour. var. *biflora* (Walter) Sarg. SWAMP TUPELO. To 15m, base of trunk swollen when growing in water. Lvs to 9cm, more leathery, oblanceolate. SE US. Z3.

NYSSACEAE Dumort. 3/8. *Davidia, Nyssa.*

O

Oak *Quercus.*

Oakesia Wats. = *Uvularia.*

Oakesiella Small = *Uvularia.*

Oak Fern *Gymnocarpium dryopteris.*
Oakleaf Fig *Ficus montana.*
Oak-leaved Banksia *Banksia quercifolia.*
Oak-leaved Dryandra *Dryandra quercifolia.*
Oak-leaved Geranium *Pelargonium quercifolium.*
Oak-leaved Hydrangea *Hydrangea quercifolia.*
Oat Grass *Arrhenatherum; Helictotrichon.*
Oats *Avena.*
Oba-giboshi *Hosta montana.*
Obedience Plant *Maranta arundinacea.*
Obedient Plant *Physostegia.*

Oberonia Lindl. Orchidaceae. 330 epiphytic stemless orchids. Lvs fleshy with bases overlapping in a fan, carinate-conduplicate, oblong or sword-shaped, acuminate. Fls small, crowded in a cylindric term. spike. OW Trop. Z10.
O. brevifolia Lindl. = *O. disticha.*
O. disticha (Lam.) Schltr. Lvs to 3.5×1cm. Infl. 4–5cm; fls bright ochre to orange-yellow. E & W Afr.
O. iridifolia (Roxb.) Lindl. Lvs 5–25×1–2.5cm. Infl. to 18cm; fls pale green or brown. Himal., Burm., Philipp., Pacific.
O. kanburiensis Seidenf. Lvs to 8.5×10cm. Infl. equalling or exceeding lvs; fls ochre to yellow. Thail.

Obregonia Fric. Cactaceae. 1 taprooted, low-growing cactus; st. mostly simple, 5–30cm diam., depressed, tubercles triangular, arranged as in a rosette, acuminate; spines 0–5, to 15mm, pale, soon decid. Fls 2–3.6×2.5cm, in woolly stem-apex, almost white; pericarpel and tube well-developed, naked; tep. narrow; sta. sometimes sensitive; fil. pink. Summer. NE Mex. Z9.
O. denegrii Fric.

Oca *Oxalis tuberosa.*
Ocean-spray *Holodiscus discolor.*

Ochagavia Philippi. Bromeliaceae. 3 stiff, shrubby, perenn. herbs. Lvs linear, spiny, in a rosette. Infl. bracteate, globose or capitate, short-stalked or sunk into rosette centre. C Chile. Z10.
O. carnea (Beer) L.B. Sm. & Looser. To 60cm. Lvs 20–50cm, deflexed, 30–50 in a dense rosette, stiff, ash-grey scaly, shiny above, toothed, with 5mm spines. Infl. many-fld, globose, on a short peduncle; bracts bright rose-pink, laciniate, forming an involucre; fls 3–5cm, pink to lavender, sta. bright yellow, exserted. Coastal C Chile.
O. lindleyana Mez = *O. carnea.*
→*Bromelia.*

Ochna L. BIRD'S EYE BUSH. Ochnaceae. 86 decid. or semi-everg. trees and shrubs. Lvs glossy. Fls solitary or in rac., pan. or umbels; sep. 5, spreading, enlarged and red to purple in fr.; pet. 5–10, yellow, caducous; sta. numerous; ovary deeply lobed, each lobe becoming a 1-seeded drupe around a swollen receptacle and subtended by cal. OW Trop. Z10.
O. atropurpurea DC. Distinguished from *O. serrulata* by the purple, not bright red cal. To 2m. Lvs ovate, sharply toothed. Fls solitary. S Afr.
O. japonica hort. = *O. serrulata.*
O. kirkii Oliv. To 5m. Lvs 5–8cm, obovate-elliptic to broadly oblong, entire or minutely ciliate-toothed. Infl. a short pan.; cal. red-purple. Trop. Afr.
O. mossambicensis Klotzsch. To 3.5m. Lvs to 25cm, obovate to oblanceolate, serrulate. Infl. a dense pan.; cal. lobes red. Moz.
O. multiflora hort. non DC. = *O. serrulata.*
O. serratifolia hort. non Bak. = *O. serrulata.*
O. serrulata (Hochst.) Walp. MICKEY-MOUSE PLANT; BIRD'S EYE BUSH. To 2.25m. Lvs to 6cm, narrowly elliptic, serrulate. Fls solitary or clustered; cal. lobes bright red in fr. Drupes glossy, black. S Afr.

OCHNACEAE DC. 37/460. *Ochna.*

Ochre Lily *Lilium primulinum.*

Ochrocarpus A. Juss. = *Mammea.*

Ochroma Sw. BALSA; DOWN-TREE. Bombacaceae. 1 fast-growing spreading tree to 30m, trunk often buttressed; wood v. light. Lvs simple or palmate with 5–7 lobes or angles, rounded, cordate, to 30cm+ across, stellate-pubescent beneath; petioles long. Fls solitary, axill.; cal. to 5cm, campanulate, lobes 5, somewhat fleshy; pet. 5, dull white to yellow-brown, to 15cm; sta. numerous, exceeding pet. Fr. an elongate angular capsule to 25cm. Lowland trop. Amer. Z10.
O. lagopus Sw.
O. pyramidale (Cav.) Urban = *O. lagopus.*

Ochrosia Juss. Apocynaceae. 23 trees or shrubs with milky sap. Lvs usually in whorls, entire. Infl. a dense, stalked corymb; cal. 5-lobed; cor. funnelform, limb flaring, 5-lobed. Fr. made up of 1 or 2 small, 1-seeded drupes. Malesia and Pacific Is., Aus. Z10.
O. elliptica Labill. POKOSOLA. Tree to 6(–12)m. Lvs elliptic, leathery. Fls to 1.2cm, fragrant. Fr. angled, red. New Caledonia to Aus.
O. mariannensis A. DC. Small tree. Lvs elongate-oblanceolate, lustrous. Fls small, white. Fr. red, compressed. Pacific Is.

Ocimastrum Rupr. = *Circaea.*

Ocimum L. Labiatae. 35 aromatic herbs and shrubs. St. erect. Infl. of 6-fld verticillasters arranged in a lax or dense spike; bracts occas. brightly coloured, sometimes forming a term. coma; cal. bilabiate, tubular, upper lip large, entire, lower lip 4-lobed; cor. bilabiate, tube straight or funnelform, subequal to cal. or exserted, upper lip subequally 4-lobed, lower lip entire. OW Trop. Z10.
O. africanum Lour. = *O. americanum* var. *pilosum.*
O. americanum L. Ann. or short-lived perenn., 15–70cm. St. woody at base, covered in long or short hairs. Lvs 1-8×0.4–4cm, narrowly ovate or elliptic, entire to shallowly serrate, glab. or with hairs beneath on veins. Verticillasters 10mm apart; cor. 4–6mm, white or pale mauve, tube straight or funnelform. Trop. & S Afr., China and India. var. *americanum.* St. with short retrorse, adpressed hairs. Lvs to 2.5cm. var. *pilosum* (Willd.) Paton. St. with long spreading hairs. Lvs longer than 2.5cm. Trop. Afr.
O. basilicum L. COMMON BASIL; SWEET BASIL. Ann. or short-lived perenn., 20–60cm. St. woody at base, minutely pubesc. on infl. axis. Lvs 1.5–5×0.5–2cm, narrowly ovate to elliptic, entire to serrate, gland. punctate. Verticillasters 8–20mm apart; cor. 5–8mm, pink, white or creamy yellow, tube straight. Trop. Asia. 'Citriodorum': lvs lemon-scented. 'Crispum': lvs curled around the edges. 'Minimum' BUSH BASIL; GREEK BASIL: 15–30cm; lvs v. small, less than 1cm long, ovate. 'Purple Ruffles': lvs purple, curled around the edges. 'Purpureum' ('Dark Opal'): lvs red-purple, clove-scented. 'Spicy Globe': compact and globose; lvs small; fls white.
O. canum Sims = *O. americanum.*
O. citriodorum Vig. = *O. basilicum.*
O. crispum Thunb. = *Perilla frutescens* var. *nankinensis.*
O. frutescens L. = *Perilla frutescens.*
O. frutescens var. *crispum* (Benth.) Decne. = *Perilla frutescens* var. *nankinensis.*
O. fruticulosum Burchell = *O. americanum.*
O. gratissimum L. Shrubby perenn., 60–250cm. St. woody at base, epidermis often peeling in strips, pubesc. at nodes and on infl. axis. Lvs 1.5–15×1–8.5cm, elliptic or ovate, sometimes glandular-punctate, pubesc., serrate. Infl. lax or dense; cor. 3–5mm, green, dull yellow or white, tube straight or funnelform. India, W Afr., or Trop. Afr. to Nam. and Natal. var. *glabrum* Paton. Wholly glab. India, W Afr. ssp. *cylindraceum* Paton. Infl. 0.7–1cm wide. Tanz.
O. graveolens R. Br. = *O. americanum* var. *pilosum.*
O. lanceolatum Schumacher & Thonn. = *O. basilicum.*
O. madagascariense Pers. = *Plectranthus madagascariensis.*
O. pilosum Willd. = *O. americanum* var. *pilosum.*
O. pusillum Forst. = *Plectranthus forsteri.*
O. sanctum L. = *O. tenuiflorum.*
O. scutellarioides L. = *Solenostemon scutellarioides.*

O. simile N.E. Br. = *O. basilicum*.

O. stamineum Sims = *O. americanum*.

O. suave Willd. = *O. gratissimum*.

O. tenuiflorum L. HOLY BASIL. Aromatic woody or suffrutescent herb to 1m. St. woody at base, with spreading hairs. Lvs 1.5–3×1.1–2cm, broadly elliptic, serrate, covered in short hairs. Infl. lax; cor. to 3mm, pink or white, tube parallel-sided. India and Malaysia.

O. verticillatum L.f. = *Plectranthus verticillatus*.

O. viride Willd. = *O. gratissimum*.

Oconee Bells *Shortia galacifolia*.

Ocotillo *Fouquieria splendens*.

Octoclinis Muell. = *Callitris*.

Octomeria R. Br. Orchidaceae. *c*50 epiphytic or terrestrial orchids. Rhiz. creeping. Secondary st. elongate, erect, enveloped by tubular sheaths, apically unifoliate. Lvs erect, fleshy to coriaceous. Fls axill., solitary or in 1–several heads or clusters; sep. subsimilar, free to shortly connate, spreading; pet. shorter; lip shorter than pet., entire or obscurely 3-lobed, disc with a shortly bilamellate callus. C & S Amer., W Indies. Z10.

O. complanata Schweinf. St. to 8.5cm. Lvs to 4cm, subterete to triquetrous-subulate. Infl. several, 1-fld; fls to 1.8cm diam.; pale golden-brown to dark maroon-red, lip edged red-maroon, midlobe ovate; keels yellow. Venez., Peru, Braz.

O. diaphana Lindl. St. to 8cm, slender, subcylindrical. Lvs to 6cm, ovate to oblong-lanceolate, convex. Infl. 1-fld; fls to 2cm diam., translucent white, unscented, lip yellow-white flecked red-maroon, dentate, slightly crisped, apex truncate. E Braz.

O. erosilabia Schweinf. St. to 19cm, subterete to tetragonal, 3–5-jointed. Lvs to 17cm, linear-elliptic or linear-oblong. Infl. numerous, subcapitate, 1- to few-fld; fls to 2cm diam.; pale cream-white to cream-yellow, subtranslucent, lip yellow with 2 purple marks, midlobe truncate, erose-dentate. Venez., Guyana.

O. graminifolia (L.) R. Br. St. to 5cm, remote. Lvs to 11cm, narrowly linear-lanceolate to linear-oblong. Infl. 1- or 2-fld; fls to 2cm diam., pale yellow to yellow-green; lip with 2 purple lamellae, midlobe denticulate. Early winter. W Indies to Colomb. & Braz.

O. grandiflora Lindl. St. to 20cm, terete or subterete, compressed above. Lvs to 20cm, linear-rhombic to linear-lanceolate. Infl. 1- or 2-fld; fls to 2.5cm diam., translucent, white to straw-yellow, lip yellow marked purple; deeply emarginate, erose. Venez., Trin., Braz., Surinam, Boliv., Parag.

O. integrilabia Schweinf. St. to 5cm. Lvs to 50mm, linear or linear-oblong to terete. Infl. 1- or 2-fld; fls to 1cm diam., rose to straw-yellow; lip ± simple. Guyana, Venez.

O. nana Schweinf. St. to 2.5cm. Lvs to 40mm, linear-lanceolate or linear-oblong. Infl. few-fld; fls to 0.8cm diam., thin-textured, pale translucent brown-yellow, the lip pale yellow, simple, ± emarginate. Venez.

O. oxycheila Barb. Rodr. St. to 11cm, erect to slightly arched. Lvs to 8cm, lanceolate or oblong-lanceolate. Fls to 1cm diam., spreading to pendent, yellow-white, faintly scented, lip midlobe truncate, 3-toothed. Braz.

O. saundersiana Rchb. f. St. to 25cm. Lvs to 6cm, terete, subulate. Infl. fasciculate; fls yellow striped purple, lip midlobe acute. Braz.

O. steyermarkii Garay & Dunsterville. St. to 5.5cm. Lvs to 5cm, narrowly lanceolate. Infl. 1-fld; fls to 2cm diam., cream tinged pink, or pink to dark puce, dors. sep. caudate. Venez.

O. surinamensis Focke. St. to 10cm, apex compressed, 3- or 4-jointed. Lvs to 14cm, linear to oblong-elliptic. Infl. several, 1- to few-fld; fls to 1.5cm diam., yellow-white to pale yellow, lip with maroon keels, midlobe denticulate, 3-toothed. Peru, Braz., Guianas, Venez., Colomb.

Octopus Plant *Aloe arborescens*.

Octopus Tree *Schefflera actinophylla*.

Odontadenia Benth. Apocynaceae. 30 climbing shrubs. Fls in large, loose cymes; cal. 5-lobed; cor. funnelform or slightly salverform. Trop. Amer. Z10.

O. grandiflora (G. Mey.) Kuntze = *O. macrantha*.

O. macrantha (Roem. & Schult.) Markgr. Lvs to 15cm, oblong-ovate, smooth, dark, leathery. Fls scented; cor. bright yellow shaded orange, limb to 8cm diam., tube 3.5–5cm. Costa Rica to Peru and N Braz.

O. speciosa Benth. = *O. macrantha*.

✕ **Odontioda**. (*Odontoglossum* ✕ *Cochlioda*.) Orchidaceae. Gdn hybrids with strap-shaped lvs and erect to arching sprays of rounded to star-shaped fls often with ruffled or crisped edges in shades of white, yellow, tan brown, pink and velvety red, often spotted or blotched red or yellow.

Odontites Ludw. Scrophulariaceae. 30 semi-parasitic annuals or dwarf shrubs. Fls in term. spike-like rac.; cal. campanulate; cor. tubular, upper lip entire to bilobed, lower lip 3-lobed. W & S Eur. to W Asia. Z6.

O. rubra Gilib. = *O. verna*.

O. verna (Bellardi) Dumort. RED BARTSIA. Ann., to 50cm. St. erect, branching or simple. Lvs lanceolate to linear-lanceolate, sessile. Fls 5–6mm, pubesc., mauve-pink. Summer. Eur.

→*Bartsia*.

✕ **Odontobrassia**. (*Brassia* ✕ *Odontoglossum*.) Orchidaceae. Gdn hybrids with upright spikes of narrow fls in shades of yellow and cream marked brown.

✕ **Odontocidium**. (*Odontoglossum* ✕ *Oncidium*.) Orchidaceae. Gdn hybrids with branching sprays of small to medium fls in shades of yellow, copper and cream mottled or banded chestnut brown to rusty red.

Odontoglossum HBK. Orchidaceae. Some 100 epiphytic or lithophytic orchids. Rhiz. short or creeping. Pbs usually ovoid or elliptic-oblong, 1–3-leaved at apex, enveloped at base by leafy sheaths. Lvs linear-lanceolate to oblong-elliptic, basically strap-like, thinly coriaceous. Rac. or pan. basal erect or arching, sep. subequal, spreading; pet. similar to sep., often shorter; lip simple or 3-lobed, basal portion often claw-like and usually parallel with column, sometimes adnate to column, lat. lobes spreading or erect, midlobe deflexed, disc lamellate, cristate or acallose. C & S Amer. Z10.

O. alexandrae Batem. = *O. crispum*.

O. angustatum Lindl. non Batem. Pan. short- or long-branched, usually exceeding lvs; fls to 7cm diam.; sep. green, marked brown, linear-lanceolate, long-acuminate, undulate; pet. yellow barred brown, lanceolate to ovate-lanceolate, broader than sep., undulate; lip white, ovate to ovate-oblong or oblong, barred brown above. Ecuad., Peru.

O. aureopurpureum Rchb. f. Pan. much-branched, erect, to 160cm, many-fld; fls to 7cm diam., golden-yellow marked and spotted purple, red or brown; sep. linear-lanceolate to ovate-lanceolate, long-acuminate, undulate-crisped, with long claws; pet. shorter and broader; lip golden-yellow with brown base and spotted brown, fleshy, lanceolate, strongly recurved, crenate and undulat at base, callus yellow. Venez., Colomb., Ecuad., Peru.

O. bictoniense (Batem.) Lindl. = *Lemboglossum bictoniense*.

O. blandum Rchb. f. Fls to 5cm diam., crowded near apex of 25cm, arching rac., tep. white spotted maroon-crimson, lanceolate, long-acuminate; lip white spotted purple, ovate, emarginate, acuminate, erose-dentate, callus yellow. Colomb.

O. brachypterum Rchb. f. = *Otoglossum brevifolium*.

O. brevifolium Lindl. = *Otoglossum brevifolium*.

O. cariniferum Rchb. f. Pan. to 1m, stout, erect or arcuate, many-fld, br. spreading, fractiflex; fls to 5cm diam., fleshy, tep. deep chestnut-brown edged yellow, lanceolate, acute or acuminate; pet. shorter than sep.; lip white, pale yellow with age, long-clawed, reniform, apiculate, callus rose-mauve. Spring. Costa Rica, Panama, Venez.

O. cervantesii La Ll. & Lex. = *Lemboglossum cervantesii*.

O. chiriquense Rchb. f. = *Otoglossum chiriquense*.

O. cimiciferum Rchb. f. = *Oncidium cimiciferum*.

O. cirrhosum Lindl. Rac. or pan. to 60cm, arching; fls to 7cm diam.; tep. white blotched red-brown; sep. narrowly lanceolate, long-acuminate, terminating in a bristle-point; pet. shorter and broader; lip white with red-brown blotches on midlobe, base yellow, 3-lobed, lat. lobes rounded, denticulate, midlobe recurved, narrow-lanceolate, long-acuminate. Spring. Ecuad., Peru, Colomb.

O. citrosmum Lindl. = *Cuitlauzina pendula*.

O. compactum Rchb. f. = *O. aureopurpureum*.

O. constrictum Lindl. Rac. or lightly branched pan. to 60cm, arching fls to 4.5cm diam.; tep. yellow or pale olive blotched and banded red-brown, oblong-lanceolate; lip white blotched pale red, pandurate, apiculate, callus with erose margins. Venez., Colomb., Ecuad.

O. convallarioides (Schltr.) Ames & Correll = *Osmoglossum convallarioides*.

O. cordatum Lindl. = *Lemboglossum cordatum*.

O. coronarium var. *chiriquense* (Rchb. f.) Veitch = *Otoglossum chiriquense*.

O. crispum Lindl. Rac. or pan., arching, to 50cm; fls to 8.5cm diam., usually sparkling white or pale rose, spotted or blotched red or purple, tep. spreading, ovate-elliptic to oblong-elliptic, obtuse to acuminate, undulate or finely dentate; lip usually white or pink with a few red spots and a yellow disc, oblong, acute, undulate, finely dentate. Winter. Colomb.

O. cristatum Lindl. Rac. to 50cm, arching; fls to 6cm diam.; tep. fleshy, cream-yellow with chestnut-brown blotches and markings, elliptic-lanceolate or ovate-lanceolate, acuminate; lip white or cream-yellow with few brown spots, fimbriate-dentate, disc denticulate. Colomb., Ecuad., Peru.

O. dormannianum Rchb. f. Rac. or short-branched pan., ascending to arching; fls to 7cm diam., tep. pale yellow to yellow-brown spotted chocolate-brown; sep. linear-lanceolate to lanceolate, acuminate; pet. linear- to ovate-lanceolate; lip yellow blotched dark brown near white callus, lanceolate, sub-acuminate. Colomb., Venez.

O. edwardii Rchb. f. Pan. much-branched, suberect, far exceeding lvs; fls to 2.5cm, fragrant, tep. bright magenta or mauve-purple, oblong, undulate; lip short, tongue-shaped, with yellow callus. Spring. Ecuad.

O. egertonii Lindl. = *Osmoglossum egertonii*.

O. epidendroides HBK. Pan. or rac. to 45cm, slightly arching; fls to 7cm, tep. bright yellow with 3–5 carmine spots; sep. lanceolate, acuminate, slightly undulate; pet. slightly wider; lip white spotted purple, clawed, elliptic-oblong, sharply reflexed, crenate-undulate. C Amer.

O. erosum Rich. & Gal. = *Lemboglossum stellatum*.

O. gloriosum Lind. ex Rchb. f. = *O. odoratum*.

O. grande Lindl. = *Rossioglossum grande*.

O. grande var. *williamsianum* Rchb. f. = *Rossioglossum williamsianum*.

O. hallii Lindl. Rhiz. short. Rac. (rarely a pan.) to 90cm, erect or arching; fls to 8.5cm diam.; tep. pale yellow blotched chocolate-brown or purple-brown; sep. lanceolate or elliptic-lanceolate, long-acuminate; pet. shorter and broader; lip white blotched purple-brown, callus deep yellow, oblong, dentate to lacerate, basal portion crenulate, callus toothed. Spring. Colomb., Ecuad., Peru.

O. harryanum Rchb. f. Rac. to 1m, erect; fls to 9cm diam.; sep. buff to chestnut brown with vein-like streaks of yellow, elliptic-oblong, undulate; pet. chestnut brown, white at base with broad lines of mauve-purple; lip lateral lobes white striped purple, midlobe white to pale yellow disc with a prominent yellow, fimbriate callus. Summer. Colomb., Peru.

O. hastilabium Lindl. = *Oncidium hastilabium*.

O. hastilabium var. *fuscatum* Hook. = *O. cariniferum*.

O. hennisii Rolfe. Infl. to 20cm; fls to 6, to 5cm diam.; tep. yellow spotted and blotched brown, lanceolate, acuminnate; lip spotted white and blotched red-brown, short-clawed, spreading, 3-lobed, lat. lobes dentate, midlobe long-acuminate. Peru, Ecuad.

O. hookeri Lem. = *Lemboglossum cordatum*.

O. hunnewellianum Rolfe. Rac. to 40cm, branched, arching; fls to 5cm diam., fleshy, tep. yellow with brown blotches, broadly lanceolate to ovate, acute; lip cream-white spotted red-brown, obovate-elliptic, crenulate to undulate, callus yellow. Autumn––spring. Colomb.

O. hystrix Batem. = *O. luteopurpureum*.

O. insleayi (Barker ex Lindl.) Lindl. = *Rossioglossum insleayi*.

O. kegeljanii Morr. Rac. to 40cm, arching, several-fld; fls to 9cm diam.; tep. lemon-yellow blotched chestnut-brown, acute; lip white blotched red-chestnut on apical lobe, oblong to sub-orbicular, crisped, callus toothed. Spring. Venez., Colomb., Ecuad., Peru.

O. koehleri Schltr. = *O. aureopurpureum*.

O. krameri Rchb. f. = *Ticoglossum krameri*.

O. lawrenceanum hort. = *Rossioglossum insleayi*.

O. laxiflorum (Lindl.) Rchb. f. = *Gomesa laxiflora*.

O. lindenii Lindl. Pan. short-branched, to 60cm, 5–7-fld; fls to 4cm diam., bright yellow; sep. lanceolate to oblanceolate, undulate; pet. shorter, undulate; lip ovate-lanceolate, callus prominent, fleshy, with toothed projections. Spring. Jam., Venez., Colomb., Ecuad.

O. lindleyanum Rchb. f. Rac. or pan. loosely several-fld; arching; fls to 6cm, fragrant, star-shaped, tep. yellow with red-brown blotch spots at base, linear-lanceolate, long-acuminate; lip red-brown tipped yellow, white at base spotted purple, lat. lobes small, midlobe linear-lanceolate, reflexed. Spring–summer. Colomb.

O. lucianianum Rchb. f. Rac. to 40cm, erect; fls to 3.8cm diam.; tep. yellow-brown spotted red-brown, lanceolate or narrowly ovate; lip yellow or yellow-white with large chestnut-brown blotch in front of white callus, triangular-lanceolate. Venez.

O. lueddemannii Reg. = *Lemboglossum cordatum*.

O. luteopurpureum Lindl. Rac. to 1m, suberect, loose; fls to 10cm diam.; tep. bright chestnut-brown tipped and marked yellow, ovate-lanceolate, acute or acuminate, undulate, sometimes fringed; lip yellow-white spotted brown, long-clawed, lat. lobes small, midlobe reniform, emarginate, fringed, callus golden-yellow. Spring. Colomb.

O. maculatum La Ll. & Lex. = *Lemboglossum maculatum*.

O. madrense Rchb. f. = *Lemboglossum maculatum*.

O. majale Rchb. f. = *Lemboglossum majale*.

O. membranaceum Lindl. = *Lemboglossum cervantesii*.

O. naevium Lindl. Rac. arching; fls star-shaped, showy, to 6cm diam., tep. white blotched deep red-brown or red-purple, lanceolate, acuminate, undulate; lip white spotted red-brown, linear-lanceolate, pubesc., disc yellow. Spring–summer. Venez., Colomb., Ecuad., Guianas.

O. nevadense Rchb. f. Rac. exceeding lvs, arching, to 15-fld; fls to 8.5cm diam., tep. cinnamon edged yellow, sometimes barred yellow at base, narrowly lanceolate or ovate-lanceolate, acuminate; lip white barred chestnut-brown, triangular, acuminate, deeply fimbriate or dentate. Spring–summer. Colomb., Venez.

O. nobile Rchb. f. Rac. or pan. to 60cm, branched, erect or arching, 10–100-fld; fls to 6cm diam., fragrant, tep. snow-white, sometimes tinged pale rose, ovate-elliptic or ovate-oblong, acute, undulate; lip white blotched purple-crimson at base, pandurate, cuspidate, undulate, callus yellow. Spring. Colomb.

O. odoratum Lindl. Rac. or pan. to 75cm; fls to 6.5cm diam., fragrant, pale to deep yellow dotted and blotched chocolate-brown; sep. ovate-lanceolate, acute or acuminate; pet. lanceolate, long-acuminate, undulate; lip white at bsae, short-clawed, lanceolate to oblong-elliptic, acuminate. Spring. Colomb., Venez.

O. oerstedii Rchb. f. = *Ticoglossum oerstedii*.

O. pendulum (La Ll. & Lex.) Batem. = *Cuitlauzina pendula*.

O. pescatorei Lindl. = *O. nobile*.

O. planifolium (Lindl.) Rchb. f. = *Gomesa planifolia*.

O. platycheilum Weatherby = *Lemboglossum majale*.

O. polyxanthum hort. = *O. kegeljanii*.

O. praestans Rchb. f. & Warsc. Pan. or rac. to 30cm, few- to many-fld; fls to 8cm diam., yellow-green spotted cinnamon-brown or purple; seg. lanceolate or linear-lanceolate, acuminate; pet. shorter and slightly wider; lip simple, lanceolate, long-acuminate. Peru.

O. pulchellum Batem. ex Lindl. = *Osmoglossum pulchellum*.

O. purum Rchb. f. = *O. wallisii*.

O. radiatum Rchb. f. = *O. luteopurpureum*.

O. ramosissimum Lindl. Pan. to 1.5m, erect, much-branched, dense; fls to 5cm diam., fragrant, tep. white spotted violet, undulate and reflexed, narrowly lanceolate, acuminate; lip white blotched violet at base, cordate or deltoid, acuminate, undulate, callus white. Spring. Venez., Colomb., Ecuad.

O. ramulosum Lindl. Pan. to 1m, erect or arching, short-branched; fls to 3cm diam., tep. yellow, base marked deep brown; sep. obovate-oblong or spathulate, undulate; pet. spathulate to elliptic-obovate; lip yellow marked brown, ovate to elliptic-oblong, acute to obtuse, callus yellow or pale yellow. Colomb., Venez., Ecuad.

O. recurvum (R. Br.) Lindl. = *Gomesa recurva*.

O. retusum Lindl. Pan. to 60cm, slender, short-branched, erect; fls to 3cm diam.; tep. orange-red tinged yellow; sep. broadly oblanceolate to narrowly obovate, acute, concave; pet. narrowly oblong-obovate; lip golden-yellow, oblong-subquadrate, recurved above, simple or slightly 3-lobed, retuse. Ecuad., Peru, Colomb.

O. rigidum Lindl. Pan. far exceeding lvs, loosely branched; fls to 3cm diam.; tep. bright canary-yellow; dors. sep. ovate-lanceolate, acuminate, lat. sep. longer and narrower; pet. slightly wider; lip deep yellow, subquadrate, apiculate. Peru, Ecuad.

O. rossii Lindl. = *Lemboglossum rossii*.

O. sanderianum Rchb. f. Pan. short-branched, suberect, arching, many-fld; fls to 7cm diam.; tep. light ochre marked brown, lanceolate, acuminate; lip white with large purple-crimson mark below callus, subpandurate, acute, undulate. Venez., Colomb.

O. schillerianum Rchb. f. Rac. erect, surpassing lvs; fls fragrant, to 5cm diam.; tep. yellow blotched brown or maroon, elliptic-lanceolate, acute to acuminate; ± finely pubesc.; lip white at base, centre purple-brown tipped yellow, clawed, deflexed, midlobe oblong, acute, undulate, pubesc. Winter–spring. Venez., Colomb.

O. spectatissimum Lindl. = *O. triumphans*.

O. stellatum Lindl. = *Lemboglossum stellatum*.

O. tetraplasium Rchb. f. = *O. angustatum*.

O. tripudians Rchb. f. & Warsc. Rac. arching, far exceeding lvs, sometimes branched, many-fld; fls to 7cm diam.; sep., maroon-brown, yellow at base and tips, elliptic-lanceolate to elliptic-oblong, acuminate; pet. smaller, golden-yellow blotched maroon-brown near base; lip white or cream blotched rose or purple-red, subquadrate to pandurate, dentate, disc white; spotted purple-red. Colomb., Ecuad., Peru.

O. triumphans Rchb. f. Rac. or pan. to 90cm, erect or arching, 5–12-fld; fls to 10cm diam., tep. golden-yellow spotted chestnut-brown; sep. oblong-lanceolate, acute or acuminate; pet. elliptic-lanceolate, acute, undulate; lip white apically blotched red-brown, oblong-ovate, long-apiculate, lacerate. Spring. Colomb., Venez.

O. uro-skinneri Lindl. = *Lemboglossum uro-skinneri*.

O. wallisii Lind. & Rchb. f.   Rac. or pan. arching, to 50cm or more; fls to 5cm diam., fleshy, tep. golden-yellow blotched cinnamon-brown, oblong-lanceolate, acute or apiculate; lip white streaked rose-purple near apex, midlobe oblong-ovate or oblong-elliptic, tip sharply reflexed, fringed. Colomb., Venez., Peru.

O. warscewiczii Rchb. f. = *Miltoniopsis warscewiczii*.

O. williamsianum Rchb. f. = *Rossioglossum williamsianum*.

O. **grexes and cvs.** There are many cvs, most with fls in shades of yellow and brown or purple-red. The many selections of *O. crispum* have broad ruffled blooms usually white with red or yellow markings.
→*Oncidium*.

Odontoloma J. Sm., nom. nud. = *Lindsaea*.

Odontonema Nees. Acanthaceae.   26 herbs and sparsely branched shrubs. Infl. a term. rac. or racemose pan.; fls short-stalked; cal. lobes 5; cor. long-tubular, 5-lobed or bilabiate; sta. 2 attached above middle of cor. tube; fil. toothed. Trop. Amer. Z10.

O. callistachyum (Schldl. & Cham.) Kuntze. Everg. pubesc. shrub to 4m. St. 4-angled. Lvs to 30cm, ovate-oblong, acute, rugulose. Infl. a term. racemose pan., strongly erect; cor. to 3cm, red, exterior glab., tube gland. within, lower lip deflexed. Mex.

O. schomburgkianum (Nees) Kuntze. Everg. shrub, erect to 2m. St. obscurely ridged. Lvs to 22cm, oblong-lanceolate, acuminate, glab. or sparsely downy at first, veins impressed. Rac. to 90cm, v. slender, pendulous; cor. to 3cm, crimson to scarlet, narrowly tubular, slightly swollen at base, then constricted, widening toward limb, lobes small, equal, rounded. Colomb.

O. strictum (Nees) Kuntze. Everg. glab. shrub to 2m. St. rigid, erect. Lvs to 15cm, oblong, acuminate, ± undulate, glossy. Infl. to 30cm, erect, slender, compact; cor. to 2.5cm, crimson, waxy, lobes small. C Amer. Sometimes misnamed *Justicia coccinea*.
→*Thyrsacanthus*.

✕ **Odontonia**. (*Odontoglossum* ✕ *Miltonia*.) Orchidaceae. Gdn hybrids with large fls on tall spikes in shades of brown, yellow, purple-red and mauve-pink or white marked brown or yellow.

Odontophorus N.E. Br. Aizoaceae. 3 succulent perennials. Low, shrub-forming plants with fleshy roots; st. ascending or forming mats. Lvs 1–2 pairs per shoot, v. thick, soft-fleshy, grey-green, tuberculate, pubesc., dentate. Fls pedicellate, yellow or white. S Afr. (Cape Prov.). Z9.

O. angustifolius L. Bol. Lvs 2.5–3.2cm, 4 per st., oblong-linear to linear-tapered, tip rhombic with 3–4 marginal teeth. Fls 0.6cm diam., lemon yellow. W Cape.

O. areolatus Marloth nom. nud. = *O. nanus*.

O. marlothii N.E. Br. Lvs 2.5–3.5cm, 2–3 pairs per st., somewhat swollen at base, side angles with 6–7 thickened, awned teeth, grey to dark green with prominent rounded tubercles tipped with fine white hairs. Fls 3cm diam., yellow. W Cape.

O. nanus L. Bol. Lvs crowded, to 1.5cm, ± ovate on upper surface, sides expanded and tuberculate, margins with stiff teeth, green-white with hair-tipped tubercles. Fls to 4.5cm diam., white. W Cape.

✕ **Odontorettia**. (*Odontoglossum* ✕ *Comparettia*.) Orchidaceae. Gdn hybrids with delicate sprays of small fls in shades of orange, pink and purple or white.

Odontosoria Fée. BRAMBLE FERN. Dennstaedtiaceae. Some 12 or more of terrestrial or lithophytic ferns. Rhiz. creeping, with many dense roots, trichomes and/or scales. Fronds stipitate, scandent, rampant, to 5✕ pinnate, glab.; pinnules entire to lobed or incised; rachis flexible, spiny. Trop. Z10.

O. aculeata (L.) J. Sm. Fronds to 3-pinnate, membranous; primary pinnae to 45✕15cm, lanceolate to ovate, final seg. narrowly wedge-shaped, to 4-lobed at margin. W Indies.

O. chinensis (L.) J. Sm. = *Sphenomeris chinensis*.

O. clavata (L.) J. Sm. = *Sphenomeris clavata*.

O. fumarioides (Sw.) J. Sm. Fronds to 5-pinnate, membranous; primary pinnae to 55✕30cm, deltoid to lanceolate, final seg. deeply lobed or fan-cut. W Indies.
→*Davallia*.

Odontospermum Necker ex Schultz-Bip.

O. aquaticum (L.) Schultz-Bip. = *Nauplius aquaticus*.

O. maritimum (L.) Schultz-Bip. = *Asteriscus maritimus*.

Oeceoclades Lindl. Orchidaceae. 30 terrestrial orchids. Pbs on woody rhiz., 1- to several-leaved at apex. Lvs stiff, leathery or fleshy, conduplicate. Rac. or pan. basal; fls resupinate, thin-textured; sep. and pet. free, spreading; lip 3- or 4-lobed, usually spurred. Trop. & S Afr., Madag., Masc. Is., Seych., Comoros Is., India to New Guinea, Polyn. and Aus., Flor., Carib., C & S Amer. Z10.

O. angustifolia (Sengh.) Garay & P. Tayl. Pbs 2cm, ovoid or pear-shaped. Lvs to 10cm, linear, acute, dull green mottled with purple. Infl. erect, racemose or with a few br., to 30cm; sep. to 0.8cm, green-white below, brown above, pet. white striped green, lip white, edge of midlobe ochre yellow, lat. lobes and disc spotted red, spur green to 3m, subglobose. Madag.

O. ecalcarata (Schltr.) Garay & P. Tayl. Pbs 4–6cm, ovoid or ellipsoid, set close together on rhiz. Lvs 20–25cm, linear, acute, decid. Infl. racemose or paniculate with a long peduncle; tep. to 0.8cm green dotted with red, lip golden yellow with red spots; spur 0. Madag.

O. maculata (Lindl.) Lindl. Pbs 2–4cm, obliquely conical. Lvs 8–32cm, lanceolate, stiff, leathery, pale grey-green mottled, darker green. Rac. to 35cm; tep. to 1cm, green-pink, lip white with 2 purple-pink blotches in throat and purple-veined lat. lobes; spur 4–5mm, bulbous at tip. Trop. Afr. (widespread), Flor., Carib., C & S Amer.

O. pulchra (Thouars) Clements & Cribb. Pbs 12–16cm, spindle-shaped. Lvs 20–70cm, lanceolate, thin-textured. Rac. lax, to 1m; fls to 1.8cm diam., yellow-green with small red-purple lines on pet and lip, throat orange-yellow; spur short, globose, sometimes slightly bifid. Madag., Masc. Is., Comoros Is., Asia and SE Asia to New Guinea, Polyn. and Aus.

O. roseovariegata (Sengh.) Garay & P. Tayl. Pbs 2.5cm, ovoid, clustered, violet-brown. Lvs to 4cm, ovate, acuminate, undulate, dark purple-black mottled pink. Infl. erect, racemose or slightly branched, to 55cm, tep. to 0.6cm, green flushed purple, lip white, densely red-spotted; spur 5mm, pendent, cylindrical. Madag.

O. saundersiana (Rchb. f.) Garay & P. Tayl. Pbs 6–20✕1.5–2cm, conical or cylindrical. Lvs 10–22cm, glossy green, leathery. Rac. longer than lvs; fls yellow-green flushed purple-brown and with purple-brown veins; sep. to 2cm; spur 5–6mm, straight, cylindrical, obtuse. Trop. Afr. (widespread).
→*Eulophia*.

Oemleria Rchb. OSO BERRY; OREGON PLUM. Rosaceae. 1 decid. shrub to 5m; bark smooth. Lvs to 10cm, oblong to oblanceolate, glossy dark green above, grey and pubesc. beneath, entire. Fls 6.5mm diam., white, fragrant, in nodding, 10cm rac.; cal. tube turbinate-campanulate, 5mm, seg. 5, 3mm; pet. 5, obovate to narrow-obovate, to 6mm; sta. 15 in 3 rings; pistils 5, free. Drupe black, glaucous, 1-seeded. Spring. W N Amer. Z6.

O. cerasiformis (Torr. & A. Gray) Greene.
→*Nuttallia* and *Osmaronia*.

Oenanthe L. Umbelliferae. 30 creeping glab. perenn. herbs of wet places. Lvs usually pinnate. Umbels compound, usually with numerous bracts and bracteoles; fls small, white. N Hemis., S Afr., Aus.

O. japonica Miq. = *O. javanica*.

O. javanica (Bl.) DC. St. 20–40cm, erect, angled, bristle from a branching base. Lvs 1–2✕ pinnate, seg. 1–3cm, ovate or narrow-ovate, irregularly toothed, sometimes deeply lobed. Umbels opposite lvs; rays 5–15, 2–5mm. Summer. India to Jap., Ryukyu, Taiwan, Malaysia, N Aus. (Queensld). 'Flamingo': lvs splashed and zoned pale pink, cream and white. Z10.

O. pimpinelloides L. St. 30–100cm, erect, branched, groove. Lvs bipinnate, seg. 0.5–3cm, ovate to lanceolate, linear-lanceolate or linear, lobes usually entire.Umbel term.; rays 6–15, 1–2cm. W & S Eur. to SW Asia. Z8.

O. stolonifera var. *japonica* (Miq.) Maxim. = *O. javanica*.

Oenothera L. EVENING PRIMROSE; SUNDROPS; SUNCUPS. Onagraceae. 124 ann., bienn. or perenn. herbs. St. erect or decumbent, with taproot or fibrous roots. Lvs someimtes in basal rosette, otherwise alt. Fls solitary in lf axils or in corymbose, racemose or spicate infl., actinomorphic, mostly opening at dawn or dusk, soon fading; floral tube cylindrical, apex flared pet. 4; sta. 8 in 2 whorls; ovary 4-locular. Fr. an elongate capsule. N & S Amer., nat. elsewhere.

O. acaulis Cav. Tufted perenn. or bienn., to 15cm, ± stemless. Lvs 12–20cm, oblanceolate, irregularly pinnatifid, hairy, term. lobe enlarged. Fls 5–8cm diam.; pet. emarginate, white ageing rose. Chile. 'Aurea': to 15cm, with prostrate br.; fls large, 5–8cm, yellow. Z5.

O. albicaulis Pursh. Decumbent ann. or bienn., 15–30cm. St. white-pubesc. Rosette lvs 2.5–5cm, spathulate to obovate, st. lvs lanceolate, pinnatifid. Fls solitary, axill.; pet. obcordate, 1–3cm, white ageing pink. Rocky Mts. 'Mississippi Primrose': fls pure white ageing through cream to shell-pink, fragrant. Z5.

O. amoena Lehm. = *Clarkia amoena*.

O. argillicola Mackenzie. Bienn. to perenn., fleshy, glab. St. 60–120cm. Rosette lvs 15–20cm, oblanceolate-linear, st. lvs linear-lanceolate. Infl. terminal, evening-flowering; pet. 2.5–3cm, yellow ageing red-orange. US (Appalachians). Z5.

O. berlandieri (Spach) Walp. = *O. speciosa* non *Calylophus berlandieri*.

O. biennis L. COMMON EVENING PRIMROSE; GERMAN RAMPION. Erect, ann. or bienn. St. erect, branched, 10–150cm. Lvs shallow-dentate, rosette lvs 10–30cm, oblong-lanceolate, st. lvs 8–15cm, lanceolate. Infl. erect, elongate, spicate or branched; pet. 1.8–2.5cm, yellow, ageing gold. E N Amer., nat. Eur. and elsewhere. Z4.

O. biennis var. *hirsutissima* A. Gray ex S. Wats. = *O. elata* ssp. *hirsutissima*.

O. brachycarpa A. Gray. Perenn., glab. to tomentose, ± stemless. Lvs 5–15cm, tufted, grey-green, narrow, entire to sinuate-pinnatifid. Pet. broadly rhombic-ovate, 2.5–5cm, pale yellow, ageing lavender. W Tex. to SE Ariz. and New Mex. Z6.

O. brachycarpa var. *typica* sensu Munz = *O. coryi*.

O. caespitosa Nutt. Tuft-forming rhizomatous bienn. or perenn. St. 10–40cm, subglabrous to villous. Lvs 2–25cm, rosulate, oblanceolate to rhombic or spathulate, irregularly sinuate-dentate. Fls fragrant, several opening together; pet. 2–5×0.5–1cm, white ageing pink. Washington. ssp. *caespitosa*. Floral tube 3.5–7.5cm; pet. fading rose-purple. ssp. *crinata* (Rydb.) Munz. Many-branched, forming dense mats. Pet. fading rose or deep purple. ssp. *macroglottis* (Rydb.) W.L. Wagner, Stockhouse & Klein. St. 4–8cm. Lvs oblanceolate to spathulate, glandular-pubesc., dentate. Pet. fading pink to pale rose. ssp. *marginata* (Nutt. ex Hook. & Arn.) Munz. Lvs oblanceolate to lanceolate or elliptic, pinnately lobed. Pet. fading pink to lavender. Z4.

O. californica S. Wats. Perenn. with creeping rhiz. St. erect, 7–10cm. Lvs narrow-lanceolate, toothed or pinnatifid, strigose or hairy. Fls fragrant, 5cm diam., white to pale pink with yellow centre. Calif. Z7.

O. cheiranthifolia Hornem. = *Camissonia cheiranthifolia*.

O. childsii hort. = *O. speciosa*.

O. clutei Nels. = *O. longissima*.

O. coryi W.L. Wagner. Tuft-forming ± stemless perenn. Lvs to 16cm, linear to narrowly lanceolate, rosulate, densely strigillose, lower half pinnately lobed. Fls 1–3, slightly fragrant; pet. to 4×4cm, yellow, fading orange, drying lavender to purple, broadly obovate, sometimes with an apical tooth. WC Tex. Z7.

O. deltoides Torr. & Frém. DESERT EVENING PRIMROSE. Ann., 5–25cm, branching from base, pubesc. above. Lvs 5–10cm, crowded, rhombic-ovate to rhombic-lanceolate, entire to pinnatifid. Fls solitary, axill., white, ageing pink, 4–8cm diam. Calif. Z9.

O. densiflora Lindl. = *Boisduvalia densiflora*.

O. drummondii Hook. Erect to procumbent ann. or perenn., densely strigulose, sometimes villous. St. 10–50cm, stiff, sometimes flushed red. Lvs grey-green, hairy to glandular-puberulent, shallowly toothed to subentire, basal lvs 5–14cm, narrowly oblanceolate to elliptic, st. lvs to 8cm, elliptic to obovate, sometimes lyrate. Fls solitary; pet. 2–4.5cm, yellow, broadly obovate, truncate to emarginate. N Amer. Z6.

O. elata Erect bienn. to perenn., to 80cm, with a basal rosette. Lvs 5–12.5cm, lanceolate. Fls many in term. spikes. ssp. *hirsutissima* (A. Gray ex S. Wats.) Dietr. St. flushed with red, without gland. hairs in the region of the infl. Z7.

O. erythrosepala Borb. = *O. glazioviana*.

O. flava (A. Nels.) Garrett. Perenn.; stemless, caespitose. Lvs to 20cm, oblong-linear to oblanceolate, runcinate-pinnatifid. Pet. 1–2.6cm, pale yellow to white, usually obovate with a term. tooth. Washington S to Calif., Ariz. and Mex. ssp. *taraxacoides* (Wooton & Standl.) W.L. Wagner. MOUNTAIN DANDELION. Sep. often flecked with red-purple, obcordate. New Mex., Mex. Z8.

O. fraseri Pursh = *O. fruticosa* ssp. *glauca*.

O. fruticosa L. SUNDROPS. Bienn. or perenn., 30–80cm, strigose to hairy overal, tinged red. Basal lvs 3–12cm, oblanceolate to obovate, toothed, st. lvs 2–11cm lanceolate. Day-flowering; pet. 1.5–2.5cm, suborbicular, shallow-toothed, deep yellow. E N Amer. 'Fireworks' ('Feuerwerkeri'): lvs tinged purple; fls yellow. 'Golden Moonlight': to 80 cm high; fls large, bright yellow. 'Highlight' ('Hoheslicht'): fls yellow. 'Illumination': lvs

leathery, tinged bronze; fls large, deep yellow. 'Lady Brookborough': fls large, pale yellow. 'Silvery Moon': to 80cm high; fls large, pale yellow. 'Sonnenwende': to 60cm; lvs red in autumn; fl. buds red-orange. 'Yellow River': st. brick red; fls bright canary yellow. 'Youngii': to 50cm; fls large, bright yellow. 'Youngii-lapsley': to 60cm; fls yellow. ssp. *glauca* (Michx.) Straley. Lvs broader, usually relatively glab. and glaucous, young foliage tinted red. Z4.

O. glauca Michx. = *O. fruticosa* ssp. *glauca*.

O. glazioviana Micheli ex Mart. LARGE-FLOWERED EVENING PRIMROSE. Hirsute bienn., to 1.5m. St. erect, spotted red, hairy. Lvs broadly lanceolate, crispate, basal lvs in a rosette, midvein red beneath. Fls 5–8cm yellow, sep. flushed red. NW Eur., widely nat. except Antarctica. Z3. 'Afterglow': st. and cal. tinted red.

O. graciliflora Hook. & Arn. = *Camissonia graciliflora*.

O. grandiflora (Lindl.) Nutt. = *Clarkia amoena* ssp. *lindleyi*.

O. heterantha Nutt. = *Camissonia subacaulis*.

O. hookeri Torr. & A. Gray = *O. elata* ssp. *hookeri*.

O. jamesii Torr. & A. Gray. Similar to *O. elata* ssp. *hookeri* but cal. tube 7–10cm, not 2–5cm. Okl. to New Mex.

O. kunthiana (Spach) Munz. Perenn. St. slender, to 60cm. Basal lvs 2–10cm, oblanceolate, sinuate-pinnatifid. Fls few; pet. to 1.5cm, white to pink. Tex. to Guat. Z8.

O. laciniata Hill. Erect to procumbent ann. or short-lived perenn., usually rosette-forming. St. to 1m, with stiff hairs. Lvs villous to strigillose, rosette lvs 4–15cm, linear-oblanceolate to oblanceolate, lobed or dentate, st. lvs 2–10cm, narrowly oblanceolate to elliptic. Fls 1 per spike; pet. 0.5–2.2cm, broadly ovate, yellow to pale yellow, truncate to emarginate. N & E US, nat. W Eur. Z3.

O. lamarckiana De Vries, non Ser. = *O. glazioviana*.

O. lavandulifolia Torr. & A. Gray = *Calylophus lavandulifolius*.

O. leucocarpa Comien ex Lehm. = *Calylophus serrulatus*.

O. lindleyi Douglas = *Clarkia amoena* ssp. *lindleyi*.

O. linearis Michx. = *O. fruticosa*.

O. longissima Rydb. Similar to *O. elata* ssp. *hookeri* but ashy-strigose, with cal. tube 7–10cm, not 2–5cm. SW US.

O. macrocarpa Nutt. OZARK SUNDROPS. Perenn., ± short-stemmed, branched from base, decumbent to erect, pubesc. Lvs 2–8cm, lanceolate to ovate or obovate, subentire to dentate, with silver midrib. Fls yellow, to 10cm diam. SC US. 'Green-court Lemon': fls lemon yellow. Z5.

O. marginata Nutt. ex Hook. & Arn. = *O. caespitosa* ssp. *marginata*.

O. missouriensis Pursh = *O. macrocarpa*.

O. muricata L. = *O. biennis*.

O. nuttallii Torr. & A. Gray. Perenn., 30cm–1m. St. glab., glandular-pubesc. in infl. Lvs 2–7.5cm, oblong-linear to lanceolate, usually entire, glab. above, strigose beneath. Fls white, 3.5–5cm diam. NW N Amer. Z5.

O. ovata Nutt. ex Torr. & A. Gray = *Camissonia ovata*.

O. pallida Lindl. Glab., rhizomatous perenn., 20–50cm, br. spreading. Lvs 2.5–7cm, lanceolate, subentire or undulate. Fls fragrant; pet. 1–2.5cm, white ageing pink. W N Amer. ssp. *trichocalyx* (Nutt. ex Torr. & A. Gray) Munz & W. Klein. Lvs grey-green, usually sinuate-dentate. Z4.

O. perennis L. SUNDROPS Perenn., 10–50cm. St. slender, simple or few branched. Basal lvs 2.5–5cm, spathulate to oblanceolate, ± entire, finely strigulose. Fls in a loose spike; pet. 0.6–0.8cm, yellow. E N Amer. Z5.

O. pilosella Raf. SUNDROPS. Erect perenn., 10–50cm, covered in spreading hairs. Basal lvs obovate, to oblanceolate, st. lvs 2.5–10cm, lanceolate. Pet. 1–2.5cm, yellow, prominently veined. Central N Amer. Z3.

O. pratensis (Small) Robinson = *O. pilosella*.

O. primiveris A. Gray Stemless winter ann., hairy. Lvs 2–10cm, oblanceolate, deeply pinnatifid, lobes toothed or lobed. Pet. 2–4cm, yellow ageing orange. SW US. Z8.

O. primuloidea H. Lév. = *Camissonia ovata*.

O. pumila L. = *O. perennis*.

O. pusilla Michx. = *O. perennis*.

O. rhombipetala Nutt. ex Torr. & A. Gray. Erect, strigillose, rosette-forming bienn. St. 30–150cm, simple or branched, hairy. Rosette lvs to 20cm, narrowly oblanceolate, crenate to lobed; st. lvs to 15cm, narrowly lanceolate to narrowly oblanceolate. Spikes elongated; pet. 3–4.5cm, yellow, broadly elliptic to rhombic-elliptic. N Amer. (Great Plains). Z4.

O. riparia Nutt. = *O. fruticosa*.

O. rosea L'Hérit. ex Ait. Erect, strigulose perenn. or ann., 15–60cm. Lvs oblong-ovate to oblanceolate, basal lvs 2–5cm, entire to pinnatifid; st. lvs 1.5–3cm, subentire to pinnatifid. Infl. spicate; pet. 0.4–1cm, pink to red-violet. Tex. to Peru, nat. S Eur. Z6.

O. rubicunda Lindl. = *Clarkia rubicunda*.

O. serotina Lehm. = *O. fruticosa* ssp. *glauca*.

O. serrulata Nutt. = *Calylophus serrulatus*.

O. sinuata L. = *O. laciniata*.

O. speciosa Nutt. WHITE EVENING PRIMROSE. Rhizomatous perenn., erect, 30–60cm, strigose. Lvs oblong-lanceolate to obovate, remotely toothed or pinnatifid, in basal rosettes. Day-flowering; pet. 2–2.5cm, white ageing rose, sometimes pink when young. SW US to Mex. 'Rosea': to 30cm; fls pale pink, opening during the day. Z5.

O. spinulosa Nutt. ex Torr. & A. Gray = *Calylophus serrulatus*.

O. stubbei Dietr., Raven & W.L. Wagner. Rosette-forming perenn. St. 30cm–3m, several, decumbent; usually flushed red, hairy, young parts villous. Lvs remotely dentate, pubesc., st. lvs 2–7cm, narrowly elliptic to narrowly lanceolate, apex acute, rosette lvs 8–23cm. Pet. 3–5cm, yellow, fading orange, drying red-purple. Mex. Z8.

O. subacaulis (Pursh) Garrett = *Camissonia subacaulis*.

O. taraxifolia Sweet = *O. acaulis*.

O. tenella Cav. = *Clarkia tenella*.

O. tetragona Roth = *O. fruticosa* ssp. *glauca*.

O. tetraptera Cav. Branched ann., to 40cm, hairy. Lvs to 9cm, lanceolate to oblanceolate or narrowly elliptic, sinuate to sinuate-pinnatifid. Pet. to 3.5cm, white, fading to pink. Tex. S to S Amer.

O. trichocalyx Nutt. ex Torr. & A. Gray = *O. pallida* ssp. *trichocalyx*.

O. triloba Nutt. Sparsely hairy ann. or bienn. Stemless st. to 15cm. Lvs 5–20cm, tufted, oblanceolate, deeply pinnatifid. Pet. 1–2cm, pale yellow, suborbicular with apical sinus and sometimes a dentate midlobe. C US. Z5.

O. whitneyi A. Gray = *Clarkia amoena* ssp. *whitneyi*.

O. youngii hort. = *O. fruticosa* ssp. *glauca*.

→*Anogra, Lavauxia, Pachylophus* and *Raimannia*.

Oenotrichia Copel. Dennstaedtiaceae. 4 terrestrial, epiphytic or lithophytic ferns. Rhiz. creeping, red-pubesc. Fronds stipitate, finely pinnatifid, deltoid, pubesc. on rachis, thin-textured, final seg. incised. Aus. Z10.

O. tripinnata (F. Muell.) Copel. HAIRY LACE FERN. Fronds erect or suberect, 20×15cm+, 3-pinnate or 2-pinnatifid, pinnae lanceolate or oblong, pinnules with to 4 obovate, obtuse lobes; stipes wiry, to 15cm, pubesc. Aus. (Queensld).

→*Davallia*.

Oeonia Lindl. Orchidaceae. 6 epiphytic orchids, most with thin, branched st. Rac. few- to many-fld; sep. and pet. ovate-oblong, free; lip with 3–6 spreading lobes. Madag., Masc. Is. Z10.

O. oncidiiflora Kränzl. St. to 80cm, pendent or ascending, sparsely branched, thin. Lvs 2–5cm, ovate-oblong or elliptic. Rac. to 15cm; fls 25mm diam., green or yellow-green, lip white spotted with bright red in the throat; lip 4-lobed, throat scattered with small hairs; spur 7–20mm, somewhat swollen at apex. Madag.

O. volucris (Thouars) Dur. & Schinz. St. long, thin and branched, pendent or ascending. Lvs to 2.5cm, ovate or elliptic. Rac. 30–35cm; fls to 30mm diam., white; papillose in throat, trilobed; spur 6mm, tapering from mouth to apex. Madag., Masc. Is.

Oeoniella Schltr. Orchidaceae. 2–3 epiphytic orchids. St. long and leafy. Rac. few- to several-fld; sep. and pet. free; lip cone-shaped at base, trilobed at apex; spur short. Madag., Masc. Is., Seych. Z10.

O. polystachys (Thouars) Schltr. St. usually to 15cm, branched, leafy. Lvs 3–11cm, ligulate or oblong. Rac. erect, 15–20cm, 7–15-fld; fls to 36mm, white; tep. linear-lanceolate; lip with lat. lobes broad, margin crenulate, midlobe linear; spur 4mm, tapering to apex. Range as for the genus.

Oerstedella Rchb. f. Orchidaceae. Some 25 epiphytic or terrestrial orchids. St. clumped, cane-like, simple or branched, leafy, with verrucose lf sheaths. Lvs numerous, distichous, coriaceous. Infl. a term. (rarely axill.) rac. or a pan.; sep. linear-lanceolate to oblong-lanceolate; pet. subsimilar to sep., lip clawed, adnate to column, 3-lobed, lateral lobes obtuse or acuminate, midlobe large, oblong to oblong-lanceolate, entire to crenulate, callus papillose. Trop. Amer. Z10.

O. endresii (Rchb. f.) Hagsater. St. to 30cm. Lvs to 4.5cm, elliptic to oblong-lanceolate. Rac., to 15cm, erect, few to several-fld; fls to 2.5cm diam., fragrant, opal-white tinged lavender to rose-purple; lip white blotched violet-purple; midlobe bilobulate. Winter. Costa Rica, Panama.

O. schumanniana (Schltr.) Hagsater. St. to 50cm. Lvs to 9cm, lanceolate to elliptic-oblong. Infl. to 60cm, erect, a rac. or a pan., loosely many-fld; fls to 2.5cm diam., fragrant, tep. fleshy; yellow spotted red-brown; lip dark lavender, midlobe bifid, entire to crenulate. Costa Rica, Panama.

O. schweinfurthiana (Correll) Hagsater. St. slender. Lvs 11cm, elliptic-lanceolate. Rac., to 10cm, few-fld; tep. brown; lip midlobe deeply bilobulate, crenulate. Guat.

O. verrucosa (Sw.) Hagsater. St. to 120cm, stout. Lvs to 23cm, narrowly lanceolate to linear-lanceolate. Infl. to 40cm, usually a pan., erect; fls fragrant, long-lived, white to cream-yellow; lip midlobe bilobulate, lobules cuneate to broadly subquadrate-flabellate, fimbriate, callus yellow. Summer. C Amer., W Indies.

O. wallisii (Rchb. f.) Hagsater. St. slender, to 70cm. Lvs to 11cm, oblong-lanceolate. Rac. arching to pendent, term. or axill.; fls to 4.5cm diam., fragrant, long-lived; tep. yellow spotted crimson; lip white marked red-purple, with radiating tuberculate lines. Autumn–early winter. Panama, Colomb.

→*Epidendrum*.

Officinal Rose *Rosa gallica*.
Ohio Buckeye *Aesculus glabra*.
Oil of Ben Tree *Moringa oleifera*.
Oil Palm *Elaeis guineensis*.
Okame-zasa *Shibataea kumasasa*.
Okinawa Pine *Pinus luchuensis*.
Okra *Abelmoschus esculentus*.
Old Calabar Fig *Ficus saussureana*.

Oldenburgia Less. Compositae. 4 shrubs, subshrubs or dwarf herbs, densely lanate below. Lvs rosulate, simple, sessile, obtuse, coriaceous, glab. above, densely pubesc. beneath. Cap. radiate, large, solitary; ray flts purple and white, bilabiate, outer lip much larger; disc flts deeply 5-fld. S Afr. (Cape Prov.). Z9.

O. arbuscula DC. = *O. grandis*.

O. grandis (Thunb.) Baill. Shrub to 3m. Lvs crowded at apices of sterile br., 15–25cm, obovate-oblong, cuneate at base, convex above, subrevolute, stiff, coriaceous, lvs of flowering br. alt., petiole lanate. Cap. to 10cm diam., peduncles to 50cm.

O. paradoxa Less. Dwarf, to 4cm. Lvs of sterile st. tufted at apex, 15–25cm, obovate-oblong, cuneate at base, strongly revolute, lvs of flowering st. 5–6cm, narrowly lanceolate. Cap. at first sessile among lf tufts, peduncles finally elongating to 30cm.

Oldenlandia L. Rubiaceae. Some 300 ann. or perenn. herbs and shrubs. Lvs with narrow stipules. Fls 1–2cm, solitary or, more usually, in cymes or pan.; cal. tube subglobose or obovoid to top-shaped, limb 4- or, occas., 5–8-toothed, teeth erect, usually distant; cor. cylindric, funnel- or salver-shaped, often pubesc. at throat, 4–5-lobed; sta. 4 or 5, anth. usually exserted. Fr. a capsule, globose, ovoid or turbinate. Trop. and subtrop. Z9.

O. natalensis (Hochst.) Kuntze. Erect shrub, to 50cm. St. somewhat pubesc. Lvs to 8cm, ovate to lanceolate. Fls in term., few-fld, umbellate clusters, pale blue to lavender or mauve. S Afr.

O. umbellata L. CHAY; INDIAN MADDER. Spreading ann. St. glab. or pubesc. woody-based. Lvs to 12cm, ovate or lanceolate or deltoid. Fls in term. or axill., to 7-fld umbellate clusters, white. Trop. Asia.

Old Field Cinquefoil *Potentilla simplex*.
Old Field Toadflax *Linaria canadensis*.
Oldham Bamboo *Bambusa oldhamii*.
Old Maid *Catharanthus roseus*.
Old Man *Artemisia absinthium*.
Old Man Cactus *Cephalocereus senilis*.
Old Man of the Andes *Oreocereus celsianus*; *O. trollii*.
Old Man's Beard *Clematis vitalba*; *Tillandsia usneoides*.
Old Man's Whiskers *Geum triflorum*.
Old Witch Grass *Panicum capillare*.
Old Woman *Artemisia stelleriana*.
Old Woman Cactus *Mammillaria hahniana*.
Old World Arrowhead *Sagittaria sagittifolia*.

Olea L. OLIVE. Oleaceae. 20 long-lived everg. trees and shrubs. St. smooth to spiny, glossy, slender and pliable at first, becoming fissured and eventually, blackened and contorted. Lvs opposite, entire or toothed, coriaceous. Pan. axill. or term.; fls inconspicuous, with a musty fragrance; cal. and cor. short, 4-lobed; sta. 2. Fr. ovoid or globose drupe containing a single, ellipsoid stone.

O. capensis L. BLACK IRONWOOD. To 20m. Lvs to 10cm, broad-lanceolate to obovate, dark, shining, coriaceous above, paler beneath. Fls white, crowded in term. pan. Fr. globose, black, 1cm. Spring. S Afr. Z9.

O. chrysophylla Lam. = *O. europaea* ssp. *cuspidata*.

O. communis Steud. = *O. europaea* var. *europaea*.

O. europaea L. COMMON OLIVE; EDIBLE OLIVE. To 7m. Lvs to 8cm, elliptic to lanceolate, grey-green above, scurfy, silver-green beneath. Fls off-white, in axill. pan. Fr. subglobose, ripening red to purple-black, to 4cm. Summer. var. *europaea* is the fr. and oil-yielding cultigen. Medit. 'Cipressino' ('Pyramidalis'): pyramidal in growth; fr. profuse when young. 'Coratina': self-fertile, erect habit. 'Frantoio' ('Frantoiana', 'Correglio', 'Razzo'): shoots pendulous; fr. large, fleshy, ovoid. 'Leccino': large mauve fr. carried on drooping br., semi-hardy. 'Moraiolo': hardy and strong-growing. (*edible*) 'Ascolana': large, yellow. 'Cucco': fr. black, prolific. 'El Greco': fr. large, stones small. 'Manzanillo': crown rounded, open-branched; lvs leathery; fr. black. 'Mission': vigorous, prolific, v. cold resistant. 'Santa Caterina': fr. large, ovate. 'Uovo di piccione': purpled, v. sweet. (*ornamental*) 'Little Ollie': bushy dwarf, fast-growing when young; lvs v. dark green, no fls; heat- and drought-resistant. 'Majestic Beauty': open and refined in growth; lvs lighter and narrower, no mature fr. 'Picholine': vigorous, medium-sized, cured olives with nut-like flavour. var. *oleaster* (Hoffm. & Link) DC. WILD OLIVE. To 5m with ridged, spinose st.; fr. small, to 1.5cm, subglobose, thinly fleshed, inedible. ssp. *africana* (Mill.) P. Green. Resembling type but fr. smaller, harder. To 8m with warty grey st. Lvs to 10cm, linear-lanceolate with yellow scurf beneath. Fr. globose, to 0.5cm. S Afr. ssp. *cuspidata* (Wall ex DC.) Cif. To 9m. Lvs 5–10cm, oblong-lanceolate, acuminate, glossy above, red-brown and scaly beneath. Fr. ovoid, black, to 0.8cm. NW Himal., Arabia. Z8.

O. laurifolia Lam. = *O. capensis*.

O. undulata Jacq. = *O. capensis*.

O. verrucosa (Willd.) Link = *O. europaea* ssp. *africana*.

OLEACEAE Hoffsgg. & Link. 24/900. *Abeliophyllum, Chionanthus, Fontanesia, Forestiera, Forsythia, Fraxinus, Jasminum, Ligustrum, Olea, Osmanthus, Phillyrea, Schrebera, Syringa.*

Oleander *Nerium.*
Oleander Podocarp *Podocarpus neriifolius.*
Oleander Spurge *Euphorbia neriifolia.*

Oleandra Cav. Oleandraceae. 40 epiphytic or terrestrial ferns. Rhiz. rigid, becoming woody, forming interwoven mats, then ascending or scandent, scaly and pubesc., rooting freely, scaly. Fronds stipitate, simple, entire, lanceolate to elliptic. Trop. Z10.

O. articulata (Sw.) Presl. Fronds to 35×5cm, lanceolate, apex caudate to narrowly acute, glab., thin-textured to leathery; stipes to 20cm, jointed. W Indies, C to S Amer.

O. mollis Presl = *O. neriiformis.*

O. neriiformis Cav. Fronds to 30×3cm, linear to lanceolate, attenuate to caudate at apex, glab. or pubesc., leathery; stipes to 2cm. Asia to Polyn.

O. nodosa (Willd.) Presl = *O. articulata.*

O. wallichii (Hook.) Presl. Fronds to 40×4cm, oblong, apex attenuate to caudate, pubesc. beneath; stipes to 5cm. India, China, Taiwan.

→*Ophiopteris* and *Neuronia.*

OLEANDRACEAE (J. Sm.) Ching ex Pichi-Serm. 4 genera. *Arthropteris, Nephrolepis, Oleandra.*

Olearia Moench. DAISY BUSH. Compositae. 130 herbs, everg. shrubs or small trees. Branchlets usually white- or buff-tomentose at first. Lvs usually alt., simple, leathery, usually white- or buff-tomentose beneath. Cap. radiate or discoid, solitary or few to several and variously compound; ray flts white, purple or blue or 0; disc flts, yellow, white or purple. Australasia. Z8 unless specified.

O. albida Hook. f. Shrub or small tree to 5m, branchlets grooved, angular. Lvs 7–10cm, oblong to ovate-oblong, glab. above when mature, white-hairy beneath, margins flat to undulate. Cap. to 7mm, radiate, v. numerous, narrow; ray-florets 1–5, white, disc flts white. NZ.

O. albida hort., non Hook. f. = *O.* 'Talbot de Malahide'.

O. algida Wakef. Shrub, to 1.5m; br. numerous slender. Lvs to 0.5cm, in dense lateral fascicles, deltoid, revolute, glaucous, fleshy. Cap. radiate, solitary, to 1.5cm diam.; ray flts 3–4, white; disc flts white. Spring. SE Aus.

O. allomii T. Kirk. Shrub to 1m; branchlets stout. Lvs 2.5–5cm, obliquely ovate-oblong, coriaceous, glab. above when mature, adpressed silvery-tomentose beneath, entire. Cap. radiate, 1.5cm diam., in branched corymbs; flts 14–20, ray flts 5–10. NZ.

O. alpina Buch. = *O. lacunosa.*

O. angustifolia Hook. f. Shrub or small tree to 6m. Lvs 7–15cm, narrowly lanceolate, acuminate, subsessile, finely crenate-dentate, becoming glab. above, teeth callused. Cap. radiate, 2.5–5cm diam.; peduncles with leafy bracts; ray flts white, disc flts purple. Summer. NZ.

O. arborescens (Forst. f.) Ckn. & Laing. Shrub to 4m; branchlets angular. Lvs 4–8cm, broad- to elliptic-ovate, acute, sinuate-

dentate to subentire, subcoriaceous, sparsely tomentose beneath. Cap. to 1.5cm diam., in large corymbs; ray flts 7–10, white, disc flts pale yellow. Summer. NZ.

O. argophylla (Labill.) Benth. MUSKWOOD. Tree or shrub to 15m; young shoots slightly ribbed. Lvs 5–15cm, oblanceolate or ovate, tapered at apex and base, denticulate, grey-green, slightly tomentose above at first, grey-tomentose beneath. Cap. numerous, in clustered corymbs to over 25cm diam.; ray flts 5mm, 3–5, narrow, cream; disc flts 6–8, yellow. Summer. S & SE Aus. 'Variegata': lvs edged yellow.

O. asterotricha (F. Muell.) F. Muell. ex Benth. Shrub to 1m, br. grooved. Lvs to 4cm, oblong-linear, ± sinuate-dentate, scabrous above. Cap. radiate, large, solitary, terminal or few in a term. corymb; flts blue or purple; ray flts 20+. Spring. S & SE Aus.

O. avicenniifolia (Raoul) Hook. f. Shrub or small tree to 7m; young shoots ribbed. Lvs 5–10cm, ovate-lanceolate, tapered at base and apex, entire, grey-white, glab. above, white- or pale yellow-tomentose beneath. Cap. cylindric, 0.5cm, in erect, rounded, term. corymbs to 5–8cm diam.; flts 2–3, white; ray flts 0–2. Summer. NZ. 'White Confusion': lvs large, slightly waxed; fls profuse, white. Z8.

O. buchananii T. Kirk. Shrub or small tree to 6m; branchlets with red bark, glab. Lvs 5–7.5cm, elliptic-lanceolate, obtuse, entire, attenuate, glab. above, thinly white-tomentose beneath. Cap. discoid, 6–7mm, clustered in small corymbs; flts 6–8. NZ.

O. capillaris Buch. Shrub to 2m; branchlets slender, zig-zagging, bark furrowed, pale-papery. Lvs silvery-tomentose beneath, those in sun 0.5–1.5cm diam., broad-ovate to suborbicular, entire, coriaceous, those in shade to 3cm, more oblong, sinuate, membranous. Cap. radiate, 5–11, in lax corymbs; flts 8–12, ray flts white, disc flts yellow. Summer. NZ.

O. chathamica T. Kirk. Shrub, to 2m. Lvs 3–8cm, oblanceolate to elliptic, acute, tapered at base, regularly and obtusely dentate, glab. above, midrib raised beneath, petioles long. Cap. to 4.5cm diam., solitary; peduncles to 25cm; ray flts numerous, 1.5cm, white or tinged purple; disc flts dark purple. Summer. NZ.

O. cheesemanii Ckn. & Allan. Erect shrub or small tree to 4m, bark somewhat flaking; branchlets grooved. Lvs 5–9cm, linear to narrowly lanceolate, sinuate, apex subacuminate, thinly coriaceous, pilose above at first, becoming pale buff-tomentose; petioles winged. Cap. 8–9mm in lax corymbs to 15cm diam.; ray flts white; disc flts yellow. Spring–summer. NZ.

O. ciliata (Benth.) F. Muell. ex Benth. Shrub to 30cm. Lvs in fascicles, 1–1.5cm, linear, rigid, mucronate, strongly revolute, scabrous-ciliate, glab. or scabrous above, minutely tomentose beneath. Cap. 5–13cm, radiate, solitary, term.; ray flts c20, white, mauve or blue; disc flts 50–80, yellow. Spring. Aus. (temp. regions, inc. Tasm.).

O. colensoi Hook. f. Shrub to 3m; branchlets stout. Lvs 8–20cm, obovate, acute, serrate, glab., rugose above, densely tomentose beneath. Cap. discoid, 2–3cm diam., dark brown to purple, in rac. of 5–8 heads to 20cm long; flts dark brown to purple tubular, outer row ♀. NZ.

O. coriacea T. Kirk. Shrub to 3m, branchlets stout. Lvs 1–2cm, broadly ovate to suborbicular, coriaceous, subglabrous above, densely pale brown-tomentose beneath, ± revolute and undulate. Cap. discoid, narrow, in small corymbose pan.; flts tubular, white. NZ.

O. cunninghamii hort. = *O. cheesemanii.*

O. cymbifolia (Hook. f.) Cheesem. = *O. nummulariifolia* var. *cymbifolia.*

O. dentata Hook. f. non hort. = *O. macrodonta.*

O. dentata hort. non Hook. f. = *O. rotundifolia.*

O. ericoides (Steetz) Wakef. Shrub to 1m, much-branched, viscid. Lvs to 0.6cm, linear to linear-obovate, tomentose beneath, with viscid yellow exudates, revolute. Cap. radiate, solitary, term., 2cm diam.; ray flts to 15, white or tinged blue, linear; disc flts white. Spring. Tasm.

O. erubescens (DC.) Dipp. Shrub to 1.5m; br. reddish. Lvs 2–4cm, lanceolate, acute, sinuate-dentate, glab., reticulate above. Cap. 2.5cm diam., solitary or 2–5 together in a leafy, oblong pan. to 45cm; ray flts 3–5, white; disc flts 6–8, yellow. Spring–summer. NSW, Vict., Tasm. var. *ilicifolia* (DC.) Bean. As for *O. ilicifolia* except lvs less spiny, broader, and cap. more numerous.

O. ×excorticata Buch. (*O. arborescens* ×*O. lacunosa.*) Shrub or small tree to 4m, bark brown, papery. Lvs to 10cm, elliptic, obscurely sinuate-dentate, acuminate, glab. above, white-tomentose beneath. Cap. radiate, 3–4mm, numerous, in rounded corymbs; flts c12, ray flts 5–7, disc flts exserted. Spring. NZ.

O. floribunda (Hook. f.) Benth. Shrub to 2m, branchlets slender. Lvs 0.2–0.3cm, in loose clusters, oblanceolate or oblong, flat or revolute, bright to dark green, tomentose beneath. Cap. radiate, narrow, numerous, in large pyramidal pan.; ray flts 3–5, white; disc flts 3–6, yellow. Summer. SE Aus.

O. forsteri Hook. f. = *O. paniculata*.

O. fragrantissima Petrie. Shrub or tree to 5m; branchlets rigid, flexuous, striate; bark dark red-brown. Lvs 0.8–3cm, elliptic to obovate, entire, membranous, becoming glab. above, white-tomentose beneath. Cap. radiate, to 2cm diam., ± sessile, in alt. clusters of 12; flts 4–8, fragrant. NZ.

O. frostii (F. Muell.) J.H. Willis. Straggling subshrub. Lvs 1–2.5cm, obovate, entire or bluntly sinuate-dentate above, densely stellate-pubesc., dark green above, paler beneath. Cap. radiate, solitary and term. or 2–3 together, axill. 2–3cm diam.; ray flts 40–50, pale mauve or lilac; disc flts numerous, yellow. Vict.

O. furfuracea (A. Rich.) Hook. f. Shrub or tree to 5m, branchlets grooved. Lvs 5–10cm, ovate to elliptic-oblong, subentire to crenate-dentate, coriaceous, glab., dark glossy green above, lustrous brown-tomentose beneath, ± undulate. Cap. to 1.5cm diam., many, in large corymbs to 12cm diam.; ray flts 2–5, 3–6mm, oblong, white; disc flts 3–7, yellow. Spring. NZ.

O. glandulosa (Labill.) Benth. Aromatic shrub or subshrub, 1–2m, glandular-tuberculate at first. Lvs 1.5–5cm, narrowly linear, acute, spreading, grooved above, convex beneath, margins glandular-tuberculate. Cap. small, radiate, in corymbose pan.; ray flts 12–20, 4mm, white or tinged blue; disc flts c20, yellow. Summer. SE Aus.

O. gunniana (DC.) Hook. f. ex Hook. = *O. phlogopappa*.

O. × haastii Hook. f. (*O. avicenniifolia* × *O. moschata*.) Shrub, 1–3m. Lvs 1–2.5cm, crowded, oval or ovate, entire, dark glossy green, glab. above, white-tomentose beneath. Cap. 8mm diam., in corymbose clusters 5–8cm diam.; ray flts white; disc flts yellow. Summer. NZ. Z8.

O. hectoris Hook. f. Shrub to 5m; branchlets slender, grooved, bark dark red-brown. Lvs 2–5cm, in fascicles of 2–4, broadly elliptic, submembranous, glab. above, thinly tomentose beneath; petioles slender. Cap. radiate, 5mm diam., in nodding fascicles of 2–5; ray flts to 15, narrow, tinged yellow; disc flts yellow. NZ.

O. 'Henry Travers' (*O. chathamica* × *O. semidentata?*.) Medium-sized shrub. Lvs lanceolate, grey-green, silvery beneath. Cap. radiate, large, slender-stalked and pendent; ray flts lilac, disc flts deep mauve. Summer. Gdn. origin.

O. hookeri (Sonder) Benth. Shrub to 1m, br. slender, viscid, glab. Lvs 3–6cm, narrow, grooved above, convex beneath, revolute. Cap. radiate, solitary, sessile; ray flts 8–10, indigo; disc flts 8–12, yellow. Summer. Tasm.

O. ilicifolia Hook. f. Tree or shrub to 5m, with musky fragrance; branchlets stout. Lvs 5–10cm, linear-oblong to lanceolate, acute to acuminate, coriaceous to glab. above, white- to yellow-tomentose beneath, undulate, serrate-dentate. Cap. radiate, fragrant, 1–1.5cm, many, in large corymbs to 10cm diam.; ray flts 10–15, white. Summer. NZ. Z8.

O. ilicifolia var. *mollis* T. Kirk = *O. × mollis*.

O. insignis Hook. f. Spreading shrub, to 2m; branchlets stout. Lvs 8–16cm, crowded at shoot apices, entire, oval or obovate, coriaceous, becoming glab. above except on midrib and margins, petiole stout. Cap. term., solitary, 3–6cm diam.; ray flts 12mm, numerous, in c2 rows, linear, emarginate, 12mm, white; disc flts crowded, yellow. Summer. NZ.

O. iodochroa (F. Muell.) F. Muell. ex Benth. Bushy shrub to 2m. Lvs to 1cm, linear to subobovate, entire or emarginate, recurved. Cap. radiate, solitary or few in a term. corymb; ray flts 15–20, white; disc flts purple. Spring. SE Aus.

O. lacunosa Hook. f. Shrub to 5m; branchlets numerous, densely tomentose. Lvs 7–16cm, linear to linear-oblong, acute to acuminate, coriaceous, rugose, midrib yellow above, sub-revolute, minutely sinuate-dentate. Cap. many, radiate, to 1cm, in corymbs; flts 8–12, white. NZ.

O. ledifolia (DC.) Benth. Shrub to 60cm, forming rounded clumps. Lvs 0.5–3cm, crowded, oblong-linear, obtuse, silver- or rusty-tomentose beneath, revolute. Cap. solitary, radiate; ray flts 10–12, white; disc flts yellow. Tasm.

O. lepidophylla (Pers.) Benth. Shrub, 1–2m, stout, erect, rigid. Lvs to 3cm, clustered, ovate to suborbicular, tomentose beneath, revolute. Cap. radiate, small, in ± racemose clusters; ray flts 3–6, white; disc flts 5–10, violet. Summer. SE Aus.

O. lineata (T. Kirk) Ckn. = *O. virgata* var. *lineata*.

O. lirata (Sims) Hutch. Shrub or small tree, to 3m. Lvs 8–12cm, lanceolate, acuminate, entire, rugose or reticulate, shiny light green above, tomentose beneath crenately undulate. Cap. 2cm diam., in dense, rounded terminal clusters; ray flts 10–14, white; disc flts yellow. Spring. Vict., NSW, Queensld, Tasm.

O. lyallii Hook. f. Shrub or tree to 10m; branchlets stout, densely white-tomentose. Lvs 10–25cm, elliptic-ovate to ovate-orbicular, abruptly acute to acuminate, irregularly crenate, densely white-tomentose beneath. Cap. radiate, 3–4cm diam., clustered in rac. to 25cm; flts dark brown. NZ.

O. lyrata (Sims) Hutch. = *O. lirata*.

O. macrodonta Bak. NEW ZEALAND HOLLY. Shrub or tree to 6m, bark peeling in long strips; branchlets slender, angular. Lvs 5–10cm, ovate-oblong, acute to acuminate, dark glossy green above, silver-tomentose beneath, musk-scented when crushed, undulate, acutely dentate-serrate. Cap. radiate to 1cm, many in corymbs 8–15cm diam.; ray flts 10+, rays short, narrow, white; disc flts few, rufescent. Summer. NZ. 'Major': lvs and fls large. 'Minor': dwarf: lvs and fls small. Z8.

O. megalophylla (F. Muell.) F. Muell. ex Benth. Shrub to 1m; branchlets grey- or brown-tomentose at first. Lvs 5–10cm, elliptic to oblong, reticulate above, grey- or brown-tomentose beneath. Cap. radiate, large, numerous, in terminal corymbs; ray flts 7–12, white. Summer. Vict., NSW.

O. × mollis (T. Kirk) Ckn. (*O. ilicifolia* × *O. lacunosa*.) Shrub to 3m. Lvs to 10cm, lanceolate, spinulose, rounded at base, veins sunken above, v. prominent beneath, densely white- to pale yellow-tomentose beneath, revolute. Cap. to c15cm diam., radiate, many, in corymbs, ray flts 8–15, white. NZ. 'Zennorensis': shrub to 2m; lvs narrow, acute, sharply dentate, 10×1–1.5cm, dark olive green above, white-tomentose below. Z8.

O. × mollis hort. = *O. ilicifolia*.

O. moschata Hook. f. Shrub to 4m, slightly viscid. Lvs 0.8–1.5cm, crowded, oval to obovate, green, tinged grey, scurfy above, tomentose beneath. Cap. radiate, 1cm diam., in axill. corymbs of 20–30; ray flts 7–9, linear, white; disc flts 4–12, yellow. Summer. NZ.

O. myrsinoides (Labill.) Benth. Low and straggling shrub; br. angled. Lvs 0.6–1.2cm, obovate, occas. narrowly oval, dentate, glossy green, glab. above. Cap. radiate, 3–5 in axill. clusters; ray flts 2–3, white; disc flts 2–5, yellow. Vict., Tasm.

O. nernstii (F. Muell.) F. Muell. ex Benth. Shrub to 2m; br. viscid. Lvs 3–7cm, oblong-lanceolate, narrow, acute, sub-membranous, glab. and glossy green above, loosely stellate-tomentose beneath. Cap. radiate, in term. clusters; ray flts 15–20, white; disc flts yellow. NSW, Queensld.

O. nitida (Hook. f.) Hook. f. = *O. arborescens*.

O. nummulariifolia (Hook.) Hook. f. Shrub to 3m. Lvs 0.5–1cm, densely alt., ovate to suborbicular, glab. above white- to buff- or yellow-tomentose beneath, revolute. Cap. solitary, 3–5mm diam., fragrant; flts 5–12, cream or pale yellow; ray flts 3–5. Summer. NZ. var. *cymbifolia* Hook. f. Lvs to 1.5cm, narrow-ovate, v. viscid, revolute almost to midrib. Z8.

O. obcordata (Hook. f.) Benth. Straggling shrub to 90cm. Lvs 0.6–1cm, cuneate, entire, apex truncate, bluntly 3–5-dentate, pale above, silver-grey beneath. Cap. radiate, solitary, axill.; flts few, white; ray flts 5 or 6. Summer. Tasm.

O. odorata Petrie. Sparse shrub to 3.5m, br. terete, wiry. Lvs 1–3cm, opposite or in opposite fascicles, spathulate, bright green, glab. above, silver-tomentose beneath. Cap. radiate, 6mm diam., in opposite fascicles of 2–5, on short br., scented; flts dull grey-brown, ray flts to 20, short, disc flts to 20, viscid-glandular. NZ.

O. oleifolia hort. = *O.* 'Waikariensis'.

O. oporina (Forst. f.) Hook. f. Like *O. chathamica*, except ray flts white, disc flts yellow. Summer. NZ.

O. Rowallan Hybrids. (*O. arborescens* × *O. macrodonta*.) Lvs sharply toothed. Cap. pendulous.

O. pachyphylla Cheesem. Shrub to 3m, branchlets stout, grooved. Lvs 7–13cm, ovate to ovate-oblong, glab. above, densely silver- to pale brown-tomentose beneath, entire, undulate; petiole stout. Cap. radiate, to 2cm, many in corymbs; flts 17–40 white to cream. NZ.

O. paniculata (Forst. & Forst. f.) Druce. Shrub or tree to 6m; branchlets grooved, angular. Lvs 4–9cm, elliptic- and ovate-oblong, glab. above, white- to buff-tomentose beneath, undulate. Cap. discoid, narrow, in pyramidal pan. to 5cm long; flts tubular, 0.5cm, dull white, fragrant. Autumn. NZ.

O. pannosa Hook. Shrub to 1.2m. Lvs 5–7.5cm, ovate-cordate to oblong, entire, veins often depressed above. Cap. radiate, large; ray flts to 2.5cm, white. Spring. SE & S Aus.

O. persoonioides (DC.) Benth. Shrub to 3m; branchlets numerous. Lvs 1.5–5cm, elliptic to obovate, obtuse, entire, tapering toward base, glab. above, white- to fawn-silky-tomentose beneath. Cap. radiate, numerous, in small groups, forming term. clusters; ray flts 3–4, white, disc flts yellow. Summer. Tasm.

O. phlogopappa (Labill.) DC. Aromatic shrub to 3m, much-branched. Lvs 1.5–5cm, oblong or narrowly obovate, sinuous or shallowly toothed, dark dull green above, white- or grey-white-tomentose beneath. Cap. 2.5–3cm diam., in erect, loose corymbs; ray flts 10–16, white, occas. pink, mauve or blue, disc flts yellow. Spring. Tasm., Vict., NSW. Splendens group includes 'Comber's Blue', 'Comber's Mauve', 'Comber's Pink': fls respectively blue, mauve and pink. 'Rosea': fls pale pink. var.

subrepanda (DC.) J.H. Willis. Lvs obovate, to 1.2cm. Cap. often solitary; peduncles v. short, leafy.

O. pinifolia (Hook. f.) Benth. Shrub to 1.5m; br. slender. Lvs 2.5–4cm, narrowly linear, rigid, pungent, revolute. Cap. radiate, usually solitary, axillary; flts numerous, white; ray flts 8–10. Tasm.

O. ramulosa (Labill.) Benth. Shrub to 1.5m; br. numerous, arching, somewhat bristly, gland. Lvs 0.2–1cm, crowded, linear to linear-obovate, glab. above, tomentose beneath, revolute, petiole to 0.3cm. Cap. radiate, solitary, sessile, 1.5cm diam.; ray flts 3–15, linear, white, occas. pale blue or pink; disc flts white. Summer. S Aus., Tasm. 'Blue Stars': lvs small; fls blue, star-like, profuse.

O. rani hort. = *O. cheesemanii.*

O. 'Rossii'. (*O. argophylla* ×*O. macrodonta.*) Vigorous. Lvs ellipsoid, green above, silver-pubesc. beneath.

O. rotundifolia (Less.) DC. Stout, much-branched shrub. Lvs 3–6cm, ovate, acute or obtuse, subentire, to 4–6-dentate, dark green and rough above, tomentose beneath; petiole 1.5cm. Cap. 2.5–6cm, 9–12 in a term. pan.; ray flts numerous, linear, often emarginate, pale rose; disc flts yellow. Spring–summer. E Aus.

O. ×scilloniensis Dorrien-Sm. (*O. lirata* ×*O. phlogopappa.*) Shrub to 3m. Lvs to 11cm, elliptic-oblong, obtuse, deep green and reticulate above, pale green and closely tomentose beneath, sinuate. Cap. radiate, 4–6cm diam., numerous, in corymbs; ray flts 10–15, pure white; disc flts yellow. Spring. Gdn origin. 'Master Michael': lvs tinted grey; fls blue, profuse. Z8.

O. semidentata Decne. Rounded shrub to 3.5m; branchlets slender. Lvs 3.5–7cm, linear to lanceolate, distantly serrate above, rugose, glab. above, white-tomentose beneath. Cap. radiate, solitary, term., to 5cm diam.; ray flts 2×0.5cm, spreading or slightly decurved, numerous, pale purple; disc flts darker violet-purple. Summer. Chatham Is., NZ.

O. semidentata hort. non Decne = *O.* 'Henry Travers'.

O. solandri (Hook. f.) Hook. f. Shrub or small tree to 4m; branchlets angular, viscid, yellow-tomentose. Lvs to 1.5cm, opposite or in opposite fascicles, midrib depressed, linear-spathulate to linear-obovate, subcoriaceous, glab. above, white-to yellow-tomentose beneath, slightly revolute. Cap. radiate, solitary, sessile, 10×5–7mm; phyllaries bright tawny yellow, viscid-pubesc.; flts 8–20, pale yellow. Summer–autumn. NZ. 'Aurea': lvs strongly tinged gold.

O. speciosa Hutch. Straggling shrub to 1m. Lvs to 10cm, oblong-elliptic, stout and coriaceous, brown-tomentose beneath, revolute, dentate. Cap. radiate, 2.5cm diam., in loose corymbs to 20cm across; ray flts 5–6, white or blue, disc flts 10–12, yellow. Summer. Vict.

O. stellulata hort. = *O. phlogopappa.*

O. subrepanda (DC.) Hutch. = *O. phlogopappa* var. *subrepanda.*

O. 'Talbot de Malahide'. V. similar to *O. avicenniifolia* except lvs more obtuse at apex and base, cap. to 1cm, ray flts 3–6. Z8.

O. tasmanica Curtis. Shrub to 1m; br. numerous, twiggy. Lvs 1–4cm, elliptic to obovate, obtuse, entire, rusty above, pale-tomentose beneath. Cap. radiate, solitary in axils of upper lvs, forming term. clusters; ray flts 5–6, white; disc flts yellow. Tasm.

O. teretifolia (Sonder) F. Muell. ex Benth. Shrub to 1.5m; br. slender, glab., glutinous. Lvs 0.2–0.5cm, linear, erect, adpressed, obtuse. Cap. small, radiate, term., in a long, narrow pan.; ray flts 4–9, 5–6mm, white; disc flts 5–10, white. Summer. SE Aus.

O. tomentosa (Wendl.) DC. ex Steud. Shrub to 2m; br. slender. Lvs 3–7cm, ovate to suborbicular, dentate, fleshy, rough or pubesc. above, tomentose beneath. Cap. radiate, solitary or few in a term. corymb; ray flts many, white to blue or mauve; disc flts yellow. Spring. SE Aus.

O. tomentosa hort. = *O. rotundifolia.*

O. ×traillii T. Kirk. (*O. angustifolia* ×*O. colensoi.*) Like *O. colensoi* but to 6m, lvs, 10–15cm, cap. radiate, with white ray flts. Summer. NZ.

O. traversii (F. Muell.) Hook. f. Shrub or tree, to 10m; bark pale, branchlets 4-angled. Lvs 4–6.5cm, opposite, oblong to ovate-oblong, apiculate, entire, glab. bright dark green above, silky white-tomentose beneath. Cap. discoid, 6mm, many, in axill. pan. of 5–12 2.5–5cm; flts 5–15, tubular outermost ♀, dull grey. NZ. 'Variegata': dwarf form; lvs variegated green and gold.

O. virgata (Hook. f.) Hook. f. Shrub to 5m; branchlets slender, wiry, tangled, usually glab. Lvs 0.5–2cm, opposite or in opposite fascicles, narrowly obovate, glab. above, white-tomentose beneath. Cap. 8–9mm diam., radiate, in opposite clusters to 4cm diam.; flts 5–12, yellow to white, ray flts 3–6, white. Summer. NZ. var. *lineata* T. Kirk. Shrub to 2m; branchlets slender, pendulous, pubesc. Lvs 2–4×0.1–0.2cm, in sparse fascicles, narrowly linear, strongly revolute. Cap. radiate, on slender peduncles to 4cm; ray flts 8–14; disc flts 6–10. Z7.

O. viscosa (Labill.) Benth. Shrub, 1–2m; branchlets viscid. Lvs 5–7cm, opposite, thin, oblong-lanceolate, silver-white-

tomentose beneath. Cap. radiate, numerous in irregular pan.; ray flts 1–2, cream-white; disc flts 3–5, yellow. Summer. SE Aus.

O. 'Waikariensis'. Hybrid of unknown origin. As for *O.* ×*haastii* except compact shrub to 2.5m. Lvs to 7.5cm, elliptic, obtuse, silver-white-tomentose beneath.

→*Arnica, Aster, Eurybia, Pachystegia* and *Solidago.*

Oleaster *Elaeagnus* (*E. angustifolia*; *E. latifolia*).

Olfersia Raddi. Dryopteridaceae. 1 terrestrial fern. Rhiz. creeping; scales tufted, apex twisted and hair-like, gold to pale brown. Fronds leathery, sterile fronds to 85×35cm, pinnate, ovate or lanceolate to oblong, glab., pinnae to 25cm, lat. pinnae 4–12 pairs, sometimes alt., ascending, ovate or lanceolate to oblong, entire or notched, cartilaginous, fertile fronds 2-pinnate, pinnae reduced pinnules to 1cm, entire, stipes to 50cm, scaly at base, straw-coloured. Trop. America. Z10.

O. cervina (L.) Kunze.

→*Acrostichum, Osmunda* and *Polybotrya.*

Olga Bay Larch *Larix gmelinii* var. *olgensis*

Olive *Olea.*

Olive Buddleia *Buddleja saligna.*

Oliverella Rose.

O. elegans Rose = *Echeveria harmsii.*

Olive Wood *Capparis odoratissima.*

Olivo *Capparis odoratissima.*

Olsynium Raf. Iridaceae. 12 fibrous-rooted perenn. herbs. Lvs mostly basal, usually linear or lanceolate. Fls term., enclosed in spathes; perianth bell-shaped; tep. equal, 6; sta. joined only at base; style with 3 short br. N & S America. Z9.

O. biflorum (Thunb.) Goldbl. St. 10–70cm. Basal lvs 1–5, 4–22cm×1–2.5mm, linear fls scented cream, striped maroon. Spring. Patagonia.

O. douglasii (A. Dietr.) E. Bickn. GRASS WIDOW; PURPLE-EYED GRASS. St. 15–30cm high. Basal lvs bract-like, st. lvs to 1cm, fls pendent, wine-red, purple-pink or white. Western N America.

O. filifolium (Gaudich.) Goldbl. St. 15–20cm; lvs rush-like. Fls erect, white with red-purple lines. Spring. Falkland Is.

O. grandiflorum (Douglas ex Lindl.) Raf. = *O. douglasii.*

O. inflatum Suksd. = *O. douglasii.*

→*Phaiophleps, Sisyrinchium* and *Synphyostemon.*

Olympic Violet *Viola flettii*

Ombú *Phytolacca dioica*

Omeo Gum *Eucalyptus neglecta*

Omoto-giboshi *Hosta rohdeifolia*

Omphalodes Mill. NAVELWORT; NAVELSEED. Boraginaceae. Some 28 ann., bienn. or perenn. herbs. Lvs simple, alt.; basal lvs long-petiolate, st. lvs smaller, ± sessile. Fls usually in term. cymes, sometimes solitary and axill., sometimes bracteate; cal. 5-parted; cor. 5-lobed, subrotate or subcampanulate, tube short, throat with 5 saccate invaginations forming an eye; sta. 5, included. Europe, N Africa, Asia, Mexico.

O. cappadocica (Willd.) DC. Perenn. to 28cm, erect or ascending. Basal lvs to 10×4.5cm, ovate to cordate, acute or acuminate, finely pilose. Cor. bright blue, eye white, tube to 2mm, limb to 5mm diam. Asia Minor. 'Cherry Ingram': vigorous, to 25cm; fls deep blue. Z6.

O. japonica (Thunb.) Maxim. Perenn., spreading-hirsute. St. to 20cm, ascending from a decumbent base. Basal lvs to 15×2.5cm, oblanceolate, acute, pubesc. Infl. a simple rac., somewhat bracteate near base; cor. to 10mm diam., blue. Japan. Z7.

O. krameri Franch. & Savat. Perenn., with white spreading hairs. St. to 40cm, simple, erect. Basal lvs to 15×3.5cm, broadly oblanceolate, acute. Infl. erect, forked; bracts usually 0; cor. to 15mm diam., blue. Japan. Z7.

O. linifolia (L.) Moench. Ann. St. to 40cm, sometimes slightly branched near base, erect. Basal lvs to 10×2cm, linear-lanceolate to spathulate, sparingly strigose-ciliate. Infl. term., loosely 5 to 15-fld; bracts 0; cor. to 12mm diam., white or blue. SW Europe.

O. luciliae Boiss. Perenn. to 25cm, tufted, glab. Basal lvs to 10×3.5cm, ovate or elliptic to oblong, obtuse or rounded, petiolate. Infl. term., bracteate; cor. to 8mm diam., rose becoming blue. Greece, Asia Minor. Z7.

O. lusitanica (L.) Pourr. ex Lange = *O. nitida.*

O. nitida Hoffsgg. & Link. Perenn. to 65cm, erect, branched, sparingly setose. Basal lvs to 20×3.5cm, lanceolate or oblong-lanceolate, acute or acuminate, slightly strigose beneath. Infl.

term., bracteate near base; cor. to 10mm diam., blue, centre yellow-white. Spain, Portugal. Z7.

O. verna Moench. CREEPING FORGET-ME-NOT. Perenn. to 20cm, stoloniferous. Basal lvs to 20×6cm, ovate or ovate-lanceolate to cordate, mucronate to acuminate, sparingly hirsute. Infl. term., bracteate near base; cor. to 12mm diam., blue. Europe. 'Alba': fls white. Z6.

→*Cynoglossum*.

Omphalogramma (Franch.) Franch. Primulaceae. 15 perenn., usually rhizomatous, herbs. Lvs arising from a sheath of scales. Scapes and outside of cor. tube covered with long articulate, gland. hairs. Fl. 6–8-merous, solitary; cor. infundibuliform, tube longer than lobes. Early summer. Himalaya, W China. Z7.

O. delavayi Franch. Rhiz. scales forming a collar around base of petioles. Lvs to 10×7cm, broadly ovate to oblong or suborbicular, slightly crenulate, ± glab., margins ciliate; petiole pubesc., to 3× longer than lamina. Scape 6–15cm, pubesc.; cor. pale to deep rose-purple, 30–35mm diam., tube to 5cm, base yellow, lobes ovate or oblong, deeply incised. China (Yunnan), NE Upper Burma.

O. elegans Forr. Rhiz. scales not forming collar. Lvs to 10×4cm, ovate to ovate-lanceolate, apex obtuse, base cuneate to cordate, usually entire, sometimes minutely denticulate, pubesc. above, less so beneath; petiole subequal to twice as long as lamina, pubesc. Scape to 15cm, pilose; cor. 2-lipped, deep-violet to dark blue-purple, to 6cm diam., tube to 35mm, colourless or creamy at base, with 6 or 7 cream bands running into upper portion, lobes oblong to obovate, bilobed, entire or toothed. SE Tibet, NW Yunnan, Upper Burma.

O. elwesianum (King ex G. Watt) Franch. Scales embracing petiole bases. Lvs to 10×3cm, oblanceolate, apex round or obtuse, entire or obscurely denticulate, glab.; petiole broadly winged, subequal to lamina. Scape to 12cm, apex with crimson hairs; cor. purple, limb to 3cm diam., lobes oblong to obovate, emarginate, slightly dentate, margins pubesc., tube pale lemon inside; outside with crimson hairs. Sikkim, SE Tibet.

O. farreri Balf. f. Scales forming collar, surrounding petioles. Lvs to 10×5cm, round to cordate, apex obtuse or acute, base deeply cordate, slightly crenulate, pubesc.; petiole to twice length of lamina. Scape to 12cm; cor. deep rose-purple or violet, tube base yellow, 4–6cm diam., hairy lobes oblong or ovate, dentate, the upper 3 reflexing, lower lobes projecting. NE Upper Burma.

O. rockii W.W. Sm. = *O. vinciflorum*.

O. souliei Franch. Scales oblong, forming collar to 10cm. Lvs to 30×7cm, ovate to elliptic or oblong, apex acute or obtuse, base tapering, entire or denticulate, usually glab., rather fleshy; petiole broadly winged, subequal to half again as long as petiole. Scape to 35cm, apex covered in red, gland. hairs; cor. 4–6cm diam., deep red-purple or blue-purple, tube base yellow with yellow bands inside, tube 2–4cm, glandular-pilose, lobes spreading, broad-obovate or oblong, deeply or slightly bilobed, entire or toothed. NW Yunnan, SE Tibet.

O. vinciflorum (Franch.) Franch. Scales surrounding base of plant. Lvs to 20×5cm, ovate-oblong to oblong, apex round, entire to crenulate, base tapering into broadly winged petiole or rounded, with narrow petiole, glandular-pubesc. Scape to 20cm, apex tinged purple, glandular-pilose; cor. deep indigo-blue or purple, outside glandular-pubesc., limb 3–5cm diam., lobes narrow or broad-obovate, entire, faintly or deeply emarginate, apex crenate or toothed, upper lobes reflexed, lower lobes pointing forward. China (Yunnan, Sichuan).

ONAGRACEAE Juss. 24/650. *Boisduvalia, Calylophus, Camissonia, Circaea, Clarkia, Epilobium, Fuchsia, Gaura, Hauya, Lopezia, Ludwigia, Oenothera*.

✕**Oncidioda**. (*Cochlioda* ✕*Oncidium*.) Orchidaceae. Gdn hybrids with branching sprays of small fls in red marked pink or yellow.

Oncidium Sw. Orchidaceae. Some 450 epiphytic, lithophytic or terrestrial orchids. Pbs clustered or distant, conspicuous or near-absent. Lvs ± strap-shaped, sheathing and terminating pb., or solitary, massive, leathery in ± non pseudobulbous spp., conduplicate and equitant. Infl. a lat. rac. or pan., often branching and elongated; fls often yellow or brown; sep. usually subequal, spreading or reflexed, ± undulate; pet. similar to dors. sep. or larger; lip entire to 3-lobed, midlobe often cleft; disc with cristate or tuberculate basal callus. Subtropical & Trop. America. Z10.

O. abortivum Rchb. f. Pbs to 4×2.5cm, ellipsoid Lvs to 16×2.5cm, thin. Pan. to 30cm, many-fld, br. 2-ranked; abortive fls consisting of linear seg., to 8mm, fertile fls to 24mm diam., bright yellow banded dark purple-brown; lip bright yellow

marked brown in centre, callus pale yellow. Venezuela.

O. acrobotryum Klotzsch = *O. harrisonianum*.

O. altissimum (Jacq.) Sw. non Lindl. Pbs to 10×5cm, ovoid-oblong. Lvs to 20×3cm. Pan. to 3m, short-branched toward apex; fls to 3.5cm diam.; tep. yellow-green barred and blotched maroon, fleshy; lip bright yellow, blotched maroon at base of midlobe. W Indies.

O. altissimum Lindl. non (Jacq.) Sw. = *O. baueri*.

O. ampliatum Lindl. Pbs to 10×8cm, ovoid to suborbicular. Lvs to 40×10cm, fleshy-coriaceous. Rac. or pan. to 60cm; fls to 2.5cm diam.; sep. bright to pale yellow spotted chocolate-brown; pet. yellow with a few brown spots; lip bright yellow; callus pale cream marked yellow. Guatemala to Peru, Venezuela, Trinidad.

O. ansiferum Rchb. f. Pbs to 14×7cm, ellipsoid or elliptic-oblong. Lvs to 45×5.5cm, subcoriaceous. Pan. to 1m, much-branched; fls to 3cm diam.; tep. red-brown edged yellow; lip bright yellow with yellow-brown claw; callus yellow-white spotted pale brown. Costa Rica, Guatemala, Panama, Nicaragua.

O. anthocrene Rchb. f. Pbs to 15×5cm, ovoid-oblong. Lvs to 38×5cm, coriaceous. Rac. rarely branching, to 1.2m; fls to 6.5cm diam., waxy; tep. brown marked yellow; lip with red-brown claw, lat. lobes yellow often spotted red-brown, midlobe bright yellow, callus yellow. Panama, Colombia.

O. ascendens Lindl. Pbs to 2×1cm, ovoid. Lvs to 80×1cm, terete. Rac. to 50cm, simple or branched; fls to 2cm diam., yellow marked and stained red-brown; lip yellow marked red near callus. C America, Mexico.

O. auriferum Rchb. f. Pbs to 6×4cm, ovoid. Lvs to 25×2.5cm, coriaceous. Pan. to 40cm, br. small; fls to 2.5cm diam.; tep. yellow with 2 or 3 pale brown bands; lip golden-yellow with a blotch of pale red-brown either side of disc; callus white. Venezuela, Colombia.

O. aurosum Rchb. f. = *O. excavatum*.

O. barbatum Lindl. Pbs to 6.5×3.5cm, ovoid to ovate-oblong. Lvs to 10×2.5cm. Pan. to 50cm, short-branched; fls to 2.5cm diam., waxy; tep. yellow barred chestnut-brown; lip bright yellow, spotted red on callus. Brazil.

O. baueri Lindl. Pbs to 15×4cm, oblong-ovoid to cylindric. Lvs to 78×6cm, slightly coriaceous. Pan. to 3m, much-branched, many-fld; fls to 3cm diam., waxy; tep. green-yellow to bright yellow barred brown. Peru, Brazil, Bolivia, Ecuador.

O. bernoullianum Kränzl. = *O. ampliatum*.

O. bicallosum Lindl. Resembles *O. cavendishianum* except infl. racemose, fls larger, yellow with green-brown suffusion, unspotted, lip lat. lobes smaller. Mexico, Guatemala, El Salvador.

O. bicolor Lindl. Pbs to 7×3cm, ovoid. Lvs to 18×6cm, coriaceous. Pan. to 1m, much-branched; fls numerous, to 2cm diam.; tep. brown-yellow marked dark red-brown; lip bright yellow; callus white marked dark red-brown, pubesc. Venezuela, Brazil.

O. bicornutum Hook. = *O. pubes*.

O. bifolium Sims. Pbs to 9cm, ovoid or ovoid-oblong. Lvs to 14×1.5cm, subcoriaceous. Infl. simple, sometimes branched, to 35cm; fls 5–20, to 2.5cm diam.; tep. yellow marked red-brown; lip rich golden-yellow; callus yellow marked, red-brown. Brazil, Uruguay, Argentina, Bolivia.

O. bifrons Lindl. = *O. warscewiczii*.

O. boothianum Rchb. f. Pbs to 8cm, ellipsoid. Lvs to 30×9cm, subcoriaceous. Pan. to 2m, arcuate to pendent, much-branched, many-fld; fls to 3cm diam.; tep. yellow marked red-brown; lip golden yellow marked red-brown; callus white, verrucose. Venezuela.

O. brachyandrum Lindl. Pbs to 8×4.5cm, ovoid to ellipsoid. Lvs to 30×2cm, grassy. Rac. or pan. slender, elongated, few- to many-fld; tep. yellow or yellow-green mottled red-brown; lip yellow, callus yellow marked red-brown. Mexico, Guatemala, Honduras.

O. bracteatum Warsc. & Rchb. f. Pbs to 7.5×3.5cm, linear to ovoid-oblong. Lvs to 40×3cm, coriaceous. Pan. to 120cm, short-branched, conspicuously bracteate; fls usually 3, to 2.5cm diam.; tep. bright yellow-green heavily blotched and spotted brown-purple; lip bright to pale yellow with red-brown claw. Costa Rica, Panama, Nicaragua, Colombia.

O. brenesii Schltr. = *O. obryzatum*.

O. brevilabrum Rolfe. Pbs to 5.25cm, ovoid. Lvs to 32cm, linear. Pan. crowded; fls to 2cm diam., golden-yellow banded chocolate brown. S America.

O. bryolophotum Rchb. f. = *O. heteranthum*.

O. cabagrae Schltr. Pbs to 11×3cm, ovoid-elliptic to sublinear. Lvs to 25×3cm, subcoriaceous. Pan. to 80cm, loosely many-fld; fls to 2.5cm diam., long-lived; tep. yellow, heavily blotched deep chestnut-brown; lip bright yellow with red-brown claw; callus white spotted brown. Costa Rica, Panama.

O. caminiophorum Rchb. f. Pbs to 4×3cm, suborbicular to

narrowly ovoid. Lvs to 12cm, linear-oblong. Pan. to 50cm, branched from base, many-fld; fls to 2.5cm diam.; sep. bright yellow, brown below; lip bright yellow spotted red, with chestnut-brown band. Venezuela.

O. candidum Lindl. = *Palumbina candida*.

O. cardiochilum Lindl. Pbs to 10×2.5cm, ovoid-cylindric. Lvs to 75×6cm, subcoriaceous. Pan. to 2m, loosely many-branched, rachis distinctly fractiflex; fls to 2cm diam., lilac-scented; tep. red-brown tipped and marked green-white; lip white tinged and spotted red-purple; callus spotted brown. Guatemala, Peru, Costa Rica, Panama, Colombia.

O. carinatum Lindl. = *Leochilus carinatus*.

O. cariniferum (Rchb. f.) Beer = *Odontoglossum cariniferum*.

O. carthagenense (Jacq.) Sw. Pbs 0 or to 2.5cm. Lvs to 50×7cm, rigid and coriaceous. Pan. to 2m, many-fld; fls to 2.5cm across, pale yellow or white, variously blotched and spotted rose-purple. Florida and W Indies, Mexico to Venezuela and Brazil.

O. cavendishianum Batem. Pbs to 2cm or 0. Lvs to 45×13cm, elliptic-oblong or broadly lanceolate, thickly coriaceous. Pan. to 2m, stout, erect, usually branched, many-fld; fls to 4cm diam., fragrant, waxy; tep. yellow or green-yellow spotted and blotched red or brown; lip deep yellow, callus white flecked red-brown. Mexico, Honduras, Guatemala.

O. cebolleta (Jacq.) Sw. Pbs to 1.5×1.5cm, conical to sub-spherical. Lvs to 40×2.5cm, subcylindric to terete. Rac. or pan. simple or short-branched, to 150cm, many-fld; fls to 3.5cm diam.; tep. green-yellow marked deep red-brown; lip bright yellow spotted red-brown, callus spotted red-brown. Mexico and W Indies to Paraguay.

O. celsium A. Rich. = *O. bifolium*.

O. cerebriferum Rchb. f. = *O. ensatum*.

O. cheirophorum Rchb. f. COLOMBIA BUTTERCUP. Pbs to 2.5×1.5cm, ovoid to suborbicular. Lvs to 15×1.5cm, thin. Pan. to 20cm, slender, densely many-fld; fls to 1.5cm diam., fragrant, bright yellow; callus white. Colombia, Panama, Costa Rica.

O. chrysomorphum Lindl. Pbs to 5cm, ovoid. Lvs to 23cm, linear, slightly coriaceous. Pan. to 55cm, erect, branched from middle, densely fld, br. short, distichous, alt., recurved; fls to 2cm diam.; tep. golden yellow; lip pale yellow. Colombia, Venezuela.

O. ciliatulum Hoffsgg. = *O. barbatum*.

O. ciliatum Lindl. = *O. barbatum*.

O. cimiciferum (Rchb. f.) Lindl. Pbs to 10×4cm, oblong-cylindrical. Lvs to 65×5cm. Pan. to 3m with many short br.; fls to 2cm diam., brown or green-yellow banded brown, callus bright yellow. Venezuela, Colombia, Ecuador, Peru.

O. cirrhosum (Lindl.) Beer = *Odontoglossum cirrhosum*.

O. citrinum Lindl. Resembles *O. altissimum* in habit. Infl. simple or slightly branched, to 40cm, slender, several-fld; fls to 3.5cm diam.; tep. pale yellow or green-yellow faintly marked brown; lip clear yellow spotted and marked pale red-brown on callus. Trinidad, Venezuela, Colombia.

O. citrosmum (Lindl.) Beer = *Cuitlauzina pendula*.

O. concolor Hook. Pbs to 5×2.5cm, ovate-oblong. Lvs to 15×2.5cm, subcoriaceous. Rac. to 30cm, pendent, loosely few-to many-fld; fls to 4cm diam., bright golden-yellow. Brazil.

O. confusum Rchb. f. = *O. ensatum*.

O. convolvulaceum Lindl. = *O. globuliferum*.

O. cornigerum Lindl. Pbs to 10cm, subcylindrical. Lvs to 15cm, fleshy, ovate or elliptic-oblong. Pan. to 30cm; fls to 2cm diam., crowded in upper reaches; tep. bright yellow spotted and banded red-brown; lip bright yellow, lat. lobes horn-like. Brazil.

O. corynephorum Lindl. = *O. volubile*.

O. crispum Lodd. Pbs to 10×5cm, oblong or ovoid. Lvs to 20×5cm, subcoriaceous. Pan. to 110cm, erect to pendent, strongly branched, many-fld; fls to 8cm across, strongly crisped-undulate; tep. chestnut-brown or copper-brown sometimes spotted yellow, lip chestnut-brown or copper-red with yellow base and callus. Brazil.

O. crispum var. *forbesii* (Hook.) Burb. = *O. forbesii*.

O. crista-galli Rchb. f. Pbs to 1.5×1cm, ovoid, concealed by thin leaflike bracts to 8×1cm. Infl. 1–4, slender, equalling lvs, filiform, 1- to few-fld; fls to 2cm diam.; sep. yellow-green; pet. bright yellow barred red-brown; lip bright yellow marked red-brown on disc. Mexico to Colombia, Peru, Ecuador.

O. cristatum (Lindl.) Beer = *Odontoglossum cristatum*.

O. cryptocopis Rchb. f. Pbs to 12cm, narrowly ovoid-conic. Lvs to 50×3cm. Pan. to 2m, cascading, br. remote, short, few-fld; fls to 7.5cm across; tep. chestnut-brown edged golden-yellow; lip chestnut-brown, midlobe yellow. Peru.

O. cucullatum Lindl. PSeudobulbs to 5cm, ovoid to oblong. Lvs to 20×3.5cm. Rac. or pan. slender, to 50cm, few- to many-fld; fls to 3.5cm diam.; sep. dark chestnut-brown or olive-green sometimes with yellow margin; lip white to rose-purple spotted purple-crimson, callus bright orange-yellow. Colombia, Ecuador.

O. cucullatum var. *nubigenum* (Lindl.) Lindl. = *O. nubigenum*.

O. cucullatum var. *phalaenopsis* (Lind. & Rchb. f.) Veitch = *O. phalaenopsis*.

O. dasystyle Rchb. f. Pbs to 5cm, ovoid. Lvs to 15×2.5cm. Rac. or pan. to 40cm, sparsely branched; fls to 4cm diam.; tep. pale yellow blotched purple-brown; lip pale yellow, callus dark purple. Brazil.

O. decipiens Lindl. = *O. crista-galli*.

O. deltoideum Lindl. Pbs to 7.5cm, ovoid. Lvs to 25×3cm, subcoriaceous. Pan. to 80cm, br. spreading, loosely many-fld; fls to 2.5cm diam., pale golden-yellow, sometimes spotted red, callus pale yellow surrounded by red band. Peru.

O. delumbe Lindl. = *O. ansiferum*.

O. diadema Lindl. = *O. serratum*.

O. dielsianum Kränzl. = *O. cheirophorum*.

O. digitatum Lindl. = *O. leucochilum*.

O. divaricatum Lindl. Pbs to 4cm, subspherical. Lvs to 30×8cm, coriaceous. pan. to 2m, much-branched, many-fld; fls to 2.5cm; tep. yellow blotched chestnut-brown; lip yellow spotted chestnut-brown, callus cushion-like. Brazil.

O. echinatum HBK = *Erycina echinata*.

O. egertonii (Lindl.) Beer = *Osmoglossum egertonii*.

O. ensatum Lindl. Pbs to 10×5cm, ovoid or ellipsoid. Lvs to 100×3cm, subcoriaceous. Pan. to 2m, many-fld; fls to 3cm diam.; tep. clear yellow or yellow marked olive-brown; lip bright yellow, callus white. British Honduras to Panama.

O. epidendroides (HBK) Beer = *Odontoglossum epidendroides*.

O. excavatum Lindl. Pbs to 10cm, ovoid-oblong. Lvs to 50×4cm. Pan. to 1.5m, stout, many-fld; fls to 3.5cm diam.; tep. golden yellow, spotted and barred red-brown basally, lip lat. lobes red-brown, midlobe yellow, red towards base. Ecuador, Peru.

O. falcipetalum Lindl. Pbs to 15×5cm, oval or ovoid-oblong. Lvs to 60×5.5cm. Pan. to 6m, short-branched, flexuous; fls to 7cm diam.; sep. russet-brown edged yellow; pet. yellow blotched chestnut-brown; lip green-brown or purple-brown with yellow base and shiny brown sides, callus bright yellow. Venezuela, Colombia, Ecuador, Peru.

O. fimbriatum Hoffsgg. = *O. barbatum*.

O. flexuosum Sims. Pbs to 9×3cm, ovoid-oblong. Lvs to 22×3cm, subcoriaceous. Pan. to 1m, usually many-fld; fls to 2cm diam.; tep. bright yellow blotched and barred red-brown; lip bright yellow marked red-brown on cushion-like callus. Brazil, Argentina, Paraguay, Uruguay.

O. flexuosum Lindl. non Sims = *O. cimiciferum*.

O. forbesii Hook. Resembles *O. crispum* except infl. simple, tep. rich chestnut-brown with yellow-marbled margins. Brazil.

O. fulgens Schltr. = *O. obryzatum*.

O. galeottianum Drapiez = *Cuitlauzina pendula*.

O. gardneri Lindl. Resembles *O. crispum* except tep. brown striped yellow marginally, oblanceolate, lip with v. small lat. lobes, midlobe yellow spotted red-brown marginally, brown at base. Brazil.

O. ghiesbreghtiana A. Rich. & Gal. = *Mexicoa ghiesbreghtiana*.

O. globuliferum HBK. Pbs to 2.5×2cm, suborbicular to elliptic. Lvs to 6×2cm, coriaceous. Infl. to 9cm, 1-fld; fls to 3.5cm; tep. basally spotted red or red-brown; lip bright yellow marked red-brown on claw and clalus. Colombia, Venezuela, Costa Rica, Panama.

O. graminifolium Lindl. = *O. brachyandrum*.

O. guttatum (L.) Rchb. f. = *O. luridum*.

O. haematochilum Lindl. Similar in habit to *O. lanceanum*. Pan. to 60cm, many-fld; fls to 5cm diam., long-lived, fragrant; tep. yellow-green blotched rich cinnamon; lip bright crimson, margin yellow spotted red, callus bright crimson, verrucose. Colombia, Trinidad.

O. haematochrysum Rchb. f. = *O. flexuosum*.

O. haematoxanthum Rchb. f. = *O. flexuosum*.

O. hallii (Lindl.) Beer = *Odontoglossum hallii*.

O. harrisonianum Lindl. Pbs to 2.5×2cm, subspherical. Lvs to 15×3cm, rigid, fleshy. Pan. to 30cm, many-fld; fls to 1.5cm diam.; tep. golden-yellow blotched red or red-brown; lip golden-yellow, lat. lobes small, faintly striped chocolate-brown. Brazil.

O. hastatum (Batem.) Lindl. Pbs to 11×6cm, ovoid-conical. Lvs to 43×3cm, linear to lanceolate. Pan. to 1.5m, loosely branched, br. suberect; fls to 4cm diam.; tep. yellow-green or yellow, heavily spotted and barred deep maroon; lip lat. lobes white, midlobe tinged and blotched rose-purple, callus white lined rose-purple. Mexico.

O. hastilabium (Lindl.) Garay & Dunsterv. Pbs to 6×4cm, ovoid. Lvs to 35×4cm. Pan. to 80cm, many-fld; fls to 7.5cm diam., fragrant; tep. pale cream-yellow or pale green, banded chocolate-brown; lip white with rose-purple base. Venezuela, Colombia, Peru.

O. hebraicum Rchb. f. = *O. baueri*.

O. heteranthum Poepp. & Endl. Pbs to 5×3cm, ovoid or

ellipsoid. Lvs to 20×3.5cm, subcoriaceous, keeled below. Pan. to 1m, erect to pendent, br. short, with 1–3 fertile fls toward apex, lower fls abortive; tep. pale yellow-green marked red-brown; lip bright yellow slightly marked red-brown; callus white marked brown. Costa Rica, Panama, Venezuela, Colombia, Ecuador, Peru, Bolivia.

O. hians Lindl. Pbs to 1.5cm, ovoid-subrotund. Lvs to 7×1cm, coriaceous. Infl. simple or slightly branched, to 25cm, v. slender, few-fld; fls to 1cm diam., ochre; lip yellow with some red-brown spots, callus white with 4 red-spotted finger-like lobes. Brazil.

O. holochrysum Rchb. f. = *O. onustum.*

O. hookeri Rolfe. Pbs to 6×1.5cm, narrowly conical. Lvs to 20×1.5cm. Pan. to 45cm, many-fld; fls to 1cm diam.; tep. yellow flushed orange-brown; lip yellow marked orange or pale chestnut at base. Brazil.

O. hyphaematicum Rchb. f. Pbs to 10cm, oblong. Lvs to 30cm, ligulate, subcoriaceous. Pan. much-branched, to 1.5m; fls to 3.5cm diam., stained red below; tep. red-brown blotched deep red-brown, tipped yellow; lip canary-yellow, pale yellow below flushed and spotted crimson. Ecuador.

O. incurvum Barker ex Lindl. Pbs to 10×3cm, ovoid. Lvs to 40×2cm. Pan. to 2m, br. distichous arching; fls to 2.5cm diam., fragrant; tep. white streaked and blotched lilac and rose-pink; lip rose-pink blotched white, callus yellow marked brown. Mexico.

O. insculptum (Rchb. f.) Rchb. f. Pbs to 12.5×5cm, ovoid. Lvs to 45cm, ensiform to narrowly linear. Pan. loosely branched in upper half, pale green-brown, flexuous, br. short, few-fld; fls to 3.5cm, diam., glossy, dark cinnamon; tep. edged yellow-white; lip apex blue-grey. Ecuador.

O. insleayi (Barker & Lindl.) Lindl. = *Rossioglossum insleayi.*

O. ionops Cogn. & Rolfe = *O. heteranthum.*

O. iridifolium Lindl. = *O. crista-galli.*

O. isthmii Schltr. Pbs to 12×4cm, narrowly ovoid to linear-oblong. Lvs to 45×3cm, subcoriaceous. Pan. to 1m, many-fld; fls to 2.5cm diam., yellow marked copper-brown. Costa Rica, Panama.

O. janeirense Rchb. f. = *O. longipes.*

O. jonesianum Rchb. f. Pbs to 1×1cm, ovoid. Lvs to 40×1.5cm, terete, fleshy. Rac. to 50cm, usually pendent, to 15-fld; fls to 7.5cm diam., tep. yellow-white spotted chestnut-brown; lip lat. lobes yellow-orange, midlobe white spotted crimson. Brazil, Paraguay, Uruguay.

O. kienastianum Rchb. f. Pbs to 8cm, oblong-ovoid. Lvs to 50×2.5cm or more. Pan. long-scandent, short-branched above, few-fld; fls to 3cm diam.; tep. rich chocolate-brown edged pale yellow; lip lat. lobes yellow spotted brown, midlobe brown, callus yellow. Peru, Colombia.

O. kramerianum Rchb. f. = *Psychopsis krameriana.*

O. kymatoides Kränzl. = *O. carthagenense.*

O. labiatum (Sw.) Rchb. f. = *Leochilus labiatus.*

O. lacerum Lindl. = *O. stipitatum.*

O. lanceanum Lindl. Pbs ± 0. Lvs to 50×10cm, thickly coriaceous. Pan. to 30cm, few- to many-fld; fls to 6cm diam., fragrant, waxy; tep. yellow or green-yellow, heavily spotted purple-brown or chocolate-brown; lip pale purple, base deep rose-purple, callus deep rose-purple. Colombia, Venezuela, Brazil, Trinidad, Guianas.

O. lankesteri Ames = *O. ansiferum.*

O. leopoldianum (Kränzl.) Rolfe. Pbs to 2.5cm, ovoid-oblong to ovoid-cylindrical. Lvs to 16×2cm. Pan. to 2.5m, scandent, many-branched; fls to 4cm; tep. white with purple central portion; lip purple-violet, callus white. Peru.

O. leucochilum Batem. ex Lindl. Psuedobulbs to 13×6cm, ovoid. Lvs to 60×4.5cm, coriaceous. Pan. to 3m, strongly branched, many-fld; fls to 3.5cm diam.; tep. bright green to white-green blotched and barred deep red-brown or green-brown; lip white tinged pink or yellow, callus tinged purple. Mexico, Honduras, Guatemala.

O. leucostomum Hoffsgg. = *O. hians.*

O. lietzii Reg. Pbs conical or subfusiform, to 12×2cm. Lvs to 20×5cm. Rac. or pan. to 70cm, arching; fls to 3.5cm diam.; tep. yellow or green-yellow barred bright red-brown; lip lat. lobes yellow with few chocolate-brown spots, midlobe chocolate-brown, callus pale orange-brown. Brazil.

O. limminghei E. Morr. ex Lindl. = *Psychopsis limminghei.*

O. longicornu Mutel. Pbs to 7×2cm, oblong-conical. Lvs to 20×3cm. Pan. to 45cm, br. elongate, slender, 2-ranked; fls to 2cm diam.; sep. pale green or red-brown; pet. red-brown, tipped yellow; lip yellow above, red below, callus red, a long, incurved horn. Brazil.

O. longifolium Lindl. = *O. cebolleta.*

O. longipes Lindl. & Paxt. Pbs to 2.5cm, ovoid-pyriform. Lvs to 15×2cm, soft. Rac. to 15cm, erect, loosely 2–6-fld; fls to 3.5cm diam., usually smaller, tep. yellow-brown or pale red-brown

spotted and sstreaked yellow, yellow-tipped; lip rich deep yellow with pale red-brown claw, callus white-spotted with 2 v. prominent teeth. Brazil.

O. loxense Lindl. Pbs to 12.5×4cm, ovoid to pyriform. Lvs to 40×5cm. Pan. to 1.8m, vine-like, several-fld; fls to 7.5cm diam., fleshy; tep. cinnamon-brown barred bright or pale yellow; lip bright orange, pale yellow-orange on disc, callus crimson-spotted. Ecuador, Peru.

O. lucasianum Rolfe. Pbs to 5cm, ovoid. Lvs to 20cm, linear-lanceolate. Pan. to 1m, fls to 3cm diam., golden-yellow. Peru.

O. lunatum Lindl. = *Solenidium lunatum.*

O. luridum Lindl. Pbs to 1.5cm. Lvs to 85×15cm, coriaceous. Pan. to 1.5m, short-branched; fls to 4cm diam., usually yellow-brown or red-brown marked and spotted yellow, callus white or yellow spotted purple. Florida, W Indies and Mexico and Guyana and Guianas.

O. luteopurpureum (Lindl.) Beer = *Odontoglossum luteopurpureum.*

O. macrantherum Hook. = *Leochilus oncidioides.*

O. macranthum Lindl. Pbs to 15cm, ovoid to oblong-conical. Lvs to 55×5cm. Pan. to 3m, short-branched, lax or twining; fls to 10cm diam.; sep. dull yellow-brown; pet. golden-yellow; lip white bordered violet-purple, callus white. Ecuador, Peru, Colombia.

O. maculatum Lindl. Pbs to 10×4cm, ovoid. Lvs to 25×5cm, coriaceous. Rac. or pan. to 1m, erect; fls to 5cm diam., fragrant; tep. bronze to yellow blotched dark chestnut-brown; lip white marked red-brown. Mexico, Guatemala, Honduras.

O. marshallianum Rchb. f. Pbs to 15×4cm, ovoid-oblong. Lvs to 30×4cm, subcoriaceous. Pan. to 1.8m, many-fld; fls to 5.5cm diam., variable; sep. dull yellow, barred pale red-brown; pet. canary-yellow spotted pale red-brown towards centre or base; lip lat. lobes bright yellow spotted red, midlobe bright yellow, claw and callus spotted red-orange. Brazil.

O. massangei Morr. = *O. sphacelatum.*

O. megalous Schltr. = *O. heteranthum.*

O. meirax Rchb. f. Pbs to 2.5×1.5cm, ovoid to ovoid-oblong. Lvs to 7.5×1.5cm. Rac. or pan. to 25cm; tep. yellow flushed maroon; lip yellow tipped maroon. Colombia, Venezuela, Ecuador, Peru.

O. microchilum Batem. & Lindl. Pbs to 3.5×3cm, ovoid or spherical. Lvs to 30×6.5cm, coriaceous, olive, keeled below. Pan. to 1.5m, erect, much-branched; fls to 2.5cm diam.; sep. pale brown marked yellow; pet. chestnut-brown or purple-brown barred and edged yellow; lip lat. lobes white flecked maroon-purple, midlobe white with a purple spot, callus yellow spotted purple above, purple below. Guatemala, Mexico.

O. microglossum Klotzsch = *O. barbatum.*

O. monoceras Hook. = *O. longicornu.*

O. naevium (Lindl.) Beer = *Odontoglossum naevium.*

O. nanum Lindl. Pbs to 1.5×1cm. Lvs to 20×4cm. Pan. to 25cm, short-branched; fls to 13cm diam.; tep. ochre spotted rust; lip bright yellow, lat. lobes marked red-brown, callus honey-brown. Venezuela, Peru, Brazil, Guianas.

O. naranjense Schltr. = *O. ansiferum.*

O. nigratum Lindl. & Paxt. Pbs to 12×6cm, ovoid to ovoid-oblong. Lvs to 35×6cm, coriaceous. Pan. to 1.8m, arcuate, lightly to much-branched, br. to 60cm; tep. white or cream heavily banded and marked deep red-chocolate; lip yellow-brown or clear yellow, marked purple-brown, callus yellow spotted red. Venezuela, Colombia, Guyana.

O. nodosum E. Morr. = *Psychopsis krameriana.*

O. nubigenum Lindl. Resembles *O. cucullatum* except smaller, fls smaller, lip white with violet spot in front of callus. Ecuador, Peru, Colombia.

O. oblongatum Lindl. Pbs to 10×3.5cm, ovoid to ellipsoid. Lvs to 45×2.5cm, subcoriaceous. Pan. to 1.4m, erect, short-branched, many-fld; fls to 3cm diam., bright yellow spotted red-brown at base of seg. Mexico, Guatemala.

O. obryzatoides Kränzl. = *O. obryzatum.*

O. obryzatum Rchb. f. Pbs to 10×4cm, ovoid to suborbicular. Lvs to 45×4cm. Pan. to 1m, many-fld; fls to 3.5cm diam., yellow marked chocolate-brown, callus white or yellow sparsely spotted chocolate-brown, surrounded by red-brown blotch. Colombia, Venezuela, Peru, Ecuador, Panama, Costa Rica.

O. ochmatochilum Rchb. f. = *O. cardiochilum.*

O. oerstedii Rchb. f. = *O. carthagenense.*

O. onustum Lindl. Pbs to 4cm, ovoid to oblong. Lvs to 12.5×2cm. Rac. or pan. to 40cm, often secund; fls to 2.5cm across, deep golden-yellow. Panama, Colombia, Ecuador, Peru.

O. ornithorhynchum HBK. Pbs to 6×3cm, ovoid to pyriform. Lvs to 35×3cm, soft. Pan. to 50cm, strongly arching, many-fld; fls to 2.5cm, fragrant; tep. white, pink or lilac; lip darker pink or lilac, callus golden-yellow or deep orange. Mexico, Guatemala, Costa Rica, El Salvador.

O. pachyphyllum Hook. = *O. cavendishianum.*

O. panamense Schltr. Pbs to 16×6cm, ovoid-oblong. Lvs to 75×4cm, subcoriaceous. Pan. to 3.5m, erect to pendent or scandent, many-fld; fls to 2.5cm diam.; tep. yellow blotched and barred olive to brown; lip yellow blotched red-brown to yellow-brown below callus, callus white. Panama.

O. papilio Lindl. = *Psychopsis papilio*.

O. papilio var. *kramerianum* Lindl. = *Psychopsis krameriana*.

O. patulum Schltr. = *O. nanum*.

O. pelicanum Lindl. = *O. reflexum*.

O. phalaenopsis Lind. & Rchb. f. Close to *O. cucullatum*. Lvs narrow. Rac. to 25cm, slender, few-fld; fls to 3cm diam. tep. white, barred and spotted dark purple; lip white tinted rose-purple, spotted purple around callus. Ecuador.

O. phymatochilum Lindl. Pbs to 12.5×2.5cm, ovoid-oblong. Lvs to 35×7.5cm, coriaceous. Pan. to 60cm, pendent, loosely many-fld; fls to 5cm diam., showy; tep. pale yellow marked red-brown, sometimes white spotted red-orange; lip white spotted red-orange on callus. Mexico, Guatemala, Brazil.

O. powellii Schltr. = *O. anthocrene*.

O. pubes Lindl. Pbs to 7×1.5cm, subcylindrical. Lvs to 12×3cm, subcoriaceous. Pan. to 60cm, br. alternately 2-ranked; fls to 2.5cm diam.; tep. usually chestnut to brick red banded and spotted yellow; lip red-brown edged yellow. Brazil, Paraguay.

O. pulchellum Hook. Pbs 0. Lvs to 20×1.5cm, equitant, flattened keeled. Rac. or pan. to 50cm, erect or arcuate, many-fld; fls to 2.5cm diam., variable in size and colour, usually white, tinged pink or lilac-rose; callus yellow. Jamaica, Guianas, Cuba, Hispaniola.

O. pulvinatum Lindl. Pbs to 5cm diam., suborbicular-oblong. Lvs to 30×8cm. Pan. to 3m, flexuous, many-fld, loosely branched, br. often compound; fls to 2.5cm diam.; tep. yellow with red-brown or red-orange base; lip pale yellow spotted red or red-orange, callus white spotted red, cushion-like. Brazil.

O. pumilum Lindl. Pbs small or 0. Lvs to 12×3.5cm, coriaceous. Pan. to 15cm, short-branched, densely many-fld; fls to 1cm diam.; tep. somewhat incurved, straw-yellow spotted red-brown; lip pale yellow marked red either side of callus. Brazil, Paraguay.

O. pusillum (L.) Rchb. f. Pbs 0. Lvs to 6×1cm, fleshy, equitant, conduplicate, bases overlapping to form a flattened fan. Infl. to 6cm, axill.; fls 1–4, to 3cm diam., yellow marked rusty-red. C & S America, W Indies.

O. pyramidale Lindl. Pbs to 7cm, ovoid to cylindrical. Lvs to 20×3cm. Pan. to 50cm, erect or pendent, loosely many-fld, br. short, often compound; fls to 2.5cm diam., fragrant, canary-yellow, often spotted red. Peru, Ecuador, Colombia.

O. quadricorne Klotzsch = *O. hians*.

O. quadripetalum Sw. = *O. tetrapetalum*.

O. racemosum (Lindl.) Rchb. f. = *Solenidium racemosum*.

O. raniferum Lindl. Pbs to 6.5×2cm, ovoid to oblong. Lvs to 17×1.5cm, thin. Pan. to 35cm, erect, br. to 11cm, spreading; fls to 1.5cm across; tep. pale or bright yellow spotted red-brown; lip yellow, callus red-brown, large. E Brazil.

O. rechingerianum Kränzl. = *O. cabagrae*.

O. reflexum Lindl. Pbs to 8×5cm, ovoid to broadly ellipsoid. Lvs to 35×4cm, chartaceous. Pan. to 75cm, slender, straggling, loosely branched; fls to 4cm diam.; tep. pale yellow-green speckled dull red-brown; lip bright yellow spotted red at base. Mexico, Guatemala.

O. rigbyanum Paxt. = *O. sarcodes*.

O. robustissimum Rchb. f. Pbs short, broadly elliptic. Lvs to 40cm, ovate-elliptic or oblong, fleshy. Pan. to 2m, br. to 15cm, numerous, spreading; fls to 2.5cm diam.; tep. tipped yellow, red-brown at base; lip yellow spotted or striped cinnamon. Brazil.

O. sanderae Rolfe. Pbs to 6cm, ovoid. Lvs to 45×8cm. Infl. to 80cm; fls to 10cm diam., produced in succession; dors. sep. red-brown, yellow marked red lat. sep.; pet. similar to dors. sep.; lip pale yellow spotted red-brown. Peru.

O. sarcodes Lindl. Pbs to 14×3cm, subfusiform. Lvs to 25×5cm, coriaceous. Pan. to 1.8m, short-branched above; fls to 5cm diam.; tep. glossy, deep chestnut-brown edged yellow; lip bright yellow spotted red-brown at base. Brazil.

O. scansor Rchb. f. = *O. globuliferum*.

O. schillerianum Rchb. f. Pbs to 5cm, ovoid-oblong. Lvs to 15×3cm. Pan. to 1.2m, scandent, loosely branched, br. short, often compound; fls to 3cm diam.; yellow-green barred brown. Peru, Brazil.

O. serratum Lindl. Pbs to 12cm, oblong-ovoid. Lvs to 55×4cm. Pan. to 4m, loosely branched above, twining, many-fld; fls to 7.5cm diam., sep. bright chestnut-brown edged yellow; pet. chestnut-brown tipped bright yellow; lip purple-brown with white margin. Ecuador, Peru.

O. sessile Lindl. ex Paxt. Pbs to 10×4cm, ovoid-oblong. Lvs to 38×3cm. Pan. to 60cm, branched above middle, erect, br. short, spreading; fls to 3.5cm diam., spreading, canary-yellow

centrally spotted red-brown. Venezuela, Colombia, Peru.

O. sphacelatum Lindl. Pbs to 15×5cm, ovoid-ellipsoid. Lvs to 100×3.5cm, subcoriaceous. Pan. to 1.5m, short-branched; fls to 3cm diam.; tep. bright yellow blotched and spotted red-brown; lip golden-yellow marked red-brown in front of callus, callus white or yellow spotted orange-brown. Mexico to El Salvador.

O. sphegiferum Lindl. Pbs to 4cm diam., broadly oval to sub-rotund. Lvs to 20×4cm. Pan. to 1.2m, many-fld; fls to 2.5cm diam., bright orange, stained red-brown at base; lip orange, callus cushion-like. Brazil.

O. spilopterum Rchb. f. Pbs to 4×2.5cm, ovoid. Lvs to 20×2.5cm, subcoriaceous.Infl. to 40cm, erect to pendent, simple, loosely several-fld; fls pendent; tep. violet-brown marked yellow-green; lip sulphur-yellow, callus violet-purple. Brazil, Paraguay.

O. splendidum A. Rich. ex Duchartre. Pbs to 5×4.5cm, rotund. Lvs to 30×4.5cm, strongly conduplicate. Pan. to 1m, erect, many-fld; fls to 6cm diam.; tep. bright yellow blotched and spotted rich red-brown; lip golden-yellow, lat. lobes tinged lavender. Guatemala, Honduras.

O. stelligerum Rchb. f. Pbs to 8×3.5cm, ovoid-ellipsoid. Lvs to 16×3.5cm, coriaceous. Pan. to 80cm, several-branched; fls to 5cm diam., stellate; tep. yellow spotted brown; lip yellow-white with dark yellow callus. Mexico, Guatemala.

O. stenotis Rchb. f. Pbs to 14×4cm, linear-oblong. Lvs to 60×5cm, subcoriaceous. Pan. to 1.5m, short-branched, usually densely many-fld; fls to 3cm diam.; tep. yellow blotched and barred red-brown; lip bright yellow with brown claw. Costa Rica, Panama, Nicaragua.

O. stipitatum Lindl. Pbs to 1×1cm, broadly truncate at apex. Lvs to 70×1cm, cylindrical. Pan. slender, equalling lvs, pendent, many-fld; fls to 2cm diam.; tep. yellow marked or tinged red-brown; lip bright yellow. Panama, Nicaragua, Honduras.

O. stramineum Lindl. Pbs inconspicuous. Lvs to 20×4cm, coriaceous, rigid. Pan. stout, exceeding lvs, short-branched; fls to 2cm diam.; tep. white or straw-coloured, lat. sep. speckled red; lip white or straw-coloured, speckled red. Mexico.

O. suave Lindl. = *O. reflexum*.

O. superbiens Rchb. f. Pbs to 10×3.5cm, elongate-ovoid. Lvs to 60×6cm, subcoriaceous. Pan. to 4m, twining, irregularly branched, br. to 15cm, few-fld; fls to 8cm diam.; sep. red-brown tipped yellow; pet. yellow banded brown toward base; lip purple or maroon, callus yellow. Colombia, Venezuela, Peru.

O. superfluum Rchb. f. = *Capanemia superflua*.

O. teres Ames & Schweinf. Habit similar to *O. stipitatum*. Pan. to 45cm, many-fld; fls to 1.5cm diam.; tep. yellow, heavily spotted red-brown; lip bright yellow, spotted red-brown below, callus yellow spotted red-brown. Panama.

O. tetrapetalum (Jacq.) Willd. Pbs 0. Lvs tufted, to 20×0.5cm, triquetrous, linear-ligulate. Rac. sometimes branched, exceeding lvs, erect; fls to 2.5cm diam.; tep. usually chestnut to rusty red barred and marked yellow or purple-rose; lip white or pink blotched red to fore of callus. W Indies to Colombia and Venezuela.

O. tigratum Rchb. f. & Warsc. Pbs to 10×4cm, variable. Lvs to 20×3.5cm. Pan. to 40cm, short-branched, br. loosely several-fld, fractiflex; fls to 2.5cm diam., showy; tep. deep yellow marked brown or crimson; lip bright yellow banded brown basally with white callus. Venezuela, Colombia, Peru.

O. tigrinum La Ll. & Lex. Pbs to 10×6cm, subglobose. Lvs to 45×2.5cm, narrowly oblong, coriaceous. Pan. to 90cm, stout, usually erect, loosely branched, many-fld; fls to 7.5cm diam., violet-scented; tep. bright yellow heavily blotched deep brown; lip bright yellow, claw often tinged brown. Mexico.

O. tricolor Hook. = *O. tetrapetalum*.

O. trilingue Sander = *O. kienastianum*.

O. triquetrum (Sw.) R. Br. Pbs 0. Lvs 4 or more, triquetrous, to 15×1.5cm, linear-ligulate. Rac. to 20cm, slender, simple or slightly branched above, 5–15-fld; fls to 1.5cm diam., long-lived; tep. white-green spotted dark purple or rose, margins white, deeply tinged and spotted crimson; lip usually white spotted and streaked purple or red-purple, callus orange-yellow. Jamaica.

O. uaipanese Schnee = *O. nigratum*.

O. unguiculatum Lindl. = *O. tigrinum*.

O. unicorne Lindl. = *O. longicornu*.

O. varicosum Lindl. Pbs to 12cm, ovate-oblong. Lvs to 25cm, rigid, ligulate. Pan. to 1.5m, loosely branched, usually pendent, many-fld; fls to 3cm diam.; tep. yellow-green spotted and barred pale red-brown; lip bright yellow. Brazil.

O. variegatum (Sw.) Sw. VARIEGATED ONCIDIUM. Pbs much reduced. Lvs 4–6, equitant, lanceolate, recurved, to 15×1.5cm. Rac. or pan. to 45cm, slender; fls to 2cm diam., white to pink richly stained brown or crimson-purple; callus white-yellow. Florida, W Indies.

O. vexillarium Rchb. f. = *O. bifolium*.

O. volubile (Poepp. & Endl.) Cogn. Pbs to 5cm, narrowly oblong-cylindrical. Lvs to 45×4cm. Pan. to 7m, scandent, br.

loose, short, simple, few-fld; fls to 5cm diam.; sep. light violet-purple or cinnamon-brown; pet. pale cinnamon or pale violet, white above middle; lip deep maroon, base yellow or white. Peru.

O. volvox Rchb. f. Pbs to 7×5cm, ovoid or oblong-pyriform. Lvs to 36×3cm, coriaceous. Pan. to 5m, loosely branched; fls to 2.5cm diam.; tep. yellow or yellow-brown, spotted and marked red-brown; bright yellow marked dark brown. Venezuela.

O. waluewa Rolfe. Pbs to 7×1.5cm, oblong-cylindrical. Lvs to 9×1cm, subcoriaceous. Infl. pendent, to 10cm, slender, densely fld above; fls to 2cm diam.; sep. green-white or cream; pet. white to green-white barrred purple; lip similar in colour to pet., callus purple, linear, tubercles forming the image of an insect. Brazil, Paraguay.

O. warscewiczii Rchb. f. Pbs to 8×3cm, ovoid. Lvs to 30×3.5cm, subcoriaceous. Rac. to 50cm, spathaceous, to 15-fld; fls to 3cm diam., golden-yellow. Costa Rica, Panama.

O. wentworthianum Batem. ex Lindl. Pbs to 10×4.5cm, ovoid-ellipsoid. Lvs to 35×3cm, subcoriaceous. Pan. to 1.5m, pendent, short-branched, many-fld; fls to 3cm diam.; tep. deep yellow blotched red-brown; lip to lateral lobes pale yellow, mid-lobe pale yellow blotched red-brown, callus fleshy, spotted red-brown. Mexico, Guatemala.

O. werckleri Schltr. = *O. globuliferum*.

O. xanthodon Rchb. f. Pbs to 12cm, ovoid to ellipsoid.Lvs to 60×6cm. Pan. to 2.7m, slender, climbing, loosely many-branched, br. slender, few-fld; fls to 5cm diam.; tep. deep brown edged yellow; lip chocolate brown with yellow callus. Ecuador, Colombia.

O. zebrinum (Rchb. f.) Rchb. f. Pbs ovoid. Lvs to 50×5cm. Pan. to 4m, much-branched, br. few- to several-fld; fls to 3.5cm diam.; tep. white barred red to violet; lip white, yellow-green at base, callus yellow, often marked red. Venezuela.

O. grexes and cvs Many cvs, both strap-lvd. and mule-ear-type plants with branching sprays of fls in shades of yellow, bronze, copper, rusty red and chocolate, variously marked.

→*Leochilus, Odontoglossum, Psygmorchis* and *Waluewa*.

Oncoba Forssk. Flacourtiaceae. 39 shrubs or small trees, sometimes spiny. Fls ♂♀; sep. 3–5; pet. 5–20, spreading, sta. numerous, in many rows borne on a fleshy ring. Fr. a leathery, pulpy berry. Trop. & S Africa; Brazil.

O. echinata Oliv. Glab. shrub. Lvs to 15cm, thin, oblong. Fls white, to 12mm diam., borne on the br. below the lvs, solitary or in twos and threes. Fr. round, to 25mm diam., densely spiny, with many seeds. Upper Guinea. Z10.

O. kraussiana (Hochst.) Planch. Much-branched thornless everg. shrub, to 4.5m. Lvs to 6cm, elliptic-oblong, downy. Fls 5cm diam., white, solitary or in twos and threes. Fr. orange, smooth, to 5cm diam. S Africa. Z9.

O. monacantha Steud. = *O. spinosa*.

O. routledgei Sprague. Spiny shrub or small tree, to 60m, similar to *O. spinosa*. Lvs ovate, crenate. Fls 5cm diam., fragrant, white, solitary or in pairs. Trop. Africa. Z9.

O. spinosa Forssk. Glab. shrub with spines to 5cm. Lvs to 9cm, thin or leathery, elliptic, serrate. Fls 5cm diam., showy, white, fragrant, resembling a gardenia or camellia, term. or lat. Fr. round, to 5cm diam., shiny, brown, smooth with a hard shell. Africa, Arabia. Z9.

→*Xylotheca*.

Oncosiphon Källersjö. Compositae. 7 ann. herbs. Lvs alt., pinnatisect. Cap. subglobose, radiate or discoid, solitary or in corymbs; disc flts white 4-lobed, tube conspicuously swollen, campanulate. S Africa, Nam.

O. africanum Källersjö. Erect or spreading, to 30cm. Lower lvs 2.5–5cm, bipinnatisect, glab. or sparsely pubesc., lobes narrow. Cap. solitary, radiate; ray flts white; disc flts yellow or tinged red. S Africa.

O. grandiflorum (Thunb.) Källersjö. Erect, much-branched, to 45cm. St. pubesc., corymbosely branched. Lvs to 6cm, bipinnatisect, lobes narrow. Cap. 7mm diam., solitary, discoid; flts yellow, lobes short. S Africa.

O. piluliferum (L. f.) Källersjö. STINK-NET. To 45cm, foul-smelling. St. much-branched. Lvs to 4.5cm, bipinnatisect, lobes narrow. Cap. variable in size, solitary, discoid; flts yellow, lobes short. S Africa.

O. suffructicosum (L.) Källersjö. Erect, to 45cm, strongly aromatic. St. corymbosely branched, rather woody. Lvs to 4cm, bipinnatisect, lobes narrow. Cap. to 6mm diam., discoid, in dense, many-headed corymbs; flts bright yellow, lobes short. S Africa.

→*Cotula, Matricaria* and *Tanacetum*.

Oncosperma Bl. Palmae. 5 palms. St. erect, clustered, becoming bare, ringed, often armed with decid., downward-pointing, black spines. Crownshaft tomentose, spiny. Lvs pinnate; petiole flat or concave above, spiny; pinnae single-fold, acuminate, held in one plane, or clustered and held in differing planes. Infl. infrafoliar, erect becoming horizontal, branched ×2 at base; peduncle tomentose, unarmed or with spines; bud enclosed in 2 woody bracts, armed with straight or twisted spines; rachillae flexuous and pendent; fls in triads. Fr. spherical, purple-black. SE Asia and Malay Archip. from Sri Lanka to Indochina and Philipp. Z10.

O. fasciculatum Thwaites. St. to 12m, clustered, densely spiny. Lvs to 2.4m; pinnae clustered in groups and held in differing planes along rachis, ascending but apices pendent. Sri Lanka.

O. filamentosum Bl. = *O. tigilarum*.

O. tigilarum (Jack) Ridl. NIBUNG PALM. St. to 25m, densely clustered, smooth. Lvs 3.5–6m with spiny bracts; pinnae pendent. Malay Penins., Borneo, Sumatra, Philipp.

O. vanhoutteanum H.A. Wendl. & Van Houtte = *Nephrosperma vanhoutteanum*.

Onion *Alliumcepa*.

Onobrychis Mill. Leguminosae (Papilionoideae). SAINFOIN; SAINTFOIN; HOLY CLOVER. 130 ann. or perenn. herbs, sub-shrubs or spiny shrubs. Lvs imparipinnate. Fls pea-like in axill. rac. or long-stalked spikes. Fr. compressed, suborbicular, margins toothed. Summer. Temp. Eurasia. Z7.

O. alba Boreau = *O. viciifolia*.

O. alectorocephale St.-Lager = *O. caput-galli*.

O. alectorolopha St.-Lager = *O. crista-galli*.

O. arenaria (Kit. ex Schult.) DC. Perenn. herb, to 80cm, pubesc. or subglabrous. Lfts usually 3–12 pairs, narrow-oblong to elliptic, glab. to pubesc., green or grey-green. Fls to 1cm, pink veined purple, in slender rac. Temp. Eurasia. Z6.

O. caput-galli (L.) Lam. Ann. to 90cm, sparsely pubesc. or glab. Lfts in 4–7 pairs, obovate to linear, mucronate, hairy. Rac. to 8-fld; fls to 1cm, pale pink to red-purple. Medit. to C Bulgaria.

O. carnea Schleich. = *O. arenaria*.

O. crista-galli (L.) Lam. Ann. resembling *O. caput-galli* but infl. 2–8-fld; fr. to 1.4cm, not 1cm, with broadly not narrowly triangular teeth. Medit., N Africa, Asia Minor.

O. laconica Orph. ex Boiss. Stemless seirceous perenn. to 30.5cm. Lfts in 7–9 pairs, linear-elliptic. Fls bright pink, large, in a dense long-stalked oblong-cylindric spike. Levant. Possibly only a variant of *O. viciifolia*.

O. montana DC. Perenn. herb to 50cm, sparsely pubesc. to sub-glab. Lfts 5–8 pairs, elliptic or ovate to oblong, green or grey-green beneath. Fls to 10 per rac., to 14mm, pink usually purple veined. Mts of C Europe, Italy and Balkan Peninsula, possibly Pyrenees. Z5.

O. ochinata St. Lager = *O. caput-galli*.

O. radiata Steud. Erect herb, to 40cm. Lfts ovate, obtuse, mucronate, hairy beneath. Spikes cylindric; fls yellow-white, lined red, standard spotted yellow. Iberian Penins.

O. sativa Lam. = *O. viciifolia*.

O. trilophocarpa Coss. & Durieu. = *O. cirsta-galli*.

O. viciifolia Scop. SAINFOIN; HOLY CLOVER; ESPARCET. Perenn. herb to 80cm, pubesc. to subglabrous. Lfts in 6–14 pairs, ovate to oblong, rarely linear. Rac. to 9cm, many-fld; fls to 1cm+, pink veined purple. C Europe. Z6.

Onoclea L. Dryopteridaceae (Athyriaceae). 1 terrestrial, perenn. fern. Rhiz. branching, creeping. Fronds dimorphic, emerging bronze to pink; sterile fronds to 1m, pinnately divided, pale green, broadly ovate-triangular, pinnae 8–12 pairs, to 8cm wide, lobed to sinuate or entire, rachis winged; fertile fronds to 60cm, stiffly erect, lanceolate, bipinnate, becoming dark brown; pinnules revolute, sori in beadlike lobes. E N Amer., E Asia. Z4.

O. orientalis Hook. = *Matteuccia orientalis*.

O. sensibilis L. SENSITIVE FERN; BEAD FERN. Occas. nat. W Europe.

O. struthiopteris (L.) Hoffm. = *Matteuccia struthiopteris*.

Ononis L. Leguminosae (Papilionoideae). 75 ann. or perenn. herbs or dwarf shrubs, usually gland., hairy. Lvs 3-foliolate, sometimes simple or imparipinnate. Fls in pan., spikes or rac. Summer. Canaries, Medit., N Africa, Iran.

O. altissima Colm. = *O. arvensis*.

O. antiquorum Willk. = *O. arvensis*.

O. aragonensis Asso. Perenn. dwarf subshrub, to 30cm. St. often tortuous, densely hairy above, sometimes with short gland. hairs. Lfts to 1cm, elliptic or suborbicular, leathery. Fls in long, loose, term. pan.; cor. to 18mm, yellow. Pyren., E & S Spain, Alg. Z8.

O. arvensis L. Perenn. herb to 1m, sometimes spiny. St. variably hairy. Lfts to 2.5cm, elliptic to ovate. Fls in a dense term. rac.; cor. to 2cm, pink, standard hairy. Norway, E Germ., Albania. Sometimes considered synonymous with *O. spinosa* and united with it under the name *O. campestris*. Z6.

O. caduca Vill. = *O. arvensis.*

O. campestris Koch. and Ziz. = *O. spinosa* and *O. arvensis.*

O. cenisia L. = *O. cristata.*

O. cristata Mill. Perenn. to 25cm. Lfts small, obovate, denticulate. Fls rose pink. Summer. S Eur. Z7.

O. dumosa Lapeyr. = *O. aragonensis.*

O. fructicosa L. Dwarf shrub to 1m. Young st. short-pubesc. lfts to 2.5cm, oblong-lanceolate, subcoriaceous, glab. Cor. to 2cm, pink. C & E Spain, C Pyren., SE France. Z7.

O. hircina Jacq. = *O. arvensis.*

O. minutissima L. Dwarf shrub to 30cm. St. often prostrate and rooting, subglabrous. Lfts to 6mm, sessile oblong-oblanceolate to obovate. Infl. a dense term. rac.; cor. to 1cm, shorter than or equal to cal., yellow. W Medit. to Balk. Z6.

O. natrix L. Perenn. dwarf shrub; erect, many-branched. St. to 60cm, with dense glands and hairs. Lower lvs sometimes pinnate; lfts ovate to long and narrow. Fls in loose, leafy pan.; cor. to 2cm, yellow, often with violet or red veins. S & W Eur., N Spain. Z7.

O. procurrens Wallr. = *O. repens.*

O. repens L. Resembles *O. spinosa*, but st. usually decumbent and rooting. Lfts usually ovate, obtuse or emarginate. Fls in loose leafy rac.; cor. to 2cm, pink or purple. W & C Europe, E Sweden to Estonia, N Balkan Penins. Z6.

O. rotundifolia L. Perenn. dwarf shrub, to 50cm, erect. St. villous and gland. Lfts 2.5cm, elliptic to orbicular, obtuse, roughly toothed, sparsely gland. Infl. a pan.; cor. to 2cm, pink or white. Mainly mts, SE Spain to E Austria and C Italy. Z7.

O. speciosa Lagasca. Dwarf glandular-hairy shrub, to 1m. Lfts to 23mm, elliptic to suborbicular, subcoriaceous, glab., sticky. Infl. a dense, oblong pan.; cor. to 2cm, golden-yellow. S Spain. Z7.

O. spinosa L. Dwarf shrub to 80cm. St. usually spiny, sparsely gland. Lfts variable. Fls in loose rac.; cor. to 2cm, pink or purple. W, C & S Europe, S Norway, NW Ukraine. Z6.

O. spinosa ssp. *procurrens* (Wallr.) Briq. = *O. repens.*

O. viscosa L. Ann. to 80cm. St. erect, eglandular, downy. Lfts to 2cm, usually elliptic to obovate, obtuse. Fls in pan.; cor. to 12mm, yellow, standard often veined red. Medit., Portugal.

Onopordon see *Onopordum.*

Onopordum L. Compositae. c40 spiny, arachnoid biennials. St. usually spiny-winged. Lvs armed, alt., simple, pinnatilobed, pinnatifid to pinnatisect. Cap. large, thistle-like, discoid, solitary or corymbose; involucre globose to hemispherical; phyllaries many in series, imbricate, spine-tipped, often recurved; flts tubular, maroon, rarely pink or white. Eur., Medit., W Asia.

O. acanthium L. GIANT THISTLE To 3m. St. yellow, pubesc., wings 2–4, with spines to 11mm. Lvs to 35cm, oblong-ovate to lanceolate or ovate, sinuate-dentate or pinnatilobed, lobes triangular, with an apical spine to 1cm, grey-green tinged grey and sparsely lanate above. Cap. solitary or in leafy, term. clusters of phyllaries gradually tapering to a 5mm spine, minutely pubesc.; flts to 2.5cm, white or purple. Summer. W Europe to C Asia. Z6.

O. acoulon L. St. 0. Lvs to 40cm, in rosettes, oblong-oblanceolate to elliptic-lanceolate, petiolate, shallowly lobed to pinnatisect, lobes with apical spine to 1cm, white- to grey-lanate above, densely white-tomentose beneath. Cap. solitary or in clusters of 2–6; phyllaries to 4mm wide, ovate-lanceolate, apical spine to 12mm, glab.; flts 2–2.5cm, white. Summer. Spain (mts), NW Africa. Z8.

O. arabicum hort. = *O. nervosum.*

O. bracteatum Boiss. & Heldr. To 180cm. St. white or tinged yellow, pubesc., wings 6–12, palmately spiny, spines to 7mm. Lvs to 30cm, oblong-lanceolate, pinnatisect to pinnatilobed, lobes triangular, palmate to dentate with an apical spine to 8mm. Cap. solitary or 2–4 phyllaries to 1cm wide, broadly lanceolate, apical spine to 8mm; flts 3–4cm, purple. Summer. E Medit. Z6.

O. deltoides Ait. = *Synurus deltoides.*

O. illyricum L. To 130cm. St. tinged yellow, pubesc., wings 2–12, spines to 7mm. Lvs to 55cm, oblong-lanceolate, pinnatifid to pinnatisect, lobes triangular-cuneate, lobulate or toothed, spiny. Cap. 1–4; phyllaries to 8mm wide, broadly lanceolate, tinged pink, attenuate to a 3–5mm spine, outer and middle phyllaries somewhat reflexed; flts 2.5–3.5cm, purple. Summer. S Eur. Z7.

O. macracanthum Schousb. To 1.5m. St. white-lanate, wings to 10mm wide, spines to 5mm. Lvs 40cm, ovate-lanceolate to lanceolate, pinnatifid, lobes triangular-acute, each with apical spine to 6mm, densely tomentose, tinged grey above, white be-

neath. Cap. subglobose; phyllaries 5–6mm wide, ovate-lanceolate, acuminate, spine to 7mm; flts 3cm, purple. Summer. SE Portugal and S Spain. Z8.

O. nervosum Boiss. To 3m. St. tinged yellow, densely pubesc., wings to 2cm wide, densely reticulate-veined, spines to 1cm. Lvs to 50cm, oblong-lanceolate, sessile, beneath, pinnatifid, lobes triangular, apical spine to 1cm, subglabrous above, sparsely wispy-hairy below. Cap. conical-ovoid; phyllaries 4–6mm wide, ovate to lanceolate, acuminate, apical spine to 4mm; flts 3–3.5cm, pink. Summer. Portugal and Spain. Z8.

O. salteri hort. To 2m, ± viscid. St. yellow-brown, wings 2–4 to 1.5cm wide, spines to 15mm. Lvs 25cm, oblong-lanceolate, pinnatilobed to pinnatifid, lobes triangular, remote apical spine to 8mm, rarely much longer, dark green, sparsely pubesc. above, more densely so beneath. Cap. in compound corymbs of 2–6; phyllaries 4–7mm wide, tapering to rigid spine to 4mm, outer usually deflexed; flts 2.5–3cm, purple-pink. Summer. SE Eur. Z8.

O. virens DC. = *O. tauricum.*

Onosma L. Boraginaceae. Some 150 hispid bienn. and perenn. herbs, often woody-based. St. lvs smaller than basal lvs. Fls in term. cymes, usually branched, bracteate; cal. deeply 5-lobed; cor. tubular to tubular-campanulate, shortly 5-lobed; styles exserted. Medit. to E Asia.

O. alborosea Fisch. & Mey. Perenn. St. to 25cm, ascending sometimes branched, setose. Lvs to 6×1.2cm, spathulate-lanceolate to obovate or oblong, green-white, densely setose. Infl. dense nodding; cor. to 30mm, white to pink-purple, becoming deep purple or violet-blue. SW Asia. Z7.

O. arenaria Waldst. & Kit. Perenn. or bienn. St. to 70cm, much-branched, puberulent, setose. Lvs to 18×1.5cm, spathulate-oblong, densely setose. Infl. branched; cor.to 17mm, pale yellow, glab. to puberulent. SE & C Europe. Z6.

O. bourgaei Boiss. Perenn. St. to 50cm, sometimes branched, patent-setose. Lvs oblong-spathulate to oblong-linear, subacute to obtuse, downy, to 15×2cm. Infl. of usually 2 cymes, weakly branched; cor. to 15mm, pale yellow, cream or white, pubesc. SW Asia. Z7.

O. caerulea Willd. = *Moltkia caerulea.*

O. cassia Boiss. Perenn. St. to 60cm, a densely patent-setose, br. numerous. Lvs to 7×3cm, oblong to oblong-lanceolate, acute, densely patent-setose, white-tuberculate. Infl. elongate, subcorymbose; cor. to 16mm, yellow, glab. SW Asia. Z7.

O. decipiens Schott & Kotschy ex Boiss. = *O. nana.*

O. echioides L. Perenn. St. to 30cm, erect, sometimes slightly branched, stellate-setose. Lvs to 6×0.7cm, oblong-linear or linear, subglabrous to densely stellate-setose, setae white, yellow or grey. Fls short-stalked; cor. to 25mm, pale yellow, pubesc. SE Europe. Z7.

O. emodi Wallich. Perenn. St. to 50cm, usually several, decumbent or ascending, hirsute. Lvs to 15×20cm, lanceolate or oblanceolate, hispid, minutely strigose. Cymes clustered, usually forked; cor. to 13mm. Himalaya. Z7.

O. frutescens Lam. Perenn. St. to 40cm, erect or ascending, simple, puberulent, patent-setose. Lvs to 7×1cm, lanceolate to oblong-lanceolate or linear, revolute, puberulent, setose. Infl. of 1 or 2 cymes, simple or slightly branched; cor. to 20mm, pale yellow tinged purple, red or brown glab.; anth. exserted. SW Asia. Z8.

O. helvetica (A. DC.) Boiss. Perenn. St. to 50cm, several, simple or branched above, puberulent, stellate-setose. Lvs to 7×0.6cm, spathulate-oblong, stellate-setose, puberulent. Fls short-stalked; cor. to 24mm, pale yellow, puberulent. C Europe. Z6.

O. heterophylla Griseb. Perenn. St. to 40cm, several, simple or branched, stellate-setose, puberulent. Lvs to 15×1cm, oblong to oblong-linear, stellate-setose. Infl. of 1 to several cymes; cor. to 30mm, pale yellow, puberulent. SE Europe to SW Asia. Z6.

O. hookeri Clarke. Perenn. St. short, several, simple, hispid or hispid-villous. Lvs to 15×1.5cm, oblanceolate, acute, revolute, hispid-villous above, villous beneath. Cymes usually solitary, simple or forked; cor. to 28mm, blue, sometimes purple or red, villous. Himalaya. Z7.

O. nana DC. Perenn. St. to 18cm, erect, simple, puberulent, patent-setose. Lvs to 5.5cm, linear-spathulate, velutinous, setose. Infl. of 1 or 2 cymes; cor. to 25mm, white to yellow, becoming pink to blue or blue-purple, campanulate-cylindric, glab. Turkey. Z8.

O. pyramidalis Hook. Bienn. St. to 60cm, several, erect or ascending, branched above, hispid. Basal lvs to 20cm, oblanceolate, hispid; cauline lvs to 8×1.5cm, lanceolate, acute. Cymes simple or forked; pedicels 20mm, slender, hispid; cal. to 11mm, lobes linear-lanceolate, acute, hispid; cor. to 13mm, red, exterior minutely pubesc., interior mostly glab., lobes to 1×2mm, recurved. Himalaya. Z7.

O. rupestris Bieb. = *O. tenuiflora.*

O. sericea Willd. Perenn. St. to 30cm, 1 to several, erect or ascending, usually simple. Lvs to 10×3cm, lanceolate or obovate, acute; cauline lvs sericeous, sessile. Infl. of scorpioid cymes, becoming elongate; pedicels to 5mm in fr.; bracts to 7mm, linear to linear-lanceolate; cal. to 16mm in fl. to 30mm in fr., lobes lanceolate; cor. to 20mm, yellow, infundibular to clavate, puberulent. SW Asia. Z7.

O. setosa Ledeb. Bienn. St. to 60cm, erect, much-branched, hispid. Basal lvs to 10×1cm, linear to linear-lanceolate, densely setose. Infl. much branched; pedicels to 5mm; cal. to 30mm in fr.; cor. to 25mm, cream or pale yellow, glab. S Russia, Caucasus. Z6.

O. sieheana Hayek. Perenn. St. to 45cm, erect, simple or branched above, patent-setose. Basal lvs narrowly lanceolate, attenuate, petiolate; cauline lvs to 6×0.6cm, linear-lanceolate or linear, acute, revolute, adpressed-setose. Cymes term. or lat., scorpioid; pedicels to 6mm; bracts narrowly linear-lanceolate; cal. to 17mm in fl. patent-setose; cor. orange or pale yellow, short-pubesc., lobes suberect; anth. sometime exserted. Turkey. Z8.

O. stellulata Waldst. & Kit. Perenn. St. to 25cm, simple, short-pubesc., stellate-setose. Basal lvs to 14×1.5cm, spathulate-oblong, sparingly stellate-pubesc. Pedicels to 14mm in fl.; cal. to 9mm, with simple or stellate setae; cor. to 18mm, light yellow, glab. Yugoslavia. Z6.

O. taurica Pall. ex Willd. Perenn. St. to 30cm, several, tufted, usually simple, puberulent, stellate-setose. Lvs stellate-setose, puberulent, often white-green, basal lvs to 12×1cm, linear-oblong, acute, attenuate, petiolate, cauline lvs linear-oblong to linear-lanceolate, obtuse, sessile or subsessile. Cymes 1 or 2, term.; pedicels to 5mm; cal. to 13mm in fl., to 18mm in fr., lobes linear, setose; cor. to 30mm, white to pale yellow, campanulate, glab. SE Europe to SW Asia. Z6.

O. tenuiflora Willd. Perenn. St. to 25cm, simple, ascending, pubesc. Lvs to 4×0.4cm, linear, obtuse, puberulent, setose. Cymes 1 or 2, terminal, many-fld; pedicels to 2mm; bracts linear, subacute; cal. to 8mm, lobes narrowly linear, densely pubesc.; cor. to 12mm, pale yellow, cylindrical, lobes acute, suberect, glab. Caucasus, Turkey. Z6.

O. tubiflora Velen. = *O. heterophylla*.

Ontario Poplar *Populus* ×*jackii* 'Gileadensis'.

Onychium Kaulf. CLAW FERN. Adiantaceae. 6 small terrestrial ferns. Rhiz. usually slender, fast-creeping, paleate. Fronds 3–4-pinnate, finely cut giving an open, lacy appearance, glab., soft or subcoriaceous. OW Trop. and Subtrop. Z10.

O. auratum Kaulf. = *O. siliculosum*.

O. japonicum (Thunb.) Kuntze. CARROT FERN. Fronds 30cm, ovate-acuminate, 4-pinnatifid, deep green above, paler beneath, glab.; pinnules to 8mm, usually deltoid, ultimate divisions linear-mucronate. Jap.

O. lucidum Spreng. Fronds 30cm+, ovate-acuminate, 3–4-pinnatifid, somewhat coriaceous, glossy; pinnules nearly uniform, narrow-linear, gradually acuminate above, tapering below. E India, Nepal.

O. siliculosum (Desv.) C. Chr. Rhiz. stout. Fronds to 40cm, ovate, finely 3- or 4-pinnate, ultimate pinnules numerous, and narrow, usually spathulate when sterile, to 5mm, often dentate at apex. India to China, S to Malaya, Philipp.

Ookow *Dichelostemma congestum*.

Oophytum N.E. Br. Aizoaceae. 2 highly succulent perennials forming dense matts of closely packed, soft, ovoid bodies concealed during resting period by dry white skins of old lvs. Fls mostly white. S Afr. (Cape Prov.). Z9.

O. nanum (Schltr.) L. Bol. Bodies to 20mm, spherical, 5–7mm across, minutely papillose. Fls 10mm diam., pet. white with reddened tips. W Cape.

O. oviforme (N.E. Br.) N.E. Br. Bodies 12–20mm, 10–12mm across, olive-green, often flame-coloured, glossy-papillose. Fls 22mm diam., pet. white below, purple-pink above. W Cape.

→*Conophytum*.

Ophiocolea H. Perrier. Bignoniaceae. 5 shrubs. St. simple or little-branched. Lvs imparipinnate, in whorls below smaller whorls of leafy bracts. Fls in rac. or pan. or cymes; cor. tubular-campanulate. Madag., Comoros Is. Z10.

O. floribunda (Bojer ex Lindl.) H. Perrier. To 12m. Pinnae 15cm, 7–17 per lf, entire. Infl. borne on old wood just above previous year's lf scars; cor. 2–5cm, tubular-campanulate, hairy inside, tube bright orange-yellow, lobes often white. Madag.

→*Colea*.

OPHIOGLOSSACEAE (R. Br.) Agardh. 3 genera. *Botrychium*, *Helminthostachys*, *Ophioglossum*.

Ophioglossum L. ADDER'S TONGUE FERN. Ophioglossaceae. 30–50 largely terrestrial or epiphytic ferns. Rhiz. short, bulbous. Fronds erect or, in epiphytic spp., dangling, bright green, simple, thinly succulent. Sporangia bead-like in 2 ranks or tiered on a long-stalked, flattened spike, forming an offshoot of the sterile frond or separate from it. Cosmop.

O. engelmannii Prantl. Terrestrial fern, 5–20cm. Stipes 5–10cm. Fronds 2–5, ovate, usually 5–7×2–3cm, elliptic to oblong, apiculate. Fertile spike 1–3.5cm×3mm; on peduncle 6–9cm. N Amer. Z4.

O. lusitanicum L. Terrestrial. Rhiz. somewhat tuberous. Fronds 1.2–2.4cm, lanceolate to linear-lanceolate, obtuse; fertile spike 6–12mm, linear, on firm peduncle 1–4cm when mature, arising near base of sterile blade. Medit. and Cauc. Z6.

O. palmatum L. Epiphytic. Rhiz. cylindric, bearing many fleshy roots; stipes flaccid, succulent, 15–30cm. Frond blades 20–75cm, arching-pendent, obdeltate, palmately lobed, lobes 2–10, occas. forked. Fertile spikes to 3cm, on 5cm stalks at top of stipe. Trop. Amer., Madag., SE Asia. Z10.

O. pendulum L. RIBBON FERN. Epiphytic, rhiz. creeping. Fronds ± sessile, 30cm–4.5m×3–8cm, pendent, strap-like, simple or forked, generally twisted. Fertile spike pendent, inserted near base of sterile blade, cylindric, 5–15cm. Australasia, Asia, Polyn. Z10.

O. petiolatum Hook. Rhiz. erect, fleshy; stipes 10–20cm, occas. to 30cm. Fronds 1.5–6cm, simple or forked at apex, ovate to broadly ovate or oblong. Fertile spike term., simple, pedunculate. Summer. Trop. Asia, Jap., Korea, Polyn., Trop. Amer. Z10.

O. reticulatum L. Rhiz. erect, cylindric, 0.5–2cm. Fronds 5–8cm, solitary or in pairs, deltate-ovate to reniform, cordate-lobed at base. Fertile spikes inserted above middle of sterile blade, 2–5cm on slender peduncle 7–15cm. Pantrop. Z10.

O. vulgatum L. ADDER'S TONGUE. Terrestrial fern to 35cm; rhiz. not tuberous; stipes 5–12cm. Fronds 15–22cm, ovate to oblong-elliptic. Fertile spike 1–4cm, inserted near middle of sterile frond, on 7–14cm peduncle. Eur., W Asia, N Amer.

Ophionella P.V. Bruyns.
O. arcuata (N.E. Br.) P.V. Bruyns = *Pectinaria arcuata*.

Ophiopogon Ker-Gawl. Liliaceae (Convallariaceae). 4 perenn., everg. tufted herbs. Lvs linear, grasslike. Fls numerous in rac.; tep. 6, overlapping, tube obconical, adnate to inferior ovary; sta. 6, joined at base to tep., fil. short. Fr. berry-like.

O. intermedius D. Don. Lvs to 60×0.5cm, margins serrulate toward base. Fls 1cm wide, white to lilac, numerous, in a loose rac. China. 'Argenteomarginatus': lvs edged white; fls white.

O. intermedius var. *argenteomarginatus* D. Don. = *O. intermedius* 'Argenteomarginatus'.

O. jaburan (Kunth) Lodd. Close to *O. japonicus*, but more robust. Roots not tuberous. Lvs to 60×0.5cm. Flowering st. to 60cm; fls tinted lilac or white in a dense 7.5–15cm rac. Fr. violet-blue, oblong. Jap. 'Aureovariegatus': lvs striped yellow. 'Caeruleus': fls violet. 'Crow's White': lvs variegated white; fls white. 'Vittatus' ('Argenteovittatus', 'Javanensis', 'Variegatus'): lvs symmetrically arranged, pale green striped and edged creamy white; fls white. 'White Dragon': lvs boldly striped white, almost no green. Z7.

O. japonicus (L. f.) Ker-Gawl. Stolons large; roots tuberous. Lvs to 40×0.3cm, rather rigid, dark green, somewhat curved. Flowering st. 5–10cm, fls white to light lilac in a loose, short rac. Fr. blue, 0.5cm diam. Jap. 'Albus': fls white. 'Compactus': miniature, dense, to 5cm. 'Kyoto Dwarf': tightly clumped, to 4cm; lvs narrow, dark green. 'Minor': compact, to 8cm; lvs curling, black-green. 'Nanus': small, to 12cm. 'Silver Dragon': lvs variegated white. Z7.

O. planiscapus Nak. Often stoloniferous; root thickened. Lvs to 35×0.3–0.5cm. Fls white or lilac, in 6.5cm rac. Fr. dull blue. Jap. 'Nigrescens' ('Arabicus', 'Black Dragon', 'Ebony Knight'): to 15cm; lvs curving, purple-black, tinted silver-green at base when young; fls white tinted pink to lilac; fr. black. Z6.

O. spicatus D. Don = *O. intermedius*.

→*Liriope*.

Ophrys L. Orchidaceae. Some 30 terrestrial tuberous herbaceous orchids. Lvs ovate to oblong-lanceolate in a loose basal rosette and on flowering st. Spike erect, clothed with bract-like lvs; sep. 3, glab.; pet. 2, usually shorter and narrower than sep.; lip flat, concave or convex, entire to trilobed, velvety above often with mirror-like patch (speculum), sometimes with swelling below and apical appendage. Eur., N Afr., W Asia.

O. apifera Huds. BEE ORCHID. To 50cm. Fls 2–11; sep. 8–15mm, oblong-ovate, green or purple-violet, rarely white, with green veins; pet. green or purple, triangular to linear-lanceolate or oblong; lip 10–13mm, trilobed, central lobe broadly ovate, convex, margins dark red-brown, sometimes ochre or bicolour, velvety, appendage deflexed, yellow, sometimes 0, lat. lobes to 3mm, triangular-ovate, villous, speculum red-brown with yellow apical spots and margins. Mid spring–mid summer. W & C Eur. Z7.

O. arachnites (L.) Reichard = *O. holoserica*.

O. araneola Rchb. To 45cm. Fls 6–10; sep. 6–10mm, green, revolute; pet. 4–8mm, green single-veined; lip 5–8mm, obscurely trilobed, pale to dark brown or olive green, entire, velvety, speculum blue, glab., loosely H-shaped. Spring–early summer. S & SC Eur. Z7.

O. bertolonii Moretti. To 35cm. Fls 3–8, sep. 8–10mm, deep pink-lilac, basally tinted green; pet. linear-lanceolate, lilac; lip 10–13mm, entire or trilobed, deep purple-black, velvety, speculum blue-violet, paler at edges; apical appendages yellow, margins glab. Late spring. S & C Eur. Z7.

O. bombyliflora Link. To 25cm. Fls 5–14; sep. 9–12mm, green, ovate, obtuse, lat. sep. spreading or deflexed; pet. triangular, purple at base, green at apex, velvety; lip to 10mm, trilobed, lobes deflexed appearing globose-inflated at tips, dark brown, velvety, speculum blue-violet with paler margin. Late spring–early summer. Medit. Z8.

O. ciliata Biv. = *O. vernixia*.

O. fuciflora (F.W. Schmidt) Moench = *O. holoserica*.

O. fusca Link. To 40cm. Fls 1–10; sep. 9–11mm, oblong or ovate, dors. slightly incurved, lat. sep. spreading, green to yellow-green, rarely pink; pet. linear to linear-oblong, green, yellow or light brown; lip 10–15mm trilobed, lat. lobes oblong-ovate (sometimes obscure), central lobe reniform, ovate, notched or bilobed, maroon, velvety above, speculum 2-segmented, iridescent blue, violet or brown, margin sometimes white or yellow. Mid–late spring. Medit., SW Rom. Z7.

O. fusca ssp. *iricolor* (Desf.) K. Richt. = *O. iricolor*.

O. holoserica (Burm. f.) Greuter. LATE SPIDER ORCHID. To 55cm. Fls 6–14; sep. 9–13mm, ovate-oblong, bright pink to magenta or white with green mid-vein; pet. triangular, rarely linear-lanceolate, pink to rose-purple, velvety; lip 9–16mm, ovate to obovate, entire, rarely incised or trilobed, dark brown to dark maroon or ochre, velvety, sometimes edged yellow; appendage upcurved, often 3-toothed. Late spring–mid summer. Eur., Medit., Russia. Z6.

O. insectifera L. FLY ORCHID. To 50cm. Fls 2–14; sep. 6–8mm, oblong-ovate, slightly concave; pet. linear, revolute, violet-black, velvety; lip 9–10mm, trilobed, central lobe emarginate, ovate, violet-black or purple, paler at tip, sometimes with yellow margin, lat. lobes spreading, speculum reniform or rectangular, pale blue or violet. Late spring–summer. Eur. inc. Scand. Z6.

O. iricolor Desf. To 30cm. Fls 1–4; sep. to 12mm, oblong to ovate, yellow-green; pet. ligulate, olive or bronze, sometimes with small projections; lip to 25mm, trilobed, velvety, brown, lat. lobes deep maroon, speculum iridescent metallic blue. Late winter–late spring. Medit. Z8.

O. litigiosa Camus = *O. araneola*.

O. lutea Cav. YELLOW BEE ORCHID. To 40cm. Fls 1–7; sep. 9–10mm, green, ovate to oblong-ovate; pet. linear-oblong, obtuse, yellow-green; lip 12–18mm, oblong, dark brown to purple-black with a deep yellow border, lat. lobes ovate, mid-lobe reniform, emarginate to spreading-emarginate, speculum entire or bilobed, iridescent blue. Late winter–late spring. Medit. Z8.

O. muscifera Huds. = *O. insectifera*.

O. scolopax Cav. WOODCOCK ORCHID. To 45cm. Fls 3–10; sep. 8–12mm, oblong to ovate, pink to mauve; pet. lanceolate to triangular, pink or red; lip 8–12mm, middle ovate, brown to black-purple, velvety, margins glab., lat. lobes triangular, dark brown with basal projections, speculum circular or loosely X-shaped, blue or violet, edged yellow or white, spotted dark brown. Early–late spring. S Eur. Z8.

O. speculum Link = *O. vernixia*.

O. sphegodes Mill. EARLY SPIDER ORCHID. 10–45cm. Fls to 10; sep. 6–12mm, oblong-ovate to lanceolate, green, rarely white or purple; pet. oblong-triangular to lanceolate, green to purple-green or brown-red, often undulate; lip ovate, rich maroon-chocolate brown, velvety, speculum H-shaped, maroon or deep indigo, often bordered yellow. Spring. Eur. Z6.

O. sphegodes ssp. *litigiosa* (Camus) Bech. = *O. araneola*.

O. tenthredinifera Willd. SAWFLY ORCHID. To 45cm. Fls 3–8; sep. 6–14mm, ovate, concave, lilac to pale rose, often veined green; pet. triangular, rose purple to pink, velvety, obtuse; lip 8–14mm, entire or obscurely trilobed, obovate or oblong with basal swelling, brown-purple, velvety, margin yellow to green, speculum small, grey-blue bordered yellow or white, bilobed, sometimes spotted brown. Late spring–early summer. Medit.

Z8.

O. vernixia Brot. To 50cm. Fls 2–15; sep. 6–8mm, oblong, green to purple-brown, forming hood; pet. purple-brown, lanceolate; lip to 13mm, trilobed, round or linear, brown to brown-purple, villous, speculum almost covering lobes, iridescent blue bordered yellow. Late spring–early summer. Medit., N Afr. Z8.

Ophthalmophyllum Dinter & Schwantes.
O. schlechteri Schwantes. ex Jacobsen = *Conophytum maughanii*.
O. triebneri Schwantes. ex Jacobsen = *Conophytum friedrichiae*.

Opithandra B.L. Burtt. Gesneriaceae. 6 herbs. Lvs radical, petiolate. Fls in an umbellate infl., on scape-like, axill. peduncles; cal. 5-partite; cor. tube elongate, limb 2-lipped, upper lip 2-lobed, lower lip 3-lobed. E Asia. Z10.
O. primuloides (Miq.) B.L. Burtt. Densely pubesc. rhizomatous perenn. Lvs to 10×7cm, ovate, elliptic or orbicular, grey-green, sharply toothed. Fls to 10, on peduncles to 20cm; cor. to 2cm, pale purple-violet, purple-striate, exterior downy. Summer. Jap.

Opiuma *Pithecellobium dulce*.
Opium Poppy *Papaver somniferum*.

Oplismenus Palib. Gramineae. 6 ann. or perenn. grasses. St. slender, trailing, leafy, rooting. Lvs lanceolate to ovate, flat. Infl. unilateral, rac. spicate on a common axis; spikelets paired, 2-fld, laterally flattened. Trop., subtrop. Z9.
O. bromoides (Lam.) Palib. = *O. burmannii*.
O. burmannii (Retz.) Palib. Ann., glab. to pubesc., to 60cm. Lvs lanceolate to elliptic, to 6cm×1.8cm, acuminate. Infl. to 10cm. Summer–winter. Trop. 'Albidus': lvs white with a pale green median stripe.
O. compositus (L.) Palib. Perenn., resembling *O. hirtellus* but more robust. Lvs narrow-elliptic to ovate, to 15×2.5cm. Infl. to 30cm. Afr., Asia, Polyn.
O. hirtellus (L.) Palib. Everg. perenn., to 90cm+. Lvs narrow-lanceolate to ovate, to 5cm×1.3cm, acuminate, pubesc.; sheaths flattened overlapping glab. to pubesc. Infl. to 15cm. Summer–winter. Trop. Amer., Afr., Polyn. 'Variegatus' ('Vittatus'): lvs striped white, sometimes tinted pink.
O. imbecillus Roem. & Schult. = *O. hirtellus*.
O. loliaceus (Lam.) HBK = *O. hirtellus*.
O. undulatifolius (Ard.) Beauv. Lvs small, ovate, strongly undulate to puckered. Trop. & Subtrop.
→*Panicum*.

Oplopanax (Torr. & A. Gray) Miq. Araliaceae. 3 decid. suckering shrubs, with branching st. to 1m or so, densely prickly. Lvs simple, ± lobed, toothed, usually slightly hairy beneath. Infl. pseudo-terminal, paniculate, compound, narrowly conic, woolly; fls green-white, in small umbel-like clusters; cal. obscurely 5-toothed; pet. 5. Fr. drupaceous, red, round. Late spring and early summer. NE Asia, N Amer. Z5.
O. elatus (Nak.) Nak. Lvs to 30cm diam.; lobes 5–7, relatively shallow, as in some states of *O. horridus*, closely double-serrate, venation bristly-pubesc. beneath. Infl. to 18cm; peduncles to 6cm; pedicels finally to 10mm. Fr. to 12mm. China, Korea, Siboie. Z5.
O. horridus (Sm.) Miq. DEVIL'S-CLUB. Lvs to 40cm diam., shallowly or deeply 5–13-lobed, conspicuously serrate. Infl. to 20cm; peduncles to 5cm; pedicels finally to 8mm. Fr. to 7mm. C & W N Amer. (esp. Pacific Coast). Z4.
O. japonicus (Nak.) Nak. As *O. horridus* but lvs somewhat smaller and more deeply lobed, with the base sometimes peltate; lobes long-acute. Jap. Z6.
→*Echinopanax*.

Opophytum N.E. Br.
O. aquosum (L. Bol.) N.E. Br. = *Mesembryanthemum hypertrophicum*.
O. dactylinum (Welw. ex Oliv.) N.E. Br. = *Mesembryanthemum cryptanthum*.
O. forskahlii (Hochst.) N.E. Br. = *Mesembryanthemum cryptanthum*.

Opsiandra Cook.
O. maya Cook = *Gaussia maya*.

×**Opsistylis**. (*Vandopsis* ×*Rhynchostylis*.) Orchidaceae. Gdn hybrids. Small plants with spreading or upright spikes of yellow to mauve or red fls overlaid with spots or veins.

Opthalmophyllum Dinter & Schwantes.
O. acutum Tisch. = *Conophytum acutum*.
O. caroli (Lavis) Tisch. = *Conophytum carolii*.
O. edithae (N.E. Br.) Tisch. = *Conophytum pillansii*.

O. friedrichiae (Dinter) Dinter & Schwantes = *Conophytum friedrichiae*.

O. herrei Lavis = *Conophytum longum*.

O. littlewoodii L. Bol. = *Conophytum devium*.

O. longum Tisch. = *Conophytum longum*.

O. maughanii (N.E. Br.) Schwantes = *Conophytum maughanii*.

O. noctiflorum L. Bol. = *Conophytum maughanii*.

O. verrucosum Lavis = *Conophytum verrucosum*.

Opulaster Medik. ex Rydb.

O. alternans Heller = *Physocarpus alternans*.

O. bracteatus Rydb. = *Physocarpus bracteatus*.

O. glabratus Rydb. = *Physocarpus glabratus*.

Opuntia Mill. PRICKLY PEAR; TUNA. Cactaceae. 200+ succulent trees and shrubs, some low; st. seg. cylindric, club-shaped, subglobose, or flattened, sometimes tuberculate, rarely ribbed; lvs where present terete or subulate, usually small, caducous; glochids present; spines 1 to many, sometimes sheathed and barbed. Fls lat. or subterm., usually solitary; perianth rotate or spreading. Fr. fleshy or dry.

O. acanthocarpa Engelm. & Bigelow. Shrub or tree to 3m; stemseg. cylindric, 12–50×2–3cm, with elongate tubercles; lvs *c*12×1.5mm; glochids minute; spines sheathed, 6–25, to 2.5cm, tinged red to white, or straw-coloured. Fl. red, purple or yellow. Fr. spiny, to 4cm, tinged brown. SW US & adjacent Mex. Z9.

O. aciculata Griffiths = *O. lindheimeri*.

O. albispina hort. = *O. microdasys*.

O. alexanderi Britt. & Rose. Subshrub to 50×50cm; stem-seg. globose to elongate, to 9×3–5.5cm, tuberculate; areoles small; glochids to 4mm, pale yellow; spines 4–15, to 4cm, white, tipped darker, or violet-grey. Fl. pink. Fr. spiny, red, dry. NW Arg. Z9.

O. andicola Pfeiff. = *O. glomerata*.

O. aoracantha Lem. Erect, to 60cm, simple or branched; stemseg. ovoid, 4–10×2–7cm, strongly tuberculate; areoles 4–10mm diam., sunken; glochids forming a ring around areoles to 5mm, red; spines 2–7, 5–16cm, flattened, yellow-brown then grey. Fl. white. Fr. spiny, 2.5–3cm, disintegrating. NW Arg. Z9.

O. arborescens Engelm. = *O. imbricata*.

O. arbuscula Engelm. Dwarf tree or shrub to 3m; stem-seg. cylindric, 5–15cm×6–9(–12)mm, smooth, tubercles inconspicuous; lvs to 9mm; areoles elliptic 3–4.5mm; spines sheathed, 1–4, 1–4cm, red- or purple-brown, sheath light brown. Fl. green, yellow or tinged brown. Fr. spineless, to 4cm. Ariz. & NW Mex. Z9.

O. arenaria Engelm. Small creeping shrub, forming groups to 15×300cm, with rhizome-like regenerative roots; stem-seg. flattened, narrowly obovate-oblong, 5–7.5×2.–2.5cm, glaucous; areoles 4.5–6mm apart; glochids to 3mm, pale brown; spines 5–7, to 3.5cm, white to grey or red-brown. Fl. yellow. Fr. spiny, 2.5–3cm. SW US, Mex. Z9.

O. articulata (Pfeiff.) D. Hunt. Dwarf shrub with brittle erect br. to 20–30cm; stem-seg. globose to oblong, usually 2.5–5×2.5–5cm; spines lacking or 1–4, to 5cm or more, flat, paper or raffia-like, pale brown or white. Fl. white or pale pink. Arg. Z9.

O. atrispina Griffiths. Sprawling subshrub, 45–60×60–100cm; stem-seg. flattened, rounded to obovate, *c*10×7.5cm; areoles to 4.5mm diam.; golchids yellow; spines 4–7, variable to 4cm, almost black. Fl. yellow, Fr. spineless, to 2cm, red-purple. S Tex. and adjacent NE Mex. Z9.

O. auberi Pfeiff. Resembling *O. cochenillifera*. Stem-seg. narrower; spines usually present, 2–3, to 3cm, off-white, tipped brown. Fl. dull red; sta. tinged pink; stigmas green. S Mex. Z9.

O. aurantiaca Lindl. Low spreading shrub to 30cm; stem-seg. almost terete at base, somewhat compressed above, to 15×1.5×1cm, not tubercled; spines usually 2–3, 1–3cm, pale brown. Fl. orange-yellow. Fr. to 3cm, purple-red, spiny. Urug. and adjacent Arg. Z9.

O. aurea Baxter = *O. basilaris*.

O. austrina Small. Resembling *O. compressa*; stem-seg. obovate to elliptic, 7.5–10(–14)×5–9(–12.5)cm; spines 3–5.6cm. SE US. Z9.

O. azurea Rose. Shrub, 1–2m; stem-seg. flattened, circular to obovate, 10–15cm diam., glaucous; areoles *c*2cm apart, lowermost spineless; spines 1–3, unequal, to 3cm, reflexed, becoming black. Fl. intense yellow; tep. carmine tipped. Fr. spineless, subglobose to ovoid, carmine, juicy and edible. NC Mex. Z9.

O. basilaris Engelm. & Bigelow Forming clumps 30–60cm or more; stem-seg. obovate to orbicular, often truncate to retuse at apex, usually 8–20×6–15cm, blue-grey often tinged purple, velvety; glochids red-brown, decid.; spines 0–1(–5), short. Fl. usually deep purple-red. Fr. dry, globose or obovoid. SW US, NW Mex. (Sonora). Z9.

O. beckeriana Schum. Low shrub, freely branching; stem-seg. to 10cm; spines 2–6, straight, yellow or with dark bands, or nearly white. Fl. deep yellow. Origin unknown. Z9.

O. bergeriana F.A. Weber. Tree-like or thicket-forming, muchbranched, 1–3.5m, trunk 30–40cm diam.; stem-seg. narrowly oblong, to *c*25cm; spines 2–5, to 4cm, ± flattened, brown or yellow below. Fl. deep red. Fr. to 4cm, red. Spring–summer. Origin unknown. Z9.

O. bigelovii Engelm. TEDDY-BEAR CHOLLA. Small tree to 2.5m; stem-seg. cylindric-ellipsoid, 7.5–12.5(–20)×3.8–6cm, tuberculate; areoles 3mm diam.; spines dense, golden-sheathed, *c*6–10, to 2.5cm, pink- to red-brown. Fl. pale green to yellow, striped with lavender. Fr. spineless, yellow, tuberculate, to 2m. SW US, NW Mex. Z9.

O. boliviana Salm-Dyck. Subshrub to 30cm; stem-seg. ovoidoblong, 5–6.3×2–2.5cm, smooth; areoles sunken; spines 1–4, to 10cm, erect, translucent pale yellow. Fl. yellow to orange. Mts of Boliv., N Arg. Z9.

O. brachyarthra Engelm. & Bigelow = *O. fragilis*.

O. bradtiana (Coult.) K. Brandg. Spreading subshrub, to 1×5m+; stem-seg. cylindric, ribbed, 4–7cm diam.; lvs linear, fleshy, 8mm, spines 15–25, 1–3cm, off-white except when young. Fl. v. short, deep shiny yellow; fil. brown. Fr. spiny, ellipsoid. NE Mex. Z9.

O. brasiliensis (Willd.) Haw. Tree-like, to 6–9m or more, with cylindric, unjointed trunk and br.; ultimate stem-seg. flat and somewhat leaf-like, obovate to oblong-lanceolate, to 15×6cm, 4–6mm thick; lvs small, subulate, spines 1–3, to 15mm, on young growth, more numerous on the trunk, or lacking. Fl. pale yellow. Fr. globose, 2.5–4cm diam. E S Amer. Z9.

O. bravoana Baxter. Shrub to 2×2m; stem-seg. flattened, oblong, to 36×14cm, green with purple markings beneath areoles; glochids yellow; spines 0–5, 2–6cm, pale yellow to grey, darker at base. Fl. yellow. NW Mex. Z9.

O. bruchii Speg. = *O. alexanderi*.

O. bulbispina Engelm. Dwarf mat-forming shrub, to 120cm diam.; stem-seg. ovoid, 20–25×10–12mm, tuberculate; spines 12–16, to 12mm, off-white, bulbous at base. Fl. purple. N Mex. Z9.

O. burrageana Britt. & Rose. Sprawling shrub, less than 1m; stem-seg. cylindric, to 15cm, tuberculate, often decid.; areoles close; glochids short, pale yellow, sometimes lacking; spines yellow-sheathed, numerous, to 2cm. Fl. tinged pink or brown with a green centre. Fr. spiny, 2cm diam., tuberculate. NW Mex. Z9.

O. camanchica Engelm. & Bigelow = *O. phaeacantha*.

O. cantabrigiensis Lynch. Densely branched shrub, forming thickets 1.2×4cm; stem-seg. flattened, 16–24×12–17cm, spines 1–3, 1–2cm, white. Fl. yellow. Fr. spineless, ovoid, 4cm, glaucous red. Summer. Origin unknown. Z8.

O. chlorotica Engelm. & Bigelow. Tree or shrub to 2×1.2m; stem-seg. flattened, rounded to broadly obovate, 15–20×12.5×17cm; areoles *c*2cm apart, elliptic; glochids to 4.5mm, yellow; spines 1–6, to 4cm, deflexed, pale yellow. Fl. yellow. Fr. spineless at maturity, 4–6cm, grey-purple. SW US, NW Mex. Z9.

O. cholla F.A. Weber. Small tree, to 5m; st. seg. cylindric, 5–30×2–3cm, tuberculate; glochids numerous, yellow; spines golden-sheathed, 5–13, 3–25mm, yellow then grey. Fl. purplepink. Fr. spineless, obovoid, green, 3–5cm, proliferous. Spring. Baja Calif. Z9.

O. clavarioides Pfeiff. Low shrub, much branched from tuberous roots; stem-seg. obconic, truncate or concave, often cristate at apex, to *c*2×1.5cm, not tubercled; lvs 1.5mm, tinged red spines 4–10, minute, adpressed, white. Fl. tinged brown, rarely seen in cult. Arg. Z9.

O. clavata Engelm. Low mat-forming shrub, 7.5–10×100–200cm; stem-seg. cylindric-clavate, 4–5×2–2.5cm, tuberculate; areoles *c*6mm apart; glochids pale yellow, 6mm; spines sheathed, 10–20, to 2.5cm, deflexed, grey. Fl. white. Fr. spineless, yellow, 4cm. US (Ariz., New Mex.). Z9.

O. cochenillifera (L.) Mill. Shrub or tree to 4m or more; stem-seg. elliptic to obovate, 8–25×5–12cm, dark green; areoles wide-spaced; spines to 1cm, 0(–3). Fl. bright red; sta. pink. Fr. ellipsoid, 2.5–3.8cm, fleshy, red. Mex. Commonly confused with *O. paraguayensis*. Z9.

O. compressa (Salisb.) Macbr. Shrub, forming clumps or mats 10–30cm×2m or more; stem-seg. elliptic to obovate to orbicular, 5–12.5×4–10cm, often tinged purple; lvs subulate 4–7mm; spines usually 0, sometimes 1–2, on marginal areoles, to 2.5cm. Fl. yellow, often with red centre. Fr. obovoid, 2.5–4cm, purple or red. Summer. E & C US. Z8.

O. corrugata Salm-Dyck. Low creeping shrub, to 10cm; stem-seg. obliquely ovate or elliptic to orbicular ± flattened, to 5×2.5×1.5cm, with low tubercles, pale blue green; lvs subulate, 2mm, tinged red; spines several, 8–12mm. Fl. red; stigmas green. NW Arg. Z9.

O. covillei Britt. & Rose = *O. littoralis*.

O. crassa Haw. Resembling spineless forms of *O. ficus-indica*; 1–2m tall, with thick, glaucous stem-seg. *c*8–12.5cm, usually spineless. Fl. and fr. not described. Origin uncertain, cult. in trop. America, but of v. uncertain status. Z9.

O. curassavica (L.) Mill. Low spreading shrub; stem-seg. somewhat flattened, 2–5cm; glochids poorly developed; spines 4 or more, to *c*2.5cm, pale yellow fading to white. Fl. yellow, streaked red. Netherlands Antilles, N Venez. Z9.

O. cylindrica (Lam.) DC. Becoming a small tree 3–4m; st. cylindric, unsegmented, 3–5cm diam., with low tubercles, green; lvs terete, acute, 10–13mm; spines (0–)2–6, to 1cm, off-white, usually mixed with fine glochids. Fl. red. Ecuad. Z9.

O. decumbens Salm-Dyck. Spreading subshrub to 40cm; stem-seg. flattened, 10–20cm, pubesc.; areoles with red markings beneath; spines 1–3, to 4cm, yellow. Fl. yellow-green. Fr. spiny, 1.2–2.5cm. S Mex. Z9.

O. dejecta Salm-Dyck. Shrub to 2m; stem-seg. somewhat flattened, lanceolate, 10–15×3–6cm, green to grey-green; spines 2, or more, to 4cm, tinged red at first, later yellow to grey. Fl. red; tep. erect. Fr. spineless, dark red. C Amer. Z9.

O. diademata Lem. = *O. articulata*.

O. dillenii (Ker-Gawl.) Haw. = *O. stricta*.

O. echinocarpa Engelm. & Bigelow. Shrub to 1.5m; stem-seg. cylindric, 5–15(–40)×2(–4)cm, tuberculate; areoles circular, 1–2cm apart, 4–5mm; spines sheathed, 3–12, to 3.8cm, pale yellow to silvery. Fl. yellow-green. Fr. spiny, 1.2–2.5cm. SW US, NW Mex. Z9.

O. engelmannii Salm-Dyck = *O. ficus-indica*.

O. engelmannii auctt., non Salm-Dyck = *O. phaeacantha*.

O. erinacea Engelm. & Bigelow. Similar to *O. polyacantha*, but with at least some of the spines flattened basally. SW US. var. **ursina** (F.A. Weber) Parish. Stem-seg. oblong or oblong-elliptic, 5–10×2.5–6cm; spines numerous, from all areoles to 10cm, slender and flexuous. Fl. orange or pink. var. *utahensis* (Engelm.) L. Bens. Stem-seg. obovate, 5–8.5×5–7.5cm; areolar areas often purple-brown; spines from upper areoles only. Fl. purple-red or pink. Z9.

O. exaltata A. Berger. Resembling *O. subulata* and perhaps only a cv. of it. Tree to 5m with a trunk 5–30cm diam. st. somewhat glaucous; lvs terete, acute, 1–7cm; spines pale brown. Mts of Peru, Boliv. Z9.

O. falcata Ekman & Werderm. Resembling *O. moniliformis* but smaller, to 1.5m, stem-seg. narrower, 35×9cm, spines to 4cm. Fl. red. Haiti. Z9.

O. ficus-indica (L.) Mill. INDIAN FIG; BARBARY FIG; PRICKLY PEAR. Large shrub or small tree to 5(–7)m with a trunk sometimes 1m diam.; stem-seg. obovate to oblong 20–60×10–40cm; spines variable, (0–)1–2 or more, the longer to 2.5cm, white or off-white. Fl. yellow. Fr. 5–10×4–(cm yellow, orange, red or purple in different cvs. Mex. Z9.

O. floccosa Salm-Dyck. Low caespitose shrub forming mounds 2m diam.; individual stem-seg. to 10×3cm, with long white areolar hair; lvs terete, 8–13×2–3mm, persistent; spines 1–3, 1–3cm, pale yellow. Fl. yellow or orange. Mts of Peru and Boliv. Z9.

O. fragilis (Nutt.) Haw. Low shrub, forming clumps 5–10cm high and 30cm or more diam.; setem-seg. variable in shape, 2–4.5×1.2–2.5cm; spines 1–6(–9). Fl. yellow or tinged green. Fr. obovoid, 12–15mm, green or red-green. US, Canada. Z8.

O. fulgida Engelm. Small tree, to 3.5m; st. seg. cylindric, 5–15×3–5cm, tuberculate, light green; areoles elliptic, *c*4.5mm, glochids pale yellow, to 2mm; spines sheathed, 6–12, to 3cm, pink to red-brown. Fl. pink to off-white. Fr. usually sterile, proliferating, green. SW US, NW Mex. Z9.

O. fuscoatra Engelm. = *O. compressa*.

O. glomerata Haw. Low caespitose shrub, forming dense mounds; stem-seg. terete-conical, to 4×2cm; sines ± flattened. Fl. yellow. N Arg. Z9.

O. gosseliniana F.A. Weber = *O. macrocentra*.

O. grahamii Engelm. = *O. schottii*.

O. grandiflora Engelm. = *O. macrorhiza*.

O. hamiltonii (Gates) G. Rowley, invalid name. = *O. rosarica*.

O. hickenii Britt. & Rose = *O. glomerata*.

O. hoffmannii H. Bravo = *O. pubescens*.

O. humifusa (Raf.) Raf. = *O. compressa*.

O. humilis Haw. = *O. tuna*.

O. hyptiacantha F.A. Weber. Small tree, to 4m; stem-seg. flattened, oblong or obovate, 20–30cm; areoles small, 2–3cm apart; glochids dark; spines 1 at first, later to 6, to 2cm, pale. Fl. red. Fr. spineless, globose, yellow to purple. C Mex. Z9.

O. hystricina Engelm. & Bigelow = *O. erinacea*.

O. imbricata (Haw.) DC. Eventually a small tree, to 3m; larger stem-seg. 12–38×2–3cm, tuberculate; lvs to 15mm; spines 8–30, to 3cm, sheath dull brown. Fl. purple. Fr. nearly globose, 3cm,

yellow, spineless. Mex., SW US. Z9.

O. inermis (DC.) DC. = *O. stricta*.

O. invicta Brandg. Low shrub, 20–50cm, forming colonies; stem-seg. obovoid to clavate, 6–10×2–6cm, tuberculate; lvs subulate, 8–14, tinged red; spines formidable *c*16–22, to 3.5cm, flattened, red becoming dull brown. Fl. yellow. Baja Calif. Z9.

O. kleiniae DC. Shrub to 2m; stem-seg. cylindric, 10–30×0.5–1cm, tuberculate, tinged purple-red; areoles 6–12mm apart; glochids tinged red; spines sheathed, 1–4, to 2.5cm, grey-pink, sheaths pale brown. Fl. red-bronze to purple. Fr. spineless, red. SW US, N Mex. Z9.

O. kuehnrichiana Werderm. & Backeb. Low-growing, caespitose; stem-seg. globose to slightly oblong, to 8cm, grey-green; areoles off-white, lowermost spineless; spines 5–12, to 3.5cm, off-white. Fl. yellow. Fr. depressed-globose. Peru. Z9.

O. kunzei Rose = *O. parishii*.

O. laevis J. Coult. = *O. phaeacantha*.

O. lagopus Schum. Mat-forming shrub; stem-seg. cylindric, 10–25×3–8cm, hidden by the extremely long glochids; glochids to 1.5cm, dense, pale yellow; spines 1, 2cm, white. Peru. Z9.

O. lanceolata Haw. V. close to *O. ficus-indica*. Stem-seg. rhomboid or lanceolate, 20–30×6–8cm. Origin uncertain. Z9.

O. leptocaulis DC. Brittle, thin-stemmed shrub to 50cm or more; stem-seg. slender-elongate, 5–15cm, scarcely tuberculate, branching at right-angles; lvs to 12mm; spines usually 1, 1–5cm, brown or white-sheathed. Fl. pale green or pale yellow. Fr. globose to obovoid, 10–18mm, orange, red or yellow, often proliferous. Mex., SW US. Z9.

O. leucotricha DC. Becoming a small tree 3–4m; term. stem-seg. oblong to broadly ovate, to 25cm, about 1cm thick, velvety; lvs small, subulate; spines 1–6, to 7.5cm, denser on older seg., setaceous or hair-like, white, almost covering the st. Fl. yellow. Mex. Z9.

O. lindheimeri Engelm. Shrub, to 3m; stem-seg. flattened, rounded to elongate, 15–25cm; lvs 3–9mm; areoles elliptic, 4.5×3mm; glochids yellow, becoming brown; spines 1–6, to 4cm, yellow or paler. Fl. yellow or red. Fr. almost spineless, 3–7cm, purple. Z9.

O. linguiformis Griffiths = *O. lindheimeri*.

O. littoralis (Engelm.) Cockerell. Sprawling shrub, 30–60×60–120cm; stem-seg. flattened, obovate, elliptic or nearly rounded, 7.5–25cm or more, glaucous; areoles 1.5–3mm diam.; glochids yellow to brown; spines 0–11, to 5cm, brown, pink or grey. Fl. yellow with a red centre. Fr. spineless, to *c*4cm, red-purple. SW US, NW Mex. Z9.

O. mackensenii Rose = *O. macrorhiza*.

O. macracantha Griseb. Small tree; trunk cylindric, to 15cm diam.; ultimate stem-seg. flattened, oblong or ovate; areoles 2–3cm apart; glochids abundant, brown; spines 1–4, to 15cm, off-white. Fl. orange-yellow. Cuba. Z9.

O. macrocentra Engelm. Sprawling shrub, 0.6–2m, sometimes tree-like; stem-seg. nearly orbicular, *c*10–20cm, persistently purple-tinged; areoles 1.5–2.5cm apart; spines 0 or 1(–3), often restricted to upper margins of seg., to 10(–17)cm. Fl. with inner tep. bright yellow, red at base. Fr. 2.5–4cm, red or purple-red. SW US, N Mex. Z9.

O. macrorhiza Engelm. Low shrub to 12×180cm; rootstock usually tuberous; stem-seg. flattened, rounded to obovate, 5–10cm, glaucous; lvs to 7.5mm; areoles 1–2cm apart; glochids yellow to brown; spines 1–6, to *c*5.5cm deflexed, off-white. Fl. yellow or yellow with a red centre. Fr. spineless, to 4cm, red-purple. US & N Mex. Z9.

O. mamillata Schott = *O. fulgida*.

O. marenae S.H. Parsons. Low shrub, 15–60cm; rootstock tuberous; stem-seg. to 20cm, faintly tubercled; lvs 5–10mm; spines several adpressed 3–10mm, fine white, and 1–2 or more stronger, decurved to 2cm. Fl. satiny white; sta. sensitive. Fr. not externally visible until tip of st. splits. NW Mex. Z9.

O. margaritana (J. Coult.) Baxter = *O. pycnantha*.

O. marnieriana Backeb. Low shrub; stem-seg. flattened, ovate to oblong, to 18cm; spines usually 2, 1–3cm, flattened and curved, red-brown, tipped brown, sometimes with 1–2 shorter spines. Fl. orange-red. Mex. Cf. *O. stenopetala*. Z9.

O. maxima Mill. Resembling *O. ficus-indica*, but stem-seg. elongate, ± spathulate, to 35cm. Fl. orange-red. Known only in cult. Z9.

O. megacantha Salm-Dyck = *O. ficus-indica*.

O. mesacantha Raf. = *O. compressa*.

O. microdasys (Lehm.) Pfeiff. Shrub, forming thickets 40–60cm; stem-seg. oblong, obovate or suborbicular, 6–15cm, green, velvety; glochids yellow, or white; spines 0, rarely 1, v. short. Fl. yellow, outer seg. often tinged red. Fr. nearly globose, *c*3cm diam., fleshy, red or purple-red. C & N Mex. Z9.

O. microdasys var. *rufida* (Engelm.) Schum. = *O. rufida*.

O. mieckleyi Schum. Erect shrub; stem-seg. flattened, narrowly oblong, 15–25cm, dark green, tuberculate; areoles large, white-woolly; spines 0–2, to 5mm, dark. Fl. brick-red. Parag. Z9.

O. miquelii Monv. Spreading shrub to *c*1×5m; stem-seg. cylindric, *c*8–20cm, tuberculate, strongly glaucous; glochids abundant, brown; spines 10 or more, eventually to 10cm, off-white. Fl. magenta. Fr. larger, off-white. N Chile. Z9.

O. missouriensis DC. = *O. polyacantha*.

O. moelleri A. Berger. Dwarf caespitose shrub; stem-seg. cylindric-clavate, 4–7cm, tuberculate; central spines 6, to 16mm, off-white; radial spines numerous. Fl. yellow-green. NE Mex. Z9.

O. mojavensis Engelm. = *O. phaeacantha*.

O. molinensis Speg. Similar to spineless forms of *O. articulata*, but seg. much smaller, with conspicuous tufts of red-brown glochids. N Arg. Z9.

O. monacantha (Willd.) Haw. Erect shrub, to 2m, sometimes with a short trunk; stem-seg. oblong to obovate, tapered towards the base, 10–30cm; spines 1 or 2, unequal, longer to 4cm, brown towards tip and base, off-white between. Fl. yellow or orange-yellow; outer tep. tinged red. Fr. pear-shaped, 5–7.5cm, red-purple. SE Braz. to Arg., nat. elsewhere. Z9.

O. moniliformis (L.) Haw. Tree, with trunk 3–4m; ultimate stem-seg. flattened, 10–30cm; areoles on small tubercles; glochids to 8mm, brown; spines 3 or more, to 2.5cm, pale yellow. Fl. orange-yellow. Fr. oblong-ovoid, *c*6cm. Hispan. to Puerto Rico. Z9.

O. munzii C. Wolf. Tree to 5m; stem-seg. cylindric, 10–25cm, tuberculate; areoles 6–9mm apart; spines sheathed, 9–12, to 2cm yellow like the sheaths. Fl. yellow-green, sometimes tinged red. Fr. spineless, often sterile, yellow. S Calif. Z9.

O. nigrispina Schum. Dwarf, mound-forming shrub, to 10cm; stem-seg. cylindric to ellipsoid, 2–3.5cm, tuberculate when young, yellow-green; glochids brown; spines 2–5, the 1–2 largest to 2.5cm, violet-black, rough, others paler. Fl. yellow. NW Arg. Z9.

O. occidentalis Engelm. & Bigelow = *O. ficus-indica*.

O. ovata Pfeiff. Dwarf, caespitose or mound-forming shrub, to 12cm; stem-seg. ovoid, 3–4cm, not tuberculate; areoles 8mm apart; spines 7–8, unequal, stiff, straight, 4–10mm, white at first. Fl. pale golden yellow. N Arg. Z9.

O. pachypus Schum. Simple, or branching candelabra-like, to *c*1m; st. cylindric, unsegmented, 3–5cm diam., tuberculate; lvs subulate, 4mm, caducous; areoles at upper edge of tubercles, 4mm diam., arranged in dense spirals; glochids yellow; spines 20–30, 5–20mm. Fl. tubular, red pericarpel spiny. Peru. Z9.

O. paediophila Cast. = *O. aoracantha*.

O. pailana Weingart. Erect, branched shrub; stem-seg. flattened, rounded to obovate, 10–14cm, blue; areoles 2cm apart; glochids yellow-grey; spines 3–8, 2–3cm, white at first, later brown. NW Mex. Z9.

O. pallida Rose = *O. rosea*.

O. papyracantha Philippi = *O. articulata*.

O. paraguayensis Schum. Stem-seg. oblanceolate or narrowly elliptic, to 30cm, dark glossy green; spines 0 or 1, to 1cm, pale yellow. Fl. orange. Parag. Cf. *O. cochenillifera*. Z9.

O. parishii Orcutt. Mat-forming or caespitose shrub, to 15cm; stem-seg. cylindric to narrowly obovoid, 7.5–15cm, tuberculate or sometimes ribbed; lvs to 6mm; areoles 2–2.5cm apart; spines mostly at areoles on upper part of seg. sheathed, 16–33, the longest directed down, to 5cm, yellow, brown or red. Fl. yellow or tinged red. Fr. spiny, to 8cm, yellow. SW US, N Mex. Z9.

O. parryi Engelm. Sprawling shrub to 40cm; stem-seg. cylindric, 7–45cm, strongly tuberculate; lvs 4.5–7.5mm; areoles 9mm apart, 6–7.5mm diam.; glochids red-brown; spines sheathed, 7–20, to 1.5(F–3)cm, grey to red-brown, sheaths sometimes paler. Fl. yellow or yellow-green, tinged purple. Fr. spiny. S Calif. and adjacent Mex. Z9.

O. pentlandii Salm-Dyck. Dwarf shrub forming mounds eventually 1m diam.; stem-seg. globose to cylindric or obovoid, 2–10cm; spines variable in number and length, acicular (not flattened), ± deflexed, sometimes 0. Fl. yellow, orange or red, rarely seen. Boliv. Z9.

O. pestifer Britt. & Rose = *O. pubescens*.

O. phaeacantha Engelm. Sprawling and spreading shrub 0.3–1m tall; stem-seg. obovate or orbicular 10–40cm, blue-green, sometimes tinged purple; spines (0–)1–8 or more, to 6cm, flattened, brown or red-brown. Fl. yellow, sometimes red-tinged within. Fr. pear-shaped, 4–8cm, purple. SW US, N Mex. Z9.

O. picardoi Marn.-Lap. Low creeping shrub; stem-seg. flattened, obliquely oval, to 7cm, glossy green; spines to 10, v. short, white, tipped yellow. Fl. 4cm diam., red. N Arg. Z9.

O. pilifera F.A. Weber. Small tree, to 5m; stem-seg. flattened, rounded, 12–35cm, pale or glaucous; areoles 2–3cm apart, with long white hairs; spines 3–6(–9), to 1.5cm, white. Fl. deep pink; pericarpel white-bristly. Fr. 4–5cm, red, juicy. S Mex. Z9.

O. platyacantha Pfeiff. Low shrub, freely branched; stem-seg. cylindric, 2.5–7.5cm, tinged brown, scarcely tuberculate; upper spines 2–3, 1.2–2.5cm, flattened, pale yellow-grey with darker bands, the lower 3–4 shorter, adpressed. Origin (Arg. or Chile). Z9.

O. pollardii Britt. & Rose = *O. austrina*.

O. polyacantha Haw. Low shrub, forming mats or clumps 15cm×0.3–1m or more; stem-seg. orbicular to broadly obovate, 5–10cm, blue-green; spines 5–10, longest to 5cm, not markedly flattened in section, mostly deflexed and largely covering the seg. Fl. 4.5–8×4.5–6cm, yellow. Fr. dry, spiny. Canada, US, N Mex. Z3.

O. polyantha Haw. = *O. tuna*.

O. polycarpa Small = *O. austrina*.

O. pottsii Salm-Dyck = *O. macrorhiza*.

O. prolifera Engelm. Small tree to 2.5m; stem-seg. cylindric, elongate-ellipsoid, 7.5–14cm, tuberculate; areoles 5–9mm apart; spines yellow or rusty-sheathed, 6–12, to 3cm, red-brown, later grey. Fl. magenta. Fr. often sterile, proliferating. S Calif. and adjacent Mex. Z9.

O. puberula Pfeiff. Resembling *O. decumbens*. Low shrub, 40–70cm, sometimes with a definite trunk; stem-seg. flat but thick, elliptic to obovate, 7.5–18cm, pubesc.; areoles with purple markings beneath; spines usually 0, or 2–4, to 8mm, off-white. Fl. yellow or tinged red. Fr. spineless, 3cm, purple-red. S Mex. Z9.

O. pubescens Wendl. ex Pfeiff. Brittle prostrate shrub, densely branched, to 40cm; stem-seg. nearly terete, 2–8cm or when young flattened and 2–3cm broad; spines 2–5 or more, 5–20(–30)mm, brown to black. Fl. yellow. Fr. spiny, 2–2.5cm, red. S Mex., Ecuad., Peru. Z9.

O. pycnantha Engelm. Low-growing, spreading shrub; stem-seg. flattened, rounded, 10–18cm, puberulous; areoles close-set, to 7mm diam.; spines 7–12, 5–30mm, yellow or red-brown. Fl. yellow, often tinged red. Fr. v. spiny, red. NW Mex. Z9.

O. quimilo Schum. Small tree to 5m; stem-seg. flattened, elliptic to obovate, to 50cm, grey-green; spines 1–3, to 14.5cm. Fl. red. Fr. pear-shaped to globose, 5–7cm, yellow-green. N Arg. Z9.

O. rafinesquei Engelm. = *O. compressa*.

O. ramosissima Engelm. Shrub to 60(–150)cm, profusely branched; stem-seg. cylindric, 5–10cm, with diamond-shaped, flattened tubercles; spines sheathed, 1–3, to 5.5cm. Fl. deep yellow to brown or some tep. lavender to red. SW US, N Mex. Z8.

O. rauppiana Schum. = *O. sphaerica*.

O. repens Bello. Thicket-forming shrub, to 50×400cm; stem-seg. flattened, oblong or linear, 5–16cm, sometimes pubesc.; spines numerous, to 3.5cm, pink to brown at first, later paler. Fl. yellow, fading to orange-pink. Fr. spineless, 2–3cm, red, few-seeded. Puerto Rico and nearby islands. Z9.

O. retrorsa Speg. Creeping shrub; stem-seg. somewhat flattened, linear-lanceolate; areoles with purple markings beneath; spines 1–3, reflexed, white, tipped pink. Fl. pale yellow. Fr. 2cm, purple. N Arg. Z9.

O. rhodantha Schum. = *O. erinacea* var. *utahensis*.

O. robusta Wendl. & Pfeiff. Shrub to 2m or more; stem-seg. orbicular or nearly so, massive, to 40cm or more, waxy pale blue; spines 2–12, unequal, to 5cm, white, pale brown or yellow below. Fl. yellow. Fr. globose to ellipsoid, 7–8cm, deep red. Summer. C Mex. Z9.

O. rosarica G. Lindsay. Caespitose shrub, to *c*1×1m, rooting on contact with the ground; stem-seg. 10–25cm, cylindric, tubercles arranged into 8–12 spiralled ribs; areoles 5–9×4mm; spines sheathed, 4–15, the central(s) 2.5–5cm, red-black. Fl. yellow, tinged red. Fr. spiny, dry. Baja Calif. Z9.

O. rosea DC. Resembling *O. imbricata* but smaller and more compact, more freely branched, spines denser, pale yellow. Fl. rose pink. C Mex. Z9.

O. rubescens Salm-Dyck. Tree to 6m; ultimate stem-seg. flattened, thin, oblong to obovate, to 25cm; areoles 1–1.5cm apart; spines to 6cm, white, or 0. Fl. yellow, orange or red; pericarpel tuberculate. Fr. spiny, obovoid or subglobose, 5–8cm diam., red. Lesser Antilles. Z9.

O. rufida Engelm. V. similar to *O. microdasys* but glochids red-brown. SW US, N Mex. Z9.

O. rutila Nutt. = *O. polyacantha*.

O. salmiana Pfeiff. Shrub 30–50cm or more, much branched; stem-seg. slender-cylindric to 25cm, not tuberculate, often tinged red; lvs 1–2mm, tinged purple; spines 3–5, to 15mm, or 0. Fls profuse, pale yellow; sta. sensitive. Fr. oblong-ellipsoid, *c*1cm diam., red, proliferous but sterile in cult. S Braz. to Arg. Z9.

O. santamaria (Baxter) H. Bravo. Resembling *O. rosarica* but tubercles shorter, spines numerous, to *c*20. NW Mex. Z9.

O. santa-rita Rose = *O. macrocentra*.

O. scheeri F.A. Weber. Shrub to 1m; stem-seg. oblong to orbicular, 15–30cm, blue-green; spines 8–12, to 1cm, yellow, intermixed with long white or yellow hairs. Fl. large, fading to salmon-pink. C Mex. Z9.

O. schickendantzii F.A. Weber. Resembling *O. aurantiaca* but to 1–2m; stem-seg. larger, somewhat tuberculate, grey-green. N Arg. Z9.

O. schottii Engelm. Mat-forming or caespitose shrub, to 10×300cm; stem-seg. cylindric-clavate, 4–6cm, tuberculate; areoles *c*6mm apart, elliptic; spines 6–12, to 2.5–5cm, tinged brown, yellow or red, flattened. Fl. yellow. Fr. spineless, 4–5.5cm, yellow. SW US, N Mex. Z9.

O. schweriniana Schum. = *O. fragilis*.

O. serpentina Engelm. = *O. parryi*.

O. setispina Engelm. = *O. macrorhiza*.

O. soehrensii Britt. & Rose. Prostrate shrub, forming mats to 1m diam.; stem-seg. erect at first, somewhat flattened, rounded, 4–6cm diam., tuberculate, often tinged purple; spines up to 8, to 5cm, yellow or brown. Fl. light yellow. Fr. spineless, 3cm. W Arg. Z9.

O. spegazzinii F.A. Weber = *O. salmiana*.

O. sphaerica C.F. Först. Low shrub, forming colonies; stem-seg. ovoid becoming globose, to 5cm diam.; areoles close-set, shortly woolly; spines few to many, unequal, 1–4cm, brown at first, fading to grey. Fl. deep orange. Peru. Z9.

O. spinosior (Engelm.) Toumey. Shrub or tree to 2m; stem-seg. cylindric, 12.5–30cm, tuberculate; lvs 9–12mm; areoles 6–9mm apart; glochids minute; spines pale brown-sheathed, 10–20, to 1.5cm, grey, pink at apex. Fl. purple, red, yellow or white. Fr. spineless, bright yellow. SW US, N Mex. Z9.

O. spinosissima (Martyn) Mill. Tree to 5m with densely spiny trunk to 20cm diam.; stem-seg. flattened, narrowly oblong, 12–40cm; areoles with conspicuous glochids and several spines, longest to 8cm, deflexed; flowering seg. usually spineless. Fl. orange; pericarpel 4–5cm. Jam. Z9.

O. stanlyi Engelm., invalid name. = *O. parishii*.

O. stenarthra Schum. Low shrub, creeping to 2m or clambering to 80cm; stem-seg. narrowly oblong, 8–25cm; spines 0–3, 0.6–3.5cm, pale brown to almost white. Fl. lemon-yellow. Fr. pear-shaped, to 2.5cm. Parag. Z9.

O. stenopetala Engelm. Creeping shrub, with some erect br.; stem-seg. flattened, rounded to obovate, 10–25cm, grey-green; areoles 1–3cm apart; spines 2–6, to 5cm, red-brown to black. Fl. orange-red. Fr. globose, 3cm diam. N Mex. Z9.

O. streptacantha Lem. Tree to 5m; stem-seg. flattened, obovate to rounded, to 30cm, dark green; spines numerous, white. Fl. yellow to orange. Fr. globose, 5cm diam., dark red or yellow. Mex. Z9.

O. stricta Haw. Sprawling or erect shrub, 0.5–2m; stem-seg. obovate to oblong, 10–40cm, blue-green; spines few or 0 in var. *stricta*, up to 11 in var. *dillenii* (Ker-Gawl.) L. Bens., usually 1.5–4cm, stout, straight or commonly curved, flattened, yellow or with brown bands. Fl. yellow. Fr. globose to pear-shaped 4–6cm, fleshy, purple. SE US to N Venez., nat. in various trop. countries. Z9.

O. strigil Engelm. Erect or sprawling shrub, 60–10×130–200cm; stem-seg. flattened, obovate, 10–12.5cm; areoles *c*9mm apart; glochids 6mm, red-brown; spines 1–8, deflexed, one much longer, to 4cm, red-brown, tipped yellow. Fl. creamy white. Fr. spineless, globose, 1.2–1.9cm, red. SW US, N Mex. Z9.

O. strobiliformis A. Berger = *O. articulata*.

O. subinermis Backeb. = *O. pentlandii*.

O. subulata (Muehlenpf.) Engelm. Becoming a small tree, 2–4m, or branched near the base; st. cylindric, unsegmented, 5–7cm diam., with low tubercles, green; lvs terete, acute, 5cm or more, persisting; spines 1–2 (or more on older growth), pale yellow. Fl. red. S Peru. Z9.

O. sulphurea G. Don. Low shrub, to 30×200cm; stem-seg. flattened, oblong to obovate, 12–25cm, tuberculate; spines 2–8, 3–10cm, brown or red-brown or paler. Fl. yellow. Fr. 1cm. Arg. Z9.

O. tardospina Griffiths = *O. lindheimeri*.

O. tenuispina Engelm. & Bigelow = *O. macrorhiza*.

O. teres Cels ex F.A. Weber = *O. vestita*.

O. tesajo Engelm. Resembling *O. ramosissima* but st. tubercles elongate. Fl. to 2, not 1.2cm diam. Fr. red. Baja Calif. Z9.

O. tetracantha Toumey = *O. kleiniae*.

O. tomentosa Salm-Dyck. Small tree 3–5m; stem-seg. flattened, oblong, 10–60cm, pubesc.; spines 0 or 1–3, pale yellow. Fl. orange. Fr. ovoid, red. C Mex. Z9.

O. tortispina Engelm. & Bigelow = *O. macrorhiza*.

O. treleasei J. Coult. = *O. basilaris*.

O. tuna (L.) Mill. Shrub to 90cm; stem-seg. flattened, obovate to oblong, to 16cm usually smaller, tinged brown above the larger areoles; spines 2–6, pale yellow. Fl. pale yellow tinged red. Fr. obovoid, *c*3cm, red. Jam. Z9.

O. tunicata (Lehm.) Link & Otto. Shrub, to 60cm, densely branched; spines 6–10, to 5cm, sheath conspicuous, yellow or off-white. Fl. yellow. Mex., SW US, and nat. in parts of S

Amer. Z9.

O. turpinii Lem. = *O. articulata*.

O. ursina F.A. Weber = *O. erinacea* var. *ursina*.

O. vaseyi (Coult.) Britt. & Rose = *O. littoralis*.

O. velutina F.A. Weber. Shrub to tree to 4m; stem-seg. flattened, obovate, oblong or pear-shaped, 15–30cm, pubesc.; glochids numerous, to 3mm; spines 0 or 1–6, to 4cm, pale yellow. Fl. yellow, orange or red. Fr. small, subglobose, dark red. S Mex. Z9.

O. verschaffeltii Cels. Low shrub, forming clumps; stem-seg. usually elongate in cult., 6–20cm, with low tubercles; lvs terete, to 3cm, persistent; spines 1–3 or more, 1–3cm, setaceous, or 0. Fl. orange to deep red. Boliv., N Arg. Z9.

O. versicolor Engelm. & J. Coult. Shrub or small tree to 2.5(–4.5)cm, stem-seg. cylindric, 12.5–35cm, tubercles elongate; areoles elliptic, 12–15mm apart; spines sheathed, 7–10, to 1.5cm, red, tipped yellow. Fl. variable in colour, red, lavender, purple-pink, orange, yellow, green. Fr. spineless, sometimes proliferous. SW US, N Mex. Z9.

O. vestita Salm-Dyck. Low, fragile-stemmed shrub; stem-seg. to 20cm, with dense, soft white areolar hair; lvs *c*1cm; spines 4–8, usually short, sometimes to 15mm. Fl. violet-red. Boliv., N Arg. Z9.

O. vilis Rose. Resembling *O. bulbispina* but stem-seg. clavate, to 5cm. N Mex. Z9.

O. violacea Engelm., invalid name. = *O. macrocentra*.

O. vivipara Rose = *O. arbuscula*.

O. vulgaris Mill., confused name. = *O. compressa*.

O. vulgaris auct., misapplied. = *O. monacantha*.

O. whipplei Engelm. & Bigelow Mat-forming shrub, usually 30–60cm×1–2m, rarely erect, to 2m tall; stem-seg. cylindric, erect, densely arranged, 7.5–15cm, tuberculate; spines silver-sheathed, 4–14, to 2.5(–5)cm, pale pink to pink-brown. Fl. pale yellow. Fr. spineless, to 3×2cm, yellow. SW US. Z9.

O. wrightiana Baxter = *O. parishii*.

O. xanthostemma Schum. = *O. erinacea*.

→*Austrocylindropuntia*, *Cereus*, *Grusonia*, *Nopalea*, *Platyopuntia* and *Tephrocactus*.

Orach *Atriplex*.

Orange *Citrus sinensis*.

Orange Ball Tree *Buddleja globosa*.

Orange Balsam *Impatiens capensis*.

Orange Berry Pittosporum *Pittosporum undulatum*.

Orange Blossom Orchid *Sarcochilus falcatus*.

Orange Browallia *Streptosolen jamesonii*.

Orange Bush Monkey Flower *Mimulus aurantiacus*.

Orange Clock Vine *Thunbergia gregorii*.

Orange Daisy *Erigeron aurantiacus*.

Orange Everlasting *Helichrysum acuminatum*.

Orange Eye *Buddleja davidii*.

Orangeglow Vine *Pseudogynoxys chenopodioides*.

Orange Grass *Hypericum gentianoides*.

Orange Immortelle *Waitzia acuminata*.

Orange Jasmine *Murraya paniculata*.

Orange Jessamine *Murraya paniculata*.

Orange Lily *Lilium bulbiferum*.

Orange Spruce *Picea asperata* var. *aurantiaca*.

Orbea Haw. Asclepiadaceae. 20 leafless succulent perenn. herbs to about 10cm. St. branching from the base, clump-forming, tetragonal, erect to decumbent, ridges prominently toothed. Fls mostly basal, unscented or slightly maldorous, solitary or cymose; cor. large, usually flattened, with a thickened annulus surrounding corona, lobes 5, rugose, margins often with club-shaped cilia; corona 1–2-whorled, whorls 5-lobed, lobes lanceolate to 2-horned. Follicle spindle-shaped. S, E Afr. Z9.

O. aperta (Masson) Sweet = *Tridentea aperta*.

O. ciliata (Thunb.) Leach. Fl. solitary, 7–8cm diam., bowl-shaped, pale yellow-green covered in a maroon-tipped, papillose verrucae above, annulus cup-shaped, dark purple, rough, lobes 3–3.2cm, ovate-acute, spreading, margins densely covered in motile white cilia; outer corona pale yellow sparsely dotted purple, inner buff dotted purple. Cape Prov.

O. cooperi (N.E. Br.) Leach. Fls 1–3, in a cyme, to 3.5cm diam., flat, glab., pale purple with yellow trasnverse rugae, annulus to 9mm diam., pink-purple, tuberculose, lobes 1–1.4cm, ovate, acute, spreading or recurved, star-like, base purple-ciliate; outer corona dark maroon, inner pale yellow with purple spots. S Afr.

O. irrorata (Masson) Leach. Fls solitary to few, 3.5cm diam., broadly campanulate, annulus indistinct, pale yellow-green spotted dark red, lobes 1.2cm, triangular, slightly recurved, cilia 0; outer corona glossy black to purple-brown, inner orange-yellow, lobes bordered maroon. Cape Prov.

O. lepida (Jacq.) Haw. Fls 1–2, basal, 3.5cm diam., glab., sulphur-yellow with small, irregular, purple-brown spots, annulus paler than lobes, tuberculose, lobes 1.2cm, broadly ovate, margins ciliate; outer corona green or green-yellow, inner pale yellow or green, sometimes dotted purple-brown. Known only in cult.

O. longidens (N.E. Br.) Leach. Fls 3.5–4cm diam., 3 together, tube campanulate, lobes 14–16mm, ovate-lanceolate, pointed, pale green-yellow blotched red-brown, more densely so toward tips. Moz.

O. macloughlinii (Verdoorn) Leach. Fls to 5cm diam. with a distinct raised annulus around corona which gradually merges, along its outer edge, lobes broad-deltoid, yellow marked red. S Afr.

O. maculata (N.E. Br.) Leach. Fls 1–3, around mid-point of st. v. deeply 5–6-lobed, green-yellow with small maroon spots, annulus small, lobes to 2.5cm, oblong, subacute, slightly rugulose, margins revolute, with 3mm, club-shaped white cilia; corona dark maroon. S Afr., Bots., Zimb.

O. namaquensis (N.E. Br.) Leach. Fls 1–4, basal, 8–10cm diam., flat, pale green-yellow, banded or blotched purple, annulus thick, 5-angled, tube with dense, purple hairs at base, lobes 2.5–3cm, broadly ovate, recurved, long-attenuate, with dense rugae, papillose, outer corona yellow with purple-brown spots, inner lobes filiform. W Cape.

O. paradoxa (Verdoorn) Leach. Fls to 5 together, 2–2.4cm diam., unshaped below the annulus, cup-shaped above it, dark glossy red, with stiff red hairs below, annulus glossy dark red, outer margins blotched white; corona green-white banded dark red, lobes 6mm, ovate to acute, green-white with dark red blotches in lines, margins with red hairs. Natal.

O. prognatha (Bally) Leach. Fl. solitary, 1.5–3cm diam., livid blue-purple, tube shallowly saucer-shaped, densely papillose, annulus thick, fleshy, lobes broadly triangular, tips recurved, margins ciliate; outer corona dark purple, inner corona pale yellow-brown. N Somalia.

O. pulchella (Masson) Leach. Fls several together, rotate, 4.5cm diam., lobes triangular-ovate, tapered minutely transversely wrinkled with minute brown spots, annulus small, minutely tuberculate with brown spots and ciliate margin. S Afr.

O. rangeana (Dinter & A. Berger) Leach. Fls 4cm diam., glab., deeply 5-cleft, lobes to 1.8cm, oblong to oblong-spathulate, yellow-green spotted wine red. Nam.

O. semota (N.E. Br.) Leach. Fls 1–3, 3.5–4.5cm diam., flat, golden yellow with chocolate-brown markings, annulus 5-angled, dark red-brown, lobes about 1.5cm, ovate-lanceolate, attenuate, spreading or slightly reflexed, marginal cilia 3mm, dark red. Tanz., Kenya.

O. speciosa Leach. Fls 1–3 together, 3.5–5cm diam., minutely tuberculate, yellow with purple-red markings denser to ward lobe tips, margins with red, clavate hairs, annulus small but distinct. S Afr. (Natal).

O. tapscottii (Verdoorn) Leach. Fls 3–4 together, 5cm diam., lobes to 2cm, ovate, tapered, red with white markings and several hairs, annulus 1cm diam. S Afr. (W Cape).

O. umbracula (Henderson) Leach. Fls solitary or several together, 2.5–3cm diam., lobes recurved from small prominent annulus, thick, glab., terracotta to tan, lobe tips transversely wrinkled, marked yellow-green. Cape Prov.

O. variegata (L.) Haw. TOAD CACTUS; STARFISH CACTUS. Fls 1–5, 5–9cm diam., flat, densely rugose, pale yellow to sulphur with dark brown blotches and transverse lines, blotches sometimes coalescing into 6 or 7 rows, annulus circular or slightly 5-angled, broad, pale yellow with small blotches, lobes broad, ovate, spreading; corona lobes yellow, with fine maroon spots; corona 2-horned. Cape Prov. 'Decora': fl. base yellow, delicate claret spots and cross lines.

O. verrucosa (Masson) Leach. Fls 1–3, basal, 4.5–6cm diam., flat to saucer-shaped, pale yellow with brown and blood-red spots, annulus 5-angled, slightly hairy, with dense spots, furrowed toward angles, lobes deltoid-ovate, sharply tapering, recurved or spreading, rough, with irregular transverse rugae, papillose; outer corona dark chocolate-brown, margins yellow, inner corona yellow, edged maroon. Cape Prov. var. *fucosa* (N.E. Br.) Leach. Fls 3cm diam., interior wrinkled, annulus 5-angled, 8–9mm diam., lobes triangular, to 1cm with dark red blotches, annulus with confluent blotches, margins deep red. S Afr.

O. woodii (N.E. Br.) Leach. Fls 3 to several together, 4cm diam., rotate, lobes ovate, tapered, dark brown sparsely blotched yellow, v. wrinkled, annulus ciliate, margins recurved. S Afr. (Natal).

→*Caralluma, Diplocyatha, Podanthes, Stapelia* and *Stultitia.*

Orbeanthus Leach. Asclepiadaceae. 2 succulent perenn. differing from *Orbea* in sprawling habit and eciliate fls. S Afr. Z9.

O. conjunctus (A. White & B.L. Sloane) Leach. Fls 2 or more, subglobose-campanulate, annulus 8mm diam., lobes 1×0.3cm, interior of tube, annulus and bottom of limb bright maroon, remainder cream-white. Transvaal.

O. hardyi (R.A. Dyer) Leach. Fls solitary or several, annulus to 2mm diam., lobes 2–2.5×1.3–1.8cm, minutely papillose, liver-coloured, rim of annulus paler. Transvaal.

→*Stultitia.*

Orbeopsis Leach. Asclepiadaceae. 10 dwarf, succulent, leafless herbs with maldorous fls resembling *Orbea.* S Afr. to Angola and Moz. Z9.

O. albocastanea (Marloth) Leach. Fls 3–6, 2.5cm diam., ivory, densely spotted purple-brown with coarse rugae, tube cup-shaped, shallow, lobes 1cm, subacute, with clavate cilia; corona dark brown. Nam.

O. caudata (N.E. Br.) Leach. Fls several, in sessile clusters yellow, mottled purple, tube shallow, saucer-shaped, 5–6mm diam., minutely papillose within, lobes 3–4.5cm, caudate, spreading, with sparse, motile, clavate purple cilia; corona yellow. Zimb., Nam., Malawi.

O. gerstneri (Letty) Leach. Fls 2–6 in clusters, 3.5cm diam., tube cupular, interior purple-red, velvety, lobes to 1.5cm, parchment-coloured with dark red spots, velvety, glossy, purple-ciliate. Natal. ssp. *elongata* (Dyer) Leach. Cor. lobes 2.5–3cm. Transvaal.

O. gossweileri (S. Moore) Leach. Fls 6–15 together, maldorous, 10cm diam., lobes 4.5cm, tapering, margins recurved, minutely pubesc., base transversely rugose, granular towards the tips. Angola, Zimb., Zam.

O. huillensis (Hiern) Leach. Fls 6–10 in clusters, 9cm diam., lobes 3–4cm, liinear-lanceolate, dark red, exterior finely pruinose, interior glab., rough. Angola.

O. knobelii (E. Phillips) Leach. Fls about 10 to 3.5cm diam., white densely blotched black-purple, tube 5-angled, shallow, lobes 1.3cm, ovate, tips green, reflexed, cilia dark purple; outer corona lobes striped. Bots.

O. lutea (N.E. Br.) Leach. Variable. Fls 3–26, in a dense cluster, 4–7.5cm diam., yellow to maroon, rugulose, tube shallow, lobes 2–3.5cm, narrow-lanceolate, attenuate, cilia purple; corona yellow. S Afr. ssp. *vaga* (N.E. Br.) Leach. Cor. lobes much broader and longer. Nam., Angola, W Cape.

O. melanantha (Schltr.) Leach. Fls 3–5, per cluster, 5cm diam. tube 0, dark black-purple, rugulose, with dense, minute hairs, lobes 1.6–1.8cm, deltoid-ovate, acute, spreading, cilia long, purple; outer corona brown-purple, inner corona dark purple. Transvaal, Moz.

O. tsumebensis (Oberm.) Leach. Fls many, in sessile bundles, about 4cm diam., exterior distinctly veined, interior dark chocolate-brown, tube 7mm, campanulate, lobes 2.5cm, lanceolate, acute. N Nam.

O. valida (N.E. Br.) Leach. Fls in dense clusters of 20–40, 4–6cm diam., deep chocolate or blood red, lobes to 2.5cm, narrowing toward tips, surface v. rough, covered with 3mm hairs. Bots., Transvaal, Zimb., Zam.

→*Caralluma* and *Stapelia.*

Orbignya Mart. ex Endl. BABASSU PALM. Palmae. c20 unarmed palms. St. subterranean to erect. Crownshaft 0. Lvs pinnate, marcescent; sheaths thick, margins fibrous; petiole channelled above; pinnae crowded, single-fold, regularly spaced or clustered along rachis, linear-lanceolate. Spikes interfoliar, ♂ or ♀, or with fls of both sexes, erect to pendent, branched once, amid 2 persistent bracts. Fr. ovoid, 1 to several-seeded, with persistent perianth and staminodal ring, epicarp scaly, mesocarp hard and fibrous or soft and pulpy. S Mex. to subtrop. S Amer. Z10.

O. barbosiana Burret = *O. phalerata.*

O. cohune (Mart.) Dahlgr. ex Standl. COHUNE PALM. Trunk to 13.5m×30cm. Lvs to 9m, pinnae regularly spaced along rachis. C Amer.

O. guayacule (Liebm.) E. Hern. Resembles *O. cohune* but ♂ pet. spathulate, not oblanceolate. W Mex.

O. macropetala Burret = *O. phalerata.*

O. martiana Barb. Rodr. = *O. phalerata.*

O. phalerata Mart. BABASSU; COCO DE MACAO. Trunk to 30m×50cm. Lvs to 9m, pinnae clustered at base of rachis, regularly spaced above. Braz.

O. speciosa (Mart.) Barb. Rodr. = *O. phalerata.*

O. spectabilis (Mart.) Burret. Trunk short or 0. Lvs erect, pinnae regularly spaced. Braz.

Orchard Grass *Dactylis glomerata.*

ORCHIDACEAE Juss. 796/17,500. *Acacallis, Acampe, Acanthephippium, Aceras, Acianthus, Acineta, Acriopsis, Ada,*

Aerangis, Aeranthes, Aerides, Aganisia, ✕ *Alexanderara,* ✕ *Aliceara, Amblostoma, Amesiella, Amitostigma, Anacamptis, Ancistrochilus, Ancistrorhynchus, Angraecopsis, Angraecum, Anguloa,* ✕ *Angulocaste, Anoectochilus, Ansellia, Arachnis,* ✕ *Aranda, Arethusa, Arpophyllum, Arthrochilus, Arundina,* ✕ *Ascocenda,* ✕ *Ascofinetia, Ascocentrum, Ascoglossum,* ✕ *Asconopsis, Aspasia, Barbosella, Barbrodria, Barkeria, Barlia, Bartholina, Batemannia, Bifrenaria, Bletia, Bletilla, Bollea, Bonatea, Brachycorythis, Brassavola, Brassia,* ✕ *Brassocattleya,* ✕ *Brassoepidendrum,* ✕ *Brassolaeliocattleya, Bromheadia, Broughtonia, Bulbophyllum, Cadetia, Caladenia, Calanthe, Calopogon, Calypso, Calyptrochilum, Capanemia, Catasetum, Cattleya, Cattleyopsis,* ✕ *Cattleytonia, Caularthron, Cephalanthera, Chamaeangis, Chaubardia, Chiloglottis, Chondrorhyncha,* ✕ *Christieara, Chysis, Cirrhaea, Cleisostoma, Cleistes, Clowesia, Cochleanthes, Cochlioda, Coelia, Coeliopsis, Coeloglossum, Coelogyne, Comparettia, Comperia, Constantia, Coryanthes, Corybas, Corymborchis, Cribbia, Cryptostylis, Cuitlauzina, Cycnoches, Cymbidiella, Cymbidium, Cynorchis, Cypripedium, Cyrtidium, Cyrtopodium, Cyrtorchis, Cyrtostylis, Dactylorhiza, Dendrobium, Dendrochilum,* ✕ *Dialaelia, Diaphananthe, Dichaea, Dimerandra, Dimorphorchis, Diplocaulobium, Diplomeris, Dipodium, Dipteranthus, Disa, Disperis, Diuris, Domingoa,* ✕ *Doritaenopsis, Doritis, Dracula, Dressleria, Dryadella, Dyakia, Elleanthus, Elythranthera, Encyclia,* ✕ *Epicattleya, Epidendrum,* ✕ *Epiphronitis, Epigeneium, Epipactis, Eria, Eriochilus, Eriopsis, Erycina, Esmeralda, Euanthe, Eulophia, Eulophiella, Eurychone, Flickingeria, Galeandra, Gastrochilus, Geodorum, Glossodia, Gomesa, Gongora, Goodyera, Grammangis, Grammatophyllum, Graphorkis, Grobya, Grosourdya, Gymnadenia, Habenaria, Hexadesmia, Hexisea, Himantoglossum, Holcoglossum, Houlletia, Huntleya, Ionopsis, Isabelia, Isochilus, Jacquiniella, Jumellea, Kefersteinia, Kegeliella, Kingidium, Koellensteinia, Laelia,* ✕ *Laeliocattleya, Laeliopsis, Lanium, Lemboglossum, Leochilus, Lepanthes, Lepanthopsis, Leptotes, Leucohyle, Liparis, Listera, Listrostachys, Lockhartia, Ludisia, Lueddemannia, Luisia, Lycaste, Lyperanthus,* ✕ *Maclellanara, Macodes, Macradenia, Malaxis, Masdevallia, Maxillaria, Mendoncella, Mexicoa, Microterangis, Microtis, Miltonia,* ✕ *Miltonidium, Miltoniopsis,* ✕ *Mokara, Mormodes, Mormolyca, Mystacidium, Nageliella, Nanodes, Neobathiea, Neobenthamia, Neocogniauxia, Neofinetia, Neogardneria, Neolauchea, Neomoorea, Nephelaphyllum, Nervilia, Nidema, Nigritella, Notylia, Oberonia, Octomeria,* ✕ *Odontioda,* ✕ *Odontobrassia,* ✕ *Odontocidium, Odontoglossum,* ✕ *Odontonia,* ✕ *Odontorettia, Oeceoclades, Oeonia, Oeoniella, Oerstedella,* ✕ *Oncidioda, Oncidium, Ophrys,* ✕ *Opsistylis, Orchis, Ornithidium, Ornithocephalus, Ornithophora, Osmoglossum, Otochilus, Otoglossum, Otostylis, Pabstia, Palumbina, Panisea, Paphinia, Paphiopedilum, Papilionanthe, Papperitzia, Paraphalaenopsis, Pecteilis, Peristeria, Pescatorea, Phaius, Phalaenopsis, Pholidota, Phragmipedium, Platanthera, Platystele, Plectorrhiza, Plectrelminthus, Pleione, Pleurothallis, Podangis, Pogonia, Polycycnis, Polystachya, Pomatocalpa, Ponerorchis, Porpax, Porroglossum,* ✕ *Potinara, Prasophyllum, Promenaea, Psychopsis, Pterostylis, Rangaeris,* ✕ *Renanopsis,* ✕ *Renantanda, Renanthera,* ✕ *Renanthopsis, Restrepia, Restrepiella, Rhinerrhiza, Rhyncholaelia, Rhynchostylis,* ✕ *Rhynchovanda, Robiquetia, Rodriguezia, Rossioglossum, Sarcochilus,* ✕ *Sarconopsis, Satyrium, Scaphosepalum, Scaphyglottis, Schoenorchis, Schomburgkia, Scuticaria, Sedirea, Seidenfadenia, Selenipedium, Serapias, Sievekingia, Sigmatostalix, Smitinandia, Sobralia, Solenangis, Solenidium,* ✕ *Sophrocattleya,* ✕ *Sophrolaelia,* ✕ *Sophrolaeliocattleya, Sophronitella, Sophronitis, Spathoglottis, Spiranthes, Stanhopea, Stelis, Stenia, Stenoglottis, Stenorrhynchos,* ✕ *Stewartara, Summerhayesia, Sunipia, Symphyglossum, Taeniophyllum, Tainia, Telipogon, Tetramicra, Teuscheria, Thelymitra, Theodorea, Thrixspermum, Thunia, Ticoglossum, Trias, Trichocentrum, Trichoceros, Trichoglottis, Trichopilia, Trichosalpinx, Trichotosia, Tridactyle, Trigonidium, Trisetella, Trudelia, Vanda, Vandopsis, Vanilla,* ✕ *Vascostylis,* ✕ *Vuylstekeara, Warmingia, Warrea, Warreella,* ✕ *Wilsonara, Xylobium, Ypsilopus, Zeuxine, Zootrophion, Zygopetalum, Zygosepalum, Zygostates.*

Orchidantha N.E. Br. Lowiaceae. 7 low-growing rhizomatous perenn. herbs. Lvs distichous, sheathing at base. Fls solitary or paired in bracteate cymes or pan.; cal. 3-lobed, tubular; cor. lobes 3, 1 enlarged, forming a lip. SE Asia. Z10.

O. maxillarioides (Ridl.) Schum. To 40cm. Lvs to 25cm, oblong, coriaceous, tufted; petioles to 10cm. Pan. 2–3-branched; cor. lobes to 3.75cm, flushed purple-violet, tipped green, lip to 2.5cm, green marked purple. Malaysia.

Orchid Cactus *Epiphyllum.*
Orchid Ginger *Alpinia mutica.*

Orchid Tree *Bauhinia* (*B. variegata*).

Orchis L. Orchidaceae. 35 decid., terrestrial orchids. Tubers globose to elliptic, 2–3. Lvs linear-lanceolate to oblong-ovate, sometimes spotted purple, basal and sheathing st. of erect, crowded term. rac.; bracts membranous; pet. and sep. ± equal, incurved, forming a hood, or lat. sep. spreading; lip entire or trilobed, central lobe entire or divided; spur usually slender, horizontal to decurved. Spring–summer. Temp. N Hemis. Z5.

O. aristata Fisch. ex Lindl. = *Dactylorhiza aristata.*

O. collina Banks & Sol. St. 10–40cm. Basal lvs sometimes spotted. Infl. cylindric or oblong; dors. sep. 10–12mm, incurved, ovate-oblong, lat. sep. spreading or erect; pet. oblong-lanceolate, dark olive green to red; lip to 10mm, ovate to obovate, undulate, green-pink often blotched white; spur conical, short. Late winter–mid spring. Medit.

O. comperiana Steven = *Comperia comperiana.*

O. coriophora L. BUG ORCHID. St. 15–60cm. Infl. oblong or cylindric, dense; pet. and sep. to 10mm, ovate-lanceolate, forming a violet-brown hood; lip trilobed, incurved, dark purple-red to purple-green, sometimes spotted dark purple, lat. lobes denticulate. Mid spring–early summer. SC & E Eur. ssp. *fragrans* (Pollini) Sudre. As *O. coriophora* but fls paler, fragrant, bracts white.

O. coriophora ssp. *sancta* (L.) Hayek = *O. sancta.*

O. elata Poir. = *Dactylorhiza elata.*

O. iberica Willd. = *Dactylorhiza iberica.*

O. incarnata Soó = *Dactylorhiza incarnata.*

O. italica Poir. St. 20–45cm. Lvs sometimes spotted. Infl. dense, conical, becoming ovoid or globose; sep. and pet. to 10mm, ovate-lanceolate, incurved, lilac-rose beneath, sometimes striped red; lip pink, trilobed, to 16mm, rose-white above, often spotted purple, central lobe narrowly cleft, lat. lobes linear, red or magenta towards tip. Summer. Medit.

O. lactea Poir. As *O. tridentata* except st. to 20cm, infl. dense, sep. spreading, veined green below, basally flushed green; lip linear-oblong to square, central lobe apically finely dentate, white, spots purple, sometimes forming a continuous line. Summer. Medit.

O. laxiflora Lam. St. to 120cm, usually shorter. Infl. lax, ovoid or cylindric; sep. rose pink, lilac or red, oblong, spreading, lat. sep. deflexed, dors. sep. almost erect; pet. oblong, incurved; lip trilobed, centre sometimes white, lat. lobes oblong, reflexed, midlobe reduced. Spring–early summer. Eur., Medit.

O. longicornu Poir. St. 10–35cm. Infl. dense, oblong; sep. to 6mm (pet. smaller), oblong, incurved, white to pale pink or maroon; lip shallowly trilobed, midlobe white, spotted purple, lat. lobes larger, recurved, deep purple-violet to pink or red, spur v. long. Late winter–mid spring. W Medit.

O. longicurris Link = *O. italica.*

O. maculata L. = *Dactylorhiza maculata.*

O. maderensis Summerh. = *Dactylorhiza foliosa.*

O. mascula L. EARLY PURPLE ORCHID. St. 20–60cm. Lvs often spotted. Infl. dense, cylindric or ovoid; fls purple; sep. 6–8mm, oblong-lanceolate or ovate, lat. sep. spreading or reflexed, dors. sep. and pet. forming hood; lip 8–15mm, trilobed, white, centrally spotted purple or crimson, lateral lobes slightly deflexed, midlobe longer, notched. Mid spring–mid summer. Eur.

O. militaris L. MILITARY ORCHID. St. 20–45cm. Infl. dense, conical, becoming cylindric; sep. and pet. to 15mm, ovate-lanceolate, forming white to grey-pink hood, veined purple above; lip to 15mm, trilobed, white to dark purple, spotted red, lat. lobes linear, falcate, mmidlobe narrow, becoming triangular, apically bilobed, lobes oblong or ovate, with short dentations between. Mid spring–mid summer. Eur., Medit., Russia.

O. morio L. GREEN-WINGED ORCHID. St. 5–50cm. Infl. pyramidal or oblong; sep. and pet. usually rose-purple, sep. veined green oblong-ovate, forming hood; lip purple to 10mm, trilobed, recurved, midlobe notched, truncate, sometimes dark-spotted, lateral lobes smaller, tinged green; spur long cylindric, horizontal or upcurved. White-fl forms occur. Spring–mid summer. Eur., Medit.

O. pallens L. St. 15–40cm. Infl. dense, ovoid or oblong; fls yellow; sep. 7–9mm, lat. sep. deflexed, ovate-oblong, dors. sep. forming hood with oblong pet; lip trilobed, lat. lobes orbicular, midlobe truncate, slightly emarginate. Mid spring–early summer. C & SE Eur.

O. palustris L. St. 80–100cm. Infl. cylindric, slightly lax; fls purple or pink; lateral sep. oblong, erect, patent; lip to 10mm, flabellate-cuneate, midlobe equal or exceeding rounded-rectangular lat. lobes, centre white, dotted purple (rarely entire, dark purple). Mid spring–mid summer. N Eur., Russia.

O. papilionacea L. BUTTERFLY ORCHID. St. 15–40cm. Infl. lax, ovoid; fls purple, rarely red or brown; sep.and pet. to 18mm, forming a lax hood, deep red or purple, prominently veined; lip

12–25mm, entire, cuneate or fan-shaped, dentate, rose to red, dark-spotted or striped. Spring–early summer. Medit.

O. praetermissa Druce = *Dactylorhiza praetermissa.*

O. provincialis Balb. PROVENCE ORCHID. St. 15–35cm. Lvs sometimes spotted. Infl. lax to dense, cylindric; fls palle yellow or white, lip deeper, centre orange-yellow, spotted maroon; sep. 9–11mm, ovate-oblong, lat. sep. spreading, deflexed, middle erect; pet. smaller; lip round-ovate, trilobed, lat. lobes ovate to round, midlobe smaller, truncate, rounded; spur cylindric, patent. Mid spring–early summer. S Eur. var. *pauciflora* (Ten.) Camus. Lvs sparsely spotted or unspotted, fls 3–7, spike lax, ovary exceeds bracts, lip 13–15mm, trilobed, lat. lobes recurved, midlobe incised. Mid spring–early summer. EC Medit.

O. purpurea Huds. LADY ORCHID. St. 30–80cm. Infl. dense, cylindric; sep. 12–14mm, forming hood with pet., brown-purple or pink beneath, sometimes spotted purple, rarely pale green with white lip; lip to 15mm, lat. lobes linear, midlobe obcordate or triangular, often toothed, pale rose or white, spotted purple. Mid spring–mid summer. Eur., Medit.

O. purpurella T. & T.A. Stephenson = *Dactylorhiza purpurella.*

O. quadripunctata Ten. St. 10–40cm. Lvs usually spotted. Spike lax, ovoid or cylindric; fls pink to violet, red or white; dors. sep. 3–5mm, ovate, forming hood, lat. sep. spreading, pet. to 5mm; lip orbicular, trilobed or entire, lat. lobes 4–7mm, oblong-ovate, midlobe oblong, blotched white with 2–6 purple spots. Late spring–early summer. Medit.

O. saccata Ten. = *O. collina.*

O. saccifera Brongn. = *Dactylorhiza saccifera.*

O. sambucina L. = *Dactylorhiza sambucina.*

O. sancta L. As *O. coriophora* except fls pink to lilac-red; dors. sep. 9–12mm, elongate, ascending; lip flat, incurved, lat. lobes rhombic, 3–4-dentate, midlobe entire. Mid spring. E Medit.

O. sesquipidaliensis Willd. = *Dactylorhiza elata.*

O. simia Lam. MONKEY ORCHID. St. 20–45cm. Infl. dense, broadly cylindric to ovoid; sep. and pet. to 10mm, ovate-lanceolate, forming hood, pale pink to red beneath, often streaked red, interior spotted or veined red; lip trilobed, to 20mm, white to rose pink, dotted purple, lat. lobes linear, obtuse, midlobe deeply divided, lobules 2, slender, tipped. Early spring–early summer. Eur.

O. traunsteineri Rchb. = *Dactylorhiza traunsteineri.*

O. tridentata Scop. TOOTHED ORCHID. St. 15–45cm. Infl. conical to ovoid, fls white to rose-pink to violet, lip spotted maroon; sep. and pet. ovate-oblong, forming veined hood; lip lat. lobes incurved, falcate, truncate, dentate, midlobe triangular, longer, bilobed or notched, lobules minutely dentate. Mid spring–early summer. C & S Eur.

O. ustulata L. BURNT ORCHID. St. 12–35cm. Infl. dense, ovoid, becoming cylindric; fls scented; sep. and pet. 3–3.5mm, forming hood, brown-purple beneath, pink above; lip 4–8mm, lat. lobes spreading, oblong, midlobe bilobed or entire, white to palle pink, spotted red. Mid spring–late summer. Eur., Russia.

Oregano *Origanum* (*O. vulgare*).

Oregon Alder *Alnus rubra.*

Oregon Ash *Fraxinus latifolia.*

Oregon Boxwood *Paxistima myrtifolia.*

Oregon Cedar *Chamaecyparis lawsoniana.*

Oregon Foetid Adder's-tongue *Scoliopus hallii.*

Oregon Grape *Mahonia aquifolium.*

Oregon Lily *Lilium columbianum.*

Oregon Maple *Acer macrophyllum.*

Oregon Myrtle *Umbellularia californica.*

Oregon Oak *Quercus garryana.*

Oregon Plum *Oemleria; Prunus subcordata.*

Oregon Sidalcea *Sidalcea oregana.*

Oregon Tea *Ceanothus sanguineus.*

Oregon White Oak *Quercus garryana.*

Oreocallis R. Br. Proteaceae. 5 everg. trees or shrubs. Lvs simple or pinnate. Fls paired in solitary or clustered rac.; perianth tube cylindrical, limb 4-lobed. S Amer., Aus., Malay Archipel. Z9.

O. pinnata (Maid. & Betche) Sleumer. DORRIGO OAK. Tree to 25m. Lvs entire to pinnately lobed, adult lvs entire, lanceolate, to 15cm. Fls to 3cm, pink-red, in short term. rac. Spring–early summer. E Aus.

Oreocarya E. Greene.

O. celosioides Eastw. = *Cryptantha celosioides.*

O. sheldonii Brand = *Cryptantha sheldonii.*

Oreocereus (A. Berger) Riccob. Cactaceae. 5–7 mostly shrubby cacti st. cylindric; areoles often developing long white hairs, densely spiny. Fls tubular-funnelform; floral areoles numerous,

± hairy; perianth-limb narrow, oblique; upper tep. suberect, lower spreading or recurved; style and sta. exserted. Fr. globose to ovoid, hollow, pericarp fleshy. Andes.

O. celsianus (Cels ex Salm-Dyck) Riccob. 1 to 3m, mainly branching near base; st. to 12–20cm diam.; ribs 10–17, tuberculate; areoles with long woolly hairs; central spines to 8cm; straw yellow to dark brown; radial spines to 2cm. Fl. 7–9cm, dull pink; tube slightly curved; anth. violet; stigmas yellow-green. Mts of NW Arg. & Boliv. Z9.

O. crassiniveus Backeb. = *Oreocereus trollii.*

O. doelzianus (Backeb.) Borg. To 1m, branching from the base; st. 6–8cm diam.; ribs 10–11; areoles naked or densely to sparsely hairy; spines to 3cm, yellow to dark brown, 4 longer centrals sometimes developing later. Fl. to c10cm, deep purple-pink; limb oblique. C Peru. Z9.

O. fossulatus sensu Backeb. non *Pilocereus fossulatus* Labouret = *O. pseudofossulatus.*

O. hempelianus (Gürke) D. Hunt. St. simple or branched from the base, globose becoming short-cylindric, erect or decumbent, to 60×10–15cm, grey- or blue-green; ribs 10–20; areoles large; spines variable; centrals to 5cm, often curved, white, brown, or nearly black, radials 1–3cm, needle-like to bristly, pale yellow to glassy white. Fl. 5–7.5cm, scarlet to purple-red; tube slightly curved. Mts of S Peru, N Chile. Z9.

O. hendriksenianus Backeb. = *O. leucotrichus.*

O. leucotrichus (Philippi) Wagenkn. Shrub to 1–2m, branching from base; st. 6–12cm diam., grey-green; ribs 10–18; areoles large, with white, brown or almost black hairs; spines pale yellow or yellow-brown to orange-red; central spines 5–8cm, radial spines shorter. Fl. 8–9.5cm, scarlet to purple-red; tube straight or slightly curved. S Peru, N Chile. Z9.

O. neocelsianus Backeb. = *O. celsianus.*

O. pseudofossulatus D. Hunt. Shrub to 4m, branching up to half-way up; st. usually 5–6cm diam.; ribs 10–13, prominently tubercled; areoles usually with numerous white trichomes to 5cm; central spine (+), 2–5cm, straw yellow to red-brown, radial spines to 6mm. Fl. to 9cm, pink, tinged green, to mauve. Boliv. Z9.

O. rettigii (Quehl) F. Buxb. = *O. hempelianus.*

O. trollii (Kupper) Backeb. Resembling *O. celsianus*, but lower-growing, to 1m; st. branching from base, c10cm diam. Fl. said to be only 4cm. S Boliv., N Arg. Z9.

→*Arequipa, Borzicactus, Cleistocactus* and *Morawetzia.*

Oreocharis Benth. Gesneriaceae. 27 low-growing perenn. herbs. Fls tubular-campanulate, 2-lipped. China and Jap.

O. aurantiaca Franch. Lvs 3.5–5cm, in rosette, lanceolate or oblong-elliptic, ± leathery, green above, rusty-hairy beneath. Scapes 2–5, to 12.5cm; cal. red; cor. yellow, white-hairy. Yunnan.

O. forrestii (Diels) Skan Lvs 3.5–14cm, in a rosette, ovate-oblong, coarsely toothed, densely rusty-hairy at least at first. Scapes 4–10 or more, 6–12cm; cor. pale yellow. Yunnan.

Oreodoxa auct. non Willd.

O. borinquena Reasoner = *Roystonea borinquena.*

O. caribaea Becc. non Dammer & Urban = *Roystonea borinquena.*

O. caribaea Dammer & Urban non Becc. = *Roystonea oleracea.*

O. princeps Becc. = *Roystonea princeps.*

O. regia HBK = *Roystonea regia.*

Oreopanax Decne. & Planch. Araliaceae. 80–100 unarmed, everg., shrubs or trees, some with dimorphous foliage. Lvs clustered towards the ends of br., simple, palmately lobed, palmatifid or digitately compound. Infl. terminal, paniculate, 1–2× compound; fls in heads; pet. usually 5 (rarely 4–6), white or tinged green. Fr. berry-like, white to black. Middle and S Amer.

O. andreanus Marchal. Shrub or small tree to 4m; st. ± simple. Shoots, petioles and lf undersurfaces covered with rusty hair. Lvs on summits of flowering shoots, entire or somewhat 3-lobed, elliptic, rounded and ± cordate in outline, elsewhere palmately lobed with pinnatifid seg. Ecuad. (Andes). Z9.

O. capitatus (Jacq.) Decne. & Planch. CABALLERA DE PALO; COAMATL. Tree to 18m, more commonly a shrub. Lvs to 25×18cm, simple or tripartite, ovate or elliptic to oblong-elliptic, entire, dark green above, pale grey beneath, sometimes with small scale-like hairs. Spring and summer. Throughout range of the genus except at high altitudes. Z9.

O. catalpifolius (Willd. ex Roem. & Schult.) Decne. & Planch. = *O. capitatus.*

O. dactyliferus auct. = *O. dactylifolius.*

O. dactylifolius Lind. ex Williams. Shrub or small tree, the st., petioles and undersurfaces of the lvs rusty-hairy. Lvs in young plants to 45cm across, deeply palmatifid; seg. usually 7, deeply pinnately lobed; lvs in fertile shoots smaller, moderately to deeply 5-lobed, lobes entire or few-toothed, smooth. Origin reported as Mex. but more likely from Andean S Amer. Z9.

O. dactylifolius var. *epremesnilianus* André = *O. epremesnilianus*.

O. echinops (Schldl. & Cham.) Decne. & Planch. CASTAÑO; CINCO HOJAS. Few-branched, coarsely yellow-hairy shrub or tree to 12m. Mature lvs 5-foliolate (becoming 5-lobed below infl.); lfts thin, soft, obovate or oblong-obovate, to 45×22cm, sharply pointed, juvenile lvs trilobed. Summer–autumn. Mex., Guat.

O. epremesnilianus (André) André. Shrub or tree. Lvs pseudo-digitately compound, long-petioled, appearing peltate, seg. 7–9, the outer oblong or lanceolate, the middle coarsely pinnatifid. Autumn. Origin undetermined. Z9.

O. jaliscanus S. Wats. = *O. peltatus*.

O. langlassei Standl. = *O. xalapensis*.

O. nymphaeifolius (Lind. ex Hibb.) Gentil. Vigorous tree to 5.5m. Lvs glab., ovate to broadly ovate, to 30cm, entire, bright green above, paler beneath, veins prominent beneath; open slenderly pointed, base obtuse to rounded. Summer. Origin undetermined, possibly Guat. Possibly conspecific with *O. capitatus*. Z9.

O. peltatus Lind. ex Reg. MANO DE LEON. Shrub or tree to 15m, crown ultimately large; densely rusty-hairy. Adult lvs palmately lobed, sometimes peltate, to 50cm or more across, darker above and sometimes glabrescent, base truncate or cordate, lobes usually 5–7, oblong or oblong-elliptic, coarsely toothed; juvenile lvs peltate. Summer. Mex., Guat. Z10.

O. reticulata hort., non (Willd.) Decne. & Planch. = *Meryta denhamii*.

O. salvinii Hemsl. = *O. peltatus*.

O. sanderianus Hemsl. COHETE; TRONADOR. Glab. shrub or small tree, with habit of *Fatsia japonica* when young. Lvs usually long-petiolate, to 25cm across, bright green, glossy, mostly 3–5-partite (those directly below infl. entire); lat. lobes mostly small, widely set, midlobe usually largest, triangular. Mex. to Hond. Z10.

O. thibautii Versch. ex Hook. f. = *O. xalapensis*.

O. xalapensis (Kunth) Decne. & Planch. BRAZIL; MACUILILLO MANO DE LEON; PATA DE GALLO. Shrub or tree to 18m, mostly glab. Adult lvs 5–10-foliolate, long-petiolate, lfts narrowly oblong-lanceolate to obovate, to 30cm, lustrous above, paler beneath, entire or somewhat toothed; juvenile lvs simple, cordate-ovate; intermediate lvs deeply lobed or with 3 lfts. Most of year. Mex. to Panama. Z10.

→*Aralia*, *Monopanax* and *Sciadophyllum*.

Oreopteris Holub. Thelypteridaceae. 3 terrestrial ferns. N Hemis.

O. limbosperma (All.) Holub. MOUNTAIN FERN. Caudex branched, 10cm, with dead frond bases and brown-scaly; stipes 5–15cm, sparsely scaly. Fronds fragrant when bruised; blade 25–75×8–25cm, lanceolate, bright green tinged yellow, golden-glandular beneath; pinnae 20–30 each side, linear-lanceolate, pinnatifid; seg. oblong, acute with incurved apex, shallowly crenate. Eur. (Sweden to Pyren. and N It., W to GB, E to Caspian Sea). (Angustifrons group) 'Radnor': frond narrow with elongate tip, 50cm. (Cristata-gracile group) 'Fernworthy': frond and pinnae lightly crested, pinnae curve towards apex of frond, 40–50cm.

→*Dryopteris*, *Lastrea* and *Thelypteris*.

Organ-pipe Cactus *Pachycereus marginatus*.
Oriental Arborvitae *Platycladus*.
Oriental Beech *Fagus orientalis*.
Oriental Bittersweet *Celastrus orbiculatus*.
Oriental Bush Cherry *Prunus japonica*.
Oriental Cherry *Prunus serrulata*.
Oriental Garlic *Allium tuberosum*.
Oriental Hornbeam *Carpinus orientalis*.
Oriental Plane *Platanus orientalis*.
Oriental Poppy *Papaver orientale*.
Oriental Spruce *Picea orientalis*.
Oriental Sweet Gum *Liquidambar orientalis*.
Oriental Thuja *Platycladus*.
Oriental White Oak *Quercus aliena*.

Origanum L. MARJORAM; OREGANO. Labiatae. Some 20 aromatic subshrubs or perenn. herbs. St. tetragonal, generally rhizomatous. Infl. a spike-like arrangement of whorled fls appearing paniculate or corymbose; bracts conspicuous, imbricate; cal. campanulate or funnel-shaped, pubesc., 5-toothed or 1–2-lipped; cor. 2-lipped, upper lip entire, lower lip 3-lobed. Medit. to E Asia.

O. acutidens (Hand.-Mazz.) Ietsw. St. to 50cm, glab. Lvs to 3cm, ovate, glaucous, obtuse. Fls to 12 per whorl; bracts yellow-green; cor. white or tinged with pink, to 16mm. Summer. Turk. Z9.

O. amanum Post. St. to 20cm, hirsute to scabrous. Lvs to 1.9cm, cordate. Fls to 10 per whorl; bracts ovate, 2cm, vivid purple; cor. pink. Late summer and autumn. E Medit., Turk. Z8.

O. bevanii Holmes = *O. syriacum* var. *bevanii*.

O. calcaratum Juss. Subshrub to 35cm, lanate or subglabrous. Lvs 0.6–3cm, suborbicular to ovate or cordate, lanate to glab. and glaucous. Spikes often pyramidal, to 4cm, erect and crowded; bracts 5–12mm; cor. to 18mm, pink. Is. of S Aegean.

O. dictamnus L. DITTANY OF CRETE; HOP MARJORAM. Dwarf shrub to 30cm. Lvs 1.3–2.5cm, woolly-white, ovate to round, veins prominent. Fls densely whorled in lax pan.; bracts hoplike, rose-purple; Mid-late summer. Crete. Z7.

O. ×hybridum Mill. (*O. dictamnus* ×*O. sipyleum*.) Tufted perenn. subshrub to 25cm. Lvs to 2.5cm, downy, ovate, grey-green. Fls pink, 12mm, solitary or in threes, drooping, in hoplike cluster of bracts. Late summer-autumn. Levant. Z8.

O. laevigatum Boiss. St. to 70cm, glab. Lvs to 3cm, ovate to elliptic, subcoriaceous. Fls purple, to 16mm. Spring, summer, early autumn. Turk., Cyprus. 'Hopleys': to 75cm; fls large, strong pink, bracts large. 'Herrenhausen': upright, to 45cm; lvs and shoots flushed purple when young and during winter; fls pale lilac, in large clusters. Z8.

O. leptocladum Boiss. St. to 65cm, glab. Lvs to 1.7cm, cordate or ovate, glaucous. Fls 2 per whorl; bracts lanceolate 5mm; cor. pink, to 14mm. Autumn. Turk. Z8.

O. libanoticum Boiss. St. to 60cm, pubesc. at base. Lvs 1.2cm, ovate, obtuse. Fls in nodding spikes; bracts deep pink; cor. to 2cm, pink. Summer. Leb. Z8.

O. majorana L. SWEET MARJORAM; KNOTTED MARJORAM. Ann., bienn. or perenn. herb to 60cm. St. glab. or tomentose, red. Lvs to 2cm, ovate, grey, pubesc. Infl. a dense term. pan.; bracts grey-green, to 4mm; cor. white, mauve or pink, to 8mm. Late summer–autumn. Originally Medit. and Turk., now widespread escape in Eur. Z7.

O. majoricum Cambess. St. to 60cm, pubesc. Lvs to 2.5cm, ovate to lanceolate. Fls to 8mm, pink, in term. pan.; bracts over half length cor. SW Eur. Possibly the sterile result of *O. vulgare* ×*O. majorana*. Z7.

O. microphyllum (Benth.) Boiss. St. to 50cm. Lvs to 0.8cm, ovate, pubesc. Fls 5mm, purple, in lax terminal pan.; bracts 4mm, spathulate. Summer. Medit.

O. onites L. POT MARJORAM. Mound-forming shrublet to 60cm. St. red, pubesc. and warty. Lvs to 2.2cm, ovate, rounded to cordate at base, bright green, aromatic. Infl. term., corymbose; bracts to 3mm; cor. to 6mm, mauve or white. Late summer. Medit. 'Aureum': tall; lvs gold. Z8.

O. pseudo-onites Lindb. = *O. syriacum* var. *bevanii*.

O. rotundifolium Boiss. Subshrub to 30cm, spreading by rhiz. St. pubesc. Lvs to 2.5cm, suborbicular or cordate, stem-clasping, blue-grey. Infl. nodding, hop-like; bracts reniform to 25mm, bright pale green tinged purple-pink; cor. to 16mm, white or pale pink. Late summer, early autumn. Armenia, Georgia, Turk. Z8.

O. scabrum Boiss. & Heldr. Perenn. to 45cm. St. rhizomatous, then erect and glab. Lvs 3cm, ovate, margins scabrous. Fls pink in lax nodding pan.; bracts to 10mm, purple. S Greece (mts). ssp. *pulchrum* Boiss. & Heldr. Lf margin smooth. Z8.

O. sipyleum L. Subshrub to 80cm. St. tomentose at base. Lvs to 2.4cm, elliptic or cordate, usually glaucous. Fls to 11mm, pink, paired in spicules to 28mm. Turk. Z8.

O. syriacum L. var. *bevanii* (Holmes) Ietsw. Subshrub to 90cm. St. pubesc. Lvs to 3.5cm, ovate. Infl. paniculate; bracts obovate, 2.5mm; cor. 5mm. Late spring, early summer. Cyprus, Turk. Z8.

O. tournefortii Ait. = *O. calcaratum*.

O. vulgare L. WILD MARJORAM; OREGANO; POT MARJORAM. Rhizomatous, woody, branched perenn. herb to 90cm, strongly aromatic. Lvs to 4cm, round to ovate, entire or slightly toothed, spotted-glandular beneath. Infl. a loose pan. or corymb; bracts to 10mm, violet-purple or green; cor. purple, to 4mm. Late summer and autumn. Eur. 'Album': to 25cm, bushy; lvs light green; fls white. 'Aureum': to 30cm, spreading; lvs small, gold; fls lavender. 'Aureum Crispum': lvs golden, curly. 'Compactum': to 15cm, compact and cushion-forming; lvs small, round, dark green; fls pink tinted violet, profuse. 'Compactum Nanum': to 10cm, compact; lvs dark green, purple in winter; fls lilac. 'Gold Tip': lvs tipped in yellow. 'Heiderose': to 40cm, bushy, upright; fls pink. 'Heideturum': to 50cm; fls light pink. 'Nanum': dwarf, to 20cm; fls purple. 'Roseum': fls pink. 'Thumble's Variety': to 35cm; lvs large, pale yellow later yellow-green; fls soft white. 'Tracy's Yellow': vigorous; lvs gold. ssp. *vulgare*. Lvs and cal. not usually glandular-punctate, st. and lvs pilose, bracts partly purple, often glabrescent. Cor. pink. Medit., E to S China. ssp. *hirtum* (Link) Ietsw. Lvs and cal.

usually glandular-punctate, st. lvs and cal. densely hirsute, bracts green-hirsute, cor. white. Infl. usually compact, br. and spikes short. Greece, Turk., Aegean Is. ssp. *gracile* (K. Koch) lets. Lvs and cal. usually glandular-punctate, glabrescent to puberulent, lvs ± glaucous, bracts green, glabrescent. Infl. usually lax, br. and spikes slender. E Anatolia. ssp. *viride* (Boiss.) Hayek. Lvs and cal. not usually glandular-punctate, st. and lvs pilose, bracts green, rarely purple-tinged, often puberulent. Fls white or pale pink. N & C Turk. Z5.

O. cvs. 'Barbara Tingey': fls pink, drooping, bracts green. 'Bucklands': upright; fls large, pink, bracts flushed pink. 'Entedank': to 50cm, loosely bushy; lvs tinted blue; fls small, lilac-pink, late-flowering. late-flowering. 'Kent Beauty': fls small, pink to mauve, bracts pink. 'Kent Pride': to 15cm; fls green flushed purple.
→*Amaracus.*

Orihou *Pseudopanax colensoi.*

Orites R. Br. Proteaceae. 6 shrubs or trees. Lvs entire, dentate or lobed. Infl. a terminal or axill. spike; fls in pairs within each bract; bracts concave; perianth seg. usually free; fil. short. E Aus.

O. excelsa R. Br. PRICKLY ASH. Tall tree, to 30m. Lvs 15–20cm, juvenile lvs tinted red, deeply pinnate, prickly toothed, adult lvs simple. Fls white in 10cm axill. spikes. Late winter–early spring. E Aus. Z10.

O. lancifolia F. Muell. ALPINE ORITES. Spreading medium shrub to 1.5m. Lvs 3cm, oblong-lanceolate, thick. Fls creamy white, in erect, 5cm spikes. Summer. E Aus. Z9.

Orixa Thunb. Rutaceae. 1 decid. shrub to 3m; new growth aromatic, puberulous. Lvs 5–12cm, obovate, rhombic-ovate or elliptic, entire, puberulous. Infl. axill., solitary and racemose, 2–3cm; fls 4-merous, 1–5mm, green. Jap., Korea, China. Z6.
O. japonica Thunb. 'Variegata': lvs tinted silver, shading to a white edge.
→*Othera.*

Ormiscus Ecklon & C. Zeyh.
O. amplexicaulis (L. f.) Ecklon & C. Zeyh. = *Heliophila amplexicaulis.*

Ormocarpum P. Beauv. Leguminosae (Papilionoideae). 20 shrubs or small trees. Lvs imparipinnate or paripinnate, or with 1 lft only. Fls pea-like, solitary, or in short rac. or clusters. Trop. Asia, Afr., Mex., Carib. Z9.

O. sennoides DC. Shrub to 2m. Lvs ending in a long spine; lvfts in 7–10 pairs. Rac. loosely 3–7-fld; fls yellow. Summer. Carib. (St Thomas Is.)

O. trichocarpum (Taub.) Engl. Shrub or small tree to 4.5m. Lvs imparipinnate, bristly; lvfts in 7–13 pairs. Fls in clusters of 1–4 along the st., violet, cream, blue or mauve-pink, veined deep purple. Autumn. Uganda, Kenya, S Afr.

Ormosia Jackson. NECKLACE TREE; BEAD TREE. Leguminosae (Papilionoideae). Some 100 trees. Lvs usually imparipinnate. Fls pea-like in clustered rac. or, usually, in downy term. pan. Fr. oblong or ovoid, laterally compressed or turgid, fleshy, becoming leathery or woody; seeds circular, large, often red, or red and black. Trop. Asia, Amer., Madag. Z9.

O. acuta Vogel = *O. monosperma.*
O. calavensis Azaola in Blanco. Lvfts to 14cm, in 2–3 pairs, elliptic or elliptic-oblong, glab., leathery. Infl. a bushy, rusty-tomentose, corymbiform pan.; cor. dull violet or purple-white, to 1.8cm. Fr. *c*3cm, 1–2-seeded, glab., black; seeds about 8mm diam., red. Summer. Philipp., nat. in Flor.
O. coarctata Jackson. BARACARO; JUMBIE BEAD. Lvfts to 15cm, 5–11, oblong-elliptic, rusty-pubesc. Cor. 15mm; dark purple. Fr. 4cm, 1–3-seeded; seeds to 13mm, red and black. Guyana, Trin.
O. coccinea (Aubl.) Jackson. PANACOCO; AGUI. Lvfts to 11.5cm, in 3–5 pairs, ovate to oblong, thick, glossy above, main veins v. prominent beneath, sometimes hairy. Infl. a pan.; cor. to 1.5cm, dark purple. Fr. to 6cm, shining, black or dark brown, 1–4-seeded; seeds 15mm, scarlet with black spot. Amaz. Basin, Guyana.
O. emarginata (Hook. & Arn.) Benth. Lvfts to 7.5cm, mostly 5–7, obovate-oblong, glab., sometimes emarginate. Pan. small; fls to 13mm; cal. black in contrast to pale pet. Fr. to 5cm; seeds to 1cm, ovoid to elliptic, shiny, scarlet. Hong Kong.
O. glaberrima Wu = *O. emarginata.*
O. krugii Urban. BOIS NAN-NON; PALO PERONIA; PERONILA. Lvfts to 20cm, 5–9, suborbicular, obtuse or abruptly acuminate, sericeous beneath. Cor. to 1.5cm, dark violet. Fr. to 10cm, sericeous, brown; seeds to 13mm, 4–6, red sometimes spotted black.

Hispan., Puerto Rico, Lesser Antilles.
O. minor Vogel = *O. monosperma.*
O. monosperma Urban. NECKLACE TREE; SNAKEWOOD; CACONIER. Lfts 15–20cm, 7–9, oblong to obovate-oblong, slender-pointed; petiolules elliptic or elliptic-oblong, to 4mm. Infl. rusty-pubesc.; cor. to 2cm blue or purple. Fr. to 4cm, velutinous; seeds about 1.5cm, black or scarlet with black spot. Summer. Lesser Antilles, NE Venez.
O. panamensis Benth. PERONIL; CORONIL. Lfts 10×5cm, 5–7 pairs, elliptic-oblong, acuminate, pubesc. Rac. gold or tawny-pubesc.; cor. to 2cm, lilac. Fr. to 7×5cm, sericeous, tawny-brown; seeds to 17mm, 1–4, dark red. Panama.
O. stipitata Schery = *O. panamensis.*
→*Layia.*

Ornamental Cabbage *Brassica oleracea* cvs.
Ornamental Maize *Zea mays* cvs.
Ornamental Pepper *Capsicum anuum* cvs.
Ornamental Yam *Dioscorea discolor.*

Ornithidium Salisb. Orchidaceae. 20 epiphytic orchids. Rhiz. sometimes ascending and stem-like. Pbs with 1 apical lf scattered or clustered, enveloped by leafy sheaths, reduced or 0 in some sp. Fls solitary on clustered stalks borne basally, small; tep. free, incurved, spreading; lip erect, 3-lobed. Trop. Amer. Z10.
O. densum (Lindl.) Rchb. f. Pbs to 7cm, compressed, ovate-oblong. Lvs to 40cm, linear-oblong. Infl. to 5cm; fls grey to green-white tinged purple to red-brown; sep. to 9mm, elliptic-linear to elliptic-lanceolate; pet. to 7mm, elliptic-lanceolate; lip to 4mm, midlobe ovate to suborbicular, obtuse. Mex., Hond., Guat., Hond.
→*Maxillaria.*

Ornithocephalus Hook. Orchidaceae. 50 epiphytic orchids. Rhiz. concealed by overlapping lf sheaths. Pbs 0. Lvs sword-like, distichous, overlapping, arranged in a fan. Rac. lat.; fls small; sep. free, concave; pet. larger, concave; lip entire or trilobed, with a basal fleshy callus. Trop. Amer. Z10.
O. bicornis Lindl. Lvs to 7cm, lanceolate to oblong-lanceolate, acute or apiculate, rigid. Infl. seldom exceeding lvs, few- to many-fld; peduncle flexuous, densely lanuginose; fls to 0.5cm diam., white-green or white-yellow. Guat., Hond., Panama, Costa Rica.
O. bonplandii Rchb. f. Lvs to 2cm, fleshy, lanceolate or oblong-lanceolate, acute. Infl. to 4cm, few-fld; peduncle minutely denticulate; fls to 1cm diam., pale green, lip white. Venez., Colomb.
O. gladiatus Hook. Lvs to 6cm, oblanceolate to oblong, acute to acuminate. Infl. to 7cm, suberect to arching, few to several-fld; peduncle glab., narrowly winged; fls to 0.8cm diam., pale cream-green or white marked green. C Amer. to Braz., Peru, Boliv.
O. grandiflorus Lindl. Lvs to 15cm, few, narrowly oblong, obtuse. Infl. surpassing lvs, arching, densely many-fld; fls to 1.8cm diam., white, with bright green marks in centre. Braz.
O. inflexus Lindl. = *O. gladiatus.*
O. iridifolius Rchb. f. Lvs to 8.5cm, fleshy, linear-ensiform, acute or acuminate. Infl. to 8cm, spreading, loosely many-fld; peduncle slender, fractiflex, winged; fls to 0.8cm diam., white. Mex., Guat.
O. myrticola Lindl. Lvs to 25cm, narrowly linear-lanceolate to ligulate-lanceolate, falcate, acute or acuminate. Infl. to 8cm, ascending, arching, densely many-fld; peduncle glandular-pubesc.; fls to 0.8cm diam., lemon-scented, glandular-pubesc., white and green, pet. almost transparent. Braz., Boliv.
O. navicularis Barb. Rodr. = *Zygostates lunata.*
O. planifolius Rchb. f. = *Dipteranthus planifolius.*

Ornithogalum L. Liliaceae (Hyacinthaceae). Some 80 bulbous perenn. herbs. Lvs linear to lanceolate or obovate, sometimes with a silver-white median stripe. Infl. a scapose rac. or corymb, pyramidal to subcylindric; bracts usually conspicuous; tep. 6, equal or unequal in 2 distinct whorls; sta. 6, fil. flattened; ovary superior, cylindric to spherical, usually yellow-green; style term. S Afr., Medit.
O. apertum (Verdoorn) Oberm. Lvs 10–20, glaucous, narrow, tightly spiralled and coiled. Scape to 20cm; tep. white or yellow, with broad green central band. S Afr. (SW Cape). Z9.
O. arabicum L. Lvs to 60cm, broadly linear, ± erect, dark green, thickly textured. Scape 30–80cm; rac. cylindric to subspherical, fls fragrant; tep. 1.5–3.2cm, white or cream; ovary black or purple-black. Medit. The name *O. çorymbosum* is usually applied to exceptionally floriferous specimens, bearing larger fls in corymbose rac. Z9.
O. aurantiacum Bak. = *O. multifolium.*
O. aureum Curtis = *O. dubium.*

O. balansae Boiss. = O. oligophyllum.

O. caudatum Ait. = O. longibracteatum.

O. conicum Jacq.   V. similar to O. thyrsoides but scapes 40–100cm, lvs with smooth margins. Early spring. S Afr. (Cape Prov.). Z9.

O. corymbosum Ruiz & Pav. = O. arabicum.

O. dichotomum Labill. = Thysanotus dichotomus.

O. dubium Houtt.   Lvs to 10cm, lanceolate to ovate-lanceolate, yellow-green, margins hairy. Scape to 30cm; rac. crowded, corymbose, cylindric to subspherical; tep. 1.2cm, orange, red, yellow or white, often tinged green or brown at base within. Winter–spring. S Afr. (Cape Prov.). Z9.

O. flavescens Lam. = O. pyrenaicum.

O. lacteum Jacq. = O. conicum.

O. longibracteatum Jacq. SEA ONION; FALSE SEA ONION; GERMAN ONION.   Lvs to 60cm, strap-shaped, long-acuminate, fleshy, flaccid, pale green. Scapes 1–1.5m; rac. triangular to cylindric; bracts far exceeding fls; tep. to 9mm, white, outside with a green stripe. S Afr. (Cape Prov., Natal). Z9.

O. maculatum Jacq. SNAKE FLOWER.   Lvs to 15cm, fleshy, blue-green. Scape 10–50cm; infl. to 8-fld; tep. yellow or orange, outer whorl often with tips blotched black or brown. Spring. S Afr. Z9.

O. miniatum Jacq. = O. dubium.

O. montanum Cyr.   Lvs linear, 10–15cm, pale green usually with a white line above. Scape to 60cm, infl. somewhat corymbose, cylindric, fls drooping; tep. 2–3cm, translucent white, outside with a broad green stripe. Eur. (Balk., It.), SW Asia. Z6.

O. multifolium Bak.   Lvs to 7cm, c10, slender, terete, glab., somewhat twisted. Scape to 25cm, usually c15cm; infl. 5–10-fld; fls fragrant, bright yellow to orange yellow. Spring. S Afr. (Cape Penins.).

O. narbonense L.   Lvs to 90cm, linear. Scape to 90cm; fls to 5cm diam. in loose, many-fld rac.; tep. keeled, milk white, midvein green. cf. O. pyramidale. Spring. Medit., Cauc., NW Iran. Z7.

O. nutans L.   Lvs 30–40cm, lorate, rather limp, pale green, with a white line above. Scapes to 60cm; rac. cylindric, 1-sided; fls nodding; tep. 2–3cm, translucent, white, broadly striped green outside. Spring. Eur., SW Asia, nat. in E US. Z6.

O. oligophyllum Clarke.   Lvs to 15cm, linear-lanceolate to narrowly obovate, broad and blunt at apex, somewhat glaucous. Rac. corymbose; tep. 1–1.6cm, white to ivory edged pure white with a broad yellow-green stripe outside. Spring. Balk., Turk., Georgia. Z6.

O. orthophyllum Ten.   Similar to O. umbellatum but not producing bulblets; pedicels spreading to ascending (not horizontal) in fr. Spring. S & C Eur. to N Iran. Z6.

O. pruinosum F.M. Leighton. CHINCHERINCHEE.   Lvs to 17cm, to 6, deep blue-green. Scape to 35cm, occas. to 60cm; infl. a dense, many-fld spike, usually 35cm; fls white, fragrant. S Afr. (Namaqualand, SW Cape). Z9.

O. pyramidale L.   Lvs to 45cm, glossy, glaucous. Scape 30–120cm; rac. cylindric to pyramidal; tep. 1.1–1.5cm, translucent white with a green stripe outside. Spring. C Eur., Balk., Rom. Z6.

O. pyrenaicum L. BATH ASPARAGUS; PRUSSIAN ASPARAGUS; STAR OF BETHLEHEM.   Close to O. pyramidale but smaller and more delicate; tep. 0.9–1.3cm, pale yellow with a narrow green stripe outside. Spring. Eur., W & S Turk., Cauc. Z6.

O. saundersiae Bak. GIANT CHINCHERINCHEE.   Lvs 60cm, erect to flaccid, lorate. Scape 30–100cm; rac. corymbose, pyramidal; tep. 1–1.5cm, white or cream; ovary black or green-black. Early spring. S Afr. Z9.

O. tenuifolium Guss. = O. orthophyllum.

O. thyrsoides Jacq. CHINCHERINCHEE; WONDER FLOWER.   Lvs to 30cm, linear to narrow-lanceolate, margins ciliate. Rac. corymbose, pyramidal to subspherical; tep. 1–2cm, translucent white to ivory tinted bronze or green at base. Spring–early summer. S Afr. (Cape Prov.). 'Album': fls snow white, with a somewhat darker 'eye' crowded in showy rac. 'Aureum': fls topaz to golden. 'Flavescens': fls golden. 'Flavissimum': fls golden to ochre. Z9.

O. umbellatum L. STAR OF BETHLEHEM.   Lvs to 30cm, linear, tapering, with a broad white midvein. Rac. broad corymbose; tep. 1.5–2.2cm, lustrous white with a green stripe outside. Spring. Eur., N Afr., Middle E. Z5.

Ornithophora Barb. Rodr. Orchidaceae.   2 dwarf epiphytic orchids. Pbs sited along slender rhiz., compressed ovoid-pyriform, apex 2-leaved; sheaths 1–2, leafy. Rac. slender, basal, erect, lax; tep. oblong-lanceolate, reflexed to spreading; lip trilobed, callus rigid. Braz. Z10.

O. radicans (Lind. & Rchb. f.) Garay & Pabst.   Lvs linear-grassy, 10–18cm. Infl. 7–15cm; fls to 0.8cm diam., white-green or green-yellow, lip white, callus yellow.

→Sigmatostalix.

OROBANCHACEAE Vent. 17/230. Aeginetia, Orobanche.

Orobanche L. BROOMRAPE. Orobanchaceae.   150 ann. and perenn. herbs, root parasites lacking chlorophyll. Aerial st. erect, scaly. Fls in coompact, term. spikes; cal. 2-lipped, 4–5-toothed; cor. tubular, curved, 2-lipped, lower lip 3-lobed, upper lip 2-lobed. Temp. regions, notably Eur. Z6.

O. alba Stephan ex Willd. THYME BROOMRAPE.   St. 8–35cm, stout, dull red, tinted ochre. Bracts similar in colour to st., glandular-pubesc. Fls to 2cm, scented of cloves, pale yellow tinted red to deep mauve-red. Eur.

O. arenaria auct. ex Wallr. = O. purpurea.

O. caerulea Vill. = O. purpurea.

O. epithymum DC. = O. alba.

O. flava Mart. YELLOW BROOMRAPE.   St. 15–60cm, stout, dull yellow-brown. Bracts same colour as st., sparse, slender. Fls to 2cm, ochre, the upper lip stained red-brown. Eur.

O. purpurea Jacq. PURPLE BROOMRAPE.   St. 15–45cm, stout, blue-grey, glandular-pubesc. above, sparsely slender-scaly below. Fls to 3cm, dull violet, cream to yellow at base of cor. Eur.

O. rubra Sm. = O. alba.

Orobus L.

O. cyaneus Steven = Lathyrus cyaneus.

O. gmelinii Fisch. ex DC. = Lathyrus gmelinii.

O. luteus L. = Lathyrus gmelinii.

O. myrtifolius (Muhlenb.) Hall = Lathyrus palustris.

O. myrtifolius Alef. = Lathyrus palustris.

O. niger L. = Lathyrus niger.

O. roseus (Steven) Ledeb. = Lathyrus roseus.

O. venetus Mill. = Lathyrus venetus.

O. vernus L. = Lathyrus vernus.

Orontium L. GOLDEN CLUB. Araceae.   1 aquatic, perenn. herb. Rhiz. thick. Lvs to 25×8cm, oblong to narrow-elliptic, submerged, aerial, or floating, with thick glaucous silvering above, often purple-tinted beneath; petiole to 35cm. Spathe v. small, soon withering; spadix to 18cm, narrowly cylindric, bright yellow, merging below into long, white stalk, breaking the surface of the water. E US. Z7.

O. aquaticum L.

Orostachys (DC.) Fisch. Crassulaceae.   10 bienn. succulent herbs. Lvs fleshy, in a dense hemispherical to globose basal rosette giving rise to an erect flowering st. with smaller, narrower lvs. Fls racemose; sep. 5, fleshy, around half pet. length; pet. 5, yellow, green or white, lanceolate, spreading; sta. 10. N Asia to Eur. Z7 unless specified.

O. aggregata (Mak.) Hara.   Similar to O. iwarenge except lvs only 20–40mm, green, tips rounded. Jap.

O. chanetii (Lév.) A. Berger.   Similar to O. fimbriata except lvs linear with a small cartilaginous spine; infl. somewhat pyramidal, to 20cm; pet. to 10mm, white-pink. Autumn. China.

O. erubescens (Maxim.) Ohwi.   To 25cm. Lvs 15–30mm, spathulate, fleshy, spine-tipped, sparsely toothed, cartilaginous. Rac. many-fld; pet. 6–8mm; anth. red turning purple. Autumn. Jap., Korea, N China.

O. fimbriata (Turcz.) A. Berger.   To 15cm. Lvs 25mm, oblong, tip cartilaginous with a long spine. Rac. dense, branched; pet. 5–6mm, tinged red. Tibet, Mong., Jap., China.

O. furusei Ohwi.   Perenn. To 10cm. Lvs 10–20mm, fleshy, obovate, flat. Rac. many-fld; pet. 4.5–5mm, pale green. Autumn. Jap.

O. iwarenge (Mak.) Hara.   To 45cm. Lvs 30–70mm, glaucous, spathulate-oblong, blunt. Rac. many-fld; 5–7mm, white. Autumn. China. Z6.

O. japonica A. Berger = O. erubescens.

O. malacophylla (Pall.) Fisch.   Lvs blunt, lanceolate-oblong or elliptic. Rac. elongated, many-fld, occas. branched; bracts covering fls; pet. 4–6mm, pale green-yellow. Late summer. Mong., China, Jap. Z6.

O. spinosa (L.) C.A. Mey.   To 35cm. Lvs 15–25mm, oblong, apical spine white, 2–4mm, margin white. Rac. many-fld, compact; pet. 6–9mm, yellow-green. E Russia to N & C Asia. Z4.

→Cotyledon, Sedum and Umbilicus.

Oroxylum Vent. MIDNIGHT HORROR; TREE OF DAMOCLES; KAMPONG; KI TONG TOKANG. Bignoniaceae.   1 glab., spreading, semi-decid. tree, 6–27m. Lvs 2–4-pinnate 0.5–2m; lfts 4–15cm, ovate to oblong. Fls nocturnal, foetid, in term. erect rac., 0.25–1.5m; pedicels 2–4cm; cal. leathery becoming woody, truncate or split, 2–4cm, brown-purple; cor. purple-red to brown outside, yellow to pink inside, 7–10cm, lobes crisped or crenate, glandular-hairy inside. Fr. a pendent capsule,

45–120×6–10cm, becoming black. Sri Lanka through Himal. to SE Asia and China. Z10.

O. flavum Rehd. = *Radermachera pentandra*.

O. indicum (L.) Kurz. TREE OF DAMOCLES.

→*Arthrophyllum*, *Calosanthes* and *Spathodea*.

Oroya Britt. & Rose. Cactaceae. 2 low-growing cacti; st. simple or offsetting, flattened-globose to v. short cylindric, many-ribbed; areoles elongate; spines pectinate. Fl. subapical, shortly funnelform or campanulate, tube v. short, fil. and style not exserted. Fr. obovoid, slightly fleshy. Peru.

O. borchersii (Boed.) Backeb. Resembling *O. peruviana*, but st. broader, fl. wholly yellow-green to yellow. N Peru. Z9.

O. gibbosa Ritter = *O. peruviana*.

O. neoperuviana Backeb. = *O. peruviana*.

O. peruviana (Schum.) Britt. & Rose. St. to 40×20cm, with up to 35 ribs; areoles to 1.5cm; central spines to c2cm, radial spines pectinate, to 1.5cm. Fl. 1.5–3cm, pale to deep pink-red, usually yellow inside. Mts of C Peru. Z9.

Orphanidesia Boiss.

O. gaultherioides Boiss. & Bal. = *Epigaea gaultherioides*.

Orphium E. Mey. Gentianaceae. 1 slightly downy shrub erect to 60cm. Lvs to 5cm, linear to oblong, thick. Fls solitary or clustered, term. or in upper axils; cal. 1.5cm, tubular; cor. to 4cm diam., pink to red, subrotate, tube short, lobes 5, rounded, mucronulate. S Afr. Z9.

O. frutescens (L.) E. Mey.

→*Chironia*.

Orpine *Hylotelephium telephium*.

Ortegocactus Alexander. Cactaceae. 1 low-growing cactus; st. 3–4cm diam., clustering, globose to short-cylindric, grey-green; tubercles low, rhomboid; spines, at least the tip, almost black; central spine 1, 4–5mm, radial spines 7–8, 5–10mm. Fls axill., funnelform, 2–3×1.8–2.5cm; pericarpel immersed in areolar wool; tube short, pale green; tep. yellow, or outermost tinged purple. Fr. globose-ellipsoid, dull red. S Mex.

O. macdougallii Alexander. S Mex. Z9.

Orthilia Raf. Pyrolaceae. 1 shrubby, perenn., everg., rhizomatous herb to 20cm. Lvs 1.5–6cm, whorled, thinly coriaceous, ovate-elliptic, entire to crenulate. Rac. secund, drooping, papillose, 8–15-fld; bracts membranous, 3–5mm; fls campanulate, pale green to ivory; styles exserted. Summer. N temp. regions. Z5.

O. secunda (L.) House.

→*Pyrola*.

Orthiopteris Copel.

O. inaequalis (Kunze) Copel. = *Saccoloma inaequale*.

Orthocarpus Nutt. Scrophulariaceae. Some 27 semi-parasitic annuals. St. erect, leafy. Spike term., bracteate; cal. 2-lobed, campanulate; cor., upper lip entire, lower lip 3-lobed. Summer. W US, S Amer. Z9.

O. erianthus Benth. To 30cm. Lvs incised at apex. Cor. tube pubesc., pale yellow. W US. var. *roseus* A. Gray. Cor. rose to cream, becoming rose-purple. W US.

O. imbricatus Torr. ex S. Wats. To 30cm. Lvs to linear-lanceolate or linear. Infl. bracts entire, ovate, closely overlapping, purple-tipped; cor. rose-purple, lower lip tipped white. SW US.

O. lithospermoides Benth. CREAM SACS. 25–60cm. Lvs pubesc., entire, lanceolate, upper lvs pinnate. Infl. bracts palmatifid; cor. tube pale yellow to cream, lower lip with 2 purple blotches. SW US.

O. purpurascens Benth. ESCOBITA. To 45cm, purple-flushed. Lvs linear to pinnatifid, often tinged brown. Infl. bracts tipped rose-purple; cor. purple or crimson, tip of lower lip white with purple and (or) yellow spots or markings. SW US.

O. tenuifolius (Pursh) Benth. To 30cm. Lvs lanceolate, entire or with 3–5 thread-like seg. Infl. bracts to 1.5cm, elliptic, entire or with side lobes, tipped purple; cor. yellow, purple-tipped or wholly purple, minutely pubesc. SW US.

→*Triphysaria*.

Orthophytum Beer. Bromeliaceae. 17 semi-succulent, stoloniferous mat-forming perenn. herbs. Lvs forming a rosette; sheaths large, clasping; blades serrate, narrowly triangular, long-attenuate, softly spiny. Infl. usually bipinnate, with several dense heads, scapose or sunken in centre of rosette; bracts leafy. E Braz. Z9.

O. navoides (L.B. Sm.) L.B. Sm. Whole plant red at floral maturity. Lvs 30cm, sparsely scaly, fairly densely toothed,

spines 1mm, upward-curving. Infl. densely capitate, sunk into rosette centre; fls white.

O. saxicola (Ule) L.B. Sm. Lvs 3–6cm, suberect, pale green, fleshy and leathery, laxly toothed, with recurved 2–3mm spines. Infl. few-fld, compact, stemless or on a short scape; fls white.

O. vagans M.B. Fost. Lvs to 12cm, green, deeply channelled, scaly beneath, toothed, spines 2mm. Infl. dense, stemless, bracts bright red or orange; fls apple-green.

Orthrosanthus Sweet. Iridaceae. 7 everg. perenn. herbs. Rhiz. short, woody. Lvs narrowly ensiform to linear, equitant, basal, or 1–2 reduced on flowering st. Fls 2 to many per spathe in clusters forming a loose pan. on slender erect stalk, ephemeral; perianth radially symmetric, tube short, seg. ovate or oblong, spreading. Trop. Amer., Aus. Z9.

O. chimboracensis (HBK) Bak. Basal lvs to 40×1cm, margins minutely toothed, rough to the touch. Fls lavender-flue, to 4cm diam., in a loose pan. composed of 3–4-fld clusters. Summer. Mex. to Peru.

O. multiflorus Sweet. Basal lvs to 45×0.4cm, margins smooth. Fls pale blue with dark midveins, 3–4cm diam. in 5–8-fld clusters forming a narrow pan. Spring–summer. SW Aus.

O. ocisapungum Ruiz. ex Diels = *O. chimboracensis*.

→*Sisyrinchium*.

Orychophragmus Bunge. Cruciferae. 2 ann. or bienn. herbs. St. simple or branching at base. Lvs thin, lyrate, pinnatifid, toothed, st. lvs entire. Fls in clustes; sep. 4, linear; pet. 4, violet, long-clawed, broadly obovate. C Asia, China. Z7.

O. violaceus (L.) Schultz. St. erect to 15cm. Pet. to 30mm, violet. China.

Oryza L. RICE. Gramineae. Some 19 ann. or perenn. rhizomatous grasses. St. flimsy to robust. Lvs linear, flat; ligules subcoriaceous to papery. Infl. a pan.; spikelets laterally compressed, 3-fld. Trop. Asia, Afr. Z10.

O. sativa L. RICE. Ann., to 180cm. St. arching. Lvs elongate, to 150×2.5cm. Pan. arching to pendent, to 45cm; spikelets to 1cm; paler scabrous mucronate to long-awned, enclosing grain. SE Asia. 'Nigrescens': lvs dark purple. var. *rufipogon* (Griff.) Watt. Awns long, red; ornamental.

Oryzopsis Michx. RICE GRASS. Gramineae. 35 perenn. grasses. St. clumped. Lvs flat to rolled. Infl. paniculate; spikelets stipitate, 1-fld. N Hemis., temp. and subtrop. Z8.

O. hymenoides (Roem. & Schult.) Ricker. SILKGRASS; INDIAN MILLET. To 60cm. Lvs slender, margins inrolled. Pan. to 15cm, br. spreading. SW US, N Mex.

O. miliacea (L.) Asch. & Schweinf. SMILO GRASS. To 1.5m. Lvs flat, smooth. Pan. linear to oblong, pendent, to 30cm, sometimes tinged purple. Summer–autumn. Medit.

→*Milium* and *Piptantherum*.

Osage Orange *Maclura*.

Osbeckia L. Melastomataceae. 40 herbs, subshrubs and shrubs, usually erect and bristly hairy. Lvs somewhat leathery, 3–7-veined. Fls term., solitary or in loose heads or pan.; cal. scaly or hairy; pet. 5, rarely 4, obovate, often ciliate. SE Asia, China, Jap., Aus., some spp. in Afr. Z9.

O. chinensis L. Shrub, 30–60cm. Lvs lanceolate-oblong, 3-veined, hispidulous, slightly toothed. Fls purple, in few-fld term. cymes; pet. long-acuminate. Summer. China.

O. glauca Benth. Shrub, about 60cm. Lvs elliptic, softly hairy, 3–5-veined. Fls red or purple in a term. pseudoraceme. Summer. India.

O. nepalensis Hook. Shrub to 35cm, branched. Lvs lanceolate, often spotted brown. Fls large, purple-rose, in term. and axill. pan. or corymbs. Early summer. Nepal. 'Albiflora': fls white.

O. parvifolia Arn. Shrub, 30–60cm. Lvs ovate, 3-veined, strigose. Fls large, in threes, rose. Summer. Sri Lanka.

O. rostrata D. Don. Shrub; st. terete. Lvs oblong-lanceolate, slender-pointed, bullate, subsessile. Fls in term. cymes, rose-pink; anth. long, curved, exserted. Bengal.

O. rubicunda Arn.. Shrub. Lvs oblong, acute. Fls 5cm across, term., solitary or in clusters, deep purple. Sri Lanka.

O. stellata Wallich. Shrub, 90–180cm. Lvs 6–15cm, thin, somewhat hispidulous, 5-veined, long-acuminate. Fls lilac-red, clustered in term., few-fld cymes. Summer. India to China.

O. wightiana Benth. Erect shrub; st. hairy. Lvs ovate, small, hairy. Fls large, purple, in close heads. India.

O. yunnanensis Franch. ex Craib. Shrub, 30–90cm. Lvs 5.5–9cm, ovate to oblong-ovate, sparsely bristly; stalk tinged red. Fls in a few-fld pan. and solitary in upper axils, bright magenta. W China.

O. zeylanica Ker-Gawl. = *O. parvifolia*.

Oscularia Schwantes.
O. caulescens (Mill.) Schwantes. = *Lampranthus deltoides*.
O. pedunculata (N.E. Br.) Schwantes = *Lampranthus deltoides*.
O. deltata Schwantes = *Lampranthus deltoides*.
O. deltoides (L.) Schwantes = *Lampranthus deltoides*.

Oshima Cherry *Prunus speciosa*.
Osier *Salix*.

Osmanthus Lour. DEVILWOOD; SWEET OLIVE; CHINESE HOLLY. Oleaceae. 30 everg. shrubs or small trees. Lvs leathery, dark, glossy above, spotted beneath with numerous gland. depressions. Fls to 1cm, usually smaller, clustered in lf axils or in term. pan., usually fragrant; cal. 4-toothed; cor. bell-shaped to tubular, limb 4-lobed; sta. 2. Fr. a drupe, dark blue to purple. S US, Middle E, E Asia.
O. americanus (L.) A. Gray DEVILWOOD. Shrub or small tree to 10m. Lvs to 20cm, elliptic to lanceolate, entire, glossy dark green, coriaceous. Fls fragrant, cream to white in short axill. pan. Fr. dark blue. Spring. SE US. Z9.
O. aquifolium Sieb. & Zucc. = *O. heterophyllus*.
O. armatus Diels. Shrub, 2–4m. Young growth densely pubesc. Lvs 7–14cm, oblong-ovate, spiny, strongly toothed, cordate at base, sometimes entire. Fls off-white, clustered in lf axils. Fr. deep violet, to 2cm. Autumn. W China. Z7.
O. aurantiacus (Mak.) Nak. = *O. fragrans* f. *aurantiacus*.
O. ×burkwoodii (Burk. & Skipw. P. Green. (*O. delavayi* ×*O. decorus*.) Compact shrub to 2m. Lvs 2–4cm, ovate-elliptic, serrate. Fls clustered in axils, white, fragrant. Late spring. Z6.
O. decorus (Boiss. & Bal.) Kasapl. Broad shrub, to 3m. Lvs to 12cm entire, oblong-acuminate, yellow beneath. Fls white in small clusters. Fr. to 1.5cm, blue-black. Spring. Cauc., Lazistan. 'Baki Kasapligil': slow-growing, more hardy, lvs narrower. Z7.
O. delavayi Franch. Stocky shrub to 2m. Lvs to 3cm, ovate, finely toothed. Fls clustered in axils or term., white, sweetly fragrant. Spring. W China. Z7. 'Latifolius': taller; lvs broader, rounded.
O. forrestii Rehd. = *O. yunnanensis*.
O. ×fortunei Carr. (*O. fragrans* ×*O. heterophyllus*.) Expansive shrub, to 3m. Lvs to 10cm, oval, acuminate, teeth to 10, large, triangular or lvs entire. Fls white, fragrant, to 10 at axils. Late summer. 'Variegatus': slow-growing; lvs variegated cream. Z7.
O. fragrans Lour. FRAGRANT OLIVE; SWEET TEA. Shrub or small tree to 12m. Lvs to 10cm, oblong-lanceolate, entire or finely toothed. Fls white, solitary or few in stalked clusters highly fragrant. Summer. Himal., Jap., China. f. *aurantiacus* (Mak.) P. Green. Lvs entire; fls orange. Z9.
O. heterophyllus (G. Don) P. Green. HOLLY OLIVE; CHINESE HOLLY; FALSE HOLLY. Erect dense shrub to 5m. Lvs to 6cm, elliptic-oblong entire or with large lobe-like teeth, both forms found together. Fls white, fragrant. Fr. 12mm, blue. Late summer. Jap., Taiwan. 'Argenteomarginatus' = 'Variegatus'. Aureomarginatus ('Aureus'): lvs bordered yellow. 'Goshiki': compact, erect; lvs thorny, cream and bronze variegated, young growth rose pink. 'Gulftide': dense in habit; lvs slightly tortuous, teeth sharp. 'Myrtifolius': lvs ovate, entire. 'Purpureus': new growth purple-red. 'Rotundifolius': lvs obovate, undulate, entire; slow-growing. 'Sasaba': lvs deeply cut into many spiny lobes. 'Variegatus': lf margins cream-white. Z6.
O. ilicifolius (Hassk.) hort. ex Carr. = *O. heterophyllus*.
O. rehderianus Hand.-Mazz. = *O. yunnanensis*.
O. serrulatus Rehd. Shrub, to 3m. Young growth finely pubesc.; lvs resemble *O. yunnanensis*, but broader with finer, forward-pointing teeth or sometimes entire. Fl. white. Spring. W China. Z8.
O. suavis King ex C.B. Clarke. Resembles *O. delavayi*, but lvs larger. Shrub or small tree to 3m. Young growth downy. Lvs to 6cm, oblong-lanceolate, finely crenate. Fls white, in axils and term. Himal. to Yunnan. Z9.
O. yunnanensis (Franch.) P. Green. Similar to *O. serrulatus* but with longer, more spiny teeth. Tall shrub to 5m. Young growth glab., yellow-grey. Lvs to 20cm, ovate-lanceolate, narrow-acuminate, spotted black beneath with to 30 sharp teeth on either side or entire. Fls waxy, off-white to light yellow, in axill. clusters, v. fragrant. Fr. to 15mm, dark purple, pruinose. W China. Z7.
→×*Osmarea* and *Phillyrea*.

×Osmarea Burkw. & Skipw.
× *O. burkwoodii* Burkw. & Skipw. = *Osmanthus* ×*burkwoodii*.

Osmaronia Greene.
O. cerasiformis = *Oemleria cerasiformis*.

Osmia Schultz-Bip.
O. odorata (L.) Schultz-Bip. = *Chromolaena odorata*.

Osmoglossum Schltr. Orchidaceae. 7 epiphytic orchids similar in habit to *Odontoglossum*. Fls fleshy, white, often tinged purple; tep. obovate to oblong-elliptic, usually concave; lip sessile, entire, callus fleshy 3-keeled. Mex., Guat., El Salvador, Hond., Costa Rica. Z10.
O. anceps Schltr. = *O. egertonii*.
O. convallarioides Schltr. Infl. to 40cm, erect, few-fld; fls to 1.5cm diam., fragrant, white, sometimes tinged pink or lavender; lip to 1×0.8cm, often spotted purple-red, obovate, apex subacute to obtuse, concave, callus yellow-orange. Spring. Mex., Guat., Hond., Costa Rica.
O. egertonii (Lindl.) Schltr. Infl. erect, to 40cm, 5–10-fld; fls to 2cm diam., white marked lilac; lip to 1.2×1cm, oblong-subquadrate or oblong-elliptic, apiculate, concave; callus yellow spotted brown. Usually spring. Mex., Guat., Hond., Costa Rica.
O. pulchellum (Batem. ex Lindl.) Schltr. LILY OF THE VALLEY ORCHID. Infl. to 50cm, erect or slightly pendent, 3–10-fld; fls to 3cm diam., fragrant, long-lived; sep. and pet. white above, tinted rose below; lip to 2×1cm, white, pointing upwards, pandurate, apex recurved, margins crisped; callus yellow spotted red. Autumn–winter. Mex., Guat., El Salvador.
→*Odontoglossum* and *Oncidium*.

Osmorhiza Raf. SWEET CICELY; SWEET JARVIL. Umbelliferae. 10 aromatic perenn. herbs, with thick, fleshy roots. Lvs 2–3-ternate or 2-pinnate, seg. serrate to pinnatifid; petioles sheathing. Umbels compound; involucral bracts few or 0; involucel of several, narrow bracteoles, or 0; pet. spathulate to obovate. Americas, Asia. Z6.
O. brachypoda Torr. To 80cm, most parts pubesc. Lvs 8–25cm, ternate-pinnate, seg. ovate, 2–6cm, coarsely serrate to deeply pinnatifid; petiole to 20cm. Rays 2–5 per umbel, 2.5–10cm; bracts often 0; bracteoles ciliate, linear; fls green-yellow. US (Calif., Ariz.).
O. brevistylis DC. = *O. claytonii*.
O. chilensis Hook. & Arn. 30–100cm, hispid. Lvs 5–15cm, 2-ternate, seg. ovate-lanceolate to orbicular, obtuse or acute, 2–6cm, hispid, serrate, incised or lobed; petiole to 16cm. Rays 3–8, per umbel; involucre and involucel 0; fls green-white occas. tinged pink. E & W US, S Amer.
O. claytonii (Michx.) C.B. Clarke. WOOLLY SWEET CICELY; SWEET JARVIL. To 1m, hairy. Lvs 10–30cm, ternate-pinnate, pubesc., seg. ovate to lanceolate, 3–7cm; petiole 5–12cm. Rays 3–5 per umbel, 1.5–8cm; bracts usually 0; bracteoles several, reflexed; fls white. E N Amer.
O. longistylis (Torr.) DC. SMOOTH SWEET CICELY; ANISEROOT. To 1m. Lvs 8–25cm, 2-ternate or ternate-pinnate, seg. serrate, cut or deeply pinnatifid, ovate, 3–10cm, hirtellous; petioles 5–16cm. Rays 3–6 per umbel, to 5cm; bracts 1 to several, ciliate; bracteoles several; fls white. N Amer.
O. occidentalis (Nutt.) Torr. To 120cm. Lvs 10–20cm, 2-pinnate, seg. ovate to oblong-lanceolate, 2–10cm, serrate and incised or lobed; petiole 5–30cm. Rays 5–12 per umbel, 2–13cm; involucre and involucel often 0; fls yellow to green-yellow. W N Amer.

Osmoxylon Miq. Araliaceae. c50 unarmed, everg. shrubs and trees. Lvs simple, lobed or digitately compound, bases sometimes with ring or spirally arranged fringe of appendages; stipular ligules also present. Infl. terminal, umbelliform, generally 2× compound, pet. 4–8, ± united, the lower part tubular; sta. 4–30. Fr. drupaceous. Borneo and Taiwan to Micronesia. Z10.
O. eminens (Bull) Philipson. Tree to 12m; br. few, stout. Lvs in term. rosettes, glabrescent; petiole to 1m; blade to 60cm dark glossy green above; lobes 9–19, lanceolate to oblong, lorate to pinnatisect, sometimes 3-parted, coarsely toothed. Infl. stout, hairy, 40cm diam.; primary rays dull red-brown; fls light orange, in heads to 2cm diam. Fr. to 1cm, indigo-black. Micronesia; Philipp. Z10.
→*Boerlagiodendron* and *Trevesia*.

Osmunda L. FLOWERING FERN. Osmundaceae. 12 terrestrial ferns; rhiz. buried or exposed and trunk-like. Fronds in large crowns, bipinnate or bipinnatifid, richly coloured in fall. Sori on strongly contracted fertile pinnules, either separate and gathered in 'panicles' on entirely fertile fronds or found in the middle or towards the end of sterile fronds. Temp. & Trop. E Asia, N & S Amer.
O. banksiifolia (Presl) Kuhn. Rhiz. erect, stout, sparsely ferruginous-lanate when young; stipes winged near base, lustrous brown. Fronds light green, 1–1.5cm; pinnate; pinnae in 10–20 pairs, 15–25×1–2cm, linear-lanceolate, acuminate, dentate, lustrous, glab., margins thickened, tinged white; fertile pinnae 7–10cm, central, linear-cylindric, dark brown. E Asia.

Z10.

O. cervina L. = *Olfersia cervina*.

O. cinnamonea L. CINNAMON FERN; FIDDLEHEADS; BUCKHORN. Whole plant densely ferruginous-tomentose at first; stipes of sterile fronds 30–45cm, of fertile fronds shorter. Sterile fronds 60–90cm, ppinnate, pinnae 8–10×2–2.5cm, ligulate-lanceolate, cut almost to rachis; fertile fronds distinct much smaller, becoming cinnamon brown, pinnae lanceolate. N & S Amer., W Indies, E Asia. Z3.

O. claytonia L. INTERRUPTED FERN. Foliage pink-tomentose when young. Fronds 30–60cm, pinnate to pinnatifid; sterile pinnae 10–15×2.5cm, lanceolate, cut almost to rachis; fertile pinnae central, much smaller pinnules dense, cylindric. N Amer., Himal., China. Z3.

O. japonica Thunb. Rhiz. ascending, short, stout, cinnamon-brown to black lanate when young; stipes winged at base. Fronds to 1m, bipinnate; pinnae 20–30cm, oblong-ovate; pinnules 4–10×1–2.5cm, oblong to broadly lanceolate, minutely dentate, distinct glaucescent beneath; fertile fronds distinct to 50cm, rusty brown. Jap., China, Himal. Z6.

O. javanica Bl. Stipes 15–30cm. Young growth clammy. Fronds 30–90cm, pinnate, lower or central pinnae fertile; sterile pinnae 10–20×1–2cm, entire, undulate or acutely dentate, occas. slightly stalked, fertile pinnae shorter, oblong, in numerous close-set clusters. Borneo, Sumatra, Java. Z10.

O. lancea Thunb. Sterile fronds to 1m, bipinnate, pinnae 20–30cm, oblong, pinnules 5×0.3cm, linear to lanceolate, acuminate, slightly dentate above; fertile fronds 20–50cm, distinct. Jap. Z6.

O. palustris Schräd. = *O. regalis*.

O. regalis L. ROYAL FERN; FLOWERING FERN. Rhiz. exceeding, massive with fibrous roots. Stipes 30–45cm. Fronds 60–180cm, bipinnate, sterile pinnae 15–30cm, pinnules 2.5–5×1–2cm, oblong, blunt, minutely serrate; fertile pinnae cylindric, forming large rusty pan. at frond apex. Cosmop. 'Crispa': 100–150cm; pinnules crisped. 'Cristata': 100–130cm; pinnules, pinnae and frond finely crested. 'Purpurascens': 120–180cm; growth purple when young, rachis purple throughout the season, possibly a form of *O. regalis* var. *spectabilis*. var. **spectabilis** (Willd.) A. Gray. Rachis of fertile pan. subglab. or glab., not black-pubesc. N & S Amer. Z2.

→*Nephrodium. Leptopteris, Osmunda, Todea*

OSMUNDACEAE Gérardin & Desv. 3 genera. *Leptopteris, Osmunda, Todea*.

Oso Berry *Oemleria*.

Osteomeles Lindl. Rosaceae. 2 everg. shrubs or trees. Lvs small, finely pinnate. Fls in small, term. corymbs; cal. tube campanulate or turbinate, cal. teeth 5; pet. 5, oval-oblong, patent; sta. 15–20. Fr. a small pome, red to blue-black. China to Hawaii and NZ. Z8.

O. anthyllidifolia auct. = *O. schwerinae*.

O. schwerinae Schneid. To 3m. Branchlets slender, pendulous, grey-pubesc. Lvs to 7cm, grey-pubesc.; lfts 15–31, elliptic to obovate-oblong, to 12mm, cuspidate. Fls to 1.5cm diam., white, in lax cymes to 6cm diam. Spring–summer. S W China (Yunnan). var. *microphylla* Rehd. & Wils. Lvs smaller, less woolly; lfts less numerous, to 5mm. Infl. smaller, more dense; cal. glab. W China.

O. subrotunda K. Koch. Resembles *O. schwerinae*, but smaller, slow-growing shrub, with tortuous br. Lfts 9–17, to 8mm, rounded to obovate, ciliate, thinly pubesc. beneath. Fls 1cm diam., in lax corymbs to 3cm diam. Summer. E China.

Osteospermum L. Compositae. *c*70 shrubs, subshrubs or ann. to perenn. herbs. Lvs usually alt., entire, toothed, pinnatifid or pinnatisect. Cap. radiate, few to many solitary term. or in loose umbellate or corymbose pan. S to trop. Afr. and Arabia. Z9.

O. amplectans (Harv.) Norl. Ann. herb to 90cm. Lvs to 12cm, lower lvs elliptic to rhombic, often auriculate, ± sinuate-dentate, upper lvs lanceolate or linear-lanceolate, dentate, often amplexicaul. Ray flts yellow to orange; disc flts yellow, purple at apex. S Afr.

O. barberiae (Harv.) Norl. Spreading, rhizomatous perenn. to 50cm, glandular-pubesc. Lvs to 15cm, oblong-lanceolate, linear-lanceolate to spathulate, sparsely dentate, acute to sub-acute, base attenuate, amplexicaul. Fls magenta above, usually light orange-brown beneath; disc flts deep purple or yellow. Autumn–early spring. S Afr. 'Compactum' ('Nanum'): to 10cm; flts deep pink with dark purple reverse.

O. ecklonis (DC.) Norl. Robust shrub or subshrub to 1m. Lvs to 10cm, linear-oblong, elliptic, or lanceolate, entire, denticulate or serrate-dentate, glandular-pubesc. Ray flts white above, indigo, often with white margin beneath; disc flts bright blue. S

Afr. 'Deep Pink Form': to 30cm; flts numerous, narrow, dark pink. Giant Mixed: to 35cm; fls in cream, orange and salmon pastels. 'Starshine': to 75cm; fls snow-white with blue eyes. 'Weetwood': to 25cm; fls white, olive green below.

O. fruticosum (L.) Norl. Perenn. to 60cm. Decumbent or ascending, woody below. Lvs to 10cm, often in basal rosettes, obovate spathulate or oblanceolate, obtuse, mucronate, amplexicaul margins entire or remotely callose-denticulate, slightly fleshy, glandular-pubesc, glabrescent. Ray flts white above, violet to rose-lilac beneath; disc flts dull violet. All year. S Afr.

O. hyoseroides (DC.) Norl. Aromatic, glandular-pubesc. erect ann., to 60cm. Lvs glandular-pubesc. to glab., lower to 10cm, oblong to oblanceolate, sinuate-dentate, semi-amplexicaul, upper oblong-linear to oblanceolate, sessile. Ray flts yellow to orange; disc flts yellow, dark violet at apex. S Afr.

O. jucundum (E. Phillips) Norl. Perenn. herb, to 50cm. Lvs to 15cm, oblanceolate-elliptic to narrowly oblong-linear, coarsely and remotely dentate-denticulate, sessile or narrowly petiolate. Ray flts red on both surfaces; disc flts black-purple at apex. S Afr.

O. jucundum hort. non (E. Phillips) Norl. = *O. barberiae*.

O. pinnatum (Thunb.) Norl. Much branched ann. to 30cm, viscid, downy. Lvs 1–2.5cm, pinnate, seg. linear, obtuse, usually entire. Ray flts about 2.5cm, orange to yellow or buff-pink. S Afr.

O. cvs. Many hybrids and cvs ranging in height from 25cm to 60cm and in a var. of bright colours; shorter cvs (to 25cm) include the white- and pink-backed 'Cannington Roy' and the pink 'Hopley's' and 'Langtrees'; taller cvs (to 60cm) include the white-fld variegated-lvd 'Silver Sparkler', the pink 'Pink Whirls' and 'Bodegas Pink' with variegated lvs, and 'Buttermilk' with pale yellow fls. 'Whirligig': foliage grey-green; ray flts powder-blue to chalky grey, strongly contracted with margins inrolled above mid-point, then expanded again at tip; disc flts dark blue-grey. The Cannington Hybrids include pink-, white- and purple-fld forms 15–30cm tall. Seed races such as the 25cm Dwarf Salmon and the 45cm Tetra Pole Star are also offered.

→*Calendula, Dimorphotheca* and *Tripteris*.

Ostericum Hoffm.
O. florenti (Franch. & Savat.) Kitag. = *Angelica florenti*.

Ostrich-feather Fern *Matteuccia struthiopteris*.
Ostrich Fern *Matteuccia struthiopteris*.

Ostrowskia Reg. Campanulaceae. 1 perenn. tap-rooted herb to 1.8m, erect, glab., unbranched. Lvs blue-green, in distant whorls, narrowly ovate, dentate, to 15cm. Rac. term.; cor. milky blue veined lilac, campanulate, tube to 5cm, lobes broadly ovate. Turkestan. Z7.

O. magnifica Reg. GIANT BELLFLOWER.

Ostrya Scop. Betulaceae (Carpinaceae). Some 9 round-headed, decid., monoecious trees to 25m. Bark grey. Lvs alt. in 2 rows. ♂ infl. resembling *Carpinus*, but forming in autumn. ♀ catkins term., bristly, with fls in 3–12 pairs subtended by caducous bracts, each fl. set in a sac-like husk, closed and inflated on fruiting, giving an overall hop-like appearance. Eur., Asia, Amer.

O. carpinifolia Scop. HOP HORNBEAM. To 20m. Young shoots downy. Lvs ovate, rounded at base, acute at apex, to 10×5cm, lustrous dark green, hairy between veins above, paler beneath with sparse hairs on veins, veins in 15–20 pairs, double-dentate. Infr. to 5cm. Autumn. S Eur., Asia Minor. Z6.

O. italica Spach = *O. carpinifolia*.

O. japonica Sarg. To 25m. Young shoots densely downy. Lvs ovate to ovate-oblong, long-acuminate, rounded to cordate at base, dark green pubesc. above, pale green, velvety, irregularly sharp-toothed. Infr. to 5cm. Autumn. Jap., China, NE Asia. Z5.

O. knowltonii Cov. To 10m. Young shoots downy, olive brown. Buds cylindric, hairy. Lvs ovate, cuneate to cordate at base, acute to obtuse at apex, to 6×3cm, irregularly biserrate, downy throughout, veins in 5–8 pairs. Infr. to 3cm. Autumn. Ariz., Utah. Z5.

O. virginiana (Mill.) K. Koch. EASTERN HOP HORNBEAM; IRONWOOD. To 20m. Young shoots glandular-pubesc. Lvs ovate-lanceolate, rounded to cordat at base, apex long-acuminate, 7×12×3–5cm; dark green, hairy on midrib and between veins above, pale, pubesc. beneath, veins in 11–15 pairs. Infr. to 6cm. Autumn. E N Amer. var. *glandulosa* (Spach) Sarg. All parts more glandular-hairy. Z4.

O. vulgaris Willd. = *O. carpinifolia*.

Ostryopsis Decne. Betulaceae (Carpinaceae). 2 decid. shrubs to 3m. ♂ fls in cylindric catkins to 2cm; anth. hairy at tip. ♀ fls in term., erect, short rac.; each fl. surrounded by a trifid involucral bract. Fr. a nut, conic, surrounded by tubular involucre to 2cm. China, Mong. Z6.

O. davidiana (Baill.) Decne. Shrub to 3m. Young shoots downy. Lvs broadly ovate, cordate at base, 3–8cm, double-dentate, dark green, sparsely hairy above, downy beneath. Spring. China. Z4. var. *cinerascens* Franch. Lvs ovate, smaller, with brown hairs. ♂ catkins to 3cm, purple. Fr. grey-hairy. W China. Z6.

O. nobilis Balf. f. & W.W. Sm. Shrub to 2m. Young shoots scabrous. Lvs rounded to ovate, to 4cm, tough, dull green above; olive-brown, hairy beneath, double-serrate, ♂ catkins rust-coloured. Spring. W China. Z7.

Oswego Tea *Monarda didyma.*

Osyris L. Santalaceae. 7 dioecious semi-parasitic shrubs. ♂ fls in rac.; sep. 3–4; ♀ fls solitary or clustered. Fr. drupaceous. Medit. to E Asia, Afr. Z9.

O. alba L. Shrub to 1.2m. Br. diffuse, slender. Lvs narrow-lanceolate, coriaceous. Sep. 3, off-white. Fr. to 7mm, red. Medit.

Otafuku-giboshi *Hosta decorata.*
Otaheite Apple *Spondias dulcis.*
Otaheite Gooseberry *Phyllanthus acidus.*
Otaheite Orange *Citrus × limonia.*

Otanthus Hoffm. & Link. Compositae. 1 white-felted tufted, creeping, perennial, maritime herb to 50cm. Lvs to 1.5cm, numerous, imbricate oblong to oblong-lanceolate, entire to crenulate, sessile, fleshy, tomentose. Cap. discoid, few, in dense, imbricate oblong clusters; flts yellow. Summer. Coasts of W Eur. to Near E. Z8.

O. maritimus (L.) Hoffm. & Link. COTTON WEED.

Otatea (McClure & E.W. Sm.) Cald. & Söderstr. Gramineae. 2 delicate, bamboos forming open clumps. Mex. to Nic. Z10.

O. acuminata (Munro) Cald. & Söderstr. Culms 2–8m×2–4cm, ultimately curving gracefully, with white powder below nodes; sheaths glabrescent, the upper sheaths decid., the lower disintegrating. Lvs 7–16×0.3–0.5cm, pendulous.
O. acuminata ssp. *aztecorum* (McClure & E.W. Sm.) Guzman = *O. acuminata.*
→*Arthrostylidium* and *Yushania.*

Oteniqua Yellowwood *Afrocarpus falcatus.*

Othera Thunb.
O. japonica Thunb. = *Ilex integra.*
O. orixa (Thunb.) Lam. = *Orixa japonica.*

Othonna L. Compositae. c150 perenn. herbs or small shrubs, usually glab. and glaucous. Lvs entire to variously dissected, lobed or toothed, membranous, leathery or fleshy. Cap. usually radiate, solitary or clustered in corymbs; involucre ± campanulate; ray flts yellow. Mostly S Afr. Z9 unless specified.
O. aeonioides Dinter = *O. furcata.*
O. amplexicaulis Thunb. Erect shrub, to 2m, glab. Lvs to 20cm, broadly obovate to oblong, mucronate, entire or minutely toothed, auriculate, amplexicaul, sessile to subdecurrent, gradually reduced above. Phyllaries 8. Spring–summer. S Afr.
O. amplexifolia DC. Somewhat ascending herb, glab. and glaucous. St. branched, woolly below. Lvs to 7cm, broadly ovate, cordate, acute or obtuse, amplexicaul, margin undulate or repand, mucronate, soft and slightly fleshy. Phyllaries 9–10. S Afr.
O. arborescens L. Succulent shrub, to 1m. St. flexuous, white-woolly on recent lf scars below. Lvs to 5cm, obovate-oblong, base attenuate, obtuse or subacute, margin entire or sinuate-toothed, fairly thick. Phyllaries 5. S Afr.
O. bulbosa L. Glab. to sparsely hairy herb. St. short, flexuous. Basal lvs to 12cm, ovate to oblong-lanceolate, acute, entire, membranous, st. lvs oblong to obovate, occas. repand, semiamplexicaul. Phyllaries 7–10. Summer. S Afr.
O. capensis L.H. Bail. LITTLE-PICKLES. Short herb. St. trailing, branched, slender. Lvs to 2.5cm, often clustered, cylindric to cylindric-obovoid, acute, grooved, pale green, succulent, apex cartilaginous. Phyllaries c9. Summer. S Afr.
O. carnosa Less. Shrub, to 30cm, fleshy, glab. St. forked. Lvs to 5cm,scattered, linear or somewhat fusiform, semiterete, spreading, thick, fleshy, glaucous. Phyllaries 8–9. S Afr.
O. cheirifolia L. Spreading everg. shrub, to 40cm. Lvs to 8cm, lanceolate-spathulate, base attenuate, apex obtusely rounded, sessile, glaucous or tinged grey, thick. Phyllaries c8–10. Summer. Alg., Tun. Z8.

O. ciliata L. f. Shrub to 40cm. St. decumbent. Lvs to 5cm, oblong, obovate or spathulate, usually pinnatifid, lobes short, broad, ciliate-toothed or entire, base attenuate. Phyllaries c8. S Afr.
O. coronopifolia L. non Thunb. Shrub, to 60cm. St. erect, flexuous, often forked and bushy, glab. Lvs to 6×1cm, lanceolate or linear-lanceolate, entire or irregularly few-toothed, base attenuate, acuminate, leathery, thick. Phyllaries 7–8. Summer–early autumn. S Afr.
O. coronopifolia Thunb. non L. = *O. arborescens.*
O. crassifolia Harv. = *O. capensis.*
O. cylindrica (Lam.) DC. Shrub, to 1m, fleshy, glab. St. laxly branched, forked, terete, leafy at first, markedly scarred later. Lvs to 8×0.2cm, scattered, linear-elongate, semiterete, spreading, base attenuate, acute, fleshy, glaucous. Phyllaries 8–9. S Afr.
O. dentata L. Shrub to 90cm, succulent and glab. Lvs to 5cm, subrosulate near br. apices, obovate, base cuneate, sessile, coarsely toothed to entire or subentire. Phyllaries c8. S Afr.
O. denticulata Dryand. in Ait. = *O. amplexicaulis.*
O. digitata L. Herb, to 45cm, glab., or pubesc. below. St. lanate in axils. Lvs to 15cm, oblong to lanceolate, cuneate, entire, toothed, dentate or coarsely 3–5-lobed, lower petiolate, st. lvs amplexicaul. Cap. discoid; phyllaries 8–10. Summer–early autumn. S Afr.
O. euphorbioides Hutch. Shrub to 1m. St. erect, v. succulent, similar in habit to some succulent *Euphorbia* spp. Lvs to 1.5cm, reduced, narrowly oblanceolate or spathulate, fleshy, glab. Cap. discoid; phyllaries c9. S Afr.
O. fructescens L. Shrub, to 90cm. St. decumbent, leafy. Lvs to 10cm, obovate, base attenuate, mucronate, entire or ciliate, petiolate, upper st. lvs gradually reduced to scales, oblong or linear, entire or toothed. Phyllaries c8. Late summer. S Afr.
O. furcata (Lindl.) Druce. Subshrub, to 1.2m. St. branched, v. pale grey or white. Lvs to 10cm, elongate-elliptic, entire, petiolate below. Cap. discoid; phyllaries 7–11. Nam.
O. integrifolia L. = *Tephroseris integrifolia.*
O. linifolia L. f. Glab. herb, to 40cm. St. bare, forked, woolly at base. Lvs to 25cm, mostly basal, linear-attenuate or linear-lanceolate, tapered to both ends, entire, rigid, ribbed, veined or striate, lower axils woolly, st. lvs few, linear, sessile. Phyllaries 9–10. Summer–early autumn. S Afr.
O. palustris L. = *Tephroseris palustris.*
O. pinnata L. f. Glab. herb, to 50cm. St. flexuous, lower axils woolly. Lvs to 15cm, pinnatisect, seg. several, paired, to 2.5cm oblong, ovate or subrotund, entire, decurrent. Phyllaries 12–13. Early summer. S Afr.
O. quercifolia DC. Shrub, to 80cm. St. erect, succulent, glab. Lvs to 10cm, pinnatifid, obtuse, base attenuate, lobes 3–4, 1 to 1.5cm, oblong, mucronate. Phyllaries 5–6. S Afr.
O. quinquedentata Thunb. Shrub, to 1.3m. St. erect, loosely branched above robust. Lvs to 15cm, oblong, sessile, semi-amplexicaul, subdecurrent, 5-toothed near apex, blunt, minutely mucronate, callous-margined, leathery. Phyllaries 7–8. S Afr.
O. retrofracta Less. Subshrub, to 60cm. St. branched, spreading or bent. Lvs to 8cm, oblong-lanceolate, base cuneate, 1-toothed or lobulate with a single tooth on each side. Cap. discoid; phyllaries c10–10. Summer. S Afr.
O. retrorsa DC. Woody herb, to 40cm. St. simple or branched, woolly and clad in dead leaf-bases below. Lvs to 8cm, rosulate at br. apices, oblong- to linear-spathulate, base attenuate, subacute, rigid, thin, reticulate-veined, ciliate. Phyllaries c8. S Afr.
O. triplinervia DC. Succulent shrub, to 1m. Lvs to 8cm, crowded toward br. apices, obovate, obtuse, base attenuate, entire or repand, reticulate-veined, slightly fleshy. Phyllaries c5. S Afr.
O. tuberosa Thunb. = *O. bulbosa.*
→*Ceradia, Hertia* and *Othonnopsis.*

Othonnopsis Jaub. & Spach.
O. cheirifolia Benth. & Hook. = *Othonna cheirifolia.*

Otites Adans. = *Silene.*

Otochilus Lindl. Orchidaceae. 4–6 epiphytic or lithophytic orchids. Pbs arising from apex of previous season's pb., thus chain-like in habit, apically bifoliate. Infl. term., bracteate, slender; tep. narrow, spreading; lip basally saccate, midlobe entire, lat. lobes erect. Himal. to SE Asia. Z9.
O. fuscus Lindl. Lvs to 12cm, ligulate. Infl. to 10cm, pendent; fls to 1.25cm diam., white or pale pink; lip basally concave, midlobe linear; column brown.

Otoglossum (Schltr.) Garay & Dunsterv. Orchidaceae. 7 epiphytic orchids, resembling *Odontoglossum* in habit. Lvs to 30cm, elliptic-oblong, coriaceous. Rac. erect, large, long-stalked; tep.

spreading, obovate to elliptic-oblong, undulate; lip pandurate, deflexed. C & S Amer. Z10.

O. brevifolium (Lindl.) Garay & Dunsterv. Infl. to 60cm; fls to 5cm diam.; sep. and pet. rich chestnut brown, margins yellow; lip bright golden yellow with central band, to 2.5cm, midlobe cuneate to obovate, bilobed or retuse, disc with a fleshy keel with a transverse frontal callus and a fleshy callus at base of each lateral lobe. Spring. Colomb., Ecuad., Peru.

O. chiriquense (Rchb. f.) Garay & Dunsterv. Infl. to 45cm; fls to 7.5cm diam., bright yellow spotted and blotched rich chestnut brown; lip to 2.5cm, midlobe obovate, obtuse or emarginate, disc tuberculate. Usually spring. Costa Rica, Panama, Colomb., Peru.

→*Odontoglossum*.

Otome-giboshi *Hosta venusta.*

Otostylis Schltr. Orchidaceae. 3 terrestrial orchids. Pbs small, with overlapping sheaths, apex 1- to several-leaved. Lvs narrowly lanceolate, plicate. Rac. lat.; sep. and pet. free, oblong to ovate-elliptic; lip often clawed, simple or trilobed, disc with a raised callus. Colomb., Venez., Trin., Guyanas to Braz. Z9.

O. brachystalix (Rchb. f.) Schltr. Pbs to 2cm, ovoid. Lvs to 70×5cm. Infl. to 90cm; tep. white, 18mm; lip white, to 12mm, trilobed, midlobe suborbicular to obovate, obtuse, callus pale yellow, dentate. Colomb., Venez., Trin., Guyana.

O. lepida (Lind. & Rchb. f.) Schltr. Pbs to 6cm, ovoid-fusiform.Lvs to 65×6cm. Infl. to 70cm; tep. to 20mm, white tipped pale rose; lip to 18mm, white, simple, ovate-suborbicular, rounded, callus yellow, crenulate. Venez., Braz., Br. Guyana.

→*Aganisia, Koellensteinia* and *Zygopetalum.*

Ottelia Pers. Hydrocharitaceae. 21 aquatic herbs. St. erect, occas. creeping or rhizomatous. Lvs usually radical; juvenile lvs linear to ovate, sessile; adult lvs petiolate, submerged or partially emersed, elliptic to orbicular, midrib prominent; petiole flexuous. Infl. subtended by a spathe of 2 fused bracts, submerged or emergent; fls unisexual or ♂; sep. 3, free, narrowly triangular to ovate; pet. 3, free, ovate to orbicular; usually clawed at base; sta. 3–15. OW trop. and temp. regions, 1 New World sp. Z9.

O. alismoides (L.) Pers. Ann. or perenn.; st. short, corm-like. Lvs submerged, narrowly elliptic to widely ovate, translucent. Pet. to 3cm, obovate to orbicular, white, pink, pale blue to light purple, usually yellow at base. N Afr., NE India to W China, SE Asia and Aus., introd. elsewhere, inc. N It., in association with irrigated crops.

O. ovalifolia (R. Br.) Rich. Ann. or perenn.; st. corm-like. Adult lvs partially emergent, elliptic to ovate, coriaceous. Pet. 3–6cm, clawed, cream with deep red base. Aus., NZ, New Caledonia.

O. tenera Benth. = *O. ovalifolia*.

→*Damasonium.*

Ougeinia Benth.
O. dalbergioides Benth. = *Desmodium ooieinense.*

Ougon-kou Chiku *Phyllostachys sulphurea.*
Ouricury *Syagrus coronata.*

Ourisia Comm. ex Juss. Scrophulariaceae. Some 25 creeping or low-growing, rhizomatous perenn. herbs or subshrubs. Lvs usually radical, petiolate. Fls axill. and solitary or in bracteate scapose corymbs or whorled rac.; cal. deeply 5-lobed; cor. slightly zygomorphic, tube short, slightly oblique, lobes 5, usually spreading. Summer–autumn. Andes, Antarc. S Amer., NZ, Tasm.

O. breviflora Benth. Lvs 0.7–1cm, basal, clustered, hairy, ovate to orbicular, obtuse, somewhat crenate. Fls solitary, or in 2–4-fld rac.; cor. tube 10–14mm, violet with darker venation, lobes 3×2mm, linear to obovate, emarginate. Summer. Z8.

O. caespitosa Hook. f. Lvs 0.4–0.8cm, on creeping st. distichous, obovate-spathulate, entire or with 2–3 notches on each side. Peduncle 2–7cm, 1–5-fld; cor. white, to 16mm diam. Spring–summer. NZ. var. *gracilis* Hook. f. Smaller; lvs 4mm; peduncles 1–2-fld; fls 12mm. NZ. Z7.

O. coccinea Comm. ex Juss. St. to 30cm. Lvs broadly elliptic or oblong, shallowly and irregularly dentate. Infl. a pan., crowded, term.; cor. to 4cm, scarlet, drooping; sta. exserted. Spring–autumn. Chile (Andes).

O. macrocarpa Hook. f. St. erect, rarely to 60cm. Lvs to 1.5cm, radical, ovate-oblong to orbicular, crenate, thick, ciliate. Peduncle stout; fls in several superposed whorls; cor. 15–25mm diam., white sometimes with yellow throat, tube broad, villous

within, lobes obovate, retuse or cupped. Spring–summer. NZ. Z7.

O. macrophylla Hook. f. Rhiz. short, robust; st. to 60cm, erect. Radical lvs 2–22cm, ovate to orbicular-oblong, shallowly crenate, membranous, sparsely pubesc. Peduncle erect; bracts subtended by a whorl of 2–4 lvs; whorls 3–8, fls 1 to many per whorl; cor. 20mm, white or white with purple streaks, lobes obovate, retuse. Summer. NZ. Z7.

O. uniflora Philippi = *O. breviflora.*

*O.***cvs.** 'Loch Ewe' (*O. coccinea* ×*O. macrophylla*): to 20cm, slowly spreading in tight rosettes; fls shell pink. 'Snowflake' (*O. macrocarpa* ×*O. caespitosa* var. *gracilis*): to 10cm; lvs dark, glossy, fls white. Z7.

→*Euphrasia.*

Our Lady's Bedstraw *Galium verum.*
Our Lady's Milk Thistle *Silybum marianum.*
Our Lord's Candle *Yucca whipplei.*
Oval Kumquat *Fortunella margarita.*
Oval-leaved Bilberry *Vaccinium ovalifolium.*
Oven's Wattle *Acacia pravissima.*
Overcup Oak *Quercus lyrata.*

Ovidia Meissn. Thymelaeaceae. 4 decid. shrubs, similar to *Daphne* but with a more slender style. S Amer. Z9.

O. andina (Poepp. & Endl.) Meissn. Shrub to 2.25m. Young shoots downy. Lvs 5–13cm, oblanceolate to narrow-ovate, tips blunt or rounded, glab. above, glaucous and hairy beneath. Fls in dense, term. umbels to 4cm diam.; cal. 6mm diam., funnel-form, 4-lobed, downy, cream-white; anth. red. Fr. to 6mm, white. Summer. Chile.

O. pillopillo (C. Gay) Meissn. Similar to *O. andina*, but shrub or small tree 3–9m. Shoots v. downy. Lvs 2.5–8cm, oblanceolate, glab., somewhat glaucous. Cal. 1.5cm diam., tubular, 4-lobed, white, v. downy. Fr. red-purple. Chile.

Owl-eyes *Huernia zebrina.*

OXALIDACEAE R. Br. 8/575. *Averrhoa, Biophytum, Oxalis.*

Oxalis L. SORREL; SHAMROCK. Oxalidaceae. 800 ann. or perenn., stemmed or stemless herbs and shrubs, often tuberous or bulbous. Lvs radical or cauline, palmate; lfts usually 3, sometimes more or phyllodic, often folding down at night. Fls axill., slender-stalked, cymose, umbellate or solitary; pet. 5, usually partly fused at base, sta. 10 in two whorls of 5, fil. fushed in a tube. Fr. a dehiscent capsule; aril fleshy, ejecting seed when ripe. Cosmop. but centres of diversity in S Afr. and S Amer.

O. acetosella L. WOOD-SORREL; CUCKOO BREAD; ALLELUIA. Creeping perenn.; rhiz. slender, scaly, pale green. Lvs trifoliate, petioles to 8cm; lfts to 1.5cm, obcordate, pale green, sparsely hairy. Fls solitary, 1.5–2cm across white, veined purple. Spring. N temp. Amer., Eur. and Asia. var. *purpurascens* Mart. Fls rose with purple veining. Z3.

O. adenophylla Gillies. SAUER KLEE. Stemless perenn., from a brown, scale-covered, tuberous base. Lvs erects to spreading; petioles 5–12cm, red-brown; lfts *c*6mm, 9–22, obcordate, silver-grey, glab. Peduncles 1–3-fld; fls *c*2.5cm across, lilac-pink to violet with darker veins and 2 purple spots in white throat. Late spring–early summer. Chile, W Arg. (Andes). 'Minima': lvs small. Z5.

O. alstonii Lourteig. FIRE FERN; RED FLAME. Similar to *O. hedysaroides* but st., petioles and flowering parts pubesc.; lvs maroon-red. Summer–autumn. Braz. Z9.

O. ambigua 4–12cm. Bulbous. Lvs to 2.5cm, tufted; petioles ciliate; lfts 3, to 0.75cm obselloid, blue green flecked purple, ciliate. Fls solitary, to 1.5cm diam., white usually with yellow in throat and exterior tinted pink. Summer. S Afr. Z9.

O. amplifolia (Trel.) Knuth = *O. drummondii.*

O. articulata Savigny. Stemless perenn.; rhiz. to 14×2cm, little-branched, dark brown, tuberous, semi-woody, becoming cylindrical, jointed. Lvs 6–25cm, petioles erect to sprawling, glab. or downy; lfts 3, 10–25mm, obcordate, green, glab. above, hairy beneath. Peduncles v. numerous, to 40cm; infl. a 5–10-fld umbellate cyme; fls to 2cm across, bright mauve-pink. Summer–autumn. Parag. var. *hirsuta* Progel. Lvs hairy above. 'Alba': fls white. Z8.

O. asinina Jacq. = *O. fabaefolia.*

O. bifida Thunb. Perenn. with a weak, erect or procumbent, branched st. to 30cm; bulb scaly. Petioles slender, 1.5–4cm, at st. apices; lfts 3, 5–6mm, narrowly obcordate, divided to the middle or more, green with black marginal spots, thinly hairy beneath. Fls solitary, *c*12mm across, purple-red with a yellow-green throat. Spring–summer. S Afr. (Cape Prov.). Z9.

O. binervis Reg. = *O. latifolia.*

O. bipunctata Graham = *O. corymbosa*.

O. bowieana Lodd. = *O. bowiei*.

O. bowiei Lindl. Stemless perenn., glandular-hairy. Bulb elongate with a smooth brown tunic and a long, white, contractile root. Petioles 5–15cm; lfts 3, to 5cm, rounded to obcordate, notched, leathery, sometimes purple beneath, ± glab. above, hairy beneath. Infl. 10–30cm, umbel 3–12-fld; fls 3–4cm across, bright rose-red to pink, with a yellow-green throat. Summer–autumn. S Afr. (Cape Prov.). Z8.

O. bupleurifolia A. St.-Hil. Erect stemmed branching perenn. to 40cm; st. woody, brown. Lvs crowded at the st. apices, glab.; petioles to 11cm and expanded into phyll. 12mm wide; lfts 3, 8mm, caducous. Umbel 2–4-fld on a flattened 8cm stalk; fls to 1cm across, yellow. Summer–autumn. Braz. Z9.

O. caprina L. GOAT'S-FOOT; WOOD-SORREL. V. short-stemmed, subglabrous perenn., 15–20cm. Bulb scaly with a slender vertical rhiz. petioles 2–5cm; lfts 3, 5–10mm, triangular in outline, divided to about the middle, lobes obovate. Peduncles to 20cm, bearing 2–4-fld umbels; fls pale violet, rarely white, with pale green throat. Spring–early summer. S Afr. (Cape Prov.). Z9.

O. carnosa Molina = *O. megalorrhiza*.

O. cathariensis N.E. Br. = *O. regnellii*.

O. cernua Thunb. = *O. pes-caprae*.

O. chrysantha Progel. V. hairy, mat-forming perenn. with slender, creeping st. to 20cm, rather woody, producing lf rosettes. Petioles 2–4cm, lfts 3, 7mm, triangular-obcordate, green with white hairs. Fls solitary, 1.5cm across, golden yellow with red markings at mouth. Summer–autumn. Braz. Z8.

O. convexula Jacq. = *O. depressa*.

O. corniculata L. PROCUMBENT YELLOW SORREL; CREEPING YELLOW OXALIS; CREEPING OXALIS. Creeping, much-branched, short-lived perenn. st. 10–30cm from a short taproot. Petioles erect, 1–8cm, somewhat hairy; lfts 3, 5–15mm, obcordate, umbels green, glab. above and hairy beneath. Peduncles 1–10cm, umbels 2–6-fld; fls c1cm across, light yellow, sometimes with a red throat. Spring–autumn. Cosmop. weed, origin unknown. var. *atropurpurea* Planch. All parts suffused purple. var. *villosa* (Bieb.) Hohen. Lvs hairy above and beneath. Z5.

O. corniculata L. (misapplied). = *O. dillenii*.

O. corniculata var. *microphylla* Hook. = *O. exilis*.

O. corniculata var. *purpurata* Parl. = *O. corniculata* var. *atro-purpurea*.

O. corymbosa DC. Stemless perenn., with round bulb producing numerous loosely scaly, sessile bulbils. Petioles 10–35cm, with white hairs; lfts 3, 25–45mm, broadly obcordate, rounded, green, with dark spots beneath, sparsely hairy. Peduncles 15–40cm, with white hairs; infl. 8–15-fld, branched cyme; fls c1.5cm across, red to purple with darker veins and a white throat. Spring–early summer. Braz., Arg. 'Aureoreticulata': lvs with yellow veining, probably virus-induced. Z9. *e*Uα, 12 – 6

O. crenata Jacq. = *O. tuberosa*.

O. cumingiana Turcz. = *Biophytum sensitivum*.

O. cymosa Small = *O. stricta*.

O. debilis Kunth = *O. corymbosa*.

O. delicata Pohl = *O. rosea*.

O. dendroides HBK = *Biophytum dendroides*.

O. deppei Lodd. = *O. tetraphylla*.

O. deppei Lodd. (misapplied). = *O. tuberosa*.

O. depressa Ecklon & Zeyh. Bulbous, nearly stemless perenn., with a vertical rhiz. from bulb to soil surface. Petioles 8–20mm, glab.; lfts 3, 3–10mm, rounded to triangular-ovate, grey-green, sometimes dark-spotted, glab. or sparsely hairy. Fls solitary, 1.5–2cm across, bright pink to rose-violet, with a yellow throat, purple and white forms are known. Summer. S Afr. (Cape Prov.). Z5.

O. dillenii Jacq. Erect, stemmed ann. to 40cm, branching freely from base. Lvs borne in whorls all over plant; petioles 3–8cm, pubesc.; lfts 3, 4–20mm, obovate, green, glab. above, pubesc. beneath. Peduncles 3–10cm, pubesc.; umbel 2–3-fld; fls c1cm across, yellow. Autumn. E N Amer.

O. dispar N.E. Br. Small, softly pubesc. shrub to about 60cm with slender br. Lvs few; petioles 7–9cm, slender, pubesc.; lfts 3, about 7cm, ovate-lanceolate, green, hairy. Peduncles 7–9cm, slender; cyme 7–10-fld; fls 2–3cm across, golden yellow, beautifully scented. Spring–winter. Guyana. Z10.

O. drummondii A. Gray. Bulbous, stemless perenn., bulb of open, papery scales. Petioles 5–16cm, erect to spreading, glab.; lfts 3, V-shaped, deeply lobed, lobes to 30mm. Umbel 3–10-fld; fls c2cm across, purple. Spring–summer. Mex. Z9.

O. elongata Jacq. = *O. versicolor*.

O. engleriana Decid. 8–18cm, similar in habit to *O. gracilis*, but with still narrower st. and lvs in strictly term. rosettes with to 6 finger-like lfts. Fls to 1.5cm diam., rose-pink. S Afr. Z9.

O. enneaphylla Cav. SCURVY GRASS. Stemless perenn. to 14cm,

rhiz. 5×2cm, covered in thick white scales with bulbils in axils. Petioles 1.5–8cm, occas. hairy; lfts 9–20, 4–12mm, obcordate, partially folded, somewhat fleshy, glaucous blue, hairy; fls solitary, held just above lvs, c2cm across, white to red, fragrant. Spring–summer. Falkland Is., Patagonia. 'Alba': fls white. 'Ione Hecker' (*O. enneaphylla* × *O. laciniata*): lvs with rather narrower seg., deeper green; fls to 3cm across, vivid blue at edge darkening to dark purple at centre. 'Minutifolia': dwarf form. 'Rosea': to 6cm, fls rose-pink. 'Rubra': fls red. Z6.

O. enneaphylla var. *patagonica* (Speg.) Skottsb. = *O. patagonica*.

O. europaea Jordan = *O. stricta*.

O. exilis A. Cunn. Resembles a small *O. corniculata*, to 4cm tall and st. to 15cm long. Petioles 6–13mm; lfts 3–5mm, green. Fls solitary. Spring–summer. Aus., NZ. Z8.

O. fabaefolia Jacq. Glab., bulbous, stemless perenn. Petioles 1.5–10mm, with leaf-like wings, lfts 2–5, 1.5–5cm, ovate to oblanceolate, rather thick. Fls solitary, to 3cm across, yellow, white or mauve. Summer–autumn. S Afr. Z9.

O. filicaulis Jacq. = *O. bifida*.

O. flabellifolia Jacq. = *O. flava*.

O. flava L. Stemless perenn. to 25cm from a brown scaly rhiz. Petioles 2–6cm; lfts (2–)5–12, 7.5mm, narrow, digitate, oblong with an apical notch, glab. Fls solitary, c2.5cm across, bright yellow, white or v. pale rose-violet with a yellow throat. A v. variable sp. Spring–early summer. S Afr. (Cape Prov.). Z9.

O. floribunda Lehm. = *O. articulata*.

O. floribunda auctt. = *O. bowiei*; *O. lasiandra*; *O. rosea*; *O. rubra*.

O. floribunda var. *alba* Nichols. = *O. articulata* var. *hirsuta* 'Alba'.

O. fontana Bunge = *O. stricta*.

O. fruticosa Knuth. Shrubby perenn., irregularly branched and sprawling to 50cm. Lvs phyllodic, lfts minute, occas. present; petioles 11–13cm, expanded to a blade 3–4mm wide. Infl. 1–3-fld, to 3cm, cymose; fls to 1–1.5cm across, yellow. Spring. Peru. Z9.

O. fulgida Lindl. = *O. hirta* var. *fulgida*.

O. furcillata Decid. 6–8cm. Similar in habit to *O. gracilis*, but with white, hairy st. and congested lvs with shorter petioles and strongly cleft lfts. Fls to 2cm diam., solitary, white, yellow in throat. Summer. S Afr. Z9.

O. gigantea Barnéoud. Erect shrub, 1–2.5m; st. long, wandering, little branched. Lvs numerous, fleshy; lfts 3, c3.5mm, obcordate, hairy beneath. Fls 1–2cm across, yellow solitary, or in 3–6-fld umbellate cymes. Spring–summer. Chile. Z9.

O. gracilis Decid. perenn. 50–30cm. Sts. simple, slender, bronze, arising from bulb, flimsy. Lvs in remote or strictly term. whorls, amber-red in fall; petioles to 2cm, wiry; lfts. 3, to 1cm, narrow, folded, cleft. Fls to 1.5cm diam., solitary or clustered, salmon pink to apricot. Summer. S Afr. Z9.

O. grandiflora Jacq. = *O. purpurea*.

O. hedysaroides HBK. Erect subshrub to 1m, much branched, st. leafy throughout. Petioles 3 to 6cm; lfts 3, c25mm, widely ovate to rounded, stalked, glaucous beneath, glab. Infl. 3–7cm, a dichasial cyme of c6 fls; fls c1cm across, yellow. Spring–summer. C Amer. 'Rubra': lvs maroon. Z9.

O. herrerae Knuth. Branching, glab. perenn. shrublet, 10–30cm, br. to 8mm thick. Petioles 2–5cm, fleshy, thick and tapering at the ends like a cigar; lfts 3, 5–10mm, obcordate, fleshy, green, caducous. Infl. to 10cm, 5–7-fld unequally branched cymes; fls 1–1.5cm across, yellow with red veins. Summer. Peru. Z9.

O. herrerae Knuth (misapplied) = *O. peduncularis*.

O. hirta L. Erect or trailing, hairy bulbous perenn.; st. to 30cm, branching above. Lvs almost sessile; lfts 3, 10–15mm, linear to oblong with an apical notch, green. Fls solitary, c2.5cm across, long-tubular, red to violet and purple, or paler to white, rarely yellow, with a yellow throat. A v. variable sp. Autumn. S Afr. (Cape Prov.). 'Gothenburg': to 25cm; fls deep pink. var. *fulgida* (Lindl.) Knuth. Fls purple. var. *rubella* (Jacq.) Knuth. Fls deep red. Z9.

O. hirtella Jacq. = *O. hirta*.

O. imbricata Decid. 6–15cm. Lvs dense, tufted; petioles to 1cm, red-tinted; lfts. 3, to 0.5cm, obcordate, rounded, retuse, blue-green. Fls solitary, to 1.5cm diam., white to magenta or red-purple on stalks far exceeding lvs. Summer. S Afr. Z9.

O. incarnata L. Bulbous, glab., perenn. with erect to sprawling slender st. 10–50cm. Petioles 2–6cm in whorls, axils sometimes bulbiliferous; lfts 3, 8–20mm, obcordate, translucent with dark marginal spots beneath; fls solitary, 2cm across, white or v. pale lilac, with darker veins and a yellow throat. Autumn. Nam. Z9.

O. inops Ecklon & Zeyh. = *O. depressa*.

O. intermedia Rich. (misapplied). = *O. latifolia*.

O. kamiesbergensis Decid. 2–3cm. Lvs in rosettes; petioles to 1.5cm; lfts 3, to 0.8cm, folded, blue-green. Fls to 1.5cm diam., pink on stalks exceeding lvs. Summer. S Afr. Z9.

O. laciniata Cav. Rhizomatous, stemless perenn., 5–10cm; rhiz. forming chain of tiny, scaly bulbils. Petioles 2.5–7cm, erect, tinged pink; lfts 8–12, to 2cm, obcordate, folded, glaucous green with purple, undulate margin. Peduncles as long as lvs; fls solitary, *c*2.5cm across, violet, crimson to lilac, blue and paler, with darker veins and green throat, sweetly scented. Late spring–summer. Patagonia. Z9.

O. lactea Hook. = *O. magellanica*.

O. lasiandra Zucc. Bulbous, stemless perenn., 15–30cm, with a thick taproot connected in bulbils at the apex. Petioles to 15cm, erect, stalks red-green, hairy; lfts 5–10, to 5cm, wedge-shaped to strap-like, apex rounded, usually notched, glab. Peduncles twice as long as petioles, succulent, hairy; infl. a 9–26-fld umbel; fls *c*2cm across, crimson to violet, with a yellow throat. Summer–autumn. Mex. Z9.

O. latifolia HBK. Bulbous, stemless perenn., 7–25cm, producing bulbils on short. Petioles 8–23cm; lfts 3, to 7cm, broadly deltoid to obcordate, dark, glab. Infl. to 2.5cm, 6–32-fld, pseudo-umbel; fls 1.5–2cm across, violet-pink or paler, with a green throat. Summer–autumn. Mex. to Peru; widely nat., can be a troublesome weed. Z9.

O. libyca Viv. = *O. pes-caprae*.

O. lobata Sims. Stemless, bulbous perenn., 8–10cm, with tuberous roots. Petioles 4–5cm; lfts 3, 5mm, obcordate, glab., usually blotched, the lateral pair somewhat folded. Fls solitary, about 1.5cm across, golden-yellow, dotted and veined red. Late summer–autumn. Chile. Z8.

O. lupinifolia Jacq. = *O. flava*.

O. magellanica Forst. f. Prostrate, stoloniferous, carpet-forming perenn. to 4cm; rhiz. slender, scaly. Petioles 2–4cm, sparsely hairy; lfts 3, 5mm, obcordate, bronze-green, glab. Fls solitary, 1cm across, pure white. Late spring–summer. S Amer., Aus.; can become a gdn pest. 'Nelson' ('Flore Pleno'): lvs tinged bronze; fls double, white. 'Old Man Range': lvs distinctive, grey tinged pink in summer; fls white, abundant. Z6.

O. martiana Zucc. = *O. corymbosa*.

O. massoniana Decid. 4–24cm. Fls brick red with yellow throat. Close to *O. pardalis*. Summer. S Afr. Z9.

O. megalorrhiza Jacq. Glab. perenn. with fleshy, erect to sprawling st., to 40cm with age, little-branched, semi-woody at base, ascending from woody rhiz. Petioles to 8cm, fleshy; lfts 3, 11–18mm, obcordate, succulent, shiny above, appearing crystalline beneath. Umbel 2–5-fld; fls to 2.5cm across, bright yellow. Summer–autumn. S Amer. (Boliv., Chile, Galapagos Is., Peru). Z10.

O. melanosticta Sonder. Small, nearly stemless, bulbous perenn. to 2.5cm. Petioles 1.5–2.5cm, v. hairy; lfts 3, 7–11mm, obcordate to rounded, thick, green with orange to black spots, usually hairy. Fls solitary, to 2cm across, yellow. Late spring–summer. S Afr. Z9. *Ja||*

O. multiflora Jacq. = *O. hirta*.

O. navieri Jordan = *O. dillenii*.

O. nelsonii (Small) Knuth. Resembling *O. tetraphylla*; plant with sparse to abundant hairs; lfts 5 or 6, usually entire; fls 1.5 to 2.5cm across, deep purple. Summer. Mex. Z9.

O. obtusa 6–10cm. Fls pink red, yellow or white. Summer. S Afr. Z9.

O. oregana Nutt. ex Torr. & A. Gray. REDWOOD SORREL. Perenn. to 6–20cm from a creeping, brown, rhiz. Petioles 3–20cm, with patent hairs; lfts 3, 2.5–3.5cm, obcordate, green, margins and undersurfaces with long hairs. Fls solitary, 2–2.5cm across, pale lilac or darker, occsionally white. Spring–autumn. W N Amer. Z7.

O. ortgiesii Reg. TREE OXALIS. Erect perenn. with persistent st. to 45cm. Hairy, green-purple. Lvs at st. apex; petioles 4–8cm, hairy; lfts 3, 6cm, obcordate, deeply divided into two large triangular lobes, purple or olive-green above, red-purple beneath, hairy. Infl. to 30cm a many-fld cyme; fls to 2.5cm across, lemon yellow with darker veins. Peru. Z8.

O. palmifrons Decid. 2–4cm. Lvs flat spread in a symmetrical, ground-hugging rosette, multifoliate with numerous lfts in palm-like arrangement. Fls white. Summer. S Afr. Z9.

O. pardalis Decid. 4–7cm. Fls white, yellow, lilac, deep pink, purple or red-purple. Summer. S Afr. Z9.

O. patagonica Speg. Stemless perenn. to 5cm with a semi-jointed, creeping rhiz. covered below with rounded orange scales. Petioles 2–5cm; lfts 10–14, 7–8mm, obcordate, divided to base folded, glaucous hairy. Fls solitary, 2.5cm across, red, pink to pink blue, somewhat hairy. Late spring–summer. Patagonia. Z8.

O. pectinata Jacq. = *O. flava*.

O. peduncularis HBK. Erect to ascending, leafy stemmed perenn. to 30cm; st. to 30cm, succulent, red-green, glab. Lvs crowded toward apex; petioles 4–15cm, fleshy, glab.; lfts 3, 12mm, obovate, fleshy, bright green, with a purple margin, pub-

esc. beneath. Infl. to 30cm, 9–16-fld cyme; fls 1.5cm across, yellow with red veins. Spring–summer. Peru, Ecuad. Z9.

O. peduncularis misapplied. = *O. herrerae*.

O. pentaphylla Sims = *O. polyphylla*.

O. pes-caprae L. BERMUDA BUTTERCUP; ENGLISH-WEED. Bulbous, stemless, glab. perenn.; bulbils prolific. Petioles 3–12cm, somewhat succulent; lfts 3, 16–20mm, obcordate, bright green often marked. Peduncles twice as long as petioles; infl. a 3–2-fld umbellate cyme; fls 2–2.5cm across, deep golden yellow. Spring–early summer. S Afr. (Cape Prov.). 'Flore Pleno': double-fld. Z9.

O. polyphylla Jacq. Erect stemmed, bulbous perenn.; st. to 20cm, rather rigid. Lvs congested at apex of st.; petioles 1–5cm; lfts 3–7, 1–3cm, linear, emarginate, with 2 conspicuous orange-red apical calli. Fls solitary, 1.5 to 3cm across, purple, rose-pink to rose-flesh colour or white, throat yellow. Summer. S Afr. (Cape Prov.). Z8.

O. pulchella Decid., 3–16cm. Lvs tufted; petioles to 2cm, slender; lfts 3, to 0.8cm, obovate-cuneate, rounded, sage green. Fls to 3cm diam., solitary, salmon- or rose-pink, throat often yellow. Summer. S Afr. Z9.

O. punctulata Knuth = *O. versicolor*.

O. purpurata Jacq. Stemless bulbous perenn. with fleshy underground stolons. Petioles to 30cm, glab. to pubesc.; lfts 3, 1.5–5cm, obcordate, rounded, dark green and glab. above, dark purple and hairy beneath. Infl. 10–30cm, a 3–10-fld umbel; fls 2.5cm across, purple to violet with a yellow throat. Summer. S Afr. (Cape Prov.). Z9.

O. purpurata var. *bowiei* (Lindl.) Sonder = *O. bowiei*.

O. purpurea L. Bulbous perenn. to 15cm with no aerial st. Petioles 2–8cm, white-pubesc.; lfts 3, 4–40mm, rhomboid to orbicular, or widely obovate, dark green above, maculate or deep purple beneath, long-ciliate. Fls solitary, 3–5cm across, rose-purple, deep rose to violet and pale violet, yellow, cream or white, with yellow throat. Autumn–winter. S Afr. (Cape Prov.). 'Bowles' White': fls white. 'Ken Aslet': to 7cm; lvs large, silky; fls yellow. Z8.

O. racemosa Savigny = *O. rosea*.

O. regnellii Miq. Stemless perenn.; rhiz. covered in tubercle-like deltoid scales. Petioles 10–15cm, glab.; lfts 3, to 25mm, broadly deltoid, emarginate, green suffused purple above, vivid purple beneath, sometimes with dark blotches. Infl. 10–20cm a 3–7-fld umbel; fls 1.5–2cm across, pale pink to white. Spring–summer. Peru, Braz., Boliv., Parag., Arg. Z8.

O. repens Thunb. = *O. corniculata*.

O. rosea Jacq. Erect stemmed ann., often reddened at base; st. 10–35cm, not thickened, much branched and leafy. Petioles to 3cm; lfts 3, to 11mm, obcordate, occas. reddened beneath. Infl. to 10cm, a lax forked, 1–3-fld; cyme; fls 1–1.5cm across, pink with darker veins and a white throat, rarely entirely white. Spring. Chile. *ever*

O. rubella Jacq. = *O. hirta* var. *rubella*.

O. rubra A. St.-Hil. Clump-forming, stemless perenn. to 40cm; tubers round to cylindrical, with red-brown scales, sometimes semi-woody, in tight clusters. Petioles to 30cm; lfts 3, c18mm, obcordate, green, maculate, particularly around sinus, hairy beneath, ciliate. Infl. to 40cm a 6–12-fld umbellate cyme; fls 1–1.5cm across, red to pink. Summer. S Braz. to Arg. 'Alba': fls white. 'Lilacina': fls lilac-purple. Z9. *sp'–frost*

O. rubra 'Delicata' (misapplied). = *O. rosea*.

O. rubra Jacq. non A. St.-Hil. = *O. rubra*.

O. scandens HBK. St. climbing to 1.5m, ± herbaceous, glab., simple to sparsely branched. Petioles to 4cm; lfts 3, to 18mm, obcordate, sharply toothed, thin, sparsely hairy beneath. Infl. a short-stemmed 3-fld cyme, br. 2–3cm; fls 1–2cm across, yellow-green. Spring. Colomb. Z9.

O. sensitivum L. = *Biophytum sensitivum*.

O. siliquosa hort. = *O. vulcanicola*.

O. smithiana Ecklon & Zeyh. Stemless, bulbous, 10–20cm. Petioles 5–18cm; lfts 3, 1–4.5cm, polymorphous, 2-lobed to middle or almost to base, obcordate to obtriangular in outline, lobes linear; spreading, densely punctate above. Fls solitary, 2–3cm across, rose-lilac or white, throat yellow-green. Spring–summer. S Afr. Z9.

O. speciosa Jacq. = *O. purpurea*.

O. squamoso-radicosa Steud. = *O. laciniata*.

O. stricta L. Stoloniferous, ann., erect, single-stemmed when young, becoming branched and decumbent with age; st. 10–40cm, leafy. Lvs in whorls; petioles 3–10cm; lfts 3, 4–20mm, obcordate, somewhat pubesc. beneath. Infl. a 2–5-fld, 3–10cm dichotomous cyme; fls *c*1cm across, pale yellow. Summer–autumn. N Amer., E Asia.

O. stricta L. (misapplied). = *O. dillenii*.

O. succulenta Barnéoud (misapplied). = *O. herrerae*.

O. suksdorfii Trel. Closely allied and similar to *O. stricta*; differing in st. trailing, infl. a 1–3-fld umbel or irregularly branched, fls somewhat larger. Summer–autumn. W US. Z7.

O. tenuifolia Jacq. Slender stemmed bulbous perenn. 6–24cm, often caespitose; st. erect, pubesc., with dense rosettes of lvs in upper parts and numerous abortive br. above. Lvs almost sessile, appearing fasiculate; lfts 3, 4–9mm, linear, folded or involute, emarginate, yellow-pubesc. beneath, marked on margins. Fls solitary, 2–3cm across, purple to white with purple margin and yellow throat. Winter. S Afr. Z9.

O. tetraphylla Cav. LUCKY CLOVER; GOOD LUCK LEAF; GOOD LUCK PLANT. Bulbous, stemless perenn.; bulb covered in hairy scales. Petioles 10–40cm, hairy; lfts 4 (rarely 3), 2–6.5cm, strap-shaped to obtriangular, entire or emarginate, usually with a V-shaped purple band pointing to apex, hairy beneath. Infl. 15–50cm, a 5–12-fld umbel; lfts 1–2cm across, red to lilac-pink, rarely white, throat green-yellow. Summer. Mex. 'Iron Cross': portion of lft. usually bordered by the coloured band, entirely purple. Z8.

O. trilliifolia Hook. Stemless perenn. Rhiz. stout, brown, 4cm or more long, covered in lf bases. Petioles 9–25cm, rather succulent; lfts 3, 2.5–4cm, obcordate, glaucous above, hairy beneath, ciliate. Infl. 10–25cm, a 2–8-fld umbellate cyme; fls c2cm across, white to pale violet. Summer. Pacific N Amer. Z8.

O. tropaeoloides Schlachter = O. corniculata var. purpurata.

O. tuberosa Molina. OCA. Erect to decumbent, succulent-stemmed perenn. to 25cm; tubers 4×3cm, covered in small scales; st. green-purple, densely pubesc. Petioles 7–10cm; lfts 3, to 25mm, obcordate, green or suffused purple, densely pubesc., thick. Infl. to 18cm, a 5–8-fld umbel; fls to 2cm across, yellow. Summer. Colomb. Root crop: three colours of tuber are grown: yellow, white and red; the red and yellow types have lost the ability to fl. Z8.

O. valdiviana hort. = O. valdiviensis.

O. valdiviensis Barnéoud. Compact, erect-stemmed ann., glab. with a thick fleshy taproot; st. 5–10cm, leafy, unbranched. Petioles 4–14cm; lfts 3, 12–20mm, obcordate with a narrow sinus, pale green, thin. Infl. to 18cm, a forked cyme of 4–14 fls; fls 1–1.5cm across, yellow, usually with brown veins. Chile. Z9.

O. varabilis Jacq. = O. purpurea.

O. versicolor L. Bulbous perenn., almost glab. or sparsely pubesc.; st. 3–15cm, erect to spreading, simple. Lvs in apical clusters; petioles 0.5–4cm; lfts 3, to 12mm, cuneate-linear to linear, emarginate, margins marked. Fls solitary, 2–3cm across, white to purple-white, throat yellow, margin purple-violet. Summer–autumn. S Afr. (Cape Prov.). 'Candy Cane': compact; lvs small, round; fls white striped red. var. *flaviflora* Sonder. Fls yellow. Z9.

O. versicolor Jacq., non L. = O. polyphylla.

O. vespertilionis Torr. & A. Gray, non Zucc. = O. drummondii.

O. vespertilionis Zucc. (misapplied). = O. drummondii.

O. vespertilionis Zucc., non Torr. & A. Gray = O. latifolia.

O. violacea L. VIOLET WOOD SORREL. Stemless, bulbous perenn. Petioles 7–13cm, erect; lfts 3, 8–20mm, obcordate, green, marked orange around sinus. Infl. to 25cm, umbellate, 2–16-fld; fls 1.5–2cm across, lavender, pink or paler, with green throat. Spring–autumn. N Amer. Z5.

O. vulcanicola J.D. Sm. Bushy perenn. with lax, succulent, persistent, red st., 20–70cm, spreading, much branched, hairy above. Lvs concentrated mid-stems upwards, v. dense at apex; petioles 3–7cm; lfts 3, to 4cm, obcordate, green flushed red and glab. above, magenta and pubesc. beneath. Infl. to 8cm, 4–7-fld umbellate cyme; fls 1–1.5cm across, yellow with purple-red veins. Summer–autumn. C Amer. Z9.

O. cvs. 'Beatrice Anderson': fls large, pink veined purple. 'Copper Glow': lvs thin, copper; fls yellow.

Oxera Labill. ROYAL CLIMBER. Verbenaceae. Some 20 shrubs, often scandent, glab. Lvs coriaceous. Fls in axill., forked cymes; cal. 4 or 5-lobed or dentate; cor. 4-lobed; sta. 2, long-exserted. New Caledonia. Z10.

O. pulchella Labill. SNOWY OXERA. Scandent, everg. shrub. Lvs to 12.5cm, entire or dentate, oblong-lanceolate. Cymes many-fld; fls pendent; cor. to 5cm, white or yellow-white; campanulate or infundibular, lobes broadly oblong. New Caledonia.

Ox Eye Buphthalmum; Heliopsis.
Ox-eye Daisy Leucanthemum vulgare.
Oxlip Primula elatior.
Ox-tongue Picris.

Oxybaphus L'Hérit. ex Willd. = Mirabilis.

Oxycoccus Hill.
O. macrocarpos (Ait.) Pers. = Vaccinium macrocarpon.
O. quadripetala Gilib. = Vaccinium oxycoccos.

Oxydendrum DC. Ericaceae. 1 decid. shrub to 9m or small tree to 20m. Trunk slender, bark rusty-red to grey; canopy arching and spreading. Lvs 8–20cm, oval, elliptic or oblong-lanceolate, acute, serrulate, thin-textured, lustrous, vivid red in fall. Fls in slender, term. pan. 15–25cm long, br. narrow, decurved then upswept, pale and persisting after lvs; cal. lobes 5, c5mm, green-white; cor. 6–9mm, white, cylindric to urceolate, finely downy, lobes 5, small. Late summer–early autumn. E & SE US. Z5.

O. arboreum (L.) DC. SORREL TREE; SOURWOOD; TITI.
→Andromeda and Lyonia.

Oxylobium Andrews. Leguminosae (Papilionoideae). 30+ everg. shrubs or prostrate subshrubs. Lvs v. short-stalked, simple. Fls papilionaceous, in term. and axill. rac.; standard suborbicular to reniform or transverse-elliptic, wings obliquely oblong, or elliptic, straight but incurved from claw, narrower than keel, auriculate, keel obliquely ovate-elliptic, incurved. Fr. a turgid legume, ovoid or oblong. SW Aus. Z9.

O. callistachys hort. = O. lanceolatum.

O. ellipticum R. Br. Everg. shrub to 3m. St. prostrate or erect. Lvs c7.5cm, oval, dark green. Fls yellow.

O. lanceolatum (Vent.) Druce. Pubesc. shrub to 3m with slightly tawny young growth. Lvs c10cm, lanceolate to ovate-lanceolate, mucronate, leathery. Fls orange or yellow, standard red-patched. Summer.

O. linariifolium (G. Don) Domin. Shrub. Lvs c8cm, narrow-oblong or linear, mucronulate. Fls yellow and red. Spring. Aus.

O. pulteneae A. DC. Bushy strigulose subshrub to 1m. Lvs c1cm, elliptic, elliptic-lanceolate, or subulate, coriaceous, margins revolute. Fls yellow or orange. Spring. Aus. (NSW).
→Callistachys.

Oxypetalum R. Br.
O. caeruleum (D. Don) Decne. = Tweedia caesulea.

Oxyria Hill. Polygonaceae. 2 glab. perenn. herbs, with stout roostocks. Lvs mostly basal, petiolate. Fls minute, in loose narrow pan.; sep. 4, inner pair enlarged in fr.; sta. 6. Fr. with 2 broad wings. Arc., mts of N Amer., Eur., Asia.

O. digyna (L.) Hill. MOUNTAIN SORREL. 10–30cm, slightly succulent. Lvs reniform to cordate, 1.5–2.5cm, entire, green-red; petiole long. Fls congested pan. 4–10cm long; inner sep. green to red, ripening to form pale brown membranous wings, surroundings achene. Summer. Range as for the genus. Z2.

Oxytropis DC. POINT VETCH; LOCOWEED; CRAZY WEED. Leguminosae (Papilionoideae). c300 perenn. herbs. Lvs imparipinnate. Fls pea-like in scapose axill. rac. or spikes, keel with an apical tooth (thus differing from Astragalus). N temp. regions.

O. albiflora (Nels.) Schum. non Bunge = O. sericea.

O. campestris (L.) DC. MEADOW MILKVETCH; YELLOW OXYTROPIS. Lvs to 15cm, in a basal rosette; lfts to 2.5cm, 10–15, elliptic or lanceolate, acuminate, pilose-tomentose. Scapes to 20cm; rac. ovoid, 5–15-fld; cor. usually light yellow, standard to 2cm, keel often violet or dark violet at apex. Summer–autumn. N Eur. and mts of C & S Eur. ssp. sordida (Willd.) Hartm. Cor. yellow or light violet. Scand., Arc. Russia. ssp. tiroliensis (Sieber ex Fritsch) Leins & Merxm. Cor. usually light violet or white. CE Alps. Z3.

O. foetida (Vill.) DC. Aromatic, gland. St. glutinous. Lfts 15–25 pairs, thick, oblong-lanceolate or lanceolate, clammy, glab. Scapes to 15cm, rather longer than lvs, lanate; rac. ovoid, 3–7-fld; cor. yellow, standard to 2cm. Summer. SW Alps. Z6.

O. halleri Bunge ex Koch. PURPLE OXYTROPIS. To 15cm, with adpressed to patent hairs. Lvs to 2.5cm; lfts to 6mm, usually 10–14, to 18m, ovate-lanceolate to lanceolate, acute. Scapes to 30cm, with adpressed hairs; rac. 5–15-fld, ovoid; cor. blue-purple, standard to 2cm, keel dark purple. Summer. Pyren., Alps, Carpath., mts of Scotland. ssp. velutina (Sieber) Schwartz. Scapes and petioles densely downy; cor. pale purple. C Alps. Z6.

O. jacquinii Bunge. Stout, caulescent herb to 40cm. Lfts 14–20 pairs, ovate-lanceolate to lanceolate, sparsely hairy. Rac. subspherical; cor. purple-violet, standard to 1.3cm. Alps. Z5.

O. lambertii Pursh. PURPLE LOCO; LOCOWEED. Tufted, sometimes silky-pubesc. Lvs to 20cm; lfts 7–15, linear to ovate, acute. Rac. 15cm, with 10–25 purple or pink to white fls; standard to 2.5cm. SW US. Z3.

O. lapponica (Wahlenb.) Gay. To 10cm, hairy. Lfts to 14 pairs, oblong-lanceolate or lanceolate, with adpressed hairs. Infl. short, 6–12-fld; rac. subspherical; cor. violet-blue, standard to 1.2cm. Summer. Mts of Lapland, Pyren., Alps. Z3.

O. lazica Boiss. Stemless, procumbent. Lvs 3–7cm; lfts 0.3–1cm, in 6–15 pairs, oblong-ovate to elliptic, pilose. Scape 7–14cm suberect; infl. dense, 4–10-fld; cor. white to purple-blue; standard 1.7–2.2cm. Asia Minor. Z5.

O. megalantha H. Boissieu. Tufted. St. procumbent to ascending, white or grey hairy. Lvs 5–8cm; eaflets 2–3cm, 17–23, oblong-ovate to broadly lanceolate, pubesc. beneath. Scape 20cm; fls to 7; cor. purple-blue to 2cm. Jap. Z6.

O. micans Freyn & Sint. = *O. lazica*.

O. montana ssp. *jacquinii* (Bunge) Hayek = *O. jacquinii*.

O. montana ssp. *samnitica* (Arcang.) Hayek = *O. pyrenaica*.

O. pilosa (L.) DC. WOOLLY MILKVETCH. Resembles *O. foetida* but nearly eglandular, to 50cm. St. and petioles with patent hairs, lfts usually 9–13 pairs, linear-oblong or oblong, with addressed hairs. Rac. ovoid to oblong, many-fld; cor. light yellow, standard to 1.4cm. C & E Eur. Z6.

O. pyrenaica Godron & Gren. Resembles *O. jacquinii* to 15cm. Lfts to 20 pairs, oblong-elliptic or lanceolate, pointed, sericeous. Scape to 20cm, stout, lanate; rac. 8–20-fld, ovoid to spherical; cor. purple or blue-violet, standard to 1.2cm. Summer. Mts of S & SC Eur., esp. Pyren. Z6.

O. sericea Nutt. ex Torr. & A. Gray non (Lam.) Simonkai. Lvs to 30cm, sericeous, canescent; lfts 9–25, to 4cm, ovate to lanceolate. Scapes to 30cm, usually stout, pilose; rac. to 18cm, 6–27-fld; cor. usually white, standard to 2.5cm. N Amer. Z3.

O. sericea (Lam.) Simonkai non Nutt. ex Torr. & A. Gray = *O. halleri*.

O. shokanbetsuensis Miyabe & Tatew. Sparsely white-hairy. St. to 15cm, procumbent. Lvs 6–10cm, white-pubesc.; lfts lanceolate, 1–1.5cm, 19–26, glab. above. Scapes to 10cm, 5-fld; cor. 2–2.3cm, purple-red. Jap. Z7.

O. sordida (Willd.) Pers. = *O. campestris* ssp. *sordida*.

O. splendens Douglas. To 45cm, densely silky-pubesc. Lvs to 25cm; lfts 2cm, in 7–15 clusters of 2–4, elliptic to lanceolate, acute. Fls pink to deep pink. W US. Z6.

O. tiroliensis Sieber ex Fritsch = *O. campestris* ssp. *tiroliensis*.

O. uralensis (L.) DC. Resembles *O. halleri*, but rac. do not elongate after flowering. Summer. Ural Mts. Z6.

→*Astragalus*.

Oyster Bay Cypress-pine *Callitris rhomboidea.*

Oyster Plant *Mertensia maritima*; *Tradescantia spathacea*; *Tragopogon porrifolius.*

Ozark Chinkapin *Castanea ozarkensis.*

Ozark Sundrops *Oenothera macrocarpa.*

Ozothamnus R. Br. Compositae. *c*50 everg. shrubs and woody perenn. herbs. Lvs small and often heath-like. Cap. discoid, often in dense corymbs; phyllaries usually imbricate, with papery appendages, often conspicuously radiate, white, simulating ray flts; flts usually white. Australasia. Z9 unless specified.

O. antennaria (DC.) Hook. f. Shrub to 3m, young br. glutinous grey- to tawny-scurfy. Lvs to 3cm, oblanceolate to obovate, dark green above, grey or tawny scurfy beneath. Cap. to 6mm diam., in dense clusters. Tasm., esp. mts Z8.

O. coralloides Hook. f. Shrub to 50cm, br. spreading, densely tomentose. Lvs closely addressed, to 5mm, oblong, obtuse, revolute, thick and leathery, concave and densely tomentose above, convex or obscurely keeled beneath, glab., lustrous. Cap. 6–8mm diam., solitary, surrounded by lvs recurved; flts 20–40. NZ. Z8.

O. depressus Hook. f. Suberect or prostrate shrub to 1m, white- to grey-tomentose, br. spreading. Lvs addressed, to 3mm, linear, concave, obtusely keeled, loosely woolly above, silky beneath. Cap. *c*4mm diam., solitary. Summer. NZ.

O. diosmifolius (Vent.) DC. Erect shrub to 3m, br. woolly to coarsely hairy. Lvs to 2cm, linear, revolute, tuberculate above, woolly beneath. Cap. in terminal corymbs; phyllaries white, outermost often tinged pink. SE Queensld, NSW.

O. ericifolius Hook. f. Everg. shrub, densely leafy, branching, to 3m. Lvs to 6mm, oblong-linear, obtuse, spreading, leathery, strongly revolute, glab. above, downy with a sweetly aromatic, yellow exudate beneath. Cap. forming v. long floral sprays; phyllaries light brown, inner with white tips. Tasm. Z8.

O. glomeratus (Raoul) Hook. f. Shrub to 3m, br. spreading, tomentose above. Lvs to 3cm, orbicular to broadly ovate or ovate-spathulate, obtuse to apiculate, entire, glab., minutely reticulate above, tomentose beneath. Cap. *c*3mm diam., in subglobose corymbs; phyllaries brown, base woolly. NZ.

O. gunnii Hook. f. Shrub to 3m, br. densely woolly-tomentose. Lvs to 4cm, linear, obtuse, revolute, tomentose above at first, woolly beneath. Cap. *c*5mm diam., in broad, dense, compound corymbs; inner phyllaries with white, radiating tips. Summer. Tasm.

O. hookeri Sonder. Erect shrub, to 2m. Lvs small, scale-like, erect, closely addressed, revolute concave above, woolly beneath. Cap. small, in dense clusters; inner phyllaries with white tips. Summer. Vict., Tasm.

O. ledifolius (DC.) Hook. f. KEROSENE WEED. Strongly aromatic, inflammable shrub to 1m, young shoots downy, older lvs and br. viscid, producing yellow exudate. Lvs to 15mm, oblong to linear, obtuse, spreading, leathery, strongly revolute, glab. above, downy beneath, rufescent at first. Cap. in dense terminal corymbs; phyllaries tawny to yellow or red, innermost with white radiating tips, downy, viscid. Tasm. Z8.

O. purpurascens DC. Like *O. ericifolius* but lvs to 2cm and acute, with curry-like odour, and phyllaries usually pink to purple. Tasm.

O. rosmarinifolius (Labill.) DC. Shrub to 3m, br. erect, woolly at first. Lvs crowded, to 4cm, linear, mucronate, woolly beneath, revolute. Cap. to 4mm diam., in dense corymbs; phyllaries light brown, usually crimson-tinged, inner with white radiating tips. Summer. NSW, Vict., Tasm. Z8. 'Silver Jubilee': lvs v. silvery.

O. scutellifolius Hook. f. Shrub to 2m, tomentose. Lvs minute, scale-like, ovate, reflexed, revolute, glab. to tomentose above, tomentose beneath. Cap. *c*4mm diam., in clusters of 3–5; phyllaries woolly pale brown, tipped white. Summer. Tasm.

O. secundiflorus (Wakef.) C. Jeffrey. CASCADE EVERLASTING. Shrub to 2m, br. white-woolly. Lvs to 12mm, oblong-linear, sparsely downy above, densely woolly beneath. Cap. numerous, pendent, in clusters forming long sprays, fragrant; phyllaries russet, inner with white radiating tips. NSW, Vict.

O. selaginoides Sonder & F. Muell. Spreading perenn. herb or subshrub, to 30cm, glab. Lvs small, obtuse, spreading to recurved, base decurrent, fleshy, convex or flat beneath. Cap. *c*4mm diam., sessile in terr. clusters; innermost phyllaries with broad, white, spreading tips. Summer. Tasm.

O. selago Hook. f. Shrub to 40cm, young shoots arching or pendulous, tomentose. Lvs minute, densely imbricate, addressed, ovate-deltoid, obtuse to subacute, thick and leathery in upper part, concave, woolly above, lustrous beneath. Cap. *c*6mm diam., solitary; phyllaries dull white or yellow-tinged. Summer. NZ. Z8.

O. thyrsoideus DC. SNOW IN SUMMER. Shrub to 3m, young shoots glutinous. Lvs to 5cm, narrowly linear, addressed, dark green, resinous above, paler beneath with fine, addressed down. Cap. *c*4mm diam., in dense, rounded corymbs to 2cm; phyllaries pale brown, papery, inner with white, radiating tips. Summer. NSW, Vict., Tasm.

O. vauvilliersii Hombron & Jacquinot ex Decne. = *Cassinia vauvilliersii.*

→*Helichrysum* and *Swammerdamia*.

P

Pabstia Garay. Orchidaceae. 5 epiphytic orchids. Pbs ovoid-cylindrical, 2-leaved at apex, sheathed by leafy bracts. Lvs lanceolate, plicate. Rac. basal, few-fld; sep. free, subequal; pet. subsimilar to sep.; lip shorter than tep., simple to trilobed, callus grooved. Braz. Z10.

P. jugosa (Lind.) Garay. Pbs 5.5–7cm. Lvs 15–25cm. Infl. 12–20cm, 1- to few-fld; fls 5.5–7.5cm diam., fleshy, fragrant; sep. white or cream, oblong or obovate-oblong, spreading; pet. white, heavily blotched, spotted or broken-banded chocolate, maroon or rose-purple, narrowly obovate-oblong, erect-spreading; lip white or cream, streaked and blotched violet-purple or rose purple, deeply 3-lobed, disc puberulent. Summer. Braz.
→*Colax* and *Maxillaria*.

Pacaya, Pacayo *Chamaedorea neurochlamys; C. tepejilote.*

Pachira Aubl. SHAVING-BRUSH TREE. Bombacaceae. 24 everg. or decid. shrubs or trees, sometimes spiny. Lvs digitate. Fls solitary or in cymes, subtended by 2–3 bracteoles, pedicel short; cal. cup-shaped, truncate or 3–5-lobed; pet. narrow, tomentose beneath; sta. v. numerous, fused below into long tube. Capsule woody, pulp fibrous or fleshy. Trop. Amer. Z10.

P. aquatica Aubl. GUIANA CHESTNUT; WATER CHESTNUT; PROVISION TREE. 5–20m. Lfts to 30cm, 5–9, obovate to elliptic-lanceolate. Pet. 35cm, green- to yellow-white, or pink to purple; staminal tube to 12.5cm, fil. white to red or scarlet, anth. red. Fr. subglobose to elliptic, to 30cm. Mex. to N S Amer.

P. fendleri Seem. To 30m; trunk with large buttresses, covered with stout spines as are br. Lfts 5, obovate, to 18cm. Pet. to 11cm, white on inner side, brown externally; sta. in 5 fascicles, to 8.5cm. Fr. to 10cm, oblong-obovoid, 5-angled. Nic. to Colomb.

P. insignis (Sw.) Savigny. WILD CHESTNUT. To 30m, resembling *P. aquatica* but lfts to 23×9cm, 5–7, obovate-oblong. Pet. to 23cm, brown-red to scarlet or purple, fil. purple, sometimes white below, anth. yellow. Fr. globose to ellipsoid, to 25cm. Braz.

P. macrocarpa (Schldl. & Cham.) Walp. = *P. aquatica.*

P. quinata hort. = *P. fendleri.*
→*Bombacopsis.*

Pachycereus (A. Berger) Britt. & Rose. Cactaceae. 9 tree-like or shrubby cacti; st. stout, erect. Flowering areoles confluent or connected by a groove, felted; fls small to medium-sized, shortly tubular, funnelform or campanulate; tube with scales; floral areoles naked or woolly and/or bristly. Mex.

P. chrysomallus (Lem.) Schum. = *P. militaris.*

P. columna-trajani (Karw. ex Pfeiff.) Britt. & Rose = *Cephalocereus columna-trajani.*

P. grandis Rose. Differs from *P. pecten-aboriginum* and *P. pringlei* in more fastigiate habit; trunk to 1m diam.; ribs 9–11; areoles discrete; central spines 3, lowest longest, to 6cm. Fl. c4cm. S Mex. Z9.

P. hollianus (F.A.C. Weber ex J. Coult.) F. Buxb. Shrub to 4–5m, ± unbranched; st. 4–6cm diam., bark grey-green; ribs 8–14; central spines 3–5, 3–5(–10)cm, flattened, red-brown, later grey to black; radial spines 12–14, 1–3.4cm. Fl. broadly tubular-campanulate, 7–10×3–3.5cm; scales of pericarpel and tube brown; outer tep. brown-green, inner white. S Mex. Z9.

P. marginatus (DC.) Britt. & Rose. Shrub 3–5(–7)m, ± unbranched; st. 8–20cm diam., dark green; ribs 4–7; central spines 1–2, 10–15mm; radial spines c7, 2–4mm. Fls tubular, 3–5×3cm; floral areoles woolly and sometimes with small spines; inner tep. pale green-white or pink. C & S Mex. Z9.

P. militaris (Audot) D. Hunt. Tree to 5–6m; br. numerous, c12cm diam., dark grey-green; ribs 5–7, later to 9–11; spines 8–14, to 1cm, weak. Flowering zone an apical cephalium, with dense golden bristles; fls 6–7×3.5–4cm; pericarpel and tube yellow-green; inner tep. pale green. SW Mex. Top cuttings of sts with 'Grenadier's Cap' cephalium are in cult. Z9.

P. pecten-aboriginum (Engelm.) Britt. & Rose. Resembling *P. pringlei*, but not glaucous when young and differing in having fewer (10–11) ribs and spines (8–12), and less woolly fls. W Mex. Z9.

P. pringlei (S. Wats.) Britt. & Rose. Massive tree to 15m, trunk short; br. erect, 25–50cm, diam., blue-green; ribs 11–17; spines 20 or more, 1–3cm, stout. Fl. 6–8cm; pericarpel and tube densely woolly in the axils of the scales; inner tep. white. NW Mex. Z9.

P. ruficeps (F.A. Weber ex Roland-Goss.) Britt. & Rose = *Neobuxbaumia macrocephala.*

P. schottii (Engelm.) D. Hunt. Large shrub, 3–7m, branching at the base; st. erect, 10–15cm diam.; ribs usually 5–7; spines 8–10, to 12mm or numerous, weak, bristly somewhat twisted, 3–7.5cm. Fl. funnelform, c4×3cm with disagreeable smell; floral areoles sparsely woolly or naked; inner tep. pink or white. NW Mex., S (S Ariz. Z9.

P. tetetzo (F.A. Weber ex Schum.) Ochot. = *Neobuxbaumia tetetzo.*

P. weberi (J. Coult.) Backeb. Massive candelabriform tree to 10m with trunk short, crown dense; br. c20cm diam., blue-green; ribs c10; central spine 1, to 10cm, stout, somewhat flattened; radial spines 6–12, 1–2cm. Fl. funnelform, 8–10cm; floral areoles with brown hairs and sparse bristles; inner tep. white. S Mex. Z9.
→*Backebergia, Cephalocereus, Cereus, Lemaireocereus* and *Lophocereus.*

Pachycymbium Leach. Asclepiadaceae. 32 succulent, leafless, perenn. herbs. St. bluntly 4-angled, dark-mottled, teeth conical or flattened-deltoid, tapering, tuberculose, apices soft, subulate. Infl. cyme 1- to few-fld, toward st. apex; cor. campanulate to flat, sometimes with a thickened annulus at tube mouth, lobed, corona variable. Afr., Arabia. Z9.

P. baldratii (A. White & B.L. Sloane) M. Gilbert. St. about 10cm, not markedly grooved between angles, often tinged purple. Fls 2–8cm diam., pale mahogany brown or cream with tiny red spots, red-hispidulous, lobes dark mahogany brown, replicate; outer corona black-purple, inner corona with cerise lobes. Most material labelled as *P. baldratii* is *P. meintjesianum.* Eritrea, Kenya, N Tanz.

P. carnosum (Stent) Leach. St. 6–15×4.5cm, grey-green spotted red, teeth 12mm. Fls to 1cm diam., campanulate, exterior grey-mauve spotted red, interior deep cream with minute and dense tuberculate hairs, spotted dark red, annulus 5-angled, red-spotted. S Afr.

P. decaisneanum (Lem.) M. Gilbert. St. 10–40×1.5cm, mottled brown, distinctly grooved between rounded angles, teeth to 1.5cm. Fls 2.5cm diam., flat, dark purple, with pale papillae, tube short, campanulate, lobes 1–1.2cm, ovate-oblong, acute. Senegal, Mauritania, Moroc., Chad, Sudan.

P. deflersianum (Lavranos) M. Gilbert. St. to 7×1.5cm, grey-green, with oblong, brown blotches, teeth to 12mm. Fls campanulate, grey-green with brown spots outside, tube cylindric, 1.3×1cm, base pink, glab., otherwise dark maroon, minutely warty, lobes 1.8cm, ovate-lanceolate, slightly ascending, dark purple-brown, with dense, hair-tipped papillae, margins revolute; outer corona pink, margins dark purple-brown, inner corona dark purple-brown. S Yemen.

P. dummeri (N.E. Br.) M. Gilbert. St. to 12×1cm, grey-green, striped dark red-brown, teeth to 10mm. Fls to 3.5cm diam., dark green, tube 6mm, saucer-shaped, smooth, mouth tuberculose, lobes 1.4cm, lanceolate or ovate-lanceolate, spreading, with dense, yellow-green, spindle-shaped papillae within, apical hairs 3mm. Uganda, Kenya, Tanz.

P. gemugofanum (M. Gilbert) M. Gilbert. St. to 22cm, teeth tuberculose, to 2.2cm. Fls flat to shallowly campanulate, fleshy, yellow to pale brown, often more brightly coloured toward centre, smooth tube 8mm diam., lobes to 12.5mm, ovate to deltoid; outer corona dull pink, margin brown or shiny dark red, inner corona dark red to amber. S Ethiop.

P. keithii (R.A. Dyer) Leach. St. 7–9×3–4.5cm, glaucous-green mottled red-brown, teeth to 1.5cm. Fls 1–2cm diam., dark maroon with sparse ivory spots, wrinkled, tube campanulate, warty, with a raised, 5-angled annulus, lobes 5mm, deltoid, papillose, with clavate cilia; corona stalked, ochre, flushed red. S Afr., Swaz., Zimb., Moz.

P. meintjesianum (Lavranos) M. Gilbert. St. to 8×2cm, glaucous-green with darker or purple-brown spots; teeth to 5mm. Fls to 3.5cm diam., flat, glaucous-green blotched purple below, green-yellow with blood-red spots above, minutely papillose, glab., lobes 1.5cm, deltoid, with a central band of denser spots, edged blood-red, tipped olive green; corona golden-yellow blotched red. S Yemen.

P. rogersii (L. Bol.) M. Gilbert. St. to 10cm×8mm, green, glab., teeth to 1.5cm. Fls 3–3.5cm diam., pale yellow, tube 5mm diam. with dense papillae, lobes slender, ascending to incurved, papillose, ciliate toward base. Bots., Zimb., S Afr. (Transvaal).

P. schweinfurthii (A. Berger) M. Gilbert. St. to 10×1.5cm, pale green, with minute, pale red spots or stripes, teeth to 1.5cm. Fls 1.5–2.5cm diam., flat, deeply lobed, pale green with pale brown blotches below, brown or yellow, spotted wine-red or purple, tuberculose and papillose above, tube flat, densely hairy, annulus at mouth, lobes deltoid-ovate, sparsely hairy; corona cream, star-shaped. C & CE Afr.

P. sprengeri (N.E. Br.) M. Gilbert. St. to 15×1.5cm, pale green with tiny red spots or stripes, teeth to 1.5cm. Fls 2.3cm diam., flat, pale green with small stripes and blotches below, light grey-brown to dark brown above, hairy, tube densely so, saucer-shaped, mouth slightly thickened, lobes 1–2cm, narrowly lanceolate to ovate, with hair-tipped papillae; corona yellow to pink-brown or dark brown. Ethiop., Somalia, Sudan.

→*Caralluma* and *Stapelia*.

Pachylophus Spach.
P. macroglottis Rydb. = *Oenothera caespitosa* ssp. *macroglottis*.

Pachyphragma Rchb. Cruciferae. 1 perenn., rhizomatous herb to 40cm. Lvs glossy dark green, mostly radical, 5–11cm, ovate-reniform to round, cordate at base, crenate; petiole to 25cm. Corymb dense, term.; fls malodorous, to 1.8cm diam., white, veined pale green. Cauc., NE Turk., nat. GB. Z7.

P. macrophylla (Hoffm.) Busch.
→*Pterolobium* and *Thlaspi*.

Pachyphytum Link, Klotzsch & Otto. Crassulaceae. 12 succulent, perenn. herbs or subshrubs; st. becoming decumbent with age. Lvs crowded, usually forming rosettes, fleshy, flattened to terete, usually glaucous, tinged purple or pink-red. Flowering st. erect, axill., bracteate; rac. pendulous; fls campanulate or cup-shaped; sep. 5; pet. 5, sometimes margin incurved below forming scale-like appendages to half length of pet. Mex. Z9.

P. aduncum (Bak.) Rose = *P. hookeri*.
P. amethystinum Rose = *Graptopetalum amethystinum*.
P. bracteosum Link, Klotzsch & Otto. St. to 30cm high, 1–2.5cm diam. Lvs 1–5×4–11×0.3–1.2cm, obovate to spathulate, white-glaucous. Infl. 15–60cm; fls white with red marking. Autumn–winter. Mex.
P. chloranthum Walth. = *Echeveria heterosepala*.
P. compactum Rose. St. to 12cm diam. Lvs 30–60, 18–30×12mm, fusiform, acute, glaucous, sometimes tinged red-purple. Infl. 30–40cm; fls orange-red with darker tips. Spring. Mex.
P. fittkaui Moran. St. glutinous, to 15mm across. Lvs 2.5–6.5×1.5–3×0.3–1.5cm, not forming rosettes, obovate, flattened, blunt to minutely pointed, with grey-white bloom. Infl. fls red. Mainly winter–early spring. Mex.
P. heterosepalum Walth. = *Echeveria heterosepala*.
P. hookeri (Salm-Dyck) A. Berger. St. to 18mm across. Lvs 25–40, 2.5–5×0.6–1.5cm, scattered, apex minutely pointed, green with blue-grey to white bloom. Infl. 10–25cm; fls dark pink to light red. Year-round. Mex.
P. longifolium Rose. St. 1–2.5cm diam. Lvs 6–11×1.5–2.5×0.9cm, not forming rosettes, broader toward tip, grooved beneath, blunt or acute, purple-green with glaucous bloom. Fls white with a red blotch. Summer–winter. Mex.
P. oviferum Purpus. MOONSTONES. St. to 12mm diam. Lvs 3–5×2–3×1.6cm, crowded, thickly obovoid, purple-glaucous, with dense white bloom. Infl. 5cm; fls pale green-white. Winter–spring. Mex.
P. roseum hort. ex Bak. = *P. hookeri*.
P. sodalis (Berger Rose = ×*Pachyveria sodalis*.
P. uniflorum Rose = *P. hookeri*.
P. viride Walth. St. 18–30mm diam. Lvs 6–14×1.5–3×1.5cm, not forming rosettes, elliptic-oblong, blunt, green to purple-red. Infl. 10–22-fld; fls white, with a red blotch. Autumn–spring. Mex.
P. werdermanii Poelln. St. decumbent, to 1m, 12mm diam. Lvs 4–10×1.5–3.5×1.2cm, scattered, oblong or ellipsoid, blunt, blue-grey or whiter bloom. Infl. 15–25cm; pale pink with a darker pink blotch. Winter–spring. Mex.
→*Cotyledon* and *Echeveria*.

Pachypodium Lindl. Apocynaceae. 17 stem-succulent, spiny, pachycaul, decid. shrublets and trees, often caudiciform. Lf bases elevated on tubercles arranged spirally; lvs scattered or in apical whorls, simple, entire, leathery. Fl. usually tubular-salverform, similar to *Adenium*. Fr. 2 large follicles. S & SW Afr., Madag. Z9.

P. baronii Costantin & H. Boissieu. Differs from *P. rosulatum* in fls brilliant red, c5.5×5cm. N Madag. var. *windsori* (Poiss.) Pichon. Smaller with a white eye to the fl.
P. bispinosum (L. f.) A. DC. Differs from *P. succulentum* in pink to dull purple fls with a much broader cup-shaped tube and short, arching lobes. E Cape.
P. brevicaule Bak. Dwarf, caudex globose, potato-like, thin flat, lobed 30cm+ diam., growing points scattered. Lvs 2–4×1.2–1.6cm, in rosettes amid spines, dark green, puberulent when young. Fls bright yellow, to 1.5×2.5cm. C Madag.
P. decaryi Poiss. Similar to *Adenium* with almost smooth br. and tiny prickles up to 5mm. Fls 0.5–0.8×12cm, white, heavily perfumed. N Madag.
P. densiflorum Bak. Differs from *P. rosulatum* in floral tube opened out almost flat. C Madag. var. *brevicalyx* Perrier. Pedicels elongated; sep. minute, scale-like.
P. geayi Costantin & H. Boissieu. Differs from *P. lamerei* in long-er, narrower lvs and soft grey indumentum. Fls smaller, on much-branched cymes. SW Madag.
P. giganteum Engl. = *P. lealii*.
P. horombense Pichon. Differs from *P. rosulatum* in broad campanulate fls, 5-scalloped in section.
P. lamerei Drake. Tree to 6m with a swollen, tapered or cigar-shaped trunk covered in low spiralled tubercles; branching dichotomous, apical; spines to 2.5cm, in 3's. Lvs 25–35×2.5–11cm, dark, lustrous, revolute. Fls 3.5×6–11cm, white, on stout, branched 5–20cm peduncles. S Madag. Cristate and variegated forms are known.
P. lealii Welw. Caudex massive, or conical to 6m, tapering into thick tuberculate br.; spines to 4cm, in 3's. Lvs 2.5–8×1.2–4cm, undulate. Fls white, 2.5–4×3–5cm, lobes undulate. S Angola, Nam.
P. namaquanum (Wyley ex Harv.) Welw. Solitary pachycaul trunk 1.5–2m×7–30cm, rarely branched, with spiralled tubercles, spines in 3's, 5–7cm. Lvs 8–12×2–6cm, pale green, downy, crisped. Fls in rings around growing point, broadly cupped, 2.5–5×1cm, yellow-green, dull purple within. NW Cape, S Nam.
P. rosulatum Bak. St. pyriform, forming a massive caudex with a crown of thick, forked br. 1–1.5–3.5m high, spines to 1cm, paired. New shoots lanate. Lvs 3–8cm, elliptic. Fls held aloft on a 7–40cm forking peduncle, yellow, 2–7×0.4–2.5cm, with rounded, 10–15mm lobes. Madag. var. *gracilius* Perrier. Smaller, to 40cm diam. with fewer, slimmer br. and narrower red-brown spines.
P. rutenbergianum Vatke. To 8m, trunk tapered or pyriform to 60cm diam. Br. thick forking spiny; spines paired, to 1.5cm. Lvs to 16×4.5cm. Fls large, white. C & S Cape.
P. saundersii N.E. Br. Differs from *P. leadii* in less hairy lvs. S Zimb. to N Natal.
P. succulentum (L. f.) A. DC. Low, twiggy shrublet arising from a massive turnip-like underground caudex. St. 20–60cm, fleshy. Lvs to 6×1cm, tomentose, stipular spines paired to 2.5cm. Fls few in short-stalked term. cymes, 1–2×1.8–4cm, tube narrow, lobes spreading, red, pink or particoloured to white. C & S Cape to OFS.
P. windsori Poiss. = *P. baronii* var. *windsori*.

Pachyptera DC. ex Meissn.
P. alliacea (Lam.) A. Gentry = *Mansoa alliacea*.
P. hymenaea (DC.) A. Gentry = *Mansoa hymenaea*.

Pachyrhizus Rich. ex DC. Leguminosae (Papilionoideae). 6 twining herbs with long, massive tuberous roots. Lvs trifoliolate. Fls pea-like in dense rac. to 20cm. Fr. flat, strigose, torulose. Summer. Trop. Amer., nat. Flor. Z10.
P. angulatus Rich. ex DC. = *P. erosus*.
P. erosus (L.) Urban. YAM BEAN. Herbaceous twiner, to 4.5m. Lfts angular, rhomboid to ovate or subreniform, usually dentate or lobed, to 19cm. Fls to 2.5cm, dark purple-violet to white. Fr. to 15cm. C Amer.
P. palmatilobus Benth. ex Hook. f. = *P. erosus*.
P. tuberosus (Lam.) A. Spreng. YAM BEAN; POTATO BEAN. Herbaceous twiner, to 7m. Lfts ovate-rhomboid, ± entire to 25.5cm. Fls to 2.2cm, white to violet, with green spot on standard. Fr. to 30cm. Amaz. Basin.

Pachysandra Michx. Buxaceae. 4 everg. or semi-everg., procumbent subshrubs or perenn. herbs, with fleshy often rhizome-like st. and short erect br. with lvs clustered at tips. Fls spicate, white, small, apetalous, sep. 4–6. Fr. a capsule or drupe. China, Jap., SE US.
P. axillaris Franch. Low everg. subshrub to 45cm, young shoots

white. Lvs 5–10cm, ovate, coarsely-toothed, base cuneate to round. Infl. to 2.5cm, axill. Fr. a capsule. Spring. China. Z6.

P. procumbens Michx. Semi-evergreen, perenn. herb; st. brown-pink, to 30cm. Lvs 5–10cm, grey-green with brown-green mottling, ovate to round, coarsely toothed above. Infl. 5–10cm, lat.; anth. pink. Fr. a capsule. Spring. SE US. Z6.

P. terminalis Sieb. & Zucc. Everg. subshrub, to 20cm. St. somewhat fleshy, green. Lvs 5–10cm, oblong-rhombic to oblong-obovate, dentate above, dark green, glossy. Infl. 2–3cm, term. Fr. a drupe. Spring. Jap., NC China. Z5. 'Green Carpet': erect, low and compact; lvs small, finely toothed, deep green. 'Silver Edge': lvs light green, narrowly edged silver-white. 'Variegata': lvs variegated white; slow-growing.

Pachystachys Nees. Acanthaceae. 12 everg. perenn. herbs and shrubs. Spike term., erect; bracts large, overlapping, often in 4 ranks; cal. lobes 5; cor. tubular, bilabiate. Trop. Amer. Z10.

P. coccinea (Aubl.) Nees. CARDINAL'S GUARD. Shrub to 2m. Lvs to 20cm, elliptic-ovate, rugulose. Infl. to 15cm, 4-sided; cor. to 5cm, scarlet. W Indies, N S Amer.

P. lutea Nees. Shrub to 1m. Lvs to 12cm, narrow-ovate to lanceolate, veins sunken above. Infl. to 10cm, 4-sided; bracts golden to amber; cor. to 4.75cm, white. Peru.

→*Beloperone*, *Jacobinia* and *Justicia*.

Pachystegia Cheesem.
P. insignis (Hook. f.) Cheesem. = *Olearia insignis*.
P. insignis var. *minor* Cheesem. = *Olearia insignis*.

×**Pachyveria** hort. Haage & Schmidt. (*Echeveria* ×*Pachyphytum*.) Crassulaceae. 8 succulents. Lvs forming rosettes or scattered, fleshy, flattened or rounded below. Infl. of 1–3 cincinni; fls bell-shaped, red to orange-red. Mex. Z9.

×*P. clavata* Walth. (*Echeveria* sp. ×*Pachyphytum bracteosum*.) Lvs c10×3cm, spathulate, grey-green.

×*P. clevelandii* Walth. (*Echeveria* sp. ×*Pachyphytum bracteosum*.) Lvs to 10×2.5cm, green-purple, fine-pointed.

×*P. glauca* Haage & Schmidt. (*Pachyphytum compactum* ×*Echeveria* sp.) Lvs to 6×1.5cm, forming a dense rosette, ± circular or slightly flattened, semi-terete, glaucous, acute. Fls yellow, tips red.

×*P. haagei* hort. = ×*P. glauca*.

×*P. mirabilis* (Delile) Walth. (*Echeveria scheeri* ×*Pachyphytum bracteosum*.) Lvs to 6×2.6cm, acute, glaucous, broader above.

×*P. pachyphytoides* (De Smet) Walth. (*Echeveria gibbiflora* 'Metallica' ×*Pachyphytum bracteosum*.) Differs from *Pachyphytum bracteosum* in lvs to 12×5cm, glaucous, tinged purple-red. Fls pink-red.

×*P. scheideckeri* (De Smet) Walth. (*Echeveria secunda* ×*Pachyphytum bracteosum*.) Lvs 6–7×1–2cm, forming a rosette, apex acute, blue-grey or whiter bloom, white-striate.

×*P. sobrina* (A. Berger) Walth. (*Echeveria* sp. ×*Pachyphytum bracteosum* or *Pachyphytum hookeri*.) Lvs to 5×9cm, somewhat broader toward tip, apex acute.

×*P. sodalis* (A. Berger) Walth. Lvs to 8.5–3.5cm, sharp-pointed, blue-grey, spathulate.

→*Diotostemon*, ×*Echephytum*, *Echeveria*, *Pachyphytum*, and ×*Urbiphytum*.

Pacific Dogwood *Cornus nuttallii*.
Pacific Fir *Abies amabilis*.
Pacific Grindelia *Grindelia stricta*.
Pacific Plum *Prunus subcordata*.
Pacific Red Coast Elder *Sambucus callicarpa*.
Pacific Silver Fir *Abies amabilis*.
Pacific Yew *Taxus brevifolia*.

Packera Löve & D. Löve Compositae. 60 perenn. herbs. Lower lvs stalked, st. lvs ± sessile, often reduced to bracts at summit. Cap. usually radiate, solitary to numerous; receptacle flat to convex; flts yellow to orange or red. Amer., E N Asia.

P. aurea (L.) Löve & D. Löve. GOLDEN GROUNDSEL; GOLDEN RAGWORT. To 80cm, becoming glab. Basal lvs to 15cm, cordate-ovate, crenate or serrate, petiole long, apex broadly obtuse, sometimes tinged purple beneath; st. lvs pinnate. Cap. 2cm diam., in corymbs; phyllaries often purple-tipped; flts yellow, ray flts rarely 0. Spring–summer. E N Amer. to Tex. Z3.

P. bolanderi (A. Gray) W.A. Weber & Löve. To 60cm, ± glab. Basal lvs to 7cm, orbicular-cordate, shallowly palmately lobed, thick; st. lvs pinnatifid or lyrate-pinnatifid, much reduced. Cap. to 4cm diam., in a compact cyme; phyllaries often loosely hairy; flts yellow. Summer. N Calif., SW Oreg. Z7.

P. cana (Hook.) W.A. Weber & Löve. To 45cm, white-tomentose. Basal lvs to 5cm, narrowly oblanceolate to elliptic or ovate, entire or dentate, glab. above, petioles to 5cm; st. lvs re-

duced, often toothed or lobed. Cap. to 4cm diam., in a flat-topped term. cluster; flts yellow. Summer. W N Amer. Z7.

P. cymbalaria (Pursh) W.A. Weber & Löve. Dwarf, to 20cm, subglabrous. Lvs elliptic to obovate, entire to lyrate-pinnatifid; upper st. lvs pinnatifid. Cap. to c3cm diam., usually solitary; flts yellow, ray flts often with violet stripes. Arc. E Asia and N Amer. Z3.

P. flettii (Wiegand) W.A. Weber & Löve. WOOLLY BUTTERWEED. To 20cm, tawny tomentose at first. Basal lvs to 8cm, ovate to obovate, pinnatifid to lyrate-pinnatifid, lobes dentate; st. lvs few, linear. Cap. to c3cm diam., in a term., compact, cymose cluster; flts dark yellow. Summer. Washington State. Z6.

P. obovata (Muhlenb. ex Willd.) W.A. Weber & Löve. To 70cm, stolons abundant. Basal lvs to 20cm, narrowly obovate to orbicular, obtuse, crenate-serrate, base sometimes deeply cut, petiole to 40cm; st. lvs often pinnatifid. Cap. c3.5cm diam., in a corymbose cyme; phyllaries often purple-tipped; flts yellow, ray flts sometimes 0. Spring–early summer. SE US. Z7.

P. pauciflora (Pursh) Löve & D. Löve. RAYLESS ALPINE BUTTERWEED. To 40cm. Lvs somewhat succulent, basal lvs 5cm, elliptic-ovate to subrotund, crenate-dentate, petiole to 10cm; st. lvs toothed to pinnatifid. Cap. usually discoid, to 1.5cm diam., in a somewhat umbellate cyme; phyllaries suffused maroon from tip; flts orange or tinged red. Summer. E Canada to W N Amer. Z3.

P. paupercula (Michx.) Löve & D. Löve. BALSAM GROUNDSEL. To 60cm. Basal lvs to 8cm, lanceolate to oblong or suborbicular, crenate-serrate to subentire, petiole to 8cm; st. lvs dissected. Cap. to c3cm diam., in a corymbose cyme; phyllaries often purple-tipped; flts yellow, ray flts sometimes 0. Summer. N Amer. Z3.

P. werneriifolia (A. Gray) W.A. Weber & Löve. ALPINE ROCK BUTTERWEED. To 15cm, sparsely hairy. Lvs to 7cm, spathulate to oblanceolate, lanceolate-elliptic or orbicular-ovate, ± entire. Cap. to c3cm diam., long-pedunculate; flts yellow. Summer. W N Amer. Z5.

→*Senecio*.

Padauk, Padouk *Pterocarpus indicus*.
Paddy's Pride *Hedera colchica* 'Sulphur Heart'.

Paederota L. Scrophulariaceae. 2 perenn. alpine herbs. Rac. spike-like, bracteate, term.; cal. 5-lobed; tube cylindrical, limb bilabiate, upper lip erect, usually entire, lower lip 3-lobed, ± patent; sta. 2. S Eur. Z6.

P. bonarota (L.) L. To 20cm; st. numerous, crispate-pubesc. Lvs ovate-suborbicular to oblong-lanceolate, hirsute to glab., toothed. Cor. 10–13mm, violet-blue, rarely pink; sta. exserted. E Alps.

P. lutea Scop. YELLOW VERONICA. Like *P. bonarota* but less hairy; lvs narrow-ovate to narrow-lanceolate, with more than 9 teeth per side. Cor. yellow; sta. usually included. E Alps, W Balk.

→*Veronica*.

Paeonia L. PEONY. Paeoniaceae. 33 perenn. herbs or shrubs with slender cane-like st. branching above ('Tree Peonies'). Lvs basal and cauline in herbaceous spp., cauline in tree peonies, compound. Fls solitary to many, term.; sep. 5; pet. 5–10; sta. numerous; fil. white to red, anth. usually yellow; carpels 2–8. Fr. 2–8 spreading follicles; seeds often with a fleshy, coloured coat. Eur., temp. Asia, NW Amer., China.

P. albiflora Pall. = *P. lactiflora*.

P. anomala L. Herb to 50cm, glab. Lvs biternate, lfts pinnatisect, seg. 2–3-lobed, narrow-oblong, 5–9cm, dark green above, glaucous beneath. Fls solitary, to 9cm diam.; pet. obovate, truncate at apex, bright red, undulate; carpels 3–5, glab. Early summer. E Russia to C Asia. var. *intermedia* (C. Mey. ex Ledeb.) B. Fedtsch. & O. Fedtsch. Carpels tomentose. Z5.

P. arborea Donn = *P. suffruticosa*.

P. arietina Anderson = *P. mascula* ssp. *arietina*.

P. bakeri Lynch. Herb to 60cm. St. villous. Lvs biternate, lfts 7–10.5cm, ovate, acute, dark green above, glaucous, tomentose beneath. Fls solitary, to 11.5cm diam.; pet. obovate or suborbicular, maroon-red; fil. red, anth. yellow; carpels 3, densely hairy. Late spring–early summer. Origin unknown. Z5.

P. banatica Rochel = *P. officinalis* ssp. *banatica*.

P. broteri Boiss. & Reut. Herb to 40cm, glab. Lower lvs biternate, term. lfts cut into 2–3 seg., upper lvs with lfts entire. Fls solitary, to 10cm diam.; pet. broadly ovate, light pink; carpels 2–4, white-woolly. Late spring–summer. Iberian peninsula. Z7.

P. brownii Douglas ex Hook. Herb to 45cm. St. glab. Lvs biternate, dark green above, glaucous beneath; lfts cut into 3seg., seg. deeply divided, to 4-lobed, lobes entire or toothed. Fls cup-shaped, to 3cm diam.; pet. broadly ovate to suborbicular, dark magenta; carpels 5, glab. Summer. W N Amer. Z7.

P. brownii ssp. *californica* (Nutt. ex Torr. & A. Gray) Abrams = *P. californica*.

P. californica Nutt. ex Torr. & A. Gray. Herb to 60cm. St. glab. Lvs biternate, dark green above, pale green beneath, glab., lfts papery, seg. narrowly oblong, lobes 2–3, occas. incised. Fls cup-shaped, to 3cm diam.; pet. ovate to suborbicular, concave, purple-maroon; carpels 3, glab. Spring. S Calif. Z7.

P. cambessedesii Willk. Herb to 45cm. St. glab., tinged red. Lvs spaced along st., biternate, to 25cm, dark green above with veins impressed, marked purple beneath; lfts lanceolate to elliptic, to 10cm, entire. Fls solitary, to 10cm diam.; pet. broadly ovate, deep pink; fil. red; carpels 5–8; glab., purple. Late spring. Balearic Is. Z8.

P. chinensis hort. = *P. lactiflora*.

P. clusii Stern & Stearn. Herb to 30cm. St. glab., pink. Lvs biternate, lfts divided, seg. 30+, narrow-oblong to elliptic, to 6cm, occas. lobed or toothed, green above, glaucous, ± glab. beneath. Fls to 10cm diam.; pet. 6–8, obovate, rounded white, rarely marked with pink; fil. pink; carpels 2–4; hoary tomentose. Spring. Aegean Is. (Crete, Karpathos). Z7.

P. corallina Retz. = *P. mascula* ssp. *mascula*.

P. corallina var. *triternata* Boiss. = *P. mascula* ssp. *triternata*.

P. coriacea Boiss. Herb to 55cm. St. glab., erect. Lower lvs biternate; lfts to 9, some cut into 14–16 seg., broadly elliptic, lanceolate to ovate, cuneate to rounded at base, acute, green, glab. above, glaucous, glab. beneath. Fls to 15cm diam.; pet. obovate, light pink. Late spring. S Spain, Moroc. var. *atlantica* (Coss.) Stern. Lfts larger, hairy beneath. Alg. Z8.

P. cretica Tausch = *P. clusii*.

P. daurica Andrews = *P. mascula* ssp. *triternata*.

P. decora Anderson = *P. peregrina*.

P. delavayi Franch. Tree peony to 1.6m, glab. St. slender, cane-like, sparsely branching above. Lvs biternate, to 27cm, deeply and gracefully dissected; lfts ovate-lanceolate, to 10cm, dark green above, blue-green beneath, entire or toothed, term. lfts trifid. Fls to 9cm diam., subtended by 8–10 leaf-like bracts; pet. obovate, to 4cm, v. dark red to maroon; fil. dark-red, anth. golden. Summer. SW China. 'Anne Rosse' (*P. delavayi* × *P. lutea* var. *ludlowii*): fls to 10cm diam., pet. lemon, exterior streaked red. Z6.

P. delavayi var. *angustiloba* Rehd. & G.H. Wils. = *P. potaninii*.

P. delavayi var. *lutea* (Franch.) Finet & Gagnep. = *P. lutea*.

P. edulis Salisb. = *P. lactiflora*.

P. emodi Wallich ex Royle. Herb to 75cm. St. erect, light green, glab. Lvs biternate; lfts 12–17cm, elliptic, acuminate, entire or bilobed, dark green, glab., term. lfts trifid. Fls to 12cm diam.; pet. obovate, to 4cm, white; carpels 1–2, densely yellow bristly. Spring. NW India. var. *glabrata* Hook. f. & Thoms. Carpels glab. Z8.

P. fragrans (Sab.) Redouté = *P. lactiflora*.

P. humilis Retz. = *P. officinalis* ssp. *humilis*.

P. intermedia C. Mey. ex Ledeb. = *P. anomala* var. *intermedia*.

P. japonica (Mak.) Miyabe & Tak. As for *P. obovata* except lvs villous beneath; fls opening less widely, pet. more concave, white. Early summer. Jap. Plants offered under this name may be Japanese cvs of *P. suffruticosa*. Z7.

P. kesrouanensis Thiéb. Differs from *P. mascula* in carpels glab. not tomentose. Spring. Syr. Z8.

P. laciniata Siev. = *P. anomala*.

P. lactiflora Pall. Herb to 60cm. St. erect, marked red. Lvs biternate, dark green, glab. above, light green, with sparse hairs on veins beneath; lfts entire or lobed, elliptic to lanceolate, margins rough-bumpy. Fls to 10cm diam., fragrant; pet. obovate, white, to 4.5cm; carpels 4–5; glab. Summer. Tibet to China and Sib. var. *trichocarpa* (Bunge) Stern. Carpels hairy. Old hybrids of *P. lactiflora* ('The Chinese Paeonies') vary in fl. colour from white to pink, deep red, crimson or maroon, and are single, double or semi-double in form. (white doubles) 'Festiva Maxima': a few pet. with basal blotch blood red. 'Kelway's Glorious': pet. base suffused cream, fls fragrant. (pink doubles) 'Auguste Dessert': salmon rose, margins silver. 'Carnival': outer pet. carmine pink, inner pet. cream and rose. 'Kelway's Lovely': bright rose-pink. 'Sarah Bernhardt': apple blossom pink. (red and purple doubles) 'Bunkers' Hill': semi-double, pet. pale crimson. 'Chocolate Soldier': rich black-red, inner pet. dotted yellow. 'Félix Crousse': deep carmine rose with a deeper red centre. 'François Ortegat': fls fragrant, semi-double, fls crimson-purple. 'Hidcote Purple': fls deep maroon-purple. 'President Roosevelt': fls large, dark pink, richly fragrant. (single) 'Lord Kitchener', 'Poetic', 'Sir Edward Elgar': deep crimson. 'Pink Delight': blush pink. 'Whitleyi Major': pure white. (so-called Imperial varieties with petaloid sta.) 'Bowl of Beauty': fuchsia-rose, petaloid sta. pale yellow. 'Calypso': fls pale carmine, petaloid sta. tipped gold. 'Instituteur Doriat':

velvet carmine, edged white. 'Kelway's Majestic': cherry rose, petaloid sta. lilac. 'Palermo': pale pink. Z6.

P. × lemoinei Rehd. (*P. lutea* × *P. suffruticosa*.) Tree peony to 2m. Fls yellow or combinations of yellow and pink. Gdn origin. 'Alice Harding': fls double, lemon yellow. 'Argosy': fls single, to 18cm diam., pet. primrose yellow, basal blotch carmine. 'Chromatella': fls double, sulphur yellow. 'La Lorraine': fls double, cream-yellow. 'L'Espérance': fls 15–20cm diam., pet. pale yellow, basal blotch crimson. 'Mme Louis Henry': fls 15–17.5cm diam., cream-yellow, suffused red. 'Souvenir de Maxime Cornu': fls double, pet. yellow, tinged brown, orange and red. 'Tria': fls in groups of 3, single; pet. 10–12, yellow; v. early. Z7.

P. lutea Delav. ex Franch. As for *P. delavayi* except bracts lacking from base of fl.; fls to 7.5cm diam.; pet. yellow; carpels 3–4. Early summer. China. 'Superba': new growth bronze, later green; fls large, tinged pink at base. var. *ludlowii* Stern & Tayl. TIBETAN PEONY. To 2.5m. Fls to 12.5cm diam., earlier. Spring. Tibet. Z6.

P. macrophylla (Albov) Lom. Herb to 90cm. Lvs biternate, lfts to 25cm, elliptic-lanceolate to ± orbicular, dark green above, glaucous, sparsely hairy on veins beneath. Fls to 7.5cm diam.; pet. white, tinged yellow; carpels 2–4, glab. Spring. W Cauc. Z7.

P. mairei Lév. Herb to 90cm. St. erect or spreading, glab. Lvs biternate; lfts elliptic to obovate, to 19cm, dark green above, light green beneath, lat. lfts occas. bifid. Fls to 11cm diam.; pet. obovate to ovate-elliptic, to 7cm, rose-pink; fil. red; carpels glab. to tawny tomentose. Late spring. SW China. Z6.

P. mascula (L.) Mill. V. variable herb, 25–60cm. St. glab. Lvs biternate, lfts 9–21, entire or cleft, elliptic to broadly obovate, glab. or pilose beneath. Fls to 13cm diam.; pet. red, pink or white; fil. red to white; carpels 2–5. ssp. *mascula* (L.) Mill. Herb to 60cm. Lvs biternate, green, glab. beneath; lfts 9–21, elliptic to obovate-elliptic, often deeply 2–3-lobed, terminal lfts broadly elliptic. Fls to 12cm diam.; pet. obovate, purple-red; fil. purple; carpels 2–5, tomentose. Summer. S Eur. ssp. *arietina* (Anderson) Cullen & Heyw. Lvs hairy beneath; lfts 12–15, narrowly elliptic. E Eur., Asia Minor. 'Mother of Pearl': fls pale pink. 'Northern Glory': lvs grey-green; fls single, deep magenta-carmine. 'Purple Emperor': fls single, rose-purple. 'Rose Gem': fls single, bright blood-red. ssp. *hellenica* Tzanoudakis. Pet. white. SW Greece. ssp. *russii* (Biv.) Cullen & Heyw. To 45cm. Lvs tinged purple, glab. to sparsely hairy beneath. W C Greece, Ionian Is., Corsica, Sardinia, Sicily. ssp. *triternata* (Boiss.) Stearn & P.H. Davis. Lfts 9–11, concave above, undulate. Late spring. NW Balk. to Asia Minor. Z8.

P. microcarpa Salm-Dyck = *P. officinalis* ssp. *villosa*.

P. mlokosewitschii Lom. Herb to 1m. St. glab. Lvs biternate, lfts to 10cm, broadly oblong to obovate, dark to silvery or blue-green, glaucous beneath. Fls to 12cm diam.; pet. concave, broadly ovate, yellow; carpels 2–4, densely hairy. Spring. EC Cauc. Z6.

P. mollis Anderson. Herb to 45cm. St. villous to glab. Lvs biternate, lfts to 10cm, cleft, lobes many, narrowly oblong to elliptic, glab. above, white-hairy beneath. Fls to 7cm diam.; pet. cupped, obovate, red or white; fil. red or pale yellow; carpels 2–3, densely hairy. Summer. Origin unknown. Z6.

P. moutan Sims = *P. suffruticosa*.

P. obovata Maxim. Herb to 60cm. St. erect, glab. Lvs biternate, lfts to 14.5cm, broadly oval or oblong, dark green above, glaucous, sparsely hairy beneath, term. leaflet obovate. Fls to 7cm diam.; pet. white to red-purple; fil. white or pink; carpels 2–3, glab. Early summer. Sib., China. var. *willmottiae* (Stapf) Stern. Lfts to 6cm+. Fls cup-shaped, to 10cm diam.; pet. obovate, white. Early summer. China. Z7.

P. officinalis L. Herb to 60cm. St. becoming glab. Lvs biternate, lfts divided into several, narrowly elliptic to oblong seg. to 11cm, sparsely hairy to glab. beneath. Fls to 13cm diam., pet. red, obovate, widespread; fil. red; carpels 2–3 densely hairy. Summer. Eur. ssp. *banatica* (Rochel) Soó. Middle leaflet incised into seg., lat. lfts entire. Carpels tomentose. Balk., Rom., Hung. ssp. *humilis* (Retz.) Cullen & Heyw. St. and petioles hairy. Lfts incised to one-third of their length. Carpels glab. SW Eur. ssp. *villosa* (Huth) Cullen & Heyw. St. and petioles somewhat floccose; lfts as for ssp. *humilis*. Carpels tomentose. Summer. S Fr., It. Cvs include: 'Alba Plena': fls double, white. 'Anemoniflora Rosea': fls deep pink, petaloid sta. yellow, margins crimson. 'China Rose': fls single, salmon pink; sta. orange-yellow. 'Crimson Globe': fls single, garnet-red, petaloid sta. crimson and gold. 'James Crawford Weguelin': fls single, garnet-red, anth. yellow. 'Lize van Veen': fls double, white flushed pink. 'Mutabilis Plena': fls deep pink fading to blush pink. 'Rosea Plena': fls double, darker pink than 'Rosea Plena'. 'Rosea Superba': fls large double, pink. 'Rubra Plena': fls double, crimson. Z8.

P. paradoxa Sab. = *P. officinalis* ssp. *humilis*.

P. parnassica Tzanoudakis. Herb to 65cm. St. hairy. Lvs biternate, lfts 9–13-lobed, obovate to narrowly lanceolate, tinged purple at first, grey-green beneath, pilose, term. leaflet entire, occas. 2–3-lobed. Fls to 12cm diam.; pet. obovate to orbicular, deep red; fil. tinged purple, carpels 2–3, tomentose. Early summer. SC Greece. Z8.

P. peregrina Mill. Herb to 50cm. St. glab. Lvs biternate, rigid, seg. to 2cm, 15–17, occas. 2–3-lobed, lustrous above, glaucous, glab. or sparsely hairy beneath. Fls to 12cm diam., cup-shaped; pet. oblong-ovate to suborbicular, deep red; fil. pink or red; carpels 1–4. Late spring–early summer. S Eur. 'Otto Froebel' ('Sunshine'): fls vermilion; early flowering. Z8.

P. peregrina Bornm. non Mill. = *P. mascula* ssp. *arietina*.

P. potaninii Komar. TREE PEONY. As for *P. delavayi* except stoloniferous, shorter, lf seg. narrower, fls to 6.5cm diam., nodding, not subtended by bracts; pet. maroon to dark velvety red. Early summer. W China. 'Alba': fls and stigmas white, fil. green. var. *trollioides* (Stapf ex Stearn) Stearn. Fls pale yellow; pet. curved inward. W China, Tibet. Z7.

P. reevesiana (Paxt.) Loud. = *P. lactiflora*.

P. rhodia Stearn. Herb to 35cm. St. glab., tinged red. Lvs biternate, divided into 9–29 seg.; lfts to 2.5cm, lobed, ovate to oblong-elliptic or lanceolate, pale green beneath. Fls to 8cm diam.; pet. 6–8, obovate to orbicular, white; fil. red, carpels 2–5, tomentose. Spring. Rhodes. Z8.

P. russii Biv. = *P. mascula* ssp. *russii*.

P. × smouthii Van Houtte. (*P. lactiflora* × *P. tenuifolia*.) Herb to 45cm. Lvs divided into many seg. Fls produced early in season, bright red, fragrant.

P. sterniana Fletcher. Herb, 30–90cm, glab. Lvs to 30cm, seg. to 10cm, glab., elliptic or oblong-elliptic, dark green above. Fls solitary, white, to 8cm diam. above; pet. obovate; fil. white; carpels 5. E Tibet. Z7.

P. suffruticosa Andrews. MOUTAN PEONY. Tree peony to 2m. Lvs biternate deeply dissected; lfts to 10cm, lanceolate to ovate, 3–5-lobed, pale green above, blue-green beneath. Fls to 15cm diam.; pet. many, concave, pink to white, with a deep purple, red-bordered basal patch, margins finely scalloped; fil. violet red; carpels 5. Spring–summer. China, Tibet, Bhutan. 'Banksii': fls double, carmine. 'Godaishu': fls semi-double, large, clear white. 'Hana-daigin': fls double, large, violet. 'Kenreimon': fls purple with pink, pet. turning inwards. 'Kintei': fls lemon streaked dark yellow. 'Koka-mon': fls large, red-brown striped white. 'Reine Elizabeth': fls fully double, large, salmon-pink tinged red, margins ruffled. 'Renkaku': fls double, dense, white, ruffled, anth. long, deep yellow. 'Yae-zakura': fls v. large, double, soft cherry-pink. ssp. *spontanea* (Rehd.) S.G. Haw & L.A. Laurier. Smaller. Fls to 11cm diam.; fil. red. China. 'Cardinal Vaughn': fls ruby-purple. 'Duchess of Kent': fls rose-scarlet. 'Duchess of Marlborough' fls rose-pink. 'Lord Selborne': fls pale salmon pink. 'Montrose': fls pale lavender-lilac. 'Mrs William Kelway': fls white. 'Raphael' fls pale pink. 'Superba': fls cherry red. ssp. *rockii* S.G. Haw & L.A. Laurier. ('Rock's Variety', 'Joseph Rock'): fls semi-double, spreading, pet. v. pale flesh pink to silvery-white blotched maroon at base. Z7.

P. tenuifolia L. Herb to 60cm. Lvs biternate; lfts dissected and lobed in a tripinnate pattern, seg. many linear, dark green above, glaucous beneath. Fls cup-shaped, to 8cm diam.; pet. oblanceolate to obovate, obtuse to emarginate, deep red; carpels 2–3, roughly tomentose. Spring. SE Eur. to Cauc. 'Early Bird': fls single, deep red. 'Latifolia': habit tall; lf seg. broad. 'Plena': fls double, longer-lasting. 'Rosea': fls pale pink. Z8.

P. triternata Boiss. = *P. mascula* ssp. *triternata*.

P. trollioides Stapf ex Stern = *P. potaninii* var. *trollioides*.

P. veitchii Lynch. Herb to 50cm. St. glab. Lvs biternate; lfts incised; seg. 2–4, cut into lobes or entire, oblong-elliptic, long-acuminate, dark green above glaucous, glab. beneath. Fls nodding to 9cm diam.; pet. obovate-cuneate, truncate to emarginate, pale to deep magenta; fil. pink; carpels 2–4. Spring to early summer. China. 'Alba': fls cream-white. var. *woodwardii* (Stapf & Cox) Stern. To 30cm. St. hairy. Lvs hairy beneath on veins and midrib. W China. Z8.

P. willmottiae Stapf = *P. obovata* var. *willmottiae*.

P. wittmanniana Hartw. ex Lindl. To 120cm. St. glab. Lvs biternate; lfts to 16cm, broadly ovate to elliptic, acute, to 16cm, villous beneath, esp. on veins. Fls to 12.5cm diam., pale yellow; carels tomentose. Spring to early summer. NW Cauc. var. *nudicarpa* Schipcz. Carpels glab. Z7.

P. woodwardii Stapf & Cox = *P. veitchii* var. *woodwardii*.

P. cvs. SAUNDERS HYBRIDS. A v. wide range of hybrid herbaceous peonies which can largely be attributed to *P. officinalis*, *P. peregrina* and *P. lactiflora*, although many more spp. have been used. They include 'Archangel' (*P. lactiflora* × *P. macrophylla*): fls single, white. 'Daystar'

(*P. mlokosewitschii* × *P. tenuifolia*): lvs pointed; fls yellow, early. 'Defender': fls red, early. 'Early Windflower' (*P. emodi* × *P. veitchii*): lvs narrow, fern-like; fls white, hanging. 'Golden Hind': lvs dark green; fls fully double, large, deep yellow. 'Renown': fls single, strawberry red suffused yellow. 'Savage Splendour': fls large, ivory splashed and edged purple, pet. twisted. 'Thunderbolt': fls single, black-crimson. 'Vesuvian': habit compact; lvs deep green, finely cut; fls fully double, black-red. 'White Innocence' (*P. lactiflora* × *P. emodi*): habit tall to 1.5m; fls white, centres green, late flowering. DAPHNIS HYBRIDS (Tree Peonies). 'Artemis': habit tall, upright, st. and petioles tinged red; fls single, large, silky yellow. 'Gauguin': fls large, yellow veined red from bold red centre. 'Kronos': fls semi-double, dark red tinged blue. 'Marie Laurencin': lvs glossy; fls semi-double, lavender, centre of darker shade, symmetrical, pet. 10–12; v. early.

PAEONIACEAE Rudolphi. 2/34. *Glaucidium, Paeonia*.

Paesia St.-Hil. Dennstaedtiaceae. 12 terrestrial or epilithic ferns. Rhiz. long-creeping, with massed roots and brown hairs or scales. Fronds stipitate, uniform, 2–4-pinnate-pinnatifid, usually gland. and rough, pinnae and pinnules oblique, seg. toothed to lobed, rachis flexuous. Malaysia to Polyn., NZ. Z7.

P. scaberula (A. Rich.) Kuhn. LACE FERN; SCENTED FERN. Frond to 45×25cm, 2–4-pinnate, ovate to lanceolate, apex narrowly acute, leathery, glandular-pubesc., pinnae to 25×5cm, sub-opposite or alt., distant, ovate to deltoid, pinnules to 2.5cm, short-stalked, lanceolate, seg. to 0.6cm, oblong, acute, entire to toothed or lobed; stipes to 30cm, rough, yellow or chestnut to brown. NZ.

→*Allosorus*.

Pagoda Dogwood *Cornus alternifolia*.
Pagoda Flower *Acmadenia tetragona*; *Clerodendrum paniculatum*; *C. × speciosum*.
Pagoda Tree *Plumeria*; *Sophora japonica*.
Pahautea *Libocedrus bidwillii*.
Painkiller *Morinda citrifolia*.
Paintbrush *Haemanthus albiflos*.
Painted Cups *Castilleja*.
Painted Daisy *Tanacetum coccineum*.
Painted Drop Tongue *Aglaonema crispum*.
Painted Fern *Athyrium nipponicum*.
Painted Fingernail *Neoregelia spectabilis*.
Painted Lady *Burtonia scabra*; *Gladiolus carneus*; *G. debilis*.
Painted Lady Fern *Athyrium nipponicum* 'Pictum'.
Painted Leaf *Euphorbia cyathophora*; *E. pulcherrima*.
Painted-leaf Begonia *Begonia rex*.
Painted Net Leaf *Fittonia verschaffeltii*.
Painted Nettle *Solenostemon scutellarioides*.
Painted Sundew *Drosera zonaria*.
Painted Tongue *Salpiglossis sinuata*.
Painted Trillium *Trillium undulatum*.
Painted Wood Lily *Trillium undulatum*.
Paint Indian *Lithospermum canescens*.
Paint Leaf *Euphorbia heterophylla*.
Pala *Marattia douglasii*.
Pala Indigo Plant *Wrightia tinctoria*.
Palas *Butea monosperma*; *Licuala*.
Pale Dog Violet *Viola lactea*.
Pale Flax *Linum bienne*.
Pale Hickory *Carya pallida*.
Pale Pink Boronia *Boronia floribunda*.
Pale Spike *Lobelia spicata*.
Palestine Oak *Quercus coccifera*.
Pale Trumpet *Sarracenia alata*.
Pale Violet *Viola striata*.

Paliavana Vand. Gesneriaceae. 3 everg. shrubs. Lvs opposite, fleshy, toothed, hairy. Fls axillary and solitary or clustered or in a term. rac.; cal. campanulate, lobes 5, acute, reflexed; cor. tubular, limb oblique, lobes 5, rounded; sta. 4, included. Braz. Z10.

P. prasinata Benth. & Hook. f. St. erect, ringed at nodes, br. villous, becoming woody. Lvs to 12×5cm, ovate-lanceolate, acuminate, tomentose above, softly white-hairy beneath. Fls 2 per axil; cal. campanulate, lobes acute; cor. to 3cm, funnelform, green, spotted black, inflated. Braz.

P. schiffneri (Fritsch) Handro = *Sinningia schiffneri*.

Palicourea Aubl. Rubiaceae. *c*125 shrubs or trees. Lvs ± glab., entire, stipulate. Fls sessile or short-pedicellate, in axill. or term. pan., cymes or corymbs, minutely bracteate; cal. tubular, truncate or 5-lobed; cor. funnel-shaped to subcylindric, lobes 5;

sta. 5, inserted at throat. Fr. a dark, globose berry to 1cm. Trop. Amer. Z10.

P. apicata HBK. Shrub, to 2m, or tree, to 10m. St. terete. Lvs to 12cm, elliptic to oblong, apex attenuate to acute, lustrous and leathery to papery. Fls in sessile, term., pyramidal pan. to 8×6cm, white or yellow to violet or purple; cor. tube to 9mm, gibbous at base, tuberculose, exterior glab., lobes to 4mm, lanceolate to oblong. Venez.

P. barbinervia DC. = *P. guianensis* ssp. *barbinervia*.

P. brevithyrsa Britt. & Standl. = *P. crocea*.

P. coccinea DC. = *P. crocea*.

P. crocea (Sw.) Roem. & Schult. Shrub, to 5m. St. terete to 4-angled. Lvs to 20cm, ovate, lanceolate or elliptic to oblong, apex attenuate to acute, stiff and leathery. Fls in axill. or term., erect, many-fld, pyramidal pan. or corymbs, yellow or orange to red; cor. to 1cm, tube gibbous at base, glab., interior pubesc. at throat, lobes to 1mm, ovate. Summer. W Indies and Cuba, C Amer., N S Amer.

P. guianensis Aubl. Shrub or tree, to 3.5m. St. 4-angled. Lvs to 25cm, ovate to elliptic, apex narrowly acute, papery. Fls in term., thyrsoid or corymbose pan., yellow to orange; cor. to 15mm, tube distended above, exterior minutely pubesc. W Indies, C Amer., N S Amer. ssp. *barbinervia* (DC.) Steyerm. Lvs densely pubesc. on veins. Cal. lobes ciliate; cor. tube pubesc. at throat. Venez., Braz.

P. nicotianifolia Cham. & Schldl. Shrub or tree. St. terete. Lvs to 20cm, obovate to elliptic, apex caudate. Fls in term., thyrsoid pan. to 18cm, yellow; cor. to 12mm, tube pubesc., lobes to 2mm, deltoid. S Amer.

P. rigida HBK. Shrub, to 3m. St. 4-angled. Lvs to 20cm, ovate to elliptic, acute or obtuse, leathery, rugose, glab. Fls in many-fld, pyramidal, cymose pan., yellow to orange; cor. to 15mm, tube exterior papillose, lobes to 5mm. Summer. Trop. S Amer.
→*Psychotria*.

Pali-mari *Alstonia scholaris*.

Palisota Rchb. ex Endl., nom. cons. Commelinaceae. 18 rhizomatous, clump-forming, perenn. herbs, some almost stemless. Infl. thyrses sometimes borne low amid lf stalks, often congested, cincinni elongate, not paired; sep. petaloid; pet. similar to sep.; fil. bearded. Fr. a berry. Trop. Afr. Z10.

P. barteri Hook. St. 0 or to 1m. Lvs 12–50cm, elliptic to obovate, semi-erect or arching, thinly coriaceous, undulate, glossy light green, downy beneath, petiole 2.5–25cm. Infl. ovoid, dense, 10–15cm, without conspicuous bracts; fls white. Fr. purple ripening bright red. Spring. W & C Trop. Afr. Z9.

P. bracteosa C.B. Clarke. St. 0. Lvs 25–40cm, elliptic to oblanceolate, often with green-white stripe along midrib, sessile or with petiole to 25cm. Infl. 4–18cm; bracts conspicuous, long-ciliate; fls pink-white or white. Fr. red, pilose, beaked. Spring. W Trop. Afr. *P. elizabethae* Gent., with lvs variegated with feathery, white midstripe, is usually treated as *P. pynaertii* 'Elizabethae', but may be referable here. Z9.

P. hirsuta (Thunb.) Schum. To 6m. Lvs *c*40cm, clustered towards apex of st., elliptic, short-petiolate, glossy green, subcoriaceous, petioles with long dark hairs. Infl. 10–30cm, lax, with numerous slender cincinni, off-white to pink-flushed; fls 1cm diam., white, tipped maroon. Fr. black-green or purple-red, glossy. Winter–spring. W & C Trop. Afr. Z9.

P. maclaudii Gand. = *P. hirsuta*.

P. mannii C.B. Clarke. St. 0 or to 1m. Lvs 40–100cm; petiole to 30cm. Infl. elongate, 7–19cm, without conspicuous bracts; fls crowded, small, white, later pale pink or lilac. Fr. green or white, turning yellow, orange-red or deep purple. Spring. Trop. Afr. Z9.

P. pynaertii De Wildeman. St. ± 0. Lvs 35–90cm, clustered or rosulate, narrowly ovate to obovate-lanceolate, acuminate, deep green above, grey and velvety beneath, undulate, petiole thick, with long rufous hairs. Infl. ovoid, *c*10cm; fls white. Fr. red. Spring. Trop. Afr. Z9. For the plant usually treated as *P. pynaertii* 'Elizabethae', see *P. bracteosa*.

P. thyrsiflora Benth. = *P. hirsuta*.

Paliurus Mill. Rhamnaceae. 8 spiny, decid. or everg. trees or shrubs. Lvs alt., 3-veined, leathery, dark above, paler beneath, usually in 2 rows, with spinescent stipules. Infl. axill., fls small, 5-merous, yellow. Fr. flat, dry, hemispherical, with a wide wing. S Eur. to E Asia.

P. aculeatus Lam. = *P. spina-christi*.

P. aubletii Benth. = *P. ramosissimus*.

P. australis Gaertn. = *P. spina-christi*.

P. hemsleyanus Rehd. To 15m, br. slender, glab. usually with black thorns. Lvs 6–10cm, obovate to oval-lanceolate, apex acute, base rounded, crenate. Fr. 3cm diam., with a russet-brown wing. S China. Z9.

P. orientalis Hemsl. = *P. hemsleyanus*.

P. ramosissimus (Lour.) Poir. 1.5–3m, br. flexuous, thorns sharp, young growth, rusty-silky. Lvs 3.5–5cm, ovate to oblong, base and apex blunt, teeth small. Fr. to 1.2cm diam., woody, obconical, truncate. China, Korea, Jap., Taiwan. Z7.

P. spina-christi Mill. CHRIST'S THORN. 3–7m, twigs flexuous, hairy, thorns paired, 1 straight, 1 curved. Lvs 2–4cm, entire to crenate-serrate, hairy on veins beneath. Fr. 1.8–3cm diam., woody, 3-lobed, subglobose, wing undulate. Spring, summer. Spain to C Asia and N China. Long cultivated as a hedging plant. Z8.

Pallensis (Cass.) Cass.

P. spinosa (L.) Cass. = *Asteriscus spinosus*.

Palma Plum. ex Mill.

P. elata Bartr. = *Roystonea elata*.

Palma Amarga *Sabal mauritiiformis*.
Palma Blanca *Sabal uresana*.
Palma Cana *Sabal parviflora*.
Palma Christi *Ricinus communis*.
Palma Corcho *Microcycas calocoma*.
Palma de Cana *Copernicia berteroana*.
Palma de Sombrero *Copernicia tectorum*.
Palma de Vaca *Sabal mauritiiformis*.

PALMAE Juss. 198/2650. Acanthophoenix, Acoelorraphe, Acrocomia, Aiphanes, Allagoptera, Archontophoenix, Areca, Arenga, Attalea, Bactris, Borassus, Brahea, Butia, Calamus, Carpentaria, Caryota, Ceroxylon, Chamaedorea, Chamaerops, Chambeyronia, Chrysalidocarpus, Coccothrinax, Cocos, Copernicia, Corypha, Cyrtostachys, Dictyosperma, Drymophloeus, Elaeis, Euterpe, Gaussia, Gronophyllum, Hedyscepe, Howea, Hydriastele, Hyophorbe, Hyphaene, Jubaea, Jubaeopsis, Laccospadix, Latania, Licuala, Linospadix, Livistona, Lodoicea, Maximiliana, Metroxylon, Nephrosperma, Normanbya, Nypa, Oncosperma, Orbignya, Parajubaea, Phoenicophorium, Phoenix, Pigafetta, Pinanga, Polyandrococos, Pritchardia, Ptychosperma, Raphia, Reinhardtia, Rhapidophyllum, Rhapis, Rhopalostylis, Roystonea, Sabal, Salacca, Schippia, Serenoa, Syagrus, Thrinax, Trachycarpus, Trithrinax, Veitchia, Verschaffeltia, Wallichia, Washingtonia.

Palma Pita *Yucca treculeana*.
Palmella *Yucca elata*.
Palmetto *Sabal*.
Palm Grass *Curculigo capitulata*; *Setaria palmifolia*.
Palmito Amargoso *Syagrus comosa*.
Palmito do Campo *Syagrus flexuosa*.
Palm-leaf Begonia *Begonia luxurians*.
Palm-like Fig *Ficus pseudopalma*.
Palm Lily *Yucca gloriosa*.
Palmyra Palm *Borassus flabellifer*.
Palo Colorado *Luma apiculata*.
Palo Cruz *Tabebuia nodosa*.
Palo de Neuz *Juglans jamaicensis*.
Palo de Velas *Parmentiera cereifera*.
Palo Hediondo *Lonchocarpus latifolius*.
Palo Madroño *Amomyrtus luma*.
Palo Peronia *Ormosia krugii*.
Palo Seco *Lonchocarpus latifolius*.
Palo Verde *Parkinsonia florida*.
Palta *Persea americana*.

Palumbina Rchb. f. Orchidaceae. 1 epiphytic orchid. Pbs elliptic, compressed, to 4.5cm. Lvs linear-lanceolate, subcoriaceous. Infl. lat., few-fld, axis purple, slender; fls white; dors. sep. erect, elliptic, round to obtuse, to 1cm, lat. sep. fused; pet. spotted violet at base, obovate, rounded or notched, to 1cm; lip ovate-elliptic, obtuse to rounded, convex, callus warty, yellow spotted red. Guat. Z10.

P. candida (Lindl.) Rchb. f.
→*Oncidium*.

Pamianthe Stapf. Amaryllidaceae. 2 bulbous herbs. Bulbs with a long stem-like neck. Lvs linear with a rounded keel. Fls 1–4 in a term. scapose umbel, spathe valves linear; perianth with a long cylindrical tube; lobes 6; fil. fused at base into a campmanulate corona with 6 short lobes; anth. 6 versatile, exserted. S Amer. Z10.

P. peruviana Stapf. Lvs to 50×4cm. Scape exceeding lvs; fls 2–4, fragrant, perianth tube to 13cm, green, lobes to 13cm, white or cream, oblanceolate with a central green stripe; corona to 8cm. Peru.

Pampas Grass *Cortaderia.*
Pampas Lily of the Valley *Salpichroa origanifolia.*
Pamplemousse *Citrus ×paradisi.*
Panacoco *Ormosia coccinea.*
Panama Hat Plant *Carludovica palmata.*
Panama Monkey Pot *Lecythis tuyrana.*
Panama Orange × *Citrofortunella microcarpa.*
Panama Rubber Tree *Castilla (C. elastica).*
Panama Tree *Sterculia apetala.*
Panamica *Pilea involucrata.*
Panamiga, Panamigo *Pilea involucrata.*
Panamint Daisy *Enceliopsis corvellei.*

Panax L. GINSENG. Araliaceae. 5 perenn. herbs with thickened or tuberous roots. St. to 1m, erect, ann., with a whorl of 3 palmate lvs and terminated by an umbel of small, green-white, 5-merous fls. Fr. drupaceous. S & E Asia, E N Amer.
P. arboreus Forst. f. = *Pseudopanax arboreus.*
P. balfourii Sander = *Polyscias scutellaria* 'Balfourii'.
P. crispatus Bull = *Polyscias* 'Crispata'.
P. davidii Franch. = *Metapanax davidii.*
P. diffissus Bull = *Polyscias* 'Diffissa'.
P. discolor T. Kirk = *Pseudopanax discolor.*
P. dissectus Bull = *Polyscias* 'Dissecta'.
P. dumosus Bull = *Polyscias* 'Dumosa'.
P. elegans (Williams = *Polyscias* 'Elegans'.
P. excelsus hort. = *Polyscias* 'Excelsa'.
P. fissus Bull = *Polyscias* 'Fissa'.
P. fruticosa L. = *Polyscias fruticosa.*
P. fruticosus var. *deleauanus* (Lind.) N.E. Br. = *Polyscias* 'Deleauana'.
P. fruticosus var. *multifida* Veitch = *Polyscias* 'Multifida'.
P. fruticosus var. *victoriae* (Bull) N.E. Br. = *Polyscias guilfoylei* 'Victoriae'.
P. ginseng C.A. Mey. GINSENG; NIN-SIN. Rootstock carrot-shaped, branching, aromatic. Lvs 5-foliolate, lfts elliptic to ovate, shortly stalked, gradually acuminate, bidentate; petioles to 12cm. Fr. red. Korea, NE China. Z6.
P. laciniatus Williams = *Polyscias guilfoylei* 'Laciniata'.
P. lepidus Bull = *Polyscias* 'Lepida'.
P. lessonii DC. = *Pseudopanax lessonii.*
P. nitidus Bull = *Polyscias* 'Nitida'.
P. ornatus Bull = *Polyscias filicifolia* 'Ornata'.
P. pinnatus Lam. = *Polyscias cumingiana.*
P. plumatus Bull ex W. Richards = *Polyscias* 'Plumata'.
P. pseudoginseng auct., non Wallich = *P. ginseng.*
P. quinquefolius L. AMERICAN GINSENG; SANG. Rootstock to 2cm diam., cigar-shaped, branching, aromatic. Lvs 3-7-foliolate; lfts stalked, ovate to obovate, acuminate, coarsely toothed; petioles to 1cm. Fr. bright red. Early summer. E N Amer. Z3.
P. quinquefolius auct., non L. = *P. ginseng.*
P. rotundatus Williams = *Polyscias* 'Rotundata'.
P. sambucifolius Sieb. = *Polyscias sambucifolia.*
P. schinseng T. Nees = *P. ginseng.*
P. serratifolius Williams). = *Polyscias* 'Serratifolia'.
P. splendens Kunth = *Schefflera morototonii.*
P. trifolius L. DWARF GINSENG; GROUNDNUT. Rootstock 12–13mm diam., nearly black, almost round. Lvs 3–5-foliolate; lfts sessile, oblanceolate or obovate, finely toothed; petioles to 4cm. Fr. yellow. Spring. E N Amer. Z3.
P. victoriae Bull = *Polyscias guilfoylei* 'Victoriae'.

Pancratium L. Amaryllidaceae. 16 bulbous perenn. herbs. Lvs basal, 2-ranked, linear to lorate. Fls 3–15 in a scapose umbel, or solitary, large, fragrant; perianth funnelform, lobes spreading or erect; staminal corona conspicuous, anth. dorsifixed. Canary Is., Medit. to Trop. Asia, W Afr. to Nam.
P. amboinense L. = *Proiphys amboinensis.*
P. aurantiacum HBK = *Stenomesson aurantiacum.*
P. australasicum Ker-Gawl. = *Proiphys amboinensis.*
P. canariense Ker-Gawl. Differs from *P. illyricum* in lvs broader, pedicels much longer (to 3cm), corona teeth shorter. Early autumn. Canary Is. Z9.
P. coccineum Ruiz & Pav. = *Stenomesson coccineum.*
P. flavum Ruiz & Pav. = *Stenomesson flavum.*
P. illyricum L. Bulb scales purple-black. Lvs 50×1.5–3cm, glaucous. Scape to 40cm; pedicels 1–1.5cm; perianth white to cream, tube *c*2cm, lobes 5cm, linear-oblong to narrowly elliptic; corona much longer than perianth, teeth paired, long and narrow. Late spring–early summer. W Medit. Is. (Corsica, Sardinia). Z8.
P. latifolium Ruiz & Pav. = *Urceolina latifolia.*
P. maritimum L. Differs from *P. illyricum* in bulb scales pale, lvs longer and narrower, persistent; perianth tube to 7.5cm, v. slender; corona two-thirds length of perianth, with short teeth. Summer. Medit., SW Eur. Z8.

P. mexicanum L. = *Hymenocallis concinna.*
P. variegatum Ruiz & Pav. = *Stenomesson variegatum.*
P. viridiflorum Ruiz & Pav. = *Stenomesson viridiflorum.*
P. zeylanicum L. Lvs not glaucous. Scape to 30cm; fls solitary; pedicels short; perianth lobes narrowly lanceolate longer than tube, fused at base. Summer. Sri Lanka. Z10.

PANDANACEAE R. Br. 3/675. *Freycinetia, Pandanus.*

Pandanus R. Br. SCREW PINE. Pandanaceae. 600 everg. trees or shrubs. St. usually cylindrical, dichotomously branched, ringed by lf scars, on thick stilt roots and producing adventitious roots. Lvs in 3 spiralling ranks, forming term. rosettes, linear with long-acuminate tips, base tough, sheathing, margin and keel usually spiny-toothed. Fls small, pale, apetalous, massed on term. spadices. Fr. an oblong-elipsoid syncarp of woody drupes. SE Asia, esp. Malaysia, Aus. Z10.
P. pygmaeus Thouars. Spreading shrub to 60cm, branched from base. Lvs 30–60× to 1.5cm, glaucous beneath, spines fine, brown. Madag.
P. sanderi Mast. Lvs 75×5cm, striped yellow or golden and green, minutely spiny. Origin uncertain; possibly from Timor. 'Roehrsianus': robust; lvs to 1m, new lvs deep golden-yellow, later striped pale yellow.
P. utilis Bory. Tree to 20m. Lvs 0.5–2m×6–10cm, somewhat rigid, glaucous, with red spines. Fr. to 15cm or slightly more, made up of 100 drupes, each 3cm. Madag.
P. veitchii Mast. & Moore. Lvs 50–100×75cm, slightly drooping, margin spiny, dark green bordered with pure or silvery-white. Origin uncertain; possibly from Polyn. 'Compactus': dwarf form.

Panda Plant *Kalanchoe tomentosa.*

Pandorea Spach. Bignoniaceae. 6 lianes. Lvs pinnate; lfts paired, ovate-lanceolate, glossy. Infl. thyrsiform, mostly term.; fls fragrant, cal. cupular to campanulate, 5-lobed or truncate; cor. tubular, lobes 5. Aus., Papuasia, E Malesia, New Caledonia. Z9.
P. amboinensis Boerl. = *Tecomanthe dendrophila.*
P. australis Spach = *P. pandorana.*
P. brycei (N.E. Br.) Rehd. = *Podranea brycei.*
P. dendrophila Boerl. = *Tecomanthe dendrophila.*
P. jasminoides (Lindl.) Schum. BOWER PLANT. To 5m. St. stout. Pinnae 2.5–5×1–2cm, 4–9. Cor. 4–5cm, white, streaked deep, rich pink within. Spring–summer. NE Aus. 'Alba': fls pure white. 'Lady Di': fls white, throat cream. 'Rosea': fls pink, throat darker. 'Rosea Superba': fls large, pink, throat darker, spotted purple.
P. pandorana (Andrews) Steenis. WONGA-WONGA VINE. To 6m. St. slender. Pinnae 3–10×1.5–6cm, usually in 6 pairs, sometimes crenate. Cor. 1–3cm, creamy yellow, streaked and splashed red or purple. Winter–spring. Aus., New Guinea, Pacific Is. 'Rosea': fls pale pink.
P. ricasoliana (Tenf.) Baill. = *Podranea ricasoliana.*
→*Bignonia* and *Tecoma.*

Paniala *Flacourtia jangomans.*
Panic Grass *Panicum.*
Panicled Dogwood *Cornus racemosa.*

Panicum L. PANIC GRASS; CRAB GRASS. Gramineae. *c*470 ann. or perenn. grasses. Lvs threadlike or linear-ovate. Infl. paniculate to racemose, open to contracted; spikelets symmetric to laterally compressed, awnless, 2-fld, upper glume as long as spikelet. Pantrop. to temp. N Amer. Z5.
P. boscii Poir. St. to 70cm, glab. or minutely puberulent. Lf sheaths glab.; lvs to 12×3cm, spreading, sparsely ciliate at base, glab. Pan. to 12cm; spikelets papillose. E US.
P. capillare L. OLD WITCH GRASS; WITCH GRASS. Ann., to 90cm. St. clumped, upright to spreading. Lvs linear to narrow-lanceolate, to 30cm×1.4cm, stiffly pubesc. Pan. open, to 45cm+, green to purple; spikelets to 3mm; equal. Summer–autumn. S Canada, US. var. *occidentale* Rydb. Spikelets slightly larger.
P. crus-galli L. = *Echinochloa crus-galli.*
P. germanicum Mill. = *Setaria italica.*
P. glaucum L. = *Setaria glauca.*
P. italicum L. = *Setaria italica.*
P. maximum Jacq. Rhizomatous perenn. to 3m, densely tufted. St. erect, simple or sparsely branched. Lvs linear, glab. or softly pubesc. with scabrous margins. Pan. erect or nodding, to 45cm, usually villous; spikelets to 5cm, glab., pale green or tinged purple. Trop. Afr., nat. US.
P. miliaceum L. MILLET; BROOM CORN MILLET; HOG MILLET. Ann., to 120cm. St. robust, erect. Lvs linear-lanceolate, to

40×2cm. Pan. open to contracted, to 30cm, br. rigid; spikelets to 6mm. C, S & E Eur., Asia. 'Violaceum': infl. purple tinged.

P. palmifolium Koenig = *Setaria palmifolia*.

P. plicatile Hochst. = *Setaria plicatilis*.

P. plicatum Willd. non Lam. = *Setaria palmifolia*.

P. plicatum hort. = *Setaria plicatilis*.

P. plicatum Lam. non Willd. = *Setaria plicata*.

P. polystachyum HBK = *Echinochloa polystachya*.

P. purpurascens Raddi. = *Brachiaria mutica*.

P. ramosum L. = *Brachiaria ramosa*.

P. sanguinale L. = *Digitaria sanguinalis*.

P. spectabile Nees ex Trin. = *Echinochloa polystachya*.

P. subquadriparum Trin. = *Brachiaria subquadripara*.

P. sulcatum Aubl. = *Setaria sulcata*.

P. teneriffae R. Br. = *Tricholaena teneriffae*.

P. tonsum Steud. = *Rhynchelytrum repens*.

P. variegatum hort. = *Oplismenus hirtellus* 'Variegatus'.

P. virgatum L. SWITCH GRASS. Perenn., to 180cm. St. clumped, flimsy to robust, purple to glaucous green. Lvs linear, flat, erect, to 60cm×1.4cm, usually glab., green, yellow in autumn. Pan. open, to 50×25cm; br. spreading, stiff; spikelets to 6mm. Summer–autumn. C Amer. to S Canada. 'Haense' ('Haense Herms'): weeping; lvs plum to rich burgundy in autumn; infl. suffused red. 'Heavy Metal': lvs stiffly erect, pale metallic blue, yellow in autumn. 'Rotbraun' ('Red Bronze'): to 80cm; lvs light brown, flushed red at tips, rich autumn colour. 'Rotstrahlbusch': lvs vivid red in autumn. 'Rubrum': to 1m; lvs flushed red, bright red in autumn; spikelets rich brown, in clouds. 'Squaw': lvs tinted red in autumn. 'Strictum': narrowly upright, to 1.2m. 'Warrior': tall, strong-growing; lvs tinted red-brown in autumn.

P. viride L. = *Setaria viridis*.

Panisea Lindl. Orchidaceae. 9 terrestrial orchids. Pbs small, clustered, narrow-lanceolate to oblong-lanceolate, plicate. Rac. lat. with few fls and membranous bracts; sep. and pet. subequal, lat. sep. basally saccate; lip fused to column base, claw sigmoid. NE India, SE Asia. Z10.

P. uniflora (Lindl.) Lindl. Pbs to 15mm. Lvs 5–10cm. Infl. short; fls solitary, yellow-brown; tep. to 20mm, oblong-lanceolate; lip undulate, midlobe ovate, with 4 elongated dark brown spots. N India. Z10.

Pansy *Viola × wittrockiana*.

Pansy Orchid *Miltonia*.

Pansy Violet *Viola pedata*.

Panterpa Miers = *Arrabidaea*.

Panther Lily *Lilium pardalinum*.

Papaver L. POPPY. Papaveraceae. 50 ann. or perenn. herbs. Latex white or yellow. St. 1 to many, simple or branched, usually bristly. Lvs basal or cauline, pinnatifid to pinnatisect, toothed. Fls solitary; sep. 2, rarely 3, concave, often bristly, short-lived; pet. 4, rarely 5 or 6, usually obovate, obtuse, creased in bud, falling early; sta. numerous, fil. pale or v. dark; stigmatic disc crenate to incised, convex to concave. Capsule clavate to globose. Eur., Asia, Aus., S Afr., N Amer.

P. aculeatum Thunb. Ann. to 1m. St. erect, few-branched, prickles yellow. Lvs to 30cm, sinuate-pinnate, lobes 4–7, ovate, obtuse, dentate. Fls racemose, few, to 3cm diam., orange-red without basal markings. Summer. S Afr., Aus. Z8.

P. alpinum L. Perenn. to 25cm. St. scapose, often v. short. Lvs basal, to 20cm, 2–3-pinnate, lobes 6–8, linear to ovate-lanceolate, acute, occas. pinnatisect, glaucous grey-green to green, glab. to sparsely bristly, toothed. Fls solitary on scapes to 25cm; pet. white, yellow or orange, to 2.5cm. Summer. Alps, Carpath., Pyren. A highly variable sp. of uncertain limitations. *Pp. burseri*, *kerneri*, *pyrenaicum* and *rhaeticum* are perhaps best treated as members of this complex. Z5.

P. amurense hort. ex Karrer = *P. nudicaule*.

P. anomalum Fedde. Perenn. to 40cm. St. v. short. Lvs basal, to 10cm, pinnatifid to lobed, glaucous, subglabrous, lobes oblong, obtuse. Scapes to 40cm, orange-pubesc.; fls solitary; pet. orange, narrow, to 2cm, margins slightly scalloped; fil. black. Summer. C China. Z7.

P. apokrinomenon Fedde. Perenn. to 60cm. St. usually solitary, densely hairy. Lvs basal and on st., 12–25cm, pinnately lobed, oblong-ovate, lobes deeply incised, crenate to serrate. Fls solitary, red. Summer. C Asia (mts). Z7.

P. apulum Ten. Ann. to 40cm. St. branching. Lvs bipinnatifid, lobes linear, obtuse, bristly. Scapes pubesc.; fls solitary, to 5cm diam., purple with pale central blotch; sta. dark purple. Summer. Medit. Z8.

P. arenarium Bieb. Ann. to 50cm. St. branching. Lvs bipinnate, seg. linear, obtuse, sometimes adpressed-pubesc. Scapes adpressed-pubesc.; fls to 6cm diam.; pet. purple with black basal blotch; anth. yellow. Summer. Asia Minor. Z8.

P. argemone L. PRICKLY POPPY. Ann. to 50cm, hispid. St. simple or branching. Lvs pinnatisect, seg. linear to oblong-lanceolate, acute. Fls orange-red; pet. to 2.5cm, occas. with maroon basal spot; sta. pale mauve. Summer. N Afr., S Eur. Z8.

P. atlanticum (Ball) Coss. Perenn. to 45cm. Rhiz. woody. Lvs to 15cm, oblong-lanceolate, jagged-toothed or pinnatisect, pilose. Scape to 45cm, simple or forked, pubesc.; pet. to 2.5cm, buff-orange to red. Summer. Moroc. Z6.

P. bracteatum Lindl. V. close to *P. orientale*. Perenn. to 1m. St. simple. Basal lvs to 45cm, pinnate, pinnatisect near apex, seg. lanceolate or oblong, serrate. Scapes white-hispid; fls to 10cm diam. or wider, subtended by 2 incised bracts; pet. red with purple spot at base. Summer. Cauc., Asia Minor. Z5.

P. burseri Crantz. Perenn. to 25cm. Lvs basal, to 20cm, 2–3-pinnate, glaucous, seg. 6–8, linear-lanceolate to narrowly linear, acute. Scapes to 25cm, setose. Fls solitary; pet. to 2cm, usually white. Summer. C Eur. (mts). 'Alpinum': lvs fine, tinged grey; fls in range of pastel colours; see *P. alpinum*. Z5.

P. californicum A. Gray. WESTERN POPPY. Ann. to 60cm. St. slender with erect br. Lvs to 7.5cm, pinnate, lobes obtuse to acute. Scapes adpressed-pubesc.; pet. to 2.5cm, 1 pair sometimes filiform, red with green or black, pink-rimmed basal spot. Summer. Calif. Z8.

P. caucasicum Bieb. = *P. fugax*.

P. commutatum Fisch. & Mey. Ann. to 40cm. St. erect, branching, sparsely hairy. Lvs to 15cm, pinnatifid, adpressed-downy, seg. to 3cm, oblong to ovate, dentate to entire. Scapes long, adpressed-pubesc.; pet. to 3cm, red with black basal spot. Summer. Cauc., Asia Minor. 'Lady Bird': to 45cm; fls scarlet splashed with black. Z8.

P. croceum Ledeb. = *P. nudicaule* 'Croceum'.

P. dubium L. Ann. to 60cm. St. robust, erect, branching, hairy. Lvs ± glaucous, basal lvs pinnatisect or lobed, seg. ovate; st. lvs bipinnate, seg. linear-lanceolate. Fls to 5cm diam., red or white with black basal spot; anth. violet. Summer. Eur., SW Asia. Z7.

P. fauriei Fedde. Perenn. to 20cm. Lvs basal, pinnatifid, ovate, lobes oblong or oblong-ovate, broadly cuneate towards apex. Pet. to 2cm, yellow. Summer. N Jap. Z8.

P. fugax Poir. Bienn. to 60cm, glaucous, sparsely hairy. Lvs to 20cm, lanceolate, pinnatifid, seg. distant, linear-lanceolate to ovate, serrate to entire. Fls to 3cm diam., dull red, yellow toward centre; sta. yellow. Summer. Asia Minor. Z8.

P. glaucum Boiss. & Hausskn. To 50cm, branching at base. St. erect. Lvs obovate-oblong, pinnatifid, glaucous, seg. triangular-oblong, serrate to dentate. Fls to 4cm diam., red, with a dull basal spot. Summer. Syr., Iraq, Iran. Z8.

P. heldreichii Boiss. Perenn. to 50cm. St. erect, leafy, hoary-hispid. Lvs pilose; basal lvs to 20×5cm, oblong, st. lvs bract-like, serrate. Rac. few-fld, corymbose; pet. to 5cm, orange-red. Summer. C Medit. Z8.

P. heterophyllum (Benth.) Greene = *Stylomecon heterophyllum*.

P. hookeri Bak. ex Hook. f. Branching, erect ann. herb, to 1.2m. Lvs to 12.5cm, sessile, ovate or lanceolate, coarsely toothed. Fls to 9cm diam., crenulate, pale rose to bright crimson, blotched blue-black at base, on long peduncles. Scarcely distinct from *P. rhoeas*. Temp. Eur., Asia.

P. horridum DC. = *P. aculeatum*.

P. ×hybridum L. ROUGH POPPY. Lvs 2–3× pinnatipartite. Fls red, usually with purple spot at base of pet. Eur., W Asia. 'Fireball': to 25cm; fls double, orange-red.

P. kerneri Hayek. Differs from *P. burseri* in pet. yellow. Summer. C Eur. (mts). Z5.

P. laevigatum Bieb. Ann. to 40cm, glab. to sparsely setose. St. ± simple. Lvs narrowly pinnate, ± glab.; seg. ovate to oblong, or linear, acute (on st. lvs). Pet. obovate, red with black basal spot; anth. yellow. Summer. C Medit. Z8.

P. lateritium K. Koch. Perenn. to 60cm, densely hairy. St. many, branching. Lvs lanceolate, irregularly deeply serrate. Fls 1–3, to 5cm diam., bright orange or red. Summer. Turk. 'Flore Pleno': fls semi-double, orange. Z8.

P. macounii Greene = *P. nudicaule*.

P. macrostomum Boiss. & Huet. Ann. to 45cm. St. erect, branching, sparsely hairy. Lvs pinnatisect, seg. oblong-lanceolate to linear-lanceolate, acute-dentate. Fls to 5cm diam., purple, sometimes with black basal spot which may be rimmed white. Summer. Armenia. Z8.

P. mairei Battand. = *P. dubium*.

P. miyabeanum Tatew. = *P. nudicaule*.

P. monanthum Trautv. Perenn. to 45cm. Lvs basal, to 20cm, linear to oblong, pinnatifid, irregularly acute-dentate. Fls solitary; pet. 3–5cm. Summer. Cauc. Z7.

P. nordhagenianum Löve. Pubesc. perenn. to 35cm. Lvs long-petiolate, trifoliolate or pinnatisect. Scapes numerous; pet. yellow. Summer. Iceland, Faeroes, Scand. Z4.

P. nudicaule L. ICELANDIC POPPY; ARCTIC POPPY. Perenn. to 30cm. St. v. short. Lvs 3–15cm, pinnatifid to pinnatisect, somewhat glaucous, pubesc., seg. 3–4, oblong, incised, occas. mucronate. Fls to 7.5cm diam., solitary, long-stalked, white with yellow basal patch, yellow, orange, peach or pale red, ruffled; anth. yellow. Summer. Subarc. regions. 'Champagne Bubbles': to 40cm; fls to 12cm wide. 'Croceum': fls orange or orange-red. Gdn Gnome Hybrids: dwarf, compact; fls in shades of yellow, orange and pink; seed race. 'Hamlet': fls large. Hybrid Matador: neat; st. firm; fls bright scarlet. Kelmscott Giant: st. long to 80cm; fls in pastel shades. Oregon Rainbows: to 55cm; fls delicate in pastel shades. 'Pacino': compact; fls abundant, pale yellow. Sparkling Bubbles Mixed: fls large, abundant, in range of rich and pastel colours; seed race. Unwins Giant Coonara: to 50cm; fls bright. Wonderland Hybrids: dwarf, hardy bienn. to 25cm; fls large, in range of whites, oranges, yellows and reds. Z2.

P. oreophilum Rupr. Perenn. to 15cm, forming dense mats. Lvs hairy, lanceolate-oblong and pinnatifid or deeply incised. Peduncles to 15cm, flexuous; fls 2 per st.; pet. to 4.5cm, deep red. Summer. Cauc. Z8.

P. orientale L. ORIENTAL POPPY. Large, robust perenn. to 90cm. St. erect, sparsely leafy. Lvs to 25cm, hispid, pinnate to pinnatisect at apex, seg. lanceolate or oblong. Fls solitary, to 10cm diam., red, orange or pale pink usually with purple basal blotch. Summer. SW Asia. Over 70 cvs, height 40–110cm, dwarf and compact to tall; st. nodding to erect; fls sometimes double, in a range of colour from white, pink and orange to deep red and purple, sometimes bicolour; pet. fringed or ruffled. 'Black and White': fls large, white with black centre. 'Cedric Morris' ('Cedric's Pink'): lvs grey-hirsute; pet. shell pink with a clear violet-black basal spot. 'Fatima': compact; fls white with pink edges, dark spots. 'Glowing Embers': to 110cm, robust, erect; fls in 10cm diam., bright orange-red, pet. ruffled. 'Harvest Moon': to 1m; fls semi-double, deep orange. 'Indian Chief': fls maroon. 'Ladybird': fls v. large, vermilion with black centre. 'May Queen': st. drooping; fls double, orange-vermilion. 'Mrs Perry': fls large, salmon-pink tinged apricot. 'Nana Flore Pleno': dwarf, to 45cm; fls double, orange-red, pet. ruffled. 'Perry's White': to 80cm; st. strong; fls grey-white with purple centre. 'Picotee': fls banded salmon and white. 'Redizelle': fls scarlet with black throat. 'Suleika': to 90cm; erect; fls deep red with blue gloss, spotted black, pet. fringed. Z3.

P. pavoninum Fisch. & Mey. Ann. to 25cm. St. branching, hairy. Lvs to 10cm, pinnate or pinnatisect, deeply incised to mucronately toothed. Fls 5cm diam., red with black basal blotch; anth. purple. Summer. C Asia. Z8.

P. persicum Lindl. Bienn. to 45cm. St. branching, leafy. Basal lvs to 25cm, oblong-lanceolate, pinnate, seg. entire or mucronately toothed. Fls to 5cm across, deep red with green basal blotch. Summer. SW Asia. Z9.

P. pilosum Sibth. & Sm. Perenn. to 1m. St. erect, leafy, hairy. Lvs adpressed-velutinous, to 15cm, oblong, lobed and toothed. Fls in a corymb, to 10cm across; pet. scarlet or bright orange with white basal spot. Summer. Asia Minor. Z6.

P. pseudocanescens Popov. As for *P. radicatum* except lf lobes broader. Summer. Sib., Mong. Z3.

P. pyrenaicum A. Kerner. Lvs pinnatipartite with oval, ovate-lanceolate or lanceolate seg., toothed or pinnately cut. Fls yellow, orange or white. Pyren. Material under this name may be *P. rhaeticum*.

P. radicatum Rottb. Densely tufted perenn. to 20cm. Lvs 5–10cm, pinnatifid or lobed, seg. lanceolate to obovate, entire or incised. Scape to 20cm, rusty or black-pubesc.; fls to 5cm across, white or yellow, rarely pink. Summer. N Eur., W Asia. Z3.

P. rhaeticum Leresche. Perenn. to 10cm, tuft-forming. Lvs basal, to 7.5cm, pinnate, adpressed-pubesc., seg. entire or bipinnate, ovate to ovate-lanceolate. Scape to 10cm; fls solitary to 4cm diam., yellow or orange. Summer. Pyren. Z7.

P. rhoeas L. CORN POPPY; FIELD POPPY; FLANDERS POPPY. Ann. to 90cm. St. erect, branching, hispid. Lvs pinnate or pinnatisect, seg. lanceolate, to 15cm. Fls solitary, to 7.5cm across; brilliant red sometimes with black basal spot. Summer. Temp. OW. Shirley Poppies: fls medium-sized, single, white to scarlet (not mauve) or double, in a wide range of colours except yellow. 'Valerie Finnis': fls grey, mauve, pink and white. Z5.

P. rupifragum Boiss. & Reut. Tufted perenn. to 45cm. Lvs oblong or lanceolate, pinnately cut, pubesc. on veins. Fls to 7.5cm diam., pale brick-red. Spain. Z7.

P. schinzianum Fedde. Hoary-pubesc. perenn. to 45cm. Lvs irregularly pinnatifid, obovate-lanceolate. Fls to 5cm diam., rusty to sealing-wax red. Origin unknown.

P. sendtneri (Kerner) Fedde As for *P. rhaeticum* except lvs glaucescent, pet. white or yellow. Z4.

P. setigerum DC. = *P. somniferum* ssp. *setigerum*.

P. somniferum L. OPIUM POPPY. Ann. to 120cm, glaucous grey-green. St. erect. Lvs to 12.5cm, obovate-oblong, deeply and jaggedly incised and toothed, base decurrent to clasping; fls to 10cm across, pale white, light mauve, purple or marked, frequently double; pet. erose, occas. with dark basal spot. Summer. SE Eur., W Asia. ssp. *setigerum* (DC.) Corb. All parts pubesc. Lf lobes acute. Peony-fld Hybrids: fls double. Z7.

P. spicatum Boiss. & Bal. = *P. heldreichii*.

P. suaveolens Lapeyr. Tufted perenn. to 10cm. Lvs basal, to 7cm, pinnatifid, adpressed-pubesc., seg. lanceolate or oblong, entire, or pinnately lobed. Scape to 10cm, hispid; fls solitary, to 3cm diam., yellow or cream. Summer. Pyren., W Medit. Z5.

P. triniifolium Boiss. Bienn. to 30cm or more, glaucous, sparsely villous, br. spreading. Basal lvs to 7.5cm, ovate to oblong, 2–3-pinnate, seg. narrow-linear, yellow-mucronate, st. lvs trifid. Fls to 2.5cm across, pale red. Summer. Asia Minor. Z8.

P. umbrosum hort. = *P. commutatum*.

PAPAVERACEAE Juss. 23/210. Arctomecon, Argemone, Bocconia, Chelidonium, Corydalis, Dendromecon, Dicranostigma, Eomecon, Eschscholzia, Glaucium, Hunnemannia, Hylomecon, Macleaya, Meconella, Meconopsis, Papaver, Platystemon, Roemeria, Romneya, Sanguinaria, Stylomecon, Stylophorum.

Papaw Asimina triloba; Carica.
Papaya Carica.
Paperbark Melaleuca (M. leucadendra).
Paperbark Maple Acer griseum.
Paperbark Tree Melaleuca viridiflora var. rubriflora.
Paper Birch Betula papyrifera.
Paper Bush Edgeworthia (E. papyrifera).
Paper Flower Bougainvillea glabra.
Paper Mulberry Broussonetia (B. papyrifera).
Paper Reed Cyperus papyrus.
Paper-shell Pinyon Pinus remota.
Paper-white Narcissus Narcissus papyraceus.

Paphinia Lindl. Orchidaceae. 3 epiphytic orchids. Pbs to 6cm, ovoid-oblong. Lvs to 26cm, elliptic-lanceolate, prominently nerved. Infl. a basal rac., pendent, to 10cm, 1- to several-fld, fls fleshy, sep. linear-lanceolate; pet. smaller; lip smaller than tep., uniguiculate, trilobed, lat. lobes erect, falcate, midlobe triangular to sagittate, disc callose or crested with gland. hairs. N S Amer., Guat. Z10.

P. cristata (Lindl.) Lindl. Tep. to 6×2cm, white to yellow, striped red or red-brown, concave; lip to 2×1.6cm, dark chocolate-purple with a white claw, margins white, midlobe ovate-hastate to subsagitatte, cristate-fimbriate, callus white, laciniate. Venez., Colomb., Trin., Guyana, Surinam.

P. lindeniana Rchb. f. Tep. to 5×2cm, white variably marked dark red-purple; lip to 2.5×1.5cm, white, shaded dark red-purple at base, slightly concave, apically dentate, midlobe semi-hastate, fimbriate-papillose, crest with white fusiform hairs. Venez., Braz., Colomb., Peru, Guyana.

Paphiopedilum Pfitz. VENUS' SLIPPER. SE Asia, India, Indon., SE China, New Guinea, Philipp., Solomon Is. Orchidaceae. 60 sympodial orchids. Pbs 0. St. v. short or 0. Lvs 2 to several, 2-ranked, in clumped growths, leathery, conduplicate, oblong, ligulate or elliptic. Fls waxy, carried one to several on a slender term. stalk; dors. sep. large, erect, lateral sep. fused to form synsepalum; pet. horizontal or pendent; lip strongly saccate, forming a pouch; column short, bearing a fleshy staminode. SE Asia, India, Indon., SW China, New Guinea, Philipp., Solomon Is. Z10.

P. acmodontum Schoser ex M.W. Wood. Lvs tessellated above, to 18×4cm. Infl. erect, 1-fld, to 25cm; dors. sep. 4×3cm, white or pink, veined dark purple or purple-green; synsepalum 3×1.5cm, white tinged purple, veined purple and green; pet. spreading, 4×1.5cm, sparsely ciliate, green beneath, purple above, veined and spotted dark purple in basal half; lip deeply saccate, 1×2cm, bronze or olive green with darker veins. Spring. Philipp.

P. adductum Asch. Lvs to 26×4.2cm, dark green. Infl. 2–3-fld, arching, to 29cm; sep. pale green-yellow or white, veined maroon; dors. sep. arching, ovate, 6.5×3cm; synsepalum ovate, 6.5×3cm; pet. arcuate-dependent, linear-tapering, to 15×1cm; lip porrect, to 5×2cm. Winter. Philipp.

P. appletonianum (Gower) Rolfe. Lvs to 25×4cm, tessellated with purple marking beneath. Infl. 1–2-fld, to 48cm; sep. pale green, veined green, dors. sep. ovate, cordate at base, apiculate above, 4.5×2.4cm; synsepalum elliptic-lanceolate, to 3×1.5cm; pet. spathulate, to 5.8×1.8cm, half-twisted above, striped darker with maroon-black spots in basal half, purple above; lip 3–5cm, ochre to pale purple, veined darker. Winter–spring. Philipp.

P. argus (Rchb. f.) Stein. Lvs narrowly elliptic, mottled pale and dark green above, purple beneath. Infl. 1-fld, to 45cm; dors. sep. to 4.5×3.5cm, white veined green, spotted purple toward base; synsepalum to 4.4×2cm, white veined green; pet. recurved, ligulate, to 6.5×1.8cm, white veined green, purple at apex, heavily spotted maroon, maroon hairs on margin; lip green flushed pink, veined green, to 4.5×2.5cm. Spring. Philipp.

P. armeniacum S.C. Chen & Liu. Lvs to 12cm×2.3cm, marbled dark and light blue-green above, spotted purple beneath. Infl. 1-fld, to 26cm; fls bright golden yellow; dors. sep. ovate, to 5×2.5cm, pubesc. near base; synsepalum ovate, to 3.5×2cm; pet. ovate, rounded, to 5×3.5cm, ciliate; lip inflated, thin textured, to 5×4cm, margins incurved, dotted purple inside. Spring–summer. SW China.

P. barbatum (Lindl.) Pfitz. Lvs to 15×4cm, mottled pale and dark green above. Infl. 1–2-fld, erect, to 36cm; dors. sep. ovate, to 5×5.5cm, white, green at base, veined purple; synsepalum narrowly ovate, to 3.5×1.5cm, pale yellow-green, veined green, flushed purple; pet. pale green beneath, purple above, veined darker, upper margin spotted dark maroon, deflexed, to 6×1.5cm, ciliate; lip to 4.5×2.5cm. Spring–summer. Penins. Malaysia and Penang Is.

P. barbigerum Tang & Wang. Lvs to 19×1.3cm, green. Infl. 1-fld, erect, about 16cm; dors. sep. subcircular, to 3.2×3cm, white with green base; synsepalum elliptic, to 3.5×1.5cm; pet. ligulate-spathulate, to 3.4×0.9cm, fawn margined cream, undulate and sparsely ciliate; lip to 3×1.5cm, tan-brown. China.

P. bellatulum (Rchb. f.) Stein. Lvs to 14×5cm, dark green mottled pale green above, spotted purple below. Infl. 1-fld, rarely 2-fld, to 4.5cm; fls round, white or cream, spotted maroon; dors. sep. concave, to 3.5×4cm, synsepalum deeply concave, to 2.2×2.7cm; pet. somewhat concave, to 6×4.5cm; lip narrowly ovoid, to 4×2cm. Summer. W Burm., Thail.

P. bougainvilleanum Fowlie. Lvs to 22×4.2cm, pale green, tessellated darker. Infl. 1-fld, to 23cm; sep. white, veined green, outer surface purple-pubesc., pet. white, veined green, apical margins flushed purple; lip green, veined darker; dors. sep. ovate, to 3.8×4cm; synsepalum concave, ovate, to 2.7×1.7cm; pet. falcate, narrowly elliptic, to 5×2cm; lip to 5×2.6cm, narrowing to apex. Autumn. Papua New Guinea.

P. bullenianum (Rchb. f.) Pfitz. Lvs to 14×5.5cm, tessellated dark green above, flushed purple beneath. Infl. erect, 1-fld, to 25cm; dors. sep. usually concave, to 3×2cm, white, veined green, marked purple at base; synsepalum lanceolate, to 2.5×1.5cm, white veined green; pet. spathulate, to 5×1.5cm, ciliate, green at base, purple above, margins spotted maroon-black; lip to 4cm, emarginate at apex, ochre-green. Winter. Borneo, Sumatra, Penins. Malaysia. var. *celebesense* (Fowlie & Birk) Cribb. Differs by having fewer spots on pet. margins and lack of emarginate apex to the lip.

P. callosum (Rchb. f.) Stein. Lvs to 20×4.5cm, tessellated above. Infl. 1-fld, rarely 2-fld, to 40cm; sep. white flushed purple in lower half, veined purple and green, dors. sep. broadly ovate, to 5.5×6cm, ciliate; synsepalum concave, to 3×2.5cm; pet. curved down and upwards at tip, to 6.5×2cm, white to yellow-green, apical third purple, maroon-spotted on upper margin; lip to 4.5×2.5cm, green, flushed maroon. Summer. Thail., Cambodia, Laos. var. *sublaeve* (Rchb. f.) Cribb. Fls smaller. Penins. Thail., NW Malaysia.

P. charlesworthii (Rolfe) Pfitz. Lvs to 15×3cm, green. Infl. 1-fld, 8–15cm; dors. sep. transversely elliptic to circular, to 5.5×6.5cm, outer surface finely pubesc., pink, veined darker; synsepalum elliptic, to 4×3cm, pale yellow, flecked and veined purple; pet. ligulate-spathulate, to 4.5×1.5cm, ciliate above; lip wide-mouthed, to 4×3cm, pink-brown, veined darker. Autumn. Burm.

P. ciliolare (Rchb. f.) Stein. Lvs to 15×5cm, mottled pale and darker green above, tinged purple beneath. Infl. 1-fld, erect, 20–32cm; sep. white at base, pale purple and green above, tinged purple beneath. Infl. 1-fld, erect, 20–32cm; sep. white at base, pale purple and green above, veined purple, dors. sep. ovate, to 5.5×5cm, ciliate; synsepalum elliptic-ovate, to 3×2cm; pet. slightly falcate, oblanceolate, to 7×2cm, ciliate, upper margins warty, white, spotted and veined dark purple; lip to 6×3.5cm, dark brown-purple. Summer. Philipp.

P. concolor (Batem.) Pfitz. Lvs to 14×4cm, tessellated dark and pale green on upper surface, finely spotted purple beneath. Infl. 1–2-fld, rarely 3-fld, to 8cm; fls yellow, rarely ivory or white, finely spotted purple; dors. sep. broadly ovate, to 3.5×3cm; synsepalum, elliptic to ovate, to 3×3cm; pet. elliptic, rounded at apex, to 4.5×2.5cm; lip fleshy, margins incurved, to 4×2cm. Summer–autumn. SE Burm., SW China, Thail., Indochina.

P. dayanum (Lindl.) Stein. Lvs to 21×5cm, tessellated dark and light yellow-green or blue-green. Infl. 1-fld, to 25cm; sep. white veined green, dors. sep. ovate, to 6×3cm, ciliate; synsepalum to

5×2cm; pet. oblanceolate-spathulate, to 8×1.5cm, purple-pink, purple-ciliate; lip deep maroon, 5×2cm, apical margin ciliate. Summer. Borneo (Sabah only).

P. delenatii Guill. Lvs to 11×4cm, mottled above, spotted purple below. Infl. 1-fld but commonly 2-fld, to 22cm; fls pale pink with red and yellow markings on staminode, pubesc.; dors. sep. ovate, to 3.5×2.5cm; synsepalum similar; pet. broadly elliptic, rounded, 4.3×5cm; lip ellipsoidal to subglobose, 4×3cm, margins incurved. Spring. Vietnam.

P. Delophyllum: attractively mottled dark green lvs; several deep pink fls are borne consecutively.

P. Delrosi: attractively mottled foliage; v. attractive fls on tall st., deep pink with deeper pink striping.

P. druryi (Bedd.) Stein. Lvs to 20×3cm, coriaceous, light green with darker veins. Infl. 1-fld, erect, to 25cm; fls green-yellow or chartreuse, a central maroon-brown streak on dors. sep. and pet., lip honey-yellow; dors. sep. curved forward, elliptic, to 4×3cm, shortly ciliate; synsepalum to 3.5×2.5cm, pubesc.; pet. incurved-porrect, narrowly oblong, slightly drooping, to 4×2cm, pubesc., undulate; lip to 4.5×1.5cm. Summer. S India.

P. emersonii Koopowitz & Cribb. Lvs to 23×4cm, green. Infl. erect, to 11.5cm, 1–2-fld; fls 8.5–9.5cm across, subcampanulate, sep. white, thick-textured, pet. white, flushed pink at base, lip creamy, rim flushed pink, spotted purple within, yellowing with age; dors. sep. elliptic-ovate, hooded, 4.5×3cm, pubesc.; sysepalum elliptic-subcircular, 3.5×3.5cm, pubesc.; pet. elliptic to subcircular, upcurved to 4.5×4.5cm, pubesc.; lip 3.5×3cm, flared at base, apical margin incurved, grooved. Spring. China.

P. exul (Ridl.) Rolfe. Lvs to 35×3cm, yellow-green. Infl. 1-fld, to 18cm; dors. sep. ovate-elliptic, 4.5×3cm, white, centre yellow with raised maroon spots; synsepalum oblong-elliptic, 4.5×2.5cm, pale yellow-green, veined darker; pet. incurved, subhorizontal, narrowly oblong, 5×1.7cm, ciliate, margins undulate, glossy, buff-yellow, veined darker; lip 3.5×2cm, glossy, buff, veined darker. Summer. Penins. Thail.

P. fairrieanum (Lindl.) Stein. Lvs to 28×3cm, v. faintly mottled. Infl. 1-fld, rarely 2-fld, to 45cm; sep. white, veined green and purple, purple suffusion on dors. sep., pet. similar; dors. sep. elliptic, to 8×7cm, ciliate, margins recurved, undulate; synsepalum ovate, 3.5×2.5cm; pet. S-shaped, 5×1.5cm, purple-ciliate, undulate; lip deep, 4×2.5cm, olive to yellow-green, veined darker. Autumn. Sikkim, Bhutan, NE India.

P. glanduliferum (Bl.) Stein. Lvs to 40×5.5cm, green. Infl. 2–5-fld, to 50cm; sep. and pet. yellow veined maroon, pet. margins maroon-warted on base, lip yellow, veined and flushed purple; dors. sep. ovate to 5.5×3cm; synsepalum to 5.5×3cm; pet. deflexed, linear-tapering, to 10×1cm, tips papillose, sparsely ciliate below usually twisted; lip to 5.5×2cm. Summer. W New Guinea and adjacent islands.

P. glaucophyllum J.J. Sm. Lvs to 28×5cm, glaucous, scarcely mottled. Infl. to 20- or more-fld; dors. sep. ovate to broad, to 3×3cm, ciliate, white or cream, centre yellow-green, veins flushed maroon; synsepalum to 3×2cm; pet. deflexed, linear, to 5×1cm, apical half twisted, long-ciliate, pubesc. at base, white, spotted purple; lip to 4×2cm, pink-purple, finely spotted, margins pale yellow. Summer. E Java. var. *moquetteanum* J.J. Sm. Lvs to 55×10cm, scape longer, fls to 10cm across; dors. sep. narrower, yellow finely speckled purple. SW Java.

P. godefroyae (Godef.-Leb.) Stein. Lvs to 14×3cm, tessellated dark and pale green above, spotted purple beneath. Infl. 1–2-fld, erect, to 8cm; fls white or ivory, usually spotted purple; dors. sep. concave, broadly ovate, to 3×3.5cm; synsepalum to 3×3cm; pet. oblong-elliptic, rounded, to 5.5×3cm, often undulate; lip ellipsoidal, to 3.5×1.5cm, margins strongly incurved. Summer. Penins. Thail., adjacent islands.

P. Goultenianum: similar to the above but fls wine red and white instead of green and white. 'Album': strong plants with beautifully mottled lvs; fls lime green and white with striped dors. sep. and down-swept warted pet.

P. Gowerianum: strong plants with mottled foliage; fls lime-green and white or wine red and white, dors. sep. boldly striped.

P. gratrixianum (Mast.) Guill. Lvs to 30×2.3cm, green, spotted purple near base beneath. Infl. 1-fld, to 25cm; dors. sep. ovate to obovate, to 5.2×4.6cm, white above, pale green below, purple-hairy; synsepalum ovate-elliptic, to 5×2.5cm, pale green, outer surface purple-pubesc.; pet. spathulate, to 5.2×2.5cm, glossy, yellow, flushed and veined purple-brown, ciliate, margins reflexed; lip to 4.2×2.8cm, tapering to apex, yellow flushed brown. Winter. Laos, possibly Vietnam.

P. Harrisianum: strong plants with mottled lvs; red-brown glossy fls with striped dors. on strong st. The first *Paphiopedilum* hybrid made and flowered in 1859.

P. haynaldianum (Rchb. f.) Stein. Lvs to 45×5cm, green. Infl. arching, 3–4-fld, to 51cm; dors. sep. obovate-elliptic, apex cucullate, to 6×2.5cm, creamy white, sides flushed purple, centre green or yellow with basal half spotted maroon;

synsepalum 4.5×2.5cm, pale green, spotted maroon at base; pet. arcuate, spathulate, half-twisted, to 8cm×14mm, ciliolate, green or yellow, basal half spotted maroon, purple above; lip to 4.5×2.3cm, ochre-green, veined darker. Spring. Philipp.

P. hirsutissimum (Lindl. ex Hook.) Stein. Lvs 5–6, to 45×2cm, green, spotted purple beneath. Infl. 1-fld, to 25cm, long-haired; sep. and lip pale yellow to pale green with glossy dark brown suffusion almost to margins, pet. pale yellow, lower half spotted purple-brown, apical half flushed rose-purple; dors. sep. ovate-elliptic, 4.5×4cm, undulate, ciliate; synsepalum, 3.6×2cm; pet. horizontal to deflexed, spathulate, 7×2cm, half-twisted toward apex, strongly undulate below, pubesc.; lip 4.5×2cm. Spring--summer. NE India. var. **esquirolei** (Schltr.) Cribb. Pet. to 8cm, pet. hairs on peduncle shorter. SW China to N Thail.

P. hookerae (Rchb. f.) Stein. Lvs 23×5cm, tessellated dark and light green above. Infl. 1-fld, to 50cm; dors. sep. ovate, 4×3cm, basal margins reflexed, cream, centre flushed green; synsepalum to 3×1.5cm, pale yellow; pet. deflexed, half-twisted in middle, spathulate, 5.5×2.2cm, pale green, basal two-thirds spotted brown, apical third and margins purple; lip 4×1.5cm, brown. Summer. Borneo (Sarawak and W Kalimantan). var. **volonteanum** (Sander ex Rolfe) Kerch. Lvs narrower, spotted purple beneath, pet. broader and more obtuse, lip slightly constricted mouth. Borneo (Sabah only).

P. insigne (Wallich ex Lindl.) Pfitz. Lvs to 32×3cm, green. Infl. 1-fld, to 25cm; dors. sep. ovate-elliptic to obovate-elliptic, 6.4×4cm, apical margins incurved, pale green, inner surface with raised maroon spots, margin white; synsepalum 5×2.5cm, pale green, spotted brown; pet. oblong-spathulate, 6×2cm, undulate in basal two-thirds, yellow-brown, veined red-brown; lip 5×3cm, yellow, marked purple-brown. Autumn–winter. NE India, E Nepal.

P. javanicum (Reinw. ex Lindl.) Pfitz. Lvs 23×4cm, pale green, veined and mottled darker. Infl. 1-fld, to 36cm; dors. sep. ovate to elliptic, to 4×3cm, shortly ciliate, pale green, veined darker, margin white-pink; synsepalum 3×1.5cm, outer surface pubesc., pale green; pet. usually deflexed, narrowly oblong, to 5×1.5cm, pale green, purple-pink above, spotted maroon below; lip 4×2cm, shortly pubesc., green, veined darker, often flushed brown. Spring–summer. Java, Bali, Flores, possibly Sumatra. var. **virens** (Rchb. f.) Pfitz. Pet. with fewer spots. Sabah.

P. kolopakingii Fowlie. Lvs to 60×8cm, green. Infl. to 14-fld, arching, to 70cm; sep. white veined dark red-brown, pet. green, veined red, lip ochre, veined darker; dors. sep. ovate, 6.5×3.5cm, finely pubesc.; synsepalum 5×2.5cm, 2-keeled; pet. falcate, linear-tapering, to 7×8cm, pubesc.; lip apex sharp, to 6×3cm. Borneo.

P. lawrenceanum (Rchb. f.) Pfitz. Lvs to 19×6.5cm, dark mottled yellow-green. Infl. 1-fld, to 31cm; dors. sep. broadly ovate-subcircular, to 6×6cm, white, veined maroon above, green, below; synsepalum to 4×1.4cm, white flushed green, veined maroon; pet. ligulate, about 6×1cm, green with purple apex, margins purple-ciliate and maroon-warted; lip 6×3cm, green overlaid dull maroon, spotted maroon within. Summer. Borneo (Sarawak and Sabah).

P. Leeanum: primary hybrid with light green lvs; fls small, yellow-brown dors. edged white, with some small spots.

P. lowii (Lindl.) Stein. Lvs to 40×5cm, green. Infl. erect to arching, 3–7-fld, to 60cm; dors. sep. elliptic-ovate, to 5.5×3cm, undulate and ciliate, pale green, basal half mottled purple, basal margins recurved; synsepalum to 4cm, 2-keeled; pet. spathulate, often once-twisted, to 9×2cm, ciliate, pale yellow, apical third purple, basal two-thirds spotted maroon; lip to 4×3cm, dull ochre brown. Spring–summer. Penins. Malaysia, Sumatra, Java, Borneo, Sulawesi.

P. Makuli: attractive mottled foliage; fls small and distinctive, lime green and white or wine red and white, some forms v. dark red with near black warts on pet.

P. malipoense S.C. Chen & Tsi. Lvs to 20×4cm, dark green, lower surface keeled and marked with purple. Infl. to 30cm, 1-fld; sep. and pet. strongly veined, green with purple stripes and spots; dors. sep. elliptic-lanceolate, to 4.5×2cm, sparsely pubesc.; synsepalum 4×2cm; pet. obovate, about 4×3cm, ciliate, pubesc.; lip pale grey spotted purple within, deeply saccate, 4.5cm, subglobose, margins inrolled. Spring. SW China.

P. mastersianum (Rchb. f.) Stein. Lvs to 30×4cm, faintly tessellated. Infl. 1-fld, to 30cm; dors. sep. broadly ovate, to 37×43mm, cream with green centre; synsepalum to 29×20mm; pet. slightly reflexed, oblong-spathulate, to 5.5×2cm, ciliate, glossy, tinged green, spotted dark maroon near base, apical half flushed brown; lip to 52×30mm, pale rosy-brown. Summer. Moluccas.

P. Maudiae: one of the best-known slipper orchids with attractive mottled lvs; fls distinctive, lime green and white with striped dors. sep. Many slipper orchids similar to this in colour and shape are known as Maudiae types. Named clones include

'Magnificum' and 'The Queen'. 'Coloratum' has attractive mottled lvs; fls on strong upright st., large, wine red and white with striped dors. sep. and green-brown lip.

P. micranthum Tang & Wang. Lvs to 15×2cm, mottled, spotted purple beneath. Infl. erect, 1-fld, to 20cm; sep. and pet. pale yellow, flushed pink, veined red-purple; dors. sep. ovate, to 2.5×3cm; synsepalum elliptic, to 24×11mm; pet. elliptic-suborbicular rounded, to 33×34mm, white-pubesc.; lip deeply inflated, elliptic-ovate, to 65×47mm, rose-pink, spotted purple within. Spring. SW China.

P. niveum (Rchb. f.) Stein. Lvs to 19×3.5cm, mottled v. dark and pale green above, heavily dotted purple beneath. Infl. 1–2-fld, to 25cm; fls white, often dotted purple near base of seg. and front of lip, pubesc.; dors. sep. v. broadly ovate, to 3×5cm; synsepalum concave, to 28×22mm; pet. elliptic, rounded, to 39×26mm, ciliate; lip ovoid to ellipsoidal, to 3×1.7cm, margins incurved. Summer. N Malaysia and S Thail.

P. papuanum (Ridl.) Ridl. Lvs to 22×4.2cm, tessellated, veined dark green. Infl. 1-fld, to 28cm; dors. sep. ovate, to 25×26mm, ciliate, pubesc., white with centre tinged yellow or green, veined purple; synsepalum, to 18×13mm; pet. oblong-lanceolate, to 42×17mm, ciliolate, dull maroon, spotted black below; lip to 3.7×1.4cm, dull crimson or brown-maroon. Spring–summer. Highland New Guinea.

P. parishii (Rchb. f.) Stein. Lvs to 45×7.5cm, green. Infl. arching to suberect, to 50cm, to 9-fld; sep. cream to green, veined darker, dors. sep. elliptic, to 4.5×3cm, incurved below; sysnepalum to 4×2.9cm, 2-keeled; pet. decurved-pendent, linear-tapering, to 10.5×1.1cm, apical half spirally twisted, ciliate, undulate, green, spotted dark maroon below, margins and apical half dark maroon, maroon spots on lower basal margin; lip apex narrow, to 4.5×2cm, green, yellow-green or flushed purple. Summer. E & NE Burm., Thail., SW China. var. **dianthum** (Tang & Wang) Cribb & Tang. Fls slightly larger, less spotted pet. SW China only.

P. philippinense (Rchb. f.) Stein. Lvs to 50×5cm. Infl. erect, 2–4-fld, to 50cm; sep. white, dors. sep. ovate, to 5×2.5cm, striped maroon; synsepalum to 5.5×3cm; pet. linear, tapering to 13×0.6cm, ciliate, white or yellow at base, maroon above, dark maroon warts on margin in basal half; lip small, rather ovoid, 3.8×1.4cm, yellow. Summer. Philipp. and islands off N Borneo coast. var. **roebelenii** (Veitch) Cribb Fls larger with pet. to 13cm. Philipp.

P. praestans Rchb. f. = P. glanduliferum.

P. primulinum M.W. Wood & Tayl. Lvs to 17×3.8cm, green. Infl. many-fld, opening in succession, to 35cm or more; fls pale yellow with yellow-green sep.; dors. sep. ovate, to 2.6×2.6cm, ciliate; synsepalum to 2.6×1.4cm; pet. linear-tapering, spreading, twisted in apical half, ciliate, to 3.2×0.8cm; lip to 3.5×1.9cm, bulbous toward apex. Summer. N Sumatra. var. **purpurascens** (M.W. Wood) Cribb. Fls flushed purple.

P. purpuratum (Lindl.) Stein. Lvs to 17×4.2cm, tessellated above. Infl. erect, 1-fld, to 20cm; dors. sep. ovate-cordate, 3.5×3.6cm, white, veined purple-maroon; synsepalum 2.7×1.5cm, green, veined darker; pet. horizontal, narrowly elliptic to oblong, to 4.6×1.3mm, ciliate, glossy maroon, green-white near base, lower two-thirds spotted black-maroon; lip to 4×2cm, incurved, lat. lobes verrucose, brown-maroon. Autumn. Hong Kong, adjacent China, Hainan Is.

P. randsii Fowlie. Lvs green, to 35×6cm. Infl. 3–5-fld, to 40cm; fls white, sep. and pet. veined maroon; dors. sep. ovate 4.2×2.2cm; synsepalum 3.2×2cm; pet. deflexed, arcuate, linear, 4.5×0.6cm; lip rounded and grooved at apex, 3.2×1.5cm, green-yellow. Summer. Philipp.

P. rothschildianum (Rchb. f.) Stein. Lvs to 60×5cm, green; infl. 2–4-fld, erect, to 45cm; dors. sep. ovate, to 6.6×4.1cm, ivory-white or yellow veined maroon; synsepalum about 5.7×3.3cm; pet. to 12.4×1.4cm, narrowly tapering to rounded apex, yellow or ivory-white marked maroon; lip subporrect, about 5.7×2.2cm, golden, heavily suffused purple. Spring–summer. Borneo.

P. sanderianum (Rchb. f.) Stein. Lvs to 45×5.3cm, shiny, green. Infl. horizontal or slightly ascending, 2–5-fld; sep. yellow striped maroon; dors. sep. lanceolate, slightly concave, to 6.5×2.5cm; synsepalum 2-keeled; to 6×2cm; pet. ribbon-like, pendent, undulate, twisted, tapering, to 90×0.9cm, off-white to yellow, spotted maroon, maroon warts on basal margins, basal half ciliate, apex minutely pubesc.; lip subporrect, pointed, to 5×2.5cm. Winter. Borneo (Sarawak).

P. spicerianum (Rchb. f. ex Mast. & T. Moore) Pfitz. Lvs to 30×6cm, glossy dark green, spotted purple toward base beneath. Infl. 1-, rarely 2-fld, to 35cm; dors. sep. curving forward, obovate to transversely elliptic, to 4.2×5cm, sides recurved, white with central maroon vein and green-tinged base; synsepalum to 3.5×2.2cm, off-white; pet. falcate, linear-tapering, to 3.9×1.3cm, undulate, ciliate toward apex, yellow-green with central brown-purple vein and flecking; lip to 4.3×3cm, glossy, pale green, flushed brown with darker veins. Winter. NE India, NW Burma.

P. stonei (Hook.) Stein. Lvs to 70×4.5cm, green. Infl. 2–4-fld, to 70cm; sep. white, lined dark maroon, dors. sep. ovate, to 6.7×4.4cm; synsepalum to 5×3.4cm; pet. linear-tapering, dependent, to 15×0.75cm, sometimes twisted, yellow, lined and spotted maroon, sometimes flushed maroon in apical half; lip forward-pointing, to 5.7×2.8cm, pale yellow, strongly flushed pink and veined darker. Summer. Borneo (Sarawak only). var. *platytaenium* (Rchb. f.) Stein. Pet. to 2cm wide.

P. sukhakulii Schoser & Sengh. Lvs 13×4.5cm, tessellated dark and yellow-green above. Infl. 1-fld; sep. white veined green, spotted purple at base, outer surface pubesc., dors. sep. concave, to 4×3cm, ciliate; synsepalum 3.4×1.6cm; pet. subhorizontal, to 6.2×2cm, green heavily spotted maroon, ciliate; lip saccate, 5×2.3cm, green, veined and flushed maroon. Autumn. NE Thail. only.

P. superbiens (Rchb. f.) Stein. Lvs to 24×5cm, tessellated above, flushed purple at base beneath. Infl. 1-fld, to 23cm; sep. white veined green and purple, marked green or purple-green at centre, pet. white, spotted maroon-purple, sometimes flushed purple, raised spots on upper margin and in basal half, lip dark maroon; dors. sep. ovate to 5.8×5.3cm, ciliate; synsepalum to 4×1.9cm; pet. recurved-falcate, to 7.5×1.9cm, ciliate, half-twisted in apical half; lip to 6.5×3cm. Summer. N & C Sumatra.

P. tonsum (Rchb. f.) Stein. Lvs to 20×4.5cm, veined green, upper surface mottled darker green. Infl. 1-fld, erect, to 35cm; sep. white, veined and tinged yellow-green, pet. olive to yellow-green, veined darker, black-warted, lip olive-brown, flushed pink, veined darker; dors. sep. obovate, about 4.5×4cm; synsepalum 3.5×1.5cm; pet. slightly drooping, about 6.5×2cm; lip saccate, 5.5×3.3cm. Autumn–winter. N & C Sumatra.

P. urbanianum Fowlie. Lvs to 20×4cm, tessellated above. Infl. erect, 1-fld, rarely 2-fld, to 25cm; dors. sep. ovate to broadly ovate, to 3.6×4.2cm, white veined green; synsepalum 3.1×1.9cm, green veined darker; pet. slightly recurved, oblanceolate, to 6×1.8cm, white lined green, basal two-thirds spotted maroon, apical half purple; lip to 4.5×3cm, dull purple, lat. lobes marked maroon, ciliate on apical margin. Spring. Philipp.

P. venustum (Wallich) Pfitz. ex Stein. Lvs to 25×5.5cm, sea green tessellated dark green, spotted purple beneath.Infl. 1-fld (rarely 2-fld), to 23cm; sep. white veined green, pet. white veined green, warted maroon-black, flushed purple in apical half; dors. sep. ovate, to 3.8×2.8cm; synsepalum similiar, to 3cm; pet. oblanceolate, recurved, ciliate, to 5.4×1.4cm; lip to 4.3×3.2cm, yellow tinged purple and veined green. Winter. NE India, E Nepal, Sikkim, Bhutan.

P. victoria-mariae (Sander ex Mast.) Rolfe. Lvs to 30×6.5cm, green mottled darker, flushed purple beneath. Infl. to 1m+, many-fld in succession; dors. sep. broadly ovate to obovate, to 2.9×3cm, ciliate, pale yellow with centre bright green; synsepalum to 2.8×1.7cm; pet. linear, horizontal-reflexed, to 4×1.1cm, ciliate, twisted above, green flushed brown to red-purple; lip tapering, to 4×2.5cm, purple, margined yellow or green. Spring. S & CW Sumatra.

P. victoria-reginae (Sander) M.W. Wood. Lvs to 28×6cm, green, flushed purple beneath. Infl. to 60cm, arching, rachis flexuous; fls to 32 in succession; dors. sep. subcircular-elliptic, to 3×3cm, yellow-green or white, lower half flushed green or yellow, veined dark purple, undulate; synsepalum to 3×2.1cm, yellow-green, veined purple; pet. horizontal, ligulate, slightly recurved, to 4×0.8cm, yellow or pale yellow, spotted and streaked dark maroon, twice twisted, ciliate; lip to 4.1×2.1cm, pink with white rim, inflated. Autumn. Sumatra.

P. villosum (Lindl.) Stein. Lvs to 42×4cm, green. Infl. suberect to arching, 1-fld, to 24cm; dors. sep. obovate, to 6.5×3.5cm, margins reflexed, green, margined white, glossy maroon areas in centre; synsepalum to 3.5×2.6cm; pet. incurved, obovate-spathulate, to 7×3cm, glossy, ciliate, red-brown with central maroon stripe; lip tapering, to 6×3.8cm, ochre, flushed pink or red. Winter–spring. NE India, Burma, Thail. var. *boxallii* Rchb. f. Sep. narrower at base, dors. sep. heavily spotted and purple marking on pet.

P. violascens Schltr. Lvs to 22×4cm, grey-green, mottled above. Infl. 1-fld, to 30cm; dors. sep. broadly ovate, to 4.3×3cm, white veined green; synsepalum to 2.6×1.6cm, green veined darker; pet. deflexed 45°, obliquely oblong, to 4.4×1.8cm, minutely ciliate, white or green-white, apical three-quarters heavily flushed purple; lip to 5×2cm, deeply saccate, margin ciliate, green to ochre. Spring. New Guinea.

P. wardii Summerh. Lvs oblong-lanceolate, to 17cm, dark blue-green mottled paler above, mottled purple beneath. Infl. 1-fld, to 20cm; dors. sep. ovate, to 5×3cm, white veined green;

synsepalum to 4.5×2.2cm; pet. oblong-lanceolate to oblong, to 6.5×1.7cm, spreading, somewhat pendulous, green-white flushed brown-purple, spotted dark maroon; lip to 5×2cm, green-tinged or ochre, finely spotted brown. Winter. N Burm., SW China.

P. wentworthianum Schoser. Lvs to 25×4.5cm, tessellated light and dark green, shortly pubesc. Infl. 1-fld, to 35cm tall; dors. sep. concave, broadly ovate, to 3.2×3.5cm, cream veined green with green centre; synsepalum to 2.5×2.6cm; pet. oblong-elliptic, spreading below horizontal, to 4.5×2.5cm, glossy purple above, brown and green toward base, ciliate, undulate; lip to 4.5×2.2cm, yellow-green flushed brown. Spring. Bougainville and Guadalcanal.

P. grexes and cvs.

Hundreds of *Paphiopedilum* cvs ranging widely in foliage from the short and mottled to the long, narrow and dark green; in number and disposition of fls from solitary short-stemmed blooms to long, arching, remote rac.; in fl. shape from the large and virtually round to the narrow- or spiral-petalled; in fl. colour from yellow to brown, green, red, pink, white or purple-black variously veined, dotted and flushed.

Papilionanthe Schltr. Orchidaceae. 11 monopodial, epiphytic orchids. St. slender, terete, scrambling, often branching and rooting. Lvs in 2 ranks, alt., terete, narrowly tapering. Infl. a short, axill. rac. or pan.; sep. obovate, undulate, alt. sep. clawed; pet. suborbicular, spreading, strongly undulate; lip trilobed, base saccate, midlobe, broad, lat. lobes large; spur saccate, conical. Himal. to Malaysia.

P. hookeriana (Rchb. f.) Schltr. To 2.2m. Lvs 7–10cm, mid-green. Infl. to 30cm; fls 2–12; dors. sep. and pet. white or pale mauve, chequered deep mauve, faintly spotted, lat. sep. nearly white, lip deep purple, midlobe pale mauve marked purple, midlobe to 3×4cm, weakly trilobed. Malaysia, China, Borneo, Vietnam. Z10.

P. teres (Roxb.) Schltr. To 1.75m scrambling.Lvs incurved, to 20cm, olive green. Infl. 15–30cm; fls 3–6 per rac., 5–10cm diam.; sep. and pet. white or ivory deepening to rose or magenta, lip buff to golden, banded or dotted blood-red or mauve, midlobe flabellate to obcordate, deeply cleft. Thail., Burm., Himal.; widely nat. Important cut fl. and parent of many grexes (see *Vanda*). Z9.

P. vandarum (Rchb. f.) Garay. To 2m, sprawling. Lvs to 10cm, ± straight, dark green often flushed purple. Infl. to 8cm; fls to 5 per infl., nocturnally fragrant, to 5cm diam., crystalline white, often tinged opal or basally flushed lilac to pink; lip midlobe clawed, broadly obcordate, apically ruffed and deflexed. India, Burm. Z9.

→*Aerides* and *Vanda*.

Papoose Root *Caulophyllum thalictrioides*.

Papperitzia Rchb. f. Orchidaceae. 1 epiphytic orchid. Pbs to 1cm, clustered. Lvs to 7cm, linear, coriaceous. Rac. basal, erect to pendent; fls to 1.5cm, green, yellow-pubesc.; dors. sep. hood-like, subcaudate, spurred, lateral sep. connate, navicular, subcaudate; pet. free, similar to dors. sep.; lip fleshy, funnel-shaped at base forming a saccate pouch, pubesc. within. Mex. Z10.

P. lieboldii (Rchb. f.) Rchb. f.
→*Leochilus*.

Paprika *Capsicum annuum* var. *annuum*.

Papuacedrus Li. Cupressaceae. 2 everg. conifers. Crown conic, bark exfoliating in scales. Juvenile lvs dimorphic; facial lvs small; lat. lvs lanceolate, flat, sharp acuminate, adnate to twig. Adult lvs smaller, decussate, scale-like, addressed; facial lvs quadrilateral in cross section, keeled above, base decurrent. Cones ovoid, scales 4, lanceolate or ovate, coriaceous. New Guinea, Moluccas. Z10.

P. arfakensis (Gibbs) Li. To 30m or more. Bark rust brown; twigs segmented, flattened. Juvenile facial lvs in widely spaced pairs, rhombic to cuneate; lat. lvs flattened, 1–2cm, overlapping facial lvs. Adult lvs to 5mm, obtuse. All lvs glossy green above, marked glaucous bands beneath.

P. papuana (F. Muell.) Li. Tree to 50m, bark dark grey, grooved; twig apices curved. Lvs as for *P. arfakensis* when young. Lvs evenly formed; lat. lvs to 3×1–2mm, only partly obscuring facial lvs, to 2×2mm.

P. torricellensis (Schltr. ex Laut.) Li = *P. papuana*.
→*Libocedrus*.

Papyrus *Cyperus papyrus*.
Pará Rubber Tree *Hevea brasiliensis*.

Parabenzoin Nak.
P. praecox (Sieb. & Zucc.) Nak. = *Lindera praecox*.

Paraboea Ridl. Gesneriaceae. 65 rosulate or caulescent perenn. herbs and shrubs; young shoots woolly. Lvs opposite or whorled, arachnoid above, densely hairy beneath. Fls paired in cymes; cal. seg. 5; cor. obliquely campanulate or with a short tube and flat limb, limb slightly bilabiate. SE Asia. Z10.
P. rufescens B.L. Burtt. Caulescent perenn. herb. Lvs to 7cm, subcoriaceous, broadly ovate, crenate-serrate. Peduncles to 13cm, flushed purple; cor. to 1×1.2cm, dark violet, broadly campanulate, limb oblique. Thail.

Paracaryum (DC.) Boiss. Boraginaceae. 15 ann., bienn. or perenn. herbs, erect or decumbent. Basal lvs usually long-petiolate; cauline lvs ± sessile, narrower. Infl. becoming elongate, sometimes bracteate; cal. deeply lobed; cor. cylindrical or infundibular to campanulate, usually with faucal appendages. NE Afr. to S Russia and Himal. Z8.
P. himalayense (Klotzsch) C.B. Clarke. Perenn. to bienn., to 60cm. Erect, long-branched, white-setose. Basal lvs to 9cm, oblong to spathulate-lanceolate, obtuse, sometimes revolute. Infl. term. or axill., lax; cor. pink to white-blue, to 4mm, campanulate-cylindric, faucal scales trapeziform. Afghan., Pak., Kashmir, NW India.
P. lithospermifolium (Lam.) Grande. Perenn. to 25cm, ascending or decumbent, grey or white sericeous-villous. Basal lvs to 4cm, obovate. Cymes mostly simple; pedicels to 5mm in fl.; cor. purple to red-violet, to 5.5mm, faucal scales emarginate, papillose. SE Eur.
P. microcarpum Boiss. Perenn. to 45cm, hirsute, ascending to procumbent. Basal lvs to 10cm, oblong-spathulate. Infl. axill. or term., lax, bracteate; cor. bright blue, to 5mm, infundibular-campanulate, lobes ovate. Kashmir, Afghan., Pak.
P. racemosum (Schreb.) Britten. Perenn., often tufted, to 40cm, ascending, villous or glabrescent. Basal lvs to 4cm, linear, tomentose or pilose above. Infl. a corymb or a pan.; cor. bright blue, to 15mm, infundibular; faucal scales linear, obtuse. Turk.
→*Cynoglossum, Lepechiniella, Mattia* and *Mattiastrum*.

Paraceterach (F. Muell.) Copel. Adiantaceae. 2 small terrestrial ferns. Rhiz. creeping. Stipes chaffy. Fronds pinnate, clad with chaffy scales. Aus. Z10.
P. muelleri (Hook.) Copel. Stipes 7.5–10cm, wiry, ferruginous-scaly. Fronds 10–25cm, erect to pendulous, pale green, thick and coriaceous; pinnae 4×1cm, oblong to ovate, entire, lower often auriculate. NE Queensld.
P. reynoldsii (F. Muell.) Tind. Stipes short, dark brown to black, scaly. Fronds to 30cm, erect, dark green, with flat pale scales beneath, becoming glab. above; pinnae 0.8–1.5cm, suborbicular to oblong, entire. Aus., except in SE.
→*Gymnogramma*.

Parachute Plant *Ceropegia sandersoniae*.

Paradisea Mazz. Liliaceae (Asphodelaceae). 2 fleshy-rooted, rhizomatous perenn. herbs. Lvs grass-like, basal. Scapes slender, bracteate; fls funnelform to campanulate, in lax rac.; tep. 6, free, clawed. Summer. S Eur. (mts). Z7.
P. liliastrum (L.) Bertol. ST BRUNO'S LILY; PARADISE LILY. To 60cm. Lvs 3–5cm. Fls white with green apical spot in secund rac.; pedicels not articulated. S Eur. 'Major': more robust, fls larger.
P. liliastrum var. *lusitanicum* Cout. = *P. lusitanicum*.
P. lusitanicum (Cout.) Samp. To 150cm, more robust than *P. liliastrum*. Lvs to 2cm wide. Fls white, to 2cm, in 2-ranked rac.; pedicels articulated. Port.
→*Anthericum*.

Paradise Apple *Malus pumila* var. *paradisiaca*.
Paradise Flower *Caesalpinia pulcherrima*; *Solanum wendlandii*.
Paradise Lily *Paradisea liliastrum*.
Paradise Nut *Lecythis pisonis*; *L. zabucaya*.
Paradise Palm *Howea forsteriana*.
Paradise Plant *Justicia carnea*.
Para Fern *Marattia fraxinea*.

Paragramma (Bl.) Moore. Polypodiaceae. 1 epiphytic fern. Rhiz. creeping, covered with roots and scales. Fronds to 90×4cm, uniform, simple, linear-lanceolate, apex acute to obtuse, base long-attenuate, entire to somewhat revolute, fleshy to leathery, glab.; stipes to 8cm, jointed to rhiz. E Asia. Z10.
P. longifolia (Bl.) Moore.
→*Grammitis*.

Paraguayan Jasmine *Brunfelsia australis*.

Paraguayan Silver Trumpet Tree *Tabebuia argentea*.
Paraguay Tea *Ilex paraguariensis*.

Parahebe W. Oliv. Scrophulariaceae. 30 prostrate or decumbent subshrubs, rarely herbs. Similar to *Hebe* but with suffruticose habit and fls in axill. rac. NZ, New Guinea, Aus.
P. ×*bidwillii* (Hook. f.) W. Oliv. (*P. decora* ×*P. lyallii*.) Shrub to 15cm, mat-forming, procumbent. Lvs to 0.6cm, oblong to obovate, coriaceous, entire or with 1–2 teeth per side. Rac. to 20cm, narrow; cor. to 8mm diam., white, veins lilac. Summer. NZ. 'Kea': lvs small; st. long; fls white, veined crimson. 'Rosea': fls pink. Z8.
P. birleyi (N.E. Br.) W. Oliv. Subshrub, sprawling to 20cm. Br. sparse, decumbent then ascending, fleshy when young, pubesc. at tips, with grey bark when mature. Lvs to 0.9cm, crowded, cuneate to obovate, glandular-hairy, crenate, 5-lobed at apex. Fls single or paired, glandular-hairy; cor. to 20mm, white. NZ. Z8.
P. canescens (T. Kirk) W. Oliv. Minute prostrate herb, forming creeping rooted mats to 20cm. St. filiform, much-branched, sparsely villous. Lvs to 0.3cm, broad-ovate, sparsely pubesc., tinged brown, entire. Fls single or paired; cor. to 6mm, blue, funnelform. Summer. NZ. Z8.
P. catarractae (Forst. f.) W. Oliv. Variable subshrub, st. to 30cm, decumbent to ascending, woody when mature, usually bifar-iously pubesc., tinged purple when young. Lvs to 4cm, ovate to lanceolate, dark above, paler beneath, glab., acute, sharply serrate, midrib pubesc. Fls v. numerous, glab. to glandular-hairy; cor. to 1cm, white, veins pink or purple. Summer–autumn. NZ. 'Alba': fls white. 'Delight': to 15cm, bushy; fls blue. 'Diffusa': to 20cm; lvs small, toothed; fls tiny, pink flushed. 'Miss Willmott': fls rose-lilac veined mauve. 'Por-lock': to 25cm; fls blue and white. 'Rosea': to 20cm; fls pink. Z8.
P. decora Ashwin. Subshrub, prostrate, mat-forming. St. slender, woody. Lvs to 5cm, ovate to suborbicular, entire, fleshy, glab., often tinged red, apex rounded. Fls in rac., to 15-fld, usually in whorls; cor. to 1cm, white to pink, venation often red. NZ. Commonly grown under the name *P.* ×*bidwillii*. Z8.
P. diffusa (Hook. f.) W. Oliv. = *P. catarractae*.
P. hookeriana (Walp.) W. Oliv. Low subshrub, much-branched. St. to 25cm, woody, prostrate to decumbent; br. ± pubesc. Lvs to 1.2cm, imbricate, ovate to suborbicular, thick-coriaceous, pale green, crenate or serrate, pubesc. to gland., often ciliate. Fls in to 8-fld rac., densely pubesc. or glandular-hairy; cor. to 1cm, white to pale blue. Summer. NZ. The limits of this sp. are ill-defined, probably due to crossing with *P. catarractae*. Z9.
P. linifolia (Hook. f.) W. Oliv. Subshrub to 12cm, much-branched, base woody, glab.; sprawling to erect. Lvs to 2cm, close-set, linear to lanceolate, glab., acute, base ciliate, midrib depressed above. Rac., to 4-fld, glab.; cor. to 15mm, white to pink, veined red. Summer. NZ. 'Blue Skies': fls blue. Z8.
P. lyallii (Hook. f.) W. Oliv. Subshrub to 20cm, much-branched. St. slender, usually woody, prostrate to decumbent; br. pubesc. Lvs to 1cm, suborbicular to linear-obovate, coriaceous, obtuse to rounded, crenate to bluntly serrate. Fls numerous in rac., occas. glandular-hairy; cor. to 1cm, white to pink. Summer. NZ. 'Rosea': fls pink. Z8.
P. perfoliata (R. Br.) B.G. Briggs DIGGER'S SPEEDWELL. Woody-based glaucous herb. St. to 1.5m, several, arching, ± un-branched. Lvs to 5cm, ovate, amplexicaul to connate-perfoliate, blue-green. Rac. to 20cm, axill., slender; fls to 1cm diam., blue-violet. Aus. Z9.
P. spathulata (Benth.) W. Oliv. Subshrub, prostrate, forming mats to 25cm., main root v. stout; br. pubesc. Lvs to 1cm, crowded, may form small rosettes, suborbicular, pubesc. or glab., obtuse, crenate. Rac. numerous, villous; cor. to 8mm, white or lavender. Summer. NZ. Z8.
P. cvs. 'Mervyn': to 8cm; lvs tinged purple; fls lilac blue.
→*Hebe*; *Veronica*.

Parajubaea Burret. Palmae. 2 palms. St. solitary, erect, grey, faintly ringed. Lvs pinnate; rachis slightly twisted, terete; pinnae single-fold, subopposite, linear, acuminate, apex shallowly divided or oblique. Colomb., Ecuad., and Boliv. Z10.
P. coccoides Burret. Trunk to 15m×25cm, swollen at base, clean. Lvs to 5m, drooping; seg. regularly spaced, reduplicate, apex acuminate, yellow-green and shiny above, dull and scurfy be-neath; rachis glab. Ecuad., Colomb.

Parakeet Flower *Heliconia psittacorum*.

Paramacrolobium Léonard. Leguminosae (Caesalpinioideae). 1 everg. tree to 40m; bark grey-black, finely striated. Lvs paripinnate; lfts to 15cm, 3–5 pairs, elliptic to oblong, acuminate, subcoriaceous, golden-sericeous beneath. Infl. to 8cm, compact, corymbose; sep. 4–5; pet. 5, 2-lobed, spathulate,

to 5cm, blue-violet with green-blue basal spot; sta. 9. Sierra Leone to Congo, Kenya, Tanz. Z10.
P. coeruleum (Taub.) Léonard.

Paramansoa Baill. = *Arrabidaea.*

Paramongaia Velarde. Amaryllidaceae. 1 bulbous herb. Lvs to 75cm, narrow-linear. Scape to 60cm; fls 1(–2), bright yellow, fragrant; perianth tube 10cm, cylindrical, lobes to 8cm, 6, spreading; corona large trumpet-like; style exserted. Peru. Z10.
P. weberbaueri Velarde. COJOMARIA.

Parana Pine *Araucaria angustifolia.*

Paranephelius Poepp. Compositae. 7 perenn. herbs or shrubs. Lvs mostly white-tomentose beneath. Cap. radiate, few to numerous in cymose clusters, or solitary; receptacle scaly, flat; phyllaries lanceolate; ray flts numerous, yellow; disc flts orange or yellow. N & S Amer. Z8.
P. ovatus Wedd. Dwarf, stemless perenn. herb, to 10cm. Lvs in a basal rosette, to 4.5cm, elliptic to rhombic-ovate, irregularly toothed, occas. lyrate-pinnatifid, green and glab. above, nerves impressed, smooth or wrinkled-bullate, white cottony-tomentose beneath. Cap. to 9cm diam.; peduncle to 6mm, thick, white-cottony, with 2 scale-like purple-tinged bracts; receptacle scales deep red-purple; phyllaries tinged purple, spathulate-oblong, apex usually rounded, innermost sharply acute, pungent; ray flts to 6cm, spreading-ascending and recurved. Andes of Peru and Boliv.
P. uniflorus Poepp. & Endl. Dwarf, stemless perenn. herb, to 12cm. Lvs in a basal rosette, c10cm, obovate to obovate-lanceolate, deeply and irregularly acutely sinuate-toothed or pinnatifid, lobes acutely toothed, dark green and rugose above, nerves impressed, snow-white adpressed-tomentose beneath. Cap. to 9cm diam.; peduncle to 10cm, stout, densely tomentose; receptacle scales shortly fimbriate, phyllaries linear-oblong, obtuse or acute, ray flts to 4cm, spreading. Andes of Peru and Boliv.
→*Liabum.*

Paranomus Salisb. Proteaceae. 18 small erect everg. shrubs. Lvs usually dimorphic, pinnate at base of shoot, entire on upper part, rarely uniform, fan-shaped and dissected. Infl. spike-like, term.; cap. 4-fld; fls actinomorphic; perianth limb elliptic, 4-partite to near base, tube short, cream to white or pink. S Afr. Z9.
P. reflexus (Phillips & Hutch.) N.E. Br. Shrub to 2.5m, densely bushy, st. long. Lvs 7–8cm, crowded, divided into slender lobes, acute, pale to mid green, red at apex, lvs at st. summits 3×2cm, entire. Infl. 12×8cm, on velvety flowering st. to 60cm; perianth yellow-green to cream tinged pale green to buff, seg. slender. Autumn–winter. S Afr.

Para-para *Pisonia umbellifera.*

Paraphalaenopsis A.D. Hawkes. Orchidaceae. 4 orchids differing from *Phalaenopsis* in lvs few, cylindrical, canaliculate. Borneo. Z10.
P. denevei (Sm.) A.D. Hawkes. Fls to 6cm diam.; tep. spreading, green-yellow to yellow-brown; lip white, spotted crimson; midlobe linear-spathulate, papillose, callus wrinkled, minutely toothed; lat. lobes oblong to triangular, falcate. W Borneo.
P. labukensis (P.S. Shim) A. Lamb & C.L. Chan. Tep. raspberry pink, dotted and edged yellow, lip yellow, spotted purple, apex dolabriform. Borneo.
P. laycockii (M.R. Henderson) A.D. Hawkes. Fls to 8cm diam., magenta to lilac, lip blotched yellow and brown; midlobe forward pointing, linear-spathulate, apical lobes triangular, disc pale yellow, striped brown, lat. lobes linear-oblong, erect, apex truncate to rounded. SC Borneo.
P. serpentilingua (Sm.) A.D. Hawkes. Fls to 4cm diam.; scented, tep. white above, lip lemon yellow, banded purple; midlobe recurved, linear, tip bifid, callus toothed, lat. lobes linear, falcate. W Borneo.
→*Phalaenopsis.*

Paraquilegia J.R. Drumm. & Hutch. Ranunculaceae. 4 tufted perenn. herbs. Lvs petiolate, 2–3-ternate, lobed. Fls large, solitary, long-stalked; sep. 5, petaloid; pet. form nectaries, orbicular, elongate or tubular, concave below, apex emarginate; sta. numerous; anth. yellow; carpels 3–7. C Asia mts to Himal. Z5.
P. anemonoides (Willd.) Ulbr. Glab., to 18cm. Lvs basal, long-petiolate, ternate, lfts 1–2cm across, divided into many deeply lobed seg., glaucous. Fls cup-shaped, 2–4cm across, white to lilac; sep. 5, broad elliptic; nectaries 5, yellow, obovate.

Summer. Himal. (Pak. to W China), C & N Asia.
P. grandiflora (Fisch. ex DC.) Drumm. & Hutch. = *P. anemonoides.*
P. microphylla (Royle) Drumm. & Hutch. = *P. anemonoides.*

Parasitaxus Laub. Podocarpaceae. 1 parasitic conifer, to 2m, specific to the host *Falcatifolium taxoides* (Podocarpaceae). Lvs spirally arranged, loosely overlapping, succulent, tinged red, lacking chlorophyll. ♂ cones ovoid, to 4×2mm, tinged red. Seed cones globose, 3–4mm, glaucous, subtended by 6 involucral bracts. New Caledonia. Z10.
P. ustus (Vieill.) Laub. PARASITE YEW.
→*Dacrydium* and *Podocarpus.*

Parasite Yew *Parasitaxus ustus.*
Parasolier *Musanga cecropioides.*
Paras Pipal *Ficus arnottiana.*

Parasyringa W.W. Sm.
P. sempervirens (Franch.) W.W. Sm. = *Ligustrum sempervirens.*

Parathelypteris (H. Itô) Ching. Thelypteridaceae. 15 terrestrial ferns. Rhiz. creeping. Stipes generally castaneous, shining, glab. or ashy hairy. Fronds oblong-lanceolate, deeply bipinnatisect, firmly herbaceous to chartaceous. Warm & Trop. Asia, Malaysia, N Amer. Z10.
P. beddomei (Bak.) Ching. Stipes 15–22cm. Fronds 15–30×7.5–10cm, oblong-lanceolate, firm; pinnae 4–5cm, dissected into numerous entire, acute lobes to 2mm, margins recurved. Sri Lanka, Java.
P. glanduligera (Kunze) Ching. Stipes slender. Fronds 15–45×5–15cm, narrowly deltoid to broadly lanceolate, acuminate, pilose above, yellow-glandular beneath; pinnae 2–8cm, spreading, linear-lanceolate, acuminate, pinnatipartite. China to India, Jap., Korea, Indochina.
P. nevadensis (Bak.) Ching. SIERRA WATER FERN. Stipes 3–20cm. Fronds rhombic, often narrowly so, pinnate-pinnatifid, acuminate and pinnatifid at apex, glab. or v. sparsely pilose on veins beneath; pinnae, pinnatifid, seg. ascending. NW Amer.
P. noveboracensis (L.) Ching. NEW YORK FERN. Stipes 5–30cm. Fronds 30–60×10–15cm, lanceolate, acuminate, pinnate, membranous; pinnae 4–9cm, lanceolate, deeply pinnatifid, long acuminate, ciliate and finely pubesc. beneath; seg. oblong, obtuse. N Amer.
P. simulata (Davenp.) Ching. Stipes 15–40cm. Fronds oblong-lanceolate, acuminate, rather thin and membranous, minutely pubesc.; pinnae lanceolate, pinnatifid; seg. obliquely oblong, obtuse, entire, slightly revolute. NE US.
→*Aspidium, Dryopteris, Lastrea, Nephrodium* and *Thelypteris.*

Paratropia DC.
P. reinwardtii Decne. & Planch. = *Schefflera longifolia.*
P. rotundifolia Ten. = *Schefflera rotundifolia.*

Pardanthopsis Lenz. Iridaceae. 1 rhizomatous perenn. herb, to 1m. Rhiz. producing swollen roots. Lvs in fans, to 30×2.5cm. Infl. branching; fls to 6 per spathe, ephemeral, to 4.5cm diam.; falls larger than standards, ivory spotted and striped maroon from base, flecked purple in centre, claw striped purple. Summer. Sib., N China, Mong. Z7.
P. dichotoma (Pall.) Lenz.
→*Iris.*

Pardanthus Ker-Gawl.
P. chinensis (L.) Ker-Gawl. = *Belamcanda chinensis.*

Paris L. Liliaceae (Trilliaceae). 4 rhizomatous herbaceous perennials. St. erect, simple, glab., to 40cm. Lvs 4–12 in a whorl near apex of st. Fls solitary, term.; sep. 4–6, green; pet. 4–6, narrow; sta. 4–10. Fr. a fleshy, purple-black capsule. Spring–summer. Eur. to E Asia.
P. apetala Hoffm. = *P. incompleta.*
P. bashanensis Wang & Tang. Differs from *P. quadrifolia* in narrower, longer lvs and narrower, reflexed sep. W China. Z7.
P. dahurica Fisch. ex Tersch. = *P. verticillata.*
P. hexaphylla Cham. = *P. verticillata.*
P. hexaphylla Cham. f. *purpurea* Miyabe & Tatew. = *P. verticillata.*
P. incompleta Bieb. St. to 33cm. Lvs 6–12, oblong-lanceolate to obovate, petiole short petiole, 6–10cm. Pedicel shorter than lvs; sep. 4, pale green, sessile, lanceolate, 2.5–4cm, spreading; pet. 0. Turk., Cauc., Armenia. Z7.
P. japonica (Franch. & Savat.) Franch. = *Kinugasa japonica.*
P. obovata Ledeb. = *P. verticillata.*
P. octyphylla Hoffm. = *P. incompleta.*

P. quadrifolia L. HERB PARIS. St. 15–40cm. Lvs usually 4, ovate, short-petiolate. Pedicel 2–8cm, yellow green; sep. 4, green, lanceolate, 2.5–3.5cm; pet. 4 equalling sep., v. narrow, flattened, acute. Eur., Cauc., Sib., temp. E Asia. Z6.

P. quadrifolia L. var. *setchuanensis* Franch. = *P. bashanensis*.

P. quadrifolia Thunb. non L. = *P. tetraphylla*.

P. tetraphylla A. Gray St. to 40cm. Lvs 4–5, sessile, oblong to elliptic, 4–10cm. Pedicel 3–10cm; sep. similar in shape to lvs, green, 1–2cm, reflexed; pet. 0. Jap. Z8.

P. verticillata Bieb. St. 40cm. Lvs subsessile, 5–8, ovate to lanceolate. Pedicel 5–15cm; sep. 4, ovate to lanceolate, 2–4cm, green; pet. 4, filiform, 1.5–2cm, reflexed, yellow. Cauc., Sib., E Asia. Z7.

P. yakusimensis Masam. = *P. tetraphylla*.

→*Daiswa*.

Paritium Juss.

P. tiliaceum (L.) Juss. = *Hibiscus tiliaceus*.

PARKERIACEAE Hook. See *Ceratopteris*.

Parkia R. Br. Leguminosae (Mimosoideae). 40 unarmed trees. Lvs bipinnate; rachis usually gland. Fls in long-stalked, usually pendent, globose or pyriform heads; pet. slender, free or basally fused, 5; sta. 10, shortly exserted, fil. connate below. Trop. Z10.

P. javanica (Lam.) Merrill. Tree to 46m, with wide-spreading crown. Pinnae in 15–30 pairs, each with 50–70 pairs of lfts, lfts 6–13mm, acute. Peduncles 25–41cm; fl. heads 4cm diam., yellow-white. Java.

Parkinsonia L. Leguminosae (Caesalpinioideae). 12 everg. shrubs or trees, usually armed; br. slender, green. Lvs usually bipinnate; pinnae narrow; lfts v. small. Fls in short rac., yellow; sta. 10, subequal, about as long as perianth. Amer., S & NE Afr. Z9.

P. aculeata L. JERUSALEM THORN. Shrub or tree to 10m, armed; branchlets yellow-green to dark green, smooth. Lvs with 2–3 pinnae; lfts to 0.5cm, ovate to oblong, Fls fragrant, 2–15 per rac., cor. 2cm diam., seg. crispate to lacerate, standard dotted orange. Spring. Trop. Amer.

P. florida (Benth. ex A. Gray) S. Wats. Tree to 8m; br. pendulous, densely armed, blue- to grey-green. Lvs with 1 pair of pinnae; petiole to 6mm; lfts to 0.7cm, ovate to obovate, somewhat pubesc. Fls 5–8 per rac.; cor. 2.5cm diam., standard blotched red at base, suborbicular. Spring. SW US.

→*Cercidium*.

Parlour Ivy *Delairea odorata*.
Parlour Maple *Abutilon*.
Parlour Palm *Chamaedorea elegans*.

Parmentiera DC. Bignoniaceae. 9 shrubs or trees. Lvs 3-foliolate; petiole winged. Fls solitary or 2–3 on trunk or older br.; cal. spathe-like, split to base; cor. funnelform to campanulate; sta. subexserted; ovary cylindrical. Fr. linear-oblong. C Mex. to Nw Colomb. Z10.

P. aculeata (HBK) Seem. COW OKRA; CAT; SAN LUIS POTOSI. To 10m. Lfts (1)–3(–4), 1.5–5×0.6–2.5cm, obovate. Cor. campanulate, 5–7×2–2.5cm at apex, white. Fr. 17×3cm+. Mex. to Hond., nat. Queensld.

P. alata (HBK) Miers = *Crescentia elata*.

P. cereifera Seem. PALO DE VELAS; CANDLE TREE. To 7m. Lfts 3, 3–6.5×1.4–3.6cm, elliptic to rhombic, midrib puberulent. Cor. 3.7–6.4×1.8–2.9cm, tubular, white. Fr. to 54×2.4cm, yellow, waxy. Panama.

→*Crescentia*.

Parnassia L. GRASS OF PARNASSUS; BOG STAR. Saxifragaceae. 15 perenn., glab., usually everg. herbs. Lvs in a basal rosette, reniform-ovate or oblong; petioles long. Flowering st. slender, erect, bearing a solitary term. fl., subtended by a single bract; sep. 5, fused to form a shallow cup; pet. 5, spreading; staminode at base of each pet.; sta. 5. Summer. N Temp.

P. americana Muhlenb. = *P. caroliniana*.

P. asarifolia Vent. To 50cm. Lvs reniform, 7.5cm broad. Bract clasping scape, half way up; fls 2.5cm diam.; pet. white, clawed, entire; staminodes 3-lobed. E US. Z6.

P. californica (A. Gray) Greene = *P. palustris* var. *californica*.

P. caroliniana Michx. To 15cm. Lvs near orbicular, paler beneath to 6cm; petiole to 10cm. Bract on lower half of scape; pet. white tinged green, 10–18mm; staminodes 3–4-lobed. C Canada to Carol. Z4.

P. fimbriata Banks in Koenig & Sims. To 30cm. Lvs reniform, 4cm; petiole 5–15cm. Bract at or above middle of scape; pet. white, clawed, margin fringed; staminodes with several finger-like lobes. Alask. to Calif. and Colorado. Z3.

P. foliosa Hook. f. & Thoms. To 30cm. Scape tetragonal, winged; pet. white, fringed; staminodes 3-lobed. India, W China, Jap. Z5.

P. glauca Raf. To 60cm. Lvs ovate-orbicular, 5cm. Bract on or below mid-point of scape, sometimes 0; fls 2–4cm; pet. entire; staminodes 3-lobed. Newfoundland to Indiana. Sometimes misidentified as *P. caroliniana*. Z3.

P. grandifolia DC. To 60cm. Lvs orbicular, 3–10cm; petiole 3–15cm. Bract borne on or below mid point of scape; pet. 15–20mm; staminode lobes 3–5, v. narrow. C & SE US. Z6.

P. montanensis Fern. & Rydb. = *P. palustris* var. *montanensis*.

P. multiseta Fern. = *P. palustris*.

P. nubicola Wallich. To 30cm. Lvs elliptic, 5–10cm. Scapes tetragonal; fls to 3.5cm diam., white; staminodes yellow. Himal. Z4.

P. nudata Raf. = *P. asarifolia*.

P. ovata Muhlenb. = *P. caroliniana*.

P. palustris L. To 15cm. Lvs ovate to 3cm; petiole 1–4× blade length. Fls white, netted green, 2.5cm diam.; staminodes divided into 5–11 fil., swollen at tips. N Temp. var. *californica* A. Gray. Staminode fil. 17–27. Sierra Nevada. var. *montanensis* (Fern. & Rydb.) C. Hitchc. Staminode fil. 5–9; st. lf not clasping. W US. Z4.

P. parviflora DC. To 30cm. Lvs oval-elliptic, narrowed at base, 1–3cm. Bract below mid point of scape; pet. elliptic, 6–10mm; staminode fil. 5–10. Quebec to BC, S to Idaho. Z2.

P. repanda Raf. = *P. caroliniana*.

P. rotundifolia Raf. = *P. caroliniana*.

P. wightiana Wallich. To 45cm. Lvs deeply cordate, 3cm. Pet pale yellow, obovate-oblong, fringed; staminodes 3–5-lobed, lobes swollen at apex. Z6.

Parochetus Buch.-Ham. ex D. Don. Leguminosae (Papilionoideae). 1 prostrate clover-like herb; st. slender, rooting. Lvs trifoliolate; lfts to 2cm, obcordate. Fls to 2.5cm, solitary or paired, pea-like, deep blue. Summer–autumn. Mts of trop. Afr., Asia to Java. Z9.

P. communis Buch.-Ham. ex D. Don. SHAMROCK PEA; BLUE OXALIS.

Parodia Speg. Cactaceae. 35–50 low-growing cacti, simple or clustering; st. mostly small, globose to shortly cylindric, ribbed or tuberculate. Fls subapical, shortly funnelform; scales narrow; floral areoles with hairs and bristles, or bristles restricted to the uppermost areoles. S Braz. to NW Arg.

P. alacriportana Backeb. & Voll. Resembling *P. buenekeri* but st. usually smaller; ribs 17–31; central spines 5–25mm, one always hooked; radial spines whiter. Spring. S Braz. Z9.

P. allosiphon (Marchesi) N.P. Tayl. Simple; st. globose, 8–12×11–13cm; ribs c15–16, v. high, straight with low tubercles below the areoles; central spines 4, 8–20mm, terete, stiff, dark red to black, then grey; radial spines 2+, thinner. Fl. 5.5×5cm, pale yellow. Urug. Z9.

P. aureicentra Backeb. Simple or clustering; st. globose to elongate, c15–40×8–15cm; ribs c13–20, spiralled, tuberculate; central spines 4–12, to 7cm, some curved to hooked; radial spines 20–40, to 12mm, setaceous, white to pale yellow. Fl. 3.5–5cm, red. Spring–summer. N Arg. Z9.

P. ayopayana Cárdenas. Simple or clustering; st. globose, 6–8×6–10cm (or in var. *elata* Ritter to 60×12cm); ribs c11, well-defined, vertical; central spines to 4, 3–3.5cm, subulate, straight, light brown to almost white; radial spines c6–11, 12–20mm, acicular, almost white. Fl. 3cm, orange-yellow. Spring. C Boliv. Z9.

P. brevihamata W. Haage ex Backeb. Resembling *P. buenekeri*, but st. usually smaller; central spines 2–10mm, 1 or more hooked. Fl. lemon-yellow. Spring. S Braz. Z9.

P. buenekeri Buining. Simple or clustering; st. globose to elongate, to 8cm or more diam.; ribs c15–29, vertical, tuberculate; spines setaceous, glassy-white, brown or orange, later grey, in an apical brush-like tuft; central spines 4–6, 5–50mm, straight or one hooked; radial spines c14–20, 4–23mm, interlaced. Fl. 2.6–4×3.5–4cm, golden-yellow. Spring. S Braz. Z9.

P. buiningii (F. Buxb.) N.P. Tayl. Simple; st. depressed-globose to globose, to 8×12cm, pale grey- or glaucous-green; ribs c16, straight, thin acute, with blade-like tubercles; central spines 3–4, c2–3cm, straight, stiff, pale yellow, dark brown at base; radial spines c2–3, smaller. Fl. to 7×8cm, yellow. Summer. N Urug., S Braz. Z9.

P. caespitosa (Speg.) N.P. Tayl. Simple or suckering; st. cylindric, 4–8×2–4cm; ribs 11–22; central spines 1–4, 3–15mm, brown or red-brown, straight to hooked; radial spines 9–17, 3–6mm, setaceous, white or pale yellow. Fl. 2.7–4.2cm, sulphur- or lemon-yellow. Summer. S Braz., Urug. Z9.

P. catamarcensis Backeb. = *P. microsperma*.

P. chrysacanthion (Schum.) Backeb. Simple; st. depressed-globose to globose, to 12×10cm, apex woolly and tufted with erect spines; tubercles spiralled; spines 30–40, to 3cm, straight, acicular to setaceous, golden-yellow or paler. Fl. *c*2cm, yellow. Spring. N Arg. Z9.

P. claviceps (Ritter) Brandt. Simple or clustering; st. depressed-globose to shortly cylindric, 10–50×8–20cm+; ribs 23–30; spines to 2–5cm, acicular, pale yellow; central spines 1–3; radial spines 5–8. Fl. to 5.5×6cm. Summer. S Braz. Z9.

P. comarapana Cárdenas. Simple or clustering; st. 5–8×7–8cm; ribs 12–21, straight or spiralled, tuberculate; central spines *c*4–8, 1–2cm, straight, white to pale yellow, brown-tipped; radial spines *c*18–35, 3–10mm. Fl. to 2.5×3cm, yellow to orange. Spring–summer. C Boliv. Z9.

P. concinna (Monv.) N.P. Tayl. Simple; st. depressed-globose to elongate when old, 3–10×4–10cm, apex depressed; ribs 15–32, low, with chin-like tubercles; spines hairlike to setaceous, curved to twisted, brown, red-brown or partly white to pale yellow; central spines 4–6 or more, *c*10–25mm; radial spines 9–25, shorter, appressed and interlaced. Fl. 5–8×5–8cm, lemon-yellow. Spring. S Braz., Urug. Z9.

P. crassigibba (Ritter) N.P. Tayl. Simple; st. depressed-globose 4–17cm diam., shining dark green; ribs 10–16, low, rounded, with chin-like tubercles; spines 5–30mm, adpressed, mostly curved, off-white to grey or pale brown; central spines 0–1; radial spines 6–14. Fl. 3.5–6×4.5–6cm, nearly white, yellow or red-purple. Spring–summer. S Braz. Z9.

P. erinacea (Haw.) N.P. Tayl. Young plants less woolly and more spiny than older specimens; simple; st. globose, or short-cylindric when old, 6–30cm diam., light to dark green; apex v. woolly in old plants; ribs 12–30, acute; spines to 2cm, almost white, grey or brown, straight to curved, subulate. Fl. 3–5×4–7cm, glossy yellow. Summer. S Braz., Urug., NE Arg. Z9.

P. erythrantha (Speg.) Backeb. Resembling *P. microsperma*, but fl. slender, to 3cm diam., red or yellow; pericarpel ± naked, floral areoles with wool and bristles throughout. Spring–summer. N Arg. Z9.

P. faustiana Backeb. Resembling *P. stuemeri*. St. globose, to 6cm diam.; ribs spiralled, tuberculate; central spines 4, stout, to more than 25mm, dark; radial spines *c*20, to 10mm, glassy-white. Fl. yellow, red outside. N Arg. Z9.

P. formosa Ritter. Resembling *P. microsperma*. St. globose, 3–8cm diam.; ribs 16–26 dissolved into spiralled tubercles; central spines 1–12, 3–25mm, finely acicular, red-brown; radial spines 8–30, 3–12mm, white or brown-tipped. Fl. 1.6–4×3.5–4.5cm, yellow. Spring–summer. S Boliv. (Tarija). Z9.

P. gibbulosa Ritter. Resembling *P. formosa*, but fl. numerous, 5 or more borne together, *c*1.8cm. Spring–summer. Boliv. Z9.

P. gracilis Ritter. Simple; st. globose to elongate, 5–10cm diam.; ribs 13–19, ± vertical, tuberculate; central spines 4–10, 7–10mm, brown, red-brown or nearly white, usually straight; radial spines 14–20, 5–20mm, acicular to hairlike. Fl. 3–3.3cm, golden- to orange-yellow. Spring–summer. S Boliv. Z9.

P. graessneri (Schum.) F. Brandt. Resembling *P. haselbergii*, but spines to 2cm+, pale to golden-yellow, some pale brown to white. Fl. yellow-green, to *c*25mm. Spring. S Braz. White-spined variants can be confused with *P. haselbergii* when not in fl. Z9.

P. gummifera Backeb. & Voll = *Uebelmannia gummifera*.

P. haselbergii (Ruempl.) F. Brandt. Simple; st. globose, 4–15cm diam., apex depressed and sometimes distorted in old plants; ribs 30–60 or more, dissolved into small tubercles; spines *c*25–60, to 1cm, covering st., straight glassy-white or tinged yellow. Fl. *c*15×9–11mm, brilliant orange-red or rarely orange-yellow. Winter–spring. S Braz. Z9.

P. herteri (Werderm.) N.P. Tayl. Simple; st. globose to elongate, 10–15cm diam., dark green, corky at base; ribs *c*20–30, straight, tubercles chin-like; central spines 4–6, to 2cm, subulate, brown; radial spines *c*8–17, to 12mm, acicular, white or brown-tipped. Fl. *c*4×5cm, shocking pink or darker, pale in throat, in a ring around st. apex. Summer. S Braz. Z9.

P. heteracantha Ritter ex Weskamp. Resembling *P. rigidispina*, but central spines to 22mm; pericarpel nearly naked. N Arg. Z9.

P. horstii (Ritter) N.P. Tayl. Simple or sparingly clustering; st. globose, to elongate, to 14cm diamm., green becoming corky from base upwards; ribs 12–19, well defined, tubercles low, 5–9mm apart; central spines 1–6, 8–30mm+, acicular, yellow to brown, straight, curved or twisted; radial spines *c*10–15, 6–30mm, finer, white to pale brown. Fl. 3–4cm, yellow-orange, red or purple. Summer–autumn, occas. spring. S Braz. Z9.

P. leninghausii (Schum.) Brandt. Simple or clustering; st. cylindric, to 60×7–10cm, green, apex usually slanted; ribs 30–35, straight; spines yellow or pale brown, straight to curved, finely setaceous; central spines *c*3–4, to 20–50mm; radial spines

15–20 or more, 5–10mm. Fl. *c*5–6cm, lemon-yellow. Summer. S Braz. Z9.

P. liliputana (Werderm.) N.P. Tayl. = *Blossfeldia liliputana*.

P. maassii (Hesse) A. Berger. Simple, seldom clustering, st. 10–50×7–25cm; ribs *c*10–21, straight or spiralled; central spines 1–6, 2–7cm, lowermost longest, strongly curved to hooked variously coloured; radial spines 6–18(18–28 in f. *maxima* (Ritter) Krainx), 1–4cm, straight to curved, acicular, paler than centrals. Fl. *c*3–4.5cm, red to yellow. Spring–summer. S Boliv., N Arg. (Jujuy). Z9.

P. magnifica (Ritter) F. Brandt. Simple, rarely clustering; st. globose to elongate, 7–15cm diam., blue-green; ribs 11–15, straight, acute; spines 12–15 or more, 8–20mm, setaceous, golden-yellow. Fl. 4.5–5.5×4.5–5.5cm, sulphur-yellow. Summer. S Braz. Z9.

P. mairanana Cárdenas. Simple, later clustering; st. depressed-globose, 4–3×4–5.5cm, dark green; ribs *c*13–14, spiralled, scarcely tuberculate; central spines 1–3, straight to hooked, light brown to nearly black, 8–20mm; radial spines *c*8–14, 3–12mm, acicular. Fl. 1–3.5×2–3.5cm, orange-red to golden-yellow. Spring. C Boliv. Z9.

P. mammulosa (Lem.) N.P. Tayl. Simple; st. globose to elongate, 5–13cm diam., v. dark; ribs 13–21, vertical, well defined, tubercles large, pointed, chin-like; central spines 2–4, to *c*2cm or more, straight, rather stout and stiff, white to grey or pale brown, one strongly flattened; radial spines *c*6–25, 5–10mm, acicular or stouter, off-white to pale brown. Fl. *c*3.5–5.5cm, pale to golden-yellow. Summer. S Braz., Urug., NE Arg. Z9.

P. microsperma (F.A.C. Weber) Speg. St. simple, rarely offsetting, depressed-globose to globose, sometimes elongate, 5–20×5–10cm; ribs *c*15–21, tubercles spiralled, central spines 3–4, 5–20(–50)mm, red, brown or darker, lowermost hoooked; radial spines 7–20, *c*4–8mm, setaceous, white. Fl. 3–3.5×4–5cm, yellow or red. Spring–summer. N Arg. Z9.

P. miguillensis Cárdenas. Simple; st. depressed-globose to cylindric, 6–30×3–8cm; ribs 8–16, well defined, vertical; central spines 4–9, 1–2.5cm, fine, straight or somewhat curved, yellow-brown to dark brown; radial spines 12–18, 2–20mm, hairlike, nearly white to yellow-brown. Fl. 1.5–2.5×0.7–2cm, light to golden-yellow. Summer. C Boliv. Z9.

P. mueller-melchersii (Backeb.) N.P. Tayl. Simple; st. globose, 5–8×5–6cm, dark green; ribs 21–24, low, tubercles small rounded; central spines 1, 3–4, 20mm, straight, subulate to acicular, pale yellow, darker at base and apex; radials 14–18+, 2–8mm, acicular, off-white. Fl. *c*3×4.5–5cm, pale golden-yellow. Summer. Urug. Z9.

P. mutabilis Backeb. Resembling *P. microsperma*; central spines 4–10, yellow, red-brown or brown; radial spines 20–50+, v. fine, white. Fl. 3–5cm diam., yellow. Spring–summer. N Arg. Z9.

P. neohorstii (Theunissen) N.P. Tayl. Simple; st. globose, 3–9cm; ribs 18–26; central spines 1–6, 1–3cm, straight, pale below, dark brown to black at apex; radial spines 14–24, 3–7mm, adpressed, slender, almost white. Fl. 2.5–4×2.5–3.5cm, shiny yellow. Summer. S Braz. Z9.

P. nivosa Backeb. Simple; st. globose to elongate, to 15×8cm; tubercles spiralled, central spines 4, to 2cm, straight, setaceous, white or one dark at base; radial spines *c*18, white, finer. Fl. *c*3×2.5–5cm, fiery red. Spring. N Arg. Z9.

P. ocampoi Cárdenas. Clustering; st. shortly cylindric, 7–20×6–11cm; ribs 13–17, straight, well defined, 5–10mm high; central spine 1, 5–25mm, straight, red-brown; radial spines 8–9, 10–25mm, red-brown. Fl. *c*3×5cm. Spring–summer. C Boliv. Z9.

P. ottonis (Lehm.) N.P. Tayl. Simple at first, later clustering; st. ± globose, tapered at base, 3–15cm diam., variable in colour; ribs 6–15, well defined, rounded or acute; spines hairlike, straight, curved or twisted; centrals 1–6, 8–40mm, brown or yellow; radials 4–15, 5–30mm, off-white to yellow or brown. Fl. 2.5–6cm, yellow or rarely orange-red. Summer. S Braz., Urug., NE Arg., S Parag. var. *ottonis*. St. mostly 3–10cm diam.; ribs 6–12, rarely more. Fl. *c*4–6cm, few. S Braz., Urug., NE Arg., S Parag. var. *tortuosa* (Link & Otto) N.P. Tayl. St. to 15cm diam.; ribs 10–15, occas. more. Fl. *c*2.5–4cm, many produced together. S Braz. Z9.

P. penicillata Fechser & Van Der Steeg. St. globose, then cylindric, to 30(–70)×7–12cm; ribs 17–20, spiralled, tuberculate; spines tufted at stem-apex; central spines to 10–20, to 5cm, straight, almost white, pale yellow or pale brown; radial spines to *c*40, shorter, glassy white. Fl. to 5×4cm, orange- to blood-red. Summer. N Arg. Z9.

P. procera Ritter. Simple; st. globose, clavate or cylindric, to 30×3–8cm; ribs somewhat spiralled, scarcely tuberculate; central spines 4, 15–35mm, straight or one curved to hooked, brown; radial spines 7–10, 7–15mm, hairlike. Fl. to 3×2.5–4cm, yellow. Spring–summer. Boliv. Z9.

P. rigidispina Krainz. Resembling *P. microsperma*; central spines

4, to 7mm, stiff, all straight or one curved, red to brown; radial spines 6–11, c5mm. Fl. slender, 3.7cm, yellow, smelling of iodine. N Arg. Z9.

P. rutilans (Daeniker & Krainz) N.P. Tayl. Simple; st. globose to elongate, c5cm diam., dark green; ribs 18–24, vertical or weakly spiralled, tubercles chin-like; central spines 2, the lower to 7mm, straight, stiff, red-brown; radial spines c14–16, to 5mm, acicular, almost white, daker tipped. Fl. 3–4×6cm, pink, becoming paler to yellow-tinged in the throat. Summer. N Urug. Z9.

P. sanagasta Weing. = *P. microsperma*.

P. sanguiniflora Backeb. = *P. microsperma*.

P. schuetziana Jajo. Simple; st. depressed-globose to elongate, to c11cm diam.; ribs c21, vertical or spiralled, tuberculate; central spines 1–4, lowermost hooked, pale brown; radial spines c15, hairlike, interlaced, white. Fl. campanulate, c2cm, dark red. Spring–summer. N Arg. Z9.

P. schumanniana (Nicolai) F. Brandt. Usually simple; st. globose to cylindric, green, to 180×30cm; ribs 21–48 (fewer in juvenile plants), straight, acute; spines golden-yellow, brown or red-brown, later grey, setaceous, straight or slightly curved; central spines 3–4, 10–30mm; radial spines c4, 7–50mm. Fl. 4–4.5×4.5–6.5cm, lemon- to golden-yellow. Summer. S Parag., NE Arg. Z9.

P. schwebsiana (Werderm.) Backeb. Usually simple; st. depressed-globose to shortly cylindric, 2.3×12×8cm, apex v. woolly; ribs 13–20, somewhat spiralled, tuberculate; central spines 1–4, 1–2cm, hooked, red-tinged to pale brown; radial spines c5–10, 5–12mm, tinged red or yellow. Fl. 2–3×2–2.5cm, dark red. Summer. C Boliv. Z9.

P. scopa (Spreng.) N.P. Tayl. Simple or clustering; st. globose to cylindric, 50×6–10cm, dark green, obscured by spines; ribs 25–40, low, finely tuberculate; central spines 3–4, 6–12mm, brown, red or white; radial spines c35–40 or more, 5–7mm, fine glassy white or pale yellow. Fl. 2–4×3.5–4.5cm, bright yellow, in a ring around st. apex. Summer. S Braz., Urug. Z9.

P. scopaoides Backeb. = *P. microsperma*.

P. setifera Backeb. = *P. microsperma*.

P. stuemeri (Werderm.) Backeb. Simple; st. globose, later cylindric, 15–25×7–12cm; ribs c15–22, rarely spiralled, tuberculate; central spines 4–8, 11–25mm, straight or curved, pale yellow or brown; radial spines 9–35, to 20mm, pale. Fl. 2.5–4×2.5–5cm, red, orange or yellow. Spring–summer. N Arg. Z9.

P. succinea (Ritter) N.P. Tayl. Resembling *P. scopa*, but st. 2.5–7cm diam.; ribs 18–26; central spines 4–12, to 25mm, yellow, brown or violet-grey; radial spines 12–40, 3–10mm, off-white, pale yellow or brown. Fl. 3–3.6×3–4cm. Summer. S Braz. Z9.

P. tilcarensis (Werderm. & Backeb.) Backeb. = *P. stuemeri*.

P. tuberculata Cárdenas. Simple, rarely clustering; st. depressed-globose, 7–11cm diam.; ribs 13–20, spiralled, strongly tuberculate at first; central spines 1–4, 15–25mm, one hooked, brown to black or grey; radial spines 7–11, to 10mm. Fl. 1.8–2.7×3cm, yellow-red. Spring–summer. Boliv. Z9.

P. warasii (Ritter) Brandt. Resembling *P. leninghausii* and *P. magnifica*; usually simple; st. to c50×10–15cm, green; ribs 15–16; spines c15–20, 1–4cm, acicular, white to pale brown. Fl. 5–6cm diam., golden- to lemon-yellow. S Braz. Z9.

P. werdermanniana (Herter) N.P. Tayl. Resembling *P. concinna*, but usually larger, to 13×10cm; ribs to 40; spines fine, straight, yellow to white, radials not depressed. Fl. c6×7cm, sulphur-yellow, produced in a ring around st. apex. Spring. Urug. Z9.

→*Echinocactus, Frailea, Notocactus* and *Wigginsia*.

Paronychia L. WHITLOW-WORT. Caryophyllaceae. c40 low-growing annuals or perennials, sometimes woody-based. Lvs paired, linear-lanceolate to ovate, with silvery stipules. Fls small, in dense axill. heads, surrounded by conspicuous silvery bracts. Perianth seg. 5 (rarely 4), sepaloid, often persistent and hardening with a strong term. awn. Widespread trop. and warmer temp. regions, common in Medit.

P. argentea Lam. Much-branched mat-forming perenn. Lvs small, ovate to lanceolate. Infl. dense, partially covered by silvery, ovate bracts; perianth seg. c2mm, awned, margins membranous. Summer. S Eur., N Afr., SW Asia. Z7.

P. capitata (L.) Lam. Like *P. argentea* but with lvs linear-lanceolate to lanceolate and fls in distinct, v. silvery heads; peri-anth seg. green, hooded, awnless. Summer. Medit. area. Z5.

P. capitata auct. = *P. kapela*.

P. chionaea Boiss. = *P. kapela*.

P. kapela (Hacq.) Kerner. Like *P. argentea* but with fls in distinct, v. silvery heads and perianth seg. green, hooded and awnless. Summer. Medit. area. Z7.

P. nivea DC. = *P. capitata*.

P. pulvinata A. Gray. Densely cushion-forming, woody at base. Lvs thick, 3–5mm. Fls solitary, inconspicuous. Summer. US (S Rocky Mts). Z5.

P. serpyllifolia Chaix = *P. kapela*.

Parrot Bush *Dryandra sessilis*.
Parrot Feather *Myriophyllum aquaticum*.

Parrotia C.A. Mey. IRONWOOD; IRONTREE. Hamamelidaceae. 1 decid. spreading or erect shrub or tree, to 10m. Bark smooth, iron-grey, flaking. Lvs 6–10cm, entire, ovate to obovate, strongly veined, wavy, ± shallowly toothed at apex, stellate-pubesc. becoming glossy, tough, deep green to bronze then crimson and yellow in fall. Fls in dense clusters before lvs, 1cm diam.; cal. 5–7-lobed; pet. 0; sta. to 15, anth. coral-pink to scar-let red. Early spring. N Iran. Z5.

P. jacquemontiana Decne. = *Parrotiopsis jacquemontiana*.

P. persica (DC.) C.A. Mey. 'Pendula': br. pendulous, forming a dense, weeping dome.

Parrotiopsis (Niedenzu) C. Schneid. Hamamelidaceae. 1 decid., erect tree, to 6m. Lvs ovate to orbicular, 5–9cm, short-toothed, yellow in fall, stellate-pubescent. Infl. c20 packed heads of yellow sta., to 5cm diam., subtended by 4–6 ovate to orbicular, white, petal-like bracts. Spring–early summer. Himal. Z7.

P. involucrata Decne. = *P. jacquemontiana*.

P. jacquemontiana (Decne.) Rehd.
→*Parrotia*.

Parrot Flower *Heliconia psittacorum*.
Parrot Plantain *Heliconia psittacorum*.
Parrot Leaf *Alternanthera ficoidea* var. *amoena*.
Parrot's Beak *Clianthus puniceus*; *Lotus berthelotii*.
Parrot's Beak Orchid *Pterostylis nutans*.
Parrot's Bill *Clianthus puniceus*.
Parrot's Feather *Myriophyllum*.

Parrya R. Br. Cruciferae. 25 perenn. herbs. Lvs simple or pinnatifid, usually glandular-pubescent, tapering to a slender petiole. Rac. term.; pet. 4, white or purple, large, long-clawed; sta. 6, free. Summer. Arc., Alpine regions, Russia, Alask. Z3.

P. grandiflora Schischkin = *P. microcarpa*.

P. menziesii Greene = *Phoenicaulis cheiranthoides*.

P. microcarpa Ledeb. 4–12cm. Lvs rosulate oblong to elliptic, white-hairy, entire or sessile on fl. st. Sep. 1–4mm, white-hairy; pet. 6–7mm. Sib., Mong.

P. nudicaulis (L.) Reg. 5–30cm; base covered by the remains of old lf bases. Lvs 1.5–12cm, entire, lobed or pinnatisect. Sep. 5–8mm, often suffused pink; pet. 12–20mm. Alask., Yukon, Eurasia.

→*Draba*.

Parry Manzanita *Arctostaphylos manzanita*.
Parry's Lip-fern *Cheilanthes parryi*.
Parry's Pinyon *Pinus quadrifolia*.
Parsley *Petroselinum* (*P. crispum*).
Parsley Fern *Botrychium australe*; *Cryptogramma*.
Parsley-leaved Bramble *Rubus laciniatus*.
Parsley-leaved Thorn *Crataegus apiifolia*.
Parsnip *Pastinaca sativa*.
Parsnip Chervil *Chaerophyllum bulbosum*.

Parsonsia R. Br. Apocynaceae. 80 soft to woody climbers. Lvs opposite; fls small, paniculate; cor. tubular, often inflated, limb 5-lobed. Asia, Australasia, Pacific.

P. capsularis R. Br. Everg. climber to 5m. St. slender, twining. Juvenile lvs 2–7.5cm, narrow-linear, entire or lobed, buff over-laid chocolate, pink or dark green, adult lvs 2.5–6cm, entire, less colourful. Pan. term. to 3mm, white, campanulate, lobes recurved. NZ. Z9.

Parthenium L. Compositae. 15 aromatic herbs and shrubs. Lvs alt., entire to pinnatisect. Cap. radiate, few to many solitary or in small corymbs; receptacle convex, scaly; ray flts white or yellow-tinged, inconspicuous, disc flts many. Summer. Trop. & subtrop. Amer. & W Indies.

P. argentatum A. Gray. GUAYULE. Shrub to 1m, much-branched. Lvs to 5×1.5cm, oblanceolate, entire or sparsely dentate. Cap. 6mm diam., many, in a compact corymb. Tex., N Mex. Z8.

P. argenteum hort. = *P. argentatum*.

P. integrifolium L. WILD QUININE; AMERICAN FEVERFEW; PRAIRIE DOCK. Perenn. herb, 0.5–1m, simple or branched above. Lvs to 20×10cm, lanceolate-elliptic to broadly ovate, crenulate-serrate or sublyrate at base. Cap. to 10mm diam., several, in a broad, flat-topped corymb. E US to Wisc. and Ark. Z3.

Parthenocissus Planch. VIRGINIA CREEPER. Vitaceae. 10 usually decid. woody vines climbing to 18m or trailing; tendrils branched, twining, usually with adhesive discs. Lvs palmately compound, 3-lobed or unlobed. Fls small; pet. 4–5 yellow-green, in term. clusters or lf-opposed cymose pan.; pet. 4–5; sta. short, erect. Fr. a berry, dark blue or black. N Amer., E Asia, Himal.

P. engelmannii Koehne & Gräbn. ex Gräbn. = *P. quinquefolia* var. *engelmannii.*

P. henryana (Hemsl.) Diels. & Gilg.   Tendrils 5–7-forked, terminating in adhesive disks. Lvs long-stalked; lfts 3–5, 4–12cm, obovate to oblanceolate or narrowly ovate, acute, coarsely dentate above, dark velvety green with pink and silvery main veins, turning red in autumn, slightly pubesc. in vein axils beneath. China. Z7.

P. henryi hort. = *P. henryana.*

P. heptaphylla (Buckl.) Britt. & Small. Tendrils long, forked. Lvs 7-parted, coarsely serrate, dark green above, paler beneath, glab.; lfts 3–6cm, oblong-obovate. Spring. Tex. Z9.

P. heterophylla (Bl.) Merrill.   Lvs compound, long-stalked; lfts 6–25cm, 3, or 1–2 on floral br., crenate-serrate, lat. lfts ovate-oblong, central oblong, petiolulate, glab. or pubesc. beneath. China. Z8.

P. himalayana (Royle) Planch.   Tendrils with term. adhesive disks. Lvs long-stalked; lfts 5–15cm, 3, short-stalked, central leaflet ovate, oval or obovate, lat. lfts ovate, v. obliquely cordate at base, dentate, abruptly tapered to apex, dark green above, (rich red in autumn), somewhat glaucous and sparsely pubesc. on main veins beneath. Late spring–summer. Himal. var. *rubrifolia* (Lév. & Vaniot) Gagnep. Lfts smaller, tinged purple when young. Taiwan, W China. Z9.

P. hirsuta Small = *P. quinquefolia* var. *hirsuta.*

P. inserens Hayek = *P. inserta.*

P. inserta (A. Kerner) Fritsch. Tendrils 3–5-branched, twining, lacking adhesive disks (cf. *P. quinquefolia*). Lvs glossy green (richly coloured in autumn), glab. to thinly pubesc. beneath, long-stalked; lfts 5, elliptic to obovate, serrate, abruptly acuminate, sessile or stalked. Summer. N Amer. 'Macrophylla': lvs large. Z3.

P. laetevirens Rehd.   Tendrils thin, 5–8-branched. Lvs 5–10cm, elliptic to obovate, coarsely serrate, light green tinged yellow, glab., or pubesc. on veins beneath. China. Z9.

P. quinquefolia (L.) Planch.   VIRGINIA CREEPER; WOODBINE. Tendrils 5–8-branched with adhesive disks. Lvs long-stalked; lfts 3–5, radiating, 2.5–10cm, elliptic to obovate, serrate, acuminate, dull green above, brilliant scarlet and flame in fall, paler and somewhat glaucous beneath, sessile or petiolulate. Summer. E US to Mex. 'Minor': 10–12 branchlets on tendrils; lvs broad, small, oval to elliptic. 'Murorum': tendrils short, abundant. var. *engelmannii* Rehd. Lvs smaller. var. *hirsuta* Planch. Lvs and young st. softly white-pubesc. var. *saint-paulii* (Koehne & Gräbn.) Rehd. Tendrils 8–12-branched; lvs persistent in autumn, lfts 12–15cm. Z3.

P. saint-paulii Koehne & Gräbn. = *P. quinquefolia* var. *saint-paulii.*

P. semicordata (Wallich) Planch. Similar to *P. himalayana* but young shoots setose; lvs smaller, setose beneath. Himal. Z9.

P. sinensis Diels & Gilg = *P. himalayana* var. *rubrifolia.*

P. spaethii Koehne & Gräbn. = *P. inserta.*

P. thomsonii (Lawson) Planch.   Slender vine similar to *P. henryana* but with rather more thickly textured glossy dark green lfts lacking silver veins. Lvs 2.5–10cm, red at first; lfts 5, ovate to obovate, apex acute, base tapered, shallowly serrate, tinted purple-red, scarlet in fall. W & C China. Z7.

P. tricuspidata (Sieb. & Zucc.) Planch. in DC. JAPANESE CREEPER; BOSTON IVY; VIRGINIA CREEPER.   Tendrils short, much-branched, with adhesive disks. Lvs to 20cm, broadly ovate, serrate, with base cordate and 3 distinct, tapering lobes, shallower in young lvs, rarely 3-foliolate, glossy green (rich crimson in autumn), glab. above, pubesc. on veins beneath. Summer. China, Jap. 'Atropurpurea': vigorous growth; lvs large, green tinged blue turning purple, red in spring and autumn. 'Aurata': lvs almost yellow, somewhat marbled green, red, rough margin. 'Beverley Brook': lvs exceptionally small, red in autumn. 'Green Spring': young lvs tinged red, later bright, glossy green above, dull beneath, to 25cm. 'Lowii': MINI-ATURE JAPANESE IVY: smaller and more slender, lvs 2–3cm, deeply and sharply 3–7-lobed, bright green tinged purple when young, colouring brilliant red in autumn. 'Minutifolia': lvs larger than 'Lowii', glossy, later purple turning pink. 'Purpurea': lvs red tinged purple. 'Robusta': strong growth; lvs glossy, often trifoliate, red and orange in autumn. 'Veitchii' JAPANESE IVY: lvs simple to jaggedly but shallowly lobed, small, puckered, dark purple when young, red-purple in fall. Z4.

P. veitchii Gräbn. = *P. tricuspidata* 'Veitchii'.

P. vitacea (Knerr) Hitchc. = *P. inserta.*

→*Ampelopsis, Cayratia, Cissus* and *Vitis.*

Partridge Berry *Mitchella repens.*
Partridge-breast Aloe *Aloe variegata.*
Partridge Pea *Pisum sativum* var. *arvense.*
Pascuita *Euphorbia leucocephala.*

Pasithea D. Don. Liliaceae (Asphodelaceae). 1 rhizomatous perenn. herb. Lvs to 25cm, mostly basal, linear, grass-like, keeled. Scape slender, erect; pan. loose, pyramidal, perianth seg. 6, basally united into a short tube, spreading, blue, inner seg. paler than outer. Chile. Z9.

P. caerulea (Ruiz & Pav.) D. Don.

Paspalum *Paspalum dilatatum.*

Paspalum L. Gramineae. 330 glab. to sparsely pubesc. ann. or perenn. grasses. Lvs narrow-linear to lanceolate or ovate; ligules membranous. Infl. solitary, paired or clustered secund rac.; rachis winged; spikelets 2-fld, solitary or paired, hemi-spherical to ovate, in 2–4 rows, awnless. New World Trop. Z8.

P. ceresia (Kuntze) Chase.   Perenn., to 75cm. Lvs to 20×1cm, glaucous. Rac. to 4, to 8cm; spikelets solitary, lanceolate to oblong, to 3mm, with silver hairs. Summer. Trop. S Amer.

P. dilatatum Poir. DALLIS GRASS; PASPALUM.   Perenn., to 180cm. Lvs to 45×1.3cm. Rac. to 5, to 11cm; central axis, to 20cm; spikelets elliptic to ovate, to 4mm, green tinged yellow. Summer. S Amer., nat. US.

P. elegans Roem. & Schult. = *P. ceresia.*

P. membranaceum Lam. = *P. ceresia.*

P. notatum Fluegge. BAHIA GRASS.   Perenn. to 50cm. Lvs flat or folded. Rac. to 7cm, recurved-ascending, mostly paired; spike-lets to 2mm, ovate to obovate, glossy. Mex., W Indies, S Amer.; introd. US.

P. racemosum Lam. Ann., to 90cm. St. nodes dark brown. Lvs to 15×2.5cm glab.; sheaths inflated. Infl. dense; rac. to 80, beige to purple; spikelets solitary, elliptic, to 3cm. Autumn. Peru.

P. stoloniferum Bosc = *P. racemosum.*

Pasque Flower *Pulsatilla vulgaris.*

Passerina L. Thymelaeaceae. 18 everg., heath-like shrubs. Lvs decussate, entire. Fls in bracteate spikes; cal. tubular, lobes 4; pet. 0; sta. 8, exserted. S Afr. Z9.

P. ericoides L.   Lvs closely adpressed, 2mm, linear to ovate-oblong, blunt, thick. Spikes 8-fld; bracts oblong, 2mm, woolly within; cal. tube ovoid, 3mm, lobes 2mm. S Afr.

P. filiformis L.   Lvs crowded, erect, clothing st., to 8mm, triangular, pointed, incurved. Spikes 12-fld; bracts ovate, 5mm, woolly within; cal. tube short, 5mm, ovoid below, cylindric, lobes 3mm. S Afr.

P. hirsuta Endl. = *Thymelaea hirsuta.*

Passiflora L. PASSION FLOWER. Passifloraceae. *c*500 vines or scandent shrubs, rarely erect herbs, shrubs or small trees. Tendrils long, axill., tightly spiralling. Lvs stipulate, usually 3–5-lobed, sometimes bilobed or entire; petioles often with stalked glands. Fls regular, usually solitary; subtended by 3 green bracts; cal. cupped to tubular, sep. 5, fleshy or membranous; pet. 5, sometimes 0; fil. in several series, forming a showy corona; sta. 5 on a gynophore, anth. linear or oblong; stigma capitate; styles 3. Fr. usually a juicy, many-seeded berry. Trop. Americas, Asia, Aus., Polyn.

P. actinia Hook.   Lvs to 10×8cm, broad-oval or suborbicular, apex notched, base rounded or tapered, entire, often glaucous beneath; petioles 4-gland. Fls to 9cm diam., fragrant; cal. campanulate, sep. to 1.5cm diam., oblong-lanceolate, obtuse; pet. to 2×1cm, white; fil. 4–5-seriate the outermost to 3cm, banded blue, white and red. Spring–summer. SE Braz. Z10.

P. adenopoda DC.   Lvs to 12×15cm, lobes 3–5 ovate, apex abruptly acuminate, base cordate, entire or denticulate, hispidulous; petioles biglandular. Fls to 7cm diam.; sep. to 1cm diam., oblong-lanceolate; pet. to 12×5mm, green-white to ivory, linear-lanceolate; fil. 1-seriate. Fr. to 2.5cm diam., minutely-pubesc. Mex. to Venez., E Peru. Z10.

P. alata C. Curtis.   St. stout, 4-winged. Lvs to 15×10cm, simple, ovate or ovate-oblong, apex acuminate, base rounded to sub-cuneate, entire or denticulate; petioles 2–4-glandular. Fls to 12cm diam., fragrant; sep. oblong, pale crimson above; pet. oblong, obtuse brilliant carmine; fil. 4-seriate to 3cm, banded purple red and white. Fr. to 10×6cm, obovoid or pyriform, glab., yellow. Spring–summer. NE Peru, E Braz. 'Ruby Glow': fr. yellow, grapefruit-sized. Z10.

P. × alato-caerulea. (*P. alata* × *P. caerulea.*)   St. narrowly winged. Lvs trilobed, entire. Fls to 10cm diam., pink to purple, white outside; sep. white inside; fil. blue-violet, white at apex.

Gdn origin. 'Imperatrice Eugénie': lvs 3-lobed; fls to 16cm diam., sep. white, pet. lilac-pink, fil. white and mauve. Z9.

P. alba Link & Otto = *P. subpeltata*.

P. × allardii Lynch. (*P. caerulea* 'Constance Elliot' × *P. quadrangularis*.) Lvs usually trilobed. Fls to 11.5cm diam., white, suffused pink; fil. deep cobalt-blue. Summer–autumn. Raised in 1907 at Cambridge Bot. Gdn. Z9.

P. × amabilis Lem. Lvs to 12×9cm, ovate-oblong or ovate-lanceolate, apex short-acute, base subcordate, entire; petioles 2–4-glandular. Fls to 9cm diam.; cal. short-tubular, bright red inside, green outside, sep. 3.5×1cm, linear-oblong or linear-lanceolate; pet. similar, bright red; fil. 4-seriate, white. Spring. S Braz. Z10.

P. amethystina Mikan. Lvs to 6×10cm, lobes 3, oblong, apex obtuse, base cordate and often peltate, somewhat glaucous beneath; petioles 5–8-glandular. Fls to 8cm diam.; cal. campanulate, sep. to 6mm diam., oblong, carinate, bright blue inside; pet. to 8mm diam., darker than sep., oblong, obtuse; fil. 4–5-seriate, to 2.5cm, dark purple. Fr. ellipsoid, to 6×2.5cm, subglabrous. Autumn. E Braz. Z10.

P. antioquiensis Karst. BANANA PASSION FRUIT. Lvs to 15×8cm, ovate to lanceolate, or with lobes 3, lanceolate, subcordate or rounded at base, sharp-serrate, lanuginose beneath; petioles lanuginose. Fls to 12.5cm diam.; cal. to 4cm, narrowly tubular, rose-red or magenta, sep. to 6.5×2.5cm, oblong-lanceolate, obtuse; pet. oblong-lanceolate, darker; fil. 3-seriate, corona small, violet. Fr. ellipsoid. Summer. Colomb. Z9.

P. arborea Spreng. Tree or shrub to 10m. Lvs to 30×15cm, oblong or obovate-oblong, apex acute, base rounded, glaucous beneath. Fls to 7.5cm diam., clustered 3–6 on nodding stalks; cal. to 1×0.5cm, cylindric-campanulate, sep. to 3×1.2cm, green-white, linear-oblong, obtuse; pet. linear-oblong, paler; fil. triseriate, yellow. Fr. to 4×2.5cm, ovoid, somewhat yellow. Summer. Colomb. Z10.

P. atomaria Planch. = *P. subpeltata*.

P. × atropurpurea Nichols. (*P. racemosa* × *P. kermesina*.) Fls dark blood-red, 7.5cm diam.; sep. purple inside; fil. violet, spotted white.

P. aurantia Forst. f. Lvs to 7.5cm, lobes 3, ovate, blunt, acute sometimes lobulate. Fls to 10cm diam., bracts setiform; sep. pale pink deepening to orange-red, linear-oblong; pet. orange to brick red; fil. deep red, inner series forming a tube, outer to 2cm. Summer. Aus. (Queensld). Z10.

P. banksii Benth. = *P. aurantia*.

P. × belottii Pépin = *P. × alato-caerulea*.

P. biflora Lam. St. 5-angled. Lvs to 10×10cm, narrowly suborbicular to reniform, sometimes bilobed, lobes lanceolate or ovate, apex usually acuminate, base truncate to cuneate, coriaceous; petioles eglandular. Fls to 3.5cm diam.; cal., campanulate, white inside, green, ± glab. outside, sep. to 12×7mm, ovate-lanceolate, obtuse; pet. 8×5mm, white; corona 2.5cm diam., yellow, fil, biseriate. Fr. to 2cm diam., globose, glab. to dense minute-pubesc. Summer. Mex. to Colomb., Venez., Ecuad. and Bahamas. Z10.

P. bryonioides HBK. St. hispidulous. Lvs to 7×9cm, lobes 3, oblong, lat. lobes sometimes bilobed, base cordate, entire or dentate, hispidulous; petioles biglandular. Fls to 3cmdiam.; cal. green-white, sep. to 13×5mm, ovat-elanceolate; pet. 4×1mm, white, linear or linear-lanceolate; corona white, fil. 1-seriate. Fr. to 3.5×2.5cm, ovoid. SW US, Mex. Often confused with *P. morifolia*, which has purple fr. at maturity. Z8.

P. caerulea L. PASSION FLOWER; BLUE PASSION FLOWER. Lvs to 10×2.5cm, lobes (3–)5(–9), oblong, apex obtuse or emarginate, base cordate, glab.; petioles 2–4-, 6-glandular. Fls to 10cm diam.; cal. cupulate, white or pink-white inside; sep. to 2×1.5cm, oblong, obtuse; pet. to 2.5×1.5cm, oblong, obtuse, thin-textured, green-white, fil. 4-seriate, broadly banded, blue at apex, white at centre, purple at base. Fr. 6×4cm, ovoid or subglobose, glab., orange or yellow. Summer–autumn. Braz., Arg. 'Constance Eliott': fls ivory white. 'Grandiflora': fls to 15cm diam. Z7.

P. × caerulea-racemosa. (*P. caerulea* × *P. racemosa*.) Lvs deeply 5-lobed, glab. Fls dark violet, solitary; fil. deep purple-violet. 'Eynsford Gem': fls pink-mauve; fil. white. Z9.

P. capsularis L. St. 3–5 angular. Lvs to 7×10cm, lobes 2, forward-pointing, lanceolate, apex acute, base cordate, pilosulous above, pubesc. beneath; petioles eglandular. Fls to 6cm diam.; cal. to 3cm×4mm, campanulate, pilose, sep. linear-lanceolate, acute, green-white; pet. to 1.5×0.4cm, ivory, narrow oblong-lanceolate, obtuse; fil. yellow-white, 1–2-seriate. Fr. to 6×2cm, ellipsoid or fusiform ridged and angled, purple-red. Summer. Nic. to C Braz. to Parag., Greater Antilles. Z10.

P. × cardinalis hort. ex Mast. (*P. alata* × *P. racemosa* (?).) Intermediate between parents. Fls red, 7.5cm diam. Z10.

P. cheilidonea Mast. St. lanuginose. Lvs to 14×8cm, oblong-lanceolate, lobes 2–3, lanceolate, (central lobe often reduced or

merely a mucro), apex acute, base subcordate or rounded, coriaceous; petioles somewhat purple. Fls to 5cm diam.; cal. glossy, sep. 2.5×1.2cm, yellow green, oblong-lanceolate; pet. 1.2×0.4cm, clearer; fil. biseriate, white, the outermost spotted violet. Fr. 1.5cm diam., globose. Summer. Colomb., Ecuad. Z10.

P. cinnabarina Lindl. Lvs to 10×10cm, lobes 3, ovate, cordate at base; petioles eglandular. Fls 6.5cm diam.; bracts setiform; sep. 2.5×1cm, bright scarlet, narrow-oblong; pet. vivid scarlet, to 1.25cm; fil. erect, corona yellow. Spring–summer. Aus. Z10.

P. coccinea Aubl. RED PASSION FLOWER; RED GRANADILLA. St. obtuse-angular, deep-furrowed. Lvs to 14×7cm, oblong, rearely suborbicular, apex acute to subobtuse, base subcordate, biserrate or crenate, tomentose beneath; petioles eglandular or biglandular. Fls to 12.5cm diam.; cal. to 2×1.3cm, cylindric-campanulate, sep. to 5×1cm, exterior yellow, interior scarlet, linear-lanceolate, acute; pet. to 4×0.8cm, vivid scarlet, linear; fil. triseriate, pale pink to white at base, deep purple twoard apex. Fr. 5cm diam., ovoid or subglobose, finely tomentose, orange or yellow, green-striate and -mottled. Guianas, S Venez., Peru, Boliv., Braz. Z10.

P. × colvillii Sweet. (*P. caerulea* × *P. incarnata*.) Lvs deep 3–5-lobed, dentate. Fls 9cm diam., white, red spotted; fil. corona banded purple, white and blue. Z7.

P. coriacea Juss. BAT-LEAF PASSION FLOWER. Lvs to 7×25cm, peltate, lobes 2(–3), oblong-ovate, acute to obtuse, broadly divergent, coriaceous. Fls to 3.5cm diam., solitary or in rac. to 6cm; cal. patelliform or campanulate, yellow-green above, sep. to 1.5×0.5cm, oblong-lanceolate, obtuse; pet. 0; fil. ivory, biseriate. Fr. to 2cm diam., globose, glab. Mex. to N Peru and N Boliv., Guyana. Z10.

P. × decaisneana Planch. (*P. alata* × *P. quadrangularis*.) Fls 10cm diam., brilliant carmine; fil. purple and white. Also arising from this cross is the hybrid named as *P. × innesii* Mast.: fls off-white, speckled red; sep. white inside; corona fil. several-sriate, white, banded red at base, spotted violet above, tipped white. Z10.

P. edulis Sims. GRANADILLA; PURPLE GRANADILLA; PASSION FRUIT. St. stout, angled. Lvs to 10×20cm, lobes 3, ovate, glandular-dentate, shiny above, glab.; petioles biglandular. Fls to 7.5cm diam.; sep. oblong, spreading, white above; pet. narrower and paler; fil. white banded purple or indigo, strongly wavy towards tips. Fr. 5cm diam., ovoid, green-yellow to dull purple. Summer. Braz. f. *edulis* Fr. yellow. 'Alice': fls abundant; fr. egg-shaped, purple. 'Crackerjack': fr. large, deep purple to black, abundant. 'Purple Passion': fls purple. 'Supreme': fr. large, rounded. Additional purple-fruited cvs include 'Black Knight', 'Edgehill', 'Frederick', 'Purple Giant', 'Red Giant', 'Red Rover' and 'Sunnypash' (usually grafted on *P. caerulea*; v. adaptable). f. *flavicarpa* Degen. Yellow-fruited cvs include 'Brazilian Golden' and 'Golden Giant'. Z10.

P. eichleriana Mast. Lvs to 8×10cm, lobes 3, oblong, apex mucronate, base cordate and subpeltate, entire, membranous; petioles 6–8-glandular. Fls to 7cm diam.; cal. campanulate, glab., sep. 1cm diam., white-green, oblong, subcoriaceous; pet. white, oblong, membranous; fil. 6-seriate. Fr. 3.5cm diam., globose, coriaceous. E Braz., Parag. Z10.

P. × exoniensis hort. ex L.H. Bail. (*P. antioquiensis* × *P. mollissima*.) St. vining, initially lanuginose. Lvs to 10×12.5cm, base cordate, lanuginose, deeply trilobed; petioles biglandular. Fls to 12.5cm diam., pendulous; cal. 6.5cm, tubular-cylindric, exterior brick red, interior rosy pink, sep. oblong-lanceolate; pet. pink tinted violet, oblong-lanceolate; corona small, pale. Z10.

P. filamentosa Cav. St. lanuginose. Lvs to 8×12cm, lobes 5–7, to 3cm diam., oblong-lanceolate, slightly toothed, base cordate, glossy above; petioles biglandular. Fls to 8cm diam.; cal. campanulate, white, sep. to 1cm diam., narrow-oblong, obtuse; pet. white tinted rose fil. several-seriate, white, the outermost banded blue. Fr. 4cm diam., globose. Autumn. C Braz. Z10.

P. foetida L. RUNNING POP; LOVE-IN-A-MIST; WILD WATER LEMON. St. malodorous when crushed, viscid, hairy. Lvs hastate, 3–5-lobed, thin-textured, glandular-ciliate; petioles eglandular. Fls to 5cm diam., subtended by 3 deeply glandular-fringed bracts; cal. white streaked green, sep. ovate; pet. oblong, ivory; fil. several striate white banded violet. Fr. to 2.5cm diam., globose, hirsute, yellow to bright red. Summer–autumn. S Amer., Puerto Rico, Jam., Lesser Antilles. Z10.

P. fulgens Wallis ex Morr. = *P. coccinea*.

P. galbana Mast. St. somewhat flexuous. Lvs to 13×6.5cm, oblong-lanceolate, entire, apex obtuse and mcuronulate, base rounded or shallow-cordate, coriaceous; petioles minutely-glandular. Fls on pedicels to 9cm, fragrant, opening at night, broadly cylindric-campanulate; sep. 4×0.7cm, narrow-oblong, white, horned; pet. 6.5mm diam., narrow-oblong, white to primrose yellow; fil. biseriate. Fr. to 7×2cm, narrow-ovoid, tapered at apex, glab. Winter. E Braz. Z10.

P. garckei Mast. Lvs to 15×25cm, lobes 3, oblong-lanceolate, apex acute to obtuse, base truncate or subcordate, subpeltate, ± entire, coriaceous, glab.; petioles 4–6-glandular. Fls to 8.5cm diam.; cal. campanulate, glab., sep. to 4×1cm, blue or purple above, oblong, cucullate; pet. to 3.5×1.2cm, lilac, oblong, obtuse; fil. several-seriate, white with a broad central violet band. Fr. subellipsoid, glab. Autumn. Fr. Guiana, Guyana, Surinam. Z10.

P. glandulosa Cav. Lvs to 15×10cm, ovate-oblong to oblong-lanceolate, apex acute or acuminate and mucronulate, base cordate to subacute, entire or undulate, glaucous, coriaceous; petioles biglandular. Fls red or scarlet; call. to 2.5×1cm, cylindric, sep. to 5cm×13mm, oblong; fil. to 1.25cm, biseriate, pink. Fr. to 6×3cm, ovoid. Spring. Guianas, Surinam, E Braz. Z10.

P. gracilis Jacq. ex Link. Lvs to 7×10cm, lobes 3, obtuse or rounded, cordate at base, entire, membranous, glaucous beneath. Fls 2cm diam.; cal. campanulate, sep. to 1×0.3cm, white to pale green, narrow-oblong, obtuse, concave; pet. 0; corona to 2cm diam., fil. bisriate. Fr. 2.5×1.5cm, ellipsoid, glab., scarlet. Summer. Venez. Z10.

P. grandiflora hort. = **P. caerulea** 'Grandiflora'.

P. hahnii (Fourn.) Mast. Lvs to 8×7cm, broadly ovate-lanceolate, entire, peltate at base, membranous, minutely toothed, purple-tinted beneath; petioles eglandular. Fls to 6cm diam., white or cream; cal. campanulate, glab., sep. and pet. to 3×1cm, oblong, obtuse; fil. biseriate, yellow. Fr. to 3.5cm diam., globose, glab. Summer–autumn. C Mex. to Costa Rica, Colomb. Z10.

P. herbertiana Ker-Gawl. Lvs 9×9cm, lobes 3, triangular, truncate, lanuginose. Fls to 10cm diam., solitary or paired, white to pale orange-yellow; sep. 4cm, linear-lanceolate; pet. to 2cm; corona broadly tubular, yellow, fil. to 1.25cm. Aus. Z10.

P. holosericea L. Lvs to 10×7cm, lobes 3, rounded, mucronulate, base cordate and bidentate, entire, velutinous above, soft-tomentose beneath; petioles biglandular. Fls to 4cm diam., fragrant, solitary or 2–4; cal. campanulate, pubesc. outside, sep. to 1.5×0.5cm, white, ovate-lanceolate, obtuse; pet. to 1.3×0.6cm, white spotted red, oblanceolate or spathulate; fil. biseriate, yellow, purple at base. Fr. 1.5cm diam., globose, glab. or soft-pubesc. Mex., C Amer. Z10.

P. imthurnii Mast. = **P. glandulosa**.

P. incarnata L. WILD PASSION FLOWER; MAY POPS; APRICOT VINE; MAY APPLE. Lvs to 15×15cm, lobes 3, lanceolate, apex acute or acuminate, base cordate, finely serrate, membranous, somewhat glaucous beneath; petioles biglandular. Fls to 7.5cm diam.; sep. pale lavender with a horn-like apical projection; pet. white or pale lavender; fil. usually pink to purple. Fr. to 5cm, ovoid, yellow. E US. Z6.

P. ×innesii Mast. = **P. ×decaisneana**.

P. insignis (Mast.) Hook. Lvs to 25×12cm, ovate-lanceolate, apex acute, base ± cordate, denticulate, coriaceous, shiny, rugulose above, rusty-woolly beneath; petioles 2–4-glandular. Fls pendulous; pedicels to 20cm; cal. to 4cm×8mm, tubular-cylindric, tomentose, violet-crimson, sep. to 9×2cm, oblong, obtuse, concave; pet. to 7×1.5cm, rose-purple, oblong, obtuse; fil. 12.5mm, 1-seriate, white, mottled blue. Summer–autumn. Boliv., Peru. Z10.

P. jamesonii (Mast.) L.H. Bail. Lvs to 8×11cm, glab., lobes 3, subelliptic, mucronate, base subcordate, spiny-dentate, subcoriaceous, glossy. Fls to 10cm diam., pendulous; pedicels to 10cm; bracts laciniate; cal. to 10cm, tubular-cylindric, bright rose glab., sep. to 5×2cm, oblong, obtuse; pet. rose to coral pink, oblong; corona tinged purple. Ecuad. (Andes). Z9.

P. jorullensis HBK. Lvs to 8.5×8cm, 2–3 (central lobe reduced to mucro) rounded or subacute, mucronulate, base subcuneate or truncate, minutely pubesc.; petioles eglandular. Fls to 4cm diam., orange turning pink; cal. campanulate, glab., sep. 1.5cm×3mm, linear-lanceolate, acute; pet. to 4×1mm, slender, linear, obtuse; fil. 1-seriate, orange then pink almost equalling sep. Fr. 1cm diam., glossy black. Autumn. C & S Mex. Z10.

P. kermesina Link & Otto. Lvs to 8×10cm, lobes 3, oblong-ovate, apex rounded or subacute, base truncate or cordate, membranous, deep green above, glaucous and purple-tinted beneath; petioles minutely 2–4-glandular. Fls to 8cm diam.; pedicels to 15cm, tribracteate; cal. 1cm, cylindric-campanulate; sep. to 4cm×7mm, linear-oblong, scarlet, obtuse, radiate, later reflexed; pet. similar to sep. fil. 3–4-seriate, violet-purple. E Braz. Z10.

P. ×kewensis hort. (**P. caerulea** × **P. kermesina**.) Fls 9cm diam., carmine, suffused-blue. Z8.

P. laurifolia L. YELLOW GRANADILLA; WATER LEMON; JAMAICA HONEYSUCKLE; BELLE APPLE; VINEGAR PEAR; POMME-DE-LIANE. Lvs to 12×8cm, ovate-oblong or oblong, subacute to obtuse, mucronate, base rounded, entire, coriaceous, glossy; petioles biglandular. Fls to 7cm diam.; cal. to 1cm, cylindric-

campanulate, glab., sep. to 2.5×1cm, green beneath, red above, oblong, obtuse; pet. similar; fil. 6-seriate, outermost purple banded red, blue and white. Fr. to 8×4cm, ovoid, yellow or orange. Summer. E Braz., Peru, Venez., Guianas, W Indies, Trin. Z10.

P. ×lawsoniana Mast. (**P. alata** × **P. racemosa**.) Lvs ovate-oblong, cordate at base. Fls to 10cm diam., somewhat red; sep. rufous. Z10.

P. ligularis Juss. GRANADILLA; SWEET GRANADILLA. St. cylindric. Lvs to 15×13cm, broadly ovate, apex abruptly acuminate, base cordate, entire, membranous, glab., blue-green beneath; petioles with 4–6 filiform glands. Fls to 9cm diam.; cal. campanulate, glab., sep. to 3.5×1.5cm, green-white beneath, white or rosy above, ovate-oblong, acute; pet. smaller; fil. 5–7-seriate, white banded, oblong, acute; pet. smaller; fil. 5–7-seriate, white banded, purple, outer series equalling pet. Fr. to 8×5cm, ovoid, glab. Autumn. C Mex., C Amer., Venez., Peru, W Boliv. Z10.

P. lutea L. Lvs to 9×15cm, lobes 3, broadly triangular-ovate, apex rounded or obtuse, base rounded to subtruncate, membranous; petioles eglandular. Fls to 2cm diam.; cal. patelliform, light green, sep. to 1×0.3cm, linear-oblong, obtuse; pet. to 0.5×0.1cm, ivory, linear, subacute; fil. biseriate, white, pink at base. Fr. 1.5×1cm, globose-ovoid, purple. Summer. E US. Z5.

P. macrocarpa Mast. = **P. quadrangularis**.

P. maculifolia Mast. = **P. organensis**.

P. maliformis L. SWEET CALABASH; SWEETCUP; CONCH APPLE. Lvs to 12×10cm, sometimes to 25×15cm, ovate, apex acute, base rounded to cordate, serrulate or undulate, membranous; petioles biglandular. Fls to 8cm diam., fragrant; cal. 1×1.2cm, campanulate, sep. 4×1.5cm, oblong, green; pet. 3×0.5cm, green-white spotted purple, linear-lanceolate; fil. several-seriate, innermost to 3cm, purple-red banded white, the outermost shorter, banded white and violet. Fr. to 4cm diam., orange-green. Summer–autumn. Venez., Colomb., N Ecuad., W Indies. Z10.

P. manicata (Juss.) Pers. RED PASSION-FLOWER. St. stout, angular. Lvs to 8×9cm, lobes 3, ovate, apex obtuse or subacute, base subcordate or rounded, serrate, tomentose beneath; petioles 4–10-glandular. Fls vivid scarlet; pedicels to 7cm; cal. to 2×1cm, urceolate-campanulate, green-white, sep. to 3.5cm×7mm, oblong-lanceolate, obtuse; pet. oblong, obtuse; fil. 3–4-seriate, corona blue and white. Fr. to 5×3.5cm, shiny deep green, glab. Colomb. to Peru. Z9.

P. maximiliana Bory = **P. misera**.

P. medusae Lem. = **P. jorullensis**.

P. membranacea Benth. Lvs to 10×10cm, orbicular, obscurely trilobed, base peltate, membranous, glab.; petioles eglandular. Fls light green or cream; pedicels to 15cm; cal. 2cm diam., broad-campanulate, sep. to 4×1cm, oblong-lanceolate, obtuse; pet. to 4×0.8cm, oblanceolate; fil. biseriate. S Mex. to Costa Rica. Z10.

P. mexicana Juss. St. obscurely 5-angled. Lvs to 8cm diam., glab., lobes 2, to 4cm, oblong, apex obtuse, base truncate or rounded, deep green above, paler beneath. Petioles eglandular. Fls to 4cm diam., maroon; cal. 1cm diam., patelliform, interior white, exterior green to red, sep. to 1.5cm×5mm, narrow-lanceolate; pet. reflexed; fil. biseriate. SW US, C Mex. Z9.

P. miersii Mast. Lvs to 8×3cm, lanceolate, apex subacute or rounded, base subpeltate, truncate or rounded, subcoriaceous, glab., dark claret or maroon with pale green veins beneath; petioles biglandular. Fls to 5cm diam.; cal. campanulate, glab., sep. to 2.5×0.7cm, green, oblong, aristate; pet. white tinted pink, obtuse; fil. 4-seriate, white, outermost banded violet. Summer. E Braz. Z10.

P. ×militaris hort. (**P. antioquiensis** × **P. manicata**.) Fls to 12.5cm diam., bright crimson. Z10.

P. misera HBK. Lvs to 13cmdiam., lobes 2 to 2.5cm, apex rounded or subacute, base cordate or subtruncate, membranous, glab. or pilosulous, flushed purple beneath; petioles eglandular. Fls to 4cm diam.; pedicels to 10cm; cal. patelliform or campanulate, interior white, sep. to 1.8×0.5cm, lanceolate-oblong to linear-oblong, obtuse; pet. to 1.3×0.4cm, white, linear-oblong, obtuse; fil. biseriate, tinted or marked purple. Autumn. Panama to N Arg. Z9.

P. mixta L. f. Lvs 10–17×13cm, lobes 3, ovate-oblong, acute, base truncate or subcordate, serrate, glab. above, glab. to velutinous beneath, coriaceous; petioles 4–8-glandular. Fls pendulous; pedicels to 6cm; bracts sometimes woolly (var. *eriantha*) cal. to 11×1cm, tubular-cylindric, sep. to 4×1.5cm, pink to orange-red, oblong, obtuse; pet. same colour; fil. 1–2-seriate, mauve, v. short. Summer–autumn. C Venez., Colomb., Ecuad., Peru, Boliv. Z10.

P. mollissima (HBK) L.H. Bail. CURUBA; BANANA PASSION FRUIT. St. golden-pubesc. Lvs to 10×12cm, lobes 3, ovate, apex acute, base subcordate, serrate, soft-pubesc. above, tomentose beneath, membranous. Fls pendulous; pedicels to 6cm; cal. to 8×1cm, olive-green, long-tubular, sep. to 3.5×1.5cm, soft pink oblong, obtuse; pet. same colour; corona a warty rim. Fr. to 7×3.5cm, oblong-ovoid, yellow-soft-pubesc. W Venez., Colomb., SE Peru, W Boliv. Z6.

P. mooreana Hook. f. Lvs to 12×10cm, glab., lobes 3, narrowly oblong-lanceolate, mucronate, base cuneate, coriaceous, glaucous beneath; petioles biglandular. Fls 6cm diam.; cal. campanulate, exterior green, sep. to 8mm diam., oblong, obtuse; pet. 1cm diam., white, oblong, obtuse; fil. biseriate, blue, banded white and indigo. Fr. ovoid, glab., yellow. Summer. S Boliv., Parag., N Arg. Z10.

P. morifolia Mast. Lvs to 11×15cm, lobes 3(-5), ovate, apex acute, base cordate, dentate or subentire, membranous, deep green, hispidulous above, pilosulous beneath; petioles biglandular. Fls to 3cm diam.; sep. to 1.5×0.4cm, white and purple-mottled, or green, linear-oblong, obtuse; pet. to 0.8×0.4cm, inconspicuous, linear-lanceolate; fil. 1-seriate. Fr. 2cm diam., purple, globose, glaucous, hispidulous. Guat., Peru, Parag., Arg. 'Scarlet Flame': fr. tasting of strawberries. Z10.

P. oerstedii Mast. Lvs to 13×9cm, lanceolate, apex acute or obtuse, rarely 2-3-lobed, base cordate, subpeltate, glab. above, glaucous and glab. to dense-tomentose beneath; petioles (2–)4-6-glandular. Fls to 6cm diam.; cal. to 8mm, campanulate, sep. to 3×1.2cm, white, ovate-lanceolate; pet. to 1.5×0.5cm white tinted pink, linear, obtuse; fil. several-seriate, purple. S Mex. to Colomb. and C Venez. Z10.

P. onychina Lindl. = **P. amethystina**.

P. organensis Gardn. Lvs to 10cm diam., dark green to brown with jagged-edged regions of silver, cream, pink or lime-green variegation, lobes divergent, broad-ovate to lanceolate, base rounded, subcoriaceous with dark, punctate nectaries above. Fls to 5cm diam., cream to dull purple, usually solitary. E Braz. Z10.

P. peltata Cav. = **P. suberosa**.

P. penduliflora Bertero ex DC. Lvs to 7.5×8cm, suborbicular to triangular-obovate, lobes 3, shallow, acute or obtuse, sometimes subentire, rounded at base; petioles slender, eglandular. Fls to 4cm diam. pendulous, pedicels to 10cm; cal. campanulate, sep. to 2×0.6cm, yellow-green, oblong-lanceolate; pet. to 0.7cm, yellow-green to ivory, oblanceolate, short-clawed; fil. 1-seriate. Spring–summer. E Cuba, Jam. Z10.

P. perfoliata L. Lvs to 6×2.5cm, oblong, lobes 2, widely divergent, rounded ovate, overlapping at base, perfoliate, subcoriaceous. Fls maroon, 1(–2); cal. to 1.3×0.8cm, turbinate-cylindric, sep. to 2×0.3cm; pet. to 0.7cm diam., oblanceolate, acute; fil. 1-seriate, corona v. short, yellow. Summer. Jam. Z10.

P. pfordtii Mast. = **P. ×alato-caerulea**.

P. picturata Ker-Gawl. Lvs to 6×7cm, lobes 3, ovate, apex rounded or subacute, bas subpeltate and rounded, glab., bright green above, somewhat purple beneath; petioles 2-6-glandular. Fls to 10cm diam.; pedicels to 12cm; cal. 0.5×1.5cm, campanulate, interior white, blue or violet, exterior green, sep. 2.5×1.5cm, linear-oblong, concave; pet. to 2.5×1.2cm, pale rose or violet, oblong, obtuse; fil. biseriate outermost white banded blue. Autumn. Surinam, Braz. Z10.

P. pinnatistipula Cav. Lvs to 10×13cm, lobes 3, lanceolate, apex acute or acuminate and mucronate, base subcordate, sharp-serrate, rugose and glab. above, densely grey-white-lanate beneath, coriaceous; stipules with pinnate, filiform lobes; petioles 4-6-glandular. Pedicels to 7cm; nodding; cal. to 5×1cm, tubular-cylindric, interior white tinged blue, exterior bright pink, densely-tomentose, sep. to 4×1cm; pet. bright rosy pink, obtuse; fil. 2.5cm, biseriate, blue. Peru, Chile. Z10.

P. princeps Lodd. = **P. racemosa**.

P. pruinosa Mast. = **P. garckei**.

P. psilantha (Sodiro) Killip. Lvs to 8×10cm, lobes 3, oblong-lanceolate, apex acuminate, base cordate, serrate-dentate, subglabrous above, soft-pubesc. beneath; petioles 8-10-glandular. Fls pale red or white; cal. to 10×0.5cm, tubular-cylindric, glab., sep. to 3×0.5cm, narrow-oblong, obtuse; pet. obtuse. Fr. 5×2.5cm, ovoid, soft-pubesc. S Ecuad. (mts). Z9.

P. punctata L. Lvs to 5×12cm, oblong, glab., lobes (2–)3, shallow, rounded and emarginate, base truncate or subcordate, somewhat glaucous beneath; petioles biglandular. Fls to 4cm diam., green-white; pedicels to 8cm; cal. campanulate, glab., glossy yellow-green; sep. to 1.8×1cm, oblong-lanceolate; pet. to 1.2×0.6cm, recurved; fil. biseriate. Ecuad., N Peru. Z10.

P. quadrangularis L. GRANADILLA; GIANT GRANADILLA. Sts 4-winged, stout. Lvs to 20×15cm, ovate-lanceolate, apex abruptly acuminate, base rounded, to cordate, entire, glab.; petioles 6-glandular. Fls to 12cm diam.; cal. shallowly campanulate, glab., sep. to 4×2.5cm, pearly grey-green tinted flesh pink, ovate or ovate-oblong, concave; pet. to 4.5×2cm, fleshy, pale mauve-pink, oblong-ovate to oblong-lanceolate, obtuse; fil. 5-seriate,

white, banded blue and red-purple, strongly twisted. Fr. to 30×15cm, oblong-ovoid, glab. Trop. Amer. 'Variegata': lvs blotched yellow. Z10.

P. racemosa Brot. RED PASSION FLOWER. Lvs to 10×11cm, ovate and simple, or with 3 oblong lobes, apex acute or subobtuse, base subpeltate, truncate or cordate, entire, coriaceous; petioles biglandular. Fls to scarlet-red or white, in pendulous rac. to 30cm; cal. to 1.5×1.2cm, cylindric, glab., throat maroon; sep. to 4×1cm, oblong, with keel-like wings; pet. oblong, obtuse; fil. triseriate, white banded dark purple, inner fil. red, short. Braz. Z10.

P. raddiana DC. = **P. kermesina**.

P. rubra L. St. 3–5-angled, grey-pubesc. Lvs to 8×10cm, bilobed (rarely with a far smaller midlobe), cordate at base, membranous, downy; petioles eglandular. Fls to 5cm diam.; cal. patelliform or campanulate, pubesc. outside, distinctly 3-veined, sep. to 3×0.6cm, ivory linear-lanceolate; pet. to 1.5×0.4cm, similar to sep.; fil. 1–2-seriate, red-purple or lavender. Autumn. Colomb., Venez., Peru, Boliv., E Braz., W Indies. Z10.

P. sanguinolenta Mast. & Lind. Lvs densely villous-hirsute, lunate-bilobed, lobes to 2cm diam., lanceolate, mucronulate, base cordate, membranous; petioles eglandular. Fls dull red or maroon; cal. to 2cm, cylindric, densely villous-hirsute, sep. to 2×0.5cm, linear-oblong, pet. to 1×0.3cm, linear; fil. biseriate. Ecuad. (mts). Z9.

P. seemannii Griseb. Lvs to 13×15cm, cordate-ovate, apex mucronate, base deeply-cordate, subentire, glaucous, glab., thin-textured; petioles 2(–4)-glandular. Fls to 10cm diam.; pedicels to 10cm; cal. 2cm, campanulate-funnelform, glab., white, tinged purple, sep. to 4×1.5cm, ovate-lanceolate, corniculate; pet. to 3.5×1.2cm, purple, oblong-lanceolate, obtuse; fil. biseriate. S Mex. to Panama, NW Colomb. Z10.

P. serratifolia L. Lvs to 12×7cm, ovate, apex acuminate, base rounded or cordate, serrulate, minutely hirsute beneath; petioles 6-glandular. Fls to 6cm diam., fragrant; pedicels to 7cm; cal. campanulate, sep. to 3×0.8cm, pink-purple, lanceolate; pet. to 2×0.6cm, oblong-lanceolate; fil. several-seriate, outermost to 3cm, blue, dark purple toward base. Fr. to 9×5cm, glab., yellow. Spring–autumn. E Mex. to Costa Rica. Z10.

P. sicyoides Schltr. & Cham. Lvs to 8×10cm, lobes 3, deltoid-acuminate, midlobe longest, mucronate, base cordate, entire or denticulate, light green above, glaucous beneath, hispidulous; petioles biglandular. Fls v. fragrant, to 4cm diam.; cal. patelliform or campanulate, hispidulous, sep. to 2×1cm, yellow-green, oblong-lanceolate; pet. to 1.2cm, white, ovate-lanceolate; fil. 8.5mm, 1-seriate, white, banded red-purple. Summer. C & S Mex. Z10.

P. stipulata Aubl. Lvs to 8×10cm, lobes 3, broad-ovate, apex subacute, base subpeltate and cordate, membranous, glab., glaucous beneath; petioles 2–5-glandular. Fls to 6cm diam., fragrant; cal. obconic-campanulate, light green inside, darker outside, sep. to 3×1cm, white-green, oblong-lanceolate; pet. white to 3cm; fil. several-seriate, white, violet at base. Fr. Guiana. Z10.

P. suberosa L. St. becoming winged and corky. Lvs entire to deeply trilobed, lobes linear-lanceolate to broad-ovate, base rounded, subcoriaceous; petioles biglandular. Fls to 3cm diam., green-yellow to ivory, solitary or paired, sometimes in term. rac.; pet. 0; fil. biseriate. Fr. to 1.5cm diam., purple or black, glaucous. Summer. Trop. Amer. Z10.

P. subpeltata Ortega. GRANADINA. Lvs to 9×12cm, lobes 3, oblong, apex obtuse, base often subpeltate or subcordate, glab.; petioles 2-4-glandular. Fls to 5cm diam.; cal. glab., sep. to 1cm diam., green-white above; pet. white, linear-oblong; fil. 5-seriate, white. Fr. to 4cm diam., ovoid or subglobose, glab., somewhat green. C Mex., C Amer., Colomb., Venez. Z10.

P. tinifolia Juss. = **P. laurifolia**.

P. trifasciata Lem. Lvs to 10×10cm, glab., lobes 3, deltoid, apex acute or subobtuse, base cordate, dull dark green mottled pale green or yellow on veins above, maroon or violet beneath; petioles eglandular. Fls to 3.5cm diam., fragrant; ivory-white. Peru, Braz. Z10.

P. tuberosa Jacq. Tuberous-rooted. St. vining. Lvs to 6×12cm, oblong, lobes 2, lanceolate, with a mucro in sinus, base rounded, subcoriaceous, glossy above, paler beneath; petioles eglandular. Fls to 5cm diam., white, solitary or paired; fil. white banded purple, biseriate. Summer–autumn. Carib. (St. Thomas, Trin.), N S Amer. Z10.

P. tucumanensis Hook. Sts ± glaucous, sulcate. Lvs to 6×1.5cm, lobes 3–5, oblong-lanceolate, mucronate, base cordate and finely serrate, membranous, deep green above, somewhat glaucous beneath; petioles eglandular. Fls to 5cm diam.; white; sep. 5mm diam., oblong-lanceolate, cucullate; pet. white; fil. 12.5mm, several-sriate, white, banded violet. Summer. NW Arg. Z10.

P. umbilicata (Griseb.) Harms. Lvs to 6×7.5cm, lobes 3, oblong-ovate, apex rounded or subacute and mucronate, base cordate, entire or undulate, subcoriaceous; petioles eglandular or minutely biglandular. Fls erect, maroon, violet or dark blue; pedicels to 9cm; cal. to 3.5×0.9cm, tubular-cylindric, sep. to 3cm×6mm, linear-oblong; pet. linear-oblong, obtuse; fil. 5-seriate. C Boliv., N Arg. Z10.

P. van volxemii Triana & Planch. = *P. antioquiensis*.

P. violacea Vell. Lvs to 12×15cm, lobes 3, oblong, base cordate and subpeltate, ± entire, membranous or subcoriaceous, glaucous beneath; petioles 3–8-glandular. Fls to 10cm diam., violet; peduncles stout, to 15cm; cal. campanulate, purple inside, pruinose outside, sep. to 1cm diam., oblong or oblong-lanceolate long-awned; pet. to 1cm diam., oblong-lanceolate, obtuse; fil. 6–7-seriate, to 4cm, violet, white at apex and base. Autumn. Boliv., E Braz., Parag. Z10.

P. viridiflora Cav. Lvs to 16×25cm, glab., lobes 3, ovate to suborbicular, obtuse, entire, peltate, coriaceous, glossy, petioles biglandular. Fls green; cal. cylindric, glabrous, glab., sep. to 1.5×0.2cm, linear; pet. 0; fil. 1-seriate. S Mex. Z10.

P. vitifolia HBK. St. rusty tomentose. Lvs to 15×18cm, vine-like, lobes 3, acuminate, truncate to cordate at base, dentate or crenate, shiny above, minutely tomentose beneath; petioles biglandular. Fls to 9cm diam., scarlet, bright red or vermilion; pedicels rusty-tomentose; cal. cylindric, subglabrous, sep. to 8×2cm, lanceolate, obtuse; pet. to 6×1.5cm, linear-lanceolate, obtuse; fil. 2-seriate, red to bright yellow. Spring–summer. C & S Amer. 'Scarlet Flame': fr. tasting of strawberries. Z10.

P. warmingii Mast. Lvs to 5×6cm, lobes 3, deltoid, acute, mucronulate, cordate at base, dentate, membranous, hispidulous above; petioles biglandular. Fls 2.5cm diam., white; cal. green-white, sep. to 1×0.5cm, lanceolate-oblong, obtuse; pet. to 7×3mm, lanceolate-oblong, obtuse; fil. biseriate, white; purple-violet at base. Fr. ovoid, pilose. Colomb., Braz., Parag. Close to *P. morifolia*. Z10.

P. watsoniana Mast. Lvs to 6×8cm, lobes 3, oblong, apex obtuse or subacute, base subpeltate and subtruncate, membranous, glab., green above, maroon beneath; petioels 2–5-glandular. Fls to 8cm diam.; cal. 4mm, campanulate, glab., sep. 7mm diam., white tinted violet above oblong-lanceolate, obtuse; pet. 4mm diam., white-tinted violet to pale lilac, thin, linear-lanceolate; fil. 5-seriate, erect, violet, banded white. Summer–autumn. C & S Braz. Z10.

P. cvs. 'Amethyst': st. thin; lvs to 10cm diam., 3-lobed; pet. intense blue, corona fil. dark purple. 'Star of Bristol': slender vine; lvs 3–5 lobed; sep. to 5×1.5cm, green, purple above; pet. mauve, to 4.5×1.6cm, fil. 4–5-seriate, deep mauve at base, centrally banded of lilac, apex mauve; fr. ovoid, bright orange. 'Star of Clevedon': slender vine; sep. white, green and white outside, to 5×1.5cm; pet. white, to 5×1.5cm; corona fil. 4-seriate, purple at base, centrally banded white then blue-lilac. 'Star of Kingston' (*P.* 'Amethyst' ×*P. caerulea*): mauve, fil. deep mauve base, banded white, apex mauve.

→*Tacsonia*.

PASSIFLORACEAE Juss. 18/600. *Adenia, Malesherbia, Passiflora.*

Passion Flower *Passiflora* (*P. caerulea*).
Passion Fruit *Passiflora edulis.*
Passion Vine *Passiflora.*

Pastinaca L. Umbelliferae. 14 stoutly tap-rooted bienn. or perenn. herbs. Lvs simple or 1–2-pinnate, seg. simple to pinnatisect. Umbels compound, with 3–30 rays; fls small, yellow. Eurasia.
P. sativa L. PARSNIP. Strong smelling bienn. to 1m, from thick, turbinate white rootstock. Lvs 10–30cm, pinnate, seg. 5–11, ovate; crenate-dentate. Umbels 5–20-rayed, to 10cm diam.; bracts 2, withering early. Summer. Eur., W Asia.

→*Peucedanum*.

Pasture Brake *Pteridium aquilinum.*
Pasture Rose *Rosa carolina.*
Pata de Gallo *Oreopanax xalapensis.*
Patagonian Cypress *Fitzroya cupressoides.*
Pate *Schefflera digitata.*

Patersonia R. Br. Iridaceae. 20 perenn. rhizomatous herbs. Lvs linear, distichous, usually forming a fan. Fls regular, short-lived, in spathaceous sessile spikelets on an erect scape; perianth tube slender, outer 3 tep. ovate, spreading, inner 3 erect, small; fil. joined into tube; style filiform, with 3 petaloid br. Aus., Borneo, New Guinea. Z10.
P. glabrata R. Br. St. to 15cm. Fls purple. Aus. (Vict., NSW, Queensld).

P. glauca R. Br. St. v. short. Spathes 2.5–3cm, glab., enclosing 2–4-fld spikes; fls blue; outer tep. c10mm. Aus. (NSW to Tasm.).
P. longiscapa Sweet. Spathes brown, spikelets 3–4-fld; fls blue-purple, tube enclosed in spathe; outer tep. about 20mm; tube velvety. Aus. (Vict., S Aus., Tasm.).
P. media R. Br. = *P. glabrata.*
P. occidentalis R. Br. St. usually 15–50cm, forming tufts. Spikelets few to several-fld; fls deep blue or purple; tube 25–35mm; outer tep. 15–35mm. Spring–summer. W Aus.
P. sericea R. Br. St. to 30cm, silky. Spikelets several-fld; fls deep violet-blue; spathes woolly. Summer. Aus. (Vict., NSW, Queensld).
P. umbrosa Endl. To 50cm. Spathes 5–7cm, keeled; fls blue; outer tep. to 30mm. Summer. W Aus. 'Xanthina': fls yellow.

Pati *Syagrus botryphora; S. cocoides; S. comosa.*
Patience Dock, Patience Herb *Rumex patentia.*
Patience Plant *Impatiens* (*I. walleriana*).
Patioba *Syagrus botryphora.*

Patrinia Juss. Valerianaceae. 15 herbaceous perennials. Lvs pinnately cut or lobed mostly basal. Fls small, in corymbose pan. to 10cm diam., cal. limb short, toothed; cor. tube v. short with 5 spreading lobes. Temp. Asia.
P. gibbosa Maxim. To 22.5cm. Lvs to 15cm, ± blistered, elliptic-ovate to broadly ovate, long-petioled, slender-pointed, pinnately cut and coarsely toothed. Fls in flat cymes, yellow. Jap.
P. triloba Miq. To 60cm. Lvs to 5cm, 3–5-pinnately lobed, upper lvs coarsely toothed. Fls golden-yellow, fragrant, in loose, 3-branched cymes. Jap. var. *palmata* (Maxim.) Hara. Fls with spurs to 3mm.
P. villosa (Thunb.) Juss. To 90cm. Lvs to 15cm, ovate, simple to pinnatifid, white-pubesc., upper lvs sessile, toothed. Fls white in corymbose pan. Jap.

Patula Pine *Pinus patula.*

Paulownia Sieb. & Zucc. Scrophulariaceae. 17 decid. trees. Shoots thick, hairy becoming glab., without terminal buds. Lvs opposite, large, cordate at the base, entire or 3–5-lobed, usually hairy at least beneath. Pan. term., erect, tomentose, buds present throughout winter; cal. deeply 5-lobed, thick, hairy; cor. large, campanulate to foxglove-like, with 5 short, spreading lobes. Capsule leathery. E Asia.
P. fargesii Franch. To 12m. Lvs 15–21×12–14cm, long-ovate, cordate at base, entire, densely hairy beneath. Pan. br. stalked; cor. foxglove-like, 5–7cm, usually violet or lilac, yellow within. W China. Z7.
P. fargesii Osborn non Franch. = *P. tomentosa* 'Lilacina'.
P. fortunei Hemsl. To 20m. Lvs 14–21×7–12cm, long-ovate, cordate, glab. and shining above, densely hairy beneath. Panicle-branches stalked; cor. foxglove-like, 8–10cm, cream flushed with lilac. China, Jap. Z6.
P. imperialis Sieb. & Zucc. = *P. tomentosa.*
P. kawakamii Itô. To 12m. Lvs 11–30×8–27cm broadly cordate, 3–5-lobed, glandular-hairy above, densely so beneath. Pan. br. not or scarcely stalked; cor. campanulate, 3–4.5cm, lilac. S China, Taiwan. Z6.
P. lilacina Sprague = *P. tomentosa* 'Lilacina'.
P. tomentosa (Thunb.) Steud. To 20m. Lvs 17–30×12–27cm, broadly ovate, entire, hairy above, densely so beneath. Pan. br. stalked; cor. foxglove-like, 5–6cm, violet with yellow stripes inside. C & W China. 'Coreana': lvs tinted yellow, woolly beneath; fls violet, throat speckled yellow inside. 'Lilacina': young shoots glandular-hairy; cor. pale lilac. Z5.

Paurotis Palm *Acoelorraphe.*

Pavetta L. Rubiaceae. 400 shrubs or subshrubs, or trees. Fls in cymes or corymbs; bracts connate; cal. tube ovoid or bell-shaped, limb lobed or truncate; cor. cylindric to salver- or funnel-shaped; lobes 4, spreading; sta. 4, exserted. Fr. a berry, lustrous, usually black. Trop. and subtrop. OW. Z10.
P. abyssinica Fres. Shrub to 2.5m or tree to 9m. Lvs to 17×7cm, obovate to elliptic, apex narrowly acute or obtuse, thin-textured, lustrous, glab. to sparsely pubesc. Fls in loose, term. corymbs to 12×6cm; cor. white, tube to 4cm, lobes to 10mm. Trop. Afr.
P. assimilis Sonder = *P. gardeniifolia.*
P. caffra L. f. = *P. capensis.*
P. capensis (Houtt.) Bremek. Shrub to 2m. Lvs to 5×2cm, obovate, apex narrowly acute, glab. Fls in dense, term., sub-umbellate corymbs, bracts laciniate and ciliate; cor. white, tube to 2cm, lobes to 7mm. Summer. S Afr.

P. gardeniifolia Hochst. ex A. Rich. COMMON BRIDE'S BUSH. Shrub or tree, to 7m. Lvs to 12×6cm, elliptic to obovate or oblanceolate, apex acute or obtuse and hard-tipped, glab. or pubesc. Fls in dense, short-pedunculate, term. corymbs to 7cm wide; cor. white to cream or pale yellow, tube to 2cm, lobes to 7mm. Trop. Afr.

P. indica L.   Shrub or tree to 3m. Lvs to 25×8cm, elliptic or lanceolate to obovate or orbicular, apex acute to caudate, membranous to leathery. Fls in dense, sessile, corymbose cymes to 12cm wide; cor. white, tube to 2cm, lobes to 12mm. Trop. Asia.

P. javanica Bl. = *Ixora javanica*.

P. montana Reinw. ex Bl.   Shrub or tree, to 4m. Lvs to 13×5cm, ovate or lanceolate to oblong, apex acute to caudate, herbaceous to leathery, glab. to pubesc. Fls in loose, subsessile, many-fld corymbs; cor. white, tube to 2cm, lobes to 6mm. Malaysia, Indon.

P. natalensis Sonder. NATAL BRIDE'S BUSH.   Shrub or tree to 4m. Lvs to 14×4cm, lanceolate or elliptic to oblong, apex and base attenuate, glossy. Fls in loose, long-stalked cymose heads to 11cm wide; cor. white; tube to 2cm, lobes to 10mm. S Afr.

P. obovata E. Mey. = *P. revoluta*.

P. quinqueflora Sessé & Moq. = *Ixora ferrea*.

P. revoluta Hochst. DUNE BRIDE'S BUSH.   Shrub or tree, to 6m. Lvs to 8×4cm, obovate to elliptic, apex attenuate or obtuse, lustrous and leathery, glab. above, pubesc. on veins beneath. Fls in dense corymbose heads to 4cm wide; cor. white, tube to 12mm, lobes to 8mm. S Afr.

P. rhodesiaca Bremek. = *P. gardeniifolia*.

P. salicifolia Bl. = *Ixora salicifolia*.

P. undulata Lehm. = *P. revoluta*.

Pavonia Cav. Malvaceae. About 150 sp. of herbs, subshrubs and shrubs, to glab. St. rod-like. Lvs simple to palmately lobed, stipulate. Fls axillary, solitary, in term. globose clusters or paniculate infl.; epical. seg., linear-lanceolate, 4 to many; cal. campanulate or cup-shaped, 5-fid; staminal column truncate or 5-toothed at apex; styles 10, stigmas capitate. Fr. a schizocarp, mericarps 5, smooth. Trop. and Subtrop. Z10.

P. ×gledhillii Cheek. (*P. makoyana* ×*P. multiflora*.)   Shrub to 2m. Lvs 10–16cm, elliptic-lanceolate, acute to acuminate, obscurely serrate, glossy light green. Fls solitary, in upper lf axils; epical. seg. 9–10, 3mm, bright red, ciliate; cal. 2cm, stellate-tomentose; teeth grey-pink; cor. to 3cm, tubular, dark purple; anth. entirely exserted, fil. bright red; pollen chalky lilac-blue. Widespread in horticulture. 'Kermesina': dwarf; fls carmine. 'Rosea': fls rose.

P. hastata Cav.   Shrub or subshrub to 2m. Lvs to 5cm, lanceolate to ovate, hastate to narrowly saggitate, dentate. Epical. seg. 5–6, to 5mm; pet. to 3cm, pale red to white, with red spots at base. Trop. S Amer., nat. in S US (Georgia and Flor.). Cvs to follow.

P. intermedia hort. non St.-Hil. = *P. ×gledhillii*.

P. mackoyana auct. = *P. makoyana*.

P. makoyana E. Morr.   Shrub to 80cm. Lvs 8–15cm, elliptic-lanceolate, acuminate, entire or obscurely sinuate, coriaceous dark green, nerves red-brown beneath. Epical. seg. rose-red; sep. 8mm; pet. 3cm, erect, dark brown-purple, linear-oblong, rounded; fil. and styles rose-red; anth. and stigmas blue-purple. Braz.

P. multiflora Juss.   Shrub to 2m. Lvs to 25cm, lanceolate-ovate to oblong, entire to dentate. Fls solitary or in upper lf axils; epical. seg. 10–24, bright red to 4cm; cal. shorter than epical., red; pet. to 4cm, purple-red; staminal column exserted, red; anth. blue. Braz.

P. praemorsa (L. f.) Willd.   Shrub to 3m. Lvs to 2.5×2.5cm, broadly obovate or fan-shaped, dentate-crenate, scabrous above, canescent beneath. Fls axill., solitary; pedicels exceeding lvs; epical. seg. 12–14; cal. canescent, seg. ovate, acute; cor. bright yellow with a dark centre. S Afr.

P. semiserrata (Schräd.) Gürke.   Tree to 7m. Lvs 2–5cm, elliptic, obscurely serrate, obtuse. Fls 2–3cm, solitary, on long peduncles; epical. seg. 5–6; cal. 1cm, campanulate; pet. 1.5×0.6cm, purple; staminal column 2.5–3cm, glab. Braz.

P. semperflorens (Nees) Gürke = *P. semiserrata*.

P. sepium St.-Hil.   Similar to *P. spinifex* but smaller, with narrower cuneate lvs; epical. and cal. about 6mm; pet. 1.2–2cm. S Amer.

P. spinifex (L.) Cav.   Shrub to 4.5m. Lvs 3–10cm, broadly ovate to ovate-lanceolate, serrate, obtuse. Fls solitary; epical. seg. 5–8; cal. to 1cm; pet. 2–3.5cm, yellow. Bermuda, Mex. to Braz. and Peru, W Indies, Greater Antilles; nat. SE US.

→*Goethea* and *Triplochlamys*.

Pawpaw *Asimina triloba*; *Carica*.

Paxistima Raf. Celastraceae. 2 dwarf, everg., glab. shrubs. Br. 4-angled, corky, warted. Lvs opposite, simple, serrulate, coriaceous. Fls 4-merous, small solitary or clustered in axils. Capsule to 4mm, oblong, compressed, 2-valved; seeds 1–2, with a white aril. N Amer.

P. canbyi A. Gray. CLIFF GREEN; MOUNTAIN LOVER.   St. to 40cm, decumbent, rooting. Lvs to 2cm, sessile, linear-oblong, obtuse, revolute, entire or finely serrate. Pedicels to 10mm; pet. green, to 2.5mm. Spring, summer. N Amer. 'Compacta': hardy, extra dwarf; lvs dark green later turning bronze. Z3.

P. myrsinites (Pursh) Raf. = *P. myrtifolia*.

P. myrtifolia Wheeler. MOUNTAIN LOVER; OREGON BOXWOOD.   Spreading, much-branched, to 1m. Lvs to 3cm, subsessile, ovate, oblong or oblanceolate, finely serrate, dark glossy green above. Pedicels to 3mm; pet. to 1.5mm, tinted red. Spring, summer. BC to Calif., eastwards to Mont., Colorado, New Mex. Z6.

Payapa *Ficus drupacea*.
Pea *Pisum*.
Peace Lily *Spathiphyllum*.
Peach *Prunus persica*.
Peach-bells *Campanula persicifolia*.
Peach Bush *Prunus texana*.
Peach Leaved Willow *Salix amygdaloides*.
Peach Palm *Bactris gasipaes*.
Peach Wood *Caesalpinia echinata*.
Peacock Fern *Selaginella willdenovii*.
Peacock-flower Fence *Adenanthera pavonina*.
Peacock Flower *Caesalpinia pulcherrima*; *Delonix regia*; *Tigridia*.
Peacock Lily *Kaempferia roscoeana*.
Peacock Moss *Selaginella unciniata*.
Peacock Plant *Calathea makoyana*; *Kaempferia atrovirens*.
Peanut *Arachis hypogaea*.
Peanut-brittle Begonia *Begonia domingensis*.
Peanut Cactus *Echinopsis chamaecereus*.
Pear *Pyrus* spp.
Pear-fruited Mallee *Eucalyptus pyriformis*.
Pearl Berry *Margyricarpus pinnatus*.
Pearlbush *Exochorda*.
Pearl Flower *Conostephium pendulum*.
Pearl Fruit *Margyricarpus pinnatus*.
Pearl Haworthia *Haworthia margaritifera*.
Pearlwort *Sagina*.
Pearly Everlasting *Anaphalis* (*A. margaritacea*).
Pear Thorn *Crataegus calpodendron*.
Pea Shrub *Caragana* (*C. jubata*).
Pea Tree *Caragana*.
Pebble Plants *Lithops*.
Pecan *Carya* (*C. illinoinensis*).

Pecluma M. Price. Polypodiaceae. 35 epiphytic ferns. Rhiz. creeping. Fronds stipitate, uniform, pinnate to pinnatifid, lanceolate to deltoid or oblong, seg. linear to strap-shaped, usually decurrent at base, glab. or puberulent. Trop. Amer. Z10.

P. pectinata (L.) M. Price.   Fronds to 90×15cm, deeply pinnate-pinnatifid, lanceolate or elliptic to linear or oblong, thin-textured, pinnae or lobes to 6×0.7cm, obtuse, entire or dentate; stipes to 15cm. W Indies, C to S Amer.

P. plumala (Humb. & Bonpl. ex Willd.) M. Price.   Fronds to 45×10cm, deeply pinnate-pinnatifid, elliptic to linear or oblong, bullate-scaly beneath, pinnae or lobes to 3×0.3cm obtuse, entire to ciliate; stipes to 8cm. W Indies, C to S Amer.

→*Goniophlebium*.

Pecteilis Raf. Orchidaceae. 4 terrestrial orchids. St. erect. Lvs cauline or, basal and rosulate. Fls racemose, few; sep. spreading, free; pet. narrower; lip midlobe entire, lat. lobes fringed, spreading; spur slender. Trop. Asia. Z10.

P. radiata (Thunb.) Raf.   To 45cm. Lvs linear-lanceolate, 2–10×0.3–0.7cm. Sep. ovate-lanceolate, to 1cm, green; pet. white, ovate, margins white, jagged; lip white, to 2×3cm, midlobe linear-ligulate, lat. lobes obovate, deeply and irregularly divided; spur decurved, green. Jap., Korea.

P. sagarikii Seidenf.   To 25cm. Lvs ovate, 10–12×6–9cm. Fls white or cream, fragrant; dors. sep. ovate, to 2.5cm, lat. sep. lanceolate; pet. smaller; lip convex, sometimes bright yellow, base obscurely trilobed, apex subobovate, rounded or obtuse, to 2–5×2cm, lateral lobes obscure, rounded; spur weakly incurved. Thail.

P. susannae (L.) Raf.   To 20cm. Lvs elliptic, to 12×5cm. Fls white to green-white, fragrant; dors. sep. subcircular, to 3cm diam., lat. sep. linear, to 3.5cm; pet. linear, falcate, to 1.5cm; lip midlobe linear-spathulate, entire to 3cm, lat. lobes deeply fringed; spur strongly decurved. China, Burm., Malaya.

→*Habenaria*.

Pectinaria Haw. Asclepiadaceae. 3 dwarf, succulent, clump-forming, leafless herbs. St. angled, prostrate, tuberculate, with small teeth. Fls in clusters or solitary; cor. tube short, campanulate, lobes triangular, acute, joined at apices. S Afr. (Cape Prov.). Z9.

P. arcuata N.E. Br. St. 5–10cm, bluntly 4-angled. Fls 12mm, ovoid-acuminate; tube hemispherical, dark red; lobes 7mm, pale yellow, exterior flushed purple, interior dark purple at base, apex white spotted maroon. Z9.

P. articulata (Ait.) Haw. St. bluntly 5–8-angled. Fls 5–8mm diam., purple, red-brown or pale yellow, exterior densely to sparsely papillose, interior with spiculate, crystalline papillae. ssp. *articulata*. St. to 6cm, 5–6-angled, often flushed red. Fls 5–8mm diam., flat-topped, bowl-shaped, purple-brown, sometimes pale yellow, exterior papillose, interior purple-black, densely papillose. ssp. *asperiflora* (N.E. Br.) P.V. Bruyns. St. 2–8cm, dark purple, 6–8-angled. Fls pendulous, conical, 6–8mm diam., exterior densely papillose, interior papillose, dark purple, tube 2–3.5mm, lobes 3.5–6mm, fused outside tube. ssp. *borealis* P.V. Bruyns. Fls 3.5mm long, 7mm diam., exterior covered in glab. papillae, interior with columnar papillae covered with round-topped spicules, dark purple brown, lobe tips jointed, conical. W Cape. ssp. *namaquensis* (N.E. Br.) P.V. Bruyns. Fls 5mm diam., shortly conical, pale grey-yellow or red-purple, interior covered with rounded dome-like papillae, covered in spinescent transparent spicules. W Cape.

P. asperiflora N.E. Br. = *P. articulata* ssp. *asperiflora*.

P. breviloba R.A. Dyer. = *Stapeliopsis breviloba*.

P. longipes (N.E. Br.) P.V. Bruyns. St. 6×1–1.5cm, brown-green, 6-angled. Fls 8–12mm diam., yellow covered with translucent spicules, lobes spreading, ovate-deltoid, 2.5–3mm. SE Cape.

P. maughanii (R.A. Dyer) P.V. Bruyns. St. 8×1–1.5cm, 6-angled, green to brown-green. Fls 1.2–1.6mm diam., covered with fine transparent spicules, lobes 5–7mm, dark purple-black, margins replicate. W Cape.

P. saxatilis N.E. Br. = *Stapeliopsis saxatilis*.

P. stayneri Bayer. = *Stapeliopsis saxatilis* ssp. *stayneri*.

P. tulipiflora Luckh. = *Stapeliopsis saxatilis*.

→*Caralluma* and *Ophionella*.

PEDALIACEAE R. Br. 18/95. *Ceratotheca, Ibicella, Martynia, Proboscidea, Pterodiscus, Sesamothamnus*.

Pedalium Royen ex L.

P. busseanum (Engl.) Stapf = *Pterodiscus angustifolius*.

Pedicularis L. LOUSEWORT; WOOD BETONY. Scrophulariaceae. c350 often semi-parasitic erect ann., bienn. or perenn. herbs. Rac. spikelike; cal. campanulate or tubular, lobed, cor. bilabiate, upper lip helmet-shaped, often extended into a beak; lower lip shorter. N Temp. regions, particularly Eur. and Asia, in New World extending S to Ecuadorean Andes.

P. canadensis L. COMMON LOUSEWORT; WOOD BETONY. Perenn. herb, 15–40cm. Lvs to 13cm, lanceolate or oblanceolate to narrowly oblong, pinnately lobed; seg. oblong-ovate, crenate. Fls creamy yellow, purple or bicoloured, occas. white. Spring–summer. SE Canada to N Mex., E to Flor. Z3.

P. densiflora Benth. ex Hook. INDIAN WARRIOR. Perenn. herb 15–55cm. Lvs 18–25cm, narrowly oblong to ovate, pinnatifid to pinnate; seg. oblong-lanceolate, dentate. Fls crimson to maroon, lower lip tinged yellow. Spring–early summer. SW US. Z6.

Pedilanthus Necker ex Poit. SLIPPER SPURGE; RED BIRD CACTUS; JEW BUSH. Euphorbiaceae. 14 shrubs. St. succulent, narrowly cylindrical, waxy. Lvs succulent. Infl. similar to *Euphorbia*, but cyathia zygomorphic. S US to trop. Amer. Z9.

P. aphyllus Boiss. ex Klotzsch & Garcke = *P. cymbiferus*.

P. bracteatus (Jacq.) Boiss. CANDELILLA. Shrub, to 3m. Lvs to 10cm, ovate to obovate. Cyathia green or pale green, glands crimson. SE Sonora.

P. cymbiferus Schldl. Low shrub to 50cm. Lvs to 1.5cm, ovate to obovate. Cyathia pink to vivid red, green at base. Summer–early winter. Mex.

P. macrocarpus Benth. Shrub, to 1.5m. Lvs caducous to 10cm. Cyathia red. W Mex.

P. smallii Millsp. = *P. tithymaloides* ssp. *smallii*.

P. tithymaloides (L.) Poit. Everg. or decid. shrub, to 3m. Lvs to 6cm, ovate to elliptic, keeled beneath. Cyathia red above, yellow-green at base. W Indies. 'Nana Compactus': br. upright; lvs dark green, dense. ssp. *retusus* Benth. Lvs retuse, ovate or obovate to elliptic, to 7.5×5cm, lvs widest below middle. ssp. *smallii* (Millsp.) Dressler. JACOB'S LADDER; DEVIL'S BACKBONE; RIBBON CACTUS. St. flexuous. 'Variegatus': lvs green,

variegated white and red.
→*Euphorbia*.

Pediocactus Britt. & Rose. Cactaceae. 6 dwarf or low-growing cacti, simple or clustering; st. tuberculate. Fls sub-apical, campanulate; tube v. short, scaly. W & SW US.

P. bradyi L. Bens. Simple; st. 3.8–6.2×2.5–5cm, obscure by spines; tubercles 3–4.5mm; central spines 0 or 4mm; radial spines 3–6mm, subpectinate, white or yellow-brown. Fl. 1.5–2×1.5–3cm, pale yellow. SW US. Z9.

P. knowltonii L. Bens. Simple or clustering; st. 0.7–5.5×1–3cm; tubercles 2–4×1–2mm; central spines 0; radial spines 1–1.5mm, adpressed, pale brown, pink or white. Fl. 1–3.5×1–2.5cm, pink. Spring. SW US. Z9.

P. papyracanthus (Engelm.) L. Bens. = *Sclerocactus papyracanthus*.

P. paradinei B.W. Bens. Simple; st. 3–7.5×2.5–3.8(–8)cm; tubercles to 5×3–5mm; spines hairlike, white to pale grey; central spines 8–28mm; radial spines 2–5mm. Fl. to 2.2×1.9–2.5cm, pale yellow or pink. Spring. SW US. Z9.

P. peeblesianus (Croizat) L. Bens. Simple; st. obovoid, globose or depressed-globose, 2.2–6×2–5.5cm; tubercles 3–7×4–6mm; central 0 or 5–21mm, white to pale grey, corky; radial spines 2–9mm. Fl. 1.5–2.5cm diam., cream, yellow or yellow-green. Spring. SW US. Z9.

P. sileri (Engelm. ex Coult.) L. Bens. Simple; st. depressed-ovoid to short-cylindric, 5–15(–25)×6–11.5cm; central spines black brown to grey, 13–30mm; radial spines 11–21mm, white. Fl. to 2.2×2.5cm, yellow; to tep. fringed. Spring. US (Ariz.). Z9.

P. simpsonii (Engelm.) Britt. & Rose. Simple or clustering; st. globose to ovoid (2.5–)5–15×(3–)5–15cm, tubercles spirally arranged, central spines 5–28mm, red-brown; radial spines 3–19mm, white. Fl. 1.2–3×1.5–2.5cm, white, pink, magenta, yellow or yellow-green. Spring. W US. Z5.

→*Mammillaria*.

Pedunculate Oak *Quercus robur*.

Peepul *Ficus religiosa*.

Peersia L. Bol.

P. macradenia (L. Bol.) L. Bol. = *Rhinephyllum macradenium*.

Peganum L. Zygophyllaceae. 6 erect herbs or subshrubs. Lvs pinnate. Fls solitary, axill.; cal. 5-parted, persistent; pet. 4–5, overlapping; sta. 12–15, inserted with pet. at base of short disc. Capsule 3-valved. Medit. to Mong., S N Amer.

P. harmala L. HARMAL. Glaucous perenn. to 1m. St. ascending, forking. Lvs 5–8cm, deeply pinnatisect, lobes-linear. Fls 1–2cm; pet. white, oblong-elliptic. SE Eur. to warm Asia. Z8.

Père David's Maple *Acer davidii*.

Pegwood *Cornus sanguinea*.

Pejibeye *Bactris gasipaes*.

Pejivalle *Bactris gasipaes*.

Peking Willow *Salix matsudana*.

Pelargonium L'Hérit. Geraniaceae. GERANIUM. 250 subshrubs, herbaceous perennials and annuals. St. sometimes succulent or swollen. Lvs alt., palmate or pinnate, simple or compound, usually lobed or toothed, sometimes aromatic; petioles often long. Fls arranged in a pseudoumbel; sep. 5; pet. 5, free or 2 or 4, usually clawed, 2 upper pet. usually larger than lower 3; sta. 10. Most from S Afr. with a few from trop. Afr., Aus. and Middle E. All cultivated sp. Zone 10 except *P. endlicherianum*.

P. abrotanifolium (L. f.) Jacq. SOUTHERNWOOD GERANIUM. Erect bushy plant to about 50cm, st. becoming woody, with petiole remains. Lvs aromatic, grey-green, finely divided, to 15×20mm. Fls 1–5, usually white or pink, 15mm diam.; pet. narrow-obovate, upper 2 marked maroon pedicel v. short. Spring–summer. S Afr.

P. acerifolium L'Hérit. = *P. cucullatum*.

P. acetosum (L.) L'Hérit. Somewhat straggling subshrub to 60cm with brittle st. Lvs glaucous with red margins, somewhat fleshy, obovate, toothed, 2–6×1–3cm. Fls 2–7, salmon pink, 4cm diam.; pet. narrow, upper 2 erect marked with darker veins; pedicel short. Spring–summer. S Afr.

P. alchemilloides (L.) L'Hérit. Hairy herb to 30cm. Lvs to 10×12cm often less, with dark circular zone, orbicular, with 5–7 toothed lobes; petiole long. Fls c5, to 2cm diam., sometimes much smaller, white to cream to pink; pet. spathulate, sometimes with darker veins. Spring–summer. E & S Afr. Most plants grown as *P. grandiflorum* should be included here.

Angel Pelargoniums show some resemblance to Regals but rarely exceed 30cm and the fls are single. 'Catford Belle': fls rose-red with darker markings; 'Mrs G.H. Smith': fls off-white with pink markings.

P. angulosum (Mill.) L'Hérit. = *P. cucullatum*.

P. ×*ardens* Lodd. (*P. fulgidum* ×*P. lobatum.*) Similar to *P. schottii* but with lvs less deeply divided and fls smaller, bright but dark red marked, dark purple-brown. Early summer. Gdn origin.

P. australe Willd. Straggling, softly hairy, herbaceous perenn. to 30cm. Lvs faintly aromatic, to 10cm diam., rounded, shallowly 5–7-lobed. Fls 5–10, pale pink to white, almost regular, to 15mm diam.; 2 upper pet. veined deep pink, often emarginate; pedicel short. Spring–summer. SE Aus., Tasm. Plants collected in Tasmania under this name are smaller with dark lvs and red petioles.

P. betulinum (L.) L'Hérit. Erect or sprawling subshrub, woody at base, 30–60cm. Lvs glaucous, usually glab., broadly ovate, toothed, often edged red, to 3×2cm. Fls 3–4, large, to 2.5cm diam., pink or purple, sometimes white; upper pet. veined darker, broadly obovate, lower pet. narrower. Late spring. S Afr.

P. 'Blandfordianum'. Spreading, branching, covered with short hairs. Lvs grey, aromatic, similar in shape to *P. graveolens*. Fls 5–8, white, sometimes tinged pink, to 2cm diam.; 2 upper pet. broadly obovate, rounded to emarginate at apex, marked red. Summer. Gdn origin.

P. burtoniae Bol. = *P. stenopetalum*.

P. capitatum (L.) L'Hérit. ROSE-SCENTED GERANIUM. Decumbent or weakly erect, softly hairy, becoming woody at base with age, to 1m. Lvs rose-scented, velvety with crinkled margin, 3–5-lobed, 2–8cm diam. Fls 10–20, 15–20cm diam., usually mauve-pink; 2 upper pet. marked with darker veins; pedicel 1mm. Spring–summer. S Afr. 'Attar of Roses'; habit more upright; lvs rougher, more strongly scented.

P. carnosum (L.) L'Hérit. To 50cm+; st. short, thick, succulent, branched, bearing remains of persistent petioles. Lvs to 15×5cm, succulent, grey-green, pinnately divided. Infl. branched with 2–8-fld pseudoumbels; pedicels short; fls under 1cm diam., white to pale yellow-green; pet. broadly ovate, 2 upper pet. marked with red veins. Summer–autumn. SW S Afr.

P. ceratophyllum L'Hérit. Similar to *P. carnosum* but much smaller with st. less swollen, lvs more fleshy and infl. less branched. Summer. S Afr.

P. cordatum L'Hérit. = *P. cordifolium*.

P. cordifolium (Cav.) Curtis. Branched, spreading, hairy subshrub, to 1m. Lvs 3–5-lobed, toothed, to 6cm, cordate dull green above, paler and hairy beneath. Infl. branched, leafy, pseudoumbels 4–8-fld; fls to 3cm diam.; 2 upper pet. to 2cm, obovate, purple with darker veins, lower pet. paler, unmarked, linear. Spring–summer. S Afr.

P. coriandrifolium (L.) Jacq. = *P. myrrhifolium* var. *coriandrifolium*.

P. cotyledonis (L.) L'Hérit. About 30cm; st. succulent, with rough bark and persistent stipules. Lvs at apices rounded, 2–5cm diam., glossy above, grey-hairy beneath; petiole to 8cm. Infl. branched, pseudoumbels 5–15-fld; fls regular, to 1cm diam.; pet. rounded, white, unmarked. Late spring–early summer. S Atlantic (St Helena).

P. crassipes Harv. Similar to *P. hirtum* but lvs less finely divided and petiole broad, persistent and reflexed with age; fls less regular, pet. oblong. Spring. Namaqualand.

P. crispum (Bergius) L'Hérit. LEMON GERANIUM. Erect, branched, subshrub, to 70cm. Lvs to 1.5cm, appearing 2-ranked, obscurely 3-lobed to reniform, rough, lemon-scented, coarsely crispate. Fls 1–2, to 2cm diam., usually pink; 2 upper pet. broadly spathulate, marked deep pink, lower pet. narrow. Spring–summer. S Afr. 'Cinnamon': compact; lvs small, crisped, lemon scent with hint of cinnamon. 'Major': lvs larger. 'Minor': habit stiff, upright; lvs v. small, crisped. 'Peach Cream': fls pink, peach scent. 'Prince Rupert: habit upright; lvs ruffled. 'Variegatum': lvs edged with cream.

P. crithmifolium Sm. Differs from *P. carnosum* in lvs more fleshy; fls white and to 1.5cm diam., peduncles and pedicels longer, becoming almost spiny. Spring. Nam.

P. cucullatum (L.) L'Hérit. Erect, hairy subshrub, to 2m+. Lvs to 5cm, rounded to triangular, toothed, sometimes lobed, hooded or cup-shaped, margin red-tinted. Infl. with several 5-fld heads; fls about 3cm diam., bright purple-pink; pet. broad, 2 upper pet. with darker veins. Spring–summer. SW S Afr.

P. denticulatum Jacq. PINE GERANIUM; FERN-LEAF GERANIUM. Erect subshrub to 1.5m. Lvs 6–8cm, balsam-scented, sticky, rough, triangular, deeply bipinnatifid; seg. narrow, toothed. Fls 6, 2cm diam., purple-pink; 2 upper pet. narrow-spathulate, emarginate, veined purple. Spring–summer. S Afr. 'Filicifolium', 'Fernaefolium': lvs even more finely divided and upper 2 pet. v. deeply bifid.

P. dichondrifolium DC. Perenn.; st. short. Lvs crowded, grey-green, aromatic, reniform, crenate; petiole long, persistent. Infl. branched, 2–5-fld; fls white, to 2cm diam.; upper pet.

oblong, marked with red lines. Summer. S Afr.

P. ×*domesticum* L.H. Bail. REGAL PELARGONIUMS. Name given to the hybrid group known as Regals; cultigens of complex ancestry, usually involving *P. grandiflorum*, *P. cucullatum* and others. St. to 45cm, thick, branching. Lvs to 10cm diam., reniform-orbicular to obscurely trilobed, hairy, undulate and coarsely denticulate, or more deeply divided. Fls usually large and showy in erect, long-stalked umbels; pet. white, salmon, pink-purple or red, upper pair with dark veins and blotches. Also known as Martha Washington, Lady Washington or Show pelargoniums. 'Carisbrooke': fls large, pink, marked with maroon, pet. ruffled; 'Grand Slam': fls rose-red with darker markings; 'Pompeii': compact plant, pet. nearly black with v. narrow pink-white margins. 'White Chiffon': fls pure white.

P. echinatum Curtis. CACTUS GERANIUM; SWEETHEART GERANIUM. Subshrub to 50cm; roots tuberous, st. succulent branched covered with spiny stipules. Lvs ovate, lobed, to 6cm diam., grey-green above, tomentose below. Fls 3–8, 15–20mm diam., white with dark red blotches on 2 upper pet. Spring. W S Afr. 'Miss Stapleton': fls bright purple-pink.

P. elongatum (Cav.) Salisb. Straggling, short-lived perenn. with gland. hairs. Lvs to 4cm, with a dark horseshoe-shaped mark, reniform with 5–7 crenate lobes. Fls 1–5, white to cream, 15mm diam.; 2 upper pet. veined red. Spring–late summer. S Afr.

P. endlicherianum Fenzl. Herbaceous rhizomatous perenn. Lvs mostly basal, rounded, lobes 5 shallow, to 6cm diam., hairy. Fls 5–15, bright purple-pink, fragrant; 2 upper pet. recurved, to 3cm, 3 lower pet. minute or 0. Summer. Turk. Z7.

P. erodioides Hook. = *P. australe*.

P. Fragrans group. Erect, much-branched subshrub, 30–40cm. Lvs with spicy scent, grey-green, velvety, cordate-ovate, 3-lobed and blunt-toothed. Infl. often with red-brown branched peduncle, each cluster 4–8-fld; fls to 15mm diam., white; 2 upper pet. erect, with red lines. Spring–summer. S Afr. 'Cody's Fragrans': similar to 'Old Spice' but with less crinkled lvs. 'Fragrans Variegatum': lvs edged with creamy yellow becoming almost green as they mature. 'Old Spice': compact form with grey-green crinkle-edged lvs. 'Snowy Nutmeg': habit low; lvs small, centre largely grey, broadly margined cream. 'Variegatum': lvs edged with creamy yellow, becoming almost green as they mature.

P. fulgidum (L.) L'Hérit. Scrambling to about 70cm; st. succulent becoming woody. Lvs pinnate or pinnatifid, to 10cm, oblong, silvery. Infl. branched with 4–9-fld pseudoumbels; fls scarlet, to 2cm diam. Spring–early summer. S Afr.

P. gibbosum (L.) L'Hérit. GOUTY GERANIUM; KNOTTED GERANIUM. Scrambling, few-branched; st. succulent to woody; nodes swollen. Lvs glaucous, slightly fleshy, pinnate to 12cm. Infl. 5–15-fld; fls to 2cm diam., green-yellow, scented at night, pet. obovate, reflexed. Summer. S Afr.

P. glutinosum (Jacq.) L'Hérit. PHEASANT'S FOOT GERANIUM. Erect, branching subshrub to 1.5m. Lvs balsam-scented, viscid, usually about 5×5.5cm, ± triangular, deeply lobed, toothed, glossy. Fls 1–8, pale to dark pink, 15mm diam. Spring. S S Afr.

P. grandiflorum (Andrews) Willd. Erect to decumbent, glab., woody below. Lvs palmately lobed ×5–7, toothed, to 8cm diam., glaucous, often with dark zone. Fls 2–3, cream to pink, large, to 4cm diam.; 2 upper pet. veined and sometimes blotched purple. Spring–summer. S Afr.

P. graveolens L'Hérit. ROSE GERANIUM; SWEET-SCENTED GERANIUM. Erect, downy subshrub, to 120cm. Lvs rose-scented, grey-green, to 4×6cm, triangular, bipinnatifid. Fls 5, white to v. pale pink, 15mm diam.; uppper pet. narrow-obovate, veined purple. Spring–summer. S & NE S Afr. The above is the plant found wild in S Afr. L'Héritier's original description represents a possible hybrid with rough lvs and small, pale pink fls. Many cvs assigned to this sp. may in fact be derived from *P. capitatum* and *P. radens*. 'Lady Plymouth': lvs margined with cream. 'Little Pet': habit compact; fls rose pink. 'Mint Rose': lvs edged pure white; peppermint scent. 'Radula': similar to *P. radens* but with less finely divided lvs and a less pungent scent. 'Red Flowered Rose': habit dwarf; lvs fingered; fls bright scarlet. 'Rober's Lemon Rose': habit vigorous; lvs soft grey-green, irregularly pinnate, lemon to rose scented; fls small, pink.

P. grossularioides (L.) L'Hérit. Spreading to weakly erect, ± glab., short-lived; st. red, internodes long. Lvs aromatic, rounded, lobed and toothed, to 4×5cm; petiole long. Infl. dense; fls deep magenta, about 8mm diam.; 2 upper pet. marked with darker blotches. Spring–summer. S & SE Afr.

P. heracleifolium Lodd. = *P. lobatum*.

P. hirtum (Burm. f.) Jacq. Low-growing subshrub with short, thick st., petiole remains persistent. Lvs hairy, finely divided, carrot-like, aromatic, to 5m. Infl. thin, leafy, branched, pseudoumbels 2–6-fld; fls bright pink, to 1.5cm diam.; pet. rounded. Late winter–spring. S Afr.

P. hispidum (L.) Willd. Erect subshrub to, 2m+, hispid, bristly. Lvs aromatic, deeply palmately lobed and toothed, to 9×10cm. Infl. leafy, with many 6–12-fld br.; fls to 15mm diam., pink; 2 upper pet. obovate, marked dark red, reflexed, lower pet. narrow, much smaller. Spring–summer. S S Afr.

P. ×hortorum L.H. Bail. GERANIUM; BEDDING GERANIUM; ZONAL PELARGONIUM. Complex group of hybrids resulting from *P. inquinans* ×*P. zonale*. St. succulent, glabrescent to 60cm; lvs orbicular to reniform to 10cm diam., sometimes basally cordate, undulate, crenate or sinuate, variegated or marked with dark, horseshoe-shaped zone. Cactus-fld pelargoniums have furled or quilled pet. Irenes, of American origin, are fast-growing, free-flowering and strong, with large flowerheads which may be used as cut fls. Stellar pelargoniums are small plants which have star-shaped, often zoned lvs. The upper pet. of the fls are forked. Startel pelargoniums, an F1 selection, are similar to the older Stellar range, with pointed, tinted pet. and comparable foliage. Miniature pelargoniums do not exceed 13cm in height but are v. free-flowering and dwarf pelargoniums are 13–20cm. Rosebud pelargoniums have fls with numerous small pet. which are so tightly arranged that they look like half-opened roses.

'A.M. Mayne' (double): fls magenta flushed scarlet in centre; 'Appleblossom Rosebud' (rosebud): pet. white-edged pink with pale green centre; 'Caroline Schmidt' (coloured lf): lvs with silver sheen, fls double, bright red; 'Dolly Vardon' (coloured lf): lvs tricoloured, edged white, rose red and green, fls single, red; 'Fantasia' (dwarf): fls double, white; 'Gustav Emich' (semi-double): fls scarlet; 'Irene': the original Irene type with bright red semi-double fls; 'Miss Burdett-Coutts' (coloured lf): lvs with carmine splashes, fls small, single vermilion; 'Mr Henry Cox' (coloured lf): lvs variable with shades of green over red with yellow border, fls small, single, rose-pink; 'Mrs Pollock' (coloured lf): lvs with green and dark red zones and yellow margin, fls small, single, vermilion; 'Mr Wren' (single): pet. orange-red, edged white; 'Mrs Quilter' (coloured lf): lf with bronze zone, fls single, pink; 'Party Dress' (Irene): fls pale rose-pink; 'Paul Crampel' (single): fls scarlet; 'Red Rambler' (rosebud): fls bright red; 'Santa Maria' (semi-double): fls salmon pink; 'Silver Kewense' (miniature): lf edged white, fls single, red with narrow pet.; 'Spitfire' (cactus): fls scarlet, lvs variegated cream; 'Stellar White' (stellar): fls single, white; 'Stellar Grenadier' (stellar): fls double, crimson; 'Stellar Snowflake' (stellar): fls double, white; 'Tangerine' (cactus): fls double orange; 'Verona' (coloured lf): lvs sage gold, fls small, single, pink.

P. incrassatum (Andrews) Sims Tuberous herb. Lvs basal, narrowly ovate, 3–6cm, deeply pinnatifid, silver-pilose to canescent. Pseudoumbel, 20–40-fld, st. to 30cm; fls bright magenta, 2 upper pet. spathulate, to 20mm, 3 lower pet. much smaller. Spring. S Afr.

P. inquinans (L.) L'Hérit. Erect, branching, velutinous subshrub, to 2m. Lvs suborbicular, to 8cm diam., lobes 5–7 dentate. Fls 10–30, usually bright scarlet; pet. rounded, to 20mm. Spring–autumn. S Afr.

P. ×kewense R.A. Dyer. (Probably *P. zonale* ×*P. inquinans*.) Similar to *P. ×salmoneum* but lvs larger and greener, not thick, sometimes with dark circular zone when young. Fls to 27, bright crimson-red with narrowly spathulate pet. Late spring–early autumn. Gdn origin.

P. ×limoneum Sweet = *P.* 'Lady Mary'.

P. lobatum (Burm. f.) L'Hérit. Tuberous herb. Lvs ± basal, softly hairy, to 30cm diam., 3- or more lobed. Infl. branched, clusters 5–20-fld; fls scented at night, 2cm diam.; pet. rounded, dark purple with yellow-green margin. Spring. S Afr.

P. malvifolium Jacq. = *P. alchemilloides*.

P. myrrhifolium (L.) L'Hérit. Erect, hairy subshrub, to 30cm. Lvs to 5cm, oblong, pinnatifid or bipinnatifid. Infl. leafy, branched; fls 2–6, white to pink; 2 upper pet. spathulate, veined deep red, to 15mm. Spring–summer. S Afr. var. *coriandrifolium* (L.) Harv. Sometimes decumbent. Lvs more finely divided. Fls larger. Spring–summer. S Afr.

P. odoratissimum (L.) L'Hérit. APPLE GERANIUM. Low-growing perenn.; flowering st. trailing. Lvs light green, apple-scented, rounded, to 4cm diam., base cordate, crenate. Infl. branched, each cluster 3–10-fld; fls to 12mm diam., white; 2 upper pet. oblong with red veins. Spring–summer. S Afr.

P. panduriforme Ecklon & Zeyh. Erect subshrub to 1.5m. balsam-scented, sometimes viscid, with long hairs. Lvs 3–5cm, grey-green, panduriform, pinnate with rounded lobes. Infl. 2–20-fld; fls 3cm diam., pale purple-pink; 2 upper pet. spathulate to 35mm, erect, marked deep purple. Spring–summer. S S Afr.

P. papilionaceum (L.) L'Hérit. Erect, hairy subshrub to 2m+, foetid. Lvs to 7×10cm, almost rounded, 3–5-lobed. Infl. with many 5–10-fld br.; fls to 2cm diam., light to dark pink; 2 upper pet. 2cm, with purple blotch and white basal area, obovate, low-

er pet. v. narrow, pale. Spring–summer. S S Afr.

P. peltatum (L.) L'Hérit. IVY GERANIUM; HANGING GERANIUM. Trailing or climbing. Lvs peltate, ± fleshy, bright green often with a darker circular zone, 3–7cm diam., lobes 5 triangular. Fls 2–9, to 4cmdiam., pale purple to pink; 2 upper pet. obovate, to 25mm, with darker veins. Spring–summer. S Afr. Plants known as *P. lateripes* have non-peltate lvs but should be assigned to *P. peltatum*. 'Saxifragoides': prostrate, glab.; lvs fleshy, to 2cm diam., with 3–5 acute lobes, dark green. Fls 2–5, 8–9mm diam., pink or white; 2 upper pet. reflexed with darker veins; spring–summer; origin unknown. 'Crocodile': lvs cream-veined, fls single, rose-pink; 'Galilee': fls rose-pink, double; 'La France': fls semi-double, mauve veined white and purple; 'L'Elégante': off-white and green lvs shaded with pink when grown in light, fairly dry conditions, fls single, white, veined purple; 'Pink Gay Baby': miniature with pink single fls; 'Rouletta': semi-double white fls striped red.

P. pinnatum (L.) L'Hérit. Tuberous herb to 25cm. Lvs to 30cm, slender, basal, erect, villous, pinnate; pinnae elliptic, to 2cm, in alt. whorls. Fls to 3cm diam., delicate; upper pet. buff, veined rose and violet, apically blotched violet, lower pet. bronze suffused pink. Winter. S Afr.

P. populifolium Ecklon & Zeyh. = *P. ribifolium*.

P. quercifolium (L.) L'Hérit. OAK-LEAVED GERANIUM; ALMOND GERANIUM; VILLAGE OAK GERANIUM. Erect, viscid subshrub to 1.5m, scented of balsam. Lvs rough with long gland. hairs, triangular, deeply pinnately or palmately divided, seg. divided and toothed. Fls 2–6, 15mm diam., purple pink, 2 upper pet. emarginate, erect to reflexed, marked darker pink. Spring–summer. S S Afr. 'Fair Ellen': low growing plant; lvs smaller more deeply cut but with more rounded lobes and a dark mark along midrib; fls pink; upper pet. toothed. 'Royal Oak': habit shrubby; lvs with rounded lobes, dark green with dark purple-brown blotch; fls purple pink with darker spots on upper pet. 'Giant Oak': lvs lobed, v. large.

P. quinquelobatum A. Rich. Straggling to prostrate, hairy, herbaceous plant. Lvs deeply 3–5-lobed term. lobe longer, to 10×8cm, dull green. Fls 5, pale yellow-green to grey-blue-green, to 15mm diam.; upper pet. veined pink. Summer. E Afr.

P. radens H.E. Moore. Somewhat similar to *P. graveolens*. Lvs rough, with strong scent, seg. strongly recurved. Fls 5, 15mm diam., pale or purple-pink. Spring–summer. S Afr. 'Dr. Livingstone': habit tall, bushy; lvs deeply cut and lobed; lemon fragrance.

P. relinquifolium N.E. Br. = *P. dichondrifolium*.

P. reniforme Curtis. Erect tuberous subshrub, becoming woody below, to 1m. Lvs reniform, to 3cm diam., grey-green velvety above, silvery grey beneath. Infl. branched, leafy; fls 1–2cm diam., deep magenta or deep pink; 2 upper pet. narrow-oblong, marked deep purple. Spring–summer. S Afr.

P. ribifolium Jacq. Similar to *P. scabrum* with rough aromatic lvs, but lvs with cordate base and rounded lobes. Fls white, upper pet. veined red; spur with conspicuous nectar gland. Spring. S Afr.

P. roseum (Andrews) DC. = *P. incrassatum*.

P. ×salmoneum R.A. Dyer. Erect subshrub, to 1m. Lvs thick, fleshy, green to glaucous, ± rounded, lobes 5 shallow-toothed, to 5cm diam. Fls 4–14, salmon pink, to 4cm diam.; pet. obovate, 2 upper pet. veined deeper red. Spring–summer.

P. scabrum (Burm. f.) L'Hérit. Erect subshrub to 1m, lemon-scented, with rough hairs. Lvs rough, rhomboidal, about 4×4cm, lobes 3, acute, toothed, sometimes narrow. Fls 6, white to pink to purple-pink, 15mm diam.; 2 upper pet. spathulate, veined deeper purple. Early spring–summer. W & SW S Afr. 'M. Ninon': lvs dark, glossy; fls deep rose-pink; apricot scent.

P. scandens hort. non Ehrh. V. similar to *P. ×kewense* but lvs with distinct narrow, dark circular zone one-third from the outer margin. Late spring to autumn.

Scented-leaved Pelargoniums. 'Attar of Roses': lvs strongly scented of roses; 'Chocolate Peppermint': lvs large, lobed with central brown blotch, somewhat scented of peppermint; fls small, pink; 'Clorinda': strong-growing with large, pungent, rose-scented, lobed lvs and large rose-pink fls; 'Joy Lucille': grey-green, deeply cut, peppermint-scented lvs and white fls; 'Mabel Grey': robust, tall-growing, with rough, serrate, strongly lemon-scented lvs with pale purple fls; 'Lady Mary': a probable hybrid involving *P. crispum*. Lvs to 5-lobed, toothed, not undulate, coarse, strongly scented of lemons. Upper pair of pet. clear lilac, tinted mauve, veined and centrally marked darker purple, lower pet. unmarked; 'Peach Cream': habit similar to *P. crispum*; lvs splashed cream, peach-scented; fls pink; 'Prince of Orange' (derived from *P. crispum*): erect with orange-scented, light green lvs and large mauve fls; 'The Boar': scrambling plant with rounded lvs and with dark brown central blotch; fls pale salmon pink. 'Viscosissimum': similar to *P. glutinosum* with v. sticky, balsam-scented lvs sometimes with a darker streak along midrib; fls pink-purple.

P. × schottii Hook. f. (*P. fulgidum × P. lobatum.*) Subshrub st. thick to 30cm. Many lvs basal, hairy, oblong, irregularly pinnately divided, toothed. Fls 6–8 to 2cm diam., v. dark crimson with distinct black blotches on pet. Early summer. Gdn origin.

P. 'Splendide'. (Probably *P. tricolor × P. ovale.*) Often incorrectly grown as *P. tricolor* var. *arboreum* or *P. violaceum.* St. short, erect, woody, clusters of grey-green, hairy, ovate, toothed lvs. Infl. branched with several 2–3-fld clusters; fls to 3cm diam.; 2 upper pet. rounded, dark red with base almost black, lower pet. white.

P. stenopetalum Ehrh. Similar to *P. zonale* but lvs only sometimes faintly zoned. Infl. to 10-fld; fls with v. narrow red pet. Spring and summer. S Afr. (Natal).

P. tabulare (L.) L'Hérit. = *P. elongatum.*

P. terebinthaceum (Cav.) Desf. = *P. graveolens.*

P. tetragonum (L.) L'Hérit. SQUARE-STACK CRANESBILL. Succulent erect to sprawling; st. long, 3–4-sided. Lvs few, hairy, cordate, to 4cm diam. Fls 2, large, cream to pale pink; 2 upper pet. spathulate, to 40mm, with red lines, 2 lower pet. much smaller. Spring. S S Afr.

P. tomentosum Jacq. Low-growing, wide-spreading, to 50cm, peppermint-scented. Lvs velvety, 4–6×5–7cm, palmate, lobes 3–5 rounded, base cordate. Infl. with several 5–15-fld br.; fls 15mm diam., white; upper pet. obovate, marked purple, lower pet. narrow longer. Spring–summer. S Afr. 'Variegatum': habit compact; lvs emerald edged with cream.

P. tongaense Vorster. Semi-erect to decumbent perenn. Lvs 4–7cm diam., thick, hairy, ivy-shaped, lobes 3–5 triangular; petioles long. Infl. 3–10-fld; fls 25mm diam., bright scarlet; pet. ovate rounded. Summer. NE Natal.

P. trilobatum Ecklon & Zeyh. = *P. ribifolium.*

P. triste (L.) L'Hérit. Tuberous herb. St. v. short. Lvs ± basal, long-stalked to 45cm, finely 2–3-pinnate or pinnatifid, hairy. Infl. 5–20-fld; fls to 1.5cm diam., scented; pet. obovate, brown-purple with a dull yellow margin. Spring–early summer. S Afr.

Unique Pelargoniums. Mostly crosses involving *P. fulgidum*, vigorous plants, woody at base, often with scented lvs and larger fls than those of the sp. 'Aurore's Unique': lvs grey-green, hairy, fls bright red with v. dark blotches and veins; 'Madam Nonin': fl. pet. twisted to give the impression of a double fl., red with paler edges; 'Rollinson's Unique': lvs lobed, aromatic, fls magenta in a rather tight head; 'White Unique': bushy plants with white fls marked with purple-pink.

P. vitifolium (L.) L'Hérit. V. similar to *P. capitatum*, strongly aromatic but more erect, to 1m; lvs less hairy and somewhat rough; fls 5–10, to 15mm diam., often paler pink. Spring–summer. S Afr.

P. zonale (L.) L'Hérit. Erect or scrambling subshrub to 1m. Lvs ± orbicular, 5–8cm diam., lobed, crenate, often with a darker horseshoe-zone. Fls to 50, to 3cm diam., pale pink, sometimes red or white; pet. narrow, 2 upper pet. erect, with darker veins, lower 3 pet. spreading. Spring–autumn. S Afr.

Pelecyphora Ehrenb. Cactaceae. 2 simple or clustering cacti. St. globose or obconic tubercled. Spiny part of areole abaxial, woolly flowering part adaxial, parts connected by a narrow groove or corky ridge. Fls subapical, shortly funnelform or campanulate; tube naked; perianth purple-pink. NE Mex.

P. aselliformis Ehrenb. Simple or clustering; individual st. globose or obconic, 5cm diam.; tubercles hatchet-shaped, c5mm high. Summer. EC Mex. Z9.

P. pectinata Stein = *Mammillaria pectinifera.*

P. pseudopectinata Backeb. = *Neolloydia pseudopectinata.*

P. strobiliformis (Werderm.) Frič & Schelle ex Kreuzinger. Usually simple; st. depressed-globose to globose or ovoid, to 6cm diam., tubercles overlapping, scale-like. Summer. NE Mex. Z9.

P. valdeziana H. Möller = *Neolloydia valdeziana.*

→*Ariocarpus.*

Pelican Flower *Aristolochia grandiflora.*
Pelican's Beak *Lotus berthelotii.*

Peliosanthes Andrews. Liliaceae (Convallariaceae). 1 perenn. rhizomatous herb. Lvs along rhiz. and in a term. tuft, 10–50×1–12cm, linear to obovate; petioles 4–50cm. Rhiz. scapose, 35(–75)cm; fls 1–6 per scale-like bract; perianth lobes 6, to 8mm, erect or spreading, basally united into a tube; stames 6; capsule trilocular; seeds blue. E Himal. to SE Asia, China, Taiwan. Z9.

P. albida Bak. = *P. teta* ssp. *humilis.*

P. humilis Andrews = *P. teta* ssp. *humilis.*

P. teta Andrews. ssp. *teta.* Fls 2–6 per bract, usually green, rarely blue. ssp. *humilis* (Andrews) Jessop. Fls 1 per bract, often

white, blue, violet or purple.

P. violacea Bak. = *P. teta* ssp. *humilis.*

Pellaea Link. Adiantaceae. 80 ferns. Rhiz. creeping or abbreviated; stipes black. Fronds pinnate to variously compound. Trop. and warm temp. regions.

P. andromedifolia (Kaulf.) Fée. COFFEE FERN. Rhiz. long-creeping; stipes stramineous, glaucous. Fronds 15–70×5–20cm, tripinnate, pinnules remote, oblong, obtuse, sterile, fertile revolute. Calif. and Baja Calif. Z9.

P. atropurpurea (L.) Link. PURPLE ROCK BRAKE. Rhiz. v. short; stipes to 10–22cm, scaly. Fronds 10–25×4–10cm, tufted, narrowly ovate-triangular to oblong or oblong-lanceolate, bipinnate, pinnules to 1.5cm, ovate to elliptic-lanceolate, auriculate at base, attenuate at tip, often glaucous-rusty-red; when young, coriaceous; rachis hard, dark, glossy. N Amer. Z4.

P. atropurpurea var. *simplex* (Butters) Morton = *P. glabella.*

P. brachyptera (Moore) Bak. Rhiz. elongate; stipes castaneous, glaucous, glab. Fronds to 40cm, linear, bipinnate or tripinnate, grey-green, pinnules 5–13, linear, revolute, crenate, subcoriaceous. S Oreg., N Calif. Z8.

P. breweri D.C. Eaton. Rhiz. short-creeping; stipes bright glossy brown, corrugate. Fronds 5–20×1.5–3.5cm, pinnate, linear-oblong, pinnae in 6–12 pairs, mostly 2-lobed; seg. linear-ovate to deltoid. W US. Z4.

P. bridgesii Hook. Rhiz. short-creeping; stipes dark, glossy chestnut. Fronds to 35cm, closely tufted, linear to linear-oblong, pinnate, grey-green, coriaceous, pinnae, pinnae ovate to cordate-oblong suborbicular; generally conduplicate; revolute. Oreg. and Idaho to Calif. Z4.

P. calomelanos Link. HARD FERN. Rhiz. tufted, hirsute; stipes 7–10cm, stout, below. Fronds 15–20×7–10cm, deltoid, 2–3-pinnate, pinnae deltoid, pinnules 4–12mm, stalked, cordate, ovate-deltoid, hastate, or pinnate, rounded, thick, glaucous, rachis wiry, shiny, black. Afr., India, China. Z9.

P. falcata (R. Br.) Fée. SICKLE FERN. Rhiz. creeping, stout; stipes 5–15cm, stout, wiry, dark brown, with dark brown scales when young. Fronds 30–40×4–7cm, dull dark green above, chaffy beneath, pinnae 2–5cm, shortly stalked, lanceolate-oblong, apiculate. India to Australasia. Z10.

P. glabella Mett. Rhiz. stout, ascending; stipes dark castaneous, mostly glab. Fronds to 20cm, tufted, oblong to lanceolate, pinnate, occas. bipinnate, blue-green, coriaceous, seg. oblong-lanceolate, 3–5-lobed, often auricled, apex obtuse to submucronate. N Amer. Z3.

P. hastata (Thunb.) Prantl = *P. calomelanos.*

P. intramarginalis (Kaulf.) J. Sm. Stipes 8–15cm, tufted, erect, darkly castaneous. Fronds 15–30cm, broadly ovate-lanceolate, tripinnatifid, pinnate 5–8cm, lanceolate, cut to rachis, pinnules linear-oblong. Mex. to Costa Rica. Z10.

P. mucronata (D.C. Eaton) D.C. Eaton. BIRD'S FOOT FERN. Rhiz. thick, woody; stipes 5–20cm, dull purple-brown. Fronds 10–30cm, 2–3-pinnate, stiff, pinnae distant, pinnules generally ternate, seg. linear-oblong to elliptic, revolute, glaucous, wrinkled. Calif. and Baja Calif. Z9.

P. occidentalis (Nels.) Rydb. = *P. glabella.*

P. ornithopus Hook. = *P. mucronata.*

P. ovata (Desv.) Weatherby. Rhiz. short-creeping; stipes 10–35cm, red tinged grey or darkly stramineous. Fronds 15–70cm, entangled, oblong, bipinnate to tripinnate, bright green, subcoriaceous, pinnae alt., seg. 1–2.5cm, triangular-ovate to suborbicular, obtuse to truncate at apex. Mex. to Peru. Z10.

P. paradoxa (R. Br.) Hook. Rhiz. medium- to long-creeping, generally buried; stipes to 15cm, dark brown. Fronds 15–20cm, broadly ovate, pinnae 4–10cm, lanceolate, attenuate at apex, deep green; rachis dark, glossy. E Aus. Z10.

P. rotundifolia (Forst. f.) Hook. Rhiz. creeping, stout; stipes 5–15cm, stout, rusty-scaly. Fronds 15–30cm, narrowly oblong, dull dark green above, coriaceous, glab., pinnae 1–2cm, narrowly oblong to suborbicular, apiculate, shortly stalked or sessile, minutely crenate. NZ, Aus. Z10.

P. sagittata (Cav.) Link. Rhiz. short-creeping, stout; stipes shorter than lamina, pale stramineous. Fronds ovate-oblong to triangular-ovate, pinnate to tripinnate, subcoriaceous, pinnae to 5.5cm, shortly stalked; pinnules ovate-triangular to sagitate, deeply cordate to sagittate at base, rounded to obtuse at apex. Mex. to Guat.; Colomb. to Boliv. var. *cordata* (Cav.) A. Tyron. Seg. rotundate-cordate. Tex., Mex. Z10.

P. suksdorfiana Butters = *P. glabella.*

P. ternifolia (Cav.) Link. Rhiz. v. short-creeping; stipes 7–22cm, dark brown to black. Fronds 15–45cm, linear, pinnate to pinnatisect below at least, stiffly erect, pinnae ternately divided, each seg. 2–3cm or entire. C & S Amer., to Arg. and N Chile. Z10.

P. viridis (Forssk.) Prantl. GREEN CLIFF BRAKE. Rhiz. short, shallowly creeping; stipes to 35cm. Fronds to 65cm+, almost as broad as long, broadly lanceolate to triangular, bipinnate or tripinnate, pinnules lanceolate to triangular or oblong, sometimes deeply lacerate, bright green, softly herbaceous to coriaceous. Afr., particularly S and adjacent islands. Z10.

P. wrightiana Hook. Rhiz. short-creeping; stipes 7–22cm, brown tinged purple. Fronds 15–45cm, narrowly triangular or linear, bipinnate, stiffly erect, pinnae to 2cm, lobed or divded. N Amer. Z6.
→*Allosurus*.

Pellionia Gaudich. Urticaceae. 50 herbs or subshrubs; st. sometimes succulent. Lvs alt., 2-ranked, subsessile, entire or dentate. Trop. & subtrop. Asia, from India to Jap. Z10.

P. daveauana (Carr.) N.E. Br. = *P. repens*.

P. pulchra N.E. Br. RAINBOW VINE. Low spreading to creeping herb; st. fleshy, tinged purple. Lvs 2–5cm, obliquely oblong to elliptic, marked dull black-green along midrib and veins above, purple beneath. Summer. Vietnam.

P. repens (Lour.) Merrill. TRAILING WATERMELON BEGONIA. Creeping herb to 60cm; st. succulent, tinged pink. Lvs 1–6cm, oblong to orbicular, scalloped, bronze-green above, tinged violet with a broad central band of pale grey-green, tinged pink beneath, purple-edged. Summer. SE Asia. 'Argentea': lvs silverwhite marked pale green.
→*Elatostema*.

Peltandra Raf. ARROW ARUM. Araceae. 3 aquatic rhizomatous perenn. herbs. Lvs sagittate or hastate; petioles long. Peduncle equalling or exceeding petioles; spathe margins overlapping below, open above, undulate; spadix shorter than spathe; sometimes with short appendix. Fr. a berry. N Amer.

P. alba Raf. = *P. sagittifolia*.

P. sagittifolia (Michx.) Morong. WHITE ARROW ARUM. Lvs to 15cm, sagittate to hastate; petioles to 50cm. Peduncle erect in fr.; spathe to 10cm, limb white, opening widely. Berries red. Early summer. SE US. Z7.

P. virginica (L.) Kunth. GREEN ARROW ARUM. Lvs to 90cm, hastate; petioles to 45cm. Peduncle recurved in fr.; spathe to 20cm, limb green edged white or yellow narrowly open; short spadix appendix sometimes present. Berries green. Early summer. E & SE US. Z5.

Peltapteris Link. Lomariopsidaceae. 4 small epiphytic ferns. Rhiz. wide-creeping, slender. Fronds erect, distant; sterile fronds flabellate, ± finely dissected, divisions dichotomous; fertile blades simple, orbicular, cordate, dentate or lobed. W Indies, C & S Amer. Z10.

P. peltata (Sw.) Morton. Rhiz. filiform, interlacing. Sterile fronds to 15cm, reniform, 4–6× dichotomously divided, 2.5–5cm broad, stipes longer than blades; fertile fronds with blades 5–20mm broad, erose-dentate, translucent; stipes longer. Trop. Amer.
→*Acrostichum* and *Elaphoglossum*.

Peltaria Jacq. Cruciferae. 7 glab. perenn. herbs. Lvs mostly basal, entire. Infl. corymbose; pet. 4, white, short-clawed. Spring–summer. E Medit. to Iran and C Asia. Z6.

P. alliacea Jacq. 20–60cm. Lvs peltate, smelling strongly of garlic when crushed, st. lvs ovate-lanceolate, cordate, sessile. Pet. 3.5–4.5mm, round-ovate. E Eur.

P. turkmena Lipsky. 50–70cm. Lvs oblong-ovate, entire to remotely toothed; petiole long; st. lvs short-petioled to sessile; pet. 6mm. C Asia.

Peltiphyllum (Engl.) Engl.

P. peltatum (Torr. ex Benth.) Engl. = *Darmera peltata*.

Peltoboykinia (Engl.) H. Hara. Saxifragaceae. 2 rhizomatous perenn. herbs to 85cm. Basal lvs peltate, lobed with long petioles, reduced, and sessile higher up st., toothed. Fls in term. cymes, 5-merous, cal. campanulate, lobes 3–6mm; pet. short-clawed, cream to pale yellow with gland. hairs, short-lived 2–3× longer than cal. lobes, sta. 10. S Jap. (mts). Z7.

P. tellimoides (Maxim.) H. Hara. Basal lvs 15–30×10–30cm, orbicular to cordate, to 13-lobed, finely dentate; petiole 20–45cm. Early summer. Jap.

P. watanabei (Yatabe) H. Hara. Differs from *P. tellimoides* in lvs to 10cm wider and longer, to 10-lobed, acutely dentate. Jap.
→*Boykinia* and *Saxifraga*.

Peltophorum (Vogel) Benth. Leguminosae (Caesalpinioideae). Some 15 everg. trees. Lvs bipinnate. Fls fragrant, yellow, in subterminal axill. rac. or term. compound rac.; cor. seg. 5, clawed, spreading, silken, frilled; sta. 10; fil. orange. Pantrop.

P. africanum Sonder. Petiole to 20cm; pinnae 4–10 pairs; lfts to 8×3.5mm, 10–20 pairs, elliptic-oblong, mucronate, pubesc. Rac. to 11cm; cor. to 2.5cm diam. Summer. S Afr.

P. brasiliense (L.) Urban = *Caesalpinia brasiliense*.

P. dubium (Spreng.) Taub. Petiole to 40cm, persistently rufous-tomentulose, usually gland.; pinnae 15–25 pairs; lfts to 11×4.5mm, 10–25 pairs, short-oblong. Rac. to 30cm; cor. to 3.5cm diam. Spring–summer. S Amer.

P. ferrugineum (Decne.) Benth. = *P. pterocarpum*.

P. linnaei Benth. = *Caesalpinia violacea*.

P. pterocarpum (DC.) K. Heyne YELLOW FLAMBOYANT. Crown umbrella-shaped. Petiole to 40cm, rusty-tomentulose, rarely gland.; pinnae 7–15 pairs; lfts to 20×10mm, 8–20 pairs, elliptic-oblong, rounded or emarginate. Rac. to 20cm; cor. to 4cm diam. Summer. Trop. Asia.

Peluskins *Pisum sativum* var. *arvense*.
Penang Sloe *Kopsia flavida*.
Pench Tree *Euphorbia tirucalli*.
Pencil Cedar *Juniperus virginiana*; *Polyscias murrayi*.
Pendent Silver Lime, Pendent White Lime *Tilia* 'Petiolaris'.
Pendulous Sedge *Carex pendula*.

Peniocereus (A. Berger) Britt. & Rose. Cactaceae. 20 prostrate or scandent shrubs; roots massive, thickened; st. slender, ribbed, sparingly-branched; spines conspicuous, or adpressed and short. Floral tube long and slender; floral areoles with bristles or spines. C Amer. to NW Mex. and SW US.

P. diguetii (F.A.C. Weber) Backeb. = *P. striatus*.

P. greggii (Engelm.) Britt. & Rose. St. 30–60×1–2cm, dark grey-brown, papillose-downy; ribs 3–6, deep; spines to 3mm. Fl to 20cm, white. C N & NW Mex., SW US. Z9.

P. johnstonii Britt. & Rose. St. 1 or more, unbranched, to 3m, 5–15mm diam.; ribs 3–5; spines 1.5–9mm. Fl. 15cm; tep. white, tinged pink outside. Baja Calif. Z9.

P. maculatus (Weingart) Cutak. Shrub to 3m or more, sparsely branched; setms seg. c50×3cm, olive-green, tinged purple, with small white spots; ribs 3–4; spines 1–3mm. Fls to 10cm, creamy white; outer tep. tinged purple red. Spring–summer. Mex. Z9.

P. serpentinus (Lagasca & Rodriguez) N.P. Tayl. St. 2–3m×3–5cm, green; ribs 10–17; spines to 30mm. Fl. 15–20cm, white, tinged red outside. Summer. Mex., widely cult. Z9.

P. striatus (Brandg.) F. Buxb. St. to 1m×5–8mm, grey or blue-green; ribs 6–9; spines to 3mm. Fl. 7.5–15cm, white to pink or purple-tinged. NW Mex., S Ariz. Z9.

P. tomentosa Bravo = *P. viperinus*.

P. viperinus (F.A.C. Weber) Klusac ex Kreuzinger. St. to 3m×1–1.5cm, dark grey-brown, papillose-downy; ribs 8–10, v. low; spines to 5mm. Fl. 3–9cm, bright pink to red. Summer. S Mex. Perhaps preferable here is *Wilcoxia papillosa* Britt. & Rose. Z9.
→*Cereus, Neoevansia, Nyctocereus* and *Wilcoxia*.

Pennisetum Rich. ex Pers. Gramineae. c80 rhizomatous or stoloniferous ann. or perenn. grasses. Lvs flat; ligule ciliate. Infl. term. to axillary, spicate, cylindric to globose; spikelets to 4 per cluster, lanceolate to oblong, sessile to short-stipitate, 2-fld, enclosed by a bristly involucre. Trop., subtrop., warm temp.

P. alopecuroides (L.) Spreng. CHINESE PENNISETUM; SWAMP FOX-TAIL GRASS; FOUNTAIN GRASS. Perenn., to 1.5m. St. clumped, slender, upright. Lvs to 60cm×1.2cm, glab., scabrous. Infl. cylindric to narrow-oblong, to 20×5cm, yellow-green to dark purple; spikelets 1–2, to 8mm. Summer–autumn. E Asia to W Aus. 'Burgundy Giant': to 1.2m; lvs broad, bronze tinted claret. 'Hameln': dwarf, to 50cm; lvs golden in autumn; fls white tinted green. 'Herbstzanber': small, to 50cm; early flowering. 'Moudry': low; lvs wide, dark green, shiny; fl. heads dark purple to black. 'Weserbergland': somewhat dwarf. 'Woodside': robust; inch. dark purple; early flowering. var. *purpurascens* (Thunb.) Ohwi. CHIKARA-SHIBA. Spikelet bristles dark purple. var. *viridescens* (Miq.) Ohwi. Spikelet bristles pale green. Z7.

P. americanum (L.) Schum. = *P. glaucum*.

P. asperifolium (Desf.) Kunth = *P. setaceum*.

P. atrosanguineum hort. = *P. setaceum*.

P. caudatum hort. = *P. alopecuroides*.

P. cenchroides hort. non Rich. = *Cenchrus ciliaris*.

P. ciliare (L.) Link = *Cenchrus ciliaris*.

P. compressum R. Br. = *P. alopecuroides*.

P. cupreum A. Hitchc. ex L.H. Bail. = *P. setaceum*.

P. japonicum Trin. = *P. alopecuroides*.

P. latifolium Spreng. URUGUAY PENNISETUM. Perenn., to 270cm. St. robust, erect, branched above. Lvs to 75×5cm, scabrous. Infl. compact, pendent, to 9cm×1.8cm, pedicels threadlike; spikelets 1, to 5mm. Summer–autumn. Braz., Peru, Arg. Z9.

P. longistylum Vilm. non Hochst. = *P. villosum*.

P. macrostachyum (Brongn.) Trin. Resembles *P. setaceum* but lvs to 2.5cm wide, infl. more compact, tinged purple-brown; bristles not plumed.

P. macrostachyum Freis. non (Brongn.) Trin. = *P. setaceum*.

P. macrourum Trin. Perenn., to 180cm. St. flimsy to robust, erect, clumped. Lvs to 60cm×1.3cm, scabrous. Infl. cylindric, compact, erect or inclined, to 30×2cm, pale brown to purple. Spikelets 1, to 6mm. Summer–autumn. S Afr. Z7.

P. orientale Rich. Rhizomatous prenn., to 90cm. St. clumped, slender, erect to decumbent. Lvs to 10×0.4cm, slightly rough. Infl. loose, to 14×2.5cm; axis pubesc.; spikelets 2–5, to 6mm. Summer–autumn. C, SW Asia to NW India. Z7.

P. rueppelianum Hochst. = *P. setaceum*.

P. ruppelii Steud. = *P. setaceum*.

P. setaceum (Forssk.) Chiov. FOUNTAIN GRASS. Perenn., to 90cm. St. erect, slender, clumped. Lvs to 30×0.3cm, rigid, v. scabrous. Infl. erect to inclined, plumed, to 30×3cm, tinged pink to purple; axis scabrous; spikelets 1–3, to 6mm. Summer. Trop. Afr., SW Asia, Arabia. 'Purpureum' ('Atropurpureum'): lvs purple, infl. deep crimson. 'Rubrum' ('Cupreum'): tall; lvs maroon tinted bronze; plumes deep burgundy. A red-leaved form, never exceeding 60cm is also grown. Z9.

P. spicatum Roem. & Schult. = *P. glaucum*.

P. typhoides (Burm.) Stapf & C. Hubb. = *P. glaucum*.

P. villosum R. Br. ex Fries. FEATHERTOP. Perenn., to 60cm. St. loosely clumped, erect to ascending. Lvs to 15cm×0.6cm. Infl. cylindric to subglobose, compact, plumed, to 11×5cm, tinged tawny brown to purple; spikelets to 15mm. Summer–autumn. NE Trop. Afr. (mts). Z8.

→*Gymnothrix*.

Pennycress *Thlaspi arvense*; *T. perfoliatum*.
Penny Flower *Lunaria annua*.
Pennyroyal *Mentha pulegium*.
Pennywort *Cymbalaria muralis*; *Hydrocotyle*; *Umbilicus rupestris*.
Pennywort Begonia *Begonia hydrocotylifolia*.

Penstemon Schmidel. Scrophulariaceae. *c*250 subshrubs or perenn. herbs. Infl. a racemose, cymose or thyrsoid pan.; cal. 5-lobed; cor. tubular, ± regular to strongly bilabiate, upper lip 2-lobed, lower 3-cleft; sta. 4, paired, fil. arching, plus 1-elongate staminode. Alask. to Guat., mostly W US, 1 sp. in Kamchatka and N Jap.

P. abietinus Pennell. Mat-forming; st. ascending, caespitose, 5–10cm. Lvs 1×0.1cm, linear, mucronate. Fls 14–18mm, deep blue or ultramarine with maroon tube, palate sparsely hirsute, deeply bilabiate. Utah. Z3.

P. acaulis L.O. Williams. Lvs 1.5–2cm, in ± radical tufts, narrowly linear-spathulate, acute, ± viscid. Fls solitary; 14–16mm, deep azure blue, moderately ampliate, limb to 10mm broad, throat golden-hirsute. Wyom. Z3.

P. acuminatus Douglas ex Lindl. SAND-DUNE PENSTEMON. To 60cm, glaucous, erect. Lvs to 7cm, lanceolate to ovate, coriaceous. Infl. thyrsoid, elongate, fls 12–18mm, throat gradually ampliate, limb obscurely bilabiate, blue-mauve. Summer. Washington and Oreg. to Idaho. Z5.

P. acuminatus ssp. *congestus* Jones = *P. pachyphyllus*.

P. adamsianus Howell = *P. fructicosus*.

P. aggregatus Pennell = *P. rydbergii* ssp. *aggregatus*.

P. alamosensis Pennell & Nisbet. St. few, 70cm, glab. Lvs lanceolate to obovate. Infl. narrow, somewhat secund; almost regular, lobes 2–2.5cm, spreading bright red, glandular-pubesc. Summer. New Mex. (mts). Z9.

P. albertinus Greene. To 40cm; st. clustered, pubesc., or glabrate. Lvs to 7cm, lanceolate, entire or shallowly dentate, thin. Infl. ± gland.; fls to 2cm, light blue to violet or rarely pink, throat dilated, palate hirsute. BC and Alberta to Idaho and Mont. Z3.

P. albidus Nutt. St. 15–40cm, minutely pubesc. Lvs 4–8cm, oblong-lanceolate, entire or remotely crenate. Infl. to 10cm, strict, gland.; fls 1.5–2cm, gradually dilated, white or faintly flushed violet, minutely glandular-pubesc. within. Summer. S Canada to Okl., Tex., Colorado and New Mex. Z3.

P. alpinus Torr. Differs from *P. glaber* in st. and lvs glab. to minutely pubesc.; fls glab. to pubesc. or villous within. Wyom. and Colorado. Z4.

P. alpinus ssp. *brandegeei* (Porter) Harrington = *P. brandegeei*.

P. amabilis G.N. Jones = *P. ovatus* and *P. pruinosus*.

P. ambiguus Torr. To 60cm, glab., shrubby. Lvs 1.5–5cm, filiform or linear, mucronate. Infl. laxly paniculate; fls rose-pink to flesh-pink becoming white, limb rotate, obscurely bilabiate, lobes suborbicular, lower lobe somewhat hairy. Early summer–early autumn. Colorado and Utah to Calif. and Tex., Mex. Z3.

P. ambiguus var. *thurberi* A. Gray = *P. thurberi*.

P. amplexicaulis Buckley = *P. buckleyi*.

P. anguineus Eastw. SISKIYOU PENSTEMON. To 80cm. Lvs 5–15cm, ovate to oblong, serrate to subentire. Infl. thyrsoid, or openly paniculate; fls 13–18mm, deep lavender to blue-violet, abruptly ampliate, upper lip short, erect, lower lip longer, spreading, palate sparingly hirsute to glab. Summer. Oreg. to Calif. Z7.

P. angustifolius Nutt. ex Pursh. To 30cm, glaucous erect, tufted. Lvs to 7.5cm, linear to lanceolate, rather fleshy. Infl. thyrsoid; fls 15–18mm, pink becoming sky-blue, glab. within, bilabiate, lobes spreading, to 12mm wide. Summer. S Dak. and Wyom. to Colorado and Kans. Z3.

P. angustifolius ssp. *caudatus* (Heller) Keck = *P. caudatus*.

P. angustifolius ssp. *venosus* Keck = *P. caudatus*.

P. angustifolius var. *caudatus* (Heller) Rydb. = *P. caudatus*.

P. antirrhinoides Benth. CHAPARRAL BEARD-TONGUE. Shrub, 1–2.5m; st. spreading, minutely pubesc. Lvs 1–2cm, crowded, elliptic, firm. Infl. a broad pan., leafy; fls 16–20×8mm, throat abruptly dilated, upper lip broad, arching, lower lip reflexed, yellow tinged red-brown, viscid. Spring–summer. Calif. and Baja Calif. ssp. *microphyllus* (A. Gray) Keck. Twigs cinereous; lvs yellow-grey-green, canescent. Calif. to Baja Calif. and Ariz. Z9.

P. aridus Rydb. 10–50cm, densely tufted. Lvs 2–4cm, linear to narrowly oblanceolate, obscurely scabrid-denticulate, stiff. Infl. glandular-pubesc.; fls 12mm, blue or tinged purple, tubular-funnelform, lower lip slightly exceeding upper. Mont., Wyom., Idaho. Z3.

P. arizonicus Heller = *P. whippleanus*.

P. arkansanus Pennell. 30–90cm, sts tufted. Lvs 5–6cm, lanceolate to oblong-lanceolate, entire or remotely dentate, membranous. Infl. paniculate, diffuse; fls v. numerous, 15–18mm, white without, purple or violet within with darker nectar-guides, throat almost tubular with prominent ventral ridges, lower lobes projecting. Late spring–summer. Missouri and Ark. to Tex. Z5.

P. attenuatus Douglas Rosulate, then, st. slender, 30–60cm. Lvs 4–10cm, linear-lanceolate to oval, entire to minutely dentate. Infl. thyrsoid, strict, glandular-pubesc.; fls ampliate, bilabiate, 14–20mm, pale yellow or blue-purple to violet, palate white-hirsute. Summer. Washington to Oreg. and Idaho. ssp. *pseudoprocerus* (Rydb.) Keck Shorter; fls smaller, blue-purple. Z4.

P. auriberbis Pennell. Erect, to 35cm. Lvs to 7.5cm, linear to lanceolate, entire or undulate-dentate, minutely pubesc. Infl. narrow, secund, gland.; fls 18–25mm, lavender to purple, gland., lobes spreading, lower lobes bearded. Summer. Colorado and Ariz. Z4.

P. australis Small. St. 40–80cm, finely pubesc. Lvs narrowly lanceolate to obovate, acuminate, serrulate, minutely pubesc. Infl. paniculate, slender; fls 20–25mm, maroon, lower lobes creamy white within with purple lines. Summer. SE US. Z7.

P. azureus Benth. Subshrub, 20–50cm. Lvs 1.5–6cm, glaucous, obovate to lanceolate. Infl. thyrsoid, strict, subsecund; fls 20–30×7mm, tubular-campanulate, gaping, indigo, buds tinged yellow. Late summer. Calif. ssp. *angustissimus* (A. Gray) Keck. Lvs v. narrow, pale yellow-green. Z8.

P. azureus var. *jeffreyanus* A. Gray = *P. azureus*.

P. barbatus (Cav.) Roth. St. stout, 1m+. Lvs lanceolate to ovate, to linear. Fls 3–4cm, red tinged pink to carmine, strongly bilabiate, throat gradually inflated, upper lobes projecting, lower lobes reflexed and yellow-hirsute at base. Summer. New Mex. to Utah, Ariz. and N Mex. 'Albus': fls white. 'Carneus': fls pale pink. 'Coccineus': to 90cm; fls bright scarlet. 'Praecox': early-flowering. 'Praecox Nanus': habit dwarf; var. of colours. 'Roseus': fls pink. ssp. *torreyi* (Benth.) Keck. St. more slender; st. lvs all linear; cal. 3–5mm, cor. scarlet, generally glab. at base of lobes. Colorado to New Mex. and Ariz. Z3.

P. barbatus var. *torreyi* (Benth.) Gray = *P. barbatus* ssp. *torreyi*.

P. barrettiae A. Gray. Forming shrubby clumps, 20–40cm tall. Lvs 4–6cm, ovate to elliptic-ovate, serrate, glaucous. Infl. 7–25cm, thyrsoid, subracemose, dense; fls 35×8mm, lips projecting, short, lilac to rosy purple, ventral ridges villous. Early summer. Washington and Oreg. Z7.

P. berryi Eastw. Differs from *P. newberryi* in fls, 27–33×8mm, with throat more ampliate, ventral ridges within bearded with longer hairs. Oreg. to Calif. Z7.

P. bicolor (Brandg.) Clokey & Keck. 60–140cm, glaucescent. Lvs 8cm, ovate, dentate, thick. Fls to 2.5cm, white, yellow or pink, gland., gradually inflated, lower lip sparsely villous. Spring. Nevada and Ariz. Z5.

P. bradburii Pursh = *P. grandiflorus*.

P. brandegeei Porter. St. stout, to 60cm, minutely pubesc. Lvs lanceolate to oblanceolate, to 10cm. Infl. spreading, secund; fls many, 3–4cm, blue or tinged purple, glab. or sparsely hairy, throat greatly expanded, lower lip deflexed or divergent. Summer. Colorado and New Mex. Z4.

P. breviflorus Lindl. GAPING PENSTEMON. Shrub, 0.5–2m; st. numerous, lax, glaucous. Lvs 1–1.5cm, lanceolate, mminutely serrate to entire. Infl. 10–55cm, thyrsoid, pyramidal; fls 15–18mm, white flushed rose, with prominent purple guide-lines, buds tinged yellow; upper lip arching, helmet-shaped, lower lip strongly reflexed, 3-parted, glandular-pubesc. Late summer–early autumn. Calif. Z7.

P. brevifolius (A. Gray) Nels. 10–30cm, creeping, tufted. Lvs 1.5–2.5cm, ovate to elliptic-ovate, thin. Infl. glandular-pubesc.; fls 8–12mm, violet-blue, minutely glandular-pubesc., bilabiate, throat not inflated above, with weak ventral ridges, upper lobes abruptly spreading, slightly exceeded by lower lobes. Summer. Utah. Z3.

P. bridgesii A. Gray. Subshrub, 30–100cm; st. erect. Lvs linear to spathulate, 2–8cm, subglabrous. Infl. a subsecund thyrse, glandular-pubesc.; fls strongly bilabiate, upper lip erect, lower sharply reflexed, 22–35×4mm, vermilion to scarlet, thinly gland. Summer. Calif. and Baja Calif. to Colorado and Ariz. Z4.

P. buckleyi Pennell. St. stout, to 40cm, glaucous. Lvs oblanceolate to lanceolate, glaucous. Infl. narrow; fls 1.5–2cm, pale lavender to light blue with prominent guide-lines within throat, throat slightly expanded, lobes spreading. Spring–summer. Kans. to Tex. and New Mex. Z5.

P. caelestinus Pennell. St. erect, 25–40cm. Lvs 3–4cm, elliptic-ovate, dentate to entire, st. lvs narrower. Infl. thyrsoid, secund; fls 15–17mm, blue-violet with purple nectar-guides, glab. or minutely glandular-pubesc. without, throat somewhat inflated, with 2 ventral ridges, base of lower lip villous, lobes bright violet-blue. Mont. Z4.

P. caeruleus Nutt. = *P. angustifolius*.

P. caeruleus hort. ex Vilm. non Nutt. = *P. hartwegii*.

P. caesius A. Gray. CUSHION PENSTEMON. Matted, tufted; st. erect, 15–45cm. Lvs 1–2cm, mostly basal, suborbicular, glaucous, coriaceous, st. lvs oblanceolate. Infl. a thyrsoid pan., lax glandular-pubesc.; fls gradually ampliate, 17–23×4mm, lips small, blue tinged purple, throat glab. within. Summer. Calif. Z8.

P. caespitosus Nutt. ex A. Gray. St. 15–40cm, decumbent to prostrate. Lvs to 1cm, linear to lanceolate, apiculate, glabrate. Infl. leafy; fls 14–18mm, light blue with purple throat, white or v. pale within, throat sparingly hirsute within, tube scarcely inflated, upper lip erect, lower spreading, exceeding upper, lobes to 2mm. Wyom., Colorado and Utah. ssp. *desertipici* (A. Nels.) Keck. Lvs densely minutely pubesc.; cor. tube abruptly inflated, pale blue without. Utah to Ariz. Z3.

P. caespitosus A. Nels. = *P. caespitosus* var. *desertipici*.

P. calcycosus Small. St. to 1m. Lvs to 15cm, lanceolate to ovate-lanceolate, serrate to subentire. Fls 2.5–3.5cm, sometimes smaller, violet-purple without, off-white within. Summer. E & C US. Z4.

P. californicus (Munz & I.M. Johnst.) Keck. St. tufted, 5–15cm, cinereous-pubesc. Lvs 0.8–1.5cm, linear-oblanceolate, mucronate, rather thick, minutely, cinereous-pubesc. Infl. a racemiform thyrse, minutely gland.; fls 14–18×4–6mm, narrowly tubular-funneliform, blue tinged purple. Summer. Calif. and Baja Calif. Z8.

P. campanulatus Willd. St. 30–60cm. Lvs linear-lanceolate, serrate, to 7cm. Infl. elongate, lax, secund; fls 2.5cm+, rosy purple or violet, glandular-pubesc. without, funnelform, bilabiate. Early summer. Mex. and Guat. 'Pulchellus': fls violet or lilac. 'Purpureus': fls purple. Z9.

P. canescens (Britt.) Britt. 30–90cm. Lvs ovate to broadly lanceolate or oblong, minutely serrate, membranous, pubesc. Infl. laxly thyrsoid; fls 2–3.5cm, purple or violet, with dark nectar-guides; throat abruptly inflated, flattened, with prominent ventral ridges, lower lobes projecting. Summer. E US. Z5.

P. canosobarbatus Kellogg = *P. breviflorus*.

P. cardinalis Wooton & Standl. St. erect, to 1m+. Lvs to 12cm, elliptic to ovate or oblong. Infl. narrow, secund; fls 2–3cm, dull red to crimson, obscurely bilabiate, throat gradually dilated, constricted at orifice, lobes 2–3mm, upper erect, lower spreading or reflexed, yellow-hirsute at base. Summer. New Mex. Z9.

P. cardwellii T.J. Howell. Forming broad clumps 10–20cm. Lvs 1.5–4cm, elliptic, serrate. Infl. racemose, few- to several-fld, strict; fls 25–38×7mm, brilliant purple, ventral ridges villous. Summer. Washington and Oreg. 'Albus': fls white. 'Roseus': fls pink. Z8.

P. carinatus Kellogg = *P. breviflorus*.

P. caudatus Heller. St. stout, to 50cm. Lvs lanceolate to spathulate, acuminate, glaucous. Infl. compact; 1.5–2.5cm, blue to violet without prominent markings, throat gradually expanded, lobes subequal, spreading, lower lip sometimes sparsely pubesc. at base. Summer. Kans. to Utah, New Mex. and Ariz. Z4.

P. centranthifolius Benth. SCARLET BUGLER. Glaucous st. 30–120cm. Lvs 4–10cm, lanceolate or spathulate. Infl. thyrsoid, virgate; fls 25–33×4–6mm, tubular, lobes scarcely spreading, scarlet, glab. Early summer. Calif. and Baja Calif. 'Pilatas Pink': fls pink. Z9.

P. cinerascens Greene = *P. laetus* ssp. *roezlii*.

P. cinereus Piper. 10–50cm, rosulate, clump-forming; st. slender, grey. Lvs to 5cm, lanceolate to linear, firm, cinereous-pubesc. Infl. thyrsoid, glandular-pubesc.; fls to 13mm, subtubular to gradually ampliate, bright blue to indigo or blue-mauve. Summer. Oreg. to Nevada. Z4.

P. clevelandii A. Gray. St. 30–70cm. Lvs ovate to deltoid-lanceolate, entire to serrate, deep green to glaucescent. Infl. a narrowly racemiform thyrse; fls tubular-funnelform, tube short-er than throat, not contracted at orifice, 17–24×5mm, lobes quadrate, rotate-spreading, crimson or maroon, limb glandular-pubesc. within. Summer. Calif. and Baja Calif. Z9.

P. clutei A. Nels. 60–140cm, glaucescent. Lvs to 5cm, lanceolate-ovate, dentate, ± coriaceous. Infl. often interrupted; fls deep pink to rosy purple, gland., throat gradually inflated, ventricose, to 2.5cm, almost regular. Summer. Ariz. 'Albiflorus': fls white. Z7.

P. cobaea Nutt. St. 30–60cm, erect, stout, minutely pubesc. Lvs 10–20cm, oblong to lanceolate, entire minutely dentate, thinly pubesc. Infl. paniculate, short, lax; fls 3.5–5cm, abruptly campanulate-ventricose above, pale to deep purple or white. Late summer. SC US. Z4.

P. coloradoensis A. Nels. = *P. linarioides* ssp. *coloradoensis*.

P. comarrhenus A. Gray. St. to 1m, minutely pubesc. Lvs 1–2.5cm, oblong-lanceolate, to linear-lanceolate, attenuate. Infl. elongate, lax, rather secund; fls 3–3.5cm, pale blue to blue-mauve, glab., strongly bilabiate, tube gibbous, upper lip projecting to erect, lower lip spreading to reflexed. Summer. Colorado to Utah, New Mex. and Ariz. Z4.

P. concinnus Keck. ELEGANT PENSTEMON. 80–200cm; st. flushed purple, minutely pubesc. Lvs 2–5cm, linear to oblanceolate, en-tire to dentate, somewhat glaucous. Infl. narrowly thyrsoid, 4–7-whorled, glandular-pubesc.; fls 8–10mm, blue-violet with dark purple nectar-guides, glandular-pubesc. without, palate white-pilose, moderately ampliate, lower lip reflexed. Nevada and Utah (mts). Z3.

P. confertus Douglas. YELLOW PENSTEMON. Glab., rosulate; st. slender, 2–5cm. Lvs 3–7cm, lanceolate to oblanceolate, thin. Infl. thyrsoid, strict; fls 8–12mm, tubular, not strongly bilabiate, pale sulphur-yellow, palate brown-hirsute. Summer. BC to Alberta, Mont. and Oreg. 'Violaceus': fls violet. Z4.

P. confertus var. *caeruleopurpureus* A. Gray = *P. procerus*.

P. congestus (M.E. Jones) Pennell = *P. pachyphyllus* ssp. *congestus*.

P. connatifolius A. Nels. = *P. pseudospectabilis* ssp. *connatifolius*.

P. cordifolius Benth. Sprawling shrub, 1–3m. Lvs 2–5cm, lanceolate-ovate to cordate, minutely toothed, lustrous, veins conspicuous. Pan. drooping pyramidal, subsecund; fls resupine, 30–40×5mm, dull scarlet, upper lip helmet-shaped, lower lip broadly spreading. Early summer. Calif. Z8.

P. corymbosus Benth. REDWOOD PENSTEMON. Shrub, 30–50cm. Lvs 1.5–4cm, elliptic, entire to remotely serrate, glab. to canescent, coriaceous. Infl. corymbose, term., many-fld, glandular-pubesc.; fls narrowly tubular, upper lip helmet-shaped, lower lip spreading, 25–35×4mm, brick-red. Summer. Calif. Z8.

P. crandallii A. Nels. St. prostrate and rooting, to ascending, 30–120cm. Lvs 0.5–2.5cm, spathulate to oblanceolate, entire, scabrous to subglabrous. Infl. elongate; fls 15–20mm, blue to blue-lavender, glandular-pubesc. without, bilabiate, flattened with 2 ventral ridges, lobes spreading, palate sparsely hirsute. Utah and Colorado. ssp. *procumbens* (Greene) Keck St. decumbent; lvs glab. Colorado. Z3.

P. crassifolius Lindl. = *P. fructicosus*.

P. cristatus Nutt. = *P. eriantherus*.

P. cusickii A. Gray. St. 20–40cm, woody at base, thyrse. Lvs 3–6.5cm, linear to narrowly oblanceolate, grey-green, hirtellous. Infl. a narrow; fls to 2.5cm, purple to blue, tube rapidly dilated into ample throat, limb gaping, clearly bilabiate, glab. Summer. Oreg. to Idaho. Z4.

P. cyananthus Hook. St. erect, 30–60cm, slightly glaucous. Lvs ovate to rounded, to 6cm broad, glaucous. Infl. thyrsoid, inter-rupted; fls 2–2.5cm, bright blue, bilabiate, tube ventricose upwards. Late summer. Mont. and Idaho to Colorado and Utah. Z4.

P. cyananthus var. *brandegeei* Porter & Coult. = *P. brandegeei*.

P. cyaneus Pennell. St. several, 40–80cm. Lvs to 10cm, lanceolate, light green. Infl. narrowly thyrsoid, secund; fls to 3cm, violet-pink becoming deep sky-blue, violet in throat, glab., tube narrow, throat inflated, somewhat contracted at orifice, upper lip projecting, lower lip exceeding upper. Summer.

Idaho, Mont. and Wyom. Z3.

P. dasyphyllus A. Gray. St. to 70cm, cinereous-pubesc. Lvs to 9cm, linear, acuminate, cinereous-pubesc. to glabrate. Infl. secund, glandular-pubesc.; fls 2.5–3.5cm, blue or tinged purple, lower lip exceeding upper. Spring–summer. Tex. to Ariz. and Mex. Z9.

P. davidsonii Greene. Differs from *P. menziesii* in lvs entire; fls 18–35mm. Washington to Calif. 'Albus': fls white. 'Broken Top': habit low and spreading to 40cm diam.; lvs neat-toothed; fls rich purple. ssp. *thompsonii* Pennell & Keck Larger in all parts. Z6.

P. deserticola Piper = *P. speciosus*.

P. desertipicti A. Nels. = *P. caespitosus* var. *desertipicti*.

P. deustus Douglas. HOT-ROCK PENSTEMON. St. erect, forming clumps 20–60cm. Lvs 1–5cm, linear-lanceolate to elliptic-ovate, serrate, bright green. Infl. thyrsoid, strict; fls 10–16mm, almost tubular, lower lip exceeding upper, yellow tinged brown with purple guide-lines, sparingly gland. Summer. Washington to Calif., E to Wyom. Z3.

P. diffusus Douglas ex Lindl. = *P. serrulatus*.

P. digitalis Nutt. St. to 15m, flushed purple, ± glaucous, glossy. Lvs 10–15cm, oblong-lanceolate to subulate, entire to dentate. Infl. paniculate, 10–30cm, glandular-pubesc.; fls 2.5–3cm, white or flushed v. pale violet, with purple nectar-guides, tube dilated abruptly near middle. Summer. Maine to S Dak., S to Tex., Alab. and Virg. 'Albus': fls white. 'Nanus': habit dwarf. 'Woodville White': fls white. Z3.

P. diphyllus Rydb. Differs from *P. triphyllus*, in lvs more regularly arranged, nearly all opposite or subopposite. Mont. to Idaho and Wyom. Z3.

P. dissectus Elliot. St. to 50cm, minutely pubesc. Lvs pinnately parted, seg. 7–11, linear, 1–2mm broad. Infl. paniculate; fls to 2cm, few purple, obscurely bilabiate. Georgia. Z8.

P. dolius M.E. Jones. St. to 12cm. Lvs minutely cinereous-pubesc., 1–5cm, ovate-lanceolate to oblanceolate. Infl. narrow; fls 1.5–2cm, blue tinged purple, sparingly glandular-pubesc. Summer. Utah to Nevada. Z4.

P. douglasii Hook. = *P. fructicosus*.

P. eastwoodiae Heller = *P. utahensis*.

P. eatonii A. Gray. EATON'S FIRECRACKER. St. 60cm. Lvs 4–18cm, oblanceolate to lanceolate-oblong, green or glaucescent, coriaceous. Infl. thyrsoid, strict, secund; fls 2.5–3×0.6–0.8cm, subtubular, throat slightly expanded, lobes erect or spreading, scarlet, glab. Late summer. Calif. to Nevada and Utah. Z4.

P. ×edithae English. (*P. rupicola* ×*P. barrettiae*.) To 25cm, mat-forming, glab. Lvs to 4.5cm, suborbicular to elliptic, dentate or entire, glaucous, glab., fls to 4cm, pink. Gdn origin. Z7.

P. ellipticus J. Coult. & E. Fisher. Forming lax mats; st. erect, 8–12cm. Lvs 2–3cm, broadly elliptic to suborbicular, serrate to entire. Infl. racemose, viscid-pubesc.; fls 3.5cm, violet-purple, strongly bilabiate, ventricose, throat narrow, lobes erose. Idaho. Z5.

P. eriantherus Pursh CRESTED-TONGUED PENSTEMON; CRESTED BEARD-TONGUE. St. 10–30cm, villous to canescent. Lvs 4–8cm, lanceolate to ovate, entire to dentate, glandular-pubesc. to canescent. Infl. 4–13cm, thrysoid, compact, glandular-pubesc.; fls 20–35×9–14mm, lilac-purple with deeper maroon-purple guidelines, throat strongly ampliate, strongly bilabiate, palate pilose. Summer. Washington to Alberta, Dak. and Neb. 'Nanus': habit dwarf. Z3.

P. eriantherus var. *whitedii* A. Nels. = *P. whitedii*.

P. erosus Rydb. = *P. rydbergii*.

P. euglaucus English. Glaucous; st. 15–50cm. Lvs 4–10cm, elliptic, rather firm. Infl. thyrsoid, strict, clusters remote, many-fld; fls 11–15mm, moderately ampliate, deep blue, palate lightly yellow-hirsute. Summer. Washington to Oreg. (Cascade Mts) Z5.

P. exilifolius A. Nels. = *P. laricifolius* ssp. *exilifolius*.

P. fendleri Torr. & A. Gray. St. to 50cm, ± glaucous. Lvs 2–9cm, lanceolate to ovate, mucronate, somewhat glaucous, thick. Infl. narrow, 12–25cm; fls 1.5–2.5cm, blue with deep violet guidelines, throat narrow, slightly expanded, lobes spreading. Spring–summer. Okl. and Tex. to Ariz. and Mex. Z3.

P. flavescens Pennell. St. 20–40cm, decumbent or erect. Lvs 3–7cm, oblong-lanceolate, light green. Infl. thyrsoid, of 2–6 fascicles, congested; fls 12–15mm, yellow, glab. without, villous at base of lower lip, throat semi-campanulate, with 2 ventral ridges, lobes light yellow, upper arched, lower deflexed-spreading. Mont. and Idaho. Z3.

P. floridus Brandg. ROSE PENSTEMON. St. 60–120cm. Lvs ovate, obtuse, spinose-dentate or subentire, to 10cm, glaucous. Infl. thyrsoid, glandular-pubesc.; fls 22–30×12–15mm, abruptly inflated, gibbous, slipper-shaped with oblique orifice, base of lower lip projecting beyond base of upper lip, lobes reflexed, rose-pink with yellow throat, with darker guide-lines. Summer. Calif.

and Nevada. Z5.

P. fructicosus (Pursh) Greene. SHRUBBY PENSTEMON. Forming shrubby clumps, to 40cm. Lvs 1–5cm, lanceolate to elliptic, entire or thinly coriaceous. Infl. strict, subsecund, glandular-pubesc.; fls lavender-blue to pale purple, ventral ridges villous. Spring–summer. Washington to Oreg., E to Mont. and Wyom. 'Albus': fls white. 'Major': fls large. ssp. *serratus* Keck. Shorter and more shrubby; lvs prominently serrate. Z4.

P. fructicosus ssp. *cardwellii* Piper = *P. cardwellii*.

P. fructicosus ssp. *scouleri* (Lindl.) Pennell & Keck = *P. scouleri*.

P. fructicosus var. *crassifolius* Krautter = *P. fructicosus*.

P. fruticiformis Coville. DEATH VALLEY PENSTEMON. Shrubby, 30–60cm. Lvs linear-lanceolate, revolute, to 6mm broad, glab. and glaucous. Infl. thyrsoid, lax, short; fls 20–27×10–13mm, tube short, throat strongly inflated, lobes reflexed, white or flesh pink, limb pale lavender, with purple guide-lines. Summer. Calif. Z8.

P. gairdneri Hook. Woody and spreading at base, 10–30cm. Lvs 1–3cm, linear, revolute, cinereous-pubesc. Infl. thyrsoid, strict, glandular-pubesc.; fls 15–20mm, throat 4–6mm broad, scarcely ampliate, limb 12–14mm diam., lobes reflexed, lavender purple, limb deep blue, gland. within. Summer. Oreg. ssp. *oreganus* (A. Gray) Keck. Lvs 2–7cm; fls pale blue or lavender to almost white. E Oreg. and adjacent Idaho. Z4.

P. gairdneri var. *oreganus* A. Gray = *P. gairdneri* ssp. *oreganus*.

P. garrettii Pennell. Subglabrous; st. several, 20–40cm. Lvs 6–10cm, lanceolate, dull, rather glaucous. Infl. narrow, secund, sparingly glandular-pubesc.; fls 2cm, blue, glab. Summer. Utah. Z4.

P. gentianoides (HBK) Poir. St. 60–120cm, erect, robust, glab. Lvs to 11cm, lanceolate, entire to dentate, in whorls of 3 above. Infl. racemose, leafy; fls 3cm, purple, tube v. short, greatly enlarged above, somewhat bilabiate, lobes ovate. S Mex. and Guat. Z9.

P. gentianoides Lindl. non (HBK) Poir. = *P. hartwegii*.

P. glaber Pursh. Caudex woody, st. 50–65cm, solitary or many. Lvs 3–12cm, linear-lanceolate. Infl. thyrsoid, congested, secund, 10–25cm; fls 2.5–3.5cm, posterior deep blue to indigo or rarely pink, anterior pale blue to white, with maroon nectar-guides, throat moderately inflated, lobes of upper lip projecting, lobes of lower lip spreading to reflexed. Late summer. Wyom. 'Roseus': fls pink. Z3.

P. glaber var. *alpinus* (Torr.) A. Gray = *P. alpinus*.

P. glaber var. *cyananthus* (Hook.) A. Gray = *P. cyananthus*.

P. glaber var. *speciosus* (Douglas ex Lindl.) Rydb. = *P. speciosus*.

P. glandulosus Douglas ex Lindl. Glandular-pubesc.; st. stout, 50–100cm. Lower lvs 4–16cm, lanceolate to lanceolate ovate, serrate, thin. Infl. of 2–5 congested remote clusters; fls 28–40×11–15mm, pale lilac to light violet, generally glab. within. Summer. Washington and Oreg. to Idaho. Z4.

P. glaucus Graham = *P. gracilis*.

P. glaucus var. *stenosepalus* Gray = *P. whippleanus*.

P. globosus (Piper) Pennell & Keck. St. 25–40cm. Lvs 5–18cm, lanceolate to oblong, thin. Infl. a subcapitate cluster; fls 15–20×7mm, gradually ampliate, bright blue to blue-purple, palate bearded. Summer. Oreg. to Idaho. Z4.

P. gordoni Hook. = *P. glaber*.

P. gormanii Greene. St. to 30cm, pubesc. or glabrate. Lvs lanceolate to spathulate, entire or minutely serrate above. Infl. gland.; fls to 2.5cm, blue-purple, throat dilated, palate hirsute. Alask. to BC. Z3.

P. gracilentus A. Gray. Compact; st. numerous, 20–70cm. Lvs 3–10cm, oblanceolate to linear-lanceolate, sometimes glaucescent. Infl. a compact thyrsoid pan., glandular-pubesc.; fls 1.5cm, purple tinged blue to maroon, slightly ampliate, somewhat bilabiate, lower lip villous within. Summer. Oreg., Calif. and Nevada. Z5.

P. gracilis Nutt. SLENDER BEARD-TONGUE. St. 30–50cm, slender. Lvs lanceolate to linear-lanceolate, serrate, 5–10cm. Infl. 5–15cm, slender, gland.; fls 15–20mm, pale violet, bilabiate, throat narrow, flattened, strongly 2-ridged, lower lobes exceeding upper, hirsute at base. Summer. Alberta to Manit., S to Wisc., Iowa, Neb. and New Mex. Z3.

P. grandiflorus Nutt. LARGE BEARD-TONGUE. To 1m; st. erect, glaucous. Lvs 2–9cm, obovate-oblong to suborbicular, thick, glaucous. Infl. 15–30cm, racemiform, interrupted; fls 3.5–4.5cm, pink to blue-lavender or pale blue with magenta nectar-guides, tube abruptly dilated, lobes of upper lip spreading to reflexed, lobes of lower lip projecting or spreading. Summer. N Dak. to Wyom., Tex. and Ill. 'Albus': fls white. Z3.

P. grinnellii Eastw. Small rounded bush, 30–100cm. Lvs ovate, spinose-dentate or subentire, to 15cm, bright green or glaucescent. Infl. 4–8cm diam., thyrsoid, lax; fls 20–30×10mm, tube short, throat strongly inflated, lobes reflexed, white or tinged pale purple or blue, paler without, with prominent guide-lines. Spring–summer. Calif. Z8.

P. hallii A. Gray. Caespitose; st. erect, to 20cm. Lvs linear to ovate-lanceolate. Infl. thyrsoid, short, 5–15-flld; fls 1.5–2cm, blue-violet, bilabiate, tube v. short, throat abruptly inflated, decurved at base. Summer. Colorado (mts). Z3.

P. harbourii A. Gray. St. 5–10cm, tufted. Lvs 0.8–1.6cm, obovate to oval, rather thick. Infl. thyrsoid, reduced to 2–3 crowded fls; fls 14–18mm, purple, slightly bilabiate, throat rather broad, short, lobes rounded, lower lip hirsute within. Colorado. Z4.

P. hartwegii Benth. St. 90–120cm. Lvs to 10cm, lanceolate to ovate-lanceolate. Infl. racemose-paniculate, glandular-pubesc.; fls 5cm, deep scarlet, minutely viscid-pubesc., tubular-funnelform, gradually dilated above. Mex. Z9.

P. havardi A. Gray. To 60cm, glaucescent. Lvs 5–10cm, obovate to elliptic or oblong, coriaceous. Infl. a racemiform thyrsus, elongate; fls 2.5cm, violet or blue, tubular, bilabiate, lips to 4mm, upper erect, lower spreading. SW Tex. and adjacent Mex. Z9.

P. haydenii S. Wats. 20–45cm; st. decumbent to ascending. Lvs to 11cm, linear to linear-lanceolate, somewhat glaucous, firm. Infl. 6–16cm, thyrsoid, v. compact, cylindric; fls fragrant; to 2.5cm, distinctly bilabiate, milky blue to milky lavender or pale rose, with magenta nectar-guides, throat inflated, lobes of upper lip arched-projecting, of lower lip projecting to spreading. Summer. Nevada. Z4.

P. heterodoxus A. Gray. SIERRAN PENSTEMON. St. slender, 8–15cm. Lvs 0.5–2cm, linear-oblanceolate to spathulate, thin. Infl. clustered, subcapitate, dense, gland.; fls gradually ampliate, 10–16mm, indigo, palate yellow-brown-hirsute. Summer. Calif. and adjacent Nevada. Z5.

P. heterophyllus Lindl. FOOTHILL PENSTEMON. Shrub, 30–50cm. Lvs 2–5cm, linear ot linear-lanceolate green or glaucous. Infl. a subracemose thyrse; fls gaping, 25–35×9–18mm, rosy violet, lobes blue or lilac. Mid-summer. Calif. 'Blue Gem': habit dwarf. 'Heavenly Blue': fls blue to mauve. 'Zuriblau': to 50cm; fls bright blue. ssp. *purdyi* Keck. Plant mat-forming, minutely pubesc. throughout; lvs 2.5–6cm; blue to light purple. Calif. Z8.

P. hians I.M. Johnston = *P. grinnellii*.

P. hirsutus (L.) Willd. St. erect, 40–80cm, minutely glandular-pubesc. above. Lvs 5–12cm, lanceolate to oblong, subentire to dentate. Infl. lax, minutely glandular-pubesc.; 2.5cm, dull purple with white lobes, tube nt broadening toward mouth, almost close by arched base of lower lip, tube pubesc. within. Late summer. E N Amer. 'Caeruleus': fls blue-tinted. 'Purpureus': fls clear purple. 'Pygmaeus': to 15cm high, floriferous; fls violet. 'Roseus': fls tinted pink. 'Rosinus': fls pink. Z3.

P. humilis Nutt. ex A. Gray. Densely tufted, forming clumps 10–30cm high, cinereous-pubesc. Lvs lanceolate to oblanceolate, firm. Infl. thyrsoid, glandular-pubesc.; fls ± tubular, lower lip exceeding upper, 12–16mm, azure to lavender-blue, tube purple. Late summer. Oreg. to Mont., S to Colorado and Calif. 'Albus': fls white. Z4.

P. humilis ssp. *brevifolius* A. Gray = *P. brevifolius*.

P. imberbis (HBK) Poir. St. 30–60cm, shrubby at base, slender. Lvs 5–10cm, linear or linear-lanceolate. Infl. laxly paniculate, elongate, few-fld; fls 2.5cm, pink to red, slightly gland. without, somewhat bilabiate, elongate-funnelform, slightly gibbous below, lobes spreading. Mex. (mts) Z9.

P. incertus Brandg. MOJAVE PENSTEMON. Shrubby, 60–80cm. Lvs narrowly linear-lanceolate, glaucous. Infl. thyrsoid, lax, somewhat gland.; fls 25–28×8mm, tube long, gradually expanded into ample throat, strongly bilabiate, lips reflexed, violet tinged red or purple, limb deep blue, lower lip villous at base. Summer. Calif. Z8.

P. intonsus Heller = *P. corymbosus*.

P. isophyllus Robinson. St. 70cm, decumbent then erect, simple, stout, purple. Lvs 3–4cm, lanceolate, revolute, rather thick. Infl. secund, 30cm; fls 4cm, red, white-pubesc., throat slightly dilated, limb 5-lobed, minutely crenate. Mex. Z9.

P. jamesii Benth. St. to 50cm, erect. Lvs linear to lanceolate or spathulate, undulate or entire. Infl. narrow, secund, glandular-pubesc.; fls 2.5–3.5cm, pale lavender to blue with prominent guide-lines, throat abruptly expanded, upper lobes erect, lower spreading or reflexed, gland. and white-pilose at base. Summer. W Tex. to Colorado and New Mex. Z4.

P. jamesii ssp. *ophianthus* (Pennell) Keck = *P. ophianthus*.

P. jeffreyanus Hook. = *P. azureus*.

P. keckii Clokey. V. similar to *P. speciosus* except infl. gland., fls gland., hirsute at base of lower lip. Nevada. Z6.

P. labrosus (A. Gray) Hook. f. SAN GABRIEL PENSTEMON. St. 30–70cm. Lvs 5–10cm, linear-oblanceolate, coriaceous. Infl. thyrsoid, strict, somewhat secund; fls 3–4cm, scarlet, glab., limb nearly hallf length of tube, upper lip erect, shallowly lobed, lower lip slit to base into reflexed linear lobes. Late summer. Calif.

and Baja Calif. Z9.

P. lacerellus Greene = *P. rydbergii*.

P. laetus A. Gray. Subshrub, 20–80cm; st. often flushed purple, pubesc. or canescent. Lvs linear to oblanceolate, 2–10cm, grey-green minutely pubesc. or canescent. Infl. lax, narrow, glandular-pubesc.; 2–3cm, blue-violet to blue-lavender, tubular-campanulate, limb bright blue, widely gaping, glab. within. Summer. Calif. ssp. *roezlii* (Reg.) Keck. Lvs much smaller; fls 1.5–2cm. Oreg. to Calif. and Nevada. Z5.

P. laevigatus Sol. St. 60–120cm, pubesc. ± often in stripes. Lvs to 15cm, lanceolate to narrowly oblong, dentate, coriaceous. Infl. sparingly gland.; fls to 2.5cm, tube abruptly dilated in distal half, pale violet without, white to pale violet within. Summer. Penn. to Miss. and Flor. Z4.

P. laevigatus var. *digitalis* (Nutt.) A. Gray = *P. digitalis*.

P. laricifolius Hook. & Arn. Cushion-like, with woody, subterranean caudex; st. erect, 10–20cm. Lvs 1.5–3.5cm, in dense rosettes, filiform, fls 15–18mm, purple, tubular-campanulate, gradually ampliate, limb regular, spreading, prominent, lower lip bearded at base. Wyom. ssp. *exilifolius* (A. Nels.) Keck Fls 12–15mm, white with green-yellow tinge. Wyom. and adjacent Colorado. Z3.

P. laricifolius var. *exilifolius* Pays. = *P. laricifolius* ssp. *exilifolius*.

P. leiophyllus Pennell. St. 15–60cm, slightly glaucous. Lvs 10–13cm, linear-lanceolate to narrowly lanceolate, dull green. Infl. narrow, secund; fls 2.5–3cm, blue, minutely glandular-pubesc. without, throat inflated. Summer. Utah. Z4.

P. lemhiensis (Keck) Keck & Cronq. To 7cm, compact, sometimes glaucous. Lvs lanceolate to oblanceolate, ± entire, to 2.5cm wide. Fls 2.5–3.5cm, blue-purple, palate glab. Idaho, Mont. Z4.

P. lentus Pennell. St. to 30cm, erect, glaucous. Basal lvs to 4cm, ovate, petioles winged, st. lvs lanceolate to ovate, amplexicaul, to 7cm. Infl. elongate, rather secund; fls 18–20mm, blue to purple, throat somewhat inflated, hirsute within on ventral side, lower lip greatly exceeding upper. Summer. Colorado to Utah, New Mex. and Ariz. Z4.

P. leptophyllus Rydb. = *P. wilcoxii*.

P. lewisii Benth. = *P. fruticosus*.

P. linarioides Gray. St. to 50cm, erect to ascending. Lvs to 2.5cm, linear, mucronate. Infl. narrow, secund, gland.; fls 1.5–2cm, purple to violet with dark purple guide-lines, tube slender, throat gibbous, 2-ridged, lower lip densely yellow-hirsute at base. Summer. New Mex. and Ariz. ssp. *coloradoensis* (A. Nels.) Keck. Older st. decumbent at base, matted, rooting at lower nodes; fls sparsely hirsute at base of lower lip. Colorado and Utah to New Mex. and Ariz. Z4.

P. linearifolius J. Coult. & E. Fisher = *P. lyallii* var. *linearifolius*.

P. lobbii hort. ex Lem. = *P. antirrhinoides*.

P. lyallii Gray. St. to 80cm. Lvs narrow, elongate, entire to minutely serrate, to 10cm+. Infl. ± paniculate, gland.; fls to 4.5cm, lavender, glab. without, conspicuously lanate-villous on prominent ventral ridges within, tube dilated. Alberta and BC to Mont. and Idaho. var. *linearifolius* (J. Coult. & E. Fisher) Krautter. Densely cinereous-pubesc.; lvs 4–5cm. Idaho. Z4.

P. menziesii Hook. Forming creeping mats; flowering st. to 10cm. Lvs 0.5–1.5cm, elliptic to orbicular, minutely serrate, ± glandular-punctate. Infl. racemose, few-fld, glandular-pubesc.; fls 25–35×7mm, violet-purple, ventral ridges villous. Summer. BC and Vancouver Is. to Washington. 'Microphyllus': habit compact, to 10cm; lvs small; fls lavender. Z7.

P. menziesii ssp. *davidsonii* (Greene) Piper = *P. davidsonii*.

P. menziesii var. *crassifolius* Schelle = *P. fruticosus*.

P. menziesii var. *douglasii* A. Gray = *P. fruticosus*.

P. menziesii var. *lewisii* A. Gray = *P. fruticosus*.

P. menziesii var. *lyallii* A. Gray = *P. lyallii*.

P. menziesii var. *newberryi* A. Gray = *P. newberryi*.

P. menziesii var. *robinsonii* Mast. = *P. newberryi*.

P. menziesii var. *scouleri* A. Gray = *P. scouleri*.

P. metcalfei Wooton & Standl. = *P. whippleanus*.

P. micranthus Nutt. non Torr. = *P. procerus*.

P. micranthus Torr. non Nutt. = *P. strictus*.

P. microphyllus A. Gray = *P. antirrhinoides* ssp. *microphyllus*.

P. miser A. Gray. GOLDEN-TONGUED PENSTEMON. St. 10–25cm, minutely cinereous-pubesc. Lvs linear-lanceolate to elliptic, entire or minutely serrate or sinuate-dentate, cinereous-pubesc. Infl. thyrsoid, compact, glandular-pubesc.; fls 1.5–2.5cm, dull purple with purple guide-lines, tube long, abruptly dilating, strongly bilabiate, palate pilose; staminode exserted, hooked, orange-hairy. Summer. Oreg., Calif. and Nevada. Z5.

P. missouliensis hort. = *P. albertinus*.

P. montanus Greene. Forming loose clumps; st. to 15cm, arising from slender caudex. Lvs oblong to ovate-lanceolate, dentate, to 3cm, minutely cinereous-pubesc. Fls in 1–3 pairs 3cm, pink-purple, tube scarcely ventricose. Idaho, Mont., Wyom. and

Utah (mts). Z3.

P. murrayanus Hook. To 90cm, glaucous; st. simple, erect. Lvs 15cm, spathulate to ovate, connate-perfoliate above. Infl. virgate, or few-fld clusters; fls to 2.5cm, deep scarlet, tubular, gradually widening upwards, lobes small. Late summer. Ark., Tex. and adjacent Okl. and Miss. Z6.

P. nelsoniae Keck & J.W. Thomps. = *P. attenuatus*.

P. nemorosus (Douglas) Trautv. Caudex simple woody, st. 30–80cm, few, erect. Lvs to 10cm, lanceolate to ovate, serrate. Infl. thyrsoid, glandular-pubesc.; fls strongly bilabiate, 2.5–3.5cm, lower lip greatly exceeding upper, rosy purple to light maroon, paler ventrally, strongly plicate, glab. within. Summer. Vancouver Is. to Calif. Z8.

P. neomexicanus Wooton & Standl. St. to 70cm. Basal lvs lanceolate to oblanceolate with winged petioles, st. lvs lanceolate to linear, 6–15mm broad. Infl. elongate, secund; fls 2.5–3.5cm, blue or tinged purple, throat broadly expanded, lobes spreading, lower lobes strongly hirsute at base. Summer. New Mex. (mts). Z4.

P. newberryi A. Gray. MOUNTAIN PRIDE. Forming mats 15–30cm tall, woody below. Lvs 1.5–4cm, elliptic to ovate, minutely serrate, coriaceous. Infl. racemose, subsecund, short, glandular-pubesc.; fls 22–30×5mm, throat slightly dilated, rosy red, ventral ridges bearded with short stiff hairs. Summer. Calif. and adjacent Nevada. f. *humilior* Sealy. Dwarf and bushy, to 15cm. Z8.

P. newberryi ssp. *berryi* (Eastw.) Keck = *P. berryi*.
P. newberryi var. *rupicola* Piper = *P. rupicola*.

P. nitidus Douglas. To 30cm; st. erect, glaucous. Lvs lanceolate to ovate, entire or shallowly dentate, to 10cm, v. glaucous, thick. Infl. thyrsoid, cylindric; fls to 2cm, bright blue, spreading-ascending, tube gradually dilated, palate glab. Summer. BC to Saskatch., S to Washington, Wyom. and N Dak. ssp. *polyphyllus* Pennell. Larger; lvs lanceolate to oblanceolate. Z3.

P. nitidus var. *major* Benth. in DC. = *P. pachyphyllus*.

P. oliganthus Wooton & Standl. St. to 60cm, erect. Basal lvs ovate to elliptic, st. lvs linear to lanceolate, erect. Infl. few-fld, gland.; fls 1.5–2.5cm, blue to maroon, throat paler, strongly 2-ridged, lower lip exceeding upper, lower lobes bearded at base, gland. without. Summer. Colorado to New Mex. and Ariz. Z4.

P. ophianthus Pennell. Differs from *P. jamesii* in fls 1.8–2.2cm. Summer. Colorado and S Utah to New Mex. and Ariz. Z4.

P. oreganus Howell = *P. gairdneri* ssp. *oreganus*.

P. osterhoutii Pennell. St. 40–80cm. Lvs conspicuously veined, glaucous, lvs 5–15cm, lanceolate-ovate to ovate. Infl. narrow; fls 2cm, blue to violet, glab. without, pubesc. at base of lower lobes within. Summer. Colorado. Z4.

P. ovatus Douglas ex Hook. BROAD-LEAVED PENSTEMON. St. 50–100cm, several. Lvs 5–15cm, ovate, serrate-dentate, bright green, sparingly hirtellous to glab. Infl. thyrsoid, glandular-pubesc.; fls to 22×7mm, ampliate, bilabiate, lower lip exceeding upper, deep blue to indigo, palate villous or occas. glab. Summer. BC to Oreg. Z3.

P. pachyphyllus A. Gray ex Rydb. St. 30–60cm, glaucous. Lvs ovate, pale green-glaucous, 5–7cm, on winged petioles; st. lvs perfoliate, 3–5×2–4cm. Infl. thyrsoid, narrowly elongate; fls 15–18mm, blue, mostly glab., throat inflated, ventrally rounded, upper lobes arched, lower lobes spreading, exceeding upper, lanate at base. Summer. Utah. ssp. *congestus* (M.E. Jones) Keck Cor. subglabrous within. Z4.

P. pallidus Small. Pubesc.; st. to 1m. Lvs to 10cm, lanceolate to oblong-lanceolate, entire or remotely dentate, pale green, firm, softly pubesc. Infl. ± paniculate, glandular-pubesc.; fls to 2.5cm, white with purple nectar-guides, throat not strongly inflated. EC US. Z4.

P. palmeri A. Gray. SCENTED PENSTEMON. St. 50–140cm, erect. Lvs ovate-lanceolate, spinose-dentate or subentire, to 15cm, uppermost connate-perfoliate. Infl. thyrsoid, secund; fls 25–35×10–20mm, tube short, throat strongly inflated, lobes reflexed, white flushed pink or lilac with conspicuous red guide-lines; lower lip villous at base. Summer. Calif. to Nevada, Utah and Ariz. Z5.

P. palmeri var. *bicolor* Brandg. = *P. bicolor*.

P. parryi A. Gray. St. 30–60cm, many, erect. Lvs oblanceolate to spathulate, 5–8cm, st lvs auriculate-semiamplexicaul at base, glaucous. Thyrse racemiform, lax; fls 1.5–2cm, rose magenta, gland., funnelform, obscurely bilabiate, lobes large, orbicular. Spring. S Ariz. Z8.

P. payettensis Nels. & Macbr. Forming clumps 15–60cm high. Lvs to 18cm, oblanceolate to narrowly obovate, bright green, rather thick. Infl. thyrsoid, often rather secund; 22–27mm, tube abruptly dilated into throat, limb ample, distinctly bilabiate, bright blue tinged purple, glab. Summer. Oreg. to Idaho. Z4.

P. peckii Pennell. Forming clumps; st. slender, 25–50cm. Lvs 2–5cm, linear-lanceolate. Infl. thyrsoid, strict, minutely glandular-pubesc.; fls 8–10mm, pale blue-mauve to white, limb expanded, palate low-ridged, rather pilose. Summer. Oreg. Z5.

P. perpulcher A. Nels. Lvs linear-lanceolate to linear-oblong, to 1.5cm broad. Fls 2–2.5cm, palate glab. Idaho. Z4.

P. phlogifolius Greene = *P. watsonii*.
P. pickettii St. John = *P. richardsonii*.
P. pilifer Heller = *P. speciosus*.
P. pinetorum Piper = *P. wilcoxii*.

P. pinifolius Greene. St. to 40cm, numerous, woody below. Lvs filiform, to 1mm wide. Infl. secund; fls 2.5–3cm, scarlet, strongly bilabiate, throat narrow, 2-ridged, upper lobes projecting, lower spreading or reflexed, yellow-pilose at base. Summer. New Mex. to Ariz. and Mex. 'Mersea Yellow': to 20cm, fls bright yellow. Z8.

P. platyphyllus Rydb. 30–70cm, ± glaucous, st. shrubby at base, minutely pubesc. when young. Lvs 4–5cm, elliptic-ovate, acuminate. Fls 2–3cm, lavender-violet, glab., shallowly bilabiate, throat broadly inflated, lobes all spreading. Summer. Utah. Z3.

P. pratensis Greene. WHITE-FLOWERED PENSTEMON. St. 25–50cm, light green, glab. Lvs linear-oblanceolate to elliptic, thin, 3–8cm, light green. Infl. thyrsoid, strict; fls 11–14mm, tubular to ampliate, white buds tipped yellow, palate hirsute with yellow hairs. Summer. Oreg. to Idaho and Nevada. Z4.

P. procerus Douglas. SMALL-FLOWERED PENSTEMON. St. 10–40cm, slender. Lvs 2–6cm lanceolate to oblanceolate or oblong, deep green, thin. Infl. thyrsoid; fls blue-purple, limb spreading, palate bearded. Summer. NW N Amer. Z3.

P. procumbens Greene = *P. crandallii* ssp. *procumbens*.

P. pruinosus Douglas ex Lindl. CHELAN PENSTEMON. St. 10–30cm, clustered, ± viscid-pubesc. Lvs 5–10cm, lanceolate to ovate, minutely serrate-dentate, ± minutely viscid-pubesc.; petioles slender. Infl. thyrsoid, glandular-pubesc.; fls 10–16×2–4mm, lower lip larger than upper, palate weakly hirsute to glab., indigo. Summer. BC to Washington. Z7.

P. pseudoprocerus Rydb. = *P. attenuatus* ssp. *pseudoprocerus*.

P. pseudospectabilis M.E. Jones. DESERT PENSTEMON. St. 60–100cm, erect, virgate. Lvs ovate, serrate, upper st. lvs connate-perfoliate forming discs to 12×6cm, thin, glaucous. Infl. thyrsoid, sparingly gland.; fls 20–26×6mm, rosy purple, often tinged yellow at throat, tinged yellow throughout in bud, with dark guide-lines within, minutely viscid-pubesc. Spring–summer. Calif. to Ariz. ssp. *connatifolius* (A. Nels.) Keck Lvs more finely serrate to subentire; infl. glab. Summer. New Mex. and Ariz. Z8.

P. pubescens Sol. = *P. hirsutus*.
P. pubescens var. *gracilis* A. Gray = *P. gracilis*.

P. pulchellus Lindl. St. rather woody at base. Lvs lanceolate to oblong, serrate, with smaller subsidiary lvs clustered in axils. Infl. lax, gland.; 2–2.5cm, violet, paler below, slightly gland. without, throat dilated, lower lobes slightly pubesc. at base. New Mex. Z9.

P. pumilus Nutt. Tufted, grey-canescent; 5cm, erect or ascending, v. leafy. Lvs to 2.5cm, lanceolate or lower spathulate, attenuate at base. Fls 1–3 per axils, to 2cm, purple or bllue, regularly funnelform, glab. within. Mont. (mts). Z3.

P. puniceus Lilja non A. Gray. = *P. hartwegii*.
P. puniceus A. Gray non Lilja. = *P. superbus*.
P. puniceus var. *parryi* A. Gray = *P. parryi*.
P. purdyi hort. = *P. heterophyllus* ssp. *purdyi*.

P. rattanii A. Gray. St. 30–120cm, stout. Basal lvs 5–25cm, lanceolate to ovate to oblong, undulate-serrate to shallowly dentate. Infl. thyrsoid, leafy below, glandular-pubesc.; fls 24–30mm, maroon to violet purple to blue-mauve, abruptly ampliate, upper lip short, erect, lower lip longer, spreading, palate hirsute. Summer. Oreg. to Calif. Z7.

P. rattanii var. *minor* A. Gray = *P. anguineus*.
P. rex Nels. & Macbr. = *P. speciosus*.

P. richardsonii Douglas. CUT-LEAVED PENSTEMON. Subshrub, 20–80cm, subglabrous to canescent. Lvs to 7cm, lanceolate, serrate to pinnately parted with lobes toothed or parted. Infl. a racemose to branched thyrse, glandular-pubesc.; fls 18–30×7mm, pink to rosy lilac or bright lavender, with white guide-lines, glandular-pubesc. without, lower lip occas. sparsely hirsute within, throat dilated. Summer. BC to Oreg. Z7.

P. roezlii Reg. = *P. laetus* ssp. *roezlii*.

P. rotundifolius A. Gray. Glaucous, woody-based. Lvs to 4cm, orbicular, lowermost with winged petioles, thickly coriaceous. Infl. paniculate; 2.5cm, red, tubular, lobes 4mm, subequal, throat glab. N Mex. Z9.

P. rubicundus Keck. WASSUK PENSTEMON. St. 50–120cm, erect, glaucous. Lvs 2.5–10cm, oblanceolate or broadly lanceolate, dentate, glaucous, fleshy. Infl. elongate, secund; fls 3–3.5cm, dark pink to deep rose with maroon nectar-guides, throat white within, minutely glandular-pubesc., palate hirsute, ventricose-ampliate, lboes short, those of lower lip reflexed. Summer.

Nevada. Z5.

P. rupicola (Piper) Howell. ROCK PENSTEMON. Mat-forming, woody below, to 10cm, v. glaucous, glab. or canescent. Lvs 0.8–2cm, elliptic to orbicular, minutely serrate-dentate, v. glaucous, thick, glab. or canescent. Infl. racemose, dense, few-fld, glandular-pubesc.; fls 27–35×8mm, throat moderately dilated, deep rose, ventral ridges sparsely villous. Late spring–summer. Washington to Calif. 'Albus': fls white. 'Diamond Lake': growth vigorous; lvs large; fls large, rich pink. 'Pink Dragon': habit compact; fls light salmon-pink. 'Roseus': fls pink. Z7.

P. rydbergii A. Nels. St. to 60cm. Lvs oblong to elliptic, entire. Infl. interrupted, of 2 or more many-fld clusters; fls to 2cm, indigo, glab. without, throat ± expanded, densely yellow-hairy at base of lower lobes. Summer. Wyom. to Colorado and New Mex. ssp. *aggregatus* (Pennell) Keck Fls paler blue to purple. Z4.

P. saliens Rydb. = *P. eriantherus*.

P. scouleri Lindl. Forming dense, broad clumps, 10–40cm tall, shrubby at base. Lvs linear-lanceolate, subentire to serrate, 2–5mm wide, lustrous, coriaceous. Infl. strict, subsecund, rather dense, glandular-pubesc.; fls 3.5–5×1cm, bright lavender-blue to pale purple, ventral ridges villous. Summer. N Washington to N Idaho and BC. 'Albus': fls white. 'Purple Gem': to 10cm; fls violet-purple. 'Roseus': fls rose-pink. Z5.

P. secundiflorus Benth. St. to 50cm, erect, ± glaucous. Lvs ovate to spathulate or linear, somewhat glaucous. Infl. narrow, secund; fls 1.5–2.5cm, blue or violet, unmarked, throat gradually inflated, lower lip hirsute. Summer. Wyom. to Colorado and New Mex. Z3.

P. sepalulus A. Nels. 60–80cm, blue-glaucous, shrubby at base. Lvs 6–9cm, linear-lanceolate, entire. Fls 2.5–3cm, pale lavender to pale violet, glab., shallowly bilabiate, throat broadly inflated, lobes all spreading. Summer. Utah. Z4.

P. serrulatus Menz. CASCADE PENSTEMON. Subshrub, 30–70cm. Lvs 2–9cm, broadly lanceolate to spathulate, subentire to serrate or shallowly laciniate. Infl. thyrsoid, of 1–5 dense clusters; fls 16–23×6mm, tubular-campanulate, deep blue to dark purple, sometimes sparsely pubesc. at base of lower lip. Late summer. S Alask. to Oreg. 'Albus': fls white. Z5.

P. shantzii A. Nels. = *P. parryi*.

P. similis A. Nels. = *P. jamesii*.

P. Six-Hills Hybrid. (*P. davidsonii* ×*P. eriantherus*.) To 15cm, bushy. Fls large, violet. Late spring–early summer. Z5.

P. smallii Heller. St. to 120cm, simple. Lvs 5–13cm, ovate to lanceolate, serrate, thin. Infl. thyrsoid, open, secund, glandular-pubesc.; fls 3cm, bright pink-purple with white stripes within, abruptly tubular-campanulate, gibbous above, upper lip entire, lower exceeding upper, 3-lobed, yellow-hirsute. N Carol. and Tenn. Z6.

P. speciosus Douglas ex Lindl. St. 20–80cm, tufted, erect. Lvs to 15cm, lanceolate to spathulate, rather thick, glab. to mostly pubesc. or glaucescent. Infl. thyrsoid, elongate, ± secund; fls 25–35×8–10mm, bright purple-blue, tube rather long, abruptly dilated into ample throat, limb strongly bilabiate. Summer. Washington to Calif., to Idaho and Utah. Z3.

P. speciosus ssp. *lemhiensis* Keck = *P. lemhiensis*.

P. spectabilis Thurber ex A. Gray non Wooton & Standl. St. 80–120cm, several, erect. Lvs 4–10cm, oblanceolate to ovate, ± connate-perfoliate, coarsely serrate, green or glaucescent. Infl. thyrsoid, lax; fls 25–33×8mm, tube abruptly expanded into ample throat, strongly bilabiate, upper lip almost erect, lower lip reflexed, lavender-purple, lobes blue, white within, lower lip sometimes weakly hirsute at base. Early summer. Calif. to N Baja Calif. Z7.

P. staticifolius Lindl. = *P. glandulosus*.

P. stenosepalus (A. Gray) T.J. Howell = *P. whippleanus*.

P. strictus Benth. STIFF BEARD-TONGUE. St. to 80cm. Basal lvs spathulate, long-petiolate, st. lvs linear to broadly lanceolate, glab. Infl. narrow, secund; fls 2–3cm, dark blue to violet, prominently bilabiate, throat moderately expanded, lower lobes exceeding upper, sometimes sparsely hairy at base. Summer. SW US. Z3.

P. subglaber Rydb. 30–100cm, erect. Lvs linear to broadly lanceolate. Infl. thyrsoid; fls 22–30mm, blue, bilabiate, tube narrow at base, then inflated, lower lobes spreading, glab. at base. Summer. Wyom. and Utah. Z3.

P. subulatus M.E. Jones. To 60cm, erect. Lvs to 7.5cm, green or glaucescent, oblanceolate to elliptic, to linear-subulate. Fls to 2.5cm, scarlet, glab., narrowly tubular, obscurely bilabiate, limb v. narrow. Spring–summer. Ariz. Z6.

P. superbus A. Nels. V. glaucous; st. to 180cm, stout. Lvs to 15cm, obovate, st. lvs ovate, sometimes connate-perfoliate, thick. Infl. thyrsoid, interrupted, many-fld; fls brilliant scarlet, almost funnelform, lobes spreading, to 6mm, rounded. Mex. Z9.

P. ternatus Torr. ex A. Gray. BLUE-STEMMED PENSTEMON. Shrub, straggly, 0.5–1.5m. Lvs 2–5cm, in whorls of 3, lanceolate, remotely serrate-dentate, rather thick. Infl. an elongated pan.; fls 23–30×4mm, narrowly tubular, upper lip helmet-shaped, lower lip spreading, scarlet, minutely glandular-pubesc. Summer. Calif. and Baja Calif. Z9.

P. teucrioides Greene. Often mat-forming, to 10cm; st. minutely cinereous-pubesc. Lvs to 1cm, crowded, linear, mucronate, revolute, minutely cinerous-pubesc. Fls 15–19mm, pale blue to blue-purple, throat somewhat ampliate with 2 ventral ridges, upper lip ± erect, lower lip spreading, often exceeding upper. Colorado. Z4.

P. thompsoniae (A. Gray) Rydb. Forming mats or tufts, 2–5cm high. Lvs 1–2cm, oblanceolate to spathulate-oblong, mucronate, pale grey, adpressed-pubesc. Infl. a racemiform thyrse, leafy, obscurely viscid; cor. 13–18mm, to 5mm diam. at throat, sub-tubular, blue-violet, palate hirsute. Summer. Calif. to Utah and Ariz. Z4.

P. thompsonii hort. = *P. davidsonii* ssp. *thompsonii*.

P. thurberi Torr. Bush, 30–60cm, woody below, intricately branched. Lvs 1–3cm, narrowly linear, mucronate, bright green, revolute, ± scabrid. Infl. a thyrsoid rac.; obliquely salverform, lobes spreading, sparsely pubesc. at base of lower lobes, with 2 ventral lines of pubesc. in throat, 12–15mm, blue to rosy lavender or maroon. Summer. Calif. and Baja Calif. to Ariz. and New Mex. Z9.

P. tidestromii Pennell. St. 30–50cm. Lvs 10–12cm, oblanceolate, obtuse, rather glaucous, minutely pubesc. Infl. narrow; fls 1.5–2cm, blue, glab. Summer. Utah. Z4.

P. tolmiei Hook. ALPINE PENSTEMON. Plant with well-developed basal rosette, st. slender, 5–15cm. Lvs 1.5–5cm, lanceolate to elliptic. Fls 1cm, clustered, somewhat ampliate, lower lip exceeding upper, indigo or pale yellow, palate, hirsute, limb spreading. Summer. NW N Amer. Z7.

P. torreyi Benth. = *P. barbatus* ssp. *torreyi*.

P. triflorus Heller. St. 60–90cm, erect, simple. Lvs to 10cm, spathulate or oblong, entire to dentate. Infl. minutely glandular-pubesc.; fls in 3's, 2.5cm+, bright rosy-purple, paler within with darker nectar-guides, gradually dilated, lobes spreading. Tex. Z8.

P. triphyllus Douglas. WHORLED PENSTEMON. Subshrub, 30–80cm. Lvs 2–5cm, largely in 3's, linear to narrowly lanceolate, subentire to pinnately dentate or cleft. Infl. thyrsoid, rather open, elongate; fls 13–17×3–4mm, pale lavender to bright blue-lilac with prominent guide-lines, lower lip sometimes sparsely hirsute within. Summer. Washington and Oreg. to Idaho. Z5.

P. triphyllus ssp. *diphyllus* (Rydb.) Keck = *P. diphyllus*.

P. tubaeflorus Nutt. St. 50–100cm. Lvs 8–12cm, elliptic or oblong-lanceolate. Infl. cylindric, slender, often interrupted; fls tube gradually dilated from base, limb nearly regular, 2–2.5cm, white, throat minutely glandular-pubesc. within. Late spring–summer. EC US. Z4.

P. unilateralis Rydb. 40–90cm, glab.; st. erect. Lvs linear to ovate-lanceolate, 6–12cm. Infl. thyrsoid, of many several-fld fascicles; fls blue, bilabiate, tube gradually much inflated from base, glab. or sparsely pubesc. within near front. Summer. Wyom., Colorado. Z3.

P. utahensis Eastw. UTAH BUGLER. St. 30–60cm. Lvs lanceolate, coriaceous, glaucous, scabrid. Infl. a racemiform thyrse; fls 18–24×4mm, subtubular, lobes rotately spreading or reflexed, carmine, glandular-pubesc. without, densely gland. within at orifice. Spring–summer. Calif. to Nevada, Utah and Ariz. Z4.

P. utahensis A. Nels. non Eastw. = *P. subglaber*.

P. variabilis Suksd. St. erect, forming clumps 20–60cm high. Lvs 1–5cm, in whorls, opposite, or scattered, narrowly linear to lanceolate-oblong, entire to finely serrate. Infl. thyrsoid, branched or rarely strict; fls 10–12mm, almost tubular, lower lip exceeding upper, yellow tinged brown with purple guide-lines, gland. Summer. Washington to Oreg. Z7.

P. venustus Douglas. LOVELY PENSTEMON. Subshrub, 30–80cm, often glaucescent. Lvs to 10cm, lanceolate to oblong, minutely serrate or hook-toothed. Infl. a spike-like pan., subsecund; fls 20–32×8mm, pale violet to violet-purple, lobes ciliate. Early summer. Washington and Oreg. to Idaho. Z5.

P. virens Pennell. Forming mats; st. to 40cm, erect, slender. Lvs to 10cm, lanceolate, entire to minutely dentate. Infl. 6–18cm; fls to 1.5cm, pale to dark blue-violet, paler within with maroon to purple nectar-guides, glandular-pubesc., lobes spreading, palate white-hirsute. Summer. Colorado. Z4.

P. virgatus A. Gray. St. to 80cm, often solitary, slender. Lvs linear to narrowly lanceolate. Infl. narrow, secund; fls 1.5–2.5cm, blue, white or pink, usually with purple guide-lines, strongly bilabiate, throat broadly inflated, lobes of upper lip spreading or projecting, lobes of lower lip spreading or reflexed. Summer. New Mex. and Ariz. Z8.

P. watsonii A. Gray. Clump-forming, glaucescent; st. 30–60cm. Lvs 2.5–5cm, oblong-lanceolate to ovate-lanceolate. Infl thyrsoid rather lax; cor. 12–16mm, violet-purple or white in part, narrowly funnelform, lower lip subglabrous at base. Summer. Colorado, Utah and Nevada (mts). Z3.

P. wherryi Pennell. To 60cm, minutely cinereous-pubesc. Lvs to 5cm, elliptic to lanceolate, entire to serrate, thin. Fls to 2cm, pale lilac; staminode yellow-hirsute. Okl. and Ark. Z6.

P. whippleanus A. Gray. St. slender, to 60cm. Basal lvs ovate to spathulate, st. lvs lanceolate to oblong-lanceolate, entire to minutely dentate. Infl. elongate, glandular-pubesc.; fls 2–3cm, dull purple, gland. without; throat abruptly expanded, lobes of lower lip exceeding those of upper, villous. Summer. Wyom. and Idaho, S to Colorado, Utah, New Mex. and Ariz. Z4.

P. whitedii Piper. St. 10–40cm. Lvs broadly linear to lanceolate or oblanceolate, entire to dentate; glab. to cinereous-pubesc. Infl. thyrsoid, glandular-pubesc.; fls 18–23×6–9mm, maroon tinged blue with darker guide-lines, throat ample, limb rather small, palate somewhat pilose. Summer. Washington. Z7.

P. wilcoxii Rydb. St. 40–100cm. Lvs 4–20cm, lanceolate to ovate, minutely serrate-dentate to subentire, rather thick. Infl. thyrsoid, or paniculate; fls 13–23×4–8mm, ampliate, lower lip greatly exceeding upper, bright blue to blue tinged purple. Summer. Oreg. to Washington and Mont. Z4.

P. wrightii Hook. Stem 40–60cm, erect, rather stout. Lvs 5–10cm, oblong or obovate. Infl. thyrsoid, elongate; fls 18mm, bright rose-pink, slightly pubesc., throat ampliate, limb expanded to 18mm diam. Early summer. W Texas, New Mexico and Arizona. Z8.

P. xylus A. Nels. = *P. crandallii*.

P. cultivars. 'Alice Hindley': mauve and white trumpets. 'Amethyst': amethyst-blue. 'Apple Blossom': small white, pink tipped fls. 'Barbara Barker': pink and white. 'Blue Spring': to 30cm; white. 'Burgundy': deep wine-purple. 'Edithae': shrubby, prostrate; fls deep lilac. 'Evelyn': neat; lvs narrow; fls slim rose-pink with pale striped throats. 'Firebird': lvs narrow; fls clear red with honey guide-lines. 'Friedhelm Hahn': fls wine-red. 'Garnet': garnet-red. 'Hidcot White': white. 'Hopley's Variegated': variegated form of 'Alice Hindley'. 'Mother of Pearl': white, flushed with purple. 'Old Candy Pink': vibrant pink. 'Pink Endurance': candy-pink, with honey guide-lines at throat. 'Prairie Fire': orange-red. 'Shoenholzeri' ('Firebird'): deep red. 'Snow Storm': white, turning pink tinted. 'Sour Grapes': tinted purple. 'Weald Beacon': tinted blue.

→*Chelone* and *Leiostemon*.

Pentachondra R. Br. Epacridaceae. 3 small, heath-like shrubs. Fls small, solitary, or clustered in upper lf axils; cor. tube short, recurved, bearded inside. Fr. a drupe. Aus., NZ and Tasm. Z8.

P. pumila (Forst. & Forst. f.) R. Br. Procumbent, everg. closely-branched, dwarf shrub to 15cm, bronze-tinted. Lvs to 0.5cm, crowded, oblong to obovate, tip callose, ciliolate. Fls to 6mm, solitary, white. Fr. red. Winter. Aus., NZ.

Pentactina Nak. Rosaceae. 1 decid. shrub to 70cm; young shoots angled, tinged red. Lvs 2–3cm, oblanceolate to obovate, apex toothed, silky beneath. Pan. term., 6–8cm, slender, arched; pet. white 5, linear; sta. 20, white, exserted. Summer. Korea. Z5.

P. rupicola Nak.

Pentadenia Wiehler. Gesneriaceae. 24 shrubby herbs or climbers. St. and lvs usually hairy. Fls axill., solitary or many in a cyme; cal. 5-lobed; cor. erect, tubular, often spurred, limb 5-lobed. Trop. Amer. Z10.

P. angustata Wiehler. St. ascending or descending. Lvs to nearly equal pairs, to 10×3.5cm, elliptic, green, hirsute above, suffused pink beneath. Fls 2–6, to 2.7cm, orange, yellow or rarely pink, puberulent. Costa Rica.

P. byrsina Wiehler. St. ascending or descending. Lvs in strongly unequal pairs, larger lf to 8×3cm, leathery, lustrous, sparsely hairy above, pink-flushed with white silky hairs beneath. Fls to 2.4cm, white, inflated and magenta toward apex, limb pale yellow, puberulent. Ecuad., Colomb.

P. colombiana Wiehler. St. to 3m, pendent. Lvs in subequal pairs, to 4×2.4cm, ovate. Fls solitary, to 3cm, spur cream, tube deep pink, glandular-hairy, limb pale green. Colomb.

P. crassicaulis Wiehler. St. to 3m, spreading or descending. Lvs in equal pairs, to 7–9×3–5.5cm, ovate, crenate. Fls solitary to 5.3cm, spur cream, tube pale yellow, lobes yellow, glab. Colomb., Ecuad.

P. ecuadorana Wiehler. St. to 60cm, erect or spreading. Lvs in equal pairs, to 5–7.5×2–4cm, elliptic or oblanceolate. Fls few, to 4cm, maroon, pink or yellow, silky. Ecuad.

P. microsepala (Morton) Wiehler. St. pendent, often prostrate. Lvs crowded, to 3.2×2.5cm, broadly elliptic, crenate, sparsely white-hairy. Fls yellow, to 1.3cm. Venez.

P. orientandina Wiehler. St. to 40cm, ascending or spreading. Lvs in strongly unequal pairs, larger lf 6–9×2.5–3.5cm, elliptic to oblanceolate, spotted red beneath, apex translucent red; smaller lf often caducous. Fls 2–8 to 2.5cm, pale yellow. Ecuad., Peru.

P. spathulata (Mansf.) Wiehler. St. upright to spreading. Lvs in unequal pairs, elliptic, crenate, marked red beneath. Fls many, cymose, yellow. Ecuad.

P. strigosa (Benth.) Hanst. Epiphyte. Lvs to 7.5cm, oblanceolate to elliptic, marked red beneath. Fls to 6.3cm, ventricose, orange-yellow. Ecuad., Colomb., Venez.

P. zapotalana Wiehler. St. to 80cm, ascending or descending. Lvs in markedly unequal pairs, larger lf to 12×5cm, oblanceolate, acuminate, red beneath. Fls 1–4 to 3.2cm, pale yellow. Ecuad.

→*Alloplectus* and *Columnea*.

Pentaglottis Tausch. Boraginaceae. 1 hispid perenn. herb; st. to 1m, branched, erect. Basal lvs to 40cm, ovate or ovate-oblong, long-petiolate; cauline lvs sessile. Cymes dense, axill. or term., bracteate; cor. blue, tube to 6mm, infundibular or cylindrical, limb to 10mm diam., rotate, with 5 scales in throat. SW Eur. Z7.

P. sempervirens (L.) Tausch ex L.H. Bail.
→*Anchusa*.

Pentapanax Seem.
P. henryi Harms = *Aralia tomentella*.
P. warmingianus (Marchal) Harms = *Aralia warmingiana*.

Pentaptera Klotzsch.
P. arjuna Roxb. ex DC. = *Terminalia arjuna*.

Pentapterygium Klotzsch.
P. rugosum Hook. = *Agapetes rugosum*.

Pentas Benth. Rubiaceae. c30 perenn. or bienn. herbs or shrubs. Lvs ovate to lanceolate; stipule seg. filiform to subulate. Fls in terminal, much-branched cymes or flat-topped corymbs; cal. tube globose to ovoid, ribbed, limb swollen, lobes 5; cor. tubular to cylindric, lobes 5, elliptic to oblong; sta. 5, included or exserted. Fr. a capsule. Trop. Arabia and Afr., Madag. Z10.

P. bussei K. Krause. Herb or shrub, to 4m, erect or scrambling. Lvs to 15cm, ovate or lanceolate to oblong, white-pubesc. beneath; Cymes to 8cm wide; fls scarlet; cal. lobes unequal, 1–3 developed and foliaceous, cor. 18×4mm; cor. tube to 1.8cm, lobes to 12×5mm. Trop. E Afr.

P. carnea Bak. = *P. lanceolata*.
P. coccinea Stapf = *P. bussei*.
P. coccinea auct., non Stapf = *P. zanzibarica* var. *rubra*.
P. flammea Chiov. = *P. bussei*.
P. klotzschii Vatke = *P. bussei*.

P. lanceolata (Forssk.) Deflers. STAR-CLUSTER; EGYPTIAN STAR-CLUSTER. Herb or subshrub, to 2m, erect or prostrate. Lvs to 15cm, ovate to elliptic or lanceolate, pubesc. Corymbs many-fld, fls pink or magenta to blue or lilac or, occas., white; cal. lobes unequal, 1–3 developed and foliaceous, to 12×3mm; cor. tube to 4cm, lobes to 10×5mm. Yemen to E Afr. ssp. *quartiniana* (A. Rich.) Verdc. Fls pink or red; cor. tube to 22mm. Ethiop. 'Avalanche': lvs streaked white; fls white. 'Kermesina': fls bright rose, throat violet. 'Quartiniana': fls rose, abundant.
P. lanceolata Robyns = *P. zanzibarica* var. *rubra*.
P. longituba De Wild. & T. Dur., non Schum. = *P. nobilis*.
P. mussaendoides Bak. Shrub, to 4m, erect, brown-pubesc. Lvs to 10cm, elliptic to oblong, apex acute. Fls in term. cymes or corymbs, pink or purple; cal. lobes strongly unequal; cor. tube to 25mm. Madag.
P. nobilis S. Moore. Herb or shrub, to 2m. Lvs to 20cm, ovate or elliptic to oblong, rough and bristly. Fls in loose, cymes or corymbs, white or red-flushed, fragrant; cal. lobes to 25×2mm, equal; cor. tube to 15cm, lobes to 20×7mm. Subtrop. Afr. (Zaire, Zam., to Tanz., Zimb.).
P. parviflora Benth. Subshrub, to 60cm, erect. Lvs to 8cm, ovate or elliptic to lanceolate, pubesc. on veins beneath. Fls in dense cymes, scarlet or blue to purple; cal. lobes to 3mm, equal; cor. tube to 6mm, lobes to 2mm. Trop. W Afr.
P. quartiniana (A. Rich.) Oliv. = *P. lanceolata* ssp. *quartiniana*.
P. stolzii Schum. & K. Krause, pro parte. = *P. zanzibarica*.
P. verruculosa Chiov. = *P. lanceolata* ssp. *quartiniana*.
P. zanzibarica (Klotzsch) Vatke. Herb or shrub, to 3m. Lvs to 15cm, ovate to lanceolate or elliptic, pubesc. Fls in dense cymes, pink or red to lilac or mauve, or white; cal. lobes to 9×2mm, unequal; cor. tube to 1cm, lobes to 6×3mm. Trop. E Afr. var. *rubra* Verdc. To 2.5m. Lvs to 17cm, bullate. Fls pink to red. Uganda, Kenya, Zaire.
P. zanzibarica = *P. zanzibarica* var. *rubra*.

P. cvs. 'California Lavender': dwarf; fls pale lavender, in large umbels, profuse. 'California Pink': compact; fls pale pink, in broad umbels. 'Orchid Star': lvs light green; fls large, lilac. 'Tu-Tone': compact; fls pink, centre red, in large round umbels. →*Manettia, Ophiorrhiza, Pentanisia* and *Sacosperma*.

Pentelesia Raf. = *Arrabidaea*.

Penwiper Plant *Notothlaspi*.
Peony *Paeonia*.

Peperomia Ruiz & Pav. RADIATOR PLANT. Piperaceae. *c*1000 largely succulent herbs. Lvs fleshy, usually long-stalked. Fls minute, white-cream in stalked erect spikes, sometimes sunk into axis; perianth 0; sta. 2, stigma often penicillate. Pantrop. Z10.

P. acuminata Ruiz & Pav. To 60cm+, erect, sparingly branched. Lvs to 12×4cm, elliptic to oblanceolate, sharply acuminate at apex, cuneate at base, veins pinnate; petiole short. Trop. Amer.

P. angulata HBK = *P. quadrangularis*.

P. argyreia Morr. WATERMELON BEGONIA; WATERMELON PEPPER. To 20cm, erect, dark red. Lvs 7×5.5cm, broadly ovate, concave, acute at apex, rounded at base, peltate, silver-grey above with dark green stripes along main veins; petiole to 12cm, red. N S Amer. to Braz.

P. arifolia Miq. St. short, thick. Lvs 6×5cm, rounded-ovate, subacute at apex, rounded to subcordate at base, green with grey variegation; petiole 12cm. SE Braz., Parag., Arg.

P. asperula P.C. Hutchison & Rauh. Erect herb, v. succulent. Lvs 18×9mm, crowded, folded along main vein, glossy and translucent above, grey-green, scabrous beneath. Peru.

P. berlandieri Miq. Creeping herb; st. minutely pubesc., to 10cm. Lvs 0.7cm, in whorls of 4, obovate, obtuse or emarginate, short-stalked. Mex. to Costa Rica.

P. bicolor Sodiro. Herb to 20cm, stoloniferous then ascending, pubesc. Lvs 3.5×3cm, ellitic or obovate, acute, tinged purple beneath. Ecuad.

P. blanda (Jacq.) HBK. Herb to 50cm, erect, fleshy, pink to red. Lvs 3.8×1.8cm, broadly elliptic to obovate, broadly acute at apex, broadly tapered to rounded at base, green above with paler pattern of veins, dark green beneath, thin, pubesc.; petiole 11mm, pink or green, hairy. S Amer., N to Flor., W Indies, S & C Afr. & Sr Lanka. var. *langsdorfii* (Miq.) Hens. Lvs 7×3cm, elliptic to elliptic-obovate or subrhombic. W Indies, Venez., Colomb. & Braz.

P. botteri C. DC. St. slender. Lvs 4×2.5cm, ovate to elliptic-lanceolate or subrhombic, acuminate at apex, acute to rounded at base, minutely pilose-pubesc., veins 5; petiole 1.5cm. Mex.

P. brevipes Benth. = *P. rotundifolia* var. *pilosior*.

P. camptotricha Miq. To 45cm; st. densely hirsute. Lvs 2.5×1.5cm, whorled, lower lvs suborbicular, 1cm diam., upper lvs obovate-rhombic, thick, green above, flushed red beneath, densely pubesc.; petioles short. S Mex.

P. caperata Yunck. EMERALD-RIPPLE PEPPER; GREEN-RIPPLE PEPPER; LITTLE-FANTASY PEPPER. Erect to 20cm, tough, dark green or tinged purple. Lvs 3.2×2.5cm, cordate, broadly acute to rounded at apex, rounded or auriculate at base, often peltate, dark glossy green, veins impressed, in rippling folds; petiole 7.5cm, green to dull red. Braz. (?). 'Emerald Ripple': lvs deep green. 'Little Fantasy': habit dwarf. 'Tricolor': lvs with wide cream edge, marked pink at base. 'Variegata' ('Variegated Ripple'): edged cream.

P. cerea Trel. St. often pendent. Lvs often whorled, 12×8mm, rounded-elliptic, revolute; petiole 2mm. Peru.

P. chachopoana Trel. = *P. microphylla*.

P. clusiifolia (Jacq.) Hook. Erect to 25cm, fleshy, green to purple. Lvs 7.5×2.7cm, obovate to elliptic, broadly acute to rounded at apex, tapered to often clasping base, green or tinged purple, margin flushed maroon, glandular-punctate above, main vein raised beneath and red at base; petiole 2.5mm, dark red. W Indies, perhaps Venez. 'Jellie': lvs green and cream flushed pink, margin red. 'Variegata': lvs light green, variegated cream towards edge, margin red.

P. columnella Rauh & P.C. Hutchison. Herb to 10cm, erect to sprawling, freely branched. Lvs in whorls, downward-pointing, cordate, sessile, v. succulent, to 8×6×5mm, green to dark green, with translucent shiny window above. N Peru.

P. cordata Trel. & Yunck. Large creeping herb. Lvs 7.5×5.5cm, rounded-ovate to elliptic-ovate, acuminate at apex, deeply cordate at base, subpeltate, dark green above, paler and granular beneath; petiole 6.5cm. Colomb.

P. crassifolia Bak. LEATHER PEPPER. Decumbent herb; st. to 30cm. Lvs 12mm, orbicular, obtuse at apex, sparsely pubesc. beneath; petioles short. Uganda.

P. cubensis C. DC. Creeping or scandent herb. Lvs to 7.5cm, ovate, acuminate at apex, cordate at base, minutely ciliate; petioles to 5cm. Cuba.

P. dahlstedtii C. DC. VINING PEPPER. Herb to 40cm, st. prostrate, angled, rufescent, glossy. Lvs 4×2cm, elliptic, broadly acute to rounded at apex, tapered to base, green, coriaceous, minutely glandular-punctate above, veins raised beneath; petiole 6.5×2mm, red-tinted. Braz.

P. dolabriformis HBK. PRAYER PEPPER. To 25cm, erect, branched. Lvs folded together and fused, 28×13mm, mucronate at apex, tapered to cuneate base, pale green, darker along line of fusion, succulent; petiole 4mm. Peru.

P. eburnea Sodiro. Sts prostrate, 35cm; slender. Lvs 5×2.5cm, ovate, acuminate at apex, rounded or cordate at base, scarcely peltate, with emerald green veins, coriaceous, white pubesc. beneath; petiole 2.5cm, white, sparsely hairy. Ecuad.

P. elongata HBK. Stoloniferous. Lvs 6×2cm, elliptic-lanceolate, acuminate, ciliate at apex, acute at base, glab.; petiole 1.5cm, ciliate. Fr. Guiana, Surinam, Venez. & Colomb.

P. emarginella (Sw.) C. DC. St. spreading, filiform. Lvs rounded obovate to obcordate, obtuse to subtruncate often emarginate, rounded to subacute at base, ± ciliate, 4mm wide, thin, petiole 3mm. W Indies, C Amer. & N S Amer.

P. fenzlei Reg. Erect, shrubby. Lvs obovate, rounded, minutely pubesc., 3-veined; petiole vry short. Origin unknown.

P. flexicaulis Wawra. Erect, st. ± flexuous, dull red. Lvs erect, oblanceolate, somewhat concave, succulent, 3×1.5cm, dark green above, flushed maroon beneath, 3 prominent veins above; petiole short. Peru ?.

P. floridana Small. Similar to *P. obtusifolium* except lvs suborbicular to elliptic, to 9cm. S Flor.

P. fosteri hort. = *P. dahlstedtii*.

P. fraseri (C. DC. FLOWERING PEPPER. To 40cm, erect; st. striate, dull red, minutely pubesc. Lvs 3.5×3.2cm, broadly ovate to suborbicular, acute at apex, cordate at base, tinged purple on veins, pale green beneath with bright red to pink veins and pink spots; petiole 4.5cm, dull red to pink. Spike to 4cm, bright white, fragrant, mignonette-like appearance. Colomb. and Ecuad.

P. galioides HBK. To 40cm, erect, branched, pubesc. Lvs in whorls, 18×6mm, elliptic, or obovate, broadly acute to rounded at apex, tapered at base, pubesc.; petiole 2mm, pubesc. C & S Amer., W Indies.

P. gardneriana Miq. Erect, rhizomatous. Lvs 4cm, rounded-ovate to subreniform, obtuse at apex, cordate to truncate at base, bright green above, paler beneath, pellucid-glandular; petiole 7cm. Braz. & Venez.

P. glabella (Sw.) A. Dietr. To 20cm, erect or sprawling, softly fleshy, glossy red. Lvs 3.8×3cm, broadly elliptic to obovate, rounded to obtusely acute at apex, broadly tapered to rounded at base, green, often black glandular-punctate, fleshy; petiole 9mm, red. C & S Amer., W Indies. 'Variegata': lvs pale green, edged or variegated off-white.

P. graveolens Rauh & Barthl. Erect to 15cm; st. red. Lvs oblong, rounded or emarginate, v. succulent, somewhat boat-shaped, folded, to 40×12mm, glossy bottle-green above, maroon beneath; petioles to 12mm, red. Winter. Peru.

P. griseoargentea Yunck. IVY-LEAF PEPPER; SILVER-LEAF PEPPER; PLATINUM PEPPER. To 20cm, erect. Lvs 3.8×3cm, cordate, broadly acute to rounded at apex, auriculate or rounded at base, often peltate, grey-green above, paler beneath, coriaceous, veins deeply impressed above; petiole 5cm, pale green to pink. Braz. 'Blackie': petioles dotted red; lvs thin, dark olive to black flushed bronze. 'Nigra': lvs corrugated, metallic black.

P. haughtii Trel. & Yunck. = *P. puteolata*.

P. hederifolia hort. = *P. griseoargentea*.

P. hirta C. DC. St. straggling, freely branched, pubesc. Lvs 4cm, ovate to obovate or rhombic-elliptic, acute, grey-green. above, ciliate, satiny; petiole 2cm. Cuba.

P. hoffmannii C. DC. St. spreading, br. erect or ascending. Lvs 6×4mm, cuneate-obovate, pale to bright green, coriaceous-fleshy; petiole 9mm. Costa Rica to Colomb. & Braz.

P. incana (Haw.) Hook. To 30cm, somewhat shrubby; sts white-lanate. Lvs 4.2×3.8cm, rounded to broadly ovate, rounded to broadly acute or down-turned mucronate at apex, rounded to cordate at base, coriaceous, white-lanate. SE Braz.

P. inquilina Hemsl. Procumbent, succulent, v. delicate; st. rooting, red. Lvs orbicular to obovate, 5mm, green, fleshy; petiole v. short. Mex. & Guat.

P. japonica Mak. Perenn. herb to 30cm, erect, sparsely branched, minutely pubesc. Lvs in whorls, 18×11mm, elliptic to obovate, rounded to obtuse, slightly fleshy; petiole 5mm. Jap.

P. lanceolata C. DC. To 1m; slender, villous at nodes. Lvs in whorls 32×12mm, elliptic-lanceolate to subrhombic, acute to acuminate at apex, acute at base, pubesc. on veins above, glab., punctate beneath; petiole 8mm, narrowly winged. Ecuad.

P. langsdorfii Miq. = *P. blanda* var. *langsdorfii*.

P. leptostachya Hook. & Arn. To 25cm, decumbent and rooting, soon ascending, hirtellous. Lvs 2.5×1.5cm, elliptic to obovate, shortly attenuate to obtuse at apex, acute to cuneate at base, hirtellous; petiole 7mm. Hawaii & other Pacific Is.

P. liebmanii C. DC. To 45cm, branched above, hirsute. Lvs in whorls, obovate to rhombic-obovate, acute at apex, cuneate at base, thick and succulent, to 3cm, green above, red beneath, densely pubesc.; petioles short. S Mex.

P. maculosa (L.) Hook. To 20cm, succulent, sparsely hairy, decumbent then ascending, green with dark red spots. Lvs 8.5×14.5cm, elliptic-ovate, abruptly acuminate at apex, rounded to subcordate at base, peltate, ± pubesc.; petiole 10cm, spotted. W Indies, Panama, N S Amer.

P. magnoliifolia (Jacq.) Dietr. Differs from *P. obtusifolia* in more upright habit and lvs more contracted to rather acute apex. Panama, N S Amer. & W Indies. 'Golden Gold': lvs irregularly spattered green and yellow. 'Golden Gates': lvs matt green and gold with bright green specks. 'USA': lvs edged yellow to cream. 'White Cloud': lvs wrinkled, edged white. 'Variegata': lvs variegated lime green.

P. marmorata Hook. f. To 30cm; st. erect, tough. Lvs 10×5cm, ovate, obtuse to acute at apex, deeply cordate at auriculate at base with overlapping lobes, green above with silver-grey or white patterns between veins, coriaceous; petiole 6mm. S Braz. 'Silver Heart': lvs dappled silver between veins.

P. meridana Yunck. To 50cm, succulent, erect to ascending, maroon or red. Lvs 24×18mm, suborbicular-ovate to ovate-elliptic, subpeltate at base, dull to bright green above; petiole 25mm. Venez.

P. metallica Lind. & Rodigas. To 15cm, erect, st. pink or red, fleshy. Lvs 2.5×1.2cm, elliptic, acute at apex, broadly tapered to rounded at base, green tinged brown with silvery-green band above, tinged red beneath, succulent; petiole 6mm, red. Peru.

P. microphylla HBK. To 30cm, st. ± prostrated, slender, pubesc. Lvs whorled, 1×0.6cm, broadly elliptic to obovate, rounded at apex, broadly tapered to rounded at base, coriaceous becoming succulent, petiole 2mm. C & NW S Amer.

P. minima C. DC. = *P. emarginella*.

P. moninii C. DC. Erect to 20cm. Lvs 3.5cm, elliptic, tapered, subcoriaceous, veins pubesc. beneath; petiole 1cm. Réunion Is.

P. nivalis Miq. To 20cm, erect or prostrate. Lvs folded upwards, but not so completely as in *P. dolabriformis*, 15×6mm, bright green above, white or flushed pink beneath, succulent; petiole 8mm. Peru.

P. nummularifolia HBK = *P. rotundifolia*.

P. obliqua Ruiz & Pav. Large lvs, ascending. Lvs 5.5×2.5cm, oblanceolate-subrhombic, acuminate at apex, cuneate at base; petiole 8mm. Peru.

P. obtusifolia (L.) Dietr. BABY RUBBER PLANT; AMERICAN RUBBER PLANT; PEPPER-FACE. Stoloniferous st. rooting, ascending, to 15cm. Lvs 10×5cm, elliptic-obovate, rounded to emarginate at apex, cuneate at base; petiole 28mm, ± winged. Mex. to N S Amer. & W Indies. 'Alba': new growth cream, st. and petioles dotted red. 'Albo-marginata': lvs small, obovate, pale green irregularly edged cream. 'Gold Tip': lvs oblique, mottled pale yellow, heavily towards tip. 'Lougenii': lvs variegated cream. 'Minima': dwarf, dense; lvs shiny. 'Variegata': lvs more pointed, variegated pale green and marked cream towards margin; st. marked scarlet.

P. orba Bunting. To 15cm, bushy, erect, dull green flecked red, hairy. Lvs ovate to elliptic, acute at apex, rounded at base, green, coriaceous, pubesc.; petiole 10mm, minutely red-punctate, hairy. Origin unknown. A juvenile form with numerous short st. and small lvs is offered as 'Pixie' or 'Teardrop'. 'Pixie' ('Teardrop'): miniature form.

P. ornata Yunck. To 20cm, erect. Lvs crowded towards st. apex, 5×3.5cm, ovate to elliptic or suborbicular, broadly acute to rounded at apex, broadly tapered, rounded or cordate at base, often tinged red on veins beneath, fleshy, minutely gland. aobve; petiole 5mm, pink to red. S Venez., N Braz.

P. pavasiana C. DC. = *P. pseudovariegata*.

P. peltifolia C. DC. St. villous. Lvs to 27×17cm, ovate, acute to shortly acuminate at apex, rounded or notched at base, peltate, hairy; petioles to 11cm, villous. W Boliv.

P. peltifolia hort. non C. DC. = *P. argyreia*.

P. pereskiifolia (Jacq.) HBK. To 30cm, st. spreading, green tinged dull red, sometimes glandular-punctate. Lvs in whorls, elliptic to broadly obovate, acute to somewhat acuminate at apex, tapered to base, 4×2.5cm, green, sometimes edged red, succulent, veins slightly paler; petiole 5mm, red-tinged, minutely punctate. Colomb. & Venez.

P. perrottetiana Miq. Trailing, succulent and fleshy; br. erect. Lvs 2.2cm, broadly elliptic to obovate, dark green above, paler beneath, glandular-punctate, 3 main veins conspicuous above; petiole 4.5mm. Maur.

P. polybotrya HBK. To 25cm, lf scars prominent. Lvs rounded-ovate, abruptly acute to acuminate at apex, truncate to cordate at base, peltate, to 9cm diam.; petiole 8cm. Colomb. and Peru.

P. prostrata hort. St. filiform, trailing, white-pubesc. Lvs 1×1cm,

rounded ovate, obtuse to subcordate at base, often subpeltate, pubesc. beneath, veins white; petiole 2mm. SE Braz.

P. prostrata Mast. & Moore = *P. rotundifolia* var. *pilosior*.

P. pseudovariegata C. DC. ± succulent; st. erect or procumbent and rooting. Lvs 12×5.5cm, oblong-lanceolate, acute at apex, subacute at base, pubesc. beneath, coriaceous; petiole 6.5cm. W Colomb. var. *sarcophylla* (Sodiro) Trel. & Yunck. Lvs glab. SW Colomb. & Ecuad.

P. pubifolia hort. Creeping, downy-pubesc. Lvs ovate, small, green with middle grey bar, fleshy.

P. pulchella Dietr. = *P. verticillata*.

P. puteolata Trel. St. to 40cm prostrate, angled, red, glossy. Lvs 6.5×2.5cm, elliptic to narrowly elliptic, acute to somewhat-acuminate at apex, tapered at base, green, with pale zones on veins, paler beneath, stiff and coriaceous, veins sunken above; petiole 5mm, red-tinted, ciliolate. Colomb.

P. quadrangularis (Thomps.) Dietr. To 20cm, prostrate, angled, wiry red-tinted, minutely pubesc. Lvs in whorls 2.1×1.6cm, broadly elliptic to orbicular, rounded, green, flushed pink when young, coriaceous to succulent; petiole 3mm, minutely pubesc. W Indies, Panama & N S Amer.

P. resediflora Lind. & André = *P. fraseri*.

P. rotundifolia (L.) HBK. To 25cm, creeping; st. rounded, green, glab. Lvs orbicular to broadly elliptic, rounded or cordate at base, 15mm, green, paler beneath, sparsely hairy, fleshy; petiole 3mm, hairy. C & S Amer., W Indies, S Afr. var. *pilosior* (Miq.) DC. More densely hairy; lvs with pale green reticulate pattern above. SE Braz.

P. rubella (Haw.) Hook. Erect to 15cm, branched, dark red, sparsely villous. Lvs in whorls 7×4mm, elliptic, broadly acute to rounded at apex, broadly tapered to rounded at base, light to dark green above, flushed pink, convex and sparsely hairy beneath; petiole to 2mm, red. W Indies.

P. sandersii DC. = *P. argyreia*.

P. sarcophylla Sodiro = *P. pseudovariegata* var. *sarcophylla*.

P. scandens hort. St. 60cm+, scandent, stout, swollen at nodes. Lvs to 7.5×6cm, ovate to suborbicular, long-acuminate at apex, truncate to subcordate at base; petiole to 3cm. Origin unknown. Perhaps synonymous with *P. serpens*.

P. scandens Ruiz & Pav. non hort. = *P. serpens*.

P. serpens (Sw.) Loud. To 50cm, trailing; st. fleshy, sometimes flecked red. Lvs 4×2.5cm, lanceolate, acuminate at apex, rounded to cordate at base, pale green, coriaceous, glab.; petiole 14mm, flecked red. Panama to Braz., Peru & W Indies. 'Variegata': lvs pale green roughly edged off-white.

P. subpeltata C. DC. Small, sometimes scandent; st. filiform. Lvs 2cm, rounded, acute at apex, cordate at base, peltate, pellucid, glab.; petioles 4–8cm. Ecuad.

P. tithymaloides Vahl = *P. magnoliifolia*.

P. trinervis Ruiz & Pav. To 25cm, stoloniferous; st. ascending, crisped-pubesc. Lvs 2.8×1.8cm, elliptic to elliptic-obovate, lower suborbicular, acute to acuminate at apex, acute to rounded at base, black-punctate, villous; petiole 8mm. Ecuad., Peru, Chile.

P. trinervula C. DC. To 15cm, stoloniferous, decumbent then ascending, somewhat succulent, villous to crisped-pubesc. Lvs rounded subrhombic-ovate, attenuate to somewhat acute apex, shortly acute at base, 18×15mm, green above, paler beneath, yellow glandular-punctate, succulent, crisped-pubesc.; petiole 6mm. N S Amer.

P. tristachya HBK. Herb, st. ascending, to 25cm, sparingly branched. Lvs 6.5×4.5cm, rounded-ovate, prolonged to acuminate apex, subsinuate-cordate at base, peltate. Colomb.

P. urocarpa Fisch. & C.A. Mey. St. rooting ascending. Lvs rounded-ovate, abruptly acuminate at apex, rounded or cordate at base, minutely ciliate toward apex, 3cm wide, membranous; petiole 3cm, crisped-pubesc. N S Amer. & W Indies.

P. variegata Ruiz & Pav. = *P. maculosa*.

P. velutina Lind. & André. To 20cm; st. erect, succulent, hirtellous. Lvs 4.5×3.8cm, elliptic, acute, dull green above with silvery stripes along veins, bright red tinged pink beneath and white-punctate, margins often tinged pink or silver, coriaceous to succulent; petiole 8mm, pink. Ecuad.

P. verschaffeltii Lem. = *P. marmorata*.

P. verticillata (L.) Dietr. Erect to 50cm; st. pale green to pink, hirsute. Lvs in whorls of 5, lowest lvs orbicular, 8mm, pale green above, tinged red beneath, thickly succulent, subsessile, upper lvs obovate, to 3×3.5cm, pale green, coriaceous, clearly veined; petiole to 3mm. W Indies.

P. viridis hort. St. decumbent, long, stout, swollen at nodes. Lvs ovate-lanceolate, acuminate at apex, truncate at base, petiolate, medium-sized, glossy green.

→*Piper* and *Rhynchophorum*.

Pepino *Solanum muricatum*.

Pepper *Capsicum*; *Piper*.

Pepper-and-salt *Erigenia bulbosa*.

Pepper-face *Peperomia obtusifolia.*
Pepper Grass *Lepidium sativum.*
Pepperidge *Nyssa sylvatica.*
Peppermint *Eucalyptus amygdalina*; *Mentha × piperita.*
Peppermint Geranium *Pelargonium tomentosum.*
Peppermint Stick *Kleinia gregorii.*
Pepper Plant *Piper nigrum.*
Pepper Root *Cardamine diphylla.*
Pepper Tree *Drimys lanceolata*; *Kirkia wilmsii*; *Macropiper excelsum*; *Schinus molle.*
Pepper Vine *Ampelopsis arborea.*
Pepperwood *Umbellularia californica*; *Zanthoxylum clava-herculis.*
Pepperwort *Lepidium sativum*; *Marsilea.*

Peranema D. Don Dryopteridaceae. 2 terrestrial ferns. Rhiz. short, erect. Fronds stipitate, uniform, 3–4-pinnate or -pinnatifid, ovate to deltoid, rough. Trop. Asia. Z9.
P. cyatheoides D. Don. Fronds to 90cm, pinnae petiolate, alt., falcate, lanceolate, pinnules to 4cm, oblong, seg. obtuse, notched; stipes to 30cm. India, Nepal, China, Taiwan.
P. formosana Hayata = *P. cyatheoides.*
→*Sphaeropteris.*

Peraphyllum Nutt. Rosaceae. 1 erect, decid. shrub to 1.5–2m. Lvs 2–5cm, lanceolate, downy at first, sometimes sparsely toothed. Fls 2–5 in term. clusters, 2cm diam., white often flushed pink; pet. 5, circular, spreading; sta. 20. Fr. a pendent, yellow-brown drupe. Late spring. NW US. Z5.
P. ramosissimum Nutt.

Peregrina *Jatropha* (*J. integerrima*).
Perennial Cornflower *Centaurea montana.*
Perennial Flax *Linum perenne.*
Perennial Honesty *Lunaria rediviva.*
Perennial Pea *Lathyrus latifolius.*
Perennial Phlox *Phlox paniculata.*

Pereskia Mill. Cactaceae. 16 trees, shrubs and woody climbers, differing superficially from most cacti in st. not conspicuously succulent, terete, unsegmented, lvs broad, flat. Glochids 0; spines numerous. Fls solit., paniculate or corymbose, floral areoles with wool, rarely spines, perianth rotate. Fr. berry-like to pear-like. S Mex., C Amer., N & W S Amer., Braz.
P. aculeata Mill. Woody climber to 10m; main st. cane-like. Lvs lanceolate to elliptic or ovate, to 11×4cm, spines stipular or at areoles on older growth only. Fls numerous, in pan., 2.5–5cm diam., scented white or nearly so. Autumn. Trop. Amer. 'Godseffiana': lvs variegated yellow to peach-coloured, purple-tinted beneath; an attractive house-plant or conservatory subject, not easily recognized as a cactus. Z9.
P. amapola F.A.C. Weber = *P. nemorosa.*
P. antoniana (Backeb.) Rauh = *P. weberiana.*
P. bleo (Kunth) DC. Shrub or small tree 2–8m. Lvs narrowly elliptic to oblong or lanceolate, acuminate, 6–20cm, fleshy, bifurcate; spines 1–5, 5–15mm. Fls in a condensed rac., 4–6cm diam., bright red or orange-red. Spring–summer. Panama, Colomb. Z9.
P. conzattii Britt. & Rose = *P. lychnidiflora.*
P. corrugata Cutak = *P. bleo.*
P. godseffiana hort. = *P. aculeata* 'Godseffiana'.
P. grandifolia Haw. Shrub or small tree 2–5(–10)m. Lvs narrowly elliptic, ovate or obovate-lanceolate, 9–20cm, rather thin; spines 0–8, 1–4cm. Fls few to many, 3–5(–7)cm diam., pink to purple-pink. Spring–autumn. Braz. Z9.
P. lychnidiflora DC. Tree to 10(–15)m. Lvs unequal, variable in shape and size, 2–8cm, oblanceolate or elliptic to obovate to orbicular, acute, rounded on emarginate; spines 0–3, 2–7cm. Fls solitary, c6cm diam., yellow-orange. Summer–autumn. S Mex. to Costa Rica. Z9.
P. nemorosa Rojas Acosta. Similar to *P. sacharosa* but with narrower and larger lvs, larger fls. Spring–summer. S Braz., Parag., Urug., Arg. Z9.
P. pereskia (L.) Karst. = *P. aculeata.*
P. pititache Karw. ex Pfeiff. = *P. lychnidiflora.*
P. sacharosa Griseb. Shrub or small tree to 7m. Lvs obovate to oblanceolate, 3–12(–20)cm, fleshy; spines 1–8, 1–6cm. Fls solitary or in clusters, 3–7cm diam., pink, white at base. Spring–autumn. NW Arg., W Parag., Boliv., W Braz. Z9.
P. sparsiflora Ritter = *P. sacharosa.*
P. weberiana Schum. Slender shrub, 1–3m, sometimes scandent; st. cane-like. Lvs 2.5–8cm, elliptic to narrowly elliptic-lanceolate, fleshy; spines 3–5, 8–13mm. Fls solitary, 1.5–2.5cm diam., pink or white. Spring. Boliv. Z9.
→*Pereskiopsis* and *Rhodocactus.*

Pereskiopsis Britt. & Rose. Cactaceae. 9 sparsely branched or scrambling shrubs; st. terete, unsegmented; lvs large, persistent, succulent; glochids present; spines usually 1 to several, acicular. Fls usually lat. Fr. fleshy. Mex. and Guat.
P. aquosa (F.A.C. Weber) Britt. & Rose. 1–2m. Lvs elliptic, 6–8cm, margin tinged red; glochids yellow; spines 1–2, 1–3cm, off-white. Fls golden-yellow, tinged red. Fr. pear-shaped, 4–5cm, edible, green-yellow. Summer. Mex. Z9.
P. chapistle (F.A.C. Weber) Britt. & Rose = *P. rotundifolia.*
P. diguetii (F.A.C. Weber) Britt. & Rose. 1m+, minutely pubesc. at first. Lvs 2–6cm, elliptic to ovate, minutely velvety-pubesc.; spines 1–4, to 7cm, almost black. Fl. c5cm diam., yellow, tinged red. Summer. Mex. Z9.
P. gatesii Baxter. Scandent to 2–3m; lvs obovate, to 3.5cm, fleshy; glochids brown; spines 1- several, 5cm, pale brown at first. Fl. 6.5cm diam., lemon-yellow. Fr. sterile, proliferous. Summer. Baja Calif. Z9.
P. pititache (Karw. ex Pfeiff.) Britt. & Rose = *Pereskia lychnidiflora.*
P. porteri (Brandg. ex F.A.C. Weber) Britt. & Rose. Scandent to 1.2m+; lvs obovate, to 3cm, fleshy; glochids brown; spines 0–8 or more, 3–5cm, pale brown. Fl. c4cm diam., yellow. Summer. NW Mex. Z9.
P. rotundifolia (DC.) Britt. & Rose. 3–4m, wide-spreading, lvs obovate or elliptic to orbicular and mucronate, 3–4cm, v. fleshy; glochids off-white; spines 1, to 6–10cm, off-white. Fl. 3cm diam. yellow, tinged pink. Summer. SW Mex. Z9.
P. spathulata hort. = *P. diguetii.*
P. velutina Rose = *P. diguetii.*

Perezia Lagasca. Compositae. 30 ann. to perenn. herbs or shrubs. Lvs basal or alt., entire, toothed or pinnatisect, margins often spinulose, often amplexicaul. Cap. solitary or many in a pan. or cyme; receptacle flat, naked; phyllaries imbricate, in 2 to many series, green to maroon, margins usually scarious; flts with a 3-toothed outer lip and shorter, 2-toothed inner lip, recurved. S Amer. Z9.
P. linearis Less. Tufted, often prostrate, perenn. herb to 30cm. Basal lvs lanceolate to spathulate, mucronate, ± glab., st. lvs to 3cm, lanceolate, densely ciliate, amplexicaul. Cap. solitary, to 4cm diam., phyllaries occas. red-tipped, apex glandular-hairy; flts blue or white. Winter–early spring. S Andes.
P. microcephala (DC.) A. Gray = *Acourtia microcephala.*
P. multiflora (Humb. & Bonpl.) Less. Erect ann., to 50cm, gland. pubesc. Basal lvs to 9cm, oblong-lanceolate, st. lvs, ovate-lanceolate. Cap. few to many, to 2.5cm diam., in corymbose or paniculate clusters; outer lip of outer flts blue or white, other lips and inner flts yellow. Winter–summer. Andes (S Colomb. to N Chile). ssp. *sonchifolia* (Bek.) Vuill. To 30cm. Basal lvs to 5cm, oblanceolate, st. lvs much smaller. Phyllaries with short apical spines. Urug.
P. recurvata (Vahl) Less. Procumbent to erect, often matforming perenn. herb to 40cm. Lvs to 2cm, linear-lanceolate, imbricate, apex, spinose base somewhat sheathing, recurved, rigid, revolute, ciliate, glab. Cap. terminal, to 3cm diam.; phyllaries often red at apex; flts blue or white. Late autumn–early spring. S S Amer.
P. sonchifolia Bak. = *P. multiflora* ssp. *sonchifolia.*
P. viscosa Less. Erect ann. to 45cm often gland. Lvs oblong-cuneate, obtuse, sinuate, ± gland., basal lvs petiolate, st. lvs sessile. Flts purple. Summer. Chile.

Perfoliate Pondweed *Potamogeton perfoliatus.*

Periboea Kunth. Liliaceae (Hyacinthaceae). 2 perenn. bulbous herbs. Lvs basal, linear, channelled, fleshy. Rac. few-fld; perianth lobes 6, basally united into a tube. S Afr. Z9.
P. corymbosa (L.) Kunth. Lvs to 12cm. Scape to 7.5cm; rac. 4–8-fld, corymbose; fls to 1.5cm; perianth lilac-rose, tube to 0.75cm; sta. exserted.
→*Hyacinthus.*

Pericallis D. Don. Compositae. 14 perenn. herbs or shrubs. Lvs alt. or in a basal rosette, simple, petiolate. Cap. radiate, solitary or in a corymb or pan. Macronesia. Z9.
P. appendiculata (L. f.) R. Nordenstam. Shrub to 1m; st. white-lanate. Lvs ovate, pinnatifid, lobes 7–9, base cordate, toothed, glab. and glossy above, white lanate beneath. Cap. 1–1.5cm, clustered in a corymb or pan.; ray flts white, disc flts yellow, tinged purple. Canary Is.
P. cruenta (L'Hérit.) R. Nordenstam. Perenn. herb to 1m; st. lanate. Lvs ovate to ovate-lanceolate or triangular-cordate, 5–15cm wide, crenate-ciliate to sinuate-dentate, base attenuate, petiole, winged, pink- to purple-tomentose beneath. Cap. 2.5–4cm diam., in open, flat pan.; ray flts pink to maroon or purple; disc flts dark purple. Spring–summer. Tenerife.

P. × *hybrida* R. Nordenstam. FLORIST'S CINERARIA. A variable complex of hybrids between *P. lanata* and *P. cruenta* and possibly other spp. Perenn. herb, often grown as ann., forming compact cushions or openly branched plants to 1m. Lvs ovate to suborbicular, often light green. Cap. to 5cm diam., clustered in corymbs; flts white to pink, red, maroon, deep purple, violet and blue, ray flts sometimes bicoloured, with white base and coloured apex. Nat. in mild coastal areas, e.g. Calif. Amigo Hybrids: v. compact, to 20cm; lvs small; flts long-lasting, to 5cm diam., bright colours. California Super Giant: habit compact, branching from base to 45cm high; flts large in range of colours from red to purple and blue. Cindy Mixture: v. compact; flts in blue, carmine, dark red and copper, several bicolours. Dwarf British Beauty Mixed: compact, to 30cm; flts in several bright colours, some with contrasting white centres; early. Elite Hybrids: compact; flts to 4cm diam. in blend of pink, rose, carmine, bright red and blue shades, some bicolours; early. Erfurt Dwarf Mixture: compact, dense, to 20cm; flts, to 4cm diam., several bright colours. 'Grandiflora': medium height; flts large, blue with white eye. 'Grandiflora nana Zwerg' ('Gmunder Zwerg'): dwarf; lvs small; flts medium in range of colours including rose, deep red, entirely blue or with white eye, and white. Jubilee Dwarf Mixture: dwarf, to 25cm; lvs small, compact; flts to 5cm diam., in formula blend of blue, red, pink and white solids and bicolours. Mini-Starlet Mixed: v. dwarf and compact, to 20cm; flts in tight clusters, to 4.5cm diam., wide range of bright colours. Mini Starlet Series: to 15cm; flts single, small. Moll Improved Hybrids: spreading, to 60cm; flts to 5cm diam., range of colours, including bright scarlet, blue with eye, strawberry red, light blue and white. Multiflora nana Goldcentre: flts small, in solid colours with centre cushion formed by protruding yellow anth. Saucer Series: flts single, exceptionally large. 'Siter's Rainbow Purple': compact; lvs small; v. large heads of magenta-purple flts with white eye. Starlet Mixture: compact, to 20cm; lvs small; flts to 4cm diam., wide colour range, solids and bicolours. 'Stellata Nana': habit compact to 45cm; flts somewhat small, pet. narrow, white with blue centre, also in blue and shades of pink. Superb Series: to 40cm; flts large, single. Tosca Hybrids: dwarf, to 25cm; lvs compact; flts large, in wide colour range, few bicolours; early. Tourette Mixture: to 26cm; flts to 4cm diam., wide colour range; early.

P. lanata (L'Hérit.) R. Nordenstam. Subshrub to 1m, ascending to procumbent, flexuous, densely pubesc. Lvs to 15cm, broadly ovate-cordate to suborbicular, sparsely dentate or pinnatifid, lobes 5–7, densely pubesc. beneath, petiolate. Cap. 3–5cm diam., solitary or clustered in loose corymbs, violet-scented; ray flts mauve, disc flts purple. S Tenerife.

P. multiflora (L'Hérit.) R. Nordenstam. Perenn. herb to 1m, erect, hairy below, glab. and glaucous above. Lvs broadly ovate to suborbicular, base cordate, wispy-hairy beneath; petioles auriculate, winged above. Cap. large, clustered in a much-branched pan.; ray flts lilac; disc flts dark purple. Canary Is.
→*Cacalia, Cineraria* and *Senecio*.

Perilla L. Labiatae. 6 ann. herbs. Lvs opposite, often variegated or coloured. Fls paired in verticillasters in spikes; cal. campanulate, 10-nerved, 5-toothed; cor. bilabiate, 5-lobed, tube shorter than cal. India to Jap. Z8.
P. crispa (Thunb.) Tan. = *P. frutescens* var. *nankinensis*.
P. frutescens (L.) Britt. To 1m, erect, pubesc. Lvs 4.5–12cm, broadly ovate, acuminate, deeply serrate, green sometimes speckled purple. Infl. to 10cm; cor. 3.5–4mm, white. Summer. Himal. to E Asia; nat. Ukraine. 'Atropurpurea' lvs deep red-purple. var. *nankinensis* (Lour.) Britt. Lvs laciniate-dentate, dark bronze or purple, margins crisped, fringed. China; nat. E US. f. *rosea* L.H. Bail. Lvs variegated red pink, crenate.
P. fruticosa D. Don = *Elsholtzia fruticosa*.
P. laciniata W. Mill. & L.H. Bail. = *P. frutescens* var. *nankinensis*.
P. ocimoides L. = *P. frutescens*.
→*Ocimum*.

Periploca L. Asclepiadaceae. 11 glab. shrubs, sometimes twining. Fls star-like in loose cymes or corymbs. Fr. 2, narrow-cylindrical, follicles. Medit. to E Asia, Trop. Afr. Z6.
P. graeca L. SILK VINE. Decid. twiner to 10m. Lvs 2.5–5cm, ovate to lanceolate, glossy dark green. Fls to 2.5cm diam., in long-stalked corymbs, malodorous, exterior yellow-green, interior maroon to chocolate, lobes 5, downy. Follicles to 12cm; seeds tufted. SE Eur. to Asia Minor.

Peristeria Hook. Orchidaceae. 7 epiphytic or terrestrial orchids. Pbs 10–15cm, oblong-ovoid to subconical, 1- to several-leaved. Lvs 50–85cm, elliptic-lanceolate, plicate, petiolate. Rac. basal, erect to pendent; fls thickly fleshy, cupped, fragrant; sep. subequal, elliptic to suborbicular; pet. smaller; lip fleshy, hypochile concave, 3-lobed, epichile rounded, simple, disc often callose. S & C Amer. Z10.

P. aspersa Rolfe. Infl. to 15cm, arching; tep. red-yellow or orange-yellow spotted red-maroon, to 3.5×3.5cm; lip orange spotted dark maroon. Venez., Braz., Colomb.
P. barkeri Batem. = *Acineta barkeri*.
P. elata Hook. Infl. to 130cm, erect; tep. white to 3×2.5cm; lip spotted red-rose. Costa Rica, Panama, Venez., Colomb.
P. pendula Hook. Epiphytic. Infl. to 20cm, pendulous; fls pale green or yellow-green, tinged and spotted red-purple; tep. to 3.5×2.5cm. Venez., Peru, Braz., Guyanas, Surinam.

Peristrophe Nees. Acanthaceae. 15 everg. perenn. herbs and subshrubs. Lvs opposite, entire. Fls solitary or clustered in axils surrounded by bracts; cor. long-tubular, limb-2 lipped. OW Trop. Z10.
P. angustifolia Nees = *P. hyssopifolia*.
P. hyssopifolia (Burm. f.) Bremek. Subshrub to 60cm. St. initially pubesc. Lvs 2–8cm, ovate-lanceolate, finely acuminate, dark green. Fls deep rose pink to magenta, in small clusters. Java. 'Aureo-variegata' (MARBLE LEAF): lf midrib and veins zoned cream to yellow.
P. salicifolia (Bl.) Hassk. = *P. hyssopifolia*.
P. speciosa (Roxb.) Nees. Subshrub to 1m. St. grey. Lvs to 12cm, ovate-elliptic, glossy dark green. Fls paired or in threes; cor. to 5cm, magenta to violet, blotched crimson. India.

Periwinkle *Catharanthus; Vinca*.
Pernambuco Wood *Caesalpinia echinata*.

Pernettya Gaudich.
P. angustifolia Lindl. = *Gaultheria mucronata* var. *angustifolia*.
P. ciliaris G. Don = *Gaultheria myrsinoides*.
P. ciliata Small = *Gaultheria myrsinoides*.
P. empetrifolia (Lam.) Gaud. = *Gaultheria pumila*.
P. furens auct. = *Gaultheria insana*.
P. furiens (Hook. & Arn.) Klotzsch = *Gaultheria insana*.
P. insana (Molina) Gunckel. = *Gaultheria insana*.
P. lanceolata (Hook. f.) B.L. Burtt & Hilliard = *Gaultheria lanceolata*.
P. leucocarpa D.C. = *Gaultheria pumila* var. *leucocarpa*.
P. mucronata (L.f.) Gaudich. ex Spreng. = *Gaultheria mucronata*.
P. mucronata var. *angustifolia* (Lindl.) Reiche = *Gaultheria mucronata* var. *angustifolia*.
P. mucronata var. *rupicola* (Phillips) Reiche = *Gaultheria mucronata* var. *rupicola*.
P. macrostigma Colenso = *Gaultheria macrostigma*.
P. nana Colenso = *Gaultheria parvula*.
P. pentlandii DC. = *Gaultheria myrsinoides*.
P. prostrata (Cav.) DC. = *Gaultheria myrsinoides*.
P. prostrata ssp. *pentlandii* (DC.) B.L. Burtt = *Gaultheria myrsinoides*.
P. pumila (L. f.) Hook. = *Gaultheria pumila*.
P. pumila var. *leucocarpa* (DC.) Kausel = *Gaultheria pumila* var. *leucocarpa*.
P. rupicola Phillips = *Gaultheria mucronata* var. *rupicola*.
P. tasmanica Hook. f. = *Gaultheria tasmanica*.
P. tasmanica var. *neozelandica* T. Kirk = *Gaultheria parvula*.

Peronil *Ormosia panamensis*.
Peronila *Ormosia krugii*.

Perovskia Karel. Labiatae. 7 perenn. subshrubs. St. erect, grey-white. Lvs aromatic, grey-felted at first, usually deeply cut. Fls tubular, 2-lipped, small in slender term. pan. Asia Minor, Iran, C Asia, Himal. Z6.
P. abrotanoides Karel. To 1m. Lvs to 7×2.5cm, oval to oblong, bipinnatisect, grey-green. Pan. to 40cm; fls 4–6 per whorl; cal. violet; cor. pink. Late summer. Afghan., W Himal. Z5.
P. artemesioides Boiss. Differs from *P. abrotanoides* in persistent pubescence. Baluchistan. Z6.
P. atriplicifolia Benth. To 150cm. Lvs to 6×3.5cm, lanceolate to cuneate, grey-green crenate or coarsely toothed. Pan. narrow; fls soft blue. Late summer. Afghan., Pak. 'Blue Mist': fls light blue, fls earlier; 'Blue Spire': lvs deeply cut; fls lavender blue in larger pan. Z6.
P. 'Hybrida'. (*P. abrotanoides* × *P. atriplicifolia*.) Lvs to 5cm, ovate, pinnatisect-bipinnatisect, grey-green. Infl. a long pan. of lavender-blue fls. Gdn origin. Z5.
P. scrophulariifolia Bunge. To 1m. Lvs to 7×3.5cm, ovate, base rounded or cordate, gland. Pan. pyramidal to 30cm. Late spring–early summer. C Asia. Z6.

Persea Mill. Lauraceae. 150 everg. trees or shrubs. Lvs entire. Fls ♀ or unisexual, inconspicuous, yellow-green, in axill. or term. pan. Fr. a berry or drupe, ellipsoid to pyriform. Trop. and subtrop. Amer., Macaronesia, SE Asia. Z10.
P. americana Mill. AVOCADO PEAR; AGUACATE; ALLIGATOR PEAR; PALTA. To 20m. Lvs 10–25cm, ovate-elliptic, subcoriaceous to

papery, dull dark-green above, paler beneath. Pan. term., rufous. Fr. to 12cm, oblong-ovoid to pyriform, skin leathery, glossy dark green, pale-punctate, to dark purple-green, tuberculate, flesh lime-green to yellow, firm; smooth and oily seed ovoid, 4cm. C Amer. Cultivated avocados will usually conform to one of three races, Guatemalan, W Indian, Mexican. Guatemalan and West Indian avocados fall within the circumscription of the typical var. *americana*. The Mexican avocados belong to var. *drymifolia* (Schldl. and Cham.) S.F. Blake, with lvs aromatic, fr. small, narrow, thin-skinned.

P. borbonia (L.) Spreng. RED BAY. Small tree. Lvs lustrous above, glaucous beneath. Fr. dark blue, red-stalked. SE US.

P. caustica Spreng. = *Lithrea caustica*.

P. gratissima Gaertn. = *P. americana*.

P. indica (L.) Spreng. To 20m. Lvs 8–20cm, lanceolate. Pan. term., corymbose to 15cm. Fr. to 26cm, ovoid-ellipsoid, ripening blue-black. Azores and Canary Is.

P. leiogyna S.F. Blate. = *P. americana*.

Persian Buttercup *Ranunculus asiaticus*.
Persian Carpet Flower *Edithcolea grandis*.
Persian Double Yellow *Rosa foetida*.
Persian Everlasting Pea *Lathyrus rotundifolius*.
Persian Ironwood *Parrotia persica*.
Persian Ivy *Hedera colchica*.
Persian Juniper *Juniperus macropoda*.
Persian Lilac *Melia azedarach*.
Persian Oak *Quercus macranthera*.
Persian Shield *Strobilanthes dyerianus*.
Persian Stone Cress *Aethionema grandiflorum*.
Persian Violet *Cyclamen*; *Exacum affine*.
Persian Walnut *Juglans regia*.

Persicaria L.

P. affinis (D. Don) Ronse Decraene = *Polygonum affine*.

P. alata (D. Don) Gross = *Polygonum alatum*.

P. amphibia (L.) S.F. Gray = *Polygonum amphibium*.

P. amplexicaulis (D. Don) Ronse Decraene = *Polygonum amplexicaule*.

P. bistorta (L.) A. Samp. = *Polygonum bistorta*.

P. campanulata (Hook. f.) Ronse Decraene = *Polygonum campanulatum*.

P. capitata (Buch.-Ham.) Gross = *Polygonum capitatum*.

P. filiformis (Thunb.) Nak. = *Polygonum virginianum*.

P. orientalis (L.) Vilm. = *Polygonum orientale*.

P. polystachya (Wallich ex Meissn.) H. Gross. = *Polygonum polystachyum*.

P. runcinata (Buch.-Ham. ex D. Don) H. Gross. = *Polygonum runcinatum*.

P. sericea (Pall. non hort.) H. Gross. = *Polygonum sericeum*.

P. vaccinifolia (Wallich ex Meissn.) Ronse Decraene = *Polygonum vaccinifolium*.

P. virginiana (L.) Gaertn. = *Polygonum virginianum*.

P. vivipara (L.) Ronse Decraene = *Polygonum viviparum*.

P. weyrichii (F. Schmidt) Ronse Decraene = *Polygonum weyrichii*.

Persimmon *Diospyros kaki*.

Persoonia Sm. GEEBUNG. Proteaceae. 75 undershrubs, shrubs or small trees. Lvs simple, entire. Fls small, solitary or rac.; perianth *c*1.5cm, often hairy, seg. usually free, recurved; anth. inserted within perianth tube. Fr. a 1- or 2-seeded drupe. Aus. Z9.

P. chamaepeuce Lhotsky ex Meissn. DWARF GEEBUNG. Prostrate shrub, 30cm high. Lvs 2cm, narrow-linear. Fls dull yellow, solitary in lf axils. Summer. E Aus.

P. comata Meissn. Erect shrub to 1.5m. Lvs 6–15cm, narrow-cuneate, revolute. Fls dull yellow in subapical rac. Spring–early summer. W Aus.

P. cornifolia Cunn. ex R. Br. BROAD-LEAVED GEEBUNG. Shrub to small tree to 6m; young growth hairy. Lvs 4–12cm, narrow-elliptic to broadly ovate. Fls dull yellow, solitary or in terminal rac. Summer. E Aus.

P. hirsuta Pers. Hairy, medium shrub to 1m. Lvs to 1.2cm, linear to oblong, revolute. Fls yellow, axill., almost sessile. Summer. E Aus.

P. lanceolata Andrews. Erect rounded shrub to 2m. Lvs 3–7cm, lanceolate to elliptic, apex abrupt. Fls yellow, solitary. Summer.

P. laurina Pers. Erect shrub to 1.5m. Lvs 4–9cm, ovate to elliptic. Fls yellow, solitary, or in clusters of 4–6. Early summer. E Aus.

P. levis (Cav.) Domin. BROAD LEAVED GEEBUNG. Medium to tall shrub to 5m with flaky red bark. Lvs 8–20cm, thick, lanceolate to narrow-ovate. Fls yellow, solitary, or in short term. rac. Summer. E Aus.

P. linearis Andrews. Tall, open shrub to 5m with black flaky

bark. Lvs 3–8cm, narrow to broad-linear. Fls yellow, solitary, axill. Summer. E Aus.

P. longifolia R. Br. SNOTTYGOBBLE. Shrub to small tree, 3–6m, with red-brown, flaky bark. Lvs 12–20cm, falcate. Fls yellow, axill. or in term. rac. Mid-spring and summer. W Aus.

P. myrtilloides Sieb. ex Schult. and Schult. f. Small to medium shrub to 1.5m with hairy br. Lvs 2–4cm, lanceolate to ovate. Fls yellow, rarely green, solitary, pendulous. Late spring–summer. E Aus.

P. nutans R. Br. Low, spreading shrub to erect, to 1m. Lvs 7–30mm, narrow-linear to broadly ovate. Fls yellow, axill., smooth. Summer. E Aus.

P. pinifolia R. Br. PINE LEAF GEEBUNG. Tall, spreading shrub 3m. Lvs 6.5cm, linear-terete. Fls yellow, solitary, axill. Summer. E Aus.

P. saccata R. Br. SNOTTYGOBBLE. Erect shrub, 0.5–2m. Lvs 5–15cm, ± terete, slender, grooved. Fls yellow or green-yellow, solitary, axill. in a subterminal. Spring–early summer. W Aus.

Peruvian Bark *Cinchona officinalis*.
Peruvian Daffodil *Hymenocallis narcissiflora*.
Peruvian Lily *Alstroemeria*.
Peruvian Mastic Tree *Schinus molle*.
Peruvian Old-man Cactus *Espostoa lanata*.
Peruvian Pepper-tree *Schinus molle*.

Pescatorea Rchb. f. Orchidaceae. 15 epiphytic orchids. Pbs 0. Lvs to 60×5cm, distichous, arranged in a fan, thin-textured to subcoriaceous, conduplicate. Fls showy, solitary, on short stalks; sep. elliptic-lanceolate to oblong-obovate, fleshy, concave; pet. narrower; lip fleshy, lat. lobes small, midlobe rounded, convex or ventricose, revolute, callus fleshy, ridged. Costa Rica to Colomb. Z10.

P. bella Rchb. f. Fls to 9cm diam.; tep. white-violet or pale violet, tips banded deep purple-violet; lip yellow-white, apex blotched purple-violet, callus marked purple. Colomb.

P. cerina (Lindl.) Rchb. f. Fls to 7.5cm diam., highly fragrant; sep. white to pale yellow, blotched yellow-green at base; pet. white; lip yellow, callus marked red-brown. Costa Rica, Panama.

P. dayana Rchb. f. Fls to 7.5cm diam., highly fragrant; tep. milk-white, often tipped rose-purple; white flushed purple-violet; callus purple-violet. Colomb.

P. lehmannii Rchb. f. Fls to 8.5cm diam., waxy, fragrant; tep. white, densely marked red-purple; lip dark purple, callus with chestnut-brown keels. Colomb., Ecuad.

→*Huntleya* and *Zygopetalum*.

Petalostemon Michx.

P. candidum Michx. = *Dalea candida*.

P. gattingeri (A.A. Heller) A.A. Heller = *Dalea gattingeri*.

P. oligophyllum Torr. = *Dalea candida* var. *oligophylla*.

P. purpureum (Vent.) Rydb. = *Dalea gattingeri*.

P. villosum Nutt. = *Dalea villosa*.

P. violaceum Michx. = *Dalea purpurea*.

Petamenes Salisb. ex J.W. London.

P. abbreviatus (Andrews) N.E. Br. = *Gladiolus abbreviatus*.

P. schweinfurthii (Bak.) N.E. Br. = *Gladiolus schweinfurthii*.

Petasites Mill. BUTTERBUR; SWEET COLTSFOOT. Compositae. 15 perenn. rhizomatous herbs. Lvs mostly basal, stalked and broad, often lobed; st. lvs spathe or scale-like. Cap. discoid or radiate, solitary to many, in a spike- or head-like pan. produced usually before basal lvs. N temp. regions.

P. albus (L.) Gaertn. Basal lvs 14–40cm diam., orbicular-cordate, regularly lobed, lobes dentate, basal lobes usually divergent, glab. above, lanate beneath. Infl. 15–30cm; cap. discoid; flts yellow-white. Spring. N & C Eur. to W Asia. Z5.

P. fragans (Vill.) Presl. WINTER HELIOTROPE. To 30cm. Basal lvs reniform-cordate, lobed, basal lobes convergent to divergent, glab. above, pubesc. beneath, margins regularly dentate. Cap. radiate; flts white-pink, vanilla-scented. Winter. C Medit. Z7.

P. frigidus (L.) Fries. Basal lvs deltoid-cordate, coarsely dentate or sparsely lobed, basal lobes divergent, glab. above, pubesc. below. Cap. radiate; flts white-yellow or red. N Eur. Z5.

P. giganteus F. Schmidt = *P. japonicus* var. *giganteus*.

P. hybridus (L.) P. Gaertn., Mey. & Scherb. BOG RHUBARB; BUTTERBUR. To 1m. Basal lvs to 60cm diam., orbicular-cordate, somewhat angular, lobed, basal lobes convergent, sparsely tomentose beneath, margin irregularly dentate. Cap. discoid; flts lilac-pink or yellow. Spring–summer. Eur., N & W Asia. Z4.

P. japonicus (Sieb. & Zucc.) Maxim. To 1m. Basal lvs to 80cm diam., reniform-cordate, lobed, basal lobes convergent, glab.

above, pubesc. beneath, irregularly dentate. Cap. discoid; flts pale mauve to almost white. Spring. Korea, China, Jap., nat. Eur. 'Variegatus': lvs with milky yellow to cream spots. var. *giganteus* (F. Schmidt) Nichols. Lvs 0.9–1.5m across; petioles to 2m. Jap. Z5.

P. niveus (Vill.) Baumg. = *P. paradoxus*.

P. paradoxus (Retz.) Baumg. Lvs deltoid-cordate to hastate, rarely bilobed at base, basal lobes usually divergent, densely white-tomentose beneath, regularly dentate. Cap. discoid; flts red-pink to white. Spring. Eur. mts. Z5.

P. spurius (Retz.) Rchb. Lvs deltoid-hastate, lobed, lobes 2–5 at each side of the base, glab. above, pubesc. beneath, regularly dentate. Cap. radiate, 10–45; flts yellow. Russia, E Rom.

P. vulgaris L. = *P. hybridus*.
→*Tussilago*.

Petastoma Miers.
P. langlasseanum Kränzl. = *Mansoa hymenaea*.
P. tonduzianum Kränzl. = *Mansoa hymenaea*.

Petiolate Fig *Ficus petiolaris*.
Petit Boux Caledonien *Schefflera elegantissima*.

Petrea L. BLUE BIRD VINE; PURPLE WREATH; QUEEN'S WREATH; SANDPAPER VINE. Verbenaceae. 30 lianes, shrubs, or small trees. Infl. racemose, axill. or terminal, elongate, cal. tube campanulate, lobes 5, blue, purple, violet or white; cor. inferior, hypocrateriform, darker than cal., lobes 5, rounded; sta. 4, included. Fr. drupaceous. Trop. Amer. and Mex.; *P. volubilis* nat. in India. Z10.

P. arborea HBK. BLUE PETREA; TREE PETREA. Subscandent shrub or small tree. Br. slender, grey, lenticellate. Lvs to 16×8cm, thin-textured, grey-green above, brighter green beneath, elliptic, asperulous. Infl. to 16cm, ascending or nodding, pubesc.; cal. to 17mm, blue, lobes longer than tube; cor. to 7mm, lobes rounded, cambridge blue. Colomb. and Venez. to Guyana and Trin. Commonly confused in hort. with *P. volubilis*. 'Broadway': flts white.

P. kohautiana Presl. FLEUR DE DIEU. Liane to 20m. Br. stout, light grey or ashy-white, lenticellate. Lvs to 20×11cm, coriaceous, dark green, broadly elliptic, glabrate. Infl. to 60cm, erect or nodding, scabrous; cal. to 2cm, violet or blue, lobes exceeding tube; cor. to 2cm, lobes rounded, violet or blue. W Indies, Antilles. var. *anomala* Mold. Fls white.

P. racemosa Nees. PURPLE WREATH. Woody vine or shrub, br. grey or brown, puberulent. Lvs to 18×8cm, membranous, elliptic, bright green, serrate or denticulate, glab. Infl. to 31cm, erect or nutant; cal. tube to 6mm, puberulent, lobes to 14mm; cor. tube to 9mm, lobes to 7.5mm, short-pubesc. N S Amer.

P. volubilis L. PURPLE WREATH; SAND PAPER. Woody vine to undershrub, to 12m. Br. twining, pale brown to ashy grey, shortly pubesc., lenticellate. Lvs to 21×11cm, oblong-elliptic, subcoriaceous, deep green above, lighter green and scurfy beneath. Infl. to 22–36cm, erect or pendent, cylindrical; cal. lilac, lobes longer than tube, to 18×6mm; cor. to 8mm, tube densely pubesc. above, indigo to amethyst. C Amer. and Lesser Antilles, introd. elsewhere. 'Albiflora': fls white.

Petrocallis R. Br. Cruciferae. 1 cushion-forming alpine perenn. herb to 5cm. Lvs to 6mm, digitately 3-lobed, grey-green in tight rosettes. Flowering st. leafless, hairy; fls few, corymbose, to 1cm diam., vanilla-scented, pink-lilac to blue. Pyren., Alps, Carpath. Z4.

P. fenestrata Boiss. = *Elburzia fenestrata*.
P. pyrenaica (L.) R. Br.
→*Draba*.

Petrocoptis A. Braun. Caryophyllaceae. 7 perenn., tussock-forming rock plants. Pyren. and mts of N Spain. Z7.

P. glaucifolia (Lagasca) Boiss. Loosely tufted, glab. perenn. with fragile, flowering st. to 15cm. Basal lvs not rosulate, ovate to lanceolate, grey-green. Cyme lax; pet. limb 12–15mm, entire or shallowly indented, pink-purple. Summer. N Spain (mts).

P. lagascae (Willk.) Willk. = *P. glaucifolia*.

P. pyrenaica (Bergeret) A. Braun. Like *P. glaucifolia* but lvs rosulate; pet. limb *c*10mm, white or pale pink. Summer. W Pyren.
→*Lychnis*.

Petrocosmea Oliv. Gesneriaceae. 29 perenn., rhizomatous herbs. Lvs rosulate, petiolate, pubesc. Fls in an axill., scapose cyme; cal. 5-partite; cor. tubular or campanulate, upper lip 2-lobed, lower lip 3-lobed. Asia (mts).

P. kerrii Craib. Lvs to 10×6cm, ovate-lanceolate to oblong, dentate. Fls 1–3 on scapes to 5cm; cor. white, tube to 0.3cm, lobes to 0.7cm, blotched yellow at base. Thail. Z10.

P. nervosa Craib. Lvs to 5.5×5.5cm, obovate to orbicular. Fls 1–3 on scapes to 6cm; cor. blue, tube to 0.3cm, lobes to 0.7cm, ciliate. Yunnan. Z9.

P. parryorum C. Fisch. Lvs to 10×3cm, orbicular or elliptic-ovate or oblong, bullate, undulate. Fls 1–12 on scapes to 7.5cm; cor. violet, tube to 0.9cm, obliquely campanulate, lobes to 0.3cm. India. Z10.

Petromarula Vent. ex Hedw. f. Campanulaceae. 1 robust perenn. herb to 50cm. Lvs to 30cm, pinnately lobed, lobes dentate to serrate. Fls clustered in a long, unbranched spike; cal. deeply 5-lobed; cor. lobes 5 linear to 1cm. Crete. Z8.

P. pinnata (L.) A. DC.

Petronymphe H.E. Moore. Liliaceae (Alliaceae). 1 perenn. herb. Lvs to 60cm, linear, keeled. Scape to 60cm, arched; fls slender-stalked, to 14 in an umbel; perianth to 5cm, tubular, pale yellow lined green, lobes short, 6; anth. blue-violet. Mex. Z9.

P. decora H.E. Moore.

Petrophila R. Br. Proteaceae. 40 shrubs. Lvs coriaceous, often divided. Infl. a dense spike or cone, usually term., subtended by an involucre of bracts; perianth tube slender, seg. 4. Aus. Z9.

P. biloba R. Br. Erect prickly shrub to 2m. Lvs to 1.5cm, rigid, 3-lobed or pinnately 4-lobed. Fls grey to pink, in small, ovoid, sessile, axill. heads; perianth 2cm, villous. Late winter–spring. W Aus.

P. brevifolia Lindl. Erect shrub to 2m. Lvs 2.5–2.8cm, terete, pungent. Fls cream-yellow in term., ovoid heads; perianth 1.6cm, silky. Mid-winter–late spring. W Aus.

P. carduacea Meissn. Erect shrub to 2m. Lvs 3–5cm, oblong-lanceolate, pinnatifid, prickly toothed. Fls yellow, in a globose to ovoid pedunculate head to 3cm. Spring.

P. circinata Kipp. ex Meissn. Dense shrub to 60cm. Lvs 7–12cm, terete, twice pinnate, young growth red. Fls white to yellow, in large term. heads. Spring. W Aus.

P. divaricata R. Br. Prickly shrub 1–1.5m. Lvs 3–8cm, divaricate, twice-pinnate, seg. terete. Fls yellow-cream in sessile, villous ovoid heads. Late winter–spring. W Aus.

P. diversifolia R. Br. Erect shrub to 2m. Lvs 3–7cm, doubly compound, trifid. Fls pale-pink to white in axill., pedunculate heads; perianth tube 12mm. Late winter–spring. W Aus.

P. drummondii Meissn. Erect, dwarf shrub to 50cm. Lvs 3–6cm, terete, 2–3× ternately divided. Fls yellow in sessile, term., ovoid to globose heads. Spring. W Aus.

P. ericifolia R. Br. Erect, rounded shrub to 1m. Lvs to 1.2cm, gland. or glab., terete, blunt, adpressed. Fls yellow in term., sessile heads; outer bracts and perianth glutinous. Late winter–spring. W Aus.

P. fastigiata R. Br. Erect, rounded shrub to 90cm. Lvs to 7cm, erect, obtuse, 2–3× ternately divided. Fls yellow in term., sessile, ovoid heads; perianth 1cm, glab. Spring. W Aus.

P. heterophylla Lindl. Straggly erect shrub, to 1–2.5m. Lvs 5–10cm, linear to linear-lanceolate, flattened with prominent veins, 2–3-fld. Fls yellow in sessile, ovoid-oblong heads; perianth to 2cm. Late winter–spring. W Aus.

P. linearis R. Br. PIXIE MOPS. Low, sparse shrub to 1m. Lvs 4–8cm, flat, thick, rigid with rounded margins, falcate. Fls pink, v. hairy, in ovoid, term. heads; perianth 2.5cm. Spring. W Aus.

P. longifolia R. Br. ± prostrate shrub, 30–45cm. Lvs 16–30cm, terete, entire. Fls cream to yellow in term., sessile heads; perianth hairy. Spring. W Aus.

P. macrostachya R. Br. Erect shrub to 1m. Lvs to 7cm, flat, deeply divided into 3-lobes each lobe often divided into 3 shorter lobes. Fls yellow in a sessile, 5cm cone. Spring. W Aus.

P. media R. Br. Erect, open shrub to 45cm. Lvs 4–10cm, rigid, thick, terete. Fls yellow, sweetly scented, in term., sessile, oval heads; perianth villous. Winter–spring. W Aus.

P. pulchella (Schräd.) R. Br. CONESTICKS. Tall, sparse shrub to 3m, sometimes dwarfed to 50cm. Lvs to 9cm, terete, 2–3× pinnate. Fls creamy-yellow, in term. clusters of 2–3 heads; perianth silky, 14mm. Late spring–summer. E Aus.

P. rigida R. Br. Divaricate, rigid shrub, to 1m. Lvs to 2.5cm, trichotomously seg. terete. Fls yellow-white in term., sessile, ovoid-oblong heads. Spring. W Aus.

P. serruriae R. Br. Erect, prickly-leaved shrub, 1–2m. Lvs to 3cm, intricately divided, 2–3× pinnate. Fls white-yellow to pink in sessile, ovoid-globose heads. Late winter–spring. W Aus.

P. shuttleworthiana Meissn. Rigid, rounded, shrub, 60cm–2m. Lvs 7cm, cuneate, deeply 3-fid, seg. linear, pungent. Fls cream-white in sessile oblong to cylindrical heads. Late winter–spring. W Aus.

P. squamata R. Br. Erect shrub, 60cm–1m. Lvs 4cm, 1–2× ternately divided in 5–10mm, flat, pungent lobes. Fls creamy-white in ovoid, sessile, axillary heads. Late winter–spring. W Aus.

Petrophytum Rydb. ROCK SPIRAEA. Rosaceae. 3 everg. subshrubs; shoots prostrate, v. short. Lvs crowded, coriaceous, entire. Fls in short, dense rac.; cal. teeth 5; pet. white, 5, overlapping; sta. 20–40. N Amer. (mts).

P. caespitosum (Nutt.) Rydb. Subshrub forming dense mats to 80cm diam.; br. sericeous. Lvs to 1.2cm, spathulate, blue-green, in rosettes, densely sericeous-pubesc. Infl. to 10cm; pet. 1.5cm, obtuse. Summer. US (Rocky Mts). Z3.

P. cinerascens (Piper) Rydb. Dense subshrub; shoots short, stout. Lvs oblanceolate to 2.5cm, coriaceous, ash-grey, sparsely pubesc. Infl. to 15cm, cinereous; pet. spathulate or oblanceolate, 2cm. Summer–autumn. N Amer. Z5.

P. elatius (S. Wats.) Heller. Dense subshrub. Lvs to 2cm, oblanceolate, sericeous-pubesc. Infl. to 10cm, often branched; pet. oblanceolate, to 3mm. Summer–autumn. Mts of W US.

P. hendersonii (Canby) Rydb. Dense grass-like subshrub; shoots short, stout. Lvs spathulate, to 2cm, thick, sparsely villous. Infl. to 8cm.; pet. obovate or oval, 2.5cm. Summer–autumn. N Amer. Z5.

→*Eriogynia, Luetkea* and *Spiraea*.

Petrorhagia (DC.) Link. Caryophyllaceae. 25–30 ann. or perenn. herbs, broadly similar to *Gypsophila*. Eurasia, esp. E Medit.

P. saxifraga (L.) Link. Subglabrous, mat-forming perenn. to 40cm. Lvs linear, keeled. Infl. a loose-fld delicate cyme; pet. 5–10mm, short-clawed, pale pink with deeper veins, limb indented. Summer. S & C Eur. 'Alba': fls white. 'Alba Plena': fls double, white. 'Lady Mary': to 8cm; fls double, soft pink. 'Pleniflora Rosea': low; fls double, pink. 'Rosea': fls light pink. 'Rosette': more compact; fls double, pink. Z6.

→*Dianthus, Kohlrauschia* and *Tunica*.

Petroselinum Hill. PARSLEY. Umbelliferae. 3 bienn. taprooted herbs. Lvs 1–3-pinnate. Umbels compound; involucre and involucels present; fls small. Eur.

P. crispum (Mill.) A.W. Hill. PARSLEY. Aromatic. St. to 80cm. Lvs triangular in outline, 3-pinnate, seg. ovate, to 3cm, toothed, 3-fid (often crispate). Umbels with 8–20 rays, to 3cm; fls yellow. Summer. Eur. Over 20 cvs; v. dwarf and compact to tall and upright, some exceptionally hardy; lvs lightly curled to flat, deeply to finely cut, v. dark green to bright emerald. 'Afro' (tall, upright; lvs tightly curled, dark green), 'Clivi' (dwarf, neat; base lvs remain green), 'New Dark Green' (v. dwarf, compact, hardy; lvs bright emerald green), 'Paramount' (hardy, vigorous growth; lvs v. dark green, dense, closely curled), 'Italian Plain Leaf' (lvs flat, plain, deeply cut, dark green), 'Darki' (v. tolerant of cold; lvs v. dark green, tightly curled), 'Crispum' (lvs plain, strong flavour), 'Champion Moss Curled' (lvs curled, finely cut, deep green). var. *neapolitanum* Danert. ITALIAN PARSLEY. Lvs not curled. var. *tuberosum* (Bernh.) Crov. TURNIP-ROOTED PARSLEY; HAMBURG PARSLEY. Root thick, fleshy, edible.

Petteria C. Presl. DALMATIAN LABURNUM. Leguminosae (Papilionoideae). 1 erect shrub to 2m. Lvs to 7cm, long-stalked, trifoliolate; lfts elliptic to rounded. Fls fragrant to 2cm, pea-like yellow, in erect, term. rac. Spring. Balk. (Dalmatia, Montenegro). Z6.

P. ramentacea (Sieber) C. Presl.
→*Cytisus.*

Petticoat Daffodil *Narcissus bulbocodium.*
Petticoat Heath *Erica glauca* var. *elegans.*
Petticoat Palm *Copernicia macroglossa.*
Petty Morel *Aralia racemosa.*
Petty Whin *Genista anglica.*

Petunia Petunia × hybrida.

Petunia Juss. Solanaceae. Some 35 ann. or perenn. herbs or shrubs. St. pubesc., viscid. Fls solitary, in upper lf axils; cal. 5-lobed; cor. salverform to funnel form, tube cylindric, limb lobes equal. Trop. S Amer. Z7.

P. axillaris (Lam.) BSP. LARGE WHITE PETUNIA. Ann. to 60cm, decumbent to erect, sticky-pubesc. Lvs ovate to lanceolate-ovate, to 5×1.5cm, sessile. Fls nocturnally fragrant; cor. buff-white, tube to 5cm, limb to 5cm diam. Fr. conic. S Braz., Urug., Arg.

P. fimbriata hort. = *P.* ×*hybrida.*
P. grandiflora hort. = *P.* ×*hybrida.*
P. ×*hybrida* hort. Vilm.-Andr. PETUNIA. A complex group of hybrids, thought to be *P. axillaris* ×*P. integrifolia.* Resembles *P. integrifolia,* but habit stouter, fls larger, to 10cm, to 13cm diam. Fls *single.* 'Appleblossom': fls soft flesh-pink, fringed.

'Blue Frost': fls large, violet blue edged white. 'Chiffon Cascade': fls light pastel mauve. 'Burgundy Star': hardy; fls wine red with white star, long-lasting. Daddy Hybrids: well-branched; fls large to 10cm, attractive veining, in range of colours from pastel pink to deep orchid purple. Dazzler Hybrids: to 20cm, compact, neat; fls large, abundant, in range of colours including white, shades of pink, orange, red and violet. 'Fluffy Ruffles': fls 15cm across, often tricoloured with contrasting veining and throat colour, ruffled; seed race. 'Flamenco': fls magenta rose. 'Lacy Sails': fls true blue, veined. 'Sheer Madness': dense to 30cm; fls pink with darker veins, large, prolific. 'Super Cascade Lilac': dwarf, compact; fls rose-lilac; early flowering. 'Super Cascade Blush Improved': dwarf, compact habit, hardy; fls large. 'White Carpet': tall, compact, uniform, hardy; fls white, early flowering. Yellow Magic': vigorous; fls large, lightly ruffled, pale yellow, abundant. Fls *double.* 'Apple Tart': hardy; fls rich scarlet red, fragrant, abundant. 'Blue Danube': fls lavender blue veined dark violet. 'Purple Pirouette': bushy, well-branched; fls bicoloured, purple edged white. 'Red Bouquet': fls large, fringed, bright scarlet. 'Snowberry Tart': fls medium, pure white, fragrant. *Picotee.* 'Blue Picotee': fls large, deep violet with white ruffled edge. 'Hoolahoop': fls intense scarlet edged white. 'Velvet Picotee': fls rich red ringed white, edged ruffled.

P. inflata R.E. Fries = *P. axillaris.*

P. integrifolia (Hook.) Schinz & Thell. VIOLET-FLOWERED PETUNIA. Ann. herb or short-lived shrublet, to 60cm, viscid-pubesc. Lvs elliptic to lanceolate, to 5×2cm, petiolate. Fls interior violet, exterior violet to rose red; peduncle to 3cm; cor. interior violet, exterior violet to rose-red, tube to 4cm, striate, limb to 3cm diam., violet. Arg.

P. multiflora hort. = *P.* ×*hybrida.*
P. nana hort. = *P.* ×*hybrida.*
P. nyctaginiflora Juss. = *P. axillaris.*
P. superbissima hort. = *P.* ×*hybrida.*
P. violacea hort. non Lindl. = *P. integrifolia.*
P. violacea Lindl. = *P. integrifolia.*
→*Nicotiana* and *Salpiglossis.*

Peucedanum L. Umbelliferae. 170 herbs or shrubs. St. hollow, striate. Lvs 1- to many times pinnate or ternate, long-stalked below, ± sessile, sheathing on st. Fls small in compound umbels. Eurasia, Trop. & S Afr.

P. angustifolium Rchb. f. = *P. ostruthium* var. *angustifolium.*

P. austriacum (Jacq.) Koch. Glab. perenn. to 120cm. Lvs 3-4-pinnate, seg. pinnately lobed, lobes oblong. Umbels 15–40-rayed; involucral bracts numerous, deflexed; fls white. Summer. C & S Eur. Z6.

P. cervaria (L.) Lapeyr. Subglabrous perenn. to 1.5m. Lvs to 50cm, 2–3-pinnate, seg. ovate to ovate-oblong, to 5cm, lower seg. 1–4-lobed, sharply dentate. Umbels with 15–30 puberulent rays; involucral bracts numerous, deflexed, some pinnatisect; fls white. C Eur. to Asia. Z6.

P. graveolens (L.) C.B. Clarke = *Anethum graveolens.*

P. ostruthium (L.) Koch. MASTERWORT. Subglabrous perenn. to 1m. Lvs triangular in outline, 1–2-ternate, seg. 5–10cm, lanceolate to ovate, irregularly toothed, middle seg. occas. 3-lobed. Umbels with 30–60 rays, to 5cm; involucral bracts few or 0; fls white or tinged pink. Summer. Mts of C & S Eur. var. *angustifolium* (Bellardi) Alef. Lvs narrow. Z5.

P. palustre (L.) Moench. MILK PARSLEY. Subglabrous or glabrescent bienn. to 1.5m; st. often tinged purple. Lvs to 50cm, 2–4-pinnate, seg. 0.5–2cm, lanceolate to ovate in outline, serrulate, pinnatifid, petiole long, canaliculate above, base sheathing. Umbels with 15–40 puberulent rays, to 5cm; involucral bracts usually 4, linear-lanceolate; fls white. Summer. Eur. to C Asia. Z6.

P. sativum Benth. & Hook. = *Pastinaca sativa.*

P. verticillare (L.) Koch ex DC. Monocarpic perenn., 1–3.5m. Lvs to 50cm, triangular in outline, ternately 2–3-pinnate, seg. 2.5–8cm, ovate to ovate-oblong, 3-lobed or irregularly toothed, petiole puberulent. Umbels with 10–30 rays; involucral bract 1 or 0; fls pale green-yellow. E & EC Alps, to Hung. and It. Z7.

Peumus Molina. Monimaceae. 1 tree or shrub, 3–6m, aromatic. Lvs 3–7cm, ovate-elliptic or oblong, acute, entire, ± coriaceous, dark green above, paler and yellow-pubescent beneath. Rac. short; fls 5–10mm across; perianth 10–12 lobed in two series, stellate-pubescent; sta. 40 or more. Drupes to 7mm, 2–9 on a receptacle. Chile. Z9.

P. boldus Molina. BOLDO.
P. fragans Pers. = *P. boldus.*
→*Boldoa* and *Ruiza.*
Peyote *Laphophora.*

Pfeiffera Salm-Dyck.
P. cereiformis Salm-Dyck = *Lepismium ianthothele.*
P. ianthothele (Monv.) F.A. Weber = *Lepismium ianthothele.*

Phacelia Juss. SCORPION WEED. Hydrophyllaceae. 150 ann.,
bienn. and perenn. downy to glandular-pubescent herbs. Lvs
pinnatisect or entire. Fls in term. cymes or rac.; cal. lobes 5,
narrow; cor. tubular at base, limb spreading 5-lobed; sta. 5. W
N Amer., E US, S Amer.
P. bipinnatifida Michx. Bienn. to 40cm, downy, gland. Lvs
pinnate, lfts 3–5, ovate, biserrate to pinnatifid. Cor. to 1.5cm
diam., violet-blue, broadly campanulate, ciliate. E N Amer. Z5.
P. campanularia A. Gray. CALIFORNIA BLUEBELL. Glandular-
hispid ann., 15–40cm. Lvs elliptic to ovate, angular-toothed to
irregularly crenate. Cor. to 2.5cm, dark blue spotted white at
the base of each lobe sinus, sometimes wholly white, broadly
campanulate-funnelform. S Calif. Z9.
P. ciliosa Rydb. = *P. sericea* ssp. *ciliosa.*
P. congesta Hook. BLUE CURLS. Hirsute to sericeous ann. to
60cm. Lvs pinnatifid to finely pinnatisect, lobes irregular, ovate,
obtuse. Cor. to 0.75cm, blue, campanulate. Tex., New Mex.
P. divaricata (Benth.) A. Gray. Downy ann. to 30cm. Lvs
2.5–7.5cm, oblong or obovate, entire, sparsely toothed near
base or 3-lobed. Cor. to 1.25cm, blue-violet, campanulate. N
Calif.
P. grandiflora (Benth.) A. Gray. Glandular-pubesc. ann. to
90cm. Lvs to 20cm, broadly elliptic to ovate-orbicular, biserrate,
base rounded to truncate. Cor. to 3.25cm, lilac or white. S Calif.
P. linearis (Pursh) Holzing. Erect ann. to 32cm, grey-downy, not
gland. Lvs to 7cm, linear to narrowly lanceolate, usually entire,
rarely pinnatifid or palmatifid. Cor. to 1.25cm, broadly
campanulate, violet or white. W N Amer.
P. minor (Harv.) Thell. ex F. Zimm. WHITLAVIA. Erect, viscid,
shortly pubesc. ann., 15–60cm. Lvs to 10cm, oblong to ovate,
coarsely biserrate. Cor. to 2cm, lilac-blue, violet or white,
tubular-campanulate. S Calif. 'Gloxinioides': fls white at centre.
P. parryi Torr. Viscid, downy ann., 15–60cm. Lvs to 10cm, ovate,
biserrate or lobed. Cor. to 2.5cm diam., purple-blue marked or
spotted yellow or white at centre, campanulate-rotate. S Calif.
to Mex.
P. purshii Buckley. MIAMI MIST. Downy ann. to 75cm. Lvs to
5cm, oblong to elliptic, pinnatifid to pinnate, seg. lanceolate to
elliptic. Cor. light blue, centre white, lobes fringed. E US.
P. sericea (Graham) A. Gray. Bienn. or short-lived perenn. to
60cm, normally shorter. Lvs to 10cm, oblong to oblong-elliptic,
deeply pinnatifid, sericeous. Cor. deep blue, indigo or mauve,
rarely white, campanulate. W N Amer. ssp. *ciliosa* (Rydb.) G.
Gillett. Lvs more broadly lobed and less silky. Cor. urceolate-
campanulate. Oreg. to NE Calif., Ariz. to Wyom. Z3.
P. tanacetifolia Benth. FIDDLENECK. Hispidulous ann.,
15–120cm. Lvs to 24cm, oblong-elliptic to ovate, 1–2×
pinnatifid to pinnate, seg. oblong to lanceolate, short-pubesc.
Cor. to 1.5cm, deeply campanulate, blue to lilac or mauve.
Calif. to Mex.
P. viscida (Benth. ex Lindl.) Torr. Densely glandular-pubesc.
ann., 7–55cm. Lvs to 7.25cm, ovate to orbicular, bidentate.
Cor. to 1.25cm, broadly campanulate, pale blue to lilac, centre
of tube flushed rose to purple, rarely pure white. Calif.
P. whitlavia A. Gray = *P. minor.*
→*Eutoca* and *Whitlavia.*

Phaedranassa Herb. QUEEN LILY. Amaryllidaceae. 7 bulbous,
herbaceous perennials. Lvs narrow to broadly oblong,
hysteranthous, petiolate. Fls drooping, in scapose umbels, perianth narrow funnel-shaped or nearly cylindric, with narrow,
spreading lobes with corona of hyaline teeth between 6 anth.
fil.; sta. exserted. S Amer.; native to Andes but cult. in Costa
Rica. Z8.
P. carnioli Bak. Scape to 60cm; fls 6–10, to 5cm, glaucous
crimson, tipped green with yellow fringe. Spring–summer. S
Amer.
P. chloracra Herb. = *P. dubia.*
P. cinerea Ravenna. Scape 25–80cm; fls 7–17, 3.2–5.5cm long,
coral-pink, green at apex, separated by narrow white band.
Ecuad.
P. dubia HBK. Scape to 45cm, fls 5cm long or more, purple-pink,
tipped green. Spring–summer. Peru. var. *obtusa* Herb. Perianth
lobes obtuse. Peru.
P. eucrosioides (Bak.) Benth. & Hook = *Eucrosia stricklandii.*
P. lehmannii Reg. Fls in 3-fld umbel, to 2.5cm, scarlet, lobes
shortly spreading. Spring–summer. Colomb.
P. rubroviridis Bak. = *Eustephia coccinea.*
P. schizantha Bak. Fls with v. short green tube; perianth lobes to
3cm, bright red, fading to pink at apices. Late autumn. Ecuad.
P. tunguraguae Ravenna. Scape to 54cm; fls 6–8, to 3.2cm,

coral-red, apex green. Ecuad.
P. ventricosa Roezl. ex Wallace = *P. dubia.*
P. viridiflora Bak. Scape to 66cm; fls 5, yellow-green,
campanulate-tubular; tube 1cm, tep. oblanceolate, to 2.4cm.
Ecuad., possibly Peru.

Phaedranthus Miers.
P. buccinatorium (DC.) Miers = *Distictis buccinatoria.*

Phaenocoma D. Don Compositae. 1 leafy, everg. shrub, to
60cm, lanate at first. Lvs v. small, ovate, acuminate, often
scale-like, imbricate. Cap. discoid, solitary, to 4cm diam.;
phyllaries red-purple; flts bright yellow. Winter. S Afr. Z9.
P. prolifera (L.) D. Don.

Phaeomeria Lindl. ex Schum.
P. magnifica (Roscoe) Schum. = *Etlingera elatior.*
P. speciosa (Bl.) Merrill = *Etlingera elatior.*

Phaius Lour. Orchidaceae. 30 terrestrial orchids. St. with or
without pbs, sometimes cylindric. Lvs few, large, plicate,
stalked. Rac. axill., erect, exceeding lvs; sep. and pet. similar,
spreading; lip entire or lobed, spurred. Indomal., S China,
Trop. Aus. Z10.
P. australis F. Muell. Pbs to 7cm. Lvs lanceolate, to 125×10cm.
Fls to 10cm diam., maroon, veined yellow above, white below;
sep. elliptic; pet. oblong-ovate; lip midlobe crisped. Aus.
P. callosus (Bl.) Lindl. Pbs 6–12cm. Lvs elliptic to oblong-
lanceolate, 60–110cm. Tep. oblong, to 5cm, yellow-brown
above, red-brown beneath, lip long-pubesc., white often golden
yellow, blotched violet or yellow, streaked red-brown, spur
yellow. Malaysia.
P. flavus (Bl.) Lindl. Pbs 10–15cm. Lvs to 50cm elliptic-
lanceolate, spotted pale yellow. Fls 6–8cm diam., tep. oblong,
yellow, rarely white, lip streaked brown, spur white. India, Malaysia, Java.
P. francoisii (Schltr.) Summerh. Similar to *P. humblotii* except lip
laterals yellow, dotted red, apical point of midlobe deeper red,
tep. narrower. Madag.
P. grandifolius Lour. = *P. tankervilliae.*
P. humblotii Rchb. f. Pbs spheric. Lvs elliptic-lanceolate,
25–40cm. Tep. to 3.5cm, ovate, rose, blotched, white and red,
lip midlobe deeper, with 2 yellow apical teeth. Madag.
P. maculatus Lindl. = *P. flavus.*
P. mishmensis (Lindl.) Rchb. f. Pbs obscure. St. fleshy. Lvs
elliptic-lanceolate to oblong-ovate, 15–30cm. Fls erect, tep. to
3.5cm, linear-oblong, pale rose, purple-brown or dark red, lip
pink or white, speckled purple. India, Burm., Thail. to Philipp.
P. roseus Rolfe = *P. mishmensis.*
P. tankervilliae (Banks) Bl. Pbs 2.5–6cm. Lvs elliptic-lanceolate,
30–100cm; fls nodding, 10–12.5cm diam.; tep. lanceolate, white,
green or rose beneath, red yellow-brown, or white above, edged
gold, lip tubular, crisped, interior pink to burgundy, base
yellow, exterior white, midlobe red-orange or white and pink.
Himal. to Aus.
P. tetragonus Rchb. f. St. to 30cm, 4-angled. Lvs ovate-
lanceolate. Fls large, tep. oblong, tinted green above, green
below, lip orange-red, streaked yellow, midlobe crisped. Maur.,
Sri Lanka.
P. tuberculosus (Thouars) Bl. Pbs small, obscured. Lvs
lanceolate, 30–60cm. Tep. elliptic-lanceolate, to 4cm, white, lip
midlobe white, margins spotted lilac or violet, lat. lobes yellow,
dotted red, disc and callus yellow, midlobe undulate, callus,
warty. Madag.
P. wallichii Hook. f. = *P. tankervilliae.*

Phalacraea DC. Compositae. 4 perenn. herbs; st. decumbent.
Lvs opposite, crenate to serrate, glandular-punctate beneath.
Cap. discoid, in loose cymes; phyllaries gland-dotted; flts white.
Colomb., Ecuad., Peru. Z10.
P. latifolia DC. To 50cm. Lvs broadly ovate to deltoid, base
truncate to cordate. Cap. 5–6mm diam.; flts tinged purple.
Peru.
→*Piqueria.*

Phalacrocarpum (DC.) Willk. Compositae. 2 perenn. woody-
based herbs. Lvs opposite, toothed to deeply divided. Cap.
radiate, solitary; ray flts ♀, white or purple; disc flts 5-lobed,
yellow, inner sometimes petaloid. SW Eur. Z9.
P. oppositifolium (Brot.) Willk. Grey-white tomentose or silky
unbranched or branched below, ascending. Lvs obovate,
pinnatipartite to pinnatisect, seg. lanceolate or 2-pinnatisect,
lobes linear. Cap. 3–5.5cm diam., on peduncles to 20cm. N & C
Port., N Spain.

Phalaenopsis Bl. MOTH ORCHID. Orchidaceae. 40 epiphytic, monopodial orchids. St. short, composed of overlapping lf bases. Lvs 2–6, fleshy, distichous, broad-obovate or oval, often glossy or papillose, sometimes mottled. Rac. lat., simple or branched; sep. spreading, elliptic to broadly spathulate, usually smaller than pet.; lip 3-lobed, midlobe fleshy with complex basal calli, apex oftenn lobed, the lobes terminating in horn-like projections or fil. Asia, Australasia. Z10.

P. amabilis (L.) Bl. Lvs to 50×10cm. Infl. to 1m; fls to 10cm diam., fragrant, sep. and pet. white, often pink below, sep. elliptic-ovate, to 4×2,5cm, pet. larger, almost circular; lip white, base red, margins yellow, midlobe cruciform, side projections triangular, with 2 yellow-tipped appendages, callus almost square, yellow, dotted red. E Indies, Aus.

P. amboinensis J.J. Sm. Lvs to 25×10cm. Fls few, cream to orange-yellow, striped cinnamon; dors. sep. elliptic to ovate-elliptic, lat. sep. broadly ovate or ovate-elliptic; pet. ovate to rhombic-ovate; lip clawed, midlobe ovate or oblong-ovate. In-don.

P. aphrodite Rchb. f. Resembles *P. amabilis* except in fls to 7cm diam.; lip midlobe subtriangular, not cruciform, callus with deeper red markings. Philipp. to Taiwan.

P. cochlearis Holtt. Lvs to 20×10cm. Infl. to 50cm; fls white to pale green or yellow, tep. with 2 light to orange-brown basal stripes, dors. sep. narrow to lanceolate-elliptic, to 2cm, lat. sep. ovate, pet. lanceolate-elliptic; lip midlobe primrose, striped red to orange-brown, orbicular, apex rounded or notched. Sarawak.

P. corningiana Rchb. f. As *P. sumatrana* except fls few, to 5cm diam.; tep. pale yellow, apex barred mahogany to crimson, dors. sep. obovate to oblanceolate, lat. sep. ovate, pet. lanceolate; lip midlobe, magenta to carmine, elliptic-oblong, narrow, callus forked, orange-yellow. Borneo, Sarawak.

P. cornu-cervi (Breda) Bl. & Rchb. f. Lvs to 25×4cm. Infl. to 40cm, axis flattened; fls waxy yellow to yellow-green; sep. marked red-brown, dors. sep. obovate-elliptic, lateral sep. elliptic to elliptic-lanceolate; pet. lanceolate; lip white, midlobe anchor-shaped, projections hooked, lat. lobes red-brown or striped cinnamon. SE Asia.

P. delicosa Rchb. f. = *Kingidium delicosum*.

P. denevei Sm. = *Paraphalaenopsis denevei*.

P. equestris (Schauer) Rchb. f. Lvs to 20×6.5cm. Infl. to 30cm; fls to 4cm diam.; tep. rose or white suffused rose, sep. oblong-elliptic, pet. elliptic; lip deep pink to purple, midlobe ovate, concave, apex fleshy, callus 6–8-sided, yellow, spotted red, lat. lobes marked yellow. Philipp., Taiwan.

P. fasciata Rchb. f. Lvs to 20cm. Fls waxy, pale to deep yellow, to 4cm diam., tep. striped red-brown; dors. sep. elliptic, lat. sep. ovate-elliptic; pet. similar; lip midlobe oblong-ovate, apex magenta, base orange-yellow, callus orange, projecting appendages forked, lat. lobes dotted orange. Philipp.

P. fimbriata J.J. Sm. Lvs 15–25cm. Infl. to 30cm, sometimes mottled; fls many, white to cream, barred magenta at centre; tep. ovate-elliptic, to 2cm; lip midlobe ovate, convex, fleshy, fringed, upcurved. Java, Sumatra.

P. gigantea J.J. Sm. Lvs to 50×20cm. Infl. to 40cm; fls scented, cream to yellow, tep. elliptic, blotched and lined maroon to dark purple; lip fleshy, white, striped, or lined magenta, midlobe ovate. Borneo, Sabah.

P. grandiflora Lindl. = *P. amabilis*.

P. hieroglyphica (Rchb. f.) H. Sweet. Lvs to 30×10cm. Tep. white lined red-purple, ovate-elliptic; lip to 2cm, midlobe truncate, apex jagged, central keel pubesc. Philipp.

P. ×intermedia Lindl. (*P. aphrodite* × *P. equestris*.) Lvs to 30×8cm. Fls white to deep rose; dors. sep. elliptic, lateral sep. ovate, to 4cm; pet. elliptic; lip midlobe obovate, apex tapering, bidentate. Philipp.

P. ×leucorrhoda Rchb. f. (*P. aphrodite* × *P. schilleriana*.) Lvs spotted silver-grey. Infl. to 70cm. Fl. pure white to deep rose, margins rose; sep. elliptic to ovate; pet. reniform to circular; lip white, dotted or lined yellow and purple, midlobe apex filamentous or anchor-shaped, callus yellow, spotted red. Philipp.

P. lindenii Loher. Lvs dappled silver-white, to 25×4cm. Fls white, dotted rose at centre; dors. sep. oblong-elliptic, lat. sep. oblong-ovate; pet. elliptic-rhombic; lip to 1.5cm, midlobe circular, tipped purple-pink, lined rose, apex pointed, lat. lobes white, dotted red or orange, with 3 purple lines at apex. Philipp.

P. lobbii (Rchb. f.) H. Sweet. Lvs to 13×5cm. Tep. cream, dors. sep. oblong-elliptic, lat. sep. ovate, pet. obovate, to 8×5mm; lip with 2 red-brown stripes, midlobe mobile, triangular, apex rounded. India, Himal.

P. lueddemanniana Rchb. f. Lvs to 30×10cm. Infl. to 30cm, flex-uous; fls to 6cm diam.; tep. white, striped brown-purple, dors. sep. elliptic to oblong-elliptic, lateral sep. ovate-elliptic, to 3cm, pet. smaller; lip to 2.5cm, carmine, base yellow, midlobe oblong to ovate, callus white, pubesc. Philipp.

P. lueddemanniana var. *hieroglyphica* (Rchb. f.) Veitch = *P. hieroglyphica*.

P. lueddemanniana var. *purpurea* (Rchb. f.) Veitch = *P. pulchra*.

P. maculata Rchb. f. Lvs to 20×4cm. Fls few; tep. white or pale rose, banded purple, dors. sep. oblong-elliptic, lat. sep. ovate-elliptic; lip white, midlobe oblong, apex purple. Borneo, Sulawesi.

P. mannii Rchb. f. Lvs to 40×7cm. Infl. pendent; fls fragrant, to 4.25cm; tep. green or yellow, blotched cinnamon, sep. ovate-lanceolate, pet. lanceolate, revolute; lip to 1cm, white and purple, midlobe anchor-shaped, callus often hirsute. Himal., Vietnam.

P. mariae Warner & Williams. Lvs to 30×7cm. Infl. pendent; fls to 5cm diam.; tep. oblong-elliptic, white or cream, striped and blotched brown-red, base rarely spotted purple; lip pale mauve to purple, midlobe expanded, apex dentate. Philipp.

P. micholitzii Rolfe. Lvs to 16×6cm. Infl. arching; fls white to pale green; dors. sep. elliptic, lat. sep. ovate; pet. ovate-elliptic, to 3cm; lip fleshy, midlobe rhombic, central patch villous, calli orange-yellow. Philipp.

P. pallens (Lindl.) Rchb. f. Lvs to 20cm. Infl. arching or erect; fls few, to 5cm diam., tep. pale lemon to yellow-green, lined brown, oblong-elliptic, to 2cm; lip to 2cm, midlobe white, ovate, narrow, callus pubesc., lat. lobes yellow. Philipp.

P. parishii Rchb. f. Lvs to 12×5cm. Infl. to 15cm; to 1cm, tep. white, sep. elliptic to circular, to 1cm, pet. elliptic to obovate; lip to 1.5cm, midlobe purple, triangular, margins fringed, lat. lobes white or yellow, spotted brown or purple. Himal., Vietnam.

P. pulcherrima (Lindl.) J.J. Sm. = *Doritis pulcherrima*.

P. pulchra (Rchb. f.) H. Sweet. Lvs to 15×5cm. Fls few, deep magenta-purple, with faint stripes or bars; dors. sep. erect, elliptic, lat. sep. ovate; pet. elliptic or ovate-elliptic; lip midlobe ovate to flabellate. Philipp.

P. reichenbachiana Rchb. f. & Sander. Lvs to 35×7cm. Infl. to 45cm; fls to 4cm diam.; tep. green-white to yellow, barred red-brown, dors. sep. elliptic-ovate, lat. sep. ovate-lanceolate, pet. ovate; lip base orange-yellow, midlobe ovate, angular, tipped magenta and pale violet, margins minutely toothed, callus yellow, bifid, lat. lobes white. Philipp.

P. sanderiana Rchb. f. Lvs marked silver-grey beneath. Infl. to 80cm; fls to 7.5cm diam., tep. ovate-elliptic, pink, dappled white, or wholly white; lip to 3cm, midlobe triangular, white or yellow, striped purple or brown, apex with 2 filiform projections, callus yellow or white, spotted red or purple, lat. lobes white, spotted pink. Philipp.

P. schilleriana Rchb. f. Lvs mottled silver-grey above, to 45×11cm. Infl. branching pendent; fls fragrant, white to pink, mauve and rose-purple; tep. edged white, dors. sep. elliptic, to 3.5cm, lat. sep. ovate, basally spotted carmine-purple, pet. rhombic; lip midlobe circular, white to magenta, appendages 2, anchor-shaped, lat. lobes yellow, dotted red-brown at base. Philipp.

P. speciosa Rchb. f. Lvs to 20×8cm. Infl. to 30cm; tep. oblong-elliptic, white-rose, blotched purple, pet. bases striped white; lip midlobe ovate, white, marked purple, lat. lobes yellow at base, tips white. Nicobar Is.

P. stuartiana Rchb. f. Lvs blotched grey above, to 35×8cm. Infl. branched, to 60cm; fls to 6cm diam., fragrant; sep. white, lat. sep. elliptic to ovate-elliptic, yellow dotted red-brown at base; pet. ± circular; lip to 2.5cm, almost circular, apex anchor-shaped, callus spotted orange. Philipp.

P. sumatrana Korth. & Rchb. f. Lvs to 30×11cm. Infl. to 30cm; fls to 5cm diam.; tep. oblong-lanceolate, white to pale yellow, banded cinnamon; lip midlobe oblong-elliptic, white, with red or purple stripes, lat. lobes cream, dotted spotted orange, margin brown or yellow. Malaysia, Sumatra, Borneo, Java.

P. violacea Witte. Lvs to 25×12cm. Infl. jointed, to 12.5cm; fls few, to 4.5cm diam., sometimes fragrant; tep. broadly elliptic, sharply acute, amethyst fading to white or lime green at apex; lip midlobe oblong, apiculate, violet tipped with white pubescence, central crest yellow. Sumatra, Borneo.

P. grexes and cvs. Many hybrids with large or small habit, plain or mottled lvs and tall, branching or arching or congested sprays of small to large, rounded to insect-like fls in white, rose, cream, pale yellow, red, green-yellow and bronze sometimes spotted or veined red, purple, rose yellow or brown, the lips often particularly marked.

Phalaris L. Gramineae. Some 15 ann. or perenn. grasses. Infl. a compact pan. N Temp. (Medit., S Amer., Calif.).

P. aquatica L. TOOWOMBA CANARY GRASS; HARDING GRASS. Perenn., to 1.5m. Lvs to 30×1cm, glab., rough to smooth, sometimes tinged blue. Infl. cylindric to ovoid-cylindric, compact, to 11×1cm, pale green or tinged purple. Summer–autumn. S Eur., Medit. Z8.

P. arundinacea L. REED CANARY GRASS; GARDENER'S GARTERS; RIBBON GRASS. Perenn., to 1.5m. Lvs to 35×1.8cm, glab. Infl. narrow, to 17cm. Summer–autumn. Eurasia, N Amer., S Afr. 'Dwarf's Garters': as 'Picta' but dwarf, to 30cm. 'Luteo-Picta': small; lvs striped golden-yellow. 'Mervyn Feesey': small; lvs light green, boldly striped white; fl. stalked tinted pink. 'Picta' ('Tricolor'): lvs striped white, usually predominantly on one side of lf. 'Streamlined': lvs mainly green, edged white. Z4.

P. canariensis L. CANARY GRASS; BIRDSEED GRASS. Ann., to 120cm. Lvs linear to linear-lanceolate, to 25×1.3cm, scabrous. Infl. ovoid to ovoid-cylindric, compact, erect, to 6×2cm. Summer–autumn. W Medit. Z6.

P. minor Retz. Ann., to 120cm. Lvs to 15×0.6cm, glab. Infl. ovoid to cylindric, compact, to 7cm×1.6cm, pale green. Summer. Medit. to NW Fr. Z6.

P. nodosa Murray = *P. aquatica.*
P. stenoptera Hackel = *P. aquatica.*
P. tuberosa L. = *P. aquatica.*
→*Digraphes* and *Typhoides.*

Phalsa *Grewia asiatica.*
Phanera *Bauhinia corymbosa.*

Phanerophlebia Presl. Dryopteridaceae. 8 terrestrial ferns. Rhiz. short-creeping to suberect. Fronds imparipinnate, chartaceous to subcoriaceous; pinnae entire to minutely spinose. Americas.

P. fortunei (J. Sm.) Copel. = *Cyrtomium fortunei.*
P. juglandifolia (Humb. & Bonpl. ex Willd.) J. Sm. Rhiz. suberect, short; stipes to 45cm. Fronds to 90cm, glab. or with few scales; pinnae 20×5cm, elliptic to ovate, entire to minutely spinose at tip. Mex. to Venez. Z10.
P. macrophylla (Mak.) Okuy. = *Cyrtomium macrophyllum.*
P. macrosora (Bak.) Underw. Rhiz. stout; stipes to 60cm. Fronds to 135cm, scaly beneath; pinnae 15–25×2–4cm, narrowly oblong-lanceolate, margins entire to minutely spinose. Mex. to Panama. Z9.
→*Cyrtomium.*

Pharbitis Choisy.
P. hederacea (L.) Choisy = *Ipomoea hederacea.*
P. imperialis hort. = *Ipomoea* ×*imperialis.*
P. nil (L.) Choisy = *Ipomoea nil.*
P. purpurea (L.) Choisy = *Ipomoea purpurea.*

Pharus P. Browne. Gramineae. 5 perenn. grasses. Lvs linear to oblong, sometimes ciliate. Infl. a delicate pan. Summer. Trop. Amer. Z9.
P. latifolius L. To 90cm. Lvs oblanceolate to narrowly-obovate, to 25×10cm; petiole to 10cm. Pan. to 30cm, loose; glumes tinged brown or purple; lemma tinged pink. 'Vittatus': lvs striped white, tinged pink.

Phaseolus L. BEAN. Leguminosae (Papilionoideae). *c*20 ann. or perenn., usually climbing herbs. Lvs trifoliolate. Fls pea-shaped in axill. rac. Fr. a linear-oblong, dehiscent legume. New World. For cvs of edible beans see *Phaseolus* and BEANS in *New RHS Dictionary of Gardening.*

P. aconitifolius Jacq. = *Vigna aconitifolius.*
P. acutifolius A. Gray. Ann. St. short, twining. Lfts to 6cm, linear or lanceolate-ovate. Fls white to pale purple, few, on v. short peduncles. Fr. to 9×1.5cm; seeds 2–10, 8.5×5.5mm, variable in colour. SW US, Mex. var. *latifolius* G. Freeman. TEPARY BEAN. Lfts larger. Fr. linear. 'Golden': yellow-seeded, v. prolific, tolerates heat and drought. 'Mitla Black': black-seeded, best for soup, two crops a year. 'Sonoran Brown': brown-seeded, early-maturing, grows well in drought and heat. Z10.
P. angularis W. Wight = *Vigna angularis.*
P. aureus Roxb. = *Vigna radiata.*
P. bipunctatus Jacq. = *P. lunatus.*
P. calcaratus Roxb. = *Vigna umbellata.*
P. caracalla L. = *Vigna caracalla.*
P. coccineus L. SCARLET RUNNER BEAN; DUTCH CASE-KNIFE BEAN. Resembles *P. vulgaris*, but perenn. (treated as an ann.), rac. many-fld and longer than lvs, fls scarlet. Lfts to 13cm, ovate-cordate. Fr. to 30cm; seeds to 2.5cm, black, mottled buff to red. Trop. Amer. 'Albus' WHITE DUTCH RUNNER: fls and seeds white. Z10.
P. giganteus hort. = *Vigna caracalla.*
P. inamuenus L. = *P. lunatus.*
P. limensis Macfad. = *P. lunatus.*
P. lobatus Hook. = *Vigna hookeri.*
P. lunatus L. LIMA BEAN. Twining or erect, grown as an ann. Lvs long-petiolate; lfts to 10cm, ovate to deltoid. Infl. to 20cm; fls

yellow-green or white to lilac. Fr. to 10cm, oblong-lunate; seeds 2–4, to 1×0.5cm, red-brown, reniform. Winter–spring. Trop. S Amer. Z10.

P. multiflorus Lam. = *P. coccineus.*
P. mungo L. = *Vigna mungo.*
P. puberulus HBK = *P. lunatus.*
P. pubescens Bl. = *Vigna umbellata.*
P. radiatus L. = *Vigna radiata.*
P. saccharatus Macfad. = *P. lunatus.*
P. sublobatus Roxb. = *Vigna radiata.*
P. vulgaris L. KIDNEY BEAN; GREEN BEAN; SNAP BEAN; HARICOT; COMMON BEAN; FRENCH BEAN; FRIJOL; RUNNER BEAN; STRING BEAN; SALAD BEAN; WAX BEAN. Erect or climbing ann. to 4m. Lfts to 10cm, ovate or ovate-orbicular. Rac. shorter than lvs, to 6-fld; cor. to 1.8cm, white, pink or purple. Fr. to 50cm, narrow, flat or subcylindric; seeds 1.3cm, elongate or globose, red, brown, black, white, or mottled. Summer. Trop. Amer. var. *humilis* Alef. The widely grown 'bush' bean. Z10.
P. xuaresii Zucc. = *P. lunatus.*

Pheasant Grass *Stipa arundinacea.*
Pheasant's Eye *Adonis annua.*
Pheasant's-eye Narcissus *Narcissus poeticus.*
Pheasant's-foot Geranium *Pelargonium glutinosum.*
Pheasant's-tail Grass *Stipa arundinacea.*

Phegopteris Fée. BEECH FERN. Thelypteridaceae. 3 terrestrial ferns. Rhiz. erect to creeping. Fronds stipitate, uniform, 1–2-pinnate or -pinnatisect; pinnae basally attached to stipes by winged rachillae. N temp. & SE Asia.

P. connectilis (Michx.) Watt. BEECH FERN; LONG BEECH FERN; NARROW BEECH FERN; NORTHERN BEECH FERN. Rhiz. long-creeping. Lamina to 20cm, emerald green, sagittate or deltoid to ovate, apex attenuate; pinnae oblong or linear to lanceolate, deeply pinnatifid, to 8×2cm, seg. oblong, entire to detate, to 5mm wide; stipes to 15cm. N Amer., Eur., W Asia. Z5.
P. decursive-pinnata (Van Hall) Fée. Rhiz. erect to short-creeping. Lamina to 60cm, pinnate or 2-pinnatifid, attenuate at apex; pinnae linear, occas. pinnatifid; stipes to 20cm. China, Taiwan, Jap., Korea, Himal. Z6.
P. dryopteris (L.) Fée = *Gymnocarpium dryopteris.*
P. effusa (Sw.) Fée = *Lastreopsis effusa.*
P. hexagonoptera (Michx.) Fée. BROAD BEECH FERN. SOUTHERN BEECH FERN. Differs from *P. connectilis* (to 35×35cm) in its broader fronds with basal pinnae not decurved but spreading. E N Amer. Z5.
P. munita Mett. = *Lastreopsis munita.*
→*Dryopteris* and *Thelypteris.*

Phellodendron Rupr. Rutaceae. 10 decid., aromatic trees. Bark corky. Lvs pinnate. Pan. term.; fls small, yellow tinged green; sep. and pet. 5–8; sta. 5–6. Fr. a drupe, pea-sized, black. Temp. and subtrop. E Asia.

P. amurense Rupr. To 15m; bark pale grey, corky; twigs yellow tinged grey. Lvs to 35cm; lfts 5–10cm, 9–13, broadly ovate to ovate-lanceolate, dark glossy green above, glaucous beneath, turning yellow in autumn. Early summer. N China, Manch. Z3.
P. amurense var. *japonicum* (Maxim.) Ohwi = *P. japonicum.*
P. amurense var. *lavallei* (Dode) Sprague = *P. lavallei.*
P. amurense var. *sachalinense* F. Schmidt = *P. sachalinense.*
P. chinense Schneid. Tree to 10m; bark thin, dark grey-brown; shoots ferruginous when young. Lfts 7–14cm, 7–13, oblong-lanceolate, acuminate at apex, yellow-green above, light green and tomentose beneath. C China. Z5. var. *glabriusculum* Schneid. Differs in ± glab. lfts.
P. japonicum Maxim. Tree, 5–10m; bark thin, finely grooved, deep brown; shoots ferruginous when young. Lvs 25–35cm; lfts 6–10cm, 9–13, ovate to ovate-oblong, dull green above, grey tomentose beneath. C Jap. Z6.
P. lavallei Dode. Tree, 7–10m+; bark thick and corky; shoots ferruginous when young. Lvs 20–35cm; lfts 5–10cm, 5–13, ovate-elliptic to oblong-lanceolate, acuminate, dull yellow tinged green above, light green and pubesc. beneath. Early summer. C Jap. Z6.
P. sachalinense (F. Schmidt) Sarg. Tree, 7m+, with broad crown; bark thin, dark brown, finely channelled, not corky; twigs ferruginous. Lvs 22–30cm; lfts 6–12cm, 7–11+, ovate to ovate-oblong, acuminate, dull green above, glaucous beneath. Sakhalin, N Jap., Korea, W China. Z3.
P. wilsonii Hayata & Kanehira. Branchlets glab. Lvs 27cm; lfts to 8cm, *c*9, ovate-oblong, acuminate, chartaceous, glab. above, pubesc. on veins beneath. Taiwan (mts).

Phellosperma Britt. & Rose.
P. tetrancistra (Engelm.) Britt. & Rose = *Mammillaria tetrancistra.*

Phenakospermum Endl. Strelitziaceae. 1 giant herb to 10m, closely resembling *Ravenala* less prominent, lvs to 1.25cm, dark glossy green, midrib often tinted coral-red. Infl. term., bracts 7, carinate, 30–45cm; fls white, seed with orange aril. Braz., Guyana. Z10.

P. guyannense (Rich.) Endl. ex Miq.
→*Ravenala*.

Pherosphaera Archer.
P. hookeriana Hook. non Archer = *Microstrobos niphophilus*.
P. fitzgeraldii F. Muell. ex Hook. = *Microstrobos fitzgeraldii*.

PHILADELPHACEAE D. Don. see HYDRANGEACEAE.

Philadelphus L. MOCK ORANGE. Hydrangeaceae (Philadelpha-ceae). 60 largely decid. shrubs. Bark peeling. Lvs opposite, simple. Fls in rac., pan. or cymes, or solitary usually white often strongly scented, disc-shaped (with pet. rounded) or cross-shaped (with pet. narrow); sep. 4; pet. 4; sta. numerous. C & N Amer., Cauc., Himal., China and E Asia.

P. argenteus Rydb. Similar to *P. argyrocalyx* but lvs ovate-oblong, strigose to hispid above. Calif., Baja Calif. Z9.

P. argyrocalyx Wooton. Erect shrub to 2m; twigs grey-brown; current growth shaggy. Lvs 1–3.5cm, ovate, ovate-lanceolate or elliptic, glab. above, sparsely shaggy-bristly. Fls solitary on short stalks, cross-shaped, to 3.5cm wide, white and slightly fragrant. Summer–late summer. US (New Mex.) Z7.

P. billiardii Koehne = *P. insignis*.

P. brachybotrys (Koehne) Koehne. Shrub to 3m; bark of the second year brown-grey; current growth shaggy becoming glab. Lvs 2–6cm, ovate, finely toothed or almost entire, sparsely adpressed-bristly. Fls 5–7 in short rac., cream, disc-shaped, c3cm across. Summer. SE China. Z7.

P. brachybotrys var. *purpurascens* Koehne = *P. purpurascens*.

P. × burkwoodii Burkw. & Skipw. (*P. mexicanus* ×?.) Dwarf shrub, bark v. dark brown, eventually peeling; current growth adpressed stiffly-hairy. Lvs 3.5–6.6cm, oval-elliptic, sparsely hairy beneath. Fls 1–5, in pan., cross-shaped, 5–6cm across, fragrant. Gdn origin. Z7.

P. californicus Benth. Erect shrubs to 3m; bark dark brown; current year's growth soon becoming glab. Lvs ovate or ovate-elliptic, 4.5–8cm, ± glab., entire or obscurely toothed. Fls 3–5 in a pan., to 2.5cm across, cross-shaped, fragrant. Summer. Calif. Z7.

P. caucasicus Koehne. Like *P. coronarius*, but disc and style pub-esc. Summer. Cauc. var. *aureus* Rehd. Smaller; lvs tinged yellow. Z6.

P. columbianus hort. = *P. inodorus* var. *grandiflorus*.

P. cordifolius Lange. Differs from *P. californicus*, in lvs larger, and fls numerous, in dense pan. Calif. Z7.

P. coronarius L. Shrubs to 3m; bark dark brown, slowly peeling; current growth downy becoming glab. Lvs 4.5–9cm, ovate, mostly glab., irregularly and shallowly toothed, apex acuminate. Fls 5–9 in short term. rac., creamy white, strongly fragrant, 2.5–3cm across. Early summer. S Eur., Cauc. 'Aureus' ('Foliisaureis'): compact; lvs golden yellow to lime green; fls fragrant. 'Bowles's var': lvs edged white. 'Deutziflorus' ('Multiflorus Plenus'): dwarf; fls double, more freely produced than 'Duplex'; pet. pointed, narrow. 'Dianthiflorus' dwarf; fls double; pet. narrow. 'Duplex' ('Nanus', 'Pumilus'): dwarf to 1m; lvs small 3–5cm, oval; fls double, solitary to groups of 5, sparse, produced only with age; pedicels hairy. 'Gracieux': fls double, creamy white; pet. sometimes fimbriate. 'Maculiformis': fls 3cm; pet. red at base; considered to be a bud mutation. 'Primuliflorus' ('Rosiflorus Plenus'): like 'Dianthiflorus', but taller to 2m; lvs to 7cm; pedicel hairy; fls solitary to groups of 5. 'Salicifolius': lvs narrower; tips of pet. bear a few hairs; may be of hybrid origin. 'Speciosissimus': dwarf, lvs small. 'Zeyheri': vigorous, to 2.5m, lvs 6–10cm; fls 2.5cm diam. unscented, poorly produced, possiblly *P. coronarius* × *P. inodorus* var. *grandiflorus*. Z5.

P. coronarius var. *tomentosus* (Royle) Hook. & Thoms. = *P. tomentosus*.

P. coulteri Wats. Shrub to 1.3m; current year's growth hairy. Lvs 1.5–3cm, ovate to ovate-eliptic, ± entire, apex obtuse or apiculate, strigose. Fls white, solitary or in threes; cor. disc-like, 2.5–3.5cm across. Summer. Mex. Z9.

P. × cymosus Rehd. Erect shrub to 2.5m; bark brown, not peeling. Lvs ovate, sparsely toothed, hairy beneath. Fls white to cream, sometimes tinted rose, 4–10cm diam., cupped to spreading, fragrant in cymes of 1–5; some sta. petal-like. Gdn origin. 'Amalthée': lvs glossy green above; fls 4cm, pink at base, slightly fragrant. 'Bannière': upright to 2m; fls abundant, semi-double. 'Bouquet Blanc': fls semi-double, milky white, fragrant borne in great profusion. 'Conquette': br. arching; lvs long, to 10cm; fls single to double v. fragrant, in cymes of 3–5; the type

of the cross. 'Dresden': low growing. 'Mer de Glace' fls double, fragrance slight. 'Monster': v. vigorous 3–8m; lvs to 15cm; fls 5cm, in rac. of 9. 'Nuée Blanche': fls single to semi-double, creamy, fragrant, profuse. 'Perle Blanche': habit compact; fls single to semi-double, fragrant. 'Rosace': fls wide opening, semi-double. 'Velleda': fls rounded with rose fragrance. 'Voie Lactée': vigorous, lvs large, fls to 5cm, freely produced; pet. reflexed. Z5.

P. delavayi Henry. Shrub to 4m; bark grey-brown, grey or chestnut-brown, not peeling; current growth glaucous. Lvs ovate-lanceolate or ovate-oblong, acuminate, 2–8cm, serrate or entire, sparsely bristly above, shaggy-hairy beneath. Fls in rac. of 5–9 (rarely more), 2.5–3.5cm across, disc-shaped, pure white, fragrant; cal. purple-tinted. Early summer. SW China. 'Nymans Variety': cal. plum-coloured. Z6.

P. × falconeri Nichols. Shrub to 3m, bark brown, peeling; br. slender, pendulous; current growth glab. Lvs 3–6.5cm, ovate or ovate-elliptic, faintly toothed. Fls 3–5 in cymes, abundant, to 3cm wide, pure white, star-shaped. Summer. Gdn origin. Z5.

P. floribundus Schräd. = *P. × cymosus*.

P. floridus Beadle. Shrub to 3m; new growth hairless, brown, second-year growth chestnut. Lvs 4–10cm, ovate-elliptic, sharply acuminate, entire or inconspicuously toothed, adpressed-bristly beneath. Fls in threes or rarely solitary or in rac., disc-shaped, 4–5cm across; pet. almost circular, c2.5cm, pure white. Early summer. US (Georgia). var. *faxonii* Rehd. Fls smaller, in the shape of a cross. Z6.

P. gloriosus Beadle = *P. inodorus* var. *grandiflorus*.

P. godohokeri Kirchn. = *P. hirsutus*.

P. hirsutus Nutt. Low, spreading shrub with slender, slightly twisted arching br., to 2.5m; bark dark brown, peeling, new growth shaggy. Lvs 2.5–7cm, ovate-elliptic or ovate-lanceolate, acuminate, sharply toothed, hirsute above, shaggy beneath. Fls 1–5 on v. short shoots, disc-shaped, white, c2.5cm across. Early summer. SE US. Z6.

P. incanus Koehne. Erect shrub to 3.5m, bark grey and smooth, later peeling; current growth hairy. Lvs oval-elliptic, 4–8.5cm, slender-pointed, bristly. Fls 7–11 in rac., white, c2.5cm across. Late summer. China. Z5.

P. inodorus L. Arching shrub to 2–3m, bark chestnut-brown, peeling; new growth hairless. Lvs 5–9cm, ovate-elliptic or elliptic, ± entire or faintly toothed, ± glab. above, hairy on veins beneath. Fls 4–5cm across, in cymes of 1, 3 or rarely 9. Summer. SE US. var. *grandiflorus* (Willd.) Gray. Fls large, campanulate when opening. E US. Z5.

P. insignis Carr. Erect shrub to 4m, bark grey or brown. Lvs 3.5–8cm, ovate or ovate-elliptic, acute or strongly acuminate, entire or faintly toothed, adpressed-hairy beneath. Fls in threes in pan., 2.5–3.5cm across. Summer. W US. Z7.

P. × insignis Carr. = *P. insignis*.

P. intectus Beadle. Erect shrub to 5m, bark silvery, not peeling, new growth glab. Lvs ovate to oblong-elliptic, 6–10cm, apex acuminate, glab. or rarely hairy beneath, sparsely serrate. Fls in rac. of 5–9, disc-shaped, c3cm across. Summer. SE US. Z5.

P. kansuensis (Rehd.) S.Y. Hu Upright shrub to 7m; new growth with curly hairs, becoming hairless, bark grey-brown, peeling. Lvs ovate or ovate-lanceolate, to 11cm, entire or faintly toothed, apex pointed, bristly-hairy. Fls 5–7 in rac., disc-shaped, c2.5cm across. Summer. NW China. Z7.

P. karwinskyanus Koehne. Like *P. mexicanus*, but pan. several-fld, fls 2.5–3cm across. Mex. Z9.

P. lasiogynus Nak. = *P. schrenkii* var. *jackii*.

P. laxiflorus Rehd. Differs from *P. brachybotrys*, in lvs uniformly bristly above, bark chestnut-brown. Summer. China. Z6.

P. × lemoinei Lemoine. (*P. coronarius* × *P. microphyllus*.) Low compact shrub, bark peeling. Lvs 1.5–2.5cm, ovate, glab. above, sparsely bristly below, apex acuminate, with c6 teeth. Fls usually in threes, fragrant, cross-shaped, c3cm across; pet. notched. Summer. Gdn origin. Cvs with habit arching to upright; lvs 2.5–15cm, mottled and variegated to smooth dark green; fls 2.5–6cm, white to creamy, fragrant to v. fragrant; pet. sometimes waved, dentate or cut. 'Avalanche': upright, fls v. fragrant. 'Candelabre': slow, compact; fls 3.5cm in dense heads; pet. waved and dentate. 'Coupe d'Argent': br. arching; fls to 3cm, flat, rose-scented. 'Dame Blanche': small, lvs to 15cm, dark smooth green; fls double, creamy, 'Erectus': upright, fls v. fragrant. 'Fimbriatus': to 80cm, fls double; pet. cut. 'Innocence': lvs mottled yellow; fls single to semi-double, v. fragrant. 'Innocence Variegatus': lvs edged cream. 'Lemoinei': spreading, fls pure white, v. fragrant. 'Manteau d'Hermine': lvs small to 2.5cm; fls creamy, double, fragrant; buds red. 'Silver Showers' ('Silberregen'): fls solitary, wide-opening, scented of strawberry. Z5.

P. lewisii Pursh. Erect shrub to 3m; bark brown-yellow to chestnut-brown, cracked not peeling; new growth glab., ciliate at nodes. Lvs 4–5.5×2–3.5cm, rounded, apex acute, entire or finely toothed, with long, rough hairs on veins above and tufts of hair in vein axils beneath, ciliate. Fls in rac. of 5–11, cross-shaped, 3–4.5cm across. Early summer. BC to Calif. var. *gordonianus* (Lindl.) Koehne. Lvs more densely hairy and more strongly toothed, fls disc-shaped. Summer. W US. 'Waterton': young shoots red-brown, fls creamy, star-like. Z5.

P. lewisii var. *californicus* (Benth.) Torr. = *P. californicus*.

P. maculatus hort. = *P. mexicanus* 'Rose Syringa'.

P. mexicanus Schldl. Climbing, everg. shrub to 5m with drooping br.; bark dark brown wrinkled; new growth long-bristly. Lvs 5–11.5cm, ovate, adpressed-bristly, apex long-acuminate, entire or with few tiny teeth. Fls solitary or in threes, yellow-white, rose-scented, 3–4cm across; pet. hairy. Summer. Mex., Guat. 'Rose Syringa': pet. with pink-purple basal marking. Z9.

P. microphyllus A. Gray. Erect shrub to 1m; new growth adpressed-pubesc., bark chestnut-brown, shiny, soon flaking. Lvs 1–1.5cm, oval-elliptic or lanceolate, entire and ciliate, glabrate above, softly shaggy-hairy beneath. Flowering shoots 1.5–4cm long, with 1 or rarely 2 pure white, v. fragrant, cross-shaped, fls *c*3cm wide. Early summer. SW US. Z6.

P. nepalensis Koehne = *P. triflorus*.

P. ×nivalis Jacques. (Probably *P. coronarius* × *P. pubescens*.) Arching shrub to 2.5m, bark dark brown, peeling; new growth hairless. Lvs 5–10cm, ovate or ovate-elliptic, apex acuminate, faintly toothed, hairless above, shaggy-hairy beneath. Rac. with 5–7 double fls, disc-shaped, 2.5–3.5cm across. Early summer. Gdn origin. 'Plenus': fls double. Z5.

P. pallidus Hayek ex Schneid. = *P. coronarius*.

P. pekinensis Rupr. Low compact shrub to 2m; bark dark brown, peeling; new growth hairless. Lvs ovate, 6–9cm, long-pointed at apex, toothed, hairless. Rac. with 3–9 yellow-white, fragrant, disc-shaped fls, 2–3cm across. Early summer. N & W China. Z4.

P. pekinensis var. *brachybotrys* Koehne = *P. brachybotrys*.

P. pekinensis var. *kansuensis* Rehd. = *P. kansuensis*.

P. pendulifolius Carr. (*P. pubescens* ×?) Medium-sized. Fls cup-shaped, racemose.

P. ×polyanthus Rehd. (*P. insignis* × *P. ×lemoinei*?.) Erect shrub, bark dark brown, peeling; new growth sparsely shaggy. Lvs 3.5×5cm, ovate, apex acuminate, entire or with a few sharp teeth, sparsely bristly beneath. Fls 3–5 in cymes or corymbs, cross-shaped, *c*3cm across. Summer. Gdn origin. 'Atlas': to 2m; lvs to 6cm, often mottled; fls 5–6cm in rac. of 5–7, wide opening, milky-white, slightly fragrant. 'Boule d'Argent': habit compact, fls 4cm in cymes of 5–7, semi-double, scarcely fragrant. 'Favourite': to 2m, fls large, cross shaped, cupped; pet. serrate; sta. yellow. 'Gerbe de Neige': v. free flowering. 'Mont Blanc': to 1m, fls cross shaped, pure white, fragrance strong. 'Norma': to 1.5m, br. arching; fls 4cm cupped, freely borne, fragrance slight. 'Pavillon Blanc': low bush, br. arching; fls creamy-white, fragrant. Z5.

P. pubescens Lois. Shrub to 5m; bark grey; new growth hairless. Lvs 4–8cm, ovate, abruptly acuminate, remotely toothed or entire, glab. above, except for veins, shaggy-bristly-hairy beneath. Fls 5–11 in rac., white, scentless, *c*3.5cm across. Early summer. SE US. Z6.

P. pubescens var. *intectus* (Beadle) Moore = *P. intectus*.

P. purpurascens (Koehne) Rehd. Shrub to 4m; bark brown or grey, smooth; hairless. Lvs ovate to ovate-lanceolate, 1.5–6cm or longer on nonflowering shoots, adpressed-bristly above and on veins beneath, finely toothed. Rac. usually with 5–9 bell-shaped fls 3–4cm wide and v. fragrant, cal. tinged purple, glaucous. Summer. S China. var. *venustus* (Koehne) S.Y. Hu. Young growth with shaggy hairs. SW China. Z6.

P. ×purpureomaculatus Lemoine. (*P. ×lemoinei* × *P. coulteri*.) Shrub to 1.5m, bark black-brown, peeling in second year; new growth hairy. Lvs 1–3.5cm, broadly ovate, tip acute, ± entire, with few scattered hairs beneath. Fls solitary or in threes or fives, fragrant, disc-shaped, 2.5–3cm across, white, purple at centre. Summer. Gdn origin. 'Beauclerk' ('Sybille' ×'Burfordiensis'): 'Belle Etoile': to 2m, fls to 8cm, centre purple; pet. broad; pineapple-scented. 'Bicolore': dwarf; lvs 3cm, fls creamy, centre purple. 'Etoile Rose': fls carmine at centre fading to apex, scarcely fragrant. 'Fantasie': to 80cm; fls rounded. 'Galathée': br. arching, fl solitary, centre pink. 'Nuage Rose': fls opening wide, centre pink. 'Oeil de Pourpre': upright and narrow; fls small cupped, centre dark. 'Ophelie': free-flowering, fl. centre purple, fragrance mild. 'Purpureo-Maculatus': fls solitary, centre pink-purple. 'Romeo': free-flowering, fl. centre wine-red. 'Sirene': fls flat, centre pale pink. 'Suprise': fls large, centre dark pink-purple. 'Sybille': free-flowering, fl. centre pink. 'Sylvanie': free-flowering, fls large, centre pink. Z5.

P. rubricaulis Carr. = *P. pekinensis*.

P. salicifolius hort. = *P. coronarius* 'Salicifolius'.

P. satsumanus Miq. Similar to *P. satsumi* but with uniformly downy lvs. Summer. Jap. Z6.

P. satsumi (Sieb.) S.Y. Hu. Upright shrub to 3m; bark brown, eventually peeling; new growth glabrate. Lvs 5–9cm, ovate to ovate-lanceolate, with coarse, forward-pointing teeth, apex long-acuminate, with sparse bristles or hairless above, with stiff hairs on veins beneath. Fls 5–7 in rac., cross-shaped, slightly fragrant; *c*3cm wide. Summer. Jap. Z6.

P. schrenkii Rupr. Upright shrub too 4m, bark grey or rarely brown, cracked, rough-hairy at first. Lvs ovate or ovate-elliptic, 4.5–13cm, tip acuminate, remotely finely toothed to entire, sparsely shaggy-hairy on veins beneath. Fls 3–7 in rac., cross-shaped, v. fragrant, 2.5–3.5cm wide. Summer. Korea to E Sib. var. *jackii* Koehne. Lvs more obviously toothed, veins hairy beneath. Summer. N China, Korea. Z5.

P. sericanthus Koehne. Shrub to 3m; new growth glab., bark grey or grey-brown, slowly peeling. Lvs 4–11cm, oval-elliptic or elliptic-lanceolate, apex acuminate, coarsley toothed, sparsely adpressed-bristly above and on veins beneath. Fls 7–15 in rac., pure white, unscented, *c*2.5cm across. Summer. W China. Z6.

P. serpyllifolius Gray. Somewhat spiny shrub to 1.5m; new growth hairy. Lvs ovate to ovate-lanceolate, entire, pubesc., lanate beneath. Fls solitary, 1–1.5cm diam. Summer. S US and Mex.

P. speciosus Schräd. ex DC. = *P. inodorus* var. *grandiflorus*.

P. speciosus misapplied = *P. satsumi*.

P. ×splendens Rehd. (Thought to be *P. inodorus* var. *grandiflorus* × *P. lewisii* var. *gordonianus*.) Upright shrub; bark dark brown, peeling; new growth glab. Lvs 6–11.5cm, oblong-elliptic, apex acuminate, finely toothed to ± entire, hairless or rough, shaggy-hairy on veins beneath. Fls in crowded rac. of 5–9, disc-shaped, *c*4cm wide, slightly scented, pure white. Gdn origin. Z5.

P. subcanus Koehne. Erect shrub to 6m; new growth brown, ± glab., bark grey-brown, smooth, peeling late. Lvs 4–14cm, ovate or ovate-lanceolate, apex acuminate, finely toothed, sparsely covered with upright hairs above, shaggy-hairy on veins beneath. Fls 5–29 in rac. 2.5–22cm long, disc-shaped, 2.5–3cm across, pure white, slightly fragrant. Early summer. W China. Most commonly seen is var. *magdalenae* (Koehne) S.Y. Hu, smaller with fl. stalks and cal. only slightly downy with curly hairs. Early summer. SW China. Z6.

P. tenuifolius Rupr. ex Maxim. Upright shrub to 3m; new growth pubesc. Lvs to 11cm, ovate, distantly toothed, glab. except for sparse hairs on veins beneath. Fls 5–9 in a rac., slightly fragrant, 2.5–3.5cm across. Summer. E Russia, Korea. Z5.

P. tomentosus Royle. Shrub to 3m, similar to *P. coronarius* apart from downy undersides of lvs; bark cinnamon, eventually peeling; new growth hairless or becoming so. Lvs 4–10cm, ovate or lanceolate, apex acuminate. Fls 5–7 in a rac., *c*3m across, cross-shaped, fragrant, cream. Early summer. N India, Himal. Z6.

P. triflorus Wallich. Differs from *P. tomentosus* in lvs hairless beneath. Summer. Indian Himal. Z6.

P. venustus Koehne = *P. purpurascens* var. *venustus*.

P. verrucosus Schräd. ex DC. = *P. pubescens*.

P. viksnei Zam. = *P. tenuifolius*.

P. ×virginalis Rehd. A stiffly upright to 2.5m; bark grey, peeling when old; new growth hairy. Lvs 4–7cm, ovate, apex shortly acuminate, becoming glab. above, shaggy beneath. Fls in rac., usually double, pure white, v. fragrant, 4–5cm wide. Summer. Gdn origin. 'Albâtre': fls pure white, profuse. 'Argentine': fls large, double. 'Burfordiensis': to 3m; lvs 11cm; fls 7cm in rac. of 5–9, sta. yellow, conspicuous; similar to 'Monster' in *P. ×cymosus*. 'Dwarf Minnesota Snowflake': v. dwarf; fls double, profuse, v. fragrant. 'Fleur de Neige': to 1m, fls 4cm, semi-double; sta. yellow. 'Fraicheur': fls large, v. double, creamy, profuse. 'Glacier': fls creamy, v. double, late. 'Le Roy': to 1m, fls cream. 'Minnesota Snowflake': to 1.5m; lvs well retained; fls double. 'Natchez' fls single, to 5cm. 'Purity': fls single, to 5cm, profuse. 'Pyramidal': vigorous, fls semi-double. 'Savilos': to 5cm, single to semi-double. 'Schneestrum': fast growing, pure white double. 'Virginal': fls double in loose heads. Z5.

P. wilsonii Koehne = *P. subcanus*.

P. cvs and hybrids. 'Buckley's Quill' ('Frosty Morn' ×'Bouquet Blanc'): 'Faxonii': habit arching; fls cross-shaped. 'Frosty Morn': fls 3cm, double; frost tolerant. 'Mrs E.L. Robinson': fls large fragrant. 'Patricia' (resembles *P. lewisii*): lvs leathery, dark green; fls in rac. of 3–7, v. fragrant. 'Slavinii': rounded bush to 3m; lvs 6.5–9.5cm; fls 6cm, cross shaped, abundant. 'Splendens' (possibly *P. inodorus* var. *grandiflorus* × *P. lewisii* var. *gordonianus*): habit full, rounded; fls single, wide opening, fragrance slight, pet. rounded. 'Stenopetalus' (possibly a form of *P. pubescens*): fls campanulate. 'Thelma' (origin unknown, possibly *P. purpurascens*): habit low, graceful; lvs 2.5cm; fls 1.5cm, campanulate.

✕ Philageria Mast. (*Philesia* ✕ *Lapageria*.) Liliaceae (Philesiaceae). Scrambling shrub. Lvs 4.5cm, lanceolate, leathery. Fls solitary or few at ends of br., drooping, outer tep. 3.8cm, fleshy, dull red or magenta, glaucous, inner tep. 6cm, bright rose; fil. spotted pink. Summer. Gdn origin. Z9.
✕ P. veitchii Mast. (*Lapageria rosea* ✕ *Philesia magellanica*.)

Philagonia Bl.
P. fraxinifolia Hook. = *Tetradium fraxinifolium*.

Philesia Juss. Liliaceae (Philesiaceae). 1 erect shrubby everg. of rather box-like habit to 1m. St. slender, purple-green, bearing scale-like lvs. Lvs 1.5–3.5cm, oblong-lanceolate, leathery, glossy above, glaucescent beneath. Fls solitary or few at ends of br., slender-campanulate, pendent; tep. 6, outer 3 1.5–2.2cm, tinged green or pink, inner 3, 4.5–6.5cm, purple-red, sometimes faintly flecked orange-pink. Summer. Chile. Z9.
P. buxifolia Willd. = *P. magellanica*.
P. magellanica Gmel.

Philippicereus Backeb.
P. castaneus (Philippi) Backeb. = *Eulychnia castanea*.

Philippine Fig *Ficus pseudopalma*.
Philippine Violet *Barleria cristata*.
Philippine Waxflower *Etlingera elatior*.

Phillyrea L. MOCK PRIVET. Oleaceae. 4 everg. shrubs. Lvs to 6cm, entire or toothed, coriaceous, glossy green, glab. Fls small, clustered in axils, cream to white, fragrant; cal. and cor. 4-lobed. Fr. a blue-black ovoid drupe. Medit. to Asia Minor. Z7.
P. angustifolia L. Shrub to 3m. Lvs linear-lanceolate, usually entire. Summer. Medit. 'Rosmarinifolia': lvs narrower, smaller, to 6×4cm, grey-green, somewhat glaucous.
P. decora Boiss. & Bal. = *Osmanthus decorus*.
P. latifolia L. Shrub or small trees to 9m. Lvs ovate to elliptic-lanceolate, dentate or entire. Late spring. Medit. 'Buxifolia' ('Rotundifolia'): lvs small, obovate, entire. 'Spinosa': lvs spiny-dentate, ovate.
P. media L. = *P. latifolia*.
P. spinosa Mill. = *P. latifolia* 'Spinosa'.
P. vilminiana Boiss. & Bal. = *Osmanthus decorus*.

Philodendron Schott. Araceae. 350+ epiphytic or terrestrial, everg., climbing shrubs, small trees or stemless herbs; juvenile phase often distinct from adult. St. stout with adventitious roots. Lvs entire or lobed to pinnatifid to pedate, coriaceous; petiole to 1.5m, occas. geniculate above or swollen below, lf scars distinct; lvs subtended by cataphylls. Peduncles axill., usually short; spathe to 30cm, fleshy, forming tube around spadix below, expanded above, hooded or cymbiform, white to green-yellow, often marked red and purple; spadix shorter than or subequal to spathe, usually white. Fr. a berry, white to orange or red. Trop. Amer.
P. andreanum Devansaye = *P. melanochrysum*.
P. angustisectum Engl. Climbing. Lvs to 60×45cm, reflexed ovate, basal sinus triangular, pinnatisect, seg. to 2.5cm across, 16 per side, linear, glossy dark green above; petiole subequal to lamina. Colomb.
P. asperatum K. Koch = *P. ornatum*.
P. auriculatum Standl. & L.O. Williams. Climbing. Lvs to 90×35cm, erect, narrow-elliptic-oblong, basally auriculate, veins paler; petiole shorter than lamina. Costa Rica.
P. bahiense Engl. Differs from *P. ruizii* in smaller lvs (35×12.5cm). Braz.
P. barrosoanum Bunting. Climbing. Lvs 40×25cm, reflexed, hastate, 3-lobed, median lobe ovate, lat. lobes 30×17.5cm, elliptic-ovate, sinus v. broad; petiole to 75cm. S Amer.
P. 'Barryi'. = *P. bipinnatifidum* ✕ ?.
P. bipennifolium Schott. HORSEHEAD PHILODENDRON; FIDDLE-LEAF PHILODENDRON. Climbing. Lvs 45–15cm, reflexed, 5-lobed, glossy dark green, terminal lobe to 25×10cm, obovate, lat. lobes angular, basal lobes broadly oblong-triangular; petiole shorter than lamina. SE Braz.
P. bipinnatifidum Endl. Arborescent to 2m, decumbent with age, lf scars prominent. Lvs to 1m, reflexed, ovate, sagittate, pinnatisect, seg. many, obtuse, pinnatifid or sinuate, flat or undulate, bright green; petioles equalling lamina. SE Braz. 'California type': arborescent; lvs v. deeply cut, scoop-shaped, dark green. 'German Selloum': graceful; lvs finely cut, seg. undulate. 'Johnsii': lvs somewhat lobed, in rosette form when young. 'Miniature Selloum': dwarf; lvs small, heavy, petioles thick. 'Uruguay': lvs large, thick, lobes frilled. 'Variegatum': lvs marbled light green to yellow.
P. brenesii Standl. Climbing. Lvs to 50×25cm, lanceolate- to ovate-oblong, deeply cordate, coriaceous, midrib prominent;

petiole subequal to lamina. Costa Rica.
P. 'British Guiana'. = *P. pinnatifidum*.
P. calophyllum Brongn. ex Lind. & André = *P. insigne*.
P. cannifolium Kunth. St. prostrate. Lvs 45×15–20cm, erect, lanceolate to ovate, base obtuse to truncate, coriaceous, glossy, petioles to 40cm, swollen, margins angular. SE Braz.
P. coerulescens Engl. = *P. inaequilaterum*.
P. cordatum (Vell. Conc.) Kunth. HEART-LEAF PHILODENDRON. Climbing. Lvs 45×25cm, reflexed, ovate-triangular, base cordate, undulate; petioles shorter than or exceeding lamina. SE Braz.
P. cordatum misapplied. = *P. scandens*.
P. ✕ corsinianum Senoner. (Probably with *P. verrucosum* in parentage.) Climbing, fibrous cataphyll remains present. Lvs 75×60cm, reflexed, ovate, base cordate, shallowly pinnate-lobed, metallic red-purple between green veins beneath when young; petiole subequal to lamina.
P. crassinervium Lindl. Climbing. Lvs to 60×10cm, narrow-elliptic-oblong, long-acuminate, cuneate at base, coriaceous, midrib convex, inflated, to 1.5cm across; petioles to 18cm. SE Braz.
P. cruentum Poepp. REDLEAF. Differs from *P. ruizii* in lamina to 40×10cm, basal lobes acute; petioles to 18cm. Peru.
P. deflexum Poepp. ex Schott = *P. myrmecophilum*.
P. deflexum hort. non Poepp. ex Schott = *P. barrosoanum*.
P. devansayeanum Lind. Prostrate or climbing. Lvs to 100cm, ovate, cordate, glossy, orange-brown when young, main veins purple-red beneath; petioles to 150cm, purple-red. Peru, W Ecuad.
P. distantilobum K. Krause. Climbing. Lvs to 40×35cm, erect, ovate-oblong, pinnatifid, seg. 5–6 per side, oblanceolate to linear, acuminate, to 5cm across, entire or bifid, sinuses wide, angular; petiole subequal to lamina. Braz.
P. domesticum Bunting. SPADE-LEAF PHILODENDRON. Climbing. Lvs 60–30cm, reflexed, elongate-triangular, sagittate, undulate, glossy bright green, basal lobes round-oblong to triangular; petiole equalling lamina, centrally ridged. Origin unknown. 'Variegatum': lvs splashed yellow, cream and acid green.
P. dubium Chodat & Visch. = *P. tweedianum*.
P. dubium hort. non Chodat & Visch. = *P. radiatum*.
P. duisbergii Epple ex Bunting = *P. fendleri*.
P. eichleri Engl. = *P. undulatum*.
P. elegans K. Krause = *P. angustisectum*.
P. erubescens K. Koch & Augustin. RED-LEAF PHILODENDRON; BLUSHING PHILODENDRON. Climbing. Sts red-purple when young, with pink-brown cataphylls. Lvs to 40cm, reflexed, ovate-triangular, base short sagittate-cordate, glossy dark green above, coppery-purple beneath; petiole equalling lamina, tinged purple. Colomb. 'Burgundy' (hybrid): lvs leathery, to 30cm, base cordate to hastate, flushed red, veins burgundy, st. claret. 'Golden Erubescens': vigorous climber; st. thin, round; lvs gold, tinted pink beneath and when young. 'Imperial Red': lvs dark purple to red. 'Red Emerald': vigorous; st. claret; lvs long-cordate, to 40cm, dark green with red ribs beneath, shiny, petioles long and rich red.
P. fendleri K. Krause. Climbing. Lvs 60cm, reflexed, triangular-ovate in outline, pinnatifid, seg. 11–23cm, 6–9 per side, oblong, obtuse, sinus wide, midrib convex; petioles to 90cm. Colomb., Venez., Trin.
P. 'Fernleaf' = *P. pinnatilobum*.
P. fibrillosum Poepp. Climbing. Fibrous cataphyll remains persistent. Lvs 40×18cm, erect, oblong-elliptic, tapering, membranous, veins prominent; petiole 18cm, apex geniculate. Peru.
P. fibrillosum hort. non Poepp. = *P. grazielae*.
P. fragrantissimum (Hook.) Kunth. Climbing when young. Adult lvs 45–60cm, oblong-cordate to sagittate, petioles deeply grooved, juvenile lvs ovate, small, petioles winged. N S Amer.
P. giganteum Schott. Climbing. St. to 10cm diam., cataphyll remains persistent. Lvs to 100×60cm, reflexed, ovate, cordate or sagittate, basal lobes rounded, overlapping; petioles exceeding lamina. Carib. Is. to Trin.
P. gloriosum André. St. prostrate, with persistent cataphyll remains. Lvs 40×33cm, reflexed, broad-ovate, cordate-sagittate, basal lobes rounded, dark velvety green above, main veins ivory-white; petioles to 75cm. Colomb. 'Terciopelo Redondo': lvs sage green with pale green venation, tinted pink beneath.
P. grandifolium (Jacq.) Schott. St. climbing, with purple spots. Lvs 50×35cm, lanceolate, cordate, acuminate to cuspidate, subcoriaceous, basal lobes ovate to quadrangular; petiole to 45cm. Venez., Fr. Guiana, Martinique.
P. grazielae Bunting. Climbing. Lvs 8.5×10.5cm, reflexed, sub-reniform, cordate, acuminate, coriaceous; petioles to 7.5cm. Amazonian Peru, Braz.
P. guatemalense Engl. = *P. inaequilaterum*.

P. guttiferum hort. non Kunth = *Monstera standleyana*.

P. hastatum hort. non K. Koch & Sello = *P. domesticum*.

P. ilsemannii Sander. Climbing. Lvs reflexed, narrow-ovate, cordate-sagittate, heavily marked white with green and grey-green patches. Origin unknown. Probably a variegated juvenile form of a sp. allied to *P. cordatum*.

P. imbe Endl. St. climbing, red-purple. Lvs 33×18cm, reflexed, ovate-oblong, cordate to sagittate, glossy above, basal lobes rounded; petiole equalling lamina. SE Braz. 'Goldiana': dense; lvs long-ovate, rich green with gold speckles, red beneath, yellow when young, petioles short. 'Variegatum': lvs blotched green, dark green and cream. 'Weber's Selfheading': climber; lvs thick, v. shiny, oblique oblanceolate, midrib light green, ribs red beneath, petioles red spotted yellow-green.

P. imperiale Schott = *P. ornatum*.

P. inaequilaterum Liebm. St. slender, woody, climbing. Lvs to 30×15cm, spreading to erect, membranous, ovate to elliptic-oblong, acuminate, base obtuse or truncate; petioles to 20cm, winged to geniculum. Mex. to Colomb.

P. inconcinnum Schott. Climbing. Lvs 20×8.5cm, oblong to narrow-obovate, acuminate, base emarginate; petioles to 20cm+. Venez.

P. insigne Schott. St. short, erect. Lvs 100×22cm, erect, oblanceolate-spathulate, acuminate, base cuneate, coriaceous; petioles to 12.5cm, thick. N S Amer.

P. krebsii Schott. Climbing. Lvs 35×20cm, spreading, ovate to oblong-elliptic or elongate-triangular, cordate, subcoriaceous, glossy, petioles 12.5cm. Carib.

P. lacerum (Jacq.) Schott. St. climbing, to 30m, internodes long. Lvs 75cm, reflexed, ovate to round in outline, cordate, pinnatisect to less than halfway to midrib, lobes cuneate, obtuse, midrib and main lat. veins prominent; petioles to 90cm. Cuba, Jam., Hispan.

P. laciniatum (Vell. Conc.) Engl. = *P. pedatum*.

P. laciniosum Schott = *P. pedatum*.

P. latilobum Schott. Climbing. Juvenile lvs entire; adult lvs 30×25cm, ovate-triangular, 3-lobed toward apex, median lobe to 15cm across, broad-ovate, acute, lateral lobes rounded. Peru.

P. lingulatum (L.) K. Koch. Slender, climbing. Lvs to 40cm, membranous, oblong-elliptic to ovate, acuminate, truncate to emarginate at base, glossy dark green above; petioles slightly exceeding lamina, widely winged below. W Indies.

P. linnaei Kunth. St. to 10cm. Lvs 50–70×8–11cm, rosulate, oblanceolate to spathulate, coriaceous, midrib prominent; petioles stout. Amazonian Braz.

P. mamei André. St. prostrate, cataphylls becoming scarious, persistent. Lvs 60×45cm, reflexed, ovate, sagittate, basal lobes angular, spotted grey-green, veins impressed; petioles subequal to lamina, red at base and apex. Ecuad.

P. martianum Engl. = *P. cannifolium*.

P. maximum K. Krause. Climbing, cataphyll remains persistent. Lvs 135×73cm, reflexed, long-ovate, sagittate, undulate to sinuate, dark green above, veins pale; petiole to 105cm. Braz.

P. melanochrysum Lind. & André. BLACK-GOLD PHILODENDRON. Climbing. Lvs 100×30cm, reflexed to pendent, oblong-lanceolate or narrow-ovate, sagittate, acuminate, velvety black-green above, veins pale green, copper-coloured when young; petioles to 50cm. Colomb.

P. melinonii Brongn. ex Reg. St. erect, with persistent cataphyll remains. Lvs 100×40cm, erect, ovate-triangular, emarginate, midrib concave, pale green; petioles stout, narrowly winged; juvenile lvs oblong, base truncate, rose-purple below. N S Amer.

P. mexicanum Engl. Climbing. Lvs reflexed, long-triangular, ± hastate, mediann lobe 38×18cm, lat. lobes 23×8.5cm, lanceolate to oblong, curved; petioles 60cm. Mex.

P. micans K. Koch = *P. scandens* ssp. *scandens* f. *micans*.

P. microstictum Standl. & L.O. Williams. Climbing. Lvs to 23×20cm, broad-triangular to reniform, long-acuminate, emarginate or truncate in juvenile phase; petioles equalling lamina. Costa Rica.

P. myrmecophilum Engl. Climbing. Lvs 25–50×17.5–30cm, erect, entire, ovate, cordate to hastate, coriaceous, basal lobes obtuse to rounded, to 17cm; petioles to 50cm, inhabited by ants in habitat. Amaz. basin.

P. nobile Bull = *P. linnaei*.

P. ochrostemon Schott. St. climbing, slender. Lvs 28×11.5cm, spreading or erect, oblong-elliptic to oblong, base truncate; petioles shorter than laminae, auriculate at apex. Mex.

P. ornatum Schott. Climbing. Cataphyll remains persistent. Lvs 60cm, reflexed, ovate, deeply cordate, glossy dark green, sometimes spotted grey, veins red beneath; petiole equalling lamina. Venez. to Peru & SE Braz.

P. oxycardium Schott = *P. scandens* ssp. *oxycardium*.

P. panduraeforme misapplied. = *P. bipennifolium*.

P. pedatum (Hook.) Kunth. Tall, climbing. Lvs reflexed, ovate,

irregularly pinnatifid, term. lobe 45×30cm, median seg. elliptic, obovate or rhombic, lat. seg. to 5 per side, oblong; petioles exceeding lamina. S Venez., Surinam to SE Braz.

P. pertusum Kunth & Bouché = *Monstera deliciosa*.

P. pinnatifidum (Jacq.) Schott. St. erect, short and stout, covered by persistent cataphyll remains. Lvs to 60cm, triangular-ovate, acuminate, pinnatifid, lat. lobes to 20×5cm, 5–6 per side, oblong, basal lobes with 2–4 divisions, glossy above; petioles equalling or exceeding lamina, spotted purple-brown. Venez., Trin.

P. pinnatilobum Engl. St. climbing, angular. Lvs to 50cm, across, erect, ovate-orbicular, pinnatifid, lat. seg. 1.5cm across, to 13 per side, narrow, basal lobes bifid; juvenile lvs with fewer seg. and basal lobes reduced; equalling lamina. Braz.

P. pittieri Engl. = *P. scandens* f. *scandens*.

P. radiatum Schott. DUBIA PHILODENDRON. Climbing. Lvs to 90×70cm, reflexed, ovate, cordate-sagittate, deeply pinnatifid, term. lobe with 8 pairs oblong or further 3-parted seg., basal lobes 5-parted; petioles exceeding lamina. C Amer.

P. rubens Schott. Erect or climbing, stout. Lvs 50×28cm, reflexed, ovate, sagittate-cordate, acuminate, basal lobes rounded; petioles to 60cm. Venez.

P. rugosum Bogner & Bunting. Climbing. Lvs to 35×30cm, ovate, cordate, apex cuspidate, coriaceous, bright green, rugose above; petioles to 40cm. Ecuad.

P. ruizii Schott. Climbing. Lvs to 60×30cm, long triangular-oblong, sagittate, subcoriaceous, glossy bright green, basal lobes to 12.5cm, triangular, obtuse; petioles subequal to lamina. Peru.

P. sagittatum hort. = *P. sagittifolium*.

P. sagittifolium Liebm. Climbing. Lvs to 60×30cm, long triangular-oblong, sagittate, subcoriaceous, glossy bright green, basal lobes to 12.5cm, triangular, obtuse; petioles subequal to lamina. SE Mex.

P. sagittifolium misapplied. = *P. ilsemannii*.

P. scandens K. Koch & Sello. HEART-LEAF PHILODENDRON. ssp. *scandens* f. *scandens*. St. slender, climbing to pendent. Lvs 10–30×6–23cm, reflexed, ovate-cordate, acuminate, glossy green above, green or red-purple beneath; petioles slender, shorter than lamina. Mex. and W Indies to SE Braz. f. *micans* (K. Koch) Bunting. Lvs bronze above, red to red brown beneath, basal lobes larger, slightly overlapping. ssp. *oxycardium* (Schott) Bunting. New lvs glossy, brown. E Mex. 'Variegatum': lvs dark green marbled off-white and green-grey.

P. schottianum H. Wendl. ex Schott. Climbing. Lvs 60×40cm, broad-ovate,'cordate; petioles exceeding lamina. Costa Rica.

P. selloum K. Koch = *P. bipinnatifidum*.

P. sellowianum Kunth = *P. imbe*.

P. sodiroi hort. ex Bellair & St. Leger. = *P. ornatum*.

P. speciosum Schott. ex Endl. Close to *P. williamsii*. St. to 1m, erect and decumbent. Lvs 60–95×45–60cm, reflexed, sagittate, glossy dark green, median seg. to 60cm, basal lobes smaller, pink to purple beneath; petiole to 100cm. Braz. 'Ballenger's Exotica' (*P. speciosum* × *P. undulatum*): lvs to 1.5m long, thick, deep green, hastate, deeply lobed, edges cut.

P. squamiferum Poepp. Close to *P. pedatum*, climbing. Lvs 60×45cm, pinnatifid, 5-lobed, lobes entire, median lobe elliptic to rhombic, lat. lobes oblong-triangular, falcate, basal lobes elliptic, separated by broad sinuses; juvenile lvs entire or 3-lobed; petioles 15–30cm, red, terete, densely covered by fleshy bristles. Surinam, Fr. Guiana, Braz. 'Florida' (*P. pedatum* × *P. squamiferum*): climber; lvs with 5 lobes, midrib pale, ribs indented, brown to red beneath; petioles thin, round, somewhat warty. 'Florida Compacta' (*P. pedatum* var. *palmisectum* or *P. quercifolium* × *P. squamiferum*): non-climbing; lvs thick, deep green; petioles, marked plum. 'Florida Variegata': lvs irregularly blotched pale cream.

P. teretipes Sprague. St. pendent. Lvs 28×6.5cm, lanceolate-oblong, acuminate, green with red margin; petioles red, to 20cm. Colomb.

P. tripartitum (Jacq.) Schott. Climbing. Reflexed, lobes 3 to 25×7.5cm, elongate ovate-elliptic, unequal; petioles slightly exceeding lamina. S Amer.

P. trisectum Standl. Close to *P. tripartium*, but smaller. Lf blades 19×3.5cm, nearly equal; petioles to 33cm. Costa Rica.

P. triumphans hort. = *P. verrucosum*.

P. tweedianum Schott. St. erect, 50–100cm, or subterranean. Lvs 30–50×25–40cm, reflexed, broad ovate-triangular, sagittate, apiculate, basal lobes obtuse, separated by oblong sinus to 10cm, somewhat glaucous, weakly undulate; petioles 40–90cm. S Braz., Urug.

P. undulatum Engl. St. erect or decumbent, to 200×20cm. Lvs 40–80×30–65cm, reflexed, ovate, sagittate, median lobe to 55×65cm, lat. seg. 4–7 per side, subtriangular to rounded, basal lobe to 25×35cm, sinuate; petiole 90cm. Braz., Parag.

P. verrucosum Schott. Climbing. Lvs 60×40cm, reflexed, ovate, sagittate-cordate, shallowly sinuate, lustrous dark green above with pale green zones along main veins, red-violet beneath; petioles equalling lamina, covered by fleshy red, green or white scales. Costa Rica to Ecuad.

P. warscewiczii K. Koch. St. v. large, climbing. Lvs reflexed, membranous, triangular, bipinnatifid, primary lobes few, deeply lobed, ultimate seg. occas. dentate. Guat.

P. wendlandii Schott. St. erect to prostrate. Lvs 75–90×20cm, rosulate, erect, narrow-obovate, truncate or with small auricles at base; petioles 30×3.5cm, spongy. Nicaragua to Panama. 'Lynette' (*P. wendlandii* ×*P. elaphoglossoides*): 'bird-nest' form; lvs thick, vivid green, ribs indented. 'Tricolor' (*P. domesticum* 'Variegatum' ×*P. wendlandii*): lvs long, lanceolate, splashed cream and white. *P. wendlandii* also crossed with *P. imbe* to give *P.* 'Wend-Imbe'.

P. williamsii Hook. f. St. erect, arborescent. Lvs to 90cm, reflexed, oblong-triangular, sagittate, median lobe to 35cm across, basal lobes to 22cm, oblong-ovate, obtuse, coriaceous, veins dull purple beneath; petioles to 90cm. Braz.

P. cvs. 'Angra dos Reis': lvs thick, broad-sagittate, v. glossy; stalks marked red. 'Beleza do Acre': climber; lvs broad sagittate, to 1m, shiny, margin wavy, ribs lighter. lighter. 'Brazilian Arrow': rosette, later tree-like; lvs lanceolate, hastate to 80cm, lobed, vivid green, thick, veins paler, petioles thin. 'Choco': climber, dense; lvs heavy, to 30cm, dark lush green, veins white. 'Edmundo Barroso': creeping; lvs thick, upright, ovate-oblong, midrib raised. 'Emerald King': lvs to 30cm long, spade-shaped, pointed. 'Emerald Queen': lvs bright green, hastate, shiny, petioles short; Fl hybrid. 'Jungle Gardens' ('São Paulo' ×*P. bipinnatifidum*): tree-like with age; lvs large, bright green, pinnately cut, seg. somewhat lobed, slightly wavy. 'Jungle Gardens Variegated': lvs blotched white to yellow. 'Majesty': dense; st. thick; lvs large, lanceolate, dark green flushed copper, red petioles and beneath. 'Minas Gerais': small epiphyte; lvs like fine arrows, edges wavy, petioles thin. 'New Red': non-climbing; lvs arrow-shaped, deep metal red. 'New Yorker': climber; lvs sagittate, dipped, thick, dark green, veins lighter, tinted red when young, petioles dotted maroon. 'Painted Lady': lvs sagittate, gold when young, later mottled green; petioles tinted red. 'Queremal': rosette; lvs cordate, erect, firm, shiny. 'Red Duchess': climber; lvs to 25cm long, cordate, dark green, shiny, tinted red beneath, petioles red. 'Santa Leopoldana': climbing; lvs long sagittate, thick, to 1m, dark green, shiny, ribs white, edges red; petioles and st. red; spathe tinted red. 'São Paulo': lvs cupped, vivid green. 'Seaside': vigorous, arborescent; lvs large, thick, heavily cut, lobes frilled; disease-resistant. 'Silver Cloud': vigorous, climbing; lvs thick, waved, splattered silver towards edge, pale beneath, petioles broad and flat, finely striped white. 'Venezuela': 'bird-nest' form; lvs thick, oblanceolate, corrugated.

Philodendron-leaf Begonia *Begonia valdensium*.

Phinaea Benth. Gesneriaceae. 9 rhizomatous perenn. herbs; st. simple, short. Lvs often clustered near st. apex, petiolate, thin and soft. Fls solitary to clustered toward st. apex; cal. turbinate-campanulate; cor. subrotate, tube to 1cm, limb to 0.8cm, spreading, broadly 5-lobed. Mex. to N S Amer. Z10.

P. albolineata Benth. ex Hemsl. To 22cm. Lvs ovate, crenate-serrate, rich velvety green above with white veins, flushed purple beneath. Fls rotate or subrotate, solitary, lobes subequal, rounded, crenate, concave, snowy white. Early autumn. D Amer.

P. multiflora C. Morton. To 13cm. Lvs ovate to rhombic, dentate, green with paler veins above, green or tinged red beneath, thinly membranous, pilose. Fls in clusters, rotate, white, pilose without, lobes equal, suberect, gland. without. Mex.

P. rubida Fritsch. = *Niphaea oblonga*.

Phlebodium (R. Br.) J. Sm. Polypodiaceae. Rhiz. creeping, fleshy and thick, rusty to golden-scaly at first. Fronds ovate, pinnatifid or subpinnate, glab., leathery or papery; stipes remote, jointed. Trop. Amer. Z10.

P. aureum (L.) J. Sm. GOLDEN POLYPODY; RABBIT'S-FOOT FERN; HARE'S-FOOT FERN. Rhiz. to 15mm wide. Fronds to 1m×50cm, deeply pinnatifid, ovate to oblong or deltoid, seg. to 30×5cm, linear to oblong or strap-shaped, sinuses ± round; stipes to 50cm. Trop. Amer. var. *areolatum* (Humb. & Bonpl. ex Willd.) Sota. Fronds erect, smaller, leathery, glaucous. 'Cristatum': fronds crested. 'Mandaianum' BLUE FERN: frond seg. curved and wavy. 'Undulatum': seg. notched and v. wavy, grey to silver.

P. decumanum (Willd.) J. Sm. Rhiz. to 2cm wide. Fronds to 120×60cm, deeply pinnatifid, oblong, leathery, glaucous, seg. to 30×7cm, strap-shaped to oblong or lanceolate, wavy, toothed in sinuses; stipes to 60cm. Trop. Amer.

P. nitidum J. Sm. ex Hook., non Kaulf. = *Microgramma nitida*. →*Chrysopteris*, *Goniophlebium* and *Polypodium*.

Phleum L. Gramineae. Some 15 ann. or perenn. grasses. Lvs flat. Infl. paniculate, spicate, cylindric to subglobose. N, S temp. regions, S Amer. Z5.

P. boehmeri Wibel = *P. phleoides*.
P. nodosum L. = *P. pratense*.
P. phlaroides K. Koch = *P. phleoides*.

P. phleoides (L.) Karst. Perenn. to 60cm. St. slender. Lvs to 13×0.4cm. Infl. cylindric, to 10×0.6cm, tinged green to purple, spikelets with rough and bristly keel, mucronate. Summer. NW Afr., Eur., N Asia.

P. pratense L. TIMOTHY; CAT'S TAIL; MEADOW CAT'S TAIL. Perenn. to 1.5m. St. robust, swollen at base. Lvs to 45×1cm. Infl. cylindric, to 30×1cm; spikelets with ciliate keel, awned. Summer. C, N, W Eur.

P. pratense var. *nodosum* (L.) Huds. = *P. pratense*.

Phlogacanthus Nees Acanthaceae. 15 perenn. herbs and sub-shrubs. Lvs usually large, thryse-like, term. or short, axill.; cor. tubular, curved, limb bilabiate. Asia. Z10.

P. thyrsiflorus Nees = *P. thyrsiformis*.
P. thyrsiformis (Hardw.) Mabb. Shrub to 2.25m. Lvs to 22cm, elliptic-lanceolate. Infl. to 30cm, terminal; fls orange. N India.

Phlomis L. Labiatae. c100 pubesc. or woolly herbs, subshrubs or evergr. shrubs. Lvs opposite, narrow to ovate, rugose. Fls in axill. verticillasters; cal. tubular, 5-toothed; cor., 2-lipped, upper lip hooded, lower 3-lobed, spreading. Medit. to C Asia and China.

P. alpina Pall. To 45cm, white-pubesc. Lvs 20cm, ovate-lanceolate to cordate. Verticillasters 20–30-fld; cor. tinted purple. Altai Mts, Mong. Z8.

P. armeniaca Willd. To 60cm. Lvs 2–10cm, ovate-oblong to linear-lanceolate, crenulate to shallow-lobed, stellate-pubesc. above, canescent beneath. Verticillasters 2–5, distant or crowded toward apex, 4–10-fld; cor. 25–35mm, yellow. Summer. Turk., Cauc., N Iran. Z7.

P. bovei Noë. Erect perenn. herb to 1m, stellate-pubesc. Basal lvs largest, 6–8cm, broadly cordate-oblong, crenate, upper surface green, bullate, lower densely pubesc., petiole to 6cm. Infl. an interrupted spike of dense distant verticillasters; cor. to 3.5cm, purple-pink, exterior yellow-tomentose, lower lip purple-spotted. Alg., Tun. ssp. *maroccana* Maire. To 1.5m. St. glandular-hairy; cor. 4–4.5cm, purple-pink, exterior white-tomentose. Moroc. Z9.

P. bracteosa Royle. Robust, to 1m. Lvs 5–10cm, ovate, cordate, coarsely serrate, rugose above, downy beneath, short-petiolate. Verticillasters many-fld; cor. blue-purple. W temp. Himal. Z8.

P. cashmeriana Royle. Robust, to 90cm. St. densely woolly. Lvs 13–23cm, ovate-lanceolate, obtuse, entire in lower part, broadly rounded at base, downy, white beneath. Verticillasters many-fld; cor. pale lilac. Summer. Kashmir, W Himal. Z8.

P. chrysophylla Boiss. Low everg. subshrub. Lvs to 6cm, broadly elliptic to oblong-ovate, truncate to cordate at base, yellow pubesc., golden, downy when young. Fls in distant, many-fld verticillasters or paired; cor. golden yellow. Summer. Leb. Z9.

P. ferruginea Ten. Shrub to 90cm. Br. rusty-tomentose. Lvs oblong-lanceolate, crenate, cordate at base, white beneath. Verticillasters 12–30-fld; cor. 25–27mm, yellow. Summer. It., Crete. Z9.

P. fruticosa L. JERUSALEM SAGE. Spreading subshrub to 130cm, tawny-pubesc. to floccose. Lvs 3–9cm, ovate-lanceolate, truncate or cuneate at base, dull green, rugose above, hoary toomentose beneath, entire or crenulate. Verticillasters cymose, 1–2, 20–30-fld; bracteoles obovate, lanate; cor. 30mm, golden yellow. Summer. Medit. W to Sardinia. 'Edward Bowles' (possibly *P. russeliana* ×*P. fruticosa*): robust; lvs to 15cm; fls pale yellow. Z7.

P. glandulosa Schenk = *P. viscosa*.

P. grandiflora H.S. Thomps. To 2m, woody at base. Lvs 3–8cm, ovate to oblong, rounded-truncate or cordate at base, entire or crenulate, dull green, short-pubesc. above, hoary tomentose beneath. Verticillasters single, many-fld; cor. 30–40mm, yellow. Spring–summer. E Medit. Z8.

P. herba-venti L. Perenn. herb to 70cm. St. green, stellate-hirsute. Lvs 9–18cm, ovate or lanceolate, base truncate or cordate, crenate or serrate, surfaces glab. or shortly hirsute. Verticillasters (6), 10–14-fld; cor. 15–20mm, purple or pink. Medit. Region, Balk., SW & C Asia. Z7.

P. herba-venti ssp. *pungens* (Willd.) Maire ex DeFilipps = *P. pungens*.

P. italica L. Subshrub to 30cm. Lvs to 5cm, oblong to oblong-lanceolate, obtuse, white-tomentose, shallow-crenate.

Verticillasters distant, 6-fld; cor. 20mm, pink or pale lilac. Summer–autumn. Balearic Is (not native to It.). Z8.

P. lanata Willd. Shrub to 50cm. Young st. golden-floccose. Lvs 1.5–2.5cm, oblong to rounded, woolly. Verticillasters 1 to several, 2–10-fld; cor. orange-yellow, 2cm. Summer. Crete. Z8.

P. latifolia Royle ex Benth. = *P. bracteosa*.

P. leonorus L. = *Leonotis leonorus*.

P. longifolia Boiss. & Bl. Eglandular shrub to 130cm. St. pubesc. Lvs 3–7cm, lanceolate to oblong or ovate, cordate or subcordate at base, crenulate or crenate-serrate, green-tomentose above, low grey to yellow tomentose beneath. Verticillasters 1–3, distant, (6) 12–20-fld; cor. 3–4cm, yellow. var. *longifolia*. Basal lvs lanceolate. S Anatolia, Leb., Syr. var. *bailanica*. (Vierh.) Huber-Morath). Basal lvs oblong or ovate. Anatolia, Syr., Leb., Cyprus. Z9.

P. lunariifolia Sm. var. *russeliana* Sims = *P. russeliana*.

P. lychnitis L. LAMPWICK PLANT. Subshrub to 70cm, white-pubesc. Lvs 5–11cm, oblong-linear, entire, clasping. Verticillasters 4–40-fld; cor. 20–30mm, yellow. Summer. SW Eur. Z8.

P. lycia D. Don. Much-branched shrub to 150cm. Lvs yellow- or golden stellate-tomentose, 2–5cm, oblong-lanceolate, sub-cordate or cordate at base, crenulate, short-petiolate; upper lvs often larger and broader. Verticillasters 1–2, 6–12-fld; bracteoles white-lanate; cor. 25–30mm, yellow. SW Anatolia. Z9.

P. nepetifolia L. = *Leonotis nepetifolia*.

P. ocymifolia Burm. f. = *Leonotis ocymifolia*.

P. pratensis Karel. & Kir. St. simple, densely pubesc. Lvs oblong, cordate, crenate. Verticillasters many-fld; cor. tinted purple. Sib. Z5.

P. pungens Willd. Perenn. herb to 70cm, short white stellate-tomentose, rarely glab. St. lvs 5–13cm, lanceolate to ovate-lanceolate, denticulate or serrate, rarely entire, hispidulous; petiole to 10cm. Verticillasters 2–7, 2–6(–15)-fld; cor. 15–25mm, purple or pink. Spain, eastwards to C Russia, inc. Cauc., N Iran, Turk. and Syr. Z7.

P. purpurea L. To 60cm. St. woolly. Lvs 5–10cm, broadly lanceolate, coriaceous, undulate, stellate-pubesc. above, floccose beneath. Verticillasters to 12-fld; cor. 25mm, rose to mauve or white, downy. Summer. Spain, Port. Z8.

P. rotata Benth. Lvs suborbicular, leathery, crenate, rugose, woolly beneath; petiole dilated. Verticillasters in a dense sub-sessile head; cor. small, purple-blue. Alpine Himal., W China. Z7.

P. russeliana (Sims) Benth. To 1m. Lvs 6–20cm, broadly ovate, obtuse, crenate, cordate at base, grey-green, thinly stellate-tomentose above, hoary beneath, long-stalked. Verticillasters 2–5, distant, 12–20-fld; cor. 25–35mm, ciliate. Summer. W Syr. 'Lloyd's Variety': upright and bushy, to 1m; lvs grey; fls 0. 'Nova': fls golden yellow. Z7.

P. samia L. To 1m. Lvs 8–23cm, subcordate, crenate or serrate, stellate-tomentose above, tomentose and glandular-pubesc. be-neath; petiole long. Verticillasters 3–5, 10–20-fld; cor. 30–35mm, purple. Spring–summer. N Afr., Balk., Greece. Z7.

P. setigera Falc. Tall, subglabrous herb. Lvs ovate, acuminate, rounded or cordate at base, crenate; petioles short. Verticillasters many-fld; cor. purple. Temp. Himal. Z8.

P. superba K. Koch = *P. russeliana*.

P. taurica Bunge = *P. pungens*.

P. tuberosa L. To 150cm. Roots producing small tubers. Lvs oblong-ovate, obtuse, sagittate, subauriculate or cordate at base, pubesc. long-stalked. Verticillasters numerous, upper crowded, lower distant, 14–40-fld; cor. purple or pink, 15–20mm, ciliate. Summer. C & SE Eur. to C Asia. Z6.

P. umbrosa Turcz. Coarsely pubesc. herb. Lvs suborbicular to cordate. Verticillasters many-fld; cor. purple. N China. Z7.

P. viscosa Poir. Much-branched shrub to 130cm. Lvs glandular-puberulent, densely toomentose beneath, lower lvs 4–15cm, broadly ovate to oblong-lanceolate, base cordate, crenate, petiole to 4cm, upper lvs oblong to lanceolate. Verticillasters 1–4, (6) 12–20-fld; cor. 25–35mm, yellow. Anatolia, SW Asia. Z8.

P. viscosa hort. non Poir. = *P. russeliana*.

Phlox L. PHLOX. Polemoniaceae. 67 herbaceous to shrubby annuals or perennials, erect, diffuse or caespitose. Lvs entire, usually opposite, fls 5-merous, in terminal pan. or corymbs, rarely solitary; cal. campanulate or tubular, ribbed; cor. hypocrateriform, tube slender; sta. usually included. Alask. to N Mex.

P. abdita Nels. = *P. alyssifolia*.

P. adsurgens Torr. ex A. Gray Slender perenn. st. prostrate to ascending, to 30cm. Lvs 1–2.5cm, rounded to narrowly ovate, glab. Infl. lax, few-fld, glandular-hairy to villous; cor. to 2.5cm diam., pink or purple, tube, 1.2–2cm, lobes obovate. Summer.

US (Oreg., N Calif.). 'Black Buttes': habit creeping; lvs grey-green; fls lavender, abundant. 'Red Buttes': fls large, deep pink, lobes overlapping. 'Wagon Wheel': st. woody; lvs oval; fls pink, lobes narrow. Z6.

P. alba Moench = *P. maculata*.

P. alyssifolia E. Greene Compact, subshrubby perenn., 3–10cm tall. Lvs to 1.2cm, elliptic-lanceolate to oblong, glandular-hairy, margins cartilaginous, ciliate toward base, apex cuspidate. Infl. 1–5-fld; fls fragrant; cor. 1–1.8cm, pink or purple, rarely white. ssp. *alyssifolia*. Infl. (1–)3(–5)-fld, densely glandular-hairy; cor. 1.1–1.5cm, lobes c1×0.7cm, blunt. Late spring–early summer. NW US, (Saskatch.). ssp. *abdita* (Nels.) Wherry. Infl. 3–5-fld, glandular-hairy; cor. 1.2–1.8cm, lobes c1.3×0.8cm, blunt to subacute. Late spring–early summer. NW US. Z5. ssp. *collina* (Rydb.) Wherry. Infl. 1–3-fld, hairy but not gland.; cor. 1–1.2cm, lobes c0.7×0.5cm, blunt. Late spring. US (W Mont.). Z3.

P. amoena hort. non Sims = *P. ×procumbens*.

P. amoena Sims non hort. Perenn., decumbent to erect, to 60cm. Lvs to 5cm, oblong-lanceolate, pilose-pubesc. Fls magenta, red-purple, pink or white, crowded in a term. cluster subtended by leafy bracts. Spring. SE US. Z8.

P. andicola Nutt. Erect perenn., 5–12cm. Lvs 1.5–2cm, linear-subulate, subaerose, glabrescent to pilose. Infl. 1–5-fld, with crisped hairs; cor. 1.7cm, white, rarely pale yellow or purple, lobes obovate. Spring–early summer. NW US. Z5.

P. ×arendsii hort. (*P. divaricata* ×? *P. paniculata*.) To 60cm. Lvs to 10cm, lanceolate-ovate to linear-lanceolate. Fls lavender or mauve, 2.5cm diam., in clusters to 15cm diam. 'Anja': fls purple tinged red. 'Hilda': fls lavender centred pink. 'Lisbeth': fls lavender-blue. 'Susanne': fls white centred red. Z3.

P. austromontana Cov. Woody-based, caespitose perenn., to 15cm. Lvs 1–1.5cm, pungent to acerose, white-hairy above. Fls solitary lavender or pink to white, cor. tube 1.1–1.4cm, lobes 5–7mm, obovate. Late spring–summer. US (S Calif. to Ariz. and Utah), Baja Calif. Z6.

P. bifida (L.) Beck. SAND PHLOX. Caespitose perenn. to 20cm. Lvs to 3cm, distant, linear to narrowly elliptic, ciliate, pilose. Infl. glandular-hairy, lax, (3–)6–9(–12)-fld; fls sweet-scented; cor. 0.9–1.4cm, lavender to white, lobes c1cm, deeply emarginate. Spring–early summer. C US. 'Alba': fls white. 'Colvin's White': mound-forming; fls white, fragrant. 'Starbright': habit low, compact, mat-forming; fls deeply divided, pale blue. Z6.

P. borealis Wherry Caespitose perenn., 6–9cm tall. Lvs 8–15mm, linear, ciliate, glabrescent. Infl. 1–3-fld, 2.5–7.5cm, with gland. and simple hairs; cor. 8–12mm, lavender, lilac or white, lobes to 14mm, broadly obovate, emarginate or entire. Summer. Alask. Z2.

P. bryoides Nutt. Cushion-forming perenn., 2–5cm. Lvs 3–5mm, broadly subulate to oblong, densely overlapping, arachnoid-pubesc. Fls solitary; cor. 4–8mm, 7–9mm diam., white or pale lilac. Spring–early summer. W US. Z3.

P. buckleyi Wherry. SWORD-LEAF PHLOX. Everg. perenn., 15–45cm tall. Lvs 5–10cm, linear-ensiform, long-acuminate, thick, glabrescent. Infl. glandular-hairy, 6–25-fld; cor. 1.7–2.3cm, pink to bright purple, glandular-hairy, lobes c10mm, obovate, blunt to erose-emarginate. Early summer. SE US. Z6.

P. caespitosa Nutt. CUSHION PHLOX. Cushion-forming perenn., erect to spreading. Lvs 4–8mm, linear overlapping, rigid, glandular-hairy to glab., apiculate, ciliate. Fls solitary; cor. 1–1.5cm, white to pale blue, lobes 4–7mm. ssp. *caespitosa*. Mounds 15–25cm tall. Summer. W US. ssp. *condensata* (A. Gray) Wherry. Mounds to 4cm tall. Lvs adpressed. Summer. US (Colorado). ssp. *pulvinata* Wherry. Mounds 3–7cm tall. Lvs spreading. Summer. C & W US. Z5.

P. canadensis Sweet = *P. divaricata*.

P. carolina L. THICK-LEAF PHLOX. Perenn. to 1.2m, glabrescent. Lvs to 15cm, narrowly oblong-lanceolate to linear, thick. Infl. a compound cyme; cor. to 2.4cm, pink to purple, rarely white. Late spring. US. 'Bill Baker': to 45cm; fls large, pink. 'Gloriosa': fls salmon-pink. Z5.

P. condensata (A. Gray) E.E. Nels. = *P. caespitosa* ssp.*condensata*.

P. cuspidata Scheele. Delicate ann., 5–55cm. Lvs to 3.5cm, oblanceolate to linear. Infl. a spiral cyme of glomerules; cor. 0.8–1.5cm, purple to pink, tube pale inside. Spring. US (E Tex., S Okl.). Z6.

P. decussata Lyon ex Pursh = *P. paniculata*.

P. diffusa Benth. Perenn. freely branching, subshrub, 10–30cm tall, prostrate to decumbent. Lvs 1–1.5cm, linear-subulate, yellow-green, acerose, subglabrous. Fls usually solitary; cor. to 1.2cm diam., white or lilac to pink, tube 9–13mm, lobes obovate. Late spring–summer. NW US. Z7.

P. divaricata L. WILD SWEET WILLIAM; BLUE PHLOX. Perenn. to 45cm, spreading. Lvs to 5cm, oblong to ovate or narrowly lanceolate. Infl. a compound cyme, minutely glandular-pubesc.; cor. 1.2–1.8cm, to 4cm diam. lavender to pale violet or white, tube sometimes darker inside, lobes emarginate to erose. Spring. SC US to Quebec. 'Alba': fls white. 'Dirigo Ice': to 30cm; fls clear blue. 'Grandiflora': fls large. Z4.

P. douglasii Hook. Perenn. to 20cm tall, usually less, laxly caespitose, glandular-hairy. Lvs 1–1.2cm, stiff, subulate to linear-subulate, pungent. Infl. 2.5–7.5cm, 1–3-fld; cor. 1–1.3cm, lobes c7.5mm, obovate. ssp. **douglasii**. 10–20cm tall. Infl. 1–3-fld; fls strongly fragrant; cor. white, lavender or pink. Spring–early summer. NW US. Z5. 'Boothman's Variety': to 6cm; fls lavender marked blue around centre. 'Concorde': fls crimson-violet with dark grey eye. 'Crackerjack': compact; fls saucer-shaped, magenta. 'Eva': habit neat; fls lavender. 'Holden Variety': fls lilac with dark purple eye. 'Iceberg': fls white tinged blue. 'Red Admiral': vigorous, compact; fls crimson. 'Rose Queen': fls pink tinged silver. 'Tycoon': fls red, abundant. 'Waterloo': fls rich crimson-red. ssp. **rigida** (Benth.) Wherry. 2.5–7.5cm tall. Fls solitary, slightly fragrant, white or pink. Spring–early summer. NW US. Z5

P. douglasii Hook. var. **austromontana** Jeps. & H.L. Mason = **P. austromontana**.

P. drummondii Hook. ANNUAL PHLOX; DRUMMOND PHLOX. Ann., 10–50cm tall, hairy, sometimes gland. Lvs narrowly oblanceolate to ovate, sessile or clasping. Infl. somewhat spiral, a group of 2–6 glomerules; cor. 1–2.2cm, pubesc., rarely glab., purple, violet, pink, lavender, red or white, rarely pale yellow, often paler inside tube with markings around throat. Spring. US (E Tex.). 'Brilliant': to 50cm; fls in dense heads, white centred rose. 'Carnival': fls large with contrasting centres. Dwarf Beauty Hybrids: habit dwarf; fls abundant in range of colours, early flowering. 'Gigantea': fls large in wide range of colours. Globe Hybrids: habit dwarf, hemispherical; fls in range of pastel and dark shades. 'Grandiflora': fls purple above, white below. Palona Hybrids: habit dwarf, compact, bushy, globe-shaped; fls including bicolors. 'Petticoat': habit dwarf to 10cm; fls in range of colours including shades of white, pink and purple, bicolors. 'Rotundata': cor. lobes broad. 'Twinkle' ('Sternenzauber'): cor. lobes cuspidate, narrow, often cut and fringed. Z6.

P. floridana Benth. Erect or ascending perenn., 20–50cm tall, glab. except infl. Lvs to 4–8cm, oblong to linear or lanceolate. Infl. dense, glandular-pubesc.; cor. 1.5–2cm, pink to purple, tube paler inside, with dark striae, lobes c1.1cm, obovate, obtuse. ssp. **floridana**. Lvs matt. Cor. pink to purple. Summer. SE US. ssp. **bella** Wherry. Lvs glossy. Cor. pastel pink. Summer. US (W Flor.). Z7.

P. glaberrima L. SMOOTH PHLOX. Perenn. to 1.5m. Lvs 5–15cm, linear-lanceolate, usually glab. Pan. cymose; cor. 1.8–2.3cm, pink to purple or white, lobes to 0.7cm, orbicular to obovate. 'Interior': to 35cm; fls rose to red-purple. ssp. **glaberrima**. Cymes few-fld. Late spring. SE US. Z4. ssp. **triflora** (Michx.) Wherry. Infl. cymes 3-fld. Late spring–summer. SE US. Z4.

P. ×henryae Wherry. (P. bifida × P. nivalis.) Vigorous perenn. to 15cm tall. Lvs to 1.5cm, narrowly linear to lanceolate. Fls to 2.5cm diam.; cor. lilac-purple, lobes emarginate. Spring–early summer. Gdn origin. Z6. 'Blanda': plant small; lvs blue-grey.

P. hoodii hort. non Richardson = **P. diffusa**.

P. hoodii Richardson Dwarf, tufted, mat-forming perenn. to 6cm high. Lvs to 1cm, subulate, tomentose. Fls solit., white to palest violet. Spring–summer. NW N Amer. Z7. ssp. **glabrata** (E.E. Nels.) Wherry is largely glab.; ssp. **muscoides** (Nutt.) Wherry is v. small, compact and mossy; ssp. **viscidula** Wherry is somewhat viscid with purple-pink fls.

P. idahonis Wherry. Perenn. 50–100cm tall, fine-hairy. Lvs to 6–8cm, oblong to ovate-cordate. Infl. a 9–50(–100)-fld compound cyme; cor. 1.5–2cm, lavender to lilac, rarely white, lobes c9mm, obovate. Early summer. US (C Idaho). Z6.

P. kelseyi Britt. Perenn. dwarf shrub, 7–15cm tall, somewhat succulent. Lvs to 1.2–2.5cm, linear-lanceolate, acuminate, thick. Infl. usually glandular-hairy, 1.5–fld; fls scented; cor. 1–1.5cm, white to lilac or lavender, somewhat blue-hued, lobes c7.5mm, obovate. Late spring. US (E Idaho, SW Mont., S Wyom.). 'Rosette': habit compact, circular; fls pink, abundant. Z5.

P. maculata L. WILD SWEET WILLIAM; MEADOW PHLOX. Rhizomatous perenn., 35–70cm tall, glab. to minutely hairy; st. often red-spotted. Lvs 6.5–13cm, linear to ovate. Infl. a 75–150-fld pan.; cor. 1.8–2.5cm, pink, purple or white, sometimes with a dark purple ring in throat, lobes c9mm, orbicular to ovate. 'Alpha': fls lilac-pink, fragrant. 'Miss Lingard': to 80cm, hardy; fls salverform, white, sometimes with pale pink ring near centre, fragrant. 'Omega': fls white centred lilac, fragrant. ssp. **maculata**. Lvs glab. above, pilose beneath. Infl. cylindric; fls often sweet-scented; cor. 1.8–2.5cm. Late spring. US (Conn. to N Carol.). ssp. **pyramidalis** (Sm.) Wherry. Lvs glab. or glabrescent throughout. Infl. cylindric to narrowly conical; fls

not scented, cor. 2–2.5cm. Summer. US. Z5.

P. mesoleuca E. Greene = P. nana.

P. missoulensis Wherry Mound-forming perenn., 5–10cm high. Lvs 1.5–2.5cm, linear-lanceolate, subacerose, glandular-pilose, ciliate. Infl. densely glandular-hairy; fls solitary, fragrant; bright pink to lavender, lobes c8mm, obovate to orbicular. Spring. US. Z4.

P. multiflora Nels. Caespitose perenn., decumbent, 8–15cm tall. Lvs 1.5–2.5cm, linear, glab. Infl. 1–3-fld; cor. 1–1.6cm, white or lilac to pink, lobes obovate. ssp. **multiflora**. Fls solitary; cor. 1–1.5cm, lobes c8mm, entire. Late spring–early summer. US (Colorado to Mont.). ssp. **patula** (Nels.) Wherry. Infl. 1–3-fld; fls on long peduncles; cor. 1.2–1.6cm, lobes c10mm, sometimes emarginate. Late spring–summer. US (Colorado to S Mont.). Z3.

P. nana Nutt. SANTA FE PHLOX. Erect or ascending perenn., 10–25cm, much-branched, glandular-pubesc. Lvs 1.2–4cm, linear-lanceolate. Fls few or solitary; cor. purple to pink, tube 1.3–1.7cm, lobes 1.2–2cm, obovate, erose. Late spring–summer. SW US. 'Arroya': fls carmine-rose. 'Chameleon': fls cream turning pink. 'Manjana': fls rose-pink. 'Mary Maslin': fls scarlet with yellow eye. 'Paul Maslin': fls lemon-yellow with chocolate eye. 'Tangelo': fls rich orange. 'Vanilla Cream': fls large, cream with dark eye. Some of these cvs are hybrids with the N Mexican P. lutea (fls yellow) and P. pururea (fls rosy-purple). Z8.

P. nivalis Lodd. ex Sweet. TRAILING PHLOX. Decumbent sub-shrub to 30cm, forming mats. Lvs to 2.5cm, lanceolate or subulate. Infl. a term., bracteate cyme, 3–6-fld, gland. to pubesc.; cor. 1.1–1.7cm, purple, pink or white, lobes c1.2cm, emarginate to erose. Spring. SE US; introd. elsewhere in US. 'Azurea': fls light blue. 'Camla': fls salmon-pink. 'Jill Alexander': fls pink. 'Nivea': habit compact; fls white. 'Sylvestris': fls to 1.5cm across, pale pink. Z6.

P. ovata L. MOUNTAIN PHLOX. Perenn.; decumbent to erect, 25–50cm tall. Lvs 5–15cm, elliptic to oblong. Infl. usually 15–30-fld, subglabrous to densely short-hairy; cor. (1.2–)1.6–2.4cm, dull magenta, pink, purple, or rarely white, lobes to 1cm, obovate. Late spring. US. Z5.

P. ovata var. **pulchra** Wherry = P. pulchra.

P. paniculata L. PERENNIAL PHLOX; SUMMER PHLOX; AUTUMN PHLOX; FALL PHLOX. Erect perenn. 60–100cm tall, subglabrous to puberulent. Lvs 1.2–12cm, subsessile, ovate or lanceolate to elliptic, toothed, ciliate. Infl. a term., compound, corymbiform cyme, many-fld; cor. 2–2.8cm, blue, lavender, pink or white, tube hairy, lobes 8–12mm. Summer. US (NY and Georgia to Ark. and Ill.); introd. elsewhere in US. 'Amethyst': fls violet. 'Balmoral': growth strong to 100cm; fls in large heads, pale pink. 'Brigadier': lvs dark green; fls deep pink suffused orange. 'Blue Ice': fl. buds pink opening white, occas. tinged blue, in large trusses. 'Eventide': fls light mauve blue. 'Fairy's Petticoat': to 75cm; fls pale mulberry with dark eye. 'Fujiyama': to 75cm; cylindrical heads of pure white fls. 'Harlequin': lvs variegated, fls purple. 'Mother of Pearl': to 75cm; fls white suffused pink. 'Nora Leigh': to 90cm; lvs variegated; fls pale lilac. 'Prince of Orange': to 80cm; habit strong; fls orange-pink. 'Prospero': hardy, to 90cm; fls pale lilac. 'Starfire': to 90cm; fls deep red. 'White Admiral': to 90cm; fls pure white. Z4.

P. pilosa L. PRAIRIE PHLOX. Perenn., to 60cm tall. Lvs to 12.5cm, linear to lanceolate. Infl. a large cymose pan.; cor. 1–2cm, glab. to pubesc. or gland., lobes 8–16mm, lavender, purple, white or pink apex blunt to apiculate. ssp. **pilosa**. Glandular-pubesc. above. Cor. 1–1.6cm. Spring. US (E Tex.). ssp. **pulcherrima** Lundell. Coarsely pubesc. but not gland. Cor. 1.2–2cm. Spring. US (E Tex.). Z5.

P. ×procumbens Lehm. (P. stolonifera × P. subulata.) Decumbent clump-forming perenn., 15–25cm tall. Lvs to 2.5cm, oblanceolate to elliptic. Infl. lax, a flat pan.; cor. bright purple. Spring. Gdn origin. 'Variegata': lvs variegated cream; fls deep pink. 'Millstream': habit dense; lvs dark, narrow; fls rich lilac-pink. 'Rosea': fls pale pink. Z4.

P. pulchra (Wherry) Wherry. Perenn., 25–50cm tall, spreading. Lvs to 3–6cm, elliptic, ciliate. Infl. 12–36-fld, glab. to sparsely pilose; cor. 2–2.4cm, pink, lilac, lavender or white, lobes 1.5cm, orbicular to obovate, blunt or erose. Late spring–early summer. Alab. Z5.

P. pyramidalis Sm. = P. maculata ssp. pyramidalis.

P. reptans Michx. = P. stolonifera.

P. rigida Benth. = P. douglasii ssp. rigida.

P. sibirica L. SIBERIAN PHLOX. Caespitose woody-based perenn., 8–15cm. Lvs 3–6cm, linear, long-acuminate, sparsely pilose, ciliate. Infl. (1–)3–6-fld, pubesc., sometimes gland.; cor. 1–1.2cm, lobes c9mm, obovate, erose-emarginate to entire. Spring–early summer. Sib. Z3.

P. speciosa Pursh. BUSH PHLOX. Shrub to 60cm. Lvs 3–7.5cm, linear to lanceolate, pilose. Infl. a 3–18-fld corymb, glandular-hairy; cor. 0.9–1.5cm, to 2.5cm in diam., pink to purple or white, tube paler and sometimes striped inside, lobes obtuse or emarginate. Spring. US. Z4.

P. stellaria A. Gray = *P. bifida*.

P. stolonifera Sims. CREEPING PHLOX. Creeping perenn., forming 15–25cm talls mats. Lvs to 4.5cm, obovate and long-stalked to oblong, sessile. Infl. lax, *c*6-fld, glandular-hairy; cor. 2.1–2.5cm, pilose, some hairs gland., violet to lavender or purple to lilac, lobes *c*1.4cm, obovate. Spring. SE US. 'Ariane': to 20cm; lvs pale green; fls in large, loose heads, white with yellow eye. 'Blue Ridge': lvs glossy; fls blue. 'Bruce's White': habit creeping, dense; fls white with yellow centres. 'Home Fires': fls rich pink. 'Mary Belle Frey': fls pink. 'Pink Ridge': fls soft pink, pet. broad. 'Rosea': fls pale pink. 'violacea': fls mauve-blue. 'Violet Vere': fls violet. Z4.

P. subulata L. MOSS PHLOX; MOUNTAIN PHLOX; MOSS PINK. Perenn., forming dense mats or cushions to 50cm, villous to hirtellous. Lvs 6–20mm, elliptic to linear, or semi-rigidly subulate apiculate. Infl. a few-fld, term., bracteate cyme; cor. 1–1.3cm, pink to lavender or white, lobes 7–10mm, emarginate. Spring. E US. 'Apple Blossom': fls pale lilac with dark eye. 'Fort Hill': fls deep pink, fragrant. 'G.F. Wilson': to 15cm; fls large, blue with pearl hue. 'Greencourt Purple': fls mauve with dark eye. 'Maiden Blush': fls pink with red eye. 'McDaniel's Cushion': fls bright pink, numerous. 'Marjorie': fls bright rose-pink. 'May Snow' ('Maischnee'): fls pure white. 'Red Wings': fls carmine-red with dark centre. 'Samson': fls large, deep rose-pink. 'White Delight': lvs pale green; fls pure white. Z3.

P. hybrids and cvs. 'Chatahoochee' (*P. divaricata* ssp. *laphamii* × *P. pilosa*): st. arching to 20cm; fls bright blue with cream eye. 'Charles Ricardo' (*P. divaricata* × *P. pilosa*): to 15cm; fls pale blue, fragrant. 'Kelly's Eye' (*P. douglasii* × *P. subulata*): fls shell pink with crimson eye. 'Laura': habit low, compact; fls pastel pink.

P. suffruticosa Vent. = *P. carolina*.

Phoberos Lour. = *Scolopia*.

Phoebe Nees. Lauraceae. 70 everg. aromatic trees and shrubs. Lvs simple. Fls ♂ , fragrant, in pan. or corymbs; perianth lobes 6, sepal-like, persistent, becoming hard and enclosing base of fr.; sta. 12. Fr. a berry. E Asia. Z10.

P. formosana (Hayata) Hayata. Tree to 15m. Bark smooth, brown.Lvs 16cm, elliptic-oblong to lanceolate-ovate, subcoriaceous, lustrous above, tomentulose beneath. Pan. to 12cm; fls to 0.4cm diam., white, sericeous. Fr. to 1cm, purple to blue-black. China, Taiwan.

P. sheareri Gamble = *P. formosana*.

Phoenicaulis Nutt. Cruciferae. 1 tufted, perenn. herb to 20cm. Lvs in a dense basal rosette, 3–10cm, lanceolate-spathulate, stellate-pubescent, entire. Rac. showy; pet. 4, pink-purple or white, long-clawed, to 10mm. Spring. W N Amer. Z5.

P. cheiranthoides Nutt.
→*Parrya*.

Phoenician Juniper *Juniperus phoenicea*.

Phoenicophorium H.A. Wendl. LATANIER PALM. Palmae. 1 palm to 16m. St. solitary, clothed with black spines when juvenile, to 10cm diam. Lvs to 2×1m, pinnately ribbed but undivided, emarginate; sheath tomentose, with large black spines at first; petiole with large black spines beneath on young plants; blade bright green or tinged red, divided along ribs to one-third depth, each lobe shallowly divided at apex, glab. above, scaly below. Seych. Z9.

P. borsigianum (K. Koch) Stuntz.
→*Stevensonia*.

Phoenix L. DATE PALM. Palmae. Some 17 palms. St. solitary or clustered, clothed with persistent lf bases or scarred. Lvs pinnate, sheath fibrous; pinnae linear-lanceolate, single-fold, regularly spaced or clustered, emerging floccose or waxy, becoming scaly, lowermost pinnae reduced to spines. Infl. interfoliar, erect to arching, branched once; fls solitary, cream-yellow or pale orange. Fr. oblong-ellipsoid to ovoid, 1-seeded, yellow, orange, green, brown or red to blue-black; mesocarp fleshy or pasty. Afr., Asia. Z9.

P. abyssinica Drude. Differs from *P. reclinata* in hard endocarp. Ethiop.

P. acaulis Roxb. Trunk to 30cm diam., squat, ovoid, usually buried. Lvs to 90cm, pinnae to 45×1cm, few, in clusters of 2–4. Fr. to 2×1cm, ovoid, red to blue-black, edible. Assam to Burm.

P. canariensis hort. ex Chabaud. CANARY ISLAND DATE; CANARY DATE PALM. Trunk to 15×0.9m, solitary with oblong scars, wider than long. Lvs to 6m, rachis sometimes twisted; pinnae crowded, regularly spaced. Fr. 2×1cm, oblong-ellipsoid, yellow

tinged red. Canary Is.

P. cycadifolia hort. ex Reg. = *P. canariensis*.

P. dactylifera L.. DATE; DATE PALM. Trunk to 30m, slender, suckering; petiole scars as long as wide or longer. Lvs to 3m; rachis rigid; pinnae 30×2cm, to 80 on each side, regularly spaced or clustered; rigid. Fr. 4–7×2–3cm, oblong-ellipsoid, yellow to brown, edible. Cultigen, probably originating in W Asia and N Afr.

P. humilis Royle = *P. loureirii*.

P. loureirii Kunth. St. 1.8–4.5m, often clustered. Lvs twisted and reflexed; pinnae clustered, oblong rachis. Fr. red, 1–2×1cm. India to China.

P. paludosa Roxb. St. to 9m, slender, clustered. Lvs spreading; pinnae paired, clustered or in 2 rows, white-waxy beneath. Fr. 1×0.5–1cm, orange, becoming black. Bengal to Malay Penins., Andaman Is.

P. pumila Reg. = *P. reclinata*.

P. pusilla Gaertn. St. to 3m, usually shorter, stout, covered in lf bases. Lvs to 2m, crowded; pinnae rigid, held in differing planes. Fr. to 1.2cm, purple-black. S India, Sri Lanka.

P. reclinata Jacq. SENEGAL DATE PALM. St. to 10m, slender, clustered, with red-brown woven sheaths. Lvs to 2.5m, arching to decurved, often twisted; petiole tinted orange, with 6mm spines; pinnae to 25×2cm, to 120 each side, clustered in fanned groups, tattering. Fr. 1.3–1.7×0.9–1.3cm, pale yellow to red. Trop. Afr.

P. roebelinii O'Brien. MINIATURE DATE PALM; PYGMY DATE PALM; ROEBELIN PALM. St. to 2m, slender at base, expanding toward crown, often leaning, roots forming a basal mass. Lvs to 1.2m; pinnae to 25×1cm, *c*50 each side, grey-green, regularly spaced; drooping, silver-scurfy. Fr. 1×0.5cm, ellipsoid, black. Laos.

P. rupicola Anderson. CLIFF DATE; WILD DATE PALM; INDIA DATE PALM; EAST INDIAN WINE PALM. St. to 7m×20cm, bare. Lvs to 3m, often twisted about rachis; pinnae 80 or morpe each side, in one plane, grey scaly beneath. Fr. 2cm, oblong-ellipsoid, glossy yellow ripening dark purple-red. Himal. India, Sikkim, Assam.

P. spinosa Schum. & Thonn. = *P. reclinata*.

P. sylvestris (L.) Roxb. WILD DATE; INDIA DATE. St. to 15m×30cm, scarred. Lvs to 4.5m, grey-green; pinnae to 45×2.5cm, in clusters in 2–4 planes. Fr. to 3cm, oblong-ellipsoid, orange-yellow, to purple-red. India.

P. tenuis hort. = *P. canariensis*.

P. zeylanica Trimen. = *P. pusilla*.

Phoenix Tree *Firmiana simplex*.

Pholidota Lindl. RATTLESNAKE ORCHID. Orchidaceae. 29 epiphytic or terrestrial orchids. Pbs cylindric or conical, basally sheathed. Lvs solitary or paired, apical, linear to elliptic, obscurely plicate, stalked. Rac. from centre of new shoots, erect then pendulous, spiralling or flexuous; bracts small, conspicuous, overlapping, closely 2-ranked, concave, papery; fls numerous, small, white to brown. Indomal., W Pacific. Z9.

P. articulata Lindl. Pbs to 15cm, borne at apex of previous year's pb. Lvs ovate to linear-lanceolate, to 20cm. Infl. to 6.5cm; bracts brown, to 1cm, falling as fls open; fls to 65, fragrant, cream, green-white to pink. India, China, Burm., Thail. to Celebes.

P. chinensis Lindl. Pbs ovoid to 11cm. Lvs to 20cm, ovate-oblong to linear-lanceolate. Infl. axis strongly flexuous, to 30cm; fls to 35, green-white to white, lip cream-white, column pale buff, tinged pink. Burm., China.

P. convallariae (Rchb. f.) Hook. f. Pbs slender to swollen to 7cm. Lvs linear-lanceolate, to 21cm. Infl. axis flexuous, to 10cm; fls 3–28, white. India, Burm.

P. imbricata (Roxb.) Lindl. Pbs cylindric, to 10cm. Lvs ovate-oblong to linear-lanceolate to 50cm. Infl. to 15cm, spiralling; bracts papery, light brown persistent, concealing fls; fls to 130, white to cream, tinted yellow to pink. Vietnam, Solomon Is., Aus. to Fiji.

P. khasiyana Rchb. f. = *P. articulata*.

Pholistoma Lilja. Hydrophyllaceae. 3 prostrate or weakly climbing ann. herbs. St. rather succulent, usually angled and spiny. Lvs pinnatifid. Fls in cymes or solitary; cal. lobes 5; cor. lobes 5, spreading. SW N Amer.

P. auritum (Lindl.) Lilja. FIESTA FLOWER. To 1.2m. Lvs oblong, hirsute, clasping at base, lobes 7–11. Fls to 2.75cm diam., blue, lilac or violet marked with deeper streaks. Calif.
→*Nemophila*.

Phoradendron Nutt. FALSE MISTLETOE. Viscaceae (Loranthaceae). Some 200 parasitic shrubs resembling mistletoe. Lvs opposite, simple, sometimes reduced to scales. Fls small. Fr. a small viscid berry. US. Z6.

P. flavescens (Pursh) Nutt. = *P. serotinum*.

P. serotinum (Raf.) M. Johnst. AMERICAN MISTLETOE. Everg. Habit densely bunching, to 1m diam.; twigs woody, brittle. Lvs to 5cm, obovate or oblanceolate, tinged yellow. Fls in spikes. Fr. small, globose, off-white, translucent. E & SC US.

Phormium Forst. & Forst. f. FLAX LILY. Agavaceae. 2 large, everg., perenn. herbs. Lvs basal, sword-shaped, folded and keeled below, equitant, 2-ranked, stiff. Pan. erect, scapose, exceeding lvs, br. 2-ranked, alt., bracteate; perianth waxy, tubular at base, seg. 6, tips reflexed; sta. 6, protruding. NZ. Z8.

P. colensoi Hook. f. MOUNTAIN FLAX. Lvs to 150×6cm, flexible, base red-tinted. Infl. to 2m, often inclined. Fls 2.5–4cm, green tinged orange or yellow. Summer. 'Apricot Queen': to 1m; lvs recurved, arching, dark green and apricot edged bronze. 'Cream Delight': to 1m, compact; lvs arching, green with wide central cream patch and several narrow stripes. 'Dark Delight': lvs to 1.2m, broad, strongly ascending but drooping at tips, dark plum. 'Duet': lvs to 30cm, narrow, stiff, bright green variegated cream. 'Jack Spratt': dwarf, compact and upright; lvs pale bronze. 'Maori Chief': vigorous; lvs to 1.2m, ascending, pink, red and buff. 'Maori Maiden': upright; lvs to 90cm, tinted bronze and striped red. 'Maori Queen': lvs deep pink, edged purple. 'Maori Sunrise': small, to 70cm; lvs arching, slender, apricot and pink edged bronze. 'Sundowner': vigorous, to 1.8m; lvs broad, erect, cream with dull purple centre, broadly edged pink fading to cream. 'Sunset': dwarf, to 30cm; lvs narrow, waved and twisted, soft bronze. 'Tricolor': lvs drooping, green striped cream and edged red; fls yellow. 'Variegatum': lvs with margins striped cream to lime.

P. cookianum Le Jolis. = *P. colensoi*.

P. hookeri Hook. f. = *P. colensoi*.

P. tenax Forst. & Forst. f. NEW ZEALAND FLAX; NEW ZEALAND HEMP. To 4.5m. Lvs to 3m×5–12cm, stiff, margin red or orange, base pale. Infl. to 5m, usually erect. Fls dull red, to 6cm. Summer. 'Aurora': lvs striped red, bronze salmon pink and yellow. 'Bronze Baby': dwarf; lvs red tinted bronze, outer lvs arching. 'Burgundy': lvs deep claret. 'Dazzler': lvs arching, to 75cm, narrow, lax, red, edged maroon. 'Goliath': growth vigorous. 'Nana Purpureum' ('Alpinum Purpureum'): dwarf, to 45cm; lvs purple tinted bronze. 'Purpureum': lvs maroon; 'Radiance': lvs variegated bright yellow. 'Tom Thumb': dwarf, to 40cm; lvs narrow, upright, bright green edged bronze. 'Variegatum': lvs striped with creamy yellow and white; 'Veitchii': creamy-white stripes on middle of lvs. 'Williamsii Variegated': vigorous; lvs large with thin marginal lines and central yellow stripe. 'Yellow Wave': to 1m; lvs broad, arching, brilliant yellow variegated green with age.

P. cvs. 'Pink Panther': lvs bright pink, edged red. 'Thumbellina': dwarf; lvs red tinted bronze.

Photinia Lindl. CHRISTMAS BERRY. Rosaceae. 60 decid. and everg. trees and shrubs. Fls small, white in dense term. corymbs or pan.; sep. 5, persistent; pet. 5, white; sta. about 20. Fr. a globose pome to 0.8cm, usually orange-red. E & SE Asia, N to Himal., W US.

P. amphidoxa auct. = *P. villosa* f. *maximowicziana*.

P. arbutifolia (Ait.) Lindl. = *Heteromeles arbutifolia*.

P. beauverdiana Schneid. Decid. shrub to narrow tree to 10m, glab.; shoots purple-brown with pale lenticels. Lvs 5–13cm, narrow-obovate to lanceolate, narrow-pointed, teeth small, dark glandular-tipped. Infl. 5×2.5cm, terminal on early shoots on 1-year-old wood. Late spring. W China. var. *notabilis* (Schneid.) Rehd. & Wils. Lvs to 12.5cm, broader and larger. Infl. 7.5–10cm wide. China. Z6.

P. benthamiana Hance. Lvs oblong, entire, glab. Infl. a much-branched corymb, hairy. N India. Z9.

P. crenatoserrata Hance = *Pyracantha crenatoserrata*.

P. davidiana (Decne.) Cordot. Large shrub or small tree, erect. Lvs lanceolate or oblanceolate, leathery, entire. Fr. crimson, in conspicuous pendent bunches along br. W China. 'Palette': lvs marked with cream-white blotches, tinted pink at first. Salicifolia group: lvs narrow-lanceolate. Undulata group: medium-sized shrub, widely spreading; lvs to 7.5cm, undulate. 'Fructuluteo': fr. bright yellow. 'Prostrata': low-growing. Z8.

P. davidsoniae Rehd. & Wils. Everg. shrub to tree to 15m, shoots downy, red becoming partly spiny. Lvs 7.5–15mm oblanceolate to narrow elliptic, thick, dark and shiny above, paler beneath. Infl. 7–10cm, downy. Late spring. C China. Z9.

P. deflexa Hemsl. = *Eriobotrya deflexa*.

P. eugeniifolia Lindl. = *P. benthamiana*.

P. ×fraseri Dress (*P. glabra ×P. serratifolia*.) Vigorous everg. shrub. Lvs 7–9cm, elliptic-ovate, small-toothed, coppery at first, becoming shiny dark green. Infl. 10–12cm diam. Gdn origin. 'Birmingham': lvs obovate, thick, leathery, coppery at first becoming dark green; the type of the cross. 'Indian Princess': dwarf compact form; lvs to 4.5cm, coppery-orange when young.

'Red Robin': lvs sharply toothed, dark red at first becoming dark shiny green. 'Robusta': young lvs coppery-red. 'Rubens': to 1.5m, habit dense; lvs bright sealing-wax red when young. Z8.

P. glabra (Thunb.) Maxim. JAPANESE PHOTINIA. Everg., glab. shrub, 3–6m. Lvs 5–8cm, elliptic to narrow obovate, red at first, becoming dark shining green. Infl. 5–10cm diam., a loose term. pan.; fls sometimes flushed pink. Late spring. Jap. 'Rosea Marginata': lvs variegated green, white, grey and pink. 'Variegata' ('Pink Lady'): lvs pink at first, becoming green edged white. Z7.

P. glabra 'Red Robin' = *P. ×fraseri* 'Red Robin'.

P. glomerata Rehd. & Wils. Decid. shrub, 6–10m, shoots long-hairy, red. Lvs 12–18cm, narrow oblong-oblanceolate, somewhat revolute, finely toothed, red at first, becoming yellow green. Infl. 6–10cm, closely long-haired; fls fragrant. SW China. Z9.

P. integrifolia Lindl.   Small tree, glab. Lvs 7.5–12.5cm, oblanceolate, tapered, entire. Fls to 1cm diam. Fr. 5mm, globose, glaucous blue. Himal. Z8.

P. japonica (Thunb.) Franch. & Savat. = *Eriobotrya japonica*.

P. koreana Lancaster = *P. villosa* f. *maximowicziana*.

P. maximowicziana (Lév.) Nak. non. Decne. = *P. villosa* var. *laevis* f. *maximowicziana*.

P. notabilis Schneid. = *P. beauverdiana* var. *notabilis*.

P. nussia (D. Don) Kalkman. Large shrub to 6m. Lvs to 10cm, oblanceolate to obovate, leathery, dark glossy, finely toothed. Fls in flattened tomentose clusters. Fr. downy, orange. Himal., SE Asia. Z9.

P. parvifolia (Pritz.) Schneid. Decid. shrub, 2–3m; young shoots glab., dark red. Lvs 3–6cm, oval to obovate, slender-pointed, small-toothed, dark green above, paler beneath, soon glab. Infl. 3cm, an umbellate pan. Late spring. China. Z6.

P. prionophylla (Franch.) Schneid. Everg. stiffy branched shrub to 2m; young shoots grey downy. Lvs 2.5–7.5cm, obovate to oval, leathery, sharply serrate, dark green above, downy beneath, veins prominent. Infl. 7.5cm, corymbose, erect. Summer. China. Z9.

P. prunifolia (Hook & Arn.) Lindl. Differs from *P. glabra* in lvs minutely spotted black beneath; fls larger. China; Vietnam.

P. 'Redstart'. (*P. davidiana* 'Fructuluteo' ×*P. ×fraseri* 'Robusta'.) Large shrub or small tree. Lvs to 11cm, bright red at first, becoming dark green, finely toothed above. Fls in dense hemispherical corymbs. Fr. orange-red, tinged yellow. From the same cross is 'Winchester' with thinner, elliptic-oblong lvs and yellow-flushed orange-red fr. Z7.

P. serratifolia (Desf.) Kalkman. Everg. shrub to tree, 5–12m. Young shoots and lvs copper-red, glab. Lvs to 10cm, ovate to obovate, saw-toothed, becoming leathery, glossy dark green. Pan. term., corymbose, 10–15cm diam. Fr. red, haw-like. Spring. China, Taiwan. 'Aculeata' ('Lineata'): lvs with larger teeth. 'Rotundifolia': lvs smaller, rounded. Some forms exhibit white-tomentose young growth, red buds and stipules and bronze newly emerged foliage. Z7.

P. serrulata Lindl. = *P. serratifolia*.

P. subumbellata Rehd. & Wils. = *P. parvifolia*.

P. variabilis Hemsl. = *P. villosa*.

P. villosa (Thunb.) DC. Decid. shrub or small tree to 5m; young shoots downy at first. Lvs 3–8cm, obovate to lanceolate dark ovate, apex long-tapered, leathery, teeth glandular-tipped, green above, 5cm diam., corymbose stalk waried, downy. Late spring. Jap., Korea, China. var. *laevis* (Thunb.) Dipp. Lvs smaller, narrower, long-pointed, soon glab. Jap. f. *maximowicziana* (Lév.) Rehd. Lvs obovate, apex rounded, turning yellow in autumn. Korea. var. *sinica* Rehd. & Wils. Narrow tree to 8m; young shoots downy. Lvs 2–8cm, oval to oblong, acuminate, finely toothed, turning red in autumn. C & W China. Z4.

→*Eriobotrya, Pyrus, Pourthiaea, Sorbus* and *Stranvaesia*.

Photinopteris J. Sm. Polypodiaceae. 1 epiphytic and terrestrial fern. Rhiz. long-creeping, 1cm wide, green to frosted and glaucous; scales decid., chestnut brown. Fronds to 70cm, pinnate, sterile (lower) pinnae to 25×10cm, to 10 pairs, ovate, glab., leathery, fertile (upper) pinnae to 25×1cm, linear; stipes to 30cm. SE Asia. Z10.

P. speciosa (Bl.) Presl.

→*Lomaria*.

Phragmipedium Rolfe. LADY-SLIPPER. Orchidaceae. 20 terrestrial or epiphytic orchids, differing from *Paphiopedium* in lvs narrower, more numerous and fls produced 1–several in succession with dors. sep. long caudate, pet. usually long, pendent and lip inflated with upper margin involute. C & S Amer. Z10.

P. Ainsworthii. Strong growing plants; fls white and pale pink, larger than in *P. Sedenii*.

P. besseae Dodson & J. Kuhn. Fls small, scarlet, strongly pouched; sep. and pet. short, broad.

P. boissierianum (Rchb. f.) Rolfe. Fls bronze or olive green veined dark green, edged white or brown, dors. sep. to 6×1.5cm, lanceolate, acuminate, undulate-crisped, pet. to 10cm, widely spreading, linear-lanceolate, twisted; lip brown, lateral lobes heavily spotted green-brown. Ecuad., Peru.

P. caricinum (Lindl. & Paxt.) Rolfe. Fls bronze to olive edged purple-green, dors. sep. to 2.5×1.5cm, ovate-lanceolate to lanceolate, undulate, pet. to 8×4cm, linear-lanceolate, acute, pendent, twisted, undulate; lip yellow-green, to 3.5cm, lat. lobes spotted dark green and purple. Peru, Boliv., Braz.

P. caudatum (Lindl.) Rolfe. Dors. sep. white to yellow-green with dark green venation, to 15×3cm, lanceolate, arched over lip, undulate to spiralled; pet. purple-brown to green-brown, to 60×1cm, linear-lanceolate, pendulous, spiralling; lip yellow near base, apex tinted pink or maroon, veined green, to 7×2cm. Mex. to Peru, Venez., Colomb., Ecuad.

P. Dominianum. Fls yellow-green, tinged copper-brown; lip deep red-brown in front, with darker reticulations, yellow-green behind, mouth incurved, yellow spotted dark purple.

P. Grande. V. large plants; tall infl. with several large fls simultaneously, green-brown with v. long pet.

P. hartwegii (Rchb. f.) L.O. Williams. Fls green-yellow; dors. sep. to 5×2cm, ovate-oblong, attenuate, undulate; pet. to 9cm, linear-ligulate or linear-lanceolate, pendent, twisted, undulate-crisped; lip slightly slipper-shaped. Ecuad., Peru.

P. klotzschianum (Rchb. f. ex Schomb.) Rolfe. Sep. pink-brown veined maroon, to 3×1cm, lanceolate, subacute, dors.; pet. pale brown veined green or maroon, to 5×1cm, pendent, linear, twisted; lip to 3×1.5cm, lat. lobes strongly incurved, yellow spotted brown, midlobe white. Venez., Guyana.

P. lindenii (Lindl.) Dressler & N. Williams. Resembles *P. caudatum* except lip simple, unpouched. Colomb., Peru, Ecuad.

P. lindleyanum (Schomb. ex Lindl.) Rolfe. Dors. sep. pale green or yellow-green, veined red-brown to 3.5×2cm, elliptic, obtuse, concave; pet. yellow-green at base, white-green toward apex, margins and veins flushed purple, to 5.5×1cm, linear-oblong, undulate; lip pale yellow-green with yellow-brown venation, to 3×1.5cm, lat. lobes spotted light purple. Venez., Guyana.

P. longifolium (Warsc. & Rchb. f.) Rolfe. Dors. sep. pale yellow-green, veined dark green or rose, edged white, to 6×2cm, lanceolate, erect or curved forward, sometimes undulate; pet. pale yellow-green, margins rose-purple, to 12×1cm, spreading, linear, twisted; lip yellow-green, to 6×1.5cm, margins spotted pale rose. Costa Rica, Panama, Colomb., Ecuad.

P. Nitidissimum. Large plants with several fls simultaneously; fls yellow-green with pink margins and brown lip.

P. sargentianum (Rolfe) Rolfe. Fls green or yellow-green veined purple-green, dors. sep. to 3×1.5cm, ovate-elliptic, acute, concave, ciliate; pet. to 6×1.5cm, oblong-ligulate, spreading, slightly twisted, ciliate, margins tinged purple; lip yellow or yellow-green veined purple, lateral lobes spotted purple. Braz.

P. schlimii (Lind. & Rchb. f.) Rolfe. Fls white flushed rose-pink, dors. sep. to 2×1cm, ovate-oblong, obtuse, concave, pet. slightly longer than sep., spreading, spotted pink at base, elliptic; lip rose-pink, lat. lobes streaked white and rose. Colomb.

P. Sedenii. Sep. ivory white, flushed pale rose, exterior rose-pink; pet. white, margins tinged rose-pink, twisted; lip rose-pink, lobes white spotted rose; staminode white, slightly dotted pink.

P. warscewiczianum (Rchb. f.) Schltr. = *P. caudatum*.

Phragmites Adans. REED. Gramineae. 4 rhizomatous perenn. grasses. St. erect, robust. Lvs linear, flat. Pan. term., large, plumed. Cosmop., trop. to temp. regions.

P. 'Gigantea' = *P. australis* ssp. *altissima*.

P. australis (Cav.) Trin. ex Steud. COMMON REED; CARRIZO. St. to 3.5m. Lvs to 60×5cm, arching, margins scabrous. Infl. oblong to ovoid, erect to pendent, sericeous, tinged brown to purple, to 45cm. Summer–autumn. Cosmop. 'Humilis': dwarf. 'Rubra': infl. tinted crimson. 'Striatopicta': less vigorous, lvs striped pale yellow. 'Variegata': lvs striped bright yellow, fading to white. ssp. *altissima* W. Clayton. To 6m; pan. to 40cm; glumes tridentate. Z5.

P. communis Trin. = *P. australis*.

P. communis var. *gigantea* (Gay) Husnot = *P. australis* ssp. *altissima*.

P. flavescens hort. = *P. australis*.

P. maxima Chiov. = *P. australis*.

P. vulgaris (Lam.) Crépin = *P. australis*.

→*Arundo*.

Phryganocydia Mart. ex Bur. Bignoniaceae. 3 lianes. Lvs 2-foliolate, often with simple tendril. Fls solitary or in lax pan.; cal. spathe-like; cor. tubular-funnelform. Costa Rica to Braz. Z10.

P. corymbosa (Vent.) Bur. ex Schum. Lfts elliptic to ovate-elliptic, obtuse, 4–20×2–11cm; tendrils 7–16cm. Fls magenta, throat white, 4–9×1–2.5cm. Panama to Braz. and Boliv.
→*Spathodea*.

Phrynium Willd. emend Schum. Marantaceae. 15 perenn. herbs. Lvs basal; petioles long, pulvinate at apex. Infl. a spike or cap.; prophylls 1–3 per fl. pair; sep. subovate-oblong; cor. tube rarely exceeding cal., lobes oblong; outer staminodes 2, petaloid. India, SE Asia. Z10.

P. allouia (Aubl.) Roscoe = *Calathea allouia*.

P. basiflorum Ridl. = *P. villosulum*.

P. coloratum Hook. = *Calathea colorata*.

P. compressum (A. Dietr.) K. Koch = *Ctenanthe compressa*.

P. cylindrica Roscoe = *Calathea cylindrica*.

P. daniellii Benn = *Thaumatococcus daniellii*.

P. flavescens (Lind.) Sweet = *Calathea flavescens*.

P. flexuosum Benth. = *Marantochloa cuspidata*.

P. houtteanum K. Koch = *P. villosulum*.

P. jagorianum K. Koch = *Stachyphrynium jagorianum*.

P. lubbersianum hort. = *Ctenanthe lubbersiana*.

P. macrostachyum Benth. = *Megaphrynium macrostachyum*.

P. metallicum K. Koch = *Calathea metallica*.

P. picturatum Lind. = *Calathea picturata*.

P. propinquum Poepp. & Endl. = *Calathea propinqua*.

P. sanguineum Hook. = *Stromanthe sanguinea*.

P. setosum Roscoe = *Ctenanthe setosa*.

P. textile Ridl. = *Ataenidia conferta*.

P. varians K. Koch & Mathieu = *Calathea varians*.

P. variegatum K. Koch = *Calathea variegata*.

P. villosulum Miq. To 2m. Lvs to 35×15cm, ovate-oblong, leathery, light green with dark bands over veins above. Infl. basal or cauline, to 4.5cm. Malaysia.

P. villosum Lodd. = *Calathea villosa*.

P. zebrinum (Sims) Roscoe = *Calathea zebrina*.

Phuopsis Griseb. & Hook. f. Rubiaceae. 1 mat-forming slender perenn. herb to 30cm. Lvs whorled, narrow-lanceolate, slender-pointed, spiny-ciliate. Fls small, pink clustered; cor. tubular-funnel-shaped with 5 oblong-ovate, lobes. Cauc. Z7.

P. stylosa (Trin.) B.D. Jackson. 'Purpurea' ('Rubra'): fls purple-red.
→*Crucianella*.

Phycella Lindl. Amaryllidaceae. 7 bulbous herbs. Lvs narrow-linear to 60cm. Fls 2–12, in drooping scapose umbels; perianth declinate, funnel-shaped with a short tube with 6 lobes; sta. 6, declinate. S Amer. Z9.

P. bicolor Herb. Scape to 40cm, spathes equalling pedicels; fls 4–9, ascending, to 5cm long, bright red, green-yellow at base, perianth tube short, lobes oblanceolate. Autumn. Chile.

P. phycelloides (Herb.) Traub. Scape to 25cm; spathes exceeding pedicels; fls to 7cm, 3–6, erect, brilliant red, yellow in the centre, perianth tube to 2cm, lobes ovate-lanceolate. Chilean Andes.

→*Amaryllis, Habranthus* and *Hippeastrum*.

Phygelius E. Mey. ex Benth. Scrophulariaceae. 2 everg. or semi-everg. shrubs and subshrubs. Lvs ovate-lanceolate, bluntly serrate. Infl. a pyramidal pan., often one-sided; fls pendulous; cor. tubular, pink to orange-red, narrowing towards base, lobes 5, recurved; sta. 4–5, exserted. Mid summer–late autumn. S Afr. Z8.

P. aequalis Harv. ex Hiern. Subshrub to 1m. Lvs to 10cm. Pedicels 1.5cm; fls dusky pink, orange near mouth, lobes crimson; tube curving inwards below, with spreading lobes. 'Yellow Trumpet' ('Aurea', 'Cream Trumpet'): dense bushy habit; fls pale cream-yellow, lobes deeper.

P. capensis E. Mey. ex Benth. CAPE FUCHSIA. Sprawling shrub to 3m. Lvs 7.5cm. Pecicels to 4cm; fls pale orange to deep red, pendulous, tube somewhat bowed, limb oblique, lobes becoming strongly recurved. 'Coccineus': lvs 8.6×3.6cm; fls rich orange, lobed orange-red.

P. ×rectus Coombes. (*P. aequalis* × *P. capensis*.) Fls pendulous, pale red; lobes deeper sharply recurved, revolute; tube straight; pedicel to 3m. Gdn origin. 'African Queen' ('Indian Chief') (*P. aequalis* × *P. capensis* 'Coccineus'): fl. buds pendulous, tips inclined to st. when open; cor. tube almost straight, upturned towards mouth, pale red; lobes orange-red. 'Devil's Tears' (*P. ×rectus* 'Winchester Fanfare' × *P. capensis* 'Coccineus'): fls pendulous, inclined to st. when open, cor. upturned towards irregular mouth, deep red-pink, deeper in bud; lobes orange-red, throat yellow. 'Moonraker' (*P. aequalis* 'Yellow Trumpet' ×*P.* ×*rectus* 'Winchester Fanfare'): lvs lanceolate, serrate; fls pendulous, pale yellow; lobes deeper; tube concave above, straight below, upturned towards irregular mouth; lobe margins sharply recurved. 'Pink Elf' (*P. aequalis* 'Yellow Trumpet' ×*P.* ×*rectus* 'Winchester Fanfare'): dwarf; infl. paniculate, sparsely flowered but recurrent flowering; fls held at 45° from st.; cor. pale pink straight, down-curved when open; lobes deep crimson, margins sharply recurved, throat yellow. 'Salmon Leap' (*P.* ×*rectus* 'Winchester Fanfare' ×*P. capensis* 'Coccineus'): fl. buds pendulous, at 45° to st.; cor. orange, lobes deeper, margins sharply recurved. 'Winchester Fanfare' (*P. aequalis* 'Yellow Trumpet' ×*P. capensis* 'Coccineus'): close to 'African Queen' but with broader lvs and pendulous, straight-tubed fls dusky red-pink with scarlet lobes.

Phyla Lour. FROGFRUIT. Verbenaceae. 15 perenn. herbs, densely creeping or procumbent, sometimes woody at base. Infl. an axill. bracteolate spike, solitary or paired in leaf-axils; fls small, numerous; cal. membranous; cor. tube straight or slightly curved, limb 4-lobed, sta. 4, included. C & S America. Z10.
P. canescens (HBK) Greene. CARPET GRASS. St. white, strigose-pubesc., rugose. Lvs to 2.5×1cm, elliptic to oblanceolate, obtuse, dentate, pubesc. above. Infl. to 8cm; bracteoles purple; white to lilac, exterior puberulent. S Amer.
P. dulcis (Trev.) Mold. = *Lippia dulcis*.
P. lanceolata (Michx.) Greene. St. glab. or strigulose, with white adpressed hairs. Lvs to 7.5×3cm, ovate or oblong-lanceolate, acute, serrate, sparsely strigulose. Infl. to 3.5cm; bracteoles adpressed-strigulose; cor. pale blue, purple or white. C & S US, Mex.
P. nodiflora (L.) Greene. MATGRASS; CAPEWEED; TURKEY TANGLE. St. glabrescent to adpressed-strigulose. Lvs to 7×2.5cm, obovate, oblanceolate or spathulate, obtuse to sub-acute, serrate, glab. to strigulose. Infl. to 2.5cm; bracteoles green or violet; cor. white or lilac with a yellow eye, slightly strigulose. Trop. and subtrop. var. *rosea* (D. Don) Mold. Fls rose, good ground cover.
P. nodiflora var. *canescens* (HBK) Mold. = *P. canescens*.
→*Lippia* and *Verbena*.

Phylica L. CAPE MYRTLE. Rhamnaceae. 150 low, everg., ericoid shrubs. Br. erect. Lvs crowded revolute, hairy. Infl. a spike, head or rac., usually terminal. Fls with 5 sep.; pet. 0 or filamentous. S Afr., Madag., Tristan da Cunha.
P. aethiopica Hill = *P. ericoides*.
P. arborea Thouars. Small dense, silvery shrub. Lvs small, crowded. Fls v. small, green-white, muskily scented. Autumn–winter. S Atlantic & Indian Ocean (Is.). Z9.
P. ericoides L. To 1m, downy. Lvs 0.6–1.2cm. Fls solitary or in globose fascicles surrounded by dense white wool. S Afr. (Cape Prov.). Z9.
P. microcephala Willd. = *P. ericoides*.
P. plumosa L. To 2m, long-pubesc. Lvs 2–3cm. Infl. 2–3cm, spicate, surrounded by many pale brown, feathery bracts. S Afr. Z10.
P. pubescens Lodd. = *P. plumosa*.
P. superba hort. = *P. arborea*.

Phyllanthus L. Euphorbiaceae. 650 trees, shrubs and herbs often with cladophylls. New growth often flushed bronze-red. Lvs simple, sometimes 2-ranked on lat. br. giving the appearance of pinnately compound lvs. Trop. and warm temp. regions. Z10.
P. acidus (L.) Skeels. OTAHEITE GOOSEBERRY; GOOSEBERRY TREE. Small shrub or tree to 10m. Lvs 6–7.5cm, 2-ranked, ovate-lanceolate to broadly ovate. Fr. angled, yellow-green, to 2cm diam. S Asia; nat. trop. Amer.
P. angustifolius (Sw.) Sw. FOLIAGE FLOWER. Shrub to *c*3m. Cladophylls to 10cm, ovate to lanceolate, tinted bronze at first, fringed with cream-pink fls. Jam., Swan Is., Cayman Is., nat. US.
P. arbuscula (Sw.) J.F. Gmel. FOLIAGE FLOWER. Shrub or small tree to 7m. Cladophylls (2.5)4–11cm, elliptic to lanceolate, often paler yellow beneath. Jam. Sometimes confused with *P. angustifolius*.
P. chantrieri André = *P. pulchroides*.
P. discoideus (Baill.) Muell. Arg. = *Margaritaria discoidea*.
P. distichus (L.) Muell. Arg. = *P. acidus*.
P. ×*elongatus* (Jacq.) Steud. (*P. arbuscula* × *P. epiphyllanthus*.) Shrub. Cladophylls to 25cm, 2-ranked, lanceolate, primary axis ending in a floriferous cladophyll 10–13cm long. Fls pink. W Indies.
P. emblica L. AONLA; EMBLIC; MYROBALAN. Much-branched shrub or tree to 15m. Lvs 1–2cm, 2-ranked, linear-oblong, obtuse, nearly sessile, tinted pink at first. Fr. somewhat lobed, yellow, to 2.5cm diam. Trop. Asia.

P. epiphyllanthus L. Shrub or small tree, 1–3m. Cladophylls (3–)5–25(–32)cm, falcate or linear-lanceolate, toothed toward tip, striately veined. Widespread in the W Indies.
P. grandifolius auct. = *P. juglandifolius*.
P. juglandifolius Willd. Tree; br. 30–60cm, resembling radius of pinnate lvs, decid. Lvs *c*10×2.5cm, oblong-lanceolate, acute to acuminate, rounded or cordate at base. Trop. S Amer.
P. linearis sensu Griseb. = *P. proctoris*.
P. mimosoides Sw. Shrub *c*1–5m, with a term. crown of leafy branchlets. Lvs pinnate, distichous, rachis filiform; lfts *c*5–11mm, oblong or oblong-obovate. Lesser Antilles.
P. montanus Sw. Shrub or tree *c*2–5m. Scale lvs minute, decid. Flowering cladophylls, in 2 vertical rows, bronze then glossy green, lanceolate to oblong or elliptic, 5–15cm, outline wavy, with shallow notches, striate. Jam.
P. niruri L. Ann. herb, 15–50cm. Lvs 7–15mm, 2-ranked on branchlets, ovate or elliptic. W Indies.
P. nivosus W.G. Sm. = *Breynia nivosa*.
P. proctoris Webster. Shrub to 3m. Branchlets crowded, 3.5–5cm, 2-ranked. Cladophylls *c*4–11cm, linear-lanceolate, toothed. Jam.
P. pulcher Wallich. Small shrub. Lvs broadly ovate, apiculate, glab., glaucous beneath, stalks v. short. Java, Sumatra, Borneo.
P. pulchroides Beille. Shrub with br. at right angles to st. Lvs apparently pinnate, glossy-green. C & S Vietnam.
P. reticulatus Poir. Shrub or small tree, 2–3.5m. Lvs well-developed, elliptic or oblong-elliptic, 1–4cm, glab. OW Trop.
P. salviifolius HBK. Similar to *P. pulcher*. Shrub with spreading br. Lvs 2-ranked, ovate-oblong, acute, hairy. Colomb., Ecuad., Venez.
P. speciosus Jacq. = *P. arbuscula*.
P. verrucosus Thunb. Much-branched shrub, 1.5–3m. Br. grey, warty. Cladophylls with 3–5 lvs. Lvs to 1.5cm, obovate to elliptic, rounded, often retuse, thin, glab. S Afr.

×**Phylliopsis** Cullen & Lancaster. (*Phyllodoce* × *Kalmiopsis*.) Ericaceae. 1 everg. subshrub to 30cm. Bark shiny brown, hirsute. Lvs 1.5–2cm, oblong-obovate, apex rounded, somewhat revolute, lustrous and dark green above. Rac. elongated; pedicels red, to 1cm; sep. 5, ciliate; cor. 1cm diam., bell-shaped, red-purple, 5-lobed. Spring. Gdn origin.
P. ×*hillieri* Cullen & Lancaster. (*Phyllodoce breweri* × *Kalmiopsis leachiana*.) 'Coppelia': fls large, cup-shaped, pink-lilac. 'Pinocchio': compact, hardy; lvs small, glossy; fls small, rich pink, in spikes. Z6.

Phyllitis Ludw.
P. sagittata (DC.) Guinea & Heyw. = *Asplenium sagittatum*.
P. scolopendrium (L.) Newman = *Asplenium scolopendrium*.

Phyllobolus N.E. Br.
P. resurgens (Kensit) Schwantes = *Sphalmanthus resurgens*.

Phyllocalyx O. Berg = *Eugenia*.

Phyllocarpus Riedel ex Endl. Leguminosae (Caesalpinioideae). 2 thornless trees. Lvs paripinnate. Fls flamboyant, in crowded, short rac. clustered at bare nodes, appearing fascicled. Trop. Amer. Z10.
P. septentrionalis J.D. Sm. To 30m. Lvs distichous; petiole to 15cm; lfts to 8cm, 4–8 pairs, elliptic, glossy above. Fls to 2cm diam., scarlet; sta. exserted. Spring. C & S Amer.

PHYLLOCLADACEAE (Pilger) H. Keng. See *Phyllocladus*.

Phyllocladus Rich. & A. Rich. CELERY PINE. Phyllocladaceae. 5 everg. coniferous trees or shrubs. Shoots dimorphic; normal shoots with a term. bund and *Phylloclades* leathery, narrowed into a petiole-like region. Lvs radial on normal shoots, subtending the phylloclades, and also in phylloclade margins, scale-like; juvenile lvs, acicular. ♂ 'cones' catkin-like; ♀ cones solitary in scale-leaf axils or margins of phylloclades. Cones berry-like with fleshy arils. Malaysia, Indon., New Guinea, Tasm., NZ.
P. alpinus Hook. f. ALPINE CELERY PINE. To 9m, sometimes shrubby. Phylloclades simple, oblong or irregular to rhombic, lacerate, lobes linear, coriaceous, 2–4×1–2cm, rarely to 6cm, glaucous grey-green. NZ. 'Silver Blades': phylloclades silvery blue-green. Z8.
P. aspleniifolius (Labill.) Hook. f. CELERY TOP PINE. To 20m. Phylloclades simple, rhombic to deltoid, lobed, 2–5×2–3cm; lobes obtuse. Tasm. Z9.
P. glaucus Carr. TOATOA. To 15m. Pinnate, 10–40cm; pinnae 9–17, rhombic in outline, cuneate to broad-ovate basally, 3–6×2–4cm, glaucous beneath, rugose above, lobed, shallow-serrate. NZ. Z10.

P. hypophyllus Hook. f. Shrub or tree to 30m. Phylloclades pinnate, to 15cm; pinnae 5–12, in whorls, ovate to cuneate, obtusely or sharply shallow-toothed, apex occas. bilobed, 2–8×1–4cm. Philipp., Indon., Papua New Guinea. Z10.

P. trichomanoides D. Don. TANEKAHA. Tree to 20m. Phylloclades 2-ranked, alt., pinnate, to 30cm, glaucous; pinnae 7–15, roughly rhombic, to 2.5cm, shallow-crenate; apical seg. cuneate, broader than laterals. NZ. Z9.

Phyllodoce Salisb. Ericaceae. 8 small, scandent to erect, everg. shrubs. Lvs linear, imbricate, leathery, minutely dentate, strongly revolute, soft-downy beneath. Fls pendulous or sub-erect in term. rac., subumbellate clusters or solitary; pedicels gland.; cal. lobes usually 5, cor. pitcher- or bell-shaped, lobes 5, short; sta. 8–12, fil. slender. Arc. & Alpine regions of N hemis.

P. aleutica (Spreng.) A.A. Heller. Small, decumbent or scandent, everg. shrub, forming thick mats. Lvs 8–14mm. Fls 6–12 in drooping, term. heads; pedicels 12–40mm, gland. soft-hirsute; cor. 7–8mm, pale yellow-green, pitcher-shaped; anth. pink. Spring–summer. Jap. 'Flora Slack': fls white. Z2.

P. aleutica ssp. *glanduliflora* (Hook.) Hult. = *P. glanduliflora*.

P. breweri (A. Gray) A.A. Heller. PURPLE HEATHER; BREWER'S MOUNTAIN HEATHER. Semi-prostrate, everg. shrub 10–40cm. Lvs 6–20mm. Fls many in erect, term. rac. 5–10cm; pedicels to 20mm, downy and sparsely gland.; cor. bell-shaped, dark rose, c8mm diam., lobes equalling or exceeding tube; anth. exserted. W US. Z3.

P. caerulea (L.) Bab. St. 10–35cm, erect or scandent. Lvs 6–12mm. Fls solitary or 3–4 in drooping umbels; pedicels to 38mm, slender, glandular-downy; cor. 7–12mm, lilac to purple-pink, pitcher-shaped, lobes short; anth. included. Spring–summer. Asia, Eur. & US. Z2.

P. empetriformis (Sm.) D. Don. PINK MOUNTAIN HEATHER. Low, diffuse, mat-forming shrub, 10–38cm. Lvs 6–15mm. Fls few to numerous, in umbellate clusters; pedicels 12–28mm, glandular-downy; cor. 5–9mm, bell-shaped, rose-pink, lobes c2mm, recurved; anth. brown-purple. Spring–summer. BC to Calif. Z3.

P. glanduliflora (Hook.) Cov. YELLOW MOUNTAIN HEATHER. 20–40cm, br. stiff and erect. Lvs 4–12mm. Fls fragrant, solitary or 3–8 in clusters; pedicels 10–30mm, thickly glandular-hirsute; cor. yellow or olive-coloured, 5–9mm, tube glandular-downy, lobes 5, minute, anth. purple. Spring–summer. Alask. to S Oreg., E to Rocky Mts. Z3.

P. hybrida Rydb. = *P. ×intermedia*.

P. ×intermedia (Hook.) Rydb. (*P. empetriformis ×P. glanduliflora*.) Dense, bushy subshrub, 15–23cm. Lvs 6–16mm. Fls solitary; pedicels 12–18mm, glandular-hirsute, slender; cor. c6mm, mauve to purple-red or yellow-pink, ovate-campanulate to pitcher-shaped, lobes rounded. Spring. W N Amer. 'Drummondii': habit flat; fls dark purple. 'Fred Stoker': fls light purple. Z3.

P. nipponica Mak. Small, branched, sub-erect shrub, 7–23cm. Lvs 5–12mm. Fls 3–7 in pendulous, subumbellate infl.; pedicels 20–25mm, erect, often red-tinged, gland. soft-hirsute and white downy; cor. 6–7×c6mm, rose to white, bell-shaped, lobes, anth. brown, included. Spring–summer. N Jap. var. *amabilis* (Stapf) Stoker. Cal. lobes red; tip of cor. limb red or pink; anth. short, crimson. var. *oblongovata* (Tatew.) Toyok. Larger. Lvs 8–12×c2mm. Summer. Z3.

P. taxifolia Salisb. = *P. caerulea*.

P. tsugifolia Nak. Small shrub to 15cm. Lvs to 12mm. Fls in term., subumbellate infl.; pedicels glandular-hirsute above; cor. white, pitcher-shaped. N Jap. Z3.

→*Bryanthus*.

Phyllostachys Sieb. & Zucc. Gramineae. Some 80 medium and large bamboos, readily recognized by their grooved culms and branching habit. Rhiz. running, in colder climes appearing pachymorph. Culms hollow and grooved, or flattened on alt. sides, where br. emerge. China, India, Burm.

P. 'Allgold' (sensu Chao) = *P. sulphurea*.

P. angusta McClure. Resembles *P. flexuosa*, but with culms straight, not flexuous, little white powder, yellow-green not black; sheaths much paler, striped and hardly dotted, with paler ligules. Z8.

P. arcana McClure. Culms somewhat ribbed, sometimes curved at base, with white powder, sometimes blackening with age; sheaths striped with no or few dots, no auricles or bristles, ligule broad, convex; nodes prominent. Z8.

P. aurea (Carr.) A. & C. Riv. FISHPOLE BAMBOO; GOSAN-CHIKU; HOTEI-CHIKU. Culms 2–10m×2–5cm, green later brown-yellow with a little waxy powder below nodes; sheaths lightly spotted and streaked, br. rather erect. Lvs 5–15×0.5–2cm, nat. Jap. 'Albovariegata': culms slender; lvs striped white. 'Holochrysa': culms yellow, sometimes striped green; lvs occas. striped. 'Violascens': culms to 6m, gouty, swollen, green thinly

striped purple or yellow in time, ultimately violet; lvs to 12cm, glossy above, glaucous beneath. Z6.

P. aureosulcata McClure. YELLOW-GROOVE BAMBOO. Culms 3–10m×1–4cm, sometimes markedly geniculate below, with white waxy powder at first, yellow-green, grooves fading to yellow; sheaths striped, with few or no spots. Lvs 5–17×1–2.5cm. NE China. 'Spectabilis': culms yellow with a green groove. Z6.

P. bambusoides Sieb. & Zucc. GIANT TIMBER BAMBOO; MADAKE; KU-CHIKU. Culms 3–30m×1.5–20cm, erect, stout, green, glab. with little or no white powder; sheaths large, thick, rather heavily marked. Lvs 9–20×2–4.5cm. China and perhaps Jap. 'Castillonis': differs from 'Holochrysa' in having green grooves to the culms. 'Castillonis Inversa': a sport from 'Castillonis' with green culms and yellow grooves. 'Holochrysa' ('Allgold'): smaller and more open, with golden-yellow culms, sometimes with green stripes. Z7.

P. bissettii McClure. Culms medium-sized, slightly scabrous, powdery at first; sheaths lightly striped, unspotted. Lvs large. Z5.

P. dulcis McClure. Culms tall, thick, strongly tapered, ribbed, striped, hairless, with abundant powder; sheaths pale, striped, with a few spots. Lvs sometimes pubesc. beneath. Z8.

P. edulis (Carr.) Houz. MOSO BAMBOO; MOUSOU-CHIKU. Culms 3–27m×4–30cm, v. thick, grey-velvety when young, ultimately green or almost orange, with white powder below nodes, curved near base; sheaths thick, mottled brown. Lvs 5–12×0.5–2cm, numerous. China, introd. Jap. f. *heterocycla* (Carr.) Muroi TORTOISESHELL BAMBOO; KIKKOUCHIKU. Lowest internodes of some culms short, bulging on alt. sides. Z7.

P. elegans McClure = *P. viridi-glaucescens*.

P. fastuosa (Marliac ex Mitford) Nichols. = *Semiarundinaria fastuosa*.

P. flexuosa (Carr.) A. & C. Riv. Culms 2–10m×2–7cm, slender, often flexuous, green-yellow, finally almost black, glab. with white powder below nodes; sheaths smooth with some dark markings. Lvs 5–15×1.5–2cm. China. Z6.

P. henonis Mitford = *P. nigra* var. *henonis*.

P. heterocycla (Carr.) Matsum. = *P. edulis*.

P. heterocycla f. *pubescens* (Mazel ex Houz.) Muroi = *P. edulis*.

P. humilis Munro. Culms small, 3–5m, rough, dark then pale green; sheaths papery, grey-white, striped. Mature lvs small, glab. Z8.

P. kumasasa (Zoll. ex Steud.) Munro = *Shibataea kumasasa*.

P. makinoi Hayata. Tall to vigorous; culms rough, glaucous for some time, with white powder; sheaths spotted, glab. Z8.

P. mazellii A. & C. Riv. = *P. bambusoides*.

P. meyeri McClure. Robust culms with little white powder; sheaths spotted and blotched with white hairs at the base. Z8.

P. mitis sensu A. & C. Riv. = *P. sulphurea* var. *viridis*.

P. mitis auctt. non A. & C. Riv. = *P. edulis*.

P. nevinii Hance = *P. nigra* var. *henonis*.

P. nidularia Munro. Culms 3–5–10m×0.5–4cm, ± flexuous to arching, slightly ribbed, yellow-brown, glabrescent, with white powder below the nodes; sheaths streaked. Lvs 6–14×0.9–2cm, rather broad. N & C China. Z7.

P. nigra (Lodd. ex Lindl.) Munro. BLACK BAMBOO; KURO-CHIKU. Culms 3–10m×1–4cm, rather thin with white waxy powder below nodes, green at turning shining black; sheaths glabrescent, unspotted except; br. rather erect. Lvs 4–13×0.8–1.8cm, thin, glab. E & C China, widely cult. elsewhere. 'Boryana': culms green blotched brown. var. *henonis* (Mitford) Stapf ex Rendle. Culms green, later yellow-green, downy and rough when young. f. *punctata* (Bean) Mak. Culms marked dark purple-brown. Z7.

P. nuda McClure. Robust; culms ribbed, glab., sometimes geniculate below, with much white powder at first; sheaths rough, striped or blotched. Z8.

P. propinqua McClure. Differs from *P. meyeri* in absence of white hairs from base of culm sheath. Z8.

P. puberula (Miq.) Nak. = *P. nigra* var. *henonis*.

P. pubescens Mazel ex Houz. = *P. edulis*.

P. quilioi (Carr.) A. & C. Riv. = *P. bambusoides*.

P. reticulata sensu K. Koch = *P. bambusoides*.

P. rubromarginata McClure. Culms slender, glab., habit rather open, sheaths unspotted and unstriped, edged red above and on fringed ligules. Lvs rather broad; sheaths with red ligules. Z8.

P. ruscifolia (Sieb. ex Munro) Satow = *Shibataea kumasasa*.

P. sulphurea (Carr.) A. & C. Riv. OUGON-KOU CHIKU; ROBERT OUGON-CHIKU. Culms 4–12m×0.5–9cm, yellow with age, sometimes striped green, lower nodes usually minutely pitted, with a little white powder below them; sheaths thick, striped, ultimately spotted and blotched brown. Lvs 6–16×1.5–2.5cm, sometimes striped. E China. var. *viridis* R.A. Young. KOU-CHIKU. Larger; culms green. Z7.

P. tranquillans (Koidz.) Muroi = *Hibanobambusa tranquillans*.

P. viridiglaucescens (Carr.) A. & C. Riv. Culms 4–12m×1–5cm, often curved at base, smooth, glab., with white waxy powder below nodes; sheaths rough, with dark spots and blotches; br. spreading. Lvs 4–20×0.6–2cm. E China. Z7.

P. viridis (R.A. Young) McClure = *P. sulphurea* var. *viridis*.

P. viridis var. *robertii* Chao & Renvoize = *P. sulphurea* var. *viridis*.

P. viridis 'Robert Young'. = *P. sulphurea* var. *viridis*.

P. vivax McClure. Culms 3–25m×2.3–12.5cm, ribbed, pale grey, glab., with white waxy powder below nodes; sheaths with many spots and blotches. Lvs 7–20×1–2.5cm. E China. Z8.

Phyllota Benth. (DC.) Leguminosae (Papilionoideae). 10 heath-like shrubs. Lvs simple, linear, revolute. Fls pea-like, solitary, axill. SW & E Aus. Z10.

P. aspera Benth. = *P. phylicoides*.

P. comosa Benth. = *P. phylicoides*.

P. phylicoides Benth. To 60cm. Lvs to 2cm in tuberculate, occas. pubesc. Fls to 1.5cm, yellow, in leafy heads or spikes. Summer. S Aus.

P. squarrosa Benth. = *P. phylicoides*.

✕**Phyllothamnus** Schneid. Ericaceae. (*Phyllodoce* ✕*Rhodothamnus*.) Gdn hybrids.

✕*P. erectus* (Lindl.) Schneid (*P. empetriformis* ✕*R. chamaecistus*). Dwarf shrublet to 45cm. Lvs narrow, crowded. Fls rose, ± funnelform in term. umbels. Spring. Z6.

Phymatodes (Willd.) Pichi-Serm.

P. bifrons Hook. = *Solanopteris bifrons*.

P. billardieri (R. Br.) Presl = *Microsorium diversifolium*.

P. crustacea (Copel.) Holtt. = *Lecanopteris crustacea*.

P. diversifolium (Willd.) Pichi-Serm = *Microsorium diversifolium*.

P. novae-zelandiae Pichi-Serm. = *Microsorium novae-zelandiae*.

P. punctatum (L.) Presl = *Microsorium punctatum*.

P. scandens (Forst. f.) Presl = *Microsorium scandens*.

P. scolopendria (Burm. f.) Ching = *Microsorium scolopendrium*.

P. sinuosa (Wallich) J. Sm. = *Lecanopteris sinuosa*.

P. vulgaris Presl = *Microsorium scolopendrium*.

Phymatosorus Pichi-Serm.

P. diversifolia (Willd.) Pichi-Serm. = *Microsorium diversifolium*.

P. nigrescens (Bl.) Pichi-Serm. = *Microsorium nigrescens*.

P. parksii (Copel.) Brownlie = *Microsorium parksii*.

Phymosia Desv. Malvaceae. 8 shrubs or small trees. Lvs palmately lobed. Fls in cymes in upper lf axils; epical. seg. 3; cor. campanulate; staminal column tubular, glab. Mex., Guat., W Indies. Z10.

P. abutiloides (L.) Desv. BAHAMAS PHYMOSIA. To 3m. Lvs to 20cm, sharply 5- or 7-lobed, lobes serrate. Fls to 2cm, pink or rose, white-veined, red-streaked at base. Bahamas.

P. rosea (DC.) Kearney. To 5m. Lvs to 20cm, deeply 3-, 5- or 7-lobed, lobes crenate-dentate. Fls to 6.5cm, rose to dark red. Mex., Guat.

P. umbellata (Cav.) Kearney To 6m. Lvs to 20cm, shallowly 3-, 5- or 7-lobed, sinuate-dentate. Fls to 4cm. Mex.

→*Sphaeralcea*.

Phyodina Raf.

P. navicularis (Ortgies) Rohw. = *Callisia navicularis*.

P. rosea (Vent.) Rohw. = *Callisia rosea*.

Physalis L. GROUND CHERRY; HUSK TOMATO. Solanaceae. *c*80 ann. or perenn. herbs. St. erect, leafy. Fls solitary, sessile, axill.; cal. campanulate, 5-lobed, accrescent, inflated in fr.; cor. campanulate to rotate, tube short, limb 5-lobed, sta. 5. Fr. a sessile, globose berry, enclosed by cal. Cosmop., esp. Americas.

P. alkekengi L. CHINESE LANTERN; WINTER CHERRY; BLADDER CHERRY. Perenn., to 60cm, thinly glandular-pubesc. Lvs deltoid-ovate to rhombic, to 12cm. Fls pendent; cal. to 2cm, becoming inflated, lantern-like to 5cm, orange, surrounding fr.; cor. to 1.5×2.5cm, yellow to cream. Fr. to 17mm, red to scarlet. Summer. C & S Eur., W Asia to Jap. 'Gigantea' ('Monstrosa'): fr. large. 'Pygmaea': dwarf. 'Variegata': lvs deeply bordered cream and yellow-green. Z6.

P. bunyardii Mak. = *P. alkekengi*.

P. edulis Sims = *P. peruviana*.

P. franchetii Mast. = *P. alkekengi*.

P. heterophylla Nees. CLAMMY GROUND CHERRY. Fls densely glandular-pubesc., to 90cm. Lvs ovate, to 10cm, sinuate to dentate. Fls to 2×2.5cm, yellow, spotted purple. Fr. small, yellow, edible, surrounded by a green-brown cal. Summer–autumn. SE US. Z8.

P. ixocarpa Brot. ex Hornem. TOMATILLO; JAMBERRY; MEXICAN HUSK TOMATO. Ann., subglabrous, to 120cm. Lvs lanceolate to ovate, entire or dentate. Cal. yellow, veined purple; cor. tube yellow, with 5 dark brown patches, to 1.5cm, throat brown to purple; limb to 2.5cm diam. Fr. to 2.5cm+, viscid; violet, almot filling cal. when mature. Mex., S US. 'Golden Nugget': fr. yellow. 'Large Green': fr. large. 'Purple': medium-sized, fr. purple. 'Purple Husk': fr. small, husks purple. 'Rendidore': fr. large, yellow-green. 'Verde Puebla': fr. large, yellow. Z8.

P. lobata Torr. Perenn. Lvs ovate to lanceolate to linear-lanceolate, pinnatifid, to 10cm, cor. violet, to 18mm diam., blue to purple, sometimes yellow to white. SW US, Mex. Z8.

P. peruviana L. CAPE GOOSEBERRY; PURPLE GROUND CHERRY. Perenn., pubesc., to 1m. Lvs ovate to cordate, to 10cm, entire or undulate, dentate. Cal. to 1cm, becoming ovoid, pubesc., to 4cm; cor. to 14×5mm, yellow, blotched brown or purple, lobes bue-green. Fr. globose, yellow to purple, to 2cm diam. Summer. Trop. S Amer. 'Giallo Grosso' ('Large Golden Italian'): fr. large. 'Goldenberry': fr. golden large, sweet. Z8.

P. philadelphica Lam. TOMATILLO; MILTOMATE; PURPLE GROUND CHERRY; JAMBERRY. Ann., subglabrous, to 60cm. Lvs ovate to broadly lanceolate, 10cm, entire or dentate at base. Cal. enlarging to 5cm, green, veined violet; cor. to 3cm diam., yellow, marked purple-brown. Fr. yellow to purple edible. Mex., nat. E N Amer. 'Purple de Milpa': fr. small, purple, sharp. Z7.

P. pruinosa L. STRAWBERRY TOMATO; DWARF CAPE GOOSEBERRY. Ann., to 45cm. St. viscid, bluntly angled. Lvs to 8cm. Fls dull yellow, to 13mm. Fr. yellow, edible. E N Amer. Z5.

P. pubescens L. GROUND CHERRY; HUSK TOMATO; STRAWBERRY TOMATO; DOWNY GROUND CHERRY. Ann., villous, erect, to 90cm, ridged. Lvs ovate, to 11cm, dentate. Cal. enlarging, to 3cm, green; cor. to 12mm diam., yellow, blotched purple at throat. Fr. to 1.5cm, yellow. Summer–autumn. Americas. 'Cossack Pineapple': fr. small, pineapple-flavoured. 'Goldie': fr. medium-sized, prolific. Z7.

P. subglabrata Mackenzie & Bush. Subglabrous perenn., to 120cm. Lvs ovate to lanceolate, to 10cm, entire to dentate. Cal. lobes lanceolate; cor. yellow to 2.5cm diam., tipped purple. Fr. red to purple. Summer–autumn. E N Amer. Z5.

→*Quincula*.

Physaria (Nutt.) A. Gray. BLADDERPOD. Cruciferae. 14 downy perenn. herbs. Rootstock elongated. Lvs usually rosulate. Flowering st. simple, few-leaved. Infl. racemose; fls small; pet. 4, spathulate. W N Amer. Z6 unless specified.

P. alpestris Suksd. Lvs 3–5×1–2cm, obovate, silvery stellate-pubesc. Flowering st. 5–15cm; rac. corymbose; pet. 12–14mm. Fr. much inflated, 10–15×7–10mm, navy.

P. didymocarpa (Hook.) A. Gray. Lvs 15–40×8–16mm, obovate, crenate to toothed, sometimes entire, petiole long. Flowering st. numerous, somewhat prostrate; rac. congested at first; pet. 10–12mm, yellow. Fr. strongly inflated, 6–9×5–7mm. Z3.

P. geyeri (Hook.) A. Gray. Lvs 30–70×8–12mm, obovate, entire, rarely sparsely broad-toothed; petiole winged. Flowering st. 10–30cm, somewhat prostrate. pet. 8–12mm. Fr. moderately inflated, 6–9×5–7mm. Z3.

P. oregana Wats. Lvs 40–60×8–15mm, obovate, broadly toothed; petiole slender. Flowering st. 1–35cm; pet. 9–12mm, lemon yellow. Fr. 18–25×10–12mm, moderately inflated to slightly compressed.

Physianthus Mart.

P. albens Mart. = *Araujia sericofera*.

P. auricarius Graham = *Araujia graveolens*.

P. megapotamicus Mart. = *Araujia angustifolia*.

Physic Nut *Jatropha curcas*; *J. multifida*.

Physocarpus Maxim. NINEBARK. Rosaceae. 10 decid. shrubs; bark exfoliating. Lvs ovate, rounded to cordate at base, palmately lobed, coarsely veined. Fls in term. corymbs; cal. tube campanulate, sep. 5; pet. to 0.7cm, white to pale pink, 5, rounded, patent; sta. 20–40. N Amer., NE Asia.

P. alabamensis Rydb. = *P. opulifolius*.

P. alternans (Jones) J.T. Howell To 1.5m; bark tawny or grey-white. Shoots stellate-pubesc. often gland. Lvs rounded to rhombic, to 18mm diam., lobes 3–7, double-crenate, stellate-pubesc. Fls 3–12 in term. corymbs. Summer. Mts of W US.

P. amurensis (Maxim.) Maxim. To 3m. Branchlets glab. to grey-pubesc. Lvs to 10×9cm, ovate, lobes 3–5, pointed, subglabrous above, white-green and somewhat lanuginose beneath, finely and doubly serrate-incised. Fls in lax corymbs to 5cm. Summer. Manch., Korea. Z5.

P. bracteatus (Rydb.) Rehd. To 180cm+; bark chartaceous, exfoliating. Shoots yellow, glab. Lvs to 7cm, broad-ovate, lobes 3, double-crenate. Fls 12mm diam., in several-fld, hemispheric, 5cm diam. cymes. US (Colorado). Z6.

P. capitatus (Pursh) Greene. Erect shrub to 3m. Lvs to 7cm, broad-ovate, glab. above, stellate-tomentose beneath, double-serrate, deeply lobed on long shoots. Fls in dense, hemispheric corymbs to 7cm diam. Spring–summer. W N Amer. Z6.

P. glabratus (Rydb.) Rehd. Differs from *P. monogynus*, in lvs not so deeply lobed, lobes double-crenate, and fls slightly larger. US (Colorado). Z4.

P. intermedius (Rydb.) Schneid. = *P. opulifolius* var. *intermedius*.

P. malvaceus (Greene) Kuntze. To 2m, of erect habit. Shoots stellate-lanuginose. Lvs to 6cm, rounded to broad-ovate, double-crenate, stellate-pubesc., often glab. above, lobes 3–5, broad-rounded, Fls in few-fld, 3cm diam., corymbs. Summer. W N Amer. Z6.

P. missouriensis Daniels = *P. opulifolius* var. *intermedius*.

P. monogynus (Torr.) Coult. MOUNTAIN NINEBARK. To 1m, usually decumbent. Br. brown, glab. to sparsely stellate-pubesc. Lvs suborbicular-ovate to reniform, to 4cm, subglabrous, deeply 3–5-lobed, incised. Fls in corymbs. Spring–summer. C US. Z5.

P. opulifolius (L.) Maxim. NINEBARK. To 3m; bark brown, shredded. Shoots glab. Lvs to 7.5cm, oval to rounded, cordate at base, glab., double-toothed, usually 3-lobed. Fls often pale pink, or white tinged with rose, in many-fld, corymbs. Summer. C & E N Amer. 'Dart's Gold': low-growing, to 1.2m; lvs bright gold; fls white, washed pink. 'Luteus': lvs golden on young growth, later olive green or tinted bronze. 'Nanus': low-growing, to 1.8m, bushy, dense; lvs small, dark green, sparsely and shallowly lobed. var. *intermedius* Rydb. To 1.5m. Young shoots glab. or subglabrous. Lvs oval-rounded, to 6cm, slightly stellate-pubesc. beneath to subglabrous, lobes 3, shallow, obtuse double-crenate. Fls 12mm diam. in dense cymes. US. Z2.

P. pauciflorus Piper = *P. malvaceus*.

P. ramaleyi Nels. = *P. opulifolius* var. *intermedius*.

P. stellatus (Rydb.) Rehd. = *P. opulifolius*.

P. torreyi (S. Wats.) Maxim. = *P. monogynus*.

→*Neillia, Opulaster* and *Spiraea*.

Physochlaina G. Don. Solanaceae. 6 erect, glab., perenn. herbs. Infl. term.; cal. tubular to campanulate, slightly 5-lobed; cor. funnelform to campanulate, with 5 broad, short, overlapping lobes. C Asia. Z8.

P. grandiflora Hook. = *P. praealta*.

P. orientalis (Bieb.) G. Don. To 45cm. Lvs deltoid-ovoid, repand or entire, downy. Fls pale purple-blue, in an erect-capitate rac. Iberia, around Narzana.

P. physaloides G. Don = *Scopolia physaloides*.

P. praealta (Decne.) Miers. Gland., downy, to 120cm. Lvs to 15cm, ovate or cuneate, entire or undulate. Fls in term. branched clustered; cor. to 3cm, green-yellow with purple veins. Pak. to C Nepal.

→*Hyoscyamus*.

Physostegia Benth. OBEDIENT PLANT; FALSE DRAGON HEAD. Labiate. 12 erect, rhizomatous, perenn. herbs. St. normally unbranched. Infl. erect, term. racemose; floral bracts overlapping lanceolate to ovate; fls packed, semi-erect, remaining fixed if moved; cal. 5-lobed, 10-nerved, campanulate; cor. bilabiate, upper lip flat to galeate, lower lip 3-lobed. N Amer.

P. denticulata (Ait.) Britt. = *P. virginiana*.

P. digitalis Small. Erect to 2m. Lvs 5–17cm, oblanceolate to elliptical, subentire to bluntly serrate. Racs pubesc. to tomentose; floral bracts 3–9mm; fls tightly packed, pale lavender to off-white, usually spotted inside with purple. Midsummer. S US. Z8.

P. latidens House = *P. virginiana*.

P. nivea Lund = *P. virginiana*.

P. nuttallii (Britt.) Fassett = *P. parviflora*.

P. obovata (Elliott) Godfrey = *P. purpurea*.

P. parviflora Nutt. ex A. Gray. Erect to 70cm. Lvs to 12cm, lanceolate to elliptical, serrate or subentire. Rac. densely puberulent, with scattered stalked glands. Floral bracts 2–4mm; fls tightly packed, lavender to red-violet, spotted and streaked inside with purple, puberulent to finely tomentose. Mid–late summer. C & W Canada and US. Z2.

P. praemorsa Shinn. = *P. virginiana* ssp. *praemorsa*.

P. purpurea (Walter) Blake. Erect to 140cm. Lvs 1–6cm, linear, spathulate, obovate, or pandurate, apex rounded, crenate to sharply serrate. Rac. less densely pubesc.; floral bracts 2–4mm; fls tightly packed or fairly loose, white to lavender-purple, usually spotted and streaked with purple inside, finely tomentose. Early–mid summer. E US. Z5.

P. serotina Shinn. = *P. virginiana* ssp. *praemorsa*.

P. speciosa (Sweet) Sweet = *P. virginiana*.

P. variegata (Vent.) Benth. = *P. virginiana* ssp. *praemorsa*.

P. virginiana (L.) Benth. Erect to 180cm. Lvs 2–18cm, elliptic, lanceolate, or spathulate, sharply serrate or entire. Rac. pub-

esc.; floral bracts 0; fls tightly or loosely spaced, red-violet, lavender or white usually spotted and streaked purple. Summer–autumn. ssp. *praemorsa* (Shinn.) Cantino. Erect, 100–180cm. Lvs elliptic-oblanceolate, obovate, ovate or spathulate, sharply serrate, rac. 1–8-fld, pubesc.; fls tightly packed. Midsummer–late autumn. C & S US and NE Mex. 'Alba': fls white. 'Bouquet Rose' ('Rose Bouquet'): to 1.2m; fls lilac-pink. 'Galadriel': dwarf, to 45cm; fls pale lilac-pink. 'Gigantea': to 2.2m, fls pink. 'Morden Beauty': lvs willow-like; fls pink. 'Pink Bouquet': to 90cm; fls rose pink, in dense term. clusters. 'Rosea': fls large, pink, in spikes. 'Snow Crown': fls large, white, in dense spikes. 'Summer Snow': short, to 1m; fls white. 'Summer Spire': to 60cm; fls rose pink. 'Variegata': to 1m; lvs tinted grey, boldly edged cream; fls pale lavender-pink. 'Vivid': fls claret-pink. Z4.

Phyteuma L. HORNED RAMPION. Campanulaceae. *c*40 perenn. herbs. Fls in bracteate term. spikes or heads; cor. lobes 5, linear, spreading to recurved, sometimes connate at tip. Eur., Asia. Z6 unless specified.

P. austriacum G. Beck = *P. orbiculare* var. *austriacum*.

P. balbisii A. DC. Erect, to 10cm. Lower lvs cordate to broadly ovate, entire to denticulate. Cor. globose to obovoid; cor. white tinged with blue. Summer. N It. Z7.

P. betonicifolium Vill. Erect, to 70cm. Lower lvs to 5cm, ovate to lanceolate, serrate. spike cylindric; bracts few; cor. violet-blue. Summer. Pyren.

P. campanuloides Bieb. = *Asyneuma campanuloides*.

P. canescens Waldst. & Kit. = *Asyneuma canescens*.

P. charmelii Vill. Erect, to 30cm. Lower lvs ovate-cordate, serrate. Fls in ovoid to globose heads; cor. curved in bud, blue. Summer. Apennines.

P. comosum L. Tufted, to 10cm. Lower lvs ovate-cordate, serrate. Fls in umbellate clusters; cor. tubular, inflated at base, violet. Summer. Alps.

P. halleri All. = *P. ovatum*.

P. hemisphaericum L. Erect or ascending, to 10cm. Lower lvs to 8cm, linear-lanceolate, acuminate, entire to serrulate. Infl. ovoid to spherical; bracts lanceolate, short; cor. blue, occas. tinged white. Alps to Austria.

P. humile Schleich. ex Gaudin. Tufted, erect, to 15cm, glab. Lower lvs crowded, linear-oblanceolate. Infl. globose; bracts lanceolate, serrate; cor. deep blue to violet. Summer. Switz.

P. limoniifolium (L.) Sibth. & Sm. = *Asyneuma limoniifolium*.

P. lobelioides Willd. = *Asyneuma lobelioides*.

P. michelii All. To 60cm. Lvs ovate to linear-lanceolate, serrate. Spikes ovoid; bracts abruptly recurved; cor. pale to deep blue. Summer. S Eur.

P. nigrum F.W. Schmidt. Erect, to 25cm. Lower lvs to 5cm, cordate, blunt. Infl. ovoid; bracts linear, acuminate; cor. curved in bud, dark violet, tinged black. Summer. C Eur.

P. orbiculare L. ROUNDHEADED RAMPION. Erect, to 50cm. Lower lvs to 10cm, lanceolate to elliptic, cordate, serrate. Infl. dense, spherical; bracts lanceolate to acuminate; cor. dark blue to violet. Summer. Eur. var. *austriacum* (G. Beck) G. Beck. Upper lvs narrow-ovate.

P. ovatum Honck. Erect, to 60cm, glab. Lower lvs ovate to deeply cordate, acuminate, dentate. Infl. dense, obovoid; bracts ovate, spreading to recurved; cor. dark violet. Alps.

P. pauciflorum L. Tufted, to 8cm. Lvs to 3cm, oblanceolate to ovate, entire or apically toothed. Infl. spherical, fls few; bracts elliptic-acuminate, serrulate; cor. blue. Alps.

P. pedemontanum R. Schulz. Erect. Lvs rosulate, ligulate-acuminate, apically denticulate, st. lvs few, small. Infl. spherical; cor. dark, blue. Summer. Alps.

P. scheuchzeri All. To 40cm, lax. Lower lvs linear to oblong-lanceolate, cuneate, bluntly dentate. Infl. spherical; bracts linear, leafy; cor. dark blue. Summer. Alps.

P. scorzonerifolium Vill. = *P. michelii*.

P. sieberi Spreng. Erect, or ascending, to 10cm. Lower lvs ovate to narrow elliptic, sinuate. Infl. globose; bracts lanceolate, serrate; cor. deep blue. Summer. Alps.

P. spicatum L. SPIKED RAMPION. Erect, to 80cm, glab. Lower lvs ovate-cordate, serrate. Infl. dense, spicate; bracts linear; cor. white, cream or blue. Summer. Temp. Eur.

P. tenerum R. Schulz. To 45cm. Lower lvs lanceolate. Fls dark blue. W Eur.

P. vagneri A. Kerner. Erect, to 30cm. Lower lvs deeply cordate, crenate to serrate. Infl. a dense ellipsoid to spherical head; bracts narrow lanceolate; cor. dark violet, tinged black. Hung.

P. zahlbruckneri Vest. Erect, to 90cm, glab. Lower lvs narrow-ovate, base cordate, crenate. Spikes obovoid, lax; cor. dark blue. E Eur., Balk.

Phytolacca L. POKEWEED. Phytolaccaceae. 35 herbs, shrubs and trees. Fls small, apetalous, in spike-like rac.; cal. 4- or 5-lobed, white, pink or red in fr.; sta. 6–33, in 1 or 2 rows. Fr. fleshy, berries packed on spike. Temp. and warm regions.

P. acinosa Roxb. INDIAN POKE. Subglabrous herbaceous perenn., to 150cm; st. succulent, stout. Lvs to 25cm, lanceolate, long-pointed, thinly succulent. Rac. to 15cm, suberect; sta. 8–10 anth. rose. Fr. fleshy, red to black. Kashmir to SW China, SE Asia. Z8.

P. acinosa var. **esculenta** Maxim. = *P. esculenta*.

P. acinosa var. **kaempferi** (A. Gray) Mak. = *P. esculenta*.

P. americana L. POKE; POKEWEED; SCOKE; GARGET; PIGEON BERRY. Herbaceous perenn., to 4m. St. purple-red, dichotomous. Lvs to 30cm, oblong or ovate-lanceolate, becoming purple in autumn. Rac. to 20cm, drooping in fr. Fr. 1.2cm diam., glossy, green becoming red then purple-black. N & C Amer. Z4.

P. clavigera W.W. Sm. Branched decid. subshrub, to 1.5m. Lvs to 15cm, ovate-elliptic or ovate-lanceolate, undulate. Rac. erect, dense, to 30cm in fr.; sta. 12. Fr. depressed, 10mm diam., black with dark juice. SW China. Z6.

P. decandra L. = *P. americana*.

P. dioica (L.) Moq. OMBU; BELLA SOMBRA. Dioecious everg. tree, to 20m; trunk broad, with a high water content, and large outgrowths at base. Lvs 10cm+, elliptic or ovate, leathery, with a prominent midrib, turning yellow then purple. Rac. erect or drooping, equalling lvs; ♂ fls with 20–30 sta. Fr. black. S Amer. Z9.

P. esculenta Van Houtte. Branched herb, to 1m, base woody. Lvs to 15cm, suborbicular to ovate-elliptic, acuminate. Rac. to 12cm; sta. 8. Fr. purple-black. China, Jap. Z6.

P. heterotepala H. Walter. Glab. shrub, suberect. Lvs to 13cm, ovate-elliptic or elliptic, papery or leathery, yellow. Infl. to 25cm, suberect, lax. Fr. red, to 11mm diam. Mex. Z9.

P. icosandra L. Herb, to 2m. Lvs to 20cm, elliptic, acuminate, mucronate, thick. Rac. to 15cm, erect; sta. 8–20. Fr. to 8mm diam., green ripening dark red, then black. Mex., S Amer. Z9.

P. kaempferi A. Gray = *P. esculenta*.

P. mexicana Gaertn. = *P. icosandra*.

P. octandra L. Spreading or erect subshrub to 2m. St. often red-tinged. Lvs to 20cm, elliptic to ovate-lanceolate. Rac. erect, to 11cm; sta. 8–10. Fr. to 8mm diam., shiny black with dark red juice. NZ. Z9.

P. volubilis Heimerl. = *Ercilla spicata*.

PHYTOLACCACEAE R. Br. 18/65. *Agdestis, Ercilla, Phytolacca, Rivina, Trichostigma*.

Piaranthus R. Br. Asclepiadaceae. 16 dwarf, succulent, leafless, perenn. herbs. St. to 4×2cm in small globose-cylindric segs., 4–5-angled, ridges toothed. Fls small, 1 to several near apex; cor. flat or campanulate, lobes lanceolate to triangular, softly hairy; corona 5-lobed. S Afr., Nam. Z9.

P. comptus N.E. Br. Fls to 4, to 2cm diam., deeply lobed, less flat, white, covered in dense hairs above, lobes ovate-lanceolate, blotched red-brown, sometimes ciliate; corona yellow, sometimes spotted maroon. W Cape.

P. cornutus N.E. Br. Fls 2, to 3cm diam., deeply lobed, primrose-yellow blotched red above, lobes lanceoalte; corona yellow. W Cape.

P. disparilis N.E. Br. Fls 1, to 2.5cm diam., flat, pale pink with fine, pale yellow bands, downy, lobes lanceolate; corona yellow. Cape Prov.

P. foetidus N.E. Br. Fls 1–6, malodorous; cor. 1.5–2cm diam., flat, flushed purple below, yellow, blotched and banded crimson to maroon, downy above; lobes ovate-lanceolate; corona dark orange-yellow, edged purple-brown. Cape Prov., Nam.

P. geminatus (Masson) N.E. Br. Fls 2, to 3cm diam., flat, deeply lobed, flushed red below, ochre to buff, flecked red, pubesc. above; lobes lanceolate, attenuate; corona yellow. Cape Prov.

P. globosus A. White & B.L. Sloane. Fls 1–2, to 1.3cm diam., flat, pale green-yellow, dappled pale red or lavender, downy below, lobes ovate-lanceolate; corona yellow, with a lavender or red-spotted crest. Known only in cult.

P. pallidus Lückh. Fls 2–4, flat, pale yellow above, lobes to 1.3cm, attenuate; corona yellow. Cape Prov.

P. parvulus N.E. Br. Fls to 12, to 1.2cm diam., flat, straw-yellow above, lobes deltoid-lanceolate; corona yellow. Cape Prov.

P. pillansii N.E. Br. Fls 2, 3.5cm diam., flat, lobed almost to base, wholly yellow to olive or heavily marked red, sometimes dark red, banded lime and downy above, lobes narrow-lanceolate; corona yellow. Cape Prov.

P. pulcher N.E. Br. Fls 1–2, to 2cm diam. dark green or brown below, pale green-yellow with dark red-brown blotches, covered in white and purple hairs above, lobes narrow; corona dark yellow. Cape Prov.

P. ruschii Nel. Fls fragrant, 2–3, to 1.8cm diam., flat, green-yellow, heavily blotched dark brown , lobes ovate-lanceolate, with dense white hairs; corona yellow. Nam.

Pica-pica *Cnidoscolus urens*.

Piccabben Palm *Archontophoenix cunninghamiana*.

Picea A. Dietr. SPRUCE. Pinaceae. c35 everg. coniferous trees. Crown conical to domed; bark, often exfoliating in flakes, becoming furrowed. Br. in whorls, ± horizontal. Buds occas. resinous. Lvs in spirals, usually pressed forward onto st., borne on a pulvinus acicular, entire. Juvenile lvs finer, adults ± flattened. Cones sessile, becoming pendulous, ovoid to cylindric with large, usually thin scales. Most of N Hemis. except Afr.

P. abies (L.) Karst. NORWAY SPRUCE. To 55m; bark red-brown to grey or purple, flaking in thin plates. Crown conical, columnar with age, br. level or drooping and upcurved, branclets pendulous. Lvs 1–2.5cm, dark green, obtuse. Cones cylindric, green or purplish, ripening brown, 8–18×3–4cm, to ×5–6cm open; scales rhombic. N & C Eur. Upright, conical selections include the slender, to 20m 'Cupressina' and 'Viminalis' and the broadly conical 'Pyramidata'; sparse forms include the irregularly branched 'Virgata' (SNAKE-BRANCH SPRUCE) and 'Cranstonii'. Weeping forms include the upright, v. pendulous 'Frohburg' and 'Inversa' and the semi-prostrate 'Lorely'; notable low-growers (to 5m) include the narrow-conic 'Concinna', the broad-conic 'Conica' and the profusely coning 'Acrocona'. Of several dwarfs (to 3m), notable selections include the v. slow-growing 'Clanbrassiliana' (3m in 180 years), the irregular 'Pachyphylla' and 'Pygmaea', and the more regular 'Elegans' and 'Humilis'; globose dwarfs include the stoutly branched 'Nana Compacta' and 'Pyramidalis Gracilis' and the finer 'Gregoryana' and 'Hystrix'; flat-topped dwarfs include the slow-growing 'Little Gem' (2cm p.a.) and the mat-forming 'Repens'. Cvs noted for needle colour include the yellow to gold 'Aurea' and 'Aurescens', the steel-blue 'Coerulea' and the dwarf gold-variegated 'Callensis' and 'Helen Cordes'. Z4.

P. abies var. **alpestris** (Brügger) P. Schmidt = *P. alpestris*.

P. albertiana S. Br. = *P. glauca* var. *albertiana*.

P. alcoquiana (Veitch ex Lindl.) Carr. ALCOCK'S SPRUCE. To 25m; bark grey, deeply furrowed, flaking in square scales. Crown broad conical, with long level to ascending br. Lvs 1–2cm, dark green with some stomata above, blue-green with distinct white lines of stomata beneath, imbricate, upward-curving. Cones sessile, purple, becoming brown, ovoid, 6–12×3.5cm; seed scales obovate, toothed. C Jap. 'Howell's Tigertail': broad-growing dwarf, br. upturned at tips. 'Prostrata': dwarf, completely prostrate. var. **acicularis** (Shiras. & Koyama) Fitschen. Shoots pubesc. Lvs curved, glaucous. Probably natural hybrid with *P. koyami*. var. **reflexa** (Shiras. & Koyama) Fitschen. Seed scales entire, apex reflexed. Z5.

P. alpestris Brügger ex Stein. To 30m. Bark grey-white; shoots densely pubesc. Lvs 1–2cm, stout, glaucous blue-green with many stomatal lines. Cones similar to *P. smithiana*, 7–14×3–4cm, open to 6cm, stout, scales smoothly rounded, shaped as *P. obovata* but 15–20mm wide. SE Switz. Z4.

P. ascendens Patschke = *P. brachytyla*.

P. asperata Mast. DRAGON SPRUCE. To 40m; bark purple-grey to grey-brown, exfoliating in thick plates. Br. decurved and upswept. Lvs glaucous blue-green to dark green, 1–2cm, stiff, somewhat curved, slightly imbricate. Cones 5–16cm, cylindrical, brown; scales obovate, obtuse, striated. W China. 'Pendula': pyramidal to 2m, convexly weeping; lvs tinged blue. var. **aurantiaca** (Mast.) Boom. ORANGE SPRUCE. Shoots deep orange, becoming grey. Cones shining brown; seeds scales rhombic-ovoid. China. var. **retroflexa** (Mast.) Cheng. TAPAO SHAN SPRUCE. Bark grey. Shoots orange-yellow, becoming grey, glab. Lvs acute, spreading. Cones 8–13×2.5–4cm. SW China. Z6.

P. aurantiaca Mast. = *P. asperata* var. *aurantiaca*.

P. balfouriana Rehd. & Wils. To 40m. Crown dense; upper shoots level; bark orange, finely flaky. Lvs 1–1.5cm, ± flattened, green-grey above, greyer beneath with more stomata. Cones 5–9×2–2.5cm, with broad, flat scales, purple with violet brown. SW China. var. **hirtella** (Rehd. & Wils.) Cheng ex Y.L. Chen. Branchlets densely hairy. Lvs longer, to 2cm, brighter blue. Cones to 10cm, purple-green. SW China. Z6.

P. bicolor (Maxim.) Mayr = *P. alcoquiana*.

P. brachytyla (Franch.) Pritz. SARGENT SPRUCE. To 40m. Bark grey or purple-grey, becoming scaly. Crown conic to domed. Br. horizontal with upward-growing apices; branchlets pendulous. Lvs 10–12.5mm, slightly imbricate, spreading, flattened, lustrous green above, vivid white beneath with 2 broad bands. Cones 6–12cm, cylindric, green or purple, ripening dark brown; scales broadly obovate, apex acute or wavy. SW China, E Assam. var. **complanata** (Mast.) Rehd. Bark light grey. Cones to 14cm; scales truncate or obtuse. SW China. Z8.

P. breweriana Wats. BREWER'S SPRUCE. To 35m, slow growing. Bark grey or purple-grey, becoming scaly. Crown ovoid-conic. Br. horizontal, upward-pointing, branchlets pendulous. Lvs flattened, obtuse, 2.5–3.5cm, glossy deep green above, 2 white stomatal bands beneath, somewhat curved. Cones 8–14×2–2.5cm, opening to 3–4cm, cylindric, purple then red-brown, resinous; seed scales large, obovate, apex rounded. N Calif. and S Oreg. Z6.

P. chihuahuana Martinez. To 30m. Bark silver-grey, flaking in large scales. Br. horizontal; shoots v. stout, densely branched, ± pendulous. Lvs blue-green, to 20mm, stout, 3–6 stomatal lines, curved, with a hard, sharp apex. Cones 7–14×3cm, fusiform-cylindric, glossy yellow-brown; scales packed, thick, obovate, rounded. NW Mex. Z8.

P. complanata Mast. = *P. brachytyla* var. *complanata*.

P. crassifolia Komar. To 25m, crown conic-columnar, br. level or ascending. Lvs stout, 12–22mm, rigid, ± radial, straight or curved forwards, green with stomata on all faces. Cones 7–11×2–3cm; scales rounded, broad. NW China. Z5.

P. engelmannii Parry ex Engelm. ENGELMANN SPRUCE. To 45m. Bark thin, buff, splitting into small plates, resinous. Crown conic to narrowly acute. Br. in dense whorls, upward-pointing, branchlets pendulous. Lvs straight or curved, blue-green or glaucous, soft, flexible 1.5–3cm, forward-pointing. Cones 3–5×1cm; ovoid-cylindric, tapering, green to light brown; scales v. thin obtuse. W N Amer. 'Argentea': lvs grey, tinged silver. 'Fendleri': br. pendulous; lvs to 3cm. 'Glauca': upright; lvs vivid blue. 'Microphylla': dwarf, bushy, compact. 'Snake': highly irregular upright; tinged blue. f. *glauca* hort. ex Beissn. Lvs intense glaucous blue. ssp. *mexicana* (Martinez) P. Schmidt. Lvs longer, 2–4cm, stiffer and sharper; cone scales slightly thicker. Mex. Z3.

P. excelsa (Lam.) Link = *P. abies*.

P. farreri Page & Rushforth. BURMESE SPRUCE; FARRER SPRUCE. To 35m, br. level, branchlets arched-drooping with pendulous shoots. Lvs forward pointing, 17–24mm, flattened, glossy green above without stomata, vivid white stomatal bands beneath. Cones 6–12×2cm, scales more rounded than *P. brachytyla*, margin wavy. Upper Burm., Yunnan border. Z8.

P. ×fennica (Reg.) Komar. (*P. abies* ×*P. obovata.*) Natural hybrid intermediate between parents. NE Sweden E to Ural Mts. Z3.

P. glauca (Moench) Voss. WHITE SPRUCE. To 25m. Bark light grey becoming darker with white cracks. Crown conic. Br. level or descending, with upward-growing tips; branchlets dense. Lvs stiff, dull blue-green, 10–18mm, imbriacate to spreading. Cones 3–5×1cm; ovoid-cylindric, tapering, green to light brown; scales vry thin obtuse. Canada, far NE US. 'Aureospicata': young shoots yellow, later green. 'Coerulea' ('Caerulea'): to 2m, densely pyramidal, lvs tinged silver-blue. 'Hendersonii': similar to 'Coerulea', young shoots lat., later pendulous. 'Parva': prostrate, dense, laterally flat crowned; lvs tinged blue. 'Pendula': weeping, upright leader with v. pendulous red br.; lvs tinged blue. 'Pinsapoides': upright strong-grower; lvs tinged blue. 'Sander's Fastigiate': dwarf, tight, narrow upright; 'Laurin' is similar. var. *albertiana* (S. Br.) Sarg. To 45m. Shoots pubesc. Buds slightly resinous. Lvs to 2.5cm. Cones ovoid, to 4cm. Canadian Rocky Mts. 'Alberta Globe': mutation of 'Conica', globose. 'Conica': to 4m, dense, conical; lvs permanently juvenile, 11–15×0.5mm, v. slender, curved. 'Elegans Compacta': mutation of 'Conica', more conical, twigs tinged yellow. 'Gnom': slow-growing mutation of 'Conica' (to 5cm p.a.). 'Laurin': small, dense, mutation of 'Conica'. var. *porsildii* Raup. Short lvs; pubesc. shoots. Alask. & Yukon. Z2.

P. glehnii (F. Schmidt) Mast. SAKHALIN SPRUCE. To 30m. Bark dark brown, flaking in thin plates. Crown narrowly conic, v. dense. Lvs crowded, green to blue-green above, with 2 white stomatal bands beneath, 0.5–1.5cm, imbricate above shoot, spreading beneath. Cones 4–8cm, cylindric, purple, bloomed violet, ripening brown; scales crowded, obtuse, waved, sometimes toothed. Jap., Sakhalin. Z4.

P. heterolepis Rehd. & Wils. = *P. asperata*.

P. hondoensis Mayr = *P. jezoensis* ssp. *hondoensis*.

P. jezoensis (Sieb. & Zucc.) Carr. YEZO SPRUCE. To 35m. Bark brown, becoming purple-brown, flaking in round plates. Crown conic. Br. level, branchlets pendulous. Lvs glossy, 1–2cm, flattened, dark green above, duller beneath with 2 white to blue-white stomatal bands, imbricate above sit., spreading below, and to sides, pointing forwards. Cones 4–7cm, cylindric, yellow-brown; scales oblong thin, fine-toothed. NE Manch., E Sib., N Korea, Jap., Sakhalin. 'Yatsubusa': dense and rounded; lvs vivid blue and green bicolor. 'Yosawa': dwarf, upright and regular. ssp. *hondoensis* (Mayr) P. Schmidt To 50m. Shoots darker, orange, to red-brown with age; buds bright purple, v. resinous. Lvs silver-white below. Cones darker red-brown. Jap. 'Aurea': young lvs gold, later brown, then green. Z2.

P. koraiensis Nak. = *P. koyamai*.

P. koyamai Shiras. To 25m. Bary grey-brown, flaking in thin, oblong scales. Crown conic. Br. dense, apices growing upwards. Lvs densely arranged, assurgent, blue-green or grey-green mostly curved, 7–15mm, stomatal lines distinct above. Cones 4–9cm, ovoid-cylindric, light green, becoming brown; scales thin, ovate, striated, small-toothed. Jap. *P. koraiensis* Nak. has slightly longer, more spreading lvs and broader cones. Z6. N Korea, NE Manch., SE Russia. Z5.

P. likiangensis (Franch.) Pritz. LIJIANG SPRUCE. To 50m. Bark grey, smooth to scaly or shallow-fissured. Crown open, broad conic. Br. level to ascending. Lvs 8–15mm, sharp, dark green to blue-green, flattened, keeled, 2 blue-white stomatal lines beneath, 2 faint bands above, forward-growing, loosely imbricate. Cones oval-cylindric, 7–13×3cm, red to purple; scales thin, obovate, finely toothed. SW China, SE Tibet, E Assam. var. *montigena* (Mast.) Cheng ex Chen. Lvs short, 6–15mm; cones intermediate between type and *P. balfouriana*. Most cultivated trees named as this are *P. asperata*. SW China. Z8.

P. likiangensis var. *balfouriana* (Rehd. & Wils.) Hillier = *P. balfouriana*.

P. likiangensis var. *hirtella* (Rehd. & Wils.) Cheng ex Y. Chen = *P. balfouriana*.

P. likiangensis var. *purpurea* (Mast.) Dallim. & Jackson = *P. purpurea*.

P. likiangensis var. *rubescens* Rehd. & Wils. = *P. balfouriana*.

P. ×lutzii Little. (*P. sitchensis* ×*P. glauca.*) Natural hybrid, intermediate between parents; used for forestry in Iceland. Alask. Z3.

P. mariana (Mill.) BSP. BLACK SPRUCE. To 20m+. Bark red-brown to grey-brown, exfoliating in thin flakes. Crown conic. Br. downswept. Lvs densely arranged, 0.5–1.5cm, blue-green above, off-white stomatal stripes beneath, stiff, obtuse. Cones 2–4×1.5cm, fusiform, mauve, becoming grey-brown, persisting; scales woody, rounded, some margins finely toothed. N N Amer. 'Argenteovariegata': some lvs almost completely white. 'Aurea': lvs tinged gold. 'Beissneri': dwarf, slow-growing to 5m, similar to 'Doumettii', broader, lvs tinged blue. 'Beissneri Compacta': dwarf to 2m. 'Doumettii': dwarf to 6m, globose-conic when young, becoming irregular; crown dense; lvs bright blue-green. 'Empetroides': dwarf, procumbent, br. sparse. 'Ericoides': dwarf, procumbent, lvs tinged blue. 'Fastigiata': conical dwarf, br. slender, ascending. 'Nana': v. dwarf and globose to 50cm, slow-growing to 3cm p.a., more than one clone in cult. 'Pendula': upright leader, br. weeping. 'Semiprostrata': short-stemmed, semi-prostrate dwarf. Z2.

P. mariorika hort. (*P. mariana* ×*P. omorika*.) 'Kobold': dense and globose to 1×1m in 20 years, shoots stiff, tinged red. 'Machala': spreading dwarf to 50cm×1m, middle br. semi-erect, lvs with blue tint.

P. martinezii Patterson. To 30m, crown open, irregular cylindric with age, scaly, grey. Lvs directed forward, 16–27mm, bright glossy green, sharply acuminate. Cones 9–16×3cm, scales thick, rigid, to 2cm wide, orange-brown. NE Mex. Z8.

P. maximowiczii Reg. ex Mast. To 25m. Bark red-brown, rough, fissured, flaking in thin scales. Crown dense, conic. Br. with upward-growing tips. Lvs sparse, to 15mm, lustrous dark green, acute, straight. Cones to 7cm, cylindric-oblong, light green, becoming brown; seeds scales entire, obtuse. Jap. Z7.

P. mexicana Martinez = *P. engelmanii* ssp. *mexicana*.

P. meyeri Rehd. & Wils. V. similar to *P. asperata*; to 3m. Lvs 1.5–3cm, slightly flattened, blue- or grey-green. Cones 6–9×3cm, pale brown, scales rounded, striated. NW China.

P. montigena Mast. = *P. likiangensis* var. *montigena*.

P. morrisonicola Hayata. TAIWAN SPRUCE. To 40m. Similar to *P. wilsonii*, but shoots sparse, pendulous. Lvs 10–20mm, slender, sharply acuminate, glossy dark green. Cones 5–8×1.5–2cm, oblong-cylindric; scales obovate, obtuse. Taiwan. Z8.

P. neoveitchii Mast. To 30m, crown conic to ovoid-columnar; bark grey-brown; scaly. Lvs similar to *P. torano*, stout, 15–20mm, curved forwards, dark yellow-green, sharp pointed. Cones 8–14×4cm, green ripening yellow-brown, v. stout, with few large, thick scales to 3cm wide, margin rounded, wavy. C China. Trees from name sometimes misapplied to *P. wilsonii*. Z5.

P. obovata Ledeb. SIBERIAN SPRUCE. To 35m. Bark purple-grey, exfoliating in fine platse. Br. level to downswept; branchlets mostly pendulous. Lvs shiny green, to 2cm, acuminate, adpressed above. Cone 5–8×2cm, ovoid-cylindric, green or purple, ripening mid-brown; scales obovate, obtuse, glossy, 10–15mm wide. N Eur. to E Sib. Z1.

P. obovata var. *alpestris* (Brügger) Henry = *P. alpestris*.

P. omorika (Pančić) Purkyne. SERBIAN SPRUCE. To 35m. Bark orange-brown to purple-brown, becoming cracked and flaking in fine plates. Crown conic to narrowly spire-like. Br. downswept to upcurved; branchlets dense, ± pendulous. Lvs 10–20mm, flattened, keeled, dark to blue-green, with 2 silver-grey bands beneath. Cones 3–7×2cm, fusiform, purple, ripening red-brown, scales closely adpressed, broadly obtuse, finely toothed. Balk. 'Expansa': vigorous procumbent dwarf, br. ends slightly ascending. 'Frohnleiten': irregular, loose dwarf, to 40cm after 10 years. 'Gnom': broadly conical dwarf, slow-growing to 3cm p.a. 'Minima': short-branched dwarf. 'Nana': globose to broadly conic-pyramidal dwarf. 'Pendula': slender and upright, br. pendulous. 'Pendula Bruns': similar to 'Pendula', br. more pendulous. 'Pimoko': dense, irregular and low-growing to 30×40cm. Z5.

P. orientalis (L.) Link. ORIENTAL SPRUCE; CAUCASIAN SPRUCE. To 50m. Bark smooth, pink-grey, becoming cracked; forming small raised plates. Crown conic, dense, to ovoid-columnar; br. slightly ascending. Lvs 0.5–0.8cm, slightly flattened, blunt, bevelled, dark green, adpressed to st. Cones 5×9–1.5cm, purple, ripening, brown, cylindric-conic to fusiform; scales obovate, obtuse, entire, to 15mm wide. Cauc., NE Turk. 'Atrovirens': lvs v. dark green. 'Aurea': young lvs gold, later dark green, with gold tint. 'Aurea Compacta': broadly pyramidal and compact semi-dwarf; upper lvs gold, lower lvs green. 'Compacta': broadly conical dwarf. 'Early Gold': mutation of 'Aurea', lvs also green-gold in winter. 'Gowdy': narrowly conical to 3.5m; lvs small, rich green. 'Gracilis': v. dense dwarf, oval in growth, to 6m, slow-growing (to 7cm p.a.). 'Nana': globose dwarf to 1m, v. slow-growing (to 2.5cm p.a.). 'Nigra Compacta': narrow and compact to 2m, lvs glossy dark green. 'Nutans': spreading, weeping and irregular in growth, lvs v. dark green. 'Pendula': compact and slow-growing; twigs nodding. Z5.

P. polita (Sieb. & Zucc.) Carr. = P. torano.

P. pungens Engelm. BLUE SPRUCE; COLORADO SPRUCE. To 40m+. Bark purple-grey, deeply grooved, forming thick scales. Crown dense, conic to columnar-conic. Lower br. downswept. Lvs 2–2.5cm, radial, assurgent, grey-green to bright pale blue, thickly glaucous, stiff, pungent. Cones 6–12×2.5–3cm, oblong-cylindric, bloomed violet, ripening light brown; scales thick based with thin tips, flexible, emarginate, finely toothed and undulate. US (S Rocky Mts). Cvs mostly with blue-tinted needles, some with green or yellow; of the blue upright selections, examples include the short-needled 'Microphylla', 'Endtz', 'Oldenburg', the v. blue 'Koster' and 'Moerheim' and the compact 'Fat Albert'; notable blue-tinted dwarfs include the globose 'Glauca Globosa' and 'Pumila' and the slow-growing 'Montgomery'. 'Glauca Procumbens' is almost recumbent and 'Glauca Pendula' an irregular, graceful weeping form; yellow and green selections include the sulphur 'Aurea', 'Lucky Strike' (also with profuse cones) and the dark green 'Viridis'. f. glauca (Reg.) Beissn. Group name for all plants with glaucous, blue-grey lvs. Z3.

P. purpurea Mast. PURPLE-CONED SPRUCE. To 45m. Bark orange-brown, flaking; scaly in old trees. Crown dense, columnar to conic. Lvs deep green above, blue-white beneath, moderately flattened, to 1.5cm, adpressed above shoot. Cones 3–6×2cm, ovoid, purple, bloomed violet ripening purple-brown; scales rhombic, undulate. China. Z5.

P. retroflexa Mast. = P. asperata var. retroflexa.

P. rubens Sarg. RED SPRUCE. To 30m. Bark purple-brown to red-brown, flaking in fine, concave plates. Crown dense, narrowly conic. Lower br. bowed, ascending at tips. Lvs grass-green, becoming darker, glossy, 10–15mm, crowded on upper part of st. Cones 2–5cm, ovoid-oblong, lustrous red-brown; scales convex, broadly obtuse, woody, finely toothed. N N Amer. 'Nana': broadly conic dwarf; young shoots spreading, v. short, tinged red. 'Virgata': similar to P. abies 'Virgata', sparse and slender. Z3.

P. schrenkiana Fisch. & Mey. To 45m. Bark grey. Crown dense, conic to columnar. Br. usually level. Lvs stiff, straight or bowed, grass-green, 2–3cm. Cones 6–11×2–3cm, ovoid-cylindric, often slightly curved, purple-brown, resinous; seed scales obovate, 12–15mm broad, rounded. C Asia. ssp. tianschanica (Rupr.) Bykov. Lvs 1–2cm. Cones less than 7cm; seed scales obovate. C Asia. Z4.

P. shirasawae Hayashi = P. alcoquiana var. acicularis.

P. sitchensis (Bong.) Carr. SITKA SPRUCE. To 90m. Bark red-grey, exfoliating in coarse scales. Crown broad, conic, br. straight, branchlets mmoderately pendulous. Lvs 15–25mm, dark green, with 2 blue-white stomatal bands beneath, sharply pointed flattened, slightly keeled. Cones 3–10×1.5cm when closed, to 3.5cm broad, cylindric-oblong, pale green, ripening beige; scales v. thin oblong-rhombic, undulate, serrate. N Amer. (Pacific Coast). 'Compacta': broadly conic, dense dwarf to 2m, br. spreading, young shoots tinted yellow. 'Microphylla': dwarf, v. slow-growing to 25cm after 10 years, upright and narrowly conic. 'Nana': slow-growing dwarf, habit open; lvs

tinted blue. 'Speciosa': br. dense and ascending; lvs tinted blue, weak in growth. 'Strypemonde': compact and v. slow-growing dwarf; lvs tinted blue. 'Tenas' ('Papoose'): broadly conical, compact dwarf to 75cm, blue striation below. Z7.

P. smithiana (Wallich) Boiss. MORINDA SPRUCE; HIMALAYAN SPRUCE. To 55m. Bark dull grey-purple, grooved, splitting into round scales. Crown conic, columnar with age. Br. horizontal, shoots pendulous. Lvs loosely radial, 3–4(–5)cm, dark green, apex acuminate. Cones 10–16cm, cylindric, curved, tapered, shiny pale green, ripening brown, resinous; scales semi-circular, woody, entire, to 2.5cm wide. W Himal. (Afghan. to C Nepal). Zone 8, selected clones hardy to Z7.

P. spinulosa (Griff.) Henry. SIKKIM SPRUCE. To 65m. Bark pale grey, rough, flaking. Crown broadly conic, to domed-columnar. Shoots arching then pendulous. Lvs 1.5–3.5cm, flattened, flexible, shiny, dark green above, 2 bright blue-white stomatal bands beneath. Cones 6–12×2.5cm, cylindric-conic, curved, green, ripening shiny red- or orange-brown; scales leathery, rhombic, finely toothed. E Himal. Z8.

P. tianschanica Rupr. = P. schrenkiana ssp. tianschanica.

P. torano (K. Koch) Koehne. TIGER-TAIL SPRUCE. To 45m. Bole to 1m diam. Bark grey-brown, rough, flaking in scales. Crown dense, conic. Br. ± ascneding, becoming pendulous. Lvs 12–25mm, v. stout, stiff, extremely sharp, shiny yellow-green. Cones 6–12×4cm, oblong-ovoid, sessile, yellow-green, ripening red- to orange-brown; scales elliptic, leathery, obtuse, sometimes finely toothed or entire. S Jap. Z6.

P. watsoniana Mast. = P. wilsonii.

P. wilsonii Mast. WILSON'S SPRUCE. To 45m. Bark red-brown, flaky, later greyer; exfoliating in large, thin scales. Crown conic, becoming columnar. Lvs grass-green, pointed, straight or slightly curved, 10–18mm. Cones 4–7×2m, oblong-cylindric, green, often tinged purple, ripening light brown; scales circular to obtuse-rhombic, sometimes finely toothed. China. Z5.

Pichi Fabiana imbricata.
Pickaback Plant Tolmiea menziesii.
Pickart's Poplar Populus ×canescens.
Pickerel Weed Pontederia cordata.

Pickeringia Nutt. ex Torr. & A. Gray CHAPARRAL PEA; STINGAREE-BUSH. Leguminosae (Papilionoideae). 1 spiny, everg. shrub, to 3m. Br. spreading, olive green. Lvs trifoliolate, crowded; lfts 0.8–1.5cm, bright green above, blue-green beneath, oblanceolate to obovate, tough. Fls axill., solitary, pea-like 1.5–2cm, crimson, red-purple or rose, with a triangle of mustard-yellow at base of standard. Late spring–summer. Calif., Baja Calif., New Mex. Z9.

P. montana Nutt. ex Torr. & A. Gray.

Picrasma Bl. Simaroubaceae. 8 decid. trees. Lvs imparipinnate, crowded at end of branchlets. Fls small, green in loose axill. cymes; sep. ovate, imbricate, persistent; pet. 4–5, oblong; sta. 4–5, longer than pet. Trop. Amer., Indomalesia. Z10.

P. ailanthoides (Bunge) Planch. Slender tree to 12m; young shoots red-brown with yellow spots. Lvs to 38cm, lfts to 10cm, 9–13, glossy green, ovate, sharp-toothed. Fls in loose clusters 15–20cm long. Spring. Jap., N China, Korea.

P. excelsa Roxb. Tree to 24m. Lvs 30cm+, glandular-hairy, lfts many, coarsely toothed. Fls in much-branched pan. India.

P. quassioides (Hamilt.) Benn = P. ailanthoides.

Picridium Desf.

P. tingitanum (L.) Desf. = Reichardia tingitana.

Picris L. BITTERWEED; OX-TONGUE. Compositae. c45 ann. to perenn. herbs with milky sap. Lvs alt., simple, entire, toothed or pinnatisect. Cap. ligulate, solitary or several in corymbs; flts yellow, outer usually with red stripe beneath. Medit., Asia, African nuts. Z6.

P. echioides L. BRISTLY OX-TONGUE. Spiny ann. or bien., to 1m. Lvs to 25cm, elliptic to lanceolate or oblanceolate, petiole winged, margin, upper lvs amplexicaul, sessile. Summer. S Eur.

P. hieracioides L. Bienn. or perenn., to 1m. Lvs to 14cm, lanceolate to oblanceolate, tapering to petiole, entire or toothed, upper lvs sessile, amplexicaul, toothed. Summer. Eur., Asia, nat. elsewhere.

P. kamtschatica Ledeb. Stout ann., to 1m, with hooked hairs. Lvs to 20cm, lanceolate to oblanceolate, bristly serrate. Summer. Transcauc.

Pie Plant Rheum ×cultorum.

Pieris D. Don Ericaceae. Some 7 everg. trees, shrubs or lianes. Bark usually grey or brown, striate. New growth often tinged red or bronze; lvs simple, leathery. Fls often scented, in erect or drooping, term. or axillary rac. or pan.; cal. lobes 5, valvate; cor. waxy, white, pitcher-shaped; lobes 5; sta. 10. E Asia, Himal., E US, W Indies.

P. bodinieri Lév. = *P. formosa.*

P. elliptica (Sieb. & Zucc.) Nak. = *Lyonia ovalifolia* var. *elliptica.*

P. floribunda (Pursh ex Sims) Benth. & Hook. FETTER BUSH. Shrub to *c*2m. Bark grey to grey-brown. Twigs initially downy and stiff hirsute. Lvs 3–8cm, elliptic to ovate, serrate and ciliate, sharp-tipped, dull green above, sparsely glandular-hirsute. Pan. 5–10cm, ± downy and glandular-hirsute; cor. 4–7×3–5.5mm, pitcher-shaped, white. Spring. SE US. 'Elongata': hardy; fls in long term. pan., later-flowering. 'Karemona': hardy. 'Spring Snow': compact, early flowering. Z5.

P. formosa (Wallich) D. Don. Shrub or small tree, 2.5–5m. Young growth glab., bark grey to grey-brown. Lvs 2.5–10cm, elliptic or obovate, finely serrate, sharp-tipped or blunt, coriaceous, lustrous, sparsely glandular-hirsute. Pan. or rac. usually axill., erect to drooping to 15cm; cor. 4–9×3.5–5.5mm, white, rarely pink-tinged, urceolate to cylindric, hairy. Spring. SW China, Vietnam, Himal., Nepal. 'Charles Michael': young growth red; fls large. 'Charles Williams': fls white in large pan. var. *forrestii* (Harrow) Airy Shaw. To 3m. New growth scarlet. Lvs 6–10cm, elliptic-lanceolate, acuminate, finely serrate. Fls in drooping, term. pan., fragrant, white. Spring. W China, Burm. Z7. 'Henry Price': lvs broad, dark green, deep red when young, deeply veined. 'Jermyns': buds red in winter, opening white. 'Wakehurst': to 5.4m, hardy, vigorous; lvs bright red fading to pink before turning deep green, oblong-elliptic to oblanceolate, margins serrated; fls in large clusters.

P. forrestii Harrow. = *P. formosa* var. *forrestii.*

P. japonica (Thunb.) D. Don ex G. Don. LILY OF THE VALLEY BUSH. Shrub or small tree, 2.7–4m. Bark grey to brown; twigs usually glab. when young. Lvs 2.5–10cm, obovate to lanceolate, serrate, coriaceous, sharp-tipped to blunt, emerging pink to red or bronze, hardening dark and lustrous green, sparsely glandular-hirsute. Rac. or pan. to 12cm, erect to drooping, axill.; cor. 5–8×3–4.5mm, urceolate to cylindric, white, rarely tinged pink. Late winter–spring. Jap., Taiwan, E China. Plants formerly known as *P. taiwanensis* usually have bronze-red young growth, tougher, matt green lvs with sparser teeth and spreading to erect pan. They include 'Crispa', a small, slow growing shrub with curled or wavy lvs. 'Bert Chandler': young lvs pale pink turning glossy yellow-white then dark green. 'Blush': fl. buds pink opening to white tinged rose. 'Cavatine': hardy; fls white, long-lasting, late flowering. 'Compacta': compact, dense, to 1.8m; lvs small. 'Christmas Cheer': fls white and deep rose, early flowering. 'Daisen': vigorous; lvs abundant; buds dark pink, fls red fading to pink. 'Debutante': habit compact; fls large, pure white. 'Firecrest': young growth bright red. 'Flamingo': young growth bronze-red; fls deep pink. 'Flaming Silver' ('Havila'): young lvs bright red, margin pink at first, soon silver-white. 'Forest Flame': (*P. formosa* 'Wakehurst' ×*P. japonica*): compact; lvs oblanceolate or oblong-oblanceolate, finely serrate; young growth red changing to pink, ivory, then pale green; pan. large spreading. 'Little Heath': resembles a smaller 'variegata'; fl. buds pink. Green reversions are called 'Little Heath Green'. 'Pygmaea': dwarf, slow-growing; lvs blade-like; fls white. 'Scarlett O'Hara': young lvs red; fls off-white splashed red. 'Snow Drift': young growth bronze-red; fls large on long, upright pan., abundant. 'Valley Valentine': buds crimson, fls deep purple-red. 'Variegata': lvs small, flushed pink at first, variegated cream to silver; fls white. 'White Caps': infl. obovate long, white. Z6.

P. macrocalyx Anthony = *Lyonia macrocalyx.*

P. mariana (L.) Benth. & Hook. f. = *Lyonia mariana.*

P. nana (Maxim.) Mak. = *Arcterica nana.*

P. nitida (Bartr.) Benth. & Hook. f. = *Lyonia lucida.*

P. ovalifolia (Wallich) D. Don. = *Lyonia ovalifolia.*

P. phillyreifolia (Hook.) DC. Shrub 50cm–1m or, more commonly, lianes. Bark brown or grey. Lvs 2–6cm, elliptic, ovate or obovate, revolute, apex serrate, v. sparsely glandular-hirsute. Rac. axill.; cor. 6–8×4–5mm, white, cylindrical-urceolate. Winter–spring. E US. Z7.

P. taiwanensis Hayata = *P. japonica.*

Pigafetta (Bl.) Becc. Palmae. 1 palm to 50m. St. erect, to 40cm diam., riged, green, becoming grey-brown, base with mass of spine-like roots. Lvs pinnate, arching to 6m; sheath tomentose, with soft spines; petioles to 2m, with soft spines beneath; pinnae crowded, linear, acuminate, margins and main veins bristly, midrib prominent. Sulawesi, Moluccas, Papua New Guinea. Z10.

P. filaris (Giseke) Becc.

Pigeon Berry *Duranta erecta*; *Phytolacca americana.*

Pigeon Pea *Cajanus cajan.*

Pigeon Plum *Coccoloba* (*C. diversifolia*).

Pigeon Wings *Clitoria ternatea.*

Pigeon Wood *Hedycarya arborea.*

Piggy-back Plant *Tolmiea.*

Pig Laurel *Kalmia angustifolia.*

Pignut *Carya glabra.*

Pignut Palm *Hyophorbe.*

Pigweed *Chenopodium.*

Pigwood *Geniostoma ligustrifolium.*

Pilea Lindl. Urticaceae. Some 600 ann. or perenn. herbs, creeping, decumbent or erect, sometimes woody at base. Lvs usually opposite, often unequal, entire to serrate with linear to stellate cystoliths giving appearance of opalescent spots. Infl. solitary or a loose pan.; fls minute, white-green becoming pink-brown. Trop. (except Aus.). Z10.

P. cadierei Gagnep. & Guillaum. Spreading to erect perenn. herb or subshrub to 50cm. Branchlets slender, green tinted pink. Lvs to 8.5×5cm, obovate to oblong-oblanceolate, dentate, silver on a dark green ground or wholly metallic. Vietnam. 'Minima': dwarf, freely branching; st. pink; lvs small, elliptic, deep olive green, raised patches of silver, margins crenate.

P. callitrichoides (Knuth) Knuth = *P. microphylla.*

P. crassifolia (Willd.) Bl. Bushy here to 120cm, ascending. Lvs to 13×4cm, thick, ovate or elliptic to lanceolate, acuminate, lustrous green above, veins often red-pink beneath, serrate; petiole to 4cm. Jam.

P. grandifolia (L.) Bl. Shrubby herb to 2m. Lvs to 22×16cm, broadly ovate to elliptic, acuminate, dentate-serrate, lustrous dark green with red veins. Jam.

P. involucrata (Sims) Urban. FRIENDSHIP PLANT; PANAMICA. Trailing to erect herb, hairy to pilose; br. 20–30cm. Lvs to 6×3cm, ovate to obovate, hairy, toothed, 3-nerved, marked bronze, silver or red. Summer. C & S Amer. 'Coral': st. tinged red; lvs long, ovate, glossy, crenate, copper above, tinged purple beneath. 'Liebmannii': lvs tinged silver. 'Moon Valley': lvs ovate, quilted, crenate, tinged bronze, broad silver band along middle, edges dotted silver, sometimes placed under *P. crassifolia.* 'Norfolk': habit small, dense; lvs broad, oval, bronze to black-green, raised silver bands. 'Silver Panamiga': st. brown, hairy; lvs ovate or rhombic, blue-silver, deeply toothed towards apex. 'Silver Tree': stalks white, hairy; lvs ovate, quilted, crenate, tinged bronze, broad silver band along middle, dotted silver on sides.

P. microphylla (L.) Liebm. ARTILLERY PLANT; GUNPOWDER PLANT; PISTOL PLANT. Ann. or short-lived perenn. to 30cm. St. slender, translucent, succulent, densely branched. Lvs v. small, crowded, mossy, obovate to orbicular, pale green, succulent. Fls minute, white tinged red, in dense cymes. Mex. to Braz. 'Variegata' ('Confetti'): lvs blotched white and pink.

P. muscosa Lindl. = *P. microphylla.*

P. nummularifolia (Sw.) Wedd. Trailing herb. Lvs to 2cm, in similar pairs, broadly ovate to suborbicular, crenate, pale green, usually strigillose. Summer. Trop. S Amer., W Indies.

P. peperomioides Diels. Erect herb superficially resembling *Peperomia.* St. elongate, glab. Lvs to 9×9cm, succulent, elliptic to suborbicular, pale green, prominently veined; petioles to 6cm. Summer. W Indies.

P. pubescens misapplied = *P. involucrata.*

P. repens (Sw.) Wedd. BLACK-LEAF PANAMICA. Creeping herb to 30cm. St. pilose, becoming glab., br. erect. Lvs to 3.5×3cm, obovate to suborbicular, obtuse or rounded, glab. or pilose, crenate dark. Summer. W Indies. 'Black Magic': dense, mat-forming; lvs small, round, wavy, somewhat crenate, green shaded bronze.

P. serpyllacea (Knuth) Liebm. Resembles *P. microphylla* except tinged red throughout. Lvs to 15×5mm, entire to crenate. Summer. Trop. N S Amer.

P. serpyllifolia misapplied = *P. serpyllacea.*

P. spruceana misapplied. = *P. involucrata.*

Pileanthus Labill. Myrtaceae. 3 everg. shrubs. Lvs entire, narrow. Fls in upper lf axils. W Aus. Z10.

P. filifolius Meissn. SUMMER COPPER CUPS. Shrub to 1m. St. slender, erect, hairy. Lvs 1.2cm, cylindrical and blunt. Fls pink-red, to 2cm diam.; pet. 5, sometimes frilled.

Pileostegia Hook. f. & Thoms. Hydrangeaceae. 4 climbing or prostrate everg. shrubs differing from *Hydrangea* and *Schizophragma* in fls all alike in term., corymbose pan. E Asia.

P. viburnoides Hook. f. & Thoms. 6–10m. St. self-clinging. Lvs 5–18cm, narrow-oblong to ovate-lanceolate, coriaceous, glossy dark green, pitted above, prominently veined beneath. Pan. to 15cm, crowded; fls 0.8cm diam., white; sta. conspicuous. India, China, Taiwan. Z9.

→*Schizophragma.*

Pilewort *Ranunculus ficaria.*

Pilgerodendron Florin.
P. uviferum (D. Don) Florin = *Libocedrus uvifera.*

Pillwort *Pilularia.*

Pilocereus Lem.
P. arrabidae Lem. = *Pilosocereus arrabidae.*
P. chrysacanthus F.A.C. Weber = *Pilosocereus chrysacanthus.*
P. coerulescens Lem. = *Pilosocereus coerulescens.*
P. glaucescens Lem. = *Pilosocereus piauhyensis.*
P. glaucochrous Werderm. = *Pilosocereus glaucochrous.*
P. hapalacanthus Werderm. = *Pilosocereus hapalacanthus.*
P. leucocephalus Poselger = *Pilosocereus leucocephalus.*

Pilosella Hill. Compositae. 18 hairy, rhizomatous and stoloniferous perenn. herbs. St. few to numerous. Lvs in basal rosettes, entire or slightly denticulate, st. lvs, if present, small. Cap. ligulate, one to several per st. Eurasia and N W Afr. Z5.
P. aurantiaca (L.) F.W. Schultz & Schultz-Bip. Lvs to 20cm, oblanceolate to elliptic, obtuse to acute, pale green or glaucous, with simple hairs. Cap. 2–25, to 2.5cm diam. in a terminal corymb, scape to 65cm, with long dark hairs; flts orange to orange-red. Summer. Eur. (a weed in N US and Pacific Coast).
P. officinarum F.W. Schultz & Schultz-Bip. Lvs 1–12cm, oblong to lanceolate or spathulate, obtuse or acute, stellate-hairy. Cap. solitary, on 5–50cm scape with gland. hairs; flts lemon, striped red below. Summer. Temp. Eurasia.
→*Hieracium.*

Pilosocereus Byles & Rowley. Cactaceae. *c*45 succulents, shrubby or arborescent, base or trunk to 10m; ribs (3–)4–30, often cross-furrowed; areoles often long-woolly. Fls tubular-campanulate, nocturnal. US (Flor.), Mex., Carib. region, and trop. S Amer. (esp. E Braz.).
P. alensis (F.A.C. Weber ex Roland-Goss.) Byles & Rowley. Shrub, 2–5m; st. to 12cm diam.; ribs 10–14; areoles with few white hairs; spines *c*10, to 2cm. Fls green-purple from densely woolly areoles. W Mex. Z9.
P. arrabidae (Lem.) Byles & Rowley. Shrub to 4m, branched near base; st. 4.5–9.5cm diam.; ribs (5–)6–8; areoles with few long hairs pale brown to yellow spines to 4cm. Flowering areoles like non-flowering; fls *c*7×5cm, creamy white. Summer. E Braz. Z9.
P. backebergii (Weingart) Byles & Rowley = *P. lanuginosus.*
P. catingicola (Gürke) Byles & Rowley. Tree to 7m, v. woody; br. whorled; st. 8–12cm diam.; ribs (3–)4–6; areoles with dense hairs; spines 15–18, to 4cm, grey to pale brown. Fls usually flattened, to *c*7×7cm, white. E Braz. Z9.
P. chrysacanthus (F.A.C. Weber) Byles & Rowley. Shrub or tree to 5m or more, with many br.; st. to 9cm diam.; ribs 9–12; spines 12–15, to 4cm, golden. Flowering areoles with dense hair and spines; fl. v. stout, to 8cm, pale pink. Summer. S Mex. Z9.
P. chrysostele (Vaup.) Byles & Rowley. Shrub to 3m, ribs 20–30; clothed in short yellow spines, areolar hairs inconspicuous. Flowering areoles with dense wool and bristles; fl. short and broad, to 5cm; tube pale pink; tep. white. NE Braz. Z9.
P. coerulescens (Lem.) Ritter. Shrub to *c*1.5m; st. 4–6cm diam.; ribs 13–17 (sometimes more); areoles copiously white-hairy and with bristles 1–3cm; spines acicular, pale golden-yellow, 5–30mm. Fl. 3.5–6cm; pericarpel and tube green or red-green; inner tep. white. E Braz. Z9.
P. collinsii (Britt. & Rose) Byles & Rowley. Shrub to 2.5m; st. 4–5cm diam.; ribs 7–10; areoles with long hairs; spines *c*10, to 2.5cm, almost black or grey. Fls slender, to 7cm, tinged green or purple. S Mex. Z9.
P. glaucochrous (Werderm.) Byles & Rowley. Narrow tree or shrub to 4m; st. to 7cm diam.; ribs 5–10; areoles white to black-felted, with long hairs; spines 12–16, to 5cm, translucent yellow or pale brown. Fl. slender, to *c*5.5cm, dirty pink, some tep. v. pale. E Braz. Z9.
P. gounellei (F.A.C. Weber) Byles & Rowley. Shrubby, with v. short trunk, branching to form low broad mass of st. to 2(–3)m high; ribs 8–13, strongly tuberculate, valleys between sinuate; central spines *c*4, 4–12cm. Fl. immersed in wool, to 9cm, white to pale pink. NE Braz. Z9.
P. hapalacanthus (Werderm.) Byles & Rowley. Differs from *P. catingicola* in ribs 6–12; areoles scarcely woolly; spines shorter and weaker. Fl. smaller. NE Braz. (coastal). Z9.
P. lanuginosus (L.) Byles & Rowley. Tree to 10m+; st. to 12cm diam.; ribs to 13; areoles woolly at first; spines pale yellow to brown. Flowering areoles v. woolly; fls to 7cm, white. N S Amer. Z9.
P. leucocephalus (Poselger) Byles & Rowley. Eventually a tree to 6m; st. 5–10cm diam.; ribs 6–9; upper areoles densely clothed

with white hairs; spines pale brown or yellow at first. Fl. 6–8cm; outer tep. purple-brown; inner tep. pale pink. Summer. E. Mex., C. Amer. Z9.
P. leucocephalus misapplied = *P. alensis.*
P. moritzianus (Otto ex Pfeiff.) Byles & Rowley. Resembling *P. lanuginosus*; st. 10cm+ diam.; ribs 7–10; areoles woolly at first; spines to 3.5cm, pale brown. Fl. *c*5cm diam., red. N. Venezuela. Z9.
P. nobilis (Haw.) Byles & Rowley. = *P. royenii.*
P. palmeri (Rose) Byles & Rowley. = *P. leucocephalus.*
P. pentaedrophorus (Labouret) Byles & Rowley. St. simple, or few-branched at base, erect or decumbent, 2–5m+ tall, *c*3–7cm diam., blue-green; ribs 4–6(–10), notched above areoles; spines to 4cm, yellow. Fl. 4–6cm, curved; inner tep. white. E Braz. Z9.
P. piauhyensis (Gürke) Byles & Rowley. Tree to 10m; st. to 10cm diam.; ribs 7–16; spines *c*18–25, 5–15mm, golden-yellow. Flowering areoles with dense white hairs; fl. 6–7cm; tube blue- or brown-green; inner tep. white to pink. E Braz. Z9.
P. purpusii (Britt. & Rose) Byles & Rowley. Simple or somewhat branched, to 3m; st. to 4cm diam.; ribs 12, areoles close-set, with long white hairs when young; spines to 3cm, pale yellow. Flowering areoles with silky white hair; fl. *c*7cm, pale pink. N Carib. Z9.
P. royenii (L.) Byles & Rowley. Tree, to 8m+, st. stout; ribs 7–11; spines variable. Fl. 5cm; tube yellow-green or tinged purple; inner tep. white. Carib. Z9.
P. werdermannianus (Buining & Brederoo) Ritter = *P. coerulescens.*
→*Cactus, Cephalocereus, Cereus* and *Pilocereus.*

Pilularia L. PILLWORT. Marsileaceae. 6 semi-aquatic ferns. Rhiz. long-creeping, slender. Fronds to 10cm, grassy, green, erect, reduced to a thin filiform or subulate stipe. sporocarps basal, globular, black. Temp. regions except Afr. Z8.
P. americana A. Br. Sporocarps to 2mm diam., usually 3-chambered. W US.
P. globulifera L. Sporocarps 4-chambered. W Eur.

Pimelea Banks & Sol. ex Gaertn. RICE FLOWER. Thymelaeaceae. 80 compact everg. shrubs or herbs. Lvs ± sessile, usually small, entire. Fls in term. heads surrounded by leaf-like coloured bracts; perianth tubular, lobes 4, spreading, petal-like, often silky; pet. 0; sta. 2, usually exceeding tube. Fr. a 1-seeded drupe or nut, green, red or black. Australasia. Z9.
P. arenaria A. Cunn. Much-branched shrub, 30–60cm, main st. creeping; shoots silky. Lvs decussate, 6–12mm, ovate to oblong or orbicular, shiny-silky beneath. Fls 6mm diam., silky, pure white in heads. Early summer. NZ.
P. drupacea Labill. Erect shrub to 2m; young shoots silky. Lvs opposite, 2.5–7cm, ovate to elliptic, dark green glab. above, paler beneath, ciliate. Fls to 8mm diam., silky, white, in term. clusters of 4–7. Summer. S & E Aus., Tasm.
P. ferruginea Labill. Erect shrub to 2m. Lvs opposite, to 12mm, ovate or oblong, shiny green above, often hairy beneath, revolute. Fls to 10mm diam., rose-pink in almmost spherical heads 2.5–4cm diam. Late spring–early summer. W Aus.
P. glauca R. Br. Erect shrub, to 1m, all parts except infl. glab. Lvs opposite, to 20mm, narrow-elliptic to ovate, blue-green, midrib prominent. Fls to 7mm diam., hairy, creamy in term. clusters. Anth. pale orange. Summer. Aus., Tasm.
P. gnidia (Forst. & Forst. f.) Willd. Erect, much-branched, glab. shrub to 1.5m; br. stout. Lvs crowded, to 20mm, oblong-lanceolate, light green, leathery. Fls to 5mm diam., in heads of to 30, pale rose, silky. NZ.
P. graciliflora Hook. = *P. sylvestris.*
P. hispida R. Br. Erect, much-branched shrub, 60–120cm; shoots glab. Lvs 12–25mm, oblong-lanceolate. Fls to 6mm diam., crowded in heads to 4cm diam., pale rose, hairy. Summer. W Aus.
P. imbricata R. Br. Shrub to 50cm; shoots, erect, downy. Lvs alt. or opposite, 6–12mm, oblanceolate to narrow-oblong. Fls 4mm diam., white, in heads 25–30mm diam., long-hairy. Spring–summer. W Aus.
P. intermedia Lindl. = *P. glauca.*
P. linifolia Sm. Upright or prostrate shrub 30–90cm, except infl. Lvs opposite, 10–35mm, linear to oblong or linear-obovate, green or blue-green. Fls silky, 6–9mm diam., white tinged pink, in erect, term., globose heads 3cm diam.; bracts to 19mm, tinged red-purple. Early summer, most of the year in the wild. Aus., Tasm.
P. linoides Cunn. = *P. linifolia.*
P. longiflora R. Br. Upright shrub to 120cm. Shoots v. slender, hairy. Lvs 6–15mm, linear, hairy. Fls to 15×8mm, white, in term., globose heads 3cm diam. Summer. W Aus.
P. lyallii Hook. f. Small, prostrate or partly erect shrub, usually white silky-hairy. Lvs overlapping, 4–8mm, narrow-oblong to

lanceolate, concave. Fls white, silky-hairy, 4–6mm diam., in heads of 3–4. NZ.

P. macrocephala Hook. = *P. suaveolens*.

P. nana Graham = *P. imbricata*.

P. nivea Labill. Erect, straggly or bushy shrub to 2m, all parts woolly except upper surface of lvs. Lvs opposite, to 15mm, round-ovate to orbicular, thick, shiny above. Fls white, cream or pink, 6mm diam., in many-fld globose heads 18–24mm diam. Summer. Tasm.

P. pauciflora R. Br. Erect, much-branched shrub, to 3m. Lvs opposite, to 20mm, narrow-elliptic to oblong; petioles 1mm. Fls white to green-yellow, terminal, 2–7 per head. Early summer. Aus., Tasm.

P. petraea Meissn. = *P. imbricata*.

P. prostrata (Forst. & Forst. f.) Willd. Low shrub; br. spreading; shoots adpressed-silky. Lvs interlacing, black, crowded, 2–12mm, ovate to elliptic-oblong, glab., grey-green above, margins often red, leathery. Fls 3–6mm diam., silky, fragrant, white, in small crowded heads of 3–10, 18mm diam. NZ.

P. rosea R. Br. Erect shrub, 30–60cm. Lvs scattered, linear-lanceolate, pointed, revolute. Fls 6mm diamm. rose to white, in crowded hemispheric heads to 4cm diam. Summer. Aus.

P. sericea R. Br. Much-branched shrub 60–120cm; shoots silvery silky. Lvs crowded, 6–15mm, round-ovate to ovate, silky beneath, glab. above. Fls many, downy 5–9mm diam., white tinged pink, in term. heads 3cm diam. Early summer. Tasm.

P. spectabilis (Fisch. & C.A. Mey.) Lindl. Erect shrub, 1–1.25m; shoots glab. Lvs crowded, to 4cm, linear to lanceolate, glaucous beneath. Fls 1.5cm diam., hairy, pale to rich pink or yellow, in crowded, globose heads to 7cm, bracts tinged pink. Early summer. W Aus.

P. suaveolens Meissn. Shrub, 30–60cm; shoots glab. Lvs ovate-lanceolate, 12–35mm, concave, glab., leathery. Fls 12mm diam., yellow opening to pale rose, downy in hemispherical heads, 5cm diam. Summer. W Aus.

P. sylvestris R. Br. Freely branched, glab. shrub, 60–90cm. Lvs 12–25mm, opposite, oblong to lanceolate. Fls 5–9mm diam., pale rose, in heads 4–5cm diam. Summer. W Aus.

P. tomentosa (Forst. & Forst. f.) Druce = *P. virgata*.

P. traversii Hook. f. Dwarf shrub to 60cm; shoots stout, glab., often twisted. Lvs overlapping, to 9mm, obovate-oblong to orbicular, blunt, thick, margins often red. Fls to 8mm diam., in heads of to 20, white to pink, v. silky. NZ.

P. virgata Vahl. Slender, upright shrub to 50cm; st. with pale hairs. Lvs to 20mm, linear to oblong-lanceolate, smooth above, hairy beneath. Fls small, in heads of 6–12. NZ.

Pimento Palm *Schippia*.
Pimpernel *Anagallis*.

Pimpinella L. Umbelliferae. 150 ann. or perenn. herbs. St. branching above. Lvs simple, ternate or 1–3-pinnate. St. branching above. Umbels compound; involucre and involucels usually 0; small fls. Eurasia, N Afr.

P. anisum L. ANISE; ANISEED. Aromatic ann. to 50cm, finely pubesc. Lower lvs 2–5cm, simple, reniform to ovate, dentate or shallowly lobed; lower st. lvs pinnate, seg. linear. Umbels 7–15-rayed; fls white or yellow-white. Summer. C & S Eur., Russia, Cyprus, Syr., Egypt.

P. magna L. = *P. major*.

P. major (L.) Huds. GREATER BURNET SAXIFRAGE. Perenn. to 1m, glab. to slightly pubesc. Lower lvs pinnate, seg. 3–9, serrate to lobed, ovate or oblong, *c*6cm; st. lvs 3-lobed. Umbels with 10–25 rays, to 4cm; fls white to pink. Summer. Eur. 'Rosea': to 60×30cm; lvs fern-like; fls pale pink, delicate. Z5.

P. peregrina L. Bienn. to 1m, finely pubesc. Lower lvs *c*15cm, pinnate, seg. 5–9, suborbicular, crenate; st. lvs 1–2-pinnate, seg. linear. Umbels with 8–50 filiform rays; fls white. Early summer. S Eur., Cauc., Crimea, C Asia. Z6.

P. saxifraga L. BURNET SAXIFRAGE. Perenn. to 1m, scarcely pubesc. Lower lvs pinnate, seg. in 4–6 pairs, ovate to lanceolate, serrate to pinnatifid, to 2.5cm; st. lvs with 3 pairs of narrow lobes; petiole tinged purple. Umbels with 6–25 rays, *c*3cm; fls white, occas. tinged pink or purple. Summer. Eur., inc. GB. Z4.

P. tragium Vill. Perenn. to 60cm, pubesc. to glab. Lower lvs oblong in outline, pinnate, seg. obovate or lanceolate, crenate to dentate, or lobed; st. lvs few, often reduced. Umbels 6–15-rayed; fls white, occas. tinged pink. Summer. S & E Eur. Z7.

→*Anisum*.

Pimple Fern *Microsorium nigrescens*.

PINACEAE Lindl. 9/194. *Abies, Cathaya, Cedrus, Keteleeria, Larix, Nothotsuga, Picea, Pinus, Pseudolarix, Pseudotsuga, Tsuga*

Pinang *Areca catechu; Pinanga*.

Pinanga Bl. PINANG; BUNGA. Palmae. Some 120 unarmed, palms. St. solitary or clustered, ringed, sometimes stilt-rooted. Crownshaft distinct. Lvs entire and pinnately ribbed, or pinnate; pinnae 1 to several fold sometimes mottled or coloured when young. Himal. and S China to Papua New Guinea. Z10.

P. bifida Bl. = *P. disticha*.

P. coronata (Bl. ex Mart.) Bl. St. 3–5(6)m×4cm, clumped. Pinnae crowded, several-fold, linear-lanceolate, slightly falcate, upper pinnae truncately toothed. Java, Sumatra.

P. dicksonii (Roxb.) Bl. ex H.A. Wendl. St. 5–6m×5cm. Lvs 1.25m; pinnae 30–60cm, crowded, broadly linear, upper pinnate confluent. India.

P. disticha (Roxb.) Bl. ex H.A. Wendl. St. 0.6–1.8m, usually clustered. Lvs 30–40cm; pinnae obovate-cuneate, simple and deeply forked, or just a few broad based pinnae. Infl. to 7.5cm, simple. Fr. elliptic, small, red. Malaya.

P. insignis Becc. St. tall, woody. Pinnae subulate, regularly spaced, rigid, apices deeply notched. Philipp.

P. kuhlii Bl. = *P. coronata*.

P. maculata Porto ex Lem. TAMY'S PALM; TIGER PALM. St. slender, smooth. Lvs entire or with 1–2 seg. each side, or pinnate with wide, pendent pinnae, mottled dark green, purple or yellow. Philipp.

P. malaiana (Mart.) R. Scheff. St. to 3m×4cm, clustered. Lvs to 1.8m or more; pinnae to 70cm, subalternate, 18–20, several-fold, linear-lanceolate, glaucous beneath. Malay Penins., Sumatra, Borneo.

P. paradoxa (Griff.) R. Scheff. St. 0.5–2m×0.6cm. Lvs 30cm, oblong, entire or with 3–6 pairs of linear-lanceolate, sigmoid seg. 10–15cm. Malacca.

P. patula Bl. St. to 2.5m×2.5cm, clustered, smooth, swollen at base. Lvs to 1.5m, oblong, irregularly pinnate; pinnae 1–5 fold, sigmoid, acuminate. Sumatra, Borneo.

P. pectinata Becc. St. to 5m×9cm, clustered. Lvs to 1.25m, pinnate, pinnae to 40×4.5cm, 1–5 fold, blue-green beneath. Malay Penins.

P. philippinensis Becc. St. to 3cm diam., stepped. Crownshaft swollen, pale. Pinnae held erect, broad, pointed, deep green. Philipp.

P. scortechinii Becc. St. to 3m. Pinnae crowded, lanceolate, acuminate, 2–5-fold. Malay Penins.

P. ternatensis R. Scheff. St. solitary. Lvs 3.5m; pinnae to 1m, lanceolate, falcate, 2-fold. Ternate Is.

Pin Cherry *Prunus pensylvanica*.
Pinchot Juniper *Juniperus pinchotii*.

Pinckneya Michx. Rubiaceae. 2 decid. shrubs or trees. Fls in term. and axill. corymbs; cal. lobes 5, 1–2 occas. enlarged, leaflike, rose-coloured; cor. salverform, tube elongate, lobes 5, recurved; sta. 5, exserted. SE US, N S Amer. Z9.

P. pubens Michx. GEORGIA BARK; FEVER TREE; BITTER-BARK. Shrub or tree to 9m. Lvs to 20cm, elliptic to oblong or oval, pubesc., dark green above, paler beneath. Fls in corymbs to 20cm wide; enlarged cal. lobe to 7cm, oval or ovate, membranous; cor. to 4cm, yellow-green, lobes oblong to linear, marked brown or purple. S Carol. to Flor.

Pincushion Cactus *Mammillaria*.
Pincushion Euphorbia *Euphorbia aggregata; E. ferox; E. pulvinata*.
Pincushion Flower *Scabiosa (S. atropurpurea)*.
Pincushion Hakea *Hakea laurina*.
Pincushion Tree *Hakea*.
Pindo Palm *Butia*.
Pine *Pinus*.
Pineapple *Ananas*.
Pineapple Broom *Argyrocytisus battandieri*.
Pineapple Flower *Eucomis*.
Pineapple Ginger *Tapeinochilos annanasae*.
Pineapple Guava *Acca sellowiana*.
Pineapple Lily *Eucomis*.
Pineapple Mint *Mentha suaveolens*.
Pineapple-scented Sage *Salvia rutilans*.
Pineapple Weed *Matricaria matricarioides*.
Pine Barrens Gentian *Gentiana autumnalis*.
Pine Fern *Anemia adiantifolia*.
Pine Geranium *Pelargonium denticulatum*.
Pine Heath *Astroloma pinifolium*.
Pine Hyacinth *Clematis baldwinii*.
Pine Leaf Geebung *Persoonia pinifolia*.
Pine Lily *Lilium catesbaei*.

Pinellia Ten. Araceae. 6 perenn. herbs. Lvs basal, simple to compound; petioles slender, bulbils sometimes borne by lvs. Peduncle solitary, distinct; spathe margins overlapping below to form a tube, limb expanded above, oblong-lanceolate; spadix usually exserted with a term. appendix. China, Jap. Z6.

P. cordata N.E. Br. Lvs 3–5cm, lanceolate, cordate, veins marked in cream; petioles short, purple, bulbiliferous. Spathes to 3cm, incurved, green with purple veins; spadix long-exserted, erect, scented of fr. Summer. China.

P. integrifolia N.E. Br. Lvs 3.5–7.5cm, ovate to oblong, acute; petiole to 15cm. Spathe to 3.5cm; spadix sigmoid, appendix exserted to 3.5cm. Summer. China, Jap.

P. pedatisecta Schott. Lvs pedate, seg. 7–11, to 18cm, ovate-lanceolate. Spathe to 19cm, limb to 15cm; appendix shorter than spathe, yellow-green. Summer. N & W China.

P. ternata (Thunb.) Breitenb. Lfts 3–12cm, ovate-elliptic to oblong; petiole bulbiliferous. Spathe to 7cm, green, tube 1.5–2cm, limb curved at apex, puberulent within; spadix appendix to 10cm, erect, purple below. Summer. Jap., Korea, China.

P. tripartita (Bl.) Schott. Lf seg. 8–20cm, 3, ovate, caudate. Spathe 6–10cm, green; purple within, tube to 3cm, limb apex slightly curved, papillose within; spadix appendix 15–25cm. Summer. S Jap.

P. tuberifera Ten. = P. ternata.

Pine Mat Ceanothus diversifolius.
Pine-mat Manzanita Arctostaphylos nevadensis.
Pine Violet Viola purpurea.
Pingle Dryandra carduacea.

Pinguicula L. BUTTERWORT. Lentibulariaceae. c50 carnivorous perenn. herbs. Lvs usually flat in a basal rosette, sometimes packed and bud-like in resting phase, longer and more expanded in summer (described below), thinly fleshy, entire, with ± inrolled margins and superficial glands. Fls solitary; axillary, scapose; cor. bilabiate with lobes spreading, spurred, upper lip 2-lobed shorter than lower, lower 3-lobed. Late spring to summer. Eur., Circumboreal, Americas to Antarc.

P. agnata Casper. Lvs 3.3–5.5cm, spathulate or obovate-oblong, thick and succulent. Scapes 5–12cm; cor. 1.8–2.2cm, white or pale mauve-blue, darker towards margins. Mex. Z10.

P. alpina L. Lvs 2.5–4.5cm, elliptic-oblong to lanceolate-oblong, yellow-green. Scapes 5–11cm; cor. 1–16cm, white with yellow spots on palate. Arc., mts of Eur. Z3.

P. bakeriana Sander = P. moranensis.

P. caerulea Walter. Lvs 1–6cm, ovate-oblong. Scapes 10–30cm; cor. 2.5–4cm, pale violet veined darker violet. E US. Z8.

P. caudata Schldl. = P. moranensis.

P. colimensis McVaugh & Michel. Lvs obovate-oblong, rounded. Scapes 6–14cm; cor. 3.5–5cm, deep rose-pink. Mex. Z10.

P. corsica Bernard & Gren. Lvs 2.5–3.5cm, ovate to obovate-oblong, yellow-green, petiolate. Scapes 4–9cm; cor. 1.6–2.5cm, pale blue to pink, veined purple in throat. Corsica. Z9.

P. cyclosecta Casper. Lvs 1–3cm, obovate-spathulate. Scapes 3–5cm; cor. to 2cm, mallow-purple, throat white. Mex. Z10.

P. ehlersae auct. = P. ehlersiae.

P. ehlersiae Speta & Fuchs. Lvs to 2cm, rounded-spathulate, pale copper-pink. Scapes 9–11cm; cor. to 2.5cm, lilac to mallow-purple, throat white. Mex. Z10.

P. filifolia Wright ex Griseb. Lvs 8–15cm, erect, linear to filiform. Scapes 12–19cm; cor. 14–16mm, white or pink or blue or purple or pale-lilac. Cuba. Z10.

P. flos-mulionis Morr. = P. moranensis.

P. grandiflora Lam. Lvs 3–4.5cm, oblong to obovate-oblong, yellow-green. Scapes 6–15cm; cor. 2.5cm, purple to pink or white, white at throat. W Eur. (SW Ireland, Spain to Fr.). Z7.

P. gypsicola Brandg. Lvs 4–7cm, erect, lanceolate-linear. Scapes 7.5–12.5cm; cor. 2–4cm, violet-purple or purple-pink, veined darker purple, lobes narrow. Mex. Z10.

P. hirtiflora Ten. Lvs 2–6cm, elliptic-oblong to ovate-oblong, apex truncate or emarginate. Scapes 5–11cm; cor. to 2.5cm, pink to blue, white and yellow in throat. C & S It., Balk. Z6.

P. longifolia Ramond ex DC. Lvs 6–13cm, lowermost elliptic, others linear-lanceolate, somewhat undulate, petiolate. Scapes, 10–15cm; cor. 2.2–4cm, lilac to pale blue, spotted white at base of lower lip. S Eur. Mts (Fr. Alps, Pyren., Apennines). Z6.

P. lusitanica L. Lvs 1–2.5cm, oblong-ovate, strongly involute, v. pale green suffused pink. Scapes 2.5–15cm, v. slender; cor. 7–9mm, pale pink to pale-lilac, throat yellow. W Eur. (inc. GB). Z7.

P. lutea Walter. Lvs 1–6.5cm, oblong-ovate, yellow-green. Scapes 10–50cm; cor. 2–3.5cm, chrome-yellow. SE US. Z8.

P. macrophylla McVaugh & Michel = P. moranensis.

P. moranensis HBK. Lvs 6–11.5cm, round-ovate or obovate-obtuse. Scapes 13–18cm; cor. 3.5–5cm, crimson to magenta or

pink, throat white with darker markings at base of lobes. Mex. Z10.

P. orchidioides DC. = P. moranensis.

P. planifolia Chapm. Lvs 3–10cm, elliptic, acute, suffused dull red to purple. Scapes 20–40cm; cor. 2–3cm, purple to pink or white, throat dark pink. SE US. Z8.

P. primuliflora Wood & Godfrey. Lvs 4–8cm, oblong, base-spathulate, apex rounded. Scapes 9–17cm; cor. to 2.5cm, rose-pink or violet-blue, white at bse of lobes, yellow in throat. SE US. Z8.

P. rosea Wats. = P. moranensis.

P. vallisneriifolia Webb. Lvs 4–20cm, suberect, ligulate, un-dulate, petiolate. Scapes 10–15cm; cor. 2.5–3.5cm, violet, throat white, hairy. S Spain. Z8.

P. vulgaris L. Lvs 2–4.5cm, oblong to obovate-oblong, yellow-green. Scapes 7.5–18cm; cor. 1.5–2cm, violet, throat white. NW & C Eur. Z3.

P. zecheri Speta & Fuchs. Lvs 6–7.5cm, narrow-elliptic, bright green, short-petiolate. Scapes 8–10cm; cor. 3.5cm, mallow-purple, darker at centre, throat white. Mex. Z10.

Pink Dianthus.
Pink Agapanthus Tulbaghia fragrans.
Pink And White Everlasting Acroclinium roseum.
Pink Arum Zantedeschia rehmannii.
Pink Bell Gladiolus ornatus.
Pink Boronia Boronia muelleri.
Pink-bracted Manzanita Arctostaphylos pringlei.
Pink Broom Notospartium.
Pink Buttons Crassula pellucida ssp. marginalis.
Pink Cedar Acrocarpus fraxinifolius; Tabebuia heterophylla.
Pink Dot Hypoestes phyllostachya.
Pink Dryandra Dryandra carlinoides.
Pink Everlasting Gnaphalium ramosissimum.
Pink Fivecorner Styphelia triflora.
Pink Fritillary Fritillaria pluriflora.
Pink Hibiscus Hibiscus cameronii.
Pink Iron Bark Eucalyptus sideroxylon.
Pink Jacaranda Stereospermum kunthianum.
Pink Manjack Tabebuia heterophylla.
Pink Mountain Bell Darwinia squarrosa.
Pink Mountain Berry Cyathodes parviflora.
Pink Mountain Heather Phyllodoce empetriformis.
Pink Mulla Mulla Ptilotus exaltatus.
Pink of my John Viola tricolor.
Pink Paper-daisy Acroclinium roseum.
Pink Porcelain Lily Alpinia zerumbet.
Pink Powderpuff Calliandra haematocephala.
Pink Root Spigelia.
Pink Root of Demerara Spigelia anthelmia.
Pink Sand Verbena Abronia umbellata.
Pink Shower Cassia grandis; Cassia javanica.
Pink Snakeweed Stachytarpheta mutabilis.
Pink Snowball Dombeya.
Pink Spire Clethra alnifolia.
Pink Sundew Drosera capillaris.
Pink Tephrosia Tephrosia glomeruliflora.
Pink Tips Callistemon salignus.
Pink Trumpet Tree Tabebuia heterophylla.
Pink Trumpet Vine Podranea ricasoliana.
Pinkwood Eucryphia lucida; E. moorei.
Pink Woodruff Asperula taurina.
Pinnate Boronia Boronia pinnata.
Pin Oak Quercus palustris.

Pinus L. Pinaceae. c110 everg. conifers. Winter buds scaly, often resinous, a single central bud surrounded by a pseudowhorl of smaller buds. Needles slender, solitary or 2–6 per fascicle, with a basal sheath, margins finely serrate or entire; stomatal lines visible on all or 1–2 surfaces. ♂ cones cylindric, catkin-like, yellow, red or orange, produced in spirally arranged clusters. ♀ cones axill. or subterminal, solitary or in pseudowhorls, ovoid to subglobose, sometimes resinous; scales spirally arranged, slightly to v. woody, imbricate, exposed part of scale with a rhombic woody scale shield (apophysis), with a central or term. protruberance, or umbo. N hemis., from the Arc. Circe S to C Amer., N Afr. and SE Asia.

P. albicaulis Engelm. WHITEBARK PINE. To 20m. Crown spreading, shrubby at higher altitudes; bark grey-white, exfoliating; br. horizontal, upcurved. Needles 5, 4–7cm×1mm, stiff, flexible, dark green; stomatal lines on all 3 surfaces. Cones 4–7×4–5cm, ovoid, matt purple when young, turning brown; scales short, thick, not opening with a sharp-pointed umbo. Seeds edible. N Amer. 'Flinck': dwarf form. 'Noble's Dwarf': shrubby, compact. Z2.

P. amamiana Koidz. Related to *P. parviflora* and *P. fenzeliana*; to 25m; bark smooth, grey, thick-scaled on old trees. Needles 5, 6–11cm, glossy dark green with indistinct stomatal lines on inner faces. Cones 4.5–7×2.5cm, glossy orange-brown; scales thick. S Jap. Z9.

P. apachea Lemmon = *P. engelmannii*.

P. apulcensis Lindl. Tree to 22m, crown domed when mature; bark v. rough, fissured. Needles 5, 15–30cm, stout, grey-green. Cones ovoid, 10–15×5cm, opening to ×9cm, buff, scales stiff, thick; umbo. E Mex. *P. estevezii* (Martinez) Perry, cones to 13cm, slightly asymmetric. E Mex. Z9.

P. aristata Engelm. ROCKY MOUNTAINS BRISTLECONE PINE. To 18m. Crown with ascending, whorled, dense br.; bark dark grey, becoming fissured, rust-brown. Needles 5, 2.5–4cm×1mm, sulcate, with flecks of white resin, bright green, blue-white on inner surface in first year of growth, darker later, densely arranged. Dark purple, maturing cylindric-ovoid, brown, 5–10cm, apophysis convex, umbo a bristle-like thorn. US (Rocky Mts). 'Cecilia': dwarf form. Z3.

P. aristata var. *longaeva* (Bail.) Little = *P. longaeva*.

P. arizonica Engelm. ARIZONA PINE. Tree to 35m, similar to *P. ponderosa* ssp. *scopulorum* but shoots slender, yellow-brown bloomed white or pink; needles 5, 4 or 3, 13–20cm. Cones 5–8cm, scales thin, shiny, flexible, umbo with a sharp spine. SW US, NW Mex. var. *stormiae* Martinez. Lvs 3–5 per fascicle, coarser, 20–28cm; cones 6–12cm, scales stiffer, less shiny, umbo with a small prickle. SW US, NE Mex. Z8.

P. armandii Franch. CHINESE WHITE PINE. To 40m. Br. horizontal, spreading widely; bark thin, grey to green-grey, smooth, becoming cracked. Needles 5, 10–18cm, bright glossy green, thin, flexible, spreading or pendulous, often kinked near the base, inner face white-green to glaucous blue, dentate. Cones cylindric to oblong-conic, in groups of 1–3, 8–20×4–11cm, erect, pendulous in the second year; scales yellow-brown, incurved, thick, acutely tapered or rounded, umbo. C & W China. var. *dabeshanensis* (Cheng & Law) Silba. Lvs 8–15cm. E China. var. *marstersiana* Hayata. To 25m. Needles to 15cm, lime green. Cones to 20×8cm; scales yellow-to red-brown, apex often slightly reflexed. Taiwan. Z7.

P. armandii var. *amamiana* (Koidz.) Hatsusima = *P. amamiana*.

P. attenuata Lemmon. KNOBCONE PINE. To 24m, often multi-stemmed; crown slender-conic, br. ascending to erect; bark dark brown, splitting. Needles 3, slender, 11–18cm, erect, yellow-green, serrate, stomatal lines on all faces. Cones reflexed, in groups of 2–4, slender-conic, 9–17×4–5cm, scales conically enlarged, umbo thick, bowed, thorned. W US. Z7.

P. ×attenuradiata Stockw. & Righter. (*P. attenuata* ×*P. radiata*.) Resembles *P. radiata* more than *P. attenuata* in habit, but hardier than *P. radiata*. Z7.

P. australis Michx. = *P. palustris*.

P. ayacahuite Ehrenb. ex Schldl. MEXICAN WHITE PINE. To 55m in wild, resembling *P. monticola* in habit. Bole to 1.5m diam.; bark smooth, light grey becoming rust-brown, fissured. Needles 5, 9–18cm×1mm, thin, pendullous, 3-sided, silver to blue-green, finely toothed. Cones pendulous, solitary or grouped, v. resinous, often slightly curved cylindric, 16–35×4–5cm; scales flexible, elliptic-oblong, apex recurved with a small, blunt umbo. C Amer. Z7.

P. ayacahuite var. *brachyptera* G.R. Shaw = *P. strobiformis*.

P. ayacahuite var. *veitchii* (Roezl) G.R. Shaw = *P. veitchii*.

P. bahamensis Griseb. = *P. caribea*.

P. balfouriana A. Murray. FOXTAIL PINE. To 25m, v. slow growing. Crown slender-conic, bark grey, ridged. Needles 5, curved, 20–50×1mm, glossy dark green, stomatal lines white, on inner surface only. Cone 7–13×2.5–3cm, opening to ×5–7cm, oblong-cylindric, purple-brown to red-brown; scales fragile, narrow, elongate, umbo bearing a short spine to 1mm. N Calif. var. *austrina* (R.J. Mastr. & J.D. Mastr.) Silba. Cones smaller 6–10cm. US (Calif., S Sierra Nevada). Z5.

P. banksiana Lamb. JACK PINE. To 23m. Crown irregular, ovoid-conic; bark scaly, fissured, orange-grey to red-brown; shoots flexible. Needles 2, twisted, spreading, 2–5cm×1.5mm, light green to yellow green, obscurely serrate. Cones 3–6.5×2cm, ovoid-conic, often in pairs, yellow-buff fading to grey, small, often curved, umbo unarmed or with a v. small spine. N Amer. 'Annae': needles tinted yellow. 'Compacta': dense and fast-growing dwarf. 'Tucker's Dwarf': denser than 'Compacta'. 'Uncle Fogy': prostrate, fast-growing. Z2.

P. benthamiana Hartweg = *P. ponderosa*.

P. bhutanica Grierson, Long & Page. EAST BHUTAN PINE. To 25+m, trunk and br. sinuous. Shoots grey-green bloomed white. Needles 5, 15–2cm, pendulous, glossy green with white stomatal band on inner faces. Cone similar to *P. wallichiana* but scales red-brown not buff, and usually smaller. E Himal. Z9.

P. bonapartea Roezl ex Gordon = *P. veitchii*.

P. brachyptera Engelm. = *P. ponderosa* ssp. *scopulorum*.

P. brutia Ten. TURKISH PINE; CALABRIAN PINE. To 30m, crown conic becoming irregular; bark thick, orange with black fissures. Needles 2–3, sparse, yellow-green, 10–29cm and pendulous,slender, indistinct stomatal lines on both sides. Cones on a thick peduncle 5–11×3.5–4.5cm closed, red-brown, scales hard and stiff. NE Greece & Turk. to Leb., Crimea & E Black Sea coast; nat. S It. ssp. *eldarica* (Medv.) Nahal. ELDAR PINE. Lvs slightly shorter, 8–13cm, cones shorter, 5–8cm. Azerbaijan, N Iraq, Iran to Pak. Z7.

P. bungeana Zucc. ex Endl. LACEBARK PINE. To 25m, often multi-stemmed, slow growing; bark white to grey-green, smooth, exfoliating to reveal cream or pale yellow. Needles 3, 5–9cm×2mm, hard, shiny, sharply acuminate, dark yellow-green on outer face, pale grey-green on inner face, smelling of turpentine when crushed. Cones solitary or in pairs, bluntly ovoid, 4–6.5×3–5cm, umbo with a reflexed spike. C & N China. Z5.

P. californiarum D. Bail. CALIFORNIA SINGLE-LEAF PINYON. Small tree to 10m. Needles 1, 4–6cm×1.5–2mm thick, dark grey-green (not glaucous blue). Cones globose, 3–4cm. SE Calif., N Baja Calif. ssp. *fallax* (Little) D. Bail. ARIZONA SINGLE-LEAF PINYON. Has only 2–7 resin ducts in the 1.2–1.7mm broad lvs. US (SW Ariz.). Z9.

P. canariensis C. Sm. CANARY ISLANDS PINE. To 60m, narrowly conical to domed, br. whorled; bark thick, dark to rust brown, scaly and deep-fissured, 15–30cm×1mm, bright green, stomatal lines on all sides. Juvenile foliage blue-green, 3–6cm. Cones brown, ovoid-conic, solitary or grouped 2–4, spreading to pendulous, 9–20×5–6cm, opening to ×7–13cm; scales thick, umbo ± flat. Canary Is. Z9.

P. caribaea Morelet. CARIBBEAN PINE. To 30m. Crown open, broad; bark grey to brown, ridged, exfoliating. Needles 3(–4), crowded, 15–25cm, olive green to dark glossy green, stomatal lines on all sides. Cones glossy rust-brown, 5–10×2.5–3.5cm, opening to ×5–7cm; scales flat to slightly swollen, umbo with a small thorn. W Cuba. var. *bahamensis* (Griseb. Barrett & Golfari BAHAMAS PINE. To 22m. Needles often 2 as well as 3 per fascicle, cones narrower, umbo more prominent. Bahama & Caicos Is. var. *hondurensis* (Loock) Barrett & Golfari HONDURAN PINE. To 44m, v. fast growing. Needles 3 to 4, occas. 5, to 33cm; cones larger, to 13cm, darker brown, umbo strong, spiny. C Amer. Z10.

P. cembra L. SWISS PINE; AROLLA PINE. To 25m. Crown dense, narrow-columnar to acute-ovate, often branched from ground; bark smooth, grey-green, becoming brown suffused grey, furrowed; br. densely twiggy. Needles stiff, 5, 6–11cm, dark green on the extior surface, serrute, stomatal lines on 2 blue-white interior surfaces. Cones resinous, obtuse-ovate, 4–7.5×4cm, purple when young; scales thick, obtuse, to 2cm; seeds edible. C Eur. 'Aurea': lvs yellow. 'Aureovariegata': lvs yellow. Compacta Glauca': compact and conic with ascending br.; needles tinted blue. 'Jermyns': compact and conic, v. slow-growing. 'Kairamo': needles profuse, dense at br. tips. 'Monophylla': slow-growing, irregular dwarf. 'Nana': tightly pyramidal dwarf; needles tinted blue. 'Pendula': br. pendulous. 'Pygmaea': dwarf form, to 40m. 'Stricta': narrowly columnar, br. ascending. 'Variegata': needles stippled yellow, sometimes entirely yellow. Z4. ssp. *sibirica* (Du Tour) Rupr. SIBERIAN PINE. Needles with 3 resin canals, not 1; cones 6–9×5cm. Sib. Z1.

P. cembra var. *pumila* Pall. = *P. pumila*.

P. cembroides Zucc. PINYON PINE; MEXICAN NUT PINE. To 15m. Crown domed; bark thick, deeply rectangular fissured, black-brown, br. outspread. Needles 2–3, clustered at shoot tips, 3–6cm, entire, olive green, stomatal lines on all 3 surfaces. Cones globose, 3–4cm, bright green when young, opening to ×5cm, orange- or buff-brown, scales 12–16mm wide, umbo, slightly protruding seed, edible. Mex., US (W Tex., rare). 'Blandsfortiana': v. slow-growing dwarf. ssp. *lagunae* (Pass.) D. Bail. To 21m. Needles 5–7.5cm, 2–3; cones ovoid 4.5×3.5cm opening to ×5cm; scales longer and narrower. S Baja Calif. ssp. *orizabensis* D. Bail. Bark as for *P. discolor*. Needles 3–4, 3.5–5.5cm, with stomata mostly on inner faces. Cones larger, 5–6×5cm, opening to ×7.5cm, scales flatter, 18–20mm wide; seed larger. Mex. Z8.

P. cembroides var. *bicolor* Little = *P. discolor*.

P. cembroides var. *edulis* (Engelm.) Voss = *P. edulis*.

P. cembroides var. *monophylla* (Torr. & Frém.) Voss = *P. monophylla*.

P. cembroides var. *parryana* (Engelm.) Voss = *P. quadrifolia*.

P. cembroides var. *remota* Little = *P. remota*.

P. chiapensis (Martinez) Andresen. CHIAPAS WHITE PINE. To 35m+, crown ovoid-conic, becoming broad with long level br.; bark smooth grey, rectangular-fissured. Needles 5, 8–13cm, slender, bright green, with glaucous stomatal bands on inner surfaces only. Cones on slender peduncles, 10–17×2.5cm, orange-brown; scales to *P. strobus* but not reflexed at tips. S Mex., Guat. Z10.

P. chihuahana Engelm. = *P. leiophylla* ssp. *chihuahana*.

P. chylla Lodd. = *P. wallichiana*.

P. clausa (Chapm.) Vasey. SAND PINE. Shrub or small tree to 10m; crown irregular, bark scaly. Needles 2, 5–9cm, slender, dark green. Cones ovoid-conic, 5–8cm; scales thin, umbo curved or straight. US (Flor.). Z9.

P. clusiana Clem. ex Arias = *P. nigra* ssp. *monspeliensis*.

P. contorta Douglas ex Loud. SHORE PINE. To 25m, shrubby on poor sites. Crown domed, columnar or ovoid; young trees conical, bushy at base; bark red to yellow-brown, fissured into small squares. Needles 2, densely arranged, twisted, yellow to dark green, 4–5cm×1.5mm. Cones ovoid, 3–7cm; scales narrow, yellow-brown, umbo with a sharp thorn. Coastal NW US. 'Compacta': upright, dense; needles dark green. 'Frisian Gold': needles with conspicuous gold tint, even in summer. 'Pendula': rare weeping form. 'Spaan's Dwarf': irregular, pyramidal dwarf to 1.5m; needles dark green. ssp. *bolanderi* (Parl.) Critchf. MENDOCINO SHORE PINE. Shrub; lvs slender, cones with thicker scales, bark v. dark brown. N Calif. coast. ssp. *latifolia* (Engelm.) Critchf. LODGEPOLE PINE. To 30m. Bark thick, ridged, rarely thin and scaly. Needles 8cm, more spreading, brighter green. Rocky Mts. ssp. *murrayana* (Grev. & Balf.) Critchf. SIERRA LODGEPOLE PINE. To 50m. Bark thin, pink-brown. Needles olive green, to 8cm, cones paler, buff, open when ripe and falling soon after, 4–6cm. SW US (Calif., Sierra Nevada Mts). Z7.

P. cooperi Blanco. To 33m. Crown ovoid-conic, becoming domed; bark rough, thick, plated and deeply fissured, dark red-brown. Needles stout, 7–11cm, 5, grey-green. Cone 5–9cm, ovoid-conic; scales stiff, nearly flat, buff to brown with brown lines radiating from prickly umbo. NW Mex. Z7.

P. coulteri D. Don. BIG-CONE PINE. To 30m. Crown broad conic, becoming ovoid; st. erect; br. spreading; bark brown to black with scaly ridges. Needles 3, 20–32cm×2mm, grey or blue-green, stiff, finely serrate, stomatal lines on all surfaces. Cones yellow-brown, ovoid-conic, 20–40×15cm, woody, scales with a hook-like umbo. NW Mex., Calif. Z8.

P. cubensis Griseb. = *P. occidentalis*.

P. culminicola Andresen & Beaman. CERRO POTOSI PINYON. Shrub, to 5m. Crown compact, widely branching; bark green-grey, scaly. Needles 5, stomatal lines white on 2 inner surfaces, outer face glossy-green. Split sheaths rolling back in a rosette at needle base. Cones subglobose, 2.5–4×2–3.5cm, opening to ×4.5cm; scales similar to those of *P. cembroides*. Mex. Z7.

P. dalatensis De Ferré. To 40m. Needles 5, 5–10cm, glossy green, with glaucous stomatal bands on inner faces. Cones similar to *P. peuce*, 6–11cm, yellow-brown bloomed glaucous. S Vietnam (mts). Z10.

P. densa (Little & Dorman) Laub. & Silba. SOUTH FLORIDA SLASH PINE. Similar to *P. elliotii*, but smaller cones and seedlings with a fire-resistant 'grass' stage. To 30m, crown narrow conic becoming rounded on long clear st.; bark thick, deeply fissured. Needles 2–3, 18–25cm, stiff, dark green. Cones 6–11×2.5cm, slender conic to ovoid to ×7cm, glossy chestnut, scales with spine on umbo. S Flor. Z10.

P. densata Mast. To 30m. Crown ovoid-conic, becoming rounded and irregular with age; bark thick, fissured, grey-brown at base. Needles 2(–3), 8–20cm, stout, dark green with indistinct lines. Cones 4–7×2.5–3.5cm, ovoid, scales v. thickened and pyramidal, or flatter; thick, woody sub-shiny, buff- or orange-brown, umbo prickly. SW China. Z6.

P. densiflora Sieb. & Zucc. JAPANESE RED PINE. To 35m. Crown conic in young trees, wide-spreading, irregular rounded when mature; bark rust-brown, scaly, fissured and grey at base. Needles 2, 7–10cm, slender, bright green. Cones buff to pale brown, ovoid, 4–6cm; scales thin; umbo with a short thorn or obtuse point. Jap., Korea. 'Alice Verkade': habit dwarf, tightly globose. 'Aurea': needles with gold tint or spots. 'Globosa': slow-growing, hardy and hemispherical to 1m. 'Jane Kluis': broadly globose dwarf to 75cm; needles compact. 'Oculus-draconis': irregular, alt., yellow and green variegated needles. 'Pendula': vigorous, semi-prostrate. 'Rezek WB Seedling': rounded, mushroom-like head. 'Umbraculifera': v. slow-growing umbrella form to 4×6m; needles bright green. Z5.

P. devoniana Lindl. MICHOACAN PINE. To 35m, crown conic to ovoid or rounded and domed with age; bark thick, deeply fissured, v. rough. Needles 5, 25–45mm, stout, light to dark green. Cones 15–35×5–6cm long cylindric-conic, opening to ×11cm ovoid-cylindric, buff to brown, matt; scales with weak spine easily lost. Listed in most texts as *P. michoacensis* and much confused with *P. montezumae*, with narrower shoots and lvs, smaller cones, and scales with stouter reflexed spine. C & S Mex., Guat. Z9.

P. discolor Bail. & Hawksw. BORDER PINYON. Small tree to 15m,

crown rounded; bark thin, becoming black with shallow fissures bright orange at centre. Needles 3, 2.5–6cm, slender, glosys green, bright white stomatal bands on inner faces. Cones ovoid-globular, 2–3×2–2.5cm, opening to ×4cm, orange-buff; scales flat; seeds edible. US (SE Ariz., SW New Mex.), NW Mex. Z8.

P. divaricata (Ait.) Dum.-Cours. = *P. banksiana*.

P. douglasiana Martinez = *P. gordoniana*.

P. durangensis Martinez. DURANGO PINE. To 40m, crown conic to rounded and domed, bark rough, deeply fissured, grey-brown. Needles usually 12–20cm, 1.5–2mm thick, dark green to grey-green, sub-shiny with indistinct stomata on all 3 surfaces. Cones 6–10×3cm, ovoid-conic to ×6cm, mid brown; scales hard, thin edged; umbo with a sharp point. W Mex. Z8.

P. echinata Mill. SHORT-LEAF PINE. To 35m. Crown conic open; bole often with epicormic shoots; bark dark grey, red-brown whem br. whorled, thin. Needles 2–3, 8–13cm×1mm, soft, flexible, yellow-green, finely serrate, stomatal lines visible on both sides. Cones pale brown, ovoid-conic, 4–7×2cm, opening to ×3–4cm, apophysis diamond-shaped, thorn incurved. SE US. Z6.

P. edulis Engelm. ROCKY MOUNTAIN PINYON. To 15m. Crown compact, domed; bark silvery grey, scaly, ridged red-brown. Needles 2, 3–6cm×2mm, outer face dark green, inner glaucous. Cones subglobose, pale brown or green-brown, 3–4.5×3–4cm; scales 4–8, umbo with a central depression and minute spine. SW US. Z5.

P. eldarica Medv. = *P. brutia* ssp. *eldarica*.

P. elliottii Engelm. SLASH PINE. To 35m, bole to 90cm diam. Crown dense, domed; bark grey, fissured, purple-brown when mature, exfoliating in large plates. Needles 2–3, crowded at br. tips, 20–30cm×1mm, stiff, dark green, glossy, finely serrate, stomatal lines visible on all surfaces. Cones shiny chestnut brown, narrow conic, 9–15×3–4cm, ovoid to ×8–10cm when open, scales with a thick, grey thorn to 3mm. SE US. Z9.

P. elliottii var. *densa* Little & Dorman = *P. densa*.

P. engelmannii Carr. APACHE PINE. To 35m; bark dark brown to v. dark grey, rough, deeply fissured, forming plates. Needles 3, rarely 4, 30–40cm, bright green or olive green, finely toothed, stomatal lines 12 on the outer face, 6 on the inner. Cones hard, heavy, ovoid to oblong-conical, 10–18×5–6cm, opening to ×10cm, yellow-brownn, scales with recurved, woody umbo. SW US, Mex. Z8.

P. estevezii Perry = *P. apulcensis*.

P. excelsa Wallich ex D. Don = *P. wallichiana*.

P. fenzeliana Hand.-Mazz. Similar to *P. amamiana* and *P. morrisonicola*. To 35m. Needles 5, 7–12cm, slender, glosys green on outer surface, 4–5 green-white rows of stomata on inner faces. Cones stalked, 6–10×2.5cm, opening to ×4–5cm, glossy yellow-brown; scales 14–18mm wide. China, Vietnam, rare and endangered in wild. Z9.

P. fenzlii Anton & Kotschy = *P. leiophylla*.

P. flexilis James. LIMBER PINE. To 25m. Crown conic to broadly rounded, bark smmooth, thin, grey; br. candelabra-like, upswept; shoots v. flexible. Needles 5, pointing toward shoot apex, 4–8cm×1mm, densely crowded; stomatal lines faintly visible on all sides, blue-green. Cones 6–14×5–6cm, erect, yellow ochre, glossy; fertile scales thick, woody, umbo dark, obtuse. SW Canada to W US. 'Extra Blue': irregular and erect to 2.5m; br. dense, tufted. 'Firmament': needles tinted blue; resistant to blister rust. 'Glauca Pendula': vigorous, prostrate; needles long, thick, blue. 'Glenmore': needles long, to 11.5cm, tinted silver. 'Nana': bushy dwarf; needles short, to 3cm. 'Pendula': st. and br. weeping. 'Tiny Temple': slow-growing dwarf; needles to 7cm, tinted blue. 'Vanderwolf's Pyramid': erect; needles tinted blue. Z3.

P. formosana Hayata = *P. morrisonicola*.

P. funebris Komar. = *P. densiflora*.

P. gerardiana Wallich ex D. Don. CHILGOZA PINE. To 21m. Crown rounded; br. short, thick, spreading; bark thin, silvery grey, exfoliating in plates. Needles 3, erect, spreading, 7–10cm×2mm, green. Cones v. resinous, 10–18×8–12cm, bluntly woody, scales pyramidal, umbo triangular; seeds edible. NW Himal., Kashmir, NW Pak., N Afghan. Z7.

P. glabra H. Walter. SPRUCE PINE. To 35m, bole to 75cm diam. Bark rust-brown, smooth, grey, thin on upper trunk, br. horizontal. Needles 2, 5–9cm×1mm, dark green, twisted, stomatal lines on all surfaces. Cones ovoid, 5–6cm, buff-brown, reflexed; scales soft, umbo with a small thorn. SE US. Z8.

P. gordoniana Hartw. ex Gordon. GORDON'S PINE. Tree to 35m, crown rounded, dense; bark thick, fissured at base, thin and exfoliating above, orange-red. Needles 5, 23–38cm×1.5mm, bright green with stomata on all sides. Cones on a stout stalk, conic 8–12×3–4cm, scales grooved, rhombic, red-brown, with a blunt umbo. SW Mex. Z9.

P. greggii Engelm. ex Parl. To 20m. Crown broadly conic, domed when mature; young bark grey, smooth, basal bark rough, ridged. Needles 3, 7–13×1mm, spreading, pale green, stomatal lines visible on all surfaces. Cones yellow-brown, 6–13cm, ovoid to conical, often in groups. Mex. Z8.

P. griffithii McClell. = *P. wallichiana*.

P. ×hakkodensis Mak. (*P. parviflora* ×*P. pumila*.) Low, 6m, slow-growing. Needles longer, more twisted, rougher than *P. pumila*. Cone as *P. pumila*, or slightly larger and rougher scaled. Jap. Z4.

P. halepensis Mill. ALEPPO PINE. To 20m. Crown conic to umbrella-shaped, becoming globose, st. often bowed or twisted; bark silver-grey, becoming red-brown, fissured.Needles 2, spreading, 6–10cm, stiff, v. slender, 0.8mm, persistent 2 years, indistinct stomatal lines on all sides. Medit. (Moroc. and Spain to Libya, Greece and Isr.). Z8.

P. halepensis var. *brutia* (Ten.) Henry = *P. brutia*.

P. hamiltonii Ten. = *P. pinaster*.

P. hartwegii Lindl. To 25m, rarely 35m. Crown columnar, domed; bark grey, thick, scaly. Needles 3–5, to 15cm, stiff, dark to glaucous green. Cone dark purple to black, cylindric-ovoid, to 16cm; scales thin, flexible, umbo prominent, thorn minute. High mts in C & S Mex. to Hond. and NW El Salvador. Z8.

P. heldreichii Christ. BOSNIAN PINE. Tree to 25m. Crown ovoid conic; bark ash grey, splitting into furrows, exposing yellow-grey patches; seeds edible. Needles 2, 6–9cm×2mm, spiny-tipped, stiff, curved forward, glossy dark green, dentate, stomatal lines on all surfaces. cones ovoid; scales soft, brittle, yellow-brown. W Balk. Penins., SE It., Greece (Thessalian mts). 'Aureospicata': broadly conic, slow-growing; needles tips yellow. 'Compact Gem': compact and slow-growing dwarf to 25 by 30cm after 10 years; needles dark green. 'Pygmy': slow-growing, mound-forming dwarf; needles dark green. 'Satellit': conic, v. narrow; needles dark green. 'Schmidtii': compact, dense and slow-growing dwarf; needles rich green. Z5.

P. henryi Mast. Similar to *P. densiflora*. Needles 2, 7–12cm, slender, dark green. Cones 2.5–5cm, conic opening ovoid to ×4.3cm, scales yellow-buff, shiny. C China. Z7.

P. herrerai Martinez. To 30m, crown conic becoming rounded; bark as in *P. teocote*. Needles 3, 11–20cm, v. slender, soft and drooping, glossy light green. Cones on a slender peduncle, ovoid-conic, 2.5–5×2cm, opening to ×3.5cm buff, shiny; scales hard and stiff. W & SW Mex. Z10.

P. heterophylla Sudw. non Koch non Presl = *P. elliotii*.

P. himekomatsu Miyabe & Kudô = *P. parviflora*.

P. ×holfordiana A.B. Jackson. (*P. veitchii* ×*P. wallichiana*.) To 30m. As for *P. wallichiana*, but with young shoots finely pub-esc., cones wider, scale end broad, acute, not reflexed. Z8.

P. ×hunnewelli A.G. Johnson. (*P. strobus* ×*P. parviflora*.) Crown open; young shoots pubesc. Needles to 9cm, arched, twisting, green tinged blue. Cones subsessile. Z6.

P. hwangshanensis Hsia ex C.H. Tsoong. Similar to *P. thunbergii*. To 25m. Needles 2, 5–8cm, 1mm broad, fresh green. Cones 4–5cm, conic opening ovoid to ×5cm, scales pale buff. E China. Z7.

P. inops Sol. = *P. virginiana*.

P. insignis Douglas ex Loud. = *P. radiata*.

P. insularis Endl. = *P. kesiya*.

P. jaliscana Pérez = *P. pringlei*.

P. jeffreyi Balf. ex A. Murray. JEFFREY'S PINE. To 55m. Crown dome-shaped, conic; bark black-brown, splitting, in large plates; br. stout, spreading. Needles 3, 14–27cm×2mm, matt grey-green, finely serrate, stomatal lines, 10–12 on outer face, 4–6 on inner. Cones ovoid-conical, 10–24×6–8cm, open ×10–15cm, scales pale buff brown, umbo with a sharp, reflexed thorn. S Oreg. to N Baja Calif. Z8.

P. johannis Pass. Multistemmed shrub or small tree to 10m, v. similar to *P. discolor*. Needles 3, 3–5cm, slender, dark green outer surface with no stomata, white stomatal bands on inner faces. Cones ovoid-globose, 3–4×2.5–3cm, opening to ×4cm, orange-buff; seeds edible. NE Mex. Z8.

P. kesiya Royle ex Gordon. To 40m. Bark thick, deeply fissured. Needles 3, 15–24×0.5mm, grey-green, stomatal lines visible on all sides. Cones 5–11×3cm, dark brown. Assam (Khasi mts) to SE Yunnan, Indochina & N Philipp. Z9.

P. khasya Royle = *P. kesiya*.

P. khasyana Griff. = *P. kesiya*.

P. kochiana Klotzsch ex Koch = *P. sylvestris* var. *hamata*.

P. koraiensis Sieb. & Zucc. KOREAN PINE. To 50m. Habit as for *P. cembra* but looser; young bark smooth, brown suffused grey, becoming furrowed; br. horizontal to erect. Needles 5, loosely arranged, 6–12cm×1mm, outer face blue green, serrulate, stomatal lines blue-white, on inner faces only. Cones erect, conical-cylindric, 8–16×5–7cm, bright green or purple; scales leathery, undulate; tips elongated; seeds edible. NE Asia, Manch., Korea to Jap. 'Silveray': needles thick, tinted blue. 'Tortuosa': needles spirally twisted, eesp. at br. tips.

'Variegata': needles tinged yellow to entirely yellow. 'Winton': bushy dwarf, to 2×4.5m after 30 years. Z3.

P. krempfii Lecomte. To 40m. Bark rust-brown, smooth. Needles 2, 4–7cm×4mm, flattened, lanceolate, sharply pointed. Cones 4–7×2–3cm, ovoid, red-brown, similar to *P. balfouriana* and *P. rzedowskii*, but smaller. S Vietnam, rare & endangered. Z10.

P. lambertiana Douglas. SUGAR PINE. To 70m in wild. Bark smooth, pale brown to grey-green, becoming thick, splitting and ridged in mature trees; br. long, whorled. Needles 5, 6–11cm×1.5mm, sharp-acuminate, rigid, twisted, dark green, stomatal lines all surfaces, inner surfaces blue-white. Cones 20–64×6–7cm opening ×9–16cm, pendulous, long pedunculate, glossy yellow or orange-brown, scales leathery. Oreg., Calif. to Baja Calif. Z7.

P. laricio Poir. = *P. nigra* var. *maritima*.

P. latisquama Engelm. = *P. pinceana*.

P. latteri Mason = *P. merkusii*.

P. lawsonii Roezl ex Gordon To 25m, crown conic becoming rounded; bark as in *P. teocote*. Needles 3–4(–5), 13–23cm, coarse and stiff, glaucous or blue-green. Cones on a slender peduncle, ovoid, 5–8cm, yellow to brown, shiny. SW & S Mex. Z10.

P. leiophylla Schiede ex Schldl. & Cham. SMOOTH-LEAF PINE. To 30m. Crown irregular, open; bark dark brown; bole with epicormic shoots. Needles 5, to 15cm, grey-green, thin, finely serrate. Cones ovoid to ovate-conic, 3–6cm, long stalked; scales to 2cm, brown. C Mex. ssp. *chihuahana* (Engelm.) E. Murray. Needles thicker and stiffer, mostly 3, sometimes 4 or 5. NW Mex. Z9.

P. leucodermis Antoine = *P. heldreichii*.

P. leucosperma Maxim. = *P. tabulaeformis*.

P. lindleyana Gordon = *P. montezumae* var. *lindleyi*.

P. longaeva Bail. ANCIENT PINE. To 20m, v. similar to *P. balfouriana*, but cone scales aristate. Crown conic, becoming rough, twisted. Bark chocolate brown, in plates; br. erect to pendulous. Needles 5, 2–4cm×1mm, green with white stomatal bands on inner faces. Cone ovoid-cylindric, red brown, 5–11cm; umbo thornlike. NW US. Often confused with *P. aristata*, but resin drops 0. 'Sherwood Compact': tight and conic. br. ascending. Z4.

P. longifolia Salisb. = *P. palustris*.

P. longifolia Roxb. non Salisb. = *P. roxburghii*.

P. luchuensis Mayr. OKINAWA PINE. To 25m, similar to *P. thunbergii*. Crown irregular; bark thin, grey, exfoliating in scales. Needles 2, 12–16cm. Cones ovoid-conic, 4–6cm, brown. S Jap. Z9.

P. lumholtzii Robinson & Fern. To 25m. Crown open; br. level, lower br. pendulous. Needles 3, rarely 2 or 4, hanging vertically, 20–30cm, bright green to olive green, finely serrate. Cones 3–6cm, ovoid, pendulous, brown. W & NW Mex. Z8.

P. lutea Walter = *P. taeda*.

P. lutea Martinez, non Walter = *P. cooperi*.

P. macrophylla Engelm. = *P. engelmannii*.

P. maritima Mill. = *P. pinaster*.

P. martinezii Larsen = *P. durangensis*.

P. massoniana Lamb. To 25m. Crown spreading, ovate or flattened; bark grey at base, forming thick, irregular plates; br. horizontal. Needles 2, 13–20cm×0.5–1mm, dark green. Cones 4–7×4cm, ovoid-oblong, chestnut brown, apophysis red-brown; umbo smooth. C & SE China, Taiwan, N Vietnam. Z7.

P. maximartinezii Rzed. MARTINEZ PINYON. To 11m. Crown open, branching from base. Needles 5, 9–20cm, pale glossy-green above, white beneath, entire or dentate. Cone 15–23×10–15cm, ovoid to oblong-ovoid, apophysis thick, pyramidal-ovoid; scales yellow-buff. Seed to 3cm, the largest of any pine. Seedlings with up to 24 cotyledons. Mex. Z10.

P. maximinoi H.E. Moore. THINLEAF PINE. Tree to 35m, crown rounded; bark thick, fissured at base, thin, flaking above, orange-red. Needles 5, v. slender, 20–30cm×0.8mm, bright green with stomata on all sides. Cones conic 7–10×3cm, rarely to 14cm, scales v. thin, rhombic, red-brown. S Mex. to Hond. Z10.

P. merkusii Jungh. & De Vries. SUMATRAN PINE. Tree to 45m, crown open, trunk often sinuous; bark thick, deeply fissured, scaly, black-brown. Needles 2, rarely 3, 15–20cm, slender pale green with indistinct stomatal bands on both faces. Cones ovoid-cylindric, 5–7.5×2.5cm, opening ovoid to ×5cm, glossy red-brown. Philipp., Sumatra. ssp. *latteri* F. Mason. TENASSERIM PINE. Differs in longer stouter needles, 18–27cm; cones cylindric-conic, 6–12×2.5cm, scales flatter, regularly rhombic. Burm. to Indochina and extreme SW China. Z10.

P. michoacaënsis Martinez = *P. devoniana*.

P. mitis Michx. = *P. echinata*.

P. monophylla Torr. & Frém. SINGLE-LEAF PINYON. To 15m, often with many st. Crown domed; bark smooth, becoming ridged with age. Needles 1–2, terete, 4–6cm, 1.7–2.3mm thick, stiff, glaucous blue-green. Cones 5–9×3–5cm, ovoid-conic, yellow buff, opening to ×4.5–8.5cm; scales woody, thickened pyramidally; seed edible. SW US. 'Tioga Pass': br. ascending; needles blue. Z6.

P. *montana* Mill. = P. *mugo*.

P. *montana* var. *uncinata* (DC.) Heering = P. *mugo* ssp. *uncinata*.

P. **montezumae** hort. non Lamb. MONTEZUMA PINE; ROUGH-BARKED MEXICAN PINE. To 35m. Crown columnar to conic, becoming rounded; bark rust-brown, rough, fissured. Needles 5, rarely 4–6, erect or pendent, 15–30cm×2mm, green, stomatal lines on all surfaces. Cones 12–25cm, broadly cylindric-conical to ovoid-conical, yellow to rust-brown, apophysis buff to glossy brown, umbo with a decid. thorn. W & NE Mex. to Guat. var. *lindleyi* Loud. Cone more cylindric, scales more numerous. Z9.

P. *montezumae* hort. = P. *rudis*.

P. *montezumae* var. *hartwegii* (Lindl.) Engelm. = P. *hartwegii*.

P. *montezumae* var. *rudis* (Endl.) G.R. Shaw = P. *rudis*.

P. **monticola** Douglas ex D. Don. WESTERN WHITE PINE. To 60m. Crown conical; bark smooth, pale brown when young, grey-brown, fissuring when mature. Needles 5, 7–10cm, glossy bright green on outer face, blue-white stomatal bands on inner faces, densely serrate. Cones stalked, becoming pendulous, to 28×5cm, narrowly conic or cylindric, gently curved, green to purple-green, yellow-brown when mature. BC to Oreg., Mont. 'Ammerland': vigorous clone, fast-growing to 50cm p.a; needles tinted blue. 'Minima': dwarf, needles short, tinted blue; witches' broom. 'Pendula': st. bowed; br. weeping. 'Skyline': slender upright; needles conspicuously blue. var. *minima* Lemmon. Cones shorter, 9–15cm, glosys yellow-ochre. W US. Z4.

P. **morrisonicola** Hayata. TAIWAN WHITE PINE. Resembles P. *parviflora*. To 25m. Bark brown, suffused grey, furrowed when mature. Needles 5, 6–10cm×1mm, glossy yellow-green, stomatal lines only on inner faces. Cones ovoid to oblong-ovoid, glossy yellow ochre, to 10×5cm. Taiwan. Z8.

P. *mughus* Scop. = P. *mugo*.

P. **mugo** Turra. MOUNTAIN PINE; DWARF MOUNTAIN PINE. Shrub, to 6m. Crown conic; br. erect or decumbent; bark grey-brown, scaly.NEedles 2, often bowed, twisted, 3–7cm×2–3mm, dark green, stomatal lines faint on both sides.Cones 2–6×3cm, ovoid to conic, apophysis dark brown, umbo grey-brown, flattened with a slight point, surrounded by a dark ring. C Eur., Balk. Penins. (mts). 'Allgau': v. flat in growth; shoots and needles short. 'Aurea': semi-dwarf to 1m; needles turning gold in winter. 'Compacta': dense and globose with ascending shoots. 'Frisia': dense irregular upright, to 2×1.5m. 'Glendale': habit depressed globose; leaders erect. 'Gnom': broad pyramidal semi-dwarf to 2×2m. 'Hesse': low, compact, cushion-forming dwarf; needles slightly tortuous. 'Humpy': v. compact, globose dwarf, slow-growing to 4cm p.a. 'Kissen': dense and flattened to 80×30cm. 'Knappenburg': irregular, broad, dense dwarf; winter buds tinted red. 'Kobold': broadly globose dwarf; br. stiff and thick. 'Kokarde': needles speckled gold; appearing in gold rings from above. 'Mops': broadly upright dwarf to 1.5m, slow-growing, dense. 'Ophir': flattened globose to 60cm, attractively yellow in winter. 'Pal Maleter': needle tips conspicuously yellow in winter. 'Prostrata': prostrate. 'Rigi': narrow-conic. 'Slavinii': broadly dwarf, mat-forming, prostrate with ascending tips; needles dense, tinted blue. 'Trompenburg': broadly globose; needles bright green. 'Variegata': needles stippled yellow. 'Winter Gold': open, wide and low in growth to 1m; needles spreading, tortuous, tinted gold in winter. ssp. *uncinata* (Ramond) Domin. Resembles P. *mugo*, but to 25m. St. usually single and erect. Cones 2.5–6cm. Switz. to W Alps, Cevennes, Pyren. 'Grune Welle': compact globose dwarf; needles bright green, coarse. 'Leuco-Like': upright conical dwarf to 50×35cm after 10 years; needles coarse, ascending, dark green. 'Paradekissen': v. compact, flattened, mat-forming dwarf to 10×3cm after 10 years; needles lat., coarse, dark green. Z3.

P. **muricata** D. Don. BISHOP PINE. To 40m. Crown broad-conic, rounded when mature; bark red-brown, deeply splitting; br. spreading. Needles 2 (–3), 12–15cm×2mm, twisted, green. Cones glossy, not-brown, 4–9×3–7cm, ovoid, scales with a thick, recurved thorn. Calif., N Baja Calif. var. *borealis* Axelrod. Crown slender, conic to old age; lvs tinged blue; cones with more numerous, smaller scales. NW Calif. coast. Z8.

P. *murrayana* Balf. = P. *contorta* ssp. *murrayana*.

P. **nelsonii** G.R. Shaw. Shrub to small tree, to 9m. Br. long, thin, open; bark smooth, grey. Needles to 3, tightly adpressed and appearing single, 4–10cm×1mm, regularly dentate. Cones in pairs, cylindric, 9–14×5cm; scales red-brown, tips red. NE Mex. Z8.

P. **nigra** Arn. BLACK PINE; AUSTRIAN PINE. To 40m+. Crown ovoid-conic, becoming flat topped or rounded, v. dense; bark grey to dark grey-brown, deeply fissured. Needles 2, dark green, stiff, 8–14cm×2mm, straight or bowed, finely toothed.

Cones 5–8×2.5cm, opening to ×5cm, yellow-grey to buff, glossy, umbo dark with a small thorn. SE Eur. 'Aurea': young shoots with gold needles, later green tinted grey. 'Balcanica': irregular, contorted, cushion-forming dwarf. 'Bujotii': dense, globose dwarf; needles dark green, slightly tortuous. 'Columnaris': columnar; br. short; needles long. 'Geant de Suisse': columnar-fastigiate; needles v. long, to 18cm. 'Globosa': semi-dwarf, slow-growing; br. short; needles to 16cm. 'Hornibrookiana': compact, globose, mound-forming dwarf. 'Jeddeloh': dense and compact; twigs and needles short. 'Nana': broadly upright and shrubby to 3m, slow-growing to 5cm p.a. 'Pyramidalis': narrowly conic; br. bowed and ascending; needles tinted blue. 'Strypemonde': vigorous, ascending; needles bright green; witches' broom. 'Variegata': needles stippled gold. 'Wurstle': compactly globose; needles long, vivid green; witches' broom. 'Zlatiborica': needles tinted gold. var. *caramanica* (Loud.) Rehd. TURKISH BLACK PINE. Single trunk. Bark pink-grey to yellow buff on old trees; lvs 8–16cm; cones 5–10cm, yellower. Turk., Cyprus, Greece, S Balk. var. *pallasiana* (Lamb.) Schneid. CRIMEAN PINE. Often 2–3 main trunks in cult. Bark as above var., lvs 12–18cm, cones 6–11cm, buff (not yellower). Crimea. ssp. *monspeliensis* (Salzm. ex Koehne) E. Murray. CEVENNES BLACK PINE. Crown more open, br. regular, level. Lvs 14–18cm, slender, 1–1.5mm, cone with flatter apophyses. S Fr., Pyren., NE Spain. var. *maritima* (Ait.) Melville. CORSICAN PINE. To 55m in wild, 45m in cult. Lvs 12–18cm, slender, 1.5mm. Cone 5–9cm. var. *mauretanica* Maire & Peyerimh. SPANISH BLACK PINE; ALGERIAN BLACK PINE. Lvs 12–18cm, 1.7mm thick, cones 5–7cm. SE Spain, N Alg., N Moroc. Z5.

P. **oaxacana** Mirov. To 30m, crown tall, rounded, bark thick and fissured at base, thin, pale brown in crown. Needles 5, 20–30cm, drooping, pale grey-green. Cones 7–15×6cm, opening to ×10cm, ovoid, dark brown, apophysis thickened, pyramidal, umbo grey. SE Mex. to Hond. Z9.

P. **occidentalis** Sw. To 40m, crown, bark, shoot and buds as for P. *caribea*. Needles 3–5 per fascicle, coarse, 2, 15–23cm. Cones erect, ovoid-conic when mature, 4–8cm, glossy nut-brown; umbo small-thorned. E Cuba, Dominican Rep., Haiti. Z10.

P. **oocarpa** Schiede ex Schldl. Tree to 25m; crown conic to rounded; bark thick, rough, grey, fissured. Needles 5, 20–28cm, coarse, stiff, 1.5–2mm wide, mid-green with indistinct stomatal lines on all faces, serrate. Cones on a long peduncle, ovoid-globular, 5–8×4–6cm, sub-shiny brown or orange-buff, to ×6–9cm. S & W Mex. to N Nic. var. *trifoliata* Martinez. Lvs 3. NW Mex. var. *manzanoi* Martinez. Probably a natural hybrid with P. *patula*; cones conic, lvs 4–5, less stiff. C Mex. Z9.

P. *oocarpa* var. *microphylla* G.R. Shaw = P. *praetermissa*.

P. *oocarpa* var. *ochoterenai* Martinez = P. *patula* ssp. *tecunumannii*.

P. *oocarpoides* Lindl. ex Loud. = P. *oocarpa*.

P. **palustris** Mill. PITCH PINE; LONGLEAF PINE; SOUTHERN YELLOW PINE. To 40m. Crown ovoid-conic; bark red-brown, deeply ridged, exfoliating in thin plates. Needles 3, to 45cm, finely toothed, bright green, falling after 2 years, densely arranged, stomatal lines visible on all surfaces. Cones cylindric to oblong-conic, 15–25cm; fertile scales thin, umbo with a short, reflexed thorn. SE US. Z8.

P. *parryana* Engelm. = P. *quadrifolia*.

P. **parviflora** Sieb. & Zucc. JAPANESE WHITE PINE. To 20m. Crown ovoid-conic in wild, compact, usually irregular and spreading; bark grey-black, smooth, exfoliating in small plates. Needles 5, 3–6cm×1mm, curved, twisted, stiff, finely toothed, exterior surface glossy dark green, stomatal lines blue-white, on 2 interior surfaces. Cones ovoid to cylindric, 4–8, rarely to 10×3cm; scales leathery-woody, rugose, incurved, rust-brown. S & C Jap. (mts). 'Adcock's Dwarf': diminutive and slow-growing, to 75cm, forms a congested bun. 'Blue Giant': vigorous and regular to 15m; br. ascending; needles tinted blue. 'Brevifolia': narrow, upright and sparse; needles dense, short, stiff, tinted blue. 'Fukusumi': asymmetrical dwarf to 75cm; needles curving, conspicuously blue. 'Gimborn's Ideal': slender, upright to 8m; needles tinted blue. 'Gimborn's Pyramid': dense, broadly compact to 3×2m; needles vivid blue in spring. 'Glauca': irregular, sparse pyramidal upright to 12m; usually less, needles blue, coarse and twisted; cones profuse; frequently used for bonsai. 'Glauca Brevifolia': sparse, narrow upright; br. ascending; needles tinted blue; cones profuse. 'Glauca Nana': semi-dwarf, to 1m; needles short, strongly tinted blue. 'Goykukasen': slow-growing; needles vividly tinted bright blue. 'Hagoromo': globose dwarf; needles coarse, bright green. 'Negeshi': slender and regular pyramidal form, dark green. 'Saentis': wide and compact in growth with long needles. 'Saphir': irregular and slow in growth; needles sapphire-blue. 'Schoon's Bonsai': rare dwarf; br. irregular, ascending. 'Tempelhof': vigorous and fast-growing; trunk thick.

'Variegata': needles speckled or bordered light yellow. var. *pentaphylla* (Mayr) Henry. Cones broader. Occurs further N. Z5.

P. parviflora var. *morrisonicola* (Hayata) Wu = *P. morrisonicola*.

P. patula Schiede ex Schldl. & Cham. PATULA PINE; MEXICAN WEEPING PINE. To 45m. Crown open, ovoid, conic or open, branching from base; bark scaly at base, exfoliating, papery above, rust-brown. Needles 3, 15–28cm, pendulous, thin, bright green to yellow-green, serrate, stomatal lines on all sides. Cones 5–10cm, ovoid to conic, umbo indented with a v. small decid. thorn. C & E Mex. ssp. *tecunumanii* (Eguiluz & Perry) Styles. To 55m. Needles 3–4 per fascicle, cones long stalked. SE Mex. to Nic. Z8.

P. patula var. *macrocarpa* Mast. = *P. greggii*.

P. pentaphylla Mayr = *P. parviflora* var. *pentaphylla*.

P. peuce Griseb. MACEDONIAN PINE; BALKAN PINE. To 35m. Crown ovoid-conic; bole often branched from base; bark smooth, grey, thick, deeply ridged. Needles 5, 7–10cm×1mm, pendulous, blue-green, finely serrate, stomatal lines on all sides, more conspicuous on inner face. Cones resinous, pendulous, 7–15×3cm, ×6–7cm, cylindric, pale brown. S Balk., Greece, Albania. 'Aurea': needles soft yellow, brighter in winter. 'Aureovariegata': needles bright yellow on young shoots, later green. 'Glauca Compacta': tight in growth; needles blue. Z5.

P. pinaster Ait. MARITIME PINE. To 35m. Crown ovoid-conic, becoming broad rounded or irregular, bark thick, rust-brown, deeply fissured; br. level to pendulous. Needles 2, stout, 2.5mm broad, yellow- or grey-green, stiff, shiny, finely dentate, stomatal lines on all surfaces. Cones 8–18×4–5cm, opening ×7–11cm, ovoid-conic, red-brown and shiny, umbo dark grey, prominent. Atlantic Eur. to Greece, Medit. 'Aberdoniae': tall with stout, spreading br.; needles rich green. 'Lemoniana': small, to 10m with broad crown; br. spreading. 'Nana': dense, globose, flat-topped dwarf; needles light green. 'Variegata': needles gold, short, to 7cm, interspersed with green needles. Z8.

P. pinceana Gordon. WEEPING PINYON. To 12m, often branched from base. Crown many-branched; bark smooth, grey; shoots hanging, blue-bloomed. Needles 3, 5–10cm, bright or glaucous green, stomatal lines only on inner faces, grey-green. Cones cylindric, 6–9cm, peduncles slender, scales few, large, orange, umbo dark, concave. Mex. Z9.

P. pinea L. STONE PINE; To 25m. Crown domed, umbrella-shaped; mature bark scaly, orange, red to yellow-brown, with deep furrows; br. horizontal, upswept. Needles 2, 12–18cm×2mm, rarely to 28cm, twisted, glossy green, stomatal lines visible on all surfaces. Juvenile foliage blue-grey, single flattened lvs 3–4cm long. Cones ovoid to subglobose, 8–15×6–10cm; fertile scales thick, apophysis rhombic, umbo flat, to dark brown, grey-white. Medit. 'Correoviana': prostrate dwarf. 'Fragilis': seeds thin-shelled; widely cultivated for edible seed in S Europe. Z8.

P. ponderosa Douglas ex Lawson. PONDEROSA PINE; WESTERN YELLOW PINE. To 50m. Bark to thick, yellow-brown, deeply fissured; br. stout, whorled, spreading. Needles 3, spreading, straight or gently curved, 11–22cm×1.5–2mm, dull green with 8–12 stomatal lines on the outer face and 4–5 on the inner faces. Cones green or purple, 6–10×4cm, opening to ×5–8cm, mid to red-brown, sub-shiny. W US & SW Canada. ssp. *washoensis* (Mason & Stockw.) E. Murray. Needles 11–17cm×2mm, stout. Cones small, 5–8cm, with numerous scales purple before ripening. W US. ssp. *scopulorum* (Engelm.) E. Murray. More compact, to 35m. Needles frequently about 2 and 3 per fascicle and shorter, 7–15cm, rarely 20cm×1.5–1.8mm. Cones green ripening buff to brown, 6–9cm. US (Rocky Mts to New Mex.). Z4.

P. ponderosa var. *arizonica* (Engelm.) G.R. Shaw = *P. arizonica*.

P. ponderosa var. *jeffreyi* (Murray) Vasey = *P. jeffreyi*.

P. ponderosa var. *macrophylla* (Engelm.) G.R. Shaw = *P. engelmannii*.

P. praetermissa Styles & McVaugh. Small tree to 20m; crown rounded or irregular in old trees. Shoots flexible, slender. Needles 5, 8–16cm, slender, light green, glossy with indistinct stomatal lines on all faces, finely serrate. Cones on a slender peduncle, ovoid-globose, 4.5–6.5×3.5–4cm, glossy green-tinged buff; scales recurved, inner surface pearly. SW Mex. Z9.

P. pringlei G.R. Shaw. Tree to 25m; crownn conic, becoming rounded; bark scaly, plated on bole, thin in upper crown, dark red-brown to grey. Needles 3, 17–26cm, coarse, stiff, 1.5–2mm wide, yellow-green with indistinct stomatal lines on all faces, serrate. Cones on a strong peduncle, ovoid-conic, 5–9×3–5cm, sub-shiny brown or yellow ochre, to ×5–7cm. S Mex. to N Nic. Z9.

P. pseudostrobus Lindl. SMOOTH-BARK MEXICAN PINE. To 40m.

Crown dense, rounded; br. whorled, bark yellow and smooth, rough, grey and fissured. Needles 5, bright or blue-green, 15–25cm×1mm, flexible, finely dentate. Cones 6–12cm, rarely 16cm, ovoid to oblong-ovoid; apophysis 4-sided, with a small, decid. thorn. SW Mex. to Hond. Z9.

P. pseudostrobus ssp. *apulcensis* (Lindl.) Stead = *P. apulcensis*.

P. pseudostrobus var. *apulcensis* (Lindl.) G.R. Shaw = *P. apulcensis*.

P. pseudostrobus var. *coatepecensis* Martinez = *P. apulcensis*.

P. pseudostrobus var. *estevezii* Martinez = *P. apulcensis*.

P. pumila (Pall.) Reg. DWARF SIBERIAN PINE. Prostrate shrub, to 3m, or small tree to 6m. Needles 5, 4–8cm×1mm, twisted densely arranged, glossy, green outer face, blue-white stomatal lines visible on interior surfaces, finely toothed or entire. Cones clustered, ovoid, 3–6×3cm, violet-black when young, red to yellow-brown when mature; scales 15–20mm wide, umbo triangular, spreading. NE Asia. 'Blue Dwarf': irregular in growth, br. vigorously ascending; needles tortuous, tinted blue. 'Chlorocarpa': cones yellow-green. 'Draijer's Dwarf': flat-growing, compact; needles tinted light silver. 'Glauca' ('Dwarf Blue'): variable, broad, bushy, slow-growing; needles light grey-blue. 'Globe': v. dense globose form to 2×2m; needles tinted silver. 'Jeddeloh': vigorous, broadly horizontal, centre depressed. 'Jermyns': compact, conic, slow-growing dwarf. 'Nana': dense and globose semi-dwarf to 3×3m; ♂ fls claret; needles tortuous, bright grey-green. 'Saentis': upright and ascending. Z1.

P. pungens Lamb. TABLE MOUNTAIN PINE; HICKORY PINE. To 15m. Crown rounded, broad; bark dark brown, exfoliating in irregular sheets. Needles 2 or 3, 4–8cm×2mm, stiff, twisted, yellow-green, smelling of lemon when crushed. Cones ovoid, 5–9×4–6cm, open ×6–8cm, pink to pale brown, mostly long persistent; scales 15mm wide, with a stout, sharp thorn. E US. Z6.

P. quadrifolia Parl. ex Sudw. PARRY'S PINYON. Small tree to 15m; crown rounded. Needles 5, 4 or 3, 2–4cm×1mm, slightly curved forwards, outer surface glossy green without stomata, or in hybrids, duller with some stomata, inner surfaces with dense white stomatal bands. Cones subglobose, 3.5–5cm, opening to ×5.5–7cm, red-brown. S Calif., N Baja Calif., hybridizing with *P. californiarum* in most of range. Z8.

P. radiata D. Don. MONTEREY PINE. To 45m. Crown ovoid-conic, becoming rounded, dense; young bark purple-grey, becoming grey to dark brown, deeply fissured. Needles 3, 10–16cm×1mm, bright green, stomatal lines obscure; cones 6×4cm to 16×11cm, sometimes 16×6cm, glossy yellow-brown, becoming grey, scales thick, swollen, umbel with a tiny decid. thorn. US (Calif.). 'Aurea': needles vivid gold when young. 'Isca': regular, globose; needles deep green. var. *binata* (Engelm.) Lemmon. Needles to 13cm×2mm, 2 occas. 3; cones metric, 6–9cm. Guadelupe I., Baja Calif. var. *cedrosensis* (Howell) Silba. Needles 2 per fascicle; cones 5–7cm. Cedros I., Baja Calif. Z8.

P. ×reflexa (Engelm.) Engelm. (*P. flexilis × P. strobiformis*.) Natural hybrid intermediate between parents; v. variable. SW US. Z7.

P. remorata Mason = *P. muricata*.

P. remota (Little) D. Bail. & Hawksw. PAPER-SHELL PINYON. Small tree or shrub to 7m; crown irregular. Needles 2, occas. 3, 3–5.5cm×1.5mm, both surfaces with stomata, grey-green. Cones subglobose, 2–4×2–3.5cm, opening to ×3–6cm, glossy yellow. US (W Tex.), NE Mex. Z8.

P. resinosa Ait. RED PINE. To 35m, br. horizontal, ascending at tips, bark thick, fissured, rust-brown. Needles 2, 10–17cm×1mm, brittle, densely covering twigs, twisted, bright olive green, sharp-acuminate. Cones 3–6×2–5cm, open ×3.5–5cm, ovoid-conic, nut-brown, umbo obtuse, darker brown. E N Amer. 'Globosa': dense, globose dwarf; shoots pale yellow. Z3.

P. ×rhaetica Brügger. (*P. mugo × P. sylvestris*.) To 20m. Bark brown suffused grey. Needles 3–5cm, dark green suffused, grey acute. Cones 3–4cm, ovoid, short-stalked, yellow-brown when mature, umbo pointed. Gdn origin; also sometimes found wild in C Eur. Z4.

P. rigida Mill. PITCH PINE; NORTHERN PITCH PINE. Tree to 25m. Crown irregular, rounded, open, bark dark grey or red-brown, deeply furrowed, br. level. Needles 3, yellow to pale green, stout, twisted, becoming dark grey-green, 7–10×2–2.5mm, occas. to 14cm, stomatal lines visible on both sides. Cones grouped, ovoid-conic, 4–7×3–4cm, pale brown, opening ×5–6cm when mature, umbo, thorn slender, sharp. NE US, extreme SE Canada. Z4.

P. rigida ssp. *serotina* (Michx.) Clausen = *P. serotina*.

P. rigida var. *serotina* (Michx.) Loud. ex Hoopes = *P. serotina*.

P. roxburghii Sarg. CHIR PINE; LONG LEAVED INDIAN PINE. To 50m. Crown broad when mature; bark grey to rust-brown, fissured, exfoliating in broad, scaly plates. Needles 3,

20–40cm×1mm, pale to yellow-green, pendulous, flexible, finely serrate, stomatal lines indistinct, on all faces. Cones ovoid-conic, 9–24×6–8cm, umbo thickened, reflexed. Himal. (Afghan. to Bhutan). Z9.

P. rudis Endl. ENDLICHER'S PINE. Tree to 24m. Crown high, rounded, umbrella-shaped; bark dark grey, rough, deeply fissured. Needles 5, rarely 4 or 6, 10–30cm×2mm, radiating like a chimney sweep's brush, blue-green to grey-green. Cones long-ovoid, 6–12cm, apex tapered, dark brown, peduncle to 1cm, umbo thorn recurved. C & N Mex. (mts). Most plants cultivated in GB as *P. montezumae* are in fact a long-foliaged form of this sp. Z8.

P. russelliana Lindl. = *P. montezumae.*

P. rzedowskii Madrigal & Caball. To 30m. Crown open, irregular; bark grey, wrinkled, fissured. Needles 3–4, flexible, 6–10cm×1mm, stomatal lines 0 on exterior, dense on glaucous inner face. Cone bright rust-brown, oblong-cylindric, pendulous 10–15×6–8cm. Mex. Z10.

P. sabiniana Douglas ex D. Don. DIGGER PINE. To 25m. Crown open, rounded; bark deeply furrowed, brown suffused grey, exfoliating in irregular scales, red-brown below, br. undulate, irregular. Needles 3, outspread or pendulous, 18–30cm×1–2mm, glaucous, pale grey-green, finely serrate, stomatal lines on all surfaces. Cones 12–25×9cm, ovoid, nut-brown, pendulous; scales to 5cm, umbo 1–3cm, sharp, deflexed or S-shaped. W US. Z8.

P. × schwerinii Fitschen. (*P. wallichiana* ×*P. strobus.*) As for *P. wallichiana*, but crown wider. To 25m or more. Needles 5, thin, pendulous, 8–14cm. Cones grouped, 10–20×4cm, cylindric, resinous, peduncle to 2.5cm. Gdn origin. Z6.

P. scopulorum Lemmon = *P. ponderosa* ssp. *scopulorum.*

P. serotina Michx. POND PINE. Tree to 30m. Bark furrowed, scaly, often with epicormic growths; buds v. resinous. Needles 3 per fascicle, yellow-green, to 20cm. Cones buff-yellow, sub-globose, variable, 6×5–9×7cm. SE US. Z8.

P. sibirica Du Tour = *P. cembra* ssp. *sibirica.*

P. sinensis Lamb. = *P. massoniana.*

P. sinensis auct. non Lamb. = *P. tabulaeformis.*

P. sinensis var. *yunnanensis* G.R. Shaw = *P. yunnanensis.*

P. × sondereggeri Chapm. (*P. palustris* ×*P. taeda.*) Natural hybrid. Bark rust-brown; young shoots beige; buds conic. Needles 3, sharp-acuminate. SE US. Z8.

P. strobiformis Engelm. SOUTHWESTERN WHITE PINE. To 35m. Crown ovoid-conic, becoming rounded. Bark grey-white, smooth when young, dark brown, furrowed. Needles 5, dark blue-green, 8–14cm, stomatal lines visible on inner surfaces, finely serrated. Cones pendulous, cylindric, 18–35cm, yellow-brown to red-brown; scales thick, umbo thornless. NW Mex. var. *carvajalii* Silba. Cones 25–50cm. SW Mex. Z8.

P. strobiformis Sudw. non Engelm. = *P. × reflexa.*

P. strobus L. WEYMOUTH PINE; EASTERN WHITE PINE. To 50m. Crown broad-conic; bark grey-green to brown, fissured; br. horizontal. Needles 5, blue-green, 7–13cm, obtuse, serrate, stomatal lines on inner faces only. Cones pink-brown, in groups, pendulous, narrow-cylindric, 8–16×2cm, peduncles to 2.5cm, umbo obtuse. SE Canada to Allegheny Mts, E US. Over 30 cvs, of the dwarfs, notable selections include the blue-tinted 'Billaw', 'Blue Shag' and 'Pumila' and the Nana group ('Nana', 'Pygmaea', 'Radiata', 'Umbraculifera') with light green needles; several dwarfs such as 'Macopin' and 'Sea Urchin' are developed from witches' brooms; larger globose forms include 'Oliver Dwarf' and 'Unconn'; upright pyramidal cvs include the tortuous 'Fastigiata' and the gold-needled 'Hillside Winter Gold'; weeping cvs include 'Inversa' and 'Pendula'; 'Alba' has pure white new growth. Z3.

P. strobus var. *chiapensis* Martinez = *P. chiapensis.*

P. subpatula Royle = *P. patula.*

P. sylvestris L. SCOTS PINE. To 30m, rarely 40m. Crown ovoid-conic, becoming rounded. Bark thin, red-brown, exfoliating to show rust-brown beneath, thick and fissuring at base with purple ridges. Needles 2, 4–6cm×2mm, rarely to 10cm, twisted, blue to pale grey-green, finely serrate, stomatal lines on both sides. Cones ovoid-conic, 3–7×2–4cm, buff grey-brown; umbo with a v. small thorn or thornless, shiny. Sib. to E Asia, Eur. Many cvs, differentiated by growth and needle habit; notable dwarfs include the blue-tinted 'Beuvronensis', 'Glauca Nana', and 'Compressa', and the vivid blue 'Doone Valley' and the 3m 'Watereri'. 'Globosa Viridis' and the yellow-needled 'Moseri' are attractive pyramidal dwarf forms; prostrate, creeping dwarfs include the blue-tinted 'Hillside Creeper' and 'Albyns' and the v. dark green of 'Repens' and 'Saxatilis'; 'Lodge Hill' and 'Oppdal' are irregular dwarfs derived from witches' brooms; 'Gold Coin' and 'Gold Medal' are richly gold in winter; notable cvs of normal growth include the pyramidal 'Fastigiata', 'Pyramidalis Glauca' and the vivid blue of 'Mt. Vernon Blue'; weeping forms include 'Mitsch Weeping' and 'Pendula'. Silver

tinted cvs include 'Argentea Compacta' and 'Alba', the gold-tinted 'Aurea', 'Beissneriana' and 'Nisbet's Gem', the soft white 'Nivea' and the stippled white 'Variegata'. var. *hamata* Steven. Remains blue-green even in cold winters. SE Eur., Turk., Crimea, Cauc. Z2. var. *lapponica* Fries ex Hartmann. Lvs shorter, 2.5–4.5cm, dark green; cones smaller, 2.5–5cm. N Scand., N Sib. Z1. var. *mongolica* Litvi. Shoots smooth, grey-green, lvs to 9cm. NE Mong., NE China, SC Sib. Z2.

P. tabulaeformis Carr. CHINESE RED PINE. Tree to 25m+, crown ovoid-conic, becoming irregular and flat-topped. Bark fissured, dark grey at base, red, scaly and thin in upper crown. Needles 2, 9–15cm, mid-green, 1.3mm thick, indistinct lines of stomata on both sides. Cones ovoid-conic, 3.5–7×3cm opening to ×4–7cm, matt buff; umbo with a small spine. N & NW China. var. *mukdensis* (Uyeki ex Nak.) Uyeki. Cones with broader scales, to 20mm, with unusual stiff card-like texture; umbo larger with a forward-pointing spine. S Manch., N Korea. Z5.

P. tabulaeformis hort. non Carr. = *P. densata.*

P. tabulaeformis var. *densata* (Mast.) Rehd. = *P. densata.*

P. tabulaeformis var. *yunnanensis* (Franch., hort. = *P. yunnanensis.*

P. taeda L. LOBLOLLY PINE. To 40m, trunk to 1m diam. Crown domed, br. spreading; bark v. dark brown, scaly when young, becoming grey to red-brown, furrowed when mature. Needles 3, occas. 2, pale green, twisted, 15–25cm×1–2mm, finely dentate, stomatal lines on all sides. Cones in groups, ovoid-conic, 6–14cm, buff rust-brown, umbo a stout recurved thorn. SE US. Z7.

P. taeda var. *heterophylla* Elliott = *P. elliottii.*

P. taiwanensis Hayata TAIWAN PINE. Tree to 35m, allied to *P. densiflora*; crown conic, flatter in old trees; bark fissured and scaly. Needles 2, 8–12cm, slender, mid-green. Cones 4.5–7×2–3cm, to ×4–6cm open, orange-brown, scales numerous, small, with a minute mucro. Taiwan (mts). Z8.

P. tecunumanii Eguiluz & Perry = *P. patula* ssp. *tecunumanii.*

P. tenuifolia Benth. non Salisb. = *P. maximinoi.*

P. teocote Schiede ex Schldl. & Cham. TWISTED LEAF PINE. To 30m. Bark thick, furrowed, in plates to thin, scaly, red-orange to brown. Needles 3, occas. 2–5, spreading, stiff, 10–15cm×1.5mm, dark green, sharp-acuminate, finely dentate, stomatal lines on all sides. cones 4–6cm, rarely to 9cm, oblong-ovoid, buff-brown to chestnut-brown. Mex. (mts). Z8.

P. thunbergii Parl. JAPANESE BLACK PINE. To 30m. Crown open, with few, long, level or sinuous br.; bark black-grey, furrowed. Needles 2, 7–14cm×2mm, densely arranged, spreading, twisted, dark green, stomatal lines on all surfaces. Cones solitary or in clusters, 3–7×3cm, ovoid-conic, scales large and few, apophysis pink-buff, rhombic, umbo with a small spine. Coastal Jap., S Korea. 'Kotobuki': small and pyramidal in growth, needles short, bright green. 'Majestic Beauty': dense and compact; resistant to salt and smog damage. 'Mt Hood Prostrate': low-growing to 2.5×4m; needles v. dark green. 'Pygmaea': compact dwarf to 1.5m; needles long, rich green 'Shioguro': compact and globose; needles long, bright green. Z6.

P. torreyana Parry ex Carr. SOLEDAD PINE. To 35m, trunk to 60cm diam. Crown conic, becoming domed; bark deeply fissured, in large scales, brown suffused grey. Needles 5 per fascicle, v. stout, densely arranged, 20–32cm×2mm, dark green, stomatal lines on all surfaces. Cones 10–15cm, ovoid, shiny, nut-brown, umbo short, occas. incurved. SW US. Z8.

P. tropicalis Morelet. Tree to 30m, crown ovoid-conic. Needles 2, 20–30cm, stiff, erect, bright green, with numerous v. large resin ducts. Cones 5–8cm, similar to *P. yunnanensis*, rufous-brown, umbo with a minute mucro. W Cuba, Isle of Pines. Z10.

P. tuberculata D. Don = *P. radiata.*

P. tuberculata Gordon non D. Don. = *P. attenuata.*

P. uncinata Ramond ex DC. = *P. mugo.*

P. uyematsui Hayata = *P. morrisonicola.*

P. veitchii Roezl. Differs from *P. strobiformis* in cones 22–45×6–7cm opening to ×10–13cm, scales woody, 3–4cm wide with long recurved or S-shaped apophysis. C Mex. Z8.

P. virginiana Mill. SCRUB PINE; VIRGINIA PINE. Tree to 15m or shrub, trunk to 50cm diam. Bark thin, furrowed; br. irregular, spreading, often twisted. Needles 2, 4–7cm, yellow-green to dark green, twisted, stiff, sharp, finely serrated. Cones oblong-conic, 3–7cm, spreading to pendulous, yellow-buff to rust-brown, apiphysis diamond-shaped, umbo with a short thorn. E US. Z6.

P. wallichiana A.B. Jackson. HIMALAYAN PINE; BLUE PINE; BHUTAN PINE. To 50m. Crown conic, or irregular. Bark grey-brown, becoming fissured; upper br. whorled, ascending. Needles 5, hanging, flexible, grey-green to waxy blue, to 20cm×1mm, stomatal lines on inner faces only. Cones long-stalked, erect, becoming pendulous, cylindric, 14–28×4cm, opening to ×10cm, green, ripening buff or yellow-brown, scales keeled. Himal. 'Densa': dense and conic; needles short.

'Glauca': needles conspicuously blue. 'Nana': globose dwarf with attractive long, pendulous silver needles. 'Silverstar': slow growing, globose to conic; needles notably blue, short. 'Umbraculifera': low-growing, mushroom-headed dwarf; needles pendulous, light green. 'Vernisson': br. ascending; needles long; hardy to zone 7. 'Zebrina': vigorous conic upright; br. ascending; needles variegated yellow. Z8.

P. wangii Hu & Cheng.   Tree to 30m, closely related to *P. parviflora*; bark smooth grey, becoming dark brown, hard and cracked into square plates. Needles 3–7cm×1mm, rigid, curved glossy dark green on outer face, blue-white stomatal bands on inner faces. Cones pedunculate, on 0.5–2.5cm, scales few, rugose red-brown becoming grey-brown. S China. Z8.

P. wilsonii G.R. Shaw = *P. densata*.

P. wrightii Engelm. = *P. occidentalis*.

P. yunnanensis Franch.   To 35m. Crown conic, becoming flat; bark thin, red-brown, exfoliating on upper trunk. Needles bright to dark green, 3, occas. 2; 15–30cm×1mm, pendulous. Cones 5–11cm, orange to yellow-brown, glossy, becoming dark brown; umbo raised, with a small spine. SW China. Z8.

Pinwheel *Aeonium haworthii*.
Pinwheel Flower *Tabernaemontana divaricata*.
Pinyon Pine *Pinus cembroides*.

Piper L. PEPPER. Piperaceae.   1000+ erect shrubs, woody climbers, trees, or herbs, often with pungent odour; st. swollen at nodes. Lvs entire, base often unequal. Spike cylindric, long-stalked, rarely compound; fls small, cream to green; perianth wanting. Fr. a small drupe usually green ripening through red. Pantrop. Z10.

P. angustifolium Lam.   Small shrub; twigs slender, pubesc. Lvs 9×2cm, narrowly lanceolate, glossy, glandular-punctate beneath. Spikes small. Fr. Guiana.

P. auritum HBK.   Tree, 4.5m, rather aromatic. Lvs 25×16cm, ovate to elliptic-ovate, acuminate at apex, cordate at base; thinly pubesc. above, densely so beneath; petiole winged. Spikes 18cm. Mex.

P. betle L. BETEL; BETLE PEPPER; PAN.   Climber to 5m, producing adventitious roots. Lvs 13.5×7.5cm, broadly ovate to cordate, acute to acuminate at apex, rounded to cordate at base, glab., coriaceous. Infl. to 15cm. Fr. embedded and coalescing into a fleshy red mass. Indian to Malay Penins.

P. bicolor Yunck. = *P. magnificum*.

P. borneense N.E. Br.   Herb, 22–30cm; st. stout, pilose. Lvs elliptic to elliptic-oblong, acute at apex, auriculate-cordate at base, large, deep green above with broad, pale silver-grey stripes, rugose, pubesc. beneath. Spikes 7cm. Borneo.

P. celtidifolium Desf. = *P. unguiculatum*.

P. cubeba L. f. CUBEB; CUBEB PEPPER.   Climber to 3m. Lvs 14×6cm, elliptic to lanceolate, acute to acuminate at apex, broadly tapered or somewhat cordate at base, paler beneath, smooth. Spike to 9cm, erect becoming pendulous. Fr. loosely arranged, red-brown. Indon.

P. decurrens DC.   Shrub, st. stout, pale green with white spots and black lines. Lvs 12×4.5cm, lanceolate, cuneate to acute at base, slightly decurrent on petiole, green with metallic iridescence. Costa Rica to Colomb.

P. elongatum Poir. = *Peperomia elongata*.

P. emarginellum Sw. ex Wikstr. = *Peperomia emarginella*.

P. futokadsura Sieb. = *P. kadzura*.

P. guineense Schum. & Thonn. GUINEA CUBEB; ASHANTI PEPPER; BENIN PEPPER.   Vine to 23m. Lvs to 10×7cm, suborbicular to oval or lanceolate, acuminate at apex, cordate or rounded at base. Fruiting spikes 7cm, tomentose; fr. red, dry. Trop. Afr. (Guinea to Uganda and Angola).

P. kadzura (Choisy) Ohwi. JAPANESE PEPPER.   Scandent shrub, with aerial roots. Lvs 6.5×3.5cm, ovate, or rounded-cordate, long-acuminate at apex, rounded at base, dark green, paler beneath, thick, sparsely pubesc. Spikes 3–8cm. Fr. red. Jap., S Korea, Ryukyus.

P. longum L.   Slender climber, 3m; st. angled or fluted, rather hairy. Lvs 7.5×4cm, broadly lanceolate to lanceolate-elliptic, acute to obtuse at apex, deeply auriculate at base, green above, paler beneath, densely glandular-punctate. Infl. erect to 6cm. Trop. E Himal.

P. macrophyllum HBK.   Large shrub, st. striate, br. erect. Lvs oblong, large, obtusely acuminate at apex, oblique at base, glab. Spikes erect, long. E Indies.

P. maculosum L. = *Peperomia maculosa*.

P. magnificum Trel. LACQUERED PEPPER.   Shrub, erect, to 1m; st. winged. Lvs 15×11.5cm, ovate to broadly elliptic or suborbicular, rounded or broadly acute at apex, cordate to auriculate at base, glossy deep green, bright maroon beneath with white margin and veins, quilted; petiole broadly winged.

Peru.

P. magnoliifolium Jacq. = *Peperomia magnoliifolia*.

P. metallicum Hallier f.   Scandent herb; st. red when young with adventitious roots. Lvs to 15×11cm, ovate, apex acuminate and mucronate, tinged red when young, metallic deep green when mature, tinted red with silvery sheen beneath, thick; veins reticulate, dark red. Borneo.

P. methysticum Forst. KAVA; KAVA-KAVA.   Shrub, erect, to 4m. Lvs 17×13cm, cordate to suborbicular, rounded, or broadly acute at apex, deeply auriculate at base, deep green above, paler beneath, smooth, minutely granular-pubesc. above, pubesc. beneath; petiole broadly winged. S Pacific.

P. nigrum L. COMMON PEPPER; PEPPER PLANT; BLACK PEPPER; WHITE PEPPER; MADAGASCAR PEPPER.   Climber to 4m. Lvs 9×6cm, broadly ovate to cordate, broadly tapered, rounded or weakly cordate at base, often shortly acuminate at apex, glab. Spikes to 7.5cm. Fr. dark red when ripe. S India & Sri Lanka, nat. N Burm. and Assam.

P. officinarum DC.   Lvs oblong-elliptic, attenuate to acuminate apex, tapered to cordate base, coriaceous; veins rather prominent beneath. Infl. cylindric, densely fld. Fr. coalescing. India, Malaysia.

P. ornatum N.E. Br. CELEBES PEPPER.   Shrub, spreading, creeping or weakly climbing, to 5m; st. wiry, glab. Lvs 9.5×7.5cm, broadly cordate to suborbicular, peltate, rounded or acute and attenuate at apex, rounded to cordate at base, finely mottled dark green, pink and silver above, flushed maroon beneath. Sulawesi. Sometimes erroneously offered as *P. crocatum*.

P. porphyrophyllum (Lindl.) N.E. Br.   Shrub spreading, creeping or weakly climbing, to 8m; st. wiry, often with lines of hairs. Lvs 12.5×10.5cm, broadly cordate to suborbicular, shortly mucronate at apex, cordate to auriculate at base, thin, dark green above with red and white spots, flushed purple beneath. Malay Penins., Borneo.

P. rubronodosum Nichols.   Shrub; st. fleshy, scabrous, red at nodes. Lvs deep sea green frosted with silver-grey, eesp. when young; petioles tomentose. Colomb.

P. rubrovenosum hort. ex Rodigas.   Woody vine. Lvs obliquely elliptic to cordate, acute to acuminate at apex, entire, bright deep green above, paler beneath, coriaceous; veins marked by irregular rose lines above. New Guinea.

P. sylvaticum Roxb. MOUNTAIN LONG PEPPER.   Climber to 4m. Lvs 9×5cm, ovate to cordate, acute to acuminate at apex, broadly tapered, rounded or cordate at base, dark green above, paler beneath, rough, glandular-pubesc. on veins beneath. Spikes long. Fr. densely arranged, individuals distinct. Subtrop. E Himal.

P. trinerve Vahl. = *Peperomia trinervis*.

P. unguiculatum Ruiz & Pav.   Shrub, 3m+. Lvs 7×2.5cm, lanceolate-oblong to oblong-ovate, acuminate at apex, rounded at base, glab. or minutely pubesc. above. Spikes to 7cm; fr., minutely velvety-pubesc. Peru.

→*Artanthe*.

PIPERACEAE Agardh. 14/1940. *Macropiper, Peperomia, Piper*.

Pipewort *Eriocaulon aquaticum*.
Pipsissewa *Chimaphila*.

Piptadenia Benth.
P. macrocarpa Benth. = *Anadenanthera colubrina* var. *cebil*.

Piptanthus D. Don ex Sweet. Leguminosae (Papilionoideae).   2 everg. shrubs or small trees to 4m. Sts dark green to grey, hollow. Lvs trifoliolate; lfts to 15cm, lanceolate to ovate, dark green. Fls yellow, in axill. or term. rac. to 15cm; cal. 5-lobed, villous; standard to 2.5cm broad, emarginate, wings and keel auriculate. Himal.

P. bicolor Craib = *P. nepalensis*.

P. concolor Craib = *P. nepalensis*.

P. forrestii Craib = *P. nepalensis*.

P. laburnifolius (D. Don) Stapf = *P. nepalensis*.

P. leiocarpus Stapf = *P. nepalensis*.

P. nepalensis (Hook.) D. Don ex Sweet.   Lfts subglabrous to puberulent beneath. Fls bright yellow, standard occas. with purplebrown or with grey marking. Summer. Himal. Z8.

P. tomentosus Franch.   Lfts thickly silky-tomentose eesp. beneath. Fls lemon-yellow. Spring–summer. SW China. Z8.

→*Baptisia*.

Piptatherum Palib.
P. multiflorum (Cav.) Palib. = *Oryzopsis miliacea*.

Piqueria Cav. Compositae.   7 erect, ann. to perenn. herbs or subshrubs. Lvs opposite. Cap. discoid, small, few in compound, loose pan.; flts white to pale yellow, occas. tinged lavender.

Trop. Amer. Z10.
P. latifolia DC. = *Phalacraea latifolia*.
P. trinervia Cav. Bushy perenn. herb, to 1m. Lvs to 7cm, narrowly ovate to lanceolate, base rounded to cuneate, serrate. Autumn–winter. Mex., C Amer., Haiti.
→*Stevia*.

Piquetia N.E. Br.
P. pillansii (Kensit) N.E. Br. = *Kensitia pillansii*.

Piriadacus Pichon.
P. hibiscifolius (Cham.) Pichon = *Arrabidaea corallina*.

Pirigara Aubl.
P. speciosa Kunth = *Gustavia speciosa*.
P. superba Kunth = *Gustavia superba*.

Piririma *Syagrus cocoides*.
Pirri-pirri Bur *Acaena novae-zelandiae*.

Pisaura Bonato = *Lopezia*.

Piscidia L. JAMAICA DOGWOOD. Leguminosae (Papilionoideae). 8 trees. Lvs imparipinnate. Fls pea-like in congested lat. pan. C Amer. to W Indies and Flor. Z10.
P. erythrina L. = *P. piscipula*.
P. piscipula (L.) Sarg. JAMAICA DOGWOOD; WEST INDIAN DOGWOOD; FISH FUDDLE. To 15m. Lvs to 25cm; lfts to 10cm, elliptic-ovate, undulate or weakly dentate. Fls to 1.5cm, blue-purple to white striped red. Fr. to 7cm, wings lobed and crispate. S Flor., W Indies.
→*Icthyomethia*.

Pisonia L. Nyctaginaceae. 35 trees and shrubs, climbing or erect. Fls in pan. or cymes: ♂ funnel-shaped, lobes short, spreading, deltoid, sta. to 40, exserted; ♀ with longer and narrower perianth tube, swollen at base, sta. rudimentary. Trop., mainly Amer. Z10.
P. umbellifera (Forst. & Forst. f.) Seem. BIRD-CATCHER TREE; PARA-PARA. Tree to 18m+. Lvs to 40cm, oblong. Fls to 8cm, pink or yellow; sta. 6–14. Maur., Aus., NZ. 'Variegata': lvs marbled pale green, margins creamy white, flushed pink eesp. when young.
P. zapallo Griseb. Lvs to 12.5cm, broadly elliptic. Fls in small clusters; sta. 5. Arg.

Pissaba Palm *Attalea funifera*.
Pistachio *Pistacia*; *P. vera*.

Pistacia L. PISTACHIO. Anacardiaceae. 9 dioecious trees and shrubs. Lvs pinnate, rarely simple or trifoliate. Fls small, apetalous in pan. or rac. Fr. a single-seeded drupe. Medit., C Asia to Jap., Malesia, Mex., S US. Z9 unless specified.
P. atlantica Desf. BETOUM; MOUNT ATLAS MASTIC. Tree to 20m. Lfts 7–11, to 6cm, lanceolate, obtuse not mucronate; rachis winged. Fr. obovoid, to 8mm. N Afr. var. *latifolia* DC. Tree to 15m. Lvs larger; lfts 6–8, occas. 9, lanceolate or oblong to broadly ovate. E Medit.
P. chinensis Bunge. Tree to 15m, occas. taller. Lvs decid., lfts 10–20, about 8cm, glossy, colouring in fall, lanceolate, acute or acuminate, mucronate to cuspidate. Fr. scarlet to purple-blue, thinly fleshy. China, Taiwan, Philipp. ssp. *integerrima* (Stewart) Rech. f. Lvs 15–25cm; lfts broadly lanceolate to oblong, to 10cm. Afghan. to Kashmir. Z8.
P. formosana Matsum. = *P. chinensis*.
P. lentiscus L. (sensu lato). MASTIC; LENTISCO; CHIOS MASTIC. Tree or shrub to 4m, everg. Lvs coriaceous; lfts 4–6, rarely more, 15–45mm, ovate, oblong-lanceolate or elliptic, obtuse to mucronate. Fr. red becoming black, globose, 4–5mm. Medit. except NE Afr.
P. mexicana HBK. COPALL. Tree to 6m. Br. angular, pubesc. at first. Lvs to 15cm; lfts 16–36, 10–26mm, thin, often alt., oblong, mucronate, occas. revolute. Fr. sessile, globose, 4–6mm, red to black. Mex., Guat.
P. narbonensis L. = *P. vera*.
P. reticulata Willd. = *P. vera*.
P. terebinthus L. CYPRUS TURPENTINE; TEREBINTE; TEREBINTHO. Tree or shrub, 2–6m, decid. Lvs glossy, aruomatic, 10–20cm; lfts 6–12, 3–5cm, ovate-lanceolate, to oblong, mucronate, glab. Fr. obovoid, to 7mm, purple, wrinkled. Iberia to Turk., Moroc. to Egypt. var. *macrocarpa* Zoh. Fr. 7–9mm, more fleshy. var. *oxycarpa* Zoh. Fr. larger (8×6mm).
P. texana Swingle. AMERICAN PISTACHIO; LENTISCO. Tree branching from base. Lvs to 10cm; lfts 9–17, oblong, mucronate, membranous 10–22mm. Fr. dark brown, lenticular, 5–6mm broad. S US, Mex.

P. vera L. PISTACHIO; GREEN ALMOND; FUSTUQ. Tree to 1m, decid. Lvs 10–20cm, coriaceous; lfts 3 or 5, 5–12cm, broadly lanceolate to ovate, shining above, dull beneath. Fr. long-stalked, oblong-linear to ovate, often red. W Asia.

Pistia L. WATER LETTUCE; SHELL FLOWER. Araceae. 1 everg. aquatic herb. Roots fine, feathery, spreading from undersides of rosettes. Lvs to 20×7cm, in floating rosettes, broadly wedge-shaped, fluted above, 7–15-ribbed below, spongy toward base, with fine water-repellent hairs, blue-green above, pearly beneath. Pantrop., now a widespread weed of rivers and lakes, first recorded on the Nile, possibly having originated from Lake Victoria. Z10.
P. stratiotes L.

Pistol Plant *Pilea microphylla*.

Pisum L. PEA. Leguminosae (Papilionoideae). 5 ann. herbs, often climbing by branched tendrils. Stipules leafy, oblong-orbicular; lfts 1–3 pairs, oval. Fls papilionaceous, solitary or 2–3. Fr. a flattened to cylindric, inflated, oblong-linear legume; seeds subglobose. Medit., W Asia. For edible cvs, see PEAS in *New RHS Dictionary of Gardening*.
P. arvense L. = *P. sativum* var. *arvense*.
P. elatius Bieb. = *P. sativum* ssp. *elatius*.
P. graecum Quézel & Contandr. = *Lathyrus grandiflorus*.
P. sativum L. GARDEN PEA. Glaucous ann. to 2m. Stipules to 10×6cm, dentate, semi-amplexicaul at base; lfts to 7×4cm, 1–4 pairs, suborbicular to oblong, entire or dentate. Fls 1–3, to 3cm; standard white sometimes suffused lilac, broad, wings white, sometimes stained dark red-purple. Fr. to 15×3cm, oblong-linear or linear; seeds 3–10, 5mm+ diam. S Eur. var. *arvense* (L.) Poir. FIELD PEA; DUN PEA; GREY PEA; MUTTER PEA; PARTRIDGE PEA; PELUSKINS. Stipules spotted red. Seeds to 8mm, frequently angled and blotched. var. *macrocarpon* Ser. EDIBLE-PODDED PEA; MANGE TOUT; SUGAR PEA; SNOW PEA. Pod edible, flat, broad. ssp. *elatius* (Bieb.) Asch. & Gräbn. Lfts 2–4 pairs, ovate-elliptic, entire or subdentate. Fr. to 7×1.2cm; seeds papillose.

Pitanga *Eugenia pitanga*.

Pitcairnia L'Hérit. Bromeliaceae. 260 terrestrial perenn. herbs, occas. epiphytic. Lvs stalked or sessile in a basal tuft or rosette, sheath small, sometimes thickened and bulbous, blade linear to broadly lanceolate, toothed or entire, scapose term. Infl. bracteate, simple or compound; fls showy, ephemeral; sep. free and rolled; pet. free, long and narrow. C & S Amer., W Afr. Z9.
P. andreana Lind. To 20cm. Lvs to 35cm, linear-lanceolate, petiolate, acute, densely white-scaly beneath, sparsely so above. Infl. laxly branched; bracts narrowly ovate; pet. orange, yellow near apex. Colomb.
P. cernua Kunth & Bouché = *P. heterophylla* var. *exscapa*.
P. ×darblayana André. (*P. corallina* ×*P. paniculata*.) Large, vigorous. Lvs to 1.7m, petiolate, entire, base and apex acute. Infl. lax; bracts oval; sep. brick-red; pet. red. Gdn origin.
P. exscapa Hook. = *P. heterophylla* var. *exscapa*.
P. flavescens Bak. = *P. xanthocalyx*.
P. funckiana A. Dietr. = *P. maidifolia*.
P. heterophylla (Lindl.) Beer. 10–20cm.Lf bases, dark brown, bulb-like; lvs to 70cm, green, linear, attenuate and filiform, glab. sometimes reduced to brown spines. Infl subspicate or compound; bracts ovate; pet. pink-red. Mex. to Venez. and Peru. var. *exscapa* Mez. Lvs homomorphic. Pet. red Guat., Colomb.
P. lepidota Reg. = *P. andreana*.
P. macrocalyx Hook. = *P. maidifolia*.
P. maidifolia (Morr.) Decne. To 1.3m. Lvs in a loose rosette; petiole to 20cm; blades lanceolate, 50–100cm scurfy then bright green. Infl. simple, one-sided; bracts broadly ovate, green or yellow, often tinged red; pet. white or white-green. Late spring. Hond. to Colomb. and Surinam.
P. maydifolia Decne. = *P. maidifolia*.
P. mazaifolia hort. ex Beer = *P. maidifolia*.
P. mirabilis Mez = *Puya mirabilis*.
P. morrenii Lem. = *P. heterophylla*.
P. spicata (Lam.) Mez. To 1m+. Lvs to 1.4m; sheaths toothed, triangular-ovate, brown-scaly; blades linear, white-scaly beneath, sometimes reduced to dark spines. Infl. 15–28cm, densely racemose; bracts narrowly lanceolate-triangular; pet. red. Martinique.
P. sulphurea K. Koch = *P. xanthocalyx*.
P. xanthocalyx Mart. To 130cm. Lvs entire or minutely spinose; sheaths suborbicular, small, brown; blades linear to linear-lanceolate, apex filiform, scurfy beneath. Infl. crowded, simple;

bracts linear-lanceolate; sep. orange; pet. primrose yellow. C Mex.

P. zeifolia K. Koch = *P. maidifolia*.

Pitch Apple *Clusia major*.
Pitcher Plant *Cephalotus*; *Heliamphora*; *Nepenthes*; *Sarracenia*.
Pitcher Sage *Lepechinia calycina*; *Salvia spathacea*.
Pitchforks *Bidens*.
Pitch Pine *Pinus palustris*; *P. rigida*.

Pithecellobium Mart. Leguminosae (Mimosoideae). 20 shrubs or trees with stipular thorns. Lvs bipinnate; petiole usually gland. Fls in capitate or spiciform; pan., mimosa-like cal. short-lobed; cor. 5-lobed; sta. 10 to numerous, fil. showy. Subtrop. & trop. Amer., introd. to Asia. Z10.

P. dulce (Roxb.) Benth. MANILA TAMARIND; HUAMUCHIL; OPIUMA; MADRAS THORN. Shrub or tree, spines to 1.2m. Pinnae 2, each with 2 lfts to 5cm, elliptic. Fls green to light yellow, in term. rac. Fr. to 10×1.5cm, oblong-falcate to circinate, torulose, red, coriaceous. Spring. Mex., C Amer., introd. Philipp.

P. flexicaule (Benth.) Coult. TEXAS EBONY. Tree to 20m, spines to 0.5cm; br. flexuous. Lfts 1cm, 3–6 pairs, elliptic-oblong, thick, shiny. Fls in yellow spikes. Fr. to 15×3cm, oblong, straight to falcate. Summer. SE US, N Mex.

P. guadalupense (Pers.) Chapm. = *P. keyense*.

P. junghuhnianum Benth. Tree. Lvs 20cm+, pinnae 2–4, term. pinna 3–4 pairs lfts; lfts to 7.5cm, oblong or rhomboidal. Fls orange-yellow. Fr. flat, contorted. W Indies.

P. keyense Britt. ex Britt. & Rose. BLACK BEAD. Spreading shrub or small tree, unarmed. Pinnae 2, each with 2 lfts to 5×4cm, obovate to narrow-elliptic, coriaceous. Fls to 2.5cm diam., white to yellow often flushed pink. Fr. to 20×1cm, narrow-oblong, curved to circinnate, turgid, dark brown. Winter--spring. Flor., W Indies, NS Amer.

P. saman (Jacq.) Benth. = *Albizia saman*.

P. unguis-cati (L.) Benth. CAT'S-CLAW; BLACKBEARD; BLACK JESSIE. Shrub or small tree, unarmed or with spines to 5mm. Pinnae 2, each with 2 lfts to 6×3.5cm, obovate to elliptic. Fls white to yellow-green. Fr. to 15×1cm, oblong to linear, curved, later circinnate, turgid, irregularly constricted, red to dark brown. W Indies, S Flor.

→*Ebenopsis*, *Inga* and *Siderocarpus*.

Pithecoctenium Mart. ex Meissn. Bignoniaceae. 12 lianes. Br. hexagonal. Lvs 2–3-foliolate, term. leaflet often replaced by trifid, sometimes adhesive tendril. Rac. or pan., term.; cal. cupular, 5-denticulate, lepidote; cor. white, tubular-campanulate, fleshy, puberulent. Fr. a capsule, bristly-spiny. Americas, Mex., to Braz. and Arg. Z10.

P. buccinatorium DC. = *Distictis buccinatoria*.

P. carolinae Nichols. Lfts apex acuminate, base cordate, lightly pubesc. Fls white, tube tinted yellow, fragrant, arcuate, tomentose, lobes slightly recurved, laciniate, crispate. Braz.

P. cinereum DC. = *Distictis laxiflora*.

P. clematideum Griseb. = *P. cynanchoides*.

P. crucigerum (L.) A. Gentry. Lfts 3.3–18cm, ovate to sub-orbicular, apex acuminate, base cordate, lepidote. Fls 3.6–6cm, often bent 90° in middle of tube, densely pubesc., yellow in throat, otherwise white. Mex. to N Arg. and Urug.

P. cynanchoides DC. Lfts 2.5–4cm, felted at first, ovate, reniform or triangular, apex acuminate, ciliate. Fls 3–6cm, white streaked yellow in throat. Braz. to Arg.

P. echinatum (Jacq.) Baill. = *Pithecoctenium crucigerum*.

P. laxiflorum DC. = *Distictis laxiflora*.

→*Bignonia*.

Pitomba *Eugenia luschnathiana*.

Pittocaulon H. Robinson & Brettell. Compositae. 5 shrubs or small trees of dry places. Lvs alt., palmate, petiolate, falling before anthesis. Cap. radiate, clustered at br. apices in corymbs or umbels; flts yellow. Mex., C Amer. Z10.

P. praecox (Cav.) H. Robinson & Brettell. Shrub or small tree, to 5m. Lvs clustered at br. apices, to 15cm, 5–7-lobed, glabrous, petiole to 12cm. Mex.

→*Cineraria* and *Senecio*.

PITTOSPORACEAE R. Br. 9/240. *Billardiera*, *Bursaria*, *Hymenosporum*, *Marianthus*, *Pittosporum*, *Sollya*.

Pittosporum Banks ex Gaertn. Pittosporaceae. *c*200 everg. trees and shrubs. Lvs alt. to whorled, usually entire. Fls 1 to many in clusters, corymbs or umbels often sweetly scented; sep. 5; pet. 5, ± fused at base; sta. 5. Fr. a dry, woody capsule, 2–3(–4)-valved. Australasia and S Afr. to S & E Asia and Hawaii. Z9.

P. bicolor Hook. f. Shrub or small tree, 5–10m, young twigs tomentose. Lvs 3–6cm, linear, leathery, dark green above, white-tomentose, beneath at first, later brown, margins somewhat inrolled. Fls axill. *c*1cm diam., yellow with dark red-brown markings, fragrant. Spring. SE Aus., (Tasm.).

P. cornifolium A. Cunn. Shrub to 2m, young twigs, glab. Lvs 3.5–8cm, in clusters at twig apices, narrowly obovate or oval-lanceolate, apex acute leathery. Infl. 2–5-fld; fls *c*8mm diam., dark red, musk-scented, ♂ long-stalked. Early spring. NZ.

P. crassifolium Banks & Sol. ex A. Cunn. CARO; KARO; EVERGREEN PITTOSPORUM. Shrub or small tree to 5(–10)m, crown columnar, young twigs tomentose. Lvs 5–7cm, oblong to elliptic or obovate, leathery, dark green above, white- or buff-tomentose beneath when young, margins thickened. Fls dark crimson to purple, in term. clusters. NZ. 'Compactum': habit dwarf, densely branched; lvs in tight whorls, grey-green; fls small, maroon, in clusters. 'Variegatum': to 2.5m; lvs variegated with white.

P. dallii Cheesem. Small tree, 4–6m, crown rounded, young twigs red-hued. Lvs 5–11cm, on red-petioles, in clusters at twigs apices, acuminate, dark green, sharply toothed. Fls 12mm diam., in dense term. clusters, white, fragrant. Summer. NZ.

P. divaricatum Ckn. Shrub to 1(–4)m, densely branched, twigs pubesc. when young. Lvs to 1.5cm, linear-obovate to ovate, tough and leathery, deeply toothed, lobed or entire. Fls term., solitary, 4mm, dark maroon. Late spring. NZ.

P. eriocarpum Royle. Small tree to 3–4m, young growth tomentose. Lvs to 15cm, oblanceolate-oblong, obovate or broadly obovate-oblong, leathery. Pan. term.; fls to 9mm, yellow, fragrant. Late spring. NZ.

P. erioloma C. Moore & F. Muell. Shrub to 5m. Lvs to 5cm, in whorls, obovate to oblanceolate, leathery, revolute. Infl. term., 2–7-fld, fls cream-white with red markings. Solomon Is.

P. eugenioides A. Cunn. TARATA; LEMONWOOD. Tree to 10m, twigs dark, glab. Lvs 5–10cm, lemon-scented when crushed, narrowly ovate to oblong, thin, glossy pale green, revolute. Infl. a term. cluster of corymbs; fls 1.5mm diam., yellow-green, honey-scented. Summer. NZ. 'Platinum': habit neat, compact, pyramidal; st. brown-purple; lvs light green margined silver. 'Variegatum': lf margins cream shaded yellow. 'Zita Robinson': habit erect; lf margins wavy.

P. flavum Hook. = *Hymenosporum flavum*.

P. floribundum Wight & Arn. Small tree, bark pale grey. Lvs to 20cm, lanceolate, glab., margins wavy. Pan. term.; fls to 6mm, yellow-green. N India, Nepal.

P. glabratum Lindl. Shrub, 1–1.5m, twigs glab. Lvs 5–12cm, clustered at twig apices, narrowly ovate, apex long-acuminate, glossy-green above, paler beneath, memebranaceous. Fls 8–12mm, fragrant, dull pale yellow, in clusters. Late spring. S China.

P. hawaiiense Hillebrand. Small tree to 6m, bark white. Lvs to 20cm, obovate-oblong, chartaceous, veins deeply impressed above. Fls cream-white clustered, axill. Hawaii.

P. heterophyllum Franch. Shrub, 1–3m, twigs glab. Lvs to 3.8cm, ovate or obovate to lanceolate, apex obtuse, base cuneate. Fls often clustered into pan., pale yellow, fragrant. Late spring--early summer. W China.

P. hosmeri Rock. Tree to 10m. Lvs to 60cm, oblong, leathery, brown-hairy beneath, revolute. Fls to 12mm, cream-white, racemose. Hawaii.

P. mayi hort. = *P. tenuifolium*.

P. napaulense (DC.) Rehd. & Wils. Shrub or small tree to 6m, occas. scandent. Lvs 7–20cm, in clusters at twig apices, elliptic, coriaceous, apex acuminate, base attenuate. Pan. clustered, white-hairy; fls sweetly scented, yellow. Late spring–summer. India (Sikkim), Bhutan, Nepal.

P. nigricans hort. = *P. tenuifolium*.

P. patulum Hook. f. Shrub or small tree, 2–5m, crown conical, twigs pubesc. at first. Young lvs 3–5cm, linear, margins lobed, at maturity 4–5cm, lanceolate, entire or shallowly toothed, leathery. Fls to 1cm, clustered, campanulate, dark crimson, strongly fragrant on slender stalks. Late spring. NZ.

P. phillyreoides DC. NARROW-LEAVED PITTOSPORUM; WEEPING PITTOSPORUM; DESERT WILLOW. Shrub or small tree to 10m, young twigs pubesc., pendulous. Lvs 2–10cm, linear-lanceolate or linear-oblong, acute, mucronate. Fls to 2.8cm diam., cream-yellow, in cymose clusters. Aus.

P. ralphii T. Kirk Shrub, 2.5–5m, young twigs tomentose. Lvs to 15cm, on slender petioles, oblong to oblong-obovate, leathery, pale tomentose beneath. Fls small, dark crimson in term. clusters. NZ.

P. revolutum Ait. Shrub, 2–3m, young twigs brown-tomentose. Lvs 3–11cm, narrowly elliptic to lanceolate, pale brown-tomentose beneath, dark green above, acuminate. Fls 8–12mm, umbellate, yellow. Spring. Aus. (NSW).

P. rhombifolium A. Cunn. ex Hook. QUEENSLAND PITTOSPORUM; DIAMOND LEAF PITTOSPORUM. Tree to 30m. Lvs 7.5–10cm, long-petiolate, rhomboid to rhombic-ovate or narrowly oval, glossy, leathery, toothed above. Infl. compound, many-fld; fls 8–12mm diam., white. Late autumn. E Aus.

P. tenuifolium Banks & Sol. ex Gaertn. TAWHIWHI; KOHUHU. Tree to 10m, trunk slender, young shoots dark. Lvs 2.5–10cm, elliptic, obovate or oblong, glab., flat, revolute or undulate, pale green. Infl. axill., 1- to few-fld; fls with a honey-like fragrance. NZ. 'Abbotsbury Gold': lvs 2–3cm, rounded-obovate, yellow with an irregular, green wavy margin. 'Deborah': lvs small, variegated white and cream. 'Elia Keightley' ('Sunburst'): 3–5m, habit slender; lvs 2–4cm, rounded-ovate, v. slightly wavy. 'Garnetii' (*P. tenuifolium* ×*P. ralphii*): to 4m, twigs grey; lvs 4–6cm, ovate-elliptic, grey-green, margin white with pink spots, slightly wavy. 'Golden King': habit upright, to 3m; lvs 3–5cm, ovate to broadly ovate, pale golden-green, margins wavy. 'Irene Paterson': to 1.2m; lvs 2.5–4cm, ovate-elliptic, white with green spots, margin v. wavy. 'James Stirling': habit open; twigs black tinged red; lvs 1–2cm, silver-green, ovate-rounded, margins wavy. 'Limelight': lvs 2–5.5cm, elliptic, lime-green with dark green, v. slightly wavy margins. 'Margaret Turnbull': to 1.8m; lvs dark green, heavily variegated with gold centre. 'Nigricans': twigs black; lvs 2.6–6cm, oblong-elliptic, margins wavy. 'Purpureum': habit open; lvs green at first, dark purple-bronze when mature, v. wavy. 'Saundersii' (*P. tenuifolium* ×*P. ralphii*): twigs dark grey; lvs 4–7cm, obovate to ovate, grey-green, margins white with pink spots, slightly wavy. 'Silver Magic': lvs small, silver turning pink. 'Sterling Gold': habit erect; lvs small, mottled gold. 'Tom Thumb': 1–2m, compact; lvs 3–6cm, oblong-elliptic, dark purple-bronze, with v. wavy margins. 'Tresederi' ('Silver Queen'): 1–4m, habit compact; lvs 3–5cm, elliptic, silver-grey. 'Variegatum': lvs 3–5cm, elliptic, green with a flat, cream margin. 'Warnham Gold': lvs 3–5cm, elliptic-ovate, golden-green at first, golden-yellow when mature; eesp. colourful in autumn. ssp. *tenuifolium*. Lvs 2.5–7cm, oblong to elliptic-ovate. Fls dark purple-black. ssp. *colensoi* (Hook. f.) T. Kirk. Young twigs finely hairy. Lvs 5–10cm, oblong-lanceolate to ovate-oblong, thick, dark green. Fl. usually solitary, purple. NZ.

P. tobira Ait. TOBIRA; MOCK ORANGE; JAPANESE PITTOSPORUM. Shrub or small tree to 5m. Lvs 3–10cm, obovate, apex rounded, base cuneate, leathery, dark green and glossy, revolute. Infl. term., umbellate, 5–7.5cm diam.; fls orange-blossom-scented, 2.5cm diam., cream-white to lemon-yellow. Spring–early summer. China, Jap. 'Compactum': habit compact. 'Variegatum': lvs variegated with ragged white margin; fls small, fragrant. 'Wheeler's Dwarf': habit miniature, mound-forming.

P. turneri Petrie. Tree, 4–9m, conical, twigs glab. Lvs 2.5–3cm, obovate or linear-oblong, thin but leathery, entire, toothed or lobed. Infl. terminal, 6–12-fld; fls pink to purple. Late spring–early summer. NZ.

P. umbellatum Banks & Sol. ex Gaertn. Tree to 10m. Lvs to 10cm, oblong-lanceolate to elliptic, leathery, revolute. Umbel term., 4–15-fld; fls 1.5cm, orange-red, fragrant. NZ.

P. undulatum Vent. VICTORIAN BOX; ORANGE BERRY PITTOSPORUM; CHEESEWOOD. Tree, 9–14m. Lvs 7–15cm, acuminate, laurel-like, shiny dark green above, pale beneath, margins wavy. Fls 1.2–1.8cm diam., fragrant, cream-white in clustered umbels. Late spring–summer. E Aus. 'Variegatum': lvs with white margins.

P. viridiflorum Sims CAPE PITTOSPORUM. Shrub to 6m, twigs hairy. Lvs 2.5–10cm, obovate, apex rounded, glossy dark green above, leathery, flat or revolute. Pan. many-fld terminal; fls to 6mm, jasmine-scented, yellow-green. Late spring. S Afr.

Pityopsis Nutt. Compositae. 8 erect perenn. herbs, usually stoloniferous and silky hairy. Lvs alt., often grass-like, entire, veins parallel. Cap. radiate, few to many in a corymb; ray flts yellow; disc flts yellow. E US to C Amer.

P. falcata (Pursh) Nutt. To 30cm. St. erect, occas. branching above, silky white-pubesc. Lvs to 7cm, broadly linear, acuminate, falcate, lower sparsely pubesc. to glab., sessile. Cap. 1–5 on white-hairy peduncles to 4cm; ray flts to 8mm. New Jersey to S New York State. Z6.

P. graminifolia (Michx.) Nutt. SILK GRASS. To 50cm. St. erect, branched above, silky white-hairy. Lvs to 25cm, linear, grass-like, silky hairy, st. lvs smaller. Cap. to 15mm diam., solitary to numerous on peduncles to 10cm; ray flts to 14mm. SE US. var. *latifolia* (Fern.) Semple & Bowers. Lvs commonly grasslike, often wider. Late summer–autumn. SE US to Hond. var. *tenuifolia* (Torr.) Semple & Bowers. Upper lvs much reduced. Ray flts to 7mm. Late summer. Tex. to N Carol. Z8.

P. microcephala (Small) Small = *P. graminifolia* var. *tenuifolia*.

P. nervosa (Willd.) Dress = *P. graminifolia* var. *latifolia*.

P. pinifolia (Elliott) Nutt. To 50cm, ± glab. St. clumped, leafy. Basal lvs in a rosette, to 4cm, linear, acute, silky-villous, sessile, st. lvs crowded, to 8cm, light green. Cap. to 2cm diam., few or several; peduncles to 4cm; ray flts to 7mm. Autumn. SE US. Z8.

→*Chrysopsis* and *Heterotheca*.

Pityrogramma Link. Adiantaceae. c40 terrestrial ferns. Rhiz. short-creeping, to ascending; stipes wiry, dark, glossy. Fronds tufted, linear to deltoid-pentagonal, pinnae to tripinnate, conspicuously silvery to golden farinaceous beneath. Americas and Afr. Z10.

P. argentea (Willd.) Domin. Stipe to 30cm, castaneous, dark brown. Lamina to 30×20cm, deltoid-ovate, 3–4-pinnatifid, white, pink or yellow farinaceous beneath; pinnae narrowly deltoid-ovate, pinnules to 5cm, alt., deltoid, pinnules cuneate to broadly oblong-ovate, pinnatifid. S Trop. Afr.

P. calomelanos (L.) Link. SILVER FERN. Stipes 20–55cm, dark purple, farinaceous when young. Lamina to 60×30cm, ovate, bipinnate or tripinnatifid at base, papyraceous, silver-white farinaceous beneath; pinnae to 17cm, deeply lobed, acuminate, pinnules narrowly deltoid, lobed, to 3cm. Trop. Amer., now pantrop. var. *aureoflava* (Hook.) Weatherby ex L.H. Bail. GOLDEN FERN. Farina golden beneath.

P. chrysophylla (Sw.) Link. GOLD FERN. Stipes to 2×length of lamina, dark brown, tinged black; lamina 20–60cm, ovate to ovate-triangular, bipinnate or more compound, bright golden-yellow or rarely white farinaceous beneath. W Indies (Lesser Antilles & Puerto Rico) and S Amer., widely nat. as a subtrop. weed.

P. decomposita (Bak.) Domin = *P. pearcei*.

P. ebenea (L.) Proctor = *P. tartarea*.

P. ×hybrida Domin. (*P. chrysophylla* ×*P. calomelanos*.) Fronds larger than *P. chrysophylla* margins doubly dentate, scarcely revolute.

P. pallida (Weatherby) Alt. & Grant. Stipes 5–25cm, black, sometimes tinged purple; lamina 2–9×2–9cm, pentagonal to broadly ovate-lanceolate, 1–2× pinnatifid, pinnae entire to pinnate-pinnatifid, white gland. above, white farinaceous beneath. Calif.

P. pearcei (Moore) Domin. Stipes 15–30cm; lamina to 30×45cm, ovate-lanceolate to elongate-deltoid, to 4-pinnate, much-dissected, white or bright yellow farinaceous beneath; pinnae 10–15cm, pinnules imbricate, seg. slender. Panama, Costa Rica, Colomb.

P. pulchella (Moore) Domin. Stipes 15–22cm, farinaceous; lamina 15–30×10–15cm, tufted, tripinnatifid, dark green above, pure white farinaceous beneath; pinnules imbricate; seg. flabellate-cuneate, dentate. Venez.

P. schizophylla (Bak. ex Jenman) Maxon. Stipes 4–7cm, dark brown tinged purple, shining; lamina 30–60cm, scarcely or not at all farinaceous, proliferous; lamina finely 4-pinnate, linear lanceolate to narrowly oblong, generally bifurcate below apex, bright green. W Indies (Jam. and Hispan.).

P. sulphurea (Sw.) Maxon. JAMAICA GOLD FERN. Stipes 2–10cm, glosys brown tinged purple; lamina 12–30×3–12cm, linear-lanceolate to ovate-lanceolate, acuminate; bipinnate-pinnatifid or tripinnate, light green, membranous, yellow farinaceous beneath; pinnae to 6×2.5cm, narrowly deltoid, pinnules trapeziform to oblong-ovate, pinnatifid to pinnate at base; seg. flabellate-cuneate. W Indies (Greater Antilles).

P. tartarea (Cav.) Maxon. Stipes equalling lamina, dark brown tinged purple, glossy, lamina 20–80×7–35cm, elongate-deltoid, acuminate, pinnate-pinnatifid to bipinnate, dark green, lustrous above, white farinaceous beneath; pinnae remote, narrowly deltoid, to 20×8cm, pinnules remote, oblong to linear-oblong, entire to crenate. Trop. Amer.

P. triangularis (Kaulf.) Maxon. CALIFORNIAN GOLD FERN. Stipes stiff, about 2× length of lamina, v. dark brown; lamina, deltoid-pentagonal, pinnate; pinnae linear-oblong, with largest pinnules on lower side; seg. rounded to obtuse, coriaceous, white or yellow to orange farinaceous beneath. N Amer.

P. triangularis var. *pallida* Weatherby = *P. pallida*.

P. viscosa (D.C. Eaton) Maxon. SILVERBACK FERN. Stipes 5–20cm, brown or mahogany, lamina 3–12×1.5–8cm, broadly lanceolate to pentagonal, pinnate-pinnatifid, or pinnate-bipinnatifid at base, pinnae entire to bipinnatifid, viscid gland. above, white to pale yellow farinaceous beneath. Calif.

→*Acrostichum, Anogramma* and *Gymnogramma*.

Pixie Caps *Acianthus fornicatus.*
Pixie Mops *Petrophila linearis.*

Placospermum C.T. White & Francis. Proteaceae. Tree to 30m. Junveile lvs oblanceolate to lobed, to 9cm, adult lvs to 17cm, spathulate to oblanceolate. Fls in term. branching rac., pink-red; perianth cylindrical, 13mm. Spring. E Aus. Z10.

P. coriaceum C.T. White and Francis. ROSE SILKY OAK.

Plagianthus Forst. & Forst. f. RIBBON WOOD. Malvaceae. 2 shrubs or trees. Young growth often downy; bark grey in fibrous ribbons. Lvs simple. Fls small, in term. or axill. pan., or solitary; epical. 0; pet. yellow or white; anth. 8–20 on staminal column. NZ. Z8.

P. betulinus A. Cunn. = *P. regius*.

P. divaricatus Forst. & Forst. f. Shrub to 2.5m. Lvs 2–3cm, linear-spathulate to narrow-obovate, entire. Fls 0.5cm diam. yellow, ♀ solitary or few in short lateral cymes; cor. 5mm diam; yellow; anth. 8–12. NZ.

P. lyallii (Hook. f.) A. Gray ex Hook. f. = *Hoheria lyallii*.

P. pulchellus (Willd.) Hook. f. = *Gynatrix pulchella*.

P. regius (Poit.) Hochr. RIBBON WOOD. Tree to 15m. Lvs 0.5–7.5cm, ovate to ovate-lanceolate, acuminate, crenate-serrate. Fls 3–4mm diam., white, mostly unisexual, in paniculate cymes to 25cm; anth. about 12, red. NZ.

P. sidoides Hook. = *Asterotrichion discolor*.

Plagiobothrys Fisch. & C.A. Mey. Boraginaceae. *c*50 ann. or perenn. herbs, usually adpressed-pubesc. Spike or rac. slender; cal. deeply lobed, cor. tube short, lobes overlapping, rounded. W Amer., Aus.

P. nothofulvus (A. Gray) A. Gray. POPCORN FLOWERS. Ann. herb to 50cm. St. erect, branched above, hairy. Basal lvs to 10cm, rosulate, oblanceolate, villous. Spike forked; cor. to 8mm wide, white. N Amer. (W coast).

→*Eritrichium*.

Plagiolirion Bak. Amaryllidaceae. 1 perenn. bulbous herb. Lvs to 15×7.5–10cm, bright green, petiolate. Fls to 12, in a scapose umbel, white, small, 1 seg. decurved, 5 ascending. Summer. Colomb. Z9.

P. horsmannii Bak.

Plagiorhegma Maxim.

P. dubium Maxim. = *Jeffersonia dubia*.

Plagiospermum Oliv.

P. sinense Oliv. = *Prinsepia sinensis*.

Plagius L'Hérit. ex DC. Compositae. 1 much-branched, ± woody-based perenn. herb, to 1m. Lvs alt., obovate to ovate-oblong, dentate, base auriculate. Cap. discoid, 1–2cm diam., in term., 4–10-headed corymbs; flts yellow. Corsica, Sardinia. Z8.

P. flosculosus (L.) Alava & Heyw.

→*Chrysanthemum*.

Plaid Cactus *Gymnocalycium mihanovichii*.
Plains Ironweed *Vernonia marginata*.
Plains Lemon Monarda *Monarda pectinata*.
Plains Violet *Viola viarum*.

Planchonella Pierre. Sapotaceae. *c*60 everg. trees or shrubs. Lvs leathery, simple. Infl. a small, axill. cluster, fls small, sep. 4(–5), small, pet. sta. and staminodes 4(–5). Fr. a berry. E Asia to W Polyn. and NZ. Z10.

P. costata (Endl. Pierre. Tree to 15m, with latex. Lvs elliptic to obovate-oblong, glossy. Infl. 1(–2)-fld, fls (3–)4(–6)mm diam., on curved peduncle to 1.2cm. Fr. to 2.5cm, ellipsoid to ovoid. NZ.

→*Sideroxylon*.

Plane *Platanus*.

Planera Gmel. WATER ELM; PLANER TREE. Ulmaceae. 1 decid. tree or shrub, to 14m; crown broad; branchlets pubesc., lenticelled. Lvs 3–7cm, 2 ranked, ovate-oblong, acuminate, serrate, base oblique, pilose and dark green above, puberulous and paler beneath, venation conspicuous, yellow; petiole 3–6mm; stipules red. Fls small, fascicled; cal. 4–5 lobed, campanulate; cor. 0; sta. 4–5. Fr. a nut-like drupe, 8–12mm, dry, ovoid, prickly-tuberculate. SE US. Z6.

P. abelicea (Lam.) Schultz = *Zelkova abelicea*.
P. acuminata Lindl. = *Zelkova serrata*.
P. aquatica (Walter) Gmel.
P. davidii Hance = *Hemiptelea davidii*.
P. ulmifolia Michx. = *P. aquatica*.

Planer Tree *Planera*.
Plane Tree *Platanus*.

PLANTAGINACEAE Juss. 3/255. *Plantago*.

Plantago (Tourn.) L. PLANTAIN. Plantaginaceae. *c*200 herbs or shrublets. Lvs basal, rosulate, broad, stalked or slender on branching st. Fls small, green to brown-purple with white, yellow or purple sta., grain-like, packed in slender scapose spikes. Cosmop.

P. affra L. Like *P. arenaria* except strongly glandular-pubesc. S Eur.

P. alpina L. Perenn. Lvs in several rosettes, 3–10cm, broadly deltoid or linear, flat, glab. Scapes exceeding lvs; spikes 10–30×3mm. Summer. C & S Eur. (mts). Z3.

P. arborescens Poir. Dwarf shrub to 60cm; st. woody, much-branched. Lvs 2–4cm, crowded, linear to filiform, dark green, pubesc., ciliate. Scapes 3–5cm; spikes ovoid, few-fld. Canary Is. Z9.

P. arenaria Waldst. & Kit. Ann.; st. to 50cm, erect, branched, pubesc. above, gland. below. Lvs 3–8cm, linear or linear-lanceolate. Scapes 1–6cm, spikes 5–15mm. Eur., except W & N.

P. argentea Chaix in Vill. Perenn., 20–50cm. Lvs rosulate, erect, 10–30cm including petiole, linear-lanceolate, sometimes seric-eous; petiole winged. Scape 10–60cm; spike ovoid to cylindric, 0.5–2cm. Summer. S & C Eur. Z6.

P. coronopus L. CUT-LEAVED PLANTAIN; BUCK'S-HORN PLANTAIN. Ann. or short-lived perenn., producing several tufts of lvs 2.5–12cm, spreading, pinnately divided or bipinnatifid, seg. line-ar. Scapes ± decumbent, 5–35cm; spikes 3–9cm. Summer. Eur. Z6.

P. cynops L. 1753 non 1762. SHRUBBY PLANTAIN. Dwarf shrub to 45cm, everg.; br. erect, downy. Lvs 2.5–6.5cm, linear, grooved, trigonous, scarious. Scape 4–9cm, downy; spikes ovoid, 1cm. Summer. C & S Eur. Z6.

P. cynops L. 1762 non L. 1753 = *P. sempervirens*.

P. lanceolata L. ENGLISH PLANTAIN; NARROW-LEAVED PLANTAIN; RIBWORT; RIBGRASS; RIPPLE-GRASS; BUCKHORN. Perenn. or bienn. Lvs rosulate, erect, 4–40cm, oblong-lanceolate, entire or minutely dentate, pubesc. beneath; decurrent to petiole, ribbed minutely dentate, pubesc. beneath. Scapes slender, 5-sulcate, 10–60cm; spike 1.5–6×0.5–1cm, ovoid to cylindric. Eur. 'Marginata': lvs edged and blotched with white. Z6.

P. major L. COMMON PLANTAIN; WHITE-MAN'S FOOT; CART-TRACK-PLANT. Perenn., sparingly pubesc. Lvs 5–20cm, rosulate, spreading, ovate, subcordate at base, entire or irregularly dentate, decurrent to petiole, ribbed. Scapes decumbent, 8–40cm including spike. Summer. Eurasia, nat. worldwide; a troublesome weed of lawns and cult. ground. 'Atropurpurea': lvs purple tinged bronze to purple. 'Nana': dwarf, lvs prostrate, green, scapes reclining. 'Rosularis' (ROSE PLANTAIN): monstrous form, scape stout, with apical coma of green lvs to 9cm diam. replacing fls. 'Rubrifolia': lvs large, dark maroon. 'Variegata': lvs variegated cream and green. Z5.

P. maxima Juss. ex Jacq. Perenn. Lvs rosulate, ovate-elliptic, en-tire or minutely dentate, narrowed to base, hairy ribbed; petiole longer than lamina. Scapes exceeding lvs; spikes 5–20cm. E Eur. (S Russia, Rom., Hung.). Z6.

P. media L. HOARY PLANTAIN. Perenn. Lvs rosulate, 5–15cm in-cluding petiole, ovate-elliptic, entire or crenate, narrowed to base, crispate-hairy; petiole equalling lamina. Scapes greatly exceeding lvs; spikes dense, 2–6cm. Eur. Z6.

P. nivalis Boiss. Perenn. Lvs rosulate, to 1cm, linear-lanceolate, contracted at base, mucronate, white-sericeous. Scapes equal-ling lvs; spikes globose, to 1cm. S Spain (mts). Z6.

P. psyllium L. 1753 non 1762. FLEAWORT; SPANISH PSYLLIUM. Ann. to 60cm, glandular-pubesc.; st. erect. Lvs linear-lanceolate to linear, entire to minutely dentate. Scapes from upper lf axils; spikes ovoid-globose, glandular-hairy. Medit.

P. psyllium L. 1762 non L. 1753. = *P. affra*.

P. ramosa Asch. = *P. arenaria*.

P. reniformis G. Beck. Perenn. Lvs rosulate, 5–17cm including petiole, ovate-cordate to suborbicular, irregularly dentate to subdigitate near base, crispate-hairy; petiole to 2× length of lamina. Scapes exceeding lvs; spikes dense. SW Balk., N Albania. Z6.

P. sempervirens Crantz. Dwarf shrub to 40cm; st. freely branched, minutely pubesc. Lvs 1–6cm, linear to linear-subulate, entire to minutely dentate, scabrid. Scapes 2–10cm; spikes 5–15mm, 5–12-fld. SW Eur. to It. Z7.

P. subulata L. Perenn. Lvs in many rosettes, 3–25cm, linear, trigonous, apiculate rigid, sometimes hairy. Scapes not exceed-ing lvs; spike 2–5cm×2–3mm. S Eur. Z6.

Plantain *Musa*; *Plantago*.
Plantain Lily *Hosta*.

Platanthera Rich. Orchidaceae. 85 tuberous, terrestrial orchids. St. erect. Basal lvs 1–3, ovate. Spike cylindric; dors. sep. and pet. forming a hood, lateral sep. spreading; lip linear-oblong to lanceolate; spur long. Summer. Temp. N and S hemis.

P. bifolia (L.) Rich. LESSER BUTTERFLY ORCHID. To 50cm. Lvs oblong-lanceolate, broadly elliptic or obovate. Fls fragrant, white, tinted green; lip 8–12mm, decurved, spur to 40mm. Late spring–summer. Medit., Russia. Z6.

P. blephariglottis (Willd.) Lindl. To 50cm. Lvs elliptic to lanceolate. Fls white; lip ovate, fringed, spur to 20mm. Mid–late summer. N Amer. Z7.

P. chlorantha (Custer) Rchb. GREATER BUTTERFLY ORCHID. As *P. bifolia* except spike lax, fls earlier, larger, stronger green, less fragrant, spur 18–40mm. Late spring–summer. Eur., Medit. Z7.

P. ciliaris (L.) Lindl. To 100cm. Lvs lanceolate, ridged. Fls orange; lip to 25mm, oblong, fimbriate, spur 25–35mm. Mid-summer–early autumn. E N Amer. Z7.

P. grandiflora (Bigelow) Lindl. To 120cm. Lvs elliptic to lanceolate. Fls white; lip to 25cm, narrowing toward base, fimbriate, spur to 25mm. Summer. E N Amer. Z7.

P. integra (Nutt.) Gray. To 60cm. Lvs lanceolate. Fls golden-yellow; lip oblong, rounded, denticulate, spur to 6mm. Summer. C & E N Amer. Z8.

P. japonica (Thunb.) Lindl. To 60cm. Lvs oblong. Fls golden to lime-green; lip ligulate, spur to 15mm. Summer. SW and E N Amer. Z8.

P. montana Rchb. f. = *P. chlorantha*.

P. nivea (Nutt.) Luer. To 60cm. Lvs white. Fls white; lip linear-elliptic, recurved; spur 15mm. Summer–early autumn. SW & N E Amer. Z8.

P. orbiculata (Pursh) Lindl. To 60cm. Lvs elliptic-oblong to orbicular, fleshy. Fls green-white; lip to 24mm, linear-oblong, pendent, spur to 50mm. Summer–early autumn. N N Amer. Z7.

P. psycodes (L.) Lindl. To 90cm. Lvs elliptic to lanceolate. Fls purple; lip 3-lobed, fimbriate, spur 12–18mm. E N Amer. Z6.

Platanus L. SYCAMORE; BUTTONWOOD; PLANE; PLANE TREE. Platanaceae. 6–7 mostly decid. trees. Bark pale, scaling off in small plates. Lvs mostly palmately lobed, soon long-petiolate. Fls small in dense globular clusters on a long peduncle in lf axil. Fr. an obovoid achene 2mm long with a ring of hairs, packed tightly into long-stalked globose fr. balls. Mostly N Amer.

P. ×acerifolia (Ait.) Willd. LONDON PLANE. (*P. occidentalis ×P. orientalis.*) To 50m; bark peeling off in flakes, cream weathering to grey. Lvs usually truncate to shallowly cordate at the base, 3- or 5-lobed, 12–25cm wide, lobes triangular, sinuately toothed to entire. Fr. globose *c*2.5cm thick, usually in groups of 2, bristly. Origin unknown. 'Augustine Henry': lower br. pendulous; lvs 25–35cm wide, 5-lobed, slightly blue-green, tomentose beneath at first. 'Cantabrigiensis': lvs smaller, more deeply lobed, more delicate in all respects. 'Hispanica': lvs to 30cm wide, normally 5-lobed, lobes toothed, veins tomentose beneath; fr. grouped 1–2. 'Kelseyana': lvs yellow variegated. 'Mirkovec': lvs becoming red-tinged in summer, purple-red in fall. 'Pyramidalis': habit upright, bark rougher; lvs mostly 3-lobed, lobes slightly toothed; close to *P. occidentalis*. 'Sutternii': lvs white-blotched speckled over the entire surface. 'Tremonia' ('Dortmund'): habit quite narrow, conical, v. fast growing. Z7.

P. ×acerifolia var. *hispanica* (Münchh.) Bean = *P. ×acerifolia* 'Hispanica'.

P. ×acerifolia f. *argenteovariegata* hort. = *P. ×acerifolia* 'Sutternii'.

P. ×acerifolia f. *pyramidalis* (Jankó) C. Schneid. = *P. ×acerifolia* 'Pyramidalis'.

P. ×aureovariegata hort. = *P. ×acerifolia* 'Kelseyana'.

P. californica Benth. = *P. racemosa*.

P. californica hort. non Benth. = *P. racemosa*.

P. cantabrigiensis Henry = *P. ×acerifolia* 'Cantabrigiensis'.

P. cretica Dode = *P. orientalis* var. *insularis*.

P. cuneata Willd. = *P. orientalis* var. *cuneata*.

P. cyprius hort. = *P. orientale* var. *insularis*.

P. densicoma Dode pro parte. = *P. occidentalis* var. *glabrata*.

P. glabrata Fern. = *P. occidentalis* var. *glabrata*.

P. ×hispanica Mill. ex Münchh. = *P. ×acerifolia*.

P. ×hybrida Brot. = *P. ×acerifolia*.

P. mexicana Moric. Tree to 20m. Lvs to 20cm wide, lobes 5, entire, acuminate, off-white-tomentose beneath. Fr. heads 1 or 2 on a peduncle, rough, tawny-hairy, 3.5cm diam. NE Mex. Z9.

P. occidentalis L. AMERICAN SYCAMORE; BUTTONWOOD; AMERICAN PLANE. To 50m. Bark exfoliating in small plates. Lvs generally 3-lobed, 10–18cm wide, coarsely sinuate, occas. entire, base obtuse to cuneate, tomentose beneath at first. Fr. usually solitary, occas. in pairs. SE US. *P. ×acerifolia* was often grown and sold under this name. var. *glabrata* (Fern.) Sarg. Lvs smaller, tougher, more deeply lobed, lobes long acuminate and often entire. Iowa to NE Mex. Z5.

P. orientalis L. ORIENTAL PLANE. To 30m. Bark exfoliating in large plates. Lvs deeply 5–7-lobed, occas. 3-lobed on younger shoots, 10–20cm wide, lobes longer than wide, base cuneate or

truncated. Fr. in groups of 3–4 or more, occas. in pairs. SE Eur. to Asia Minor. var. *insularis* A. DC. CYPRIAN PLANE. Lf lobes 5, deep, further lobed with ascending teeth, long acuminate. Fr. only *c*1.5cm thick, usually 2–3 together. Crete. 'Cuneata' lvs deeply incised, lobes entire to lobulate. Z7.

P. orientalis var. *cretica* Dode = *P. orientalis* var. *insularis*.

P. racemosa Nutt. CALIFORNIA SYCAMORE; ALISO. 30(40)m. Lvs usually cordate to truncate, 15–30cm wide, deeply 3–5-lobed, tough, deep green above, lighter and tomentose beneath, lobes narrow, entire or sparsely dentate. Fr. 3–7 together. Calif., Baja Calif. Z8.

P. wrightii S. Wats. ARIZONA SYCAMORE. To 25m. Lvs deeply 5–7-lobed, tomentose beneath, lobes lanceolate, entire to sparsely dentate. Fr. grouped 2–4, individual heads stalked. N Amer.; Ariz. to NW Mex. Z8.

Platinum Pepper *Peperomia griseo-argentea*.

Platter Leaf *Coccoloba uvifera*.

Platycarya Sieb. & Zucc. Juglandaceae. 1 decid. tree or shrub to 12m. Br. pubesc., later glab., yellow-brown. Lvs imparipinnate, 15–30cm; lfts 7–15, ovate to oblong-lanceolate, acuminate, biserrate, 4–10cm, glabrescent. ♂ infl. a slender, erect catkin, 5–8cm; ♀ infl. solitary, cone-like, about 3cm. Summer. C & S China.

P. strobilacea Sieb. & Zucc.

→*Fortunaea*.

Platycerium Desv. STAGHORN FERN; ELKHORN FERN; ANTELOPE EARS. Polypodiaceae. 18 epiphytic ferns. Rhiz. short concealed by fronds. Sterile fronds sessile, flat, broad, clasping and overlapping, becoming brown and papery; sterile fronds at base of sterile fronds, erect to pendent, stalked, cuneate, repeatedly forked. Trop. Z10.

P. aethiopicum Hook. = *P. stemaria*.

P. alcicorne Auct., Hook. non Desv. = *P. andinum*.

P. alcicorne hort. non Desv. = *P. bifurcatum*.

P. andinum Bak. SOUTH AMERICAN STAGHORN. Sterile fronds 60×30cm+, erect, cuneate and 2–3-lobed at upper margin, entire at lower margin; fertile fronds to 3m, pendent, cuneate to linear, narrowly and forking into 3 or more br., pale grey to green. Peru, Boliv.

P. angolense Welw. ex Bak. = *P. elephantotis*.

P. biforme (Sw.) Bl. = *P. coronarium*.

P. biforme var. *erecta* Ridl. = *P. ridleyi*.

P. bifurcatum (Cav.) C. Chr. COMMON STAGHORN FERN; ELKHORN FERN. Sterile fronds to 60×45cm, sessile, erect, rounded, entire, wavy, or shallowly lobed, papery; fertile fronds to 90cm, pendent, base cuneate, 2 or 3 (occas. to 5) times forked, leathery, seg. strap-shaped, obtuse, stellate-pubesc. SE Asia, Polyn., subtrop. Aus.

P. bifurcatum var. *hillii* (T. Moore) Domin = *P. hillii*.

P. bifurcatum var. *quadridichotomum* Bonap. = *P. quadri-dichotomum*.

P. bifurcatum var. *veitchii* (Underw.) Hennipman & Roos = *P. veitchii*.

P. bifurcatum var. *willinckii* Hennipman & Roos = *P. willinckii*.

P. coronarium (J.G. Koenig ex Muell.) Desv. Sterile fronds to 100×50cm, sessile, erect to recurved, elliptic, lobed above, basally fleshy, bright green; fertile fronds to 3m, pendent, narrowly elliptic to obovate, to 7 times narrowly forked, sterile central lobe, 2 spreading, sterile strap-like and forking divisions at base, fertile lobe horizontal, semicircular to reniform, fleshy, on stalk to 7cm. SE Asia.

P. coronarium var. *cucullatum* v.A.v.R. = *P. ridleyi*.

P. diversifolium Bonap. = *P. ellisii*.

P. elephantotis Schweinf. CABBAGE FERN; ELEPHANT'S EAR FERN. Sterile fronds to 90×45cm, sessile, erect, rounded to oblong, truncate at apex, entire to wavy above, membranous and prominently veined; fertile fronds to 75×55cm, pendent, obovate to obcuneate, rounded, entire, leathery. Trop. Afr. (Sudan to Moz.).

P. ellisii Bak. Sterile fronds to 30×20cm, sessile, adpressed, rounded, entire to shallowly lobed; fertile fronds to 60cm, erect, obovate to cuneate, entire or 2-lobed above, light green. Madag.

P. ellisii var. *diversifolium* C. Chr. = *P. ellisii*.

P. grande (Fée) Kunze. STAGHORN FERN. Sterile fronds to 110×180cm, sessile, spreading, suborbicular to reniform, upper margin to 5 times deeply and irregularly dichotomously lobed, lower margin entire, papery, bronze to green, strongly veined; fertile fronds to 180cm, pendent, cuneate, forked, leathery, dividing into strap-shaped seg. to 30cm. Malaysia, Aus., Philipp.

P. grande var. *bambourinense* Domin = *P. superbum*.

P. hillii T. Moore. NORTHERN ELKHORN FERN. Sterile fronds to 40×24cm, sessile, adpressed, rounded and shallowly lobed at upper margin; fertile fronds to 70cm+, erect or suberect, broadly cuneate to spathulate in lower part, irregularly forked or palmately lobed above, dark green, seg. narrowly elliptic to obovate. Aus. (Queensld), New Guinea. Cvs include 'Bloomei', 'Drummond', 'Drummond Diversifolium', 'Pumilum'. 'Drummond': fertile fronds to 30cm, pendent, broadly fan-shaped, to 10 or more times dichotomously divided.

P. holttumii De Joncheere & Hennipman. Sterile fronds to 115×135cm, sessile, spreading, cuneate and truncate, to 6 times lobed above, wavy below, green; fertile fronds to 125cm, cuneate, 2-lobed, and to 5 times forked, pale grey to green, lobes cuneate, forks pendent. Thail. to Malaysia.

P. madagascariense Bak. Sterile fronds to 35×22cm, subsessile, adpressed, rounded, minutely toothed, prominently veined; fertile fronds to 30cm, erect to pendent, cuneate to fan-shaped, to 3 times forked. Madag.

P. madagascariense var. *humblotii* Poiss. = *P. madagascariense*.

P. quadridichotomum (Bonap.) Tard. Sterile fronds to 40×17cm, sessile, erect to adpressed, cuneate and truncate, entire or toothed or wavy above; fertile fronds to 40cm, pendent, cuneate, to 4 times forked, densely stellate-pubesc. Madag.

P. ridleyi Christ. Sterile fronds to 50×40cm, stipitate, adpressed, rounded and shallowly lobed, entire, veins prominent; fertile fronds to 17×15cm, erect, kidney-shaped, to 8 times forked, seg. to 7 times forked, stalk to 10cm. Thail., Malaysia to Indon.

P. stemaria (Beauv.) Desv. TRIANGULAR STAGHORN FERN. Sterile fronds to 60×3cm, sessile, erect, cuneate, apex truncate, entire or irregularly toothed or wavy; fertile fronds to 90cm, spreading or, in var. *laurentii*, pendent, broadly cuneate to triangular, once or twice forked. Trop. Afr.

P. sumbawense Christ = *P. willinckii*.

P. superbum De Joncheere & Hennipman. STAGHORN FERN. Sterile fronds to 160×150cm, sessile, spreading, cuneate, apex truncate, to 4 times forked or lobed, grey to green; fertile fronds to 2m, spreading to pendent, cuneate, to 5 times forked, seg. often twisted. Aus.

P. veitchii (Underw.) C. Chr. SILVER ELKHORN FERN. Sterile fronds to 45×18cm, sessile, adpressed, elliptic, twice forked or lobed, seg. strap-like; fertile fronds to 70cm, erect to spreading, narrowly cuneate, to 3 times forked, seg. triangular to linear, stellate-pubesc., silver-white. Aus. (Queensld).

P. velutinum C. Chr. = *P. elephantotis*.

P. wallichii Hook. Sterile fronds to 65×50cm, sessile, erect, cuneate, truncate at apex, to 5 times lobed, above; fertile fronds to 70cm, pendent, cuneate, 3-lobed, to 3 times forked, densely yellow stellate-pubesc. E India, China, Malaysia.

P. wandae Racib. Sterile fronds to 125×135cm, sessile, spreading, cuneate, truncate at apex, to 6 times forked, wavy and laciniate below; fertile fronds to 2m, 2-lobed, lobes one to 4 times laterally forked, seg. pendent. New Guinea.

P. wilhelminae-reginae v.A.v.R. = *P. wandae*.

P. willinckii T. Moore. JAVA STAGHORN FERN. Sterile fronds to 70×50cm, sessile, erect, rounded, to 4 times forked; fertile fronds to 90cm, pendent, cuneate to spathulate in lower part, to 5 times forked, seg. narrowly triangular to strap-shaped; pale-stellate pubesc. Indon., New Guinea. 'Lemoinei': fronds initially with white and woolly stellate pubescence, and more rigid. 'Payton': fertile fronds to 38cm with to 8 seg., rigid. 'Scofield': fertile fronds wider than sp. type, more widely forked, seg. to 3cm wide.

→*Alcicornium*.

Platycladus Spach. ORIENTAL THUJA; BIOTA. Cupressaceae. 1 everg. conifer to 15m. Bark rust-brown, fibrous. Crown conic to broadly ovate. Lvs scale-like, closely adpressed, 2mm, in lat. and facial pairs, grooved, obtuse, light or dull green, tinted bronze in winter. Cones erect, oblong, 10–20mm, fleshy, becoming woody, blue-green; scales usually 6, apices with a recurved thick, fleshy bract. W China, N Korea; also a small wild population in NE Iran. Z6.

P. orientalis (L. f.) Franco. Numerous cvs., ranging from dwarf forms to small trees; some with juvenile, needle-like lvs., others green, golden, slightly variegated, or with filamentous br. 'Elegantissima': slow-growing, dense, yellow green, the commonest form in cult.

→*Biota* and *Thuja*.

Platyclinis Benth. = *Dendrochilum*.

Platycodon A. DC. BALLOON FLOWER; CHINESE BELLFLOWER. Campanulaceae. 1 erect perenn. herb, to 70cm. Lvs whorled below, alt. above, elliptic-lanceolate, dentate. Fls term., in few-fld corymbs or solitary; cor. broadly campanulate, with abruptly acuminate lobes, much inflated in bud, grey to slate blue, interior sky blue, azure, white or pink. Summer. D China, Manch., Jap. Z4.

P. glaucus (Thunb.) Nak. = *P. grandiflorus*.

P. grandiflorus (Jacq.) A. DC. 'Albus': fls white, often veined blue. 'Apoyama': habit dwarf; fls large, deep mauve. 'Baby Blue': habit dwarf, bushy; fls blue. Balloon Series: habit dwarf, compact; fls blue. 'Hakone Double Blue': fls double, deep violet-blue. 'Komachi': fls remaining balloon-shaped, blue. 'Perlmutterschale' ('Mother of Pearl'): fls large, pale pink. 'Plenum': fls semi-double, pale blue. 'Shell Pink': fls delicate pink.

→*Campanula* and *Wahlenbergia*.

Platycrater Sieb. & Zucc. Hydrangeaceae. 1 low, decid. shrub to 1m. Lvs 10–20cm, oblong to lanceolate, narrow-acuminate, finely sinuate-serrate, thin-textured, pubesc. beneath. Fls small, white, 5–10 per term. flat-topped cyme, the outer, fls sterile, showy, disc-like. Jap. Z8.

P. arguta Sieb. & Zucc. 'Hortensis': infl. reduced to 3–5 enlarged fls.

Platykeleba N.E. Br.
P. insigne N.E. Br. = *Sarcostemma insigna*.

Platylobium Sm. Leguminosae (Papilionoideae). 4 low-growing, everg. shrubs or subshrubs. Lvs 1-foliolate, ovate to cordate. Fls 1 to several, axill.; standard orbicular or reniform, much longer than the other pet. E Aus. Z9.

P. angulare hort. = *P. triangulare*.

P. formosum Sm. FLAT PEA. Lvs to 5×4cm, cordate or ovate, cuspidate. Fls solitary; standard 2.5cm diam., deeply notched, bright yellow, blotched dark red at base. Summer. Aus., Tasm.

P. murrayanum Hook. = *P. triangulare*.

P. obtusangulum Hook. COMMON FLAT-PEA; NATIVE HOLLY. Lvs to 3×3cm, broadly triangular to ovate-cordate. Fls 1–3 per axil, ± sessile; standard 1.4–2cm, pink-red or brown beneath, orange-yellow above. Autumn. S Aus.

P. parviflorum Sm. = *P. formosum*.

P. triangulare R. Br. IVY FLAT-PEA. Readily distinguished from the closely related *P. obtusangulum* by the pedicels to 1.5cm. Summer. Aus. (Vict., Tasm.).

Platylophus D. Don. Cunoniaceae. 1 everg. tree to 18m. Lvs trifoliate, lfts to 7.5cm, sessile, usually serrate. Fls loosely clustered, axill., small, white or cream, strongly sweet-fragrant; pet. 4 or 5. S Afr. Z9.

P. trifoliatus (Thunb.) D. Don. WHITE ALDER.
→*Weinmannia*.

Platymiscium Vogel Leguminosae (Papilionoideae). Some 20 trees and shrubs. Lvs imparipinnate. Fls fragrant in clustered axill. rac.; standard orbicular or ovate, wings obliquely oblong, keel straight or incurved. Trop. Amer. Z10.

P. floribundum Vogel. Tree. Lfts 6×2.5cm, 5, oblong, acuminate. Fls in rac. to 10cm, yellow, standard erect. Braz.

P. pinnatum (Jacq.) Dugand. Erect shrub to 4m. Lfts to 7.5cm, ovate, acuminate. Fls in rac. to 10cm, yellow, fragrant, standard reflexed. Colomb.

P. trinitatis Benth. ROBLE. Tree to 30m. Lfts to 12×7cm, 3–5, elliptic, obtuse. Rac. yellow-pubesc.; fls yellow, standard minutely puberulous. Trin., Guyana.

Platyopuntia Engelm.
P. corrugata (Salm-Dyck) Ritter = *Opuntia corrugata*.

Platyosprion Maxim.
P. platycarpum (Maxim.) Maxim. = *Cladrastis platycarpa*.

Platystele Schltr. Orchidaceae. 12 small epiphytic orchids, st. v. short, slender, tufted, apically unifoliate. Rac. or fascicle term. or lat., slender, usually many-fld; fls small; tep. somewhat spreading, lat. sep. shortly connate; lip minute, fleshy, simple. C & S Amer. Z10.

P. compacta (Ames) Ames. Lvs to 55×35mm, linear-oblanceolate, obtuse. Infl. to 10cm, many-fld; fls to 5mm diam., yellow-green, usually spotted purple. Guat., Hond., Costa Rica.

P. johnstonii (Ames) Garay. Lvs to 6×4mm, oblong-lanceolate to oblong-elliptic, rounded. Infl. to 22mm, 1 to few-fld, erect or arching; fls minute, cream-white; lip to 1mm, papillose. Venez., Colomb., Ecuad.

P. misera (Lindl.) Garay. Lvs to 60×10mm, oblanceolate or oblong-spathulate, acute or subobtuse. Infl. to 17cm, filiform, few to many-fld; fls to 6mm diam., tan or green suffused purple; lip velvety. Colomb.

P. ornata Garay. Lvs to 22×3mm, ovate-spathulate or oblanceolate, rounded or obtuse. Infl. usually shorter than lvs, many-fld; fls to 3mm diam., purple; finely gland. Venez.

P. ovalifolia (Focke) Garay & Dunsterv. Lvs to 8×4mm, elliptic to obovate, ± fleshy, acute or apiculate. Infl. to 15mm, erect or ascending, 1 to few-fld; fls to 4mm diam., pale cream or pale yellow. W Indies, Trin., Venez., Surinam, Guyana, Braz.

P. stenostachya (Rchb. f.) Garay. Lvs to 35×5mm, obovate to linear-spathulate, obtuse.Infl. to 1.5cm, axillary, few to several-fld; fls to 3mm diam.; tep. yellow-green or yellow-brown, lip dark maroon edged white, fleshy, papillose. Mex. to Panama, Venez. & Colomb.

→*Humboldtia, Pleurothallis* and *Stelis.*

Platystemon Benth. CREAMCUPS; CALIFORNIAN POPPY. Papaveraceae. 1 ann. herb to 30cm, erect or decumbent, branching at base. Lvs to 7.5cm, linear to oblong-lanceolate, entire, pubesc. Fls solitary, to 2.5cm diam., yellow or yellow and white on stalks to 7.5cm; pet. 6; sta. many. Summer. Calif. Z8.

P. californicus Benth.
P. leiocarpus Fisch. & Mey. = *P. californicus.*

Platythyra N.E. Br.
P. barklyi (N.E. Br.) Schwantes = *Mesembryanthemum barklyi.*

Plectocephalus D. Don. Compositae. 6 erect, ann. to perenn. herbs. Lvs alt., simple. Cap. discoid, solitary or few, term. on thickened peduncles; involucre cylindrical to globose; phyllaries laciniate-fringed; outer disc flts larger, ligulate, central flts tubular. C & S Amer. Z9.

P. chilensis G. Don ex Loud. Perenn. to 1.2m. Lvs to 7cm, pinnatifid, lobes linear, entire to slightly dentate. Involucre c2cm diam.; flts red. Autumn. Chile.

→*Centaurea.*

Plectorrhiza Dockr. Orchidaceae. 3 epiphytic orchids. Roots tangled. St. long, wiry. Fls small, fragrant, infl. racemose; sep. and pet. subequal; lip trilobed, saccate, spurred. Aus., Lord Howe Is. Z9.

P. tridentata (Lind.) Dockr. TANGLE ORCHID. To 30cm. Lvs to 10cm, 4–20, linear-oblong, falcate. Rac. to 12cm, 3–15-fld; fls green, sometimes marked red-brown; spur to 3cm. Late summer–mid winter. E Aus.

Plectostachys Hilliard & B.L. Burtt. Compositae. 2 white-tomentose subshrubs. Lvs cobwebby to glab. above, white-tomentose beneath, ± sessile. Cap. radiate, in small, rounded, corymbose clusters; phyllaries tipped white; flts yellow. S Afr. Z9.

P. serphyllifolia (A. Berger) Hilliard & B.L. Burtt. Straggling, to 1.5m, young br. sparsely white-tomentose. Lvs to 1cm, broadly elliptic to suborbicular, glab. above, sparsely tomentose beneath, subsessile. Spring. Cape Penins.

→*Helichrysum.*

Plectranthus L'Hérit. Labiatae. 350 annuals, perenn. herbs or shrubs. St. and lvs semi-succulent or succulent. Infl. paniculate, racemose or spicate, usually term., fls whorled or cymose; cor. tubular, bilabiate, upper lip usually 4-lobed, lower longer than upper. Afr., Asia & Aus. Z10.

P. amboinicus (Lour.) Spreng. SOUP MINT; MEXICAN MINT; INDIAN MINT; COUNTRY BORAGE; FRENCH THYME; SPANISH THYME. Decumbent, many-stemmed, aromatic, perenn. herb. St. to 1.5m. Lvs 4.5cm, ovate, pubesc. gland-dotted, rounded, crenulate. Infl. spicate, fls in dense glomerate verticils; 7–9mm, lilac, mauve or white. Trop. to S Afr.; widely cult. A form with white-edged lvs is in cult.

P. argentatus S.T. Blake. Spreading ± hairy shrub to 1m. Br. ascending, with silvery hairs. Lvs 5–11cm, canescent, ovate, acute or acuminate, crenate, gland. Infl. racemose to 30cm, verticillasters 9–11-fld; fls pale blue-white, 9–11mm. Aus. 'Green Silver' is a widely cultivated clone.

P. arthropodus Briq. = *P. fruticosus.*
P. behrii Compton = *P. fruticosus.*
P. charianthus Briq. = *P. fruticosus.*
P. coleoides hort. non Benth. = *P. forsteri.*
P. forsteri Benth. Decumbent, aromatic, perenn. herb. St. straggling, to 1m, pubesc. above. Lvs 1.5–3.5cm, ovate to broad-ovate, pubesc., gland. beneath, crenate or crenate serrate. Infl. racemose; verticillasters 6–10-fld, fls pale to mid-blue or mauve, 3–8mm. New Caledonia, Fiji, E Aus. Is. 'Marginatus' ('Variegatus'): lvs variegated cream; fls small, white. A golden-variegated form is widely cultivated under the name *P. coleoides*; this name however applies to another Asian sp. which is little known.

P. fruticosus L'Hérit. Erect, shrub to 2m, sparingly pubesc. or gland. Lvs 4–14cm, broadly ovate to ovate-elliptic, obtuse or acute, crenate-dentate, underside gland-dotted and suffused purple. Infl. paniculate, fls in 1–3-fld cymes forming 2–6-fld verticillasters; 5–13mm, blue-mauve or pink or pale blue speckled purple. S Afr.

P. galpinii Schltr. = *P. fruticosus.*

P. madagascariensis (Pers.) Benth. Procumbent or decumbent semi-succulent herb. St. to 1m, rooting, ± tomentose often gland. Lvs 1.5–4.5cm, slightly succulent, voate to subrotund, strigose above, undersurface tomentose beneath, gland-dotted, obtuse to rounded, crenate to dentate. Infl. simple or with 2 branchlets near base; fls in 3–8-fld cymes, forming 6–16-fld verticillasters; 5–18mm, white or mauve to purple, often dotted with red glands. S Afr., Moz. & Madag. A fragrant-lvd variegated form is grown as a trailing plant under the name 'Variegated Mintleaf' or incorrectly as *P. coleoides* 'Variegata'.

P. nummularius Briq. = *P. verticillatus.*

P. oertendahlii T.C.E. Fries. Freely branching, semi-succulent, perenn. herb. St. decumbent, to 1m, rooting, glandular-tomentose. Lvs 3–4cm, semi-succulent, ovate to suborbicular, sparingly villous, purple, beneath acute to obtuse, crenate dentate, ciliate. Infl. simple or branched, fls in sessile 3-fld cymes forming 6-fld verticils, white or suffused with mauve, 8–13mm. S Afr. (Natal). 'Variegatus': lvs to 4cm, green-bronze, variegated silver and off-white, particularly at edges.

P. peglerae Cooke = *P. fruticosus.*

P. saccatus Benth. Erect, soft-stemmed, shrub to 1.2m. St. tinged purple, glandular-puberulous. Lvs 2–7cm, semi-succulent, ovate-deltoid, subglabrous to glandular-puberulous, acute, with few large teeth. Infl. simple or branched near base; rac. to 12cm with few large, saccate fls in sessile 1–3-fld cymes forming 2–6-fld verticils mauve, pale blue rarely white. E S Afr. var. *longitubus* Codd. Lvs larger and cor. tube longer, 2–2.6cm, but narrower at base.

P. scutellarioides (L.) R. Br. = *Solenostemon scutellarioides.*
P. thunbergii Benth. = *P. verticillatus.*
P. thyrsoideus (Bak.) B. Mathew. FLOWERING BUSH COLEUS. Woody-based viscid, shrubby perenn. to 1m. Lvs 5–7.5cm, broadly ovate, crenately toothed to ± erose, matt green above, grey-green beneath. Fls many in long-stalked whorls in pan. to 35cm; cor. to 1cm, bright blue to indigo. C Afr.

P. urticaefolius (Lam.) Salisb. = *P. fruticosus.*
P. verticillatus (L.f.) Druce. Semi-succulent, procumbent, perenn. herb. St. glab. or slightly pubesc., more than 1m. Lvs 1.5–4cm, succulent, ovate to rotund, glab. to pubesc., undersurface red, gland-dotted, acute to rounded, crenate-dentate with 3–6 pairs of teeth. Infl. simple or with pair of br. near base; fls in sessile 1–3-fld cymes forming 2–6-fld verticils; 1–2.5cm, white to pale mauve, speckled purple. E S Afr., Swaz., Moz. Variegated forms are grown.

→*Coleus* and *Ocimum.*

Plectrelminthus Raf. Orchidaceae. 1 epiphytic monopodial orchid. St. short, leafy. Lvs 10–35cm, ligulate, light yellow-green. Rac. axill., pendent, to 60cm, rachis flexuous; fls scented, fleshy, tep. to 5cm, lanceolate, pale green, usually tinged bronze, lip 6cm, pandurate-acuminate, undulate, ivory-white, tipped green, pointing upwards; spur 17–25cm, coiled. W Afr., from Fr. Guinea to Zaire. Z10.

P. caudatus (Lindl.) Summerh.
→*Angraecum.*

Plectritis DC. Valerianaceae. 4 ann. herbs. Lvs opposite. Fls in capitate or dense interrupted spikes; cor. with a basal spur and 5 lobes. W N Amer.

P. congesta (Lindl.) DC. To 45cm. Lvs to 5cm, obovate to oblong-ovate. Fls to 8mm, pink to rose, in headlike clusters. BC to N Calif.

Pleioblastus Nak. Gramineae. 20 dwarf to medium-sized bamboos; rhiz. short or far-running. Culms erect, almost always hollow, usually with br. upper nodes. Lvs scaberulous, tessellate, with smooth white bristles or none. China, Jap.

P. akebono (Mak.) Nak. Culms slender, 20–50×1–2cm, glab.; br. erect, 1–2 from low down. Lvs 5–7cm×1–1.5mm in 2 rows, mostly suffused white or yellow. Origin unknown. Z7.

P. angustifolius (Mitford) Nak. = *P. chino* f. *angustifolius.*
P. argenteostriatus (Reg.) Nak. Differs from *P. variegatus* in being sturdier and more upstanding with culms to 1m. Lvs 1.4–2.2×1.0–2.1cm; sheaths hairy only at base. Unknown in the wild; cult. in Jap. Z7.

P. argenteostriatus f. *akebono* (Mak.) Muroi = *P. akebono.*
P. argenteostriatus f. *pumilus* (Mitford) Muroi = *P. humilis* var. *pumilus.*

P. auricoma (Mitford) D. McClintock. KAMURO-ZASA. Culms 1–3mm×2–4mm, sometimes purple-lined, softly hairy; nodes prominent with white waxy powder below; br. usually 1–2 from low down. Lvs 12–22×1.5–3.5cm, softly hairy, brilliant yellow with green stripes; sheaths downy, ciliate, purple, bristles few or none. Cult. and nat. Jap. f. *chrysophyllus* Mak. Lvs entirely golden-yellow. Z7.

P. chino (Franch. & Savat.) Mak. Culms 2–4m×0.5–1cm, sometimes purple, glab. with white wax below nodes; br. 3 or more. Lvs 12–25×1–3cm, green, sometimes slightly downy beneath, or ciliate; sheaths often tinted purple, ciliate with bristles. C Jap. f. *angustifolius* (Mitford) Muroi & H. Okamura in Sugimoto. Lvs to 1.3cm across, often downy beneath, striped white or entirely green. f. *gracilis* (Mak.) Nak. Lvs to 0.6cm across, glab., usually variegated white. Z6.

P. chino var. *argenteostriatus* (Reg.) Mak. = *P. argenteostriatus*.

P. chino var. *viridis* f. *pumilus* (Mitford) S. Suzuki = *P. humilis* var. *pumilus*.

P. distichus (Mitford) Muroi & H. Okamura = *P. pygmaeus* var. *distichus*.

P. fortunei (Van Houtte) Nak. = *P. variegatus*.

P. gramineus (Bean) Nak. Differs from *P. linearis* in its glab. culm sheaths; culms 2–5m×0.5–2cm, glab. with white powder below nodes; br. many above. Lvs 15–30×0.8–2cm, long-acuminate, glab., pendulous, sheaths glab., often lacking bristles. Jap., E China. Z7.

P. humilis (Mitford) Nak. Culms 1–2m×2–3mm, glab.; nodes with white powder below; br. 1–3, low down. Lvs 10–25×1.5–2.3cm, glabrescent; sheaths slightly downy, with or without bristles. C Jap. var. *pumilus* (Mitford) D. McClintock. More robust and compact, upper culm sheaths leave bearded scars.

P. kongosanensis 'Auricoma'. = *P. auricoma*.

P. linearis (Hackel) Nak. Differs from *P. gramineus* in hairy culm sheaths and shorter lvs. C Jap. Z7.

P. maximowiczii (A. & C. Riv.) Nak. = *P. chino*.

P. pygmaeus (Miq.) Nak. DWARF FERN-LEAF BAMBOO; KE-OROSHIMA-CHIKU. St. v. small and slender, 10–20cm×1mm, glab. with white powder; br. 1–2, low down. Lvs 2–4cm×0.2–0.5cm, in 2 close ranks, slightly downy; margins sometimes withering papery white. Unknown in the wild; cult. in Jap. var. *distichus* (Mitford) Nak. Often misnamed *P. pygmaeus*, and sometimes under cv. names such as 'Mine-zuzme' 'Orishimazasa' or 'Tsuyuzasa'. Taller, to 1m; sheaths, nodes and lvs usually hairless; lvs 3–7×0.3–1cm, to 8 pairs in 2 close ranks atop st. Z6.

P. pygmaeus var. *distichus* 'Akebono'. = *P. akebono*.

P. shibuyanus 'Variegatus'. = *P. variegatus*.

P. simonii (Carr.) Nak. SIMON BAMBOO; MEDAKE. Culms 3–8m×1.2–3cm, stout, glab.; nodes with white powder below; br. numerous above. Lvs 13–27×1.2–2.5cm, often half-glaucous beneath, sometimes white-striped at first; sheaths glab. C & S Jap. f. *variegatus* (Hook. f.) Muroi. Less robust, lvs variable, some white-striped. Z6.

P. simonii var. *heterophyllus* (Mak. & Shirasawa) Nak. = *P. simonii* f. *variegatus*.

P. vaginatus (Hackel) Nak. = *P. chino* f. *gracilis*.

P. variegatus (Sieb. ex Miq.) Mak. DWARF WHITE-STRIPED BAMBOO; CHIGO-ZASA. Culms 20–75×0.5–2cm; nodes glab. with white powder; br. 1–2, from low down. Lvs 10–20×0.7–1.8cm, dark green with cream stripes of varying breadth; sheaths purple-lined, minutely downy, ciliate, bristles few or none. var. *viridis* (Mak.) D. McClintock (*P. shibuyanus* Nak.): lvs green. Unknown in the wild. Z7.

P. viridistriatus (Reg.) Mak. = *P. auricoma*.

→*Arundinaria, Nippocalamus, Sasa* and *Yushania*.

Pleiogynium Engl. Anacardiaceae. 3 trees. Lvs usually imparipinnate. Fls small, 4–6-merous in axillary rac., pan. or spikes, ♂ infl. longer than ♀; sta. twice as many as pet. Fr. a drupe. Pacific Is., Malaysia, NE Aus. Z10.

P. cerasiferum (F.J. Muell.) Parker = *P. timoriense*.

P. pleiogyna F. Muell. = *P. timoriense*.

P. popuanum C.T. White = *P. timoriense*.

P. solandri (Benth.) Engl. = *P. timoriense*.

P. timoriense (DC.) Leenh. To 48m, sometimes buttressed. Bark peeling, fissured. Lfts 3.5–13.5cm, 6–12, stalked elliptic-oblong to elliptic-lanceolate. ♂ infl. to 30cm. Fr. about 1.5×2cm, red to dark brown, smooth. Pacific Is., Malaysia, NE Aus.

→*Spondias*.

Pleione D. Don. INDIAN CROCUS. Orchidaceae. 16 dwarf epiphytic or terrestrial orchids. Pbs clustered, usually only 2 seasons' growth persisting, ovoid to pyriform. Lvs sometimes white-striped at first, plicate. Infl. term. in emerging growth (appearing basal); fls 1–2; tep. spreading, lanceolate; lip rolled-tubular,

entire to obscurely trilobed, irregularly toothed, laciniate or fimbriate, callus hirsute lines or lamellae. India to Taiwan, Thail. Z8.

P. aurita Cribb & Pfennig. Pbs conical, to 4.5cm. Fls pale pink to rose or purple, paler at base; pet. ligulate, obtuse, to 4.5cm, sharply reflexed; lip obscurely trilobed at apex, undulate, toothed, larcellae 5, orange-yellow, pubesc. SW China.

P. bulbocodioides (Franch.) Rolfe. Pbs pyramidal or conical, to 3cm. Tep. to 4.5cm, pink to rose-purple or magenta, lip marked dark purple; obovate, obscurely trilobed, margins irregular, notched, lamellae 4–5, toothed. China.

P. formosana Hay. Pbs globose to ovoid, to 3cm, green to dull dark purple. Tep. to 5cm, white, lilac or magenta, lip white, typically stained or marked yellow; entire or trilobed, tip notched, margin undulate, fimbriate, lamellae 2–5, entire or jagged. E China.

P. forrestii Schltr. Pbs narrow-ovoid or conical, to 3cm, flushed purple at base. Tep. to 4cm, golden yellow or white, lip spotted brown or crimson; elliptic-obovate, fimbriate, notched, lamellae 5–7, entire. China.

P. hookeriana (Lindl.) Williams. Pbs ovoid or conical, to 3cm, purple or green. Tep. lilac-pink to rose, sometimes dotted pale violet, rarely white, lip white, dotted yellow-brown or purple; lip cordate, obscurely trilobed, notched, fringed, lamellae 7, barbed, yellow. C Nepal to S China.

P. humilis (Sm.) D. Don. Pbs olive green, pyriform, to 6cm. Fls to 8cm diam., white, lip spotted and streaked bronze or blood red, oblong-elliptic, base saccate, apex notched, obscurely trilobed, margins jagged, lamellae yellow, 5–7, barbed. Burm., NE India.

P. × lagenaria Lindl. (*P. maculata × P. praecox*.) Pbs squat-ellipsoid, to 2.5cm. Tep. to 4cm, pink to rose-purple, lip white, central patch yellow, margins blotched purple; obscurely trilobed, midlobe almost rectangular, toothed, lamellae 5, papillose. Asia, SW China.

P. limprichtii Schltr. Pbs conical to ovoid, pale to deep green or purple, to 4cm. Tep. to 4cm, rose-pink to magenta, lip paler, spotted ochre or crimson, almost orbicular, apex obscurely trilobed, laciniate, lamellae 4, white, toothed or jagged. SW China, N Burm.

P. maculata (Lindl.) Lindl. Pbs turbinate, beaked, covered in the netted, sheath remains. Fls to 8cm diam., fragrant, cream, rarely streaked pink, lip white, central blotch yellow, apical margins blotched purple, oblong, obslcurely trilobed, midlobe notched, undulate, jagged, 5–7 papillose. India, Bhutan, Burm., SW China, Thail.

P. pogonioides (Rolfe) Rolfe = *P. bulbocodioides*.

P. praecox (Sm.) D. Don. Pbs turbinate, beaked, green, dappled red-brown; fls. to 10cm diam., white to rose-purple, lip midlobe cleft, toothed or fringed, lamellae 3–5 papillose, yellow. Indochina, Burm.

P. pricei Rolfe = *P. formosana*.

P. speciosa Ames & Schltr. Pbs ovoid to conical, to 3cm. Tep. to 7cm, bright magenta, lip blotched peach, almost rhombic to obovate, truncate, minutely toothed, lamellae 2–4 toothed, yellow. China.

P. yunnanensis (Rolfe) Rolfe. Pbs squat, conical, to 2cm. Tep. to 4cm, pale lavender to rose pink, rarely white; lip flecked red or purple; obscurely trilobed, midlobe subrectangular, undulate, lacerate, lamellae 5, entire. N Burm., China.

P. cvs.
Many grexes and selections, either spring- or winter-flowering, fls white to pink, pale mauve, purple-rose, apricot, gold or yellow, lip sometimes paler often frilled or fimbriate and variously spotted or blotched red.

Pleiospilos N.E. Br. LIVING GRANITE; LIVING ROCK; STONE MIMICRY PLANT. Aizoaceae. 4 highly succulent, stemless perennials. Lvs similar in texture to lumps of granite paired and decussate, v. thick, flat above, apex obtuse to acute, grey-green or dark green with translucent dots. Fls ± sessile solitary or several together. Late summer. S Afr. Z9.

P. archeri (Ait.) Schwantes = *Tanquana archeri*.

P. bolusii (Hook. f.) N.E. Br. MIMICRY PLANT; LIVING ROCK CACTUS. Usually solitary with 1 pair of lvs, 4–7cm long, 3–3.5cm thick, upper surface broader than long, lower surface rounded, apex thickened and drawn over upper surface, red or brown-green with numerous dots. Fls 1–4, 6–8 diam., golden-yellow. Karroo.

P. borealis L. Bol. = *P. compactus* ssp. *canus*.

P. clavatus L. Bol. = *Tanquana archeri*.

P. compactus (Ait.) Schwantes. Lvs 4–6 per shoot, 2–5cm, convex below, blunt-carinate blow tip, brown-green or red-green with a purple tinge, densely spotted. Fls solitary, 2.5–3cm diam., light yellow. Cape. SW Cape. ssp. *canus* (Haw.) Hartm. & Liede. Lvs 4–8 per shoot, 3–9cm, triquetrous, acutely carinate below.

Fls 3.5–8cm diam., golden to pale yellow. Karroo. ssp. *minor* (L. Bol.) Hartm. & Liede. Lvs 4–6 per shoot, 2.5–8cm, underside keeled above, expanded toward the tip, with prominent dots, margins sometimes reddened. Fls 4.5–7cm diam., glossy yellow. W Cape.

P. dekenahii (N.E. Br.) Schwantes = *P. compactus* ssp. *canus*.

P. dimidiatus L. Bol. = *P. compactus* ssp. *minor*.

P. hilmarii L. Bol. = *Tanquana hilmarii*.

P. kingiae L. Bol. = *P. compactus* ssp. *canus*.

P. latipetalus L. Bol. = *P. compactus* ssp. *canus*.

P. loganii L. Bol. = *Tanquana archeri*.

P. minor L. Bol. = *P. compactus* ssp. *minor*.

P. multipunctatus hort. = *P. compactus* ssp. *canus*.

P. nelii Schwantes. SPLITROCK; CLEFTSTONE; MIMICRY PLANT. Resembling *P. bolussi* in stature. Lvs 2–4, rounded below, drawn over upper surface so that lf is hemispherical, dark greygreen, densely dotted. Fls solitary, 7cm diam., salmon pink to yellow to orange. SW Cape.

P. nobilis (Haw.) Schwantes = *P. compactus* ssp. *canus*.

P. optatus (N.E. Br.) Schwantes = *P. compactus*.

P. pedunculata L. Bol. = *P. nelii*.

P. prismaticus (Schwantes) Schwantes = *Tanquana prismatica*.

P. roodiae (N.E. Br.) Schwantes = *Tanquana prismatica*.

P. simulans (Marloth) N.E. Br. Lvs 6–8cm, usually paired, ovate-triangular, tip thickened beneath, not drawn over upper surface, red-, yellow-, or brown-green, spotted, undulating and tuberculate. Fls 1–4, yellow, sometimes orange, fragrant. E Cape.

P. sororius (N.E. Br.) Schwantes = *P. compactus* ssp. *minor*.

P. tricolor N.E. Br. = *P. nelii*.

P. willowmorensis L. Bol. = *P. compactus* ssp. *canus*.

→*Punctillaria*.

Pleiostachya Schum. Marantaceae. 3 caulescent, rhizomatous herbs, 1–3m. Lvs 1–2 at base, otherwise cauline, ovate to oblong, pulvinately inserted on long sheathing petioles. Infl. paniculate, laterally compressed; bracts distichous, overlapping, fls 2 per cymule; cor. tube white, 2.5–5cm; outer staminode, 1, purple, callose staminode yellow, tipped purple, fleshy. Trop. Amer. from Mex. to Ecuad. Z10.

P. pruinosa (Reg.) Schum. Erect. to 2m. Lvs to 45cm, oblong to lanceolate, dark green above, purple beneath. Infl. to 10cm. C Amer.

→*Maranta*.

Pleomele Salisb.

P. deremensis (Engl.) N.E. Br. = *Dracaena deremensis*.

P. gracilis hort. = *Dracaena cincta*.

P. reflexa (Lam.) N.E. Br. = *Dracaena reflexa*.

P. thalioides (hort. Makoy ex E. Morr.) N.E. Br. = *Dracaena thalioides*.

Pleonotoma Miers. Bignoniaceae. 14 lianes. Br. tetragonal. Lvs pinnate with trifid tendrils. Fls in term. rac.; cor. tubularfunnelform, ventricose, bilabiate, 5-lobed. Americas. Z10.

P. variabilis (Jacq.) Miers. Lower lvs twice trifoliate, upper lvs ternate, with trifid tendril; lfts 2–16cm, ovate-elliptic. Rac. short; cor. 6–10×1–3cm, tube pale yellow, limb white to cream. Guat. to Venez. and Trin.

→*Bignonia*.

Pleopeltis Humb. & Bonpl. ex Willd. Polypodiaceae. 40 epiphytic ferns. Rhiz. slender, long-creeping, scaly. Fronds uniform, simple, rarely pinnatifid, membranous to rigid. Trop. Amer. to Afr., Asia, Jap., Hawaii. Z10.

P. accedens (Bl.) Moore = *Lemmaphyllum accedens*.

P. alternifolia (Willd.) Moore = *Microsorium nigrescens*.

P. diversifolia (Willd.) Melvaine = *Microsorium diversifolium*.

P. hemionitidea (Presl) Moore = *Colysis hemionitidea*.

P. iridoides (Poir.) Moore = *Microsorium punctatum*.

P. lima v.A.v.R. = *Selliguea lima*.

P. lycopodioides (L.) Presl = *Microgramma lycopodioides*.

P. macrocarpa (Bory ex Willd.) Kaulf. Fronds to 30×1cm, linear to elliptic, apex attenuate, undulate, leathery to rigid, scaly beneath; stipes to 15cm. Trop. S Amer.

P. musifolia (Bl.) Moore = *Microsorium musifolium*.

P. nigrescens (Bl.) Carr. ex Seem. = *Microsorium nigrescens*.

P. normalis (D. Don) Moore = *Microsorium normale*.

P. percussa (Cav.) Hook. & Grev. Fronds to 30×3cm, lanceolate, apex narrowly acute, entire, leathery, sparsely scaly beneath; stipes to 7cm. Trop. S Amer.

P. phyllitidis (L.) Alston = *Campyloneurum phyllitidis*.

P. phymatodes (L.) Moore = *Microsorium scolopendrium*.

P. pteropus (Bl.) Moore = *Microsorium pteropus*.

P. punctata (L.) Bedd. = *Microsorium punctatum*.

P. subnormalis (D. Don) v.A.v.R. = *Microsorium normale*.

Pleurisy Root *Asclepias tuberosa*.

Pleurosorus Fée. Aspleniaceae. 3 terrestrial ferns. Rhiz. short and erect. Fronds stipitate, uniform, pinnate to pinnatifid, herbaceous, pubesc. Chile; Spain and Moroc.; Aus. and NZ. Z9.

P. rutifolius (R. Br.) Fée. Fronds to 10×3cm, oblong, occas. gland., white- to rusty-pubesc., pinnae to 15×10mm, to 4 pairs, obovate to flabellate, subentire to lobed; stipes to 5cm, occas. gland., rusty-pubesc. Aus., Tasm., NZ.

→*Ceterach*, *Grammitis* and *Gymnogramma*.

Pleurospermum Hoffm. Umbelliferae. 3 bienn. or perenn. herbs. Lvs 2–3-pinnate. Umbels compound; bracts few to many, often compound; bracteoles entire to toothed or pinnatifid, often white; fls small. E Eur., Asia. Z7.

P. brunonis (DC.) C.B. Clarke. Perenn. to 170cm. Lvs pinnate, seg. lanceolate, 3-lobed, toothed. Umbels with 10–25 rays, to 20cm diam.; bracteoles 5–8 oblong, large4, with white, toothed margins; fls white-pink. Summer. Pak. to W Nepal.

Pleurothallis R. Br. Orchidaceae. Some 900 epiphytic and lithophytic orchids. Slender st., tufted, erect, usually unifoliate. Lvs term., coriaceous to fleshy, rac., term. or, rarely, lat.; fls small; dors. sep. free or briefly connate with lat. sep., lat. sep. ± connate, concave pet. smaller; lip usually shorter than pet., entire or 3-lobed. Trop. Amer. Many of the larger sp. described here will be considerably smaller in cult. Z10.

P. acrisepala Ames & Schweinf. = *P. brighamii*.

P. amethystina Ames = *P. segoviensis*.

P. angustisegmenta Schweinf. = *Barbosella cucullata*.

P. araguensis Ames = *P. secunda*.

P. astrophora Rchb. f. ex Kränzl. = *Lepanthopsis astrophora*.

P. atropurpurea (Lindl.) Lindl. = *Zootrophion atropurpureum*.

P. barboselloides Schltr. = *P. brighamii*.

P. brighamii S. Wats. St. to 6mm. Lvs to 9×1cm, oblanceolate to elliptic-oblong. Infl. to 10cm, 1- to several-fld, filiform; fls to 1cm diam., yellow striped red-brown or with green and brown markings. Guat. and Br. Hond. to Panama.

P. calerae Schltr. = *P. immersa*.

P. cardiostola Rchb. f. St. to 20cm. Lvs to 14×4cm, lanceolate to narrowly ovate. Fls usually solitary, successive, brown or pale green-brown, to 3cm diam., interior downy lip. Venez., Colomb., Ecuad.

P. cerea Ames = *P. octomerioides*.

P. ciliaris (Lindl.) L.O. Williams = *Trichosalpinx ciliaris*.

P. ciliata Knowles & Westc. = *P. lanceana*.

P. compacta (Ames) Ames & Schweinf. = *Platystele compacta*.

P. dura Lindl. = *Trichosalpinx dura*.

P. endotrachys Rchb. f. = *P. platyrachis*.

P. floripectin Rchb. f. = *Lepanthopsis floripectin*.

P. fulgens Rchb. f. St. minute. Lvs to 8.5×2cm, elliptic to obovate-spathulate; fls bew, fasciculate, to 1.5cm diam., bright cinnabar-red. Costa Rica, Panama.

P. gelida Lindl. St. to 35cm. Lvs to 25×7cm, ovate-elliptic to oblong-elliptic. Infl. 1- to several-fld, to 30cm, erect; fls second, to 1cm, pale yellow to green-yellow. Flor., Mex. to Panama, W Indies, S Amer.

P. ghiesbreghtiana Rich. & Gal. = *P. quadrifida*.

P. glomerata Ames = *P. ruscifolia*.

P. grobyi Batem. ex Lindl. St. to 1cm. Lvs to 7×1cm, obovate, spathulate or oblanceolate. Infl. to 15cm, loosely few- to several-fld; fls to 1cm, membranous, green, white or yelloworange, marked red-purple. Mex. and W Indies to Peru and Braz.

P. immersa Lind. & Rchb. f. St. to 7cm. Lvs to 19×4cm, oblongoblanceolate. Infl. to 40cm, erect, loosely many-fld; peduncle slightly compressed; fls to 1.5cm, usually pendent, yellow-green or purple-brown with dark venation. Mex., Guat., Hond., Costa Rica, Venez., Colomb., Panama.

P. intermedia Schltr. = *P. loranthophylla*.

P. johnstonii Ames = *Platystele johnstonii*.

P. krameriana Rchb. f. = *P. immersa*.

P. lanceana Lodd. St. short. Lvs to 9×3cm, elliptic-oblong, fleshy. Infl. exceeding lvs, many-fld; fls to 1cm, dors. sep. yellow flecked purple-crimson, lat. sep. yellow; pet. tinged pink; lip yellow-brown spotted maroon. Guat., Costa Rica, Trin., trop. S Amer.

P. lasiosepala Schltr. = *P. immersa*.

P. lindenii Lindl. = *P. secunda*.

P. longissima Lindl. = *P. quadrifida*.

P. loranthophylla Rchb. f. St. to 10cm. Lvs to 10×3.5cm, elliptic-oblong. Infl. loosely several-fld; fls to 1cm, light brown tinged maroon, spotted maroon. Venez., Colomb., Ecuad., Peru, Boliv.

P. marginata Lindl. = *P. grobyi*.

P. mathewsii Lindl. = *P. phalangifera*.

P. megachlamys Schltr. = *P. tuerckheimii*.

P. miersii Lindl. = *Barbrodria miersii*.

P. misera Lindl. = *Platystele misera*.

P. octomeriae Schltr. = *P. octomerioides*.

P. octomerioides Lindl. St. to 15cm. Lvs to 12×2cm, narrowly elliptic to oblong-lanceolate. Fls in clusters, fleshy, pale yellow, to 1cm. Mex. to Panama.

P. ophiocephala Lindl. = *Restrepiella ophiocephala*.

P. ornata (Garay) Foldats = *Platystele ornata*.

P. ospinae R.E. Schult. = *Restrepia antennifera*.

P. ovalifolia (Focke) Rchb. f. = *Platystele ovalifolia*.

P. pauciflora Schltr. = *P. pruinosa*.

P. periodica Ames = *P. brighamii*.

P. pfavii Rchb. f. = *P. platyrachis*.

P. phalangifera (Presl) Rchb. f. St. to 34cm. Lvs to 17×8cm, ovate to ovate-elliptic. Infl. 1–3, to 30cm, few- to many-fld; fls to 6cm diam., yellow-green to purple. Venez. and Colomb. to Peru.

P. picta Lindl. = *P. grobyi*.

P. pittieri Schltr. = *P. velaticaulis*.

P. platyrachis (Rolfe) Rolfe. St. to 2cm, stout. Lvs to 20×3cm, oblanceolate-ligulate, fleshy. Infl. to 35cm, erect; fls fleshy; sep. bright red or orange-red, white toward base, verrucose laterals to 2cm; pet. bright red. Mex. to Panama, Colomb., Venez.

P. plumosa Lindl. = *P. lanceana*.

P. prolifera Herb. ex Lindl. St. to 20cm. Lvs to 8×4cm, fleshy, ovate to ovate-lanceolate. Infl. shorter than lvs, few- to many-fld sometimes proliferous; fls to 1cm, deep purple or red-brown. Venez., Braz.

P. pruinosa Lindl. St. to 8cm. Lvs to 5×1cm, elliptic-oblong or lanceolate. Infl. 1–3, few-fld, usually exceeding lvs; fls to 1cm diam., pale yellow or white-green. C. Amer., Venez., Colomb., Ecuad., Peru, Guianas, W Indies.

P. punctata (Karst.) Schltr. = *P. loranthophylla*.

P. quadrifida (La Ll. & Lex.) Lindl. St. to 17cm. Lvs to 16×3cm, oblanceolate to elliptic-oblong. Infl. to 40cm, many-fld; fls to 2cm diam., fragrant, pendent, yellow or pale yellow-green. Mex. to Panama, W Indies, Venez., Colomb.

P. ruscifolia (Jacq.) R. Br. St. to 40cm. Lvs to 20×6cm, elliptic-oblong to lanceolate. Fls clustered, slightly fragrant, to 2cm, pale green to pale yellow. W Indies, Guat., Costa Rica, Panama, N S Amer.

P. secunda Poepp. & Endl. St. to 40cm. Lvs to 30×6cm, elliptic or oblong. Infl. to 20cm, pendent, few-fld; sep. translucent yellow-green, laterals striped purple; pet. red or yellow, to 15×3mm; lip yellow. Venez., Colomb., Ecuad., Peru.

P. segoviensis Rchb. f. St. to 6cm. Lvs to 13×1.5cm, oblanceolate to ligulate. Infl. to 17cm, few- to several-fld, slender-stalked; fls to 2cm diam., yellow-green blotched brown to dark red-purple. Mex. to Panama.

P. sertularioides (Sw.) Spreng. St. to 5mm. Lvs to 4×0.4cm, linear-oblanceolate to linear-spathulate. Infl. filiform, usually shorter than lvs, 1- or 2-fld; fls to 1cm diam., strew-yellow. Mex., Guat., Hond., Nic.

P. stenopetala Lodd. ex Lindl. St. to 14cm. Lvs to 10×3cm, elliptic-oblong or oblanceolate. Infl. to 27cm, many-fld; fls to 2cm, narrow, yellow-white or green-white. Braz.

P. stenostachya Rchb. f. = *Platystele stenostachya*.

P. tribuloides (Sw.) Lindl. St. to 1cm. Lvs to 7×1.5cm, obovate to oblanceolate. Infl. a fascicle of 1–3 fls; peduncle to 1cm; fls to 8mm, brick-red or dark maroon. C Amer., W Indies.

P. tuerckheimii Schltr. St. to 35cm. Lvs to 25×7cm, elliptic to lanceolate. Infl. to 35cm, erect, loosely many-fld; fls to 3cm diam., purple-maroon and white or cream, papillose-puberulent. Mex. to Panama.

P. velaticaulis Rchb. f. St. to 30cm. Lvs to 22×9cm, oblanceolate-ligulate. Rac. shorter than lvs, many-fld; fls to 1cm diam., fragrant, pale green or yellow-green. Costa Rica, Panama, W Indies, Venez. to Peru.

P. verrucosa (Rchb. f.) Rchb. f. = *Scaphosepalum verrucosum*.

P. wercklei Schltr. = *P. segoviensis*.

Plover's Eggs *Adromischus cooperi*.

Plum *Prunus* (*P. × domestica*).

Plumbagella Spach. Plumbaginaceae. 1 ann. herb to 50cm. St. erect or ascending, 3- or 4-angled, tinged red, branching and spinose below. Lvs 3–15cm, ovate-lanceolate, acuminate, entire, base cordate, slightly decurrent, blotched or spotted beneath. Infl. compact, spiciform, 3–5-fld, borne in axil of bracts; cal. about 4mm, 5-ribbed; cor. 5-lobed, narrowly campanulate, slightly exceeding cal., blue-violet. C Asia.

P. micrantha (Ledeb.) Spach.
→*Plumbago*.

PLUMBAGINACEAE Juss. 22/440. *Acantholimon, Armeria, Ceratostigma, Goniolimon, Limoniastrum, Limonium, Plumbagella, Plumbago, Psylliostachys*.

Plumbago L. LEADWORT. Plumbaginaceae. 15 shrubs or perenn. or ann. herbs. Lvs simple, entire, often auriculate. Infl. a spicate term. rac.; cal. tubular, 5-parted; cor. tube slender, limb 5 lobed, spreading; style 1, pubesc. below, usually long and slender. Warm and trop. regions.

P. aphylla Bojer ex Boiss. Herb. Lvs to 2.5cm, on young st. only, oblong-ovate. Rac. to 6cm; cor. white 1.5cm, edged red. Madag. Z10.

P. auriculata Lam. CAPE LEADWORT. Shrub; st. long-arching, somewhat scandent. Lvs to 7cm, oblong to oblong-spathulate, tapering into petiole. Spikes short; cor. 4cm, pale blue. S Afr., nat. S Eur. Z9.

P. auriculata Bl. non Lam. = *P. zeylanica*.

P. caerulea HBK. Ann., 30–50cm, erect; st. arching. Lvs ovate-oblong to rhomboidal, acuminate; petiole winged. Spikelets 1-to few-fld; cor. to 1.5cm; tube rich purple, lobes deep blue with central dark line. Peru.

P. capensis Thunb. = *P. auriculata*.

P. coccinea Salisb. = *P. indica*.

P. europaea L. Slender, erect perenn. herb to 1m. Lvs to 8cm, broadly elliptic to lanceolate, glaucescent, short-petioled. Fls subsessile; cor. to 1.2cm, violet to deep pink. W Medit. to Balk. and C Asia. Z6.

P. flaccida Moench = *P. zeylanica*.

P. floridana Nutt. = *P. scandens*.

P. glandulosa Willd. ex Roem. & Schult. = *P. caerulea*.

P. humboldtiana Roem. & Schult. = *P. caerulea*.

P. indica L. Herb or subshrub, semiscandent or erect. Lvs 5–11cm. Spikes 10–30cm, lax; cor. deep rosy pink to pale red or purple to 2.5cm. SE Asia. Z10.

P. lactea Salisb. = *P. zeylanica*.

P. larpentiae Lindl. = *Ceratostigma plumbaginoides*.

P. mexicana HBK = *P. scandens*.

P. micrantha Ledeb. = *Plumbagella micrantha*.

P. occidentalis Sweet = *P. scandens*.

P. pulchella Boiss. Subshrub, slender, erect to 1m. Lvs ovate-oblong, acuminate, mucronate; petiole cor. clasping. Spikes lax; cor. about 1.5cm, blue-violet. Mex. Z10.

P. rhomboidea Hook. non Lodd. = *P. caerulea*.

P. rhomboidea Lodd. non Hook. = *P. pulchella*.

P. rosea L. = *P. indica*.

P. scandens L. DEVIL'S HERB; TOOTHWORT. Shrub, decumbent to scandent; br. grooved. Lvs to 10cm, oblong-lanceolate, mucronate, tapering to short petiole. Infl. paniculate; cor. to 2cm, white or blue, lobes mucronulate. Summer. S US to Trop. S Amer. Z10.

P. virginica Hook. f. = *P. zeylanica*.

P. viscosa Blanco = *P. zeylanica*.

P. zeylanica L. Shrub to 1m, somewhat scandent; br. angled. Lvs 3–12cm, ovate to oblong, tapering to petiole. Spikes dense, gland.; cor. 2.5cm, white, anth. blue to violet. SE Asia to Aus. Z10.

Plume Albizia *Albizia lophantha*.

Plume Bush *Calomeria amaranthoides*.

Plumed Lanolin Bush *Franklandia triaristata*.

Plumed Maidenhair *Adiantum formosum*.

Plumed Tussock *Cortaderia richardii*.

Plumed Tussock Grass *Chionochloa conspicua*.

Plume Flower *Justicia carnea*.

Plume Hyacinth *Muscari comosum* 'Monstrosum'.

Plume Poppy *Macleaya cordata*.

Plumeria L. FRANGIPANGI; TEMPLE TREE; NOSEGAY; WEST INDIAN JASMINE; PAGODA TREE. Apocynaceae. 8 decid. shrubs and small trees. Br. candelabriform, cylindrical, swollen, grey-green, with petiole scars and milky sap. Lvs petiolate, oblong or lanceolate-elliptic. Fls fragrant in termminal thyrses; cor. slaverform or funnelform, lobes 5, spreading, ovate-elliptic. Trop. Amer. Z10.

P. alba L. WEST INDIAN JASMINE. To 6m tall. Lvs to 30cm, lanceolate, often rather bullate, usually finely pubesc. beneath. Cor. to 6cm diam., yellow with white centre, tube to 2.25cm. Puerto Rico, Lesser Antilles.

P. emarginata Griseb. = *P. obtusa*.

P. obtusa L. To 8m. Lvs to 20cm, obovate to oblong, obtuse, often emarginate. Cor. white, yellow at centre; salverform; limb to 7cm diam., tube to 2.5cm. Bahamas, Greater Antilles. var. *sericifolia* (C.H. Wright) Woodson. Lf undersurfaces and infl. pubesc. Hispan., Cuba, Yucatan.

P. pudica Jacq. To 4m. Lvs to 30cm, oblong-spathulate, apex blunt or briefly tapering. Cor. near-funnelform, white or ivory marked yellow, limb to 1.8cm diam., tube to 2.5cm. Colomb., Venez.

P. rubra L. To 7m. Lvs to 40cm, obovate, broadly elliptic or oblong-lanceolate. Cor. typically rose-pink with a yellow throat, but highly variable in colour, fragrant; to 10cm diam., salverform, tube to 2.5cm. Mex. to Panama. f. *acutifolia* (Poir.) Woodson. Lvs narrow. Cor. white, throat golden. f. *lutea* (Ruiz & Pav.) Woodson. Cor. yellow, exterior often suffused pale red. f. *tricolor* (Ruiz & Pav.) Woodson. Cor. white, edged rose, throat yellow.

Plume Smokebush *Conospermum incurvum.*
Plume Thistle *Cirsium.*
Plum-fruited Yew *Prumnopitys andina.*
Plum Tree *Eucryphia moorei.*
Plum Yew *Cephalotaxus.*
Plush Plant *Echeveria pulvinata.*
Plymouth Strawberry *Fragaria moschata.*

Pneumatopteris Nak. Thelypteridaceae. 80+ terrestrial or rupestral ferns. Rhiz. short and erect or long-creeping. Fronds usually large, attenuate at base, sparsely short-pubescent or glab. and pustular beneath, pinnae many, lobed, lobes often cartilaginous at margin; stipes scaly at base. OW Trop. to Hawaii. Z10.

P. pennigera (Forst. f.) Holtt. Rhiz. short, trunk-like, to 10cm wide. Foliage sometimes mucillaginous. Stipes to 50cm. Fronds to 1m×30cm, pinnae to 20×30cm, distant, oblong, acute, lobes to 2cm, oblong, entire to notched or undulate. NZ, Aus.
→*Dryopteris* and *Thelypteris.*

Poa L. MEADOWGRASS; BLUE GRASS; SPEAR GRASS. Gramineae. *c*500 mostly perenn. grasses. St. slender to robust. Lvs narrow, folded to flat, ligules membranous. Infl. paniculate, open to compact; spikelets stipitate, 2- to several flowered. Cool temp. regions.

P. abbreviata R. Br. Habit v. dwarf, to 2cm. Lvs dark green. Spikelets minute, soft.

P. alpina L. ALPINE MEADOW GRASS; BLUE GRASS. Perenn., tufted. St. to 50cm, somewhat thickened at base. Lvs to 5×0.3cm, linear, thick, flattened; ligules to 4mm. Pan. to 7cm, ovoid, dense, shortly branched. C Asia, Russia. var. *vivipara* (L.) Tzvelev. Spikelets replaced by numerous plantlets.

P. annua L. Ann. or bienn. St. to 30cm, smooth, creeping or erect. Lvs to 3.5mm diam., narrowly linear, flat, smooth; ligules to 2mm. Pan. to 7cm, pyramidal, loose. Eur., US.

P. bulbosa L. BULBOUS MEADOW GRASS. Perenn., densely tufted to 55cm. Basal sheaths swollen, forming a bulb. Lvs to 1.5mm diam., narrow-linear, involute; ligules to 2mm, hyaline. Pan. to 6cm, oblong, compact; br. scabrous, short. Eurasia, N Afr.; nat. US.

P. caesia Sm. = *P. glauca.*

P. chaixii Vill. BROAD-LEAVED MEADOWGRASS; FOREST BLUE-GRASS. Perenn., to 120cm. Lvs to 45×1cm, flat or folded, bright green. Pan. ovoid to ovoid-oblong, open, to 25×11cm. Spring–summer. Eur., SW Asia. Z5.

P. colensoi Hook. f. Perenn., to 25cm. St. erect or arching, flimsy, blue-green. Lvs to 16cm×0.2cm, threadlike, blue-green, involute. Pan. lax, to 5cm; spikelets blue, becoming brown-tinged. NZ. Z7.

P. curvula Schräd. = *Eragrostis curvula.*

P. fertilis Host = *P. palustris.*

P. glauca Vahl. GLAUCOUS MEADOWGRASS. Glaucous perenn., to 40cm. Lvs to 8cm×0.4cm, glab.; ligules to 3mm. Pan. erect, stiff, to 10×4cm, sometimes tinted purple. Summer–autumn. N Eurasia, N N Amer. Z5.

P. iridifolia Hauman. Perenn., to 90cm. Lvs flat or folded, erect, to 50cm×1.8cm, glab.; ligules to 3mm. Pan. ovoid, erect to pendent, to 30×7cm. Summer. Urug., Arg. Z8.

P. labillardieri Steud. Perenn. to 1m. Lvs to 30cm or more, slender, grey-green. Spikelets tinged purple. Aus.

P. mexicana Hornem. = *Eragrostis mexicana.*

P. nemoralis L. WOOD MEADOWGRASS Perenn., to 90cm. Lvs to 12cm×0.3cm, glab.; ligules v. short, membranous. Pan. ovoid to cylindric, to 20cm; br. spreading. Summer. Eur., temp. Asia, NE Amer. Z5.

P. palustris L. SWAMP MEADOWGRASS. Perenn., to 1.5m. Lvs to 20cm×0.4cm, scabrous; ligules to 5mm. Pan. ovoid to oblong, to 30×15cm, tinged yellow-green or purple. Summer. N temp. Z5.

P. pilosa L. = *Eragrostis pilosa.*

P. plumosa Retz. = *Eragrostis tenella.*

P. pratensis L. KENTUCKY BLUE GRASS; JUNE GRASS. Perenn., loosely tufted. Lvs to 4mm diam., narrow-linear, flattened, smooth or scabrous; ligule to 1.5mm, rounded to truncate. Pan. to 20cm, pyramidal. Eurasia, N Afr. Z3.

P. serotina Ehrenb. = *P. palustris.*
P. sudetica Haenke = *P. chaixii.*
P. trichodes Nutt. = *Eragrostis trichodes.*
→*Agrostis.*

POACEAE Barnhart. See *Gramineae.*

Poached Egg Flower *Limnanthes douglasii.*
Pocketbook Flower *Calceolaria.*
Pocket Handkerchief Tree *Davidia involucrata.*
Pocket Handkerchief Tree *Davidia.*

Podachaenium Benth. ex Ørst. Compositae. 2 trees or shrubs. Lvs opposite, occas. alt. above, pinnatifid or dentate, petiolate. Cap. radiate, in corymbose pan.; ray flts white; disc flts yellow. C Amer. Z10.

P. eminens (Lagasca) Schultz-Bip. Shrub or small tree, to 8m, br. softly tomentose. Lvs to 30cm, broadly ovate to suborbicular, lobes angular, ± glab. above, pale grey- to brown-tomentose beneath. Cap. to 2.5cm diam. Spring–summer. Mex. to Costa Rica.
→*Ferdinanda.*

Podalyria Willd. Leguminosae (Papilionoideae). 25 downy shrubs. Lvs simple, linear to suborbicular, usually subcordate at base, revolute, often caducous. Fls pea-like, fragrant 1–2, on axill. stalks. S Afr. Z9.

P. calyptrata (Retz.) Willd. To 3m. Lvs to 5×4cm, elliptic or obovate, grey-green, thinly pubesc. Fls to 3cm; buds enveloped by bracts; pet. light pink to lavender-purple, purple at base, keel white. Spring–summer.

P. sericea (Andrews) R. Br. To 1m. Lvs to 2×2cm, obovate, submucronate, initially silvery-, later golden-sericeous. Fls to 1cm; buds not enveloped by bracts; pet. lavender. Winter.

P. styracifolia Sims = *P. calyptrata.*
→*Sophora.*

Podangis Schltr. Orchidaceae. 1 epiphytic monopodial orchid. St. short. Lvs 4–16cm×5–12mm, fleshy. Rac., shorter than lvs, subcapitate; fls white; tep. 3.5–5mm, elliptic, obtuse; lip 6mm, ± orbicular, entire, crenulate; spur 11–14mm, swollen and often bifid at apex. Trop. Afr. Z10.

P. dactyloceras (Rchb. f.) Schltr.

Podanthes Haw.
P. pulchellus Haw. = *Orbea pulchella.*

PODOCARPACEAE Endl. 12/155. *Acmopyle, Afrocarpus, Dacrycarpus, Dacrydium, Falcatifolium, Halocarpus, Lagarostrobus, Lepidothamnus, Microcachrys, Microstrobos, Nageia, Parasitaxus, Podocarpus, Prumnopitys, Retrophyllum, Saxegothaea, Sundacarpus.*

Podocarp *Podocarpus.*

Podocarpus L'Hérit. ex Pers. PODOCARP; YELLOW-WOOD. Podocarpaceae. *c*100 everg., coniferous tress or shrubs. Lvs spirally arranged, often twisted at base, apparently in 2 ranks, or in dense clusters, broadly acicular, sometimes falcate, coriaceous, base decurrent. ♂ cones solitary or in groups to 5, axill., or many in narrow elongate spicate infl., yellow. ♀ cones with 1–2 seeds on fused scales swelling to become a fleshy receptacle. Mex., C & S Amer., C & S Afr., Asia (Himal. to Jap.), Australasia.

P. acicularis Van Houtte ex Gordon = *P. elatus.*
P. acutifolius T. Kirk = *P. lawrencei.*

P. alpinus R. Br. ex Hook. f. TASMANIAN PODOCARP. Shrub, to 3m. Br. level or upswept. Lvs linear-oblong, 6–12×1.5–2mm, dark buff green above, tinged blue beneath, obtuse to apiculate; midrib keeled. Receptacle fleshy, to 6×5mm, vivid red. SE Aus. (NSW, Vict., Tasm.). Z7.

P. amarus Bl. = *Sundacarpus amarus.*
P. andinus Poepp. ex Endl. = *Prumnopitys andina.*
P. antillarum R. Br. = *P. coriaceus.*
P. appressus Maxim. = *P. macrophyllus.*
P. bidwillii Hooibr. = *P. spinulosus.*
P. bracteata Bl. = *P. neriifolius.*
P. chilinus Rich. = *P. salignus.*
P. chinensis Wallich ex Parl. = *P. macrophyllus.*

P. coriaceus Rich. YACCA PODOCARP. Tree, to 20m. Lvs linear-lanceolate, straight to bowed, 8–18×1–2cm, coriaceous; long acuminate; midrib conspicuous, receptacle to 10mm, red, often tinged blue, fleshy. W Indies (Puerto Rico to Trin.). Z10.

P. cunninghamii Colenso. Name of uncertain application; Colenso's description suggests the hybrid *P. totara* ×*P. hallii*, occas. found wild in New Zealand. Lvs and shoots as *P. totara*;

bark as *P. hallii.* NZ.

P. cunninghamii sensu Laub., non Colenso = *P. hallii.*

P. cupressina R. Br. ex Mirb. = *Dacrycarpus imbricatus.*

P. dacryoides A. Rich. = *Dacrycarpus dacryioides.*

P. discolor Bl. = *P. neriifolius.*

P. dispermus C.T. White. Tree, to 18m. Lvs linear to narrow-lanceolate, 10–20×2–3cm, acuminate, dark green, shiny above, midrib clearly visible. Receptacle v. fleshy, scarlet. Aus. (N Queensld). Z11.

P. drouynianus F. Muell. Shrub, resembles *P. spinulosus* in habit, to 2m. Lvs linear, 5–8cm×2–3mm, green above, tinged blue beneath, sharp-acuminate, revlute, midrib conspicuous. Receptable fleshy, 12–25cm, purple, glaucous. W Aus. (extreme SW, 250km S of Perth). Z10.

P. elatus R. Br. ex Mirb. ROCKINGHAM PODOCARP; BROWN PINE. Tree, to 30m. Lvs oblong to lanceolate, straight or bowed, 5–15cm×7–12mm, pale green above, midrib clearly visible, apex obtuse or mucronate. Receptacle globose, to 12mm, blue-black. E Aus. Z10.

P. elongatus (Ait.) L'Hérit. ex Pers. CAPE YELLOWWOOD; AFRICAN YELLOWWOOD. Tree to 30m, or shrub. Lvs narrow-oblong or elliptic, 3–6cm×3–5mm on mature trees, to 12cm×12mm on young trees, green tinged blue above, some stomata above as well as beneath. Receptacle 10–15mm, fleshy, red to purple, bifid. S Afr. Z10.

P. elongatus Carr. non L'Hérit. = *Afrocarpus falcata.*

P. ensifolius R. Br. = *P. elatus.*

P. ensisculus Melville = *P. henkelii.*

P. eurhyncha Miq. = *Sundacarpus amarus.*

P. falcatus (Thunb.) R. Br. ex Mirb. = *Afrocarpus falcata.*

P. falcatus Engl. non (Thunb.) R. Br. ex Mirb. = *Afrocarpus gracilior.*

P. falciformis Parl. = *Falcatifolium falciforme.*

P. ferrugineus D. Don ex Laub. = *Prumnopitys ferruginea.*

P. ferruginoides Compton = *Prumnopitys ferruginoides.*

P. fleuryi Hickel = *Nageia fleuryi.*

P. forrestii Craib & W.W. Sm. = *P. macrophyllus.*

P. gracilior Pilger = *Afrocarpus gracilior.*

P. gracillimus Stapf = *Afrocarpus falcata.*

P. hallii T. Kirk. Resembles *P. totara.* Tree to 20m, bark papery, exfoliating in large sheet; shoots nodding in young specimens. Lvs on mature trees 25–40×4–5mm, linear-lanceolate, stiff, glaucous beneath, on young trees to 9cm, long acuminate, apex sharp. NZ. Z8.

P. henkelii Stapf. FALCATE YELLOWWOOD. Tree, to 35m; bark charcoal grey, exfoliating in long strips; br. pendent. Lvs similar to *P. salignus,* drooping, attenuate, falcate, 5–15cm×4–91mm. Receptacle green tinged glaucous blue, fleshy. S Afr. Z10.

P. horsfieldii Wallich = *Dacrycarpus imbricatus.*

P. imbricatus Bl. = *Dacrycarpus imbricatus.*

P. ladei Bail. = *Prumnopitys ladei.*

P. lambertii Klotzsch. Tree to 25m, br. whorled, numerous. Lvs erect, crowded, narrow oblong to linear-lanceolate, 25–35×2–4mm. Receptacle fleshy, 4mm. NE Arg., SE Braz. Z10.

P. latifolius (Thunb.) R. Br. ex Mirb. YELLOWWOOD. Tree to 30m, or shrubby; bark dark grey, smooth, exfoliating in long strips. Lvs linear-elliptic, 4–10cm×6–10mm on mature trees, to 20cm×18mm on young trees, straight or falcate, rigid, dark glossy green to green tinged blue above, midrib distinct beneath. Receptacle red tinged purple, fleshy, 8–14mm. Afr. (S Sudan to S Natal). Z10.

P. lawrencei Hook. f. Spreading shrub to small tree, to 10m. Lvs narrow-linear, 15–25×1.5–3mm, green suffused bronze, mucronate. Receptacle, bright red. NZ. Z7.

P. lawrencei auct. non Hook. f. = *P. alpinus.*

P. leptostachya Bl. = *P. neriifolius.*

P. longifoliolatus Pilger. Tree, to 12m. Bark furrowed, red or grey-brown. Lvs lanceolate, 5–10cm×6–10mm, to 14–11mm on young trees. Receptacle to 8mm, fleshy. New Caledonia. Z10.

P. longifolius Parl. = *P. macrophyllus.*

P. macrophyllus (Thunb.) D. Don. BIGLEAF PODOCARP; KUSAMAKI. Tree to 15m, or shrub to 2m. Lvs broad linear-lanceolate, 8–10cm×9–11mm on mature trees, to 18cm×14mm on young trees, green tinged yellow beneath, flexible, midrib distinct, bluntly acute. Receptacle 12–15mm, fleshy, red. S China, Jap. 'Angustifolius': lvs narrower. 'Argenteus': lvs narrow, bordered white. 'Maki': fastigiate, lvs shorter, 5–9cm. var. *nakai* (Hayata) Li & Keng. Lvs 6–8cm×8–12mm, lanceolate, more tapered. Taiwan. Z7.

P. mannii Hook. f. = *Afrocarpus mannii.*

P. matudae Lundell. Tree to 30m. Lvs 4–9cm×10–15mm, to 15cm×18mm on vigorous shoots; lanceolate, sometimes falcate, midrib raised above and beneath. Receptacle 6×6mm, red-brown. NE Mex., S to Costa Rica. Z9.

P. meyerianus Endl. = *Afrocarpus falcata.*

P. milanjianus Rendle = *P. latifolius.*

P. minor (Carr.) Parl. = *Retrophyllum minor.*

P. montanus (Willd.) Lodd. = *Prumnopitys montana.*

P. nageia R. Br. ex Mirb. = *Nageia nagi.*

P. nagi (Thunb.) Mak. = *Nageia nagi.*

P. neriifolius D. Don. OLEANDER PODOCARP; THITMIN. Tree, to 40m+. Bark brown, suffused grey or red, exfoliating in strips. Lvs narrow-lanceolate, 4cm×5mm to 24cm×28mm, coriaceous, flexible, glossy aove, paler beneath, midrib slightly raised above and beneath. Receptacle 8mm, 10mm. SE Asia to W Pacific. Z10.

P. nivalis Hook. ALPINE TOTARA. Resembles *P. alpinus,* but lvs elliptic, wider. Shrub, erect to prostrate or procumbent, to 2m×3m wide. Lvs 6–18×3mm, obtuse, rigid margin thickened. Receptacle red, to 7mm. S NZ (mts). Z7. 'Bronze': lvs tinged yellow-bronze, esp. when young.

P. nubigenus Lindl. CLOUD PODOCARP; CHILEAN PODOCARP. Tree to 20m, resembles *P. totara.* Lvs lanceolate to slightly falcate, 2–4cm×3–4mm, stiff, pungent, coriaceous, bright green above, 2 blue-white stomatal bands beneath. Receptacle fleshy red. S Chile, SW Arg. Z7.

P. oleifolius D. Don. Tree to 20m, bark yellow-brown. Lvs broad lanceolate, 3–8cm×6–12mm, apex acuminate, midrib groove above and ridge beneath. Receptacle fleshy, bright red-purple, 6–9×4mm. S Mex. to Boliv. Z10.

P. pedunculata Bail. = *Sundacarpus amarus.*

P. pungens D. Don = *P. spinulosus.*

P. richei Buchholz & Gray = *P. matudae.*

P. rospigliosi Pilger = *Retrophyllum rospigliosi.*

P. salignus D. Don. WILLOWLEAF PODOCARP; WILLOW PODOCARP; MAÑIO. Tree, to 20m, or shrub in cold areas. Bark fibrous. Br. ± arching. Adult lvs narrow-lanceolate, ± falcate, 8–12cm×5–7mm, shiny above, paler beneath; juvenile lvs straighter, 5–10cm. Receptacle fleshy, 8mm, dark red to violet. S Chile. Z8.

P. spicatus R. Br. ex Mirb. = *Prumnopitys taxifolia.*

P. spinulosus (Sm.) R. Br. ex Mirb. SPINY LEAF PODOCARP. Shrub, to 1.5m. Lvs 2–8cm×2–4mm, lanceolate, long acuminate, sharply spined, dark yellow-green. Receptacle violet, bloomed waxy blue, 10×8mm. Aus. (New S Wales). Z10.

P. taxifolius Kunth = *Prumnopitys montana.*

P. taxifolius Sol. ex D. Don non Kunth = *Prumnopitys taxifolia.*

P. taxodioides Carr. = *Falcatifolium taxoides.*

P. thunbergii Hook. = *P. latifolius.*

P. totara G. Benn ex D. Don TOTARA. Tree, to 30m. Bark dark brown, to silver-grey, thick, exfoliating in strips. Lvs 15–25×3–4mm, linear-lanceolate, straight to falcate, sharply spined, coriaceous, stiff, green tinged yellow-grey ridged above and raised, midrib beneath. Receptacle fleshy, orange-red to bright red, 5–6mm. NZ. Z9. 'Aureus': lvs yellow-green.

P. totara var. *alpina* Carr. = *P. alpinus.*

P. totara var. *hallii* (T. Kirk) Pilger = *P. hallii.*

P. ulgurensis Pilger = *P. latifolius.*

P. usambarensis Pilger = *Afrocarpus usambarensis.*

P. ustus (Vieill.) Brongn. & Griseb. = *Parasitaxus ustus.*

P. vitiensis Seem. = *Retrophyllum vitiense.*

P. wallichiana Presl = *Nageia wallichiana.*

Podocytisus Boiss. & Heldr. Leguminosae (Papilionoideae). 1 unarmed shrub to 2m. Lvs trifoliolate; lfts 0.5–1.5cm, obovate, mucronulate, grey-green. Fls pea-like, to 1cm, yellow, 5–10 in term., erect, often pyramidal rac. to 15cm. Fr. 1cm, ovate-oblong, compressed, winged. Late summer. Balk., Turk., Greece. Z8.

P. caramanicus Boiss. & Heldr.

→*Cytisus* and *Laburnum.*

Podolepis Labill. Compositae. 18 ann. to perenn. herbs, usually cobwebby-hairy. Lvs rosulate and cauline, linear to lanceolate, entire. Cap. discoid or radiate, solitary, numerous, term. or axill.; phyllaries in several series, often clawed and scarious. Aus. Z9.

P. acuminata R. Br. = *P. jaceoides.*

P. aristata Benth. = *P. canescens.*

P. canescens Cunn. ex DC. Ann., to 80cm. Lvs to 8×15mm, mostly basal, oblanceolate, base attenuate, petiolate; st. lvs elliptic to lanceolate, sessile. Cap. several, in loose pan.; phyllaries light brown to red-brown; ray flts to 1cm, yellow. Summer–autumn. S Aus.

P. gracilis (Lehm.) Graham. Ann., to 50cm. Lvs usually cauline, to 8×1cm, oblanceolate to broadly linear, white-woolly beneath, sessile. Cap. solitary to many on flimsy peduncles; phyllaries light brown to red-brown, shining; ray flts to 1.5cm, pink. Summer. W Aus.

P. jaceoides (Sims) Voss. Perenn., to 70cm. Basal and lower st. lvs to 20×2cm, linear to oblanceolate, glab. to scabrous above, sparsely white-woolly beneath, upper lvs linear to lanceolate, clasping. Cap. solitary to few in a loose cyme; ray flts to 2.5cm; yellow. E & SE Aus., Tasm.

P. robusta (Maid. & Betche) J.H. Willis. Robust perenn., to 60cm. Basal lvs to 20×4.5cm, spathulate, glab., amplexicaul, margins crinkled; st. lvs broad-linear, densely white-woolly above, clasping, decurrent. Cap. few in a dense, term. cluster; ray flts to 2cm, yellow. E Aus.

P. rosea Steetz = *P. gracilis*.

P. rugata Labill. Perenn., often to 60cm, glab. Basal lvs to 8cm, narrowly lanceolate to oblanceolate, often 0; st. lvs to 10×1.5cm, elliptic, linear or oblanceolate. Cap. solitary to few in a loose cyme; phyllaries red-brown; ray flts to 1.5cm, yellow. Summer. S Aus.

Podophyllum L. Berberidaceae. 7 perenn., stoutly rhizomatous herbs. Lvs large, peltate, palmately lobed, radical and long-stalked or 1-several, ruff- or parasol-like subtending or overtopping fls on erect thick st. to 40cm. Fl. term., solitary or several; sep. 6; pet. 6-9; sta. 6-18. Fr. a berry, large, fleshy, ovoid. E N Amer. to E Asia and Himal.

P. aurantiocaule Hand.-Mazz. Differs from *P. hexandrum* in lvs 4-7-lobed, fine-toothed, fls 2-4, cream-yellow. SW China. Z7.

P. emodi Wall. ex Hook. f. & Thoms. = *P. hexandrum*.

P. hexandrum Royle. Lvs to 25cm across, 3-5-lobed, each lobe further 3-lobed at tip often flushed red-bronze at first (marbled red-bronze or brown in cv Majus). Fls solitary, term., erect, appearing before lvs mature; pet. 6, 25-40mm, white-rose pink. Fr. 2-5cm, red. W China, Himal. Z6.

P. japonicum Itô = *Ranzania japonica*.

P. peltatum L. MAY APPLE; WILD MANDRAKE. Lvs 30cm across, lobes 5-9, bifid, finely hairy beneath. Flowering st. with 2-3 lvs or leafless. Fls nodding, fragrant, pet. 25-40mm, white to rose, apex toothed. Fr. green-yellow, rarely red, 2-5cm. Spring. E N Amer. S to Tex. Z4.

P. pleianthum Hance. Differs from *P. versipelle* in lvs glossy mid-green, to 60cm diam., shallowly and bluntly lobed and fls v. malodorous, dark amber with pet. 6-9, to 6cm. C & SE China. Z7.

P. versipelle Hance. Lvs 40cm across, irregularly deeply divided, 5-8 lobed, finely toothed; flowering st. lvs 2. Fls to 8, nodding below spreading st. lf., dull orange-bronze to deep crimson, malodorous; pet. 6, 1.8-4cm. Fr. less than 4cm. China, Tibet. Z7.

→*Diphylleia*.

Podranea Sprague. Bignoniaceae. 2 climbing shrubs. Lvs imparipinnate. Thyrse term., pyramidal; cal. campanulate; cor. funnelform-campanulate; sta. included. S Afr. Z9.

P. brycei (N.E. Br.) Sprague. QUEEN OF SHEBA; ZIMBABWE CLIMBER. St. 4-angled. Lfts 9-11, 2-4cm, serrulate. Infl. to 10cm; cor. 3.8×1.8cm at throat, lobes 1.3-2.3cm, pale purple, throat villous. Zimb.

P. ricasoliana (Tanf.) Sprague. PINK TRUMPET VINE. Lfts 5-11, entire. Fls to 6cm, pale pink striped red, throat glab. S Afr.

→*Pandorea* and *Tecoma*.

Poellnitzia Uitew. Liliaceae (Asphodelaceae). 1 succulent perenn. herb. Lvs 2.5-4cm, 4-ranked, ovoid-triangular, squarrose-imbricate, triquetrous, pungent, thick, hard, yellow-green to glaucous, striate, margins minutely scabrid. Scapes to 30cm; rac. subsecund, to 12cm; fls 2-2.5cm narrowly tubular, pale red, seg. with brown midveins, minutely crenate. Summer. S Afr. Z9.

P. rubrifolia (L. Bol.) Uitew.

→*Aloe* and *Apicra*.

Poet's Daffodil *Narcissus poeticus*.
Poet's Ivy *Hedera helix*.
Poet's Narcissus *Narcissus poeticus*.

Pogonia Juss. Orchidaceae. 10 tuberous terrestrial orchids. Lf. solitary. Infl. scapose, 1 to 3-fld; sep. usually erect; pet. held over lip, wider than sep.; lip simple or 3-lobed, inrolled round column, bearded or fringed. Widely distrib., mostly temp. Asia and N Amer. Z3.

P. divaricata (L.) R. Br. = *Cleistes divaricata*.

P. ophioglossoides (L.) Juss. To 40cm. Lvs to 12cm, ovate to ovate-lanceolate. Fls rose to white, fragrant; dors. sep. to 2cm, elliptic-oblong, lat. sep. to 2.7cm, linear-oblong to linear-lanceolatel; pet. to 2.5cm, obovate-elliptic, rounded; lip to 2.5cm, narrowly oblongspathulate, lacerate-dentate, callus yellow-white beared. US.

P. rosea (Lindl.) Rchb. f. = *Cleistes rosea*.

→*Arethusa*.

Pogonopus Klotzsch. Rubiaceae. 5 shrubs or trees. Pan. loose, term., cymose; cal. turbinate, 5-toothed, one tooth enlarged, leaflike, coloured; cor. tubular, lobes 5; sta. 5, anth. exserted. Trop. Amer. Z10.

P. exsertus Ørst. = *P. speciosus*.

P. speciosus (Jacq.) Schum. Shrub or tree, to 10m. Lvs to 22cm, obovate to elliptic-obovate, pubesc. beneath. Enlarged cal. lobe ovate, to 5cm, crimson to purple, petiole to 2.5cm; cor. to 3cm, pubesc., purple or pink. Summer. C to N S Amer.

→*Macrocnemum*.

Pohutukawa *Metrosideros excelsus*.
Poinciana *Caesalpinia gilliesii*.

Poinciana L.
P. gilliesii Wallich ex Hook. = *Caesalpinia gilliesii*.
P. pulcherrima L. = *Caesalpinia pulcherrima*.
P. regia Bojer. = *Delonix regia*.

Poincianella Britt. & Rose.
P. mexicana (Gray) Britt. & Rose = *Caesalpinia mexicana*.

Poinsettia *Euphorbia pulcherrima*.

Poinsettia Graham = *Euphorbia*.

Pointed-leaf Maple *Acer argutum*.
Point Reyes Ceanothus *Ceanothus gloriosus*.
Point Reyes Creeper *Ceanothus gloriosus*.
Point Vetch *Oxytropis*.
Poison Arrow Plant *Acokanthera oblongifolia*.
Poisonberry *Solanum nigrum*.
Poison Bulb *Crinum asiaticum*.
Poison Bush *Acokanthera*.
Poison Camas *Zigadenus nuttallii*.
Poison Hemlock *Conium maculatum*.
Poison Ivy *Toxicodendron radicans*.
Poison Mercury *Toxicodendron radicans*.
Poisonous Nightshade *Solanum dulcamara*.
Poison Peas *Gastrolobium*.
Poison Primrose *Primula obconica*.
Poison Sumac *Toxicodendron vernix*.
Poison Tree *Acokanthera*.
Poke *Phytolacca americana*.
Poker Plant *Kniphofia*.
Pokeweed *Phytolacca* (*P. americana*).
Pokosola *Ochrosia elliptica*.

Polanisia Raf. Capparidaceae. 6 ann. or perenn. herbs. Lvs trifoliate. Rac. elongate, terminal; sep. free, decid.; pet. clawed to subsessile, truncate or emarginate, erose orlaciniate; sta. 8-27; style slender. N Amer., Mex.

P. dodecandra (L.) DC. To 1m, sparsely branched. Petioles to 6cm; lfts to 6cm, narrowly lanceolate to obovate. Infl. to 4cm, many-fld; pet. to 3cm, white to deep pink, obcordate to spathulate, emarginate to truncate; sta. 10-27, fil. to 5cm, purple. C & E N Amer. Z5.

P. graveolens Raf. = *P. dodecandra*.

P. tenuifolia Torr. & A. Gray. To 90cm, closely branched. Petioles to 2cm; lfts to 5cm, linear or filiform. Infl. to 15cm, few-fld; pet. to 0.8cm, white, sometimes tinged purple, broadly ovate to spathulate, emarginate or truncate, sta. 8-13, fil. to 0.6cm, white. SE N Amer. Z9.

Polar Willow *Salix polaris*.

Polaskia Backeb. Cactaceae. 2 succulent small, broad-crowned trees. St. ribbed. Fls urceolate or campanulate. Fr. globose, 2-4cm, red, juicy, edible. S Mex. Z9.

P. chende (Roland-Goss.) Gibson & Horak. To 7m, trunk to 30cm diam., crown broad; st. 5-7cm diam.; ribs 7-9; central spines 0 or 1, rudimentary; radial spines 5(-6), 5-30mm, pale brown at first. Fl. campanulate, to 5×5cm, scented; outer tep. tinged purple-red, inner pale pink.

P. chichipe (Roland-Goss.) Backeb. To 5m, trunk to 1m diam.; crown candelabriform; st. to 7cm diam.; ribs 9-12, central spine 1, longer than radial; radial spines 6-9, 3-10mm, grey with dark tip. Fl. urceolate-rotate, c3×3cm; tep. creamy white.

→*Heliabravoa* and *Lemaireocereus*.

Polecat Bush *Rhus aromatica*.
Polecat Weed *Symplocarpus*.

POLEMONIACEAE Juss. 20/275. *Cantua, Cobaea, Collomia, Eriastrum, Gilia, Ipomopsis, Langloisia, Leptodactylon, Linanthus, Navarretia, Phlox, Polemonium*.

Polemonium L. JACOB'S LADDER; SKY PILOT. Polemoniaceae. 25 erect, or spreading annuals or rhizomatous perennials with tufted lvs and erect flowering st. Lvs pinnate or pinnatifid. Infl. axill. or term., cymose; cal. 5-lobed, (sub)campanulate; cor. narrowly funnelform to rotate-campanulate, lobes 5, sta. and style included to exserted. Temp. to Arc. regions.

P. acutiflorum Willd. ex Roem. & Schult. = *P. caeruleum* ssp. *villosum*.

P. amoenum Piper = *P. carneum*.

P. boreale Adams. NORTHERN JACOB'S LADDER. Perenn. 8–30cm, erect, pubesc. or gland. Lvs mostly basal, lfts. 13–23, 4–12mm, oval to oblong. Infl. capitate; cor. 1.5–2cm, campanulate, blue to violet, lobes slightly longer than tube. Summer. Circumboreal. Z3 'Album': fls white.

P. brandegei (A. Gray) E. Greene. Erect perenn. 10–30cm, densely glandular-pubesc. Lvs mostly basal, lfts many, appearing whorled, oval to narrowly oblong, entire or divided. Infl. a short raceme-like cluster; cor. 2–2.5cm, funnelform with a v. narrow tube. W U.S. ssp. *brandegei*. Lvs aromatic. Cor. yellow or golden-yellow. Late spring–summer. Z4. ssp. *mellitum* (A. Gray) Wherry. Lvs musky-scented. Fls pleasantly scented white to yellow. Summer–early autumn. SW & W US. Z3.

P. caeruleum L. JACOB'S LADDER; GREEK VALERIAN; CHARITY. Perenn., 30–90cm tall, glandular-pubesc. above. Lvs to 40cm, lfts 17–27, lanceolate to oblong-lanceolate. Infl. lax; cor. 8–15mm, 10–25mm diam., rotate-campanulate, blue, rarely white, lobes ovate. 'Album': fls white. ssp. *caeruleum*. Basal lvs with 17–27 lfts. Infl. many-fld; cor. 8–15mm, blue; sta. exserted. Late spring–summer. N & C Eur., N Asia. ssp. *amygdalinum* (Wherry) Munz. Basal lvs with 19–27 lfts. Infl. strict; cor. 13–15mm, blue; sta. included. Summer. Alask. to Calif., Yukon and BC. Z2. ssp. *himalayanum* (Bak.) Hara. Cal. v. densely glandular-hairy; cor. to 4cm diam., lilac-blue, lobes to 2cm, ovate. Spring–summer. Pak. to W Nepal. var. *lacteum* (Lehm.) Benth. Cor. white. N & C Eur., N Asia. ssp. *van-bruntiae* (Britt.) J.F. Davidson. Sta. and style long-exserted. Summer. NW US. ssp. *villosum* (J.D. Rudolph ex Georgi) Brand. Basal lvs with to 17 lfts. Infl. lax; cor. 18–22mm. Summer. Alask. and BC to Arc. and Subarc. Eur. and N Asia. Z2.

P. caeruleum var. *grandiflorum* Manning = *P. caeruleum* ssp. *himalayanum*.

P. caeruleum L. var. *album* hort. = *P. caeruleum* ssp. *himalayanum* var. *lacteum*.

P. caeruleum L. var. *yezoense* Miyabe & Kudô = *P. yezoense*.

P. californicum Eastw. Perenn., 10–30cm, glandular-hairy. Lfts 11–23, 5–20m, ovate to lanceolate, glandular-pilose to subglabrous. Infl. cymose, bracteate, cor. 8–15mm diam., rotate-campanulate, tube white, lobes blue. Summer. NW US. Z6.

P. carneum A. Gray. Erect perenn., 10–40cm. Lfts. 11–19 elliptic to ovate, 1.5–4.5cm. Infl. lax; cor. 1.8–2.8cm, campanulate, pink or yellow, sometimes dark purple to lavender, rarely pink or blue. Late spring–summer. W US. Z6. 'Album': fls white. 'Rose Queen': fls deeper pink.

P. confertum A. Gray = *Polemonium viscosum*.

P. delicatum Rydb. SKUNKLEAF JACOB'S LADDER. Slender perenn., 10–20cm, glandular-hairy. Lvs 3–8cm, lfts. 5–11, 3–20mm, oblong or ovate-lanceolate. Infl. compound; cor. *c*7×8mm, campanulate, blue to violet; sta. included. Summer. US (Idaho to New Mex. and Ariz.). Z6.

P. elegans E. Greene. Dwarf, tufted perenn., to 15cm, glandular-pubesc. Lvs mostly basal, base expanded and papery, lfts 13–27, 2.5–6mm. Infl. capitate-cymose; cor. 1.2–1.5cm, tubular-funnelform blue, lobes shorter than tube; sta. exserted. Summer. Washington to BC. Z5.

P. filicinum E. Greene = *P. foliosissimum*.

P. flavum E. Greene = *P. foliosissimum* var. *flavum*.

P. foliosissimum A. Gray. LEAFY JACOB'S LADDER. Erect perenn., 40–120cm, sparsely villous, gland. above. Lvs 3–15cm, lfts 5–25, 0.8–5cm, narrowly oblong to elliptic in ranks. Infl. term. and axill., corymbiform, dense; cor. 1–1.8cm, campanulate, blue-violet, cream or white; sta. included or exserted. W US. var. *foliosissimum*. 50–90cm tall. Cor. blue to violet, rarely white. Summer–early autumn. Z4. C & S US. var. *alpinum* Brand. 80–120cm tall. Cor. white. Summer. Z5. var. *flavum* (E. Greene) Davidson. Stout, 40–70cm tall. Cor. yellow, tawny-red outside. Summer–early autumn. Z3.

P. haydenii Nels. = *P. pulcherrimum*.

P. himalaiacum hort. = *P. caeruleum* ssp. *himalayanum*.

P. himalayanum Bak. = *P. caeruleum* var. *himalayanum*.

P. humile Salisb. = *P. reptans*.

P. lindleyi Wherry = *P. pulcherrimum*.

P. mellitum A. Gray = *P. brandegei* ssp. *mellitum*.

P. mexicanum Cerv. ex Lagasca. Erect perenn., 30–40cm, glandular-hairy. Lvs mostly cauline lfts 23–27, ovate to lanceolate, 1–1.2cm. Infl. corymb-like, axillary, few-fld; cor.

1–1.2cm diam., broadly campanulate, violet-blue. Summer early autumn. Mex. Z7.

P. occidentale E. Greene = *P. caeruleum* ssp. *amygdalinum*.

P. pauciflorum S. Wats. Perenn. to 50cm. Lvs to 15cm, mostly cauline, lfts 11–25, to 25mm, elliptic or lanceolate, glangular-pubesc. Infl. at apical, 1–2-fld; cor. to 3(-4)cm, funnelform, yellow or yellow-green, often purple-hued; sta. equalling tube. Summer. SW US, Mex. Z7.

P. pulcherrimum Hook. Perenn., 0.5–3m, erect. Lfts 11–37, to 3.5cm. Infl. glangualr, dense; cor. 7–13mm, campanulate, blue to violet or white, tube yellow inside. Late spring–summer. NW Amer. Z4.

P. reptans L. GREEK VALERIAN. Erect or spreading perenn., 30–70cm. Lfts 7–19, elliptic or oblong-lanceolate. Infl. lax; cor. 1.5–2cm diam., blue. Spring–early summer. E US. Z4. 'Album': fls white. 'Blue Pearl': to 25cm; fls blue. 'Lambrook Manor': mound-forming to 45cm; fls lilac-blue.

P. × richardsonii hort. (?*P. caeruleum* × *P. reptans*.) Perenn. to 50cm. Fls to 4cm diam., sky-blue. Late spring–summer. Gdn origin. Z6. 'Album': fls white.

P. sibiricum D. Don = *P. caeruleum*.

P. van-bruntiae Britt. = *P. caeruleum* ssp. *van-bruntiae*.

P. villosum J.D. Rudolph ex Georgi = *P. caeruleum* ssp. *villosum*.

P. viscosum Nutt. Perenn., to 20(-40)cm tall, densely gland. Lvs to 20cm, mostly basal, lfts many, usually 2–5-lobed, seg. 1.5–6mm. Infl. densely cymose-capitate; cor. 1.7–2.5cm, tubular-funnelform, blue to violet. Summer. NW Amer. Z5.

P. viscosum ssp. *mellitum* (A. Gray) Davidson = *P. brandegei* ssp. *mellitum*.

P. yezoense (Miyabe & Kudô) Kitam. Perenn. 25–45cm tall. Lvs 13–16cm lfts 19–23, ovate-lanceolate, mucronate. Infl. lax, corymbose, glandular-hairy; cor 2.2–2.5cm, blue. Late spring–summer. Jap. Z5.

P. cvs. 'Hopley's': fls pale pink. 'Sapphire': fls small, light blue. 'Pink Beauty': fls tinged purple.

Polianthes L. Agavaceae. 13 thickly rhizomatous perenn. herbs. Lvs basal, thinly succulent, tough, lanceolate or linear. Fls waxy, scented, usually paired in erect spike-like rac. with leaf-like bracts; perianth tube cylindric to funnel-shaped, seg.6, erect to spreading. Mex. Z9.

P. geminiflora (La Ll. & Lex.) Rose. To 70cm. Lvs 30–40cm, linear. Fls to 2.5cm, bright orange red, nodding in a lax rac. Summer.

P. maculosa (Hook.) Shinn. = *Manfreda maculosa*.

P. runyonii Shinn. = *Manfreda longiflora*.

P. tuberosa L. TUBEROSE. To 1.2m. Lvs to 45cm, linear, bright to grey-green. Fls v. fragrant, in a lax spike to 1m, pure waxy white, 3–6cm. Only known as a cultigen: cultivated in pre-Columbian Mexico. 'Excelsior Double Pearl': an improved form of 'The Pearl'. 'Single Mexican': fls single, to 5 spikes, long-lasting; possibly typical. 'The Pearl': fls double, highly fragrant. var. *gracilis* Link & Otto. Habit more slender, lvs narrower, perianth with long slender tube, seg. linear.

P. variegata (Jacobi) Shinn. = *Manfreda variegata*.

P. virginica (L.) Shinn. = *Manfreda virginica*.

→*Bravoa* and *Coetocapnia*.

Policeman's Helmet *Impatiens glandulifera*.

Poliothyrsis Oliv. Flacourtiaceae. 1 decid. tree, to 15m. Lvs broadly ovate, to 15cm, dentate, hairy beneath. Pan. loose term., to 20cm, white-hairy; fls fragrant, 8mm diam., long-pedicelled, white becoming yellow; sep. 5; pet. 0; sta. many. C China. Z7.

P. sinensis Oliv.

Polished Willow *Salix laevigata*.
Polish Larch *Larix decidua*.
Polka-dot Plant *Hypoestes phyllostachya*.
Pollyanna Vine *Soleirolia soleirolii*.

Polyandrococos Barb. Rodr. BURI PALM. Palmae. 1 rusty-hairy palm. St. closely ringed, rough. Lvs pinnate, erect, sheaths; pinnae single-fold, regularly spaced or clustered, held in one or differing planes, waxy-tomentose beneath, emarginate to praemorse or acuminate. Braz. Z10.

P. caudescens (Mart.) Barb. Rodr.

Polyanthus see *Primula* Pruhonicensis Hybrids.
Polyanthus Narcissus *Narcissus tazetta*.

Polyarrhena (L.) Cass. Compositae. 4 perenn. herbs and subshrubs. Cap. radiate, solitary. S & W Cape Prov.

P. reflexa (L.) Grau. Straggling subshrub, to 1m. Lvs oblong to lanceolate, reflexed, sessile, serrate. Ray flts white, tinged red

beneath. Summer. SW Cape Prov.
→*Aster* and *Felicia*.

Polybotrya Willd. Dryopteridaceae. 25–35 terrestrial or epiphytic ferns. Rhiz. creeping or ascending with massed roots and scales. Frongs stipitate, dimorphous. Trop. Amer. Z10.

P. apiifolia J. Sm. = *Psomiocarpa apiifolia*.

P. aristeguietae Brade = *P. osmundacea*.

P. cervina (L.) Kaulf. = *Olfersia cervina*.

P. cyathifolia Fée & L'Hermin. = *P. osmundacea*.

P. latifolia Meyen = *Hemigramma latifolia*.

P. osmundacea Willd. Rhiz. ascending. Fronds arched, sterile fronds to 1.8×1m, 3-pinnate or -pinnatifid, ovate to deltoid or lanceolate, papery, pinnae to 40cm, 13–18 pairs, lanceolate to deltoid, pinnules to 14cm, lanceolate, seg. ovate to rhomboid or oblong, subentire to toothed, fertile fronds shorter, 3-pinnate or -pinnatifid, deltoid, seg. to 12mm, falcate, linear; stipes to 50cm, erect. Mex., W Indies, to Braz.

→*Acrostichum* and *Dorcapteris*.

Polycarpa Lind. ex Carr.

P. maximowiczii Lind. ex Carr. = *Idesia polycarpa*.

Polycycnis Rchb. f. Orchidaceae. 7 epiphytic orchids. Pbs to 6cm, ovoid to subcylindrical. Lvs 35–50cm, elliptic-lanceolate, plicate, conduplicate, sheathing and apical, petiolate. Rac. basal, fls on curving stalks with elongate columns, thus swan-like in outline; sep. to 2.5cm, spreding or reflexed; pet. sometimes with an elongate, stalked base; lip c2cm, usually with a trilobed hypochile, lat. lobes erect or spreading, apex usually pubesc., epichile inserted on under-surface of hypochile, simple or obscurely 3-lobed; column slender, arched. Panama and Costa Rica to Colomb., Guyana and Peru. Z10.

P. barbata (Lindl.) Rchb. f. Infl. to 32cm, pendent, fls thin-textured, pale, clear yellow spotted red, lip white spotted red or purple. Lip epichile obscurely 3-lobed, ovate, acuminate, lat. lobes subauriculaqte, disc with a densely pubesc. callus. Costa Rica, Panama, Colomb., Venez., Braz.

P. muscifera (Lindl. & Paxt.) Rchb. f. Infl. to 60cm, erect to arching; fls, thin-textured, pale brown marked light maroon, lip light brown-green spotted maroon. Lip epichile simple or obscurely 3-lobed, ovate-hastate, acute or acuminate, disc with a fleshy, subelliptic, pubesc. keel. Panama, Venez., Colomb., Ecuad., Peru, Boliv.

P. vittata (Lindl.) Rchb. f. Infl. to 20cm, erect or suberect; fls white or cream, striped deep red-maroon or chocolate; lip epichile rhombic or ovate-rhombic, acute or rounded, glab., disc with a longitudinal, sulcate callus. Colomb., Venez., Guianas, Braz., Peru.

→*Cycnoches* and *Houlletia*.

Polygala L. MILKWORT; SENECA; SNAKEROOT. Polygalaceae. c500 ann. or perenn. shrubs and herbs, rarely trees. Fls in term. or axill. rac., varying in colour sometimes on the same plant; sep. 5, the inner 2 petal-like (wings); pet. 3–5, often united, the lower pet. (keel) often crested; sta. 8, rarely 6. Subcosmopolitan.

P. alba Nutt. Perenn. herb, to 30cm. Lvs to 2.5cm, alt., linear. Fls white with green centres, crest often purple. N Amer. Z4.

P. alpestris Rchb. f. St. 7–15cm, arising from basal rosettes. Basal lvs 15–35, elliptical to obovate, the upper lanceolate to oblong, acute. Rac. 8–25-fld; fls blue, violet, pink or white; cor. 3.5–6.5mm. S & SC Eur., from the Alps to the Pyrennees and Greece. Z6.

P. alpestris Spach = *P. chamaebuxus*.

P. amara L. St. 5–20cm, arising from basal rosettes. Basal lvs 15–35mm, elliptical to obovate, the upper lanceolate to oblong, acute. Rac. 8–25-fld; fls blue, violet, pink or white; cor. 3.5–6.5mm. Mts of EC Eur. and N Balk. Z6.

P. amarella Crantz. Differs from *P. amara* in cauline lvs obtuse. Much of Eur., but 0 from most of the S. Z6.

P. amarella Coss. & Germain = *P. calcarea*.

P. apopetala Brandg. Shrub or small tree, to 5m. Lvs to 8cm, alt., lanceolate to ovate. Fls pink-purple. N Amer. Z4.

P. arillata Buch.-Ham. ex D. Don). Shrub, 1–3m. Lvs 10–15cm, ovate-lanceolate. Fls in drooping, branched rac., wings red-purple, keel yellow, amply crested. India, Sri Lanka, SE Asia. Z10.

P. calcarea F.W. Schultz. Stolons terminating in leaf-rosettes, flowering st. erect to 20cm, rosette lvs spathulate to obovate, st. lvs smaller, linear-lanceolate. Rac. 6–20-fld.; fls usually blue or white. W Eur., inc. S Engl. 'Bulley's Variety': infl. lax.; fls large, deep blue. 'Lillet': fls bright blue. Z7.

P. chamaebuxus L. Everg. shrub, ±procumbent, 5–15cm. Lvs 1.5–3cm, elliptic to obovate, leathery, somewhat glossy. Fls solitary or in 10–14mm, wings cream-white, keel yellow, with a 2- to 6-lobed crest. C Eur. to It. 'Kamniski': to 20cm; fls white, pink, purple or yellow, occas. with second flush of fls. 'Loibe': mat-forming, dark green; fls deep purple and yellow. var. *grandiflora* Neilr. Wings purple, pet. yellow. Z6.

P. chamaebuxus var. *purpurea* Neilr. = *P. chamaebuxus* var. *grandiflora*.

P. cowellii (Britt.) S.F. Blake. VIOLETA; VIOLET TREE; TORTUGUERO. Small to medium-sized, decid. tree, 5–13m. Lvs 5–13cm, alt., elliptic, leathery, yellow-green. Fls in short, lat. rac., violet, c2cm diam. Puerto Rico. Z10.

P. ×dalmaisiana hort. (*P. oppositifolia* ×*P. myrtifolia*.) Shrub, 1–3m. Lvs to 2.5cm, alt. or opposite, elliptic, lanceolate to ovate. Fls purple-red or rosy red. Gdn origin.

P. diversifolia L. = *Securidaca diversifolia*.

P. lutea L. YELLOW MILKWORT; CANDYWEED; YELLOW BACHELOR'S-BUTTON. Bienn., to 30cm. Lvs 2.5–5cm, in a rosette, lanceolate, obovate or spathulate. Fls in dense spike-like rac. to 4cm, orange-yellow. N Amer. Z6.

P. myrtifolia L. Erect, much-branches shrub, 1–2.5m. Lvs 2.5–5cm, alt., elliptic-oblong or obovate. Fls 1.8cm in short, term. rac., green-white veined purple, keel crested. S Afr. var. *grandiflora* Hook. Fls large, rich purple. Z9.

P. paucifolia Willd. FLOWERING WINTERGREEN; BIRD-ON-THE-WING; FRINGED POLYGALA; GAY-WINGS. Perenn., to 18cm, stoloniferous. Upper lvs to 4cm, clustered, ovate to oblong, lower lvs remote, scale-like. Fls 1–4 together, rose-purple or white, keel fringed. N Amer. Z2.

P. senega L. SENGA ROOT. St. glandular-puberulent, to 45cm, from a thick root. Lvs to 5cm, alt., linear-lanceolate. Fl. in term. rac., white or green-white, v. small. N Amer. Z2.

P. speciosa Sims = *P. virgata* var. *speciosa*.

P. vayredae Costa. Perenn., to 5cm. Lvs 2–2.5cm, alt., linear-lanceolate. Fls axillary, solitary to paired, wings and upper pet. pink-purple, keel tinged yellow, with 5–9-lobed, crests. E Pyren. Z6.

P. virgata Thunb. ± decid. shrub or small tree, 1.5–2m; br. erect. Lvs 2–2.5cm, alt., linear to lanceolate. Fls in term. rac., purple or pink. S Afr. var. *speciosa* (Sims.) Harv. Lvs more obovate-cuneate to linear, obtuse. Fls in rac., c15cm long, purple-violet. S Afr. Z9.

P. vulgaris L. GAND FLOWER; MILKWORT. Small perenn. st. numerous spreading or ascending, tufted 7–35cm. Lvs alt., obovate to linear-lanceolate. Rac. 10–40-fld, rather dense, conical at first; fls blue, pink or white. Eur. and Medit. Z6.

POLYGALACEAE R. Br. 18/950. *Polygala, Securidaca*.

POLYGONACEAE Juss. 51/1150. *Antigonon, Atraphaxis, Coccoloba, Eriogonum, Homalocladium, Muehlenbeckia, Oxyria, Polygonum, Rheum, Rumex, Ruprechtia, Triplaris*.

Polygonatum Mill. Liliaceae (Convallariaceae). SOLOMON'S SEAL. c30 stoutly rhizomatous, perenn. herbs. St. erect to arching. Lvs alt., opposite, or whorled. Fls tubular-campanulate, solitary, paired or several nodding or hanging from each axil or in loose rac. or subumbels; seg. 6. N US, Eur., Asia.

P. biflorum (Walter) Elliott. St. 40cm–2m, erect or arched. Lvs 4–18cm, alt., narrow-lanceolate to broadly elliptic, glaucous beneath. Fls drooping, solitary or 1–4, 1.1–2.3cm, green-white. E US, SC Canada. Z3.

P. canaliculatum (Muhlenb.) Pursh = *P. biflorum*.

P. commutatum (Schult.) Dietr. = *P. biflorum*.

P. falcatum Gray. St. to 85cm. Lvs to 23cm, narrow-lanceolate to ovate-elliptic, alt., sickle-shaped. Fls 2–5, drooping, 1.1–2.2cm, white. Jap., Korea. Z6.

P. giganteum Dietr. = *P. biflorum*.

P. hirtum (Poir.) Pursh. St. 20–120cm, erect, angular, puberulent above. Lvs 7–15cm, alt., lanceolate to ovate, puberulent beneath. Fls drooping, 1–5 per axil, to 2cm, white with green tips. EC & SE Eur., W Russia, NW Turk. Z5.

P. hookeri Bak. St. to 10cm. Lvs crowded-alternate, 1.5–2cm, linear to narrow-elliptic, glab. beneath. Fls solitary, erect, c2cm, purple or lilac-pink. E Himal., China. Z6.

P. humile Maxim. Differs from *P. hirtum* in fls solitary or paired. Z5.

P. ×hybridum Bruegger. (*P. multiflorum* ×*P. odoratum*.) Intermediate between parents; common in cult. 'Flore Pleno': fls double. 'Striatum' ('Variegatum'): lvs striped creamy white, somewhat undulating. Z6.

P. japonicum Morr. & Decne. = *P. odoratum*.

P. latifolium (Jacq.) Desf. = *P. hirtum*.

P. macranthum (Maxim.) Koidz. = *P. stenanthum*.

P. macrophyllum Sweet = *P. verticillatum*.

P. multiflorum (L.) All. St. to 90cm, arched. Lvs 5–15cm, alt., elliptic-oblong to ovate, amplexicaul. Fls 1–2cm, drooping, 2–5 per axil, white tipped green. Eur., Asia. Z4.

P. odoratum (Mill.) Druce. St. to 85cm, angular, arched. Lvs 10–12cm lanceolate to ovate, alt., ascending, glab. beneath. Fls 2–4 per axil, drooping, fragrant 1–2cm, white tipped green. Eur., Asia. 'Gilt Edge': lvs edged yellow. 'Grace Barker': lvs striped creamy white. 'Variegatum': st. red when young; lvs narrowly edged creamy white. var. *thunbergii* (C. Morris & Decne.) Hara St. to 1.1m. Lvs to 15cm. Z4.

P. officinale All. = *P. odoratum*.

P. pubescens (Willd.) Pursh. Differs from *P. odoratum* in fls yellow-green, minutely warty inside. E to SC Canada, S to Georgia and N Carol. Z3.

P. roseum (Ledeb.) Kunth. St. to 70cm, sulcate. Lvs 7–15cm, ascending, linear to narrow-lanceolate, opposite to whorled, often minutely rough beneath. Fls erect, rose, 1–2 per axil, 1–1.2cm. W Sib., C Asia. Z3.

P. sibiricum Delaroche. Close to *P. verticillatum*. St. to 1m. Infl. solitary or clustered to 30 per peduncle. W Sib., C Asia. Z3.

P. stenanthum Nak. St. to 120cm. Lvs 8.5–17.5cm, lanceolate to ovate, alt. Fls drooping, 1–4 per axil, 2.1–3.6cm, white. Jap., Korea. Z7.

P. stewartianum Diels. Close to *P. verticillatum*. Lvs always whorled, 5–10cm, tips tendril-like. Fls. purple-pink. Eur., temp. Asia. Z6.

P. verticillatum (L.) All. St. 20–100cm, erect, angular. Lvs 6.5–15cm, opposite or whorled, linear-lanceolate to narrow ovate, minutely rough beneath. Fls to 1.5cm, drooping, 1–3 per axil, green-white. Eur., temp. Asia, Afghan. Z5.

P. vulgare Desf. = *P. odoratum*.

Polygonum L. KNOTWEED; SMARTWEED; FLEECE VINE; SILVER LACE VINE. Polygonaceae. c150 ann. or perenn. herbs, occas. aquatic or scramblers, some woody or woody based. Lf. stipules sheating. Fls small, clustered in axils or in term. pan. or spikes; perianth funnel- or bell-shaped, seg. 3–6, commonly 5; sta. 3–9; stigmas 2–3. Fr. a 2–3-angled achene, enclosed by persistent perianth. N temp. regions.

P. affine D. Don. Low, mat-forming perenn. to 25cm. Lvs 3–10cm, mostly basal, elliptic to oblanceolate, petiole short, dark green, red-bronze in autumn, sometimes v. finely toothed. Fls in dense, erect spikes, 5–7.5cm, pink or red. Late summer–autumn. Himal. 'Border Jewel': low, spreading; lvs dark, glossy; fls pink. 'Darjeeling Red': lvs elongated, tapering and leathery; fls turning dark red. 'Dimity': lvs red in autumn; fls white. 'Donald Lowndes': spreading, compact; fls salmon pink ageing to dark pink. 'Himalayan Border Jewel': low-creeping, to 10cm; fls small, light pink. 'Superbum': vigorous growth; lvs rich brown in autumn; fls pale pink to crimson, cal. red. Z3.

P. alatum D. Don. Perenn. to 1m; st. erect or low and procumbent, leafy. Lvs 3–7cm, ovate to deltoid-ovate, base cordate; petile winged. Fls in heads, to 1.5cm diam., pale pink. Summer. Himal. China (NW Yunnan). Z8.

P. alpinum All. ALPINE KNOTWEED. Perenn. to 1m; st. ± glab. Lvs 3–8cm, ovate to lanceolate, hairy. Fls in loose pan., white. Summer. Alps to SW Asia. Z5.

P. amphibium L. WILLOW GRASS. Perenn., semi-aquatic. Aquatic plants floating, st. 30–100cm. Lvs 7–10cm, oblong or lanceolate, truncate to cordate at base; petiole 2–4cm. Terrestrial plants with lvs 7–12cm, oblong to lanceolate, strigose, ± sessile. Fls in dense spikes, 2–5cm, pink or red. Summer. N temp. regions. Z5.

P. amplexicaule D. Don. Perenn. to 1m; rootstock woody. Lvs 8–25cm, ovate to lanceolate, acuminate, cordate at base, downy beneath; petiole long; st. lvs clasping. Fls in loose spikes to 8cm, rose-red to purple or white. Summer–early autumn. Himal. 'Album': fls white. 'Arun Gem': low, to 30cm; fls curving downward, dark pink, with bronze tips. 'Atrosanguineum': bushy; fls deep rich crimson. 'Fire Tail': low; fls bright crimson. 'Inverleith': dwarf; fls on short spikes, dark crimson. 'Roseum': fls pale pink. 'Rubrum': fls red. Z5.

P. aubertii L. Henry. RUSSIAN VINE; CHINA FLEECE VINE; SILVER LACE VINE. Rampant, twining, woody vine to 15m. Lvs 3–10cm, ovate to ovate-oblong, acute, slightly cordate at base ± glab. Fls in pan., white or green-white to pink. Later summer–autumn. W China, Tibet, Tadzhikistan. Z4.

P. baldschuanicum Reg. MILE-A-MINUTE VINE; RUSSIAN VINE. Differs from *P. aubertii* in more woody habit; fls larger in broader, drooping pan., white tinged pink. Late autumn–autumn. Iran. Z4.

P. bistorta L. BISTORT; SNAKEWEED; EASTER LEDGES. Perenn., to 60cm; rootstock stout. Lvs 10–20cm, ovate to oblong, obtuse, truncate at base, wavy; petiole long, winged; st. lvs triangular, sessile. Fls in dense, cylindrical spikes, rose or white. Summer. Eur., N & W Asia. ssp. *carneum* (Koch) Coode & Cullen. Fls in conical to spherical spikes, 2–3cm. Cauc., Turk. 'Superbum': over 75cm; fls in dense spikes, pink. Z4.

P. bistortoides Pursh. Differs from *P. bistorta* in basal lvs 10–25cm, lanceolate to oblong, petioles not wings. Fls in dense rac., white. Summer. NW US. Z5.

P. brunonis Meissn. = *P. affine*.

P. campanulatum Hook. f. LESSER KNOTWEED. Creeping perenn. to 1m; st. branched, pubesc. Lvs 3.5–12cm, lanceolate to elliptic, white- to pink-brown hairy beneath; petiole short. Fls in loosely branched, nodding pan., pink-red or white, fragrant. Summer–early autumn. Himal. Z8. var. *lichiangense* (W.W. Sm.) Steward. Lvs grey-white hairy beneath; fls white. W China. Z5. 'Album': spreading; fls white, in loose pan. 'Rosenrot' ('Roseum'): habit upright; fls dark rose. 'Southcombe White': fls white.

P. capitatum Buch.-Ham. ex D. Don. Perenn. to 7.5cm with creeping st. to 30cm, rooting, glandular-hairy. Lvs 2–5cm, ovate to elliptic, green with purple V-shaped band; petiole short. Fls pink in dense, stalked heads. Summer. Himal. 'Magic Carpet': creeping, compact, to 10cm high, fast growing; fls pink. Z8.

P. carneum Koch = *P. bistorta* ssp. *carneum*.

P. chinense misapplied = *P. dibotrys*.

P. coccineum Muhlenb. WATER SMARTWEED. Semi-aquatic perenn.; st. 50–500cm, rooting at nodes, shoots slightly pubesc. Lvs 3–10cm, oblong or elliptic, obtuse or acute. Fls. pale rose in a dense, cylindrical spike. Summer. N US. Z5.

P. compactum Hook. f. = *P. japonicum* var. *compactum*.

P. cuspidatum Sieb. & Zucc. = *P. japonicum*.

P. cymosum Trev. = *P. dibotrys*.

P. dibotrys D. Don. Pubesc. perenn. to 1m; resembling *P. fagopyrum* but st. more robust. Lvs 6–15cm, broadly triangular, cordate, sparsely pubesc.; petiole long. Fls clustered at tips of open branched pan., white. Late summer. Pak. to SW China. 'Variegatum': new growth bright red; lvs pink and yellow when young, later marbled green and butter yellow; large.

P. emodi Meissn. Low trailing perenn. resembling *P. affine* but lvs 3–8cm, narrower, linear-lanceolate, entire. Fls in loose, slender spikes, red. Summer. Kashmir to SW China. Z7.

P. equisetiforme hort. non Sm. = *P. scoparium*.

P. fagopyrum L. BUCKWHEAT. Erect ann. to 60cm; st. hollow, few-branched. Lvs to 7cm, triangular-ovate, base cordate, dark green. Fls in pan., white, fragrant. Late summer to early autumn. C & N Asia.

P. filiforme Thunb. = *P. virginianum*.

P. griffithii Hook. f. Woody-based tufted perenn. to 45cm, resembling *P. macrophyllum*. Basal lvs 10–15cm, oblong or elliptic, hairy beneath, undulate; st. lvs small, slightly clasping. Fls in simple or branched, drooping spikes, rich crimson. Summer. N India, W China. Z7.

P. hayachinense Mak. = *P. macrophyllum*.

P. japonicum Meissn. JAPANESE KNOTWEED; MEXICAN BAMBOO. Massive, freely suckering rhizomatous perenn. to 2m; st. stout, branched above, occas. red-brown. Lvs broad-ovate, acuminate, base truncate, 6–12cm; petioles short. Pan. axill.; fls cream-white. Late summer–early autumn. Jap. var. *compactum* (Hook. f.) Bail. Compact form to 70cm, lvs nearly circular, undulate; fls in denser, erect pan., to 6cm, red-brown. E Asia. 'Spectabile': lvs red later marbled with yellow. Z4.

P. lanigerum R. Br. Perenn. to 2m, resembling *P. orientale* but lvs 10–15cm, narrower, ovate-lanceolate, silvery, white-hairy. Fls in pan., pink or white. Summer–early autumn. Trop. Z9.

P. lichiangense W.W. Sm. = *P. campanulatum* var. *lichiangense*.

P. macrophyllum D. Don. Perenn., 5–15cm, rootcrown stout. Lvs 3–12cm, mostly basal, oblong acute to broadly linear, rounded at base; petiole long, st. lvs clasping. Fls in dense spikes, pink or red. Summer. Himal. to W China. Z5.

P. milletii (Lév.) Lév. St. to 50cm. Lvs to 30cm, linear-lanceolate to oblong; petiole winged; upper lvs clasping. Fls in broad-cylindrical to rounded heads, crimson. Summer–early autumn. Himal. to SW China. Z5.

P. molle D. Don. Shrubby perenn. to 2.5m, softly tomentose. Lvs 10–20cm, lanceolate to elliptic-lanceolate, hairy. Fls in tomentose pan., white or cream, slightly fragrant. Late summer. Himal. Z7.

P. muhlenbergii (Meissn.) S. Wats. = *P. coccineum*.

P. multiflorum Thunb. Climbing perenn., 1–2m+; root tuberous; st. slender, red. Lvs 3–6cm, ovate-cordate, green, shiny; petiole long. Pan. loose, tomentose; fls white. Autumn. China. Z7.

P. orientale L. PRINCE'S FEATHER; PRINCESS FEATHER; KISS-ME-OVER-THE-GARDEN-GATE. Pilose ann., 1–1.5m, st. stout, branching. Lvs 10–20cm, broadly ovate, base slightly cordate. Fls in dense, branched, nodding spikes, pink to rose-purple or white. Late summer–autumn. E & SE Asia, Aus., nat. N Amer.

P. oxyphyllum Wallich ex Meissn. = *P. amplexicaule*.

P. paniculatum Bl. = *P. molle*.

P. polystachyum Wallich. HIMALAYAN KNOTWEED. Shrubby perenn. to 2m. Lvs 10–25cm, lanceolate to oblong-lanceolate, acuminate, slightly cordate or truncate at base, veins tinged red, hairy beneath; petiole 1–3cm, often red. Fls in much-branched, leafy pan., white or pale pink, fragrant. Late summer. Himal. Z6.

P. regelianum Komar. = *P. bistorta.*

P. reynoutria hort. non Mak. = *P. japonicum* var. *compactum.*

P. rude Meissn. = *P. molle.*

P. sachalinense Schmidt. GIANT KNOTWEED; SACALINE. Perenn. resembling *P. japonicum* but 2–4m; st. more robust, red-brown, forming a coarse thicket. Lvs 15–30cm, ovate-oblong, base cordate. Fls in shorter, denser pan., white-green. Late summer–autumn. Sakhalin Is. Z4.

P. scoparium Req. ex Lois. Perenn., slender 50–120cm; rootstock, woody; st. erect, slender. Lvs to 1.5cm, narrow, caducous; stipules short, red-brown. Fls in loose term. spikes, white-pink. Late summer. Corsica, Sardinia. Z7.

P. senegalense misapplied. = *P. lanigerum.*

P. sericeum hort. non Pall. = *P. alpinum.*

P. sieboldii De Vriese = *P. japonicum.*

P. spaethii Dammer = *P. orientale.*

P. speciosum Meissn. = *P. amplexicaule.*

P. sphaerostachyum Meissn. = *P. macrophyllum.*

P. sphaerostachyum auct. non Meissn. = *P. milletii.*

P. tenuicaule Bisset & Moore. Perenn. with short, thick rhiz. Lvs mostly basa, 3–8cm, ovate-elliptic, cordate to cuneate at base; petiole long, narrowly winged. Fls in loose spike, white, fragrant. Spring-summer. Jap. Z6.

P. tinctorium Ait. Ann. to 80cm; st. erect, sparingly branched. Lvs to 8cm, oval or ovate; stipules, tinged red. Fls in compact spikes, forming a leafy pan., red or pink. Summer. Russia.

P. undulatum Murray = *P. alpinum.*

P. vacciniifolium Wallich ex Meissn. Trailing perenn.; st. woody, much-branched, to 30cm. Lvs 1–2.5cm, ovate or elliptic, glaucous beneath; petiole short. Fls in loose, erect spikes, pink. Early autumn. Himal. Z7.

P. virginianum L. Perenn. to 120cm, glab. to roughly hairy. Lvs 8–15cm, ovate to elliptic, acuminate to rounded, glab. to roughly pubesc.; petiole to 3cm. Fls in slender spikes, green-white or tinged pink. Late summer–early autumn. Jap., Himal., NE US. 'Painter's Palette': lvs variegated with gold, overlaid by area of pink brown. 'Variegatum': lvs broad, variegated ivory and primrose yellow. Z5.

P. viviparum L. ALPINE BISTORT; SERPENT GRASS. Perenn. to 30cm, with thick bulb-like rootstock; st. erect. Lvs 2–10cm, linear-lanceolate to oblong, margins inrolled, lower lvs longpetioled. Fls in slender term. spikes, 2–10cm, pink to rosewhite, lower fls replaced with purple-brown bulbils. Summer. N US, Eur., Arc. to temp. Asia. Z3.

P. weyrichii Schmidt ex Maxim. Robust perenn. to 1.5m; st. sparsely branching, hairy. Lvs 8–17cm, ovate, acuminate, white-tomentose beneath, upper lvs revolute, shorter-stalked. Panickles, dense, pubesc; fls pale green-white. Summer. Sakhalin Is. Z5.

→*Bilderdykia, Bistorta, Fagopyrum, Fallopia, Persicaria, Reynoutria* and *Tovara.*

POLYPODIACEAE Bercht. & J. Presl. 51 genera. *Aglaomorpha, Anarthropteris, Arthromeris, Belvisia, Campyloneurum, Colysis, Crypsinus, Dictymia, Drymoglossum, Drymotaenium, Drynaria, Drynariopsis, Goniophlebium, Lecanopteris, Lemmaphyllum, Lepisorus, Leptochilus, Merinthosorus, Microgramma, Microsorum, Niphidium, Paragramma, Pecluma, Phlebodium, Platycerium, Pleopeltis, Polypodium, Pseudodrynaria, Pyrrosia, Selliguea, Solanopteris.*

Polypodium L. POLYPODY. Polypodiaceae. *c*75 epiphytic, lithophytic or terrestrial ferns. Rhiz. creeping, red-brown, scaly. Fronds stipitate, uniform to slightly dimorphous, entire to pinnate or pinnatifid; stipes jointed to phyllopodia. Mainly temp. N hemis.

P. accedens Bl. = *Lemmaphyllum accedens.*

P. adnatum Klotzsch. Fronds to 75×30cm, ovate, membranous, hoary-pubesc., pinnae to 20×5cm, spreading distant, elliptic to lanceolate, apex acute, base attenuate and decurrent, notched to dentate; stipes to 30cm, lustrous brown. C to S Amer. Z10.

P. areolatum Humb. & Bonpl. ex Willd. = *Phlebodium aureum* var. *areolatum.*

P. arisanense Hayata = *Goniophlebium amoenum.*

P. aspidistrifrons Hayata = *Microsorium steerei.*

P. aureum L. = *Phlebodium aureum.*

P. aureum var. *reductum* (Humb. & Bonpl. ex Willd.) Jennean. = *Phlebodium aureum* var. *areolatum.*

P. australe Fée = *P. cambricum.*

P. brasiliense Poir. Fronds to 80×40cm, erect or arching, lanceolate or ovate, leathery, glab., pinnae to 22×3cm, to 18 pairs, short-petiolate to adnate, erect to spreading, lanceolate or

oblong, long-acuminate, base cuneate or obtuse; stipes to 55cm, glab. S Amer. Z10.

P. brownii Wikstr. = *Dictymia brownii.*

P. californicum Kaulf. Fronds to 30×15cm, ascending, deeply pinnatifid, oblong to deltoid, herbaceous to membranous, seg. to 6×1cm, spreading, oblong to linear, base decurrent, entire to dentate; stipes to 20cm, straw-coloured. Calif. Z9.

P. cambricum L. WELSH POLYPODY. Differs from *P. vulgare* its broader, softer fronds. 13–50×7–10cm, pinnatifid, deltoid or oblong, base truncate, seg. to 9mm wide; stipes to 20cm, brown. Eur. 'Cambricum': plumose form; pinnae lacerated, sterile, 30–40cm; 'Barrowii': frond more leathery than 'Cambricum', pinnae seg. crisped and elongated, 25–35cm; 'Hadwinii': frond narrow, not greatly congested, 15–25cm; 'Prestonii': frond narrow, congested, pinnae seg. overlapping, 15–25cm; 'Oakleyae': similar to 'Cristatum' but lamina short, 20cm; 'Whilharris': tall, leathery, frond narrow with pinnae deeply lacerated, 30–40cm. 'Cristatum': pinnae and frond tip crested, 20–30cm. 'Grandiceps': pinnae crested, crest at frond tip large, three named forms: 'Foster': small term. crest, frond narrow, 20–30cm; 'Fox': large curled crest, frond broader, 20–30cm; 'Parker': entire frond absorbed into enormous crest, 10–20cm. 'Macrostachyon': tip of frond elongated, 20–35cm. 'Omnilacerum' ('Oxford Superbum'): pinnae irregularly pinnatifid, 20–40cm. 'Pulcherrimum': pinnae broad, nearly and regularly pinnatifid, 20–35cm. 'Semilacerum': pinnae irregularly pinnatifid along part of frond, usually the basal half, 20–30cm; there are several named forms: 'Falcatum O'Kelly': narrow form with pinnae curving toward apex, rare, 30cm; 'Jubilee': pinnae seg. broad and even, 25cm; 'Robustum': seg. irregularly pointed or rounded, twisted and dark green, 30cm. Z6.

P. capitellatum Wallich = *Arthromeris wallichiana.*

P. carnosum Kellogg = *P. scouleri.*

P. catharinae Langsd. & Fisch. Fronds to 30×10cm, deeply pinnatifid, ovate, narrowly acute, glab., membranous to leathery, seg. to 8×1cm, spreading, oblong, apex obtuse, base somewhat decurrent, entire to undulate; stipes to 15cm, lustrous, straw-coloured. C to S Amer. Z10.

P. coronans Wallich ex Mett. = *Pseudodrynaria coronans.*

P. ensato-sessilifrons Hayata = *Colysis hemionitidea.*

P. fauriei Christ. Resembles *P. formosanum* but the slender, more scaly rhiz. Fronds to 20×8cm, arching to pendent, lanceolate to ovate, attenuate at base, grass-like to papery, pubesc. beneath, pinnae to 5mm wide, to 25 pairs, spreading, lanceolate to linear, somewhat notched above, stipes to 6cm, straw-coloured. Jap., Korea. Z9.

P. feei (Bory) Mett. = *Selliguea feei.*

P. formosanum Bak. GRUB FERN; CATERPILLAR FERN. Fronds to 50×15cm, arching to pendulous, ovate to oblong, thin, pale green, minutely pubesc., pinnae to 7×2cm, to 30 pairs, spreading to midrib, spreading, lanceolate to linear, ± entire; stipes to 30cm, lustrous, straw-coloured to brown. China, Taiwan, Jap. Z9.

P. fortunei Kunze = *Drynaria fortunei.*

P. fraxinifolium hort. = *P. menisciifolium.*

P. glycyrrhiza D.C. Eaton. LICORICE FERN. Fronds to 35×15cm, pinnate to pinnatifid, lanceolate to elliptic or oblong, caudate or attenuate, thin-textured, seg. to 6×1cm, alt., falcate, linear, base dilated, notched, stipes to 15cm, straw-coloured. Alask. to Calif. 'Grandiceps': large bunched crests, 30cm. 'Malahatense': pinnae lacerated. 'Longicaudatum': Frond apex greatly elongated, 30cm. Z7.

P. hemionitideum (Presl) Mett. = *Colysis hemionitidea.*

P. hesperium Maxon. WESTERN POLYPODY. Fronds to 20×5cm, deeply pinnatifid, deltoid to linear or oblong, herbaceous to membranous, pale green to glaucous, seg. to 30×8mm, spreading, alt., spathulate to elliptic, entire to dentate, stipes to 10cm, straw-coloured. N Amer. Z5.

P. interjectum Shivas. Differs from *P. cambricum* in tough lvs and from *P. vulgare* in broad lf seg. Fronds to 25cm, pinnatifid, deltoid or lanceolate to linear or strap-shaped, subcoriaceous, grey to green, seg. obtuse, entire or notched. W Eur. Z5.

P. intermedium Hook. & Arn. = *P. californicum.*

P. iridoides Poir. = *Microsorium punctatum.*

P. japonicum (Franch. & Savat.) Maxon, non Houtt. = *P. fauriei.*

P. juglandifolium D. Don = *Arthromeris wallichiana.*

P. kuhnii Fourn. Fronds 65×30cm+, pinnatifid, lanceolate to ovate, scaly beneath, membranous, seg. to 23×1cm, plane to falcate attenuate. C to N S Amer. Z10.

P. latipes Langsd. & Fisch. = *P. mosenii.*

P. lepidopteris (Langsd. & Fisch.) Kunze. Fronds to 45×8cm, linear to lanceolate, apex caudate or narrowly acute, base attenuate, pubesc.-scaly, subcoriaceous, seg. spreading, close, ovate to linear or spathulate, decurrent at base, entire or undulate; stipes to 8cm, scaly. S Amer. Z10.

P. lepidotrichum (Fée) Maxon. Fronds to 65×23cm, ovate to deltoid, scaly, seg. to 12×1cm, to 18 pairs, adnate, deltoid to linear, base decurrent; stipes to 20cm, scaly, straw-coloured. C & S Amer. Z10.

P. linguaeforme Mett. = Microsorium linguaeforme.

P. liukiuense Christ = *P. formosana*.

P. loriceum L. Fronds to 50×25cm, erect, oblong to lanceolate, apex caudate or narrowly acute, base truncate or attenuate, thin-textured, seg. to 10×2cm, close falcate, horizontal, oblong or strap-shaped, base dilated, ± entire; stipes to 20cm, glab. W Indies, C to S Amer. Differs from *P. formosanum* in larger, erect fronds. Z10.

P. maritimum Hieron. Fronds to 60cm, oblong to deltoid, pinnae spreading, oblong, obtuse at apex, dilated at margin; stipes remote. C to S Amer. Z10.

P. membranaceum D. Don = Microsorium membranaceum.

P. menisciifolium Langsd. & Fisch. Fronds to 70×30cm, arching, ovate or obovate to lanceolate, dark green, leathery or membraneous to papery, seg. to 20×3cm, sessile, spreading, subfalcate, close to overlapping, oblong or lanceolate, stipes to 40cm. Braz. Cultivated plants are frequently more compact with shorter fronds. Z10.

P. meyenianum (Schott) Hook. = Aglaomorpha meyeniana.

P. mosenii C. Chr. Fronds to 90cm, seg. to 20×2cm, plane or falcate, linear or oblong to lanceolate, apex acute, base attenuate and dilated; stipes to 30cm. S Amer. Z10.

P. neriifolium Schkuhr = *P. triseriale*.

P. normale D. Don = Microsorium normale.

P. normale var. *madagascariense* Bak. = Microsorium pappei.

P. novae-zelandiae Bak. = Microsorium novae-zelandiae.

P. occidentale (Hook.) Maxon = *P. glycyrrhiza*.

P. owariense Desv. = Micrograma owariensis.

P. pachyphyllum D.C. Eaton = *P. scouleri*.

P. palmeri Maxon = Micrograma nitida.

P. pappei Mett. ex Kuhn = Microsorium pappei.

P. parksii Copel. = Microsorium parksii.

P. persicifolium Desv. = Goniophlebium persicifolium.

P. piloselloides L. = Micrograma piloselloides.

P. plebeium Schltr. & Cham. Fronds to 30×15cm, ovate or oblong to deltoid, somewhat fleshy, leathery to membranous, scaly beneath, seg. to 9mm wide, spreading, linear to oblong or spathulate, entire or notched, stipes to 20cm, red-brown. C to S Amer. Z10.

P. polypodioides (L.) Watt. RESURRECTION FERN. Fronds to 15×6cm, deltoid or oblong, apex attenuate to acute, margins rolling inwards during dry weather, somewhat leathery, seg. to 25cm×5mm, distant, spreading, linear or oblong, apex obtuse, base dilated, entire or notched, scaly; stipes to 10cm, scaly. Americas, S Afr. Z7.

P. propinquum Wallich = Drynaria propinqua.

P. pteropus Bl. = Microsorium pteropus.

P. ptilorhizon Christ. Fronds to 24×12cm, deltoid to lanceolate, scaly, seg. to 22 pairs, apex acute or obtuse, base dilated; stipes remote. Costa Rica. Z10.

P. punctatum (L.) Sw. = Microsorium punctatum.

P. pyrrholepis (Fée) Maxon. Fronds to 50×7cm, lanceolate to linear or oblong, apex attenuate, seg. to 35cm×6mm, to 40 pairs, oblong to linear, obtuse, scaly; stipes to 20cm, scaly, chestnut. Mex. Z10.

P. rhodopleuron Kunze. Fronds to 32×13cm, deltoid or lanceolate to linear or ovate, scaly beneath, seg. to 33 pairs, lanceolate or oblong, veins, red; stipes to 15cm, red. C Amer. Z10.

P. rubidum Kunze = Microsorium rubidum.

P. scouleri Hook. & Grev. COAST POLYPODY; LEATHERY POLYPODY. Fronds to 40×15cm, ovate to deltoid, thick-textured and rigid, seg. to 14 pairs, spreading, linear to oblong, margin entire to notched or undulate and cartilaginous; stipes to 10cm, glab. N Amer. (W coast). Z9.

P. sparsisora Desv. = Drynaria sparsisora.

P. splendens (J. Sm.) Hook. = Aglaomorpha splendens.

P. squamulosum Kaulf. = Micrograma squamulosa.

P. steerei Harr. = Microsorium steerei.

P. subauriculatum Bl. = Goniophlebium subauriculatum.

P. subpetiolatum Hook. Fronds to 45×30cm, lanceolate or deltoid to ovate or oblong, leathery or membranous, seg. to 10×1cm, sessile to short-petiolate, remote, alt., lanceolate, notched, glab. or sparsely pubesc.; stipes to 30cm, glab. C Amer. Z10.

P. thyssanolepis A. Braun ex Klotzsch. SCALY POLYPODY. Fronds to 25×10cm, erect, deltoid or oblong, apex attenuate, base truncate, leathery, pinnae to 4×1.1cm, distant, ascending, oblong to lanceolate or elliptic, entire, pubesc. above, scaly beneath; stipes to 30cm, scaly. W Indies, Tex. to Peru. Z9.

P. triseriale Sw. Fronds to 60×40cm, arching or pendent, ovate to oblong, herbaceous to leathery, pinnae to 15×2cm, sessile, distant, erect to spreading, linear or strap-shaped to lanceolate or

elliptic, entire; stipes to 35cm, lustrous straw-coloured to red-brown. W Indies, C to S Amer. Z10.

P. vacciniifolium Langsd. & Fisch. = Micrograma vacciniifolia.

P. virginianum L. ROCK POLYPODY; AMERICAN WALL FERN. Fronds to 25×7cm, arching or pendent, lanceolate or deltoid to oblong, leathery to thin-textured, seg. to 4×1cm, to 25 pairs, alt. to subopposite, lanceolate to linear or oblong, entire to notched and undulate; stipes to 15cm, straw-coloured. N Amer., E Asia. 'Bipinnatifidum' pinnae regularly and deeply lacerated, plumose. Z5.

P. vulgare L. COMMON POLYPODY; ADDER'S FERN; WALL FERN; GOLDEN MAIDENHAIR. Fronds to 30×15cm, ascending to erect, lanceolate to ovate or oblong or linear, glab., thin-textured to subcoriaceous, seg. to 6cm×7mm, close, spreading, horizontal to ascending, oblong to linear, obtuse, entire to dentate; stipes to 10cm, straw-coloured. N Amer., Eur., Afr., E Asia. 'Bifidograndiceps': regularly crested, each pinna tip bi- or trifid, 30–40cm. 'Bifidum': basal seg. cleft. 'Cornubiense': pinnae broad, neatly and regularly pinnatifid (as with *P. australe* 'Pulcherrimum'), but some fronds, or parts of fronds revert, 30–40cm. 'Cornubiense multifidum': pinnae and frond tip slightly crested, 30cm. 'Cornubiense Grandiceps': term. crests large, 25–30cm. 'Cristatum': seg. crested at tip. 'Elegantissimum': a refined form of 'Cornubiense', pinnae divisions finer, 30cm. 'Glomeratum': fronds branched and pinnae crested, no two fronds alike, 20–30cm. 'Jean Taylor' ('Congestum Cristatum'): finely cut dwarf grandiceps form; like 'Cornubiense', some fronds or parts of fronds revert to normal, 10–20cm. 'Ramosum': rachis branched many times, 20–30cm. 'Ramosum Hillman': seg. forking and crested. 'Trichomanoides Backhouse': a finely cut form, a non-crested form of 'Jean Taylor', 20cm. Z3.

P. vulgare var. *columbianum* Gilbert = *P. hesperium*.

P. vulgare var. *japonicum* Franch. & Savat. = *P. fauriei*.

P. vulgare var. *occidentale* Hook. = *P. glycyrrhiza*.

P. wrightii (Hook.) Mett. ex Diels = Colysis wrightii.

→Goniophlebium, Marginaria and Synammia.

Polypody *Polypodium*.

Polypogon Desf. Gramineae. 18 ann. or perenn. grasses. Lvs flat, scabrous. Infl. paniculate, contracted to spicate, bristled. Summer–autumn. Warm Temp. Z8.

P. fugax Nees ex Steud. Ann. to 60cm. St. loosely clumped. Lvs to 20×1cm; ligules to 0.5cm. Infl. cylindric, compact, to 15×3cm, silky, tinged green to purple. Warm temp. Asia, NE Afr.

P. littoralis hort. = *P. fugax*.

P. monspeliensis (L.) Desf. ANNUAL BEARD GRASS; BEARD GRASS; RABBIT'S FOOT GRASS. Ann. to 60cm. St. solitary or clumped. Lvs to 15×0.8cm; ligules to 1.5cm. Infl. narrow-ovoid to cylindric, to 15×3cm, tinged light green to yellow green, silky. Cosmop. in Eur., nat. N Amer.

Polyscias Forst. & Forst. f. Araliaceae. c100 everg. shrubs or trees to 25m. Lvs simple, trifoliolate or pinnately compound. Infl. term., pseudolateral or on short shoots, paniculate, sometimes umbelliform or racemiform, once or more times compound; fls small, solitary or more commonly in umbels or heads, racemosely or spicately arranged; pet. 4–15. Afr., Madag., Masc. Is., S Asia, Ceylon, Malesia, Micronesia, Pacific Is. (except Hawaii and Marquesas), Aus.

P. balfouriana (Sander ex André) L.H. Bail. = *P. scutellaria* 'Balfourii'.

P. cumingiana (C. Presl) Fernandez-Villar. Shrub or tree to 4m, scarcely branched. Lvs crowded at br. ends, scarcely pinnate, to 100cm, lfts 5–9, ovate-oblong or elliptic, to 30×13cm, apex narrowed, base obtuse to rotund or truncate or slightly cordate, entire or minutely toothed. Infl. term., paniculate, to 140cm; fls in small umbels. C & E Malesia, mainly near coasts. *P. filicifolia* and *P. guilfoylei* are probably derivatives. Z10.

P. elegans (C. Moore ex Muell.) Harms. CELERY WOOD; MOWBULAN WHITEWOOD; SILVER BASSWOOD. Tree to 20m, at first unbranched, crown later spreading. Lvs twice pinnate, glabrescent, to 110cm; lfts ovate or elliptic, entire, to 6×3cm. Infl. term., paniculate, twice compound; main axis to 30cm; fls racemose. E Aus., S & SE New Guinea. Z10.

P. filicifolia (C. Moore ex Fourn.) L.H. Bail. ANGELICA; CHOTITO; FERN-LEAF ARALIA. Large erect shrub, bark at first olive or tinged purple with white spots. Lvs in younger plants 9–17-foliolate, blades narrowly elliptic, stalked, deeply cut or pinnatifid, to 10cm, bright green, midribs tinted purple, shallowly toothed; adult lvs with longer lfts, followed by lvs more as in *P. cumingiana*. Infl. as *P. cumingiana* but less well developed. Probable cultigen originating in E Malesia or the W Pacific, now widespread in warmer regions. 'Ornata': juvenile lfs soon passing into adult lfts; these oblong, entire, closely spaced. 'Marginata' and 'Variegata': lfts white-margined. Z10.

P. fruticosa (L.) Harms. MING ARALIA. Glab. erect shrub or small tree to 8m. Lvs 1–3-pinnate, to 75cm, petiole spotted; lfts shortly stalked, linear-lanceolate, narrow-ovate or oblong, to 20cm, apices acute, toothed, lobed or irregularly pinnatisect, teeth spiny, with a red tinge. Infl. paniculate, diffuse, to 15cm; fls in small umbels. Possible cultigen originating in E Malesia or the W Pacific, now widespread in warmer regions. Z10.

P. fruticosa 'Elegans'. = *P.* 'Elegans'.

P. guilfoylei (Bull) L.H. Bail. GERANIUM ARALIA; WILD COFFEE; COFFEE TREE. Erect shrub or treelet to 6m, little-branched, young st. striped. Lvs to 60cm; lfts 5–9, stalked, rotund to broadly ovate or oblong-elliptic, to 15cm, irregularly spiny-toothed often obscurely lobed, marginal areas white or cream. Infl., term., paniculate, somewhat umbelliform, br. to 50cm; fls in small umbels at ends of secondary br. Probable cultigen originating in E Malesia or the W Pacific, now widespread in warmer regions. 'Crispa': compact; lvs glossy, tinged bronze, sharply toothed. 'Laciniata': lvs twice-pinnate, drooping; primary pinnae 5, seg. lanceolate with white margins, toothed and cut. 'Monstrosa': lvs pinnate, 3–7-foliolate, lfts elliptic with grey-blotched surfaces and creamy-white margins, irregularly cut. 'Variegata': lfts with irregular white or cream patches. 'Victoriae' LACE ARALIA: compact; lvs 3–5-foliolate, pinnae deeply divided; seg. elliptic, margins with a pure white border, toothed or cut. Z10.

P. murrayi (F. Muell.) Harms. PENCIL CEDAR; UMBRELLA TREE. Straight-trunked pachycaul tree to 20m, resembling *P. elegans*. Lvs pinnate, to 122cm, rachis jointed; lfts 13–51, shortly stalked, oblong to narrowly oblong, to 20cm, soft, finely toothed to entire. Infl. term., paniculate, pyramidal; fls in umbels, racemosely arranged. E Aus. The usual here of *Aralia splendidissima* Bull ex. Richards, a juvenile form, is doubtful. Z10.

P. nodosa (Bl.) Seem. BINGLIU; RANGIT; WILD PAPAYA. Similar to *P. murrayi*, but to 25m and with lvs to 3m, sessile lfts to 15cm, fls in heads. Malesia, Solomon Is. Z10.

P. paniculata auct., non (DC.) Bak. The plants initially recognized as *Terminalia elegans* Bull ex Hibb. A juvenile form with coloured, trifoliolate lvs, have been placed here. They belong, however, to a recently described sp. of *Gastonia* from Mauritius.

P. paniculata hort., non (DC.) Bak. = *P. guilfoylei*.

P. pinnata Forst. & Forst. f. = *P. scutellaria*.

P. sambucifolia (Sieb.) Harms. ELDERBERRY PANAX. Glab. shrub or small spindly tree to 6m. Lvs once or twice compound; undifferentiated lvs to 40cm; lfts 9–11, broadly elliptic to linear-lanceolate, to 8cm, entire or remotely toothed; more differentiated lvs sometimes glaucous, once- or twice-compound, lfts pinnatifid, rachis winged. Infl. term. or on short shoots, paniculate, 1–3 times compound, columnar to pyramidal. Spring and early summer. Vict. to S Queensld. Z9.

P. scutellaria (Burm. f.) Fosb. Shrub or small narrow tree to 6m. Lvs to 30cm; lfts 1–3(-5), broadly elliptic or orbicular, often shield-like, to 28cm wide, apex rounded, the base obtuse to cordate, entire or minutely spine-toothed sometimes lobed, some forms with white margins or points. Infl. terminal, paniculate, somewhat umbelliform, to 60cm; fls in small umbels. Possible cultigen originating in E Malesia or the W Pacific, now widespread in warmer regions. 'Balfourii' BALFOUR ARALIA: tree to 7m; st. speckled grey; lfts 1–3, broadly ovate to orbicular, to 10cm wide, toothed or cut, often white. 'Cochleata': lvs unifoliolate, shield-like. 'Pennockii': lfts 1–3, yellow green with white midrib and veins, margins upturned. 'Tricochleata': lfts 3, possibly not distinct from 'Balfourii'. Z10.

P. tricochleata (Miq.) Fosb. = *P. scutellaria* 'Tricochleata'.

P. cvs. 'Balfourii': see *P. scutellaria*. 'Crispa': similar to 'Crispata', but more crinkly. 'Crispata' CHICKEN GIZZARD: compact; lfts 3, overlapping, triangular-rotund, lat. bifid, toothed and sometimes incised. 'Deleauana': lvs pinnately 3–5-divided, the primary divisions again and again split into smaller seg., linear to wedge-shaped or, outwardly, oblique-subelliptic, variously serrate and lobate, teeth white-apiculate. 'Diffissa': lvs bipinnate, crisped, bright green; lfts linear-oblong, lobed and spiny-toothed. 'Dissecta': erect, branching; lvs drooping, bipinnate; lfts wedge-shaped, obovate, often bilobed, the margins long-toothed. 'Dumosa': to 50cm, with short, densely foliaged st.; lvs pinnately divided, green, the outline round-ovate, primary divisions closely spaced, ultimate seg. v. variable spiny-toothed; petiole brown or olive-green, mottled brighter green. 'Elegans': dense; lvs leathery, finely divided; resembles 'Deleauana'. 'Excelsa': see 'Plumata'. 'Fissa': st. erect, branching, with pallid spots; lvs tripinnate, blades linear-lanceolate, white-toothed, the teeth few, incurved. 'Laciniata': see *P. guilfoylei*. 'Lepida': dense; lvs twice-ternately divided, the

term. seg. largest, lateral pinnules of secondary seg. obliquely obovate, but central one much reduced and distinctly covered by the lat. pinnules; margins deeply incised and spinosely toothed. 'Marginata' DINNER-PLATE ARALIA: shrub; lvs 1–3-foliolate; blades ± rotund, green with margins white-bordered or pointed, the venation somewhat palmate. 'Monstrosa': see *P. guilfoylei*. 'Multifida': compact, with feathery crown of tripinnatisect lvs, the seg. to 1cm or so, linear or linear-lanceolate, tipped with a short white bristle; margins often also with bristly teeth. 'Nitida': compact shrub; lvs round-obovate, margins with slightly spinulose teeth and 1–2 incisions towards the base. 'Ornata': see *P. filicifolia*. 'Plumata': shrub; lvs bipinnate, the pinnules pinnatisect, sharply toothed; ultimate seg. small, narrow, v. fine; more finely cut than *P. guilfoylei* and possibly like 'Elegans'. 'Quercifolia': compact; lvs 5-foliolate; blades large, dark coppery green, pinnatifid, oblong or rotund in outline. 'Rotundata': lvs closely set; 3–5-pinnate, the main divisions further divided, ultimate pinnules variegated, somewhat round, spiny-serrate. 'Serratifolia': st. and petioles marked with brown; lvs compound, lfts serrate. 'Spinulosa': st. and petioles spotted and suffused with crimson; lvs odd-pinnate, 5–7-foliolate, blades dark green, oblong, acute; margins spinulose, the teeth tinged red. 'Victoriae': see *P. guilfoylei*.

→*Aralia, Nothopanax, Panax* and *Tieghemopanax*.

Polystachya Hook. Orchidaceae. *c*200 largely epiphytic orchids. Pbs globose to stem-like with 1 to several lvs. Infl. term. racemose or paniculate. Fls resupinate, usually not opening wide; lat. sep. forming mentum with column foot; lip entire or trilobed. Afr., Madag., E to Philipp., Indon. and New Guinea, S US, Carib., C & S Amer. Z10.

P. adansoniae Rchb. f. Pbs 2.5–9cm, oblong, conical or cylindrical. Lvs to 20cm, linear or ligulate. Spike 5–12cm; fls yellow-green or almost white, anth. and tip of lip purple or brown, lat. sep. 4–5.5mm, obliquely ovate; lip to 4×3mm, with fleshy, pubesc. callus, lat. lobes rounded, midlobe lanceolate, lacuminate. Widespread, Trop. Afr.

P. affinis Lindl. Pbs ± orbicular, compressed 1–5cm wide. Lvs 9–28cm, oblanceolate or oblong. Infl. racemose or paniculate, to 40cm; fls fragrant, white or yellow with red-brown markings, outside pubesc.; lat. sep. to 8mm, obliquely triangular-ovate; lip 6.5–7.5mm, lat. lobes erect, midlobe ovate to suborbicular; disc with fleshy, puberulent ridge. Trop. Afr.

P. bella Summerh. Pbs to 4cm, oval, compressed. Lvs 5–16cm, elliptic or ligulate. Infl. racemose or paniculate, erect, pubesc., to 25cm; fls yellow or golden yellow, the lip with deep orange central streak; lateral sep. 15–17mm, obliquely lanceolate; lip 9.5–11.5mm, lateral lobes erect, 1mm, midlobe 4.5×2.5mm, triangular-lanceolate, acuminate, fleshy, recurved. Kenya.

P. bracteosa Lindl. = *P. affinis*.

P. buchananii Rolfe = *P. concreta*.

P. campyloglossa Rolfe. Pbs 1–2cm, ovoid or globose. Lvs 5–10cm, oblanceolate or linear, sometimes edged purple. Rac. slightly longer than lvs, pubesc.; tep. green, yellow-green or yellow, lip white, lateral lobes purple-veined; lat. sep. to 14mm, obliquely triangular; lip 8–11mm, recurved, with pubesc. disc and conical callus, lat. lobes erect, rounded, midlobe ovate, fleshy. E Afr., Malawi.

P. concreta (Jacq.) Garay & Sweet. Pbs 1–5cm, ovoid or conical. Lvs to 30cm, oblanceolate or elliptic. Pan. to 50cm, many-fld; fls rather fleshy, small, yellow, pale green, pink or dull red-purple with white or cream lip; lateral sep. 3–5.5mm, obliquely ovate, apiculate; lip 3.5–5mm, with fleshy longitudinal callus, lat. lobes triangular or oblong, midlobe suborbicular. Widespread in trop. Afr.; Flor., C & S Amer.

P. cultrata Lindl. = *P. cultriformis*.

P. cultriformis (Thouars) Spreng. Pbs 2–18cm, conical or cylindrical. Lf 3–36cm, elliptic. Infl. racemose or paniculate, to 30cm; fls cupped, scented, usually white tinted pink or purple, sometimes green, yellow or wholly mauve; lat. sep. 5–8mm; lip 4–8mm, with fleshy yellow central callus, lat. lobes rounded, midlobe oblong, apiculate. Widespread in trop. Afr.; S Afr., Madag., Masc. Is., Seych.

P. dendrobiiflora Rchb. f. Pbs 1.5–5cm, conical. Lvs 8–25cm, linear, grass-like. Infl. paniculate, borne on old pbs, to 80cm; fls in clusters, opening over a long period, pale to deep lilac-pink or white, lip sometimes with red or lilac spots; lat. sep. 6.5–12mm long, oblong; lip 7–11mm, entire, with yellow, slightly pubesc. callus, ovate-oblong, often undulate; anth. cap deep lilac. C & E Afr.

P. flavescens (Lindl.) J.J. Sm. = *P. concreta*.

P. foliosa (Hook. f.) Rchb. f. Pseudobulbs to 2cm, ovoid. Lvs to 20cm, narrowly elliptic. Pan. with several br.; fls fleshy, green or yellow-green; lat. sep. 4mm, obliquely triangular, acuminate; lip to 4mm, trilobed, with farinose disc and ovoid callus, midlobe oblong, recurved, emarginate, lateral lobes triangular-falcate. Trop. C & S Amer., Grenada.

P. galeata (Sw.) Rchb. f. Pbs 6–14cm cylindrical. Lf 8–27cm, oblanceolate or ligulate. Rac. shorter than lf, pubesc.; fls white, green, yellow-green, yellow or pink, with some purple spots; lat. sep. 10–22mm, obliquely triangular, pubesc., apiculate; lip 10–21.5mm, fleshy, lat. lobes erect, midlobe pubesc. in centre, quadrate to orbicular, reflexed-apiculate. W Afr., Zaire, Angola.

P. gerrardii Harv. = *P. cultriformis*.

P. goetzeana Kränzl. Pbs 5–15mm, obliquely conical. Lvs 8–22cm, linear, grass-like. Rac. erect, shorter than lvs; sep. lime green or yellow-green, purple-veined, pet. and lip white, lip with yellow central line; lat. sep. 13–15mm, obliquely triangular; lip 11–15mm, recurved, with yellow, pubesc. keel, lat. lobes erect, rounded, midlobe subquadrate, apiculate, undulate. Tanz., Malawi.

P. kermesina Kränzl. Pbs to 2cm, slender, arising from middle or previous growth. Lvs 2–4cm, linear. Rac. shorter than lvs, 1–3-fld; fls rather fleshy, orange or scarlet, opening almost flat, lat. sep. 5mm, obliquely ovate-orbicular; lip 8–9mm, fleshy, with long, hairy claw, lat. lobes rounded, midlobe; orbicular, with a tooth-like callus. Zaire, Uganda.

P. lawrenceana Kränzl. Pbs 2.5–5.5cm, conic-elliptic with 2–3 nodes. Lvs to 15cm, ligulate. Rac. to 16cm, laxly 6–8-fld; peduncle pubesc.; fls fleshy, pubesc.; tep. yellow-green flushed maroon, lip pink with white callus; lat. sep. 11mm, obliquely ovate-triangular, acuminate; lip 9mm, lat. lobes erect, oblong, midlobe broadly ovate, obtuse, with central groove. Malawi.

P. leonensis Rchb. f. Pbs subglobose, 1cm diam. Lvs 7–20cm, lanceolate. Rac. to 20cm, laxly several-fld; tep. pale green, usually flushed purple-brown, lip white, lat. lobes tinged purple; lat. sep. 4–5mm, obliquely triangular, obtuse; lip 6mm, lat. lobes triangular-oblong, obtuse, midlobe ovate, obtuse; disc pubesc. W Afr.

P. luteola (Sw.) Hook. = *P. concreta*.

P. melliodora Cribb. Pbs about 3cm, oblong, flattened. Lf to 15cm, narrowly oblong-elliptic. Rac. to 10cm; fls honey-scented, waxy, white, lip purple-edged with yellow callus, anth. cap pink; lat. sep. 15mm, obliquely triangular, acuminate; lip 11mm, obscurely trilobed. Tanz.

P. minuta (Aubl.) Frappier ex Cordm. = *P. concreta*.

P. modesta Rchb. f. Pbs 8–25mm, conic or ovoid. Lvs to 8mm, lanceolate, edged purple. Infl. racemose or with a few short br.; fls fleshy, pale yellow tinged purple, lip usually darker yellow; lat. sep. 5mm, obliquely triangular; lip 4mm, with a pubesc. cushion, lat. lobes erect, midlobe suborbicular, bullate, obtuse or emarginate. Widespread, trop. Afr.

P. mystacidioides De Wildeman. Pbs narrowly cylindrical with lvs 2-ranked or swollen with lf 1, term. Lvs fleshy, bilaterally compressed, 2–15cm. Fls solitary, white with red or purple marks, or pale brown; sep. 8–9mm, pubesc.; lip 10–11mm, lat. lobes small, midlobe oblong. Ivory Coast, Cameroun, Zaire.

P. odorata Lindl. Pbs 2–4.5cm, globose to narrowly conical. Lvs 13–26cm, oblanceolate to elliptic. Pan. 10–30cm; fls scented, pubesc., white, pale green or dull red-brown; sep. flushed red or purple, lip white, midlobe pink-tinged, callus yellow; lat. sep. 8–9mm, obliquely ovate, apiculate; lip 7–8mm, recurved, lat. lobes erect, midlobe, suborbicular, emarginate, crenulate; callus fleshy. W Afr., Zaire, Uganda, Tanz., Angola.

P. ottoniana Rchb. f. Pbs 10–20mm, conical, in chains or clustered. Lvs 7–12cm linear-lanceolate. Rac. erect, 1–6-fld; fls white tinged with pink or lilac, lip with yellow central stripe; lat. sep. 12–14mm, obliquely lanceolate; lip obscurely trilobed, 10–11mm, anth. cap violet. S Afr., Swaz.

P. paniculata (Sw.) Rolfe. Pbs 5–18cm, cylindric, 3–4 nodes. Lvs 10–30cm, distichous, ligulate. Pan. to 21cm; fls small, orange or vermilion, lip marked darker red; lat. sep. 3–4mm, lanceolate, acute; lip 2.5–3mm, entire, ovate or elliptic. W Afr. to Zaire.

P. pubescens (Lindl.) Rchb. f. Pbs conical. Lvs 6–7cm, broadly lanceolate or elliptic. Rac. erect, pubesc.; fls golden yellow, lat. sep. and lip with red lines; lat. sep. obliquely ovate, 14mm; lip 9–12mm, lat. lobes 1–2mm, silky, miblobe 5–6mm. S Afr., Swaz.

P. rufinula Rchb. f. = *P. concreta*.

P. tayloriana Rendle = *P. dendrobiiflora*.

P. tessellata Lindl. = *P. concreta*.

P. villosa Rolfe. Pbs to 4cm, oblong or conical with 2–3 nodes. Lvs to 18cm, oblanceolate or ligulate. Rac. 15–20cm, pubesc; fls densely hairy on outside, primrose-scented, pale green, white or cream, lip white with purple spots on side lobes and at base of midlobe; lip 5–8mm, rather fleshy, callus yellow, lat. lobes erect, rounded, midlobe, bullate, ovate. Tanz., Zam., Malawi.

P. virginea Summerh. Pbs 5–11cm, cylindrical or conical. Lf 12–26cm, lanceolate. Rac. 4–9cm; fls white, scented; lat. sep. 8.5–12mm, obliquely triangular; lip 11.5–15.5mm, with central

fleshy callus, lat. lobes erect, rounded, midlobe triangular to subquadrate, apiculate. C Afr.

P. vulcanica Kränzl. Pbs 1–9cm, narrowly cylindrical. Lf 2.5–11cm, linear. Rac. 2–9cm; sep. creamy white flushed rose-pink, pet. and lip wine red or purple; lat. sep. 4–8mm, obliquely triangular, apiculate; lip 5–10mm, fleshy, sometimes callused lat. lobes erect, midlobe suborbicular, apiculate, anth. cap rose-purple. Zaire, Uganda.

P. zambesiaca Rolfe. Pbs 1–2cm, ovoid. Lvs 3–8cm, lanceolate or oblanceolte, glaucous often purple-edged. Rac. 5–7.5cm, pubesc.; fls pubesc. on outside, yellow or yellow-green, lip white or pale yellow, purple-veined on lat. lobes; lat. sep. 9–12mm; lip 6–7mm, fleshy, with brown, pubesc. callus at base, lat. lobes erect, rounded, midlobe bullate, ovate. Tanz., Malawi, Zam.

Polystichopsis (J. Sm.) Holtt.

P. mutica (Franch. & Savat.) Tag. = *Arachniodes mutica*.

P. nipponica (Rosenst.) Tag. = *Arachniodes nipponica*.

Polystichum Roth. HOLLY FERN. Dryopteridaceae. 175+ terrestrial ferns. Rhiz. erect or decumbent, woody, densely scaly-scurfy; stipes chaffy. Fronds usually tufted, mostly 1–3-pinnate, rarely almost simple linear to oblong in outline with a tapered or truncate base; ultimate divisions ± auriculate, generally serrate. Cosmop.

P. acrostichoides (Michx.) Schott. CHRISTMAS FERN. Stipes 10–25cm, green, scaly. Fronds 20–50×5–12cm, linear-lanceolate, pinnae alt., 20–35 each side, linear-oblong, acutely auriculate at base, minutely spinose-dentate, dark green with hair-like scales beneath. N Amer. Z4.

P. aculeatum (L.) Roth. Stipe short, brown scaly. Fronds 30–90×5–22cm, lanceolate, rigid, pinnae to 50 per side, pinnate or pinnatifid; pinnules serrate, decurrent. Eur. Z5.

P. adiantiforme (Forst. f..) J. Sm. = *Rumohra adiantiformis*.

P. andersonii L.S. Hopk. Stipes 5–25cm, paleaceous. Fronds 40–80×8–20cm, in a close crown, narrowly lanceolate-oblong to lanceolate-elliptic, pinnae numerous, narrowly deltoid, subpinnate, at base, seg. elliptic, decurrent, strongly serrate. NW Amer. Z4.

P. angulare (Kit. ex Willd.) C. Presl = *P. setiferum*.

P. aristatum Hook. non (Forst.) Presl. = *P. richardii*.

P. aristatum (Forst.) Presl = *Arachniodes aristata*.

P. aristatum var. *simplicium* (Mak.) Matsum. = *Arachniodes simplicior*.

P. auriculatum (L.) Presl. = *P. harpophyllum*.

P. australiense Tind. Stipes papery, scaly. Fronds to 120×120cm, 2–3-pinnate, dark green, harsh and coriaceous, with a proliferous bud near apex of main rachis, pinnules serrate, with short apical spine. Aus. (NSW). Z10.

P. braunii (Spenn.) Fée. Stipes thick, 13–18cm, densely scaly. Fronds to 80×20cm, oblong-lanceolate, soft, pinnae 30–40 per side, pinnate to pinnatifid, pinnules 9–15 per side, ovate-deltoid to ovate-oblong, acute, minutely spinose-dentate, softly pubesc. above. N Amer., Eurasia. Z5.

P. californicum (D.C. Eaton) Underw. Stipes to 35cm, brown-paleaceous below. Fronds 20–75×5–20cm, linear-oblong to narrowly linear-lanceolate, subcoriaceous, pinnae numerous, linear, pinnatifid to incised, seg., elliptic, decurrent, aristate. W US. Z8.

P. capense (Willd.) J. Sm. = *Rumohra adiantiformis*.

P. caryotideum (Wallich) Diels = *Cyrtomium caryotideum*.

P. coriaceum (Sw.) Schott = *Rumohra adiantiformis*.

P. craspedosorum (Maxim.) Diels. Stipes 0.5–5cm, clad in rusty brown scales. Fronds 5–18×1.5–3.5cm, lanceolate, pinna 1–1.5cm, in 15–35 pairs, narrowly oblong, obtuse at apex, broadly auriculate at base, dentate; rachis proliferous and rooting at apex. NE Asia. Z4.

P. cystostegia (Hook.) Cheesem. Stipes 5–15cm, stout, densely scaly below. Fronds 8–15×3–5cm, lanceolate to oblong-lanceolate, pale green, soft pubesc., pinnae to 4×1.5cm, rather distant, ovate, pinnules ovate to lanceolate, crenate, to 1cm; rachis winged. NZ. Z7.

P. dudleyi Maxon. Stipes 15–45cm, paleaceous. Fronds 25–75×8–25cm, oblong-lanceolate to narrowly ovate, pinnae linear to narrowly oblong-lanceolate, attenuate, filiform-paleaceous, pinnules obliquely ovate or ovate-oblong, auriculate, serrate to incised. Calif. Z8.

P. falcatum (L. f.) Diels = *Cyrtomium falcatum*.

P. falcinellum Moore. Stipes 10–30cm, clad in glossy brown scales. Fronds 30–150cm, everg., lanceolate, pinnae 2.5–10cm, numerous, linear biserrate, auriculate on upper side at base, paleate beneath. N Amer. Z5.

P. fallax Tind. Stipe papery brown-scaly below. Fronds to 70×20cm, 2–3-pinnate, with no proliferous buds, pinnules ovate, margins irregularly serrate, apical spine longer than marginal ones. Aus. (NSW, Queensld). Z10.

P. fortunei (J. Sm.) Nak. = *Cyrtomium fortunei*.

P. hispidum (Sw.) J. Sm. = *Lastreopsis hispida*.

P. imbricans (D.C. Eaton) Wagner. Stipes 5–20cm, dark-brown-scaly. Fronds 20–45×4–9cm, linear, pinnae 2–4.5cm, entire, minutely spinose, auriculate. NW Amer. Z7.

P. ×kruckebergii Wagner. (*P. lonchitis* ×*P. lemmoni*.) Stipes 2–10cm, with long, pale scales. Fronds 8–20×1.5–3cm, linear-lanceolate, pinnae oblong, short, lobulate with larger auricle on upper side. N Amer. Z4.

P. ×kurokawae Tag. Stipes stout, 25–30cm, scaly. Fronds 40–80×20–25cm, broadly lanceolate to oblong-ovate, pinnae 2–2.5cm wide, pinnules oblong-ovate to ovate, obtuse to sub-acute, mucronate, spinose-dentate, scaly. Jap. Z8.

P. lachenense (Hook.) Bedd. Rhiz. rather stout; stipes erect, 3–10cm, brown-scaly below. Fronds 8–20×1.5–2.5cm, linear-lanceolate, pinnae to 15–25 pairs, ovate, coarsely awned-dentate or lobed, sparsely scaly beneath. NE Asia. Z8.

P. lemmoni Underw. Stipes 3–15cm, stramineous, v. chaffy below. Fronds 10–30×1.5–5cm, linear to narrowly lanceolate-oblong, succulent, pinnae usually overlapping, deltoid-oblong to deltoid-ovate, seg. close, trapeziform-ovate to obliquely ovate, crenate. NW Amer. Z7.

P. lentum (D. Don) T. Moore. Differs from *P. proliferum* in fronds 2-, never 3-pinnate. Himal. Z8.

P. lepidocaulon (Hook.) J. Sm. Stipes 10–40cm, with dull brown scales. Fronds 15–40×6–15cm, narrowly ovate, often rooting and proliferous at apex, pinnae 3–10cm, 10–20 per side, lanceolate, subentire to undulate-dentate, scaly beneath. NE Asia. Z8.

P. lobatum (Huds.) Chevall. = *P. aculeatum*.

P. lobatum var. *chinense* Christ = *P. neolobatum*.

P. lonchitis (L.) Roth. NORTHERN HOLLY FERN. Fronds 20–60×3–7cm, linear-lanceolate, rigid, coriaceous, pinnae 25–40 each side, lanceolate, slightly curved, auriculate on upper side at base, serrate, dark green above, scaly beneath, v. shortly stipitate. Eur. Z4.

P. macleayi (Bak.) Diels. Stipes 30–55cm, pale brown, with scales. Fronds 40–60×20–24cm, narrowly oblong, with triangular term. seg. to 4cm, coriaceous, rigid; pinnae in 25–40 pairs, alt., linear-lanceolate, serrate, dark green above, minutely brown-scaly beneath. S Afr. Z9.

P. macrophyllum (Mak.) Tag. = *Cyrtomium macrophyllum*.

P. makinoi (Tag.) Tag. Stipes 20–40cm, with brown scales. Fronds 30–60×10–20cm, pinnules 7–15×3–6mm, ovate, obtuse with short apical spine, spinose-dentate, coriaceous, scaly beneath. Jap. Z8.

P. mayebarae Tag. Stipes dark-scaly. Fronds 30–40×10–18cm, ovate-lanceolate, pinnae lanceolate, 1.5–3cm wide, pinnules 8–15×5–8mm, rhombic-ovate, spinose-dentate, with short apical spine. Jap. Z8.

P. mohrioides (Bory ex Urv.) C. Presl. Stipes to 18cm, densely dark-scaly. Fronds 20–60×6–15cm, elliptic-lanceolate to ovate-lanceolate, pinnae 3–8cm, lanceolate to oblong-lanceolate, pinnules 8–12mm, ovate to subrhomboid, lobed to shallowly pinnatifid. Tierra del Fuego, Falkland Is. Z5.

P. monotis Christ = *P. tsussimense*.

P. munitum (Kaulf.) Presl. Stipes to 18cm, densely scaly below. Fronds to 90cm, linear, rigid, coriaceous; pinnae to 40 per side, linear, serrate to biserrate. N Amer. Z4.

P. neolobatum Nak. Stipes stout, brown below, densely scaly. Fronds 20–80cm, broadly lanceolate, pinnae in 15–40 pairs, lanceolate to ovate, coriaceous, scaly, pinnules 7–15mm, ovate, acute, mucronate, remotely spinose-dentate, lustrous. NE Asia. Z8.

P. nipponicum Rosenst. = *Arachniodes nipponica*.

P. plicatum (Poepp. ex Kunze) Hicken = *P. mohrioides*.

P. polyblepharum (Roem.) Presl. Stipes stout, 20–30cm, with brown scales. Fronds 30–80×15–25cm, narrowly oblong-ovate, deep green and slightly lustrous above, pinnate 15–25mm wide, pinnules 8–15×4–6mm, oblong-ovate, mucronate, spinose-dentate, scaly beneath. Jap., S Korea. Z5.

P. prescottianum (Wallich) Moore. Stipes 2–7cm, pale-scaly. Fronds 15–30×3–3.5cm, pinnatifid to subpinnate, pinnae 1–2×0.5–1cm, ovate-oblong to elongate-lanceolate, truncate at base, serrate, soft, scaly beneath. Himal. Z5.

P. proliferum (R. Br.) Presl. MOTHER SHIELD FERN. Rhiz. trunk-like with age; stipes brown-scaly below. Fronds to 100×30cm, bipinnate to tripinnate, dark green, with proliferous buds near apex, pinnule spiny-serrate. Aus. (NSW, Vict., Tasm.). Z10.

P. retrorsopalaeceum (Kodama) Tag. Stipes 20–40cm, scales membranous brown. Fronds 40–100×15–30cm, abruptly acuminate, pinnules ovate to ovate-oblong, obtuse, mucronate, dentate. Jap. Z8.

P. rhomboideum Schott = *Arachniodes amabilis*.

P. richardii (Hook.) J. Sm. NZ, Fiji. Rhiz. stout, erect; stipes stout, 15–30cm, chaffy below, hairy above. Fronds

25–30×10–15cm, lanceolate to deltoid-oblong, dark green above, somewhat scurfy beneath, coriaceous, pinnae 5–10cm, lanceolate, pinnules to 15mm, lanceolate- to ovate-oblong, serrate to crenate or subentire. Z9.

P. rigens Tag. Stipes 20–40cm, dark brown below, with long brown to black scales. Fronds 30–45×10–20cm, narrowly ovate-oblong, acuminate, coriaceous, pinnae 15–25mm broad, lanceolate, pinnules 10–12mm, ovate, mucronate, spinose-dentate to subentire, decurrent on narrowly winged rachis. Jap. Z7.

P. schkuhrii Presl = *Lastreopsis hispida*.

P. scopulinum (D.C. Eaton) Maxon. WESTERN HOLLY FERN. Stipes 2–12cm, densely scaly. Fronds 10–30×2.5–4cm, linear-lanceolate, paleaceous beneath; pinnae 30–40 per side, alt., obtuse to acute, auriculate. N Amer. Z2.

P. setiferum (Forssk.) Woyn. SOFT-SHIELD FERN. Stipes to 12cm, clad in pale orange-brown scales. Fronds 30–120×10–25cm, lanceolate, soft, pinnae to 11×2.5cm, to 40 per side, pinnules serrate, stipitate; rachis bearing bulbils. S, W & C Eur. 'Acutilobum': 50–70cm; pinnules narrowed and pointed, un-divided except for a 'thumb' on some basal pinnules; frond texture hard. 'Congestum': 30–50cm; frond congested, often combined with cresting. 'Cristato-gracile Moly': 30–50cm; pinnae and frond lightly crested, dark green. 'Cristato-pinnulum': 70–80cm; pinnules fan-shaped, notched margin; frond slightly depauperate, bulbiferous. 'Divisilobum': 50–70cm; texture hard, bulbiferous; pinnules narrowed and pointed (as with 'Acutilobum') but pinnules clearly divided. There are many named forms of which the following are dis-tinct: 'Divisilobum Bland': the best wild find of 'Divisilobum', 50–70cm; bottom half of frond feathery with pinnae overlap-ping, bulbiferous. (Divisilobum grandiceps group): forms of 'Divisilobum', 30–60cm, with enormous term. ramose heads, some pinnae branched at tips, bulbiferous. 'Divisilobum In-veryanum': 50cm; a crested form of 'Divisilobum', frond spread-ing, bulbiferous. 'Divisilobum laxum': 50–60cm; pinnae and pinnules well separated, an airy form of 'Divisilobum'. 'Foliosum Walton': 30–50cm; a fine foliose form. 'Gracillimum': raised form 'Plumosum Bevis', 30–50cm; pinnules greatly elongated with some tasselling at tips, frond spreading and v. open. 'Lineare' ('Confluens'): 30–80cm; pinnules narrow, pinnules at base of pinnae often missing. 'Multilobum': 60–80cm; akin to 'Divisilobum' but pinnules divide into seg. which are not narrowed, frond not glossy. 'Plumosum Bevis': 60–90cm; pinnules elongated into fine points, toward tip of frond pinnae curve toward apex, dark green, glossy. 'Plumosum Drueryi': 60–70cm; pinnules divided, dark green, completely sterile. 'Plumosum Green': 60–70cm; pinnules deeply divided into narrow seg., frond quadri-pinnate and completely sterile. 'Plumosum Moly': 100–120cm; tall feathery fronds with broad pinnules, tri-pinnate completely sterile. 'Rotundatum': 50cm; pinnules rounded. 'Wakeleyanum': 50–90cm; pinnae cruciate in mid section of frond, frond narrow. Z7.

P. ×setigerum (Presl) Presl. (*P. braunii* ×*P. munitum*.) ALASKAN HOLLY FERN. Stipes 6–20cm, pale brown-scaly below. Fronds 25–90×8–20cm, rhombic, pinnate-pinnatifid to sub-bipinnate, acute to acuminate at apex, pinnae oblong-lanceolate, deeply lobed to subpinnate at base. Alask. to BC. Z3.

P. silvaticum (Colenso) Diels. Stipes 5–25cm, with broad, shiny, dark brown scales. Fronds 15–40×5–18cm, elliptic, dark green above, pale green beneath, pinnae 3–10cm, pinnules elliptic to ovate, deeply dissected, with long apical points. NZ. Z8.

P. simplicius (Mak.) Tag. = *Arachniodes simplicior*.

P. standishii (Moore) C. Chr. = *Arachniodes standishii*.

P. tripteron (Kunze) Presl. Stipes erect, 10–40cm, pale green, laxly scaly. Fronds 20–45×5–10cm, lanceolate, pinnae 2.5–5×0.5–1cm, 20–35 per side, lanceolate, often falcate, dentate, occas. lobulate, with soft awn, glab. above, sparsely scaly beneath, pinnules in 8–15 pairs. NE Asia. Z6.

P. tsussimense (Hook.) J. Sm. Stipes pale green to stramineous, brown below with black to brown scales. Fronds 25–40×10–20cm, broadly lanceolate to oblong-ovate, acuminate, pinnules 7–15mm, ovate to oblong-ovate, mucronate, spinose-dentate, glab. and glaucous above. NE Asia. Z7.

P. tsussimense var. *mayebarae* (Tag.) Kurata = *P. mayebarae*.

P. vestitum (Forst. f.) Presl. Stipes to 45cm, stout, densely brown-peleate. Fronds 30–75×10–25cm, oblong-lanceolate, dark green above, rather harsh; pinnae to 12×2.5cm, lanceolate-oblong, pinnules to 15mm, v. close-set, ovate-oblong to subrhombic, dentate, v. shortly stalked. S Atlantic (NZ, Tasm., Tierra del Fuego). Z7.

→*Aspidium*.

Polyxena Kunth. Liliaceae (Hyacinthaceae). 5 dwarf, bulbous perennials. Lvs 10–15cm, ovate to linear. Fls *c*2cm, fragrant in a term. corymb; scape concealed by sheathing lf bases; tep. 6 fused into a narrow tube, lobes spreading. Early spring. S Afr. Z9.

P. angustifolia Bak. Lvs 10×2.5cm. Scape 7.5–16cm; fls white. Cape Prov.

P. corymbosa (L.) Jessop. Lvs linear. Scape to 5cm; fls carmine, outside paler. Cape Penins.

P. odorata Nichols. Lvs 10–12.5×0.6cm. Fls white, held between lvs on v. short scape. Cape Prov.

P. pygmaea Kunth. Lvs to 10×2.5cm. Scape 10–15cm; fls lilac. Cape Prov.

→*Massonia* and *Neobakeria*.

Pomaderris Labill. Rhamnaceae. *c*40 everg. shrubs or small trees. Lvs oblong to aciform, stellate-pubesc., fls small in term. cymose or corymbose pan., cal. 5-lobed, tube fused to ovary; pet. 0 or 5; sta. 5. Spring–summer. Aus., NZ. Z9.

P. apetala Labill. Shrub or small tree to 4m. Lvs 5–7cm, oval or oval-oblong, rugose and glab. above, densely felted beneath. Infl. 7–25cm, paniculate, subpyramidal; fls *c*6mm diam., apetalous, pale yellow. Aus.

P. elliptica Labill. Shrub to 2m, with young growth, lower lf surfaces white-downy. Lvs 5–10cm, ovate to elliptic-lanceolate. Infl. 5–7cm-wide, flat; fls pale yellow; pet. broad. Aus., NZ.

P. kumeraho A. Cunn. Rounded shrub, 2–3m. Lvs to 6cm, oval or elliptic, glaucous above, stellate-pubesc. beneath. Infl. to 10cm diam., dense; fls yellow. NZ.

P. phylicifolia Lodd. Shrub to 1m, ericoid, young growth densely lanate. Lvs to 1.2cm, oblong to linear, revolute, stellate pubesc. beneath. Pan. large, leafy; fls small, apetalous, pale yellow. Spring. Aus., NZ.

P. rugosa Cheesem. Erect, much-branched shrub to 3m. Lvs 1–5.5cm, oblong-lanceolate to elliptic, rugose above, stellate-hairy beneath, rusty near veins. Infl. axill. or term., cymose; fls *c*4mm diam., apetalous. NZ.

Pomatocalpa Breda. Orchidaceae. 60 epiphytic, monopodial orchids. Lvs oblong or lorate, coriaceous. Rac. nodal, often branched; fls small; spreading, ovate-oblong; lip fleshy, midlobe ovate-triangular or semi-orbicular, lat. lobes triangular, broad; spur saccate, crested within. China, Malaysia, Aus., Polyn. Z9.

P. latifolia (Lindl.) J.J. Sm. 5–30cm. Lvs oblong, to 20×4cm. Infl. to 40cm; fls. to 1.8cm diam., tep. green-yellow, speckled or edged maroon; lip yellow, lamellae, crenate, white, suffused violet, interior of lat. lobes spotted red; spur yellow-green, speckled brown. Malaya, Sumatra, Java.

P. siamensis (Rolfe ex Downie) Summerh. St. to 35cm. Lvs linear-oblong, to 17×2cm. Infl. to 50cm; fls to 1.5cm diam., minutely pubesc.; lip callus oblong, erect, with 2 backward-pointing lamellae. Thail.

P. spicata Breda. St. short, stout. Lvs oblong-lorate, undulate, to 28×2cm. Infl. to 15cm; fls to 1.8cm diam., pale yellow, tep. blotched maroon, spur lamellae violet, tipped white; spur interior with dentate, 2-ridged lamellae. India to Vietnam, Philipp.

→*Cleisostoma*.

Pomegranate *Punica granatum*.
Pomelo *Citrus ×paradisi*.
Pomme Blanche *Psoralea esculenta*.
Pomme-de-liane *Passiflora laurifolia*.
Pomme De Prairie *Psoralea esculenta*.
Pommette Bleue *Crataegus brachyacantha*.
Pom-pom Darwinia *Darwinia vestita*.

Poncirus Raf. Rutaceae. 1 small decid. tree, with tangled, rigid, green br. and stout green spines to 6cm. Lvs trifoliolate; lfts 3–6cm, obovate-elliptic, cuneate at base; petiole 1–2.5cm winged. Fls to 3cm, axill., solitary, scented, subsessile, generally 5-merous, waxy white; sta. 20+. Fr. globose to somewhat pyriform, 3–5cm diam., green to dull lemon-yellow, fragrant when ripe, acid, inedible; peel thick, rough, with oil glands. C & N China. Z5.

P. trifoliata (L.) Raf. TRIFOLIATE ORANGE; BITTER ORANGE. →*Citrus*.

Pond Apple *Annona glabra*.
Pond Cypress *Taxodium ascendens*.
Ponderosa Pine *Pinus ponderosa*.
Pond Lily *Nymphaea odorata*.
Pondoland Palm *Jubaeopsis caffra*.
Pond Pine *Pinus serotina*.
Pondweed *Elodea*.

Ponerorchis Rchb. f. Orchidaceae. 24 tuberous terrestrial orchids. China, Jap.

P. graminifolia Rchb. f. 8–15cm. Lvs linear, to 12cm. Rac. secund; fls few, rose-purple; sep. oblong; pet. ovate, erect, forming a hood with dors. sep.; lip ascending, deeply trilobed; spur to 2cm. China, Jap. Z8.

Pongamia Vent. Leguminosae (Papilionoideae). 1 spreading everg. tree to 25m. Lvs imparipinnate, emerging pink-bronze, hardening bright green, glossy; lfts 5–9, ovate. Fls in axill. rac. to 12.5cm, fragrant, pea-like, pink-mauve or cream. Indomal., Aus. Treated by some authors as a sp. of *Millettia* Wight & Arn. Z10.

P. pinnata Pierre. INDIAN BEECH; KARANJA; THINWIN; KARUM TREE; POONGA OIL TREE.

Pongelia Raf. = *Dolichandrone*.

Pontederia L. PICKEREL WEED; WAMPEE. Pontederiaceae. 5 perenn., aquatic or marginal herbs. Rhiz. branched, often submerged; aerial st. erect or prostrate. Lvs lanceolate or sagittate or reniform, entire, dark green glaucous; petioles long, clasping at base. Infl. spicate subtended by 1 lf and spathe; fls small, zygomorphic, with bilabiate tubular perianth, each lip with 3 basally connate lobes, largest lobe spotted yellow, fil. gland. hairy. N & S Amer., mostly E.

P. cordata L. PICKEREL WEED; WAMPEE. Aquatic perenn. to 1.3m. Lvs emergent erect cordate, sagittate, ovate or lanceolate, to 18cm; petioles to 60cm. Infl. 2–16cm, on peduncle to 35cm; fls many to 17mm across, in a cylindric spike blue to white. Summer. E N Amer. to Carib. Z3.

PONTEDERIACEAE Kunth. 7/31. *Eichhornia, Heteranthera, Monochoria, Pontederia*

Pontine Oak *Quercus pontica*.
Pony Tail *Nolina recurvata*.
Poonga Oil Tree *Pongamia pinnata*.
Poor Knights Lily *Xeronema callistemon*.
Poor Man's Cibotium *Pteris tremula*.
Poor Man's Orchid *Schizanthus*.
Poor Man's Pulse *Macrotyloma uniflorum*.
Poor Man's Rhododendron *Impatiens sodenii*.
Poor Man's Weatherglass *Anagallis arvensis*.
Pop-a-gun *Cecropia peltata*.
Popcorn Flowers *Plagiobothrys nothofulvus*.
Poplar *Populus*.
Poplar Box *Eucalyptus populnea*.
Poplar Gum *Eucalyptus platyphylla*.
Poppy *Papaver*.
Poppy Mallow *Callirhoë* (*C. papaver*).

Populus L. POPLAR; COTTONWOOD; ASPEN. Salicaceae. Some 35 decid., trees, often resinous. Lvs alt., ovate to triangular, long stalked, often with glands at junction with lf lamina. Infl. a pendulous catkin, borne before lvs; ♂ catkins denser and shorter than ♀. Capsule 2–4 valved; seed minute with cotton wool-like apical tuft. Eur., Asia, N Afr., N Amer.

P. ×acuminata Rydb. (*P. angustifolia* ×*P. deltoides*.) To 20m, crown spreading, flat-topped, bark pale brown. Young twigs slender, glab., orange-brown; buds v. resinous, sparsely bristled. Lvs to 13.5cm, lanceolate to rhombic-lanceolate, long-acuminate, base broadly cuneate, sometimes with 1 or 2 glands, crenate-serrate, pale green; petioles 2–4.5cm. Spring. Canada (Alberta) to W Tex. Z3.

P. alba L. WHITE POPLAR; SILVER-LEAVED POPLAR; ABELE. To 30m, crown broad, bark smooth, grey suckering. Young twigs, white-tomentose. Lvs 6–12cm, ovate, base subcordate, those on long shoots lobed, coarsely toothed, on short shoots serrate, ovate to elliptic-oblong, dark green and glab. above, white-woolly beneath; petioles 1.2–3.7cm. Late winter. S, C & E Eur., N Afr. to C Asia. 'Globosa': tall shrub with a broadly rounded habit and young lvs pink. 'Intertexta': young lvs dull white, becoming yellow-speckled. 'Nivea': juvenile form; young twigs, lf underside and petiole chalk white; lvs deeply lobed. 'Paletzkyana': lvs deeply lobed. 'Pendula': br. pendent. 'Pyramidalis': tall tree, narrowly conical; lvs large, lobed, often glab. beneath. 'Raket' ('Rocket'): slender, columnar; st. grey; lvs glossy green above, silver-grey beneath. 'Richardii': lvs golden-yellow above. var. **subintegerrima** Lange. Lvs almost entire. Z3.

P. angulata Ait. = *P. deltoides*.

P. angustifolia James. NARROWLEAF COTTONWOOD; WILLOW-LEAVED POPLAR. To 20m, narrowly conical. Young twigs glab., later orange-brown. Lvs 8–10cm, willow-like, oval-lanceolate, round glandular-toothed, pale green beneath; petioles *c*1cm. W US, N Mex. Z3.

P. balsamifera L. BALSAM POPLAR; HACKMATACK; TACAMAHAC.
To 30m; suckering from base. Young twigs slnd.; buds and new
growth covered in a fragrant resin. Lvs glossy mid-green, subcoriaceous, ± crenate, glab., ciliate, venation reticulate. var.
balsamifera. Lvs 7–12cm, oval to ovate-lanceolate, acute, base
rounded or broadly cuneate, dark glossy above, white or pale
green beneath. N US, Canada, Russia. 'Aurora': lvs yellow
white, spotted dark green. var. *michauxii* (Dode) Henry. Lvs
ovate, base rounded or subcordate, major veins beneath, twigs
and petioles slightly hairy beneath. N US. var. *subcordata*
Hylander. Lvs 12–16cm, broadly ovate to triangular,
acuminate, base cordate, dark green and glossy above, metallic
white, beneath. Capsules stalked. NE US, Canada. Z2.

P. balsamifera var. *viminalis* Loud. = *P. laurifolia*.
P. balsamifera var. *candicans* (Ait.) A. Gray = *P. ×jackii*
'Gileadensis'.

P. ×berolinensis K. Koch. (*P. laurifolia* ×*P. nigra* 'Italica'.) To
25m, slenderly columnar. Young downy, yellow-brown. Lvs
7–12cm, broadly ovate or rhombic-ovate, long-acuminate, base
rounded or cuneate, crenate to serrate, bright glossy green
above, paler beneath, ± glab.; petioles 2–4cm, hairy. BERLIN
POPLAR. Z2.

P. bolleana Lauche = *P. alba* 'Pyramidalis'.

P. ×canadensis Moench. (*P. deltoides* ×*P. nigra*.) CANADIAN
POPLAR. Tall, fast-growing tree to 30m, crown broad. Young
twigs glab. or slightly hairy. Lvs 7–10cm, triangular to ovate,
long-acuminate, base truncate, sparsely toothed, and sometimes
with 1 or 2 glands, margins crenate, initially ciliate; petioles
tinged red. Spring. 'Aurea': lvs golden yellow, becoming
yellow-green, petiole red. 'Eugenei': to 50m, columnar, bark
pale; lvs coppery-brown when young, 5–8cm, triangular to
rhombic, short-acuminate. 'Gelrica': trunk slightly crooked,
bark white with pale spots and rings, crown dense; lvs red-
brown when young, later pale green, broadly deltoid, base
shallowly cordate; petioles tinged red; ♂. 'Marilandica' (MAY
POPLAR): trunk short, crown broad, rounded, br. spreading,
often crooked, growing downwards; young lvs brown, soon pale
green, to 10cm, rhombic to triangular-ovate, apex slenderly
acute, entire. 'Regenerata': trunk straight, br. whorled, spreading, bark pale grey; young twigs slender, pendulous, young lvs
pale brown, soon pale green, lvs triangular; petioles tinged red;
♀. 'Robusta': columnar, br. ascending, almost whorled; young
twigs green, becoming red, finely hairy; lvs red-brown when
young, 10–12cm, glossy, tough, triangular, with to 2 basal
glands, teeth rounded, regular, apex entire; petioles becoming
red. 'Serotina' (LATE POPLAR; BLACK ITALIAN POPLAR): to 40m,
crown broadly conical, open; young twigs brown, flexible, glab.;
young lvs not borne until late spring, 7–10cm, red-brown,
ovate-triangular to equilaterally triangular-ovate, base truncate, matt
dark green when mature; petioles tinged red; ♂. Z4.

P. candicans Ait. = *P. ×jackii* 'Gileadensis'.

P. ×canescens (Ait.) Sm. (*P. alba* ×*P. tremula*.) GREY POPLAR.
To 45m; crown rounded, bark yellow-grey, scarred. Young
twigs grey-woolly, soon glab. Lvs 6–12cm, triangular-ovate,
base cordate, dark green above, grey-woolly beneath, ciliate,
teeth gland., rounded; petioles 1–7.5cm, woolly to glab. Early
spring. Natural hybrid, Russia (Georgia), Iran to C Eur.
'Aureovariegata': lvs marbled yellow; slow growing. 'Macrophylla' PICKART'S POPLAR: 'Pyramidalis': crown broadly conical,
bark grey-green, upper br. steeply ascending, lower br. spreading. Z4.

P. carolinensis hort. = *P. deltoides* 'Carolin'.

P. cathayana Rehd. Tree to 30m. Young shoots olive-green,
becoming orange-yellow to grey-yellow. Lvs on short shoots
ovate, often narrow, 6–10cm, acuminate, base rounded, rarely
cordate, glossy green above, white beneath; lvs on long shoots
10–20cm, slightly cordate. NW China to Korea. Z4.

P. davidiana Dode = *P. tremula* var. *davidiana*.

P. deltoides Bartr. ex Marshall EASTERN COTTONWOOD; NECKLACE
POPLAR. To 30m; crown broad, bark pale green-yellow. Young
twigs ribbed, glab.; buds sticky, balsam-scented. Lvs 7–18cm,
deltoid-ovate to rhombic, base cordate to truncate, often with
2–5 glands, apex acute, densely ciliate, teeth coarse, gland.;
petioles tinged; red. E & C US. 'Carolin': long br. conspicuously angled; lvs thick, cordate at base. 'Cordata': lf base
cordate; petioles yellow-green. ssp. *monilifera* (Ait.) Eckenw.
Br. pale yellow, glossy. Buds downy-hairy. Lvs deltoid-ovate,
wide with 2 basal glands, abruptly acuminate, teeth few, large,
esp. toward base, ± glab., yellow-green. Ont. to Tex. ssp.
wislizenii (S. Wats.) Eckenw. Lvs 5–10cm, triangular to broadly
ovate, short-acuminate, base slightly cuneate or rounded, lacking glands, coarsely crenate, teeth few, ± glab. Early spring.
Colorado to N Mex. Z2.

P. eugenei hort. (Simon-Louis). = *P. ×canadensis* 'Eugenei'.

P. ×euroamericana (Dode) Guinier = *P. ×canadensis*.

P. fremontii S. Wats. COTTONWOOD. To 30m, trunk short,

straight or dividing near base, crown conical. Young twigs thick,
smooth. Lvs 4–14cm, broadly deltoid-ovate to rhombic, sharply
acuminate, apex entire, base slightly cordate or cuneate, lacking
glands, yellow-green, teeth coarse, rounded, margins
translucent, ciliate or glab.; petiole 4–7cm. Late winter–spring.
Calif. to Ariz., N Mex. Z7.

P. gelrica (Houtz.) Houtz. = *P. ×canadensis* 'Gelrica'.

P. ×generosa Henry. (*P. deltoides* ×*P. trichocarpa*.) To 35m,
crown narrowly cylindrical, br. ascending. Young twigs dark
red, hairy to glab.; buds red, downy, yellow-resinous. Lvs
7–15cm, rhombic-ovate to broadly deltoid-ovate, base broadly
cuneate or truncate, finely crenate-serrate, basal glands 2;
petioles 3–6.5cm. Spring. W US. Z6.

P. ×gileadensis Roul. = *P. ×jackii* 'Gileadensis'.

P. glauca Haines. Lvs broad, ovate, to 18×20.5cm, base weakly
cordate, finely serrate, glaucous finely pubesc. beneath; petiole
to 14cm. Nepal. Z7.

P. grandidentata Michx. BIG-TOOTHED ASPEN; CANADIAN ASPEN.
To 20m; crown narrow, rounded. Young twigs grey-woolly. Lvs
7–10cm, ovate, coarsely sinuate on long shoots, elliptic with
sharper teeth on shorter shoots, pale grey-woolly at first, midrib
yellow; petioles 2.5–6cm. E N Amer. Z3.

P. hickeliana Dode = *P. alba* var. *subintegerrima*.

P. ×jackii Sarg. (*P. balsamifera* ×*P. deltoides*.) 10–30m, crown
obovoid, dark grey-brown, tinted orange. Young twigs red-
brown, hairy or glab.; buds v. resinous. Lvs 2.5–11.5cm,
deltoid-ovate, acuminate, base subcordate with 2–3 prominent
glands, blue-green above, pale beneath, finely crenate-serrate;
petioles 2–5.5cm. Spring. C & E N Amer. 'Aurora': lvs boldly
variegated pale pink, eesp. on strong shoots. 'Gileadensis' BALM
OF GILEAD: lvs to 17cm, deltoid-ovate, base cordate, petioles
covered in stiff, dense hairs ♀. Z2.

P. jacquemontiana var. *glauca* (Haines) Kimura = *P. glauca*.

P. koreana Rehd. = *P. maximowiczii*.

P. lasiocarpa Oliv. CHINESE NECKLACE POPLAR. To 25m, crown
rounded. Young twigs angular, densely woolly at first. Lvs to
15–35cm, ovate, acute, base cordate, glandular-crenate, glossy
grey-green above, paler and downy beneath, veins red; petioles
5–10cm, red. SW China. Z5.

P. laurifolia Ledeb. LAUREL POPLAR. To 20m, crown spreading.
Young twigs angled, grey-yellow, somewhat pubesc. when
young. Lvs on long shoots ovate-lanceolate to lanceolate,
acuminate, base rounded, minutely glandular-serrate, glossy
green above, white-pubesc. beneath (often only midrib). NW
India to NE Sib., Jap. f. *lindleyana* (Carr.) Rehd. Lvs
narrower, often lanceolate on the long shoots, base round to
broad-cuneate. Z6.

P. lindleyana Carr. = *P. laurifolia* f. *lindleyana*.

P. marilandica Bosc ex Poir. = *P. ×canadensis* 'Marilandica'.

P. maximowiczii Henry. DORONOKI; JAPANESE POPLAR. To 40m,
crown broad, bark grey, deeply fissured. Young twigs red,
hairy. Lvs 6–12cm, elliptic to oval-elliptic, apex abruptly
acuminate to a twisted cusp, base slightly cordate to rounded,
matt dark green and wrinkled above, pale green beneath, gland.
serrate and ciliate, veins hairy, somewhat leathery; petioles
2–4cm. NE China, Jap., Korea. Z4.

P. michauxii Dode = *P. balsamifera* var. *michauxii*.

P. monilifera Ait. = *P. deltoides* ssp. *monilifera*.

P. nigra L. BLACK POPLAR. To 30m; crown broad, rounded, trunk
often thickly knotted, bark deeply fissured. Young twigs
cyklindrical. Lvs 5–10cm, rhombic, triangular or ovate, sometimes wider than long, apex slenderly acuminate, base cuneate
or truncate, green, paler beneath, finely crenate, glands 0;
petioles 3–7cm. Spring. W Eur., N Afr., Sib. 'Afghanica':
columnar; bark almost white with age; young twigs grey, initially hairy; lvs triangular-ovate, base broadly cuneate. var.
betulifolia (Pursh) Torr. DOWNY BLACK POPLAR; MANCHESTER
POPLAR. Young twigs initially hairy, brown-orange. Lvs hairy
when young, smaller, tapering gently to acute apex; petioles
yellow-green. Spring. W Eur. 'Charkowensis': crown oblong,
broad, pyramidal, br. ascending; young br. sparsely pubesc.
'Italica' LOMBARDY POPLAR; ITALIAN POPLAR; PYRAMIDAL
POPLAR: columnar, br. steeply ascending; young twigs brown at
apex, later grey; lvs small, rounded-rhombic; petioles tinged
red; ♂. 'Gigantea': as 'Italica' but broader; winter twigs
orange; ♀. 'Lombardy Gold': lvs golden. 'Plantierensis': habit
columnar (less so than 'Italica'); young twigs hairy; lvs small;
petioles tinged red, hairy. 'Vereeken': crown columnar-conic.
'Vert de Garonne': as 'Italica' but broader and densely leafy.
Z2.

P. nigra var. *thevistina* Dode Bean = *P. nigra* 'Afghanica'.

P. picardii hort. = *P. ×canescens* 'Macrophylla'.

P. plantierensis Simon-Louis = *P. nigra* 'Plantierensis'.

P. pyramidalis Salisb. = *P. nigra* 'Italica'.

P. regenerata hort. ex C. Schneid. = *P. ×canadensis* 'Regenerata'.

P. robusta C. Schneid. = *P. ×canadensis* 'Robusta'.

P. sargentii Dode = *P. deltoides* ssp. *monilifera*.

P. serotina Hartig = *P.* ×*canadensis* 'Serotina'.

P. sieboldii Miq. JAPANESE ASPEN.   Tree to 20m, suckering. Young twigs thick, initially white-downy. Lvs 5–8cm, apex short-triangular, base short, cuneate, with 2 prominent glands, dark green, glab. above, white-hairy beneath, glandular-serrate; petioles 1–4cm. Jap. Z4.

P. simonii Carr. Tree to 30m, slender, crown narrow, bark grey-green, branch-lets pendulous. Young twigs red-brown, glab., angular. Lvs 6–12cm, rhombic-elliptic, acute, crenate, bright green above, pale green beneath; petioles 1–2cm, red. N & WC China. 'Fastigiata': columnar; young twigs dark brown, v. steeply ascending; lvs small, obovate, base long-cuneate. 'Pendula': br. weeping. Z2.

P. suaveolens C. Schneid. non Fisch. = *P. cathayana*.

P. suaveolens Fisch. non C. Schneid. To 30m in wild. Young twigs yellow-brown, cylindrical, hairy above nodes; buds fragrantly resinous. Lvs 5–12cm, oblong-elliptic, apex short, abruptly acuminate, often twisted, leathery, crenate, hairy beneath; petioles 1–4cm. N China, N Jap., Korea, E Sib. Z3.

P. szechuanica C. Schneid. To 40m in wild. Young twigs red-brown, angular. Lvs 7–20cm, tinged red at first, ovate-oblong broadly ovate, crenate, teeth with apical glands, apex acuminate, base rounded or slightly cordate, bright green above, white-silver beneath, veins red; petioles 2–7cm. W China. Z4.

P. tacamahaca Mill. = *P. balsamifera*.

P. ×*tomentosa* Carr. (*P. alba* ×*P. adenopoda.*) To 40m. Young twigs grey-woolly. Lvs to 15m, triangular-ovate, acuminate, biserrate, grey-woolly beneath, later glab., lacking lobes. CHINESE WHITE POPLAR. N China. Z4.

P. tremula L. ASPEN; QUAKING ASPEN. To 20m; crown broad, much-branched, bark fissured and dark grey with age, suckering. Lvs 3–12cm, oval to suborbicular, acute, base with 2 glands, truncate or cordate, undulate, crenate, grey-green above, v. pale beneath; petioles 4–7cm, slender. Late winter. NW Eur. to N Afr., Sib. 'Erecta': narrow, upright; br. dense. 'Pendula': small tree, twigs pendulous. 'Purpurea': lvs tinged red. 'Tapiau': v. vigorous, growing by to 2m per season. var. *davidiana* (Dode) Schneid. Habit lax. Lvs shallowly dentate. var. *villosa* (Láng) Wesm. Young leaves hairy. Lvs persistently hairy. Z2.

P. tremuloides Michx. AMERICAN ASPEN. To 20m, trunk slender, bark v. pale yellow-grey, suckering. Young twigs red-brown. Lvs 3–7cm, broadly oval to suborbicular, short-acuminate, base truncate to broadly cuneate, finely serrate, ciliate, dark glossy above, blue-green beneath, pale yellow in autumn; petioles 3–9cm. Canada to Mex. Z1.

P. trichocarpa Torr. & A. Gray. BLACK COTTONWOOD; WESTERN BALSAM POPLAR. To 35m, slenderly pyramidal, crown open, bark smooth, yellow-grey. Young twigs olive-brown, glab. to hairy, slighty angular. Lvs 8–25cm, ovate to rhombic-oblong, slenderly acuminate, base rounded or truncate, leathery, shallowly toothed, dark green and glab. aove, white or pale brown beneath; petioles 3–6cm. Spring. W N Amer. 'Fritz Pauley': a ♀ clone. 'Pendula': br. weeping. 'Scott Pauley': a ♂ clone. Z5.

P. tristis Fisch. Shrubby. Twigs dark red-brown, pubesc. Lvs oblong-ovate, acuminate, crenate and ciliate, 7–12cm, base round to cordate, black-green above, white and finely-pubesc. beneath; dead lvs persistent. Russia. Z1.

P. vernirubens Henry = *P.* ×*canadensis* 'Robusta'.

P. villosa Láng = *P. tremula* var. *villosa*.

P. violascens Dode. Differs from *P. lasiocarpa* in shoots thinner, buds smaller. Lvs 10–22cm, violet-red when young, becoming dull green, venation red, pubesc. beneath; petiole violet. China. Z6.

P. wilsonii C. Schneid. To 25m, crown regularly conical. Young shoots red; buds large, glossy-resinous. Lvs 8–18cm, broadly cordate, apex truncate, crenate, glab., dull green above, blue or tinged grey beneath; petioles to 15cm. C & W China. Z5.

P. wislizenii (S. Wats.) Sarg. = *P. deltoides* ssp. *wislizenii*.

P. yunnanensis Dode. To 25m or more. Young twigs glab., strongly angular. Lvs 6–15cm, ovate to obovate-lanceolate, acute, base broadly cuneate, red when young, teeth gland., bright green above, pale green beneath, midrib red; petioles 6–12mm, red. SW China. Z5.

Porana Burm. f. Convolvulaceae. 20 slender, twining herbs or shrubs. Fls small, in term. pan. or cymes or solitary, 1 or more sep. enlarged; tubular-campanulate to funnelform, lobes broad, spreading, plicate. Trop. Asia, Aus. Z10.

P. paniculata Roxb. BRIDAL-BOUQUET; CHRIST VINE; SNOW CREEPER; SNOW-IN-THE-JUNGLE; WHITE CORALLITA. Liane to 9m. Lvs cordate, to 15cm, slender-acuminate, white-pubesc. beneath. Pan. large, pendulous; fls to 8mm, white, tubular-campanulate. Summer. N India, Upper Burm.

Porcelain Flower *Hoya*.

Porcupine Palm *Rhapidophyllum hystrix*.

Pork and Beans *Sedum rubrotinctum*.

Porlieria Ruiz & Pav. Zygophyllaceae. 6 shrubs or small trees; br. rigid, spreading; branchlets stout. Lvs pinnate, with sleep movements. Fls axill., sometimes clustered, short-stalked; sep. 4–5, sometimes joined at base; pet. 4–5, slightly exceeding cal.; sta. 8–10. Fr. a globose capsule, somewhat fleshy, 4-angled. Tex. to S Amer. Z10.

P. angustifolia Gray. TEXAS PORLIERIA; SOAP BUSH.   Shrub or small tree, to 7m. Lfts about 12×3mm, 4–8 pairs, linear, coriaceous. Fls solitary or in clusters; pet. 5, violet to purple; sta. 10. Fr. yellow to red. Tex., Mex.

P. hygrometra Ruiz & Pav. Shrub to 2m. Lfts about 8×2mm, 9–10 pairs, linear to linear-oblong, sometimes mucronate, subcoriaceous, ciliate. Fls to 8mm, solitary; pet. 5; sta. 8. Fr. brown. Peru.

Poroporo *Solanum uporo*.

Porpax Lindl. Orchidaceae. 10 minute epiphytic orchids. Pbs turbinate or spherical, clustered. Fls 1–3, at apex of pb.; lat. sep. forming tube with pet., dors. sep. forming a hood. Trop. Asia. Z10.

P. meirax King & Pantl. Pbs to 10mm diam. Lvs elliptic-oblong, to 2.5cm. Fls solitary, dull brown. Autumn. Sikkim.
→*Eria*.

Porroglossum Schltr. Orchidaceae. 25 epiphytic or terrestrial orchids differing from *Masdevallia* in fls small, several on lat. rac., often resupinate with porrect lip. Venez., Colomb., Ecuad., Peru to Boliv. Z9.

P. amethystinum (Rchb. f.) Garay. Lvs to 10cm. Infl. to 25cm, few-fld; sep. bright rose, dors. sep. to 5×7mm, tail to 2mm, lat. sep. to 9×7mm, tails to 14mm, orange; pet. to 4×2mm, translucent; lip white tinged and spotted dark purple. Ecuad.

P. echidnum (Rchb. f.) Garay. Lvs to 14cm. Infl. to 20cfm, few-fld; peduncle downy; sep. brown or green with brown venation, slightly verrucose, dors. sep. to 7×6mm, tail to 25mm, lat. sep. to 8×8mm, tails to 25mm, reflexed; pet. 4×1.5mm, translucent brown; lip to 8×4mm, light brown flecked red, or dark brown, apex ciliate. Colomb.

P. meridionale Ortiz. Lvs to 4.5cm. Infl. to 10cm; sep. clear pale purple spotted purple, dors. sep. to 7×5mm, subverrucose, tail to 9mm, lat. sep. to 7×6mm, tails to 8mm, orange-brown; pet. translucent, to 4×1mm; lip to 4×4mm, purple, pubesc. Peru.

P. mordax (Rchb. f.) Sweet. Lvs to 8cm. Infl. to 15cm; sep. pale green tinged purple, erose, subverrucose, dors. sep. to 20×8mm, tail 0, lat. sep. to 18×4mm; pet. to 5×2mm, translucent; lip to 5×5mm, pale green, ciliate, callus deep purple. Colomb.

P. muscosum (Rchb. f.) Schltr. Lvs to 15cm. Infl. to 26cm, few-fld; peduncle pubesc.; sep. light brown to brown or green, glab. to subverrucose, dors. sep. to 8×6mm, tail to 30mm, lat. sep. to 10×6mm, tails to 30mm, slender; pet. to 5×1.5mm, clear yellow-white to brown; lip to 5.5×4mm, white tinged rose or purple, apex ciliate. Colomb., Ecuad., Venez.

P. olivaceum Sweet. Lvs to 10cm. Infl. to 27cm, several-fld; sep. light brown to light yellow-brown, veined dark brown, dors. sep. to 5×6mm, tail to 3mm, lateral sep. to 4×7mm, tails to 13mm; pet. to 5×2mm, clear pale yellow or pale brown; lip to 5×4mm, yellow distal portion purple, short-pubesc. Ecuad., Colomb.

P. portillae Luer & Andreetta. Lvs to 6cm. Infl. to 11cm, few-fld; fls non-resupinate; sep. yellow tinged rose-pink, minutely spotted purple, dors. sep. to 7×6mm, tail to 5mm, lat. sep. to 6×8mm, tails to 7mm; pet. to 5×1mm, rose-pink; lip to 5×5mm, rose flecked purple, apex ciliate. Ecuad.

P. rodrigoi Sweet. Lvs to 4.5cm. Infl. to 7cm; sep. purple, dors. sep. to 5×6mm, tail to 1.5mm, lat. sep. to 4×5mm, tails to 5mm, light yellow; pet. to 3×1.5mm, red-purple; lip to 3×3mm, white tinged rose-pink. Colomb.

P. xipheres (Rchb. f.) Garay = *P. muscosum*.
→*Masdevallia* and *Scaphosepalum*.

Portea Brongn. ex K. Koch. Bromeliaceae (Bromelioideae). 7 perenn., terrestrial herbs, to 2m in fl. Lvs in a basal rosette, stiff, scaly, sword-shaped. Infl. erect, terminal, much-branched, scapose with brightly coloured bracts; sep. fused, pungent; pet. free, symmetric, with 2 fimbriate basal scales. E Braz. Z9.

P. petropolitana (Wawra) Mez. Lvs to 80cm, spines 4mm, black to brown. Infl. to 50cm, subcylindric, laxly 3-pinnate, br. to 12cm; scape stout, bracts red-brown; sep. pink-orange; pet. 30mm, lavender-blue, narrowly elliptic.

P. tillandsioides (Reg.) Nichols. = *Aechmea recurvata* var. *ortgie-sii.*

Portenschlagia Vis.
P. australis (Vent.) Tratt. = *Cassine australis.*

Portia Tree *Thespesia*; *T. populnea.*
Portio Oil Nut *Thespesia populnea.*
Port Jackson Fig *Ficus rubiginosa.*
Port Jackson Heath *Epacris purpurascens.*

Portlandia P. Browne. Rubiaceae. 20+ everg. shrubs or small trees. Lvs leathery, often connate at base. Fls axill. or term., solitary or few; cal. tube obovoid or campanulate, 4–7-lobed; cor. campanulate or funnelform to tubular, lobes usually 5, triangular; sta. usually 5, anth. exserted or included. W Indies, Mex., C Amer.
P. coccinea Sw. To 3m, often less. Lvs to 12×7cm, ovate to ellip-tic, acute at apex, lustrous 5–7-veined. Fls solitary or paired; cor. funnel-shaped, to 7×5cm, scarlet to crimson, interior lined white. Jam.
P. coriacea Sw. = *P. coccinea.*
P. grandiflora L. To 3m. Lvs to 16×10cm, ovate to oblong or elliptic, sharp-pointed at apex, 7–10-veined. Fls fragrant, solitary; cor. funnel-shaped to tubular, to 20×6cm, white and pink-flushed to cream. Summer. W Indies.
P. grandiflora var. *latifolia* DC. = *P. grandiflora.*
P. hexandra Jacq. = *Coutarea hexandra.*
P. platantha Hook. Differs from *P. grandiflora* in lvs ovate to elliptic, lustrous, dark green; cor. to 3cm. Summer. Amer.

Portland Rose *Rosa* ×*damascena* var. *semperflorens.*
Portland Spurge *Euphorbia portlandica.*
Port Lincoln Mallee *Eucalyptus lansdowneana.*
Port Macquarie Cypress-pine *Callitris macleayana.*
Port Orford Cedar *Chamaecyparis lawsoniana.*
Portugal Laurel *Prunus lusitanica.*
Portuguese Broom *Chamaecytisus albus.*
Portuguese Cypress *Cupressus lusitanica.*
Portuguese Heath *Erica lusitanica.*
Portuguese Laurel Cherry *Prunus lusitanica.*
Portuguese Oak *Quercus faginea.*
Portuguese Quince *Cydonia oblonga.*

Portulaca L. PURSLANE; MOSS ROSE. Portulacaceae. 40 fleshy or trailing, mostly ann. herbs. Lvs flat or cylindrical, often with bristles in axils, uppermost forming floral involucre. Sep. 2; pet. 4–6, usually 5; sta. 8 to many. Widely distrib. in warm and trop. regions.
P. arachnoides Haw. = *Anacampseros arachnoides.*
P. filamentosa Haw. = *Anacampseros filamentosa.*
P. grandiflora Hook. ROSE MOSS; SUN PLANT; ELEVEN-O'CLOCK. St. prostrate or ascending, to 30cm. Lvs cylindrical, to 2.5cm, thick, fleshy. Fls single to double, rose, red, yellow, white, often striped, 2.5cm diam, opening in sunlight. Braz., Arg., Urug. 'Afternoon Delight': dwarf, spreading; fls large, double, in wide range of colours including pink, orange, scarlet and white. 'Aztec Double': fls double, bicolored gold and fuchsia. Calypso Hybrids: fls mainly double. Cloudbeater Hybrids: fls double, gold, carmine, scarlet, apricot, white and pink; seed race. Dwarf Double Minilacea Hybrids: compact; fls large in shades of scarlet, rose pink, apricot, cream and gold, abundant. Extra Double Hybrids: spreading; fls double, small, rose shaped in range of bright colours; seed race. 'Jewel': br. tinged red; lvs small and narrow; fls large, double, rose-pink with darker centre. Magic Carpet Hybrids: fls double, in range of colours in-cluding white, pink, orange, red and yellow, occas. striped. Peppermint Candy: fls single, bicolored red and white. Sun-dance Hybrids: neat, spreading; fls double in range of bright colours. Sunny Boy Hybrids: dwarf, spreading; fls mainly double. 'Swanlake': fls large, double, white. Wildfire Hybrids: low-lying; fls in bright colours; seed race.
P. lanceolata Haw. = *Anacampseros lanceolata.*
P. oleracea L. PURSLANE; PUSSLEY. St. soft, prostrate, forming mats. Lvs to 3cm, spathulate to obovate. Fls bright yellow, to 1cm diam.; sta. sensitive. Cosmop., probably originally from In-dia. 'Giganthes': prostrate; fls double, yellow, 2.5cm diam. var. *sativa* DC. KITCHEN-GARDEN PURSLANE. Potherb. st. to 45cm, erect, v. succulent. Lvs obovate. Fls 1.2cm diam.
P. oleracea var. *giganthes* L.H. Bail. = *P. oleracea* 'Giganthes'.
P. pilosa L. St. thick, red, with tufts of white hairs. Lvs 1.2cm, cylindrical, red-margined. Fls yellow, to 1.2cm diam. SE US and Mex. 'Hortualis': (SHAGGY GARDEN PURSLANE): fls red-purple, to 2cm diam.

PORTULACACEAE Juss. 21/400. *Anacampseros, Ceraria, Clay-tonia, Lewisia, Montia, Portulaca, Portulacaria, Spraguea, Tali-num.*

Portulacaria Jacq. Portulacaceae. 1 much-branched fleshy shrub to 3m; br., spreading segmented, succulent. Lvs to 2cm, smooth glossy green, obovate, upper surface flat, lower surface convex. Fls in small clusters, 1mm diam., pale pink. Late spring–early summer. S Afr. Z9.
P. afra Jacq. ELEPHANT BUSH. 'Tricolor': br. pendulous; lvs small, variegated with cream, edges rose; fls pale pink. 'Variegata': dense; st. tinged red; lvs pale green broadly margined cream with thin pale-red edge. var. *foliis-variegatis* Jacobsen. Lvs mottled yellow. var. *macrophylla* Jacobsen. Lvs to 2.5cm. var. *microphylla* Jacobsen. Lvs circular, 0.6cm diam.
P. namaquensis Sonder = *Ceraria namaquensis.*
P. pygmaea Pill. = *Ceraria pygmaea.*
→*Crassula.*

Posadaea Cogn. Cucurbitaceae. 1 pubesc. herb climbing by tendrils. Lvs ovate to orbicular, entire or shallowly 3–7-lobed, occas. denticulate, to 18×19cm. ♂ fls racemose, cor. yellow, rotate, lobes 5, sparsely dentate, to 1cm; sta. 3. ♀ infl. to 5cm; fls with 5 staminodes. Fr. a berry, globose, rugose, to 10cm diam. Guat. to Ecuad. and Braz. Z10.
P. sphaerocarpa Cogn.

Posoqueria Aubl. Rubiaceae. 16 shrubs or trees. Lvs entire, leathery. Fls many in terminal, corymbs, fragrant; cal. tube obovoid, lobes 5; cor. salver-shaped, tube slender, pendent, lobes 5; sta. 5, anth. exserted. Trop. Amer. Z10.
P. acuminata Mart. = *P. longiflora.*
P. coriacea Mart. & Gal. Tree, to 20m. Lvs to 27×16cm, ovate or to suborbicular, leathery to fleshy, 5–8-veined. Fls in 10–25-fld cymes or corymbs; cor. salver-shaped, tube to 25cm, lobes to 2.5cm, strap-shaped to oblong. Mex. and C Amer. to Colomb. and Venez. ssp. *formosa* (Karst.) Steyerm. Cal lobes smaller, ciliate. Colomb., Venez.
P. formosa (Karst.) Planch. = *P. coriacea* ssp. *formosa.*
P. gracilis (Rudge) Roem. & Schult. = *P. latifolia* ssp. *gracilis.*
P. latifolia (Rudge) Roem. & Schult. Shrub to 2m or tree to 6m. Lvs to 25×13cm, ovate or oblong to lanceolate, leathery, 6–8-veined. Fls in dense, few- to many-fld, terminal pedunculate corymbs, white; cor. tube to 17cm, pubesc. at throat, lobes to 3cm, oblong. Spring. W Indies, Mex. to Braz. ssp. *gracilis* (Rudge) Steyerm. Cor. tube shorter.
P. longiflora Aubl. Shrub, to 2.5m. Lvs to 14×6cm, lanceolate to oblong, undulate, thick-textured and lustrous, 8-veined. Fls in 6–12-fld, term., umbellate corymbs, white; cor. tube to 15cm, curved and pendent, pubesc. at throat, lobes to 3cm, linear. Summer. Guyana to Braz.
P. trinitatis DC. Tree to 6m. Lvs to 26×12cm, ovate or elliptic to oblong, lustrous. Fls in pedunculate corymbs; cor. tube to 17cm, pubesc. at throat, lobes to 3cm, oblong. W Indies.
→*Solena.*

Possum Grape *Cissus trifoliata.*
Possum Haw *Ilex decidua.*
Possumwood *Diospyros virginiana.*
Post Oak *Quercus stellata.*
Post-oak Grape *Vitis linecumii.*

Potamogeton L. Potamogetonaceae. *c*90 freshwater, perenn., pondweeds. Shoots upright, usually arising from bottom-rooting rhiz. Lvs submerged and/or floating, varying according to flow and depth of the water. Fls produced either above the water or submerged, small, green, in pedunculate, interrupted or contin-uous fleshy spikes. Cosmop.
P. acutifolius Link. SHARP-LEAVED PONDWEED. Rhiz. 0. St. flat, branched, to 1m. Lvs to 7cm, submerged, sessile, linear, poiinted, 2–4mm wide. Summer. Eur., Asia and Aus.
P. americanus Cham. & Schldl. = *P. nodosus.*
P. coloratus Hornem. FEN PONDWEED. St. cylindric, to 1m. Floating lvs to 10×5cm, ovate to lanceolate, translucent, often tinged red, petiolate; submerged lvs to 18cm, narrower and thinner, obtuse, often tinged red. Summer. W & C Eur., N Afr.
P. crispus L. CURLED PONDWEED. St. terete, resting buds produced at st. ends. Lvs submerged, to 10cm×15mm, sessile, narrow-oblong, crisped or undulate, young lvs flat, lightly toothed. Summer. Eur., nat. E US and Calif.
P. densus L. = *Groenlandia densa.*
P. filiformis Pers. St. thread-like, to 40cm. Lvs submerged, to 20cm, slender, to 1–1.5mm wide, tubular at base at first sub-merged. N Eur., N US, Asia, Egypt, Aus.
P. gayii A. Bennett. St. thread-like, much-branched. Floating lvs

to 7cm, oval; submerged lvs to 8cm, sessile, light green to red-brown. Summer. S Amer.

P. gramineus L. VARIOUS-LEAVED PONDWEED. St. to 1m+. Floating lvs to 7×3cm, elliptic or elliptic-ovate, not transparent, petiole often longer than lamina; submerged lvs. to 8×3cm, sessile, usually narrow-elliptic, finely denticulate, undulate, acuminate or acute. Summer. Widespread in Eur. except Medit., N US.

P. lucens L. SHINING PONDWEED. St. stout, to 2m+. Lvs submerged, to 20×6cm, narrow-elliptic to obovate-elliptic, tips acuminate or cuspidate, translucent, undulate, petiolate. Summer. Eur., W Afr.

P. malaianus Miq. St. ± unbranched. Lvs submerged, to 12cm, linear-oblong to lanceolate, wavy and indistinctly toothed; petioles 3cm. Jap., China to India, Malaysia.

P. natans L. BROAD-LEAVED PONDWEED. St. ± unbranched. Floating lvs to 12.5×7cm, broad-oval, with flexible joint at base; petioles often longer than blade; submerged lvs reduced, linear. Summer. Eur., N US.

P. nodosus Poir. LODDON PONDWEED. Floating lvs to 15×6cm, elliptic to broad-elliptic, opaque, petiole; submerged lvs to 20×4cm, petiolate, narrower, longer, lanceolate, finely denticulate at first, net-veined. Summer. Eur., N US.

P. pectinatus L. FENNEL PONDWEED. St. and lvs filiform. Lvs submerged, to 2mm wide, deep green, linear, margins often inrolled. Summer. Eur., E US to S Amer., Afr.

P. perfoliatus L. PERFOLIATE PONDWEED. St. branched. Lvs submerged, to 10×6cm, sessile, deep green, ovate to lanceolate, base cordate and clasping, tips rounded or blunt. Summer. Eur., N US.

P. rutilus Wolfg. SHETLAND PONDWEED. Rhiz. 0. Winter buds produced on ends of side br. Lvs submerged, to 1.5mm wide, stiff, finely pointed. Summer. N, C & E Eur.

POTAMOGETONACEAE Dumort. 2/90. *Groenlandia, Potamogeton*

Potato *Solanum tuberosum*; for cvs, see POTATO in *New RHS Dictionary of Gardening.*

Potato Bean *Apios americana*; *Pachyrhizus tuberosus.*

Potato Creeper *Solanum seaforthianum.*

Potato Fern *Marattia salicina*; *Solanopteris.*

Potato Tree *Solanum wrightii.*

Potato Vine *Solanum jasminoides*; *S. wendlandii.*

Potentilla L. CINQUEFOIL; FIVE-FINGER. Rosaceae. *c*500 mostly perenn. herbs and shrubs. Lvs stipulate, palmate, pinnate or trifoliate. Fls usually saucer-shaped, solitary or in term. or axill. clusters; epical. of 5 green bractlets alt. with (4–)5 sep.; pet. 5; receptacle hairy; sta. 10–30. N hemis.

P. alba L. Low-growing, spreading perenn. herb to 10cm. Basal lvs palmate, lfts 5, 2–6cm, oblong to obovate-lanceolate, apex toothed, glab. above; st. lvs simple or divided into lfts, silvery silky beneath at first. Fls to 2.5cm diam., white in groups of to 5. Spring–summer. C, S & E Eur. Z5.

P. alchemilloides Lapeyr. Perenn. herb to 30cm. St. woody below. Basal lvs palmate, long-petioled, lfts 5–7, obovate or oblong, deep green above, white silky beneath, apex lightly toothed; st. lvs with fewer lfts. Fls white many, to 4cm diam. in compact corymbs. Pyren. Z6.

P. alpestris Haller. f. = *P. crantzii.*

P. ambigua Cambess. = *P. cuneata.*

P. andicola Benth. Tufted, silky hairy perenn. Lvs few; basal lvs pinnate, lfts 3–5, ovate, toothed. Fls many yellow. Colomb. Z8.

P. ×anglica Laich. (*P. erecta* ×*P. reptans.*) Similar to *P. erecta* but st. trailing, rooting; lvs not falling early, lfts obovate, coarsely toothed; fls 1 to few in cymes, yellow to apricot, blotched brown at base. W Eur. Z5.

P. anserina L. SILVERWEED; GOOSE-GRASS; GOOSE-TANSY. Perenn. St. procumbent, to 80cm. Lvs to 10–20cm, rosulate, pinnate, lfts to 5cm, oblong to ovate, serrate, green above, silver silky beneath. Fls to 2.5cm diam., solitary, axill., yellow. N US, Eur., Asia. Z5.

P. apennina Ten. Perenn. to 20cm, white-tomentose. Lfts 3 to 1.5cm, obovate, apex toothed, silvery downy, sometimes hairless above. Balk. Z6.

P. arbuscula D. Don. = *P. fruticosa* var. *arbuscula.*

P. argentea L. HOARY CINQUEFOIL; SILVERY CINQUEFOIL. Much-branched, somewhat tomentose woody-based perenn. to 50cm. Basal lvs petiolate, palmate, lfts 5, rarely 7, to 2.5cm, upper lvs sessile lfts 3, 5, or 7, obcordate, deeply toothed, green above, white hairy beneath. Fls 12mm diam., term. in leafy cymes, sulphur-yellow. Early summer. Eur., Asia Minor, Sib. Z4.

P. argentea var. *calabra* (Ten.) Fiori & Paol. = *P. calabra.*

P. arguta Pursh. TALL CINQUEFOIL. Perenn. herb, 30–100cm, st. woody at base, glandular-hairy. Basal lvs petiolate, pinnate, lfts

7–11, ovate to obovate, hairy, serrate, upper lvs with lfts 3, lanceolate. Fls 2cm diam., in narrow capitate cymes, white or cream. Summer. N Amer. Z3.

P. argyrophylla Wallich ex Lehm. = *P. atrosanguinea* var. *argyrophylla.*

P. atrosanguinea Lodd. ex D. Don. Hairy perenn. to 90cm; st. few-branched. Lvs long-petioled, lfts 3, to 7.5cm, elliptic-ovate to obovate, toothed, silky above, white hairy beneath. Fls to 3cm diam. in paniculate cymes on slender pedicles, deep purple-red. Late summer. Himal. var. *argyrophylla* (Lehm.) A.J.C. Grierson & D.G. Long. Fls yellow or yellow-orange. Hybrids derived from these and (in some cases) *P. nepalensis* include: 'Etna': to 45cm; lvs tinted silver; fls deep crimson. 'Firedance': habit small, to 30cm; fls deep coral; long flowering. 'Gibson's Scarlet': to 45cm; lvs soft green; fls bright scarlet. 'Mons. Rouillard': to 45cm; fls double, dark copper. Z5.

P. aurea L. Mat-forming perenn. to 30cm, silvery hairy. Lvs digitate, lfts 5, silver hairy on margins and veins beneath, oblong, toothed at tip; st. lvs smaller. Fls few in lax clusters, to 2cm diam., golden yellow, base deeper. Summer. Alps, Pyren. 'Aurantiaca': to 15cm; fls sunset yellow. 'Flore Pleno': fls double, light gold. 'Goldklumpen' ('Gold Clogs'): fls bright gold with orange ring. 'Rahboneana': fls semidouble, golden yellow. ssp. *chrysocraspeda* (Lehm.) Nyman. Lfts 3, teeth often obtuse. Fls to 12, yellow. Upper Carpath. Z5.

P. beanii hort. = *P. fruticosa* 'Beanii'.

P. ×bicolor Lindl. (*P. atrosanguinea* var. *argyrophylla* ×*P. atrosanguinea.*) Fls yellow with orange and red. Z6.

P. blaschkeana Turcz. ex Lehm. = *P. gracilis.*

P. brauniana Hoppe in Sturm. Hoppe in Sturm. Dwarf perenn.; st. to 5cm, slender, spreading, slightly hairy. Lfts 3, to 1.5×1cm; obovate, shallow toothed, lightly hairy beneath. Fls solitary, to 5, to 2.5cm diam., yellow. Summer. E Pyren., Alps. Z6.

P. ×brennia Huter ex A. Kerner (*P. crantzii* ×*P. nivea.*) Basal lvs with 4–5 lfts. Z5.

P. breweri Wats. Similar to *P. drummondii* but lamina not as wide, thickly white hairy when young, lfts to 2.5cm, 8–12, paired. US. Z7.

P. buccoana Clementi. Ascending perenn. to 60cm. Lfts 3, coarsely toothed, 5cm. Fls numerous in cymes, 1.2cm diam., yellow. W Asia. Z6.

P. calabra Ten. Ten. Similar to *P. argentea*; lvs smaller, silver, lfts narrower. Sicily. Z6.

P. canadensis L. Silky-hairy, small, creeping perenn.; st. prostrate. Lvs not completely opened at flowering; lfts 5, cuneate-obovate, toothed toward apex. Fls 1.2cm diam., yellow. N Amer. Z3.

P. caulescens L. Silky perenn. to 30cm. Lvs digitate, lfts 5–7, to 3cm, oblong, apex-toothed, silky beneath. Fls to 2cm diam., many, in loose cymes, white to light pink. Alps. Z5.

P. chrysantha Trev. Perenn. Ls digitate, lfts 5–9, to 10×5cm, obovate to elliptic, serrate. Fls 2.5cm diam., in term. cymes on lat. hairy st., golden yellow. C & S Eur. Z6.

P. cinerea Chaix ex Vill. Dwarf clump-forming perenn. to 10cm; st. procumbent, rooting, lfts 3–5, to 2×0.9cm, narrow obovate, dentate, grey-green above, grey beneath. Fls to 6, 2cm diam., in cymes, pale yellow. Summer. C, E & S Eur. Z3.

P. clusiana Jacq. Pubesc. perenn. to 15cm; st. hairy, base somewhat woody. Lvs digitate, lfts 5 or 3, to 12mm, obovate, apex rounded 3–5-toothed, silky beneath. Fls 3, 2.5cm diam., white. Summer. Alps. Z6.

P. coccinea Hoffmeister = *P. nepalensis.*

P. comarum Nestl. = *P. palustris.*

P. concolor Rolfe. Perenn. to 30cm, upright, hairy. Basal lvs pinnate, upper lvs trifoliate, lfts 2.5–5cm, obovate-ellipotic, Fls 5cm diam., in few-fld cymes, dark yellow, base orange. Summer. W China. Z6.

P. coriandrifolia D. Don. Perenn. to 15cm, slightly hairy to glab. Basal lvs to 10cm, many short-petioled, pinnate, lfts many, 5mm wide, cut into linear hair-pointed lobes, lobes again divided. Fls to 2cm diam., in terminal, few-fld loose clusters, yellow, base red. Summer. Himal. Z7.

P. corsica Sieber ex Lehm. = *P. rupestris.*

P. crantzii (Crantz) G. Beck. ALPINE CINQUEFOIL. Perenn. herb, to 20cm; rootstock woody. Lvs digitate, lfts 3 or 5, 2cm, obovate to cuneate, toothed at apex, green, hairless above, hairy beneath. Fls 1–12, to 2.5cm diam., yellow, often orange spotted at base. Spring. N US, N, C & S Eur. Z5.

P. crassinervia Vis. Perenn. to 40, ascending, hairy. Basal lvs palmate, petioles long, lfts 5, broad-obovate, tips rounded, deeply bluntly-toothed, velvety, veins prominent. Fls in many-fld cymes, white. Summer. Corsica, Sardinia. Z7.

P. crinita A. Gray. Perenn. to 30cm, silky hairy. lvs many, pinnate; lfts to 17, to 2cm, oblong, toothed at apex, silky beneath. Fls many, 1cm diam., yellow. C & S US. Z4.

P. cuneata (Wallich) Lehm. Woody-based tufted peren., upright or creeping, silky to hairless. Lvs 6–15cm, short-petioled, lfts 3, obovate or rounded-cuneate, tips broad, 3-toothed, leather, green above, glaucous beneath. Fls solitary, to 2.5cm diam., yellow. Summer. Himal. Z5.

P. dahurica hort. = *P. fruticosa* var. *davurica*.

P. davurica Nestl. = *P. fruticosa* var. *davurica*.

P. delphinensis Gren. & Godron. Perenn. to 45cm. Lvs digitate, lfts 5, to 2cm, obovate, green, roughly toothed above. Fls 2.5cm diam., many, on laterally hairy peduncles to 50cm, yellow. SW Alps. Z6.

P. diversifolia Lehm. Perenn. to 30cm; rootstock woody. Lvs usually digitate, lfts 5 or 7, to 5cm, oblanceolate, toothed toward apex, hairless to strigose beneath. Fls 12mm diam., yellow. W US. Z3.

P. dombeyi Nestl. Tufted perenn. to 15cm, green-brown, scantily hairy. Lvs to 1.2×0.5cm, orbicular, toothed, 3-lobed or 3-foliate. Fls 1cm diam., yellow. Peru. Z8.

P. drummondii Lehm. Perenn. to 45cm, lightly hairy. Lvs ovate-oblong, lfts paired, 4–10, 6cm, cuneate-obovate, serrate. Fls few, 2cm diam. US. Z3.

P. dubia (Crantz) Zimmeter = *P. brauniana*.

P. egedii Wormsk. Differs from *P. anserina* in subglabrous petioles, peduncles and stolons. Lvs 50cm, lfts to 30, to 5cm, oblong to obovate, white-tomentose to glab. beneath. Fls 3–4cm diam. yellow. Coastal W US, E Asia. Z4.

P. erecta (L.) Räusch. Perenn. to 50cm. Lvs in term. rosettes, lfts 3–5, to 3cm, wedge shaped to lanceolate, apex dentate, hairless or lightly hairy above. Fls 1cm diam., in term. cymes. Summer. Eur. except Medit. Z5.

P. eriocarpa Wallich ex Lehm. Perenn.; rhiz. ascending, covered in sheathing stipules; st. to 45cm. Lvs long-petioled, lfts 3, to 4cm, cuneate, toothed and incised toward apex. Fls to 4cm diam., yellow. Himal. Z7.

P. fissa Nutt. To 30cm, glandular-hairy. Lvs pinnate, lfts to 13, rounded, deeply cut. Fls numerous in cymes, to 2cm diam., cream-white. US. Z4.

P. flabellifolia Hook. ex Torr. & A. Gray. St. narrow, to 30cm. Lvs mostly basal, lfts 3, to 4cm, cuneate, deeply saw-toothed. Fls in cymes, 2cm diam., pet. yellow. BC to Calif. Z7.

P. flagellaris Willd. ex Schldl. Diffuse perenn.; br. prostrate, slender, downy, rooting. Lvs palmate, lfts 5, lanceolate, sharp-toothed, smooth. Fls solitary on axill. peduncles, yellow. Sib. Z2.

P. formosa D. Don = *P. nepalensis*.

P. fragiformis Willd. ex Schldl. = *P. megalantha*.

P. frondosa Greene = *Horkelia frondosa*.

P. fruticosa L. SHRUBBY CINQUEFOIL; GOLDEN HARDHACK; WIDDY. Decid., much-branched shrub, to 150cm; bark brown, peeling. Lvs pinnate or trifoliate, lfts 3 or 5, to 2.5cm,ovate to lanceolate, light to mid-green, silky revolute. Fls to 4cm diam., solitary or in groups of 2–3, bright yellow or white. Late spring–summer. N hemis. var. *albicans* Rehd. & Wils. Lfts 5, elliptic-oblong, grey-green and pubesc. above, white-tomentose beneath. Fls to 2cm diam., medium yellow. W China. var. *arbuscula* (D. Don) Maxim. Low shrub to 60×100cm. St. ascending or procumbent; stipules large, brown, lfts usually 5 occas. 3, 1cm+, lobed, light to mid-green, thick, white hairy beneath, veins reticulate beneath. Fls 3cm diam., in lax clusters, rich yellow. Summer–autumn. Himal., N China. f. *rigida* (D. Don) Hand-Mazz. To 60cm. Lvs 3cm, leaflet 3, elliptic, to 2.5×1cm, green above, blue-green beneath. Fls to 3cm diam., deep yellow. Himal. var. *davurica* (Nestl.) Ser. To 50cm; st.: upright; twigs red, pendulous. If stipules brown; lvs pinnate, hairless, lfts 5, to 2.5cm, obovate, without stalks, light to mid-green. Fls solitary to few, 2.5cm diam., white to pale yellow. Summer–autumn. China, E Sib. var. *mandschurica* (Maxim.) Wolf. Low-growing, to 45cm; lvs grey silky hairy; fls to 2.5cm diam., white. Manch. A clone in cult. is sometimes named 'Manchu'. var. *subalbicans* Hand-Mazz. Close to var. *davurica*. To 1.5m; st. stiffly hairy. Lvs sparsely whtie hairy above, more thickly hairy beneath. Fls many in compact cymes, large, white. W China. var. *tenuiloba* Ser. Slow-growing; to 45×90cm. Lvs small, lfts 5, linear. Fls to 2.5cm diam., golden-yellow. WN Amer. var. *unifoliolata* Ludl. To 1m; st. densely leafly. Lvs simple, or occas. with 2 lfts, 0.7–1.5cm. Fls solitary, 2–3cm diam., golden-yellow. Bhutan. 'Abbottswood Silver': unstable sport: lvs edged cream-white. 'Beanii': st. upright; lvs deep green; fls to 2.5cm diam., white. 'Beesii': slow-growing, compact, to 60cm; lfts 3–5, to 1cm, elliptic, silvery silky above, veins hairy beneath; fls 2.5cm diam., in a conical cluster, golden-yellow. 'Daydawn': fls salmon pink; sport from 'Tangerine'. 'Donard Gold': prostrate, to 50cm tall, but much wider; lvs green; fls golden-yellow. 'Elizabeth' ('Arbuscula'; 'Sutter's Gold'): to 1×1m; fls to 3.5cm diam., golden-yellow. 'Farreri' ('Gold Drop'): to 60×90cm; lvs small, lfts 7, 0.5–0.8cm; fls 2–3cm, golden-yellow; 'Farrer's White' is a

derivative of this, with lvs yellow-green and fls white. 'Farrer's Red Form': refers to a collection of seed made by Farrer in W China from red-fld plants, but at first the seedlings flowered yellow; eventually the gene for redness surfaced in *P.* 'Tangerine'; red-fld cvs are now common. 'Friedrichsenii' ('Berlin Beauty') (*P.f.* var. *fruticosa* ×*P.f.* var. *davurica*): a grex of several clones of which this is the nominate plant): upright, to 1.5m. Lvs pinnate, ovate to oblong, large, lfts 5–7, to 3cm, pale green above, paler beneath; fls 3cm diam., light yellow to white. 'Goldstar': semi-erect, to 80cm, spreading; fls 4–5cm diam., golden-yellow, abundant. 'Jackman': st. erect, to 1.2m; lvs to 6cm, lfts 7, lanceolate to elliptic, deep green above, blue green beneath; fls 3.5–4cm diam., golden-yellow, abundant. 'Katherine Dykes': to 1.5m, spreading widely; lvs 3cm, lfts 5, grey-green, densely pubesc. beneath; fls 3cm diam., primrose yellow. 'Klondike': resembling 'Farreri' but lfts larger, 1–1.8cm; fls 3.5–4cm diam., bright yellow. 'Lady Daresbury': to 90cm; lfts 5, blue-green, densely pubesc. beneath; fls to 3.5cm diam., mid-yellow. 'Longacre': low-growing, spreading widely; lfts 5, blue-green; fls 3cm diam., sulphur-yellow. 'Maanelys' ('Moonlight'): to 1.2m; lvs 4cm, lfts 5, blue-green; fls 2.5–3cm diam., soft yellow, paler beneath. 'Mount Everest': st. upright, to 1m; lfts 5, narrow, yellow-green; fls 3–3.5cm diam., white. 'Ochroleuca': to 1.2×1.8m, st. spreading; lvs 3cm, lfts 5–7, oblong-elliptic, narrow, green above, blue-green beneath; fls 3cm diam., pale yellow, white beneath. 'Parvifolia': to 80cm; lfts 7, v. small, green above, blue-green beneath; fls 2cm diam., yellow. 'Primrose Beauty': br. spreading or drooping; lfts to 1.5cm, grey-hairy; fls deep cream with darker centre. 'Princess': lvs green; fls clear pink. 'Pyrenaica' ('Farreri Prostrata'): procumbent, to 20cm; lvs 2cm, lfts 3, oblong-elliptic, green above blue-green beneath; fls 2.5cm diam., golden-yellow. 'Red Ace': to 75×120cm; fls bright vermilion above, pale yellow beneath; colour fades in bright sunlight. 'Rhodocalyx': a selection from var. *davurica*; low growing; fls nodding; pedicels and cal. crimson; cor. white. 'Royal Flush': resembling 'Red Ace' but fls deep pink. 'Snowflake': lvs large, deep green; fls white single to double. Sulphurascens group (*P.f.* var. *arbuscula* ×*P.f.* var. *davurica*): variable; fls usually pale yellow; some of the best cvs are derived from this parentage; originally found wild in W China (Yunnan). 'Sunset': low-growing, resembling 'Tangerine'; fls orange-yellow to brick-red, depending on age and climatic conditions. 'Tangerine': low-growing, lax habit; lvs small, lfts 7, green; fls 3cm diam., orange to copper- to golden-yellow. 'Veitchii' to 1.5m; lvs 2.5cm, lfts 5, 1cm, pale green; fls 2.5cm, white with sta. bud red. 'Vilmoriniana': to 90–120×150cm; lvs grey-hairy above, white-tomentose beneath; fls ivory-white to pale yellow. 'Walton Park': to 60cm, spreading; lvs to 4cm, deep green above, blue-green beneath; fls in clusters of 1–5, 3.5–4cm diam., golden-yellow. 'William Purdom' ('Purdomii'): to 1m; lvs 3cm, lfts 7, oblong-elliptic, pale green above, grey-green beneath; fls 2–2.5cm diam., pale yellow.

P. fulgens Wallich ex D. Don. To 60cm. Lvs 5–15cm, lfts paired, many, to 4cm, toothed, spreading hairs beneath. Fls silvery pubesc. in pan. or corymbs, 1cm diam., yellow. Himal. Z7.

P. glabra Lodd. = *P. fruticosa* var. *davurica*.

P. glabrata Willd. ex Schldl. = *fruticosa* var. *P. davurica*.

P. glandulosa Lindl. Perenn. to 60cm; st. gland. Lvs pinnate, lfts 5–7, downy, toothed, round-ovate or obovate, lfts usually 3. Fls 1.5cm diam., in open leafy cymes, light yellow or crimson. Summer. W US. Z7.

P. gordonii (Hook.) E. Greene = *Ivesia gordonii*.

P. gracilis Douglas ex Hook. Upright perenn. to 60cm; st. slender, downy. Basal lvs long-stalked, palmate, lfts 5–7, to 5cm, obovate or oblanceolate, sharply toothed, green and smooth above, white-hairy beneath. Fls many, to 2cm diam. in pan., yellow. Late summer. W US. Z4.

P. grandiflora L. Pubesc. perenn. herb, to 45cm; st. upright, branching, velvety. Lfts 3, 1.2–3.5cm, obovate, apex toothed. Fls few, 2.5cm diam., in upright few-fld cymes, gold-yellow. Summer. C Eur., S Fr. to Austria. Z6.

P. haematochroa Lehm. Softly hairy upright tufted perenn. to 60cm; rootstock woody. Lvs palmate, long-petioled; lfts 3–7, to 9cm, elliptic oblong, crenate. Fls to 20, 3.5cm diam., brown-red. Mex. Z8.

P. heptaphylla L. Perenn.; st. short, ascending. Lvs digitate, lfts 5–7, to 2.5cm, ovate-lanceolate, dentate. Fls to 1.6cm diam., yellow 1–10 on slender peduncles with red gland. hairs. C & E Eur. Z6.

P. hippiana Lehm. Perenn.; st. 30–60cm, upright, silky. Basal lvs petiolate, pinnate; lfts 7–10, upper three 1–4cm, joined, oblong or oblong-lanceolate, obtusely and deeply toothed, silky-hairy. Fls 1–3cm diam., in loose term. cymes, bright yellow. Summer. W US. Z6.

P. hirta L. Similar to *P. recta* but without gland. hairs on st. and lvs. Lfts linear to oblanceolate, toothed at apex. Fls large, yellow, in term. pan. Summer. C & S Eur., Asia Minor, N Afr. Z6.

P. ×hopwoodiana Sweet. (*P. nepalensis* × *P. recta.*) Perenn. herb to 45cm. Lvs palmate, lfts 5. Fls rose-red at base with pink zone, edges white. Z5.

P. longifolia Willd. Perenn., st. to 50cm, bristly hairy and gland. Lvs pinnate, lfts to 13, to 2cm, lanceolate, toothed. Fls abundant in term. pan., almost pin-headed, yellow. Summer. C Asia. Z6.

P. matsumurae T. Wolf. Perenn.; st. to 15cm, ascending. Lfts 3, to 1.2cm, obovate or rounded, toothed, lightly hairy. Fls 12mm diam., yellow. Jap. Z7.

P. megalantha Tak. Softly hairy tufted perenn. to 30cm. Basal lvs to 8cm wide, lfts 3, broad obovate, coarsely crenate, hairy beneath. Fls solitary, to 4cm diam., bright yellow. Summer. Jap. Z5.

P. meifolia Wallich = *P. coriandrifolia.*

P. menziesii Paxt. = *P. ×bicolor.*

P. micrantha Ramond ex DC. Dwarf tufted perenn.; st. to 15cm, thickly pubesc. lfts 3, to 5cm, obovate, serrate, green above, grey-downy beneath, st. lvs simple. Fls 8mm diam., 1–3 interior white, exterior flushed rose. Spring. S & C Eur. to Iran. Z6.

P. minima Hallier f. = *P. brauniana.*

P. montana Brot. Perenn., usually stoloniferous. St. to 20cm, pubesc. Basal lvs of 3–5 lfts, st. lvs with 1–3 lfts to 3cm, obovate or oblong, crenate-dentate at tip, grey-silky beneath and on margins. Fls 1–4, 2.5cm diam. Summer. W & C Fr. Z6.

P. multifida L. Perenn. herb; st. to 30cm, upright, tomentose. Lvs pinnate to almost digitate, tomentose, lfts to 9, to 4cm, pinnatisect, lobes to 5, narrow, silvery beneath. Fls many, 12mm diam. in term. corymbs, yellow. Summer. SE Fr., Lapland, Russia to Tibet and Korea. Z3.

P. nepalensis Hook. Perenn. herb; st. leafy, erect, to 60cm. Basal lvs with petioles to 30cm, lfts 5, 3–8cm, obovate or elliptic-obovate, coarsely toothed, hairy. Fls 2.5cm diam. in long branching pan.; purpled-red or crimson, base deeper. Summer. W Himal. 'Flammenspiel': to 40cm; fls red narrowly edged yellow. 'Miss Willmott' ('Willmottiae'): to 40cm; fls cherry red; name often misapplied. 'Roxana': to 40cm; buds red, fls salmon pink. Z5.

P. neumanniana Rchb. Mat-forming, perenn. to 10cm; st. woody, procumbent. Lvs digitate, lfts 5–7, to 4cm, obovate, dentate. Fls to 12, 2.5cm diam., on axill. peduncles, yellow. Spring onwards. N, W & C Eur. 'Goldrausch': to 10cm; fls bright gold. 'Nana': to 7.5cm; lvs vivid green; fls gold. Z5.

P. nevadensis Boiss. Tufted silky perenn.; st. to 30cm, procumbent. Basal lvs digitate, lfts 5, to 2cm, round-toothed, green and almost smooth above, silky hairy beneath; upper lvs trifoliate. Fls to 4, term. or axill., 2.5cm diam., yellow. Summer. S Spain (Sierra Nevada). Z7.

P. nitida L. Tufted, silver-grey, downy perenn. to 10cm. Lfts 3, to 1cm, oblanceolate to obovate, apex usually 3-toothed, silvery-silky. Fls 2.5cm+ diam., 1–2, term., white or pink, base deeper. Summer. SW & SE Alps. 'Alannah': fls pale pink. 'Alba': fls white. 'Compacta': v. dwarf, to 5cm; fls large, gold. 'Lissadel': fls vivid pink. 'Rubra': fls deep rose, free-flowering. Z5.

P. nivalis Lapeyr. Perenn. herb to 30cm, thickly pubesc. Lvs digitate, lfts 5–7, to 2cm, obovate, toothed above, velvety pubesc., grey-green to green. Fls many, to 2.5cm diam., white. Summer. N & E Spain, Pyren., SW Alps. Z6.

P. nivea L. Perenn. to 20cm, subglabrous to silky. Lfts 3, to 2.5cm, ovate, toothed, green and slightly hairy above, thickly white-tomentose beneath. Fls to 2cm diam., to 12 in term. cymes, yellow. Summer. N hemis. Z2.

P. norvegica L. Ann. or perenn. to 45cm. Lvs in threes or pinnate, lfts to 7cm, elliptic, oblong or obovate, green, serrate. Fls 6–12mm diam., roughly hairy, in clusters in upper lf axils. Late spring–summer. N & C Eur., N US. Z3.

P. nuttallii Lehm. = *P. gracilis* var. *glabrata.*

P. opaca L. = *P. heptaphylla.*

P. pacifica T.J. Howell = *P. egedei.*

P. palustris (L.) Scop. Rhiz. long and creeping. Lvs pinnate, lfts 3, 5 or 7, to 6cm, oblong, serrate, subglabrous beneath. Fls to 3.5cm diam., on st. to 45cm in loose term. cyme, purple. Eur., N US. Z3.

P. peduncularis D. Don. Perenn.; st. 10–20cm, erect or ascending. Lvs 10–20cm, lfts 1–4cm, numerous, oblong, serrate, silky beneath. Fls 2cm diam., few, in corymbs, yellow. Himal. Z7.

P. pensylvanica L. Perenn. herb, grey-hairy; st. to 80cm, upright. Lvs pinnate, leaflets 5–19, to 7cm, lanceolate, roughly toothed, bristly above, grey-hairy beneath. Fls 12mm diam., abundant, in term. pan., yellow. Summer. Spain, N US. Z4.

P. pyrenaica Willd. = *P. fruticosa* 'Pyrenaica'.

P. quinquefolia Rydb. Ascending or spreading somewhat pubesc. perenn. to 20cm. Basal lvs digitate, lfts 3 or 5, to 2.5cm,

oblanceolate or obovate, cut into lanceolate or oblong lobes, silky green above, white-tomentose beneath. Fls to 12mm diam., few to many, yellow. NW & C US. Z4.

P. recta L. Perenn.; st. to 45cm, velvety hairy, with gland. hairs. Lvs digitate, lfts 5–7, to 3.5cm, oblong-lanceolate, green, serrate to pinnatisect. Fls many, to 2.5cm diam., in corymbs. Summer. 'Macrantha' ('Warrenii'): fls bright yellow, in loose clusters. Z4.

P. reptans L. Rampant pubesc. perenn.; st. to 100cm, trailing, rooting. Lvs in rosette, gland. hairy, lfts 5 or 7, to 7cm, obovate, toothed. Fls 25mm diam., solitary, axill., yellow. Eur., Asia. Z5.

P. rupestris L. Pubesc. perenn. to 45cm. Lvs pinnate, lfts 5–7, to 4cm, ovate to nearly rounded, doubly crenate, green, pubesc. Fls to 2.5cm diam., 1 to many on st. to 60cm, white. N US, W & C Eur. 'Alba': fls white. 'Nana' ('Pygmaea'): habit dwarf, st. erect; fls in clusters, white. Z5.

P. salesoviana Stephan. Few-branched, decid., upright shrub to 1m. Lfts 7–13, to 4cm, linear-oblong, serrate, deep green above, white-tomentose beneath. Fls 3cm diam., nodding, to 7 in cymes, white flushed red. Summer. Turkestan, SE Sib., Himal., W China. Z4.

P. saxifraga Ardoino ex De Not. Tufted perenn. herb. Lvs digitate; lfts 3–5, to 3cm, linear to obovate, apex 3-toothed, margin revolute, leathery, almost glab. above, silver downy beneath. Fls to 20 in loose term. cymes, white. Early summer. SE Fr., Alps. Z6.

P. simplex Michx. OLD FIELD CINQUEFOIL. Differs from *P. canadensis* in tuberous swellings on stolons at end of season. Lvs usually fully developed at flowering. Fl. st. arching. E & C US. Z3.

P. speciosa Willd. Perenn. lfts 3, 3cm, broad to elliptic obovate, crenate-dentate, white-tomentose beneath. Fls on short pedicels, 15–25mm diam., white. W & S Balk. Z6.

P. splendens Buch.-Ham. ex Trev. = *P. fulgens.*

P. splendens Ramond ex DC. = *P. montana.*

P. ×sulphurascens Hand-Mazz. = *P. fruticosa* Sulphurascens group.

P. sulphurea Lam. = *P. recta.*

P. tabernaemontani Asch. = *P. neumanniana.*

P. ternata Lehm. = *P. aurea* ssp. *chrysocraspeda.*

P. thurberi A. Gray. Perenn. to 75cm, pubesc. and glandular-hairy. Lvs palmate; lfts 5–7, 2.5–5cm, broadly obovate, tips rounded, roughly toothed. Fls 2cm diam. in lax clusters. S US and Mex.

P. tommasiniana F.W. Schultz = *P. cinerea.*

P. ×tonguei hort. ex Baxt. (*P. anglica* × *P. nepalensis.*) St. procumbent, not rooting. Lfts 3–5, obovate, dark green. Fls apricot with carmine-red eye. Z5.

P. tormentilla Stokes = *P. erecta.*

P. tormentilla-formosa hort. = *P. ×tonguei.*

P. transcaspia T. Wolf = *P. recta.*

P. valderia L. Perenn. to 40cm, shortly grey-tomentose; st. weak. Lvs digitate, lfts 5–7, to 3cm, linear-obovate, dentate velvety beneath. Fls many, 1cm diam., in dense corymbs. Summer. Maritime Alps, Balk. Z6.

P. veitchii Wils. = *P. fruticosa* 'Veitchii'.

P. villosa Dulac = *P. crantzii.*

P. vilmoriniana hort. = *P. fruticosa* 'Vilmoriniana'.

P. viscosa Donn ex Lehm. = *P. longifolia.*

P. visianii Pančić. Perenn. herb.; st. to 40cm, pubesc., gland. Lvs pinnate, lfts 5–17, to 1.5cm, obovate to ovate, hairy, 2–7-toothed. Fls 5cm diam., abundant in loose term. cymes, yellow. NW Balk., Serbia. Z5.

Poterium L.

P. canadense (L.) A. Gray = *Sanguisorba canadensis.*

P. caudatum Ait. = *Bencomia caudata.*

P. sanguisorba L. = *Sanguisorba minor.*

P. tenuifolium Franch. & Savat. = *Sanguisorba tenuifolia.*

Pothos L.

P. aureus Lind. & André = *Epipremnum aureum.*

P. celatocaulis N.E. Br. = *Rhaphidophora celatocaulis.*

P. tricolor hort. = *Epipremnum aureum* 'Tricolor'.

P. wilcoxii hort. = *Epipremnum aureum* 'Wilcoxii'.

✕Potinara. (*Brassavola* × *Cattleya* × *Laelia* × *Sophronitis*.) Orchidaceae. Gdn hybrids, usually vigorous plants, compact to large with fls in shades of purple, crimson, red, yellow, gold or apricot, the lip often velvety, ruffled and differently coloured.

Pot Marigold *Calendula officinalis.*
Pot Marjoram *Origanum onites*; *O. vulgare.*
Pot-of-gold Lily *Lilium iridollae.*
Pouch Flower *Calceolaria.*

Poupartia Comm. ex Juss. Anacardiaceae. 12 reeds or shrubs; bark thick, resinous. Lvs imparipinnate, crowded at ends of br. ♂ infl. a cluster, ♀ a rac. Fls small; 4–5(–6) parted; sta. 8–20. Fr. a drupe, ± fleshy. Trop. Afr. to Trop. Asia. Z10.

P. borbonica Lam. HOG PLUM. To 15m. Lfts 7–19 elliptic to ovate, acuminate, basally oblique, initially hairy and red tinted. Sta. 10. Fr. purple, plum-like. Madag.

P. caffra (Sonder) H. Perrier = *Sclerocarya birrea* ssp. *caffra*.

P. pinnata Blanco = *Spondias pinnata*.

→*Spondias*.

Pourouma Aubl. Cecropiaceae. 23 lactiferous trees, often with stilt roots. Lvs spiral, palmate. Infl., 1–2 per axil, 1–3-branched. ♂ fls clustered or solitary, perianth seg. 3–4, sta. 4; ♀ fls solitary or clustered, perianth tubular, 3–4-lobed. Fr. with fleshy perianth, endocarp crustaceous. C & Trop. S Amer. Z10.

P. cecropiifolia Mart. TANARIBE; UVA DEL MONTE; To 20m. Branchlets short, annulate, wrinkled. Lvs digitate; petiole to 20cm; lfts 9–11, oblanceolate, to 20cm, slightly rough above, white-tomentellous beneath. Fr. ovoid velutinous when young, ultimately glab., yellow-green, about 2cm, mucilaginous. Upper Amaz. Basin.

Pourthiaea Decne.

P. arguta Lav. non Decne. = *Photinia villosa* var. *laevis*.

P. parvifolia Pritz. = *Photinia parvifolia*.

P. villosa (Thunb.) Decne. = *Photinia villosa*.

Pouteria Aubl. Sapotaceae. 50 everg., woody shrubs and trees, to 30m. Lvs often in spirals, entire. Inflorescence an axill. cluster or solitary; cor. cyathiform to tubular, green or white to yellow, lobes usually erect; sta. 4–6(–9), alt. with staminodes, usually included. Fr. a berry, usually fleshy; seeds 1 to several, ellipsoid, dark. Pantrop. Z10.

P. campechiana (HBK) Baehni. CANISTEL; EGGFRUIT; SAPOTE BORRACHO/AMARILLO. Tree to 17m usually shorter. Lvs 7.9–25cm, narrowly elliptic to oblanceolate, vein pairs 9–18. Infl. a 2–3-fld axill. fascicle, cor. side.; cor. 0.75–1.35cm, cylindrical, lobes 5–7, rounded or truncate. Fr. 2.5–7cm, ellipsoid to subglobose, yellow to green or brown smooth skin, pulp mealy, orange or yellow, sweet, edible. Mex. to Panama.

P. mammosa Jacq. = *P. sapota*.

P. sapota (Jacq.) H.E. Moore & Stearn. SAPOTE; MAMMEE SAPOTE; MARMALADE PLUM. Tree to at least 30m. Lvs 10–35cm, oblanceolate, vein pairs 20–25. Fls in 3–6-fld fascicles; cor. broadly tubular, 0.7–1cm, lobes 5, 2.5–4mm, broadly oblong or spathulate. Fr. 9–12cm, ovoid to ellipsoid, roughened, brown to grey-brown, pulp bright orange, buttery, v. sweet. Mex. to Nic. Most cvs have medium-sized fr. (0.5–1kg) e.g. 'Mayapan', 'Pantin', 'Tazumal'; 'Magana' has fr. to 2.5kg.

→*Lucuma*.

Poverty Grass *Corema conradii*; *Hudsonia tomentosa*.
Powder-puff Cactus *Mammillaria bocasana*.
Powder-puff Tree *Calliandra*.

Praecitrullus Pang. Cucurbitaceae. 1 climbing or trailing herb. St. hairy. Tendrils slender, 2–3-fld. Lvs sparingly pinnately lobed, hispid, toothed to entire. Fls solitary, yellow, campamulate, to 1cm diam. Fr. a subspherical berry, to 6cm diam., light or dark green. Early spring–autumn. India, Pak. Z10.

P. fistulosus (Stocks) Pang.

→*Citrullus*.

Prairie Coneflower *Ratibida columnifera*.
Prairie Cord Grass *Spartina pectinata*.
Prairie Crab *Malus ioensis*.
Prairie Dock *Parthenium integrifolium*; *Silphium*.
Prairie Fire *Castilleja*.
Prairie Flax *Linum perenne*.
Prairie Gentian *Eustoma grandiflorum*.
Prairie Grass *Schizachyrium scoparium*.
Prairie Iris *Nemastylis acuta*.
Prairie Mallow *Sidalcea*; *Sphaeralcea coccinea*.
Prairie Mimosa *Desmanthus illinoensis*.
Prairie Onion *Allium stellatum*.
Prairie Phlox *Phlox pilosa*.
Prairie Rose *Rosa arkansana*; *R. setigera*.
Prairie Smoke *Geum triflorum*.
Prairie Sunflower *Helianthus petiolaris*.
Prairie Willow *Salix humilis*.

Prasophyllum R. Br. Orchidaceae. Some 70 terrestrial herbaceous orchids. Spike or rac. slender-stalked; fls. resupinate; dors. sep. lanceolate, erect, recurved or hooked, lat. sep. free or partially fused; lip sessile or attached to a projection at column base, fimbriate, entire or denticulate. Winter–summer. Aus., NZ. Z9.

P. australe R. Br. To 75cm. Dors. sep. to 8mm pet. striped red-brown, yellow-green; lip white. Aus.

P. despectans Hook. f. SHARP MIDGE ORCHID. To 40cm. Fls to 45, pale yellow-green, brown or purple; dors. sep. to 2mm. SE Aus., Tasm.

P. rufum R. Br. RED MIDGE ORCHID. To 40cm. Fls few to many, green or red-brown to dark maroon, rarely grey-green and red; dors. sep. to 3mm. SE Aus.

Pratia Gaudich. Campanulaceae. About 20 mostly prostrate, small perenn. herbs. St. slender, creeping; rooting. Lvs usually smaller than 1cm. Fls small, solitary; cor. bilabiate. Fr. a berry, red to blue-black. Aus., NZ, trop. Afr., S Amer.

P. angulata (Forst. f.) Hook. f. Lvs suborbicular, succulent, serrate. Fls to 1cm, subsessile, white with purple veins. Summer. NZ. 'Ohau': fls large, white; fr bright red. Z7.

P. arenaria Hook. f. Habit like *P. angulata* but lvs larger, denticulate and fls pure white, short-pedicellate. Summer. NZ. Z8.

P. begoniifolia (Wallich ex Roxb.) Lindl. = *P. nummularia*.

P. linnaeoides Hook. f. = *Lobelia linnaeoides*.

P. littoralis R. Cunn. = *P. angulata*.

P. macrodon Hook. f. Lvs to 0.8cm, ovate to elliptic, base cuneate, irregularly serrate. Fls short-stalked to sessile to 1cm, white-cream. NZ. Z7.

P. nummularia (Lam.) A. Braun & Asch. Lvs orbicular to cordate, dentate. Fls to 1cm, mauve, pale pink, to yellow or green, lower lip marked purple. Summer. Trop. and subtrop. Asia. Z9.

P. pedunculata (R. Br.) F. Muell. ex Benth. Lvs to 9mm diam., ovate or orbicular, with few teeth. Fls small, blue, to 7mm, on pedicels longer than lvs. Aus. 'County Park': fls blue. 'Jack's Pass': habit creeping; fr deep red. 'Tom Stone': fls pale blue. Z7.

P. perpusilla (Hook. f.) Hook. f. Lvs minute, oblong or ovate-oblong, acute or obtuse, fleshy, deeply dentate, glab. or short-pubesc. Fls to 6mm, white, ± subsessile; cor. lobes narrow. NZ. 'Fragrant Carpet': fls white, fragrant. 'Summer Meadows': lvs bronze-coloured; fls fragrant, white. Z8.

P. physaloides (A. Cunn.) Hemsl. St. to 130cm. Lvs to 17cm, ovate, serrate, glab. or sparsely pubesc. Rac., term., shorter than lvs fls. to 5cm, pale blue, pubesc. NZ. Z8.

P. repens Gaudich. Lvs reniform, sinuate. Fls 1cm+, long-pedicellate, white suffused with violet. Summer. Falkland Is. Z7.

→*Lobelia*.

Prayer Pepper *Peperomia dolabriformis*.
Prayer Plant *Maranta leuconeura*.
Pregnant Onion *Ornithogalum longibracteatum*.
Preiss's Paperbark *Melaleuca preissiana*.

Prenanthes L. Compositae. 15 erect, much branched, perenn. herbs, with latex. Lvs alt., pinnatisect, base sagittate-cordate, those below petiolate, those above sessile. Cap. ligulate, numerous nodding, in rac. or pan. N temp. to African mts. Z5.

P. alba L. = *Nabalus albus*.

P. aspera Michx. = *Nabalus asper*.

P. autumnalis Walter = *Nabalus autumnalis*.

P. purpurea L. RATTLESNAKE ROOT. To 1.5m. Lvs to 18cm, elliptical to oblong, rarely pinnatisect, entire to dentate. Cap. in a pan.; involucre to 15×5mm; flts purple, rarely white. Summer. C & S Eur.

P. serpentaria Pursh = *Nabalus serpentarius*.

P. virgata Michx. = *Nabalus autumnalis*.

Prepodesma N.E. Br.

P. orpenii (N.E. Br.) N.E. Br. = *Aloinopsis orpenii*.

P. uncipetala N.E. Br. = *Hereroa uncipetala*.

Preserving Melon *Citrullus lanatus* var. *citroides*.

Prestonia R. Br. Apocynaceae. 65 woody vines with milky sap. Fls in dense lat. corymbose cymes or umbels; cor. funnelform, limb 5-lobed, flaring, with 5 scale-like seg. in throat. Trop. Amer. Z10.

P. quinquangularis (Jacq.) Spreng. Lvs to 15cm, oval-ovate, thin-textured, veins red or purple, ultimately white. Fls in clusters of 6–20, cor. 1.5×1.8cm, yellow-green, lobes obovate, reflexed. Summer. Lesser Antilles to Guyana, Venez.

Prickleweed *Desmanthus illinoensis*.
Prickly Ash *Orites excelsa*; *Zanthoxylum*.

Prickly Bottlebrush *Callistemon brachyandrus.*
Prickly Cardinal *Erythrina zeyheri.*
Prickly Cucumber *Echinocystis lobata.*
Prickly Custard Apple *Annona muricata.*
Prickly Cycad *Encephalartos altensteinii.*
Prickly Gooseberry *Ribes cynosbati.*
Prickly Hakea *Hakea amplexicaulis.*
Prickly Juniper *Juniperus oxycedrus.*
Prickly Lettuce *Lactuca serriola.*
Prickly Moses *Acacia pulchella*; *A. verticillata.*
Prickly Myrtle *Rhaphithamnus spinosus.*
Prickly Palm *Bactris major.*
Prickly Pear *Opuntia.*
Prickly Phlox *Leptodactylon californicum.*
Prickly Plume Grevillea *Grevillea annulifera.*
Prickly-pole *Bactris guineensis.*
Prickly Poppy *Argemone*; *Papaver argemone.*
Prickly Rasp-fern *Doodia aspera.*
Prickly Shield Fern *Polystichum aculeatum.*
Prickly Thrift *Armeria pungens.*
Pride of Bolivia *Tipuana tipu.*
Pride of California *Lathyrus splendens.*
Pride of India *Koelreuteria paniculata*; *Lagerstroemia speciosa*; *Melia azedarach.*
Pride of Madeira *Echium candicans.*
Pride of Tenerife *Echium simplex.*
Prima de Sierra *Gaussia princeps.*
Primavera *Cybistax donnell-smithii.*
Primrose *Primula vulgaris.*
Primrose Jasmine *Jasminum mesnyi.*
Primrose-leaved Violet *Viola primulifolia.*
Primrose Peerless *Narcissus* ×*medioluteus.*

Primula L. Primulaceae. 400 perenn. herbs usually with short rhiz., a few shrub-like. Lvs in basal rosettes, many sp. with waxy farina. Fls. solitary, axill. and pedicellate, or in scapose rac., umbels or superposed whorls, 5 lobed; cor. tube usually exceeding cal., lobes 5, usually overlapping, emarginate; most sp. heterostylous, bearing fls with short styles and anth. at mouth of lower (thrum-eyed), or with long styles and anth. down inside fl. (pin-eyed). N Hemis., Ethiop., Trop. mts to Java and New Guinea, S S Amer.

P. acaulis (L.) Hill = *P. vulgaris.*
P. albocincta Widm. = *P. auricula.*
P. algida Adams. Farinose or efarinose. Lvs oblong or oblanceolate, denticulate, rarely entire, 1.5–7cm, apex obtuse to rounded, tapering to winged petiole. Peduncle 3–20cm, farinose or efarinose. Umbel 3–12-fld; cor. to 1.5cm diam., flat, violet to violet-pink, sometimes white, tube white or yellow. Spring. Cauc., mts of E & NE Turk., N Iran. Z5.
P. allionii Lois. Lvs 1.5–4.5cm, oblanceolate to suborbicular, entire, crenulate or finely serrate, fleshy, viscid, densely pubesc., withered lvs persistent, petiole narrow to winged. Scapes v. short, 1- to 5-fld; cor. 1.5–3cm diam., pale pink to red-purple with white eye, sometimes white, lobes obovate, emarginate, overlapping; tube 1–1.5cm. Early spring. Fr. and It. Maritime Alps. 'Anna Griffith': lvs bright green, dentate; fls v. pale pink, lobes with several notches. 'Alba': white fls. 'Apple Blossom': lvs mid-green, crenate; fls relatively large, rose-pink, shading to white; pet. edges wavy; thrum-eyed. 'Avalanche': lvs crenate; large flowered albino, pin-eyed. 'Celia': pet. 7–8, overlapping, cor. deep lilac-pink, thrum-eyed. 'Crowsley Variety': lvs small, grey-green, v. slightly toothed; cor. deep crimson with white eye. 'Margaret Earle': fls to 3cm diam.; pet. wavy; similar to seed parent, except thrum-eyed. 'Mary Berry': lvs light green, slightly crenate; fls to 3cm diam., cor. dark red-purple, thrum-eyed. 'Pinkie': dwarf, forming a tight cushion, early-flowering; fls pink, thrum-eyed. 'Praecox': autumn-flowering; fls lilac-pink, thrum-eyed. 'Snowflake': fls white, crystalline, flushed with pink, thrum-eyed; pet. overlapping, undulate, lip emarginate. 'Superba': parent of 'Margaret Earle', which it resembles; fls relatively large, rose with white eye, pin-eyed; pet. broad, overlapping. 'Viscountess Byng': lvs grey-green, subentire; fls purple-pink, with white eye, thrum-eyed; pet. broad, wavy. 'William Earle': fls to 3cm diam., lilac-pink, with white eye, thrum-eyed; pet. v. broad (5 may form complete disc), wavy. Many hybrids produced in cult. but only that with *P. marginata* found wild. In most cases the hybrid offspring are intermediate between the parents to varying degrees. The following are the most frequently encountered: *P. allionii* ×*P. auricula.* See *P.* ×*loiseleurii.* *P. allionii* ×*P. hirsuta.* Lvs glandular-hairy. Peduncle short or 0. 'Ethel Barker': Lvs long-petiolate, pubesc.; peduncle v. short; fls 3–5, bright carmine with white eye. *P. allionii* ×*P. marginata.* Both wild and artificially produced clones are grown; most resemble a compact, few-fld *P. marginata.* 'Miniera': was a clone collected in the wild; the

name was not published as a grex-name but has been widely used. 'Sunrise': lvs serrate, glossy green, efarinose; peduncle short; fls to 20, pale lilac-pink with centre white, lobes irregularly toothed. 'Beatrice Wooster': lvs larger than *P. allionii*, less gland.; peduncle shortly exceeding lvs; fls clear pink with white centre. 'Clarence Elliott' (*P. allionii* ×'White Linda Pope'): lvs resembling those of *P. allionii*; peduncle 5–7cm; fls to 7, 2.5–4cm diam., bright lilac with small white eye and yellow throat, lobes 5, overlapping. 'Fairy Rose': lvs deeply and irregularly serrate; peduncle v. short; fls large, rose-pink, with v. narrow white eye. 'Joan Hughes': lvs resembling those of *P. marginata*, regularly toothed; peduncle short, gland.; fls to 20, to 1.5cm diam., deep magenta-pink, darker at lobe-margins, with white centre. 'Linda Pope': see under *P. marginata.* *P. allionii* ×*P.* ×*pubescens.* Offspring v. variable. 'Margaret': rosettes compact; lvs ovate to broadly lanceolate, grey-green, margins finely dentate and ciliate; peduncle 2cm; fls to 20, to 2.5cm diam., lilac-pink, centre white, lobes overlapping. Z7.
P. alpicola Stapf. Lvs to 10cm, elliptic, apex rounded, base cuneate or cordate, denticulate or crenulate, petiole winged. Peduncle 15–50cm, farinose above; bracts, to 2cm, cor. white, yellow, purple or violet, to 2.5cm diam., broadly funnel-shaped, eye farinose, fragrant, lobes round, emarginate. Summer. SE Tibet. var. *alba* W.W. Sm.: fls white; var. *luna* (Stapf) W.W. Sm.: fls soft yellow; var. *violacea* (Stapf) W.W. Sm.: fls violet, variable in shade. Z6.
P. amoena Bieb. Lvs 5–16cm, elliptic, ovate, obovate, spathulate, irregularly crenate or denticulate, usually pubesc. beneath, apex round or obtuse, base usually tapering to winged petiole. Peduncle 5–15cm, hirsute; infl. usually secund, 6–10-fld; cor. 1.5–2.5cm diam., flat to shallowly funnel-shaped, violet-blue to lavender-blue to purple with yellow yee (albinos known), lobes obovate, deeply emarginate. Early spring. Cauc., NE Turk. (mts). Z5.
P. angustifolia Torr. Lvs upright, entire or denticulate, oblanceolate to lanceolate, 0.5–7cm, usually curled inwards, apex round, base tapering to winged petiole. Peduncle 0.5–10cm. Fls 1–(2–4); cor. 0.7–2cm diam., flat to funnel-shaped, rose-lilac to purple-pink, eye yellow with white margin, albinos known, lobes obovate, emarginate, slightly overlapping. Spring. Rocky Mts. Z6.
P. anisodora Balf. f. & Forr. Aromatic. Lvs to 25cm, obovate, apex obtuse, denticulate; petiole winged. Peduncle stout, to 60cm; 3–5 8–10-fld whorls; cor. brown-purple, to 15mm diam., eye green, lobes crenulate. Summer. SW China. Z6.
P. appenina Widm. Lvs 2.5–6.5cm, denticulate above obovate or broadly oblanceolate, apex rounded or obtuse, base tapering into petiole, yellow to brown-glandular-hairy. Peduncles 1–9cm; infl. gland., 1–8-fld; cor. to 2.5cm diam., exannulate, lilac to magenta-pink, eye white, lobes, obovate, emarginate, sometimes overlapping, tube 20–23mm. Spring. It. (mts). Z7.
P. atrodentata W.W. Sm. V. close to *P. denticulata* but smaller. Lvs 1–4cm, white- or yellow-farinose beneath. Peduncle to 10cm; cal. nearly black; cor. to 2cm diam., lavender, with a yellow eye, fragrant, lobes emarginate. Himal.
P. aurantiaca W.W. Sm. & Forr. Lvs oblanceolate to obovate, to 20cm, denticulate, apex rounded. Peduncle to 30cm, tinged red; infl. 2–6 whorls, 6–12-fld; cal. dark red; cor. red-orange, 15mm diam., lobes narrowly obovate, emarginate. Summer. SW China. Z6.
P. aureata Fletcher. Lvs broad-spathulate to oblong, to 10cm, toothed, apex obtuse, white-farinose, base tapering to short, red-tinged petiole. Peduncle v. short; infl. 10-fld; cor. cream to yellow, to 4cm diam., eye dark yellow, lobes broad-obovate, toothed, recurved. Spring. Nepal. ssp. *fimbriata* A. Richards ex Gould. Lvs finely dentate. Cor. to 3cm diam., pale cream-yellow, with orange eye, lobes deeply toothed. Nepal.
P. auricula L. Lvs 1.5–12cm, suborbicular to lanceolate, usually obovate, sometimes furinose, entire to dentate, fleshy. Peduncle 1–16cm, often farinose; infl. 2–30-fld; cor. 1.5–2.5cm diam., deep yellow, lobes obovate, emarginate, throat white-farinose, fragrant. Spring. Alps, Carpath., Apennines. Wild forms of *P. auricula* have in the past been given subspecific or varietal rank based on the presence or absence or degree of characters such as farina, lf ciliation, and fragrance. Amongst these are: ssp. *bauhinii* (Beck) Ludi. (short cilia on lf margin, fls lemon-yellow, scented, farinose or efarinose); var. *albocincta* Widmer (heavily farinose in cor. and on lf-margins); ssp. *ciliata* (Moretti) Ludi (efarinose, lf-margins long-ciliate, fls deep yellow, unscented, Italy). Some true cvs of *P. auricula* have been selected, including 'Blairside Yellow': plant compact, 5–10cm, efarinose; lvs to 5×2cm, shallowly dentate; fls to 1.5cm diam., yellow. 'Broadwell Gold': vigorous, farinose; peduncles to 10cm; fls deep golden-yellow with farinose centre, lobes undulate. *P. auricula* hybridizes with many spp. in cult. They are usually intermediate between the parents in appearance. The exception

is the hybrid with *P. hirsuta*, *P.* ×*pubescens* and the immense complex of Show, Border and Alpine Auriculas. *P.* ×*venusta* Host. is the wild hybrid with *P. carniolica*. Z3.

P. auriculata H.J. Lam. Rosettes scantily farinose, overwintering as bud scaly. Lvs 12–30cm, broadly oblanceolate to lanceolate, serrate-dentate, apex rounded or obtuse, narrowing to a broad petiole. Peduncles 8–60cm. Infl. globose, 8–20-fld, cor. 1.5–2.5cm diam., lilac, 9–12mm, throat pale green. Spring. S Cauc., Turk. (mts). Z5.

P. balbisii Lehm. = *P. auricula*.

P. beesiana Forr. Lvs to 22cm, oblanceolate to obovate, attenuate to base, dentate. Peduncle to 40cm, farinose above; infl. of 2–8 whorls of 8–16 fls; cor. to 2cm diam., rose-carmine with yellow-eye, lobes obovate, emarginate, tube yellow. W China.

P. bellidifolia King ex Hook. f. Lvs 5–15cm, oblanceolate to spathulate, obscurely toothed, narrowed to winged petiole. Peduncle 10–30cm, farinose above; infl. 10–15-fld; cor. mauve to blue-violet, to 16mm diam., eye farinose, lobes obovate, emarginate. Spring. Tibet, Bhutan, Sikkim. Z5.

P. ×*berninae* Kerner. (*P. latifolia* × *P. hirsuta*.) 'Windrush': fls large, red-purple.

P. bhutanica Fletcher. = *P. whitei*.

P. biflora Huter = *P.* ×*floerkeana*.

P. ×*bilekii* Sunderm. = *P.* ×*forsteri* f. *bilekii*.

P. boothii Craib. Lvs 3–15cm, broadly spathulate to elliptic, toothed, short-petiolate. Peduncle ± 0; pedicels, to 5cm; cor. pink, 3cm diam., eye brown-yellow, lobes obovate, often 3-toothed. Spring. E Himal. 'Alba': fls white. 'Edrom': fls pale pink with white eye, lobes finely toothed. Z6.

P. bracteosa Craib. Lvs 5–16cm, spathulate to obovate-spathulate, tapering to broad-winged petiole, dentate, farinose. Peduncle v. short; pedicels 4.5cm; cor. pale lilac, to 2.5cm diam., eye yellow, lobes obovate, 2–3-toothed. Spring. Bhutan. Z6.

P. ×*bulleesiana* Janson. (*P. bulleyana* × *P. beesiana*.) Intermediate between parents: fls orange-yellow to mauve. 'Asthore Hybrids' were a selected seed strain of this. Hybrids of the Section Proliferae (Candelabra) are now likely to be of v. complex parentage, with parents also including *P. aurantiaca*, *P. chungensis*, *P. cockburniana*, *P. burmanica* and *P. pulverulenta*. Selected seed strains have been named, such as Sunset Shades and Harlow Carr, often with v. vivid fls.

P. bulleyana Forr. Lvs 12–35cm, ovate to ovate-lanceolate, dentate, apex rounded, base narrowed. Peduncle to 60cm; infl. 5–7-whorls, many-fld; cor. deep orange, to 2cm diam., lobes broad obovate, emarginate. Summer. SW China. Z6.

P. burmanica Balf. f. & Kingdon-Ward. Lvs to 30cm, oblanceolate, dentage, apex obtuse, petiole winged. Peduncle to 60cm; infl. 3–6 whorls, 10–18-fld; cor. red-purple, 2cm diam., eye yellow, lobes obcordate, entire or shallowly emarginate. Summer. Upper Burm., China. Z6.

P. calderiana Balf. f. & R. Cooper. Lvs 5–30cm, oblanceolate to spathulate, denticulate. Peduncle 5–30cm, brown-purple, pubesc. Inf. 5–10-fld cor. maroon to purple, to 3cm diam., eye yellow, lobes broad, irregularly indented. Spring. Himal. ssp. *strumosa* (Balf. f. & Cooper) A. Rich. Lvs to 10cm, lanceolate or oblanceolate, serrate, apex obtuse, petiole short, winged. Peduncle to 20cm, infl. 15-fld; cor. yellow, to 2.5cm diam., eye golden yellow, lobes oblong. Summer. Bhutan, Nepal, SE Tibet. Z6.

P. Candelabra Hybrids. See also *P.* ×*bulleesiana*. 'Bonfire': to 35cm; peduncle deep brown; fls apricot-red. 'Inverewe' ('Ravengalss Vermilion'): to 45cm; peduncles v. numerous; fls bright orange-scarlet, sterile. 'Red Hugh': fls bright orange-red, fertile.

P. capitata Hook. Lvs to 12.5–15cm, oblong, denticulate, oblanceolate or oblong-spathulate, white-farinose beneath. Peduncle 15–30cm, farinose; infl. crowded, somewhat flattened; cor. violet, to 12mm diam., Summer. SE Tibet, Bhutan. ssp. *crispata* (Balf. f. & W.W. Sm.) W.W. Sm. & Forr. Lvs efarinose. Fls open, in a flattened head. ssp. *mooreana* (Balf. f. & W.W. Sm.) W.W. Sm. & Forr. Lvs densely whitefarinose beneath, apex rounded, never acute. Sikkim. Z5.

P. capitellata Boiss. Rhiz. short, thick. Lvs 1.5–10cm, oblong-lanceolate to spathulate, tapering to short, broad petiole, subentire to dentate, white-farinose beneath. Peduncle 2.5–25cm. Umbel 5–12-fld cor. to 0.7cm diam., rose-pink, lobes obcordate, shallowly emarginate, tube to 8mm. Iran, Afghan.

P. carniolica Jacq. Lvs efarinose, 2–15cm, obovate to oblanceolate, subentire or shallowly toothed above, shining, fleshy, tapering to winged petiole. Peduncle 5–20cm; infl. 2–15-fld; cor. purple-pink, to 2cm diam., throat white-farinose, lobes obcordate. Balk. (mts). Z6.

P. carpathica (Griseb. & Schenk) Fuss = *P. elatior*.

P. ×*caruelii* Porta. (*P. glaucescens* ×*spectabilis*.) Intermediate between parents. It. Alps.

P. cawdoriana Kingdon-Ward. Lvs to 4cm, obovate to spathulate, dentate, pubesc. Peduncle 7.5–15cm, farinose above; infl. 3–6-fld; bracts tinged purple; cor. pale mauve, to 3cm long, 3cm diam., funnel-shaped, eye white, lobes oblong, 2–3-notched. Spring. SE Tibet. Z6.

P. chionantha Balf. f. & Forr. Lvs 15–25cm, lanceolate, toothed or subentire, white farinose beneath, tapering to winged petiole. Peduncle 35–70cm; infl. of 1–4 many-fld whorls; cor. 2.5cm diam., white, fragrant, lobes elliptic, entire. Early summer. SW China. Z6.

P. chungensis Balf. f. & Kingdon-Ward. Lvs to 30cm, elliptic to oblong-obovate, toothed and shallowly lobed, glab. Peduncle to 60cm; infl. 2–5 whorls, 10-fld; cor. pale orange, to 18mm diam., tube red, fragrant, lobes broadly obovate. Summer. China, Bhutan, Assam. Z6.

P. ciliata Moretti = *P. auricula*.

P. clarkei G. Watt. Lvs scattered, to 5cm, orbicular to broadly ovate, dentate, base cordate or truncate. Peduncle usually 0; pedicels 4–6cm; coir. rose-pink, to 2cm diam., eye yellow, lobes obovate, deeply emarginate. Spring. Kashmir. 'Johanna' (*P. clarkei* × *P. warshenewskiana*): lvs to 3cm, ovate, serrate; petiole relatively long, red; peduncle to 20cm; fls clear pink with yellow eye, lobes emarginate. 'Peter Klein' (*P. clarkei* ×*rosea*): 10–15cm; lvs resembling peduncle stout; fls deep pink. Z7.

P. clusiana Tausch. Lvs 1–9cm, oblong to elliptic, ovate or obovate, leathery, entire, ciliate, shiny above, grey-green beneath, apex acute, obtuse or rounded, base tapering into short, winged petiole. Peduncle 1–5cm, glandular-hairy; umbel 1–4-fld; bracts narrowly linear or lanceolate, stained purple; cal. sometimes tinged red; cor. 1.5–4cm diam., bright rose, fading to lilac, throat gland., eye white, lobes obcordate, deeply cleft. Spring. W Austrian Alps. Z6.

P. cockburniana Hemsl. Lvs to 15cm, oblong to oblong-obovate, obscurely lobulate and denticulate. Peduncle to 30cm, slender. Infl. of 1–3, few-fld whorls; cor. dark orange-red, to 15mm diam., lobes oblong-obovate. Summer. China. Z5.

P. comberi W.W. Sm. = *P. magellanica*.

P. commutata Schott. = *P. villosa* ssp. *commutata*.

P. concholoba Stapf & Sealy. Lvs to 2–8cm, oblanceolate-oblong to oblong, pubesc. tapering to winged petiole. Peduncle to 18cm; infl. 10- to 20-fld; cor. bright violet, exterior white-farinose, to 12mm, lobes concave and connivent. Late spring–early summer. Himal. Z5.

P. cortusoides L. Lvs 5–10cm, ovate, lobulate, irregularly dentate, pubesc., base cordate, petioles, slender winged, with long hairs. Peduncle 15–30cm, pubesc., infl. 2–15-fld; cor. pink to red-violet, rarely white, to 2cm diam., lobes obcordate, deeply emarginate. Early summer. W Sib. Z3.

P. crispa Balf. f. & W.W. Sm. = *P. glomerata*.

P. crispata Balf. f. & W.W. Sm. = *P. capitata* ssp. *crispata*.

P. cuneifolia Ledeb. Lvs 1–3cm, fleshy, coarsely dentate above, oblanceolate, obovate or cuneate, apex rounded tapering to winged petiole. Peduncle 4–30cm; infl. discoid, 1–9-fld; cor. to 2cm diam., rose red to magenta, eye yellow, occas. with white margin, albinos known. Spring–early summer. E Sib., N Jap., Aleutian Is., W & S Alask. to BC. Z3.

P. cusickiana A. Gray. Lvs 2–5cm, oblanceolate to oblong, obtuse, entire or sparsely dentate, ± succulent, petiole winged. Peduncle 3–9cm; fls 1–4 in umbel; cor. to 1.5cm diam., deep violet or occas. white, fragrant, eye yellow, lobes obovate, undulate or emarginate. Oreg., Idaho.

P. daonensis Leyb. Lvs 1.8cm, narrowly cuneate-obovate, rarely ovate, dentate above, fleshy, with gland. hairs producing an orange secretion. Peduncle 1.5–9cm; infl. 2–8-fld; cor. pink to lilac, throat usually white, 1–2cm diam., lobes obovate, emarginate. Spring. E Alps. Z5.

P. darialica Rupr. Lvs 2–8cm, obovate, oblong or spathulate, apex rounded to obtuse, attenuate to base, denticulate, cream-white-farinose or efarinose beneath, petiole winged. Peduncle 2.5–10cm; fls 2–15 in erect umbel; cor. to 1.4cm diam., pink to carmine-red, with yellow eye, lobes obovate, deeply emarginate, overlapping. Cauc. Plants in cult. as *P. darialica* are almost always *P. frondosa*.

P. decipiens Duby = *P. magellanica*.

P. denticulata Sm. DRUMSTICK PRIMULA. Lvs to 10cm, oblong-obovate or spathulate, later to 30cm, when oblong to oblanceolate, denticulate, farinose beneath, narrowing to winged petiole. Peduncle 10–30cm; infl. crowded, subglobose; cor. pale purple to red-purple, sometimes white, to 17mm, eye yellow, lobes obcordate, emarginate. Spring–early summer. Afghan. to SE Tibet and Burm. 'Alba': fls white with yellow eye. 'Cashmeriana': lvs and peduncles farinose. 'Karryann': lvs with cream-variegated margins. 'Rubra': fls red-purple; many red-fld forms have been named. Z5.

P. deorum Velen. Lvs 2–15cm, narrowly oblanceolate to oblong, coriaceous, with short pale gland. hairs above, entire. Peduncle 5–20cm, viscid, violet above; infl. 3–18-fld; cal. tinged purple; cor. deep red to violet-purple, to 2cm diam., lobes obovate, emarginate. SW Bulg. (mts). Z5.

P. × deschmannii Gusmus = *P. × vochinensis.*

P. deuteronana Craib. Lvs 1.5–5cm, oblong-obovate to oblong-ovate, irregularly denticulate; petiole short. Peduncle 0; pedicels 1–2cm; cor. to 3cm diam., pale purple with annulus yellow, lobes obovate, toothed or lobed. Himal. (C Nepal to Sikkim).

P. × digenea Kerner. (*P. elatior* × *P. vulgaris.*) A wide range of forms between parents. Z5.

P. × discolor Leyb. (*P. auricula* × *P. daonensis.*) Fls purple to pale yellow. Those resembling *P. auricula* may be distinguished by lvs having red gland. hairs. Those resembling *P. daonensis* distinguished by lvs subentire, or farinose. Z6.

P. edgeworthii (Hook. f.) Pax. Young lvs 5–7.5cm, spathulate, irregularly serrate or lobulate, undulate; mature lvs to 15cm, ovate, base truncate or cordate, petiolate. Peduncle ± 0; pedicels 2.5–8cm; cor. blue, lilac, pink or white, to 3cm diam., eye orange-yellow edged white, lobes obovate, acute, entire to emarginate. Spring. W Himal. 'Ghose's': lvs light green, farinose; fls pale mauve or blue, with yellow eye. Z4.

P. elatior (L.) Hill. OXLIP. Lvs 5–20cm, ovate to oblong or elliptic, crenate, often erose, pubesc. beneath, apex rounded, base contracting abruptly into long, broad, winged, petiole. Peduncle 10–30cm; infl. secund, many-fld; cor. yellow, 2–2.5cm, throat green-yellow to orange, lobes obcordate, emarginate. Spring–early summer. Eur. to Near E. ssp. *leucophylla* (Pax.) H. Harrison ex W.W. Smith & Forr. Lvs gradually attenuate to petiole, grey-tomentose beneath when young, entire to crenulate. Rom. ssp. *pallasii* W.W. Sm. & Forr. Lvs gradually attenuate to petiole, glab., dentate. Fls few. N Asia, S to N Iran. ssp. *ruprechtii* (Kusn.) H. Harrison. Close to ssp. *leucophylla*, differing in lvs persistently tomentose. Cauc., Armenia. Z5.

P. elatior ssp. *meyeri* (Rupr.) Valent. & Lamond. = *P. amoena.*

P. Elatior Hybrids see *P.* Pruhonicensis Hybrids.

P. erythrocarpa Craib. Close to *P. denticulata.* Lvs oblanceolate, ± farinose beneath. Peduncles 10–35cm, farinose above; fls mauve, eye yellow. E Himal.

P. exigua L. = *P. farinosa* ssp. *exigua.*

P. × facchinii Schott (*P. minima* × *P. spectabilis.*) V. variable. Z6.

P. farinosa L. Usually farinose. Lvs 1–10cm, oblanceolate to elliptic, obtuse, entire or denticulate, white farinose beneath; winged. Peduncle 3–20cm; infl. 2-many-fld cal. tinged black or purple; cor. 8–16mm diam., lilac-pink, rarely purple or white, throat yellow, lobes obcordate, deeply emarginate, tube 5–8mm. Scotland and C Sweden to C Spain to Bulg., N Asia and N Pacific. ssp. *exigua* Velen. Usually smaller, efarinose; fls 2–6 on longer pedicels. Bulg. (mts). Z4.

P. fauriae Franch. = *P. modesta* var. *fauriae.*

P. fauriae var. *samanimontana* Tatew. = *P. modesta* var. *fauriae.*

P. fedschenkoi Reg. Lvs obovate-elliptic to spathulate, to 6cm, attenuate to broad petioles, dentate. Peduncle 4–12cm; infl. a few-fld umbel; cor. purple-pink, with darker eye, lobes entire or emarginate. Afghan., C Asia.

P. finnmarchica Jacq. = *P. nutans.*

P. firmipes Balf. f. & Forr. Lvs 2.5–7.5cm, ovate or rounded, base cordate, deeply crenate-dentate, petiole to 20cm, winged. Peduncle 10–40cm, yellow-farinose above; infl. a 2–10-fld umbel; cor. 2cm diam., soft yellow, nodding, farinose within, lobes obovate, emarginate. E Himal. to W China, N Burm.

P. flaccida Balakr. Lvs 10–20cm, elliptic or obovate, denticulate, downy, apex acute, base narrowed to winged petiole. Peduncle 20–40cm; infl. densely 5–15-fld; cor. lavender to violet, to 2.5cm diam., broadly funnel-shaped, farinose, downward-pointing. Summer. China.

P. × floerkeana Schröd. (*P. glutinosa* × *P. minima.*) Fls deep purple to bright pink. V. common in Alps. V. common in Alps. Z5.

P. floribunda Wallich. Pubesc. Lvs ovate to elliptic, coarsely dentate, petiole broadly winged. Peduncle 5–25cm; infls of 2–6 superposed umbels of 3–6 fls, cor. to 1cm diam., yellow, lobes entire or emarginate, tube long. W Himal. (Afghan. to W Nepal).

P. florindae Kingdon-Ward. Lvs 5–20cm, broadly-ovate, dentate, shining, base deeply cordate; petiole 4–20cm, often tinged red. Peduncle to 90cm; infl. 40+-fld; pedicels, slender; cal. yellow-farinose; cor. yellow, creamy-farinose within, to 2cm diam., fragrant, funnel-shaped, lobes broad-ovate. Summer. SE Tibet. 'Rubra': fls orange to crimson; often sold as *P. florindae* Orange or Red Hybrids: probably of hybrid origin, with *P. waltonii* usually smaller than *P. florindae*. Z6.

P. forrestii Balf. f. Subshrub with long woody rhiz., glandular-hairy. Lvs 3–8cm, ovate-elliptic, crenate to serrate, apex obtuse, base rounded or subcordate, rugose above, pale farinose beneath; petiole to 10cm. Peduncle 15–22cm; infl. 10–25-fld; bracts leafy; cor. yellow, to 2cm diam., eye orange, lobes broad-obcordate, emarginate. Summer. China. Z6.

P. × forsteri Stein. (*P. hirsuta* × *P. minima.*) V. variable. f. *bilekii* (Sunderm.) Widm. Differs from *P. minima* in lvs glandular-pubesc., more teeth with shorter-cartilaginous tips. Infl. to 3-fld; fls brighter red, lobes broader. f. *kelleri* (Widm.) Widm. Similar to *P. hirsuta* but lvs with cartilaginous tips, bracts longer, shortly glandular-pubesc. f. *steinii* (Obrist) Widm. Intermediate between *P. hirsuta* and *P. minima*. 'Dianne' lvs broadly spathulate, with 6–7 sharp teeth at apex; fls deep magenta-crimson. Z5.

P. frondosa Janka. Lvs to 10cm, spathulate or obovate, denticualte or crenulate, farinose beneath, apex rounded, base tapering to winged petiole. Peduncle 5–12.5cm; infl. 1–30-fld; cor. rose-lilac to red-purple, to 1.5cm diam., eye yellow, lobes obcordate, deeply emarginate, tube yellow. Late spring. Balk. Z5.

P. gambeliana Watt. Lvs 2–30cm, ovate to orbicular, apex rounded, base cordate, crenate, petiole slender. Peduncle 3–25cm; umbel solitary or 2 superimposed, cor. to 2.5cm diam., purple-pink to violet-pink, throat yellow, lobes broadly obcordate, deeply emarginate. E Himal.

P. geraniifolia Hook. f. Lvs 5–20cm, orbicular, pubesc., lobes 7–9, rounded, crenate, base cordate; petiole 5–7.5. Peduncle 10–30cm, pubesc.; infl. 2–12-fld, lax; cor. pink to pale purple, 1–2cm diam., semi-pendent, lobes obcordate. Summer. E Himal., Yunnan. Z5.

P. glaucescens Moretti. Lvs 1–10cm, broadly lanceolate to oblong, coriaceous, stiff, shining, minutely crenulate, apex acute, base narrowed. Peduncle 3–12cm; infl. 2–6-fld; cal. tinged red cor. min-red to lilac, to 2.5cm diam., lobes obcordate, deeply notched. Spring. It. Alps. Z6.

P. glomerata Pax. Lvs 3–15 cm, oblong, oblanceolate or obovate-spathulate, erose to denticulate, white-farinose when young, tapering to winged petiole usually tinged red at base. Peduncles 10–30cm, with a rosette of raggedly toothed lvs. Infl. compact, globose; cor. purple-blue, to 1.5cm diam., funnel-shaped, lobes obcordate, deeply emarginate. Late summer–early autumn. Himal. Z6.

P. glutinosa Wulf. Lvs 1.5–6cm, narrowly oblanceolate to oblong, coriaceous, with minute, pale gland. hairs above. Peduncle 1.5–9cm; infl. 2–8-fld; cor. deep violet, rarely white, to 2cm diam., fragrant, lobes ovate, emarginate. Early summer. E Alps, C Balk. Z4.

P. gracilipes Craib. Lvs 4–15cm, oblong-spathulate to elliptic, irregularly toothed, tapering to broad-winged petiole. Peduncle 0); pedicels 1–6cm; cor. bright pink-purple, eye small, orange-yellow with narrow white border, lobes 2–4cm, obovate, toothed, spreading. Late spring–early summer. C Nepal, SE Tibet. 'Winter Jewel': to 15cm; lvs finely dentate; fls bright rose-pink. Z5.

P. grandis Trautv. = *Sredinskya grandis.*

P. griffithii (Watt) Pax. Lvs 6–30cm, ovate to sagittate, base attenuate to broad petiole, or rounded to cordate, sparsely farinose beneath, irregularly dentate. Peduncle 10–20cm; umbel 5–12-fld. cor. to 2.5cm diam., deep purple with yellow eye lobes obcordate, shallowly emarginate. E Himal.

P. halleri J.F. Gmel. Lvs 2–8cm, elliptic to obovate, subentire to denticulate, yellow farinose. Peduncle 8–18cm; cor. 15–20mm diam., lilac, tube 20–30mm. Spring. Alps, Carpath., Balk. Penins. (mts). Z5.

P. × heerii Brügger. (*P. hirsuta* × *P. integrifolia.*) distinct from *P. hirsuta* by absence of white eye to cor.; distinct from *P. integrifolia* by teeth on lf margins. Natural hybrid. Z5.

P. × helenae Arends. = *P.* Pruhonicensis Hybrids.

P. helodoxa Balf. f. = *P. prolifera.*

P. heucherifolia Franch. Lvs to 6–15cm, orbicular, with 7–11, broadly triangular lobes, somewhat pilose, base cordate; petiole red-villous. Peduncles 15–30cm; infl. 3–9-fld; cal. red; cor. mauve-pink to deep purple, to 2.5cm diam., pendent, lobes obovate, emarginate. Early summer. Tibet, China. Z5.

P. hirsuta All. Lvs 2–9cm, ovate, obovate or suborbicular, dentate, fleshy, glandular-pubesc., producing a pale or red-brown secretion, petiole winged. Peduncle 1–7cm; infl. 1–15-fld; cor. to 2.5cm diam., pale lilac to deep purple-red, usually with white centre, lobes obovate, emarginate. Spring. C Alps, Pyren. Z5.

P. hyacinthina W.W. Sm. Lvs 16–18cm, oblanceolate to oblong, obtuse, base attenuate to winged petiole, dentate, white-farinose beneath. Peduncle 20–45cm; infl. a compact spike or cap. cor. to 2.7cm, violet, pendent, strongly hyacinth-scented. SE Tibet.

P. ianthina Balf. f. & Cave. Lvs to 25cm, oblong-oblanceolate, rounded, petiole winged, glandular-punctate, finely denticulate. Peduncle to 60cm, yellow-farinose at nodes; infl. of 3 many-fld whorls; cor. to 2cm diam., violet, lobes obcordate, rounded, emarginate. Sikkim.

P. imperialis Jungh. = *P. prolifera*.

P. incana M.E. Jones. Lvs 1.5–8cm, elliptic to spathulate, usually denticulate, farinose beneath, obtuse; petiole winged or 0. Peduncle 5–45cm, farinose above; infl. capitate, 2–14-fld; cor. to 1cm diam., lilac fading toward centre, eye yellow. Spring–early summer. E Alask. to E Colorado. Z4.

P. integrifolia L. Slightly viscid, secretion sometimes drying to form white crust. Lvs 1–4cm, elliptic to spathulate, ± entire, fleshy to coriaceous, hair gland. Peduncle 0.5–5cm; infl. 1–3-fld; cor. red-purple or pink-lilac, to 2cm diam., lobes obovate, deeply cleft. Early summer. C Alps, E to C Pyren. Z5.

P. × intermedia Porta. (*P. clusiana* × *P. minima*.) Fls large, rose. Natural hybrid. Z5.

P. involucrata Wallich. Lvs 3–15cm, ovate to oblong, entire or denticulate, glab., long-petiolate, base rounded. Peduncle 10–30cm; infl; cor. white, 1–2cm diam., eye yellow, tube purple, 1–1.5cm, lobes obcordate, notched. Summer. Pak. to SW China. Z5.

P. ioessa W.W. Sm. Lvs to 6–20cm, narrowly oblong or oblanceolate to spathulate, deeply toothed, base narrowed to long petiole. Peduncle 10–30cm; infl. 2–8-fld; pedicles yellow-farinose; cal. almost black, farinose; cor. pink-mauve to violet or white, fragrant, to 2.5cm diam., funnel-shaped. Spring–early summer. SE Tibet. Z6.

P. irregularis Craib. Lvs to 8–12cm yellow-farinose, at first, oblong-elliptic to elliptic-obovate, apex rounded, base cuneate or attenuate, deeply dentate, sometimes lobed. Peduncle 1–2cm at anthesis, farinose; umbel 10–20-fld; cal. farinose, gland.; cor. to 2.5cm diam., pink with yellow eye surrounded by white zone, lobes broadly oblong-ovate, toothed. Himal. (Nepal to Sikkim).

P. japonica A. Gray. Lvs to 25cm, obovate, oblong or broad-spathulate, finely crenate-dentate, tapering to winged petiole. Peduncle to 45cm; infl. of 1–6 many-fld whorls; cor. purple-red, crimson, pink to white, to 2cm diam., lobes obcordate. Early summer. Jap. 'Fuji': 'Millers Crimson': to 45cm; abundant crimson fls. 'Postford White': to 45cm; fls white with yellow eye. 'Valley Red': to 50cm; fls bright red. Z5.

P. jesoana Miq. Lvs to 35cm, orbicular-cordate, 7–9-lobed, tinged purple, tapering to winged petiole. Peduncle 10–30cm; infl. 2–6-fld; cor. pink or pink-purple or white, to 2cm diam., eye yellow, lobe obcordate, emarginate. Spring. Jap. Z6.

P. juliae Kuzn. Stoloniferous. Lvs round, 2–10cm, crenate, base deeply cordate; petioles narrow marked red. Peduncle 0; pedicels equal to or longer than petioles; cor. 2–3cm diam., mauve to deep blue-magenta, darker red around yellow eye. Spring. Cauc. Z5.

P. × juliana Rosenheim & May. = *P.* Pruhonicensis Hybrids.

P. × juribella Sunderm. (*P. minima* × *P. tyrolensis.*) Resembling *P. minima* but lvs incurved and cal. tinged purple, features of *P. tyrolensis*. Dolomites.

P. × kelleri Widm. = *P. × forsteri* f. *kelleri*.

P. 'Kewensis'. (*P. floribunda* × *P. verticillata* ?) Lvs 15–20cm, obovate to spathulate, denticulate, sparingly farinose, tapering to winged petiole. Peduncles to 30cm; infl. of 2–5 6- to 10-fld whorls; cor. yellow, fragrant, to 2cm diam., lobes broad-obcordate. Early spring. Z9.

P. kisoana Miq. Short red-hairy. Lvs to 15cm, orbicular-cordate, with 6 pairs of broad-crenate lobes; petiole 7.5–10cm. Peduncle 5–20cm; infl. 2–6-fld; cor. 2.5–3cm diam., deep rose or rose-mauve, lobes obcordate, deep emarginate. Spring. Jap. Z6.

P. kitaibeliana Schott. Viscid. Lvs 2–9cm, elliptic to obovate, mostly with shallow, distant teeth, fleshy, malodorous, hairy. Peduncle 2–5cm; infl. 1–3-fld; cor. pink to lilac, to 2.5cm diam., lobes obcordate, emarginate. Late spring. W and C Balk. Z7.

P. latifolia Lapeyr. Lvs 3–15cm, oblanceolate to obovate, with teeth near apex or subentire, fleshy, viscid, glandular-pubesc. Peduncle 3–18cm; infl 2–20-fld, secund; cor. 1–2cm diam., purple or dark violet, fragrant, lobes oblong to obovate, emarginate, throat ± farinose. Late spring–early summer. S, W and C Alps. Z5.

P. laurentiana Fern. = *P. mistassinica* var. *macropoda*.

P. lichiangensis Forr. = *P. polyneura*.

P. × loiseleurii Sunderm. (*P. allionii* × *P. auricula*.) Intermediate between parents; fls pink or yellow. Gdn origin. 'Lismore Yellow' (*P. allionii* 'Alba' × *P. auricula*): lvs dentate, glossy dark green, glandular-pubesc.; fls 2.5cm diam. with cream-yellow with darker yellow eye.

P. longiflora All. = *P. halleri*.

P. luteola Rupr. Lvs 10–30, lanceolate to elliptic to oblanceolate, denticulate, base tapering to winged petiole. Peduncle 15–35cm, white-farinose above; infl. symmetrical to globose; pedicels farinose; cor. to 1.5cm diam., exannulate, yellow. Spring. E Cauc. Z5.

P. macrocalyx Schur = *P. veris*.

P. macrophylla D. Don. Lvs 15–25cm, lanceolate to oblanceolate, entire or crenulate, white-farinose beneath, tapering to petiole. Peduncle 12.5–25cm, farinose above; infl. 5–25-fld; cor. purple, violet or lilac, eye usually darker or tinged yellow, to 2cm diam., lobes obovate, entire. Summer. Himal. Z6.

P. magellanica Lehm. Lvs 1–10cm, rhombic to obovate to spathulate, serrulate-dentate, apex rounded, base tapering gradualy, usually farinose beneath. Peduncles 5–15cm, farinose above; infl. tight, symmetrical, cor. 1–2cm diam., usually white, cream or lilac to purple, fragrant, eye yellow, lobes obovate, emarginate. Spring. S S Amer., Falklands. Z7.

P. malacoides Franch. FAIRY PRIMROSE; BABY PRIMROSE. Lvs 2–4cm, broad-oblong to ovate, with shallow, dentatge lobes, base cordate; petiole 5–7.5cm. Peduncle 20–30cm; infl. of 2–6, 4–6-fld whorls, cor. mauve to pink, red, or white, to 1.5cm diam., lobes obcordate. Winter. China. Z8.

P. marginata Curtis. Lvs 1.5–10cm, obovate to oblong, serrate-dentate, leathery, fleshy, apex obtuse or rounded, base tapering to a winged petiole, ultimately farinose on margins. Peduncle 2–12cm, farinose above; infl. 2–20-fld; cal. often flushed red; cor. lilac to lavender or blue, sometimes violet or pink, shallow funnel-shaped, 1.5–3cm diam., faintly fragrant, eye white-farinose. Spring. Maritime, Cottian Alps. 'Alba': cor. usually small, pale pink, fading to white. 'Barbara Clough': cor. pink to lilac, eye white, lobes rounded. 'Beamish Variety': fls blue, eye white-farinose. 'Beatrice Lascaris': compact, slow-growing; cor. blue, eye white-farinose, flat. 'Caerulea': cor. blue, funnel-shaped. 'Clear's Variety': cor. small, lilac, eye white. 'Correvon's Variety': vigorous, lvs deeply incised; cor. large, lavender. 'Drake's Form': large cor. pale lilac to lavender. 'Elizabeth Fry': cor. large, silvery lavender. 'Highland Twilight': cor. rich purple to blue. 'Holden's Variety': compact; fls small; cor. blue, funnel-shaped. 'Inschriach Form': fls blue. 'Ivy Agee': fls large; lilac to blue, eye cream. 'Kesselring's Variety': similar to 'Pritchard's Variety' but lvs white-farinose throughout; fls smaller, deep lavender. 'Pritchard's Variety': lvs to 9cm sparingly farinose; cor. lilac to purple, eye white-farinose. 'Rosea': fls lilac to pink. 'Rubra': fls deep rose to lilac. 'Waithman's Variety': fls pale blue. Hybrids include: 'Barbara Barker' ('Linda Pope' × *P. × pubescens* 'Zuleika Dobson'): lvs green with white-farinose dentate margins. Fls to 2cm diam., lavender-blue with white eye. 'Hyacinthia': fls to 3cm diam., hyacinth blue, lobes 6, overlapping. 'Linda Pope' (*P. marginata* × *P. allionii*): lvs large, heavily white-farinose; fls rounded, mauve-blue with white-farinose eye. 'Marven' (*P. marginata* × *P. × venusta*): lvs light green, farinose; fls deep violet-blue with dark eye bordered by white-farinose zone. 'White Linda Pope' ('White Lady'): fls to 2.5cm, pale-green becoming white with pale yellow-green eye. Z7.

P. matsumurae Petitm. = *P. modesta* var. *matsumurae*.

P. megaseifolia Boiss. Lvs 2.5–15cm, ovate to round, crenate-dentate to subentire, apex rounded, base cordate, dark green, glab. above, paler beneath, pubesc.; petiole 1–10cm, stained red. Peduncle 1–10cm, pubesc., stained red; infl. secund, 2–9 fld; cor. 1.5–2.5cm diam., magenta-rose to rose-pink, eye white, throat yellow, lobes obovate, deeply emarginate. Early spring. Black Sea Coast, N Turk. 'John Fielding' (*P. megaseifolia* × *P. juliae*): lvs 4.5cm, elliptic, dentate; peduncle 10cm; fls to 2.3cm diam., orchid-purple. Z7.

P. melanops W.W. Sm. & Kingdon-Ward. Lvs to 25cm, lanceolate, crenate-serrate, farinose beneath, resovolute tapering to a winged petiole. Peduncle 20–35cm, farinose above; infl. of 1–2 umbels 6–12-fld; cor. purple, eye black, to 2cm diam., fragrant, lobes ovate. Early summer. China. Z5.

P. minima L. Lvs 0.5–3cm, cuneate, shining, coriaceous, entire, apex truncate or rounded, sharply dentate, glandular-pubesc. Peduncle 0.2–4cm; infl. 1–2-fld; cor. 1.5–3cm diam., bright pink, lilac or white, lobes deeply emarginate, appearing Y-shaped. Late spring. S Eur. (mts). Z5.

P. mistassinica Michx. Lvs 0.5–7cm, narrow, oblanceolate to spathulate, usually dentate or denticulate above, apex rounded; petiole usually 0, or distinct. Peduncle 3–21cm; infl. 1–10-fld; pale pink, lilac, blue-purple, rarely white, tube yellow, to 2cm diam., eye yellow to orange, lobes obovate, notched. Spring–early summer. Canada, NE US. var. *macropoda* (Fern.) Boiv. Farinose. Lvs 1–25cm, oblanceolate to spathulate, denticulate, apex subacute to rounded, white-farinose beneath. Peduncle, 1–45cm; cor. to 1.5cm diam., lilac to purple-pink, eye orange-yellow fading to orange, tube yellow, lobes obcordate. Spring. E Canada, N US (mts). Z3.

P. modesta Bisset & S. Moore. Lvs 2.5–7.5cm, elliptic to spathulate, undulate-crenate or serrate, yellow-farinose beneath, tapering to winged petiole. Peduncle 2.5–12.5cm; infl. 2–15-fld; cor. pink-purple, to 1.5cm diam., lobes obcordate, deeply emarginate. Spring. Jap. var. *fauriae* (Franch.) Tak. Smaller. Lvs broadly ovate, ± entire, revolute. Hokkaido, Honshu. var. *matsumurae* (Petitm.) Takeda. Lvs oblanceolate, obscurely dentate. Peduncle robust; fls to 10 per umbel. Hokkaido. Z6.

P. mollis Nutt. ex Hook. softly pubesc. Lvs to 7.5cm, broad-ovate, obscurely lobed, crenate, base cordate; petiole 7.5–10cm. Peduncle 10–60cm; infl of 2–10, 4–9-fld umbels; cal. tinted red; cor. rose to crimson, to 2cm diam., eye yellow, lobes obovate, emarginate. April. Himal. Z7.

P. moorcroftiana Wallich = *P. macrophylla*.

P. mooreana Balf. f. & W.W. Sm. = *P. capitata* ssp. *mooreana*.

P. ×*muretiana* Moritzi (*P. integrifolia* ×*P. latifolia*.) Fls more brilliantly coloured than parents. Z5.

P. muscarioides Hemsl. Lvs 10–20cm, obovate or elliptic, crenate or dentate, slightly pubesc. above, tapering gradually to winged petiole. Peduncle to 40cm, farinose above; infl. dense heads or short spikes; cor. deep purple-blue, to 10mm diam., fragrant, tubular, pendent. Early summer. China. Z5.

P. nipponica Yatabe. Lvs 2–4cm, cuneate or obovate-cuneate, apex obtuse, dentate, rather fleshy. Peduncle 7–15cm; infl. a 1–8-fld umbel; cor. to 1.5cm diam., white with yellow eye, lobes emarginate. Jap.

P. nivalis Pall. Lvs to 15–25cm, lanceolate or narrowly elliptic, crenate or dentate, glab., sometimes farinose beneath; petiole short, winged. Peduncle 15–20cm; infl. 8–12-fld; cor. purple 2–2.5cm diam., lobes oblong, entire. Spring. C Asia. Z4.

P. nivalis var. *macrophylla* (D. Don) Pax = *P. macrophylla*.

P. nutans Georgi. Lvs 1–12cm, oblong to ovate to orbicular, en-tire or obscurely denticulate, fleshy, apex rounded, petiole narrowly winged. Peduncle 2–30cm; infl; 1–10-fld; cal. some-times tinged red; cor. 1–2cm diam., lilac to pink-purple, eye yellow, lobes obovate to cuneate. Early summer. Mts of N Asia, N Russia, N Scand., Alask., SW Yukon. Z5.

P. nutans Delavay ex Franch. non Georgi. = *P. flaccida*.

P. obconica Hance. GERMAN PRIMROSE; POISON PRIMROSE. Lvs to 15cm, ovate or elliptic to oblong, dentate or lobulate, base cordate; petiole 5–10cm, downy. Peduncles 15–17.5cm; pubesc.; infl. 10–15-fld; cor. pale-lilac or purple, to 2.5cm diam., eye yellow, lobes obovate emarginate. Winter. China. Z8.

P. oenensis Thomas ex Gremli = *P. daonensis*.

P. officinalis (L.) Hill = *P. veris*.

P. palinuri Petagna. Lvs efarinose, 3–20cm, broadly spathulate to oblong-ovate, ± dentate, fleshy, viscid, aromatic, glandular-hairy. Peducnles 8–20cm; infl. 5–25-fld; cal. densely farinose; cor. to 3cm diam., deep yellow, throat with white, farinose ring, lobes obovate, not spreading. S It. Z5.

P. parryi A. Gray. Lvs 6–33cm, foetid, obovate to oblanceolate, recurved, leathery, frequently contorted, entire or denticulate, covered in short glands; petiole obsolete to v. short, winged. Peduncle 8–40cm; infl. secund; pedicels often long, drooping, often tinged purple; cor. to 3cm diam., purple-red to magenta, eye yellow with dark halo, tube yellow, lobes obovate to orbicular. Early summer. W US. Z4.

P. pedemontana Thom. ex Gaudin. Lvs 1.5–10cm, obovate, oblong-lanceolate to spathulate, entire or shallowly dneticulate above, margins with red gland. hairs, base tapering to winged petiole or 0. Peduncle 2.5–12cm; infl. 1–16-fld; cor. pink, eye white, tube white inside, slightly gland., lobes obovate, emarginate. Early summer. Alps, Pyren.. Z6.

P. petiolaris Wallich. Lvs to 15cm, spathulate, denticulate, apex obtuse, base tapering to distinct petiole. Peduncle 3–5cm; infl. many-fld; cor. 1.5cm diam., pink, eye yellow with thin white border, lobes deep obovate, 3-toothed. Early summer. Himal.

P. Petiolares Hybrids. 'Linnet': close to *P. petiolaris* and *P. gracilipes*; lvs finely dentate; fls v. numerous, farinose in bud, deep pink with white zone surrounding yellow markings at base of each lobe. 'Soup Plate (*P. sonchifolia* ×*P. whitei*): over-wintering buds v. large; fls numerous, ice-blue. 'Tantallon' (*P. whitei* ×*P. edgeworthii*): Lvs 5×1.5cm, lanceolate, acute, dentate, sparsely farinose; peduncle 1cm, farinose; fls to 3cm diam., violet-blue, with yellow-green eye surrounded by narrow white zone. 'Tinney's Appleblossom' (*P. boothii* ×*P. aureata*): lvs oblong, finely dentate, stained red beneath; fls numerous, white with yellow eye, pink-tinged toward end of dentate lobes. 'Tinney's Dairymaid': (*P. boothii* ×*P. aureata*): lvs mid-green; fls numerous, to 3.5cm diam., milk-white with yellow eye, throat green, lobes overlapping, finely dentate. Z5.

P. poissonii Franch. Lvs to 18cm, oblong-obovate, denticulate, usually revolute, glaucous, base tapering to winged petiole. Peduncle to 45cm; infl. of 2–6 whorls; cor. purple to crimson to 2.5cm diam., eye yellow, lobes obcordate, notched. Summer. China. Z6.

P. ×*polyantha* Mill. Hybrids between *Pp. veris, elatior, vulgaris.*

See *P.* Pruhonicensis Hybrids.

P. polyneura Franch. Softly pubesc. or subglabrous. Lvs 4–30cm, ovate to orbicular, obulate, obtuse; petiole 2.5–20cm. Peduncle to 23cm; infl. of 1 or 2–3 superimposed 10–50-fld umbels; cor. pale rose to rich rose-red to crimson or purple, to 2.5cm diam., eye yellow, lobes obcordate, emarginate. Summer. China. Z5.

P. prolifera Wallich emend Benth. Lvs to 35cm, oblanceolate, oblong-obovate or lanceolate, denticulate, tapering to winged petiole. Peduncle to 90cm. Infl. of 4–6, 12–20-fld whorls; cal. creamy-farinose; cor. to 2.5cm diam., golden-yellow, fragrant, lobes obovate, cleft. Early summer. E Himal. to Indon.

P. Pruhonicensis Hybrids. POLYANTHUS. The name is here taken to cover several groups of hybrids between *P. juliae, P. veris, P. elatior* and *P. vulgaris,* which have interbred producing a vast range of plants in many colours and conforming, ±, to either the primrose-type habit or the cow-/oxlip with stalked umbels. *P.* ×*pruhoniciana* (*P. juliae* ×P. vulgaris) (*P.* ×*helenae*) are the early spring primulas with fls in red, purple, pink and white, often with white or yellow eyes. *P.* ×*margotae* (*P. juliae* ×P.Elatior Hybrids) have lvs often flushed purple-bronze and pink, red or purple fls in short-stalked umbels. For example 'Garryarde Guinevere' (lvs bronze; fls pink). Elatior Hybrids (*P.* ×*polyantha*) are strictly hybrids between members of *Primula* sect. *Vernales.* These are the polyanthuses with scapose umbels of fls in shades of gold, pale yellow, bronze, brown and red. Included here are the gold and silver-laced forms with small, virtually black fls edged in golden yellow and silver-white. 'Betty Green': fls crimson, eye clear yellow. 'Blue Cushion': vigorous; fls blue. 'Blue Horizon': vigorous, free-flowering, fls bright grey-blue, eye yellow. 'Blue Riband': vigorous, fls deep blue, centre shade red. 'Bunty': free-flowering; fls purple to blue, eye yellow. 'Craddock White': fls white, eye yellow. 'Crimson Cushion': fls blood red. 'Crimson Queen': fls large, red. 'Crispii': fls mauve-pink. 'Dinah': fls burgundy red, eye olive green. 'E.R. Jones': fls salmon pink, flushed orange. 'Gloria': fls scarlet, eye yellow, lobes with white marks on in-side. 'Groenekens Glory': fls bright mauve-pink, eye green. 'Icombe Hybrid': fls large, rose to mauve, eye white 'Iris Main-waring': compact; fls pale blue, flushed pink. 'Jill': compact; fls mauve-purple, eye white tinged green. 'Lilac Time': fls on short polyanthus-like st., pale rose-lilac. 'Lingwood Beauty': fls red, eye deep orange. 'Morton Hybrid': v. dwarf; fls red, eye yellow, large. 'Mrs Frank Neave': fls small, red. 'Mrs Macgillavry': fls rich violet-mauve. 'Pam': fls small, long, red-purple. 'Perle Von Bottrop': fls vivid red-purple. 'Purple Cushion': similar to 'Wanda', lvs tinged red. 'Purple Splendour': fls large, purple-red, eye pale yellow. 'Queens of the Whites': fls large, clear white. 'Romeo': vigorous, prolific; fls v. large, violet. 'Snow Cushion': fls small, pure white. 'Snow White': vigorous; fls white. 'Wendy': fls pale pink, flushed mauve, lobes frilled. 'Wanda': most popular var., fls purple-red. Cvs of *polyanthus habit* 'Beamish Foam': fls pink, splashed pale yellow. 'Ideal': fls purple, eye yellow. 'Kinlough Beauty': fls salmon-pink, lobes with cream stripe. 'Lady Greer': fls small, pale yellow. 'McWatts Cream': fls small, cream. 'Tawny Port': dwarf, long-flowering, lvs tinged red; fls wine-red. 'The Bride': fls pure white. *Double primroses* Plants with double fls (often calycantheris, i.e. with corolla-like cal.). They include 'Alba Plena': fls white. 'Arthur du Moulin': fls v. deep violet; one of few doubles to produce pollen in quantity. 'Bon Accord Gem': vigorous; fls rose-red, shaded with mauve. 'Bon Accord Lilac': fls lilac, lobes yellow at base. 'Bon Accord Purple': fls large, creamy-white tinged green, lobes frilled. 'Castlederg': fls deep yellow, splashed pink and brown. 'Chevithorne Pink': pedicels short; cor. pink. 'Cloth of Gold': lvs large pale green; fls yellow. 'Crimson King': fls large, deep red. 'Double Sulphur': fls sulphur-yellow. 'Double White': vigorous, with primrose habit; fls white. 'Lady Isobel': fls deep yellow. 'Marie Crousse': fls vio-let, splashed and edged white. 'Mrs A.M. Wilson': vigorous; fls large, red. 'Our Pat': lvs tinged crimson-bronze; fls sapphire blue. 'Quakers Bonnet': vigorous; fls pink-lilac. 'Red Paddy': fls small, red, flushed pink, edged silver.

P. pruhonicensis Zeeman ex Bergmans = *P.* Pruhonicensis Hybrids.

P. ×*pruhoniciana* Zeeman = *P.* Pruhonicensis Hybrids.

P. ×*pruhonictziana* Zeeman = *P.* Pruhonicensis Hybrids.

P. ×*pubescens* Jacq. (*P. auricula* ×*P. hirsuta.*) Distinguished from *P. hirsuta* by lvs sometimes entire, farinose. Cal. slightly farinose. Cor. white, yellow, pink, red, purple, brown, often appears faded. 'Alba': usually compact with heads of white fls. 'Bewerly White': fls creamy-white. 'Boothmans Variety' ('Car-men'): fls crimson red, eye white, lobes overlapping, notched. 'Christine': compact; lvs shallowly crenate; cor. deep rose, eye white. 'Faldonside': fls red-pink, eye white. 'Freedom' ('Belluensis'): lvs denticulate; fls deep lilac. 'The General': vigorous, lvs lanceolate, shallowly denticulate; cor. rich red, eye yellow. 'Harlow Car': lvs shallowly denticulate; fls large, creamy white. 'Mary Curle': lvs broad-lanceolate, denticulate; cor. trumpet-shaped, eye white-farinose, long narrow tube. 'Mrs J.H. Wilson': lvs grey-green, serrate at tip; cor. purple, centre white, fragrant. 'Ruby': fls small, wine-red, centre white. 'Rufus': lvs shallowly denticulate; cor. brick-red, to 3cm diam., eye golden yellow, lobes notched. 'Wharfedale Buttercup': fls to 3cm diam., sulphur-yellow, throat darker yellow. Z5.

P. pulverulenta Duthie. Lvs to 30cm, obovate or oblanceolate, dentrate, tapering to winged petiole. Peduncle to 90cm, farinose; infl. with many whorls; pedicels farinose; cor. deep red, to 2.5cm diam., eye darker red or purple lobes obcordate, notched. Summer. China. Z6.

P. redolens Balf. f. & Ward. Low subshrub. Lvs 6–12cm, elliptic to oblong, apex rounded, petiole distinct, rugose to bullate above, ± farinose beneath. Peduncle 10–20cm; umbel 5–12-fld; cor. to 2.5cm diam., pale purple-pink or lilac-pink to pinkish-cream, or white, fading pale violet, eye yellow, lobes obcordate or rounded, emarginate. SW China.

P. reidii Duthie. Lvs 3–20cm, oblong or lanceolate, crenate or lobulate, obtuse, petiole winged with long hairs. Peduncles 6–15cm, farinose above; infl. 3–10-fld, compact, fragrant; cor. white, 2–2.5cm diam., urceolate, pendent, lobes broad ovate, emarginate. Early summer. Himal. (Kashmir to C Nepal). var. *williamsii* Ludlow. More robust. Fls pale blue to white. W & C Nepal. Z6.

P. reinii Franch. Lvs 2–26cm, orbicular to reniform, shallowly 7–9-lobed, crenate to dentate, villous beneath, base cordate. Peduncle 2–10cm; infl. 1–3-fld; cor. rose to purple, 1.5–3cm diam., eye yellow, lobes obcordate, emarginate. Early summer. Jap. Z7.

P. renifolia Volg. Lvs 3–5cm diam., rounded to reniform, base cordate, dull green and rugose above, white-tomentose beneath, crenate-dentate to subentire, petiole slender, narrowly winged. Peduncle short, fls 2–3 in finely hairy umbel; cor. to cm, blue-violet with yellow eye, lobes obovate, emarginate, tube yellow-green. Cauc.

P. reptans Hook. f. ex Watt. Forming mats. Lvs 0.4–0.6cm, ovate to rounded, revolute, dentate, petiole short. Fls sessile, solitary; cor. to 1.5cm diam., pale purple to pink, eye white, lobes obcordate, emarginate. Himal. (Pak. to C Nepal).

P. reticulata Wallich. Lvs to 4–40cm, oblong to ovate, dentate, base cordate, petiole to 30cm. Peduncle 20–40cm; infl. lax, pedicels farinose cor. yellow or white, 1–2cm diam., funnel-shaped, farinose within, lobes obovate, emarginate. Summer. C Nepal to SE Tibet. Z6.

P. rosea Royle. Lvs tinted red-bronze at first, emerging after fls., ultimately to 20cm, obovate to oblanceolate, crenate or denticulate, base narrowed. Peduncle 3–10cm; infl. lax, 4–12-fld; cor. rose-pink to red, 1–2cm diam., eye yellow, lobes obcordate, cleft. Summer. NW Himal. 'Gigas': to 10cm; fls large, bright pink. 'Grandiflora': to 20cm; fls large, rich pink. 'Micia Visser de Geer' ('Delight'): fls clear soft pink.

P. rotundifolia Wallich = *P. roxburghii*.

P. roxburghii Balakr. Lvs 5–20cm ovate to orbicular, crenate, sometimes farinose beneath, apex obtuse, base cordate; petiole thick, long. Peduncle 10–30cm; infl. 2–16-fld, lax; cor. pink to purple, 1.5–2cm diam., eye golden-yellow, lobes obcordate, entire or ± crenate. Early summer. W Nepal to Sikkim.

P. rubra J.F. Gmel. = *P. hirsuta*.

P. rusbyi Greene. Lvs 3–8cm, elliptic to spathulate, entire or denticulate, gland., apex acute or rounded; petiole winged, short. Peduncle 6–20cm, white-farinose above; infl. secund, 4–12-fld; tinged purple; cor. rose-red to magenta to deep purple, to 2cm diam., eye yellow bordered crimson, tube pale green, lobes obcordate, incurved. Spring. SE Ariz., SW New Mex. Z7.

P. sapphirina Hook. f. & Thoms. Lvs 0.5–1cm, oblanceolate to obovate, white-hairy above, dentate; petiole short, broad. Peduncle to 5cm; fls 1–4, nodding; cor. to 0.5×0.6cm, violet-purple to blue, lobes ovate, emarginate. E Himal.

P. saxatilis Komar. Lvs 6–20cm, oblong to ovate-oblong, shallowly dissected into irregular, rounded, entire or dentate lobes, crisped, with long hairs, base cordate; petiole narrowly winged. Peduncles to 30cm; infl. 3–15-fld; cor. rose-lilac, to 2.5cm diam., eye white, lobes obovate, emarginate. Summer. NE Asia. Z4.

P. scandinavica Bruun. Lvs 2–3cm, narrowly obovate to spathulate, apex rounded, denticulate to subentire, white-farinose beneath; petiole winged. Peduncle 4–10(–18)cm; umbel 2–10-fld, cal. dark-tinged, gland.; cor. 0.9–1.5cm, purple-violet, eye yellow, lobes obovate, emarginate. Norway, W Sweden.

P. scapigera Craib. Lvs to 15cm, oblong to spathulate, to elliptic or obovate, dentate or lobulate, apex obtuse, base narrowed to petiole. Peduncle to 4cm, elongating later; infl. few-fld; cor. pink to purple, to 3cm diam., yellow eye bordered white, lobes

broad-obovate, toothed. Spring. W Himal. Z5.

P. scotica Hook. Lvs 1–5cm, elliptic, oblong or spathulate, entire or crenulate-denticulate, thickly farinose beneath. Peduncles 0.5–6cm; infl. 1- to 6-fld; cor. 5–8mm diam., dark purple with yellow throat, rarely white, lobes obcordate, notched. Spring–autumn. N Scotland. Z4.

P. secundiflora Franch. Lvs 25–30cm, oblong to obovate or oblanceolate, crenae to serrate, farinose beneath when young, base narrowed to short petiole. Peduncle 30–60cm, farinose above. Infl. 10–20-fld, secund; cor. red-purple or deep rose-red, 1.5–2.5cm diam., pendent, lobes obovate to oblong, rounded. Summer. W China. Z6.

P. serratifolia Franch. Lvs to 20cm, oblong-ovate to obovate, apex rounded, base attenuate to petiole, coarsely and irregularly dentate. Peduncle to 45cm; umbels 1 or 2, 5–10-fld.; cor. to 2.5cm diam., yellow, with streaks of orange, lobes obovate, entire or emarginate. W China, N Burm.

P. sibirica Jacq. = *P. nutans*.

P. sibthorpii Koch non Hoffssg. = *P. vulgaris*.

P. sibthorpii Hoffssg. non Koch = *P. vulgaris* ssp. *sibthorpii*.

P. sieboldii E. Morr. Lvs 10–40cm, ovate to oblong including petiole, with numerous dentate lobes, base cordate. Peduncle 30cm; infl. 6–10-fld; cor. white, pink or purple, 2.5–3cm diam., eye white, lobes broad-obcordate, cleft. Early summer. Jap., NE Asia. 'Alba': fls white, pet. entire. 'Fimbriated Red': fls bright cerise, pet. deeply cut and notched. 'Istaka': fls white edged and backed purple-pink, deeply fimbriate. 'Kuisakigarri': fls white, v. finely cut, resembling a snowflake. 'Musashino': fls large, pale rose above, darker beneath. 'Shi-un': fls finely fimbriate, red-lavender fading to lavender blue. 'Snowflake': fls scarcely cut, wide-petalled, snow white. 'Sumina': fls deep wisteria blue, pet. slender-clawed and retuse. 'Yubisugata': fls broad, jaggedly cut, undersurface white, upper surface lavender with a white spot.' Z5.

P. sikkimensis Hook. f. Lvs 10–40cm, elliptic or oblong to oblanceolate, shining, serrate or dentate, base tapering to winged petiole. Peduncle 15–90cm; infl. many-fld, sometimes superposed; cal. yellow-farinose; cor. yellow or cream-white, to 2.5cm diam., pendent, funnel-shaped, lobes oblong to obcordate, entire or emarginate. Early summer. W Nepal to SW China. 'Tilman no. 2': 45–60cm; fls rich yellow, strongly scented. var. *pudibunda* (Balf. f. & Cooper) W.W. Sm. & Fletcher. A high altitude extreme; in cultivate indistinguishable from the type. var. *hopeana* (Balf. f. & Cooper) W.W. Sm. & Fletcher. Plants smaller. Fls white or pale yellow becoming white. Bhutan, Tibet. Z6.

P. sinensis Sab. ex Lindl. Softly pubesc. Lvs 7.5–10cm, broad-ovate to orbicular, with 4–5 pairs of dentate lobes, often red beneath, base cordate; petiole to 18cm. Peduncle 10–15cm; infl. or 1 or more 6–10-fld whorls; cor. in many colours, usually purple to pink, 2–5cm diam., eye yellow, lobes obovate, entire or incised. Winter–spring. China. 'Filicifolia': lvs crisped. 'Fimbriata': fls fringed or crested. 'Stellata': fls in superposed umbels. Z8.

P. sinopurpurea Balf. f. Lvs to 5–35cm, oblong-lanceolate, serrate, yellow-farinose beneath, base narrowed to winged petiole. Peduncle 30–45cm, farinose above; fls 6–12, nodding; cal. purple; cor. violet, to 3cm diam., eye pale, lobes round, overlapping. Summer. China. Z5.

P. smithiana Craib. = *P. prolifera*.

P. soldanelloides Watt. Minute, mat-forming. Lvs 0.8–1.5cm, pinnateliy lobed, tapering to long petiole. Peduncle 2.5–4cm; fls solitary, nodding, cal. black-green, deeply incised; cor. 1–1.5cm lonb, white, campanulate, lobes oblong-ovate, emarginate or dentatge. E Himal.

P. sonchifolia Franch. Lvs to 20cm, oblong to obovate, serrate, lobulate, apex obtuse, base narrowed to short, winged petiole. Peduncle elongating to 30cm in fr.; infl. 3–20-fld; cor. blue to purple, to 2.5cm diam., eye yellow, edged white, lobes obovate to suborbicular, entire or toothed. Early spring. W China. Z6.

P. spectabilis Tratt. Lvs 1.5–10cm, broad oval-rhomboid to obovate to oblong, shining, punctate above. Peduncle 2–15cm; 2–5-fld; cal. stained purple; cor. 2–4cm diam., pink-red to lilac, lobes obovate, emarginate, gland. beneath. Early summer. It. Alps. Z6.

P. specuicola Rydb. Lvs 4–13cm, spathulate, sinuate-dentate, crisped, white-farinose beneath, narrowing to short petiole. Peduncles 10–16cm, infl. 2–10-fld; cor. violet, to 1cm diam., eye yellow, tube yellow. Spring. SE US. Z7.

P. ×steinii Obrist. = *P. forsteri* f. *steinii*.

P. strumosa Balf. f. & Cooper = *P. calderiana* ssp. *strumosa*.

P. stuartii var. *purpurea* (Royle) Watt = *P. macrophylla*.

P. suffrutescens A. Gray. Gland. throughout. Rhiz. and st. long, branching, woody. Lvs 1.5–3cm, cuneate to spathulate, fleshy, crenate to dentate or serrate above, pale beneath, tapering to a short, winged petiole. Peduncles 3–13cm; infl. 2–10-fld; cor.

rose pink to red or purple, to 2cm diam., eye and tube yellow, lobes obovate, emarginate. Spring. Calif. Z8.

P. takedana Tatew. Lvs 8–16cm, orbicular to reniform, cordate at base, 5–7-lobed, dentate, hairy, petiole long. Peduncle 8–15cm; umbels 1(–2), 2–3-fld.; pedicels long; cor. to 1.5cm diam., white, campanulate to funnel-shaped, lobes obovate-oblong. Jap.

P. tanneri King ssp. **tsariensis** (W.W. Sm.) A. Richards. Lvs 8–13cm, elliptic to ovate-lanceolate, crenate, apex obtuse, base cuneate, rounded or subcordate. Peduncle to 15cm; infl. 1–8-fld; cor. blue to purple, to 3cm diam., eye yellow, lobes broad-ovate, emarginate. Spring. SE Tibet.

P. tibetica Watt. Lvs 1–5cm, ovate, elliptic or spathulate, entire, fleshy, base tapering to winged petiole. Peduncles 3–15cm; infl. 1–10-fld; cor. pink, 5–10mm diam., eye yellow, lobes obcordate, deeply notched. Mid summer. Tibet, Nepal, Sikkim. Z6.

P. tsariensis W.W. Sm. = *P. tanneri* ssp. *tsariensis*.

P. tschuktschorum Kjellmann. Lvs lanceolate to spathulate, 3–8cm, dentate or entire, base tapering to winged petiole. Peduncles to 20cm; infl. usually 3–5-fld, cal. sometimes black, white-farinose within; cor. pink, to 2cm diam., lobes entire, subspathulate. Summer. N Asia, Alask. Z5.

P. tyrolensis Schott. Lvs 1–3cm, suborbicular to broadly obovate, finely dentate, ciliate, fleshy, with pale gland. hairs, withered lvs persistent. Peduncle 0.5–2cm; infl. 1–2-fld; cor. rose, 1–2.5cm diam., lobes obovate, emarginate. Summer. S Tyrol. Z5.

P. uralensis Fisch. = *P. veris*.

P. ×variabilis Goupil. (*P. veris* ×*P. vulgaris*.) V. variable, intermediate between parents.

P. veitchii Duthie = *P. polyneura*.

P. ×venusta Host. (*P. auricula* ×*P. carniolica*.) Fls red with white, centre, to rose, to crimson, to purple or brown. Otherwise v. variable. Z6.

P. veris L. COWSLIP. Lvs 5–20cm at fl., ovate to oblong-ovate, crenate to erose-crenate, or entire, apex rounded, base narrowing abruptly to winged petiole, subglabrous to white-tomentose beneath. Peduncle 6–30cm, pubesc.; infl. 2–16-fld, fragrant; cor. yellow, 1–1.5cm diam., orange mark at base of each lobe, lobes obcordate. Late spring–early summer. Eur., W Asia. ssp. *canescens* (Opiz) Hayek. Lvs grey-tomentose. Cor. 0.8–2cm diam. SC Eur., S Fr., N Spain. ssp. *columnae* (Ten.) Ludi. Lvs ovate, cordate at base, white-tomentose beneath. Cor. 1–2.2cm diam., flat. S Eur., N Turk. ssp. *macrocalyx* (Bunge) Ludi. Lvs elliptic, often hairless. Cal. 1.5–2cm, v. hairy; cor. 1.8–2.8cm diam. SE Russia, N Asia, E Turk. Z5.

P. verticillata Forssk. Lvs 10–30cm, lanceolate to ovate-lanceolate, acute, sharp-serrulate, white-farinose beneath, petiole short, broad-winged. Peduncle 10–60cm; infl. of 2–4 many-fld whorls; cor. to 2cm diam., yellow, fragrant, lobes broad-ovate, emarginate. SW Arabian Penins., NE Afr.

P. vialii Delav. ex Franch. Lvs 10–30cm, broad-lanceolate to oblong, pubesc., dnetate, base tapering to winged petiole. Peduncle stout, 30–40cm, farinose above; spikes dense, narrowly conical; cal., red in bud, later pink; cor. blue to violet, to 1cm diam., deflexed, lobes ovate. Summer. China. Z7.

P. villosa Wulf. Lvs 2–15cm, obovate or spathulate to oblong, dentate, entire, fleshy, glandular-pubesc., producing red to brown secretion. Peduncle 2–15cm, red-glandular-pubesc.; infl. 4–12-fld; cor. pink to lilac, to 2.5cm diam., centre white, lobes obovate, emarginate. Early summer. Tyrol, Switz. Z5.

P. viscosa Vill. non All. = *P. hirsuta*.

P. viscosa All. non Vill. = *P. latifolia*.

P. vittata Franch. = *P. secundiflora*.

P. ×vochinensis Gusmus. (*P. minima* ×*P. wulfeniana*.) Wide range of forms, all small, 1–2-fld. Those resembling *P. wulfeniana* with brilliantly coloured fls. E Dolomites. Z6.

P. vulgaris Huds. PRIMROSE. Lvs 5–25cm, obovate or oblanceolate, dentate to crenate, often erose, pubesc. beneath, base tapering to short, winged petiole. Peduncle 0; infl. to 25-fld, sometimes fragrant; pedicels 6–20cm; cor. pale yellow, 2.5–4cm diam., lobes ovate, emarginate, base orange. Spring. W & S Eur. ssp. *balearica* (Willk.) W.W. Sm. & Forr. Fls white, v. fragrant. ssp. *sibthorpii* (Hoffsgg.) W.W. Sm. & Forr. Fls usually red or purple. E Balk. Penins. Cvs include forms with single, double or hose-in-hose fls, in a wide range of colours. 'Jack in the Green': abnormality with cal. leafy. Z6.

P. waltonii G. Watt ex Balf. f. Lvs 8–30cm, elliptic-oblong to oblanceolate, toothed, base cuneate, petiole winged. Peduncle to 60cm; infl. few to many-fld; bracts tinged purple, farinose; cal. tinged purple, farinose; cor. pink to deep wine-purple, to 2cm diam., pendent, funnel-shaped, with farinose bands. Early summer. SE Tibet, Bhutan. Z6.

P. warshenewskiana B. Fedtsch. Lvs 1.5–7cm, oblong to oblanceolate, apex obtuse, base attentuate to short winged petiole, denticulate. Peduncle short; umbel 1–8-fld; cor. to 1.2cm diam., bright rose or pink, with yellow eye surrounded by narrow white zone, lobes obcordate, deeply emarginate. C Asia to N Himal.

P. wettsteinii Wiem. = *P. ×intermedia*.

P. whitei W.E. Sm. Lvs 2–10cm in fl., spathulate to oblong-spathulate, denticulate, slightly farinose, base tapering to winged petiole. Peduncle short; infl. 5–10-fld; cal. lobes fringed; cor. blue to violet, to 2.5cm diam., eye white or yellow-green, lobes obovate, toothed. Spring. E Himal. *P. bhutanica* Fletcher (*P. whitei* 'Sheriff's Variety') with more conspicuously dentate cor. is a form of *P. whitei*. 'Arduaine': vigorous, sterile; lvs narrow, serrate; fls ice-blue, with pale yellow eye. Z6.

P. wilsonii Dunn. Lvs to 20cm, oblanceolate, denticulate, glaucous, base narrowing to winged petiole. Peduncle to 70cm; infl. of 3–6, whorls; cor. purple, to 2cm diam., concave, lobes round, entire to emarginate. Summer. China.

P. winteri Will. Watts. = *P. edgeworthii*.

P. wollastonii Balf. Lvs 2.5–5cm, oblanceolate to obovate, dentate, crenate or subentire, pubesc., sometimes farinose beneath, tapering to short, winged petiole. Peduncle 12–20cm; infl. 2–6-fld; cal. purple or green; cor. light or dark purple, or blue, to 2.5cm diam., bell-shaped, fragrant, tube farinose. Spring. C to E Nepal, Tibet. Z6.

P. wulfeniana Schott. Lvs 1.5–4cm, lanceolate or elliptic to oblanceolate to obovate, coriaceous, entire, glandular-pubesc. Peduncle 0.5–7cm; infl. 1–2-fld; cor. rose-red to lilac, to 2.5cm diam., lobes obovate, deeply cleft. Spring. Austrian Alps to S Carpath. Z5.

P. yuparensis Tak. Lvs 1.5–3cm, oblanceolate to elliptic, narrowing to short, winged petiole, sparsely white-farinose beneath when young, finely denticulate. Peduncle 4.5–6cm; fls 2–3 in umbel; cor. to 1.5cm diam., purple, lobes obcordate, emarginate. Jap. Z6.

PRIMULACEAE Vent. 22/800. *Anagallis, Androsace, Ardisiandra, Coris, Cortusa, Cyclamen, Dionysia, Dodecatheon, Douglasia, Hottonia, Lysimachia, Omphalogramma, Primula, Samolus, Soldanella, Sredinskya, Trientalis, Vitaliana.*

Prince Albert's Yew *Saxegothaea conspicua.*
Prince of Wales Heath *Erica perspicua.*
Prince of Wales Fern *Leptopteris superba.*
Prince of Wales Plume *Leptopteris superba.*
Prince Rupprecht Larch *Larix principis-rupprechtii.*
Prince's Feather *Amaranthus cruentus; Polygonum orientale.*
Prince's Pea *Psophocarpus tetragonolobus.*
Prince's Pine *Chimaphila.*
Prince's Plume *Stanleya.*
Princess Feather *Polygonum orientale.*
Princess Flower *Tibouchina.*
Princess Palm *Dictyosperma.*
Princess Pea *Psophocarpus tetragonolobus.*
Princess Pine *Crassula muscosa; Lycopodium obscurum.*
Princess Tree *Paulownia tomentosa.*
Princess Vine *Cissus sicyoides.*
Prince Wood *Hamelia ventricosa.*

Prinos L.
P. ambiguus Michx. = *Ilex ambigua.*
P. dubia G. Don = *Ilex amelanchier.*
P. lucidus Ait. = *Ilex coriacea.*
P. glaber L. = *Ilex glabra.*
P. laevigatus Pursh. = *Ilex laevigata.*
P. verticillatus L. = *Ilex verticillata.*

Prinsepia Royle. Rosaceae. 3–4 spreading, decid. spiny shrubs. Bark grey-brown peeling, spines to 1cm. Fls in short, axill. rac.; pet. 5, rounded, spreading; sta. 10–30. Fr. an ellipsoid, cherry-like, red-purple drupe, 1.5cm diam. Himal. to N China and Taiwan.

P. sinensis (Oliv.) Oliv. To 2m+. Lvs to 8×1.3cm, ovate-lanceolate to lanceolate, acuminate, bright green, fine-ciliate, entire or serrulate. Fls bright yellow, 1.5cm diam., clustered. Spring. Manch. Z4.

P. uniflora Batal. To 1.5m. Lvs to 6×0.8cm, linear-oblong to narrow-oblong, somewhat acute or rounded, dark above, lighter beneath, glab., entire or serrulate. Fls white, 1.5cm diam., solitary or clustered. Spring. NW China. Z5.
→*Plagiospermum.*

Prionopsis Nutt. Compositae. 1 erect, ann. or bienn. herb, to 1.5m. Lvs alt., to 8cm, ovate, serrate-ciliate, sessile. Cap. radiate, to 4cm diam., solitary or few in a loose cyme; ray flts yellow; disc flts yellow. Tex., New Mex. Z9.

P. ciliata (Nutt.) Nutt.
→*Donia* and *Haplopappus.*

Prionotes R. Br. Epacridaceae. 1 small, epiphytic, scandent shrub. Br. intertwining. Lvs to 2cm, elliptic or oblong, dark green, thick, minutely callose-serrate. Fls solitary, pendulous on slender pedicels, cor. rose pink to scarlet; to 2.5cm, inflated-tubular, constricted at throat. Summer. Tasm. Z9.
P. cerinthoides R. Br. CLIMBING HEATH.

Pritchardia Seem. & H.A. Wendl. LOULU PALMS. Palmae. 37 palms to *c*20m. St. solitary, erect, ringed. Lvs costapalmate, blade divided to half radius into seg., seg. single-fold, shallowly divided at apex, rigid and held in one plane along rachis, or pendent. Infl. interfoliar, branched ×3; fls cream to orange. Fr. to 2cm, ripening black. Fiji, Hawaii, Pacific Is. Z10.
P. pacifica Seem. & H.A. Wendl. FIJI FAN PALM. Trunk to 10m×30cm. Petioles exceed 1m; lf blades 1m diam., seg. *c*90, acuminate, rigid. Tonga, introd. to Fiji before Eur. colonization.

Pritzelago Kuntze. Cruciferae. 1 tufted, perenn. herb, to 10cm. Lvs pinnately cut, lobes to 2.5cm, entire, hairy or glab. Flowering st. straight usually leafless. Fls v. small, 4-merous, white. Spring–summer. C & S Eur. (mts). Z7.
P. alpina (L.) Kuntze. CHAMOIS CRESS. As above. ssp. *auerswaldii* (Willk.) Greuter & Burdet. To 15cm. Flowering st. flexuous, leafy. ssp. *brevicaulis* (Spreng.) Greuter & Burdet. To 5cm.
→*Lepidium* and *Noccaea.*

Privet *Ligustrum.*

Proboscidea Keller in Schmidel. UNICORN PLANT; DEVIL'S-CLAW; ELEPHANT-TUSK; PROBOSCIS FLOWER. Pedaliaceae. 9 ann. or perenn. herbs, viscid-pubesc. or gland. Infl. terminal, open, lax; cal. 'spathe-like' 4–5-dentate; cor. funnelform-campanulate, lobes 5, spreading. Fr. a 2-valved capsule, with prominent incurved horns, sculpted. S Amer. N to C US. Z10.
P. arenaria (Engelm.) Decne. SAND DEVIL'S CLAW. St. spreading, 30–50cm. Lvs 3–6cm, suborbicular to reniform, lobed. Fls. 3–4cm diam., yellow or copper, often with purple spots. Fr. body 5–6cm, horns 10–12cm, crested both sides. S US to Mex.
P. fragrans (Lindl.) Decne. SWEET UNICORN PLANT. Similar to *P. louisianica* except lvs 5-lobed; fls fragrant violet- to red-purple, upper lobes often blotched with darker purple, lower lobe with bright yellow band. Mex.
P. jussieui Keller in Schmidel = *P. louisianica.*
P. louisiana Wooton & Standl. = *P. louisianica.*
P. louisianica (Mill.) Thell. COMMON UNICORN PLANT; COMMON DEVIL'S CLAW; RAM'S HORN. Ann., glandular-viscid 30–100cm, prostrate or ascending. Lvs 6–20cm, ovate to suborbicular, cordate, entire to sinuate. Fls. 3.5–5cm, white to cream to purple, throat yellow, blotched or flecked rose-purple. Fr. body 4–6cm, crested on upper side, horns 1–3× length of body. S US to Mex.; nat. Aus.
P. lutea Stapf. = *Ibicella lutea.*
P. petiolaris hort. A listed name of no botanical standing.
→*Martynia.*

Proboscis Flower *Ibicella; Martynia; Proboscidea.*
Procumbent Yellow Sorrel *Oxalis corniculata.*

Proiphys Herb. Amaryllidaceae. 3 perenn. bulbous herbs. Infl. scapose, umbellate; spathes 2–4; perianth funnel-shaped, white, lobes 6, elliptic to obovate, apiculate, spreading; sta. 6, inserted at throat of perianth tube, fil. united and expanded below into a distinct corona. NE Aus. Z10.
P. alba (R. Br.) Mabb. Lvs 10–35cm, elliptic to ovate, base cuneate; petiole 7–35cm. Scape to 60cm; umbel 10–30-fld; perianth tube 8–15mm, lobes 6–24mm. Queensld.
P. amboinensis (L.) Herb. Lvs 20–30cm, reniform or broadly ovate, base cordate, undulate; petiole 15–60cm. Scape 15–90cm; umbel 5–25-fld; perianth tube 2.5–3cm, lobes 2.5–4cm. W Aus.
P. cunninghamii (Ait. ex Lindl.) Mabb. BRISBANE LILY. Lvs 10–25cm, ovate, base rounded; petiole 10–25cm. Scape 25–80cm; umbel 5–12-fld; perianth tube 8–12mm, lobes 15–18mm. SE Queensld, NSW.
→*Eurycles* and *Pancratium.*

Promenaea Lindl. Orchidaceae. 15 diminutive epiphytic orchids. Pbs small, clustered, ovoid, compressed. Lvs ovate-lanceolate, short-petioled, veined, sea-green. Rac. 3-10cm, basal, 1–2-fld; fls rounded, fleshy; tep. ovate-lanceolate; lip triblobed, lat. lobes erect, midlobe obovate. Braz. Z10.
P. citrina D. Don. = *P. xanthina.*
P. rollissonii (Lindl.) Lindl. Pbs to 2.5cm. Lvs to 9×2.5cm, thin. Fls to 4.5cm diam., pale yellow, lip yellow spotted red-purple, column yellow-green unspotted. Braz.

P. stapelioides (Lindl.) Lindl. Pbs to 2.5cm. Lvs 3–10×0.75–2.5cm. Fls to 5cm diam.; tep. cream to buff with broken, concentric bands of maroon, lip dark purple. Braz.
P. xanthina (Lindl.) Lindl. Pbs to 2cm. Lvs 2.5–7×0.75–1.5cm. Fls to 5cm diam., strongly fragrant, long-lived; tep. yellow lip yellow spotted brick red, column spotted red. Braz.
→*Maxillaria.*

Pronephrium Presl. Thelypteridaceae. 65 terrestrial rupestral ferns. Rhiz. creeping. Lamina uniform or dimorphous, pinnate or simple. India & Ceylon, S China to Queensld, E to Fiji. Z10.
P. asperum (Presl) Holtt. Rhiz. short-creeping. Stipes to 70cm, glab. Lamina simply pinnate, 60cm+, glab. to short-pubesc., pinnae to 35×6cm, 6–16 lat. and 1 term., sessile, elliptic to oblong crenate or slightly toothed. Philipp. & Malay Penins. S to Queensld.
P. triphyllum (Sw.) Holtt. Rhiz. long-creeping. Rhiz. long-creeping. Stipes to 20cm, scaly at base. Lamina pinnately trifoliate, to 25cm, pinnae to 10×3cm, 2 lateral and 1 term., stalked lanceolate or oblong, sinuate, entire. India & Ceylon & SE Asia to Jap. & Queensld.
→*Meniscium* and *Thelypteris.*

Propeller Banksia *Banksia candolleana.*
Propeller Plant *Crassula cultrata* (*C. perfoliata* var. *falcata*).
Prophet Flower *Arnebia pulchra.*

Proserpinaca L. MERMAID WEED. Haloragidaceae. 5 aquatic herbs. St. creeping. Lvs uniform or dimorphic with submerged lvs pinnatifid; emersed lvs serrate to pinnatifid. Fl. minute, solitary or clustered, white to green. N & C Amer., W Indies. Z10.
P. palustris L. St. to 1m. Submerged lvs to 6cm, seg. 8–14, to 3cm, linear-filiform, emersed lvs to 8.5×1.5cm, lanceolate to oblanceolate, entire to serrate. N & C Amer., W Indies.
P. pectinata Lam. St. to 40cm. Lvs uniform, to 3cm, pectinate or pinnatifid, seg. linear to filiform, entire to serrate. N & C Amer., W Indies.

Prosopis L. MESQUITE. Leguminosae (Mimosoideae). 44 usually spiny trees, shrubs and subshrubs. Lvs bipinnate. Fls in axill., spike-like rac., usually green-white to yellow; cal. campanulate; pet. linear, mostly connate; sta. 10, slender, showy. Fr. a loment. Warm Amer., SW Asia, Afr. Z10.
P. alba Griseb. Tree to 15m. Branchlets pendulous; spines few, to 4cm. Petiole to 8cm; pinnae to 14cm; lfts to 1.7cm, 25–50 pairs, linear. Rac. to 11cm. Fr. to 25×2cm, yellow. Subtrop. Arg. to Peru.
P. atacamensis Philippi = *P. alba.*
P. chilensis auct. non (Molina) Stuntz = *P. glandulosa.*
P. chilensis var. *glandulosa* (Torr.) Standl. = *P. glandulosa.*
P. glandulosa Torr. HONEY MESQUITE. Shrub or tree to 9m; spines to 4.5cm. Petiole to 15cm; pinnae to 17cm; lfts to 6.5cm, 6–17 pairs, linear or oblong. Rac. to 14cm. Fr. to 20×1.3cm, yellow or violet-tinged. SW US, Mex.
P. horrida Kunth = *P. juliiflora* var. *horrida.*
P. juliiflora (Sw.) DC. Tree to 12m, occas. shrub-like spreading; spines to 5cm, sometimes 0. Petiole to 7.5cm; pinnae to 11cm; lfts 2.3cm, 6–29, elliptic-oblong. Rac. to 15cm. Fr. to 30×1.7cm, yellow to brown. N S Amer., C Amer. var. *horrida* (Kunth) Burkart. To 8m; spines to 7.5cm. Petiole to 7cm; pinnae to 10cm; lfts 1.5cm, 10–15 pairs per pinna, elliptic, ovate to oblong, pubesc. Rac. to 12cm. Fr. to 24cm×12mm, brown. Peru. var. *inermis* (HBK) Burkart. Spines 0. Lfts finely pubesc. Ecuad.
P. juliiflora var. *constricta* Sarg. = *P. glandulosa.*
P. juliiflora var. *glandulosa* (Torr.) Cockerell = *P. glandulosa.*
P. odorata Torr. = *P. pubescens.*
P. pubescens Benth. SCREWBEAN. Shrub or tree to 10m. Spines to 8cm. Lfts to 12×4mm, 5–9 pairs per pinna, elliptic-oblong, subacute. Fls pubesc. yellow. Fr. to 5.5×0.6cm, puberulous or glabrescent, yellow. SW US, NW Mex.
P. siliquastrum var. *longisiliqua* Philippi = *P. alba.*
→*Algarobia, Mimosa, Neltuma* and *Strombocarpa.*

Prosopostelma Baill.
P. aculeatum Descoings = *Folotsia aculeatum.*
P. grandiflorum Choux = *Folotsia floribundum.*

Prostanthera Labill. AUSTRALIAN MINT BUSH. Labiatae. 50 everg. shrubs or small trees, viscid, aromatic. Fls in leafy rac. or term. pan.; cal. bilabiate, 10-nerved; cor. bilabiate, tube short, upper lip 2-lobed, erect, hooded, lower lip 3-lobed, patent, middle lobe largest. SE Aus., Tasm. Z9.
P. baxteri A.M. Cunn. ex Benth. Erect shrub to 2m. Lvs 1–2cm,

linear, terete, silver-pubesc. Fls large, axill. lavender, densely pubesc.

P. cuneata Benth. Dense shrub, to 1m. Lvs to 0.6cm, ovate to orbicular, shiny-green, evolute, v. fragrant when crushed. Fls numerous, term. in leafy rac., white with purple or violet blotches in throat. Summer. SE Aus., Tasm.

P. denticulata R. Br. Shrub, prostrate or erect to 1m. Lvs to 2cm, shiny green, setose, toothed. Fls mauve-violet in distant pairs forming interrupted terminal rac. Summer. E Aus.

P. empetrifolia Sieb. ex Spreng. = *P. scutellarioides*.

P. lasianthos Labill. VICTORIA DOGWOOD; VICTORIA CHRISTMAS BUSH. Woody, to 8m. Lvs 5–8cm, lanceolate, serrate. Fls fragrant, in short rac. forming term. pan. to 15cm pubesc., white or cream, rarely tinted violet or lilac, spotted brown or yellow in throat. Summer. SE Aus., Tasm.

P. linearis R. Br. Erect shrub to 3m. Lvs to 2.5cm, linear, somewhat revolute. Fls in leafy term. rac., white to mauve, pubesc., throat sometimes spotted brown. SE Aus.

P. melissifolia F. Muell. BALM MINT BUSH. Slender shrub to 2m. Lvs 2.5cm, ovate-elliptic, dentate, rarely entire, highly aromatic. Fls in term. rac., mauve, purple or pink. SE Aus.

P. nivea A.M. Cunn. ex Benth. Tall bushy shrub to 3m. Lvs to 4cm, linear, revolute. Fls solitary in axils forming leafy rac. to 15cm, snow-white or tinted blue. Spring. SE Aus., Tasm.

P. ovalifolia R. Br. Erect shrub, to 4m. Lvs to 1.5cm, oval to ovate-lanceolate glaucous. Fls numerous in short term. rac., purple, mauve or white tinted lilac. E Aus.

P. rotundifolia R. Br. MINT BUSH. Shrub to 3m. Lvs orbicular to ovate, obscurely dentate or crenate, dark green above. Fls in short, loose, rac., violet or lilac. Spring. SE & S Aus. 'Chelsea Pink': lvs aromatic, grey-green, cuneate at base; fls pale rose, anth. mauve.

P. scutellarioides (R. Br.) Briq. Spreading, divaricate shrub, 60–100cm. Lvs to 1.5cm, linear, short-setose, revolute. Fls solitary, axill., violet or mauve. Autumn. E. Aus.

P. sieberi Benth. Shrub, spreading or erect to 2m. Lvs to 2.5cm, ovate to oblong, dentate, strongly aromatic. Fls 4–8 in short, term. rac., pale mauve to violet. Spring. SE Aus.

P. striatiflora F. Muell. Erect to 2m. Lvs 1.5–2.5cm, rigid, lanceolate to linear-lanceolate. Fls axill., crowded in a leafy term. rac., cream streaked crimson.

P. violacea R. Br. Slender shrub, to 2m. Shoots rough, pubesc. Lvs to 0.5cm, ovate to orbicular, crenate, slightly revolute. Fls 4–6, in small racemose heads, violet or lavender. Spring. SE Aus.

Prostrate Blue Violet *Viola walteri*.
Prostrate Coleus *Plectranthus oertendahlii*.
Prostrate Southern Violet *Viola walteri*.
Prostrate Speedwell *Veronica prostrata*.

Protea L. Proteaceae. 115 shrubs or small trees. Br. erect or prostrate. Lvs tough, coriaceous. Infl. term., usually solitary, subtended by coloured involucral bracts; fls perianth seg. 4, tubular in bud, packed in a cone-like or flat head. Afr. (mostly S Afr.). Z9.

P. aurea (Burm.) Rourke. Shrub to 5m. Lvs to 4cm, ovate to oblong, glabrescent. Infl. to 12cm, cylindric in bud, obconical when open; inner bracts to 9cm, cream with green tinged to crimson, margins pubesc. Spring–summer. S Afr. (Cape Prov.).

P. burchellii Stapf. St. subterranean, branched, rising slightly above ground. Lvs 15–22cm, linear-oblanceolate, glossy, glab. or minutely pubesc. near base. Infl. subglobose, to 6.5cm; bracts ovate to oblong, obtuse or subobtuse, dark chestnut-brown, glabrescent. Spring–summer. S Afr.

P. compacta R. Br. Erect shrub to 3.5m. Lvs 5–13cm, oblong to elliptic, glabrescent, margins horny. Infl. oblong to obovoid 7–10cm diam.; bracts 8-seriate, inner to 10cm, narrowly oblong, longer than outer, bright pink or white, ciliate. Spring–summer. S Afr. (Cape Prov.).

P. cynaroides (L.) L. KING PROTEA. Shrub to 2m. Lvs 8–14cm, orbicular to elliptic, glab. Infl. 12–30cm, goblet-shaped resembling globe artichoke; bracts to 12cm, 12–13-seriate, lanceolate, deep crimson to pink or cream, silky. Late spring–summer. S Afr. (Cape Prov.).

P. eximia (Knight) Fourc. Shrub or small tree to 5m, erect. Lvs 6–10cm, ovate, cordate at base, glaucous to green tinged purple, glab. Infl. oblong to obconic, to 14cm; bracts 4–10cm, in 2 series, ciliate, spathulate, pink tinted red. Spring–summer. S Afr. (Cape Prov.).

P. grandiceps Tratt. Shrub to 2m. Lvs 8–13cm, erect, ovate to obovate, sometimes somewhat cordate at base often with red, ciliate margins. Infl. oblong to goblet-shaped, to 14cm; bracts to 8cm, 8-seriate, spathulate, coral pink (greenin poor light), tips incurved with white or purple hairs. Summer. S Afr. (Cape Prov.).

P. lacticolor Salisb. Shrub or small tree to 6m. Lvs 7–11cm, lanceolate, blue-green. Infl. oblong, to 8cm; bracts to 5cm, incurved, ivory, cream or rich pink, pubesc., margins pilose. Spring–summer. S Afr. (Cape Prov.).

P. longiflora Lam. = *P. aurea*.

P. magnifica Link. Small shrub, villous. Lvs to 10cm, oblong or lanceolate, narrowed or subcordate at base, undulate, sub-glaucous, hairy on margins. Infl. turbinate-obovoid, to 15cm; bracts in 7–8 series, creamy pubesc. to tomentose, ovate-lanceolate to linear-lanceolate white-ciliate. Spring–summer. S Afr. (Cape Prov.).

P. minor Compton = *P. pudens*.

P. mundi Klotzsch in Otto & Dietr. Small shrub. Lvs 4–10.5cm, lanceolate or elliptic-lanceolate, sometimes loosely pilose when young. Infl. 7.5cm; bracts 11–12 seriate, outer ovate, green, ciliate, pubesc., inner oblong or oblong-spathulate, white-pubesc. to tomentose, white-ciliate. Spring–summer. S Afr.

P. nana (Bergius) Thunb. MOUNTAIN ROSE. Small compact shrub, 60–120cm. Lvs to 2.5cm, linear, mucronate soft, occas. flushed red. Infl. pendulous, cupulate, 4cm diam.; bracts 2.5cm, smooth, brilliant rose to crimson, to wine or mahogany, buff in centre, occas. tinged green; fls crowded in cone red, hirsute. Late spring. S Afr.

P. neriifolia R. Br. Shrub to 3m, erect. Lvs 10–18cm, narrowly oblong, glabrescent. Infl. goblet-shaped, to 13cm; bracts 14cm, oblong to spathulate, incurved, pink to dark rose, apex densely black-hirsute. Spring–summer. S Afr. (Cape Prov.).

P. obtusifolia Meissn. Shrub or small tree to 4m. Lvs 10–15cm, oblanceolate to elliptic, glabrescent. Infl. goblet-shaped bracts to 10cm, deep pink to creamy green, margins fringed. Spring–summer. S Afr. (Cape Prov.).

P. pudens Rourke. GROUND ROSE. Procumbent, to 40cm. Lvs 6–10cm, crowded, linear, grey-green. Infl. resting on ground, campanulate, 5–8cm; bracts red-brown to deep dusky rose; fls white, hairy, with purple-black awns. Winter. S Afr.

P. repens (L.) L. Shrub or small tree to 4m. Lvs 5–15cm, erect, linear to lanceolate, glab. Infl. to 6cm, goblet-shaped, to 9cm diam.; bracts to 11cm, creamy white, sometimes tinged dark red or pink, glab., resinous. Spring–summer. S Afr. (Cape Prov.).

P. scolymocephala (L.) Reichard. Shrub to 1.5m. Lvs 3.5–9cm, linear to spathulate. Infl. bowl-shaped, to 4.5cm diam.; bracts to 2.5cm, concave at apex, creamy green, pink at apex, ciliate. Late spring–summer. S Afr. (Cape Prov.).

P. susannae Phillips. Shrub to 4m. Lvs 8–16cm, oblong, glabrescent, margins horny. Infl. goblet-shaped, to 10cm; bracts to 8cm, spathulate, concave at apex, pink tinged brown, brown-resinous. Spring–summer. S Afr. (Cape Prov.). Lvs have a sulphurous odour when bruised.

PROTEACEAE Juss. 75/1350. *Adenanthos, Agastachys, Banksia, Bellendena, Buckinghamia, Conospermum, Dryandra, Embothrium, Franklandia, Gevuina, Grevillea, Hakea, Hicksbeachia, Isopogon, Knightia, Lambertia, Leucadendron, Leucospermum, Lomatia, Macadamia, Mimetes, Oreocallis, Orites, Paranomus, Persoonia, Petrophila, Placospermum, Protea, Roupala, Serruria, Stenocarpus, Stirlingia, Synaphea, Telopea, Xylomelum.*

Protowoodsia Ching.
P. manchuriensis (Hook.) Ching = *Woodsia manchuriensis*.

Provence Broom *Cytisus purgans*.
Provence Orchid *Orchis provincialis*.
Provence Rose *Rosa ×centifolia*.
Provision Tree *Pachira aquatica*.

Prumnopitys Philippi. Podocarpaceae. 10 everg., coniferous trees. Lvs similar to those of *Taxus*, petiole often twisted to give 2-ranked effect. ♂ cones solitary or in groups, cylindric to ovoid, 1–3cm. Fr. 1–8 on a 2–4cm racemose peduncle, drupe-like, 0.8–2.5cm, with soft pulp, enlarged receptacles 0. S Amer., NZ, E Aus., New Caledonia.

P. amara Bl. Laub. = *Sundacarpus amara*.

P. andina (Poepp. ex Endl.) Laub. PLUM-FRUITED YEW. Tree to 25m or shrub; bark smooth, grey-brown tinged red. Crown dense, rounded to irregular. Lvs 10–25mm, soft, often curved or twisted, bright green above, 2 pale green stomatal bands beneath, bluntly acute. Fr. 1–4, ovoid, pale green ripening dark purple, mucronate. S Chile, SW Arg. Z8.

P. elegans Philippi = *P. andina*.

P. ferruginea (D. Don) Laub. MIRO. Tree to 25m; bark brown suffused grey, exfoliating in scales. Lvs 13–25mm, dark green above, yellow green beneath, slightly revolute, bluntly acute. Fr. solitary, ovoid-acute, bright red bloomed pink. NZ. Z9.

P. ferruginoides (Compton) Laub. Tree to 15m or more, similar to *P. ladei*. Lvs 15–20mm, leathery, blunt acute. Fr. rounded or ovoid, not acute or mucronate. New Caledonia. Z10.

P. ladei (Bail.) Laub. Tree to 30m, bark smooth, brown tinged red. Lvs 12–16mm, obtuse. Fr. solitary, ellipsoid, purple, pruinose, acute. Aus. (NE Queensld) Z10.

P. montana Willd.) Laub. Tree to 25m. Lvs 10–20mm, green above, 2 pale stomatal bands beneath acute. Fr. solitary, apiculate. N Andes. Z10.

P. spicata (R. Br. ex Mirb.) Mast. = *P. taxifolia*.

P. standleyi (Buchholz & Gray) Laub. Tree to 25m, br. pendent or spreading; twigs green to brown, tinged red. Lvs 12–25mm, glaucous beneath, acute or mucronate. C Costa Rica. Z10.

P. taxifolia (Sol. ex D. Don) Laub. MATAI. Tree to 25m. Crown rounded; br. erect to drooping. Bark blue-black or bron tinged purple. Lvs 7–15mm, dark green above, glaucous tinged bronze beneath, obtuse, or apiculate. Fr. 5–8, globose, mucronate, black, pruinose. NZ. Z9.

→*Podocarpus*.

Prunella L. SELF HEAL; HEAL ALL. Labiatae. 7 spreading, decumbent then ascending perenn. herbs. Infl. of dense spikelets or subcapitate; verticillasters 4–6-fld, subtended by leaf-like bracts; cal. tubular-campanulate, 10-nerved 2-lipped; cor. tubular, 2-lipped, upper lip erect, somewhat hooded, lower lip shorter, deflexed, 3-lobed. Eurasia, N Afr., N Amer.

P. alba Pall. ex Bieb. = *P. laciniata*.

P. grandiflora (L.) Scholler. Sparsely pubesc. to 60cm. Lvs to 10cm, ovate to ovate-lanceolate, entire or crenulate. Infl. not subtended by leafy bracts; fls 18–30mm, lips deep violet, tube off-white. Eur. ssp. **grandiflora**. Lvs cuneate at base. Infl. not more than 5cm. Eur. except Port. and SW Spain (calcicole). ssp. **pyrenaica** (Gren. & Godron) Bolós & O. Bolós. Lvs hastate. Infl. to 8cm. SW Eur. 'Alba': fls pale to white. 'Rosea': fls pink. 'Rotkäppchen' ('Red Cap'): fls carmine. 'Loveliness': fls pale lilac. 'Loveliness White': fls white. 'Loveliness Pink': fls pink. Z5.

P. hyssopifolia L. Glab. or sparsely pubesc. to 40cm. Lvs 3–8cm, linear- to elliptic-lanceolate, entire. Fls. 15–18mm, violet, rarely off-white. SW Eur. Z6.

P. laciniata (L.) L. Densely pubesc. to 30cm. Lvs to 7cm, lobed or pinnatifid. Fls to 18mm, yellow-white, rarely rose-pink or purple. SW & C Eur. Z6.

P. latifolia Brot. = *P. grandiflora*. ssp. *pyrenaica*.

P. vulgaris L. Glab. or sparingly pubesc. to 50cm. Lvs 5cm, ovate to broadly ovate, usually entire. Fls 10–15mm, upper lip sparingly pubesc., dark blue, purple, rarely white. Eur. Z3.

Prunus L. PLUM; CHERRY; PEACH; ALMOND; APRICOT. Rosaceae. 430 decid. and everg. shrubs or trees. Fls usually white, often pink to red, solitary or in clusters or rac.; cal. 5-lobed; pet. 5; sta. many. Fr. a fleshy, usually 1-seeded, pruinose drupe. N Temp. regions, S Amer.

P. acida Ehrh. = *P. cerasus* var. *caproniana*.

P. acida sensu K. Koch, non Ehrh. = *P. cerasus* var. *frutescens*.

P. acuminata Michx. = *P. maritima*.

P. 'Affinis'. = *P. 'Jo-nioi'* (Sato-Zakura group).

P. 'Albo-rosea'. = *P. 'Shiro-fugen'* (Sato-Zakura group).

P. alleghaniensis Porter. NORTHERN SLOE; ALLEGHANY PLUM; SLOE. Shrub or small tree to 3.5m. Br. smooth, dark grey. Lvs to 9cm, lanceolate to oval-lanceolate, apex acute or acuminate, serrate, glab. above, pale and pubesc. beneath; stipules linear, with bright red glands. Fls to 12mm diam., white, in sessile, 2–4-fld umbels; pedicels to 1cm. Fr. 1cm diam., subglobose or obovoid, dark purple, blue-pruinose, fleshy yellow. Spring. NE US. Z5.

P. americana Marsh. WILD PLUM; AMERICAN RED PLUM; AUGUST PLUM; GOOSE PLUM; HOG PLUM. Tree to 10.5m. Bark dark brown, exfoliating; br. spiny. Lvs to 10cm, oval to narrow-obovate, apex acuminate, glab. above, pale and glab. beneath, serrate; stipules linear. Fls to 2.5cm diam., in subsessile, 3–4-fld umbels; pedicels to 1.5cm. Fr. to 2.5cm, subglobose, red-orange to red, blue-pruinose, flesh yellow. Spring. E & C N Amer. Edible cvs, known as 'American plums', include hybrids (usually with *P. salicina*): 'Grenville', red mottled yellow, large, dessert quality; 'South Dakota', yellow, dessert quality, cold-hardy. Z3.

P. americana var. *nigra* Waugh = *P. nigra*.

P. ×amygdalo-persica (Weston) Rehd. (*P. dulcis* × *P. persica*.) Tree or shrub. Intermediate to *P. dulcis*, scabrous-serrate. Fls to 5cm diam., light pink. Fr. peach-like, dry. 'Pollardii': fls large, rich pink, March; type of the cross. Z4.

P. amygdalus Batsch = *P. dulcis*.

P. angustifolia Marsh. CHICASA PLUM; CHICKASAW PLUM. Shrub or small tree to 3m. Bark dark rufous, somewhat smooth. Lvs to 5cm, lanceolate or oval-lanceolate, condupulicate, acute, glandular-serrate, lustrous above, pale beneath; stipules linear,

gland., serrate. Fls to 9mm diam., in 2–4-fld umbels; pedicels to 6mm, glab. Fr. subglobose, small, flesh yellow. Winter–spring. S US. var. *watsonii* (Sarg.) Waugh. SAND PLUM. Shrub to 2m. Branchlets spiny. Lvs to 4.5cm, oval or oblong-oval. Fls with anth. sometimes red. Spring. US (Kans. to New Mex.). Z6.

P. ansu (Maxim.) Komar. = *P. armeniaca* var. *ansu*.

P. apetala Franch. & Savat. CLOVE CHERRY. Decid. small tree to 7mm. Bark grey brown or dark purple. Lvs to 9.5cm, obovate or obovate-elliptic, acuminate, incised, adpressed pubesc. above, pilose beneath. Fls apetalous in 1–3-fld umbels; pedicels to 16mm, cal. tube tubular, to 1cm, pale brown, sep. to 4mm. Fr. 8mm diam., round-ovoid, black. Spring. Jap. Z6.

P. armeniaca L. APRICOT. Tree to 10m, with spherical-flat or somewhat elongate crown. Bark rufous. Lvs to 12cm, orbicular or ovate, glab., serrate to subcrenate. Fls to 4cm diam., white or pink, usually solitary; sta. 25–45, anth. yellow. Fr. to 5.5×5cm, globose, or ovoid, white to orange-red or yellow, pubesc. Spring–summer. N China. var. *ansu* Maxim. Small tree. Shoots flushed purple. Lvs rounded. Fls pink. Often confused with *P. mume*. 'Flora Pleno': shoots flushed purple in spring; fls semi-double, buds carmine opening pink, in dense clusters. 'Pendula': br. weeping. 'Variegata': lvs variegated white. Z5.

P. armeniaca var. *sibirigantiaca* (Vill.) Dipp. = *P. brigantina*.

P. armeniaca var. *mandshurica* Maxim. = *P. mandshurica*.

P. armeniaca var. *sibirica* K. Koch = *P. sibirica*.

P. ×arnoldiana Rehd. (*P. cerasifera* × *P. triloba*.) Differs from *P. triloba* in lvs, larger, thicker, less coarsely serrate, and less pubesc.; fls white, appearing with lvs. Gdn origin. Z4.

P. 'Asano' = *P. 'Geraldinae'* (Sato-zakura group).

P. avium L. BIRD CHERRY; SWEET CHERRY; GEAN; WILD CHERRY; MAZZARD. Tree to 20m, crown conical. Lvs 10.5cm, oblong-ovate, acuminate, crenate-serrate, pubesc. on veins beneath. Fls 2.5cm diam., white, in sessile, several-fld umbels. Fr. 2cm, cordate-ovoid, dark maroon. Spring. Eur. to Asia Minor, Cauc., W Sib. 'Asplenifolia': lvs deeply cut. 'Decumana': lvs to 30cm; fls large. 'Fastigiata': habit narrowly upright to conic. 'Nana': dwarf; br. short; fls solitary. 'Pendula': br. semi-pendulous. 'Plena' ('Multiplex', 'Grandiflora'): to 17m; br. wide-sweeping with age; bark brown, shiny, peeling horizontally, silver and rough with age; lvs orange and red in autumn; fls double, pure white, early May. 'Premorsa' ('Praemorsa'); lvs notched at apex, deformed. 'Rubrifolia': lvs purple flushed red. 'Salicifolia': lvs deeply cut, v. narrow. Z3.

P. 'Benifugen' = *P. 'Fugenzo'* (Sato-zakura group).

P. besseyi Bail. WESTERN SAND CHERRY; ROCKY MOUNTAINS CHERRY. Bushy shrub to 120cm, erect or prostrate. Lvs to 4.5cm, oval-elliptic or oblong-obovate, serrate below, glab.; stipules linear, gladular-serrate. Fls to 12mm diam., 3–4-clustered; pedicels to 7mm. Fr. to 18mm diam., globose to oblong, black to red and yellow. Spring. 'Black Beauty': small, black, sweet, crops well. 'Hansen's': large, purple-black, good flavour. Z3.

P. bifrons Fritsch. Low shrub to 2m, semi-erect. Lvs dimorphic, silver-tomentose beneath, to 3.5×2cm, broad-ovate to obovate, lvs on previous year's shoots 2.2×1cm, nearly oblanceolate, blunt. Fls 2cm diam., pink, solitary or paired; pedicel v. short. Fr. 8mm diam., cordate-rotund, amber-crimson, glabrescent. Himal. (SW Afghan., Kashmir). Z7.

P. ×blireana André. (*P. cerasifera* 'Atropurpurea' or 'Pissardii' ×double form of *P. mume*.) Shrub or small tree to 4.5m. Branchlets nodding. Young lvs to 6cm, oval, bronze-red, green by summer. Fls 3cm diam., bright rose, double, solitary. Spring. Gdn origin (Lemoine, 1906). 'Moseri': lvs light red flushed brown; fls small, pale pink, sep. without glands; vigorous. Z5.

P. borealis Poir. = *P. nigra*.

P. bracteata Franch. & Savat. = *P. maximowiczii*.

P. brigantiaca Vill. = *P. brigantina*.

P. brigantina Vill. BRIANCON APRICOT. Decid. shrub or small tree to 6m. Lvs to 7.5cm, ovateor oval, short-acuminate, biserrate, pubesc. beneath. Fls 2cm diam., 2–5-clustered, white or pale pink. Fr. a small clear yellow, smooth apricot. SE Fr. Z7.

P. buergeriana Miq. Tree to 9m. Lvs to 11cm, elliptic to oblong-elliptic, acuminate, ± glab. Fls 7mm diam., white, in thin, pub-erulous rac. to 8cm. Fr. subglobose, black. Jap., Korea. Z5.

P. bungei Walp. = *P. humilis*.

P. campanulata Maxim. TAIWAN CHERRY; FORMOSAN CHERRY; BELL-FLOWERED CHERRY. Decid. small tree. Bark purple-brown. Lvs to 11cm, elliptic, acuminate, double-serrate, glab.; stipules long, much-divided. Fls to 3cm diam., claret, campanulate, cernuous in 5–6-fld umbels; pedicels to 1.5cm. Fr. 11mm diam., subglobose, black-purple. Spring. S Jap., Taiwan. 'Okame' (*P. campanulata* × *P. incisa*): habit broadly ovate, to 8m high; lvs small, dark green, flaming orange in autumn; fls shocking pink, in clusters to 3. 'Plena': fls double, small, carmine. 'Shosar' (*P. campanulata* × *P. sargentii*): tall, broadly columnar; lvs grass green, later yellow flushed copper; fls single, to 4cm across, dark pink. Z7.

P. 'Campanuloides' = *P.* 'Shujaku' (Sato-zakura group).

P. 'Candida' = *P.* 'Ariake' (Sato-zakura group).

P. canescens Bois. HOARY CHERRY; GREYLEAF CHERRY. Shrub to 3m. Bark exfoliating, leaving a shiny brown, mirror-like reflecting trunk. Lvs 6cm, ovate to ovate-lanceolate, acuminate, serrate, pubesc., often stalked gland. near base; stipules dentate. Fls 12mm diam., tinted pink, in 2–5-fld, compact corymbs; pedicels 0.5cm. Fr. 1cm, subspherical, cherry-red. Spring. China. Z6.

P. capollin Zucc. = *P. salicifolia*.

P. caproniana (L.) Gaudin = *P. cerasus* var. *caproniana*.

P. capuli Cav. ex Spreng. = *P. salicifolia*.

P. caroliniana (Mill.) Ait. CHERRY LAUREL; LAUREL CHERRY; WILD ORANGE; MOCK ORANGE. Everg. tree to 12m. Lvs to 12cm, oblong-elliptic to elliptic-lanceolate, mucronate, coriaceous, dark green. Fls to 5mm diam., cream, minute, in congested rac.; pedicel to 4mm. Fr. to 13mm, ovoid to subglobose, lustrous, black. Spring. S US. Z7.

P. 'Cataracta' = *P.* 'Taki-nioi' (Sato-zakura group).

P. ceraseidos Maxim. = *P. apetala*.

P. ceraseidos var. *kurilensis* Miyabe = *P. nipponica* var. *kurilensis*.

P. cerasifera Ehrh. CHERRY PLUM; MYROBALAN. Decid. tree-like shrub to round-headed tree to 9m, often spiny. Lvs to 6.5cm, ovate, oval or obovate, dentate, lanuginose on veins beneath. Fls to 2.5cm, pure white, solitary. Fr. to 3cm diam., round red to yellow, somewhat pruinose. Spring. Asia Minor, Cauc. 'Diversifolia' ('Asplenifolia'): lvs irregularly lobed or toothed, purple tinted bronze; fls white; a sport of 'Pissardii'. 'Festeri': lvs large; fls large, pink; related to 'Pissardii'. 'Hessii' ('Hessei'): habit small, shrubby; shoots purple; lvs narrow, purple tinted bronze, toothed and mottled cream; fls pure white. 'Hollywood' ('Trailblazer') ('Nigra' × 'Shiro'): lvs green, later red-brown, to 9cm long; fls pale pink, appearing before lvs; fr. large red. 'Frankthrees': broadly globe-shaped, to 7m high; lvs large, dark purple; fls pink. 'Lindsayae': habit slender; shoots nearly black when young; lvs red-brown; fls to 2cm across, light almond pink. 'Louis Asselin': small, shrubby, lvs green speckled white. 'Mount St. Helens': sport and improved form of 'Newport'. 'Newport' ('Newportii'): habit shrubby, to 3m high; lvs brown tinged bronze; fls small, white to light pink. 'Pendula': weeping; lvs green; fls white. 'Pissardii': lvs large, dark red, later purple; fls white, buds pink, profuse, appearing before foliage; fr. maroon, globose, to 3cm diam. 'Purpusii': lvs turning red-brown, later pink and yellow along midrib. 'Rosea' (*P. cerasifera* 'Vesuvius' × *P. spinosa*): lvs fading from purple flushed bronze, to green flushed bronze; st. purple; fls salmon pink. 'Spencer Thundercloud': habit compact, dwarf; fls pink, fragrant; fr. large, edible. 'Thundercloud': habit tall, broadly ovate, to 10m; lvs rusty brown, dull bronze in autumn; fls pink. 'Vesuvius' ('Krauter's Vesuvius'): habit broadly globe-shaped, to 5m; st. red-black; lvs large, red-black; fls pink fading to blush. 'Woodii': lvs small, deep red-black; fls pink. ssp. *divaricata* (Ledeb.) Schneid. Slender looser. Fls smaller. Fr. globose, 2cm diam., yellow, not indented at stalk insertion. Balk., Asia Minor, Cauc., C Asia. Z4.

P. cerasifera var. *blireana* (André) Bean = *P.* × *blireana*.

P. cerasifera var. *gigantea* Späth = *P.* × *gigantea*.

P. cerasoides D. Don. Semi-pendulous tree. Bark grey-brown, glossy. Lvs to 12cm, obovate-elliptic or obovate, acuminate, double-serrate, light green beneath; stipules short, viscid. Fls 4cm diam., pale red in 2–3-fld umbels; pedicels to 2.5cm. Fr. 1.5cm diam., flattened, broad-ellipsoid, yellow-brown. Autumn–winter. Himal., SW China, N Burm. var. *rubea* F.B. Ingram. To 30m. Shoots glab. Lvs to 11cm, broad oval-oblong to obovate, caudate, teeth uneven, gland-tipped. Fls in 2–4-fld, to 3cm diam., pink-red, pendulous umbels. Fr. 1.5cm, red. Spring. Himal., N India, Upper Burm., SW China. Z8.

P. cerasoides var. *campanulata* Koidz. = *P. campanulata*.

P. cerasus L. SOUR CHERRY. Bushy shrub or small round-headed tree to 6m. Lvs 6.5cm, narrow-ovate to elliptic-obovate, acute, finely serrate, dark glossy, glab. Fls 23mm diam., white, in sessile, several-fld umbels; pedicels to 3cm. Fr. 18mm diam., subglobose, dark red. Spring. SE Eur. to N India, Iran, Kurdistan. var. *austera* L. MORELLO CHERRY. Tree to 9m, somewhat pendulous. Fls to 6cm; pedicels longer. Fr. black-red. 'Bunyardii': lvs small, obtuse; fl. stalks to 5cm. 'Cucullata': lvs convex. 'Laciniata': lvs deeply cut. 'Persiciflora': fls double, soft pink. 'Plena': fls semi-double, white. 'Polygyna': spreading, semi-pendulous; fls and fr. profuse. 'Pulverulenta': lvs variegated yellow and white. 'Rhexii': round-headed, to 10m high, lvs dark green, glossy; fls large, white, early May. 'Salicifolia': lvs narrow lanceolate, to 12cm, doubly serrate. 'Semperflorens': habit dense to pendulous; fls loosely grouped, white; fr. small, dark red, sour. 'Umbraculifera': dwarf, dense,

rounded; lvs narrow. 'Variegata': lvs blotched white. var. *caproniana* L. AMARELLE CHERRY; KENTISH RED CHERRY. Tree to 9m, round-headed. Br. erect. Lvs to 12cm, broad-elliptic, acuminate or short-mucronate, crenate-serrate, shiny, glab. Fls in 2–4-fld umbels, white. Fr. globose, light red. var. *frutescens* Neilr. BUSH SOUR CHERRY. Shrub to 1m, suckering. Branchlets slender, cernuous. Lvs to 7.5cm, elliptic or obovate. Fls in 2–3-fld umbels. Fr. 1cm, globose, dark red. C Eur. var. *marasca* (Host) Viv. MARASCHINO CHERRY. Tree. Br. arching. Fls in compact infl. Fr. black-red, v. small. Z3.

P. cerasus var. *humilis* Bean = *P. cerasus* var. *frutescens*.

P. changangensis (F.B. Ingram) F.B. Ingram. CHINESE SPRING CHERRY. Small tree to 10.5m. Lvs 5cm, ovate to oblong-obovate, abruptly acuminate, pilose beneath; stipules to 1cm, linear-lanceolate, serrate. Fls 23mm diam., pink-white, in 3–5-fld corymbs; pedicels to 3cm, villous, pet. incised. Fr. 1cm diam., subglobose, purple-black. China. Z6.

P. 'Cheal's Weeping' = *P.* 'Kiku-shidare' (Sato-zakura group).

P. chicasa Michx. = *P. angustifolia*.

P. × *cistena* (Hansen) Koehne. (*P. cerasifera* 'Atropurpurea' × *P. pumila*.) Shrub to 2.5m, weakly growing. Lvs to 6cm, obovate-lnaceolate, red-brown, serrate, lustrous. Fls 1 or 2, white; cal. and pedicel red-brown. Fr. black-purple. Gdn origin. 'Crimson Dwarf': habit dense, upright, to 1.2m high; lvs red tinted bronze, crimson when young; shoot tips red; fls shell pink, cal. dark red, spring. 'Schmidteis': broadly globe-shaped, to 5m high; lvs large, purple, green when young; fls single, pink. Z3.

P. cocomilia Ten. Shrub or small tree to 5m. Lvs to 4cm, elliptic to obovate-elliptic, glandular-crenulate, glab. or addpressed-pubesc. Fls to 1.5cm diam., white, 2–4-clustered; pedicels to 4mm. Fr. 2cm, ovoid-globose, yellow, flushed red. N It. Z6.

P. communis (L.) Arcang. non Huds. = *P. dulcis*.

P. conadenia Koehne. Tree to 10m. Lvs to 9cm, obovate, caudate, glandular-biserrate. Fls in 5–8-fld rac.; pedicels to 1.5cm. Fr. ovoid, red. W China. Z5.

P. concinna Koehne. Shrub or small tree, 2–4m. Lvs to 7cm, oval-oblong, long-acuminate, scabrous, simple to biserrate, venation pubesc. beneath; stipules linear, small. Fls 2.5cm diam., white or occas. tinted soft pink, solitary or grouped in sessile clusters of 2, sometimes 4; pedicel 1cm, with leafy bracts; cal., pet. 12mm, incised. Fr. ovoid purple-black. April. C China. Z6.

P. conradinae Koehne = *P. hirtipes*.

P. consociiflora Schneid. Small decid. tree. Lvs to 7.5cm, oblanceolate to obovate, acuminate, teeth gland., veins lanuginose beneath. Fls 13mm diam., white, 2–3-clustered in 2.5cm diam. fascicles; pedicels 6.5mm. Fr. globose. Spring. China. Z6.

P. cornuta (Royle) Steud. HIMALAYAN BIRD CHERRY; BIRD CHERRY. Tree to 15m. Lvs to 15cm, elliptic, acuminate, finely serrate, glab. or pubesc. beneath; stipules to 1.5cm, linear-lanceolate. Fls to 7mm diam., white, in term. rac. to 25cm; pedicels to 5mm;. Fr. ellipsoid to subglobose. Spring–summer. Himal. (Bhutan, Sikkim). Z5.

P. crassipes Koidz. = *P. apetala*.

P. crenata Koehne = *P. apetala*.

P. cuneata Raf. = *P. pumila* var. *susquehanae*.

P. cyclamina Koehne. Tree to 9m. Lvs 10cm, oblong-obovate to oblong, abruptly acuminate, teeth often gland-tipped, slightly rugose; stipules occas. fimbriate, stalked-glandular. Fls 3.5cm diam., rose-pink, in usually 4-fld corymbs; pedicels 17.5mm, sep.; pet. deeply incised. Fr. ovoid, red. Spring. C China. Z6.

P. damascena Ehrh. = *P.* × *domestica*.

P. × *dasycarpa* Ehrh. (*P. armeniaca* × *P. cerasifera*.) BLACK APRICOT. Small tree to 6m. Lvs to 6cm, oval to orbicular-ovate, finely-crenate, pubesc. on veins beneath, somewhat rugose. Fls white, pink-tinged; pedicels to 7mm. Fr. 3cm diam., subglobose, violet-black, velutinous, purple pruinose. Spring. C Asia, Asia Minor. Z5.

P. davidiana (Carr.) Franch. DAVID'S PEACH. Decid. tree to 9m. Branchlets erect, rod-like. Lvs to 1cm, lanceolate, long-acuminate, dark green and shiny above, sharp-tootehd. Fls 2.5cm diam., white or pale pink, solitary. Fr. 3cm diam., spherical, yellow, lanuginose. Winter–spring. China. 'Alba': br. upright; lvs and shoots light green; fls white. 'Rubra': fls pink tinted red. Z4.

P. × *dawyckensis* Sealy (*P. canescens* × *P. dielsiana*.) Tree to 9m; bark dark brown, shining. Lvs to 9cm, elliptic or narrowly ovate, coarsely serrate, pubesc. Fls 2–4 in short corymbs, to 2cm diam., pale pink. Fr. ellipsoid, to 1.5cm, amber-red. China. 'Dawsar': upright, small; pubesc.; fls large, pink-purple, cal. tinted red, pet. incised. Z6.

P. dehiscens Koehne = *P. tangutica*.

P. demissa Nutt. ex Dietr. = *P. virginiana* var. *demissa*.

P. depressa Pursh = *P. pumila* var. *depressa*.

P. dielsiana Schneid. Tree to 6m. Bark tawny brown. Lvs 10cm, oblong-obovate to oblong, abruptly acuminate, pubesc. beneath on veins; stipules gland-tipped, fimbriate. Fls 3.5cm diam., white or pale pink, in corymbose rac.; pedicels with gland-fimbriate bracts; pet. incised. Fr. 8mm diam., ovoid. China. Z6.

P. divaricata Ledeb. = *P. cerasifera* ssp. *divaricata*.

P. 'Diversifolia'. = *P.* 'Kirigayatsu' (Sato-zakura group).

P. ×*domestica* L. (*P. spinosa* × *P. cerasifera* ssp. *divaricata*.) Decid. tree to 12m, sometimes spiny. Lvs to 10cm, elliptic or oblong, pubesc., later glab. Fls to 2.5cm diam., white, 2–4-clustered; pedicels to 2cm. Fr. to 8cm, ovoid or subglobose, yellow or red to violet and dark blue, flesh green or yellow. Spring. PLUM; COMMON PLUM. S Eur., Eurasia. 'Plantierensis': fls semi-double, white; fr. violet. ssp. *insititia* (L.) Schneid. BULLACE. Br. often spiny. Lvs pubesc. Fr. smaller, usually dark purple. See also BULLACE; DAMSON; PLUMS. Z5.

P. domestica var. *cerasifera* Ser. = *P. cerasifera*.

P. domestica var. *myrobalan* L. = *P. cerasifera*.

P. dulcis (Mill.) D.A. Webb. ALMOND; ALMOND TREE. Decid. trees to 9m. Lvs to 13cm, lanceolate, long-acuminate, glab. above, fine toothed. Fls rose or almost white, to 5cm, solitary or paired; pedicel short. Fr. to 6.5cm, ovoid, velutinous. Syr. to N Afr. 'Alba': fls single, white. 'Alba Plena': fls double, white. 'Erecta': to 6m, habit broadly columnar; br. erect; fls pink. 'Macrocarpa': fls to 5cm diam., palest pink; fr. to 8cm long, large, edible. 'Pendula': br. pendulous. 'Praecox': fls pale pink, 2 weeks earlier than type. 'Purpurea': lvs red flushed purple. 'Roseoplena' ('Rosea Plena'): fls double and dense, to 4cm diam., dark pink. Z7.

P. ×*dunbarii* Rehd. (*P. americana* × *P. maritima*.) Resembles *P. maritima*, but shoots later glab., lvs larger, more acuminate, less pubesc. beneath, and serrations more scabrous. Fr. purple, larger. US. Z3.

P. ×*effusa* (Host) Schneid. = *P.* ×*gondouinii*.

P. emarginata Walp. = *P. nigra*.

P. ×*eminens* Beck. (*P. cerasus* × *P. fruticosa*.) Erect shrub to 3m. Intermediate between parents, but lvs and flks larger, and petioles and pedicels longer than those of *P. fruticosa*. Z4.

P. 'Erecta'. = *P.* 'Amanogawa' (Sato-zakura group).

P. eriogyna C. Mason = *P. fremontii*.

P. fasciculata (Torr.) A. Gray. DESERT ALMOND. Divaricately much-branched decid. shrub to 3m. Lvs to 1.5cm, fascicled, oblanceolate-spathulate, entire, pale green, minutely pubesc. Fls 6mm diam., subsessile, 2–3-clustered. Fr. to 12mm, ovoid, dry brown-tomentose. Spring. SW US. Z7.

P. fenzliana Fritsch. Shrub or tree to 1.5m. Br. divaricate, long, purple. Lvs to 8cm, elliptic-lanceolate, orbicular, subcoriaceous, smooth, paler beneath, crenate-serrate. Fls 1–5-clustered; cal. red; pet. pink, incised. Fr. rounded, velutinous. Spring–summer. Cauc. Z4.

P. fremontii S. Wats. DESERT APRICOT. Decid. shrub or small tree to 4m. Branchlets rigid, often spine-tipped. Lvs to 2cm, round to broad-ovate, serrate. Fls to 1.2cm, white, solitary or few-clustered; pedicels to 12mm. Fr. to 14mm, elliptic-ovoid, yellow, puberulent, dry. Spring. US (Calif.) Z7.

P. fruticosa Pall. STEPPE CHERRY. Shrub to 1m, rarely to 2m, suckering. Lvs to 5cm, oblong-elliptic, obovate or lanceolate, acute or obtuse, shiny dark green above, paler beneath; stipules, linear, dentate. Fls to 1.4cm diam., white, in 3–4-fld umbels; pedicels to 2.5cm, glab., recurved; pet. incised. Fr. to 1.5cm, subglobose, usually mucronate, dark red. Spring. C & E Eur. to Sib. 'Pendula': br. slender, pendulous. 'Variegata': br. slender, pendulous; lvs green speckled cream. Z4.

P. ×*gigantea* (Späth) Koehne. (*P. dulcis* × *P. persica* × *P. cerasifera*.) Closely resembles *P. cerasifera*. Lvs to 12cm, elliptic-oblong to elliptic-lanceolate. Fls light pink, subsessile. Z4.

P. glandulosa Thunb. DWARF FLOWERING ALMOND. Shrub to 2m. Term. shoots, virgate. Lvs to 7cm, oblong-oval or lanceolate, thin-mucronate, pubesc. midrib beneath, fine-serrate; stipules gland. Fls to 2cm diam., red becoming pink or white, solitary or 2–3-clustered; pedicels to 2cm, glandular-dentate. Fr. 1cm, globose, dark red. C & N China, Jap. 'Alba': fls single, pure white. 'Alba Plena' ('Alboplena'): shoots pendulous; lvs to 12cm; fls double, large, white, profuse. 'Sinensis' ('Rosea Plena'): shoots large, pendulous, dark green; lvs to 12cm, dark green; fls large, double, bright pink, profuse. Z4.

P. glandulosa (Hook.) Torr. & A. Gray non Thunb. = *P. texana*.

P. glauciphylla Ghora & Panigr. = *P. cornuta*.

P. ×*gondouinii* (Poit. & Turpin) Rehd. (*P. avium* × *P. cerasus*.) Lvs like *P. avium*. Fr. large, resembling a heart cherry. DUKE CHERRY. Gdn origin. 'Schnee': small tree or shrub, globose; lvs to 7cm, elliptic, dark green; fls single, dazzling white, v. profuse. For edible cvs see CHERRIES. Z4.

P. gracilis Engelm. & A. Gray. Straggling shrub to 120cm. Bark grey. Lvs to 5cm, oval, rarely ovate, pointed, pale and strongly

pubesc. beneath, teeth gland-tipped when young. Fls to 1cm diam., in 2–4-fld umbels; pedicels to 1cm, fine-pubesc. Fr. to 18mm diam., globose to ovoid, usually red, light pruinose. Spring. SW US. Z6.

P. 'Grandiflora' = *P.* 'Ukon' (Sato-zakura group).

P. gravesii Small. Unarmed shrub to 1m. Bark dark, rough. Lvs to 3cm, oblong-orbicular, serrate, paler and pubesc., beneath; stipules linear, gland. Fls to 1.5cm diam., solitary, or in 2–3-fld umbels; pedicels 6mm, pubesc. Fr. to 1.5cm diam., globose, deep purple, blue pruinose. US (Conn.). Z5.

P. grayana Maxim. JAPANESE BIRD CHERRY. Small, compact tree to 9m. Lvs 9cm, oblong-ovate to oblong-obovate, acuminate, finely bristle-toothed; petioles 1cm. Fls 1cm diam., white, in many-fld rac. Fr. 8mm diam., black. Jap. Z6.

P. haussknechtii Schneid. = *P. webbii*.

P. helenae Koehne = *P. hirtipes*.

P. ×*hillieri* hort. (*P. incisa* × *P. sargentii*.) Small, densely branched tree to 9m. Lvs bronze, double-serrate. Fls 3cm diam., blue-pink, 1–4-grouped; pedicels long; cal. bronze-red, dentate. Spring. Gdn origin (Hillier, c1928). 'Hilling's Weeping': small tree; br. slender, almost perpendicularly weeping; fls pure white, profuse in early April. 'Kornicensis': tree to 5m; shoots glab., red-brown; lvs to 12cm, elliptic-acuminate; fls clustered, light pink; fr. dark red. 'Spire': tree to 8m, basal width to 3m, conical, upright; lvs richly tinted in autumn; fls single, almond pink; early-flowering. Z6.

P. himalaica Kit. = *P. rufa*.

P. hirtipes Hemsl. Loosely branched tree to 12m+. Lvs 7.5cm, usually obovate to obovate-oblong, abrupt-acuminate, glab. Fls 2cm diam., 3–4-clusters; pet. white, occas. pink, incised. Fr. 1cm, ovoid, red. Spring. C China. 'Malifolia': fls to 4cm wide, late-flowering. 'Semiplena': fls semi-double, milky pink, fading to white, long-lasting. Z8.

P. 'Hokusai' = *P.* 'Uzuzakura' (Sato-zakura group).

P. hortulana Bail. Tree to 9m. Bark thin, exfoliating in plate-like scales, dark brown. Lvs to 11cm, ovate-lanceolate, acuminate, yellow-green, glab. and slightly lustrous above, pubesc. beneath, glandular-serrate to subcrenate; stipules linear, glandular-serrate. Fls to 1.5cm diam., in 2–5-fld umbels; pedicels 14mm. Fr. to 2.5cm diam., globose, red to yellow, usually with white dots. C US. 'Mineri': lvs thick, coarsely toothed; fr. firm, produced late. Z6.

P. 'Hosokawa' = *P.* 'Shirotae' (Sato-zakura group).

P. hosseusii Diels = *P. cerasoides* var. *rubea*.

P. humilis Bunge. HUMBLE BUSH CHERRY. Shrub to 1.5m. Lvs 4cm, obovate to elliptic, fine-serrate. Fls 14mm diam., pink-white, solitary or paired. Fr. 13mm diam., subglobose, red. N China. Z5.

P. 'Ichiyo'. = *P.* 'Hizakura' (Sato-zakura group).

P. ilicifolia (Nutt.) Walp. HOLLY-LEAVED CHERRY; ISLAY. Dense everg. shrub or small tree to 8m. Lvs to 5cm, ovate to round, coarsely spiny-toothed, coriaceous. Fls to 0.6cm, white in rac. to 6cm. Fr. to 1.5cm, ovoid-ellipsoid, red, rarely yellow. Calif. Z9.

P. incana (Pall.) Batsch. Erect shrub to 2m. Branchlets slender, lanuginose. Lvs to 4cm, elliptic to narrow-oblanceolate, serrate, white-tomentose, sometimes later glab. beneath. Fls to 1.4cm diam., pink, solitary or paired; pedicels 2mm. Fr. to 7mm diam., subglobose, dark red. Spring. SE Eur., Asia Minor. Z6.

P. incisa Thunb. FUJI CHERRY. Small tree to 5m. Lvs to 5cm, obovate or ovate, short-acuminate, pubesc. above and on veins beneath, double-serrate. Fls to 2cm diam., white to rose, 1–3; pedicels to 2.5cm; pet. retuse. Fr. to 8mm, ovoid, purple-black. Spring–summer. Jap. 'February Pink': fls light pink flowering by February. 'Moerheimii': habit small, weeping, wide-spreading, dome-shaped; fls pink in bud, fading to blush-white; late March. 'Okame' (*P. incisa* × *P. campanulata*): habit neat; fls carmine, cal. and stalks red tinted; March. 'Praecox': fls pale pink, January. Z6.

P. insititia L. = *P.* ×*domestica* ssp. *insititia*.

P. integrifolia Sarg. non Walp. = *P. lyonii*.

P. intermedia Host non Poir. = *P.* ×*eminens*.

P. involucrata Koehne = *P. pseudocerasus*.

P. iwagiensis Koehne = *P. nipponica*.

P. jacquemontii Hook. f. Straggling shrub to 3m+. Lvs to 6cm, ovate-elliptic to obovate-oblong, or to 3cm, oblanceolate, serrate, dark above, paler beneath; stipules branched filiform on young shoots, minute on old st. Fls 19mm diam., rose pink, solitary or paired; pedicels 5mm. Fr. 1.5cm diam., subglobose, red. NW Himal. Z7.

P. jacquemontii var. *bifrons* Ingram = *P. bifrons*.

P. jamasakura Sieb. ex Koidz. = *P. serrulata* var. *spontanea*.

P. jamasakura var. *speciosa* Koidz. = *P. speciosa*.

P. 'James H. Veitch'. = *P.* 'Fugenzo' (Sato-zakura group).

P. japonica Thunb. ORIENTAL BUSH CHERRY. Shrub to 1.5m. Br. thin, elongate. Lvs to 7cm, ovate acuminate, double-serrate, completely glab. or pubesc. on veins beneath; stipules long, laciniate. Fls white or pale pink, single, small, 2–3-clustered; pedicels to 1cm. Fr. 14mm, subglobose, dark red. C China to Korea, Jap. 'Alba': fls white. 'Engleri': lvs long-acuminate; stalks long; fls, pale pink; fr. to 1.5cm diam. 'Thunbergii': lvs long-acuminate, fls light pink. var. *nakaii* (Lév.) Rehd. Small shrub, to 50cm. Lvs broadly ovate, pubesc. beneath. Fls few, light pink Fr. large, plum-like. Manch. Z4.

P. ×*juddii* E. Anderson. (*P. sargentii* ×*P. yedoensis.*) Similar to *P. sargentii* but lvs copper-tinted when young, crimson in fall. Fls larger, abundant, pale to intense pink. Z6.

P. 'Kajima' = *P.* 'Shirotae' (Sato-zakura group).

P. kansuensis Rehd. Decid. shrub or small tree to 6m. Bark smooth, brown. Lvs to 10cm, lanceolate, fine-serrate, pubesc. on midrib. Fls 2cm diam., white, mostly paired, in infl. to 4.5cm; cal. grey, ciliate. Fr. globose, velutinous, fleshy white. Winter–spring. NW China. Z4.

P. 'Kanzan' = *P.* 'Sekiyama' (Sato-zakura group).

P. kurilensis Miyabe ex Tak. = *P. nipponica* var. *kurilensis*.

P. 'Kwanzan' = *P.* 'Sekiyama' (Sato-zakura group).

P. lanata Mackenzie & Bush = *P. americana*.

P. lannesiana (Carr.) Wils. The wild type with fragrant white fls, now known as *P. speciosa*, was named *P. lannesiana* f. *albida*. The name *P. lannesiana* has been used to cover the flowering gdn cherries. See *P.* Sato-Zakura group.

P. latidentata Koehne = *P. mugus*.

P. ×*laucheana* Bolle ex Lauche. (*P. padus* ×*P. virginiana*.) Tree to 15m. Lvs almost round, short-acuminate, fine adpressed-scabrous serrate, pale beneath. Fls in short, upright rac. Fr. 12mm, diam., black-red. Gdn origin. Z3.

P. laurocerasus L. CHERRY LAUREL; LAUREL CHERRY. Everg. shrub or tree to 6m. Lvs to 25cm, oblong-elliptic, acuminate, glossy and dark green, coriaceous. Fls white, small, in dense cylindrical rac. to 10cm. Fr. 8mm, globose-ovoid, black. Spring. SE Eur., Asia Minor. 'Aureovariegata': lvs striped yellow. 'Camelliifolia': lvs curled. 'Caucasica': vigorous, upright shrub; lvs large, light green, glossy. 'Castlewellan': narrow to 2m; lvs slightly contorted, speckled white. 'Herbergii': pyramidal, to 2m; lvs narrow, bright green above. 'Magnifolia' ('Latifolia'): tall, wide-spreading, vigorous; lvs v. large, deep green, shiny. 'Marbled White': broadly conical; lvs marbled grey or white. 'Mischeana': growth flat and low; lvs dark green, glossy, undulate. 'Otto Luyken': compact and broad-growing shrub, to 1; lvs narrow glossy dark green; free-flowering. 'Reynvaanii': dense, erect, to 2m; lvs dull green; fls sparsely on older plants. 'Schipkaensis': broad, goblet shaped, to 2m; lvs large; v. hardy. 'Zabeliana': growth almost horizontal; lvs light green; v. hardy. Z7.

P. litigiosa Schneid. TASSEL CHERRY. Small tree to 7.5m+, ascending. Lvs 7cm, narrow-obovate to oblong-ovate, acuminate, finely serrate, pubesc. on veins beneath. Fls white, 22.5mm diam., in 2–3-fld, subsessile umbels. Fr. to 1cm diam., ellipsoid, semi-translucent, scarlet-red. China. Z6.

P. lobulata Koehne. RIBBED CHERRY. Tree to 9m, with broad crown. Lvs 7cm, narrow-ovate, apex acuminate, double-serrate, initially setose-pubesc. above, pilose on veins beneath; stipules small glandular-fimbriate. Fls 1.5cm diam., white, cernuous, solitary or paired; pedicels 13mm, pilose, with small gland-toothed bracts at base. Fr. 12mm, dark crimson. China. Z6.

P. lusitanica L. PORTUGUESE LAUREL CHERRY; PORTUGAL LAUREL. Everg. shrub of wide, bushy habit, or tree to 20m. Branchlets red. Lvs to 12cm, oblong-ovate, acuminate, somewhat serrate, thinly coriaceous dark green and shiny above. Fls to 13mm diam., white, erect, in rac. to 15cm. Fr. 8mm, ovoid, dark purple. Summer. Iberian Penins. ssp. *azorica* (Mouill.) Franco. AZORES LAUREL CHERRY. Shrub or small tree to 4m. Lvs to 10cm, ovate-elliptic. Fls in shorter, fewer-fld rac. Fr. to 13mm. Azores. 'Angustifolia': lvs to 8cm, oblong-lanceolate. 'Myrtifolia': habit rounded, neat; lvs to 6cm, nearly ovate. 'Ormistonensis': habit compact; lvs dark green, leathery. 'Variegata': lvs small, margined white, sometimes flushed pink in winter. Z7.

P. lyonii (Eastw.) Sarg. CATALINA CHERRY. Resembles *P. ilicifolia*, but lvs larger. Narrow-ovate, mostly entire. Rac. many-fld to 12cm. Fr. to 2.5cm, globose, nearly black. Spring. US (Calif.) Z8.

P. maackii Rupr. MANCHURIAN CHERRY; AMUR CHERRY. Decid. tree to 16m. Bark golden to russet, pellucid, papery, peeling. Lvs 10cm, elliptic or oblong, mucronate; stipules to 7mm, linear, dark purple, with oblong glands. Fls small, white, in dense term. rac. Fr. 4mm, ovoid-globose, dry, black. Spring. Korea, Manch. 'Amber Beauty': habit uniform; bark golden; br. slightly ascending. Z5.

P. macradenia Koehne. Small tree to 10m, close to *P. maximowiczii*. Lvs 4.5–6.5cm, ovate to oval-elliptic, entire to biserrate. Fls in 3- to 4-fld, pubesc., corymbose rac. Fr. globose, dark red. W China. Z5.

P. mahaleb L. ST. LUCIE CHERRY. Patent tree to 9m+. Lvs 4.5cm, broad-ovate to robund-obovate, occas. pubesc. on midrib beneath, crenate-serrulate. Fls 14mm diam., white, in 5–7-fld, corymbose rac. Fr. 6mm, round-ovoid, black. Eur., Asia Minor. 'Albomarginata': lvs broadly margined off-white. 'Aurea': lvs heavily splashed yellow. 'Bommii': habit v. pendulous. 'Monstrosa' ('Globosa'): dwarf, habit rounded and bushy; slow-growing. 'Pendula': br. nodding. 'Xanthocarpa': fr. yellow. Z5.

P. mandshurica (Maxim.) Koehne. Tree to 15m, wide crown. Lvs to 12cm, oval-lanceolate to broad-oval, abruptly acuminate, scabrous-serrate, deep green above. Fls 3cm diam., pale pink, solitary; pedicels to Fr. 2.5cm diam., globose, yellow. Spring. Manch., Korea. Z6.

P. maritima Marsh BEACH PLUM. Straggling shrub to 180cm. Bark v. dark grey or brown. Lvs to 6.5cm, usually ovate or elliptic, acute, serrate, dull green above, paler and soft-pubesc. beneath. Fls to 14mm diam., in 2–3-fld umbels; pedicels 7mm. Fr. 1.5cm diam., globose, dull purple, sometimes crimson or yellow. Spring–summer. E US. 'Eastham': large well-flavoured fr., heavy cropper; 'Hancock': sweet, juicy, early ripening; 'Squibnocket': selected for high quality, also ornamental and a good soil binder. Z3.

P. maximowiczii Rupr. MIYAMA CHERRY. Tree to 7.5m. Br. patent. Lvs 4.5cm, obovate, abrupt-acuminate, coarse-serrate, single- or double-incised. Fls 1.5cm diam., cream-white, in erect, 5–10-fld, corymbose rac.; pedicels with leafy bracts. Fr. 5mm diam., globose, black. Spring. Jap. Korea, Manch. Z4.

P. melanocarpa Rydb. = *P. virginiana* var. *melanocarpa*.

P. mexicana Wats. BIG-TREE PLUM. Tree to 12m. Bark exfoliating in platelike scales. Lvs to 1.5cm, oblong-obovate, acute, rounded or subcordate at base, serrate, yellow-green above, paler beneath; stipules usually lobed. Fls to 18mm diam., in subsessile, 2–4-fld umbels. Fr. to 3cm diam., globose, magenta, blue-pruinose. SW US to Mex. Z6.

P. microlepis Koehne = *P.* ×*subhirtella*.

P. 'Mikuruma-gaeshi' = *P.* 'Kirigayatsu' (Sato-zakura group).

P. mira Koehne. Shrub or tree to 10m. Shoots slender, green. Lvs to 10cm, lanceolate, sparse-crenate, entire toward apex. Fls to 2.5cm diam., white-pink, solitary or paired, subsessile; cal. red. Fr 3m ciam., globose, dense-tomentose, with white flesh. SW China. Z5.

P. monticola K. Koch = *P. cerasifera* ssp. *divaricata*.

P. 'Mount Fuji'. = *P.* 'Shirotae' (Sato-zakura group).

P. 'Moutan'. = *P.* 'Botanzakura' (Sato-zakura group).

P. mugus Hand.-Mazz. TIBETAN CHERRY. Shrub to 90cm. Lvs 4cm, broad-ovate, dark green, sparsely setose-pubesc. above, glabrescent beneath, doubly serrate; stipules 1cm, linear-subulate, dentate. Fls 1.5cm diam., shell-pink, solitary or paired; pedicel 2cm. Fr. 9mm, ellipsoid, dark red. SE Tibet. Z5.

P. mume Sieb. & Zucc. JAPANESE APRICOT; MEI. Decid. tree to 9m, of rounded habit. Branchlets lustrous. Lvs to 10cm, rounded or broadly ovate, serrate, sparse-pubesc., later glab. Fls to 3cm, pale rose, solitary or paired, subsessile. Fr. to 3cm diam., globose, somewhat pubesc., yellow. Spring. S Jap. 'Alba': fls single, pure white, abundant; strong growing. 'Alboplena' ('Alba Plena'): fls semi-double, white; early-flowering. 'Alphandii': fls double, clear pink; fls in March. 'Benishidori' ('Beni-shidon'): fls double, to 1cm diam., intense pink, fading later, fragrant. 'Bonita': to 6m; fls semi-double, rose red. 'Dawn': fls large, double, pale pink, ruffled; late-flowering. 'Kobai': fls double, light pink, profuse. 'O-moi-no-wac': fls semi-double, cup-shaped, white, occasional pet. or even whole fl. pink; fls late March. 'Peggy Clarke': fls double, deep rose, cal. red. 'Pendula': habit small, weeping; fls single or semi-double, light pink; fls late February. 'Rosemary Clarke': fls semi-double, white, cal. red, fragrant; early-flowering. 'W.B. Clarke': weeping; fls double, pink. Z6.

P. munsoniana Wight & Hedr. Tree to 8m. Young shoots glab., later dark red. Lvs to 10cm, lanceolate to oblong-lanceolate, finely glandular-serrate, lustrous above, paler beneath; stipules linear, glandular-serrate. Fls to 1.5cm diam., 2–4-clustered; pedicels to 12mm. Fr. globose or oval, bright red, light-pruinose. C US. Z6.

P. mutabilis Miyoshi = *P. serrulata* var. *spontanea*.

P. myrobalana Lois. = *P. cerasifera*.

P. myrtifolia (L.) Urban. Lvs small. Fr. small, spherical. Jam., Greater Antilles. Z10.

P. nakai Lév. = *P. japonica*.

P. nana (L.) Stokes, non Duroi = *P. tenella*.

P. napaulensis (Ser.) Steud. Tree to 20m. Lvs 18cm, narrow elliptic lanceolate, fine-serrate. Fls to 1cm diam., in rac. to 25cm. Fr. to 1.5cm, ovoid. Himal. (Bhutan, Sikkim). Z7.

P. napaulensis var. *sericea* Batal. = *P. sericea*.

P. nigra Ait. CANADIAN PLUM; CANADA PLUM. Small tree to 9m. Bark dark, grey. Lvs to 13cm, oval or obovate, green and glab.

above, paler and pubesc. on veins beneath, coarsely serrate; stipules linear or lobed, margins gland. Fls to 3cm diam., white to pink, in subsessile, 2–3-fld umbels; pedicels to 2cm, usually glab.; cal. red; pet erose. Fr. to 3cm, oblong-ovoid, crimson to orange-yellow. NE Amer. 'Princess Kay': habit upright; bark black; fls double, white; fr. red. Z2.

P. ×*nigrella* W.A. Cumming. (*P. nigra* ×*P. tenella.*) Shrub to 3m, habit rounded. Lvs to 4cm diam., oblanceolate to oblong, sometimes lanceolate. Fls 3.5cm diam., lilac. Spring. Gdn origin. 'Muckle': type of the cross. Z3.

P. nikkoensis Koehne = *P. nipponica.*

P. nipponica Matsum. JAPANESE ALPINE CHERRY; NIPPONESE CHERRY. Shrub to small tree to 5m. Lvs to 8cm, obovate, caudate-acuminate, pilose and pale green beneath, incised and double serrate. Fls to 2.5cm diam., pink, in 1–3-fld, sessile umbels or in umbellate corymbs; pedicels to 3cm. Fr. 8mm diam., globose, purple-black. Spring–summer. Jap. var. *kurilensis* (Miyabe) Wils. KURILE CHERRY. Petioles or pedicels pilose. Jap. 'Kursar' (*P. nipponica* var. *kurilensis* ×*P. sargentii*): habit upright, spreading to 6m high, vigorous; lvs rich orange tints in autumn; fls deep cerise pink. 'Ruby': lvs carmine in autumn; fls lilac-pink, later fading. Z5.

P. oeconomica Borkh. = *P.* ×*domestica.*

P. pachyclada Zab. = *P. cornuta.*

P. padus L. BIRD CHERRY; COMMON BIRD CHERRY. Decid. tree to 15m. Bark dark brown; br. drooping. Lvs to 9cm, obovate to elliptic or narrow-obovate, serrate, pubesc. on veins beneath. Fls to 1.5cm diam., white, in many-fld, glab. to puberulent rac. to 12cm; pedicels to 12mm; pet. dentate. Fr. pea-sized, black. Eur., W Asia to Korea and Jap. 'Alberti': habit broadly conical, dense; fls profuse, on long rac.; free-flowering. 'Aucubifolia': lvs speckled yellow. 'Aurea': lvs flushed yellow when young; fls large. 'Bracteosa': floral bracts exceeding pet. 'Chlorocarpos': fr. green tinted yellow. 'Colorata': st. deep purple; lvs purple flushed copper, later dark green, tinted purple beneath; fls pink, carmine in bud; fr. dark maroon. 'Heterophylla': lvs deeply incised. 'Leucocarpos': twigs somewhat pubesc.; fr. off-white. 'Nana': habit almost hemispherical, to 3m high, densely branched. 'Pendula': br. drooping. 'Plena': fls semi-double, large, long-lasting. 'Purple Queen': habit small, to 7m; lvs purple flushed copper when young, on dark shoots; fls pale pink. 'Spaethii': habit broad; fls to 2cm wide, on elongated rac. 'Stricta': fls in erect rac. 'Wateri' ('Grandiflora'): habit broadly conical at first, later rounded, to 10m; lvs oval, light green; fls white, in pendulous, rac., almond-scented; fr. small, black. var. *commutata* Dipp. Medium-sized tree. Lvs coarser, crenate; fls in long rac. to 15cm. Z3.

P. padus sensu F.B.Ingram non L. = *P. cornuta.*

P. padus var. *rotundifolia* hort. ex Koehne = *P.* ×*laucheana.*

P. palmeri Sarg. = *P. americana.*

P. paracerasus Koehne = *P.* ×*yedoensis.*

P. pedunculata (Pall.) Maxim. Shrub to 2m. Lvs to 5cm, oblong-obovate or oblong-oval, serrate, ciliate-pubesc.; stipules narrow, to 4mm. Fls to 2cm, pink, solitary; pedicels to 8mm, ciliate. Fr. 1cm, ovoid or oblong-ovoid, pubesc. Spring –summer. Sib. Z4.

P. pendula Maxim. Decid. tree to 15m. Bark grey; branchlets pendulous. Lvs to 10cm, elliptic, short caudate, pubesc., serrate. Fls 3cm diam., white, single, in umbels; pedicels to 3cm, pubesc. Fr. 1cm diam., subglobose, black-purple. Spring. Jap. var. *adscendens* Mak. Br. elongate, slender, light grey-brown, pilose when young. Jap. Z6.

P. pensylvanica L. f. BIRD CHERRY; PIN CHERRY; RED CHERRY. Tree to 9m. Lvs 9cm, narrow-ovate, acuminate, with gland., incurved teeth. Fls 1.5cm, white, in 4–8-fld umbellate clusters. Fr. 6mm diam., globose, red. N Amer. Z2.

P. persica (L.) Batsch. PEACH. Small tree to 8m. Lvs to 15cm lanceolate to broad-oblanceolate, long-acuminate, glabrescent, serrulate. Fls pink to white, to 3.5cm diam., in groups of 1–2; pedicels v. short. Fr. to 7cm diam., cordate, globose, downy, yellow blushed red, fragrant, v. juicy. Spring–autumn. China. *Habit.* 'Nana' (dwarf, to 1m; lvs large, pendulous; fls light pink, profuse), 'Alboplena Pendula' (weeping; fls double, white, abundant), 'Crimson Cascade' (weeping; fls carmine), 'Windle Weeping' (umbrella-forming; fls cup-shaped, semi-double, pink; vigorous); cvs notable for foliage include 'Royal Redleaf' (lvs brilliant red, later green tinted red). Fls. fls are 'Alba' (wood green; lvs light green; fls single, white), 'Alboplena' (fls double, white, profuse), 'Iceberg' (fls semi-double large, pure white), 'Helen Borchers' (fls semi-double, clear pink; vigorous), 'Cardinal' (fls semi-double, rosette, deep burgundy), 'Klara Mayer' (shrub-like; fls double, to 4cm, strong red-pink; fr. pale green, tinted red), 'Russel's Red' (habit dense; fls double, striking red), 'Palace Peach' (fls double, small, deepest red), 'Peppermint Stick' (fls double, white, striped red), 'Dianthifolia' (fls v. large, semi-double, pet. narrow, striped deep red),

'Versicolor' (lvs light green; fls double, white usually striped rust red, profuse; slow-growing). Z5.

P. pilosiuscula Koehne. Semi-erect tree to 9m. Lvs 6.5cm, oval to oblong-obovate, short setose-pubesc. above, serrate, aristate. Fls white or tinted pink, in 2–3-fld, rarely 5-fld, corymbose umbels. Fr. 1cm, ellipsoid, red. Spring. C & W China. Z5.

P. pissardii blireana fl. pl. Lemoine = *P.* ×*blireana.*

P. polytricha Koehne = *P. pilosiuscula.*

P. pseudoarmeniaca Heldr. & Sart. = *P. cocomilia.*

P. pseudocerasus Lindl. YING TAO CHERRY. Small tree to 5.5m. Lvs 9cm, broad-obovate to obovate-ovate, coarse-serrate. Fls 2cm diam., white, in elongated racemose corymbs. Fr. 1.5cm, cordate-globose to ellipsoid, amber-red. Spring. China. 'Wadai' (*P. pseudocerasus* ×*P. subhirtella*): shrub-like, tall multi-stemmed; twigs aerial roots; lvs elliptic-acuminate, to 8cm; fls small, pale pink, darker in bud. Z6.

P. pseudocerasus var. *spontanea* Maxim. = *P. serrulata* var. *spontanea.*

P. pubescens Pursh = *P. maritima.*

P. pubigera Koehne. Medium-sized tree. Fls small, creamy white, in pendulous rac. to 18cm. W China.

P. puddum Kingdon-Ward, non DC. = *P. cerasoides* var. *rubea.*

P. pulchella Koehne = *P. pilosiuscula.*

P. pumila L. SAND CHERRY. Shrub to 80cm, occas. semi-prostrate. Lvs 4cm, oblanceolate to narrow-obovate, shallow-serrate toward apex, grey-green above, glaucescent beneath; stipules linear, pinnatifid. Fls to 2cm diam., white, 2–4-clustered; pedicels 12mm. Fr. 1cm diam., subglobose, dark red. Spring. NE US. var. *depressa* (Pursh) Bean. Prostrate, to 30.5cm. Lvs more slender, blue-white beneath. Fr. rounded-ellipsoid. var. *susquehanae* (Willd.) Jaeger To 90cm. Lvs obovate, blunt-serrate toward apex, white-green beneath. Fr. smaller, astringent. Z2.

P. pumila var. *besseyi* (Bail.) Waugh = *P. besseyi.*

P. pumila var. *cuneata* (Raf.) Bail. = *P. pumila* var. *susquehanae.*

P. 'Purpurascens' = *P.* 'Sekiyama' (Sato-zakura group).

P. 'Purpurea' = *P.* 'Yae-marasakizakura' (Sato-zakura group).

P. racemosa Lam. = *P. cornuta.*

P. racemosa Lam. = *P. padus.*

P. reflexa hort. = *P.* ×*eminens.*

P. rehderiana Koehne = *P. litigiosa.*

P. reverchonii Sarg. = *P. rivularis.*

P. rivularis Scheele. CREEK PLUM. Shrub to 2.5m. St. slender. Lvs to 7.5cm, ovate to oblong-ovate, glandular-serrate, glab. above, pubesc. beneath; stipules linear or lobed, gland. Fls 1cm diam., in 2–5-fld umbels; pedicels to 8mm. Fr. 1.5cm diam., subglobose, red. Spring. US (Tex.). Z8.

P. 'Rosea' = *P.* 'Kiku-shidare' (Sato-zakura group).

P. 'Roseaplena' = *P.* 'Uzuzakura' (Sato-zakura group).

P. rufa Hook. f. HIMALAYAN CHERRY. Tree to 6m+. Shoots rusty-fawn lanuginose. Lvs to 7cm, narrow-oval to obovate-lanceolate, finely glandular-serrate. Fls 16mm diam., white or pink-white, mostly solitary, sometimes 2–3 together; cal. red-tinted, serrulate. Fr. 1mm, ellipsoid, dark red. Himal. var. *tricantha* (Koehne) Hara. Lvs more elongate. Pedicels and cal. tube pubesc. Z8.

P. rufomicans Koehne = *P. sericea.*

P. 'Ruiran' = *P.* 'Taguiarashi' (Sato-zakura group).

P. sachalinensis Miyoshi = *P. sargentii.*

P. salasii Standl. Tree. Lvs to 14cm, oblong-lanceolate, sharpserrate, pale beneath. Fls to 1cm diam., white, in rac. to 18cm; pedicels to 4.5mm. Fr. 13mm, globose. C Guat. (mts). Z7.

P. salicifolia Kunth. MEXICAN BIRD CHERRY. Tree to 12m. Lvs 8.5cm, lanceolate, acuminate, coriaceous, glab., finely serrate. Fls 1cm diam., white, in loose, cernuous rac. Fr. 17.5mm diam., subglobose. Mex. to Peru. 'Ecuadorian': large sweet fr., tree drooping, heavy cropper; 'Fausto': large sweet fr., good cropper; 'Harriet': large fr., tree dwarf; 'Huachi Grande': large mild-flavoured fr., v. heavy cropper. Z6.

P. salicina Lindl. JAPANESE PLUM. Small tree to 10m. Shoots red. Lvs to 12cm, oval-obovate to broad-oval, double-crenate, glossy above, dull beneath. Fls to 2cm diam., 2–4- clustered, white, pedicels to 1.5cm. Fr. to 7cm diam., globose to ovoid, yellow or red, sometimes violet. Spring. China, Jap. Z6.

P. salzeri Zdarek = *P. padus.*

P. sargentii Rehd. Spreading tree to 18m+. Lvs 10.5cm, broad oblong-elliptic to obovate-oblong, acuminate, with sharp red teeth, glaucescent beneath. Fls to 4cm diam., blue-pink, in 2–4-fld, sessile umbels; pedicel to 2cm; pet. incised. Fr. to 1cm, elongate-ovoid, glossy crimson. Jap. 'Columnaris' ('Rancho'): columnar, to 10m; bark mahogany; lvs flaming red and gold in autumn; fls single, pink, early-flowering. 'Accolade' (*P. sargentii* ×*P. subhirtella*): habit flat topped, older plants somewhat pendulous; lvs to 10cm, elliptic-oblong, long acuminate, serrate; fls semi-double, to 4cm diam., shocking pink in pendulous groups to 3, early April. Z4.

P.Sato-zakura group. The Japanese flowering cherries, currently collected under the name 'The Sato-zakura group'. Most probably derived from *P. serrulata*. This collective name encompasses the sp. *P. donarium* Sieb., *P. lannesiana* Wils. (this name was sometimes used by Japanese botanists for the many hybrids of *P. serrulata* var. *spontanea* × *P. pseudocerasus* Lindl. 'Amanogawa' ('milky way' or 'celestial river') ('Erecta'): narrowly fastigiate, to 6m high, to 120cm wide; lvs tinted when young, yellow marked red in autumn; fls densely clustered, single, occas. semi-double, pale pink, fragrant, freely produced, early to mid May; fr. small, black, infrequently produced. 'Ariake' ('dawn') ('Candida'): to 6m; lvs tinted bronze when young; fls single, to 6cm diam., pink in bud, opening blush. 'Asagi': strong-growing; lvs flushed red when young; fls abundant, single, to 4.5cm diam., pale yellow; mid-April to early May. 'Benden': narrowly upright, strong-growing; br. ascending; lvs pale copper when young, coral red in autumn; fls single, pink-lilac; mid-April. 'Botanzakura' ('Botan-sakura', 'Moutan'): habit broadly upright, small, weakgrowing; lvs serrate, pale bronze when young, flame orange in autumn; fls grouped to 4 in loose corymbs, single, to over 5cm diam., blush pink fading to white. 'Daikoku': habit small, br. sharply ascending; lvs bright green, with awned teeth, flushed yellow when young; stalks long, rigid; fls in pendulous, loose corymbs, double, to 5cm diam., bright lilac pink, cluster of leafy carpels at centre; late spring. 'Edozakura' ('Yedo Zakura', 'Yedo-sakura', 'Nobilis'): habit small, broadly upright; lvs broadly oblong to obovate, short-acuminate, golden brown when young; fld semi-double, to 5cm diam., cal. lobes short, pet. to 12, carmine in bud opening almond pink; early April. 'Fudanzakura' ('Fudan Zakura'): habit small; fls single, to 4cm diam., cal. red, buds soft pink, opening white, in sessile clusters; November to April, precocious fls smaller. 'Fugenzo' ('goddess on a white elephant') ('Benifugen', 'James H. Veitch'): habit spreading, crown rounded; lvs finely toothed, copper when young; fls in long pendent clusters to 3, double, large, rose pink, 2 leafy carpels at centre; mid-May, profuse. 'Fukurokuju': habit spreading, to 6m high, to 10m wide, weak-grower; lvs bronze when young, later dark green; fls in loose corymbs to 4, single with a few extra pet., soft pink fading to white; late April.

'Geraldinae' ('Asano'): habit small, narrowly upright; br. ascending; lvs narrow lanceolate, green flushed bronze when young; fls double, to 5cm diam., freely produced in short-stemmed clusters; pet. to 100, pointed, deep pink flushed mauve. 'Gyoiko' ('Tricolor'): inverted cone-shaped; fls semi-double, to 4cm diam., cream slashed green; pet. tips burgundy; free-flowering, early May. 'Hatazakura' ('Hatasakura'): fls single, small, white with ragged edges. 'Hizakura' ('Hisakura', 'Ichiyo'): to 6m, habit open, br. wide spreading; fls single to semi-double, wreathed along main growths in corymbs to 4, large, deep rose pink; cal. purple; mid-April. 'Horinji': to 5m, erect, sparsely branched; lvs lanceolate, ochre when young; fls clustered at shoot tips, semi-double, to 4.5cm diam., cal. purple, pet. to 14, pale pink; late April. 'Imose': to 9m, strong and free-growing; lvs pale copper when young, to lobster red, gold by lf drop; fls in long, loose clusters, abundant, double, to 4.5cm diam., pet. to 30, mauve pink. 'Itokukuri': habit erect, bushy; lvs flushed bronze when young; fls in loose clusters at br. tips, semi-double, light pink. 'Jo-nioi' ('Affinis', 'Elegant Fragrance'): habit tall, to 11m, br. widely ascending; lvs goldenbrown when young; fls grouped to 5, single, small, pure white, almond-scented, profuse; late April. 'Kaba': fls double, white strongly flushed green. 'Kiku-shidare' ('weeping chrysanthemum cherry') ('Kiku-shidare-sakura', 'Cheal's Weeping', 'Rosea'): small tree, to 3cm diam., br. steeply pendulous; lvs lanceolate, dark green, pale green at first; fls densely clustered, double, to 3cm diam., clear deep pink, pet. pointed; April. 'Kikuzakura': shrub-like, erect; lvs flushed bronze when young; fls double, globose, pet. to 200, soft pink; weak grower. 'Kirigayatsu' ('Mikuruma-gaeshi', 'Diversifolia'): habit open, small tree to 7m, with long ascending br.; lvs short-toothed, pale brown when v. young, copper red with yellow markings in autumn; fls densely packed in clusters, mainly on main st., single or semi-double, to 5cm, pale pink edged in deeper pink. 'Kirin': fls densely double, pet. thin, buds carmine later deep pink; late flowering. 'Kokonoe' ('Kokonoye-sakura'): small tree; lvs flushed bronze when young; fls semi-double, large, to 4.5cm diam., soft pink, profuse; earlyflowering.

'Ojochin' ('large lantern') ('Senriko'): habit stiff, stout, to 7m; lvs large, broadly elliptic, leathery, bronze at first; fls in longstalked clusters to 8, single, to 5cm diam., pink in bud, opening blush; late May. 'Okiku-sakura' ('Okiku'): habit stiff and upright; lvs flushed bronze when young; fls in dense and hanging clusters, double, to 5cm diam., pale pink, carpel leaf-like. 'Okumiyako' ('Shimidsu', 'Shimidsu-sakura'): habit small, wide-spreading, flattened crown; fls grouped to 6 in pendulous corymbs to 20cm

long, double, large, to 5cm diam., buds flushed pink opening white, pet. fringed at margin, with 2 leafy carpels in centre; mid-May. 'Oshokun' ('Conspicua'): habit broad and flat, to 3m; br. twisted; lvs tinted bronze when young; fls in short-stalked clusters, double, carmine in bud, opening malmaison pink, profuse. 'Pink Perfection': habit vase-shaped; lvs pale bronze when young; fls in long pendulous clusters, double, to 4.5cm diam., bright rose in bud, opening clear pink (sometimes fls show 2 shades); mid-April; from a seed of 'Okumiyako' and possibly 'Sekiyama'.

'Sekiyama' ('Kanzan', 'Kwanzan', 'Purpurascens'): br. stiffly ascending, eventually spreading, to 12m, vigorous; lvs large, short-toothed serrations, lightly tinted red, yellow copper in autumn; fls grouped to 5 in pendulous clusters, fully double, v. large, buds maroon opening cyclamen pink, sometimes tinged blue, often with 2 leaf-like carpels. 'Shiro-fugen' ('white god') ('Albo-rosea'): habit wide and spreading, flat-topped, to 10m high; bark dark brown; lvs brown, crimson flushed bronze when young; fls in loose hanging clusters, double, pink in bud, opening white, fading to pink-mauve with darker centre, bracts often leaflike; mid May. 'Shirotae' ('snow white' or 'double white') ('Hosokawa', 'Mount Fuji', 'Kojima'): small tree, br. spreading horizontally, occas. pendulous; lvs deeply serrate, teeth with long tips, pale green, tinted bronze with young, golden in autumn; fls grouped to 3 in pendulous corymbs, freely produced before lvs, single (sometimes semi-double on older plants), large, to 5.5cm diam., snow white, hawthorn fragrance; early April. 'Shogun': lvs richly tinted in autumn; fls semi-double, deep pink, profuse on older plants; vigorous. 'Shosar' (*P. campanulata* × *P. sargentii*): habit broadly fastifiate, strong growing; lvs bright green, yellow tinted copper in autumn; fls single, large, to 4cm diam., clear cerise pink, fl. stalks and cal. darked red; late March. 'Shujaku' ('a southern constellation') ('Campanuloides'): to 5m; lvs small, short-aristate teeth, stipules and bracts small, bronze when young; fls grouped to 6, semi-double, profuse, somewhat bell-shaped, to 4cm diam., pet. to 15, pale pink; late April. 'Sumizome' ('ink dye', referring to shadow pattern): lvs tinted bronze when young; fls semi-double, to 4.7cm diam., pet. to 14, gentle pink.

'Taguiarashi' ('Ruiran'): habit broadly upright; lvs 1-toothed, tinted brown when young, stipules and bracts small and incised; fls grouped to 4 on long stalks, single, plate-shaped, to 4.7cm diam., soft pink fading later. 'Taihaku' ('great white cherry') ('Taihaku'): habit tall and spreading, to 12m; bark with prominent brown tinted lenticels; lvs large when mature, to 20×12cm, with pronounced 'drop-tips'; bright green, red flushed bronze when young, gold by lf fall; fls to 6cm diam., single, saucer-shaped, pet. tips distinctly notched, pure white, blush pink in bud; mid-April; tetraploid. 'Taizanfukan': habit shrub-like, tightly erect and wellbranched; shoot's bark rough when older; lvs small, leathery, dark green, bronze when young; stalks of lvs and fls downy; fls densely clustered, v. double, pale pink, many buds but few bloom. 'Takinioi' ('fragrant cloud', 'fragrance of a waterfall') ('Cataract'; 'Gozanoma-nioi'): habit widely spreading, to 7×7m; lvs red tinted bronzed when young, appearing with fls; fls single, loosely arranged, v. abundant, small, snow white, hawthorn fragrance. 'Taoyame' ('Tao-yoma', 'Taoyame Zakura'): habit low and spreading; lvs brown flushed red or copper when young; fls semidouble, fragrant, shell pink fading to blush, cal. and pedicels purple-brown. 'Temari': fls single or semi-double, to 4.5cm diam., light pink, in rounded infl. at shoot tips.

'Ukon' ('yellowish') ('Grandiflora'): funnel-shaped, horizontally spreading, to 7m high, to 10m wide, vigorous; lvs pale bronze when young, flame red and plum in autumn; fls semi-double, large, to 4.5cm diam., primrose or sulphur tinted green; late April. 'Umineko' ('seagull') (*P. incisa* × *P. speciosa*): habit narrow and upright, to 8m high, to 3m wide; lvs large, bright green, orange and red in autumn; fls abundant, single, to 2.5cm, cupshaped, pure white, sta. gold; April. 'Uzuzakura' ('Hokusai', 'Roseaplena' 'Spiralis'): habit wide-spreading, vigorous, to 8m high, to 10m wide; lvs dark green, leathery, tinted brown when young, rich autumn shades; fls in long-stalked corymbs, semidouble, to 4.5cm diam., pet. to 12, shell pink, dark spot developing at centre with age; mid-April. 'Washinoo' ('eagle's tail') ('Washi-no-o'): habit vigorous, stout branched, wide open head; fls single, to 4cm diam., clustered on short peduncles to 5, buds shell pink opening pure white, scented; freely produced; early April. 'Yae-akebono': habit open, small; fls profuse, semi-double, pink; late April. 'Yae-marasakizakura' ('Purpurea', 'Yae Murasakai Zakura'): habit small, to 3m, slow growing; lvs deep green, copper red when young, brilliant orange in autumn; fls semi-double, with to 10 pet., buds red in winter, opening pinkpurple, v. abundant; late April, free flowering. 'Yokihi': medium tree, br. spreading or widely ascending; lvs green flushed bronze when young; fls freely produced in loose clusters, semi-double, large, to 4.5cm diam., pale pink with outer ring of pet. slightly darker; late April.

P. × schmittii Rehd. (*P. avium* × *P. canescens.*)   Resembles

P. canescens in narrow habit and bark, and *P. avium* in taller growth. Small tree of erect habit with a vase-shaped crown. Bark shiny, mahogany-coloured. Lvs to 8cm, elliptic-oblong, acuminate. Fls to 2cm diam., pale pink; pedicels to 1.5cm, with large bracts at base. Gdn origin. Z5.

P. scoparia (Spach) Schneid. Shrub or small tree to 6m. Br. slender, broom-like. Lvs 2–4cm, narrowly linear, fine-dentate to subentire, red-brozne when young. Fls 2.5cm diam., pale-pink. Fr. 2cm, oval, pubesc. Iran.

P. scopulorum Koehne. Tree of upright habit, 11–12m. Fls v. small, fragrant, white flushed pink in spring. China.

P. 'Senriko' = *P.* 'Ojochin' (Sato-zakura group).

P. seoulensis Nak. = *P. padus* var. *commutata*.

P. sericea (Batal.) Koehne. Tree to 18m. Lvs 9cm, narrow elliptic-obovate to narrow-oblong, brown-tomentose beneath, serrate. Fls 8mm diam., white, in congested, cylindric rac. Fr. 12.5mm, ovoid, black. W China. Z6.

P. serotina Ehrh. BLACK CHERRY; RUM CHERRY. Tree to 30m. Lvs 8.5cm, lanceolate-oblong to narrow-ovate, vivid shiny green, pubesc. on midrib beneath, fine-serrate. Fls 8mm diam., white, in cylindric, 12cm rac. Fr. 9mm diam., round, black. N Amer. 'Asplenifolia': Lvs narrow, deeply cut. 'Cartilaginia': br. more erect; lvs, to 15cm, glossy. 'Pendula': br. drooping, twigs delicate; slow-growing. 'Pyramidalis': habit conical. 'Phelloides': lvs narrow-lanceolate, pendulous. Z3.

P. serrula Franch. BIRCH-BARK TREE. Tree to 15m. Bark shiny maghogany-brown, peeling and birch-like. Lvs 7.5cm, lanceolate, fine-serrate, pubesc. on venation beneath; stipules linear. Fls 2cm diam., white, in subsessile, 1–4-fld umbels; pedicels 12mm. Fr. 1cm, ovoid, bright red. Spring. SW China. Z5.

P. serrulata Lindl. ORIENTAL CHERRY. Decid. tree to 3m. Lvs to 13cm, ovate, long-acuminate, smooth, serrulate. Fls 3.5cm diam., pure white, double, 3–5-clustered; pedicels to 4cm. Fr. a small, black cherry. Spring. China. var. *spontanea* (Maxim.) Wils. HILL CHERRY; JAPANESE MOUNTAIN CHERRY; YAMAZAKURA. To 18m. Bark brown or grey with conspicuous lenticels. Lvs to 11.5cm, elliptic-ovate to obovate-oblong, apex acuminate, bristly, double-serrate. Fls to 2.5cm diam., white or pink, in few-fld corymbs; pet. incised. Fr. magenta. Jap. Z5.

P. 'Shimidsu'. = *P.* 'Okumiyaku' (Sato-zakura group).

P. sibirica L. Shrub or small tree to 3m. Br. spreading, grey-brown or rufous, glab. Lvs to 10cm, ovate to orbicular, long-acuminate, fine-serrate. Fls white and pink-veined or pink. Fr. to 2.5cm, globose, pubesc., yellow or orange. Spring. E Sib., Manch., N China. Z5.

P. ×*sieboldii* (Carr.) Wittm. (*P. speciosa* ×*P. apetala*.) Slow-growing small tree. Shoots glossy. Lvs to 10cm, obovate, long slender-pointed, lanuginose beneath, double-serrate. Fls to 4.5cm diam., pink, semi-double, in 3–4-fld corymbs; pedicels to2.5cm, pubesc. Spring. Jap. 'Caepitosa' ('Naden', 'Waterer's Cherry', *P.* 'Takasago' (Sato-zakura group)): habit round-topped, to 8m; lvs tinted bronze or red when young, mid green, deep red in autumn; fls semi-double, to 4.5cm diam., pale pink, profuse, mid-April. Z6.

P. simonii Carr. Shrub or small tree with pyramidal crown. Lvs to 10cm, ovate-lanceolate, acuminate, fine-crenate, glab. Fls to 2.5cm diam., white, 3-clustered; pedicels to 4mm. Fr. to 6cm diam., globose, red, flesh yellow. N China. Z6.

P. sinensis Pers. = *P. glandulosa*.

P. ×*skinneri* Rehd. (*P. japonica* ×*P. tenella*.) Subshrub to 1m. Lvs to 5cm, ovate-oblong, acuminate, double-serrate. Fls many, bright pink, small. Gdn origin. 'Baton Rouge': fls profuse. Z6.

P. 'Snofozam' ('Wayside White Weeper', 'Snow Fountains'). Moderately weeping, to 4m high. Lvs dark green, orange and gold in autumn. Fls single, white, profuse. Fr. small black.

P. speciosa (Koidz.) Ingram. OSHIMA CHERRY. Loosely branched tree to 12m+. Lvs 10cm, elliptic-ovate to narrow-obovate, abruptly acuminate, bronze-green. Fls whtie, in lax, 3.5cm diam. corymbs. Spring. Jap. Z6.

P. spinosa L. SLOE; BLACKTHORN. V. spiny shrub or small tree to 8m. Lvs to 5cm, elliptic to oblong-obovate, fine-serrate to crenate. Fls to 2cm diam., white, solitary, rarely paired; pedicels to 1.5cm. Fr. to 1.5cm, globose, black, pruinose. Spring. Eur., N Afr., Asia Minor. 'Plena': fls double, small, white. 'Purpurea': lvs red when young, later green tinted purple; fls pale pink. 'Variegata': lvs variegated white. Z4.

P. 'Spiralis'. = *P.* 'Uzuzakura' (Sato-zakura group).

P. ssiori F. Schmidt. JAPANESE BIRD CHERRY. Tree to 23m+. Lvs 9.5cm, oblong to oblong-obovate, acuminate, rounded to cordate at base, bristly serrulate. Fls 9mm diam., white, in many-fld rac. Fr. black. C Jap. Z5.

P. subcordata Benth. PACIFIC PLUM; WESTERN WILD PLUM; OREGON PLUM. Shrub to 8m. Bark grey-brown, furrowed, scaly. Lvs to 5cm, orbicular to ovate, apex rounded, base subcordate, incised-serrate, later glab.; stipules lanceolate, with gland.

margins. Fls to 18mm diam., in 2–4-fld, umbellate clusters; pedicels to 13mm. Fr. to 3cm, oblong, marroon or yellow. Spring. W N Amer. Z7.

P. subcordata var. *kelloggii* Lemmon = *P. subcordata*.

P. subhirtella Miq. WINTER FLOWERING CHERRY; SPRING CHERRY; HIGAN CHERRY; ROSEBUD CHERRY. Decid., broad-crowned tree to 18m. Bark gre; branchlets slender, cascading. Lvs to 8cm, ovate to lanceolate, acuminate, serrate. Fls in groups of 2–5, pale pink to white, appearing before lvs, to 18mm diam.; cal. red-purple; pet. incised. Fr. to 9mm, ovoid, purple-black. Autumn, winter and early spring, often remontant. Jap. 'Ascendens Rosea': br. widely ascending, fls clear shell pink, cla. tinted red. 'Autumnalis' ('Jugatsu Sakura'): habit spreading, to 5m; lvs deeply serrate, red and orange in autumn; fls semi-double, pet. somewhat frilled, opening white, pink in bud, sta. dark pink, almond-scented, November to April, winter fls in sessile clusters, spring fls on stalks to 4cm. 'Autumnalis Rosea': as white form but fls soft pink centre. 'Elfenreigen' (*P. subhirtella* ×*P. concinna* ?): habit narrow, open branched; lvs brown tinted when young, intense pale colour; fls white, pet. narrow, loose stellate form; fls late April. 'Florepleno': habit dome-shaped; fls fully double, to 3cm diam., opening palest pink, pink in bud. 'Fukubana': br. broadly ascending, to 8m; fls semi-double, 12–14 pet., deeply notched, striking deep pink, darker in bud, mid-May; fertile. 'Grandiflora' ('Dai Higan Sakura'): br. widely ascending; fls large, to 5cm, palest pink, not profuse, late March. 'Hally Jolivette' (*P. subhirtella* ×*P. yedoensis*) ×*P. subhirtella*): habit rounded, to 4m, densely branched; shoots slender, tinted red; lvs to 4.5cm, narrow-ovate, sharply toothed, hairy above and more so beneath; fls double, small, buds pink, opening white with pink centre; fls for 3 weeks. 'Pandora' (*P. subhirtella* 'Rosea' ×*P. yedoensis*): habit shrub-like, broadly fastigiate, to 7m high, to 4m wide; shoots loose, nodding; lvs ovate-elliptic, to 7cm long, pubesc. beneath; fls single pale pink with darker edge; v. abundant. 'Pendula' ('Ito Sakura', 'Shidare Higan'): habit weeping; br. slender; lvs wide; fls small, faded pink; abundant, freely produced, early April. 'Pendula Plena Rosea' ('Sendai Ito Sakura', 'Pendula Flore Pleno'): habit weeping; fls double, rosette form, strong pink. 'Pendula Rosea': habit weeping, dome-shaped; fls rich pink in bud, fading later, profuse. 'Pendula Rubra' ('Ibara Ito Sakura'): habit weeping; br. slender; lvs lanceolate, red and yellow in autumn; fls deep pink, ruby in bud, early April. 'Plena': fls double, flat, pink in bud, opening paler, profuse. 'Rosea' ('Beni Higan Sakura'): habit upright; fls cup-shaped, pedicels short, bracts serrated, rose pink, in umbels to 4. 'Rosy Cloud': habit spreading, upright, to 6m; fls double, soft pink, fragrant, long-lasting. 'Stellata' ('Pink Star'): habit erect, slightly spreading, to 7m high, to 7m wide; fls single, 3.5cm across, pet. narrows oblong, clear shell pink, clustered to 5 at end 15cm of shoots so appears to form single pan. 'Whitcombii': habit broadly globe-shaped, to 10m high, to 12m wide; lvs green, opening light green; fls single, pink fading to white. Z5.

P. subhirtella var. *changyangensis* Ingram = *P. changyangensis*.

P. ×*sultana* Voss. (*P. salicina* ×*P. simonii*.) Tree of narrow, erect habit. Lvs elongate-lanceolate. Fr. v. large, maroon, flesh yellow. WICKSON PLUM. Gdn origin. 'Wickson': habit narrow and upright; lvs lanceolate; fr. large, maroon, flesh yellow. Z6.

P. susquehanae Willd. = *P. pumila* var. *susquehanae*.

P. sweginzowii Koehne. Shrub to 1.5m. Lvs to 7.5cm, linear-lanceolate or lanceolate, glab., biserrate, scabrous; stipules to 1cm linear-lanceolate, leaflike. Fls to 2cm diam. dark pink; cal. glandular-fimbriate. Fr. to 2.5cm, orbicular-ovoid. Spring-–summer. Turkestan. Z6.

P. szechuanica Batal. Small tree. Lvs to 4cm; petiole black-purple. Fl. bracts to 8mm, disc-shaped, compressed. W China. Z6.

P. tangutica (Batal.) Koehne. Dense, spiny shrub to 4m. Lvs to 3cm, oblanceolate to oblong, acute dark green, paler beneath, fine-crenate. Fls 2.5cm diam., pink-red, solitary. Fr. 2cm diam., tomentose. W China. Z5.

P. tatsienensis Batal. Closely resembles *P. litigiosa*, but lvs caudately acuminate, glab., teeth with large, conical glands at tips, floral bracts glandular-toothed. W China. Z6.

P. tenella Batsch DWARF RUSSIAN ALMOND. Low, decid. shrub to 1.5m, of bushy habit. Lvs to 9cm, obovate or oblong, somewhat thick, scabrous-serrate, dark above, paler beneath. Fls 13mm+ diam., rose-red, sessile, 1–3-clustered. Fr. 2.5cm, ovoid, grey-yellow, velutinous. Spring. C Eur. to E Sib. 'Alba': lvs light green; fls pure white. 'Fire Hill': habit dwarf, to 75cm high, forms thickets of thin erect st.; fls intense red, profuse; a selection of *f. gessleriana*. 'Speciosa': to 0.8m, fls large dark pink in bud, opening lighter. Z2.

P. texana Dietr. TEXAS ALMOND; PEACH BUSH. Bush. Bark grey; br. v. irregular. Lvs to 3cm, ovate to oblong-elliptic, green and pubesc. above, grey-tomentose beneath, glandular-serrulate.

Fls to 12mm diam., white, solitary or paired; pedicels to 4mm. Fr. small, velutinous. Summer. US (Tex.). Z6.

P. tomentosa Thunb. DOWNY CHERRY. Shrub to 2.5m. Young shoots dense-tomentose. Lvs 5.5cm, obovate to oblong, slightly rugose, green, pubesc. above, dense-lanuginose beneath, serrate. Fls 23mm diam., white or pink-white, solitary or paired. Fr. 12.5mm, subglobose, pubesc. red. N & W China, Tibet, Kashmir. 'Leucocarpa': fr. white. Z2.

P. tricantha Koehne = *P. rufa* var. *tricantha*.

P. 'Tricolor' = *P.* 'Gyoiko' (Sato-zakura group).

P. triflora Roxb. = *P. salicina*.

P. triloba Lindl. FLOWERING ALMOND. Decid. shrub or small tree to 4.5m. Branchlets brown, rod-like, at first velutinous-pubesc. Lvs to 6.5cm, ovate or obovate, often trilobed, coarsely biserrate. Fls to 2.5cm diam., pink-white, solitary or paired, often double. Fr. 13mm diam., globose, red, lanuginose. Spring. China. 'Petzoldii': twigs glab.; lvs elliptic to ovate; fls to 2cm diam., pet. pink. var. *simplex* (Bunge) Rehd. The wild form. Fls simple small, pink. Z5.

P. umbellata Elliott. SLOE. Tree to 6m. Bark dark brown. Lvs to 7cm, lanceolate to oval, fine-serrate, pubesc. on veins beneath. Fls to 18mm diam., in 2–4-fld umbels; pedicels to 1cm. Fr. to 2cm diam., globose, red, yellow or dark purple, pruinose. Spring. E US. Z8.

P. undulata D. Don, non sensu F.B. Ingram. Everg. shrub or tree to 12m. Lvs to 15cm, elliptic or oblong, long-acuminate, entire or shallow-serrate. Fls to 0.8cm diam., white or cream, in rac.; pedicels to 7mm. Fr. ovoid. Himal. (Bhutan, Sikkim). Z6.

P. ×utahensis Koehne. (*P. angustifolia* var. *watsonii* ×*P. besseyi*.) Closely resembles *P. besseyi*, but lvs to 6cm, elliptic to oblong-obovate, fine-serrate, shiny above, and fr. dark, red, pruinose. W N Amer. Z4.

P. vaniotii Lév. Tree to 15m. Lvs to 11cm, oblong to ovate-oblong, short-acuminate, serrulate. Fls to 0.8cm diam., white, many, in rac. to 14cm. Fr. to 6mm, ovoid. W China to Taiwan. Z5.

P. verecunda Koehne. Tree to 20m. Bark grey-brown or purple-brown. Lvs to 12cm, obovate or obovate-elliptic, caudate, biserrate, shiny, soft pubesc. Fls to 3cm diam., white to pale red in 2–4-fld corymbs; pedicels to 2cm, pubesc.; pet. incised. Fr. to 1cm diam., purple-black. Spring. Jap., Korea. Z8.

P. vilmoriniana hort. = *P. scopulorum*.

P. virginiana L. Shrub to 3.5m, or rarely small tree. Lvs 8cm, broad-obovate or broad-elliptic, vein axils sandy-pubesc., v. fine-serrate. Fls 1cm diam., white, in dense, rac. Fr. round, dark red to black. W N Amer. 'Canada Red': broadly pyramidal, well-branched, to 8m; lvs purple. 'Duerinckii': lvs broadly elliptic. 'Leucocarpa': fr. pale amber. 'Nana': habit dwarf. 'Pendula': br. drooping. 'Schubert': habit dense, spreading, to 6m high, to 7m diam.; lvs green, later brown tinted maroon, eventually dark brown. var. *demissa* (Torr. & A. Gray) Torr. WESTERN CHOKEBERRY. Erect shrub or small tree to 3m. Branchlets glab. or pubesc. Lvs to 9cm, shorter acuminate, sometimes lanuginose beneath; petiole bi-glandular. Fr. dark red. NW US. var. *melanocarpa* (A. Nels.) Sarg. Shrub or small tree. Branchlets smooth. Lvs glab. beneath; petiole eglandular. Fr. almost black. US (Rocky Mts). 'Xanthocarpa': fr. yellow. Z2.

P. wallichii Steud. = *P. undulata*.

P. watsonii Sarg. = *P. angustifolia* var. *watsonii*.

P. wattii Ghora & Panigr. = *P. cornuta*.

P. webbii (Spach) Vierh. Shrub or small tree to 6m. Short shoots spiny, young shoots red. Lvs to 4.5cm, oblong-linear, glandular-crenate, paler beneath. Fls 2cm diam., white, solitary, sometimes clustered; fil. becoming pink. Fr. 2cm, conical, velutinous. Sicily to Asia Minor. Z6.

P. wilsonii (Schneid.) Koehne. Tree to 10m. Lvs to 13cm, obovate, acuminate, round at base, fine-serrate, sericeous-pubesc. beneath. C China. Z6.

P. ×yedoensis Matsum. (*P. subhirtella* ×*P. speciosa*.) Small tree to 15m, broadly upright. Bark smooth. Lvs to 10cm, elliptic, acuminate, biserrate, pubesc. beneath; petiole yellow with red pubesc. Fls to 3.5cm diam., pure white, in 5–6-fld, rac. Fr. pea-sized, black. Spring. TOKYO CHERRY. Jap. 'Akebono': fls pure pink. 'Erecta': fastigiate, compact; fls to 4cm diam., somewhat cup-shaped, pale rose, faintly scented; late March. 'Ivensii': br. horizontal, branchlets slender and nodding; fls to 2cm diam., pink in bud, opening white. 'Moerheimii': shrub-like, to 3m, weeping; twigs pendulous, grey; fls pink fading to white; to 2cm diam.; late-flowering. 'Shidare Yoshino' ('Pendula'): habit weeping; fls snow white, profuse. Z5.

→*Laurocerasus* and *Persica*.

Psammophora Dinter & Schwantes. Aizoaceae. 6 highly succulent perennials, st. mat-forming or subterranean. Lvs short, thick, decussate, ± triquetrous to semicylindric, slightly glossy, blue-green to grey-green viscid. Fls terminals, solitary, pedicellate. Nam. Z10.

P. herrei L. Bol. Lvs 2×1cm, short-triangular, upper surface convex, lower surface rounded, acutely carinate toward tip, surface rough, brown-grey. Fls 2.5cm diam., white. W Cape.

P. longifolia L. Bol. Lvs 4–4.5×1.2cm, linear, rounded to rounded-carinate below, v. rough, light grey-green to grey-brown. Fls 3.5cm diam., white. Nam.: Great Namaqualand.

P. modesta (Dinter & A. Berger) Dinter & Schwantes. Lvs 1.2×0.5cm, rounded-triangular, acute, grey-green, faintly flushed red, rough. Fls 1.5cm diam., violet. Nam.

P. nissenii (Dinter) Dinter & Schwantes. Lvs 1.2–4×0.6cm, tip expanded-triangular, lower surface semicylindric or with rounded keel, grey-green, tinged white or red. Fls 1.2cm diam., white or violet. Nam.

Pseudepidendrum Rchb. f.

P. spectabile Rchb. f. = *Epidendrum pseudepidendrum*.

Pseuderanthemum Radlk. Acanthaceae. Some 60 everg. herbs subshrubs and shrubs. Fls in erect bracteate spikes, cal. lobes 5, narrow; cor. long-tubular, lobes 5, spreading. Trop. Z10.

P. alatum (Nees) Radlk. CHOCOLATE PLANT. Low-growing herb. Lvs ovate-cordate, bronze to chocolate brown, blotched silver along midvein above, leaden grey beneath petioles winged. Fls small, purple. C Amer.

P. atropurpureum L.H. Bail. Slender shrub to 1.5m. Lvs 10–15cm, ovate-elliptic, purple to deep metallic green. Fls to 2.5cm, white, spotted rose or purple at base. Polyn., nat. trop. Amer. 'Variegatum': lvs bronze-purple, marked pink, variegated cream-yellow; fls magenta marked red.

P. reticulatum (Hook. f.) Radlk. Subshrub to 1m. Lvs to 27cm, ovate-lanceolate, undulate, dark green net-veined cream-yellow. Fls to 3cm, flushed and spotted damson. Polyn.

P. seticalyx (C.B. Clarke) Stapf = *Ruspolia seticalyx*.

→*Chamaeranthemum* and *Eranthemum*.

Pseudobombax Dugand. Bombacaceae. 20 decid. shrubs or trees. Lvs simple or digitate, clustered at end of short twigs, inarticulate (unlike *Bombax*). Fls before lvs, clustered at branch-ends, or solitary; cal. cup-shaped to subtubular, truncate to shortly 5-lobed; pet. 5, united with staminal tube, erect, fleshy, with tufts of hairs; sta. many united below to form short staminal tube. Fr. a dehiscent woody capsule, seeds embedded in fibres. Trop. Amer. Z10.

P. ellipticum (HBK) Dugand. SHAVING-BRUSH TREE. To 10m. Lvs with 3–6 lfts, elliptic, apiculate, to 31×17.5cm. Fls solitary or paired; pedicel to 3.5cm; cal. 1.5cm; pet. 9–16×1–2cm, oblong-linear, white to pink, densely pubesc. externally; sta. to 13cm. Fr. to 15cm, yellow-brown. Mex. to Guat.

P. grandiflorum (Cav. (Robyns To 40m. Lvs with 5–9 lfts, obovate to subelliptic, obtuse to sub-acuminate to 28×10cm. Fls solitary or paired; pedicel to 5cm; cal. to 3cm; pet. to 18×2cm, linear-lanceolate, dark black-purple, paler within, densely pubesc. externally; sta. to 10cm. Fr. to 30cm, brown. Braz.

→*Bombax* and *Pachira*.

Pseudocalymma Samp. & Kuhlm.

P. alliaceum var. *microcalyx* pro parte Sandw. = *Mansoa hymenaea*.

P. alliaceum (Lam.) Sandw. = *Mansoa alliacea*.

P. hymenaeum (DC.) Sandw. = *Mansoa hymenaea*.

P. laevigatum (Bur. & Schum.) A. Samp. & Kuhlm. = *Mansoa hymenaea*.

P. macrocarpum Sandw. = *Mansoa hymenaea*.

P. pachypus (Schum.) Sandw. = *Mansoa hymenaea*.

P. pohlianum Bur. & Schum. = *Mansoa hymenaea*.

Pseudocyclosorus Ching. Thelypteridaceae. 11 terrestrial ferns. Rhiz. Young fronds mucilaginous. Pinnae deeply lobed. Trop. Afr., Madag., Masc. Is., Trop. & Subtrop. Asia to Jap. & Indon. Z10.

P. canus (Bak.) Holtt. & Grimes. Rhiz. suberect or creeping. Stipes 20cm+, short-hairy. Frond blade lanceolate to obovate, 70cm+, pinnae to 15×3cm, to 28 pairs, apex attenuate, base truncate, lobes obtuse, veins hairy. N India.

P. repens (Hope) Ching = *P. canus*.

→*Nephrodium*.

Pseudocydonia Schneid. Rosaceae. 1 shrub or small decid. to semi-everg. tree to 18m. Bark peeling; br. hairy, becoming shiny. Lvs 5–8cm, obovate to oval, bristly-serrate, glossy above,

hairy beneath, red or yellow in fall. Fls 2.5–3cm diam., solitary, pale pink. Fr. 10–15cm, ovoid, yellow. Spring. China. Z6.
P. sinensis (Dum.-Cours.) Schneid.
→*Chaenomeles, Cydonia* and *Malus.*

Pseudodrynaria C. Chr. Polypodiaceae. 1 epiphytic fern. Rhiz., creeping, stout, woolly. Fronds to 2m, leathery to membranous, dark green turning brown at base, sessile, lower part shallowly pinnately lobed or sinuate, cordate, dilated, scarious, upper part deeply pinnatifid or pinnatisect, seg. 30×3cm, lanceolate to linear. India to Taiwan. Z10.
P. coronans (Wallich ex Mett.) Ching.
→*Aglaomorpha* and *Polypodium.*

Pseudoespostoa Backeb.
P. melanostele (Vaupel) Backeb. = *Espostoa melanostele.*

Pseudogaltonia Kuntze. Liliaceae (Hyacinthaceae). 1 bulbous perenn. herb. Lvs in a rosette, erect, broadly linear , glaucous, soft. Fls in a scapose dense rac., far exceeding lvs; tep. pale glaucous green, basally united into a curved cylindric tube, lobes spreading, ovate; sta. 6, slightly exserted. S Afr., Nam., Bots., Angola. Z10.
P. clavata (Mast. ex Bak.) Phillips.

Pseudognaphalium Kirpiczn. Compositae. 10 ann. to peennial herbs. Cap. disciform, few in corymbose or cymose clusters; phyllaries cream-white to yellow, glandular-hairy; outer flts filiform or narrowly tubular, inner flts, tubular. Warm regions.
P. obtusifolium (L.) Hilliard & B.L. Burtt. Ann. to 50cm, woolly to puberulent or glandular-villous. Lvs to 10cm, lanceolate to linear, glab. above, gland., sessile. Involucre 6–7mm high; phyllaries spreading, white, rust-tinged. Autumn. SE US.
→*Gnaphalium.*

Pseudogynoxys (Greenman) Cabr. Compositae. 13 perenn. shrubs or climbers. Lvs alt. Cap. radiate or discoid, solitary or few to many in term. or axill. corymbose clusters; flts pale to deep orange or red. Trop. S Amer. Z10.
P. chenopodioides (Kunth) Cabr. MEXICAN FLAMEVINE; ORANGEGLOW VINE. Liane or climbing shrub to 6m. Lvs narrowly ovate, dentate, light green, glab. Cap. radiate, to 5cm diam., few, in term. and axillary corymbs, fragrant. Colomb.
→*Senecio.*

Pseudolarix Gordon. GOLDEN LARCH. Pinaceae. 1 decid., larch-like conifer to 40m. Crown broadly conic; bark rust-brown, narrow-ridged, becoming grey and fissured. Br. whorled. Lvs in open spiral on long shoots, in pseudowhorls on short shoots, 3–5(–7)cm×2–3mm, linear, keeled beneath, pale green becoming rich gold in autumn. ♂ 'cones' in umbels of 10–20, cylindric, 1cm; ♀ cones solitary, ovoid, short stalked, 5–7.5×5cm, grren, pruinose, ripening rusty-brown. E China. Z6.
P. amabilis (J. Nels.) Rehd. 'Annesleyana': dwarf, spreading; br. crowded and drooping at tips. 'Dawsonii': dwarf, conical, compact. 'Nana': dwarf, tiered, to 1m.
P. fortunei Mayr = *P. amabilis.*
P. kaempferi (Lamb.) Gordon = *P. amabilis.*
→*Chrysolarix.*

Pseudolithos Bally. Asclepiadaceae. 4 leafless, succulent, dwarf herbs. St. unbranched, erect, v. soft, swollen, often compressed above. Umbels many-fld, lat. shoot, fls small. Somalia, Kenya, Arabia. Z9.
P. cubiformis (Bally) Bally. St. 3–5×4–6cm, obtusely quad-rangular, pale green, tessellated. Fls 4.3cm diam. to 30 per umbel, tube glab. pale green outside, tinged brown inside, lobes 9mm, grey-green, purple or pink, with clavate hairs at tip. Somalia.
P. migurtinus (Chiov.) Bally. St. hemispherical, to 12×6.5cm, pale green or yellow-green to grey, covered in flat, blunt tubercles. Fls to 1cm diam., to 10 per umbel, tube, pale, lobes 3mm, exterior pale green, interior purple-maroon, papillose, ciliate, with cluster of trap-shaped cilia. E Somalia.
→*Lithocaulon.*

Pseudolobivia Backeb.
P. aurea (Britt. & Rose) Backeb. = *Echinopsis aurea.*

Pseudolopezia Rose = *Lopezia.*

Pseudolysimachion Opiz.
P. longifolium (L.) Opiz = *Veronica longifolia.*
Pseudolysimachion spicatum (L.) Opiz = *Veronica spicata.*

Pseudomertensia Riedl.
P. echioides (Benth.) Riedl = *Mertensia echioides.*
P. elongata (Decne.) Riedl = *Mertensia elongata.*

Pseudomuscari Garb. & Greuter = *Muscari.*

Pseudonephelium Radlk. = *Dimocarpus.*

Pseudopaegma Urban = *Anemopaegma.*

Pseudopanax K. Koch. Araliaceae. 12–20 unarmed, everg. trees or shrubs. Lvs simple or palmately compound sometimes dimorphic. Infl. lat. or terminal, simple or compound; fls small, green to yellow in umbels, clusters or rac. Fr. purple-black, round. LANCEWOODS. NZ and associated islands, Tasm., Chile.
P. arboreus (Murray) K. Koch. FIVE-FINGER; PUAHOU; WHAU-WHAUPAKU. Round-headed tree to 8m; trunk slender, br. pointed upwards. Lfts 3–7, thick, narrowly oblong to oblong-obovate, to 20cm, coarsely toothed, dark glossy green above. NZ. Z10.
P. chathamicus T. Kirk. HOHO. Stoutly branched tree to 7.5m. Lvs simple; in adults thick, linear-obovate, to 20cm, toothed near blunt apex. Summer. Chatham Is. Z9.
P. colensoi (Hook. f.) K. Koch. MOUNTAIN IVY-TREE; ORIHOU. Similar to *P. arboreus* but lvs 3–5-foliolate with thick, ± sessile lfts. NZ.
P. crassifolius (Sol. ex A. Cunn.) K. Koch HOROEKA; LANCE-WOOD. Tree to 15m. Juveniles unbranched, wand-like, with fierce-downward-pointing armour-lvs. Lvs simple or 3(–5) foliolate; adult lvs simple, upright, linear to linear-obovate leathery, to 20cm, sinuate or coarsely toothed; seedling lvs ovate-lanceolate, membranous, to 60cm, coarsely toothed or lobed; armour lvs linear, rigid, to 100cm somewhat variegated, spine-toothed. Summer. var. *trifoliolatus* T. Kirk (*Aralia trifoliae* hort.) (North Is.) early adult lvs 3-foliolate, lfts to 30cm. var. *pentadactylus* Voss (*Panax pentadactylus* Decne. & Planch.) lvs 5-foliate. NZ. Z9.
P. davidii (Franch.) Philipson = *Metapanax davidii.*
P. delavayi (Franch.) Philipson = *Metapanax delavayi.*
P. discolor (T. Kirk) Harms. Much-branched shrub or small tree to 6m. Lvs 1–5-foliolate, blades or lfts narrowly obovate, to 7.5cm, sharply toothed, stalked paler, lustrous beneath. NZ. Z10.
P. ferox (T. Kirk) T. Kirk. TOOTHED LANCEWOOD. Resembling *P. crassifolius* but to 7m. Lvs always simple, in adults to 15cm or so; intermediate lvs to 45cm, jaggedly toothed. Summer. NZ. Z9.
P. laetus (T. Kirk) Philipson. Shrub or small tree, to 6m or so. Lvs 5–7-foliolate; petioles purple-red, to 25cm, lfts obovate, thick, to 30cm, stalked, toothed above. NZ. Z10.
P. lessonii (DC.) K. Koch. HOUMSPARA; HOUPARA. Shrub or small tree to 6m. Lvs 3–5-foliolate, lfts in adults sessile, thick, to 10cm, narrowly obovate, entire or ± toothed, lfts in juveniles 5, linear-lanceolate, coarsely toothed. NZ. Z9. 'Gold Splash': lvs variegated with gold.
P. linearis (Hook. f.) K. Koch. Similar to *P. chathamicus* but adult lvs smaller and narrower, to 10cm. Shrub to 4m; lvs in pseudowhorls; juvenile lvs to 25cm; midrib in adult lvs yellow. NZ. Z9.
P. simplex (Forst. f.) K. Koch. HAUMAKAROA. Much-branched shrub or small tree to 8m. Juvenile lvs thin, 3–5-foliolate, lfts pinnatifid; adult lvs simple, narrowly ovate, elliptic or obovate, to 12.5cm, serrate, glossy. NZ. (inc. Stewart and Auckland Is.) var. *sinclairii* (Hook. f.) Edgar. MOUNTAIN PANAX. Lvs 3(–5)-foliolate, lfts to 7cm, dull; no juvenile lvs present. Z10.
→*Neopanax, Nothopanax, Panax.*

Pseudopectinaria Lavranos.
P. malum Lavranos = *Echidnopsis malum.*

Pseudorhipsalis Britt. & Rose = *Disocactus.*
P. alata (Sw.) Britt. & Rose = *Disocactus alatus.*
P. himantoclada (Roland-Goss.) Britt. & Rose = *Disocactus himantocladus.*
P. macrantha Alexander = *Disocactus macranthus.*

Pseudosasa Mak. ex Nak. Gramineae. 6 bamboos with running rhiz. (clumped in colder climates). Culms erect; sheaths longer than the internodes, bristles white and smooth or 0; nodes not prominent, with white waxy powder below; br. 1–3 from the upper nodes. Lvs tessellate, glab. China, Jap., Korea. Z6.
P. amabilis (McClure) Keng f. TONKIN CANE. Culms 5–13m×2–7cm, bristly when young, thick-walled; sheaths bristly-hairy; br. usually 3. Lvs 10–35×1.2–3.5cm; sheaths usually with bristles. S China; cult. throughout SE Asia.

P. japonica (Sieb. & Zucc. ex Steud.) Mak. ex Nak. ARROW BAMBOO; METAKE. Culms 3–6m×1–2cm, thin-walled, glab.; sheaths with few or no bristles; br. 1 per node. Lvs 20–36×2.5–3.5cm, two-thirds glaucous beneath; sheath lacking bristles. Distinguished from *Sasamorphaborealis* in the white powder and the bicoloured undersides to the lvs. Jap., Korea.
→*Arundinaria, Sasa* and *Yadakea.*

Pseudotaxus Cheng. Taxaceae. 1 everg. conifer resembling *Taxus* to 4m. Br. whorled. Lvs apparently distichous, 10–25×3–4mm, linear or subfalcate, deep shining green above, paler beneath with 2 grey-blue stomatal bands. Seeds with cuplike, white aril. SE China (Zhejiang to Guangxi). Z8.
P. chienii (Cheng) Cheng. WHITE BERRY YEW.
→*Nothotaxus* and *Taxus.*

Pseudotsuga Carr. DOUGLAS FIR. Pinaceae. 8 everg. coniferous trees. Crown conic, becoming irregular with age. Bark smooth, with resin blisters when young, becoming fissured corky. Br. spreading or sweeping slightly down. Lvs (needles) radially arranged, short-petiolate, the petiole twisted often in a pectinate arrangement, linear, soft, flattened, two white or grey stomatal bands beneath. ♂ cones ovoid, yellow or pink; ♀ cones ovoid, composed of long tridentine bracts. Mature cones pendulous on a bract-covered stalk, ovoid, ovoid-cylindric or ovoid-conic, often bloomed, ripening brown, resinous. W N Amer. S to Mex., and E Asia from S Jap. to Taiwan and SW China.
P. brevifolia Cheng & Fu = *P. sinensis* var. *brevifolia.*
P. douglasii (Lindl.) Carr. = *P. menziesii.*
P. flahaultii Flous = *P. menziesii* var. *flahaultii.*
P. forrestii Craib. To 40m. Bark scaly grey-brown; crown broad conic, open. Shoots slightly hairy; lvs sparse, moderately pectinate, 2.5–5cm, green with white bands beneath, emarginate or blunt. Cones as *P. japonica* but longer and much stouter, 4.5–7×3.5–4cm. SW China. Z8.
P. glauca (Beissn.) Mayr = *P. menziesii* ssp.*glauca.*
P. guinieri Flous. MEXICAN DOUGLAS FIR. To 45m. Bark as *P. menziesii.* Crown slender conic, open, br. level or downswept. Shoots glab.; lvs all round shoot except underneath, strongly forward-pointing at basal end, curved outward at apex, 13–20mm, green with two green-white bands on outer surface acute. Cones on 1cm st., slender-cylindric, 4–8×1.5cm violet bloomed white. US (W Tex.), Mex. Z8.
P. japonica (Shiras.) Beissn. JAPANESE DOUGLAS FIR. To 40m. Bark smooth grey, fissured brown; crown broad conic, irregular in cult. Shoots glab.; lvs moderately pectinate, 2–3cm, yellow-green above, two white bands beneath, emarginate or rounded. Cone on a 1cm stalk, ovoid-conic, 4–5.5×2cm closed, purple bloomed violet. S Jap. Z7.
P. macrocarpa (Vasey) Mayr. BIG-CONE DOUGLAS FIR. to 25m. Bark broad purple-brown corky plates separated by pale orange-buff vertical fissures. Crown broad open conic, br. gently downswept, branchlets pendulous. Shoots finely pubesc.; lvs all round shoot, parted beneath on stronger shoots, straight or gently curved forward and down, 3–5cm, to on strong shoots, deep glossy green above, two grey-white bands beneath, acute. Cones on a 5–10mm stalk, long ovoid-conic to cylindric, 11–13×3cm, green-brown. US (SW Calif. mts). Z8.
P. macrolepis Flous = *P. guinieri.*
P. menziesii (Mirb.) Franco. DOUGLAS FIR; GREEN DOUGLAS FIR. To 100m. Bark green-brwon with resin blisters, becoming red-brown, corky, fissured; crown dense, conic, more slender and open in vigorous trees, spire-like; br. level or gently downswept, branchlets drooping. Shoots thinly pubesc., strongly aromatic; lvs pectinate in several ranks, 1.5–4cm, bright green above, two dull white bands beneath, blunt, rounded. Cone on a 5–12mm stalk, ovoid-cylindric to cylindric, 6–11.5×2cm, green. SW BC, to WC Calif. ssp. *glauca* (Beissn.) E. Murray BLUE DOUGLAS FIR; COLORADO DOUGLAS FIR. Smaller tree to 40m. Shoots greyer, less aromatic; lvs strongly upswept, 1.5–2.5cm, grey-green to blue-green, stomatal bands above as well as beneath. Cone 4–7cm. C & S US. About 15 cvs; 'Argentea' and 'Candida' brilliant white-blue lvs; several dwarf. var. *caesia* (Schwerin) Franco. GREY DOUGLAS FIR; FRASER RIVER DOUGLAS FIR. Lvs slightly pectinate, dull grey-green with some stomata above, grey-white bands beneath. Cone 4–6cm. SE BC to Idaho. Several cvs; 'Fretsii' frequent, dull shrub with short broad lvs. var. *flahaultii* (Flous) Silba. ARIZONA DOUGLAS FIR. Lvs 1.7–3cm; cones purple, 5–9cm. S US to Mex. Z7.
P. menziesii var. *glauca* (Beissn.) Franco = *P. menziesii* ssp. *glauca.*
P. sinensis Dode. CHINESE DOUGLAS FIR. To 40m in wild, shrub in cult. V. similar to *P.forestii* and *P. wilsoniana.* Lvs 20–40×1.5–2mm, shiny green above, emarginate. SC China. var. *brevifolia* (Cheng & L.K. Fu) Farjon & Silba. Lvs

7–20×2–3mm. SW Guanxi. Z8.
P. taxifolia (Lamb.) Britt. ex Sudw. = *P. menziesii.*
P. wilsoniana Hayata. TAIWAN DOUGLAS FIR. To 40m in wild, shrub in cult. Differs from *P.forrestii* in shorter lvs, mostly 15–25mm but occas. to 45mm. Taiwan. Z8.

Pseudowintera Dandy. Winteraceae. 2 glab., everg. shrubs or small trees to 8m. Lvs entire, coriaceous. Fls solitary and axillar, or clustered, yellow-green; cal. cupular; pet. 5–6; sta. 5–15, fil. laterally compressed. Fr. a berry. NZ.
P. axillaris (Forst. & Forst. f.) Dandy. Lvs to 13cm, narrow-ovate to oblong, lustrous deep green above, glaucous beneath. Fr. red.
P. colorata (Raoul) Dandy. Lvs 2–6cm, elliptic-oblong, green, flecked or edged purple-red or orange and red above, pearly beneath. Fr. black.
→*Drimys* and *Wintera.*

Psidium L. GUAVA. Myrtaceae. 100 everg. trees or shrubs. Lvs opposite, simple. Fls to 2.5cm diam., white, cal. tube prolonged above the ovary, splitting irregularly; pet. 5 rounded; sta. many. Fr. a globose or pear-shaped berry, sometimes large and edible. Americas. Z10.
P. araca Raddi = *P. guineense.*
P. cattleianum Salisb. = *P. littorale* var. *longipes.*
P. friedrichsthalium (O. Berg) Niedenzu. Shrub or small tree to 8m. Branchlets 4-angled. Lvs to 7cm, glossy above, pubesc. beneath. Fls solitary. Fr. to 6cm, sulphur-yellow, with white flesh. C Amer.
P. guajava L. COMMON GUAVA; YELLOW GUAVA; APPLE GUAVA. Shrub or small tree, to 10m. Branchlets 4-angled. Lvs to 15cm, ovate to oblong-elliptic, pubesc. beneath. Fls solitary or clustered. Fr. ovoid to pear-shaped, 2–10cm, with yellow or dark pink flesh. Trop. Amer.; cult. throughout the tropics and subtrop. 'Beaumont': pink-fleshed. 'Detwiler': yellow-fleshed. 'Pear': flesh cream-white.
P. guineense Sw. GUAVA. Shrub or small tree to 7m. Branchlets ± cylindrical. Lvs to 13cm or more, ovate to oblong-elliptic, rusty-pubesc. beneath. Fls solitary or clustered, fragrant. Fr. ovoid, brown-green, turning to pale yellow when ripe, acid. Trop. Amer.
P. littorale Raddi. Shrub or small tree to 8m. Lvs to 7.5cm, elliptic to obovate, glab. Fls solitary, 2.5cm diam. Fr. to 4cm with white flesh. Braz. var. *littorale.* YELLOW STRAWBERRY GUAVA; YELLOW CATTLEY GUAVA; WAIAWI. Fr. sulphur-yellow, somewhat translucent, acid. var. *longipes* (O. Berg) McVaugh. PURPLE GUAVA; PURPLE-STRAWBERRY GUAVA; CATTLEY GUAVA. Fr. globose, purple-red, sweet. 'John Riley': fr. large, dark red.
P. littorale var. *lucidum* (Deg.) Fosb. = *P. littorale* var. *littorale.*
P. lucidum hort. = *P. littorale* var. *littorale.*
P. molle Bertol. = *P. guineense.*
P. montanum Sw. MOUNTAIN GUAVA; SPICE GUAVA. Shrub to about 2m. Branchlets flat rounded. Lvs ovate to oval, rounded at both ends or cordate at base. Fls solitary or clustered. W Indies.

Psiguria Necker ex Arn. Cucurbitaceae. 15 slender vines or lianes. Tendrils simple. Lvs 3–5-foliolate to entire. ♂ fls racemose, cal. cylindrical, 5-lobed, cor. rotate, sta.; ♀ fls solitary staminodes 2. Trop. Amer. Z10.
P. warscewiczii (Hook. f.) Wunderlin. Lfts. 3, central 11–17cm, obovate-oblong, laterals somewhat hastate, smaller; petioles 3–6cm. Fls orange to scarlet, cor. ventricose lobes rounded to obovate, 5–8mm, pubesc. Fr. oblong-ellipsoid, 5.5–7cm, pale green with darker stripes. S Mex. to Colomb.

Psilanthus Hook. f. Rubiaceae. 18 shrubs and small trees. Fls axill. or term. white; bracts and bracteoles 0 or forming chaff-like calyculus; cal. tubular, irregularly 5-toothed; cor. salverform, tube elongate, membranous, exterior and throat glab. or pubesc., lobes 4–5, spreading; sta. 4–5. Fr. a berry. Trop. Afr., Asia, and Aus. Z10.
P. bengalensis (Roem. & Schult.) J. Leroy. Shrub. Lvs to 13cm, ovate or elliptic, acute to acuminate; stipules subulate. Fls 1–3 per axil; cor. to 4cm wide, tube to 2.5cm, lobes ovate-oblong. Fr. to 13mm, black. India, Burm.
→*Coffea.*

Psilocaulon N.E. Br. Aizoaceae. 70 annuals biennials or shrubs. St. cylindrical, often constricted at nodes, internodes. Lvs short-lived, small, soft, cylindrical, united in sheath at base. Fls c1cm diam., solitary or many together, shortly pedicellate. S Afr. (Cape Prov.), Nam. Z10.
P. arenosum (Schinz) L. Bol. Shrubby, erect, 60–90cm. St. 4-angled, internodes 7–18×4–7mm, jointed, green. Lvs 7–10mm, papillose. Fls numerous, white. Namaqualand.

P. ciliatum (Ait.) Friedr. Low-growing. St. green, jointed inter-nodes 3–7×3–4mm, spherical. Lvs 2–5mm, papillose with cilia at base. Fls in a cyme, white. W Cape, Nam.

P. dinteri (Engl.) Schwantes. Forming large mats to 75cm; st. v. fleshy, jointed, 4–10mm diam., barrel-shaped, swollen. Lvs 10×2–3mm. Fls 3–5 together, red. Nam.

P. gymnocladum (Schltr. & Diels) Dinter & Schwantes = *P. arenosum*.

P. marlothii (Pasc.) Friedr. Forming dense cushions; st. cylindrical, internodes 4×4mm, nodes not conspicuously jointed, covered by ciliate, lf remains, red-brown. Lvs 6–8mm with cilia at base. Fls white or pink. Namaqualand.

→*Brownanthus*.

PSILOTACEAE Kanitz. See *Psilotum*.

Psilotum Sw. FORK FERN; WHISK FERN. Psilotaceae. 2 rootless, primitive, terrestrial or epiphytic clump-forming herbs of skeletal, broom-like appearance; st. erect to pendulous, dichotomously branched, angular, rigid, green, bearing minute scale-like lvs. Sporangia term., to 2mm diam. yellow-brown. Subtrop. and Trop. Z10.

P. complanatum Sw. St. to 70cm, spreading or flaccid-pendulous, br. elliptic in cross-section, with distinct midrib, young st. some-times triquetrous, dark green. Pantrop. rainforest.

P. nudum (L.) Beauv. SKELETON FORK FERN. St. to 60cm, erect or pendulous. Br. triquetrous, pale green fading to dull yellow. Pantrop. (Amer., Jap., Australasia).

P. triquetrum Sw. = *P. nudum*.

Psomiocarpa Presl. Dryopteridaceae. 1 terrestrial fern. Rhiz. ascending. Fronds dimorphic: sterile fronds to 15×12cm, short-stipitate, rosette-forming, 2–3-pinnate or -pinnatifid, ovate, pubescent on veins, pinnules to 3mm, wide, obtuse, entire, fertile fronds smaller, modified to much-reduced, narrow blade, above, stipitate, 3-pinnate or -pinnatifid at base. Trop. Asia (Philipp.). Z10.

P. apiifolia (J. Sm.) Kunze.

→*Acrostichum* and *Polybotrya*.

Psophocarpus Necker ex DC. Leguminosae (Papilionoideae). 10 climbing herbs. Lvs 1- or 3-foliolate. Fls pea-like, solitary, clustered or in rac. Fr. a 4-winged, oblong, dehiscent legume. Trop. Asia and Afr.

P. tetragonolobus (L.) DC. WINGED BEAN; WINGED PEA; GOA BEAN; MANILA BEAN; ASPARAGUS PEA; PRINCE'S PEA; PRINCESS PEA; DAMBALA; FOUR-ANGLED BEAN. Tuberous-rooted twining herb. Lfts to 15cm, 3, ovate, acute. Infl. a lax rac.; fls to 3cm, red-brown. Fr. to 25×2.5cm with thin, leafy wings to 0.6cm deep. Asia, Maur.

Psoralea L. SCURF PEA. Leguminosae (Papilionoideae). 130 glandular-scurfy, perenn. herbs or shrubs. Lvs 1–3-foliolate to imparipinnate. Fls pea-like in heads, rac. or spikes, occas. clustered or solitary. N & S Amer., S Afr.

P. acaulis Steven ex Bieb. Stemless perenn. herb to 25cm. Lfts 3, hairy, ovate-elliptic, dentate. Fls cream in solitary heads. Cauc. Z6.

P. aphylla L. BLOUKEUR; FONTEINBOS. Shrub to 3m. Br. erect or drooping, nearly leafless. Lfts 3 narrow or lvs scale-like. Standard blue, keel and wing white. Summer. S Afr. Z9.

P. esculenta Pursh. POMME BLANCHE; POMME DE PRAIRIE; INDIAN BREADROOT. Perenn. to 50cm. Tuberous roots edible. St. hairy. Lfts 5, 5.5cm, oblong to oblanceolate, hairy beneath. Fls yellow to blue in a spike to 10cm. Spring to early. N Amer. Z4.

P. glandulosa L. CULEN. Shrub to 3m, black-glandular. Lfts 3, to 7.5cm, lanceolate, rounded or wide-cuneate at base, deep green. Fls white blotched blue in a spike-like, downy rac. to 13cm. Summer–autumn. Peru, Chile. Z9.

P. hypogaea Torr. & A. Gray. Perenn. herb, white-pubesc. Lfts 3–7 to 5cm, elliptic-linear to narrowly obovate, glabrescent above. Spike to 3cm, 3–7 fls white to lavender. Mont. to Tex. and New Mex. Z4.

P. linearis Burm. f. = *Aspalathus linearis*.

P. pinnata L. BLUE PEA. Shrub to 2m. Lfts 5–11, 3cm, linear-lanceolate, ± puberulous. Fls numerous, solitary or clustered, violet or blue, wings white. Summer. S Afr. Z9.

P. tetragonolobus L. = *Cyanopsis tetragonolobus*.

Psychopsis Raf. BUTTERFLY ORCHID. Orchidaceae. 5 epiphytic orchids. Rhiz. short. Pbs to 4cm, orbicular to subquadrate, strongly laterally compressed, wrinkled. Lvs oblong-elliptic, erect, coriaceous, often dotted or mottled maroon. Rac., erect basal remontant; fls 1–3 in succession; dors. sep. erect, spathulate, narrow, revolute and undulate, lat. sep. ovate-oblong, crispate to undulate; pet. similar to dors. sep.; lip

pandurate, 3-lobed, lat. lobes orbicular, midlobe large, transversely subquadrate, disc fleshy, with calli; column long, with antennae-like processes. C & S Amer. Z10.

P. krameriana (Rchb. f.) H. Jones. Lvs to 16×6cm. Peduncle to 1m; terete; fls to 12cm diam.; tep. deep red-brown with golden yellow margins, undulate-crisped; lip yellow blotched deep red-brown, to 4.5×4cm, sub pandurate, lat. lobes suborbicular, erose, midlobe transversely oblong, with conspicuous yellow central blotch, bilobulate, margins mottled red-brown, undulate-crisped, callus deep bronze-purple. Costa Rica, Panama, Ecuad., Peru, Colomb.

P. limminghei (E. Morr. ex Lindl.) E. Luckel & G.J. Braem. Lvs to 3.5×3.5cm. Peduncle terete, to 10cm; fls to 3.5cm diam., sep. dull red-brown; pet. bright red-brown barred with pale yellow-brown; lip cream-yellow spotted orange-brown, to 2.5×2.5cm, lateral lobes large, oblong, recurved, midlobe larger, triangular, bilobulate. Braz., Venez.

P. papilio (Lindl.) H. Jones. Lvs to 25×7cm. Peduncle to 120cm strongly compressed, fls to 15cm diam.; dors. sep. and pet. purple-brown mottled yellow-green, slightly undulate, lat. sep. bright chestnut red barred yellow, strongly undulate; lip to 4×3.5cm, lat. lobes small, semi-orbicular, yellow spotted orange-brown, midlobe, emarginate, golden yellow mottled red-brown, undulate-crisped, disc pale yellow or white spotted red-brown. Trin., Venez., Colomb., Ecuad., Peru.

P. picta Raf. = *P. papilio*.

→*Oncidium*.

Psychotria L. WILD COFFEE. Rubiaceae. 500–900 shrubs, trees or perenn. herbs. Lvs stipulate, domatia and nodules usually present. Fls sessile or pedicellate, in sessile or pedunculate, term., or lat. infl.; bracteate and bracteolate, often involucrate; cal. tube cup-shaped, truncate or toothed or lobed; cor. tubular to bell-shaped, lobes 4–5, sta. 4–5. Fruita berry, to 1cm globose to ovoid. Trop. and Subtrop. Z10.

P. bacteriophila Val. = *P. punctata*.

P. berteriana Bello, non DC. = *P. pubescens*.

P. capensis (Ecklon) Vatke. Shrub to tree, to 7m. Lvs to 15cm, obovate to elliptic, lustrous and leathery, pubesc. on veins beneath. Pan. or corymbs to 15cm; cor. cream to yellow; tube to 5mm, pubesc. at throat, lobes to 3mm, deltoid to oblong. Fr. red to black. S Afr.

P. crocea Sw. = *Palicourea crocea*.

P. cyanocarpa Ruiz & Pav. Perenn. herb. Lvs elliptic, entire to undulate. Fls white. Fr. blue. C Amer.

P. emetica L. f. FALSE IPECAC. Shrub or subshrub, to 60cm. Lvs to 17cm, lanceolate or elliptic to obovate, minutely pubesc. beneath. Pseudoracemes few-fld; cor. white; tube to 5mm, interior minutely pubesc.; lobes acute. Fr. blue. Guat. to Boliv.

P. hirsuta Spreng., non Sw. = *P. undata*.

P. ipecacuanha (Brot.) Stokes. Shrub or perenn. herb, to 50cm. Lvs to 15cm, ovate or elliptic to oblong, lustrous, occas. pubesc. beneath. Cap. globose; cor. white to 1cm, tube interior minutely pubesc., lobes 5, falcate. Fr. red to blue. Winter. C to S Amer.

P. jasminiflora (Lind. & André) Mast. Shrub. Lvs to 8cm, ovate to oblong, white-pubesc. beneath. Pan. terminal corymbose; cor. white to 3cm, tubular to funnel-shaped, distended above, exterior pubesc., lobes 4. Braz.

P. nervosa Sw. Shrub to 2.5m, or tree to 6m. Lvs to 16cm, ovate or lanceolate to elliptic, entire to undulate, glab. to minutely pubesc. Pan. terminal; cor. white tube to 3mm. Fr. yellow to red. Flor., W Indies.

P. oligotricha DC. = *P. undata*.

P. peduncularis (Salisb.) Steyerm. Shrub or herb, to 4m. Lvs to 27cm, elliptic or lanceolate to oblong or obovate, thinly leathery, pubesc. beneath. Cap. term., many-fld; bracts white, yellow or blue, cor. white cylindric to funnel-shaped, tube to 7mm, lobes to 3mm, lanceolate to deltoid Fr. white to blue or black. Trop. Afr.

P. pilosa Ruiz & Pav. Herb, to 60cm. Lvs oblong. Fls in short-pedunculate pan., white; bracts pubesc. Fr. blue. C Amer.

P. portericensis DC. = *P. undata*.

P. pubescens Sw. Shrub to 3m, or tree to 5m. Lvs to 20cm, elliptic or lanceolate to oblong, membranous, pubesc. Pan. many-fld to 9cm, cor. to 7mm, white to yellow or pink, tube exterior and throat pubesc., lobes 5, oblong. Fr. purple to black. W Indies and Cuba, C Amer.

P. punctata Vatke. Shrub or tree, to 3m. Lvs to 15cm, ovate to elliptic, obtuse leathery to fleshy, glab. to minutely pubesc. pan. dense to 8cm; cor. white tube to 6mm, lobes to 4mm, elliptic to oblong. Fr. red. Trop. Afr.

P. racemosa (Aubl.) Rausch. Shrub, to 2m. Lvs to 20cm, elliptic to oblong, apex attenuate. Pan. term. to 5×5cm, cor. white to green to 6mm, tube exterior papillose and pubesc., lobes spreading, cucullate, interior papillose. Fr. orange to purple or black. Summer. C & N S Amer.

P. rigida (HBK) Willd. ex Roem. & Schult. = *Palicourea rigida*.

P. tabacifolia J. Muell. = *Palicourea nicotinaefolia*.

P. undata Jacq. Shrub, to 3m. Lvs to 12cm, elliptic to oblong, papery, glab. to pubesc. pan. term., few- to many-fld; cal. tube to 1mm, limb ± truncate; cor white to 4mm. Fr. red. Flor., W Indies, C Amer.

P. venosa (Hiern) Petit. Shrub, to 4.5m. Lvs to 20cm, elliptic to oblong, lustrous above. Cymes many-fld, paniculate, cor. white to 4mm. Trop. W Afr.

→*Cephaelis* and *Grumilea*.

Psydrax Gaertn. Rubiaceae. 75 shrubs or trees, erect or climbing. Fls in branched or umbellate, cymose clusters, or solitary; cal. tube hemispheric or ellipsoid, 4–5-toothed, or truncate; cor. cylindric, lobes 4–5, spreading, eventually reflexed; sta. 4–5, anth. exserted. Fr. a drupe. Trop. Afr., Asia, Oceania. Z10.

P. subcordata (DC.) Bridson. Tree; br. spreading. Lvs to 20cm, ovate or oval, apex truncate or obtuse, base cordate or obtuse, leathery, glab., bristly or hairy. Fls in branched, pedunculate cymes. Trop. Afr.

→*Canthium*.

Psygmorchis Dodson & Dressler.

P. pusilla (L.) Dodson & Dressler = *Oncidium pusillum*.

Psylliostachys (Jaub. & Spach) Nevski Plumbaginaceae. 6 annuals. Lvs pinnately cut or entire, usually basal. Infl. a slender-stalked pan. of 2–4-fld spikelets; cal. tubular, 5-lobed, scarious; cor. funnelform, lobes 5, small. Syr. to Iran and C Asia.

P. leptostachya (Boiss.) Roshk. 10–20cm. Lvs 4–10cm, oblanceolate, pinnatisect, glossy green. Peduncles exceeding lvs, rarely branched; spike slender simple; cal. to 2mm, glandular-pubesc., 5-ribbed; cor. white. Iran, Afghan.

P. ×myosuroides (Reg.) Roshk. (*P. leptostacha* ×*P. suworowii.*) Fls larger, cal. more densely pubesc., 10-ribbed; cor. white to dark pink. Iran, N. Afghan.

P. spicata (Willd.) Nevski. 10–40. Lvs 5–15cm, oblanceolate, pinnatisect, glossy green, pubesc. on midrib. Peduncles far exceeding lvs, pubesc.; term. spikelet to 9cm, lat. spikelets shorter, sessile; cal. 3mm, 10-ribbed, glandular-pubesc.; cor. about 4mm, rose. Spring. Crimea, Cauc., Iran.

P. suworowii (Reg.) Roshk. Similar to *P. spicata* but lvs glab.; peduncles, pubesc. toward infl.; lat. spikelets sometimes stalked; fls larger, pink or bright pink. C Asia, Iran, N Afghan.

→*Limonium* and *Statice*.

Ptelea L. HOP TREE; SHRUBBY TREFOIL Rutaceae. 11 shrubs or small trees. Lvs generally 3-foliolate, lat. lfts shorter and narrower than term., muskily aromatic, pellucid-punctate. Infl. of corymbose or paniculate cymes; fls, pale green or white tinged green; sep. 4–5, occas. 6; pet. 4–5(–6), exceeding pet. Fr. a samara, 2- or occas. 3-celled, body broadly winged. N Amer.

P. angustifolia (Benth.) V.L. Bail. Shrub to 4m; young twigs glab. to slightly pubesc. Lfts oblong-lanceolate, pubesc. to glab. above, ± glaucous beneath. Fr. rounded, wings refuse. Summer. Mex., S US.

P. aptera Parry. Shrub, 2–5m, young twigs adpressed-pubesc. Lfts 2+cm, narrowly obovate, obtuse, crenulate becoming revolute. Fr. to 1cm, unwinged, ovate to subcordate-ovate, emarginate, sinously ridged. Calif., Baja Calif. Z9.

P. baldwinii Torr. & A. Gray. Shrub 3–8m, bark white. Lfts 1–2cm, ovate, pale green, ciliate, later glab. Fr. oblong to suborbicular, retuse or subulate-tipped, 1–2cm, thin, body usually strongly reticulate. Spring. S US. Z6.

P. crenulata Greene. Shrub or small tree, to 6.5m; young twigs glandular-punctate, sparingly hairy. Lvs vivid minutely pubesc., glandular-punctate; lfts cuneate-obovate crenulate term. 4–7cm, lat. 1.5–4.5cm. Fr. 1.5–2.5cm, orbicular, body 2× width of wing, glandular-punctate, minutely pubesc. Calif. Z8.

P. isophylla Greene = *P. trifoliata*.

P. jucunda Greene = *P. angustifolia*.

P. lutescens Greene = *P. baldwinii*.

P. microcarpa Small. Shrub, 1.5–3m, branched. Lvs glab.; lfts 4–10cm, elliptic to oblong-lanceolate, entire to undulate, beneath. Fr. 8–11mm, orbicular-obovate to suborbicular, rounded or truncate at base, pitted, wings slightly crisped. Spring. SE US. Z7.

P. mollis M.A. Curtis = *P. trifoliata* var. *mollis*.

P. monticola Greene. Young twigs minutely velvety. Lvs somewhat glaucous beneath, subcoriaceous, punctate, lfts 3–5cm, term. leaflet broadly cuneate-obovate, crenate becoming revolute. Fr. 1.5cm, obovate-orbicular, truncate to emarginate, obscurely punctate, wing narrower than body. Tex. Z8.

P. neomexicana Greene = *P. angustifolia*.

P. pallida Greene. Young twigs minutely pubesc., older twigs cinereous. Lvs glaucescent beneath, subcoriaceous, scarcely glandular-punctate; lfts crenulate-serrulate, term. 3.5–5.5cm, elliptic-lanceolate. Fr. 1.5–2cm, orbicular, obtuse to subtruncate, body oval, narrower than wing, transversely sinuous-ridged, sparingly glandular-punctate. Ariz. Z8.

P. polyadenia Greene. Young twigs rusty-velvety. Lvs 6cm, subcoriaceous, glossy above, minutely pubesc. and dark glandular-punctate; lfts slightly crenate, term. ovate-elliptic. Fr. 1.5cm, rounded obovate, retuse or emarginate, thick and hard, body orbicular-ovate, rugose and distinctly punctate, wing broader than body. SW US. Z6.

P. serrata Small. Shrub, 1–2m. Lvs glab.; lfts elliptic, term. 2.5–7cm, serrate, dark above, v. pale beneath. Fr. obovate, acute at base, 16–19mm, body glandular-punctate, wing delicate. Georgia. Z8.

P. straminea Greene. Twigs polished, pale, scarcely glandular-punctate. Lvs glab., sparingly punctate; lfts 4–6.5cm, obovate, crenate. Fr. 2cm, broadly suborbicular, cordate, somewhat 2-lobed, body narrower than wing, faintly rugose, glandular-punctate. Ariz. Z8.

P. tomentosa Raf. Shrub or small tree. Lvs tomentose beneath; lfts 2.5–8cm, elliptic to obovate; petiole densely tomentose. Fr. 1.3–2.5cm, ovate, cordate or truncate at base, emarginate or subulate at apex, strongly reticulate. E US. Z7.

P. trifoliata L. HOP-TREE; STINKING ASH; WATER ASH. Shrub or tree to 8m. Lvs glab. or pubesc.; lfts 4–12cm, ovate to oblanceolate, entire to undulate or minutely crenate, lustrous above, paler beneath. Fr. 2–2.5cm, ovate-orbicular to suborbicular, rounded or notched at base. Early summer. E & C US. 'Aurea': lvs soft yellow, later lime. 'Fastigiata': habit upright. 'Glauca': lvs tinted blue. 'Monophylla': lfts only 1. 'Pentaphylla' ('Heterophylla'): lfts narrow, sometimes 4–5. var. *mollis* Torr. & A. Gray. Lvs broader, grey-tomentose beneath. Z5.

P. trifoliata var. *angustifolia* (Benth.) M.E. Jones = *P. angustifolia*.

PTERIDACEAE Spreng. ex Jameson. 6 genera. *Acrostichum, Anopteris, Pteris.*

Pteridium Gled. ex Scop. (nom. cons.). Dennstaedtiaceae. 4–8 terrestrial ferns. Rhiz. long-creeping, subterranean, woody with red-brown hairs. Fronds stipitate, uniform, 2–4-pinnate-pinnatifid, ovate to deltoid, coarse, firm-textured, pubesc. or glab., pinnae with nectaries at base (at least initially), opposite to subopposite, pinnules alt., revolute. Cosmop.

P. aquilinum (L.) Kuhn. BRACKEN; BRAKE; PASTURE BRAKE. Fronds to 1m, erect, 2–4-pinnate, ovate or deltoid to oblong, pubesc. beneath, pinnae to 80cm, ovate to deltoid, pinnules to 15cm, ovate to lanceolate, caudate or obtuse, entire to incised, seg. linear to oblong, attenuate to obtuse, brown. N Hemis. 'Cristatum': all pinnae and pinnules crested. 'Grandiceps': raised from 'Cristatum', far less invasive, foliage reduced to large grandicipital crests (Grandiceps), a curiosity, 50–70cm. var. *latiusculum* (Desv.) Underw. ex A.A. Heller. Fronds with oblique pinnae, seg. glab. to sparsely pubesc. at margin and on costa beneath. E N Amer., Eur., E Asia. var. *pseudocaudatum* (Clute) A.A. Heller. Fronds to 70cm, seg. ± glab. but hair-tipped at proliferous and caudate apex. E US. var. *pubescens* Underw. WESTERN BRACKEN. Fronds pubesc. above, pubesc. to tomentose beneath, pinnules horizontal. W N Amer. Z4.

P. aquilinum Copel., non (L.) Kuhn = *P. esculentum*.

P. aquilinum var. *japonicum* Nak. = *P. aquilinum* var. *latiusculum*.

P. esculentum (Forst. f.) Nak. Fronds to 3m, erect, 2–4-pinnate-pinnatifid, deltoid, initially pubesc. to glab., eesp. on veins beneath, pinnae to 1m, ovate to deltoid, pinnules to 14cm, lanceolate, caudate, lobed at base, seg. linear to oblong, obtuse. Malaysia to Australasia, Polyn. Z10.

P. latiusculum (Desv.) Hieron. ex Fries = *P. aquilinum* var. *latiusculum*.

Pteridophyllum Sieb. & Zucc. Fumariaceae. 1 rhizomatous perenn. herb. Lvs radical lanceolate in outline, 5–15×2.5cm, finely pinnatisect, lobes oblong, blunt to truncate. Fls white, nodding and slender stalked in erect rac.; pet. 4, elliptic-oblong, to 1cm. Spring. Jap. Z7.

P. racemosum Sieb. & Zucc.

Pterilema Reinw.

P. aceriflorum Reinw. = *Engelhardia spicata*.

Pteris L. BRAKE; DISH FERN; TABLE FERN. Pteridaceae. 280 terrestrial ferns; rhiz. erect to creeping. Fronds pinnate to 4-partite, basal pinnae often forked and as large as the rest of the blade; stipes slender, erect, equalling blade. Subtrop. and Trop. Z10.

P. altissima Poir. Frond blade deltate-ovate, somewhat pentagonal, to 1.5×1.2m, basal pinnae 2-pinnate-pinnatifid, the apical portion 1-pinnate-pinnatifid, terminating in a broad pinnatifid apical pinna, pinnules broadly pinnatifid, caudate seg. elongate-deltate. Trop. Amer.

P. argyraea Moore. Frond-blade 1-pinnate-pinnatisect, green with a broad white central line, term. pinna 15–30×3–5cm, seg. linear-oblong. Trop.

P. atrovirens Willd. Frond-blade 50–100cm, 1-pinnate-pinnatisect term. pinna 15–22×4–7cm, seg. linear, dentate, lowest lat. pinnae forked with similar pinnules below; rachis spinose beneath. Trop. Afr.

P. aurea Poir. = *Cheilanthes bonariensis*.

P. biaurita L. Frond blade oblong or deltate-oblong, to 1.3m, 1-pinnate-pinnatisect, lower pinnae forked; pinnae 5–15 pairs. Pantrop.

P. catoptera Kunze. Fronds blade pinnate, pinnae subsessile, seg. oblong-linear, entire, confluent at base, thin, coriaceous. S Afr. & S Trop. Afr.

P. childsii hort. = *P. cretica* 'Childsii'.

P. comans Forst. f. NETTED BRAKE; COASTAL BRAKE. Frond-blade to 2m, 2–3-pinnate at base; term. pinna to 30cm+, cut to rachis, lat. pinnae to 45×15cm, few, pinnules to 5cm, oblong, dentate, veins netted. Aus., NZ.

P. cretica L. Frond blade ovate or rotund in outline, with 1–5 pairs of simple or forked pinnae, term. pinnae similar glab. or with a few castaneous, filiform scales pinnae 10–20cm, linear-lanceolate. OW Trop. & Subtrop. 'Albolineata': seg. wider with a broad white stripe. 'Childsii': fronds lobed, waved or frilled, bright green. 'Major': to 30cm; pinnae in to 6 pairs, linear, entire, sessile, term. pinna elongate. 'Maxii': similar to 'Albolineata' but dwarfer, with seg. narrower, crested. 'Ouvardii': to 60–90cm; seg. dark green, narrowly linear. 'Parkeri': robust; fronds lustrous; seg. broadly lanceolate, finely undulate-dentate. 'Rivertoniana': pinnae in 4–5 pairs, deeply lobed. 'Whimsettii': a vigorous grower; fronds 45–60cm, with chestnut stripes, pinnae variously lobed or toothed. 'Wilsonii': fronds compact, bright green, lobed, heavily crested, giving a fan-like appearance.

P. dentata Forssk. Frond-blade deltoid to ovate, 2–3-pinnate-pinnatisect, 50–100×30–30cm, bright green, pinnae 15–30cm, cut into many lobes, to 5cm, linear, crenate-dentate. Trop. & S Afr.

P. dispar Kunze. Frond-blade 25–40×8–15cm, lanceolate to narrowly oblong-ovate, bipinnatifid, chartaceous, term. pinna 10–20cm, triangular-lanceolate, dentate, lat. pinnae 5–10cm, in 3–7 pairs, narrowly deltoid, pinnatifid or entire, pinnules 10–30mm, linear to oblong-lanceolate. China, Jap. to Taiwan.

P. ensiformis Burm. f. SWORD BRAKE. Frond-blade bipinnate 15–30×8–15cm, term. pinna 5–10cm slightly compound with central portion entire, lat. pinnae to 4–5 pairs, cut into 2–6 obovate-oblong pinnules to 12mm wide, dentate. Himal. to Jap., Philipp., Polyn. & Trop. Aus. 'Arguta': lvs dark green, with central, silver-white markings. 'Evergemiensis': fronds with silvery white central band and dark green margins. 'Victoriae': fronds with a white zone flanking the midrib on either side, sterile fronds small, prostrate, fertile fronds 40–45cm, erect, with pinnae to 4mm wide.

P. fauriei Hieron. = *P. quadriaurita*.

P. flabellata Thunb. = *P. dentata*.

P. grandifolia L. Frond blade narrowly oblong, 1–2×0.4–0.7m, 1-pinnae 2–6cm apart, narrowly oblong-linear to linear-ligulate, entire and narrowly cartilaginous. Trop. Amer.

P. heterophylla L. = *Anopteris hexagona*.

P. hirsuta (L.) J. Sm., non Poir. = *Lonchitis hirsuta*.

P. incisa Thunb. = *Histiopteris incisa*.

P. laciniata Willd. = *Lonchitis hirsuta*.

P. longifolia L. Frond blade oblong to oblanceolate-elliptic or oblanceolate, 18–80×8–25cm, pinnae narrowly linear, base cordate or hastate, crenulate-serrulate. W Indies, Central Amer. to Braz.

P. macilenta A. Rich. SWEET FERN. Frond-blade ovate, 3-pinnate at base, 30–90×15–50cm, terminal pinna 10–20cm, cut into oblong lobes, deeply toothed, numerous, lat. pinnae cut into deeply lobed deltoid pinnules. NZ.

P. microphylla A. Cunn. = *Paesia scaberula*.

P. microptera Mett. Frond blade large, pinnate, primary pinnae 30–60+cm, secondary pinnae 10–25cm, deeply pinnatifid, seg. linear or oblong-lanceolate, lower sometimes shortly pinnatifid, dentate decurrent. Australasia, Pacific Is.

P. multifida Poir. SPIDER BRAKE; SPIDER FERN. Frond blade ovate, pedate, 2-pinnate at base, pinnatisect above, 20–50cm long, 10–25cm broad, pinnae elongate-pinnatisect, decurrent, to 5mm broad, long-attenuate. E Asia, introd. Amer. 'Cristata':

smaller, more compact; seg. slender, more branched, with broad, crests.

P. nipponica Shieh. Fronds dimorphous, simply pinnate, sterile fronds with blade consisting of a term. pinna, 1–3 pairs of lat. pinnae, these linear-oblong, 10–20cm, sessile, serrate, term. pinnae longer. Fertile lat. pinnae linear, 20–30cm, short-stalked.

P. nitidula Wallich = *Pellaea nitidula*.

P. orientalis v.A.v.R. Frond blades to 1m, erect, arching, pinnate, dark green, pinnae to 20×1cm, linear ± equal. SE Asia, Ryuku Is.

P. pacifica Hieron. Frond-blade 30–50cm, erect, pinnate, the basal pair of pinnae basicopically bipinnate, pinnae 10–25cm, linear, perpendicular to rachis. Aus.

P. quadriaurita Retz. Frond-blade to 90×45cm, term. pinna bipinnate, tripinnate in lower part, cut into numerous lobes 2.5cm+, linear-oblong, lower pinnae forked at base giving 4 distinct divisions at base of frond. OW Trop.

P. ryukyuensis Tag. Frond-blade ternate or occas. with 1 remote pair of basal pinnae, glab., sterile pinnae 2–7×1cm, lanceolate to oblong-ovate, lower sometimes divided, fertile pinnae 4–15×0.3–0.4cm, linear. Jap.

P. scaberula A. Rich. = *Paesia scaberula*.

P. semipinnata L. Frond-blade 30–45×15–22cm, ovate-lanceolate, apex cut to rachis into numerous linear lobes, entire, lowest 4–8cm, lower two-thirds of frond with 6–8 opposite pinnae, pinnatisect below, largest 7–15cm, winged on upper side, and 4–6 linear pinnules to 5cm along basiscopic side. SE Asia, inc. Ryukyu Is.

P. serrulata Forssk. Frond blades to 60×30cm, ovate, pinnate, pinnae in to 11 pairs, pinnatisect, lowest sometimes forked, seg. oblong-lanceolate, serrate above. Azores, Canary Is., Madeira, N Afr.

P. tremula R. Br. TENDER BRAKE; SHAKING BRAKE; TURAWERA; AUSTRALIAN BRACKEN; POOR-MAN'S CIBOTIUM. Frond-blade ovate, 3–4-pinnate at base, 30–90×20–70cm; pinnules to 2cm, narrowly oblong to linear, dentate, ultimate seg. linear to 3.5×0.5cm, toothed. NZ, Aus., Fiji.

P. trichomanoides L. = *Cheilanthes trichomanoides*.

P. tripartita Sw. GIANT BRACKEN. Frond-blades 2–2.5m pinnae 3 equal, middle pinna 1-pinnate-pinnatifid, shortly caudate, with one large basiscopic 1-pinnate-pinnatisect pinnule, lobes. SE Asia, New Guinea, Aus. & Polyn.

P. umbrosa R. Br. JUNGLE BRAKE. Frond-blade 30–50cm, erect, pinnatifid, pinnae 10–30cm, linear-lanceolate, decurrent with rachis wing, entire or minutely dentate, lat. pinnae 6–9 each side, lowermost with 2 or 3 linear, large basiscopic lobes. Aus.

P. vespertiliensis Labill. = *Histiopteris incisa*.

P. victoriae Bull = *P. ensiformis* 'Victoriae'.

P. vittata L. Frond-blade oblong elongate, 1-pinnate, 20–100cm long, 20–40cm broad, pinnae linear-ligulate, 10–18×1–2cm, glab. or with brown scales. Trop. and temp. regions of Eur., Afr., Asia and Australasia; introd. in Amer.

P. wallichiana J. Agardh. Frond-blade to 1m, tripartite, soft, pale green, central pinna 60×30cm, pinnate, pinnules lanceolate, cut into oblong lobes, subentire when sterile, lat. pinnae forked again. Trop. Asia to Pacific New Guinea.

Pterisanthes Bl. Vitaceae. 20 vines climbing by tendrils. Infl. pendulous, flat fleshy bodies with lobed margins, attached to rachis along one side, with sessile or immersed fls (sometimes long-pedicelled). Fr. a berry. Burm., W Malaysia. Z10.

P. polita (Miq.) Lawson. Slender, glab. apex. Lvs 10–20cm, elliptic-oblong to ovate, base subcordate, acute, entire or remotely spinose-serrate. Infl. body red; fls 4-merous. Borneo, Sumatra.

→*Vitis*.

Pterocactus Schum. Cactaceae. 9 dwarf succulent shrubs; rootstock usually tuberous; st. seg. globose, cylindric or clavate, often suffused brown or red; lvs small, subulate, caducous; glochids present; spines few. Fls terminal, immersed in the apex of stem-segments; perianth rotate; staments touch-sensitive. Arg.

P. fischeri Britt. & Rose. St. unbranched, cylindric, to 10(−15)×1–1.5cm, tuberculate, brown-green; central spines usually 4, 1–3(−5)cm, flat and somewhat papery, base yellow; radial spines 12+, 6mm, bristly, off-white. Fl. 2.5cm diam. coppery yellow to clear brown or purple. S Arg. (Rio Negro, Neuquen). Z7.

P. kuntzei Schum. St. seg. 7–20×8–15mm, brown or brown-green, with a vertical violet line below areoles; spines 8–12, 5–10mm, terete, off-white. Fl. 3–5cm diam., pale yellow, or tinged orange-brown or brown. Arg. Z7.

P. pumilus Britt. & Rose = *P. valentinii*.

P. tuberosus (Pfeiff.) Britt. & Rose = *P. kuntzei*.

P. valentinii Speg. St. seg. little-branched, cylindric, 4–8×1–1.5cm, green; central spines 0; radial spines 25–30, 4–5mm, hyaline. Fl. yellow to coppery. W Arg. Z7.

Pterocarpus Jacq. Leguminosae (Papilionoideae). 20 trees or climbers. Lvs imparipinnate. Fls in massed rac. or pan., often produced before lvs; standard and wings crisped. Fr. a legume, often broadly winged. Trop. Amer., India, Trop. & S Afr. Z10.

P. angolensis DC. BLOODWOOD TREE; KIAAT; MUNINGA. Tree to 12m. Lfts 2.5–5cm, 4–12 pairs, pubesc. at first, petiolules 8mm. Fls to 1.5cm wide, orange-yellow, fragrant. Fr. 8–10cm diam., discoid, hispidulous. Autumn. S Afr. to Nam., Angola and Tanz.

P. echinatus Pers. = *P. indicus*.

P. indicus Willd. PADAUK; PADOUK; BURMESE ROSEWOOD. Tree to 9m. Lfts to 10cm, 5–9, glab., short-stalked. Fls to 1.3cm wide, yellow. Fr. 5cm diam., orbicular, sericeous. Spring. India to China, Malay Archipel., Philippine Is.

Pterocarya Kunth. WINGNUT. Juglandaceae. 10 decid. trees. Lvs pinnate, infl. a pendulous catkin; fls small green, with wing-like bracteoles. Fr. a small winged nutlet, 1-seeded. Cauc. to E & SE Asia.

P. caucasica C.A. Mey. = *P. fraxinifolia*.

P. delavayi Franch. To 20m. Bark grey, young twigs pubesc. Lvs 20–30cm; lfts oblanceolate, 11cm, coriaceous, midrib and petiole pubesc. Fr. SW China. Z8.

P. dumosa Lav. = *P. fraxinifolia* var. *dumosa*.

P. fraxinifolia (Lam.) Spach. CAUCASIAN WALNUT. To 25m, often multistemmed. Bark grey-black, deeply furrowed; twigs olive-brown, slightly pubesc. Lvs 20–40cm; lfts 11–21, oval-oblong to oblong-lanceolate, 8–12cm, midrib pubesc. beneath. Cauc. to N Iraq. 'Albomaculata': young lvs speckled white. var. *dumosa* (Lav.) Schneid. Shrubby, br. yellow-brown. Lfts 5–7cm. Cauc. Z7.

P. fraxinifolia K. Koch non Spach = *P. fraxinifolia* var. *dumosa*.

P. hupehensis Skan. To 20m. Bark pale grey, becoming deeply fissured; twigs scurfy. Lvs 15–20cm; lfts 5–9, oblong to oblong-lanceolate or slightly obovate, to 14cm. C China. Z6.

P. japonica hort. = *P. stenoptera*.

P. laevigata hort. = *P. fraxinifolia*.

P. macroptera Batal. To 20m. Bark dark brown; twigs glab. Lvs 70–160cm; petiole rusty tomentellous; lfts 9–11, narrowly oblong-lanceolate, serrate, midrib rust-red tomentellous beneath. China. Z7.

P. paliurus Batal. = *Cyclocarya paliurus*.

P. ×rehderiana C. Schneid. (*P. fraxinifolia ×P. stenoptera*.) To 20m, suckering. Young shoots red-brown. Lvs about 20cm; rachis partially winged; lfts 11–21, narrow-oblong, 6–12cm. Gdn origin (Arnold Arboretum, 1908). Z6.

P. rhoifolia Sieb. & Zucc. To 30m. Twigs finely pubesc. at first. Lvs 20–40cm; rachis finely pubesc.; lfts 11–21, ovate-oblong, 6–12cm, finely serrate, veins sometimes pubesc. beneath. Jap. Z6.

P. sinensis hort. = *P. stenoptera*.

P. sorbifolia Dipp. = *P. fraxinifolia*.

P. spachiana Lav. = *P. fraxinifolia*.

P. stenoptera C. DC. To 25m. Young shoots tawny pubesc. Lvs 20–40cm; rachis winged, sometimes serrate; lfts 11–23, oval-oblong to narrow-oblong, serrulate, veins sometimes pubesc. beneath. China. Z7.

Pteroceltis Maxim. Ulmaceae. 1 decid. tree to 10m; crown broad; bark pale grey, peeling in flakes. Lvs 3–10cm, ovate-oblong to ovate-lanceolate, serrate, acuminate, base broad-cuneate, 3-nerved, downy in vein axils beneath. Fls inconspic-uous, ♂ clustered, ♀ solitary. Fr. a samara, 1.5–2cm wide, broad winged, suborbicular. N & C China. Z5.

P. tartarinowii Maxim.

Pterocephalus Adans. Dipsacaceae. Some 25 ann. or perenn. herbs, subshrubs and shrubs. Fl. heads discoid, flattened, long-stalked, subtended by narrow bracts; outermost fls 2-lipped and larger than those at centre. Medit. to C & E Asia. Z6.

P. parnassi Spreng. = *P. perennis*.

P. perennis Coult. Cushion-forming perenn. To 10cm, usually shorter, tufted. Lvs to 4cm, ovate to oblong, crenate to lyrate. Fls purple-pink in heads to 4cm diam., on 5–7cm peduncles. Greece.

P. pyrenaicus hort. = *Scabiosa pyrenaica*.

→*Scabiosa*.

Pterodiscus Hook. Pedaliaceae. 18 shrubs or small perenn. herbs, often semi-succulent with a swollen caudex and tuberous roots. Fls solitary from the lf axils; cal. small; cor. tube funnel-shaped, limb spreading, 2-lipped. Trop. E Afr., Angola, Nam., S Afr. (W Cape). Z9.

P. angustifolius Engl. Br. basal, spreading, fleshy, 9–20cm, purple. Lvs 2.5–13cm, fleshy, oblong-lanceolate, gland. at first, dark green, entire or undulate, rarely dentate above. Fls yellow or orange, with purple blotches in tube. Tanz.

P. aurantiacus Welw. Caudex bottle-shaped, to 30cm with several thick br. Lvs oblong-lanceolate or ovate-spathulate, sinuate, tinged blue. Fls brilliant red. Angola, Nam. Kalahari.

P. coeruleus Chiov. St. simple or branched, 5–20cm. Lvs 1.3–4cm cuneate at base. Fls white or white suffused mauve in throat, lobes with red veins. Somalia, Kenya.

P. heterophyllus Stapf = *P. kellerianus*.

P. kellerianus Schinz. Caudex fleshy, edible. Basal lvs elliptic, undulate, upper lvs narrowly lanceolate, entire or somewhat in-cised, sometimes pinnatisect. Somalia.

P. luridus Hook. Caudex obconical, 50×7–8cm; br. 15–20cm. Lvs 7–8cm, oblong, basally spathulate, apically laciniate, glaucous. Fls yellow, outside dotted red. S Afr., Nam.

P. ruspolii Engl. Caudex thick at base, 4–8×0.5–2cm; br. around 20, 4–20cm. Lvs 1.5–6.5cm, obovate to elliptic, gland. beneath, entire or undulating. Fls light yellow to orange, with red or purple blotches in the centre. Kenya, Ethiop., Sudan, Somalia.

P. somaliensis (Bak.) Stapf = *P. ruspolii*.

P. speciosus Hook. Caudex conic to cylindric, 15–50×6cm; br., few, to 15cm. Lvs 3–6cm, linear to linear-oblong, dentatge or in-cised. Fls light purple-red. S Afr.

P. welbyi Stapf = *P. ruspolii*.

→*Harpagophytum* and *Pedalium*.

Pterolobium R. Br. ex Wight & Arn. Leguminosae (Caesalpinoi-deae). 10 lianes, shrubs or trees, with paired spines. Lvs bipinnate. Flowrs in pan. or term. rac., almost regular; pet. 5, oblong or obovate; sta. 10, exceeding pet. Fr. a samaroid legume. S & E Afr. to SE Asia. Z9.

P. biebersteinii Andrz. = *Pachyphragma macrophyllum*.

P. exosum (J.F. Gmel.) Bak. = *P. stellatum*.

P. stellatum (Forssk.) Brenan. Climbing shrub to 5m. Lvs to 20cm; pinnae in 8–12 pairs; rachis prickly; lfts to 1cm, oblong, in 9–16 pairs. Fls small, cream or yellow, in dense, spike-like rac. Fr. to 5cm, crimson. Spring. E & SE Afr. (Ethiop. to Zimb.).

Pteroneuron Fée = *Humata*.

Pteropogon DC. Compositae. 10 ann. herbs; st. solitary or few, slender, erect. Lvs alt., entire, sessile, arachnoid-pubescent above. Cap. few, discoid, in a compact term. corymb, encircled by crowded lvs; phyllaries in many series, oblong, scarious, out-er dark brown, inner petaloid, slightly exceeding outer; flts pale. Aus., S Afr.

P. humboldtianum (Gaudich.) F. Muell. Ann. to 60cm. Lvs to 3cm, linear to narrowly oblanceolate, dark green, revolute. Cap. small, many, subsessile, in subglobose clusters; phyllaries yellow. Summer–autumn. S Aus.

→*Helichrysum* and *Helipterum*.

Pterospermum Schreb. BAYUR. Sterculiaceae. 25 trees or shrubs, stellate-pubescent, often with suckers. Lvs leathery scaly or pubesc. Fls nocturnal, fragrant, often long and conspic-uous, axill., solitary or in clusters; cal. tubular, sep. linear, fleshy; pet. soon falling; androgynophore short; sta. 15, anth. long. Fr. a woody capsule. Trop. Asia. Z10.

P. acerifolium (L.) Willd. MAPLE-LEAVED BAYUR. Tree to 30m. Lvs ovate to orbicular, palmately lobed, apex truncate-mucronate, peltate to cordate at base. Fls 8–15cm; sep. rusty-tomentose, slightly exceeding white pet. India to Java.

P. suberifolium Willd. CORK-LEAVED BAYUR. Small tree. Lvs oblong, obliquely cordate at base, coarsely toothed near apex, pubesc. beneath. Fls in term. or axill. few-fld rac.; sep. pubesc.; pet. white. E Indies.

Pterostylis R. Br. GREENHOOD. Orchidaceae. 60 terrestrial, tuberous orchids. Lvs in a basal rosette or reduced to bracts on st. Fls scapose, usually solitary; dors. sep. incurved, forming a hood with pet. and projecting as a slender curved tip. Lat. sep. deflexed or erect; lip with mobile claw and basal appendage. Aus., NZ, W Pacific. Z9.

P. acuminata R. Br. To 25cm. Lvs 4–8, ovate to oblong. Fl. pale green, marked white; pet. and dors. sep. tipped pink, tip to 1cm. Mid spring–early summer. E Aus., New Caledonia, New Guinea.

P. australis Hook. f. = *P. banksii*.

P. banksii Hook. To 35cm. Lvs 4–6, linear. Fls pale green, stripes darker, tep. tipped orange-pink, lip with red ridge above, margins green, tip. tubular, apically pubesc. Autumn–winter. NZ.

P. baptistii Fitzg. To 40cm. Lvs 4–8, oblong to ovate. Fls to 6cm, pale green, marked dark green and white, tep. tipped pink; dors. sep. erect, sharply curved at mid point, tip to 1.5cm. Mid summer–mid autumn. C & SE Aus.

P. coccinea Fitzg. SCARLET GREENHOOD. To 22cm. Lvs ovate to oblong-elliptic, lanceolate. Fls green to scarlet, hood sharply incurved; to 4.5cm; lip red-brown, to 20mm. Mid winter–mid spring. NE Aus.

P. concinna R. Br. To 30cm. lvs 4–6, ovate to oblong. Fls striped dark green, tips tinged brown; hood erect, incurved; lip to 10mm, dark brown. SE Aus.

P. cucullata R. Br. To 15cm. Lvs oblong to elliptic, several. Fl. ̨red-brown, often green and white at base, incurved, exterior downy; tip to 1cm; lip, brown. Summer–autumn. C & SE Aus.

P. curta R. Br. To 30cm. Lvs ovate or oblong. Fl to 4.5cm, white, striped green, tinted brown and green, hood erect, becoming incurved, tip to 1.2cm; lip to 20mm, brown. Summer–autumn. C & SE Aus.

P. nutans R. Br. PARROT'S BEAK ORCHID. To 30cm. Lvs 3–6, ovate to oblong. Fls translucent, striped green, sometimes tipped red, hood arched; lat. sep. fimbriate, tip exceeding hood; lip to 15mm, green, central ridge red-brown, fringed. Spring–autumn. E Aus., NZ.

P. pedunculata R. Br. MAROONHOOD. To 25cm. Lvs 4–6, ovate to oblong. Fls green and white, tipped dark red-brown; hood erect, basally incurved, tip to 3cm; lip to 5mm, dark red-brown. Summer–autumn. E Aus.

Pterostyrax Sieb. & Zucc. Styracaceae. 3 decid. shrubs or trees. Fls in open pan. on short lateral shoots; cal. campanulate, 5-toothed; pet. 5, distinct or barely fused at base, overlapping in bud; sta. 10, exserted. Fr. a dry oblong drupe, ribbed or winged. Summer. EPAULETTE TREE. Jap., China, Burm. Z6.

P. corymbosa Sieb. & Zucc. Shrub or tree to 12m. Lvs 6–11cm, elliptic or ovate to ovate-oblong, apex acuminate, base cuneate, to subcordate, bristly-serrulate, sparsely pubesc. Pan. corymbose, 8–15cm; fls white; cor. stellate-pubesc., lobes 14mm. Fr. 1–1.5cm, 5-winged, downy. Jap.

P. hispida Sieb. & Zucc. FRAGRANT EPAULETTE TREE. Tree to 15m or shrub to 4.5–6m; bark grey, peeling, aromatic. Lvs 7–17cm, oval or obovate, rounded or cuneate at base, bristly denticulate sparsely pubesc. beneath. Fls white, in downy, pendulous pan. 12–25cm; cor. lobes 8–10mm, oval, finely downy. Fr. 1cm, not winged, bristly. Jap., China.

P. psilophylla Perkins. Shrub to 7m. Distinguished from *P. corymbosa* by its ascending br. and shorter lvs and pan. Lvs oval or obovate-elliptic, 8–9cm, minutely serrate. Infl. 8–12cm, many-fld; fls white; cor. lobes 8–10mm, minutely stellate-tomentose. China.

Pterygota Schott. & Endl. Sterculiaceae. 15 trees, differing from *Sterculia* and *Brachychiton* mainly in having winged seeds. Trop. regions, esp. OW. Z10.

P. alata (Roxb.) R. Br. Tree to 45m high; trunk buttressed. Lvs to 35cm, cordate-ovate, sometimes lobed above. Fls in short pan.; cal. *c*2.5cm, rusty-tomentose; males with slender staminal column. Fr. to 12×10cm on 10cm woody stalk, laterally compressed, pubesc. Trop. Asia.
→*Sterculia.*

Ptilomeris Nutt.
P. coronaria Nutt. = *Lasthenia coronaria.*

Ptilopteris Hance. Adiantaceae. 1 fern. Rhiz. ascending, short, with persistent stipe bases. Stipes slender, 6–20cm, lustrous brown. Fronds 20–50×2–4cm, linear-lanceolate, apex long-attenuate, pinnate, membranous, pinnae scurfy beneath when young; pinnae –2.5cm, numerous, broadly lanceolate, obtusely dentate. Jap., China, Taiwan.

P. maximowiczii (Bak.) Hance.
→*Monachosorum.*

Ptilostemon Cass. Compositae. 14 ann. to perenn., spiny herbs or small, unarmed shrubs. Lvs alt., tufted or rosulate on sterile shoots, spiny, ± glab. above, densely white-tomentose beneath. Cap. discoid, in clusters; receptacle hairy; phyllaries imbricate, rigid, with a sharp apical spine; flts tubular, purple, rarely white. Medit.

P. afer (Jacq.) Greuter. Usually bienn., to 1m. St. white-tomentose to nearly glab. Lvs oblong-lanceolate, pinnatifid, seg. with 2–3 lobes each narrowly triangular, with spines to 1.5cm. Cap. in a term. corymb or cylindric rac.; involucre 20–50mm, campanulate. C & S Balk. Z5.

P. casabonae (L.) Greuter. Perenn. herb to 1.5m. St. sparsely hairy to glabrescent. Lvs lanceolate to linear-lanceolate, ± entire, marginal spines slender, to 1.5cm. Cap. numerous, in a

term. spike; involucre 16–24mm, cylindric-campanulate. W Medit.
→*Carduus* and *Cnicus.*

Ptilotrichum C.A. Mey.
P. lapeyrousianum (Jordan) Jordan = *Alyssum lapeyrousianum.*
P. peyrousianum Willk. = *Alyssum lapeyrousianum.*
P. purpureum (Lagasca & Rodr.) Boiss. = *Alyssum purpureum.*
P. pyrenaica (Lapeyr.) Boiss. = *Alyssum pyrenaicum.*
P. spinosum (L.) Boiss. = *Alyssum spinosum.*

Ptilotus R. Br. Amaranthaceae. Some 100 ann. or perenn. herbs and shrubs. Lvs cauline. Fls in dense, shaggy spikes, often in compound corymbs; bracts and bracteoles membranous, pilose; perianth a short tube of 5 villous seg. Australasia. Z9.

P. exaltatus Nees. PINK MULLA MULLA. Tender ann. or perenn., erect, to 1m. Lvs thick, apiculate, oblong-lanceolate, undulate, blue-green, tinged red, to 8cm. Spikes conical to cylindric, to 15×5cm, cream-yellow tinged pink. Winter–summer. Aus.

P. manglesii (Lindl.) F. Muell. Decumbent to ascending perenn. or ann. To 30cm. Lvs obtuse or acute, basal, ovate to linear, lower lvs to 8cm. Spikes globose or ovoid, villous, pink to violet-purple, to 10×6cm. Summer. Aus.

P. spathulatus (R. Br.) Poir. PUSSYTAILS; CAT'S PAWS. Low procumbent perenn. to 40cm. Lvs fleshy, basal lvs to 10cm, spathulate to ovate. Spikes cylindric, yellow, green or golden, tipped pink, 12×2.2–2.7mm. Winter–summer. Aus.

P. stirlingii (Lindl.) F. Muell. Procumbent to ascending, to 1m. Lvs 1.5–3cm, lanceolate to linear, undulate. Spikes globose, solitary or in pan., 2.5cm across, deep pink to mauve. Summer. W Aus.
→*Trichinium.*

Ptychosperma Labill. Palmae. 30 solitary or clump-forming, unarmed palms. St. slender, smooth, ringed. Crownshaft distinct. Lvs pinnate; pinnae slender-pointed, jagged or entire at tip. Aus. and New Guinea to Solomon Is. and Micronesia.

P. alexandrae F.J. Muell. = *Archontophoenix alexandrae.*

P. cunninghamiana H.A. Wendl. = *Archontophoenix cunninghamiana.*

P. elegans (R. Br.) Bl. ALEXANDER PALM; SOLITAIRE PALM. St. solitary, to 12m. Crownshaft, woolly. Lvs to 2.5m; petioles to 30cm; pinnae to 60cm, regularly arranged, toothed or notched at apex. NE Aus.

P. macarthurii H.A. Wendl. St. to 7m, clumped. Crownshaft, woolly. Lvs to 2m, arched; pinnae regularly arranged, broad, apically toothed. New Guinea.

P. propinquum (Becc.) Becc. St. to 8m. Crownshaft green-brown. Lvs to 1m; petioles 30cm, scaly; pinnae irregularly arranged in groups of 2–3, apically notched. Aru Is.

P. salomonense Burret. Lvs *c*1.2m. New Guinea.

P. sanderianum Ridl. St. clumped, to 4m. Crownshaft green-brown. Lvs to 1.2m; petioles to 20cm; pinnae long, narrow, regularly arranged, apically concave and toothed. New Guinea.

P. waitianum Essig. St. solitary, to 4.5m. Lvs to 7cm; pinnae regularly arranged, coarsely toothed, apically concave. New Guinea.
→*Actinophloeus, Seaforthia* and *Strongylocaryum.*

Puahou *Pseudopanax arboreus.*
Puccoon *Lithospermum canescens.*
Pudding Berry *Cornus canadensis.*
Pudding Pipe Tree *Cassia fistula.*

Pueraria DC. Leguminosae (Papilionoideae). 20 herbaceous or woody twiners. Lvs trifoliolate or pinnate. Infl. long, axill., or clustered as rac. at br. ends; standard obovate or round. SE Asia, Jap. Z5.

P. lobata (Willd.) Ohwi. JAPANESE ARROWROOT; KUDZU VINE. Woody, hairy-stemmed vine to 20m; root tuberous. Lfts ovate to rhomboid, 14–18cm, pubesc.; petiole 10–20cm. Rac., erect, to 25cm; fls to 1.5cm, purple. Autumn. China, Jap.

P. thunbergiana (Sieb. & Zucc.) Benth. = *P. lobata* (Willd.) Ohwi.

Puerto Rican Hat Palm *Sabal causiarum.*
Puerto Rican Royal *Roystonea borinquena.*
Puka *Meryta sinclairii.*
Pukanui *Meryta sinclairii.*
Pukaponka *Brachyglottis repanda.*
Pukatea *Laurelia novae-zealandiae.*

Pulicaria Gaertn. FLEABANE. Compositae. 40 erect, ann. to perenn. herbs. Lvs alt., simple, cordate, ± amplexicaul and auriculate. Cap. radiate, occas. discoid, solitary or arranged in pan. or corymbs; ray flts yellow; disc flts yellow. Temp. Eurasia and warm S Afr. Z7.

P. dysenterica (L.) Bernh. Stoloniferous perenn. St. 20–75cm, branched, lanate or tomentose. Lvs to 6cm, oblong-lanceolate, undulate and remotely serrate, green and scabrid above, grey-tomentose beneath, lower lvs petiolate, withered at anthesis. Cap. 15–30mm diam., in corymbs. Summer–early autumn. Eur., N Afr.

→*Inula*.

Pulmonaria L. LUNGWORT. Boraginaceae. 14 rhizomatous, bristly-hairy perenn. herbs. Basal lvs ovate to linear-lanceolate, long-petiolate, cauline lvs ± sessile, few. Infl. of term., forked cymes, bracteate; cal. 5-lobed; cor. 5-lobed, infundibular, throat with 5 tufts of hairs, faucal scales 0; sta. 5, included. Eur., Asia. Z4.

P. affinis Jordan. Lvs to 18×9cm, spotted white, setose, glandular-pubesc., rough. Infl. glandular-pubesc., setose; fls purple to blue-violet. Eur.

P. alpina Torr. = *Mertensia alpina*.

P. angustifolia L. Lvs to 40×5cm, unspotted, setose, sparingly gland.; fls bright blue. Eur. 'Azurea': to 25cm; lvs dark green; fls bright blue, tinted red in bud. 'Beth's Blue': to 25cm; lvs fresh green, faintly spotted; fls rich blue. 'Beth's Pink': to 25cm; lvs broad, spotted; fls coral red. 'Blaues Meer': fls large, gentian blue. 'Johnson's Blue': habit small, to 20cm; fls blue. 'Munstead Blue': habit low, to 15cm; lvs small, dark green; fls clear blue, early-flowering. 'Rubra': to 25cm; fls soft red, early spring. 'Variegata': lvs narrow, variegated white. Z3.

P. azurea Besser = *P. angustifolia*.

P. ciliata James = *Mertensia ciliata*.

P. lanceolata Pursh = *Mertensia lanceolata*.

P. longifolia (Bast.) Boreau. Lvs to 50×6cm, usually spotted white, setose and sparingly gland. above, setose and gland. beneath. Infl. long-setose, sparingly glandular-pubesc.; fls violet to blue-violet. Eur. 'Bertram Anderson': lvs long and narrow, spotted silver; fls vivid blue. 'Lewis Palmer': to 35cm; lvs wide, faintly spotted; fls soft blue faintly tinted pink, profuse. 'Mournful Purple' ('Mourning Widow', 'Mournful Widow'): lvs faintly spotted silver; fls purple. 'Patrick Bates': lvs well spotted; fls dusky mauve. Z6.

P. maculata Dietr. = *P. officinalis*.

P. maritima L. = *Mertensia maritima*.

P. mollis C.F. Wolff ex Heller = *P. montana*.

P. montana Lej. Lvs to 50×12.5cm, usually unspotted, setose and sparingly glandular-pubesc. above. Infl. densely setose, glandular-pubesc.; fls violet to blue. Eur. 'Albocorollata': to 30cm; lvs pale green; fls pure white, early spring. 'Bowles' Red': lvs spotted white; fls coral red. 'David Ward': to 30cm; lvs edged white; fls coral red. 'Barfield Pink': to 30cm; lvs soft green; fls brick red, edged and veined in white. 'Red Start': to 40cm; lvs fresh green; fls large, pale red. Z6.

P. oblongifolia Nutt. = *Mertensia oblongifolia*.

P. officinalis L. JERUSALEM SAGE. Lvs to 16×10cm, spotted white, setose. Infl. setose and glandular-pubesc.; fls red to rose-violet or blue. Eur. 'Alba': fls white. 'Bowles' Blue': fls v. pale blue. 'Brentor': lvs lightly spotted silver; fls magenta. 'Cambridge' ('Cambridge Blue'): to 30cm; lvs heart-shaped, spotted; fls pale blue, tinted pink in bud, profuse. 'White Wings': to 30cm; fls white, eye pink, late-flowering. Z6.

P. paniculata Ait. = *Mertensia paniculata*.

P. rubra Schott = *P. montana*.

P. saccharata Mill. JERUSALEM SAGE. Lvs to 27×10cm, green, usually spotted white, long-setose, glandular-pubesc. fls white or red-violet to dark violet. Eur. 'Alba': to 30cm; lvs variegated white, forms rosettes; fls large, snow white. 'Argentea': to 30cm; lvs frosted silver. 'Frühlingshimmel' ('Blauhimmel', 'Spring Beauty'): lvs spotted; fls pale sky blue, cal. purple. 'Highdown': to 30cm, vigorous; lvs frosted silver; fls rich blue, nodding. 'Leopard': lvs spotted white; fls red tinted pink. 'Margery Fish': lvs spotted silver, fading to white; fls pink tinted blue. 'Mies Stam': lvs spotted silvery; fls soft carmine pink tinted lilac, profuse. 'Mrs Moon': lvs well spotted in silver; fls lilac tinted red. 'Pink Dawn': lvs spotted silver; fls deep pink. 'Reginald Kaye': to 30cm; lvs spotted silver at border and central patch. 'Sissinghurst White': to 30cm, vigorous; lvs large, well spotted; fls white, early-flowering. 'Tim's Silver': to 30cm high; lvs silver sheened except for rim; fls mid blue. Z3.

P. stiriaca A. Kerner. Lvs to 22×8cm, spotted white, setose and glandular-pubesc. above. Infl. short-setose, long-glandular-pubesc; fls bright blue. Eur. Z5.

P. suffruticosa L. = *Moltkia suffruticosa*.

P. virginica L. = *Mertensia virginica*.

P. cvs. 'Beth Chatto': tall; lvs well spotted; fls dark blue. 'Blue Ensign': to 30cm; lvs broad, dark green; fls large, rich blue. 'Blue Mist': lvs well spotted; fls palest clear blue. 'Glacier': to

30cm; lvs spotted; fls palest blue, occas. pink or white. 'Mawson's Blue': to 40cm; lvs deep green, low; fls gentian blue, in tall sprays, later-flowering. 'Weetwood Blue': fls clear true blue.

Pulsatilla Mill. Ranunculaceae. 30 perenn. hairy, tufted herbs. Lvs long-stalked in a basal rosette or forming an involucre below fls, pinnately or palmatelky dissected. Fls solitary, scapose; perianth wide-spreading or campanulate, seg. usually 6, rarely 5–8, petal-like, exterior silky; sta. in a central boss surrounded by a ring of staminodes. Fr. heads with long feather styles. Eurasia, N Amer.

P. alba Rchb. Short hairy perenn. Basal lvs long-stalked, bipinnate, hairy at first. Fls bowl-shaped, 2.5–4.5cm diam., white sometimes flushed blue. C Eur. Z5.

P. albana (Steven) Bercht. & Presl. 5–18cm at anthesis. Basal lvs 2.5–6cm, bipinnatisect with 3–4 pairs of primary seg., secondary seg. deeply pinnate, lobes lanceolate or linear, entire or slightly incised-dentate, villous. Fls nodding campanulate, to 2.5cm, yellow, exterior densely sericeous. Cauc., NE Turk. var. **andina** Rupr. Fls suberect; seg. wide spreading, yellow, red after pollination. var. **georgica** Rupr. Lf seg. v. narrow. Fls pale pink-lilac or pale lilac, sometimes white within. var. **violacea** (Rupr.) Asch. & Gräbn. Fls white, flushed blue. Z5.

P. alpina (L.) Delarb. ALPINE PASQUE FLOWER. 20–45cm. Basal lvs bipinnate, term. seg. strongly incised, lobes often reflexed. Fls ± erect 4–6cm diam., white flushed blue-purple and seric-eous outside. C Eur. (mts). ssp. **apiifolia** (Scop.) Nyman. Fls pale yellow. Z5.

P. andina (Rupr.) Woron. = *P. alpina* var. *apiifolia*.

P. armena (Boiss.) Rupr. 5–10cm at anthesis. Basal lvs 1.5–4cm, densely white-hairy, bipinnatisect, secondary seg. deeply pinnate, lobes narrowly linear-oblong. Fls nodding to suberect, campanulate, to 3.5cm, purple-lilac, exterior densely white-villous. Cauc., Transcauc. Z5.

P. aurea (Somm. & Levier) Juz. 6–35cm an anthesis. Basal lvs ternate with seg. ovate, pinnatisect, secondary seg. pinnate, lobes acute, deeply incised, pilose beneath; fls suberect, 3.5–6cm diam., golden-yellow, exterior addressed-pilose. Cauc., Transcauc. Z6.

P. bungeana C.A. Mey. 1.5–5cm at anthesis. Basal lvs pinnatisect, with secondary seg. entire or dentate, subobtuse, broad, somewhat pilose. Fls erect, campanulate, blue-violet, seg. to 1.5cm. Sib., Altai Mts. Z5.

P. cernua (Thunb.) Bercht. & Presl. 4–20cm at anthesis. Basal lvs pinnatisect with 2 pairs sessile lateral lfts, lfts. broad-rhombic, 2–3-lobed, secondary seg. short, ovate-lanceolate, incised or dentate, densely hairy beneath. Fls pendulous, not opening widely, bright violet-red or dark purple-brown, seg. to 3.5cm, exterior grey-villous. Jap., Korea, China (Manch.). Z5.

P. chinensis (Bunge) Reg. 7–25cm at anthesis. Basal lvs, ternate, seg. deeply 2–3-lobed, lobules rounded, pinnate, pilose fls erect, blue-lilac or violet, seg. 2.5–4.5cm, hairy externally. NE Asia. Z6.

P. dahurica (Fisch.) Spreng. 15–40cm at anthesis. Basal lvs pinnatisect, with 2 distant pairs of narrow-rhombic seg., term. seg. broader, all 2–3-lobed, with secondary seg. cuneate, incised into linear-lanceolate, entire or dentate lobules, pilose beneath. Fls pendulous, blue-violet, seg. to 3cm. NE Asia. Z6.

P. flavescens (Zucc.) Juz. Closely related to *P. patens*, but fls to 8cm diam., sulphur-yellow, occas. flushed blue without. Late spring. Urals to C Asia. Z5.

P. grandis Wender. = *P. vulgaris* ssp. *grandis*.

P. halleri (All.) Willd. To 15cm at anthesis. Basal lvs densely hairy pinnately divided into 3–5 seg., lobes oblong-lanceolate, pinnately dissected. Fls erect or nearly so, 4–9cm diam., campanulate or shallowly bell-shaped, violet-purple to lavender blue. Late spring–early summer. C & SE Eur., Crimea. ssp. **halleri**. Basal lvs 3–7cm, pinnately dissected into 5 primary lobes, usually less than 50 lobes in all, woolly. Fls dark violet. SW & C Alps. Forms with lacinate pet. are cultivated, as well as others with semi-double fls. ssp. **rhodopaea** K. Krause. Basal lvs with 50–100 lobes, densely woolly. Balk., S Bulg., N Greece. ssp. **slavica** (Reuss) Zam. Basal lvs pinnately dissected into 3 primary divisions, lvs usually with less than 50 lobes, woolly. Fls dark violet. W Carpath. ssp. **styriaca** (Pritz.) Zam. Basal lvs 5–11cm, pinnately dissected into 5 primary divisions, lvs usually with less than 50 lobes, ± woolly. SE Austria. ssp. **taurica** (Juz.) K. Krause. Basal lvs with 50–100 lobes, primary lobes of basal lvs usually sessile, densely woolly. Crimea. Z5.

P. hirsutissima (Britt.) MacMill. = *P. patens*.

P. montana (Hoppe) Rchb. to 15cm in fl., to 45cm in fr. Basal lvs 3-parted, lfts further finely cut, forming c150 lobes, pubesc. Fls pendent, 3–4cm, bell-shaped, blue-purple to dark violet. SW Switz., E Rom., Bulg. Z6.

P. nigricans Stork = *P. pratensis*.

P. occidentalis (Wats.) Freyn. 10–60cm. Basal lvs 4–8cm wide, ternate, with seg. bipinnate, lobes linear to lanceolate-linear, long-sericeous. Fls erect, white or cream-white, sometimes flushed purple or blue, perianth seg. 2–3cm, exterior villous. N Amer. Z4.

P. patens (L.) Mill. EASTERN PASQUE FLOWER. St. 8–15cm in fl. Basal lvs palmately lobed, each lobe divided into 2–3 linear-lanceolate, toothed seg., coriaceous, with spreading hairs when young. Fls erect, 5–8cm diam., blue-violet or lilac, exterior yellow or white, with spreading hairs. Spring–early summer. N Eur., Russia (Sib., N Amer.). Z4.

P. patens 'Nuttaliana'. = *P. patens*.

P. pratensis (L.) Mill. St. to 12cm in fl. Basal lvs usually 3× pinnate, lobes cut, forming *c*150 lobes. Fls 3–4cm diam., narrow-campanulate, pale or dark purple to purple-green, exterior thickly hairy. Spring–early summer. C & E Eur. (to Denm. and S Norway). ssp. *nigricans* (Stork) A. Kerner Perianth seg. to 3cm, black-violet, outward curved. N & C Eur. ssp. *hungarica* Soó. Fls pale yellow. S Eur. Z5.

P. rubra (Lam.) Delarb. Fls dark red-purple, brown-red or black-red, rarely dark violet. Spring–early summer. C & S Fr., C & E Spain. ssp. *hispanica* Zimm. ex Asch. & Gräbn. Fls black-violet or purple violet; lvs appearing with fls. Spain. Z6.

P. sulphurea (DC.) Sweet = *P. alpina* ssp. *apiifolia*.

P. turczaninowii Krylov & Sergiewskaja. 5–35cm. Basal lvs, 4–14cm, bipinnate, primary seg. in 3 pairs, secondary seg. divided into linear lobes. Fls suberect, not opening fully, blue-violet, seg. 2.5–3.5cm, adpressed pilose. Sib., NE Asia. Z6.

P. vernalis (L.) Mill. St. to 15cm in fl. Basal lvs pinnately divided into 3–5-seg., seg. oblong, toothed, ± glab. Fls pendent, becoming erect, 4–6cm, campanulate, with brown silky hairs outside, white, outer seg. usually flushed pink or violet-blue outside. Spring–summer. Eur. (mts from Scand. to S Spain, E to Bulg.), Sib. Z4.

P. vulgaris Mill. PASQUE FLOWER. St. 3–12cm. Basal lvs silky at first, pinnately dissected into 7–9 lobes, seg. divided 2–3× almost to the midrib, lobes linear-lanceolate. Fls erect or slightly pendent, 4–9cm diam., bell-shaped or narrowly campanulate, pale or dark violet, rarely white. Spring–early summer. GB and W Fr. to Sweden, eastwards to Ukraine. 'Alba': fls white. 'Albocyanea': fls blue-white. 'Bartons Pink': lvs pale green; fls a true clean pink. 'Gotlandica': 30cm, fls purple, large. 'Ena Constance': dwarf, fls deep red, later than other cvs. 'Mallenderi': fls deep purple. 'Mrs Van der Elst': the first pink var., perhaps no longer in cult. 'Rode Klokke' ('Rote Glocke'): fls deep red. 'Rubra': fls rust red to red-purple. 'Weisser Schwan' ('White Swan'): fls white. Many of the darker cvs may be hybrids of *P. montana* × *P. halleri*. ssp. *vulgaris*. Basal lvs v. dissected, with over 100 lobes. Perianth seg. narrow-elliptic. W & C Eur., S Scand. ssp. *grandis* (Wender.) Zam. Basal lvs with *c*40, 3–7mm wide lobes; lvs appearing after fls. Fls to 9cm diam. Buds covered with silvery gold brown hairs. Spring. C Eur., Ukraine. Z5.

→*Anemone*.

Pultenaea Sm. Leguminosae (Papilionoideae). 120 evergeen shrubs. Lvs simple. Fls axill. and soliary, crowded toward br. tips or in dense heads. Aus., Tasm. Z9.

P. daphnoides Wendl. LARGE-LEAF PEA BUSH. Shrub to 2m. Lvs to 4cm, oblanceolate, obtuse, mucronate. Fls yellow and scarlet in dense, sessile involucrate heads. Summer. Aus.

P. obcordata Andrews = *P. daphnoides*.

P. stipularis Wendl. Shrub to 1m. Lvs 2–4cm, narrowly linear, pointed, ciliate. Fls yellow in sessile term. heads, yellow. Spring. Aus. (NSW).

Pulza *Jatropha curcas*.
Pummelo *Citrus maxima*.
Pumpkin *Cucurbita maxima*; *C. moschata*.
Pumpkin Ash *Fraxinus tomentosa*.

Punctillaria N.E. Br.

P. optata (N.E. Br.) N.E. Br. = *Pleiospilos compactus*.
P. roodiae N.E. Br. = *Tanquana prismatica*.
P. sororia (N.E. Br.) N.E. Br. = *Pleiospilos compactus* ssp. *minor*.

Punica L. Punicaceae. 2 densely branched shrubs or small trees. Fls in clusters, axillary, and term.; cal. fleshy, leathery tubular or campanulate, sep. 5–8; pet. 5–7, overlapping; sta. many. Fr. a globose, berry with numerous fleshy seeds in leathery shell. E Medit. to Himal. Z9.

P. granatum L. POMEGRANATE. Decid., branching shrub to 2m, or small tree to 6m. Lvs 2–8cm, obovate to oblong, pale green, glossy, subcoriaceous, tinted red in autumn. Fls to 3cm diam., silky, crumpled. Fr. to 12cm diam., globose, brown-yellow to purple-red, with persistent cal.; seeds with fleshy crimson coat. 'Nana': dwarf, intricately branched tree with small lvs, fls and fr. *P. sempervirens* hort. = *P. granatum*.

PUNICACEAE Horan. 1/2. *Punica*.

Pupunha *Bactris gasipaes*.
Purau Teruere *Hibiscus hastatus*.
Purging Cassia *Cassia fistula*.
Purging Nut *Jatropha curcas*.

Purgosea Haw.
P. hemisphaerica (Thunb.) G. Don = *Crassula hemisphaerica*.

Purple Allamanda *Allamanda blanchetii*.
Purple Amaranth *Amaranthus cruentus*.
Purple Anise *Illicium floridanum*.
Purple Avens *Geum rivale*; *G. triflorum*.
Purple Beard Grass *Bothriochloa caucasica*.
Purple Beech *Fagus sylvatica* f. *purpurea*.
Purple Broomrape *Orobanche purpurea*.
Purple Clover *Trifolium pratense*.
Purple-coned Spruce *Picea purpurea*.
Purple Coneflower *Echinacea purpurea*.
Purple Coral Pea *Hardenbergia violacea*.
Purple Crab *Malus* ×*purpurea*.
Purple-eyed Grass *Olsynium douglasii*.
Purple-flowering Raspberry *Rubus odoratus*.
Purple-fruited Chokeberry *Aronia* ×*prunifolia*.
Purple Glory Plant *Sutera grandiflora*.
Purple Goosefoot *Chenopodium purpurascens*.
Purple Granadilla *Passiflora edulis*.
Purple Ground Cherry *Physalis peruviana*; *P. philadelphica*.
Purple Guava *Psidium littorale* var. *longipes*.
Purple Heart *Setcreasea*.
Purple Heather *Phyllodoce breweri*.
Purple Leaf Plum *Prunus cerasifera* 'Pissardii'
Purple-leaved Ivy *Hedera helix* 'Atropurpurea'
Purple Loco *Oxytropis lambertii*.
Purple Loosestrife *Lythrum salicaria*.
Purple Milk Vetch *Astragalus danicus*.
Purple Moor-grass *Molinia caerulea*.
Purple Mountain Saxifrage *Saxifraga oppositifolia*.
Purple Mullein *Verbascum phoeniceum*.
Purple Needlegrass *Stipa pulchra*.
Purple-net Toadflax *Linaria reticulata*.
Purple Nightshade *Solanum xantii*.
Purple Osier *Salix purpurea*.
Purple Oxytropis *Oxytropis halleri*.
Purple Pea *Hovea*.
Purple Poppy Mallow *Callirhoë involucrata*.
Purple Prairie Violet *Viola pedatifida*.
Purple Rock Brake *Pellaea atropurpurea*.
Purple Sage *Salvia dorrii*.
Purple Sanicle *Sanicula bipinnatifida*.
Purple Saxifrage *Saxifraga oppositifolia*.
Purple Silkweed *Asclepias purpurascens*.
Purple-stemmed Cliff Brake *Pellaea atropurpurea*.
Purple-strawberry Guava *Psidium littorale* var. *longipes*.
Purple Toadflax *Linaria purpurea*.
Purple Top *Verbena bonariensis*.
Purple Velvet Plant *Gynura aurantiaca*.
Purple Viper's Grass *Scorzonera purpurea*.
Purple Willow *Salix purpurea*.
Purple Wreath *Petrea*

Purshia DC. ex Poir. ANTELOPE BUSH. Rosaceae. 2 decid. shrubs or small trees. Lvs small, congested, 3-cleft, revolute. Fls to 1.6cm diam., white to creamy yellow, solitary, at the ends of short br.; cal. tube turbinate to funnel-shaped, teeth 5; pet., 5, spathulate; sta. 25. W N Amer. Z6.

P. glandulosa Curran. Erect shrub to 5m. Branchlets glab., gland. Lvs to 1cm, gland. and sparsely pubesc. above, ± tomentose beneath, lobes 3(–5), linear, sometimes dentate. Spring–summer. US (Colorado to Nevada).

P. tridentata (Pursh) DC. Erect shrub to 3m. Branchlets gland., tomentose. Lvs to 3cm, fine-pubesc. above, white-tomentose beneath, lobes 3, oblong-linear. Spring–summer. US (Oreg. and Calif. to New Mex.).

P. tridentata var. *glandulosa* Jones = *P. glandulosa*.

Purslane *Claytonia*; *Portulaca* (*P. oleracea*).
Pururi *Vitex lucens*.

Puschkinia Adams. Liliaceae (Hyacinthaceae). 1 perenn. bulbous herb. Lvs to 15×0.5cm, 2–3, basal, linear-lorate.

Scapes 5–20cm; rac. loose; perianth pale blue with darker stripes, short-tubular, 7–10mm, lobes 6, erect or slightly spreading. Spring. Cauc., Turk., N Iran, N Iraq, Leb. Z5.

P. hyacinthoides Bak. = *P. scilloides*.

P. libanotica Zucc. = *P. scilloides* var. *libanotica*.

P. scilloides Adams. As above. 'Alba': fls pure white. var. *libanotica* (Zucc.) Boiss. Fls smaller.

Pussley *Portulaca oleracea*.

Pussy-ears *Cyanotis somaliensis; Kalanchoe tomentosa*.

Pussy-paws *Spraguea umbellatum*.

Pussy-tails *Ptilotus spathulatus*.

Pussy-toes *Antennaria*.

Pussy Willow *Salix caprea*.

Putaputawheta *Carpodetus serratus*.

Putoria Pers. Rubiaceae. 3 foetid dwarf shrubs; st. tetragonal, divaricately branched. Lvs opposite, somewhat leathery. Fls solitary or in term. clusters, subsessile, bracteate; cor. funnel-shaped with 4–5 oblong lobes; sta. 4–5, exserted. Medit. Z8.

P. calabrica (L. f.) DC. STINKING MADDER. St. prostrate or spreading, mat-forming, 30cm. Lvs to 20mm, obovate to elliptic-lanceolate, revolute and papillose, leather. Fls in a dense term. cluster, pink; cor. lobes 4 linear-lanceolate to 4mm. Fr. dark red, black when ripe. Spring–summer. Medit.

→*Asperula* and *Ernodea*.

Putterlickia Endl. Celastraceae. 2 everg., glab., spiny shrubs. Fls cymose; sep. 5, unequal, laciniate; pet. 5, oblong or obovate, ciliate. Capsule 3-valved; seeds black with orange aril. S Afr. Z9.

P. pyracantha (L.) Endl. To 3m. Br. curved, v. spiny. Lvs to 4cm, elliptic to obovate-cuneate, emarginate or acute, revolute. Pet. to 5mm, creamy-white. Fr. to 2cm, obovoid, red, bristly; seeds black, aril orange. Summer. S Afr.

P. pyracantha (L.) Endl. = *Celastrus pyracanthus*.

P. verrucosa Sim. St. curved, warty-spiny; spines to 5cm on br. Lvs 2.5cm, obvate, undulate, minutely spiny dentate. Pan. to 5cm; pet. to 2mm, tinged green. Summer. S Afr.

→*Celastrus*.

Puya Molina. Bromeliaceae. 168 perenn., terrestrial herbs with long, stout st. or stemless. Lvs tough, forming a dense rosette, with narrowly triangular blades, margins normally toothed and spinose. Infl. terminal, erect, tall, simple or paniculate. Andean S Amer., N Braz., Guyana, Costa Rica.

P. alpestris (Poepp.) Gay. 1.2–1.5m in fl. Lvs to 60cm, arching, covered in white scales beneath, hooked-spinose. Infl. sparsely branched on a stout scape, loosely bipinnate, pyramidal; blue-green. SC Chile. Z8.

P. alpestris (Poepp.) Gay (in part). = *P. berteroniana*.

P. berteroniana Mez. To 4.5m in fl. Lvs 1m, arching, marginal spines to 1cm, stout, hooked. Infl. and scape tomentose, bipinnate, much branched; pet. blue-green. C Chile. Z8.

P. chilensis Molina. Resembles *P. berteroniana* except in its almost straight glab. lvs and leathery marginal spines. Infl. and scape subglabrous; pet. sulphur-yellow to yellow-green. C Chile. Z9.

P. coarctata Philippi = *P. berteroniana*.

P. coarctata (Ruiz & Pav.) Fisch. non Philippi = *P. chilensis*.

P. coerulea Lindl. 1–2m in fl. Lvs 40–60cm, covered with ash-grey scales, distant-serrate, with rusty hooked spines. Infl. white-floccose, bipinnate, much-branched, occas. simple; pet. dark blue. var. *violacea* (Brongn.) L.B. Sm. & Looser. To 1m in fl. Infl. axis red, nearly glab.; pet. violet. C Chile. Z8.

P. ferruginea (Ruiz & Pav.) L.B. Sm. To 4m in fl. Lvs to 1m. Infl. laxly pyramidal, covered with rusty brown scales; br. one-sided; pet. white-green to purple. Ecuad., Peru, Boliv. Z8.

P. floccosa (Lind.) E. Morr. To 2m in fl. Lvs to 1m, sublinear, white-scaly beneath, hooked-spinose. Infl. on a white-floccose scape, loosely bipinnate; fls erect, on all sides of infl.; pet. blue. Costa Rica, Colomb., Venez., N Braz. Z9.

P. grandiflora Hook. = *P. ferruginea*.

P. hortensis L.B. Sm. 1–2m in fl. Lvs 60–70cm, pale-scaly when young, ± glab. later, serrate, hooked-spinose. Infl. loosely bipinnate, villous, scurfy; pet. maroon. Early summer. Origin unknown. Z8.

P. laxa L.B. Sm. To 1m in fl. Lvs to 60cm, apex thread-like, sheaths thickly felted with scaly hairs, marginal spines 5mm, hooked. Infl. pyramidal, loosely compound; fls spirally arranged, white woolly; pet. dark violet with green stripe. Arg.

P. medica L.B. Sm. To 20cm in fl. Lvs 12cm, densely scaled, marginal spines 2mm, brown. Infl. simple, cylindrical, 10×2cm; bracts pink; pet. dark blue. N Peru.

P. mirabilis (Mez) L.B. Sm. 1.5m+ in fl. Lvs 60–70cm, white to

brown, finely toothed. Infl. erect, in simple loose rac. to 50cm; pet. green to white. Arg., Boliv.

P. raimondii Harms. To 2m in fl. Lvs 1–2m, stiff, in a dense, rounded rosette, undersides densely scaly, marginal spines 1.5cm, hooked, brown. Infl. compound, racemose, tapering; pet. yellow-green. Peru.

P. saxatilis Mart. = *Encholirium spectabile*.

P. spathacea (Griseb.) Mez. To 1m in fl. Lvs 60–110cm, glab. and grey-green above, pale-scaly beneath, margins hooked-spinose. Scape glab., red; infl. much-branched, bipinnate, stellate-pubesc. becoming gland.; sep. pink; pet. blue to dark green. NC Arg. Z8.

P. violacea (Brongn.) Mez = *P. coerulea* var. *violacea*.

P. whytei Hook. f. = *P. alpestris*.

→*Pitcairnia*.

Puzzle Bush *Ehretia hottentotica*.

Pycnanthemum Michx. AMERICAN MOUNTAIN MINT. Labiatae. 21 aromatic, mint-scented perenn. herbs. Infl. simple or branched, of compact glomerules, pedunculate, usually subtended by a pair of leaflike bracts; cal. regular or 2-lipped; cor. tube expanding to form two lips, upper lip longer; sta. 4, lower pair slightly longer, all usually exserted. E N Amer. and Calif.

P. arkansanum Fres. = *P. muticum*.

P. flexuosum Britt., Sterns & Pogg. Upright perenn. herb, 60–100cm. St. glab. branching above. Lvs linear, 2.2–5.6mm, entire, involucral bracts with prominent midveins, bracts apiculate, cor. tube rapidly enlarging, 3–4.5mm, pubesc. within the throat, upper lip 2–2.5mm. E US. Z5.

P. lanceolatum Pursh = *P. virginianum*.

P. linifolium Pursh = *P. flexuosum*.

P. muticum Pers. Upright perenn. herb, 70–110cm. St. pubesc., branching above. Lvs 3–8cm, narrowly ovate to ovate-lanceolate, usually serrate. Bracts velvety, cor. tube pink, gradually enlarging to 3.5mm, upper lip 1.5–2mm. E US. Z5.

P. muticum var. *pilosum* Gray = *P. pilosum*.

P. ovatum Nutt. ex Benth. = *P. muticum*.

P. pilosum Nutt. Upright perenn. herb, 100–150cm. St. pilose branching in the infl. Lvs 3–7cm, lanceolate, entire or shallowly serrate, pilose beneath, bracts canescent; cor. tube pink, gradually expanded, 3–5mm, upper lip 2–3mm. C & E US. Z4.

P. tenuifolium Schräd. = *P. flexuosum*.

P. virginianum Dur. & Jackson. Upright perenn. herb, 70–100cm. St. with short leafy br., with pubescence on st. angles. Lvs 3.5–6.5cm, lanceolate to linear-elliptic, entire or shallowly serrate, bracts without prominent midveins; cor. pink and white, tube gradually enlarging 2–4mm, upper lip 1.5–2.5mm. E US. Z5.

P. virginicum Pers. = *P. virginianum*.

→*Satureja*.

Pycnostachys Hook. Labiatae. About 40 erect perenn. herbs or soft shrubs with minutely pubes. lvs. Fls in dense bracteate term. spikes; cal. 5-dentate, teeth spine-like; cor. 2-lipped, tube cylindric widening campanulate, upper lip 4-lobed, shorter than lower, lower lip compressed, boat-shaped. Trop. & S Afr., Madag. Z9.

P. coerulea Hook. To 120cm. Lvs 7–10cm, linear-lanceolate, distantly and shortly dentate. Fls 4–5mm, blue in single spike, 25–50×8–10mm. Summer. Madag.

P. dawei N.E. Br. To 180cm. Lvs to 30cm, linear-lanceolate, serrate, red-glandular beneath. Fls to 25mm, cobalt blue in spikes to 13×4.5cm. Summer. Trop. C Afr.

P. stuhlmannii Gürke. To 120cm. Lvs to 18cm, linear-lanceolate, minutely serrate, pubesc. beneath, malodorous when crushed. Fls blue, to 12mm, in spike to 30×10mm. Zimb.

P. urticifolia Hook. To 2.5m. Lvs 45–120m, ovate, crenate to deeply incised-dentate, subglabrous to densely pubesc. fls 12–20mm, gentian blue, rarely white tinted blue in thyrse-like spike, 5–10×2.5–3cm; cal. purple-red. Trop. & S Afr.

Pycreus P. Beauv. Cyperaceae. 70 perenn., grasslike herbs. St. terete or 3-angled, leafy. Lvs grasslike, linear umbel, spicate, subtended by leaflike bracts fls in spikelets hermaphrodite, minute, spirally arranged, subtended by scalelike glumes. Cosmop.

P. congestus (Vahl) Hayek = *Cyperus congestus*.

P. filicinus (Vahl) T. Koyama. NUTTALL'S CYPERUS. Slender, tufted ann., 0–35cm. Bracts unequal, 1–2 v. much exceeding the rest; umbel compound, with 0–2 rays; spikelets linear-lanceolate, 3mm, golden yellow to brown. Summer. N Amer. Z7.

P. longus (L.) Hayek = *Cyperus longus*.

→*Cyperus*.

Pygmy Chain Sword Plant *Echinodorus intermedius.*
Pygmy Date Palm *Phoenix roebelinii.*
Pygmy Rose *Rosa chinensis.*
Pygmy Water Lily *Nymphaea tetragona.*
Pyinma *Lagerstroemia speciosa.*
Pyjama Flower *Androcymbium melanthoides.*
Pyjama Lily *Crinum macowanii.*
Pyracanth *Pyracantha coccinea.*

Pyracantha Roem. FIRETHORN. Rosaceae. 7 everg. thorny shrubs of dense spreading habit, to 6; thorns leafy. Lvs alt., glossy above, paler ± downy beneath. Fls 0.5–1cm, white, in corymbs on leafy shoots; cal. persistent; pet. rounded; sta. *c*20, anth. yellow. Fr. orange to red. SE Eur. to China.

P. angustifolia (Franch.) Schneid. Shoots stiff, densely downy in the first year. Lvs 1.5–5cm, linear-elong to obovate, apex rounded and sometimes toothed. Fls 0.5cm diam., in 5cm corymbs. Fr. to 1cm, felted at first, later yellow-orange. SW China. 'Gnome': v. hardy, habit erect, dense; fls profuse; fr. orange. 'Yukon Belle': habit dense; fr. orange, persistent. Z7.

P. atalantoides (Hance) Stapf. Br. olive-brown, downy only at first. Lvs 3–7cm, lanceolate to elliptic or obovate, mostly entire, sometimes small-tootehd. Fls 1–1.5cm diam., in 3–4cm corymbs. Fr. 7–8mm, scarlet-crimson. Spring–early summer. SE to W China. 'Aurea': fr. yellow. 'Bakeri': fr. red. 'Nana': dwarf, to 1m; fr. red. Z7.

P. coccinea Roem. PYRACANTH; FIRETHORN; BUISSON ARDENT. Shoots downy at first. Lvs 2–4cm, elliptic to lanceolate. Fls 8mm diam., in 3–4cm corymbs. Fr. 5–6cm, bright scarlet. Early summer. It. to Asia Minor. 'Baker's Red': hardy; fr. bright red. 'Kasan': compact, upright, fast-growing to 5m; fr. orange. 'Lalandei': upright to 5m, hardy; fr. profuse, bright orange. 'Lalandei Monrovia': upright dense; fr. orange. 'Sparkler': slow-growing; lvs variegated white; fr. red. 'Walker's Pride': v. hardy, compact, berries well when young; fr. orange. Z6.

P. crenatoserrata (Hance) Rehd. Closely resembling *P. atalantoides* and *P. rogersiana*; shoots red-brown downy at first. Lvs 2–7cm, oblong-lanceolate, toothed, apex rounded. Fls 1cm diam. in 3–4cm corymbs. Fr. 2cm, red. Early summer. C & W China. 'Graberi': vigorous; fr. red, in large clusters which last well. Z7.

P. crenulata (D. Don) Roem. NEPALESE WHITE THORN. Closely resembling *P. coccinea*; shoots red-brown, downy. Lvs to 5cm, oblong-oblanceolate, apex rounded, tip bristled, crenate. Fls 8mm diam. in 3cm corymbs. Fr. 6–8mm, orange. Spring to early summer. Himal. var. *kansuensis* Rehd. Lvs narrower, to 2.5cm; fr. smaller. NW China. Z7.

P. crenulata var. *rogersiana* A.B. Jacks. = *P. rogersiana.*
P. crenulata var. *yunnanensis* Vilm. = *P. crenatoserrata.*
P. discolor Rehd. = *P. atalantoides.*
P. formosana hort. = *P. koidzumii.*
P. fortuneana (Maxim.) Li = *P. crenatoserrata.*
P. gibbsii A.B. Jacks. = *P. atalantoides.*
P. gibbsii var. *yunnanensis* Vilm. = *P. crenatoserrata.*
P. gibbsii var. *yunnanensis* Osborn = *P. crenatoserrata.*
P. kansuensis hort. = *P. crenulata* var. *kansuensis.*

P. koidzumii (Hayata) Rehd. Resembling *P. rogersiana*; shoots red, downy, becoming glab. and purple. Lvs 2.5–4.5cm, oblanceolate, apex rounded, entire or short-toothed. Fr. 7mm, orange-red. Taiwan. 'Rosedale': br. arching; fr. large, bright red. 'Santa Cruz': habit prostrate; fr. large, red. 'Victory': vigorous, to 5m; fr. large, late to colour, lasting well. Z8.

P. rogersiana (A.B. Jacks.) Chitt. Shoots pale downy at first becoming glab., red-brown. Lvs 2–3.5cm, oblanceolate to narrow obovate, apex rounded and shallow toothed. Fls 0.5cm diam., in corymbose rac. Fr. 8–9mm, yellow to orange-red. SW China. 'Flava': fr. bright yellow. Z8.

P. rogersiana var. *aurantiaca* Bean = *P. rogersiana.*
P. yunnanensis Chitt. = *P. crenatoserrata.*

P. **cvs.** 'Alexander Pendula': to 1.8m, br. weeping; fr, coral red. 'Andenken an Heinrich Bruns' (*P. coccinea* ×*P. rogersiana*): variable seedling mix, parent of 'Orange Charmer' and 'Golden Charmer'. 'Apache': habit compact spreading mound 1.5×2m; fr. bright red resistant to scab and fireblight. 'Brilliant': fr. bright red. 'Buttercup' (*P. coccinea* ×*P. rogersiana*): habit spreading; fr. small, yellow. 'Fiery Cascade': habit upright, 2.5×3m; lvs small, shining; fr. small, red; resistant to disease. 'Golden Charmer' (*P. coccinea* ×*P. rogersiana*): to 2.4m; fr. large, golden yellow; resistant to scab. 'Golden Dome': habit low; lvs bright green; fr. yellow. 'Harlequin': lvs variegated; fr. red. 'Knap Hill Lemon': habit vigorous, dense; fr. small, pale yellow. 'Lavinia Rutgers': habit spreading, br. thorny; lvs small, narrow; fr. orange. 'Mohave' (*P. koidzumii* ×*P. coccinea* 'Wyatt'): habit upright, to 4×5m; fr. bright orange, unaffected by bird feeding; resistant to scab and fireblight. 'Morettii' (hybrid of *P. coccinea*): 'Navajo': habit low, dense; fr. orange-

red; resistant to scab. 'Orange Giant': fr. bright orange. 'Orange Charmer' (*P. coccinea* ×*P. crenatoserrata*): habit vigorous, dense; fr. bright orange; resistant to scab. 'Pueblo': habit spreading, compact; fls 1cm; fr. orange red; resistant to scab and fireblight. 'Red Column': habit upright; fr. small, red. 'Red Cushion': habit dense, to 1×2m; fr. mid-red. 'Red Elf' ('Monelf'): habit dwarf, compact, mounding; lvs dark green; fr. bright red. 'Red Pillar': habit vigorous, upright; fr. orange-red. 'Renault d'Or': fr. yellow. 'Ruby Mound': habit low, dense; fr. orange-red; resistant to scab. 'Rutgers 3': habit low, creeping to 3m in width; fr. orange; resistant to disease. 'Shawnee' (*P. crenatoserrata* ×*P. koidzumii*): habit dense, spreading to 3.5m; fr. abundant, yellow-orange, colouring early; resistant to scab and fireblight. 'Soleil d'Or' ('Sungold') mutation of 'Morettii': habit semi-spreading; lvs pale green; fr. yellow. 'Sunshine' (*P. coccinea* ×*P. rogersiana*): habit open, br. lax; fr. orange. 'Taliensis' (*P. crenatoserrata* ×*P. rogersiana*): fr. yellow, abscising early. 'Teton 15': habit upright; lvs medium green; fr. orange-yellow; resistant to scab and fireblight. 'Tiny Tim' (*P. crenatoserrata* hybrid): habit dwarf, to 1m, densely leafy; fr. profuse. 'Watereri' ('Waterer's Orange') (*P. atalantoides* ×*P. rogersiana*): habit compact, vigorous to 2.5m; fr. profuse, orange.

→*Cotoneaster, Mespilus* and *Photinia.*

✕Pyracomeles Rehd. ex Guillaum. (*Pyracantha* ×*Osteomeles.*) Rosaceae. Gdn origin.

✕*P. vilmorinii* Rehd. ex Guillaum. (*Osteomeles subrotunda* ×*Pyracantha crenatoserrata.*) Semi-everg. shrub to 1.5m. Branchlets slender. Lvs to 3.5cm, grey-pubesc., soon glab., pinnatisect above, pinnate below; lfts or lobes oval, crenate-serrulate at apex. Fls 1cm diam., in many-fld term. corymbs; pet. broad-obovate; sta. 12–15. Fr. globose, 4mm diam., red-pink. Spring. Gdn origin. Z6.

Pyramidal Poplar *Populus nigra* var. *betulifolia.*
Pyramid Bugle *Ajuga pyramidalis.*
Pyramid Orchid *Anacamptis pyramidalis.*
Pyrenean Dead-nettle *Horminum.*
Pyrenean Oak *Quercus pyrenaica.*
Pyrenean Saxifrage *Saxifraga longifolia.*

Pyrethrum Zinn.
P. achilleifolium Bieb. = *Tanacetum achilleifolium.*
P. atrosanguineum hort. = *Tanacetum coccineum.*
P. carneum Bieb. = *Tanacetum coccineum.*
P. cinerariifolium Trev. = *Tanacetum cinerariifolium.*
P. clusii Fisch. ex Rchb. = *Tanacetum corymbosum* ssp. *clusii.*
P. corymbosum (L.) Scop. = *Tanacetum corymbosum.*
P. densum Labill. = *Tanacetum densum.*
P. foeniculaceum Willd. = *Argyranthemum foeniculaceum.*
P. gayanum Coss. & Dur. = *Chrysanthemopsis gayana.*
P. hybridum Wender. = *Tanacetum coccineum.*
P. maresii Coss. = *Chrysanthemopsis maresii.*
P. parthenifolium Willd. = *Tanacetum parthenifolium.*
P. parthenium (L.) Sm. = *Tanacetum parthenium.*
P. poteriifolium Ledeb. = *Tanacetum poteriifolium.*
P. ptarmiciflorum Webb non Willd. = *Tanacetum ptarmiciflorum.*
P. ptarmicifolium Willd. non Webb = *Achillea ptarmicifolia.*
P. radicans Cav. = *Leucanthemopsis radicans.*
P. roseum Bieb. = *Tanacetum coccineum.*
P. tchihatchewii (Boiss.) Bornm. = *Tripleurospermum oreades* var. *tchihatchewii.*
P. uliginosum (Waldst.) & Kit. ex Willd. = *Leucanthemella serotina.*

+Pyrocydonia Winkl. ex Daniel. Rosaceae. Graft hybrids between *Pyrus* and *Cydonia.*

+*P. danielii* Winkl. ex Daniel. (*Cydonia oblonga* + *Pyrus communis* 'Williams' Bon Chrétien'.) Resembles *Cydonia oblonga* with lvs ovate, to 7.5cm, roiunded at base, dentate, pubesc., and petiole to 6mm. Gdn origin. 'Winkleri': hybrid sprung not from the graft-union but from a root of the stock, which had arisen from the graft-union many years before; habit shrubby; lvs to 4.5cm, elliptic-ovate, acuminate, obtuse at base, slightly navicular, more tomentose beneath, and white-dentate. Z6.

+*P. winkleri* Guill. = +*P. danielii* 'Winkleri'.
→*Pyronia.*

Pyrogennema Lunell = *Epilobium.*

Pyrola L. WINTERGREEN; SHINLEAF. Pyrolaceae. 15 perenn., rhizomatous, glab. herbs. Rhiz. creeping. Lvs in basal clusters, simple, usually long-petioled. Scapes erect, bracteate, fls nodding 0.5–2cm diam., waxy, in loose rac.; pet. 5, concave; style exserted, curved, sta. 10. Summer. N temp. region. Z5.

P. americana Sweet. 12–30cm. Lvs ovate to broadly elliptic, 6.5cm, coriaceous. Fls numerous, white. E N Amer.

P. aphylla Sm. = *P. picta*.

P. asarifolia Michx. To 65cm. Lvs broiadly elliptic to reniform, to 10cm, entire or crenate, often purple beneath. Pink to crimson. Canada, E US, Asia. var. *purpurea* (Bunge) Fern. Lvs ovate-elliptic, to 7cm, sometimes red beneath. Fls bright violet or rose, large, fragrant. N Amer. ssp. *asarifolia*, BOG WINTERGREEN. Lvs ovate, round or obovate, entire or obscurely crenate. ssp. *bracteata* (Hook.) Haber. Bracts and sep. longer. Z4.

P. bracteata Hook. = *P. asarifolia* ssp. *bracteata*.

P. californica Krisa = *P. asarifolia* ssp. *asarifolia*.

P. chlorantha Sw. GREEN-FLOWERED WINTERGREEN. 15–25cm. Lvs ovate-elliptic, to 2.5cm, entire or ± crenate. Fls 1–10, pale green. N Amer. Z5.

P. dentata Sm. = *P. picta*.

P. elata Nutt. = *P. asarifolia* ssp. *asarifolia*.

P. elliptica Nutt. To 20cm. Lvs ovate to elliptic, 3–6cm, scarcely toothed. Fls 5–10, white, campanulate. N Amer. Z3.

P. grandiflora Radius. Resembles *P. asarifolia* but pet. white with edges tinged pink. N Amer. Z5.

P. media. L. Resembles *P. minor* but to 30cm. Lvs ovate to obovate, to 4.5cm diam. Fls white tinged red. N Amer. Z5.

P. menziesii R. Br. ex D. Don = *Chimaphila menziesii*.

P. minor L. LESSER WINTERGREEN. To 15cm. Lvs to 3cm, ovate to oblong-obovate, entire to obscurely crenate. Fls many, spherical, small, white or tinged rose. Eur., N Amer. Z5.

P. picta Sm. WHITE-VEINED WINTERGREEN. Lvs to 8cm, often glaucous beneath, ovate-elliptic, entire, dark green above, purple beneath, veins white, or oblanceolate, entire to prominently toothed, dull green above, veins not white. Fls 4–24, pale green, creamy-white or white flushed pink. Eur., W N Amer. 'Dentata': lvs spathulate-oblong, sometimes sharp-toothed, veins without white borders. Z6.

P. rotundifolia L. To 25cm. Lvs round to oval, fls 10–20 white. Eur., N Amer. Z4.

P. rotundifolia auct. non L. = *P. americana*.

P. secunda L. = *Orthilia secunda*.

P. uliginosa (Torr.) Torr. & A. Gray = *P. asarifolia* var. *purpurea*.

P. umbellata L. = *Chimaphila umbellata*.

P. uniflora L. = *Moneses uniflora*.

P. virens Schreb. in Schweig. & Körte = *P. chlorantha*.

PYROLACEAE Dumort. 4/42. *Chimaphila, Moneses, Orthilia, Pyrola*.

Pyrolirion Herb. Amaryllidaceae. 4 perenn. bulbous herbs. Fl. solitary, scapose; spathe tubular and sheathing below; perianth tube erect, narrow, upper part swollen, limb of 6 subequal lobes, reflexed fil. erect. Andes. Z9.

P. aureum (Ruiz & Pav.) Herb. GOLDEN FLAME LILY. Lvs to 10cm, channelled. Perianth golden, tube to 3.5×0.8cm, throat with denticulate scales, lobes to 6×0.8cm, lanceolate, deflexed; fil. shorter than lobes. Peru.

P. aureum Edwards = *Zephyranthes flava*.

P. flavum Herb. = *Zephyranthes flava*.

→*Amaryllis* and *Zephyranthes*.

✗Pyronia Veitch. Rosaceae.

✗*P. danielii* (Winkl. ex Daniel) Rehd. = +*Pyrocydonia danielii*.

✗*P. veitchii* (Trabut) Guillaum. (*Cydonia oblonga* ×*Pyrus communis.*) Resembles *Cydonia* in habit. Shoots brown, spotted. Lvs to 10cm, elliptic, tapered, tough, entire to crenulate, lanuginose when young. Fls pink-white, 5cm diam. Fr. rounded, to 8cm, green. Spring–autumn. Gdn origin. Z6.

→*Cydonia*.

Pyrostegia Presl. Bignoniaceae. 4 lianes; br. angled. Lvs bifoliate with or without terminal trifid tendril; sometimes trifoliate. Thyrses term.; cor. tubular, curved; sta. exserted. Americas. Z10.

P. ignea (Vell.) Presl = *P. venusta*.

P. venusta (Ker-Gawl.) Miers. Lfts to 11cm, ovate to oblong-lnaceolate, apex obtuse, base rounded, papery or leathery, glab. to pubesc. and scaly. Cor. tube 3.5–6×0.3cm, orange, lobes linear, 1–1.5cm, puberulent. Braz., Parag., Boliv., NE Arg.

→*Bignonia*.

Pyrrheima Hassk.

P. fuscata (Lodd.) Hassk. = *Siderasis fuscata*.

Pyrrhocactus Backeb.

P. bulbocalyx (Werderm.) Backeb. = *Neoporteria bulbocalyx*.

P. dubius Backeb. = *Neoporteria strausiana*.

P. horridus Backeb. invalid name = *Neoporteria horrida*.

P. intermedius Ritter = *Neoporteria taltalensis*.

P. mammillarioides (Hook.) Backeb. = *Neoporteria curvispina*.

Pyrrocoma Hook. Compositae. 10 perenn. herbs. St. several, decumbent. Lvs chiefly radical, usually simple, sometimes pinulose-dentate. Cap. term. or in lf axils radiate; involucre hemispheric; phyllaries usually foliaceous; ray flts many; disc flts yellow. W US.

P. apargioides (A. Gray) Greene. St. to 20cm, decumbent to ascending, glab. or villous, red-tinged. Basal lvs to 10×1cm, linear-lanceolate to oblanceolate, laciniate and spinulose-dentate to entire, coarsely ciliate toward base, petiolate, coriaceous. Cap. usually solitary, long-pedunculate; involucre *c*12mm, ray flts yellow. Summer–autumn. Calif., Nevada. Z3.

P. clementis Rydb. St. to 40cm, decumbent to ascending, somewhat villous, esp. above. Lvs to 15cm, linear-oblong, entire or dentate, ciliate, otherwise glab., petiolate, upper lvs lanceolate or ovate-lanceolate, sessile. Cap. sessile, solitary or few, sessile, terminal; involucre *c*12mm; ray flts bright yellow. Summer. Wyom., Colorado, Utah. Z3.

P. crocea (A. Gray) Greene. St. to 60cm, several, sparingly villous above. Basal lvs to 20cm, spathlate, rarely dentate, glab., firm, petiolate. Cap. usually solitary, term.; involucre *c*2cm, ray flts to 2cm, orange-yellow. Summer–autumn. Wyom., Colorado, Utah, New Mex. Z3.

→*Haplopappus*.

Pyrrosia Mirb. FELT FERN. Polypodiaceae. 100 epiphytic, lithophytic, or terrestrial ferns. Rhiz. creeping, branched. Fronds stipitate or sessile, uniform or dimorphous with fertile fronds longer than sterile, usually simple and entire, fleshy to leathery, stellate pubesc. and scaly, often becoming glab. above, felted beneath. Trop. OW. Z10.

P. adnascens (Sw.) Ching = *P. lanceolata*.

P. africana (Kunze) Ballard. Rhiz. to 4mm wide, short-creeping. Fronds to 33×3cm, uniform, pendent, falcate, linear to lanceolate, acute, leather, veins obscure; stipes 0. S Afr.

P. angustata (Sw.) Ching. Rhiz. to 2mm wide, long-creeping. Sterile fronds narrowly acute at apex, decurrent at base, lustrous above, fertile fronds to 45×4cm, veins distinct, stipes to 15cm. Malaysia to Polyn.

P. confluens (R. Br.) Ching. ROBBER FERN. Rhiz. to 2mm wide, long-creeping, much-branched. Blades fleshy to leathery, sterile fronds linear to oblong or obovate, obtuse or subacute, fertile fronds 5–18×1.5cm, elliptic or lanceolate to linear, midvein prominent; stipes to 5cm. Aus.

P. eleagnifolia (Bory) Hovenkamp. Rhiz. to 2mm wide, long-creeping. Sterile fronds obtuse at apex, attenuate or truncate at base, fertile fronds to 13×2cm, acute or obtuse at apex, attenuate base, veins obscure; stipes to 5cm. NZ.

P. flocculosa (D. Don) Ching. Rhiz. to 6mm wide, short-creeping. Fronds to 32×8cm, uniform, acute or narrowly acute at apex, cuneate or truncate at base, veins distinct; stipes to 20cm. India to SE Asia.

P. hastata (Thunb.) Ching. Rhiz. to 7mm wide, short-creeping. Fronds to 15×10cm, uniform, pedately or palmately 3–5-lobed, hastate, truncate or cordate at base, leather, lobes, lanceolate, term. lobe spreading, ovate to deltoid; stipes to 20cm. China, Jap., Korea.

P. lanceolata (L.) Farw. Rhiz. to 2mm wide, long-creeping. Sterile fronds linear or spathulate to obovate or lanceolate, obtuse at apex, to 6×2cm, fertile fronds lanceolate to linear, caudate, to 20cm×5mm; stipes to 5cm. India to China, Malaysia, New Guinea, Polyn., Aus.

P. lingua (Thunb.) Farw. TONGUE FERN; JAPANESE FELT FERN. Rhiz. to 3mm wide, long-creeping. Fronds to 30×5cm, uniform, lanceolate to ovate, narrowly acute at apex, cuneate at base, leathery; stipes to 5cm. China, Taiwan, Jap. 'Eboshi' ('Contorta'): fronds twisted. 'Monstrifera': fronds deeply and irregularly cut. 'Nana': fronds short. 'Nankin-Shisha' ('Kujuku'): fronds cristate and contorted. 'Nokogiri-ba' ('Serrata'): fronds crenate and crinkled. 'Shisha' ('Cristata'): fronds forked at tips, appearing crested. 'Tsunomata': frond tips 2–3× branched. 'Variegata': fronds crenate, with oblique, variegated stripes.

P. longifolia (Burm. f.) Morton. Rhiz. to 3mm wide, long-creeping. Fronds to 1m×2cm, uniform, strap-shaped, acute or obtuse at apex, fleshy, glossy deep green, often arching and puckered, veins distinct, stipes to 20cm. Malaysia, Aus. (Queensld). Polyn.

P. macrocarpa (Hook. & Arn.) Shing = *P. serpens*.

P. nummulariifolia (Sw.) Ching. CREEPING BUTTON FERN. Rhiz. to 2mm wide, long-creeping. Sterile fronds to 5×4cm, ovate to circular, thin-textured, fertile fronds to 12×1cm, linear or oblanceolate, apex obtuse, veins obscure; stipes to 3cm. Indochina to Malaysia, Philipp.

P. polydactyla (Hance) Ching. Rhiz. to 6mm wide, short-creeping. Fronds to 20×18cm, uniform, pedately or palmately 6–8-lobed, cuneate at base, deep lustrous green, lobes to finger-like; stipes to 10cm. Philipp.

P. serpens (Forst. f.) Ching. Rhiz. to 2mm wide, long-creeping. Sterile fronds to 15×2cm, obovate to circular, apex obtuse, fertile fronds to 25×2cm, linear to oblong; stipes to 5cm. Australasia.

P. stigmosa (Sw.) Ching. Rhiz. to 5mm wide, short-creeping. Fronds to 45×5cm, uniform, narrowly acute at apex, cuneate at base, leather, veins prominent; stipes to 25cm. Indochina to New Guinea.

P. subfurfuracea (Hook.) Ching. Rhiz. to 7mm wide, short-creeping. Fronds to 90×8cm, uniform, narrowly acute at apex, attenuate at base, veins distinct; stipes to 30cm. Indochina, SE Asia.

P. tricuspe (Sw.) Tag. = *P. hastata*.

P. varia (Kaulf.) Farw. = *P. lanceolata*.

Pyrularia Michx. Santalaceae. 4 large parasitic shrubs. Br. initially pubesc. Lvs alt., short-petiolate. Fls unisexual in spikes; sep. 5, pubesc., ovary distinctly narrowed stalk-like. Fr. drupaceous, pyriform. N Amer., Himal. Z4.

P. pubera Michx. BUFFALO NUT; ELK. To 4m. Lvs obovate to oblong, acute. Infl. a sparse spike. Drupe 2.5cm or longer. E US.

Pyrus L. PEAR. Rosaceae. *c*30 decid. trees and shrubs; shoots occas. thorny. Lvs decid., alt., simple, commonly serrate or scalloped, occas. lobed; stipules reduced to a bristle-like protrusion or awl-shaped. Fls white, sometimes tinted yellow, green or rose, usually fading to white, in umbels or corymbs on lateral shoots, cal. and pet. 5, sta. usually 20, rarely 25–30, carpels 5 or rarely 2, separate or slightly fused, styles usually distinct or basal part tightly grouped near the disk. Fr. slender-stalked globose to pyriform, often with persistent cal., flesh embedded with grit cells; seed cavity with tough parchment-like walls, seeds black-brown. Eur. to E Asia and N Afr.

P. achras Gaertn. = *P. pyraster*.

P. alpina Willd. = × *Sorbaronia alpina*.

P. amygdaliformis Vill. Shrub or small tree to 6m; shoots slender, thorny. Lvs 2.5–7cm, ovate-obovate, pointed or blunt, ± coriaceous, entire or finely scalloped, grey-felted at first becoming shiny green, glab. Fls 2–2.5cm diam., in corymbs of 8–12. Fr. 2–3cm, rounded, yellow-brown. S Eur., Asia Minor. var. *cuneifolia* (Guss.) Bean. Lvs smaller and narrower. var. *lobata* (Decne.) Koehne. Shrub. Lvs entire or with 1–2 lobes. var. *oblongifolia* (Spach) Bean. Lvs elliptic to oblong, apex blunt, base rounded. Fr. larger, yellow flushed red. S Fr. Z6.

P. amygdaliformis var. *persica* (Pers.) Bornm. = *P. persica*.

P. arbutifolia (L.) L. f. = *Aronia arbutifolia*.

P. aria 'Kumaonensis'. = *Sorbus japonica*.

P. auricularis Kroop = × *Sorbopyrus auricularis*.

P. austriaca Kerner = *P. nivalis* f. *austriaca*.

P. balansae Decne. Resembles *P. communis* but lvs 5–10cm, ovate to oblong, long tapered, base rounded, serrate becoming entire or scalloped on mature specimens. Fr. 2.5cm, almost triangular on long pedicels. Asia Minor. Z6.

P. bartramiana Tausch = *Amelanchier bartramiana*.

P. betulifolia Bunge. Tree, 5–10m, erect, narrow, br. ± arching. Lvs 4–7cm, ovate-oblong or slightly rhombic, long-tapered, roughly serrate, base rounded or slightly heart-shaped, glossy green above, grey-green and sparsely downy beneath. Fls 2cm diam. in downy corymbs of 8–10. Fr. 1–1.5cm, subglobose, brown speckled white. N China. Z5.

P. bollwylleriana DC. = × *Sorbopyrus auricularis*.

P. botryapium L. f., in part. = *Amelanchier canadensis*.

P. bourgaeana Decne. Tree, erect at first, later spreading; bark becoming finely plated with age. Lvs 2–7cm, ovate-lanceolate to broadly ovate, scalloped. Fr. 17–25mm, globose or angular, matt yellow, brown spotted in places. W Spain, Port., Moroc. Z6.

P. bretschneideri Rehd. Medium tree resembling *P. ussuriensis* var. *ovoidea*. Lvs 5–11cm, ovate to elliptic, long-tapered, base triangular to rounded, bristly-serrate woolly at first. Fls 3cm diam., in tomentose clusters. Fr. 2.5–3cm, subglobose to more oval, yellow, flesh white, edible. N China. Z5.

P. bucharica Litv. = *P. korshinsky*.

P. calleryana Decne. CALLERY PEAR. Tree, shoots thorny. Lvs 4–8cm, ovate, short tapered, undulate-scalloped, shiny, glab. Fls 2–2.5cm diam. Fr. 1cm, rounded, brown, pitted. China. 'Aristocrat': fast-growing to 13m, broadly pyramidal; br. thornless; lvs wavy-edged, glossy, brilliant red in autumn, plum when young; fr. red to yellow. 'Autumn Blaze': fast-growing, to 12m,

habit asymmetrical and open; lvs glossy, crimson autumn colour. 'Bradford': to 13m, crown broadly ovate, dense; lvs red to maroon in autumn. 'Capital': to 12m, loosely pyramidal, dense; lvs rich glossy green, purple in autumn. 'Chanticleer' ('Cleveland Select', 'Select'): to 13m, crown narrow-conical, evenly branched; lvs glossy green, becoming carmine scarlet in autumn; spiny. 'Redspire': to 12m, crown moderately pyramidal, upright, well-branched; lvs long, thick, glossy, coloured crimson to purple in autumn; fls profuse. 'Stone Hill': to 12m, upright, crown oval; lvs deep green, shiny, brilliant orange in autumn. 'Trinity': to 10m, somewhat globe-shaped, crown rounded; lvs light green, somewhat serrate, orange to red in autumn. 'White House': to 10m, upright, compact, moderately ovate; br. upward-arching; lvs red to plum in early autumn. f. *tomentella* Rehd. Lvs soon glab. except for wooly midrib, finely serrate. Infl. downy, tufted in axils. China. Z5.

P. calleryana var. *fauriei* (Schneid.) Rehd. = *P. fauriei*.

P. × *canescens* Spach (*P. nivalis* × *P. salicifolia*.) Resembling *P. nivalis* but lvs lanceolate or narrow-elliptic, apex scalloped, grey-white downy at first; fr. pale green. Z6.

P. communis L. COMMON PEAR. Tree to 15m, crown conical, broad, often thorny. Lvs 2–8cm, oval-elliptic, pointed, scalloped, soon glab., autumn colour red-yellow. Fls 3cm diam., in smooth or downy corymbs. Fr. 2.5–5cm, pyriform or sub-globose, yellow green, flesh bitter. Eur., Asia Minor. var. *sativa* DC. A collective name for all edible pear cvs. Z4.

P. communis var. *cordata* (Desv.) Briggs = *P. cordata*.

P. communis var. *pyraster* L. = *P. pyraster*.

P. cordata Desv. Shrub 3–4m, spreading, densely thorny. Lvs 1–4cm, oval, base cordate, scalloped, glab.; petiole long. Fls to 2cm diam. in small clusters with long axes. Fr. 10–18mm, sub-globose, red waxy. S Eur., SW Engl. Z8.

P. cossonii Rehd. Small tree with occasional thorns. Lvs 2.5–5cm, elliptic or ovate, apex blunt or short tapered, crenulate, eventually green shiny, felted when young. Fls 3cm diam., in clustered to 7cm. Fr. 1.5cm, rounded, brown lightly pitted. Alg. Z8.

P. delavayi Franch. = *Docynia delavayi*.

P. depressa Lindl. = *Aronia arbutifolia* var. *pumila*.

P. elaeagrifolia Pall. Small tree, resembling *P. nivalis* but br. thorny. Lvs 4–7cm, lanceolate-elliptic, narrower than *P. nivalis*, entire, grey-white felted, occas. becoming smooth above. Fr. 2cm, rounded to angular, green. Asia Minor. var. *kotschyana* (Decne.) Boiss. Thornless shrub. Lvs 3–6cm, wider. Asia Minor. Z5.

P. fauriei Schneid. Tree or large shrub, becoming thorny with age. Resembles *P. calleryana* but smaller. Lvs 2.5–5cm, elliptic. Korea. Z9.

P. ferruginea Koidz. = *P. ussuriensis* var. *hondoensis*.

P. firma hort. = *Sorbus hybrida* 'Gibbsii'.

P. glomerulata (Koehne) Bean = *Sorbus glomerulata*.

P. grandifolia Lindl. = *Aronia melanocarpa* var. *grandifolia*.

P. heterophylla Reg. & Schmalh. non Poir. non Steud. = *P. regelii*.

P. hondoensis Kikuchi & Nak. = *P. ussuriensis* var. *hondoensis*.

P. hybrida Moench = × *Sorbaronia hybrida*.

P. indica Wallich = *Docynia indica*.

P. japonica Thunb. = *Chaenomeles japonica*.

P. japonica Sims non Thunb. = *Chaenomeles speciosa*.

P. kawakamii Hayata. EVERGREEN PEAR. Shrub or small tree 4–10m, bark black-brown with sharp thorns. Lvs 6–10cm, ovate or obovate, everg. coriaceous, crenulate. Fls sparse in small clusters. Fr. to 11mm, rounded, smooth. China, Taiwan. Z8.

P. korshinskyi Litv. Tree, closely resembling *P. communis*, shoots felted (not thinly downy) at first; lvs 5–8cm, oval-oblong to lanceolate, upper surface only slightly pubesc., crenulate below. Fr. 2cm, globose. Turkestan. Z6.

P. kumaoni Decne. = *P. pashia* var. *kumaoni*.

P. × *lecontei* Rehd. (*P. communis* × *P. pyrifolia*.) Sturdy medium-sized tree. Lvs 8cm, ovate-elliptic, long tapered, crenulate. Fls to 3cm diam., in flattened clusters of 7–10. Fr. 6–8cm, ellipsoid, yellow, pitted, flesh granular, white, sour. LE CONTE PEAR. Gdn origin (pre-1850). Z6.

P. lindleyi Rehd. Resembles *P. ussuriensis*, but lvs ovate, apex abruptly tapered, base rounded to cordate, with short adpressed teeth. Fr. on long stalks, ellipsoid. China. Z6.

P. lobata Decne. = *P. amygdaliformis* var. *lobata*.

P. longipes Coss. and Dur. = *P. cossonii*.

P. malifolia Spach. = × *Sorbopyrus auricularis* 'Bulbiformis'.

P. malus L. pro parte = *Malus sylvestris*.

P. maulei (T. Moore) Mast. = *Chaenomeles japonica*.

P. melanocarpa (Michx.) Willd. = *Aronia melanocarpa*.

P. × *michauxii* Bosc. (*P. amygdaliformis* × *P. nivalis*.) Unarmed small tree, crown almost globose. Lvs 3–7cm, ovate to elliptic-oblong, blunt or abruptly tapered entire, felted at first then shiny above. Fls in short crowded corymbs. Fr. 3cm rounded or rather angular, yellow-green, sour. Asia. Z6.

P. ×*mixta* Fern. = × *Sorbaronia sorbifolia*.

P. nivalis Jacq. SNOW PEAR. Small tree to 10m, without thorns. Lvs 5–8cm elliptic to obovate, base triangular, entire or slightly scalloped only at tip, white-felted becoming dark green above, autumn colour dark red. Fls 2.5–3cm diam., in felted corymbs of 6–9. Fr. 3–5cm, globose or more angular, yellow-green. SE Eur. f. *austriaca* (Kerner) Schneid. Lvs elliptic, glab. when mature. Austria, Hung. Z6.

P. nivalis var. *elaeagnifolia* Schneid. = *P. elaeagnifolia*.

P. oblongifolia Spach = *P. amygdaliformis* var. *oblongifolia*.

P. ovoidea Rehd. = *P. ussuriensis* var. *hondoensis* var. *ovoidea*.

P. parviflora Desf. = *P. amygdaliformis*.

P. pashia Hamilt. Tree 10–12m, young shoots felted, thorny. Lvs 6–12cm, ovate-oblong, apex long-tapered, base rounded, crenate serrate, felted at first. Fls 2–2.5cm diam. Fr. 2cm, subglobose, brown with irregular pits. Himal. to W China. var. *kumaoni* (Decne.) Stapf. Young sts and infl. glab. Z5.

P. persica Pers. Small tree. Lvs 3–6cm, held horizontally, elliptic-oblong, thick, blue-green above, sparsely tomentose beneath, finely scalloped. Infl. a felted umbel of 6–12 fls. Fr. 3cm, globse or angular, green flushed red. Asia Minor, Greek Is. Z7.

P. phaeocarpa Rehd. Tree. Lvs 6–10cm, elliptic-ovate to oval-oblong, long-tapered, base broadly triangular, widely dentate, downy-tufted at first. Fls 3cm diam. in tomentose corymbs of 3–4. Fr. 2–2.5cm, pyriform, brown speckled white-yellow. N China. f. *globosa* Rehd. Lvs usually ovate, base rounded. Fr. 1.5–2cm subglobose. Z5.

P. pinnatifida var. *fastigiata* Bean = *Sorbus* ×*thuringiaca* 'Fastigiata'.

P. pollveria L. = × *Sorbopyrus auricularis*.

P. pyraster Burgsd. Small or medium tree, bark thick, thorny. Lvs 3–5cm, ovate or more rounded, thin, downy at first. C to SW Eur. Z6.

P. pyrifolia (Burm.) Nak. SAND PEAR. Tree 5–12m. Lvs 7–12cm, oval oblong, rarely ovate, long tapered, base rounded or somewhat cordate, finely bristle-serrate, smooth or woolly. Fls 3–3.5cm diam., in corymbs of 6–9, often woolly. Fr. 3cm, subglobose, brown, slightly pitted. C & W China. var. *culta* (Mak.) Nak. Lvs longer and wider. Fr. pyriform or globose, brown or yellow. China, Jap. f. *stapfiana* (Rehd.) Rehd. Serrations more open; fr. to 5cm, pyriform. China. Z6.

P. regelii Rehd. Shrub or small tree to 9m, thorny. Lvs ovate-oblong, simple or lobed, with rough teeth, sometimes almost pinnate. Fls 2–2.5cm diam. in flattened corymbs, white. Fr. 2–3cm, globose or pyrimiform. Turkestan. Z6.

P. rhamnoides Hook. = *Sorbus rhamnoides*.

P. salicifolia Pall. Tree 5–8m, shoots slender, almost pendulous. Lvs 3–9cm, narrow oblong-elliptic, apex acuminate, entire or sparsely toothed, silvery grey-downy becoming ± glab. above. Fls cream 2cm diam., in small clusters of 6-8. Fr. 2–3cm, pyriform, green. SE Eur., Asia Minor, Cauc. 'Pendula': doubtfully distinct from type. 'Silfrozam': to 4.5×3.5m, crown broadly weeping; lvs willow-like, silver-grey. Z4.

P. ×*salviifolia* DC. (*P. communis* ×*P. nivalis*.) Resembles *P. nivalis* but lvs smaller; shoots with large, thick thorns. Lvs to 5cm, elliptic to ovate, pointed or tapered, finely scalloped, grey downy at first. W & C Eur. Z6.

P. serotina Rehd. = *P. pyrifolia*.

P. serrulata Rehd. Closely resembles *P. pyrifolia* but lvs finely serrate 5–11cm, ovate to oval-oblong, woolly at first. Fls 2.5cm diam., in tomentose flattened clusters. Fr. 1.5cm, subglobose, brown, speckled. China. Z6.

P. simonii Carr. = *P. ussuriensis*.

P. simonii hort. non Carr. = *P. ussuriensis* var. *hondoensis* var. *ovoidea*.

P. sinaica Dum.-Cours. = *P. persica*.

P. sinensis Lindl. non Poir. = *P. lindleyi*.

P. sinensis sensu Decne. = *P. ussuriensis*.

P. sinensis var. *maximowicziana* Lév. = *Photinia villosa* var. *laevis* f. *maximowicziana*.

P. sorbifolia (Poir.) Wats. = × *Sorbaronia sorbifolia*.

P. syriaca Boiss. Small erect thorny tree. Lvs 2.5 to 10cm, oblong or more lanceolate ± glab., finely scalloped. Fls in densely felted corymbs. Fr. 3cm, pyriform. Cyprus, Asia Minor. Z7.

P. ursina Wallich ex G. Don = *Sorbus ursina*.

P. ussuriensis Maxim. Tree to 15m. Lvs 5–10cm, ovate or more rounded, long-tapered, base rounded cordate, with bristle-like teeth, glab., yellow-green above, paler beneath, crimson in fall. Fls to 3cm diam., 6–9 in domed clusters. Fr. 3–4cm subglobose, green-yellow. Fowering early. NE Asia. var. *hondoensis* (Kikuchi & Nak.) Rehd. Shoots and lvs woolly at first, later dark orange brown, margins with fine, less tapered, less adpressed teeth. var. *ovoidea* (Rehd.) Rehd. Shoots spreading. Lvs narrow ovate to oblong-ovate; fr. ovoid to pyriform, yellow. N China, Korea. Z4.

P. variolosa Wallich = *P. pashia*.

P. vestita Wallich = *Sorbus cuspidata*.

P. wilhelmi Schneid. = *P. pashia* var. *kumaoni*.

P. yunnanensis Bean pro parte. = *Malus yunnanensis* var. *veitchii*.

Q

Qat *Catha edulis.*
Quail Bush *Atriplex lentiformis.*
Quaker-ladies *Houstonia caerulea.*
Quaking Aspen *Populus tremula.*
Quaking Grass *Briza.*
Quamash *Camassia.*

Quamoclit Moench.
Q. coccinea var. *hederifolia* (L.) House = *Ipomoea hederifolia.*
Q. coccinea (L.) Moench = *Ipomoea coccinea.*
Q. hederifolia (L.) G. Don = *Ipomoea hederifolia.*
Q. lobata (Cerv.) House = *Ipomoea multifida.*
Q. pennata (Desr.) Bojer = *Ipomoea quamoclit.*
Q. ×sloteri House = *Ipomoea ×sloteri.*
Q. vulgaris Choisy = *Ipomoea quamoclit.*

Quaqua N.E. Br. Asclepiadaceae. 13 dwarf, succulent, perenn. herbs. St. thick, glab., bluntly angled, tinged grey or purple, angles toothed, tuberculose. Fls solitary or in clusters usually short-stalked, between st. angles toward st. tips; cor. tube deep, conical to bowl-shaped, lobes ovate-lanceolate to linear; outer corona lobes bifid or entire. Nam., S Afr. Z9.
Q. acutiloba (N.E. Br.) P.V. Bruyns. Clump-forming; st. 4–20×1.2–2cm, 4-angled, pale blue-grey green, teeth hard-tipped. Cor. glab., exterior pale green-purple, interior purple-black or marked purple-black on yellow ground or uniformly yellow, area around corona paler, lobes 3–6×2–3.5mm, deltoid. W Cape.
Q. armata (N.E. Br.) P.V. Bruyns. Forming dense mats. St. 10–20×2–3cm, 4–6-angled, dark grey-green, mottled purple, teeth with a blunt, hard, conical tip. Cor. 2.2cm diam., glab., lobes 8–15×4mm, brown becoming yellow-brown toward the pale yellow tube. Cape Prov. ssp. *arenicola* (N.E. Br.) P.V. Bruyns. St. to 15cm, usually 4-angled, green to grey-purple with a sharp tip to each tubercle. Cor. with short papillate hairs in the mouth of the tube, otherwise glab., lobes 12mm diam., 3× longer than wide, margins recurved for three-quarters of length. S Cape. ssp. *maritima* P.V. Bruyns. Cor. 9mm diam., with papillate hairs in tube mouth, lobes 6–8mm, purple-black becoming off-white in the tube, margins replicate. W Cape. ssp. *pilifera* P.V. Bruyns. St. mostly 4-angled, to 10cm, green-purple with a sharp tip to each tubercle. Cor. 11–13mjm diam., covered with fine spicules and usually L-shaped papillae, each topped by a thick hair, dark purple-brown within, tinged green outside, tube 2–3mm deep, 4mm wide at mouth, lobes usually slightly replicate for most of their length, 8×4mm. SE Cape.
Q. framesii (Pill.) P.V. Bruyns. Forming dense clumps; st. to 40×2cm, grey-green to purple with small red spots, 4–6-angled, angles irregular to spiralled, with hard, short-tipped, yellow teeth. Cor. to 18mm diam., exterior yellow-green, interior bright yellow, tube cupular, 3×3mm with stiff hairs in mouth, lobes 8×2mm, apex obtuse often slightly incurved, margins folded back. W Cape.
Q. hottentotorum N.E. Br. = *Q. incarnata.*
Q. incarnata (L. f.) P.V. Bruyns. St. 10–30×2.5cm, erect, grey to purple-green, 4-angled, teeth conical, stout. Cor. white to pale pink, interior pale yellow to cream-white, tube 2mm, cup-shaped, campanulate or shallowly conical, lobes to 8mm, tube mouth and lobes stiffly hairy; corona enclosed by tube. Namaqualand. var. *tentaculata* P.V. Bruyns. Cor. lobes 8–10×2mm, margins replicate. W Cape. ssp. *aurea* (Lückh.) P.V. Bruyns. Cor. 2–2.2cm diam., exterior off-white, mottled pale pink, glab., interior yellow, paler in tube, minutely hairy, tube V-shaped, 2mm diam., lobes 6–9×2.5–3mm. W Cape.
Q. inversa (N.E. Br.) P.V. Bruyns. St. 25×1.5–2.5cm, 4-angled, grey-green to purple-green with stout acute tteh on tubercles. Cor. to 1.5cm diam., tube 1.5–2mm deep, yellow or white, sometimes triped purple, lobes 3–8×2–4mm, margins with flattened purple hairs, yellow to green at tip, purple-brown to red in lower half. W Cape. var. *cincta* (Lückh.) P.V. Bruyns. Cor. 2.1cm diam., tube off-white with concentric purple bars or lines, lobes 5–8×2–4mm, dark purple brown, ciliate except near tips and base. W Cape.
Q. linearis (N.E. Br.) P.V. Bruyns. St. 6–15×1–2.5cm, grey to dark purple-black, angles rounded, obtuse, teeth 1–3mm. Cor. 3–4mm, campanulate, glab., white, occas. suffused purple, lobes 8–10mm, tips incurved, deep purple-brown. W Cape.

Q. mammillaris (L.) P.V. Bruyns. St. 12–50×4cm, erect, spirally 4–6-angled, teeth to 2cm, stout, irregular. Cor. exterior pale green and glab., interior with hair-tipped papillae, tube 3–4mm, campanulate, pale yellow with purple-black spots, lobes 1.2–2cm, purple to red-black; corona dark purple-brown. Namaqualand.
Q. marlothii (N.E. Br.) P.V. Bruyns. St. forming dense clusters, 9×2–2.5cm, 4–5-angled, green speckled purple, teeth 3–5mm. Cor. 7–10mm diam., exterior pale green, interior yellow blotched purple, with stiff purple hairs, lobes 4×2mm, recurved. W Cape.
Q. parviflora (Masson) P.V. Bruyns. St. clustered, 10–30×1–2cm, branching, 4-angled, grey to purple, teeth with a hard yellow point. Cor. 8–10mm diam., lobes lanceolate with purple bars or a green to yellow or off-white ground, finely ciliate. W Cape. ssp. *bayeriana* P.V. Bruyns. Cor. 6–7mm diam., interior covered with purple, twisted hairs, pale yellow-green with light purple blotches, lobes 2.5×2mm, deltoid, tube small. W Cape. ssp. *dependens* (N.E. Br.) P.V. Bruyns. Cor. 7–11mm diam., tube ± lacking, lobes broad to midpoint then narrowing to a broadly acute tip, pale yellow barred purple near the centre, becoming plain purple nearer the tips, margins slightly reflexed, ciliate with soft, twisted, purple hairs. W Cape. ssp. *gracilis* (Lückh.) P.V. Bruyns. Cor. 14–19mm diam., upper surface glab., mostly spreading, tube lacking, lobes v. variable in width, 5–7×2mm, central area off-white with scattered brown dots, lobes becoming brown or yellow toward tips, margin with purple hairs. W Cape. ssp. *pulchra* P.V. Bruyns. 10–16mm diam., interior with purple hairs over red part of fl., central part deep to pale red with a white ring around base of lobes, lobes bright yellow, rarely white, abruptly acute, 4–8×2mm, margins with purple twisted hairs. W Cape. ssp. *swanepoelii* (Lavranos) P.V. Bruyns. Cor. 10–12mm diam., glab., tube virtually 0, off-white with purple to red-brown spots, lobes 3–4×2–3mm, ovate-deltoid to ovate-lanceolate, margins slightly reflexed with twisted red-purple hairs. W Cape.
Q. pillansii (N.E. Br.) P.V. Bruyns. St. 20–40×3cm, 4-angled, grey-green, spotted red, angles flattened, teeth to 1.5cm. Cor. tube to 6mm, purple-brown, campanulate, with dense papillae with purple apical hairs, lobes 6–10mm, oblong-ovate, papillose, grey-purple with maroon spots; outer corona lobes dark purple-brown. Cape Prov.
Q. pruinosa (Masson) P.V. Bruyns. Forming sprawling clumps; st. 50×1.5cm, grey-green to dark purple-grey, 4-angled, with rounded tubercles armed with a minute tooth. Cor. 10–13mm diam., exterior glab., grey-green to mottled purple-brown, interior with fine, crinkled, white hairs, surface dark brown, rugulose, tube short, lobes 4–5×3mm, deltoid. W Cape, Nam.
Q. ramosa (Masson) P.V. Bruyns. St. 12–30cm, bluntly 4-angled, grey-green or tinged purple, teeth to 3mm. Cor. tube 3–4mm, campanulate, base white, mouth dark purple with dense, hair-tipped papillae, lobes 1cm, attenuate, black-purple, covered with slender spicules, outer corona cup-shaped, dark purple-black. Cape Prov.
→*Caralluma, Sarcophagophilus, Stapelia* and *Tromotriche.*

Quartervine *Bignonia capreolata.*

Quassia L. Simaroubaceae. 35 trees or shrubs. Lvs pinnate or simple, lfts usually with pitted glands above. Infl. a rac., pan. or umbel. Fr. 1–6 from each fl., drupaceous or woody, sometimes v. large. Trop. Afr., SE Asia, Aus. Z10.
Q. amara L. BITTERWOOD. Erect shrub, to 3m. Lvs emerging purple-red, rachis winged; lfts opposite, entire, usually 5. Pan. to 25cm, red-stalked; cal. 7–8mm, red; pet. to 3cm, exterior bright red, interior white; sta. 3.5–4cm, exserted. Fr. purple-black. Braz.

Quatre Saisons Rose *Rosa ×damascena* var. *semperflorens.*
Quebrahacha *Caesalpinia punctata.*
Queen Anne's Double Daffodil *Narcissus* 'Eystettensis'.
Queen Anne's Jonquil *Narcissus jonquilla* 'Flore Pleno'.
Queen Cup *Clintonia uniflora.*
Queen Lily *Curcuma petiolata*; *Phaedranassa.*
Queen of Sheba *Podranea brycei.*
Queen of the Meadows *Filipendula ulmaria.*
Queen of the Night *Selenicereus grandiflorus.*

Queen of the Prairie *Filipendula rubra.*
Queen Palm *Syagrus romanzoffianum.*
Queen's Crape Myrtle *Lagerstroemia speciosa.*
Queensland Arrowroot *Canna indica.*
Queensland Bottletree *Brachychiton rupestris.*
Queensland Ebony *Bauhinia carronii.*
Queensland Kauri *Agathis robusta.*
Queensland Lace-bark *Brachychiton discolor.*
Queensland Lily *Doryanthes guilfoylei.*
Queensland Nut *Macadamia tetraphylla.*
Queensland Pittosporum *Pittosporum rhombifolium.*
Queensland Poplar *Homalanthus populifolius.*
Queensland Pyramid Tree *Lagunaria patersonii.*
Queensland Silver Wattle *Acacia podalyriifolia.*
Queensland Umbrella Tree *Schefflera actinophylla.*
Queen's Tears *Billbergia nutans.*
Queen's Wreath *Petrea.*

Quekettia Lindl.
Q. micromera (Barb. Rodr.) Cogn. = *Capanemia micromera.*

Quercifilix Copel. Dryopteridaceae. 1 terrestrial fern. Rhiz. creeping or suberect; stipes tufted, scaly at base, hairy throughout, those of sterile fronds to 5cm, those of fertile fronds to 15cm. Sterile fronds oak leaf-like, ± trifoliate, shallowly lobed, apical seg. to 5cm, lat. seg. to 1.5cm, rounded; fertile fronds fls thinner, trifoliate, with apical seg. to 3cm. Asia. Z10.
Q. zeylanica (Houtt.) Copel.
→*Leptochilus.*

Quercus L. OAK. Fagaceae. 600 everg. or decid. trees or shrubs. Bark usually fissured; branchlets downy at first. Lvs entire, toothed or lobed, short-stalked. ♂ fls in slender pendulous catkins, perianth 4–7-lobed, sta. 4–6(–12), usually with a vestigial ovary. ♀ fls solitary or 2 to many in a spike, perianth lobes 6, inconspicuous; ovary inferior, 3-locular, styles 3. Fr. a single-seeded nut (acorn), ovoid to globose, partly or almost wholly enclosed by a cup-shaped involucre (cupule), composed of adpressed scales. N Amer. to W trop. S Amer., N Afr., Eur. and Asia.
Q. aegilops L. probably referrable to a form of *Q. ithaburensis.*
Q. acuta Thunb. JAPANESE EVERGREEN OAK. Everg. tree to 25m, usually a large shrub in cult. Lvs 10–17×4–6cm, oblong-ovate to lanceolate-oblong or elliptic, apex acuminate, base rounded to cuneate, usually undulate, coriaceous, deep lustrous green above, matt yellow-green beneath. Acorns to 2cm, ellipsoid, clustered; cupule surrounding one-third of acorn, conspicuously ringed, finely downy. Jap., N Korea, China. Z7.
Q. acuta Raf. non Thunb. = *Q. coccinea.*
Q. acutissima Carruth. SAWTHORN OAK. Decid. tree, seldom exceeding 25m. Bark ashen to black corky, fissured. Lvs 6–20×2.5–6.5cm, lanceolate, lanceolate-oblong, to obovate, apex long acuminate, base cuneate to rounded, teeth broadly triangular, bristle-tipped, lustrous green above, paler and glab. beneath. Acorns to 2.5cm, solitary, ovoid, sometimes dorsally depressed; cupule to 3.5cm diam., concealing two-thirds of acorn, covered with long, hairy scales. China, Korea, Jap. ssp. *chenii* (Nak.) Camus. Fr. smaller, cupule scales more slender. S & C China. Z5.
Q. acutissima (Michx.) Sarg. non Roxb. = *Q. muehlenbergii.*
Q. aegilops Willd. non L. = *Q. ithaburensis* ssp. *macrolepis.*
Q. aegilops Boiss. non L. = *Q. ithaburensis* ssp. *macrolepis.*
Q. afares Pomel = *Q. castaneifolia* var. *incana.*
Q. agrifolia Née. CALIFORNIA LIVE OAK. Everg. tree to 25m, often shrubby in cult. Crown borad; bark thick, smooth or grooved, grey, red or black. Lvs 2.5–7×2.5×4cm, ovate-elliptic or broadly elliptic, apex acute, base rounded, spiny-toothed, deep glossy green and rather concave above, paler beneath, glab. except for tufted hairs in axils of veins. Acorns 2–3.5cm, ovoid, acute, solitary; cupule enclosing one-quarter to one-third of acorn, sericeous. Calif. Z8.
Q. alba L. WHITE OAK. Decid. tree in 45m. Crown rounded. Bark pale grey to brown, exfoliating in plates. Lvs 10–20×6.5–14cm, obovate, oblong or elliptic, apex abruptly acute, base cuneate, lobes 3–4 per side, entire or sparsely toothed, initially pubesc., dull mid-green above, orange to burgundy in fall, paler glaucous beneath. Acorn 1–3cm, ovoid-oblong, short or long-stalked; cupule enclosing quarter to one-third of acorn, grey-white, composed of adpressed, compacted, hairy scales. E US. f. *elongata* Kipp. Lvs slender, to 25×8cm, orange to purple red in fall. f. *pinnatifida* (Michx.) Rehd. Lvs deeply pinnatisect, lobes slender, dentate. f. *repanda* (Michx.) Trel. Lvs v. shallowly lobed. Hybrids between *Q. alba* and *Q. bicolor* are referred to as *Q. ×jackiana.* Z4.
Q. aliena Bl. Decid. tree to 25m. Lvs 10–20cm, obovate to oblong, apex acute to rounded, base cuneate, sinuately dentate,

teeth coarse, blunt, 10–15 per side, yellow-green glab. above, grey-white to blue-green and tomentellous beneath. Acorns 2–2.5cm, ovoid, solitary or grouped 2–3; cupule enclosing one-third of acorn, grey-tomentose with scales adpressed. Jap., Korea. var. *acuteserrata* Maxim. Lvs smaller and narrower, teeth acute, rather incurved, gland. tipped. Jap., C China. Z5.
Q. alnifolia Poech. GOLDEN OAK. Everg. shrub to 2m or tree to 8m. Bark coarsely textured, grey. Lvs 2.5–6×1.5–5cm, broadly obovate to suborbicular, apex and base rounded to subtruncate, denticulate above, glossy dark or livid green above, with ochre or ash-coloured felty pubescence beneath. Acorns 2.5–3.5cm, obovoid, mucronate, solitary or paired; cupule small, enclosing to half acorn, scales spreading, long-pubesc., arranged in a broad band. Cyprus. Z8.
Q. ambrozyana Simonkai = *Q. ×hispanica* 'Ambrozyana'.
Q. ×andleyensis Henry. (*Q. ilex* × *Q. petraea.*) Decid. or semi-evergreen tree. Lvs 8–9cm, variable on same shoot, obovate-oblong, entire and undulate, or with 4–5 teeth or lobes per side, lobes sometimes toothed at tips, scurfy, becoming dark glossy-green above, paler beneath with indumentum persisting on veins. Gdn origin.
Q. aquatica Walter. = *Q. nigra.*
Q. aquifolioides Rehd. & Wils. = *Q. semecarpifolia.*
Q. arizonica Sarg. ARIZONA WHITE OAK. Semi-evergreen shrub or small tree to 17m, crown rounded. Lvs 3–8cm, entire or spiny-toothed in juveniles, oblong-lanceolate to broad ovate, margin slightly revolute, dark blue-green above, pale tomentose beneath. Acorns 2–2.5cm; ovoid-oblong; cupule with thick, corky scales, covering a third to half of the acorn. Ariz., New Mex., NW Mex. Z7.
Q. arkansana Sarg. Decid. tree to 18m. Crown slender. Bark deeply fissured, grey-black. Lvs 3.5–12×2–6.25cm, broadly elliptic to obovate, apex rounded, base tapering, margins entire or sinuately 3-lobed; initially white pubesc. above, olive-green, brown-tomentose beneath, ultimately glab. except for tufts of hairs in vein axils. Acorns 1–1.5cm, subglobose to ovoid, solitary or paired; cupule shallow, enclosing a quarter or rarely one-third of acorn. SE US. Z7.
Q. armeniaca Kotschy = *Q. hartwissiana.*
Q. aucheri Jaub. & Spach. BOZ PIRNAL OAK. Everg. shrub or tree to 5(10)m. Lvs 1–4×1–2.5cm, entire to spiny-serrate, oblong to ovate, coriaceous, glab. grey-green above, stellate-tomentose and waxy grey-white beneath. Acorns to 2×1.5cm, ovoid-acute, sweet, edible; cupule stout, to 2.5cm broad, covering two-thirds to three-quarters of acorn, scales adpressed but rough. Greek Is., SW Turk. Z8.
Q. austriaca Willd. = *Q. cerris* var. *austriaca.*
Q. austrina Small. Decid. tree to 20m. Bark pale grey, exfoliating. Lvs 6.5–15×2.75–8.5cm, obovate-elliptic, entire, sinuate or with 2 to 3 broad lobes per side, deep green above, pale and glab. beneath (not glaucous, cf. *Q. alba*). Acorns 1.2–2cm, short-stalked, solitary; cupule thin, downy, enclosing one-third to one-half of acorn. S US. Z5.
Q. ×auzendii Gren. & Godron. (*Q. coccifera* × *Q. ilex.*) Foliage like *Q. coccifera*, but felty-pubesc. beneath. Acorns in clusters of 2–3; cupule scales adpressed; stalk to 2.5cm.
Q. ballota Desf. = *Q. ilex* var. *ballota.*
Q. balsequillana Trel. = *Q. emoryi.*
Q. bambusifolia Hance non Fort. nec Mast. BAMBOO-LEAVED OAK. Everg. tree to 12m, or large shrub. Young br. crimson. Lvs 3.5–8×0.6–1.6cm, linear-lanceolate to nearly elliptic, apex obtuse or rounded, base attenuate or cuneate, entire, or with 1 or 2 weak teeth, revolute, leathery, glossy green above, sparsely silky pubesc. becoming glaucous beneath. Acorn 1.5–2.4cm, ovoid, mucronate, silky becoming glab.; cupule enclosing to half of acorn, puberulent or glabrescent outside, silky inside, with scales forming 5 or 6 close rings. S China, Hong Kong, Tonkin. Plants grown under this name may also be *Q. myrsinifolia, Q. salicina, Q. stenophylla* or *Q. glauca.* Z8.
Q. bambusifolia Fort. non Hance nec Mast. = *Q. myrsinifolia.*
Q. banisteri Michx. = *Q. ilicifolia.*
Q. baronii Skan. Everg. or semi-everg. shrub to 3m or more. Lvs 2–6×1–3cm, oblong-lanceolate with numerous triangular, aristate teeth tomentose at first. Acorn subsessile, 1.5×1cm ovoid; cupule with reflexed scales. SW China. Z8.
Q. ×bebbiana C. Schneid. (*Q. alba* × *Q. macrocarpa.*) Close to *Q. alba* but with lvs far larger, usually broadly 5-lobed on each side, downy beneath. Acorns solitary or a few, clustered and malformed; cupule deeper than in *Q. alba* not so densely fringed. Natural hybrid.
Q. ×benderi Baenitz. (*Q. coccinea* × *Q. rubra.*) Close to *Q. rubra.* Shoots tinted red at first. Lvs obovate, apex acuminate, base truncate, lobes 5–7 per side, deep, bristle-toothed, ultimately glab. except for hair tufts in vein axils beneath, purple-red or yellow in fall. Acorns ovoid or malformed; cupule turbinate, enclosing half acorn. Gdn origin.

Q. bicolor Willd. SWAMP WHITE OAK. decid. tree to 25m. Crown rounded; bark pale grey-breown, fissured, exfoliating. Lvs 6.5–16×3–7cm, oblong-obovate or obovate, apex rounded or abruptly acute, base tapering, bluntly toothed or deeply lobed, dark glossy green above (turning orange to fiery red in fall), hoary or velutinous beneath. Acorn 2–3cm, oblong-ovoid, solitary or paired on stalk to 8cm; cupule with many, slender, hairy, compacted scales, enclosing one-third of acorn. NE N Amer. Z4.

Q. blakei var. *variotii* Chun = *Q. glauca*.

Q. boissieri Reut. = *Q. infectoria* ssp. *veneris*.

Q. borealis Michx. = *Q. rubra*.

Q. borealis var. *maxima*. = *Q. rubra*.

Q. brantii Lindl. Decid. or semi-evergreen shrub or small tree to 10m. Lvs 6–10×3–6cm, ovate-oblong, base cordate, serrate, teeth short-aristate; dull green above, densely stellate-tomentose beneath. Acorn similar to that of *Q. ithaburensis* but smaller, cupule 2.5–3.5cm, with large rhomboid elongated scales, uppermost scales filiform, covering two-thirds to almost all of the acorn. Kurdistan S to SW Iran. Z7.

Q. brevifolia Sarg. = *Q. incana*.

Q. ×brittonii W.T. Davis. (*Q. ilicifolia* ×*Q. marilandica*.) Divaricately branching small tree or shrub. Lvs 9–10cm, obovate to broadly obovate, apex broad, rounded, base taper-ing, rounded-cuneate or lyrate, margins broad, sinuate teeth and 3–4 lateral lobes, ultimately lustrous dark green above with veins pubesc., thinly tawny to ashy-tomentose beneath. Natural hybrid.

Q. brutia Ten. = *Q. robur* ssp. *brutia*.

Q. bungeana Forbes = *Q. variabilis*.

Q. ×bushii Sarg. (*Q. marilandica* ×*Q. velutina*.) Decid. tree to 10m. Lvs 10–13cm, typically obovate, deeply and sinutely 3–5-lobed, lobes with sparse, inconspicuous spines extending from veins on somewhat slanted margins, glossy dark green above, olive to yellow-green beneath, glab. except tufts in vein axils. US.

Q. californica Cooper = *Q. kelloggii*.

Q. calliprinos Webb = *Q. coccifera* ssp. *calliprinos*.

Q. canariensis Willd. ALGERIAN OAK; MIRBECK'S OAK. Decid. tree to 40m in habitat. Bark thick, rugged, black. Lvs 5–18×4–12cm, oval or obovate, apex rounded, base tapering, rounded or subcordate, margins obtusely lobed or coarsely toothed, coriaceous, rusty floccose at first, becoming dark green and glab. above, paler beneath, glab. except for rusty residual hairs on veins. Acorns to 2.5cm, solitary, paired or in small clusters; cupule with adpressed downy scales, enclosing one-third of acorn. N Afr., Iberian peninsula (*not* Canaries). Z7.

Q. castanea Willd. = *Q. muehlenbergii*.

Q. castaneifolia C.A. Mey. Decid. tree to 35m. Crown large, rounded; bark brown, rough-textured and corky. Lvs 6–16×2.5–4cm, narrowly elliptic to oblong-lanceolatem, apex acute, base cuneate or rounded, with coarse triangular aristate saw-teeth, deep glossy green above, dull grey-green beneath, glab. or minutely downy. Acorns 2–3cm, ovoid, often dorsally compressed, solitary or to 5 on a stout stalk; cupule clothed with slender sclaes (sometimes reflexed), enclosing one-third to half of acorn. Cauc., Iran. var. *incana* Batt. & Trabut. Less vigorous, to 25m; bark more densely fissured. ♀ fls with 4–5 slender, spreading styles (not 3 short, erect styles as in *Q. castaneifolia*). Alg., Tun. Z6.

Q. castaneifolia var. *algeriensis* Bean = *Q. castaneifolia* var. *inca-na*.

Q. catesbaei Michx. = *Q. laevis*.

Q. cerris L. TURKEY OAK. Decid. tree to 43m. Crown conical. Bark grey-white, spolitting into thick plates. Lvs 5–12×1.5–3cm, oblong-lanceolate, tapered to an acute apex and a rounded or truncate base, lobes or teeth triangular to lobulate, mucronulate, dark green and stellate-pubesc. initially above, lighter and pubesc. to tomentose beneath, yellow-brown in fall. Acorns in groups of 1–4, to 3.5cm, ellisoid, apex subtruncate and mucronate; cupule of subulate often spreading or reflexed scales, enclosing one-third of acorn. C & S Eur., Asia Minor. var. **cerris**. Lobes on lvs lobulate, sinuses deep. 'Argenteovariegata': lf margins irregularly variegated cream-white. 'Aureovariegata': lvs yellow variegated. f. **laciniata** (Loud.) Schneid. Lvs irregularly pinnately lobed or divided, lobes acute, sometimes further pinnately divided, pale green and sparsely pubesc. beneath. 'Pendula': branchlets long, pendulous. var. **austriaca** (Willd.) Loud. Lvs ovate, regularly and deeply dentate, triangularly lobed, lobes not lobulate. var. **haliphlaeos** (Lam.) DC. Lvs larger, 10–14×3.5–5cm, base roiunded or subcordate, lightly puberulent beneath, slightly leathery, usually lyrately lobed. S Fr.

Q. cerris 'Ambrozyana'. = *Q. ×hispanica* 'Ambrozyana'.

Q. cerris var. *ciliata* Kotschy = *Q. cerris* ssp. *tournefortii*.

Q. cerris f. *argenteo-variegata* Ottol. = *Q. cerris* 'Argenteovariegata'.

Q. cerris f. *asplenifolia* hort. = *Q. cerris* f. *laciniata*.

Q. cerris f. *dissecta* hort. = *Q. cerris* var. *haliphloeus* f. *laciniata*.

Q. cerris f. *variegata* hort. = *Q. cerris* 'Argenteovariegata'.

Q. chapmanii Sarg. Small semi-evergreen shrub on tree to 9m in habitat. Crown spreading, bark separating into large irregular plates. Lvs 5–12×3.5–4.5cm, oblong-obovate or subelliptic, attenuate and rounded at base, apex rounded or obtuse, entire or iregularly sinuate with a few rounded lobes, initially tawny-tomentose, becoming leathery, dark green, and glab. above, puberulent beneath. Acorns solitary or in clusters of to 3, 1.5–1.7×–1.4cm, pale brown, silky tomentose toward apex; cupule scarcely pubesc. inside, scales oblong, pale-tomentose with red-brown margins, enclosing one-third of acorn. SE US.

Q. chinensis Bunge = *Q. variabilis*.

Q. chinquapin Pursh = *Q. prinoides*.

Q. chrysolepis Liebm. CANYON; LIVE OAK; MAUL OAK. Everg. tree to 25m. Bark white-grey or tinted red, breaking into small scales. Lvs 2.5–5(–10)×1–4(–5)cm, oval to elliptic or lanceolate, apex acute or subobtuse, mucronate, base rounded or cordate, usually entire, rarely with 4–10 short, spiny teeth each side, gland. and tomentose at first, becoming leathery and shining above, pale glaucous-waxy beneath. Acorns solitary or paired, 2.5–3.5cm, ovoid, apex rounded or attenuate and mucronate, puberulent; cupule short and thick, pale green or red-brown in-side, scales oval or triangular, with fawn to white tomentum, en-closing one-third of acorn. SW US, NW Mex. Z7.

Q. chrysolepis var. *vacciniifolia* (Kellogg) En-gelm. = *Q. vacciniifolia*.

Q. chrysophyllus Kellogg = *Q. chrysolepis*.

Q. cinerea Michx. = *Q. incana*.

Q. coccifera L. KERMES OAK; GRAIN OAK. Everg. bushy shrub, usually 0.25–1.5m, rarely a tree 4.5m. Bark smooth and grey at first, cracked with age. Lvs 1.2–3.5×0.6–2cm, oval, elliptic or oblong, apex acute or rounded, mucronate, base rounded or cordate, becoming leathery, dark and glab. above, paler and glab. or with a few hairs in nerve axils beneath, margin un-dulate, with 4–6 pairs of spreading, spine-like teeth. Acorns 1.5–3cm, ovoid or oblong-ovoid, apex attenuate with an apical spine light brown striped darker; cupule enclosing one-half to two-thirds of acorn, scales spiny, often reflexed, lightly pub-erulent. W Medit., S Eur., NW Afr. ssp. **calliprinos** (Webb) Boiss. PALESTINE OAK; SIND OAK. Tree to 12m. Lvs larger and more oblong, to 5×3cm. Acorn to three-quarters enclosed by cup. E Medit., SW Asia. Z6.

Q. coccifera var. *pseudococcifera* (Desf.) A. DC. = *Q. coccifera*.

Q. coccinea Münchh. SCARLET OAK. Decid. tree to 30m. Bark pale grey-brown, cracked into irregular, scaly plates. Lvs 8–12×6–12(–15)cm, oval or obovate, rarely oblong, base truncate, rarely cuneate, silky at first, becoming glab. and glossy, paler and with tufts of hair in vein axils beneath, scarlet in fall, margin deeply pinnately sinuate-dentate or serate, lobes usually 7. Acorns 1.5–2.5cm, ovoid to subspherical, apex and base rounded, with thin red-brown tomentum; cupule turbinate, scales yellow-brown, oval, subglabrous, enclosing one-third to one-half of acorn. E US, S Canada. 'Splendens': lvs brilliant scarlet in fall. Z4.

Q. coccinea Sarg. non Münchh. = *Q. ellipsoidalis*.

Q. conferta Kit. = *Q. frainetto*.

Q. congesta Presl. Decid. large shrub or tree. Lvs 7.5×14×4–9cm, ovate to oblong-ovate, base cordate to attenuate, deeply sinuately lobed or pinnatifid, lobes 6–8 each side, glab. and shining above, grey-green pubesc. beneath. Acorns 1.4–3×1–2.4cm, ovoid, obtuse; cupule with pedicel to 4cm, scales spreading to erect, not adpressed, with pale shaggy hairs. Sicily, Sardinia, S Fr. Z7.

Q. crassifolia Humb. & Bonpl. Decid. tree to 25m in habitat. Lvs 8–14×4–5(–9)cm, obovate to suborbicular, rarely subelliptic, apex obtuse, sometimes acuminate, base cordate, fawn-velvety at first becoming leathery, hard bright. above, tomentum pers-ists beneath, sometimes sinuate-dentate, teeth few, mucronate, rigid. Acorns 1.5–2cm, ovoid, with a thick mucro and persistent styles, brown; cupule scales brown-hairy to apex, often becom-ing glab., enclosing one-third or more of acorn. C Mex. Z8.

Q. crassipes Humb. & Bonpl. Everg. tree to 25m. Shoots tomentose. Lvs 5–9cm, oblong-elliptic, coriaceous, entire or sinate, glab. above, tomentose beneath. Acorns 2–2.5cm, ovoid; cupule with adpressed scales. C Mex. Z8.

Q. crassipocula Torr. = *Q. chrysolepis*.

Q. cuneata Dipp. non Wangenh. non Dipp. = *Q. falcata*.

Q. cuneata Wangenh. = *Q. marilandica*.

Q. daimio K. Koch. = *Q. dentata*.

Q. dalechampii Ten. Small tree. Lvs 8–13cm, oblong to obovate-lanceolate, base truncate to subcordate, sinuately lobed to pinnatifid, lobes 5–7 each side ovate to lanceolate, acute, soon becoming glab. Acorns in groups of 1–3, ovate, to 2cm; cupule scales thick, rough, white-grey tomentose, enclosing one-third to a half of acorn. S It. Z7.

Q. dalechampii Wenz. non Ten. = *Q. virgiliana*.

Q. ×*deamii* Trel. (*Q. macrocarpa* ×*Q. muehlenbergii*.) Closely resembles *Q. muehlenbergii* but lvs finely pubesc. beneath, margins more deeply lobed, lobes 7–9 each side, acute. Acorn pedicellate. US (Indiana).

Q. dentata Thunb. DAIMIO OAK; JAPANESE EMPEROR OAK. Decid. tree, fast-growing to 20–25m. Crown large, rounded. Bark brown, fissured and split into grey-scaly plates. Lvs 15–50×8–30cm, orbicular-obovate to oblong-obovate, base attenuate to cordate, apex attenuate or rounded, sinuately lobed, lobes large, rounded, often mucronulate, pale yellow tomentose at first, becoming dark green and glab. except on nerves above, paler and densely tomentose beneath. Acorns 1.2–2.4cm, ovoid to subglobose, glab., apex rounded, mucronate; cupule scales adpressed, upper scales erect to recurved, enclosing more than half of acorn. Jap., Manch., Korea, Mong., China, Taiwan. 'Pinnatifida': lvs crispate, deeply and narrowly lobed. Jap. var. *oxygloba* Franch. Lvs narrower at base, lobes more abruptly acuminate and triangular. SW China. Z5.

Q. douglasii Hook. & Arn. BLUE OAK. Decid. tree to 20m. Crown dense, rounded. Bark white-grey, slightly with small brown or red scales. Lvs (2.5–)5–8(–10)×2.5–4cm, oblong to elliptic, base cuneate or slightly rounded, apex obtuse or rounded, bluntly or sinuately toothed, sometimes 3–5(–7) lobed, initially soft-pubesc., becoming blue-green, glabrescent, above, fawn-pubesc. beneath. Acorns 2–3.5cm, solitary, ovoid, apex sometimes attenuate, mucronate; cupule flat, thin pale-green pubesc. inside, scales adpressed, subacute, enclosing acorn base. W US. Z7.

Q. douglasii var. *gambelii* (Nutt.) A. DC. = *Q. gambelii*.

Q. dschorochensis sensu Wenz. non Koch = *Q. iberica*.

Q. dumosa Nutt. CALIFORNIA SCRUB OAK. Semi-everg. shrub or small tree to 4m. Lvs 1.5–2.5cm, often entire on mature plants, spiny toothed on young and some mature plants, coriaceous, glab. above, tomentose beneath. Acorn 2–3cm, ovoid; cupule thick, lower scales tuberculate, covering half of acorn. W Calif., N Baja Calif. Z8.

Q. durandii Buckl. DURAND OAK. Tree to 25m, closely allied to *Q. austrina*. Lvs 7–15cm, entire or slightly lobed, yellow-green. Acorns 1.5–2cm; cupule thin, enclosing acorn only at base. SE US. Z7.

Q. durandii var. *austrina* (Small) Palmer = *Q. austrina*.

Q. durata Jeps. LEATHER OAK. Everg. shrub or small tree to 4m, similar to *Q. dumosa*; differs in lvs stiff and thickly coriaceous, dull (not glossy) above and with revolute margins. Calif. Z7.

Q. duraznillo Trel. = *Q. emoryi*.

Q. ehrenbergii Kotschy. Decid. shrub or small tree. Bark shallowly cracked, grey-brown. Lvs 5–8×3–5cm, ovate or short-elliptic, apex obtuse, base truncate or subcordate, stellate-pubesc. occas. dentate, more usually deeply lobed to pinnatifid, lobes acute, apiculate or with a bristle-like apex. Acorn solitary, 3–4cm, subcylindrical, truncate, mucronate; cupule scales thick, erect to slightly recurved, finely pubesc., enclosing at least half of acorn. Syr., Leb. Z7.

Q. ellipsoidalis E.J. Hill. NORTHERN PIN OAK. Decid. tree to 20m. Bark grey-brown, fissured into narrow places. Lvs 6–15×5–12cm, obovate or elliptic, base truncate or cuneate, margin deeply lobed, lobes 5–7, oblong, coarsely dentate with 1–3 teeth, silky-tomentose at first, becoming glab. except on vein axils beneath, dark green and shining above, paler beneath, yellow to light brown with red markings in fall. Acorns 1.2–2cm, solitary or paired, ellipsoid, mucronate, puberulent, chestnut-brown with darker lines; cupule turbinate to obconical, light red-brown, scales adpressed, finely pubesc., enclosing one-third to one-half of acorn. NE US. Z4.

Q. emoryi Torr. EMORY OAK. Decid. tree 9–12m, rarely to 21m. Bark dark brown-black, split into oblong plates, scaly. Lvs 2.5–6×1–2.5cm, oblong-lanceolate to oblong, apex acute, mucronate, base rounded to cordate, margin slightly revolute, entire or with a few, acute teth, white-tomentose often tinted red at first, rapidly becoming dark green and shining above, with a few tufts of hair on midrib beneath, leathery. Acorns 1.5–2cm, oblong-ellipsoid, apex rounded, mucronate, dark chestnut to black; cupule deep, pale green pubesc. inside, scales adpressed, ovate, pale brown, white-tomentose, enclosing one-third of acorn. SW US, Mex. Z7.

Q. engleriana Seemen Everg. tree 6–9(–10)m. Bark dark brown. Lvs 6–10×(2.5–)3.5–4.5cm, ovate to lanceolate, apex long-acuminate, base rounded, teeth small, acute, sharp, dark green, glab. and shining above, paler and brown-lanate beneath. Acorns in groups of 1–3, 1.2–3cm, oblong-ovoid, pale brown, apex puberulent attenuate; cupule sessile, hemispherical, silky inside, scales grey-pubesc. outside, enclosing only base of acorn.

China. Z7.

Q. esculus L. nomen ambiguum.

Q. esculus auct. non L. = *Q. frainetto*.

Q. fabri Hance. Decid. tree to 25m, usually smaller in cult. Lvs 6–17×2.5–6(–10)cm, oblong-obovate or ovate, apex rounded or obtuse, base rounded or subauriculate, margin undulate with 7–10 lobes each side, becoming glab. above, densely yellow-white tomentose beneath. Acorns 1.8–2.2cm, oblong or cylindrical, apex mucronate and crowned with persistent styles; cupule scales adpressed, obtuse, erect, brown, puberulent, enclosing one-third of acorn. China, Korea. Z5.

Q. faginea Lam. PORTUGUESE OAK. Semi-evergreen shrub or tree to *c*20m in habit, usually smaller in cult. Bark grey to brown, broken into subrectangular plates. Lvs 3–7×1.5–4cm, ovate-elliptic or oblong-obovate, apex rounded or obtuse, base rounded, truncate or subcordate, margin undulate, dentate, slightly revolute, initially stellate-pubesc. above, grey-tomentose slowly becoming glab. beneath. Acorns to 2.5cm, ovoid-oblong, apex usually apiculate, yellow, subglabrous; cupule scales adpressed, slightly rough, tomentose, enclosing one-fifth to one-third of acorn. Spain, Port. ssp. *tlemcenensis* (A. DC.) Maire & Weiller. Intermediate between type and *Q. canariensis*, possibly of hybrid origin: Lvs to 12×5cm, mostly 5–10cm, elliptic-oblong, shallow-lobed or toothed, thinly tomentose at first. NW Afr. Z7.

Q. falcata Michx. SOUTHERN RED OAK; SWAMP RED OAK. Decid. tree to 30m. Crown rounded or ovoid. Bark dark red-brown arching into scaly plates. Lvs 7–20×5–12cm, obovate or oblong, apex acute or acuminate, base rounded, sometimes cuneate, pubesc. at first above, becoming dark green, lustrous, densely silver-white tomentose beneath, margins sinuately lobed, lobes 3–7, entire or with a few teeth. Acorns 1.2–1.4cm, subglobose, mucronate, puberulent at first; cupule obconical or a flat cup, red-brown, shining, scales adpressed, mostly glab., enclosing only base or to one-third of acorn. SE US. var. *pagodifolia* Ellis. CHERRY-BARK RED OAK. Tree to 30m, rarely more; bark scaly, cherry-like. Lvs 15–20cm, lobes 5–11, shallower than lobes of type, white-tomentose or tinted red beneath. Z6.

Q. fallax Palmer = *Q.* ×*deamii*.

Q. farnetto Ten. = *Q. frainetto*.

Q. ×*fernaldii* Trel. see *Q. ilicifolia*.

Q. ferruginea var. *hybrida* Dipp. = *Q.* ×*brittonii*.

Q. fontanesii Guss. = *Q.* ×*hispanica*.

Q. frainetto Ten. HUNGARIAN OAK. Decid. tree to 30m. Bark smooth with small scale-like plates, dark grey. Crown large. Br. sometimes pendulous. Lvs 8–25×5–12cm, obovate or oblong-obovate, apex rounded, base subcordate or truncate, margin pinnatifid, lobes 6–10(–12) pairs, sometimes lobulate or sinuate, initially white-yellow tomentose, becoming glab. or stellate-pubesc., above, paler glaucescent beneath. Acorns 1.25–3.5cm, oblong ellipsoid or ovoid-oblong, apex rounded, mucronate; cupule densely tomentose outside, scales adpressed, enclosing up to one half of acorn. S It., Turk., Balk. Z6.

Q. fruticosa Brot. Small semi-evergreen shrub to 2m, usually low and spreading. Lvs 2.5–5(–9)×1.2–3cm, oblong-obovate or obovate-elliptic, apex obtuse, base rounded or cordate, entire or sinuate-crenate and often dentate at apex, teeth 4–7 pairs, flat or curved, usually mucronate, leathery, sparsely hairy above, white-grey pubesc. beneath. Acorns 1–1.5cm, oblong, glabrescent; cupule scales overlapping, triangular, pubesc., enclosing to two-thirds of acorn. S Spain and Port., Moroc. Z8.

Q. fulhamensis Zab. = *Q.* ×*hispanica* 'Fulhamensis'.

Q. fulvescens Kellogg = *Q. chrysolepis*.

Q. gambelii Nutt. GAMBEL OAK. Decid. shrub 1 or small tree to 8m. Bark deeply fissured, dark grey often tinted red-brown. Lvs 7–12×3–6cm, obovate, base attenuate, rounded, margin deeply lobed, lobes 3–6 each side, rounded, entire, term. lobe sometimes lobed, glab. or sparsely hairy above, paler and finely puberulent beneath. Acorns 1.5–2cm, ovoid, tomentose, apex rounded, mucronate; cupule sometimes turbinate, enclosing half of acorn. Wyom., Colorado, Utah, New Mex. Z4.

Q. ×*ganderii* C. Wolf. (*Q. agrifolia* ×*Q. kelloggii*.) Intermediate between parents, but with tufts of hairs in vein axils beneath.

Q. garryana Douglas ex Hook. OREGON WHITE OAK. Decid. tree 10–18(–20 or 30)m. Crown rounded. Br. crooked, ascending, or pendulous. Bark pale grey, shallowly cracked. Lvs 10–15×5–12cm, obovate or oblong-obovate, apex rounded, base cuneate, rounded, or subcordate, margins slightly revolute, lobes 3–5 per side, entire or dentate, dark green and glab. above, paler and soft pubesc. beneath. Acorns 2–2.5cm, ovoid, base truncate, apex rounded, mucronate, glab.; cupule shallow, puberulent inside, scales adpressed, pubesc., apices free, acute. W N Amer. Z5.

Q. genuensis nom. illegit. = *Q. warburgii*.

Q. georgiana M.A. Curtis. GEORGIA OAK; STONE MOUNTAIN OAK. Shrub or small tree, 1.5–4m. Bark light brown. Ls 3–12×2–9cm, ovate or obovate, apex acute, base attenuate or cuneate, lobes 3–7, triangular, term. lobe entire or trilobed, initially green tinted red, veins tomentose, margins ciliate, becoming green and shining above, paler and with tufts of hair in axils beneath, orange to scarlet in fall. Acorns 1–1.25cm, oblong or subglobose, light red-brown, apex mucronate, glab. and shining; cupule light red-brown, shining inside, scales adpressed, ovate, obtuse, slightly silky. E US, localized in Georgia. Z6.

Q. gilliana Rehd. & Wils. Everg. shrub or tree to 8m. Lvs 2.5–6×1–3cm, ovate, rounded to cordate base, entire, or spiny-toothed in juveniles, glab. above, pubesc. at first beneath. Acorns 2–4 on a short stout peduncle; cupule enclosing about half, scales adpressed, pubesc. SW China. Z8.

Q. gilva Bl. Everg. tree to 30m. Crown cylindrical, rounded at top. Lvs 6–7.5×2–2.5(–3)cm, lanceolate or oblong-lanceolate, apex short-acuminate, base attenuate or rounded, shallowly dentate in upper half, teeth rigid, yellow-tomentose at first, becoming glab. above, white and tomentose beneath. Acorn 1.5–1.7cm, ovoid, mucronate; cupule tomentose outside, scales forming 5–6 bands, enclosing one-third or more of acorn. Jap., C China. Z7.

Q. glabrescens Benth. Everg. shrub or small tree to 10m. Lvs 5–10×2–3cm, oblong-elliptic, base entire, cuneate, rest coarsely mucronate-toothed, often wavy, rarely entire dark, rough green above, pale, almost glab. beneath. Acorns 1.5cm, clustered 1–3; cupule with adpressed pubesc. scales, covering a third to half of the acorn. C Mex. Z8.

Q. glandulifera Bl. Decid. tree to 15m. Bark fissured. Lvs 5–15×2–4.5cm, obovate to oblong-ovate, apex acute, base acuminate, sharply serrate, glab. and green above, blue-green and lightly pubesc. beneath. Acorns in groups of 1–3; cupule shallow, scales adpressed, white-tomentose, enclosing one-third of cup. Jap., Korea, China. Z5.

Q. glauca Thunb. medium sized everg. tree, sometimes to 18m. Lvs 8–10(–15)×4–5(–6)cm, lanceolate-obovate to obovate, rarely oblanceolate, apex acuminate, base attenuate, rarely rounded, silky-pubesc. at first, ultimately glaucous, glab. or puberulent, entire below, dentate above. Acorns 1.3–2cm, cylindrical or conic-ovoid, apiculate, shining, sometimes with dark stripes; cupule enclosing one-third of acorn, scales forming 6–7 flat bands, puberulent. Jap., China. var. *micrococca* Maxim. Lvs glaucous, hairy beneath. Acorn 10–12×7–8mm, ovoid; cupules small, with 4–5 rings. Jap., China. var. *gracilis* A. Camus. Resembles *Q. myrsiniifolia*, but lvs pubesc., beneath, smaller and narrower, 4.5–8×1.5–2.5cm, oblong-elliptic to oblong or oblong-lanceolate, apex slightly acuminate, base cuneate to rounded, margins shallowly dentate, pubesc. beneath. China. var. *linearifolia* Koidz. Lvs 1–7×0.7–1cm, narrowly linear, acute, margins with irregular, spiny teeth. Jap. var. *lacera* Matsum. Lvs obovate, oval or lanceolate, apex acuminate-cuspidate, margins deeply lobed, tips of lobes with cartilaginous point. ssp. *annulata* Sm. Lvs oval or lanceolate, apex acuminate, base rounded, wider at middle than type, teeth more acuminate, waxy and often abundantly hairy beneath. Cupules larger, silky-pubesc. Himal. from Kashmir to Bhutan, Nepal, Sikkim, Burm., Tonkin. Z7.

Q. glauca Loud. non Thunb. = *Q. glauca* ssp. *annulata*.
Q. glauca var. *caesia* Bl. = *Q. glauca*.
Q. glauca var. *stenophylla* Bl. = *Q. stenophylla*.
Q. glauca f. *gracilis* Rehd. & Wils. = *Q. glauca* var. *gracilis*.
Q. graeca Kotschy = *Q. ithaburensis* ssp. *macrolepis*.
Q. grisea Liebm. Shrub to medium-sized tree, to 4m. Twigs densely pubesc. Lvs to 5cm, coriaceous, grey-green, downy throughout, oblong, minutely and sparsely dentate. SW US, N Mex.
Q. grosseserrata Bl. = *Q. mongolica* var. *grosseserrata*.
Q. haas Kotschy. Decid. tree related to *Q. robur*. Bark dark grey. Lvs 10–20×4–7cm, obovate, apex rounded or slightly truncate, base auriculate or subcordate, margin with 3–5 rounded lobes each side, dark green and glab. above, paler blue-green and tomentose beneath. Acorns 4–5cm, ellipsoid, apex rounded mucronate, almost glab.; cupule flattened-hemispherical, scales adpressed, tips free, erect, tomentose, enclosing one-third to one-quarter of acorn. Asia Minor. Z5.
Q. haliphoeos Lam. = *Q. cerris* var. *haliphloeos*.
Q. hartwissiana Steven. Decid. tree to 25m. Bark furrowed. Lvs 7–12(–15)×3.5–6.5(–9.5)cm, oblong to obovate-oblong or subelliptic, apex rounded or obtuse, base auriculate, subcordate, margin with 5–9 short, rounded lobes each side, dark green, glab. and shining above, paler, glab. or with hairs on veins beneath. Acorns in groups of 1–3 on a 1.8–3cm, almost obovoid, mucronate, glab., yellow-brown; cupule scales adpressed in overlapping rings, tomentose, enclosing one-third of acorn. SW Bulg., Asia Minor, Cauc., W Transcauc. Z5.
Q. hastata Liebm. = *Q. emoryi*.

Q. ×heterophylla Michx. f. (*Q. phellos* ×*Q. rubra*.) Decid. tree 20–25m. Bark smooth, pale-grey or brown. Lvs 10–18×2–4.3cm, oblong-lanceolate to obovate, apex mucronate, base cuneate, entire or with few shallow teeth, or with 4–6 shallow or deep, often mucronate lobes each side, ultimately glab. or slightly hairy on veins beneath; petiole 1.25–2.5cm, pubesc. becoming glab. Acorns closely resembling *Q. rubra*. First observed near Philadelphia.

Q. ×hickelii Camus. (*Q. pontica* ×*Q. robur*.) Decid. shrub, larger than *Q. pontica*. Lvs 15×10cm, either obovate, base attenuate and cordate, or subelliptic, base cuneate, coarsely dentate, teeth obtuse, mucronate, dark green and shining above, paler beneath. Gdn origin, Fr.

Q. hinckleyi C.H. Mull. Rare everg. shrub, forming low thickets in the wild. Lvs glaucous rigid, short-stalked, bearing 2–3 sharp spines on each side, base often auriculate. SW Tex.

Q. hindsii Benth. = *Q. lobata*.

Q. ×hispanica Lam. (*Q. cerris* ×*Q. suber*.) Semi-evergreen tree or shrub to 30m. Bark less corky than in *Q. suber*. Lvs 4–10×2–4cm, oblong-elliptic, acute, margin sinuate-dentate, teeth small, mucronulate, dark green and sparsely hairy above, densely yellow-white tomentose beneath. Acorns 3–4cm, oblong-ovoid, mucronate, mostly glab.; cupule hemispherical to ovoid, tomentose scales erect to reflexed, enclosing half or more of acorn. S Fr. to Port. and It., Balk. 'Ambrozyana': lvs 6–10cm, usually rather small, oblong-obovate, lobes subulate-mucronate, dark green and shining above, grey tomentose beneath. 'Crispa': compact shrub or small tree; bark more corky; lvs 5–8cm, crispate, densely white tomentose beneath. 'Dentata': bark corky; lvs more closely resembling *Q. cerris*, coarsely dentate, dark green above, grey-tomentose beneath; sometimes confused with 'Fulhamensis'. 'Diversifolia': small tree; bark v. corky; lvs 5×2cm, ovate, each side with conspicuous sinus, thus resembling *Q. cerris* lvs, margin lobed in lower half, entire to denticulate above; acorn cup hemispherical, scales more adpressed than hybrid type. 'Fulhamensis': graceful tree; br. more slender and bark less corky; lvs 7.5–9×3.5cm, ovate, apex acute, base rounded to subcordate, margin dentate, teeth 5–8 each side, apex acute, tomentum white; often confused with and grown as cv. Dentata. 'Fulhamensis Latifolia': lvs to 8×6cm, larger than 'Fulhamensis', apex obtuse, margin teeth wider and shallower than 'Fulhamensis', tomentum grey. 'Heterophylla': closely resembles *Q. cerris* var. *haliphloeos*; lvs oblong, irregularly lobed, sometimes with conspicuous broad sinus each side of midrib. 'Lucombeana': crown conical; bark only slightly corky; lvs resemble those of *Q. cerris*, 6–12×2.5–4cm, oblong, coarsely dentate, teeth 6–7(9) each side, green, glab., shining above, paler and tomentose beneath; acorn to 2.5cm, cupule with lower scales reflexed, upper scales erect, enclosing more than half of acorn. Z7.

Q. humilis Lam. non Walter = *Q. fruticosa*.
Q. hybrida Bechst. non Houba = *Q. ×rosacea*.
Q. hybrida Houba non Bechst. = *Q. ×runcinata*.
Q. hypoleuca Engelm. non Miq. = *Q. hypoleucoides*.
Q. hypoleucoides Camus. SILVER-LEAF OAK; WHITE-LEAF OAK. Semi-evergreen tree 6–10(–20)m, sometimes shrub 2–3m. Bark brown-black, split into large plates. Lvs 5–12×1–3cm, lanceolate or oblong – lanceolate to sublelliptic, base rounded or attenuate, apex attenuate and often mucronate, margin revolute, entire or sinuate-dentatge above, rarely with several rigid teeth, tomentose at first, becoming glab. above, pale-wooly beneath, rigid. Acorns 1–1.2cm, conic-oblong, rounded or acute, dark green; cupule scales adpressed, light chestnut-brown, silky-tomentose, enclosing one-third of acorn. S US, Mex. Z7.

Q. iberica Steven ex Bieb. Decid. tree related to *Q. petraea*, but generally shorter. Lvs 8–12×4–4.5cm, oblong-obovate to subelliptic, apex rounded or attenuate, base rounded or truncate, with 6–10 shallow, rounded, entire lobes each side, green and glab. above, paler and scattered short-pubesc. beneath. Acorns grouped 1–3 together, 1.4–1.6cm, ovoid, glab., apex subacute; cupule scales adpressed, velvety or puberulent. Balk., Asia Minor to N Iran (not Iberian Penins.). Trees from SE Turkey with larger lvs, to 17cm, more deeply lobed, are sometimes separated as *Q. pinnatiloba*. Z5.

Q. ichangensis Nak. = *Q. glauca*.
Q. ilex L. HOLM OAK; EVERGREEN OAK; HOLLY-LEAVED OAK. Everg. tree to 20(–27)m. Crown broad, rounded. Bark smooth, grey, becoming shallowly split. Lvs 2–9×1–3cm, sometimes wider, narrowly elliptic, ovate-lanceolate or suborbicular, slighly concave beneath, apex acute or obtuse, base attenuate or slightly cordate, entire or with mucronate, acuminate teeth, leathery, subglabrous, above, densely pubesc. beneath. Acorns groups of 1–3, 1.5–3×1–1.5cm, oblong-ovoid to subglobose, mucronate, grey-brown with darker lines, lightly lanate becoming pulverulent; cupule scales adpressed, triangular, obtuse,

tomentose except at apex of cupule, enclosing about half of acorn. Medit. region. 'Rotundifolia': lvs suborbicular. Often confused with *Q. ilex* var. *ballota*, which has the synonym *Q. ilex* var. *rotundifolia*. var. *angustifolia* DC. Lvs lanceolate, subentire. var. *ballota* (Desf.) A. DC. Lvs 1.25–5cm, obong, rounded, apex mucronate. Acorns large, sweet, eaten roasted. N Afr., S Spain. 'Crispa': lvs 1.5cm, suborbicular, margins slightly revolute. 'Fordii': crown narrow. Lvs 2.5–3.75cm, oblong, apex and base attenuate, margin undulate, entire or dentate. 'Genabii': lvs to 12.5×6.75cm, v. leathery, rigid, upper half coarsely toothed, entire beneath. 'Latifolia': lvs like 'Genabii' but thinner textured, softer. f. *microphylla* Trabut. Lvs 2–2.7cm, elliptic, margins spiny-dentate. Alg. Z7.

Q. ilicifolia Wangenh. BEAR OAK. Dense, decid. shrub or small tree, 1–5(–8)m. Bark smooth, dark brown. Crown rounded. Lvs 5–12×3–9cm, obovate, sometimes obovate-oblong, apex obtuse, mucronate, base cuneate, marginal lobes 3–7, triangular with bristle-like tips, dark red and pubesc. at first, becoming green, glab. above, white-tomentose and bullate beneath, yellow or scarlet in fall. Acorns 1.2–1.6cm, ovoid to subglobose, apex mucronate, base rounded, grey- or olive-brown striped darker, glab.; cupule cupular or turbinate scales ovate, truncate, obtuse, light-grey, slightly overlapping, enclosing half of acorn. E US. Hybrids of *Q. ilicifolia* × *Q. rubra* have occurred naturally and are referred to as *Q.* × *fernaldii* Trel. Z5.

Q. imbricaria Michx. SHINGLE OAK. Decid. tree 15–20cm. Crown conical to rounded. Bark light brown, smooth, split by narrow cracks into plates. Lvs 10–17×(2.5–)5–7cm, oblong-lanceolate to ovate, apex acuminate, apiculate, base attenuate or cuneate, entire, often crispate undulate, revolute, occas. lobed, initially red-puberulent above and thick white-tomentose beneath, becoming dark green, glab. above, soft-tomentose beneath. Acorns 1–1.5cm, subglobose, mucronate, subglabrous to silky-pubesc.; cupule scales adpressed, hairy, enclosing up to half of acorn. E & C US. Z5.

Q. incana Bartr. non Roxb. BLUEJACK OAK. Decid. to semievergreen tree or shrub, 4–8m. Crown narrow, irregular. Lvs 5–9cm, oblong, apex acuminate, bristle-like, base rounded, entire, puberulent at first becoming lustrous above, whitetomentose beneath. Acorns solitary, sessile, 1.5cm, ovoid; cupule turbinate, enclosing almost half of acorn. SE US. Z7.

Q. incana Roxb. non Bartr. = *Q. leucotrichophora*.

Q. infectoria Olivier. Semi-evergreen tree to 4(6)m. Bark grey, deeply fissured, scaly. Lvs 4–6×1.56cm, oblong, base rounded or cordate, apex rounded, margin undulate, dentate or crenatedentate, teeth 4–8 each side, mucronate, glossy above, paler, sometimes glaucescent, sometimes sparsely hairy beneath. Acorns usually solitary, 2.5–4×1.2–1.8cm, cylindrical, mucronate, glab., pale yellow-brown; cupule scales adpressed, grey-tomentose, enclosing one-fifth or one-third of acorn. NW Turk., Greece. ssp. *veneris* (A. Kerner) Holmb. Larger tree, to 16m. Lvs 4–9cm, entire or with 5–7 pairs of teeth, soft pubesc. beneath, nerves 8–10 pairs. Asia Minor, Syr., Kurdistan, Persia, Cyprus. Z6.

Q. ithaburensis Decne. VALLONEA OAK. Semi-evergreen to decid. tree to 18(25)m. Bark furrowed, dark brown. Lvs 4–9×2–5cm, ovate to lanceolate-elliptic, apex acuminate, base subcordate, teeth 5–9 each side, triangular, aristate, greytomentose becoming glab. above, persistent grey-tomentose beneath. Acorns clustered 1–3, 2.5–4.5cm, ovoid, apex obtuse or depressed; cupule to 5×5cm, with borad, thick, flattened, woody scales to 20×5mm enclosing two thirds to nearly all of the acorn. Syr., Palestine. Z7. ssp. *macrolepis* (Kotschy) Hedge & Yaltirik. Lvs more deeply incised; acorn cupule scales more flexible and less woody. Specimens from SE Turkey with woody scales like the type are sometimes separated as var. *vallonea* (Kotschy) Zoh. (*Q. vallonea* Kotschy). SE It., Balk., Greece and Turk.

Q. × *jackiana* hort. = *Q. alba*.

Q. jacobi R. Br. = *Q. garryana*.

Q. kelloggii Newberry. CALIFORNIA BLACK OAK. Decid. tree to 35m, sometimes a shrub to 5m. Crown spreading, rounded. Bark smooth and grey at first, becoming almost black, cracked. Lvs 10–25×6–16cm, obovate, sinuately 5–7, lobed, lobes dentate, leathery, pubesc. becoming glab. and glossy above, glab. or sparsely tomentose beneath. Acorn solitary or paired, 2.5–3cm, ovoid; cupule of loosely adpressed, glab. scales, enclosing half of acorn. W US.

Q. × *kewensis* Osborn. (*Q. cerris* × *Q. wislizeni*.) Everg. tree to c15m. Lvs 5–8cm, ovate-oblong, teeth 5–6 each side, triangular, acute, base truncate or subcordate, glab. and matt green above, with a few hairs on veins beneath. Acorn to 2.5cm. Grown from acorns of *Q. wislizenii* at Kew, 1914.

Q. koehnei Ambrozy = *Q.* × *andleyensis*.

Q. laevigata Bl. = *Q. acuta*.

Q. laevis Walter. AMERICAN TURKEY OAK. Small, slow-growing,

decid. tree or shrub, 6–12m, rarely to 20m. Crown narrow. Young branchlets often flushed red. Lvs 10–20cm, obovate to triangular, base cuneate, margin deeply 3–5–(7)-lobed, lobes triangular to oblong with 1–3 aristate teeth, green, glab. above, glab. except for red-brown hairs in nerve axils beneath. Acorns usually solitary, 2cm, ovoid to ellipsoid, with mucro surrounded by white scurfy ring; cupule enclosing one third of acorn. SE US. Z6.

Q. lamellosa Sm. Evergen tree to 36m, usually shorter in cult. Bark rough, grey-brown. Lvs 15–45×5 22cm, ovate or ovatelanceolate to elliptic, apex acute or acuminate, base rounded or attenuate, leathery, pubesc. at first, becoming glab., glossy above, silvery-white waxy beneath, margin dentate except at base. Acorn solitary or in groups of 2–4, 3–4cm, turbinate to globose; smooth; cupule much wider, made up of 10 concentric rings, enclosing two-thirds to four-fifths of acorn. Himal.: Nepal, Assam, SE Tibet, N Burm., SW China. Z8.

Q. lanuginosa (Lam.) Thuill. non D. Don = *Q. pubescens*.

Q. laurifolia Michx. LAUREL OAK. Decid. to semi-evergreen tree to 25(–30)m. Bark smooth, dark brown to balck, fissured. Lvs 6–13×1.2–4cm, oblong to obovate, apex acute to rounded, base tapered, acute or rounded, margin entire or with to 3 hallow teeth at apex, glossy above, paler and initially pubesc. beneath, midvein and petiole yellow. Acorns solitary or paired, 1–1.5cm, ovoid-globose, black-brown; cupule scales adpressed, obtuse, enclosing only the base of acorn, subsessile. SE US. Z7.

Q. × *leana* Nutt. (*Q. imbricaria* × *Q. velutina*.) Large, decid. tree resembling *Q. imbricaria*. Lvs 8–17cm, narrowly obovate to obovate, apex acute, base rounded, margin entire but for 3-lobes at apex or 1–3 irregular lobes each side of apex, glab. above, lightly pubesc. beneath. Acorn solitary or paired, 2cm; cupule encloses half of acorn. Natural hybrid.

Q. leucotrichophora A. Camus. Everg. tree 10–24(30)m in habitat. Bark rough, fissured, exfoliating in large flakes. Lvs 7–18×3.5–5cm, lanceolate, apex acuminate or acute, base rounded or attenuate, entire at base, with widely spaced teeth above, white-pubesc. at first, becoming leathery, rigid, glab. above, white-tomentose beneath. Acorns solitary or to 3 together, 2–2.25cm, ovoid brown, shining, mucronate; cupule campanulate, of adpressed white-brown scales, enclosing half of acorn. Himal. Z8.

Q. liaotungensis Koidz. Large decid. tree. Bark ash-grey. Lvs 3–13×1–6.5cm, obovate to oblong, apex obtuse, base attenuate and rounded or cordate, margin with 4–9 pairs of rounded lobes, leathery, dull or glossy green above, paler, glab. or sparsely hairy beneath. Acorns 1–2cm, ovoid or roundedellipsoid, mucronate, light brown, apex sily-pubesc.; cupule scales adpressed, smooth, upper scales pubesc., enclosing onethird to one-half of acorn. China, Mong., Korea. Z4.

Q. × *libanerris* Boom. (*Q. cerris* × *Q. libani*.) Decid. tree resembling *Q. cerris*. Gdn origin. 'Trompenburg': lvs 7–13×2–4cm, oblong, apex acute, base cuneate, margins with 10–16 pairs of spreading lobes, lobes forward pointing with needle like tips, ± glab. above, grey-pubesc. beneath; acorn similar to those of *Q. cerris* but broader, cup scales shorter. Z6.

Q. libani Olivier. LEBANON OAK. Decid. rarely semi-evergreen, slender, densely branched shrub or tree, 7–8(–10)m. Bark grey, smooth at first becoming fissured. Lvs 4.5–11×1–3.5cm, apex acuminate, base attenuate, rounded or subcordate, teeth tips bristle-like, dark green and glab. above, paler and glab. to pubesc. beneath. Acorns solitary or paired, 2.5cm diam., ovoid to cylindrical; cupule campanulate or a shallow cup, scales adpressed or upper scales spreading, enclosing two-thirds of acorn. Syr., N Iran, N Iraq, Turk. Z6.

Q. lineata var. *oxyodon* (Miq.) Wenz. = *Q. oxyodon*.

Q. lobata Née. CALIFORNIA WHITE OAK; VALLEY OAK. Decid. tree to 35m. Crown symmetrical, rounded. Bark light-grey or dark brown, split into rectangular plates. Lvs 5–12×2.5–8cm, obovate or obovate-oblong, apex obtuse, base cuneate, rounded or cordate, margin slighly thickened, revolute, 3–5-lobed each side, papery, dark green glab. or sparsely hairy above, paler, grey-pubesc. beneath. Acorns 3–5.5cm, ellipsoid to elongateovoid, apex attenuate, umbonate; cupule base rounded, paletomentose, lower scales thick, adpressed, convex, tuberculate, lanceolate, upper scales with apex free, acute, enclosing onethird of acorn. W US. Z7.

Q. lodicosa Warb. Allied to *Q. leucotrichophora*; tree to 25m; distinguished by larger acorns to 3×2cm with a depressed apex, and stout cupules to 2.5cm wide. SE Tibet to Upper Burm. Z8.

Q. lucombeana Sweet = *Q.* × *hispanica* 'Lucombeana'.

Q. × *ludoviciana* Sarg. (*Q. falcata* var. *pagodifolia* × *Q. phellos*.) Large decid. tree. Lvs 7–12cm, entire, or 12–15cm, with 1–4 irregular, triangular lobes, slightly pubesc. beneath. Acorn 1.2cm, oblong-ovoid, rounded; cupule enclosing one-third of acorn. S & E US. 'Microcarpa': lvs 7–9cm, lanceolate, lobes shallow.

Q. lusitanica Webb non Lam. = *Q. faginea*.

Q. lusitanica auct. non Webb nec Lam. = *Q. fruticosa*.

Q. lusitanica ssp. *veneris* (A. Kerner) Holmb. = *Q. infectoria* ssp. *veneris*.

Q. lusitanica var. *baetica* Webb = *Q. canariensis* or *Q. faginea*.

Q. lyrata Walter. OVERCUP OAK. Decid. tree to 30m. Crown rounded. Bark light-grey tinted red-brown, breaking into large plates. Lvs 17–20×3.5–12cm, obovate, apex acute or obtuse, lyrate, lobes 3–4 pairs, acute, uppermost lobes often further divided, dark green, glabrescent above, soft-pubesc. or white-tomentose beneath. Acorns 1.5–2.5cm, subglobose, mucronate; cupule grey-tomentose outside, enclosing two-thirds or more of acorn. C & S US. Z5.

Q. 'Macon'. (*Q. macranthera* ×*Q. frainetto*.) Lvs smaller than those of *Q. frainetto*, more distinctly obovate. Young branchlets tomentose like *Q. macranthera*. Acorns 3–4×0.5–0.8cm.

Q. macedonica A. DC. = *Q. trojana*.

Q. macranthera Fisch. & Mey. CAUCASIAN OAK; PERSIAN OAK. Decid. tree 25–30m. Lvs 8–20×5–11cm, obovate, apex rounded or blunt, base rounded, subcordate or subcuneate, serrate, teeth 7–11 each side, rounded or obtuse, rarely mucronate, dark green, glab. above, densely yellow or red-brown tomentose beneath. Acorns 1.6–2.5cm, ovoid-ellipsoid, almost glab.; cupule scales erect to spreading, lanceolate, pubesc., enclosing half of acorn. Cauc., N Iran. Z6. ssp. *syspirensis* (K. Koch) Menitsky. Lvs smaller, 5–13cm.

Q. macrocarpa Michx. BURR OAK; MOSSY CUP OAK. Decid. tree to 50m. Crown rounded. Bark rugose, split into irregular plates, light grey-brown. Lvs 10–45×5–16cm, obovate or obovate-oblong, base attenuate, cuneate or cordate, lyrately lobed, lobes 5–7 each side, dark green and glab. above, paler, glaucous or white-tomentose beneath, pale-yellow to brown in fall. Acorns 2.5–4cm, ovoid to hemispherical, mucronate, soft-tomentose; cupule hairy, lower scales adpressed, upper scales with free, spreading apices, enclosing half or more of acorn. C & NE US, SE Canada. Z3. var. *olivaeformis* (Michx. f.) Gray. Lvs more deeply divided, lobes narrower, more irregular. Acorns oblong-ellipsoid, like an olive, smaller; cupule encloses more of acorn. E US.

Q. macrolepis Kotschy see *Q. ithaburensis* ssp. *macrolepis*.

Q. marilandica Münchh. BLACKJACK OAK. Small decid., slow-growing tree, 6–15m. Bark rough, black-brown, split into square plates. Lvs 10–17×7–12cm, broadly obovate, apex obtuse, often divided into 3 mucronate lobes, base rounded to cordate, dark green, shining above, paler and red-brown tomentose beneath, yellow to brown in fall. Acorns solitary or paired, 1–2cm, ovoid; cupule hairy, made up of broad, adpressed scales, enclosing one- to two-thirds of acorn. C & SE US. Z5.

Q. mas Thore. Closely resembles *Q. petraea*, but lf margins regularly sinuately lobed, lobes at least 4 each side, young lvs more abundantly hairy beneath. Fr. Pyren. to N Spain. Z6.

Q. michauxii Nutt. SWAMP CHESTNUT OAK. Decid. tree to c30m. Bark pale grey, scaly. Lvs 10–16cm, obovate to oblong-obovate, apex acute, base attenuate to rounded, coarsley dentate, teeth 10–14 pairs, obtuse and gland., lustrous above, grey-velvety beneath. Acorns 3cm, oblong-elliptic; cupules made of thickened scales at base, upper scales stiff, fringed, enclosing one-third of acorn. SE US. Z6.

Q. mirbeckii Durieu = *Q. canariensis*.

Q. mongolica Fisch. ex Turcz. Large decid. tree to 30m. Lvs 10–20cm, obovate, apex obtuse, base attenuate, cordate, teeth rounded, glab. above, glab. or pubesc. on venation beneath. Acorns 2cm, ovoid; cupule made up of tuberculate scales, uppermost scales acuminate, ciliate, enclosing one-third of acorn. NE Asia. var. *grosseserrata* (Bl.) Rehd. & Wils. This tree is largely represented in cult. by var. *grosseserrata* (Bl.) Rehd. & Wils. Lvs 10–12cm, teeth acute, sometimes themselves dentate. Acorn cupule made of closely adpressed eciliate scales. Jap., Sakhalin, Kuriles. Z3.

Q. montana Willd. = *Q. prinus*.

Q. moreliana Trel. = *Q. crassifolia*.

Q. muehlenbergii Engelm. YELLOW CHESTNUT OAK; CHINKAPIN OAK. Decid. tree to 20m, rarely 45m. Bark grey, split into thin, flaky scales. Lvs 10–18×5–12cm, oblong, obovate or lanceolate, apex acute or acuminate, base cuneate, serrate, teeth acute, pale green flushed bronze at first, subglabrous above, tomentose beneath, becoming glab. above, white silky-pubesc. beneath, orange or scarlet in fall. Acorns solitary, 1.3–2cm, ovoid, mucronate, silky-pubesc.; cupule made up of tomentose scales, uppermost scales acute, forming fring, enclosing half of acorn. E US. Z4.

Q. myrsinifolia Shiras. non Bl. = *Q. stenophylla*.

Q. myrsinifolia Bl. non Shiras. Everg. tree 12–25m. Lvs, 5–15×2–4cm, lanceolate or lanceolate-elliptic, apex long-acuminate, base rounded or shortly acuminate, leathery, dark green above, glaucescent beneath, slightly papillose beneath, margin

with fine teeth in upper half. Acorns 17–25×7–10mm, narrowly ovoid, puberulent at first, becoming glab., crowned with persistent styles; cupule slightly glaucous, ashy-puberulent outside, silky inside, with scales forming 7–9 rings. Jap., China, Laos. Z7.

Q. myrtifolia Willd. MYRTLE OAK; SEASIDE SCRUB OAK. Small, densely branched, everg. shrub or tree, 1–6mm. Bark grey, smooth, slightly cracked. Lvs 3.5–4×1.5–2.5cm, ovate, obovate or subelliptic, apex rounded, apiculate, base slightly attenuate, margin revolute, sometimes undulate, rarely sinuate-dentate, dark red and sparsely hairy beneath at first, becoming leathery, glab. and glossy above, yellow-green to pale orange-brown beneath. Acorns solitary or paired, 0.8–1.2×0.5–1cm, ovoid, attenuate, mucronate, silky; cupule scales slightly overlapping, obtuse, uppermost scales ciliate, enclosing one-quarter of acorn. SE US. Z8.

Q. nana (Marsh) Sarg. = *Q. ilicifolia*.

Q. neglecta Koidz. = *Q. bambusifolia*.

Q. nigra L. non Wangenh. nec Duroi. WATER OAK. Decid. tree 20–35m. Bark brown, smooth initially, becoming black-brown, deeply channelled. Lvs 3–15×1.5–6cm, obovate with shallowly lobed apex, lobe tips bristle-like, or oblong and entire, leathery, matt blue-green and glab. above, glab. but for tufts of hair in axils of veins beneath. Acorns solitary, 1–1.5cm, globose to ovoid, black; cupule made up of short, adpressed scales, enclosing up to half of acorn. SE US. Z6.

Q. nigra Wangenh. non L. = *Q. marilandica*.

Q. nobilis Koch = *Q. falcata*.

Q. nuttallii Palmer. NUTTALL'S OAK. Closely similar to *Q. palustris*; to 30m. Lvs 8–15cm, as *Q. palustris* but vein axil tufts yellow. Acorns 2–3cm, ovoid-oblong, enclosed for one third in a bowl-shaped cupule. S US. Z6.

Q. oblongifolia Torr. MEXICAN BLUE OAK. Everg. or semi-evergreen shrub or small tree to 8m, crown rounded. Lvs 2.5–5cm, entire, often undulate, rarely few-toothed, margin revolute, blue-green and glab. and glaucous beneath. Acorns 1.5–2cm, ovoid, sweet; cupule covering one third of acorn, scales thin, woolly, with red tips. SW US, NW Mex. Z7.

Q. oblongifolia R. Br. non Engelm. nec Torr. = *Q. chrysolepis*.

Q. obovata Bunge = *Q. dentata*.

Q. obscura Seemen = *Q. engleriana*.

Q. obtusiloba Michx. = *Q. stellata*.

Q. olivaeformis Michx. f. = *Q. macrocarpa* var. *olivaeformis*.

Q. oxyodon Miq. Small everg. tree, to 7m. Crown flattened. Lvs 12–22×3.5–5cm, ovate or ovate-lanceolate, apex cuspidate, base attenuate, teeth rigid, leathery, glab. above, white-waxy beneath. Acorns 1.5–1.7cm, subglobose except at apex, apex umbonate; cupule sometimes white-waxy, scales forming 5–8 concentric rings, enclosing half of acorn. W China, Upper Burm., E Himal. Z8.

Q. pagoda Raf. = *Q. falcata* var. *pagodifolia*.

Q. pagodifolia Ashe = *Q. falcata* var. *pagodifolia*.

Q. palustris Münchh. PIN OAK. Decid. tree, 20–25(–35)m. Crown dense, ovoid-conical. Bark smooth, grey-brown becoming fissured and ridged. Lvs 8–15cm, obovate, apex acute, base attenuate or truncate, pinnately lobed, lobes oblong to triangular, tips slightly lobed and bristle-like, glab. and glossy above, paler and glab. except for tufts of green-white hair in vein axils beneath. Acorns 1.2–1.7cm, mucronate; cupule saucer-shaped, puberulent, red-brown, enclosing only base of acorn. NE US, SE Canada. 'Crownright': crown narrowly conical. 'Pendula': br. pendent. 'Reichenbachii': young lvs and shoots flushed red. 'Umbraculifera': crown rounded, symmetrical. Lvs shining green, colouring red in autumn.

Q. palustris f. *nuttallii* (Palmer) Mull. = *Q. nuttallii*.

Q. pannonica Booth ex Gordon = *Q. frainetto*.

Q. pedunculiflora K. Koch. Decid. tree resembling *Q. robur*. Lvs 8–17×6–9cm, obovate or oblong-obovate, apex rounded, base rounded to cordate, margin with 4–5 pairs of rounded, entire or shallowly divided lobes, puberulent above and white-tomentose beneath at first. Acorns 2–3cm, ovoid, mucronate and tomentose, otherwise glab.; cupule made up of tightly adpressed or spreading yellow-tomentose scales, enclosing one-third of acorn. Asia Minor, Cauc. to Balk. Z6.

Q. pendunculata Ehrh. = *Q. robur*.

Q. petraea (Mattuschka) Liebl. Decid. tree to 45m. Crown regular, trunk reaching far into crown. Bark grey to black-brown, furrowed. Lvs 6–17×3–9cm, broadly or narrowly obovate, base attenuate or truncate to subcordate but not auriculate as is *Q. robur*, apex rounded, margin with 4–6 pairs of even, rounded lobes, glossy, glab. above, paler, glaucous, glab. to pubesc. beneath. Acorns clustered, 2–3cm, ovoid to oblong-ovoid; cupule made up of closely adpressed, pubesc. scales. Eur. to W Russia. 'Albovariegata': lvs variegated with white. 'Aurea': young branchlets yellow; lvs initially yellow, becoming green but petiole and nerves persistently yellow.

'Aureovariegata': lvs yellow-green variegated. 'Cochleata': lvs more leathery, slightly convex. 'Columna': crown columnar. Lvs narrower, more oblong, margins irregularly lobed, grey-green. 'Falkenbergensis': lvs shorter, apex rounded, lobes flat, 5–7 pairs, green and glab. above, white-green beneath with pubescence on venation. 'Giesleri': lvs long, narrowly oblong, margin entire or shallowly lobed. 'Insecata': lvs much longer and narrower, sometimes thread-like, margin irregularly divided, sometimes white. 'Laciniata': lvs more deeply divided than sp. 'Mespilifolia': lvs narrowly oblong-lanceolate, undulate, entire, leathery. 'Muscaviensis': lvs of first branchlets subentire, lvs of secondary growth resemble those of sp. 'Pendula': br. and branchlets pendent. 'Pinnata': lvs pinnatisect. 'Purpurea': lvs crimson-purple becoming grey-green flushed red, veins red. Z4.

Q. petraea 'Rubicunda'. = *Q. petraea* 'Purpurea'.

Q. petraea ssp. *iberica* (Steven ex Bieb.) Krasslin. = *Q. iberica*.

Q. petraea f. *laciniata* Späth non Schwarz = *Q. petraea* 'Insecta'.

Q. petraea f. *laciniata* (Lam.) Schwarz non Späth = *Q. petraea* 'Laciniata'.

Q. petraea f. *pinnata* Schneid. = *Q. petraea* 'Pinnata'.

Q. phellos L. WILLOW OAK. Decid. tree to 40m. Crown rounded to columnar. Bark grey tinted red-brown, glab. Lvs 7–12×0.8–2.5cm, oblong-lanceolate, apex acute, base attenuate, entire, often undulate, dark green above, paler beneath, almost glab. Acorns to *c*1cm, subglobose, pale yellow-brown; cupule shallow, scales adpressed, grey-tomentose, enclosing only base of acorn. SE US. Z6.

Q. phillyreoides Gray. Everg. shrub or small tree, 5–9m. Habit rounded. Lvs 3–6cm, obovate to oval, apex rounded to acuminate, base rounded to subcordate, entire below upper half with shallow, blunt teeth, dark green and shining above, paler, glab. and shining beneath. Acorns 1.5–2cm, ovoid, apex slightly tomentose; cupule scales short, adpressed, white-tomentose, enclosing one-third to half of acorn. China, Jap. 'Chirimen': slow-growing; lvs small, crisped. Z7.

Q. phullata Hamilt. apud D. Don = *Q. glauca* ssp. *annulata*.

Q. pinnatifida Franch. & Savat. = *Q. dentata* var. *oxygloba* 'Pinnatifida'.

Q. platanoides (Lam.) Sudw. = *Q. bicolor*.

Q. polycarpa Schur. = *Q. iberica*.

Q. 'Pondaim'. (*Q. pontica* ×*Q. dentata*.) Tree. Lvs obovate, marginal teeth large, acute. Gdn origin.

Q. pontica K. Koch. ARMENIAN OAK. Decid. shrub or small tree, to 6m, rarely 10m. Lvs 15–25×5–13cm, obovate to elliptic, apex acute, base attenuate, margin shallowly and irregularly dentate, teeth mucronate, dark green and shining above, paler with sparse pubescence on veins beneath, midrib yellow. Acorns 2cm, ovoid; cupule of triangular, pubesc., adpressed scales, enclosing to half of acorn. NE Turk., Cauc. Z5.

Q. prinoides Willd. DWARF CHINKAPIN OAK. Decid., suckering, small tree or shrub to 4m. Bark grey. Lvs 6–12cm, obovate, apex acute, base attenuate, margin undulate, dentate, teeth 4–7 pairs, acute, short, green and glab. above, paler and finely pubesc. beneath. Acorns solitary, 1–1.5cm, ovoid; cupule made of tuberculate scales, half enclosing acorn. NE & C US. Z5.

Q. prinus L. CHESTNUT OAK; BASKET OAK. Decid. tree to 25(30)m. Bark dark grey-black, furrowed. Lvs 10–23×4–11.5cm, oblong to narrowly obovate, apex rounded, attenuate or acute, base attenuate or rounded, margin with 10–5 regular, shallow, obtuse lobes, tips not gland., yellow-green, glab. and glossy above, grey-white tomentose beneath, orange in fall. Acorns solitary or paired, 2.5–4cm, ovoid; cupule made up of adpressed, tuberculate scales, one-quarter to one-third enclosed in cupule. E US. Z5.

Q. pseudococcifera Desf. = *Q. coccifera*.

Q. pseudosuber Santi = *Q. ×hispanica*.

Q. pubescens Willd. DOWNY OAK. Decid. tree to 20m in habitat, to rarely 27m in cult. Crown broad, rounded. Bark brown to black. Lvs 4–9×2–5cm, obovate to elliptic, apex rounded, base rounded or subcordate, margin with 4–8 rounded lobes each side, dark green and glab. above, grey-tomentose beneath. Acorns solitary or in groups of 4, 1.5–2cm, ovoid; cupule sessile or fr. cluster pedunculate, tomentose, scales adpressed. S Eur., to Turk. and the Crimea. 'Pinnatifida': lvs 3–6cm, pinnatisectly lobed, lobes rounded, often dentate, veins soft-pubesc. ssp. *palensis* (Pall.) Schwartz. Shrub or tree; lvs 4–7cm, sinutaely toothed to slightly blobed, tomentose beneath. Cupule scales irregular, basal scale short, thick, connate, apical scales longer, discrete, cuspidate. Z5.

Q. pubescens var. *pinnatifida* (Gmel.) Spenn. = *Q. pubescens* 'Pinnatifida'.

Q. pungens Liebm. SANDPAPER OAK. Semi-evergreen shrub to tree. Lvs 9×4cm, oblong-elliptic, apex acute or obtuse, base rounded to subcordate, margin with mucronate, coarse teeth, undulate-crispate, shining and scabrous above, tomentose be-

neath. Acorn ripe in first year, 1cm. SW US. Z7.

Q. pyrami Kotschy = *Q. ithaburensis*.

Q. pyrenaica Willd. PYRENEAN OAK; SPANISH OAK. Decid. tree or shrub 10–15(–30)m. Br. spreading to pendulous. Bark brown-black, furrowed. Lvs obovate to narrowly-obovate, 7–16×4–8cm, apex rounded, base rounded to cordate, margin with 4–7 pairs of deep lobes, lobes oblong, tips rounded or acute, sometimes dentate, scurfy at first, sparsely pubesc. above, densely grey-tomentose beneath. Acorns in clusters of 2–4, 1.5–3cm, oblong-ovoid, apex hairy; cupule subhemi-spherical, made up of free, lanceolate, pubesc. scales, enclosing half of acorn; peduncle 1.25–3.75cm. SW Eur., Moroc. 'Pendula': twigs pendent. Lf lobes deeper with few teeth. Z7.

Q. ransomii Kellogg = *Q. douglasii*.

Q. ×rehderi Trel. (*Q. ilicifolia* ×*Q. velutina*.) Decid. shrub to small tree. Young branchlets soon glab., lenticellate. Lvs 6–11cm, obovate, apex obtuse, base cuneate, margin with 2–3 pairs of spreading lobes, lobes deeper than *Q. ilicifolia*, velvety but becoming subglabrous beneath; petiole 8–12mm. US.

Q. reticulata HBK. NETLEAF OAK. Everg. shrub or small tree. Lvs 7–10×to 7cm, obovate to oblong-obovate, apex rounded to obtuse, base rounded to subcordate, margin undulate-dentate, teeth usually mucronate, semi-rigid, leathery, dark green, subglabrous, with conspicuous reticulate venation above, yellow-tomentose beneath. Acorns in clusters of 2–6, 1.5cm; cupule hemispherical, made up of adpressed, tomentose scales, enclosing one-quarter of acorn. N Mex., SW US. Z7.

Q. ×richteri Baenitz. (*Q. palustris* ×*Q. rubra*.) Closely resembles *Q. palustris* but lvs more like *Q. coccinea*, deeply 4–5 lobed each side. Acorn cupule shallower than in *Q. coccinea*. E US.

Q. ×robbinsii Trel. (*Q. coccinea* ×*Q. ilicifolia*.) Tree to 12m, differing from *Q. ×rehderi* by less pubescence on lvs and branchlets and a deeper acorn cupule enclosing one half of acorn. E US.

Q. robur L. ENGLISH OAK; COMMON OAK; PEDUNCULATE OAK. Decid. tree 20–30(45)m. Crown broad, spreading, irregular. Trunk often not straight and extending only a short distance into crown. Bark grey-brown, deeply fissured. Lvs 5–14×3.5–6cm, oblong to obovate, apex rounded, base attenuate, auriculate, margin with 3–6 pairs of deep, rounded lobes, glab. dark green above, paler blue-green beneath. Acorns solitary or clustered, 1.5–2.5cm, shape variable, ovoid to oblong-ovoid, apex mucronate; cupule subhemispherical, made up of tightly adpressed, velvety scales, enclosing one-quarter to one-third of fr.; peduncle 3–10cm. Eur. to W Russia. var. *thomasii* (Ten.) Wenz. Lvs to 12×5cm, obovate, base attenuate, margin with 3–5 pairs of deep lobes, glab. Acorn usually solitary, 3.5–4×2.5cm; peduncle 2–4cm. C & S It. ssp. *brutia* (Ten.) O. Schwarz. Lvs pubesc. beneath, lobes long with narrow sinuses. Acorn cupule to 2.3cm, made up of adpressed scales with free tips. S It. Cvs vary in habit, from dwarf to columnar, in colour from variegated to yellow or purple throughout, and in lf from flat to convex, entire to deeply incised and crispate. *Habit*: 'Contorta': dwarf; lf lobes twisted. 'Cupressoides': columnar tree; lvs smaller than in 'Fastigiata'. 'Fastigiata': columnar; branchlets erect. 'Pendula': vigorous; br. pendent. 'Tortuosa': dwarf, with twisted br. 'Umbraculifera': crown globose. *Lf colouring*: 'Argenteomarginata': lf margins white. 'Argenteovariegata' ('Variegata'): branchlets lined red and white, lvs white-variegated, flushed red. 'Atropurpurea': to 10m; lvs plum purple. 'Aureobicolor': first lvs sparsely yellow-dotted, late lvs yellow-variegated, flushed red. 'Concordia': lvs golden. 'Nigra': lvs deep purple. *Lf form*: 'Cucullata': lvs elongate, convex, margin shallowly divided. 'Cristata': lvs small, curled and twisted. 'Fennessii': lvs flat or convex, margins deeply incised, lobes irregular, narrow. 'Filicifolia': slow-growing tree; lvs often incised to midrib, lobes regular, acute, sometimes crispate. 'Strypemonde': slow-growing; lvs irregularly incised, lobes sharp or 0, mottled yellow. 'Salicifolia' ('Halophylla'): slow-growing; lvs elliptic, entire. Z6.

Q. robur var. *haas* (Kotschy) Boiss. = *Q. haas*.

Q. robur var. *tenorei* DC. = *Q. virgiliana*.

Q. ×rosacea Bechst. (*Q. petraea* ×*Q. robur*.) naturally occurring hybrid. Decid. tree to 35m. Lvs obovate to subelliptic, subcordate, base narrow. Acorn peduncle 1–3cm. Scattered in parts of parents' range. Scattered in parts of parents' range.

Q. rotundifolia Lam. = *Q. ilex* var. *ballota*.

Q. rubra L. RED OAK; NORTHERN RED OAK. Decid. tree 30(45)m. Crown rounded. Lvs 10–22×10–15cm, oblong to obovate, base attenuate or rounded, margin with 3–5 pairs of lobes, lobes triangular or ovate, acute, sinuses run to midrib, lobe margins irregularly toothed, dark green, glab. and matt above, paler yellow-green and glab. except for red-brown hairs in nerve axils, colouring dull red or yellow-brown in fall. Acorns 2–3cm, ovoid; cupule made up of tightly adpressed, short scales, enclosing one-third of acorn. E N Amer. 'Aurea': lvs golden yellow, becoming slightly green towards autumn. 'Heterophylla': lvs oblong-ovate to linear-lanceolate, often falcate, margin with a few shallow teeth. 'Schrefeldii': lf margins deeply divided, lobes often imbricate. Z3.

Q. rubra sensu Sarg. non L. = *Q. falcata.*

Q. rubra var. *nana* Marsh = *Q. ilicifolia.*

Q. ×*rudkinii* Britt. (*Q. marilandica* ×*Q. phellos.*) Lvs oblong, entire, or with a few, flat, rounded teeth, leathery, pubesc. at first, red-brown beneath. Breeds true from seed. SE US.

Q. ×*runcinata* (A. DC.). Engelm. (*Q. imbricaria* ×*Q. rubra.*) Lvs 10–13(17)cm, oblong-obovate, base rounded or truncate, margin with 3–4 pairs of lobes, lobes falcate, acute, irregular, brown puberulent beneath; petiole 1.5–2.5cm. Acorns resemble those of *Q. rubra.* E US.

Q. rysophylla Weatherby. Everg. tree, strong-growing. Lvs downy, young lvs red, mature lvs to 25×8cm, elliptic, base auriculate, margins undulate, shallowly lobed to dentate above, glossy-green and conspicuously bullate above, subglabrous beneath, bearing tufts of hair in vein axils. Mex.

Q. sadleriana R. Br. DEER OAK. Small semi-evergreen shrub to 2(3)m, forming thickets. Lvs 8–13×4–5(–7)cm, obovate, ovate or subelliptic, apex acute or obtuse, base rounded to cuneate, margin dentate, teeth curved, flat, acute, erect, initially green tinted bronze, puberulent above, white-pubesc. beneath, becoming glab. dark green above, paler and sometimes glaucous-pubesc. beneath. Acorns solitary or clustered in lf axils, 1.7–2×1.2–1.5cm, ovoid; cupule light brown, soft-tomentose, made up of adpressed, ovate, acute scales with free tips, enclosing to one-third of acorn. W US. Z6.

Q. salicina Bl. non Seem. nec. Yabe. Close to *Q. bambusifolia* in habit. Lvs 4–10×(0.8)1.5–2.2(–2.5)cm, narrowly oblong-lanceolate, apex obliquely acuminate, base attenuate, margins usually entire, rarely serrulate with widely spaced teeth at tip, leathery, younglvs white-puberulent beneath, becoming glab., green above, white-waxy beneath. Jap. Z8.

Q. salicina Seem. non Bl. nec Yabe = *Q. bambusifolia.*

Q. salicina Yabe non Seem. non Bl. = *Q. stenophylla.*

Q. ×*sargentii* Rehd. (*Q. prinus* ×*Q. robur.*) Closely resembles *Q. prinus* but lvs dentate, base cordate to auriculate.

Q. ×*saulii* Schneid. (*Q. alba* ×*Q. prinus.*) Decid. tree to 15m. Lvs 20–24×10cm, apex narrower than *Q. prinus*, margin irregularly 6–9 lobed each side, lobes deeper than those of *Q. prinus*, glabrous or pubesc. beneath. Acorn cupule encloses more of acorn than in *Q. prinus.*

Q. schneckii Britt. = *Q. shumardii* var. *schneckii.*

Q. ×*schochiana* Dieck. (*Q. palustris* ×*Q. phellos.*) Decid. tree. Lvs resemble those of *Q. phellos*, but margins undulate or with small, rounded, irregular lobes, glab. above and beneath but for a few hairs in nerve axils beneath. Sterile. First noticed at Wörlitz, Germ.; also noted occurring naturally in E US.

Q. semecarpifolia Sm. Large everg. or semi-evergreen tree to 30m in habitat, much smaller in cult. Bark grey-brown, roughened. Lvs 5–9×3.5–6cm, oblong-elliptic to suborbicular, apex rounded, base rounded to cordate, margin spiny-dentate at first, old lvs entire, glab. above excepting midrib, brown-tomentose beneath. Acorns solitary or paired, subglobose to ovoid, 2.5cm diam., mucronate; cupule flat or shallow, made up of adpressed scales, tips free, erect, ciliate. Himal., Afghan., W China. Z8.

Q. serrata Sieb. & Zucc., non Thunb. = *Q. acutissima.*

Q. serrata Thunb. nomen ambiguum; possibly *Q. glandulifera.*

Q. sessiliflora Salisb. = *Q. petraea.*

Q. sessilis Ehrh. = *Q. petraea.*

Q. shumardii Buckl. SHUMARD OAK. Decid. tree resembling *Q. palustris*, to 30(50)m. Bark grey-brown, mottled or spotted, furrowed. Lvs 10–15×8–10cm, obovate, apex acute, base truncate, white-puberulent at first, becoming glab., except for a few tufts in nerve axils beneath, paler beneath, not bullate, margin 7–9 lobed, lobes spiny-dentate, sinuses deep. Acorns 1.8–2.5cm, ovoid, mucronate, puberulent; cupule shallow, made up of ovate, obtuse, often tuberculate and tomentose scales, enclosing base of acorn; peduncle short. SE US. var. *schneckii* (Britt.) Sarg. To 40m or more. Bark smoother, less deeply furrowed. Lf margins more shallowly divided. Acorn cupule almost flat. C US. Z5.

Q. shumardii var. *texana* (Buckl.) Ashe = *Q. texana.*

Q. sonomensis DC. = *Q. kelloggii.*

Q. spinulosa Martens & Gal. = *Q. crassifolia.*

Q. stellata Wangenh. POST OAK. Decid. tree, 10–20m. Crown rounded. Bark grey to red-brown, fissured and split into scaly plates. Lvs 8–20×4–8cm, obovate, apex rounded, base cuneate, attenuate or rounded, margin deeply 5(7) lobed, central lobes largest, often further shallowly lobed, leathery, dark green, rough-hairy above, sparsely grey-pubesc. beneath. Acorns solitary or paired 1–2.5cm, ovoid, apex rounded, mucronate, pale yellow-brown; cupule hemispherical to top-shaped, made up of closely adpressed, ovate, acute, pubesc. scales, enclosing

one-third of acorn. E US. Z5.

Q. stenophylla (Bl.) Mak. Everg. shrub or tree. Lvs 6–8×1.5–2.5(–3)cm, lanceolate, apex acuminate, asymmetrical, base attenuate, leathery, glab. or slightly hairy, glaucous and waxy beneath, margin entire at base, dentate in upper half or three-quarters, teeth thin, erect, acuminate. Acorn 1.5–2cm, ovoid, apex mucronate, light brown, glab.; cupule silky outside and inside, enclosing at least half of acorn, scales forming 6–8 rings, hardly dentate. Often confused with *Q. glauca* and *Q. salicina* in cult. Jap., Korea. var. *angustata* Nak. Lvs 3–12×0.7–2.2cm, linear-lanceolate, apex attenuate, base cuneate; petiole long 5–12mm, young br. less hairy than *Q. salicina.* var. *stenophylloides* A. Camus. Lvs leathery, thick, oblong-oval to oval, lanceolate, v. glaucous beneath, margins with long ascending to erect or recurved teeth. var. *hypargyrea.* Lvs 7–11×3.5cm, lanceolate to lanceolate-oval, apex acuminate, asymmetrical, white-silky beneath at first, becoming almost glab., v. waxy beneath, dentate, teeth acuminate; erect. Z7.

Q. stenophylla var. *salicina* (Bl.) Mak. = *Q. salicina.*

Q. stenophylloides Hayata = *Q. stenophylla* var. *stenophylloides.*

Q. stipularis Humb. & Bonpl. = *Q. crassifolia.*

Q. suber L. CORK OAK. Everg. tree to 20(26)m. Bark to 15cm thick, corky, deeply fissured. Lvs 3.5×1.5×4cm,ovate to ovate-oblong or ovate-lanceolate, apex acute, base sometimes slightly cordate, margin dentate, teeth 5–7 each side, mucronate, dark green, shining, glabrous above, paler, grey-tomentose beneath. Acorns solitary or paired, 2–4.5cm, ovoid or ellipsoid, apex slightly mucronate; cupule subhemispherical, lower scales closely adpressed, upper scales spreading, enclosing half or more of acorn. N Afr., S Eur. Z8.

Q. subfalcata Trel. = *Q.* ×*ludoviciana.*

Q. sutchuensis Franch. = *Q. engleriana.*

Q. texana Buckl. SPANISH OAK. Small decid. tree resembling *Q. shumardii* to 10(20)m. Trunk branched almost from the base, spreading. Bark light brown, scaly. Lvs 8–11×8–9cm, obovate, base truncate, or slightly attenuate, lightly pubesc. at first, becoming yellow-green, glab. above, glab. with a few hairs in nerve axils beneath, margin deeply lobed, lobes 2–3 each side, tips bristly-dentage. Acorns 1.5–2cm, ovoid-ellipsoid, rounded, mucronate, pale-brown, puberulent; cupule conical, made up of ovate, obtuse, puberulent scales, enclosing base of acorn. Tex., S Okl. Z7.

Q. texana sensu Sarg. non Buckl. = *Q. shumardii.*

Q. thomasii Ten. = *Q. robur* var. *thomasii.*

Q. tinctoria Michx. = *Q. velutina.*

Q. tinctoria var. *californica* Torr. = *Q. kelloggii.*

Q. tlemcenensis (A. DC.) Villar = *Q. faginea* ssp. *tlemcenensis.*

Q. toumeyi Sarg. TOUMEY'S OAK. Everg. shrub, similar to *Q. arizonica* but with smaller lvs 1.5–3cm and acorns only 1.5cm long. Ariz. Z7.

Q. toza Bast. = *Q. pyrenaica.*

Q. triloba Michx. = *Q. falcata.*

Q. trojana Webb Decid. or semi-evergreen tree to 18m, to 25m in cult. Lvs 4–6(9)×1.5–2.5cm, oblong-ovate, apex acute, base rounded to cordate, undulate-dentate, teeth incurved, often mucronate, leathery, metallic-shiny, glab. or sparsely hairy above, glab. or sparsely hairy beneath. Acorns 2.7–4.5cm, ovoid to ellipsoid, light brown, glab.; cupule hemispherical or campanulate, made up of adpressed scales, tips erect to reflexed, enclosing half of acorn. SE Eur. to W Turk. Z6.

Q. ×*turneri* Willd. (*Q. ilex* ×*Q. robur.*) Semi-evergreen tree to 15(25)m. Lvs 6–8cm. Lvs obovate of elliptic, apex acute or obtuse, base rounded to subcordate, margin sinuately-lobed, lobes 5–6, obtuse, leathery, dark green and glab. above, paler and subglabrous but pubesc. on veins beneath. Acorns, where produced in clusters of 3–7, to 2cm, ovoid; cupule subhemispherical, pubesc., enclosing half of acorn. 'Pseudoturneri': lvs narrowly oblong-obovate, lobes narrower, more glab. beneath, remaining green for longer.

Q. undulata Torr. WAVYLEAF OAK. Decid. or semi-evergreen shrub 1–3m, or small tree to 9m. bark grey, rough, scaly. Lvs 2.5–8×1.5–3cm, oblong to elliptic, apex acute or obtuse, base rounded, cordate or cuneate, margin sinuate-dentate, teeth 2–5 each side, acute, often mucronate, grey-tomentose becoming blue-green and pubesc. above, then glab. and shining, yellow-tomentose beneath. Acorns 1.5–2cm, ovoid or cylindrical, apex rounded or mucronate, light brown, glab.; cupule hemispherical, made up of ovate, acute, glabrescent, ciliate scales, enclosing one third or half of acorn. SW US, Mex. Z5.

Q. undulata var. *gambelii* (Nutt.) Engelm. = *Q. gambelii.*

Q. utahensis (A. DC.) Rydb. = *Q. gambelii.*

Q. vacciniifolia Kellogg. HUCKLEBERRY OAK. Prostrate or erect shrub, 0.5–1.8m. Lvs 2–3×0.8–1.5cm, lanceoalte, oblong-lanceolate or ovate, apex obtuse or subacute, base rounded or attenuate, margin entire or serrate at apex, pale green, glab. above, glaucous, sometimes sparsely hairy beneath. Acorns

1.2–1cm, ovoid, pale, with persistent perianth and stigmas; cupule made up of ovate, slightly overlapping, grey-tomentose scales, enclosing only the base or up to half acorn. W US. Z6.

Q. vallonea Kotschy = *Q. ithaburensis* ssp. *macrolepis*.

Q. vaniotii Lév. = *Q. glauca*.

Q. variabilis Bl. CHINESE CORK OAK. Decid. tree to 30m. Bark to 10cm thick, grey, corky. Lvs 6.5–20×4–10cm, oblong or narrowly elliptic, apex acute or acuminate, base rounded to subcordate, margin dentate, teeth 9–16(22) each side, tips bristle-like, marking the end of lat. nerves, rich glossy green, glab. above, pale silver-grey tomentose beneath. Acorns 1.5–2cm, ovoid to subglobose; cupule made up of long, curled scales, enclosing most of acorn. China, Jap., Korea. Z4.

Q. velutina Lam. BLACK OAK. Decid. tree 20–30m, rarely to 45m. bark black-brown, deeply fissured, fissures orange at centre. Lvs 6–25×4.5–15.5cm, narrowly ovate to obovate, often misshapen, apex acute, base truncate, deeply 5 or 7 lobed, lobes ovate to triangular, 1–3 bristle-tipped teeth, dark green, glab. and glossy above, paler, densely tomentose at first beneath, becoming scurfy with a few hairs in nerve axils. Acorns solitary or paired, 1.5–2.5cm, ovoid to subglobose, pale brown; cupule made up of loosely overlapping, hairy scales, enclosing half of acorn. E US, SE Canada. 'Albertsii': lvs much larger, to 35×24cm, obovate, shallowly lobed. 'Macrophylla': young branchlets flushed purple, lvs with 4 pairs of wide lobes, densely pubesc. becoming glab. above, veins red. 'Magnifica': lvs 17–25×12–20cm, apex rounded, mucronate, sinuses rounded. 'Nobilis': lvs with 2–4 pairs of rounded lobes, grey pubesc. at first, becoming glab., dark green above, paler and usually persistently tomentose beneath, venation red-brown.

Q. veneris A. Kerner = *Q. infectoria* ssp. *veneris*.

Q. vibrayeana Seem. = *Q. glauca* var. *gracilis*.

Q. vibrayeana Franch. & Savat. non Seem. = *Q. myrsinifolia*.

Q. virgiliana Ten. Decid., medium sized tree, resembling *Q. pubescens*. Lvs 7–15×4–7cm, sometimes more, obovate or oblong-obovate, base cordate, margin 5–7 lobed, lobes obtuse or rounded, middle lobes sometimes further lobed, loose tomentose at first becoming glaucous, glabrescent or sparsely hairy beneath. Acorns in groups of 2–4, ovoid; cupule hemispherical, made up of adpressed, grey-white tomentose scales, peduncle 3–8cm. SE Eur., N Turk. Z6.

Q. virginiana Mill. LIVE OAK; SOUTHERN LIVE OAK. Everg. tree 12–20m; crown v. broad, to 45m. Bark red-brown, slightly channelled, scaly. Lvs 3–12×0.8–2cm, elliptic to oblong-obovate, apex rounded or obtuse, often mucronate, base rounded, attenuate or cordate, entire or with few obtuse teeth, revolute, dark green, glab., shining above, grey-pubesc. (rarely glab.) beneath. acorns 2.5–3cm, ovoid, apex attenuate and mucronate, glab.; cupule hemispherical, made up of adpressed, oblong to ovate, tomentose scales, enclosing one-quarter to one-third of acorn. SE US. Z7.

Q. vulcanica Kotschy. Decid. tree to 30m, allied to *Q. frainetto*. Lvs with persistent 10mm stipules, 9–17×5–10cm, with 4–7 deep lobes each side, on young trees lobes often secondarily lobed; glarbous dark green above, yellow-green to grey stellate-tomentose beneath. Acorns 2–2.5cm; cupule hemispherical, scales flat, adpressed; covered a third to a half of the acorn. SW & C Turk., 1300–1800m. Z6.

Q. warburgii Camus. CAMBRIDGE OAK. Semi-evergreen tree to 20m. Lvs 8–12×3–8cm, ovate to oblong, apex rounded, base attenuate to subcordate, margin shallowly and irregulary lobed, lobes small, mucronate, matt green, glab., rugose above, paler and glab. beneath. Acorn solitary or paired, 2.5cm; ovoid; cupule hemispherical, made up of closely adpressed, grey-pubesc. scales, enclosing one-third of acorn. Origin unknown; may be of hybrid origin, possibly with the Mexican *Q. rugosa* as one of the parents.

Q. wislizeni A. DC. INTERIOR LIVE OAK. Everg. shrub or tree 20–25m. Crown rounded. Bark black-brown or red-brown, fissured. Lvs 2.5–3.8×1.3–3cm, ovate to oblong-lanceolate, apex rounded, base rounded to cordate, margin shallowly dentate to entire, teeth spine-tipped, dark green, glab. and shining on both faces. Acorns oblong-ellipsoid, apex acute; cupule top-shaped, made up of thin, flat, pubesc. scales, enclosing two-thirds of acorn. Calif., NW Baja Calif.

→*Cyclobalanopsis*.

Quesnelia Gaudich. Bromeliaceae. 14 perenn., rhizomatous, terrestrial herbs, to 2.5m in fl. Lvs usually ligulate, denticulate, pungent, in a rosette. Infl. scapose, simple or few-branched, with vivid floral bracts. E Braz. Z9.

Q. liboniana (De Jonghe) Mez. To 1m in fl. Lvs to 80cm, in a slender, funnel-shaped rosette, pale-scaly, sometimes banded beneath, marginal spines to 2mm, straight or curved. Infl. usually simple, pendent; scape slender; floral bracts orange, papery; sep. to 23mm, orange-red; pet. to 50mm, dark blue.

Q. marmorata (Lem.) Read. GRECIAN URN PLANT. To 60cm in fl. Lvs 40–50cm, in 2 rows, forming a near-circular rosette, blue-green, thick, scaly beneath with brown or maroon blotches or bands, marginal spines 1.5mm, straight, pink-grey. Infl. sub-pyramidal, base bipinnate, apex simple; scape red; bracts pink, elliptic; sep. to 10mm, purple; pet. to 25mm, blue or purple.

Q. quesneliana (Brongn.) L.B. Sm. 70–250cm in fl., sometimes long-stemmed. Lvs to 90cm; sheaths inflated, white-scaly; blades scaly, banded grey or white beneath, spines 1–3mm, dark. Infl. narrow-ellipsoid or cylindric, simple, scape erect; floral bracts rose-pink, erect, in 6–10 ranks, margins white-scaly, undulate; sep. 10mm, crimson; pet. 20–25mm, white, margins blue.

Q. rufa Gaudich. = *Q. quesneliana*.

Q. seideliana L.B. Sm. & Reitz. To 50cm in fl. Lvs 35–40cm, in a bundle-like rosette, scales white; sheaths large, flushed purple; blades green, spines dark. Infl. simple, cone-like; scape slender, tomentose; floral bracts yellow, thin, broadly ovate; sep. 15mm, white; pet. 25mm, sky blue.

Q. testudo Lindm. To 45cm in fl. Lvs 50–80cm, scaly; sheaths flushed purple, blades linear, banded white beneath, spines to 1.5mm. Infl. cylindric, simple; scape short; floral bracts bright red-pink, overlapping, oblong, undulate; sep. 9–10mm; pet. 18–20mm, blade pale violet to white.

→*Aechmea* and *Billbergia*.

Quiabentia Britt. & Rose. Cactaceae. 2 or more sp. of shrubs 2–3m or trees to 15m; br. often verticillate, cylindric-terete. Lvs broadly ovate, obovate or spathulate, flat, fleshy, decid.; areoles with glochids and spines, including tube; perianth rotate, showy. S Amer.

Q. zehntneri (Britt. & Rose) Britt. & Rose. Shrub to 3m; br. ascending, readily detached; lvs ovate to circular, to 4cm; spines numerous, thin. Fl. 4–8cm, purple-red. NE Braz. Z9.

Quick-set Thorn *Crataegus laevigata*.

Quillaja Molina. SOAP-BARK TREE. Rosaceae. 3 everg. shrubs or trees. Lvs simple, glab. Fls actinomorphic; cal. coriaceous, pubesc., 5-lobed, disc fleshy, red; pet. 5, sta. 10, biseriate; ovary semi-inferior, carpels. Temp. S Amer. Z10.

Q. saponaria Molina. SOAP-BARK TREE; QUILLAY; SOAP BUSH. Shrub or tree to 10m. Lvs to 5cm, elliptic or ovate, obtuse or subacute, shallowly dentate, shiny. Fls to 1.5cm diam., in corymbs; cal. thick, lanate; pet. white, oval-elliptic, 7mm, unguiculate. Chile.

Quillay *Quillaja saponaria*.
Quillwort *Isoetes*.
Quilt Plant *Hoffmannia bullata*.
Quince *Cydonia* (*C. oblonga*).

Quincula Raf.
Q. lobata (Torr.) Raf. = *Physalis lobata*.

Quinine *Cinchona*.
Quinine Bush *Garrya fremontii*.
Quinoa *Chenopodium quinoa*.

Quintinia A. DC. Grossulariaceae. Some 25 trees or shrubs. Lvs coriaceous. Infl. a rac. or a pan., usually many-fld; fls small; cal. tubular, 4 or 5-lobed; pet. 4 or 5, free, overlapping; sta. 4 or 5. Fr. a capsule, 3–5-valved. New Guinea, Aus., NZ. Z9.

Q. acutifolia T. Kirk. To 12m; trunk to 50cm diam. Lvs to 16×5cm, broadly obovate-elliptic to obovate-cuneate, often undulate, slightly serrulate. Rac. to 7cm; pet. to 3.5mm, pale lilac, ovate to oblong-ovate. NZ.

Q. serrata A. Cunn. To 9m; trunk to 50cm diam., Lvs to 12.5×2.5cm, narrowly lanceolate of oblanceolate to narrowly oblong, serrate. Rac. to 8cm; pet. to 3cm, pale lilac, oblong-obovate. NZ.

Quisqualis L. Combretaceae. 17 scandent shrubs. Lvs simple, entire; petioles sometimes persisting, becoming woody, thorn-like. Infl. a rac. or pan., bracteate, few- to several-fld; cal. tube pubesc. to glab., lobes 5, triangular; cor. tubular, lobes 5, oblong-elliptic, spreading; sta. 10, in 2 series. Fr. oblong, 5-angled or 5-winged, 1-seeded. Trop. and S Afr., Indomal. Z10.

Q. indica L. RANGOON CREEPER. Rampant climber; branchlets hairy, sometimes gland. Lvs to 18.5×9cm, elliptic or elliptic-oblong, acuminate, cordate to rounded at base, glab. to pubesc., veins sunken above; petiole to 5cm. Infl. to 10cm, sometimes paniculate, pendent; fls fragrant; cor. tube long, slender, lobes to 2×0.6cm, white changing to pink then brick red, often white beneath, somewhat silky. OW Trop.

R

Rabbit Brush *Chrysothamnus.*
Rabbit-eye Blueberry *Vaccinium ashei; V. virgatum.*
Rabbit's Fern *Phlebodium aureum.*
Rabbit's Foot *Maranta leuconeura* var. *kerchoveana.*
Rabbit's Foot Fern *Davallia fejeensis.*
Rabbit's Grass *Polypogon monspeliensis.*
Rabbit's Pea *Tephrosia virginiana.*
Rabbit Tracks *Maranta leuconeura* var. *kerchoveana.*

Rabiea N.E. Br. Aizoaceae. 7 dwarf, compact succulents. Lvs 4–8 per shoot, ascending or spreading, acute or acuminate, one lf often broadened at the tip. Fls solitary, subsessile. S Afr. Z9.
R. *albinota* (Haw.) N.E. Br. Lvs to 10×1cm, sabre-shaped, triquetrous above, apiculate, with spots and dots. Fls 3.5–6cm diam., yellow, sometimes tipped red. E Cape.
R. *albipuncta* (Haw.) N.E. Br. Lvs to 4×0.7cm, apiculate, carinate beneath, glossy green, rough, with white tuberculate dots. Fls 3cm diam., straw- to flesh coloured wit a red median line. OFS.
R. *lesliei* N.E. Br. Lvs to 1.2×0.5cm, bluntly carinate beneath, green to red with prominent, often blue dots. Fls 2.5cm diam., orange. OFS.
→*Aloinopsis* and *Nananthus.*

Radermachera Zoll. & Moritzi. Bignoniaceae. *c*15 everg. trees or shrubs. Lvs 2–3-pinnate. Infl. a term. thyrse; cal. irregularly lobed; cor. funnelform or tubular, lobes 5, unequal, rounded. Indomalesia, S China, Hainan, Taiwan, Ryukyu Is. Z10.
R. acuminata Merrill = *R. pinnata.*
R. amoena Gamble non Steenis = *R. pinnata* ssp. *acuminata.*
R. amoena Steenis non Gamble = *R. gigantea.*
R. banaibana Bur. = *R. pinnata.*
R. corymbosa Steenis = *R. pinnata* ssp. *acuminata.*
R. elmeri Merrill = *R. gigantea.*
R. fenicis Merrill = *R. pinnata.*
R. *gigantea* (Bl.) Miq. Shrub or tree. Lvs 12–80cm, 2-pinnate, lfts 4–15cm, oblong to elliptic, acuminate, gland. at base. Cor. to 6cm, pink or white, splashed yellow inside, abruptly dilated above, lobes ciliate. SE Asia and Malesia.
R. gigantea Burkwood. = *R. pinnata* ssp. *acuminata.*
R. *glandulosa* (Bl.) Miq. To 12m. Lvs simple-pinnate, lfts to 30×17cm, 2–5 pairs, papery, elliptic or elliptic-lanceolate, base dark-glandular below. Cor. pale purple, white inside, lobes 4cm, ciliate, tube glandular-hairy within. SE Asia and Malesia.
R. lobbii Miq. = *R. pinnata* ssp. *acuminata.*
R. mindorensis Merrill = *R. pinnata.*
R. palawanensis Merrill = *R. gigantea.*
R. *pentandra* Hemsl. Everg. tree to 7m. Lvs 2-pinnate, to 1m, lfts oblong, to 17cm. Fls in pan., to 30cm; fls yellow, *c*5×7.5cm. SE Asia.
R. *pinnata* (Blanco) Seem. To 20m. Lvs 25–70cm, 1–3-pinnate, lfts 3–16cm, acuminate, oblong-elliptic, papery, gland. at base. Cor. pink to purple, streaked yellow in throat. W & C Malesia to Philipp. and Taliabu Is. ssp. *acuminata* (Merrill) Steenis. Lvs 2-pinnate or biternate, pinnae 8–15cm, leathery, obovate to elliptic, rounded or truncate, rarely acuminate. SE Asia.
R. quadripinna Seem. = *R. pinnata.*
R. *sinica* (Hance) Hemsl. Shrub or tree. Lvs to 75cm, triangular-delloid in outline, 2-pinnate; pinnules ovate-rhomboid, ± lobed or toothed, glossy. Fls scented; cor. to 7.5cm, deep yellow, lobes 2.5cm, crisped. Spring–summer. S & E Asia.
R. stricta Zoll. & Moritzi ex Zoll. = *R. glandulosa.*
R. triternata Merrill = *R. gigantea.*
R. *xylocarpa* (Roxb.) Schum. Tree or shrub. Lvs to *c*1.3m, 2- or 3-pinnate, lfts *c*12cm, oblong to cordate, rigid, glab. Fls white tinted yellow, fragrant; cor. tube short, lobes rounded, curled. Spring–summer. E India.
→*Millingtonia, Oroxylum, Spathodea* and *Stereospermum.*

Radiator Plant *Peperomia.*

Radicula Moench.
R. armoracia (L.) Robinson = *Armoracia rusticana.*

Radish *Raphanus sativus.*

Radyera Bullock. Malvaceae. 2 tomentose, soft-woody shrubs. Lvs entire to shallowly palmatifid, toothed. Fls axill. or term. clusters; epical. seg. 8–10; cal. campanulate, pet. 5; staminal column slender. S Afr. and Aus. Z10.
R. *farragei* (F. Muell.) Fryx. & Hashmi. BUSH HIBISCUS; KNOBBY HIBISCUS. To 1m. Lvs 4–15cm, suborbicular to ovate. Pet. 4–5cm, purple. S & W Aus., N Territ., NSW, Vict.
→*Hibiscus.*

Raffenaldia Godron. Cruciferae. 2 dwarf, perenn. herbs. Lvs obovate-lanceolate, lyrate or pinnatifid, toothed. Fls solitary, axill., pet. long-stalked; 4, obovate-oblong, clawed. Moroc., Alg. Z9.
R. *primuloides* Godron. Lvs 2.5–10cm. Fls many, about 3cm diam.; sep. flushed lilac; pet. yellow or lilac, dark-veined. Winter.

Raffia *Raphia.*
Raffia Palm *Raphia farinifera.*
Ragged Robin *Lychnis flos-cuculi.*
Rag Gourd *Luffa.*
Ragi *Eleusine coracana.*
Railroad Vine *Ipomoea pes-caprae.*
Railway Fence Bauhinia *Bauhinia pauletia.*

Raimannia Rose.
R. drummondii (Hook.) Rose ex Sprague & Riley = *Oenothera drummondii.*

Rainbow Fern *Selaginella uncinata.*
Rainbow Plant *Billbergia chlorosticta.*
Rainbow Shower *Cassia javanica.*
Rainbow Star *Cryptanthus bromelioides.*
Rainbow Vine *Pellionia pulchra.*
Rain Daisy *Dimorphotheca pluvialis.*
Rain Lily *Zephyranthes.*
Rain Tree *Albizia saman; Brunfelsia undulata.*
Raisin Tree *Hovenia dulcis.*
Rakkyo *Allium chinense.*
Ramie *Boehmeria nivea.*
Ramo-giling *Schefflera longifolia.*

Ramonda Rich. ex Pers. Gesneriaceae. 3 perenn., stemless pubesc. herbs. Lvs withering in drought, rugose, canescent above, villous beneath. Fls solitary or few in scapose, axill. umbels; cal. seg. 4–6, exceeding cor. tube; cor. 4–6-merous, rotate, often slightly 2-lipped. S Eur. (mts). Z6.
R. *myconi* (L.) Rchb. Lvs to 6×5cm, elliptic to rhombic-orbicular, deeply toothed, red-brown-pilose, crenate. Fls to 4cm diam., 1–6 on glandular-pubesc., red-tinged scapes to 12cm, violet to pink or white with a yellow centre. Pyren. 'Alba': fls white; 'Carnea': fls pink; 'Rosea': fls pink.
R. *nathaliae* Pančić & Petrovič. Lvs to 5×3cm, elliptic-ovate to suborbicular, entire or slightly crenate, truncate at base. Fls to 3.5cm diam., 1–3 on glandular-pubesc. scapes to 8cm, white to lilac to purple, orange-yellow at centre. Balk. 'Alba': fls white.
R. pyrenaica Rich. ex Pers. = *R. myconi.*
R. *serbica* Pančić. As for *R. nathaliae* except lvs spathulate to narrowly obovate, deeply dentate or crenate, cuneate at base. Anth. violet-blue, not yellow tinged blue. Balk. Penins. 'Alba': fls white.
R. serbica var. *nathaliae* hort. = *R. nathaliae.*

Ramontchi *Flacourtia indica.*
Ramp *Allium tricoccum.*
Rampion *Campanula rapunculus.*
Ram's Head *Cypripedium arietinum.*
Ram's Horn *Proboscidea louisianica.*
Ramsons *Allium ursinum.*

Ranalisma Stapf. Alismataceae. 1 small, perenn., aquatic herb. Lvs to 3cm, basal, long-petiolate, ovate or oblong-elliptic, rounded at base; submerged lvs linear-lanceolate, to 10cm. Fls 3-merous, 1–3 per infl. Summer. W Afr. Z9.
R. *humile* (Kunth) Hutch.

Randia L. Rubiaceae. 200+ shrubs or trees, often spiny. Fls solitary or in cymes or corymbs; cal. tube ovoid to turbinate, limb tubular to 5-lobed; cor. bell- to funnel- or salver-shaped, lobes usually 5; sta. usually 5. Fr. a berry, globose to ellipsoid, usually succulent. Trop. Z10.

R. buchananii Oliv. = Rothmannia manganjae.

R. dumetorum (Retz.) Poir. = Catunaregam spinosa.

R. formosa (Jacq.) Schum. Shrub or tee, to 4m. Lacking spines. Lvs to 10cm, ovate to rhomboid or oblong, membranous, ± glab. Fls sessile, term., solitary, white to green; cal. tube to 1cm, silky, lobes to 1cm, linear to subulate; cor. to 15cm, interior papillose, lobes 5, ovate to oblong; anth. short-exserted. Fr. to 3×2cm, green and white-striped. Trop. C & S Amer.

R. kraussii Harv. = Catunaregam spinosa.

R. lachnosiphonium Hochst. = Catunaregam spinosa.

R. macrantha (Schult.) DC. = Euclinia longiflora.

R. maculata DC. = Rothmannia longiflora.

R. nilotica Stapf = Catunaregam nilotica.

R. stenophylla K. Krause = Rothmannia urcelliformis.

R. vestita S. Moore = Catunaregam spinosa.

→Gardenia and Mussaenda.

Rangaeris (Schltr.) Summerh. Orchidaceae. 6 epiphytic, monopodial orchids. Lvs tough, 2-ranked, ligulate, conduplicate. Rac. axill., arching; fls mostly white, scented at night; sepal and pet. subsimilar; lip entire or triblobed, spurred. Trop. & S Afr. Z10.

R. amaniensis (Kränzl.) Summerh. Lvs to 11×2cm, fls white, sometimes tinged green, spur apricot; tep. lanceolate, spreading 11–13mm; lip 13mm, obscurely lobed below. Ethiop., Rift Valley, Zimb.

R. brachyceras (Summerh.) Summerh. = Cribbia brachyceras.

R. muscicola (Rchb. f.) Summerh. Lvs to 18×2cm, fls white, turning apricot with age; sep. 8–9mm, ovate; pet. 8×3mm, lanceolate; lip 9mm, entire, broadly ovate or sub-quadrate, apiculate. Trop. Afr. (widespread), S Afr.

R. rhipsalisocia (Rchb. f.) Summerh. Lvs 7–8×0.5–1cm. Fls white or cream, spur tinged green; ovary hairy; tep. 8–9mm, lanceolate; lip of similar length, ovate acute, entire to 1.4cm. W Afr., Zaire, Angola.

Rangiora Brachyglottis repanda.

Rangit Polyscias nodosa.

Rangoon Creeper Quisqualis indica.

Rangpur, Rangpur Lime Citrus ×limonia.

Rangpur Lime Citrus ×limonia.

RANUNCULACEAE Juss. 58/1750. Aconitum, Actaea, Adonis, Anemone, Anemonella, Anemonopsis, Aquilegia, Callianthemum, Caltha, Cimicifuga, Clematis, Clematopsis, Consolida, Coptis, Delphinium, Eranthis, Helleborus, Hepatica, Hydrastis, Isopyrum, Laccopetalum, Naravelia, Nigella, Paraquilegia, Pulsatilla, Ranunculus, Semiaquilegia, Thalictrum, Trautvetteria, Trollius, Xanthorhiza.

Ranunculus L. BUTTERCUP; CROWFOOT. Ranunculaceae. c400 ann., bienn. or perenn. herbs. Lvs mostly forming basal rosette, laciniate to palmately lobed to entire. Fls solitary or in cymose pan., term. or axill.; sep. 3–7; pet. usually 5, rounded, occas. reduced or 0, often with nectariferous depression at base; sta. numerous, spirally arranged, shorter than pet. Fr. a head of compressed or subglobose achenes, often beaked. Temp. and boreal regions worldwide, mts in Trop.

R. aconitifolius L. Perenn. to 60cm. Basal lvs dark green, palmately, 3–5-lobed. Fls few to many, white, to 2cm, across; sep. red or purple beneath. Spring. W to C Eur. 'Flore Pleno' (WHITE BACHELOR'S BUTTONS; FAIR MAIDS OF FRANCE; FAIR MAIDS OF KENT): fls fully double, long-lasting. 'Luteus Plenus': fls double, yellow. Z6.

R. acriformis A. Gray. Perenn. to 60cm. Lvs 2-ternate, seg. narrow. Fls many, yellow, to 2cm across. Spring–summer. Rocky Mts. Z4.

R. acris L. MEADOW BUTTERCUP. Perenn. to 1m. Basal lvs with 3–7 deep lobes simple or further divided, dentate, hairy, sometimes marked with black. Fls several, glossy golden yellow, to 2.5cm across. Spring. Eur., Asia, nat. elsewhere. 'Flore Pleno' ('Multiplex') (YELLOW BACHELOR'S BUTTONS): to 90cm; fls double; 'Hedgehog': lvs marked dark brown; fls pale. Z5.

R. adoneus A. Gray. Low tufted perenn. to 15cm. Basal lvs 2–3-ternate, seg. linear. Fls 1–3 per st., golden yellow, to 4cm across. Spring–summer. Mts W US Z4.

R. alpestris L. Glab. perenn., 3–12cm. Lvs basal, glossy dark green, orbicular, lobes 3–5, deeply crenate. Fls 1–3, white, to 2cm across; sep. tinged red-brown 3–5. Spring–summer. Eur. (mts). Z5.

R. amplexicaulis L. Perenn. 8–30cm. Basal lvs ovate-lanceolate, glaucous, blue-grey; st. lvs amplexicaul. Fls several, white, occas. pink, 2–2.5cm diam.; pet. sometimes more than 5.

Spring. Pyren., N Spain. Z6.

R. anemonoides Zahlbr. = Callianthemum anemonoides.

R. aquatilis L. WATER CROWSFOOT. Ann. or perenn., aquatic; st. slender, branched, submerged. Submerged lvs finely dissected, 3–8cm; floating lvs rounded, deeply lobed. Fls emergent, white, to 1.8cm diam., with yellow centre. Spring–summer. Eur. Z5.

R. asiaticus L. Pubesc. perenn. to 45cm. Basal lvs 3-lobed, lobes stalked, divided and toothed. Fls few to several, red, pink, purple, yellow to white, 3–5cm across; anth. purple-black. Spring–summer. SE Eur., SW Asia. Bloomingdale Hybrids: habit dwarf; fls double in shades of pink, yellow, rose, red and white; seed race. 'Color Carnival': tall, robust; fls large, double, in wide range of colours; 'Picotee': compact; fls double, v. large, ruffled, in pink, red, orange, white and yellow, picotee edge; 'Pot Dwarf': fls semi-double and double, in scarlet, pink, salmon, orange and white; 'Superbissimus': tall; fls large. Tecolote Hybrids: robust; fls exceptionally large. Victoria Hybrids: fls large, fully double in wide range of colours. Z9.

R. bilobus Bertol. Close to R. crenatus, differing in basal lvs bright green, with prominent veins. Pet. emarginate deeply notched. Spring. It. Alps. Z7.

R. brevifolius Ten. Close to R. thora, but smaller; to 10cm. Basal lvs grey. Fls 1–2, to 2.5cm across. Spring–summer. It., Balk. Z7.

R. breyninus Crantz = R. montanus.

R. broteri Freyn = R. bulbosus ssp. gallecicus.

R. buchananii Hook. f. Perenn., white-pilose, to 30cm. Basal lvs reniform, 5–15cm across, lobes 3, stalked, cuneate, divided and toothed. Fls 1–4, white, 3–7cm across; pet. 15–20. Spring–summer. NZ. Z8.

R. bulbosus L. Pubesc. perenn.; rootstock swollen; st. 15–50cm. Basal lvs ovate, seg. 3, divided and toothed. Fls several, golden yellow, to 3cm across, glossy. Spring–summer. Eur. to W Asia, N Afr., nat. N Amer., NZ. Z5. 'F.M. Burton': fls single, light lemon. 'Pleniflorus' ('Flore Pleno'): fls double, chrome-yellow with green centre, to 4cm across. ssp. gallecicus (Freyn ex Willk.) P.W. Ball & Heyw. Rootstock scarcely swollen. Fls solitary or few. Spring. NW Spain. Z7.

R. bullatus L. Perenn.; roots tuberoius; st. to 30cm. Lvs basal, ovate, crenate, bullate. Fls 1–2, yellow, 2.5cm across, violet scented; pet. 5–12. Autumn–spring. Medit. to NW Spain and Port. Z7.

R. calandrinioides Oliv. Perenn. to 15cm. Lvs to 6.5cm, long-petiolate, lanceolate to ovate-lanceolate, entire, undulate, glaucous. Fls 1–3, white or flushed pink, to 5cm across. Winter–spring. Moroc. Z7.

R. californicus Benth. Perenn. to 70cm. Basal lvs ovate to orbicular, 2–7cm broad, 3-lobed or with 3–5 lobed and toothed lfts., hairy. Fls several, golden-yellow, to 3cm across. Spring. Calif., Oreg. Z7.

R. carpaticus Herbich. Perenn., 15–40cm. Basal lvs to 15cm broad, lobes 3–5 rhombic-ovate, dentate. Fls several, golden-yellow, to 5cm across. Spring. E Carpath. Z6.

R. chaerophyllos sensu Coste, non L. = R. paludosus.

R. cortusifolius Willd. Villous perenn., sometimes tuberous; st. to 1.2m. Basal lvs leathery, orbicular-cordate, lobes shallow divided and toothed. Fls numerous in corymb, golden-yellow, to 5cm across, sweetly scented. Summer. Azores, Canaries, Madeira. Z9.

R. crenatus Waldst. & Kit. Glab. perenn. to 15cm. Basal orbicular, weakly cordate, crenate or 3-lobed at apex. Fls 1–2, white, to 2.5cm across. Spring. E Alps, Apennines to Balk. and Carpath. Z7.

R. creticus L. Pubesc. perenn., sometimes tuberous, to 30cm. Basal lvs reniform, crenate, shallowly lobed. Fls several, yellow, to 3cm across. Spring. Crete. Z8.

R. delphiniifolius Torr. = R. flabellaris.

R. eschscholtzii Schldl. Glab. perenn. to 15cm. Basal lvs orbicular, 2.5cm broad, lobes 3, divided or entire, seg. obtuse. Fls 1–3 per st., soft yellow, to 3cm across. Spring–summer. Mts W N Amer. var. eximius (Greene) L. Bens. Basal lvs with middle lobes entire, seg. acute. Fls 4–5cm across. Mont., Idaho, Utah. Z4.

R. eximius Greene = R. eschscholtzii var. eximius.

R. fascicularis Muhlenb. ex Bigelow. EARLY BUTTERCUP. Perenn. to 30cm. Lvs lobes to ternate or pinnate, lobes 3–5, oblong to linear. Fls 1–4 per st., yellow, to 3cm across. Spring. E N Amer. Z3.

R. ficaria L. LESSER CELANDINE; PILEWORT. Glab. perenn., 5–30cm with clustered tubers. Basal lvs cordate, angled or crenate, 1–4cm, dark green, long-petiolate. Fls solitary to few, brilliant golden-yellow, fading to white, 2–3 across; pet. 8–12. Spring. Eur., NW Afr., W Asia, nat. N Amer. 'Albus': lvs with a dark mark; fls v. pale yellow, fading white, blue-green below. 'Bowles Double': fls double, green centre on opening, later paler yellow. 'Brazen Hussy': lvs chocolate brown; fls golden. 'Collarette': anth. petaloid, forming a tight anemone centre.

'Cupreus' ('Aurantiacus'): lvs heavily silvered with a prominent dark mark; fls coppery-orange. 'Double Bronze': fls double, yellow, with bronze backs to pet. 'Double Cream': fls double, upper surface of pet. creamy, lower surface tinged grey. 'E.A. Bowles': fls golden yellow, anemone-centred. 'Flore Pleno': fls double, yellow, pet. reverse tinged green. 'Green Petal': many narrow, wavy-edged green and yellow staminodes; pet. 0. 'Hoskin's Miniature': small; lvs slightly marked silver. 'Lemon Queen': fls simple, pale yellow, pet. reverse tinged bronze. 'Major' ('Grandiflorus'): v. large in all parts; fls to 42mm across. 'Randall's White': lvs without a dark mark; upper surface of pet. pale cream, lower surface purple-blue. 'Salmon's White': lvs with a dark mark; upper surface of pet. v. pale cream, lower surface purple-blue. 'Whiskey Double Yellow': fls double, yellow, pet. reverse tinged yellow and bronze. ssp. *bulbilifer* (L.) Lambinon. Bulbils borne in st. lf axils. ssp. *ficariiformis* Rouy & Foucaud. Large in all parts. Fls 3–5cm across; sep. white-yellow. S Eur. Z5.

R. flabellaris Raf. YELLOW WATER CROWFOOT. Aquatic perenn.; st. slender, submerged or floating. Submerged lvs cut into filiform seg.; emergent lvs thicker, seg. broad. Fls 1–7, yellow, 2–3cm across. Spring–summer. N Amer. Z4.

R. flabellatus Desf. = *R. paludosus*.

R. flammula L. LESSER SPEARWORT. Variable semi-aquatic perenn.; st. erect, ascending or creeping, rooting, 880cm. Lvs to 4cm, broad-ovate to linear-lanceolate. Fls solitary or few in cyme, yellow, 1–2.5cm across. Summer. Eur., temp. Asia. Z5.

R. fumariifolius Desf. ex DC. = *R. millefoliatus*.

R. glaberrimus Hook. Glab. perenn. prostrate or ascending, 5–15cm. Basal lvs to 3cm, rounded to obovate, entire or 3–5-lobed. Fls 1–6 per st., yellow, fading white, 2.5cm across; sep. tinged lavender. Spring. Calif. to BC, S Dak. Z4.

R. glacialis L. Prenn., 4–25cm. Basal lvs dark-green, somewhat fleshy, lobes 3, stalked, deeply segmented. Fls 1–3, white or pale pink, red after pollination, 2–3cm across. Spring–summer. Alps, Pyren., Sierra Nevada, Arc. Eur., Iceland, Greenland. Z4.

R. gouanii Willd. Close to *R. montanus*. Pubesc. perenn. to 30cm. Basal lvs 3–5-lobed, lobes obovate, dentate. Fls 1–5 per st., rich yellow, to 4cm across. Spring. Pyren. Z6.

R. gouanii 'Plenus'. = *R. bulbosus* 'Pleniflorus' ('Flore Pleno').

R. gouanii hort. non Willd. = *R. carpaticus*.

R. gramineus L. Perenn., 20–50cm. Basal lvs linear to lanceolate, flat, glaucous. Fls 1–3 per st., citron-yellow, to 2cm across. Spring–summer. S Eur., N Afr. 'Flore Pleno': fls double. Z7.

R. graminifolius hort. = *R. gramineus*.

R. haastii Hook. f. Fleshy, glaucous perenn. to 15cm. Basal lvs reniform to suborbicular, 5–10cm across, lobes 5–7, irregularly incised. Fls 1–5, yellow, 2–4cm, acorrs; pet. 5–15. Summer. NZ. Z8.

R. hirtellus Royle ex D. Don. Pubesc. perenn., erect or decumbent, to 15cm. Basal lvs rounded to reniform, 1–3cm across, lobes 3, broad and divided. Fls solitary or several, yellow, 1–1.5cm across. Spring–summer. Afghan. to SW China. Z7.

R. illyricus L. Sericeous tuberous perenn. to 50. Lvs linear-lanceolate, lobes to 3, entire or further divided, linear-lanceolate. Fls numerous, pale yellow, 3cm across. Spring. C & SE Eur. Z6.

R. insignis Hook. f. Perenn.; st. branched, 10–90cm. Basal lvs to 14cm, ovate-cordate, crenate, coriaceous, dark green, villous beneath. Fls 5–20, yellow, 2–5cm across; pet. 5–6. Summer. NZ. Z8.

R. kochii Ledeb. Close to *R. ficaria*, 5cm. Lvs rounded, entire. Fls golden-yellow, to 2cm across. Spring. Mts Turk., Iraq, Iran. Z6.

R. lanuginosus L. Pubesc. perenn.; st. hairy, 30–50cm. Basal lvs with 3–5 ovate, toothed lobes. Fls many, deep orange-yellow, to 4cm across. Spring. C & S Eur., Cauc. 'Pleniflorus': lvs heavily marked; fls double, orange-yellow. Z5.

R. lappaceus Sm. Caespitose perenn., hairy, to 5cm. Basal lvs ovate to suborbicular, to 4cm broad, 3-lobes, toothed. Fls solitary, pale to golden yellow, to 4cm acrooss. Spring–autumn. Aus., Tasm., NZ. Z8.

R. lingua L. GREATER SPEARWORT. Semi-aquatic stoloniferous perenn.; st. stout, 50–200cm. Basal lvs to 20cm, ovate to ovate-oblong, long-petiolate, st. lvs oblong-lanceolate, usually toothed. Fls in lax cyme, bright yellow, to 5cm across. Summer. Eur. to Sib. 'Grandiflorus': fls large, fleshy. Z4.

R. lyallii Hook. f. MOUNT COOK LILY; MOUNTAIN LILY. Perenn.; rootstock thick, roots fleshy; st. stout, to 1.5m. Basal lvs peltate, 12–40cm broad, crenate, leathery, dark green, long-petiolate. Fls 5–15 in pan., white, 5–8cm across. Summer. NZ. Z7.

R. macaulayi A. Gray. Perenn., to 15cm. Basal lvs to 5cm, oblong to spathulate, truncate and toothed at apex, glossy. Fls 1–2, bright-yellow, 2.5cm across; sep. black-hairy; pet. 5–8. Spring–summer. Colorado, New Mex. Z4.

R. macranthus Scheele. Perenn.; st. robust, hairy, to 60cm. Basal lvs with 3–7 lfts, to 15cm. Fls numerous, yellow, 3cm across; pet. 8–18. Spring. Ariz., N Mex. Z6.

R. millefoliatus Vahl Tuberous pubesc. perenn, 15–30cm. Basal lvs 2–3-pinnatisect, lobes linear-lanceolate. Lvs usually entire, golden-yellow, 2–3cm across, almost flat. Spring–summer. S & EC Eur., N Afr., W Asia. 'Grandiflorus': fls larger. Z6.

R. monspeliacus L. Tuberóus white-woolly perenn. to 50cm. Basal lvs ovate-cordate, with 3 toothed or laciniate lobes. Fls several, golden yellow, 2.5cm across. Spring. W Medit. Z8.

R. montanensis Rydb. = *R. acriformis*.

R. montanus Willd. Glab. to pubesc. rhizomatous perenn., 16–30cm. Basal lvs 3–5-lobed, lobes obovate, dentate. Fls 1–3, glossy golden-yellow, 2–3cm across. Spring–summer. Eur. (mts). 'Molten Gold': dwarf, robust; lvs dark; fls large, rounded, gold. Z6.

R. nemorosus DC. Perenn.; st. 20–80cm, erect, pubesc. Basal with 3 deeply lobed and dentate lobes. Fls to 4cm diam., golden-yellow. Eur. Z5.

R. nyssanus Leichtlin = *R. psilostachys*.

R. occidentalis Nutt. WESTERN BUTTERCUP. Perenn.; st. branched, hairy, 20–70cm. Basal lvs pubesc., 2–5cm across, lobes 3 ovate or further dissected. Fls several, yellow, 2.5cm across; pet. 5+. Spring. W Amer. (BC to Calif.). Z7.

R. paludosus Poir. Tuberous pubesc. perenn. to 50cm. Basal lvs 3-lobed, middle lobe stalked, lobes further divided, seg. narrow, dentate. Fls few, golden-yellow, to 2cm across. Spring. W Eur. (to Channel Is.), Medit. Z7.

R. parnassifolius L. Perenn. 4–10cm. Basal lvs entire, ovate cordate to broad-lanceolate, ± pubesc., deep green, leather. Fls 1–several, white or pink, to 2.5cm across. Spring–summer. Alps, Pyren., N Spain. Z5.

R. 'Phethora'. (*R. thora* × *R. brevifolius*.) Intermediate between parents. Austrian Alps. Z6.

R. phthora hort. = *R. 'Phethora'*.

R. platanifolius L. Close to *R. aconitifolius*, but larger. Basal lvs 5–7-lobed, middle lobe not free to base. Spring–summr. C & S Eur., Scand. Z5.

R. psilostachys Griseb. Tuberous perenn. to 30cm. Basal lvs to 10cm across, suborbicular and 3-lobed or cut, seg. obovate-cuneate, dentate, sericeous beneath. Fls 1–14, glossy yellow, 2–3cm across. Spring. Balk., W Turk. Z6.

R. pyrenaeus L. Glab. perenn. to 15cm. Lvs linear to broad-lanceolate, sessile, dark green. Fls 1–10, white, 2cm across; pet. sometimes 0. Spring–summer. Alps, Pyren., Spain (mts), Corsica. Z6.

R. repens L. CREEPING BUTTERCUP. Glab. to pubesc. stoloniferous perenn., 15–60cm. Basal lvs triangular-ovate, lfts 3, lobed and dentate. Fls usually solitary, golden-yellow, 2–3cm across. Spring–summer (sporadically autumn and winter). Eur., nat. N Amer., NZ. 'Flore Pleno' ('Pleniflorus'): fls double; said to be less invasive. 'Joe's Golden': lvs golden green. 'Nanus': habit dwarf. Z3.

R. rupestris Guss. Tuberoius pubesc. perenn. to 30cm. Basal lvs reniform or orbicular, lobes 3, shallowly-divided, crenate, hirsute. Fls 1–4, yellow, to 4cm across. Spring. Spain, Port., Sicily. Z7.

R. saxicola Rydb. = *R. eschscholtzii* var. *eximius*.

R. seguieri Vill. Perenn. 8–20cm, glabrescent. Basal lvs palmate, lobes 5–7, further divided. Fls solitary, white, 2.5cm across. Spring–summer. Eur. (mts Spain to Balk.). Z5.

R. speciosus 'Plenus'. = *R. bulbosus* 'Pleniflorus' ('Flore Pleno').

R. spicatus Presl = *R. rupestris*.

R. thora L. Tuberous perenn. 10–30cm. Basal lvs reniform, coarsely toothed above, glaucous, emerging after flowering. Fls 1-few, yellow, 1–2cm across. Spring. Eur. (mts, Spain to Balk.). Z5.

R. traunfellneri Hoppe. Close to *R. alpestris*, but smaller, to 7cm. Basal lvs 3-lobed, midlobe with 3-segments, laterals with 2. Fls solitary, 1.5cm across. Austria, It. (SE Alps). Z6.

R. villarsii L. = *R. montanus*.

Ranzania Itô. Berberidaceae. 1 perenn., rhizomatous herb, 15–40cm. Lvs 2–3 per st.; lfts 3, ovate to round, 3-lobed, 8–12cm across. Fls 2.5cm across, nodding, appearing before lvs, pale lavender-violet on a stalk to 8cm, subtended by 3 bracts; sep. 6, petaloid, ovate, pet. 6, much reduced. Summer. Jap. Z8.

R. japonica (Itô) Itô.

→*Podophyllum* and *Yatabea*.

Raoulia Hook. f. Compositae. *c*20 low growing perenn., herbs or subshrubs, often forming cushions or mats. Lvs crowded, usually, small, imbricate. Cap. discoid, sessile or subsessile, solitary, or few in a term. cluster; phyllaries tipped. NZ. Z7.

R. australis Hook. f. St. branched, rooting creeping, prostrate, forming mats to 1m diam. Lvs to 2mm, spathulate, densely imbricate, silver-pubesc. Cap. to 5mm diam.; phyllaries tipped bright yellow; flts yellow. Spring. N & S Is. 'Calf': prostrate, compact, mat-forming; lvs in v. tight rosettes, to 1mm diam., silver-green. 'Saxon Pass': v. low-growing, to 4mm; lvs in tight rosettes, to 2mm diam., silver-grey.

R. australis auct. = *R. hookeri.*

R. glabra Hook. f. St. lax, rooting, prostrate, apices ascending. Lvs to 5mm, laxly imbricate, ovate to linear-oblong, pale green, glab. Cap. to 9mm diam.; phyllaries tipped white or yellow; flts yellow. Late spring. N & S Is.

R. haastii Hook. f. St. creeping, apices ascending. Lvs to 5mm, laxly imbricate, ovate to linear-oblong, pale green, glab. Cap. to 9mm diam.; phyllaries tipped white or yellow; flts yellow. Late spring. S Is.

R. hectoris Hook. f. St. prostrate, apices ascending, forming mats to 80cm diam. Lvs to 4mm, densely imbricate, ovate, base glab., apex tomentose. Cap. to 4mm diam.; phyllaries green; flts pale yellow. S Is.

R. hookeri Allan. St. much-branched, prostrate, rooting, forming flat patches to 50cm diam. Lvs to *c*2mm, closely imbricate, narrowly obovate-spathulate, membranous toward base, leathery toward apex, woolly above, white-tomentose toward apex beneath. Cap. to 7mm diam.; phyllaries green or straw-coloured; flts yellow.

R. leontopodium hort. = *Leucogenes leontopodium.*

R. lutescens Beauv. = *R. australis.*

R. monroi Hook. f. St. prostrate, rooting, apices ascending. Lvs to 3mm, densely imbricate, linear-oblong to oblong-spathulate, tomentose. Cap. to 5mm diam.; phyllaries pale yellow-green, apex dark brown; flts yellow. S Is.

R. parkii Buch. St. creeping, prostrate, rooting, apices erect or ascending. Lvs to 5mm, densely imbricate, obovate-spathulate, apex tomentose, base glab. Cap. to 7mm; phyllaries tipped white, flts yellow. S Is.

R. × *petrimia* Kit Tan & McBeath. St. densely tufted, forming a compact hemispherical cushion, to 6cm tall and 12cm diam. Lvs to 5mm, narrowly oblong-lorate, densely golden- to white-silky villous toward apex above, long white-silky beneath. Cap. to 3mm diam.; flts red. N and S Is.

R. subsericea Hook. f. St. branched, prostrate, rooting, apices erect or ascending. Lvs to 6mm, imbricate, linear-oblong, pale green, base silvery- to golden-tomentose, becoming glab. toward apex, except for term. tuft. Cap. to 1cm diam.; phyllaries with white, radiate tips; flts yellow. S Is.

R. tenuicaulis Hook. f. St. creeping, rooting, densely branched, apices ascending, forming mats. Lvs to 5mm, imbricate, sub-lanceolate, thin white-tomentose at apex. Cap. to 6mm diam. N & S Is.

Rapanea Aubl.

R. chathamica (F. Muell.) Oliv. = *Myrsine chathamica.*

R. nummularia (Hook. f.) Oliv. = *Myrsine nummularia.*

Rape, Rape Kale *Brassica napus.*

Raphanus L. Cruciferae. 8 ann., bienn. or perenn. herbs. Roots often swollen. Lvs pinnatifid, lyrate. Rac. long, leafy, term., fls 4-merous, white or yellow with purple veins. Fr. a silique, jointed. Eur., temp. Asia.

R. caudatus L. RAT-TAIL RADISH. Ann. St. tinged purple, glaucous, becoming prostrate. Lvs pinnatisect or lyrate, coarsely toothed. Fr. 20–75cm, slender-acuminate, torulose, edible. Summer–autumn. Java; possibly of gdn origin. Z8.

R. sativus L. RADISH. Ann. or bienn. Taproot red, white or yellow, spindle- or turnip-shaped. Lvs lyrate, lobed. Fr. smooth, beaked. Early summer. Gdn origin. Z6.

R. tenellus Pall. = *Chorispora tenella.*

Raphia P. Beauv. RAFFIA. Palmae. 28 monocarpic palms. St. subterranean to erect, partly clothed with persistent lf bases, occas. bearing spine-like roots. Lvs pinnate; sheath unarmed; pinnae crowded, single-fold, linear. Infl. branched ×2. Fr. ellipsoid, 1-seeded; epicarp scaly, mesocarp thick, oily. C & S Amer., Afr., Madag. Z10.

R. farinifera (Gaertn.) N. Hylander. RAFFIA PALM. Trunk to 10m×60cm. Lvs to 20m, erect to arching; rachis orange-brown; pinnae to 150 per side, to 1m×8cm, held in differing planes along rachis, rigid, white-waxy beneath, lightly waxy above, margins spiny. Fr. to 10cm, with reflexed orange scales.

R. kirkii Becc. = *R. farinifera.*

R. lyciosa Kunth. = *R. farinifera.*

R. pedunculata Beauv. = *R. farinifera.*

R. polymita Kunth. = *R. farinifera.*

R. ruffia (Jacq.) Mart. = *R. farinifera.*

→*Sagus.*

Raphidophora Hassk.

R. laciniosa hort. = *Monstera subpinnata.*

R. pinnata Schott. = *Epipremnum pinnatum.*

Raphiolepis *Rhapiolepsis.*

Raphionacme Harv. Asclepiadaceae. 30 caudiciform succulent perennials. Roots tuberous, solitary and napiform or clustered and fusiform. Shoots imple or branched, sometimes twining, sap milky. Lvs narrow, grey-green. Fls in axillary cymes, small. E S Afr., Trop. W Afr. Z10.

R. brownii Scott-Elliot. Tuberous, shoots to 30cm. Lvs linear. Fls in term. or lat. cymes; cor. tube 3mm, lobes 5–7mm, pink; corona lobes, filiform. W Afr.

R. burkei N.E. Br. Shoots to 156cm. Lvs 3cm, linear. Fls in small axill. clusters all along st.; cor. 9–10mm diam., lobes 3mm, exterior hirsute, interior green to olive-green; corona purple-tinged. S Afr., Bots.

R. daronii Berhaut. Shoots herbaceous. Lvs 8–12 elliptic to lanceolate. Fls 2–3 together in axils; cor. to 1.6cm diam., violet. W Afr. (Senegal, Ghana).

R. divaricata Harv. = *R. hirsuta.*

R. elata N.E. Br. Shoots to 90cm. Lvs to 6cm, narrow-ovate, short-hairy. Fls in 1 or 2 clusters at the ends of st.; cor. 9mm diam., lobes green to olive-green; corona tinged purple. S Afr. (Natal, Transvaal).

R. hirsuta (E. Mey.) Dyer. St. 15–20cm. Lvs 3cm, orbicular, glab., or smaller, thinner, hirsute. Fls in scattered clusters along st.; cor. 1.5cm diam., lobes 8mm, purple-red; corona white. S Afr.

R. keayi Bullock Shoots to 1m. Lvs to 12cm, oblong-oblanceolate, crispate-pubesc. Fls numerous in lat. cymes; pedicels 4–6mm; cor. tube 2mm, lobes triangular, 5–6mm, green with a deep red zone at base, minutely papillate inside; corona banded red and white. Somalia.

→*Brachystelma.*

Raspa Lengua de Hoja Chiza *Bourreria succulenta* var. *revoluta.*

Raspberry *Rubus idaeus.*

Raspy Root *Rhinerrhiza divitiflora.*

Rata *Metrosideros robustus.*

Rathbunia Britt. & Rose. Cactaceae. 2 sprawling or thicket-forming shrubs; st. ribbed, v. spiny. Fls narrowly tubular, zygomorphic, diurnal; sta. numerous, exserted. NW Mex.

R. alamosensis (J. Coult.) Britt. & Rose. Shrub to 4m; br. arching to prostrate, to 1–2m×6–10cm, dark green, tinged red; ribs 5–8, somewhat sinuate; to 4cm. Fl. 7–10×2–3cm, bright red; fil. white, anth. purple. NW Mex. Z9.

Ratibida Raf. PRAIRIE CONEFLOWER; MEXICAN HAT. Compositae. 6 erect, rough, hairy biennials or perenn. herbs to 1m. Lvs alt., pinnate to pinnatifid. Cap. solitary, radiate, showy, long-pedunculate; receptacle globose to cylindrical and cone-like; ray flts yellow or partly brown-purple; disc flts yellow-brown. N Amer., Mex. Z3.

R. columnifera (Nutt.) Wooton & Standl. LONG-HEAD CONEFLOWER. PRAIRIE CONEFLOWER. Gland. perenn., branched above. Lvs pinnate, seg. 5 or more, linear or oblong, often pinnatifid. Receptacle cylindric to columnar; ray flts to 2.5cm, yellow to red or partly to entirely brown-purple. Summer–early autumn. BC to New Mex.

R. pinnata (Vent.) Barnhart. GREY-HEAD CONEFLOWER; DROOPING CONEFLOWER. Gland. to eglandular perenn. Lvs pinnate, seg. lanceolate, seg. of lower lvs serrate or dentate. Receptacle globose; ray flts to 5cm, yellow. Late spring–early autumn. Central N Amer.

R. tagetes (James) Barnhart. Often gland., short perenn. much branched. Basal lvs to 6cm, entire or 1–2-pinnate, st. lvs pinnate, seg. linear, hirsute. Receptacle subglobose; ray flts *c*1cm, yellow to purple-brown. Summer. C to SW US.

→*Lepachys.*

Rat-tail Cactus *Aporocactus flagelliformis.*

Rat-tail Cypress *Crassula muscosa.*

Rat-tail Radish *Raphanus caudatus.*

Rattan Cane *Calamus rotang.*

Rattan Palm *Calamus; Rhapis humilis.*

Rattlebox *Crotalaria* (*C. spectabilis*); *Ludwigia alternifolia.*

Rattlesnake Crassula *Crassula barklyi.*

Rattlesnake Fern *Botrychium virginianum.*

Rattlesnake Grass *Briza.*

Rattlesnake-master *Eryngium yuccifolium.*

Rattlesnake Orchid *Pholidota.*

Rattlesnake Plant *Calathea lancifolia.*

Rattlesnake Plantain *Goodyera pubescens.*

Rattlesnake Root *Chamaelirion luteum*; *Nabalus*; *Prenanthes purpurea*.
Rattlesnake Violet *Viola fimbriatula*.
Rattletop *Cimicifuga*.
Rattle Weed *Baptisia tinctoria*.
Rauli Beech *Nothofagus procera*.

Rauvolfia L. Apocynaceae. Some 60 shrubs and small trees. Infl. a few-fld, ± term., dichasial cyme; fls small; cal. short, 5-parted; cor. salverform, tube constricted at throat, lobes 5. Fr. 2 drupes, distinct or fused. Trop. & Subtrop. Z10.
R. canescens L. = *R. tetraphylla*.
R. chinensis (Spreng.) Hemsl. = *R. verticillata*.
R. tetraphylla L. Everg. shrub to 2.5m. Lvs to 15cm, ovate to ovate-elliptic, downy. Cor. to 1cm, white to ivory or pink. Fr. to 1.5cm, red ripening black. Subtrop. & Trop. Amer.
R. verticillata (Lour.) Baill. Everg. shrub to 2m. Lvs to 12cm, elliptic to oblanceolate. Cor. to 0.5cm, white. Fr. to 1.25cm, red, usually paired. Indochina, China, Taiwan.
R. vomitoria Afzel. Shrub or small tree to 7m. Lvs to 18cm, lanceolate to elliptic, cor. 0.5–1.5cm, ivoiry, throat pubesc. within. Fr. to 0.75cm, scarlet, solitary or paired. Trop. Afr.

Ravenala Adans. TRAVELLER'S TREE. Strelitziaceae. 1 giant tree-like herb, to 16m. St. simple, stout, clothed above by lf bases, otherwise ring-scarred and smooth. Lvs to 4m, 2-ranked, becoming torn along veins, petiole bases overlapping to form a distinctive fan. Madag. Z10.
R. guyanensis (Rich.) Benth. = *Phenakospermum guyanense*.
R. madagascariensis Sonn.

Ravine Orchid *Sarcochilus fitzgeraldii*.

Ravnia Ørst. Rubiaceae. 4 everg. epiphytic shrubs. Fls in term. clusters; cal. top-shaped, lobes 5–6; cor. tubular, lobes 5–6, anth. short-exserted. C Amer. Z10.
R. triflora Ørst. To 1m. Lvs to 10cm, lanceolate- or elliptic-oblong, apex acuminate. Cor to 5cm, rose-red, lobes 3mm. Costa Rica.

Rayless Alpine Butterweed *Packera pauciflora*.
Ray Water Fern *Blechnum fluviatile*.

Rebutia Schum. Cactaceae. c40 low-growing cacti, simple or clustering; st. small, globose to shortly cylindric, tuberculate or weakly ribbed; spines relatively weak, often scarcely differentiated into radial and central. Fls funnelform, comparatively small; pericarpel and tube with small scales naked or hairs and sometimes bristles; tube often slender, often curved. Mts of Boliv., NW Arg.
R. albiflora Ritter & Buining. Clustering; st. globose to short cylindric, to 2.5×1.8–2.5cm, bright green; tubercles in 12+ rows; central spines to 15mm, white, pale brown at base; raidal spines 3–5mm, hairlike. Fl 2.5×2.5cm; tube v. slender; tep. white or rose white with deeper rose midstripe. Boliv. Z9.
R. albopectinata Rausch. St. to 2–3×2–3.5cm; radial spines to 3mm, pectinate; central spines 0 or 1. Fl. 2.5–5×3–4.5cm; tube 3–4mm diam.; perianth pure red to crimson. Boliv. Z9.
R. arenacea Cárdenas. Simple or clustering; st. depressed-globose, apex umbilicate, 2–3.5×2.5–5cm; tubercles in c30 spiral series; spines raidal, c5mm, pectinate, white to yellow or brown-tinged. Fl. 3×3cm, inner tep. orange-yellow. Boliv. Z9.
R. auranitida (Wessner) Buining & Donald = *R. einsteinii*.
R. aureiflora Backeb. Clustering; st. depressed-globose to globose, to 6cm diam., often red-tinged; tubercles c6mm; central spines to 1cm, bristly; radial spines to 0.6cm. Fl. broadly funnelform, c4cm diam., yellow with white throat, sometimes orange, red or purple; tube pale, scales tipped green-red. NW Arg. Z9.
R. brachyantha (Wessner) Buining & Donald = *R. steinmannii*.
R. calliantha Bewerunge = *R. wessneriana*.
R. candiae Cárdenas. Clustering; st. globose, 2–3×4–5cm; tubercles in c15–20 spirals; spines raidal, to 7mm, pectinate, yellow to brown. Fl. 2.5–3×3–3.5cm, yellow. Boliv. Z9.
R. canigueralii Cárdenas. Clustering; st. globose, 1×2cm, slate-grey; tubercles in 13 series; central spines 0–2, erect; radial spines 1.5–2mm, bristly. Fl. 3–4×3–4cm; tube upcurved; throat yellow, limb orange-red. Boliv. Z9.
R. chrysacantha Backeb. = *R. senilis*.
R. costata Werderm. = *R. steinmannii*.
R. cylindrica (Donald) D. Hunt. Tuberous. Simple or offsetting; st. cylindric, to 12×4.5cm; central spines to 15mm, tipped red-brown; radial spines 5–10mm, pale. Fls 3×3.5–4cm, deep yellow, with musty scent. Boliv. Z9.
R. deminuta (F.A.C. Weber) A. Berger. Simple or clustering; st. subcylindric, 5–6×3.5cm; tubercles in 11–13 spirals; spines

3–5mm, bristly. Fl. 2.5–3×3cm; tube 15mm, solid; tep. red to orange or dark purple. NW Arg. Z9.
R. einsteinii Frič. Clustering; st. slender-cylindric, to 8×3.5cm, often bronze-tinted; tubercles in 13–15 vertical or spiral rows; spines all radial, 8–12, 2–5mm, bristly brown to almost white. Fl. 3×3.5cm, golden-yellow to orange. NW Arg. Z9.
R. elegans Backeb. = *R. einsteinii*.
R. euanthema (Backeb.) Buining & Donald, invalid name. = *R. aureiflora*.
R. famatinensis (Speg.) Speg. Usually simple; roots tuberous; st. subcylindric, umbilicate at apex, 30–35×25–38mm; ribs c24, straight; spines 1.5–2mm, weak, white or pectinate, addpressed. Fl. woolly, tubular-campanulate, 3cm; tube densely woolly; outer tep. purple, inner orange above, yellow below. W Arg. (La Rioja and San Juan). Z9.
R. fidaiana (Backeb.) D. Hunt. Usually simple; st. globose to short-columnar, tuberculate, 30×15cm, grey-green; spines upcurved, straw-coloured to violet black, to 5cm. Fl. to 3×3cm, tube short, yellow, tep. yellow. Spring. Boliv. Z9.
R. fiebrigii (Gürke) Britt. & Rose. Variable; st. globose, depressed at apex, 5cm tall, tuberculate; central spines to 2cm, brown-tipped; radial spines shorter, white or all bristly. Fl. funnelform, 2–3cm; tube slender, upcurved, bright orange to red. Boliv., NW Arg. Z9.
R. glomeriseta Cárdenas. Clustering; st. globose, c5–6cm diam.; tubercles in c20 series; spines 2–3, bristly, interlacing, pale brown at first. Fl. 2.5×1.5cm, golden-yellow. Boliv. Z9.
R. grandiflora Backeb. = *R. minuscula*.
R. haagei Fric & Schelle = *R. pygmaea*.
R. heliosa Rausch. Simple at first, later clustering; st. flattened-globose to short cylindric, to 2×1.5–2.5cm; tubercles in 35–40 spirals, v. small; spines 1mm, pectinate, white. Fl. 4.5–5.5×4cm; tube to 3cm, deep rose to orange-pink; inner tep. orange with lilac midstripe. Boliv. Z9.
R. kesselringiana Bewerunge = *R. senilis*.
R. knuthiana Backeb. = *R. minuscula*.
R. krainziana Kesselr. St. depressed-globose, c4–5×3–4cm; spines c1–2mm, bristly, white. Fl. c3×4cm, bright red with violet sheen and violet throat. Probably gdn origin. Z9.
R. krugeri (Cárdenas) Backeb. Resembling *R. arenacea*. Spines bristly, pectinate, usually brown, occas. with 1–2 short erect central spines. Fl. yellow or orange and yellow. Boliv. Z9.
R. kupperiana Boed. Resembling *R. deminuta*. St. tinged purple; spines strongly projecting, chocolate brown. Fl. larger, dark crimson. Boliv. Z9.
R. margarethae Rausch. St. simple to 4×6cm; spines dark brown with yellow base, to 30mm. Fl. c4×3.5cm, orange-red. N Arg. Possibly of hybrid origin. Z9.
R. marsoneri Werderm. Usually simple; st. to 3×4.5cm, pale green; tubercles, 2mm; spines c30–35, the lower 20, c3–5mm, white upper 9–15, longer, thicker, red-brown or white with brown tip. Fl. 3.5–4.5cm; tube 2–2.4cm, tep. yellow to orange-yellow. N Arg. Z9.
R. mentosa (Ritter) D. Hunt. Simple at first; st. to 9–10×6–7cm; central spines 5–35mm; radial spines 5–25mm, pectinate and ascending, brown or yellow. Fl. 3×3.5cm, purple or magenta. Boliv. Z9.
R. minuscula Schum. Soon clustering; st. globose, to c5cm diam.; tubercles in 16–20 spirals; spines 2–3mm, bristly. Fl. to 4cm; pericarpel pale red; tep. variable in colour. N Arg. Z9.
R. muscula Ritter & Thiele = *R. fiebrigii*.
R. neocumingii (Backeb.) D. Hunt. Simple; st. depressed-globose to globose, to 10cm diam.; tubercles in 16–18 spiral series; spines c1cm, pale yellow, tipped darker. Fl. 2.5cm, orange or yellow. Boliv. Z9.
R. neumanniana (Backeb.) D. Hunt. Simple often tuberous; st. subglobose, to 7×5cm, grey-green, velvety; ribs c14, obscurely hexagonal tubercles; spines, 1–3cm, dark brown to red-black, rigid. Fl. c2.5×2.5cm, yellow or orange-red. NW Arg. Z9.
R. pseudodeminuta Backeb. Resembling *R. deminuta*; st. to 7×5–6cm; spines to 3cm, interlacing, white to yellow, orange or brown. Fl. to 3.5×4cm; pure orange through scarlet to light crimson. NW Arg., Boliv. Z9.
R. pseudominuscula (Speg.) Donald & Buining = *R. deminuta*.
R. pulchra Cárdenas. Clustering; st. 1.5×3cm, dark green to violet; tubercles in c16 spiral series; spines 1–3mm, subulate, addpressed, tinged yellow to black. Fl. 3×3cm, magenta-pink, usually with paler or white throat. Boliv. Z9.
R. pulvinosa Ritter = *R. albiflora*.
R. pygmaea (R.E. Fries) Britt. & Rose. Simple, or clustering; st. ovoid to short-cylindric, 1–3×1.2–2cm; tubercles in 8–12 spiral rows; spines radial, 2–3mm, addpressed. Fl. curved-erect, 18–25mm, rose-purple; floral aeroles hairy; tube c3mm diam. NW Arg. Z9.
R. senilis Backeb. St. to 8×7cm, deep green; spines c25, to 3cm, chalky white or tinged yellow. Fl. 3.5cm, carmine with white

throat or citron yellow (*R. kesselringiana*). N Arg. Z9.

R. spegazziniana Backeb. Resembling *R. deminuta*; ribs well-defined with conic tubercles. Fl. dark red. NW Arg. Z9.

R. spinosissima Backeb. Resembling *R. fiebrigii*. Spines bristly, white, the most central brown-tipped. N Arg. Z9.

R. steinbachii Werderm. Clustering; st. depressed-globose; tubercles in *c*13 spirals; spines to 2.5cm, almost black. Fl. *c*3.5×3.5cm; tube well-developed; limb scarlet to magenta, rarely yellow, musty-scented. Boliv. Z9.

R. steinmannii (Solms-Laubach) Britt. & Rose. Clustering; st. oblong, 2–3×1–2.2cm; ribs often spiralled, tuberculate; spines to 4mm, bristly. Fl. lat., 3.5×2.5cm; tube *c*3mm diam., tep. scarlet. Boliv. Z9.

R. stuemeriana (Backeb.) Backeb. = *R. senilis*.

R. taratensis Cárdenas. Clustering; st. globose 2–2.5×2–3.5cm, dark green or tinged purple tubercles in *c*15 spiral series; spines radial, 3–4mm, white, tipped dark brown. Fl. 4×3.5cm, magenta red. Boliv. Z9.

R. tiraquensis Cárdenas. Resembling *R. mentosa*; central spines red-brown, contrasting with the glassy white radials. Boliv. Z9.

R. violaciflora Backeb. = *R. minuscula*.

R. vizcarrae Cárdenas. Rootstock tuberous, *Dahlia*-like; st. globose, 3–3.5×4–5cm, grey-green, sometimes tinged purple; ribs *c*18; areoles grey-felted; spines almost white to yellow to or pale brown; 11mm, spreading; radial spines to 11mm, spreading; radial spines, pectinate. Fl funnelform, 3.5cm, clove-scented; tube short; tep. magenta. Boliv. Z9.

R. wessneriana Bewerunge. Freely offsetting; st. depressed-globose, to 7(–15)×8cm; spines *c*15–25, to 2cm, white, brown-tipped. Fl. 4.5–5.5cm diam., bright red. N Arg. Z9.

R. xanthocarpa Backeb. Offsetting; st. subglobose, to 4.5×*c*5cm; spines 15–20, 1–7mm, tinged yellow. Fl. 2cm diam., scarlet to carmine or salmon-pink, lighter inside. N Arg. Z9.

→*Gymnocalycium, Lobivia, Mediolobivia, Sulcorebutia* and *Weingartia*.

Rechsteineria Reg.
R. aggregata (Ker-Gawl.) Kuntze = *Sinningia aggregata*.
R. allagophylla (Mart.) Reg. = *Sinningia allagophylla*.
R. canescens (Mart.) Kuntze = *Sinningia canescens*.
R. cardinalis (Lehm.) Kuntze = *Sinningia cardinalis*.
R. cooperi (Paxt.) Kuntze = *Sinningia cooperi*.
R. incarnata (Aubl.) Leeuwenb. = *Sinningia incarnata*.
R. lindleyi (Hook.) Fritsch. = *Sinningia sceptrum*.
R. lineata Hjelmqv. = *Sinningia macropoda*.
R. macropoda (Sprague) Curtis = *Sinningia macropoda*.
R. macrorrhiza (Dumort.) Kuntze = *Sinningia macrorrhiza*.
R. purpurea hort. = *Sinningia verticillata*.
R. ramboi Hoehne = *Sinningia sellovii*.
R. reitzii Hoehne = *Sinningia reitzii*.
R. sellovii (Mart.) Kuntze = *Sinningia sellovii*.
R. sulcata (Rusby) Fritsch = *Sinningia sulcata*.
R. tuberosa (Mart.) Kuntze = *Sinningia tuberosa*.
R. verticillata (Vell.) L.B. Sm. = *Sinningia verticillata*.

Red Alder *Alnus rubra*.
Red Alpine Blueberry *Vaccinium scoparium*.
Red Amaranth *Amaranthus cruentus*.
Red-and-green Kangaroo Paw *Anigozanthos manglesii*.
Red Angels' Trumpet *Brugmansia sanguinea*.
Red Apple *Acmena australis*.
Red Ash *Fraxinus pennsylvanica*.
Red Baneberry *Actaea rubra*.
Red Bark *Cinchona pubescens*.
Red-barked Dogwood *Cornus alba*.
Red Bartsia *Odontites verna*.
Red Beak *Lyperanthus nigricans*.
Red Beech *Nothofagus fusca*.
Red-berried Elder *Sambucus pubens; S. racemosa*.
Redberry *Rhamnus croceus*.
Red Bilberry *Vaccinium parvifolium*.
Red Birch *Betula nigra*.
Red Bird Cactus *Pedilanthus*.
Redbird Flower *Pedilanthus tithymaloides* 'Variegatus'.
Red Bloodwood *Eucalyptus gummifera*.
Red Bonnets *Burtonia hendersonii*.
Red Bopple Nut *Hicksbeachia pinnatifolia*.
Red Boronia *Boronia heterophylla*.
Red Box *Eucalyptus polyanthemos*.
Red Bryony *Bryonia dioica*.
Red Buckeye *Aesculus pavia*.
Redbud *Cercis canadensis*.
Redbud Maple *Acer heldreichii*.
Red Bush Monkey Flower *Mimulus puniceus*.
Red Buttons *Hoya pubicalyx*.
Red Calla *Sauromatum venosum*.

Red Campion *Silene dioica*.
Red Cap Gum *Eucalyptus erythrocorys*.
Red Cedar *Acrocarpus fraxinifolius; Thuja*.
Red Cherry *Prunus pensylvanica*.
Red Chokeberry *Aronia arbutifolia*.
Red Clover *Trifolium pratense*.
Redcoats *Utricularia menziesii*.
Red Cole *Armoracia rusticana*.
Red Currant *Ribes silvestre*.
Red Cypress-pine *Callitris endlicheri*.
Red Dragon Flower *Huernia schneideriana*.
Red Elm *Ulmus rubra; U. serotina*.
Red False Mallow *Sphaeralcea coccinea*.
Red Fescue *Festuca rubra*.
Red Fir *Abies magnifica*.
Red Flame *Oxalis alstonii*.
Red Flame Ivy *Hemigraphis alternata*.
Red-flowered Mallee *Eucalyptus erythronema*.
Red-flowered Moort *Eucalyptus nutans*.
Red-flowered Silky Oak *Grevillea banksii*.
Red-flowering Gum *Eucalyptus ficifolia*.
Red Fox *Celosia argentea*.
Red Ginger *Alpinia purpurata*.
Red Ginger Lily *Hedychium coccineum*.
Red Gram *Cajanus cajan*.
Red Granadilla *Passiflora coccinea*.
Red Grape *Vitis palmata*.
Red Gum *Liquidambar styraciflua*.
Red-heart *Ceanothus spinosus*.
Red Helleborine *Cephalanthera rubra*.
Red Hickory *Carya ovalis*.
Red Horsechestnut *Aesculus ×carnea*.
Red Horse Chestnut *Aesculus ×carnea*.
Red-hot Cat's Tail *Acalypha hispida*.
Redhot Poker *Kniphofia*.
Redhot Poker Aloe *Aloe aculeata*.
Redhot Poker Tree *Erythrina abyssinica*.
Red Huckleberry *Vaccinium parvifolium*.
Red Ink Plant *Phytolacca americana*.
Red Ink Sundew *Drosera erythrorrhiza*.
Red Ironbark *Eucalyptus sideroxylon*.
Red Ivy *Hemigraphis alternata*.
Red Ixora *Ixora coccinea*.
Red Justicia *Megaskepasma erythrochlamys*.
Red Latan *Latania lontaroides*.
Redleaf *Philodendron cruentum*.
Red-leaf Philodendron *Philodendron erubescens*.
Red Mahogany *Eucalyptus resinifera*.
Redmaids *Calandrinia ciliata*.
Red Manjack *Cordia nitida*.
Red Maple *Acer rubrum*.
Red Martagon of Constantinople *Lilium chalcedonicum*.
Red Midge Orchid *Prasophyllum rufum*.
Redmint *Mentha ×gracilis*.
Red Mombin *Spondias purpurea*.
Red Moonseed *Cocculus carolinus*.
Red Morning Glory *Ipomoea coccinea*.
Red Mountain Spinach *Atriplex hortensis* var. *rubra*.
Red Mulberry *Morus rubra*.
Red Oak *Quercus rubra*.
Redondo Creeper *Lampranthus filicaulis*.
Red Orach *Atriplex hortensis* var. *rubra*.
Red Orchid Cactus *Nopalxochia ackermanii*.
Red Osier Dogwood *Cornus stolonifera*.
Red Passion Flower *Passiflora coccinea; P. manicata; P. racemosa*.
Red Pepper *Capsicum annuum* var. *annuum*.
Red Pine *Dacrydium cupressinum; Pinus resinosa*.
Red Pineapple *Ananas bracteatus*.
Red Pokers *Hakea bucculenta*.
Red Puccoon *Sanguinaria*.
Red Raspberry *Rubus idaeus*.
Red Ribbons *Clarkia concinna*.
Red Rose *Rosa gallica*.
Red Rose of Lancaster *Rosa gallica*.
Red Sandalwood Tree *Adenanthera pavonina*.
Redshanks *Adenostoma sparsifolium*.
Red Silk-cotton Tree *Bombax ceiba*.
Red Silver Fir *Abies amabilis*.
Red-skinned Onion *Allium haematochiton*.
Red Sorrel *Hibiscus sabdariffa*.
Red Spider *Grevillea speciosa*.
Red Spider Lily *Lycoris radiata*.
Red Spike Ice Plant *Cephalophyllum alstonii*.
Red Spruce *Picea rubens*.
Red Star *Rhodohypoxis baurii*.

Red Stem-fig *Ficus variegata.*
Red-stemmed Wattle *Acacia myrtifolia*; *A. rubida.*
Red Stopper *Eugenia confusa.*
Red Stringybark *Eucalyptus macrorhyncha.*
Red St. Wattle *Acacia myrtifolia.*
Red Swamp Banksia *Banksia occidentalis.*
Red Toothbrushes *Grevillea hookeriana.*
Red Tussock Grass *Chionochloa rubra.*
Red Twig *Leucothoë recurva.*
Red Valerian *Centranthus ruber.*
Red-veined Pie Plant *Rheum australe.*
Red-white-and-blue Flower *Cuphea ignea.*
Red Willow *Salix laevigata.*
Redwood *Adenanthera pavonina*; *Sequoia sempervirens.*
Red-wooded Fig *Ficus racemosa.*
Redwood Penstemon *Penstemon corymbosus.*
Redwood Sorrel *Oxalis oregana.*
Redwood Violet *Viola sempervirens.*
Red Zebrina *Calathea ecuadoriana.*
Reed *Phragmites.*
Reed Canary Grass *Phalaris arundinacea.*
Reed Grass *Calamagrostis.*
Reedmace *Typha.*
Reed Meadow Grass *Glyceria maxima.*
Reed Rhapis *Rhapis humilis.*
Reed Sweet Grass *Glyceria maxima.*

Reevesia Lindl. Sterculiaceae. 4 decid. shrubs or small trees. Lvs simple, entire. Fls in many-fld term. cymes or corymbs; cal. 3–6-toothed; pet. 5, clawed; androgynophore with 5 groups of 3 sessile anth., alternating with 5 small staminodes. Fr. a woody capsule. Himal. to Taiwan. Z9.
R. thyrsoidea Lindl. THYRSE-FLOWERED REEVESIA. Tree to 18m. Lvs to 25cm, ovate-lanceolate to broadly oblong, glossy. Pet. to 1.2cm, white or cream, often yellow-spotted above the claw. Fr. to 2.5cm, obovoid. S China to Java.
R. wallichii R. Br. Tree to 15m. Lvs to 10cm, broadly ovate, thinly stellate-pubesc. Fls scented; pet. to 4cm diam., white. Fr. 4–5cm, oblong. E Himal.

Reeves Spiraea *Spiraea cantoniensis.*
Reflexed Stonecrop *Sedum reflexum.*
Regal Lily *Lilium regale.*
Regal Pelargoniums *Pelargonium ✕domesticum.*

Regelia Schauer. Myrtaceae. 5 everg. shrubs. Lvs small, entire. Fls in term. spike. Sta. numerous. W Aus. Z9.
R. ciliata Schauer. Shrub to 1.5m, erect, rigid, and open-textured. Lvs 0.5cm, broad, blunt. Fls purple, globose heads.
R. cymbifolia (Diels) C. Gardn. Shrub to 2.5m, erect and densely textured. Lvs 0.6cm, dull green, crowded. Fls bright purple, in loose term. spikes.
R. inops (Schauer) Schauer. Shrub to 1m, erect and open-textured. Lvs 0.3cm, triangular, stiff. Fls pink-purple, in dense, term. heads.
R. megacephala C. Gardn. Shru to 3m, erect, rigid. Lvs small and finely hairy. Fls dark purple, in term. heads.
R. velutina (Turcz.) C. Gardn. Shrub to 3m, erect and slender, open. Lvs 1–1.5cm, elliptic, grey-blue, in 4 rows. Fls scarlet-orange, with golden tips in term. heads.

Regnellidium Lindm. Marsileaceae. 1 aquatic or semi-aquatic fern. Rhiz. slender, creeping, rooting. Fronds clover-like, blades 2, each with 2 ovate-reniform segs. to 5cm, glossy bright green, terminating slender stipes to 20cm. S Braz. Z10.
R. diphyllum Lindm.

Rehderodendron Hu. Styracaceae. 9 decid. shrubs or trees; branchlets stellate-pubesc. Fls white, in axill. leafless pan. or rac.; cal. lobes 5, short; pet. 5, connate at base, broadly obovate; sta. 10, unequal, equalling pet. S & W China.
R. hui Chun. Shrub to 2.5m. Lvs to 10cm, elliptic, denticulate. Fls to 7 per pan.; cor. to 4cm diam. China. Z7.
R. macrocarpum Hu. Tree to 9m; br. red, sparsely hairy. Lvs 8–11cm, elliptic to oblong, minutely serrate, stellate-pubesc. on veins beneath. Fls 6–10 per rac., fragrant, appearing before lvs. Cor. to 5cm diam., finely pubesc. Spring. W China. Z8.

Rehmannia Libosch. Gesneriaceae. 9 hairy perenn. herbs. Fls in term., bracteate rac.; cal. ovoid-campanulate, 5-fld; cor. hairy, tube broadly ventricose, limb 2-lipped, lobes 5, spreading. China. Z9.
R. angulata (D. Don) Hemsl. As for *R. glutinosa* except lvs sessile or subsessile, deeply pinnately lobed, lobes deltoid, irregularly dentate. Cor. to 6cm. C China.
R. angulata hort. non (D. Don) Hemsl. = *R. elata.*

R. elata N.E. Br. Perenn. to 1.5m; st. branched. Lvs to 25cm, lobes 2–6, usually entire, sometimes toothed, densely hairy. Cor. 7–10cm, bright rose-purple, throat yellow, spotted red.
R. glutinosa Libosch. ex Fisch. & C.A. Mey. Viscid erect perenn. herb to 30cm, purple-pubesc. Lvs rosulate, obovate, to 7.5cm, coarsely toothed. Cor. to 7.5cm, red-brown to yellow, purple-striate, lobes pale yellow. Spring. China.
R. oldhamii Hemsl. = *Titanotrichum oldhamii.*

Reichardia Roth. Compositae. 8 ann. to perenn., latex-producing herbs, usually branched and leafy. Cap. ligulate, few to numerous, solitary at br. apices; flts yellow, sometimes base and back of outer ligules purple-stained; anth. yellow, pink or purple. Medit., to India. Z8.
R. picroides (L.) Roth. Glab., erect perenn. to 60cm. Lvs thin or slightly leathery, sparingly white-papillose; basal lvs to 13×2.5cm, spathulate to oblanceolate, attenuate, entire to pinnatisect, upper st. lvs smaller, ovate-lanceolate, entire to lobed, cordate, amplexicaul. Involucre 5.5–15×5–14mm; ligules yellow, outer ones with a green stripe on back; anth. yellow. Medit.
R. tingitana (L.) Roth. Glab. ann. or rarely bienn., to 60cm. Lvs densely white-papillose, basal lvs to 17×7cm, spathulate to oblanceolate, dentate to pinnatisect-dentate, base attenuate, middle st. lvs ovate-lanceolate, cordate, amplexicaul, upper-most bract-like. Involucre 8.5–18×4.5–21mm; ligules yellow, usually with a purple stain at base, outer ones usually with a purple stripe on back; anth. usually purple. Macaronesia, Medit., to W India.
→*Picridium* and *Scorzonera.*

Reineckea Kunth. Liliaceae (Convallariaceae). 1 perenn. herb. St. prostrate, clump-forming. Lvs 15–35cm, 2-ranked appearing tufted, linear-lanceolate, arching. Scapes 6–10cm; fls fragrant in a dense term. spike; perianth 8–12mm, pale to fleshy pink, tep. united below, reflexed at tips. Fr. a scarlet berry. Early summer. China, Jap. Z7.
C. carnea (Andrews) Kunth. 'Variegata': lvs striped cream.

Reinhardtia Liebm. Palmae. 6 palms. St. erect, slender solitary or clustered, scarred, sometimes with stilt roots. Lvs entire and pinnately ribbed with an apical notch, or pinnately divided; pinnae single-fold, emarginate, or several-fold, sharply toothed. S Mex. to N Colomb. Z10.
R. gracilis (H.A. Wendl.) Burret. WINDOW PALM. St. solitary or clustered, to 2.5m. Petiole to 60cm; pinnae 2–4 each side of rachis, with small holes at bases between main veins. var. *gracilior* (Burret) H.E. Moore. Fr. with sharp pointed apex. S Mex. to Hond. var. *rostrata* (Burret) H.E. Moore. Fr. with porminent truncate hump at apex. E Nic. and Costa Rica.
R. simplex (H.A. Wendl.) Burret. St. to 1.2m, slow to sucker and appearing solitary. Petiole to 16cm; lower 2 pinnae oblanceolate, term. pinnae united in a toothed fan. Hond. to Panama.
→*Malortiea.*

Reinwardtia Dumort. Linaceae. 1 glab. shrub or subshrub, to 90cm. Lvs elliptic-obovate or oblong-obovate, membranous, often serrate. Fls golden yellow, 2.5–5cm diam., in short, clustered rac., solitary or in dense term. corymbs; pet. 5, broad, spreading, united below. N India, China. Z9.
R. indica Dumort. YELLOW FLAX. Sometimes erroneously grown as *Linum flavum.*
R. tetragyna Planch. = *R. indica.*
R. trigyna (Roxb.) Planch. = *R. indica.*
→*Linum.*

Remusatia Schott. Araceae. 4 tuberous perenn. herbs often producing a scape of hooked bulbils instead of fertile infl. Lvs solitary, entire, peltate, long-petiolate. Infl. solitary; spathe thick, convolute-tubular at base, limb erect or reflexed; spadix short. Fr. small red berries. Trop. Afr., Himal. through SE Asia to N Aus. Z10.
R. vivipara Schott. Bulbiliferous shoots to 30cm, bulbils many, hooked. Lf 12.5–45cm, orbicular-ovate or cordate dark green with paler viens; petiole to 50cm. Peduncle to 15cm; spathe tube 5cm, limb to 7.5cm, green to golden yellow; spadix to 3.5cm, cream-white. Late spring.

✕ Renanopsis. (*Renanthera* ✕*Vandopsis.*) Orchidaceae. Gdn hybrids with strap-like lvs and branching sprays of large, thickly textured fls in shades of red, often with darker spotting.

✕ Renantanda. (*Renanthera* ✕*Vanda.*) Orchidaceae. Tall gdn hybrids with strap-shaped lvs and erect to arching, branched sprays of large fls in shades of red, orange and pink often marked or spotted red, purple or yellow.

Renanthera Lour. Orchidaceae. 10 robust, monopodial, epiphytic orchids. Lvs oblong-ligulate, conduplicate, coriaceous, 2-ranked. Rac. sometimes branching; dors. sep. and pet. similar, spreading, often clawed, lat. sep. almost parallel, larger; lip smaller, triblobed, base saccate or spurred, midlobe ligulate. Indomal. Z10.

R. angustifolia Hook. f. = *R. matutina*.

R. annamensis Rolfe. Fls. to 4cm diam.; spur and base of sep. and pet. yellow, spotted crimson, lip lobes and pet. apex deep crimson; lat. sep. spathulate, concave, obtuse, to 1.8cm; lip midlobe cordate to orbicular, obtuse. Vietnam.

R. bella J.J. Wood. Fls to 4cm, yellow-cream to pink or crimson, blotched dark crimson, yellow to apricot at centre, lip yellow, densely blotched dark red and maroon; lat. sep. undulate; narrow-elliptic; lip midlobe oblong, reflexed. Malaysia.

R. coccinea Lour. Fls. to 5cm diam.; dors. sep. pale pink, speckled bright red or cinnabar red, speckled orange-yellow, lat. sep. ovate-oblong; claw linear, weakly undulate, bright red, lip pale yellow at base, midlobe deep red-purple, lat. lobes edged and streaked red; lip midlobe ovate. SE Asia.

R. elongata (Bl.) Lindl. Fls to 5cm diam. dull red or yellow, blotched red, lip red, calli yellow; lat. sep. ovate, elongate, undulate; lip midlobe oblong-spathulate. Java.

R. imschootiana Rolfe. Fls 3–4cm diam.; sep. red or orange, base yellow, pet. yellow, spotted red, lip and column red; lat. sep. oblong, clawed, weakly undulate, lip midlobe elliptic, concave. India, Burm., Indochina.

R. matutina (Bl.) Lindl. Fls 2.5–5cm diam., crimson or vermilion, spotted scarlet, lip white and orange-yellow, spotted red, midlobe red-brown; sep. arching, narrow-oblong or clavate, revolute; lip midlobe ligulate, revolute. Thail. to Sumatra.

R. micrantha Bl. = *R. matutina*.

R. monachica Ames. Fls some 2.5cm diam., yellow, spotted red; lat. sep. lanceolate; lip minute, fleshy, to 0.15cm, midlobe oblong. Philipp.

R. storiei Rchb. f. Fls 4–7.5cm diam., dors. sep. and pet. orange, mottled deep red, lat. sep. rose-purple, spotted crimson, lip red, lobesyellow, striped red, midlobe base and callus white; lat. sep. oblong, undulate, clawed; lip midlobe ligulate, obtuse. Philipp.

✕Renanthopsis. (*Renanthera* ✕ *Phalaenopsis*.) Orchidaceae. Gdn hybrids with leathery 2-ranked lvs and long sprays of fls in shades of yellow, bronze, pink and purple.

Renealmia L. f. Zingiberaceae. 70 aromatic rhizomatous perenn. herbs. Lvs in 2 ranks, forming reed-like pseudostem. Infl. bracteate, paniculate or racemose, terminal on leafy st. or carried on a separate scape; cor. fused at base to staminodal tube; lip erect, 3-lobed. Trop. Amer. and Afr. Z10.

R. amoena Rich. = *R. jamaicensis*.

R. antillarum var. *puberula* Gagnep. = *R. jamaicensis* var. *puberula*.

R. cernua (Sw. ex Roem. and Schult.) Macbr. 1–5m. Sheaths prickly-pubesc. Lvs 10–43cm, narrowly elliptic, glab. Infl. 4–27cm; bracts red to yellow; cal. red to yellow; cor. to 2.2cm, yellow to white. Mex. to S Amer.

R. jamaicensis (Gaertn.) Horan. 0.4–3m. Sheaths usually glab. Lvs 6–40cm, narrowly elliptic, glab. Infl. 3–17cm, glab. or hairy; bracts pink to scarlet; cal. red; cor. 1.5–2.5cm, white, lip sometimes flushed purple. Jam., Cuba, Bahamas. var. *puberula* (Gagnep.) Maas. 1–3m. Lvs 10–40cm. Infl. 6–17cm; axis hairy; bracts subglabrous; cor. 2–2.5cm. Hispan.

R. nicolaiodes Loes. 2–5m. Sheaths glab. or pubesc. and prickly. Lvs 95–250cm, narrowly elliptic, hairy beneath. Infl. 5–10×4–12cm, spike-like bracts, red to orange, cal. red to orange; cor. 3.7–5cm, yellow to yellow flushed red. W S Amer.

R. pauciflora Griseb. ex Petersen = *R. jamaicensis*.

R. ventricosa Griseb. Lvs 30cm, linear-lanceolate. Infl. term., dense, elliptoid; cor. small, red. Hispan. Sometimes misnamed *Alpinia vittata* in cult.

→*Alpinia, Costus* and *Zingiber.*

Renge-giboshi *Hosta fortunei.*

Reseda L. MIGNONETTE. Resedaceae. 55 herbs, sometimes partially woody, ascending or erect. Lvs alt., entire or pinnatifid. Infl. a rac., simple or branched, term.; sep. 4–8; pet. 4–8, entire or laciniate, alternating with sep.; sta. 7–40, merging with fleshy disc. Medit., E Afr., SW Asia to NW India.

R. alba L. WILD MIGNONETTE; WHITE UPRIGHT. Ann. or perenn., to 80cm, erect. Lvs to 15cm, ovate to ovate-oblong, pinnatifid. Rac. 20–75cm, erect; fls white or cream; sep. 3–4mm; pet. 5–6, 3.5–6mm wide, papillose. Medit. origin; widespread weed

throughout temp. and trop. regions. var. *alba.* ssp. *decursiva* (Forssk.) Maire. Pet. with slightly auriculate claw. Z8.

R. complicata Bory. Perenn., to 50cm, glaucous. Lvs 1.5–2.5cm, linear, scarcely toothed below. Infl. erect, to 15cm; fls white; sep 1–1.5mm; pet. 6, 2–4mm. Spain (Sierra Nevada). Z8.

R. decursiva Forssk. = *R. alba* ssp. *decursiva.*

R. dimerocarpa Rouy & Foucaud = *R. luteola* ssp. *dimerocarpa.*

R. luteola L. Ann. or perenn., 50–130cm, erect. Lvs 2.5–12cm, linear to ovate or oblong, entire. Infl. sometimes branching, to 60cm; fls yellow or yellow-green; pet. 4–8-lobed; sta. 20–40. Eur., C Asia. ssp. *luteola.* Ovaries usually 3-carpellate. ssp. *dimerocarpa* (Muell.) & De Wit. Ovaries bicarpellate. Z6.

R. odorata L. MIGNONETTE; SWEET RESEDA; BASTARD ROCKET. Ann., erect to ascending, to 80cm. Lvs to 10cm, oblanceolate obovate, upper lvs with 1–2 lat. lobes. Infl. to 15cm; fls white, sometimes tinged green or yellow or buff, intensely fragrant; sep. to 4mm, 6; pet. to 5mm, divided. Mediterranean. var. *odorata.* Erect, stout. Limb of superior pet. flabellate. var. *neilgherrensis* (J. Muell.) Abdallah & De Wit). Slender, ascending. Superior pet. with central lobes of limb shorter than adjacent lobes.

→*Luteola.*

RESEDACEAE Gray. 6/75. *Reseda.*

Rest-harrow *Ononis.*

Restio Rottb. Restionaceae. 88 perenn. herbs superficially resembling *Equisetum* or *Ephedra.* St. slender erect to arching, clumped, tough, with whorled br. and lvs reduced to scales or persistent leathery sheaths. Fls minute, in brown spikelets in dense, spathaceous term. pan. S Afr., Aus. Z9.

R. compressus Rottb. St. to 1m, erect, compressed, branching from centre. S Afr. (Cape Prov.).

R. tetraphyllus Labill. St. to 1m, erect, terete, with filiform dichotomous br. E Aus., Tasm.

RESTIONACEAE R. Br. RESTIO FAMILY. 38/400. *Restio.*

Restrepia HBK. Orchidaceae. 30 epiphytic orchids, resembling *Pleurothallis* in habit. Fls small to large, often lying on or held barely clear of lf surface, dors. sep. free, erect, narrow, antenna-like, lat. sep. usually forming a boat-like synsepalum; pet. similar to dors. sep., smaller; lip smaller than sep., simple to trilobed. Mex. to Arg. Z10.

R. antennifera HBK. St. to 15cm. Lvs to 9cm, fleshy-coriaceous, elliptic-ovate to ovate-suborbicular. Infl. to 10cm; fls translucent; sep. pale yellow striped maroon, tails tinged green, dors. sep. to 40mm, concave, tail-like, lat. sep. to 40mm, forming a synsepalum, narrowly elliptic; pet. to 23mm, similar to dors. sep.; lip to 15mm, pale brown spotted maroon, papillose. Venez., Colomb., Ecuad.

R. cucullata Lindl. = *Barbosella cucullata.*

R. elegans Karst. St. 2–6cm. Lvs 2.5–6cm, elliptic or ovate-elliptic. Infl. 1.75–4cm; dors. sep. to 25mm, white lined maroon, lanceolate, long-attenuate, lat. sep. to 24mm, orange-brown marked maroon, oblong elliptic, forming a synsepalum; pet. similar to dors. sep., smaller; lip to 11mm, pale brown marked maroon, glandular-granulose. Venez.

R. guttulata Lindl. St. 5.5 to 11cm. Lvs 4–8cm, lanceolate or ovate-lanceolate. Infl. to 7cm; dors. sep. to 25mm, wite, veined and tipped rose-purple, lanceolate to long-attenuate at apex, lat. sep. to 25mm, light orange-brown spotted dark maroon, forming an ovate-lanceolate synsepalum; pet to 13mm; lip to 10mm, light brown spotted rose, fleshy, apex verrucose. Venez., Colomb., Ecuad.

R. lansbergii Rchb. f. & Wagner. St. to 6.5cm, usually shorter. Lvs 3.25–6cm, oblong to elliptic, often flushed purple-red. Infl. surpassing lvs; dors. sep. to 30mm, apex purple-maroon, base white lined dark maroon-purple, lanceolate, papillate, lat. sep. to 30mm, forming an obovate synsepalum, cream-white spotted dark maroon; pet. to 19mm, similar to dors. sep.; lip to 9mm, pale yellow-brown spotted dark maroon-purple, sometimes suffused maroon, erose-crenulate,. Venez.

R. leopardina hort. = *R. guttulata.*

R. maculata Lindl. = *R. guttulata.*

R. miersii (Lindl.) Rchb. f. = *Barbrodria miersii.*

R. pardina Lem. = *R. guttulata.*

R. punctulata Lindl. = *R. elegans.*

→*Pleurothallis.*

Restrepiella Garay & Dunsterv. Orchidaceae. 7 epiphytic orchids resembling *Pleurothallis* in habit. Infl. short, fasciculate; fls velutinous; dors. sep. free, lat. sep. free or briefly connate; pet. smaller; lip simple to obscurely 3-lobed. Costa Rica and Venez. to Peru. Z10.

R. ophiocephala (Lindl.) Garay & Dunsterv. St. to 20cm. Lvs to 20cm, oblong to lanceolate; fls dull yellow or yellow-white blotched purple, fleshy, papillose-pubesc.; dors. sep. to 2.8cm, elliptic-oblong to ligulate-oblong; pet. rounded, white-fimbriate; lip to 0.3cm, elliptic-oblong. Mex., Guat., El Salvador, Costa Rica.
→*Pleurothallis*.

Resurrection Fern *Polypodium polypodioides*.
Resurrection Lily *Kaempferia rotunda*; *Lycoris squamigera*.
Resurrection Plant *Anastatica*; *Selaginella lepidophylla*.
Retam *Retama raetam*.

Retama Raf. Leguminosae (Papilionoideae). 4 erect, unarmed, many-branched shrubs. Lvs linear, sericeous, usually 0 in mature plants. Fls pea-like in dense axill. rac. Medit., Canaries. Z9.
R. monosperma (L.) Boiss. Straggling, unarmed shrub, to 3m. Br. slender, pendent, grooved, v. pubesc. when young. Fls highly fragrant; cal. purple; cor. white. Spain, N Afr.
R. raetam (Forssk.) Webb. RETAM; WHITE BROOM; JUNIPER BUSH. Graceful shrub to 3m. Br. slender, persistently appressed-pubesc. Cal. finely pubesc.; cor. white. Spring. Syr., Isr.
R. sphaerocarpa (L.) Boiss. Decid. shrub to 1.3; st. erect slender, ribbed, ± glab. Cal. glab.; cor. yellow. Early summer. Spain, N Afr.
→*Genista* and *Lygos*.

Retinispora Sieb. & Zucc.
R. obtusa Sieb. & Zucc. = *Chamaecyparis obtusa*.
R. pisifera Sieb. & Zucc. = *Chamaecyparis pisifera*.

Retrophyllum Page. Podocarpaceae. 5 everg. coniferous shrubs or trees, crown columnar in trees, bark rough furrowed brown. Branchlets flattened, pinnate. Lvs in two or four ranks, decussate, flattened, thick fleshy-coriaceous, larger on juvenile plants, stomata on both surfaces. ♂ cones solitary or grouped 2–5, short-pedunculate, 6–10×mm. ♀ cones solitary or paired, term.; mature fr. subtended by a non-swollen, fleshy drupe-like, red to purple-blue, pruinose. Oceania, trop. S Amer. Z10.
R. minor (Carr.) Page. Shrub to 3m. Lvs 1–2mm on strong shoots. 10–20mm, on lat. shoots, in four ranks, ascending. New Caledonia.
R. rospigliosi (Pilger) Page. Tree to 35m. Lvs opposite in two ranks, ovate-lanceolate, 20–25mm. S Amer. (N Andes).
R. vitiense (Seem.) Page. Tree to 45m. Lvs opposite in two ranks, narrowly lanceolate, 15–20mm, to 30mm on young plants; 2mm on strong shoots. Fiji, Solomon Is., Celebes, New Guinea.
→*Decussocarpus* and *Podocarpus*.

Rewa Rewa *Knightia excelsa*.
Rex Begonia *Begonia rex*.
Rex Begonia Vine *Cissus discolor*.

Reynoutria Houtt.
R. japonica var. *compacta* (Hook. f.) Buchheim = *Polygonum japonicum* var. *compactum*.
R. japonica (Meissn.) Houtt. = *Polygonum japonicum*.
R. sachalinensis (Schmidt) Nak. = *Polygonum sachalinense*.

RHAMNACEAE Juss. 53/875. *Berchemia, Ceanothus, Colletia, Discaria, Hovenia, Noltea, Paliurus, Phylica, Pomaderris, Rhamnus, Ziziphus*.

Rhamnus L. BUCKTHORN. Rhamnaceae. *c*150 decid. or everg. trees, frequently thorny. Infl. racemose or fasciculate; fls small, 4(–5) merous, yellow-green. Fr. a globose drupe, to 1cm diam., red ripening black. Widely distrib. in N temp. areas, with a few sp. in E & S Afr. and Braz.
R. alaternus L. Thornless, everg. shrub, 1–5m. Branchlets grey. Lvs 3–7cm, ovate to elliptic, coriaceous, ± serrate, glab. Early spring. S Port. to N Afr. and SE Russia. 'Argenteovariegatus' ('Variegatus'): lvs narrower with broad creamy-white margins on leaden green. Z7.
R. alnifolius L'Hérit. Decid. shrub to 1m, twigs finely downy. Lvs 4–10cm, elliptic to ovate, base cuneate, apex acute, unevenly toothed, glab. above. Late spring, early summer. N Amer. Z2.
R. alpinus L. Erect, decid., thornless shrub to 4m. Lvs to 4–10cm, elliptic, apex rounded to ruspidate, base rounded to slightly cordate, finely serrate. Late spring, early summer. Spain to Greece. Z6.
R. alpinus ssp. *fallax* (Boiss.) Maire & Petitmengin = *R. fallax*.
R. californicus Eschsch. COFFEEBERRY. Everg. shrub to 4m, twigs tinged red. Lvs 3–8cm, oblong to elliptic, apex acute to obtuse, margins sometimes revolute, toothed or entire, glossy and glab. W US. Z7.

R. carolinianus Walter. CAROLINA BUCKTHORN. Decid. shrub or small tree to 6m, bark grey. Lvs 3–11.5cm, golden-yellow in autumn, obovate or narrowly ovate, apex acute or acuminate, glab. or pubesc., often velvety beneath, margins with small, irregular teeth. Late spring, early summer. US (NY and Neb. to Tex. and Flor.). Z6.
R. catharticus L. Decid. shrub or small tree, 4–6m, twigs grey-green or brown, spiny. Lvs 3–7cm, ovate to elliptic, apex cuspidate or blunt, glab. or slighly hairy beneath, denticulate. Late spring, early summer. Temp. Eur. and Asia, NW Afr., introd. E US. Z3.
R. costatus Maxim. Decid. shrub to 3–4m, twigs stout. Lvs 8–14cm, opposite, oval-oblong, margins with rounded teeth, apex acuminate, pubesc. beneath. Late spring. Jap. Z6.
R. crenatus Sieb. & Zucc. Decid. shrub to 3m, twigs and lvs rusty-brown hairy at first. Lvs 5–10cm, lanceolate or obovate-oblong to oblong-ovate, pale green above, pubesc on veins beneath, finely toothed. Early summer. Jap. and Korea to C China. Z4.
R. croceus Nutt. REDBERRY. Everg. spreading shrub to 2m, bark grey-green, twigs often spiny. Lvs 5–15cm, obovate or broadly ovate to elliptic, glossy, leathery, ± glab. or almost so, with small, gland. teeth. Calif., Ariz., Baja Calif. Z8.
R. dahuricus Pall. Large decid. shrub, or small tree, to 7m; twigs thick, spiny. Lvs 5–10cm, oblong to elliptic, apex acuminate, glab., somewhat leathery, grey-green beneath. Late-spring. E Russia, Jap., China, N Korea. Z5.
R. erythroxylon Pall. Much-branched shrub to 2m; twigs red, shiny, spinose. Lvs 3–10cm, leathery, subglabrous, linear to oblong-linear, grey-green beneath. Late spring. E Russia, Mong. Z3.
R. fallax Boiss. Erect shrub to 0.5m, glab. Lvs 4–14cm, decid., 4–14cm, ovate-elliptic to oval, dark green, crenate-serrulate. Late spring, early summer. SE Eur., Turk., Leb. Z6.
R. frangula L. ALDER BUCKTHORN. Shrub or small tree, to 2–5m. Lvs 3–7cm, decid., oblong-lanceolate or obovate-elliptic, short-acuminate, entire, dark glossy green above, paler beneath. Late spring, early summer. Eur., Turk., N Afr. 'Asplenifolius': lvs dissected. 'Tall Hedge' ('Columnaris'): to 3–4×0.8cm, forming a dense columnar shrub. Z3.
R. heterophyllus Oliv. Decid. shrub to 1.5m, twigs slender, short-pubesc. at first. Lvs 0.5–3cm, with spinescent stipules, oblong-ovate or lanceolate to rounded, acute, glab. above, with long hairs on veins beneath, margins with few, small teeth. Summer. W China. Z6.
R. ×hybridus L'Hérit. (*R. alaternus* ×*R. alpinus*.) Semi-evergreen shrub to 4m, twigs glab. Lvs 5–10cm, elliptic-oblong or ovate to elliptic, glossy and glab., yellow-green beneath, with small, shallow teeth. Gdn origin. 'Billardii': lvs 4–7cm, lanceolate-ovate, narrow, teeth large and coarse. Z6.
R. imeretinus Booth. Decid. shrub to 2(–4)m, twigs green-pubesc., not spiny. Lvs 8–15(–25)cm, bronze-purple in autumn, elliptic or oval to broadly lanceolate, apex mucronate or short-acuminate, finely toothed, glab. and dull green above, pale and velutinous beneath. Early summer. E Turk., Georgia, Armenia. Z6.
R. infectorius L. = *R. saxatilis* ssp. *saxatilis*.
R. japonicus Maxim. Decid. spreading shrub to 3m, twigs thorny, shiny yellow-brown. Lvs 5–8cm, oblong to obovate, apex short-acuminate, finely toothed, glab., glossy. Fls. fragrant. Late spring. Jap. Z4.
R. lanceolatus Pursh. Decid. erect shrub or small tree to 4m. Lvs 3–5(–7)cm, elliptic, apex short-acuminate, glab. or sparsely pubesc., with small teeth. Late spring. US. Z5.
R. leptophyllus Schneid. Decid. shrub to 2m. Lvs 4–7cm, obovate-elliptic, apex acuminate, glab., paler beneath, margins with few small teeth. Late spring. C & W China. Z6.
R. pallasii Fisch. & C.A. Mey. Decid. shrub, 1–3m, twigs spiny, brown, glab. or puberulous. Lvs 2–3cm, linear-oblanceolate, subentire or with few teeth, glab. or puberulous. NE Turk., Georgia, Armenia, Azerbaijan, NW Iran. Z6.
R. pumilus Turra. Procumbent shrub to 20cm, with downy young twigs. Lvs 1.5–6(–7.5)cm, elliptic or obovate, acute, acuminate or rarely obtuse, finely toothed. Montane areas from Spain to Albania. Z5.
R. purshianus DC. CASCARA SAGRADA. Decid. lax shrub to small tree, to 12m, twigs sparsely hairy. Lvs 5–5cm, obovate or boradly elliptical, apex obtuse to subtruncate, margins irregularly toothed, hairy to subglabrous. Late spring, summer. BC, Calif. Z7.
R. rupestris Scop. Decid. spreading, procumbent or ascending shrub to 80cm. Lvs 2–5cm, elliptic to suborbicular, apex obtuse or acute, entire or with small teeth, pubesc. on veins beneath. Summer. NE It. to Greece. Z6.
R. saxatilis Jacq. Erect to procumbent shrub to 2m, much-branched, decid., lat. twigs often spine-tipped. Lvs 1–5cm,

lanceolate, ovate or obovate, apex acute, crenate-serrate. S &
SC Eur. ssp. *saxatilis*. AVIGNON BERRY; ROCK BUCKTHORN.
Habit procumbent. Twigs glab. Lvs 1–3cm, glab. Spring. ssp.
tinctorius (Waldst. & Kit.) Nyman. DYER'S BUCKTHORN. Habit
erect, twigs pubesc. Lvs 2–5cm, downy on veins beneath at
maturity. Spring. EC & SE Eur. Z6.

R. utilis Decne. Decid. shrub to 2–3m, twigs not spinescent, glab.
Lvs 6–12cm, narrowly oblong, glossy dark green above, yellow-
green beneath, finely toothed. E & C China.
→*Frangula*.

Rhaphidophora Hassk. Araceae. 70 everg. climbers or creepers,
sometimes with juvenile and adult phases. St. stout, with
adventitious roots. Lvs in 2 ranks when juvenile (shingle plant),
entire or pinnatifid, sometimes perforate; petioles long,
geniculate at apex. Peduncle solitary; spathe, cymbiform,
yellow to green; spadix shorter than spathe. SE Asia. Z10.

R. aurea (Lind. & André) Birdsey = *Epipremnum aureum*.

R. celatocaulis (N.E. Br.) Knoll. SHINGLE PLANT. Juvenile lvs
8.5–10cm, in 2 ranks, closely adpressed, overlapping and
obscuring st., entire, elliptic-ovate, blue-green; adult lvs to
40cm, entire, pinnatifid or pinnatisect, occas. perforate, seg.
obliquely truncate. Borneo.

R. decursiva (Wallich) Schott. Lvs (adult; juvenile phase not usually cultivated) 90cm, oblong pinnatisect, seg. lanceolate,
attenuate above, constricted at base. Sri Lanka to N Burm.
→*Pothos*.

Rhaphiolepis Lindl. Rosaceae. 15 everg. shrubs or small trees.
Lvs coriaceous, glossy dark green, serrate to entire. Fls in erect
term. rac. or pan. to 10cm; cal. lobes, subulate or triangular;
pet. 5, obovate, clawed; sta. 15–20. Early spring. Subtrop. E
Asia.

R. × delacourii André. (*R. indica* × *R. umbellata*.) To 2m. Lvs
3.25–7cm, obovate, dentate toward apex, base tapered or
rounded. Fls to 1.8cm diam., rose-pink. Gdn origin. 'Coates'
Crimson': fls crimson. 'Majestic Beauty': open, branching; lvs
large, dark green; fls milky pink, scented, in clusters to 25cm
across. 'Springtime': compact, vigorous, new growth flushed
pink-brown; fls broad, candy pink. Z8.

R. indica (L.) Lindl. To 1m. Lvs to 7cm, lanceolate-acuminate,
strongly serrate. Fls to 1.6cm diam., white tinted pale pink
toward centre; sta. bright red-pink. S China. 'Charisma': small,
tightly branched; lvs rich green; fls double, soft pink, abundant,
late winter–spring. 'Enchantress': dwarf, compact; lvs glossy
green; fls small, rose, late winter–early summer. 'Indian
Princess': broadly mounding, compact, densely branched; lvs
large, bright green; fls bright pink fading to white, in broad
clusters, spring-flowering. 'Jack Evans': upright, to rounded; lvs
leathery; fls pink, in large clusters. 'Rosea': fls deep pink. 'Snow
White': spreading, vigorous; lvs dark green; fls white, in loose
clusters, in early spring. 'Spring Rapture': compact and mounding; fls rose, abundant. 'White Enchantress': dwarf, compact;
lvs glossy green; fls small, white, spring-flowering. Z8.

R. japonica Sieb. & Zucc. = *R. umbellata*.

R. ovata Briot = *R. umbellata*.

R. umbellata (Thunb.) Mak. Lvs to 9cm, broad-oval or obovate,
obtuse or abruptly acute, subentire to bluntly toothed, floccose
beneath when young. Fls fragrant to 2cm diam.; white; sta.
bright pink-red. Jap., Korea. 'Minor': dwarf, mounding; lvs
small, elongated at far tip; fls small, white, scented, early spring.
Z8.

Rhaphithamnus Miers. Verbenaceae. 2 spiny, everg. shrubs and
low trees. Rac. short, between larger spines or in lf axils; cal.,
urceolate, 5-toothed, accrescent, becoming pulpy; cor. gunnel-
shaped, 5-lobed, bilabiate; sta. 4, 2 anterior anth. exserted. Fr.
drupaceous, blue. Chile, Peru, Arg., Juan Fernandez Is. Z9.

R. cyanocarpus (Hook. & Arn.) Miers = *R. spinosus*.

R. spinosus (Juss.) Mold. PRICKLY MYRTLE. To 7m. Spines to
4cm; twigs densely pubesc. Lvs to 4cm, glossy, bright green,
elliptic ovate, apex acute, base rounded or cordate, entire
leathery, gland. Infl. axill.; cor. to 20mm, lilac, pubesc. Fr.
(cal.) to 1.2cm, blue-violet. Distribution as for the genus. Distrib. as for the genus.
→*Citharexylum* and *Volkameria*.

Rhapidophyllum H.A. Wendl. & Drude NEEDLE PALM. Palmae.
1 palm to 1.5m. St. decumbent or erect, with persistent lf bases,
dark fibres and erect spines, becoming bare. Lvs to 1m,
costapalmate; seg. semi-rigid, linear, with 2 midribs, waxy
above, silvery glaucous beneath. E coastal US. Z8.

R. hystrix (Pursh) H.A. Wendl. & Drude NEEDLE PALM;
PORCUPINE PALM; BLUE PALMETTO.

Rhapis L. f. ex Ait. LADY PALM. Palmae. 12 palms. St. clumped,
slender, cane-like, clothed with fibrous lf sheaths. Lvs palmate,
deeply divided; seg. several-fold, apices ± truncate, toothed.
China, Jap. Z9.

R. aspera var. *foliisvariegatus* hort. = *R. excelsa* 'Variegata'.

R. excelsa (Thunb.) Henry. GROUND RATTAN; BAMBOO PALM;
LADY PALM; MINIATURE FAN PALM; FERN RHAPIS. St. to
5m×4–5cm, reed-like clothed with coarse fibres, becoming
smooth. Lvs divided 3–10 times to within 5–8cm of rachis, seg.
20–30×1.5cm, tip truncate; petiole equals or exceeds blade.
Probably originally from China but introd. from Jap.
'Variegata': lvs palmate, leathery; seg. striped white. Many
other variegated forms are cultivated and highly prized,
particularly in Japan.

R. flabelliformis L'Hérit. ex Ait. = *R. excelsa*.

R. humilis Bl. REED RHAPIS; SLENDER LADY PALM. Differs from
R. excelsa in slender st. and finer sheath fibres. Lf seg. at least 9,
15–18× to 2cm, tip more acuminate; petiole equalling blade. S
China.

Rhazya Decne.

R. orientalis (Decne.) A. DC. = *Amsonia orientalis*.

Rhea *Boehmeria nivea* var. *tenacissima*.

Rheedia L. = *Garcinia*.

Rhektophyllum N.E. Br. Araceae. 1 tall everg. climber to
10m+. St. rooting, thick. Juvenile lvs to 30cm, entire, hastate to
sagittate, undulate, dark green variegated white between veins;
petiole to 40cm; adult lvs. oblong-ovate, perforated or laciniate
to form cuneate seg.; petioles to 90cm. Peduncle 5cm; spathe to
10cm, cylindric, green externally, red-purple within; spadix
shorter than spathe. Fr. an obovoid berry, 1cm, red. Trop. W
Afr. Z10.

R. mirabile N.E. Br.

Rheum L. RHUBARB. Polygonaceae. 50 stout perenn. herbs with
tough or woody rhiz. Lvs in basal clumps, large, sinuately
toothed or palmatifid; petioles often thick; stipular sheaths
(ochreae) conspicuous. Fls small, 6-merous clustered in large
pan. on erect st. with conspicuous bracts. Fr. 3-winged. Eurasia,
Asia. Z7.

R. acuminatum Hook. f. & Thoms. SIKKIM RHUBARB. To 1m,
resembling *R. australe* but smaller. Lvs to 20cm diam.,
triangular to broadly cordate, dull green above, downy beneath;
petiole slender. Pan. sparsely branched, tinted dark red-brown.
Summer. Nepal to SE Tibet. Z6.

R. alexandrae Batal. To 1.5m. Lvs to 22×13cm, ovate-oblong,
basally cordate, entire, dark green in neat rosettes, glab.;
petiole slender, equals blade. Bracts to 10cm, yellow-green,
subcordate. Fls green-yellow in remote axillary pan. Summer.
W China, Tibet. Z5.

R. australe D. Don. HIMALAYAN RHUBARB; RED-VEINED PIE PLANT.
To 3m. Lvs 40–75×30–60cm, rounded to broadly ovate, obtuse,
base cordate, hairy beneath, margins wavy; petiole stout,
300–45cm, tinged red. Infl. 20–30cm; fls in white to wine-red in
a congested, fastigiate pan. Fr. purple. Summer. Himal. Z6.

R. collinianum Baill. Habit robust, to 90cm. Lvs ovate, subcordate, deeply cut into broad lobes red beneath at first, with
unequally cut margin. Infl. dull red. China. Z6.

R. compactum L. Lvs 20–40cm diam., broadly ovate, cordate,
obtusely lobed, glab., tough and shining above, toothed, wavy.
Bracts orbicular; fls white, in a broad congested pan. Fr. red-
brown. Summer. China. Z6.

R. × cultorum Thorsrud & Reis. RHUBARB; GARDEN RHUBARB; PIE
PLANT. Resembles *R. australe*, but lvs ovate, cordate, glab.
above, hairy on veins beneath; petiole flushed red. Flowering st.
to 1.5m; fls in dense pan.; br. erect, red. An ancient and
complex hybrid, probably involving *R. rhaponticum* L. Z3.

R. emodi Wallich = *R. australe*.

R. forrestii Diels. To 80cm. Lvs slightly lobed, somewhat cordate
at base and slightly pointed. Fls white, in a long pan. on slender
pedicels. W China. Z6.

R. hybridum hort. = *R. × cultorum*.

R. moorcroftianum Royle. Robust, to 60cm. Lvs 15–30cm diam.,
glabrescent, rounded, base cordate; petiole to 15cm. Infl. shorter than in most spp., composed of erect, dense, hairy spikes,
red-green, becoming bright red in fr. Summer. C Nepal. Z7.

R. nobile Hook. f. & Thoms. SIKKIM RHUBARB. Bold, erect, to
2m. Lvs to 30cm diam., rounded, base cuneate to rounded,
glossy, leather, dark green veined red, entire, edged red; petiole
stout, red; ochreae fragile, pink. Flowering st. wiith drooping
and overlapping cream bracts; fls green. Summer. Nepal to SE
Tibet. Z7.

R. officinale Baill. Resembles *R. australe* but to 3m. Lvs reniform-orbicular, to 90cm diam., unequally cut into 5 shallow, coarsely toothed lobes. Fls in dense, branched pan., white to green-white. Summer. W China, Tibet. 'Dissectum': lvs deeply lobed. Z7.

R. palmatum L. To 1.5m. Lvs 50–90×50–70cm, ± orbicular, palmately lobed, lobes ovate to lanceolate, base cordate, hairy onveins beneath, entire to coarsely toothed. Fls in loose, pub-esc. pan., deep red. Summer. NW China. 'Atrosanguineum' ('Atropurpureum'): plant suffused blood-red. 'Bowles Crimson': lvs crimson beneath; fr. red. 'Hadspen Crimson': to 4.5m; lvs to 100×75cm, deep red; fls deep crimson. 'Irish Bronze': lvs broad, bronze, deeply cut; fls v. small, pink, along stout fl. st. 'Red Select': to 1.5m; lvs red; fls deep red. 'Rubrum': lvs flushed dark maroon-red, eesp. when young. var. *tanguticum* Reg. More robust. Lvs v. deeply lobed. Z6.

R. rhabarbarum L. = *R. ×cultorum*.

R. ribes L. St. thick, to 1.5m, leafy below. Lvs 14–42×18–70cm, rounded to reniform, base deeply cordate, dull grey-green roughly hairy or papillose beneath, finely toothed; fls in broad, erect, much-branched pan., green-white. Early-summer. SW Asia. Z6.

R. tanguticum (Reg.) Maxim. = *R. palmatum* var. *tanguticum*.

R. undulatum hort. = *R. ×cultorum*.

R. webbianum Royle. Stout, 30–20cm. Lvs 10–60cm diam., rounded-cordate to reniform with deep basal sinus. Fls in spikes forming much-branched, terminal infl., pale yellow. Summer. Himal. Z6.

R.cvs. 'Ace of Hearts' ('Ace of Spades'): lvs large, veined, crimson beneath; fls pink. 'Green Knight': to 120cm; fls white.

Rheumatism Root *Jeffersonia diphylla.*

Rhexia L. MEADOW BEAUTY; DEER GRASS. Melastomataceae. 10 erect herbs or subshrubs. Lvs opposite, simple, 3–5-veined. Fls solitary or in term. cymes; cal. tube along, bell- or urn-shaped, lobes 4, pet. 4, obovate; sta. 8. E N Amer.

R. ciliosa Michx. To 30–45cm; st. simples, smooth, 4-angled toward apex. Lvs to 2.5cm, ovate, bristly above. Fls 1–2.5cm diam., purple. Summer. SE US. Z6.

R. mariana L. To 60cm; st. terete or 6-angled, glandular-pubesc. Lvs to 3cm, elliptic to lanceolate, acute, bristly toothed. Fls 3.5–5cm diam., purple or white, exterior purple. Summer. E coastal N Amer. W to Iowa, Tex. Z4.

R. virginica L. Tuberous-rooted; st. to 45cm, 4-angled, slightly pubesc. Lvs to 5cm, ovate to lanceolate, serrulate-ciliate. Fls to 3.5cm diam., rose-purple. Summer. Nova Scotia to Flor., Iowa, Tex. Z3.

Rhigozum Burchell. Bignoniaceae. 9 spiny shrubs or trees. Lvs imparipinnate or with one pair of lfts only, from cushion-like swellings on branchlets. Fls solitary or clustered, borne from similar swellings; pedicels short; cal. 5-dentate, campanulate; cor. campanulate, 5-lobed; sta. 5. Afr., Madag. Z9.

R. obovatum Burchell. Spiny shrub or tree to 4.5m. Lvs simple or with one pair of lfts to 2cm, oblong to obovate, grey-green, apex often serrate, revolute. Fls in groups of 1–3; cor. 1.5cm, yellow funneliform-campanulate, throat hairy, lobes 9–16mm, orbicular, ciliate. Zimb., Nam., S Afr.

Rhinanthus L. Scrophulariaceae. 45 ann. herbs, semi-parasitic on grasses. Lvs sessile, opposite. Rac. spike-like term.; cal. 4-toothed, flattened; cor. tubular, 2-lipped. Summer. N Hemis., esp. Eur. Z6.

R. minor L. sensu lato. YELLOW RATTLE; HAY RATTLE. To 50cm. Lvs ovate-oblong to linear-lanceolate, crenate to dentate, dark green. Fls 12–15mm, yellow or brown, lip violet or white.

Rhinephyllum N.E. Br. Aizoaceae. 12 short-stemmed succulent perennials or shrublets. Lvs 2–4 per st., opposite, upper surface flat, lower surface round or keeled. Fls solitary, term. S Afr. (Cape Prov.). Z9.

R. broomii L. Bol. Lvs 10×7mm, lower lvs spathulate, minutely tuberculate at the tip with 4–5 marginal teeth, upper lvs hemi-spheric, densely tuberculate, olive green. Fls 1–2cm diam., yellow. W Cape.

R. macradenium (L. Bol.) L. Bol. Lvs 25–60×6–8mm, semicylindric, swollen-triquetrous ± obtuse at tip. Fls 2.5cm diam., yellow-white. S Cape.

R. muirii N.E. Br. Lvs 10–24×5–10mm, thick above, lower sur-face drawn slightly forward over the tip, covered above with white tubercles, margins and keel white, cartilaginous. Fls 12–14mm diam., yellow-white. W Cape.

R. schonlandii L. Bol. 20×12mm, broadly spathulate, square below, ± rounded and expanded above, lower surface convex, margins usually with 1–3 indistinct teeth or lobes above. Fls 16mm diam., yellow, tipped red. W Cape.
→*Peersia.*

Rhinerrhiza Rupp. Orchidaceae. 2 short-stemmed epiphytic, monopodial orchids. Roots dark, rough, papillose. Lvs 5–15cm, oblong, rigid, coriaceous. Rac. axill., pendent; fls ephemeral; tep., axill., pendent; fls ephemeral, almost filiform; lip trilobed, spur pouch-like. NE & SW Aus. Z10.

R. divitiflora (Muell. ex Benth.) Rupp. RASPY ROOT. St. 6–8cm. Lvs slightly undulate. Fls pale orange, dotted and blotched red; tep. filiform; lip white, spur to 1mm. Mid summer-mid autumn. NSW, Queensld.

R. moorei (Rchb. f.) M. Clements, B. Wallace & D. Jones. St. to 12cm. Lvs tinged pink or mauve. Fls, fragrant, tawny yellow, dotted and blotched brown; tep. spathulate; lip fleshy, white or yellow, spur to 3mm, conical. NE Aus.
→*Sarcochilus.*

Rhipogonum hort. = *Ripogonum.*

Rhipsalidopsis Britt. & Rose.
R. gaertneri (Reg.) Moran = *Hatiora gaertneri*.
R. ×graeseri (Werderm.) Moran = *Hatiora ×graeseri*.
R. rosea (Lagerh.) Britt. & Rose = *Hatiora rosea*.

Rhipsalis Gaertn. Cactaceae. To 50 epiphytic cacti, often pendulous, st. cylindric, ribbed, angled, winged or flat, usually segmented and spineless. Fls small, rotate; tube v. short or 0. Fr. small, berry-like. Trop. Amer., with one sp. extending to trop. Afr., Madag. and Sri Lanka, the only cactus sp. which occurs spontaneously outside Amer.

R. alata (Sw.) Schum. not of Steud. = *Disocactus alatus*.

R. baccifera (J.F. Mill.) W.T. Stearn. St. cylindric, pendent, 1–4m, slender, 4–6mm diam. Fl. 5–10mm diam., almost white. Fr. globose, white or pink. Winter–spring. Trop. Amer., Afr., Madag., Ceylon. Z9.

R. cassutha Gaertn. = *R. baccifera*.

R. cassytha auct. = *R. baccifera*.

R. cavernosa Lindb. = *Lepismium cruciforme*.

R. cereoides (Backeb. & Voll) Cast. Stem-seg. 3–4-angled, 4–10× up to 1–7cm, not crenate. Fls 2cm diam., white. Fr. pale pink. E Braz. Z9.

R. cereuscula Haw. St. dimorphic, the longer cylindric, 10–30cm×3–4mm, the shorter in apical clusters, branching above, 1–3cm×3–4mm, obscurely 4–5-angled. Fls campanulate, 8–15×10–20mm, white. Fr. white. NE Braz. to Arg. Z9.

R. clavata F.A.C. Weber. St. seg. cylindric-clavate, slender, truncate, to 5cm×2–3mm with whorled branchlets. Fl. campanulate, c15mm, white. Fr. white. SE Braz. Z9.

R. coriacea Polak. = *Disocactus ramulosus*.

R. crispata (Haw.) Pfeiff. Br. v. slender-cylindric then divided into flat or 3-winged, seg. 6–13×2–4cm, margins crenate or repand. Fl. 10–12mm diam., creamy white. Fr. white or tinged red. SE Braz. Z9.

R. crispimarginata Loefgr. = *R. crispata*.

R. cruciformis (Vell. conc.) Cast. = *Lepismium cruciforme*.

R. dissimilis (G.A. Lindb.) Schum. Stem-seg. variable, usually with 5–9 low ribs, sometimes 3–5-angled or terete, 5–14cm×4–10mm. Fl. buds tinged red; fls 10–15mm diam., pale yellow. Fr. pink or purple. SE Braz. Z9.

R. elliptica G.A. Lindb. ex Schum. Like *R. pachyptera*, but stem-segments less robust, 7–13×3.5–7cm, reddening in strong light. Fls. with outer tep. deep yellow. Fr. red. Winter. E Braz. Z9.

R. floccosa Salm-Dyck ex Pfeiff. Stem-seg. in whorls of 2–6, cylindric, to 25cm×5–10mm, often tinged purple, near felted areoles. Fl. 0.8–2cm diam., creamy white, buds surrounded by woolly hairs. Fr. white or pink-tinged. Winter-spring. Braz., N Parag., Arg., Boliv. Z9.

R. gaertneri (Reg.) Vaupel = *Hatiora gaertneri*.

R. gibberula F.A.C. Weber = *R. floccosa*.

R. gracilis N.E. Br. Variable, st., v. slender, main br. elongate, 10–15cm or more ×2–3mm, branchlets arising in clusters, short, 1–1.5mm diam. Fls 6–8mm diam., white. Fr. white to deep red. Autumn. E Braz. Also called *R. cribrata* (Lem.) Ruempl., *R. capilliformis* F.A.C. Weber, *R. prismatica* (Lem.) Ruempl. and *R. virgata* F.A.C. Weber. Z9.

R. grandiflora Haw., confused name. = *R. hadrosoma*.

R. hadrosoma Loefgr. Stems-seg. elongate, cylindric, to 25cm×6–12mm, tinged purple near the areoles. Fl. *c*12×20mm, creamy white. Fr. white or tinged pink to purple. Spring. Braz. Z9.

R. heteroclada Britt. and Rose = *R. gracilis*.

R. houlletiana Lem. = *Lepismium houlletianum*.

R. knightii Pfeiff. = *Lepismium cruciforme*.

R. lindbergiana Schum. = *R. baccifera*.

R. lumbricoides (Lem.) Lem. = *Lepismium lumbricoides*.

R. megalantha Loefgr. St. to 35cm×8–10mm; areoles prominent, purple-tinged. Fl. 3–4cm diam., white with pink or orange sta. Fr. off-white, tinged pink purple-red, surrounded by woolly hairs. Autumn-winter. SE Braz. Z9.

R. mesembryanthoides Haw. St. dimorphic; primary st. cylindric, elongate, 10–20cm×1–2mm, becoming woody; lat. br. numerous, terete-cylindric, stubby, 7–15×2–4mm, remaining green; areoles with a few fine bristles, c2mm. Fls lat. on the short br. (rarely on the long shoots), c8×15mm, white. Fr. white or tinged red. SE Braz. Z9.

R. micrantha (Kunth) DC. Stem-seg. flat or 3- to 5-angled, shallowly crenate. Fl. c7mm diam. Fr. white or red-tinged. Ecuad., N Peru. Z9.

R. oblonga Loefgr. Resembling *R. crispata*, but stem-seg. scarcely cylindric at base, 12–20×2–3.5cm, only 0.5–0.6mm thick. Winter. E Braz. Z9.

R. pachyptera Pfeiff. Branching dichotomous or whorled, stem-segments flat or 3–4 winged, elliptic to orbicular, to 20×9cm, thick, deeply crenate. Fl. 12×13mm, white, fragrant. Fr. white. Summer-autumn. SE Braz. Z9.

R. paradoxa (Salm-Dyck ex Pfeiff.) Salm-Dyck. St. pendent, to 5m, juveniles with bristly spines; adult branching whorled; seg. 3-angled, stiff, in a string-like arrangement. Fl. lat., rotate, 1 per areoles, 11×12–20mm, off-white. Spring. SE Braz. Z9.

R. pentaptera Pfeiff. St. to 40×6–15mm, segmented, 5–8-ribbed. Fls 7–8×12mm, white. Fr. translucent white or tinged pink. Winter-spring. S Braz., Urug. Z9.

R. pilocarpa Loefgr. St. slender-cylindric, seg. to 40×6mm, with whorled br. above, areoles tinged purple, with fine white bristles. Fl. 2.5–4cm diam., white. Fr. wine-red, bristly. Spring. SE Braz. Z9.

R. pulvinigera G.A. Lindb. Resembling *R.floccosa*, but more slender, stem-segments 3–5mm diam. Fr. deep red-pink. Winter. SE Braz. Z9.

R. puniceodiscus G.A. Lindb. Resembling *R.floccosa* but st. branched dichotomously; areoles woolly. Fl. white; sta. pink or orange. Fr. becoming orange-yellow. Winter-spring. SE Braz. Z9.

R. ramulosa (Salm-Dyck) Pfeiff. = *Disocactus ramulosus*.
R. rhombea Salm-Dyck = *R. elliptica*.
R. rosea Lagerh. = *Hatiora rosea*.
R. salicornioides Haw. = *Hatiora salicornioides*.
R. shaferi Britt. & Rose = *R. baccifera*.
R. squamulosa (Salm-Dyck) Schum. = *Lepismium cruciforme*.
R. swartziana Pfeiff. = *Disocactus alatus*.
R. teres (Vell.) Steud. = *R. baccifera*.
R. tonduzii F.A.C. Weber = *R. micrantha*.
R. trigona Pfeiff. St. to 2m or more pendent; seg. 3-winged, to 10×1.5cm, often curved or twisted. Fl. to 2cm, white or pale pink. Fr. red. Autumn-winter. SE Braz. Z9.
R. tucumanensis F.A.C. Weber = *R.floccosa*.
R. warmingiana Schum. = *Lepismium warmingianum*.
→*Erythrorhipsalis*, *Hatiora* and *Lepismium*.

Rhizobotrya Tausch. Cruciferae. 1 perenn., tuft-forming herb, 2–4cm. Lvs spathulate to oblong, blunt; petiole long. Fls small, racemose, pet. 4, short-clawed, white. S Alps. Z6.

R. alpina Tausch. ALPINE SCURVY GRASS.
→*Kernera*.

Rhodanthe Lindl. Compositae. 60–100 xerophytic, ann. to perenn. herbs and shrubs. Lvs alt., simple, ± entire. Cap. discoid, solitary or few to many in somewhat xerophyte clusters; phyllaries in many imbricate series, often petaloid and brightly coloured; receptacle flat; flts tubular. S Afr., Aus.

R. manglesii Lindl. SWAN RIVER EVERLASTING. Erect, glab. ann., to 80cm. Lvs to 10cm, oblong to ovate, base cordate, amplexicaul, glaucous. Cap. c4cm diam., solitary; phyllaries radiating, light pink, persistent; flts pink. W Aus. 'Maculatum': phyllaries spotted red.
→*Helipterum*.

Rhode Island Bent *Agrostis canina*.
Rhodesian Cycad *Encephalartos manikensis*.

Rhodiola L. Crassulaceae. c50 perenn. herbs; rhiz. thick, fleshy and branching, bearing brown, scaly radical lvs and/or foliage lvs. Ann. flowering st. arising laterally, lvs fleshy. Infl. term., a dense or spreading cyme; fls solitary to numerous; sep. 4 or 5, rarely 3 or 6, fleshy, fused near base; pet. same number as sep., free; sta. usually 8 or 10, most twice as long as pet., anth. usually dark purple. Himal., NW China, C Asia, N Amer., Eur. Z4.

R. asiatica D. Don = *R. quadrifida* or *R. wallichiana*.
R. atropurpurea Trautv. Differing from *R. rosea* in rhiz. not prominently aerial; lvs sharply dentate towards tip; pet. dark purple. Early summer. Sib., Arc., Far E. Z3.
R. atropurpurea (Turcz.) Trautv. = *R. integrifolia*.
R. bupleuroides (Wallich ex Hook. f. & Thoms.) S.H. Fu 7–90cm; rhiz. short, stout to elongate, not distinctly aerial. Flowering st. 5–45cm, erect, curving. Lvs 1–4×0.5–2cm, scattered, sessile, ovate or ligulate, apex obtuse or acute, slightly clasping cordate base, glaucous, entire or shortly dentate. Infl. a lax, 7- to numerous-fld cyme; fls. to median diam.; sep. marked purple; pet. 5. Early summer. Nepal, Yunnan. Z6.
R. dumulosa (Franch.) Fu. To 18cm. Scaly radical lvs 4–7mm, triangular; ann. st. 5–15cm, tinged red. Lvs alt., 5–25mm, linear to lanceolate-elliptic, obtuse. Infl. 4–20-fld, corymbose; fls to 8mm diam.; pet. 5, oblong-oblanceolate to narrowly ovate, cream to pale green, fleshy, finely mucronate; sta. shorter than pet., anth. dark red to purple becoming yellow. Summer. Tibet, Burm., China, Mong., Manch., N Korea. Z6.
R. elongata (Ledeb.) Fisch. & Mey. = *R. rosea*.
R. fastigiata Fu. To 15cm high, aerial parts with scaly radical lvs. Flowering st. 6–15cm, erect. Lvs 1–1.5mm, lanceolate to linear-elliptic, obtuse, entire. Infl. a 6–15-fld compound cyme; fls to 6mm diam.; sep. purple; pet. 4, linear-obovate, obtuse, red-purple. Early summer. Himal., Tibet, SW China. Z6.
R. heterodonta (Hook. f. & Thoms.) Boriss. To 40cm; rhiz. robust, branching, not clearly aerial, bearing scaly radical lvs toward top. Flowering st. few, clustered. Lvs to 10mm, ovate, acute, base cordate, clasping toothed above. Infl. dense, corymbose; fls to 3mm diam.; pet. 4, purple above, green below. Late spring. Afghan. to Nepal. Z5.
R. himalensis (D. Don) Fu. To 22cm; rhiz. thick, elongate, aerial parts with scaly radical lvs. Flowering st. 20–30cm, pubesc. Lvs alt., 5–20mm, oblanceolate, obovate, acute to obtuse, somewhat fleshy, entire. Fls to 7.5mm diam.; sep. dark red; pet. 5, ovate or broader towards tip, dark red-purple; sta. slightly shorter than pet. Summer. Bhutan, E Himal., Yunnan, Sikkim, Nepal. Z6.
R. hobsonii (Hamet) S.H. Fu. Forming a 3–4cm hummock; rhiz. branching, thick, scales 0; radical lvs 1–2cm, elliptic, petiolate, acute, entire. Flowering st. to 13cm, prostrate. Lvs 8–12mm, elliptic. Infl. a 3–12-fld, lax cyme; fls 4–5mm diam.; sep. tinged red; pet. 5, pale pink; sta. shorter than pet. or equal. Summer. Tibet. Z5.
R. integrifolia Raf. To 30cm, rhiz. sparsely branched; radical lvs scaly, 4–10mm, ovate to triangular-lanceolate. Flowering st. 5–30cm, often red-green. Lvs 5–30mm, sessile, oblanceolate to narrowly obovate-oblong ovate, glaucous, serrate toward tip. Infl. usually a 15–50-fld dense cyme; fls to 6mm diam.; sep., tinged or dotted red; pet. 4 or 5; green, red to deep purple. Early summer. Arc., Sib., Alask., W N Amer. Z2.
R. kirilowii (Reg.) Maxim. To 90cm; rhiz. branched, thick, with scaly radical lvs. Flowering st. stout, erect. Lvs 40–90mm, linear to lanceolate, crowded, sharp-toothed towards tip. Infl. a many-fld. corymbose cyme; fls to 6mm diam.; sep. red-green; pet. 5, obovate-oblanceolate, yellow-green or brown-red. Early summer. C Asia, Tibet, China, Mong. Z5.
R. minor Mill. = *R. rosea*.
R. pinnatifida Boriss. = *R. stephanii*.
R. pleurogynantha (Hand.-Mazz.) Fu = *R. primuloides*.
R. primuloides (Franch.) S.H. Fu. 3–10cm; rhiz. branching, stout or slender; radical lvs 2–3.5cm wide in rosettes of 30–50, ± orbicular entinre, minutely warty. Flowering st. 3–5cm; lvs 3–5mm, narrowly obovate to oblong, rounded apex; fls 6–8mm diam., usually solitary or to 3; pet. 5, to 6.5mm, pale pink to white; sta. 10, shorter than pet., anth. yellow. Summer. SW China. Z6.
R. purpureoviridis (Praeger) S.H. Fu. Papillose perenn., 15–40cm; rhiz. rarely branched, scaly above, radical lvs broadly ovate, rounded. Flowering st. 15–40cm. Lvs 2.5–4mm, narrowly oblong-lanceolate, margin hairy, slightly toothed. Infl. an 80–200-fld. cyme; fls 4–5mm diam.; sep. hairy outside; pet. 5, light green-yellow; anth. pale orange to purple-red. Early summer. W China, Tibet. Z6.
R. quadrifida (Pall.) Fisch. & C.A. Mey. To 12.5cm; rhiz. branching, aerial parts densely scaly radical lvs 4–8mm deltoid. Flowering st. 1–5cm, delicate. Lvs alt., 3–7mm, linear, obtuse, entire, red with age. Infl. usually solitary, fls to 4mm diam.; pet. 4, yellow or red-purple sometimes red-tipped, anth. red-yellow. Summer. C Asia, Himal., Arc., Sib., Russia. Z2.
R. rhodantha (Gray) Jacobsen. To 40cm; rhiz. branching, thick, aerial part with scaly radical lvs. Flowring st. erect, stout. Lvs 15–25mm, oblong, fleshy, acute, entire. Infl. a dense rac.; fls to 3mm diam., bell-shaped; sep. tinged red; pet. 5, pink-red to white; sta. shorter than pet., anth. purple. Summer. W US. Z4.
R. roanensis Britt. = *R. rosea*.
R. rosea L. ROSE-ROOT. 5–30cm; rhiz. thick, branching; scaly radical lvs 2–5mm, triangular to ovate. Flowering st. 1–3, rarely more. Lvs 7–40mm, glaucous, variably oblong, apex obtuse to

acuminate, tinged red, base round or slightly cordate, entire to irregularly serrate. Infl. a 25–50- or as many as 70-fld corymbose to umbellate cyme; fls to 6mm diam.; sep. green-yellow; pet. 4, green-yellow; sta. 8, anth. deep yellow. Early summer. N hemis.; extremely variable. Z1.

R. semenowii Boriss. To 60cm; rhiz. branching, thick, aerial parts with scaly radical lvs. Flowering st. erect, fleshy, stout. Lvs 30–70mm, linear-elongate, acute, entire; infl. dense, racemose cyme; fls to 9mm diam.; sep. red; pet. 5, green-white to red-tinged; sta. equal pet., anth. yellow to red. Summer. C Asia. Z6.

R. sinica Diels = *R. yunnanensis* ssp. *yunnanensis*.

R. sinuata (Royle ex Edgew.) S.H. Fu. 5–30cm; rhiz. to 20cm, branched; foliage radical lvs 0; scaly radical lvs 1.5–5×1–4mm, deltoid. Flowering st. 15–30cm. Lvs alt., 15–40mm, papillate, deflexed, blunt, crowded at tips, sessile, narrowly oblanceolate, dentate to lobed above, papillate, grooved above. Infl. a 3- to many-fld cyme, lax to compact, leafy; pedicel hairy; fls. to 12mm diam.; sep., deltoid, obtuse; pet. 5, white-tinged, red or green below, sometimes deep pink; sta. 10, shorter than pet. with anth. pale to deep red-purple. Late summer. Kashmir to Tibet. Z6.

R. stephanii (Cham.) Trautv. & Mey. To 25cm; rhiz. branching, aerial part scaly, foliage radical lvs 0; scaly radical lvs 3–5mm, ovate to oblong. Flowering st. 10–25cm. Lvs alt., 2.5–4mm, larger towards tip of st., scattered, broadly oblanceolate or narrower, obtuse to acute, glab., yellow-green, deeply toothed. Infl. a dense, 30–60-fld cyme; fls to 9mm diam.; sep. 4 or 5, fleshy, cream, red-tinged; pet. 4, occas. 5, pale cream-white, obtuse; sta. 8, same length as pet. anth. deep brown-red. Summer. Sib., Far E. Z5.

R. tibetica S.H. Fu. 7–25cm; rhiz. often branched, scaly radical lvs dense towards top, broadly triangular. Flowering st. 7–25cm. Lvs alt., 5–12mm, scattered, oblong-ovate, glab., entire to serrate. Infl. a 20–40-fld cyume; fls 4–6mm diam.; sep. 5, fleshy, triangular to subulate; pet. usually 5, oblong, sta. longer than pet., 0 in females. Summer. W Himal., Tibet. Z6.

R. wallichiana (Hook.) S.H. Fu. To 30cm; rhiz. sometimes stoloniferous, aerial part scaly. Flowering st. 15–30cm. Lvs 10–30mm, along st., paired, linear, glab., toothed towards apex, grooved above. Infl. a dense few-fld cyme; fls to 12mm diam.; sep. 5, almost free; pet. 5, elliptic, concave, white to pale yellow, sometimes tinged pink; sta. same length as pet., anth. orange turning dark purple. Summer-early autumn. Himal., W China. Z6.

R. yunnanensis (Franch.) S.H. Fu. to 60cm, sometimes 100cm; rhiz. branched, scaly above. Lvs whorled, 2–14cm, ovate to linear-oblong, obtuse to acute, base rounded or cordate, somewhat dentate, glab. Infl. a many-fld paniculate cyme; fls 2.5–3.5mm diam.; sep. (4–)5(–6), rounded; pet. 5, occas. 4 or 6, obovate to oblanceolate, apex rounded, reflexed, yellow-green; sta. shorter than pet. anth. dark red. Summer. SW China. ssp. *yunnanensis* Franch. Lvs variably ovate, more than 1.5mm wide. Summer. Widespread, SW & C China, Burm., SE Tibet, Assam. ssp. *forestii* (Hamet) H. Ohba. Lvs narrow to oblong-linear, 19–44×4–11mm. Summer. SW China. Z6.
→*Chamaerhodiola, Clementsia* and *Sedum*.

Rhodocactus (A. Berger) F. Knuth.
R. antonianus Backeb. = *Pereskia weberiana*.

Rhodochiton Otto & Dietr. Scrophulariaceae. 3 perenn., climbing herbs. St. slender, twining. Lvs cordate to deltoid, serrulate; petioles twining. Fls pendulous, solitary; cal. inflated, cup-like, divisions shallow, lobes acute; cor. tube slender, lobes 5 obtuse; sta. 4, anth. exserted. Summer. Mex. Z9.

R. atrosanguineum (Zucc.) Rothm. To 6m. Lvs to 4cm, cordate or obscurely 5-lobed. Cal. to 3cm diam. acutely 5-lobed, membranous, shallow-campanulate, rose-pink or mauve; cor. blood-red to maroon-black, to 6.5cm, minutely glandular-pubesc.; sta., slender, anth. ash-white.

R. volubile Otto & Dietr. = *R. atrosanguineum*.

Rhodocistus Spach.
R. berthelotianus Spach = *Cistus symphytifolius*.
R. osbekiifolius Webb ex Christ = *Cistus osbekiifolius*.

Rhododendron L. Ericaceae. 700–800 trees and shrubs, largely everg. Lvs usually entire, sometimes revolute, veins obscure or sunken, conspicuous, glossy or bristly and/or with hairs and scales. Fls in lat. or term. rac., sometimes solitary; bracteoles 2, bract- or thread-like, usually caducous; cal. lobes 5+ or ± 0; cor. tubular, campanulate, funnelform or ± rotate, usually 5-lobed, sometimes with dark basal nectar pouches; sta. (5–)10(–27), radial or declinate, ovary 5-celled, style straight, declinate or deflexed. Cosmopolitan. For Azalea and Rhododendron

hybrids and cvs, see *Rhododendron* in *The New RHS Dictionary of Gardening*.

R. aberconwayi Cowan. To 2m. Lvs 3–6cm, thick, elliptic. Cor. 2.8–3.5cm, open-campanulate, white to pale rose with purple spots. SW China. 'His Lordship': fls white with crimson streaks. Z7.

R. achroanthum Balf. f. & W.W. Sm. = *R. rupicola* var. *rupicola*.

R. adenogynum Diels. Shrub or small tree to 4m. Lvs 6–11cm, elliptic or narrowly so lower surface with a usually dense spongy covering of ramiform hairs, yellowish at first, olive-brown when mature; cor. 3–4.5cm, campanulate, white flushed pink or pale pink. SW China. Adenophorum Group: br. and petioles gland., 'Kirsty': fls white, upper pet. and outside of fls flushed and spotted with purple. Z6.

R. adenophorum Balf. f. & W.W. Sm. = *R. adenogynum*.

R. aechmophyllum Balf. f. & Forr. = *R. yunnanense*.

R. aeruginosum Hook. = *R. campanulatum* ssp. *aeruginosum*.

R. aganniphum Forr. & W.W. Sm. To 3m. Lvs 4–12cm, elliptic to broadly ovate-lanceolate, lower surface with densely covering of compacted, ramiform hairs, white-yellow at first, becoming brown. Cor. 3–3.5cm, campanulate, white, often flushed with pink. SW China. var. *aganniphum*. Lf hairs pale. var. *flavorufum* (Balf. f. & Forr.) Chamberl. Lf hairs becoming deep red-brown and patchy. Z7.

R. agapetum Balf. f. & Kingdon-Ward = *R. kyawi*.

R. aiolosalpinx Balf. f. & Forr. = *R. stewartianum*.

R. alabamense Rehd. Shrub to 5m. Lvs 3–7.5×2–2.5cm, oblong-elliptic, obovate or elliptic, ciliate, usually hairy, pale or grey-green beneath with usually dense hairs. Fls fragrant, opening with the lvs 3–3.5cm, funnel-shaped white with a yellow blotch. SE US. Z7.

R. albiflorum Hook. to 2m. Lvs 2.5–7cm, oblong-elliptic, oblong or obovate, hairy above when young, glab. beneath except for long, adpressed hairs on the midrib. Fls to 2cm, open-campanulate, white, rarely spotted yellow or orange. N Amer. Z4.

R. albrechtii Maxim. To 2m. Lvs 4–12cm, obovate, ciliate, finely toothed, densely grey-tomentose beneath. Before or with the lvs. Fls to 5cm, openly campanulate, red-purple. Jap. 'Michael McLaren': fls purple, spotted with yellow-green. Z5.

R. album Buch.-Ham. = *R. arboreum* ssp. *cinnamomeum* var. *roseum*.

R. alutaceum Balf. f. & W.W. Sm. To 4.5m. Lvs 5–17cm, oblong to oblanceolate, lower surface with a 2-layered indumentum, brown or reddish. Fls 3–4cm, campanulate to funnel-campanulate, white to pink with crimson spots, sometimes with a purple basal blotch. SW China. Z7.

R. amagianum Mak. To 5m. Lvs 4.5–11.5×3–9cm, rhomboid to ovate, minutely toothed, with long, slender hairs above, lower surface pale green, sparsely strigose. Fls 2.5–4cm, openly campanulate, red or orange-red. Late spring. Jap. Z7.

R. amoenum (Lindl.) Planch. = *R. ×obtusum* 'Amoenum'.

R. annae Franch. To 6m. Lvs 6–15cm, elliptic to oblanceolate, glab. when mature with punctate hair bases on veins beneath. Fls 2.5–4cm, open-campanulate, white with a flush, sometimes with purple spots. SW China, NE Burm. 'Folks Wood': fls white. Z7.

R. anthopogon D. Don. Small shrub to 1m. Lvs 1–3.5cm, ovate or elliptic, dark scaly beneath. Fls 1–2cm, usually white or pink, rarely cream or yellowish. Himal., W China. 'Betty Graham': fls deep pink. var. *anthopogon*. Lf bud-scales quickly decid. var. *hypenanthum* (Balf. f.) Cullen. Lf bud-scales persistent. 'Annapurna': compact, fls yellow foliage dark. Z7.

R. anthosphaerum Diels. Shrub or tree to 12m. Lvs 6–16cm, elliptic-obovate to oblong, glab. at maturity with punctate hair bases beneath. Fls 3–4.5cm, 6–7-lobed, tubular-campanulate, pink, crimson, magenta or peach-coloured, sometimes with darker spots and basal blotch. SW China, NE Burm. Z8.

R. anwheiense Wils. = *R. maculiferum* ssp. *anwheiense*.

R. aperantum Balf. f. & Kingdon-Ward. Dwarf matted shrub to 1.5m. Lvs 1.4–2.4cm, obovate to oblanceolate, glab. when mature glaucous beneath. Fls 3–4.5cm, tubular-campanulate, white or yellow flushed with pink to orange or red. SW China, NE Burm. Z8.

R. apiculatum Rehd. & Wils. = *R. concinnum*.

R. apodectum Balf. f. & W.W. Sm. = *R. dichroanthum* ssp. *apodectum*.

R. araiophyllum Balf. f. & W.W. Sm. Differs from *R. annae* in lvs without punctate hair-bases. SW China, NE Burm. 'George Taylor': fls white with red-purple blotch and spots. Z8.

R. arborescens Torr. Shrub to 3m, rarely tree-like and to 6m. Lvs 3–8×1.5–2.5cm, obovate to oblong-lanceolate, bright green and glab. above, glaucous, sparingly strigose or glab. beneath. Fls opening with or after the lvs, fragrant, 4–5cm, funnel-shaped, white or pink. S US. 'Ailsa': fls white with yellow blotch. Z4.

R. arboreum Sm. Tree to 50m. Lvs 6.5–19cm, glab. and wrinkled above, densely hairy beneath; fls. 3–5cm, tubular-campanulate, fleshy, pink to deep crimson or rarely white, often with dark spots. Himal., China to Thail., S India and Sri Lanka. ssp. *arboreum* Lvs ± flat, 8–19cm, with a silvery or white indumentum beneath. Himal. 'Goat Fell': fls cherry red with some spots in throat. 'Rubaiyat': fls red with darker spots. ssp. *cinnamomeum* (Lindl.) Tagg. Lvs flat, 6.5–11cm. var. *cinnamomeum* Lindl. Lvs off-white or fawn hairy cor. pink to red, rarely white. Himal. 'Sir Charles Lemon': fls creamy white; lvs dark green above with bright orange-brown indumentum beneath. var. *roseum* Lindl. Similar to var. *cinnamomeum*, but the lvs have a 1-layered, fawn to off-white compacted indumentum, fls tinged red. Himal. 'Tony Schilling': fls deep pink with darker spots. ssp. *delavayi* (Franch.) Chamberl. Lvs 7–15.5cm, off-white to fawn – hairy beneath; cor. red. E India, Burm., China to Thail. ssp. *nilagiricum* (Zenk.) Tagg. Leaf-apex rounded. S India. ssp. *zeylanicum* (Booth) Tagg. Lvs strongly concave; cor. red. Sri Lanka. Z7.

R. argenteum Hook. = *R. grande*.

R. argyrophyllum Franch. To 12m. Lvs 1.8–6cm, elliptic to oblanceolate, glab. above, with thin, silvery to fawn hairs beneath. Fls 3–5.5cm, funnel-campanulate or open-campanulate, white to pale pink with purple spots. SW China. ssp. *argyrophyllum* Ovary and pedicels eglandular. ssp. *hypoglaucum* (Hemsl.) Chamberl. Pedicels gland. 'Heane Wood': fls white, flushed and spotted with purple, opening from pink buds. Z6.

R. arizelum Balf. f. & Forr. = *R. rex* ssp. *arizelum*.

R. artosquameum Balf. f. & Forr. = *R. oreotrephes*.

R. astrocalyx Balf. f. & Forr. = *R. wardii* var. *wardii*.

R. atlanticum Rehd. Low stoloniferous shrub to 60cm. Lvs obovate or oblong-obovate, bright blue-green above, sparingly strigose beneath. Fls v. fragrant; cor. 3–4cm, funnel-shaped, white or flushed with pink or purple. Late spring. US (Delaware to S Georgia). 'Seaboard': fls white, cor. tube pink. Z6.

R. aucklandii Hook. = *R. griffithianum*.

R. augustinii Hemsl. Shrub or small tree to 10m. Lvs narrowly elliptic to elliptic, uusally everg., 4–11×1.5–4cm, glab. above, golden scaly beneath. Fls 2.8–4cm, openly funnel-shaped, purple, lavender or almost blue, rarely white, with greenish or brownish spots inside, outside of the tube scaly or sparsely hairy. China. 'Electra' (ssp. *augustinii* × ssp. *chasmanthum*): fls large, deep blue. 'Magor's Form': fls lavender-blue, white at base with green eye. 'Tower Court form': fls large, lavender-blue, red veins and anth. ssp. *augustinii*. Lvs mostly everg.; cor. lavender to blue. E Sichuan, Hubei. ssp. *chasmanthum* (Diels) Cullen. Lvs mostly everg.; cor. lavender to blue, tube hairy, not scaly outside. N Yunnan, NW Sichuan, Xizang. Exbury form: fls blue-purple with some yellow spots. Z6.

R. aureum Georgi. To 1m. Lvs 2.5–15cm, ovate to broadly elliptic, glab. when mature. Fls 2.5–3cm, widely campanulate, usually yellow, often spotted. E Russia, Korea, Jap., N China. Z2.

R. auriculatum Hemsl. Shrub or tree to 6m. Lvs 15–30cm, oblong-oblanceolate, base auriculate, margin fringed with small glands, villous and gland. beneath. Fls 8–11cm, fragrant, 7-lobed, funnel-shaped, white or cream to pink, tinged green at the base. Late spring. W China. Z6.

R. auritum Tagg. To 2m, bark grey, rough. Lvs 5–10cm, oblong-elliptic to elliptic, brown-green above, brown and scaly beneath. Fls 1.8–2.8cm, narrowly campanulate, v. pale yellow or cream, occas. with a pink flush. SW China. Z8.

R. austrinum Rehd. To 3m. Lvs 3–9cm, elliptic to oblong-obovate, finely pubesc. Fls 3.5cm, funnel-shaped, tube abruptly expanded at the apex, usually tinged purple or with 5 purple stripes, lobes yellow and orange. Late spring. SE US. Z6.

R. bachii Lév. = *R. ovatum*.

R. baeticum Boiss. & Reut. = *R. ponticum*.

R. baileyi Balf. f. To 2m. Lvs 2–5cm, elliptic, with persistent dark brown and overlapping scales beneath. Fls 1.2–1.5cm, magenta to purple, ext. usually densely scaly. Himal., W China. Z7.

R. bainbridgeanum Tagg & Forr. To 2m. Lvs 8–12cm, obovate to elliptic, glab. above and with a continuous, felted, dark brown indumentum with glands beneath. Fls 3–3.5cm, campanulate, white to cream-yellow, usually flushed pink. SW China, NE Burm. Z8.

R. bakeri Lemmon & McKay = *R. calendulaceum*.

R. balfourianum Diels. To 4.5m. Lvs 4.5–12cm, ovate-lanceolate to elliptic, densely hairy beneath, silver to pink-brown, glossy. Fls 3.5–4cm, campanulate, pale to deep pink, with purple spots. SW China. Z6.

R. barbatum G. Don. Shrub or tree to 6m; bark usually smooth. Lvs 9–19cm, elliptic to obovate, glab. above, with scattered hairs and glands beneath. Fls 3–3.5cm, fleshy, tubular-campanulate, crimson to blood-red or rarely pure white. Himal. Z7.

R. basilicum Balf. f. & W.W. Sm. Shrub or tree to 10m. Lvs 17–25cm, obovate to oblanceolate, glab. above with deeply

impressed veins, grey, later red-brown, hairs beneath. Fls 3.5–5cm, fleshy, 8-lobed, obliquely campanulate, pale yellow with a crimson blotch. SW China, NE Burm. Z8.

R. bathyphyllum Balf. f. & Forr. To 1.5m. Lvs 4–7cm, elliptic to oblong, dark red-brown hairy beneath. Fls 3–3.5cm, campanulate, white flushed pink, with red spots. SW China. Z8.

R. bauhiniiflorum Hutch. = *R. triflorum* var. *bauhiniiflorum*.

R. beanianum Cowan. To 3m. Lvs 6–9cm, obovate to elliptic, finely wrinkled above with dense, brown hairs. Fls. 3.5cm, fleshy, tubular-campanulate, carmine to blood-red. NE India, NE Burma. 'Compactum': lvs more glossy above, with thicker, paler hairs beneath. Z8.

R. beesianum Diels. Shrub or tree to 9m. Lvs 9–19cm, oblanceolate to elliptic, with thin fawn to brown hairs beneath. Fls. 3.5–4.5(–5.5)cm, broadly campanulate, white flushed pink or red, sometimes with purple spots and a purple basal blotch. SW China. Z7.

R. benthamianum Hemsl. = *R. concinnum*.

R. blandfordiiflorum Hook. = *R. cinnabarinum* ssp. *cinnabarinum*.

R. bodinieri Franch. Material in cult. under this name may be *R. rigidum* and *R. siderophyllum*.

R. boothii Nutt. To 2m, often epiphytic. Lvs 7.5–11.5cm, narrowly ovate to ovate-oblong, lower surface dark brown with close, equal scales. Fls 2.5–2.7cm, campanulate, dull yellow, scaly. E India, W China. Z9.

R. brachyanthum Franch. To 2m. Lvs 3.5–5.5cm, narrowly elliptic to narrowly obovate. Scaly beneath. Fls 1–2cm, campanulate, pale or green-yellow. NE Burm., W China. 'Jaune': fls primrose yellow. ssp. *brachyanthum*. Scales on lower leaf-surface sparse. C Yunnan. ssp. *hypolepidotum* (Franch.) Cullen. Scales on lower lf surface much closer. NE Burm., NW Yunnan. 'Blue Light': fls translucent yellow. Z6.

R. brachycarpum G. Don. To 3m. Lvs 7–11cm, oblong to obovate, glab., often with compacted grey to fawn, hairs beneath dumentum. Fls to 2.5cm, broadly funnel-campanulate, white to pale pink, with green-spots. Jap., Korea. ssp. *brachycarpum* Lvs with persistent hairs beneath. ssp. *fauriei* (Franch.) Chamberl. Lvs glab. beneath when mature. Z6.

R. brachysiphon Hutch. = *R. maddenii* ssp. *maddenii*.

R. bracteatum Rehd. & Wils. To 2m, with thin, scaly br. Lvs to 3.5cm, ovate to elliptic, scaly beneath with somewhat distant, golden scales. Fls 1.5–2.5cm, openly funnel-shaped, white with many red-purple spots, sparsely scaly. Spring. W China. Z8.

R. brevistylum Franch. = *R. heliolepis* var. *brevistylum*.

R. brookeanum Lindl. Shrub to 2m. Lvs 12–25cm, in false whorls of 3–4(–5), oblong to lanceolate-oblong, pitted, ultimately scaleless. Fls funnel-shaped, 5–9cm, orange-pink with a white or cream centre, more rarely white, brick-red or yellow. Winter. Borneo, Sumatra. 'Kinabalu Mandarin': fls red, bright yellow in throat. 'Raja': fls yellow. Z10.

R. bullatum Franch. = *R. edgeworthii*.

R. bureavii Franch. Shrub to 3(–6)m. Lvs 4.5–12cm, elliptic, dense, woolly-hairy beneath, hairs pink when young, becoming rich rusty red. Fls 2.5–4cm, campanulate, white flushed with pink to pink, sometimes with purple spots. SW China. 'Ardrishaig': fls pale pink flushed with deeper pink, red-spotted inside, opening from deep pink buds. Z6.

R. burmanicum Hutch. To 2m. Lvs 5–5.5cm, obovate, dark green and densely scaly above scaly beneath. Fls 3–3.5cm, funnel-campanulate, green-yellow, ext. scaly. Late spring. C Burm. Z9.

R. caeruleum Lév. = *R. rigidum*.

R. caesium Hutch. To 2m.Lvs ± everg., 3–4.2cm, oblong-elliptic or oblong-ovate, glab. above, white-papillose with distant distant, golden scales beneath. Fls 1.8–2cm, funnel-campanulate, scaly outside, yellow. Late spring. SW China. Z8.

R. calendulaceum (Michx.) Torr. Much-branched shrub to 3m. Lvs 3.5–9cm, elliptic to broadly elliptic or ovate-oblong, finely pubesc. above, more densely so beneath. Fls scarcely fragrant; appearing with the lvs to 5cm, funnel-shaped, ext. pubesc., orange, red or yellow, more rarely pink. Late spring. SE US. Involved in the parentage of the decid. azalea hybrids. 'Alhambra': fls bright orange-red. 'Burning Light': fls coral red, orange in throat. 'Camp's Red': fls rich red. 'Croceum': fls rich yellow. 'Luteum': fls yellow. 'Roseum': fls pink. 'Smoky Mountaineer': fls almost scarlet. Z5.

R. californicum Hook. = *R. macrophyllum*.

R. callimorphum Balf. f. & W.W. Sm. To 2m. Lvs 3.5–7cm, broadly ovate to orbicular, glab. above, and gland. beneath. Fls 3–4cm, campanulate, white to rose-pink, sometimes with purple spots and a faint basal blotch. SW China. var. *callimorphum*. Fls pink. var. *myiagrum* (Balf. f. & Forr.) Chamberl. Fls white. Z7.

R. calophytum Franch. Tree to 12m. Lvs 14–30cm, oblong-oblanceolate, glab. when mature. Fls 4–6cm, 5–7-lobed, open-campanulate, glab., pink-white with purple spots and a bsal blotch. SW China. Z6.

R. calostrotum Balf. f. & Kingdon-Ward. Prostrate, matted or erect shrub, 5–150cm. Lvs 1–3.3cm, oblong-ovate to almost circular, upper surface usually matt with persistent, dried-out scales, margins bristly, lower surface with dense overlapping scales. Fls 1.8–2.8cm, magenta or rarely pink or purple, often with darker spots on the upper lobes, ext. hairy and occas. scaly; ovary scaly but glab. NE India, N Burm., W China. 'Gigha': compact, v. free-flowering fls large, rosy-crimson. Rock's form: fls large, blue-purple; foliage purple-tinged. ssp. *calostrotum*. Lvs 1.2–2.2cm×7–20mm, persistently scaly above, obtuse. N Burm., W China. ssp. *riparium* (Kingdon-Ward) Cullen. Like ssp. *calostrotum* but fls 2–5 in each rac., flower-stalks 1–1.5cm. NE India, NE Burm., W China. 'Calciphilum': pink fls and smaller lvs. 'Nitens': pink-purple fls in June-July, later than other cvs; lvs green. ssp. *keleticum* (Balf. f. & Forr.) Cullen. Prostrate shrublet; lvs 2–9mm wide, acute, without scales, shining dark green above. NE Burm., W China. Variants of this ssp. have been called *R. radicans*; one of these is a parent of 'Radmosum' (×*R. racemosum*). Z6.

R. caloxanthum Balf. f. & Farrer = *R. campylocarpum* ssp. *caloxanthum*.

R. camelliiflorum Hook. Shrub. Lvs 6–10cm, narrowly elliptic to oblong-elliptic, shining dark green above, pale green to brown-tinged beneath with dense scales. Fls 1.4–2cm, waxy with a short broad tube, white to deep pink, scaly outside. Late spring. Himal. Z9.

R. campanulatum D. Don. Shrub or small tree to 4.5m. Lvs ovate to broadly elliptic, 7–14cm, glab. above when mature, dense, brown, woolly-hairy beneath. Fls open-campanulate, 3–5cm, white to pale mauve or pink, usually with purple spots. Himal. 'Knaphill': fls lavender blue. 'Roland Cooper': fls white, tinged with mauve. 'Waxen Bell': fls purple, spotted with deeper purple. ssp. *campanulatum*. Lvs 9.5–14cm, without blue, metallic bloom when young. ssp. *aeruginosum* (Hook.) Chamberl. Lvs 7–10cm, with a blue metallic bloom when young. Z5.

R. campbelliae Hook. = *R. arboreum* ssp. *cinnamomeum* var. *cinnamomeum*.

R. campylocarpum Hook. Shrub or small tree to 5m. Lvs 3–10cm, orbicular to elliptic, glab., rarely with a few red-tinged glands near base beneath. Fls 2.5–4cm, campanulate, pale sulphur yellow, sometimes tinged with red in bud, with or without a basal blotch. Himal., SW China, NE Burm. ssp. *campylocarpum*. Lvs elliptic. Himal. and W China. Elatum group: taller plants; fls spotted and blotched with red. ssp. *caloxanthum* (Balf. f. & Farrer) Chamberl. Lvs orbicular. W China, NE Burm. Z6.

R. campylogynum Franch. Creeping, prostrate or decumbent shrub to 60cm, rarely rather erect and to 1m. Lvs 1–3.5cm, obovate or narrowly elliptic, dark green above, papillose, often off-white or silver beneath. Fls 1–2.5cm, pink to red or purple, bloomed and scaleless outside. E India, NE Burm., W China. 'Album': fls white. 'Beryl Taylor': fls red-purple. 'Crushed Strawberry': fls strawberry pink. 'Esther Berry': v. dwarf form with plum pink fls. 'Hillier's Pink': fls pink. 'Leucanthum': fls white. 'Patricia': fls plum red. Celsum Group: erect plants, growing to almost 2m. Charopeum Group: fls large, c2.5cm. Cremastum Group: erect plants over 1m high; lvs pale green on both surfaces; 'Bodnant Red': fls almost a true red; 'Thimble': fls salmon pink. Myrtilloides group: c15cm high; fls dusky pink, c1cm long. Z7.

R. camtschaticum Pall. Creeping shrublet to 20cm. Lvs 2–5cm, ± obovate, midrib and margins at first with gland-tipped hairs. Fls to 2.5cm, v. openly campanulate, pink-purple, ext. hairy. Late spring. Alask. and adjacent Russia. Z5.

R. canadense (L.) Torr. Slender shrub to 1m. Lvs 1.5–6cm, elliptic to oblong, dull blue green and sparsely strigose above, thinly hairy beneath. Fls to 2cm, v. openly campanulate, 2-lipped, rose purple or white. E N Amer. 'Albiflorum': fls white, lvs glaucous. Z3.

R. canescens (Michx.) Sweet. Slender shrub to 5m. Lvs 2–8cm, oblong-obovate to oblanceolate, sparsely pubesc. above, densely pubesc. beneath. Fls 3–4cm, funnel-shaped, tube wide-ning abruptly, etxt. villous, pink throughout or lobes white. SE US. Z7.

R. cantabile Hutch. = *R. russatum*.

R. capitatum Maxim. Compact or rounded shrub to 1.5m. Lvs 1–2.2cm, elliptic or oblong-elliptic, undersurface pale brown with darker speckling. Fls 1–1.5cm, broadly funnel-shaped, pale lavender to blue-purple or deep purple. W China. Z8.

R. cardiobasis Sleumer = *R. orbiculare* ssp. *cardiobasis*.

R. carolinianum Rehd. = *R. minus*.

R. catacosmum Tagg. Shrub to 3m. Lvs 8–10cm, obovate, glab. above, brown-tomentose beneath. Fls to 4.5cm, tubular-

campanulate, crimson. SW China. Z7.

R. catawbiense Michx. Shrub to 3m. Lvs 6.5–11.5cm, broadly elliptic to obovate, glab. when mature. Fls 3–4.5cm, funnel-campanulate, usually lilac-purple with faint spots. Late spring. E US. 'Album': fls large, white, opening from lilac buds; foliage mid-green; heat resistant. 'English Roseum': fls bright pink, faintly tinged with lilac; heat resistant. 'Lavender Queen': medium-sized; fls pale lavender. 'Lee's Dark Purple': fls deep purple. 'Powell Glass': fls pure white. 'Roseum Elegans': vigorous fl.; fls purple-pink. Some of the above forms, widely grown in the US, may be hybrids. Z4.

R. caucasicum Pall. Small shrub to 1m. Lvs 4–7.5cm, obovate to elliptic, glab. above, beneath with dense fawn to brown hairs. Fls 3–3.5cm, broadly campanulate, white to yellow, sometimes flushed with pink, and with green spots. Late spring. Turk., Russia (Cauc.). 'Cunningham's Sulphur': fls pale sulphur yellow with green marks inside; lvs glossy green. Z6.

R. cephalanthoides Balf. f. & W.W. Sm. = *R. primuliflorum*.

R. cephalanthum Franch. Variably sized, often contorted and sometimes prostrate shrub, 10–120cm high. Lvs 1.5–4.5cm, broadly elliptic to almost circular, dark, glossy green above, lower surface fawn to brown or rusty with dense golden scales. Fls 1–2.2cm, white or pink, rarely yellow, lobes often with a few scales outside. N India, NE Burm., W China. Z7.

R. cerasinum Tagg. Shrub to 3.5m. Lvs 4.5–7cm, narrowly obovate to elliptic, glab. except for a few hair-bases beneath. Fls campanulate, 3.5–4.5cm, crimson, scarlet or white with a deep pink border. SW China, NE Burm. 'Cherry Brandy': fls creamy white with red margins. 'Coals of Fire': fls scarlet. Z7.

R. chaetomallum Balf. f. & Forr. = *R. haematodes* ssp. *chaeto-mallum*.

R. chamaethomsonii (Tagg & Forr.) Cowan & Davidian. Dwarf shrub, rarely to 1m. Lvs 2–6cm, broadly obovate to elliptic, glab. above, glab. or sparsely addpressed off-white tomentose be-neath. Fls 2.5–4.5cm, fleshy, campanulate, pink to deep crimson. SW China. Z7.

R. chameunum Balf. f. & Forr. = *R. saluenense* ssp. *chameunum*.

R. chapmanii Gray = *R. minus* var. *chapmanii*.

R. charianthum Hutch. = *R. davidsonianum*.

R. charidotes Balf. f. & Forr. = *R. saluenense* ssp. *saluenense*.

R. charitostreptum Balf. f. & Kingdon Ward = *R. cephalanthum*.

R. chartophyllum Franch. = *R. yunnanense*.

R. chasmanthoides Balf. f. & Forr. = *R. augustinii* ssp. *chasman-thum*.

R. chasmanthum Diels = *R. augustinii* ssp. *chasmanthum*.

R. chloranthum Balf. f. & Forr. = *R. mekongense* var. *melinan-thum*.

R. chrysanthum Pall. = *R. aureum*.

R. chryseum Balf. f. & Kingdon-Ward = *R. rupicola* var. *chry-seum*.

R. ciliatum Hook. Shrub to 2m. Lvs 4.5–9cm, elliptic to narrowly elliptic, upper surface bristly, lower surface with scattered scales. Fls 3–4.5cm, campanulate to funnel-campanulate, white or white flushed pink. Himal. Z7.

R. ciliicalyx Franch. V. similar to *R. dendricola*, but lvs with rather dense but not overlapping scales beneath; cor. white or pink, 5–6cm. Late spring. W China. Z7.

R. ×cilpinense hort. An early-flowering hybrid between *R. moupinense* and *R. cilatum*.

R. cinnabarinum Hook. Straggling shrub to 7m. Lvs 3–9cm, usu-ally everg., broadly to narrowly elliptic, scaly or scaleless above, beneath with rather fleshy scales which are often tinged red or purple. Fls 2.5–3.5cm, tubular-campanulate to campanulate, yellow, orange (sometimes with a purple flush), red, red and yellow or purple, usually with a waxy bloom, ext. sometimes scaly. Himal. to N Burm. ssp. *cinnabarinum*. Most lvs everg., usually without scales above; cor. tubular-campanulate, not scaly outside, usually with some red, never purple. Himal. to W China. 'Aestivale': a late-flowering form (July) with narrow lvs. 'Mount Everest': fls apricot, more open than usual. 'Nepal': fls red at base, yellow towards margin. Blandfordiiflorum Group: fls narrowly tubular, red on outside, yellow, apricot or green in-side; late-flowering, hardy; 'Bodnant': fls vermilion red at base on outside, paling towards rim. Roylei group: fls rose-red to purple-red, relatively wide open; lvs glaucous blue-green. 'Crarae Crimson': fls plum-crimson; 'Magnificum': fls large, red-purple tinged with orange; 'Vin Rosé': fls red with a waxy bloom. ssp. *xanthocodon* (Hutch.) Cullen. Most lvs everg., without scales above; cor. campanulate, not scaly outside, yellow, orange, orange with a purple flush or purple. E India, Bhutan, China. Concatenans group: fls bell-shaped, apricot to coral; lvs glaucous white below, blue-green above. 'Copper': fls coral-red flushed with orange and red. Pallidum group: fls pale pink-purple, broadly funnel-shaped. Purpurellum group: fls pink-purple, broadly funnel-shaped. Purpurellum group: fls bright mauve-pink or plum-purple, bell-shaped.

R. cinnabarinum has been widely used in hybridization; some of the hybrids, previously thought to be interspecific, are now within the sp., e.g. 'Conroy' (*R. cinnabarinum* ssp. *cinnabarinum* 'Roylei' ×ssp. *xanthocodon*); others involve other sp., e.g. 'Cinnkeys' (×*R. keysii*); 'Royal Flush' and 'Rose Mangles' (both ×*R. maddenii* ssp. *maddenii*) and 'Yunncinn' (×*R. yunnanense*). Z6.

R. cinnabarinum var. *purpurellum* Cowan = *R. cinnabarinum* ssp. *xanthocodon*.

R. cinnamomeum G. Don = *R. arboreum* ssp. *cinnamomeum* var. *cinnamomeum*.

R. citriniflorum Balf. f. & Forr. To 1.5m. Lvs 4–7.5cm, obovate to elliptic, glab. above when mature, beneath with dense, thick, grey-brown ramiform hairs. Fls 3.2–4.5cm, thin, tubular-campanulate, yellow, orange or carmine. SW China. var. *citriniflorum*. Cal. rarely more than 5mm. var. *horaeum* (Balf. f. & Forr.) Chamberl. Cor. tinged yellow to red, cal. rarely less than 7mm. Z8.

R. clementinae Forr. To 3m. Lvs 6.5–14cm, ovate-lanceolate, glab. above, off-white to buff, hairy beneath. Fls 4–5cm, 7-lobed, campanulate, white to deep pink with purple spots. W China. Z6.

R. coelicum Balf. f. & Farrer. To 2m. Lvs 6–8.5cm, obovate, glab. above, with thick, brown hairs beneath. Fls 3.8–4.5cm, fleshy, tubular-campanulate, crimson. W China, NE Burm. Z8.

R. complexum Balf. f. & W.W. Sm. Much-branched shrub to 60cm. Lvs 3.5–11mm, broadly or narrowly elliptic to ovate, lower surface red-brown with contiguous scales. Fls 9–13mm, narrowly funnel-shaped, pale lilac to rosy purple, occas. pubesc. outside. W China. Z7.

R. concatenans Hutch. = *R. cinnabarinum* ssp. *xanthocodon*.

R. concinnum Hemsl. Shrub to 2m. Lvs 3.5–6cm, ovate or elliptic, rounded or cordate at base, scaly above, grey or brown beneath, numerous contiguous or overlapping large, flat scales. Fls 2–3cm, purple or red-purple, scaly on the tube outside. W China. Z7.

R. coombense Hemsl. = *R. concinnum*.

R. coreanum Rehd. = *R. yedoense* var. *poukhanense*.

R. coriaceum Franch. Shrub or small tree to 7.5m. Lvs 12–25cm, oblanceolate, becoming glab. above, densely off-white to brown-hairy beneath. Fls 3.5–4cm, funnel-campanulate, white sometimes flushed with pink and with a red basal blotch, occas. also spotted red. W China. 'Morocco': fls white with a crimson blotch and few spots. Z9.

R. coryphaeum Balf. f. & Forr. = *R. praestans*.

R. cosmetum Balf. f. & Forr. = *R. saluenense* ssp. *chameunum*.

R. crassum Franch. = *R. maddenii* ssp. *crassum*.

R. crebreflorum Hutch. & Kingdon-Ward = *R. cephalanthum*.

R. cremastum Balf. f. & Forr. = *R. campylogynum*.

R. crinigerum Franch. Shrub or small tree to 5m. Lvs 7–17cm, obovate to oblanceolate, glab. above when mature, beneath with matted, fawn to red brown hairs and a few glands. Fls 3–4cm, campanulate, white flushed pink, with a purple basal blotch and usually some spots. W China, NE Burm. Z7.

R. croceum Balf. f. & W.W. Sm. = *R. wardii* var. *wardii*.

R. cubitii hort. A hybrid of *R. dendricola* and some other unknown sp. of Subsection *Maddenia*. The name *R. cubitii* Hutch. is a synonym of *R. veitchianum*. Z10.

R. cubitii Hutch. non hort. = *R. veitchianum*.

R. cucullatum Hand.-Mazz. = *R. roxieanum* var. *cucullatum*.

R. cumberlandense E. Braun. V. similar to, and difficult to distinguish from *R. calendulaceum*, but flowering after the lvs have expanded, lf lower surface often glab. Late spring. E US. Z6.

R. cuneatum W.W. Sm. Shrub 1–2m+. Lvs 1–7cm, narrowly to broadly elliptic, ± scaly above, fawn to deep red-brown beneath with dense scales. Fls 1.5–3cm, funnel-shaped, often pubesc. and/or scaly outside, deep purple to rose-lavender, often with darker purple spots, rarely almost white. W China. Z5.

R. cuthbertii Small = *R. minus*.

R. cyanocarpum (Franch.) W.W. Sm. Shrub or small tree to 4m. Lvs 6.5–12.5cm, broadly elliptic to orbicular, glab. above, glab. and ± glaucous beneath. Fls 4–6cm, campanulate to funnel-campanulate, white or cream to clear pink, with dark nectar-pouches. Spring. W China. Z6.

R. cyclium Balf. f. & Forr. = *R. callimorphum* var. *callimorphum*.

R. dalhousiae Hook. Large epiphytic or free-growing shrub. Lvs 7.5–17cm, narrowly elliptic, lower surface grey- or brown-green with small red-ringed scales. Fls fragrant; 8.5–10.5cm, narrowly funnel-shaped, white or cream, often tinged yellow inside, sometimes with 5 red lines running from lobes to base. Late spring. Himal. var. *dalhousiae*. Cor. without red lines. var. *rhabdotum* (Balf. f. & Cooper) Cullen. Cor. with 5 red lines. Z9.

R. dasycladum Balf. f. & W.W. Sm. = *R. selense* ssp. *dasycladum*.

R. dauricum L. Straggling shrub to 1.5m. At least some lvs overwintering, leathery, densely scaly beneath, 1–3.5cm, elliptic. Fls 1.4–2cm, pink or violet-pink. Late winter–early spring. E Sib., Mong., N China, Jap. 'Arctic Pearl': fls white. 'Hokkaido': fls large, white, later-flowering than usual. 'Midwinter': fls bright rose-purple, open in winter; semi-evergreen. 'Nanum': dwarf form. Sempervirens group: plants everg. Sometimes split into 3 spp.: *R. dauricum* has lvs dark green above, rusty brown beneath, most overwintering, flowering in spring while covered in last year's lvs. *R. ledebourii* Pojark. (lvs pale above and beneath, mostly falling in late autumn, with a few scales on the upper surface) and *R. sichotense* Pojark. (similar but without scales on the upper leaf-surface) are two names used in gardens; it is uncertain what they really represent. Z5.

R. davidsonianum Rehd. & Wils. Shrub to 5m. Lvs 3–6.5cm, often V-shaped in section, lower surface densely scaly with small brown scales. Fls 2.3–2.7cm, pink, pink-lavender or lavender. W China. 'Caerhays Blotched': fls pale pink with darker spots. 'Exbury': fls pink. 'Ruth Lyons': fls rich pink with few spots, becoming deeper coloured with age. 'Serenade': lvs small, rounded; fls clear pink. Z7.

R. decorum Franch. Shrub or small tree to 6m. Lvs 6–20cm, oblanceolate to elliptic, glab. when mature with punctate hair bases beneath. Fls 4.5–11cm, 6–7-lobed, funnel-campanulate, sparsely gland. outside, densely so within, white to pale pink, with or without green or crimson spots. W China, NE Burm., Laos. ssp. *decorum*. Fls 4–6.5cm, and lvs to 12cm. 'Cox's Uranium Green': fls chartreuse green. ssp. *diaprepes* (Balf. f. & W.W. Sm.) Chamberl. Lvs and cor. larger. 'Gargantua': fls v. large, white, flushed green below. Z7.

R. degronianum Carr. Shrub to 2.5m. Lvs 8–14cm, elliptic to oblanceolate, with dense grey to fawn hairs beneath. Fls 3–4.5cm, 5–7-lobed, widely funnel-campanulate, pink with conspicuous darker spots. Late spring. Jap. ssp. *degronianum*. Indumentum generally velvety, heavily felted or spongy; cor. funnel-shaped, 5-lobed. N Jap. 'Gerald Loder': fls white, spotted and flushed with red-purple. ssp. *heptamerum* (Maxim.) Hara. Indumentum thin or thick; cor. funnel-shaped, 7-lobed. C & S Jap. ssp. *yakushimanum* (Nak.) Hara. Indumentum v. thick and dense; cor. broadly-based, campanulate, 5-lobed. Yakushima Is, at the extreme S of Jap. This las ssp. has been much used in recent hybridization as a parent of a range of striking, v. hardy hybrids. 'Ken Janeck': plants and lvs larger than usual; fls pink. 'Koichiro Wada': fls white opening from pink buds, in dense trusses, freely produced. 'Overstreet': fls white opening from pink buds; lvs v. narrow. 'Tremeer': a tall form. Z7.

R. delavayi Franch. = *R. arboreum* ssp. *delavayi*.

R. deleiense Hutch. & Kingdon-Ward = *R. tephropeplum*.

R. dendricola Hutch. Tall epiphytic or free-growing shrub. Lvs 7–12cm, narrowly elliptic to narrowly obovate, scaly beneath. Fls to 7cm, funnel-shaped white, often with a yellow, green or orange blotch, often flushed pink. Himal., SW China, Burm. Cultivated under a var. of names (including *R. ciliicalyx*, see above). Z8.

R. desquamatum Balf. f. & Forr. = *R. rubiginosum*.

R. diacritum Balf. f. & W.W. Sm. = *R. telmateium*.

R. diaprepes Balf. f. & W.W. Sm. = *R. decorum* ssp. *diaprepes*.

R. dichroanthum Diels. Dwarf shrub to 2m. Lvs 4–9.5cm, oblanceolate to elliptic, glab. above, with loose to compacted, silvery to fawn hairs beneath. Fls 3.5–5cm, fleshy, tubular-campanulate, orange red, or occas. yellow flushed red. W China, NE Burm. ssp. *apodectum* (Balf. f. & W.W. Sm.) Cowan. Young shoots and ovary without glands. ssp. *scyphocalyx* (Balf. f. & Forr.) Cowan. Young shoots and ovary gland. Z8.

R. didymum Balf. f. & Forr. = *R. sanguineum* ssp. *didymum*.

R. dilatatum Miq. = *R. reticulatum*.

R. diphrocalyx Balf. f. Shrub to 5m. Lvs 9–14cm, elliptic to obovate, glab. except for a few bristles at the base of the midrib beneath. Fls 3–4cm, funnel-campanulate, pale to deep crimson, without spots. Gdn origin. Perhaps a hybrid between *R. habrotrichum* and *R. neriiflorum* or one of its allies.

R. discolor Franch. = *R. fortunei* ssp. *discolor*.

R. drumonium Balf. f. & Forr. = *R. telmateium*.

R. dryophyllum Balf. f. & Forr. See *R. phaeochrysum* var. *phaeochrysum*. Much material in gardens named as *R. dryophyllum* is *R. phaeochrysum* var. *levistratum*.

R. dryophyllum Balf. f. & Forr. = *R. phaeochrysum* var. *phaeochrysum*.

R. dryophyllum misapplied. = *R. phaeochrysum* var. *levistratum*.

R. eclecteum Balf. f. & Forr. Shrub to 4.5m; bark smooth and peeling. Lvs 4–14.5cm, obovate-lanceolate to elliptic, glab. except for a few hairs near the midrib beneath, veins conspicuous. Fls 3–5cm, campanulate to widely funnel-campanulate, white or cream, or more usually, deep crimson, with or without purple spots. W China, NE Burm. Z8.

R. edgarianum hort. Name applied to gdn hybrids between unknown sp. of Subsection *Lapponica* (though *R. tapetiforme* is one likely parent). Z6.

R. edgeworthii Hook.   Epiphytic shrub to 2.5m. Young lvs covered in orange to pale beige hairs, upper surface wrinkled. Fls fragrant; 3.5–6.5cm, broadly funnel-shaped, white, sometimes flushed pink, usually with a yellowish blotch at the base; scaly outside. Himal., SW China. Z9.

R. elaeagnoides Hook. f. = *R. lepidotum*.

R. elliottii Watt. Small shrub. Lvs 8.5–10cm, lanceolate to elliptic, becoming glab. Fls 4–5cm, funnel-campanulate, purple with darker spots. NE India. Z9.

R. eriogynum Balf. f. & W.W. Sm. = *R. facetum*.

R. eritimum Balf. f. & W.W. Sm. = *R. anthosphaerum*.

R. erubescens Hutch. = *R. oreodoxa* var. *fargesii*.

R. euchaites Balf. f. & Forr. = *R. neriiflorum*.

R. eudoxum Balf. f. & Forr. Small shrub to 1.2m. Lvs 3.5–9cm, elliptic, glab. above, with sparse off-white to brown-tinged hairs beneath. Fls 2.5–4cm, tubular-campanulate to campanulate, pink to carmine. W China. Z7.

R. eximium Nutt. = *R. falconeri* var. *eximium*.

R. exquisetum Hutch. = *R. oreotrephes*.

R. facetum Balf. f. & Kingdon-Ward. Shrub or tree to 10m. Lvs 10–18.5cm, oblanceolate to elliptic, glab. when mature. Fls 4–5cm, tubular-campanulate, sparingly tomentose or glab. outside, deep pink to scarlet. W China, NE Burm. Z8.

R. falconeri. Hook. Tree to 12m. Lvs 18–35cm, broadly elliptic to obovate, upper surface glab. or scurfy, wrinkled, lower surface with white and red tinged hairs. Fls 4–5cm, fleshy, obliquely campanulate, off-white to pink or pale cream with darker tips and purple basal blotch. Himal. var. *falconeri*. Lvs glab. above at maturity, cor. white to cream. var. *eximium* (Nutt.) Chamberl. Lvs scurfy above, cor. pink with darker tips. Z9.

R. fargesii Franch. = *R. oreodoxa* var. *fargesii*.

R. fastigiatum Franch. Prostrate or cushion-forming shrub to 1.5m. Lvs 5–16mm, broadly elliptic to ovate, lower surface fawn to grey with opaque, pink or grey scales. Fls 1–1.8cm, funnel-shaped, bright lavender-blue to pink-purple or rich purple, scaleless outside, but sometimes finely hairy. W China. A parent of many hybrids; its influence can generally be detected by the presence of opaque, pink or grey scales on the lf undersurface, e.g. R.'Intrifast' (×*R. intricatum*). 'Blue Steel': compact; lvs v. blue-green. 'RBG': fls rich blue-violet. Z6.

R. fauriei Franch. = *R. brachycarpum* ssp. *fauriei*.

R. ferrugineum L. Small shrub to 1.5m with erect or ascending br. Lvs 2.8–4cm, narrowly elliptic to elliptic, margins slightly revolute, dark green above, red-brown beneath with dense, overlapping scales. Fls 1.2–1.7cm, deep pink (rarely pale or off-white), scaly and pubesc. outside. Late spring. C Eur. 'Album': fls white. 'Coccineum': fls crimson. 'Glenarn': fls deep rose-pink; attractive, twisted foliage. Z4.

R. fictolacteum Balf. f. = *R. rex* ssp. *fictolacteum*.

R. fimbriatum Hutch. = *R. hippophaeoides*.

R. flavantherum Balf. f. & W.W. Sm. Shrub to 1m, usually epiphytic. Lvs 3–4.5cm, ovate-elliptic to elliptic, dark green and with dried-out scales above, somewhat papillose beneath, with distant pale scales. Fls 1.4–2cm, tubular-funnel-shaped to tubular-campanulate, bright yellow. W China. Doubtfully in cult.

R. flavidum Franch. Erect shrub to 2.5m. Lvs 7–15mm, broadly elliptic to oblong, lower surface pale grey-green with well-spaced scales. Fls 1.2–1.8mm, broadly funnel-shaped, yellow, pubesc. outside. W China. 'Album': fls large, white; habit fairly lax. Z6.

R. flavorufum Balf. f. & Forr. = *R. agganiphum* var. *flavorufum*.

R. flavum G. Don = *R. luteum*.

R. fletcherianum Davidian. Similar to *R. valentinianum* but lvs crenulate above, scales beneath distant, surface green, midrib usually not bristly above. SW China. 'Yellow Bunting': fls primrose-yellow. Z7.

R. floccigerum Franch. Shrub to 3m. Lvs 3.5–11cm, narrowly elliptic to oblong or elliptic, glab. above, beneath glauc. with loose, red-tinged, patchy hairs. Fls 3–4cm, tubular-campanulate, usually crimson to scarlet, rarely yellow or pink. W China. Z6.

R. floribundum Franch. Shrub or small tree to 5m. Lvs 10–18cm, oblanceolate to elliptic, glab. above when mature, beneath with a 2-layered indumentum of off-white woolly hairs. Fls broadly campanulate, to 4cm, magenta-pink, with crimson spots and a basal blotch. W China. 'Swinhoe': fls rose-purple with a deep red blotch. Z8.

R. formosum Wallich. Erect shrub to 2m. Lvs 4–7.5×1–2.1cm, narrowly elliptic to linear-elliptic or linear-obovate, sparsely scaly beneath. Fls funnel-capanulate, 4–5.5cm, white or white flushed pink, usually with a yellow blotch at the base. Himal. 'Khasia': fls strongly scented, white with yellow blotch. Iteophyllum Group: fls white, sometimes tinged with pink; lvs v.

narrow. Z8.

R. forrestii Diels. Dwarf, creeping shrub, st. to 60cm long, though rarely more than 10cm high. Lvs 1–2.8cm, obovate to orbicular, upper surface glab., lower surface purple or green, glab. or sparsely gland.-hairy beneath. Fls 3–3.5cm, fleshy, tubular-campanulate, crimson. W China, NE Burm. Repens Group: prostrate form; fls deep red; lvs pale green underneath. Tower Court form: fls scarlet-crimson. Tumescens group: dome-shaped plants; fls and lvs usually larger. Z8.

R. fortunei Lindl. Shrub or tree to 10m. Lvs 8–18cm, broadly oblanceolate to obovate, glab. when mature except for persistent hair-bases beneath. Fls 5.5–7cm, 7-lobed, open-campanulate or funnel-campanulate, pale pink to almost pure white, ext. gland. or glab. China (widespread). 'Mrs Butler': fls pink. ssp. *fortunei*. Lvs obovate. ssp. *discolor* (Franch.) Chamberl. Lvs oblanceolate. 'John R. Elcock': fls purple-pink, yellow in throat. Z6.

R. ×fragrantissimum hort. (*R. edgeworthii* ×*R. formosum*.) See also *R. ×sesteriamum*.

R. fulgens Hook. Shrub to 4.5m. Lvs 7–11cm, broadly ovate to obovate, glab. above, with a dense, woolly, brown hairs beneath. Fls 2–3.5cm, tubular-campanulate, scarlet to blood red. Himal., W China. Z7.

R. fulvum Balf. f. & W.W. Sm. Shrub or small tree to 8m. Lvs 8–22cm, oblanceolate to elliptic, glab. above when mature, velvety brown hairy beneath, appearing granular. Fls 2.5–4.5cm, campanulate, white to pink, usually with a dark basal blotch, with or without crimson spots. W China, NE Burm. Z7.

R. fumidum Balf. f. & W.W. Sm. = *R. heliolepis* var. *heliolepis*.

R. galactinum Tagg. Tree to 8m. Lvs 14–20cm, ovate-lanceolate, glab. and smooth above, beneath with off-white and cinnamon-brown hairs. Fls 3–5cm, 7-lobed, campanulate, pale pink with a crimson basal blotch. W China. Z5.

R. genestierianum Forr. Shrub to 5m, bark of older shoots smooth, tinged purple. Lvs 6.5–12×2.5–4cm, narrowly elliptic to narrowly elliptic-oblanceolate, dark green above, white-papillose beneath with distant, golden yellow to brown scales. Fls 1.2–1.7cm, fleshy, red-purple, bloomed, scaleless and glab. outside. Late spring. NE Burm., W China. Z9.

R. gibsonii Paxt. = *R. formosum*.

R. giganteum Tagg = *R. protistum* var. *giganteum*.

R. glaucopeplum Balf. f. & Forr. = *R. agganiphum* var. *agganiphum*.

R. glaucophyllum Rehd. Shrub to 1.5m. Lvs 3.5–6×1.3–2.5cm, narrowly elliptic to elliptic, upper surface dark brown-green, lower surface white, with pale and dark scales. Fls 1.8–3.2cm, campanulate to tubular-campanulate, pink or white flushed with pink, rather densely scaly outside. Himal., W China. 'Branklyn': fls pale pink, bell-shaped. Glenarn form: fls deep rose pink. 'Prostratum': low-growing. var. *glaucophyllum*. Style sharply deflexed. Himal. Material in cult. as *R. shweliense* is usually this. var. *tubiforme* Cowan & Davidian. Cor. tubular-campanulate; style declinate, not deflexed. E Himal., W China. Z8.

R. glaucum Hook. non Sweet = *R. glaucophyllum* var. *glaucophyllum*.

R. glischroides Tagg & Forr. = *R. glischrum* ssp. *glischroides*.

R. glischrum Balf. f. & W.W. Sm. Shrub or small tree to 8m. Lvs 11.5–30cm, obovate to elliptic, ciliate, upper surface smooth to wrinkled, with some glandular-bristles, lower surface with a dense covering of bristles, sometimes also with a thin brown covering of hairs. Fls 3–5cm, campanulate, pink to scarlet or occas. white flushed pink, with purple spots and usually also a basal blotch. W China, NE Burm. ssp. *glischrum*. Lvs smooth and glab. above. ssp. *glischroides* (Tagg & Forr.) Chamberl. Lf upper surface wrinkled, the veins beneath with a thin covering of short hairs. ssp. *rude* (Tagg & Forr.) Chamberl. Upper surface of the lvs with a sparse covering of bristles. 'Frank Kingdon Ward': fls purple-pink, spotted purple. Z8.

R. globigerum Balf. f. & Forr. = *R. roxieanum* var. *cucullatum*.

R. glomerulatum Hutch. = *R. yungningense*.

R. grande Wight. Tree to 12m. Lvs 15–27cm, elliptic to oblanceolate, glab. above, with a thin, silvery hairs beneath. Fls 5–7cm, 8-lobed, ventricose-campanulate, pale yellow (rarely with a purple tinge) with purple nectar-pouches. Himal., W China. Z8.

R. griersonianum Balf. f. & Forr. Shrub to 3m. Lvs 10–20cm, elliptic, glab. above at maturity, beneath densely woolly, off-white to pale brown. Fls 5.5–8cm, tubular-campanulate to funnel-campanulate, tube ext. densely hairy, deep pink to crimson or scarlet. Late spring. W China, NE Burm. Z8.

R. griffithianum Wight. Shrub or tree to 10m. Lvs 10–30cm, oblong, glab. Fls 4.5–8cm, 5-lobed, open-campanulate, pale pink fading to white. Late spring. Himal. Z8.

R. gymnocarpum Tagg = *R. microgynum*.

R. habrotrichum Balf. f. & W.W. Sm. Shrub to 4m. Lvs 7–16cm, ovate to obovate, with bristly-ciliate, glab., bristles on veins beneath. Cor. 4–5cm, campanulate, white flushed pink, with or without purple spots and basal blotch. W China, NE Burm. Z8.

R. haemaleum Balf. f. & Forr. = *R. sanguineum* ssp. *sanguineum* var. *haemaleum*.

R. haematocheilum Craib = *R. oreodoxa* var. *oreodoxa*.

R. haematodes Franch. Shrub to 1.8m, young shots densely tomentose or bristly. Lvs 4.5–10cm, ovate to oblong, glab. above, beneath with densely matted, fawn to red-brown hairs. Fls 3.5–4.5cm, fleshy, tubular-campanulate, scarlet to deep crimson. W China, NE Burm. ssp. **haematodes**. Young shoots tomentose, bristles few or 0. ssp. **chaetomallum** (Balf. f. & Forr.) Chamberl. Young shoots covered in stout bristles. Glaucescens group: lvs glaucous above. Z7.

R. hanceanum Hemsl. Shrub to 2m. Lvs 7–11×3–5.5cm, narrowly ovate or oblong-elliptic, narrowing to a drip tip, lower surface pale green with flat or golden-brown scales. Fls in a long rac., c2cm, narrowly funnel-campanulate, white. W China. Most material cult. is a low-growing selection ('Nanum'). 'Canton Consul': fls cream opening from green-cream buds. Z8.

R. heliolepis Franch. Shrub to 3m. Lvs 5–11×2–4cm, oblong-ovate to oblong-elliptic, scurfy above, with golden or brown scales beneath. Fls 2.2–3.4cm, funnel-shaped, white to pink or pink-purple, with red, green or brown spots on the upper lobes. Late spring–early summer. W China, N Burm. var. **heliolepis**. Lvs truncate or rounded at the base. var. **brevistylum** (Franch.) Cullen. Lvs tapered to the base. Z8.

R. hemitrichotum Balf. f. & Forr. Shrub to 2m. Lvs 2.5–4×0.7–1.3cm, narrowly elliptic, finely hairy, white-papillose beneath. Fls 9–15mm, openly funnel-shaped, pink or white edged with pink. W China. Z8.

R. hemsleyanum Wils. Shrub or small tree to 8m. Lvs 10–20cm, ovate to ovate-elliptic, ± glab. Fls 4.5–6cm, 6–7-lobed, campanulate, pure white. W China. Z8.

R. herpesticum Balf. f. & Kingdon-Ward = *R. dichroanthum* ssp. *scyphocalyx*.

R. hippophaeoides Balf. f. & W.W. Sm. Erect, openly branched shrub to 1.2m. Lvs 5–12×2–6mm, elliptic, oblong or narrowly obovate, grey-green above, yellow-green or grey-green with numerous scales beneath. Fls broadly funnel-shaped, pale lavender to deep purple (rarely white). W China. 'Bei-ma-shan': tall, with fls lavender-blue. 'Haba-shan': fls lavender in large trusses. Z6.

R. hirsutum L. Small shrub to 1m. Lvs 1.3–3.3×0.7–1.4cm, narrowly obovate to obovate or almost circular, flat, scaleless above, golden scaley beneath, margins with long bristles. Fls 1.2–1.8cm, pink, sparsely scaly and hairy outside. Late spring. C Eur. (Alps). Z4.

R. hirtipes Tagg. Low shrub to small tree to 8m. Lvs 5–11cm, broadly ovate, glab. above, beneath with scattered shortly stalked glands and sparsely floccose, sometimes ciliate towards base. Fls to 4cm, campanulate, white to pink, usually with a few purple spots. W China. Z6.

R. hodgsonii Hook. Shrub or small tree to 11m. Lvs 17–24cm, obovate to oblanceolate or elliptic, upper surface becoming glab., lower surface with dense silvery to cinnamon-brown hairs. Fls fleshy, 7–8(–10)-lobed, tubular-campanulate, 3–5cm, pink to magenta or purple, with a darker basal blotch. Himal., W China. 'Poet's Lawn': fls white, tinged with purple. Z9.

R. hookeri Nutt. Shrub or small tree to 4m, bark smooth. Lvs to 13cm, broadly oblanceolate, glab. except for sparse, large hairs on veins beneath. Fls 3.5–4.5cm, tubular-campanulate, deep pink to crimson with darker nectar pouches and a few spots. NE India. Z8.

R. horaeum Balf. f. & Forr. = *R. citriniflorum* var. *horaeum*.

R. hormophorum Balf. f. & Forr. see *R. yunnanense*.

R. houlstonii Hemsl. & Wils. = *R. fortunei* ssp. *discolor*.

R. hunnewellianum Rehd. & Wils. Shrub or small tree to 6m. Lvs 7–15cm, narrowly oblanceolate, glab. above, with white to yellow hairs and scattered glands beneath. Fls 4–5cm, widely campanulate, white to pink or purple, with purple spots. W China. Z9.

R. hypenanthum Balf. f. = *R. anthopogon* var. *hypenanthum*.

R. hyperythrum Hayata. Shrub ultimately. Lvs 8–12cm, elliptic, glab. Fls 3.5–4.5cm, funnel-campanulate, white with red spots. Late spring. Taiwan. 'Omo': fls white. Z8.

R. hypoglaucum Hemsl. = *R. argyrophyllum* ssp. *hypoglaucum*.

R. hypolepidotum (Franch.) Balf. f. & Forr. = *R. brachyanthum* ssp. *hypolepidotum*.

R. impeditum Franch. Compact, much-branched shrub to 1m. Lvs 4–14×2.5–7mm, lower surface pale grey-green speckled with brown or more uniformly brown. Fls 8–15mm, broadly funnel-shaped, violet to purple, rarely lavender. W China. An important sp. in hybridization, contributing its low habit to a series of blue-fld hybrids, e.g. 'Blue Tit' (×R. augustinii). Z4.

R. imperator Kingdon-Ward = *R. uniflorum* var. *imperator*.

R. indicum (L.) Sweet. Low shrub to 2m, sometimes prostrate. Lvs 1.8–3.5×0.8–1cm, crowded, persistent, narrowly lanceolate to oblanceolate, crenate-serrulate, ciliate with scattered brown hairs. Fls 3–5cm, broadly funnel-shaped, bright red to scarlet or rarely pink-red. Late spring. Jap. A variable sp., widely cultivated in Japan. The 'Indian Azalea' of nurseries is *R. simsii*. 'Balsaminiflorum': a dwarf, c10cm; fls double, salmon-red. 'Crispiflorum': fls bright pink, the pet. undulate. 'Variegatum': lvs variegated. Z6.

R. insigne Hemsl. & Wils. Shrub to 3.5m. Lvs 7–13cm, elliptic, glab. above, fawn-hairy beneath. Fls to 4cm, widely campanulate, pink with a darker median line on each lobe. W China. Z6.

R. intricatum Franch. Compact and intricately branched shrub to 1.5m. Lvs 5–12×3–7mm, oblong to elliptic or almost circular, upper surface ± scaly, lower surface buff to pale yellow with dense scales. Fls 8–14mm with a short parallel-sided tube and spreading lobes, pale lavender to dark purple-blue; sta. included. W China. A parent of a few hybrids including 'Bluebird' (crossed with *R. augustinii*) and 'Intrifast' (crossed with *R. fastigiatum*). Z5.

R. irroratum Franch. Shrub or small tree to 9m. Lvs 7–14cm, oblanceolate to elliptic, ultimately glab. with red, punctate hair-bases on the veins beneath. Fls 3.5–5cm, campanulate to tubular-campanulate, white or cream to violet-pink with green or purple spots. W China, Vietnam, Indon. 'Polka Dot': fls pale pink, copiously spotted purple. Z7.

R. ixeuticum Balf. f. & W.W. Sm. = *R. crinigerum*.

R. japonicum (A. Gray) Sur. Shrub to 2m. Lvs 5–10cm, obovate to oblanceolate, ciliate, with scattered bristles above and on veins beneath. Fls 5–6cm across, broadly funnel-shaped, tube shorter than lobes, orange or salmon to brick red, with a large orange blotch made up of small dots. Late spring. C & E Jap. Z5.

R. japonicum (Bl.) Schneid. = *R. degronianum*.

R. japonicum (Bl.) Schneid. = *R. degronianum* ssp. *degronianum*.

R. japonicum var. **pentamerum** (Maxim.) Hutch. = *R. degronianum* ssp. *degronianum*.

R. japonicum (Bl.) Schneid. = *R. degronianum* ssp. *heptamerum*.

R. jasminiflorum Hook. Shrub to 2.5m. Lvs 2.5–6cm, in false whorls of 3–5, broadly obovate-elliptic to suborbicular, scaly above when young, persistently scaly beneath. Fls 3.5–4.5cm, salver-shaped, v. fragrant, tube cylindric, narrow, lobes spreading, white sometimes flushed pink. Winter. Malaysia, Philipp., Sumatra. Z10.

R. javanicum (Bl.) Benn. Shrub or small tree, 2–3m. Lvs 4–20cm, in false whorls of 5–8, broadly oblong, elliptic-oblong or ovate-oblong, densely scaly at first. Fls 3–3.5cm, funnel-shaped, fleshy, orange, yellow or scarlet. Winter. Widespread in SE Asia, from mainland Malaysia to Indon. (Bali). Z10.

R. johnstoneanum Hutch. Variable-sized shrub. Lvs 5.5–7.5cm, elliptic to broadly elliptic, margins bristly, undersurface green-brown with dense scales. Fls 4.5–5.5cm white, usually with a yellow blotch at the base, often with a pink or purple flush. India (Manipur, Mizoram). 'Demi-John': fls white, flushed with yellow-green in throat. 'Double Diamond': fls double, pale yellow; rather tender. 'Rubeotinctum': fls white with a pink stripe on each pet. and a pink or yellow blotch in centre. Z7.

R. kaempferi Planch. Shrub to 3m. Lvs 1–5×1–2.5cm, entire, strigose. Fls 2–3cm, funnel-shaped, pink or red. Jap. V. similar to *R. indicum*, but with broader lvs. 'Mikado': fls red with darker spotting in throat. Z5.

R. keiskei Miq. Small shrub, 30–300cm, often creeping or almost so. Lvs 2.5–7.5×0.8–2.8cm, lanceolate or oblong-lanceolate to narrowly elliptic, dark green and variably scaly above, lower surface with distant, large scales. Fls 1.8–2.5cm, pale yellow, unspotted, funnel-shaped. Jap. 'Ebino': dwarf form, free-flowering; fls clear, pale lemon yellow. 'Yaku Fairy': v. dwarf plant with large, lemon yellow fls. Z5.

R. keleticum Balf. f. & Forr. = *R. calostrotum* ssp. *keleticum*.

R. keysii Nutt. Straggling shrub to 6m. Lvs 6–15×2–3.5cm, elliptic, scaly. Fls 1.5–2.5cm, tubular, lobes slightly flaring, deep red to salmon-pink, lobes usually yellow. Himal. 'Unicolor': fls uniformly red. Z7.

R. kiusianum Mak. Dwarf shrub to 1m. Lvs 0.5–2×0.2–1.5cm, decid., obovate, red-brown strigose. Fls 1.5–2cm, funnel-shaped, usually rose-pink, occas. purple. Jap. The Obtusum group of cvs (see *R. obtusum*) and the Kurume Azaleas had their origin in this sp. and its hybrids with *R. kaempferi*. 'Album': fls white. 'Benichidori': fls salmon orange. 'Betty Muir': fls bright pink; lvs dark green. 'Chidori': fls white. 'Hanejiro': fls white. 'Harunokikari': fls lavender-blue. 'Harusame': fls bright pink. 'Hillier's Pink': fls pink. 'Komokul-shan': fls pale pink, pet. tipped with rose pink. 'Muraski Shikibu': fls hose-in-hose, red-purple. Z6.

R. komiyamae Mak. = *R. tosaense*.

R. kongboense Hutch. Spindly, branched shrub to 1m. Lvs 1.3–2.8×0.6–1.2cm, oblong or elliptic-oblong, scales persistent above, dense, fawn to pale brown beneath. Fls 8.5–12mm, pink to red, rarely pink-white, tube variably hairy outside. W China. Z8.

R. kotschyi Simonkai = *R. myrtifolium*.

R. kyawi Lace & W.W. Sm. Shrub to 9m. Lvs 9–22(–30)cm, elliptic to oblong, upper surface glab., lower surface with cinnamon-brown hairs. Fls 4.5–6cm, tubular-campanulate, bright crimson to scarlet, without spots. W China, NE Burm. Z9.

R. lacteum Franch. Shrub or small tree to 7.5m. Lvs 8–17cm, elliptic to obovate, with grey-brown hairs beneath. Fls 4–5cm, widely campanulate, pure yellow, without spots though sometimes with a purple basal blotch. W China. 'Blackhills': fls clear yellow, without spots or blotches. Z7.

R. laetevirens Hutch. = *R. concinnum*.

R. lanatum Hook. Shrub usually to 4m. Lvs 6.5–11cm, elliptic to obovate, ± glab. above undersurface with ± crisped indumentum, off-white when young, later deep red-brown or brown. Fls 3.2–5cm, campanulate, cream-yellow with crimson spots. Himal., W China. Z7.

R. lanigerum Tagg. Shrub or small tree to 7m. Lvs 16–22cm, elliptic to oblanceolate, wrinkled and ± glab. above, with a dense white to fawn, woolly hairs beneath. Fls to 3.5cm, campanulate, deep pink to pink-purple, with darker nectar-pouches. W China and adjacent NE India. 'Chapel Wood': fls rose-pink in v. large trusses. 'Round Wood': fls crimson. 'Silvia': fls pale crimson flushed with white, with crimson ring in throat. 'Stonehurst': fls pale cherry-red in large trusses. Z7.

R. lapponicum (L.) Wahlenb. Much-branched prostrate or erect shrub to 1m. Lvs 4–25×2–9mm, oblong-elliptic to elliptic-ovate, lower surface fawn to red-brown, scaly. Fls 6.5–15mm, broadly funnel-shaped, violet-rose to purple, rarely off-white. Circumpolar, scattered. Z2.

R. laticostum J. Ingram = *R. keiskei*.

R. latoucheae Franch. Shrub to 2m. Lvs 5–10×1.8–5cm, elliptic or obovate to elliptic-lanceolate, glab. Fls 3.5–4cm, the tube forming about one third of the total length, pink with darker spots. China, Ryukuyu Is. Differs from *R. moulmainense*, in shorter cor.-tube. Z9.

R. laxiflorum Balf. f. & Forr. = *R. annae*.

R. ledebourii Pojark. = *R. dauricum*.

R. ledifolium G. Don = *R. mucronatum*.

R. ledoides Balf. f. & W.W. Sm. = *R. trichostomum*.

R. lepidanthum Balf. f. & W.W. Sm. = *R. primuliflorum*.

R. lepidostylum Balf. f. & Forr. Shrub to 1.5m. Lvs 3–3.5×1.5–2cm, everg., leathery, margins ± rolled downwards, with bluish grey bloom, obovate or obovate-elliptic, with bristles and golden scales beneath. Fls 2–3.3cm, clear yellow, sometimes with orange spots, scaly and sparsely bristly outside. W China. Z6.

R. lepidotum G. Don. Small everg. shrub to 2m. Lvs 6–30×3–16mm, narrowly elliptic, obovate or rarely lanceolate, dark green and densely scaly above, pale grey-green and scaly beneath. Fls 1–1.7cm; white, yellow, pink or red-purple, usually densely scaly outside. Himal., NE Burm., W China. 'Reuthe's Purple': fls purple-violet. Z6.

R. leptothrium Balf. f. & Forr. Shrub to 8m. Lvs 3.5–12cm, narrowly elliptic to lanceolate. Fls to 5cm across, v. openly campanulate, pink to magenta-purple with darker spots. W China, NE Burm. Z7.

R. leucaspis Tagg. Shrub to 1m. Lvs 3–4.5×1.8–2.2cm, broadly elliptic, upper surface and margins bristly, lower surface pitted. Fls 2.5–3cm, v. broadly bell-shaped to almost disc-like, white, often tinged with pink, scaly outside, eesp. on lobes. W China. Z7.

R. levistratum Balf. f. & Forr. = *R. phaeochrysum* var. *levistratum*.

R. lindleyi T. Moore. Epiphytic shrub to 4m. Lvs 8.5–13×2.5–4.5cm, narrowly elliptic to oblong-elliptic, lower surface grey-green with rather distant, red-tinged scales. Fls 6.5–9.5cm, openly funnel-campanulate, white or cream with an orange-yellow blotch at the base. Late spring. Himal. 'Dame Edith Sitwell': fls white, tinged pale pink. 'Geordie Sherriff': fls white with a strong red-purple flush on outside. Z9.

R. linearifolium Sieb. & Zucc. Shrub to 1m. Lvs 3.5–8cm, linear to linear-lanceolate, gland. hairy, esp. beneath. Fls divided into linear-lanceolate seg., pink or purple. Late spring. C & S Jap. The cultivated plant which bears the sp. name is a monstrous cv., juss grown in Japan. The wild type is known as var. *macrosepalum* (Maxim.) Mak. (*R. macrosepalum* Maxim.): this has a broadly funnel-shaped cor., 3.5–5cm, across. Z6.

R. litangense Hutch. = *R. impeditum*.

R. litiense Balf. f. & Forr. = *R. wardii* var. *wardii*.

R. lochae F. Muell. Small shrub. Lvs 4–9cm, in false whorls, obovate, dull, dark green above, paler and persistently scaly beneath. Fls to 3.5cm, tubular, deep red, lobes somewhat spreading, sparsely scaly outside. Winter. Aus. (N Queensld). 'Down Under': fls geranium red. Z10.

R. ×lochmium Balf. f. A hybrid betwen *R. trichanthum* and probably *R. davidsonianum*, widely cultivated.

R. ×loderi hort. (*R. griffithianum* × *R. auriculatum*.) Fls usually highly fragrant. 'Helen': fls pale pink, turning white with age. 'Julie': fls creamy-yellow. 'King George': v. large white fls marked with green inside, opening from pink buds. 'Pink Diamond': fls pink with red mark inside. 'Pink Topaz': fls pink with green flash inside. 'Sir Edmund': fls v. pale pink. 'Venus': fls pale pink, opening from deep pink buds. 'White Diamond': fls white, opening from pale pink buds. Z7.

R. longesquamatum Schneid. Shrub to 3m+. Lvs 6–11cm, elliptic to oblanceolate, gland. and red-tomentose above when young, midrib red-tomentose beneath. Fls 4–4.5cm, open-campanulate, rose-pink. W China. Z5.

R. longistylum Rehd. & Wils. Shrub to 2m. Lvs 3.5–5.5×0.9–1.5cm, obovate or oblong-obovate, lower surface pale green with golden and brown scales, upper surface sparsely scaly. Fls to 2cm, narrowly funnel-shaped, sta. projecting well beyond the cor.; style equalling or exceeding sta. W China. Z8.

R. lopsangianum Cowan = *R. thomsonii*.

R. lowndesii Davidian. Small creeping shrub to 25cm. Lvs 1.5–2×0.6–1.1cm, decid., thin, narrowly elliptic to oblanceolate, crenulate and bristly, upper surface bristly, dark green, sparsely scaly, lower surface pale green, with distant yellow scales. Fls 1.3–1.5cm, yellow, sometimes spotted or streaked with red, ext. scaly. Nepal. Z6.

R. ludlowii Cowan. Small, spreading shrub to 30cm. Lvs 1.5–1.6×0.9–1cm, broadly obovate or oblong-obovate, margins ± pale green with distant, brown scales. Fls 2–2.3cm, broadly funnel- to bell-shaped, yellow drying green-yellow, sometimes with red spots on the inside of the tube, ext. densely pubesc. and scaly. W China. Z6.

R. lutescens Franch. Straggling shrub to 6m with grey bark. Lvs 5–9×1.3–3.5cm, mostly everg., lanceolate to oblong, variably scaly above, golden scales beneath. Fls 1.8–2.5cm, pale yellow with green spots in the inside of the upper lobes, funnel-shaped. Winter–early spring. W China. 'Bagshot Sands': hardy and free-flowering; fls primrose yellow with darker spots. 'Exbury': fls clear lemon yellow; red new growth, rather tender. Z7.

R. luteum (L.) Sweet. Shrub to 4m. Lvs 5–10cm, oblong to oblong-lanceolate, sticky with adpressed bristles. Fls to 3.5cm, funnel-shaped, tube cylindric, lobes about as long as tube, ext. densely glandular-sticky. Late spring. E Eur. to Cauc. Z5.

R. lysolepis Hutch. A hybrid between two spp. of Subsection *Lapponica*.

R. macabeanum Balf. f. Tree to 15m. Lvs 14–25cm, broadly ovate to broadly elliptic, glab. above when mature, beneath with dense woolly hairs. Fls to 5cm, tubular-campanulate to narrowly funnel-campanulate, lemon yellow with a purple blotch at the base. NE India. Z8.

R. macgregoriae F. Muell. Shrub to 5m, more rarely tree-like. Lvs 4–8cm, in false whorls, ovate to ovate-elliptic, scales persistent beneath. Fls 2–2.8cm, ext. tube narrow, lobes widely spreading, yellow, dark orange or red, and divided to ½ length, loosely scaly outside. Winter. New Guinea. Z10.

R. mackenzieanum Forr. = *R. moulmainense*.

R. macranthum Griff. = *R. maddenii* ssp. *maddenii*.

R. macrophyllum G. Don. Shrub to 4m. Lvs 6.5–17cm, broadly elliptic, ultimately, glab. Fls 3–4cm, broadly campanulate, white to pink with yellow spots. W N Amer. Z6.

R. macrosepalum Maxim. = *R. linearifolium*.

R. maculiferum Franch. Shrub or small tree to 10m. Lvs 5–10cm, elliptic or oblong to obovate, glab. except for midrib beneath. Fls 2.5–3cm, open-campanulate, white suffused with pale pink, with a purple blotch at the base and a few spots. China. ssp. **maculiferum**. Fls-stalks, cal. and ovary tomentose. ssp. **anwheiense** (Wils.) Chamberl. Fls-stalks, ovary and cal. glab. Z9.

R. maddenii Hook. Shrub to 2m, often epiphytic. Lvs 6–18cm, elliptic to broadly obovate, densely scaly beneath, often tinged brown, fls fragrant; usually 6–10cm, white, often flushed pink or purple, rarely wholly pink, usually with a yellow blotch at base, funnel-shaped, often with more than 5 lobes, ext. scaly. Late spring. Himal., Burm., SW China, Vietnam. ssp. **maddenii**. Lvs usually 6–15×2.8–5.5cm, often obovate. Himal. ssp. **crassum** (Franch.) Cullen. Lvs usually 9–18×5.5–8cm, usually ± elliptic. NE India, Burm., W & SW China, Vietnam. Z9.

R. magnificum Kingdon-Ward. Tree to 18m. Lvs 20–32cm, broadly obovate, glab. above, fluffy-hairy beneath. Fls 4.5–6cm, funnel-campanulate, 8-lobed, pink-purple with dark nectar-pouches. W China, NE Burm. Z9.

R. makinoi Tagg. Shrub to 3m. Lvs 7–17cm, v. narrowly

lanceolate, often sickle-shaped, finally glab. above, woolly beneath. Fls 3.5–4cm, 5-lobed, funnel-campanulate, soft pink with or without red spots. Late spring. Jap. Similar to *R. degronianum*, but with narrow lvs. Z8.

R. malayanum Jack. Shrub to 5m. Lvs 4–15cm, in false whorls, oblong-elliptic to lanceolate-elliptic, green and shining above, red beneath with dense, persistent scales. Fls 1.5–2.4cm, tubular, expanded above, waxy and glossy, bright red to purple or more rarely pink. Winter. Thail. to Malaysia and Indon. Z10.

R. mallotum Balf. f. & Kingdon-Ward. Shrub or small tree to 6.5m, usually with a well-defined trunk. Lvs 10–13cm, broadly oblanceolate to obovate, glab. above, beneath with dense, red, woolly hairs. Fls 4–4.5cm, fleshy, tubular-campanulate, crimson. W China, NE Burm. Z7.

R. manipurense Balf. f. & Watt = *R. maddenii* ssp. *crassum*.

R. mariae Hance. Shrub to 3m. Lvs 1–9cm, elliptic-lanceolate to elliptic or obovate, almost glab. Fls 1–2cm, tubular-campanulate, lilac, glab. Late spring. E China. Z9.

R. mariesii Hemsl. & Wils. Upright shrub to 3m. Lvs 3–9×2.5–4cm, decid., ovate-lanceolate to broadly elliptic, with yellow, silky hairs when young. Fls 2.5–3cm, openly funnel-shaped, rose-purple with red-purple spots, glab. Late spring. SE & C China, Taiwan. Z8.

R. martinianum Balf. f. & Forr. Shrub to 2m, with punctate hair bases, beneath. Lvs 4.5–5cm, elliptic to obovate, glab. Cor. to 3cm, funnel-campanulate, pale yellow or white flushed with pink, or entirely pink, usually dark pink in bud, spotted or not. W China, NE Burm. Z7.

R. maximum L. Shrub or small tree to 3.5m. Lvs 10–16cm, oblanceolate to elliptic, glab. above, thinly hairy beneath. Cor. 2.5–3cm, campanulate, white to pink-purple', with yellow-green spots. Late spring. E N Amer. 'Summertime': fls white, tips of pet. flushed with red-purple; yellow-green spots in throat. Z3.

R. maxwellii Millais = *R. ×pulchrum* var. *maxwellii*.

R. meddianum Forr. Shrub to 2.3m; bark slightly rough. Lvs 8–11(–15)cm, obovate to broadly elliptic, glab. Fls 4.5–6cm, fleshy, tubular-campanulate, deep pink to deep black-crimson. W China, NE Burm. var. *meddianum*. Ovary ± glab. var. *atrokermesinum* Tagg. Ovary densely gland. and sticky. Z7.

R. megacalyx Balf. f. & Kingdon-Ward. Shrub to 5m. Lvs 10–16cm, elliptic to obovate, upper surface glab., the lower tinged brown with dense golden or golden-brown scales. Fls funnel-campanulate, white or cream, rarely flushed pink or purple; cal. large, cup-like, glaucous, enlarged and papery infr. Late spring. NE India, W China, NE Burma. Z9.

R. megeratum Balf. f. & Forr. Usually free-growing shrub to 1m. Lvs 2–3.6cm, elliptic or elliptic-obovate to almost circular, upper surface ± glab., margins bristly, lower surface white-papillose. Fls 1.6–2.3cm, broadly campanulate, yellow or rarely cream, sometimes with darker spots, scaly outside. NE India, NE Burm., W China. Z9.

R. mekongense Franch. Shrub to 2m. Lvs 2–5(–6)cm, mostly decid., flat, thin, obovate; bristly and scaly beneath; pubesc. along the midrib above, rarely scaly. Fls 1.7–2.3cm, yellow to green-yellow, sometimes flushed red, scaly outside. Late spring. Himal., N Burm., W China. var. *mekongense*. Lvs not bristly above, rather densely so beneath; cal. and fl. stalks bristly. Himal., NE Burm. W China. 'Doshang La': fls yellow flecked with olive green, outside of pet. flushed with rose-pink at tips. var. *melinanthum* (Balf. f. & Kingdon-Ward) Cullen. Lvs not bristly above, rather densely so beneath; flower-stalks not bristly or bristly only at the extreme base. NE Burm., W China. var. *rubrolineatum* (Balf. f. & Forr.) Cullen. Lvs with v. sparse bristles only on margins and midrib beneath. E India, W China. Z9.

R. melinanthum Balf. f. & Kingdon-Ward = *R. mekongense* var. *melinanthum*.

R. metternichii Sieb. & Zucc. = *R. degronianum* ssp. *degronianum*.

R. metternichii var. *pentamerum* Maxim. = *R. degronianum* ssp. *degronianum*.

R. metternichii Sieb. & Zucc. = *R. degronianum* ssp. *heptamerum*.

R. metternichii var. *heptamerum* Maxim. = *R. degronianum* ssp. *heptamerum*.

R. micranthum Turcz. Shrub to 2m. Lvs 1.6–5cm, oblong-elliptic to narrowly oblong-elliptic, sparsely scaly above, pubesc. along the midrib, brown-scaly beneath. Fls 20+ per rac., 5–8mm, white, unspotted, densely scaly outside. Late spring. N China, Korea. Z3.

R. microgynum Balf. f. & Forr. Small shrub to 1.6m. Lvs 5.5–7.5cm, elliptic, glab. above, densely cinnamon-brown to buff, hairy beneath. Fls 3–3.5cm, ± fleshy, pale pink to deep crimson, sometimes with faint spots. W China. Z8.

R. microleucum Hutch. = *R. orthocladum* var. *microleucum*.

R. minus Michx. Shrub to 5m. Lvs 5–11cm, elliptic to broadly elliptic, dark green and hairy along the midrib above, densely

scaly beneath. Fls 2–3.5cm, funnel-shaped, sparsely scaly. Fls 2–3.5cm, funnel-shaped, ext. sparsely scaly or hairy. SE US. var. *chapmanii* (A. Gray) Duncan & Pullen (*R. chapmanii* A. Gray), of more erect habit and with leaf-apex obtuse or notched. 'Epoch': tetraploid (Carolinianum group). Z4.

R. mishmiense Hutch. & Kingdon-Ward = *R. boothii*.

R. molle (Bl.) G. Don. Small shrub to 2m. Lvs 4–13×1.8–3cm, decid., oblong to oblong-lanceolate, softly pubesc. above when young, beneath with more persistent, grey-white hairs. Fls 5–7cm, broadly funnel-shaped, yellow, golden yellow or orange, with a large basal green blotch composed of contiguous spots, hairy outside. E & C China. Z7.

R. mollicomum Balf. f. & W.W. Sm. Similar to *R. hemitrichotum* but lower surface of lvs covered with fine hairs. Fls 2–3cm, pale to deep pink, narrowly funnel-shaped. W China. Uncommon in cult. Z8.

R. mollyanum Cowan & Davidian = *R. montroseanum*.

R. monosematum Hutch. = *R. pachytrichum*.

R. montroseanum Davidian. Tree to 15m. Lvs 2–3cm, oblanceolate, glab. above, beneath with a thin, silvery, compacted indumentum. Fls to 5cm, ventricose-campanulate, 8-lobed, pink with a crimson blotch at the base. W China, NE Burm. 'Benmore': fls fuchsia pink with a crimson blotch. Z8.

R. morii Hayata. Shrub or small tree to 8m. Lvs 7–14cm, lanceolate to elliptic, glab. except for floccose-tomentose hairs on midrib. Fls widely campanulate, 3–5cm, white sometimes tinged with pink, usually with a red basal blotch and some spots. Late spring. Taiwan. Z7.

R. moulmainense Hook. Shrub or small tree to 15m. Lvs 6–17cm, glab. or with sparse marginal bristles. Fls 4.6–6.2cm, with a narrow tube and broad, spreading lobes much longer than tube, white, pink, violet or magenta, with a yellow basal blotch. Widely distrib. in E & SE Asia, from India and Thail. to China and Malaysia. Z10.

R. moupinense Franch. Shrub to 1m. Lvs 3–4cm, narrowly ovate, elliptic or obovate, green and scaleless above, pale green or tinged brown beneath with rather dense scales, margins bristly. Fls 3–4cm, white, often flushed pink and with dark red spots on the upper part of the tube inside. Early spring. W China. Z7.

R. mucronatum G. Don. Shrub to 2m. Lvs 3–5.5cm, lanceolate to ovate-lanceolate or oblong-lanceolate, with appressed hairs on both surfaces. Fls 3.5–5cm, widely funnel-shaped, white or rarely pink, fragrant. Late spring. Origin uncertain. Long cult. in China and Jap. 'Bulstrode': fls white with faint chestnut spots opening from lilac-tinged buds. 'Delaware Valley White': hardy form with white fls. 'Narcissiflorum': fls double, white. 'Noordtianum': fls large, sometimes tinged with pink; a large, spreading plant. 'Plenum': fls double, red. 'Roseum': fls pale pink. Z5.

R. mucronulatum Turcz. Straggling, open shrub to 2m. Lvs 4–6cm, decid., thin, bristly above towards margins, sparsely scaly beneath. Fls 2–2.6cm, openly funnel-shaped, bright mauve-pink, rarely white, hairy outside towards base. Late winter. E Russia, N & C China, Mong., Korea, Jap. 'Alba': fls white. 'Cornell Pink': fls large, clear pink. 'Crater's Edge': fls deep pink. 'Dwarf Cheju': small, to c60cm; fls pale rose pink. 'Mahogany Red': fls rich wine-red; lvs tinged with bronze. 'Roseum': fls bright rose pink. 'Winter Brightness': fls rich purple-pink. Z4.

R. muliense Balf. f. & Forr. = *R. rupicola* var. *muliense*.

R. myiagrum Balf. f. & Forr. = *R. callimorphum* var. *myiagrum*.

R. myrtifolium Schott & Kotschy. Similar to *R. ferrugineum*, but rarely exceeding 50cm; lvs narrowly obovate, less densely scaly beneath, obscurely crenulate. Fls more densely hairy and less scaly outside. Late spring. E Eur. Z5.

R. myrtilloides Balf. f. & Kingdon-Ward = *R. campylogynum*.

R. neriiflorum Franch. Shrub or small tree to 6m. Lvs 4–11cm, elliptic to oblong or oblanceolate, usually glab., lower surface glaucous. Fls 3.5–4.5cm, fleshy, tubular-campanulate, usually bright red, occas. pale yellow. W China, NE Burm. Z7.

R. nigropunctatum Franch. = *R. nivale* ssp. *boreale*.

R. nikoense Nak. = *R. pentaphyllum*.

R. nilagiricum Zenk. = *R. arboreum* ssp. *nilagiricum*.

R. niphargum Balf. f. & Kingdon-Ward = *R. uvarifolium*.

R. nipponicum Matsum. Upright shrub to 2m. Lvs 5–18cm, obovate to obovate-oblong, adpressed-pilose, fls to 1.8cm, tubular to tubular-campanulate, white, glab., with 5 rounded, short slightly spreading lobes. Late spring. C Jap. V. distinctive and without close allies. Z7.

R. nitens Hutch. = *R. calostrotum* ssp. *riparium*.

R. nivale Hook. Low, compact, much-branched shrub, prostrate or to 1m. Lvs 3.5–12mm, broadly ellipptic, ovate or almost circular, undersurface yellow to fawn, often with dark brown speckling, scales gold. Fls 7–16mm, broadly funnel-shaped, pink-magenta to purple, often ± pubesc. outside. Himal., W China. ssp. *nivale*. Leaf-apex rounded; cal. lobes with scaly margins. Himal. to W China. ssp. *australe* Philipson & Philipson. Leaf-apex ± acute; cal. lobes with hairy margins. W China. ssp. *boreale* Philipson & Philipson. Cal. rim-like, unlobed. W China. Nigropunctatum group: lvs densely covered with yellow-green scales; fls yellow-purple. Stictophyllum group: lvs dark green and scaly above, covered with overlapping red and yellow beneath. Z5.

R. niveum Hook. Tree to 6m. Lvs 11–17cm, oblanceolate-elliptic, glab. above, with dense, compacted, fawn hairs beneath. Fls 3–3.5cm, tubular-campanulate, deep magenta to purple. Himal. (Sikkim, Bhutan). 'Clyne Castle': lvs large; fls rich purple. Z7.

R. nudiflorum Torr. = *R. periclymenoides*.

R. nuttallii Booth. Shrub or small tree to 10m. Lvs 17–26cm, oblong-elliptic or oblong-obovate, wrinkled above, conspicuously veined beneath. Fls 7.5–12.5cm, funnel-campanulate, white with a yellow blotch at base. Late spring. NE India, W China. Z10.

R. oblongifolium (Small) Millais = *R. viscosum*.

R. obovatum Hook. f. = *R. lepidotum*.

R. ×obtusum Planch. Small shrub to 1m. Lvs 1–3.5cm, ovate to elliptic-ovate or oblong-lanceolate to obovate, with scattered, adpressed pale hairs. Fls to 2.5cm, funnel-shaped, white through pink and pink-red to purple-red. Late spring. A collection of cvs known only in cult., derived from *R. kiusianum*, *R. kaempferi* and perhaps other sp. 'Amoenum': lvs thin, elliptic, 1–2.5cm; cor. usually double, magenta. 'Amoenum Coccineum': fls red, tinged with magenta, sometimes double. Z6.

R. obtusum f. *amoenum* (Lindl.) Wils.) = *R. ×obtusum* 'Amoenum'.

R. occidentale A. Gray. Shrub to 3m. Lvs 3–9cm, elliptic to oblong-lanceolate, ciliate, thinly pubesc. Fls 3.5–5cm, funnel-shaped, white or sometimes pink, with a yellow blotch, villous and glandular-hairy outside. Late spring. W US. 'Crescent City Double': compact; fls semi-double, cream flushed with apricot. 'Humboldt Picotee': habit erect; fls white, edged with rose carmine. 'Leonard Frisbee': fls white with broad, frilly pet. with pink mid-line, upper pet. with yellow flare. 'Miniskirt': dwarf; fls white, v. small, with long red style. 'Stagecoach Frills': fls frilly, white flushed with pink, with orange-yellow flare. Z6.

R. odoriferum Hutch. = *R. maddenii* ssp. *crassum*.

R. oldhamii Maxim. Shrub to 3m+. Lvs 1.5–8×0.8–2.5cm, elliptic to elliptic-ovate or lanceolate, red-brown-hairy when young, becoming ± glab. above. Fls 2.5–3.5cm, funnel-shaped, orange-red to pink, glab. Late spring. Taiwan. Z9.

R. oleifolium Franch. = *R. virgatum* ssp. *oleifolium*.

R. oporinum Balf. f. & Kingdon-Ward = *R. heliolepis* var. *heliolepis*.

R. orbiculare Decne. Shrub or tree to 15m. Lvs 7–12.5cm, orbicular to ovate-orbicular, glab. Fls 3.5–4cm, 7-lobed, campanulate, rose-pink, unspotted. W China. ssp. *orbiculare*. Lvs 7–9.5cm. ssp. *cardiobasis* (Sleumer) Chamberl. Lvs to 12.5cm. Z6.

R. oreodoxa Franch. Shrub or small tree to 5m. Lvs 6–8.5cm, obovate-elliptic to elliptic, glab. when mature except for punctate hair bases beneath. Fls 3.5–4cm, usually (5–6-)7-lobed, campanulate, deep pink, glab. or hairy within. W China. var. *oreodoxa*. Ovary glab. var. *fargesii* (Franch.) Chamberl. Ovary covered with shortly stalked glands. 'Budget Farthing': fls white, flushed with red-purple, opening from red-purple buds. Z6.

R. oreotrephes W.W. Sm. Shrub to 8m. Lvs 2–8cm, mostly everg., circular to elliptic or oblong, blunt, lower surface with dense purple, red-brown or grey scales. Fls 2.5–3.4cm, rose or rose-lavender. W China. 'Exquisetum': fls pale mauve-pink, spotted red. 'James's White Form': fls white. Z6.

R. orthocladum Balf. f. & Forr. Much-branched, erect shrub to 1.3m. Lvs 8–16mm, narrowly elliptic to lanceolate, yellow-brown to fawn beneath, usually with darker speckling. Fls 7–13.5mm, funnel-shaped, pale to deep lavender-blue to purple or white, sometimes sparsely scaly outside. W China. var. *orthocladum*. Cor. blue to purple, style 3.5–5mm. N Yunnan, SW Sichuan. var. *longistylum* Philipson & Philipson. Cor. blue to purple; style 1.5–1.6cm. N & NW Yunnan. var. *microleucum* (Hutch.) Philipson & Philipson. Cor. white. Known only in cult. Z6.

R. ovatum (Lindl.) Maxim. Shrub to 4m. Lvs broadly ovate or ovate-elliptic, glab. except for a few hairs along the midrib above. Fls 4–5cm, v. openly campanulate, with a v. short tube, white, pink or pale purple, spotted above. C & S China, Taiwan. Z7.

R. oxyphyllum Franch. = *R. moulmainense*.

R. pachypodum Balf. f. & W.W. Sm. Shrub to 4m. Lvs 7–12cm, ± elliptic, brown-tinged beneath. Fls 5.5–7.5cm, funnel-campanulate, white or rarely flushed pink, with a yellow blotch at the base, sparsely scaly. Late spring. W China. The name *R. supranubium*, a synonym of *R. pachypodum*, has been

wrongly used for *R. dendricola*. Z8.

R. pachysanthum Hayata. Compact, rounded shrub to 1.5m. Lvs 4–10×1.5–5cm, lanceolate to ovate, thick, indumentum pale to deep buff. Fls to 4cm, widely campanulate, white to pale pink, sometimes strongly flecked purple-red within. Spring. Taiwan. Z8.

R. pachytrichum Franch. Shrub or small tree to 6m. Lvs 9–15cm, elliptic to obovate, glab. except for a few hairs toward midrib beneath. Fls 3.5–4cm, narrowly campanulate, white suffused with pink and with a purple basal blotch and spots. W China. 'Sesame': fls white, tinged with purple. Z6.

R. paludosum Hutch. & Kingdon-Ward = *R. nivale* ssp. *nivale*.

R. parryae Hutch. A name applied to a plant known only in cult. close to *R. johnstoneanum*. Z10.

R. parviflorum Schmidt = *R. lapponicum*.

R. patulum Kingdon-Ward = *R. pemakoense*.

R. pemakoense Kingdon-Ward. Prostrate or erect dwarf shrub. Lvs 1.7–2.6mm, obovate or obovate-elliptic, upper surface ± persistently scaly, lower surface with unequal golden to brown scales. Fls 2.4–3cm, campanulate, pink to pale purple-mauve, densely hairy and sparsely scaly outside. E Himal., China. Plants with cor. pale purple-mauve have been called *R. patulum*. Z6.

R. pendulum Hook. Similar to *R. edgeworthii* but smaller, hairs off-white to beige; lf upper surface smooth and shining; cor. 1.5–2.2cm, almost radially symmetric. Himal. Z8.

R. pentaphyllum Maxim. Shrub to 4m. Lvs 2.5–6cm, elliptic to elliptic-lanceolate, ciliate and finely toothed, midrib villous. Fls 4.5–5cm, v. widely campanulate with a short tube and spreading lobes; rose pink, unspotted. Late spring. C & S Jap. Z7.

R. periclymenoides (Michx.) Shinn. Shrub to 2m. Lvs 3–8cm, elliptic to oblong to obovate, ± glab. above, strigose beneath. Fls 2.5–4cm, funnel-shaped, tube longer than lobes, pink or off-white, usually pubesc. outside. Late spring. E US. Z3.

R. phaeochrysum Balf. f. & W.W. Sm. Shrub to 4.5m. Lvs elliptic to ovate-oblong, glab. above, beneath with dense brown hairs. Fls 2–5cm, funnel-campanulate, white flushed with pink and with crimson spots. W China. var. *phaeochrysum*. Lvs 8–14.5cm. Cor. 3.2–5cm. var. *levistratum* (Balf. f. & Forr.) Chamberl. Lvs 4–9cm. Cor. 2–3.5cm. Z8.

R. pholidotum Balf. f. & W.W. Sm. = *R. heliolepis* var. *brevistylum*.

R. planetum Balf. f. A name applied to a gdn hybrid of an unknown sp. of Subsection *Fortunea*, much material in cult. under this name is a variant of *R. oreodoxa*. Z7.

R. plebeium Balf. f. & W.W. Sm. = *R. heliolepis* var. *heliolepis*.

R. pleistanthum Wilding Differs from *R. yunnanense* in the absence of bristles on even young lvs. W China. Some material cultivated as *R. yunnanense* or as *R. hormophorum* is this sp. Z8.

R. pocophorum Tagg. Shrub to 3m. Lvs 8–15cm, oblong to obovate, glab. above and with a thick red-brown hairs beneath. Fls 4–5cm, fleshy, tubular-campanulate, pale to deep crimson. NE India, W China. 'Cecil Nice': fls deep red with darker markings in throat. Z7.

R. polyandrum Hutch. = *R. maddenii* ssp. *maddenii*.

R. polycladum Franch. Erect shrub to 1.25m. Lvs 6–18mm, narrowly elliptic to elliptic, undersurface ± grey with brown dots or more uniformly red-brown. Fls 7.5–13mm, broadly funnel-shaped, lavender to purple-blue, rarely off-white, occas. hairy outside. W China. Scintillans group: fls lavender-blue, rose-purple or almost royal blue, not hairy nor scaly on outside. Z8.

R. polylepis Franch. Shrub to 6m, usually smaller. Lvs 5–10cm, narrowly to v. narrowly elliptic, upper surface dark green, ± scaly, lower surface v. densely covered with flaky yellow-brown or dark brown scales. Cor. 2.5–3cm, purple, scaly outside. W China. Z6.

R. ponticum L. Shrub to 8m, young shoots glab. Lvs 6–18cm, oblanceolate to broadly elliptic, glab. when mature. Fls 3.5–5cm, campanulate, lilac-pink to purple, usually with green-yellow spots. Late spring. W & E Medit., widely nat. in Britain and Ireland. 'Aucubifolium': lvs spotted with yellow. 'Cheiranthifolium': lvs v. narrow, undulate; fls small, insignificant. 'Foliis-purpureis': lvs green in summer, coppery-purple in winter. 'Variegatum': compact; lvs narrow, bordered with creamy-white; fls purple. Z6.

R. ×praecox hort. A widely-grown, early-flowering hybrid between *R. ciliatum* and *R. dauricum*; 'Emasculum': sta. 0. Z6.

R. praestans Balf. f. & W.W. Sm. Shrub or small tree to 10m. Lvs 20–30cm, oblong-obovate to oblanceolate, glab. above, silver-haired beneath. Fls 3.5–5cm, 7–8-lobed, obliquely campanulate, pale yellow or white flushed with pink, with a crimson basal blotch and spots. W China. Z7.

R. praevernum Hutch. Shrub to 2m or more. Lvs 10–18cm, elliptic-oblanceolate, glab. Fls 5–6cm, campanulate, 5-lobed, white (occas. suffused with pink) and with a purple blotch and spots. W China. Z6.

R. primuliflorum Bur. & Franch.   Small shrub to 1.5m. Lvs 1–3.5cm, narrowly elliptic or somewhat oblong, dark glossy green and ± scaly, pale brown to brown beneath, scales golden. Fls 9–18mm, white, rarely flushed with pink, often yellow-orange toward base. W China. Z6.

R. primulinum Hemsl. = **R. flavidum**.

R. prinophyllum Millais = **R. austrinum**.

R. probum Balf. f. & Forr. = **R. selense** ssp. *selense*.

R. prostratum W.W. Sm. = **R. saluenense** ssp. *chameunum*.

R. proteoides Balf. f. & W.W. Sm.   Small shrub to 1m. Lvs 2–4cm, elliptic, apex cucullate, glab. above, with loose woolly, brown hairs beneath. Fls 2.5–3.5cm, campanulate, white to cream flushed with pink, and with purple spots. W China. Z7.

R. protistum Balf. f. & Forr.   Tree to 30m in the wild. Lvs 20–40cm, glab., sometimes developing buff hairs beneath. Fls 5–7.5cm, funnel-campanulate, 8-lobed, pink or sometimes off-white at the base, with a dark basal blotch and nectar-pouches. W China, NE Burm. var. *protistum*.   Mature lvs with the sparse band of marginal hairs beneath. var. *giganteum* (Tagg) Chamberl.   Mature lvs with the indumentum ± continuous; possibly a juvenile phase of var. *protistum*. Z9.

R. pruniflorum Hutch.   Shrub to 1m, with shredding, brown bark. Lvs 3–4.5cm, obovate or narrowly obovate, dark green and ± scaleless above, with dense pale yellow, clouded or milky scales beneath. Fls 1–1.3cm, campanulate, dull crimson to plum-purple. NE India, NE Burm. Z7.

R. prunifolium (Small) Millais.   Shrub to 2m. Lvs 3–12cm, elliptic or obovate to oblong, ciliate, glab. or sparingly strigose above, sparingly so on the midrib and veins beneath. Fls 3.5–5cm, funnel-shaped, crimson, finely villous and sometimes glandular-pilose outside, hairy inside. Late spring. SE US. 'Summer Sunset': fls vermilion red. Z6.

R. przewalskii Maxim.   Shrub to 3m. Lvs 5–10cm, broadly elliptic, glab. above, beneath with pale brown hairs. Fls 2.5–3.5cm, campanulate, white to pale pink with purple spots. W China. Z6.

R. pseudochrysanthum Hayata.   Shrub to 3m. Lvs 3–8cm, ovate to elliptic, glab. above when mature, beneath with soon-falling floccose. Fls 3–4cm, campanulate, pink with deeper lines outside and spots within. Taiwan. Ben Nelson's form: lvs longer and broader than usual. Exbury form: fls white, tinged with pink and spotted with red; good, silvery new growth. Z8.

R. pseudoyanthinum Hutch. = **R. concinnum**.

R. pubescens Balf. f. & Forr.   Small shrub to c1m. Lvs 1.8–2.5cm, v. narrowly elliptic to v. narrowly lanceolate, margins strongly rolled downwards, upper surface scaly and with a covering of short hairs. Fls 6–11mm, funnel-shaped, rose pink, hairy inside. W China. Z6.

R. ×pulchrum Sweet. (*R. indicum* ×*R. mucronatum*.)   Shrub to 2m. Lvs 2.5–6cm, elliptic to elliptic-lanceolate or oblong-lanceolate, at first with brown-tinged hairs, later glab. above. Fls to 6.5cm, broadly funnel-shaped, red-purple spotted dark purple. Late spring. var. *pulchrum*. 'Tebotan': habit fairly erect; fls large, semi-double lavender-rose, often with the malformed stigma protruding like a green knob. var. *maxwellii* (Millais) Rehd.   Fls carmine-red. Z7.

R. pumilum Hook.   Creeping small shrub to 10cm high. Lvs 9–19mm, elliptic to broadly elliptic, dark green, margins rolled under, pale grey above, green with distant golden scales beneath. Fls 1–2cm, campanulate, pink or purple, densey hairy. Himal. Z6.

R. punctatum Andrews = **R. minus**.

R. puralbum Balf. f. & W.W. Sm. = **R. wardii** var. *puralbum*.

R. purdomii hort.   A name applied to hybrids involving sp. of Subsection *Taliensia* in cult. Genuine **R. purdomii** Rehd. & Wils. is not in cult. Z6.

R. quinquefolium Bisset & Moore.   Shrub or small tree to 8m. Lvs 3–6cm, broadly elliptic to obovate, ciliate and often edged red-purple, glab. above except along midrib, villous beneath twoards base. Fls to 2cm, v. openly campanulate, white with green spots above, lobes longer than tube. Late spring. C Jap. 'Five Arrows': fls white spotted with olive-green. Z6.

R. racemosum Franch.   Shrub to 3m. Lvs 1.5–5cm, broadly obovate to oblong-elliptic, glab. above, shining white-papillose beneath, with dense scales. Fls 7–17mm, openly funnel-shaped, white to pale or deep pink. W China. 'Forrest': dwarf; fls pink. 'Glendoick': taller, with deep pink fls. 'Rock Rose': fls bright purple-pink. 'White Lace': fls white. Z5.

R. radicans Balf. f. & Forr. = **R. calostrotum** ssp. *keleticum*.

R. radinum Balf. f. & W.W. Sm. = **R. trichostomum**.

R. ravum Balf. f. & W.W. Sm. = **R. cuneatum**.

R. recurvoides Tagg & Kingdon-Ward.   Shrub to 1.5m. Lvs 3–7cm, lanceolate to oblanceolate, upper surface rough, lower surface with dense cinnamon-brown hairs. Fls to 3cm,

campanulate, white flushed pink, spotted with crimson, though without a basal blotch. NE Burm. Z9.

R. repens Balf. f. & Forr. = **R. forrestii**.

R. reticulatum D. Don.   Shrub to 8m. Lvs 3–6cm, broadly ovate or rhombic, at first covered in grey or yellow hairs, soon glab. above, hairs persisting on the midrib and veins beneath. Fls 3.5–5cm, funnel-campanulate, with a short white tube and spreading lobes, red-purple to magenta, usually unspotted, 2-lipped. Late spring. Jap. Z6.

R. retusum (Bl.) Benn   Shrub to 7m, but usually much smaller in cult. Lvs 1.5–6.5cm, in false whorls, obovate to oblong-obovate, scales persistent beneath. Fls 2–2.5cm, tubular, red to crimson, scarlet or orange-red, variably scaly and hairy outside. Winter. Java, Sumatra. Z10.

R. rex Lév.   Large shrubs or small trees to 12m. Lvs 10–37cm, obovate to oblanceolate, 1.5–3.8× as long as broad, ± glab. above, smooth or finely wrinkled, lower surface with a dense fawn to red hairs. Fls obliquely campanulate or campanulate, 7–8-lobed, white, pale yellow or pink, with a crimson basal blotch and spots. W China, NE Burm. ssp. *rex*.   Lvs 2.4–3.1× as long as broad with fawn hairs. Cor. white flushed pink. S Sichuan, NE Yunnan. 'Quartz': fls pink with crimson blotch and spots. 'Roseum': fls pale rose pink with small dark blotch, opening from deeper pink buds. ssp. *arizelum* (Balf. f. & Forr.) Chamberl.   Like ssp. *fictolacteum*, but lvs 1.5–2× as long as broad, hairs strongly fimbriate, cor. yellow. W Yunnan, NE Burm. 'Brodick': fls purple with red and black blotch. ssp. *fictolacteum* (Balf. f.) Chamberl.   Lvs 2–3.8× as long as broad, brown. Cor. white or pink. W Yunnan, SE Xizang, NE Burm. 'Cherry Tip': fls white, edged with pink, and with crimson blotch and spots. Z7.

R. rhabdotum Balf. f. & Cooper = **R. dalhousiae** var. *rhabdotum*.

R. rhantum Balf. f. & W.W. Sm. = **R. vernicosum**.

R. rhodora Gmel. = **R. canadense**.

R. rhombicum Miq. = **R. reticulatum**.

R. rigidum Franch.   Shrub to 10m. Lvs 3–6.5cm, thick and hard, elliptic to narrowly elliptic, scaleless above, sparsely scaly beneath. Fls 2.4–3cm, usually white, sometimes rose-pink or lilac, unspotted or spotted with red. W China. Z7.

R. riparium Kingdon-Ward = **R. calostrotum** ssp. *riparium*.

R. rirei Hemsl. & Wils.   Small tree, 3.5–16m. Lvs 9.5–17cm, elliptic to oblanceolate, glab. above, with a thin white film of compacted hairs beneath. Fls 4–5cm, campanulate, purple to violet with darker nectar-pouches. W China. Z7.

R. roseotinctum Balf. f. & Forr. = **R. sanguineum** ssp. *sanguineum* var. *didymoides*.

R. roseum Rehd. = **R. austrinum**.

R. roxieanum Forr.   Shrub, to 2.5m. Lvs 5–12cm, linear to elliptic, ± 2× as long as broad, glab. above, beneath with thick woolly, red-brown hairs. Fls 2–4cm, funnel-campanulate, white or rarely pale yellow, sometimes flushed with pink, with purple spots. W China. var. *roxieanum*.   Lvs more than 4× as long as broad, acute. Oreonastes group: lvs v. narrowly linear. var. *cucullatum* (Hand.-Mazz.) Chamberl.   Lvs to 4× as long as broad, apex acute or cucullate. Z7.

R. roylei Hook. = **R. cinnabarinum** ssp. *cinnabarinum*.

R. rubiginosum Franch.   Shrubs or small trees to 10m or more. Lvs 5–11.5cm, narrowly elliptic to elliptic or almost lanceolate, glab. and scaleless above, scaly beneath. Fls 1.7–3.8cm, openly funnel-shaped, pink, mauve-pink or rarely white flushed with pink-purple, scaly outside. W China, NE Burm. 'Wakehurst': fls mallow purple with crimson spots. Desquamatum group: fls usually larger and flatter; often more compact plants with slightly larger lvs. Z7.

R. rubrolineatum Balf. f. & Forr. = **R. mekongense** var. *rubrolineatum*.

R. rubroluteum Davidian = **R. mekongense** var. *mekongense*.

R. rude Tagg & Forr. = **R. glischrum** ssp. *rude*.

R. rufescens Franch.   Small shrub to 1m. Lvs 1–2cm, elliptic-oblong or ovate, dark glossy green above, with dark brown scales beneath. Fls 9–15mm, white, tube scaly outside, mouth pilose. W China. Z8.

R. rufum Batal.   Shrub to 4.5m. Lvs 6.5–11cm, glab. above, beneath with off-white and red-brown hairs. Fls 2–3.2cm, campanulate, white to pink, with crimson spots. W China. Z7.

R. rupicola W.W. Sm.   Much-branched shrub to 1.2m. Lvs 6.5–20mm, broadly elliptic to elliptic, oblong or almost ovate, undersurface fawn, heavily stippled red-brown, scales dark brown, golden or amber. Fls 8–18mm, broad funnel-shaped, intense purple or yellow, occas. tinged red or almost white. N Burm., W China. var. *rupicola*.   Cor. purple or tinged red, rarely white. N Burm., W China. var. *chryseum* (Balf. f. & Kingdon-Ward) Philipson & Philipson.   Cor. yellow, cal. lobes margined with hairs only. N Burm., W China. var. *muliense* (Balf. f. & Forr.) Philipson & Philipson.   Cor. yellow, cal. lobes margined with hairs and scales. W China. Z5.

R. russatum Balf. f. & Forr. Shrub to 1.5m. Lvs 1.6–4cm, narrowly to broadly elliptic or oblong, lower surface heavily speckled or uniformly brown or red-brown, scales pale gold to deep brown. Fls 1–2cm, broadly funnel-shaped, purple, pink or rose, often pubesc. outside. W China. 'Collingwood Ingram': a taller plant with rich purple fls. 'Keillour': a compact form with deep blue-purple fls. 'Maryborough': intermediate size; fls blue-purple, later than other forms. 'Night Editor': lvs relatively large, twisted; fls bright purple. Z5.

R. salignum Hook. f. = *R. lepidotum*.

R. saluenense Franch. Prostrate to upright shrubs, 5–150cm. Lvs 8–30mm, oblong-circular to oblong-elliptic or rarely oblong-obovate, upper surface usually scaleless, dark, glossy green, margins bristly, lower surface fawn to brown with dense scales. Fls 1.7–2.8cm, widely spreading, magenta to purple, rarely blue-purple, hairy and with a few scales outside. NE Burm., W China. ssp. *saluenense*. Erect to 1.5m; lvs persistently scaly above and usually bristled. NE Burm., SW China. ssp. *chameunum* (Balf. f. & Forr.) Cullen. Prostrate or mat-forming shrub, rarely 1m high; lvs usually glossy green and scaleless above, without bristles there. W China. Prostratum group: prostrate, less than 50cm; fls crimson or deep rose-purple with darker spots. Z6.

R. sanctum Nak. Shrub to 5m. Lvs 3–8×2.5–6cm, broadly rhombic to rhombic-ovate, with long red-brown hairs above, and midrib and veins beneath. Fls funnel-campanulate, 2.5–3.5cm, glab., deep pink. Late spring. Jap. Z7.

R. sanguineum Franch. Small shrub to 1.5m. Lvs 3–8cm, elliptic to obovate, glab. above, with silvery to grey hairs beneath. Fls 2.5–3.5cm, fleshy, shortly tubular-campanulate, yellow to pink or crimson or blackish crimson, rarely white. W China. ssp. *sanguineum* var. *sanguineum*. Small shrub to 1.5m. Lvs 3–8cm, elliptic to obovate, glab. above, with silvery to grey hairs. Fls 2.5–3.5cm, fleshy, shortly tubular-campanulate, yellow to pink or crimson or blackish crimson, rarely white. var. *haemaleum* (Balf. f. & Forr.) Chamberl. Cor. deep black-crimson. var. *didymoides* Tagg & Forr. ssp. *didymum* (Balf. f. & Forr.) Cowan. Bud scales persistent and cor. deep black-crimson. Z8.

R. sargentianum Rehd. & Wils. Small shrub to 60cm. Lvs 9–15mm, elliptic, dark green and scaleless above, lower surface brown or pale brown with scales golden. Fls to 1.2cm, off-white to yellow-white, scaly outside and ± pubesc. W China. 'Whitebait': fls white. Z8.

R. scabrifolium Franch. Shrub to 3m. Lvs narrowly elliptic to oblanceolate, 1.5–9cm, with fine hairs above, scaly and with dense bristles beneath. Fls shape and size, white to deep pink. W China. var. *scabrifolium*. Cor. openly funnel-shaped, 9–15mm. N Yunnan. var. *spiciferum* (Franch.) Cullen. Cor. narrowly funnel-shaped, 1.2–1.5cm. C & S Yunnan. var. *pauciflorum* Franch. Cor. 1.6–2.3cm, narrowly funnel-shaped. C & S Yunnan. Z8.

R. scabrum G. Don Shrub to 2m. Lvs 3–10cm, elliptic-lanceolate, lanceolate or oblanceolate, ciliate and slightly crenulate, with scattered grey hairs, falling, except from midrib and veins. Fls to 6.5cm, broadly funnel-shaped, pink-red to scarlet, with dark dots on the upper lobes. Late spring. Ryuku Is. Z9.

R. schlippenbachii Maxim. Shrub to 5m, often less spreading. Lvs 2.5–11×0.9–7.2cm, obovate or broadly ovate, truncate, rounded or notched at apex, sparsely pubesc. at first. Fls 3–6cm, v. openly funnel-shaped, pale pink, upper lobes spotted with red-brown. Late spring. Korea, E Russia. 'Prince Charming': fls rhodamine pink, flushed with deeper pink and spotted with crimson. Z4.

R. scintillans Balf. f. & W.W. Sm. = *R. polycladum*.

R. scyphocalyx Balf. f. & Forr. = *R. dichroanthum* ssp. *scyphocalyx*.

R. searsiae Rehd. & Wils. V. similar to *R. concinnum* but lvs *c*7×2cm, narrowly elliptic, grey or silver beneath with golden and milky or clear scales. Fls *c*2.2cm, white or pale purple. W China. Z6.

R. selense Franch. Shrub or small tree to 5m. Lvs 3.5–9cm, ovate to obovate or elliptic, glab. above; sparsely hairy beneath. Fls 2.5–4cm, funnel-campanulate, white or cream to deep pink, with or without purple spots. W China. ssp. *selense*. Young shoots with shortly stalked glands. SW China. Probum group: fls white, unspotted. ssp. *dasycladum* (Balf. f. & W.W. Sm.) Chamberl. Young shoots with gland-tipped bristles. W Yunnan, SW Sichuan. Z8.

R. semibarbatum Maxim. Shrub to 3m. Lvs 1.8–5cm, elliptic to elliptic-oblong or elliptic-ovate, minutely crenulate, dark green and glab. above, pale green and glab. beneath except for sparse bristles on midrib and veins. Fls to 2cm, widely campanulate, yellow-white or white flushed with pink, and with red dots. Late spring. C & S Jap. Z6.

R. semnum Balf. f. & Forr. = *R. praestans*.

R. serpyllifolium Miq. Low shrub. Lvs 3–10mm, decid., obovate,

elliptic or obovate-oblong, sparcely strigose above, with few flattened brown hairs on midrib beneath. Fls funnel-shaped, to 2.5cm, pink. Late spring. C & S Jap. Z6.

R. serrulatum (Small) Millais = *R. viscosum*.

R. × *sesterianum* hort. A hybrid between *R. edgeworthii* and *R. formosum*; see also *R.* × *fragrantissimum*.

R. setosum D. Don Small, intricate shrub to 30cm. Lvs 1–1.5cm, elliptic, oblong or obovate, dark green above with persistent golden scales, margins bristly, pale green with dense golden and brown scales beneath. Fls 1.5–1.8cm, openly funnel-shaped, purple or purple-pink beneath. Himal. Z6.

R. sheltonii Hemsl. & Wils. = *R. vernicosum*.

R. sherriffii Cowan. Shrub or small tree to 6m. Lvs *c*7.5cm, obovate, glab. above, densely brown-tomentose beneath. Fls 3.5–4cm, funnel-campanulate, deep carmine with darker nectar-pouches. W China. Z8.

R. shweliense Balf. f. & Forr. Like *R. brachyanthum* but lvs 3.2–4cm, narrowly elliptic to narrowly obovate, fls about 1.2cm, yellow flushed with pink. W China. Most material in cult. under this name is *R. glaucophyllum*. Z6.

R. sichotense Pojark. = *R. dauricum*.

R. siderophyllum Franch. Shrub to 7m. Lvs 4.6–8.5cm, broadly elliptic to elliptic, scaleless above, with dense flat scales beneath. Fls 1.8–2.5cm, white or pale pink-violet. W China. Much material so-named belongs to other spp. (*R. tatsiense*, *R. davidsonianum* and *R. yunnanense*). Z8.

R. sigillatum Balf. f. & Forr. = *R. phaeochrysum* var. *levistratum*.

R. silvaticum Cowan = *R. lanigerum*.

R. simsii Planch. INDIAN AZALEA. Shrub to 3m. Lvs 1–7×0.5–1.2cm, elliptic, oblong-elliptic, ovate to obovate or oblanceolate, sparsely strigose above, more densely so beneath. Fls 2.5–5cm, broadly funnel-shaped, red, spotted. Late spring. NE Burm., China, Taiwan. Z7.

R. sinense hort. A name applied to cultivated specimens of *R. japonicum* or *R. molle*.

R. sinogrande Balf. f. & W.W. Sm. Tree to 10m. Lvs 20–70(–100)cm, oblong-oblanceolate to oblong-elliptic, glab. and wrinkled above when mature, with silvery or fawn, indumentum beneath. Fls 4–6cm, ventricose-campanulate, 8–10-lobed, pale cream with a crimson blotch at the base. Spring. W China, NE Burm. Trewithen form: fls ivory white with large crimson blotch. Z8.

R. sinolepidotum Balf. f. = *R. lepidotum*.

R. sinonuttallii Balf. f. & Forr. = *R. nuttallii*.

R. smirnowii Trautv. Shrub to 4m. Lvs 7.5–14cm, oblanceolate to elliptic, upper surface glab. when mature, lower with dense white to brown woolly hairs. Fls 3.5–4cm, funnel-campanulate, pink with yellow spots. Late spring. NE Turk. and adjacent Georgia. Z4.

R. smithii Hook. Shrub or small tree to 7.5m. Lvs 8–13cm, elliptic to obovate-lanceolate, glab. above, with thin pale brown hairs beneath. Fls 3–4.5cm, tubular-campanulate, scarlet to crimson with darker nectar-pouches. NE India, Bhutan, SW China. Z8.

R. sordidum Hutch. = *R. pruniflorum*.

R. souliei Franch. Shrub to 5m. Lvs 5.5–8cm, broadly ovate, glab. Fls 2.5–4cm, openly saucer-shaped, pale purple-pink. W China. 'Exbury Pink': fls deep rose pink. 'Windsor Park': fls white, edged with pink, the 3 upper pet. with small red blotch at base. Z6.

R. speciosum (Willd.) Sweet = *R. calendulaceum*.

R. sperabile Balf. f. & Farrer. Shrub to 2m. Lvs 5–10cm, elliptic, glab. above, beneath with loose, off-white to brown hairs. Fls 3.5–4cm, fleshy, tubular-campanulate, crimson. W China, NE Burm. Z8.

R. sperabiloides Tagg & Forr. Dwarf shrub to 1.5m. Lvs 5.5–6.5cm, elliptic, glab. above, beneath with thin patchy hairs. Fls 2.5–3.5cm, fleshy, tubular-campanulate, deep red. W China. Z8.

R. sphaeranthum Balf. f. & W.W. Sm. = *R. trichostomum*.

R. spiciferum Franch. = *R. scabrifolium* var. *spiciferum*.

R. spinuliferum Franch. Shrub to 3m, similar vegetatively to *R. scabrifolium*, but lvs larger, ultimately glab. above with short fine hairs persisting along midrib. Fls 1.7–2.3cm, erect, tubular to v. narrowly funnel-shaped, filled with watery nectar, bright, deep red. W China. Z8.

R. stamineum Franch. Shrub or small tree to 13m. Lvs 6–14cm, elliptic to oblanceolate, glab. Fls 2.5–3.5cm, funnel-shaped, with a narrow tube and spreading or reflexed lobes, white or pink, with a yellow blotch. W China. Z9.

R. stenaulum Balf. f. & Farrer = *R. moulmainense*.

R. stenoplastum Balf. f. & Farrer = *R. rubiginosum*.

R. stereophyllum Hutch. = *R. tatsiense*.

R. stewartianum Diels. Shrub to 2.5m; bark peeling on younger br. Lvs 4–12cm, obovate to elliptic, upper surface glab., lower with thin gland. hairs. Fls 3.5–5.5cm, campanulate to tubular-campanulate, white or cream to pale pink, with or without purple spots. W China, NE Burm. Z9.

R. stictophyllum Balf. f. = *R. nivale* ssp. *boreale*.

R. strigillosum Franch. Shrub to 2.5m. Lvs 7.5–14cm, elliptic to oblanceolate, sometimes ciliate, ± glab. above, bristly beneath. Fls 4–6cm, tubular-campanulate, deep red, with deep, darker nectar-pouches. W China. Exbury Pink form: fls pink, opening from red buds. Z8.

R. sulfureum Franch. Epiphytic or free-growing shrub to 1.6m, with pitted scales. Lvs 3.5–7.5cm, obovate, sometimes broadly so, upper surface scaleless, margins bristly, at least when young, lower surface. Fls 1.5–2cm, green-tinged to bright yellow, unspotted, sparsely to densely scaly outside, sometimes pubesc. on tube. NE Burm., W China. Z9.

R. supranubium Hutch. = *R. pachypodum*.

R. sutchuenense Franch. Shrub to 5m. Lvs 11–25cm, oblong-lanceolate, glab. above, floccose along midrib beneath. Fls 5–7.5cm, 5–6-lobed, widely campanulate, pink with darker spots but no basal blotch. W China. 'Seventh Heaven': fls red-purple, white in centre. Z6.

R. taggianum Hutch. Differing from *R. lindleyi* only in the cal. lobes margined with quickly decid. scales rather than fine hairs. Spring. W China, NE Burm. Z10.

R. taliense Franch. Shrub to 4m. Lvs 5–11cm, glab. above, brown-hairy beneath. Fls 3–3.5cm, campanulate, white or rarely yellow, sometimes flushed with pink, with crimson spots. W China. Z6.

R. tanastylum Balf. f. & Kingdon-Ward. Shrub or small tree, to 4m. Lvs 7.5–15cm, elliptic to oblanceolate, ± glab. throughout. Fls 4.5–5.5cm, tubular-campanulate, deep pink to deep crimson, with black nectar-pouches and few to many spots. NE India, W China. Z9.

R. tapetiforme Balf. f. & Kingdon-Ward. Low, matted or densely rounded shrub, prostrate or to 90cm. Lvs 4–15mm, broadly elliptic to circular, lower surface dark red-brown with contiguous scales. Fls 9–16mm, broadly funnel-shaped, usually purple or·purple-blue, occas. violet or lavender, exceptionally yellow, sometimes pubesc. outside. NE Burm., W China. Z5.

R. taronense Hutch. = *R. dendricola*.

R. tatsienense Franch. Shrub to 5m, usually much smaller in cult. Lvs 2–5×1.2–2.5cm, broadly elliptic to elliptic, scaly above, densely scaly beneath. Fls 1.6–2.1cm, off-white, rose-pink or lavender. W China.

R. telmateium Balf. f. & W.W. Sm. Much-branched shrub forming dense cushions or mats, or erect to 1m. Lvs 3–14mm, narrowly elliptic or lanceolate, undersurface golden-fawn to orange-brown or red-brown with densely overlapping scales. Fls 7–14mm, broadly funnel-shaped, lavender-pink to purple, often pubesc. outside, always scaly. W China. Z8.

R. telopeum Balf. f. & Forr. = *R. campylocarpum* ssp. *caloxanthum*.

R. tephropeplum Balf. f. & Farrer. Shrub to 1.3m, bark scaling. Lvs 4–10cm, narrowly oblanceolate to narrowly elliptic, dark green above, brown-grey beneath, papillose and with sunken black-brown scales. Fls 2–2.5cm, campanulate, pink to red, variably scaly outside, glab. NE India, NE Burm., W China. Z8.

R. teysmannii Miq. V. like *R. javanicum*, but ovary densely hairy. Winter. Malaysia, Indon.

R. thayerianum Rehd. & Wils. Shrub to 4m. Lvs 8–13cm, narrowly oblanceolate, glab. above, beneath with a dense, compacted fawn hairs. Fls 2.5–3cm, funnel-shaped, white tinged with pink, with red spots. W China. Z7.

R. thomsonii Hook. Shrub or small tree to 3.5m. Lvs 3–11cm, orbicular to obovate or elliptic, glab., glaucous beneath, sometimes with some red glands. Fls 3.5–5cm, campanulate, fleshy, deep crimson, usually without darker spots. Himal., W China. Z6.

R. timeteum Balf. f. & Forr. = *R. oreotrephes*.

R. tosaense Mak. Shrub to 2m. Lvs 7–40×0.2–1cm, lanceolate, oblanceolate or elliptic-lanceolate, with scattered, appressed grey hairs. Fls to 1.8–2.5cm, funnel-shaped, lilac-purple. Late spring. S Jap. 'Ralph Clarke': fls rich purple, fading to white at base on outside. Z7.

R. traillianum Forr. & W.W. Sm. Shrub or small tree to 8m. Lvs 7–13cm, obovate to elliptic, glab. above, beneath with dense, red-brown hairs. Fls 2.5–4.5cm, funnel-campanulate, white, sometimes flushed with pink, with crimson spots. W China. Z7.

R. trichanthum Rehd. Shrub to 6m. Lvs 5.5–8cm, everg., ovate-elliptic, upper surface glab. or bristly, lower surface hairy at least on midrib, scales brown. Fls 3–3.6cm, light to dark purple, funnel-shaped, ext. with ± flattened bristles. W China. 'Honey Wood': fls violet-purple, paler in throat, mottled with green. Z7.

R. trichocladum Franch. Shrub to 1.5m. Lvs 2.4–4cm, decid., flat, thin, obovate or obovate-elliptic, lower surface covered with dense, curled or twisted bristles, and golden scales, upper

surface with straight bristles and/or fine, short hairs. Fls 1.8–2.3cm, yellow or green-yellow, occas. somewhat orange, scaly and variably bristly outside. Late spring. NE Burm., W China. Z6.

R. trichostomum Franch. Small, intricately branched shrub, 30–150cm, often forming rounded bushes. Lvs 1.2–3cm, linear, oblong or oblanceolate, upper surface green; scaly or not, margins usually revolute, lower surface pale brown with golden scales. Fls 6–15mm, white or pink, tube glab. outside, lobes with a few scales on their backs. W China. Ledoides group: cor. not scaly. 'Collingwood Ingram': fls red-purple, paler in throat. 'Lakeside': fls white, flushed with red-purple. 'Quarry Wood': fls white, flushed with red-purple. 'Rae Berry': fls clear, pale pink. 'Radinum group': cor. densely scaly on outside. 'Sweet Bay': fls white flushed with rose, appearing pale pink. Z7.

R. triflorum Hook. Straggling shrub to 7m, bark of mature shoots usually smooth, red-brown, peeling. Lvs 4–6.5cm, usually everg., ovate or lanceolate, dark green above, grey-brown beneath with small scales. Fls 2–3cm, variable in shape, pale yellow, yellow suffused red-brown, or with dark red spots, densely scaly, and pubesc. at the sinuses between the lobes outside. Himal. var. *triflorum*. Cor. without basal blotch. Himal. Variants with the cor. suffused red-brown have been called var. *mahogani* Hutch.. var. *bauhiniiflorum* (Hutch.) Cullen. Cor. v. widely open, almost flat. India (Manipur). Z6.

R. trinerve Franch. = *R. tschonoskii* var. *trinerve*.

R. tsarongense Kingdon-Ward = *R. primuliflorum*.

R. tschonoskii Maxim. Shrub to 2m. Lvs 1–3.5×0.3–1cm, narrowly lanceolate to elliptic-lanceolate or oblanceolate, with adpressed, off-white or red-brown hairs. Fls to 9mm, funnel-shaped, sometimes 4-lobed, white. Late spring. Jap., S Korea, E Russia. var. *trinerve* (Franch.) Mak. Lvs strongly 3-veined. Z6.

R. ungernii Trautv. Shrub or small tree to 7m. Lvs oblanceolate to obovate, glab. above when mature, beneath with dense, white or fawn, woolly hairs. Fls to 3.5cm, funnel-campanulate, white, sometimes flushed pink, with green spots. NE Turk., Georgia. Z5.

R. uniflorum Kingdon-Ward. Dwarf, ± prostrate shrub, ascending to c5cm high. Lvs 1.3–2.5cm, oblong-elliptic, upper surface scaleless, margins rolled downwards, lower surface with small, golden, later dark brown to black scales. Fls 2–2.5cm, campanulate, purple, densely hairy and sparsely scaly outside. NE Burm., W China. var. *uniflorum*. Lvs rounded at the apex. W China. var. *imperator* (Kingdon-Ward) Cullen. Lvs acute at the apex. NE Burm. Z8.

R. uvarifolium Diels. Small shrub to small tree, 2–10m. Lvs 10–22cm, oblanceolate to elliptic or oblong, glab. above, silvery-hairy beneath. Fls 3–3.5cm, campanulate, white to pale pink, with crimson spots and usually also a purple basal blotch. W China. 'Reginald Childs': fls white, flushed with red-purple and blotched with red. 'Yangtze Bend': fls rose pink, spotted and blotched with crimson. Z7.

R. vaccinioides Hook. Small, epiphytic shrub. Lvs spathulate-oblanceolate, notched at apex, with v. scattered scales beneath. Fls to 6mm, campanulate, lilac-pink or white tinged pink, sparsely scaly outside. Late spring. Himal. Z10.

R. valentinianum Hutch. Small shrub to 1.3m. Lvs 2.5–5cm, elliptic, bristly along midrib above, bristly-ciliate, lower surface brown with dense scales. Fls 2–3.2cm, funnel-campanulate, bright yellow, tube pubesc. outside, lobes scaly outside. Spring. NE Burm., SW China. Z9.

R. vaseyi A. Gray Upright shrub to 5m. Lvs 5–12cm, elliptic to elliptic-oblong, dark green and glab. above except for short hairs along midrib, pale green and glab. or sparsely pilose on the midrib beneath. Fls 2.5–3cm, v. openly campanulate, ± 2-lipped, lobes deep, spreading, pink or rarely white, with orange or orange-red spots. Late spring. E US. 'Suva': fls red-purple, fading to almost white in throat, spotted with darker red-purple. 'White Find': fls white. Z4.

R. veitchianum Hook. Epiphytic or free-growing shrub to 2m. Lvs 6.5–10cm, obovate or narrowly elliptic, upper surface dark green, scaleless, lower surface pale with distant, golden scales. Fls 5–6.5cm, openly funnel-campanulate, white, usually with a yellow blotch at the base, margins of the lobes v. waxy. Burm., Laos, Thail. Material cultivated as *R. cubitii* is generally a hybrid between *R. dendricola* and an unknown sp. Z9.

R. venator Tagg. Shrub to 3m. Lvs 8.5–14cm, elliptic to lanceolate, glab. except for hairs on midrib beneath. Fls 3–3.5cm, fleshy, tubular-campanulate, crimson with darker nectar-pouches. W China. Z8.

R. vernicosum Franch. Shrub or small tree to 8m. Lvs 5–10cm, elliptic or ovate-elliptic to obovate-elliptic, glab., punctate hair bases beneath. Fls broadly funnel-campanulate, 6–7-lobed, pale pink to pinkish purple with crimson spots. W China. 'Loch Eck': fls pure white. 'Spring Sonnet': fls white, flushed and spotted with red. Z7.

R. verruculosum Rehd. & Wils. A hybrid involving *R. flavidum*.

R. villosum Hemsl. & Wils. = *R. trichanthum*.

R. virgatum Hook. Shrub to 1.5m. Lvs to 5cm, narrowly oblong or oblong-elliptic, loosely scaly above, densely scaly beneath, papillose. Fls 1.5–3.7cm, white, pink or mauve, tube pubesc. and sparsely scaly outside, lobes scaly. Himal., W China. 'Album': fls white; a less hardy form. ssp. *virgatum* Fls 2.5–3.7cm, the tube 1.1–2cm, all pale to deep pink or mauve. Himal., SW China. ssp. *oleifolium* (Franch.) Cullen. Fls 1.5–2.5cm, tube 8–15mm, the whole white or pink. W China. Z9.

R. viridescens Hutch. = *R. mekongense* var. *mekongense*.

R. viscosum (L.) Torr. Shrub to 3m. Lvs 1.8–3cm, ovate or elliptic-obovate to oblong-oblanceolate, glab. above (except for short hairs along the midrib), strigose and pale to almost glaucous beneath. Fls 2–3cm, funnel-shaped, tube longer than lobes, white or white flushed pink (rarely deep pink), villous and finely glandular-hairy outside. Late spring. E US. Z3.

R. wallichii Hook. Shrub to 4.5m. Lvs 7–12cm, elliptic to ovate, glab. above, with sparse, dark brown hairs beneath. Fls 2.5–5cm, funnel-campanulate, white to pale mauve or lilac, with or without darker spots. Himal., W China. Z7.

R. wardii W.W. Sm. Shrub or small tree to 8m. Lvs 6–11cm, narrowly obovate to broadly ovate, entirely glab. somewhat glaucous beneath. Fls 2.5–4cm, saucer-shaped, white to pale yellow, with or without a purple basal blotch. W China. var. *wardii*. Fls yellow. 'Ellestee': fls lemon yellow with crimson blotch. Litiense group: lvs oblong, wavy-glaucous on underside. 'Meadow Pond': fls primrose yellow with crimson blotch. var. *puralbum* (Balf. f. & W.W. Sm.) Chamberl. Fls white. Z7.

R. wasonii Hemsl. & Wils. Small shrub to 1.5m. Lvs 7–8cm, ovate-lanceolate, glab. above when mature, beneath with sparse to dense red-brown hairs. Fls 3.5–4cm, openly campanulate, yellow or white to pink, with purple spots. W China. 'Rhododactylum': fls white and pink lines and large crimson blotch. Z7.

R. watsonii Hemsl. & Wils. Shrub or small tree to 6m. Lvs 10–20cm, glab. above, beneath with thin, white, compacted hairs. Fls 3.5–4cm, campanulate, 7-lobed, white with a crimson basal blotch. W China. Z9.

R. wattii Cowan. Shrub or small tree to 7m. Lvs 11–16cm, obovate to oblong, glab. above, with sparse, white, felted hairs beneath. Fls 3.5–5.5cm, tubular-campanulate, 6-lobed, pink with darker spots and purple basal patches. NE India. Z9.

R. websterianum Rehd. & Wils. Much-branched shrub to 1.5m. Lvs 6–15mm, ovate or oblong-elliptic to ovate-lanceolate, straw-coloured beneath, with dense scales. Fls 1.3–2cm, funnel-shaped, pale purple or yellow, glab. or pubesc. outside. Spring. W China. Z4.

R. weyrichii Maxim. Shrub to 5m, sometimes three-like. Lvs 3.5–8×1.5–6cm, suborbicular to broadly ovate or rhombic-ovate, with red-brown hairs when young. Fls 3–4cm, funnel-campanulate, with a short, narrow tube, pink. Late spring. S Jap. & S Korea (Quelpaert Is.). Z5.

R. wightii Hook. Shrub to 4.5m. Lvs 5–14cm, broadly elliptic to obovate, glab. above when mature, beneath with dense rusty red hairs. Fls 3.5–4.5cm, 5(–7)-lobed, ± campanulate, pale yellow with brown or purple spots. Himal., W China. Z7.

R. williamsianum Rehd. & Wils. Dwarf shrub to 1.5m. Lvs 2–4.5cm, ovate-orbicular, ± glab. Fls 3–4cm, campanulate, pale pink with darker spots. W China. 'Exbury White': fls white. Z7.

R. wilsonae Hemsl. & Wils. = *R. latoucheae*.

R. wiltonii Hemsl. & Wils. Shrub to 4.5m. Lvs 5–12cm, oblanceolate to broadly elliptic, upper surface glab. with deeply impressed veins, lower surface with dense, brown or rusty red hairs. Fls 3–4cm, campanulate, white to pink with red spots. W China. Z6.

R. xanthocodon Hutch. = *R. cinnabarinum* ssp. *xanthocodon*.

R. xanthostephanum Merrill. Shrub to 2m, mature bark smooth, red-brown, bloomed. Lvs 5–10cm, oblong-elliptic to elliptic, upper surface brown-green, lower surface silvery brown with pitted scales. Fls 1.8–2.8cm, narrowly campanulate, deep yellow, lemon-yellow or yellow-orange, variably scaly and sometimes slightly pubesc. outside. E India, NE Burm., SW China. 'Yellow Garland': fls translucent yellow. Z8.

R. yakushimanum Nak. = *R. degronianum* ssp. *yakushimanum*.

R. yanthinum Bur. & Franch. = *R. concinnum*.

R. yaragongense Balf. f. = *R. nivale* ssp. *boreale*.

R. yedoense Maxim. Compact, densely branched shrub to 2m. Lvs 3–8×1–2.5cm, elliptic-lanceolate to oblanceolate, ciliate, with adpressed, shining, grey or brown hairs. Fls to 3.5–4cm, broadly funnel-shaped, pink to pale lilac, spotted with purple-brown, fragrant. Late spring. S & C Korea. Above description represents var. *poukhanense* Nak. var. *yedoense* has fls double, rose-purple. Z5.

R. yungningense Balf. f. Erect shrub to c1m. Lvs 7–20mm, elliptic to broadly elliptic or oblong, lower surface brown to red-brown, scaly. Fls 1.1–1.4cm, broadly funnel-shaped, deep purple blue, rose-lavender or off-white, rarely pubesc. outside. W China. Z8.

R. yunnanense Franch. Shrub to 6m. Lvs 3–7×1.2–2cm, everg. or decid., narrowly elliptic or elliptic, scaly beneath, margins and upper surface with bristles, at least when young. Fls 2–3cm, white, pink or lavender, usually densely spotted above with red or yellow. Burm., W China. Decid. plants have been called *R. hormophorum*. Z7.

R. zaleucum Balf. f. & W.W. Sm. Shrub to 8m or more. Lvs 4–6.5cm, lanceolate to oblong-lanceolate, midrib finely hairy above, lower surface shining, white-papillose, with golden scales, margins bristly, at least when young. Fls white, sometimes flushed pink or lavender, finely hairy at the base of the tube outside. N Burm., W China. A yellow-fld variant is occas. found. Z9.

R. zeylanicum Booth = *R. arboreum* ssp. *zeylanicum*.

Rhodohypoxis Nel. Hypoxidaceae. 6 perenn. herbs. Lvs basal, spreading or erect, elliptic to filiform, hairy. Fls solitary or few, scapose or near-stemless; perianth lobes 6, fused at base as tube. SE Afr. Z8.

R. baurii (Bak.) Nel. RED STAR. Pseudostem to 3cm. Lvs 2.5–11cm, linear to lanceolate, folded, keeled, hairy.Scape to 15cm, hairy; fls 1–2, white, pink or red; perianth tube to 2.5mm, lobes to 2cm, hairy. Late spring. S Afr. var. *baurii*. Lvs narrower, suberect; fls red or deep pink. var. *confecta* Hilliard & B.L. Burtt. Lvs to 7.5cm, erect bright green. Fls white to red, often white ageing to red. var. *platypetala* (Bak.) Nel. Lvs broader, spreading, grey/green; fls white pale pink. *R. baurii* ×*Hypoxis parvula* Burtt. is a natural hybrid. White variants of *Hypoxis parvula* are known to cross with *R. baurii* var. *baurii* and *R. baurii* var. *platypetala*. Yellow forms of *Hypoxis parvula* have crossed with *R. baurii* var. *confecta*.

R. milloides (Bak.) Hilliard & B.L. Burtt. Pseudostem 1–5cm. Lvs 2.5–17cm, lanceolate, keeled, folded, erect, hairy, light green. Fls solitary or in twos, deep crimson or cerise, sometimes white or pink; seg. 10–20mm, elliptic, hairy at base. S Afr. (Natal).

R. platypetala (Bak.) Gray = *R. baurii* var. *platypetala*.

→*Hypoxis*.

Rhodoleia Champ. ex Hook. Hamamelidaceae. 7 everg., small trees. Lvs at tips of branchlets, thickly leathery, glaucous beneath. Fls in axill., stalked, nodding heads, surrounded by multicoloured bracts; pet. 2–4, to 2.5cm, narrow-spathulate, clawed rose; sta. 7–10. S China to Sumatra. Z9.

R. championii Hook. Lvs to 9cm, elliptic-obovate, bright green, outer bracts brown, silky, inner bracts tomentose; pet. dark pink. Late winter–early spring. Tibet, China, Hong Kong.

R. forrestii Chun ex Exell. Lvs to 15cm, elliptic, red-hairy at first, eventually glossy above. Bracts brown and rose; pet. bright rose. Spring. Upper Burm., Yunnan.

Rhodolirion Philippi.
R. andinum Philippi. = *Rhodophiala rhodolirion*.

Rhodomyrtus (DC.) Hassk. Myrtaceae. 11 shrubs or small trees. Fls solitary in axils or in 3–7-fld pedunculate cymes; cal. turbinate to globose, lobes 4–5, broad; pet. 4–5, free, spreading; sta. numerous. Fr. a berry. S China, SE Asia, E Aus. Z10.

R. tomentosa (Ait.) Hassk. To 4m. Young lvs and infl. tomentose. Lvs 4.5–8cm, coriaceous, elliptic or oblong-elliptic, tomentose beneath. Fls solitary or in 3's; pet. 15–18mm, 5, red or pink, broadly obovate, tomentose beneath; sta. 10–15mm, fil. pink, anth. yellow. Fr. 10–15mm, purple-black, tomentose, edible. S & SE Asia to S China, Philipp. and Sulawesi; an escape in Flor.

→*Myrtus*.

Rhodophiala C. Presl. Amaryllidaceae. 31 bulbous perennials. Lvs 15–40cm, narrow-linear, ± glab. Scape hollow; spathe-valves 2; fls in an umbel, funnel-shaped or nearly tubular; perianth tube v. short, seg. unequal; sta. 6, declinate-ascending. Summer to autumn. Andes (Chile, Arg., Boliv.). Z9.

R. advena (Ker-Gawl.) Traub. Scape to 50cm; fls 2–6, open-funnel-shaped, to 5cm, red, pink or yellow; seg. oblong, acute; sta. to two-thirds length perianth, style subequal to perianth. Chile.

R. andicola (Poepp.) Traub. Scape 15–20cm; fl. solitary, erect, 5cm; seg. subequal, brilliant violet; sta. short, deflexed. S Chile.

R. araucana (Philippi) Traub. Scape 30cm; fls 2, erect, funnel-shaped, rose pink; sta. and style much shorter than perianth. Chile.

R. bagnoldii (Herb.) Traub. Scape 30cm; fls 4–6, erect or ascending, openly funnel-shaped, 3–5.5cm, yellow, often tinged red; seg. oblong; sta. shorter than perianth, style equal to perianth. Chile.

R. bifida (Herb.) Traub. Scape 9–30cm; fls 2–6, erect or ascending, 5cm, bright red; perianth tube with corona, seg. oblanceolate; sta. half length seg., exceeded by style. Arg., Urug.

R. chilensis (L'Hérit.) Traub. Scape 15–23cm; fls 2, erect or ascending, to 5cm, bright red or yellow; seg. oblong; sta. shorter than seg., style equalling seg. S Chile.

R. elwesii (C.W. Wright) Traub. Scape to 20cm; fls 2, yellow with throat red; perianth tube 1cm, seg. elliptic, 4cm; sta. shorter than seg., style long-exserted. Arg.

R. pratensis (Poepp.) Traub. Scape 30–60cm; fls 2–5, ascending or horizontal, bright red or violet-purple, seg. oblanceolate, to 6cm; sta. half length perianth seg., style equalling seg. Chile.

R. rhodolirion (Bak.) Traub. Scape to 45cm; fls solitary, funnel-shaped to 7.6cm long, red to pink with darker veins or white, yellow in throat; perianth tube 2cm, green; sta. half length seg., exceeded by style. Chile.

R. rosea (Sweet) Traub. Scape 15cm; fls 1–2, nearly horizontal, 5cm long, bright red; seg. oblong-lanceolate; sta. shorter than seg., exceeded by style. Chile.

→*Amaryllis, Habranthus, Hippeastrum* and *Rhodolirion.*

Rhodosphaera Engl. Anacardiaceae. 1 tree to 20m. Lvs imparipinnate; lfts entire, oblong-acuminate. Infl. usually 10–20cm, pubesc.; sep. ovate, ciliate, *c*7mm; pet. oblong-obovate, recurved, *c*7mm, rose-pink; sta. 10 (staminodes in ♀ fls). Fr. a dark red-brown drupe. NE Aus. Z9.

R. rhodanthema (F. Muell.) Engl. YELLOWWOOD.
→*Rhus.*

Rhodostachys Philippi.
R. urbaniana Mez. = *Bromelia urbaniana.*

Rhodothamnus Rchb. Ericaceae. 1 ascending, scantily pubesc., everg., dwarf shrub to 40cm. Lvs 5–15mm, elliptic-oblanceolate, ± entire, white-ciliate, leathery, dark green above, slightly paler beneath. Fls solitary or 2–3 in term. clusters; pedicels and cal. glandular-downy; cor. 2–30mm diam., rose to lilac, flatly rotate; sta. *c*12mm, 10, anth. red-purple. E Alps. Z6.

R. chamaecistus (L.) Rchb.

Rhodotypos Sieb. & Zucc. Rosaceae. 1 decid. spreading shrub to 5m. Lvs to 6cm, ovate, acuminate, rounded at base, membranous, biserrate, corrugated above. Fls to 4cm diam., solitary, term.; pet. 4, white, orbicular, patent; sta. numerous. Fr. 1–6 shiny, black, tumid berries to 8mm. Spring–summer. China, Jap. Z5.

R. kerrioides Sieb. & Zucc. = *R. scandens.*
R. scandens (Thunb.) Mak.
R. tetrapetala (Sieb.) Mak. = *R. scandens.*
→*Kerria.*

Rhoeo Hance ex Walp.
R. discolor (L'Hérit.) Hance = *Tradescantia spathacea.*
R. spathacea (Sw.) Stearn = *Tradescantia spathacea.*

Rhoicissus Planch. Vitaceae. 12 shrubs or vines. Tendrils generally opposite lvs. Lvs simple or digitately 3–5-foliolate. Fls inconspicuous in thyrsoid cymes. Fr. a black-red berry. Trop. & S Afr. Z9.

R. capensis Planch. Everg. vine. St. terete, striate, tomentose when young; tendrils v. long, forked. Lvs orbicular to reniform, broadly cordate at base, obtuse at apex, obtusely 5-angled, repand-dentate, 10–20cm across, coriaceous, red-tomentose when young. S Afr.
→*Cissus* and *Vitis.*

Rhombophyllum (Schwantes) Schwantes. Aizoaceae. 3 succulent perennials, usually mat-forming. Lvs crowded, opposite and decussate, united at base, semicylindric, keeled. Fls 3–7 together, to 4cm diam., yellow. Early summer–early autumn. S Afr. (Cape Prov.). Z9.

R. dolabriforme (L.) Schwantes. Lvs 2.5–3cm, long-tapered on the upper surface, semi-cylindric below, expanded above to 11–15mm with a hatchet-shaped keel pulled forward with a tooth-like tip, grass-green with translucent dots. W Cape.

R. nelii Schwantes. Similar to *R. dolabriforme* but lvs bifid, 1.5cm long, 4–6mm wide, pale blue-green or grey-green with dark dots. Karroo.

R. rhomboideum (Salm-Dyck) Schwantes. Lvs in 4–5 pairs resting on the soil, 2.5–5×1–2cm, rhombic above, rounded below, thickened and keeled toward tip and pulled forward, chin-like,

margins pale, rarely 1–2-toothed, dark grey-green with white dots. E Cape.
→*Bergeranthus* and *Hereroa.*

Rhopalocyclus Schwantes.
R. weigangianus (Dinter) Dinter & Schwantes = *Leipoldtia weigangiana.*

Rhopalostylis H.A. Wendl. & Drude. NIKAU PALM. Palmae. 3 palms. St. erect, grey-green, closely ringed, smooth. Crownshaft prominent. Lvs pinnate, erect to arched; petiole v. short; rachis densely brown scaly, often twisted; pinnae linear-lanceolate, single-fold, directed to lf apex, rigid, tomentose beneath. Australasia. Z10.

R. baueri (Seem.) H.A. Wendl. & Drude. NORFOLK PALM. St. to 6m×15cm. Crownshaft to 50cm, scurfy. Lvs 3m, arching; pinnae to 60×4.5cm. Norfolk Is.

R. cheesmanii Becc. KERMADEC NIKAU PALM. To 19m. Resembles *R. sapida*, but lvs to 3m; pinnae to 80×5cm. Raoul Is.

R. sapida H.A. Wendl. & Drude. NIKAU PALM; FEATHER DUSTER PALM. St. 6–10m×25cm. Crownshaft to 60cm, smooth. Lvs 1.2–1.8m, erect; pinnae 0.8–1m×1–1.5cm. NZ.
→*Areca, Eora* and *Kentia.*

Rhubarb *Rheum* (*R.* ×*cultorum*).

Rhus L. SUMAC; SUMACH; TAAIBOS. Anacardiaceae. *c*200 aromatic trees and shrubs, decid. or everg., sometimes climbing with clinging roots. Lvs simple to odd-pinnate or palmatifid often beautifully coloured in fall. Fls inconspicuous in packed term. pan. Fr. a small drupe, thinly fleshy, often red and hairy. Temp. and subtrop. N Amer., S Afr., subtrop. E Asia, NE Aus.

R. ambigua Lav. ex Dipp., non Unger = *Toxicodendron radicans* ssp. *orientale.*
R. americana (Nutt.) Sudw. = *Cotinus obovatus.*
R. aromatica Ait. FRAGRANT SUMAC; LEMON SUMAC; POLECAT BUSH. Shrub to 1m, prostrate. Lfts 3, to 6.5cm, ovate, serrate. Spike term., to 2cm; fls yellow. Spring. SE Canada to S & E US. var. *serotina* (Greene) Rehd. Upright shrub. Lfts pilose to glabrate beneath. Indiana to Tex. 'Gro-Low': v. low and spreading; fls golden yellow, fragrant. 'Laciniata': lfts ovate-lanceolate. Z3.
R. canadensis Marshall non Mill. = *R. aromatica.*
R. caustica Hook. & Arn. = *Lithrea caustica.*
R. chinensis Mill. CHINESE GALL; NUTGALL. To 7m, decid. Lfts 3–7, to 11cm, ovate-oblong, crenate, brown-pubesc. beneath. Pan. large, term.; fls cream. Late summer. China, Jap. Z8.
R. clausseniana Turcz. = *Lithrea molleoides.*
R. copallina L. DWARF SUMAC; MOUNTAIN SUMAC; SHINING SUMAC. To 6m, decid. Lfts 9–12, to 10cm, oblong-lanceolate, entire, glaucescent above, pubesc. beneath. Pan. dense; fls green. Late summer. E US. Z5.
R. coriaria L. SICILIAN SUMAC; TANNER'S SUMAC; ELM LEAVED SUMAC. Shrub to 3m, decid. Twigs densely pubesc.; lfts 9–15, to 7cm, elliptic to oblong, serrate, pubesc., grey-green. Pan. term., 10–25cm; fls yellow-green. Late summer. S Eur. Z9.
R. cotinoides Nutt. = *Cotinus obovatus.*
R. cotinus L. = *Cotinus coggygria.*
R. diversiloba Torr. & A. Gray = *Toxicodendron diversilobum.*
R. elegans W. Hill = *Rhodosphaera rhodanthema.*
R. glabra L. SMOOTH SUMAC; SCARLET SUMAC; VINEGAR TREE. Decid. shrub or tree, to 3m. Br. pruinose. Lfts 11–31, to 11cm, oblong-lanceolate, serrate, blue-green beneath, red in autumn. Pan. dense, to 25cm; fls green. Late summer. NE US to S Canada. var. *cismontana* (Greene) Cockerell. Lfts fewer, smaller, lanceolate. 'Flavescens': lvs yellow in autumn. 'Laciniata': lfts deeply pinnatisect. 'Morden's': to 1.8m; seed heads bright red. Z2.
R. henryi Diels = *R. potaninii.*
R. hirsuta (L.) Sudw. = *R. typhina.*
R. hypoleuca Champ. ex Benth. Shrub to 3m. Lfts 11–17, ovate-lanceolate, acute, veins tomentose. Infl. a pan. China.
R. integrifolia (Nutt.) Benth. & Hook. f. ex S. Wats. LEMONADE BERRY; LEMONADE SUMAC; SOURBERRY. Everg. shrub or tree, to 10m. Lvs simple, to 5cm, elliptic, entire or serrate. Pan. pubesc.; fls white to pink. Spring. S Calif. Z9.
R. javanica Thunb. non L. = *R. chinensis.*
R. laevigata L. Shrub or bushy tree to 4m, sometimes spiny. Lfts 3, lanceolate to obovate, glossy above, paler beneath, apex rounded, base tapering, entire, term. lft to 4cm, others smaller, veins conspicuous. Pan. to 7cm, fls yellow-green. Summer. S & E coast of S Afr. Z9.
R. lancea L. f. KAREE; WILLOW RHUS. Everg. tree, to 8m; br. russet-red. Lfts 3, linear-lanceolate, entire, rarely serrate, glab.,

coriaceous, terminal lft to 12cm, others smaller. Pan. dense, term.; fls v. small, pale green-yellow. Winter. S Afr. Z9.

R. laurina (Nutt.) ex Torr. & A. Gray = *Malosma laurina*.

R. lobata Hook. = *Toxicodendron diversilobum*.

R. lucida L. SHINY LEAVED RHUS. Shrub or tree to 7m; twigs russet or grey, white-pubesc.; lfts 3, glab. obovate to oblong, entire, dark green, often glossy, term. lft to 7cm. Infl. a head, sparsely branched, to 7cm; fls ivory. Spring. S & E coast of S Afr. Z9.

R. michauxii Sarg. Shrub to 1m, decid., stoloniferous; br. densely pubesc. Lfts 9–15, to 10cm, oval-oblong, serrate, brown-pubesc. beneath, pan., to 20cm; fls green-yellow. SE US. Z6.

R. microphylla Engelm. DESERT SUMAC; SCRUB SUMAC; CORREOSA. Shrub to 4m; br. glab. or puberulent. Lfts 5–9, ovate to ovate-lanceolate, adpressed-pilose. Infl. a head or spike; fls white. S US, N Mex. Z9.

R. mucronata Thunb. = *R. laevigata*.

R. orientalis (Greene) C. Schneid. = *Toxicodendron radicans* ssp. *orientale*.

R. osbeckii Decne. = *R. chinensis*.

R. ovata S. Wats. SUGAR BUSH; SUGAR SUMAC. Everg. shrub, to 3m. Lvs to 7cm, simple, ovate, acute, often conduplicate, usually entire, spike, short, dense; fls light yellow. SW US. Z9.

R. potaninii Maxim. Decid. tree, to 8m; crown rounded. Lfts 7–11, oval-oblong to oblong-lanceolate, acuminate, basally rounded, serrate to entire. Pan. pendulous, to 20cm; fls off-white. Early summer. C & W China. Z5.

R. punjabensis Stewart var. *sinica* (Diels) Rehd. & Wils. Decid. tree, to 12m; br. pubesc. lfts 7–11, to 12cm, oval-oblong, entire veins pubesc. beneath. Pan., pubesc. to 20cm, pendulous; fls cream-white. C & W China. Z6.

R. quercifolia Steud. = *Toxicodendron diversilobum*.

R. radicans L. = *Toxicodendron radicans*.

R. rhodanthema F. Muell. = *Rhodosphaera rhodanthema*.

R. semialata Murray = *R. chinensis*.

R. sinica Koehne non Diels = *R. potaninii*.

R. sinica Diels = *R. punjabensis* var. *sinica*.

R. succedanea L. = *Toxicodendron succedaneum*.

R. terebinthifolia Schltr. & Champ. TEMAZCAL. Everg. shrub, to 2.5m; br. rusty-pubesc. to glabrescent. Lfts 3–15, 2–4.5cm, elliptic to lanceolate, mucronate or acuminate, entire, pilose, dark, lustrous above, paler beneath. Pan. to 10cm. Mex., Guat. var. *loeseneri* F. Barkley. St. and lvs glab.; lfts larger. Guat. Z10.

R. toxicodendron L. = *Toxicodendron radicans*.

R. toxicodendron ssp. *diversiloba* (Torr. & A. Gray) Engl. = *Toxicodendron diversilobum*.

R. toxicodendron var. *hispida* Engl. = *Toxicodendron radicans* ssp. *hispidum*.

R. toxicodendron var. *pubescens* Engelm. ex Wats. = *Toxicodendron radicans* ssp. *pubescens*.

R. trilobata Nutt. SKUNKBUSH. Decid. shrub, to 2m; young shoots pubesc. Lvs trifoliate, lfts to 2cm, ovate, serrate, term. lft trilobed. Infl. a spike, clustered; fls pale green. Spring. W US. var. *malacophylla* Munz. SQUAWBUSH. To 1.5m; br. diffuse, pubesc. Lfts cuneate-obovate. Fls yellow. Calif. Z5.

R. typhina L. STAGHORN SUMAC; VELVET SUMAC; VIRGINIAN SUMAC. Spreading decid. tree or shrub to 10m; twigs densely pubesc.; lfts 11–31, to 11cm, oblong-lanceolate, serrate, coarsely pubesc., colouring vividly in autumn; petiole densely rusty- to golden-pubesc. Infl. a rusty-red, dense, term. pan. Summer. E N Amer. 'Dissecta': lfts pinnately dissected. 'Laciniata': lfts laciniate. Z3.

R. venenata DC. = *Toxicodendron vernix*.

R. vernicifera DC. = *Toxicodendron verniciiluum*.

R. verniciflua Stokes = *Toxicodendron verniciiluum*.

R. vernix L. = *Toxicodendron vernix*.

R. viminalis Vahl. Shrub or shrub to 10m. Lvs trifoliate; lfts lanceolate, entire, thin, term. lft to 11cm, others smaller. Infl. an axill. or terminal head, densely pubesc. to 8cm; fls small, yellow-green. Winter. S Afr. Z9.

R. virens Lindh. ex A. Gray. EVERGREEN SUMAC; TOBACCO SUMAC; LENTISCO. Shrub to 3m. Lfts usually 5–9, to 3cm, rhombic-ovate, dark green above, lighter and sparsely pilose beneath. Infl. a term. pan.; fls white, to 3cm. SW US. Z9.

→*Schmaltzia* and *Toxicodendron*.

Rhynchelytrum Nees. RUBY GRASS. Gramineae. 14 ann. or perenn. grasses. Lvs linear to threadlike; ligules short-ciliate. Pan. racemose, compact to open; spikelets short-stipitate, flattened, keeled, 2-fld. Trop. Afr. to SE Asia. Z8.

R. repens (Willd.) C. Hubb. NATAL GRASS; RUBY GRASS. Perenn. or ann., to 120cm. Lvs to 30×1cm, flat, long-acute. Pan. cylindric to ovoid, to 20×10cm; spikelets to 4mm, densely silky-pubesc., hairs white, tinged purple to red. Summer–autumn. Trop. Afr.

R. roseum (Nees) Stapf & C. Hubb. = *R. repens*.

→*Panicum* and *Tricholaena*.

Rhynchoglossum Bl. Gesneriaceae. 17 ann. or perenn. herbs. Lvs alt. Fls in secund rac.; cal. 5-lobed, tube angled, winged; cor. 2-lipped, upper lip short, 3-lobed, lower larger, subentire, tube slender, somewhat flattened. Ceylon, India.

R. notianum (Wallich) B.L. Burtt. To 45cm. Lvs to 20cm, elliptic, strongly veined. Cor. to 2.5cm; tube cylindric, white, upper lip white, lower deep blue patched yellow near a hooded basal depression. Ceylon, India. Z10.

Rhyncholaelia Schltr. Orchidaceae. 2 epiphytic orchids. Pbs to 10cm, compressed-claviform with papery sheaths, unifoliate. Lvs to 20cm, oblong, rigidly coriaceous, grey-green. Fls term., 1–3, fragrant, waxy. Mex., C Amer.

R. digbyana (Lindl.) Schltr. Tep. to 10×3cm, pale yellow-green; lip to 7.5×8cm, white to cream-white, tinged green, emarginate, obscurely 3-lobed, midlobe deeply and heavily lacerate-fimbriate. Mex., Belize.

R. glauca (Lindl.) Schltr. Tep. to 6.5×1.5cm, white, olive-green or v. pale lavender; lip to 5.5×4cm, white to yellow-cream, with a rose-pink or purple mark at base, throat sometimes striped red-purple, obscurely 3-lobed, midlobe slightly undulate. Mex., Guat., Hond.

→*Brassavola*.

Rhynchophorum (Miq.) Small.

R. floridanum (Small) Small = *Peperomia floridana*.

R. obtusifolium (L.) Small = *Peperomia obtusifolia*.

Rhynchospermum Reinw.

R. asiaticum hort. = *Trachelospermum asiaticum*.

R. jasminoides Lindl. = *Trachelospermum jasminoides*.

Rhynchospora Vahl. Cyperaceae. 200 perenn., grasslike herbs. Lvs linear. Infl. a pan. or peduncle subtended by slender bracts; spikelets 2–3-fld, borne in the axils of spirally arranged, scale-like bracts. ± Cosmop.

R. nervosa (Vahl) Böckeler. Tufted or rhizomatous, 8–150cm, erect or arching. Lvs basal, hairy or glab. Bracts 3–8, brilliant white at base, 4–22cm. C Amer., Carib., N S Amer. ssp. *ciliata* Kayama. Bracts white for 10–35cm, glumes with red striations. Z9.

Rhynchostylis Bl. FOXTAIL ORCHID. Orchidaceae. 15 epiphytic, monopodial orchids to 30cm. Lvs to 35cm, 2-ranked, coriaceous, linear to linear-oblong. Rac. axill., dense cylindrical, to 40cm; sep. spreading, obtuse, pet. narrower, smaller; lip entire or trilobed, basally saccate or spurred. Trop. Asia. Z10.

R. coelestis (Rchb. f.) Rchb. f. Fls to 2cm diam., waxy; tep. ovate-oblong, obtuse, white, apically blotched indigo; lip obovate-oblong, white tipped mauve or indigo, spur saccate. Thail.

R. gigantea (Lindl.) Ridl. Fls to 4cm diam., fragrant, white, basally spotted violet to dark purple; lip white, term. lobes bright purple; tep. elliptic-oblong, rounded or obtuse; lip apically trilobed, fleshy, spur short. Burm., Indochina, Thail.

R. retusa (L.) Bl. Fls to 3cm diam., fragrant, white, spotted purple; dors. sep. oblong, lat. sep. ovate, obtuse; pet. narrower, oblong, basally saccate. Trop. Asia.

✗**Rhynchovanda**. (*Rhynchostylis* × *Vanda*.) Orchidaceae. Gdn hybrids with strap-shaped lvs and spikes of mauve to blue fls.

Rhytidocaulon Bally. Asclepiadaceae. 6 highly succulent, perenn. herbs. St. fleshy, few-branched, cylindrical, 4–6-angled, grey or dull green, tessellated, papillose and wrinkled. Lvs small, fleshy, caducous, in apical clusters. Fls subsessile or on short pedicels, cor. with 5 spreading lobes; corona variable, usually dark purple. Ethiop., Somalia, Arabia. Z9.

R. fulleri Lavranos & Mortimer. Main st. to 15cm tall, 20mm thick, sparingly branched, cylindrical. Cor. 10mm long, 4.5mm diam. at base, erect, lobes joined at tips, margins revolute, ciliate. SE Arabia (Muscat, Oman).

R. macrolobum Lavranos. St. to over 25cm, erect or sprawling, to 4cm diam., slightly 4-angled. Cor. 1.5cm diam., broadly campanulate, exterior white below, lobes 6.5–8mm, deltoid, pale yellow with dark purple margins and blotches, interior yellow-white toward base, basal half of lobes banded, edged and tipped dark purple, minutely ciliate, with a cluster of 2–5 motile hairs. S Yemen.

R. paradoxum Bally. St. and br. to 110cm×15mm, 4–6-angled or -ridged. Cor. 9–9.6mm across, tube shallow, lobes broadly ovate, 2.5–3mm, apex thickened, red-pink, changing half way down to white dotted and dashed red. Ethiop., Kenya.

R. piliferum Lavranos. St. and br. erect or ascending, to 40cm×5–12mm, 4–6-angled or sulcate. Cor. rotate-campanulate, 10mm across, glab., lobes v. narrow, 4mm, lower part off-white with dark purple transverse bands, apices dark purple, bearing a tuft of dark purple, simple, vibratile hairs 1mm long. N Somalia.

R. sheilae D.V. Field. Low-growing, spreading to around 20cm; main st. to 2cm×14mm. Cor. rotate, 8mm diam., exterior papillose, interior glab., lobes 3.25mm long, deltoid, basal half green with purple-green margin and transverse bands, upper part pale cream, bearing 1 or a few vibratile hairs. Saudi Arabia.

R. subscandens Bally. St. and br., to 110cm tall, to 15mm thick, 4–6-angled or -ridged. Cor. 9mm diam., broadly cup-shaped, lobes spreading, triangular, 3mm, exterior papillose, interior glab., banded red and white, sparsely fringed with short hairs. Somalia.

Ribbed Cherry *Prunus lobulata.*
Ribbed Hakea *Hakea costata.*
Ribbon Bush *Hypoestes aristata.*
Ribbon Cactus *Pedilanthus tithymaloides.*
Ribbon Fern *Campyloneurum phyllitidis; Ophioglossum pendulum.*
Ribbon Grass *Phalaris arundinacea.*
Ribbon Gum *Eucalyptus viminalis.*
Ribbon Plant *Chlorophytum comosum.*
Ribbonwood *Adenostoma sparsifolium; Hoheria sexstylosa; Plagianthus regius.*

Ribes L. CURRANT; GOOSEBERRY. Grossulariaceae. 150 shrubs, mainly decid., often thorny. Lvs usually alt., often 3–5-lobed, crenate or dentate, frequently gland. Fls small, solitary or in rac., 4–5-partite; sep. longer than pet., spreading. Fr. a juicy, many-seeded berry, gland. or bristled. N temp.

R. aciculare Sm. To 1m, st. bristled with 5–7 small nodal thorns. Lvs to 3cm wide, rounded, 3–5-lobed, shiny above, occas. pitted. Fls pink or pale green. Fr. red, green or yellow. Sib. Z3.

R. affine Douglas = *R. laxiflorum.*

R. albidum Paxt. = *R. glutinosum* 'Albidum'.

R. albinervum Michx. = *R. triste.*

R. alpestris (Decne.) A. Berger. HEDGE GOOSEBERRY. To 3m, st. tinged red at first; spines to 2.5cm, 2-parted. Lvs 2–5cm, wide, 3–5-lobed, rounded, toothed, glab. or downy. Fls solitary or paired on short stalks, green or red-green. Fr. to 1.5cm, purple-red, glandular-bristly. Himal., W China. var. *giganteum* Jancz. Shrub to 5m, thorns to 3cm. Fr. green, smooth. W China. Z6.

R. alpinum L. ALPINE CURRANT; MOUNTAIN CURRANT. To 1–2m; st. glab., light grey. Lvs to 5cm, 3-, rarely 5-lobed, broadly ovate-rounded, downy above, glab. beneath. Fls small, green-yellow in upright rac. Fr. scarlet, pruinose, sour. N Eur. (Mt Forest). 'Compactum': low-growing, dense. 'Verno-Aureum': lvs yellow when young. 'Aureum': lvs bright yellow at first becoming green-yellow later. 'Laciniatum': lvs deeply lobed and incised, dentate. 'Pumilum': only 1m in height, spreading; lvs smaller. Z2.

R. alpinum var. *mandshuricum* Maxim = *R. distans.*

R. ambiguum Maxim. To 60cm, lvs 2–5cm wide, reniform lobes 3–5 short, blunt, gland. beneath, rather gummy, smooth above. Fls solitary or paired, 12mm, green. Fr. gland. downy, translucent. Jap., China (Sichuan). Z6.

R. americanum Mill. Shrub, 1–1.5m; st. slender, yellow, gland. Lvs 5–8cm, orbicular, lobes 3, pointed and serrate, with yellow gland. spots, scarlet or red-brown in fall. Fls in pendulous rac. to 10cm, yellow-white. Fr. black, glab., flesh green. N US. 'Variegatum': lvs variegated cream; fls yellow. Z2.

R. amictum Greene = *R. roezlii.*

R. appendiculatum Krylof. = *R. petiolare.*

R. aureum Pursh. GOLDEN CURRANT; BUFFALO CURRANT; MISSOURI CURRANT. To 2m; st. brown, smooth or downy. Lvs 3–5cm wide, lobes 3, wide, coarsely toothed, smooth but often ciliate, red. Rac. pendent, 5–15-fld; fls strongly & sweetly scented, yellow, pet. often flushed red. Fr. purple-black. W US to Mex. var. *chrysococcum* Rydb. Fr. yellow. var. *gracillimum* (Cov. & Britt.) Jeps. Fls becoming red-yellow, not fragrant; fr. yellow. C & S Calif. Z2.

R. aureum hort. = *R. odoratum.*

R. ×bethmontii Jancz. (*R. malvaceum* ×*R. sanguineum.*) Differs from *R. sanguineum* in more furrowed lvs with gland. hairs, downy beneath. Infl. a pendent rac. of 10–20 fls; fls carmine, downy; pollen sterile. Fr. black. Fr. Z6.

R. biebersteinii Berl. = *R. petraeum* var. *biebersteinii.*

R. billiardii Carr. = *R. fasciculatum* var. *chinense.*

R. bracteosum Douglas ex Hook. STINK CURRANT; CALIFORNIAN BLACKCURRANT. 1.5–2m, shoots downy and gland. at first. Lvs 5–20cm, orbicular, thin, lobes 5–7, ovate to lanceolate,

biserrate, glutinous beneath. Rac. long erect to 20cm; fls green-red. Fr. black with a white bloom and yellow gland spots. Alask., N Calif. Z7.

R. burejense F. Schmidt. To 1m, br. thorned and bristled. Lvs 2–6cm, rounded, base cordate, with 3–5 deep blunt lobes, toothed, downy and gland. Fls solitary or paired, 3–6mm, bell-shaped; sta. exserted. Fr. bristled, green, palatable. NE Asia, Alask., N Calif. Z5.

R. californicum Hook. & Arn. Closely related to *R. menziesii*, differing in glab. br. and lvs. Fls green-red; sta. twice as long as pet. Fr. globose, bristly. Calif. var. *hesperium* (McClat.) Jeps. Shoots and lvs downy. Pet. off white, flushed red, almost equalling sta. Z7.

R. caucasicum Bieb. = *R. petraeum* var. *biebersteinii.*

R. cereum Douglas. SQUAW CURRANT; WHITE FIELD CURRANT. 1–2m, br. unarmed, gland. downy at first. Lvs rounded, reniform, 1–4cm wide with 3–5 obtuse lobes, crenate, smooth above, gland. downy, rather grey beneath. Rac. short, pendent; fls 6–8mm, tubular, white, green or yellow. Fr. scarlet, shiny. W US. var. *farinosum* Jancz. Br. pendulous; shoots violet at first. Lvs grey, viscid. Fls pink or white. Z5.

R. ciliatum Humb. & Bonpl. ex Roem. & Schult. To 2m; shoots thin, glandular-pubesc.; petioles and pedicels with black-stalked glands. Lvs 3–5cm wide, 3–5-lobed, biserrate, with flat bristles above, glandular-pubesc. beneath. Rac. pendent, 6–10-fld; fls 1.5cm, green. Fr. black, glossy. Mex. Z9.

R. coloradense Cov. To 50cm, resembling *R. glandulosum*, shoots downy at first. Lvs 5–8cm wide, thin, lobes obcuneate, crenate, base cordate, smooth above, veins downy beneath. Rac. to 5cm, erect, pet. green-purple. Fr. black, glands few. US. Z5.

R. cruentum Greene = *R. roezlii* var. *cruentum.*

R. ×culverwellii Macfarl. (*R. nigrum* ×*R. uva-crispa.*) To 1m, resembling *R. nigrum*. Lvs like those of *R. uva-crispa*, but glutinous glands 0. Fr. in clusters, black-red, finely downy; seedless. Gdn origin. Z6.

R. curvatum Small. To 1m; br. glab., purple, thorns 0.5cm, simple or 3-parted. Lvs 3cm wide, 3–5-lobed, dentate, lightly pubesc. Fls solitary or in pairs (rarely to 5), on slender pedicels, small, white. Fr. purple, smooth. SE US. Z7.

R. cynosbati L. DOGBERRY; DOGBRAMBLE; PRICKLY GOOSEBERRY. 1–1.5m; br. slender, pendent, thorns to 1cm, simple or 3-parted. Lvs 3–5cm, rounded with 3–5 lobes, incised serrate, hirsute. Rac. 2–3-fld; fls bell-shaped, green; sta. slightly exserted. Fr. wine-red, bristled, edible. E US. f. *inerme* Rehd. Fr. not bristled. Z2.

R. ×darwinii F. Koch. (*R. menziesii* ×*R. niveum*.) 2–3m; spines simple and 3-parted. Lvs with 5 crenate lobes, finely downy and brown-speckled at first. Rac. pendulous, 1–4-fld; sep. white, flushed red at the tip, strongly reflexed; pet. white; style long, red. Fr. black, smooth, sour. Gdn origin. Z6.

R. davianum hort. = *R. glutinosum* 'Albidum'.

R. diacanthum Pall. Erect shrub to 2m, br. smooth, with nodal paired thorns. Lvs 2.5–3–5cm, ovate or obovate, with three shallow blunt lobes, dentate, shiny. Fls in erect reacemes to 5cm, green or green-white. Fr. green-scarlet, glab. N Asia, Sib., Manch. Z2.

R. dikuscha Fisch. = *R. petiolare.*

R. distans Jancz. 60–70cm, resembling *R. alpinum*. Lvs 5cm, rounded, with 3–5 sharp lobes. Rac. 1–2cm erect; fls green. Fr. scarlet. Manch. Z5.

R. divaricatum Douglas. To 3m, shoots often bristled, grey-brown, with hooked thorns. Lvs 2–6cm wide, rounded-cordate, usually 5-lobed, venation downy. Fls inclusters, green-purple. Fr. red-black, pruinose. W US. Z4.

R. echihellum (Cov.) Rehd. To 1m, armed with thorns to 1.5cm. Lvs to 2.5cm. Fls solitary or paired, green or green-white. Fr. green, sharp bristled. SE US. Z7.

R. echinatum Lindl. = *R. lacustre.*

R. emodense Rehd. V. similar to *R. petraeum*, shoots glab., red at first. Lvs to 12cm wide, base cordate, with 3–5 sharp lobes, gland. downy beneath. Rac. 10–12cm; fls bell-shaped, green flushed red. Fr. red to black. Himal., SW China. Z6.

R. fasciculatum Sieb. & Zucc. 1–1.5cm; br. thick, furrowed, glab. Lvs 4–7cm, rounded, 3–5-lobed, dentate, downy. ♂ fls in clustered 4–9-fld rac., ♀ fls paired, cup-shaped, yellow, scented. Fr. erect, red, smooth, flesh yellow. Jap., Korea. var. *chinense* Maxim. Larger. Lvs to 10cm, some persisting throughout the winter. N China, Korea, Jap. Z5.

R. floridum Mill. = *R. americanum.*

R. ×fontenayense Jancz. (*R. sanguineum* ×*R. uva-crispa*.) 1m thornless. Lvs 6–8cm, orbicular, base slightly cordate, coriaceous, lobes 3–5, downy beneath. Rac. spreading or pendulous 3–6-fld; fls cup-shaped, wine red; style downy. Fr. purple-black with white bloom, gland. Z5.

R. fragrans Pall. non Lodd. 30–70cm resembling *R. hudsonianum*, whole plant aromatic, reminiscent of balm.

Lvs 5–6cm, reniform, 3-lobed, gland. and downy beneath. Rac. loose, upright, to 10cm. Fr. 8mm diam., brown. Manch., Sib. Z3.

R. fragrans Lodd. = *R. odoratum.*

R. 'Frühe Hochrote'. = *R.* ×*gonduinii.*

R. ×*fuscescens* (Jancz.). (*R. bracteosum* ×*R. nigrum.*) Differs from *R. bracteosum* in red-brown fls in rac. shorter, upright to pendent; fr. larger. Z6.

R. gayanum (Spach) Steud. Everg. to 1.5m, shoots gland. or softly downy at first. Lvs 3–6cm, rounded, coriaceous, with 3–5 blunt lobes, crenate, shaggy. Rac. 3–6cm upright, fls bell-shaped, yellow, honey-scented. Fr. black, downy, edible. Summer. Chile (mts). Z8.

R. giraldii Jancz. To 1m, br. spreading, bristled, nodally thorned, downy at first. Lvs 3.5cm, reniform, lobes 3–5, gland., downy. Rac. 3–7cm erect or slightly pendent; fls green-brown. Fr. red, gland., downy. N China. Z6.

R. glaciale Wallich. To 4m, resembles *R. alpinum*, shoots smooth red at first. Lvs rounded-ovate with 3–5 sharp lobes, glandular-bristly. Fls small, in 3–20-fld, 2–5cm rac., purple-brown. Fr. scarlet, sour. SW China. Z5.

R. glandulosum Grauer ex Weber. FETID CURRANT; SKUNK CURRANT. To 40cm, br. prostrate. Lvs 3–8cm, rounded, thin, with 5–7 lobes, downy beneath, malodorous. Rac. erect; fls 8–12, red-white, downy. Fr. red, gland. bristly. US (mts). Z2.

R. glutinosum Benth. 3–4m, young shoots glandular-resinous softly downy. Lvs 4–8cm, rounded, 3–5-lobed, downy beneath. Rac. 4–11cm, pendent, glandular-pubesc. Fr. black, pruinose, lightly downy. Calif. 'Albidum': fls white, flushed pink. Z6.

R. 'Gondouin'. = *R.* ×*gonduinii.*

R. ×*gonduinii* Jancz. (*R. petraeum* ×*R. silvestre.*) To 2m, young shoots red, smooth. Lvs to 10cm wide, base ± subcordate, 3–5-lobed, downy beneath. Fls campanulate in spreading rac. to 5cm. Fr. red. Z6.

R. ×*gordonianum* Lem. (*R. odoratum* ×*R. sanguineum.*) 1.5–2.5cm, shoots brown, smooth. Lvs 3–5-lobed, incised, toothed, shiny with light gland. down. Fls in erect rac. to 7cm, yellow-red. Z6.

R. gracile sensu Jancz. = *R. hirtellum.*

R. gracile sensu Britt. & Brown = *R. missouriense.*

R. gracile sensu Pursh = *R. rotundifolium.*

R. gracillimum Cor. & Britt. = *R. aureum* var. *gracillimum.*

R. grossularia L. = *R. uva-crispa* var. *reclinatum.*

R. grossularia var. *pubescens* Koch = *R. uva-crispa.*

R. grossularia var. *uva-crispa* Sm. = *R. uva-crispa.*

R. grossularioides Maxim. GOOSEBERRY; CATBERRY. To 2m, spiny, closely related to *R. alpestre*, snoots glab. or glandular-bristly. Lvs to 4cm, rounded, base cordate, 3–5 lobed, smooth or silky. Fls in rac. to 1.5cm, bell-shaped, red-green. Fr. bristly. Jap. (mts). Z6.

R. grossularioides Michx. = *R. lacustre.*

R. henryi Franch. Unarmed shrub, closely resembling *R. laurifolium* but only 1.2m high; shoots glandular-downy. Lvs larger, 5–10×3–5cm, blade thinner, margins with gland. teeth, glandular-bristly beneath. Infl. a 3–5cm rac.; fls 8mm, green. Early spring. C China. Z8.

R. hesperium McClat. = *R. californicum* var. *hesperium.*

R. himalayense Decne. non Royle = *R. emodense.*

R. hirtellum Michx. To 1m, shoots slender, grey becoming dark brown, occas. bristled and/or small-thorned. Lvs widely oval or rounded, base widely triangular, 3–5-lobed. Fls paired, solitary or in threes, in a short rac.; narrowly bell-shaped, green, often flushed red. Fr. purple-black, smooth. N US. Z4.

R. ×*holosericeum* Otto & Dietr. (*R. petraeum* var. *biebersteinii* ×*R. spicatum.*) 1–1.5m, shoots red at first. Lvs 6–7cm diam., rounded, 3-lobed, downy beneath; petiole felted. Rac. 3–7cm, 10–25-fld; fls campanulate, red-brown. Fr. small, black-red, acid. 'Pallidum' lvs to 8cm wide, 3–5-lobed, less downy beneath; fls brown; fr. large, red. Z4.

R. 'Houghton Castle'. = *R.* ×*houghtonianum.*

R. ×*houghtonianum* Jancz. (*R. silvestre* ×*R. spicatum.*) Br. slightly glandular-downy. Lvs 6cm diam., 3–5-lobed, base cordate. Rac. 3–5cm, 8–18-fld; fls larger than those of *R. spicatum*, green flushed brown. Fr. red, edible. Gdn origin (Holland, pre-1901). Z5.

R. hudsonianum Richards. NORTHERN BLACK CURRANT. To 1.5m, with scattered resinous glands. Lvs broad, reniform, downy, lobes acute, coarsely toothed. Rac. 3–6cm, erect, loose; fls woolly, white. Fr. black. Hudson Bay to Alask. Z2.

R. indecorum Eastw. WHITE FLOWERED CURRANT. Differs from *R. malvaceum*, in smaller white fls, to 2.5m, shoots densely gland. downy. Lvs ribbed above, felted beneath, with stalked glands. Fr. downy. S Calif., N Baja. Z8.

R. inebrians Lindl. Closely resembling *R. cereum*, but much branched and erect to 1.5m. Lvs smaller, 3–5 lobed, gland. beneath. Fls in sparse, rac., pink. Fr. smooth, pale red. W US (mts). var. *spaethianum* (Koehne) Jancz. Small shrub to 50cm,

all features smaller. Shoots slender, smooth. Lvs shiny. Fls v. numerous, pink. Fr. dark red. US (Colorado, Utah, Mont.). Z4.

R. inerme Rydb. 1–2m, rarely-armed. Lvs 1–6cm diam., lobes 3–5, blunt with rounded teeth, smooth or slightly glandular-downy beneath. Fls in clusters of 1–4, sep. green-red; pet. pink or white. Fr. purple-red, smooth, edible. US. Z6.

R. irriguum Douglas. 1–3m, shoots glab. or downy at first, grey with numerous thorns. Lvs 3–7cm diam., 3–5-lobed, glab. above, downy and slightly gland. beneath. Fls in pendent clusters of 1–3. Fr. glab., black. W US (mts). Z4.

R. japonicum Maxim. Unarmed shrub to 2m. Rac. erect, fls green or brown. Fr. glab., black. Jap. Z7.

R. jessoniae Stapf = *R. maximowiczii* var. *floribundum.*

R. jorullense HBK = *R. ciliatum.*

R. ×*kochii* Krüssm. (*R. niveum* ×*R. speciosum.*) To 1m, thorns like those of *R. speciosum*. Fls paired or in threes, white-red. Fr. rarely set, bristly, red-brown. Gdn origin (Switz.). Z7.

R. ×*koehneanum* Jancz. GARDEN CURRANT. (*R. multiflorum* ×*R. silvestre.*) Lvs to 6.5cm diam., 3–5-lobed. Rac. 10cm, to 35-fld; fls brown; sta. pink. Fr. red. Gdn origin. Z6.

R. lacustre (Pers.) Poir. BRISTLY BLACK CURRANT; SWAMP GOOSE-BERRY. To 1m, slender, somewhat pendent, bristled, spines 2–4mm, in a semi-circle around each node. Lvs 3–6cm, orbicular, lobes 5, strongly incised, smooth or glandular-downy. Rac. open, pendent to 9cm; fls green-red. Fr. small, with gland. bristles, black. N US. Z4.

R. lacustre var. *molle* A. Gray = *R. montigenum.*

R. lasianthum Greene. To 1m, br. stout, thorned. Fls in clusters of 2–4, yellow. Fr. red, smooth. US (Calif., mts). Z8.

R. laurifolium Jancz. Everg. shrub to 1.5m; shoots gland. only when young. Lvs 5–10×2.5cm, oval or ovate, apex pointed, base rounded, coarsely toothed, coriaceous, glab. Rac. 3–6cm; fls 6–12, clustered, green-yellow. Fr. strigose, red-black, downy. Late winter–early spring. W China. Z9.

R. laxiflorum Pursh. Low sprawling shoots, downy. Lvs 6–8cm diam., rounded, base cordate, lobes 5, ovate, serrate, glab. above, downy beneath. Rac. 6–8cm, lax, upright; fls 6–12, red, glandular-downy; pet. fan-shaped. Early summer. Alask. to N Calif. Z5.

R. lentum Cov. & Rose = *R. montigenum.*

R. leptanthum A. Gray. To 2m; br. slender with solitary thorns to 1cm. Lvs 2cm diam., rounded or reniform, lobes 3–5, narrow, slightly gland. Fls borne singly or in pairs, white or pale pink. Fr. black, glossy. Late spring. SW US. Z6.

R. leptanthum var. *lasianthum* (Greene) Jeps. = *R. lasianthum.*

R. lobbii A. Gray. GUMMY GOOSEBERRY. Shrub to 2m; shoots downy at first, 3-thorned. Lvs 2–3.5cm diam., rounded cordate, lobes 3–5, blunt, ± gland. beneath. Fls large, solitary or in pairs on a pendent, gland. pedicel; cal. dark purple; pet. pink. Fr. glandular-pubesc., purple. Late spring. US (BC to Calif.). Z7.

R. longeracemosum Franch. Unarmed to 3m. Lvs to 14cm, cordate, base rounded, lobes 3–5, pointed, glab. Rac. pendent, to 30cm; fls tubular-bell-shaped, red-green; style long protruding. Fr. shiny, black, edible. W China, Tibet. Z6.

R. luridum Hook. f. & Thoms. To 1m, closely resembling *R. glaciale*; shoots smooth, red, bark peeling. Lvs to 6cm long and wide, rounded to reniform, base cordate, lobes 3–5, shallow, blunt, coarsely toothed, thinly gland., silky hirsute beneath. Rac. 3–5cm upright, fls turbinate, dark purple. Fr. black, pulp purple, acid. Early summer. Himal. (Tibet, Sikkim, Nepal). Z5.

R. ×*lydiae* F. Koch. (*R. leptanthum* ×*R. quercetorum.*) Vigorous, erect to 1m+; shoots grey, nodally 1–3 thorned. Lvs small, bright green, resembling those of *R. leptanthum*. Fls usually paired, pale yellow. Fr. black. Z7.

R. ×*magdalenae* F. Koch. (*R. leptanthum* ×*R. uva-crispa.*) More closely resembling *R. leptanthum*, to 1.5m. Fls pink and white. Fr. ellipsoid, black. Z6.

R. malvaceum Sm. CHAPARRAL CURRANT. To 2m, resembling *R. sanguineum*, shoots covered with grey gland. hairs. Lvs 2–5cm, 3-lobed, dull green, roughly downy, glandular-felted beneath. Rac. horizontal or drooping, to 7cm, fls pink. Calif. var. *viridiflorum* Abrams. Lvs rough, covered with coarse, green-white down beneath. Fls larger. Z7.

R. mandschuricum (Maxim.) Komar. To 2m; br. black-brown. Lvs to 11cm, lobes 3, pointed. Rac. to 20cm, pendent. Fr. blue-green, ripening red. NE Asia. Z6.

R. maximowiczianum Komar. = *R. distans.*

R. maximowiczii Batal. Closely resembling *R. luridum*, differs in gland. bristly shoots. Lvs 4–6cm, ovate, entire or 3–5-lobed, toothed, beneath. Rac. 3–5cm, slender, erect; fls red. Fr. downy, glandular-downy, red, yellow or green. Early summer. C China. var. *floribundum* Jesson. Rac. 10–15cm. Fr. thinly and finely bristly, red-yellow. Z6.

R. menziesii Pursh. CANYON GOOSEBERRY. To 2m, softly hirsute, bristled, thorns 1–2cm, in threes. Lvs 2–4cm diam., rounded-ovate, 3–5-lobed, coriaceous, glab. above, glandular-downy beneath. Fls borne singly or in pairs, tubular to bell-shaped, sep. purple; pet. white, sta. protruding. Fr. bristly, black. W US. Z7.

R. meyeri Maxim. To 1m+, akin to *R. petraeum*; shoots smooth, red. Lvs to 9cm diam., base cordate, lobes 5, pointed or blunt. Rac. 3–5cm, horizontal, lax; fls small, red; style protruding. Fr. shiny, black. C Asia. var. *turkestanicum* Jancz. Lvs blunt, glab. beneath. C Asia. Z7.

R. meyeri sensu Schneid. non Maxim. = *R. emodense*.

R. missouriense Nutt. MISSOURI GOOSEBERRY. 1–2m, br. grey-white, densely bristly; thorns 1–2cm, straight, red-brown. Lvs 2–6cm diam., rounded, lobes 3–5, deeply blunt-toothed, downy beneath. Fls in twos or threes, tubular, green-white. Fr. purple-brown, smooth. Early summer. US. Z5.

R. mogollonicum Greene = *R. wolfii*.

R. montigenum McClat. 0.5–1m; thorns 3–5 per node, stout; br. bristly. Lvs 1–4cm diam., reniform, 5-cleft, glandular-downy. Rac. sparse pendent, fls brown-green. Fr. dark red, glandular-bristly. Early summer. W US (mts). Z6.

R. moupinense Franch. 1–5m; br. rather twisted. Lvs to 16cm diam., 3- or 5-lobed, with scattered gland. bristles. Rac. 4–12cm; fls bell-shaped, red or green-red. Fr. shiny, black. Tibet, W China. Z5.

R. multiflorum Kit. 160–200cm; shoots grey downy at first. Lvs to 10cm, ± cordate, lobes 3–5, blunt, toothed, grey-white downy beneath. Rac. 12cm, spreading or nodding; fls bell-shaped, yellow-green, sta. exserted. Fr. dark red. Early summmer. Balk. Penins., mts. Z6.

R. nevadense Kellogg. SIERRA CURRANT. 1–1.5m, shoots soon glab. Lvs 3–6cm diam., rounded, lobes 3–5, blunt with rounded teeth, slightly downy beneath. Rac. pendent, similar to but smaller than *R. sanguineum*; cal. pink; pet. ovate, white. Fr. blue, gland., pruinose. Summer. US (Calif., Sierra Nevada). Z7.

R. nigrum L. BLACK CURRANT; EUROPEAN BLACK CURRANT. Aromatic shrub 2m; shoots vigorous, downy at first, with yellow glands. Lvs 5–10cm, rounded, 3–5-lobed, lower lf. surfaces downy and glandular-pitted. Rac. downy, pendent; fls bell-shaped, green outside, red-white within. Fr. glab., black, edible. Eur. to C Asia and Himal., W Kazakstan. 'Apiifolium' (f. *dissectum*): lvs v. deeply incised, lobes further dissected. 'Chlorocarpum': fr. green. 'Coloratum': lvs variegated white. 'Heterophyllum' (f. *aconitifolium*, f. *laciniatum*): lvs deeply cleft. 'Marmoratum' (var. *reticulatum*): lvs deeply cut, marbled cream. 'Xanthocarpum' (f. *albidum*, f. *fructeo-luteo*): fr. yellow to white. Z5.

R. niveum Lindl. Shrub 1–3m; shoots glab., red-brown, thorns nodal 1–3 to 2cm, brown. Lvs 3cm diam., rounded, shallowly lobed, crenate, usually glab. Infl. a nodding cluster of 2–4 fls; fls campanulate, white; sta. protruding. Fr. blue-black, smooth. Early summer. W US. Z6.

R. odoratum H.L. Wendl. CLOVE CURRANT; BUFFALO CURRANT; MISSOURI CURRANT. Closely resembling *R. aureum*, differs in downy shoots. Lvs 3–8cm, oval-rounded, 3–5-lobed, toothed. Rac. pendent, 5–10-fld; fls large, scented, yellow, tube to 1.5cm, cal. lobes; reflexed. Fr. globose, black. Early summer. C US. 'Crandall': fr. large, edible. Usually grown as this form. 'Leiobotrys': young lvs and fls glab. 'Xanthocarpum': fr. yellow-orange. Z5.

R. orientale Desf. 1–2m; shoots glandular-resinous, red. Lvs 4.5cm, rounded, 3-lobed, bright green, downy beneath, aromatic. Rac. 1–5cm, upright, 5–20-fld; fls green, becoming red-green. Greece to Himal. & Sib. in the mts. var. *heterotrichum* (C.A. Mey.) Jancz. Shoots red-brown at first. Lvs shiny. Fls red. Fr. without glands. Sib. Z5.

R. oxyacanthoides L. AMERICAN MOUNTAIN GOOSEBERRY; HAWTHORN LEAVED GOOSEBERRY. Shrub to 1m; br. slender, bristly with thorns to 1cm. Lvs 2–4cm, cordate, glab., deeply 5-lobed, becoming rugose, shiny green. Fls solitary or in pairs, tubular, green-white. Fr. purple-red, glab. US. Z2.

R. oxyacanthoides sense Hook. f. non L. = *R. hirtellum*.

R. oxyacanthoides L. sensu Jancz. = *R. inerme*.

R. petiolare Fisch. To 1.5m; shoots glab. Lvs 10–15cm diam., rounded, cordate base, lobes 3–5, ovate, pointed, slightly serrate, occas. downy when young, resinous beneath. Rac. erect 5–12cm; fls downy, white. Fr. blue-black. E Sib., China (Manch.), W US. Z3.

R. petraeum Wulf. 1.5m+; br. stout, glab., grey-brown. Lvs 7–10cm diam., rounded, base cordate, lobes 3, pointed, toothed, downy beneath. Rac. densely fld to 10cm; fls small, green, pink or red-green; sep. ciliate. Fr. red or red-black, acid. W & C Eur. (in the mts). var. *altissimum* (Turcz.) Jancz. To 3m. Lvs to 15cm diam., 3–5-lobed. Rac. 5–7cm, fls small, pale red. Fr. black-red. Sib. var. *atropurpureum* (C.A. Mey.) Schneid. Lvs to 15cm diam., 3-lobed, glab., not rugose. Rac.

2–4cm; fls purple without, paler within. Fr. black-red. Sib. var. *biebersteinii* (Berl.) Schneid. Lvs to 12cm, lobes 5, shallow, blunt, downy beneath. Rac. 10cm; fls red. Fr. nearly black. E Eur. (Cauc.). var. *carpathicum* (Schult.) Scheidw. Lvs to 9cm diam., 3-lobed, glab., not rugose. Rac. short, open rac.; fls pink. E Eur. (Tatras and Carpath. mts). Z6.

R. petraeum var. *bullatum* (Otto & Dietr.) Schneid. = *R. petraeum*.

R. pinetorum Greene. To 2m; br.; thorns to 2cm, borne singly or in groups of up to 3. Lvs 2–3cm, cordate, strongly lobed, glab. above, downy beneath. Fls usually solitary, large, bell-shaped, orange-red. Fr. stoutly bristled, black-purple. Late spring to early summer. US (Ariz. to New Mex.). Z6.

R. procumbens Pall. Low spreading shrub related to *R. fragrans*, differs in lvs to 8cm diam., reniform, coriaceous, 3–5-lobed. Rac. 1–6cm erect; fls gland. red. Fr. glab., brown. Sib. Z3.

R. prostratum L'Hérit. = *R. glandulosum*.

R. pulchellum Turcz. Shrub 1–2m, similar to *R. diacanthum*, differing in larger lvs to 5cm, deeply 3-lobed; br. armed with small paired prickles, these red at first. Infl. a 2.5–6cm erect rac. of 12–20 red fls; rachis gland., red. Fr. smooth, red. China. Often confused with *R. orientale* var. *heterotrichum*. Z5.

R. pumilum Nutt. = *R. inebrians*.

R. punctatum Lindl. = *R. orientale*.

R. quercetorum Greene. 1–1.5m, br. stoutly thorned. Lvs 1–2cm diam., rounded, lobes 3–5, toothed, finely downy. Fls slightly honey-scented, yellow or white. Fr. glab., black. Early summer. US (Calif. – mts). Z8.

R. reclinatum L. = *R. uva-crispa*.

R. resinosum Pursh = *R. orientale*.

R. ×robustum Jancz. (*R. niveum* × *R. inerme*.) Thorns small. Fls white or pink-white. Fr. glab., black, edible, sour. Z6.

R. roezlii Reg. SIERRA GOOSEBERRY. To 1.5m, br. spreading, rather twisted, downy at first; thorns in threes, to 1.5cm, slender. Lvs to 1.5cm, orbicular, base ± cordate, 3–5-lobed, deeply crenate, densely downy beneath. Fls solitary, paired or in threes, purple. Fr. 1–1.5cm, bristled, red-purple. Calif. var. *cruentum* (Greene) Rehd. Whole plant glab. Lvs coriaceous. Fr. densely bristly. NW US. Z7.

R. rotundifolium Michx. To 1m, br. slender, sparsely short spined. Lvs 25cm diam., base cordate or broadly triangular, lobes 3, blunt, thinly downy. Fls in groups of 1–3, green-purple; sta. protruding. Fr. glab., purple. E & C US. Z6.

R. rubrum L. p.p. = *R. silvestre*.

R. rubrum L. p.p. = *R. spicatum*.

R. sanguineum Pursh. WINTER CURRANT. To 4m, br. softly downy, gland., aromatic, red-brown. Lvs 5–10cm, diam., rounded, base cordate, 3–5-lobed, dark green and slightly downy above, felted beneath. Rac. to 8cm, gland., erect to pendent; fls tubular, red or rosy red. Fr. gland., blue-black with white bloom. Spring. W US to Calif. 'Albescens': fls white flushed pink, appearing 3 weeks earlier than other cvs. 'Brocklebankii': to 1m, slow growing, lvs yellow. 'King Edward VII': to 1m, compact, fls deep pink. 'Plenum': slow-growing, fls double, red. 'Pulborough Scarlet': to 1.8m, fls bright mid-pink. 'Pulborough Scarlet Variegated': lvs variegated yellow. 'Red Pimpernel': lvs rich green, fls deep red. 'Tydemans White' fls bright white. Z6.

R. santae-luciae Jancz. = *R. glutinosum*.

R. sativum (Rchb.) Syme = *R. silvestre*.

R. saxatile Pall. = *R. diacanthum*.

R. saximontanum E. Nels. = *R. setosum*.

R. schlechtendahlii Lange = *R. spicatum*.

R. setosum Lindl. MISSOURI GOOSEBERRY. To 1m, br. bristly, thorns to 2cm, awl-shaped. Lvs 1–4cm diam., rounded, somewhat cordate, 3–5-lobed, finely downy. Fls in groups of 1–3, tubular or bell-shaped, white. Fr. glab. or bristly, red or black. Early summer. NW US. Z2.

R. silvestre (Lam.) Mert. & Koch. RED CURRANT. Erect broad shrub, br. slightly glandular-pubesc. at first. Lvs to 6cm, rounded, base cordate, lobes pointed, soon glab. Rac. pendent or horizontal; fls green or red. Fr. translucent, red. W Eur. (Upper Rhine, Fr., Belgium, Engl). 'Macrocarpum' GARDEN CURRANT: 'Variegatum': lvs edged and marbled white. Z6.

R. spaethianum Koehne = *R. inebrians* var. *spaethianum*.

R. spaethianum f. *majus* Koehne = *R. inebrians*.

R. speciosum Pursh. FUCHSIA-FLOWERED GOOSEBERRY. Everg. to 4m, br. gland. bristly, thorns 1–2cm in groups of 2–3. Lvs 1–4cm, rounded, 3–5-lobed, bluntly toothed, smooth. Fls hanging in rows, usually in groups of 3; cal. broadly bell shaped, red, glandular-bristly, purple-red; sta. long-exserted 4, red, anth. ovate. Fr. gland. bristled, red. Early summer. Calif. Z7.

R. spicatum Robson. NORDIC CURRANT. To 2m, br. smooth. Lvs to 10cm diam., rounded, base slightly cordate, 3–5-lobed, glab., or slightly downy beneath. Racs upright to nodding, gland. and lightly downy. Fls green flushed red-brown. Fr. translucent, red.

Early summer. Scand. to Manch. Z3.

R. stenocarpum Maxim. To 2m, br. curving, bristly and thorny. Lvs to 3cm, rounded, 3–5-lobed. Fls in groups of 1–3, red; pet. white. Fr. translucent, green or red. NW China. Z6.

R. subvestitum Hook. & Arn. = **R. menziesii**.

R. ×succirubrum Zab. (*R. divaricatum ×R. niveum*.) Br. glab., thorns to 2cm. Lvs 3–5cm diam., rounded, 3–5-lobed, slightly blunt, smooth. Fls 2–4, tinged pink-red with long-exserted sta. in pendent rac. Fr. black, pruinose.

R. tenue Jancz. To 2.5m. Fls brown-red in rac. Fr. red. W Asia. Z7.

R. tenuiflorum Lindl. = **R. aureum**.

R. triflorum Willd. = **R. rotundifolium**.

R. triste Pall. SWAMP RED CURRANT. Creeping to 0.5m. Lvs 6–10cm diam., rounded-reniform, 3-lobed, deeply toothed, paler and downy beneath. Rac. pendent, shorter than the lvs, slightly gland.; fls red. Fr. glab., red. N US. Z2.

R. ×urceolatum Tausch. (*R. multiflorum ×R. petraeum*.) Closely resembling *R. multiflorum*. Lvs to 8cm diam., rounded, 3–5-lobed. Rac. 7–12cm; fls bell shaped, brown. Fr. dark red. Z6.

R. ussuriense Jancz. To 1m, shoots downy at first, densely gland., resinous, camphor-scented. Lvs 5–8cm diam., 3–5-lobed. Rac. 5–9-fld; fls yellow-green, bell-shaped; sta. protruding. Fr. blue-black. Manch. to Korea. Z5.

R. uva-crispa L. GOOSEBERRY. To 1m, br. with 1–3 stout nodal thorns to 1cm, grey. Lvs 2–6cm, base rounded, cordate, 3–5-lobed, deeply round-toothed, lightly downy beneath. Fls in stalked clusters of 1–3, green or pink-red. Fr. translucent yellow-green, bristly to downy. NE & C Eur. var. *reclinatum* (L.) Berl. Fr. spherical to ellipsoid, glab. or glandular-bristly, red or yellow. Eur., N Afr., Cauc. Z3.

R. viburnifolium A. Gray. Unarmed everg. shrub to 1.5m, st. lax often rooting. Lvs 2–4cm, broadly ovate-oval, apex blunt, base rounded, entire or slightly dentate, with gland pits, turpentine-scented. Rac. erect to 2.5cm; fls pink. Fr. red. Spring. Calif. Z9.

R. villosum Gay non Nutt. = **R. gayanum**.

R. villosum Wallich = **R. orientale**.

R. vilmorinii Jancz. To 2m, resembling *R. alpinum*, br. slender, red at first. Lvs 2–3cm, base cordate, 3–5-lobed. Rac. to 2cm; fls v.-small, green-brown fls. Fr. glab. or gland., black. W China. Z6.

R. viscosissimum Pursh. To 1m, shoots glandular-downy. Lvs 5–8cm, diam., rounded-reniform, with short broad lobes, glandular-downy. Rac. erect, sparsely fld to 10cm; fls 6–7mm, green to red. Fr. glandular-bristly, black. Summer. W US. Z7.

R. vulgare Lam. = **R. silvestre**.

R. ×wallichii auct. (*R. glaciale ×R. luridum*.) Lvs resembling those of *R. luridum*. Fls more similar to those of *R. glaciale*, brown-purple.

R. warszewiczii Jancz. To 1.5m, resembling *R. spicatum*. Lvs to 9cm, rounded, 3–5-lobed, base cordate, lightly downy beneath. Rac. 5–7cm pendent; fls pale red. Fr. black-red. Early summer. E Sib. Z3.

R. wolfii Rothr. To 3m, shoots glab. or slightly downy. Lvs 4–9cm diam., rounded, 3–5-lobed, sharply serrate, veins glandular-downy beneath. Rac. erect, 2–4cm; rachis glandular-downy; fls green-white. Fr. glandular-bristly, black, bloomy. Early summer. SW US. Z6.

→*Grossularia*.

Ribgrass, Ribwort *Plantago lanceolata*.
Rice *Oryza*.
Rice Flower *Pimelea*.
Rice-grain Fritillary *Fritillaria affinis*.
Rice Grass *Oryzopsis*.
Rice-paper Plant *Tetrapanax*.
Rice's Wattle *Acacia riceana*.

Richardia L. Rubiaceae. 15 ann. or perenn. herbs, erect or prostrate, usually pubesc. Fls in dense, term., involucrate cymes; involucre of 2–4 lvs; cal. tube subglobose or top-shaped, lobes usually 4–6; cor. funnel- or salver-shaped, lobes 3–5; anth. exserted. Fr. a capsule, crowned with persistent cal. Widespread throughout tropics, but esp. trop. and subtrop. Amer. (S US, W Indies, S to Arg.), often as weeds; 1 sp. Fiji.

R. brasiliensis Gomes. Ann. or perenn. herb, often mat-forming from thick, woody taproot, to 40cm; br. densely hairy. Lvs 4cm or more, elliptic to oblong-lanceolate, acute, pubesc. Fls in heads to 1.5cm wide; cor. tube 3mm, white, lobes spreading, 4–6, purple at margin. Summer–autumn. S Amer., nat. subtrop. and trop.

R. scabra L. MEXICAN CLOVER. Ann. herb, to 1m. Resembling *R. brasiliensis*, but lvs to 7cm, occas. ovate, mainly glab. Cor. tube 6mm, white or pink, lobes hair-tipped. Summer–autumn. Distrib. as *R. brasiliensis*, and Fiji.

→*Richardsonia*.

Richardia Kunth. non L.
R. africana Kunth. = *Zantedeschia aethiopica*.
R. elliotiana Wats. = *Zantedeschia elliotiana*.
R. pentlandii Wats. = *Zantedeschia pentlandii*.
R. rehmannii (Engl.) N.E. Br. ex W. Harrow = *Zantedeschia rehmannii*.

Richardsonia Kunth.
R. brasiliensis (Gomes) Hayne = *Richardia brasiliensis*.
R. scabra (L.) A. St.-Hil. = *Richardia scabra*.

Richea R. Br. Epacridaceae. 11 everg. trees or shrubs. Leaves parallel-veined, narrow, stiff, base sheathing st., resembling those of a monocot such as *Dracaena*. Fls to 1.5cm, crowded in simple term. clustes, spikes or pan.; cor. closed at the apex except for a small opening. Aus., Tasm.

R. pandanifolia Hook. f. TREE HEATH. Gaunt everg. tree or shrub to 10m. Lvs to 1m, at br. tips, linear-lanceolate, acuminate, arching-recurved, smooth-waxy, entire or serrulate. Fls cream, in erect axill. pan. Summer. Tasm. Z9.

R. scoparia Hook. f. Bushy erect everg. treelet or shrub to 1.5m. Lvs to 5cm, lanceolate-subulate, semi-rigid, glab., glossy, slender-pointed. Fls in dense cylindric term. rac. to 30cm long, white, pink or orange. Summer. Tasm. Z9.

R. sprengelioides F. Muell. Low-growing shrub to 1m. Lvs 0.6–1.25cm, broadly elliptic, apex rigidly pointed. Fls red-tinted, in leafy, spherical heads. Summer. Tasm. Z9.

→*Cystanthe*.

Ricinus L. Euphorbiaceae. 1 glab. shrub to 12m, usually to 4m and treated as an ann. in cult. Br. regular. Lvs to 60cm diam., peltate, leathery, palmately lobed, dentate; petioles to 30cm. Infl. term., subpaniculate, to 15cm; ♂ fls at base, ♀ fls toward apex; cal. caducous; styles 3, forked, vivid red. Capsule ovoid, to 25mm diam., smooth or spiny. Summer. NE Afr. to Middle E, nat. throughout tropics. Z9.

R. communis L. CASTOR OIL PLANT; PALMA CHRISTI; CASTOR BEAN PLANT. 'Borboniensis': habit v. large. 'Borboniensis Arboreus': habit tall; st. red; lvs glaucous. 'Cambodgensis': st. purple-black; lvs dark. 'Carmencita': to 1.8m; lvs large, deep brown; fls early, bright red. 'Coccineus': to 12m; lvs tinged bronze, palmately lobed. 'Gibsonii': dwarf to 120cm; st. black-purple; lvs dark purple-red with metallic lustre. 'Gibsonii Mirabilis': habit dwarf, compact to 120cm; st. and lvs red. 'Impala': to 120cm; young growth maroon to carmine; fls sulphur yellow in clusters; pods maroon. 'Major': lvs large. 'Red Spire': st. red; lvs tinged bronze. 'Sanguineus': fast growing; lvs large, tinged red. 'Scarlet Queen' ('Carmineus'): lvs burgundy; fls bright orange-red. 'Zanzibarensis': lvs to 50cm wide, green veined white; seeds v. large. 'Zanzibarensis Enormis': lvs entirely green. 'Zanzibarensis Viridis': dwarf to 3m; lvs entirely green.

Ricotia L. Cruciferae. 9 usually glab. herbs. Lvs basal and cauline. Fls in long rac.; pet. 4, cordate, clawed. Fr. a silicle, much compressed. E Medit.

R. aegyptica L. = **R. lunaria**.

R. lunaria (L.) DC. EGYPTIAN HONESTY. Ann., to c23cm. Lvs 2–3× pinnately divided; lfts oblong, undulate. Fls lilac, claw white. Fr. obovate-lanceolate, septum translucent, resembling *Lunaria annua*. Spring. Syr., Leb. Z7.

→*Cardamine*.

Ridge-fruited Mallee *Eucalyptus angulosa*.

Rienga Lily *Arthropodium cirrhatum*.

Riesenbachia C. Presl = *Lopezia*.

Riga Pea *Lathyrus sativus*.
Rigid Buckler Fern *Dryopteris submontana*.

Rigidella Lindl. Iridaceae. 4 perenn. bulbous herbs. Lvs radical, long, broadly lanceolate, plicate, reduced on st. to narrowly acuminate bracts. Flowering st. erect, simple or sparsely branched; fls 1 to many per spathe, fugacious, on slender nodding pedicels, cup-shaped at base, outer lobes 3, slender-clawed, ovate-acute, inner lobes small, erect; sta. 3, fil. fused at a cylindrical tube; stigmas 3, deeply cleft. Mex. to Guat. Z9.

R. flammea Lindl. Flowering st. 1–1.5m; fls pendent in pseudo-umbels, outer seg. to 6cm, scarlet spotted or striped purple or black, inner seg. to 1cm, yellow tipped red. Mex.

R. immaculata Herb. Differs from *R. flammea* in shorter flowering st. and unmarked scarlet fls. Mex., Guat.

R. orthantha Lem. Fls scarlet, erect, outer seg. to 6cm, inner seg. to 3cm. Capsule to 4cm. Mex., Guat.

Rimaria N.E. Br.
R. divergens L. Bol. = *Vanheerdia divergens*.
R. dubia N.E. Br. = *Gibbaeum heathii*.
R. heathii (N.E. Br.) N.E. Br. = *Gibbaeum heathii*.
R. luckhoffii L. Bol. = *Gibbaeum luckhoffii*.
R. microsperma (Dinter & Derenb.) N.E. Br. = *Dinteranthus microspermus*.
R. pole-evansii (N.E. Br.) N.E. Br. = *Dinteranthus pole-evansii*.
R. primosii (L. Bol.) L. Bol. = *Vanheerdia primosii*.

Rimu *Dacrydium cupressinum*.
Ring Bellflower *Symphyandra*.
Ringed Beard Grass *Dichanthium annulatum*.
Ringworm Shrub *Senna alata*.
Rio Grande Vervain *Verbena runyonii*.
Rio Nunez Coffee *Coffea canephora*.

Ripogonum Forst. & Forst. f. Liliaceae (Smilacaceae). 8 climbing shrubs, lacking tendrils. Fls small, in axill. or terminal rac.; perianth seg. 6; sta. 6, fil. v. short. Fr. a berry. Aus., NZ. Z10.
R. scandens Forst. & Forst. f. Tall, glab. climber; st. knotted, interwoven. Lvs 7.5–12.5cm, narrowly ovate-oblong to oblong-lanceolate, coriaceous. Rac. axill., simple or branched, 7.5–15cm; fls tinged green, 0.8cm diam. Fr. bright red. NZ.

Ripple-grass *Plantago lanceolata*.
Risdon Peppermint *Eucalyptus risdonii*.
Riverbank Grape *Vitis riparia*.
River Beauty *Epilobium latifolium*.
River Birch *Betula nigra*.
River Bottlebrush *Callistemon paludosus*.
River Calabash *Amphitecna latifolia*.
River Peppermint *Eucalyptus elata*.
River Red Gum *Eucalyptus camaldulensis*.
River Teatree *Melaleuca leucadendra*.

Rivina L. Phytolaccaceae. 3 slender, shrubby, erect perenn. herbs, often grown as ann. Fls small, 4-merous, many in pendulous rac. Fr. a pea-like berry. Trop. & subtrop. Amer. Z9.
R. humilis L. ROUGE PLANT; BLOOD BERRY; BABY PEPPER. St. glabrescent, dark green, angular, to 60cm, branching divaricately. Lvs 3–10cm, cordate-ovate, acute, dark green, puberulent. Fls white to pale pink, in rac. to 15cm, ascending then pendulous, elongating in fr. Berries yellow to scarlet. S US, W Indies, S Amer.
R. laevis L. = *R. humilis*.

Roast Beef Plant *Iresine*; *Iris foetidissima*.
Robber Fern *Pyrrosia confluens*.
Robert Ougon-chiku *Phyllostachys sulphurea*.

Robinia L. Leguminosae (Papilionoideae). 20 decid. trees and shrubs. Lvs imparipinnate; shoots and pods often glandular-bristly. Fls pea-like in pendulous rac., often fragrant; standard large, reflexed. Fr. flat, elongated. US.
R. ×ambigua Poir. (*R. pseudoacacia ×R. viscosa*.) Differs from *R. pseudoacacia*, in the somewhat glutinous br. with small thorns. Lfts 7–23. Fls pale pink. 'Bella-rosea': br. more viscid, thorns shorter; fls larger, darker pink. 'Decaisneseana': br. viscid, thorns short or 0; fls large, pale pink; cal. densely pubesc. 'Idahoensis': fls pink to lavender. Z3.
R. boyntonii Ashe. Unarmed shrub, to 3m; branchlets ± glab., lfts 2–2.5cm, 7–15, elliptic to oblong-obtuse. Fls pink or rose-purple and white in rather loose, 8–10-fld rac., 6–10cm long. Early summer. SE US. Z5.
R. dubia Foucault = *R. ×ambigua*.
R. elliottii (Chapm.) Ashe. Shrub to 1.5m; branchlets tomentose. Branchlets with thorny lat. twigs at tips. Lfts to 2.5cm, 11–15, elliptic, grey-pubesc. beneath. Fls rose-purple, or purple and white, in 5–10-fld, grey-pubesc. rac. Summer. SE US. Z5.
R. fertilis Ashe = under *R. hispida*.
R. frutex L. = *Caragana frutex*.
R. glutinosa Sims = *R. viscosa*.
R. hartwegii Koehne. Glandular-pubesc. shrub or tree to 8m. Lfts to 4cm, 11–23, broadly lanceolate to narrowly ovate, sparsely pubesc. above, sericeous beneath. Rac. to 10cm, crowded, glandular-downy; fls white, magenta or mauve. Summer. SE US. Z6.
R. hispida L. ROSE ACACIA; MOSS LOCUST; BRISTLY LOCUST. Shrub to 2.25m, suckering, br. covered with long red bristles. Lfts to 5cm, 7–15, ovoid or broadly ovate, bristle-tipped, dark green above, grey-green beneath. Fls 3–5 in short rac., pale purple or rose. Late spring. SE US. 'Macrophylla': more robust br. less bristly. 'Monument': to 4m, compactly conical, sparsely bristled; rac. to 10cm, fls large, delicate lilac-pink. *R. fertilis*

Ashe is distinguished from *R. hispida* by its shorter habit (it seldom exceeds 2m), narrower lfts elliptic-oblong and thinly hairy beneath, smaller fls and more readily produced fr. rank. Z5.
R. hispida var. *rosea* hort. non Elliott & Chapm. = *R. boyntonii*.
R. hispida var. *rosea* Elliott & Chapm. non hort. = *R. elliottii*.
R. hispida f. *nana* Torr. & A. Gray = *R. nana*.
R. ×holdtii Beissn. (*R. pseudoacacia ×R. luxurians*.) Tree to 6m; crown domed, br. thorny. Lfts to 5cm, dark green, coriaceous. Rac. looser than in *R. luxurians*; fls with standard pale rose, keel and wing pale pink to white. Gdn origin. 'Britzensis': lvs initially pale green becoming grey-green; fls v. pale rose to almost white. Z4.
R. ×hybrida Audib. ex DC. = *R. ×ambigua*.
R. jubata Pall. = *Caragana jubata*.
R. kelseyi Kelsey ex Hutch. ALLEGHANY MOSS. Shrub to 3m, br. initially hispid. Lfts 2–3cm, oblong, acute, 7–11 dark green above, pale grey-green beneath. Rac. to 6cm, crowded, glandular-pubesc.; fls lilac to rose. SE US. Z5.
R. luxurians (Dieck) C. Schneid. Shrub or tree to 10m; br. thorny, initially glandular-pubesc. Lfts to 3cm, 13–21, elliptic-oblong, sericeous beneath; rachis villous. Rac. dense, glandular-pubesc.; fls pale rose or white. Summer. SE US. Z5.
R. maculata Kunth = *Gliricidia sepium*.
R. ×margaretta Ashe. (*R. hispida ×R. pseudoacacia*.) Shrub, 3–4m. Lfts downy, pubesc. beneath. Rac. to 15cm, downy; fls pale pink. N Carol. 'Idaho': habit tree-like, open, broad; fls deep red-purple, the darkest of the genus. 'Pink Cascade': vigorously suckering; fls large, pink, prolific. Z5.
R. nana Elliott. Shrub to 1.25m, frequently unarmed, branchlets hispidulous. Lfts to 2.5cm, 9–15, elliptic to ellitic-ovate, downy or glab. Rac. 3–5-fld; fls pink. W & S Carol. Z5.
R. neomexicana A. Gray. Shrub to 2m; young growth finely grey-pubesc. Lfts to 3.5cm, in 4–7 pairs, elliptic-lanceolate. Infl. pubesc. and glandular-hispid; fls rose. Summer. SW US. Z5.
R. pseudoacacia L. BLACK LOCUST; YELLOW LOCUST. Tree, to 27m, nearly glab.; bark deeply furrowed; young br. thorny, olive green to glossy dark red-brown. Lfts to 5cm, 9–19, elliptic to ovate-obtuse. Rac. dense, nodding, to 20cm; fls white to ivory, fragrant, blotched with yellow at base. Summer. E & C US, widely nat. in temp. regions. Numerous cvs include those ranging in habit from narrowly upright ('Appalachia') to rounded ('Bessoniana'; 'Inermis') to pendulous ('Pendula') to dwarf ('Nigra Nana'); br. v. thorny ('Purpurea') to thornless ('Bessoniana'), v. thin ('Bullata') to clustered like witches' brooms ('Nigra Nana') or twisted ('Tortuosa'); lvs larger than the sp. ('Inermis') to smaller and narrower ('Crispa'), bullate ('Bullata') to incised ('Dissecta'), elliptic ('Coluteoides') to oblong ('Amorphifolia') to linear ('Linearis'), lfts 1 ('Unifolia') to 19 ('Myrtifolia'), green-yellow ('Aurea') to golden yellow ('Frisia'), grey-green ('Glaucescens') to initially tinged with red ('Purpurea'); thorns 0 ('Inermis') to wine red ('Frisia'); blooms erratic ('Bessoniana') to profuse and prolonged ('Semperflorens'). Z3.
R. pygmaea L. = *Caragana pygmaea*.
R. schiediana Schldl. = *Willardia schiediana*.
R. sinica Buc'hoz = *Caragana sinica*.
R. ×slavinii Rehd. (*R. kelseyi ×R. pseudoacacia*.) Shrub. Lfts wider than *R. kelseyi*, acute to obtuse. Rac. slightly villous but not gland.; fls rosy pink. 'Hillieri': compact tree, crown rounded; fls mauve-pink. Z5.
R. spinosa L. = *Caragana spinosa*.
R. viscosa Vent. CLAMMY LOCUST. Tree to 13m, young growth glandular-pubesc., branchlets viscid, black-brown, with small thorns. Lfts to 5cm, ovate, in 6–12 pairs, dark green above, often grey-pubesc. beneath. Rac. to 8cm, crowded, pendulous; fls pink, standard speckled yellow. Late spring. SE US. Z3.

Robin-redbreast Bush *Melaleuca lateritia*.

Robinsonella Rose & Bak. f. Malvaceae. 14 shrubs and trees. Lvs unlobed or palmately lobed. Fls in pan., rac. or cymose clusters; epical. 0; pet. 5; styles as many as the mericarps, stigmas capitate. Mex. and C Amer. Z9.
R. cordata Rose & Bak. f. Tree to 12m, pilose. Lvs to 15cm, ovate, rarely 3-lobed, base cordate. Fls in racemose infl., on short axill. branchlets; pet. to 2.5cm, white to lavender. Mex. and Guat.
R. edentula Rose & J.D. Sm. = *R. lindeniana* ssp. *divergens*.
R. lindeniana (Turcz.) Rose & Bak. f. Shrub or tree to 8m. Lvs to 20cm, 3- or 5-lobed or unlobed. Fls in paniculate leafy inf.; pet. to 1.2cm, white, often veined lavender. Mex. to Costa Rica. ssp. *divergens* (Rose & Bak. f.) Fryx. Tree-like; lvs unlobed or slightly 3-lobed. Infl. congested. Mex. to Costa Rica.

Robin's Plantain *Erigeron pulchellus*.

Robiquetia Gaudich. Orchidaceae. 20 epiphytic, monopodial orchids. Lvs distichous, to 20cm, elliptic-oblong, narrow. Rac. axill., pendent, racemose; fls small, many; lip midlobe linear or tapering, concave, fleshy, lat. lobes small with fleshy thickenings; spur cylindric. Indomal. to Fiji. Z10.

R. bertholdii (Rchb. f.) Schltr. Infl. to 20cm; fls white, pink or dark pink, apical margins green; spur apex dark pink, swollen. Vanuatu, Solomon Is., Fiji.

R. mooreana J.J. Sm. Infl. oblong or ovoid; fls dense, green-white to rose purple. New Guinea, Solomon Is.

R. spathulata (Bl.) J.J. Sm. Infl. pendent, to 25cm; fls dense, tep. burnt sienna, edged bronze-yellow with similar central line, lip ochre. Java, Malaysia.

→Cleisostoma and Saccolabium.

Roble Platymiscium trinitatis.
Roblé Beech Nothofagus obliqua.
Roble Blanco Tabebuia heterophylla.
Roble Cimarron Tabebuia haemantha.
Roble de Chile Eucryphia cordifolia.
Roble de Olor Catalpa punctata.
Roble Guayo Bourreria succulenta.
Roble Negro Tabebuia dubia.
Roblillo Catalpa punctata.
Robusta Coffee Coffea canephora.
Robust Marsh Orchid Dactylorhiza elata.
Rocambole Allium sativum var. ophioscorodon.

Rochea DC.
R. coccinea (L.) DC. = Crassula coccinea.
R. jasminea (Sims) DC. = Crassula obtusa.
R. subulata (L.) Adams = Crassula fascicularis.

Rock Bell Wahlenbergia.
Rockberry Empetrum eamesii.
Rock-brake Cryptogramma.
Rock Buckthorn Rhamnus saxatilis.
Rock Cranberry Vaccinium vitis-idaea var. minus.
Rockcress Arabis; Barbarea vulgaris.
Rock Elm Ulmus thomasii.
Rocket Salad Eruca.
Rock Geranium Heuchera americana.
Rock Hare's Ear Bupleurum petraeum.
Rock Harlequin Corydalis sempervirens.
Rockingham Podocarp Podocarpus elatus.
Rock Jasmine Androsace.
Rock Lily Arthropodium cirrhatum.
Rock Maple Acer glabrum; A. saccharum.
Rock Nettle Eucnide bartonioides.
Rock Palm Brahea.
Rock Penstemon Penstemon rupicola.
Rock Polypody Polypodium virginianum.
Rock Purslane Calandrina umbellata.
Rock Rose Cistus; Helianthemum.
Rock Speedwell Veronica fruticans.
Rock Spike Moss Selaginella rupestris.
Rock Spiraea Holodiscus dumosus; Petrophytum.
Rock Violet Viola flettii.
Rocky Mountain Bee Plant Cleome serrulata.
Rocky Mountain Dogbane Apocynum pumilum.
Rocky Mountain Bristlecone Pine Pinus aristata.
Rocky Mountain Cherry Prunus besseyi.
Rocky Mountain Flowering Raspberry Rubus deliciosus.
Rocky Mountain Juniper Juniperus scopulorum.
Rocky Mountain Maple Acer glabrum.
Rocky Mountain Pinyon Pinus edulis.
Rocky Mountain Raspberry Rubus deliciosus.
Rocky Mountain Woodsia Woodsia scopulina.

Rodgersia A. Gray. Saxifragaceae. 6 stoutly rhizomatous perenn. herbs. Lvs basal, emerging, felty, palmately or pinnately compound; lfts leathery, irregularly serrate. Fls numerous, small, packed in dense pan.; sep. 5–6; pet. usually 0; sta. 10. Summer. Nepal, China, Jap. Z7.

R. aesculifolia Batal. To 2m. Lvs palmate; lfts 5–9, to 25cm, obovate, acute, coarsely toothed; stalk and veins rusty-tomentose. Pan., to 60cm, compressed; fls white. China. Z5.

R. henrici (Franch.) Franch. Similar to R. aesculifolia except in lfts long-acuminate and fls red-purple. China, N Burm., SE Tibet. Z6.

R. japonica Reg. = R. podophylla.

R. pinnata Franch. To 120cm. Lvs pseudo-pinnate; lfts 5–9, to 20cm, obovate-lanceolate. Fls red. SW China. 'Alba': fls white. 'Elegans': fls cream tinted pink. 'Rosea': fls rose. 'Rubra': fls deep red. 'Superba': tall; lvs tinted bronze to purple; fls rose, in infl. to 50cm. Z6.

R. podophylla A. Gray. To 120cm. Lvs palmate, turning bronze in autumn; lfts cleft and toothed at apex. Infl. 30cm, fls cream. Jap., Korea. 'Pagode': fls white, profuse. 'Parasol': to 90cm; lvs large; fls pink. 'Rotlaub': lvs tinted red. 'Smaragd': lvs broadly spreading; fls cream. Z5.

R. sambucifolia Hemsl. To 90cm. Lvs pinnate; lfts 3–11, acute. Pan. flat-topped, fls white or pink. China. Z6.

R. tabularis (Forbes & Hemsl.) Komar. = Astilboides tabularis.

Rodriguezia Ruiz & Pav. Orchidaceae. 35 epiphytic orchids. Pbs small, compressed, enveloped by overlapping leaf-sheaths, apex unifoliate or bifoliate. Lvs rigidly coriaceous, often scabrid, narrowly ligulate to elliptic-lanceolate, conduplicate, carinate beneath. Rac. basal; fls often crystalline-textured; dors. sep. free, spreading, concave, lat. sep. connate, often geniculate or gibbous; pet. similar to dors. sep.; lip clawed, simple, short-spurred. Trop. Amer. Z10.

R. batemanii Poepp. & Endl. Pbs to 5cm. Lvs to 35cm. Infl. to 25cm; fls to 6cm diam., fragrant, thin-textured, white, white marked yellow or pale lilac spotted lilac; lip to 48×25mm, obovate-cuneate, emarginate. Peru, Venez., Braz.

R. candida Batem. ex Lindl. Pbs to 5cm. Lvs to 15cm. Infl. to 30cm, fls to 6cm diam., fragrant, white; lip to 54×27mm, narrowly obovate, bilobulate, involute, callus yellow. Venez., Braz., Guyana.

R. compacta Schltr. Pbs to 2.5cm. Lvs to 14cm. Infl. to 4.5cm, fls to 5cm, fragrant; tep. pale yellow or green-yellow; lip to 2.5×1cm, yellow, obovate-spathulate, deeply emarginate. Nic., Costa Rica, Panama.

R. decora (Lem.) Rchb. f. Pbs to 2.5cm. Lvs to 15cm. Infl. to 40cm; fls to 3.5cm, slightly fragrant; tep. white or yellow-white, spotted or mottled dark red-purple; lip to 28×14mm, white, orbicular, apex bilobed, keels spotted red. Autumn–winter. Braz.

R. granadensis (Lindl.) Rchb. f. Pbs to 3cm. Lvs to 15cm. Infl. to 15cm; fls to 3cm diam., white, lip marked yellow; to 3.5cm, ovate or obovate, emarginate, base tubular, callus yellow. Colomb.

R. lanceolata Lodd. Pbs to 4cm. Lvs to 25cm. Infl. 8–40cm; fls to 4cm diam., pink to rose-red, sparkling; lipto 18×9mm, obovate-oblong, undulate, emarginate; callus sometimes white. Panama, Colomb., Venez., Peru, Braz., Trin., Guyana, Surinam.

R. lindenii Cogn. = R. pubescens.

R. lindmanii Kränzl. = Solenidium lunatum.

R. maculata (Lindl.) Rchb. f. Pbs to 2.5cm. Lvs to 15cm. Infl. 6–15cm; fls to 3cm, fragrant; tep. yellow spotted cinnamon; lip to 25×10mm, yellow-brown blotched dark brown, base white, long-clawed, obovate-cordate, cleft. Braz.

R. maculata Lindl. = Leochilus oncidioides.

R. pubescens (Lindl.) Rchb. f. Pbs to 3.5cm. Lvs to 13cm. Infl. 5–15cm; fls to 3.5cm diam., fragrant, pure white; lip to 17×10mm, long-clawed, subcordate to subdeltoid, deeply emarginate, undulate, disc yellow; column pubesc. Braz.

R. secunda HBK = R. lanceolata.

R. venusta (Lindl.) Rchb. f. Pbs to 3cm. Lvs to 15cm. Infl. 8–17cm; fls to 3.5cm, strongly fragrant, white; lip to 22×14mm, long-clawed, obovate-obcordate to triangular-obcordate, deeply emarginate, undulate, base narrow, disc yellow. Braz., Peru.

Rodrigueziella Kuntze = Theodorea.

Roebelin Palm Phoenix roebelinii.

Roemeria Medik. Papaveraceae. 6 ann. herbs, to 50cm. Latex yellow. Lvs deeply and irregularly pinnatisect; seg. linear. Fls solitary; peduncles opposite lvs; pet. 4; sta. numerous. Fr. a linear, cylindric capsule. Summer. Medit. to Afghan.

R. hybrida (L.) DC. VIOLET-FLOWERED HORNED POPPY; WIND ROSE. To 50cm. St. erect, branched, sparsely hairy. Lvs 2–3-pinnate, seg. mucronate. Pet. to 2.5cm, violet, with a dark purple blotch at base. Fr. to 7.5cm, setose. Medit. region.

R. refracta DC. As for R. hybrida except to 30cm. Pet. red, with a black blotch at base. Fr. red, glab., with 4 bristles at apex. Armenia, Turk., escape in S US.

R. violacea Medik. = R. hybrida.

Roezliella Schltr. = Sigmatostalix.

Rogiera Planch.
R. amoena Planch. = Rondeletia amoena.
R. cordata (Benth.) Planch. = Rondeletia cordata.
R. gratissima Lind. = Rondeletia gratissima.
R. latifolia (Hook. f.) Decne. = Rondeletia latifolia.

Rohdea Roth. Liliaceae (Convallariaceae). 1 rhizomatous perenn. herb. Lvs to 28–45×5–7cm, in a basal rosette, oblanceolate, coriaceous, suberect. Scape 5–7.5cm, axillary, spike 2.5–5cm dense; perianth to 0.5cm, fleshy white or yellow-green, campanulate. Fr. a berry, red or yellow. Early spring. SW China, Jap. Z7.

R. japonica (Thunb.) Roth. 'Aureo-striata': lvs distichous, striped creamy yellow. 'Marginata': lvs leathery, edged white. 'Striata': lvs thick, dark green edged white.

Roldana La Ll. & Lex. Compositae. 48 large, erect ann. to perenn. herbs or subshrubs. St. slender often with linear blotches. Lvs alt., to 12×12cm, usually palmate or peltate, petiolate. Cap. discoid or radiate, in terminal corymbose or paniculate infl.; involucre narrowly campanulate to cylindrical; flts yellow. Mex., C Amer. Z9.

R. petasites (Sims) H. Robinson & Brettell. Ann. to perenn. herb, to c1m. Lvs numerous, ovate to orbicular, lobes 7+, un-dulating shallow, regular and often sharp, with numerous callose teeth, base peltate or cordate, truncate, petiolate, densely pale tomentose beneath. Cap. in leafy paniculate infl.; ray flts usually 6, sometimes 0. Mex. to Nic.

R. platanifolia (Benth.) H. Robinson & Brettell. Ann. to perenn. herb, to 1m. Lvs few, ovate to orbicular, sometimes peltate, base cordate or truncate, sparsely hirsute or hispidulous, toothed or lobed, lobes 7+, angular and remotely callose-denticulate, petioles of lowest lvs 10–12.5cm, glab. or densely hirsute. Cap. few, in lax corymbs, or in elongated spike. Mex.
→Cineraria and Senecio.

Roman Candle Yucca gloriosa.
Roman Coriander Nigella sativa.
Roman Nettle Urtica pilulifera.
Roman Wormwood Artemisia pontica; Corydalis sempervirens.

Romanzoffia Cham. Hydrophyllaceae. 4 dwarf perenn. herbs with swollen rootstocks. Lvs mostly basal, long-petioled, reni-form to orbicular; palmatifid or deeply crenately incised. Fls solitary or in long-stalked, racemose, term. cymes; cor. campanulate to funnelform, white, off-white or pale purple, usually with a yellow ring, broadly ovate, sta. 5. W N Amer., Aleutian Is.

R. californica Greene = R. suksdorfii.
R. sitchensis Bong. To 10cm, most parts glab. or thinly hoary-pubesc. Lvs to 5cm diam. Infl. to 15cm; cor. white. W N Amer. Z5.

R. suksdorfii Greene. Frequently confused with R. sitchensis but attaining 30cm. Infl. held well clear of lvs. Z7.

R. tracyi Jeps. To 10cm, markedly succulent, hairy. Infl. scarcely exceeding lvs. Fls white. Washington, Oreg., Calif. Z7.

Romneya Harv. MATILIJA POPPY; CALIFORNIAN TREE POPPY. Papa-veraceae. 1 woody-based, glaucous-blue perenn. herb to 2.5m. Lvs to 15cm, irregularly pinnatifid, somewhat palmate, lobes spreading, with tough apices, toothed or entire. Fls to 15cm diam., solitary at br. tips, white, fragrant; sep. 3, 3cm, apiculate; pet. 6, obovate, silky; sta. many. Summer–autumn. Calif., Mex. Z7.

R. coulteri Harv. var. **trichocalyx** (Eastw.) Jeps. Lvs thinner-textured, more finely divided; sep. bristly. A hybrid, R.×hybrida hort. (R.×vandedenii Correv.) exists between R. coulteri var. coulteri and R. coulteri var. trichocalyx, with apiculate but slightly bristly sep. R. 'White Cloud' of the same parentage has large, scented fls with smooth, apiculate sep.; lvs v. glaucous and the habit vigorously spreading.

R. trichocalyx Eastw. = R. coulteri var. trichocalyx.

Romulea Maratti. Iridaceae. 80 small, crocus-like, perenn., cormous herbs. Basal lvs 1–6, linear to narrow-subulate, 4-ridged or -grooved. Scapes erect or elongate-recurved; fls erect, 1 per spathe; perianth tube shortly funnelform. Spring. Medit. to SW Engl.; S Afr., and at high altitudes in C & E Afr. N to the Medit.

R. atranda Lewis. Fls 3–4cm diam., magenta-rose, with dark purple zone above yellow throat. S Afr. (Cape Prov.).

R. bulbocodioides auct. = R. flava.

R. bulbocodium (L.) Sebast. & Mauri. Perianth 2.25–5cm, bright violet, rarely white, tube 0.3–0.8cm, yellow, orange or white within or at throat. Medit., Port., NW Spain, Bulg. var. **crocea** (Boiss. & Heldr.) Bak. Fls yellow. var. **leichtliniana** (Heldr.) Bég. Fls white, throat yellow. var. **subpalustris** Bak. Fls tinted purple-blue, throat white. Z7.

R. clusiana (Lange) Nyman = R. bulbocodium.

R. columnae Sebast. & Mauri. Flowering st. short; fls 1–3; peri-anth 1–1.5cm, white tinted lavender or blue or violet, often with darker veins, tube 0.25–0.5cm, yellow within. W Eur. (SW

Engl. to Medit.). Z8.

R. corsica Jourd. & Fourr. = R. ligustica.

R. dichotoma (Thunb.) Bak. Flowering st. 4.5–30cm; fls several, term. on branching scapes; perianth 2.5–4cm, pink with darker veins in throat, tube 0.3–0.5cm, yellow within and at throat. S Afr. (Cape Prov.). Z9.

R. flava (Lam.) De Vos. Flowering st. concealed by lf bases or elongate; fls 1–4; perianth 2.25–4cm, yellow-green, occas. white or tinted blue or pink, tube 0.3–0.7cm, yellow within and at throat, seg. 0.3–1.2cm across. S Afr. (Cape Prov.). Z9.

R. grandiflora Tod. = R. bulbocodium.

R. hirta Schltr. Flowering st. short, concealed by lf bases; fls 1–4; perianth 1.6–3.5cm, pale yellow, usually banded brown at centre of seg., tube to 0.5cm, seg. 0.5–0.8cm across. S Afr. (Cape Prov.). Z9.

R. ligustica Parl. Fls 1, rarely 2–3 per st.; perianth 2–3.25cm, mauve to violet, tube 0.5–0.7cm, striped violet within and at throat. Corsica, Sardinia, It. Z9.

R. linaresii Parl. Fls 1–2 per st.; perianth 1.25–2.25cm, violet, tube 0.4–0.7cm, deep purple within and at throat, seg. erecto-patent, oblanceolate, acute or obtuse. Sicily, Greece, W Turk. Z8.

R. longituba Bol. = R. macowanii.

R. longituba var. **alticola** Burtt. = R. macowanii var. alticola.

R. macowanii Bak. Flowering st. short, concealed by lf bases; fls 1–3 per st.; perianth 3–10cm, golden yellow, tube 2–6cm, deep orange-yellow within and at throat, seg. 0.5–1.5cm across, acute or obtuse. S Afr., Les. var. **alticola** (Burtt) De Vos. Perianth tube to 6.5cm; seg. to 3.5×1cm. S Afr., Les. (mts). Z9.

R. nivalis (Boiss. & Kotschy) Klatt. Fls 1–3 per st.; perianth to 2.5cm, lilac to mauve, tube to 0.3cm, yellow within and at throat, seg. lanceolate-obtuse. Leb. Z9.

R. ramiflora Ten. Flowering st. to 30cm; fls 1–4 per st.; perianth 1–2.5cm, exterior yellow-white or green-tinted, deepening to pale lilac, throat white or yellow, seg. purple. Medit. ssp. **gaditana** (Kunze) Marais. Fls 2–3cm, violet-purple, throat pale green, outer seg. green externally, inner seg. violet externally, reflexed at apex. SW Spain. Z9.

R. requienii Parl. Fls 1–3 per st.; perianth to 2.5cm, dark violet, tube to 0.8cm, sometimes paler or white within and at throat, seg. to 0.6cm across, oblanceolate-obtuse. Corsica, Sardinia, It. Z8.

R. rosea (L.) Ecklon var. **rosea**. Flowering st. short, simple, not lengthening at fruiting stage; perianth 1.25–4cm, rosy-purple, pink or white, tube to 0.5cm, tinted yellow within and at throat, sometimes suffused blue, seg. 0.3–1cm across. S Afr. var. **australis** (Ewart) De Vos. Fls pale lilac-pink, occas. white, throat yellow; outer seg. yellow externally, sometimes with 3–5 longitudinal streaks. Cape Prov., nat. Aus., St Helena, Channel Is. var. **elegans** (Klatt) Beg. Fls white, throat yellow; outer seg. red, red-purple or red-green externally. S Cape Prov. var. **reflexa** (Ecklon) Beg. Fls magenta to pink-lilac, or occas. white, throat orange or yellow, sometimes tinged violet-blue, outer seg. green-red with dark markings or longitudinal lines extern-ally. W Cape Prov. Z9.

R. sabulosa Bég. Sts short; perianth to 3–5.5cm, bright scarlet, tube 0.2–0.4cm, with a dark white- or pink-edge blotch within and at throat, seg. 1.25–2cm across, acute or obtuse. S Afr. (Cape Prov.). Z9.

R. saldanhensis De Vos. Flowering st. to 35cm. Fls 3cm diam., glossy deep- or golden-yellow, with narrow dark streaks in throat; seg. obovate, 3×1.4cm, outer seg. yellow, marked brown. S Afr. Z9.

R. tempskyana Freyn. Fls 1 per st.; perianth 2–3.5cm, mauve to violet, tube 0.8–1.7cm, slender, mauve within and at throat, seg. to 0.5cm across, lanceolate, ultimately reflexed. Greece, SW Turk., Cyprus, Isr. Z8.

Rondeletia L. Rubiaceae. c150 shrubs or trees; br. slender. Fls in axill. or term. pan., cymes or capitate corymbs, rarely solitary; cal. subglobose to ovoid or oblong, limb lobes 4–6; cor. funnel- to salver-shaped, lobes 4–6, spreading; sta. 4–6, inserted or exserted. C to S Amer., Polyn. Z10.

R. amoena (Planch.) Hemsl. Shrub to 1.5m, or tree to 14m. Lvs to 15cm, ovate or elliptic to oblong, apex narrowly acute, base obtuse to cordate, glab. to pubesc. beneath; axill. or term., many-fld, corymbose cymes or pan., white to pink; cor. tube to 12mm, exterior and throat pubesc., lobes to 3mm, spreading, emarginate. Summer. Mex., Panama, Guat.

R. asiatica L. = Tarenna zeylanica.

R. backhousei Hook. f. Shrub. Lvs to 10cm, ovate to oblong, apex acute or obtuse, base cordate, herbaceous, rough and glab. to pubesc. Fls in axill. and terminal cymes, pink or red to purple; cor. tube to 1cm, exterior pubesc., lobes to 4mm, obtuse. W Indies, C Amer.

R. cordata Benth. Shrub or tree, to 2.5m. Lvs to 13cm, ovate or lanceolate to oblong, apex acute to narrowly acute, base cordate, leathery, pubesc. to tomentose beneath. Fls in dense, axill. or term., many-fld corymbs or cymes, pink to red and yellow-throated; cor. tube to 1cm, pubesc., lobes to 2mm, obtuse. Summer. Guat.

R. erythroneura Karst. Shrub, to 2.5m. Lvs to 15cm, ovate or lanceolate to elliptic, membranous, glab. above, pubesc. beneath, veins red. Fls in loose, terminal, many-fld pan. or cymes, pink; cor. funnel-shaped, tube glab. at throat, lobes ovate to suborbicular. Venez.

R. gratissima (Lind.) Hemsl. Shrub. Lvs to 7cm, opposite, lanceolate or elliptic to oblong, apex narrowly acute to mucronate, base obtuse, leathery, glab. Fls fragrant in dense, term. cymes or corymbs, white to pink; cor. tube to 12mm, minutely pubesc., lobes to 2mm, obtuse, mealy. Mex.

R. latifolia Hook. f. Shrub. Lvs to 15cm, ovate to oblong, apex narrowly acute, base cordate, pubesc. Fls in term., corymbose cymes, pink and white-tipped. Nic., Guat.

R. odorata Jacq. Shrub, to 3m. Lvs to 10cm, ovate to oblong, apex acute or obtuse, base obtuse to cordate, margin rough, undulate and falcate, bullate and leathery. Fls fragrant in dense, term., many-fld cymes, corymbs or pan., orange to red and yellow-throated; cor. tube to 15mm, lobes to 5mm, elliptic to suborbicular. Cuba, Panama.

R. purdiei Hook. f. Shrub, to 1.5m. Lvs to 20cm, ovate to lanceolate to oblong, apex obtuse, base attenuate to cordate, glab. to sparsely pubesc. on veins beneath. Fls in dense, axill. or term., pyramidal corymbs, yellow; cor. tube pubesc. at throat. Summer. Colomb.

R. speciosa Lodd. = *R. odorata*.

R. thyrsoidea Sw. Shrub or tree, to 6m. Lvs to 12cm, ovate or elliptic to oblong, apex and base attenuate to acute, base decurrent, glab. to sparsely and minutely pubesc. on veins beneath. Fls in axill. pan. to 7cm, yellow; cor. tube to 5mm, pubesc., lobes to 2mm, interior minutely pubesc. Jam.

R. cvs. 'Splendens': compact and bushy; fls red, in term. clusters, profuse.

R. versicolor Hook. = *R. amoena*.

→*Rogiera* and *Willdenovia*.

Roodia N.E. Br.

R. digitifolia N.E. Br. = *Argyroderma fissum*.

R. brevipes (Schltr.) L. Bol. = *Argyroderma fissum*.

Roof House Leek *Sempervivum tectorum*.

Roof Iris *Iris tectorum*.

Rooibos *Aspalathus linearis*.

Rooikrans *Acacia cyclops*.

Rooster Flower *Aristolochia labiata*.

Ropebark *Dirca palustris*.

Roquette *Eruca*.

Roridula Burm. f. ex L. Roridulaceae. 2 carnivorous, viscid, suffruticose or shrubby perennials to 2m. Lvs to 6.5cm, crowded at br. ends, linear-lanceolate, entire to dentate, densely glandular-ciliate. Fls in short term. rac., large; pet. 5, pink to white, ovate or oblong; sta. 5, sensitive and motile. S Afr. Z9.

R. dentata L. Lvs to 6.5cm, pinnatifid-dentate, teeth filiform. Fls 4–6 in rac.; sep. equalling pet., margins gland.; pet. obtuse.

R. gorgonias Planch. Lvs to 6.5cm, entire, densely glandular-ciliate. Rac. spiciform; sep. exceeding pet., eglandular; pet. acute.

RORIDULACEAE Engl. & Gilg. See *Roridula*.

Rorippa Scop. Cruciferae. 70 ann. and rhizomatous perenn. herbs. Lvs pinnate, lyrate or simple, rac. corymbose; pet. 4, yellow, occas. white or lavender. Cosmop. except Antarctica.

R. amphibia (L.) Besser. GREAT YELLOWCRESS. Marginal stoloniferous perenn., 40–120cm. St. hollow, branching. Lvs oblanceolate to elliptic, bright green, entire, toothed or pinnatisect. Fls 6mm diam. Eur., N Afr., Sib. Z6.

R. armoracia (L.) Hitchc. = *Armoracia rusticana*.

R. microphylla (Boenn.) B. Hyland = *Nasturtium microphyllum*.

R. nasturtium-aquaticum (L.) Hayek = *Nasturtium officinale*.

R. officinalis (R. Br.) P. Royen = *Nasturtium officinale*.

→*Nasturtium*.

Rosa L. Rosaceae. ROSE. 100–150 mostly decid. shrubs with erect, arching or scrambling st., usually with prickles and/or bristles. Lvs usually stipulate, imparipinnate, 3-foliolate or simple; lfts toothed. Receptacle globose to urn-shaped. Fls solitary or in corymbs, usually at end of short br., single to double; sep. (4–)5, entire or with lat. lobes; pet. (4–)5 in single fls, usually obovate, tip often notched; sta. (in single fls)

c30–200, in several whorls; styles free or united into a column, sometimes exserted. Fr. (hip or hep) containing many achenes, usually red or orange, enclosed by fleshy receptacle. Summer-flowering unless specified. Temp. and subtrop. zones of the N hemis. For horticultural classification of roses and descriptions of hybrids and selections, see *Rosa* in *The New RHS Dictionary of Gardening*.

R. acicularis Lindl. St. 1(–2.5)m, prickles straight or slightly curved, weak, slender, intermixed with dense, slender bristles. Lfts 1.5–6cm, (3–)5–7(–9), ovate to elliptic, acute, blue-green above, downy beneath, toothed. Fls 1(–3), single, fragrant, 3.8–6.2cm across; sep. entire, gland., erect; pet. rose-pink to purple-pink. Fr. 1.5–2.5cm, ellipsoidal to pear-shaped, with a neck, red, smooth. Early summer. var. *nipponensis* (Crépin) Koehne. Lfts 7–9, oblong, obtuse. Fls bright pink. C & S Jap. Z2.

R. ×alba L. (possibly *R. gallica × R. arvensis* or *R. corymbifera* or even *R. canina × R. damascena*.) WHITE ROSE; WHITE ROSE OF YORK. St. stout, arching, 1.8–2.5m, prickles scattered, hooked, often mixed with bristles. Lfts 5(–7), dull green, ovate to round, shortly acuminate to obtuse, glab. above, downy beneath, toothed. Fls 1–3, semi-double or double, 6–8cm across, fragrant; sep. with lobes and leafy tips, glandular-bristly, reflexed; pet. white to pale pink. Fr. 2–2.5cm, ± spherical, red. Gdn origin. 'Incarnata' (MAIDEN'S BLUSH): st. with few prickles but densely bristly below infl.; lfts usually 7; fls double, pale pink. 'Maxima' (GREAT DOUBLE WHITE ROSE; JACOBITE ROSE; CHESHIRE ROSE): fls double, pink fading to creamy white. 'Semiplena': fls semi-double, white. Z4.

R. ×alba var. *incarnata* (Mill.) Weston. = *R. ×alba* 'Incarnata'.

R. 'Alba Maxima' = *R. ×alba* 'Maxima'.

R. alpina L. = *R. pendulina*.

R. alpina var. *oxyodon* (Boiss.) Boulenger = *R. oxyodon*.

R. 'Anemone' = *R. ×anemonoides*.

R. anemoniflora Fort. ex Lindl. = *R. ×beanii*.

R. ×anemonoides Rehd. (Probably *R. laevigata × R. ×odorata*.) Less vigorous than *R. laevigata*, with pet. pale pink with deeper veins. Early summer. Gdn origin. Z8.

R. arkansana Porter. PRAIRIE ROSE. St. erect, suckering, 50–120cm tall, with dense, straight prickles, and bristles. Lfts 2–6cm, (3–)9–11, obovate to elliptic, acute or obtuse, shiny above, sometimes downy on veins beneath, toothed. Fls in lat. clusters, single 2.5–4cm across; sep. entire or with lobes, smooth or glandular-bristly, spreading to erect; pet. deep pink. Fr. 1–1.5cm, pear-shaped to subglobose, red, smooth to gland. C US. Z4.

R. arkansana var. *suffulta* (Greene) Cockerell = *R. suffulta*.

R. arvensis Huds. FIELD ROSE. St. trailing or climbing, 1–2m, with adpressed, stout prickles. Lfts 1–4cm, (3–)5–7, deep green, elliptic to broadly ovate or rounded, acute or subacute, ± glab., toothed. Fls 1–8, single, usually fragrant, 2.5–5cm across; sep. with lobes, smooth or sparsely gland., reflexed; pet. white to pink. Fr. 0.6–2.5cm, spherical to ovoid, red, usually smooth. SW & C Eur., S Turk. Z6.

R. banksiae 'Albo-Plena' = *R. banksiae* var. *banksiae*.

R. banksiae Ait. BANKSIAN ROSE; BANKSIA ROSE. St. strong climbing to 12m, ± unarmed. Lvs everg.; lfts 2–6.5cm, 3–7, oblong-lanceolate to elliptic-ovate, acute or obtuse, glossy above, sometimes downy beneath, margin wavy, toothed. Fls many in umbels, single or double, fragrant, 2.5–3cm across; sep. entire, reflexed; pet. white or yellow. Fr. c0.7cm, spherical, dull red. Early summer. W & C China. var. *banksiae* Fls double, white, violet-scented. var. *normalis* Reg. Fls single, white, v. fragrant, and st. usually prickly. 'Lutea': st. generally unarmed; lfts usually 5; fls double, yellow, slightly fragrant. 'Lutescens': fls single, yellow, highly scented. Z7.

R. banksiae 'Banksiae' = *R. banksiae* var. *banksiae*.

R. banksiae var. *albo-plena* Rehd. = *R. banksiae* var. *banksiae*.

R. banksiae var. *lutea* Lindl. = *R. banksiae* var. *normalis* 'Lutea'.

R. banksiae f. *lutescens* Voss = *R. banksiae* var. *normalis* 'Lutescens'.

R. banksiopsis Bak. Differs from *R. caudata* in receptacle and sep. being smooth, not glandular-bristly and fls 2–3cm across. W China. Z6.

R. ×beanii Heath. St. spreading, prickles small, scattered, hooked. Lvs decid.; lfts 3.8–7.5cm, 3–5, ovate to narrowly ovate, acute or acuminate, glab., toothed. Fls in loose clusters, double, 2.5–4.5cm across; sep. with lobes; pet. pale pink, innermost narrow and ragged. Gdn origin (E China). Possibly a hybrid between *R. multiflora* and either *R. laevigata* or *R. banksiae*, or between *R. banksiae* and *R. moschata*. Z7.

R. beggeriana Schrenk ex Fisch. & Mey. St. erect, sometimes climbing 1.8–3m, red-tinged when young, prickles paired, pale, somewhat flattened, hooked. Lvs aromatic; lfts 0.7–3cm, 5–9, narrowly elliptic to obovate, obtuse, grey-green above, gland. and sometimes downy beneath, toothed. Fls in clusters of 8 or more, single, slightly malodorous, 2–3.8cm across; sep. entire, sometimes gland. or hairy. Fr. 0.6–1cm, spherical, red, turning purple, smooth. SW & C Asia. Z4.

R. bella Rehd. & Wils. Br. spreading, purple-green to 3m, prickles few slender, straight, intermixed with bristles. Lvs decid.; lfts 1–2.5cm, 7–9, elliptic to broadly ovate, acute, hairless, sometimes gland. onn veins beneath, toothed. Fls 1–3, single, 4–5cm across; sep. entire, expanded at the tip, gland.; pet. bright pink. Fr. 1.5–2.5cm, ovoid or ellipsoidal, orange-red, glandular-bristly. NW China. Z6.

R. berberifolia Pall. = *R. persica*.

R. bicolor Jacq. = *R. foetida* 'Bicolor'.

R. bierbersteinii Lindl. = *R. horrida*.

R. bifera Poir. = *R. ×damascena* var. *semperflorens*.

R. blanda Ait. St. erect, brown st. 1–2m, unarmed or with few, scattered, slender prickles. Lfts 2–6cm, 5–7(–9), elliptic to oblong- obovate, acute to obtuse, dull green and hairless above, usually downy beneath, toothed. Bracts large. Fls solitary or 3–7, single, 4.5–6.5cm across, fragrant; sep. entire, downy and gland.; pet. rosy pink. Fr. c1cm, ovoid to pear-shaped, red, smooth. Early summer. E & Central N Amer. Z2.

R. bracteata Wendl. MACARTNY ROSE. St. procumbent or climbing, brown-downy 3–6m tall, prickles stout, broad-based, hooked in pairs, bristles numerous gland. Lvs everg.; lfts 1.5–5cm, 5–11, dark green, obovate to elliptic or oblong, obtuse, glossy above, downy beneath, toothed. Bracts large, deeply toothed, downy. Fls usually solitary, single, smelling of fr., 5–8cm across; sep. entire, brown-hairy; pet. white. Fr. 2.5–3.8cm, spherical, orange-red, hairy. Summer–late autumn. SE China, Taiwan; nat. US. Z7.

R. britzensis Koehne. St. erect 2–3m tall, prickles sparse, small, scattered, slender. Lfts 2.5–3.5cm, 7–11, grey-green, elliptic to ovate, hairless above, with sparse glands on midrib beneath. Fls 1 or 2, single (3–)7–10cm across; sep. with lobes, glandular-bristly; pet. pale pink fading to white, notched. Fr. 2.5–3cm, ovoid, dark red or brown, slightly glandular-bristly. Early summer. Kurdistan. Z6.

R. brunonii Lindl. HIMALAYAN MUSK ROSE. St. arching or climbing 5–12m tall, prickles short, stout, hooked. Lvs 17–21cm, drooping; lfts 3–6cm, 5–7(–9), narrowly ovate to oblong-eliptic, acute grey-green or blue-green, downy beneath, sometimes gland., toothed. Fls in clusters, combined into a large compound infl., single, fragrant, 2.5–5cm across; sep. lobed, hairy and slightly gland. on the back; pet. white. Fr. 0.7–1.8cm, subglobose to obovoid, red-brown, smooth. Himal., from Afghan. to SW China. Many plants grown in gardens as *R. moschata* are *R. brunonii*. 'La Mortola': v. strong-growing. Z7.

R. californica Cham. & Schldl. St. erect, 1.5–3m tall, ultimately red-brown, prickles stout, broad-based, recurved in pairs, with bristles on young shoots. Lfts 1–3.5cm, 5–7, ovate to broadly elliptic, obtuse, hairless or downy above, downy and often gland. beneath, toothed. Fls in clusters, single, fragrant, 3.7–4cm across; sep. entire, hairy on the back, erect; pet. deep pink to bright crimson. Fr. 0.7–1.5cm, spherical with a neck, smooth. W US, S to Mex. (Baja Calif.). 'Plena': fls semi-double. The rose usually cultivated under this name is *R. nutkana*. Z5.

R. californica f. *plena* Rehd. = *R. californica* 'Plena'.

R. canina L. DOG ROSE; COMMON BRIER; DOG BRIER. St. arching, sometimes climbing 1.5–5.5m tall, prickles scattered, strong, hooked. Lfts 1.5–4cm, 5–7, narrowly elliptic to ovate, acute or obtuse, usually glab., sometimes gland. beneath, toothed. Fls solitary or 2–5, single, fragrant, 2.5–5cm across; sep. lobed, usually hairless on the back, reflexed; pet. white or pale pink. Fr. 1–3cm, ovoid to subglobose, red to orange, smooth. Cooler parts of Eur. and SW Asia, NW Afr., nat. N Amer. Z3.

R. 'Cantabrigiensis' (*R. xanthina* f. *hugonis* ×*R. sericea*.) Medium-sized. St. arching, v. bristly. Lvs ferny, aromatic; lfts 7–11. Fls to 5cm diam., yellow fading to cream. Gdn orig.

R. carolina L. CAROLINA ROSE; PASTURE ROSE. St. 1–1.5m tall, prickles scattered, straight, slender in pairs, bristles dense. Lfts 5–9, lanceolate to narrowly ovate or almost round, glab. or downy beneath, toothed. Fls solitary or a few in a cluster, single, 3.8–5cm across; sep. lobed, glandular-bristly, spreading; pet. pale to mid-pink. Fr. 0.7–0.9cm, subglobose, red, glandular-bristly. E & Central N Amer. 'Alba': lfts hairy beneath; fls white. 'Plena': to 50cm; fls double, outer pet. ageing almost to white. Z4.

R. cathayensis (Rehd. & Wils.) Bail. = *R. multiflora* var. *cathayensis*.

R. caudata Bak. St. erect, red-tinged 1–4m tall, prickles few, stout, scattered, broad-based. Lfts 2.5–5cm, 7–9, elliptic to ovate, acute, glab. except for midrib beneath, toothed. Fls few in a tight cluster, single, 3.5–5cm across; sep. entire, glandular-bristly, expanded at tip; pet. deep pink. Fr. 2–2.5cm, ovoid-oblong with long neck, orange-red, glandular-bristly. China. V.

close to *R. setipoda*. Z6.

R. ×centifolia L. PROVENCE ROSE; CABBAGE ROSE; HOLLAND ROSE. St. to 2m, prickles many small, lamost straight and larger, hooked. Lfts 5–7, dull green, broadly ovate to almost round, acute to obtuse, ± glab. above, downy beneath, glandular-toothed. Fls 1 to few, double, globose, v. fragrant, 6–8cm across; sep. lobed, gland., spreading; pet. usually pink, more rarely white or dark red. Fr. ellipsoidal or spherical, red. Gdn origin. A complex hybrid involving *R. gallica*, *R. moschata*, *R. canina* and *R. damascena*. 'Bullata': lfts crinkled, tinged brown above when young; fls pink. 'Cristata': sep. with many marginal seg. which provide each pink fl. with a green fringe; fls less globular. 'Muscosa' (COMMON MOSS ROSE): cal. and flower-stalks bearing much-branched scented glands which form the so-called 'moss'. 'Parvifolia' (BURGUNDY ROSE): st. to 1m; lfts small, dark green; fls fragrant, deep pink suffused with purple and with a paler centre; possibly not related to *R. chinensis*. Z5.

R. centifolia var. *cristata* Prévost = *R. ×centifolia* 'Cristata'.

R. centifolia var. *muscosa* (Mill.) Ser. = *R. ×centifolia* 'Muscosa'.

R. centifolia var. *parvifolia* (Ehrh.) Rehd. = *R. ×centifolia* 'Parvifolia'.

R. centifolia var. *sancta* (Rich.) Zab. = *R. ×richardii*.

R. cerasocarpa Rolfe. St. climbing to 4.5m, prickles few, stout, scattered, recurved. Lvs 17–20cm; lfts 5–10cm, (3–)5, narrowly ovate to elliptic, leathery, acute to acuminate, glab., toothed. Fls many in clusters, single, fragrant, 2.5–3.5cm across, buds abruptly pointed; sep. usually lobed, downy and gland., reflexed; pet. white. Fr. 1–1.3cm, spherical, deep red, downy. W & C China. Z5.

R. chinensis Jacq. CHINA ROSE; BENGAL ROSE. Dwarf to ± climbing shrub to 6m. Prickles 0 or scattered, hooked, flattened. Lvs everg.; lfts 2.5–6cm, 3–5, lanceolate to broadly ovate, acuminate, glossy and hairless above, hairless beneath except for downy midrib, margins with simple teeth. Fls solitary orin clusters, single or semi-double, c5cm across, often fragrant; sep. entire or lobed, smooth or gland., reflexed; pet. pale pink to scarlet or crimson. Fr.1.5–2cm, ovoid to pear-shaped, green-brown to scarlet. Summer to early autumn. Gdn origin (China). A repeat-flowering rose which contributed this feature to European roses when it was introduced around 1800. 'Minima' (FAIRY ROSE; PYGMY ROSE): st. 20–50cm; fls c3cm across, rose red, single or double, usually solitary; pet. pointed. 'Rouletii': st. 10–25cm; fls double, rosy pink, 1.9–2.5cm across; thought by some botanists to be synonymous with 'Minima'. 'Mutabilis': st. 1–1.7m; lfts tinged purple or coppery when young; fls single, fragrant, 4.5–6cm across, pet. yellow with an orange back, turning coppery salmon-pink and eventually deep pink. 'Pallida': st. to 1m or more; fls in clusters, semi-double, fragrant, blush-pink. 'Semperflorens': st. 1–1.5m; fls semi-double, deep pink or crimson-scarlet, delicately scented. 'Viridiflora' (GREEN ROSE): pet. green streaked with crimson or purple-green, sta. and pistils mutated to leafy, narrow, toothed seg. var. *spontanea* (Rehd. & Wils.) T.T. Yu & Ku. Climber or bush usually 1–2.5m tall. Lfts lanceolate. Fls 1–3, single, pink, turning red, 5–6cm across; sep. entire. Fr. orange. W China. Z7.

R. chinensis var. *minima* (Sims) Voss = *R. chinensis* 'Minima'.

R. chinensis var. *semperflorens* (Curtis) Koehne = *R. chinensis* 'Semperflorens'.

R. chinensis var. *viridiflora* (Lév.) Dipp. = *R. chinensis* 'Viridiflora'.

R. chinensis f. *mutabilis* (Correv.) Rehd. = *R. chinensis* 'Mutabilis'.

R. chinensis f. *spontanea* Rehd. & Wils. = *R. chinensis* var. *spontanea*.

R. cinnamomea L. 1759 not 1753 = *R. majalis*.

R. cinnamomea L. 1753 not 1759 = *R. pendulina*.

R. cinnamomea var. *plena* Weston = *R. majalis*.

R. ×collina Jacq. (Possibly *R. canina* ×*R. gallica*.) St. erect 1.5–2m, prickles strong, hooked, red when young. Lfts 5(–7), downy on veins beneath, toothed. Fls 1–3, ± double, fragrant, c5cm across; sep. lobed, with leafy tips; pet. pink. Fr. ovoid, orange-red, sometimes gland. Gdn origin. Z6.

R. coriifolia Fries. St. erect or arching, c2m, densely branched, prickles curved. Lfts 5–7, oblong to broadly elliptic, obtuse, downy beneath, toothed. Fls 1–4, single; sep. lobed, sometimes hairy; pet. white or pink. Fr. to 2.5cm, ovoid to spherical, red, smooth. Eur., Russia (Cauc.). V. similar to *R. dumalis*. Z5.

R. ×coryana Hurst. ((?) *R. roxburghii* ×*R. macrophylla*.) Differs from *R. roxburghii* in having shorter, less prickly st. (up to 2m), and fls bright carmine. Gdn origin. Z6.

R. corymbifera Borkh. Br. spreading or erect, 1.5–3m tall, prickle stout, hooked. Lfts 2.5–6cm, 5–9, broadly ovate to rounded, obtuse, downy, toothed. Fls in clusters, single, 4–5cm across; sep. lobed, usually glab., sometimes slightly gland.; pet. white to pale pink. Fr. 1.2–2cm, ovoid to subglobose, orange-red.

Cooler parts of Eur. and SW Asia, N Afr. Z6.

R. corymbosa Ehrh. = R. palustris.

R. corymbulosa Rolfe. St. erect, prostrate or climbing to 2m, prickles 0 or few, slender, straight. Lvs turning purple in autumn; lfts 1.3–5cm, 3–5, elliptic to ovate-oblong, acute, dark green and sparsely downy above, glaucous and downy beneath, biserrate. Fls in clusters of up to 12, single, 1.9–2.5cm across; sep. entire, downy and glandular-bristly; pet. deep pink, paler at the base. Fr. 1–1.3cm, ovoid-spherical, coral-red, glandular-bristly. China. Z6.

R. cymosa Tratt. Differs from R. banksiae in having st. more prickly, infl. larger and branched, fls single, white, c1.5cm across, with lobed sep. Early summer. C & S China. Z8.

R. dalmatica Kerner = R. pulverulenta.

R. ×damascena Mill. (R. gallica ×R. moschata.) SUMMER DAMASK ROSE. Shrub; st. to 2.2m, prickles dense, stout, curved, bristles stiff. Lfts 5(–7), grey-green, ovate to elliptic, acute to obtuse, downy beneath, toothed. Fls in clusters of up to 12, semi-double, fragrant; sep. lobed, with slender tips, gland. and hairy, reflexed; pet. pink. Fr. to 2.5cm, turbinate, red, bristly. Asia Minor. var. *semperflorens* (Duhamel) Rowley. AUTUMN DAMASK ROSE; FOUR SEASONS ROSE; QUATRE SAISONS ROSE; MONTHLY ROSE. Fls produced in autumn. 'Versicolor' (YORK AND LANCASTER ROSE): fls loosely double, pet. deep pink or v. pale pink or partly deep pink and partly pale pink. 'Trigintipetala' (KAZANLIK ROSE): fls semi-double, c8cm across, with c30 red pet. 'Portlandica' PORTLAND ROSE: fls semi-double, bright red, faintly scented, produced from midsummer to autumn. Z4.

R. damascena var. *trigintipetala* (Dieck) Keller = R. × damascena 'Trigintipetala'.

R. damascena var. *versicolor* Weston = R. × damascena 'Versicolor'.

R. davidii Crépin. St. erect or arching, 1.8–4m, prickles broad-based, stout, straight or slightly curved, red-tinged. Lfts 0.6–5cm, (5–)7–9(–11), dark green, ovate to elliptic, acute, wrinkled above, downy beneath, teeth sometimes gland. Fls 3–12 or more, single, fragrant, 3.8–5cm across; sep. entire, often downy and gland., erect; pet. rosy pink. Fr. 1.5–2cm, ovoid with a slender neck, scarlet, pendulous. W & C China inc. SE Xizang. var. *elongata* Rehd. & Wils. lfts 5–7.5cm, sometimes hairless beneath; fls fewer (3–7); fr. to 2.5cm, more elongated. Z6.

R. davurica Pall. St. 1–1.5m, prickles large, ± straight, paired. Lfts 2.5–3.5cm, c7, oblong-lanceolate, acute, hairy and gland. beneath, compound-toothed. Fls 1–3, single; sep. entire, margin, erect; pet. pink. Fr. 1–1.3cm, ovoid, red. NE Asia, N China. V. close to R. majalis. Z5.

R. dumalis Bechst. St. ± erect, often pruinose 1–2m, prickles hooked, broad-based. Lfts 1.2–3.5cm, 5–7, broadly ovate to rounded, acute or obtuse, often pruinose above, hairless or downy beneath, teeth simple or compound. Fls 1 to many, single; sep. lobed, hairless or slightly gland., the margin downy, erect; pet. pink. Fr. 1.5–2.2cm, ovoid to spherical, red, long, smooth or glandular-bristly. Eur., Asia Minor. Z4.

R. dumetorum Thuill. = R. corymbifera.

R. 'Dupontii'. DUPONT ROSE; SNOW-BUSH ROSE. Differs from R. moschata in the smaller size (2–3m tall), leaflets with compound teeth, fls single, 6–7.5cm across, creamy pink with sep. gland. beneath. Gdn origin. Z6.

R. ×dupontii Déségl., in part = R. 'Dupontii'.

R. ecae Aitch. St. much-branched, erect, suckering, to 1.5m, prickles dense, straight, flattened, red-tinged. Lvs aromatic; lfts 0.4–0.8cm, 5–9, elliptic to obovate or ± orbicular, obtuse, gland. beneath, teeth often gland. Fls solitary, single, 2–3m across; sep. entire, hairless, spreading or deflexed; pet. deep yellow. Fr. 0.5–1cm, spherical, shiny red-brown, smooth and hairless. NE Afghan., NW Pak. and adjacent Russia, N China. 'Golden Chersonese' (R. ecae ×R. 'Canary Bird'): to 2m, with the aromatic lvs and deep yellow fls of R. ecae. 'Helen Knight' (R. ecae ×R. pimpinellifolia 'Grandiflora'): st. red-brown too 3m with support; fls large, yellow. Z7.

R. ecae ssp. *primula* (Boulenger) A.V. Roberts = R. primula.

R. eglanteria L., in part = R. foetida.

R. eglanteria L., in part = R. rubiginosa.

R. elegantula Rolfe. St. 1–2m, unarmed or bearing a few prickles and dense, red bristles, suckers densely prickly. Lvs glaucous green, turning purple to crimson in fall; lfts 1–2.5cm, 7–11, narrowly ovate to elliptic, acuminate or obtuse, downy on mid-rib beneath. Fls 1 to few, single, 2–3.8cm across; sep. entire, hairy inside and on margin; pet. white to pale pink or rose-pink. Fr. 1.2–1.3cm, ovoid to top-shaped, smooth or gland. Early summer. NW & WC China. 'Persetosa' (FARRER'S THREEPENNY-BIT ROSE): sts more prick;y lfts smaller; fls white to salmon-pink to 1.2–2cm across, opening from coral-pink buds, fr. orange-red, c7mm long. NW China. Z6.

R. elegantula f. *persetosa* Stapf = R. elegantula 'Persetosa'.

R. ernestii Stapf ex Bean = R. rubus.

R. ernestii f. *nudescens* Stapf = R. rubus.

R. ernestii f. *velutescens* Stapf = R. rubus.

R. fargesii hort. non Boulenger = R. moyesii 'Fargesii'.

R. farreri Stapf ex Stearn = R. elegantula.

R. farreri 'Persetosa'. = R. elegantula 'Persetosa'.

R. fedtschenkoana Reg. Sts suckering, vigorous erect 1–2.5(–3)m, prickles slender, straight or curved in pairs, tinged pink when young. Lfts 5–9, glaucous, broadly elliptic to obovate, downy beneath, toothed. Fls 1–4, single, slightly malodorous, c5cm across; sep. entire, glandular-bristly, margin and inner surface downy, erect; pet. usually white, rarely pink. Fr. 1.5–2.5cm, pear-shaped, orange-red, long, glandular-bristly. Summer–early autumn. C Asia, NW China. Z4.

R. fendleri Crépin = R. woodsii var. fendleri.

R. filipes Rehd. & Wils. St. arching and climbing to 9m, purple when young, prickles few, small, hooked. Lvs coppery when young; lfts 3.5–8cm, 5–7, narrowly ovate to narrowly elliptic, acuminate, hairless or downy on veins beneath, toothed. Fls to 100 or more in large clusters up to 30cm or more wide, single, fragrant, 2–2.5cm across; sep. lobed; gland. and slightly downy or hairless, reflexed; pet. creamy or white, sometimes downy. Fr. 0.8–1.5cm, spherical to ellipsoid, orange to crimson-scarlet. W China. 'Kiftsgate': infl. to 45cm across. Z5.

R. foecundissima Münchh. = R. majalis.

R. foetida Herrm. AUSTRIAN BRIAR; AUSTRIAN YELLOW ROSE. St. erect or arching, 1–3m, then grey-brown, prickles few, straight or curved, mixed with bristles. Lfts 1.5–4cm, 5–9, elliptic to obovate, obtuse to subacute, bright green and subglabrous aobve, dull green, downy and somewhat gland. beneath, teeth few, compound, gland. Fls solitary or 2–4, single, 5–7.5cm across, malodorous; sep. entire or lobed, apex expanded, hairless or glandular-bristly, erect; pet. deep yellow. Fr. 0.8–1cm, spherical, red, smooth or bristly. SW & WC Asia. 'Bicolor' (AUSTRIAN COPPER BRIAR): possibly a hybrid between R. kokanica and R. hemispherica; pet. coppery red inside and yellow-buff on the back; br. occas. revert to the yellow-fld form. 'Persiana' (PERSIAN DOUBLE YELLOW): fls v. double, yellow, freely produced, smaller than those of R. foetida. Z4.

R. foetida var. *bicolor* (Jacq.) Willmott = R. foetida 'Bicolor'.

R. foetida var. *persiana* (Lem.) Rehd. = R. foetida 'Persiana'.

R. foliolosa Nutt ex Torr. & A. Gray. LEAFY ROSE; WHITE PRAIRIE ROSE. St. rather weak, red-tinged 50–100cm, unarmed or with sparse slender prickles, rarely bristly. Lfts 1–5cm, 7–9(–11), narrowly oblong, acute, glossy above, downy on midrib beneath, teeth fine simple. Fls 1–5, single, fragrant, 5–6.5cm across; sep. entire, glandular-bristly, spreading; pet. white to rose-pink. Fr. c8mm wide, subglobose, red, glandular-bristly. Summer to early autumn. SE US. Z6.

R. forrestiana Boulenger. St. erect or spreading, 1–2m, prickles paired, straight, brown. Lfts 1–1.3cm, 5–7(–9), elliptic to round, obtuse, hairless or hairy to gland. on veins beneath, toothed. Fls 1–5, single, fragrant, 2–3.8cm across; sep. entire, often gland.; erect; pet. pale to bright pink. Fr. to 1.3cm, ovoid with a distinct neck, red, smooth or glandular-bristly. W China. Z8.

R. ×fortuneana Lindl. (Possibly R. banksiae ×R. laevigata.) Differs from R. banksiae in having lfts 3–5, rather thin lfts, and solitary, double, creamy white fls 5–10cm across. Gdn origin (China). Z8.

R. ×francofurtana Münchh. (Probably R. gallica ×R. majalis.) St. erect to 2m, grey-green, unarmed or bearing a few prickles and bristles. Lfts 5–7, grey-green, broadly ovate to round, obtuse, downy on veins beneath, coarsely toothed. Fls solitary or 2–6, usually double, slightly fragrant, 5–7cm across; sep. entire or lobed, hairy and gland., erect or reflexed; pet. purple-pink with darker veins. Fr. turbinate, red. Gdn origin. Z6.

R. gallica L. FRENCH ROSE; RED ROSE. Low, erect shrub, suckering. St. 50–200cm, green to dull red; prickles slender, curved to hooked, bristles gland. Lfts 3–5(–7), leathery, broadly elliptic to almost orbicular, dark green above, hairy and gland. beneath, teeth compound, usually gland. Fls solitary, or 2–4, single or semi-double, fragrant, 4–8cm across; sep. lobed, gland., reflexed; pet. rose-pink or crimson. Fr. c1.3cm, spherical to ellipsoid, brkc-red, glandular-bristly. S & C Eur. to Cauc.; nat. E N Amer. 'Officinalis' (APOTHECARIES' ROSE; OFFICINAL ROSE; RED ROSE OF LANCASTER): to 70cm; fls semi-double, crimson, v. fragrant. 'Versicolor': a sport of 'Officinalis' with st. 100–200cm and fls semi-double 7–9cm across, striped white, pink and red; often reverts; frequently confused with R. damascena 'Versicolor'. Z5.

R. gallica var. *officinalis* Thory = R. gallica 'Officinalis'.

R. gallica var. *versicolor* L. = R. gallica 'Versicolor' ('Rosa Mundi').

R. gentiliana sensu Rehd. & Wils. pro parte, non Lév. & Vaniot = R. cerasocarpa.

R. gentiliana Lév. & Vaniot = *R. multiflora* var. *cathayensis*.

R. gigantea Collett ex Crépin. St. climbing 8–12(–30)m. Prickles stout, scattered, uniform, hooked. Lvs everg. or semi-evergreen; lfts 3.8–9cm, 5–7, elliptic to ovate, acuminate, glossy above, hairless, teeth often gland. Fls 1(–3), single, fragrant, 10–15cm across, opening from slender, pale yellow buds; sep. entire, reflexed; pet. white or cream. Fr. 2–3cm, spherical or pear-shaped, red, or yellow flushed with red. Early summer. NE India, Upper Burma, W China. Z9.

R. giraldii Crépin. Differs from *R. webbiana* in acute or obtuse lfts with compound teeth, v. short flower-stalks often concealed by large bracts, smaller pink fls 1.2–2.5cm across with a white centre, and fr., rarely exceeding 1cm. China. Z5.

R. glauca Pourr. St. erect, sparsely branched, arching 1.5–3m tall, dark red and bloomy when young, prickles sparse, straight or decurved, broad-based, bristles sometimes present. Lfts 2–4.5cm, 5–9, grey-green, often tinged brown or purple, waxy, ovate to narrowly elliptic, acute, hairless, toothed. Fls solitary or 2–12, single, 2.5–4cm across; sep. entire or lobed, smooth or glandular-bristly, spreading; pet. deep pink, white at the base. Fr. 1.3–1.5cm, ovoid to subglobose, brown-red, smooth or with sparse gland. bristles. Mts of C and S Eur. Z2.

R. glauca Vill. ex Lois., non Pourr. = *R. dumalis*.

R. glutinosa Sm. = *R. pulverulenta*.

R. glutinosa var. *dalmatica* (Kerner) Keller = *R. pulverulenta*.

R. gymnocarpa Nutt. ex Torr. & A. Gray. WOOD ROSE. St. erect, slender 1–3m, unarmed or with slender, straight prickles and bristles. Lfts 1–4cm, 5–9, elliptic to ovate or rounded, obtuse, usually hairless, sometimes with glands beneath, teeth compound, often gland. Fls 1–4, single, 2.5–3.8cm across; sep. entire, hairless; pet. rose-pink. Fr. spherical, ellipsoidal or pear-shaped, red, 6–10mm, smooth. W N Amer. Z6.

R. × hardii Cels. (*R. persica* × *R. clinophylla*.) To 2m. Lvs simple or with up to 7, dark green, hairless lfts. Fls c5cm across; sep. lobed; pet. deep yellow. Fr. yellow-orange, shortly hairy with a few bristles. Early summer. Gdn origin. Z8.

R. × harisonii Rivers. (*R. pimpinellifolia* × *R. foetida*.) Erect shrub to 2m with occasional suckers. Lfts 5–9, elliptic, gland. beneath, teeth compound, somewhat gland. Fls solitary, loosely double, 5–6cm across, malodorous; sep. lobed at apex, slightly hairy, margin gland.; pet. sulphur-yellow. Fr. almost black, bristly. Gdn origin. Z4.

R. helenae Rehd. & Wils. St. rambling, 5–6m tall, purple-brown when young, prickles short, stout, hooked. Lfts 1.9–6cm, (5–)7–9, ovate to elliptic or obovate, acute, grey beneath and downy on veins, toothed. Fls many in somewhat flat clusters, single, fragrant, 2–4cm across; sep. lobed, gland.; pet. white. Fr. 1–1.5cm, ovoid, ellipsoid or pear shaped, scarlet or orange-red, gland. C China. Z5.

R. hemispherica Herrm. SULPHUR ROSE. St. erect, much-branched, bristly when young, to 2m, prickles scattered, slender decurved with broad bases. Lvs slightly aromatic; lfts 5–9, obovate, obtuse to retuse, grey-green above, glaucous and downy on veins beneath, toothed above. Fls solitary, single, 4–5cm across, often sweetly scented; sep. toothed above, erect; pet. sulphur-yellow. Fr. 1.2–1.5cm, spherical, dark red, smooth. Gardens of SW Asia. 'Flore Pleno': double-fld; more commonly cult. than sp. itself. Z6.

R. hemsleyana Täckh.. V. close to *R. setipoda*. It differs in its smaller size (up to 2m) and lobed sep. N & C China. Z6.

R. × hibernica Templeton. IRISH ROSE. (*R. pimpinellifolia* × *R. canina*.) St. 4m+. Lfts 5–7, sparsely hairy beneath. Fls single; sep. lobed with apex expanded; pet. pale pink, paler toward the base. Fr. dark red, obovoid. Natural hybrid, now thought to exist only in gardens. Z4.

R. × highdownensis Hillier. A hybrid of *R. moyesii* with clusters of mid-red to deep pink fls. Z6.

R. hirtula (Reg.) Nak. Differs from *R. roxburghii* in lfts elliptic to oblong-elliptic, downy beneath, and single, pale pink or lilac-pink fls. Jap. Z6.

R. horrida Fisch. Low, stiffly branched shrub, prickles short, stout, hooked, interspersed with gland. bristles. Lfts 0.8–2.2cm, 5–7, broadly elliptic to rounded, ± hairless, gland. beneath, teeth compound. Fls solitary, simple, 2.5–3cm across; sep. lobed, gland., reflexed; pet. white. Fr. 1–1.6cm, ovoid to spherical, red, glandular-bristly. SE Eur. to Turk. and Cauc. Z6.

R. hugonis Hemsl. = *R. xanthina* f. *hugonis*.

R. humilis Marshall = *R. carolina*.

R. incarnata Mill. = *R. × alba* 'Incarnata'.

R. indica sensu Lour., non L. = *R. chinensis*.

R. × iwara Sieb. ex Reg. (*R. multiflora* × *R. rugosa*.) Differs from *R. multiflora* in large, hooked prickles, and lfts grey-downy beneath. Fls single, white. Jap. Z5.

R. × jacksonii Bak. (*R. wichuraiana* × *R. rugosa*.) Differs from *R. wichuraiana* in larger, wrinkled lfts and bright crimson fls.

Gdn origin. Z5.

R. jundzillii Besser. St. erect or trailing, suckering 1–2.4m, prickles few slender, scattered, straight or decurved, sometimes intermixed with bristles. Lfts 2.5–4.5cm, 5–7, obovate to broadly elliptic, acute or acuminate, somewhat gland. and downy beneath, teeth compound gland. Fls usually solitary, sometimes 2–8, single, slightly fragrant, 5–7.5cm across; sep. lobed, gland., spreading to reflexed; pet. pale to rosy pink, fading with age. Fr. 1.5–2.5cm, ovoid to spherical, red, smooth or glandular-bristly. W Eur. to S Russia (inc. Cauc.), Turk. Z5.

R. × kamtchatica Vent. A hybrid involving *R. rugosa*, *R. davurica* or *R. amblyotis*. Differs from *R. rugosa* in more slender st. with fewer prickles, less wrinkled lfts, and smaller fls and fr. E Sib., Kamchatka. Z4.

R. kokanica (Reg.) Juz. St. erect, suckering, to 2m, red-brown when young. Lvs aromatic; lfts 5–7, broadly elliptic to obovate or orbicular, gland. beneath, teeth compound gland. Fls solitary, single, c5cm across; sep. entire, hairless, erect; pet. bright yellow. Fr. spherical, brown. Early summer. C Asia, possibly extending into China. Z6.

R. × kordesii Wulff. (*R. wichuraiana* × *R. rugosa*.) Differs from *R. wichuraiana* in the deep pink to red, recurrent fls which are single to semi-double and 7–8cm across. Gdn origin. cf. *R. × jacksonii*. Z5.

R. koreana Komar. St. to 100cm, densely branched, dark red, bristles dense. Lfts 1–2cm, 7–11(–15), elliptic to elliptic-obovate, obtuse, sometimes slightly downy beneath, teeth gland. Fls solitary, single, 4–6cm across, scented; sep. entire, gland., erect; pet. white tinged with pink. Fr. 1–1.5cm, ovoid to oblong, orange-red. N Korea. Z6.

R. laevigata Michx. CHEROKEE ROSE. St. climbing, green to 10m or more, prickles scattered, stout, red-brown, hooked. Lvs everg.; lfts 3–6(–9)cm, 3(–5), lanceolate to elliptic or ovate, leathery, acute or acuminate, glossy above, hairless, midrib sometimes prickly beneath, toothed. Fls solitary, single, fragrant, 5–10cm across; sep. entire, bristly, erect; pet. white or creamy white. Fr. 3.5–4cm, pear-shaped, orange-red to red, bristly. Early summer. S China, Taiwan, Vietnam, Laos, Cambodia, Burm., nat. S US. 'Cooperi' (COOPER'S BURMA ROSE): Z7.

R. latebracteata Boulenger. Similar to *R. forrestiana* but lfts to 2.5cm and styles not exserted. W China. Z8.

R. laxa Retz. St. slender, arching to 2.5m tall, prickles few, large, recurved, hooked or straight, intermixed with bristles. Lfts 1.5–4.5cm, 5–9, ovate to elliptic or oblong, obtuse, usually hairy beneath, teeth simple or compound. Fls 1–6, single, 4–5cm across; sep. entire, usually gland., erect; pet. white to pale pink, notched. Fr. c1.5cm, ellipsoid to spherical, red, smooth. Sib. S to Tien-Shan and Pamir-Alai, NW China. Z6.

R. × lheritiana Thory. (Possibly *R. pendulina* × *R. chinensis*.) St. red-tinged climbing to 4m, prickles 0 or few. Lfts 3–7, ovate-oblong. Fls many, in clusters, semi-double; sep. entire; pet. purple-red, white at the base toothed, glab. Fr. subglobose, smooth. Gdn origin. Z4.

R. longicuspis Bertol. St. scrambling and climbing to 6m, tinged red when young, prickles short, curved or hooked or 0. Lvs everg. or semi-evergreen, tinged red when young; lfts 5–10cm (3–)5–7, narrowly ovate to elliptic, leathery, acuminate, occas. downy on midrib beneath, toothed. Fls to 15 in a loose cluster, single, smelling of banans, c5cm across; sep. lobed, hairy and gland.; pet. white, silky beneath. Fr. 1.5–2cm, broadly ellipsoidal to spherical, red to orange, often hairy and gland. Early to mid-summer. NE India, W China, Burma. var. *sinowilsonii* (Hemsl.) T.T. Yu & Ku. Lvs to 30cm, lfts slightly downy beneath, flower-buds broadly ovoid, sep. ± hairless. SW China. Z9.

R. lucens Rolfe = *R. longicuspis*.

R. luciae Franch. & Rochebr. & Crépin. St. prostrate or climbing to 3.5m, prickles small, scattered, pale brown, flattened, slightly hooked. Lvs everg. or semi-evergreen; lfts 2–4.5cm, 5(–7), thin, term. longer than others, acute to acuminate, hairless, toothed. Fls 3–30 in clusters, single, fragrant, 2–3cm across, opening from short, rounded buds; sep. reflexed; pet. white. Fr. ovoid to spherical, red to purple, c7mm long, smooth or gland. Early summer and again in late summer. E China, Jap., Korea. V. similar to *R. wichuraiana*. Z7.

R. lucida Ehrh. = *R. virginiana*.

R. lutea Mill. = *R. foetida*.

R. 'Lutea Maxima'. (*R. pimpinellifolia* × *R. foetida*.) Shows influence of *R. foetida* in buttercup-yellow fls, sep. sometimes lobed, and fr. smooth. Z4.

R. macounii Greene = *R. woodsii*.

R. × macrantha hort., non Desp. (? *R. gallica* × *R. canina*.) St. 1.5–2m, arching or spreading, green, prickles sparse, sctatered, straight or slightly curved, mixed with bristles and stalked glands. Lfts 3–5(–7), dull green, ovate to oblong-ovate, acute to acuminate, hairless, gland. beneath with tiny prickles onn mid-rib, toothed. Fls 2–5 in clusters, single to semi-double, fragrant, c7.5cm across; sep. with many lobes, hairy inside and on margin, slightly gland.; pet. pale pink, fading to white.Fr. to 1.5cm wide, subspherical, red. Gdn origin. Z6.

R. 'Macrantha' = R. × macrantha.

R. macrophylla Lindl. St. erect and arching, dark red to purple 2.5–4(–5)m tall, prickles 0 or few stout, upward-pointing, straight often paired. Lfts 2.5–6.5cm, (7–)9–11, elliptic to narrowly ovate, acute or acuminate, downy and sometimes gland. beneath, toothed. Fls 1–5, single, 5–7.5cm across; sep. entire, bristly and gland., expanded at tip; pet. mid-pink or deep pink to mauve pink. Fr. 2.5–4(–7.5)cm, subglobose to bottle-shaped with a neck, red, glandular-bristly. Himal. from Pak. E to W China. Z7.

R. majalis Herrm. CINNAMON ROSE; MAY ROSE. St. erect, sucker-ing, slender, red-brown, 1.5–3m, much-branched towards the top, bristly, prickles slender, hooked, paired and scattered. Lfts 1–1.5cm, 5–7, elliptic to obovate, obtuse to acuminate, downy beneath, toothed above. Bracts large. Fls 1 to few, single or double, c5cm across; sep. entire, with woolly margins; pet. mid-pink to purple-pink. Fr. spherical or slightly elongated, dark red, 1–1.5cm long, smooth. Early summer to summer. N & C Eur., Russia (Sib.). Z6.

R. majalis 'Foecundissima' = R. majalis.

R. marginata auct., non Wallr. = R. jundzillii.

R. × mariae-graebneriae Asch. & Gräbn. (R. virginiana ×(probably) R. palustris.) Erect rounded shrub to 1.6m, prickles slightly curved. Lfts glossy green, toothed. Pet. rose-pink. Fr. subglobose, red. Summer–early autumn. Gdn origin. Z5.

R. maximowicziana Reg. St. arching and climbing, prickles few, small, scattered, straight and hooked, young br. bristly. Lfts 2.5–5cm, 7–9, ovate-elliptic to oblong, acute to acuminate, glab., toothed. Fls many in small clusters, single, 2.5–3.5cm across; sep. lobed; pet. white. Fr. 1–1.2cm, ovoid, red, smooth. Manch. Z6.

R. micrantha Sm. St. much-branched, arching, to 3.5m, bearing curved or hooked prickles. Lfts 1.5–4cm, 5–7, elliptic to broadly ovate, acute, densely hairy and gland. beneath, teeth gland. compound. Fls 1–4(–8), single, 2.5–3cm across; sep. lobed, tip expanded, gland.; pet. pale pink or white. Fr. 1.2–1.8cm, ovoid to subglobose, red, smooth or glandular-bristly. Eur., except extreme N, NW Afr., SW Asia; nat. N Amer. Z6.

R. microcarpa Lindl., non Besser non Retz. = R. cymosa.

R. microphylla Lindl. = R. roxburghii f. normalis.

R. × micrugosa Henkel. (R. rugosa × R. roxburghii.) Fls pale pink, (8–)10–12.5cm across. Fr. orange-red, subglobose with prickles. 'Alba': fls white, fragrant, produced over a long period. Z5.

R. minutifolia Engelm. Low bushy shrub to 1.2m. St. covered with red-brown spines, hairy. Lvs to 2cm, pinnate. Lfts to 0.4cm, oval, closely incised and toothed, gland. Fls to 2cm diam., single, rose purple or white. US Calif., Baja Calif. Z9.

R. mirifica Greene = R. stellata var. mirifica.

R. mollis Sm. Differs from R. villosa in young st. pruinose, lfts, 1.2–3.5cm long, ± round, and fr., 1–1.5cm. Eur., W Asia. Z6.

R. moschata Herrm. MUSK ROSE. St. arching or semi-climbing, purple- or red-tinged 3–10m, prickles few, scattered, straight or slightly curved. Lfts 3–7cm, 5–7, broadly ovate to broadly ellip-tic, acute or acuminate, shiny and hairless above, downy or not on veins beneath, toothed. Fls in few-fld loose clusters, single, with a musky scent, 3–5.5cm across; sep. entire lobed, hairy, reflexed; pet. white or cream, reflexing with age. Fr. 1–1.5cm, subglobose to ovoid, orange-red, usually downy and sometimes gland. Late summer to autumn. Unknown in the wild; cult. in S Eur., Medit. and SW Asia. var. nastarana Christ. Lfts smaller, always hairless beneath; fls larger, more numerous, tinged pink. Z6.

R. moschata var. napaulensis Lindl. = R. brunonii.

R. moyesii Hemsl. & Wils. St. erect, bristly below, stout, red-brown 2–3.5m, prickles pale, scattered, stout, broad-based. Lfts 1–4cm, 7–13, broadly elliptic to ovate, acute, dark green above, somewhat glaucous beneath, hairless except for midrib beneath, toothed. Fls 1–2(–4), single, 4–6.5cm across; sep. entire, expanded at tip, hairy and sparsely gland.; pet. pink to blood-red. Fr. 3.8–6cm, bottle-shaped, with a neck, orange-red, glandular-bristly at least towards the base. W China. 'Fargesii': fls pink to rose red; lfts shorter and wider, obtuse. 'Geranium': compact; lfts paler green; fls scarlet, and a broader crimson fr. with a shorter neck. 'Sealing Wax': fls pink; fr. large, bright red. f. rosea Rehd. & Wils., with pink fls and coarsely toothed lfts, appears to be closer to R. davidii. However, some botanists give it as a synonym of R. holodonta. R. holodonta Stapf is closely related to R. moyesii but has lfts up to 5cm. W China.

Z5.

R. moyesii sensu Stapf in part, non Hemsl. & Wils. = R. sweginzowii.

R. moyesii var. fargesii Rolfe = R. moyesii 'Fargesii'.

R. mulliganii Boulenger. Similar to R. rubus, but st. 6m or more, lfts 5–7, fls 4.5–5.5cm across in loose clusters; sep. always lobed. W China. Z5.

R. multibracteata Hemsl. & Wils. St. arching 2–4m, green turning red-brown, prickles slender, straight usually in pairs. Lfts 0.6–1.5cm, (5–)7–9, obovate to elliptic or ± round, obtuse, dark green above, grey-green beneath, downy on midrib, teeth compound. Fls 1 to many in terminal clusters, single, slightly malodorous, 2.5–3.8cm across; sep. entire, downy inside, gland.; pet. bright pink to lilac-pink. Fr. 1–1.5cm, spherical to ovoid or bottle-shaped, orange-red, with a few gland. bristles. W China. Z7.

R. multiflora Thunb. ex Murray. JAPANESE ROSE; BABY ROSE. St. arching, trailing or sometimes climbing 3–5m, prickles many small, stout, decurved. Stipules laciniate, glandular-bristly. Lfts 1.5–5cm, (5–)7–9(–11), obovate or elliptic, acute, acuminate or obtuse, sometimes downy beneath, toothed. Fls few to many in branched clusters, single, fruit-scented, 1.5–3cm across; sep. lobed, glandular-bristly; pet. cream, fading to white, occas. pink. Fr. 0.6–0.7cm, ovoid to spherical, red. Jap., Korea, nat. in US. 'Carnea': fls double, flesh-pink. 'Grevillei' (SEVEN SISTERS ROSE): lfts large, wrinkled; fls in clusters of 25–30(–50), usually double, deep pink-purple fading to white. 'Wilsonii': fls single, white, c5cm across. var. cathayensis Rehd. & Wils. Fls single, rosy pink, to 4cm across, in rather flat clusters. China. 'Nana': dwarf; fls single, fragrant, pale pink or cream. Z5.

R. multiflora 'Platyphylla' = R. multiflora 'Grevillei'.

R. multiflora var. carnea Thory = R. multiflora 'Carnea'.

R. multiflora var. platyphylla Thory = R. multiflora 'Grevillei'.

R. multiflora var. watsoniana (Crépin) Matsum. = R. watsoniana.

R. murieliae Rehd. & Wils. St. red-tinged, erect or arching 1.5–3m tall, prickles 0 or few slender, straight intermixed with pink bristles. Lfts 1–4cm, 9–15, elliptic to oblong, acute, downy on midrib beneath, teeth gland. Fls 3–7, single, 2–2.5cm across; sep. entire, expanded at tip, hairy or not on the back; pet. white. Fr. bottle-shaped, orange-red, 1–2cm long, smooth. W China. Z6.

R. muscosa Mill. = R. × centifolia 'Muscosa'.

R. mutabilis Correv. = R. chinensis 'Mutabilis'.

R. nanothamnus Boulenger = R. webbiana var. microphylla.

R. nitida Willd. St. erect, suckering often red-tinged 50–100cm, prickles sparse, straight, bristles dense purple-brown or red. Stipules broad, with gland. teeth. Lfts 1–3cm, 5–9, elliptic, acute, shiny above, ± hairless beneath, teeth fine. Fls 1(–3), single, fragrant, 4.5–6.5cm across; sep. entire, bristly or gland.; pet. deep pink. Fr. 0.8–1cm, spherical or almost so, dark scar-let, glandular-bristly. E N Amer. Z3.

R. nivea Dup. ex Lindl., non DC. = R. 'Dupontii'.

R. nutkana C. Presl. NOOTKA ROSE. St. stout, purple-brown 1.5–3m tall, prickles stout, usually straight, broad-base in pairs, bristles slender. Lfts 1.9–5cm, 5–7(–9), dark green, ovate to elliptic, acute or obtuse, gland. and sometimes downy beneath, compound gland. Fls 1(–3), single, (4–)5–6.5cm across, with glandular-bristly stalks; sep. entire, glandular-bristly or not and somewhat downy; pet. bright red to purple-pink, occas. white. Fr. 1.5–2cm, spherical to almost so, red, smooth. Alask. to N Calif. var. hispida Fern. Lfts downy beneath, teeth simple non-glandular, flower-stalks glab.; fr. glandular-bristly. BC to Utah. Z4.

R. × odorata (Andrews) Sweet. TEA ROSE. (? R. chinensis × R. gigantea.) Differs from R. gigantea in single or double fls 5–8cm across, with white, pale pink or yellow pet. Mid to late summer. Gdn origin (China). Z7.

R. odorata 'Gigantea' = R. gigantea.

R. × odorata var. gigantea (Collett ex Crépin) Rehd. & Wils. = R. gigantea.

R. omiensis Rolfe = R. sericea ssp. omeiensis.

R. omiensis f. pteracantha (Franch.) Rehd. & Wils. = R. sericea ssp. omeiensis f. pteracantha.

R. oxyodon Boiss. Differs from R. pendulina in st. 2–4m, sep. usu-ally gland. on the back, fr. smooth. E Cauc. Z6.

R. palustris Marshall. SWAMP ROSE. St. erect to spreading, suck-ering slender red-tinged or purple-brown to 2m, prickles stout, somewhat curved, broad-based in pairs. Lfts 2–6cm, 5–7(–9), dull green, oblong to elliptic, acute, hairless above, downy be-neath, toothed. Fls usually in clusters, rarely solitary, single, 4–5.5cm across; sep. expanded at tips, glandular-bristly; pet. pink. Fr. c0.8cm, spherical, red, smooth or glandular-bristly. E N Amer. Z4.

R. parvifolia Ehrh. (1791), non Pall. (1788) = R. × centifolia 'Parvifolia'.

R. × *paulii* Rehd. (*R. rugosa* × *R. arvensis.*) St. vigorous, trailing to 4m. Fls in clusters, single, white, fragrant, to 6cm across; sep. entire, gland. 'Rosea': fls pink with paler centres. Z4.

R. 'Paulii' = *R.* × *paulii.*

R. pendulina L. St. suckering, green or red-brown 60–200cm, bristles and prickles 0 or slender. Lfts 2–6cm, 5–9(–11), elliptic, acute or obtuse, downy beneath and sometimes gland., teeth compound gland. Fls 1(–5), single, 3.8–6.5cm across; sep. entire, tip expanded, sometimes gland.; pet. deep pink or purple-pink. Fr. 1.5–3cm, pendulous, subglobose to ovoid, usually with a neck, red, smooth or glandular-bristly. Early summer. Mts of S & C Eur. 'Nana': dwarf, freely suckering. Z5.

R. pendulina var. *oxyodon* (Boiss.) Rehd. = *R. oxyodon.*

R. persica Juss. St. straggling, often decumbent, suckering 40–90cm, yellow-brown, hairless or downy, prickles straight or curved, slender, yellow or red. Lvs 1.3–3.2cm, decid., simple, sessile, grey-green, broadly elliptic to obovate, toothed toward apex, usually downy, rather prickly; pet. yellow with a basal crimson spot. Fr. spherical, almost black, v. prickly. Early summer. Iran, Afghan., C Asia, SW Sib. Z5.

R. phoenicia Boiss. St. slender, climbing, 3–5m tall, prickles few, short, curved or hooked, broad-based. Lfts 2–4.5cm, (3–)5(–7), elliptic to rounded, downy, teeth simple or compound. Fls 10–14 in clusters, single, 4–5cm across, opening from ovoid, rounded buds; sep. lobed, often downy; pet. white. Fr. 1–1.2cm, ovoid, red, smooth. NE Greece, Cyprus, Turk., Syr., Leb. Z9.

R. pimpinellifolia L. BURNET ROSE; SCOTCH ROSE. St. suckering, 90–200cm, purple-brown, prickles dense straight, slender, bristles stiff. Lfts 0.6–2cm, (5–)7–9(–11), broadly elliptic to broadly obovoate to orbicular, obtuse, midvein sometimes downy beneath, teeth gland. Fls solitary, single or double, 3.8–6cm across; sep. entire, narrow, margin woolly, erect; pet. creamy white. Fr. 7–15mm, spherical or almost so, dark brown becoming black, smooth, glab. W & S Eur., SW & C Asia E to China and Korea. 'Andrewsii': fls double, rose-pink. 'Grandiflora' ('Altaica'): st. less bristly, fls 7–7.5cm across. 'Hispida': lfts 19–32mm; fls 5–7.5cm across, opening pale yellow, fading to cream. 'Nana': fls semi-double, white. Z4.

R. pisocarpa A. Gray. CLUSTER ROSE. St. erect, slender, arching 90–250cm tall, unarmed or prickles few, straight, weak in pairs and some bristles towards base. Lfts 1.3–4cm, 5–7(–9), elliptic to ovate, obtuse or somewhat acute, downy beneath, toothed. Fls (1–)4–5, single, 2.5–3cm across; sep. entire, glandular-bristly; pet. rosy pink to purple-pink. Fr. to 1.3cm, ellipsoid to spherical, purple-red to red or orange, smooth. BC to N Calif. Z6.

R. × *polliniana* Spreng. (*R. arvensis* × *R. gallica.*) Differs from *R. arvensis* in rather leathery, lfts, slightly downy beneath, fls 5–6cm across. N It. Z7.

R. polyantha Sieb. & Zucc. = *R. multiflora.*

R. pomifera Herrm., nom illegit. = *R. villosa.*

R. pomifera f. *duplex* (Weston) Rehd. = *R. villosa* 'Duplex'.

R. prattii Hemsl. St. erect purple- or red-tinged 1.2–2.5m, prickles 0 or few, straight, yellow or pale brown. Lfts 0.6–2cm, (7–)11–15, obovate to narrowly ovate or elliptic, acute, downy on veins beneath, teeth obscure. Fls (1–)3–7, single, 2–2.5cm across; sep. entire, downy, erect; pet. pale to more usually deep pink. Fr. 0.6–1cm, ovoid to bottle-shaped, scarlet to orange-red, glandular-bristly. W China. Z6.

R. primula Boulenger. St. erect, slender, to 3m, red-brown when young, prickles stout, straight, somewhat compressed, broad-based. Lvs v. aromatic; lfts 0.6–2cm (7–)9–13, elliptic to obovate or oblanceolate, acute or obtuse, with large glands beneath, teeth compound gland. Fls solitary, single, 2.5–4.5cm across; sep. entire, hairless, erect; pet. primrose-yellow. Fr. 1–1.5cm, spherical to turbinate, brown-red to maroon, smooth. Early summer. C Asia to N China. Z5.

R. provincialis Mill., in part (1788) non Herrm. (1762). = *R.* × *centifolia.*

R. provincialis Herrm. = *R. gallica.*

R. × *pruhoniciana* Schneid. (*R. moyesii* × *R. willmottiae* or *R. multibracteata.*) Differs from *R. willmottiae* in maroon-crimson fls, and fr. persisting after lvs have fallen. Gdn origin. Z6.

R. pulverulenta Bieb. Compact shrub, st. 30–70cm, prickles numerous stiff, straight or decurved, off-white intermixed with small gland. bristles. Lfts 0.7–1.5cm, (3–)5–7(–9), elliptic to obovate or rounded, hairless or somewhat downy, margins and teeth gland. Fls 1 or 2, single, 2.5–3.8cm across; sep. with gland-edged lobes, tips slightly expanded; pet. rose-pink. Fr. to 2.5cm, ellipsoidal or subglobose, dark red, smooth or glandular-bristly. S Eur. to Asia Minor, Leb., Iran, Afghan., Russia (Cauc.). Z6.

R. pyrenaica Gouan = *R. pendulina.*

R. rapinii Boiss. & Bal. = *R. hemispherica.*

R. reducta Bak. = *R. multibracteata.*

R. × *reversa* Waldst. & Kit. (*P. pimpinellifolia* × *R. pendulina.*) Lfts densely gland. Pet. carmine. Fr. *c*2cm, spherical-ovoid, deep purple-red, drooping. S Eur. N to Switz. and S Fr. Z6.

R. × *richardii* Rehd. HOLY ROSE. (*R. gallica* ×possibly *R. phoenicia* or *R. arvensis.*) St. low, spreading to 1.3m, prickles small, scattered, hooked. Lfts 3–5, ovate to narrowly elliptic, acute, wrinkled above, downy beneath, teeth gland. Fls several in loose clusters, single, 5–7.5cm across; sep. lobed, apex leafy, downy and gland.; pet. pale pink. Gdn origin. Z7.

R. 'Rosa Mundi' = *R. gallica* 'Versicolor'.

R. roulettii Correv. = *R. chinensis* 'Rouletii'.

R. roxburghii Tratt. CHESTNUT ROSE; CHINQUAPIN ROSE. Fls double, pink, darker in the centre. Originally introduced from Chinese gardens and rarely grown. f. *normalis* Rehd. &Wils. St. spreading, rather stiff st. to 5m+, bark peeling grey or pale brown, prickles few, straight, hooked in parts. Lfts 1–2.5cm, (7–)9–15(–19), narrowly ovate to obovate, hairless, toothed. Fls usually solitary, single, fragrant, 5–7.5cm across; sep. lobed, downy and prickly, erect; pet. mid-pink to deep pink. Fr. 3–4cm long, flattened-spherical, yellow-green, prickly. W China. Z5.

R. roxburghii var. *hirtula* (Reg.) Rehd. & Wils. = *R. hirtula.*

R. rubiginosa L. SWEET BRIER; EGLANTINE. Br. arching, 2–3m, dense, bearing many, stout, hooked prickles and stiff bristles on flowering br. Lvs aromatic; lfts 1–3cm, 5–9, dark green, ovate to runded, gland. and downy beneath, teeth compound. Fls 1–7, single, fragrant, 2.5–5cm across; sep. lobed, glandular-bristly, erect; pet. pale to deep pink. Fr. 1–2.5cm, ovoid to subglobose, red or orange, smooth or glandular-bristly. Eur., N Afr., W Asia, nat. N Amer. Z4.

R. rubra Lam. = *R. gallica.*

R. rubrifolia Vill. = *R. glauca.*

R. rubus Lév. & Vaniot. St. spreading or semi-climbing, often purple-tinged, 2.4–5m, prickles few, short, hooked (young shoots, sometimes hairy). Lfts 3–9cm, (3–)5, elliptic-ovate to oblong-obovate, acute, glossy above, grey-green and usually downy beneath, purple-tinged when young, teeth simple. Fls to 12 in tight clusters, single, fragrant, 2.5–3.8cm across, on stalks 1–2.5cm long; sep. sometimes lobed, downy and gland.; pet. white, yellow at the base. Fr. 0.9–1.5cm, spherical or ovoid, dark red, glandular-bristly. Late summer. W & C China. Z8.

R. rugosa Thunb. JAPANESE ROSE; TURKESTAN ROSE. St. erect, stout, 1.2–2.5m, downy when young, densely prickly and bristly. Lfts 2.5–5cm, 5–9, dark green, oblong to elliptic, acute, wrinkled above, downy beneath with conspicuous veins, teeth shallow. Fls 1 to few, single, fragrant, 6–7.5(–9)cm across; sep. entire, expanded at tip, downy, erect; pet. purple-pink. Fr. 2–2.5cm, subglobose, with a neck at the top, red to orange-red, smooth. Early summer to autumn. E Russia, Korea, Jap., N China, nat. GB and NE US. 'Alba': fls single, white, opening from pale pink buds; v. free-fruiting. var. *alboplena* Rehd. Fls double, white. var. *rosea* Rehd. Fls single, rose-pink. Z2.

R. rugosa var. *kamtchatica* (Vent.) Reg. = *R.* × *kamtchatica.*

R. rugosa var. *ventenatiana* (C. Mey.) = *R.* × *kamtchatica.*

R. sancta Rich., non Andrews = *R.* × *richardii.*

R. sempervirens L. EVERGREEN ROSE. St. prostrate, trailing or scrambling 6–10m, prickles 0 or straight or hooked. Lvs everg. or semi-evergreen; lfts 1.5–6cm, (3–)5–7, narrowly ovate to elliptic, term. larger than upper laterals, acuminate, hairless except for midrib beneath, toothed. Fls (1–)3–10 in clusters, single, slightly fragrant, 2.5–4.5cm across, opening from blunt, ovoid buds; sep. entire, glandular-bristly; pet. white. Fr. 1–1.6cm, ovoid or spherical, orange-red, often glandular-bristly. S Eur., NW Afr., Turk. Z7.

R. serafinii Viv. St. branched shrub to 1.2m, prickles stout, curved or hooked, often intermixed with bristles. Lvs aromatic; lfts 0.5–1.2cm, 5–7(–11), ovate to rounded, obtuse, glossy above, gland. beneath, teeth gland. compound. Fls 1(–3), single, 2.5–5cm across; sep. lobed, often gland.; pet. pale pink. Fr. 0.8–1.2cm wide, obovoid to spherical, red, smooth. Early summer. It., Sicily, Corsica, Sardinia, Bulg. and S Balk. Z7.

R. sericea Lindl. St. upright or somewhat spreading 2–4m, grey or brown, prickles straight or curved, often upward-pointing, red-tinged with broad bases, mixed with slender bristles. Lfts 0.6–3cm, 7–11, elliptic, oblong or obovate, obtuse or acute, hairy or not beneath, toothed above. Fls solitary, on shrt lat. shoots, single, 2.5–6cm across; sep. entire, hairless or silky; pet. usually 5, white or cream, notched. Fr. 0.8–1.5cm, spherical to pear-shaped with a narrow stalk, dark crimson, scarlet, orange or yellow, smooth. Early summer. Himal., NE Indian, N Bhutan, SW & C China. ssp. *omeiensis* (Rolfe) A.V. Roberts. Lfts 11–19, silky beneath. Pet. usually 4, white. Fr. with a fleshy stalk. W China. f. *pteracantha* Franch. St. with v. broad-based prickles forming interrupted wings, bright red at first, hardening grey-brown. W China. Z6.

R. sericea var. *omiensis* (Rolfe) Rowley = *R. sericea* ssp.

omeiensis.

R. sericea var. *pteracantha* (Franch.) Boulenger = *R. sericea* ssp. *omiensis* f. *pteracantha*.

R. sertata Rolfe. Differs from *R. webbiana* in lfts obtuse to acute, fls deep pink to purple-pink on longer stalks (1.5–3cm rather than 1–1.3cm), and fr. dark red. W & C China.

R. setigera Michx. PRAIRIE ROSE; SUNSHINE ROSE; CLIMBING ROSE. St. slender, spreading, trailing or rambling 2–5m, prickles stout, straight, broad-based, scattered. Lfts 3–8cm, 3–5, ovate to ovate-oblong, long, acute, deep green above, pale green and downy on veins beneath, teeth coarse. Fls 5–15 in loose clusters, single, sometimes fragrant, 5–7.5cm across; sep. lobed, downy and glandular-bristly; pet. deep pink fading to pale pink or nearly white. Fr. c0.8cm, spherical, red to green-brown, glandular-bristly. E & Central N Amer. Z4.

R. setipoda Hemsl. & Wils. St. stout, red tinged, erect or arching 2.4–3m tall, prickles sparse, short, straight, broad-based, intermixed with bristles. Lvs slightly aromatic; lfts 3–6cm, 7–9, elliptic to elliptic-ovate, acute to obtuse, mid-green above, grey, gland. and downy on veins beneath, toothed. Fls in loose clusters of up to 20, single, smelling of unripe apples, 3–5cm across; sep. entire, expanded at the tip, margin gland.; pet. mid-pink to deep purple-pink, shading to white at the base, slightly downy on the back. Fr. 2.5–5cm, bottle-shaped with a neck at the top, dark red, glandular-bristly. W China. Z6.

R. sherardii Davies. Br. dense to 2m, pruinose when young, prickles straight or curved. Lfts (3–)5–7, blue-green, elliptic to broadly ovate, hairy, teeth compound. Fls several in a cluster, single, 3–5cm across; sep. lobed, glandular-hairy; pet. deep pink. Fr. 1.2–2cm wide, ovoid to turbinate, red, glandular-bristly. N & C Eur. Z5.

R. shweliense hort. non Balf. f. & Forr. = *R. glaucophyllum*.

R. sicula Tratt. St. dense, suckering 50–150cm tall, red when young, prickles sparse, slender, straight or slightly curved, intermixed with gland. bristles. Lvs slightly aromatic; lfts 0.6–2cm, 5–9, broadly ovate to rounded, gland. and sometimes downy beneath, teeth gland. compound. Fls usually solitary, sometimes 2 or 3, single, 2.5–3.3cm across; sep. lobed, gland., ciliate; pet. bright pink. Fr. 1–1.3cm, ovoid to subglobose, red to black, sparsely glandular-bristly. Medit. Z8.

R. simplicifolia Salisb. = *R. persica*.

R. sinowilsonii Hemsl. = *R. longicuspis* var. *sinowilsonii*.

R. soulieana Crépin. St. erect, spreading or semi-climbing, 3–4m, prickles stout, decurved, compressed, broad-based. Lfts 1–3cm, (5–)7–9, grey-green, obovate to elliptic, somewhat downy on midrib beneath, toothed. Fls in many-fld branched clusters 10–15cm across, single, with a fruity scent, 2.5–3.8cm across, opening from yellow buds; sep. entire or lobed, hairless or downy, often gland.; pet. white. Fr. c1cm, ovoid to subglobose, pale to dark orange, gland. W China. Z7.

R. spaldingii Crépin = *R. nutkana* var. *hispida*.

R. spinosissima L. 1771, non L. 1753 = *R. pimpinellifolia*.

R. spinosissima var. *andrewsii* Willmott = *R. pimpinellifolia* 'Andrewsii'.

R. spinosissima var. *hispida* (Sims) Koehne = *R. pimpinellifolia* 'Hispida'.

R. spinosissima var. *lutea* Bean = *R.* 'Lutea Maxima'.

R. spinosissima var. *nana* Andrews = *R. pimpinellifolia* 'Nana'.

R. stellata Wooton. DESERT ROSE. St. erect, slender, stellate-hairy 60–120cm, prickles dense, straight, slender, pale yellow, often paired intermixed with gland. bristles. Lfts 0.5–1.2cm, 3–5, wedge-shaped to obovate, stellate-hairy, toothed above. Fls solitary, single, 3.5–6cm across; sep. lobed, gland. and spiny, margin woolly; pet. soft pink to bright rose or dark purple-red; sta. to 160 or more. Fr. to 2cm, hemispherical, flat-topped, not fleshy, dull red to brown-red, prickly. SW US. var. *mirifica* (Greene) Cockerell. Lacks stellate hairs and fls with fewer (up to 150) sta. Z6. SW US.

R. stellata ssp. *mirifica* (Greene) Lewis = *R. stellata* var. *mirifica*.

R. stylosa Desv. St. arching to 3m, prickles stout, hooked, wide-based. Lfts 1.5–5cm, 5–7, dark green, narrowly elliptic to ovate, acute or acuminate, glossy above, downy beneath, toothed. Fls 1–8 or more, single, 3–5cm across; sep. lobed, often slightly gland.; pet. usually white, sometimes pale pink. Fr. 1–1.5cm, ovoid to spherical red, smooth. W Eur., Bulg., W Asia. Z6.

R. suffulta Greene. St. to 50cm, bristly, prickles dense, straight. Lfts 1.5–4cm, 7–11, ovate-oblong to broadly elliptic, obtuse, bright green and hairless or downy above, downy beneath, toothed. Fls in clusters, single, c3cm across; sep. entire or sometimes lobed; pet. mid-pink. Fr. c1cm, spherical, red, smooth. E & Central N Amer. Z5.

R. × suionum Almqv. A hybrid of uncertain origin; *R. virginiana* may be involved. Lfts 5 or 7, and with a much smaller pair of lfts below the terminal one. Fls double, clear pink. Gdn origin. Z5.

R. sulphurea Ait. = *R. hemispherica* 'Flore Pleno'.

R. sweginzowii Koehne. St. red-tinged, spreading too 3.5(–5)m

tall, bristly, prickles 0 or dense, 3-angled. Lvs decid.; lfts 2.5–5cm, 7–11, elliptic to broadly so, acute, hairless above, downy on veins beneath, margins with compound teeth. Fls 1–3(–6), single, 3.5–5cm across; sep. entire, glandular-bristly on the back, erect and persistent in fr.; pet. bright pink. Fr. bottle-shaped, glossy red or orange-red, c2.5cm long, glandular-bristly. N & W China. Z6.

R. 'Tipo Ideale' = *R. chinensis* 'Mutabilis'.

R. tomentosa Sm. St. often flexuous, arching, to 3m, green when young and often pruinose, prickles sparse, straight or slightly curved, often in pairs. Lvs smelling resinous when crushed; lfts 5–7, light green to grey-green, elliptic to ovate, obtuse, acute or acuminate, hairy on both sides and gland. beneath, teeth compound gland. Fls solitary or few, single, fragrant, 3.8–5.5cm across; sep. lobed, tips expanded, glandular-bristly; pet. pale pink or white. Fr. 1.8–2.5cm, ovoid to spherical, orange-red, with stalked glands. Eur., Asia Minor, Russia (Cauc.), occ. nat. in US. Z6.

R. triphylla Roxb. = *R. × beanii*.

R. turbinata Ait. = *R. × francofurtana*.

R. villosa L. Br. dense, stiff, straight, 1–2.4m, tinged red when young, prickles scattered, slender, straight or slightly curved. Lfts 3.2–6.5cm, 5–9, blue-green, elliptic, acute or obtuse, hairy, often with dense, apple-scented glands beneath, teeth compound gland. Fls 1–3 or more, single, slightly fragrant, 2.5–6.5cm across; sep. lobed, gland.; pet. deep pink. Fr. 1–3cm, spherical to pear-shaped, dark red, glandular-bristly. C & S Eur., Asia Minor, Cauc. 'Duplex': Lfts grey-green; fls semi-double, clear pink, c6.5cm across, more free-flowering; possibly a hybrid between *R. villosa* and a tetraploid rose of gdn origin. Z5.

R. villosa auct. non L. = *R. mollis*.

R. vilmorinii Bean = *R. × micrugosa*.

R. virginiana Herrm. St. erect, often suckering, brown-red to 1.5m, bristly when young, prickles 0 or straight or decurved, paired. Lfts 2–6cm, 5–9, obovate to oblong-elliptic, acute, glossy green above, hairless or downy on midrib beneath, coarsely toothed above. Fls 1–8, single, 5–6.5cm across, fragrant; sep. entire or lobed, tips leafy, gland. and hairy; pet. pale pink to bright pink. Fr. 1–1.5cm wide, subglobose, red, smooth or glandular-bristly. E N Amer. Z3.

R. virginiana var. *alba* Bak. = *R. carolina* 'Alba'.

R. wardii Mullig. Differs from *R. sweginzowii* in lacking prickles and bristles, smaller lfts (1.3–1.9cm), and white fls. SW China. Z7.

R. watsoniana Crépin. St. arching, trailing or climbing to 1m, prickles small, scattered. Lfts 2.5–6.5cm, 3–5, linear-lanceolate, mottled yellow or grey near midrib, downy beneath, margins wavy toothed. Fls in clusters, single, 1–1.7cm across; sep. entire, hairy back; pet. pale pink, occas. white. Fr. 0.6–0.7cm, spherical, red. Gdn origin (Jap.). The fr. are usually sterile. Any seedlings produced are normal *R. multiflora*: *R. watsoniana* may be a mutant. Z5.

R. webbiana Royle. St. slender, 1–2m, purple brown, often pruinose when young, prickles few straight, slender, yellow, broad-based. Lfts 0.6–2.5cm, 5–9, obovate to broadly elliptic or rounded, obtuse, glaucous and hairless above, often slightly downy beneath, toothed above. Fls 1(–3), single, faintly fragrant, 3.8–5cm across; sep. entire, gland. and often hairy; pet. white to pale pink or lilac-pink, sometimes pink with a white base. Fr. 1.5–2.5cm, spherical to broadly bottle-shaped, with a neck, shiny red, smooth or glandular-bristly. Early summer. Himal., Xizang, Afghan., C Asia. var. *microphylla* Crépin. St. to 50cm, lfts to 16mm, fls 2.5–3.8cm across. C Asia, Afghan., Kashmir. Most common in cult. Z6.

R. wichuraiana Crépin. MEMORIAL ROSE. St. procumbent, trailing or climbing 3–6m, strong, curved. Lvs everg. or semi-evergreen; lfts 5–9, dark green, elliptic to broadly ovate or rounded, obtuse, hairless except for midrib beneath. Fls 6–10 in loose clusters, toothed single, fragrant, 2.5–5cm across; sep. entire or lobed, downy or slightly gland.; pet. white. Fr. 1–1.5cm, ovoid or spherical, orange-red to dark red. Summer–early autumn. Jap., Korea, E China, Taiwan, nat. in N Amer. 'Variegata': lfts cream with pink tips when young, turning green, marked with cream. Z5.

R. willmottiae Hemsl. St. erect or arching to 3m, glaucous-pruinose, becoming red-brown, prickles slender, straight, mostly in pairs. Lfts 0.6–1.5cm, 7–9, obovate to oblong or almost round, obtuse, hairless, toothed. Fls usually solitary, single, slightly fragrant, 2.5–3.8cm across; sep. entire, hairless; pet. purple-pink. Fr. 1–1.8cm, ovoid, pear-shaped or ± spherical, orange-red. Early summer. W & NW China. 'Wisley': fls deeper pink with narrower pet. and the sep. persistent in fr. Z6.

R. × wintoniensis Hillier. (*R. moyesii* × *R. setipoda*.) Differs from *R. moyesii* in clusters of 7–10 fls with pet. crimson, white at base, and aromatic lvs. Z6.

R. woodsii Lindl. WESTERN WILD ROSE. St. stiffly branched, to 2m, purple-brown or red-brown, becoming grey, prickles many, straight or slightly curved, sometimes intermixed with bristles. Lfts 1–3cm, 5–7(–9), obovate to elliptic, acute to obtuse, toothed, hairless or downy beneath. Fls 1–3(–5), single, 3–4.5cm across; sep. entire, hairless or downy; pet. mid-pink, occas. white. Fr. 0.5–1.5cm, ovoid to spherical, usually with a neck at the top, smooth. W & Central N Amer. var. *fendleri* (Crépin) Rydb. Differs in glandular-bristly flower-stalks, biserrate lfts, smaller lilac-pink fls and smaller fr. W N Amer. to N Mex. Z4.

R. xanthina Lindl. St. 1.5–3.5m, erect, brown to grey-brown, prickles straight or slightly curved, broad-based, sometimes much flattened on non-flowering shoots. Lfts 0.8–2cm, 7–13, broadly elliptic to obovate to orbicular, obtuse, hairy beneath, toothed. Fls solitary, rarely 2, semid-ouble, 3.8–5cm across; sep. entire, acuminate, leafy and toothed, ± hairless; pet. bright yellow. Fr. 12–15mm, spherical or broadly ellipsoid, brown red or maroon, smooth and hairless. Early summer. N China, Korea. f. *hugonis* (Hemsl.) A.V. Roberts. Lfts elliptic to obovate, lower-stalks hairless bearing single fls 4–6cm across. Early summer. C China. f. *spontanea* Rehd. Fls single, 5–6cm across. One of the parents of 'Canary Bird', the other parent being f. hugonis. Z5.

R. xanthina var. *ecae* (Aitch.) Boulenger = *R. ecae*.

R. xanthina var. *kokanica* (Juz.) Boulenger = *R. kokanica*.

R. xanthina f. *normalis* Rehd. & Wils., in part. = *R. xanthina* f. spontanea.

R. yunnanensis (Crépin) Boulenger = *R. longicuspis*.

ROSACEAE Juss. 107/3100. *Acaena, Adenostoma, Agrimonia, Alchemilla, Amelanchier,* ✕ *Amelasorbus, Aronia, Aruncus, Bencomia, Cercocarpus, Chaenomeles, Chamaebatia, Chamaebatiaria, Cotoneaster, Cowania,* +*Crataegomespilus, Crataegus,* ✕ *Crataemespilus, Cydonia, Dichotomanthes, Docynia, Dryas, Duchesnea, Eriobotrya, Exochorda, Fallugia, Filipendula, Fragaria, Geum, Gillenia, Heteromeles, Holodiscus, Horkelia, Ivesia, Kageneckia, Kelseya, Kerria, Luetkea, Lyonothamnus, Maddenia, Malus, Margyricarpus, Mespilus, Neillia, Neviusia, Oemleria, Osteomeles, Pentactina, Peraphyllum, Petrophytum, Photinia, Physocarpus, Potentilla, Prinsepia, Prunus, Pseudocydonia, Purshia, Pyracantha,* ✕ *Pyracomeles,* +*Pyrocydonia,* ✕ *Pyronia, Pyrus, Quillaja, Rhaphiolepis, Rhodotypos, Rosa, Rubus, Sanguisorba, Sibbaldia, Sibiraea, Sorbaria,* ✕ *Sorbaronia,* ✕ *Sorbocotoneaster,* ✕ *Sorbopyrus, Sorbus, Spenceria, Spiraea, Stephanandra, Waldsteinia.*

Rosa de Montana *Antigonon leptopus.*
Rosa Mundi *Rosa gallica* 'Versicolor'.
Rosary Vine *Ceropegia linearis* ssp. *woodii*; *Crassula rupestris.*

Roscoea Sm. Zingiberaceae. 17 perenn. rhizomatous herbs. St. reed-like with smooth linear-lanceolate lvs in 2 ranks or spiralling, bases sheathing, often auricled. Fls in term. condensed spikes or on distinct scapes; cor. tubular, pet. 3, posterior erect, hooded, laterals narrower, spreading, lip showy, staminodes petaloid. China, Himal. Z8.

R. alpina Royle. To 30cm. Lvs 1–4, 10cm. Fls in short hidden infl.; pink or mauve; posterior pet. circular, 2cm diam.; lip narrow, 2-lobed; staminodes 0.6–1.2cm, circular. Summer. Kashmir, Nepal. Z6.

R. alpina hort. non Royle = *R. scillifolia*.

R. auriculata Schum. To 55cm. Lvs to 25cm, 3–10, auriculate at base. Fls bright purple, enclosed in upper lf sheath; posterior pet. 3.5cm; staminodes 1.5–2cm, white. Summer–autumn. E Nepal, Sikkim. 'Beesiana' (*R. auriculata* ✕ *R. cautleoides*): st. to 45cm; lf bases strongly auriculate; fls yellow, sometimes streaked mauve. Z6.

R. capitata Sm. To 40cm. Lvs 20cm, usually 7. Fls 5–7, blue or purple, in dense capitate, spikes; cor. 5cm; lip 2cm. Himal. Z8.

R. cautleoides Gagnep. To 55cm. Lvs 15cm, 1–4. Infl. carried clear of lvs; fls 6–7, pale yellow; cor. tube longer than cal.; posterior pet. to 4cm, obovate; lip 3–4cm, obovate, 2-lobed; staminodes 1–2cm. 'Kew Beauty': lvs dark green; fls orchid-like, pale yellow. Z6.

R. chamaeleon Gagnep. = *R. cautleoides*.

R. humeana Balf. & Sm. To 34cm. Lvs 2–20cm, 4–6. Fls 2–4, purple or lilac, in short infl. hidden in lf sheaths; posterior pet. 2.5–4.5cm, longer than lateral pet.; lip large, obovate, deeply 2-lobed; staminodes 2.5cm diam., square. Spring–summer. SW China. Yellow-fld forms occur. Z7.

R. intermedia Gagnep. = *R. alpina*.
R. longifolia Bak. = *R. alpina*.
R. procera Wallich = *R. purpurea*.

R. purpurea Sm. To 30cm. Lvs to 25cm, 4–8. Infl. hidden in upper lf sheaths, pale purple or white with dark purple mark-

ings; posterior pet. 3–6cm, narrow, lip to 6cm, obovate, 2-lobed; staminodes slender, 2.5–4cm. Summer–autumn. Himal., Sikkim. Z6.

R. purpurea var. *procera* (Wallich) Bak. = *R. purpurea*.

R. scillifolia (Gagnep.) Cowley. To 37cm. Lvs 6–12cm, 1–6. Infl. carried clear of lvs on an exposed stalk; fls pink; posterior pet. 1.4–2cm, elliptic; lip to 2cm, narrow, 2-lobed or entire. Summer. SW China. Z8.

R. yunnanensis Loes. = *R. cautleoides*.

Rose *Rosa.*
Rose Acacia *Robinia hispida.*
Rose Apple *Syzygium jambos.*
Rose Balsam *Impatiens balsamina.*
Rose Banksia *Banksia laricina.*
Rose Bay *Nerium.*
Rosebay Willowherb *Epilobium angustifolium.*
Rosebud Cherry *Prunus subhirtella.*
Rosebud Orchid *Cleistes.*
Rose Cactus *Pereskia grandifolia.*
Rose Campion *Lychnis coronaria.*
Rose Coneflower *Isopogon dubius.*
Rose Geranium *Pelargonium graveolens.*
Rosegold Pussy Willow *Salix gracilistyla.*
Rose Gum *Eucalyptus grandis.*
Rose Leek *Allium canadense.*
Roselle *Hibiscus sabdariffa.*
Rose Mallee *Eucalyptus rhodantha.*
Rose Mallow *Hibiscus.*
Rose Mandarin *Streptopus roseus.*
Rosemary *Rosmarinus officinalis.*
Rosemary Willow *Salix elaeagnos.*
Rose Moss *Portulaca grandiflora.*

Roseocactus A. Berger.
R. lloydii (Rose) A. Berger = *Ariocarpus fissuratus*.

Roseocereus Backeb.
R. tetracanthus (Labouret) Backeb. = *Harrisia tetracantha*.

Rose of China *Hibiscus rosa-sinensis.*
Rose of Jericho *Anastatica; Selaginella lepidophylla.*
Rose of Sharon *Hypericum calycinum.*
Rose Penstemon *Penstemon floridus.*
Rose Periwinkle *Catharanthus roseus.*
Rose Pincushion *Mammillaria zeilmanniana.*
Rose Pink *Sabatia angularis.*
Rose Plantain *Plantago major.*
Rose-root *Rhodiola rosea.*
Rose Sage *Salvia pachyphylla.*
Rose-scented Geranium *Pelargonium capitatum.*
Rose Silky Oak *Placospermum coriaceum.*
Rose Vervain *Verbena canadensis.*
Rose Wood *Tipuana tipu.*
Rosilla *Helenium puberulum.*
Rosin-weed *Grindelia; Silphium.*

Rosmarinus L. Labiatae. 2 aromatic everg. shrubs. Lvs linear. Fls whorled, in short axillary rac.; cor. to 1.5cm, pale blue to lavender, rarely white or pink, 2-lipped, upper lip concave, 2-lobed, lower lip 3-lobed; sta. 2, strongly exserted. S Eur., N Afr.

R. eriocalyx Jordan & Fourr. Prostrate to erect to 1m. Lvs 5–15×1–2mm, glab. Infl. stellate-glandular-pubesc. N Afr., S Spain. ssp. *tomentosus* (Huber-Morath & Maire) Fernandez Casas. Lvs grey-tomentose, infl. densely tomentose. Z8.

R. lavandulaceus Noë = *R. officinalis*.
R. laxiflorus Noë = *R. officinalis*.

R. officinalis L. ROSEMARY. To 2m, erect or procumbent. Lvs 15–40×1.2–6mm, white-tomentose beneath, revolute. Infl. tomentose. Medit. 'Aureus': lvs speckled yellow. 'Albus': fls white. 'Arp': lvs light green, lemon-scented. 'Benenden Blue' ('Collingwood Ingram'): lvs narrow, dark green. 'Blue Boy': dwarf; lvs small. 'Golden Rain': lvs lush green, streaked gold. 'Lockwood de Forest': procumbent form of 'Tuscan Blue'. 'Majorca Pink': fls bright pink. 'Miss Jessop's Upright' ('Erectus'): tall, erect. 'Pinkie': erect; lvs narrow; fls bright pink. 'Prostratus': st. procumbent. 'Roseus': fls pink. 'Severn Sea': spreading, br. arching; fls deep violet. 'Tuscan Blue': lvs narrow; fls dark blue. Z6.

R. tournefortii (Murb) Jahandiez & Maire = *R. eriocalyx*.

Rossioglossum (Schltr.) Garay & Kenn. Orchidaceae. 6 epiphytic orchids. Pbs 5–10×3.5–6cm clustered, ovoid, laterally compressed. Lvs to 40×7cm, broadly elliptic to lanceolate, blue-green, scurfy at first, narrowing to short conduplicate petioles. Rac. lat., erect or bowed, few-fld; tep. subequal or with pet. wider; lip often pandurate or 3-lobed, deflexed, lat. lobes small, auriculate, midlobe large, callus prominent, fleshy or with protuberant horns. Mostly autumn–winter. Mex. to Panama. Z10.

R. grande (Lindl.) Garay & Kenn. CLOWN ORCHID. Rac. 14–30cm, 2–8-fld; fls to 15cm diam., wide-spreading, long-lived, waxy; sep. to 8.5×2cm, yellow, barred and flecked rust to glossy chestnut brown, lanceolate, acute to acuminate, undulate; pet. to broader, yellow, basal half deep red-brown, undulate; lip cream-white or cream-yellow, flecked or banded red-brown, to 4.5cm, pandurate, midlobe suborbicular to quadrate, ruffed, callus yellow, protuberances eye-like, ringed red. Late autumn–winter. Guat., Mex.

R. insleayi (Barker ex Lindl.) Garay & Kenn. Differs from *R. grande* in its revolute, slender tep. and broken banding on pet. Fls to 10cm diam.; tep. yellow or yellow-green, broken-banded chestnut-red, obtuse; lip bright yellow spotted red-cinnamon near margins, orbicular-reniform, midlobe narrowly clawed, spathulate, undulate; callus fleshy, obscurely bilobed. Mostly autumn. Mex.

R. powellii Schltr. = *R. schlieperianum*.

R. schlieperianum (Rchb. f.) Garay & Kenn. Fls to 10cm diam.; tep. pale yellow to bronze, blotched and barred yellow-ochre to rust, sep. ovate-lanceolate, subacute, margins incurved, pet. oblong-elliptic; lip similar colour to sep., pandurate, midlobe oblong-spathulate, obtuse to retuse, callus bright yellow marked red, with short central keel. Autumn. Costa Rica, Panama.

R. warscewiczii Bridges ex Stein = *R. schlieperianum*.

R. williamsianum (Rchb. f.) Garay & Kenn. Differs from *R. grande* in fls more numerous, smaller, with little red-brown blotching, pet. shorter, broader, broadly rounded. Spring. Costa Rica, Guat., Hond., Mex.

→*Odontoglossum* and *Oncidium*.

Rostraria Trin. Gramineae. 10 ann. grasses. St. bases occas. swollen. Lvs linear; ligule membranous. Infl. paniculate; br. rough; spikelets laterally flattened, to 10-fld. Summer. Temp. Eur., Asia, N Afr. Z6.

R. cristata (L.) Tzvelev. CAT TAIL GRASS. Ann. to 45cm. St. solitary to loosely clumped, erect or bent. Lvs flat, pubesc., to 18×0.8cm. Infl. cylindric to narrowly oblong, compact, to 12×1.5cm, pale green; spikelets to 0.8cm, to 8-fld.

→*Koeleria* and *Lophochloa*.

Rosularia (DC.) Stapf. Crassulaceae. 25 succulents. St. short, forming caudex with taproot. Lvs flat or keeled, oblong to spathulate in usually flat rosettes. Fls in terminal or lat. pan., tubular to funnel-shaped, 5-merous, campanulate. Asia Minor to Himal., Iberian Penins. and N Afr. Z7.

R. adenotricha (Wallich ex Edgew.) Jansson. Polymorphic with rosettes to 3cm, caudex 0. Lvs to 8×18mm, spathulate. Fls to 6mm, glandular-hairy, white to pale pink, veins purple. W slopes of Himal. ssp. **adenotricha**. Smaller and less glandular-hairy than ssp. *viguieri*. Rosette to 1.5cm. Lvs to 6×15mm, minutely serrate. ssp. **viguieri** (Raym.-Hamet) Jansson. Rosette to 3cm. Lvs spathulate, to 8×18mm, glandular-hairy, viscid. Infl. wholly gland.

R. aizoon (Fenzl) A. Berger. Rosettes to 3.5cm, in groups of 3–5. Lvs to 4×13mm, oblong to narrow-elliptical, fresh to blue-green, apex rounded, glandular-hairy. Fls to 9mm, to 8 per rac., densely glandular-hairy; yellow with coloured veins. Asia Minor. ssp. **alpestris** (Karel. & J. Kir.) Boriss. Rosettes to 4cm, caudex beetroot-shaped. Lvs to 5×20mm, oblong-acute, mucronate, glab. Fls white. C Asia. ssp. **marnieri** (Raym.-Hamet ex H. Ohba) U. Eggli. Resembles ssp. *aplestris* but slightly larger; infl. glab. below; pet. in erose, occas. rose.

R. chrysantha (Boiss.) Takht. Rosettes depressed-globose, to 2.5cm, caudex 0. Lvs to 4×14mm, fresh green, fleshy, oblong to narrow-elliptic, subglabrous to glandular-hairy, margin glandular-hairy. Rac. term.; fls to 14mm, sometimes villous, white to pale yellow, veins coloured. Summer. E Medit. (mts).

R. cypria (Holmb.) Meikle = *R. globulariifolia*.

R. globulariifolia (Fenzl) A. Berger. Rosettes to 8cm. Lvs to 9×28mm, oblong-spathulate, apex truncate or rounded, densely glandular-hairy, viscid, fresh to dull pale green, pine-scented. Fls in a spicate rac., wholly gland., to 7mm, white to pale yellow, veins coloured. Spring. E Medit. coasts.

R. haussknechtii (Boiss. & Reut.) A. Berger. Rosettes to 2cm. Lvs spathulate, to 4×18mm, subglabrous to glandular-hairy, ciliate. Fls to 9mm, in lat. rac., gland. Asia Minor.

R. libanotica (L.) Samuelsson = *R. serrata*.

R. lineata (Boiss.) A. Berger. Rosettes to 5cm. Lvs to 7×28mm, oblong-spathulate, apex truncate or rounded, fleshy, glandular-hairy, deep to dark green. Fls to 10mm, sweetly scented or malodorous, in lat. gland. rac., pink, veins darker. Jord. valley.

R. marnieri (H. Ohba) H. Ohba = *R. aizoon* ssp. *marnieri*.

R. pallida (Schott & Kotschy) Stapf = *R. aizoon*.

R. parvifolia Fröd. & Samuelsson ex Rech. f. = *R. sempervivum* ssp. *libanotica*.

R. persica (Boiss.) A. Berger = *R. sempervivum* ssp. *persica*.

R. pestalozzae (Boiss.) Samuelsson & Fröd. = *R. sempervivum* ssp. *amanensis*.

R. pestalozzae var. *glaberrima* (Bornm.) D.F. Chamberl. & Muirhead = *R. sempervivum* ssp. *glaucophylla*.

R. radiciflora ssp. *glabra* (Boiss.) D.F. Chamberl. & Muirhead = *R. sempervivum* ssp. *persica*.

R. radiciflora ssp. *kurdica* D.F. Chamberl. & Muirhead = *R. sempervivum* ssp. *kurdica*.

R. rechingeri Jansson. In cult. mostly called *R. turkestanica*. Rosettes to 20mm, semi-globular, forming compact cushions. Lvs to 3×10mm, ovate to spathulate, apex rounded, glab., margin gland. Fls to 15mm, red-glandular-hairy; pale yellow to green, venation red or purple. Asia Minor.

R. rosae Fed. = *R. sempervivum* ssp. *sempervivum*.

R. sedoides (Decne.) H. Ohba. Rosettes semi-globose, to 35mm, caudex 0, resinous scent when bruised. Lvs to 10×20mm, spathulate to ovoid, apex rounded, glandular-hairy, sometimes succulent. Fls to 8mm, in lat. gland. rac., white to green-tinged. S Himal.

R. sedoides var. *alba* (Edgew.) P.J. Mitch. = *R. sedoides*.

R. sempervivum (Bieb.) A. Berger. Rosettes flat to semi-globose, caudex usually present. Fls in lat. rac., outline paniculate. Asia Minor to Iran. ssp. **sempervivum**. Rosette to 4cm, on branched caudex. Lvs to 15×45mm, oblong-truncate, sometimes spathulate, dull or shiny. Fls to 10mm; pink, veins tinged purple. Summer. Irano-Turkey. ssp. **amanensis** U. Eggli. Pine-scented. Rosettes to 8cm, caudex 0. Lvs to 11×40mm, spathulate to obtrullate, gland., dark green. Fls to 8mm, in decumbent or pendulous rac., white or pale pink. Summer. E Medit. ssp. **glaucophylla** U. Eggli. Rosette to 5cm. Lvs to 12×24mm, glaucous-blue, serrulate or denticulate. Fls to 9mm on viscid rac., pale pink. Summer. E Medit. ssp. **kurdica** U. Eggli. Rosette to 8cm. Lvs to 10×30mm, pale to grey-green, never glaucous, serrate. Fls to 9mm, pale yellow to ivory, venation occas. red. Irano-Turkey. ssp. **libanotica** (Labill.) U. Eggli. Rosette to 6cm. Lvs to 6×30mm, semi-erect, oblong-truncate or spathulate, glandular-hairy, viscid, pine-scented. Fls to 10mm, viscid, pale pink. E Medit. ssp. **persica** (Boiss.) U. Eggli. Rosettes to 6cm. Lvs to 8×25mm, glab., serrulate to dentate. Fls to 11mm, pink with darker venation. Middle East. ssp. **pestalozzae** (Boiss.) U. Eggli. Rosette flat, to 5cm. Lvs to 11×32mm, glandular-hairy. Fls to 8mm in gland. rac., pale pink.

R. sempervivum var. *lineata* (Boiss.) Thiéb. = *R. lineata*.

R. serpentinica (Werderm.) Muirhead. Closely related to *R. chrysantha*, distinguished by the glab. sterile rosettes and by the darker lvs with a blue tinge, and apical hydathode. E Medit. var. **serpentinica**. Rosettes to 2cm, forming compact mats. Lvs to 3×10mm, gland. with red venation. var. **gigantea** U. Eggli Rosettes to 7cm, not mat-forming. Lvs to 9×35mm. Fls to 15mm.

R. serrata (L.) A. Berger. Rosettes to 6cm, forming loose cushions. Lvs to 10×30mm, spathulate, glaucous, in dry periods tinged purple or brown, margin horny, denticulate to serrate. Fls to 8mm, white to pale pink. E Medit.

R. setosa M. Bywater = *R. lineata*.

R. spatulata Hort. plur. angl. = *R. sempervivum* ssp. *glaucophylla*.

R. turkestanica hort. non *R. turkestanica* (Reg. & Winkl.) A. Berger = *R. rechingeri*.

→*Sedum* and *Umbilicus*.

Rosy Baeckea *Baeckea ramosissima*.
Rosy Garlic *Allium roseum*.
Rosy Maidenhair Fern *Adiantum hispidulum*.
Rosy Sunray *Acroclinium roseum*.

Rotala L. Lythraceae. 44 semi-aquatic ann. herbs; st. branched. Lvs whorled or opposite, ± sessile, entire, base attenuate. Fls small, axillary or in term. spikes, sometimes umbellate; cal. 3–6-lobed; pet. 3–6 or 0, inconspicuous; sta. 1–6. S Asia.

R. indica (Willd.) Koehne. To 30cm. Lvs opposite, obovate to spathulate, to 17mm, translucent, margins thickened. Fls solitary, purple. Summer. Jap. to India and Malay Penins., nat. Calif. through rice culture.

Rotanger Boehm. = *Calamus*.

Rothmannia Thunb. Rubiaceae. 30 shrubs or small trees. Lvs usually prominently veined. Fls sessile or short-pedicellate, axill. or term., solitary, clustered or in cymes; cal. tube top-shaped to cylindric, limb fleshy, truncate or 5-lobed; cor. bell- or funnel-shaped, lobes usually 5, spreading, oval to lanceolate;

sta. and anth. included or short-exserted. Trop. Afr., Madag., Asia. Z10.

R. capensis Thunb. CANDLEWOOD. Tree to 14m. Lvs to 10×4cm, oval to elliptic or broadly lanceolate, glab., lustrous, dark green above and paler below. Fls solitary, white or cream to yellow, fragrant, to 8cm, funnel-shaped. S Afr.

R. fratrum K. Krause = R. manganjae.

R. globosa (Hochst.) Keay. SEPTEMBER BELLS. Shrub or tree to 7m. Lvs to 12×4cm, elliptic to oblanceolate, midrib and lat. veins yellow or pink to maroon. Fls axill. or terminal, solitary or 2–4 in cymes, white, occas. pink-tinged, fragrant, bell-shaped, to 3×4cm. S Afr.

R. longiflora Salisb. Shrub or tree, to 5m+. Lvs to 14×6cm, elliptic to elliptic-obovate, glab., lustrous, dark green. Fls term., solitary, fragrant, to 22×9cm, funnel-shaped, pubesc., lobes white, interior red- or purple-patched. Trop. W Afr.

R. macrantha (Schult.) Robyns = Euclinia longiflora.

R. manganjae (Hiern) Keay. SCENTED BELLS. Shrub or tree, to 7m+. Lvs to 11×5cm, elliptic or lanceolate, glab., lustrous. Fls axill. or term., solitary or to 3 in clusters, to 8×5cm, funnel- to bell-shaped, pubesc., white to cream and red- or purple-flecked. Trop. E Afr., S Afr.

R. urcelliformis (Hiern) Robyns. Shrub or tree to 9m. Lvs to 13×5cm, oblanceolate or elliptic, glab., occas. pubesc. in axils beneath. Fls solitary, funnel- or bell-shaped, to 10cm, pubesc., white to cream or pale green, mottled pink, red, or purple. Trop. Afr.

→Gardenia and Randia.

Rottnest Island Cypress-pine Callitris preissii.
Rouen Lilac Syringa ×chinensis.
Rouen Pansy Viola hispida.
Rouge Plant Rivina humilis.
Rough-barked Apple Angophora floribunda.
Rough-barked Manna Gum Eucalyptus viminalis.
Rough-barked Mexican Pine Pinus montezumae.
Rough Bristle Grass Setaria viridis.
Rough Brome Bromus squarrosus.
Rough Dog's-tail Grass Cynosurus echinatus.
Rough Hawkbit Leontodon hispidus.
Rough Horsetail Equisetum hyemale.
Rough-leaf Fig Ficus hispida.
Rough Maidenhair Fern Adiantum hispidulum.
Rough Net-bush Calothamnus asper.
Rough Pea Lathyrus hirsutus.
Rough Poppy Papaver ×hybridum.
Rough Rubber Tree Ficus hispida.
Rough Saxifrage Saxifraga aspera.
Rough Tree Fern Cyathea australis.
Rough Velvet-seed Guettarda scabra.
Rough Wattle Acacia aspera.
Round Cardamom Amomum compactum.
Round-fruited Banksia Banksia sphaerocarpa.
Round-fruited Rush Juncus compressus.
Round-headed Club-rush Scirpoides holoschoenus.
Round-headed Leek Allium sphaerocephalum.
Round-headed Rampion Phyteuma orbiculare.
Round Kumquat Fortunella japonica.
Round-leafed Gum Eucalyptus perriniana.
Round-leafed Moort Eucalyptus platypus.
Round-leaved Dogwood Cornus rugosa.
Round-leaved Mallee Eucalyptus orbifolia.
Round-leaved Mint Bush Prostanthera rotundifolia.
Round-leaved Saxifrage Saxifraga rotundifolia.
Round-leaved Sundew Drosera rotundifolia.
Round-leaved Synthyris Synthyris reniformis.
Round-leaved Willow Salix rotundifolia.
Round-leaved Wintergreen Pyrola rotundifolia.

Roupala Aubl. Proteaceae. 50 trees or shrubs. Lvs leathery, rigid, entire or toothed, simple or ppinnate (sometimes on same tree). Fls in axill. or term. rac. to 20cm; perianth cylindrical; pet. 4, recurved at tips with a sta. inserted at the middle of each. Capsule hard, short-stalked. Trop. Amer. Z10.

R. aurea Lind. Shrub or small tree. Young shoots and lf stalks densely clothed with golden hairs. Braz.

R. complicata HBK. Shrub 2–3m. Lvs 3.5–12.5cm, ovate, glaucous, entire or bluntly toothed, slender-pointed, base rounded. Colomb.

R. corcovadensis hort. en Meissn. = R. macrophylla.

R. heterophylla Pohl. Shrub or small tree, 3m. Lvs 50cm, pinnate, lfts 9–13, 7–12.5cm, ovate, pointed, bluntly toothed, lustrous above, veins prominent. Braz.

R. macrophylla Pohl. Tree to 10m. Young shoots rusty-tomentose. Lvs aromatic, to 30cm, simple or pinnate, with lfts

5–8 pairs, to 12.5cm, ovate, acuminate, coarsely toothed, simple lvs to 15cm, broadly ovate, coarsely toothed. Braz.

R. montana Aubl. Shrub or small tree, 2.5–3m. Lvs 5–10cm, ovate to oval, slender-pointed, rather plicate. Fr. Guyana, Costa Rica, W Indies.

R. obovata Kunth. Tree 6–8m. Lvs simple, 7.5–15cm, obovate, shortly pointed, sparsely toothed or entire, glab. Colomb., Ecuad.

R. pohlii Meissn. in part. = R. macrophylla.

Rowan Sorbus aucuparia.
Rowan Sorbus aucuparia.
Rowe Ceanothus Ceanothus papillosus var. roweanus.
Roxburgh Fig Ficus auriculata.
Royal Agave Agave victoriae-reginae.
Royal Climber Oxera.
Royal Fern Osmunda regalis.
Royal Jasmine Jasminum officinale f. grandiflorum.
Royal Kafferboom Erythrina latissima.
Royal Paint Brush Scadoxus puniceus.
Royal Palm Roystonea.
Royal Poinciana Delonix regia.
Royal Red Bugler Aeschynanthus pulcher.
Royal Trumpet Vine Distictis 'Rivers'
Royal Velvet Plant Gynura aurantiaca.
Royal Water Lily Victoria amazonica.

Roystonea Cook. ROYAL PALM. Palmae. 10–12 solitary, unarmed palms. St. columnar, straight or swollen, ringed. Crownshaft distinct. Lvs pinnate; pinnae single-fold, regularly spaced along rachis in 1 plane, or clustered and in several planes, often hairy, midrib or sometimes scaly. Carib.

R. borinquena Cook. PUERTO RICAN ROYAL. To 18m. Trunk, spindle-shaped, c60cm diam. at base. Lvs to 3×2m, arched, pinnae 1m×3–6cm, crowded, in 2 rows, scurfy beneath, apex divided. Puerto Rico, Viques, St. Croix.

R. caribaea P. Wils. = R. borinquena and R. oleracea.

R. elata (Bartr.) F. Harper. Differs from R. regia, in nerves each side of midrib inconspicuous or 0. S Flor.

R. floridana Cook = R. elata and R. regia.

R. hispaniolana Bail. HISPANIOLAN ROYAL PALM. Trunk to 15m, not swollen, often leaning or crooked. Lvs to 20 in a crown, dull green, lower lvs pendent. Hispan.

R. jenmanii (C.H. Wright) Burret. To 9m. Trunk somewhat swollen at centre. Rachis triangular; pinnae 7.5×2.5cm, linear-lanceolate, nerves 10. Known only in cult.

R. oleracea (Jacq.) Cook. To 30m. Trunk swollen at base to 1m diam., narrowing to 45cm diam. above. Crownshaft 2–5m, bright green; lvs 3–7×2cm, horizontal or erect; pinnae to 1m×5cm, in one plane, ribs 4 pairs. Trin., Barbados.

R. princeps (Becc.) Burret. MORASS ROYAL. Trunk to 12m, base to 30cm diam., thickened in middle or narrowed in upper half. Lvs to 3×2m, spreading; pinnae to 90×2–4cm, 165–F170 per side, ribs prominent beneath, grey beneath, apex shallowly divided. Jam.

R. regia (HBK) Cook. CUBAN ROYAL. Trunk to 25m, thickened in middle, often swollen at base, sometimes leaning or crooked. Lower lvs decurved or pendent, covering crownshaft and infl., shorter than in R. oleracea; pinnae to 1m×2–4cm in 2 rows and differing planes, ribs 2–3. Cuba.

R. venezuelana L.H. Bail. Trunk to 30m, swollen at base. Lvs to 4m, ascending or horizontal, clearing crownshaft and infl., grey-glaucous beneath; pinnae to 1m×3–4cm, in 2–4 rows per side, apex divided. E Venez.

→Euterpe, Gorgasia and Oreodoxa.

Rubber Euphorbia Euphorbia tirucalli.
Rubber Plant Ficus elastica; Hevea.
Rubber Vine Cryptostegia grandiflora.

Rubia L. Rubiaceae. Some 60 herbs or subshrubs. St. climbing, diffuse, or erect, 4-angled, glab., rough or prickly. Lvs whorled or opposite. Fls in axill. or term. pan. or cymes; cal. tube globose to ovoid, limb 0 or forming a swollen rim; cor. rotate, bell- or funnel-shaped, lobes 4–5, ovate-lanceolate, anth. 4–5, exserted. Fr. red to black berry-like. Eur., Afr., Asia.

R. conotricha Gand. = R. cordifolia.

R. cordifolia L. INDIAN MADDER; MUNJEET. Perenn. herb to 6m, climbing or creeping, usually rough, prickly and pubesc., 4-angled. Lvs to 8cm, lanceolate to ovate or cordate, glab. to rough and pubesc., prickly, petiolate. Fls to 3×1mm, in loose, trichotomous cymes to 3cm or more, cream to yellow or green. Eur., Afr., Asia. Z6.

R. longipetiolata Bullock = R. cordifolia.

R. peregrina L. WILD MADDER; LEVANT MADDER. Perenn., everg. herb, climbing, scrambling or creeping, to 120cm, woody, below, 4-angled above, rough, prickly. Lvs to 6cm, sessile, linear, lanceolate, elliptic, or ovate, leathery, lustrous, rough and prickly beneath, prickly or toothed and cartilaginous at margin. Fls to 6×6mm many in cymose pan. to 10cm, light yellow-green. W & S Eur., N Afr., Middle E. Z7.

R. tinctoria L. MADDER. Perenn. herb. Climbing or scrambling, to 1m, woody below, rough and prickly or hairy; rhiz. red. Lvs to 10×3cm, subsessile, lanceolate to oblong, leathery, rough and prickly or toothed on nerves beneath and at margin. Fls to 3×5mm, in loose, much-branched, leafy cymes to 30cm, yellow-green to honey-coloured. E Medit. to C Asia. Z6.

RUBIACEAE Juss. 630/10,400. *Alibertia, Anthospermum, Asperula, Bouvardia, Burchellia, Canthium, Catesbaea, Catunaregam, Cephalanthus, Chiococca, Chomelia, Cinchona, Coffea, Coprosma, Cosmibuena, Coutarea, Craterispermum, Crucianella, Crusea, Damnacanthus, Emmenopterys, Euclinia, Galium, Gardenia, Genipa, Gonzalagunia, Guettarda, Hamelia, Hoffmannia, Houstonia, Hydnophytum, Isertia, Ixora, Leptodermis, Lindenia, Luculia, Manettia, Mitchella, Mitragyna, Mitriostigma, Morinda, Mussaenda, Myrmecodia, Nauclea, Nertera, Oldenlandia, Palicourea, Pavetta, Pentas, Phuopsis, Pinckneya, Pogonopus, Portlandia, Posoqueria, Psilanthus, Psychotria, Psydrax, Putoria, Randia, Ravnia, Richardia, Rondeletia, Rothmannia, Rubia, Sarcocephalus, Serissa, Sherardia, Spermadictyon, Tarenna, Vangueria, Warszewiczia, Wendlandia.*

Rubus L. Rosaceae. *c*250 erect, scrambling, trailing or prostrate shrubs, often prickly and bristly. Lvs entire, lobed or divided, usually toothed; stipules often conspicuous. Fls in clusters, rac. or pan., sometimes solitary; sep. 4–5+; pet. 4–5 or rarely more (occas. 0), spreading or erect; sta. numerous. Fr. a 'berry' composed of 5 to many coherent fleshy drupelets, which may separate from the receptacle as a (hollow) unit. Cosmopolitan.

R. adenophorus Rolfe. Robust decid. shrub, 2.5m or more. St. stout, erect or arching, villous and stipitate-glandular, with stiff, short prickles. Lvs to 30cm, pinnate, or simple above; lfts 3–5, to 12.5×9cm, ovate, acuminate, rounded or cordate at base, biserrate, dull and pubesc. above, grey-green beneath. Fls pink, small, in term. cylindrical pan. to 12.5cm; pet. dentate; pedicels and cal. densely setose and gland. Fr. 12.5mm diam., black. Summer. C China. Z6.

R. albescens Roxb. = *R. niveus.*

R. allegheniensis L.H. Bail. ALLEGHANY BLACKBERRY; SOW-TEAT BLACKBERRY. Decid. shrub to 3m. St. erect to arching, glandular-woolly, with hooked prickles. Lvs 3–5-foliolate, petioles glandular-woolly; lfts to 20.5cm, ovate, acuminate, biserrate, woolly beneath. Fls white in rac. to 20cm; cal. pubesc., gland.; pet. narrow. Fr. conic, black, to 12.5mm. N Amer. Z3.

R. almus (L.H. Bail.) L.H. Bail. MAYES DEWBERRY. Prostrate to 2m. St. terete, glab., with scattered prickles. Lvs soft-pubesc. beneath; lfts 3–7, elliptic-ovate, to 8cm, acute, finely serrate. Fls in rac.; cal. dense-pubesc.; pet. broad. Fr. oblong, 3cm. SW US. Z8.

R. amabilis Focke. Decid. shrub to 2m. Young shoots woolly, with small prickles. Lvs pinnate, to 20cm; petiole and rachis with needle-like prickles; lfts to 5×2.5cm, ovate, acute, sharply toothed, woolly on veins. Fls white, to 5cm diam., solitary, nodding; pedicel sericeous, prickly; sep. cuspidate, hairy and gland.; pet. suborbicular. Fr. conic, to 16mm, red. Summer. W China. Z6.

R. andersonii Hook. f., non Lef. = *R. splendidissimus.*

R. arcticus L. CRIMSON BRAMBLE; ARCTIC BRAMBLE. Herbaceous, to 30cm, without prickles. Lvs long-stalked, with 3–5 ovate lfts, serrate, glab. Fls pink or red, to 2.5cm diam., in 1–3-fld infl.; sep. glab., pet. ovate, often emarginate; sta. purple. Fr. dark red. Summer. Circumpolar. *R. stellatus* Sm. (NAGOONBERRY; KNESHENEKA) is conspecific, but smaller, with deeper red pet. and v. small globose fr. Z1.

R. armeniacus Focke = *R. procerus.*

R. australis Forst. See under *R. cissoides.*

R. australis sensu auct., in part, non Forst. = *R. cissoides.*

R. australis var. *cissoides* (A. Cunn.) Hook. = *R. cissoides.*

R. bambusarum Focke = *R. henryi* var. *bambusarum.*

R. barbatus Edgew. ex Rehd. non Fritsch = *R. nepalensis.*

R. bellobatus L.H. Bail. Erect, to 2m. Lvs, soft-pubesc. to tomentose beneath, sharply toothed; lfts 5, ovate, to 10cm, abruptly acuminate, cordate to subcordate at base. Fls 6–9 per rac.; pet. oblong, blunt. Fr. oblong to subglobose, to 3cm. NE US. Z4.

R. 'Benenden' (*R. deliciosus* × *R. trilobus.*) Erect, vigorous to 3m. Br. arching. Bark peeling. Lvs 3–5-lobed. Fls to 5cm diam., solit., axill.; pet. broad, bright white; sta. golden. Gdn origin.

R. biflorus Buch.-Ham. ex Sm. Decid. shrub to 3m. St. erect, white-glaucous, with straight prickles. Lvs to 25cm; petiole and rachis bristly; lfts 3–5, ovate to elliptic, to 10cm, acute or acuminate, sharply toothed, dark green above, white-tomentose beneath. Fls white, 1–1.7cm diam., terminal and axill.; cal. glab. Fr. round, to 2cm diam., yellow. Summer. Himal. Z9.

R. bifrons Vest ex Tratt. Semi-evergreen. St. much-branched, stout, tinged red, with needle-like prickles. Lfts orbicular or shortly obovate, shortly acuminate or cuspidate, truncate or subcordate at base, dark green, glab. 3–5, above, white-tomentose beneath. Fls light pink to red, in long woolly, prickly racs; pet. suborbicular, large; sta. white or light pink. Carpels sparsely pubesc. W & C Eur. Z6.

R. buergeri Miq. Shrub. St. slender, creeping, sometimes prickly, short-pubesc. Lvs to 10cm, suborbicular, rounded to subacute, cordate at the base, deep green, serrate, shortly pubesc. on veins above, pilose beneath. Fls in clusters; cal. yellow-pubesc.; pet. to 8mm. Fr. hemispheric, to 2.5cm, red. S Korea, Taiwan, China. Z6.

R. caesius L. DEWBERRY; EUROPEAN DEWBERRY. Decid. shrub. St. slender, creeping, pruinose when young, prickly. Lfts 3, rhombic-ovate, 2–3-lobed, to 7cm, subcordate at base, coarsely serrate, green, somewhat pubesc. Fls white, to 3cm diam., in small clusters; pedicels long, pubesc., gland.; pet. broadly elliptic; sta. green. Fr. large, black, pruinose. Eur., N Asia. Hybrids of this sp. are often referred to as *R.* × *dumetorum*. Z5.

R. calycinoides hort. non Kuntze = *R. pentalobus.*

R. calycinoides Hayata non Kuntze = *R. pentalobus.*

R. canadensis L. AMERICAN DEWBERRY. Decid. shrub to 4m. St. erect, recurved, furrowed, puberulous initially, tinged purple, with few or no prickles. Lfts 3–5, ovate to obovate, to 15cm, acute or acuminate, rounded or subcordate at base, serrate, term. lft long-stalked. Fls white, in villous or pubesc., leafy rac. to 15cm; pet. obovate, to 1.5cm. Fr. round, black. Summer. N Amer. Z3.

R. candicans Lasch = *R. linkianus.*

R. chamaemorus L. CLOUDBERRY; MALKA; SALMONBERRY; YELLOW-BERRY; BAKE APPLE; BAKED-APPLE; BAKED-APPLE BERRY. To 20cm. St. dying back each year, without prickles, gland. Lvs simple, reniform, to 7cm, deep green, rugose, 3–5-lobed, crenate-serrate. Fls white, solitary; pedicels and cal. shortly gland.; pet. to 1cm. Fr. yellow or orange. Summer. N hemis. Z2.

R. chroosepalus Focke. Semi-evergreen straggling shrub. St. slender, glab., with short prickles. Lvs simple, to 18cm, cordate, long-acuminate, finely serrate, shallowly lobed, glab., with few prickles. Fls to 1.2cm diam., in pan. to 23cm; cal. woolly, purple inside; pet. 0. Fr. small, black. C China. Z6.

R. cissoides A. Cunn. BUSH LAWYER. Scandent, everg., shrub. St. stout, unarmed; br. with reddish prickles. Lfts 3–5, variable, to 15×2cm, linear-lanceolate to ovate-lanceolate, glab. and shiny above, toothed, petioles and petiolules with prickles. Fls white, to 1.2cm diam., in much-branched pan. to 60cm. Fr. red-orange. NZ. Some material cultivated under this name may belong to the juvenile phase of the true *R. australis* Forst.. Z9.

R. clemens Focke = *R. setchuenensis.*

R. cockburnianus Hemsl. Decid. shrub to 3m. St. erect, much-branched, strongly white-glaucous, sparsely prickly; br. arching. Lvs pinnate, to 20cm; petioles woolly, with hooked prickles; lfts 9, to 6cm, ovate, or rhomboid or oval-lanceolate, acuminate, serrate, white-tomentose beneath. Fls purple, small, in term. pan. to 12cm. Fr. black. N & C China. Z6.

R. corchorifolius L. f. Decid. shrub to 2.5m. St. erect, terete, finely woolly when young, prickly. Lvs simple, oval, to 18cm, cordate at base, sometimes deeply 3-lobed, serrate, dull dark green above, paler and woolly beneath. Fls white, to 3cm diam., solitary or 2–3 together; pet. oblong, to 1cm. Fr. globose, bright red, shortly pubesc. Summer. C China, Korea, Jap. Z6.

R. coreanus Miq. Decid. shrub, to 3m. St. erect or arching, angled, with stout prickles, blue-white-glaucous. Lfts 5–7, ovate or elliptic, to 7cm, acute, broadly tapered or rounded at base, serrate, dark green above, white-tomentose beneath. Fls pink, rather small, in 3–5-fld corymbs to 7cm. Fr. small, red or black. Summer. Korea, Jap., China. Z6.

R. coronarius Sweet = *R. rosifolius* 'Coronarius'.

R. cuneifolius Pursh. SAND BLACKBERRY. Shrub to 50cm, of stiff habit. St. erect, branched, prickly. Lvs white-pubesc. beneath; petiole stout, to 5cm, pubesc.; lfts 3–5, usually obovate, to 5cm, obtuse to acute, toothed. Fls white or pink, to 3cm diam., in 3–5-fld clusters. Fr. oblong, black, to 9mm. E US. Z6.

R. deliciosus Torr. ROCKY MOUNTAIN FLOWERING RASPBERRY; ROCKY MOUNTAIN RASPBERRY. Decid. shrub to 3m. Bark peeling; br. spreading or arching, lacking prickles. Lvs to 7cm, reniform to orbicular-ovate, truncate or cordate at base, lobes 3–5, broad, rounded, toothed, gland. and sparsely pilose on the veins beneath. Fls pure white, to 5cm diam., usually solitary; sep.

candate, woolly. Fr. hemispheric, to 1.5cm diam., dark purple. Spring. W US (Rocky mts). V. similar to *R. trilobus*. Z5.

R. discolor misapplied non Weihe & Nees = *R. procerus.*

R. ellipticus Sm. Strongly-growing, scrambling everg. shrub to 4.5m. St. red- or brown-pubesc., with bristles and stout prickles. Lfts 3, broadly elliptic, rounded at the apex, serrate, grey-tomentose beneath, midrib prickly. Fls white, small, in few-fld pan. Fr. yellow. Himal., SW China. Z8.

R. flagellaris Willd. DEWBERRY; AMERICAN DEWBERRY; NORTHERN DEWBERRY. Shrub to 2m. St. prostrate, glab., with scattered prickles. Lfts 3–5, to 10cm, ovate or rhombic-ovate to oblanceolate, acute or abruptly acuminate, tapered or rounded at the base, serrate, pubesc. on veins beneath. Fls solitary, rarely 2–4 together; pet. elliptic-obovate, to 1.5cm. Fr. rounded to oblong, to 1.5cm, black, glab. E N Amer. Z3.

R. flagelliflorus Focke. Scrambling or procumbent everg. shrub to 2m. St. slender, white-tomentose when young, with minute prickles. Lvs simple, to 18cm, broadly ovate, acuminate, cordate at base, scarcely lobed, finely serrate, yellow-tomentose beneath. Fls white, in short axill. clusters. Fr. to 12.5mm diam., black. Summer. C & W China. Z7.

R. flosculosus Focke. Decid. shrub to 3.5m. St. stout, erect, arching purple-brown, with a few prickles. Lvs pinnate, to 18cm; lfts 5–7, ovate, to 4cm, term. leaflet to 7.5cm, often 3-lobed, white-tomentose beneath, coarsely serrate. Fls pink, to 6.5mm diam., in narrow cylindric rac. to 10cm. Fr. small, dark red or black. Summer. Z6.

R. ×*fraseri* Rehd. (*R. odoratus* ×*parviflorus*.) Vigorous, compact shrub to 2.5m. Branchlets and petioles less glandular-pubesc. than *R. odoratus*, lobes of lvs acuminate. Fls rose, later pale purple. Gdn origin. Z5.

R. frondosus Bigelow. St. erect or recurved, glab., with stout, prickles. Lfts 5, to 14cm, thick, suborbicular, or obovate, abruptly acuminate, cordate, or broadly cuneate at the base, serrate, subglabrous above, softly-pubesc. beneath, term. lft long-stalked. Fls white, in leafy, villous, eglandular corymbs; pet. broadly oval or suborbicular, to 1cm. Fr. black, glab. E N Amer. Z5.

R. fruticosus agg. L. A group name applied to all the micro-species of Subgenus *Rubus* collectively. Z6.

R. glaucus Benth. Similar to *R. occidentalis* but lfts finely toothed, hairless above, fr. red-black. C & S Amer. Z8.

R. gracilis Roxb. non Presl = *R. hypargyrus* var. *niveus.*

R. henryi Hemsl. & Kuntze. Scrambling everg. shrub to 6m. St. slender, with a few prickles, tomentose-floccose when young. Lvs trilobed, to 15cm, glab. above, white-tomentose beneath, lobes to 2.5cm, narrow, long-acuminate, serrate. Fls pink, to 2cm diam., in 6–10-fld; gland. rac. to 7.5cm; pet. acuminate, glandular-pubesc. Fr. 6.5mm diam., shiny, black. C & W China. var. *bambusarum* (Focke) Rehd. Branchlets with more, small, hooked prickles; lfts 3, narrowly lanceolate, to 12.5cm. C China. Z7.

R. hispidus L. SWAMP DEWBERRY; RUNNING BLACKBERRY; SWAMP BLACKBERRY. Semi-evergreen shrub to 1.5m. St. prostrate, wiry, with minute prickles, bristly. Lfts 3, obovate, to 4.5×2cm, coarsely serrate above, ± glab. Fls white, to 3cm in diam., in finely pubesc., few-fld corymbs to 30cm, pet. obovate, to 8mm. Fr. to 12mm, red, later almost black. Summer. E N Amer. Z3.

R. hupehensis Oliv. Prostrate or scrambling everg. shrub, st. thin, dark, woolly when young, with minute prickles. Lvs simple, to 11.5cm, oblong-lanceolate, long-acuminate, finely serrate, ± smooth above, grey-tomentose beneath. Fls in short, term., glandular-pubesc. rac.; cal. grey-tomentose; pet. caducous. Fr. red at first, later purple-black. C China. Z8.

R. hypargyrus Edgew. Shrub to 3m. Branchlets pubesc., eglandular, with weak prickles. Lfts 3, to 10cm, ovate, the term. long-stalked, acuminate, rounded or cuneate at base, serrate, thinly pubesc. above, hairy or subglabrous beneath. Fls pink or red, solitary or in 2–5-fld, short axillary rac.; pet. obovate, to 6mm. Fr. to 1cm, red or orange. E Himal. var. *niveus* (Wallich ex G. Don) Hara. Lvs white-tomentose beneath. E Himal. Z8.

R. ichangensis Hemsl. & Kuntze. Decid. shrub. St. long, thin, with small prickles and dark gland. bristles. Lvs to 18cm, narrowly ovate-cordate, acuminate, cordate at base, ± glab., sparsely serrate. Fls white, to 6.5mm diam., in elongate, term. pan. to 30cm or more. Fr. small, bright red. C & W China. Z6.

R. idaeus L. RASPBERRY; WILD RASPBERRY; RED RASPBERRY; EUROPEAN RASPBERRY; FRAMBOISE. To 1.5m. St. erect, bloomed, bristly and softly hairy, usually with weak prickles. Lvs usually pinnate; lfts 3–7 ovate or oblong, occas. somewhat lobed, all shortly acuminate, cordate at the base, glabrescent above, white-tomentose, beneath. Fls white, to 1cm diam., in few-fld, leafy, term. and axill. rac. Fr. red or orange. Eur., N Asia, Jap. 'Aureus': low-growing; lvs clear bright yellow. 'Phyllanthus': fls replaced by tasselled green shoots, infl. divided. var. *strigosus* (Michx.) Maxim. AMERICAN RASPBERRY.

Densely glandular-bristly. N Amer. 'Albus': fr. orange-yellow. Z3.

R. illecebrosus Focke. Subshrub to 90cm. St. creeping, bearing erect, angled, green, prickly shoots. Lvs pinnate; lfts 5–7 to 7.5×2cm, lanceolate, acuminate, serrate, usually woolly beneath. Fls white, to 4.5cm in diam., solitary or 2–3 in bracteate corymbs. Fr. rounded or broadly ellipsoid, to 3cm diam., red. Summer. Jap. Z5.

R. incisus Thunb. = *R. microphyllus.*

R. innominatus hort. = *R. kuntzeanus.*

R. irenaeus Focke. Prostrate everg. shrub. St. terete, thin, grey-tomentose, with many small prickles. Lvs simple, rounded and to 15cm, abruptly acuminate, cordate at base, margins bristly-serrate, occas. obscurely lobed, dark glab. above, pale brown-tomentose beneath. Fls white, to 2cm in diam., in few-fld axill. clusters. Fr. large, red. C & W China. Z9.

R. koehneanus Focke = *R. microphyllus.*

R. kuntzeanus Hemsl. Decid. shrub to 3m. St. erect, grey-velutinous, with few, short prickles. Lvs to 30cm; lfts 3–5, to 10×6.5cm, ovate, acute, rounded or cordate at base, toothed, dark shiny green above, white-tomentose beneath. Fls pink, to 1.2cm in diam., in term. pan. to 45cm. Fr. rounded, to 2cm, orange-red. C & W China. Z6.

R. laciniatus Willd. CUT-LEAVED BRAMBLE; CUT-LEAF BLACK-BERRY; PARSLEY-LEAVED BRAMBLE. Scrambling, decid. shrub. St. robust, angled, pubesc. with stout, recurved prickles. Lfts 3–5, divided into pairs of laciniate seg., glab. or pubesc. beneath. Fls pink-white, in large term. pan.; pet. toothed. Fr. to 2cm, black. Origin unknown. 'Elegans': lvs small, upper lf hairy; fls and fr. rare. Z5.

R. lambertianus Ser. Semi-evergreen shrub. St. angled, with few prickles, tomentulose then glab. Lvs ovate to oblong-ovate, to 12cm, cordate at base, crenate-dentate and somewhat lobed or occas. 3-lobed, pilose beneath. Fls white, to 8mm diam., in pan. to 14cm. Fr. small, red. Summer. C China. Z6.

R. lasiostylus Focke. Decid. shrub to 2m. St. erect, with bristle-like prickles, glaucous-white. Lfts 3–5 ovate, to 10cm, term. leaflet larger, all acute or acuminate, rounded or subcordate at the base, often 3-lobed, serrate, white-tomentose beneath. Fls maroon, 2.5–3.5cm in diam., in few-fld clusters. Fr. ± spherical, red with long, off-white hairs. Summer. C China. Z7.

R. laudatus A. Berger. Tall, vigorous shrub. St. erect, woolly then glab., dark brown, prickly. Lfts 3–5, obovate-oblong to oblanceolate, acuminate, tapered or subcordate at the base, green and glab. above, paler and pubesc. beneath, serrate. Fls white in 7–8-fld, infl. Fr. oval, black. C US. Z4.

R. leucodermis Torr. & A. Gray. Decid. shrub to 2m. St. erect, bluish-white pruinose, with compressed prickles. Lfts 3–5, to 10cm, ovate, acute, subcordate or rounded at base, coarsely dentate, white-tomentose beneath. Fls white in few-fld, tomentose corymbs with hooked prickles. ER; MUNJEET. Perenn. herb to 6m, climbing or creeping, usually rough, prickly and pubesc., 4-angled. Lvs to 8cm, lanceolate to ovate or cordate, glab. to rough and pubesc., prickly, petiolate. Fls to 3×1mm, in loose, trichotomous cymes to 3cm or more, cream to yellow or green. Eur., Afr., Asia. Z6.

R. longipetiolata Bullock = *R. cordifolia.*

R. peregrina L. WILD MADDER; LEVANT MADDER. Perenn., everg. herb, climbing, scrambling or creeping, to 120cm, woody, below, 4-angled above, rough, prickly. Lvs to 6cm, sessile, linear, lanceolate, elliptic, or ovate, leathery, lustrous, rough and prickly beneath, prickly or toothed and cartilaginous at margin. Fls to 6×6mm many in cymose pan. to 10cm, light yellow-green. W & S Eur., N Afr., Middle E. Z7.

R. tinctoria L. MADDER. Perenn. herb. Climbing or scrambling, to 1m, woody below, rough and prickly or hairy; rhiz. red. Lvs to 10>. <Z8.

R. louisianus A. Berger. Shrub to 2m. St. erect, angled, gland., with few prickles, woolly then glab. Lfts 5, lanceolate or oblanceolate, to 10cm, long-acuminate, serrate, green above, lighter and pubesc. beneath. Fls white, in open, leafy rac. Fr. cylindric, white. C US. Z8.

R. macropetalus Douglas ex Hook. = *R. ursinus.*

R. malifolius Focke. Decid. shrub to 3m. St. prostrate or scrambling, with few, short prickles. Lvs simple, ovate, to 12cm, rounded at the base, abruptly pointed at the apex, serrate, glab. above, woolly on veins beneath. Fls white, to 2.5cm diam., in eglandular term. rac. to 10cm. Fr. black. Summer. W China. Z6.

R. mesogaeus Focke. Strongly growing decid. shrub to 3m. St. erect, slender, arching, woolly-velvety, with curved prickles. Lfts 3–5, to 18cm, ovate or rounded, the term. slender, acuminate, all serrate, woolly above, grey-velvety beneath. Fls small, pink-white, in 5-fld term. and axill. pan. Fr. rounded, to 8mm diam., black, sparsely pubesc. at the tip of each drupelet.

Summer. C & W China. Z6.

R. microphyllus L. f. Br. slender, usually purple-brown, with slender prickles. Lvs simple, ovate to orbicular, to 5cm, rounded to acute at apex, rounded to cordat at base, shallowly 3-lobed, serrate, glaucous beneath. Fls white, usually solitary; cal. maroon; pet. to 12mm. Fr. red. Spring. China, Jap. Material grown as *R. koehneanus* is taller, with more prickly st. 'Variegatus': lvs to 8cm, 3-lobed, marbled pink and off-white. Z9.

R. mirus L.H. Bail. MARVEL DEWBERRY. Arching or scrambling shrub. St. with stout prickles. Lvs glab.; lfts 3–5, ovate or elliptic, to 6cm, shortly acuminate, broad or subcordate at the base, finely serrate. Fls white, to 3cm in diam., in 3–4-fld rac. Fr. oblong, 2.5cm or more, black. US (Flor.). Z8.

R. moluccanus hort. non L. = *R. reflexus*.

R. nepalensis (Hook. f.) Kuntze. Everg. shrub. St. creeping, covered with soft purple bristles, prickles 0. Lfts 3, rhomboid, to 6.5cm, often rounded at apex, serrate, shiny above, bristly on veins beneath. Fls pure white, to 4cm in diam.; cal. red, bristly. W Himal. (NW India to Sikkim). Z9.

R. nigrobaccus L.H. Bail. = *R. allegheniensis*.

R. niveus Thunb. HILL RASPBERRY; MYSORE RASPBERRY. To 4m. St. cylindric, shortly hairy, later glab., glaucous, prickly. Lfts 5–7, elliptic-ovate, to 6.5cm, acute or acuminate, broadly cuneate at base, serrate, ± glab. above, white-tomentose beneath. Fls rose-purple, small, in paniculate, terminal clusters with up to 25 fls. Fr. red, pubesc. India, W China. Z9.

R. niveus Wallich ex G. Don non Thunb. = *R. hypargyrus* var. *niveus*.

R. nutans Wallich ex Edgew., non Vest = *R. nepalensis*.

R. nutans var. *nepalensis* Hook. f. = *R. nepalensis*.

R. nutkanus Moc. ex Ser. = *R. parviflorus*.

R. occidentalis L. BLACK RASPBERRY; BLACKCAP; THIMBLEBERRY. Decid. shrub to 3m. St. arching, blue-white-glaucous, with few, short prickles. Lvs dark green, lfts 3–5, to 10cm, ovate, abruptly acuminate, rounded or cordate at base, coarsely serrate, white-tomentose beneath. Fls white, to 12mm diam., in few-fld term. corymbs with straight. Fr. hemispheric, to 1.5cm in diam., purple-black, glaucous. Summer. E & Central N Amer. Z3.

R. odoratus L. FLOWERING RASPBERRY; PURPLE-FLOWERING RASPBERRY; THIMBLEBERRY. Vigorous decid. shrub to 3m. St. woody, erect, with pale brown, peeling bark, gland., pubesc., without prickles. Lvs simle, to 25cm, 5-lobed, cordate at base, serrate, pubesc. beneath. Fls fragrant, pink-purple, to 5cm diam., in many-fld pan. Fr. flat and broad, red or orange. Summer–autumn. 'Albus': bark light; lvs pale; fls white. Z3.

R. omeiensis Rolfe = *R. setchuenensis*.

R. palmatus Thunb. Decid. shrub to 2m. St. with small prickles. Lvs usually 5-lobed, to 7.5cm, serrate, green, veins sericeous. Fls white, to 4cm in diam., solitary. Fr. rounded, to 2cm diam., yellow. Spring. China, Jap., Korea. Z8.

R. parkeri Hance. Scrambling decid. shrub. St. thin, with few, short prickles, grey-glandular-pubesc. Lvs simple, broadly lanceolate, to 18cm, acuminate, cordate at base, sinuously reddish-woolly beneath. Fls white, to 8mm diam., in elongate, villous and glandular-bristly open pan. Fr. small, black, with few drupelets. Summer. China. Z6.

R. parviflorus Nutt. THIMBLEBERRY; SALMON BERRY. Vigorous decid. shrub to 5m. St. erect, unarmed; bark peeling; young shoots woolly, gland. Lvs simple with 3–7 (usually 5) lobes, reniform, to 20cm+ diam., serrate, woolly, particularly beneath. Fls pure white, to 5cm in diam., in 3–10-fld racemose corymbs. Fr. hemispherical, compressed, to 2cm diam., red. Summer. N Amer., N Mex. Z3.

R. parvifolius L. Low decid. shrub. St. tangled, woolly, with prickles. Lfts 3–5, orbicular or broadly obovate, to 5cm, serrate, dark green and glab. above, white-tomentose beneath. Fls bright rose, in few-fld, prickly and pubesc. corymbs. Fr. rounded, red. Summer. Jap., China. Z6.

R. parvus Buch. Prostrate everg. shrub. St. slender, rooting, ultimately without prickles. Lvs simple, linear to linear-lanceolate, to 7.5cm, acute, cordate, glab., serrate. Fls white, to 2.5cm diam., in few-fld pan. Fr. to 2.5cm, red. Summer. NZ. Z9.

R. pedunculosus auct., non D. Don = *R. hypargyrus* var. *niveus*.

R. peltatus Maxim. Shrub. Br. robust, glab., often glaucous, loosely prickly. Lvs simple, peltate, ovate-orbicular, to 25cm, cordate at base, lobes 3–5, acuminate, serrate and pubesc. on veins beneath. Fls solitary. Fr. shortly cylindric, to 4cm, densely spreading hairy. Summer. W China. Z7.

R. pentalobus Hayata. Spreading or prostrate shrub. St. brown-pubesc., eglandular, sparsely prickly. Lvs simple, wrinkled, ovate to orbicular, to 20cm, cordate, lobes 3–5, sharply serrate, pilose to glab. above, tomentose or subglabrous beneath. Fls white, solitary; sep. brown- or yellow-sericeous. Fr. red. Taiwan. 'Emerald Carpet': habit carpet-forming, to 2cm diam.

'Almus': br. unarmed; fls from lat. buds. 'Geophilus': lvs large, serrate. 'Roribaccus' ('Lucretia'): habit robust; lvs doubly serrate, cuneate-obovate; fls large; fr. large. Z9.

R. phoenicolasius Maxim. WINEBERRY. Decid. shrub to 3m. St. spreading, red-glandular-bristly, sparsely prickly. Lvs to 18cm; lfts 3, orbicular to broadly ovate, term. much larger than laterals, rounded or cordate at base, coarsely serrate and lobed, white-tomentose beneath. Fls to 1.5cm diam., pale pink in term. rac. Fr. conical, to 2cm, bright red. Summer. Jap., Korea, China. Z5.

R. playfairianus Focke. Scrambling everg. or semi-evergreen shrub. St. terete, thin, dark, with minute prickles, woolly when young. Lfts 3–5, lanceolate, to 15cm, serrate, shiny above, pale grey-tomentose beneath. Fls to 12mm diam., in small term. pan. Fr. black. Summer. C & W China. Z7.

R. polytrichus Franch. non Progel = *R. tricolor*.

R. procerus P.J. Muell. St. arching, dull purple, prickly. Lfts 3–5, obovate or elliptic, to 7cm, cuspidate, serrate, dark green, shiny above, white-tomentose beneath. Fls pink, to 2.5cm, in prickly rac. Fr. small, round. S, W & C Eur. 'Himalaya Giant' ('Theodore Reimers'): lvs and fls larger, grown for fr. Z6.

R. reflexus Ker-Gawl. Scrambling decid. shrub. St. with dense brown hairs and sparse minute prickles. Lvs deeply 3–5-lobed, lobes triangular or narrowly triangular, acute, serrate, densely brown-hairy beneath. Fls to 1.5cm diam., in axill. clusters. Fr. spherical, purple-black. Summer. S China. Z9.

R. roribaccus Rydb. Vigorous shrub to 2m. St. stout, eglandular, with sparse prickles, erect or prostrate. Lvs glab. above, softly pubesc. beneath, serrate; lfts 3–5, ovate to oblong, to 8.5cm, long-acuminate, subcordate at the base. Fls to 4cm, diam., in 2–5-fld corymbs. Fr. globose or shortly oblong, to 1.5cm+ diam. S US. Z6.

R. rosa L.H. Bail. Robust, erect, shrub to 3m. St. angled, glab. or gland., prickly. Lvs pubesc. above, soft-pubesc. beneath; lfts 5, ovate to elliptic, to 12cm, shortly acuminate, cordate to sub-cordate at base, serrate. Fls to 4cm diam., in short, compact, 10–20-fld corymbs. Fr. shortly conical, to 2×1.5cm. NW N Amer. Z7.

R. rosifolius Sm. MAURITIUS RASPBERRY. Trailing shrub to 2.5m. St. pubesc. when young, with few prickles. Lvs thinly pubesc., with scattered yellow glands beneath, serrate; lfts 5–7, lanceolate, long-acuminate. Fls to 3cm diam., white, solitary on long pedicels. Fr. globose to oblong, red. E Asia. 'Coronarius': fls double. Z9.

R. saxatilis L. Prostrate, to 50cm. St. pubesc., with small, straight prickles. Lfts 3, ovate-elliptic, serrate, subglabrous above, pub-esc. beneath. Fls white, in 3–10-fld corymbs; pet. erect, narrow, small. Fr. of 2–6 drupelets, glossy, red. N Eur. Z4.

R. setchuenensis Bur. & Franch. Large, straggling, decid. shrub. St. stellate-pubesc., unarmed. Lvs 5- or obscurely 7-lobed, to 18×8cm, cordate at base, serrate, stellate-hairy above, densely so beneath. Fls purple, to 2cm diam., in many-fld, term. pan. Fr. black. Summer. W China. Z5.

R. sorbifolius hort. non Maxim. = *R. illecebrosus*.

R. spectabilis Pursh. SALMONBERRY. Decid. shrub to 2m. St. erect, glab., with fine prickles. Lvs to 15cm; lfts 3, ovate, to 10cm, long-acuminate, serrate, glab. Fls pink to maroon, 2–3.5cm diam., usually solitary. Fr. ovoid, large, orange-yellow. Spring. W N Amer. 'Flore Pleno': fls large, double. Z5.

R. splendidissimus Hara. V. similar to *R. lineatus* but lvs always with 3 lfts, and the indumentum more woolly and containing a few glands. Nepal, Bhutan. Z9.

R. squarrosus Fritsch. Sprawling everg. shrub. St. slender, glossy, red-brown, prickly. Lvs to 15cm, slender-stalked; lfts 3–5, linear-lanceolate, toothed, often reduced to midrib only or a vestigial blade terminating midrib. Fls yellow-white, to 8mm, in pan. Fr. orange-red. NZ. Z9.

R. stellatus Sm. See under *R. arcticus*.

R. strigosus Michx. = *R. idaeus* var. *strigosus*.

R. thibetanus Franch. GHOST BRAMBLE. Decid. shrub to 2m, resembling a shorter, finer *R. cockburnianus*. St. slender, silver to purple-pruinose, with slender bristles. Lvs to 23cm; lfts 7–13, oval or ovate, to 5cm, coarsely serrate, shiny above, white-tomentose beneath; terminal leaflet pinnately lobed. Fls purple, to 12mm diam., solitary or in few-fld term. rac. Fr. rounded, to 16mm in diam., black, pruinose. W China. 'Silver Fern': twigs pruinose; lvs silver-grey; fls purple; fr. red to black. Z6.

R. thyrsoideus Wimm. = *R. linkianus*.

R. trianthus Focke. Spreading, decid. shrub to 2m. St. erect, much-branched, prickly, glab., blue-white. Lvs trilobed, central lobe long, ovate to triangular, to 15cm, dark green above, white with hooked prickles beneath, serrate. Fls pink-white, in few-fld term. rac. Fr. dark red. C China. Z7.

R. tricolor Focke. Prostrate, semi-evergreen shrub. St. with dense, buff bristles. Lvs simple, to 10cm, acute, cordate at base, serrate, dark green above, tomentose and bristly beneath. Fls white, to 2.5cm diam., solitary or in small, few-fld term. pan. Fr. bright red. W China. 'Betty Ashburner' *R. tricolor* ×*R. fockeanus:* similar to *R. fockeanus* but lvs large, rounded, crinkled edges, shiny. 'Kenneth Ashburner': similar to *R. tricolor* but st. long; lvs pointed, shiny; vigorous. Z7.

R. 'Tridel' = *R.* 'Benenden'.

R. trifidus Thunb. Shrub to 1.5m. St. unarmed; br. elongate, terete, glandular-pubesc. Lvs orbicular, cordate or truncate at base, lobes 3–7, acute, serrate, shiny above. Fls white, to 4cm diam., in few-fld rac. Fr. globose, yellow. Spring–summer. Jap. Z6.

R. trilobus Ser. V. like *R. deliciosus,* but lvs 4–7.5×4–7cm, darker green and with more acute lobes, sep. less gland., red outside in fr. S Mex. Z6.

R. triphyllus Thunb. = *R. parvifolius.*

R. trivialis Michx. SOUTHERN DEWBERRY. Scrambling shrub to 1m+. St. ascending, becoming prostrate, prickly, bristly and glandular-pubesc. Lvs glab., often leathery and persistent; lfts 3–5, narrowly elliptic to narrowly ovate, to 7cm, acuminate or obtuse, toothed, glab. Fls white to pink, to 3cm diam., solitary. Fr. oblong, to 3cm, black. N Amer. Z6.

R. ulmifolius Schott. BRAMBLE. St. robust, arching, bloomed, with straight or hooked prickles. Lfts 3–5, white-hairy beneath. Infl. raceme-like. Pet. pink or white, crumpled. W & C Eur. 'Bellidiflorus': fls double. 'Variegatus': lvs variegated. Z7.

R. ursinus Cham. & Schltr. Procumbent or erect, everg. shrub. Branchlets grey-pubesc. when young, with straight prickles. Lfts 3–5, broadly ovate, to 6cm, acute, rounded at base, serrate, pubesc. above, white-tomentose or villous beneath. Fls to 2cm diam., white, in prickly corymbs. Fr. oblong, black, pubesc. W US. 'Loganberry': shoots long; lvs densely pubesc. beneath; fr. to 4cm, sour, abundant. Z7.

R. veitchii Rolfe = *R. thibetanus.*

R. velox L.H. Bail. V. like *R. roribaccus,* but lfts oblong. SW US. Z8.

R. vitifolius Cham. & Schltr. = *R. ursinus.*

R. xanthocarpus Bur. & Franch. Subshrub to 50cm. St. erect, angular, prickly. Lfts 3–5, ovate to lanceolate, to 7cm. Fls white, small, in clusters of 1–3.Fr. to 1.5cm, golden yellow, shiny. Summer. W China. Z6.

Ruby Grass *Rhynchelytrum repens.*

Rudbeckia L. CONEFLOWER. Compositae. 15 usually perenn. herbs; st. simple or branched. Lvs alt., entire to 2-pinnatifid. Cap. few, usually solitary, radiate; receptacle hemispheric to conic; ray flts mostly yellow or orange. N Amer., now widespread as gdn escape.

R. amplexicaulis Vahl = *Dracopis amplexicaulis.*

R. bicolor Nutt. = *R. hirta.*

R. californica A. Gray. Perenn. to 2m; st. simple. Lvs to 25cm, lanceolate to elliptic, glab. above, pubesc. beneath, entire, dentate or incised; upper lvs entire, sessile. Cap. to 13cm diam.; peduncle glab.; receptacle to 5cm, ovoid to columnar; ray flts yellow. Late summer. Calif. Z6.

R. deamii S.F. Blake = *R. fulgida* var. *deamii.*

R. echinacea var. *purpurea* hort. = *Echinacea purpurea.*

R. flava Moore = *R. hirta.*

R. fulgida Ait. Perenn. herb to 1m; st. branched. Lvs to 12cm, oblong to lanceolate, mid-green. Cap. to 7cm diam.; receptacle hemispherical to conic; ray flts yellow to orange; disc flts purple-brown. Late summer–autumn. SE US. var. *deamii* (S.F. Blake) Perdue. To 60cm, st. simple. Lvs ovate or oval-ovate, hirsute-pilose. Cap. few; ray flts to 12–14. var. *speciosa* (Wunderlin) Perdue. To 1m; st. branched above. Lvs elliptic to elongate-lanceolate, often falcate, hirsute-pilose. Cap. few to several; ray flts to 3.5cm, 12–20. var. *sullivantii* (Boynt. & Beadle) Cronq. To 1m; st. branched above. Lvs oval, ovate to narrowly ovate-lanceolate, ± pubesc. Cap. several; ray flts to 4cm, 10–15. 'Goldsturm': to 60cm; cap. to 12cm diam. Z4.

R. glaucescens Eastw. = *R. californica* var. *glauca.*

R. glorioisa hort. = *R. fulgida* var. *speciosa.*

R. grandiflora (D. Don) J.F. Gmel. ex DC. Rhizomatous perenn. herb to 1.5m. Lvs to 15cm, oval or ovate, 3–5-ribbed, lower petiolate, upper lvs ± sessile. Cap. to 9cm diam.; receptacle hemispheric to conical; ray flts yellow to orange. C & SE US. Z6.

R. hirta L. BLACK-EYED SUSAN; MARGUERITE JAUNE. Bienn. or short-lived perenn. herb to 2m. Lvs to 10cm, narrowly lanceolate or oblanceolate, mostly 3-ribbed, entire or remotely toothed, petiolate. Cap. solitary, long-stalked; receptacle conic; ray flts to 4cm, pale yellow, darker at base; disc flts purple-brown. Late summer. C US. Autumn Lvs: to 75cm, fls large, in shades of bronze, brown and red, all with dark centres. 'Bambi': to 30cm; fls in shades of bronze, chestnut and gold. 'Gloriosa' and Double Gloriosa: tetraploid races, single and double-fld ,

coarse, heads to 15cm across, fls in shades of yellow and mahogany, also bicolours, usually perenn. but flowering from seed in first year. 'Golden Flame': to 30cm; fls gold, cones crimson. 'Green Eyes' ('Irish Eyes'): flts acuminate, yellow, eyes olive green. 'Kelvedon Star': fls deep gold with a mahogany zone, cones dark brown. 'Superba': fls large, ray flts beneath maroon. Z4.

R. laciniata L. Perenn. herb to 3m, mostly glab. and glaucous. Lvs to 10cm, pinnate or ternate, strigose or hirsute beneath, petiolate, upper lvs, sessile. Cap. solitary; receptacle hemispheric to conic; ray flts to 6cm, yellow; disc flts yellow-green or grey-green. Late summer–early autumn. N Amer. 'Golden Glow' ('Double Gold', 'Gold Ball', 'Goldkugel', 'Hortensia'): tall and branching to 180cm; fls double, yellow. 'Goldquelle' ('Gold Drop'): compact and branching to 75cm; fls large, double, yellow. 'Soleil d'or': ray flts large, golden. Z3.

R. laevigata Pursh = *R. nitida.*

R. lanceolata Bisch. = *R. hirta* var. *pulcherrima.*

R. maxima Nutt. Perenn. herb to 1.5m. Lvs to 12cm, rhombic to ovate or lanceolate, entire, coriaceous. Cap. solitary; receptacle cylindric, pubesc. Late summer. C & S US. Z7.

R. monticola Small. Perenn. to 1m, ± densely hirsute or hispid. St. simple or branched. Lvs to 10cm, ovate to ovate-lanceolate or elliptic, entire or serrate. Cap. solitary; receptacle hemispherical to ovoid, to 2cm; ray flts to 3.5cm, 10–14, yellow. SE US. Z4.

R. newmanii Boynt. & Beadle = *R. fulgida* var. *speciosa.*

R. nitida Nutt. Perenn. herb to 2m. Lvs to 15cm, pinnatisect. Cap. solitary, to 10cm diam.; receptacle conic; ray flts yellow; disc flts green. Late summer–early autumn. N Amer. 'Autumn Glory': to 1.5m; fls gold. 'Herbsonne' ('Autumn Sun'): to 180cm; flts large, yellow; receptacle tall, green. 'Juligold': to 180cm; fls deep gold. Z3.

R. occidentalis Nutt. Perenn. herb to 2m; st. simple. Lvs to 12cm, ovate to ovate-elliptic, base rounded or cordate, entire or irregularly toothed. Cap. solitary, to 8cm diam.; receptacle columnar, to 6cm. Summer. W US. Z7.

R. palustris Eggert. Perenn. herb to 70cm; st. usually branched. Lvs to 20cm, lanceolate to elliptic-lanceolate, base cuneate, remotely crenate-toothed, long-petiolate, st. lvs ± sessile. Cap. solitary, several; receptacle to 12mm. C & SC US. Z4.

R. serotina Nutt. = *R. hirta.*

R. speciosa Wunderlin = *R. fulgida* var. *speciosa.*

R. subtomentosa Pursh. SWEET CONEFLOWER. Perenn. herb to 70cm; st. usually branched. Lvs to 13cm, ovate, mid-green, often ternate, grey-pubesc. Cap. solitary, to *c*8cm diam.; receptacle hemispheric to ovoid-conic; ray flts yellow; disc flts deep brown-purple. Autumn. C US. Z5.

R. sullivantii Boynt. & Beadle = *R. fulgida* var. *sullivantii.*

R. triloba L. BROWN-EYED SUSAN. Perenn. herb to 1.5m; st. simple to branched. Lvs to 12cm, ovate to oblong-ovate, often 3–7-lobed, subglabrous or strigose. Cap. solitary; receptacle subglobose to conic-globose; ray flts yellow to orange; disc flts black to purple. CE US. Z5.

R. cvs. Races with all types of size and fl. colour represented. Goldilocks: to 60cm; fls double and semi-double, to 10cm diam., bright gold, long-lasting; seed race. compact to 60cm; fls large, golden orange, cones black. Monarch Mix: compact to 60cm; fls in shades of orange, yellow and bi-colours, to 12cm diam.; seed race. 'Nutmeg': compact and low-growing to 75cm; fls double, long-lasting, rich autumnal colours, contrasting red and brown cones. Rustic Colour and Rustic Dwarf Hybrids: 50 to 75cm; fls large, in shades of yellow, gold, bronze and mahogany with contrasting black cones; seed race.

Ruddles *Calendula officinalis.*

Rue *Ruta* (*R. graveolens*).

Rue-anemone *Anemonella thalictroides.*

Ruellia L. Acanthaceae. 150 perenn. herbs, subshrubs or shrubs. Fls solitary or in axillary clusters or term. pan.; cal. deeply 5-cut; cor. funnelform, tube straight, curved or abruptly bent, lobes 5, ovate or rounded, spreading. Trop. Amer., Afr., Asia and temp. N Amer.

R. amoena Nees non Sessé & Moc. = *R. graecizans.*

R. caroliniensis (J.F. Gmel.) Steud. Perenn. herb to 1m. Lvs to 12cm, narrowly oblong-ovate. Fls axillary, 5cm, pale violet-blue. E & SE US. var. *dentata* (Nees) Fern. Lf margins wavy-toothed. Z5.

R. ciliosa Pursh. Rosulate, hairy; perenn. herb, to 30cm. Lvs 2.5–7.5cm, oblong-ovate, rough, ciliate. Fls in dense, axill. clusters; 2.5–5cm pale blue with purple veins. Summer. SE US. Z7.

R. devosiana hort. Makoy ex E. Morr. Pubesc. subshrub to 45cm. St. flushed purple. Lvs to 7.5cm, broadly lanceolate, pale veins above, purple beneath. Fls solitary, axill. 4.5cm, white flushed lavender, tube slender, lobes veined purple. Spring–summer. Braz. Z10.

R. graecizans Backer. Bushy subshrub to 60cm or more, spreading. Lvs 10–18cm, narrowly ovate to oblong, glab., usually entire. Fls in stalked axill. clusters, 2.5cm, scarlet. S Amer. Z10.

R. humilis Nutt. Perenn. pubesc. herb to 60cm. Lvs 7.5cm, ovate to oblong-ovate. Fls in clusters from upper lf axils; 5cm, violet-blue. S Penn. to Neb., Flor. and Tex. Z4.

R. hybrida Pursh = R. caroliniensis.

R. longifolia (Pohl) Griseb. ex Lindau non Rich. = R. graecizans.

R. macrantha Mart. ex Nees. CHRISTMAS PRIDE. Bushy erect subshrub 1–2m. Lvs to 15cm, lanceolate, dull dark green, veins impressed above. Fls solitary, axill. to 7.5cm, crimson to lavender-rose, throat paler with red veins. Braz. Z10.

R. makoyana hort. Makoy ex Closon. MONKEY PLANT; TRAILING VELVET PLANT. Spreading herb to 60cm. Lvs to 7.5cm, ovate, tinted violet above, purple beneath, veined silvery-grey. Fls solitary, 5cm, rosy-carmine. Braz. Z10.

R. strepens L. Pubesc. spreading perenn. herb to 30–90cm. Lvs 8–15cm, ovate or oblong-ovate, rough, ciliate. Fls 1–3 in lf axils to 5cm, light blue to purple, veined purple. NJ to Tex. and Flor. Z6.

Ruffle Palm Aiphanes (A. caryotifolia).
Ruil Nothofagus alessandrii.

Ruizia Ruiz. & Pav.
R. fragans Ruiz & Pav. = Peumus boldus.

Rukam Flacourtia jangomans; F. rukam.

Rulingia R. Br.
R. arachnoides Haw. = Anacampseros arachnoides.
R. rufescens Haw. = Anacampseros rufescens.

Rum Cherry Prunus serotina.

Rumex L. DOCK; SORREL. Polygonaceae. 200 ann., bienn. or perenn. herbs, rarely shrubs. Lvs usually basal. Fls small, clustered in dense, erect, term. pan., green often flushed pink, red or rust; tep. 6, inner 3 becoming enlarged in fr. Fr. brown, 3-angled with a papery pericarp. N temp. regions.

R. abyssinicus Jacq. SPINACH RHUBARB. Perenn. to 3m; st. erect, glab. Lvs 5–25×4–20cm, triangular or ovate, hastate at base, glab. to slightly pubesc. below; petioles of lower lvs to 10cm, blood-red. Ethiop.

R. acetosa L. GARDEN SORREL; SOUR DOCK. Somewhat succulent, glab., perenn. tufted herb to 60cm. Lvs to 14cm, basal, sagittate, long-petioled to sessile. N temp. & arctic regions. 'Blonde de Lyon': lvs large, slightly acidic. Z3.

R. alpinus L. MONK'S RHUBARB; MOUNTAIN RHUBARB. Rhizomatous creeping perenn. to 1.5m; st. erect, often tinged red. Lvs 20–40×20–35cm, mostly basal, ovate to orbicular, base cordate, hairy on veins beneath, undulate; petiole long. Summer. Eur. (mts). Z5.

R. flexuosus Sol. ex Hook. f. Glab., spreading perenn. herb to 50cm; st. much-branched, slender, flexuous. Basal lvs to 10cm, linear to lanceolate, acute, red-brown, undulate, st. lvs 2–5cm. Summer. NZ. Z7.

R. hydrolapathum Huds. GREAT WATER DOCK. Robust, glab. perenn. to 2m; rootstock stout. Basal lvs to 1m, broad oblong-lanceolate, acute, base cuneate or slightly cordate, dull green, entire or minutely toothed, undulate; st. lvs smaller, narrower. Summer. Eur. Z6.

R. hymenosepalus Torr. CANAIGRE; GANAGRA; TANNER'S DOCK; WILD RHUBARB. Perenn. to 1m, roots swollen, fusiform; st. glab. Lvs to 30cm, oblong-lanceolate, crisped to undulate; petiole short. Spring–summer. W US. Z6.

R. lunaria L. Everg. shrub, to 1.5m. Lvs 5–7cm, ovate, base truncate to slightly cordate, fairly thick, bright green; petiole 4–5cm. Winter–mid spring. Canary Is. Z9.

R. patentia L. PATIENCE DOCK; SPINACH DOCK; PATIENCE HERB. Perenn. to 2m, erect, glab., sometimes branching above. Basal lvs 15–45×5–12cm, elliptic ovate to lanceolate, acute, truncate to slightly cuneate, undulate; petioles to 30cm. Summer. Eur., Asia, nat. N US. Z6.

R. roseus L. Ann., 30–60cm; st. spreading, branched, slightly glaucous. Lvs oblong-deltoid, base truncate to cuneate sometimes lanceolate above, entire. Late spring. Egypt to Iran.

R. sanguineus L. Perenn. to 1m; st. erect, slender, often tinged purple or red. Lvs 5–15×2–5cm, oblong, acute, veined purple or blood red. Eur., SW Asia, N Afr. Z6.

R. scutatus L. FRENCH SORREL; GARDEN SORREL. Low perenn. to 45cm; st. ascending or prostrate, branching below, sometimes slightly woody. Lvs 1–5.5cm, ovate to cordate becoming hastate, acute to pandurate and obtuse on st.; petiole long.

Summer. Eur., W Asia, N Afr. 'Silver': habit spreading, forming a mound to 60cm; lvs pale, heart-shaped, edged and veined green. 'Silver Shield': habit low, dense, to 45cm; lvs silver, heart-shaped; fls green. Z6.

R. venosus Pursh. WILD BEGONIA; WILD HYDRANGEA; SOUR GREENS. Perenn. to 45cm; rootstock woody; st. stout, branched. Lvs 3–12cm, ovate to ovate-lanceolate, entire, pale green. Summer. NW US. Z4.

R. vesicarius L. Ann., st. branching at base. Lvs to 2.5×2cm, deltoid or ovate, commonly cordate at base, fleshy; petioles to 2.5cm. Late spring. N Afr., SW Asia.

Rumohra Raddi. Dryopteridaceae. 6 epiphytic or terrestrial ferns. Rhiz. long-creeping, scaly. Fronds stipitate, uniform, 1–3-pinnate-pinnatifid, ± deltoid, leathery, seg. aristate to obtuse. S hemis. (1 sp.), Madag.

R. adiantiformis (Forst. f..) Ching. LEATHER FERN; LEATHERLEAF FERN; IRON FERN. Rhiz. to 15mm diam. Fronds to 90×75cm, ovate or deltoid to lanceolate, base dilated, leathery, pinnae to 15×10cm, 7–15 pairs, petiolate, alt., distant, stiff, ovate or deltoid to lanceolate, pinnules 3–11 pairs, petiolate, alt., ovate to lanceolate, seg. sessile to short-petiolate, alt., ovate to rhomboid, toothed to notched; stipes to 50cm, ± scaly. C & S Amer., S Afr. and Madag., Aus., NZ, New Guinea. 'Cape-form': fronds to 1.5m arising from a thick, short-jointed rhiz.

R. hispida (Sw.) Copel. = Lastreopsis hispida.
→Aspidium, Dryopteris and Polystichum.

Rumphius's Ivy-palm Schefflera littorea.
Runaway Robin Glechoma hederacea.
Runner Bean Phaseolus vulgaris.
Running Blackberry Rubus hispidus.
Running Box Mitchella repens.
Running Pine Lycopodium clavatum.
Running Pop Passiflora foetida.
Running Postman Kennedia prostrata.
Running Strawberry Bush Euonymus obovatus.

Runyonia Rose.
R. longiflora Rose = Manfreda longiflora.

Rupicapnos Pomel. Fumariaceae. Some 32 variable, ± stemless, everg., perenn. herbs. Lvs pinnate; lfts pinnatisect. Fls sub-corymbose; pedicels becoming v. long; sep. 2, v. small; pet. 4, uppermost spurred. Spain, N Afr. Z8.

R. africana (Lam.) Pomel. Lvs fern-like, mostly basal, vivid glaucous-blue; lfts ovate, oblong or linear. Fls in delicate rac., rose-purple with dark purple tips, rarely white, to 1.5cm, spur downcurved. Spring–summer. N Afr. Z8.
→Fumaria.

Ruprechtia C.A. Mey. Polygonaceae. 17 trees and shrubs. Lvs alt., simple; stipules tubular. Fls in clusters or short spikes; sep. petal-like, winged. Fr. 3-angled. Trop. Amer. Z10.

R. coriacea (Karst.) S.F. Blake. BISCOCHITO. Everg. shrub or small tree to 6m. Lvs ovate to elliptic, 5–10cm, leathery, undulate. Fls red: ♂ inconspicuous; ♀ showy, abundant. Fr. to 2cm, with red, wing-like lobes. Venez.

Rupture-wort Herniaria.

Ruschia Schwantes. Aizoaceae. 360 succulent shrubs or prostrate perennials; br. covered by lf remains. Lvs shortly united, forming a tube-like sheath, blades 3-angled, long and narrow or small and hemispheric, firm-textured, blue-green, usually with darker transparent spots. Fls usually small, axill. or term., solitary or several together. S Afr. (Cape Prov.), Nam. Z10.

R. acuminata L. Bol. Shrublet to 20cm. Lvs 15–25×7×6mm, apiculate, keel blunt, rarely dentate, tinged blue, spotted, rough papillose. Fls 3cm diam., white to pale pink. E Cape.

R. banardii L. Bol. = R. odontocalyx.

R. crassa (L. Bol.) Schwantes. Shrub ascending or prostrate. Lvs blue-green, covered in short hairs, 1–2cm long and slightly less wide, swollen, obtuse, apiculate, keel beneath with 1 distinct tooth. Fls 2.2cm diam., white. W Cape.

R. derenbergiana (Dinter) Weber = Ebracteola derenbergiana.

R. dualis (N.E. Br.) L. Bol. Forming ± stemless clumps 3–5cm tall. Lvs 20×5mm, upper surface flat, lower surface semicylindric at base, swollen toward apex, white-grey with cartilaginous margins. Fls 1.5cm diam., deep pink. W Cape.

R. evoluta (N.E. Br.) L. Bol. St. numerous, forming dense small mats. Lvs small, hemispheric, blue-green. Fls 1.5cm diam., brilliant pink. Cape.

R. foliolosa (Haw.) Schwantes = R. tumidula.

R. granitica (L. Bol.) L. Bol. St. slender or creeping to erect. Lvs 5–11×4–5mm, oblong, obtuse, apiculate, blue-green, keeled beneath with red angles. Fls 1–2cm diam., pink. W Cape.

R. jacobseniana L. Bol. = *Astridia longifolia.*

R. karrooica (L. Bol.) L. Bol. Robust erect shrub to 30cm. Lvs 8–21×3–5mm, tapered, apiculate, with the clavate sheath enclosing internodes. Fls 5cm diam., purple-pink striped purple. Karroo.

R. longifolia (L. Bol.) L. Bol. = *Astridia longifolia.*

R. macowanii (L. Bol.) Schwantes. Shrub, 15–20cm, lax prostrate. Lvs 21–35×4×4mm, swollen, slightly oblique, carinate beneath. Fls 2.2cm diam., pink with a darker stripe. Cape Penins.

R. mollis (A. Berger) Schwantes. Low shrub, prostrate. Lvs 12–15×4–6mm, triquetrous with rounded sides, angles with a distinct line, obtuse, minutely hirsute, grey-green. Fls 1.5cm diam., red. Cape Prov.

R. mucronata (Haw.) Schwantes. V. small shrub, prostrate, spreading. Lvs 6mm, semicylindrical, triquetrous above, mucronate, grey-green with large dots, minutely rough. Fls 2cm diam., purple-pink. W Cape.

R. multiflora (Haw.) Schwantes. Large shrub to 1m; st. erect, freely forking, ± hexagonal at first. Lvs 3cm×3–4mm, triquetrous, apiculate, slightly grey-green with translucent spots. Fls to 3cm diam., white. SE Cape.

R. nivea L. Bol. = *R. odontocalyx.*

R. odontocalyx (Schltr. & Diels) Schwantes. Loosely branched shrub to 30cm, softly white-papillose. Lvs thick, indistinctly keeled, oblique, with a blunt tooth at tip, margins with 2–3 indistinct teeth, blue-green. Fls 2–3cm diam., white. Nam.

R. pseudorupicola (Dinter) Dinter & Schwantes = *R. odontocalyx.*

R. pygmaea (Haw.) Schwantes. St. v. short, mat-forming. First fl pair 4–5×2–3mm united, green, shrivelling; second lf pair free, ovate or lanceolate, roundly carinate beneath. Fl. 1.8mm diam., pink. SW Cape.

R. renniei (L. Bol.) Schwantes apud Jacobsen = *Ebracteola montis-moltkei.*

R. rostella (Haw.) Schwantes. St. prostrate, with numerous short shoots. Lvs 12–18×4mm, united and sheathing, grey-green with minute dots, semicylindric. Fls 2–2.5cm diam., white to purplepink. W Cape.

R. rubricaulis (Haw.) L. Bol. Small shrub with angular, red st. Lvs 25–40×4–8mm, triquetrous, swollen below, margins hairy, keel denticulate, grey-green. Fls 3cm diam., light purple. S Cape.

R. rupicola (Engl.) Schwantes = *R. odontocalyx.*

R. sabulicola (Dinter) Dinter = *R. odontocalyx.*

R. schollii (Salm-Dyck). Shrub 10–12cm. St. erect, curved, slender. Lvs 15–20×2×2mm, subcylindrical, tapered, tip recurved, fresh green, spotted. Fl. 1.8cm diam., red. SE Cape. var. *caledonica* (L. Bol.) Schwantes. St. creeping, lvs triquetrous, acute. Fls 1.5–3.2cm diam., pink-purple. W Cape.

R. semidentata (Salm-Dyck) Schwantes. Shrub with erect forking st. Lvs 2–3cm, triquetrous, tapered, the keel angle with 2–4 teeth, white-grey. Fls 4cm diam., red. W Cape.

R. steingroeveri (Pax) Schwantes = *R. odontocalyx.*

R. stenophylla (L. Bol.) L. Bol. Mat-forming with a napiform root. Lvs 4.5cm, narrow, semicylindrical, spotted. Fls 3.5cm diam., pink-purple. W Cape.

R. strubeniae (L. Bol.) Schwantes. Erect shrub to 75cm. St. red. Lvs 40–60×5–6×12mm, navicular to triquetrous, laterally compressed, margins serrate, green. Fls 3.2cm diam., pink striped purple. W Cape.

R. tumidula (Haw.) Schwantes. Freely branching shrub to 60cm. Lvs 2.5cm×4mm, swollen at base, linear-triquetrous, obtuse, apiculate with smooth angles, grey-green, spotted. Fls 2cm diam., pink. W Cape, Nam.

R. umbellata (L.) Schwantes. Shrub, 60–80cm. Lvs 5–7cm×4–6mm, obtusely triquetrous, recurved at tip, fresh green, spotted, sheath thickened. Fls 3cm diam., white. Karroo.

R. uncinata (L.) Schwantes. St. elongate, prostrate; br. and shoots secund. Lvs with a long sheath, 4–8mm, triquetrous to cylindrical, apiculate, with 1–2 short teeth on the keel, grey-green, spotted. Fls 2cm diam., pink-red. W Cape, Nam.

R. uncinella (Haw.) Schwantes = *R. uncinata.*

R. vereculata (L.) G. Rowley = *Scopelogena vereculata.*

R. vulvaria (Dinter) Schwantes. Densely branching rounded shrub, to 40cm. Lvs sheathing and united, free parts 15–20mm, apiculate with slender papillae, scarcely spotted, with 1 tooth on keel beneath. Fls 2cm diam., violet-pink. Nam.: Great Namaqualand.

→*Antimima, Argyroderma* and *Mesembryanthemum.*

Ruschianthus L. Bol. Aizoaceae. 1 low shrubby succulent. St. covered with lf remains. Lvs in unequal pairs, those of larger pair 30–45×5–6×18mm, falcate, acute, convex toward base,

compressed above, indistinctly carinate, minutely rough, pale blue-green. Fls to 3cm diam., lemon yellow. Nam. Z10.

R. falcatus L. Bol.

Ruscus L. BUTCHER'S BROOM. Liliaceae (Asparagaceae). 6 rhizomatous everg. perenn. herbs. St. erect, produced annually, tough and shrubby, dark green with flattened, sharp rigid cladophylls (fine lvs reduced to scales). Fls small, green-white, seated on cladophyll midrib. Fr. a red berry. Azores, N Afr., Madeira, W Eur. to Caspian Sea.

R. aculeatus L. BUTCHER'S BROOM; BOX HOLLY; JEW'S MYRTLE. To 125cm, erect, densely branched. Cladophylls to 2.5cm, ovate, mucronate to pungent, crowded dark glossy green, dry and matt, usually twisted. Medit. and Black Sea N to GB, W to Azores. var. *angustifolius* Boiss. Low-growing, slender. Z7.

R. colchicum Yeo. To 60cm, simple, usually arching. Cladophylls 4.5–13.5cm, to 30 per st., ovate or elliptic. Autumn. S Cauc., NE Turk. Z7.

R. hypoglossum L. To 40cm, usually far shorter, simple, arching to near procumbent. Cladophylls 3–10cm, obovate-rhombic to broadly ovate, mucronate to pungent, coarsely textured, olive to deep green, usually slightly twisted. Spring. It., Czech. to N Turk. Z7.

R. hypophyllum L. 35–75cm, erect, sometimes with 1 br. Cladophylls 5–9cm, to 16 per st., usually ovate, acute, dark green. S Spain, N Afr., SE Fr. Z8.

R. × microglossum Bertol. (*R. hypoglossum* × *R. hypophyllum.*) To 50cm, simple, usually arching. Cadlophylls 4.5–10cm, to 19 per st., obovate-lanceolate to oblanceolate, apex long, acute, sharp, slightly twisted, pale green. Throughout the year. Gdn origin, widely nat. Z7.

R. streptophyllum Yeo. To c60cm, simple, usually arching. Cladophylls 5–18cm, to c18 per st., broadly elliptic to ovate to lanceolate, in 2 rows, twisted at base. Madeira. Z9.

Rush *Juncus.*
Rush Broom *Viminaria.*
Rush Fern *Schizaea.*
Rushgrass *Sporobolus.*
Rush-leaved Jonquil *Narcissus assoanus.*
Rush Rose *Helianthemum scoparium.*

Ruspolia Lindau. Acanthaceae. 4 low-growing shrubs. Lvs opposite, ovate. Fls in spikes or pan.; cal. deeply 5-lobed; cor. tube much exceeding lobes; sta. 2, slightly exserted. Afr. Z10.

R. hypocrateriformis (Vahl) Milne-Redh. Br. tetragonal. Lvs to 7.5cm, glab. Infl. term.; cor. tube golden-yellow; lobes deep red-pink outside, yellow within.

R. seticalyx (C.B. Clarke) Milne-Redh. Br. terete. Lvs hairy. Fls paler than in *R. hypocrateriformis*; cor. lobes light orange red above, paler beneath.

→*Pseuderanthemum.*

Russelia Jacq. Scrophulariaceae. Some 52 everg. shrubs and subshrubs. St. erect, pendent or scandent. Lvs whorled or opposite, simple, rarely viscid, often scale-like, on pendulous st. Fls in axill. cymes or, solitary; cal. seg. 5; cor. tube slender, 5-lobed, 2-lipped. Summer. Mex., Cuba to Colomb. Z9.

R. campechiana var. *lilacina* Lundell = *R. lilacina.*

R. equisetiformis Schldl. & Cham. CORAL PLANT; FOUNTAIN PLANT; FIRECRACKER PLANT. Shrub to 1.5m with weeping horsetail-like habit. Br. green, slender, whorled or pendulous. Lvs caducous, scale-like. Fls red, to 3cm. Mex.

R. floribunda HBK = *R. rotundifolia.*

R. juncea Zucc. = *R. equisetiformis.*

R. lilacina (Lundell) Lundell. Arching to scandent subshrub. Lvs to 10cm, cordate, serrate or entire. Fls purple, to 2cm. Hond.

R. multiflora Sims = *R. sarmentosa.*

R. rotundifolia Cav. Shrub to 1.2m. Lvs pubesc., ovate, basally cordate. Fls red; throat beardèd below lip. Mex.

R. sarmentosa Jacq. Shrub to 1.8m. St. glab. to tomentose, angled. Lvs to 8cm, ovate, basally cordate, dentate, viscid. Fls red. Mex., Cuba to Columbia.

Russian Dandelion *Taraxacum glaucanthum.*
Russian Juniper *Juniperus semiglobosa.*
Russian Olive *Elaeagnus angustifolia.*
Russian Pea Shrub *Caragana frutex.*
Russian Rock Birch *Betula ermanii.*
Russian Sage *Perovskia.*
Russian Vine *Polygonum aubertii, P. baldschuanicum.*
Russian Violet *Viola suavis.*
Rusty Back Fern *Asplenium ceterach.*
Rusty Fig *Ficus rubiginosa.*
Rusty Foxglove *Digitalis ferruginea.*
Rusty Leaf *Menziesia ferruginea.*

Rusty-leaved Fig *Fiscus rubiginosa.*
Rusty Lyonia *Lyonia ferruginea.*
Rusty Pods *Hovea longifolia.*
Rusty Sallow *Salix cinerea.*
Rusty Woodsia *Woodsia ilvensis.*

Ruta L. RUE. Rutaceae. 8 aromatic woody-based, shrubby perenn. herbs. Lvs usually 2- or 3-pinnatisect, gland-dotted, often glaucous. Infl. cymose; sep. and pet. 4, frequently 5 in central fl., pet. to 1cm, cucullate, yellow; sta. 2× number of pet. Macaronesia, E Eur., SW Asia.

R. angustifolia Pers. Subshrub, 25–57cm. Lower lvs short petiolate, 2- or 3-pinnatisect, ultimate seg. 1.2–3.5mm wide, obovate lanceolate to narrowly oblong. Infl. rather lax, gland. puberulent; pet. oblong, with cilia longer than width of pet. W Medit., E to Balk. Z8.

R. bracteosa DC. = *R. chalapensis.*

R. chalapensis L. Glaucous subshrub, 20–60cm. Lvs long-petiolate, 2- or 3-pinnatisect, ultimate seg. 1.5–6mm wide narrowly oblong-lanceolate or obovate. Infl. lax; rarely with a few glands; pet. oblong, with cilia shorter than width of pet. Arabia, Somalia, S Eur. 'Dimension Two': prostrate; lvs divided, blue, fragrant; fls yellow, frilled. Z8.

R. corsica DC. Shrub, 25–60cm. Lower lvs with petioles to 8cm, ultimate seg. 1.5–7mm wide, obovate to cuneate-orbicular. Infl. lax, twiggy; pet. broadly ovate, denticulate, undulate. Corsica, Sardinia. Z8.

R. divaricata Ten. = *R. graveolens.*

R. graveolens L. RUE; HERB OF GRACE. Glaucous blue shrub 20–50cm. Lower lvs long petiolate, seg. usually bipinnatisect, ultimate seg. 2–9mm wide, lanceolate to obovate. Infl. lax; pet. oblong-ovate, denticulate, undulate. Balk. Penins., SE Eur. 'Blue Curl': dwarf, bushy; lvs lacy, blue. 'Blue Mound': mound-forming; lvs tinted blue. 'Curly Girl': dwarf, compact; lvs lacy, blue. 'Jackman's Blue': lvs distinctly glaucous. 'Variegata': lvs edged with creamy white. Z5.

R. hortensis Mill. = *R. graveolens.*

R. montana. (L.) L. Low subshrub 15–50cm, st. glaucous. Lower lvs petiolate, 2- or 3-pinnatisect, seg. thick, to 1mm wide, linear, on upper lvs to 12mm. Infl. dense, gland.; pet. oblong, undulate, scarcely denticulate. NW Afr., S Eur., Turk. Z7.

RUTACEAE Juss. 161/1700. *Acmadenia, Acradenia, Acronychia, Agathosma, Boenninghausenia, Boronia, Calodendron, Casimiroa, Choisya,* × *Citrofortunella,* × *Citroncirus, Citropsis, Citrus, Clausena, Correa, Dictamnus, Diosma, Eremocitrus, Eriostemon, Fortunella, Glycosmis, Limonia, Melicope, Microcitrus, Murraya, Orixa, Phellodendron, Poncirus, Ptelea, Ruta, Severinia, Skimmia, Tetradium, Triphasia, Zanthoxylum.*

Rutland-beauty *Calystegia sepium.*

Ruttya Harv. Acanthaceae. 3 shrubs. Lvs opposite, ovate. Fls in short spikes with small, linear bracts; cal. 5-parted, lobes narrow; cor. broadly tubular, 2-lippped, lobes 5. E Afr. Z10.

R. fruticosa Lindau. Everg., to 4cm. Lvs 5–6cm, wrinkled. Spike term., cone-like; cor. 5cm, yellow or orange-red, lower lip deflexed with dark brown blotch, upper lip erect. E Afr. 'Scholesei': fls yellow, spotted glossy black.

Ryegrass *Lolium.*

S

Sabal Adans. PALMETTO. Palmae. 14 palms. St. ± subterranean or erect, clothed with lf bases or becoming bare, smooth grey. Lvs costapalmate, induplicate, marcescent; petiole slender, convex beneath, blade flat to arched, deeply divided, seg. single-fold, further divided at apex, pendent. Infl. shorter than or equal to lvs, branched to ×4; rachillae slender, fls cream. Fr. globose to pyriform. SE US and E Tex. to W Indies and Colomb. Z10 unless specified.

S. beccariana L.H. Bail. = S. princeps.
S. bermudana L.H. Bail. BERMUDA PALMETTO. St. to 13m. Lf blades to 3m diam., bright green, paler beneath, central undivided portion to 30cm, seg. 60×5cm, single-fold. Bermuda.
S. blackburniana (Cook) Glazebr. ex Schult. & Schult. f. non Hemsl. HISPANIOLAN PALMETTO. To 20m. Trunk bare, cement-grey. Lvs grey-green, blade to 2m, central undivided portion to 1m, seg. to 1×5cm, midrib conspicuous beneath. Hispan., Santo Domingo, Haiti.
S. blackburniana Hemsl. non (Cook) Glazebr. ex Schult. & Schult. f. = S. bermudana.
S. causiarum (Cook) Becc. PUERTO RICAN HAT PALM. To 16m, trunk becoming smooth, grey, constricted at base, to 20cm diam. Lvs to 2m, bright green or grey-blue, sinuses containing, fil., seg. to 60, to 1m×5cm, apices filamentous. Puerto Rico.
S. deeringiana Small = S. minor.
S. domingensis Becc. = S. blackburniana.
S. etonia Swingle ex Nash. SCRUB PALMETTO. Trunk subterranean, prostrate or erect, to 2×1m. Lvs bright green, blade to 1m diam., central undivided portion to 0.25m, seg. 60, to 90×4cm, with many fil. Penins. Flor.
S. florida Becc. = S. parviflora.
S. glabra Sarg. = S. minor.
S. glaucescens Lodd. ex H.E. Moore = S. mauritiiformis.
S. guatemalensis Becc. = S. mexicana.
S. haitensis Becc. = S. blackburniana.
S. jamaicensis Becc. JAMAICAN PALMETTO; BULL THATCH. Trunk erect, bare, to 13m. Lvs green, to 1m diam., central undivided portion to 90cm, seg. to 1m, 80, fil. few or 0. Jam., W Indies.
S. jamesiana Small = S. palmetto.
S. japa Wright ex Becc. CANA JATA. To 10m, st. ringed. Lvs green, with no central undivided portion, divided into c60 unequal seg. to 1m×5cm lacking fil. W Cuba.
S. mauritiiformis (Karst.) Griseb. & Wendl. PALMA AMARGA; PALMA DE VACA. To 24m. St. to 40cm diam., ringed. Lvs soft, glossy green above, blue-green beneath, central unidivided portion to 80cm, seg. to 1m×10cm, 60, midrib and 2 side ribs marked, fil. inconspicuous or 0. Colomb.
S. mayarum Bartlett = S. yapa.
S. megacarpa Small = S. etonia.
S. mexicana Mart. TEXAS PALMETTO. To 18m. Trunk bare, rough, ringed. Lf blade to 1mm diam., bright green, central undivided portion to half total length, seg. to 1m×5cm, with fil. Mex., Tex., Guat. Z9.
S. mexicana Mart. = S. parviflora.
S. minima Nutt. = S. minor.
S. minor (Jacq.) Pers. DWARF PALMETTO; SCRUB PALMETTO; BUSH PALMETTO. Trunk subterranean or erect, to 3m×30cm, bare. Lvs blue-green, rigid, blade to 1.5m diam., central undivided portion to half blade length, seg. to 40, to 150×5cm with many lat. veins, fil. few or 0. SE US. Z9.
S. neglecta Becc. = S. blackburniana.
S. palmetto (Walter) Lodd. ex Schult. & Schult. f. BLUE PALMETTO; CABBAGE PALMETTO; CABBAGE TREE; COMMON PALMETTO. To 30m; trunk rough, to 60cm diam. Lvs to 2m, usually broader, green, seg. 60, to 80×4cm, with many fil. SE US. Z8.
S. parviflora Becc. CUBAN PALMETTO; PALMA CANA; GUANO CANA. Trunk to 16m, irregularly swollen, bare pale grey. Lvs to 1m diam., rigid, pale grey-green, central undivided region to one-quarter of blade, seg. to 1m×5cm with prominent fil. Cuba.
S. peregrina L.H. Bail. = S. yapa.
S. princeps hort. ex Becc. Trunk to 10m, clothed with persistent lf bases. Lf blade to 1.5m, central undivided portion to half length of blades, seg. to 100, green throughout, to 6cm across. Cuba.
S. pumila Elliott = S. minor.
S. schwarzii Becc. = S. palmetto.
S. serrulata (Michx.) Schult. & Schult. f. = Serenoa repens.
S. texana (Cook) Becc. = S. mexicana.

S. umbraculifera (Jacq.) Mart. = S. blackburniana.
S. uresana Trel. PALMA BLANCA; SONORAN PALMETTO. To 1m, bare and obscurely ringed. Lvs to 2m, glaucous, blue-waxy, seg. single-fold, central undivided portion to half blade length, lat. veins not tessellated. NW Mex.
→Corypha.

Sabatia Adans. ROSE PINK. Gentianaceae. 17 ann., bienn. or perenn. glab. herbs. St. erect, usually branching. Lvs basal, rosulate and cauline, opposite, sessile, sometimes amplexicaul, rather fleshy. Fls in term. cymes; cor. and cal. tubes short; cal. 5–12-lobed; cor. lobes 5–12, deeply divided, ovate or narrow, rotate. E N Amer., Carib., C Amer.
S. angularis (L.) Pursh. ROSE-PINK; BITTER BLOOM. Ann. to 1m. Lvs to 3.5cm, ovate to oblong, amplexicaul. Fls 3.5cm diam., solitary, rose-pink to white, eye yellow-green, cor. lobes. Summer. Flor., Tex. to NY and Missouri. Z6.
S. bartramii Wilbur. Perenn. to 75cm. Lvs ovate, succulent, to narrow. Fls to 6cm diam., solitary, rose-pink to magenta, eye yellow, edged red; cor. lobes 10–12. SE & C US. Z8.
S. campanulata Torr. ex Griseb. Perenn. to 60cm. Cauline lvs oblong to linear-lanceolate, to 3.5cm, rounded at base. Fls 2.5cm diam., solitary, pink with yellow eye; cor. lobes 5. Summer. Mass. to Flor. and Ark., Bahamas, Cuba. Z6.
S. dodecandra (L.) BSP. Perenn. to 60cm. Lvs to 7.5cm, spathulate to oblong-lanceolate or linear. Fls to 5cm diam., clustered, rose-pink to rose-purple, eye yellow, edged red; cor. lobes 8–12. Summer. Louisiana to Conn. Z6.
S. gentianoides Ellis. Ann. to 60cm, st. simple. Lvs ovate to narrow, thick, succulent. Fls to 5cm diam., clustered, pink with green-yellow eye; cor. lobes 7–12. Summer. SE US. Z8.
S. kennedyana Fern. Perenn. to 75cm, closely resembling S. bartramii but with br. opposite not alt. Lvs to 5cm, linear-lanceolate. Summer–autumn. Nova Scotia to S Carol. Z4.
S. macrophylla Hook. Perenn. to 1.3m. Lvs to 5cm, elliptic to ovate-lanceolate, succulent, glaucous. Fls to 2.5cm diam., white, clustered; cor. lobes 5. Summer. SE US. Z8.
S. paniculata auct. non (Michx.) Pursh = S. quadrangula.
S. quadrangula Wilbur. Ann. to 45cm+; st. 4-angled. Lvs to 3.5cm, lanceolate to oblong. Fls to 2.5cm diam., clustered, white; cor. lobes 5. Summer. Virg. to Flor.

SABIACEAE Bl. 3/48. Meliosma.

Sabicu Lysiloma sabicu.

Sabinea DC. Leguminosae (Papilionoideae). 3 small decid. trees or shrubs. Lvs paripinnate. Fls pea-like large. W Indies.
S. carinalis Griseb. CARIB WOOD. Lfts to 1.5cm, in 6–8 pairs, oblong. Fls borne before lvs, 3–5 per cluster, scarlet to crimson, standard to 3.5cm. Dominica. Z10.

Sabi Star Adenium.
Sabuguero Aralia warmingiana.
Sacahuista Nolina microcarpa.
Sacaline Polygonum sachalinense.

Saccharum L. Gramineae. c37 clumped or rhizomatous perenn. grasses. St. stout, clumped, hard, cane-like, jointed, ringed. Lvs flat, linear-lanceolate to ligulate, in 2 ranks. Infl. term., paniculate, often plumed; spikelets lanceolate, paired, 2-fld. OW Trop., warm temp. Z9 unless specified.
S. arundinaceum Retz. To 3.6m. Lvs linear, to 180×5cm, dark green, midrib stout, margins scabrous.Infl. to 90cm, compact to diffuse, silky pubesc., white, tinged silver or pink. India to Malay Is.
S. barberi Jesw. = S. officinarum.
S. bengalense Retz. MUNJ. To 5m. Lvs to 2m×2.5cm, glaucous, scabrous. Infl. cylindric, compact, to 90cm, pearly white sometimes tinged purple. Summer. N & NW India, Pak., to Iran.
S. ciliare Anderss. = S. bengalense.
S. munja Roxb. = S. bengalense.
S. officinarum L. SUGAR CANE. To 6m. Lvs to 180×5cm+, erect to pendent, margins spiny, rough. Infl. pyramidal, to 90cm+, compact to open, brittle. Summer. Trop. SE Asia, Polyn. 'Violaceum': st. and lvs purple to violet.

S. procerum Roxb. Resembles *S. arundinaceum*, but larger. Infl. larger, more lax and silky. NE India, Burma. Z8.

S. ravennae (L.) Murray. To 2m, lvs linear, lower over 90cm, upper to 60cm, long white-pubesc., rough. Infl. to 60cm, erect, dense or somewhat loose, tinged grey or purple. N Afr., Medit. Z8.

S. sara Roxb. = *S. bengalense*.

S. sinense Roxb. = *S. officinarum*.

S. spontaneum L. To 3m+. Lvs 12.5cm, linear, tapering, glaucous, margins v. scabrous with rigid midrib. Infl. oblong, to 45cm+, dense, somewhat contracted, silvery. Trop. Afr.

Saccolabium Bl.

S. bellinum Rchb. f. = *Gastrochilus bellinus*.

S. bertholdii Rchb. f. = *Robiquetia bertholdii*.

S. calopterum Rchb. f. = *Ascoglossum calopterum*.

S. curvifolium Lindl. = *Ascocentrum curvifolium*.

S. gemmata Lindl. = *Schoenorchis gemmata*.

S. micranthum Lindl. = *Smitinandia micrantha*.

S. mooreanum Rolfe = *Robiquetia mooreana*.

Saccoloma Kaulf. Dennstaedtiaceae. 10 terrestrial ferns. Rhiz. erect to creeping, woody, covered with scales, hairs and massed roots. Fronds stipitate, uniform, erect, 1–5-pinnate or -pinnatifid, ± glab. Trop. (Amer., Madag., SE Asia to Samoa). Z10.

S. inaequale (Kunze) Mett. Rhiz. erect or creeping. Fronds to 1m×80cm, 3–4-pinnate or -pinnatifid, deltoid, firm, pinnae to 65×35cm, petiolate, alt., deltoid, pinnules petiolate, seg. to 2cm, distant, lanceolate or deltoid to oblong, toothed to lobed; stipes to 1m, brown. Trop. Amer. Z10.

→*Davallia, Ithycaulon, Microlepis* and *Orthiopteris*.

Sacosperma G. Tayl.

S. parviflorum (Benth.) G. Tayl. = *Pentas parviflora*.

Sacred Bamboo *Nandina domestica*.

Sacred Bark *Cinchona*.

Sacred Fig *Ficus religiosa*.

Sacred Fir *Abies religiosa*.

Sacred Flower of the Incas *Cantua buxifolia*.

Sacred Lotus *Nelumbo nucifera*.

Sad-coloured Linaria *Linaria tristis*.

Sadleria Kaulf. Blechnaceae. 7 ferns. Rhiz. stout. Fronds uniform, pinnate, large, coriaceous. Hawaii. Z10.

S. cyatheoides Kaulf. Rhiz. to 1.5m+. Fronds to 90cm, bipinnate, dark green above, glaucous beneath; pinnae 30×1–2cm; pinnules to 1.5cm, numerous, linear, revolute; stipes to 60cm, erect. Hawaii.

Saelanthus Forssk.

S. rotundifolius Forssk. = *Cissus rotundifolius*.

Safflower *Carthamus tinctorius*.

Saffron *Crocus sativus*.

Saffron Buckwheat *Eriogonum crocatum*.

Saffron Spike *Aphelandra squarrosa*.

Saga *Tectona grandis*.

Sage *Salvia officinalis*.

Sage Brush *Artemisia*; *A. arbuscula*.

Sagebrush Violet *Viola trinervata*.

Sagenia Presl.

S. cicutaria (L.) Moore = *Tectaria cicutaria*.

S. gemmifera Fée = *Tectaria gemmifera*.

S. macrodonta Fée = *Tectaria macrodonta*.

S. mexicana Fée = *Tectaria mexicana*.

S. pachyphylla Moore = *Tectaria crenata*.

S. pteropus (Kunze) Moore = *Tectaria decurrens*.

S. subtriphylla (Hook. & Arn.) Bedd. = *Tectaria subtriphylla*.

Sage Rose *Turnera ulmifolia*.

Sage, Russian *Perovskia*.

Sage Willow *Salix candida*.

Sagina L. PEARLWORT. Caryophyllaceae. *c*20 small, low-growing, ann. or perenn. herbs. Lvs linear-subulate, paired. Fls small, solitary or in cymes; sep. 4 or 5; pet. (0–)4–5, white; sta. 4–10. Widespread in N Temp. regions, and also occurring on Trop. mts.

S. boydii Buch.-White. Densely cushion-forming, glab. perenn. Lvs crowded, rigid, recurved. Fls solitary; sep. 4 or 5, not opening widely; pet. ± 0. Summer. Said to have been collected in Scotland. Z5.

S. caespitosa auct. = *S. subulata*.

S. glabra auct. = *S. subulata*.

S. pilifera auct. = *S. subulata*.

S. procumbens L. Differs from *S. subulata* in looser habit, with v. inconspicuous, almost apetalous, 4-partite fls. Z4.

S. subulata (Sw.) Presl. Mat-forming perenn.; st. much-branching, slender, rooting. Lvs 1–1.2cm, ending in a white mucro. Fls usually solitary, on slender stalks to 4cm; sep. 5, *c*2mm; pet. 5, white. Summer. W & C Eur. 'Aurea': foliage yellow-green; in many nursery catalogues this plant is given as *Minuartia verna* 'Aurea'. Z4.

→*Arenaria*.

Sagittaria L. Alismataceae. 20 aquatic, sometimes tuberous, perenn. herbs. Lvs basal floating or submerged, submerged lvs reduced phyllodes, emersed lvs linear to sagittate. Fls in (usually) whorled, scapose pan. or rac.; sep. 3, green; pet. 3, white, sometimes blotched purple; sta. 7 to many. Summer. Temp. and Trop. regions.

S. cuneata E. Sheldon. WAPATO. Tubers large. Emersed lvs to 30cm, sagittate, linear to ovate with basal lobes about as long. Scape to 50cm; flls to 2cm diam. N Amer. Z6.

S. engelmanniana Sm. J.G. Sm. Emersed lvs linear to lanceolate, to 25cm, base usually sagittate; petioles to 70cm. Scape to 70cm; fls to 3cm diam. E US. Z6.

S. gigantea hort. = *S. lancifolia* 'Gigantea'.

S. gracilis Pursh = *S. latifolia*.

S. graminea Michx. Ann. or perenn. Emersed lvs linear to ovate, usually without basal lobes, 5–20cm, long-petiolate. Scape to 50cm+: fls 1.2cm diam. E US. var. *platyphylla* Engelm. Lvs broader. E & S US. var. *teres* (S. Wats.) Bogin. Submerged lvs reduced to spongy, cylindrical phyllodes. E US. Z6.

S. guyanensis HBK. Lvs usually floating, thin, broadly ovate, cordate at base, to 12cm. Fls inconspicuous. Pantrop. Z9.

S. hastata Pursh = *S. latifolia*.

S. isoetiformis J.G. Sm. = *S. graminea*.

S. japonica hort. = *S. sagittifolia* 'Flore Pleno'.

S. lancifolia L. Lvs mostly emersed, 15–45cm, narrowly to broadly lanceolate, leathery; petioles to 1m. Scape to 2m; fls 3–5cm diam. Trop. and subtrop. Amer. 'Gigantea': larger in all respects. Z9.

S. latifolia Willd. WAPATO; DUCK POTATO. Perenn., with large tubers. Emersed lvs 10–30cm, broadly sagittate, or linear to ovate with basal lobes. Scape to 1.2m; 3–4cm diam. US. 'Flore Pleno': double-fld . Z7.

S. longiloba Engelm. ex Torr. Lvs emersed, linear to triangular-ovate, to 18cm, sagittate, basal lobes to twice length of lamina; petioles to 90cm. Scape to 1.4m; fls to 1.2cm diam. W N Amer., Mex. Z8.

S. macrophylla Zucc. Lvs emersed, to 25cm, lanceolate to ovate, truncate or hastate at base, submerged lvs linear, to 40cm. Scape to 1m; fls white, 3–4cm diam. Mex. Z9.

S. montevidensis Cham. & Schldl. Lvs to 15cm, linear to broadly ovate, sagittate, basal lobes nearly as long as rest of blade, submerged lvs linear, to 40cm; petioles to 20cm. Scape to 1m; fls 5cm diam., spotted purple. S Amer. Z10.

S. natans Pall. Lvs floating, sometimes emersed, linear to ovate-oblong, cuneate to rounded at base, or cordate with 2 short, obtuse lobes. Fls to 2cm diam. US. Z6.

S. papillosa Buchenau. Lvs floating or emersed, linear to linear-lanceolate, to 30cm, leathery, base not sagittate; petioles to 48cm. Scape to 1m; fls to 3cm. S US. Z7.

S. rigida Pursh. Emersed lvs linear to elliptic or ovate, sometimes with 2 short basal lobes, to 40cm. SCapes geniculate; fls in rac. to 3cm diam. US, nat. SW Engl. Z7.

S. sagittifolia L. OLD WORLD ARROWHEAD. Tuberous. Emersed lvs sagittate, to 25cm, with 2 long, basal lobes; submerged lvs linear, to 80cm, petioles to 45cm; floating lvs lanceolate to ovate. Scape to 1m; fls to 2.5cm diam., spotted purple. Eurasia. 'Flore Pleno': double-fld . Z7.

S. simplex Pursh = *S. latifolia*.

S. sinensis Sims = *S. graminea*.

S. subulata (L.) Buchenau. Lvs mostly linear, to 100cm, submerged lvs ovate-oblong, rarely terminating in floating blade. Scape to 30cm; fls 1.5–2cm diam. E US. Z7.

S. teres Wats. = *S. graminea*.

→*Lophotocarpus*.

Sago *Cycas*; *Metroxylon*.

Sago Fern *Cyathea* (*C. medullaris*).

Sago Palm *Caryota urens*; *Cycas circinalis*; *Metroxylon sagu*.

Saguaro *Carnegiea gigantea*.

Sagus Gaertn.

S. farinifera Gaertn. = *Raphia farinifera*.

S. ruffia Jacq. = *Raphia farinifera*.

Saharan Cypress *Cupressus sempervirens* var. *dupreziana*.
Saho *Trithrinax brasiliensis*.
Sahuaro *Carnegiea gigantea*.
Saigun *Tectona grandis*.
Sailor-caps *Dodecatheon hendersonii*.
Sainfoin *Onobrychis*; *O. viciifolia*.
Saint John's Wort *Hypericum*.

Saintpaulia Wendl. AFRICAN VIOLET. Gesneriaceae. 20 perenn. herbs. St. 0 to v. short with a dense term. rosette of lvs or procumbent, elongated. Lvs petiolate, ± succulent, suborbicular to elliptic, usually hairy. Fls solitary or hairy in cymes; cal. seg. 5, linear or lanceolate; cor. with a short tube opening into a 2-lipped limb, upper lip 2-lobed, lower lip 3-lobed, sta. 2(–3–5), yellow, style exserted. Trop. E Afr. Z10.

S. amaniensis E. Roberts = *S. magungensis*.
S. brevipilosa B.L. Burtt. Lvs to 4×4cm, suborbicular, rounded at apex, cordate at base, shortly erect-hairy above, pale green, patent-hairy beneath; petiole to 4cm. Fls 2–6 on peduncle to 6cm, pilose; cor. purple, glandular-hairy, lower lobes 1.5×2.3cm. Tanz.
S. confusa B.L. Burtt. Lvs to 3×2.8cm, elliptic to ovate, crenate, obtuse, with hairs of 2 lengths on either side, pale green beneath. Fls 1–4 on peduncles to 3cm; cor. to 2.8cm diam., blue-violet. Tanz.
S. difficilis B.L. Burtt. Lvs to 8.5×5.5cm, ovate to ovate-elliptic, acute to subacute, base narrowed to subcordate, serrate-crenate hairy. Fls on peduncles to 7cm; cor. violet-purple, lower lobes 1×0.8cm. Tanz.
S. diplotricha B.L. Burtt. As for *S. confusa* except lf hairs of both lengths erect; lvs tinged purple above. Cor. to 2.5cm diam., pale violet. Tanz.
S. goetzeana Engl. St. creeping, rooting. Lvs to 2.6cm, orbicular, ± entire, hairs uniform above, flushed-purple above, red beneath. Fls white; lower cor. lobes marked rose-lilac. Tanz.
S. grandifolia B.L. Burtt. Lvs 10×8cm, broadly ovate, apex rounded, base cordate, crenate-serrate, erect-hairy above, pale green beneath, short-pilose. Fls on peduncles to 7cm; cor. to 2.5×2.5cm. Tanz.
S. groetii Engl. St. creeping, branching. Lvs to 8.3cm, orbicular, crenate, with hairs of 2 lengths above; petiole to 22cm. Fls 2–4; cor. to 3cm diam., pale mauve, throat violet. Tanz.
S. inconspicua B.L. Burtt. Lvs to 5×3cm, elliptic, rounded or obtuse, base rounded, pilose above, except at margins, pale pilose-pubesc. beneath; petiole to 3.5cm, pilose. Fls 1–6; cor. purple, upper lobes to 6mm, lower lobes to 5mm. Tanz.
S. intermedia B.L. Burtt. St. creeping, rooting. Lvs to 5×4cm, ovate to ovate-orbicular, apex rounded, base rounded or subcordate, crenate-serrate, deep green and pilose above, red-purple and short-pubesc. beneath. Fls many on peduncles to 6cm; cor. limb to 2.5×2.5cm. Tanz.
S. ionantha Wendl. AFRICAN VIOLET; USAMBARA VIOLET. Lvs to 5cm, ovate or ovate-ovate, obtuse, crenate, with mixed hairs of 2 lengths, pale green beneath. Fls 8–10; cor. to 2.2cm diam., light blue to blue-violet, or white with a violet throat. Tanz.
S. kewensis C.B. Clarke = *S. ionantha*.
S. magungensis E. Roberts. St. creeping. Lvs to 3.5cm, broadly ovate to orbicular, obtuse, slightly crenate, with mixed adpressed hairs of 2 lengths; petiole to 5cm. Fls 2–4, deep purple. Tanz. var. *minima* B.L. Burtt. Lvs to 2cm. Fls smaller. var. *occidentalis* B.L. Burtt. St. flushed purple. Lvs fleshy, less densely hairy.
S. nitida B.L. Burtt. St. v. short, simple or compactly branched. Lvs 5.5×5cm, ovate or suborbicular, apex rounded, base cordate, lustrous dark green above, crenate, cor. deep violet, upper lobes 7×8mm, lower lobes to 1×1cm. Tanz.
S. orbicularis B.L. Burtt. Lvs ovate-orbicular, to 6cm, dentate, adpressed-hairy; petioles to 7.5cm. Fls 8–10; cor. to 2.2cm diam., pale violet to white with blue-violet throat. Tanz. var. *purpurea* B.L. Burtt. Fls deep purple.
S. pendula B.L. Burtt. St. creeping, rooting. Lvs to 4.5×3.5cm, ovate or orbicular, apex obtuse, base subcordate, erect-pilose above, short-pilose beneath, crenate-serrate; petiole to 3.5cm. Fls usually solitary on peduncles to 5cm; cor. limb to 2.5×2.5cm, purple. Tanz.
S. pusilla Engl. Differs from *S. goetzeana* in st., narrower often ascending; lvs ovate-orbicular; lower cor. lobes almost entirely mauve. Tanz.
S. rupicola B.L. Burtt. Lvs to 6.5×4.5cm, ovate, apex obtuse, base cordate, short erect-pilose above, patent-pilose beneath, obscurely crenate-serrate; petiole to 9cm. Fls 6 per cyme; cor. limb to 2.3cm diam., purple. SE Kenya.
S. shumensis B.L. Burtt. Lvs to 3.5×3cm, ovate or ovate-orbicular, serrate-dentate, hairy, veins often red-tinged beneath. Fls to 5 on peduncles to 6cm; cor. v. pale mauve to white, lower lip sometimes marked violet. Tanz.

S. teitensis B.L. Burtt. Lvs to 7.5×5.5cm, broadly elliptic to sub-orbicular, apex rounded, base subpeltate, erect-pilose, crenate-dentate. Fls on peduncles to 5cm; cor. lower lip to 1.5×2cm. Kenya.
S. tongwensis B.L. Burtt. As for *S. iomantha* except lvs elliptic or ovate-elliptic, apex subacute, dark green above, often maroon beneath. Fls purple. Tanz.
S. velutina B.L. Burtt. Lvs to 4cm, suborbicular, base cordate, velvety, slightly crenate-serrate, with erect hairs of 2 lengths above, red-maroon beneath. Fls on peduncles to 5cm; cor. pale mauve, glandular-ciliate, edged white. Tanz. *Standard* (foliage) 'Amazen Grace': lvs dark green, cordate, wavy, serrate; 'Blue Border': lvs edged white; 'Claret Queen': lvs dark green, conspicuously serrate; 'Pink Miracle': lvs orbicular, red beneath. (fls) 'Dupont Blue': fls violet-blue; 'Glacier': fls single to semi-double, star-shaped, white with pale cream sta.; 'Hawaii': fls single, star-shaped, deep royal-blue, fringed silver-white; 'Marguerite': fls v. large, pale pink with wavy pet.; 'Porcelain': fls single, white with blue blotches. *Dwarf and Miniature* 'Little Jewel': lvs tiny, dark green, waxy; 'Love Bug': fls semi-double, wine-red; 'Mini Marina': lvs miniature, serrate; 'Pip Squeak': fls tiny, free, pale pink; 'Wee Hope': fls semi-double, white with a blue centre. *Trailing* 'Dancin' Trail': lvs dark green, red beneath; 'Ding Dong Trail': fls single, campanulate, pale pink with deeper shading on throat; 'Magic Trail': lvs mid-green, quilted; 'Snowy Trail': fls semi-dwarf, semi-double, white; 'Trail's Delight': lvs cordate, entire, edged and blotched white; 'Winding Trail': habit dwarf, fls double, blue and white.

Sakaki *Cleyera japonica*.
Sakhalin Fir *Abies sachalinensis*.
Sakhalin Spikenard *Aralia schmidtii*.
Sakhalin Spruce *Picea glehnii*.

Salacca Reinw. ex Bl. SALAK. Palmae. 10 palms. St. subterranean or short, often with adventitious roots. Lvs entire, emarginate and pinnately ribbed or pinnate, sheath armed, spiny; petiole densely spiny; pinnae single-fold, linear or sigmoid, pubesc. beneath. Infl. axill., spicate or branched ×2. Fr. 1-seeded, globose to ellipsoid, with rows of smooth or spine-like scales. Burm. and Indochina through to Borneo, Java and Philipp. Z10.
S. edulis Reinw. non Whitm. nec Wallace = *S. zalacca* and *S. wallichiana*.
S. wallichiana Mart. 6–7m. St. to 50×10cm, creeping. Lvs 5–7.5m, pinnae held in differing planes, apex fused, obtriangular, petiole spines flat, triangular, in regular rows.
S. zalacca (Gaertn.) Voss. Petioles to 6m, acaulescent, *c*2m, studded with flat, glittering, dark brown spines; pinnae numerous, arranged irregularly, reflexed, glossy green above, white-green below, term. pair fused, truncate, upper margin tattering. Fr. 6–8cm, with rust-coloured scales, flesh yellow-brown, edible. Malay Archipel., much cult., origin unknown. →*Calamus*.

Salad Bean *Phaseolus vulgaris*.
Salak *Salacca*.
Salal *Gaultheria shallon*.

Salazaria Torr. BLADDER-SAGE. Labiatae. 1 grey-pubesc. shrub to 1m, densely branched, branchlets spinescent. Lvs 1–5.5cm, bract-like, oblong or broadly lanceolate. Verticillasters 1–3-fld, in loose spikes; cal. inflating to a papery bladder in fr.; cor. to 2cm, purple, tubular, upper lip arched, lower lip recurved. Winter–spring. SW US, NW Mex. Z9.
S. mexicana Torr.

SALICACEAE Mirb. 2/435. *Populus, Salix*

Salix L. WILLOW; OSIER; SALLOW. Salicaceae. *c*300 trees and shrubs, most decid. and dioecious. Winter buds with a single scale. Lvs simple. Fls v. small, apetalous, subtended by scales in a dense catkin; catkin usually erect, appearing before or with foliage, often silver-pubescent when immature; ♂ fls with 2–9 sta.; ♀ fl. a flask-shaped ovary, stigmas 2. Cosmop. except Aus.
S. acutifolia Willd. Similar to *S. daphnoides* but shorter; lvs 8–12cm, narrow, 15 or more pairs of lat. veins. Catkin hairs longer and whiter. Russia to E Asia. 'Blue Streak': st. black, glossy with blue-white bloom. 'Pendulifolia': to 6m, lvs pendent. Z5.
S. adenophylla Hook. = *S. cordata*.
S. aegyptiaca L. Tree or tall shrub to 4m. Twigs red, grey-pubesc. when young. Lvs 6–15cm, obovate-oblong, downy at first above, glaucous beneath, toothed. Catkins 5–6cm, ♀ catkins to 8cm in fr. Late winter. Turk., Armenia, Iran. Z6.

S. *alba* L. WHITE WILLOW. Tree to 25m. Twigs light grey-pink to olive brown, silky-hairy at first. Lvs 5–10cm, lanceolate, acuminate, silky white-pubesc., dull green above, blue-green beneath, serrulate. Catkins dense, 4–6cm, on leafy stalks. Eur., N Afr. to C Asia. 'Aurea': br. yellow-green; lvs yellow-green. 'Liempde': vigorous, narrowly conical ♂ tree. var. *caerulea* (Sm.) Sm. CRICKET-BAT WILLOW. Lvs 10–11cm, near glab. when mature, blue green above, glaucous beneath. 'Britzensis' (CORAL BARK WILLOW; SCARLET WILLOW), syn. 'Chrysostela': br. bright orange-red in winter. var. *sericea* Gaudin. SILVER WILLOW. Lvs 10cm, silver-white. var. *vitellina* (L.) Stokes. GOLDEN WILLOW. Twigs bright yellow-orange, showy in winter. Z2.

S. *alba* 'Vitellina Pendula' see *S.* ×*sepulcralis* 'Chrysocoma'.
S. *alba* f. *argentea* Wimm. = *S. alba* var. *sericea*.
S. *alba* 'Tristis' = *S.* ×*sepulcralis chrysocoma*.
S. *albicans* Bong. = *S. laggeri*.
S. *alpina* Scop. Similar to *S. myrsinites* but ± prostrate; lvs entire; dead lvs not persistent, catkins slender. Carpath., E Alps. Z5.
S. ×*ambigua* Ehrh. (*S. aurita* × *S. repens.*) Mat-forming shrub to 1.5m. Twigs becoming glab., dark red-brown. Lvs to 4.5cm, obovate-oblong, dark green above, grey beneath, entire, undulate, revolute. Catkins to 12mm, precocious. Br. Isles, Eur. Z7.
S. *amygdalina* L. = *S. triandra*.
S. *amygdaloides* Anderss. PEACH LEAVED WILLOW. Tree to 20m. Twigs yellow or red-brown, glab. Lvs 8–12cm, oval-lanceolate, pubesc. when young, pale, glaucous beneath, serrulate. ♂ catkins to 5cm; ♀ 4–10cm. W N Amer. Z5.
S. *andersoniana* Sm. = *S. myrsinifolia*.
S. *anglorum* Cham. = *S. arctica*.
S. *anglorum* var. *araioclada* Schneid. = *S. arctica* var. *petraea*.
S. *angustifolia* Willd. = *S. wilhelmsiana*.
S. *annularis* Asch. = *S. babylonica* 'Crispa'.
S. *apoda* Trautv. Differs from *S. hastata* in lvs more obovate, bright green above. NC Eur., Cauc. Z6.
S. *appendiculata* Vill. Tree or tall shrub to 6m. Twigs shorthaired, becoming glab. Lvs toothed to entire, lanceolate-obovate, glabrescent above, pubesc. beneath, veins sunken above. Catkins 3cm, lax. C Eur., Balk. Penins. Z7.
S. *aquatica* Sm. = *S. cinerea*.
S. *arbuscula* L. Small, dense shrub to 50cm. Twigs soon glab. Lvs 0.5–4cm, elliptic-lanceolate, veins 7–12 pairs, glossy above, glaucous beneath, glandular-toothed. Catkins 1–2cm, appearing with lvs; anth. red. Scotland, Scand., N Russia. Z3.
S. *arbuscula* 'Erecta' = *S. waldsteiniana*.
S. *arbutifolia* Pall. Large tree; br. long, slender white-bloomed. Lvs lanceolate, bright green, initially glaucous. ♂ catkins pendulous, not erect. N Asia. Z8.
S. *arctica* Pall. ARCTIC WILLOW. Creeping shrub to 10cm. Twigs thick, glossy. Lvs entire, obovate-ovate, leathery, becoming glab., veins reticulate, prominent beneath. Catkins 2–4cm, scales dark purple; hairy. Arc. Eur., Asia and Amer. var. *petraea* Anderss. St. often buried, young twigs yellow. Z1.
S. *arenaria* L. Shrub to 1m. Lvs obovate, hairs hooked, 5–8 pairs of lat. veins, sparsely glandular-toothed. Atlantic Eur. and Poland. Z6.
S. *atrocinerea* Brot. = *S. cinerea* ssp. *oleifolia*.
S. *aurita* L. EARED WILLOW. Bushy shrub to 2.5m. Twigs dark red-brown, slender, becoming glab. Lvs 2–6cm, obovate to obovate-lanceolate, serrate, pubesc., dull green above, grey-green beneath, tip often twisted; stipules ear-shaped, serrate. Catkins 1–2.5cm, cylindrical, precocious. Eur., except Arc. and Medit. Z5.
S. *babylonica* L. BABYLON WEEPING WILLOW. Tree 10–12m. Bark tinged green, twigs long, pendulous, often drooping to ground. Lvs 8–16cm, linear-lanceolate, acuminate, deep green above, grey green beneath, glab., serrulate. Catkins to 2×0.4cm. Asia, China, Manch. 'Crispa': lvs curled into rings, slow growing. 'Pendula': graceful, weeping, canker and scab-resistent. 'Ramulis Aureis' see *S.* ×*sepulcralis* 'Chrysocoma'. 'Tortuosa' see *S. matsudana* 'Tortuosa'.
S. *babylonica* Franch. non L. = *S. matsudana*.
S. *babylonica* 'Pekinensis' = *S. matsudana*.
S. *bakeri* Seemen = *S. lasiolepis*. Z5.
S. ×*balfourii* Linton. (*S. lanata* × *S. caprea*.) Shrub to 3m. Lvs 2.5–7.5cm, broad-elliptic, hairy beneath. Catkins 5×2.5cm, silky. N Eur. Z4.
S. *balsamifera* (Hook.) Barratt = *S. pyrifolia*.
S. 'Basfordiana' = *S.* ×*rubens* 'Basfordiana'.
S. ×*bebbii* Gand. (*S. eriocephala* × *S. sericea*.) Differs from *S. eriocephala* in twigs brittle at base; lvs long-acuminate, glaucous beneath. N Amer. var. *glaucophylla* (Bebb). Lvs thicker. Z4.
S. *bicolor* Willd. non Ehrh. = *S. schraderiana*.
S. ×*blanda* Anderss. = *S.* ×*pendulina*.

S. *bockii* Seemen. Shrub to 3m. Twigs slender, grey downy. Lvs 0.6–1.5cm, oblong-obovate, obovate, bright green above, glaucous and silky beneath, ± entire. ♀ catkins to 4cm, ♂ shorter. Autumn. W China. Z6.
S. ×*boydii* Linton. (*S. lapponum* × *S. reticulata.*) Dwarf shrub. Twigs persistently hairy. Lvs nearly circular, grey-pubesc., veins prominent. Br. Isles. Z5.
S. *brachycarpa* Nutt. Shrub to 1.4m. Twigs yellow or red-brown, glab. with many lf scars. Lvs 4.5cm, entire, elliptic-oblong, base obtuse, grey-pubesc. Catkins to 2cm. N Amer., S Greenland. Z4.
S. *brachystachys* Benth. = *S. scouleriana*.
S. *breviserrata* Flod. Differs from *S. myrsinites* in lvs densely glandular-toothed, withered lvs not persistent. Alps, Pyren., N Spain. Z5.
S. *caerulea* Sm. = *S. alba* var. *caerulea*.
S. *caesia* Vill. BLUE WILLOW. Shrub to 1m. Twigs glossy brown. Lvs 2–3cm, entire, obovate-elliptic, obtuse to subcordate at base, tip acuminate, glab., dull green above, paler beneath. Catkins 1–2cm. Alps, S Urals. Z6.
S. ×*calliantha* Kern. (*S. daphnoides* × *S. purpurea*.) Large shrub to small tree. Lvs lanceolate to oblanceolate, glossy deep green above, sea green beneath. Z5.
S. ×*calodendron* Wimm. (*S. caprea* × *S. cinerea* × *S. viminalis*.) Shrub or small tree, 3–10m. Twigs ascending, felty at first. Lvs to 18cm, glandular-toothed, revolute, oblong-elliptic, dull green above, grey-green, more densely pubesc. beneath, veins tinged red. Catkins cylindrical, 3–7cm. ♂ unknown. Gdn origin, escaped in N. Eur. Z6.
S. *candida* Fluegge SAGE WILLOW; HOARY WILLOW. Shrub to 2m. Twigs tomentose, becoming glossy, red brown. Lvs to 12cm, linear to oblong-lanceolate, thick, rugose, tomentose beneath, entire to denticulate. Catkins 2.5cm; anth. red. N Amer. Z5.
S. *caprea* L. GOAT WILLOW; PUSSY WILLOW; FLORIST'S WILLOW; SALLOW. Tree or shrub to 10m. Twigs stout, glab., yellow-brown.Lvs to 12cm, toothed, broadly elliptic-obovate, dark green above, grey-green, hairy beneath. Catkins to 2.5×2cm, ovoid-cylindrical; anth. golden. Eur. to NE Asia. Cvs of weeping habit include 'Kilmarnock', 'Pendula', 'Weeping Sally'. var. *sphacelata* (Sm.) Wahlenb. Lvs subentire; grey-sericeous. Z5.
S. *caspica* Pall. Large shrub or small tree to 6m. Twigs brown becoming yellow-white, glossy. Lvs to 8cm, serrate or entire, linear-lanceolate, acute, becoming glab., venation prominent beneath. Catkins 2.5cm. SE Russia to W and C Asia. Z6.
S. *chilensis* Molina. Shrub or small tree. Twigs slender, drooping. Lvs to 15cm, linear-lanceolate, bright green, glab. persistent. Mex. to S Amer. Z8.
S. *chlorolepis* Fern. GREEN-SCALED WILLOW. Shrub to 1m. TWigs red-brown. Lvs 1–3cm, elliptic-lanceolate, bright green above, glaucous beneath, usually entire. Catkins 5–13mm. Canada. Z2.
S. *cinerea* L. GREY WILLOW. Shrub 4–6m. Twigs becoming glab. Lvs to 11cm, lanceolate-obovate, dull green, sparse-pubesc. above, grey-pubesc. beneath, crenate to irregularly serrate. Catkins 2–4×1–2cm, v. silky. Eur. to W Asia. 'Tricolor' ('Variegata'): lvs marked yellow and cream. ssp. *oleifolia* (Sm.) Macreight. RUSTY SALLOW. Twigs dark red-brown; lvs dark green above, grey beneath with rusty hairs. Z2.
S. *columbiae* Nels. & Macbr. = *S. pyrifolia*.
S. *commutata* Bebb. Shrub to 3m. Twigs yellow-brown, thick, subglabrous. Lvs 6–8cm, obovate-lanceolate or elliptic, woolly at first, entire to finely gland. serrate. Catkins appearing with lvs; ♂ to 3cm, ♀ to 6cm. Calif. to Alask. Z4.
S. *cordata* Michx. FURRY WILLOW. Differs from *S. syrticola* in lvs 6–12cm, glandular-serrate. Only ♀ in cult. NE N Amer. Z2.
S. *cordata* var. *lutea* Bebb = *S. lutea*.
S. *cordata* Muhlenb. = *S. eriocephala*.
S. ×*cottetii* Lagger ex Kern. (*S. myrsinifolia* × *S. retusa.*) Vigorous low-growing shrub. St. prostrate. Lvs dark glossy green above, paler beneath. Catkins precocious. ♂ clones are in cult. Early spring. Z5.
S. *cutleri* Tuckerm. = *S. uva-ursi*.
S. *cyclophylla* Seemen = *S. yezoalpina*.
S. *dahurica* Turcz. ex Kakschewitz = *S. miyabeana*.
S. *daphnoides* Vill. VIOLET WILLOW. Tree or tall shrub to 10m. Bark smooth, grey; twigs erect to spreading, red-brown, glaucous. Lvs 5–10cm, oblong-lanceolate, 8–12 pairs veins, dark green above, glaucous beneath, glandular-serrate. Catkins 3cm, densely silky, precocious. Eur. to C Asia, Himal. 'Aglaia': catkins large, bright silver in early spring, st. not glaucous in winter. Z5.
S. *daphnoides* var. *acutifolia* (Willd.) Doell = *S. acutifolia*.
S. ×*dasyclados* Wimm. Parentage obscure. Similar to *S.* ×*stipularis* except lvs broadly lanceolate, thinly silky beneath; catkin scales dark brown. N Eur. 'Grandis': v. vigorous. Z6.
S. *discolor* Muhlenb. Shrub or small tree, 4–7m. Twigs becoming glab., purple-brown. Lvs 4–10cm, oblong-lanceolate, tapering,

bright green above, glaucous beneath, entire to serrate. Catkins dense, oblong, 3–7cm, precocious. N Amer. Z2.

S. ×doniana Sm. (*S. purpurea* ×*S. repens.*) Shrub to 1.5m. Twigs red-brown, glab. Lvs 2–4cm, lanceolate, glossy green above, glaucous beneath, subentire. Catkins precocious. Eur. Z6.

S. dracunculifolia Boiss. = *S. wilhelmsiana.*

S. drummondiana Barratt ex Hook. Shrub to 4m. Twigs dark, slender, puberulent. Lvs 2–4cm, lanceolate, glossy green above, glaucous beneath, subentire. Catkins precocious. W N Amer. Z3.

S. ×ehrhartiana Sm. (*S. alba* ×*S. pentandra.*) Large shrub to medium tree. Branchlets glossy, olive brown. Lvs oblong-lanceolate, glossy, green. Catkins with or after lvs. Eur.

S. elaeagnos Scop. HOARY WILLOW; ROSEMARY WILLOW. Tall shrub or small tree to 6m. Twigs grey-velvety then glab., red-yellow to brown. Lvs 6–15cm, linear-lanceolate, dark glossy green above, felted-white beneath, entire or toothed near apex. Catkins 6×1cm, precocious. C Eur. to Asia Minor. Z4.

S. elegantissima Koch = *S. ×pendulina* var. *elegantissima.*

S. ×erdingeri Kern. (*S. caprea* ×*S. daphnoides.*) Similar to *S. caprea* except lvs obovate-oblong, silky when young. N Eur. Z5.

S. eriocephala Michx. Shrub to 4m. Twigs finely hairy or glab. Lvs 5–14cm, oblong-lanceolate, subcordate at base, silky when young, serrate. ♂ catkins to 5cm, ♀ to 6cm. N Amer. Z6.

S. ×erythroflexuosa Rag. = *S. ×sepulcralis* 'Erythroflexuosa'.

S. eucalyptoides Pall. = *S. arbutifolia.*

S. exigua Nutt. COYOTE WILLOW. To 9m. Twigs finely hairy or glab. Lvs 5–14cm, linear to oblong-lanceolate, subcordate at base, silky when young, serrate. ♂ catkins to 5cm, ♀ to 6cm. N Amer. Z2.

S. fargesii Burkh. Shrub to 3m. Twigs glab., glossy purple; buds large, red. Lvs 7–16cm, elliptic, glossy, dark green above, silky beneath, serrulate. Catkins to 12cm. China. Z6.

S. finnmarchica Willd. (*S. myrtilloides* ×*S. repens.*) Dwarf, carpet-forming shrub; br. ascending. Lvs small. Catkins massed along br. before lvs. Early spring. Nat. hybrid N & C Eur. Z5.

S. flavescens Nutt. = *S. scouleriana.*

S. foetida Schleich. Differs from *S. arbuscula* in lvs to 3cm, 5–10 pairs of veins, densely serrate with large white glands', malodorous when crushed. Eur. Z6.

S. formosa Willd. = *S. arbuscula.*

S. fragilis L. CRACK WILLOW; BRITTLE WILLOW. Tree to 25m. Twigs glab., olive-brown, snapping at junctions. Lvs 9–15cm, lanceolate, dark green above, glaucous beneath, glandular-serrate; petioles with 2 glands. Catkins drooping, 3–7cm. Eur., N Asia, nat. N Amer. var. *decipiens* (Hoffm.) Koch. 2nd-year twigs ochre, lvs to 9cm, bright green above. var. *russelliana* (Sm.) Koch. Lvs narrower, 13–15cm, apex attenuate. Z5.

S. franciscana Seemen = *S. lasiolepsis.*

S. ×friesiana Anderss. (*S. repens* ×*S. viminalis.*) Differs from *S. rosmarinifolia* in lvs more broadly lanceolate, persistently silky beneath. ♂ catkins ovoid, silky. Eur. Z8.

S. fruticulosa Anderss. = *S. hylematica.*

S. glabra Scop. Shrub to 1.5m. Twigs glab., dark red-brown. Lvs to 8cm, broad-elliptic to oblong, crenate to dentate, glab., leathery, glaucous beneath. Catkins 7×1cm, lax, appearing with lvs. Alps. Z6.

S. glacialis Anderss. Prostrate shrub. Lvs to 2cm, obovate-ovate, becoming glab., toothed at base. ♀ catkins round, scales black. Arc. Amer., Alask. Z1.

S. glauca L. ARCTIC GREY WILLOW. To 1m. Twigs dark red, hirsute when young, knotted grey brown. Lvs to 7cm, obovate-lanceolate, thin, entire, blue-green beneath, densely pubesc. esp. when young, veins 5–6 pairs. Catkins stout, developing with lvs. Late summer. N Eur., N Asia, NW Amer. Z2.

S. glaucosericea Flod. ALPINE GREY WILLOW. Differs from *S. glauca* in lvs pale green, glossy above, silky throughout, veins in 7–9 pairs. Alps. Z3.

S. gracilis Anderss. = *S. petiolaris.*

S. gracilistyla Miq. ROSEGOLD PUSSY WILLOW. Shrub to 3m. Br. erect, twigs hoary becoming glab. Lvs 5–12cm, linear-oblong, silky becoming glab. above, hairy beneath, entire to serrulate. Catkins 2–5cm. Jap., Korea, Manch. var. *melanostachys* (Mak.) C. Schneid. Lvs glab. Catkin scales dark brown to black. ♂. Z6.

S. ×grahamii Borrer ex Bak. (*S. herbacea* ×*S. aurita* ×*S. repens.*) GRAHAM'S WILLOW. Dwarf shrub to 50cm. Twigs densely pubesc. at first. Lvs to 5cm, ovate to round, hairy, crenate to toothed. Catkins to 2cm, stigma red. ♀. Eur. 'Moorei': catkin scales narrow-oblong. Z4.

S. grandifolia Ser. = *S. appendiculata.*

S. hastata L. HALBERD-WILLOW. Upright, dense shrub to 1.5m. Twigs becoming glab., sometimes red or purple-green in second year. Lvs 2–8cm, elliptic-obovate or lanceolate, cordate to rounded at base, becoming glab. above, glaucous beneath, veins

reticulate, midrib yellow-green, entire to serrulate. Catkins 6cm. C Eur. to NE Asia, Kashmir. 'Wehrhanii': slow-growing, spreading small to medium shrub. Catkins profuse, silver-grey becoming yellow. ♂ clone. Z6.

S. hastata var. *apoda* (Trautv.) Laksch. = *S. apoda.*

S. hegetschweileri Heer. Shrub to 4m. Twigs dark, glossy, tomentose to glab. Lvs obovate or ovate, glab., glossy, dark green above, glaucous beneath, 7–10 pairs veins, with occasional gland. teeth. Catkins to 4×2cm, precocious. Alps. Z6.

S. helvetica Vill. SWISS WILLOW. Similar to *S. lapponum* except lvs shorter, not crowded toward end of the st., widest above midpoint, becoming glab. and glossy above. Alps. Z6.

S. herbacea L. DWARF WILLOW. 2–15cm. St. v. slender, prostrate or buried. Twigs 2–3cm. Lvs to 2cm, ovate-reniform, emarginate, bright green, glossy, serrate. Catkins to 1.5cm. Arc. Circle, Eur. and N Asia (mts). Z2.

S. heteromera Hand.-Mazz. = *S. babylonica.*

S. hippophaifolia Thuill. = *S. ×mollissima* var. *hippophaifolia.*

S. hondoensis Koidz. = *S. jessoensis.*

S. hookeriana Barratt. Shrub to 1m, occas. prostrate; twigs lanate. Lvs 5–15cm, ovate to broad-ovate, white-pubesc. becoming glab., blue-green beneath, entire to finely toothed. ♀ catkins 8–12cm in fr., ♂ 3–5cm. NW Amer. Z6.

S. humboldtiana Willd. = *S. chilensis.*

S. humilis Marsh. PRAIRIE WILLOW. Shrub to 3m. Twigs woolly. Lvs 5–10cm, lanceolate-oblong, serrulate, downy at first, veins prominent beneath. Catkins red, precocious. N Amer. Z4.

S. hylematica Schneid. Dwarf shrub; shoots short, thick, red-brown, initially villous. Lvs to 1cm, lanceolate to oblanceolate, denticulate or entire. ♂ catkins to 1.5×0.9cm, ♀ catkins shorter. W Himal. Z7.

S. incana Michx. non Schrank = *S. candida.*

S. incana Schrank non Michx. = *S. elaeagnos.*

S. integra Thunb. Differs from *S. purpurea* in lvs light green. Korea, Jap. 'Itakuro Nishiki': lvs blotched white. Z6.

S. interior Rowlee = *S. exigua.*

S. irrorata Anderss. Shrub to 3m. Twigs smooth, purple-yellow, waxy. Lvs 5–10cm, oblong-lanceolate, acuminate, glossy above, glaucous beneath, entire to sparsely serrate. Catkins dense, 2–3cm. N Amer. Z5.

S. japonica Thunb. Tall shrub. Br. slender, brown. Lvs 5–12cm, elliptic-oblong, apex acuminate, scabrous, gland., serrate, silky at first, bright green above, blue green beneath. Catkins 8–10cm, slender, appearing with lvs. Japan. Z8.

S. jessoensis Seemen. Tree to 8m. Bark light grey-brown, scaly; twigs hairy at first. Lvs 5–10cm, lanceolate, silky when young, blue-green silky beneath, serrate. Catkins 2–3cm. Jap. Z6.

S. kinuyanagi Kimura. A ♂ clone cultivated in Japan, differing from *S. viminalis* in papery lvs to 20cm. Jap. (only in cult.). Also known as *S.* 'Kishu'. Z6.

S. kitaibeliana Willd. Similar to *S. retusa* except lvs 2–3cm, glossy, obtuse acute, catkin to 4cm. SE Europe. Z2.

S. koriyanagi Kimura. Similar to *S. purpurea* except lvs 1cm across, coriaceous, deep green above, blue-green beneath. Jap., Korea. Z6.

S. laevigata Bebb. RED WILLOW; POLISHED WILLOW. Tree to 15m, twigs red to yellow-brown, glab. Lvs 5–13cm, oblong-lanceolate, light green above, glaucous beneath, serrulate. Catkins 3–10cm. SW US. Z5.

S. laggeri Wimm. Shrub 2–3m. Twigs spreading, knotty, thick, villous becoming glab. Lvs lanceolate-narrow elliptic, large, glabrescent deep green above, lanate beneath, toothed. Catkins 2–4×1–2cm, golden-silky. Alps. Z6.

S. lanata L. WOOLLY WILLOW. Shrub to 1.5m. Twigs lanate, ascending, gnarled with age. Lvs 2–7cm, round-oval or obovate, apex deflexed, silky hairy then glossy, dull green above, glaucous beneath, 5–6 pairs veins, undulate. ♂ catkins golden yellow, 2.5–5cm, ♀ to 8cm in fr. Arc., Subarc. Asia and Eur. 'Stuartii': dwarf shrublet with gnarled br.; twigs yellow, buds orange in winter. Lvs smaller, catkins larger than in *S. lanata* – possibly a hybrid with *S. lapponicum.* Z2.

S. lancifolia Anderss. = *S. lasiandra.*

S. lapponum L. DOWNY WILLOW; LAPLAND WILLOW. Low, densely branched shrub, 20–150cm. Twigs thin, dark red-brown. Lvs 2.5–6cm, lanceolate-ovate, crowded toward end of twigs, olive green, downy above, grey-tomentose beneath, entire. Catkins dense, 2–4×1–1.5cm, precocious. N Eur. to N Asia. Z3.

S. lasiandra Benth. Similar to *S. pentandra* except to 15m; twigs woolly at first; lvs oval-lanceolate, midrib yellow. W N Amer. Z5.

S. lasiolepis Benth. ARROYO WILLOW. Shrub or small tree to 12m. Twigs yellow dark brown, hairy. Lvs 6–10cm, oblong-lanceolate, dark green, glab. above, glaucous beneath, subentire. Catkins 3–7cm, precocious. W N Amer. Z5.

S. laurifolia Wesm. = *S. pentandra.*

S. lindleyana Wall. Dwarf procumbent shrubs, sometimes confused with *S. hylematica*, but glab. throughout. Lvs 0.5–1.2cm, ovate-spathulate, glossy, leathery above, paler beneath; petiole yellow-brown, glossy. ♂ catkins to 1cm. Nepal, Yunnan. Z7.

S. livida Wahlenb. = *S. starkeana*.

S. longifolia Muhlenb. = *S. exigua*.

S. lucida Muhlenb. SHINING WILLOW. To 8m. Twigs glossy, glab., yellow-brown. Lvs 7–12cm, ovate-lanceolate, glossy, pale beneath, glandular-serrate. Catkins 2–7cm, sta. golden. N Amer. Z2.

S. lutea Nutt. Shrub to 5m. Twigs yellow-brown, glab. Lvs 4–11cm, lanceolate, rounded at base, yellow-green above, glaucous beneath, entire to finely serrate. Catkins to 4cm, precocious. W N Amer. Z5.

S. lyallii Heller = *S. lasiandra*.

S. magnifica Hemsl. To 6m. Twigs purple, becoming red; buds purple. Lvs 10–25cm, oval-obovate, cordate at base, tough, grey-green above, glaucous beneath, veins red, entire. Catkins long, slender, red-tinted, ascending. China. Z7.

S. makinoana Seemen = *S. udensis*.

S. 'Mark Postill' (*S. hastata* 'Wehrhanii' × *S. lanata*.) Dwarf spreading shrub; shoots purple-brown in winter. Lvs pale green at first, then thinly white-pubesc., later dark green. Catkins thick, silvery then green, produced with and after lvs. Gdn orig. Z6.

S. matsudana Koidz. PEKING WILLOW. Differs from *S. babylonica* in twigs erect to pendulous; lvs blue-green beneath. China, NE Asia. 'Tortuosa' (DRAGON'S CLAW WILLOW): main br., branchlets and lvs strongly tortuous. Z5.

S. medemii Boiss. = *S. aegyptiaca*.

S. medwedewii Dode. Small shrub closely related to *S. triandra* with lvs long, narrow, v. glaucous beneath. Catkins produced with lvs. Spring. Asia Minor.

S. melanostachys Mak. = *S. gracilistyla* var. *melanostachys*.

S. × meyeriana Rostk. ex Willd. (? *S. pentandra* × *S. fragilis*.) Similar to *S. pentandra* except bark fissured; lvs long-acuminate; catkins 4–5×1cm. Eur. Z5.

S. mielichhoferi Saut. Shrub to 2m. Twigs black to brown-green, pubesc. at first, becoming gnarled. Lvs to 8cm, obovate-lanceolate, dense-pubesc. becoming glab., dull green above, pale green beneath, usually toothed. Catkins lax, appearing with lvs. Alps. Z6.

S. missouriensis Bebb = *S. eriocephala*.

S. miyabeana Seemen. Shrub or small tree. Twigs glab., pale brown. Lvs 5–15cm, narrow-lanceolate, glab., somewhat glaucous beneath, undulate. Catkins 3–5cm, precocious. N Jap. Z6.

S. × mollissima Hoffm. ex Elwert. (*S. triandra* × *S. viminalis*.) To 6m. Differs from *S. viminalis* in lvs soon glab. ♀ catkins to 5mm wide. Eur. var. *hippophaifolia* (Thuill.) Wimm. Large shrub to small tree; twigs olive brown; lvs long, narrow. Catkins differ from those of *S. triandra* in red-tinted anth. ♂. var. *undulata* (Ehrh.) Wimm. Similar to *S. triandra* except lf tip much longer and thinner; catkins 3–4×0.5cm. Z6.

S. moupinensis Franch. Differs from *S. fargesii* in twigs slender, orange-red; lvs to only 10cm. ♀ only in cult. W China. Z6.

S. multinervis Franch. & Savat. = *S. integra*.

S. muscina hort. = *S. aegyptiaca*.

S. × myricoides auct. non Muhlenb. = *S. × bebbii*.

S. myrsinifolia Salisb. WHORTLE WILLOW. Variable, to 4m. Bark dark, fissured; twigs dull green-brown. Lvs 2–7cm, elliptic-obovate or oblong, dark green above, glaucous beneath, serrate to subentire. Catkins 1.5–4×1–1.5cm, appearing with lvs. Eur., Asia Minor, W Sib. Z5.

S. myrsinites L. MYRTLE WILLOW. Prostrate or ascending to 60cm. Br. slender, glossy, pubesc., becoming, glab., crooked, dark brown with age. Lvs 1–5cm, round-oval, tough, bright green, glossy, glandular-toothed. Dead lvs persist to second season. Catkins dark purple, 2.5cm, dense. N & E Eur., W Asia. Z5.

S. myrtilloides L. SWAMP WILLOW. 15–60cm. St. creeping, rooting; twigs ascending, soon glab., yellow-brown. Lvs 1.5–2cm, obovate-lanceolate, entire or sparsely toothed, involute, glab., dull, dark green above, glaucous to purple-green beneath. Catkins 1–2cm; scales tipped red, anth. yellow-red. N & C Eur., N Asia, NW Amer. Z2.

S. napoleonis Schultz = *S. babylonica* 'Crispa'.

S. nigra Marsh. BLACK WILLOW. Large shrub to small tree to 3m. Bark rough; twigs yellow-brown. Lvs 6–12cm, narrow-lanceolate, becoming glab. except for midrib and petiole, serrulate. Catkins 3–8cm. N Amer. Z4.

S. nigricans Sm. = *S. myrsinifolia*.

S. nitida Ser. = *S. arenaria*.

S. oleifolia Sm. = *S. cinerea* ssp. *oleifolia*.

S. opala Anderss. ex Seemen = *S. udensis*.

S. pallasii Anderss. = *S. arctica*.

S. × peasei Fern. (*S. herbacea* × *S. uva-ursi*.) To 60cm; lvs elliptic to narrow-ovate, dark green. NW Amer. Z4.

S. pedicellata Desf. To 10m. Twigs lanate, becoming glab. Lvs 6–8cm, lanceolate-obovate or oblong, near glab. above, thin-pubesc. beneath, 10+ pairs of veins, subentire or toothed. Catkins 3–6×1–1.5cm. N Medit. Z8.

S. × pendulina Wender. WISCONSIN WEEPING WILLOW; NIOBE WILLOW. (*S. babylonica* × *S. fragilis*.) To 12m. Bark fissured, twigs pendulous, glab., olive-brown. Lvs 10–12cm, lanceolate, tip slender, base cuneate, soon glab., dark green above, pale, glaucous beneath, glandular-serrate; petiole glandualr towards blade. Catkins usually ♀, 30×5mm. Gdn origin. var. *blanda* Anderss. Not strongly weeping. var. *elegantissima* (Koch) Meikle. Strongly weeping. Z4.

S. pentandra L. BAY WILLOW; LAUREL WILLOW. To 10m. Twigs glossy, brown-green; buds yellow. Lvs 5–12cm, elliptic, base cordate or rounded, glossy dark green above, pale beneath, leathery, finely glandular-serrate, apex gland. Catkins 2–5×1cm. Widespread Eur., nat. E US. Z5.

S. petiolaris Sm. Shrub to 3m. Twigs thin, soon glab., purple. Lvs 4–8cm, oval-lanceolate, soon glab., dark green above, glaucous beneath, serrulate. Catkins 2cm, precocious. E N Amer. Z2.

S. petrophila Rydb. = *S. arctica*.

S. phylicifolia L. Differs from *S. hegetschweileri* in lvs elliptic-lanceolate, broadest at or below mid point, 9–12 pairs veins. Catkins 3cm. Eur. Z8.

S. pilgeriana Seemen = *S. udensis*.

S. polaris Wahlenb. POLAR WILLOW. 3–5cm. St. creeping or sub-terranean, twigs short, slender. Lvs 1.5cm, elliptic-ovate, retuse, glossy, dark green above, matt pale green beneath, entire. Catkins ovoid, scales purple-black; fil. purple. Arc. Eur. Z2.

S. pontederiana Willd. = *S. sordida*.

S. praecox Hoppe = *S. daphnoides*.

S. pruinosa Bess. = *S. acutifolia*.

S. prunifolia Sm. = *S. arbuscula*.

S. pubescens Schleich. = *S. laggeri*.

S. pulchra Cham. Low shrub. Twigs prostrate to ascending, glossy, purple-brown. Lvs 4–6cm, narrow-lanceolate, glab., glandular-toothed. Catkins 4–5×1.5cm, stalks leafless. Arc. Amer., Russia, Asia. Z2.

S. pulchra Wimm. = *S. daphnoides*.

S. purpurea L. PURPLE WILLOW; BASKET WILLOW; PURPLE OSIER. To 5m. Bark grey; twigs, slender, pubesc. at first then shiny, often purple when young. Lvs 2–10cm, lanceolate-oblong, glab., dull blue-green above, paler, ± glaucous beneath, serrulate above. Catkins narrowly cylindrical, often curved, 1.5–3cm; sta. red becoming purple-black. Eur., N Afr. to C Asia, Jap. 'Gracilis': dwarf, twigs v. slender, lvs narrow. 'Pendula': br. pendulous, v. thin. ssp. *lambertiana* (Sm.) A. Neumann ex Rech. f. Lvs broad-obovate, serrate for most of their length. Z5.

S. purpurea var. *japonica* Nak. = *S. koriyanagi*.

S. pyrenaica Gouan. To 50cm. Twigs red-brown, becoming glab., ascending or creeping. Lvs to 3cm, elliptic-ovate, rounded at base, with 8 pairs veins, glossy, sparsely pubesc. above, glaucous, pubesc. beneath, becoming glab. except on margin, entire. Eur. (Pyren.). Only females known in cult. Z6.

S. pyrifolia Anderss. BALSAM WILLOW. To 8m, usually shorter. Twigs glab., red-brown, glossy. Lvs 5–8cm, ovate-obovate, dark green above, glaucous beneath, glab., shallow-toothed. Catkins 2–5cm. E N Amer. Z6.

S. pyrolifolia Ledeb. Tall shrub or small tree. Twigs thick, glab. to pubesc., glossy, red-brown. Lvs 5cm, round-ovate or elliptic, glab., white-green, midrib tinged brown orpink. Catkins small, dense. N Finland, N Russia, Urals. Z3.

S. rehderiana Schneid. Shrub or small tree to 10m. Twigs slender, dark brown-olive green, soon glab. Lvs 5–13cm, lanceolate-obovate, acuminate, rounded at base, glab. above, grey silky beneath, crenate. Catkins 2.5cm; anth. purple. W China. Z6.

S. repens L. CREEPING WILLOW. To 1.5m. St. creeping, twigs slender, ascending, downy at first.Lvs 1–3.5cm, narrowly elliptic-ovate or oblong, tip often twisted, 4–6 pairs veins, silky, often becoming glab., bright green above, entire to glandular-toothed. Catkins 1–2.5×0.5–1cm, precocious; scales tipped red-brown. Eur., Asia Minor, Sib. Highly variable sp., influenced by hybridization. 'Voorthuizen': prostrate; st. slender; lvs small, silky; catkins v. small, ♀. Z5.

S. repens var. *angustifolia* Neilr. = *S. rosmarinifolia*.

S. repens var. *argentea* (Sm.) Wimm. & Grab. = *S. arenaria*.

S. repens var. *nitida* (Ser.) Wender. = *S. arenaria*.

S. repens var. *rosmarinifolia* (L.) Wimm. & Grab. = *S. rosmarinifolia*.

S. repens var. *subopposita* (Miq.) Seemen = *S. subopposita*.

S. reptans Rupr. ARCTIC CREEPING WILLOW. Low shrub. Twigs prostrate, tinged red, becoming glab. Lvs 1.5–3cm, lanceolate-ovate, rounded-cordate at base, becoming glab., glaucous beneath. Catkins 2–4, 5cm, scale tips black. Arc. Russia and Asia.

Z2.

S. reticulata L. Dwarf creeping shrub to 15cm high. St. creeping, mat-forming. Lvs 1–4cm, orbicular-ovate, base cordate, apex rounded, rugose, dark green above, white beneath, nearglabrous, entire. Catkins 1–3cm. N Eur., N Amer., N Asia. Z1.

S. retusa L. To 10cm. St. creeping, rooting; twigs glab., dark green-brown. Lvs 1–3cm, ovate-oblong, clustered toward twig tips, obtuse or retuse, sometimes downy beneath, entire. Catkins 1–2×0.5–1cm. C Eur. Z2.

S. rigida Muhlenb. = S. eriocephala.

S. rosmarinifolia L. non Hook. To 1.5m. St. creeping, twigs ascending, tomentose. Lvs 2–5cm, linear-lanceolate, ± erect, dark green above, grey silky beneath, entire to undualte. Catkins globose. C & E Eur. Z5.

S. rosmarinifolia auct. non L. nec Hook. = S. ×petiolaris.

S. rosmarinifolia Hook. non L. = S. petiolaris.

S. rotundifolia Trautv. ROUND LEAVED WILLOW. To 10cm. St. long, creeping, not rooting. Lvs 0.5–1.5cm across, orbicular, base subcordate, light green, hairy at first, base serrulate. Catkins short. Arc. Russia. Z2.

S. ×rubens Schrank. (S. alba ×S. fragilis.) To 10m. Twigs olive, tinged yellow or red. Lvs 8–16cm, lanceolate, bright green above, glaucous beneath, glandular-toothed. Catkins 3–6cm, cylindric. C Eur. 'Basfordiana': branchlets long, orange-red in winter; lvs narrow; catkins yellow, slender, ♂. 'Sanguinea': differs from 'Basfordiana' in smaller lvs, shoots more strongly red-tinted. Z6.

S. ×rubra Huds. (S. purpurea ×S. viminalis.) To 6m. Bark grey, fissured; twigs long, flexible, yellow-brown. Lvs 4–15cm, lanceolate, dull green above, blue-green beneath, soon glab., undulate. Catkins 2–4×1cm, often crowded towards ends of br.; anth. red. Eur. 'Eugenei': slender, erect, conical small tree; catkins grey-pink, profuse. Z5.

S. russelliana Sm. = S. fragilis.

S. sachalinensis F. Schmidt = S. udensis.

S. salviifolia Brot. To 6m. Twigs grey-tomentose. Lvs linearlanceolate to obovate, 3–5 times longer than wide, lat. veins numerous, tomentose, toothed to entire. Catkins 3–4×1cm, precocious. Spain, Port. Z7.

S. savatieri Camus = S. integra.

S. schraderiana Willd. Shrub to 4m. Twigs dark, glossy; bud yellow-orange. Lvs ovate, obtuse, silky-pubesc. then glossy above, glaucous beneath. Catkins 1–2cm, nodding in fr. Eur., mts but not Alps. Z5.

S. scouleriana Barratt ex Hook. To 10m. Twigs thick, yellow, becoming brown. Lvs 3–10cm, oblong-obovate, dull green above, glaucous with prominent veins beneath, entire, sometimes shallow-toothed. Catkins precocious. New Mex. to Alask. Z6.

S. ×sepulcralis Simonkai. WEEPING WILLOW. (S. alba 'Tristis' ×S. babylonica.) Similar to S. babylonica except slightly less weeping, bark fissured; petiole gland. at apex. Catkins similar to S. alba. Gdn origin, Eur. var. **chrysocoma** (Dode) Meikle. Weeping tree, twigs yellow, lvs bright green above. The most commonly cultivated weeping willow. var. **salamonii** Carr. Sturdy, not strongly weeping; twigs olive; lvs dull green above. 'Erythroflexuosa': br. pendulous, orange-yellow, twisted and contorted; lvs twisted. Z6.

S. ×sericans Kerner. (S. caprea ×S. viminalis.) Shrub to 9m. Twigs white hairy, then glab., yellow to red-brown. Lvs lanceolate, acuminate, grey-pubesc., veins prominent beneath. Catkins 2–5cm, precocious, terete, hirsute. Spring. Eur.

S. ×seringeana Gaud. (S. caprea ×S. elaeagnos.) Large erect shrub or small tree. Branchlets grey-tomentose. Lvs lanceolate to narrow-oblong, grey-downy, pale beneath.

S. serpyllifolia Scop. THYME-LEAVED WILLOW. Similar to S. retusa except lvs pressed v. close to soil, to 1cm, overlapping. Catkins to 0.5cm, appearing after foliage. Alps. Z2.

S. sibirica var. **subopposita** C. Schneid. = S. subopposita.

S. sikokiana Mak. = S. udensis.

S. silesiaca Willd. SILESIAN WILLOW. To 3m. Twigs soon glab. Lvs lanceolate-obovate, almost glab., green above, blue-green beneath, serrate to entire. Catkins 1–4×0.5–1cm, scales dark redbrown. Eur. (Carpath., Balk.). Z6.

S. sitchensis Sanson ex Bong. Shrub or small tree to 7m. Twigs thin, yellow-brown, woolly at first, sometimes waxy. Lvs 4–10cm, obovate-lanceolate, dull green above, silky with prominent veins beneath, entire. Catkins 3–5cm, precocious. W N Amer. Z4.

S. ×smithiana Willd. Parentage obscure, probably involving S. cinerea ×S. viminalis. To 9m. Twigs densely hairy at first, red-brown. Lvs 6–11cm, narrowly lanceolate, dull green becoming glab. above, grey-pubesc. to glab. beneath, sparsely serrate. Catkins crowded towards tips of br., precocious. Eur. Z5.

S. ×sordida A. Kerner. (S. cinerea ×S. purpurea.) To 5m. Br. erect or spreading; twigs thin, or glab., red-brown. Lvs 4–7cm,

elliptic-obovate, soon glab., glossy above, grey, sparselypubesc. beneath, gland. serrate. Catkins to 3×1cm, precocious, anth. orange-red at first. Eur. Z5.

S. speciosa Nutt. = S. lasiandra.

S. starkeana Willd. To 1m. Twigs thin, ascending, soon glab., buds green-orange. Lvs obovate-ovate to broadly lanceolate, with 5–7 pairs veins, thinly pubesc., red becoming bright green above, grey-green with raised veins beneath, glandular-toothed. Catkins precocious. N & C Eur., Ukraine, C Russia. Z5.

S. ×stipularis Sm. Parentage obscure. To 6m. Twigs densely white pubesc., becoming glab. Lvs 10–13cm, narrow-lanceolate, tapering, sparsely pubesc. above, white silky beneath. Catkins 4–5cm, scales light brown, tip dark. N Eur. Z6.

S. 'Stuartii' = S. lanata 'Stuartii'.

S. subopposita Miq. To 30cm. Twigs thin, erect, grey hairy when young. Lvs 2.5–4cm, broad-lanceolate to narrow-oblong, ± glab. above, glaucous, hairy, prominently veined beneath, entire. Catkins to 2cm, dense. Jap., Korea. Z5.

S. syrticola Fern. To 2m. Twigs white-silky when young. Lvs 4–9cm, oblong-ovate, green above, sometimes paler beneath, white-pubesc. finely glandular-serrate. Catkins 6–8cm, slender, glabrescent. NE Amer. Z2.

S. thunbergiana Bl. ex Anderss. = S. gracilistyla.

S. treviranii Spreng. = S. ×mollissima.

S. triandra L. ALMOND-LEAVED WILLOW. To 10m, usually shorter. Twigs glabrescent, red or green-brown, bark smooth, flaking. Lvs 5–10cm, lanceolate-ovate, glossy dark-green above, dull pale-green beneath, serrate, petiole gland. above. ♂ catkins 3–7cm, ♀ shorter. Eur. Z5.

S. ×tsugaluensis Koidz. (S. integra ×S. vulpina.) Similar to S. purpurea except twigs yellow-green; lvs silver-haired beneath. Gdn origin (Eur.). 'Ginme': medium-sized to large spreading shrub. Lvs oblong, tinted orange at first, later bright green. Catkins narrow, recurved, silver, profuse, precocious. ♀ clone. Z5.

S. udensis Trautv. & Meyen. To 5m. Twigs glab., brown, hoary at first. Lvs 6–10cm, narrowly lanceolate, dark green above, blue-green, slightly hairy beneath, entire to wavy. Catkins 20–30×5–6mm. Jap., E Russia. 'Sekka': br. fastigiate. Z5.

S. undulata Ehrh. = S. ×mollissima.

S. uva-ursi Pursh. BEARBERRY WILLOW. Mat-forming shrub. Twigs brown, glab. Lvs 0.5–2.5cm, elliptic-obovate, pointed or rounded at tip, glossy above, glaucous beneath, shallowtoothed. Catkins cylindrical. Arc. Canada, W Greenland. Z1.

S. veriviminalis Nasarov = S. viminalis.

S. vestita Pursh. Similar to S. reticulata except ascending to 1m; twigs downy; lvs silky, becoming sparsely pubesc., above; petiole long. E N Amer. Z4.

S. viminalis L. COMMON OSIER. To 6m+. Twigs long, straight, flexible, grey-villous at first soon glab., olive to yellow-brown. Lvs 10–10cm, linear, acuminate, green sparsely pubesc. above, silver, densely silky beneath, sometimes undulate. Catkins precocious, scales black-brown. Eur. to NW Asia. Z4.

S. vitellina L. = S. alba var. vitellina.

S. waldsteiniana Willd. Medium, ± erect shrub, differing from S. arbuscula in longer lvs and catkins. SE Eur.

S. wilhelmsiana Bieb. To 7m. Twigs flexible, spreading, silky or glab. Lvs 2–6cm, linear, silky, later glab., entire to glandularserrate. Catkins 2–3cm, slender. SE Russia to E Asia. 'Microstachya': lvs larger. Z5.

S. xerophila Flod. To 6m. Twigs much branched, woolly, dull; bark grey; buds glossy, red-brown. Lvs oblong-obovate, thinly lanate with 7–8 pairs veins, entire to toothed. Catkins precocious, cylindrical. Lapland to Urals. Z3.

S. yezoalpina Koidz. St. prostrate, creeping, rooting; tips purplebrown, becoming glab. Lvs 2–4.5cm, elliptic to rounded, shallowly cordate at base, silky when young, glaucous beneath, entire. Catkins 1.5–3cm. Summer. Jap. Z5.

Sallow Salix (S. caprea).
Sallow Wattle Acacia longifolia.
Sally Wattle Acacia binervia; R. floribunda.

Salmalia Schott & Endl. = Bombax.

Salmonbark Wandoo Eucalyptus lanepoolei.
Salmonberry Rubus chamaemorus; R. parviflorus; R. spectabilis.
Salmon Bush Monkey Flower Mimulus longiflorus.
Salmon Gum Eucalyptus salmonophloia.
Salmwood Cordia alliodora.

Salpichroa Miers. Solanaceae. 17 herbs, sometimes scrambling. Lvs entire, long-petiolate. Fls solitary, axill.; cal. 5-parted; cor. tubular to urceolate, lobes 5; sta. 5, protruding. SW US, temp. S Amer. Z8.

S. glandulosa Hook. To 60cm. St. densely branched. Lvs to 2.5cm, cordate to ovate, glandular-pubesc. Fls slender-stalked; cor. yellow to 3cm. Summer. Chile.

S. origanifolia (Lam.) Baill. COCK'S EGGS; PAMPAS LILY OF THE VALLEY. Aromatic ann. or perenn. st. slender, pubesc. Lvs to 1.5cm, rhomboid-ovoid, subglabrous, ciliate. Fls slender-stalked, white to 1cm. Fr. a yellow-white ovoid berry to 2cm. Arg.

S. rhomboidea (Gillies & Hook.) Miers = *S. origanifolia.*

Salpiglossis Ruiz & Pav. Solanaceae. 2 erect, sticky or clammy-pubescent ann., bienn. or perenn. herbs. Lvs alt. Fls solitary; pedicels long; cal. tubular, 5-lobed; cor. funnel-shaped, limb plicate, lobes 5, emarginate. S Andes. Z8.

S. acutiloba I.M. Johnst. To 30cm. Lvs to 3cm, linear-oblong to spathulate. Fls to 1.5×1.8cm, pale yellow striped purple, exterior glandular-pubesc., limb purple. Summer–autumn.

S. gloxiniiflora hort. = *S. sinuata.*
S. grandiflora hort. = *S. sinuata.*
S. integrifolia Hook. = *Petunia violacea.*
S. linearis (Hook.) I.M. Johnst. = *S. acutiloba.*
S. sinuata Ruiz & Pav. PAINTED TONGUE. To 60cm. Lvs to 10cm, elliptic to narrow-oblong, sinuate, toothed or pinnatifid. Fls to 6×5cm, yellow to ochre, mauve-scarlet or violet-blue with darker purple veins and marking. Summer.

S. cvs (mostly derived from *S. sinuata*). Bolero Hybrids: dwarf, vigorous; fls in range of rich colours. Casino Hybrids: dwarf, compact; fls veined in shades of red, yellow, orange, rose and purple. and purple. 'Kew Blue': dwarf; fls rich blue veined golden-yellow, abundant. Splash Hybrids: compact, tolerant; fls in range of colours, abundant.

S. superbissima hort. = *S. sinuata.*
S. variabilis hort. Vilm. = *S. sinuata.*

Salpingia (Torr. & A. Gray) Raim. = *Calylophus.*

Salsify *Tragopogon porrifolius.*
Salt-and-pepper Ivy *Hedera helix.*
Saltbush *Atriplex.*
Salt Cedar *Tamarix.*
Saltillo Juniper *Juniperus saltillensis.*
Salt Marsh Mallow *Kosteletzkya virginica.*
Salt River Gum *Eucalyptus sargentii.*
Salt Rush *Juncus leseurii.*
Salt Tree *Halimodendron halodendron.*
Salt-water Paperbark *Melaleuca cuticularis.*

Salvadora L. Salvadoraceae. 5 everg. trees or shrubs. Fls numerous, small, paniculate; cal. campanulate, 4-toothed; cor. campanulate, lobes 4, elliptic, sta. 4, inserted on corolla-tube. Fr. a drupe. Afr. through Arabia to India and China. Z10.

S. persica L. TOOTHBRUSH TREE; MUSTARD TREE. Thicket-forming, to 6m; st. grey to white, usually arching. Lvs to 10cm, lanceolate to elliptic or orbicular, mucronate, coriaceous, ± succulent, bright green. Infl. to 10cm; fls green-white, fr. red or dark purple, aromatic. Afr., Arabia to India and Sri Lanka.

SALVADORACEAE Lind. 3/11. *Salvadora.*

Salvia L. SAGE. Labiatae. c900 perenn. or ann. or bienn. herbs, shrubs or subshrubs. Lvs sessile or petiolate, simple or lyrate or pinnatisect. Fls in verticillasters disposed in term. or axill. rac., spikes, pan., or cymes; bracteoles and bracts usually present; cal. tubular or ovoid to bell- or funnel-shaped, often dilated and membranous in fr., upper lip truncate to obsoletely or distinctly 3-toothed, lower lip 2-toothed; cor. 2-lipped, tube plane or curved, upper lip hooded, erect or plane, entire to bifid, lower lip spreading, 3-lobed, middle lobe often emarginate; sta. 2, included or exserted. Cosmop.

S. acuminata Vent. = *S. azurea.*

S. aethiopis L. AFRICAN SAGE. Perenn. or bienn. herb, to 60cm. Lvs to 20cm, ovate or elliptic to oblong, apex, acute, base cordate and perfoliate (cauline lvs) or attenuate, toothed to erose, rugose, white-pubesc.; petioles to 9cm. Verticillasters 4–10-fld, in much-branched, candelabriform pan.; bracts 1cm, concave, persistent. Cal. white-tomentose, teeth spiny; cor. to 15mm, white or lip sometimes yellow. Summer. C & S Eur. to W Asia. Z7.

S. affinis Schltr. & Cham. = *S. purpurea.*
S. africana L. = *S. africana-caerulea.*
S. africana-caerulea L. Shrub to 2.5m, grey-tomentose. Lvs 0.8–4cm, elliptic to obovate, entire to erose-dentate, grey-green beneath, often gland. Verticils 2–6-fld, to 12; bracts ovate, persistent; cal. campanulate-funnelform, expanding to 14mm, becoming purple, hirsute; cor. 16–28mm, bright blue, violet or pink. S Afr. Z9.

S. africana-lutea L. Diffuse shrub to 90cm, tomentose. Lvs 1–3.5cm, suborbicular to narrowly obovate, entire or occas. minutely crenate, shortly petiolate, white-tomentose and glandular-punctate. Verticillasters 2-fld, crowded in term. rac.; cal. 12–16mm, campanulate, greatly enlarged in fr., tinged purple, villous; cor. 3–5cm, golden brown, red-brown or mauve, glandular-pubesc. Late summer–autumn. S Afr. Z9.

S. albocaerulea Lind. Shrub to 3.5m. Lvs 10–20cm, oblong-lanceolate, long-acuminate, serrate, sparsely pubesc. Verticillasters 3–6-fld, distant, in infl. 15–30cm; cal. 12mm, glandular-hispid; cor. to 4cm, upper lip white, lower lip indigo. Winter. Mex. Z9.

S. albopileata Epling = *S. wagneriana.*

S. algeriensis Desf. Ann. herb, to 50cm. Glandular-pubesc. Lvs to 11cm, lanceolate or ovate to linear-oblong, subentire to notched, pubesc., on veins beneath. Verticillasters to 14, 4–8-fld, distant in branched rac.; cal. to 1cm, tubular to bell-shaped, glandular-pubesc.; cor. blue or violet and white-flecked, tube to 2cm. Spring–summer. NW Afr.

S. amarissima Ortega. Perenn. 60–180cm, gland. Lvs 2.5–10cm, deltoid, often cordate at base, acute at apex, crenate-serrate, hispid above, villous beneath. Verticillasters c6-fld, remote; cal. 5-nerved; cor. about 12mm, blue. Summer. Mex. Z9.

S. amasiaca Franch. & Bornm. = *S. verticillata* ssp. *amasiaca.*
S. ambigens Briq. = *S. guaranitica.*
S. amoena Sims. = *S. lamiifolia.*
S. angustifolia Michx., non Cav., non Salisb. = *S. azurea.*
S. angustifolia Cav., non Michx., non Salisb. = *S. reptans.*

S. apiana Jeps. BEE SAGE; CALIFORNIA WHITE SAGE. Perenn. shrub, to 3m. St. tomentose. Lvs to 10cm, ovate or elliptic to oblong, subentire to notched, pubesc., silver-tomentose. Verticillasters in erect, much-branched, thyrsoid pan. to 1.5m; cal. to 8mm; cor. white, flecked lavender, tube to 7mm. Calif. Z8.

S. argentea L. Perenn. or bienn. herb, to 1m, gland., ± glab. Lvs to 20cm, ovate to oblong, base cuneate, toothed to erose or lobed, rugose and sparsely pubesc.; petioles to 20cm. Verticillasters to 10, 4–10-fld, distant in spreading pan.; bracts to 1.7cm, persistent, concave; cal. to 12mm, bell-shaped, glandular-pubesc., teeth mucronate; cor. to 3cm, white to yellow, flecked pink to violet. Spring–summer. Medit. (S Eur. and N Afr.). Z5.

S. aristulata Mart. & Gal. = *S. longistyla.*

S. arizonica A. Gray. Perenn. herb, to 60cm. Lvs to 5cm, ovate to deltoid, apex acute, base cuneate or truncate, notched, glab. to sparsely pubesc.; petioles to 15mm. Verticillasters 6-fld, in rac.; cal. to 6mm, dilated in fr., pubesc.; cor. to 1.7cm, blue. Ariz., Tex. Z9.

S. atriplicifolia Fern. = *S. cacaliifolia.*
S. aurea L. = *S. africana-lutea.*
S. austriaca L. Perenn. herb to 1m, somewhat foetid, glandular-hairy. Lvs basal, ovate, coarsely dentate, large, ± glab. above, pubesc. beneath. Verticillasters 4–9-fld; cal. 8–10mm, campanulate, often tinged violet at base, pilose; cor. 12–17mm, pale yellow; sta. long-exserted. Summer. E Eur. Z6.

S. azurea Michx. ex Lam. Perenn. herb to 1.5m. Lvs 5–10cm, linear to elliptic or lanceolate, entire or serrate, glab. or pubesc.; petioles to 1cm. Verticillasters 2–24, 3–6-fld, approximate or distant, in pan. or spicate rac.; cal. to 8mm, tubular to bell-shaped, pubesc.; cor. 7–12mm, white or blue. Summer–autumn. SE US. ssp. *pitcheri.* var. *grandiflora* Benth. St. pubesc. Verticillasters 6–12, approximate, in dense spicate rac.; cal. densely pubesc.; cor. to 12mm. S US. Z4.

S. barrelieri Etling. Bienn., or perenn. herb, 60–90cm. Lvs to 25cm, ovate, dentate or lobulate or pinnatifid, cordate at base. Verticillasters 4–6-fld, in slender, erect, simple or sparingly branched infl.; cal. gland.; cor. to 3cm lower lip white, upper lip blue-violet. Summer. N Afr., SW Spain. 'Magnifica': fls large. Z8.

S. baumgartenii Heuff. = *S. pratensis* 'Baumgartenii'.
S. bethellii hort. = *S. involucrata* 'Bethellii'.
S. bertolonii Vis. = *S. pratensis.*
S. bicolor Lam. = *S. barrelieri.*
S. bicolor Sessé & Moq., non Lam. = *S. leucantha.*

S. blancoana Webb & Heldr. Shrub, 50cm–1m. Lvs to 9cm, oblong-elliptical, rugulose, pubesc. Verticillasters 2–6-fld, on ± leafless st.; cal. 10–14mm, glandular-viscid; cor. to 4cm, pale to violet blue, occas. streaked white. Moroc., S Spain. Z8.

S. blepharophylla Brandg. ex Epling. Perenn. herb or subshrub to 40cm, ascending, glandular-pubesc. Lvs to 5cm, ovate to deltoid, apex obtuse, base attenuate to subtruncate, notched and ciliate, glab. Verticillasters 2–6-fld, in loose rac. to 12cm; cal. to 14mm, glandular-pubesc., purple; cor. red, tube to 2cm. Summer. Mex. Z9.

S. blinii Lév. = *S. brevilabra.*
S. bodinieri Vaniot = *S. yunnanensis.*
S. bolleana Noë = *S. broussonetii.*

S. boucheana Kunth = *S. fulgens*.

S. brachycalyx Boiss. = *S. indica*.

S. bracteata Banks & Sol. Perenn. subshrub to 50cm, glandular-pubesc. Lvs pinnatifid, term. seg. to 7cm, petiolulate, ovate to oblong, lat. seg. 1–2 pairs, smaller. Verticillasters 5–10-fld, distant; bracts 3cm, ovate, membranous, bracteoles to 16×8mm, glandular-pubesc.; cal. to 16mm, tubular to funnel-shaped, glandular-pubesc.; cor. pink to purple, tube to 2cm. Spring–summer. Middle East. 'Rosea': fls rose. Z9.

S. bracteata Sims, non Banks & Sol. = *S. sclarea*.

S. brandegei Munz. Shrub to 1m. St. pubesc. Lvs subsessile, linear, obtuse, notched, bullate and tomentose. Verticillasters distant, in spikes; bracts ovate, pubesc.; cal. to 8mm; cor. lavender, tube to 8mm, interior pubesc. Calif. Z9.

S. brevilabra Franch. Perenn. herb to 1m. Lvs to 11cm, ovate to deltoid, base cordate to sagittate, toothed to erose, rugose and sparsely pubesc. Verticillasters 2–6-fld, in branched rac.; cal. bell-shaped, glandular-pubesc.; cor. violet to purple, flecked white, tube to 1.8cm. China. Z8.

S. broussonetii Benth. Perenn. shrub, to 75cm, glandular-pubesc. Lvs to 15cm, ovate, base cordate, notched to erose, pubesc. above, glandular-pannose beneath; petioles to 5cm. Verticillasters 2–6-fld, approximate, in branched pannicles or rac.; cal. to 8mm, gland.; cor. to 15mm, white to pink, glandular-pubesc. Winter–summer. Canary Is. Z9.

S. buchananii Hedge. Woody-based perenn. to 60cm. Lvs 1–7cm, spathulate to ovate-lanceolate, crenate or serrate, firm, slightly fleshy, subglabrous. Verticillasters 3–6-fld; cal. tubular, slightly glandular-pubesc.; cor. 5cm, rose-purple, densely pilose. Summer–autumn. Not known in the wild, described from Mex. Occas. sold as *S. bacheriana*. Z9.

S. bulleyana Diels. Perenn. herb to 1m. Lvs mostly basal, ovate or deltoid-ovate, cordate to hastate at base, crenate, to 12cm, sparsely pilose. Verticillasters 2-fld, in simple infl.; cor. 2–3cm, yellow with purple spot on lower lip to almost wholly. China. Z6.

S. cacaliifolia Benth. Perenn. herb to 1m, erect, glandular-pubesc. Lvs 5–10cm, deltoid, apex acute, base cordate to hastate, subentire, glab. to sparsely pubesc.; petioles to 8cm. Verticillasters 2-fld, distant, in branched paniculate rac. to 25cm; cal. to 6mm, glandular-pubesc.; teeth acute to spiny; cor. blue, tube to 2cm, pubesc. Summer. Mex., Guat. Z9.

S. caerulea L. = *S. africana-caerulea*.

S. caespitosa Montbret & Aucher ex Benth. Subshrub, 8–15cm, forming mats to 60cm diam. Lvs obovate, crenate, pinnatisect, term. seg. lanceolate, to 2cm, lat. seg. 2 pairs, oblong; petioles to 2cm, long-ciliate. Verticillasters 2–6-fld, in v. short term. rac.; bracts to 12mm, ovate; cal. 10–14mm, often tinged purple, ± pilose and gland.; cor. 2–3cm, violet-blue to lilac-pink or white. Summer. W Asia Minor (Anatolia). Z7.

S. calycina Sibth. & Sm. = *S. pomifera*.

S. campanulata Wallich ex Benth. Perenn. herb to 1m, viscid-hirsute. Lvs broadly ovate, cordate at base, crenate, lower lvs to 12cm, pilose; petioles to 25cm. Verticillasters 2-fld, in much-branched infl.; cal. short-campanulate, 12mm; cor. 2.5cm, yellow, blue or purple. Himal. Z7.

S. canariensis L. Shrub to 2m, glandular-pubesc. to white-tomentose. Lvs to 11cm, lanceolate to deltoid, base hastate to sagittate, subentire to notched, white-pubesc.; petioles to 5cm. Verticillasters 4–8-fld, in branched pan. or rac.; bracts lanceolate to ovate, membranous to papery, purple; cal. to 12mm; cor. to 18mm, white to violet or purple, glandular-pubesc. Winter–spring. Canary Is. Z9.

S. candelabrum Boiss. Herb or subshrub, to 1m, erect, glab. to pubesc. Lvs to 9cm, lanceolate or elliptic to oblong, apex obtuse, base occas. lobulate, notched, rugose and pubesc. to tomentose beneath, glandular-punctate. Verticillasters 3–5-fld, in loose, paniculate cymes; cal. to 13mm, glandular-pubesc.; cor. to 4cm, blue to violet, flecked white. Summer. Spain. Z7.

S. candidissima Vahl Perenn. herb or subshrub, to 90cm, papillose, glandular-pubesc. Lvs to 15cm, ovate or lanceolate to oblong, apex acute, base cordate or obtuse, subentire to notched or erose, rugose and pubesc. to pannose; petioles to 11cm. Verticillasters 2–6-fld, in much-branched pan. or rac. to 30cm; bracts to 10m, persistent; cal. to 15mm, papillose and glandular-pubesc.; cor. to 27mm, white, sometimes tipped yellow and flecked purple. Summer. E Medit. Z7.

S. candidissima Bieb. non Vahl = *S. verbascifolia*.

S. canescens Mey. Perenn. St. erect, to 30cm, woody at base. Lvs mostly basal, oblong-lanceolate, dentate, densely white lanate. Verticillasters 4–6-fld, in simple infl.; cor. violet. Cauc. Z6.

S. cardinalis HBK = *S. fulgens*.

S. carduacea Benth. THISTLE SAGE. Perenn. or ann. herb, to 65cm. St. scape-like, white-tomentose. Lvs to 3cm, basal, rosulate, petiolate, pinnatifid, oblong-spathulate, white-undulate to toothed and spiny. Verticillasters in dense head; bracts imbricate, ovate to lanceolate, apex spiny, tomentose; cal. to 15mm, tomentose; cor. to 3cm, lavender. Summer. Calif. Z8.

S. carnosa Douglas. Perenn. shrub to 75cm, much-branched, pubesc. Lvs to 12mm, obovate to spathulate, apex obtuse or retuse, base attenuate, entire or notched, glandular-pubesc.; petioles to 12mm. Verticillasters in dense, terminal pan. to 15cm; bracts to 6mm, pubesc., purple; cal. to 6mm, tomentose; cor. blue, tube to 7mm. Summer. W US. Z7.

S. castanea Diels. Perenn. herb to 1m, robust, downy. Lvs to 18cm, narrowly ovate to linear-lanceolate, dentate, truncate to cordate or hastate at base; petioles to 25cm. Verticillasters 2–6-fld, in elongate rac.; cal. about 12mm, gland.; cor. to 4cm, maroon to purple, tinged yellow below. Summer. China, Himal. Z7.

S. ceratophylla L. Bienn. herb, lemon-scented, erect to 30cm. Lvs 12–25cm, mostly basal, oblong, pinnatifid to pinnatisect, white-lanate, seg. linear; rachis winged; petiole ± 0. Verticillasters 2–5-fld, in infl. with few lat. br.; cal. to 12mm; cor. 15–20mm, cream or sulphur-yellow, upper lip occas. tinged violet. Summer. W Asia (Turk., Syr., Armenia, Iran, N Iraq, Afghan.). Z7.

S. chamaedrifolia André = *S. chamaedryoides*.

S. chamaedryoides Cav. Woody-based perenn., minutely stellate-hairy. St. to 45cm, ascending. Lvs 0.8–2cm, elliptic to deltoid or obovate, entire or finely crenate. Verticillasters 4–6-fld, in simple rac.; cal. 9–12mm; cor. 2–2.5cm, deep violet-blue. Summer. Tex., Mex. Z8.

S. chamelaeagnea Bergius. Aromatic shrub to 1m. St. scabrid. Lvs 3.5cm, obovate, dentate, coriaceous, scabrid, veins prominent. Verticillasters 2-fld, in much-branched, glandular-pubesc. pan.; cal. 8mm, scabrid; cor. 3cm, pale purple tinged blue. S Afr. Z9.

S. chia Sessé & Moc. = *S. hispanica*.

S. chinensis Benth. = *S. japonica*.

S. clandestina L. = *S. verbenaca*.

S. clevelandii (A. Gray) Greene. JIM SAGE. Shrub to 60cm. Lvs to 25mm, ovate or oblong to elliptic to lanceolate, apex obtuse, base attenuate, toothed, rugose above. Verticillasters solitary, term., capitate, or 2–3, in spikes; bracts to 8mm, pubesc.; cal. to 1cm, glandular-pubesc.; cor. white or blue to violet, tube to 12mm. Calif. Z8.

S. coccinea Juss. ex Murray. Ann. herb to 1m. St. erect, branched. Lvs to 6cm, ovate to deltoid, subacute, bas eobtuse to cordate or truncate, crenate-serrate, undersurface cinereous; petioles to 3cm. Verticillasters 4–8-fld, in branched rac. to 10cm; bracts to 1cm, green; cal. to 6mm, green or purple; cor. red, occas. white, tube to 17mm. Summer. Trop. S Amer.; in widespread cult. 'Bicolor': upper lip white, lower lip pink. 'Lactea': fls white. 'Nana': dwarf. 'Nana Compacta': compact, busy dwarf shrub. 'Punicea': fls purple-red. 'Splendens': to 1.5m, robust; fls scarlet.

S. coerulea Benth. = *S. guaranitica*.

S. columbariae Benth. Perenn. or ann. herb to 70cm. Lvs to 7cm, pinnate-pinnatifid, rugose, pubesc., seg. irregular, oblong, obtuse, subentire to toothed; petioles to 5cm. Verticillasters in many-fld, glomerulate heads to 3cm; bracts imbricate, ovate, apex spiny, ciliate; cal. to 6mm, teeth bristly; cor. to 13mm, blue. Summer. SW US. Z7.

S. compacta Munz = *S. pachyphylla*.

S. concolor Lamb. ex Benth. Shrubby perenn. to 180cm. St. often tinted blue. Lvs 7–15cm, deltoid-ovate, long-attenuate, acute, serrate, pubesc. Verticillasters 6–10-fld, in showy, simple infl.; cal. tinged blue; cor. about 3cm, deep blue. Mex. Z9.

S. confertiflora Pohl. Woody-based perenn. herb to 1m. Lvs to 20cm, ovate, acute at apex, tapered to base, crenate, tawny-tomentose, foetid when crushed. Verticillasters 6–15-fld, in long, simple infl. to 30cm; cal. deep red, tomentose; cor. to 12mm, red, pubesc. Late summer–autumn. Braz. Z9.

S. controversa Willk., non Ten. = *S. verbenaca*.

S. costaricensis Ørst. Herb erect or ascending, glandular-pubesc. Lvs 3–10cm, deltoid, base hastate or peltate, notched, crenate-serrate, glab. to pubesc.; petioles 2–12cm. Verticillasters in simple or branched rac. to 20cm; cal. much dilated in fr., glandular-pubesc.; cor. 8–9mm, dark blue. Costa Rica. Z10.

S. cryptantha Montbret & Aucher ex Benth. Subshrubby perenn., forming mats, to 30cm, hairy, gland. Lvs 2–5cm, mostly basal, ovate-elliptic to suborbicular, minutely crenate, pale green, rugose, white- to grey-tomentose; petiole 2–6cm. Verticillasters 4–1-fld, several in simple infl.; bracts broadly ovate, to 15mm; cal. to 15mm, lime green, occas. tinged purple; cor. to 18mm, white, sometimes tinged pink or purple. Summer. Turk. Z8.

S. cyanea Benth. = *S. concolor*.

S. cyanescens Boiss. & Bal. Slender perenn. erect to 1m. Lvs to 8cm, ovate-lanceolate cordate at base, acute at apex, silvery-white tomentose, lower lvs petiolate. Verticillasters 2–6-fld, in long rac.; bracts green; cal. to 12mm, tinted lilac or violet-blue, glandular-pubesc.; cor. to 20m; upper lip tinged pale blue, occas. purple-spotted, lower lip sometimes flushed pale lemon, fragrant. Mid- to late summer. C Anatolia. Z7.

S. decipiens Mart. & Gal. = *S. patens*.

S. deltoidea Pers. = *S. regla*.

S. deserta Schang. = *S.* × *sylvestris*.

S. dichroa Hook. = *S. barrelieri*.

S. discolor Kunth. Perenn. herb to 45cm. Lvs 3–6cm, oblong-ovate, entire, coriaceous, green and sparsely hairy above, densely white-tomentose beneath. Verticillasters 3–9-fld, infl. axis glab. or gland.; cal. thickly hoary; cor. to 2.5cm, deep indigo verging on black. Peru. Z9.

S. dombeyi Epling. Herb or shrub to 2m. Lvs to 20cm, ovate, apex acute, base cordate, notched, pubesc.; petioles to 6cm. Verticillasters 3–6-fld; in interrupted, spicate rac. to 20cm; bracts to 2cm, ovate, membranous; cal. to 4cm, purple; cor. tube to 9cm. Peru, Boliv. Z9.

S. dominica L. Much-branched aromatic shrub to 1m. Lvs 5cm, oblong-lanceolate, crenate, rugose, hirsute. Verticillasters 3–6-fld, numerous; cal. expanding in fr., v. hispid; cor. 2× length of cal., white tinged yellow, often with brown markings. Middle East. Z9.

S. dorisiana Standl. Perenn. to 1m, shrubby, freely branched. Lvs 8–18cm, ovate, apex acuminate, base cordate with lobes overlapping, serrate, petiolate, thin pubesc. Verticillasters 2–10-fld, in gland. infl. to 15cm; cor. 5–6cm, magenta, villous. Winter. Hond. Z10.

S. dorrii (Kellogg) Abrams. PURPLE SAGE; DESERT SAGE; GREY BALL SAGE. Shrub to 1m. Lvs to 3cm, linear or spathulate to obovate or oblanceolate, apex obtuse, base attenuate entire, rough, glandular-punctate, and pubesc.; petioles to 1cm. Verticillasters 3–4, to 2cm in dense or interrupted spikes; bracts to 1cm, pubesc., pink to violet; cal. to 7mm; cor. blue, tube to 1cm. N Amer. Z5.

S. elegans Vahl. Perenn. herb or subshrub to 2m, glandular-pubesc. Lvs to 10cm, ovate to deltoid, apex acute to attenuate, base usually truncate or cordate, notched, glab. to pubesc.; petioles to 3cm. Verticillasters 2–6-fld; in loose, branched rac. to 15cm; bracts ovate, caudate; cal. to 7mm, dilated in fr.; cor. scarlet, tube to 27mm. Winter–spring. Mex., Guat. Z8.

S. eremostachya Jeps. Shrub to 1m much branched, pubesc. Lvs to 3.5cm, deltoid or lanceolate to oblong, apex obtuse, base obtuse or truncate, sometimes notched, rugose and glandular-punctate; petioles to 6mm, winged. Verticillasters to 4 in interrupted spikes; bracts ovate to lanceolate, cuspidate, pubesc.; cal. to 11mm, pubesc.; cor. to 25mm, blue to purple or pink. Calif. Z8.

S. esquirolii Lév. = *S. yunnanensis*.

S. evansiana Hand.-Mazz. = *S. mekongensis*.

S. farinacea Benth. MEALY SAGE. Perenn. herb to 50cm, erect, pubesc. Lvs to 8cm, ovate or lanceolate to linear or oblong, apex obtuse to acute, base obtuse or attenuate, undulate to notched, minutely pubesc. on veins beneath; petioles to 1cm. Verticillasters 10–16-fld, subsecund, in interrupted, spicate rac. to 20cm; bracts ovate to oblong; cal. to 8mm, pubesc.; cor. blue or lavender to purple, tube to 8mm. Summer–autumn. Tex., Mex.; in widespread cult. 'Alba': fls white, middle lobe of lower lip obcordate, bifid. 'Blue Bedder': more compact; fls dark blue. 'Rhea': compact and low; fls intense dark blue, early-flowering. 'Silver' ('Argent'): fls silvery white. 'Victoria': dense basal branching; fls intense deep blue. Z9.

S. farinosa Mart. & Gal. = *S. purpurea*.

S. fimbriata Kunth = *S. tiliifolia*.

S. fistulosa Sessé & Moq. = *S. sessei*.

S. flava var. *megalantha* Diels = *S. bulleyana*.

S. formosa L'Hérit. Shrub to 1.5m. Lvs to 5cm, ovate, cordate at base, subentire, coriaceous, tomentose beneath. Verticillasters 3–6-fld; cor. 2–3cm, deep blood red. Late summer. Peru. Z9.

S. forskaohlei L. Perenn. herb 25–100cm. St. erect, simple or branched. Lvs 5 to 30cm, mostly basal, ovate or lyrate, cordate at base, serrate or crenate, glandular-strigose, long-petiolate. Verticillasters 4–8-fld; cal. 8–12mm, teeth rather spinose, glandular-pilose; cor. 20–30mm, violet-blue to pinkish-magenta, with white or yellow markings. Summer. SE Eur. & W Asia. Z7.

S. fruticosa Mill. Shrub to 1m, much-branched, glandular-pubesc. to tomentose. Lvs to 5cm, simple or pinnatifid, ovate or lanceolate to oblong, ± rugose, white-tomentose beneath, term. seg. elliptic to oblong, lateral seg. 1–2 pairs, margin notched; petioles to 3cm. Verticillasters 2–8-fld, in pan. or rac. to 20cm; bracts to 7mm, to 9mm, glandular-pubesc.; cor. to 25mm, pink to mauve, or, white. Spring–summer. Canary Is. and N Afr. to Middle E. Z9.

S. fulgens Cav. Perenn. herb or subshrub to 1m, much-branched,

glab. to glandular-pubesc. Lvs to 12cm, ovate to deltoid, apex obtuse or acute, base obtuse or cordate, toothed ot notched, white-tomentose beneath, petioles to 4cm. Verticillasters 2–6-fld, in interrupted spikes or rac. to 25cm; bracts to 6mm, ovate; cal. to 17mm, dilated in fr., glandular-pubesc.; cor. red, tube to 28mm. Summer. Mex. Z9.

S. gesneriiflora Lindl. & Paxt. Perenn. herb or subshrub to 60cm, glandular-pubesc. Lvs to 10cm, ovate, apex narrowly acute, base obtuse or cordate, notched, rugose above, pubesc.; petioles to 8cm. Verticillasters 2–8-fld, in rac. to 20cm; bracts to 1cm, ovate; cal. to 21mm, dilated in fr., pubesc.; cor. to 5cm, red, globose, pubesc. Spring and autumn. Mex. Z9.

S. gigantea Desf. = *S. virgata*.

S. glutinosa L. JUPITER'S DISTAFF. Perenn. herb to 1m, erect, simple or branched, glandular-pubesc. Lvs to 14cm, ovate or deltoid to oblong, apex acute, base hastate to cordate, notched, thin, glandular-pubesc.; petioles to 11cm. Verticillasters 2–6-fld, distant, in simple rac.; bracts to 10mm, ovate; cal. to 12mm, dilated in fr.; cor. to 4cm, yellow, flecked brown. Summer. Eur. to W Asia. Z5.

S. glutinosa auct., non L. = *S. nubicola*.

S. gossypina Benth. = *S. carduacea*.

S. goudotii Benth. = *S. rufula*.

S. grahamii Benth. = *S. microphylla*.

S. grandiflora Sessé & Moq., non Etling. = *S. fulgens*.

S. grata Vahl = *S. oppositiflora*.

S. graveolens Vahl = *S. dominica*.

S. greggii A. Gray. AUTUMN SAGE. Perenn. herb or shrub, 30–50cm, ascending, glandular-pubesc., branchlets pendent. Lvs to 3cm, ovate or elliptic to oblong or linear, apex obtuse, base attenuate, entire, leathery, gland. punctate and glab. to pubesc., petioles to 5mm. Verticillasters 2-fld, in rac. to 15cm; bracts pubesc.; cal. to 12mm, glandular-pubesc.; cor. red to purple, pink, yellow and violet, tube to 22mm. Summer–autumn. Tex., Mex. 'Alba': fls white. See also *S. microphylla* × *S. greggii*. Z7.

S. guaranitica St.-Hil. ex Benth. Perenn. subshrub (sometimes grown as an ann.), to 1.5m+. Lvs to 13cm, ovate, acuminate at apex, rounded or cordate at base, crenate-serrate, sparsely hirsute. Verticillasters 2–8-fld, in infl. to 25cm; cal. 12mm, tinged violet-blue; cor. to 5cm, dark blue. Late summer. Braz., Urug., Arg. 'Blue Ensign': lvs bright green, aromatic; fls large, Cambridge blue; cal. green. 'Blue Enigma': perenn. to 1.5m; lvs glab. above; cal. green; fls blue. 'Black and Blue': subshrub to 3m; lvs large, pubesc.; cal. v. dark violet-blue. 'Purple Splendour': lvs smooth; cor. purple. Z9.

S. hablitziana Willd. = *S. scabiosifolia*.

S. haematodes L. = *S. pratensis*.

S. halophila Hedge. Perenn. herb to 50cm, erect, branched above, glandular-pilose. Lvs 6–9cm, ovate-lanceolate to ovate-oblong, entire or crenate-dentate, cordate-truncate at base, succulent, pubesc.; petioles 4–7cm. Verticillasters 4–6-fld, numerous in erect infl.; bracts ovate-acuminate, to 6mm; cal. 6–8mm, glandular-pilose; cor. 12–17mm, pale lilac to lavender, midlobe pale. Summer–autumn. Turk. Z8.

S. heerii Reg. Subshrub, 90–150cm, hairy. Lvs 5–13cm, ovate, apex acuminate, cordate to rounded at base, serrate, softly pubesc. Verticillasters 1–3-fld, in branched infl.; cal. 12mm; cor. 3–4cm, bright scarlet. Winter. Peru. Z10.

S. hempsteadiana Blake = *S. cacaliifolia*.

S. hians Royle ex Benth. Perenn. herb to 1m, erect, robust, pubesc. Lvs to 25cm, ovate to lanceolate, apex acute, base cordate to hastate or truncate, toothed; petioles to 25cm. Verticillasters 2–6-fld, in simple or branched, spicate rac.; bracts ovate; cal. to 15mm, glandular-pubescent, cor. to 4cm, blue, often tipped white. Summer. India. var. *exannulata* Stibal. Fls smaller, lacking hairs in cor. tube, deep blue to violet. Z6.

S. hierosolymitana Boiss. Perenn. herb, to 1m, erect, branched, glandular-pubesc. Lvs to 25cm, ovate to oblong, apex obtuse, undulate to toothed, somewhat pubesc. Verticillasters 2–6-fld, racemose; bracts ovate to deltoid, glandular-pubesc.; cal. to 13mm, dilated in fr., glandular-pubesc.; cor. to 3cm, pink or red to purple. Spring–summer. Middle East. Z8.

S. hirta Kunth. Shrub to 1.5m, slender, branching, densely pubesc. Lvs 4–8cm, narrowly ovate to ovate-lanceolate, apex acute, base rotund to subcordate, crenate-serrate, hirtellous above, villous beneath; petioles 1.3cm. Verticillasters of 1–3 fls; bracts 5–8mm, ovate, ciliate; cal. 10–11mm, with gland. hairs; cor. 2.5–3cm, bright scarlet. Peru, Ecuad. Z9.

S. hispanica L. Ann. herb, to 1m, erect or ascending, branched, pubesc. Lvs to 8cm, ovate or lanceolate to oblong, apex acute, base attenuate to obtuse, notched, glab. or pubesc.; petioles to 3cm. Verticillasters 6–10-fld, in dense, term., rac. to 15cm; bracts to 8mm, ovate; cal. to 7mm, dilated in fr., pubesc.; cor. blue, tube to 6mm. Summer. C Mex., widely nat. Many plants cultivated as *S. hispanica* are *S. lavendulifolia*. Z9.

S. horminoides Pourr. = *S. verbenaca*.

S. horminum L. = *S. viridis*.

S. hoveyi hort. (misapplied. = *S. ianthina*.

S. hypargeia Fisch. & Mey. Perenn. forming tufts to 60cm diam. St. 25–40cm, simple, erect, woody at base, arachnoid-lanate below, glandular-pilose above. Lvs 4–8cm, mostly basal, linear-oblong, white-lanate beneath; petiole indistinct. Verticillasters 4–8-fld, in simple infl.; bracts ovate, to 15mm, lanate; cal. to 12mm, lanate, gland.; cor. 25mm, lavender to blue tinged purple. Summer. C Anatolia. Z7.

S. ianthina Otto & Dietr. Perenn., 60–90cm. Lvs ovate, crenate, apex attenuate. Verticillasters 1–6-fld, in simple infl.; bracts violet-purple; cal. deep violet-purple; cor. 4–4.5cm, deep violet-purple. Summer–autumn. Known only in cult.; possibly *S. splendens* ×*S. mexicana*. Z10.

S. incarnata Cav., non Etling. = *S. elegans*.

S. indica L. Perenn. herb, to 1.5m, erect, branched, glandular-pubesc. Lvs to 30cm, ovate, apex truncate or cordate, toothed to erose, glandular-pubesc.; petioles to 10cm. Verticillasters 4–6-fld, in much-branched pan. to 50cm; bracts to 8mm, ovate; cal. to 1cm, glandular-pubesc.; cor. to 3cm, white and blue or violet to lilac-tipped. Spring–summer. Middle East. Z9.

S. interrupta Schousb. Perenn. herb or subshrub, to 1m ± erect, much-branched. Lvs to 25cm, pinnate, rugose above, white-tomentose beneath, term. seg. to 11cm, ovate to oblong, notched, lat. seg. reduced, 1–3 pairs, petioles to 6cm. Verticillasters 10, 5–10-fld, to 10cm distant, in branched rac.; cal. to 15mm, glandular-pubesc.; cor. to 35mm, blue, shading to white at throat, flecked pink. Spring to summer. Moroc. Z9.

S. involucrata Cav. Perenn. herb, to 1.5m, erect, sparsely branched, woody at base, glandular-pubesc. Lvs to 14cm, ovate, apex attenuate to acute, base cuneate to cordate or obtuse, entire to notched, glab. to short-pubesc.; petioles to 9cm. Verticillasters 3–6-fld, in dense spicate rac. to 30cm; bracts ovate to suborbicular; cal. to 13mm, tubular to bell-shaped, glandular-pubesc.; cor. pink or red to purple, tube to 3cm. Summer–autumn. Mex. 'Bethellii': base of lvs cordate; fls red. 'Deschampsiana': to 1m; lvs narrowly acute at apex; fls in ovoid-spicate rac.; bracts red, cal. red, cor. rose pink, tube v. distended. Z9.

S. japonica Thunb. Perenn. herb, to 75cm erect, branched or simple. Lvs pinnate, with terminal leaflet and 2–3 pairs of laterals; lfts 2–5cm, ovate to rhombic, dentate; petioles long. Verticillasters 4-fld, in terminal spike-like infl., 10–25cm, minutely pubesc.; cal. about 6mm, pilose within; cor. about 12mm, dark lilac. Summer–autumn. NE Asia. 'Alba': cor. white. Z8.

S. judaica Boiss. Perenn. herb erect, much-branched towards infl., scabrid. Lvs lyrate or ovate-cordate, crenate or irregularly dentate, petiolate. Verticillasters 6–10-fld; in much-branched infl.; cal. maroon to purple, scabrid; cor. to 12mm, violet. Palestine. Z9.

S. jurisicii Košanin. Perenn. herb to 60cm, much-branched, white-pubesc. Lvs pinnate to pinnatifid, ovate to oblong, seg. 4–6 pairs, linear, notched to lobed. Verticillasters 2–7-fld, in loose, branched rac. to 20cm; cal. to 5mm, pubesc.; cor. white to pink or violet, to 12mm. Summer. Balk. (Macedonia). 'Alba': fls white. Z6.

S. lamiifolia Jacq. Shrubby perenn., 2.5m, freely branched. Lvs 8–20cm, ovate, apex acuminate, base subcordate, serrate, bright green above, paler beneath, glab. Verticillasters 3–6-fld; cal. hirtellous; cor. 2cm, blue tinged purple. Flowering season variable. W Indies. Z10.

S. lanata Roxb. Perenn. herb, erect to 30cm. Lvs 15–20cm, mostly basal, oblong or oblanceolate, obtuse, crenulate, sessile, loosely hairy above, white-lanate beneath. Verticillasters 4–8-fld, in remote, clammy-hairy spikes; cal. 6mm, spinose, glandular-pubesc.; cor. 16mm, lavender-blue. Himal. (Nepal to NW Pak.). Z7.

S. lanceaefolia A. Gray = *S. reflexa*.

S. lanceolata Rydb. = *S. reflexa*.

S. laterifolia Fern. = *S. riparia*.

S. latifolia Vahl = *S. algeriensis*.

S. lavandulifolia Vahl. Perenn. woody-based herb to 30cm. Lvs to 2.5cm, mostly basal, narrowly oblong, entire, grey- to white-tomentose; petioles long. Verticillasters 6–9-fld; cal. often coloured; cor. blue-violet. Spain. Z5.

S. lemmonii A. Gray = *S. microphylla* var. *wislizenii*.

S. leptophylla Benth. = *S. reptans*.

S. leucantha Cav. Perenn. herb or subshrub, to 1m. Lvs to 10cm, linear or oblong to lanceolate, apex acute, base obtuse, notched, rugose, pubesc. to tomentose beneath; petioles to 17mm. Verticillasters 6–8-fld, in purple-tomentose rac. to 24cm; cal. to 12mm, violet- to lavender-tomentose; cor. white, tube to 12mm, tomentose. Winter. Mex. and Trop. Amer.; in wide-

spread cult. Z10.

S. leucophylla Greene CHAPARRAL SAGE; SAN LUIS PURPLE SAGE. Shrub to 1mm, much-branched, white-tomentose. Lvs to 6cm, ovate or lanceolate to oblong, apex obtuse, base cordate to truncate, notched, rugose, grey-tomentose above, white-tomentose beneath. Verticillasters 3–5, in interrupted spikes; bracts to 15mm, white-tomentose sometimes purple-tinted; cal. to 11mm; cor. to 2cm, pink to blue or purple. Calif. Z8.

S. libanotica Boiss. & Gaill. = *S. fruticosa*.

S. lobryana Aznav. = *S. fruticosa*.

S. longiflora Ruiz & Pav., non Willd. = *S. dombeyi*.

S. longiflora Willd. = *S. tubifera*.

S. longistyla Benth. Perenn. herb or subshrub, to 5m, erect, branched, pubesc. to tomentose. Lvs to 25cm, ovate, apex narrowly acute, base cordate, notched, glab. to pubesc.; petioles to 15cm. Verticillasters 3–6-fld, in interrupted, branched spikes to 50cm; bracts ovate, ciliate; cal. to 24mm, glandular-pubesc., bristle-tipped; cor. pink or red to purple, tube to 35mm. Winter. Mex. Z10.

S. lycioides A. Gray. Low shrub, 30–50cm. Lvs to 3cm, oblong-elliptic, entire to obscurely serrulate, glab. to hispidulous, often glandular-punctate; petioles 2–5mm. Infl. racemose, fls 4–6, in verticillasters; bracts decid.; cal. 7–8mm, glab. or glandular-hispid, often tinted blue; cor. 1cm, deep blue. Tex., New Mex., N Mex. Z6.

S. lyrata L. CANCER WEED. Perenn. herb, to 60cm, erect, sparsely branched, pubesc. Basal lvs to 8cm, lyrate, toothed to erose, membranous, pubesc., cauline lvs few, lyrate to pinnatifid, undulate to lobed, seg. orbicular. Verticillasters 3–10-fld, in interrupted, sparsely branched pan.; bracts linear to oblong; cal. pendent, pubesc.; cor. to 3cm, violet to purple. Summer. US Z5.

S. macrostachya Kunth. Shrubby perenn. to 2m, erect, hirsute. Lvs orbicular-cordate with overlapping basal lobes, crenate, to 20cm, pubesc. Verticillasters many-fld, in dense infl.; bracts 5cm, broadly ovate, tips recurved, pale green; cal. broadly tubular; cor. pale blue. Early spring. Ecuad. Z9.

S. mandarinorum Diels = *S. przewalskii*.

S. mariae Sennen = *S. algeriensis*.

S. mekongensis Stibal. Perenn. herb, to 60cm. Lvs to 15cm, mostly basal, ovate, deeply cordate at base, crenate, pilose, long-petiolate. Verticillasters 2–4-fld, lower distinct, upper compacted, in dense infl.; cor. 3cm, deep red. SW China. Z8.

S. mellifera Greene. CALIFORNIA BLACK SAGE. Shrub, to 2m. Lvs to 6cm, lanceolate to oblong, apex acute or obtuse, base attenuate, notched, rugose, tomentose beneath; petioles to 2cm. Verticillasters to 6, in dense, interrupted spikes or heads; bracts to 1cm, cuspidate; cal. to 8mm, spiny- to bristle-tipped; cor. white to blue or lavender, tube to 9mm. Calif. Z8.

S. mentiens Pohl. Perenn., 45–60cm, sparingly branched. Lvs ovate, acute, finely dentate, glab. Verticillasters 1–3-fld, in dense infl.; bracts brightly coloured; cal. scarlet, pubesc.; cor. 5–6.5cm, rosy-scarlet. Autumn. Braz. Z9.

S. mexicana L. Perenn. shrub to 4m, erect, pubesc. Lvs to 15cm, ovate to rhomboid, apex narrowly acute, base truncate or cuneate, notched and gland., glab. to pubesc., or tomentose beneath; petioles to 5cm. Verticillasters 6–10-fld, in loose, term. spikes to 50cm; bracts to 2cm; cal. to 17mm, pubesc.; cor. blue to violet or purple, tube to 25mm. Winter. Mex. var. *minor* Benth. Cor. white. Z9.

S. microphylla Kunth. Shrubby herb to 120cm. Lvs 1.5–4cm, deltoid-ovate to elliptic, serrate-crenate, pubesc. or sub-glabrous. Verticillasters 2- or 4-fld, in an extended rac. 10–15cm; bracts 3–6mm; cal. tinged purple; cor. 2.5cm, deep crimson, pink, purple or magenta. Late summer–autumn. Mex. 'Blush Pink': fls rich pink. var. *neurepia* (Fern.) Epling. Lvs 3.5–5cm. Verticillasters 2-fld, rac. to 20cm; cor. cherry-red. Autumn. Mex. 'Newby Hall': to 2m, robust; lvs ovate, to 5cm, pubesc. on both surfaces; fls larger than in var. *neurepia*. 'Oxford': fls dark pink. 'Ruth Stungo': lvs variegated white. var. *wislizenii* (Gray) Gray. Lvs 1.5–3cm, acute to acuminate, canescent. Infl. shorter than var. *neurepia*, fls often vermilion or magenta. Mex. *S. microphylla* ×*S. greggii*: 'Pat Vlasto': lvs entire; fls peach-orange. 'James Compton': lvs ovate, serrate; fls large, dark crimson. Z9.

S. montbretii Boiss. = *S. hypargeia*.

S. moorcroftiana Wallich ex Benth. Perenn. herb, to 90cm erect, branched, robust, glandular-pubesc. Lvs to 25cm, ovate, lanceolate or elliptic to oblong, apex obtuse, base obtuse or cordate, toothed to erose, pannose or white-tomentose beneath; petioles to 14cm. Verticillasters 4–10-fld, in loose, branched pan.; bracts to 15mm, membranous; cal. to 14mm, dilated in fr., glandualr and bristly; cor. blue to lilac or violet, or white, tube to 15mm. W Himal., Kashmir. Z7.

S. multicaulis Vahl. Subshrubby perenn. to 50cm, forming mats, generally glandular-pilose. Lvs 2–5cm, mostly basal, broadly ovate-elliptic to suborbicular, occas. with small basal lobes, crenulate, rugose, white- to grey-tomentose; petiole 2–6cm. Verticillasters 4–10-fld, several in simple infl.; bracts to 15mm; cal. to 15mm, purple or lime green, gland. pilose; cor. to 18mm, violet or white. Spring–summer. SW Asia. Z8.

S. munzii Epling. Shrub, to 2.5m. Lvs to 3cm, ovate to oblong or oblanceolate, apex obtuse, base attenuate, notched, bullate above, minutely pubesc. beneath; petioles to 3mm. Spikes to 15cm; bracts to 4mm, acute or aristate, ciliate; cal. to 6mm, glandular-pubesc., teeth aristate; cor. blue, tube to 1cm. Calif. Z8.

S. napifolia Jacq. Perenn. herb erect, branched above, villous, gland. above. Lvs 3–8cm, ovate or lyrate, crenate to erose, base cordate, villous, gland.; petiole 1–5cm. Verticillasters 8–20-fld, distant; bracts to 5mm; cal. 8mm, purple-violet, pilose, gland.; cor. 12mm, purple-violet. Spring–summer. Turk. Z8.

S. nemorosa L. Perenn. herb, to 1m, erect, much-branched. Lvs to 10cm, ovate or lanceolate to oblong, apex attenuate, base obtuse or cordate, notched, rugose and glandular-pubesc.; petioles to 4cm. Verticillasters 2–6-fld, in dense, term., stiff, branched spikes to 40cm; bracts to 10mm, imbricate, ovate, violet ot purple; cal . to 6mm, dilated in fr., pubesc.; cor. 8–12mm, violet to purple, or white to pink. Summer–autumn. Eur. to C Asia. ssp. **tesquicola** (Klokov & Pobed.) Soó. Cal. long-pubesc.; cor. 10–14mm. Z5.

S. nemorosa Mottet, non L. = **S. superba**.

S. neurepia Fern. = **S. microphylla** var. **neurepia**.

S. nitidifolia Ortega = **S. mexicana**.

S. nubicola Wallich ex Sweet. Perenn. herb to 1.2m, erect, robust, glandular-pubesc. Lvs to 18cm, ovate or deltoid to oblong, apex narrowly acute, base hastate or cordate and lobulate, serrate or crenate, thick-textured, rugose, pubesc.; petioles to 10cm. Verticillasters 4–6-fld, distant, in simple rac. or branching at base; bracts 10mm; cal. to 12mm; cor. yellow or flecked orange or brown, tube 2–3cm. Summer. C Asia, Himal. Z7.

S. nutans L. Perenn. herb, to 1m erect, unbranched. Lvs to 15cm, ovate to oblong, base cordate, notched, pubesc.; petioles to 13cm. Verticillasters 4–7-fld, in initially pendent, paniculate or spicate rac. to 4cm; bracts to 6mm; cal. to 5mm, dilated in fr., pubesc.; cor. violet, tube to 8mm. Summer. Balk. to Sib. Z5.

S. odorata Willd. = **S. candidissima**.

S. officinalis L. COMMON SAGE. Perenn. shrub, to 80cm erect, much-branched. Lvs to 6cm, oblong to elliptic, base obtuse or attenuate, occas., lobulate, entire, rugose, white-pubesc., eesp. beneath; petioles to 2.5cm. Verticillasters 4–20-fld, approximate, in simple rac.; bracts ovate, membranous; cal. to 14mm, glandular-punctate and pubesc., teeth subulate; cor. white or pink to violet or purple, tube to 15mm. Summer. Medit. (Iberia and Balk.) and N Afr.; nat. S Eur.; widespread in cult. 'Albiflora': fls white. 'Aurea': lvs golden. 'Berggarten': broad and low; lvs v. wide; fls blue. 'Compacta': dwarf, to 20cm high. 'Crispa': lvs variegated, crisped. 'Grete Stolze': lvs pointed, pale grey; fls mauve-blue. 'Icterina': lvs golden-green. 'Kew Gold': lvs golden yellow. 'Latifolia': lvs to 2× longer than wide. 'Milleri': lvs red, blotched. 'Purpurascens': lvs red-purple. 'Rubriflora': lvs to 4× longer than wide. Fls red. 'Salicifolia': lvs to 7× longer than wide. 'Sturnina': lvs white-green. 'Tenuior': lvs to 4× longer than wide; fls blue. 'Tricolor': lvs grey-green zoned yellow, and pink to red. Z5.

S. officinalis var. **lavandulifolia** (Vahl) Bolós & Vigo = **S. lavandulifolia**.

S. oppositiflora Ruiz & Pav. Small shrub, 20–60cm, sparsely hairy. Lvs 2.5–5cm, broadly ovate to suborbicular, cordate to truncate, crenate or serrate, subglabrous above, viscid beneath. Verticillasters 2-fld, in simple infl.; cal. 1–2cm, glandular-hispid; cor. 2–4cm, red tinged orange, downy. Winter. Peru. Z10.

S. pachyphylla Epling. ROSE SAGE. Shrub to 90cm, decumbent, spreading. Lvs too 3cm, ovate to oblong or oblanceolate, apex obtuse, base attenuate, entire, rough, glandular-punctate, tomentose; petioles to 15mm. Verticillasters 2–4, approximate, in interrupted spikes or heads to 10cm; bracts to 2cm, membranous, purple; cal. to 12mm; cor. to 22mm, blue to violet. Calif. Z8.

S. papilionacea Cav. = **S. mexicana**.

S. patens Cav. Perenn. herb to 1m, erect, gland. pubesc. Lvs to 20cm, ovate to deltoid or pentagonal, base hastate or peltate, notched, pubesc.; petioles to 10cm. Verticillasters 2-fld, distant, decussate, in pan. to 40cm; bracts linear; cal. to 2cm, glandular-pubesc.; cor. blue, tube to 25mm. Summer–autumn. Mex. 'Alba': fls white. 'Cambridge Blue': fls pale blue. 'Chilcombe': fls mauve-blue. Z8.

S. patula Desf. = **S. argentea**.

S. paui Maire = **S. interrupta**.

S. peloponnesiaca Boiss. & Heldr. = **S. verticillata**.

S. pilosa Merrill = **S. dorrii**.

S. pitcheri Torr. ex Benth. = **S. azurea** var. **pitcheri**.

S. pomifera L. Much-branched, canescent shrub to 1m. Lvs to 4cm, canescent when young, lanceolate-ovate, apex obtuse, crenate-undulate, rugose. Verticillasters 2–4-fld; bracts green, large; cal. to 15mm, accrescent, often red-purple; cor. to 35mm, violet blue, lower lip mid-blue. Greece, Crete. Z8.

S. porphyrantha Decne. = **S. roemeriana**.

S. porphyratra Hook. = **S. roemeriana**.

S. pratensis L. MEADOW CLARY. Perenn. herb to 1m erect, simple or branched, glandular-pubesc. Basal lvs to 15cm, petiolate, ovate to oblong, apex obtuse, base cordate, toothed to notched, rugose, pubesc., cauline lvs sessile, red, maculate. Verticillasters 5–10, 4–6-fld, in loose, simple or branched spikes to 45cm; bracts to 3mm; cal. to 11mm, glandular-pubesc.; cor. to 3cm, violet or white to pink. Summer. Eur. (inc. GB). 'Alba': fls white. 'Atroviolacea': fls dark blue to violet. 'Baumgartenii':: fls blue to violet. 'Haematodes': fls lilac-blue. 'Lupinoides': to 60cm; fls blue to purple, flecked white. 'Mittsommer': fls sky blue. 'Rosea':: fls rose-pink to purple. 'Rubicunda': fls rose-red. 'Tenorii': to 60cm; fls blue. 'Variegata': fls blue to white-tipped. Z3.

S. privoides Benth. = **S. riparia**.

S. prunelloides Kunth. Tuberous perenn., 30–45cm, sparingly branched, pilose. Lvs 2.5–9cm, ovate-oblong to rhomboid, crenate, obtuse, subglabrous. Verticillasters about 3–6-fld, distinct; cal. silky-hairy; cor. 2cm, bright blue. Late summer–early autumn. Mex. Z9.

S. przewalskii Maxim. Perenn. herb, to 1.5m, ascending, glandular-pubesc. Basal lvs ovate or lanceolate to oblong, apex acute, base cordate, toothed to notched, cauline lvs hastate. Verticillasters 2–4-fld, distant, in branched, spicate rac.; bracts ovate; cal. glandular-pubesc.; cor. blue to violet or purple. Summer. China. var. **mandarinorum** (Diels) Stibal. Lvs yellow or tawny beneath. China. Z8.

S. pseudococcinea Jacq. = **S. coccinea**.

S. purpurea Cav. Perenn. herb or subshrub to 3m erect, glab. to minutely pubesc. Lvs to 12cm, ovate, apex narrowly acute, base attenuate to cordate, notched, glab. above, minutely pubesc. beneath; petioles to 6cm. Verticillasters 3+-fld, in dense, paniculate spikes or rac.; cal. to 8mm, purple-tomentose; cor. to 25mm, pink to purple. Mex., Guat. Z9.

S. recognita Fisch. & Mey. Shrubby herb, 40–90cm, erect, branching, glandular-villous. Lvs 4–13cm, pinnate, rarely simple, term. leaflet oblong-ovate, lateral lfts 1–2 pairs, rugose, glandular-hairy, crenulate; petiole 4–8cm. Verticillasters 4–6-fld, distant; bracts to 12mm; cal. to 18mm, glandular-hairy; cor. 3.5–4cm, lilac-pink. Turk. Z6.

S. rectiflora Vis. = **S. longistyla**.

S. reflexa Hornem. Ann. herb to 75cm, erect, branched. Lvs to 8cm, linear to elliptic or lanceolate, base attenuate, entire to notched, short-pubesc.; petioles to 15mm. Verticillasters 2–6-fld, in interrupted rac. or spikes; bracts to 6mm; cal. to 6mm, dilated in fr., pubesc.; cor. to 12mm, blue to lilac. N to C Amer.; widespread in cult.

S. regla Cav. Compact shrub to 1.5m. Lvs to 2–5cm, deltoid-ovate to subreniform, acuminate, crenate-serrate, sparsely pubesc. Verticillasters few-fld, infll. lax; cal. 1–2cm, inflated, scarlet; cor. 5cm, scarlet, downy. Autumn. Tex. to Mex. Z9.

S. reptans Jacq. Perenn. herb, to 1m erect to ascending, woody at base. Lvs to 8cm, linear, subentire to notched, glab. to glandular-pubesc. Verticillasters 2–6-fld, to 4cm distant, in interrupted spikes to 30cm; cor. blue, tube to 1cm. Mex. Z9.

S. rhombifolia Ruiz & Pav. Ann. herb to 50cm, much-branched. Lvs broadly ovate-deltoid, crenate, subglabrous. Verticillasters 3–6-fld, distinct, in lax rac. to 12cm; cal. 8–12mm, expanding in fr., often coloured; cor. 12mm, blue. Late summer. Peru, Boliv., Chile.

S. ringens Sibth. & Sm. Perenn. herb, to 60cm, erect, ± simple, woody at base, basal lvs pinnate to pinnatifid, rugose and pubesc., term. seg. to 12cm, ovate to elliptic, obtuse, lat. seg. reduced, 2–3-pairs, cauline lvs simple. Verticillasters 5–10, 4–6-fld, distant, in simple rac.; bracts ciliate, membranous; cal. to 17mm, pendent, glandular-pubesc.; cor. to 4cm, blue to violet or purple. Summer. Balk. Z7.

S. riparia Kunth. Ann. herb to 50cm ascending, pubesc. Lvs to 3cm, ovate, apex acute, base attenuate to cuneate, notched, pubesc.; petioles to 1cm. Verticillasters 2–24-fld, in interrupted spikes to 20cm; bracts to 4mm, ovate; cal. to 4mm, dilated in fr., glandular-pubesc.; cor. pink to red, tube to 3mm. W Indies and Cuba, C to S Amer.

S. roemeriana Scheele. Perenn. herb, to 60cm, sparsely branched, glab. to pubesc. Lvs to 2.5cm, simple to pinnate, suborbicular to cordate or reniform, undulate and toothed to notched. Verticillasters few-fld, in loose rac.; cal. pubesc., green to purple; cor. to 3cm, red. Summer. US (Tex.). Z8.

S. roezlii Scheidw. = **S. sessei**.

S. rosea Vahl = *S. coccinea*.

S. rosifolia Sm. Perenn. herb or dwarf shrub, 25–50cm, ascending, unbranched, pubesc. Lvs pinnatisect, entire to minutely serrate, pilose, gland., term. seg. 2–4cm, oblong-elliptic, lat. seg. in 2 pairs, smaller. Verticillasters 4–10-fld, in short rac.; bracts to 12mm; cal. 10–15mm, strongly tinged violet, villous; cor. 20–24mm, lilac-pink to violet. Summer. Turk. Z8.

S. rubescens Kunth. Perenn. herb or shrub, to 1m. St. 4-angled, pubesc. to tomentose. Lvs to 16cm, ovate, apex acute, base cordate, notched, tomentose beneath; petioles to 8cm. Verticillasters 3–12-fld, to 5cm distant, in dense, branched, pyramidal pan. to 30cm; bracts to 4mm, glandular-pubesc.; cal. to 1cm, glandular-pubesc., purple to brown; cor. red, tube to 2.4cm. Venez., Columbia. Z10.

S. rubicunda Wender. = *S. pratensis* 'Rubicunda'.

S. rufida Willd. ex Schult. = *S. rufula*.

S. rufula Kunth. Herb or subshrub, to 1m. St. branched. Lvs to 8cm, ovate to lanceolate, apex acute, bas attenuate to obtuse, toothed to notched, pubesc. to tomentose; petioles to 12mm. Verticillasters 3–8-fld, subsecund, in interrupted, simple spikes or rac. to 15cm; bracts to 8mm; cal. to 8mm; cor. red, tube to 16mm. Columbia. Z10.

S. russellii Benth. Erect perenn. herb to 60cm, forming tight clumps. Lvs 5–8cm, linear-oblong, occasionaly sublyrate, pilose, gland.; petiole 2–8cm. Verticillasters 20–30-fld, distant, in unbranched infl.; bracts to 6mm; cal. 6mm, blue-violet, pilose; cor. 10mm, violet or blue-violet. Summer. SW Asia. Z8.

S. rutilans Carr. PINEAPPLE-SCENTED SAGE. Subshrub to 90cm. Lvs petiolate, ovate, notched, pubesc. Verticillasters 2–8-fld, in pan. or spicate rac.; cal. to 5mm; cor. to 3cm, pink to red, pubesc. Winter. Known only in cult., probably a form of *S. elegans* Vahl. Z10.

S. salvatori hort. = *S. pratensis* 'Rosea'.

S. scabiosifolia Lam. Perenn. herb or subshrub to 50cm ascending, much-branched. Lvs to 9cm, pinnate-pinnatifid, elliptic, pubesc., lat. seg. to 4cm, 3–8 pairs, opposite or 3-whorled, linear to oblong, term. seg. larger. Verticillasters 5–11, 6–10-fld, in rac. to 15cm; cal. to 15mm, dilated in fr., glandular-pubesc.; cor. to 3cm, white, flecked violet to purple. Summer. Crimea, Bulg. Z6.

S. scapiformis Hance. Perenn. herb to 75cm, erect. Lvs almost all basal, simple ternate or pinnate with 2 pairs of lat. seg.; lfts 2–5cm, ovate to rhombic, dentate; petioles long. Verticillasters 4-fld, numerous, in terminal spike-like infl., 10–25cm; cal. about 6mm; cor. about 12mm, dark lilac. Summer–autumn. NE Asia. Z7.

S. schiediana Stapf = *S. hispanica*.

S. schimperi Benth. in DC. Perenn. herb to 1m, erect, stout, much-branched. Lvs to 18cm, oblong to ovate-lanceolate, minutely crenate, petiolate, bracts sparsely tomentose above, densely so beneath. Verticillasters about 6-fld, in large lax paniculate infl. with stiffly spreading br.; bracts large spine-tipped, white with green veins; cal. 1.5cm, green, pubesc.; cor. to 5cm, white. Summer. Ethiop. Z10.

S. sclarea L. CLARY. Perenn. or bienn. herb to 1m erect, much-branched, glandular-pubesc. Lvs to 23cm, ovate to oblong, base perfoliate or cordate, notched to erose, rugose; petioles to 9cm. Verticillasters 2–6-fld, distant, in many-fld pan. or rac.; bracts to 35mm, concave, or lilac; cal. to 1cm, glandular-punctate; cor. to 3cm, cream and lilac to pink or blue. Spring–summer. Eur. to C Asia. 'Turkestanica': st. pink; lvs petiolate; fls in spikes to 75cm, white, flecked pink. Z5.

S. semperflorens La Ll. = *S. sessei*.

S. sessei Benth. Subshrub to 5m. Lvs to 13cm, ovate or lanceolate to oblong, apex acute, base attenuate to cuneate, subentire to notched, leathery, gland. beneath; petioles to 3cm. Verticillasters few-fld, in loose, paniculate rac.; cal. to 25mm in fr., red; cor. red, tube to 35mm, pubesc. Summer. Mex. Z9.

S. sibthorpii Sibth. & Sm. = *S. virgata*.

S. similata Hausskn. = *S. virgata*.

S. simsiana Roem. & Schult. = *S. sclarea*.

S. sinaloensis Fern. Procumbent, perenn. herb, 15–30cm, sometimes purple tinted. Lvs 3–6cm, elliptic-obovate, subsessile, apex acute, serrulate, smooth to densely hairy. Verticillasters 3-flld in interrupted spikes; cal. to 7.5mm, hairy; cor. 1–2cm, deep blue, lower lip spotted white. Mex. Z9.

S. sonomensis Greene. CREEPING SAGE. Shrub, to 30cm, creeping and mat-forming, pubesc. Lvs to 5cm, spathulate to oblong or obovate, apex obtuse, base attenuate, notched, rugose, white-tomentose beneath; petioles to 2cm. Verticillasters 3–8, distant, in rac.; cal. to 8mm; cor. violet, tube to 8mm. Calif. Z8.

S. souliei Duthie = *S. brevilabra*.

S. spathacea Greene. PITCHER SAGE. Perenn. herb to 1m. St. erect, simple or sparsely branched, glandular-pubesc. Lvs to 20cm, subsessile to petiolate, ovate or lanceolate to oblong, apex obtuse, base hastate to cordate or truncate, notched,

rugose, white-tomentose beneath. Verticillasters 5–22, 2–20-fld, in dense, term. spikes to 30cm; bracts to 4cm, purple; cal. to 25mm; cor. to 3cm, red. Calif. Z8.

S. spectabilis Kunth = *S. patens*.

S. spielmannii Willd. = *S. verbenaca*.

S. splendens Sell ex Roem. & Schult. SCARLET SAGE. Perenn. or ann. herb, to 1m erect. Lvs to 7cm, ovate, apex attenuate, base obtuse or cordate to cuneate, notched, glab. to minutely pubesc.; petioles to 3cm. Verticillasters 2–6-fld, in terminal, spicate rac. to 20cm; bracts to 12mm, ovate to lanceolate, scarlet; cal. to 22mm, scarlet; cor. scarlet, tube to 35mm. Summer–autumn. Braz.; in widespread cult. 'Alba': fls white. 'Atropurpurea': fls dark violet to purple. 'Atrosanguinea': fls dark red. 'Bicolor': fls white and red. 'Bruantii': small; fls red. Cleopatra series: fls dark violet-purple. 'Compacta': small; fls in many-fld, dense rac., white or red. Dress Parade: dwarf, compact; fls white, pink, rose and purple, in abundant spikes, early-flowering, seed race. 'Grandiflora': tall; fls large. 'Issanchon': small; fls white, striped pink to red. 'Nana': fls red, early flowering. 'Scarlet Pygmy': v. dwarf; fls intense scarlet, early-flowering, seed race. 'Semperflorens': continual flowering. 'Souchetii': small; fls white or red. 'St. John's Fire': dwarf, dense; fls bright red, abundant, long-lasting, early-flowering, seed race. 'Violacea': fls violet to purple. Z10.

S. strictiflora Hook. = *S. oppositiflora*.

S. ×superba Stapf. (*S. ×sylvestris* ×*S. villicaulis*.) Perenn. herb, 60–90cm, much-branched. Lvs lanceolate to oblong, crenate, rugose, somewhat pubesc. beneath, short-stalked to amplexicaull. Verticillasters 6-fld, numerous, distant, in long, slender term. rac.; cal. tinged purple, hairy, resinous, punctate; cor. 9–12mm, bright violet or purple. Summer–autumn. Gdn origin. Z5.

S. ×sylvestris L. (*S. pratensis* ×*S. nemorosa*.) Perenn. herb. Lvs to 7cm oblong-lanceolate, rounded to cordate at base, crenate, rugose, pubesc. beneath, lower lvs petiolate. Verticillasters 4–6-fld, slightly seperated; bracts green or violet-tinged, orbicular; cor. dark violet, white pubesc. C Asia, W Sib., Eur.; nat. in N Amer. 'Alba': cor. white. Cvs grouped here are of uncertain origin and may be *S. nemorosa*. 'Blauhügel': dwarf; fls clear blue, abundant. 'Blaukönigin' ('Blue Queen'): compact; fls violet. 'Kew Gold': lvs gold, sometimes spotted green. 'Lubeca': tall; fls deep violet, early-flowering. 'Lye End': lvs dark green; fls lilac-blue; sep. plume-like, brown. 'Mainacht' ('May Night'): low; fls blue to black. 'Negrito': fls dark blue. 'Ostfriesland' ('East Friesland'): fls deep purple flushed blue. 'Primevere': fls violet-blue. 'Rose Queen': lvs tinted grey; fls pale pink, red. 'Rubin': fls plum. 'Ruegen': habit compact; fls blue. 'Senior': fls violet. 'Tänzerin': tall; fls purple. 'Viola Klose': fls rich blue, early-flowering. 'Wesuwe': fls purple tinted blue, early-flowering. Z5.

S. sylvestris Boiss., non L. = *S. nemorosa*.

S. sylvestris var. *superba* hort. = *S. superba*.

S. taraxacifolia (Coss.) ex Hook. f. Perenn. herb to 45cm. Lvs to 8cm, in rosettes, lyrate to pinnate, terminal seg. to 3cm, ovate to oblong, toothed to notched and undulate, white-pubesc. beneath; petioles to 6cm. Verticillasters to 9, 5–12-fld, distant, in rac.; bracts bristle-tipped; cor. white to pink, flecked yellow to purple, tube to 2cm. Spring–summer. Moroc. Z9.

S. tatsiensis Franch. = *S. przewalskii*.

S. tenorii Spreng. = *S. pratensis* 'Tenorii'.

S. tetragona Moench = *S. hispanica*.

S. thibetica Lév. = *S. przewalskii*.

S. tiliifolia Vahl. Perenn. or ann. herb, to 1m erect, much-branched. Lvs to 7cm, ovate or rhomboid or suborbicular, apex acute, bse obtuse to truncate or cuneate, notched, rough and somewhat bullate, pubesc.; petioles to 6cm. Verticillasters 3–12-fld, to 2cm distant, in pan. or rac. to 20cm; cal. to 6mm, gland.; cor. white to blue or lilac, tube to 4mm. Summer. Mex. to Trop. S Amer. Z10.

S. tmolea Boiss. = *S. argentea*.

S. tomentosa Mill. Similar to *S. officinalis*, which has narrower, oblong-cuneate lvs. Lvs 2–11cm, narrowly oblong to ovate, rounded to cordate at base, entire to minutely crenate; petiole 2–5cm. Verticillasters 4–10-fld, distant or rather crowded above; bracts to 8mm, broadly ovate; cal. 12–16mm, violet, pilose; cor. 25–30mm, lilac to purple or white. Summer. E Eur. to W Asia. Z6.

S. tonduzii Briq. = *S. wagneriana*.

S. traxillensis Briq. = *S. rubescens*.

S. tricolor hort., non Lem. = *S. officinalis* 'Tricolor'.

S. triloba L. f. = *S. fruticosa*.

S. tubifera Cav. Perenn. to 1m, woody. Lvs to 10cm, broadly ovate, acuminate at apex, base crenate, grey-pubesc. beneath. Verticillasters 3–4-fld, in rac. to 15cm; cor. to 2.5cm, rosy-purple. Mex. Z9.

S. tubiformis Klotzsch ex Otto & Dietr. = *S. longistyla*.

S. uliginosa Benth. Perenn. herb to 2.5m erect, branched. Lvs to 9cm, lanceolate to oblong, apex acute, base attenuate to cuneate or subtruncate, subentire to notched, glab. or pubesc.; petioles to 2cm. Verticillasters 6–20-fld, in dense, branched, cylindric to spicate rac. to 12cm; bracts to 12mm; cor. blue, tube to 7mm. Summer–autumn. Braz., Urug., Arg. Z9.

S. variegata Waldst. & Kit. = *S. pratensis* 'Variegata'.

S. vaseyi (Porter) Parish. Shrub to 1.5m, erect, minutely pubesc. Lvs to 4cm, ovate to deltoid, apex subacute or obtuse, base cuneate or truncate, notched, rough, silver; petioles to 3cm. Verticillasters 5–10, distant, in simple spikes; bracts aristate; cor. white, tube to 14mm. Calif. Z8.

S. verbascifolia Bieb. Perenn. herb to 60cm, erect, unbranched, gland. and short-pubesc. Lvs to 6cm, ovate, apex obtuse, base cordate, undulate and toothed to erose, rugose, white-tomentose; petioles to 6cm. Verticillasters 2–6-fld, to 3cm distant, in simple or branched pan.; bracts concave, ovate, glandular-pubesc.; cor. to 25mm, white to yellow. Spring–summer. Cauc. Z6.

S. verbenaca L. VERVAIN; WILD CLARY. Perenn. herb to 70cm, erect to ascending, simple or branched, glandular-pubesc. Lvs to 10cm, ovate to oblong, base attenuate to obtuse or cordate, undulate and notched to erose, rugose and glandular-pubesc.; petioles to 8cm. Verticillasters to 10, 4–10-fld, in simple or branched spicate rac.; bracts to 6mm, ovate or orbicular; cor. to 16mm, lavender or lilac to purple. Summer–autumn. Eur. to W Asia; widely nat. Z6.

S. verticillata L. Perenn. herb to 90cm, erect to ascending, glandular-pubesc. Lvs to 13cm, simple or lyrate, ovate or elliptic to oblong, apex acute, base obtuse to truncate, basal lobes unequal, 1–2 pairs, ovate to suborbicular, subentire to notched, glandular-pubesc.; petioles to 8cm. Verticillasters 20–40-fld, distant, in branched rac. to 30cm; bracts to 7mm; cal. glandular-pubesc., violet; cor. violet to lilac or white, tube to 8mm. Summer. Eur. to W Asia; nat. in N Eur. and N Amer. 'Alba': fls white. ssp. *verticillata* 50–90cm, much-branched. Lvs broadly ovate, base clearly cordate, ssp. *amasiaca* (Franch. & Bornm.) Bornm. 15–50cm, little-branched. Lvs oblong-elliptic or oblong-ovate, base rounded or subcordate. Z6.

S. villosa Fern. Perenn. woody-based herb to 40cm, ascending, glandular-pubesc. Lvs to 3cm, deltoid, apex obtuse, base truncate, notched, glandular-pubesc.; petioles to 1cm. Verticillasters 2–6-fld, to 3cm distant, in rac.; bracts gland.; cor. tube to 7mm. Mex. Z9.

S. virgata Jacq. Perenn. herb to 1m erect, pubesc. Lvs to 30cm, ovate or lanceolate to oblong, base perfoliate or cordate, subentire to notched or erose, rugose and glandular-pubesc.; petioles to 15cm. Verticillasters 2–6-fld, in simple or branched pan. or rac.; bracts to 8mm, purple; cal. to 1cm, glandular-pubesc., purple or white, tube to 9mm. Summer. E Medit. to C Asia. 'Alba': fls white. Z7.

S. virgata hort., non Jacq. = *S.* ×*superba*.

S. viridis L. Ann. or bienn. herb to 45cm, erect, glandular-pubesc. Lvs to 5cm, ovate to oblong, apex obtuse, base obtuse or cordate to cuneate, somewhat notched, pubesc.; petioles to 5cm. Verticillasters 4–8-fld, in simple, spicate rac.; bracts to 1cm; cal. to 1cm, glandular-pubesc., green or purple; cor. to 15mm, white to lilac, violet, or purple. Summer. Medit. 'Alba': bracts white. 'Bluebeard': bracts pale violet-blue with darker veins. 'Oxford Blue': bracts broad and blue. 'Purpurea': bracts rose-red to purple. 'Rose Bouquet': bracts pink. 'Violacea': bracts violet with darker veins. 'Vulgaris': bracts violet.

S. viscosa Sessé & Moq. = *S. riparia*.

S. wagneriana Polak. Perenn. herb or subshrub 1–3m erect, st. often tinged red. Lvs to 13cm, ovate, apex narrowly acute, base obtuse, notched, glandular-punctate and glab.; petioles to 5cm. Verticillasters 5–7-fld, to 2cm distant, in rac.; bracts to 8mm; cal. to 15mm, glandular-pubesc.; cor. to 35mm, red. Costa Rica, Panama. Z10.

S. wardii Stibal. Perenn. herb to 75cm, st. branched, hairy, gland. Lvs 7–16cm, ovate to subhastate, apex acute, crenate, rugose. Infl. simple or slightly branched; cal. 12–15mm, suffused violet, gland. hairy; cor. 3.5–4cm, blue, lower lip white or pale violet. Tibet. Z8.

S. yunnanensis C.H. Wright. Perenn. tuberous herb to 30cm. Lvs to 7.5cm, entire to pinnate-pinnatifid, glab. to sparsely pubesc. and purple beneath, terminal seg. ovate to linear or oblong, toothed to notched, lat. seg. 2–3 pairs. Verticillasters 3–6-fld, in simple spikes; cor. to 25mm, blue or violet to purple, pubesc. China. Z8.

→*Audibertia*.

Salvinia Adans. Salviniaceae. 10 free-floating aquatic ferns. St. short, thread-like. Lvs dimorphic, in whorls of 3, 2 floating, entire and flat or folded, with papillate hairs, 1 filamentous, root-like, submerged. Sporangia in sporocarps below floating lvs.

Widespread in trop. and warm-temperate zones, esp. in trop. Amer. & Afr. Z10.

S. auriculata Aubl. Lvs 1–2cm×0.8–4.0cm, orbicular-cordate with deeply cordate base, folded. Lat. veins 20 or more on each side. C & S America.

S. auriculata auct. = *S. molesta*.

S. cucullata Roxb. ex Bory = *S. molesta*.

S. minima Bak. Differs from *S. auriculata* in many papillae onn upper lf surface, each tufted with free, not fused hairs. C & S America.

S. molesta Mitch. Lvs ovate to suborbicular, with numerous papillae above; trichomes at ends of papillae fused at apex. Sterile. OW Trop.

S. natans (L.) All. Lvs 10–14×6–9mm, broadly elliptic rounded or subcordate at base, flat, with 3–8 lat. veins each side. S Eur., Asia, N Afr., introd. in N Amer.

S. rotundifolia Willd. = *S. auriculata*.

S. rotundifolia hort. non Willd. = *S. minima*.

SALVINIACEAE T. Lestib. See *Salvinia*.

Samaipaticereus Cárdenas. Cactaceae. 1 tree-like cactus, 3–3.5m, trunk 10–15cm diam.; st. erect, unsegmented, dark green; ribs 4–6; spines few, subulate. Fls narrowly funnelform, 4.5–5cm; tep. c1cm, white. Boliv. Z10.

S. corroanus Cárdenas. Boliv. Z9.

Saman *Albizia saman*.

Samanea Merrill.

S. saman (Jacq.) Merrill = *Albizia saman*.

Sambucus L. ELDER; ELDERBERRY. Caprifoliaceae. *c*25 perenn. herbs, decid. shrubs or small trees. Br. often covered with lenticels. Lvs imparipinnate. Fls small, white to ivory, 3–5-merous, crowded in flat-topped term. umbel-like corymbs or pan. Fr. a berry-like drupe. Temp. and subtrop. N Hemis., E & NW Afr., S Amer., E Aus., Tasm.

S. caerulea Raf. BLUE ELDER; BLUE ELDERBERRY. Shrub or small tree to 8m. Lvs to 25.5cm, glab. to hispidulous beneath; lfts 5–9, to 15×5cm, blue-green, serrate. Infl. to 18cm diam.; fls yellow-white. Fr. black, pruinose, to 6mm diam. Summer. W N Amer. var. *neomexicana* (Wooton) Rehd. Lfts 3–5, narrow-lanceolate, grey-green. Fr. richly pruinose. Ariz., New Mex. var. *velutina* (Dur.) Schwein. Young shoots white-pubesc.; lfts larger. Calif. Z5.

S. californica hort. ex K. Koch = *S. caerulea* var. *velutina*.

S. callicarpa Greene. PACIFIC RED COAST ELDER. Shrub or small tree to 3m. Lfts 5–7, to 10×2cm, oblong-lanceolate, coarsely serrate, initially pubesc. beneath. Fls yellow-white, in long-branched pan. to 10cm diam. Fr. 5mm diam., scarlet. Spring. W US. Z6.

S. canadensis L. AMERICAN ELDER; SWEET ELDER. Shrub to 3.5m, often suckering. Lfts (5–)7(–11), serrate, lowermost often lobed, glab. or lanuginose beneath. Infl. to 20.5cm diam.; fls ivory. Fr. to 5mm diam., purple-black. Summer. E N Amer. 'Acutiloba': lfts finely dissected, deep green. 'Argenteomarginata': lvs edged silver. 'Aurea': shoots pale green; lvs golden yellow; fr. red, sweet-tasting. 'Chlorocarpa' ('Speer's Elderberry'): lvs pale yellow-green; fr. light green. 'Maxima': robust, tall-growing; umbels to 40cm diam., stained red. 'Rubra': fr. pale red. var. *submollis* Rehd. Lvs grey-pubesc. beneath. Z3.

S. chinensis Lindl. Perenn. herb to 2m. St. stout, erect. Lvs to 30cm; lfts 3–11, to 18×6cm, oblong-lanceolate to elliptic-ovate, serrate, glab. or minute-pubesc. on veins. Infl. to 30cm diam.; fls white. Fr. to 4×4mm, red. Jap., C, W & S China, N Thail. Z8.

S. ebulus L. DWARF ELDER; DANE'S ELDER; DANEWORT; WALLWORT. Perenn. herb to 2m. Lfts 5–9, to 15×6cm, lanceolate to elliptic, dentate, somewhat pubesc. Fls white, sometimes tinged pinmk, in umbels to 10cm diam. Fr. 6mm, black. Summer. Eur., N Afr., Asia Minor to Iran. 5.

S. glauca Nutt. ex Torr. & A. Gray = *S. caerulea*.

S. intermedia Carr. = *S. caerulea* var. *neomexicana*.

S. kamtschatica E. Wolf = *S. racemosa* ssp. *kamtschatica*.

S. melanocarpa A. Gray. Shrub to 4m. Lfts 5–7, 7–16cm, oblong-lanceolate, serrate, deep green, pubesc. beneath. Fls yellow-white, in congested, rounded cymes to 7cm diam. Fr. 6mm diam., black. Summer. W N Amer. 'Fuerstenbergii': fr. brick red.

S. microbotrys Rydb. Shrub to 2m. Lfts 5–7, to 10cm, oval-lanceolate, long-acuminate, serrate, glab. Fls off-white, in small domed pan. to 5cm diam. Fr. 4mm diam., scarlet. SW US. Z6.

S. neomexicana Wooton = *S. caerulea* var. *neomexicana*.

S. nigra L. BLACK ELDER; BOURTREE; COMMON ELDER; ELDER-BERRY; EUROPEAN ELDER. Shrub or small tree to 10m. Bark becoming corky. Lvs to 30.5cm; lfts 3–9, to 12×6cm, ovate-lanceolate to ovate-elliptic, serrate, sparsely pubesc. on veins beneath, dark green above. Fls cream, muskily scented, in flat-topped infl. to 20cm diam. Fr. to 8mm, shiny purple-black. Summer. Eur., N Afr., SW Asia. 'Alba': fr. pellucid chalky white. 'Albopunctata': lvs splashed white, eesp. at margins. 'Albovariegata': lvs coarsely speckled white. 'Argentea': lvs white, somewhat reverse variegated green. 'Asplenifolia': lvs fern-like. 'Aurea': lvs golden to lime green, petioles flushed pink. 'Aureomarginata': lvs edged gold to yellow-green. 'Bimble': to 3m; lvs spotted and splashed yellow; fls white; fr. black. 'Cae Rhos Lligwy': bark grey; fr. large, green, goose-berry tasting. 'Dwarf Form': to 30cm, shoots densely suckering; lvs trifoliolate, lfts broadly obovate. 'Fructo-Luteo': fr. creamy gold, sometimes tinted red; slow to mature. 'Guincho Purple': to 3m; lvs tinted purple; fls flushed red. 'Hessei': habit arching; lfts to 12cm, sessile, v. slender, untoothed, glossy green. 'Heterophylla': see 'Linearis'. 'Laciniata' (f. *laciniata* (L.) Zab.): lfts not filamentous but consistently and finely laciniate. 'Latisecta': lfts 4–5-lobed per side, oak-like. 'Linearis': lfts irregularly cut to midrib, blade often reduced to midrib. 'Luteovariegata': lvs initially dark golden-yellow, lightening to white-yellow. 'Marginata': lfts broadly edged gold at first, later margined pale yellow to cream. 'Nana': to 1m, slow-growing, habit laxly rounded. 'Pendula': br. procumbent, or pendulous if grafted as a standard. 'Plena': fls double. Porphyrifolia group (f. *porphyrifolia* E.C. Nels.): a group name for purple-lvd forms. 'Pulvurentula': lvs striped and splashed pure white, appearing wholly white at first. 'Purpurea': lvs metallic maroon-bronze flecked pale green; fl. buds flushed pink, anth. pink. 'Pygmy': habit v. compact, to 60cm. 'Pyramidalis': habit erect, broad-based; lvs crowded. 'Roseaplena': fls double, flushed pink. 'Roseiflora': fls single, blushing pink. 'Rotundifolia': slow-growing; lvs often trifoliolate, lfts broad, bright green; infl. sparsely fld. 'Viridis': infl. pale green throughout; fr. pale green turning white or translucent-striped. 'Witches Broom': dwarf, to 45cm, clump-forming; fls 0; semi-evergreen. Z5.

S. pubens Michx. AMERICAN RED ELDER; RED-BERRIED ELDER; STINKING ELDER. Shrub to 4m, sometimes a small tree. Lvs finely pubesc. when young; lfts 5–7, to 10cm, long-ovate to oblong-lanceolate, serrate. Infl. loose, longer than broad, br. ray-like, not bowed as in *S. racemosa*; fls yellow-white. Fr. 5mm diam., scarlet. Summer. N Amer. 'Dissecta': lfts deeply dis-sected. 'Leucocarpa': fr. white. 'Maxima': cymes large. 'Xanthocarpa': fr. tawny-yellow. Z5.

S. racemosa L. EUROPEAN RED ELDER; RED-BERRIED ELDER. Shrub to 3.5m. Lvs to 23cm; lfts 5, to 10×4.5cm, oval or ovate, acuminate, scabrous, serrate. Fls pale green to yellow-white in bluntly pyramidal pan. to 7.5cm, br. curved. Fr. to 4mm diam., scarlet. Spring. Eur., Asia Minor, Sib., W Asia. 'Aurea': lvs bright yellow. 'Goldenlocks': to 75cm, a seedling of 'Plumosa Aurea'; lvs golden-yellow, deeply cut, lasting well in bright sun. 'Laciniata': lvs green, lfts deeply slashed, in narrow seg. 'Moreheimii': close to 'Plumosa' but more delicate. 'Ornata': first flush of lvs resembling 'Plumosa', thereafter similar to 'Laciniata', new growth purple. 'Plumosa': new growth purple, lfts deeply incised with fine, slender teeth. 'Plumosa Aurea': form resembling 'Plumosa' but foliage a striking gold through-out, new growth often tinted purple-red. 'Sutherland Gold': a seedling of 'Plumosa Aurea'; its colour, though not so fine, lasts better in full sunlight. 'Tenuifolia': dwarf suckering shrub; lvs finely incised, lfts filiform, curling in frothy masses, new growth purple. f. *simplicifolia* Hylander. Lvs often simple, sometimes trifoliolate; lfts ovate. Sweden. ssp. *kamtschatica* (E. Wolf) Hult. Shrub or tree to 8m. Lfts larger, coarsely serrate, usually pubesc. Pan. minutely pilose. Fr. larger. Jap., N & C Korea, Kamchatka. Z4.

S. racemosa var. *melanocarpa* McMinn = *S. melanocarpa*.
S. racemosa var. *pubens* (Michx.) Koehne = *S. pubens*.
S. racemosa var. *sieboldiana* Miq. = *S. sieboldiana*.

S. sieboldiana Miq.) Gräbn. Shrub or small tree to 6m. Young shoots brown, glab. Lvs to 30cm; lfts 7–11, 7–20cm, oblong-lanceolate, finely tapering, serrate, light green, glab. Pan. to 7×5cm, ovate; fls yellow-white. Fr. 4mm diam., scarlet, rarely yellow or orange-yellow. Spring. Jap., China. Z6.

Samolus L. Primulaceae. 15 glab. perenn. herbs of wet places. Lvs alt., lower lvs larger, rosulate, entire. Infl. a many-fld terminal rac. or corymb; fls small, bracteolate, 5-merous; cor. subcampanulate, with short tube, limb rotate, lobes emarginate. Summer. Cosmop. Z6.

S. floribundus HBK = *S. parviflorus*.
S. parviflorus (Nees) Raf. St. to 40cm. Lvs to 8×3cm, obovate,

obtuse. Fls white in loosely branched rac. S US, C Amer., W In-dies, S Amer.
S. valerandii L. St. to 60cm. Lvs to 8×2cm, obovate to spathulate, obtuse. Fls white in branched or simple rac. W & SW Eur., Russia, Middle E, China.

Samphire Crithmum maritimum.
San Angelo Yucca Yucca reverchonii.

Sanchezia Ruiz & Pav. Acanthaceae. 20 perenn. herbs and soft-stemmed shrubs. Infl. a term. spike or pan.; bracts often con-spicuous; cal. lobes 5, almost free; cor. tube long, cylindric or slightly inflated above midpoint, lobes 5, rounded, patent; sta. 2, exserted. C & S Amer. Z10.

S. glaucophylla hort. = *S. speciosa*.
S. nobilis hort. non Hook. = *S. speciosa*.
S. speciosa Léonard. Everg., glab. shrub to 2.25m. St. glossy, erect, sparsely branched. Lvs to 30cm, ovate-elliptic to oblong-lanceolate, acuminate, glossy dark green with midrib and principal veins sunken and outlined white or yellow. Pan. term., axis tinted purple; bracts 2.5–3.25cm, bright red, each subtend-ing 6–10 fls; cor. to 5cm, yellow. Ecuad., Peru.
S. spectabilis hort. = *S. speciosa*.

Sandalwood Santalum.
Sand Bent Mibora.
Sandberry Arctostaphylos uva-ursi.
Sand Blackberry Rubus cuneifolius.
Sand Bottlebrush Beaufortia squarrosa.
Sandbox Tree Hura crepitans.
Sand Cherry Prunus pumila.
Sand Coprosma Coprosma acerosa.
Sand Corn Zigadenus paniculatus.
Sand Devil's Claw Proboscidea arenaria.
Sand Dropseed Sporobolus cryptandrus.
Sand-dune Penstemon Penstemon acuminatus.

Sandersonia Hook. Liliaceae (Colchicaceae). 1 tuberous-rooted perenn. herb. St. to 75cm, erect. Lvs to 10cm, cauline, often tendril-tipped. Fls solitary, axill.; pedicels 2–3cm, decurved; perianth 2–2.5cm, rounded-campanulate to urceolate, orange, lobes 6, fused except at outward-curving tips. Summer. S Afr. Z9.
S. aurantiaca Hook. CHINESE LANTERN LILY; CHRISTMAS BELLS.

Sand Grape Vitis rupestris.
Sand Hickory Carya pallida.
Sandhill Sage Artemisia pycnocephala.
Sand Holly Ilex ambigua.
San Diego Ceanothus Ceanothus cyaneus.
Sand Leek Allium scorodoprasum.
Sand Lily Leucocrinum.
Sand Myrtle Leiophyllum buxifolium.
Sand Paper Petrea volubilis.
Sandpaper Oak Quercus pungens.
Sandpaper Vine Petrea.
Sand Pear Pyrus pyrifolia.
Sand Phlox Phlox bifida.
Sand Pine Pinus clausa.
Sand Plum Prunus angustifolia var. watsonii.
Sand Sage Artemisia filifolia.
Sand Sedge Carex arenaria.
Sand Spurrey Spergularia.
Sand Strawberry Fragaria chiloensis.
Sand Verbena Abronia.
Sandwort Arenaria; Minuartia; Moehringia.
Sang Panax quinquefolius.
San Gabriel Penstemon Penstemon labrosus.

Sanguinaria L. BLOODROOT; RED PUCCOON. Papaveraceae. 1 perenn. rhizomatous herb to 60cm. Lvs radical, emerging from a basal sheath; blade cordate to reniform, palmately lobed, to 30cm across, scalloped, glaucous blue-grey; petiole to 15cm. Fl. solitary, scapose, to 7.5cm diam.; pet. 8–12, oblong or obovate, white sometimes tinted rose; sta. many. Spring. E N Amer. Z3.
S. canadensis L. 'Flore Pleno' ('Multiplex'): to 20cm; fls double.

Sanguisorba L. Rosaceae. 18 rhizomatous perenn. herbs or small shrubs. Lvs imparipinnate. Fls small, sessile, ind ense term. spikes; cal. tube ovoid, lobes 4, petaloid, small; cor. 0; sta. 4 to 15. Temp. N hemis.
S. canadensis L. CANADIAN BURNET. To 2m. Lfts 7–17, to 10cm, lanceolate-oblong to ovate, obtuse, truncate or cordate at base, serrate-dentate. Fls white, in cylindric spikes to 20cm; cal. teeth tinged red. Summer. N Amer. Z4.

S. dodecandra Moretti.　To 1m. Lfts 9–21, linear-lanceolate to ovate, light green beneath, sharply serrate. Fls in cylindric, white to green-yellow spikes to 7cm. Summer. N It. Z7.

S. gaillardotii (Boiss.) Hayek = *S. minor*.

S. garganica (Ten.) Bertol. = *S. minor*.

S. hakusanensis Mak.　To 80cm. Lvs to 6×3.5cm; lfts 9–13, oblong or ovate-oblong, obtuse, cordate to obtuse at base, serrate, glaucescent beneath. Fls deep rose-purple, in pendulous, elongate-cylindric spikes to 10cm. Summer. Jap., Korea. Z7.

S. menendezii (Svent.) Nordb. Lvs glaucous; lfts crenate; stipules large, Lf-like. Fls in slender, green elongate spikes. Canary Is.

S. minor Scop. BURNET; GARDEN BURNET.　To 90cm. Lfts 2–12, to 2.2cm, orbicular to elliptic, crenate to incised-serrate. Fls in rounded heads to 2.5cm, green-white. Summer. S, W & C Eur., N Afr., Canary Is., SW & C Asia. Z5.

S. obtusa Maxim. To 50cm. Lvs usually brown-pubesc. on midrib beneath; lfts 13–17, to 5×3cm, ovate or elliptic, obtuse, cordate at base. Fls pale rose, in nodding spikes to 7cm. Summer–autumn. Jap. 'Alba': to 60cm; lvs tinted grey-blue; fls curly, white. Z5.

S. officinalis L. GREAT BURNET; BURNET BLOODWORT.　To 1m. St. erect, often red. LEaflets 7–25, to 5×3.5cm, oblong-ovate or elliptic, obtuse, cordate or truncate at base, glossy above, glaucescent beneath, serrate; petioles to 3cm, red. Fls dark red to black-purple, in oval or short-cylindric heads to 3cm; peduncles long. Summer–autumn. W Eur., Mong., Jap., China, N Amer. Z4.

S. sitchensis Mey. = *S. canadensis*.

S. tenuifolia Fisch. ex Link.　To 120cm. Lfts 13–21, to 7.5cm, narrow-linear, deeply serrate. Fls white to purple, in cylindric spikes to 8cm. Summer. Jap., China. 'Alba': fls white. 'Rosea': fls pink. Z4.

S. vallistellinae Masson = *S. dodecandra*.

→*Poterium*.

Sanicle *Sanicula*; *S. europaea*.

Sanicula L. SNAKEROOT; SANICLE. Umbelliferae.　37 glab. perennials or biennials. Lvs mostly radical, palmately divided to decompound; petioles sheathing flowering st. Umbels arranged in cymes, appearing as compound umbels; involucre leafy; bracteoles entire to lobed; cal. teeth conspicuous; pet. emarginate. Cosmop. except Australasia. Z6.

S. arctopoides Hook. & Arn. FOOTSTEPS-OF-SPRING.　Prostrate, clumps 10–30cm diam.; st. branched near base. Basal lvs 2–6.5cm, forming low rosettes, palmately 3-parted, yellow-green, dentate to laciniate. Umbels with 1–4 rays, 3–12cm; bracteoles 8–17; fls yellow. Early summer. NW US.

S. bipinnatifida Douglas. PURPLE SANICLE.　Erect to 60cm, branched near base, tinged purple. Basal lvs in rosettes, suborbicular to ovate-oblong, entire to 5-lobed, toothed, mature lvs 2-pinnatifid, long-stalked. Umbels 3–5-rayed; bracteoles 6–8; fls yellow, red or purple. Early summer. BC to Calif.

S. europaea L. SANICLE.　Perenn. to 60cm. Basal lvs 2–6cm, palmately 3–5-lobed, seg. cuneate, shallowly 3-lobed, serrate, petiole longer than blade. Umbels simple, arranged in cymes; bracteoles 6–8, fls white to pale pink. Summer. Eur., Asia.

Saniella Hilliard & B.L. Burtt. Hypoxidaceae.　1 dwarf fleshy-rooted perenn. herb. Lvs 4–8×0.2–0.4cm fleshy, glab. Fls solitary, axill.; perianth tube 2–4mm, seg. 25×8–14mm, elliptic. S Afr. (Cape Prov.), Les. Z9.

S. verna Hilliard & B.L. Burtt.

San José Hesper Palm *Brahea brandegeei*.

San Luis Potosi *Parmentiera aculeata*.

San Luis Purple Sage *Salvia leucophylla*.

Sansevieria Thunb. BOWSTRING HEMP; SNAKE PLANT; MOTHER-IN-LAW'S TONGUE. Agavaceae.　*c*70 everg., xerophytic perennials, tufted or shrubby, rhizomatous or stoloniferous. Lvs tough, fibrous, succulent, often pungent. Rac. simple or compound, rarely seen; fls fragrant, white to green; perianth tube slender, lobes 6. Fr. a berry, red, yellow or orange. Trop. and subtrop. Afr., Madag., India, E Indies. Z10.

S. abyssinica N.E. Br. Lvs 1–2 per growth, to 60×7.5cm, linear-lanceolate, stiffly erect. C-shaped in section, rough below, mottled dark green when young, with hard red-green margins. Ethiop.

S. aethiopica Thunb.　Lvs 1.5–4×1–1.5cm, 13–30 in a rosette, erect, linear, channelled, with a withered tip, dark green banded paler green. S & Trop. Afr.

S. angustiflora Lindb. Differs from *S. hyacinthoides* in lvs to 12 per rosette, longer and narrower. S Afr.

S. arborescens Cornu ex Gérôme & Labroy. St. erect, to 120cm. Lvs 20–45×2–4.5cm spirally arranged, flat or semiterete, linear-lanceolate, bright green, somewhat glaucous. Trop. E Afr.

S. aubrytiana Carr. Lvs to 1.5m×17cm, thick, sword-shaped, erect with hard white edges, mottled with white and pale green spots. Gabon.

S. bacularis Pfennig = *S. canaliculata*.

S. bagamoyensis N.E. Br. Differs from *S. arborescens* in thinner st. and narrower lvs. Trop. E Afr.

S. bracteata Bak. = *S. aubrytiana*.

S. caespitosa Dinter. Differs from *S. hyacinthoides* in lvs shorter and more coriaceous.

S. canaliculata Carr. Differs from *S. cylindrica* in lvs fewer, shorter and more flexible.

S. caulescens N.E. Br. St. to 60cm+. Lvs arranged spirally, 45–80cm×20–33mm, terete, brittle, slightly recurved, grooved above, banded, when young. E Afr.

S. conspicua N.E. Br. Differs from *S. abyssinica* in smoother, arching lvs in more marked rosettes.

S. cornui Gérôme & Labroy = *S. senegambica*.

S. cylindrica Bojer. Lvs 3–4 to a shoot, in 2 ranks, 75cm+, 25mm thick, semi-terete, straight or slightly arching, banded when young. Angola.

S. dawei Stapf. Lvs 2–3 per shoot, 30–150×15cm, erect, rigid, thick, elongate-lanceolate, C-shaped in section, glaucous and rough, dark blue-green with paler mottling. Uganda.

S. deserti N.E. Br. Lvs to 8 in fans, to 105×3cm, semi-terete, coarse, dull green, pungent, with to 12 longitudinal grooves. Bots., Transvaal, Zimb.

S. dooneri N.E. Br. = *S. parva*.

S. ehrenbergii Schweinf. ex Bak. St. to 25cm. Lvs in fan, spiralled in youth, to 1.5m×4cm, thick with flattened sides, channelled above, dark grey green, margins papery white, pungent. Libya, Eritrea, Saudi Arabia.

S. fasciata Cornu ex Gérôme & Labroy. Related to *S. aubrytiana* but lf margin narrower and lvs less evidently in rosettes.

S. fischeri (Bak.) Marais. Lvs solitary or few, to 45cm or taller, straight, terete, banded, arising like tusks from soil. E Afr.

S. fragrans Jacq. = *Dracaena fragrans*.

S. gracilis N.E. Br. St. short, to 7.5cm. Lvs 25–80cm, to 9mm diam., to 12 per terminal whorl, slender, terete, flexible, pungent, dark green.

S. grandicuspis Haw. Lvs 17–50×3.5cm, to 15 in open rosettes, recurved, flattened, dull green banded pale green, apex cusped to 5cm.

S. grandis Hook. f. SOMALI HEMP.　Lvs few, rosulate, 30–60×8–15cm, elliptic to oblong to broad-lanceolate, flat, acute with soft short tip, leathery, dull green with paler flecks at first. Trop. Afr., Somalia.

S. guineensis (L.) Willd. = *S. hyacinthoides*.

S. humbertiana Guill. = *S. volkensii*.

S. hyacinthoides (L.) Druce. AFRICAN BOWSTRING HEMP.　Lvs 2–4, 15–45×2.5–8cm, semi-erect, flattened, lanceolate to oblanceolate, dark green banded pale green, usually with a withered white tip. S Afr. 'Variegata': lvs green banded grey-green, broadly edged yellow.

S. indica Herter = *S. zeylanica*.

S. intermedia N.E. Br. = *S. volkensii*.

S. kirkii Bak. Lvs 1–3, crowded, 1m+, 7.5cm wide, linear-lanceolate to broadly ligulate, nearly flat, channelled at base, grey-green with paler mottling, with an 8–12mm tip, margins wavy, red-brown. Trop. E Afr. var. *pulchra* N.E. Br. Lvs dappled with off-white elongated spots, edged white. Zanzibar.

S. latifolia Bojer = *S. hyacinthoides*.

S. liberica Gérôme & Labroy. Lvs 1–6 per rhiz., 45–100×5–12cm, flat, erect to spreading, strap-shaped or lanceolate tapering to a channelled base, usually ± banded, dark and silvery green, tip subulate, margins wavy, withered. Trop. W Afr.

S. longiflora Sims. Similar to *S. hyacinthoides* but fls to 10cm, not 3.5cm. Trop. W Afr.

S. metallica Gérôme & Labroy Differs from *S. hyacinthoides* in lvs thicker, strap-shaped, to 1.5m×5cm. Trop. E Afr.

S. nilotica Bak. Lvs 2–5 together, 75–120×5cm, strap-shaped, linear, channelled below, dark green with some cross-banding. Trop. Afr.

S. parva N.E. Br. Lvs to 45cm×8–14mm, flat, narrow-lanceolate, 6–14 in a rosette, arching, grooved, banded, apex long, sub-ulate. Trop. E Afr.

S. pearsonii N.E. Br. Lvs 3–5 per fan, 60–90cm, erect, terete, linear, tapered to a short white tip with several furrows, channelled above, dark glaucous green, faintly mottled. Trop. Afr.

S. phillipsiae N.E. Br. Differs from *S. gracilis* in lvs thicker (12–18mm), less tapered, duller green. Somalia.

S. pinguicula Bally. Lvs 5–7, to 30cm (usually far less), in a rosette, spreading, highly succulent, semi-cylindrical at the base, concave above, tapering to a spiny tip, dark green, glaucous. Kenya.

S. ×*powellii* N.E. Br. Differs from *S. caulescens* in lvs broad, crescent-shaped in section. Probably a natural hybrid between *S. arborescens* and *S. robusta*.

S. *raffillii* N.E. Br. Lvs 2–4 to a shoot, 60–100×7–12cm, 6–8mm thick, rigidly upright, strap-shaped, with pale spots or bars at least when young, sometimes glaucous. var.(var. *glauca* N.E. Br.) Trop. E Afr.

S. *rhodesiana* N.E. Br. = *S. pearsonii*.

S. *robusta* N.E. Br. = *S. ehrenbergii*.

S. *roxburghiana* Schult. Differs from *S. zeylanica* in its shorter, paler lvs with more numerous dark bonds beneath. India.

S. *scabrifolia* Dinter. Rosettes clustered, bearing arching, ± linear lvs, 10–35cm×15–25mm, semi-terete, grooved, with broad peeling margins and withered tips, rough, dark green, cross-banded in youth. Nam.

S. *schweinfurthii* Täckh. & Drar. Similar to *S. cylindrica* but with shorter, soft-tipped, uniformly dark green lvs, to 6 per shoot.

S. *senegambica* Bak. Lvs 3–4, 30–60×3–6cm, arching, oblanceolate, acute, broad, flat blade tapering to sulcate petiole, dark green, banded. Trop. W Afr.

S. *singularis* N.E. Br. = *S. fischeri*.

S. *spicata* Haw. = *S. hyacinthoides*.

S. *stuckyi* Godef.-Leb. Mature lvs to 2.7m, upright, cylindrical, single or paired along rhiz., 5cm thick; juvenile lvs 4–6 per rosette, strap-shaped, in section crescent-shaped to semi-terete, banded. Trop. E Afr.

S. *subspicata* Bak. Lvs 4–8 per rosette, 23–60×2.5–5cm, erect or recurving, oblanceolate, relatively thin, flat, narrowed into a slender petiole below, pale to dark green. S Afr.

S. *suffruticosa* N.E. Br. St. prostrate, branching to 30cm. Lvs 7–18 per rosette, to 60×2cm, cylindrical, deep green, stiff, shallow-grooved, mucronate, obscurely banded. Trop. E Afr.

S. *sulcata* Bojer = *S. canaliculata*.

S. *thyrsiflora* Thunb. = *S. hyacinthoides*.

S. *trifasciata* hort. ex Prain. MOTHER-IN-LAW'S TONGUE; SNAKE PLANT. Lvs to 75+ ×7cm, erect, stiff, linear-lanceolate, in clusters of 1–2 or more per shoot, sometimes forming rosettes, flat, with a green awl-shaped tip, tapering below into channelled petiole, ± glaucous, banded pale and dark green. Nigeria. 'Bantel's Sensation': lvs variable, slender, variously mottled in white and green. 'Compacta': dwarf mutant of 'Laurentii'. 'Craigii': as 'Laurentii', but lf margins broader and paler, and some narrow pale vertical strips also present. 'Goldiana': as 'Laurentii' but lf margins creamy white. 'Hahnii': dwarf sport with thinner, broader lvs in open rosettes, itself the basis of further colour variants of which the two finest are 'Golden Hahnii' (lvs banded grey, margins banded cream) and 'Silver Hahnii' (lvs pale green tinted silver). 'Hoop's Pride': compact; lvs short, fleshy, deep green flecked grey. 'Laurentii': lf margins bright yellow. 'Laurentii Compacta': to 40cm; lvs stiff, abundant, dark dull green edged gold. 'Silbersee': tall; lvs strap-like, silver with faint green banded lines.

S. *volkensii* Gürke. Lvs 45–120×2cm, 2–7, spirally clustered, stiffly erect, cylindrical with a V-shaped channel, slightly curved, furrowed, spine-tipped, dull green, sometimes obscurely banded. Trop. E Afr.

S. *zeylanica* (L.) Willd. CEYLON BOWSTRING HEMP. Lvs 45–75cm×25mm, in rosettes of 5–11, thick, strap-shaped, channelled, banded light and dark green, recurved, keeled beneath. Sri Lanka.

Santa Barbara Ceanothus *Ceanothus impressus*.
Santa Barbara Daisy *Erigeron karvinskianus*.
Santa Cruz Cypress *Cupressus abramsiana*.
Santa Cruz Water Lily *Victoria cruziana*.
Santa Fé Phlox *Phlox nana*.

SANTALACEAE R. Br. 36/500. *Buckleya, Comandra, Leptomeria, Osyris, Pyrularia, Santalum*.

Santa Lucia Fir *Abies bracteata*.

Santalum L. SANDALWOOD. Santalaceae. 9 everg., semi-parasitic trees and shrubs. Lvs thick. Fls 4–5-merous, paniculate, small. Fr. a drupe. SE Asia, Australasia, Pacific.

S. *album* L. INDIAN SANDALWOOD; WHITE SANDALWOOD. Small tree with highly fragrant wood. Lvs 4–8cm, ovate to broadly lanceolate, undulate, glaucous beneath. Fr. to 1cm, dark red to black. Habitat unknown, possibly Malaysia or Indon.; cult. throughout Trop. Asia.

S. *obtusifolium* R. Br. Shrub to 2m. Lvs 5–8cm, narrow-oblong to lanceolate, not undulate, glaucous. Fr. to 8mm, black. Aus. (NSW).

Santa Maria *Calophyllum brasiliense*.

Santolina L. Compositae. 18 aromatic, small, everg. shrubs. Lvs alt., entire to finely dentate or pinnatisect. Cap. discoid, small to medium, long-pedunculate; flts tubular, yellow to white. Medit. Z7.

S. *alpina* L. = *Anthemis cretica*.

S. *canescens* Lagasca = *S. rosmarinifolia* ssp. *canescens*.

S. *chamaecyparissus* L. LAVENDER COTTON. 10–50cm, erect or ascending, densely white-tomentose at first. LVs 2.5–4×0.3cm, crowded, densely pectinate-dentate to pinnatisect, seg. in 2–4 pairs, to 2mm, grey- to white-tomentose. Cap. 1.5–2cm diam., hemispheric; flts deep yellow. Summer. W & C Medit. 'Lambrook Silver': lvs silver. 'Lemon Queen': dwarf, mound-forming to 60×60cm; lvs grey. 'Little Ness': small, tight and compact. 'Plumosus': lvs lacy, tinted silver. 'Pretty Carol': compact, to 40cm; lvs soft grey. 'Weston': dwarf, to 15cm; lvs bright silver.

S. *chamaecyparissus* var. *etrusca* Lacaita = *S. pinnata* ssp. *etrusca*.

S. *elegans* Boiss. ex DC. 10–20cm, grey-tomentose, erect. Lvs linear to oblong-spathulate, incised-crenate to pinnatisect, plicate, shortly petiolate, upper lvs entire, flat, sessile. Cap. to 1cm diam., villous, subglobose; flts yellow. Summer. S Spain.

S. *ericoides* Poir. non hort. = *S. chamaecyparissus*.

S. *ericoides* hort. non Poir. = *S. pinnata*.

S. *incana* Lam. = *S. chamaecyparissus*.

S. *leucantha* Bertol. = *S. pinnata* ssp. *pinnata*.

S. *neapolitana* Jordan & Fourr. = *S. pinnata* ssp. *neapolitana*.

S. *pectinata* Lagasca = *S. rosmarinifolia* ssp. *canescens*.

S. *pinnata* Viv. 45–80cm, subglabrous. Lvs 2.5–4cm, pinnate, seg. in 2–4 pairs, 3–5mm, green. Cap. to 15mm diam.; flts off-white. Summer. It. 'Edward Bowles': to 35cm; lvs grey-green; fls pale primrose yellow. 'Sulphurea': lvs silver; fls pale yellow. ssp. *etrusca* (Lacaita) Guinea. Like ssp. *neapolitana* but to 60cm, more dense; lvs to 3cm, green, glab.; flts cream-yellow. Summer. It., Sicily. ssp. *neapolitana* (Jordan & Fourr.) Guinea. St. 60–75cm, slender, erect, closely packed, white-tomentose. Lvs to 5×0.6cm, pinnate or with lfts in 4 rows, seg. to 6×1mm, cylindric, white-tomentose on vegetative shoots, green and less downy on fertile shoots. Cap. to 2cm diam.; flts bright yellow. Summer. S It.

S. *rosmarinifolia* L. 35–60cm, erect or ascending, glab. to sparsely tomentose. Lvs to 5×0.3cm, narrowly linear, shortly and remotely tuberculate-denticulate to pectinate-pinnatifid at first, with closely adpressed teeth later, uppermost lvs entire. Cap. 2cm diam., hemispherical; flts bright yellow. Summer. Iberian Penins. to S Fr. 'Primrose Gem': to 30cm; lvs thread-like; fls pale lemon. ssp. *canescens* (Lagasca) Nyman. Densely white tomentose throughout. Lvs pinnate, lobes more crowded, linear, spreading. Summer. SE Spain.

S. *rosmarinifolia* hort. non L. = *S. pinnata*.

S. *tomentosa* Pers. = *S. pinnata* ssp. *neapolitana*.

S. *virens* Mill. non Willd. = *S. rosmarinifolia*.

S. *virides* Willd. non Mill. = *S. rosmarinifolia*.

Sanvitalia Lam. Compositae. *c*7 ann. to perenn. herbs. Cap. radiate, receptacle hemispheric to narrowly conic, scaly; ray flts white or yellow; disc flts purple or white with a green tinge. SW US, Mex.

S. *procumbens* Lam. ± procumbent, branched, sparsely hairy ann., to 20cm. Lvs to 6cm, lanceolate-ovate, entire, strigose. Cap. to 2cm diam.; ray flts bright yellow to orange; disc flts dark purple. Summer. Mex. to Guat. 'Gold Braid': dwarf to 15cm, spreading to 40cm; fls double, gold, centres brown. 'Golden Carpet': dwarf, to 10cm; lvs dark green; fls small, single, orange washed gold, centres black. 'Mandarin Orange': dwarf, in 10cm; fls vivid orange, centres black. 'Yellow Carpet': dwarf to 10cm; lvs v. dark green; fls small, single, lemon-yellow, centres black.

SAPINDACEAE Juss. 144/1325. *Alectryon, Blighia, Cardiospermum, Dimocarpus, Dodonaea, Harpullia, Koelreuteria, Lepisanthes, Litchi, Melicoccus, Sapindus, Schleichera, Serjania, Trigonachras, Ungnadia, Xanthoceras*.

Sapindus L. SOAPBERRY. Sapindaceae. 13 decid. or everg. shrubs and trees. Lvs pinnate, or simple. Infl. axill. or term. rac. or pan.; fls small; pet. obovate, 4 or 5, with 1–2 scales over claw; sta. 8–10. Fr. a subglobose, fleshy, leathery drupe. New and OW tropics and subtrop.

S. *abruptus* Lour. = *S. mukorossi*.

S. *acuminatus* S. Wats. & Coult. = *S. drumondii*.

S. *attenuatus* Wallich ex Hiern = *Lepisanthes senegalensis*.

S. *detergens* Roxb. = *S. mukorossi*.

S. *drumondii* Hook. & Arn. WILD CHINA TREE. Decid. tree to 16m. Lvs to 20cm, pinnae 8–18, obliquely lanceolate, 4–7cm, glab. above, pubesc. beneath. Pan. to 25cm, downy; fls yellow-white. Fr. to 1.5cm thick, yellow, ripening black. Summer. SW US. Z8.

S. edulis (Roxb.) Bl. = *Lepisanthes rubiginosa.*

S. emarginatus Vahl. = *S. trifoliatus.*

S. indicus Poir. = *S. saponaria.*

S. marginatus Torr. & Gray = *S. drumondii.*

S. mukorossi Gaertn. CHINESE SOAPBERRY. Everg. tree. Lvs to 40cm, pinnae 8–13, to 15cm, oval-oblong to oblong-lanceolate, glab. beneath. Pan. to 25cm; fls white. Fr. 2cm-diam., yellow or orange-brown. E Asia, Himal. Z9.

S. rubiginosa Roxb. = *Lepisanthes rubiginosa.*

S. saponaria L. SOAPBERRY; FALSE DOGWOOD; JABONCILLO. Everg. tree to 10m. Lvs to 30cm, pinnae usually 7–9, elliptic to oblong-lanceolate, to 10cm. Pan. axis winged; fls white. Fr. orange-brown, 2cm diam. Winter. Trop. Amer. Z10.

S. saponaria Torr. non L. = *S. drumondii.*

S. saponaria Lour. non L. = *S. mukorossi.*

S. trifoliatus L. Everg. tree. Pinnae (3–)4–6, 4–20×2–10cm, oval-oblong, emarginate. Fls white. Fr. fleshy, 2–3-lobed, to 2cm diam. OW Trop. Z10.

Sapium P. Browne. TALLOW TREE. Euphorbiaceae. 100 trees and shrubs, sap milky and poisonous. Lvs entire; petiole with 2 glands at apex. Fls small in term. or lat. spikes. Fr. a fleshy capsule. Trop. and warm temp. regions N to Patagonia. Z9.

S. japonicum (Sieb. & Zucc.) Pax & Hoffm. Small glab. tree, br. grey. Lvs 7–12×5–10cm, broad-ovate, blue-green beneath, turning carmine in autumn. Infl. 5–10cm, catkin-like, yellow-green. Capsules flat, globose, yellow with brown spots, pendulous. China, Korea, Jap.

S. sebiferum (L.) Roxb. CHINESE OR VEGETABLE TALLOW-TREE. Tree to 12m or more, resembling a poplar. Lvs to 7×3–7cm, rhombic-ovate, acuminate, yellow-red in autumn; petioles long. Infl. 5–10cm, yellow-green. Capsules 3-lobed, black, with a thick layer of white wax. China, Jap.

Sapodilla *Manilkara zapota.*

Saponaria L. SOAPWORT. Caryophyllaceae. *c*20 perenn. herbs, sometimes woody-based, or rarely annuals differing from *Lychnis* and *Silene*, in styles 2(–3), not 3 or 5. Widespread in Eur. and SW Asia; most sp. in the mts of S Eur.

S. bellidifolia Sm.. Loosely tufted, ± perenn. to 50cm, with woody stock. Basal lvs spathulate. Infl ± capitate; pet. *c*5mm, spathulate, notched, pale yellow; stam. long-projecting, fil. yellow. Early summer. Eur. (mts), from Pyren. to Balk. Z7.

S. caespitosa DC. Densely tufted, slightly hairy perenn. to 15cm, with woody stock. Basal lvs linear. Infl. of few, ± fls; pet. 4–7mm, obovate, entire, pink-purple; coronal scales conspicuous. Late summer. C Pyren. Hybrids with *S. ocymoides* (*S.* × *boissieri*) have been involved in the breeding of *S.* × *olivana* Wocke; see *S. pumilio.* Z7.

S. calabrica Guss. Ann. to 30cm, glandular-hairy above. Basal lvs ± spathulate. Infl. widely branching; pet. pale purple, sometimes white or red. Summer. Medit., from S It. eastwards.

S. haussknechtii Simmler see *S. sicula.*

S. lutea L. Tufted, hairy perenn. to 10cm. Basal lvs linear-lanceolate. Infl. capitate; pet. 4cm, yellow; sta. long-projecting, fil. violet. Early summer. SW & C Alps, confined to limestone. Z6.

S. ocymoides L. Much-branched, mat-forming, hairy perenn. to 15cm. Lvs ovate-lanceolate. Infl. loose, spreading, with numerous fls in small clusters offering coverings; pet. 3–5mm, red, pink or white. Summer. Mts of S Eur., Spain to Balk. Hybrids with *S. caespitosa* (*S.* × *boissieri*) have been involved in the breeding of *S.* × *olivana* Wocke; see *S. pumilio*. 'Alba': fls white. 'Bressingham' (*S. ocymoides* × *S. olivana*): compact, to 3cm high; lvs narrow, green; fls bright pink. 'Carnea': fls flesh pink. 'Rosea': fls rose. 'Rubra': fls rich red. 'Rubra Compacta': habit neater; fls deep red. 'Splendens': fls large, deep pink. 'Versicolor': fls rose, opening white. Z4.

S. officinalis L. SOAPWORT. Robust, ± glab. perenn. to 60cm. Lvs ovate, with 3 prominent veins. Infl. a condensed dichasian, of several fls; pet. *c*1cm, narrowly ovate, ± entire, pink, red or white. Late summer–autumn. Widespread in Eur. Double-fld cvs are often grown, and a variegated plant is also available. 'Alba Plena': fls double, white, pink in bud, abundant. 'Dazzler' ('Taff's Dazzler', 'Variegata'): lvs splashed gold to cream; fls pink. 'Rosea Plena': tall; fls double, soft pink. 'Rubra Plena': fls double, red fading to pink. Z4.

S. pulvinaris Boiss. = *S. pumilio.*

S. pumila (St.-Lager) Janch. = *S. pumilio.*

S. pumilio (L.) Densely tufted, glab. perenn. with woody stock and crowded, linear, fleshy lvs. Fls solitary or paired on v. short stalks, around tussock; pet. 7–10mm, ovate, entire or notched,

pink-purple (rarely white), with conspicuous coronal scales. Summer. E Alps, SE Carpath. The hybrid *S.* × *olivana* wocke, with *S. pumilio, S. caespitosa* and *S. ocymoides* in its parentage, is easier to grow; it has the attractive cushion habit of *S. pumilio*, and large pale pink fls. Z6.

S. sicula Raf. Tufted, variably hairy perenn. to 50cm, with woody stock and narrowly obovate basal lvs. Infl. usually of several large fls; pet. limb to 8mm, deeply bifid, red. Summer. Balk. Penins. (mts). Dwarf variants (*S. haussknechtii*) are usually cultivated. Hybrids of dwarf variants with *S. cypria* Boiss., *S.* × *lambergii* hort., are more frequently grown, esp. 'Max Frei'; fls pale pink, early-flowering. Z7.

S. vaccaria L. = *Vaccaria hispanica.*

→*Silene.*

SAPOTACEAE Juss. 107/1000. *Bumelia, Chrysophyllum, Manilkara, Mastichodendron, Mimusops, Planchonella, Pouteria, Synsepalum.*

Sapote *Pouteria sapota.*

Sapote Borracho *Pouteria campechiana.*

Sapphire Berry *Symplocos paniculata.*

Sapphire Flower *Browallia speciosa.*

Sapree Wood *Widdringtonia nodiflora.*

Sapucaia Nut *Lecythis zabucaya.*

Saraca L. Leguminosae. 8 shrubs or trees, to 25m. Bark lenticellate. Lvs pinnate; lfts ± leathery. Fls in dense, subglobose corymbs, sometimes cauliflorous; bracteoles yellow to red; cal. tubular, lobes 4–6, petaloid yellow to red and purple in throat; pet. 0; sta. (3–)4–8(–10), fil. exserted, yellow to red, anth. purple-grey. India to China and Malesia. Z10.

S. arborescens Burm. = *S. indica.*

S. indica L. Lvs 10–50cm, sessile; lfts 5–30cm, elliptic, ovate or lanceolate. Infl. 3–15(–20)cm; cal. tube 7–16mm, lobes 5–12mm, rounded. Thail. to Java and Sumatra.

Sarcandra Gardn. Chloranthaceae. 3 trop. shrubs. E Asia. Z10.

S. glabra (Thunb.) Nak. Small everg. Lvs oblong. Fr. bright orange in spikes.

→*Chloranthus.*

Sarcanthus Lindl.

S. pallidus Lindl. = *Cleisostoma racemiferum.*

Sarcobatus Nees. GREASEWOOD. Chenopodiaceae. 1 spreading, spiny shrub, to 3m. Br. arching, thick and grey when mature, yellow-white, glab. or with short white hairs when young. Lvs linear, fleshy, 0.5–3cm. Fls inconspicuous. Fr. leathery, winged. W N Amer. Z5.

S. maximilianii Nees = *S. vermiculatus.*

S. vermiculatus (Hook.) Torr.

Sarcocapnos DC. Fumariaceae. 4 dwarf, tufted, perenn. herbs. St. stout with lax br. Lvs 3-ternate or simple, somewhat succulent. Rac. term.; sep. reduced; pet. 4, upright, converging apically, one outer pet. spurred at base, the other flat, inner pet. narrow, tips coherent; sta. 6. SW Eur., N Afr.

S. enneaphylla DC. 5–12cm high. Lvs 3-ternately cut, lfts ovate-orbicular, sometimes cordate; petioles slender. Fls in 10-fld rac., yellow, marked purple above, 2cm. Summer. var. *speciosa* (Boiss.) O. Bolos & Vigo. Lvs simple or 3-sect; lfts ovate. Fls pale yellow. Z9.

Sarcocaulon (DC.) Sweet. Geraniaceae. 14 decumbent to semi-upright subshrubs; st. succulent; br. spreading, succulent, spiny; bark waxy. Lvs small, entire or pinnately divided; petioles of first flush of lvs, becoming spines, 2nd flush of lvs borne in their axils. Fls axill., solitary; sep. 5, oblong-elliptic; pet. 5, clawed, overlapping, free, unequal; sta. 15. S Afr. Z9.

S. burmannii (DC.) Sweet = *S. crassicaule.*

S. crassicaule Rehm. Erect subshrub to 50cm. Br. thick, 10mm diam., spines straight to curved, 30mm; lvs obovate, 15×10mm, irregularly pinnately divided. Fls to 55mm diam.; pet. 20mm+, white, light pink, yellow or white with pink base. Spring and summer. S Afr.

S. l'heritieri Sweet. Much-branched subshrub to 75cm. Br. 5–10mm diam.; spines 25mm+ long, thin, v. dark; 1st lvs 7×6mm, obovate to orbicular, sometimes notched, base rounded, entire; 2nd lvs 11×9mm, broadly ovate. Fls to 35mm diam.; pet. obovate, yellow. Spring–early summer. S Afr.

S. patersonii (DC.) G. Don. Subshrub to 50cm. Spines to 20mm; lvs 12×8mm, obovate. Fls to 35mm diam.; pet. obovate, sometimes notched, rose pink, light magenta or purple. Spring–early summer. S Afr.

S. patersonii auct. non (DC.) G. Don = *S. salmoniflorum*.

S. rigidum Schinz = *S. patersonii*.

S. salmoniflorum Moffett. Much-branched subshrub or dwarf plant to 40cm. Long spines straight or curved; 1st lvs 5×4mm, entire, narrow to broadly elliptic, notched, base wedge-shaped; 2nd lvs 6×4mm, elliptic to broad ovate, tips notched or acute. Fls 30mm diam.; pet. narrow obovate, salmon pink to orange. Summer. SW S Afr.

S. spinosum (Burm. f.) Kuntze = *S. crassicaule*.

Sarcocephalus Sab. Rubiaceae. 2 trees. Fls in pedunculate, term., globose heads; cal. pubesc., lobes 4–5, deltoid; cor. funnel-shaped, lobes 4–5, oblong; sta. 4–5. Fr. syncarp. Trop. Afr. Z10.

S. cordatus Miq. = *Nauclea orientalis*.

S. diderrichii De Wildeman = *Nauclea diderrichii*.

S. esculentus Sab. = *S. latifolius*.

S. latifolius (Sm.) Bruce. Tree to 9m. Br. pendent. Lvs to 21×14cm, ovate to elliptic, lustrous above. Fl. heads to 5cm wide, fragrant; cor. white or yellow, tube to 1cm, lobes to 3mm, obovate to suborbicular, ciliate. Fr. to 1cm, globose to ovoid, rugose, fleshy, red. Trop. Afr.

S. ovatus Elmer. = *Nauclea orientalis*.

→*Nauclea*.

Sarcochilus R. Br. Orchidaceae. 12 small, lithophytic or epiphytic, monopodial orchids. St. short, often becoming tufted. Lvs somewhat fleshy, carinate. Rac. axillary, tep. ± equall; lip stalked, saccate, with short, spur, midlobe small. Papuasia, Aus., Polyn., SE Asia. Z10.

S. australis (Lindl.) Rchb. f. Lvs 2–7cm, linear to falcate. Rac. pendulous; fls fragrant; to 3cm diam.; tep. pale yellow-green to brown. Lat. sep. lanceolate; lip white tinted yellow, calli prominent, lat. lobes with fine red or white lines. Mid autumn–mid winter. E Aus., Tasm.

S. barkleyanus F. Muell. = *S. australis*.

S. ceciliae F. Muell. Lvs to 10cm, linear to lanceolate, often marked brown. Infl. erect, narrow lvs; fls pink to purple to 2.5cm diam.; lat. sep. ovate; lip midlobe downy, lat. lobes ciliate, disc with golden yellow calli. Late autumn–mid winter. NSW, Queensld.

S. divitiflorus F. Muell. ex Benth. = *Rhinerrhiza divitiflora*.

S. falcatus R. Br. ORANGE BLOSSOM ORCHID. Lvs to 10cm, oblong-falcate. Rac. arching; fls to 3cm diam., fragrant, white, sep. striped purple below, ovate; li midlobe narrow, yellow, lat. lobes oblong, orange spotted or banded garnet. Mid summer–mid autumn. E Aus., NSW, Vict., Queensld.

S. fitzgeraldii F. Muell. RAVINE ORCHID. Lvs to 14cm, linear to narrow-oblong, falcate. Infl. erect to arching; fls to 3.5cm diam., white or pink, blotched cerise or crimson at centre; sep. ovate; lip less midlobe triangular, yellow or orange. Mid-late autumn. NSW, Queensld.

S. hartmannii F. Muell. Lvs to 20cm linear to narrow oblong, falcate. Rac. dense; fls to 3cm diam.; tep. white, basally spotted maroon, ovate; lip small, waxy, midlobe conical, lat. lobes striped garnet. Autumn. NSW, Queensld.

S. hillii (F. Muell.) F. Muell. Lvs to 10cm, linear, spotted. Infl. narrow; fls 3cm diam., pale pink or white, fragrant; sep. ovate-oblong or ovate; lip interior white-pubesc., lateral lobes striled purple, calli yellow or orange. Late autumn–mid winter. NSW, Queensld.

S. Fitzhart. (*S. fitzgeraldii* ×*S. hartmanii*.) Lvs to 10cm, narrow-lanceolate to falcate. Rac. ascending; fls to 3cm diam., white centrally spotted pink or maroon. Winter–spring. Gdn origin.

S. minutiflos Bail. = *S. hillii*.

S. muscosus Rolfe = *Grosourdya muscosa*.

S. olivaceus Lindl. Lvs to 15cm, 2–8, oblong, rarely falcate, often undulate. Fls olive to golden green; tep. linear-oblong; lip white marked maroon. Mid summer–early autumn. NSW, Queensld.

S. roseus (Clemesha) Clemesha. Resembles *S. ceciliae* except lvs shorter with fewer markings, fls bright rose pink, lip lat. lobes entire. Late autumn–mid winter. NE Aus.

Sarcococca Lindl. SWEET BOX. Buxaceae. 11 everg., dwarf and medium shrubs or small trees, often suckering freely or spreading as if rhizomatous. Lvs glab., entire, leathery. Infl. a compact axill. cluster or an erect spike; fls small, off-white to cream, apetalous, unisexual; ♂ fls with sep., 4, sta., 4, ♀ fls with sep. 4–6, styles 2–3. Fr. a globose drupe. SE Asia, Himal., W China.

S. confusa Sealy. Everg. shrub to 2m. Young br. puberulous. Lvs 3–6.5cm, elliptic, elliptic-lanceolate to elliptic-ovate, apex acuminate to acute, base cuneate to obtuse, thinly leathery, dark green above, pale green below. Infl. v. fragrant; ♂ fls with anth. cream-coloured; ♀ fls 5–5.5mm, styles 2–3. Fr. ripening from red to black. Winter. Origin unknown. Z6.

S. hookeriana Baill. Everg. shrub to 1.8m, often suckering. Young br. pubesc. Lvs 5.5cm, coriaceous, rugose, dull green, apex acuminate, base cuneate. Infl. fragrant, white; ♂ fls with deep pink anth; ♀ fls with 3 stigmas. Fr. black. Autumn. Himal. var. *digyna* Franch. Spreading and suckering shrub, 0.3–1m. Lvs 4–8cm, narrowly elliptic to narrowly oblong-elliptic. Infl fragrant; ♂ fls with anth. cream- or rose-coloured; ♀ fls with 2 styles. Fr. purple-black. W China. 'Purple Stem': st. tinted purple when young. var. *humilis* Rehd. & Wils. Spreading and suckering shrub, 0.2–0.5m. Lvs 3.5–7cm, elliptic, acute. Infl. fragrant; ♂ fls with pink anth.; ♀ fls with 2 styles. Winter. China. Z6.

S. humilis hort. non Stapf = *S. confusa*.

S. humilis Stapf non hort. = *S. hookeriana* var. *humilis*.

S. orientalis C.Y. Wu = *S. hookeriana* var. *digyna*.

S. pruniformis Lindl. in part. = *S. saligna*.

S. ruscifolia Stapf. Spreading and suckering shrub to 1m. Young br. pubesc. Lvs 3–5.5cm, dark green, broad-ovate, apex acuminate, base cuneate. Infl. fragrant; ♂ fls with cream-coloured anth.; ♀ fls with 3 styles. Fr. red. Winter. W China, Tibet. Z9.

S. ruscifolia var. *chinensis* hort. non (Franch.) Rehd. & Wils. = *S. confusa*.

S. saligna (D. Don) Muell. Rhizomatous, everg. shrub, 0.6–1.2m. Young br. glab. Lvs 7–12cm, pale green, linear-lanceolate. Infl. 10–15mm; ♂ fls green, scentless, with yellow anth.; ♀ fls with 3 styles. Fr. dark purple or black. Winter. W Himal. (Afghan. to Kumaon). Z9.

Sarcocyphala Harv.

S. gerrardii Harv. = *Cynanchum aphyllum*.

✕Sarconopsis. (*Sarcanthus* (*Cleisostoma*) ✕*Phalaenopsis*.) Orchidaceae.
Gdn hybrids with branching sprays of rounded white, pink or lilac fls.

Sarcophagophilus Dinter.

S. armatus (N.E. Br.) Dinter = *Quaqua armata*.

Sarcostemma R. Br. Asclepiadaceae. 10 succulent subshrubs; st. jointed. Lvs 0 or reduced to scales. Fls in shortly pedunculate umbels or clusters, small white to pink; cor. rotate with projecting lobes; corona double. Trop. & subtrop. Afr., Madag., India, Malaysia, Aus. Z10.

S. aphyllum (Thunb.) R. Br. = *Cynanchum aphyllum*.

S. australe R. Br. Shrub, 1–2m; st. cylindrical, br. 5–10mm thick, grey-grene, often pruinose, erect or climbing. Fls 6–10 in nodal clusters. Aus.

S. brunonianum Wight & Arn. Twining to prostrate shrub, dichotomous, joints 5–6cm, cylindrical, green. Fls 8–12 in umbels. Penins. India.

S. decorsei Costan & Gallaud. Shoots 50–100cm, branched, cylindrical, 0.4cm, thick, distinctly nodal, tinged blue. Infl. of 4–10-fld. Madag.

S. insigne (N.E. Br.) Descoings. Erect shrub, 30–50cm, branched, shoots cylindrical, 0.2–0.3cm diam., grey-green to purple-brown with faint pale stripes. Fls 2–4 per infl., veined maroon. C Madag.

S. madagascariense Descoings. Liana-like, sap milky. Fls in groups of 2–3. Madag.

S. pearsonii N.E. Br. Shrubby, to 30cm; st. branching dichotomously, suberect, 0.3–0.4cm diam., young growth pubesc. Fls 3–6 in term. or lateral umbels 7–8mm diam., sweetly scented, yellow, corona white. S Afr., Nam.

S. resiliens Adams & Holland. Low-growing to 50cm; st. several from a thickened base, to 70×0.35–0.5cm, finely pubesc. when young, tinted purple when mature. Fls 2–7 together in clusters, sweetly scented, light purple tinged green. Kenya.

S. socotranum Lavranos. Small, shrubby, succulent perenn.; st. to 150×0.2–0.5cm, minutely pubesc. at first, trailing or pendulous, nodes much constricted. Fls 2–8 together. Socotra.

S. stoloniferum Adams & Holland. Low-growing to 15cm. St. 10–40×0.9cm, congested, mid-green to tinted purple, becoming prostrate and rooting. Fls 7–9 in clusters, sweetly scented, green-brown; corona white. Kenya Highlands, N Tanz.

S. subterraneum Adams & Holland. To 20cm; rhiz. subterranean. St. arising singly, 10–15×0.2–0.3cm, freely branching, mid-green to tinted purple. Fls 2–12mm, 2–8 together, purple-pink, corona pale pink to white. Kenya Highlands, N Tanz.

S. tetrapterum Turcz. = *Cynanchum aphyllum*.

S. vanlessenii Lavranos. Shrubby; st. to 100×0.3–0.4cm, rooting at nodes. Fls 5–7 together, dark pink or brown-pink. S Yemen.

S. viminale R. Br. Br. erect or pendulous, 0.4–0.5cm thick, jointed, dichotomous. Fls umbellate, 1cm across, white. Trop.

& subtrop. Afr., Nam., Cape Prov.
→*Decanemopsis, Drepanostemma* and *Platykeleba*.

Sarcothea Turcz. = *Schinus*.

Sargale Lily *Lilium* ×*imperiale*.
Sargent Cherry *Prunus sargentii*.

Sargentodoxa Rehd. & Wils. Sargentodoxaceae. 1 climbing decid. shrub to 7m. Lvs long-petiolate, 3-foliolate, lfts to 12cm, rhombic-ovate, dark glossy green above, pale beneath. Rac. pendulous to 15cm; fls to 1.2cm, v. fragrant; sep. in 2 whorls of 3, petaloid, green-yellow; cor. lobes 6, reduced to scale-like nectaries; ♂ with sta. 6; ♀ with carpels numerous, spirally arranged on enlarged receptacle. Fr. of stipitate berries, 8mm, dark blue, on fleshy receptacle. Late spring. China, Laos, Vietnam. Z9.
S. cuneata Rehd. & Wils.

SARGENTODOXACEAE Stapf. ex Hutch. See *Sargentodoxa*.

Sargent Spruce *Picea brachytyla*.
Sargent's Rowan *Sorbus sargentiana*.

Saritaea Dugand. Bignoniaceae. 1 liane. Lvs 2-foliate, often with a tendril; lfts to 6cm, obovate, papery, lepidote; petiole to 3cm. Pan. cymose; cal. cupular, truncate, lepidote; cor. red-purple, white in throat with purple-red nectaries; tubular-campanulate, tube 5.6–6.3cm, lobes 2.2–3.1cm. Colomb. and Ecuad.
S. magnifica (Sprague ex Steenis) Dugand.
→*Arrabidaea*.

Saro *Trithrinax brasiliensis*.

Sarracenia L. PITCHER PLANT. Sarraceniaceae. 8 carnivorous herbaceous perennials. Lvs basal, clumped or rosulate, blade-like and spreading or, more usually, erect to arching pitchers, hollow-cylindrical with a longitudinal wing or ridge, dilating toward apex into an open-mouthed funnel with a waxy rim and erect lid. Fl. pendulous, solitary, scapose; sep. (4–)5, overlapping, persistent, green to red; pet. 5, ovate to oblong, large, yellow to red, decid.; style dilated into peltate, umbrella-like structure with 5 ribs. Spring. Flor. to Canada. Z8 unless specified.
S. alabamensis F.W. & R.B. Case. = *S. rubra* ssp. *alabamensis*.
S. alata (Alph. Wood) Alph. Wood. PALE TRUMPET. Pitchers to 75cm, trumpet-shaped, narrow at mouth, with lid angled towrds mouth, yellow-green, sometimes red, veins red, reticulate above. Fls cream-yellow to white, to 6.5cm across. Alab. to Tex.
S. ×*catesbaei* Elliot. (*S. flava* ×*S. purpurea*.) Pitchers to 75cm, erect, lid erect, rounded, green to dark-purple, veined red or maroon. Fls brick-red, large. Natural hybrid, SE US. Z5.
S. ×*chelsonii* hort. Veitch. (*S. purpurea* ×*S. rubra*.) Pitchers to 45cm, semi-decumbent, somewhat curved, narrow with narrow lid, veined dark red. Fls dark mahogany. Gdn origin.
S. ×*courtii* hort. (*S. psittacina* ×*S. purpurea*.) Pitchers prostrate, somewhat inflated, crimson-purple with dark veins when young, blood-red with black-purple veins when older, with translucent patches above. Fls garnet red. Gdn origin.
S. drummondii Croom = *S. leucophylla*.
S. ×*excellens* hort. ex Nichols. (*S. leucophylla* ×*minor*.) Pitchers erect, with translucent white spots above, veins red-brown, lid horizontal. Fls mahogany red. Natural hybrid.
S. ×*farnhamii* hort. = *S.* ×*readii*.
S. flava L. YELLOW TRUMPET; YELLOW PITCHER PLANT; TRUMPETS. Pitchers 30–120cm, erect, wide at mouth, lid erect, rounded, yellow green, often veined red on lid, eesp. at base, sometimes wholly red or maroon. Fls to 10cm across, yellow. Virg. to Flor., Louisiana. 'Maxima': pitchers to 75cm, yellow-green, marked and veined maroon above and on lid, glaucous below. 'Red Burgundy': pitchers deep burgundy. Z7.
S. jonesii Wherry = *S. rubra* ssp. *jonesii*.
S. leucophylla Raf. WHITE TRUMPET. Pitchers to 120cm, erect, slender, green below, white netted with green, maroon or red veins above, lid erect, undulate, hairy within. Fls red-purple, to 10cm across. SE & C US.
S. ×*melanorhoda* hort. ex Veitch (*S. purpurea* ×*S.* ×*catesbaei*.) Pitchers to 30cm, ± decumbent, enlongate-funnel-shaped, widest at mouth, blood-red, veined black-crimson at maturity, wing broad, lid erect, crispate. Fls red. Gdn origin.
S. minor Walter. HOODED PITCHER PLANT. Pitchers 25–45(–100)cm, erect, trumpet-shaped, green with purple veins and translucent white patches above, wings broad, lid concave,

bending over mouth. Fls yellow, to 6.5cm across. S Carol. to Flor.
S. ×*mitchelliana* hort. ex Nichols. (*S. purpurea* ×*S. leucophylla*.) Pitchers to 45cm, erect or sprawling, wide-funnel-shaped, olive-green below, rich dark-red with dark veins above, some-times with green-white patches, lid erect, undulate. Fls large, dark red. Gdn origin.
S. ×*mooreana* hort. = *S.* ×*moorei*.
S. ×*moorei* hort. ex Veitch. (*S. flava* ×*S. leucophylla*.) Pitchers to 60cm, erect, green marked white above, lid rounded, undulate, veined crimson. Fls to 10cm across, red-orange to apricot or peach. Wild hybrid.
S. oreophila (Kearney) Wherry. Pitchers 30–75cm, erect, green, mouth rounded, lid erect; non-trapping lvs numerous, sickle-shaped. Fls to 7cm diam., yellow-green. Alab., Georgia.
S. ×*popei* hort. (*S. flava* ×*S. alata*.) Pitchers resembling *S. flava*, but smaller, with fine maroon veins, reticulate in lid. Gdn origin.
S. psittacina Michx. LOBSTER-POT PITCHER PLANT. Pitchers to 15cm, prostrate, rosulate, slightly curved, green, veined and marked red purple above, translucent patches, wings broad, lid forming inflated, round hood, fls red-purple, to 5cm across. SE US.
S. purpurea L. COMMON PITCHER PLANT; HUNTSMAN'S CUP. Pitchers 10–30cm, rosulate, decumbent, curved and erect above, inflated above, narrowed below, green with red or purple veins and markings, or entirely green, wing broad, lid en-tire, erect. Fls dark red or yellow, to 5cm across. NJ N to Canadian arctic, nat. Eur., esp. Eire. Z3. ssp. *venosa* (Raf.) Wherry. Pitchers squatter, lid broad, auricled, undulate, green with red markings to red throughout. Fls soft pink to deep crimson. Louisiana to NJ. Z6.
S. ×*readii* Bell. (*S. leucophylla* ×*S. rubra*.) Pitchers erect, slender, marked white and veined red above, lid incurved. Fls small, blood red. Gdn origin.
S. rubra Walter. SWEET TRUMPET PLANT; SWEET PITCHER PLANT. Pitchers to 45cm, erect to sprawling, narrow, green, becoming bronze- to copper-coloured with maroon veins above, wing broad, lid bending over pitcher mouth, elliptic. Fls to 4.5cm across, red to maroon. ssp. *rubra*. Carolinas, Georgia. ssp. *jonesii* (Wherry) Bell. MOUNTAIN PITCHER PLANT. Pitchers to 60cm, mouth broad, lid with pronounced column, veins usually purple. W N & S Carol. ssp. *alabamensis* (F.W. Case & R.B. Case) D.E. Schnell. ALABAMA CANEBRAKE PITCHER. Pitcher to 50cm, green with little or no red pigmentation, lid large, un-dulate. C Alab.
S. ×*swaniana* hort. ex Nichols. (*S. minor* ×*S. purpurea*.) Pitchers funnel-shaped, incurved, green-purple, heavily veined crimson, or crimson throughout, wings broad, lid ovate, notched. Gdn origin.
S. ×*willisii* hort. Differs from *S.* ×*mitchelliana* in young pitcher coral-pink, becoming pink-red above, without paler markings. Fls large, dark red. Name also applied to *S.* ×*courtii* ×*S.* ×*melanorhoda*. Gdn origin, GB 19th century.
S. ×*wrigleyana* hort. Veitch. (*S. psittacina* ×*S. leucophylla*.) Pitchers ascending, green below, white, strongly veined red above. Fls dark red. Gdn origin.
S. cvs. 'Ahlsii' (*S. rubra* × *S. alata*): pitchers large, lightly veined; fls plum red. 'Evendine': pitcher golden green ageing dark red with prominent veining. 'Gulf Rubra': hoods pointed with prominent veining.

SARRACENIACEAE Dumort. 3/18. *Darlingtonia, Heliampho-ra, Sarracenia*.

Sarviceberry *Amelanchier*.
Sarvis Holly *Ilex amelanchier*.

Sasa Mak. & Shib. Gramineae. *c*40 small or medium-sized bamboos; rhiz. running. Culms terete, ascending; sheaths persistent, shorter than the internodes; nodes with white waxy bloom below; br. 1 or non. Lvs large and broad, mostly thick, tessellate. Jap., Korea, China.
S. albomarginata (Franch. & Savat.) Mak. & Shib. = *S. veitchii*.
S. argenteostriata (Reg.) Camus = *Pleioblastus argenteostriatus*.
S. auricoma (Mitford) Camus = *Pleioblastus auricoma*.
S. borealis (Hackel) Nak. = *Sasamorpha borealis*.
S. cernua auctt., non Mak. = *S. palmata*.
S. disticha (Mitford) Camus = *Pleioblastus pygmaeus* var. *distichus*.
S. humilis (Mitford) Camus = *Pleioblastus humilis*.
S. japonica (Sieb. & Zucc. ex Steud.) Mak. = *Pseudosasa japonica*.
S. kurilensis (Rupr.) Mak. & Shib. Culms stout, 1–4m×2–3mm. Lvs 15–30×1.2–4.8cm, dark shining green above, sacbrous mostly oin one margin only. Jap., Korea. 'Shimofuri': lvs

striped white. Z7.

S. masumuneana (Mak.) Chao & Renvoize = *Sasaella masumuneana*.

S. nipponica Mak. (Mak. & Shib.). MIYAKO-ZASA. Culms 50–80cm, slender, unbranched, often purple. Lvs 8–20×1.4–3cm, small, thin, typically pubesc. beneath, edged white in winter. Jap. Z7.

S. palmata (Burb.) Camus. Rhiz. rampant. Culms stout, 1.5–4×2–5mm, usually soon streaked purple (f. *nebulosa* (Mak.) Suzuki). Lvs 25–40×5–9.5cm, well tapered, bright shining green. Jap. Z7.

S. paniculata Mak. & Shib. = *S. palmata*.

S. pumila (Mitford) Camus = *Pleioblastus humilis* var. *pumilus*.

S. purpurascens var. *borealis* (Hackel) Nak. = *Sasamorpha borealis*.

S. pygmaea (Miq.) Rehd. = *Pleioblastus pygmaeus*.

S. ramosa (Mak.) Mak. & Shib. = *Sasaella ramosa*.

S. senanensis auctt., non (Franch. & Savat.) Rehd. = *S. palmata*.

S. tessellata (Munro) Mak. & Shib. = *Indocalamus tessellatus*.

S. tsuboiana Mak. Rhiz. v. shortly running. Culms 1–2m×1–2mm. Lvs 12–26×2.4–4.6cm, glab. C Jap. Z6.

S. variegata (Sieb. ex Miq.) Camus = *Pleioblastus variegatus*.

S. veitchii (Carr.) Rehd. KUMA ZASA. Rhiz. gently running. Culms 80–150×2–3cm, purple-lined, glaucous. Lvs 15–25×3.2–6cm, shortly tapered, developing a broad, papery white margin. Jap. Z8.

Sasaella Mak. Gramineae. Some 12 bamboos, differing from *Sasa* in thinner culms with longer, more horizontal br. and small, narrower, thinner lvs. Jap. Z7.

S. glabra (Nak.) Nak. ex Koidz. = *S. masumuneana*.

S. masumuneana (Mak.) Hatsusima & Muroi in Sugimoto. SHIYA-ZASA. Culms 0.5–2m×3–4mm. Lvs 10–19×1.5–3.5cm, glab.; sheaths purple-lined. f. *albostriata* (Muroi) D. McClintock. Lvs striped white maturing yellow. f. *albostriata* (Muroi) D. McClintock. f. *aureostriata* (Muroi) D. McClintock. Lvs always striped yellow.

S. ramosa (Mak.) Mak. AZUMA-ZASA. A variable rampant spreader. Culms 1–1.5m×3–4mm, sometimes purple. Lvs 10–20×1.4–3cm, pubesc. beneath, margins scaberulous, withering white.

→*Arundinaria* and *Sasa*.

Sasamorpha Nak. Gramineae. 6 medium-sized bamboos, differing from *Sasa* in less rampant rhiz., culms erect, longer sheaths than the internodes; nodes flattened, rarely with any white powder. Far E. Z7.

S. borealis (Hackel) Nak. Culms 1–3m×5–8mm, well-branched above; nodes pubesc. Lvs 10×20×2–3cm, scaberulous, paler beneath, usually tinted purple toward base of stalk. Mistaken for *Pseudosasa japonica*. Jap., China.

S. purpurascens (Hackel) Camus = *S. borealis*.

S. tessellata (Munro) Nak. = *Indocalamus tessellatus*.

→*Arundinaria* and *Sasa*.

Sasa-yuri *Lilium japonicum*.
Sassafras *Sassafras albidum*.

Sassafras Trew. Lauraceae. 3 decid. aromatic trees to 30m. Bark deeply fissured. Lvs entire or 1–3 lobed. Fls small, yellow-green, apetalous clustered rac. Fr. an ovoid drupe. E N Amer., E Asia.

S. albidum (Nutt.) Nees. SASSAFRAS. Tree to 20m, multistemmed in old age. Lvs 6–15cm, ovate, 1–3-lobed above initially downy beneath, dark green, gold and red in autumn. Infl. to 5cm. Fr. to 1.5cm, deep blue, stalk red. E N Amer. Z5.

S. officinale Nees Eberm. = *S. albidum*.

S. variifolium (Salisb.) Kuntze = *S. albidum*.

Satin Everlasting *Helichrysum leucopsideum*.
Satin Flower *Clarkia amoena*.
Satin Leaf *Chrysophyllum oliviforme*.
Satin Poppy *Meconopsis napaulensis*.
Satin Potho *Scindapsus pictus*.
Satin-wood *Murraya paniculata*.
Satsuma *Citrus reticulata*.
Satureja *Acinos*.

Satureja L. SAVORY. Labiatae. 30 ann. herbs or perenn. subshrubs. Lvs entire, subsessile. Fls whorled subtended by floral lvs in loose cymes or spikes; cal. tubular, 5-toothed; cor. bilabiate, tube straight, lower lip trilobed. Temp. and warm temp. N hemis. Z8.

S. acinos (L.) Scheele = *Acinos arvensis* and *A. alpinus*.

S. calamintha (L.) Scheele = *Calamintha nepeta*.

S. calamintha ssp. *glandulosa* (Req.) Gams = *Calamintha nepeta* ssp. *glandulosa*.

S. calamintha ssp. *officinalis* sensu Gams = *Calamintha sylvatica* ssp. *sylvatica*.

S. capitata L. = *Thymus capitatus*.

S. chinensis (Benth.) Briq. = *Clinopodium chinense*.

S. coccinea (Nutt.) Bertol. = *Calamintha coccinea*.

S. coerulea Jankó in Velen. Woody-based perenn. to 25cm. St. puberulent. Lvs 20×2mm, linear, glab., ciliate. Bulg., Rom. Z6.

S. cuneifolia Ten. Woody-based perenn. to 50cm. St. hispidulous. Lvs to 16×4mm, obovate to linear-spathulate. Autumn. Medit. Z8.

S. georgiana (Harper) Ahles = *Clinopodium georgianum*.

S. glabella (Michx.) Briq. = *Clinopodium glabellum*.

S. glabra hort. non Thell. = *Clinopodium glabellum*.

S. graeca L. = *Micromeria graeca*.

S. graeca ssp. *garganica* Briq. = *Micromeria graeca* ssp. *garganica*.

S. grandiflora (L.) Scheele = *Calamintha grandiflora*.

S. hortensis L. SUMMER SAVORY. Aromatic, puberulent, shrubby ann. to 25cm. Lvs 30×4mm, linear to linear-lanceolate. Fls white or pink. Autumn. SE Eur., nat. elsewhere.

S. intermedia C.A. Mey. var. *laxior* Benth. = *S. spicigera*.

S. juliana L. = *Micromeria juliana*.

S. kitaibelii Wierzb. = *S. montana* ssp. *kitaibelii*.

S. laxiflora K. Koch = *S. hortensis*.

S. mimuloides (Benth.) Briq. = *Calamintha mimuloides*.

S. montana L. WINTER SAVORY. Shrublet to 50cm. Lvs linear to obovate, coriaceous, smooth to sparsely pubesc. Fls white to pale violet. Summer and autumn. S Eur. ssp. *illyrica* Nyman. St. glab., infl. whorls dense. ssp. *intricata* Lange. Lvs ciliate, infl. whorls dense. ssp. *kitaibelii* (Wierzb.) P.W. Ball. St. glab. on 2 sides. 'Nana' habit dwarf. 'Procumbens': creeping, to 15cm high; lvs bright green. Z6.

S. pachyphylla K. Koch = *S. hortensis*.

S. postii Aznav. = *S. hortensis*.

S. reptans hort. = *S. spicigera*.

S. rumelica Velen. Woody perenn. to 20cm. St. pubesc. Lvs 15×5mm, spathulate, obtuse, pubesc. to scabrid. Bulg. Z6.

S. rupestris Wulf. ex Jacq. = *Micromeria thymifolia*.

S. spicigera (K. Koch) Boiss. Diffuse procumbent subshrub. St. pubesc. on 2 sides. Lvs 10–25×2.5mm, linear to oblanceolate, glab. Fls to 10mm, white. Autumn. Anatolia, Iran, Cauc. Plants in gardens called *S. reptans* are *S. spicigera*. Z7.

S. thymbra L. Doomed, much-branched shrublet to 40cm. St. pubesc. Lvs to 14×3.5mm, linear to spathulate, scabrid. Spring. Balk. Z7.

S. thymoides Sol. = *Micromeria varia*.

S. virginiana L. = *Pycnanthemum virginianum*.

S. vulgaris (L.) Fritsch = *Clinopodium vulgare*.

→*Micromeria*.

Satyrium Sw. Orchidaceae. 100+ tuberous terrestrial orchids. Lvs 2 to several, broadly ovate, to 20cm, basal, or reduced to sheaths on flowering st. Spike terminal; sep. joined at base to pet. and lip; pet. narrower; lip forming hood with 2 spurs, 2 extra vestigial spurs occas. present. Mainland Afr., particularly S Afr.; Madag. (5 spp.), Asia (2 spp.). Z9.

S. bicorne (L.) Thunb. 15–60cm. Fls dull yellow or green-yellow, tinged with purple-brown, fragrant; sep. 6–9mm, pet. slightly shorter; lip 6–9mm, forming hood with mouth facing down; spurs 10–22mm, slender. S Afr. (Cape Prov.).

S. carneum (Ait.) R. Br. To 80cm. Fls fleshy, pale to deep rose pink, lip darker than tep.; tep. 13–18mm, lanceolate-oblong, tips rolled back; lip 15mm, wide-mouthed with reflexed apical flap; spurs 18–25mm, slender. S Afr.

S. ciliatum Lindl. = *S. nepalense*.

S. coriifolium Sw. 20–75cm. Fls nodding or held horizontally, bright orange or yellow, tinged with red; 7–13mm, oblong; lip 10–13mm with reflexed apical flap, v. hooded, the mouth facing downwards; spurs 9–12mm, slender. S Afr. (Cape Prov.).

S. erectum Sw. 10–50cm. Fls pale to deep pink with darker marks and sweet, pungent scent; tep. 10–15mm, obovate-oblong; lip 10–15mm, wide-mouthed, with partly reflexed apical flap; spurs 5–11mm, tapering from wide mouth. S Afr. (Cape Prov.).

S. macrophyllum Lindl. To 1m. Fls pale to deep pink; tep. 7–14mm; lip 10–12mm with short apical flap, wide-mouthed; spurs 13–26mm, slender. S & C Trop. Afr., S Afr., Swaz.

S. membranaceum Sw. To 50cm. Fls pale to deep pink, rarely white; tep. 9–11mm, oblong, pet. serrate; lip 9–11mm, wide-mouthed, with apical flap serrate, reflexed; spurs 20–30mm, standing away from st. S Afr. (Cape Prov.).

S. nepalense D. Don. 50–75cm. Fls bright pink, 10–13mm diam. Summer. Pak. to SW China. Plants known as *S. cilatum*, from Nepal and Tibet, have ciliate tep. these are now usually included in *S. nepalense*.

S. odorum Sonder. To 50cm. Fls pale green or yellow-green tinged with purple-brown, with strong, sweet pungent scent; sep. 4–8mm, oblong exceeding pet.; lip 8–10mm, wide-mouthed, with apical flap; spurs 13–18mm, slender, arched, occas. with small extra spurs. S Afr. (Cape Prov.).

Saucer Magnolia *Magnolia ×soulangiana.*
Saucer Plant *Aeonium undulatum.*
Sauer Klee *Oxalis adenophylla.*

Sauromatum Schott. Araceae. 2 tuberous, perenn. herbs. Tuber depressed globose; growing point, narrowly conical, enclosed in tightly rolled, maroon-flecked bracts, developing v. rapidly. Lf solitary, produced after fls, pedate, long-stalked. Spathe short-stalked, base bulbous, then tubular, blade oblong-lanceolate, soon withering; spadix appendage long, slender, fleshy, exceeding spathe and emitting a foul stench. E & W Afr., E Asia. Z10.
S. guttatum (Wallich) Schott = *S. venosum.*
S. nubicum Schott. V. close to *S. venosum*, but lf seg. broader, spathe blade narrower. E & W Afr.
S. venosum (Ait.) Kunth. MONARCH OF THE EAST; VOODOO LILY; RED CALLA. Tuber to 12cm diam. Petiole to 70cm, pale green mottled dark green or maroon, lf seg. to 40×12cm, laterals smaller, 7–15, oblong-lanceolate, glossy green, veins impressed. Peduncle to 6cm; spathe tube 5–10cm, blade 30–70×8–10cm, fleshy, soon reflexed, twisted and undulate, interior yellow-green to ochre spotted and mottled blood-red to maroon; spadix appendage to 35cm, fleshy pink to metallic maroon. Himal., S India.

SAURURACEAE E. Mey. 5/7. *Anemopsis, Houttuynia, Saururus.*

Saururus L. LIZARD'S TAIL. Saururaceae. 2 perenn. herbs of wet places. St. erect, clump-forming, simple or sparsely branched, leafy. Lvs ovate-lanceolate, strongly cordate at base, petiolate. Fls v. small, white or ivory, fragrant, each subtended by a small, pale bract crowded in a slender nodding rac. N Amer., E Asia.
S. cernuus L. SWAMP LILY. St. to 1.25m. Lvs 7.5–15cm, downy at first. Infl. to 30×1.5cm; fil. slender, anth. held above stigmas. E N Amer. Z5.
S. chinensis (Lour.) Baill. Differs from *S. cernuus* in rac. to 12cm, fls ivory, not white, fil. thick, anth. held below stigmas. E Asia. Z6.

Sausage Crassula *Senecio articulatus.*
Sausage Tree *Kigelia.*

Saussurea DC. Compositae. c300 perenn. herbs. Lvs alt., simple, entire to pinnatisect. Cap. discoid, solitary or in corymbs or pan.; receptacle usually scaly; involucre ovoid, campanulate or cylindric; phyllaries imbricate in many series, often hairy. Eurasia, N Amer. Z7 unless specified.
S. albescens (DC.) Hook. f. & Thoms. To 3m. Lvs to 30cm, entire to sinuate-lobed, acute or acuminate, apex and teeth apiculate, glab., scabrid or arachnoid-lanate above, tomentose beneath, lower lvs narrowly oblong, petiolate, upper lvs smaller, sessile. Cap. numerous, term. and axill. in flat-topped corymbs, long-pedunculate; receptacle v. narrow; outer phyllaries tinged purple; flts pink. Summer. Pak. to C Nepal.
S. alpina (L.) DC. To 50cm. Lvs to 25cm, ovate- to linear-lanceolate, base rounded to cuneate, entire to somewhat dentate, petiole narrowly winged, upper st. lvs sessile. Cap. several to many, in contracted term. corymbs or a corymbose pan.; flts purple, sweetly scented. Summer. Eur. to NW Asia. ssp. *macrophylla* (Saut.) Nyman. Lvs ovate to broadly lanceolate, base rounded or only slightly cordate. Cap. usually clustered in a compact corymb. E Alps, Carpath. Z2.
S. angustifolia (L.) DC. To 50cm, often tinged purple. Lvs few, to 15cm, linear to elliptic-lanceolate, dentate, acute to obtuse, shortly petiolate, glabrate to densely viscid-pubesc., often lanate beneath, upper st. lvs usually reduced. Cap. 3 to many, in racemose corymbs; flts pink to purple. Arc. of E Asia to Alask. and Canada. Z2.
S. ceratocarpa Decne. To 60cm, or 0, minutely scabrid. Lvs to 12cm, linear-oblong to lanceolate, entire or pinnatifid, sometimes white-tomentose beneath, petiolate below, sessile and auriculate at base above. Cap. solitary to many, in corymbs; flts purple. Summer. Kashmir.
S. costus (Falc.) Lipsch. To 3m. Lvs deltoid, basal lvs to 40cm, pinnate, term. lobe largest, often triangular, long petiolate, irregularly winged, st. lvs to 30cm, entire or irregularly dentate, semi-amplexicaul. Cap. few, in a dense, rounded term. corymbose cluster; phyllaries purple; flts purple. Summer. E Himal.

S. densa (Hook.) Rydb. To 20cm, sparsely arachnoid-villous. Lvs to 30cm, narrowly elliptic to lanceolate, dentate, usually petiolate. Cap. numerous, in dense, crowded capitate clusters; flts usually purple. Sib. to Canada. Z1.
S. discolor (Willd.) DC. To 20cm. Lvs to 35cm, triangular-lanceolate, dentate, base truncate to cordate at base, petiolate, densely white-tomentose. Cap. few, in a compact, term. corymb; flts violet-blue. Alps, Carpath., Apennines. Z4.
S. elegans Ledeb. To 60cm, slender. Lvs scabrid above, white wispy-pubesc. to tomentose beneath, lower lvs to 30cm, lyrate-pinnatifid or dentate, upper lvs smaller, oblong, subentire, acute, base tapered. Cap. many or numerous, in corymbs; flts pink. Summer. Cauc.
S. gossypiphora D. Don. Globose cushion forming, to 30cm, v. densely white- to yellow-lanate. St. clothed at base with shiny black lf bases. Lvs to 15cm, linear, remotely toothed or runcinate-pinnatifid, sessile, usually glab. above, glab. or lanate beneath. Cap. many, in a dense cylindric cluster to 2.5cm long; flts purple. Summer. Himal.
S. japonica (Thunb.) DC. To 150cm, minutely glandular-pubesc. Lvs to 35cm, oblong, usually pinnatifid, rarely entire, tapered to both ends, long-petiolate, lobes in c8 pairs, term. lobes oblong-lanceolate, obtuse, usually pinnately lobed, minutely glandular-pubesc., st. lvs gradually reduced upwards. Cap. many, in a corymbose pan.; flts purple. Summer–autumn. S & SE Jap., Korea and China.
S. lappa (Decne.) Schultz-Bip. = *S. costus.*
S. nuda var. *densa* Hook. = *S. densa.*
S. pulchella Fisch. ex DC. To 150cm, minutely pubesc. Lvs to 20cm, oblong to narrowly oblong or elliptic, pinnatipartite, petiolate, seg. in 6–10 pairs, lanceolate, minutely pubesc., densely glandular-punctate beneath. Cap. many, in a dense cluster; flts purple. Summer–autumn. Jap. to N Manch. and E Sib. Z3.
S. pygmaea (Jacq.) Spreng. To 15cm. Lvs to 20cm, linear to linear-lanceolate, entire or rarely obscurely dentate, sessile, pilose. Cap. solitary and term.; flts pink to purple. Summer. E Eur. to Sib. Z3.
S. stella Maxim. St. 0. Lvs to 20cm, rosulate, linear, entire, apex attenuate from an expanded ovate base, deep green, glab., leathery inner lvs tinged mauve or maroon at base. Cap. few to many, in a lax or dense cluster; flts purple; anth. blue. Himal.
S. triptera Maxim. To 55cm, st. winged, minutely pubesc. Basal lvs to 12cm, ovate or ovate-oblong, base cordate or truncate, acuminate- or dentate-mucronate to undulate-lobulate, lobes dilated above, apex rounded, crisped-pubesc., upper st. lvs shortly winged-petiolate, or sessile and decurrent. Cap. 7–24, in corymbs; flts purple. Summer. Jap.
S. veitchiana Drumm. & Hutch. To 50cm, woolly above. Basal lvs to 25cm, many, narrowly oblong-lanceolate, ± entire, st. lvs narrower, uppermost lvs much smaller, ovate-lanceolate, undulate, finely dentate, dilated at base; grading into pink- or purple-tinged scales. Cap. solitary or few in a lax cluster; flts deep purple. C China.
S. wernerioides Schultz-Bip. Cushion forming, to 3cm. Lvs to 2cm, densely imbricate, erect or somewhat spreading, lanceolate, base attenuate to a sheathing petiole, tip subulate, margins revolute often to midrib, dentate, leathery, glab. and glossy above, densely tomentose beneath. Cap. solitary, sessile; flts pale pink to purple. Himal. (Sikkim–Tibet frontier).
S. yakla C.B. Clarke. St. 0. Lvs to 30cm, linear-oblong, pinnate or pinnatifid, lobes or seg. broadly ovate or subdeltoid, sinuate-dentate, apex and teeth dentate, membranous, minutely pubesc. above, white-tomentose beneath. Cap. 1–3, sessile; flts usually purple. Sikkim.
→*Jurinea.*

Savana Calabash *Amphitecna latifolia.*
Savin *Juniperus sabina.*
Savory *Micromeria juliana; Satureja.*
Sawara Cypress *Chamaecyparis pisifera.*
Saw Banksia *Banksia serrata.*
Saw Cabbage Palm *Acoelorraphe.*
Sawfly Orchid *Ophrys tenthredinifera.*
Saw-leaved Holly *Ilex aquifolium* 'Crassifolia'.
Saw-leaf Zelkova *Zelkova serrata.*
Saw Palmetto *Serenoa repens.*
Sawthorn Oak *Quercus acutissima.*
Sawwort *Serratula tinctoria.*

Saxegothaea Lindl. Podocarpaceae. 1 yew-like coniferous everg. tree or shrub to 20m. Bark brown suffused grey, exfoliating; br. in whorls of 3–5, tips often pendulous. Lvs spirally arranged on long shoots, in 2 ranks on lateral br., linear to linear-lanceolate, 15–30×2–3mm, coriaceous, dark green, twisted stomatal bands blue-white below, midrib conspicuous, apex spined. Cones to

10×5mm; fertile scales fleshy, thickened, outcurved, blue-grey to glaucous brown. Chilean Andes, Patagonia. Z8.

S. **conspicua** Lindl. PRINCE ALBERT'S YEW.

Saxifraga L. SAXIFRAGE. Saxifragaceae. *c*370 ann. to perenn. herbs, everg. or decid., tall and leafy-stemmed to mat and cushion-forming. Lvs rosulate to alt., entire, dentate or lobed, some with lime-secreting hydathodes, thus ± chalk-encrusted. Fls in cymes, rac., pan. or solitary, generally actinomorphic; sep. 4 or 5, forming a shallow cup; pet. 4 or 5, alternating with sep., overlapping; sta. usually 10. Eur., Asia, N Amer., S Amer. Andes. Those described below are perenn. and everg. unless otherwise stated.

S. **aconitifolia** (Nutt.) Fielding & Gardn. = *Boykinia aconitifolia*.

S. **adenophora** K. Koch = *S. exarata*.

S. **affinis** D. Don = *S. rosacea*.

S. **aizoides** L. YELLOW MOUNTAIN SAXIFRAGE; YELLOW SAXIFRAGE. St. 7–20cm, branched, forming loose cushions. Lvs 4–22mm, linear to oblong, fleshy, ciliate, hydathodes usually 1, chalky crust slight. Flowering st. densely hairy; fls in short cymes of 2–15; pet. 3–7mm, yellow, often spotted orange, sometimes orange or brick red. Iceland, Scand., N Britain, Alps, Apennines. var. **atrorubens** (Bertol) Sternb. Fls dark red. Z5.

S. **aizoon** Jacq. = *S. paniculata*.

S. **ajugifolia** L. = *S. pedemontana*.

S. **alberti** hort. = *S.* ×*apiculata*.

S. **allionsii** Gaudich. = *S. exarata*.

S. ×**amabilis** Stapf = *S.* ×*bertolonii*.

S. **amplexifolia** Sternb. = *Leptarrhena pyrolifolia*.

S. **ampullacea** Ten. = *S. exarata*.

S. **andersonii** Engl. Cushion-forming. Lvs 5–10mm, spathulate, tips erect or recurved, hydathodes 5. Infl. branched, fls in whorls of 4–6; pet. to 6mm, white or pink. Sikkim, Nepal, Bhutan, Tibet.

S. ×**andrewsii** Harv. (Probably *S. paniculata* ×*S. spathularis?*) Compact perenn. to 12cm. Lvs linear, dentate. Flowering st. to 25cm, red; pet. white with red spots. Z3.

S. ×**anglica** Horńy, Soják & Webr. (*S. aretoides* ×*S. lilacina* ×*S. media.*) Cushion-forming perenn. Lvs dark green, linear. Peduncle short; fls 6mm wide, deep rose pink. Spring. 'Aubrey Prichard': small, compact cushion with tight glaucous-green rosettes; fls pale carmine-pink. 'Beatrix Stanley': fls violet. 'Beryl': fls rich pink-lilac. 'Brenda Prichard': fls bright rose. 'Christine': cushion small, with groups of firm rosettes; pet. bright cerise in bud, later dull pink. 'Cranbourne': lvs dark green; fls purple-violet. 'Delight': slow-growing, cushions small, compact; lvs dark green; fls large, soft pink, on short st. 'Desire': lvs bright green, st. short; fls pink. 'Elysium': dwarf, cushions small, domed; rosettes silvery; fls star-like, soft rose-pink. 'Felicity': cushions dense, silvery; pet. rich rose-carmine. 'Grace Farewell': cushions small, dense, slightly domed; pet. rich wine-red with violet venation. 'Jan Amos Komensky': dwarf, cushions small, slightly domed; rosettes flat; pet. dark purple fading to pale pink-lilac. 'Jan Hus': dwarf, cushions small, domed; fls cupular; pet. red-purple. 'Myra': cushions small, dividing into groups of rosettes; fls pale red-lilac or deep pink. 'Myra Cambria': cushions firm, domed; pet. large, deep cherry-red. 'Pearl Rose': cushions slow-growing, compact; pet. soft lilac-pink. 'Prichard's Glorious': fls bright ruby-red. 'Priory Jewel': cushions small, compact, glaucous; pet. deep pink. 'Quarry Wood': cushions small, tight, slightly domed; pet. pink-lilac. 'Sparkling': cushions v. small, low; rosettes closed; pet. deep rose. 'Winifred': cushions flat to slightly domed; pet. v. deep purple-violet. Z6.

S. ×**apiculata** Engl. (*S. marginata* ×*S. sancta.*) Cushion-forming, to 10cm. Lvs to 12mm, linear-lanceolate, with slight encrustation in tight rosettes. Infl. a 10–12-fld cyme; fls to 8mm diam., yellow. Spring. 'Alba': fls white. 'Albert Einstein': v. hardy, vigorous; lvs dark green. 'Gregor Mendel': lvs glossy pale green; fls pale yellow. 'Primrose Bee': rosettes open, flat; lvs glossy pale green; fls large pale yellow. 'Spartakus': vigorous, rosettes spiny; lvs dark conspicuously crusted. Z6.

S. **aquatica** Bieb. = *S. irrigua*.

S. **arachnoidea** Sternb. Perenn., densely glandular-arachnoid. Lvs to 2cm, fan-shaped to elliptic, apically divided into 3–5 ovate lobes, petioles to 1cm. Flowering st. 10–20cm; fls to 5 in a lax cyme; pet. 2.5–3mm, cream. It. Alps. Z7.

S. ×**arco-valleyi** Sünderm. (*S. lilacina* ×*S. marginata.*) Forming small domed cushions. Lvs oblong to obovate in dense rosettes to 11mm diam., silver-grey. Fls usually solitary on st. to 25mm, pale pink to bright red. 'Arco': lvs grey; fls pale pink. 'Dainty Dame': lvs narrow; fls bright rose lilac fading to white flushed pink. 'Hocker Edge': fls pale lilac. 'Ophelia': fls white. 'Sara Sinclair': fls deep pink-lilac. 'Silver Edge': lvs grey-green edged white; fls pale lilac. Z6.

S. **arenarioides** Brign. = *S. tenella*.

S. ×**arendsii** Engl. (*S. exarata* ×*S. rosacea* and other sp.) Similar to *S. caespitosa*. Lvs to 5cm, slightly thickened. Flowering st. to 20cm, gland. pilose; pan. cymose; pet. 10mm, purple to rose. Z6.

S. ×**aretiastrum** Engl. & Irmsch. = *S.* ×*boydii*.

S. **aretioides** Lapeyr. Like *S. ferdinandi-coburgi* but lvs shorter and wider, often obtuse, mucronate tips straight, cymes flatter-topped, pet. narrower. Z6.

S. **aspera** L. ROUGH SAXIFRAGE; STIFF-HAIRED SAXIFRAGE. Rosettes compact, in mats. Leafy shoots prostrate, lvs 5–8mm, narrow, entire, margins hairy. Flowering st. 7–22cm, leafy; fls 2–7 on long pedicels; pet. 5–7mm, white or pale cream, often with a deep yellow zone at base and spotted yellow, orange or crimson. Alps, Apennines. Z6.

S. **aspera** ssp. **bryoides** (L.) Engl. & Irmsch. = *S. bryoides*.

S. **atrorubens** Bertol. = *S. aizoides*.

S. **aurea** Steud. = *Chrysosplenium oppositifolium*.

S. **australis** Moric. = *S. callosa*.

S. **autumnalis** Jacq. = *S. aizoides*.

S. **baborensis** Battand. = *S. cymbalaria*.

S. **baumgartenii** Schott. = *S. retusa*.

S. ×**bertolonii** Sünderm. (*S. sempervivum* ×*S. stribrnyi.*) Cushion-forming to 8cm. Rosette lvs oblanceolate, st. lvs spathulate, obtuse and hirsute. Rac. short, nodding; pet. deep pink. 'Amabile': fls carmine. 'Antonio': fls dark violet-purple to red-purple. 'Berenika': fls large, light violet-purple edged pink. 'Samo': lvs deep purple beneath; fls violet-rose. Z6.

S. ×**biasolettii** Sünderm. (*S. federici-augusti* ×*S. sempervivum.*) Robust vigorously spreading. Lvs silvery, narrow-spathulate, acute. Infl. racemose on st. to 20cm., pet. crimson. 'Crystalie': pet. rose. 'Feuerkopf': pet. deep pink. Z6.

S. **biflora** All. Shoots woody-based, hairy forming loose cushions. Lvs 5–9mm, opposite, obovate to suborbicular, tapered to petiole, fleshy, entire, rounded apex, ciliate, hydathodes 1(3–5), chalk crust usually 0. Fls at ends of shoots resembling leafy shoots, 2–3 per shoot; pet. 5–10mm, dull purple or white, disc yellow. Alps. var. **kochii** Kittel. Pet. to 9mm. 'Alba': fls white. Z6.

S. **biternata** Boiss. Glandular-hairy. St. sprawling or prostrate, woody below; leafy shoots to 15cm. Lvs to 4cm, deeply 3-lobed, primary lobes 3-lobed. Flowering st. to 10cm; fls 2–6, funnel-form to campanulate; pet. 1.2–2cm, white veined green. S Spain. Z7.

S. **blepharophylla** Hayek = *S. oppositifolia*.

S. **blepharophylla** A. Kerner ex Hayek = *S. oppositifolia* ssp. *blepharophylla*.

S. ×**borisii** Kellerer ex Sünderm. (*S. ferdinandi-coburgi* ×*S. marginata.*) Cushion-forming, to 8cm high. Lvs to 10mm, linear, grey-green. Infl. a red-tinted cyme; fls to 20mm diam., pale yellow. 'Alderbaran': cushions small to large; fls large, cupular to flat. 'Becky Foster': cushions small, packed, dark green. 'Blanca': fls white. 'Claudia': cushions packed, matt green. 'Josef Manes': cushions closely packed; fls deep bright yellow, long-lasting. 'Marianna': cushions small, tight, domed; fls large, v. long-lasting. 'Marie Stivinova': large, robust; fls warm yellow. 'Mona Lisa': cushions dense, hard; rosettes, almost hemispherical, glossy green; pet. delicate, bright yellow. 'Vincent Van Gogh': cushions dense; dark green; fls rich yellow. Z6.

S. **boryi** Boiss. & Heldr. = *S. marginata*.

S. ×**boydii** Dewar. (*S. aretoides* ×*S. burseriana.*) Low-growing, forming tight cushions, to 8cm. Lvs linear to lanceolate, silver-green. Cyme irregular, loose, 1–4-fld; fls to 25mm diam., vivid yellow. Spring. 'Aretiastrum': cushions small, dense; fls deep sulphur-yellow, long-lasting. 'Cherry trees': cushions small, compact; fls pale yellow. 'Cleo': fls clear white, long-lasting. 'Corona': vigorous; fls large, pale yellow. 'Faldonside': cushions small, domed; fls strong yellow. 'Friar Tuck': fls pale yellow becoming white. 'Hindhead Seedling': fls light yellow. 'Kelso': dwarf; rosettes closed; fls light yellow. 'Nottingham Gold': vigorous; fls large, circular, long-lasting, bright light yellow. 'Old Britain': lvs dark grey-green; fls dark yellow. 'White Cap': fls white. Z6.

S. **brunoniana** Wallich nom. nud. = *S. brunonis*.

S. **brunonis** Wallich ex Ser. Decid. mat-forming perenn. herb with thread-like, red runners. Lvs in small rosettes. Flowering st. to 15cm; infl. a pan.; pet. yellow. Summer. Himal. Z7.

S. **bryoides** L. MOSSY SAXIFRAGE. Forming dense mats of spherical lf rosettes. Lvs 3.5–5mm, oblong-lanceolate, mucronate, margins translucent, hairy. Flowering st. 2–5cm; fls solitary; pet. 5–7mm, white spotted orange, with orange patch at base. Eur. mts. Z6.

S. ×**burnatii** Sünderm. (*S. cochlearis* ×*S. paniculata.*) To 15cm, rosette-forming. Lvs lanceolate to obovate, silver-green. Pan. lax, tinged red; fls white, to 1.5cm diam. 'Esther': fls yellow. Z5.

S. **burseriana** L. BURSER'S SAXIFRAGE. St. numerous, woody at base, forming dense cushions. Lvs 6–12mm, suberect, packed in low cones, narrow-lanceolate, margin translucent, silver-grey, hydathodes 5–7, chalk crust thin. Flowering st. 2.5–5cm, crimson, glandular-hairy; fls solitary; pet. 7–12mm, spreading white. Early summer. E Alps. 'Crenata': smaller; pet. crenate. 'Gloria': st. brilliant red; fls large, white with deep yellow centres. 'His Majesty': rosettes silver-grey; fls large, rounded, pink, flushed white. 'Major': fl. st. green; fls large, white. 'Prince Hal': fl. st. salmon-pink; fls large, white. 'Speciosa': fl. st. red; fls large, white. Z6.

S. ×*bursiculata* E.H. Jenkins. (*S. burseriana* ×*S. marginata* ×*S. sancta.*) Flowering st. to 7cm. Lvs glaucous, oblong. Corymb 4-fld, pet. 10mm, white. Gdn origin (1911). Z6.

S. caerulea Pers. = *S. oppositifolia.*

S. caesia L. BLUE GREEN SAXIFRAGE. Leafy shoots crowded, forming low cushions. Lvs 4mm, alt., oblong-spathulate, pale, upper part curved, bluntly keeled beneath, hydathodes 7, chalk crust thick. Flowering st. 4–12cm; pet. 4–6mm, white. SC Eur. 'St. John': rosettes dense, silver; fls white. Z5.

S. caesia var. *squarrosa* (Sieber) Gortani = *S. squarrosa.*

S. '**Calabrica**'. TUMBLING WATERS. (*S. callosa* ×*S. longifolia.*) Lvs ligulate, silver, in rosettes. Infl. a lax cylindrical pan. to 80cm; fls white. Gdn origin (1919). Z7.

S. calabrica hort. = *S.* 'Calabrica'.

S. callosa Sm. LIMESTONE SAXIFRAGE. Lf rosettes to 16cm diam. Lvs 4–7cm, linear, glaucous, grooved above, hydathodes many, chalk crust slight to moderate. Flowering st. to 40cm; pan. many-fld, covering more than half st.; pet. 6–12mm, white. NE Spain, SW Alps, Apennines. 'Alberti': rosettes silver; fls white. 'Leichtlinii': fls rose-red. 'Rosea': fls rose-red. 'Superba': fls large, in arching, plume-like infl.; cream-white. var. *australis* (Moric.) D.A. Webb. Lvs oblanceolate, tip diamond-shaped. Includes plants usually grown as var. *lantoscana.* ssp. *callosa* var. *callosa.* Lvs linear, not expanded at tip. ssp. *callosa* var. *australis* (Moric.) D.A. Webb. Lvs oblanceolate or linear tip expanded. ssp. *catalaunica* (Boiss. & Reut.) D.A. Webb. Infl. glandular-hairy. Z7.

S. calyciflora Lapeyr. = *S. media.*

S. canaliculata Boiss. & Reut. ex Engl. Gland. St. branched, forming loose cushions. Lvs 12mm, fan-shaped, seg. 3–11, channelled. Flowering st. 8–15cm; fls 5–12 in a compact cyme; pet. 8–10mm, white. N Spain. Z7.

S. canis-dalmatica misapplied. = *S.* ×*gaudinii.*

S. cartilaginea Willd. = *S. paniculata.*

S. castellana Reut. nom. nud. = *S. granulata.*

S. catalaunica Boiss. & Reut. = *S. callosa.*

S. caucasica Somm. & Levier. Differs from *S. juniperifolia* in lvs to 3cm, infl. glab.; fls solitary. Cauc. Z5.

S. cebennensis Rouy & Camus. Leafy shoots many, forming a cushion. Lvs 6mm, 3–5-lobed, lobes furrowed, pale green, short glandular-hairy, petiole as long as lamina. Flowering st. 5–8cm, glandular-hairy, fls 2–3; pet. 6–8mm, white. S Fr. Z7.

S. ceratophylla Dryand. = *S. trifurcata.*

S. cespitosa auct. non L. = *S. exarata.*

S. chlorantha Schur = *S. corymbosa.*

S. chrysosplenifolia Boiss. = *S. rotundifolia.*

S. clusii Gouan. Rhizomatous. Lvs in basal rosettes, 4–12cm, oblanceolate to elliptic, coarsely toothed, thin, hairy. Flowering st. to 40cm, hairy, branched; lower bracts leaflike; fls paniculate, slender-stalked sometimes replaced by leafy buds; pet. to 7mm, base spotted mustard-yellow. SW Eur. ssp. *clusii.* Flowering st. sparsely hairy; infl. without leafy buds. ssp. *lepismegena* D.A. Webb. Flowering st. thickly hairy; fls replaced by leafy buds expanded into small rosettes. Z7.

S. cochlearis Rchb. Lf rosettes numerous, 1.5–8cm diam., forming a dense cushion. Lvs to 4.5cm, spathulate to oblanceolate, fleshy, subcoriaceous, glaucous, hydathodes numerous, chalk crust marked. Infl. glandular-hairy; flowering st. 5–30cm, branched; fls many; pet. 7–11mm, white, sometimes spotted red. Maritime Alps. 'Major': fls larger. 'Minor': tight silvery hummocks. Z6.

S. compacta Sternb. = *S. valdensis.*

S. conifera Coss. & Durieu. Leafy shoots 1–4cm, forming a dense mat. Lvs 3–10mm, linear-lanceolate, pale silvery green, ciliate; buds summer-dormant. Flowering st. 4–8cm; fls 3–7 in compact pan.; pet. 3–4mm, white. N Spain. Z6.

S. coriophylla Griseb. = *S. marginata.*

S. corsica (Ser.) Gren. & Godron. Differs from *S. granulata* in basal lvs deeply 3-lobed, flowering st. strongly branched from base. Corsica & Sardinia. ssp. *cossoniana* (Boiss. & Reut.) D.A. Webb. More robust; basal lvs more deeply 3-lobed.

S. cortusifolia Sieb. & Zucc. Decid. perenn. herb similar to *S. stolonifera* but without runners. Lvs glossy, round, fleshy. Flowering st. to 40cm, fls white; upper pet. 3, to 4mm, spotted, lower 2 pet. longer. Jap. Z7.

S. corymbosa Boiss. St. sparingly branched, forming dense cush-

ions. Lvs in flattened rosettes, 7–22mm, oblong-oblanceolate, acute to mucronate, glaucous, tinged pink at base, margins translucent, hydathodes 9–15, chalk crust becoming heavy. Infl. glandular-hairy; flowering st. 3–8cm; cyme crowded; pet. 3mm, pale green-yellow. Mts of SW Eur. Z6.

S. cossoniona Boiss. & Reut. = *S. corsica* ssp. *cossoniona.*

S. cotyledon L. GREAT ALPINE ROCKFOIL; GREATER EVERGREEN SAXIFRAGE. Lf rosettes 7–12cm diam. with daughter-rosettes on short runners. Basal lvs 2–8cm, oblong to oblanceolate, hydathodes in centre of fine marginal teeth, chalk crust marked. Flowering st. to 70cm, pan. pyramidal to 25cm wide at base, glandular-hairy; fls 8–40 per br.; pet. 7–10mm, white, sometimes spotted or veined red. Scand. and Iceland, Pyren., Alps. 'Caterhamensis': to 90cm; fls white spotted red. 'Icelandica': to 105cm; rosettes large, flat; lvs bronze, coriaceous. 'Montavonensis': dwarf. 'Norvegica': lvs spathulate; infl. with numerous side shoots; fls pure white. 'Pyramidalis': branching from base; lvs long and narrow. 'Southside Seedling': fls red, spotted and edged with white. Z6.

S. crocea Gaudin = *S. aizoides.*

S. crustacea Hoppe = *S. crustata.*

S. crustata Vest Rosettes 2.5–8cm diam., forming thick cushions. Lvs 10–25mm, linear, obtuse, entire or obscurely crenate, decurved, hydathodes numerous, sunk in margin, chalk crust heavy. Flowering st. 12–35cm, glandular-hairy; fls in pan., 1–3 ending each branchlet; pet. 5–6mm, white, rarely spotted red. E Alps, N & C Balk. Z6.

S. cultrata Schott = *S. paniculata.*

S. cuneata Willd. St. branching, covered with dead lvs, forming loose tufts. Lvs to 22mm, rhombic to fan-shaped, stiff and leathery, lobes 3, often further divided. Flowering st. 7–30cm; fls 7–15 in a narrow pan.; pet. 5–8mm, pure white. N Spain. Z6.

S. cuneifolia L. SHIELD-LEAVED SAXIFRAGE. St. prostrate, lf rosettes compact at intervals. Lvs 0.8–2.5cm, ovate to orbicular, often truncate, fleshy, coriaceous, red-purple beneath, toothed to subentire; petiole flat. Flowering st. 10–25cm, forming a pan. of (3–)12(–20) fls; pet. *c*3.5mm, white, often with yellow basal patch and sometimes red spots. Mts of S & SC Eur. 'Variegata': lvs variegated cream-white. 'Infundibuliformis': lvs spathulate. var. *capillipes* Rchb. Lvs to 2cm including petiole, subentire; pan. to 10-fld. ssp. *robusta* D.A. Webb. Compact; lvs to 2.5cm including petiole, crenate-serrate; flowering st. stout; pan. to 10-fld. Z6.

S. cuneifolia Cav. non L. = *S. cuneata.*

S. cuscutiformis Lodd. DODDER-LIKE SAXIFRAGE. Resembles *S. stolonifera* but smaller. Stolons long, red. Lvs round, bronze, fleshy, netted white. Pan. to 10cm, pet. white spotted yellow and red. China. Z5.

S. cymbalaria L. Ann. or bienn. glab. or sparsely glandular-hairy. Lvs mostly alt., 22mm, reniform to circular, 5–9-lobed, bright shinging green; petiole to 35mm. Flowering st. 10–15cm, branched, leafy; cymes lax 2–6-fld.; pet. 4.5–6mm, dull orange yellow, bright yellow toward tip. Cauc. var. *huetiana* (Boiss.) Engl. & Irmsch. Lvs sometimes opposite, 5–7-lobed or subentire. Z6.

S. cymbalaria Sibth. & Sm. non L. = *S. sibthorpii.*

S. cymosa Waldst. & Kit. = *S. pedemontana.*

S. decipiens J.F. Ehrh. = *S. rosacea.*

S. decipiens ssp. *boreali-atlantica* Engl. & Irmsch. = *S. hypnoides.*

S. demissa Schott & Kotschy = *S. mutata.*

S. diapensioides Bellardi. Forming dense hard cushions. Lvs 3–5mm, alt., oblong, thick, glaucous, obtuse or mucronate, margin translucent, base tinged red, hydathodes 5, chalk crust heavy, dead lvs persistent. Flowering st. 3–8cm, glandular-hairy; cymes flat-topped; pet. 7–9mm, white. W Alps. 'Lutea': fls yellow. Z6.

S. diversifolia Wallich. Mat-forming. Lvs 3cm, oval, long-petiolate, or sessile on st. Flowering st. to 20cm, branched; fls 2cm diam., golden to dull yellow. Himal. Z6.

S. '**Dr. Ramsay**'. (*S. longifolia* ×*S. cochlearis.*) Rosette-forming. Lvs spathulate, silver. Pan. to 20cm; fls white. Summer. Z6.

S. ×*edithae* Sünderm. (*S. marginata* ×*S. stribrnyi.*) Lvs 6mm, spathulate-cuneate, shiny green, purple below glandular-pubesc. Infl. a corymb; pet. to 5mm, rose or white. Spring. Gdn origin. 'Arabella': lvs large, flat; fls small, deep pink. 'Karel Stivin': lvs wide; infl. short, compact, deep purple. Z6.

S. ×*edwardsii* Engl. (*S. exarata* ×*S. rosacea* ×*S. granulata.*) Mat-forming perenn. herb with bulbils. Infl. 1–2-fld; sep. purple; pet. 20mm, white. Z6.

S. elegans Mackay = *S. hirsuta.*

S. ×*elegantissima* Engl. & Irmsch. (*S. exarata* ×*S. rosacea.*) Forming loose mats. Lvs 3–5-lobed. Flowering st. to 20cm, sub-erect; fls. 1–2, purple. Z6.

S. ×*elizabethae* Sünderm. (*S. burseriana* ×*S. sancta.*) Cushion-forming. Lvs to 5mm, lanceolate, spiny, blue-green. Fls 1–2 on red peduncles, to 6mm diam., yellow. Spring. Gdn origin. 'Boston Spa': lvs dark glossy green; fls bright yellow. 'Brno': infl. tall; fls pale yellow. 'Icicle': cushions small, tight; fls white veined green. 'Lorelei': cushions dense; fls white. 'Millstream Cream': fls yellow-cream. 'Mrs Leng': cushions growing into mats; fls pale yellow. 'Primrose Dame': rosettes robust; lvs wide, stiff, green; fls pale yellow. Z6.

S. elongella Sm. = *S. hypnoides.*

S. ✕*engleri* Huter. (*S. crustata* ✕ *S. hostiana.*) Rosette-forming perenn. herb. Lvs linear, silvery. Infl. 8-branched; fls whte. C Eur. Z6.

S. eschscholtzii Sternb. Forming rounded cushions. Lvs 1–3mm, oblong to obovate, overlapping, bristle-fringed. Flowering st. to 1cm, naked; fls yellow or white. Yukon, Alask. to E Sib. Z3.

S. ✕*eudoxiana* Kellerer & Sünderm. (*S. ferdinandi-coburgi* ✕ *S. sancta.*) Forming tight cushions, 10cm. Lvs to 12mm, linear, dark green, spiny, cyme globose; pet. yellow. Spring. 'Eudoxia': cushions tight, domed; pet. light yellow. 'Gold Dust': fast growing; pet. solid yellow. 'Haagii': cushions extending as large mats; pet. warm yellow. Z3.

S. exarata Vill. FURROWED SAXIFRAGE. Leafy shoots to 4cm, erect, forming a compact cushion. Lvs 4–20mm, glandular-hairy, or glab., 3–5-lobed. Flowering st. 3–10cm, branched above; pet. 2.5–6mm, white to dull green-yellow, occas. tinged red. Mts of C & S Eur., Cauc., NW Iran. ssp. *exarata.* Lf lobes widely divergent, furrowed. Fls pale cream. ssp. *moschata* (Wulf.) Cav. Lf seg. not furrowed. Fls yellow-cream, sometimes tinged red. Z6.

S. exarata var. *intricata* (Lapeyr.) Engl. = *S. intricata.*

S. 'Faldonside' = *S.* ✕ *boydii.*

S. federici-augusti Biasol. Like *S. sempervivum* but lvs 12–35mm, always widened above, hydathodes to 25, chalk crust often heavy; infl. leafy, simple, erect, bright red to dark purple-red, pet. concealed by sep. Balk. Penins. 'Wisley': more vigorous and brightly coloured. ssp. *federici-augusti.* Rosette lvs to 18mm, gradually widened at tip; infl. dark purple-red. ssp. *grisebachii* (Degen & Dörfl.) D.A. Webb. Rosette lvs to 35mm, abruptly widened at tip; infl. crimson to cherry red. Z7.

S. ferdinandi-coburgi Kellerer & Sünderm. Leafy shoots crowded, forming dense irregular cushions. Lvs 4–8mm, alt., oblong-lanceolate, tips mucronate turned inwards, entire and glab. except for hairs at base, hydathodes 5–13, chalk crust thick. Flowering st. 3–12cm, tinged red, glandular-hairy, leafy; fls 3–5; sep. red, gland.; pet. 5–8mm, bright yellow. E Macedonia. 'Drakula': rosette lvs narrow; fls large. 'Radoslavoffii': more vigorous, fls large. 'Pravislawii': fls golden, many. Z6.

S. ferruginea Graham. Short-lived perenn., red-hirsute. Basal lvs 1.5–5cm, toothed, spathulate. Flowering st. to 30cm, fls in a diffuse pan., occas. replaced by bulbils; upper 3 pet. clawed with 2 yellow spots, lower 2 not clawed, unspotted. Summer. Alask. to Mont. Z4.

S. flagellaris Willd. in Sternb. Decid., spreading by long slender, runners. Lvs mainly in basal rosette, 7–16mm, oblong-lanceolate, ciliate. Flowering st. to 10cm, red glandular-hairy; fls 1(–2–4); pet 6–10mm, bright yellow. Summer. Circumpolar arctic. Z1.

S. florulenta Moretti. Monocarpic. Rosettes dense. Basal lvs 3–6cm, broader above, tip spinose, margin translucent, hairy at base, dull dark green, hydathodes few, chalk crust 0. Flowering st. 10–25cm, stout; pan. cylindrical; pet. 5–7mm, flesh-pink. Maritime Alps. Z7.

S. fortunei Hook. f. Lvs basal large, glossy, fleshy, round, obscurely toothed, brown-red beneath, slender-stalked. Flowering st. to 50cm; infl. in a pan., fls to 12mm on drooping red st.; pet. white, lanceolate or linear, lower 2 pet. longer than upper, deflexed. Late autumn. Jap. Z7.

S. ✕*gaudinii* Brügger (*S. cotyledon* ✕ *S. paniculata.*) Low-growing perenn. herb to 15cm. Lvs strap-shaped to spathulate, coriaceous. Fls white, flecked purple.

S. geoides Lacaita = *S. hirsuta.*

S. geranioides L. Forming loose cushions. Lvs 15mm, light green, semicircular, tribobed, lobes divided and toothed, seg. 17–25, glandular-hairy, appearing warty. Flowering st. 15–25cm, usually branched; fls to 20; pet. 12mm, white. E Pyren. Z7.

S. geranioides var. *irrigua* (Bieb.) Ser. non Willk. = *S. irrigua.*

S. geranioides var. *irrigua* Willk. non (Bieb.) Ser. = *S. latepetiolata.*

S. ✕*geum* L. (*S. hirsuta* ✕ *S. umbrosa.*) Lvs reniform, crenulate; petioles far exceeding blades. Pan. loose. Z3.

S. geum L. (1762), non L. (1753). = *S. hirsuta* ssp. *hirsuta.*

S. gibraltarica Boiss. & Reut. = *S. globulifera.*

S. ✕*gigantea* Kotek = *S.* ✕ *apiculata.*

S. glauca Clairv. = *S. diapensioides.*

S. glaucescens Boiss. & Reut. = *S. granulata.*

S. globulifera Desf. Leafy st. 4–8cm, ± erect, branched, forming large cushions. Lvs to 8mm, semicircular, deeply 5-lobed, glandular-hairy. Summer-dormant buds numerous. Flowering st. 5–15cm; pet. 5–7mm, white. S Spain, N Afr. var. *oranensis* (Munby) Engl. Summer-dormant buds on long stalks. Z7.

S. granatensis Boiss. & Reut. = *S. globulifera.*

S. granulata L. MEADOW SAXIFRAGE; BULBOUS SAXIFRAGE; FAIR MAIDS OF FRANCE. Rosette-forming, bulbiliferous. Basal lvs 0.6–2cm, reniform, cordate or toothed, glandular-hairy, slightly fleshy, petiole to 0.5cm. Flowering st. 10–30cm, branched to form compact pan.; pet. 7–16mm, white, sometimes red-veined. Eur. ssp. *granulata.* Basal lvs to 1.2cm wide. Infl. br. stout; pet. 12mm. 'Flore Pleno': fls sterile with many pet. ssp. *graniticola* D.A. Webb. Lvs smaller, flowering st. to 25cm. Z5.

S. granulata ssp. *russii* Engl. & Irmsch. not *S. russii* of Presl = *S. corsica.*

S. granulata var. *corsica* Ser. in Duby = *S. corsica.*

S. granulata var. *gracilis* Lange pro parte = *S. granulata* ssp. *graniticola.*

S. grisebachii (Degen & Dörfl.) D.A. Webb = *S. federici-augusti* ssp. *grisebachii.*

S. groenlandica L. non Lapeyr. = *S. cespitosa.*

S. ✕*gusmusii* Sünderm. (*S. corymbosa* ✕ *S. sempervivum.*) Lvs 16mm, spathulate. Infl. a cyme or rac.; peduncle to 12cm; pet. pale orange-red. Z6.

S. ✕*haagii* Sünderm. = *S.* ✕ *eudoxiana.*

S. ✕*hadaceki* Kotek = *S.* ✕ *anglica.*

S. hedwigii hort. = *S.* ✕ *kelleri.*

S. heucherifolia Griseb. & Schenk = *S. rotundifolia.*

S. hibernica Haw. = *S. rosacea.*

S. hirsuta L. KIDNEY SAXIFRAGE. St. prostrate, sprawling. Lvs distinctly petiolate, semi-erect to horizontal, 1.5–4cm, reniform, orbicular to broad-elliptic, soft, purple-red beneath, shallow-crenate or toothed. Flowering st. 12–40cm, pan. narrow; pet. 3.5–4mm, white, usually with yellow basal patch and faint pink spots. SW Eur. and Ireland. ssp. *hirsuta.* Lvs narrower, to 1.5cm wide, base cordate. ssp. *paucicrenata* (Leresche ex Gillot) D.A. Webb. Smaller and more compact. Lvs densely hairy, base truncate. Z6.

S. hirta Sm. non Haw. = *S. rosacea.*

S. hookeri Engl. & Irmsch. Tufted, rhizomatous with numerous ascending st. Lvs to 30mm, linear-lanceolate, obtuse, entire. Flowering st. to 35cm; fls in lax corymb or solitary; pet. to 16mm, bright yellow with red spots. Himal., Tibet. Z7.

S. ✕*hornbrookii* Horný, Soják & Webr. (*S. lilacina* ✕ *S. stribrnyi.*) Forming silvery mounds to 5cm. Lvs oblong-spathulate, gland., cyme few-fld; pet. wine-red to violet-purple. 'Ariel': infl. 3 to 8-fld; fls wine-red. 'Delia': cushions small; lvs chalk-encrusted, often flushed purple beneath; fls deep violet-pink. 'Ellie Brinckerhoff': cushions dwarf; fls violet-purple. 'Romeo': robust, free-flowering, cushions tight; fls light violet-purple. Z6.

S. hostii Tausch. Lf rosettes, with long offsets. Lvs 3–10cm, oblong to broadly linear, finely toothed, glaucous, tip usually decurved, hydathodes numerous, chalk crust marked. Flowering st. 25–50cm, branched; pet. 4–8mm, white, often spotted purple-red. E Alps. Z6.

S. huetiana Boiss. = *S. cymbalaria.*

S. hypnoides L. MOSSY SAXIFRAGE. Leafy shoots 6–12cm, prostrate, forming loose mats. Lvs widely spaced, lanceolate, entire, sometimes 3-lobed. Flowering st. 5–20cm, branched above; pet. 7–10mm. NW Eur. 'Gemmifera': compact, summer buds formed. 'Kingii': lvs tinted red. 'Whitlavei': fls more profuse. Z6.

S. hypnoides All. non L. = *S. exarata.*

S. imbricata Lam. non Bertol. = *S. retusa.*

S. imbricata Bertol. non Lam. = *S. squarrosa.*

S. incrustata Vest = *S. crustata.*

S. intricata Lapeyr. Short glandular-hairy. Leafy shoots forming low cushions. Lvs 5–9mm, rigid, dark green, seg. (0–)3(–9), furrowed above, young lvs sometime interwoven. Flowering st. 7–10cm, usually branched; pet. 5–6mm, white. E & C Pyren. Z6.

S. iranica Bornm. Cushion-forming with thick leafy shoots. Lower lvs to 4mm, crowded, hirsute, somewhat fleshy, obovate, st. lvs linear-spathulate. Flowering st. to 2.5cm; corymb –4-fld; pet. 6mm, white to purple. Cauc., N Iran. Z6.

S. iratiana F.W. Schultz = *S. pubescens.*

S. irrigua Bieb. Forming compact tuft of short, erect, leafy shoots, glandular-hairy, slightly sticky. Basal lvs semicircular, 2.5–3cm, primary lobes 3, subdivided into 11–35 seg.; petiole 4–7cm, st. lvs few, petioles shorter, seg. longer and fewer. Flowering st. 10–20cm, term.; cymes 5–12-fld; pet. 12–16mm, translucent white. Crimea. Z6.

S. ✕*irvingiena* Engl. & Irmsch. = *S.* ✕ *petraschii.*

S. ✕*irvingii* ex May et al. (*S. burseriana* ✕ *S. lilacina.*) Carpeting, to 3cm. Lvs to 7mm, in rosettes, cuneate, grey-green. Fls to 2cm diam., stemless or on short peduncles, pink or lilac. Spring. Gdn origin. 'Gem': cushions small, v. tight; fls v. pale lilac-pink to white. 'His Majesty': fls white or tinted pink. 'Jenkinsiae': looser; pet. light pink. 'Lusanna': cushions small, v. tight; pet. light lilac-pink to white with lilac veins. 'Mother of Pearl': fls shell-pink to bright rose, nacreous. 'Mother Queen': cushions slow growing, tight; fls dark rose. 'Timmy Foster': pet. deep lilac-pink, often undulate. 'Walter Irving': cushions v. tight; fls pale lilac-pink. Z6.

S. ×*jenkinsae* hort. = S. ×*irvingii*.

S. *juniperifolia* Adams. St. freely branched below, columnar, forming dense cushions. Lvs many, long-persistent when dead, 9–13mm, linear to linear-lanceolate, tapered to a narrow point, margin translucent, toothed toward base, hydathodes often only 1, chalk crust 0. Flowering st. 3–6cm, thickly hairy; cymes 3–8-fld., oblong, short; pet. 5–6mm, bright yellow; sta. exceeding pet. Bulg. Z6.

S. *juniperifolia* ssp. *sancta* (Griseb.) D.A. Webb = S. *sancta*.

S. *juniperina* Bieb. = S. *juniperifolia*.

S. **'Kathleen Pinsent'**. (S. *callosa* ×S. *paniculata*.) Lvs spathulate, silvery, apex recurved. Infl. of rose-pink fls on 20cm peduncle. Gdn origin. Z6.

S. ×*kelleri* Sündern. (S. *burseriana* and S. *stribrnyi*.) Mound-forming to 15cm. Lvs 17mm, cuneate, grey-green. Fls 3, to 12mm diam., pink. Late winter. 'Johan Kellerer': cushions small, becoming loose and irregular, forming groups of rosettes; pet. deep pink-lilac. 'Kewensis': cushions dense; rosettes open, flat; pet. pale pink with deep pink centres and deep rose veins. 'Suendermannii': cushions small, dense; fls small, long-lasting, pale pink. Z6.

S. *kewensis* W. Irv. = S. ×*kelleri*.

S. ×*kochii* Hornung. (S. *biflora* ×S. *oppositifolia*.) Close to S. *oppositifolia* but fls much larger. Z6.

S. *kochii* Bluff, Nees & Schauer = S. *biflora*.

S. *kolenatiana* Reg. = S. *paniculata*.

S. *kyrilli* Kellerer ex Sündern. = S. ×*borisii*.

S. *lactiflora* Pugsley = S. *hirsuta*.

S. ×*landaueri* Sündern. ex Horný, Soják & Webr. (S. *burseriana* ×S. *marginata* ×S. *stribrnyi*.) Lvs to 2cm in robust, cushion-forming rosettes. Spathulate-linear, glaucous. Fls loosely cymose, light rose. 'Leonore': cushions loosely packed; lvs heavily chalk-encrusted; st. and st. lvs red-purple. 'Schleicheri': flowering st. shorter, slightly tinged red; fls few; pet. slightly darker rose. Z6.

S. *lantoscana* Boiss. & Reut. = S. *callosa* var. *australis*.

S. *lasiophylla* Schott = S. *rotundifolia*.

S. *latepetiolata* Willk. Lvs gland., in a domed hemispherical group to 6cm tall, 0.8–1.5cm, reniform to semicircular, divided into 5–7 oblong-cuneate lobes, sometimes further divided; petiole 1.5–5cm. Flowering st. 15–25cm, pan. narrow-pyramidal, 15–20cm; pet. 7–10mm, white. E Spain. Z7.

S. *leptophylla* D. Don = S. *hypnoides*.

S. *leucanthemifolia* Lapeyr. et auct., non Michx. = S. *clusii*.

S. *ligulata* ssp. *cochlearis* (Rchb.) Rouy & Camus = S. *cochlearis*.

S. *ligulata* var. *cochlearis* (Rchb.) Engl. = S. *cochlearis*.

S. *lilacina* Duthie. Rosettes minute, mat-forming. Lvs to 3mm, cuneate, down-turned, mid-green, silver-glaucous. Fls solitary, scapose; pet. 8–11mm, lavender, dark-centred. Spring. Himal. Z5.

S. *lingulata* Bellardi = S. *callosa*.

S. *lingulata* var. *crustata* (Vest) D. Don = S. *crustata*.

S. *longifolia* Lapeyr. PYRENEAN SAXIFRAGE. Monocarpic. Lvs 6–11cm, linear in a single broad rosette, acute, entire, fleshy, glaucous, pale green, hydathodes, numerous on margins, chalk crust heavy. Pan. cylindrical to 60×15cm, term. glandular-hairy; pet. 7mm, white, sometimes spotted red. Pyren. 'Magnifica': rosettes to 15cm diam.; pan. large. 'Walpole's Variety': smaller, blue-grey rosettes; fls in short white spikes. Z6.

S. *longifolia* var. *minor* Sternb. = S. *crustata*.

S. *losae* Sennen = S. *pentadactylis*.

S. ×*luteola* Engl. & Irmsch. = S. ×*boydii*.

S. *luteoviridis* Schott & Kotschy = S. *corymbosa*.

S. *lyallii* Engl. Lvs to 8cm, in rosettes, cuneate to spathulate, coarsely toothed. Pan. long, loose, cylindrical, few-fld; pet. to 5mm, white with 2 yellow spots. N Amer. (Rocky Mts). Z5.

S. *macedonica* Degen = S. *juniperifolia*.

S. ×*macnabiana* R. Lindsay. (S. *callosa* ×S. *cotyledon*.) Lvs broad, dark green. Infl. much-branched on st. to 50cm; fls numerous, white flecked-red. Gdn origin (1895). Z6.

S. *macropetala* A. Kerner = S. *biflora*.

S. *maderensis* D. Don. Cushion-formng. Lvs reniform, soft, divided into 5 lobes, these further subdivided; petiole exceeding lamina. Flowering st. to 15cm; fls in a 6–13-fld open cyme; pet. to 10mm, white. Madeira. Z7.

S. *malyi* hort. = S. ×*apiculata*.

S. *manschuriensis* (Engl.) Komar. To 10cm. Lvs to 7cm wide, reniform, radical, margin scalloped. Flowering st. to 35cm; fls closely aggregated in a cyme; pet. soft pink. N China, Manch., Korea. Z5.

S. *marginata* Sternb. Forming low cushions, old lvs sometimes persisting below. Lvs 3–13mm, obovate to narrow-elliptic, usually hyaline, hydathodes 3–13, chalk crust usually conspicuous; st. lvs numerous. Flowering st. 3–12cm, glandular-hairy; fls in pan. of to 12; pet. 5–12mm, usually white, sometimes pale pink. S It., Rom., Balk. peninsula. var. *rocheliana* (Sternb.) Engl. & Irmsch. Differs from var. *marginata* in short leafy shoots and large lvs. var. *coriophylla* (Griseb.) Engl. Leafy shoot long, lvs small. var. *karadzicensis* (Deg. & Košanin) Engl. & Irmsch. is probably not distinct from var. *coriophylla*. Z7.

S. *mauscoides* Wulf. non All. = S. *moschata*.

S. *maweana* Bak. Lvs in loose rosetts, reniform, 3–5-lobed, lobes further divided; petioles twice length of lamina. Flowering st. to 20cm; pet. 12–14mm, white. Moroc. Z7.

S. *media* pro parte, auct. non Gouan = S. *porophylla*.

S. *media* Gouan. St. freely branched, leafy shoots short, crowded. Lvs 6–17mm, linear-oblong to oblanceolate, acute, glaucous, hyaline, hairy below, hydathodes 7–17, chalk crust moderate. Infl. densely hairy, red-pink, tinged green; flowering st. 3–12cm, leafy; fls 2–12, nodding at first; pet. bright pink-purple. E & C Pyren. Z6.

S. *media* Sibth. & Sm., non Gouan = S. *sempervivum*.

S. *media* ssp. *porophylla* sensu Hayek pro parte = S. *sempervivum*.

S. *media* var. *sibthorpiana* Griseb. = S. *sempervivum*.

S. ×*megaseiflora* hort. ex May, Musgrave et al. (S. *aretioides* ×S. *burseriana* ×S. *lilacina* ×S. *media*.) Resembling S. *burseriana*. Fls large, rose-pink with deeper-coloured centre. Early spring. Many cvs, divided into 2 groups. 'Prichard Monument' group: fls pink to purple; includes 'Dana'. 'Holenka's Miracle' group: fls yellow; includes 'Galaxie'. Z6.

S. *melaeana* Boiss. = S. *pubescens*.

S. *meridionalis* A. Terracc. = S. *oppositifolia*.

S. *mixta* pro parte Lapeyr. = S. *pubescens*.

S. *moschata* Wulf. = S. *exarata* ssp. *moschata*.

S. *murithiana* Tiss. = S. *oppositifolia*.

S. *muscoides* Wulf. non All. = S. *exarata*.

S. *mutata* L. Sometimes bienn. Rosettes compact, 5–15cm diam. Lvs 2.5–7cm, oblong-oblanceolate, jagged-toothed, fleshy, soft, dark green, hydathodes variable, chalk crust thin or 0. Flowering st. 10–50cm, stout, glandular-hairy; fls in narrow pan.; pet. 6–8mm, golden-yellow or orange. Alps. Z6.

S. *nervosa* Lapeyr. = S. *intricata*.

S. *nitida* Schreb. = S. *tenella*.

S. *obscura* Gren. & Godron = S. *pubescens*.

S. *occidentalis* S. Wats. Lvs 1.5–3cm, ovate, elliptic or rhombic, coarsely toothed, petiole distinct. Flowering st. 8–20cm; infl. pyramidal to rounded, fls in clusters at ends of ascending br.; pet. 1.5–3.5mm, white. W N Amer. Z6.

S. *olympica* Boiss. = S. *rotundifolia*.

S. *oppositifolia* L. PURPLE SAXIFRAGE. St. woody, freely branched, forming dense mats or a loose cushion. Lvs 0.5–0.8cm, usually opposite, oblong, elliptic or obovate, obtuse, margin bristly, concave above, rigid, dark dull green, hydathodes 1–3(–5), light to moderate. Flowering st. 1–2cm, leafy; fls solitary; pet. to 12mm, pink to deep purple fading to white. Arc., high mts of Eur., Asia and N Amer. ssp. *oppositifolia*. Lvs always opposite oblong to narrow-obovate. ssp. *blepharophylla* (A. Kerner ex Hayek) Engl. & Irmsch. Leafy shoots often columnar. Lvs broadly obovate; pet. 5–8mm. ssp. *rudolphiana* (Hornsch.) Engl. & Irmsch. Leafy shoots compressed to form a dense cushion; flowering st. almost 0. ssp. *speciosa* (Dörfl. & Hayek) Engl. & Irmsch. Lvs broadly obovate to suborbicular, tip broad and rounded, margin wide and cartilaginous. Flowering st. v. short. 'Alba': fls white. 'Latina': lvs silver-grey; fls deep rose-pink. 'Skye Form': v. small; fls brilliant magenta. 'Splendens': vigorous; fls purple. 'Vaccarina': fls deep red-purple. 'W.A. Clarke': fls large, rich pink. 'Wetterhorn': fls rose-red. Z2.

S. *oranensis* Munby = S. *globulifera*.

S. *orientalis* Jacq. = S. *cymbalaria*.

S. *palmata* Lapeyr. non Sm. = S. *geranoides*.

S. *paniculata* Mill. LIFELONG SAXIFRAGE. Mat-forming, to 25cm. Lvs to 40mm, oblong to lanceolate, in hemispherical rosettes, margins inrolled, chalky. Pan. to 30cm; fls to 12mm diam.; pet. creamy-white, sometimes red-spotted. Summer. 'Alba': fls white. 'Atropurpurea': fls rose-purple. 'Balcana': pet. white spotted red; rosettes dense. 'Baldensis': lvs short, thick, ash-grey. 'Brevifolia': pet. white; foliage silvery. 'Californica': pet. white. 'Churchillii': lvs in stiff rosettes, grey. 'Correvoniana': rosettes minute, flattened. 'Cristata': lvs narrow, silvery; pet. cream. 'Cultrata': to 35cm; basal lvs narrow, serrate; pet.

cream. 'Densa': rosettes small, intensely silvery. 'Emarginata': to 25cm; pet. cream. 'Flavescens': pet. lemon-yellow. 'Hainoldii': to 30cm, rosettes large; pet. rose. 'Labradorica': rosettes v. small; pet. white. 'Lagraveana': to 15cm; rosettes small; silvery; pet. waxy, cream. 'Lutea': pet. yellow. 'Minima': small; pet. white. 'Notata': lvs margined silver. 'Paradoxa': lvs blue-green; pet. white. 'Pectinata': lvs margined silver; pet. white spotted red. 'Punctata': dark green; silvered rosettes. 'Rex': to 25cm; fls large; pet. cream. 'Rosea': pet. bright pink. Z2.

S. parryi Torr. = *Jepsonia parryi*.

S. ×*paulinae* Sünderm. (*S. burseriana* ×*S. ferdinandi-coburgi*.) Forming dense cushions to 5cm. Lvs lanceolate, spiny. Fls large yellow, loosely cymose. Early spring. 'Bettina': cushions dense; rosettes open; lvs longer, narrower; infl. tall. 'Franzii': robust; fls rounded; pet. deep yellow. 'Paula': cushions v. dense, domed; lvs glaucous; infl. few-fld; fls light yellow. Z6.

S. pectinata Pursh non Schott, Nyman & Kotschy = *Luetkea pectinata*.

S. pectinata Schott, Nyman & Kotschy = *S. paniculata*.

S. pedatifida auct. non Sm. = *S. pedemontana*.

S. pedemontana All. Leafy shoots long, forming loose cushions. Lvs 8–15mm, fleshy or leathery, palmately divided, seg. 3–9, narrow-elliptic to linear-oblong, short glandular-hairy. Flowering st. 5–18cm, pan. narrow; pet. 9–21mm, tips recurved, pure white. Mts of SE & SC Eur., N Afr. ssp. *pedemontana*. Lvs densely hairy. Flowering st. to 18cm; pet. sometimes tinged pink at base. SW Alps. ssp. *cervicornis* (Viv.) Engl. Lvs abruptly tapered to petiole. Flowering st. to 15cm; pet. 10–13mm. Corsica & Sardinia. ssp. *prostii* (Sternb.) D.A. Webb. Lvs densely hairy, tapered abruptly to petiole, seg. acute to mucronate. Flowering st. to 18cm. C Fr. Z6.

S. petraea L. Gland.-hairy, bienn. Basal lvs rosulate, 1.2–3cm, semicircular to diamond-shaped in outline, deeply divided lobes 3, toothed and lobed into 19–23 seg., petioles 1.5–5.5cm. Flowering st. to 35cm, branched; fls in lax cymes; pet. to 11mm, notched, pure white. NW It. and NW Balk. Z6.

S. petraea auct. non L. = *S. irrigua*.

S. ×*petraschii* Sünderm. ex W. Irv. (*S. burseriana* ×*S. tombeanensis*.) Lvs lanceolate to linear, grey-green, with incurved, hooked apices. Infl. to 5cm; peduncle and buds red pet. white. Spring. 'Ada': cushions dwarf; rosettes flat; lvs glaucous. 'Affinis': cushions small, domed; rosettes closed; lvs lime-spotted beneath. 'Flush': cushions dense, flat; fls tinted pink to purple-violet. Z6.

S. planifolia Lapeyr. non Sternb. = *S. exarata*.

S. platypetala Sm. = *S. hypnoides*.

S. platysepala (Trautv.) Tolm. = *S. flagellaris*.

S. ×*polita* (Haw.) Link. (*S. hirsuta* ×*S. spathularis*.) Lvs sub-orbicular to obovate, slightly hirsute, deeply dentate. Infl. a lax pan.; pet. white. Z6.

S. poluniniana H. Sm. Lvs to 6mm, petiolate. Fls solitary; pet. to 10mm, white turning pink. Nepal. Z7.

S. ponae Sternb. = *S. petraea*.

S. porophylla Boiss. in part, non Bertol. = *S. sempervivum*.

S. porophylla Bertol. Leafy shoots short, forming dense cushions 4–8cm diam. Lvs 4–10mm, obovate-spathulate to oblong-oblanceolate, glaucous, hydathodes 5–11, chalk crust. Flowering st. 3–8cm; fls in a slender spike; sep. pale pink to green-pink; pet. 1.5mm, concealed by sep. C & S Apennines. Z6.

S. porophylla auct., non Bertol. = *S. federici-augusti*.

S. porophylla var. *stribrnyi* Velen. = *S. stribrnyi*.

S. '**Primulaize**'. (Possibly *S. umbrosa* ×*S. aizoides* or *S. paniculata*.) Resembles *S.* ×*urbium* but smaller. Lvs linear. Fls carmine or salmon-pink. Summer. Z6.

S. prostiana (Ser.) Luizet = *S. cebennensis*.

S. prostii Sternb. = *S. pedemontana*.

S. ×*pseudoborisii* Sünderm. = *S.* ×*borisii*.

S. ×*pseudokyrillii* Sünderm. = *S.* ×*borisii*.

S. ×*pseudopungens* Sünderm. = *S.* ×*apiculata*.

S. pseudosancta Janka = *S. juniperifolia*.

S. pubescens Pourr. Leafy shoots short, forming flat rosettes or long and columnar. Basal lvs to 18mm including petiole, lobes 5–9 oblong, dark green, glandular-hairy, furrowed above. Flowering st. 3–10; cyme flat-topped; pet. 4–6mm, white, rarely veined red. Pyren. ssp. *pubescens*. Lax in habit. Pet. pure white. ssp. *iratiana* (F.W. Schultz) Engl. & Irmsch. Compact, with persistent dead lvs on columnar shoots. Pet. sometimes veined red. Z6.

S. pubescens var. *prostiana* Ser. in DC. = *S. cebennensis*.

S. pulvinaria H. Sm. Forming dense cushions with columnar leafy shoots. Lvs 2–4mm. Pet. 4–5mm, white. Kashmir to Nepal. Z7.

S. pulvinata (Small) Small = *S. oppositifolia*.

S. pulvinata Small = *S. oppositifolia*.

S. ×*pungens* Sünderm. = *S.* ×*apiculata*.

S. pungens Clairv. = *S. vandellii*.

S. purpurea All. = *S. retusa*.

S. pyramidalis Lapeyr. = *S. cotyledon*.

S. pyrolifolia D. Don = *Leptarrhena pyrolifolia*.

S. quadrifaria Engl. & Irmsch. Dense mat-forming. Lvs to 2.5mm, ovate, perfoliate, densely imbricate, fleshy, hydathode 1, apical. Flowering st. to 3cm, fls solitary; pet. 4.5mm, white. E Himal., Tibet. Z7.

S. ranunculifolia Hook. = *Suksdorfia ranunculifolia*.

S. ranunculoides Haw. = *S. irrigua*.

S. recurvifolia Lapeyr. = *S. caesia*.

S. repanda Willd. = *S. rotundifolia*.

S. reticulata Willd. = *S. cymbalaria*.

S. retusa Gouan. St. woody at base, forming dense cushions. Lvs 2–4mm, opposite, oblong, obtuse, glab., sharply bent, upper half horizontal and rigid, shining dark green above, hydathodes 3–5, chalk crust heavy or 0. Flowering st. 0.5–5cm, glandular-hairy; fls in an umbel-like cyme; sep. dark red-purple; pet. 4.5mm, pink-purple. C & S Eur. ssp. *augustana* (Vaccari) Fourn. Cal. glandular-hairy. Flowering st. to 5cm, with 3–5 fls. ssp. *retusa*. Flowering st. to 1.5cm; cal. glab. Z6.

S. rhodopea Velen. = *S. rotundifolia*.

S. rocheliana Sternb. = *S. marginata*.

S. rosacea Moench. High variable, low-growing plant found in many gardens. St. short and forming dense, compact cushions or longer and trailing in mats with dead lvs persistent. Lvs 1–2cm, obovate-cuneate, bright green to red-tinted, usually cut into 5 or more seg., these deep and narrow or short and broad, glab. or pubesc. Scapes erect, slender, to 6cm, 2–5-fld, often tinted; fls 1–1.5cm diam., white to pink to dark red. Many forms and and hybrids. Spring–summer. NW & C Eur. Z6.

S. rotundifolia L. ROUND-LEAVED SAXIFRAGE. Rhiz. stout. Lvs mostly basal, in a lax rosette, 1.5–4.5cm, reniform to orbicular, base deeply cordate, subglabrous to hairy, crenate to mucronate-toothed or palmately lobed; petiole 4–18cm. Flowering st. 15–70cm; pan. spreading, cymose; pet. 6–11mm, white, usually spotted crimson-purple, shading to orange-yellow at base. Summer. Eur. (SW Fr. to Black Sea and Aegean), Cauc. ssp. *rotundifolia* var. *rotundifolia*. Fls star-like; pet. to 9mm, lightly spotted. var. *heucherifolia* (Griseb. & Schenk) Engl. Pet cupped, to 11mm, heavily spotted. ssp. *chrysosplenifolia* (Boiss.) D.A. Webb. Petiole expanded at junction with lamina; lvs without translucent border, usually fringed with hairs. Pet. as in var. *heucherifolia*. Z6.

S. rotundifolia ssp. *taygetea* (Boiss. & Heldr.) Maire & Petitmengin = *S. taygetea*.

S. rotundifolia var. *taygetea* (Boiss. & Heldr.) Engl. = *S. taygetea*.

S. rouyana Magnier = *S. granulata*.

S. ×*rubella* Sünderm. = *S.* ×*irvingii*.

S. rudolphiana Hornsch. ex Koch = *S. oppositifolia*.

S. rupestris Willd. = *S. petraea*.

S. ×*salmonica* Jenk. (*S. burseriana* ×*S. marginata*.) Cushion-forming. Lvs to 11mm, lanceolate to spathulate-linear, glaucous. Flowering st. to 8cm; cyme few-fld; pet. white. 'Friesei': cushions small to large, domed; infl. loose; pet. dentate. 'Kestoniensis': cushions dense; st. slender, red; st. lvs red. 'Maria Luisa': cushions small to large, dense; lvs widely lanceolate; pet. sometimes suffused bright rose. 'Meirose': cushions becoming loose irregular hummocks; lvs blue-green; pet. pendent to reflexed. Z6.

S. sancta Griseb. Differs from *S. juniperifolia* lvs shorter (to 10mm), flowering st. and infl. glab., sta. only slightly longer than pet. NE Greece. Z7.

S. sarmentosa L. f. = *S. stolonifera*.

S. sartorii Heldr. ex Boiss. = *S. scardica*.

S. scardica Griseb. Leafy shoots to 5cm, forming dense cushions. Lvs 5–15mm, oblong, acute, glaucous, fleshy, margin hyaline, toothed toward apex, hydathodes 9–15, chalk crust moderate. Flowering st. 4–12cm, glandular-hairy; st. lvs dark red beneath; pet. 7–12mm, white or pale pink. SW Balk. Penins. Z7.

S. ×*schraderi* Sternb. (*S. trifurcata* ×*S. continentalis*.) Resembles *S. trifurcata*. Z6.

S. sempervivum K. Koch. Leafy shoots forming loose cushions or mats. Lvs 5–20mm, linear to linear-oblong, acute, glaucous, margin narrow, translucent, hydathodes 9–19, chalk crust light. Flowering st. 6–20cm, glandular-hairy, dark red, st. lvs numerous; spike 10–20-fld.; sep. dark purple-red; pet. 2.5mm, red-purple. NE Greece. Z7.

S. sibthorpii Boiss. Bienn. (occas. ann. or perenn.), resembling *S. cymbalaria* but more compact with a tuft of basal lvs. Lvs 7–15mm, reniform and 3–5-lobed or orbicular and crenate, long-stalked. Flowering st. to 8cm; fls solitary on long pedicels; pet. 5–7mm, golden-yellow to orange. SW Greece. Z8.

S. speciosa Dörfl. & Hayek = *S. oppositifolia*.

S. sponhemica auct. non Gmel. = *S. hypnoides*.

S. spruneri Boiss. Leafy shoots to 7cm, forming deep cushions with dead lvs below. Lvs 5–7mm, oblong spathulate to obovate-oblanceolate, glandular-hairy, somewhat fleshy, hydathodes 7. Flowering st. 3–8cm, glandular-hairy; cymes compact, flat-topped; pet. 4–6mm, white. S Balk., Penins., SC Greece. Z8.

S. **squarrosa** Sieber. Close to S. *caesia* but leafy shoots more crowded, forming taller, more compact cushion; lvs narrower with fewer hydathodes, translucent margin more conspicuous. SE Alps. Z6.

S. **stellaris** L. STARRY SAXIFRAGE. Short and compact or mat-forming. Lvs in loose rosettes, to 7cm, oblanceolate to broadly elliptic, bluntly toothed, fresh green, slightly fleshy, margins hairy; petioles distinct. Flowering st. 5–20cm; pan. lax, 5–15-fld., pet. 3–8mm, white with 2 mustard-yellow spots near base. Eur. Z6.

S. **sternbergii** Willd. = S. *rosacea*.

S. **stolitzkae** Duthie ex Engl. & Irmsch. Cushion-forming, sub-shrubby. Lvs to 7mm, linear to spathulate, obtuse, densely packed, coriaceous, encrusted. Fls 4–7 in a pan.; pet. 5–9mm, white or pink. Autumn. W Himal. 'Duncan Lowe': faster growth; cushions dense, usually domed. Lvs smaller. Z7.

S. **stolonifera** Meerb. MOTHER OF THOUSANDS; STRAWBERRY GERANIUM. Spreading by long, thin, red stolons. Lvs rosette- or tuft-forming, round, mid-green with silvery veins above, flushed red beneath, bristly, long-stalked. Flowering st. to 40cm, branched; pet. white, upper 3 to 3mm, lower pair 10–20mm, narrowly elliptic. Late summer–autumn. China, Jap. 'Tricolor' ('Magic Carpet'): Lvs variegated. Z5.

S. **stribrnyi** (Velen.) Podp. Leafy shoots numerous. Lvs 12–25mm, oblanceolate to spathulate, obtuse or shortly mucronate, margins translucent with a few stout hairs at base, v. glaucous, hydathodes 7–13, chalk crust heavy. Infl. glandular-hairy and crimson; 3–9cm, pan. lax; pet. c3mm, deep violet-purple. Balk. Penins. Z6.

S. ×**sundermannii** Kellerer ex Sündern. = S. × *kelleri*.

S. ×**sündermannii** W. Irv. = S. × *petraschii*.

S. **tantoscana** Boiss. & Reut. = S. *callosa* ssp. *callosa* var. *australis*.

S. **taygetea** Boiss. & Heldr. Lvs in small rosettes, similar to S. *rotundifolia*, 5–13mm, reniform to suborbicular, base truncate or slightly cordate, shallow-crenate, glossy, sometimes sparsely hairy; petioles 0.5–7cm, hairy. Flowering st. to 25cm; pet. 7–9mm, white spotted purple-red. Mts of SW Greece and Balk. Z7.

S. **tellimoides** Maxim. = *Peltoboykinia tellimoides*.

S. **tenella** Wulf. Shoots prostrate to ascending, hairy, mat-forming. Lvs 8–11mm, linear, tapering to a long, translucent, bristle-tipped point, straw-coloured or silver-grey, shiny. Flowering st. to 15cm, slender, glab.; fls 3–9, cymose; pet. 3mm, creamy-white, 3-veined. E Alps. Z6.

S. **tenuifolia** Rouy & Camus = S. *exarata*.

S. **thessalica** Schott = S. *sempervivum*.

S. **tombeanensis** Boiss. ex Engl. Leafy shoots to 5cm, forming dense, rounded cushions. Lvs 2–4.5mm, narrow-oblong to elliptic-lanceolate, short-mucronate, margin translucent, hydathodes 1–3, chalk crust 0 or slight. Flowering st. 3–7cm, glandular-hairy; fls 1–4, cymose; pet. 8–12mm, white. SE Alps. Z6.

S. **transsilvanica** Fuss = S. *mutata*.

S. **tricuspidata** Rottb. Lvs 6–15mm, cuneate or oblanceolate, with 3 mucronate apical teeth, margins gland. hairy. Flowering st. 4–10cm, branched above; pet. 4–7mm, white to cream, spotted yellow, orange and red toward apex. NE Canada, Alask. Z3.

S. **tridactylites** L. Glandular-hairy ann., to 20cm, often shorter. Young lvs spathulate, basal lvs and lower st. lvs usually 3-lobed. Pan. lax; pet. to 4mm, white. Spring. Widespread in Eur., N Afr., SW Asia. Z5.

S. **trifurcata** Schräd. St. branched, forming large open cushions, glab., gland., not sticky. Lvs 2cm, rigid, dark green, shiny, semicircular, divided into 3 lobes, these further divided into 9–17 triangular seg.; petiole exceeds lamina. Flowering st. to 30cm; fls 5–15, cymose; pet. 8–11mm, white. N Spain. Z6.

S. **umbrosa** L. St. short, bearing crowded lf rosettes forming loose cushions. Lvs 1.5–3×1–2cm, oblong-elliptic to obovate, crenate, thinly fleshy and coriaceous, usually glab.; petiole to half length of lamina, margin hairy. Flowering st. to 35cm, tinted red; fls in narrow, lax pan.; pet. c4mm, white with 2 yellow spots near base and crimson spots near middle. Pyren. var. **hirta** D.A. Webb. Smaller, lvs. ciliate. 'Clarence Elliott': compact; fls minute, rose-pink. 'Covillei': to 15cm; fls numerous; pet. pink and white. 'Primuloides': to 15cm; lvs primrose-like; pet. rose-pink. Z7.

S. **uniflora** R. Br. = S. *cespitosa*.

S. ×**urbium** D.A. Webb. (S. *umbrosa* × S. *hirsuta*.) LONDON PRIDE. Like S. *umbrosa* but petioles longer and less hairy, and lvs more strongly crenate-toothed. Z7.

S. **valdensis** DC. Lf rosettes 1–3cm diam., crowded. Basal lvs

3–8mm, obovate to oblanceolate, entire; tip somewhat down-curved, covered with hydathodes, appearing pitted. Flowering st. 3–11cm, branched; pet. 4–5mm, white. SW Alps. Z6.

S. **vandellii** Sternb. Leafy shoots to 5cm, crowded, forming deep, hard cushion. Lvs 7–9mm, narrowly triangular-lanceolate, tapered to a sharp point, dark green, margin translucent ecept near base, where hairy, hydathodes 5–7, chalk crust slight. Flowering st. 4–6cm, glandular-hairy; fls cymose; pet. 7–9mm, white, sometimes veined red. It. Alps. Z6.

S. **varians** Sieb. = S. *exarata*.

S. **varians** Sieber incl. = S. *moschata*.

S. **vayredana** Luizet. Glandular-hairy throughout. Leafy shoots forming dense cushions. Lvs balsam-scented, 5–9×8–13mm, lobes 3, further divided into 5–9 seg., petiole longer than lamina. Flowering st. 7–12cm; pan. narrow; pet. to 7mm, pure white. NE Spain. Z7.

S. **watanabei** Yatabe = *Peltoboykinia watanabei*.

→*Leptasea*.

SAXIFRAGACEAE Juss. 36/475. *Astilbe, Astilboides, Bensoniella, Bergenia, Bolandra, Boykinia, Chrysosplenium, Darmera, Elmera, Francoa, Heuchera,* ×*Heucherella, Jepsonia, Leptarrhena, Lithophragma, Mitella, Mukdenia, Parnassia, Peltoboykinia, Rodgersia, Saxifraga, Suksdorfia, Sullivantia, Tanakaea, Tellima, Tiarella, Tolmiea.*

Saxifrage *Saxifraga*.

Sazanami-giboshi *Hosta crispula*.

Scabiosa L. PINCUSHION FLOWER; SCABIOUS. Dipsacaceae. *c*80 ann. or perenn. herbs. Lvs basal, rosulate and cauline, opposite, entire to much divided. Fls in long stalked, hemispherical, term. heads subtended by 1–2 series of involucral bracts; cal. cupular, bristly; cor. with 5 unequal lobes and a short tube, lobes often 2-lipped. Eur., Asia, Afr., mainly Medit.

S. **alpina** L. = *Cephalaria alpina*.

S. **anthemifolia** Ecklon & Zeyh. Ann. or bienn. to 75cm, st. decumbent. Lvs obovate to ovate-spathulate or oblong-lanceolate, toothed to 2–3-pinnatifid. Fls mauve or rose to violet, in heads to 6.5cm diam. S Afr.

S. **atropurpurea** L. MOURNFUL WIDOW; SWEET SCABIOUS; PINCUSH-ION FLOWER; EGYPTIAN ROSE. Ann., 60–90cm; st. erect. Basal lvs lanceolate-ovate, lyrate, coarsely toothed, st. lvs pinnatifid. Fls dark purple to deep crimson, fragrant, in heads to 5cm diam. S Afr. 'Blue Cockade': to 90cm; fls double, globe-shaped, rich blue, fragrant. 'Grandiflora': large flower-heads. 'Nana': slightly dwarf; much-branched.

S. **caucasica** Bieb. Perenn. to 60cm; st. simple or sparsely branched. Basal lvs lanceolate, entire, grey-green, glaucous, st. lvs pinnatifid. Fls pale blue, in heads to 7.5cm diam. Cauc. 'Alba': fls white. 'Blue Beauty': to 35cm; fls small, blue. 'Blue Perfection': fls lavender-blue, abundant. 'Bressingham White': fls white. 'Clive Greaves': to 60cm; fls lavender-blue, abundant. 'Compliment': to 37cm; fls blue, large. 'Fama': to 50cm; fls bright blue, large. 'Floral Queen': to 76cm, strong grower; fls pale blue. 'Goldingensis': fls large, rich lavender-blue. 'Isaac House Hybrids': fls in compact groups, crested, shades of blue and lavender. 'Loddon White': fls creamy-white. 'Miss Willmott': to 90cm; fls off-white. 'Moerheim Blue': fls dark blue. 'Moonstone': to 90cm; fls light blue. 'Perfecta': fls large, with fringe. 'Perfecta Alba': to 37cm; fls pure white. 'Penhill Blue': to 90cm; fls blue tinged mauve. 'Staefa': to 70cm; fls blue. Z4.

S. **columbaria** L. Densely lanate, bienn. or perenn. to 60cm. Basal lvs oblanceolate or obovate to lyrate, entire or divided, st. lvs pinnatifid, seg. often cut. Fls red-purple to lilac-blue in heads to 4cm diam. Eur., Afr., Asia. 'Butterfly Blue': to 70cm; fls lavender-blue. Z6.

S. **columbaria** var. **anthemifolia** hort. = S. *anthemifolia*.

S. **fischeri** DC. Perenn. to 60cm, much-branched. Lvs pinnately divided, seg. linear, entire. Fls deep violet-blue in heads to 6cm diam. SE Sib. Z4.

S. **graminifolia** L. Bushy perenn. to 40cm forming loose mats. Lvs grasslike, linear-lanceolate, entire, silver-pubesc. Fls blue-violet to rose in heads to 4cm diam. S Eur. 'Pinkushion': fls rose. Z7.

S. **japonica** Miq. Bienn. to 30cm; st. soft hairy. Lvs pinnatifid to 2-pinnatisect. Fls lavender, in heads to 5cm diam. Jap. Z7.

S. **lucida** Vill. Perenn. to 30cm. Basal lvs ovate or rhombic, coarsely cut to lyrate, silvery. Fls rose-lilac in dense heads to 4cm diam. C Eur. 'Rosea': fls pale pink. Z5.

S. **macedonica** (Griseb.) Vis. = *Knautia macedonica*.

S. **ochroleuca** L. Bienn. or perenn. to 75cm. Basal lvs obovate, crenate, st. lvs pinnatifid, seg. oblong or linear, entire. Fls primrose yellow in heads to 6cm diam. Eur., W Asia. var. **webbiana** (D. Don) Boiss. To 15cm. Fls cream-white. SE Eur. to Asia Minor. Z6.

S. palaestina L. Erect ann. to 45cm; st. pubesc. Lvs oblong to oblong-spathulate, sometimes lyrate-pinnatifid, entire to toothed. Fls pale yellow, rarely lilac, in heads to 3cm diam. Balk. to Iraq. Z7.

S. prolifera L. CARMEL DAISY. Ann. to 60cm, adpressed-hairy; st. stout. Lvs oblong to oblong-lanceolate or linear. Fls cream, in subsessile heads to 5cm diam. N Afr. to Asia Minor.

S. pterocephala L. = *Pterocephalus perennis*.

S. pyrenaica All. White-tomentose perenn. to 75cm. Basal lvs elliptic, crenate to incised, st. lvs pinnately divided. Fls blue-lilac. S Eur. Z8.

S. rotata Bieb. Ann. to 30cm. Lvs oblong-lanceolate or linear-lanceolate, entire, upper lvs linear, with 1–2 basal lobes. Fls red. Asia Minor.

S. rumelica hort. = *Knautia macedonica*.

S. silenifolia Waldst. & Kit. Perenn. to 25cm; st. erect. Basal lvs sessile, spathulate, entire, st. lvs lanceolate to pinnatifid, seg. linear. Fls blue-violet in heads to 3cm diam. SC Eur. Z6.

S. sosnowskii Sulak. Perenn. to 75cm. St. lvs pinnate to lyrate-pinnatifid, seg. sometimes toothes. Fls pale yellow in heads to 1.5cm diam. Cauc. Z6.

S. stellata L. Ann. to 45cm, st. branched, short-hairy. Lvs almost lyrate, terminal lobe largest, obovate, toothed. Fls pink or blue-white, in heads to 3cm diam. Medit. 'Drumstick': to 30cm; fls in round heads, light blue turning bronze. 'Ping Pong': fls in round heads, small, white.

S. succisa L. = *Succisa pratensis*.

S. ucranica L. Bienn. or perenn. to 75cm. Lvs entire to pinnatisect, seg. linear, entire. Fls white, pale yellow or pale blue in heads to 2.5cm diam. S Eur. to W Asia. Z7.

S. varifolia Boiss. Perenn. to 30cm. Lvs to 7.5cm, oblong or oblong-lanceolate, entire to few toothed or 3-lobed, glab. Fls pale blue. Greece (Rhodes, Karpathos). Z8.

S. vestita Facch. ex Koch Like *S. silenifolia* but st. more branching, st. lvs more numerous, fls lilac. It. Alps. Z7.

S. cvs. 'Blue Snowflake': fls v. large, sky-blue with pink anth. Dwarf Double Hybrids: fls clumped, double, wide colour range; seed race. Giant Imperial Hybrids: to 90cm; fls double, ball-shaped, blue, white, rose, pink, salmon, crimson, lavender; seed race.
→*Pterocephalus*.

Scabious *Scabiosa*.

Scadoxus Raf. Amaryllidaceae. 9 bulbous or rhizomatous herbs. Lvs spirally arranged (not 2-ranked as in *Haemanthus*), elliptic to ovate; petioles spotted, forming a neck. Scape lat., angular above, spotted; spathe valves 4 to many; infl. conical to spherical; fls crowded, mostly erect; perianth tubular, tep. 6, linear to lanceolate; sta. 6, exserted. Fr. an orange to red berry. Trop. Arabia and Afr. to S Nam. and E Cape. Z10.

S. multiflorus (Martyn) Raf. Lvs to 32×20cm. Neck to 60cm. Scape to 75cm; perianth tube 0.5–2.6cm, tep. linear, spreading, scarlet, fading pink. Spring–summer. Trop. & S Afr., Yemen. ssp. *multiflorus*. Perianth tube to 1.5cm. ssp. *katherinae* (Bak.) Friis & Nordal. To 1.2m. Lvs undulate. Perianth tube 1.6–2.6cm. ssp. *longitubus* (Wright) Friis & Nordal. To 65cm. Perianth tube 1.5–2.6cm. W Afr.

S. pole-evansii Oberm. Lvs 24–52×3–12cm; neck to 85cm. Scape to 120cm; perianth pink or scarlet tube 4–5mm, tep. elliptic, spreading. E Zimb.

S. puniceus (L.) Friis & Nordal. ROYAL PAINT BRUSH. Lvs to 12×3cm, undulate; neck to 50cm. Scape to 40cm; perianth tube to 1.2cm, tep. linear, scarlet to green-yellow. Spring–summer. E & S Afr.
→*Haemanthus*.

Scaevola L. Goodeniaceae. *c*90 herbs or shrubs. Fls solitary in lf axils or in few-fld cymes; cor. tube slit to base on upper side, lobes 5, subequal, spreading, wings equal; sta. 5. Mostly Aus., Polyn. Z10.

S. aemula R. Br. To 70cm, ascending or procumbent, glab. to pubesc. Lvs to 4.5cm, lanceolate to obovate, sharply dentate, puberulent; petiole to 1cm. Fls solitary, axill.; cor. to 30cm, white, pale blue or lilac, exterior pubesc. S & E Aus.

S. albida (Sm.) Druce. To 50cm, adpressed-pubesc., prostrate or ascending. Lvs to 3.5cm, ovate or obovate-cuneate, dentate, pubesc.; petiole to 2cm. Fls solitary, axill., sessile; cor. to 13mm, lilac to blue or white, exterior pubesc. S & E Aus.

S. anchusifolia Benth. To 20cm, erect or prostrate. Lvs to 5cm, linear or oblanceolate, entire to coarsely dentate. Fls in a term., leafy spike; cor. to 15mm, blue, exterior pubesc. W Aus.

S. attenuata R. Br. To 60cm, erect, hirsute. Lvs to 7cm, linear or linear-lanceolate, entire. Fls in term. leafy spikes; cor. to 20mm, blue, interior pubesc. W Aus.

S. calendulacea (Andrews) Druce. Procumbent, puberulent. Lvs to 5cm, succulent, obovate-oblong, usually entire, puberulent; petiole to 2.5cm. Fls solitary, axill., fragrant; cor. to 18mm, blue, throat yellow, exterior pubesc. to glab. SE & E Aus.

S. crassifolia Labill. To 1m, prostrate or decumbent, glab., often viscid. Lvs to 5cm, fleshy, obovate, orbicular or spathulate, obtuse, dneticulate; petiole to 2.5cm. Fls in dense, term. pan.; cor. to 13mm, blue to pale violet, interior pubesc. W & S Aus.

S. hookeri (De Vriese) Hook. f. To 30cm, prostrate or creeping, much branched, hirsute to glab. Lvs to 5cm, succulent, ovate, obovate or oblong, entire to dentate, short-petiolate. Fls solitary, axill.; cor. blue-purple to white, exterior pubesc. NSW, Vict.

S. microcarpa Cav. = *S. albida*.

S. pilosa Benth. To 70cm, scabrous to pilose. Lvs to 6.5cm, ovate or obovate to oblong, cordate to auriculate at base, coarsely dentate, sessile. Fls solitary, axill.; cor. to 25mm, blue, pink or purple, exterior slightly pubesc., interior densely pubesc. W Aus.

S. platyphylla Lindl. Shrub to 1m, erect, pubesc. Lvs to 4.5cm, ovate to elliptic, slightly pilose, entire to coarsely dentate, sessile. Fls in a terminal spike or rac.; cor. to 40mm, blue, exterior adpressed-pubesc., interior lanate. W Aus.

S. plumieri (L.) Vahl Shrub to 180cm. Lvs to 9cm, fleshy, obovate to spathulate, rounded, entire. Fls in axill. cymes, 3-fld; cor. to 25mm, white, exterior glab., interior lanate, lobes sublinear. W Indies, Flor. to Tex.

S. suaveolens R. Br. = *S. calendulacea*.

S. taccada (Gaertn.) Roxb. BEACH BERRY; NAUPAKA. Shrub erect, pubesc. to glab. Lvs to 10cm, obovate-oblong, rounded or obtuse, fleshy, lustrous green, serrate. Fls in axill. cymes, shorter than lvs; cor. to 20mm, white, exterior pubesc. Shores of Indian & trop. Pacific Oceans.
→*Goodenia* and *Lobelia*.

Scallops *Hakea cucullata*.

Scaly Polypody *Polypodium thyssanolepis*.

Scammony *Convolvulus scammonia*.

Scaphochlamys Bak. Zingiberaceae. *c*30 perenn. rhizomatous herbs. Shoots leafy. Lvs lanceolate. Infl. term., compact-ovoid or ellipsoid; bracts to 3cm, green to white, spirally arranged; fls 1–7 per bract; cal. 3-lobed; pet. spreading, cor. tube narrow; staminodes oblong, obtuse, spreading; lip obovate, 2-lobed. SE Asia. Z10.

S. kunstleri (Bak.) Holtt. Lvs to 45×18cm, purple-pubesc. beneath. Infl. 6–10×4cm; cor. white or pale brown; tube to 2cm, lip 2.5cm, pale orange with lemon-yellow stripe; staminodes pale orange, puberulent. Malaysia.

S. lanceolata (Ridl.) Holtt. Lvs to 12×3–5cm, with white bars above. Scape short; fls-fragrant; cor. white, tube 2.7cm; pet. 1.5cm; lip white with yellow margin, sometimes lined lilac or purple. Malaysia.

S. malaccana Bak. Lvs to 20×6cm. Scape 5–12cm; cor. white, tube 2.5cm; pet. 1.3cm; lip 1.8cm, white with yellow stripe sometimes with lilac or purple line on either side. Malacca.
→*Boesenbergia*, *Curcuma* and *Kaempferia*.

Scaphosepalum Pfitz. Orchidaceae. 30 epiphytic or terrestrial orchids. Close to *Masdevallia* but with fused lat. sep. (synsepalum) largely concave, bearing 2 fleshy distal calli. Trop. Americas. Z10.

S. amethystinum (Rchb. f.) Schltr. = *Porroglossum amethystinum*.

S. anchoriferum (Rchb. f.) Rolfe. Infl. to 20cm, ascending to pendent, several-fld; dors. sep. to 15×6mm, ovate, acute, revolute, lat. sep. to 12×12mm, elliptic, callus to 7×6mm, pubesc., yellow or yellow-orange spotted red-purple, tails to 5mm, slender, recurved. Costa Rica, Panama.

S. antenniferum Rolfe = *S. reversum*.

S. breve (Rchb. f.) Rolfe. Infl. to 25cm, loosely several to many-fld, flexuous; peduncle filiform, verucose; sep. yellow to yellow-green marked purple, dors. sep. to 18×4mm, ovate, acute, revolute, lat. sep. to 12×7mm, oblong, obtuse, callus to 6×4mm, ovate, yellow to orange marked red, tails to 13mm. Venez., Colomb., Ecuad., Guyana.

S. clavellatum Luer. Infl. to 20cm, several-fld, erect to pendent; sep. yellow-brown or orange to red, dors. sep. to 13×3mm, narrowly oblong-pandurate, obtuse, lat. sep. to 10×6mm, ovate, acute, slightly recurved, callus to 5×1mm, ovoid. Panama, Costa Rica, Ecuad.

S. echnidnum (Rchb. f.) Schltr. = *Porroglossum echnidnum*.

S. elasmotopus Schltr. = *S. microdactylum*.

S. gibberosum (Rchb. f.) Rolfe. Infl. to 50cm, loosely many-fld; peduncle slender, verrucose; sep. light green to green-white, tinged and spotted purple, dors. sep. to 57×4mm, ovate, acute, tail dark purple, lat. sep. to 10×10mm, ovate, callus to 13×3mm, narrowly falcate-triangular, fleshy, white spotted purple, tails to 25mm, white, slender. Colomb.

S. microdactylum Rolfe. Infl. to 15cm, slender, distichous; sep. light yellow or yellow-green tinged and spotted red to brown, dors. sep. to 8×3cm, fleshy, oblong, obtuse, lat. sep. to 9×6mm, oblong to broadly elliptic, bifid, carinate, callus to 3×1mm, ovoid. Mex., Guat., Hond., Costa Rica, Panama, Colomb.

S. ochthodes (Rchb. f.) Pfitz. = *S. verrucosum*.

S. ovulare Luer. Infl. to 4cm, few-fld, pendent; sep. purple or yellow marked purple, dors. sep. to 3×5mm, ovate, acute, largely fused to lat. sep. to 5×6mm, ovate, acute, callus obliquely triangular. Ecuad.

S. pulvinare (Rchb. f.) Rolfe. Infl. to 60cm, many-fld; peduncle erect, densely verrucose; sep. green tinged or spotted red-purple, dors. sep. to 15×5mm, basal portion ovate, apex linear, revolute, slightly pubesc., lat. sep. to 15×9mm, ovate, acute, minutely pubesc., callus to 8×2mm, narrowly elliptic, yellow-grey, tails to 6mm, green, slender, verrucose. Colomb.

S. punctatum (Rolfe) Rolfe = *S. anchoriferum*.

S. rapax Luer. Infl. to 4cm, few-fld; sep. purple spotted deep purple, dors. sep. to 9×3mm, ovate-triangular, sep. to 9×3mm, ovate-triangular, apiculate, revolute, serrulate, lat. sep. to 7×6mm, ovate, minutely ciliate, obtuse, callus to 3.5×1.5mm, fleshy, oblong, tails to 4mm, slender, decurved, slender. Ecuad.

S. reversum Kränzl. Infl. to 60cm, many-fld, erect; peduncle stout, verrucose; sep. dull green to yellow-green, marked and tinged purple, dors. sep. to 18×7mm, ovate-linear, apiculate, revolute, gland., lat. sep. to 15×10mm, ovate, truncate to obtuse, apical calli to 7×3mm, lunate, tails to 12mm, slender, verrucose. Colomb., Ecuad., Peru.

S. rolfeanum Kränzl. = *S. pulvinare*.

S. swertiifolium (Rchb. f.) Rolfe. Infl. to 15cm; peduncle filiform; sep. white to pale yellow marked and spotted red to brown, dors. sep. to 14×5mm, basal portion ovate-triangular, apical portion linear, acute, lat. sep. to 11×12mm, elliptic, callus to 8×5mm, rose and purple, lunate, tails to 40mm, slender. Colomb., Ecuad.

S. verrucosum (Rchb. f.) Pfitz. Infl. to 50cm, slender, many-fld; peduncle verrucose; sep. yellow to green tinged or spotted red-brown, dors. sep. to 8×4mm, fleshy lanceolate, revolute, narrowly obtuse, lat. sep. to 7×6mm, elliptic, obtuse, callus to 3×2mm, ovoid, tails to 1.5mm, recurved. Colomb.

S. xipheres (Rchb. f.) Schltr. = *Porroglossum muscosum*.

→*Masdevallia* and *Pleurothallis*.

Scaphyglottis Poepp. & Endl. Orchidaceae. *c*30 epiphytic or lithophytic orchids. St. linear to slender-fusiform where pseudobulbous, 1 to many-lvd above. Lvs narrow, fleshy-coriaceous. Infl. term. or axill., a rac. or fascicle; sep. erect or spreading, ovate to oblong; lateral sep. strongly oblique, pet. smaller; lip entire to 3-lobed. Trop. Amer. Z10.

S. amethystina (Rchb. f.) Schltr. St. simple or branching, pseudobulbous, to 12×1cm, bifoliate. Lvs to 12×1cm. Fls fascicled white to violet; sep. to 8×3mm; lip cuneate-flabellate, to 9×5mm, midlobe subquadrate, undulate. Guat., Costa Rica, Panama, Colomb., Venez.

S. brachyphylla (Rchb. f.) Schweinf. = *Hexadesmia fusiformis*.

S. crurigera (Batem. ex Lindl.) Ames & Correll = *Hexadesmia crurigera*.

S. fusiformis (Griseb.) R.E. Schult. = *Hexadesmia fusiformis*.

S. lindeniana (A. Rich. & Gal.) L.O. Williams. Pbs stem-like, to 30×2.5cm, narrow fusiform, bifoliate. Lvs to 25×4.5cm. Fls fascicled, yellow-green to red-green often veined purple; sep. to 11×4mm; lip to 11×6mm, pandurate to oblong-cuneate, retuse, finely erose. Mex. to Panama.

S. lindeniana (Rich. & Gal.) L.O. Williams = *Hexadesmia fasciculata*.

S. livida (Lindl.) Schltr. St. fasciculate-branched, pseudobulbous, narrowly fusiform-cylindrical, to 12×0.5cm. Lvs to 20×0.5cm. Fls fascicled, green to pale yellow-green striped purple; sep. to 5×2mm, lip to 3×3mm, subquadrate to ovate-quadrate, emarginate. Mex., Guat., Hond.

S. micrantha (Lindl.) Ames & Correll = *Hexadesmia micrantha*.

S. prolifera (R. Br.) Cogn. St. fasciculate-branching, erect or ascending, to 20cm, fusiform-cylindrical, bifoliate. Lvs to 4×0.5cm. Fls fasciculate, white to yellow; sep. to 5×1mm; lip to 5×2mm, oblong, fleshy, retuse. Braz., Venez., Guyana, Surinam.

S. reedii (Rchb. f.) Ames = *Hexadesmia sessilis*.

S. sessilis (Rchb. f.) Foldats = *Hexadesmia sessilis*.

S. violacea (Lindl.) Lindl. St. to 15cm, slender, branched, cylindrical or fusiform-cylindrical, striate, bifoliate. Lvs to 17×1cm. Fls solitary or in v. sparse fascicles, rose to purple-violet; sep. to 4×2mm; lip to 3×2mm, fleshy, oblong-obovate,

to elliptic-obovate, obtuse to retuse. Venez., Guyana, Braz., Peru.

→*Hexadesmia*.

Scarborough Lily *Cyrtanthus elatus*.
Scarce Marsh Helleborine *Epipactis veratrifolia*.
Scarlet Ball Cactus *Parodia haselbergii*.
Scarlet Banana *Musa coccinea*.
Scarlet Banksia *Banksia coccinea*.
Scarlet Bottlebrush *Callistemon macropunctatus*.
Scarlet Bugler *Penstemon centranthifolius*.
Scarlet Bush *Hamelia patens*.
Scarlet Feather Flower *Verticordia grandis*.
Scarlet Fritillary *Fritillaria recurva*.
Scarlet Fritillary *Fritillaria recurva*.
Scarlet-fruited Gourd *Coccinia grandis*.
Scarlet Gilia *Ipomopsis aggregata*.
Scarlet Ginger Lily *Hedychium coccineum*.
Scarlet Greenhood *Pterostylis coccinea*.
Scarlet Gum *Eucalyptus phoenicea*.
Scarlet Larkspur *Delphinium cardinale*; *D. nudicaule*.
Scarlet Maple *Acer rubrum*.
Scarlet Monkey Flower *Mimulus cardinalis*.
Scarlet Musk Flower *Nyctaginia capitata*.
Scarlet Oak *Quercus coccinea*.
Scarlet Paintbrush *Crassula perfoliata* var. *falcata*.
Scarlet Pimpernel *Anagallis arvensis*.
Scarlet Plume *Euphorbia fulgens*.
Scarlet Root Blossom *Agalmyla parasitica*.
Scarlet Runner *Kennedia prostrata*.
Scarlet Runner Bean *Phaseolus coccineus*.
Scarlet Sage *Salvia splendens*.
Scarlet Strawberry *Fragaria virginiana*.
Scarlet Sumac *Rhus glabra*.
Scarlet Trompetilla *Bouvardia ternifolia*.
Scarlet Trumpet Honeysuckle *Lonicera* ×*brownii*.
Scarlet Turk's-cap Lily *Lilium chalcedonicum*.
Scarlet Wistaria Tree *Sesbania grandiflora*.

Sceletium N.E. Br. Aizoaceae. 21 succulent subshrubs. Lvs ovate-lanceolate, acute or tapered, united at base, withering and persisting as skeleton. Fls terminal, 1–3 together on pedicels or elongated flowering br. S Afr. (Cape Prov.). Z9.

S. compactum L. Bol. Compact shrub to 7cm. Lvs 1.2–1.5×0.6–1cm, imbricate, narrow-ovate, tapered. Fls 3cm diam., ivory. Laingsburg District.

S. emarcidum (Thunb.) L. Bol. Laxly branched shrub, to 30cm. Lvs 2–4×1–2cm, ovate to ovate-lanceolate, acute. Fls 4cm diam., white. W Cape.

S. expansum (L.) L. Bol. St. to 30cm, fleshy, prostrate. Lvs 4×1.5cm, lanceolate, tapered, carinate beneath, fresh green, glossy-papillose. Fls 4–5cm diam., yellow. SW Cape.

S. namaquense L. Bol. Shrubby; br. to 26cm, prostrate. Lvs 2.5–3.2×0.6–1.2cm, imbricate, linear-lanceolate to ovate-lanceolate, green with slender veins. Fls to 4cm diam., pale pink. Little Namaqualand.

S. tortuosum (L.) N.E. Br. Br. slender, curved. Lvs 2.5×1cm, ovate-lanceolate, obtusely tapered, channelled above, carinate beneath, fresh green, minutely papillose. Fls 4–5cm diam., yellow. Karroo.

S. varians (Haw.) L. Bol. = *S. tortuosum*.

→*Mesembryanthemum*.

Scented Bells *Rothmannia manganjae*.
Scented Boronia *Boronia megastigma*.
Scented Fern *Mohria caffrorum*; *Paesia scaberula*.
Scented Heath *Erica denticulata*.
Scented Paperbark *Melaleuca squarrosa*.
Scented Penstemon *Penstemon palmeri*.
Scented Wattle *Acacia farnesiana*.
Scentless False Camomile *Tripleurospermum*.
Scentless Hayweed *Tripleurospermum inodorum*.

Schaffneria Fée. Aspleniaceae. 1 terrestrial or rupestral fern. Rhiz. short, erect; scales black. Fronds to 5×5cm, simple, fleshy, orbicular to flabellate or obovate, entire; stipes to 5cm, minutely pubesc., lustrous, black. C Amer. Z10.

S. nigripes Fée.

→*Asplenium* and *Scolopendrium*.

Schaueria Nees Acanthaceae. 8 herbs and subshrubs. Lvs opposite, entire. Infl. terminal; bracts and cal. lobes bristly or linear, giving a dense, brush-like appearance to thyrse or spike; cor. tube slender, bilabiate. Braz.

S. calicotricha Nees = *S. flavicoma*.

S. flavicoma (Lindl.) N.E. Br. Subshrub to 1m. Lvs broadly ovate to lanceolate, glossy green, principal veins sometimes ivory. Infl. short, dense, subspicate; bracts and cal. yellow- to grey-green, downy to gland., bristly; cor. to 3cm, yellow. Braz.

Schefflera Forst. & Forst. f. IVY TREE; SCHEFFLERA; UMBRELLA TREE. Araliaceae. 700+ trees, shrubs, subshrubs or vines. Lvs usually palmately compound; petiole slender, base ± girdling twig; lfts usually stalked; juvenile lvs sometimes distinct. Infl. compound, paniculate or umbellate, term.; fls in small umbels, heads, rac. or spikes; cal. rim lobed, or uniform; pet. 4–5 or more, small. Fr. drupaceous, usually black. Warmer regions of the world, with the greatest numbers of sp. in the Americas (over 200) and from S & E Asia to the Pacific (500 or more); poorly represented in Afr. and with only three sp., none endemic, in Aus. 0 from the Masc. and Hawaiian Is.

S. actinophylla (Endl.) Harms. AUSTRALIAN IVY-PALM; OCTOPUS-TREE; (QUEENSLAND) UMBRELLA-TREE. Erect, glab. shrub or small tree to 12m. Lvs in term. rosettes; petioles to 80cm; lfts to 7–16, to 30×10cm, oblong, ± entire, stalked, bright green and glossy above, obtuse; juvenile lfts fewer, smaller, toothed, acute. Infl. term., paniculate, 2× compound; primary br. 6–13, to 80cm, purple-black, stout, radiating from main axis; fls pink to red, in shortly stalked heads racemosely arranged along primary br. Aus. (N and NE parts), New Guinea (S and SE parts), nat. elsewhere. Z10.

S. arboricola (Hayata) Hayata. Glab. epiphytic shrub or liane. Lfts 7–11, in adults obovate, entire, to 11×4.5cm, stalked, bright green and semi-glossy above, obtuse; in juveniles with short, widely spaced teeth. Infl. terminal, paniculate, 2× compound; fls in small, stalked umbels, racemosely arranged along primary br. Taiwan. Several cvs formally recognized, based on leaflet shape, serration, division and variegation. The narrowly elliptic lfts intermediate between juvenile and adult forms persist in some cultivated plants. *S. leucantha* R. Vig. (*S. kwangsiensis* Merrill ex Li) small, rather narrowly elliptic lfts, widely grown in SE Asia for medicinal purposes and as an ornamental. Z10.

S. aruensis Ridl. = *S. bractescens*.

S. bractescens Ridl. Large, much-branched shrub. Lfts 10+, bases and ligules brown-hairy when young; lfts to 28×11cm, elliptic to oblong-elliptic, shortly acuminate, somewhat glossy, bright green above. Infl. term., paniculate, 2× compound; main axis to 35cm, primary br. numerous, widely spreading, to 38cm; fls green-white, in small, stalked umbels racemosely arranged along the br. NE Aus., New Guinea, Aru Is. Z10.

S. delavayi (Franch.) Harms. Sparsely branched shrub or tree to 8m, white- to brown-tomentose at first. Lfts 4–7, to 24×12cm, ovate to elliptic, stalked, entire or irregularly dentate to lobed, softly textured, dark green and glab. above, densely white-tomentose or floccose beneath. Infl. large, white-tomentose to glabrescent, paniculate, 1–2× compound; main axis to 60cm, primary br. many to 15cm; fls small, crowded, spicately arranged. SC China, NW Vietnam. Lfts variable in form, size and pubescence. Z9.

S. digitata Forst. & Forst. f. PATE. Spreading shrub or tree to 8m, soon glabrescent. Young br. and petioles red-purple to purple. Lfts 7–10, thin, to 20×6(–7)cm, narrowly obovate, shortly stalked, sharply toothed, in juvenile plants 5, ± pinnatifid, lobes toothed, pink beneath. Infl. 2× compound, paniculate; main axis to 9cm+, primary br. 8–23, to 35cm, closely spaced; fls green in racemosely arranged umbels, fascicles or solitary. NZ (inc. Stewart Is.). Z10.

S. digitata hort., non Forst. f. & Forst. = *S. venulosa*.

S. elegantissima (Veitch ex Mast.) Lowry & Frodin. FALSE ARALIA; PETIT BOUX CALEDONIEN. Glab., sparsely branching trees to 15m with dark bark. Juvenile stage to 2m, unbranched; st. and petioles dark green spotted white; lfts 7–11, linear, to 23×3cm, coarsely serrate, somewhat pendulous, dark green above, dark brown-green beneath, midrib white. Adults with larger, long-petiolate lvs and branching; lfts oblong, to 25×8cm, stalked, obtuse, broadly toothed, sinuate or entire. Infl. term., umbelliform, 3× compound; primary br. to 30cm, radiating, secondary br. from ends of primary br. or in 1–2 whorls; fls in term. umbels or stalked in whorls. Autumn. New Caledonia. 'Castor': whole plant more compact; juvenile lfts shorter and broader, the margins v. irregularly notched or toothed, the teeth rounded. Other compact forms exist. Sometimes misidentified as *S. kerchoveana*. Z10.

S. elliptica (Bl.) Harms. GALAMAI-AMO. Glab., freely branching hane to 10m or more; st. ± slender, sometimes cane-like. Lfts (4)5–7 to 17.5×10cm, elliptic to broadly elliptic or ovate, entire, glossy green above, shortly acuminate; petiole to 15cm. Infl. paniculate, 2× compound, to 15cm+, appearing conical; main axis elongate, primary br. spreading; fls v. small, green, in umbels. SE Asia to NE Aus. Z11.

S. farinosa (Teijsm. & Binnend.) Dakkus, non (Bl.) Merrill = *S. littorea*.

S. grandifolia (Koord. & Val.) Koord. = *S. longifolia*.

S. heptaphylla (L.) Frodin. CHIANG MAO; FUKANOKI; IVY-TREE. Spreading semi-deciduous or everg. tree to 25m, bark grey-white; young growth and infl. pale brown-puberulent. Lvs in loose rosettes, long-petioled; lfts usually 6–8, elliptic to oblong-elliptic, to 20×6cm, acute to obtuse, glossy and green above, often white beneath. Infl. term., paniculate, 2–3× compound, main axis to 30cm with shorter br.; fls in small umbels, term. at the ends of primary (and secondary) br. or racemosely disposed. Late summer and autumn. E Asia, Philipp. Z9.

S. kerchoveana (Veitch ex W. Richards) Frodin & Lowry. Differs from *S. elegantissima* in lfts 9–12, elliptic oblong or elliptic-lanceolate, to 8cm, spreading, serrate or undulate, deep glossy green, midrib pale; petioles spotted white. Probably Vanuatu. Plants grown as *Dizygotheca kerchoveana* are usually *S. elegantissima* or *S. veitchii*.

S. littorea (Seem.) Frodin. LAU TAKKA; RUMPHIUS'S IVY-PALM. Shrub or small tree to 5m, lvs in rosettes; young growth coated with white waxy hairs. Petioles to 90lcm; lfts 12–15, oblanceolate, to 40×9cm, stalked, base attenuate, glossy, green above, paler beneath. Infl. as *S. bractescens* but primary br. to 30 or more. Moluccas. Z10.

S. longifolia (Bl.) R. Vig. LAMPANGIT; RAMO-GILING. Shrub or small tree to 10×0.35m; not or but little-branched; young growth brown-hairy. Lvs in rosettes, petiole to 125cm; lfts 6–12, oblong, entire, to 40×15cm, long-stalked, base rounded to truncate. Infl. paniculate, 2× compound; primary br. to 60cm, brown-hairy, radiating; fls white in numerous small, stalked, racemosely arranged umbels. Sumatra, Java. Z10.

S. lucescens auct., non (Bl.) R. Vig. = *S. longifolia*.

S. morototonii (Aubl.) Maguire, Steyerm. & Frodin. MOUNTAIN TRUMPET; LUCIFERSHOUT; MANDIOQUEIRA. Slender-trunked tree to 30×0.4m+, lvs in rosettes at br. ends; lfts 7–13, moderately thick, oblong, to 45×19cm usually smaller, acute to obtuse, base obtuse to slightly cordate, glab. above, finely grey-to brown-hairy beneath, appearing metallic; lfts fewer in juvenile lvs, v. thin, toothed, hispid above, silvery beneath. Infl. term., paniculate, usually 3× compound, hairy; primary br. to 7, to 30cm, radiating, secondary br. numerous, to 12cm; fls in small umbels terminating secondary br. or racemosely arranged along them. Late summer. C & S Amer. Z10.

S. neo-ebudica Guillaum. = *S. kerchoveana*.

S. octophylla (Lour.) Harms = *S. heptaphylla*.

S. odorata (Blanco) Merrill & Rolfe = *S. elliptica*.

S. pubigera (Brongn. ex Planch.) Frodin. Large shrub to 7m, eventually scandent or spreading, lower br. sometimes rooting. Young growth and petioles red-purple, petiole to 20cm; lfts 7–9, elliptic to oblong-ovate, glab., to 17.5×8cm, tip acuminate to subcaudate, somewhat recurved, base cuneate to rounded, rich green, distinctly reticulated. Infl. term., paniculate, 2× compound; axes red-purple, puberulous to glab., primary br. about 10, to 15cm; fls red to 5mm in small, racemosely arranged, head-like umbels. E Himal. to SW Yunnan. Z10.

S. pueckleri (K. Koch) Frodin. Erect, glabrescent, spreading tree to 18×0.6m or scandent; young parts brown-floccose. Lvs in large rosettes; petioles to 45cm; lfts 5–10, narrowly oblong, to 25×8cm, resembling *S. actinophylla* but upper surface darker and glossier, yellow-green beneath, always entire. Infl. pseudolateral, paniculate, somewhat umbelliform, 2× compound, relatively few-fld; primary br. or rays about 3, to 10cm, with large basal bracts; umbels stalked, 3–5-fld, at br. ends and sometimes also paired along them; fls green, 1.5cm or more diam. Winter. S & SE Asia. Resembles *S. actinophylla* when young. Z10.

S. rotundifolia (Ten.) Frodin. Related to *S. roxburghii*. Lfts 5–7, nearly round, petiolules to 5cm. Fls yellow.

S. roxburghii Gamble. Diffusely branching shrub, scandent or spreading by br. rooting. Young growth green, glab. Lvs in term. rosettes, petiole to 15cm; lfts 5–7, narrowly ovate to shortly oblong to oblong-elliptic, glab., on stalks to 2.5cm, apex obtuse, the tip acuminate, base obtuse to rounded. Infl. paniculate, 2× compound, somewhat open, axes green, primary br. spreading, to 20cm or more; fls yellow in small, racemosely arranged umbels. Summer. N India. Z10.

S. stelzneriana hort. Calif. = *S. venulosa*.

S. stelzneriana hort. ex Guillaum. = *S. pubigera*.

S. tomentosa (Bl.) Harms. Shrub to 3m, st. hairy when young. Petiole to 30cm; lfts 5–7, oblong-elliptic, to 30×10cm, caudate-acuminate, dull, bullate, thickly brown-hairy beneath. Infl. term., paniculate, 2× compound, hairy; primary br. 2–3, to 37.5cm; fls in racemosely arranged umbels. SE Asia, Sumatra, Java and Borneo. Z11.

S. umbellifera (Sonder) Baill. BASTARD CABBAGE TREE;

CABBAGE-WOOD. Tree to 20m, crown rounded; bark resinous. Lvs crowded towards br. ends; lfts 5 (rarely 3), glab., oblong-obovate to elliptic, to 18×6cm, apex acute to rounded or notched; stalks to 5cm; petiole to 30cm. Infl. paniculate, in 20cm, 2× compound, axis elongate; fls small, yellow-green, in racemosely arranged umbels. S & SE Afr. Z10.

S. veitchii (Veitch ex Carr.) Frodin & Lowry. Tree to 12m with slender, ascending br. Juvenile lvs with lfts 9–11, linear, to 15×0.4cm, closely wavy, glossy dark green above, dark red beneath; petiole to 10cm; adult lvs with lfts 5–9, oblong-elliptic, to 8×3cm, entire. Infl. similar to *S. elegantissima* but smaller, less umbelliform and 2× compound. New Caledonia. 'Gracillima': juvenile lvs filiform. Z10.

S. venulosa (Wight & Arn.) Harms. See also *S.s pubigera*, *roxburghii*. Plants grown in Hawaii and N America (California and Florida) under this name, or as *S. digitata* or *S. stelzneriana*, cannot, however, be referred to either. They are distinguished by obovate or oblong-obovate lfts, slender infl. with small green-white fls.

S. venulosa auct., non (Wight & Arn.) Harms = *S. pubigera* and *S. roxburghii*.

S. venulosa var. *erythrostachys* (Hook. f.) A. Berger = *S. pubigera*.

→*Aralia, Brassaia, Cussonia, Didymopanax, Dizygotheca, Heptapleurum, Neocussonia, Paratropia, Sciodaphyllum* and *Tupidanthus*.

Schima Reinw. ex Bl. Theaceae. 1 variable everg. tree to 40m. Lvs 7–24cm, spirally arranged, elliptic to oblong-lanceolate, entire or shallowly crenate-serrate, red-purple when young, later dark green, sometimes glaucous beneath, thinly coriaceous. Fls axill. or subterminal, solitary or subracemose, scarlet in bud, opening purple-cream to white, to 6.5cm diam., fragrant; sep. 5–6, circular, small; pet. 5–6 shortly connate, unequal, concave; sta. many in a central boss, fil. to 1cm, yellow. S & SE Asia.

S. argentea Pritz. = *S. wallichii*.
S. kankaoensis Hayata = *S. wallichii*.
S. khasiana Dyer = *S. wallichii*.
S. noronhae Reinw. ex Blume = *S. wallichii*.
S. superba Gardn. & Champ. = *S. wallichii*.
S. wallichii (DC.) Korth.

Schinus L. Anacardiaceae. c30 resinous everg. shrubs and trees. Fls many, small, in rac. or pan.; pedicels slender; sep. 4–5; pet. 4–5, lanceolate to broadly ovate, truncate; sta. 8–10, unequal, inserted on disc. Drupe small, lavender to deep red, exocarp papery, endocarp bony; seeds 1, suspended. S Amer., Urug. to Mex., nat. S US, Canary Is., China.

S. areira L. = *S. molle* var. *areira*.
S. aroeira Vell. = *S. chichita* var. *rhoifolius*.
S. bituminoides Salisb. = *S. molle* var. *areira*.
S. brasiliensis Marchand. ex Cabr. = *Lithrea molleoides*.
S. chichita Speg. AROEIRA BLANCA. Shrub or small tree. Lvs 7–19cm, pinnate rust-red-pilose, later glab.; lfts obscurely crenate or serrate, sessile. Fr. pink. Braz. var. *rhoifolius* (Mart.) Engl. Small tree, br. densely pilose at first. Lvs 7–15cm; lfts ovate or obovate, emarginate or mucronate, entire. C Braz. Z10.
S. dentatus DC. = *S. polygamus*.
S. dependens DC. = *S. longifolius*.
S. dependens var. *alpha* Hook. = *S. latifolius*.
S. dependens var. *crenatus* Arech. = *S. latifolius*.
S. dependens var. *latifolius* Marchand. = *S. latifolius*.
S. dependens var. *subintegra* = *S. longifolius*.
S. huigan Molina = *S. molle*.
S. latifolius (Gillies) Engl. MOLLE. Small tree. Lvs 3–5×1–2.5cm, simple, subacute, coriaceous. Infl. short-pilose. Fr. lavender. C Chile. Z10.
S. lentiscifolius Marchand. COROBA; MOLLE. Shrub to 2.5m. Lvs paripinnate, glab., subcoriaceous, to 6cm; lfts 1–2.8cm, usually 8, subopposite, oblanceolate, entire or irregular sessile; rachis extends beyond upper lfts. Fr. lavender-pink. Summer. S Braz., Urug., Arg. Z10.
S. lithi Domb. ex Marchand = *Lithrea caustica*.
S. longifolius (Lindl.) Speg. Shrub or small tree. Br. slender, glab., light brown when young, eventually dark grey. Lvs 2.5–5cm, spathulate, obtuse, cuneate, usually entire, becoming glab. Fr. lavender. Spring. S Braz., Parag., Urug., Arg. var. *paraguariensis* (Hassl.) F. Barkley. Br. coarser. Lvs lanceolate, 5–8cm, subcoriaceous, acute. Z9.
S. molle L. non hort. ex Engl. PEPPER TREE; PERUVIAN MASTIC TREE; MOLLE. Tree to 15m. Br. slender, hanging. Lvs 10–30cm, imparipinnate, membranous; lfts 19–41, lanceolate, acuminate, serrate. Pan. highly branched, 8–15cm; fls pale yellow. Fr. rose-pink. Summer. Braz., Urug., Parag., N Arg. var. *areira* (L.) DC. Lfts 17–35, 1.5–5cm, coriaceous, mucronate. Boliv., S

Braz., Parag. Z9.
S. molle hort. ex Engl. non L. = *Lithrea molleoides*.
S. molleoides Vell. = *Lithrea molleoides*.
S. ovatus Lindl. = *S. polygamus*.
S. paraguariensis (Hassl.) F. Barkley = *S. longifolius* var. *paraguariensis*.
S. polygamus (Cav.) Cabr. HUIGEN. Shrub or small tree to 5m. Br. pale brown to dark grey. Lvs 1–4cm, simple, glab., oblanceolate, obovate or oblong, acute to obtuse, rarely serrate. Fr. deep purple. Late spring. W S Amer. var. *parviflorus* (Marchand) F. Barkley. MOLLE. Lvs coriaceous, 2–3.5cm, truncate to obtuse, entire to crenate or serrate. C Chile. Z10.
S. rhoifolius Mart. = *S. chichita* var. *rhoifolius*.
S. terebinthifolius Raddi. BRAZILIAN PEPPER TREE; CHRISTMAS BERRY TREE; AROEIRA. Shrub or small tree to 7m. Lvs 10–17cm, pinnate; rachis winged; lfts 5–13, 3–6cm, oval-lanceolate to obovate, acute or rounded, pubesc. when young, deep green above, lighter beneath, pan., 5–15cm; fls white. Fr. red. Venez. to Arg. var. *acutifolius* Engl. AROEIRA MANSA. Lvs imparipinnate, 7–22cm; lfts 7–15, broadly lanceolate. Fr. pink. S Braz., Parag., Arg. Z9.
→*Lithrea, Mauria, Amyris, Molle* and *Sarcothea*.

Schippia Burret. PIMENTO PALM. Palmae. 1 palm to 10m. St. to 10cm diam., striate, rough, scarred. Lvs palmate to costapalmate, to 3m; sheath split at base, forming fibrous mat, tomentose; petiole to 2m, blade to 1m, deeply divided, seg. 32 narrow, acuminate, apex shallowly divided. Hond.
S. concolor Burret.

Schisandra Michx. Schisandraceae. 25 decid. or everg. twining shrubs. Lvs entire or dentate, mostly oblong-lanceolate, cuneate at base, tapering to slender petiole. Fls solitary or in axill. clusters; perianth cupped, seg. 5–12; sta. 5–15, ± united in a disc or column. Fr. berry-like on an elongate spike. E Asia, E N Amer.
S. chinensis (Turcz.) Baill. To 8m. Lvs 5–14cm, elliptic to obovate, apex acute, base narrow, cuneate, denticulate or serrulate, glossy deep green, glab. except for young veins. Fls to 1.25cm diam., pale rose to bright pink, fragrant, on pendulous pedicels to 2.5cm; sta. 4–6. Fruiting spike to 10cm, fr. scarlet. China. Z4.
S. coccinea Michx. BAY STAR VINE; WILD SARSPARILLA. To 5m. Lvs 5–14cm, ovate to elliptic, somewhat fleshy, ultimately glab., entire or remotely and obscurely waxy-toothed. Fls to 1cm diam., crimson, on slender pedicels to 5cm; sta. 5. Fruiting spike to 3.5cm; fr. red. SE US. Z7.
S. glabra (Brickell) Rehd. = *S. coccinea*.
S. glaucescens Diels. Decid., to 7m. Lvs 5–10cm, obovate, apex acuminate, base cuneate, finely and remotely shallow-toothed, glab., glaucous beneath. Fls to 2cm diam., orange-red on pedicel to 4cm; sta. 18–25. Fruiting spike to 10cm; fr. scarlet. W China. Z8.
S. grandiflora Hook. & Thoms. Decid., to 7m. Lvs 6–15cm, lanceolate to oblanceolate, obscurely denticulate, to subentire. Fls 2.5cm diam., fragrant, white, cream or pale rose on pedicels to 5cm; sta. 33–60. Fruiting spike to 12cm; fr. red. N India, Bhutan, Nepal. var. *rubriflora* (Rehd. & Wils.) Schneid. Fls scarlet to dark red. India, Burm., W China. Z9.
S. propinqua (Wallich) Baill. Decid., to 10m. Lvs 4–16cm, lanceolate or narrowly ovate-elliptic, apex briefly acuminate, base somewhat rounded, sparsely toothed or entire. Fls to 1.5cm diam., orange, on slender pedicels to 1.25cm; sta. 6–16. Fruiting spike to 15cm, fr. red. C & W China, Himal. var. *sinensis* Oliv. Lvs narrower; fls smaller and somewhat yellow. Cold-resistant. Z8.
S. rubriflora Rehd. & Wils. = *S. grandiflora* var. *rubriflora*.
S. sphenandra auct. = *S. sphenanthera*.
S. sphenanthera Rehd. & Wils. Differs from *S. glaucescens* in lvs 3–11cm, obovate to elliptic, not glaucous beneath. Fls orange, concave; sta. 10–15. S & W China. Z7.

SCHISANDRACEAE Bl. 2/47. *Kadsura, Schisandra.*

Schismatoglottis Zoll. & Moritzi DROP-TONGUE. Araceae. c100 everg. herbs. St. rhizomatous and subterranean, or aerial and erect. Lvs oblong to ovate, sometimes lanceolate, cordate to hastate; petiole long. Peduncles shorter than petioles; spathe cylindric, convolute below, expanded above, to 12cm, green to yellow-green or white. Trop. Asia with some in trop. Amer. Z10.
S. calyptrata (Roxb.) Zoll. & Moritzi. St. decumbent, becoming erect, to 90cm. Lvs to 30×15cm, long-triangular, cordate to subsagittate, somewhat coriaceous; petiole 30–60cm, dark green, sheaths pink. Spathe to 11cm. Burm., Malaysia, to Indon. and Philipp.

S. concinna Schott. St. erect, to 20cm, often red or pink. Lvs to 15×4cm, ovate-lanceolate, base rounded to emarginate, green with grey-green marks above, green or purple beneath; petiole to 15cm. Spathe 6.5cm. Borneo, Java, Sumatra. 'Immaculata': lvs not spotted, bright green above, purple beneath and on petioles. 'Purpurea': lvs variegated above, deep purple beneath and on petioles.

S. lavalleei Lind. misapplied = *S. concinna*.

S. neoguineensis André. St. subterranean. Lvs ovate, acute, base cordate, 12–25×7–16cm, membranous, bright green with pale yellow-green blotches above, pale green beneath; petiole to 50cm, green or purple, spathe 7cm. New Guinea.

S. ornata Alderw. St. erect, to 20cm. Lvs to 15×3.5cm, reflexed, lanceolate, acute, velvety dark green above, with grey-green band along midrib; petiole equalling lamina, spathe 2.5cm. Borneo

S. picta Schott. St. subterranean. Lvs 15–35×7.5–26cm, narrow-ovate to oblong-ovate, cordate, membranous, bright green above, with pale glaucous band between midrib and margin; petiole 20–60cm. Spathe to 6cm. Indon. (Borneo, Sumatra, Java, Sulawesi).

S. rutteri Alderw. St. erect, to 50cm. Lvs oblong, sagittate, to 30×18cm, basal lobes triangular, bright green; petioles to 30cm, spathe to 10cm. Molucca Is.

Schivereckia Andrz. ex DC.
S. iberidea Boiss & Hurt. = *Bornmuellera cappadocica*.

Schizachyrium Nees. Gramineae. *c*100 perenn. grasses differing from *Andropogon* in the solitary, term. rac. with oblique br., stout rachis and pedicels and stalked spikelets. Cosmop.
S. littorale (Nash) C. Bickn. = *S. scoparium* .
S. scoparium (Michx.) Nash. BLUE STEM; BROOM BEARD GRASS; PRAIRIE GRASS; WIRE GRASS; BUNCHGRASS. St. 80–150cm, clumped, slender, erect, branched above. Lvs green or glaucous often tinted bronze in autumn, to 0.5cm across. Rac. to 15cm; peduncle sheathed, rachis flexuous, weakly hairy. N Amer. var. *littorale* (Nash) Gould. St. narrower, crowded, decumbent. Lower lf sheaths blue-green, glaucous. Infl. villous. E N Amer. Z5.
→*Andropogon*.

Schizaea J. Sm. COMB FERN; RUSH FERN. Schizaeaceae. *c*30 small ferns. Rhiz. short-creeping or tufted. Fronds erect, crowded, somewhat rush-like, simple or dichotomous, lamina reduced to a narrow wing; fertile seg. at frond apex, with sporangiophores pinnate in comb-like arrangement. Cosmop., mostly in Trop.
S. dichotoma (L.) J. Sm. Fronds 20–45cm, erect, numerous, repeatedly dichotomously branched into a fan, stipes 15–45cm, firm, dark, sterile fronds whorled. Asia, Aus., Polyn., Madag. Z10.
S. pusilla Pursh. CURLY GRASS. Fronds numerous; sterile 2–6cm, linear, twisted, somewhat flattened, unbranched, fertile 8–12cm, erect, terete, wiry, with pinnate fertile seg. near apex. E N Amer. Z4.

SCHIZAEACEAE Kaulf. 4 genera. *Anemia, Lygodium, Mohria, Schizaea.*

Schizanthus Ruiz & Pav. POOR MAN'S ORCHID; BUTTERFLY FLOWER. Solanaceae. 12 glandular-pubescent ann. or bienn. herbs. Lvs lobed. Pan. cymose, term.; cal. lobes 5 linear or spathulate; cor. tube log or short, limb spreading, zygomorphic, bilabiate, lips tripartite. Chile. Z10.
S. grahamii Gillies. Ann. glandular-hirsute, 30–50cm. Lvs to 8cm, pinnatisect to bipinnatisect. Cal. 6–7mm; cor. tube 1cm, upper lip 2cm with subrhombic central lobe, lower lip to 1.5cm, with acute divisions, violet to pink, occas. tinged orange, central lobe of upper lip yellow; sta. short. Summer. 'Roseus': cor. rose-pink. 'Trimaculatus': cor. purple-red with 3 golden, purple-edged spots.
S. hookeri Gillies. Ann., 40–80cm, glandular-hirsute. Lvs 6–8cm, pinnatisect to bipinnatisect. Cal. 6–7mm; glandular-hirsute; cor. purple, violet or pink, central lobe of upper lip deep yellow, tube to 1.8cm; sta. to three-quarters length of lower lip. Summer.
S. pinnatus Ruiz & Pav. Ann., 20–50cm. Lvs to 12cm, lanceolate to oblanceolate. Cal. 5mm; cor. tube shorter than cal., limb violet to pink, middle upper lip with yellow throat with violet markings, lat. division of lower lip linear-spathulate, obtuse; sta. prominently exserted. Summer–autumn. Angel's Wings: compact to 45cm; fls large in range of colours. 'Candidissimus': fls white. 'Carmineus': fls flesh-pink. Dr Badger's Hybrids: to 45cm; fls in range of colours excluding white, all centred golden-yellow. 'Excelsior': habit tall. 'Grandiflora': fls large. 'Lilacinus': cor. mauve-blue. Morning Mist: fls in wide range of

colours with distinctive yellow centres. 'Roseus': fls rose-pink. 'Sweet Lips': fls with picotee edge, in strong colours.
S. retusus Hook. = *S. grahamii.*
S. × wisetonensis hort. (*S. pinnatus* × *S. grahamii.*) Habit and foliage and *S. pinnatus*. Fl. shape as *S. grahamii*, but with cor. tube shorter than cal. and sta. slightly exserted, fls white, pale blue, pink or carmine-brown, with central lobe of upper lip often flushed yellow. Gdn origin. 'Compactus': dense, low-growing. 'Cherry Shades': fls single to 5cm across, pink to red with purple and maroon stripes.
S. seed races. Disco: habit compact, neat, vigorous; fls in shades of pink and crimson. Dwarf Bouquet: habit dwarf; fls in shades of crimson, amber and pink. Hit Parade: habit bushy, to 30cm; fls in shades of pink and mauve. Star Parade: habit v. dwarf, to 20cm, pyramidal; fls abundant in range of colours.

Schizobasopsis Macbr.
S. kilimandscharica (Mildbr.) Barschus = *Bowiea kilimandscharica.*
S. volubilis (Harv. & Hook. f.) J.F. Macbr. = *Bowiea volubilis.*

Schizocarya Spach = *Gaura.*

Schizocodon Sieb. & Zucc.
S. ilicifolium Maxim. = *Shortia soldanelloides* var. *ilicifolia.*
S. soldanelloides f. *alpinum* Maxim. = *Shortia soldanelloides* f. *alpina.*
S. soldanelloides var. *macrophyllum* hort. = *Shortia soldanelloides* var. *magna.*
S. soldanelloides Sieb. & Zucc. = *Shortia soldanelloides.*

Schizolobium Vogel. Leguminosae (Caesalpinioideae). GUAPIRUVU. 2 everg. trees. Lvs large, bipinnate. Fls in axill. rac. or term. pan., v. showy; pet. 5, spreading, clawed, ovate or rounded; sta. 10. S Mex. to S Braz.
S. excelsum Vogel = *S. parahybum.*
S. parahybum (Vell. Conc.) S.F. Blake. Tree to 30m; trunks buttressed; crown spreading. Lvs to 95cm; pinnae to 10 pairs; lfts in 15–20 pairs, narrow, oblong. Fls in large, erect pan.; pet. to 2cm, pale yellow.

Schizoloma Gaudich.
S. clavata (L.) Kuhn = *Sphenomeris clavata.*

Schizonotos Lindl. ex Wallich.
S. tomentosus Lindl. = *Sorbaria tomentosa.*

Schizopetalon Sims. Cruciferae. 5 hairy herbs, erect to 50cm. Lvs alt., pinnatifid. Fls in leafy rac.; pet. 4, clawed, toothed to cut. Chile. Z8.
S. walkeri Sims. To 45cm. Lvs to 14cm, deeply pinnatifid. Fls almond-scented; pet. white, fimbriate. Spring–summer.

Schizophragma Sieb. & Zucc. Hydrangeaceae. 4 decid. shrubs, creeping and climbing by means of short, adhesive roots. Bark exfoliating. Lvs long-petioled, ovate, entire or toothed. Fls white in flat-topped term. cymes, peripheral fls bearing a long-stalked petal-like enlarged sep., and forming a showy ring encompassing smaller fertile fls; sep. and pet. 4–5. Himal. to Jap., Taiwan.
S. flueggeoides J. Muell. = *S. integrifolium.*
S. hydrangeoides Sieb. & Zucc. To 10m. Lvs 8–12.5cm, broadly ovate, shortly acuminate, base subcordate, coarsely toothed. Infl. to 20cm diam., enlarged sep. 2.5–3.5cm, ovate, cordate to rhombic, white to ivory. Jap., Korea. 'Roseum': enlarged sep. snow-white blushing rose. Z5.
S. integrifolium Oliv. Lvs 10–18cm, ovate, apex narrowly acuminate, base rounded or cordate, entire or sparsely toothed. Infl. to 30cm diam.; enlarged sep. 6.5–7.25cm, narrowly ovate to rhombic, white. C & W China. Z7.
S. ramiflora J. Muell. = *S. integrifolium.*
S. viburnoides (Hook. & Thoms.) Stapf = *Pileostegia viburnoides.*

Schizostylis Backh. & Harv. KAFFIR LILY. Iridaceae. 1 perenn. rhizomatous herb to about 60cm. Lvs to 40×1cm, basal, distichous, ribbed, sword-shaped, glaucescent. Spike distichous, 4–10-fld; fls salver-shaped, scarlet, pink or white; tube to 30mm, slender, abruptly widened at throat, lobes subequal, about 35×15mm, ovate; sta. 3. Summer to early winter. S Afr., Les., Swaz. Z6.
S. coccinea Backh. & Harv. 'Alba': fls white faintly tinged pink. 'Cardinal': fls large, red. 'Jennifer': fls large, clear pink. 'Major' ('Gigantea', 'Grandiflora'): to 60cm; fls scarlet, abundant. 'November Cheer': to 60cm; growth strong; fls deep pink. 'Pallida': fls large, v. pale pink. 'Professor Barnard': to 50cm; fls dusky red. 'Rosalie': fls pink. 'Sunrise': fls large, pink.

'Tambara': fls large, soft rose-pink. 'Viscountess Byng': fls red; late flowering. 'Zeal Salmon': hardy; fls large, clear salmon-pink.
S. pauciflora Klatt = *S. coccinea*.

Schleichera Willd. Sapindaceae. 1 decid. tree to 20m. Lvs to 35cm, pinnate, bright red when young, lfts usually 6, elliptic, 5–9cm, term. leaflet 10–22cm. Fls small, yellow-green in interrupted spike-like rac. to 15cm; cal. 4–6-lobed; pet. 0; sta. 5–8. Seeds with fleshy, edible aril. SE Asia. Z10.
S. oleosa (Lour.) Oken. GUM LAC; LAC TREE; CEYLON OAK.
S. trijuga Willd. = *S. oleosa*.

Schlumbergera Lem. Cactaceae. 6 epiphytic or lithophytic cacti; st. seg. flattened, compressed or terete, oblong or obovate, new seg. and fls arising from the apices; spines bristly, short, or 0. Fl. nearly regular to strongly zygomorphic, with a distinct tube bearing tepaloid scales; sta. inserted on the tube, lowermost united below to form a short tube around style, stigmas erect, connivent. SE Braz.
S. bridgesii (Lem.) Loefgr., misapplied. = *S.* ×*buckleyi*.
S. ×*buckleyi* (T. Moore) Tjaden. (*S. truncata* × *S. russelliana.*) CHRISTMAS CACTUS. Stem-seg. flattened, oblong or obovate, truncate, 2–4.5×1.3–2.5cm, crenate (not serrate as in *S. truncata*): areoles apical and marginal, between crenations. Fl. purple, pink, white, red, orange or yellow, slightly zygomorphic, 5.5–6.5×3–4cm; limb somewhat oblique; sta. and style long-exserted. Winter. Gdn origin. Over 200 cvs of the christmas cactus have been named. Z9.
S. gaertneri (Reg.) Britt. & Rose = *Hatiora gaertneri*.
S. obtusangula (Schum.) D. Hunt. Similar to *S. opuntioides*, but stem-segments terete or obtusely angled. Fl. nearly regular, 5×2.5cm. Spring. SE Braz. Z9.
S. opuntioides (Loefgr. & Dusen) D. Hunt. Small *Opuntia*-like shrub; st. erect or arching to 40cm; stem-segments obovate to oblong, compressed, 5–7×1.5–4cm; areoles generally distributed in diagonal rows; spines to 5mm, bristly. Fl. strongly zygomorphic, resembling those of *S. truncata*, c6×4.5cm, deep pink. Spring. SE Braz. Z9.
S. orssichiana Barthlott & McMillan. Resembling *S. truncata*; stem-segments c5×3cm, margins curled and dentate; areoles apical and marginal. Fl. 9×9cm, tube 1cm, tep. purple-pink towards tip, white below. Autumn–winter. SE Braz. Z9.
S. russelliana (Hook.) Britt. & Rose. St. to 1m+, arching and pendent, woody at base; stem-seg. 2–3.5×0.5–1.5cm, crenate with 1–2 notches each side; areoles apical and marginal, bearing 1–2 weak bristles. Fl. nearly regular, to 5×3cm, deep pink; sta. and style shortly exserted. Winter. SE Braz. Z9.
S. truncata (Haw.) Moran. St. to 30cm+, becoming pendulous, scarcely woody at base; stem-segments oblong, truncate, 2.5–8×1–4cm, sharply serrate-dentate, midrib prominent; areoles apical and marginal. Fl. zygomorphic, 7×4.5cm; limb strongly oblique; tep. recurved, magenta to rose or red; sta. and style long-exserted. Autumn–winter. SE Braz. Often confused with *S.* ×*buckleyi*. Z9.
→*Epiphyllanthus, Epiphyllum* and *Zygocactus*.

Schmaltzia Desv. ex Small.
S. trilobata (Nutt.) Small = *Rhus trilobata*.

Schnittlaugh *Allium schoenoprasum.*

Schoenia Cass. Compositae. 1 erect, branched, ann., to 60cm, pubesc. to lanate-tomentose. Lvs to 7cm, linear to lanceolate, elliptic or spathulate, mostly basal. Cap. discoid, in lax corymbs; involucre to 1cm, turbinate or campanulate; outer phyllaries radiate, usually brown, inner usually white or pink; flts tubular, off-white to pink. Temp. Aus.
S. cassiniana (Gaudich.) Steetz.
S. chlorocephala Turcz. = *Helipterum chlorocephalum*.
→*Helichrysum*.

Schoenlandia L. Bol.
S. algoense hort. = *Delosperma lehmannii*.
S. lehmannii (Ecklon & Zeyh.) L. Bol. = *Delosperma lehmannii*.

Schoenoplectus (Rchb.) Palla. Cyperaceae. 80 ann. or perenn., grasslike, rhizomatous herbs. St. terete or 3-angled, not leafy. Lvs with reduced blades. Infl. subtended by 1–2 bracts, the lowest stem-like, erect; spikelets sessile or stalked. Cosmop. Z7.
S. hudsonianus (Michx.) Palla. 1.5–4m. St. slender, rough, leafless, sheaths bristle-tipped. Summer. N Amer. Z7.
S. lacustris (L.) Palla. 1–3m. St. to 15mm diam., terete. Sheaths brown, membranous; lower bract much exceeding infl., upper bract spike-like. Spikelets in a dense head, 5–8mm, red-brown. Eur., Asia, Afr., N S Amer. ssp. *tabernaemontani* (C. Gmel.)

Löve & D. Löve. St. usually less than 160cm. 'Zebrinus': st. banded white. Z4.
S. validus (Vahl) Löve. 50–250cm. St. 8–25mm diam., thick at base, sheaths with hyaline margins; bracts solitary, round, shorter than infl. Summer. N Amer. Z7.
→*Scirpus*.

Schoenorchis Bl. Orchidaceae. *c*20 epiphytic, monopodial orchids. Lvs terete, linear-lanceolate. Infl. simple or branched; tep. oblong to linear-obovate, free; lip spurred, trilobed, midlobe straight, fleshy, lat. lobes erect. Indomal. to China, Fiji. Z10.
S. densiflora Schltr. St. to 15cm. Lvs filamentous, awl-shaped, 3–5×0.2cm. Infl. dense, secund; fls to 0.4cm diam. New Guinea.
S. gemmata (Lindl.) J.J. Sm. St. 15–30cm. Lvs linear, subterete, curved, 6.5–12.5×0.5cm. Infl. branched; fls purple, pet. interior and lip apex white. N India, Nepal.
S. micrantha Bl. St. tufted, to 15cm. Lvs fleshy, arched, to 3.5×0.2cm. Infl. horizontal, to 5cm; fls to 0.5cm diam., white, becoming yellow. Vietnam, Malaysia, Java to Fiji.
→*Saccolabium*.

Schoenus L. Cyperaceae. *c*80 perenn. or ann. rushes. Culms simple, nodeless, tufted. Lvs basal, narrowly linear. Infl. capitate, 1–10 spikelets; bracts 1–2; glumes distichous; perianth setae 3–5; sta. 3. Aus., S Asia, Afr.
S. pauciflorus Hook. f. To 90cm. Culms v. slender, pale, angled, grooved. Lvs linear-subulate, grooved, rigid, erect; sheaths long, dark brown. Infl. a short lat. pan., spikelets lanceolate, 6.5mm, few, slender, 3–4-flld, dark brown. NZ.

Schomburgkia Lindl. Orchidaceae. 12 epiphytic orchids. Pbs fusiform to cylindric, short-stalked and laterally compressed (resembling *Laelia* spp.) the larger thickly cylindrical, ribbed, hollow and colonized by ants. Lvs 2–4 at or near apex of pbs, rigidly coriaceous. Pan. or rac. term., elongate, erect; fls showy; sep. free, spreading, undulate; pet. broader; lip 3-lobed, lat. lobes erect, midlobe spreading, recurved, undulate, callus carinate. Trop. Amer., W Indies. Z10.
S. crispa Auct. = *S. gloriosa*.
S. gloriosa Rchb. f. Pbs to 30cm, clavate. Lvs to 32×6cm, narrowly oblong, obtuse. Rac., to 75cm; tep. to 4×1.2cm, light yellow-brown tinged purple, veined claret to dark brown narrowly oblong; lip to 2×1.8cm, white edged pale yellow-brown to pink edged pink-brown, midlobe yellow-brown to pink-brown, ovate-elliptic, obtuse. Venez., Guyana, Surinam.
S. humboldtii (Rchb. f.) Rchb. f. Pbs to 25cm, narrowly ovoid-conical or pyriform. Lvs to 20×7cm, oblong to elliptic-ovate. Rac. to 120cm; tep. rose-violet, to 4×1cm, elliptic-lanceolate to oblong-lanceolate; lip to 4×4cm, white veined violet, midlobe suborbicular to subquadrate, emarginate or rounded, disc yellow. Venez.
S. lyonsii Lindl. Pbs to 35×3cm, narrowly fusiform, compressed. Lvs to 30×6cm, oblong. Rac. to 1m; tep. white spotted purple, to 2.5×1cm, ovate-oblong, obtuse, apiculate; lip to 1.6×1.2cm, edged yellow, ovate, obtuse. Autumn. Jam.
S. rosea Lindl. ex Lindl. Pbs to 15cm, fusiform. Lvs to 25×6cm, elliptic-oblong, rounded. Rac. to 55cm; tep. dark purple-violet, oblong-lanceolate to elliptic-lanceolate; lip to 1.7×1.2cm, rose, midlobe suborbicular, rounded, disc yellow. Venez., Colomb.
S. superbiens (Lindl.) Rolfe. Pbs to 30cm, fusiform to ellipsoid, compressed. Lvs to 30cm, oblong to linear-lanceolate. Rac. to 80cm; tep. mauve-purple marked yellow: sep. to 7cm, linear-oblong to oblong-lanceolate; pet. to 4.5cm, narrowly oblong-oblanceolate; lip to 5.5×3.5cm, midlobe obovate to obcordate, emarginate, undulate-crisped, disc yellow. Mex., Guat., Hond.
S. tibicinis (Batem.) Batem. Pbs to 55cm, stoutly cylindric, hollow. Lvs to 35×7cm, usually shorter, oblong or elliptic-oblong, obtuse. Rac. or a pan. elongate; tep. maroon to bright purple-magenta; sep. to 5×1.7cm, elliptic-oblong to elliptic-oblanceolate, undulate; pet. subequal to sep., linear-spathulate to oblanceolate, undulate-crisped; lip to 4×4cm, yellow-white to purple, midlobe small, suborbicular-obcordate, retuse, subentire to cirpsed. Mex., C Amer. to Panama.
S. undulata Lindl. Pbs to 25cm, fusiform. Lvs to 30×5cm, oblong to oblong-ligulate. Rac. to 150cm; tep. to 3.5×1.5cm, deep maroon, oblong to narrowly elliptic, rounded, undulate, twisted; lip to 2.7×2cm, bright rose-purple marked white, midlobe oblong, shortly apiculate, disc white. Early spring. Trin., Venez., Colomb.
S. weberbaueriana Kränzl. Pbs to 37cm, cylindric, grooved. Lvs to 26×6cm, oblong or elliptic-oblong. Rac. to 75cm; tep. yellow-brown streaked dark brown, sep. to 3cm, oblong, acute or apiculate, undulate, pet. shorter, obtuse or truncate; lip to 2×1.3cm, white, broadly obovate, obscurely 3-lobed, slightly

retuse, apiculate. Peru.
→*Cattleya* and *Laelia*.

Schotia Jacq. BOERBOON. Leguminosae (Caesalpinioideae). 5 trees and shrubs. Lvs paripinnate. Fls packed in axill. or terminal pan., sometimes cauliflorous; cal. 4-lobed; pet. 5; sta. 10, of 2 lengths. Fr. flat, oblong, leathery. S Afr. Z9.

S. afra (L.) Bodin. HOTTENTOT'S BEAN; KAROO BOERBOON. Densely branched, to 6m. St. sometimes twisted. Lfts to 2.5cm in 4–16 pairs, linear to oblong or obovate. Pan. axill., crowded at br. tip; pet. to 1.5cm, oval, bright red or occas. pink. S Afr., Nam.

S. brachypetala Sonder. WEEPING BOERBOON; TREE FUCHSIA; AFRICAN WALNUT. Wide-spreading, to 15m. Lvs pink-red when emerging, becoming copper and lime; lfts 2–6cm, in 4–7 pairs, oblong or oval. Pan. terminal and axill. often on old wood; fls fragrant; cal. to 2cm, long-tubular, crimson; pet. minute, obscured by cal. Summer. Zimb., Moz., S to Transvaal, Natal, Swaz.

S. capitata Bolle. DWARF BOERBOON. To 6m; br. slender. Lfts 1.3–2.5cm; in 3–5 pairs, round or oval with sharply pointed tip. Fls densely clustered; pet. to 1.5cm+, narrowly obovate, brilliant scarlet, exceeding cal. E S Afr., Moz.

S. latifolia Jacq. ELEPHANT HEDGE BEAN TREE. Domed or columnar, 5–14m. Lfts 2.5 to 6cm, in 3–5 pairs, oblong to oval, tips rounded or pointed. Pan. to 13cm, term.; cal. red-brown; pet. 0.5–0.8cm, pale pink or flesh-coloured, recurved. E S Afr.

S. speciosa Jacq. = *S. afra*.
S. transvaalensis Rolfe = *S. capitata*.

Schouwia DC. Cruciferae. 1 variable ann. herb, to 30cm. St. branched. Lvs simple, oblong-ovate, 6×4cm, fleshy, tapering to the base, entire, st. lvs clasping rac. somewhat corymbose at first; pet. 4, purple, exceeding sep.; sta. 6. Summer. Sahara to Arabia. Z6.

S. arabica DC. = *S. purpurea*.
S. purpurea (Forssk.) Schweinf.
→*Subularia*.

Schrebera Roxb. Oleaceae. 8 trees and shrubs. Lvs opposite, glab., coriaceous, simple or pinnate. Pan. term.; cor., tube extended, 6-lobed. Afr., Peru, India.

S. alata (Hochst.) Welw. To 8m. Lvs pinnate; lfts 5, elliptic, to 8cm, term. pinna to 12cm; rachis winged. Cor. white with dark centre, tube to 1 cm. Trop. Afr. Z10.

Schubertia Mart.
S. albens Mart. = *Araujia sericofera*.
S. graveolens Lindl. = *Araujia graveolens*.

Schwantesia Dinter. Aizoaceae. 10 cushion-forming succulents. Br. clothed with dried lf remains. Lvs paired, unequal, entire or dentate or lobulate, keeled, margins and keel often reddened, upper surface flat, glab. or velvety. Fls solitary. S Afr. (Cape Prov.), Nam. Z9.

S. acutipetala L. Bol. Lvs 52×15×5mm, sharply tapered, flat above, semicircular beneath, acutely angled, blue-grey. Fls 4cm diam., yellow. W Cape.

S. chrysoleuca (Schltr.) L. Bol. = *Monilaria chrysoleuca*.

S. herrei L. Bol. Lvs 25–35×16mm with an entire, acute keel pulled forward, chin-like towards obtuse tip, with several teeth, pale blue-green to chalky, smooth. Fls 3–4cm diam., yellow. W Cape, Nam. f. *major* G. Rowley. Fls to 5.5cm diam. Nam.: Great Namaqualand. var. *minor* L. Bol. Lvs 9–20×10mm. Fls 2–2.5cm diam. Nam.

S. loeschiana Tisch. = *S. herrei* f. *major*.
S. moniliformis (Haw.) L. Bol. = *Monilaria moniliformis*.

S. pillansii L. Bol. Lvs 53×5×8mm, blue-green, obliquely acute to tapered, obliquely keeled beneath with a red line along the keel. Fls 3cm diam., yellow. Cape.

S. pisiformis (Haw.) L. Bol. = *Monilaria pisiformis*.

S. ruedebuschii Dinter. Lvs erect, 30–50×10–12mm, navicular, margins ± rounded, suffused blue-green with white mottling, tip expanded and obtuse, with 3–7 broad teeth. Fls 3.5–4cm diam., light yellow. Nam.: Great Namaqualand.

S. triebneri L. Bol. Lvs 40–60×1×5mm, v. expanded and mucronate above, rounded beneath, keeled toward tip, white-green to blue-green or yellow-green with red dots and angles. Fls 4–5cm diam., yellow. W Cape.

Sciadophyllum P. Browne.
S. capitatus (Jacq.) Griseb. = *Oreopanax capitatus*.

SCIADOPITYACEAE Hayata. See *Sciadopitys*.

Sciadopitys Sieb. & Zucc. UMBRELLA PINE; JAPANESE UMBRELLA PINE. Sciadopityaceae. 1 everg. conifer to 40m; crown conic; br. slender, whorled when young; bark rich brown, peeling in vertical strips. Needles whorled 10–30, 7–12cm×3–6mm, linear, emarginate, midrib sunken, glossy green above, olive green beneath with 2 white stomatal bands. Cones solitary, oblong-ovoid, 5–9×7cm; scales spirally arranged, leathery, cuneate, apex obtuse. Jap. Z6.

S. verticillata (Thunb.) Sieb. & Zucc.
→*Taxus*.

Sciaphyllum Bremek. Acanthaceae. 1 perenn., woody-based herb to 60cm. Lvs to 15cm, ovate, opposite, glab., purple beneath; petioles long, cable to 12cm, terminal, rigid; cor. purple, tube cylindric, limb 5-lobed, bilabiate. Origin unknown. Z9.

S. amoenum Bremek.

Scilla L. Liliaceae (Hyacinthaceae). *c*90 bulbous herbs. Lvs basal, linear to elliptic. Fls few to numerous, in term. scapose rac. or corymbs; tep. 6, nearly equal, distinct, or v. shortly connate towards the base; sta. 6. S Afr., Asia, Eur.

S. adlamii Bak. = *S. Ledebouria cooperi*.
S. amethystina Vis. = *S. litardieri*.
S. amoena L. Bulb 1.5–2cm diam., dark purple-brown. Scapes 15–20cm, angled. Lvs 15–22×1–2cm, flaccid, strap-shaped, ascending, emerging before flowering, tinged red near base. Fls rotate, erect, 3–6 in a loose rac., blue; tep. 9–12mm, lanceolate, mauve-blue with deeper blue midribs. Origin uncertain but nat. SE Eur. Z7.

S. apertiflora (Bak.) C.A. Sm. = *Ledebouria apertiflora*.
S. autumnalis L. Bulb 1.5–3cm diam., brown or pink tinged. Scapes 5–30cm, scabrous. Lvs 2–18cm×1–2mm, grooved above, almost terete, emerging after flowering. Fls 5–25 in an open rac., tep. 3–5mm, spreading, lilac to pink. S, W & C Eur., NW Afr. to S Russia, Iran, Iraq. 'Alba': fls white. 'Praecox': fls large, purple-blue; v. robust. 'Rosea': fls pink. Z6.

S. bifolia L. Bulb 5–25mm diam., brown pink beneath. Scape 7.5–15cm, terete. Lvs 5–20×0.3–1.5cm, linear to linear-lanceolate, tip incurved, appearing with fls, concave above. Fls 1–10 in a narrowly 1-sided or deltoid, mostly nodding rac., 2.5–4cm diam.; tep. 5–10mm, ovate to elliptic, tips incurved, blue to purple-blue. Summer–autumn. C & S Eur., Turk. Z6.

S. campanulata Ait. = *Hyacinthoides hispanica*.
S. chinensis Benth. = *S. scilloides*.
S. cilicica Siehe. Bulb 1.25–2.5cm diam., dull violet. Lvs 13–40×1–2cm, broadly linear, appearing before fls. Scapes 14–38cm. Rac. lax; fls 2–8 ascending; seg. 9–16mm, spreading, pale or lavender-blue. Turk.

S. concolor Bak. = *Ledebouria concolor*.
S. cooperi Hook. f. = *Ledebouria cooperi*.
S. floribunda Bak. = *Ledebouria floribunda*.
S. hispanica Mill. = *Hyacinthoides hispanica*.
S. hohenackeri Fisch. & Mey. Bulb 1.5–2cm diam., grey-brown. Lvs 10–25×0.3–1cm, linear, V-shaped in section, emerging at flowering. Scape 5–20cm. Fls 4–12, on spreading or curved stalks in a fringed-bracteate rac.; tep. 1–1.5cm, oblanceolate, pale blue. S Iran, Russia. Z6.

S. hypoxidioides Schönl. = *Ledebouria hypoxidioides*.
S. inquinata C.A. Sm. = *Ledebouria inquinata*.
S. italica L. = *Hyacinthoides italica*.
S. lilio-hyacinthus L. Bulb 3–5cm, composed of yellow tinged scales. Scapes 5–10cm. Lvs 15–30×1–3cm, linear, acute, shiny, emerging at flowering. Fls 5–20, campanulate, in a dense, conical rac., 3–8cm, on ascending, blue-violet stalks; tep. 9–12mm, ovate to elliptic, bright violet-blue, or white. Fr., Spain. Z6.

S. litardieri Breistr. Bulb 1.5cm diam., brown. Scape 5–15cm. Lvs 25–30×0.4–0.8cm, narrow-ligulate, glab., narrowed at both ends, emerging at flowering. Fls 3–15, campanulate, in dense, narrow, conical rac., 5–15cm, on ascending, blue-violet pedicels; tep. 4–6mm, ovate, tinged pink or blue-violet. Balk. Z6.

S. messeniaca Boiss. Bulb 2–3cm diam., pale brown. Scapes 5–15cm, angled. Lvs 15–25×1–2.5cm, broadly linear, emerging at flowering. Fls 7–20, sheathing below in a dense, ovate-oblong rac., 4–12cm long; tep. 6–8mm, lilac-blue, linear, obtuse. S Greece. Z8.

S. mischtschenkoana Gross. Bulb 1.5–3cm diam., grey-brown. Scapes 1–3, 5–10cm, terete. Lvs 4–10×0.4–2cm, linear to oblanceolate, flat, emerging at flowering. Fls 2–6, widely campanulate, in a loose 6–12cm rac.; tep. 1–1.5cm, oblong-elliptic, obtuse, white-blue with a darker stripe. Iran, Russia. Z6.

S. monophyllos Link. Bulb 1–2cm diam., pale brown. Scape 5–15cm, slender, flexuous. Lf usually solitary, 10–25×1–3cm, broadly lanceolate to elliptic, strap-shaped. Fls 3–15, campanulate, ascending in a loose rac., 5–10cm; bracts 4–7mm, linear-lanceolate, acuminate; tep. 6–9mm, elliptic, pale violet-blue. Spain, Port., NW Afr. Z9.

S. natalensis Planch. Bulb 7–10cm diam., brown. Scape 30–45cm, stout, terete. Lvs 20–60×7–10cm, lanceolate, strap-shaped, acuminate, ascending. Fls 50–100 in a dense rac., 15–30cm, on ascending, blue pedicels; tep. 6–10mm, elliptic-oblong, obtuse, spreading, light violet-blue or pink or white. E S Afr., Les. Z9.

S. non-scripta (L.) Hoffssg. & Link = *Hyacinthoides non-scripta*.

S. nutans Sm. = *Hyacinthoides non-scripta*.

S. ovalifolia (Schräd.) C.A. Sm. = *Ledebouria ovalifolia*.

S. ovatifolia Bak. = *Ledebouria ovatifolia*.

S. persica Hausskn. Bulb 2.5–3cm diam., with purple inner tunic, dark brown outer. Lvs 30–45×1–1.5cm, slightly keeled, linear, emerging at flowering. Scapes 1–3, 20–40cm. Fls 20–80, in a compact, conical rac. 5–10cm; tep. 7–8mm, lanceolate to elliptic, narrow-concave, spreading, bright blue. W Iran, N Iraq. Z8.

S. peruviana L. Bulb 6–8cm diam., brown with woolly outer scales. Scapes 15–25cm, sparsely stout. Lvs 40–60×1–4cm, linear to lanceolate, strap-shaped, bristly-ciliate. Fls 40–100, long-stalked in a v. dense, deltoid rac., 5–20cm; tep. 8–15mm, deep violet-blue to dull purple-brown, or white. SW Eur., W Afr. *S. hughii* Tinco ex Guss., differs in its larger habit and deep violet fls. 'Alba': fls white. Z8.

S. pratensis Waldst. & Kit. = *S. litardieri*.

S. puschkinioides Reg. Bulb 1–2cm diam., grey-tinged. Scape 10–15cm, terete. Lvs 10–15×0.3–0.6cm, broadly linear, obtuse, emerging at flowering. Fls 2–8, erect, 'starry', in a short rac.; tep. 1–1.5cm, oblong, acute, tinged white or pale blue, with darker stripe. Russia. Z6.

S. rosenii K. Koch. Bulb 1–2.5cm diam., dark brown-violet. Lvs 10–15×0.6–1.5cm, tips incurved, ovoid, emerging at flowering. Scapes 10–25cm, terete. Fls in short rac.; on arching pedicels; tep. 1.5–2.5cm, oblong, obtuse, pale blue with a darker stripe on the outside, tinged white inside near base. Russia. Z6.

S. scilloides (Lindl.) Druce. Bulb 1.5–2cm diam., black tinged. Scape 20–40cm, slender, straight or slightly angled. Lvs 15–25×0.4–0.7cm, linear, flaccid, channelled, tip blunt, slightly incurved. Fls 40–80, in a dense, oblong rac., 7–12cm, on ascending, often twin pedicels; tep. 3–4mm, narrow-oblong, acute, spreading, mauve-pink. China, Korea, Taiwan, Jap., Ryukyu Is. Z5.

S. siberica Haw. Bulb 1.5–2cm diam., dark purple brown. Scapes 10–20cm, fleshy, tinged mauve above, finely ribbed. Lvs 10–15×0.5–1.5, narrowly strap-shaped, ascending. Fls mauve-stalked in loose, bracteate rac., to 1.5cm diam., rotate or broadly bowl-shaped, pendent; tep. 1–2cm, elliptic-oblong, obtuse, bright-blue with a darker median band. S Russia, nat. C Eur. 'Alba': fls white. 'Spring Beauty' ('Atrocaerulea'): upright, to 20cm; fls deep blue, long-lasting, scented. ssp. *armena* (Grossh.) Mordak. Bulb 0.7–2cm diam. Lvs 5–6×0.4–0.5cm, linear. Scapes 6–8cm; fls 1–2; tep. pale blue with dark blue line. Turk., Georgia, Armenia. Z5.

S. sinensis (Lour.) Merrill = *S. scilloides*.

S. socialis Bak. = *Ledebouria socialis*.

S. tubergeniana Stearn = *S. mischtschenkoana*.

S. verna Huds. Bulb 1–2cm diam. Scapes shorter than lvs. Lvs 3–20cm×2–5mm, linear, falcate, concave, obtuse, slightly channelled, emerging at flowering. Fls 2–12, in a dense, short, subcorymbose or deltoid rac.; tep. 5–8mm, narrow-oblong-ovate, light violet-blue. W Eur. *S. ramburei* Boiss. differs in its larger, more robust habit. Z7.

S. violacea Hutch. = *Ledebouria socialis*.

Scindapsus Schott. Araceae. *c*40 everg. herbs to lianes climbing by adventitious roots. Lvs entire, ovate to oblong or oblong-lanceolate, acuminate; petioles geniculate at apex, often winged. Peduncles solitary or clustered, equalling petiole; spathe cymbiform, to 15cm, green or white; spadix densely covered with hermaphrodite fls. SE Asia, Pacific, Braz. Z10.

S. aureus (Lind. & André) Engl. = *Epipremnum aureum*.

S. pictus Hassk. St. to 12m+, slender, verrucose. Lvs to 18× 12.5cm, ovate-lanceolate to broad-ovate, coriaceous, dull green; petiole to 3cm, winged. Spathe to 6.5cm. Java to Borneo. 'Argyraeus' (SATIN POTHO): juvenile phase, often cult.; lvs to 7–10×5–8cm, ovate, cordate, satiny dark green with silver spots.

Sciodaphyllum P. Browne.

S. pulchellum Griff., nom. nud. = *Schefflera pueckleri*.

S. pulchrum Wallich ex Voigt, nom. nud. = *Schefflera pueckleri*.

Scirpoides Ség. Cyperaceae. Perenn. rush. St. 30–50cm, cylindrical, erect. Spikelets small, ovoid, brown, awned in compact spherical heads. Eur., SW Asia. Z7.

S. holoschoenus (L.) Soják. ROUND-HEADED CLUBRUSH. 'Vareigatus': st. banded cream.

→*Holoschoenus* and *Scirpus*.

Scirpus L. Cyperaceae. *c*100 rhizomatous, perenn., grasslike herbs. St. jointed, leafy. Lvs broad-linear, with a membranous ligule. Bracts 2–4, lf.- to bristle-like; infl. a term. pan. with many br. (rays); spikelets stalked or in clusters; fls minute. Cosmop.

S. cernuus Vahl = *Isolepis cernua*.

S. cyperinus (L.) Kunth. WOOL GRASS. 1–1.5m. St. subterete. Lvs narrow-linear, ridged. Bracts exceeding infl., 15–30cm; rays somewhat drooping; spikelets 3–10cm, red-brown, bristles making spikelets appear woolly. Late summer. E N Amer. Z7.

S. cyperoides L. = *Cyperus cyperoides*.

S. filiformis Savi non Burm. f. = *Isolepis cernua*.

S. holoschoenus L. = *Scirpoides holoschoenus*.

S. hudsonianus (Michx.) Fern. = *Schoenoplectus hudsonianus*.

S. lacustris L. = *Schoenoplectus lacustris*.

S. maritimus L. = *Bolboschoenus maritimus*.

S. palustris L. = *Eleocharis palustris*.

S. parvulus Roem. & Schult. = *Eleocharis parvula*.

S. prolifer Rottb. = *Isolepis prolifera*.

S. romanus L. = *Scirpoides holoschoenus*.

S. setaceus L. = *Isolepis setacea*.

S. sylvaticus L. WOOD CLUB RUSH. 30–120cm. St. 3-angled. Lvs to 2cm wide, margins rough. Bracts unequal, the long bracts just equalling infl., shorter bracts bristle-like; infl. to 15cm; spikelets to 0.4cm, green-brown, bristles 1mm+. Eur. to Sib. Z6.

S. tabernaemontani C. Gmel. = *Schoenoplectus lacustris*.

S. validus Vahl = *Schoenoplectus validus*.

Scleranthus L. KNAWEL. Caryophyllaceae. 10 low-growing much-branched ann. or perenn. herbs. Lvs in opposite pairs, slightly joined at the base, linear to subulate. Fls v. small, apetalous, solitary, paired or in branched cymes; sep. 4 or 5, on cup-shaped receptacle; sta. 1–10. Widely distrib. in the temp. regions of both hemispheres, though not native in N Amer.

S. biflorus (Forst. & Forst. f.) Hook. sensu lato. Mat-forming, yellow-tinged perenn. Fls usually in pairs, sometimes solitary, on an axill. peduncle; each fl. with 2 small bracts at base; sep. 4–5; sta. 1. Summer. NZ, Tasm., S Amer. Z7.

S. brockiei Williamson = *S. biflorus*.

S. uniflorus Williamson = *S. biflorus*.

Sclerocactus Britt. & Rose. Cactaceae. 15–18 low-growing cacti; st. small, depressed-globose to cylindric, tuberculate-ribbed, spiny. Fls apical, shortly funnelform or campanulate; floral areoles naked. N Mex. and SW US.

S. brevihamatus (Engelm.) D. Hunt. St. globose to obovoid, 5–10×5–7.5cm; ribs usually 13, compressed; tubercles with, woolly grove, central spines 4, hooked; radial spines to 14, white, 1–2cm. Fl. 25–32mm long; inner tep. 15×4mm, pink with darker mid-stripe. SW US. Z9.

S. erectocentrus (J. Coult.) N.P. Tayl. Differs from *S. johnsonii* in central spines 1, or 2–4, upper 1–3 like radials, lowermost 1 much longer; radial spines 11–15, 1.2–2.5cm. Fl. 4–5×3.8–5cm, pale to orange-pink or rarely white. N Mex., S Ariz. Z9.

S. glaucus (Schum.) L. Bens. St. ovoid to globose, 4–6×4–5cm+, often glaucous; ribs *c*12, well-defined areoles with nectar-secreting glands; central spines 1–3, straigh to curved, rarely hooked, to 2.5cm, brown; radial spines 6–8, acicular, to 2cm, white or some brown. Fl. 3–3.8×4–5cm, magenta; stigmas pink-tinged, erect. Summer. SW US. Z9.

S. intermedius Peebles = *S. whipplei*.

S. intertextus (Engelm.) N.P. Tayl. St. globose to shortly cylindric, 5–15×4–7.5cm; ribs *c*13, tuberculate; spines pink-tinged or grey to pale yellow with pink tips, central spines 4, lowermost projecting, v. short, uppermost 3 adpressed, to 12–15mm (lowermost projecting and upper 3 less adpressed, to 2(–4)cm in var. *Dasyacanthus* (Engelm.) N.P. Tayl.); radial spines 13–25, 9–15mm, adpressed. Fl. 2–3×2.5–3cm, pale pink or salmon to white; stigmas 6–12, pink to crimson, erect. Summer. N Mex., SW US. Z9.

S. johnsonii (Parry ex Engelm.) N.P. Tayl. St. ovoid to cylindric, 10–15(–25)×5–10cm; ribs 17–21, acute; central spines 4–9, similar, straight or curved, pink to red-brown, to 3–4cm; radial spines *c*9–10, paler, 1.2–2cm. Fl. 5–6×5–7.5cm, magenta with red throat, or yellow with deep green throat; stigmas *c*10, light yellow-green to brown-green, erect. Summer. SW US. Z9.

S. mariposensis (Hester) N.P. Tayl. St. depressed-globose to ovoid, 6–10×4–6cm; ribs to *c*21, poorly defined, tuberculate; central spines 2–4, pale brown with darker tips, lowermost down-curved, 0.7–1.5cm, other(s) curving upwards, to 2cm, slender; radial spines *c*26–32, 6mm, interlaced, obscuring st., off-white. Fl. *c*2.5–4cm; tep. white to pale pink, with darker or pale green midstripe; stigmas 5–8, green, erect. Summer. N Mex. SW Tex. Z9.

S. papyracanthus (Engelm.) N.P. Tayl. Simple or clustering if grafted; st. 2.5–10×1.2–3.5cm; ribs 0 or dissolved into small tubercles; areoles nectar-secreting; central spines 1–4, 1–5cm, curved, not hooked, flattened, papery, brown; radial spines 5–9, 0.3–0.4cm, white. Fl. to 2.5×2–2.5cm; tep. almost white or outer tinged brown; stigmas c5, pale green, erect. Summer. SW US. Z9.

S. polyancistrus (Engelm. & Bigelow) Britt. & Rose. St. cylindric, 10–15×5–7.5cm; ribs c13–17, well defined; central spines c9–11, mostly hooked, to 7.5–9cm, upper 3 flattened, white, others red or red-brown, rarely yellow; radial spines 10–15, to 2cm, white. Fl. c5–6×5cm, magenta; stigmas c10, pink. Summer. S Calif., SW Nevada. Z9.

S. scheeri (Salm-Dyck) N.P. Tayl. St. globose to elongate-clavate, 2.5–15×2.5–7cm, dark green; ribs c13, tuberculate; areoles grooved, nectar-secreting; central spines 1–4, lowermost strongly hooked, 1–4.5cm, pale yellow or brown, uppermost 1–3, ± straight, flattened, white to pale yellow; radial spines 12–20-, to c1cm, straight, white to pale yellow. Fl. 2.5–3cm, yellow-green; stigmas c10, pale green. Summer. NE Mex., SW US. Z9.

S. tobuschii (W.T. Marshall) D. Hunt. Simple; st. flat-topped to turbinate or obconic, to 5×5cm; spines finely hairy, yellow tipped red; central spines 3, upper 2 to 2.2cm, lowermost strongly hooked, shorter; radial spines 7–9, to 12mm. Fl. to 3–4×3–4cm, pale yellow; stigmas 6–7, pale green. SW US. Z9.

S. uncinatus (Gal. ex Pfeiff. & Otto) N.P. Tayl. St. depressed-globose to shortly cylindric, 7.5–20×5–7.5cm (to 15cm or more diam. in var. crassihamatus (F.A.C. Weber) N.P. Tayl.), glaucous; ribs c13, well-defined; areoles on large tubercles, nectar-secreting; central spines 1–4, lowermost strongly hooked, 5–11cm, slender (stout in var. crassihamatus), ascending, red-brown, upper 3, straight incurved, red-brown or white, often flattened; radial spines 7–11, to 5cm, the upper and lat. nearly straight, pale at first, the lower hooked, red-brown. Fl. 2–4×2.5–3cm; tep. deep pink to brown-red, white in var. crassi-hamatus; stigmas c10, almost white, pale yellow or pink, spreading. Summer. N Mex., SW US. Z9.

S. unguispinus (Engelm.) N.P. Tayl. St. depressed-globose to shortly cylindric, 7–14×7–15cm; ribs 13–21, acute, strongly tuberculate; central spines 3–9, to 3.5cm, pale yellow to grey tipped dark brown to almost black, lowermost stout and strongly down-curved, recurved at apex, others ascending, stout or finer (all much finer, lowermost scarcely recurved in var. du-rangensis (Runge) N.P. Tayl.): radial spines 15–30, 1–3.3m, nearly straight, interlaced, white to pale yellow, tipped darker. Fl. to c3cm; tep. green-brown or somewhat red-brown, with pale margins; stigmas c10–15, pale yellow to green-yellow, erect. Summer. N Mex. Z9.

S. warnockii (L. Bens.) N.P. Tayl. St. ovoid to elongate, 7–11(–15)×5–7.5(–10)cm; ribs 13–21; central spines 1–6, 1.2–2.5cm; tep. white to pale pink, with pale green midstripe; stigmas 5–10, light green, erect. Summer. SW US. Z9.

S. whipplei (Engelm. & Bigelow) Britt. & Rose. St. depressed-globose to cylindric, 7.5–15(–20)×5–9cm; ribs c13–15, well-defined; areoles nectar-secreting; central spines c4, 2.5–4.5cm, lowermost hooked, purple-pink to red, uppermost to 5cm, flattened, white; radial spines 7–11, to 2.5cm, off-white. Fl. 1.5–5×2.5–5.5(–7)cm, yellow, pink, pale purple or white; stigmas 5–6, green, erect. Summer. SW US. Z9.

S. wrightiae L. Bens. St. depressed-globose to obovoid, 5–9×5–7.4cm; ribs c13; central spines 4, to 1.2cm, lowermost hooked, dark brown; radial spines 8–10, to 0.6–1.2cm, white. Fl. 2–2.5(–4)×2–2.5(–4)cm; tep. almost white to pale pink, midstripe brown; stigmas 5–8, green. Summer. W US. Z9.

→Ancistrocactus, Echinocactus, Echinomastus, Ferocactus, Hamatocactus, Neolloydia, Pediocactus and Toumeya.

Sclerocarya Hochst. Anacardiaceae. 3 trees or shrubs. Bark grey, peeling, lenticular. Lvs at ends of branchlets, imparipinnate. Infl. a pan. or rac.; sep. 4–5, oblong or orbicular; pet. 4–5, oblong or obovate, obtuse, imbricate. Fr. a drupe, 2–3-seeded. S Afr., Nam. Z10.

S. birrea (A. Rich.) Hochst. MARULA. Tree to 10m, decid. Lfts 7–13 rarely more, 3–10cm, ovate or circular to elliptic, acute, entire, dark green above, paler beneath, lower lfts sessile; petiole often winged. Infl. simple, 8–22cm; (♂ catkin-like); sep. red; pet. yellow; sta. 15–20. Fr. to 3.5cm diam. Summer. Ethiop. to S Afr., Madag. ssp. caffra (Sonder) Kokw. Lfts 7–11, 3–11cm, ovate to elliptic, acuminate or cuspidate, lower lfts shortly petiolate. Infl. to 22cm. ssp. multifoliata (Engl.) Kokw. Lfts 25–37, to 1.5cm, circular to broadly elliptic, entire or sinuate-lobed.

S. caffra Sonder = S. birrea ssp. caffra.
→Poupartia.

Sclerothamnus R. Br.
S. microphyllus R. Br. = Eutaxia microphylla.

Scobinaria Seib. = Arrabidaea.

Scoke Phytolacca americana.

Scoliopus Torr. Liliaceae (Trilliaceae). 2 small ± stemless perenn. herbs. Lvs generally 2, oblong to elliptic, purple spotted and blotched. Umbel unstalked fls malodorous; pedicels red-tinted, angled; tep. 6, outer broad, spreading, inner erect, narrow; sta. 3; ovary narrow, 3-angled, 1-celled. NW US. Z7.

S. bigelowii Torr. FOETID ADDER'S-TONGUE; STINK POD; BROWNIES. Lvs 10–20×5–10cm. Fls 3–12; pedicels 10–20cm; tep. 14–17mm, outer ovate-lanceolate, tinged green, veins flushed red. Spring. Calif.

S. hallii S. Wats. OREGON FOETID ADDER'S-TONGUE. Lvs 8–15×3–5cm. Fls 1–8; pedicels 3–6cm; tep. 8mm, outer lanceolate or oblanceolate, mottled yellow-green and purple. Spring. Oreg.

Scolopendrium Adans.
S. hybridum Milde = Asplenium hybridum.
S. nigripes (Fée) Hook. = Schaffneria nigripes.
S. officinarum Sw. = Asplenium scolopendrium.
S. sagittatum DC. = Asplenium sagittatum.
S. vulgare Sm. = Asplenium scolopendrium.

Scolopia Schreb. Flacourtiaceae. 37 small trees or shrubs, sometimes spiny. Lvs alt., crenulate or entire. Fls small in axill. rac. or pan., sep. and pet. 4–6, imbricate; sta. many. Fr. a fleshy berry. Trop. of Afr., Asia and Aus. Z9.

S. braunii (Klotzsch) Sleumer. Tree, to 30m. Lvs to 8cm, papery, ovate to lanceolate, entire or slightly toothed, sometimes with 2 or 3 marginal glands below, pan. to 5cm. Fr. to 12mm diam., dark red. Queensld, New S Wales.

S. brownii F. Muell. = S. braunii.

S. ecklonii (Nees) Harv. THORN PEAR. Much-branched shrub or tree, to 25m, with long spines bearing lvs & fls. Lvs to 8cm, obovate to elliptic, pink becoming dark green and leathery. Rac. to 3cm; fls cream or yellow, fragrant. Fr. to 8mm diam., purple-red. S Afr.

S. zeyheri (Nees) Harv. = S. ecklonii.
→Phoberos.

Scolymus L. Compositae. 3 ann. to perenn. spiny herbs; st. erect, solitary, branched, usually winged. Lvs sinuate-dentate or pinnatifid, often spotted white above. Cap. ligulate, few to numerous, term. or axill., sessile; receptacle conic or elongate, with decid. scales; phyllaries mucronate; flts 5-toothed, yellow. S Eur. Z7.

S. grandiflorus Desf. Perenn., 20–40cm, ± hairy, st. wings continuous, spinose-dentate. Lvs ovate-lanceolate to linear-oblong, pinnatisect, 6–12cm, spiny, margins scarcely thickened; upper st. lvs sparsely long spinose-dentate. Cap. in a subcorymbose pan. Spring. Medit.

S. hispanicus L. GOLDEN THISTLE; SPANISH OYSTER THISTLE. Bienn. or perenn., 20–80cm, somewhat hairy, st. wings interrupted, spinose-dentate. Lvs 4–20cm; basal lvs oblanceolate, pinnatisect, long-petiolate, soft, spines few; st. lvs linear-oblong to ovate, sinuate-pinnatifid, rigid, spiny, margins scarcely thickened, uppermost lvs irregularly spiny. Cap. clustered in a narrow pan. Summer. S Eur. northwards to NW Fr.

S. maculatus L. Ann., 15–90cm, subglabrous, st. wings continuous, irregularly spinose-dentate, with thickened white margins. Lvs 4–20cm, sometimes spotted white above, margins white, thickened; basal lvs oblanceolate, pinnatifid, stiff, spines few; st. lvs oblong-lanceolate to ovate, sinuate-pinnatifid, rigid, spiny, uppermost lvs regularly pectinate-spiny. Cap. clustered in a sub-corymbose pan. Summer. S Eur.

Scoot Berry Streptopus amplexifolius.

Scopelogena L. Bol. Aizoaceae. 2 compact to mat-forming succulent shrubs. Lvs triquetrous to cylindrical fleshy, falcate, upper surface flat to convex, lower surface rounded or bluntly carinate. Fls 7–15 together in a loosely branched infl., yellow. S Afr. (Cape Prov.). Z9.

S. gracilis L. Bol. Slender shrub, to 120cm diam. St. to 2.5cm thick, branched, erect to prostrate. Lvs to 5×0.3cm slender, obtuse. Fls small, scented. Swellendam and Riversdale Districts.

S. vereculata (L.) L. Bol. Woody, to 30cm. St. stout, erect. Lvs 2.5–3.5×0.6–0.8cm, crowded, apiculate, soft, grey-pruinose. Fls 1.5cm diam., yellow. S Cape.
→Lampranthus and Ruschia.

Scopolia Jacq. Solanaceae. 5 perenn. herbs. Rhiz. fleshy. St. erect, sparsely branched. Lvs membranous, entire, petiolate.

Fls solitary, pendent; pedicels filiform; cal. 5-lobed, accrescent; cor. cylindric to campanulate, limb 5-lobed; sta. 5, included. Eur., Jap., Himal., Sib.

S. carniolica Jacq. To 60cm+. Lvs ovate or ovate-oblong, entire, to 20×8cm, apex long-acute; petioles to 1.3cm. Fls solitary, axill.; pedicel to 4cm; cor. brown-purple to vivid red, interior yellow or green, to 2.5cm. Spring. C & SE Eur., Russia. Z5.

S. physaloides Dunal. To 45cm. Lvs ovate, weakly sinuate. Fls term., in a capitate corymb, purple violet. Spring. Sib. Z5.

S. sinensis Hemsl. = *Atropanthe sinensis.*
→*Hyoscyamus.*

Scorpion Grass *Myosotis.*
Scorpion Orchid *Arachnis.*
Scorpion Senna *Coronilla emerus.*
Scorpion Weed *Phacelia.*

Scorzonera L. Compositae. *c*150 ann. to perenn. herbs, rarely shrubby. St. solitary to several, from a thick rootstock. Lvs alt., entire to pinnatisect. Cap. ligulate, solitary to many. Medit. to C Asia. Z6.

S. aristata Ramond ex DC. Perenn., 10–50cm, subglabrous or sparsely woolly on st., lf bases and phyllaries. St. solitary or few, erect, simple or rarely forked, leafless or with 1 small lf, rather fleshy. Lvs to 40cm, linear or linear-lanceolate. Involucre 2–3cm; flts 3–6cm, yellow, sometimes tinted red beneath. S Eur. mts.

S. brevicaulis Vahl. Like *S. hispanica* but 15–50cm, st. often 1-branched at base and ± leafless, lvs to 20cm, linear to linear-lanceolate, acuminate, lacerate-dentate. S Fr., SE Spain, NW Afr.

S. coronopifolia Desf. = *S. brevicaulis.*

S. hispanica L. COMMON VIPER'S GRASS. Perenn. 25–130cm, sub-glabrous or sparsely hairy. St. solitary or few, usually branched from middle upward, erect, leafy, particularly below. Lvs 15–40cm, linear to ovate-elliptic, acuminate, entire to weakly dentate, base attenuate, sometimes petiolate. Cap. solitary; involucre 2–3cm; flts 2.5–6cm, yellow, sometimes purple on outer surface. Summer. C & S Eur., S Russia and Sib.

S. laciniata L. Ann. to perenn., 5–60cm, subglabrous to tomentose. St. several, usually branched up to middle, erect. Lvs 3–20cm, pinnatisect, seg. remote, obovate and subobtuse or pinnatisect, upper lvs entire. Cap. solitary; involucre 7–20mm; flts to 2.5cm, yellow. Summer. Eur., NW Afr. to Iran.

S. mollis Bieb. Perenn., 5–30cm, woolly-tomentose. St. solitary or few, erect, simple or branched near base. Lvs 5–15cm, linear, acute, entire, sometimes undulate, expanded at base, usually crowded in lower or middle part of st. Involucre 18–27mm; flts 1.5–4.5cm, yellow, red beneath. Summer. E Medit., Cauc., Iraq and Iran.

S. picroides L. = *Reichardia picroides.*

S. purpurea L. PURPLE VIPER'S GRASS. Perenn., 10–70cm, sub-lgabrous to woolly. St. solitary, erect, often branched above. Lvs 3–40cm, grass-like, entire, caniculate, keeled, erect, st. lvs smaller, amplexicaul. Involucre 1.5–3cm; flts 3.5–5cm, pale lilac. Late spring–early summer. C & CS Eur., SE Russia. ssp. *rosea* (Waldst. & Kit.) Nyman. St. simple. Lvs flat, scarcely keeled. Flts pale purple. Summer. EC Eur., Balk., N & C It.

S. rosea Waldst. & Kit. = *S. purpurea* ssp. *rosea.*

S. tingitana L. = *Reichardia tingitana.*

Scotch Asphodel *Tofieldia pusilla.*
Scotch-Attorney *Clusia rosea.*
Scotch Broom *Cytisus scoparius.*
Scotch Heather *Calluna.*
Scotch Laburnum *Laburnum alpinum.*
Scotch Marigold *Calendula officinalis.*
Scotch Moss *Sagina.*
Scotch Rose *Rosa pimpinellifolia.*
Scotch Thistle *Onopordum acanthium.*
Scot Lovage *Ligusticum scoticum.*
Scots Heather *Calluna.*
Scots Lovage *Ligusticum scoticum.*
Scots Pine *Pinus sylvestris.*
Scottish Flame Flower *Tropaeolum speciosum.*
Scottish Maple *Acer pseudoplatanus.*
Scott River Jugflower *Adenanthos detmoldii.*
Scouring Rush *Equisetum hyemale.*
Screwbean *Prosopis pubescens.*
Screw Pine *Pandanus.*
Scribbly Gum *Eucalyptus haemastoma; E. racemosa.*

Scrophularia L. FIGWORT. Scrophulariaceae. Some 200 often foetid herbs and subshrubs. St. angled, erect. Lvs opposite or alt., entire to compound. Fls in term., paniculate cymes, axill. among leaflike bracts; cal. 5-lobed; cor., limb 2-lipped; sta. 4,

staminode 1. N temp. Z7.

S. aquatica L. = *S. auriculata.*

S. auriculata L. WATER BETONY; WATER FIGWORT. Perenn. to 1m, st. winged. Lvs 5–25cm, simple or bearing 1 (rarely more) pairs of lobes at base. Fls 5–9mm, red-brown. W Eur. 'Variegata': lvs dark green marked cream. Z5.

S. californica Cham. & Schldl. Perenn. to 1.5m. Lvs to 13cm, ovate, cordate to truncate, once- to twice-serrate. Infl. often viscid; fls to 15mm, dull red. Winter to summer. N Amer.

S. canina L. Perenn. sparingly branched, to 60cm. Lvs linear to oblong, once- to twice-dentate. Pan. cylindric, glandular-pubesc. Summer. C & S Eur.

S. chrysantha Jaub. & Spach. Viscid perenn. or bienn. to 60cm. Lvs ovate to orbicular, cordate, twice-serrate. Fls yellow, to 13mm. Summer. Cauc.

S. marilandica L. CARPENTER'S SQUARE. Glab. perenn. to 3m. St. bluntly 4-angled. Lvs ovate to ovate-lanceolate, cordate, serrate. Fls dull green-purple, to 11mm. Summer–autumn. Central N Amer.

S. nodosa L. Perenn. St. to 1.5m, angled, rarely winged. Lvs to 12cm, ovate to ovate-lanceolate, basally cordate to truncate, acute, serrate. Fls 7–10mm, green, upper lip purple-brown. Summer. Eur.

SCROPHULARIACEAE Juss. 222/4450. *Agalinis, Alonsoa, Anarrhinum, Angelonia, Antirrhinum, Asarina, Aureolaria, Bacopa, Bartsia, Besseya, Bowkeria, Buchnera, Calceolaria, Campylanthus, Castilleja, Chaenorrhinum, Chelone, Collinsia, Craterostigma, Cymbalaria, Dermatobotrys, Diascia, Digitalis, Erinus, Euphrasia, Freylinia, Galvezia, Gratiola, Halleria, Hebe, Hebenstretia, Hemiphragma, Isoplexis, Jovellana, Kickxia, Lagotis, Lathraea, Leucocarpus, Leucophyllum, Limnophila, Linaria, Lindenbergia, Manulea, Mazus, Micranthemum, Mimulus, Misopates, Mohavea, Nemesia, Odontites, Orthocarpus, Ourisia, Paederota, Parahebe, Paulownia, Pedicularis, Penstemon, Phygelius, Rhinanthus, Rhodochiton, Russelia, Scrophularia, Selago, Sibthorpia, Sopubia, Sutera, Synthyris, Teedia, Tetranema, Tonella, Torenia, Verbascum, Veronica, Veronicastrum, Wulfenia, Zaluzianskya*

Scrub Beefwood *Stenocarpus salignus.*
Scrub Bottletree *Brachychiton discolor.*
Scrub Kauri *Agathis ovata.*
Scrub Palmetto *Sabal etonia; S. minor; Serenoa repens.*
Scrub Pine *Pinus virginiana.*
Scrub Sumac *Rhus microphylla.*
Scurf Pea *Psoralea.*
Scurvy Grass *Oxalis enneaphylla.*

Scutellaria L. SKULLCAP; HELMET FLOWER. Labiatae. *c*300 sub-shrubs. Fls axill. and solitary or in pairs, or in terminal spikes and rac.; bracts decid. or persistent, sometimes coloured; cal. hairy, bell-shaped, 2-lipped; cor. tube long, curving from base, expanding above, upper lip dilated and entire or notched, with laterally spreading lobes, lower lip broader and flat to recurved; anth. pubesc., included below hood of cor. Cosmop., through temp. regions and trop. montane, with the exception of S Afr.

S. albida L. Vigorous, branching adpressed-hairy, erect perenn., 20–35cm. Lvs 2–3cm, triangular-ovate, cordate at base, obtuse, coarsely crenate. 1-sided rac. branched, 22–31cm, densely hairy; cor. 12–19mm, cream to mauve, lower lip streaked mauve. SE Eur. to C Asia. Z7.

S. alborosea Lem. Unbranched, erect subshrub to 45cm, densely hairy above. Lvs 6cm, hairy, ovate-oblong, cordate at base, acuminate, undulate rac. crowded 5–12cm; cor. 17–18mm, white to lilac, abruptly dilated above. Upper Amaz., Ecuad. Z9.

S. alpina L. Sprawling perenn. to 35cm. St. ascending, often rooting at nodes, ± hairy. Lvs to 2.5cm, ovate, cordate at base, obtuse, crenate. Rac. crowded, 4-angled, purple-tinged; bracts overlapping, longer than cal.; cor. 25–37mm, hairy, purple, lower lip sometimes yellow. Mts of S Eur. to Sib. 'Alba': fls white. 'Bicolor': fls purple and white. 'Greencourt': to 25cm, upright, dense; lvs fresh green; fls mauve, abundant. 'Lupulina': fls yellow. 'Rosea': fls pink. Z5.

S. altissima L. Erect, simple or branched perenn., 50–100cm. Lvs 5–15cm, ovate to ovate-lanceolate, base cordate, apex acuminate, crenate to serrate, glab. or hairy on veins beneath. Rac. lax, 1-sided, hairy; cor. 12–23mm, cream to pale blue-mauve, with lower lip whiter; sometimes striped white and deeper mauve. SE Eur., Cauc., S Russia. Z5.

S. angustifolia Pursh. Creeping perenn., 15–30cm, hairy and branching at base. Lvs 1–2cm, ovate-oblong to oblong, entire to crenate, hairy or nearly glab. above. Fls solitary, axill.; cor. 20–32mm, violet-blue, tube slender. NW Amer. Z5.

S. *antirrhinoides* var. *californica* A. Gray = S. *californica*.

S. *argentata* Léon = S. *costaricana*.

S. **atriplicifolia** Benth. Erect subshrub, 30–50cm, hairy above. Lvs 4–9cm, broadly ovate, cordate to rounded at base, acuminate to obtuse, entire to sinuate or serrate, finely hairy to glab. above, softly hairy with purple veins beneath. Rac. loose, hairy 5–10cm; cor. to 2.5cm, red, lower lip violet. Ecuad. Z7.

S. **aurata** Lem. Perenn. to 45cm, scarcely branched, short-hairy above. Lvs 8–10cm, ovate, base auricled and cordate, apex obtuse-acuminate, ± entire, veins hairy beneath. Rac. erect, crowded, 5–10cm; cor. yellow or scarlet, long and tubular to funnel-shaped. Braz., Peru. 'Sulphurea': fls smaller, pale yellow. Z9.

S. **baicalensis** Georgi. Erect perenn., 3 to 38cm. St. simple or branched at base, glab. or with short hairs, often suffused purple. Lvs 1.5–4cm, ovate-lanceolate to linear-lanceolate, base orbicular or tapering, apex obtuse to acute, entire, glab. to finely hairy, ciliate. Rac. secund, sometimes branched; cor. to 25mm, blue-purple, densely hairy. Sib. (Lake Baikal), Mong., China, Jap. 'Amoena': lvs oblong; fls blue, larger than type. Z5.

S. *bolanderi* var. *californica* (A. Gray) Penland = S. *californica*.

S. **brittonii** Porter. Perenn. 15–20cm. Lvs 1.7–3.5cm, oval to ovate-elliptical, entire to crenate-serrate. Fls axill., mostly on upper st.; cor. 23–32mm, deep violet-blue to white with glab. lower lip. Colorado, New Mex., Wyom. Z5.

S. *brittonii* var. *virgulata* Rydb. = S. *brittonii*.

S. **californica** A. Gray. Perenn. 15–25cm, basally branching, hairy. Lvs to 1.5cm, ovate to oblong-elliptic, entire to crenate-serrate. Fls axill., mostly on upper st.; cor. 14–21mm, creamy-white. Calif. Z7.

S. *campestris* Britt. = S. *parvula*.

S. *canescens* Nutt. = S. *incana*.

S. **columnae** All. Erect perenn. to 1m. Lvs 4–8cm, ovate, base cordate, apex acute, crenate-serrate, glab. to densely hairy. Rac. 1-sided, to 20cm; cor. to 2.5cm, white to purple with whiter lower lip, strongly curved. Balk. N to Hung., It., Cilicia. Z6.

S. *commutata* Guss. = S. *altissima*.

S. **costaricana** Wendl. Erect perenn. to 2m, suffused dark purple. Lvs 8–14cm, elliptic to ovate-elliptic, base shallowly cordate, apex acuminate, sinuate to dentate, glab. above. Rac. crowded; cor. to 4cm, orange-scarlet, deep yellow within lip, erect. Costa Rica. Z9.

S. *epilobiifolia* A. Hamilt. = S. *galericulata*.

S. *felisberti* Nees & Mart. = S. *purpurascens*.

S. **formosana** N.E. Br. Erect, shrubby perenn., 30–60cm. Lvs 6–7.5cm, ovate-lanceolate, acuminate, slightly serrate, minutely hairy above, veins sunken. Rac. loose, almost 1-sided to 10cm; cor. to 2.5cm, dark violet-blue, green below, erect. China. Z7.

S. **galericulata** L. Erect or procumbent stoloniferous perenn., 30–70cm, finely hairy to glab.; st. sometimes suffused purple. Lvs 3–5cm, ovate-elliptic, to oblong-lanceolate, basally truncate to subcordate, apex acuminate, crenate-serrate. Fls solitary and axill. or remote in 1-sided downy rac.; cor. 14–20mm, lavender-blue, rarely pink, marked white within, lower lip sometimes paler, speckled darker blue, tube strongly curved. Temp. Eurasia, N Amer. to Alask. Z5.

S. *hartwegii* Benth. = S. *atriplicifolia*.

S. **hastifolia** L. Habit similar to S. *galericulata*. Lvs narrower, ± hastate. Fls axill., in pairs; cor. 15–20mm, violet-blue, tube strongly curved. C Eur. and Turk. Z5.

S. **hirta** Sibth. & Sm. Densely hairy, subshrubby perenn. to 20cm. Lvs 1–2cm, ovate to deltate, base truncate to cordate, apex obtuse, crenate. Rac. few-fld; cor. 9–10mm, cream, upper lip tinged red. Crete. Z6.

S. **incana** Spreng. Perenn. to 120cm, hairy above. Lvs 6.5–12cm, cordate or ovate, crenate-serrate, thinly hairy above, evenly hairy beneath. Pan. corymbose; cor. 18–25mm, blue, grey-hairy. NE US. Z5.

S. **incarnata** Vent. Grey-hairy perenn., 30–50cm. Lvs 2.5–5cm, narrowly ovate to elliptical, base rounded and narrow, apex acute, subentire to dentate-serrate, dark green above, grey-hairy (sometimes tinged purple) beneath. Rac. 10–20cm, 1-seeded; cor. 17–20mm, cream to pale red-violet or scarlet. C Amer. Z9.

S. **indica** L. Slender, v. white-hairy, procumbent perenn., 20–40cm. Lvs to 2.5cm, deltoid-cordate to broadly ovate, cordate at base, obtuse, crenate-serrate. Rac. dense, 3–8cm; cor. 18–22mm, pale purple-blue. Jap., Korea, China. 'Japonica': fls larger lilac to blue. Z5.

S. **integrifolia** L. Erect, hairy perenn., 30–60cm. Lvs 2–6cm, ovate to narrowly elliptic, entire, adpressed-hairy. Rac. occas. branched below, 5–10cm; cor. 18–26mm, blue to white. E US. Z5.

S. *javanica* var. *playfairi* Jungh. = S. *formosana*.

S. **longifolia** Benth. Erect perenn., 40–50cm. Lvs 8–10cm, ovate to ovate-lanceolate, base rounded, apex acuminate, sinuate-serrate, glab. above, veins minutely hairy beneath. Rac. branched, 10–30cm; cor. 26–30mm, scarlet. Mex. to El Salvador. Z9.

S. *macrantha* Fisch. = S. *baicalensis*.

S. *mociniana* hort. non Benth. = S. *costaricana*.

S. **orientalis** L. Sprawling, subshrubby perenn. to 45cm, grey-woolly. Lvs 1–1.5cm, ovate-oblong to broadly ovate, base attenuate to truncate, apex obtuse, weakly crenate to pinnatifid, dark green above, grey-woolly beneath. Rac. dense, 4-angled; bracts yellow-green to purple-tinged; cor. 15–32mm, hairy, yellow, sometimes spotted red or with lip slightly red, occas. pink or bright red to purple. SE Eur., mts of SE Spain. Z7.

S. **parvula** Michx. Erect, glandular-hairy perenn., 10–30cm, branching at base. Lvs 0.8–2cm, ovate to deltoid-ovate, slightly dentate, with golden gland. hairs beneath. Fls solitary, axill.; cor. 7–10mm, blue. N Amer. Z5.

S. *peregrina* L. = S. *rubicunda*.

S. *polymorpha* A. Hamilt. = S. *integrifolia*.

S. *pubescens* Muhlenb. = S. *incana*.

S. **purpurascens** Sw. Perenn., 15–40cm, st. few from small caudex, erect or sprawling, minutely hairy. Lvs 3–6cm, broadly ovate, base rounded to truncate, apex obtuse to acuminate, sinuate-dentate, sparsely hairy to glab. above, veins adpressed-hairy beneath. Rac. lax, 3–8cm; cor. 13–15mm, tube and upper lip blue, lower lip deep violet, centrally striped white. S Amer. Z9.

S. **resinosa** Torr. Perenn., st. to 20cm, many from large, woody, minutely glandular-hairy. Lvs 0.8–1.6cm, oval to rounded, base tapering, apex obtuse, entire, minutely hairy and resinous. Rac. 1-sided; cor. 17–22mm, deep violet-blue, densely hairy. US (Kans. to Tex. and Ariz.). Z5.

S. **rubicunda** Hornem. Sprawling to erect perenn., 5–50cm, usually branched, woolly or felted, sometimes suffused purple. Lvs 1–6cm, ovate-triangular, base truncate to cordate, serrate to crenate, glab. to felted. Rac. lax to 20cm; cor. 12–17mm, purple-red to blue-tinged, or white. S Eur., Asia Minor. Related closely to S. *albida*. Z5.

S. *scarlatina* Planch. & Lind. = S. *ventenatii*.

S. **scordiifolia** Fisch. ex Schrank. Erect, basally branched perenn., 10–30cm, hairy. Lvs 1–3.5cm, oblong or lanceolate, base rounded to tapering, apex obtuse, entire to sparingly denticulate, glab. above, adpressed-hairy beneath. Rac. short, lax, 1-sided; cal. usually coloured, gland.; cor. 18–22mm, violet-blue, glandular-hairy. E Eur., Sib. Z5.

S. *serrata* Spreng. = S. *incana*.

S. *speciosa* Epling non Fisch. = S. *aurata*.

S. *speciosa* Fisch. non Epling = S. *baicalensis*.

S. **splendens** Link ex Klotzsch & Otto. Erect, branching perenn. to 1m, densely hairy. Lvs 4–11cm, broadly ovate, base cordate, apex obtuse, crenulate-serrate or sinuate, paler beneath. Rac. 15–30cm; cal. glandular-hairy; cor. 21–25mm, scarlet. Autumn. Mex. Z7.

S. **tuberosa** Benth. Hairy perenn., 5–20cm, creeping by tuberous rhiz. Lvs 1–2cm, ovate, dentate, long-hairy and sticky. Fls solitary, axill., borne nearly to plant base; cor. 12–21mm, blue. Early summer. US (Oreg., Calif.). Z5.

S. **ventenatii** Hook. Perenn. to 1m, branched above, grey- or purple-hairy. Lvs 4–8cm, broadly ovate, cordate at base, obtuse to acuminate, entire to denticulate, softly hairy, paler beneath. Rac. crowded, ± 1-sided, 10–25cm, glandular-hairy; cor. 18–20mm, scarlet. Colomb. Z9.

S. *veronicifolia* Rydb. = S. *angustifolia*.

S. *villosa* Elliott = S. *incana*.

S. **violacea** Heyne. Erect, downy perenn., 45–60cm, branching from base. Lvs 3.5–7.5cm, ovate, base cordate to rounded, apex subacute, coarsely crenate or sinuate, downy beneath. Rac. many-fld, 1-sided to 15cm; cor. to 7mm, violet with white markings. India, Burm., Sri Lanka. Z7.

S. *virgulata* Nels. = S. *brittonii*.

Scuticaria Lindl. Orchidaceae. 4 epiphytic or lithophytic orchids. Rhiz. short. Pbs v. small, terete, apically unifoliate. Lvs whip-like, elongate, fleshy, pendent, terete. Infl. to 5cm, lat., pendent 1- to few-fld; fls large waxy, fragrant; sep. free, erect to spreading; pet. similar; lip concave, lat. lobes erect, midlobe smaller, rounded or emarginate. Braz., Guyana, Venez., Colomb. Z10.

S. **hadwenii** (Lindl.) Hook. Lvs to 45×1cm. Fls to 7.5cm diam., yellow blotched chestnut-brown, lip white or pale yellow, blotched and spotted bright red or chocolate; sep. to 4.5×1.5cm, oblong; lip to 3.5×3cm, suborbicular to obovate, concave, callus 3-toothed, pilose, column flushed red, slightly pilose. Spring–autumn. Braz., Guianas.

S. *keyseriana* hort. = S. *steelii*.

S. steelii (Hook.) Lindl. Lvs to 145×1cm. Fls to 7.5cm diam., yellow or pale green-yellow, marked maroon-brown or red, lip pale green-white or pale yellow striped chestnut or rusty red; sep. to 5×1.5cm, elliptic-oblong to obovate; lip to 4×4.5cm, concave, midlobe oblong to obovate, emarginate, callus, 5-toothed, pilose; column yellow-white marked pink-purple. Colomb., Venez., Braz., Guianas, Surinam.

Scypholepia J. Sm. = *Microlepia*.

Scyphularia Fée. Davalliaceae. 8 epiphytic or lithophytic ferns. Rhiz. long, creeping, branched, scales dense, dark. Fronds stipitate, uniform, 1–2-pinnate or simple, deltoid to ovate, glab., sterile pinnae wider than fertile. SE Asia to Polyn. Z10.
S. pentaphylla Fée. BLACK CATERPILLAR FERN. Rhiz. thickly black-pubesc. Fronds to 15×1cm, somewhat drooping, tough shiny dark green, 1–2-pinnate, term. pinna linear, lat. pinnae to 6, paired, linear to lanceolate, entire and undulate or dentate, lowest occas. forked; stipes to 10cm. Java to New Guinea.
S. pycnocarpa (Brackenr.) Copel. Rhiz. with scales, bristle-like, brown to black. Fronds bright green, subcoriaceous, 1–2-pinnate, term. pinna to 20×1.5cm, lat. pinnae to 8, lanceolate, entire and undulate to notched, to 10×2cm, lowest forked; stipes to 10cm. Fiji.
→*Davallia*.

Scytala E. Mey. ex DC.
S. rubra Roxb. = *Lepisanthes senegalensis*.

Scythian Lamb *Cibotium barometz*.
Sea Apple *Syzygium grandis*.
Sea Ash *Zanthoxylum clava-herculis*.
Sea Buckthorn *Hippophaë*.
Sea Campion *Silene uniflora*.
Sea Daffodil *Pancratium maritimum*.
Sea Eryngium *Eryngium maritimum*.
Sea Fig *Ficus superba*.

Seaforthia R. Br.
S. cunninghamii hort. ex L.H. Bail. = *Archontophoenix cunninghamiana*.
S. elegans Hook. = *Ptychosperma elegans*.

Sea Grape *Coccoloba* (*C. uvifera*).
Sea Heath *Frankenia laevis*.
Sea Holly *Eryngium* (*E. maritimum*).
Sea Hollyhock *Hibiscus moscheutos*.
Sea Holm *Eryngium maritimum*.
Sea Island Cotton *Gossypium barbadense*.
Sea Kale *Crambe maritima*.
Sea Lavender *Limonium*.
Sea Lily *Pancratium maritimum*.
Sealing-wax Palm *Cyrtostachys lakka*.
Sea Lyme Grass *Leymus arenarius*.
Sea Oats *Chasmanthium latifolium*.
Sea Onion *Ornithogalum longibracteatum*; *Urginea maritima*.
Sea Pea *Lathyrus japonicus*.
Sea Pink *Armeria*.
Sea Poppy *Glaucium*.
Sea Rocket *Cakile maritima*.
Sea Samphire *Crithmum maritimum*.
Seashore Mallow *Kosteletzkya*.
Seaside Alder *Alnus maritima*.
Seaside Daisy *Erigeron glaucus*.
Seaside Oats *Uniola paniculata*.
Seaside Scrub Oak *Quercus myrtifolia*.
Sea Spleenwort *Asplenium marinum*.
Sea Spurge *Euphorbia paralias*.
Sea Spurrey *Spergularia*.
Sea Squill *Urginea maritima*.
Sea Urchin *Hakea laurina*.
Sea Urchin Cactus *Echinopsis*.

Sebaea Sol. ex R. Br. Gentianaceae. *c*60 erect, ann. or perenn. herbs. St. quadrangular. Lvs opposite, sessile, usually small. Fls in corymbose cymes, few and long-stalked or solitary; cor. tube cylindric, then inflated, lobes 4–5, spreading, twisted. Trop. & S Afr., Madag., Himal., Australasia, NZ. Z9.
S. albens R. Br. Ann. to 15cm. Lvs cordate-oblong. Fls white, lobes elliptic, nearly equalling tube. Summer. S Afr.
S. aurea R. Br. Ann. to 15cm. Basal lvs cordate-triangular, upper lvs ovate-lanceolate. Fls golden-yellow, lobes elliptic-oblong, equalling tube. Summer. S Afr.
S. ovata R. Br. Ann. to 20cm. Lvs to 1.5cm, ovate to orbicular-ovate. Fls 0.7cm, pale yellow, lobes ovate, acute, half length of tube. Summer. Aus., NZ.

S. thodiana Gilg. Low perenn. Lvs to 3.5cm, round-spathulate. Fls to 2cm diam., bright yellow. Summer. S Afr.

Sebestena (Dill.) Gaertn.
S. officinalis Gaertn. = *Cordia myxa*.
S. silvestris P. Alp. = *Cordia crenata*.

Sechium P. Browne. CHAYOTE; CHACO, CHOCHO. Cucurbitaceae. *c*8 climbers. Tendrils 1–5-parted. Lvs palmately angled or lobed, base cordate; petiole long. ♂ fls in elongate rac., white, cal. 5-lobed, cor. 5-lobed, sta. 3; ♀ fls solitary, pet. 3, axill. Fr. fleshy with fleshy spines or unarmed. C Amer. Z10.
S. edule (Jacq.) Sw. CHAYOTE; CHOYOTE; CHOCHO; CHOW CHOW; CHRISTOPHINE; VEGETABLE PEAR. Perenn. climbing from tuberous roots. Lvs 5–18cm, ovate to suborbicular, 3–5-angled or -lobed, entire to minutely toothed, scabrous above, glabrate beneath; petioles 4–15cm. ♂ fls to 3cm diam., pale yellow in racs to 30cm, ♀ fls tinged green. Fr. obovoid-pyriform, to 18cm, green-yellow. Summer. C Amer.

Securidaca L. Polygalaceae. 80 trees or scandent shrubs. Lvs simple, entire, with stipular glands. Fls in sometimes branched rac., irregular; sep. 5, inner 2 petal-like (wings), lower-most usually keeled, clawed, with a fringed crest; sta. 8, fil. united into a sheath split on upper side. Z10.
S. diversifolia (L.) S.F. Blake. Trailing or climbing shrub. Lvs to 13cm, elliptic-oblong to ovate or elliptic, thick, pubesc., above. Fls pink to magenta or mauve, keel tipped yellow tip. W Indies and Mex., S to Ecuad.
S. erecta Jacq. = *S. diversifolia*.
S. longipedunculata Fres. VIOLET-TREE. Slender shrub to tree, 3–10m+. Young shoots puberulous. Lvs 2.5–5.5(–9)cm, oblong to linear-lanceolate to oblong-ovate, glab. or glabrescent. Rac. to 15cm; fls red or purple, fragrant. Trop. Afr. var. *parvifolia* Oliv. Lvs on young br. transformed or reduced to spines bearing lvs and rac.; young shoots densely pubesc.
S. virgata Sw. High climber. Lvs rounded or somewhat notched, *c*2cm wide. Fls white and rose-pink scented, in slender drooping rac. W Indies.
→*Polygala*.

Securigera L.
S. securidaca (L.) Degen & Dörfl. = *Coronilla securidaca*.

×**Sedadia** Moran. (*Sedum* ×*Villadia*.) Crassulaceae. Glab. sub-shrub, to 30cm, branching, decumbent. Lvs to 1.8×0.6cm, sessile, flat, broader toward tip. Infl. terminal, dense; fls to 1.5cm diam., pale yellow. Mex. Z9.
×**S. amecamecana** (Praeger) Moran. (*Sedum dendroideum* ×*Villadia batesii*.)
→*Sedum*.

Sedastrum Rose = *Sedum*.

Sedge *Carex*.

Sedirea Garay & H. Sweet. Orchidaceae. 1 epiphytic, mono-podial orchid to 12cm. Lvs 5–7cm, 2-ranked, leathery, strap-like, keeled. Rac. to 15cm axill.; tep. to 13mm, spreading, oblong, obtuse, green to white, sometimes basally striped maroon or brown; lip 3-lobed, midlobe obovate-spathulate, concave, basally inflated, white, callus ridged dark violet, spotted, spur conical, tapering. Jap., Korea, Ryukyu Is. Z10.
S. japonica (Lind. & Rchb. f.) Garay & H. Sweet.
→*Aerides*.

Sedum L. Crassulaceae. 300+ usually succulent, ann. to perenn. herbs and subshrubs. St. erect or decumbent, sometimes tufted or creeping. Lvs fleshy, flat to terete. Infl. usually term., compound cymose, sep. usually 5, often fleshy, green; pet. usu-ally 5, free, spreading often with a tinted keel; sta. usually 10 or double the number of pet. N temp. and trop. mountain regions.
S. acre L. STONE CROP; WALL PEPPER. Loosely tufted or mat-forming perenn., 5–12cm. St. slender, erect or trailing. Lvs 3–6mm, overlapping, triangular, blunt, thick; cyme small; pet. 6–8mm, pointed, bright yellow, horizontal. Summer. Wide-spread Eur., Turk. and N Afr., nat. E US. 'Aureum': lvs variegated pale yellow. 'Elegans': 7cm; shoots striped silver at tips. 'Minor': to 2.5cm; lvs green; fls yellow. Z5.
S. acutifolium Ledeb. = *S. subulatum*.
S. adenocalyx Blatter & J. Fernandez = *Rosularia adenotricha*.
S. adolphii Hamet. Loose bushy, everg., perenn., to 30cm. St. arising singly, erect, branching. Lvs 36–50mm, v. fleshy, elongate-oblong, ± pointed, yellow-green, margins red. Cyme lat., paniculate, v. loose, pale pink; fls long-stalked, 15mm

across; sep. tinged pink; pet. white. Spring. Mex. Z8.

S. aggregatum (Mak.) Mak. = *Orostachys aggregata*.

S. aizoon L. Herbaceous perenn., 30–40cm. St. few, erect, mostly unbranched. Lvs 50–80mm, oblong-lanceolate, midrib prominent beneath, irregularly toothed. Cyme dense, flat, compound; fls numerous; pet. 7–10mm, golden yellow. Summer. N Asia, nat. N & C Eur. 'Euphorbioides': more compact and robust than sp. type; fls stronger yellow. Z7.

S. alamosanum S. Wats. Small glaucous perenn., 8–13cm. St. tufted, erect. Lvs 6mm, densely packed at first, linear-oblong, spurred, blunt, glaucous then tinged red, becoming terete. Cyme or rac. few-fld; pet. 5mm, green-white, tipped pink; anth. tinged purple. Spring. Mex. Z8.

S. alaskanum (Rose) Henry = *Rhodiola integrifolia*.

S. albescens Haw. = *S. reflexum*.

S. albiflorum (Maxim.) Maxim. ex Komar. & Alis = *Hylotelephium pallescens*.

S. alboroseum Bak. = *Hylotelephium erythrostictum*.

S. album L. Creeping, mat-forming, everg. perenn., to 15cm. Br. ascending. Lvs 4–20mm, spreading, linear-oblong, blunt, contracted at base, ± terete, flattened above, tinged red. Cyme dense; pet. 1.5–4mm, white. Summer. Eur., Sib., W Asia, N Afr. 'Chloroticum': minute, to 5cm; lvs pale yellow-green, carpet-forming; fls white. 'Murale': 10cm; lvs rust-red; fls pale-pink. 'Coral Carpet': 5cm; lvs coral-pink; fls pale pink. Z6.

S. allantoides Rose. Everg., perenn. subshrub to 30cm. St. branching from base, ascending, clustered. Lvs 25mm, obovate, blunt, ± cylindrical, in ascending, glaucous-blue. Pan. loose, few-fld, term.; fls 15mm across, green-white. Summer. Mex. Z8.

S. alpestre Vill. Differs from *S. acre* in non-flowering st. short; flowering st. to 8cm; lvs oblong to oblanceolate, tinged red; pet. to 4mm, dull yellow. Summer. C & S Eur. (mts). Z6.

S. alsinefolium All. Tufted ann. or delicate perenn., 10–15cm. St. few, weak, spreading, branched. Lvs 10–20mm, in flat rosettes, glandular-hairy, elliptic-oblong, blunt, pan. v. lax; fls somewhat campanulate, white, keeled green. Summer. NW It. Z7.

S. altaicum Stephan ex Fröd. = *Hylotelephium ewersii*.

S. altissimum Poir. = *S. sediforme*.

S. ×amecamecanum Praeger. = *× Sedadia amecamecana*.

S. amplexicaule DC. = *S. tenuifolium*.

S. anacampseros (L.). = *Hylotelephium anacampseros*.

S. anglicum Huds. Mat-forming, everg. perenn., to 15cm. St. slender, creeping, rooting. Lvs 3–6mm, crowded, ovoid-globose, terete, tinged red. Infl. few-fld, leafy, 2–3 branched; pet. 2.5–4.5mm, white-pink, bristle-tipped; anth. purple. Summer. W Eur. Z6.

S. annuum L. Ann. or bienn., 4–20cm. St. solitary, erect, many-branched, upper part flexuous. Lvs *c*6mm, oblong-linear, thick, blunt, cyme lax, many-fld, compound; pet. yellow. Summer. Iran to Scand. Z6.

S. anopetalum DC. Differs from *S. reflexum* in lvs to 20mm, bright green, glaucous or dark green, flushed red. Cyme flat; pet. white-bright yellow, 7–10mm. Summer. S & C Eur., Turk., nat. N Amer. Z7.

S. arboreum hort. non Mast. = *S. sediforme*.

S. arboreum (L.) Hegi = *Aeonium arboreum*.

S. athoum DC. = *S. album*.

S. atlanticum Maire. Hummock-forming, everg. perenn., to 15cm. St. short from stolons, branching, prostrate. Lvs *c*4mm, ovate-obovate, blunt, fleshy, tapering below, rosulate, glaucous blue, spotted pink. Infl. few-fld, simple; fls slender 9mm diam., white, keeled purple; anth. purple. Spring. Moroc. Z7.

S. atratum L. Ann., 3–12cm. St. erect, branched, solitary. Lvs 3–6mm, semi-terete, crowded, longer at base, green, turning red-yellow, corymbs few-fld, crowded; fls 6mm diam., white-green, keeled red. Summer. C & S Eur. (mts). Z7.

S. atropurpureum Turcz. = *Rhodiola integrifolia*.

S. aureum Wirtg. ex F.W. Schultz = *S. forsterianum*.

S. azureum Royle = *Hylotelephium ewersii*.

S. balticum Hartm. = *S. album*.

S. batallae Barocio. Mat-forming. St. creeping, branching, with aeriall roots. Lvs 3–7mm, overlapping in dense term. rosettes, elliptic-ovoid, obovate, clasping at base, occas. spotted red. Fls solitary or in v. few-fld rac.; pet. 3–5mm, yellow, sta. red. Summer. Mex. Z9.

S. bellum Rose. Everg. perenn., to 15cm. St. clustered, simple, tinged pink. Lvs to 25mm, spathulate, flat, blunt, glaucous, cyme many-fld, flat, leafy; fls 12mm diam., white anth. purple. Spring. Mex. Z8.

S. beyrichianum hort. non Mast. = *S. glaucophyllum*.

S. bicolor HBK = *Echeveria bicolor*.

S. bithynicum Boiss. = *S. pallidum* var. *bithynicum*.

S. boloniense Lois. = *S. sexangulare*.

S. borissovae Balk. Mat-forming, stoloniferous everg. perenn. St. branched, withered lvs persistent below. Lvs *c*5mm, oblong, blunt, clasping, thick, glaucous green. Infl. 2-branched, few-fld,

dense; fls 6mm diam., yellow tipped red. Ukraine. Z7.

S. borschii R.T. Clausen. Low, everg. perenn. St. numerous, horizontal, tinged red. Lvs *c*6mm, in dense rosettes, obovate, blunt, thick, glaucous green. Infl. few-branched, compact; fls 12mm diam., bright yellow. Summer. NW US. Z6.

S. brevifolium DC. Differs from *S. dasyphyllum* in st. woody; lvs round, tightly packed in 4 rows, never hairy; infl. not glandular-hairy. Summer. SW Eur., Moroc. Z9.

S. brissemoretii Hamet. Differs from *S. mudum* in straggling habit st., lvs crowded toward st. tips, subterete; fls *c*12mm across, yellow keeled green. Madeira. Z9.

S. brownii hort. = *S. kamtschaticum*.

S. bupleuroides Wallich ex Hook. f. & Thoms. = *Rhodiola bupleuroides*.

S. bupleuroides var. *purpureoviride* (Praeger) Fröd. = *Rhodiola purpureoviridis*.

S. caducum R.T. Clausen. Perenn. St. papillose, horizontal, clustered. Lvs 7–22mm, obovate, blunt, channelled above, green, spotted red, 1–3mm thick. Cyme term., 2–3-branched, few-fld; fls 9–10mm diam. Mex., Tamaulipas. Z9.

S. caeruleum L. Bushy ann., 5–20cm. St. erect, hairy above. Lvs *c*10mm, oblong-linear, subterete, slightly flat above, suffused red. Pan. loose, many-fld; pet. white at base, blue above. Summer. W Medit. Is. Z8.

S. caespitosum (Cav.) DC. Erect, glab. ann., to 5cm. St. erect in clusters, simple or branched. Lvs 4–8mm, overlapping, broadly ovoid, subterete. Cyme short; pet. 3–4mm, bristle tipped; white suffused red. Summer. S & C Eur., Turk. Z8.

S. carpaticum Reuss = *Hylotelephium telephium*.

S. caucasicum (Grossh.) Boriss. = *Hylotelephium caucasicum*.

S. cauticolum Praeger = *Hylotelephium cauticolum*.

S. cavaleriei Lév. = *Sinocrassula indica*.

S. cepaea L. Bushy ann., to 30cm. St. usually solitary, erect, much-branched, hairy, dotted red. Lvs 12–25mm, linear-obovate, blunt, tapering below, flat, fleshy, smooth, spotted red. Fls long-stalked in small cymes or solitary; pet. 5mm, pink with red midvein; anth. pale purple. Early summer. S & SC Eur. Z7.

S. chanetii Lév. = *Orostachys chanetii*.

S. chilonense Kuntze = *Echeveria chilonensis*.

S. chontalense Alexander. Differs from *S. versadense* in lvs 20mm, bright green above, purple-green beneath; fls 9mm across, pale pink. Spring. Mex. Z9.

S. clavatum R.T. Clausen. Everg. perenn. subshrub, to 8cm. St. horizontal, br. ascending. Lvs *c*3mm, obovate to clavate, pointed, tapering below, thick, crowded toward tips of br. Cyme lat., convex, few-fld; fls 12mm across, white anth. dark purple. Summer. Mex. Z9.

S. clusianum Guss. = *S. album*.

S. coccineum Royle = *Rhodiola quadrifida*.

S. cockerellii Britt. Perenn., to 5cm. Roots thick, white, creeping. St. erect, simple, sparsely leafy. Basal lvs to 6mm, rosulate, spathulate; st. lvs 25mm, long-obovate, pointed. Cyme 2–3-branched; pet. 6–8mm, white, anth. brown-pink. Autumn. New Mex. (mts). Z7.

S. coerulescens Haw. = *S. sediforme*.

S. coeruleum auct. = *S. caeruleum*.

S. commixtum Moran and Hutch. Everg. perenn., to 13cm. St. numerous, erect, sparsely branched, bare below. Lvs *c*18mm, obovate, pointed, concave above, thick, fleshy, glaucous. Infl. few-fld, lat.; fls campanulate, crowded, green, maroon above, tipped yellow; anth. red-purple. Spring. Mex. Z9.

S. compactum Rose. Differs from *S. humifusum* in lvs glab.; fls cup-shaped; pet. white, pink at base. Summer. Mex. Z9.

S. compressum Rose. Differs from *S. palmeri* in lvs narrower, oblong, often suffused red, distinctly pointed; fls to 15mm across. Spring. Mex. Z9.

S. confertiflorum Boiss. Small ann., 5–10cm. St. erect, branched or simple. Lvs 4–6mm, overlapping, oblong, terete. Corymb crowded; pet. white 3–4mm, somewhat pointed. Early summer. Turk., Greece. Z8.

S. confusum Hemsl. Differs from *S. praealtum* in lvs 25–38mm, blunt. Infl. compact, 5cm diam. Spring. Origin obscure, probably Mex. Z8.

S. corsicum Duby = *S. dasyphyllum*.

S. corynephyllum Fröd. = *S. viride*.

S. craigii R.T. Clausen Hummock-forming, everg. perenn., to 15cm. St. erect, thick, horizontal, rooting, little-branched. Lvs 25–50mm, oblong-elliptic, crowded toward ends of br., round at tip, glaucous, tinged purple. Cyme lat., pink, few-fld; fls campanulate, 9mm across, white-cream, occas. streaked purple; anth. red. Autumn. Mex. Z8.

S. crassiflorum Kuntze = *Crassula vaginata*.

S. crassipes Wallich = *Rhodiola wallichiana*.

S. crassularia Raym. and Hamet. Ann., to 10cm. St. slender, erect, simple. Lvs 4–5mm, obovate, blunt, concave above, crowded, often tinged red. Cyme few-fld; pet. 2mm, purple-pink. Ethiop. Z8.

S. cremnophilum R.T. Clausen = *Cremnophila nutans*.

S. crista-galli nom. illegit. = *S. reflexum*.

S. cristatum Schräd. = *S. reflexum* 'Cristatum'.

S. cupressoides Hemsl. Everg., much-branched perenn., 8–15cm. St. erect, flimsy, slender, woody below. Lvs 4mm, closely overlapping and adpressed to st., fleshy, triangular, blunt, persisting once withered and ashy grey. Infl. v. few-fld; fls 12mm across, off-white to bright yellow; anth. yellow. Summer. Mex. Z9.

S. cuspidatum Alexander. Loose, everg., perenn. subshrub. St. few, erect, branched below. Lvs 12–18mm, ascending, elongate-obovate, cuspidate, tapering below, crowded toward tips of st., tinged purple, cyme few-fld, compact; fls 12mm across, white. Spring. Mex. Z9.

S. cyaneum Rudolph = *Hylotelephium cyaneum*.

S. cymosum (Nutt.) Fröd. = *S. smallii*.

S. dahuricum Stephan ex Boriss. = *Hylotelephium cyaneum*.

S. dasyphyllum L. Everg., cushion-forming perenn., to 3–12cm. St. numerous, branching, horizontal to erect, pink-grey. Lvs decussate, overlapping, grey to glaucous, sometimes hairy. Cyme glandular-pubesc., simple, few-fld; pet. 3mm, white streaked pink; anth. purple. Summer. Medit., SW US. 'Riffense': lvs fleshy, silver-grey; fls pink. Z8.

S. debile S. Wats. Small, everg. perenn., 2–3cm. St. ascending, few-branched. Lvs in a dense basal rosette, broadly obovate, v. fleshy, glaucous, tinged blue, corymb small, few-fld; pet. bristle-tipped, 6–8mm, yellow. W US. Z6.

S. dendroideum Moc. & Sessé ex DC. Perenn. subshrub, 10–30cm. St. solitary, much-branched, smooth. Lvs 20–40mm, spathulate-obovate, flat, apex rounded. Cyme many-fld, loose, paniculate; pet. 5, 5–6mm, yellow. Spring. Mex. Z8.

S. diffusum S. Wats. Everg., glab. perenn. Rootstock fleshy. St. 15cm, creeping, branched. Lvs 3–12mm, ± terete, blunt tip, papillose pink above, clasping, spike 1-sided; fls 9–12mm across, white. NE Mex. Z8.

S. divaricatum S. Wats. non Ait. = *S. liebergii*.

S. divaricatum Ait. = *Aichryson divaricatum*.

S. divergens S. Wats. Glab., everg. perenn., 9–15cm. St. prostrate or ascending, rooting, tinged red. Lvs decussate, crowded, horizontal, round, blunt, clasping, 6mm across, sometimes tinged red-yellow. Cyme compact, 5cm across; fls 18mm across, yellow. Summer. W N Amer. Z6.

S. diversifolium Rose = *S. greggii*.

S. douglasii hort. = *S. stenopetalum* 'Douglasii'.

S. dumulosum Franch. = *Rhodiola dumulosa*.

S. ebracteatum Sessé & Moc. Downy perenn., to 25cm. Rootstock fleshy. Lvs 12mm, in a compact basal rosette or scattered on st., ascending, ovate, pointed, fleshy, flat above, rounded beneath. Flowering st. marked with purple dashes; infl. loose, few-fld; fls 12mm across, white, keeled green; anth. red-purple. Spring. Mex. Z8.

S. edule Nutt. = *Dudleya edulis*.

S. elegans Lej. = *S. forsterianum*.

S. ellacombianum Praeger = *S. kamtschaticum*.

S. eriocarpum Sibth. & Sm. = *S. hispanicum*.

S. erubescens (Maxim.) Ohwi = *Orostachys erubescens*.

S. erythrostictum Miq. = *Hylotelephium erythrostictum*.

S. euphorbioides Schltr. ex Ledeb. = *S. aizoon* 'Euphorbioides'.

S. ewersii Ledeb. = *Hylotelephium ewersii*.

S. farinosum Lowe. Mat-forming, everg. perenn. St. woody, arching, rooting at nodes; br. ascending. Lvs 2–6mm, oblong to obovoid, blunt. Cyme crowded; fls 12mm across, white; anth. purple, nectary scales conspicuous, red. Summer. Madeira. Z8.

S. farreri W.W. Sm. = *Rhodiola dumulosa*.

S. fastigiatum Hook. & Thoms. = *Rhodiola fastigiata*.

S. flexuosum Wettst. = *S. grisebachii* ssp. *flexuosum*.

S. floriferum Praeger. Glab., herbaceous perenn. Lvs spathulate-oblanceolate, blunt, 25–40mm. Cymes term. and lat., dense, flat, 25–50mm across; fls 15mm across, yellow. China. Z7.

S. formosanum N.E. Br. Sprawling perenn., 10–15cm. St. ascending, stout, sparsely branched. Lvs 15–22mm, orbicular to obovate, tip rounded, flat, tapering below, pale green. Cyme long, many-fld; fls bright yellow, 10mm across, with leaflike bracts; anth. red. Early summer. Korea, E China, Taiwan, Jap., Philipp. Z7.

S. forsterianum Sm. Differs from *S. reflexum* in lvs flat above, sterile shoots bearing lvs in obconical rosettes 18–25mm across. Summer. W Eur. Z7.

S. frutescens Rose. Tree-like, decid. perenn., to 30cm. St. stout, woody, branching above, bark papery. Lvs *c*12mm, elliptic, pointed, tapering below, bright green. Infl. few-fld, term.; fls 9mm across, white; anth. red. Summer. Mex. Z9.

S. furfuraceum Moran. Loose, hummock-forming everg. perenn., to 8cm. Lvs 9mm, ovate, blunt, clasping, ± terete,

waxy, crowded. Infl. term., simple, few-fld; fls 9mm across, white tipped pink-purple; anth. pink. Spring. Mex. Z8.

S. furusei (Ohwi) Ohwi = *Orostachys furusei*.

S. fusiforme Lowe. Everg. perenn., to 8cm. Base stout, woody; st. erect, several; branched. Lvs *c*6mm, crowded, lanceolate to oblong, subterete, blunt, glaucous green. Infl. compact, few-fld; fls 9mm across, pale yellow, keeled green, spotted red. Summer. Madeira. Z9.

S. garwalicum Fröd. = *Rhodiola sinuata*.

S. gemmiferum Woron. ex Grossh. = *S. obtusifolium*.

S. gerardianum Wallich = *Hylotelephium ewersii*.

S. glabrum Rose. Everg. perenn., to 20cm. Lvs 30mm, in rosettes, oblong-obovate, bluntly acute, v. fleshy; flowering st. erect with lvs adpressed. Infl. compact, few-fld; fls campanulate, 6mm across; white veined purple. Summer. Mex. Z8.

S. glanduliferum Guss. = *S. dasyphyllum*.

S. glandulosum Moris = *S. villosum*.

S. glaucophyllum R.T. Clausen. Differs from *S. nevii* in lax, spreading habit; lvs to 20mm, glaucous. Fls to 12mm across. E US (Appalachian Mts). Z6.

S. glaucum Lam. non Waldst. & Kit. = *S. dasyphyllum*.

S. glaucum Waldst. & Kit. non Lam. = *S. reflexum* 'Minus'.

S. globeriferum Pourr. = *S. brevifolium*.

S. gorisii Hamet = *Rhodiola bupleuroides*.

S. gracile C.A. Mey. Differs from *S. tenellum* in infl. many-fld; fls white, veined green; anth. black. Cauc., N Iran. Z7.

S. grandiflorum hort. = *S. reflexum*.

S. grandipetalum Fröd. Mat-forming, everg. perenn., to 5cm. St. creeping, red-brown, branching. Lvs *c*6mm, overlapping, ascending, ovate, pointed, round at base, glandular-papillose, narrower, longer and pink-tinged on flowering st. Cyme term., 3-branched, many-fld; fls 15mm across, yellow. Spring. Mex. Z8.

S. grandyi Hamet = *Villadia grandyi*.

S. greggii Hemsl. Tufted, glab. perenn., to 15cm. St. branching, prostrate or ascending. Lvs 4–7mm, obovate-oblong, elliptic, overlapping, blunt, ± papillose. Infl. few-fld; fls 10mm across, yellow. Spring. Mex. Z8.

S. grisebachii Heldr. Similar to *S. laconicum* except ann. or perenn.; lvs 5–6mm, bright green, papillose at tip; infl. usually lat.; pet. 4–6mm, pale yellow. E Albania to SW Bulg. and Greece. ssp. *flexuosum* (Wettst.) Greuter and Burdet. Perenn.; st. less than 6cm. Infl. 8-fld. Z8.

S. griseum Praeger. Everg. perenn. subshrub, to 18cm. St. solitary, much-branched, woody; br. arching. Lvs 12mm, crowded, thick, linear, pointed. Cyme few-fld, compact; pet. white, keeled green; anth. red. Spring. Mex. Z8.

S. guadalajaranum S. Wats. Differs from *S. griseum* in rootstock thickened, tuberous, st. thin, wiry; infl. lax; pet. white above, red. Summer. Mex. Z8.

S. guatemalense hort. non Hemsl. = *S. rubrotinctum*.

S. gypsicolum Boiss. & Reut. Differs from *S. album* in lvs flat, ovate-rhombic, grey-green, densely short-hairy, overlapping in 5 rows. C & S Spain. Z8.

S. haltif Britt. = *S. obtusatum*.

S. hemsleyanum Rose. Similar to *S. ebracteatum* except lvs ± completely round. Mex. Z8.

S. heterodontum Hook. f. & Thoms. = *Rhodiola heterodonta*.

S. hidakanum Tatew. & Kawano = *Hylotelephium pluricaule*.

S. hillebrandtii Fenzl = *S. urvillei*.

S. himalense D. Don = *Rhodiola himalensis*.

S. hintonii R.T. Clausen. Compact, hummock-forming, everg. perenn., 5–9cm. St. few, branched, short. Lvs in basal rosettes, thick, fleshy, oblong, blunt, broad at base, hairy, or cauline, reduced. Cymes dense, hairy, term. and lat. on erect flowering st.; fls 9mm across, white; anth. red. Spring. Mex. Z8.

S. hispanicum L. Ann. or perenn. St. glandular-hairy, branched below. Lvs 12–25mm, linear, pointed, green, glaucous, often tinged red, ± flat. Cyme unilateral, many-fld; pet. 5–7mm, bristle-tipped, white veined pink; sta. red-purple. Early summer. Switz. to Iran. 'Albescens': lvs glab., fleshy, green with pink tinges. 'Aureum': lvs light green, tinged yellow. 'Pewter': lvs grey. Z8.

S. hobsonii Prain ex Hamet = *Rhodiola hobsonii*.

S. hookeri (Fu) Balakr. = *Rhodiola bupleuroides*.

S. horridum Praeger = *Rhodiola quadrifida*.

S. hultenii Fröd. Everg., perenn. subshrub, to 30cm. St. arching, rooting, branching, tinged red. Lvs *c*18mm, elliptic, pointed, petioled, slightly broad-toothed. Pan. term., scapose; fls pale yellow. Summer. Mex. Z9.

S. humifusum Rose. Minute, carpet-forming perenn. St. creeping, branching. Lvs 3–4mm, in tight rosettes, obovate, blunt, overlapping, red with age, ciliate. Fls term., solitary, 9mm across, bright yellow; anth. yellow. Early summer. Mex. Z9.

S. hybridum L. Creeping perenn. St. woody, mat-forming. Lvs *c*2.5cm, spathulate, tapering below, with coarse, red-tipped teeth above. Corymb lax, term., 5–8cm across; fls numerous; pet. yellow, 6–9mm. Summer. C & S Urals, N Asia; nat. N & C Eur. Z7.

S. hyperaizoon Komar. Similar to *S. aizoon* except to 85cm; lvs broader, 8–10×3–4cm; cyme convex not flat-topped. Summer. E Sib. Z6.

S. hyperboreum Fisch. = *Hylotelephium cyaneum*.

S. ibericum Bieb. = *S. stoloniferum*.

S. indicum var. *yunnanense* Hamet = *Sinocrassula yunnanensis*.

S. involucratum Bieb. = *S. spurium* var. *involucratum*.

S. iwarenge (Mak.) Mak. = *Orostachys iwarenge*.

S. japonicum Sieb. Everg. perenn., to 15cm. St. numerous, branching, arching and rooting. Lvs 5–10mm, ± terete, oblong, apex round. Flowering fr. slender, pink; cyme 3–4-branched, many-fld, fls 9mm across; light yellow; anth. yellow. Summer. Jap. and E China. Z7.

S. jepsonii nom. illegit. = *S. laxum*.

S. kamtschaticum Fisch. Similar to *S. aizoon* except 5–30cm; rhiz. stout, st. branched below; lvs 20–40mm, obovate-oblanceolate, apex coarsely toothed. Summer. Jap. 'Variegatum': lvs edged white, tinged pink; fls yellow, turning crimson. 'Weihenstephaner Gold': trailing; fls golden-yellow, turning orange. Z7.

S. kirilowii Reg. = *Rhodiola kirilowii*.

S. kirilowii var. *rubrum* Praeger = *Rhodiola kirilowii*.

S. kvajinae Domin = *S. acre*.

S. laconicum Boiss. & Heldr. Perenn., 5–15cm. St. ascending. Lvs 6–8mm, ± terete, obovate-oblanceolate, overlapping, often tinged red, blunt. Cyme paniculate, much-branched; pet. 5, 3–5mm, bright yellow, midrib red. Greece, Turk. Z8.

S. laggeri nom. illegit. = *S. aizoon*.

S. lampusae (Kotschy) Boiss. Monocarpic herb, 20–50cm. St. simple, erect. Lvs 40–100mm, rosulate, spathulate, pointed or blunt, glaucous, becoming reduced and thicker higher up st. Pan. many-fld to 30cm; pet. 4mm. Summer. Cyprus. Z8.

S. lanceolatum Torr. Similar to *S. stenopetalum* except not creeping; lvs blunt, finely papillose; infl. always branched. Summer. NW N Amer. ssp. *nesioticum* (G.N. Jones) R.T. Clausen. Lvs to 21mm, glab., pet. c7mm, bright yellow. Z6.

S. lancerotense R.P. Murray. Differs from *S. nudum* in lvs becoming larger towards st. apex; fls to 12mm across. Summer. Canary Is. Z8.

S. laxum (Britt.) A. Berger. Stout, everg. perenn., to 30cm. Lvs 25mm, decussate, spathulate, blunt, notched, clasping st., in loose rosettes at st. tips, sometimes tinged pink. Cyme many-fld, 5–17cm; fls campanulate, 6mm across, deep pink. Summer. S Oreg. and N Calif. ssp. *eastwoodiae* (Britt.) R.T. Clausen. To 10cm, pet. 4–6mm. ssp. *heckneri* (M.E. Peck) R.T. Clausen. St. woody. Lvs 24×18mm, somewhat leathery. 'Silver Moon' (*S. laxum* ssp. *heckneri* ×*S. spathifolium*): lvs yellow-green; fls yellow. Z7.

S. leibergii Britt. Tufted, glab. perenn., to 25cm. St. simple. Lvs 10–15mm, obovate-spathulate to oblanceolate, bluntly pointed, rosulate. Cyme unilateral, 5–10cm across, many-fld; fls 12mm across, pale yellow, keeled green. Spring. E Oreg., Washington, Idaho. Z5.

S. leptorhizum Fisch. & C. A. Mey. ex Boriss. = *Hylotelephium pallescens*.

S. liebmannianum Hemsl. Glab., bushy perenn., 5–15cm. St. ascending, green, branching, with persistent, white lf bases below. Lvs 4–6mm, semi-deciduous, clustered toward st. tips, ovate. Infl. term., crowded, few-fld; fls 9mm across, white. Summer. Mex., W Tex. Z8.

S. lilacinum Ledeb. = *Hylotelephium cyaneum*.

S. lineare Thunb. Straggling, glab., everg., perenn., to 25cm. St. usually horizontal, tinged red, rooting. Lvs 18–24mm, in whorls of 3, linear-lanceolate, blunt, flat, narrower and more terete higher up st. Flowering st. ascending, cyme large, many-fld; fls 15mm across, bright yellow. Summer. SE China, Jap. 'Variegatum': lvs edged white or cream. Z7.

S. linearifolium Royle = *Rhodiola sinuata*.

S. linifolium Nutt. = *S. pulchellum*.

S. listoniae Vis. = *S. obtusifolium*.

S. litorale Komar. Herbaceous perenn., to 32cm. St. ascending, slightly wavy. Lvs 40–60mm, in whorls of 3, obovate-lanceolate or ovate, blunt, broadly serrate. Corymb compact, flat; fls 12mm across. Summer. E Sib.

S. littoreum Guss. Ann., 4–15cm. St. erect, solitary, few-branched, brown-red, withered lvs persistent. Lvs 10–20mm, spathulate-obovate, elliptic in section, blunt. Cyme long, loose; fls 6mm across, yellow, keeled red. Spring. Coastal Syr., Turk., Cyprus to Fr. Z8.

S. longicaule Praeger = *Rhodiola kirilowii*.

S. longipes Rose. Loose, mat-forming perenn., to 20cm. St. erect then arching to trailing. Lvs to 6mm, ± remote, obovate or spathulate. Infl. simple, 1–2-fld; fls on long stalks; hooded, white-green, spotted purple-red; anth. red-brown. Winter. Mex.

Z8.

S. lucidum R.T. Clausen. Everg., perenn. subshrub, to 20cm. St. horizontal, clustered, branched. Lvs c25mm, elliptic, pointed, tapering below, semiterete. Cyme lat., convex, many-fld; fls white. Spring. Mex. Z7.

S. luteoviride R.T. Clausen. Low, everg. perenn., to 10cm. St. horizontal, branching, naked below, brown-purple. Lvs c9mm, elliptic, blunt, tapering below. Infl. flat, few-fld, branched; fls 15mm across, bright yellow. Summer. Mex. Z9.

S. lydium Boiss. Differs from *S. tenellum* in st. rooting; lvs linear, to 6mm, tips red; corymb many-fld. W & C Turk. Z9.

S. macrophyllum hort. = *S. dasyphyllum*.

S. magellense Ten. Everg. perenn., 8–11cm. St. slender, woody, horizontal to erect, rooting. Lvs 6–10mm, alt. or opposite, oblong-ovate, flat, fleshy, blunt. Racemose, 6mm across, white tinged purple. Early summer. It., Greece, Turk. ssp. *olympicum* (Boiss.) Greuter and Burdet Lvs to 8mm, broadly ovate, always opposite. Z8.

S. makinoi Maxim. Mat-forming, everg. perenn., to 20cm. St. creeping, rooting; br. ascending. Lvs 7–5mm, decussate, spathulate, flat. Infl. much-branched, large; fls around 12mm across. Summer. Jap. Z7.

S. martinii Lév. = *Sinocrassula indica*.

S. maximowiczii Reg. = *S. aizoon*.

S. maximum var. *caucasicum* Grossh. = *Hylotelephium caucasicum*.

S. mellitulum Rose. Slender, tufted perenn., 8–12cm. St. occas., tinged red, branched, horizontal erect or arching. Lvs 6–8mm, glaucous, ageing red, linear, blunt. Infl. 2–3-forked; fls 12mm across; anth. red-white. Late summer. Mex. Z8.

S. mexicanum Britt. Everg., mat-forming perenn., 10–20cm. St. many from creeping rhiz., brittle. Lvs 8–20mm, linear, compressed, tapering to a blunt tip. Cyme branched 4–8cm; fls crowded; pet. 5–6mm, golden yellow. Early summer. Mex. Z8.

S. micranthum Bast. = *S. album*.

S. middendorffianum Maxim. Herbaceous perenn., to 30cm. Rhiz. creeping, branched, woody. St. many, erect, branching below. Lvs linear-spathulate, narrow, grooved, blunt, tips toothed. Cyme lax, paniculate, many-fld; fls 18mm across, yellow; anth. orange. Summer. E Sib., Mong., Manch. Z7.

S. minus Haw. = *S. reflexum* 'Minus'.

S. mirabile H. Ohba = *Rhodiola hobsonii*.

S. monregalense Balb. Everg., perenn. 2–6cm. St. horizontal, tips erect. Lvs 6mm, lanceolate-oblong, flat above, in whorls of 4, crowded, spreading, thick, blunt, spotted pink on st. Pan. many-fld, glandular-hairy. Pet. white, keel dark; anth. black. Summer. SW Alps, Apennines. Z8.

S. moranense HBK. Bushy, everg. perenn., 7–12cm. St. with numerous wiry br. Lvs 3mm, crowded, triangular, green. Rac. secund; pet. 5mm, white, tinged red at tip; anth. purple. Summer. Mex. Z9.

S. moranii R.T. Clausen. Everg., hummock-forming perenn., to 3cm. St. v. short, branching. Lvs 15mm, obovate, blunt, tip recurved, tapering below, in dense basal rosettes, soemtimes flushed purple; flowering st. erect, stout, glandular-hairy, deep red; fls few, campanulate, pale yellow. Summer. W US. Z6.

S. morganianum Walth. BURRO'S TAIL; DONKEY'S TAIL. Everg. perenn., to 6cm. St. numerous, prostrate or pendulous, sparsely branched. Lvs to 18mm, v. succulent, glaucous, spirally arranged, overlapping, oblong-lanceolate, acute, subcylindric, incurved. Infl. term., simple; fls pendent, on long stalks, 12mm across, deep pink. Spring–summer. Cult. Mex., origin obscure. Z9.

S. multiceps Coss. & Durieu. Much-branched, bushy perenn., 8–12cm. St. with perisstent withered lvs below, horizontal, woody, terete. Lvs clustered near tips of st., linear-oblong, blunt, 6mm, fleshy, flat above, ± papillose beneath. Infl. 3 branched, few-fld; fls 9mm across, yellow. Alg. Z8.

S. neglectum Ten. = *S. acre*.

S. nevadense Coss. Glab. ann., 4–10cm. St. erect, sometimes branched below. Lvs c5mm, linear or oblong. Cyme raceme-like; pet. 3–4mm, white, suffused red. Summer. Spain, N Afr. Z8.

S. nevii A. Gray. Glab., tufted perenn., to 9cm. Lvs 12mm, in dense rosettes at ends of st., pale green, spathulate, tapering below, apex rounded to acute. Cyme 3-forked; fls 6–8mm across, white; anth. dark purple. Virg. to Alab. Z7.

S. nicaeense All. = *S. sediforme*.

S. niveum A. Davis. Prostrate, glab. perenn., to 6cm; br. short, ascending. Lvs 5–6mm, in small, lax, basal rosettes, obovate-oblong, pointed, tapering below, 6mm. Cyme v. few-fld; fls 12mm across, white veined pink. Summer. SW Calif. Z8.

S. nudum Ait. Loose, perenn. subshrub, to 10cm. St. several, straggling, rooting, woody; br. ascending. Lvs 9mm, green or glaucous, obovate-oblong, blunt. Infl. loose, few-fld, 2-forked; fls yellow-green. Summer. Madeira. Z8.

S. nussbaumerianum Bitter. Everg., perenn. subshrub, to 15cm. St. few, horizontal, branching. Lvs 3cm, elliptic, poiunted, tapering below, crowded toward tips of st. Cyme lat., many-fld; fls long-stalked, 15mm across, white. Spring. Mex., Vera Cruz. Z9.

S. nutans Rose = Cremnophila nutans.

S. nuttallianum Raf. Small, glab. ann., 5–10cm. St. branching below, ± horizontal. Lvs 4–15mm, oblong-linear, subterete, blunt. Cyme 2–5-forked; pet. 3mm, yellow. Missouri to Tex. Z7.

S. oaxacanum Rose. Mat-forming, everg. perenn., to 9cm. St. rough, to 15cm, rooting. Lvs 3–6mm, densely overlapping, oblong to obovate, blunt. Infl. 2-branched, few-fld; fls 12mm across, yellow. Summer. Mex., Oaxaca. Z9.

S. obcordatum R.T. Clausen. Everg., perenn. subshrub, to 15cm. Base woody; st. few, arching, rooting, twisted, branched, glossy. Lvs 18mm, decussate, cordate, blunt, notched, glaucous, in loose term. rosettes. Infl. dense, flat, few-fld; fls campanulate, 12mm across, yellow. Summer. Mex., Vera Cruz. Z9.

S. obtusatum A. Gray. Loose hummock-forming perenn., 3–30cm. Lvs 5–25mm, decussate, in loose rosettes at st. tips, spathulate, glaucous, blunt to rounded, tinged red. Cyme paniculate, to 10cm across; fls campanulate, pale yellow-orange. Summer. Calif. Z8.

S. obtusifolium C.A. Mey. Glab. perenn., 10–40cm. St. at first bulb-like, subterranean, lengthening to produce lf rosette and runners. Lvs 10–40mm, obovate, sparsely broad-toothed to entire; flowering st. erect; pet. 8–10mm, red-pink. Summer. N Iran to Armenia. Z7.

S. oppositifolium Sims = S. spurium var. album.

S. oreganum Nutt. Creeping, glab. perenn., to 15cm, with numerous ascending br. Lvs 10–20mm, spathulate, shining, often tinged red. Cyme flat, compact; fls cup-shaped; pet. 10–12mm, yellow. Summer. NW Amer. Z6.

S. oregonense (S. Wats.) M.E. Peck. Differs from S. obtusatum in forming compact hummocks; lf tips broad, emarginate. Summer. W US. Z6.

S. oxypetalum HBK. Tree-like, somewhat decid., perenn., 60–90cm. St. solitary, woody, erect, branched. Lvs 25–35mm, scattered, flat, obovate-spathulate, rounded. Cyme leafy, few-forked; fls crowded; pet. 6mm, purple-red. Summer. Mex. Z8.

S. pachyphyllum Rose. Differs from S. allantoides in st. not tightly packed; lvs tipped red; infl. dense, flat-topped; pet. bright yellow. Spring. Mex. Z8.

S. pallescens Freyn = Hylotelephium pallescens.

S. pallidum Bieb. Differs from S. hispanicum lvs light green; pet. to 7mm; ± erect, follicles dark red, gland. not pink-white. S Albania to N India. var. *bithynicum* (Boiss.) Chamberl. Perenn. Some st. sterile. Pet. spreading.

S. palmeri S. Wats. Sprawling, everg. perenn., 15–22cm. St. arching, branching, naked below, scarred. Lvs 2.5–15mm, spathulate, glaucous, in loose rosettes. Pan. few-fld, compact; fls 9mm across, deep orange. Spring. Mex. Z8.

S. paraguayense (N.E. Br.) Bullock = Graptopetalum paraguayense.

S. pilosum Bieb. Rosette-forming bienn., to 15cm. Lvs 8mm, in a dense, basal rosette, incurved, oblong to linear-spathulate, flat, blunt, dark green, rough-hairy. Corymb many-fld; fls campanulate; pet. 6–8mm; anth. tinged red. Early summer. Turk. to Iran. Z7.

S. pleurogynanthum Hand.-Mazz. = Rhodiola primuloides.

S. pluricaule Kudô = Hylotelephium pluricaule.

S. populifolium Pall. = Hylotelephium populifolium.

S. potosinum Rose. Low, everg. perenn., 7–15cm. St. weak, ascending, branched, tinged pink. Lvs 15mm, linear or linear-lanceolate, often tinged pink, flattened. Infl. lat., few-fld; fls 15mm across, white, keeled red; anth. red. Summer. Mex. Z9.

S. praealtum A. DC. Everg. shrub, 30–60cm, much-branched, bushy. Lvs 50–65mm, lanceolate-spathulate, green, shining, blunt, v. fleshy convex beneath. Pan. large, term.; fls 7–10mm across, bright yellow. Mex., nat. Medit. and S Engl. Z6.

S. praegerianum W.W. Sm. = Rhodiola hobsonii.

S. primuloides Franch. = Rhodiola primuloides.

S. proponticum Aznav. = S. obtusifolium.

S. pruinatum Link ex Brot. Slender, everg. perenn., to 15cm. St. 15–20cm, horizontal, rooting. Lvs c18mm, linear, flat above, pointed, crowded, toward ends of shoots. Fls crowded, sessile; pet. 8–12mm, straw yellow. Summer. Port. Z8.

S. pruinosum Britt. = S. spathulifolium ssp. pruinosum.

S. pseudospectabile Praeger = Hylotelephium spectabile.

S. pulchellum Michx. Everg., tufted perenn., 7–15cm. Br. slender, trailing or ascending, red. Lvs 6–25mm, narrow linear-lanceolate, crowded, ascending, half-clasped. Infl. 3–5-branched; fls 8–12mm across, rose-purple; anth. red. Summer. E & SE US. Z8.

S. pulvinatum R.T. Clausen. Everg., perenn. subshrub, to 15cm. St. numerous, creeping, rooting, br. ascending, tinged red. Lvs 8mm, elliptic, pointed, clasping, thick, tips purple. Fls sessile, solitary, 12mm across, white tipped red. Spring. Mex. Z8.

S. purdyi Jeps. = S. spathulifolium ssp. purdyi.

S. purpureoviride Praeger = Rhodiola purpureoviridis.

S. purpureum (L.) Link = Hylotelephium telephium.

S. quadrifidum Pall. = Rhodiola quadrifida.

S. quadrifidum var. *himalense* (D. Don) Fröd. = Rhodiola himalensis.

S. quevae Hamet. Tree-like, decid. perenn., to 18cm. Roots swollen. St. few, erect, many-branched, woody, bark peeling. Lvs c12mm, scattered, oblanceolate, flat, blunt. Cyme dense, few-fld; fls 15mm across. Autumn. Mex. Z9.

S. quitense HBK = Echeveria quitensis.

S. racemiferum (Griseb.) Hal. = S. grisebachii.

S. radiatum S. Wats. Ann. or perenn., 7–15cm. St. simple or branching, horizontal below. Lvs 5–12mm, in a basal rosette, ovate-oblong, blunt or slightly pointed, flat, papillose. Cyme few-forked; pet. 7–12mm, yellow. Calif. to Oreg. Z8.

S. rariflorum N.E. Br. = Rhodiola dumulosa.

S. reflexum L. Mat-forming, everg. perenn., 15–35cm. St. horizontall, ± woody. Lvs 12mm, linear, terete. Cyme umbellate, drooping at first, then concave; pet. 6–7mm, bright yellow. Summer. C & W Eur. 'Cristatum': lvs crested. 'Minus': dwarf variant. 'Monstrosum Cristatum': fasciated form; st. thin at base, widening towards the top edge, along which grey-green lvs are borne. 'Viride': lvs green, fls yellow. Z7.

S. rendlei Hamet = Rhodiola dumulosa.

S. reticulatum Schrank = S. dasyphyllum.

S. retusum Hemsl. Shrubby, everg. perenn. St. branched, erect or ascending. Lvs 12mm, gathered toward apex of st., obovate-oblong or spathulate, tip rounded, retuse. Cyme few-fld; pet. 6mm. Summer. Mex. Z8.

S. rhodanthum Gray = Rhodiola rhodantha.

S. rhodiola DC. = Rhodiola rosea.

S. rhodocarpum Rose. Clustered perenn., to 15cm. St. numerous, horizontal then ascending, triangular. Lvs 15mm, in whorls of 3, ovate-cordate, blunt, tapering below. Infl. few-fld, branched; fls 12mm across, white-green, suffused purple; anth. purple. Winter. Mex. Z7.

S. roseum (L.) Scop. = Rhodiola rosea.

S. roseum ssp. *atropurpureum* Turcz. = Rhodiola atropurpurea.

S. rotundifolium Lam. = Hylotelephium anacampseros.

S. rubens L. Bushy ann., 2–15cm. St. erect, branched above. Lvs 18mm, oblong to linear, blunt, crowded, terete, glaucous, later tinged red. Cyme compact, few-fld, corymbose; pet. 5mm, white, keeled red-purple; anth. red. Early summer. S & W Eur., Canary Is., N Afr. Z8.

S. rubricaule (Rose) Praeger = S. ebracteatum.

S. rubroglaucum Praeger = S. obtusatum.

S. rubrotinctum R.T. Clausen. Everg., perenn. subshrub, to 24cm. St. numerous, arching, rooting, branching. Lvs c15mm, elliptic, blunt, terete, tapering below, often suffused red, crowded. Cyme loose, many-fld; 12mm across; pet. pale yellow, keel green. Spring. Cult. Mex., origin obscure. Z9.

S. rubrum (L.) Thell. non Royel. = S. caespitosum.

S. rubrum Royle non (L.) Thell. = Hylotelephium ewersii.

S. rupestre L. = S. reflexum.

S. ruwenzoriense Bak. Everg., perenn., tree-like subshrub, to 20cm. St. few, horizontal to erect, woody, branching, leafless below. Lvs clustered toward st. tips, ovate, blunt, tapering below. Cyme flat, dense, few-fld; fls 9mm across, pale yellow, keeled green. Spring. Uganda. Z9.

S. sarmentosum Bunge. Everg., prostrate perenn., to 9cm. St. horizontal, red-brown, rooting. Lvs 10–25mm, in whorls of 3 or 2, broad lanceolate, fleshy, pointed. Flowering st. ascending. Cyme few-fld with leaflike bracts; fls 12mm across; pet. bright yellow; anth. yellow, tinged purple. Jap., W China, Korea. Introd. US. Z7.

S. sartorianum Boiss. = S. urvillei.

S. scabridum Franch. = Rhodiola quadrifida.

S. scalliana Diels = Sinocrassula indica.

S. sediforme (Jacq.) Pall. Everg. perenn., 15–60cm. St. woody, branching below. Lvs 12–18mm, lanceolate, compressed, pointed, flat above, often bristle-tipped. Cyme corymbose; pet. 4–7mm, straw yellow to green-white. Summer. Medit. Z8.

S. selskianum Reg. & Maack. Densely hairy, herbaceous perenn., to 40cm. St. erect, many, woody, tinged red, branched or simple. Lvs 30–60mm, narrowly lanceolate-spathulate, densely grey-hairy, serrate. Infl. corymb-like, many-fld, 3–7cm across; fls 12mm across, yellow; anth. yellow. Summer. Sib., Manch., Jap., China. Z6.

S. semenowii Mast. = Rhodiola semenowii.

S. sempervivoides Bieb. Erect, hairy bienn., to 20cm. Lvs 10–30mm, ovate, pointed, tinged purple, basal, rosulate. Pan.

loose, many-fld, corymbose; pet. 5, 6–8mm, bright red. Armenia, Georgia, Cauc. Z6.

S. senanense Mak. = *S. japonicum.*

S. serratum Jacq. = *Rhodiola heterodonta.*

S. sexangulare L. Everg., loosely tufted, stoloniferous perenn., 5–15cm. St. numerous, stolons wiry. Lvs 4mm, linear, terete, crowded in 6–7 rows, spreading or ascending. Flowering st. v. slender. Cyme spreading, loose; pet. 4–5mm, bright yellow. Summer. W Russia, Poland, Balk., C Eur. Z7.

S. sichotense Vorosh. Woody-based herbaceous perenn., to 10cm. St. many, horizontal to ascending. Lvs 25mm, oblanceolate, blunt, tapering, flat, toothed. Cyme flat, many-fld; fls 12mm across, bright yellow. Summer. E Ukraine. Z7.

S. sieboldii Sweet ex Hook. = *Hylotelephium sieboldii.*

S. smallii (Britt.) Ahles. Frail, loosely clustered ann., to 5cm. St. solitary, erect, rarely branched, slightly hairy. Lvs *c*3mm, 4-whorled, spathulate, blunt, finely hairy, longer, elliptic, scattered on st. Cyme term., few-fld, compact; fls 9mm across, white tipped pink, keels purple, hairy; anth. red. Summer. E US. Z7.

S. sordidum Maxim. = *Hylotelephium sordidum.*

S. spathulifolium Hook. Tight, clump-forming perenn., 9–15cm. St. short, often forming long runners. Lvs *c*18mm, in compact rosettes at st. tips, spathulate, ascending, flat, blunt. Cyme 3-forked, many-fld, flat; fls crowded, 15mm across, yellow; anth. yellow. Early summer. W N Amer. 'Aureum': lvs grey, tinged pink, flecked yellow. 'Cape Blanco': compact; lvs pale silver-grey; fls yellow. 'Carnea': lvs tinged crimson. 'Purpureum': lvs flushed purple. 'Roseum': fls rose. ssp. *pruinosum* (Britt.) R.T. Clausen & Uhl. More vigorous; lvs v. pruinose. Coastal BC to Calif. ssp. *purdyi* (Jeps.) R.T. Clausen. Compact, cushion-forming, to 30cm. Infl. much-branched. ssp. *yosemitense* (Britt.) R.T. Clausen. Small rosettes forming on a number of runners. Z7.

S. spectabile H. Ohba = *Hylotelephium spectabile.*

S. spurium Bieb. Everg., mat-forming, perenn., to 15cm. St. much-branched, finely hairy, creeping. Lvs 25mm, opposite, obovate, abruptly tapering below, toothed, fringed. Flowering st. red; corymb dense; pet. 10–12mm, white, pink or red-purple. Summer. Cauc., N Iran, nat. Eur. 'Atropurpureum': lvs burgundy; fls rose-red. 'Bronze Carpet': lvs bronze. 'Coccineum': fls scarlet-red. 'Fuldaglut': lvs dark maroon; fls deep burgundy. 'Erdblut': lvs green, edged crimson; fls vivid carmine. 'Green Mantle': lvs forming fresh green ground cover; fls 0. 'Purpurteppich' ('Purple Carpet'): habit compact; lvs plum purple. 'Roseum': fls rose-pink. 'Schorbuser Blut' ('Dragon's Blood'): lvs bronze with age; fls large, v. dark red. 'Tricolor': trailing; lvs striped pink, cream, and cream. 'Variegatum': compact; lvs edged pink and cream. var. *album* Trautv. Fls white. var. *involucratum* (Bieb.) Fröd. Uppermost lvs exceeding infl. Pet. cream, erose. Z7.

S. stahlii Solms-Laub. CORAL BEADS. Downy, everg. perenn., 10–20cm. St. red-brown, erect or spreading, woody below, rarely branched above base. Lvs 12mm, decussate, pruinose grey-green to coral pink, bluntly ovoid. Cyme 2-forked, recurved, 6cm; pet. around 8mm, bright yellow, bristle-tipped. Summer. Mex. Z9.

S. stefco Stef. Small, mat-forming, everg. perenn., 7–10cm. St. numerous, horizontal, much-branched. Lvs 4–5mm, terete, oblong, somewhat clustered at tips, lower lvs suffused bright red-pink. Infl. few-fld, dense 2–3 branched; pet. 4–5mm, pale pink-white; anth. black. Late summer. Bulg., N Greece. Z8.

S. stellatum L. = *S. littoreum.*

S. stenopetalum Pursh. Glab., tufted, everg. perenn., 8–18cm, often bearing bulbils in lf axils. St. erect, somewhat branched, withered lvs persistent. Lvs 12–18mm, crowded, lanceolate, blunt to pointed. Cyme 3–7-forked, compact; fls 8–10mm across, yellow. Summer. Rocky Mts to Colorado. 'Douglasii': to 90cm; st. creeping, br. ascending. Lvs lanceolate, bright green, tips red, turning red-yellow. Z6.

S. stephanii Cham. = *Rhodiola stephanii.*

S. stevenianum Rouy & Camus. Tuft-forming perenn. Rhiz. slender, branched. St. much-branched, creeping or ascending. Lvs 2–6mm, opposite, ovate-spathulate, flat, fleshy, blunt. Infl. umbellate, few-fld; pet. pink-white, 5–7mm; anth. red. Summer. Cauc. Z7.

S. stoloniferum S.G. Gmel. Similar to *S. spurium* except to 20cm; lvs 12–20mm; infl. lax; pet. 5–8mm. Cauc., N Iran. Z7.

S. stribrnyi Velen. = *S. urvillei.*

S. suaveolens Kimnach. Everg. perenn., to 8cm. Lvs in a large, loose, basal rosette, spathulate, mucronulate, incurved. Cyme lat., flat, many-fld; fls campanulate, 9mm across, white; anth. brown-red. Mex. Z8.

S. subulatum (C.A. Mey.) Boiss. Differs from *S. album* in lvs 10mm, subulate to linear, acute; infl. compact; pet. 5–6mm. Summer. Cauc., Turk., Armenia, N Iran. Z8.

S. takasui Kudô = *Hylotelephium cyaneum.*

S. tatorinowii Maxim. = *Hylotelephium tatorinowii.*

S. telephioides Michx. = *Hylotelephium telephioides.*

S. telephium L. = *Hylotelephium telephium.*

S. telephium ssp. *alboroseum* (Bak.) Fröd. = *Hylotelephium erythrostictum.*

S. telephium ssp. *purpureum* var. *pluricaule* Maxim. = *Hylotelephium pluricaule.*

S. telephium var. *kirinerise* Komar. = *Hylotelephium spectabile.*

S. telephium var. *pallescens* (Freyn) Komar. = *Hylotelephium pallescens.*

S. telephium f. *verticillatum* (L.) Fröd. = *Hylotelephium verticillatum.*

S. tenellum Bieb. Ascending, tufted perenn., 5–8cm. St. woody, bare below, creeping and ascending. Lvs 3mm, overlapping, oblong, terete, smooth; flowering st. ascending or arched. Infl. few-fld; pet. 3–4.5mm, white suffused red. N Iran, Cauc. Z7.

S. tenuifolium (Sibth. and Sm.) Strobl. Mat-forming perenn., to 20cm. St. procumbent, diffusely branching, tinged red. Lvs crowded toward tips of st., terete, erect, glaucous, soon withering, persistent. Flowering st. erect; cyme term., few-fld; pet. 6–8mm, yellow, midvein red. Summer. Medit. Z8.

S. ternatum Michx. Tufted, everg. perenn., 7–20cm. St. prostrate, rooting. Lvs 12–25mm, in whorls of 3 and in term. rosettes, orbicular to v. broadly spathulate, rounded; flowering st. lvs oblong, pointed. Cyme 2–4-forked; fls 1cm across. Summer. E US. Z6.

S. texanum J.G. Sm. = *Lenophyllum texanum.*

S. tibeticum Hook. f. & Thoms. = *Rhodiola tibetica.*

S. torulosum R.T. Clausen non hort. To 85cm. St. stout, irregularly thickened. Lvs 5–52mm, ovate-spathulate, glaucous, crowded in rosettes at tips of br. Cyme term., corymb-like, 55mm across; pet. 5–6mm; anth. red. Mex. Z8.

S. torulosum hort. non R.T. Clausen = *S. lucidum.*

S. treleasei Rose. Differs from *S. allantoides* in st. erect, stout; lvs shorter and broader, to 20mm, oblong, pointed; infl. lat.; fls yellow. Spring. Mex. Z8.

S. trifidum Wallich = *Rhodiola sinuata.*

S. trullipetalum Hook. f. and C. Thomps. Herbaceous, tuft-forming perenn., to 10cm. St. numerous, creeping, rooting, old lvs persistent below. Lvs 6mm, alt., elongated-triangular, pointed, clasping, glab. Cyme term., rounded, few-fld; fls 12mm across; pet. triangular, clawed, pale yellow; anth. red-brown. Autumn. Himal., Nepal to SW China. Z8.

S. tuberiferum Stoj. & Stef. Carpet-forming, everg. perenn., to 12cm. Roots tuberous. St. many, little-branched. Lvs 3–4mm, overlapping, spathulate, lanceolate, papillose, 6–8mm, linear-oblong on flowering st. Infl. few-fld, lax; pet. light yellow. Summer. Eur., Bulg., N Greece. Z7.

S. turgidum Urv. = *S. album.*

S. urvillei DC. To 15cm. Shoots thick at base, ascending. Lvs terete, linear, blunt to acute, grey-green. Flowering st. erect, branching or simple; cyme 2-branched, 3–2-fld; pet. 5–8mm, pink. Greece. Z9.

S. ussuriense Komar. = *Hylotelephium ussurinse.*

S. vaginatum (Ecklon & Zeyh.) Kuntze = *Crassula vaginata.*

S. valerianoides Diels = *Rhodiola yunnanensis* ssp. *yunnanensis.*

S. verlotii Jordan = *S. anopetalum.*

S. versadense C. Thomps. Loosely clustered, everg. perenn., 12–15cm. St. decumbent, hairy below, ascending, unbranched. Lvs 25mm, spathulate, blunt to pointed, downy, edged red, convex beneath. Infl. many-fld, 2–3-branched; fls 12mm across, white flushed pink; anth. red. Spring. Mex. Z9.

S. verticillatum L. = *Hylotelephium verticillatum.*

S. villosum L. Offsetting ann. to bienn. or perenn., 5–15cm. St. erect, red, branching from base. Lvs 4–7mm, erect, linear-oblong, glandular-hairy, semiterete. Pan. loose; fls 6mm across, light blue to pale pink. Summer. Eur., Greenland. Z5.

S. virens Ait. = *S. reflexum.*

S. viride (Rose) Berger non Mak. Shrubby, everg. perenn., to 25cm. St. branching below, thick, ascending, scarred. Lvs 25mm, corwded toward tips of br., thick, elliptic, blunt, glaucous-green, tip tinged red. Cyme lax, many-fld; fls 12mm across, yellow-green. Spring. E Mex. Z9.

S. wallichianum Hook. = *Rhodiola wallichiana.*

S. watsonii (Britt.) Tidestr. = *S. oregonense.*

S. weinbergii (Rose) A. Berger = *Graptopetalum paraguayense.*

S. woodii Britt. = *S. spathulifolium.*

S. woodwardii N.E. Br. = *S. aizoon.*

S. wrightii A. Gray. Everg., glab. perenn. Lvs 9mm, rosulate, basal, during winter, spreading along flowering st. in summer, v. fleshy, ovate or obovate to elliptic, yellow-green, pointed, tapering below. Cyme compact; fls campanulate, 9mm across, tinged rose. Tex., Mex. Z8.

S. yezoense Miyabe & Tatew. = *Hylotelephium pluricaule.*

S. yosemitense Britt. = *S. spathulifolium* ssp. *yosemitense.*

S. yunnanense var. *forestii* Hamet = *Rhodiola yunnanensis* ssp. *forestii*.
→*Clementsia* and *Sedastrum*.

Seed Box *Ludwigia alternifolia*.
Seersucker Plant *Geogenanthus poeppigii*.
Sego Lily *Calochortus*.

Seidenfadenia Garay. Orchidaceae. 1 monopodial, epiphytic orchid. St. short. Lvs to 60cm, closely 2-ranked, narrow, linear, acuminate, keeled beneath. Rac. erect, dense, to 26cm; fls to 2cm diameter, white; tep. oblong, spreading; lip purple, obtuse, flat, with 2 filamentous basal projections, spur laterally compressed, obtuse. Burm. Z10.
S. mitrata (Rchb. f.) Garay.
→*Aerides*.

Seim Bean *Lablab purpureus*.

Selaginella Beauv. LITTLE CLUB MOSS; SPIKE MOSS. Selaginella-ceae. 700+ everg. rhizomatous moss-like plants, similar to *Lycopodium*. St. frond-like, creeping to erect or scandent, with pinnate or flabellate br. clothed with small, ± overlapping scale-like lvs and bearing root-like rhizophores. Sporophylls either ordinary lvs or modified lvs clustered in strobili. Trop. and subtrop. worldwide, with a few spp. also in temp. zones, extending rarely to Arc.
S. africana A. Br. = *S. vogelii*.
S. albonitens Spring = *S. tenella*.
S. albospica hort. = *S. stenophylla*.
S. amoena Bull = *S. pulcherrima*.
S. apoda (L.) Spring. MEADOW SPIKE MOSS; BASKET SPIKE MOSS. St. 2.5–10cm, prostrate, slender, weak, forming dense mats to 40cm diam.; br. short, forked, erect. Lvs in 4 ranks, pale green. E N Amer. Z3.
S. apus Spring = *S. apoda*.
S. australiensis Bak. St. prostrate, slender, branched. Lvs dark green. Aus. (Queensld). Z10.
S. azorica Bak. = *S. kraussiana*.
S. bellula Moore = *S. plana*.
S. biformis A. Br. St. 15–30cm, trailing, pinnately compound branched. Lvs bright green. E Himal. Z9.
S. braunii Bak. TREELET SPIKE MOSS. St. 30–45cm, erect, decompound, triangular and flexuous above. Br. erecto-patent, deltoid. W China. Z8.
S. brownii hort. = *S. kraussiana* 'Brownii'.
S. canaliculata hort. = *S. delicatula*.
S. caulescens hort. = *S. involens*.
S. chinensis hort. = *S. delicatula*.
S. cuspidata (Link) Link = *S. pallescens*.
S. delicatula (Desv.) Alston. St. 90–120cm, suberect; br. 10–15cm, deltoid, flexuous; lower branchlets compound. Lvs bright green. E Himal. Z9.
S. densa hort. = *S. apoda*.
S. denticulata (L.) Link. St. to 15cm, pinnately branched, trailing, forming dense mats, lower branchllets flabellately compound. Medit. region. Z9.
S. douglasii (Hook. & Grev.) Spring. St. 15–40cm, prostrate, pinnately branched, lower br. v. compound. Lvs pale lime green. BC and Idaho to Oreg. and N Calif. Z6.
S. emiliana Bull = *S. pallescens*.
S. emmeliana Bull = *S. pallescens*.
S. eremophila Maxon. DESERT SELAGINELLA. St. 5–12cm, prostrate, lower br. spreading, 2–3-pinnate. Calif. Z9.
S. erythropus (Mart.) Spring. St. to 25cm, simple below, deltoid and pinnately decompound above, bright crimson; br. deltoid, 3-pinnate. Lvs bright dark green. Trop. Amer. Z10.
S. erythropus var. *major* Spring = *S. umbrosa*.
S. filicina Spring = *S. haematodes*.
S. flabellata Spring. St. 30–60cm, erect, pinnately decompound, deltoid above; br. deltoid, 3–4-pinnate. Lvs bright green. Trop. Amer. Z10.
S. flagellifera hort. = *S. biformis*.
S. grandis Moore. St. 45–60cm, erect, simple in lower part, deltoid and decompound above, branching pinnate to flabellate. Lvs bright green. Borneo. Z10.
S. griffithii Spring. St. 15–30cm, erect, deltoid and decompound above; br. 3× pinnate, cuspidate. Trop. Asia. Z10.
S. haematodes (Kunze) Spring. St. 30–60cm, deltoid and pinnately decompound above, bright crimson; br. 3–4-pinnate. W C & S Amer. Panama to Boliv. Z10.
S. helvetica (L.) Spring. St. 5–8cm, trailing, forked at base, remotely pinnately branched, densely matted, slender, pale. N Eurasia. Z5.
S. involens (Sw.) Spring. St. 5–15cm, much-branched, branching flabellate to pinnate, v. densely tufted, deltoid, green. Lvs v.

crowded, bright green. E Asia. The plant known as IRISH MOSS is a dwarf form from the Azores. 'Aurea': young lvs golden, becoming yellow-green. Z6.
S. japonica Spring = *S. involens*.
S. karsteniana A. Br. = *S. haematodes*.
S. kraussiana (Kunze) A. Braun. SPREADING CLUBMOSS; TRAILING SPIKE MOSS; MAT SPIKE MOSS. St. 15–30cm, trailing, jointed, copiously pinnate; br. erect-patent, compound. Lvs bright green. S Afr. 'Aurea': foliage bright golden green. 'Variegata': foliage splashed ivory to pale yellow. Z9.
S. lepidophylla (Hook. & Grev.) Spring. RESURRECTION PLANT; ROSE-OF-JERICHO. St. 5–10cm, rosulate, branched to base, primary branching closely pinnate; br. ascending, sub-flabellately compound, cuneate, broad. Lvs dark green drying or ageing rusty brown. Tex. and Ariz. S to Peru. Z9. Dried, the fronds will roll into a tight brown ball, unfurling if wet.
S. longipinna Warb. Rhiz. creeping, subterranean, wiry, long. St. erect, much-branched, fan-shaped with spreading seg.; rachis stramineous. Lvs dark, metallic green. Aus. (NE Queensld).
S. martensii Spring. St. 15–30cm, trailing. Br. decompound, flabellate to pinnate. Lvs bright green. Mex. 'Albolineata': some lvs wholly or partially white. 'Albovariegata': lvs white-tipped. Z9.
S. mutabilis hort. = *S. serpens*.
S. pallescens (Presl) Spring. MOSS FERN; SWEAT PLANT. St. to 15cm, densely tufted, branched from base, br. pinnate; pinnae rhomboid, copiously compound, short. Lvs pale green with white margins. N Amer. S to N Colomb. & Venez. 'Aurea': lvs golden-green. Z10.
S. pervillei Spring = *S. vogelii*.
S. pilifera A. Br. St. 8–10cm, densely tufted, compound, cuneate, branching pinnate to flabellate, br. erecto-patent. Tex. Z9.
S. plana (Desv. ex Poir.) Hieron. St. to 30cm, suberect; br. pinnate, deltoid, to 12cm; branchlets erecto-patent, compound, branchlets ascending. Lvs bright green. E Himal. Z9.
S. platyphylla hort. = *S. grandis*.
S. plumosa (L.) C. Presl = *S. biformis*.
S. pulcherrima Liebm. ex Bak. St. to 30cm, erect, tinged yellow, triangular and pinnately branched above; br. bipinnate, horizontal. Lvs bright light green. Mex. Z10.
S. rotundifolia Spring. St. 5–10cm, trailing, v. slender, forming close mats; br. remote, simple, short. Lvs pale green, sub-orbicular, not overlapping. W Indies (St Vincent, Martinique, Guadeloupe). Z10.
S. rupestris (L.) Spring. ROCK SPIKE MOSS; DWARF LYCOPOD. St. to 12cm, tufted, forming loose, spreading mats. Lvs with white or tawny awns, ciliate. E N Amer. Z5.
S. sanguinolenta (L.) Spring. St. laxly tufted, strongly branched. NE Asia. Z10.
S. selaginoides (L.) Link. St. trailing, short, slender, sparingly branched, br. ascending, short. Lvs bright green. GB, N Amer. Z7.
S. serpens (Desv. ex Poir.) Spring. St. 15–20cm, trailing, densely matted, pinnately branched; br. numerous, erecto-patent, slightly compound. Lvs bright green in morning, silvery and pale in late afternoon. W Indies. Z10.
S. setosa hort. = *S. erythropus*.
S. sibirica (Milde) Hieron. St. 2–6cm, tufted or matted; br. ascending, short, divaricate-branched. Lvs rather thick, dark dull green, with pale awns. NE Asia. Z4.
S. sinensis hort. = *S. delicatula*.
S. spinosa Beauv. = *S. selaginoides*.
S. stenophylla A. Br. St. 15–30cm, suberect, pinnately branched, lower br. v. compound above. Mex. Z9.
S. tenella (Beauv.) Spring. St. trailing, slender, copiously pinnate, lower br. slightly compound, upper simple. Lvs bright green. W Indies. Z10.
S. uliginosa (Labill.) Spring. SWAMP SELAGINELA. Rhiz. sub-terranean, much-branched. St. 10–15cm, erect, simple or pinnately branched, usually fan-shaped. Aus. Z10.
S. umbrosa Lem. ex Hiern. St. 25cm+, simple below, deltoid and decompound above, bright crimson; br. deltoid, 3-pinnate; branchlets ascending. Lvs bright dark green. Trop. Amer. Z10.
S. uncinata (Desv. ex Poir.) Spring. PEACOCK MOSS; RAINBOW FERN; BLUE SPIKE MOSS. St. 30–60cm, trailing, rooting, slender; br. alt., pinnate, short. Lvs iridescent blue. China.
S. underwoodii Hieron. Prostrate; st. to 15cm, 2–3-pinnately branched, rooting; br. spreading; branchlets short, recurved. Lvs bright green when young, tinged brown with age, awn white. S US. Z4.
S. variabilis hort. = *S. serpens*.
S. varians hort. = *S. serpens*.
S. victoriae Moore. St. 90–120cm, suberect; pinnae 15–22cm, lanceolate-deltoid, caudate, lower pinnules forked or somewhat pinnate, upper simple, erecto-patent. Lvs bright dark green. Borneo. Z10.

S. viticulosa Klotzsch. St. to 22cm, simple below, deltoid and decompound above; pinnae deltoid, 2–3-pinnate, branchlets ascending, 12–25mm, bright green. C Amer. to Colomb. and Venez. Z10.

S. vogelii Spring. St. 30–60cm, erect, simple below, deltoid and decompound above, often tinged pink; pinnae 6–18mm, deltoid, 3–4-pinnate, branchlets erecto-patent. Lvs bright green. W Afr. Z10.

S. wallacei Hieron. St. loosely tufted, 5–15cm, prostrate, much-branched; br. 1–4cm, decompound, ascending. NW Amer. Z4.

S. wallichii Spring. St. 60–90cm, sub-erect; pinnae 15–22cm, lanceolate; pinnules 2.5–4cm, crowded, generally simple, erecto-patent, term. pinnule occas. to 10cm. Lvs dark bright green. India. Z10.

S. willdenovii (Desv. ex Poir.) Bak. PEACOCK FERN. St. 3–6+m, scandent, branched from base; pinnae 30–60cm, deltoid, spreading; pinnules deltoid and decompound. Lvs bronze green with an iridescent sheen to kingfisher blue. OW Trop. Z10.

SELAGINELLACEAE Willk. in Willk. & Lange. See *Selaginella*.

Selago L. Scrophulariaceae. 150 shrubs, subshrubs and herbs. Fls tiny in spikes or heads often arranged in corymbs or pan.; cal. 5-lobed, cor. nearly equally 5-lobed or somewhat 2-lipped; sta. 4, exserted. Trop. & S Afr. Z10.

S. bolusii Rolfe. Subshrub, 30–50cm, much-branched, shoots minutely downy. Lvs 0.5–1cm, clustered, linear, subglabrous, spikes 2–3cm, terminating lat. twigs; cor. white, tube short. S Afr.

S. corymbosa L. Subshrub, 30–60cm, shoots erect, downy. Lvs 0.2–1cm, clustered, linear to filiform. Fls white, small and v. numerous, in corymbose clusters to 10cm across. S Afr.

S. fructicosa Rolfe. Subshrub, 30–50cm; st. minutely downy, much-branched. Lvs 0.2–1cm, linear to oblong; not clustered, downy. Spikes 1–3cm, broad oblong; cor. white or purple, tube 0.5cm, slender. S Afr.

S. galpinii Schltr. Bushy perenn. to 25cm, becoming glab. Lvs to 1.5cm, somewhat clustered, linear, entire. Fls pink to purple, in densely paniculate heads. S Afr.

S. hyssopifolia E. Mey. Erect unbranched perenn. Lvs to 3cm, linear, spreading. Fls white in round-topped pan. *c*2–2.5cm across. S Afr.

S. serrata Bergius. Glab. shrub to 20cm; st. erect or decumbent. Lvs to 2.5cm, 1 per node, crowded, sessile, obovate or oblong, toothed. Fls pale blue to purple, in compact corymbs of heads. S Afr.

S. spuria L. BLUE HAZE. Ann. or perenn. to 60cm; st. glab. or finely hairy. Lvs to 3cm, 1 per node, linear or linear-lanceolate, toothed. Fls white, pink or purple, corymbose. S Afr.

S. thunbergii Choisy. Much-branched perenn. to 60cm+; st. hairy. Lvs to 1cm, linear clustered. Fls blue in paniculate heads. S Afr.

Selenia Nutt. Cruciferae. 6 ann. herbs. Lvs pinnatifid. Rac. term.; fls small, 4-merous, yellow; sta. 6, 4 long, 2 short. Silique narrow-elliptic to broad-oblong, compressed or inflated, translucent. S N Amer.

S. aurea Nutt. To 25cm. Lvs linear-oblong, lobes entire or toothed, in 5–7 pairs. Rac. corymbose; fls 2cm diam.; pet. golden yellow, obovate to spathulate, clawed. Fr. 1.2cm. Spring. Mont., Kans. to Tex. Z6.

Selenicereus (A. Berger) Britt. & Rose. Cactaceae. *c*20 scandent, lithophytic or epiphytic cacti; st. slender and ribbed or flattened and winged; often bearing aerial roots; spines short. Fl. funnelform, nocturnal; floral areoles with hair-spines, bristles or spines. Trop. Amer., Carib.

S. anthonyanus (Alexander) D. Hunt. Climbing and epiphytic; primary st. to 2m+, flattened, shallowly lobed; lat. br. to 1m, 2-winged, broadly and deeply dentate-lobed; areoles in sinuses; spines 3, short. Fl. salverform, 12×10–15cm, fragrant; outer tep. purple, inner pale yellow. Summer. Mex. Z9.

S. atropilosus Kimnach. Sprawling to scandent, to 3m+, profusely branched; st. 1.5–2(–4)cm diam.; ribs (3–)4(–6), serrate to crenate; areoles 3–6cm apart; spines 2–6, 1–6mm, off-white, red-tinged or almost black. Fl. funnelform, upcurved, 12×9–11cm; outer tep. yellow-green, tinged red, inner pale yellow or green-tinged. Summer. Mex. Z9.

S. boeckmannii (Otto ex Salm-Dyck) Britt. & Rose = *S. grandiflorus*.

S. brevispinus Britt. & Rose = *S. grandiflorus*.

S. coniflorus (Weing.) Britt. & Rose = *S. grandiflorus*.

S. donkelaarii (Salm-Dyck) Britt. & Rose. St. to 8m×1cm diam.; ribs 9–10 or fewer, v. low, rounded; spines 10–15, 1–4mm,

adpressed. Fl. 18cm; outer tep. tinged red, inner white. SE Mex. (Yucatan). Z9.

S. grandiflorus (L.) Britt. & Rose. QUEEN OF THE NIGHT. St. 1.2–2.5cm diam.; ribs 5–8(–10), low; areoles 5–20mm apart; spines 6–18, 4.5–15mm, setaceous, young growth with white, pale yellow or brown hairs. Fl. 17.5–30×12.5–17.5cm; outer tep. pale yellow or brown-tinged, inner white. Summer. Jam., Cuba, widely nat. Z9.

S. hamatus (Scheidw. ex Pfeiff.) Britt. & Rose. St. slender, *c*1.5cm diam., angles 3–4 with prominent spurs to 1cm long beneath areoles; spines short and weak. Fl. 20–35cm, white. Summer. Mex. Z9.

S. hondurensis (Schum.) Britt. & Rose = *S. grandiflorus*.

S. inermis (Otto ex Pfeiff.) Britt. & Rose. St. 1–2.5cm diam., 3–5-angled or ribbed; ribs acute, sinuate-crenate, or v. low; areoles to 6cm apart; spines usually 0. Fl. 15×10cm; outer tep. yellow-green, tinged purple at base; inner tep. white, tinged pink at base. Venez., Colomb. Z9.

S. innesii Kimnach. St. clambering, *c*12mm diam.; ribs 6, low, tuberculate; areoles *c*1cm apart; spines 3–9, 1–2mm, the central subulate, yellow-brown, others hair-like. Fl. perfect or pistillate, 4–4.5cm long, the pistillate not expanding, the perfect rotate, *c*5cm; outer tep. tinged magenta; inner white. Windward Is. (St Vincent). Z9.

S. kunthianus (Otto ex Salm-Dyck) Britt. & Rose = *S. grandiflorus*.

S. macdonaldiae (Hook.) Britt. & Rose. Differs from *S. grandiflorus* in areoles seated on tubercles 2–3mm high. Hond. (?). Z9.

S. maxonii Rose = *S. urbanianus*.

S. megalanthus (Schum. ex Vaup.) Moran. Differs from *S. setaceus* in larger fls. Stem-seg. to 1–2m×3–6cm, 3-angled or winged; areoles 3–5cm apart; spines 2–3, 3–5mm, broad-based. Fls. funnelform, 30(–38)cm; tep. white. Fr. not known. Peru, Boliv. Possibly the plant cultivated in Columbia and Ecuador for 'pitaya', an ovoid edible fr. to 11×6cm, with thick yellow, tuberculate rind, short, decid. spines and white pulp. Z9.

S. mirandae Bravo = *Weberocereus glaber*.

S. murrillii Britt. & Rose. Slender vine to 6m+; st. 8mm diam., dark green; ribs 7–8, low, obtuse, tinged purple; areoles 1–2cm apart; spines 5–6, 2 lowest 1–2cm, others v. small, conic, tinged green to black. Fl. 15×15cm; outer tep. green-yellow; inner tep. white. Mex. Z9.

S. nelsonii (Weing.) Britt. & Rose = *S. donkelaarii*.

S. nycticalus (Link & Otto) W.T. Marshall = *S. pteranthus*.

S. pringlei Rose = *S. grandiflorus*.

S. pteranthus (Link & Otto) Britt. & Rose. Differs from *S. grandiflorus* in st. stouter, 2.5–5cm diam., 4–6-angled; areoles 2–2.5cm apart, with 1–5 short, hard, conic spines 1–3mm. Summer. Mex. Z9.

S. setaceus (DC.) Werderm. St. 3(–4–5) angled, 2–4(–8)cm diam.; areoles 2–3cm apart; spines 1–3, 1–2mm, conic, brown. Fl. 25–30cm. Braz. to Arg. Z9.

S. spinulosus (DC.) Britt. & Rose. St. 1–2cm diam., with 4–5 ribs; areoles 1.5–2.5cm apart; spines 6–8, only 1mm. Fl. 10–12.5×7–8.5cm; outer tep. pale brown-green, inner white to pale pink. Spring–summer. SW US, Mex. Z9.

S. testudo (Karw. ex Zucc.) F. Buxb. St. clambering to 5m, irregularly segmented and ribbed; seg. elongate, with 3–4 equal ribs or much broader, to semi-ovoid, to 10–15cm, v. unequal ribs folded and parted over aother; areoles 1–2cm apart; spines 10, 1–2cm, brown or pale yellow to white. Fl. *c*28cm, creamy white. C Amer. Z9.

S. urbanianus (Gürke ex Weing.) Britt. & Rose. Resembling *S. grandiflorus*. St. to 3cm diam.; ribs usually 4–5, prominent; areoles *c*1cm apart; spines several, to 1cm, brown with longer, white hairs. Fl. 20–30cm; outer tep. brown to orange; inner tep. white. Hispan., Cuba. Z9.

S. vagans (Brand) Britt. & Rose. St. 1–1.5cm diam.; ribs *c*10, low; areoles 1–1.5cm apart; spines numerous, to 1cm, acicular, yellow-brown. Fl. 15cm; tube 9cm; outer tep. white, tinged brown or green; inner tep. white. W Mex. Z9.

S. vaupelii (Weing.) A. Berger = *S. grandiflorus*.

S. wercklei (F.A.C. Weber) Britt. & Rose. St. elongate, slender, 5–15mm diam.; ribs 6–12, v. low; areoles small; spines 0. Fl. 15–16cm; outer tep. tinged red; inner tep. white. Costa Rica. Z9.

S. wittii (Schum.) G. Rowley. Epiphyte climbing by aerial roots from the midrib; st. elongate, 2-winged, *c*10cm broad, green or red or purple when in full sun; areoles marginal, 6–8mm apart; spines to 12mm, acicular, yellow-brown. Fl. 25cm; white; limb relatively short. Amazon (Braz., Colomb. and Peru). Z9.

→*Cereus, Cryptocereus, Deamia, Mediocactus* and *Strophocactus*.

Selenipedilum Pfitz. = *Selenipedium*.

Selenipedium Rchb. f. Orchidaceae. 4 terrestrial orchids. St. slender, reed-like. Lvs alt., remote on st., lanceolate, chartaceous, plicate. Spike term., bracteate; fls to 10; dors. sep. free, lat. sep. fused in synsepalum; pet. free, narrower than dors. sep.; lip prominent, inflated, slipper-like. Trop. Amer. Z10.

S. chica Rchb. f. To 5m. Infl. pubesc.; fls red-green to dull orange-brown; dors. sep. ovate, acute; pet. drooping, lanceolate; lip strongly inflated, like *Cypripedium*. Panama.

Self Heal *Prunella.*

Selinum L. Umbelliferae. 6 perenn. herbs. Lvs 2–3-pinnatisect, seg. filiform to oval. Umbels with few rays; involucre of few bracts or lacking; involucel of linear to divided bracteoles; fls small, white to purple-white; pet. obcordate. Eur. to C Asia.

S. wallichianum (DC.) Nasir. Glab. perenn. to 1.5m. Lower lvs to 20cm, 2–3-pinnate, lacy, bright green, petiole long. Umbels flat, to 20cm diam., rays 15–30; bracts 0–2; bracteoles 5–10, margins white; fls white. Summer. Kashmir, Himal., India, W Pak. Z8.

Selliguea Bory. Polypodiaceae. 5 epiphytic ferns. Rhiz. long-creeping, scaly. Fronds stipitate, dimorphous (fertile fronds narrower and longer), simple, lanceolate to ovate, entire to notched and cartilaginous at margin, lustrous, leathery, conspicuously veined; stipes remote. SE Asia to Polyn. Z10.

S. feei Bory. Rhiz. to 3mm wide; scales to 0.8cm, light golden-brown. Sterile fronds to 10×5cm, ovate to oblong, notched, fertile fronds to 15×2cm; stipes 10cm+. Malaysia to New Guinea, Philipp.

S. lima (v.A.v.R.) Holtt. Rhiz. to 2mm wide; scales to 1cm, light red-brown. Sterile fronds to 30×4cm, elliptic, entire, fertile fronds to 30×3cm; stipes to 25cm. Malaysia to Indon.
→*Pleopeltis* and *Polypodium.*

Selu *Cordia myxa.*
Semaphore Plant *Codariocalyx motorius.*

Semecarpus L. f. Anacardiaceae. About 60 trees, some pachycaul. Lvs simple, entire, large. Pan. terminal or axill.; cal. seg. usually 5; pet. usually 5, imbricate; sta. 5–6; disc broad, annular. Fr. a drupe, fleshy, oblique, hypocarp fleshy. Trop. Asia to Aus. Z10.

S. anacardium L. f. MARKING NUT TREE. To 25m. Lvs to 50cm, oblong-obovate, clustered at ends of br., coriaceous, tomentose beneath. Infl. term., compressed; fls to 1cm diam.; pet. oblong, yellow-green. Fr. purple-black, glaucescent to 2.5cm; hypocarp orange. Summer. Trop. Asia to Aus.

Semele Kunth. CLIMBING BUTCHER'S BROOM. Liliaceae (Asparagaceae). 1 everg., perenn. herb like a giant, climbing *Ruscus*. St. clumped, arising annually 5–7m×1–2cm, terete, snaking then twining, becoming rigid; br. spreading. True lvs scale-like, soon withering and becoming prickly; cladophylls dark green, glab., rigid to semi-pliable, 2.5–7×1.5cm, broadly ovate to ovate-lanceolate, pungent. Fls to 0.6cm diam., cream drying brown, persistent, 1 to several, clustered on margins or face of cladophylls, berry to 2cm diam., orange-red. Early summer. Canary Is. Z9.

S. androgyna (L.) Kunth.

Semiaquilegia Mak. Ranunculaceae. 7 perenn. herbs differing from *Aquilegia* in pet. gibbous or slightly saccate at base, not spurred; some sta. staminodal, thus differing from *Isopyrum*. E Asia. Z6.

S. adoxoides (DC.) Mak. Slender perenn. to 30cm. Basal lvs to 5cm, ternate, lfts 2–3-fid, puberulent, glaucescent above, tinged purple beneath, long-petiolate. Fls pale rose; sep. to 0.6cm; pet. tubular to 0.3cm. Carpels 3–5. Spring. Jap., Korea, China.

S. ecalcarata (Maxim.) Sprague & Hutch. Slender perenn. to 45cm. Basal lvs to 30cm, 2-ternate, lfts 3-fid, glab.; long-petiolate. Fls wine-red to purple, sep. to 1.5cm; pet. oblong, to 1.5cm. Carpels 3–10. Summer. W China. 'Flore Pleno': fls double, rounded, deep maroon.

S. simulatrix J.R. Drumm. & Hutch. = *S. ecalcarata.*
→*Aquilegia* and *Isopyrum.*

Semiarundinaria Mak. ex Nak. Gramineae. Rhiz. typically running. Culms terete or with the upper internodes grooved or flattened on one side; sheaths soon falling; br. short, 3–7 developing from the base upwards, lowest nodes branchless. Far E.

S. fastuosa (Marliac ex Mitford) Mak. ex Nak. NARIHIRADAKE. Culms erect, 3–12m×2–7cm, lined purple-brown with white powder below nodes; sheaths thick, glab. interior, usually wine-coloured and shining. Lvs 9–21×1.5–2.7cm, glab. S Jap.

var. *viridis* Mak. Culms green, lvs longer. Z7.
S. tranquillans Koidz. = *Hibanobambusa tranquillans.*
S. yamadorii Muroi. More slender than *S. fastuosa* with longer br., some lvs to 24×5cm, culm sheaths hairy at base. Jap. Z8.
S. yashadake (Mak.) Mak. Differs from *S. yamadorii* in being rather more stiffly erect, with more open growth, short br. and paler, smaller lvs. Jap. Z8.
→*Arundinaria* and *Phyllostachys.*

Seminole Bread *Zamia pumila.*

Semnanthe N.E. Br. Aizoaceae. 1 succulent. St. spreading, robust, 60–80cm. Lvs ± sabre-shaped, 30–50×8–11mm, acute, apiculate, strongly laterally compressed, triquetrous, margins cartilaginous, denticulate, keel laciniate or cartilaginous-dentate, grey-pruinose with translucent dots. Fls 4–5cm diam., pink-purple. Summer. S Afr. Z9.

S. lacera (Haw.) N.E. Br.
→*Mesembryanthemum.*

Sempervivum L. HOUSE LEEK. Crassulaceae. 42 small, fleshy, rosette-forming, perenn. herbs. Lvs succulent, in tight basal rosettes, sessile, pointed, ciliate. Flowering st. erect, leafy. Infl. a paniculate cyme; sep. 6–20, fleshy, cup-shaped; pet. as many as and exceeding sep., free; sta. twice as many as sep., fil. thin. Eur., N Afr., W Asia.

S. altum Turrill. To 35cm; rosettes around 4cm diam. Lvs 1.9cm, oblanceolate, short bristle-tipped, green, gland. hairy, ciliate, cauline. Infl. many fls subsessile, 2.5–3cm across, glandular-hairy, puprle-red, margins white. Cauc. Z6.

S. annuum Chr. Sm. = *Aichryson laxum.*

S. arachnoideum L. Rosettes around 5cm diam., dense, with dense arachnoid hairs. Lvs 7–12mm, obovate-oblong or oblanceolate; flowering st. 4, 12cm cauline, lvs tipped red. Fls 1–1.5cm diam.; pet. bright rose-red. Summer. Pyren. to Carpath. 'Clairchen': lvs pale green, densely webbed white. 'Cristate': cristate form. 'Kappa': lvs becoming red (in spring). 'Stansfieldii': lvs webbed, becoming red. Z5.

S. arboreum L. = *Aeonium arboreum.*

S. arenarium Koch = *Jovibarba hirta* ssp. *arenaria.*

S. armenum Boiss. & Huet. Stolons few; rosettes 2–6cm diam. Lvs 1–3cm, tip dark purple, spathulate to lanceolate-ovate, ± glab., cauline lvs gland. hairy. Fls 1.5–2cm diam., pale yellow-green, centre purple. Summer. Turk. Z7.

S. atlanticum Ball. To 30cm; stolons short; rosettes 4–8cm diam. Lvs 2–3.5cm, oblong-spathulate, blunt with a short pointed tip, some hairy with red tips. Fls 3–4cm across, light pink. Moroc. Z7.

S. ballsii Wale. To 12cm. Stolons thick, 10–15mm; rosettes around 3cm diam., somewhat globose, lvs erect near centre. Lvs 1.8cm, obovate, blunt with a small point, glab., yellow-green, ciliate below; cauline lvs 1.7cm, erect, slightly overlapping. Infl. 4cm diam., hairy; fls c2cm diam., pink, red in centre, keeled green. Summer. Greece, Cauc. Z7.

S. balsamiferum (Webb & Berth.) Webb & Berth. ex Christ = *Aeonium balsamiferum.*

S. barbatum C. Sm. ex Hornem. = *Aeonium simsii.*

S. barbatum C. Sm. ex Otto = *Aeonium spathulatum.*

S. barretii Menez ex Praeger = *Aichryson villosum.*

S. bentejui (Webb ex Christ) Christ = *Aeonium spathulatum.*

S. berthelotianum (Bolle) Christ = *Aeonium tabuliforme.*

S. bollei Christ = *Aichryson bollei.*

S. borisii Degen & Urum. = *S. ciliosum.*

S. borissovae Wale. To 15cm; stolons short, red-brown; rosettes 3cm diam. Lvs 2.2cm, numerous, dense, obovate, bristle-tipped, tinged red-brown, ciliate; cauline lvs 1.5cm, few, erect, lanceolate. Infl. 4cm diam., compact; fls 2.3cm diam. on red pedicels, rose-red, edged white, serrate. Summer. Cauc. Z6.

S. caespitosum C. Sm. ex Otto = *Aeonium simsii.*

S. calcareum Jordan. Similar to *S. tectorum* except lvs broad, glaucous, light green, tipped brown-purple, flowering st. lvs somewhat clasping, broad-based; pet. green to white-pink. Summer. SW Alps. 'Greenii': rosettes small, to 4cm diam. 'Limelight': rosettes medium to large, pale yellow-green, inconspicuously tipped brown. 'Monstruosum': lvs cylindrical. 'Mrs Guiseppi': habit compact, lvs with deep red tips. 'Sir William Lawrence': habit vigorous; lvs with conspicuously dark red tips. Z5.

S. canariense ssp. *christi* (Praeger) Burchard = *Aeonium canariense* var. *palmense.*

S. canariense ssp. *latifolium* Burchard = *Aeonium canariense* var. *subplanum.*

S. canariense ssp. *longithrysum* (Praeger) Burchard = *Aeonium canariense* var. *palmense.*

S. canariense ssp. *virgineum* (Webb ex Christ) Burchard = *Aeonium canariense* var. *virgineum*.

S. candollei Rouy & Camus = *S. montanum*.

S. cantabricum Huber. Stolons few, leafy, hairy; rosettes 5–7cm across, half open. Lvs olive or dull green, linear, pointed, tip dark purple, glandular-hairy; cauline lvs brown-purple, loosely overlapping. Flowering st. 12–16cm; fls 1.8–2.4cm diam., red to white. N & C Spain. Z7.

S. castello-paivae (Bolle) Christ = *Aeonium castello-paivae*.

S. caucasicum Rupr. ex Boiss. 12–20cm. Rosettes 3–5cm diam. Lvs obovate-oblong, pointed, finely hairy to glab., ciliate, green; cauline lvs 1.5–2cm, lanceolate, glandular-hairy. Infl. many-fld, 2–7cm diam.; fls to 1.5cm diam., violet. Summer. Cauc. Z6.

S. christi Praeger = *Aeonium canariense* var. *palmense*.

S. ciliare Haw. = *Aeonium simsii*.

S. ciliatum Willd. = *Aeonium ciliatum*.

S. ciliatum Sims non Willd. = *Aeonium simsii*.

S. ciliosum Craib. Stolons slender; rosettes 2–5cm diam., somewhat closed. Lvs 2.4cm, grey-green, hairy, incurved, convex onn both surfaces; flowering st. lvs overlapping. Flowering st. *c*10cm; pet. 1–1.2cm, yellow. Summer. Bulg. Z6.

S. complanatum A. DC. = *Aeonium tabuliforme*.

S. cruentum (Webb & Berth.) Webb ex Christ = *Aeonium spathulatum*.

S. cuneatum (Webb & Berth.) Webb & Berth. ex Christ = *Aeonium cuneatum*.

S. davisii Muirhead. Stolons few, 2–3cm; rosettes 3–4cm diam. Lvs 1.5–2cm, obovate-lanceolate, blunt with a short tip, grey-green, red-brown toward apex, ciliate; cauline lvs glandular-hairy. Fls *c*2cm diam., off-white. Summer. NE Turk. to NW Iran. Z8.

S. decorum (Webb ex Bolle) Christ = *Aeonium decorum*.

S. dicotomum DC. = *Aichryson laxum*.

S. divaricatum var. *politum* Lowe = *Aichryson divaricatum*.

S. dolomiticum Facch. Stolons short, slender; rosettes *c*3.5–4cm diam., half open. Lvs 1–1.5cm, lanceolate-oblong, pointed, bright green, tip red with small apical tufts of cilia, sparsely hairy. Flowering st. *c*10cm; pet. 0.9–1.2cm, deep pink, centrally striped red-brown above, green beneath. Summer. E Alps. Z5.

S. erythraeum Velen. To 23cm, stolons v. short; rosettes flat, 3–6cm diam. Lvs *c*2cm, spathulate-obovate, with a short point, glandular-hairy, grey-purple. Fls *c*2cm diam., red-purple, dashed white above, red on back. SW Bulg. 'Red Velvet': lvs velvety, pale purple-pink. 'Glasnevin': lvs blue-purple, tinged green, pink, and grey. Z6.

S. foliosum C. Sm. ex Otto = *Aeonium smithii*.

S. gaudinii Christ = *S. grandifolium*.

S. × giuseppii Wale. Stolons slender, *c*2cm; rosettes 2cm diam., compact. Lvs 1.6cm, obovate, hairy, green, apex brown; cauline lvs 2cm, sparse, ovate-oblong or ovate-lanceolate, sharp-pointed, short-hairy, tinged purple. Infl. 3.5cm diam., hairy; fls 2.3cm diam., red, edged white. Summer. Spain. Z7.

S. glabrifolium Boriss. Differs from *S. armenum* in stolons numerous; lvs swollen, glossy, outer lvs purple above, curved inwards. Summer. Turk. Z8.

S. glandulosum Ait. = *Aeonium glandulosum*.

S. glutinosum Ait. = *Aeonium glutinosum*.

S. gomerense Praeger = *Aeonium gomerense*.

S. goochiae Webb & Berth. = *Aeonium goochiae*.

S. grandifolium Haw. Stolons stout, long; rosettes 5–10cm (rarely to 24cm) diam., lax, flat. Lvs oblong-triangular, abruptly pointed, hairy, dark green, tinged red at tip, smelling of resin. Flowering st. 15–30cm; pet. 1–1.8cm, yellow, stained purple at base. Summer. W & C Alps. 'Fasciatum': habit congested and cristate. 'Keston': lvs large, pale. Z6.

S. haworthii Salm-Dyck = *Aeonium haworthii*.

S. heuffelii Schott = *Jovibarba heuffelii*.

S. hierrense R.P. Murray = *Aeonium hierrense*.

S. hirtum L. = *Jovibarba hirta*.

S. hispicaule Haw. = *Aeonium smithii*.

S. hybridum Sweet. = *Aeonium × hybridum*.

S. ingwersenii Wale. To 15cm, stolons numerous, 5–10cm, red; rosettes 3cm diam., dense, flat. Lvs 1.5–7cm, ovate or obovate, narrow at base, tapering to short red tip; cauline lvs 1.3cm, ovate or oblong. Infl. 3cm diam., compact; fls around 2cm across, red, edged white. Summer. Cauc. Z6.

S. italicum I. Ricci. An invalid name.

S. kindingeri Adamovič. Similar to *S. zeleborii* except to 25cm; lvs to 3cm, spathulate, glandular-hairy; pet. cream-yellow, base red-purple. Macedonia. Z7.

S. kosaninii Praeger. To 20cm; stolons long; rosettes 5–8cm across, open, dense. Lvs 1.5–4cm, dull or dark green, apex dark, hairy, oblanceolate; cauline lvs linear-lanceolate, overlapping. Infl. compact; fls around 25mm across, rose-purple. Summer. SW Balk. Z6.

S. lancerottense Praeger = *Aeonium lancerottense*.

S. laxum Haw. = *Aichryson laxum*.

S. leucanthum Pančić. To 25cm; stolons stout, to 9cm; rosette 4–8cm diam., somewhat flattened. Lvs many, 2cm, spathulate-oblong, apex purple, abruptly acute, glandular-hairy; cauline lvs abruptly pointed. Infl. comapct, 5–8cm diam.; fls 25mm diam., pale green-yellow. Summer. Bulg. Z6.

S. ligulare Haw. = *Aeonium simsii*.

S. lindleyi (Webb & Berth.) Webb ex Christ = *Aeonium lindleyi*.

S. lineolare Haw. = *Aeonium spathulatum*.

S. macedonicum Praeger. 7–10cm; rosettes 3–5cm diam., somewhat flat. Lvs 1.5–2cm, oblanceolate-obovate, poiunted, edged short hairy, tips red. Fls 12–18mm diam., dull rose, edges pale. SW Balk. Z7.

S. marmoreum Griseb. Similar to *S. tectorum* except to 20cm; rosettes to 6cm diam.; lvs to 2.5cm, fine-hairy, dull green-purple; pet. red, margin white. SE & EC Eur. 'Brunneifolium': habit compact; lvs pink-brown, glabrescent. 'Chocolate': lvs dark chocolate-brown. 'Rubrifolium': lvs vivid red, tipped and edged green. Z5.

S. masferreri Hillebrand = *Aeonium sedifolium*.

S. meyerheimii (Bolle) Murray = *Aeonium glandulosum*.

S. minus Turrill. Stolons short, few; rosetes 0.8–3cm diam. Lvs 0.8cm oblong-elliptic to lanceolate, short bristle-tipped, green, suffused red-brown above, pruple near base, glandular-hairy or glab., ciliate. Fls 1.6cm diam., light yellow. Summer. Turk. Z5.

S. monanthes Ait. = *Monanthes polyphylla*.

S. montanum L. To 10cm; rosettes dense, open, clustered, 1.5–3.5cm diam. Lvs *c*1cm, dark green, dull, v. fleshy, finely hairy, oblanceolate, pointed. Infl. 3–10-fld; fls 3–3.5cm diam., red-purple, white, hairy below. Summer. C Eur. ssp. *stiriacum* Wettst. ex Hayek. Rosettes 2.5–5cm diam., open. Lf tips red-brown, fine-pointed. E Alps. 'Lloyd Praeger': rosettes slightly flattened; lvs heavily tipped with dark brown. Z5.

S. nevadense Wale. 3–12cm; stolons short, slender; rosettes 1.8–3.5cm diam., hummock-forming, compact, many-lvd, red in winter, pink-bronze at flowering, offsets numerous, rounded. Lvs 1.2–1.8cm, thick, obovate, pointed, bristle-tipped, gland., short-hairy at first; cauline lvs tinged rose. Fls red-pink. Spain (Sierra Nevada). Z7.

S. nobile Praeger = *Aeonium nobile*.

S. octopodes Turrill. To 9cm; stolons slender; rosettes *c*2cm diam. Lvs *c*0.7cm, ovate-oblanceolate, suberect, hairy, tips tinged red. Infl. few-fld; pet. 8mm, yellow, base light blue-purple. Balk. Z6.

S. ossetiense Wale. Differs from *S. ingwersenii* in rosettes not flat; lvs succulent, erect, few; pet. tinged red. Late summer. Cauc. Z5.

S. paivae Lowe = *Aeonium castello-paivae*.

S. palmense (Webb ex Christ) Christ = *Aeonium canariense* var. *palmense*.

S. patina Lowe = *Aeonium glandulosum*.

S. percarneum R.P. Murray = *Aeonium percarneum*.

S. percarneum var. *guiaense* Kunkel = *Aeonium percarneum*.

S. pittonii Schott, Nyman & Kotschy. To 8cm; stolons *c*2.5cm, slender; rosettes dense, somewhat flattened, 2–5cm diam., crowded. Lvs 2.5cm, crowded, incurved, grey-green, glandular-hairy, tips dark purple.Infl. flat, 5–8cm diam.; fls 2.5cm diam., pale green-yellow. E Alps. Z6.

S. porphyrogennetos Christ = *Aichryson porphyrogennetos*.

S. × praegeri G. Rowley. (*S. ciliosum × S. erythraeum*.) Rosettes similar to *S. erythraeum* but hairs longer. Pet. hairy beneath, green-yellow, red at tip. Summer. Bulg. Z6.

S. pulchellum (C.A. Mey.) Walp. = *Aeonium spathulatum*.

S. pumilum Bieb. To 20cm; rosettes 1–2.5cm diam. Lvs 1cm, glandular-hairy or subglabrous, oblong-lanceolate, short-pointed, ciliate, green, pet. midribs dark. Fls 2–4cm diam., light blue-purple. Summer. Cauc. Z6.

S. reginae-amaliae Bak. = *Jovibarba heuffelii*.

S. retusum Haw. = *Aeonium urbicum*.

S. saundersii (Bolle) Christ = *Aeonium saundersii*.

S. simsii Sweet = *Aeonium simsii*.

S. smithii Sims = *Aeonium smithii*.

S. soboliferum Sims = *Jovibarba sobolifera*.

S. sosnowskyi Ter-Chatsch. Differs from *S. armenum* in rosettes to 15cm diam.; lvs 6–8cm, gland. hairy on st.; fls to 3.5cm diam. Cauc. Z6.

S. spathulatum Hornem. = *Aeonium spathulatum*.

S. strepsicladum var. *cruentum* (Webb & Berth.) Burchard = *Aeonium spathulatum*.

S. tabuliforme Haw. = *Aeonium tabuliforme*.

S. tectorum L. Rosettes large, 5–10cm diam., open, rather flat, offsets numerous. Lvs 2–4cm, apex with distinct dark markings, glab., oblanceolate, thick, bristle-tipped. Flowering st. to 30cm, v. hairy; infl. large, many-fld; fls 3cm diam., dull rose, with short red lines. Summer. C Eur. 'Atropurpureum': lvs dark violet. 'Boissieri': lvs bronze-green, with red-brown tips. 'Nigrum':

lvs with conspicuous red-purple tips. 'Red Flush': lvs flushed red. 'Royanum': rosettes v. large; lvs yellow-green, tipped red. 'Sunset': lvs orange-red. 'Triste': lvs red-brown. Z4.

S. **thompsonianum** Wale. To 10cm; stolons few, to 4cm; rosettes 1.5–2.5cm diam., rounded. Lvs 1.4cm, ovate-lanceolate, narrow below, short-hairy, convex, long-ciliate, tip short; cauline lvs nearly erect, triangular-lanceolate, tip dark brown. Infl. 25mm diam., hairy; fls c2cm diam.; pale purple, margins broad, white. Summer. Balk. Z6.

S. **tortuosum** DC. = Aichryson ×domesticum.

S. **tortuosum** var. **goochiae** (Webb & Berth.) Kuntze = Aeonium goochiae.

S. **tortuosum** var. **lindleyi** (Webb & Berth.) Kuntze = Aeonium lindleyi.

S. **tortuosum** var. **viscatum** (Bolle) Kuntze = Aeonium lindleyi var. viscatum.

S. **transcaucasicum** Muirhead. Differs from S. davisii in lvs glandular-hairy, yellow-green; pet. yellow, blue at base. Summer. Georgia. Z6.

S. **undulatum** (Webb & Berth.) Webb & Berth. ex Christ = Aeonium undulatum.

S. **urbicam** Lindl. non C. Sm. ex Hornem. = Aeonium arboreum var. holochrysum.

S. **urbicum** C. Sm. ex Hornem. non Lindl. = Aeonium urbicum.

S. ×**vaccarii** Wilcz. (S. arachnoideum ×S. grandifolium.) Differs from S. grandifloium in lvs with arachnoid hairs; pet. red or pale purple, tipped yellow. It. and Swiss Alps. Z5.

S. **valverdense** Praeger = Aeonium valverdense.

S. **velenovskyi** Cesm. = Jovibarba velenovskyi.

S. **villosum** Lindl. non Ait. = Aeonium spathulatum.

S. **villosum** Ait. non Lindl. = Aichryson villosum.

S. **virgineum** (Webb ex Christ) Christ = Aeonium canariense var. virgineum.

S. **viscatum** (Bolle) Christ = Aeonium lindleyi var. viscatum.

S. ×**widderi** Lehm. and Schnittsp. (S. tectorum ×S. wulfenii.) Differs from S. tectorum in pet. yellow above, red near base or yellow streaked red. N Spain. Z8.

S. **wulfenii** Hoppe ex Koch. 15–25cm; stolons long, stout; rosettes c10cm diam. Lvs c3cm, spathulate-oblong, glaucous grey-green, rosy purple at base, margin, revolute above. Infl. compact, flat; pet. 1cm, yellow or green-yellow, purple at base. Summer. Austrian and Swiss Alps. Z5.

S. **youngianum** (Webb & Berth.) Webb & Berth. ex Christ = Aeonium undulatum.

S. **zeleborii** Schott. To 18cm; stolons short; rosettes c4cm diam., rounded. Lvs c2cm, obovate-oblong, short-pointed, grey-green, pet. 9mm, green-yellow, tinged dark-purple below. SE Eur. Z6.

S. **Cvs.** 'Aldo Moro': lvs green, orange, and red, velvety. 'Beta': rosettes pubesc., heavily flushed red. 'Commander Hay': rosettes v. large, red and green. 'Director Jacobs': lvs large, deep red, with white hairs and cilia. 'Highland Mist': rosettes frosted grey-green, flushed rose-pink. 'Marmalade': rosettes vivid pink-red. 'Night Raven': lvs almost black. 'Nouveau Pastel': rosettes small, compact, bronze-pink. 'Pekinese': lvs light apple green, woolly. 'Pippin': lvs deep purple. 'Red Mountain': lvs mahogany-red in Summer. 'Shirley's Joy': lvs covered with dense, white hairs. 'Virgil': lvs grey-blue-purple, with dark tips. 'Zakenrone': lvs dark purple, tipped green-gold.

Seneca Polygala.

Senecio L. Compositae. c1000 trees, shrubs, lianes and herbs. Lvs alt., entire to variously lobed. Cap. usually in corymbs, rarely solitary, usually radiate; receptacle flat; disc flts yellow, rarely white or purple. Cosmop.

S. **abrotanifolius** L. Perenn., to 40cm; st. leafy, ± glab. Lower lvs to 8cm, 2–3-pinnatisect, seg. linear, rachis narrow, subglabrous; upper st. lvs 1-pinnatisect, linear or small and bract-like. Cap. to 4cm diam., radiate, few or solitary, v. showy; ray flts yellow to orange-scarlet, with brown stripes. Summer. C & E Eur. ssp. **carpathicus** (Herbich) Nyman. Uppermost lvs simple, bract-like. Cap. solitary. SE Eur. Z6.

S. **acaulis** (L. f.) Schultz-Bip. ± stemless, succulent perenn. to 30cm. Lvs clustered, to 15cm, linear, semi-terete, elongate, mucronate, channelled above, clasping at base, glab. Cap. to 2.5cm diam., discoid, solitary, scapes erect, with a few scattered, subulate lvs. S Afr. Z9.

S. **achyrotrichus** Diels = Ligularia achyrotricha.

S. **adonidifolius** Lois. Perenn., to 70cm, subglabrous; st. erect, leafy. Lower lvs 3-pinnatisect, seg. linear, upper lvs 1-pinnatisect, linear. Cap. small, radiate, numerous, in a term. compound corymb; ray flts bright yellow to orange. C Fr. to C Spain. Z7.

S. **aloides** DC. Dwarf shrub to 50cm, glab. Lvs 5cm, broadly linear, subobtuse, entire. Cap. to 2cm diam., radiate, subsessile, in clusters of 2–4. S Afr. Z9.

S. **alpinus** hort. = S. cordatus.

S. **altaicus** (DC.) Schultz-Bip. = Ligularia altaica.

S. **amaniensis** (Engl.) Jacobsen = Kleinia amaniensis.

S. **ambraceus** Turcz. ex DC. Erect, branched perenn. to 1m. Lvs to 7.5cm, pinnatisect, sessile or amplexicaul, upper lvs reduced, entire. Cap. to 2.5cm diam., radiate, few in term. pan.; ray flts yellow. NE Asia. Z3.

S. **ampullaceus** Hook. TEXAS GROUNDSEL. Ann. to 70cm; st. erect, stout, leafy, glab. Lvs to 12cm, remotely dentate to entire, thick, fleshy, basal lvs spathulate to broadly ovate, tapering to a flattened petiole, st. lvs oblong to lanceolate, amplexicaul. Cap. to 4cm diam., radiate, in lax long-stalked clusters to 7.5cm diam.; ray flts yellow. Spring–summer. S US. Z8.

S. **angulatus** L. f. Branched perenn. to c3cm, glab. Lvs to 5cm, ovate to lanceolate, acute, cuneate at base, lobed or repand, lobes few, short and broad or tooth-like. Cap. to 2.5cm diam., radiate, many, in compound corymbs or pan. 8–12cm across; ray flts yellow. S Afr., nat. N It., S Spain. Z9.

S. **anteuphorbium** (L.) Schultz-Bip. = Kleinia anteuphorbium.

S. **arenarius** Thunb. Branched, weak-stemmed viscid-pubesc. Ann. to 50cm. Lvs oblong or obovate, subentire or toothed, lyrate or 1–2-pinnatifid or bipinnatifid, lobes cuneate, dentate or incised, base ± clasping. Cap. radiate, in a lax corymb; peduncles long, scaly; ray flts purple, rarely white. S Afr.

S. **argentinus** Bak. Subshrubby white-tomentose, leafy perenn. to 50cm. Lvs to 6cm, deeply pinnatisect or bipinnatisect, seg. linear, acute. Cap. to 1cm diam., discoid, mostly on peduncles in corymbs; flts white. Urug., Arg. Z9.

S. **argyreus** Philippi. Woody-based perenn., to 30cm; st. procumbent to ascending, densely white-lanate. Lvs to 3cm, oblanceolate- to obovate-spathulate, obtuse, base long-attenuate, dentate or rarely subentire, revolute, densely pubesc. Cap. to 3.5mm diam., radiate, solitary, term.; ray flts yellow. Summer. Arg., Chile. Z9.

S. **arnicoides** Wallich = Cremanthodium arnicoides.

S. **artemisiifolius** Pers. = S. adonidifolius.

S. **articulatus** (L. f.) Schultz-Bip. CANDLE PLANT; HOT-DOG CACTUS; SAUSAGE CRASSULA. Perenn. succulent to 60cm; st. with cylindric, swollen joints to 2×1.2cm, glaucous blue with dark lines. Lvs to 5cm, deeply 3–5-lobed, fleshy, glaucous, petiolate. Cap. to 1.5cm diam., usually discoid, few, in corymbs, on peduncles to 25cm, malodorous; flts white. Winter. S Afr. Z9.

S. **aurantiacus** (Willd.) Less. = Tephroseris integrifolius ssp. aurantiacus.

S. **aureus** L. = Packera aurea.

S. **auriculatissimus** Britten. Everg., perenn., scandent shrub, climbing to 3m, subglabrous. Lvs to 7cm, transversely oblong or rounded-reniform, petiolate, coarsely, obtusely dentate, petiole to 5cm, base dilated into wide auricle. Cap. to 2.5cm diam., radiate, in lax clusters to 15cm diam.; ray flts golden-yellow. Spring. C Afr. Z10.

S. **australis** Willd. = S. linearifolius.

S. **balsamitae** Muhlenb. ex Willd. = Packera paupercula.

S. **barbertonensis** Klatt = S. barbertonicus.

S. **barbertonicus** Klatt. Perenn., succulent, shrub to 2m, glab.; st. much branched, leafy becoming naked. Lvs to 5.5cm, terete, sessile, mucronate, slightly curved, base attenuate. Cap. discoid, in small corymbose clusters forming term. pan.; flts bright golden-yellow. Summer. Zimb. and Moz. to S Afr. Z9.

S. **bicolor** (Willd.) Tod. = S. cineraria.

S. **bidwillii** Hook. f. = Brachyglottis bidwillii.

S. **bolanderi** A. Gray = Packera bolanderi.

S. **bonariensis** Hook. & Arn. Perenn. herb to 2m, lanate at first; st. thick. Lower lvs to 35cm, ovate-deltoid, acute, dentate, cordate or sagittate at base, fleshy, long-petiolate; mid-stem lvs ovate-lanceolate, petiole shorter, auriculate. Cap. to 2cm diam., radiate, in a dense compound corymb; ray flts white. Urug. to C Arg. Z9.

S. **buchananii** J.B. Armstr. = Brachyglottis buchananii.

S. **buchananii** hort. non J.B. Armstr. = Brachyglottis elaeagnifolia.

S. **calamifolius** Hook. = S. scaposus var. caulescens.

S. **campestris** (Retz.) DC. = Tephroseris integrifolia.

S. **candicans** Wallich = S. cineraria.

S. **cannabifolius** Less. Perenn. to 2m; st. erect, often tinged red. Lower lvs to 20cm, pinnatisect, seg. lanceolate, acuminate, serrulate, crisped-puberulent beneath, petioles auriculate at base; upper st. lvs 3-cleft to entire. Cap. c2cm diam., many, in large corymbs on slender peduncles; ray flts yellow. Summer. Jap. and N China to Sib. Z5.

S. **canus** Hook. = Packera cana.

S. **capitatus** (Wahlenb.) Steud. = Tephroseris integrifolia ssp. capitata.

S. **carniolicus** Willd. = S. incanus ssp. carniolicus.

S. **carpathicus** Herbich = S. abrotanifolius ssp. carpathicus.

S. **chenopodioides** Kunth = Pseudogynoxys chenopodioides.

S. chordifolius Hook. f. Perenn. subshrub to 30cm, glab., sparingly branched. Lvs to 24cm, ± terete, acute, flattened above toward base. Cap. to 2cm, few, narrow, in v. slender cymes to 25cm; flts yellow. Summer. S Afr. Z9.

S. cineraria DC. Shrub to 50cm+, much-branched, stout, densely white-tomentose. Lvs to 15cm, mostly crowded at base, ovate or ovate-lanceolate, dentate to pinnate, ± arachnoid-tomentose above at first, densely white-tomentose beneath. Cap. to 1cm diam., radiate, many, in dense compound corymbs on short peduncles; ray flts yellow. W & C Medit. 'Alice': to 30cm; lvs deeply cut, white stained silver. 'Cirrus': habit v. dwarf; lvs rounded, bright silver. 'New Look': habit neat, compact; lvs large, oak-leaf shape, pure white. 'Ramparts': lvs almost entirely silver. 'Silverdust': habit uniform, compact to 30cm; lvs finely divided, dusted silver. 'Silver Filigree': lvs cut, grey. 'Silver Queen': compact to 20cm; lvs lacy, silver-white. 'White Diamond': lvs silver-grey. Z8.

S. cinerascens Ait. Perenn. subshrub to 60cm; st. erect, corymbosely branched, thinly white-lanate. Lvs to 12cm, pinnatipartite or pinnatifid, lobes linear or lanceolate-oblong, obtuse, revolute, glabrate or tomentose above, white-tomentose beneath. Cap. to 1cm diam., often discoid, 3–8 in a simple corymb, on peduncles. S Afr. Z9.

S. citriformis G. Rowley. Perenn., succulent, densely tufted subshrub to 1m; st. short, suberect. Lvs to 2cm, numerous, ovate to obovate, acute, base attenuate, shortly petiolate, blue-grey with narrow, vertical, translucent lines. Cap. to 1.5cm diam., in loose corymbs; flts cream to white. S Afr. Z9.

S. clivorum Maxim. = *Ligularia dentata*.

S. compactus T. Kirk = *Brachyglottis compacta*.

S. concolor Harv. = *S. speciosus*.

S. confusus (DC.) Britten = *Pseudogynoxys chenopodioides*.

S. cordatus Koch. Perenn., to 70cm, erect, rarely branched, leafy. Lvs to 15cm, ovate, sometimes lyrate, cordate or rounded at base, strongly dentate, crenate-dentate or doubly dentate, glab. above, grey arachnoid-tomentose beneath; upper st. lvs sometimes subpinnatifid. Cap. to 4cm diam., 5–20, in a corymb; ray flts yellow, sometimes tinged orange. Mts of C Eur. Z6.

S. crassissimus Humb. Succulent perenn. shrub, to 80cm, glab.; st. much-branched, with prominent lf scars. Lvs to 5.5cm, obovate, rounded at apex, abruptly mucronate, cuneate at base, margins red-tinted, green, glaucous, thick, fleshy. Cap. radiate, several, in a term. corymb, on elongate scape; ray flts yellow. Madag. Z9.

S. cremeiflorus Mattf. Perenn. herb, to 1m stout. Lvs to 45cm, oblong-ovate, ± cordate, sinuate, obtusely dentate, glaucous or tinged purple beneath. Cap. to 2.5cm diam., radiate, in clusters 4–5cm diam., forming a large pan.; ray flts pale yellow to cream. Summer. Chile, Arg.

S. cruentes hort. = *Pericallis × hybrida*.

S. cruentus (L'Hérit.) DC. = *Pericallis cruenta*.

S. × crustii hort. = *Brachyglottis* Dunedin Hybrids.

S. cuneatus Jacobsen = *S. kleiniiformis*.

S. delavayi Franch. = *Cremanthodium delavayi*.

S. diversifolius Harv. = *S. scapiflorus*.

S. doria L. Perenn. to 1m; st. erect, herbaceous, branched above. Lvs to 40cm, ovate to linear-elliptic, subentire or patent-dentate, long-petiolate, thick, glaucous. Cap. to 2.5cm diam., many, in compound corymbs; ray flts yellow. Eur. to W Asia. Z6.

S. doronicum (L.) L. Perenn., to 60cm; st. erect, stout, simple, or branched above, arachnoid-lanate or glabrescent. Lvs to 25cm, elliptic to ovate, finely repand-dentate to subentire, subacute, rounded or cuneate at base, arachnoid-lanate beneath. Cap. to 6cm diam., radiate, solitary or in a lax corymb; ray flts yellow or orange. Summer. Medit. Z5.

S. douglasii DC. Perenn. to 2m; st. numerous, branched, woody; young shoots thinly tomentose. Lvs to 12cm, narrowly linear, tapered, many with a few long, lat. seg., principal lvs often with fascicles of smaller lvs in axils. Cap. to 5cm diam., several, in a corymb. Summer. Calif. Z8.

S. dryadeus Sieber = *S. linearifolius*.

S. elaeagnifolius Hook. f. = *Brachyglottis elaeagnifolia*.

S. elegans L. Ann. to 60cm, viscid-pubesc., erect or diffuse, branched. Lvs to 8cm, oblong, subentire or toothed, lyrate, pinnatifid or 1–2-pinnatipartite, auriculate-clasping at base, petiolate, lobes toothed or incised. Cap. to 2.5cm diam., radiate, several in lax corymbs, on long peduncles; ray flts purple, rarely white. S Afr.

S. faberi Hemsl. Perenn. herb to 1.5m, subglabrous; st. several, stout, hollow, angular. Lvs pinnatifid, coarsely dentate, semiamplexicaul, basal lvs to 60cm, uppermost lvs reduced. Cap. radiate, in a corymb to 20cm diam.; ray flts deep yellow. W China. Z7.

S. ficoides (L.) Schultz-Bip. Succulent perenn. subshrub to 1m, glab., pruinose; st. erect, branched, green, white-punctate. Lvs

to 15cm, flattened-terete, ±, acuminate, sessile, fleshy, powdery-glaucous. Cap. usually discoid, many, long-stalked in term. cymes; flts white. S Afr. Z9.

S. flammenus Turcz. ex DC. = *Tephroseris flammea*.

S. flettii Wiegand = *Packera flettii*.

S. fluviatilis Wallr. Perenn. herb to 2m; stolons fleshy above, st. erect, branched densely leafy. Lvs to 20cm, elliptic to linear-lanceolate, 1–2-serrate, glab. Cap. 3cm diam., radiate, many, in compound corymbs; ray flts yellow. C & E Eur. Z6.

S. forsteri Schldl. = *Brachyglottis repanda*.

S. fremontii Torr. & A. Gray DWARF MOUNTAIN BUTTERWEED. Perenn. to 1.5m; st. branched decumbent below, glab. Lvs to 4cm, mostly obovate to spathulate or broadly oblanceolate, dentate, ± succulent, petiole narrow, short. Cap. radiate, term.; peduncles short. Summer. W N Amer. Z7.

S. fulgens (Hook. f.) Nichols. = *Kleinia fulgens*.

S. galpinii (Hook. f.) Hook. f. = *Kleinia galpinii*.

S. glastifolius L. f. Perenn. subshrub to 1m, erect, much-branching, glab. Lvs to 7.5cm, oblong or lanceolate-oblong, acute, coarsely and unequally dentate, tapered to base, semi-amplexicaul, rigid. Cap. radiate, long-stalked, 3–5 per corymb in loose pan.; ray flts purple. S Afr. Z9.

S. gnaphaloides Sieb. Shrub to 50cm, branched below, densely white-tomentose. Lvs to 15cm, linear, entire or with to 4 pairs of distant lobes, arachnoid-lanate or glabrescent above, densely white-tomentose beneath. Cap. 12–15mm diam., radiate, many, in compound corymbs; ray flts yellow. Crete. Z8.

S. grandiflorus A. Berger. Perenn. herb to 1.5m; st. simple, mostly leafy. Lvs to 15cm, pinnatipartite, sessile, semi-amplexicaul, lobes linear, entire or dentate, revolute, sparsely pilose or subglabrous. Cap. to 3cm diam., radiate, in a loose, spreading pan. of partial corymbs of 3–5 heads; ray flts purple. Summer. S Afr. Z9.

S. grandifolius Less. = *Telanthophora grandifolia*.

S. gregorii (S. Moore) Jacobsen = *Kleinia gregorii*.

S. greyi Hook. f. non hort. = *Brachyglottis greyi*.

S. greyi hort. non Hook. f. = *Brachyglottis* Dunedin hybrids 'Sunshine'.

S. haastii Hook. f. = *Brachyglottis haastii*.

S. halleri Dandy. Woody-based perenn., to 10cm; st. erect, simple. Basal lvs to 5cm, oblong-obovate, entire, dentate or incised, st. lvs linear to lanceolate, simple, semi-amplexicaul. Cap. to 2.5cm diam., radiate, solitary; ray flts orange to yellow. Alps. Z6.

S. hallianus G. Rowley. Succulent perenn. to 30cm; st. prostrate, viscid, with wiry aerial roots producing fusiform tubers. Lvs to 2.5cm, cylindric-fusiform, glaucous, with a translucent line above and narrower inconspicuous stripes. Cap. to 2cm diam., solitary or few to several in corymbs; flts white. S Afr. Z9.

S. harfordii Piper = *Packera bolanderi*.

S. haworthii (Sw.) Steud. COCOON PLANT. Succulent subshrub, to 30cm+, densely soft white-lanate or -tomentose; st. suffruticose-fleshy. Lvs spirally arranged, to 5cm, cylindric to fusiform, tapered. Cap. to 2cm diam., discoid, solitary, term. on stout, bracteate scapes; flts orange to yellow. Summer. S Afr. Z9.

S. hectoris Buch. = *Brachyglottis hectoris*.

S. henryi Hemsl. = *Sinacalia tangutica*.

S. herreianus Dinter. Succulent perenn. to 60cm; st. prostrate, slender, rooting. Lvs to 1.2cm, elliptic, attenuate at both ends, green with many translucent lines, fleshy. Cap. small, discoid, peduncles to 7.5cm; flts white. Nam. Z10.

S. huntii F. Muell. = *Brachyglottis huntii*.

S. × hybridus (Willd.) Reg. = *Pericallis × hybrida*.

S. incanus L. Perenn., to 20cm, grey- or white-sericeous-lanate; st. erect, from a short, woody stock, branched above. Lvs sericeous-lanate beneath and often above; basal lvs to 10cm, usually pinnatifid or lobed, long-petiolate, uppermost simple. Cap. radiate, several in a dense corymb; ray flts yellow. Summer. Mts of C Eur. ssp. *carniolicus* (Willd.) Braun-Blanquet. Basal lvs oblanceolate, sometimes arachnoid-lanate. Cap. larger. Z5.

S. integrifolius (L.) Clairv. = *Tephroseris integrifolia*.

S. jacobaea L. Bienn. or perenn. to 1.5m; st. erect, subglabrous to floccose, branched above. Lvs to 20cm, lyrate-pinnatifid, petiolate, middle and upper st. 1–2-pinnatifid, perpendicular to rachis, semi-amplexicaul, sparsely floccose beneath. Cap. to 2cm diam., usually radiate, in a dense corymb; ray flts yellow. Eur. Widespread weed. Z5.

S. jacobsenii G. Rowley = *Kleinia petraea*.

S. japonicus Thunb. ex A. Murray = *Ligularia japonica*.

S. kaempferi DC. = *Farfugium japonicum*.

S. kirkii Hook. f. ex T. Kirk = *Brachyglottis kirkii*.

S. kleinia (L.) Less. = *Kleinia neriifolia*.

S. kleiniiformis Süsseng. SPEARHEAD. Succulent perenn. subshrub to 30cm, glab., white-pruinose. St. prostrate, giving off pungent odour when broken; br. erect, to 30cm. Lvs to 10cm, somewhat boat-shaped, often coarsely remotely dentate, narrowed toward base, petiolate, involute. Cap. discoid, 10–30 clustered in a pan.; flts white or yellow. S Afr. Z9,

S. lagopus Raoul = *Brachyglottis lagopus.*

S. lautus Willd. Ann. or short-lived perenn., to 60cm, erect to prostrate, simple to much-branched, leafy. Lvs to 6cm, oblong-lanceolate, entire to pinnatifid, serrate, entire toward tip, petiolate, sometimes amplexicaul, fleshy or membranous. Cap. to 2cm diam., radiate, in loose corymbs; ray flts yellow. Year round. NZ.

S. laxifolius Buch. non hort. = *Brachyglottis laxifolia.*

S. laxifolius hort. non Buch. = *Brachyglottis* 'Dunedin Hybrids'.

S. ledebourii Schultz-Bip. = *Ligularia macrophylla.*

S. leucophyllus DC. Perenn. to 20cm, grey- or white-sericeous-lanate, erect, robust, branched above. Lvs sericeous-lanate to 10cm, pinnatifid, lobes cuneate, petiolate, thick. Cap. radiate, in a dense corymb; ray flts yellow. Pyren., S Fr. Z6.

S. leucostachys Bak. = *S. viravira.*

S. leucostachys hort. non Bak. = *S. argentinus.*

S. linearifolius A. Rich. Perenn., to 1.5m glab., branched. Lvs to 15cm, linear to lanceolate, base sessile, entire or dilated into acuminate auricles, rarely thinly white-tomentose beneath. Cap. radiate, small, numerous, in a large term. corymb. SE Aus. Z9.

S. longiflorus (DC.) Schultz-Bip. = *Kleinia longiflora.*

S. longipes Bak. = *Kleinia grantii.*

S. macroglossus DC. NATAL IVY; WAX VINE. Slender, twining perenn. herb to 2m; st. somewhat succulent, glab. Lvs to 8cm, deltoid, hastate, 3-lobed, lobes acute to acuminate, lower pair spreading, somewhat succulent; petiole to 3cm. Cap. radiate, solitary or to 3 in a corymb; peduncles to 10cm; ray flts cream or pale yellow. Summer. W & S Afr. to Moz. and Zimb. 'Variegatus': climber; lvs dark green, ivy-like; fls bright yellow. Z10.

S. magellanicus Hook. & Arn. Perenn. herb to 20cm, ascending to erect, branched, sericeous. Lvs to 12cm, linear-lanceolate, acute, amplexicaul, ± revolute, sericeous. Cap. to 2cm diam., discoid, solitary, term. on scape-like st.; flts yellow. Summer. Tierra del Fuego. Z8.

S. magnificus F. Muell. Shrub or subshrub to 2m, erect, glab. and glaucous, erect. Lvs to 5cm, obovate-oblong, coarsely and acutely dentate and tapered to base to ovate-lanceolate, entire or nearly so, deeply cordate-auriculate and amplexicaul. Cap. large, radiate, in a loose term. corymb. Autumn. S Aus. Z9.

S. mandraliscae (Tineo) Jacobsen. Succulent perenn. subshrub to 30cm. Lvs to 10cm, semicylindric, somewhat flattened above, glaucous. Cap. mostly discoid, 10–13 in a forked cyme, on peduncles to 10m+; flts white. S Afr. Z9.

S. maritimus Koidz. = *S. cineraria.*

S. medley-woodii Hutch. Shrub to 1.5m; st. well-branched, thick, succulent. Lvs to 6cm, crowded, obovate, obtuse or subacute, mucronate, entire to coarsely dentate at apex, slightly undulate, narrowed to a flat, petiole-like base, tomentose at first, succulent. Cap. radiate; ray flts bright yellow. Summer. S Afr. (Natal). Z9.

S. mikanioides Otto ex Harv. = *Delairea odorata.*

S. monroi Hook. f. = *Brachyglottis monroi.*

S. multiflorus (L'Hérit.) DC. = *Pericallis multiflora.*

S. mweroensis Bak. = *Kleinia mweroensis.*

S. nemorensis L. Perenn. herb to 2m, sometimes stoloniferous; st. erect, branched above, densely leafy. Lvs to 20cm, acute, dentate, glab. above, often pubesc. beneath. Cap. to 3.5cm diam., radiate, many, in ± compound corymbs; ray flts yellow. Summer. Eur. Z6.

S. neowebsteri Blake. Perenn. to 20cm, at first ± arachnoid-villous. Lvs to 7cm, broadly oblanceolate to subrotund, dentate, petiolate. Cap. to 5.5cm diam., radiate, solitary, rarely 2, mostly pendulous; ray flts yellow. Late summer–early autumn. NW US. Z7.

S. neriifolius (Haw.) Baill. = *Kleinia neriifolia.*

S. nobilis Franch. = *Cremanthodium nobile.*

S. nudicaulis Buch.-Ham. Perenn. to 90cm, glab. or sparsely pubesc. Lvs to 18cm, variable, basal lvs often rosulate, sessile or narrowed to petiole, obovate or linear-oblong to spathulate, obtuse, crenate, st. lvs sessile, linear-oblong or obovate, crenate, lobulate or dentate, base contracted or dilated and auriculate. Cap. to 1cm diam., many. Temp. Himal. Z8.

S. obovatus Muhlenb ex Willd. = *Packera obovata.*

S. oxyriifolius DC. Perenn. herb to 1m, fleshy, glab., sometimes glaucous; st. solitary or a few, from crown, branched above. Lvs 4–9cm variable, peltate or orbicular to deltoid, or sinuate, coarsely and irregularly and sharply callose-dentate or angled, rarely entire, fleshy; petioles to 15cm. Cap. discoid in a corymbose pan.; peduncles long, naked; flts bright yellow. Winter. SE Afr. Z10.

S. palmatus Pall. ex Ledeb. = *S. cannabifolius.*

S. palmeri A. Gray. Perenn., to 60cm, densely white-tomentose.

Lvs to 5cm, oblong-lanceolate, entire or irregularly and shallowly dentate above, narrowed to base, long-petiolate, canescent above, densely white-tomentose beneath. Cap. to 2.5cm diam., few, in a pedunculate corymb; flts yellow. Spring. SW US, Baja Calif. Z9.

S. paludosus L. Perenn. herb to 2m; st. erect, from a short stock, simple below, arachnoid-lanate to glabrescent. Lvs to 20cm, linear-lanceolate to lanceolate, acute, serrate, petiole short, glab. above, arachnoid-lanate beneath. Cap. to 4cm diam., radiate, many, in a pan. or corymb; ray flts yellow. C & E Eur. Z6.

S. palustris (L.) Hook. = *Tephroseris palustris.*

S. pauciflorus Pursh. = *Packera pauciflora.*

S. pauperculus Michx. = *Packera paupercula.*

S. pendulus (Forssk.) Schultz-Bip. = *Kleinia pendula.*

S. pentactinus Klatt. Perenn. herb to 1.5m, woody; st. simple, erect, leafy above. Lvs to 8cm, subsessile to shortly petiolate, lanceolate, serrate, arachnoid-lanate at first. Cap. radiate in a flat-topped corymbose pan.; ray flts cream or v. pale yellow. Winter. S Afr. (Natal, Transvaal). Z9.

S. perdicioides Hook. f. = *Brachyglottis perdicioides.*

S. petraeus Muschl. = *Kleinia petraea.*

S. petrocallis E. Greene = *Packera werneriifolia.*

S. picticaulis Bally = *Kleinia picticaulis.*

S. platanifolius Benth. = *Roldana platanifolia.*

S. populifolius DC. = *Pericallis appendiculata.*

S. praecox (Cav.) DC. = *Pittocaulon praecox.*

S. przewalskii Maxim. = *Ligularia przewalskii.*

S. pseudoarnica Less. Perenn. herb to 50cm, fleshy, rhiz. thick; st., stout, simple, arachnoid-lanate. Lvs to 15cm, oblanceolate to obovate, obtuse, mucronate-dentate, semi-amplexicaul. Cap. to 4.5cm diam., radiate, usually few in pedunculate corymbs; ray flts yellow. Summer. Canada to N & NE Asia. Z3.

S. pteroneurus (DC.) Schultz-Bip. = *Kleinia anteuphorbium.*

S. pulcher Hook. & Arn. Perenn. herb to 60cm, lanate at first; st. erect, simple or branched above. Basal lvs to 20cm, rosulate, elliptic, crenate-lobed, tapered to petiole-like base, st. lvs lanceolate, dentate. Cap. large, radiate, usually in loose term. corymbs; ray flts violet or purple. Autumn. S Braz., Urug., Arg. Z8.

S. purdomii Turrill = *Ligularia achyrotricha.*

S. purshianus Nutt. = *Packera aurea.*

S. pusillus hort. = *S. citriformis.*

S. pyramidatus DC. Subshrub to 60cm; st. erect, simple, thick, fleshy. Lvs 7.5cm, sessile, subterete, fleshy, glab. or arachnoid-lanate. Cap. 5cm diam., radiate, many, in a thyrsoid rac. to 30cm, on lanate peduncles. Summer. S Afr. Z9.

S. radicans (L. f.) Schultz-Bip. CREEPING BERRIES. Succulent perenn. herb to 20cm, forming diffuse mats. Lvs to 5cm, fusi-form, acute, narrowed to petiole-like base, glab. Cap. discoid, solitary or in pairs, term., fragrant; peduncles erect to 15cm; flts white. Spring. S Afr. Z9.

S. reinoldii Endl. = *Brachyglottis rotundifolia.*

S. reniformis Wallich = *Cremanthodium reniforme.*

S. repens (L.) Muschl. = *S. serpens.*

S. resedifolius Less. = *Packera cymbalaria.*

S. riddellii Torr. & A. Gray. Shrub or woody-based perenn. to 1m; st. several, branched, leafy, glab. Lvs to 10cm, irregularly pinnatifid, seg. 3–9, filiform, entire, thick. Cap. 1–2cm diam., radiate, 5–20, in a terminal, corymbose cyme; ray flts yellow. Summer. W US. Z7.

S. rotundifolius Hook. f. = *Brachyglottis rotundifolia.*

S. rowleyanus Jacobsen. STRING-OF-BEADS. Succulent perenn. to 20cm, forming creeping mats; st. prostrate, slender, rooting. Lvs 8mm diam., succulent, globose, with a narrow translucent line. Cap. c1cm diam., discoid, solitary; flts white. Nam. Z9.

S. rufiglandulosus Colenso = *S. solandri* var. *rufiglandulosus.*

S. sagittifolius Bak. = *S. bonariensis.*

S. sarracenicus L. = *S. fluviatilis.*

S. saxifragoides Hook. f. = *Brachyglottis saxifragoides.*

S. scandens Buch.-Ham. ex D. Don. Perenn. to 5m, woody at base; st. branched, scandent, densely pubesc. at first. Lvs to 10cm, ovate or elongate-deltoid, acuminate, truncate to hastate at base, irregularly incised-toothed to subentire or lobed, pub-esc. Cap. c1.5cm diam., radiate; in spreading, terminal paniculate corymbs, ray flts yellow. Winter. E Asia. Z9.

S. scapiflorus (L'Hérit.) C.A. Sm. Perenn. to 50cm, white-lanate when young; st. branched. Lvs mostly basal, usually simple, deltoid, dentate, long sometimes with a few lobes along upper portion of petiole. Cap. discoid, solitary, long-pedunculate; flts white. S Afr. Z9.

S. scaposus DC. Perenn. subshrub to 50cm; st. fleshy, sometimes 0. Lvs 7.5cm, crowded at st., apices blunt, broadly linear to sub-spathulate, arachnoid-lanate at first. Cap. radiate, (1–)3–5; peduncles 30–45cm, scape-like, arachnoid-lanate. S. Afr. var. *caulescens* Harv. St. to 30cm. Z9.

S. scorzoneroides Hook. f. = *Dolichoglottis scorzoneroides*.

S. scottii Balf. f. = *Kleinia scottii*.

S. sempervivus Schultz-Bip. = *Kleinia semperviva*.

S. serpens G. Rowley. BLUE-CHALKSTICKS. Succulent shrub; to 30cm, glaucous blue, branched below. Lvs linear-lanceolate, ± cylindric, obtuse, grooved above. Cap. discoid, few, in a corymb; flts white. S Afr. Z9.

S. smithii DC. Perenn. to 1.2m; st. erect, stout, usually branched above, floccose-lanate to glabrescent. Basal lvs to 35cm, oblong-ovate, base truncate to subcordate, dentate, floccose-lanate, petiolate, upper lvs smaller, ovate-triangular. Cap. to 5cm diam., radiate, many, in a corymb; ray flts. white. Summer. Is Chile, Falklands. Z7.

S. solandella A. Gray. Perenn. to 20cm; st. tinged purple, glab. Lvs to 4cm, mostly basal, few, suborbicular to oblong-obovate, entire or denticulate, truncate to cuneate at base, attenuate to long petiole. Cap. radiate, solitary, erect to pendulous; ray flts yellow. C US. Z4.

S. solandri Allan. Perenn. herb to 1m; st. woody, br. flexuous. Lower lvs to 20cm, broadly ovate to ovate-oblong, lobes broad, dentate, acute, membranous, sparsely glandular-pubesc., upper lvs smaller and narrower. Cap. to 2cm diam., radiate, in corymbs, peduncles slender; ray flts yellow. Summer. NZ. var. *rufiglandulosus* (Colenso) Allan. St. stout. Lvs sometimes entire, densely glandular-pubesc. Corymbs large. Summer. Z9.

S. speciosus Willd. Perenn. to 70cm; st. several, base often decumbent, simple except above. Lvs to 20cm, mostly in a basal rosette, spathulate to elliptic, margins pinnately or sinuately lobed, lobulate or coarsely deltoid-toothed, tapering to broad, clasping peitole-like base, usually glandular-pubesc. beneath. Cap. to 1.5cm diam., radiate, few to many in a corymb; ray flts deep pink to purple. Summer. SE Afr. Z9.

S. sphaerocephalus Greene. Perenn., to 80cm; st. solitary, becoming glab. Lvs to 25cm, entire or slightly denticulate, basal lvs oblanceolate or elliptic, petiolate, uppermost sessile. Cap. to 3.5cm diam., radiate, 3–25, in a compact cyme. Summer. N & E US. Z5.

S. spiculosus (Sheph.) G. Rowley. Succulent perenn. herb to 50cm, glab., resinous; st. erect, sparsely branched. Lvs to 4×5mm, variable, succulent, oblanceolate to obovate, acute, laterally compressed. Cap. discoid, on term. peduncles to 3cm; flts white. S Afr. (Cape Prov.). Z9.

S. stapeliiformis E. Phillips = *Kleinia stapeliiformis*.

S. stenocephalus Maxim. = *Ligularia stenocephala*.

S. subalpinus Koch. Perenn., 30–70cm; st. erect, rarely branched, leafy, subglabrous. Basal lvs to 6cm, cordate to triangular-ovate, glab. or sparsely hairy beneath, mid-stem lvs ± lyrate, uppermost laciniate, auriculate. Cap. to 4cm diam. radiate, 5–20, in corymbs; ray flts, yellow, sometimes tinged orange. Mts of C & SE Eur. Z6.

S. subscandens Hochst. ex A. Rich. = *Solanecio angulatus*.

S. succulentus Schultz-Bip. = *S. serpens*.

S. sylvaticus L. Ann. to 70cm; st. erect, sulcate, br. ascending, usually floccose, glandular-pubesc. Lvs to 12cm, irregularly pinnatifid, lower oblanceolate, shortly petiolate, middle and upper oblong, auriculate-amplexicaul. Cap. to 6mm diam., radiate, numerous, in a large term. corymb; ray flts yellow. Summer. Eur., nat. NW Amer. Z6.

S. takedanus Kitam. = *Tephroseris takedanus*.

S. tanguticus Maxim. = *Sinacalia tangutica*.

S. tirolensis A. Kerner = *S. abrotanifolius*.

S. tomentosus hort. = *S. haworthii*.

S. triangularis Hook. Perenn., to 150cm; st. several, glab. to villous-puberulent. Lvs to 20cm, numerous, strongly dentate, lower triangular to deltoid-hastate or cordate, long-petiolate, upper lvs becoming sessile, and narrower. Cap. radiate, few or numerous, in a short, flat-topped infl. Summer. NW Amer. Z7.

S. uniflorus (All.) All. = *S. halleri*.

S. veitchianus Hemsl. = *Ligularia veitchiana*.

S. veravera hort. = *S. viravira*.

S. viravira Hieron. Subshrubby perenn. to 40cm, densely white-tomentose, branched. Lvs deeply pinnatisect, acute, rachis to 6cm, seg. to 2cm, in 2–4 pairs, linear, entire. Cap. to 7mm diam., discoid, rarely sessile, in loose corymbs; flts white, yellow or pink. C Arg. Z8.

S. vulgaris L. Ann. to 40cm, subglabrous to floccose, ± succulent; st. weak. Lvs 10cm, coarsely pinnatifid, lobes obtuse, dentate, lower lvs oblanceolate, short-petiolate, upper lvs oblong, auriculate-amplexicaul. Cap. c5mm diam. usually discoid, subsessile in dense subcorymbose clusters; ray flts yellow. Summer–autumn. Eur. Z6.

S. websteri Greenman = *S. neowebsteri*.

S. werneriifolius A. Gray = *Packera werneriifolia*.

S. wilsonianus Hemsl. = *Ligularia wilsoniana*.

→*Cineraria, Jacobea, Kleinia* and *Ligularia*.

Senegal Date Palm *Phoenix reclinata*.

Senga Root *Polygala senega*.

Senna (K. Bauhin) Mill. Leguminosae (Caesalpinioideae). 260+ shrubs, trees and herbs. Lvs pinnate, usually stipulate. Fls in simple or paniculate rac.; sep. mostly oblong-obovate; pet. 5, flabellate to obovate-elliptic, often clawed, yellow or more rarely, white; sta. usually 9–10. Legume variable in length, compression and texture, becoming angulate, swollen or rounded. Trop. and subtrop., few temp. Z10 unless specified.

S. aculeata (Benth.) Irwin & Barneby. Spreading or ascending thorny shrub to 3m. Lvs 12–31cm, almost glaucous; lfts 2.5–7cm, 6–14, oblong or oblong-lanceolate, tapering to a small apical spine, rounded or subcordate at base, coriaceous, semi-rigid, glab. Fls 13–16mm, many, in erect, axillary rac. to 40cm, yellow veined dark-yellow. Fr. 8.5–12.5cm, linear-oblong compressed. Braz., Boliv., Parag., Venez., W Cuba.

S. alata (L.) Roxb. SEVEN GOLDEN CANDLESTICKS; RINGWORM SHRUB; EMPRESS CANDLE PLANT; CHRISTMAS CANDLE. Shrub, 1–4m or tree 4–10m with a trunk to 7cm diam. Lvs 20–75cm; lfts 7–21cm, in 7–14 pairs, term. pair largest, broad oblong or obovate, base rounded or cordate, apex rounded or almmost notched, with a short, sharp point, dull or somewhat glossy, above, paler beneath, usually glab. Fls 15–24mm many, in erect, axill. rac. 15–60cm long. Fr. 11–19cm, straight or somewhat decurved. Trop. Amer., Afr., Aus., SE Asia.

S. alexandrina Mill. ALEXANDRIAN SENNA; TRUE SENNA; TINNEVELLY SENNA. Erect, scandent herb to 1m; thinly hirsute. Lvs 5–16cm, pale green; lfts 25–50mm, in 3–8 pairs, lanceolate to lanceolate-oblong, apex acute, base cuneate. Fls 10–15mm, 10–30 in erect, axill. rac. 20cm long, yellow or thinly, tawny. Fr. 3–7cm, oblong to elliptic, straight or incurved. Spring–summer. Mex., Trop. Afr. (esp. N of Equator), Near E, India.

S. angulata (Vogel) Irwin & Barneby. Shrub, erect to 2m, or bearing slender, procumbent runners or br. to 10m. Lvs 5–13cm; lfts dark green or tinged brown-purple, paler and hirsute beneath, term. pair 3–8cm, ovate to lanceolate-elliptic, blunt, notched or tapering to a short, blunt point. Fls 24–33.5mm, 4–12 in axill. rac.; pet. yellow lined or flecked red, pubesc. on veins. Fr. c17–20cm, slender-cylindrical, drooping. Braz.

S. armata (S. Wats.) Irwin & Barneby. Bushy herbs or subshrubs, 40cm–1.4m, leafless and rush-like for much of the year. St. silver-pubesc. Lvs 20–90cm; lfts 2–9mm, 0–10, paired or scattered, rhombic-, oblique- or reniform-ovate, apex blunt to sharp-tipped; stipules 0. Fls appearing single, paired or axill., stalks delicate; sep. frequently petal-like, yellow, 5–7mm; pet. rich yellow, 7.5–13mm. Fr. 2–4.5cm, linear-elliptic, later swollen, almost glossy. Ariz., Nevada, Colorado, Calif. Z4.

S. artemisioides (DC.) Randell. WORMWOOD SENNA; SOLVER CASSIA; FEATHERY CASSIA. Shrub 1–3m. Lvs 3–6cm, grey-green; lfts 6–40mm, in 0–10 pairs, narrowly linear, downy. Fls fragrant, 4–12 in axillary rac.; pet. 7–10mm, rich yellow. Fr. 4–10cm, oblong, flat, occas. brown-lustrous. Aus.

S. auriculata (L.) Roxb. AVARAM; TANNER'S CASSIA. Everg. shrub or small tree, 1–7.5m. Lvs 7.6–10.2cm, finely grey-pubesc. beneath; lfts 8–37mm, in 6–13 pairs, oblong- to obovate-elliptic, apex rounded with a hard, sharp point, subcoriaceous; stipules leafy, reniform. Fls 2–8, in corymbose rac.; pet. 17–30mm, vivid yellow. Fr. 6–18cm, linear-oblong, flat, straight, downy. Tanz., India, Sri Lanka.

S. australis (Vell.) Irwin & Barneby. Spreading-scandent or erect shrub, 1–4m. Young st. rusty-pubesc. Lvs 10–18cm; lfts in usually 4, pairs, broadly obovate, blunt or notched 4.5–8.5cm, conspicuously veined, papery, glossy. Fls 5–25 in axill., downy rac.; pet. 12.5mm. Fr. c15–20cm, linear, compressed-tetragonal, rusty-downy. SE Braz., Aus.

S. bicapsularis (L.) Roxb. Shrub 1.5–9m, often scandent, scrambling or diffuse. Lvs 25–90cm, thick, dull yellow-green; lfts 9–40mm, in 2–4 pairs, broad or narrowly obovate, blunt, notched or mucronulate. Rac. 3–18cm long, lax, axill.; 3–30-fld, pet. 10–16mm, yellow. Fr. 5–17cm, linear-oblong, straight, cylindrical; apex rounded. Trop. regions worldwide.

S. birostris (Vogel) Irwin & Barneby. Bushy shrub to 6m, rarely tree-like. Lvs 4–21cm, dull yellow-green; lfts 6–32mm, 5–16 pairs, ovate or oblong-ovate to oblong-lanceolate. Fls 4–40 in axill. rac., 2–14cm; pet. yellow, 7–14mm. Fr. decurved or straight, compressed. S Amer. var. *hookeriana* (Hook.) Irwin & Barneby. Shrub 2m. Leaflet margins and young st. sparsely downy. Lvs 4–12cm; lfts 10–30mm, in 5–11 pairs, elliptic or oblong-lanceolate. Rac. 4–19-fld lat. or packed in corymb-like pan.; pet. 7.5–12.5mm, yellow. Fr. 3.5–7cm, straight or somewhat decurved, stalk 2–4.5mm.

S. candolleana (Vogel) Irwin & Barneby. Small trees and shrubs, 1–5m. Lvs 7.5–14cm; lfts 23–45mm, in 4–8 pairs, oblong or oblong-obovate with marginal notches, apex blunt or sharp-tipped. Fls 15–30, packed in axill. rac.; sep. yellow almost petal-like; pet. rich yellow, 12–17mm. Fr. 6–10cm, linear usually somewhat decurved, swollen at maturity. Chile.

S. *corymbosa* (Lam.) Irwin & Barneby Shrub or small tree to 4m, erect or producing procumbent runners. Lvs 40–95cm, dull yellow-green, glab.; lfts 25–80mm, (2–)3, lanceolate to oblong-obovate, apex blunt or terminating in a sharp point. Fls 4–20 in axill. rac.; pet. golden-yellow 8–16mm. Fr. 12cm, cylindric-oblong, straight to incurved. S US, Urug., Arg. Z8.

S. *covesii* (A. Gray) Irwin & Barneby. DESERT SENNA. Erect, perenn., ash-grey herb, 30–60cm. St. downy, lfts 1–3cm, in 2–4 pairs, elliptic to elliptic-lanceolate, mucronate, villous or downy. Fls to 2.8cm diam., yellow, 4–8 in axillary rac. Fr. 2–3.5cm, lanceolate to falcate-oblong, swollen, beaked, thickly chartaceous, sparsely hirsute. Calif., Baja Calif., Ariz., S New Mex. Z7.

S. *cumingii* (Hook. and Arn.) Irwin & Barneby. Shrub, spreading or erect, 30cm–3m. Lvs 3.5–12cm, dull green-yellow; lfts in 4–8 pairs, linear to obovate, notched or blunt, ciliolate, glab. above, sparsely downy beneath. Fls 5- to 30, in corymbose pan.; pet. orange- or golden-yellow, 9–26mm. Fr. 4–10cm, linear to linear-oblong, compressed, torulose, straight or somewhat decurved. C Chile. var. *coquimbensis* (Vogel) Irwin & Barneby. Lfts 10–31mm, in 4–7 pairs, obovate-elliptic or oblanceolate-elliptic, blunt or mucronate.

S. *didymobotrya* (Fres.) Irwin & Barneby. Diffuse shrub 60cm–5m. Lvs 10–50cm; lfts in 8–18 pairs, elliptic-oblong to obovate-oblong, apex rounded or triangular, mucronate, downy. Fls many in erect, spike-like rac.; pet. yellow, 17–27mm. Fr. 7–12cm, linear-oblong, compressed, soft-hirsute. S India, Sri Lanka, Malesia, Trop. Afr. naturalised neotrop.

S. ×*floribunda* (Cav.) Irwin & Barneby. (*S. multiglandulosa* × *S. septemtrionalis*.) Shrub 1–3m. Lvs 6–8cm; lfts 3.2–7cm, in 4–5 pairs, oblong-elliptic, remote, abruptly sharp-tipped, somewhat hirsute. Fls 4–20 in axill. rac., frequently corymbose-paniculate; pet. to 8mm, rich yellow. Fr. 7–8cm, irregularly cylindrical, obtuse. Summer–winter. Aus. (Queensld, NSW, S Aus.), nat. Mex. and elsewhere.

S. *fruticosa* (Mill.) Irwin & Barneby. Shrub or small tree, 2–7.5m. Branchlets somewhat drooping, downy. Lvs 10–24cm; lfts 4–16cm, obliquely ovate, lanceolate-elliptic or elliptic-obovate, apex acuminate, acute or abruptly pointed, dull green-yellow above, paler and thickly downy beneath. Fls 8–35, densely packed in rac. 1.5–8cm; pet. yellow, 8.5–33mm. Fr. 10–27cm, ± cylindrical straight or incurved. Kenya, Tanz., Mex.

S. *hebecarpa* (Fern.) Irwin & Barneby. WILD SENNA. Similar to S. *marilandica*, lacking curled or short adpressed hairs; petiole and st. sparsely bristly. Lvs 13–23cm; lfts c3–6cm, in 6–10 pairs, elliptic or oblong or lanceolate-elliptic, blunt or sharp-tipped. Fls to 25 in rac. 1–7cm; pet. 8–12mm. Fr. 6–11.5cm, sparsely setose. N Amer. Z5.

S. *helmsii* (Symon) Randell. Shrub, 1–2m. Lvs 2.5–5cm, usually woolly; lfts 8–25mm, in 2–4 pairs, obovate, blunt. Fls 4–10 in axill., almost umbellate rac.; pet. 8–12mm, yellow. Aus.

S. *hirsuta* (L.) Irwin & Barneby. Woody-based herb or shrub, 20cm–2.5m, spreading or erect, malodorous, sparsely pubesc. Lvs 8–33cm; lfts 3–10cm, in 3–7 pairs, thin, ovate to obovate, sharp-tipped or tapering to a point, dull yellow-green, thickly downy. Fls usually 2–8, sometimes in short rac.; sep. yellow or green-brown; pet. yellow, 8–16mm. Fr. 10–28cm, linear, thick-hirsute. Trop. Amer. var. *leptocarpa* (Benth.) Irwin & Barneby. Lfts finely stiff-hirsute beneath, glab. or minutely downy above. Fls 7–20 in rac.; pet. 12–14mm. Fr. 16–27cm. Braz. var. *hirta* Irwin & Barneby. Hirsute; lfts in 3–5 pairs, 4.5–10.5cm, downy. Fls 2–8 in rac.; pet. 10–15mm. Fr. 14–27cm.

S. *italica* Mill. Subshrub; shoots erect herbaceous 60–120cm. Lvs 5–12.5cm, glaucous; lfts 1.25–3cm, in 3 to 7 pairs, obovate to obovate-elliptic, rounded, mucronate. Fls crowded in erect, axill. rac., 2cm across, pale yellow. Fr. 3.25–5cm, compressed, falcate. Afr.

S. *ligustrina* (L.) Irwin & Barneby. Woody based herb or shrub 40cm–3m. Lvs 10–27cm, slightly maldorous; lfts in 4–8 pairs, 3–7cm, lanceolate, acuminate or ovate, abruptly acute, usually glab. Fls 3–30 in rac.; sep. yellow or dark-hued; pet. yellow, 12–15mm. Fr. 7–14cm, ascending, compressed, flat. Flor., W Indies, C & S Amer.

S. *lindheimeriana* (Scheele) Irwin & Barneby. V. leafy herbs. St. 20cm–1.5m, 1 to several, ± erect, downy or velutinous. Lvs 6–16cm; lfts 2–5cm, in 4–8 pairs, usually 5–7, ovate-, obovate- or oblong-elliptic, bluntly mucronate, base cordate or rounded, ash-grey beneath, downy. Fls 5–25 in loose rac.; sep. pink, pale green or yellow; pet. 10.5–16mm, pale vivid yellow. Fr. 3–6.5cm, linear, laterally compressed, stiff-hirsute. Tex., Ariz., New Mex. Z7.

S. *macranthera* (DC. ex Colladon) Irwin & Barneby. Small trees

or shrubs, 1–3m, or delicate trees to 9m; branchlets hirsute. Lvs 2–26cm; lfts 1.2–16cm, ovate or obovate to obliquely lanceolate-elliptic, apex sharp-tipped to blunt and short-acuminate, downy or glab., papery. Fls 3–17 in paniculate rac.; sep. often pale, tinted yellow; pet. 20–50mm. Fr. 6–26cm. S Amer. var. *micans* (Nees) Irwin & Barneby. 1.5–6m, shrubby. Lvs small. Fr. 5–11cm. C & S Amer. var. *nervosa* (Vogel) Irwin & Barneby. Indumentum on lvs and infl. looser and longer, often yellow. Lfts elliptic and sharp-tipped or obovate or elliptic-ovate, blunt. SW US, C & S Amer. Z8.

S. *marilandica* (L.) Link. WILD SENNA. Perenn. herb, 60cm–2m. St. several to many, erect then scandent. Lvs 12–27cm; lfts 3–6cm, in 5–9 pairs, narrow and tapering, elliptic or oblong-elliptic, thin-textured, dull yellow-green above, paler and almost glaucous beneath, sharp-tipped or blunt, mucronate. Fls 3–19 in rac.; sep. pink-brown; pet. 8–14mm, yellow. Fr. 6.5–11cm, linear, compressed, glab. or sparsely stiff-hirsute. Midwest & SE US. Z4.

S. *montana* comb. nov.. Shrub. Lvs to 15cm; lfts 10–15 pairs, 3cm, oblong, bristle-tipped. Fls yellow in axill. corymbs or term. pan. Fr. to 12.5cm, glossy. India.

S. *multiglandulosa* (Jacq.) Irwin & Barneby. Leafy shrubs or small trees, 80cm–6m. Lvs 6–17.5cm; lfts 2–5cm, in 5–9 pairs, linear to lanceolate, papery, abruptly mucronate or triangular, sharp-tipped. Fls 3–20 in rac.; sep. tinged dark or yellow; pet. 12–19mm, rich yellow. Fr. 7–13.5cm, linear, drooping, black, hirsute, rugose. S & C Amer., Temp. SW US, E Aus., Macronesia, S Afr., Malaya, India, Hawaiian Is. Z8.

S. *multijuga* (Rich.) Irwin & Barneby. Tree, 6–40m, glab. to thickly soft-hirsute. Lvs 6–35cm; lfts in 10–56 pairs, narrow-lanceolate, 7.5–53mm, linear, oblong or oblong-lanceolate, apex triangular and almost sharp-tipped, dark green and dull or almost glossy above, paler beneath. Fls c5 in downy pan., term. corymbs or axill. rac.; sep. yellow, green or brown; pet. yellow, 7–21mm. Fr. 6.5–20cm, broadly linear, flat, black, chartaceous, transversely. Autumn. New and OW tropics.

S. *nemophila* comb. nov. (awaiting publication). Tall bushy shrub. Lfts to 2.5cm+, in 1–2 pairs, thick, terete or channelled above, lower lvs sometimes reduced to flattened phyllode. Fls in corymbose rac.; pet. 8mm. Fr. straight or curved, compressed. Aus.

S. *nicaraguensis* (Benth.) Irwin & Barneby. Tree-like shrubs, 1.5–9m. Br. covered with large, subcordate stipules when young. Lvs 16–52cm; lfts 3.5–8cm, in 7–19 pairs, elliptic to elliptic-oblong, subacute, mucronate or blunt, green-yellow and almost glossy throughout. Fls 8–70 in term. pan. 6–40cm; pet. yellow, 16–28mm. Fr. 7–12.5cm, flat, linear, oblong, chartaceous, glossy. Trop. Amer., C Amer., Mex.

S. *nitida* (Rich.) Irwin & Barneby. Shrub-like, producing delicate, procumbent br. or runners, to 7m. Lvs 8–17cm; lfts often sparsely downy beneath, 6–11cm. Fls 7–20 in rac.; sep. tinted yellow; pet. 16–22mm yellow. Fr. 8–18cm. Puerto Rico, Leeward Is., Virgin Is.

S. *obtusifolia* (L.) Irwin & Barneby. Herb or subshrub, 10cm–2m. Lvs 3.5–17cm, thin, foetid; lfts 1.7–7cm, usually in 3 pairs, obovate, blunt, mucronate, dark green above and paler beneath, ciliolate, glab. or downy. Fls 1–2 in rac.; sep. pale green; pet. pale yellow, 9–15mm. Fr. 6–18cm, usually curved downwards and outwards, linear, becoming brown and swollen. Trop., subtrop.

S. *occidentalis* (L.) Link. COFFEE SENNA; STYPTIC WEED; STINKING WEED. V. leafy, malodorous shrub, 50cm–2.2m, usually shorter. Lvs 11–26cm, initially hairy; lfts 4.5–10cm usually, in 4 or 5 pairs, broadly elliptic to ovate, acute to sharply acuminate, thin-textured ciliolate. Fls 1–5, in short or subumbellate rac.; sep. pale, tinged pink or dark-hued; pet. yellow 12–17mm. Fr. 8–13.5cm, linear, incurved or straight, valves with a central red or blue-black band at first. Trop. Afr., Sri Lanka, Indochina, India, Malesia, S China, Micronesia, Hawaiian Is., N Aus.

S. *odorata* (Morris). Shrub, 1–3m. Lvs 8–15cm; lfts 1–3.5cm, in 8–13 pairs, narrow and tapering to both ends, apex blunt to sharp, sparsely hirsute beneath. Fls 3–5 in axill., corymbose rac.; sep. brown, paler at margins; pet. yellow, 12–20mm. Fr. 8–12cm, oval. NSW.

S. *oligophylla* (F. Muell.) Randell. Strigose or sericeous shrub 1–2m. Lfts 1–3cm, in 2–3 pairs, ovate to obovate, apex rounded, blunt or obcuneate, leathery, subglabrous. Fls 6–20 in erect, downy rac.; pet. 8–10mm, yellow. Fr. 7cm, flat, oblong or curved. Aus.

S. *pallida* (Vahl) Irwin & Barneby. Shrubs 0.5–4m or treelets to 7m. Lvs 3.5–18cm, falling under stress and replaced by simpler axill. lvs; lfts 6–60mm, 2–31 pairs, oblanceolate, elliptic- or oblanceolate-oblong, blunt, notched, or usually sharply but abruptly pointed. Fls solitary or few in rac. or packed in clusters, rich yellow. Fr. 5–20cm, linear, straight, decurved or twisted, valves papery, brown or black. Summer. W Indies.

S. pendula (Humb. & Bonpl. ex Willd.) Irwin & Barneby. Shrubs or small trees to 5m. Lvs 5–13cm green-yellow or dull bright green above, paler beneath; lfts 1.8–6.5cm, 2–7 pairs (usually 4–5), obovate to oblanceolate or oblong-elliptic, blunt, mucronulate, broadly rounded or shallowly notched. Fls 2–35, rarely to 50, in paniculate rac.; pet. orange- or golden-yellow, notched 11–26mm. Fr. 7–18cm, drooping, cylindric. S Amer. var. *glabrata* (Vogel) Irwin & Barneby. Spreading shrub, 1–3m. Lvs thinly hirsute; lfts 2–6.5cm, in 3–6 pairs, obovate to oblanceolate, blunt or rarely notched. Fls 15–20 in rac. Fr. 9–16cm. Temp. US, Bahamas, S Penins. Flor. and S Amer.

S. phyllodinea comb. nov. SILVER CASSIA. Small diffuse shrub, 50cm–2m. St. thickly downy when young. Young lvs have 1–2 pairs of lfts to 1cm, most lvs reduced to phyll. to 5cm, narrowly oblanceolate, falcate canescent. Fls 2–5 in short rac., often subumbellate; pet. 6mm, yellow. Fr. 3–8cm, flat, occas. curved, deep brown. Summer–autumn. Aus. (N Territ., Queensld, NSW, S Aus.).

S. pleurocarpa comb. nov. Erect, glab. shrub. Lvs with 4–5 pairs of lfts to 5cm, linear-elliptic. Fls yellow in loose, axill. rac. Fr. 1–25cm, compressed, ridged above each seed. Aus.

S. polyantha (Colladon) Irwin & Barneby. Slender trees and shrubs, 1.5–7m. Lvs 4.5–14cm; lfts in 5–19 pairs, usually oblong-elliptic, 1–2.5cm, mucronulate, vividly olivaceous or dark green above, paler beneath. Fls 7–50, densely packed in rac.; sep. yellow or edged yellow; pet. vivid yellow. Fr. 7.5–11.5cm, oblong linear-compressed, becoming rigidly papery. Mex., Baja Calif. Z9.

S. polyphylla (Jacq.) Irwin & Barneby. Shrubs or small trees to 8m, br. many, stiff, many-lvd, scandent. Lvs 1.2–6cm; lfts 0.5–1cm, in 3–13 pairs, obovate-oblong or broadly elliptic, blunt, mucronulate or retuse, occas. sparsely downy and ciliolate beneath, olive above, paler beneath. Fls 1–3 in rac.; pet. yellow, 12–26mm. Fr. 4.5–14cm, linear, compressed, drooping. S Puerto Rico, US Virgin Is., N Hispan., Is. of Anegada.

S. racemosa (Mill.) Irwin & Barneby. Tree-like shrubs or trees, 3–10m. Lvs 7–26cm, golden yellow-pubesc. when young; lfts 2–6cm, in 4–12 pairs, obovate-elliptic, sharp-tipped or blunt to subretuse, dull or glossy green above, paler beneath. Fls 15–20, densely packed in numerous axillary rac.; pet. deep golden-yellow, 9–16.5mm. Fr. 8–19.5cm, linear, compressed, drooping, chartaceous, red-brown, sometimes becoming black. C & S Amer. var. *liebmannii* (Benth.) Irwin & Barneby. Thickly downy throughout. Lvs 7–16cm; lfts in 6–9 pairs, obovate-elliptic or elliptic-oblong, 2–3.7cm, blunt or subretuse, mucroonulate; pet. to 18mm. Fr. 11–19×1cm. C & S Amer.

S. reticulata (Willd.) Irwin & Barneby. Downy shrub or tree to 9m. Lvs 20–85cm; lfts 6.5–19cm, in 6–15 pairs, oblong to oblong-obovate, mucronate or subretuse, deep green, paler beneath. Fls in dense, axill. rac.; sep. petal-like; pet. yellow, 12–22mm. Fr. 8–16cm, broad, linear, compressed, stiffly chartaceous, glossy, black. C & S Amer.

S. roemeriana (Scheele) Irwin & Barneby. Perenn. herbs, 15–70cm. St. simple or few-branched, downy. Lvs 2.5–9.5cm; lfts 2–7cm, 2, lanceolate or oblong-lanceolate, sharp-tipped or blunt, olive green above, pale- or blue-green beneath, hirsute or glab. Fls ephemeral 1–5 in axill. rac.; sep. pale, or pink-tinged, brown or pale green; pet. 11–17mm, orange-yellow or yellow. Fr. 2–3cm; straight or incurved, compressed laterally, bristly. NE Mex., SW US. Z9.

S. septemtrionalis (Viv.) Irwin & Barneby. Small trees and shrubs, 1–6m; br. smooth, green to maroon, often pipe-like. Lvs 8–25cm, rich green, papery, somewhat malodorous; lfts 3.5–10.5cm, in 3–5 pairs, broadly ovate to narrow and tapering, glossy and dark green above, duller and paler beneath. Fls 3–13 in paniculate, axill. rac.; sep. tinged mahogany, sometimes vivid yellow; pet. vivid yellow, notched, 12–16mm. Fr. 6–10.5cm, cylindrical, straight or somewhat incurved, chartaceous and ± rugose. C & S Amer., India.

S. siamea (Lam.) Irwin & Barneby. KASSOD TREE. Diffusely branched, swift-growing trees. Lvs 10–35cm; lfts in 5–14 pairs, ovate-, oblong- or lanceolate-elliptic, bluntly mucronate or notched 4–8cm, stiffly papery, dark yellow-green and glab. aobve, paller, thinly hirsute beneath. Fls densely packed 10–60 in rac.; sep. yellow or, more usually, dark-hued; pet. yellow, 10–17mm. Fr. 15–30cm, linear and plano-compressed, leathery or almost woody, brown. C & S Amer.

S. singueana (Del.) Lock. WILD CASSIA. Small tree or shrub 1–15m. Lvs 12–30cm; petiole swollen at base; lfts 1.5–7.5cm, in 5–12 pairs, oblong or obovate-elliptic, apex rounded and often notched, rarely sharp-tipped, glabrescent above, hirsute beneath. Fls fragrant, 6 to many in subcorymbose rac.; pet. vivid yellow, conspicuously veined, 15–35mm. Fr. 5.5–26cm, straight or somewhat contorted, linear, cylindrical to compressed, glab. to downy. Trop. Afr.

S. sophera (L.) Roxb. Woody-based bushy herb to 2m. Lvs 7–21cm, mildly malodorous; lfts 2–6cm, in 3–8 pairs, lanceolate to oblong or ovate-lanceolate, sharp-tipped, ± glab. Fls 1–5 in glab., subumbellate rac.; pet. yellow, 10–12.5mm. Fr. 5–10.4cm, cylindrical, or linear-ellipsoid, straight or slightly incurved. S & C Amer., Carib., Australasia, Trop. Afr.

S. spectabilis (DC.) Irwin & Barneby. Shrubs or trees, 2–20m. Lvs 17–45cm; lfts in 8–20 pairs, elliptic or ovate, blunt, mucronate or acuminate, lanceolate or narrow-ovate, glossy above, paler beneath. Fls 6–60 in rac.; pet. vivid yellow, 13–36mm. Fr. drooping, linear, swollen, straight, 16–30cm. C & S Amer. var. *excelsa* (Schräd.) Irwin & Barneby. Weakly tree-like and shrubby, rarely exceeding 7m. Lvs 17–32cm; lfts 12–20 pairs, 2.6–5.5cm. Pet. 29–38.5mm. C & S Amer.

S. splendida (Vogel) Irwin & Barneby. GOLDEN WONDER. Spreading shrubs or small trees; br. to 5m, slender, scandent. Lvs 5–15.5cm, glossy and green-yellow above, paler, duller beneath; lfts 4–10.5cm, ovate to lanceolate-elliptic; apex blunt or notched, frequently mucronulate. Fls 1–12 in rac., long and lax if over 3 fls, almost umbellate if less than 3; sep. dark-hued, yellow-green, brick red r red-speckled; pet. yellow, 2.8–4.4cm. Fr. 17–49cm; rounded and almost cylindrical, drooping, ultimately glossy. Braz.

S. sturtii (R. Br.) Randell. Shrub 1–2m, canescent or lanuginose. Lvs 4–5cm; lfts 15–2.5cm, in 2–8 pairs, linear to elliptic, concave. Fls 4–5, in short, axill. rac.; pet. 7–8mm, yellow. Fr. 4–6cm, thin, flat. Aus.

S. surattensis (Burm. f.) Irwin and Barneby. Tall shrub or small tree. Lvs with 6–10 pairs lfts, each 3cm, obovate. Fls large, yellow, in umbel-like rac. Fr. 15cm, compressed. Trop. Asia, Aus., Polyn.

S. versicolor (Meyen ex Vogel) Irwin & Barneby. Subshrub, sprawling shrub or small weak tree, to 4m; lf stalks, rac. and branchlets downy, lfts in 6–15 pairs, narrow and tapering, elliptic or narrowly ovate, 1.8–3.6cm, mucronulate, darker beneath than above. Fls 7–45 in rac.; sep. pale yellow, often with darker tints; pet. yellow, 11.5–16mm. Fr. 5–11cm, straight or curved, broadly linear, ultimately brown, stiffly chartaceous. Peru. Z8.
→*Cassia*.

Sen-no-ki *Kalopanax septemlobus.*
Sensitive Fern *Onoclea sensibilis.*
Sensitive Plant *Mimosa pudica; M. sensitiva.*
Sentry Palm *Howea forsteriana.*
September Bells *Rothmannia globosa.*
September Elm *Ulmus serotina.*

Sequoia Endl. CALIFORNIA REDWOOD; COAST REDWOOD. Cupressaceae. 1 everg. coniferous tree to 110m. Crown conic becoming columnar; bole to 8.5m diameter. Bark red-brown, thick, fibrous, spongy, deeply ridged. Br. whorle dwhen young weak branchlets falling. Lvs dimorphic, scale-like, alt., arranged spirally on long shoots and appressed or spreading, to 6mm; or distichous on weak shoots, linear-lanceolate or narrow-oblong, acute, 6–20mm, deep green to blue-grey. Cones dark brown, oblong-ovoid, 2–3.5×1–2cm, terminal on 1–6cm shoots; scales 7–10mm wide, peltate, rigid, with a short central, forward pointing awn-like bract. W US. Z8.

S. gigantea (Lindl.) Decne. = *Sequoiadendron giganteum.*

S. sempervirens (D. Don) Endl. Cvs include: 'Adpressa': needles grey-green, to 1cm; shoot tips white; dwarf, slow growing but eventually 25m. 'Cantab': dwarf, prostrate; needles glaucous, to 13×5mm. 'Pendula': br. arching; branchlets pendulous. 'Nana Pendula' ('Prostrata'): dwarf, weeping.

S. wellingtonia Seem. = *Sequoiadendron giganteum.*
→*Taxodium*.

Sequoiadendron Buchholz. GIANT SEQUOIA; BIG TREE; SIERRA REDWOOD. Cupressaceae. 1 everg., coniferous tree to 95m, bole to 10m diam.; bark thick, spongy, fibrous, rust or dark brown, v. soft; crown conic, spreading with age; br. curved downward with upturned tips. Lvs 4–6mm, spirally arranged in 3 rows, scale-like to subulate, acute, green suffused grey, overlapping, in sprays pointing toward apex, cones ellipsoid, 35–55×25–40mm, maturing brown, woody, pendulous on 2–6cm peduncles; scales 30–40, to 20–27mm wide at mid-cone, rhombic, cross-ridged and rugose, depressed-mucronate. Calif. Z7.

S. giganteum (Lindl.) Buchholz. 'Glaucum': narrowly conical, glaucous. 'Pendulum': to 35m, main st. sinuous to undulate, br. and shoots pendulous. Often creates bizarre shapes, including 'looping the loop'. 'Pygmaeum': bushy dwarf, to 2×2.5m with low apical dominance. 'Variegatum': foliage flecked white.
→*Sequoia* and *Wellingtonia*.

Serapias L. TONGUE ORCHID. Orchidaceae. *c*10 terrestrial tuberous orchids. Lvs lanceolate, erect, shiny. Spike term., with bracts equal or to exceeding fls; pet. and sep. forming a deep hood, conspicuously veined; lip midlobe tongue-like, protruding, usually pubesc. above. Azores to Medit. Z8.

S. azorica Schltr. = *S. cordigera.*

S. cordigera L. St. 15–50cm. Spike dense, 5–15-fld; bracts tinted dull purple, veins maroon; hood to 2.5cm, ash-grey to purple, pet. black-purple; lip almost dark purple with 2 ridges, lat. lobes red or purple, midlobe cordate, pubesc., pale to deep yellow, sometimes orange. Mid spring–early summer. Medit.

S. lingua L. To 30cm. Spike 2–8-fld; bracts violet or green, equalling fls; hood light pink or purple, to 2cm, with red or purple veins; lip yellow, violet-pink to magenta or white with purple-black ridges, midlobe to 2cm, lanceolate to ovate. Late spring––summer. Medit.

S. neglecta de Notaris. To 30cm. Spike 2–8-fld; bracts green, tinted purple with maroon veins; hood lilac; lip cordate, ×3 longer than other seg., pubesc., lat. lobes red or purple, margins purple-black, midlobe deep yellow, rarely orange, with 2 maroon ridges. Late spring–early summer. W & C Medit.

S. vomeracea (Burm.) Briq. To 50cm. Spike lax, 3–20-fld; bracts exceeding fls, lanceolate, terracotta pink to brown; hood grey-purple or pale red, with red or maroon veins, pointing upward; lip basally ridged, lat. lobes ochre edged purple-black, midlobe pubesc., triangular-lanceolate, red or brown (rarely white), often with yellow blotch. Late spring–summer. Medit.

Serbian Spruce *Picea omorika.*

Serenoa Hook. f. Palmae. 1 palm, 1–4m. St. usually subterranean, prostrate, rarely erect, with persistent lf sheaths. Lvs to 2m, palmate, induplicate, marcescent; sheaths becoming a brown, fibrous mat; petiole to 1m, shortly toothed; blade blue-green to yellow-green, to 1m diam., seg. 20 single-fold, linear-lanceolate. Fls cream, fragrant in closely branched infl. to 60cm. Fr. to 2.5cm, blue-black. SE US. Z8.

S. arborescens Sarg. = *Acoelorraphe wrightii.*

S. repens Small. SAW PALMETTO; SCRUB PALMETTO.

→*Corypha* and *Sabal.*

Sericographis Nees.

S. incana Nees = *Justicia leonardii.*

S. pauciflora Nees = *Justicia rizzinii.*

Seriphidium Polj. Compositae. *c*60 aromatic ann. to perenn. herbs and shrubs, often grey-, white- or silvery-tomentose. Lvs usually deeply dissected. Cap. small, discoid, in spikes, pan. or rac.; flts yellow or tinged purple. N temp. regions.

S. caerulescens (L.) Soják. Perenn. to 2m, strongly aromatic, pale grey- to white-tomentose throughout. Lvs to 4.5×3cm, entire to 2-pinnatisect, petiolate, seg. to 1.5cm, spathulate to linear, subacute to obtuse, often auriculate; uppermost lvs simple. Autumn. W & C Medit., SW Port. Z8.

S. canum (Pursh) W.A. Weber. Shrub to 1m, aerial shoots often rooting, bark of older br. brown, fibrous. Lvs silvery grey-pubesc., to 6cm, linear to linear-oblanceolate, acute or acuminate, entire or occas. irregularly 3-dentate or pinnatifid, sometimes viscid. Late summer–early autumn. W N Amer. Z7.

S. maritimum (L.) Soják. Perenn. herb to 1.5m, strongly aromatic, pale grey- to white-tomentose, occas. glabrescent. Lvs to 4.5×3cm, 2–3-pinnatisect, seg. to 15mm, spathulate to linear, subacute to obtuse, petiolate, often auriculate, upper lvs sessile, entire. Summer. W & N Eur. coasts. Z7.

S. nutans (Willd.) Bremer & Humphries. Perenn. herb to 2m. Lvs to 8mm, 2–3-pinnatisect, lobes linear to subspathulate, upper lvs entire or auriculate. SE Russia. Z5.

S. palmeri (A. Gray) Bremer & Humphries. Subshrub to 3m, bark green or yellow below, tinged red above, heavily striate, becoming grey-yellow. Lvs to 12cm, pinnatifid, lobes 3–9, linear to linear-lanceolate, revolute, densely tomentose beneath. Summer. Calif., Baja, Calif. Z8.

S. rothrockii (A. Gray) Bremer & Humphries. Shrub to 60cm, aerial shoots often rooting, br. tomentose at first, bark light yellow-grey to dark brown. Lvs lanceolate or oblanceolate, broadly cuneate to flabelliform, pinnatifid, toothed or entire. Late summer–early autumn. Calif. Z8.

S. tridentatum (Nutt.) W.A. Weber. Shrub to 3m, with short trunk or few st. ascending from base, densey white-tomentose at first, later clad in pale shredded bark. Lvs to 4×1cm, cuneate, obtuse, apex 3-toothed or 4–9-toothed or -lobed, or linear and entire, silvery canescent and slightly viscid. Autumn. W Baja Calif. Z8.

S. tripartitum (Rydb.) W.A. Weber. Shrub to 80cm, with short trunk or numerous st. from base, often aerial-rooting, bark light brown or grey. Lvs to 3cm, linear, entire, or usually deeply

trifid, lobes linear to linear-lanceolate, occas. trifid. Summer. NW US. Z7.

S. vallesiacum (All.) Soják. Strongly aromatic perenn. to 2m, densely grey- to white-tomentose. Lvs 3–4-pinnatisect, lobes to 5mm, linear, often pinnatisect, auriculate; upper lvs usually with basal lobes, occas. entire. S Switz. and S Fr. to N It. Z7.

→*Artemisia.*

Serissa Comm. ex Juss. Rubiaceae. 1 densely branched everg. shrub. Lvs to 2×0.8cm, ovate, acute, subcoriaceous, dark green, foetid when crushed. Fls terminal or axill., solitary or clustered, white; cor. funnel-shaped, to 1cm, lobes 4–6, obscurely trilobate; style short-exserted. Berry 2-seeded. SE Asia.

S. foetida (L. f.) Lam. 'Flore Pleno': dwarf; lvs small; fls double, small, rose-like, white. 'Kyoto': dwarf; lvs small, lush green; fls single, small, white. 'Mount Fuji': compact; lvs edged and striped white. 'Variegata': lvs variegated off-white; fls single, white. 'Variegata Pink': lvs edged off-white; fls single, pink.

S. japonica Thunb. = *S. foetida.*

→*Lycium.*

Serjania Mill. Sapindaceae. 215 lianes. Lvs pinnate, biternate or 3-ternate. Rac. or pan. axill. or term., often bearing spring-like tendrils; fls small, fragrant, irregular; sep. 4–5; pet. 4, disc with 4 glands; sta. 8, exserted. Fr. a 3-winged schizocarp. Trop., subtrop. Amer. Z10.

S. cuspidata Cambess. Climber; br. triangular, ridges densely brown-pubesc. Lvs ternate, pinnae cordate, 3-lobed, coarse-toothed. Fls white tinged yellow; sta. tightly whorled around pistil. Braz.

Serpent Cucumber *Trichosanthes cucumerina* var. *anguina.*
Serpent Garlic *Allium sativum* var. *ophioscorodon.*
Serpent Grass *Polygonum viviparum.*

Serratula L. Compositae. *c*70 erect, perenn. herbs. Lvs alt., pinnate, toothed. Cap. discoid, solitary to many in a paniculate, corymbose cluster; involucre campanulate; phyllaries spine-tipped or crispate-erose; outermost often enlarged. Eur. to N Afr. and Jap.

S. atriplicifolia Benth. & Hook. f. = *Synurus deltoides.*

S. babylonica L. = *Centaurea babylonica.*

S. behen Lam. = *Centaurea behen.*

S. centauroides L. St. to 75cm, often branched above. Lvs linear-oblong to lanceolate, pinnatipartite, entire to remotely and coarsely serrate or pinnatifid, scabrous, uppermost lvs scarcely larger than those at base. Cap. few, 2–3cm diam.; flts pink to purple. Sib. Z3.

S. coronata L. St. 30–140cm. Lvs oblong-elliptic, pinnatipartite, coarsely serrate-dentate, acuminate, upper decurrent, serrate. Cap. few, to 3cm; flts maroon, outer few ray-like. NE Asia. Z5.

S. gmelinii Tausch. St. 60–100cm, scabrid-pubesc. Lvs deeply and irregularly pinnatifid, lobes remotely and irregularly dentate, upper lvs entire. Cap. solitary; flts tinged purple. C & SE Russia. Z5.

S. humilis Desf. = *Jurinea humilis.*

S. macrocephala Bertol. = *S. tinctoria* ssp. *macrocephela.*

S. marginata Tausch St. to 75cm. Lower lvs ovate to oblong, dentate to pinnatisect, subcordate, petiolate, upper lvs sessile, seg. oblong, entire, glab., slightly glaucous. Cap. solitary; flts purple. Sib. Z3.

S. monticola Boreau = *S. tinctoria* ssp. *macrocephela.*

S. noveboracensis L. = *Vernonia noveboracensis.*

S. nudicaulis (L.) DC. St. to 75cm, glabrate. Lvs mostly basal, rosulate, narrowly elliptic to narrowly lanceolate, subentire to coarsely serrate, uppermost bract-like. Cap. solitary, 2–2.5cm diam.; flts pink, tinged purple. Summer. SW Eur. Z6.

S. pinnatifida (Cav.) Poir. St. to 25cm, pubesc. Lvs often floccose beneath; basal lvs broadly lanceolate, denticulate to pinnatisect, often with a large terminal lobe; st. lvs broadly elliptic, usually pinnatifid. Cap. solitary or few, 2–3cm diam.; flts pink, tinged purple. Spain and Port. Z8.

S. quinquefolia Bieb. ex Willd. St. to 90cm, glab. to sparsely hairy, usually branched, winged. Lower and middle lvs lyrate-pinnatisect, seg. to 5, elliptic-oblong, attenuate, acuminate, dentate to entire at base; uppermost lvs 3-partite or reduced, entire. Flts deep purple. Cauc. Z6.

S. scariosa L. = *Liatris scariosa.*

S. seoanei Wilk. Like *S. tinctoria*, but smaller; lf seg. v. narrow. SW Eur. Z7.

S. shawii hort. = *S. seoanei.*

S. spicata L. = *Liatris spicata.*

S. squarrosa L. = *Liatris squarrosa.*

S. tinctoria L. SAWWORT. St. to 1m, subglabrous to minutely pubesc. Lvs ovate-lanceolate, finely serrate to deeply pinnatifid.

Cap. few to many, 1.5–2cm diam.; flts purple-pink. Eur. ssp. *macrocephala* (Bertol.) Rouy ex Hegi. Cap. fewer; 6–12mm diam. Eur. Z6.

Serruria Burm. ex Salisb. Proteaceae. 55 everg. shrubs. Lvs crowded, finely dissected into cylindric, seg., or entire. Infl. paniculate or corymbose, or cap. solitary; receptacle conic or subglobose, hairy; bracts usually villous; parenth seg. free or slightly connate at base, claw slender, limb short oblong; sta. 4. Fr. a nut, ovoid or subglobose. S Afr. Z9.

S. artemisiifolia Knight = *S. pedunculata.*
S. barbigera Knight = *S. phylicoides.*
S. florida Knight. BLUSHING BRIDE. Br. erect or ascending, tinged purple, glab. Lvs 4.5–6cm, pinnate to bipinnate, rather broad at base, glab., ultimate seg. v. acute. Cap. 3–4×4cm; bracts lanceolate to obovate, pure white, membranous; floral bracts linear, flushed pink, ciliate; perianth tube 3mm, ellipsoid, seg. 9mm, limb thinly villous. Summer. S Afr.
S. pedunculata R. Br. Br. erect, pilose or villous. Lvs 5–10cm, fan-shaped, bipinnate above, pilose to subglabrous, seg. narrow, mucronate, 6–12mm. Cap. globose, 2.5cm diam.; bracts 5–7mm, ovate to spathulate-obovate, recurved-acuminate, pink, tomentose; perianth lilac, tube 4mm, glab., seg. 9–10mm, villous, limb 2–3mm, elliptic, villous. Summer. S Afr. (Cape).
S. phylicoides R. Br. Br. erect, minutely pubesc. to glab. Lvs 4–5cm, bipinnate above, glab., seg. 12–18mm, subterete. Cap. corymbose, 2–2.5cm diam.; involucral bracts 123mm, linear, acute, outer glab. but for apical tuft of hairs, inner sparingly villous; floral bracts 6–9mm, narrowly lanceolate, villous; perianth tube v. short, seg. 10mm, claw glab., limb villous. S Afr. (Cape Prov.).

Serviceberry *Amelanchier.*
Service Tree of Fontainebleau *Sorbus latifolia.*

Sesamothamnus Welw. Pedaliaceae. 5 decid. thorny shrubs or small trees. St. smooth, often caudiciform, swollen at base; br. leafless at flowering time. Lvs clustered on short shoots in thorn axils. Fls large, often sweetly scented in a few-fld rac.; cal. gland.; cor. tube long, cylindric or cup-shaped, mouth dilated, spurred or tuberculate at base, lobes entire or fringed. Trop. Afr. Z10.
S. benguellensis Welw. Caudex 60cm or more diam., barely projecting above the ground; br. to 1.5m, thick, with thorny shoots. Lvs 10–15mm, oval. Fls white-pink. Trop. E Afr.
S. busseanus Engl. Shrub or small tree, 2–5m; st. swollen, with papery bark; thorns to 15mm, with 2 subsidiary thorns below. Lvs 2–5cm, obovate, densely gland. beneath. Fls white or white with a pink tube, pet. fringed. Kenya, Somalia.
S. erlangeri Engl. = *S. rivae.*
S. guerichii (Engl.) Bruce. St. succulent, to 6m with papery bark; br. and shoots thorny. Fls golden yellow. Nam.
S. lugardii N.E. Br. Caudex club-like, over 2m diam. squat, graduating above to ascending succulent br., bark peeling. Lvs oval, folded along midrib, blunt. Fls white. Nam., S Zimb.
S. rivae Engl. Shrub or small tree 2–6m tall, swollen below; br. virgate, thorns 5–9mm. Lvs 2–8cm, obovate, gland. throughout. Fls white or white-brown. Kenya, Ethiop.
S. smithii (Bak.) Stapf = *S. rivae.*

Sesbania Scop. Leguminosae (Papilionoideae). *c*50 herbs, shrubs and small trees. Lvs paripinnate. Fls pea-like, in lax, axill. rac. Fr. linear-oblong, 4-winged. Summer. Trop., Subtrop. Z9.
S. grandiflora (L.) Poir. SCARLET WISTARIA TREE; VEGETABLE HUMMING-BIRD. Short-lived tree, to 12m, lfts to 5cm, in 10–30 pairs. Fls red, pink or white, 2–4 per rac. Trop. Asia, N Aus., nat. S Flor. and W Indies.
S. punicea (Cav.) Benth. Shrub to 1.8m. Lfts to 2.5cm, in 6–20 pairs. Rac. to 10cm; fls to 2cm, vermilion. S Braz., Urug., NE Arg., nat. in SE US.
→*Daubentonia.*

Seseli L. MOON CARROT. Umbelliferae. *c*65 bienn. or perenn. herbs. Lvs 1–4-pinnate, or -ternate, seg. slender, filiform or border and incised; st. lvs usually simpler with short, sheathing petioles. Umbels compound; bracts 0–16; bracteoles several; cal. teeth small or 0; pet. broad. Eur. to C Asia.
S. dichotomum Pall. ex Bieb. Downy perenn. to 1m. Lvs 3–15cm, 2-pinnate, seg. narrow-linear, 10–20mm, silky, petioles short, sheathing. Umbels with 5–9 puberulent rays, to 2cm; bracts 0; bracteoles connate to middle; fls white. Summer. Cauc. Z6.
S. glaucum Bieb. non L. = *S. pallasii.*
S. gummiferum Pall. ex Sm. Bienn. or perenn. to 1m; st. resinous, finely pubesc., stout. Lvs 2–3-pinnatisect, seg. variable, 8–30mm, cuneate or oblong, glaucous, short-hairy.

Umbels with 20–60 densely pubesc., rays, to 5cm; bracts 0–10, linear-lanceolate; bracteoles several, basally connate; fls white or red. Summer. Crimea, S Aegean. Z6.
S. libanotis (L.) K. Koch. Bienn. or perenn. to 120cm; st. glab. to pubesc., ridged, to 30cm, 2-pinnate, seg. 5–15mm, ovate to lanceolate, serrate to pinnatifid. Umbels with 20–60 rays; bracts *c*8, linear; bracteoles 8–15, free; fls white or pink, pubesc. Summer. Eur., Sib., Cauc., N Iran. Z4.
S. montanum L. Ann. to perenn., 10–60cm. Lvs 2–3-pinnate, seg. 3–50mm, linear. Umbels with 3–25 puberulent rays; bracts usually 0; bracteoles several, narrow, free or connate; fls white or tinged pink. Summer. S Eur. to Balk. Penins. Z5.
S. pallasii Besser. Bienn. or perenn., 30–120cm, glab. Lvs triangular in outline, 2–4-pinnate, seg. 5–15mm, linear. Umbels with 7–25 glab. rays, to 6cm; in bracts 0–2; bracteoles free, margin white, membranous; fls white. Summer. Czech. to C Ukraine. Z6.

Sesleria Scop. Gramineae. MOOR GRASS. 33 tufted or clump-forming perenn. grasses. Lf blades narrow. Pan. dense, spicate, globose to cylindric. Eur., W Asia. Z6.
S. albicans Kit. ex Schult. BLUE MOOR GRASS. Vigorous, clump-forming. Lvs 2–5mm across, flat or channeled, midvein distinct. Infl. 10–40cm, spikelets to 3cm, spicate, oblong-oval, mauve to steely blue. Spring. Eur. Z4.
S. autumnalis (Scop.) F.W. Schultz. AUTUMN MOOR GRASS. Vigorous, clump-forming. Lvs to 4mm across, scabrous. Infl. to 40cm, narrow, lax, silver-white. Autumn. Ital. to Albania. Z6.
S. caerulea (L.) Scop. BLUE MOOR GRASS. Differs from *S. albicans* in more rigid infl. and blue-bloomed upper lvs. Scand., E Eur. Z4.
S. caerulea hort. non (L.) Scop. = *S. albicans.*
S. heufleriana Schur. GREEN MOOR GRASS. Loosely clump-forming to 50cm. Lvs to 5mm across, strongly glaucous at first, later bright green above, glaucous beneath. Infl. to 70cm; spikelets purple-black; anth. yellow-green. Spring. SE Eur. Z5.

Sessile Oak *Quercus petraea.*

Setaria Palib. Gramineae. *c*100 ann. or perenn. grasses. Infl. paniculate, setaceous; spikelets 2-fld, short-stipitate, gibbous, subtended by 1 to many rough bristles. Trop., subtrop., warm temp. zones.
S. glauca (L.) Palib. YELLOW BRISTLE GRASS; GLAUCOUS BRISTLE GRASS. Glaucous ann. to 75cm. St. solitary or loosely clumped, upright. Lvs linear, flat, to 30×1cm, glab. Infl. cylindric, erect, to 13cm×0.8cm, brsitles conspicuous yellow or red-tinged. Summer–autumn. OW warm temp. Z6.
S. italica (L.) Palib. FOXTAIL; ITALIAN MILLET; JAPANESE MILLET. Ann., to 1.5m. St. stout, upright, branching below. Lvs linear to narrow-lanceolate, flat, to 45×2cm, glab., scabrous. Infl. erect to pendent, cylindric or lobed, compact, to 30×3cm; bristles to 12mm. Autumn. Warm temp. Asia. Z6.
S. lutescens Hubb. = *S. glauca.*
S. palmifolia (Koenig) Stapf. PALM GRASS. Coarse perenn., to 3m. St. v. stout, upright; nodes pubesc. Lvs narrow-elliptic, long-acute, to 90×13cm, glab. to pubesc., scabrous. Infl. ovoid to cylindric, to 90×30cm; br. to 30cm, bristles solitary, inconspicuous. Summer. Trop. Asia. One of a group of tall sp. with similar lvs; others suitable for cult. include *S. chevalieri* Stapf. *S. megaphylla* (Steud.) Schinz, *S. paniculifera* (Steud.) Fourn., *S. poiretiana* (Schult.) Kunth and *S. pumila* Roem. & Schult. Z9.
S. persica hort. ex Rchb. Differs from *S. glauca* in purple-brown, spikelike fl. heads.
S. plicata (Lam.) Cooke. Resembles *S. plicatilis*, but spikelets and upper glumes larger than 3mm upper lemma transversely wrinkled, not smooth. India. Z9.
S. plicatilis (Hochst.) Hackel. Perenn., to 1.5m. St. loosely clumped, slender to stout. Lvs linear to linear-lancolate, to 35×2.5cm. sheaths flattened, scabrous. Infl. linear to cylindric, to 30×6cm, bristles to 16mm. Summer. E Afr. (mts). Z6.
S. verticillata (L.) Palib. Similar to *S. viridis* but bristles recurved.
S. viridis (L.) Palib. GREEN BRISTLE GRASS; ROUGH BRISTLE GRASS. Ann., to 60cm. St. upright, slender, loosely clumped. Lvs to 20×1cm, slightly scabrous, apex long-acute. Infl. narrow, cylindric, spicate, compact, erect, v. bristly, to 10×1cm, tinged green to purple; bristles to 3 together, to 1cm. Summer–autumn. Warm temp. Eurasia. Z6.
→*Chaetochloa* and *Panicum.*

Setcreasea Schum. & Sydow.
S. purpurea Boom = *Tradescantia pallida.*
S. striata hort. = *Callisia elegans.*

Seticereus Backeb.
S. humboldtii (Kunth) Backeb. = *Cleistocactus icosagonus*.
S. icosagonus (Schum.) Backeb. = *Cleistocactus icosagonus*.
S. roezlii (F. Haage ex Schum.) Backeb. = *Cleistocactus roezlii*.

Setiechinopsis (Backeb.) De Haas.
S. mirabilis (Speg.) De Haas = *Echinopsis mirabilis*.

Setterwort *Helleborus foetidus*.
Seuvla *Cassia*.
Seven Golden Candlesticks *Senna alata*.
Seven Sisters Rose *Rosa multiflora*.

Severinia Ten. BOX-ORANGE. Rutaceae. 6 shrubs or small trees.
Lvs simple, strongly veined; petioles v. sort. Fls small, 3–5-
merous in axill. clusters, corymbs or pan.; sta. 6–10. Fr. small,
berry-like, juicy or semi-dry, peel, thick, dotted with oil glands.
SE Asia to Malaysia. Z10.
S. buxifolia (Poir.) Ten. CHINESE BOX-ORANGE. Low shrub or
small tree to 1m, everg.; br. spiny. Lvs 2.5–4cm, ovate, obtuse
at apex, cuneate at base, coriaceous, glandular-punctate. Fls
axill., 2–3 together, 5-merous; cal. broadly campanulate, lobes
rounded, short; pet. 4mm, oblong, erect, white. Fr. depressed-
globose, black when ripe. S China, Hong Kong, Vietnam.
→*Atalantia*.

Seville Orange *Citrus aurantium*.
Seychelles Nut *Lodoicea*.

Seyrigia Keraudren. Cucurbitaceae. 4 climbing herbs. St.
slender, occas. succulent, ribbed, often becoming leafless.
Tendrils simple. Lvs to 5-fid, small. ♂ fls small, in short rac.,
pet. lanceolate; ♀ fls solitary. Fr. a small berry, bright red when
ripe. Madag. Z10.
S. humbertii Keraudren. St. to 3m, cylindrical, ribbed, white-
pubesc. Tendrils 5–20cm, white-pubesc. Lvs 3-lobed, small. Fr.
ovoid, c1.5cm. Madag.

Shad, Shadblow *Amelanchier*.
Shadbush *Amelanchier*.
Shaddock *Citrus maxima*.
Shagbark Hickory *Carya ovata*.
Shaggy Dryandra *Dryandra speciosa*.
Shaggy Garden Purslane *Portulaca pilosa*.
Shag-spine *Caragana jubata*.
Shajrat Al'asal *Tecomella*.
Shaking Brake *Pteris tremula*.
Shallon *Gaultheria shallon*.
Shallot *Allium cepa*.
Shamel Ash *Fraxinus uhdei*.
Shame Plant *Mimosa pudica*.
Shamrock *Oxalis*; *Trifolium dubium*; *T. repens*.
Shamrock Pea *Parochetus communis*.
Shantung Maple *Acer truncatum*.
Sharp-leaved Pondweed *Potamogeton acutifolius*.
Sharp Midge Orchid *Prasophyllum despectans*.
Sharp-pointed Fig *Ficus parietalis*.
Shasta Daisy *Leucanthemum* ×*superbum*.
Shatterwood *Backhousia sciadophora*.
Shaving-brush Tree *Pachira*; *Pseudobombax ellipticum*.
Shawnee Salad *Hydrophyllum virginianum*.
Shawnee Wood *Catalpa speciosa*.
Sheepberry *Viburnum lentago*.
Sheep Laurel *Kalmia angustifolia*.
Sheep's Bit *Jasione* (*J. laevis*; *J. montana*).
Sheep's Burrs *Acaena*.
Sheep's Fescue *Festuca ovina*.
Shellflower *Chelone*; *Pistia*.
Shell Ginger *Alpinia zerumbet*.
Shensi Fir *Abies chensiensis*.
She Oak *Casuarina*.

Shepherdia Nutt. BUFFALO BERRY. Elaeagnaceae. 3 decid. or
everg., dioecious shrubs. Twigs and lvs scaly. Fls apetalous: ♂
with 4 sep. and 8 sta., in precocious spikes or rac.; ♀ tubular
with single, elongated style, solitary or paired. Fr. a fleshy
drupe. N Amer.
S. argentea (Pursh) Nutt. SILVERBERRY; BUFFALO BERRY.
Arborescent shrub to 4m. Twigs red-brown, with dense silver
scales. Lvs 3–5cm, oblong, silvery. Fls small, white-yellow. Fr.
pea-sized, bright red, glossy with silvery scales, edible. Spring.
N Amer. Z2. 'Xanthocarpa': fr. yellow.
S. canadensis (L.) Nutt. BUFFALO BERRY. Spreading shrub to
2.5m. Twigs lustrous red-brown, scaly, thornless. Lvs 4–6cm,
dark yellow-green above with scattered white hairs, with white-
tufted hairs and brown scales beneath. Fls cream-yellow. Fr. to

5mm, yellow to red. Spring. N Amer. Z2. 'Rubra': fr. red.
'Xanthocarpa': fr. yellow.
S. ×*gottingensis* (Rehd.) Rehd. Intermediate hybrid between
S. argentea ×*S. canadensis*. Gdn origin.

Shepherd's Clock *Anagallis arvensis*; *Tragopogon pratensis*.
Shepherd's Purse *Capsella bursa-pastoris*.
Shepherd's Scabious *Jasione laevis*.

Sherardia L. Rubiaceae. 1 ann. herb to 40cm, st. smooth or with
deflexed prickles or spreading hairs along angles. Lvs lanceolate
or elliptic, long-pointed at apex, to 2×0.5cm, rough beneath,
cartilaginous and somewhat spinose at margin. Fls pale blue to
lilac, to 10 per 2cm wide cluster; cal. teeth erect, lanceolate to
subulate, somewhat hairy; cor. to 5mm, lobes ovate, to 2mm.
Eur., N Afr., Middle E, nat. S Afr., Americas.
S. arvensis L. FIELD MADDER; SPURWORT.

Shetland Pondweed *Potamogeton rutilus*.

Shibataea Mak. ex Nak. Gramineae. 8 squat shrubby bamboos;
rhiz. running (appearing clumped). Culms slender, flattened on
one side; sheaths thin, glab.; nodes prominent; br. 3–5, v. short.
Lvs tessellate, 1–2 per br., without sheaths but with narrow
membranous bracts at lower nodes. Far E.
S. kumasasa (Zoll. ex Steud.) Mak. ex Nak. OKAME-ZASA.
Compact, bushy. Culms 0.5–1.8m×2–5mm. Lvs
5–11×1.3–2.5cm, short and broad, long-stalked, dark shining
green, glab. above, glabrescent beneath, often withering at the
apex. China, Jap. Z6.
→*Phyllostachys*.

Shield Fern *Dryopteris*.
Shield Ivy *Hedera hibernica*.
Shield-leaved Saxifrage *Saxifraga cuneifolia*.
Shiho-chiku *Chimonobambusa quadrangularis*.
Shikakudake *Chimonobambusa quadrangularis*.
Shimpaku *Juniperus sargentii*.
Shingle Oak *Quercus imbricaria*.
Shingle Plant *Monstera acuminata*; *Rhaphidophora celatocaulis*.
Shingle Tree *Acrocarpus fraxinifolius*.
Shining Club Moss *Lycopodium lucidulum*.
Shining Gum *Eucalyptus nitens*.
Shining Pondweed *Potamogeton lucens*.
Shining Spleenwort *Asplenium oblongifolium*.
Shining Sumac *Rhus copallina*.
Shining Willow *Salix lucida*.
Shinleaf *Pyrola*.
Shiny Filmy Fern *Hymenophyllum flabellatum*.
Shiny-leaved Fig *Ficus callosa*.
Shiny-leaved Rhus *Rhus lucida*.
Shiny Lyonia *Lyonia lucida*.
Shiny Shield Fern *Lastreopsis acuminata*.
Shisham *Dalbergia sissoo*.
Shiso *Perilla*.
Shittimwood *Bumelia lanuginosa*; *B. lycioides*.
Shiya-zasa *Sasaella masumuneana*.
Shoe Black *Hibiscus rosa-sinensis*.
Shoofly *Alternanthera ficoidea* var. *amoena*; *Nicandra physaloides*.
Shooting Star *Dodecatheon* (*D. media*).
Shore Juniper *Juniperus conferta*.
Shore Pine *Pinus contorta*.
Shore Spurge *Euphorbia glauca*.
Short Blue Hesper *Brahea armata*.

Shortia Torr. & A. Gray. Diapensiaceae. 6 rhizomatous everg.
perenn. herbs. Lvs radical, orbicular or cordate, toothed, long-
petioled. Fls scapose, solitary or racemose; cal. 5-parted with
scaly bracts; cor. broadly campanulate, lobes 5, obovate, clawed
free or fused and lacerate; staminodes 5, scale-like, alternating
with 5 sta. N Amer., E Asia.
S. galacifolia Torr. & A. Gray. OCONEE BELLS. Lvs to 5cm
diam., suborbicular, bluntly toothed, coriaceous, glossy green
turning bronze-red in autumn; petioles to 10cm, ascending.
Scapes to 12cm; fls solitary; cor. to 2.5cm diam., white and
ultimately flushed rose, or pink or blue, tube funnelform, lobes
ovate-oblong, crenate. N Amer. Z5.
S. soldanelloides (Sieb. & Zucc.) Mak. FRINGED GALAX; FRINGE-
BELL. Lvs to 5cm diam., ovate or orbicular, cuneate or
cordate, coarsely toothed; petioles to 5cm, spreading. Scape
6.5–10cm; fls to 6; cor. to 2.5cm diam., broadly campanulate,
deep rose at centre fading to white on lobes, lobes deeply
lacerate. Jap. f. *alpina* (Maxim.) Mak. Smaller, v. compact.
var. *ilicifolia* (Maxim.) Mak. Lvs coarsely and sparsely toothed.
var. *magna* Mak. Lvs larger with many small, wavy, marginal
teeth. Z7.

S. uniflora (Maxim.) Maxim. NIPPON BELLS. Differs from *S. galacifolia* in its more broadly cordate and sinuately toothed lvs. Fls to 2.5cm diam., rose veined white. Spring. Jap. 'Grandiflora': fls to 3cm diam., white to shell-pink, borne in profusion. Z6.
→*Schizocodon*.

Short-leaf Fig *Ficus citrifolia*.
Short-leaf Pine *Pinus echinata*.
Short-spurred Fragrant Orchid *Gymnadenia odoratissima*.
Shot Huckleberry *Vaccinium ovatum*.
Shower Orchid *Congea tomentosa*.
Shower Tree *Cassia*.
Showy Banksia *Banksia speciosa*.
Showy Dryandra *Dryandra formosa*.
Showy Everlasting *Helichrysum subulifolium*.
Showy Lady's Slipper Orchid *Cypripedium reginae*.
Showy Sunray *Helipterum splendidum*.
Showy Wattle *Acacia decora*.
Shrimp Begonia *Begonia radicans*.
Shrimp Bush *Justicia brandegeana*.
Shrimp Plant *Justicia brandegeana*.
Shrimp Tree *Koelreuteria*.
Shrubby Bittersweet *Celastrus*.
Shrubby Cinquefoil *Potentilla fruticosa*.
Shrubby Evening Primrose *Calylophus serrulatus*.
Shrubby Germander *Teucrium fruticans*.
Shrubby Hare's Ear *Bupleurum fruticosum*.
Shrubby Penstemon *Penstemon fructicosus*.
Shrubby Plantain *Plantago cynops*.
Shrubby Restharrow *Ononis fruticosa*.
Shrubby Trefoil *Ptelea*.
Shrub Verbena *Lantana*.
Shrub Vinca *Kopsia flavida; K. fruticosa*.
Shumard Oak *Quercus shumardii*.
Shuttlecock Fern *Matteuccia struthiopteris*.
Siamese Ginger *Alpinia galanga*.
Siamese White Ixora *Ixora finlaysonia*.

Sibbaldia L. Rosaceae. 8 procumbent, woody-based perennials. Lvs trifoliolate, lfts dissected, toothed at apex. Fls 5-merous, small, in corymbs; pet. shorter than hairy sep.; sta. usually 5(–10), alternating with pet. N Temp. zones.
S. parviflora Willd. To 8cm. Lfts oblong-cuneate or obovate, to 2.5cm, densely grey-pubesc. Fls in dense, capitate, later corymbiform infl.; pet. obovate, to 2.5mm, yellow, veins anastomosing. Summer. S Balk., Asia Minor, Iran. Z6.
S. procumbens L. To 20cm. Lfts oblong or obovate, to 2cm, sparsely adpressed-pubesc. above, densely glandular-pubesc. beneath. Fls in few-fld, dense, corymbose infl.; pet. lanceolate or oblong-spathulate, to 2mm, yellow or yellow-green, veins not or scarcely anastomosing. Summer. Arc. and Alpine Eur., S Asia, N Amer. Z1.

Siberian Bugloss *Brunnera macrophylla*.
Siberian Crab *Malus baccata*.
Siberian Dogwood *Cornus alba*.
Siberian Elm *Ulmus pumila*.
Siberian Flag *Iris sibirica*.
Siberian Ginseng *Eleutherococcus senticosus*.
Siberian Kale *Brassica napus*.
Siberian Larch *Larix russica*.
Siberian Melic *Melica altissima*.
Siberian Pea-tree *Caragana arborescens*.
Siberian Phlox *Phlox sibirica*.
Siberian Pine *Pinus cembra*.
Siberian Purslane *Montia sibirica*.
Siberian Spruce *Picea obovata*.
Siberian Squill *Scilla sibirica*.
Siberian Wallflower *Erysimum* ×*allionii*.

Sibiraea Maxim. Rosaceae. 2 decid. shrubs, to 2m. Lvs narrow-ovate to lanceolate, entire. Fls white to cream, small, in term., long-branched rac.; cal. campanulate, lobes 5; pet. round-obovate; sta. 25; carpels 5, connate at base. SE Eur., Sib., W China.
S. altaiensis (Laxm.) Schneid. Br. erect, purple-brown or red, glab. Lvs to 10×2cm, oblong to lanceolate, mucronulate, soft blue-green, glab. Fls white in slender pan. to 12cm. Spring–summer. Sib., W China, Balk. Z2.
S. laevigata (L.) Maxim. = *S. altaiensis*.
S. tomentosa Diels. Lvs to 7×2.5cm, oblong-obovate to oblanceolate, mucronate, glab. above, silky beneath. Fls green-white, in dense, 5cm pan. SW China. Z6.
→*Spiraea*.

Sibthorpia L. Scrophulariaceae. 5 creeping perenn. herbs. Lvs petiolate, orbicular. Fls axillary, pedicellate; cal. 4–8-lobed; cor. short-tubular, 5–8-lobed, rotate. Summer. Trop. & S Amer., Afr., Eur., Macronesia.
S. europaea L. CORNISH MONEYWORT. St. creeping, to 40cm. Lvs 1–6cm, reniform to orbicular, pubesc. Fls solitary, white or cream tinted pink, 1–2.5mm diam. W Eur., Greece. 'Variegata': lvs gold-green, speckled and edged with silver. Z8.
S. peregrina L. Differs from *S. europaea* in larger, yellow fls. SW Eur. Z9.

Sicana Naudin. Cucurbitaceae. 2 climbing perennials. Tendrils 3–5-parted. Lvs alt., palmately lobed, glab.; petiole long. Fls solitary, large, unisexual; cor. 5-lobed, yellow. C & S Amer., W Indies. Z10.
S. atropurpurea André = *S. odorifera*.
S. odorifera (Vell.) Naudin. CURUBÁ; CURUA; COROA; CASSABANANA. St. to 15m, puberulent when young. Tendrils c4-parted. Lvs suborbicular, 3–5-lobed, base cordate, 10–20cm; petiole 4–15cm. Fr. sweetly scented, ellipsoid, to 30cm, yellow turning orange, or purple-red, flesh pale yellow. S Amer.

Sichuan Juniper *Juniperus saltuaria*.
Sicilian Fir *Abies nebrodensis*.
Sicilian Honey Garlic *Nectaroscordum siculum*.
Sicilian Sumac *Rhus coriaria*.
Sickle Fern *Pellaea falcata*.
Sickle-leaved Fig *Ficus punctata*.
Sickle-leaved Hare's Ear *Bupleurum falcatum*.
Sickle Medick *Medicago falcata*.
Sickle Plant *Crassula perfoliata* var. *falcata*.
Sickle Spleenwort *Asplenium polyodon*.

Sicydium Schldl.
S. lindheimeri A. Gray = *Ibervillea lindheimeri*.

Sicyos L. Cucurbitaceae. 25 ann. climbers and trailers. Lvs simple or palmately lobed. Tendrils 2–5-fid. ♂ infl. a rac.; ♀ fls solitary, smaller; fls small, white to pale green; pet. (3–4–)5, fused at base; sta. usually 3. Fr. small, ovoid or fusiform, usually spiny, dry. Americas, Pacific Is., Australasia.
S. angulatus L. BUR CUCUMBER; STAR CUCUMBER. To 6m. Lvs cordate to orbicular, sharply angled or lobed. Fr. spiny. N America.
S. oreganus Torr. & A. Gray = *Marah oreganus*.

Sida L. Malvaceae. 150 ann. and perenn. herbs or subshrubs. Lvs serrate or lobed. Fls solitary or in axill. clusters, spikes, rac. or pan.; epical. usually 0; cal. 5-toothed or lobed; pet. obovate, ± clawed; sta. united in a tubular column. Trop. and warm temp. regions, esp. Amer.
S. abutilon L. = *Abutilon theophrasti*.
S. alcaeoides Michx. = *Callirhoë alcaeoides*.
S. dioica (L.) Cav. = *Napaea dioica*.
S. discolor Hook. = *Asterotrichion discolor*.
S. graveolens Roxb. ex Hornem. = *Abutilon hirtum*.
S. hermaphrodita (L.) Rusby. VIRGINIA MALLOW. Perenn. glab. herb to 3m. Lvs to 25cm, deeply palmately lobed, lobes 3, 5 or 7 long-acuminate, dentate to serrate. Fls to 2.5cm diam., white in loose axill. cymes. Delaware, westwards to Ohio and Tenn. Z6.
S. hirta Lam. = *Abutilon hirtum*.
S. indica L. = *Abutilon indicum*.
S. purpurascens Link = *Abutilon purpurascens*.
S. radiata L. = *Malachra radiata*.
S. rhombifolia L. Ann. or perenn. herb to 1.2m, br. glabrate or finely stellate-hairy. Lvs to 8cm, lanceolate to rhombic-oblong, acute to obtuse at apex, serrate-dentate, glabrate or tomentose beneath. Fls large, solitary, yellow to orange-yellow, becoming pink. Trop. and subtrop. Z10.
S. rosea Link & Otto = *Abutilon purpurascens*.

Sidalcea A. Gray. PRAIRIE MALLOW; CHECKER MALLOW. Malvaceae. 20 ann. and perenn. herbs, lobes 5, lvs rounded, palmately lobed or dissected, basal lvs coarsely toothed or shallowly lobed. Fls in term. spikes or rac.; epical. 0; cal. lobes 5, united at base; pet. 5, spreading, sta. united into a tubular column, in 2 series. Fr. a schizocarp; mericarps 5–9. W N Amer.
S. campestris Greene. MEADOW SIDALCEA. Perenn. erect to 1.8m. Lower lvs to 15cm diam., rounded, lobed, upper lvs 5–7-parted, lobes narrow. Fls to 7.5 diam., in loose rac.; pet. white to pale pink. Oreg. Z7.
S. candida A. Gray. WHITE PRAIRIE MALLOW. Perenn. erect to 80cm. Lvs glossy above, sparsely hirsute beneath, basal lvs to 20cm diam., orbicular, 5–7-lobed, coarsely crenate, upper lvs deeply 3-, 5- or 7-lobed, lobes linear-lanceolate, ± entire. Fls

1.5–2.5cm diam., in dense spike-like term. rac.; pet. white or cream. Wyom., Colorado, Nevada, New Mex. Z5.

S. hendersonii S. Wats. HENDERSON'S CHECKER MALLOW. Perenn. to 1.5m. Lower lvs to 15cm diam., shallowly 5-lobed, upper lvs deeply divided in 3 or 5 laciniate lobes. Fls 2–3cm diam., in dense spike-like rac.; cal. pale purple; pet. pink-lavender to deep rose. BC, Washington, Oreg. Z7.

S. malviflora (DC.) A. Gray. CHECKERBLOOM. Perenn. erect to 80cm. Lvs 2–6cm diam., often fleshy, hairy, basal lvs rounded to reniform, shallowly 7–9-lobed, crenate, upper lvs deeply lobed. Rac. elongate many-fld; pet. 1–2.5cm, pink or lilac, usually white-veined. Oreg., Calif., Baja Calif. 'Brilliant': fls pure carmine red. 'Candida': fls white. 'Crimson King': fls ruby red. 'Croftway Red': to 1m; fls rich red. 'Elsie Heugh': low-growing; fls shell pink, fringed. 'Listeri': fls pearly pink. 'Loveliness': habit compact; fls pale pink. 'Oberon': fls soft rose. 'Puck': habit upright, compact; fls deep pink. 'Rev. Page Roberts': fls silvery pink. 'Rose Bouquet': tall; fls dark pink. 'Scarlet Beauty': fls deep purple. Stark's Hybrid Mixture: habit erect, clump-forming; fls to 3cm diam., in long spikes, in a wide range of shades of pink; seed strain. 'Sussex Beauty': fls clear pink. 'The Duchess' and 'Rose Gem': fls deep rose. 'William Smith': fls bright rose tinted salmon. ssp. *californica*. (Nutt. ex Torr. & A. Gray) C. Hitchc. All parts more densely pubesc. Z6.

S. neomexicana A. Gray. NEW MEXICO PRAIRIE MALLOW. Perenn. erect to 80cm. Lvs 2–7cm diam., rounded, pubesc. throughout, ciliate, basal lvs coarsely crenate to shallowly 5–7-lobed, upper lvs deeply 5–9-segmented, each seg. 3–5-lobed. Rac. simple or compound, many-fld; pet. 1.5–2mm, purple, magenta, palle rose or white. Wyom., Idaho, New Mex., Ariz., Calif. Z5.

S. nervata Nels. = *S. oregana*.

S. oregana (Nutt. ex Torr. & A. Gray) A. Gray. OREGON SIDALCEA. Perenn. erect to 1.8m. Lower lvs to 15cm diam., shallowly 5- or 7-lobed, crenate, upper lvs deeply divided. Rac. spike-like; pet. to 2cm, pink to deep pink. Washington, Idaho, Utah, Calif. ssp. *spicata* (Reg.) C. Hitchc. St. hirsute. Infl. densely fld. Oreg., Calif., Nevada. Z5.

S. spicata Reg. = *S. oregana* ssp. *spicata*.

Sideoats Grass *Bouteloua curtipendula*.

Siderasis Raf. Commelinaceae. 2 rhizomatous perenn. herbs. Lvs in a basal rosette. Infl. of single axill. concinni; fls actinomorphic; sep. and pet. free, equal; sta. 6. Braz.

S. fuscata (Lodd.) H.E. Moore. ± stemless, densely and softly rufous-pubesc. Lvs 15–25×5–9cm, elliptic to elliptic-obovate, with silvery midstripe above, flushed red beneath; petiole to 5cm. Infl. axill., 3–10cm, 1–4-fld; fls 2.5–4cm diam., violet to purple-pink. Summer. E Braz. Z9.
→*Pyrrheima*.

Sideritis L. Labiatae. *c*100 ann. or perenn. herbs, subshrubs, or shrubs. St. hairy. Lvs opposite, entire to notched. Fls in verticillasters, these in term. spikes; bracts leaf-like; cal. 2-lipped, tubular to bell-shaped, teeth 5; cor. 2-lipped, tube included, upper lip erect to spreading, flattened, entire to bifid, lower lip spreading, 3-lobed. Medit., Atlantic Is.

S. argosphacelus (Webb & Berth.) Clos. Subshrub, white-tomentose. Lvs cordate, notched, pubesc. Verticillasters distant, in dense, eventually pendent spikes; cor. yellow, tipped brown. Canary Is.

S. canariensis L. Shrub. Lvs to 10cm, ovate, base cordate, toothed to notched, rugose and pubesc. Verticillasters 20–30-fld, distant, in loose, erect, simple spikes; bracts linear; cor. yellow, upper lip bifid. Canary Is.

S. candicans Ait. Shrub, to 90cm, much-branched, white-tomentose. Lvs ovate to linear-lanceolate, base truncate to cordate, somewhat notched, white-tomentose. Verticillasters 10-fld, distant, in erect, simple or branched spikes; bracts linear to lanceolate; cor. pubesc., yellow, tipped red to brown. Canary Is., Madeira. Z8.

S. glandulifera Post = *S. perfoliata*.

S. hyssopifolia L. Perenn. shrub to 80cm. St. glab. to pubesc. Lvs to 3.5cm, ovate or obovate to linear or spathulate, entire to toothed or notched. Verticillasters 5–15, 6-fld, approximate, in dense spikes; bracts ovate to linear, entire or toothed; cor. to 1cm, yellow, occas. flecked purple. S Eur. (Port. to Fr.). Z8.

S. incana L. Subshrub, to 60cm. Lvs to 4cm, linear, spathulate or oblong to ovate or lanceolate, apex obtuse, base cordate, entire or minutely toothed, white-tomentose. Verticillasters to 10, 6-fld, distant, in spikes; bracts ovate, entire or toothed; cor. to 1cm, yellow or pink. Spain. Z8.

S. libanotica Labill. Shrub to 1m. St. occas. gland., white-tomentose. Lvs to 8cm, lanceolate to linear, apex acute to mucronate, entire to toothed or notched. Verticillasters 2–15, 6-fld, to 9cm distant, in spikes; bracts oblong to reniform, cor.

to 13mm, pubesc., yellow to purple, interior brown-striate. E Medit. Z8.

S. macrostachys Poir. Shrub, to 1m. Lvs ovate, base cordate, margin notched, pubesc. Verticillasters in dense, erect, branched spikes; bracts and cal. white-tomentose; cor. white, tipped brown. Canary Is. Z9.

S. montana L. Ann., to 40cm. St. pubesc. Lvs to 4cm, linear or oblong to lanceolate or elliptic, apex acute to mucronate, entire to toothed or notched, sparsely pubesc. Verticillasters 4–6-fld, in dense spikes; bracts oblong, mucronate, margin entire, yellow; cor. to 0.7cm, yellow to brown-black. Medit. (S Eur. to Cauc.).

S. nervosa C. Chr. Shrub, to 50cm. Lvs ovate, apex obtuse, base cordate, entire to notched, pubesc., veins prominent beneath. Verticillasters in branched spikes, fls yellow. Canary Is. Z9.

S. perfoliata L. Herb or subshrub, to 60cm+. St. glandular-pubesc. Lvs to 9cm, ovate to lanceolate to oblong, base semi-amplexicaul and perfoliate, entire to toothed or notched, soft-pubesc. Verticillasters 6–17, 6–15-fld, to 7cm distant, in spikes; bracts ovate to orbicular, margin membranous, yellow; cor. to 15mm, yellow pubesc., interior brown-striate. E Medit. Z8.

S. scordioides L. Perenn. subshrub, to 30cm. St. tomentose. Lvs to 3cm, ovate to linear or oblong, toothed or notched, tomentose. Verticillasters 3–10, 6-fld, distant, in spikes to 8cm; bracts to ovate, spiny, minutely toothed or notched; cor. to 1cm, yellow. S Eur. (Fr., Spain). Z8.

S. scythica Juz. = *S. taurica*.

S. steneni Zef. = *S. taurica*.

S. syriaca L. Perenn., to 40cm. St. usually simple, white-tomentose. Lvs to 6cm, linear or oblong to lanceolate or ovate, apex obtuse, entire to toothed or notched. Verticillasters 20, 4–10-fld, to 5cm distant, in spikes; bracts to 1cm, suborbicular; cor. to 15mm, yellow, pubesc., interior brown-striate. Crete. Z8.

S. taurica Stephan ex Willd. ± unbranched, ascending subshrub, to 40cm. St. white-tomentose. Basal lvs to 8cm, petiolate, oblong or spathulate to lanceolate, apex subacute or obtuse, toothed or notched, rugose and somewhat pubesc., cauline lvs to 7cm, 3–6 pairs, ± sessile, obovate to oblanceolate, apex acute. Verticillasters 18, to 3cm distant, in spikes to 20cm; bracts ovate or cordate to orbicular, apex narrowly acute, entire, tomentose; cor. to 12mm, yellow, pubesc., interior brown-striate. Summer–autumn. Crimea. Z7.

Siderocarpus Small.
S. flexicaulis (Benth.) Small = *Pithecellobium flexicaule*.

Sideroxylon L.
S. foetidissimum Jacq. = *Mastichodendron foetidissimum*.
S. mastichodendron Jacq. = *Mastichodendron foetidissimum*.
S. novo-zeylandicum (F. Muell.) Hemsl. = *Planchonella costata*.

Sidra *Cucurbita ficifolia*.
Sierra Currant *Ribes nevadense*.
Sierra Gooseberry *Ribes roezlii*.
Sierra Juniper *Juniperus occidentalis* var. *australis*.
Sierra Laurel *Leucothoë davisiae*.
Sierra Leone Coffee *Coffea stenophylla*.
Sierra Lily *Lilium parvum*.
Sierra Lodgepole Pine *Pinus contorta*.
Sierran Penstemon *Penstemon heterodoxus*.
Sierra Redwood *Sequoiadendron*.
Sierra Shooting Star *Dodecatheon jeffreyi*.
Sierra Water Fern *Parathelypteris nevadensis*.
Sierra White Fir *Abies concolor*.

Sievekingia Rchb. f. Orchidaceae. 9 epiphytic orchids. Pbs to 3cm, ovoid, furrowed, enveloped at base by papery bracts, apically 1–2-leaved. Lvs to 25cm, elliptic-lanceolate, plicate, petiolate, rac. basal, erect to pendent, few- to many-fld; fls thin-textured; sep. elliptic-lanceolate, concave, spreading; pet. narrower, entire to fimbriate; lip concave, simple or trilobed, disc callose, dentate or lamellate. Costa Rica to Guyana, Colomb. to Ecuad. and Peru. Z10.

S. dunstervilleorum Foldats. = *S. jenmanii*.

S. jenmanii Rchb. f. Infl. deflexed, few-fld; fls fleshy to 5cm diam.; sep. white to pale yellow; pet. pale orange-yellow, linear-oblong or oblong-lanceolate, acute; lip to 16×20mm, orange-yellow, midlobe ligulate, apiculate, smaller than lat. lobes, disc 3-keeled, toothed. Venez., Guyana.

S. reichenbachiana Rolfe. Infl. to 10cm, 5-fld, sharply pendent; fls to 5cm diam.; sep. yellow-green; pet. green flushed orange-yellow; lip green spotted purple on disc, with orange-yellow keels. Colomb.

S. suavis Rchb. f. Infl. short-few, to several-fld; fls to 2.5cm diam.; sep. pale lemon-yellow; pet. orange; lip to 11×10mm,

orange spotted dark red-purple, ovate or obovate-rhombic, acute, 3-ridged, central keel cleft. Mostly summer. Costa Rica, Panama.
→*Cynoglossum*.

Sieversia Willd.
S. paradoxa D. Don = *Fallugia paradoxa*.

Sigmatostalix Rchb. f. Orchidaceae. 20 epiphytic orchids. Pbs small, elliptic to oblong-ovoid, compressed, with several distichous, overlapping, lf sheaths, apically unifoliate or bifoliate. Lvs narrow. Rac. lat., few- to many-fld, usually surpassing lvs; peduncle slender, erect or arching; fls small, thin-textured; sep. and pet. similar; lip simple to trilobed, disc with a fleshy, basal callus. Mex. and C Amer. to Braz., Peru, Boliv. and Arg. Z10.
S. amazonica Schltr. Pbs to 4cm. Lvs to 15×1.5cm. Infl. often surpassing lvs, loosely few-fld; fls spreading, to 1.5cm; sep. green-yellow, to 7×2mm, oblong-lanceolate; pet. yellow-green barred brown; lip to 7×6mm, rich yellow, simple, obovate-cuneate, rounded; callus large, elliptic-ligulate. Peru, Braz., Surinam.
S. graminea (Poepp. & Endl.) Rchb. f. Pbs to 1.2cm. Lvs to 5×0.2cm. Infl. to 6cm, erect to spreading, loosely few-fld; fls pale yellow spotted or striped purple to red; sep. to 2.5×1mm, elliptic-lanceolate or oblong; lip to 3×3mm, ovate-subquadrate, retuse, base truncate, callus suborbicular, carinate. Peru.
S. guatemalensis Schltr. Pbs to 4cm. Lvs to 13×1.5cm. Infl. to 34cm, erect, loosely several-fld; fls to 1.5cm diam., pale green to yellow, often marked brown, lip deep yellow, heavily marked red-brown; sep. to 9×2.5mm, ligulate-lanceolate; lip to 6×5mm, simple to 3-lobed, ovate-suborbicular, base auriculate-sagittate, apex truncate or apiculate, callus small, suberect. Mex. to Panama.
S. hymenantha Schltr. Pbs to 3.5cm. Lvs to 14×1cm. Infl. to 14cm, erect; fls minute, pale brown or green marked tan; tep. to 2mm, oblong, often reflexed; lip to 1.5×2mm, simple to obscurely 3-lobed, ovate-elliptic, callus bilobulate. Costa Rica, Panama.
S. peruviana Rolfe. Pbs to 1.5cm. Lvs to 5×0.4cm. Infl. equalling lvs, loosely few-fld; fls spreading, pale yellow, often striped dark purple; sep. to 3.5×1.5mm, oblong or oblong-lanceolate; lip to 4×5mm, orbicular-reniform, undulate, callus large, lobulate. Peru.
S. radicans Lind. & Rchb. f. = *Ornithophora radicans*.

Signet Marigold *Tagetes tenuifolia*.
Sikkim Fir *Abies densa*.
Sikkim Larch *Larix griffithiana*.
Sikkim Rhubarb *Rheum acuminatum*; *R. nobile*.
Sikkim Spruce *Picea spinulosa*.

Silene L. CAMPION; CATCHFLY. Caryophyllaceae. *c*500 ann., bienn. or perenn. herbs, often woody-based. Fls few or solitary, cal., ± tubular with 5 teeth, sometimes strongly inflated; pet. with entire, notched or bifid (rarely 4-fid) limb and narrow claw, with or without coronal scales; sta. 10; styles 3–4, more rarely 5. Widespread in N Hemis., from the arctic to some Trop. African mts and also in S Afr. and S Amer.; the greatest concentration of sp. in the Medit. area.
S. acaulis (L.) Jacq. MOSS CAMPION. Dwarf, glab. perenn., forming moss-like tufts or mats. Lvs packed, subulate. Fls solitary, ± sessile to shortly stalked; cal. 8–10mm, usually tinged red; pet. limb *c*5mm, obovate, notched, deep pink or white; coronal scales small. Summer. Circumpolar arctic regions, mts of W & C Eur. and N Amer. 'Alba': fls white. 'Cenisia': fls double. 'Floribunda': fls abundant. 'Frances': cushion-forming; lvs gold. 'Mount Snowdon': v. compact. 'Pedunculata': fls vivid pink, abundant. Z2.
S. alba (Mill.) E.H.L. Krause = *S. latifolia*.
S. alpestris Jacq. Loosely tufted, ± hairy perenn. to 20cm. St. slender, branched. Lvs linear-lanceolate. Infl. a loose, gland. dichasium; cal. *c*6mm, pet. limb *c*6mm, triangular, fringed, white flushed pale pink. Early summer. E Alps, Balk. 'Flore Pleno': fls double, white. Z5.
S. armeria L. Ann. or bienn. to 40cm, glaucous. St. erect, usually unbranched, viscid above. Basal lvs spathulate, withering early; st. lvs ovate to lanceolate, amplexicaul. Corymb compact; cal. 1.2–1.5cm; pet. limb *c*6mm, obovate, shallowly notched, bright pink; coronal scales acute. Summer. C & S Eur.
S. californica Dur. Weak-stemmed, glandular-hairy perenn. to 40cm. Lvs ovate to narrowly obovate. Infl. loose; cal. 1.5–2cm; pet. limb 1–1.5cm, deeply 4-fid, crimson, claw long, coronal scales conspicuous. Summer. Calif., Oreg. Z7.
S. caroliniana Walter Loosely tufted, hairy, ± gland. perenn. to 20cm. Basal lvs spathulate, st. lvs linear-lanceolate. Fls long-stalked, corymbose; cal. *c*1.5cm; pet. limb 8–12mm, entire or

slightly notched, pink, claw long. Summer. Widespread and variable in E & Central N Amer. Z5.
S. coeli-rosa (L.) Godron. Glab. ann. to 50cm. Lvs linear-lanceolate. Infl. loose, fls long-stalked; cal. 1.5–2.5cm, deeply grooved with 5 long, spreading teeth; pet. limb 1–2cm, deeply notched, pink-purple with white 'eye'; coronal scales acute. Summer. Medit.; casual as an arable weed elsewhere in Eur. 'Blue Angel': fls clear blue with dark eye. 'Candida': fls white. 'Kermesina': fls red. 'Nana': dwarf. 'Oculata': fls light pink with purple eye. 'Rose Angel': fls bright rose with dark eye.
S. compacta Fisch. Differs from *S. armeria* in shorter st. and broader lvs, uppermost pair of st. lvs closely subtending ± capitate infl.; fls larger. Summer. SE Eur., SW Asia.
S. dioica (L.) Clairv. RED CAMPION. Perenn. with spreading leafy shoots and erect flowering st. to 80cm. Basal lvs obovate, long-stalked; st. lvs oblong-obovate, acute. Cal. in ♂ cylindric, 10-veined, in ♀ ovoid and 20-veined; pet. limb 8–10mm, broady obovate, deeply bifid, red; coronal scales narrow, acute. Spring and early summer. Eur. Hybridizes freely with the white-fld *S. latifolia*. 'Compacta': neat, low and dense. 'Flore Pleno' ('Rubra Plena'): fls double. 'Graham's Delight': tall, to 90cm; lvs striped cream. 'Minikin': compact; st. short; fls bright dusky pink. 'Richmond': fls deep rose pink. 'Rosea Plena': tall, to 60cm; fls double, large, dusky pink. 'Tresevern Gold': lvs variegated gold. 'Variegata': lvs striped white; fls pale pink. Z6.
S. elisabethae Jan. Tufted, hairy woody-based perenn. to 25cm. Basal lvs lanceolate, acute, thick, subglabrous. Fls often solitary; cal. 1.5–2cm, inflated; pet. with narrow projecting claw and deeply cut, white limb; coronal scales present. Summer. It. Alps, confined to limestone rocks and screes. Z7.
S. exscapa All. = *S. acaulis*.
S. fimbriata Sims. Hairy perenn. to 60cm with erect, leafy st. Lvs ovate-cordate, lower stalked, upper sessile. Pan. loose, few-fld; cal. 1.5–2cm, inflated; pet. with narrow projecting claw and deeply cut, white limb; coronal scales present. Summer. Cauc. Z6.
S. fruticosa L. Robust, ± glab., woody-based perenn. to 50cm. Lvs shiny, lanceolate to spathulate. Infl. few-fld, dense; fls erect, short-stalked; cal. *c*2.5cm, gland.; pet. limb pink or red, bifid, with conspicuous, acute coronal scales. Spring. Medit. Z9.
S. gallica L. var. *quinquevulnera* (L.) Mert. & Koch. Hairy ann. to 40cm; st. terminating in a long, leafy, raceme-like infl. of small fls, usually viscid. Basal lvs spathulate, stalked; st. lvs lanceolate, sessile. Cal. 7–10mm; pet. limb 3–5mm, entire or notched, pink with a deep crimson blotch; coronal scales present. Summer. Common arable weed in S & C Eur. Only the var., with the attractively-coloured fls, is worth cultivating.
S. hifacensis Willd. Like *S. fruticosa* but hairy. Infl. sometimes with several opposite, 3-fld, br. Cal. hairy, not gland. Spring. (Balearic Is.), S Spain. Z9.
S. hookeri Torr. & A. Gray. Tufted, grey-hairy prostrate perenn. Lvs oblanceolate, acute. Fls usually 3–7 in a condensed, leafy dichasium, sometimes solitary; cal. *c*2cm; pet. limb deeply bifid, each lobe usually cut, pink or purple with white rays; coronal scales linear. Early summer. Oreg., Calif. Z5.
S. ingramii Tidestr. & Dayton = *S. hookeri*.
S. keiskii Miq. Tufted, hairy perenn. to 15cm. Lvs lanceolate, subglabrous. Infl. few-fld; cal. *c*1cm; pet. limb *c*1cm, obovate, shallowly bifid, pink; coronal scales conspicuous, oblong. Late summer-autumn. N Jap. (mts). var. *minor* (Tak.) Ohwi & Ohashi: dwarf. Z6.
S. laciniata Cav. Differing from *S. californica* in linear to lanceolate (not ovate) lvs and the somewhat smaller, scarlet (not crimson) fls. Summer. Mex., Calif. Z7.
S. latifolia Poir. Ann. to short-lived perenn. to 80cm, usually softly hairy and gland. above. Lvs ovate or ovate-lanceolate, st. lvs sessile. Infl. a loose dichasium; fls opening in the evening and slightly scented; ♂ cal. 1.5–2cm, 1-veined, ♀ cal. 2–3cm, 20-veined, inflated; pet. white limb *c*1cm, obovate, deeply bifid; coronal scales bilobed, conspicuous. Summer. Throughout much of Eur. and W Asia, also in N Afr.; introd. in N Amer. See *S. dioica*. Z6.
S. longiscapa Kerner = *S. acaulis*.
S. maritima With. = *S. uniflora*.
S. mollissima L. pro parte. = *S. hifacensis*.
S. multifida (Adams) Rohrb., non Edgew. = *S. fimbriata*.
S. nutans L. Perenn. to 50cm; st. hairy below, glab. and viscid above. Basal lvs spathulate, long-stalked, pan. loose, one-sided with opposite 3- to 7-fld br.; fls drooping on short stalks, opening and fragrant in the evening; cal. *c*1cm, gland.; pet. white, often tinged green-yellow and pink, deeply bifid with narrow, inrolled lobes; coronal scales small. Summer. Most of Eur., also N Asia, N Afr. and Cauc. Z6.
S. pendula L. Glandular-hairy ann. with weak, branching, ascending st. to 20cm. Lvs ovate-lanceolate, acute, cyme loose, raceme-like; fls erect to spreading; cal. 1.2–1.8cm, inflated, with

wide colourless bands between prominent veins; pet. limb 7–10mm, bifid, usually pink. Summer. Medit. often nat. elsewhere. 'Compacta': dense, to 10cm high. 'Ruberrima': compact; fls deep pink. 'Ruberrima Bonnettii': st. glab., flushed purple; fls bright pink. 'Triumph': to 20cm; fls double, red.

S. pratensis (Raf.) Godron & Gren. = *S. latifolia*.

S. pumilio Wulf. = *Saponaria pumilio*.

S. quadridentata hort. = *S. alpestris*.

S. quadrifida hort. = *S. alpestris*.

S. schafta S. Gmel. ex Hohen. Mat-forming, hairy perenn. with ascending flowering st. to 25cm. Basal lvs linear-lanceolate, stalked; st. lvs lanceolate, sessile, dichasium few-fld; cal. 2–2.5cm, narrow; pet. limb *c*1cm, obovate, bifid, red-purple; coronal scales conspicuous. Late summer to autumn. Cauc. 'Deep Rose': fls rosy magenta. 'Shelly Pink': fls palest pink. 'Splendens': tall; fls rose pink.

S. uniflora Roth. Woody-based, ± glab., mat-forming perenn. Lvs lanceolate, fleshy, grey-green, ciliate. Flowering st. to 20cm, ascending, with 1–4 large fls; cal. 20-veined, inflated; pet. limb deeply bifid, usually white; coronal scales small. Summer. Coasts of Atlantic and Arc. Eur. 'Robin Whitebreast' ('Weisskehlehen'): large white double fls, split cal. and resemble a small carnation. 'Rosea': fls palest pink. 'Silver Lining': prostrate, to 20cm; lvs finely edged silver. Z3.

S. vallesia L. Mat-forming, glandular-hairy perenn. to 15cm. Lvs oblong-lanceolate. Fls solitary or in 2- to 3-fld infl.; cal. 2–2.5cm; pet. limb *c*1cm, bifid, usually pink tinged red; coronal scales small. Summer. W Alps, Apennines (ssp. *vallesia*). Z6.

S. virginica L. Glandular-hairy perenn. to 50cm, st. weak, viscid. Basal lvs ± spathulate; st. lvs lanceolate, sessile. Infl. loose, bracts leafy, fls few, long-stalked; cal. *c*2cm; pet. limb to 2cm, deeply bifid, toothed, dark red to crimson. Late summer and autumn. E N Amer. Z5.

S. vulgaris ssp. *maritima* (With.) A. & D. Löve = *S. uniflora*.

S. wherryi Small = *S. caroliniana*.

S. zawadzkii Herb. Tufted, hairy woody-based perenn. to 20cm. Basal lvs elliptic, acute, thick, ciliate with wavy hairs. Fls solitary or in few-fld infl.; cal. 1.5–1.7cm, hairy but not or scarcely gland.; pet. limb 1cm+, bifid, white. Summer. E Carpath. Z5.

→*Agrostemma, Eudianthe, Heliosperma, Lychnis, Melandrium* and *Otites*.

Silesian Willow *Salix silesiaca*.

Silk-cotton Tree *Bombax; Ceiba; Cochlospermum religiosum*.

Silkgrass *Oryzopsis hymenoides; Pityopsis graminifolia*.

Silk Oak *Grevillea robusta*.

Silk Tassel *Garrya*.

Silk Tree *Albizia julibrissin*.

Silk Vine *Periploca graeca*.

Silkweed *Asclepias*.

Silky Bent *Apera*.

Silky Camellia *Stewartia malacodendron*.

Silky Dogwood *Cornus obliqua*.

Silky Elm *Heritiera trifoliolata*.

Silky Net-bush *Calothamnus villosus*.

Silky Oak *Grevillea robusta*.

Silky-spike Melic *Melica ciliata*.

Silky-white Everlasting *Helipterum splendidum*.

Silky Wisteria *Wisteria venusta*.

Silphium L. ROSIN-WEED; PRAIRIE DOCK. Compositae. 23 coarse perenn. herbs. Cap. radiate, medium to large; receptacle flat, scaly; involucre hemispheric; ray flts ♀, yellow, rarely white; disc flts yellow. E N Amer.

S. albiflorum A. Gray. St. to 1m, simple, scabrous. Lvs linear to ovate, 1–2 pinnatifid, upper lvs 5–12cm, linear, lobes linear, coriaceous. Cap. to 7.5cm diam.; ray flts cream or white. Late spring–summer. Tex.

S. integrifolium Michx. St. 0.5–1.5m, finely tomentose to scabrous, or glab., sometimes glaucous. Lvs usually opposite, to 15cm, lanceolate to ovate or elliptic, sessile, dentate or entire, scabrous above, tomentose to glab. beneath. Cap. several, in a short, open or dense infl.; receptacle 1.3–2.5cm diam.; ray flts 15–35, yellow. Summer. E & C US. Z5.

S. lacinatum L. COMPASS-PLANT. St. 1.5–3m, hispid or hirsute, sometimes gland. Lvs alt., deeply 1–2-pinnatifid, basal lvs to 40cm, uppermost lvs to 10cm, hirsute beneath. Cap. several in a narrow racemose infl.; receptacle 2–3cm diam.; ray flts 15–30, yellow. Summer. C US. Z4.

S. perfoliatum L. CUP-PLANT. St. 1–2.5m, glab. or nearly so. Lvs to 30cm, connate-perfoliate, deltoid to ovate, coarsely dentate, scabrous above, scabrous or hispidulous beneath. Cap. several to many, in an open branched infl.; receptacle 1.5–2.5cm diam.; ray flts 20–30, yellow. Summer–early autumn. CE Canada to SE US. Z4.

S. terebinthinaceum Jacq. St. to 3m. Lvs mostly basal, to 4cm, long-petiolate, ovate, oblong or elliptic, usually cordate at base, sharply dentate to pinnatifid, glab. or scabrous. Cap. several to numerous, in an open corymb; receptacle 1.5–2.5cm diam.; ray flts 12–20, yellow. Summer. CE Canada to SE US. Z4.

S. trifoliatum L. St. 1–2m, glab., glaucous. Lvs usually in verticillate groups, to 20cm, lanceolate, subentire to irregularly dentate, base attenuate, usually scabrous above, hirsute beneath, petiole short. Cap. several numerous in an open to branched infl.; receptacle 0.7–1.7cm diam; ray flts 8–15, yellow. Summer–early autumn. S & E US. Z5.

Silverback Fern *Pityrogramma viscosa*.

Silverballs *Styrax*.

Silver Banksia *Banksia marginata*.

Silver Basswood *Polyscias elegans*.

Silver Beads *Crassula deltoidea*.

Silver Beard Grass *Bothriochloa saccharoides*.

Silver Beech *Nothofagus menziesii*.

Silverbell Tree *Halesia*.

Silver Berry *Elaeagnus angustifolia; E. commutata; Shepherdia argentea*.

Silver Birch *Betula pendula*.

Silver Buffaloberry *Shepherdia*.

Silverbush *Convolvulus cneorum; Sophora tomentosa*.

Silver Cassia *Senna phyllodinea*.

Silver Chain *Dendrochilum glumaceum*.

Silver Crown *Cacaliopsis nardosmia; Cotyledon undulata*.

Silver Dollar *Lunaria annua*.

Silver Dollar Cactus *Astrophytum asterias*.

Silver Dollar Gum *Eucalyptus polyanthemos*.

Silver Dollar Maidenhair Fern *Adiantum peruvianum*.

Silver Dollar Plant *Crassula arborescens*.

Silver Elkhorn Fern *Platycerium veitchii*.

Silver Fern *Pityrogramma calomelanos*.

Silver Fir *Abies* (*A. alba*).

Silver Fittonia *Fittonia verschaffeltii* var. *argyroneura*.

Silver-flowered Everlasting *Cephalipterum*.

Silver Gum *Eucalyptus cordata*.

Silver Hair Grass *Aira caryophyllea*.

Silver Heart *Peperomia marmorata*.

Silver Hedgehog Holly *Ilex aquifolium* 'Ferox Argentea'.

Silver Inch Plant *Tradescantia zebrina*.

Silver Jade Plant *Crassula arborescens*.

Silver King *Artemisia ludoviciana* var. *albula*.

Silver Lace *Tanacetum ptarmiciflorum*.

Silver Lace Vine *Polygonum; P. aubertii*.

Silver-leaf Oak *Quercus hypoleucoides*.

Silver-leaf Pepper *Peperomia griseo-argentea*.

Silver-leaved Mountain Gum *Eucalyptus pulverulenta*.

Silver-leaved Nettle *Solanum elaeagnifolium*.

Silver-leaved Nightshade *Solanum elaeagnifolium*.

Silver-leaved Poplar *Populus alba*.

Silver Lime *Tilia tomentosa*.

Silver Mallee *Eucalyptus crucis*.

Silver Mallet *Eucalyptus falcata*.

Silver Maple *Acer saccharinum*.

Silver-margined Holly *Ilex aquifolium* 'Argentea Marginata'.

Silver Morning Glory *Argyreia nervosa*.

Silver Nerve *Fittonia verschaffeltii* var. *argyroneura*.

Silver Net-leaf *Fittonia vershaffeltii* var. *argyroneura*.

Silver Net Plant *Fittonia verschaffeltii* var. *argyroneura*.

Silver Oak *Grevillea parallela*.

Silver Palm *Coccothrinax; C. argentata*.

Silver Peppermint *Eucalyptus tenuiramis*.

Silver Princess *Eucalyptus caesia*.

Silver Rod *Solidago bicolor*.

Silver Ruffles *Cotyledon undulata*.

Silver Sage *Salvia argentea*.

Silver Saw Palm *Acoelorraphe*.

Silver-seed Gourd *Cucurbita argyrosperma*.

Silver Speedwell *Veronica incana*.

Silver Star *Cryptanthus lacerdae*.

Silversword *Argyroxiphium*.

Silver Thatch *Coccothrinax fragrans*.

Silver Threads *Fittonia verschaffeltii* var. *argyroneura*.

Silvertop Ash *Eucalyptus sieberi*.

Silver-topped Gimlet *Eucalyptus campaspe*.

Silver Torch *Cleistocactus strausii*.

Silver Tree *Leucadendron argenteum*.

Silver Trumpet Tree *Tabebuia argentea*.

Silver Vase Plant *Aechmea fasciata*.

Silver Vine *Actinidia polygama*.

Silver Wattle *Acacia dealbata*.

Silverweed *Potentilla anserina*.

Silver Willow *Salix alba* var. *sericea*.

Silvery Cinquefoil *Potentilla argentea.*
Silvery Spleenwort *Athyrium pycnocarpon.*
Silvery Wormwood *Artemisia filifolia.*

Silybum Adans. Compositae. 2 robust ann. or bienn. herbs. St. erect, often simple. Lvs sinuately lobed or pinnatifid, white-veined or variegated, strongly spiny. Cap. discoid, solitary; involucre ovoid; outer phyllaries with an apical, setose-dentate appendage usually terminating in a spine; flts 5-fid, purple. Medit., Eur. and mts of E Afr. Z7.

S. eburneum Coss. & Dur. Like *S. marianum* but st. white or pale green, basal lvs hispid, st. lvs with yellow-brown spines 7–15mm, cap. to 6cm, peduncles with more, oblong-lanceolate bracts, phyllary spines to 7cm. Spring. NE & C Spain, NW Afr.

S. marianum (L.) Gaertn. BLESSED THISTLE; HOLY THISTLE; OUR LADY'S MILK THISTLE. St. to 1.5m, glab. or slightly arachnoid-pubesc. Lvs dark, glossy, marbled white, basal lvs 25–50×12–25cm, pinnatifid, obovate, petiolate, subglabrous, deeply triangular lobed, st. lvs smaller, less deeply dissected, auriculate-amplexicaul, with pale yellow spines to 8mm. Cap. 2.5–4cm diam.; peduncles ebracteate or with a few small bracts; spines 2–5cm. Spring–summer. Medit., SW Eur. to Afghan.

SIMAROUBACEAE DC. 22/170. *Ailanthus, Kirkia, Picrasma, Quassia.*

Simbuleta Forssk. = *Anarrhinum.*

Simethis Kunth. Liliaceae (Asphodelaceae). 1 rhizomatous fleshy-rooted perenn. herb. Lvs 15–60×2.5–7.5cm, mostly basal, linear, grass-like. Scape to 40cm; pan. term., bracteate; tep. 8–11mm, 6, free, white tinted purple, oblong, obtuse; fil. white, hairy, anth. yellow. Summer. W Medit., N Afr. Z7.

S. bicolor (Desf.) Kunth = *S. planifolia.*
S. planifolia (L.) Gren.

Simmondsia Nutt. Simmondsiaceae. 1 glab., multi-stemmed shrub to 2m; young br. grey-green, slender. Lvs to 4cm, coriaceous, ± thickened, oblong-ovate, opposite, green, yellow-green to blue-green, short-petioled to subsessile. Fls unisexual, axill., sep. 5–6, pet. 0; ♂ clustered, yellow, sep. to 5mm, ♀ solitary, pale green, sep. to 15mm. Capsule ovoid, 3-angled. SW US, N Mex. Z10.

S. californica (Link) Nutt. = *S. chinensis.*
S. chinensis (Link) C. Schneid. GOAT NUT; JOJOBA.
S. chrysophylla Hook. & Jackson = *S. chinensis.*
S. pabulosa Kellogg = *S. chinensis.*
→*Brocchia* and *Buxus.*

SIMMONDSIACEAE Tieghem. *Simmondsia.*

Simon Bamboo *Pleioblastus simonii.*

Simsia Pers. Compositae. *c*35 erect, branched, ann. to bienn. herbs. Lvs opposite, dentate to pinnatifid, petiolate. Cap. radiate or discoid, on elongate peduncles, in a loose pan.; flts usually yellow. Trop. and warm temp. Amer. Z9.

S. calva (A. Gray ex Engelm.) A. Gray. To 1m. Lvs to 7cm, deltoid-ovate to hastate, base broadly cuneate to cordate, serrate, scabrous to minutely hispid. Cap. radiate; ray flts *c*1cm. Tex. and adjacent Mex.
→*Encelia.*

Simul *Bombax ceiba.*

Sinacalia H. Robinson & Brettell. Compositae. 4 erect perenn. herbs. Lvs simple, ovate to subrotund, base cordate to sub-truncate; petioles somewhat expanded, amplexicaul. Cap. radiate, solitary to numerous in loose term. corymbs or pan.; ray flts oblong or linear-oblong, yellow; disc flts yellow. China.

S. tangutica (Maxim.) B. Nord. St. to 1m, robust, simple, brown-pubesc. above. Lvs to 16cm, ovate to truncate or almost cordate, pinnatisect, dark green, sparsely hispid above on veins, minutely pubesc. and sparsely arachnid beneath, lobes oblong, dentate. Cap. small, numerous, in a terminal, compound cluster; involucre cylindric; ray flts 2–3, 14mm; disc flts few. C China. Z5.

Sinapis L. Cruciferae. 10 ann. or perenn. herbs. Lvs pinnately cut to lobed, hairy. Fls small, 4-merous, yellow-white; sta. 6, free, silique linear to cylindrical, long-beaked. S Eur., N Afr., SW Asia.

S. alba L. WHITE MUSTARD. Ann., 20–60cm. St. erect, branching above. Lvs bright green, occas. spotted violet, pinnatifid to hyrate, term. lobe toothed. Rac. 35–50-fld; pet. 11–5mm. Fr. 20–45×2–4.5mm including beak, beak compressed, often

curved, seeds 1–8, paye yellow. Medit., C Asia, N Afr., nat. elsewhere in Eur. Z6.

S. alba L. = *Brassica hirta.*
S. arvensis L. CHARLOCK. Similar to *S. alba* except less leafy; beak of fr. only slightly compressed, often subulate; seeds red-brown or black. Medit., widely nat.; persistent ann. weed, esp. of farmland.
S. arvensis L. = *Brassica kaber.*
S. erucoides L. = *Diplotaxis erucoides.*
S. nigra L. = *Brassica nigra.*

Sinarundinaria Nak. Gramineae. 12+ clumping bamboos. Culms with white powder below nodes; br. many. Lvs tesellate. China, Himal.

S. anceps (Mitford) Chao & Renvoize = *Yushania anceps.*
S. falcata (Nees) Chao & Renvoize = *Drepanostachyum falcatum.*
S. falconeri (Hook. ex Munro) Chao & Renvoize = *Drepanostachyum falconeri.*
S. hookeriana (Munro) Chao & Renvoize = *Drepanostachyum hookerianum.*
S. maling (Gamble) Chao & Renvoize = *Yushania maling.*
S. murielae (Gamble) Nak. = *Thamnocalamus spathaceus.*
S. nitida (Mitford) Nak. FOUNTAIN BAMBOO. Culms 3–4m×4–8mm, with greyish powder at first, finally lined purple-brown, branchlets produced in 2nd yr., usually tinted purple, heavy and cascading; sheaths persistent, purple-green, pubesc. at first. Lvs 4–11×0.5–1.1cm, dark green, finely tapered, scarcely scaberulous, flickering in the breeze; stalks purple. C China. Z5.
→*Arundinaria* and *Fargesia.*

Sindaloa Hesper Palm *Brahea aculeata.*
Sind Oak *Quercus coccifera.*
Singapore Holly *Malpighia coccigera.*
Sing-kwa *Luffa acutangula.*
Single-leaf Pinyon *Pinus monophylla.*
Single-leaf Strawberry *Fragaria vesca* var. *monophylla.*
Singletary Pea *Lathyrus hirsutus.*

Sinningia Nees. Gesneriaceae. 40 perenn. herbs and shrubs. Tubers stout, depressed-globose, rarely lacking or an elongate rhiz. St. v. short with lvs basal, tufted, or ascending with lvs paired. Fls solitary or clustered in lf axils; cal. 5-partite; cor. campanulate to cylindric, limb broad, spreading, 2-lipped, lower lip 3-lobed, upper lip 2-lobed; lips often indistinct. Mex. to Arg. and Braz. Z10.

S. aggregata (Ker-Gawl.) Wiehler. To 60cm. Lvs to 12.5×6.2cm, opposite, ovate, glandular-pubesc. Fls solitary or in pairs; cor. tube to 2.5cm, horizontal, inflated dorsally below, red-orange, throat yellow-orange, spotted red, lobes 5, acute, equal. Braz.
S. allagophylla (Mart.) Wiehler. St. to 1m. Lvs in whorls of 3, elliptic, crenate. Fls solitary or in cymes of 2–3; cor. to 1.2cm, barely exceeding cal., bright red. Braz.
S. barbata (Nees & Mart.) Nichols. St. erect, to 60cm, marked red. Lvs to 15cm, oblong-lanceolate, tapering, dark green above, maroon beneath. Fls solitary or in pairs; cor. to 3cm, white-pubesc., inflated dorsally at base, lobes short. Braz.
S. bulbosa (Ker-Gawl.) Wiehler. St. erect, to 60cm. Lvs ovate-cordate, dentate, ± succulent. Fls bright red, in term. pan.; cor. tube narrow, opening toward throat, uppermost lobes exceeding others. Braz.
S. canescens (Mart.) Wiehler. St. to 25cm, tomentose. Lvs to 15×10cm, whorled, obovate, densely white-pubesc. Fls in cymes of 3–5 at each axil; cor. cylindric, pink to orange to red, hairy, to 3cm, obtuse, maroon-violet, brown-black-striate. Braz.
S. cardinalis (Lehm.) H.E. Moore. St. to 30cm. Lvs paired, to 15×11cm, ovate-cordate, densely short-pubesc. Fls solitary or several in cymes in axils of upper lvs; cor. to 5cm, bright red, pubesc. limb distinctly 2 lipped. Braz. Dwarf Hybrids: habit small; flts trumpet-shaped, plum, magenta, carmine, purple, lilac, bicolour. 'Feuerschein': fls pale tangerine-red to carmine. 'Innocence': habit compact; lvs bright green, pubesc.; fls snow white. 'Splendens': br. rambling; lvs heart-shaped, broad; fls bright scarlet-red.
S. carolinae (Wawra) Benth. & Hook. = *S. barbata.*
S. clayberghiana H.E. Moore = *S. sceptrum.*
S. concinna (Hook.) Nichols. Lvs to 6×2cm, ovate, crenate, red-veined, otherwise green, hairy above. Fls sparse, solitary; cor. trumpet-shaped, horizontal, lilac above, pale mauve to yellow-brown below, purple-spotted inside tube, limb spreading, upper 2 lobes deep purple; lower 3 lobes paler. Braz.
S. cooperi (Paxt.) Wiehler. Differs from *S. cardinalis* in cor. limb broadly spreading, heavily marked with purple at margin. Braz.
S. eumorpha H.E. Moore. St. pubesc. marked red. Lvs to 10×9.5cm, ovate-cordate, crenate, pubesc. petiolate. Fls solitary or few in cymes, on peduncles to 11cm; cor. to 3.5cm,

horizontal, curved, white or faintly flushed mauve, lobes to 1cm, throat with a purple-bordered, red-spotted yellow streak. Braz.

S. guttata Lindl. St. short, erect. Lvs closely set, oblong-lanceolate, pale green, crenate. Fls in uppermost lf axils; cor. tube white, widening to throat, lobes cream, spotted purple. Braz.

S. helleri Nees. St. fleshy, to 30cm. Lvs to 6cm, opposite, cordate-ovate, serrate, slightly pubesc.; cor. to 5cm, funnel-form, glandular-hairy, inflated between upper limb lobes, pale green-yellow tube purple-striate inside, lobes obtuse, unequal. Braz.

S. hirsuta (Lindl.) Nichols. Lvs to 15×10cm, broadly ovate, crinkled, finely pubesc. Fls many; cal. lobes to 0.5cm; cor. mauve outside, darker inside, white striped and red-maculate inside tube, tube to 1.2cm, limb broadly spreading. Braz.

S. incarnata (Aubl.) Denh. St. to 1.5cm. Lvs paired or in 3's, elliptic, to 12×4cm, crenate. Fls red or yellow, in term. infl.; cor. tubular, somewhat inflated, to 5cm, spurred. C Arg. to C Mex.

S. leucotricha (Hoehne) H.E. Moore = *S. canescens*.

S. macropoda (Sprague) H.E. Moore. St. to 60cm, striped red. Lvs paired, broadly ovate, to 20×15cm, crenuate, pubesc. Fls clustered at apex, axill. on red-spotted, gland. peduncles to 15cm; cor. tube to 3cm, gland. hairy, red; lower limb lip marked with purple spots or lines. Braz.

S. macrorrhiza (Dumort.) Wiehler. Similar to *S. cardinalis*. St. to 120cm. Lvs 10–15×8–13cm, ovate, in pairs. Fls bright red; lower limb lip red-purple spotted. Braz.

S. magnifica (Otto & Dietr.) Wiehler. Differs from *S. cardinalis* in fls held in a dense term. cluster above foliage. Braz.

S. ×pumila Clayb. (*S. pusilla* ×*S. eumorpha*.) Fls to 3cm, light mauve, shading to deep purple. Gdn origin.

S. pusilla (Mart.) Baill. St. v. short. Lvs ovate to suborbicular, to 1.2cm, short, hairy above, pale, hairy, red-veined beneath. Fls on hairy pedicels to 2.5cm; cor. to 2cm, lilac, spurred, lobes unequal, lined purple, throat white. Braz. 'White Sprite': dwarf; fls tubular, glistening snow-white.

S. regina Sprague = *S. speciosa*.

S. reitzii (Hoehne) Skog. St. to 1m. Lvs cordate, dark green above, red beneath, veins white. Fls clustered in axils; cor. horizontal, maroon, tubular, to 4.5cm; lobes marked dark purple. Braz.

S. richii Clayb. St. ascending, swollen, 5–15cm. Lvs to 20cm, opposite, oblong, pale green, lustrous. Fls 1 or 2 in each upper lf axil on peduncles to 8cm; cor. white with lined maroon, pubesc. Mex.

S. ×rosea (Moore & Wils.) H.E. Moore. (*S. eumorpha* ×*S. macropoda*.) As for *S. eumorpha* except pink fls borne in an axill. infl.

S. sceptrum (Mart.) Wiehler. St. to 1.5m, often marked purple. Lvs to 15×6cm, opposite or whorled, elliptic, crenate, pubesc., pale-pubesc. beneath. Fls in clusters near apex; cor. to 3cm, rose, pubesc., spurred, limb distinctly 2-lipped. Braz.

S. schiffneri Fritsch. Erect shrub to 1.5m, lacking tubers. Lvs to 15×7.5cm, lanceolate, dentate, pubesc. Fls solitary or 2–3 in axils; cor. funnel-shaped, to 2.5cm, cream, tube lined and spotted red inside. Braz.

S. sellovii (Mart.) Wiehler. St. erect, to 75cm. Lvs elliptic, paired. Fls in long term. spikes; cor. red, hairy, nodding, to 7cm, swollen at base, then constricted and inflated once more toward apex, lobes obtuse. SE Braz., Arg., Parag., E Boliv. Plants grown under this name maybe *S. sceptrum*.

S. speciosa (Lodd.) Hiern. FLORISTS' GLOXINIA; GLOXINIA. St. to 30cm. Lvs to 20×15cm, on short petioles, ovate to oblong, crenate, finely pubesc., green above, flushed with red below. Fls solitary or 2–3 or more in axils; cor. horizontal, to 4cm; somewhat compressed near base with a central, hairy ridge above, swollen dorsally, occas. erect and bell-shaped, purple, lavender, red or white. Braz. Fyfiana group. Fls large, campanulate, erect, white, through pink, yellow and orange, to red and violet, variously blotched and striped. 'Blanche de Meru': fls white, fringed pink; 'Boonwood Yellow Bird': lvs dark, acuminate, fls yellow; 'Chic': fls numerous, flame-red; 'Mont Blanc': fls pure white; 'Violacea': fls deep violet-blue. Maxima group. Fls large, nodding. 'Buell's Blue Slipper': lvs velvety, fls trumpet-shaped, curved, numerous; 'Buell's Queen Bee': fls lobed, white with a bright pink blotch on either side of throat; 'Kiss of Fire': fls erect, numerous, velvety with wavy lobes; 'Pink Slipper': lvs soft, light green, crenate; fls rose-pink with a dark centre and spotted throat.

S. sulcata (Rusby) Wiehler. Similar to *S. tubiflora*; lower part of st. with elliptic lvs, upper part with a term. infl. of nodding, yellow, tubular fls. Boliv.

S. tuberosa (Mart.) H.E. Moore. ± stemless. Lvs to 45×30cm, ovate or oblong, crenate, sparsely pubesc. Fls 1–6 in a rac. to

15cm; cor. cylindric, to 3.5cm, bright red, throat marked yellow. Braz.

S. tubiflora (Hook.) Fritsch. St. to 60cm+, pubesc. Lvs to 12.5×4cm, oblong-elliptic, crenate, sparsely pubesc. Fls in a term. cyme, scented; cor. white, tube cylindric, slightly curved toward apex, lobes spreading, to 1.2cm. Arg., Parag., Urug.

S. verticillata (Vell.) H.E. Moore. St. to 60cm, flushed red, downy. Lvs in a pseudowhorl of 2–6, to 19×10cm, cordate-ovate, acutely dentate; petiole to 7cm; reduced lvs in pseudo-whorls toward apex. Fls many in axils; cor. to 3.8cm, cylindric, red, marked with purple, lowermost lobe largest. Braz.

S. warscewiczii (Bouché & Hanst.) H.E. Moore = *S. incarnata*.

S. ×youngeana Marnock. (*S. speciosa* ×*S. velutina*.) Similar to *S. guttata* except cor. deep violet, lvs oblong, cordate at base, densely tomentose.

→*Achimenes*, *Besleria*, *Corytholoma*, *Gesneria*, *Paliavana* and *Rechsteineria*.

Sinobambusa Mak. ex Nak. Gramineae. 20 medium-sized bamboos. Rhiz. running. Culms terete, with v. long internodes; nodes prominent, hairy when young. Lvs tessellate, scaberulous. China, Vietnam. Z9.

S. tootsik (Sieb. ex Mak.) Mak. Culms 5–12m×2–6cm, glab.; sheaths unmarked, hairy, with prominent auricles and bristles. Lvs 8–20×1.3–3cm, sometimes pubesc. beneath; sheaths hairless with auricles and bristles. China. f. *albostriata* Muroi. Lvs striped white or yellow.

Sinocalamus McClure.
S. giganteus (Munro) Keng f. = *Dendrocalamus giganteus*.
S. oldhamii (Munro) McClure = *Bambusa oldhamii*.

Sinocalycanthus Cheng & Chang.
S. chinensis Cheng & Cheng = *Calycanthus chinensis*.

Sinocrassula A. Berger. Crassulaceae. 5 ann., bienn. or perenn. herbs. Lvs forming low dense rosettes, linear to broad-lanceolate or suborbicular, mucronate, thick and rounded or convex beneath. Infl. corymbose or paniculate; sep. 5; cor. urceolate, pet. 5, sta. 5 in 1 whorl. Summer. Himal., W China. Z9.

S. indica (Decne.) A. Berger. Glab. herb. Lvs 35–60×10–15mm, somewhat broader near tip, or gradually narrowing, occas. sub-orbicular, blotched red or red-brown. Infl. to 45cm; fls white stippled red. India, W China, Yunnan.

S. yunnanensis (Franch.) A. Berger. Glab. herb. Lvs 12.5–25×4.5–6mm, 50–70, rounded above, more so beneath, gradually narrowing to short point, deep blue-green, covered in short white hairs. Yunnan.

→*Crassula* and *Sedum*.

Sinofranchetia (Diels) Henry. Lardizabalaceae. 1 fast-growing, decid. twining shrub to 10m, glab. Lfts 3, to 14cm, stalked, ovate, entire, papery, dark green above, blue-green beneath, central leaflet larger, rhombic-obovate, short-acuminate. Rac. pendulous 10–30cm; fls white, to 8mm across; sep. 6; nectaries 6; ♂ with 6 free sta., ♀ with 3 carpels. Berry globose, 1.5–2cm, in threes, lavender-purple. Summer. C & W China. Z6.

S. chinensis (Franch.) Hemsl.

Sinoga S.T. Blake = *Asteromyrtus*.

Sinojackia Hu. Styracaceae. 2 decid. trees, to 6m. Lvs serrulate, elliptic to elliptic-obovate. Fls to 2.5cm diam., white in lat. leafy rac.; pedicels slender; cal. turbinate with 5–7 lobes; pet. 5–7, elliptic-oblong, cohering at base; sta. 10–14, stellate-pilose. E China. Z7.

S. rehderiana Hu. To 5m. Lvs 2–9cm, acuminate, cuneate to rounded or subcordate at base, minutely serrate, sparsely pubesc. on veins. Pet. 5–6. E China.

S. xylocarpa Hu. To 6m. Lvs 3–7cm, short-acuminate, cordate to rounded at base, denticulate, glab. above except midrib, stellate beneath. Pet. 6–7. E China.

Sinowilsonia Hemsl. Hamamelidaceae. 1 decid. shrub or small tree to 6m. Shoots stellate-pubescent. Lvs to 18×11cm, alt., stellate-pubescent, broadly ovate, base almost cordate, tips acuminate, bristle-toothed; petioles short. Fls apetalous, in drooping, term. rac.; ♂ to 5cm, catkin-like, appearing before lvs; sep. 5; sta. 5; ♀ 2–3cm, lengthening to 15cm at fruiting, floral tube urceolate, sep. spathulate, staminodes 5. Capsule 2cm, ovoid, woody, 2-valved. Late spring. C China. Z6.

S. henryi Hemsl.

Siphonanthus L.
S. indica L. = *Clerodendrum indicum*.

Siphonia Rich.
S. brasiliensis Willd. ex A. Juss. = *Hevea brasiliensis*.

Siphonochilus J.M. Wood & Franks. Zingiberaceae. 7 perenn. rhizomatous herbs, often tuberous. Lvs oblong-lanceolate to elliptic, bases sheathing, forming a pseudostem. Infl. lat., scapose, distinct from leafy shoots; fls subtended by a single bract; bracteoles 0; cal. lobes 3; cor. tubular, pet. 3; lip 3-lobed, central lobe divided; fertile sta. 1. Trop., S & E Afr. Z10.
S. aethiopicus (Schweinf.) B.L. Burtt. Lvs oblong-lanceolate to lanceolate. Infl. 4–12-fld, scape to 2cm; cor. tube to 5.5cm, white, pet. linear; lip 5–11.5cm, rose-purple to purple with a yellow basal blotch. Trop. Afr.
S. brachystemon (Schum.) B.L. Burtt. Lvs lanceolate-, acuminate. Infl. 5–12-fld; scape to 4cm; cor. tube 4.5–10cm, pet. 2–4cm, blue; lip 3–5cm, pale blue. E Afr.
S. decorus DWARF GINGER LILY. Lvs lanceolate, glossy dark green above, grey beneath. Fls v. fragrant, funnel-shaped, bright yellow. Moz.
S. kirkii (Hook. f.) B.L. Burtt. Lvs oblong to elliptic. Infl. 7–20-fld; scape to 35cm; fls fragrant; pet. to 2.6cm, white; lip 3cm, pale rose-purple, spotted yellow at base. Trop. S & E Afr.
S. natalensis Wood & Franks = *S. aethiopicus*.
→*Kaempferia*.

Siphonostelma Schltr.
S. stenophyllum Schltr. = *Brachystelma stenophyllum*.

Siris Tree *Albizia lebbeck*.
Sisal *Agave sisalana*.
Siskiyou-lily *Fritillaria glauca*.
Siskiyou-mat *Ceanothus pumilus*.
Siskiyou Penstemon *Penstemon anguineus*.
Sissoo *Dalbergia sissoo*.

Sisymbrium L. Cruciferae. 80 ann., bienn. or perenn. herbs. Lvs entire to pinnate. Fls 4-merous, racemose; sta. free. Silique slender, straight to curved. Eurasia, Medit., S Afr., Americas. Z6.
S. barbarea (L.) Crantz = *Barbarea vulgaris*.
S. luteum (Maxim.) Schultz. Perenn., 80–120cm. Lower lv spetiolate, pinnate, seg. in 1–3 pairs, pet. 12–13mm, yellow. Fr. to 10cm, narrow-linear. Late spring. Jap., Korea, Manch.
S. nasturtium-aquaticum L. = *Nasturtium officinale*.
S. tanacetifolium L. = *Hugueninia tanacetifolia*.
→*Hesperis*.

Sisyranthus E. Mey.
S. schizoglossoides Schltr. = *Brachystelma schizoglossoides*.

Sisyrinchium L. Iridaceae. *c*90 usually perenn. rhizomatous herbs. Lvs linear to sword-shaped, distichous, mostly basal forming a fan. St. usually flattened and winged, often branched, with lvs. Infl. composed of 2–8-fld clusters enclosed by a pair of bracts, fls regular, short-lived, stellate or cup-shaped; perianth tube v. short; tep. 6, free; style with 3 undivided br. Americas, widely nat. elsewhere.
S. alatum Hook. = *S. vaginatum*.
S. albidum Raf. St. 15–50cm, flattened, winged; lvs narrowly linear, fls pale violet-blue or almost white with a yellow centre; tep. 6–11mm, apiculate. S E N Amer. Z4.
S. anceps Cav. = *S. angustifolium*.
S. angustifolium Mill. BLUE-EYED GRASS. St. 15–45cm, flattened, narrowly winged. Lvs narrowly linear, fls blue, yellow in centre; tep. spreading, 7mm obovate, mucronate. Summer. SE US; nat. Europe. Z3.
S. atlanticum E. Bickn. St. 10–70cm, branched, narrowly winged. Lvs narrowly linear, glaucous. Fls violet-blue with a yellow centre; tep. 8–12mm, apiculate. E N Amer. Z6.
S. bellum S. Wats. CALIFORNIAN BLUE-EYED GRASS. St. 10–50cm, branched, narrowly winged. Lvs narrowly linear; fls violet-blue veined purple; tep. 10–17mm, apiculate. Calif. Z8.
S. bermudianum L. BLUE-EYED GRASS. St. 15–45cm, flattened, narrowly winged. Lvs narrowly linear. Fls starry; blue, yellow in centre; tep. 7mm, emarginate, mucronate. Summer. W Indies. Z8.
S. birameum Piper = *S. idahoense*.
S. bogotense Kunth = *S. tinctorium*.
S. boreale (C. Bickn.) J. Henry = *S. californicum*.
S. brachypus (C. Bickn.) J. Henry = *S. californicum*.
S. californicum Ait. f. St. to *c*40cm, broadly winged, lvs grey-green, sword-shaped, starry, bright yellow, tep. 6–18mm. Late spring–summer. W US, nat. Ireland. Z8.
S. campestre E. Bickn. St. to 50cm, often shorter, flattened, narrowly winged, glaucous. Lvs narrow. Fls pale blue to white with a yellow centre; tep. 8–10mm, apiculate. C US. Z5.

S. chilense Hook. St. 15–30cm. Lvs linear. Fls purple, yellow in centre; tep. *c*13mm. Summer. Mex. to S S Amer., nat. in Maur. Z9.
S. convolutum Nocca. To 30cm. St. winged, usually branched. Lvs narrow, curved. Fls yellow veined brown; tep. to 15mm. C Amer. Z9.
S. cuspidatum Poepp. St. 30–60cm. Lvs linear. Infl. spicate, with many-fld clusters; fls yellow, *c*20mm diam. Chile. Z9.
S. cyaneum Lindl. = *Orthrosanthus multiflorus*.
S. douglasii A. Dietr. = *Olsynium douglasii*.
S. eastwoodiae E. Bickn. = *S. bellum*.
S. ensigerum E. Bickn. St. 15–35cm, winged, branched. Lvs narrowly linear or sword-shaped, fls pale blue-violet, *c*20mm diam.; tep. 10–15mm, apiculate. Okl. to Tex. and Mex. Z6.
S. filifolium Gaudich. = *Olsynium filifolium*.
S. graminoides E. Bickn. = *S. angustifolium*.
S. grandiflorum Douglas = *Olsynium douglasii*.
S. idahoense C. Bickn. St. to 50cm, winged, usually unbranched, glaucous. Lvs linear. Fls light to dark violet-blue, yellow in centre; tep. 8–20mm, apiculate. W US and SW Canada. 'Album': fls white. Z3.
S. inflatum (Suksd.) St. John = *Olsynium douglasii*.
S. iridifolium HBK = *S. micranthum*.
S. iridoides Curtis = *S. angustifolium*.
S. laxum Otto. Ann. to *c*20cm. Fls blue or white; tep. about 10mm. Temp. S Amer.
S. littorale Greene. St. to *c*50cm tall, winged sometimes branched. Lvs linear. Fls violet-blue, yellow in centre; tep. 11–20mm, apiculate. Alask. to Washington. Z2.
S. lutescens Lodd. = *S. striatum*.
S. macrocephalum Graham. St. robust to *c*1m, somewhat winged. Lvs to 1cm diam. Infl. usually branched; fls yellow, tep. about 10mm. Urug., E Braz., Boliv., N Arg. Z8.
S. micranthum Cav. Ann., 5–25cm, branched at base. St. flattened, narrowly winged. Fls blue or white, yellow at base of tep., with red-purple eye; tep. *c*6mm. Capsule small, *c*3mm, globose. C Amer. to NW Arg., nat. Aus.
S. montanum E. Greene. St. to *c*50cm, pale green, narrowly winged. Lvs narrowly linear. Fls starry, bright violet-blue, yellow in centre tep. 9–15mm, apiculate. Summer. E N Amer., widely nat. in Eur. Z6.
S. mucronatum Michx. St. slender, dark green, to *c*40cm, v. narrowly winged. Lvs narrowly linear. Fls violet-blue, rarely white with yellow centre; tep. 8–10mm, apiculate. E N Amer. 'Album': fls white. Z5.
S. pachyrhizum Bak. Roots fleshy. St. 30–60cm high, flattened, winged, much branched, leafy. Lvs linear, fls yellow; tep. 6mm. Braz., Parag., Arg. Z9.
S. palmifolium L. Infl. sessile, crowded at apex of st.; fls yellow. Z9.
S. pedunculatum Hook. = *Solenomelus pedunculatus*.
S. sarmentosum Suksd. St. 15–30cm, v. slender. Lvs to 3mm wide. Fls pale blue with a yellow centre; tep. 6–11mm, apiculate. Washington. Z7.
S. striatum Sm. St. 40–80cm, narrowly winged. Lvs lanceolate; fls somewhat cup-shaped, cream or pale yellow, veined purple-brown, in dense clusters on slender spikes; tep. to 15mm. Late summer. Arg., Chile. 'Aunt May' ('Variegatum'): to 60cm; lvs narrow, green tinged grey, striped cream; fls pale yellow striped purple, trumpet-shaped, in slender spikes. Z8.
S. tenuifolium Kunth. Slender or robust, branched or unbranched; roots tuberous, lvs linear. Fls yellow, starry; tep. *c*15mm, acute. C Amer. Z8.
S. tinctorium Kunth. St. to 5cm tall, slender, unbranched, often broadly winged. Lvs narrow; fls pale yellow, somewhat bell-shaped. S Mex. to Colomb. and Venez. Z8.
S. vaginatum Spreng. St. 30–50cm, winged, leafy, much branched, forming dense tufts. Fls yellow, tep. to 10mm. Braz., Boliv., S to Urug. and Parag. Z8.
S. cvs. 'Biscutella': to 35cm; lvs grass-like; fls yellow stained and veined dusky purple. 'E.K. Balls' ('Ball's Mauve'): lvs in fan-shaped sprays; fls mauve. 'Mrs Spivey': fls pure white, abundant. 'Pole Star' ('North Star'): to 15cm; fls white; long-flowering. 'Quaint and Queer': habit small, vigorous; fls centred yellow, outer tep. dull purple.

Sitka Alder *Alnus sinuata*.
Sitka Spruce *Picea sitchensis*.

Sitolobium Desv.
S. rubiginosum (Kaulf.) J. Sm. = *Dennstaedtia cicutaria*.

Sium L. Umbelliferae. 10 slender tap-rooted glab. perennials of wet places; st. spreading, striate, branching and rooting. Lvs often heteromorphic according to season, pinnate. Umbels compound; involucral bracts often reflexed; involucels narrow;

cal. teeth small; fls small white. N Hemis.

S. cicutifolium Schrank = *S. suave*.

S. latifolium L. GREATER WATER PARSNIP. Perenn. to 2m, st. hollow, grooved. Submerged lvs 2–3-pinnate (in spring); aerial lvs pinnate; lfts to 10×3cm, 3–6 pairs, ovate to lanceolate, serrate; upper lvs with sheathing petioles. Umbels to 8cm diam., 20–30-rayed; bracts 2–6; 3–6. Summer. Eur. Z6.

S. sisarum L. SKIRRET. Perenn. to 1m; st. striate, resembling *S. latifolium*. Lvs all aerial, pinnate; lfts 3–9cm, lanceolate, serrate. Umbels *c*20. Summer. Eur. to E Asia. var. *sisarum*. Roots tuberous. Origin unknown. Z6.

S. suave Walter. WATER PARSNIP. To 120cm, stout. Lvs 6–25cm, pinnate, rarely, simple; lfts linear to lanceolate, 3–8cm, serrate to incised. Umbels 5–15-rayed, to 6cm diam.; bracts 5–10; bracteoles 4–8. Summer. N US, Asia. Z4.

Skeleton Fork Fern *Psilotum nudum*.

Skimmia Thunb. Rutaceae. 4 aromatic dioecious or hermaphrodite everg. shrubs or small trees. Lvs ± clustered, alt., simple, obovate to oblanceolate, elliptic, base often cuneate, chartaceous to coriaceous, dark green above paler beneath, gland dotted; petiole to 3cm. Infl. a terminal paniculate thyrse, globose to pyramidal; sep. 1–2mm, 4–5, rarely 7, ovate to orbicular; pet. 3–7mm, 4–5, rarely 7, oblong-elliptic to oblong-lanceolate, off-white to yellow; sta. inserted around a green disc. Drupes red or black, globose, fleshy. Himal. through E & SE Asia.

S. anquetilia N.P. Tayl. & Airy Shaw. Creeping or erect shrub, 30cm–2m, strongly aromatic. Lvs to 18cm, elongate-oblanceolate to oblong-elliptic entire, apex rounded or gradually acuminate, leathery, often pale green or yellow-green. Infl. compact, globose 5cm diam., fls 5-merous; pet. erect, green-yellow to yellow, unpleasantly scented. Fr. to 20 orange or red. Afghan., Pak., India, Nepal. Z7.

S. arborescens Gamble. Shrub or tree, 3–15m, never suckering. Lvs in dense distal clusters, to 21cm, obovate, oblong-elliptic to oblanceolate, caudate, thin, papery to leathery. ♂ infl. slender with 0–4 sub-basal br., ♀ infl. globose to ovoid, to 10-fld; fls 5-merous, scented, white, green or yellow. Fr. *c*50 black. Nepal, India, Bhutan, China, SE Asia. Z7.

S. ×confusa N.P. Tayl. (*S. anquetilia* ×*S. japonica*.) Spreading shrub, 0.5–3m, strongly aromatic. Lvs 7–15cm, oblanceolate to narrowly elliptical, entire, apex acute to acuminate, leathery. Infl. to 15cm, pyramidal, much-branched; fls sweetly scented, ♂ 5-merous, creamy white, not fully expanded, ♀ 4–5-merous, fully expanded, white. Fr. up to 50 usually sterile, red. Gdn origin. 'Kew Green': fls all ♂, creamy-yellow. 'Isabella': fls ♀, white, berries red. Z7.

S. foremanii hort. = *S. japonica* 'Veitchii'.

S. fragrans Carr. = *S. japonica* ssp. *japonica*.

S. japonica Thunb. Erect or low shrub, 0.5–7m, weakly aromatic. Lvs oblanceolate-obovate to elliptic, entire to obscurely crenate, apex rounded, acute or acuminate, dark to yellow-green, leathery. ♂ infl. well developed, ♀ and hermaphrodite 1–5-fld; fls 4–5-merous, v. sweetly scented white, sometimes flushed pink or red. Fr. 1 to many red. Jap., China. ssp. *japonica*. Low-suckering shrub, 0.5–3(–5)m. Lvs oblanceolate-obovate or oblong. Fls usually 4-merous. var. *intermedia* Komatsu. Creeping, low and densely branched, 50–100cm. Kuril Is., Sakhalin & Jap. ssp. *reevesiana* (Fort.) N.P. Tayl. & Airy Shaw. Erect, low shrub or small tree, 1–7m. Lvs elliptic-obovate to elliptic oblanceolate. Fls 5-merous. China & E Asia. 'Bowles Dwarf Male': dwarf, to 30cm; lvs wide, tinted red in winter; fls abundant. 'Bronze Knight': habit open, tall; lvs long tinted red in winter; fls red in bud; ♂. 'Cecilia Brown': habit open, slender and tall; lvs long; fr. soft red, in large clusters below lvs. 'Dunwood': wide-growing, to 60×120cm; lvs light green. 'Fortunei': habit angular, slow-growing; fr. abundant. 'Fragrans': tall, dense; lvs short; fls in large heads. 'Fructo Alba' ('Alba'): low and compact; lvs small; fr. creamy white; ♀. 'George Gardner': to 1m; lvs broad, bright green; fls prominent; strong growing. 'Helen Goodal': mushroom-form, flat-topped; brs ascending, spreading; lvs deep green, chlorotic in full sun; fr. small, dark glossy red; ♀, independent primary hybrid. 'Nana Femina' ('Rogersii', 'Rogersii Femina'): habit stiff, dense, mound-forming; lvs large, broad, thick, twisted, deep green; fls in large, round heads; fr. abundant; ♀. 'Nana Mascula' ('Rogersii Nana', 'Rogersii Mascula'): as 'Nana Femina', but more erect, smaller, slow-growing; lvs small, less twisted; fls white, in dense heads. 'Nymans': dome-forming; br. slender; lvs oblanceolate; fr. large, abundant. 'Red': tall, upright; lvs wide; fr. large, non-depressed, abundant. 'Rockyfield Green': small, to 80cm; fls abundant. 'Rubella': lvs bright red in winter, eesp. upper lvs; fls red in bud; pan. loose; ♂. 'Ruby Dome': dense and compact; lvs small, flushed red in winter; fls in large, rounded clusters; ♂. 'Snow Dwarf': dwarf, decumbent; lvs small, dark green, chlorotic in full sun; fls pure white; ♂. 'Veitchii' ('Foremanii', 'Fischeri'): lvs wide, tinted yellow; fr. orange, abundant. 'Winifred Crook': habit dense, wide and procumbent when mature; ♀. Z7.

S. laureola (DC.) Sieb. & Zucc. Low, creeping shrub or erect tree, 0.5–13m, strongly aromatic. Lvs oblanceolate to narrowly elliptic, entire, v. dark green, apex acute, acuminate or cuspidate, leathery. Infl. globose to pyramidal, branched at base; fls 5-merous, sweetly scented, creamy or green-white. Fr. 5–50, black. Nepal, Burm., China. 'Fragrant Cloud': dwarf, wide-spreading, to 45cm; lvs more pointed, bright green, aromatic; fls abundant. 'Kew Green': habit low, horizontal, compact. ssp. *laureola*. Creeping shrub to 1m. Lvs to 10×3.5cm; petiole to 8mm. Fr. with up to 15 drupes. ssp. *multinervia* (C.C. Huang) N.P. Tayl. & Airy Shaw. Erect shrub or small tree, 1–13m. Lvs to 24×6cm; petiole to 3cm. Fr. usually more than 15 drupes. Nepal, India, Burm., China, Vietnam. Z7.

S. melanocarpa Rehd. & Wils. = *S. laureola* ssp. *laureola*.

S. oblata Hoare = *S. japonica* ssp. *japonica*.

S. repens Nak. = *S. japonica* var. *intermedia*.

S. rogersii hort. = *S. japonica* 'Nana Femina'.

Skinner Maple *Acer saccharinum* f. *laciniatum*.
Skirret *Sium sisarum*.
Skullcap *Scutellaria*.
Skunk Bush *Garrya fremontii*; *Rhus trilobata*.
Skunk Cabbage *Lysichiton*; *Symplocarpus*.
Skunk Currant *Ribes glandulosum*.
Skunk Grape *Vitis labrusca*.
Skunkleaf Jacob's Ladder *Polemonium delicatum*.
Sky Flower *Duranta erecta*; *Thunbergia grandiflora*.
Sky Pilot *Polemonium*.
Sky Plant *Tillandsia ionantha*.
Skyrocket *Ipomopsis aggregata*.
Sky Vine *Thunbergia grandiflora*.
Slash Pine *Pinus elliottii*.
Sleepy Daisy *Xanthisma texana*.
Sleepy Mallow *Malvaviscus arboreus*.
Slender Banksia *Banksia attenuata*.
Slender Beard-tongue *Penstemon gracilis*.
Slender Bird's Foot Trefoil *Lotus angustissimus*.
Slender Boronia *Boronia filifolia*.
Slender Cliff-brake *Cryptogramma stelleri*.
Slender False Brome *Brachypodium sylvaticum*.
Slender Lady Palm *Rhapis humilis*.
Slender Smokebush *Conospermum huegelii*.
Slender Spike Rush *Eleocharis acicularis*.
Slender-tufted Sedge *Carex acuta*.
Slender Wattle *Acacia elongata*.
Slender Weathgrass *Elymus trachycaulos*.
Slender Wild Oats *Avena barbata*.
Slimstem Lily *Lilium callosum*.
Slipper Flower *Calceolaria*.
Slipper Orchid *Cypripedium*; *Paphiopedilum*; *Phragmipedium*.
Slipper Spurge *Pedilanthus*.
Slipperwort *Calceolaria*.
Slippery Elm *Ulmus rubra*.

Sloanea L. Elaeocarpaceae. 100 everg. or decid. trees. Lvs simple, entire or toothed. Fls in axill. or term. rac., pan. or clusters, rarely solitary; sep. 4 or 5; pet. usually 0; sta. numerous, capsule valved, prickly. Madag., Trop. Asia to Aus. and Amer. Z10.

S. hemsleyana (Itô) Rehd. & Wils. Tree to 18m. Lvs 12–25cm, oblong-lanceolate, apex finely acuminate, base broadly cuneate or rounded, thin-textured. Fls white, fragrant, in crowded term. corymbs. Fr. globose, olive to yellow, ripening maroon, prickly; seeds glossy black, aril red. W China.

S. sterculiacea (Benth.) Rehd. & Wils. Tree to 15m. Lvs 20–25cm, serrulate, glab. above, finely downy beneath, with prominent veins. Fls white. Fr. to 9cm diam,. including prickles. Sikkim, Bhutan, Yunnan.

→*Echinocarpus*.

Sloe *Prunus alleghaniensis*; *P. spinosa*; *P. umbellata*.
Slough Grass *Spartina pectinata*.
Small Alpine Lovage *Ligusticum mutellinoides*.
Small Cluster Blueberry *Vaccinium tenellum*.
Small Cranberry *Vaccinium oxycoccos*.
Small-flowered Penstemon *Penstemon procerus*.
Small-fruited Hickory *Carya glabra*.
Small Knobwood *Zanthoxylum capense*.
Small-leaved Box *Buxus microphylla*.
Small-leaved Elm *Ulmus alata*.

Small-leaved Huckleberry *Vaccinium scoparium.*
Small-leaved Lime *Tilia cordata.*
Small-leaved Moreton Bay Fig *Ficus obliqua.*
Small-leaved Rubber Plant *Ficus benjamina.*
Small Rasp-fern *Doodia caudata.*
Small Rata Vine *Metrosideros diffusus.*
Small Shell Ginger *Alpinia mutica.*
Small White Paper Daisy *Helipterum corymbiflorum.*
Small Yellow Onion *Allium flavum.*
Smartweed *Polygonum.*

Smelowskia C.A. Mey. Cruciferae. 6 tuft-forming perenn. herbs. Lvs simple, pinnatisect or pinnate. Fls 4-merous, racemose; pet. spathulate; sta. 6, 4 long, 2 short. Arc. regions of NW Amer., E Asia.

S. calycina (Stephan) C.A. Mey. Rootstock covered with old lf bases. St. simple, several to many. Lvs usually pinnatifid, seg. triangular-oblong, canescent. Pet. 5–7mm, white. Alask., E Asia. Z2.

S. ovalis M.E. Jones. Similar to *S. calycina* except loosely tufted. Lf seg. obovate, 1–8mm, petiole not ciliate. Pet. white tinted lavender or cream. Washington, Oreg. (Cascade range). Z5.

SMILACACEAE Vent. See LILIACEAE.

Smilacina Desf. FALSE SOLOMON'S SEAL; SOLOMON'S FEATHERS; SOLOMON'S PLUME. Liliaceae (Convallariaceae). 25 perenn. herbs. Rhiz. creeping. St. simple, erect, leafy. Lvs alt., sessile or v. short-stalked, ovate or lanceolate. Fls small, in a term. rac. or pan.; tep. 6, free. Fr. berry. N Amer., C Amer., Asia.

S. amplexicaulis Nutt. = *S. racemosa.*

S. japonica A. Gray. Like *S. racemosa* but lower lvs with petioles 1–1.5cm and fls with longer densely hairy stalks (i.e. 2–5mm). Late spring–summer. Jap., China, Korea. Z6.

S. oleracea (Bak.) Hook. Like *S. racemosa* but tep. 0.5–0.7cm, white, pink or purple-red; sta. shorter than tep.; fr. rose-purple with darker spots. Summer. Himal., N Burm. Z6.

S. paniculata Martens & Gal. St. 60–100cm, glab. Lvs to 13cm, narrowly ovate-lanceolate, slender-acuminate, conspicuously veined, short-stalked, glab. Pan. broad-based, lacy to 15cm; tep. 3–4mm, ivory, white or green-white faintly flushed rose. Fr. green at first, spotted purple, later red. Spring. S Mex. to Panama. Z9.

S. racemosa (L.) Desf. FALSE SPIKENARD; SOLOMON'S ZIGZAG; TREACLEBERRY. St. to 90cm, downy. Lvs to 15×7.5cm, oblong-lanceolate or elliptic to narrowly ovate, acuminate, clasping on (lower lvs) with petioles 1–4mm, finely pubesc. beneath. Pan. to 15cm, many-fld, oblong to deltoid, br. ascending; tep. 1–3mm, white, sometimes tinged green; sta. longer than tep. Fr. green to red, sometimes mottled red or purple. Summer. N Amer., Mex. var. *amplexicaulis* (Nutt.) S. Wats. FAT SOLOMON. Lvs ovate, clasping, usually sessile. Z4.

S. sessilifolia (Bak.) S. Wats. = *S. stellata.*

S. stellata (L.) Desf. STAR-FLOWERED LILY OF THE VALLEY; STAR-FLOWER. St. 20–60cm, downy. Lvs to 15×5cm, lanceolate to oblong-lanceolate, apex acuminate, base sessile, amplexicaul, glaucous and minutely pubesc. or scurfy beneath. Rac. 6–20-fld, short-stalked, crowded; tep. 3–6mm, white or white-green. Fr. green at first, striped blue-black, later dark red or dark blue. Summer. N Amer., Mex. Z3.

Smilax L. Liliaceae (Smilacaceae). *c*200 dioecious, perenn., everg. or decid., vines. St. somewhat woody, branched, spiny, prickly or bristly. Lvs alt., the lower reduced to scales, prominently veined, simple, papery to leathery, stipules basal, usually terminated by a curling tendril. Fls small, lat., solitary or in small axill. umbels or rac.; tep. 6, free. Fr. a berry. Trop., temp. Asia, US.

S. argyrea Lind. & Rodigas St. climbing, wiry with short, rigid spines. Lvs to 25cm, bright green with white or pale green spots, acute or acuminate, 3-veined, short-stalked. Peru, Boliv. Z9.

S. aspera L. Everg. to 15m; st. zigzag, angled, spiny. Lvs 4–11cm, narrowly to broadly lanceolate, triangular, ovate, oblong or kidney-shaped, base cordate, 5–9-veined, shiny with margins and main veins prickly; petiole usually spiny. Fls pale-green, fragrant, in rac. Fr. black or red, to 6mm. Canary Is., S Eur. to Ethiop. and India. Z9.

S. china DC. Decid. to 5m, st. sparsely prickly or unarmed. Lvs to 8cm, broadly ovate to orbicular, apex abruptly acuminate, base ± cordate, leathery or papery, 5–7-veined. Fls yellow-green, in umbels. Fr. red, to 9mm diam. Korea, Jap. Z6.

S. discotis Warb. Decid. to 7.2m; st. angled, with hooked spines. Lvs 4–10cm, ovate, apex acute to obtuse, base cordate, glaucous beneath, 3–5-veined. Fls green-yellow in umbels. Fr. blue-black. China. Z9.

S. excelsa L. Decid. to 20m; st. terete with slightly raised lines, spines straight. Lvs 5–13cm, broadly ovate to orbicular, apex acuminate, base cordate or truncate, thinly textured or slightly leathery, margins rough or serrulate, 5–7-veined. Fls green, in umbels. Fr. red, 8–10mm. E Bulg. to Russia. Z6.

S. glauca Walter. Decid. or semi-evergreen; st. spiny, terete, often glaucous; br. angled, prickly. Lvs 4–13cm, ovate to lanceolate, broadly tapered or cordate at base, glaucous and papillose beneath, 7-veined, often variegated. Fls yellow to brown, umbels with an arched, flat stalk. Fr. 5–8mm diam., black, glaucous. SE US. Z4.

S. grandifolia Reg. = *S. regelii.*

S. herbacea L. Herbaceous, to 3m; st. glab., unarmed, much-branched. Lvs 5–12cm, triangular-ovate to lanceolate, rounded to shortly acuminate, rounded to truncate or cordate at base, leathery, 7–9-veined. Fls carrion-scented, green, in rounded umbels. Fr. blue-black, to 1cm diam. E US. Z4.

S. hispida Muhlenb. Decid. to 15m; st. prickly below, terete or slightly angled; br. angled, unarmed. Lvs 5–15cm, ovate to circular, apex abruptly acuminate, base cordate, 5–9-veined, serrulate, shiny. Fls in umbels. Fr. blue-black, to 6mm diam. S & C US. Z5.

S. laurifolia L. Everg., st. terete, prickly below; br. angled, ± unarmed. Lvs 5–20cm, narrowly ovate to oblong-lanceolate, leathery, thick, cuneate, margins inrolled, 3-veined. Fls green, in umbels. Fr. black, 6–8mm diam. SE US. Z8.

S. maculata Roxb. = *S. aspera.*

S. officinalis F.J. Hanb. & Flueck. = *S. regelii.*

S. ornata Hook. = *S. regelii.*

S. regelii Killip & Morton. To 15m; st. with 4 sharp angles and long spines below, 4 angled or winged above. Lower lvs variable to 30cm, ovate to oblong, apex rounded or acuminate, base cordate or hastate, upper lvs much smaller, lanceolate to oblong, tapered below. ♂ fls solitary or in umbellate rac., ♀ fls solitary. Fr. black, to 1.5cm diam. NC Amer. Z9.

S. rotundifolia L. Decid. or partly everg., to 10m; st. 4-angled, with spines on angles. Lvs 5–15cm, broadly ovate to circular, base round to cordate, thick and leathery, 5-veined, dark green, lustrous, margins entire or roughened. Fls green-yellow, in umbels. Fr. blue to black, 5–8mm diam. E US. Z4.

S. saluberrima Gilg = *S. regelii.*

S. smallii Morong. Everg. to 3m; st. terete, spiny below. Lvs to 15cm, usually much smaller, lanceolate to ovate, abruptly acuminate, gradually tapered below, thin-textured, glab., 5-veined, shiny dark green above, duller and paler beneath. Fls green, in umbels, spikes or rac. Fr. black, 5–7mm diam. SE US, C Amer. Z8.

S. utilis Hemsl. = *S. regelii.*

S. walteri Pursh. Decid.; st. slightly angled, spiny below; br. square in section, unarmed. Lvs 5–12cm, ovate to ovate-lanceolate, apex obtuse or abruptly acute, base broadly cuneate to cordate, 5–7-veined. Fls in umbels, yellow, green or brown, drying brown-orange. Fr. red, occas. white, 8–12mm diam. E US. Z7.

Smilo Grass *Oryzopsis miliacea.*

Smitinandia Holtt. Orchidaceae. 1 epiphytic, monopodial orchid to 20cm. Lvs to 10×1.5cm, 2-ranked. Rac. to 7cm; fls to 1cm diam., spurred; tep. to 3mm, subequal, ovate, obtuse, pale pink, sometimes spotted purple; lip mobile, 3-lobed, purple, midlobe ligulate, fleshy, lat. lobes smaller, rounded. SE Asia. Z10.

S. micrantha (Lindl.) Holtt.
→*Cleisostoma* and *Saccolabium.*

Smodingium E. Mey. ex Sonder. Anacardiaceae. 1 dioecious tree or shrub to 6m. Bark grey to brown. Lvs trifoliolate; lfts narrowly ovate, acute, serrate, coriaceous, dark green, about 9×3cm, term. leaflet larger; petiole slender. Pan. axill., to 30cm; fls pale green; cal. 5-lobed; pet. 5, reflexed; sta. 5. Fr. a nut, to 1cm with chartaceous wing. Summer. S Afr. Z9.

S. argutum E. Mey. ex Sonder. AFRICAN POISON OAK.

Smoke Bush *Conospermum; Cotinus.*
Smoke Tree *Cotinus coggygria.*
Smokewood *Cotinus.*
Smoking Bean *Catalpa bignonioides.*
Smooth Alder *Alnus serrulata.*
Smooth Arizona Cypress *Cupressus arizonica* var. *glabra.*
Smooth-bark Apple *Angophora cordifolia.*
Smooth-bark Kauri *Agathis robusta.*
Smooth-bark Mexican Pine *Pinus pseudostrobus.*
Smooth Cypress *Cupressus arizonica* var. *glabra.*
Smooth Darling Pea *Swainsona galegifolia.*
Smooth-leaf Pine *Pinus leiophylla.*

Smooth-leaved Elm *Ulmus carpinifolia*.
Smooth Phlox *Phlox glaberrima*.
Smooth Rambutan *Alectryon subcinereus*.
Smooth Rock Spleenwort *Asplenium fontanum*.
Smooth Shield Fern *Lastreopsis glabella*.
Smooth Sumac *Rhus glabra*.
Smooth Sweet Cicely *Osmorhiza longistylis*.
Smooth Tasmanian Cedar *Athrotaxis cupressoides*.
Smooth Winterberry *Ilex laevigata*.
Smooth Woodsia *Woodsia glabella*.
Smooth Yellow Violet *Viola pubescens* var. *eriocarpa*.

Smyrnium L. Umbelliferae. 7 glab. bienn. or monocarpic herbs. Lower lvs 2–3-ternate, seg. broad, rounded, upper lvs often simple. Umbels compound, in branched infl.; involucre and involucel usually 0; fls small, bright yellow. W Eur., Medit. Z9.
S. olusatrum L. ALEXANDERS; BLACK LOVAGE; HORSE PARSLEY. To 1.5m; st. ridged. Lvs to 30cm, 2–3-pinnate or -ternate, seg. rhombic-ovate, 2–8cm, dark green and shiny, serrate, occas. lobed; upper lvs ternate or ternatisect, with inflated petiole. Umbels with 7–15 rays. Spring. W & S Eur., Medit., nat. Bermuda.
S. perfoliatum L. 40–150cm; st. angled and narrowly winged, lvs 2–3-pinnate or -ternate, seg. c1.5cm, ovate, toothed to slightly lobed bright green; upper lvs simple, ovate-cordate, 3–10cm, strongly amplexicaul, crenate-serrate. Umbels with 7–12 rays, 1–4cm. Spring. S Eur. to Czech.
S. rotundifolium Mill. To 1.5m, resembling *S. perfoliatum* but st. unwinged. Lower lvs 3-ternate, seg. oblong-cuneate; upper st. lvs orbicular, base cordate, entire to slightly serrate. Spring. SE Eur., E Medit.

Snail Bean *Vigna caracalla*.
Snail Flower *Vigna caracalla*.
Snail Seed *Coccoloba diversifolia*.
Snailseed *Cocculus carolinus*.
Snail Vine *Vigna caracalla*.
Snake Bark Maple *Acer pensylvanicum*; *A. davidii*.
Snakeberry *Actaea rubra*.
Snake-branch Spruce *Picea abies*.
Snake Bush *Duvernoia adhatodoides*.
Snake Fern *Lygodium microphyllum*.
Snake Flower *Ornithogalum maculatum*.
Snake Gourd *Trichosanthes cucumerina* var. *anguina*; *T. ovigera*.
Snakehead *Chelone glabra*.
Snake Lily *Dichelostemma volubile*.
Snake Orchid *Diuris lanceolata*.
Snake Palm *Amorphophallus* (*A. rivieri*).
Snake Plant *Sansevieria* (*S. trifasciata*).
Snake Polypody *Microgramma piloselloides*.
Snakeroot *Liatris* (*L. punctata*); *Polygala*; *Sanicula*.
Snake's-head Fritillary *Fritillaria meleagris*.
Snake's Head Iris *Hermodactylus tuberosus*.
Snakeskin Plant *Fittonia verschaffeltii* var. *pearcei*.
Snake Tree *Ficus elastica*.
Snake Vine *Hibbertia scandens*.
Snakeweed *Gutierrezia*; *Polygonum bistorta*; *Stachytarpheta* (*S. urticifolia*).
Snakewood *Cecropia peltata*; *Ormosia monosperma*.
Snakewood Tree *Cecropia palmata*.
Snap Bean *Phaseolus vulgaris*.
Snapdragon *Antirrhinum majus*.
Snappy Gum *Eucalyptus racemosa*.
Sneezeweed *Helenium autumnale*.
Sneezewort *Achillea ptarmica*.
Snottygobble *Persoonia longifolia*; *P. saccata*.
Snowball Pincushion *Mammillaria candida*.
Snowbell *Styrax*.
Snowberry *Gaultheria hispida*; *Symphoricarpos* (*S. albus*).
Snow Brake *Pteris ensiformis*.
Snow Bush *Breynia nivosa*; *Ceanothus cordulatus*.
Snow-bush Rose *Rosa* 'Dupontii'
Snow Camellia *Camellia japonica*.
Snow Creeper *Porana paniculata*.
Snowdon Lily *Lloydia serotina*.
Snowdrop *Galanthus* (*G. nivalis*).
Snowdrop Tree *Halesia*.
Snowdrop Windflower *Anemone sylvestris*.
Snowflake *Leucojum*.
Snowflower *Spathiphyllum floribundum*.
Snow Garland Spiraea *Spiraea* ×*multiflora*.
Snow Grass *Chionochloa*.
Snow Gum *Eucalyptus pauciflora*.
Snow-in-summer *Cerastium tomentosum*; *Ozothamnus thyrsoideus*.
Snow-in-the-jungle *Porana paniculata*.

Snow Myrtle *Calytrix alpestris*.
Snow On The Mountain *Euphorbia marginata*.
Snow Pea *Pisum sativum* var. *macrocarpon*.
Snow Pear *Pyrus nivalis*.
Snow Poppy *Eomecon*.
Snow-queen *Synthyris reniformis*.
Snow Rush *Luzula nivea*.
Snows Of Kilimanjaro *Euphorbia leucocephala*.
Snow Trillium *Trillium nivale*.
Snow Tussock *Chionochloa rigida*.
Snow Wreath *Neviusia*.
Snowy Mespilus *Amelanchier*.
Snowy Oxera *Oxera pulchella*.
Snowy Woodrush *Luzula nivea*.
Snuffbox Fern *Thelypteris palustris* var. *pubescens*.
Soap Aloe *Aloe saponaria*.
Soap-bark Tree *Quillaja saponaria*.
Soapberry *Sapindus saponaria*.
Soap Bush *Porlieria angustifolia*; *Quillaja saponaria*.
Soap Tree *Gymnocladus chinensis*; *Yucca elata*.
Soap Weed *Yucca elata*.
Soapwort *Saponaria* (*S. officinalis*).

Sobolewskia Bieb. Cruciferae. 4 ann. or perenn. herbs, branching at base. Lvs large, round or cordate, lobed or toothed. Fls small, 4-merous, racemose; pet. white, ovate, short-clawed; sta. 6, free, silique usually 1-seeded, clavate or oblong. E Medit. to Cauc. Z6.
S. clavata (Boiss.) Fenzl. Perenn., 25–50cm, smelling of garlic. Basal lvs cordate to reniform, broadly lobed; petioles 5–10cm; st. lvs subsessile. Infl. large, spreading; pet. 3–4mm, narrow-clawed; pedicels recurved. Fr. 6–10mm, curved. Early summer. Turk., Armenia, Kurdistan.
S. lithophila Bieb. = *S. sibirica*.
S. sibirica (Willd.) P.W. Ball. Differs from *S. clavata* in st. lvs petiolate, pedicel not recurved; fr. nearly straight. Crimea.
→*Cochlearia*.

Sobralia Ruiz & Pav. Orchidaceae. 35 epiphytic or terrestrial orchids. St. leafy, usually simple, reed- or cane-like, slender, clumped usually. Lvs alt., 2-ranked, tough, plicate-ribbed, usually lanceolate. Rac. short, bracteate, term. (rarely longer, lat.); fls produced in succession, large, often short-lived; sep. subequal, elliptic-oblong to lanceolate; pet. usually wider and undulate; lip entire or obscurely trilobed, margins involute, enveloping column, appearing funnelform with a spreading, crisped limb, disc with a smooth, lamellate or crested callus. Trop. C & S Amer. Z10.
S. candida (Poepp. & Endl.) Rchb. f. To 90cm. Lvs to 22cm, fls 1, white or cream-white; sep. to 3×0.6cm, lanceolate; lip to 3×1.5cm, white to pale pink, obscurely 3-lobed above. Peru, Venez.
S. cattleya Rchb. f. To 2m. Lvs to 30cm. Fls several, fragrant; sep. to 5.5×1.5cm, oblong-elliptic to oblong-ligulate, white or cream, margins rose-pink or maroon-pink; pet. maroon-pink marked white; lip to 4.5×5cm, maroon-purple, base and margins white, midlobe oblong, emarginate, undulate, disc yellow. Venez., Colomb.
S. chlorantha Hook. = *S. macrophylla*.
S. decora Batem. To 75cm. Lvs to 22cm, fragrant tep. white or white-lavender, sep. to 5×1.5cm, linear-oblong, apiculate, recurved, pet. to 4×1cm; lip to 3.5×4.5cm, rose-purple or lavender, tubular, base cucullate, apex rounded, apiculate, undulate, disc streaked yellow and brown. Spring–summer. Mex., Hond., Guat., Nic., Costa Rica.
S. dichotoma Ruiz & Pav. To 3m. Lvs to 35cm. Infl. lat., sometimes branching, few- to many-fld; fls fragrant, fleshy, exterior white, interior red to violet-red or rose; sep. to 6×1.5cm, elliptic-oblong to oblanceolate-oblong; lip to 6×6cm, ovate-subquadrate, midlobe cleft, undulate-crisped. Colomb., Venez., Boliv., Peru.
S. fragrans Lindl. To 45cm. Lvs to 25cm, fls 1–2, fragrant; sep. to 4×1cm, dull purple-green or ivory, linear to oblong-lanceolate, acute; pet. pale yellow; lip to 3.5×2cm, bright yellow, obovate to elliptic-obovate, apex deeply fimbriate, disc deep yellow. Spring. Guat. to Panama, Colomb.
S. leucoxantha Rchb. f. Differs from *S. micrantha* in fls smaller, tep. white, lip to 7×5cm, white marked yellow to orange in centre. Summer–early autumn. Costa Rica, Panama.
S. liliastrum Lindl. To 3m. Lvs to 25cm. Fls to 10cm diam., produced in succession on a flexuous axis amid spathe-like bracts, fleshy, fragrant, white veined or tinged yellow or rose; sep. to 7×1.5cm, oblong-lanceolate; lip to 6.5×5.5cm, infundibular, emarginate, undulate-crisped, disc yellow. Summer–early autumn. Venez., Colomb., Braz., Guianas.

S. lindleyana Rchb. f. To 60cm. Lvs to 13cm. Fls 1, fragrant, fleshy; tep. white, fading yellow-topaz, sep. to 5×1cm, elliptic-oblong to elliptic-lanceolate; lip to 5×4cm, white spotted red, obovate or cuneate-flabellate, dentate-lacerate. Mostly summer. Costa Rica, Panama.

S. macrantha Lindl. To 2m. Lvs to 30cm. Fls produced in succession, fleshy, fragrant; tep. rose-purple, sep. to 10×3cm, linear-oblong; lip to 11×7cm, rose-purple, white and tubular at base; centre tinged yellow, apical portion rotund, bilobulate, crisped to undulate. Spring–autumn. Mex. to Costa Rica. Many cvs recorded, most now probably lost. These include white, deep magenta, crimson, large-fld and dwarf-growing variants.

S. macrophylla Rchb. f. To 1.2m. Lvs to 21cm. Fls 1–2 opening at a time, fleshy, fragrant, pale yellow-green; sep. to 7×1.5cm, forming a partial tube, lanceolate; pet. broader, recurved; lip to 8×4cm, obovate-spathulate, rounded, recurved, disc golden-yellow. Costa Rica, Venez., Panama, Colomb., Braz.

S. mandonii Rchb. f. = *S. dichotoma*.

S. powellii Schltr. = *S. leucoxantha*.

S. rosea hort. non Poepp. & Endl. = *S. ruckeri*.

S. ruckeri Lind. ex Lindl. To 2m. Lvs to 38cm. Infl. to 25cm, erect, bearing to 4 fls at any time on an elongated, flexuous rachis; fls fleshy, fragrant, long-lived, pale rose-lilac to rose-purple; sep. to 11×2.5cm, oblanceolate to oblong-oblanceolate; lip to 11×5.4cm, margins deep rose-purple, centre yellow-white, infundibular, truncate to emarginate, dentate-lacerate. Summer–early autumn. Venez., Colomb., Ecuad., Peru.

S. sessilis Lindl. non Hook. To 1.2m. Lvs to 30cm, broad. Fls several produced in succession, fleshy, fragrant, white to dark rose; sep. to 5.5×2cm, lanceolate to oblong-lanceolate; lip to 5×3.5cm, infundibular, tinted yellow at base, apex erose-denticulate. Autumn. Braz., Venez., Guianas.

S. sessilis Hook. non Lindl. = *S. decora*.

S. suaveolens Rchb. f. To 45cm. Lvs to 20cm. Fls 1–2, waxy, fragrant, yellow-cream; sep. to 3×0.5cm, ligulate to linear-lanceolate; lip to 2.5×1.5cm, elliptic to obovate, fimbriate-lacerate, disc pale brown, with several yellow keels. Summer. Venez., Panama.

S. Lucasiana. Tall plants with reedy st. and lvs. Fls pale lilac with a darker pale purple lip, short-lived.

S. violacea Lind. To 1.2m. Lvs to 27cm; fls several opening in succession, fleshy, fragrant; sep. to 7.5×2cm, usually dark rose-purple, oblong to oblong-oblanceolate; pet. paler; lip to 7.5×5cm, deep yellow-orange toward base, margins deep rose-purple, slightly crisped. Mostly summer. Colomb., Venez., Peru, Boliv. A variant is sometimes offered with white fls and a rich orange-yellow disc.

S. warszewiczii Rchb. f. St. to 1m, becoming warty. Lvs to 18cm. Fls 1 bright purple; sep. to 5×2cm, broadly oblanceolate; lip to 5×3cm, flabellate, emarginate, undulate-crisped. Panama.

S. xantholeuca Rchb. f. St. 1–2m. Lvs to 17cm. Fls produced 1 at a time, nodding; to 10cm, narrow-lanceolate, ivory to lemon yellow; lip tubular strongly crisped, deep yellow flushed and streaked dark orange-yellow in throat. C Amer. 'Albescens': fls pale primrose. 'Nana': to 75cm. 'Superba': fls rich ivory, lip marked orange to red in throat. 'Wigan's Variety': tep. ivory tinted primrose, lip ivory flushed yellow; fls tinted rose at first.

Society Garlic *Tulbaghia.*
Socotrine Aloe *Aloe perryi.*

Soehrensia (Backeb.) Backeb.
S. bruchii (Britt. & Rose) Backeb. = *Echinopsis bruchii.*
S. formosa (Pfeiff.) Backeb. = *Echinopsis formosa.*

Soft Boronia *Boronia mollis.*
Soft Flag *Typha angustifolia.*
Soft Love Grass *Eragrostis pilosa.*
Soft Rush *Juncus effusus.*
Soft-shield Fern *Polystichum setiferum.*
Soft Sunray *Helipterum molle.*
Soft Tree Fern *Cyathea smithii; Dicksonia antarctica.*

Soja Moench.
S. max (L.) Piper = *Glycine max.*

Soja Bean *Glycine max.*

SOLANACEAE Juss. 90/2600. *Anthocercis, Atropa, Atropanthe, Browallia, Brugmansia, Brunfelsia, Capsicum, Cestrum, Cyphanthera, Cyphomandra, Datura, Dyssochroma, Fabiana, Grabowskia, Hyoscyamus, Iochroma, Jaborosa, Juanulloa, Lycianthes, Lycium, Lycopersicon, Mandragora, Nicandra, Nicotiana, Nierembergia, Petunia, Physalis, Physochlaina, Salpichroa, Salpiglossis, Schizanthus, Scopolia, Solandra, Solanum, Streptosolen, Vestia.*

Solander's Banksia *Banksia solandri.*

Solandra (L.) Sw. CHALICE VINE. Solanaceae. 8 shrubby climbers. Lvs entire, usually coriaceous, shiny. Fls heavily nocturnally fragrant, v. large, axill., solitary, short-stalked; cal. long-tubular, to 5-lobed at apex; cor. tube cylindric to funnel-shaped, limb campanulate with 5 reflexed lobes. Trop. Amer. Z10.

S. grandiflora Sw. To 5m+. Lvs to 17cm, glab. or pubesc., elliptic to elliptic-oblong or obovate, apex acute. Cal. tubular, to 8cm, glab. or pubesc., appearing 2-lipped; cor. white, becoming yellow to pink tinged yellow, to 23cm, funnel-shaped, lobes undulate to crenate. Spring. Jam., Puerto Rico, Lesser Antilles.

S. guttata D. Don. To 2m+. Lvs to 15cm, broad-elliptic to ovate or obovate, soft-pubesc. beneath, apex acute to acuminate. Cal. 3-lobed, to 9cm, soft pubesc.; cor. to 26cm, throat pale yellow, spotted or striped purple, limb spreading, crispate. Mex. Much material labelled as *S. guttata* is *S. maxima.*

S. hartwegii N.E. Br. = *S. maxima.*

S. laevis Hook. = *S. longiflora.*

S. longiflora Tussac. Resembles *S. grandiflora*, but cal. to half length of cor. tube. Lvs to 10cm, elliptic to obovate-oblong, cor. white tinged purple, to 32cm, apex contracted, lobes dentate, undulate. Winter. Jam., Cuba, Hispan.

S. macrantha Dunal = *S. longiflora.*

S. maxima (Sessé & Moc.) P. Green. To 4m. Lvs to 15cm, elliptic, glab., apex short-acuminate or acute to obtuse. Cal. to 7cm, glab., to 4-lobed; cor. yellow, urceolate, to 20cm, tube with 5 purple veins (5 purple ridges within). Mex., C Amer., Colomb., Venez.

S. nitida Zuccagni = *S. grandiflora.*

S. viridiflora Miers = *Dyssochroma viridiflora.*

Solanecio (Schultz-Bip.) Walp. Compositae. *c*15 subsucculent or succulent, tuberous-rooted herbs, softly woody shrubs, climbers or epiphytes. Cap. discoid, several to many in term., compound cymes; flts yellow. Trop. Afr., Madag., Yemen. Z10.

S. angulatus (Vahl) C. Jeffrey. Perenn. climbing herb, to 3m, shrubby below, glab., shining. Lvs to 12×6cm, ovate or oval, deeply dissected, base auriculate, lobes to 3cm, 2–5 on each side, linear, oblong-ovate or obovate, entire, toothed or undulate, term. lobe largest. Cap. to 1cm, in rounded, often dense cymes. Trop. Afr.

→*Cacalia* and *Senecio.*

Solanopteris Copel. POTATO FERN. Polypodiaceae. 4 epiphytic ferns. Rhiz. woody, long-creeping, bearing tuber-like swellings; scales sparse. Fronds stipitate, dimorphous (sterile shorter, wider than fertile), simple and entire to pinnatifid, glab. or scaly, thin-textured. Trop. Amer. Z10.

S. bifrons (Hook.) Copel. Sterile fronds to 10×3cm, sessile, pinnatifid, lanceolate to elliptic, attenuate, seg. obtuse; fertile fronds to 15×0.6cm, short-stipitate, simple, linear, entire. S Amer.

→*Microgramma* and *Phymatodes.*

Solanum L. NIGHTSHADE. Solanaceae. *c*1400 herbs, shrubs, trees or vines. Infl. cymose, umbellate, paniculate or racemose; cal. campanulate or rotate, 5-dentate, sometimes enlarged in fr.; cor. rotate or broadly campanulate, regular, 5-angled or 5-lobed, tube v. short; sta. 5, fil. v. short, anth. oblong to linear, connivent or connate around style. Fr. a berry, fleshy or coriaceous. Cosmop., esp. Trop. Amer.

S. abyssinicum Jacq. ex Vitm. = *S. marginatum.*

S. aculeatissimum Jacq. Spiny undershrub, 30–60cm. Lvs ovate-oblong, pinnately 5-lobed, minutely pubesc. Fls solitary or paired, lat.; cal. lobes pubesc., prickly in fr.; cor. 12mm diam., white. Fr. 3+cm diam., yellow tinged brown to scarlet, smooth. Trop. & S Afr. Z10.

S. aculeatissimum Clarke non Jacq. = *S. capsicoides.*

S. acutilobum Dunal ex Poir. Undershrub, to 60cm, br. tomentellous, sparsely prickly. Lvs cordate, sinuate-angled, lobes acute, tomentose; white beneath; petiole long. Infl. cymose, subterminal, tomentose; cal. deeply acutely lobed, tomentose; cor. 3–4× size of cal., white. Braz., Parag. Z10.

S. aethiopicum L. Shrub to 2.5m. St. tomentose when young, spiny. Lvs 5–12cm, ovate, irregularly 4–5-lobed, acute at apex, tomentose, with compressed spines. Infl. cymose, few-fld; cal. lobes lanceolate, 4–6mm, tomentose, sometimes spiny, enlarged in fr.; cor. 2–2.5cm diam., shallowly acutely 5-lobed, violet. Fr. to 2.5cm diam., yellow. Afr.; nat. W Indies. Z10.

S. ajanhuiri Juz. & Buk. (*S. stenototum* × *S. megistacrolobum* ?) Plant semirosulate when young, tuberiferous. Lvs pinnatifid to pinnate, lfts in 5–6 lat. pairs, acute, softly pubesc. Infl. simple or forked, downy; cal. 6–8mm, lobes acuminate; cor. pentagonal,

2.5–3.5cm diam., indigo. Boliv., Peru. Z10.

S. alatum Seem. & Schmidt = *S. robustum*.

S. albidum Dunal. Tree to 7m+; trunk straight, thick, branched, spiny, br. tomentose. Lvs to 60cm, 7–9-lobed to sinuate, glossy above, softly white-tomentose beneath. Infl. lat., subcorymbose, many-fld, tomentose; cal. small; cor. small, spreading, white. Fr. globose, small, yellow then black. Summer. Peru. Z10.

S. angustifolium Lam. = *S. rostratum*.

S. anthropophagorum Seem. = *S. uporo*.

S. arboreum Humb. & Bonpl. ex Dunal. Tree to 12m, unarmed; br. angled. Lvs to 20cm, in unequal pairs, larger oblong, entire, acuminate, bright green, glossy, membranous, short-stalked. Infl. cymose; cal. suburceolate lobes ovate; cor. 5-lobed, white, 8mm diam. Venez. Z10.

S. ascasabii Hawkes = *S. phureja*.

S. atropurpureum Schrank. Herb or small shrub, low-growing, armed; spines yellow, purple at base. St. flexuous, dark blood red. Lvs 8–15cm, ovate, lobes about 7, acute, entire; petioles long. Infl. 2.5cm, extraxillary, simple, 6–8-fld; cal. flushed purple; cor. 2cm diam., deeply lanceolate-lobed, purple, tinged yellow towards base. Fr. 1.5cm diam., globose, white, ripening orange. Braz. Z10.

S. auriculatum Ait. = *S. mauritianum*.

S. aviculare Forst. f. KANGAROO APPLE. Shrub, 1–3.5m, glab. Lvs to 20cm, linear-lanceolate, entire to irregularly pinnatifid with 1–3 lanceolate lobes each side, dark green, thin, veins often tinged purple or brown. Infl. cymose, 5–15cm, 3–8-fld; cor. 3–3.5cm, broadly lobed, tinged purple. Fr. 2.5cm, subglobose to ovoid, yellow-green ripening scarlet. Australasia. Z9.

S. balbisii Dunal = *S. sisymbrifolium*.

S. bracteatum Thunb. = *Teedia lucida*.

S. ×burbankii Bitter. SUNBERRY; WONDERBERRY. Ann., to 60cm, minutely pubesc. Lvs to 6.5cm, ovate to rhombic, dentate. Infl. axill., cymose, few-fld; cor. 6mm diam., white, with green centre star, flushed mauve. Fr. 1cm diam., globose, orange or black, dull. Of uncertain origin.

S. capsicastrum Link ex Schauer. FALSE JERUSALEM CHERRY. Small shrub, 30–60cm; young st. stellate-tomentose. Lvs in unequal pairs, larger 4–7cm, oblong-lanceolate, entire to undulate, slightly tomentose. Infl. racemose, short, few-fld; cor. 5-parted, 1cm diam., white. Fr. 1–2.5cm, ovoid, pointed, red-orange to scarlet. Braz. 'Craigii': fr. white or red. 'Melvinii': habit compact, to 30cm. 'Nanum': habit dwarf 'Variegatum': lvs variegated or edged cream-white. Z10.

S. capsicoides All. COCKROACH BERRY. Undershrub, 30–40cm. St. ascending from rhiz., tough, prickly. Lvs 8–11cm, broadly ovate, acutely lobed, pilose above, subglabrous beneath, with scattered spines. Fls pendulous; cal. spiny, teeth broadly triangular; cor. 12–20mm diam., white. Fr. 2.5cm diamm., globose, ripening orange to red. Trop. S Amer.; widely nat. W Indies, Trop. Asia and Afr. Z10.

S. cardenasii Hawkes = *S. phureja*.

S. carolinense L. HORSE NETTLE; BALL NIGHTSHADE. Perenn. St. to 1m, erect, laxly stellate-pubesc., with slender yellow spines. Lvs 7–12cm, ovate, lobes or large teeth 2–5 per side, yellow stellate-pubesc., spiny along major veins. Infl. a racemose cluster, several-fld; cor. 2–3.5cm diam., white or flushed pale violet. Fr. 1–1.5cm diam., yellow or flushed orange. Summer. SE US; nat. through much of N Amer. Z3.

S. ciliatum Lam. = *S. capsicoides*.

S. citrullifolium A. Br. MELON-LEAF NIGHTSHADE. Ann. herb. St. 50–100cm, extensively branched, stellate-pubesc., spiny. Lvs to 15cm, lobes 5–7, obtuse, deeply dentate, stellate-pubesc. Infl. cymose, few-fld; cal. v. spiny, lobes accrescent; cor. 3cm diam., violet or blue. Fr. enclosed in spiny cal. Summer. US, Mex. Z4.

S. coccineum Jacq. Small shrub, straggling, grey-velutinous. St. bent, prickly. Lvs to 7cm, broadly ovate to orbicular, deeply irregularly lobed, sinuses rounded. Infl. cymose, few-fld; cal. prickly; cor. 1cm diam., pale blue. Fr. 1.5cm diam., globose, dull orange to shiny scarlet. Trop. Afr. and Amer. Z10.

S. cornutum hort. = *S. rostratum*.

S. crispum Ruiz & Pav. Shrub, climbing to 3–4m. Lvs 7–12cm, ovate to lanceolate, acute at apex, rounded to cordate at base, undulate-crispate, dark green, finely pubesc. Corymbs term. 7–10cm diam.; fls fragrant, to 3cm diam., lilac-blue, anth. yellow. Fr. pea-sized, white tinged yellow. Summer. Chile. 'Glasnevin': habit vigorous; fls deep blue with golden-yellow sta., in large clusters. Z8.

S. cupuliferum Greene = *S. xantii*.

S. cyananthum Dunal in DC. Shrub, to 2m; br. pale, spiny, pubesc. Lvs to 35cm, elliptic-ovate, sinuate-repand or lobed, base cordate, ± spineless; petiole to 8cm, hairy. Infl. racemose, 10cm, about 5-fld; peduncles 5cm, prickly, hairy; cor. 5–6cm diam., stellate, blue. Braz. Z10.

S. dasyphyllum Schum. & Thonn. Undershrub to 90cm, coarsely

hairy, usually spiny. Lvs elliptic-obovate, pinnately lobed, often decurrent at base, pilose, spiny on veins, cal. with long sharp bristles, strongly accrescent in fr.; fls 2.5–4cm diam., purple tinged blue. W Trop. Afr. Z10.

S. dimidiatum Raf. V. similar to *S. carolinense*, except often less spiny; infl. often branched, forming 2–3 racemose clusters. Summer. US (Kans. to Ark. and Tex.). Z6.

S. donnell-smithii J. Coult. Tall, hairy vine, spines stout recurved yellow. Lvs 7–15cm, oblong to elliptic, angular-lobed, midvein spiny beneath. Infl. axill., cymose, lax; cal. lobes prickly; cor. 2.5+cm diam., lobes linear-lanceolate, white or tinged pale blue, densely pubesc. without. Fr. 2cm diam., globose, orange. Mex. to San Salvador. Z10.

S. douglasii Dunal. Perenn., herbaceous or shrubby, 60–200cm, minutely pubesc. to subglabrous. St. rough-hairy, angled or v. narrowly winged. Lvs 2–10cm, ovate, sinuate-dentate, apex acute to shortly acuminate, base cuneate to subtruncate; petioles slightly winged. Peduncles 1–3cm, several-fld; cor. white with pale green spots near base, lobes lanceolate, 6–9mm. Fr. 6–9mm, black. Summer. SW US., Mex. Z8.

S. dulcamara L. BITTERSWEET; CLIMBING NIGHTSHADE; DEADLY NIGHTSHADE; POISONOUS NIGHTSHADE. Highly toxic, perenn. vine, 2–4m, woody below. Lvs 5–12cm, simple or deeply lobed, deep green above, paler beneath, subglabrous, ovate, acuminate at apex, rounded or subcordate at base. Infl. laxly branched, cymose, drooping; cor. 1–1.5cm diam., lobes reflexed, pale violet or blue to white. Fr. ovoid to globose, 8–12mm, bright red. Summer. Eurasia, nat. in N Amer. 'Variegata': lvs variegated; fls pale purple-blue. Z4.

S. duplosinuatum Klotzsch = *S. dasyphyllum*.

S. elaeagnifolium Cav. SILVER-LEAVED NETTLE; SILVER-LEAVED NIGHTSHADE; WHITE HORSE NETTLE; BULL NETTLE. Perenn., silvery-canescent throughout. St. branched, stout, to 1m, spines few or 0. Lvs 5–15cm, linear to oblong or oblanceolate, entire to sinuate. Infl. cymose, clad with yellow spines; cor. 2–3cm diam., voilet or blue, pubesc. without. Fr. globose, 10–14mm, yellow or tinged brown. Summer. C & SW US, S Amer. Z4.

S. englerianum Dammer. Shrub, 1–1.5m, rusty-hairy when young, with recurved spines. Lvs to 9cm, lanceolate, sometimes sinuate, green, minutely scabrous and spiny above, rusty and spiny beneath. Rac. few-fld; cor. to 3cm diam., pale blue, pubesc. without, lobes lanceolate. Fr. ellipsoid, 1.5cm, yellow. Trop. E Afr. Z10.

S. erianthum D. Don. Shrub, 2–3m. St. erect, branched above to form spreading crown; br. yellow-pubesc., when young. Lvs 10–35cm, lanceolate-elliptic, acuminate, dark green above, paler beneath, pubesc. Infl. axill., cymose, tomentose, fls pendulous; cor. 1–1.5cm diam., creamy white, lobes reflexed. Fr. globose, 1cm diam., yellow, sparsely hairy. S Amer., nat. throughout Trop. Z10.

S. flavidum Torr. = *S. elaeagnifolium*.

S. giganteum Jacq. AFRICAN HOLLY. Shrub or small tree, 2–4m; trunk stoutly spiny, br. silvery white, prickly. Lvs to 25cm, oblong-lanceolate, acute to acuminate at apex, cuneate at base, glossy dark green above, silvery- pubesc. beneath.Infl. corymbose-paniculate, congested, white-pubesc.; cor. 1cm, mauve. Fr. globose, 9mm diam., glossy red. Trop. Afr., S India, Sri Lanka. Z9.

S. glaucophyllum Desf. = *S. melanoxylon*.

S. glaucum Dunal = *S. melanoxylon*.

S. globiferum Dunal in DC. = *S. mammosum*.

S. goniocalyx Juz. & Buk. = *S. tuberosum*.

S. havanense Jacq. Shrub, 1–2m, unarmed; br. grey, pubesc. when young. Lvs 4–9cm, elliptic-oblong, narrowed to obtuse apex, base decurrent, chartaceous to subcoriaceous, veins pubesc. when young. Infl. few-fld; cor. 1cm, campanulate, deeply 5-lobed, pale blue, lobes elliptic, pubesc. at apex. Fr. to 1.5cm, ovoid, shiny blue. Cuba, nat. elsewhere in W Indies. Z10.

S. hendersonii hort. ex Wright = *S. pseudocapsicum*.

S. hermanii Dunal = *S. linnaeanum*.

S. heterandrum Pursh = *S. rostratum*.

S. heterodoxum Britt. = *S. citrullifolium*.

S. hispidum Pers. DEVIL'S FIG. Stout shrub or broadly spreading low tree to 3m, densely ferruginous-hispid; bark grey, with fierce down-curved spines. Lvs to 30cm, broadly lanceolate, deeply pinnately lobed, dark green above, ferruginous-pubesc., with scattered spines along main vein. Peduncle stout, 1–3cm, ferruginous; cor. 3cm diam., white. Fr. 1.5cm diam., globose, brown tinged yellow. Mex., Guat.; widely nat. Z10.

S. integrifolium Poir. in Lam. CHINESE SCARLET EGG-PLANT. Ann. herb to 90cm. St. woody, grey-brown, v. minutely pubesc.; spines stout, hooked, yellow. Lvs ovate, sinuate, obtuse, smooth above, thinly tomentose beneath, with a few short spines, on veins. Infl. axill., umbellate, 2–6-fld; cor. small, white, lobes lanceolate. Fr. 2.5–5cm diam., ovoid-globose, yellow or scarlet. Origin probably Afr. Z10.

S. intrusum Soria = *S. melanocerasum.*

S. jamesii Torr. WILD POTATO. Perenn., 10–50cm, subglabrous to glandular-pilose, stoloniferous, tuber-bearing; tubes 0.5–2cm diam., globose to ellipsoid, pale brown to cream. Lvs 6–15cm, odd-pinnate, lfts 7–11, lanceolate, to 6cm. Infl. pseudoterminal, cymose, few-fld; cor. stellate, 15–30mm diam., white. Summer. SW US, Mex. Z9.

S. jasminoides Paxt. POTATO VINE. Decid. vine, densely branched, shoots slender, glab., unarmed. Lvs 3–5-parted, lfts ovate, 4–6cm, uppermost lvs simple, ovate-lanceolate, subcordate at base. Rac. 2.5–3cm in a cluster 5–7cm diam.; cor. stellate, 2–2.5cm diam., white tinted lilac-blue; sta. lemon-yellow. Summer. Braz. 'Album': lvs dark green, purple-tinted; fls pure white, long-lasting. Z9.

S. khasianum C.B. Clarke = *S. myriacanthum.*

S. laciniatum Ait. KANGAROO APPLE; LARGE KANGAROO APPLE. Shrub, 1–3m, soon glab. St. sometimes tinged purple, to 10cm diam. Lvs 15–30cm, broadly ovate and deeply pinnatisect, with 1–9 lanceolate lobes, to lanceolate and entire. Infl. 5–15cm, cymose, to 1-fld; cor. rotate, 3–5cm diam., showy, indigo, lobes emarginate. Fr. 1.5–2cm diam., ellipsoid, yellow tinged orange. Aus. Z9.

S. lanceolatum Cav. Shrub, 1–2.5m. St. tomentose, with stout short spines, or spineless. Lvs 8–18cm, oblong, elliptic-lanceolate or oblanceolate, lower irregularly lobed towards base, upper entire, densely stellate tomentose, glabrescent above. Infl. cymose, 3–10cm, many-fld; cor. 1.5–2.5cm diam., pale blue or tinged purple. Fr. globose, orange tinged yellow. Mex. Z10.

S. lasiophyllum Dunal ex Poir. FLANNEL BUSH. Shrub, 20–100cm, erect, rounded, densely pubesc. throughout. St. with fine spines; new growth flushed purple. Lvs 2.5–8cm, ovate, entire or shallowly lobed, apex rounded, base rounded or truncate, occas. sparsely spiny. Infl. cymose, 2–6-fld; cor. pentagonal-rotate, 2.5–3cm diam., purple. Fr. 10–13mm diam., globose to ovoid, yellow, enclosed in enlarged cal. Aus. Z9.

S. latifolium Poir. in Lam. = *S. aethiopicum.*

S. laurifolium Mill. = *S. subinerme.*

S. leprosum Ortega = *S. elaeagnifolium.*

S. linnaeanum Hepper & Jaeger. APPLE OF SODOM; YELLOW POPOLA; DEAD SEA APPLE. Shrub to 1m, diffusely branched; br. shiny green or purple with yellow spines. Lvs to 8cm, ovate, deeply pinnately lobed, spiny. Infl. internodal, cymose, to 6-fld; cal. densely prickly, somewhat enlarged in fr.; cor. rotate-stellate, 2cm diam., pale mauve with darker purple streak towards base of lobes. Fr. 2–3cm diam., globose, grey-yellow ripening black to brown, dry when mature. S Afr. Z9.

S. macranthum Dunal = *S. wrightii.*

S. macrocarpon L. Undershrub, semi-woody, to 1.5m, generally unarmed. St. stout, hairy or glabrescent. Lvs elliptic-obovate, lobed, often decurrent, glab. Infl. lat.; fls 2–2.5cm diam., white or purple tinged blue. Trop. W Afr. Z10.

S. mammosum L. LADY NIPPLES; NIPPLE FRUIT. Ann. to shrubby perenn., to 1.5m. St. flexuous, pubesc., spiny. Lvs 6–14cm, orbicular, angular or sinuate-dentate, apex acute, base ± cordate, white pilose, spiny on veins beneath. Infl. umbellate, crowded, 1–6-fld; cal. villous; cor. 18–24mm, purple, lobes acuminate. Fr. 3–6cm, globose to ovoid, mammose, often with additional nipple-like lobes at base, shiny orange. Trop. Amer. Z10.

S. marginatum L. f. WHITE-MARGINED NIGHTSHADE. Shrubby bienn., 1–1.5m robust. St. velvety, with scattered yellow spines. Lvs 8–20cm, broadly ovate, coarsely sinuate-lobed, tomentose and spiny, indumentum falling above, leaving white marginal band, ultimately green and subglabrate. Peduncles few-fld, 1–2cm; cor. 2.5–3.5cm diam., white with purple star extending to lobe tips, pubesc. Fr. to 4cm diam., yellow. Summer. Afr. (Ethiop.). Z10.

S. maroniense Poit. = *S. wrightii.*

S. mauritianum Scop. Shrub or small tree, 2–4m. St. several, br. brittle, grey-green, floccose. Lvs to 30cm, ovate-elliptic, acuminate at apex, cuneate at base, dark green above, paler beneath, softly pubesc. Infl. of corymbose cymes, to 15cm diam.; cor. 1cm, tinged blue, pubesc. without. Fr. 1.5cm diam., globose, deep yellow tinged orange, pubesc. Arg., widely nat. Z10.

S. melanocerasum All. GARDEN HUCKLEBERRY. Ann. herb, to 75cm. St. ± angled, smooth. Lvs 8–18cm, broadly ovate, entire to subentire, glab. above, glab. or sparsely pilose beneath. Cor. to 1cm diam., thick, white; anth. brown. Fr. 1–1.5cm diam., black. Origin unknown; widely cult. W Trop. Afr.

S. melanoxylon Link. Perenn. to 2m, erect, unbranched, glaucous. Lvs 12–15cm, ovate- to oblong-lanceolate, acute to acuminate at apex, tapered to base, glaucous, margins white; petiole winged; white. Infl. term. then lateral, corymbose, to 8cm; cor. stellate, to 2.5cm diam., blue, lobes ovate. Fr. 2cm,

oblong-ovoid, yellow to purple or violet. S Braz., Urug. Z10.

S. melongena L. EGG-PLANT; AUBERGINE; BRINJAL; JEW'S APPLE; MAD APPLE. Ann. St. erect, 0.5–2m, stellate-pubesc., spines few or 0. Lvs 10–20cm, ovate, coarsely dentate or shallowly lobed, stellate-pubesc., main vein often spiny. Fls lat., solitary or in few-fld clusters; cal. enlarged in fr.; cor. 1.5–4cm diam., violet or light blue. Fr. globose to oblong-cylindrical to 3cm diam., yellow in wild, or elongated to 20cm and purple or black in edible cultivated forms. Summer. Sri Lanka. 'Moorea': lvs large-lobed, tinged silver; fls pale violet-blue; fr. large, oblong, orange-yellow.

S. muricatum Ait. PEPINO; MELON PEAR; MELON SHRUB. Herb or shrub, erect or ascending, to 1m+. Lvs to 15cm, simple or with 1–2 pairs of lat. lfts, ovate-lanceolate, base rounded and oblique. Infl. pseudoterminal, few- to 12-fld, simple or forked, 5–8cm; cor. rotate, to 4cm diam., violet-purple or white with purple markings. Fr. pendent, to 10cm, ovoid to ellipsoid, white or pale green marked purple, flesh yellow, aromatic, edible. Andes. 'Colossal': fr. v. large. 'Ecuadorian Gold': long season. 'El Camino': almost seedless. 'Rio Bamba': good flavour, climbing or trailing. 'Temptation': large. 'Vista': vigorous, heavy cropper, self-fertile. Z9.

S. muticum N.E. Br. Shrub, to 1.5m. St. angular, pilose. Lvs to 8cm, lanceolate, undulate, acute to acuminate at apex, tapered to base, softly pubesc. Infl. axill., cymose; cor. violet, broadly funnelform, pentagonal, 2.5–4cm diam., lobes apiculate. Parag. Z10.

S. myriacanthum Dunal. Perenn., 60–120cm. St. erect, cinereous, pubesc., with weak spines. Lvs cordate, sinuate-angled, acuminate, v. hairy, spiny. Fls 2–3 together on slender stalks, shorter than petioles; cor. lobes linear-lanceolate, acute, hairy beneath. N India. Z10.

S. nigrum L. BLACK NIGHTSHADE; COMMON NIGHTSHADE; POISON-BERRY. Ann. herb, ± glab. St. 30–60cm, erect or ascending, broadly branched. Lvs 3–8cm, ovate-lanceolate to ovate, acuminate. Infl. lat., umbellate, 3–8-fld; cal. broadly shallowly campanulate, to 2mm; cor. 5–9mm diam., white or flushed pale violet. Fr. 6–9mm, globose, yellow to black, toxic. Summer. Eurasia, nat. N Amer.

S. nigrum var. *douglasii* A. Gray = *S. douglasii.*

S. nigrum var. *guineense* L. = *S. melanocerasum.*

S. pendulum Link = *S. pensile.*

S. pensile Sendt. High-climbing vine. Lvs 5–10cm, ovate, cordate at base, glossy above, paler beneath. Infl. large, paniculate, pendulous, hairy; cor. to 4cm diam., lobes incurved, bright violet to pale blue with white centre star. Fr. 1–2cm, globose, pale violet. Guyana, Surinam. Z10.

S. phureja Juz. & Buk. Plant tuberiferous. Lvs pinnatifid to pinnate, delicate; lat. lfts in 3–8 pairs, term. leaflet often larger, glossy above, sparsely pubesc.; cor. rotate, with distinct lobes, size variable, white to dark purple. W Venez. to Colomb., Ecuad., Peru and Boliv. Z9.

S. pseudocapsicum L. WINTER CHERRY; JERUSALEM CHERRY; MADEIRA WINTER CHERRY. Shrub, 1–2m, thinly tomentose when young. Lvs 5–8cm, elliptic, acute or acuminate at apex, undulate, veins impressed, dark to mid green. Infl. 1-few-fld, short; cor. stellate, 1cm diam., white. Fr. 1–1.5cm diam., globose, bright orange, when ripe, succulent, toxic. Madeira, widely nat. 'Cherry Jubilee': fr. white, yellow and orange. 'Giant Red Cherry': fr. to 2.5cm, orange-scarlet. 'Patersonii': habit dwarf, spreading; fr. abundant. Z9.

S. pseudolycoides Rusby. Shrub, much branched, glab.; br. v. pale, with rigid spine-like br. leafy at first. Lvs to 2.5cm, oblong to oblanceolate, entire, obtuse at apex, tapered to base, somewhat fleshy. Fls solitary, term.; pedicels v. slender, 1cm, winged; cal. 7mm, turbinate, tinged blue; cor. 2cm diam., blue. Fr. 7–8mm diam., compressed globose, green. Boliv. Z10.

S. pyracanthum Jacq. Bienn. or shrubby perenn., 90–180cm, armed. Lvs 12–15cm, oblong, pinnatifid, lobes ovate-lanceolate, acute, spiny along main vein. Rac., to 15cm, many-fld; cor. 2.5cm diam., violet tinged blue, lobes cuspidate. Trop. Afr., Madag. Z10.

S. quitoense Lam. NARANJILLA; LULO. Shrubby scrambler or shrub, to 2m, densely stellate-pubesc., sometimes armed. St. flushed purple. Lvs 20–50cm, broadly ovate, sinuate-angled, purple. Infl. axill., cymose, cor. 6mm diam., white. Fr. tomato-shaped, 4+cm diam., orange, fleshy juicy, green. S Amer. Z10.

S. rantonnetii Carr. = *Lycianthes rantonnetii.*

S. robustum Wendl. Shrub, 60–120cm, armed with stout spines, rusty-woolly. Lvs 34cm, elliptic, sinuate-angled, acute, velvety green beneath, spiny on veins. Rac. 4–5cm, secund; cor. 2–2.5cm diam., deeply lobed. Braz. Z10.

S. rostratum Dunal. BUFFALO-BUR. Ann. to 60cm, broadly branched, stellate-pubesc., yellow-spiny. Lvs to 12cm, ovate or oblong in outline, pinnately 3–7-lobed, seg. sometimes lobed again on larger lvs, stellate-pubesc., spiny on veins. Infl. lat., soon becoming racemose, 5–8-fld; cal. tube spiny, accrescent, to 3cm diam.; fls 2–3cm, yellow. Fr. 1cm, globose, enclosed in spiny cal. Summer. C & S US; Mex.

S. scabrum Lam. = *S. muricatum.*

S. seaforthianum Andrews. ST VINCENT LILAC; GLYCINE; ITALIAN JASMINE. Vine to 6m, glab. or sparsely pubesc. Lvs 5–10cm, broadly elliptic, entire or pinnately divided into ovate-acuminate lobes. Infl. paniculate, pendulous; cor. campanulate to rotate, to 2cm diam., lobes elliptic-oblong, blue, purple, pink or white, ciliolate. Fr. 6–10mm, globose, red. S Amer.; widely cult. and nat. in Trop. Z10.

S. sisymbrifolium Lam. VISCID NIGHTSHADE; STICKY NIGHTSHADE. Ann. herb, viscid stellate-pubesc. St. freely branched, to 1m, stoutly yellow-spiny. Lvs 3–8cm, ovate, deeply pinnatifid, seg. dentate or lobed, stellate-pubesc. Infl. cymose, glandular-villous; cal. densely spiny, accrescent; cor. 3cm diam., violet to blue or white, pubesc. Fr. 1–2cm, globose, orange to scarlet, enclosed in cal. Summer. S Amer.; nat. coastal N Amer.

S. sodomeum L. = *S. linnaeanum.*

S. subinerme Jacq. Shrub to 4m, spines to 6mm, pubesc. Lvs to 10cm, ovate to oblong, acuminate, glab. above, pubesc. beneath. Infl. axill., tomentose, many-fld; cal. accrescent; cor. blue or violet. Fr in pendulous clusters, to 14mm, depressed-globose, yellow. Carib. Z10.

S. texanum Dunal = *S. integrifolium.*

S. tomentosum L. = *S. coccineum.*

S. torreyi Gray = *S. dimidiatum.*

S. tuberosum L. POTATO; WHITE POTATO; IRISH POTATO. Ann. or short-lived perenn. herb, sparsely pubesc., with tuber-bearing underground stolons. Tubers variable, edible. St. 30–80cm, erect, branched, thinly succulent, ± winged. Lvs pinnately compound; lfts in 3–5 pairs, ovate, acuminate, alternating with much smaller sessile lfts. Infl. cymose, axill., many-fld; 5–10cm; cor. rotate to pentagonal, 2–3cm diam., white to pink, purple or blue. Fr. 2–4cm diam., globose, green to purple, succulent. Summer. S Amer.

S. umbelliferum Eschsch. BLUE WITCH. Suffruticose perenn., 50–120cm, rounded to straggling, finely pubesc. St. ridged or angled. Lvs 1.5–5cm, elliptic-ovate, entire to pinnatifid, rather thick. Peduncles to 1cm; cor. 1.5–2cm diam., shallowly 5-lobed, blue or rarely white, with pair of green glands near base opposite each lobe. Fr. 8–15mm, globose, white, dark green near base. Summer. Calif. Z8.

S. uporo Dunal. CANNIBAL'S TOMATO; BORO DINA; POROPORO. Erect shrub, 1.5m, much branched. Lvs ovate, repand-dentate to subentire, acuminate, dark glossy green, membranous. Infl. cymose, lateral, 4–6-fld; cor. rotate, white, pubesc., lobes ovate, acuminate; anth. yellow, greatly exceeding style. Fr. resembling tomato in colour and form. Fiji, Tahiti. Z10.

S. vacciniifolium Dunal = *S. havanense.*

S. valdiviense Dunal. Shrub to 3m, br. drooping; twigs angular, pubesc. Lvs 2–4cm, ovate-lanceolate, acute at apex, tapered or rarely rounded at base, with sparse, stiff; cor. 12mm diam., lilac to white; anth. yellow. Fr. pea-sized, olive-green, ± translucent. Summer. Chile. Z10.

S. variegatum Ruiz & Pav. = *S. muricatum.*

S. verbascifolium L. = *S. erianthum.*

S. wallacei (A. Gray) Parish. CATALINA NIGHTSHADE. Suffruticose perenn., 1.5–2m, tawny-villous and evil-smelling glandular-pubesc. Lvs 3–15cm, oblong-ovate, apex acute, base acute to subcordate, entire to crenate or shallowly lobed. Peduncles several-fld, branched, 1–3cm; cor. 2–4cm diam., indigo. Fr. 1.5–2.5cm, globose, dark purple. Calif. Z8.

S. warszewiczii hort. ex Lambertye = *S. hispidum.*

S. wendlandii Hook. f. POTATO VINE; GIANT POTATO CREEPER; PARADISE FLOWER. Vine to 5m+, sparsely armed with short hook-like spines. Lvs variable, 10–25cm, bright green, pinnate lvs with large term. leaflet and 8–12 laterals, simple lvs oblong-cordate, or 3-lobed, entire. Infl. term., cymose, pendulous, 15+cm diam.; cor. rotate, 5cm diam., lilac-blue. Summer. Costa Rica. 'Albescens': fls off-white. Z10.

S. wrightii Benth. POTATO TREE; BRAZILIAN POTATO TREE. Shrub or small tree to 6m, sometimes armed. Lvs 30cm, broadly ovate, sinuate-dentate to irregularly pinnatifid, hispid above, coarsely stellate-pubesc. beneath. Cymes axill., forked, to 12cm; cor. 5-lobed, 6–7cm, diam., dark violet to pale lilac or white. Braz. to Boliv.; widely cult. in Trop. Z10.

S. xantii A. Gray. PURPLE NIGHTSHADE. Suffruticose perenn., 2–100cm, short villous, glandular-pubesc. or glab. Lvs 2–4cm, ovate, subentire to hastately lobed at base, slightly decurrent on petiole. Peduncles 4–9-fld, 0.5–1cm, glandular-pubesc.; cor. 1.5–2.5cm diam., purple to deep lavender, finely pubesc. Fr. 6–8mm, globose, green, subtended by enlarged cal. Summer. Calif., Ariz., Baja Calif. Z9.

S. xantii var. **wallacei** A. Gray = *S. wallacei.*

→Androcera.

Soldanella L. Primulaceae. 10 diminutive, alpine, perenn. herbs. Lvs in basal rosettes, entire, leathery, everg., long-petiolate. Fls 5-merous, pendent, scapose, often penetrating snow cover; cal. lobes linear or lanceolate; cor. far exceeding cal., infundibuliform to campanulate, with 5 wide, shallow, fringed lobes. Spring. Alps, Carpath., Balk. Z5 unless specified.

S. alpina L. Lvs to 4cm wide, orbicular-reniform; petioles with sessile glands when young. Scapes to 15cm, fls 2–4; pedicels with sessile glands; cor. violet or blue-violet, with crimson marks inside, to 15mm, cut to middle or beyond, lobes cut into 4–5 lobules. Pyren., Alps to the Tirol.

S. ×aschersoniana Vierh. (*S. austriaca* ×*S. montana.*) Highly variable hybrids exhibiting characters of both parents. NE Alps.

S. austriaca Vierh. Lvs to 1cm wide, orbicular, base subcordate. Scape to 1.5cm, glandular-pubesc.; fls solitary; pedicels with subsessile glands; cor. tubular-campanulate, to 15mm, blue to violet, lined with violet streaks, cut to about a quarter of its length. NE (Austrian) Alps. 'Alba': fls white.

S. carpatica Vierh. Lvs to 5cm wide, suborbicular, basal sinus narrow, shallow; petioles sparsely sessile-glandular, when young. Scape to 15cm; fls 2–5; pedicels glandular-pubesc.; cor. to 15mm diam., divided to two-thrids of its length, violet, lobes 3–4-partite, or 3-dentate. W Carpath.

S. clusii Gaudin non F.W. Schmidt = *S. pusilla.*

S. clusii F.W. Schmidt. non Gaudin = *S. alpina.*

S. dimoniei Vierh. Similar to *S. hungarica*, but lvs to 1.7cm diam., blue-grey, pruinose beneath, covered in gland. pits. Scape to 9cm; fls 2–3; cor. divided to more than half its length, violet, lobes crenately lobulate. Mts of Macedonia, E Albania, Bulg. Z6.

S. ×ganderi Huter. (*S. alpina* ×*S. minima.*) Lvs orbicular; petiole subglabrous. Scape to 9cm; fls 1–2; pedicels minutely gland.; cor. to 15mm, campanulate, pale violet to white, cor. to middle. S Alps.

S. ×handel-mazzettii Vierh. = *S. ×aschersoniana.*

S. hungarica Simonkai. Lvs to 2.5cm diam., orbicular-reniform, base cordate with a narrow sinus, tinted violet beneath. Scape to 10cm, glandular-hairy; fls 1–3, cor. widely campanulate, to 15mm, lilac to violet, lobes cut to middle or beyond. Mts of EC Eur., Balk. Penins. Z6.

S. ×hybrida Kerner. (*S. alpina* ×*S. pusilla.*) Lvs cordate-reniform; petioles gland. at first. Scape to 14cm; fls 1–2; pedicels with sessile glands; cor. to 2cm, cut to a third of its length. Alps.

S. ×janchenii Vierh. (*S. minima* ×*S. pusilla.*) Lvs orbicular; petiole subglabrous. Scape to 9cm, gland.; fls 1; cor. to 15mm, cut to a third of its length. S Alps.

S. ×lungoviensis Vierh. (*S. montana* ×*S. pusilla.*) Lvs intermediate between parents, base cordate; petiole densely glandular-pubesc. Fls 5; pedicels shortly glandular-puberulent; cor. irregularly divided. Alps.

S. minima Hoppe in Sturm. Lvs to 1cm diam., suborbicular, lacking basal sinus, glandular-pitted beneath. Scape to 10cm; fls usually solitary; cor. to 15mm, campanulate, divided to quarter of its length, pale violet or lilac to almost white, tinted with lilac streaks. S Alps. 'Alba': fls white. Z6.

S. ×mixta Vierh. (*S. austriaca* ×*S. pusilla.*) Highly variable hybrids exhibiting characters from both parents. Alps.

S. montana Willd. Lvs to 6cm wide, orbicular or orbicular-reniform, sometimes shallowly dentate or crenate, often tinted violet beneath; basal sinus deep, narrow; petiole covered with persistent gland. hairs. Scape to 25cm; fls to 6; cor. to 15mm, divided to three-quarters of its length, blue to lilac, lobes deeply, divided into 3–4 narrow lobules. N Alps, Carpath., Balk. Penins. Z6.

S. neglecta O. Schulz in Vierh. = *S. ×janchenii.*

S. pindicola Hausskn. Similar to *S. carpatica* but with glands on peduncles and pedicels ± 0. Lvs with wide basal sinus, blue-grey, pruinose beneath. Fls rose-lilac. N Greece, Albania. Z6.

S. pindicola var. **dimoniei** (Vierh.) Markgr. = *S. dimoniei.*

S. pusilla Baumg. Lvs to 1cm wide, orbicular to rounded-reniform; petiole covered with decid. sessile glands. Scape to 10cm, with decid. sessile glands; fls usually solitary; cor. to 15mm, narrowly campanulate, divided to quarter of its length, blue to pale violet, lobes obtuse. Alps.

S. ×richteri Wettst. = *S. ×transsilvanica.*

S. ×transsilvanica Borb. (*S. hungarica* ×*S. pusilla.*) Highly variable hybrids, intermediate between parents. Alps.

S. villosa Darracq. Rhiz. long. Lvs to 7cm wide, orbicular-reniform, basal sinus narrow; petiole with persistent gland. hairs. Scape to 30cm, densely villous; fls 3–4; cor. to 15mm, violet, divided to three-quarters length, lobes deeply cut into 3–5 lobules. Pyren. Z6.

S. ×wettsteinii Vierh. (*S. alpina* ×*S. austriaca.*) Lvs intermediate between parents in size. Fls 2–3; cor. usually cut to middle, inside not streaked. Alps.

S. ×wiemanniana Vierh. (*S. alpina* ×*S. austriaca.*) V. variable hybrids, intermediate between parents. Alps.

Soldier Rose Mallow *Hibiscus militaris.*
Soldier's-cap *Aconitum napellus.*
Soledad Pine *Pinus torreyana.*

Soleirolia Gaudich. Urticaceae. 1 dwarf, creeping, mat-forming, everg., perenn. herb; st. delicate, intricately branching, rooting, translucent. Lvs 2–6mm, suborbicular, minutely papillose-pubescent, short-stalked. Fls solitary, axill., minute. Summer. W Medit. Is., nat. W Eur.; can become an invasive weed. Z9.
S. soleirolii (Req.) Dandy. MIND YOUR OWN BUSINESS; BABY'S TEARS; POLLYANNA VINE; ANGEL'S TEARS; IRISH MOSS; CORSICAN CURSE. 'Aurea' ('Golden Queen'): lvs golden green. 'Variegata' ('Argentea', 'Silver Queen'): lvs variegated silver.
→*Helxine.*

Solena Lour. Cucurbitaceae. 1 tuberous climbing herb. St. slender, glab. Tendrils simple. Lvs subsessile, ovate-cordate, entire or remotely dentate to deeply lobed, scabrid and gland. above. Fls to 0.6×0.4cm, yellow-white; ♂ umbellate; ♀ solitary. Fr. ovoid, scabrous or villous, fleshy, 2.5×1.5cm. Asia to Malaysia. Z10.
S. amplexicaulis (Lam.) Gandhi.
S. gracilis Rudge = *Posoqueria latifolia* ssp. *gracilis.*
S. latifolia Rudge = *Posoqueria latifolia.*
→*Bryonia.*

Solenangis Schltr. Orchidaceae. 5 epiphytic monopodial orchids. St. elongated, scandent. Lvs elliptic-lanceolate or 0. Rac. axill.; fls small; sep. and pet. free, subsimilar; lip entire or obscurely trilobed, spurred. Trop. Afr. Z10.
S. clavata (Schltr.) Schltr. Lvs 1.5–5×0.5–1.5cm. Rac. tep. ovate-oblong, many-fld; fls to 0.5cm diam. white, or tep. green and lip white; lip v. small, trilobed; spur 0.7cm, stout. W Afr.
S. scandens (Schltr.) Schltr. Lvs 3–9×1–2.5cm. Rac. 2–9cm, several-fld; fls to 1.4cm diam., white, green-white or yellow-green, sometimes tinged pink; tep. ovate; lip 0.6cm, entire; spur to 2.5cm. W Afr., Zaïre.
S. wakefieldii (Rolfe) Cribb & Joyce Stewart. Lvs 1.5–3×0.5–1.5cm. Rac. 4–6cm, laxly 4–6-fld; fls to 0.8cm diam., white; tep. oblong-lanceolate; lip 1cm, trilobed; spur 0.7cm, slender. slender; spur Kenya, Zanzibar.
→*Angraecum* and *Tridactyle.*

Solenanthus Ledeb. Boraginaceae. *c*15 erect perenn. or bienn. herbs. Basal lvs simple, long-petiolate, st. lvs sessile. Pan. axill., cymose, cal. lobes elliptic-oblong, usually accrescent; cor. infundibular to cylindrical, slightly lobed, with triangular to sub-quadrate scales; sta. 5, exserted. Eur. to C Asia. Z7.
S. apenninus (L.) Fisch. & C.A. Mey. To 120cm. Basal lvs to 50×12cm, ovate-oblong or elliptic to broadly lanceolate. Cal. to 10mm, lobes short, lanceolate; cor. to 9mm, blue to purple; scales pubesc. It., Sicily.
S. circinatus Ledeb. To 1m, robust. Basal lvs to 30×20cm, broadly ovate, acute, cordate at base, scabrous above, tomentose to strigose beneath. Cal. lobes to 4mm, ovate or obovate to oblong; cor. to 7mm, blue-purple, scales minute, narrowly triangular. W Asia to C Asia.
→*Cynoglossum.*

Solenidium Lindl. Orchidaceae. 3 epiphytic orchids. Pbs ellipsoid to cylindrical, compressed, grooved, apically bifoliate. Rac. lat., erect or ascending; tep. obovate to oblong-lanceolate subequal; lip sometimes with a pair of small basal lobes; disc callose. N S Amer. Z10.
S. lunatum (Lindl.) Kränzl. Pbs to 3.5×2cm. Lvs to 13×2cm, coriaceous, oblong or oblong-lanceolate. Infl. to 25cm, few- to many-fld; fls to 2cm diam.; tep. light yellow-brown marked red-brown, slightly fleshy; lip white spotted brown, reniform, ciliate, with a narrow claw bearing small auriculate lobes. Venez., Guyana, Braz.
S. racemosum Lindl. Pbs to 6×2.5cm. Lvs to 30×2cm, linear or linear-lanceolate. Infl. to 35cm, loosely many-fld; fls to 2.5cm diam.; tep. yellow blotched and barred chestnut brown; lip entire, broadly ovate or obovate, callus white. Winter. Colomb., Venez.
→*Leochilus, Oncidium* and *Rodriguezia.*

Solenomelus Miers. Iridaceae. 2 tufted perenn., rhizomatous herbs related to *Sisyrinchium.* St. terete. Lvs distichous, mostly basal. Fls with slender perianth tube and spreading tep.; fil. united; style unbranched. Temp. S Amer. Z9.
S. chilensis Miers = *S. pedunculatus.*
S. pedunculatus (Gillies) Hochr. 30–50cm. Basal lvs 15–30cm,

linear, grass-like. Infl. 1–3-fld; spathes *c*2.5cm, edged white. Fls yellow; tube 25mm; tep. to 25mm. Summer. Chile.
S. segethii (Philippi) Kuntze. 10–30cm. Basal lvs 10–30cm, terete. Infl. 1–2-fld; spathes to 3cm, edged white; fls blue; tube 5mm; tep. to 14mm. Summer. Chile.
S. sisyrinchium (Griseb.) Diels = *S. segethii.*
→*Sisyrinchium.*

Solenostemon Thonn. Labiatae. 60 shrubby, often succulent herbs, often hairy and gland. Lvs often blotched or variegated. Infl. term., racemose or paniculate; fls in glomerate dichasia; cal. bilabiate, uppermost tooth forming an erect ovate lobe, 2 lowermost teeth fused long, lateral teeth rounded; cor. bilabiate, tube sigmoid, upper lip obscurely 4-lobed, lower lip larger, navicular; sta. 4, declinate. Trop. Afr. and Asia. Z10.
S. blumei (Benth.) Launert = *S. scutellarioides.*
S. scutellarioides (L.) Codd. COLEUS; PAINTED NETTLE. Perenn. aromatic herb or subshrub, procumbent or erect to 1m. St. semi-succulent, 4-angled. Lvs petiolate, membranous, large, ovate-deltoid or ovate-oblong, crenate, dentate or incised. Infl. terminal, simple or with a pair of branchlets at base; fls in sessile several-fld dichasia; cal. 7mm, upper lip 2mm, erect, ovate; cor. 8–10mm, blue-violet. Malaysia, and SE Asia. The 'coleus' of florists, ranging in habit from dwarf or trailing to tall; height from 20–60cm; lvs 3–15cm long, shape oak-leafed to elongated heart-shaped or saber-like, edges sometimes deeply serrated or frilled. Bellevue Hybrid Blend: lvs striking bi- and tri-coloured in bright pink, rose, scarlet, ivory, dark green, etc. Dragon Series: lvs oak-shaped, scarlet to purple and black with golden edge. Jazz Series: dwarf; lvs brightly coloured with streaks or edging. Milky Way Mixed: v. dwarf; lvs pronounced oak-shaped, bright colours, edged. Old Lace Mixed: lvs centre rose, white, lilac or crimson, salmon, laced and edged in lemon. Saber Type: lvs long, deeply cut, green and cream. Striped Rainbow: lvs heart-shaped, irregularly striped yellow, red, burgundy, copper and green. Superfine Rainbow Fringed Mix: lvs edges cut and frilled, rainbow colours. Wizard Mixed: dwarf, compact, much base branching; lvs with pink, black, scarlet, and ivory combinations.
S. shirensis (Gürke) Codd. Robust, shrubby perenn. to 2m. Lvs 8–15cm, ovate, acuminate, crenate, puberulous, petioles hispid. Infl. paniculate of loose verticillasters; cor. blue-mauve. E Trop. Afr.
→*Coleus, Ocimum* and *Plectranthus.*

Solidago L. GOLDENROD. Compositae. *c*100 perenn. herbs; st. erect, simple at base, branching below pan. Lvs usually narrow becoming reduced further up st. and withering below. Cap. small, radiate, usually many, in fascicles, thyrses, or scorpioid or corymbose pan.; involucre ± cylindric; ray flts yellow; disc flts tubular, yellow. N Hemis., particularly N Amer., a few in S Amer., Eurasia and Macaronesia.
S. algida Piper = *S. multiradiata.*
S. alpestris Waldst. & Kit. = *S. virgaurea* ssp. *alpestris.*
S. altissima L. = *S. canadensis* var. *scabra.*
S. angusta Torr. & A. Gray. To 1.5m. Lvs to 12×3cm, lanceolate-linear to ovate, entire or rarely remotely dentate, firm, strongly glutinous, usually glab., or scabrous along veins, rarely sparsely hairy beneath. Cap. in narrow, elongate, often bracteate pan., lower clusters sometimes stiffly ascending; ray flts 5–13, 3-5mm. Late summer–autumn. C & S US. Z5.
S. arborescens Forst. f. = *Olearia arborescens.*
S. arendsii hort. = *Solidaster luteus.*
S. arguta Ait. To 1.3m. Lvs to 30×12cm, narrowly to broadly elliptic or ovate, abruptly contracted to petiole, acuminate, sharply and finely dentate except toward base, thin, glab. or slightly scabrous above. Cap. in an elongate, narrow, or broad open pan. with recurved-secund, divergent br.; ray flts 5–8. Late summer–autumn. NE US.
S. aspera Ait. = *S. rugosa* var. *aspera.*
S. bicolor L. SILVERROD. Like *S. hispida* except ray flts white or v. pale yellow. Late summer–autumn. E N Amer. Z4.
S. brachystachys hort. = *S. cutleri.*
S. buckleyi Torr. & A. Gray. To 1.2m. Lvs 14×5cm, elliptic to ovate or obovate-elliptic, more or less serrate, sessile or shortly petiolate, thin, glab. or nearly so above, hirsute on main veins beneath, rarely sparsely hairy. Cap. in a series of short, sometimes elongate clusters; ray flts 5–7, *c*3–5mm. Late summer–autumn. SE US. Z6.
S. caesia L. To 1m. Lvs to 12×3cm, lanceolate or lanceolate-elliptic, tapered to base, sessile or obscurely petiolate, serrate, acuminate, glab. or slightly pubesc. above and on midrib beneath. Cap. in an elongate series of axill. clusters; ray flts 3–4. Late summer–autumn. C & E N Amer. Z4.
S. californica Nutt. To 1.2m. Lvs to 12×3.5cm, spathulate to obovate or ovate, base attenuate, crenate to serrate, firm. Cap.

in a dense, narrow thyrse, or sometimes a pyramidal pan. with spreading br.; ray flts 8–13. Autumn. SW US, New Mex. Z8.

S. cambrica Huds. = *S. virgaurea*.

S. canadensis L. To 1.5m. Lvs to 13×2cm, lanceolate, base long-attenuate, sharply serrate, with conspicuous lat. veins, glab. above, partially glab. to pubesc. or scabrid beneath. Cap. strongly secund in a broad pyramidal pan.; ray flts 10–17, to 2mm. Late summer–autumn. N Amer., nat. Eur. ssp. *elongata* (Nutt.) Keck. St. minutely pubesc. to pilose, at least above. Lf margins scabrid, glab. to minutely scabrous-pubesc. Summer. (Nutt.) Keck. var. *scabra* (Muhlenb.) Torr. & A. Gray. To 2m. Involucre 3–5mm; disc flts 3–4mm. Z3.

S. cutleri Fern. To 50cm. Lvs to 15×4cm, oblanceolate to spathulate or elliptic, dentate, rounded to acute, glab. or ciliate, long-petiolate below, sessile above. Cap. few in a corymb or in a more elongate, bracteate infl; ray flts 10–13. Summer–early autumn. NE US. 'Pyramidalis': to 40cm; fls bright yellow. Z4.

S. drummondii Torr. & A. Gray. To 1mm. Lvs to 9×7cm, broadly or elliptic-ovate, shortly petiolate, pinnately veined, minutely pubesc. or subglabrous, or minutely scabrous above. Cap. sometimes pendulous, in pan. with recurved-secund br.; ray flts 3–7. Summer–autumn. SE & SC US. Z6.

S. elongata Nutt. = *S. canadensis* var. *elongata*.

S. flexicaulis L. To 1.3m. Lvs to 15×10cm, ovate to elliptic, sharply dentate, acuminate, base abruptly narrowed to broad, winged petiole, glab. or sparsely hairy above, hirsute beneath at least on main veins. Cap. in a series of short clusters, lowest cap. axill.; ray flts 3–4. Summer–autumn. E N Amer. 'Variegata': to 60cm; lvs stippled brown and gold. Z4.

S. gattingeri Chapm. To 1m. Lvs to 12×6cm, linear-oblanceolate, serrate to subentire, petiole of basal lvs sometimes ciliate. Cap. in a pan., commonly as broad as long, with recurved-secund br.; ray flts 3–6. Autumn. SE US. Z8.

S. gigantea Ait. Like *S. canadensis* var. *scabra* but to 2.5m; lvs glab. above, pubesc. on veins beneath. Late summer–autumn. N Amer., widely nat. Eur. ssp. *serotina* (Kuntze) McNeill. Lvs usually glab. Involucre 3–5mm. Z6.

S. glaberrima Martens = *S. missouriensis* var. *fasciculata*.

S. glomerata Michx. To 1.2m. Lvs to 35×7.5cm, oblanceolate, sharply serrate, acuminate, base attenuate, long-petiolate, ciliate, otherwise glab. Cap. clustered on ascending axill. br., forming a narrow term. thyrse; ray flts many. Late summer–autumn. E US. Z6.

S. graminifolia (L.) Salisb. To 1.5m. Lvs to 15×2cm, linear-lanceolate, entire, with 2–4 conspicuous lat. veins. Cap. in a corymbose pan., mostly sessile; ray flts 15–25. Autumn. N Amer. Z3.

S. hispida Muhlenb. ex Willd. To 1m. Lvs to 20×5cm, broadly oblanceolate to obovate or elliptic, dentate to entire, lamina and petiole. Cap. in elongate, narrow, often leafy bracteate infl., lower clusters often elongate, stiffly ascending; ray flts 7–14, deep yellow. Summer–autumn. E & Central N Amer. Z5.

S. ×hybrida hort. = *Solidaster luteus*.

S. juncea Ait. To 1.2m. Lvs to 40×8cm, narrowly elliptic, acuminate, serrate, margins scabrous or ciliate, sometimes short-hirsute. Cap. in a dense pan. with recurved-secund br.; ray flts 7–12, minute. Summer–early autumn. E N Amer. Z3.

S. latifolia L. = *S. flexicaulis*.

S. linoides Torr. & A. Gray = *S. uliginosa* var. *linoides*.

S. microcephala (Greene) Bush. To 1m. Lvs to 6cm, filiform-subulate, glab., or hirtellous on midrib beneath, thin. Cap. usually pedunculate, in small glomerules, glutinous; ray flts 7–13, short. Autumn. E US. Z5.

S. milleriana Mackenzie = *S. petiolaris*.

S. minor (Michx.) Fern. = *S. microcephala*.

S. minuta L. = *S. virgaurea* ssp. *alpestris*.

S. minutissima (Mak.) Kit. = *S. virgaurea* ssp. *alpestris* var. *minutissima*.

S. missouriensis Nutt. To 50cm. Lvs to 20×5cm, oblanceolate, entire or dentate above, base attenuate, scabrid-ciliate, sometimes early decid. Cap. usually in a rhombic or oblong pan., br. erect; ray flts 8–13. Late summer–autumn. W US, W Canada. var. *fasciculata* Holzing. To 1m. Lvs often in reduced axill. fascicles. Z7.

S. missouriensis hort. = *Solidaster luteus*.

S. mollis Bartling. To 60cm. Lvs crowded, lower lvs to 10×4cm, broadly oblanceolate, obscurely petiolate, rounded to acute, 3-nerved, firm. Cap. in a dense pan. or compact thyrse, lower br. often somewhat recurved- secund; ray flts usually 8, 3–4mm. Late summer. Central N Amer. Z5.

S. multiradiata Ait. To 40cm. Lvs to 10×2cm, basal oblanceolate to elliptic, entire to crenate-serrulate, base attenuate, petiolate, margins scabrid. Cap. few to numerous, in a dense, term. corymb; ray flts commonly 13. Summer. N Amer. to E Sib. var. *scopulorum* A. Gray. Margins of lower lvs ciliate. Cap. in open corymbs; phyllaries often subobtuse. Z2.

S. nemoralis Ait. To 1m. Lvs to 25×4cm, oblanceolate or slightly broader, dentate, basal lvs persistent, petiolate. Cap. in a long, narrow, apically pendulous pan., or pan. broader with long, divergent br.; ray flts 5–9, short. Summer–autumn. Canada, E US. Z3.

S. odora Ait. To 2m. Lvs to 10×1.5cm, lanceolate or oblong to linear-lanceolate, entire, acute, sessile, margins scabrous, finely translucent-punctate, aniseed-scented when crushed. Cap. in a pan. with recurved-secund br.; ray flts 3–5, showy. Summer. E & SE US. Z3.

S. pallida (Porter) Rydb. To 1.2m. Lvs to 12×2.5cm, lanceolate to ovate-lanceolate, usually entire, margins strongly ciliate; basal lvs sometimes crenate. Cap. in a narrow, dense, simple or branched thyrse; ray flts few. Late summer–autumn. C & E N Amer. Z4.

S. petiolaris Ait. To 1.5m. Lvs to 20×6cm, lanceolate-elliptic to ovate-oblong, sessile or short-petiolate, entire to remotely dentate, often prominently veined, firm, scarcely glutinous, glab. or scabrous above, minutely pubesc. beneath. Cap. in a narrow, elongate infl.; ray flts 5–8, 4–7mm. Summer–autumn. SE US. Z8.

S. puberula Nutt. To 1m. Lvs to 15×3.5cm, broadly oblanceolate to elliptic or obovate, serrate, petiolate, st. lvs lanceolate-linear. Cap. in terminal, dense, often bracteate infl. with stiffly ascending, scarcely secund or branched; ray flts 9–16. Summer–autumn. E N Amer. Z3.

S. pulcherrima Nels. = *S. nemoralis*.

S. riddellii Frank ex Riddell. To 1m. Lvs to 12×1cm, narrowly elongate, entire, often 3-nerved, firm, margins scabrous; basal lvs often long-petiolate and early decid.; st. lvs numerous, often arcuate. Cap. often numerous, crowded, in a corymb; ray flts 7–9. Summer–autumn. NE N Amer. Z4.

S. rigida L. To 1.5m. Lvs to 25×10cm, elliptic, elliptic-oblong to broadly ovate, rounded to somewhat acute, slightly dentate or entire, petiole equalling lamina, firm. Cap. in a dense corymb; ray flts 8–14. Autumn. E & NE US. Z4.

S. rugosa Mill. To 1.5m. Lvs crowded, to 13×4cm, elliptic to ovate-lanceolate, sharply dentate, acuminate, subsessile, not clasping, not 3-nerved, rugose-veined, thin, glab. or scabrous above, hirsute at least on main veins beneath. Cap. in a pan. with recurved-secund br.; ray flts 8–11, small. Summer–autumn. E N Amer. var. *aspera* (Ait.) Fern. Lvs usually obtusely dentate, strongly rugose-veined, thick and firm. Ray flts 6–8. C & E N Amer. Z3.

S. scopulorum Nels. = *S. multiradiata* var. *scopulorum*.

S. sempervirens L. To 2m. Lvs 30×6cm, entire, obtuse, apiculate, margins usually smooth, rarely minutely scabrid, rather fleshy; basal lvs elliptic-lanceolate to ovate, petiole wide; st. lvs narrower, ± amplexicaul. Cap. in a thyrsoid pan. or lower br. patent with ± secund cap.; ray flts 7–11, 3–5mm. Autumn. NE Amer., Azores. Z4.

S. serotina Kuntze = *S. gigantea* ssp. *serotina*.

S. shortii Torr. & A. Gray. To 1.5m. Lvs to 10×1.5cm, crowded, narrowly elliptic, acuminate or sharply acute, 3-nerved, attenuate to subsessile or obscurely short-petiolate base, remotely minutely serrate, firm, glab., gradually reduced above. Cap. in a pan. with recurved-secund br.; phyllaries acute to somewhat obtuse, firm; ray flts 5–8, 2.5–3mm. Fr. pubesc. Autumn. E US. Z6.

S. spathulata DC. To 60cm. Lvs to 12×7cm, broadly obovate to spathulate-oblanceolate, blunt or rounded, crenate-serrate, attenuate to petiole. Cap. in a simple or compound, sometimes racemiform thyrse to 25cm; ray flts 7–9, scarcely exceeding disc. Spring–autumn. W coast US. Z8.

S. speciosa Nutt. To 1.5m. Lvs numerous, entire, lower lvs to 30×10cm, elliptic or ovate, slightly dentae, often broad and abruptly petiolate. Cap. in a usually dense, rather crowded infl. with stiffly ascending br., sometimes simple; ray flts 6–8, 3–5mm. Summer–autumn. C & E US. Z5.

S. spectabilis (Eaton) A. Gray. To 50cm. Lvs to 30×4cm, usually entire, oblanceolate, attenuate to long, decurrent petiole, upper lvs linear-lanceolate, scabrid-ciliate. Cap. in v. dense, oblong pan. to 10cm; ray flts 11–15, short. Summer. W US. Z7.

S. squarrosa Muhlenb. ex Nutt. To 1.5m. Lvs to 20×10cm, broadly oblanceolate to elliptic-ovate, sharply on main veins beneath, rarely hairy above. Cap. in a narrow, elongate, bracteate infl.; ray flts 10–17. Late summer–autumn. E N Amer. Z5.

S. stricta Ait. To 2m. Lvs to 30×2cm, oblanceolate or elliptic-oblanceolate, entire or obscurely serrate, thick and firm. Cap. in narrow, elongate, minutely bracteate infl., sometimes pendulous at apex, with short, recurved- secund br.; ray flts 5–7. Summer–autumn. E & SC US. Z5.

S. uliginosa Nutt. To 1.5cm. Lvs to 35×6cm, oblanceolate to narrowly elliptic, elongate, subentire to serrate, attenuate to long petiole, sheathing; basal lvs generally persistent, often sharply dentate. Cap. in a long, narrow infl., br. often recurved-secund; ray flts 1–8. Late summer–autumn. E N Amer. var. *linoides* (Torr. & A. Gray) Fern. Lower lvs narrowly oblanceolate, to 2.5cm wide. Cap. in a narrow, minutely pubesc. pan. Z5.

S. ulmifolia Muhlenb. ex Willd. To 1.2m. Lvs to 12×5.5cm, rhombic-ovate to lanceolate-elliptic, acute or acuminate, broadly short-petiolate or attenuate and subsessile, thin, hirsute or scabrous-hirsute or less often glab. above, loosely hirsute at least on main veins beneath; basal lvs elliptic to elliptic-ovate. Cap. crowded in a pan., br. few, long, divergent; ray flts 3–5, minute. Summer–autumn. E & Central N Amer. Z4.

S. uniligulata (DC.) Porter = *S. uliginosa*.

S. virgaurea L. To 1m. Lvs generally serrate, glab. above, generally pubesc. beneath; basal lvs to 10cm, oblanceolate to obovate, st. lvs to 3×6cm, linear-lanceolate to elliptic, acute, gradually reduced above. Cap. in a thyrse or pan. with ascending racemose br.; ray flts 6–12, 4–9mm. Summer–autumn. Eur. ssp. *alpestris* (Waldst. & Kit. ex Willd.) Gaudin. St. 20cm. Lvs usually glab., somewhat coriaceous; cap. few, large, in compact, spike-like rac. Arc., W Eur. var. *minutissima* Mak. St. to 10cm. Lower lvs to 3.5cm, ovate or oblong-lanceolate. Jap. Z5.

S. virgaurea ssp. *minuta* L. = *S. virgaurea* ssp. *alpestris*.

S. cvs. Many cvs from 30 to 80cm, light to dark yellow; smaller cvs include the 30cm yellow 'Golden Dwarf', the 30cm 'Queenie' ('Golden Thumb') with variegated gold and green lvs, the 40cm light gold 'Laurin', the deep gold 50cm semi-dwarf 'Golden Gate', and the early-flowering 50cm 'Praecox'; notable taller cvs include the 70cm buttercup-yellow 'Leraft', the 80cm deep yellow 'Ledsham' and 'Lemore', the paler gold 80cm 'Goldschleier' and the 120cm light yellow 'Super'.

✕ **Solidaster** Wehrh. (*Aster* ✕*Solidago*.) Compositae. Perenn. to 1m. Lvs to 15cm, lanceolate to linear-elliptic to narrowly oblanceolate, remotely serrate, apex acute, base attenuate, long-petiolate. Cap. to 1cm diam., radiate, numerous, in a branched corymbose pan.; ray flts canary-yellow, becoming creamy yellow with age; disc flts golden-yellow. Gdn origin. Z6.

✕*S. luteus* Green ex Dress. Found 1910 as a natural hybrid in the nurseries of Léonard Lille, Lyons. 'Lemore': to 80cm; cap. massed, flts pale lemon.
→*Aster* and ✕ *Asterago*.

Solisia Britt. & Rose.
S. pectinata (Stein) Britt. & Rose = *Mammillaria pectinifera*.

Solitaire Palm *Ptychosperma elegans*.

Sollya Lindl. Pittosporaceae. 3 everg. slender climbers or scandent shrubs. Lvs small, narrow, entire or slightly undulate. Fls small, bell-like, blue, nodding, slender-stalked in cymes, or solitary, term., lax; sep. small; pet. obovate, erect to spreading. Fr. a berry. Aus. Z9.

S. drummondii Morr. = *S. parviflora*.
S. fusiformis (Labill.) Briq. = *S. heterophylla*.
S. heterophylla Lindl. BLUEBELL CREEPER; AUSTRALIAN BLUEBELL. Slender climber to 1.5m. Lvs 2.5–5cm, on short petioles, ovate to linear-oblong or oblanceolate, paler beneath. Infl. 4–12-fld; pet. 8mm. Summer. W Aus.
S. parviflora Turcz. Slender thinly downy climber to 2m. Lvs to 25cm, subsessile, lanceolate to oblong-linear, thinner than in *S. heterophylla*. Infl. 1–3-fld; pet. c6mm. Summer. W Aus.

Solomon's Feathers *Smilacina*.
Solomon's Plume *Smilacina*.
Solomon's Seal *Polygonatum*.
Solomon's Zigzag *Smilacina racemosa*.
Solver Cassia *Senna artemisioides*.
Somali Hemp *Sansevieria grandis*.

Sonchus L. MILK THISTLE. Compositae. c60 ann. to perenn. herbs and shrubs, with white latex. St. lvs amplexicaul. Cap. lingulate, few to many; involucre campanulate to cylindrical; flts yellow. Eurasia to trop. Afr., esp. Macaronesia. Many widespread weeds.

S. alpinus L. = *Cicerbita alpina*.
S. arboreus DC. Erect, tree-like shrub, 1–2.5m. St. thick. Lvs rosulate at br. apices, petiolate, glab., pinnatisect, lobes in 5–12 pairs, filiform, linear or linear-lanceolate. Cap. 5–10×1.5–3mm, clustered in a dense corymb; flts 15–20, ligule c5mm. Spring. Canary Is. Z9.
S. congestus Willd. Erect shrub to 1.5m. Lvs in rosettes at br. apices lanceolate, pinnatifid, with at least 4 pairs of acuminate, triangular lobes, margin serrulate, glab. Cap. 2–2.5cm diam., in densely congested infl.; flts numerous. Spring–summer. Canary Is. Z9.

S. gummifer Link. Perenn. to 80cm, base woody. St. to 15cm. Lvs in small, rosettes, pruinose, pinnatifid, lobes ovate or triangular, angular. Cap. few, 1–1.5cm diam., in a corymbose infl.; flts numerous. Early summer. Canary Is. Z9.
S. leptocephalus Cass. Slender shrub, to 2m. St. lvs in apical tufts, often pendent, pinnatifid to pinnatisect, lobes to 6cm, in 6–12 pairs, linear, glab. Cap. numerous, to 5mm diam., in dense pan.; flts, 12–20, ligule to 1mm. Summer. Canary Is. Z9.
S. pinnatus Ait. Shrub, to 2m. St. smooth, much branched. Lvs deeply pinnatisect, lobes lanceolate to oblong- or ovate-lanceolate, to 5×2cm, entire to denticulate. Cap. to 1.5cm diam., few to many, in a pan.; flts 18–30, ligule to 7mm. Spring–summer. Madeira. Z9.
S. plumieri L. = *Cicerbita plumieri*.
S. radicatus Ait. Perenn. herb, to 80cm. St. usually simple, woody at base. Lvs mostly in a basal rosette, lyrate-pinnatisect, lobes ovate, entire to denticulate, st. lvs few, lyrate. Cap. to 2cm diam., few in a corymbose cluster; flts numerous. Summer. Canary Is. Z9.

Sonerila Roxb. Melastomataceae. c100 herbs and subshrubs. Lvs simple, entire or toothed, 3- or 5-veined. Fls in spikes or scorpioid rac., 3-merous; cal. tubular; pet. ovate, obovate or oblong, usually rose-pink; sta. usually 3, equal, or 6 unequal. SE Asia, S China. Z10.

S. grandiflora R. Br. To 30cm, woody-based. Lvs 2.5–5cm, crowded, oblong or elliptic, glab., bristle-toothed. Fls mauve, in dense-fld, term., short-stalked rac.
S. laeta Stapf. Erect herb, to 15cm; st. glandular-pubesc. Lvs to 10cm, ovate or elliptic-ovate, spotted white, purple spotted green beneath. Fls tinged purple. China. *S. maculata* (Roxb.) differs in lvs ciliate.
S. margaritacea Lindl. Procumbent red-stemmed herb to 30cm. Lvs to 12cm, oblong or ovate-lanceolate, slender-pointed, dark green with pearly-white spots in lines between veins above, pale with red-purple veins beneath. Fls to 1.5cm diam. in an 8–10-fld corymb, rose. Java to Burm. 'Argentea': lvs claret, densely overlaid with silver. 'Hendersonii': compact, 15–20cm; lvs dark olive, densely covered with pearly-white spots. 'Marmorata': lvs banded silver-grey. 'Mme Baextele': dwarf; lvs rounded, pale grey spotted cream above, maroon below; fls pink.

Song of India *Dracaena reflexa*.
Sonoma Manzanita *Arctostaphylos densiflora*.
Sonoran Palmetto *Sabal uresana*.

Sophora L. Leguminosae (Papilionoideae). 52 decid. or everg. trees, shrubs or woody-based herbs. Lvs imparipinnate; lfts opposite, often numerous. Fls pea-like in terminal rac. or pan.; cal. tubular-campanulate, slightly bilabiate; standard spreading or forward-pointing in 'tubular' fls, sta. 10, free. Legume ± 4-winged, torulose. Cosmop.

S. affinis Torr. & A. Gray. Decid. tree to 6m. Lvs 15–23cm, lfts 2.5–3.9cm, 13–19, oval, tapering towards both ends. Rac. 7.6–15.2cm, slender, downy; fls 1.25cm, white tinged rose. Summer. SW US. Z8.
S. calyptrata Retz. = *Podalyria calyptrata*.
S. chathamica Ckn. = *S. microphylla*.
S. chrysophylla (Salisb.) Seem. MAMANE. Decid. shrub to 3m. Lfts to 3.2cm in 7–9 pairs, obovate, retuse. Fls to 1.9cm, bright yellow, in short axill. rac. Late spring–summer. Hawaii, Sandwich Is. Z10.
S. davidii (Franch.) Skeels. Spreading decid. shrub to 3m; br. ultimately spiny. Lvs 3.2–6.4cm; lfts 0.6–1cm, in 7–10 pairs, oval or obovate, sericeous beneath. Rac. 5–6.4cm, term., 6–12-fld; fls to 1.9cm white marked and tinted violet or pale lilac-blue. Summer. China. Z6.
S. flavescens Ait. Decid. shrub to 1.5m. Lvs 15–23cm; lfts 3.8–6.4cm, 19, narrowly ovate. Fls 1.3cm, yellow-white in cylindrical rac. or pan. to 30cm. Summer. China. Z6.
S. grandiflora (Salisb.) Skottsb. = *S. tetraptera*.
S. japonica L. JAPANESE PAGODA TREE; CHINESE SCHOLAR TREE. Decid. tree to 25m; bark glossy dark grey-green with paler lenticels, ultimately grey, corrugated. Lfts 2.5–5cm, in 3–8 pairs, ovate-lanceolate, dark green above, glaucous or pubesc. beneath. Pan. term., 15–25cm; fls to 1.3cm, creamy-white fragrant; cal. to 3mm. Late summer. China, Korea. var. *pubescens* (Tausch) Bosse. Lfts to 8cm, downy beneath, fls tinted lilac. 'Columnaris': habit columnar. 'Dot': habit stunted; br. somewhat pendulous, tortuous; lvs crispate. 'Pendula': habit weeping; br. stiff; slow-growing; should be grafted on to a standard. 'Princeton Upright': habit compact and upright, to 18m tall. 'Regent': habit vigorous, oval-crowned, to 18m tall; lvs large, glossy dark green; fls white, from an early age; heat-tolerant. 'Tortuosa': br. twisted. 'Variegata': lvs edged in pale cream. 'Violacea': lvs light green; cor. wing and keel flushed violet,

late-flowering. Z5.

S. korolkowii (Koehne) Dieck = *S. japonica*.

S. macrocarpa Sm. Everg. shrub or small tree, 6–12m; young wood. Lvs 8–13cm; lfts 2–4cm, 13–25, minutely red-brown-pubesc. Rac. short, axillary, to 12-fld; fls yellow, 2.5–3cm. Summer. Chile. Z9.

S. microphylla Ait. Everg. tree to 9m, br., flexuous, tangled, arching, twiggy. Lfts to 0.8cm, to 30 pairs, closely opposite, ovate or elliptic-oblong, dark green above, sericeous beneath. Fls to 4.5cm, golden-yellow, rather tubular, pendulous, clustered in rac. Summer. NZ. 'Dragon's Gold': small and bushy; lvs small; fls autumn and winter. 'Earlygold': small and compact; lvs fern-like; fls lemon yellow. 'Goldilocks': small, upright; lvs fine, rich green; fls yellow. 'Sun King': bushy with bright yellow fls in profusion from winter to spring. Hardy. Z8.

S. mollis (Graham ex Royle) Bak. Low shrub; br., lfts and cal. grey-downy. Lfts to 2cm, in 10–12 pairs, stiff, emarginate, silver-pubesc. to grey-green. Rac. abundant, to 8cm; fls to 2cm, yellow. Himal. Z8.

S. moorcroftiana auct. = *S. davidii*.

S. platycarpa hort. = *Cladrastis platycarpa*.

S. prostrata Buch. Prostrate or ascending everg. shrub, to 2mm; br. wiry, tortuous, interlaced. Lvs to 2.5cm; lfts 0.5–0.6cm, in 6–8 pairs, oblong. Fls to 2cm, orange to brown or bright yellow, to 2cm, 1–3 on slender, sericeous stalks. NZ. 'Little Baby': growth twiggy and v. angular, rather golden; lvs v. fine; fls yellow, in early spring. Z8.

S. secundiflora (Ortega) Lagasca ex DC. MESCAL BEAN; FRIJOLITO; TEXAS MOUNTAIN LAUREL. Everg. tree, 8–11m. Lvs 10–15cm; lfts to 5cm, in 3–5 pairs, oblong or obovate, notched, sericeous beneath. Rac. 3–5cm; fls 2.5cm, violet-blue, highly fragrant. Spring. Tex., New Mex., N Mex. Z8.

S. sericea Andrews = *Podalyria sericea*.

S. sinensis hort. = *S. japonica*.

S. tetraptera J.F. Mill. KOWHAI. Everg. or semi-deciduous shrub or tree, 4.5–12m; branchlets yellow-tomentose, slender. Lvs 4–15cm; lfts 1.5–3.5cm, 10–20 pairs, ovate or elliptic-oblong, sericeous. Rac. 4–10-fld; fls 2.5–5cm, somewhat tubular, golden-yellow, pendulous. Summer. NZ, Chile. 'Gnome': compact, to 1.3m high; fls golden yellow. 'Goughensis': shrubby; fls tubular, yellow tinted orange. 'Grandiflora': lfts large; fls yellow, in drooping clusters. Z8.

S. tetraptera var. *microphylla* (Ait.) Hook. f. = *S. microphylla*.

S. tomentosa L. SILVERBUSH. Tall decid. shrub or tree, white-pubesc. throughout. Lfts 2.5–5cm, to 9 pairs, broadly ovate to obovate, obtuse or retuse. Rac. 15cm, lax; fls pale yellow, 2cm wide. OW tropics. Z10.

S. treadwellii (Allan) hort. = *S. microphylla*.

S. viciifolia Hance = *S. davidii*.

S. violacea (Koehne) hort. = *S. japonica* 'Violacea'.

✕ Sophrocattleya. (*Sophronitis* ✕ *Cattleya*.) Orchidaceae.
Dwarf *Cattleya*-like hybrids with fls in shades of yellow, orange and flame-red.

✕ Sophrolaelia. (*Sophronitis* ✕ *Laelia*.) Orchidaceae.
Small gdn hybrids with clustered fls in lavender-pink, red, flame and yellow.

✕ Sophrolaeliocattleya. (*Sophronitis* ✕ *Laelia* ✕ *Cattleya*.) Orchidaceae.
Gdn hybrids; usually compact plants with small to medium-size *Cattleya*-like fls in shades of red, purple, cerise, scarlet, orange and yellow often with lip velvety and veined or blotched red or purple.

Sophronitella Schltr. Orchidaceae. 1 epiphytic orchid. Pbs spindle-shaped or narrow-ovoid, 1.5–3cm, clustered. Lf 1, term., 4–7cm, linear, coriaceous, folded along the axis. Infl. term., 1–2-fld; fls purple-violet, fleshy; sep. to 2cm, oblong-lanceolate; pet. oblong; lip obovate, narrow, entire. E Braz. Z10.

S. violacea (Lindl.) Schltr.
→*Sophronitis*.

Sophronitis Lindl. Orchidaceae. 7 dwarf epiphytic or lithophytic orchids. Pbs clustered, apically unifoliate. Lvs fleshy or coriaceous, ovate-oblong to elliptic, dark green tinted purple. Rac. short, apical; fls showy; sep. subequal, elliptic-oblong, spreading; pet. wider; lip smaller than pet. E Braz., Parag. Z10.

S. cernua (Lindl.) Lindl. Pbs to 2cm, ovoid or subcylindrical. Lvs to 2.5×2cm, ovoid. Infl. to 5cm, few-fld; fls to 3cm diam., fleshy deep cinnabar-red, the lip a deeper tone fading to white or orange-yellow at base; pet. to 12×6mm, ovate or ovate-rhombic; lip to 10×7mm, entire. Autumn–winter. E Braz.

S. coccinea (Lindl.) Rchb. f. Pbs to 4cm, fusiform or ovoid-cylindrical. Lvs to 6×2.5cm. Infl. to 6cm, suberect, usually 1-fld; fls to 7.5cm diam., fleshy, usually vivid scarlet, lip marked yellow at base (white and magenta-fld forms occur); pet. to 30×30mm, ovate-orbicular to rhombic; lip to 20×22mm, trilobed. Autumn–winter. E Braz.

S. grandiflora Lindl. = *S. coccinea*.

S. militaris Rchb. f. = *S. coccinea*.

S. modesta Lindl. = *S. cernua*.

S. violacea Lindl. = *Sophronitella violacea*.

Sopubia Buch.-Ham. ex D. Don. Scrophulariaceae. *c*60 subshrubs and ann. herbs. Lvs narrow. Racs or spikes terminal, bracteate; cal. campanulate, cut or lobed ×5; cor. lobes 5, spreading; sta. 4. Summer. OW Trop. Z9.

S. angolensis Engl. White-pubesc. herb or subshrub erect, to 60cm. Lvs linear, 4-whorled. Orange excrescences on cal. interior; cor. red to blue-purple, 7–8mm, lobes broadly ovate. Trop. Afr.

S. delphinifolia G. Don. St. spotted purple, 90–120cm. Lvs linear, finely pinnatisect. Fls 25–40mm, subcampanulate, rose-coloured. India.

S. leprosa S. Moore. St. scurfy, becoming glab. Lvs linear, usually opposite. Trop. Afr.

→*Gerardia*.

Sorbaria (DC.) A. Braun. FALSE SPIRAEA. Rosaceae. 4 decid. shrubs. St. slender, erect, branching above and suckering profusely. Lvs stipules persistent; lfts usually biserrate. Fls white, small, in usually large, term. pan.; pet. 5, circular; sta. 17–50. E Asia.

S. aitchisonii (Hemsl.) Rehd. = *S. tomentosa* var. *angustifolia*.

S. alpina (Pall.) Dipp. = *S. grandiflora*.

S. angustifolia (Wenz.) Zab. = *S. tomentosa* var. *angustifolia*.

S. arborea Schneid. = *S. kirilowii*.

S. assurgens Vilm. & Boiss. = *S. kirilowii*.

S. grandiflora (Sweet) Maxim. To 50cm. Shoots pubesc., red-grey. Lvs to 18cm; stipules to 1cm×7mm; lfts 7–21, oblong-acute, to 7×2cm, glab. above, stellate-pubesc. beneath. Fls to 1.5cm diam., in few-fld corymbs to 13×11cm; sta. 45–50. Summer. E Sib. Z5.

S. kirilowii (Reg.) Maxim. To 7m. Shoots shortly simple-pubesc. or glandular-pubesc.; stipules to 14×12mm; lfts 7–32, to 13×4cm, oblong-ovate to lanceolate, acuminate, stellate-lanuginose beneath. Fls 6.5mm diam., in fine, often pyramidal pan. to 42×33cm; sta. 20–25. Summer. SE Tibet; SW, C & NE China.

S. lindleyana (Wallich ex Loud.) Maxim. = *S. tomentosa*.

S. sorbifolia (L.) A. Braun. To 3m. Shoots brown, glab. or fine-pubesc. Lvs to 25cm; stipules to 1cm×4.5mm; lfts 9–25 to 9×2.5cm, subsessile, lanceolate or oblong, acuminate, glab. or stellate-pubesc. Fls 8mm diam., in erect pan. to 34×14cm; sta. 20–45. Summer. E Sib., Manch., N China, Korea, Jap. Z2.

S. stellipila (Maxim.) Schneid. = *S. sorbifolia*.

S. tomentosa (Lindl.) Rehd. To 6m. Shoots glab. or glandular-pubesc. Stipules to 9×1.5mm; lfts 11–21, to 11×3.5cm, lanceolate, narrow-acuminate, glab. above, veins usually simple-pubesc. beneath. Fls yellow-white, 6mm diam.; in pan. to 41×20cm; sta. 17–30. Summer. Himal. Z8. var. *angustifolia* (Wenz.) Rahn. Lfts narrow-lanceolate, often simple-serrate, glab. Afghan., Pak. Z6.

→*Schizonotus* and *Spiraea*.

✕ Sorbaronia Schneid. (*Sorbus* ✕ *Aronia*.) Rosaceae. Decid. shrubs or small trees. Lvs simple where *Sorbus aria* is the parent, otherwise partly pinnate, finely serrate. Fls *c*1cm diam., white, in small, crowded corymbs. Fr. *c*1cm diam., red to almost black. Gdn origin. Z5.

✕ S. alpina (Willd.) Schneid. (*Aronia arbutifolia* ✕ *Sorbus aria*.) To 3m. Lvs to 7.5cm, oval to obovate, acuminate, tapering at base, glandular-serrate, glabrescent above, pale-lanuginose beneath. Fls in terminal, grey-tomentose corymbs to 5cm. Fr. ovoid to obovoid, red to brown. Spring.

✕ S. dippelii (Zab.) Schneid. (*Aronia melanocarpa* ✕ *Sorbus aria*.) Bushy-headed shrub, a small tree if grafted on a standard. Lvs to 9cm, narrow-oval or oblanceolate, tapering at base, glandular-serrate, bright green above, grey-tomentose beneath. Fls in small, lanuginose corymbs. Fr. obconic or round, blue-black.

✕ S. fallax (Schneid.) Schneid. (*Aronia melanocarpa* ✕ *Sorbus aucuparia*.) Shrub of tree-like habit. Lvs to 8cm, simple, base sometimes pinnately lobed or with 1–2 pairs pinnae, ovate to oval-oblong, obtuse, dark green above, grey-green, tomentose beneath, crenate. Fls in small, glabrescent corymbs. Fr. ovoid, red-black. Spring–summer.

✕ *S. hybrida* (Moench) Schneid. (*Sorbus aucuparia* ✕ *Aronia arbutifolia*.) Loosely branched shrub to ± arching small tree. Lvs to 8.5×5cm, simple, pinnatisect or lobed at base, obtuse, occas. acute or acuminate, crenate near apex, lat. lfts or lobes obtuse, glab. above, pubesc. beneath. Fls in white-pubesc. many-fld, corymbs 3cm diam. Fr. globose to ovoid, dark purple.

✕ *S. sorbifolia* (Poir.) Schneid. (*Aronia melanocarpa* ✕ *Sorbus americana*.) Closely resembles ✕ *S. hybrida*, but nearly glab. in all its parts, lvs, lfts or lobes more acuminate and ovate; peduncles more slender.

→ *Aronia, Mespilus, Pyrus* and *Sorbus*.

Sorbet *Cornus mas*.

✕ **Sorbocotoneaster** Pojark. (*Sorbus* ✕ *Cotoneaster*.) Rosaceae. Z3.

✕ *S. pozdnjakovii* Pojark. (*Sorbus sibirica* ✕ *Cotoneaster niger*.) Shrub to 3m, sparsely branched. Shoots slender, woolly red at first, later shiny. Lvs to 7.5cm, pinnate, dull green above, pubesc. beneath; lat. lfts 1–3 pairs, uppermost 3, often term. leaflet to 5×2.5cm, elliptic or obovate, entire or serrate. Fls white, in sparse term. infl. Fr. globose, 13mm diam., dark red or red-black. Discovered as a naturally occurring hybrid in Sib.

✕ **Sorbopyrus** Schneid. (*Sorbus* ✕ *Pyrus*.) Rosaceae. Z5.

✕ *S. auricularis* (Kroop) Schneid. (*Sorbus aria* ✕ *Pyrus communis*.) BOLLWYLLER PEAR. Round-headed, decid. tree to 18m. Lvs to 10cm, ovate or oval, acute, obtuse to cordate at base, glabrescent above, grey-tomentose beneath, serrate, petiole to 4cm, lanate. Fls to 2.5cm diam., white, in white-tomentose corymbs to 7.5cm diam.; anth. rose-red. Fr. to 3×3cm, pyriform, yellow flushed red, flesh sweet, yellow. Spring. Gdn orig. 'Malifolia' ('Bulbiformis'): closer to *Pyrus*, lvs broader, elliptic to orbicular, basally cordate, only thinly tomentose beneath, more finely toothed; fls to 3cm diam.; fr. to 5cm, pyriform, yellow-amber.

→ *Pyrus*.

Sorbus L. MOUNTAIN ASH. Rosaceae. c100 decid. trees or shrubs. Buds large, scales overlapping. Lvs simple to pinnate. Fls in term. corymbs, usually, white; sep. and pet. 5, sta. 15–20. Fr. a pome. N Hemis.

S. alnifolia (Sieb. & Zucc.) K. Koch. Tree, to 20m, erect becoming thick and rounded with age, young st. red-brown, shiny. Lvs 5–10cm, ovate-elliptic, acuminate, serrate, glab. beneath, scarlet to orange in fall. Fls in corymbs 5–7cm diam. Fr. pea-sized, red and yellow. 'Skyline': erect, columnar, fall colour yellow. var. *submollis* Rehd. Lvs broader, downy beneath. Late spring. Jap., Korea. Z6.

S. alpina (Willd.) Heynh. = ✕ *Sorbaronia alpina*.

S. americana Marsh. AMERICAN MOUNTAIN ASH. Tree to 10m or shrubby, br. red-brown. Buds swollen, glutinous. Lvs to 25cm, lfts +10cm, 11–17 oblong-lanceolate, pointed, serrate, bright green, slightly downy when young, grey-green beneath, golden-yellow in fall. Fls in crowded clusters to 14cm. Fr. globose to 0.5cm, scarlet-red. Late spring. C & E US. 'Belmonte': crown ovoid, dense, lfts curved at apex during senescence; fr. large, slightly flattened. Z2.

S. amurensis Koehne. Resembles *S. aucuparia*. Lfts acuminate, apex incisely serrate, young foliage ± pubesc. beneath. Fr. 0.5cm, orange-red. NE Asia. Z7.

S. anglica Hedl. Shrub, 1–2m, shoots stout. Lvs 7–11cm, 5–6cm, obovate to rhomboidal, blunt or pointed, lobes incised, serrate, deep green, glab. above, white-grey felted beneath, golden-brown in fall. Infl. variable in size. Fr. 7–12mm, subglobose, carmine-red, pitted. Engl., Ireland. Z7.

S. arbutifolia (L.) Heynh. = *Aronia arbutifolia*.

S. aria (L.) Crantz. WHITEBEAM. Tree 6–12m, broad-conical, young shoots and buds grey-felted at first. Lvs elliptic-ovate, 8–12cm, coriaceous, silvery to dull green above, white felted beneath. Fls in branched corymbs to 5cm. Fr. 10–12mm, oval-rounded, orange-red, powdery. Eur. (mts). 'Aurea': vigorous. Lvs white at first becoming golden yellow, colour retained until fall. 'Chrysophylla': lvs tinted yellow throughout summer, deep yellow in fall. 'Cyclophylla': lvs broad, rounded. 'Decaisneana': see 'Majestica'. 'Gigantea' (*S. aria* ✕ *S. aria* 'Majestica'.) 'Lutescens': crown dense, conical, becoming wider. Young lvs silvery, slightly yellow above becoming silver-green, lower lf surfaces remaining white. 'Magnifica': crown narrow at first spreading later; lvs large, dark green waxy above, white felted below, tough, rigid, long lasting; fr. 'Majestica': crown wide spreading, lvs large, dull green above, white beneath becoming green-tomentose. Fr. dark orange-red. 'Pendula': small tree; br. weeping; lvs smaller, narrower. 'Quercoides': dense compact shrub, slow growing; lvs oblong, lobed, rough, margins incurled. 'Salicifolia': graceful lax tree; lvs narrow. 'Wilfred Fox':

to 12m, dense, crown wide; br. ascending; lvs to 20cm, biserrate, glossy; fr. rounded, to ×2cm, green later gold dotted with grey. f. *longifolia* (Pers.) Rehd. Lvs 7–14cm, elliptic to oblong. Fr. ovoid, orange. Z5.

S. aria var. *angustifolia* Dipp. = *S. aria* f. *longifolia*.

S. aria var. *decaisneana* (Lav.) Rehd. = *S. aria* 'Majestica'.

S. aria var. *edulis* Wenz. = *S. aria* f. *longifolia*.

S. aria var. *flabellifolia* Wenz. = *S. umbellata*.

S. aria f. *chrysophylla* Zab. = *S. aria* 'Aurea'.

S. aria suecica Koehne = *S. intermedia*.

S. ✕ *arnoldiana* Rehd. (*S. aucuparia* ✕ *S. discolor*.) Differs from *S. aucuparia* in glab. buds, lfts smaller, soon glab., dark green above, grey-green beneath. Fr. pink or white-pink. Gdn origin. 'Schouten': to 8m, columnar, broadens with age, compact; lvs fresh green; fr. golden. The 'Lombarts Hybrids', developed from *Ss. pratti, discolor* and *aucuparia*: 'Carpet of Gold': upright; br. thin; fr. golden yellow flecked red. 'Chamois Glow': vigorous; lvs large, fls mauve in bud, pubesc. white; fr. oatmeal. 'Golden Wonder': low, to 7m, pyramidal; lvs dark, orange and yellow in autumn; fr. gold. 'Kirsten Pink': shrubby; petiole tinted red; fr. pink. 'White Wax': shrubby; fr. white, early. Z5.

S. arranensis Hedl. Medium tree. Lvs 8–12cm, deeply lobed, apex tapered, base cuneate, lightly covered in white hairs beneath. Fr. 10mm, globose, red. Scotland, Arran Is., Norway. Z6.

S. aucuparia L. COMMON MOUNTAIN ASH. Tree, 5–15m. Shoots soon glab., grey-brown; buds tomentose. Lvs to 20cm, lfts 9–15 to 6cm, oblong-lanceolate, pointed, serrate, dull green, galbrous, grey-green, slightly hairy beneath. Corymbs 15cm. Fr. 0.75cm, bright red. Eur. to Asia Minor, Sib. 'Asplenifolia' ('Laciniata'): lfts deeply incised, often 1- to 2-lobed, thickly hairy beneath. 'Beissneri': densely erect; trunk and br. copper to russet; young shoots and petioles deep coral-red; lvs yellow green, lfts variably lobed and incised. 'Cardinal Royal': erect; fr. profuse, bright red. 'Dirkenii': lvs yellow, becoming green. 'Edulis' ('Moravia'): lvs ± glab., lfts 4–7cm ± entire, serrate in the centre; petiole red; rachis slightly hairy; fr. 1cm, sweet, edible. 'Fastigiata': crown narrow; shoots rigid, stout; fr. large. 'Integerrima': crown tightly ascending; lfts entire or nearly so. 'Nana': shrubby; fr. larger than the type. 'Pendula': br. pendulous if grafted on upright stock. 'Pendula Variegata': weeping; lvs variegated yellow. 'Rossica': lfts more obtuse, slightly bullate, entire below. Fr. 12–15mm. 'Rossica Major': vigorous; br. tightly ascending; lfts 8×2.5cm, petiole and rachis red, woolly, apical lfts serrate, slightly felted beneath, slightly puckered; fr. 15mm+. 'Sheerwater Seedling': vigorous erect small tree, crown compact, ovoid; fr. orange-red in large clusters. 'Variegata': lvs variegated yellow. 'Xanthocarpa' ('Fructo Luteo', 'Fifeana'): fr. orange-yellow. Z2.

S. aucuparia var. *dulcis* Kränzl. = *S. aucuparia* 'Edulis'.

S. aucuparia var. *morevica* Zengerl. = *S. aucuparia* 'Edulis'.

S. aucuparia f. *laciniata* Hartm. = *S. aucuparia* 'Asplenifolia'.

S. austrica Hedl. Small tree, resembles *S. intermedia* but crown more pyramidal. Lvs 9×7cm, strongly serrate, broadly elliptic, deeply lobed, grey-white felted beneath. Fr. 13mm, subglobose, red, pitted. Switz. to Aus., Hung. Z6.

S. bakonyensis (Jav.) Karpati. Small tree close to *S. latifolia*. Lvs broadly elliptic-ovate, biserrate above, glossy above, thickly grey-tomentose beneath. Fr. large, red, lenticellate. Hungary. Z6.

S. bristoliensis Wilm. Small tree, compact rounded crown. Lvs 7–9×5–5.5cm, obovate or oblong rhombic, apex triangular lobed, finely serrate, bright green waxy above, grey felted beneath. Infl. small; anth. pink. Fr. 9–11mm, ovoid, pale orange, pitted. SW Engl. Z7.

S. californica E. Greene. Differs from *S. sitchensis* in lfts ovate, fr. rosy-pink. Calif. Z7.

S. caloneura (Stapf) Rehd. Shrub or small tree to 4–5m; shoots and buds glab., black-brown. Lvs 5–9cm, elliptic-oblong, pointed, crenate soon glab. Corymbs crowded corymbs to 7cm, anth. violet purple. Fr. 1cm, pyriform, brown, pitted. C China. Z6.

S. cascadensis G.N. Jones. Shrub 2–5m, young shoots downy. Lfts 9–11, 5–7cm, oblong-elliptic, sharply pointed, deeply serrate above, green, waxy above. Fr. 0.5cm, globose, scarlet. N Calif. to BC. Z6.

S. cashmeriana Hedl. Tree to 10m; shoots glab., red. Lfts 15–19, 2–3cm, oval-elliptic, to oblong, long-tapered, rough, serrate above, dark green glab. above, pale green beneath. Rachis brown downy at first becoming red. Infl. 7–12cm; pet. dark pink in bud, opening pink-white. Fr. to 18mm, white. Himal., Kashmir. Z5.

S. chamaemespilus (L.) Crantz. DWARF WHITEBEAM. Shrub 1–2m. Lvs 3–7cm, elliptic, pointed or blunt, finely serrate, coriaceous, dark green above, yellow green beneath, glab. or felted ovoid. Fls pale red in crowded corymbs to 3cm. Fr. ovoid, red. C Eur. (mts). var. *sudetica* (Tausch) Wenz. Lvs larger, ovate, doubly serrate, felted beneath at first; fls larger, cal. cup shaggy; or to 1cm. N Czech., W Germ. Z6.

S. commixta Hedl. Tree to 7m+, upright at first. Buds glab., gummy, shoots red brown. Lfts 11–15, 4–8cm, elliptic-lanceolate, long-tapered, serrate, emerging brown, becoming pale green, blue green beneath, yellow-red in fall. Corymbs loose, glab., 8–12cm. Fr. 0.75cm, globose, scarlet. Korea, Jap. 'Ethel's Gold': lvs pinnate, fresh green; fr. golden amber, long-lasting. 'Embley': small tree; lvs glowing red in winter, colouring and persisting later in season. Fr. shiny, orange-red in large bunches. 'Jermyns': fall colour excellent. Fr. amber to fiery red in large bunches. var. *rufoferruginea* Shirai ex Schneid see S. *rufoferruginea*. 'Serotina': lfts 15–17, sharply toothed, colouring well in fall. Fr. small, orange-red. Z6.

S. ×confusa Gremli ex Rouy = S. ×vagensis.
S. conradinae Koehne = S. esserteauiana.
S. conradinae hort. non Koehne = S. pohuashanensis.
S. cretica (Lindl.) Fritsch = S. umbellata var. cretica.
S. cuspidata (Spach) Hedl. = S. vestita.

S. ×decipiens (Bechst.) Hedl. (S. aria ×S. torminalis.) Differs from S. latifolia, in thinner more flexible lvs, 12×8cm, base cuneate to rounded, thinly felted. with veins distinct beneath. E Germ., Switz., NE Fr. Z6.

S. decora Sarg. & Schneid. Shrub or tree to 10m. Lfts 11–17, to 7cm, elliptic to oval-lanceolate, blunt or slightly tapered, dark blue-green, glab. above, paler beneath, rachis red. Fls in loose clusters to 10cm, lightly hairy. Fr. 7–10mm, subglobose, red. NE US. Z2.

S. decurrens (Koehne) Hedl. = S. ×thuringiaca 'Decurrens'.
S. devoniensis Warb. Tree, resembling S. latifolia. Crown dense, rounded. Lvs 9–12×5–8cm, elliptic-ovate, pointed, deeply biserrate above, dark green waxy above, grey-green felted beneath. Infl. to 10cm. Fr. 1.5cm, globose, orange-brown, pitted. SW Engl. Z7.

S. discolor (Maxim.) Maxim. Small tree 7–10m, buds and shoots glab. or slightly downy, red; stipules leaf-like, palmately toothed. Lfts 11–15, 3–8cm, oblong-lanceolate, pointed to tapered, deeply serrate, dark green above, blue-green beneath, red in fall. Fls in 10–14cm, clusters. Fr. 6–7mm, globose, white-yellow to pink. China. Z6.

S. domestica L. Tree to 20m, bark deeply furrowed, buds gummy, shiny. Lfts 11–21, 3–8cm, narrowly oblong, serrate, woolly beneath. Fls in conical corymbs to 10cm. Fr. to 3cm, globose-pyriform, yellow-green ripening red. C S Eur., N Afr., Asia Minor. 'Signalman' (S. domestica ×S. scopulorum): low, narrowly pyramidal; lvs small; fr. large, pale orange. f. *pomifera* (Hayne) Rehd. Fr. globose, 2–3cm var. *pyrifera* Hayne. Fr. pyriform, 3–4cm. Z6.

S. dumosa E. Greene. Differs from S. scopulina in white (not rust-coloured) hairs. SW US. Z7.
S. edulis (Willd.) K. Koch = S. aria f. longifolia.
S. epidendron Hand.-Mazz. Tree or shrub to 10m. Lvs 8–15cm, narrowly elliptic, long tapered, serrate, rusty-tomentose beneath. Fls cream-white, in crowded corymbs, brown-tomentose. Fr. to 8mm, globose. W China. Z6.

S. esserteauiana Koehne. Tree, 8–15m. Buds red, white-pubesc.; stipules 1–2cm wide, dentate. Lvs 18–29cm; lfts 11–13, 6–10cm, oblong-lanceolate, coriaceous, bright green above, downy beneath, red in fall. Pan. crowded to 15cm; tomentose. Fr. 8mm, globose, bright red. W China. 'Flava': fr. orange-yellow. 'Winter Cheer': fr. yellow later orange-red, long-lasting. Z6.

S. fennica Fries = S. hybrida.
S. filipes Hand.-Mazz. Shrub to 4m, differs from S. vilmorinii in glab. shoots, lfts 19–27, 1.8–2.5cm, elliptic, sparsely toothed. Fr. 7mm, red. W China. Z6.
S. flabellifolia Schauer = S. umbellata.
S. folgneri (C. Schneid.) Rehd. Tree or graceful shrub to 10m. Shoots slender, arched, white tomentose at first. Lvs 5–10cm, lanceolate to narrowly ovate, acuminate, serrate, white tomentose beneath. Croymbs crowded to 10cm. Fr. 12mm, red. China. 'Lemon Drop': fr. glossy yellow. Z6.
S. foliolosa (Wallich) Spach = S. ursina.
S. foliolosa Wenzig = S. vilmorinii.
S. foliolosa var. *ursina* Wenig. = S. ursina.
S. forrestii McAllister & Gillham. Resembles S. hupehensis. Fr. v. large, white, persisting until mid-winter. Z7.
S. fruticosa Steud. Shrub 2–3m. Differs from S. cashmeriana in lfts smaller, crimson in fall. Fr. white, retained until mid-autumn. Shoots chocolate-brown. Tibet. Z7.
S. glabra (Thunb.) Zab. = Photinia glabra.
S. glomerulata Koehne. Small tree or shrub. Shoots and buds glab. Lvs 5–12cm, lfts 10–14 pairs, oblong or narrow-ovate, toothed above, midrib occas. downy beneath; rachis winged. Fr. 0.6cm in corymbs to 7cm. Fr. 0.5cm, globose, white-cream. China. Z6.
S. gracilis (Sieb. & Zucc.) K. Koch. Shrub to 2m, shoots slender,

bronze-red at first, as are lvs. Lfts 7–9, basal lfts 1–2cm, apical lfts 2–6cm, elliptic-oblong, blunt, serrate above.Infl. 2–4cm, bracts large. Fr. 1cm, red, pyriform. Jap. Z6.
S. graeca Lodd. = S. umbellata var. cretica.
S. 'Grondesia' hort. = S. hybrida.
S. harrowiana (Balf. & W.W. Sm.) Rehd. Tree 7–10m, often cultivated as a shrub. Shoots stout, glab. Lfts 5–9, 6–20cm, narrowly oblong, glaucous beneath, minutely toothed, term. lft long-stalked. Fls in lax infl. Fr. 8mm, pyriform, pink. W China. Z9.

S. hedlundii Schneid. Close to S. vestita. Lvs large, silver-tomentose beneath, veined rusty brown. E Himal. Z8.
S. ×hostii (Jacq. f.) K. Koch. (S. chamaemespilus ×S. mougeotii.) Shrub to 4m, differing from S. mougeotii in lvs longer to 10cm, narrow-oblong, sharply bi-serrate, shallowly lobed. Fls pink, resembling S. chamaemespilus. Fr. ovoid, red. Eur. (Alps, Jura). Z6.

S. hupehensis Schneid. Tree to 10m. Buds glab. Lfts 13–17, 2–5cm, elliptic-oblong, blunt or slightly acuminate, serrulate above, ± glab., grey-green beneath. Infl. lax, to 12cm, fls long-stalked, white-yellow. Fr. 6–8mm, globose, white to pink. C & W China. 'Coral Fire': bark red; lvs thick, bright red in autumn, petioles red; fr. coral red. 'Rufus': fr. deep pink-red, abundant. 'November Pink': vigorous small, crown globose. Lvs dull, dark green above, blue-green beneath. Fr. 1cm, white-pink becoming purple-red. var. *aperta* Schneid. Lfts 9–11, 3–6cm, pointed. var. *obtusa* Schneid. Lfts 9–11, 3–5cm, obtuse, serrate below. Z6.

S. hybrida (L.) L. (S. aria ×S. aucuparia ?.) Tree 10–12m, spreading with age. Young twigs tomentose. Lvs 7–10cm, oval-oblong, apex widely rounded, basal lfts 1–2 pairs, becoming coriaceous, coarsely serrate, blue-green above, yellow-white, downy beneath. Infl. downy, 6–10cm. Fr. 10–12mm, globose, red. NW Eur. 'Gibbsii': small tree to 7m, br. ascending. Lvs 10–15cm, with 8 lobes per side, 1–2 free lfts at base. Fr. deep red. Z5.
S. hybrida hort. non L. = S. ×thuringiaca.
S. hybrida 'Fastigiata' = S. ×thuringiaca 'Fastigiata'.
S. hybrida var. *meinichii* (Lindeb.) Rehd. = S. ×meinichii.
S. insignis (Hook. f.) Hedl. Small tree. Lvs to 30cm, lfts 9–13, 5–10cm, elliptic-oblong, blunt, central lfts larger, lightly toothed, apical lfts sessile, others stalked; petiole base large, clasping. Infl rusty-silky. Fr. pink. Himal., Sikkim. Z8. 'Bellona': shrubby, conical; lfts to 5 pairs, oblong obovate, to 9cm, glab., grey beneath; fr. coral red. 'Ghose': small, erect; lvs flushed blue beneath, lfts to 19, oblong-lanceolate; fr. red to pink, abundant. Z7.

S. intermedia (Ehrh.) Pers. Tree to 12m, occas. shrubby. Young shoots densely tomentose. Lvs 6–10m broadly ovate, blunt, base rounded, lobe or pinnatisect below, serrate, waxy above, grey woolly beneath. Infl. 8–10cm, much branched. Fr. 13mm, ellipsoid, orange-red. Scand. 'Brouwers': crown erect, compact. Z5.
S. intermedia var. *minima* (Léy.) Bean = S. minima.
S. japonica (Decne.) Hedl. Tree to 20m. Twigs downy. Lvs 7–10cm, ovate to elliptic, acuminate, biserrate, shallowly lobed, dark green above, grey felted beneath. Infl. dense woolly. Fr. 12mm, ellipsoid, scarlet, sparsely pitted. Jap., Korea. var. *calocarpa* Rehd. Lvs white-felted beneath, yellow in fall. Fr. larger, orange. C Jap. Z6.
S. japonica Koehne non Sieb. = S. commixta.
S. 'Joseph Rock'. Erect, to 9m. Lvs to 16cm, vibrant orange to plum in autumn; lfts 15–19, narrow-oblong, serrate. Fr. cream to gold. Z6.
S. kamunensis Schauer = S. lantana.
S. keissleri Rehd. Large shrub or small tree to 12m, crown tightly ascending. Lvs 5–8cm, obovate, coriaceous, crenate, waxy green. Cymes crowded, terminal, woolly, fragrant. Fr. globose, apple green, tinted red. China. Z6.
S. koehneana Schneid. Erect shrub, 2–3m. Shoots and buds red-brown. Lfts 17–25, 2–3cm, oblong to ovate, sharply toothed, bright green, grey-green beneath. 6–8cm corymbs axis, slightly winged. Fr. 7mm, globose, white, stalks red. C China. Z6.
S. koehnei Zab. = S. japonica.
S. lanata hort. non (D. Don) Schau = S. vestita.
S. lancifolia Hedl. Shrub to 4m. Lvs 8–10cm, narrow-oblong, each with 6 pairs of large triangular lobes, deeply incised. Fr. 8–9mm. Early summer. N Norway. Z6.
S. latifolia (Lam.) Pers. Vigorous tree to 15m+, broadly conical, br. shiny olive-brown. Lvs 7–10cm, round-ovate, pinnately lobed, serrate, dull dark green above, yellow grey tomentose beneath, umbel to 10cm, woolly. Fr. 1.5cm, ellipsoid, brown speckled. Eur. 'Henk Vink': crown narrowly pyramidal, fast-growing; lvs simple, wide, light green, grey tomentose beneath; fr. rusty red. 'Red Tip': upright, crown pyramidal; lvs small; fr. white spotted red. Z5.
S. matsumurana (Mak.) Koehne. JAPANESE MOUNTAIN ASH. Small tree, shoots red-brown, buds glab. Lfts 9–13, 3–6cm,

oblong, apex rounded or acuminate, serrate, dark green above, paler beneath, orange in fall. Fls in wide, 5–7cm clusters. Fr. 12mm, ovoid, scarlet. Jap. Z6.

S. megalocarpa Rehd. Large shrub or small tree to 16m, shoots stout, red-brown. Lvs 12–25cm, ovate, obovate or oval, crenate, bronze at first, scarlet in fall. Fls in crowded clusters to 12cm diam. Fr. 1.5–3.5cm, rusty brown. China. Z6.

S. × meinichii (Lindeb.) Hedl. (*S. aria* × *S. aucuparia*.) Differs from *S. aucuparia* in spreading crown, thicker darker lvs, lvs with 4–6 pairs, term. lfts rhombic, blunt, often 3-lobed. Fr. red. Norway. Z5.

S. melanocarpa (Michx.) Heynh. = *Aronia melanocarpa*.

S. meliosmifolia Rehd. Small tree 5–10m, shoots red-brown, glab. Lvs 10–18×5–9cm, ovate-elliptic, slender pointed, bright green. Fls in clusters 5–10cm. Fr. 12mm, subglobose, red-brown. W China. Z6.

S. microphylla Wenzig emend. Hedl. Tree or shrub to 7m. Branchlets purple-brown, ultimately glab.; buds with apical tuft of brown hair. Lfts in 10–15 pairs, 1–1.5cm, oblong, acute, deeply serrate, pubesc. above, densely so beneath; rachis narrowly winged above. Infl. narrow, lax, br. red-brown, hairy; fls pink to red. Fr. to 1cm, globose, white or pink-tinted. Nepal to Yunnan. Z8.

S. minima (Lév.) Hedl. Shrub to 3m, br. sparse, fine. Lvs 4–8cm, elliptic to oval, acute, shallowly lobed, toothed, dull grey, sparsely grey tomentose beneath. Fls in small ± downy clusters. Fr. 6–8mm, subglobose, scarlet, punctate. Engl., Wales. Z6.

S. 'Mitchellii' = *S. thibetica* 'John Mitchell'.

S. mougeotii Soy.-Willem. & Godron. Large shrub or small tree. Lvs ovate to obovate, broad, shallowly lobed, open above, white-grey tomentose beneath. Fr. to 0.8cm, ellipsoid, red, sparsely speckled. N Eur. (Alps, Jura). Z6.

S. munda Koehne = *S. prattii*.

S. neglecta Hedl. Shrub to 3m. Lvs 7×3–4cm, elliptic with 5–6 toothed lobes each side, deeply incised. Fr. 1cm. Norway. Z5.

S. nepalensis hort. = *S. cuspidata*.

S. norvegica Hedl. = *S. obtusifolia*.

S. obtusifolia (DC.) Hedl. Shrub to 4m. Lvs ovate, blunt, base broadly wedge-shaped, serrate, grey felted beneath. Fr. to 1cm. Norway, S Sweden. Z6.

S. occidentalis (S. Wats.) Greene. Shrub 1–3m. Young twigs finely downy. Lfts 7–11, 2–4cm, elliptic to oblong, obtuse, ± entire, slightly toothed above, dull blue green. Fls 15–40 in compact clusters 3–6cm diam. Fr. 6–8mm, ellipsoid, red-purple, glaucescent. N Amer. Z6.

S. ochrocarpa Rehd. = *S. pallescens*.

S. oligodonta (Cardot) Hand.-Mazz. = *S. hupehensis*.

S. pallescens Rehd. Small tree, br. sharply ascending, bark flaking. Lvs 4–10×2–5cm, elliptic-lanceolate, long-tapered, biserrate, grey-green, white felted beneath, veins distinct. Infl. small, sessile. Fr. 6mm, ovoid globose, green turning red. China. Z5.

S. paucicrenata (Ilse) Hedl. Differs from *S. latifolia* in thin elliptic lvs, shallowly lobed above, light green. Fr. rarely ripens. Alps, E Germ. Z6.

S. pekinensis Koehne = *S. discolor*.

S. pinnatifida 'Gibbsii'. = *S. hybrida* 'Gibbsii'.

S. pinnatifida (Ehrh.) Bean = *S. × thuringiaca*.

S. pluripinnata (Schneid.) Koehne. Resembles *S. scalaris*, differs in smaller more densely arranged lfts and smaller infl. Young shoots grey felted. Lvs 8–12cm, lfts 21–25, linear-lanceolate, apex rounded to lightly acute, serrate, blue-grey tomentose beneath. Fls small in 5–8cm, clusters. Fr. 0.5cm, ovoid, red. W China. Z6.

S. pohuashanensis (Hance) Hedl. Small tree, twigs pubesc., buds densely tomentose. Lfts 11–15, 3–6cm, elliptic to oblong-lanceolate, acute, toothed above, grey-green downy beneath. Stipules v. large, ovate. Fls 1cm, in woolly clusters to 10cm. Fr. 6–8mm, subglobose, orange-red. N China. 'Chinese Lace': small tree; lfts deeply toothed giving lace-like effect, rich autumn colour; fr. red, glossy, in wide clusters. 'Pagoda Red': shrubby; lfts coarsely toothed. 'Kewensis' (*S. pohuashanensis* × *S. esserteauiana*): low; lvs pinnate, lfts 19–23, long, deeply cut, rich green, purple in autumn, grey beneath; fr. oval, bright red. Z5.

S. poteriifolia Hand.-Mazz. Shrub 10cm–2.5m. Shoots sharply ascending, purple-brown. Lvs 5–10cm, lfts 9–19, 1–2cm, elliptic, serrate, deep green, pale green downy beneath. Fr. globose, deep pink. SW China, Upper Burm. 'Edwin Hillier' (*S. poteriifolia* × ?): small tree or shrub; fls ovate to lanceolate, elliptic, to 3 pairs serrate lobes on basal section, grey tomentose beneath; fr. pink. 'Lowndes': shoots stout, upright, buds red; lfts 15–21, elliptic-lanceolate, cut, veins prominent; fr. white flushed pink. Z7.

S. prattii Koehne. Tree to 8m. Twigs glab. Lfts 21–27, 2–3cm, entire below, blue-green beneath, usually downy beneath. Infl. to

7cm, glab. or downy, fls small. Fr. 6–8mm, white. W China. var. **subarachnoidea** (Koehne) Rehd. Lvs with rust coloured web-like down beneath. var. **tatsienensis** (Koehne) Schneid. Lfts 1–2cm, glab. beneath. Z6.

S. pumila Raf. = *S. occidentalis*.

S. pygmaea hort. Dwarf shrub 7–25cm, shoots slender. Lvs 7cm, lfts 9–15, 12×6mm, oval, pointed, serrate. Fls few in term. clusters, pale pink-carmine. Fr. 8mm, globose, pearly white. Early summer. Burm., Tibet, W China. Z5.

S. randaiensis (Hayata) Koidz. Small tree, 3–8m, br. erect, buds light brown, glab., slightly gummy. Lvs to 17cm, lfts 15–19, 2.5–4cm, oblong lanceolate, long-tapered, sharply toothed, grey beneath. Fls in terminal clusters to 8cm. Fr. 6–7mm, rounded, red. Taiwan. Z7.

S. reducta Diels. Dwarf shrub 15–40cm, suckering; shoots slender, thinly bristled. Lvs 7–10cm; petioles red; lfts 9–15, 1.5–2.5cm, ovate to elliptic, serrate, slightly downy above, glab. beneath, carmine in fall. Fls sparse, in term. corymbs, white; cal. glab. outside, interior downy. Fr. 6mm, globose, carmine. W China, Burm. Z6.

S. rehderiana Koehne. Shrub or small tree differing from *S. hupehensis* in stouter shoots to 8mm, lfts 15–19, 2.5–5cm, oblong-lanceolate, finely serrate. Infl. lax to 7cm, brown-downy. Fr. 6–7mm, white-red. W China. Z6.

S. rhamnoides (Decne.) Rehd. Shrub or small tree, shoots soon glab. Lvs 13–15cm, elliptic, serrate, green above, glabrescent beneath; petiole slender. Fr. green. Sikkim. Z6.

S. rufoferruginea (Schneid.) Schneid. Differs from *S. commixta*, in ragged brown buds, pedicel and lower surface of midrib. Z6.

S. rufopilosa Schneid. = *S. microphylla*.

S. rupicola (Syme) Hedl. Shrub to 2m, resembles *S. aria*, but lvs wider above middle, blunt, coriaceous, finely serrate, white-felted beneath, petiole red-brown. Infl. tomentose. Fr. sub-globose, 12–15mm, green and carmine, pitted. S Scand. Z7.

S. salicifolia (Myrin) Hedl. = *S. rupicola*.

S. sambucifolia sensu. Dipp. = *S. decora*.

S. sargentiana Koehne. Tree 7–10m, buds gummy, slightly downy; shoots stout. Lvs 20–25cm; stipules large; lfts 7–11, 8–13cm, oblong-lanceolate, serrate, green above, green downy beneath, brilliant red to orange in fall. Fls white in shaggy clusters to 15cm. Fr. 6mm, red. W China. 'Warleyensis': lfts smaller than sp. type; rachis red; infl. larger, lax; fr. smaller. Z6.

S. × sargentii (Poir.) Hedl. = × *Sorbaronia sorbifolia*.

S. scalaris Koehne. Large shrub or small tree to 6m, shoots downy. Lvs 10–20cm, lfts 21–37, 2–3cm, narrowly-oblong, slightly toothed above, grey felted beneath, red-purple in fall. Fls in crowded, branched clusters to 14cm, downy, axis red. Fr. 5–6mm, globose, bright red. China. Z5.

S. scandica Fries = *S. intermedia*.

S. scopulina Greene. Shrub to 4m, erect, rigid. Buds black, downy. Lfts 11–15, 3–6cm, oblong-lanceolate, subacuminate, serrate, blue-green beneath. Infl. large, slightly downy. Fr. 0.5cm, globose, glossy red. W US. Z5.

S. scopulina Hough non Greene = *S. decora*.

S. semipinnata (Roth) Hedl. = *S. × thuringiaca*.

S. serotina Koehne = *S. commixta* 'Serotina'.

S. sitchensis Roem. Shrub to 1.8m, or small tree. Lvs large, lfts 7–11, 6–8cm, ovate to oblong, pointed or blunt, coriaceous, serrate below, dull green above, glab. beneath. Infl. globose becoming corymbose to 10cm, red-brown pubesc. Fr. red, pruinose. NW US. Z5.

S. sitchensis Piper pro parte. = *S. scopulina*.

S. × splendida Hedl. (*S. americana* × *S. aucuparia*.) Differs from *S. americana*, in wider lfts, 2.5–3× longer than wide; fr. larger, winter buds downy, glutinous. Z2.

S. subarrensis Hylander = *S. arrensis*.

S. subpinnata Hedl. To 5m, differs from *S. intermedia* in narrower lvs, basal lobes narrowly and deeply incised. Fr. to 1cm. Norway. Z6.

S. subsimilis Hedl. Tree to 6m. Lvs similar to *S. intermedia* but with lobes more deeply incised, coriaceous. Fls 15mm wide. Fr. to 12mm. Norway. Z5.

S. theophtasta Lombarts = *S. devoniensis*.

S. thibetica (Cardot) Hand.-Mazz. Represented in gardens by 'John Mitchell' (*S. 'Mitchellii'*) a broad-crowned medium to large tree. Lvs to 15×15cm, rounded, green above, white-tomentose beneath. Fr. pyriform, orange tinted red. China. Z8.

S. thibetica hort. non (Cardot) Hand.-Mazz. = *S. wardii*.

S. thomsonii (King) Rehd. Large tree. Lvs elliptic-lanceolate or oblanceolate, glab., serrate above. Infl. glab. Fr. 1.8cm, red, spotted white. India. Z7.

S. × thuringiaca (Ilse) Fritsch. (*S. aria* × *S. aucuparia*.) Resembles *S. hybrida* but lvs narrowing towards apex with 10–14, not 7–9, vein pairs, finely serrate, lvs rarely with 1–4 basal pinnae. Fr. small, red. Germ. 'Decurrens': transitional form between *S.* ×*thuringiaca* and *S. aucuparia*. Lvs pinnate to apex, lfts in 5–7 pairs, the basal portion of term. lfts deeply incised, otherwise with decurrent bases, finely serrate, stipules reduced, slender. 'Fastigiata': (*S. aria* f. *longifolia* ×*S. aucuparia*): crown narrow, upright at first; lvs oval-oblong with 1–4 basal lfts with free or decurrent base, coriaceous, dark green; fr. abundant dark red. 'Leonard Springer': lvs with 4–5 pairs lfts, 3–5cm, deeply serrate, apical lfts slightly decurrent, term. lfts 6–7cm, base coarsely toothed, becoming shallower towards apex; petiole red; fr. to 12mm, long lasting. 'Neuillyensis': lvs similar to 'Leonard Springer', petiole green. Z6.

S. tianschanica Rupr. Tree or shrub 5m, br. becoming glossy-red brown. Buds thickly downy. Lfts 9–15, 3–5cm, lanceolate, tapered, serrate toward tip, dark green waxy above, glab., grey beneath. Corymbs 8–12cm. Fr. 8mm, rounded, red. Early summer. Turkestan, Tian Shan Mts. 'Red Cascade' ('Dwarf Crown'): crown oval, dense; lvs lustrous green; fr. orange-red. Z6.

S. torminalis (L.) Crantz. CHEQUER TREE; WILD SERVICE TREE. Tree 10–15m+, crown globose, br. glab., olive brown. Lvs to 10cm, broadly ovate with deep acute lobes, serrate, bright green waxy above, pale green beneath, red in fall. Fls in lax corymbs to 12cm. Fr. 1.5cm, ellipsoid, speckled brown. Eur., Asia Minor, N Afr. Z6.

S. umbellata (Desf.) Fritsch. Tree, 5–7m. Lvs 3.5–6cm, sub-circular to broadly elliptic, short lobed, base tapered, bluntly rounded above, coriaceous, dark green above, white woolly beneath. Fls flattened-globose, orange-red. SE Eur., Asia Minor. var. *cretica* Schneid. Crown wider. Lvs 5–9cm, elliptic obovate, apex not lobed, entire to bi-serrate. Fr. globose, brown-green to brown-red. Greece, Syr., Asia Minor. Z6.

S. ursina (G. Don) Schauer. Tree to 7m, occas. shrubby. Young shoots thinly tomentose, grey-brown. Lfts 8–11, 2–2.5cm, oblong, obtuse, apex awned, base rounded or truncate, finely serrate, dark green, glab. above, midrib densely tomentose beneath at first. Fls in branched clusters to 12cm, brown tomentose at first. Fr. 1cm, green-purple to white with pink flush. Himal. Z7.

S. vestita (G. Don) Lodd. HIMALAYAN WHITEBEAM. Medium-sized tree. Lvs 10–25cm, broadly elliptic, base decurrent to petiole, green above, silver to buff-tomentose beneath. Fr. to 2cm diam., depressed globose to pyriform, green speckled and stained brown to russet. Himal. 'Sessilifolia': lvs large, elliptic, apex and base tapering, ± sessile, sea-green above, hoary-tomentose beneath.

S. ×*vagensis* Wilmott (*S. aria* ×*S. torminalis*.) Compact small to medium tree. Lvs ovate to elliptic, lobed, glossy above sparsely grey-tomentose beneath. Fr. obovoid, green-brown speckled brown.

S. vilmorinii Schneid. Dainty shrub or small tree to 6m, br. spreading, buds and shoots downy, red-brown. Lvs 8–12cm, lfts 11–31, 1.5–2.5cm, elliptic, tips serrate, glab. above, grey-green beneath. Infl. lax, to 10cm, axis winged. Fr. 8mm, globose, rose-red to white flushed pink. W China. 'Pearly King': small; lvs elegantly pinnate, glossy green, yellow to red in autumn; fr. v. large, white flushed pink, in large clusters. Z6.

S. wardii Merr. Large, erect columnar tree. Lvs elliptic to obovate, green, ribbed above, sparsely hairy beneath, grey-downy at first. Fr. globose, large, amber speckled olive-brown in loose clusters. Tibet, Bhutan. Z8.

S. wilsoniana Schneid. Tree 7–10m, shoots stout. Bud tips silver-downy. Lvs to 25cm, lfts 11–15, 6–8cm, oblong lanceolate, pointed or tapered, grey green beneath, midrib downy. Fls in clusters 10–15cm. Fr. globose, carmine. C China. Z6.

S. xanthoneura Rehd. Differs from *S. pallescens* in larger fr., heavily punctate, lower lf. veins glab., yellow. Lvs 8–13×3.5–5.5cm, oblong to obovate, tapered, bi-serrate, densely white felted beneath. Fr. 8mm, depressed-globose, red. China. Z6.

S. zahlbruckneri Schneid. Tree. Br. ± glab., purple. Lvs 6–10×3.5–5cm, elliptic-ovate, short lobed, sharply toothed, waxy green above, white-grey beneath. W China. Z6.

S. cvs. 'Apricot Lady': close to *S. aucuparia*; lvs finely cut, bright green colouring well in fall; fr. large, apricot yellow. 'Autumn Glow' (*S. commixta* 'Embley' ×*S. vilmorinii*): small upright tree. Lvs pinnate, purple then orange-red in fall. Fr. white-pink, then yellow-red. 'Easter Promise' (*S. commixta* 'Embley' ×*S. vilmorinii*): small oval-crowned tree; lvs with 15–19 lfts, dark green, purple to flame in fall; rachis red-tinted. Fr. strong rose pink in heavy hanging clusters. 'Leonard Messel' (*S. aucuparia* ×*S. harrowiana*): small tree; br. upright, crown oval. Lvs large with pink rachis, turning red-purple in fall, lfts 9–11, to 11cm, oblong, serrate above, glaucous beneath. Fr. bright pink in large hanging clusters.

→*Pyrus* and *Micromeles*.

Sorghastrum Nash. Gramineae. *c*16 ann. or perenn. grasses. St. clumped, flimsy to robust. Lvs narrow, flat or rolled. Infl. narrow, term., single-digitate or paniculate; spikelets solitary, 2-fld. Trop. Afr., Americas. Z5.

S. avenaceum (Michx.) Nash = *S. nutans*.

S. nutans (L.) Nash. INDIAN GRASS; WOOD GRASS. To 2m. Lvs linear, to 60×1cm, scabrous, attenuate. Pan. to 35cm, tinged yellow to brown; spikelets hirsute, golden brown. Autumn. E & C US. Sometimes offered under the name *Chrysopogon nutans*. 'Sioux Blue': v. erect; lvs metallic blue.

S. secundum (Elliot) Nash. To 2m. Lvs less than 0.5cm diam. Pan. to 40cm, 1-sided; spikelets pilose, tinged brown. SE US.

Sorghum *Sorghum bicolor*.

Sorghum Moench. Gramineae. MILLET. *c*20 ann. or perenn., grasses. St. clumped, usually robust. Infl. paniculate; br. racemose, internodes pubesc.; spikelets in pairs, one sessile, fertile, one stipitate, ♂ or sterile; fertile spikelet awned. OW Trop., subtrop., 1 sp. endemic to Mex. Z8.

S. bicolor (L.) Moench. SORGHUM; GREAT MILLET; KAFIR CORN. Ann., to 6m. Lvs to 90×10cm, flat, midrib white. Pan. v. dense, to 60×25cm; fertile spikelets to 1cm. Grains large, variously coloured. Summer. China, S Afr.

S. halapense (L.) Pers. JOHNSON GRASS; ALEPPO GRASS; MEANS GRASS. Perenn., to 1.5m. Lvs to 60×2.5cm, flat, midrib white. Pan. compact, to 25×8cm; fertile spikelets to 0.5cm, cream to yellow. Summer–autumn. Medit.

S. vulgare Pers. = *S. bicolor*.

→*Andropogon* and *Holeus*.

Sorrel *Hibiscus sabdariffa*; *Oxalis*; *Rumex*.
Sorrel Tree *Oxydendrum arboreum*.
Sotol *Dasylirion*.
Soup Mint *Plectranthus amboinicus*.
Sourai Nut *Caryocar nuciferum*.
Sourberry *Rhus integrifolia*.
Sour Cherry *Prunus cerasus*.
Sour Dock *Rumex acetosa*.
Sour Greens *Rumex venosus*.
Sour Gum *Nyssa sylvatica*.
Sour Orange *Citrus aurantium*.
Soursop *Annona muricata*.
Sourtop *Vaccinium myrtilloides*.
Sourwood *Oxydendrum arboreum*.
South African Sage Wood *Buddleja salviifolia*.
South African Wisteria *Bolusanthus speciosus*.
South American Air Plant *Kalanchoe fedtschenkoi*.
South American Apricot *Mammea americana*.
South American Staghorn *Platycerium andinum*.
South American Vervain *Verbena bonariensis*.
Southern Arrow Wood *Viburnum dentatum*.
Southern Beech *Nothofagus*.
Southern Beech Fern *Phegopteris hexagonoptera*.
Southern Black Blueberry *Vaccinium virgatum*.
Southern Black Haw *Viburnum rufidulum*.
Southern Blueberry *Vaccinium tenellum*.
Southern Blue Flag *Iris virginica*.
Southern Blue Gum *Eucalyptus globulus*.
Southern Broom *Notospartium*.
Southern Buckthorn *Bumelia lycioides*.
Southern Coast Violet *Viola septemloba*.
Southern Dewberry *Rubus trivialis*.
Southern Gooseberry *Vaccinium melanocarpum*.
Southern Harebell *Campanula divaricata*.
Southern Japanese Hemlock *Tsuga sieboldii*.
Southern Lady Fern *Athyrium filix-femina*.
Southern Live Oak *Quercus virginiana*.
Southern Magnolia *Magnolia grandiflora*.
Southern Mahogany *Eucalyptus botryoides*.
Southern Maidenhair *Adiantum capillus-veneris*.
Southern Marsh Orchid *Dactylorhiza praetermissa*.
Southern Mountain Cranberry *Vaccinium erythrocarpum*.
Southern Plains Banksia *Banksia media*.
Southern Rata *Metrosideros umbellatus*.
Southern Redcedar *Juniperus silicicola*.
Southern Red Oak *Quercus falcata*.
Southern Swamp Crinum *Crinum americanum*.
Southern Washingtonia *Washingtonia robusta*.
Southernwood *Artemisia abrotanum*.
Southern Wood Fern *Dryopteris ludoviciana*.
Southernwood Geranium *Pelargonium abrotanifolium*.
Southern Yellow Pine *Pinus palustris*.
South Florida Slash Pine *Pinus densa*.
South Island Edelweiss *Leucogenes grandiceps*.
South Sea Arrowroot *Tacca leontopetaloides*.

Southsea Ironwood *Casuarina equisetifolia.*
Southwestern White Pine *Pinus strobiformis.*
Sowbread *Cyclamen.*

Sowerbaea Sm. Liliaceae (Asphodelaceae). 5 tufted fibrous-rooted perenn. herbs. Lvs basal and on lower part of st., narrow-linear or filiform. Flowering st. simple, occas. branching; umbel term. subtended by small, scarious bracts; perianth seg. to 0.8cm, 6, free, outer 3 free and shorter, inner 3 free or basally connate; fertile sta. Aus. Z9.
S.juncea Sm. Lvs linear-filiform, terete. Flowering st. 15–30cm; perianth seg. oval-oblong, pink. Early summer. Aus.
S.laxiflora Lindl. Lvs comvex beneath, to 1.5mm wide, tapering. Flowering st. 15–45cm; perianth seg. broadly ovate, purple. Summer. W Aus.

Sow-teat Blackberry *Rubus allegheniensis.*
Soya *Brahea.*
Soybean, Soya Bean *Glycine max.*
Spade-leaf Philodendron *Philodendron domesticum.*
Spangle Grass *Chasmanthium latifolium.*
Spangle Grass *Uniola.*
Spanish Bayonet *Yucca aloifolia; Y. baccata.*
Spanish Black Pine *Pinus nigra* var. *mauretanica.*
Spanish Bluebell *Hyacinthoides hispanica.*
Spanish Broom *Spartium junceum.*
Spanish Cherry *Mimusops elengi.*
Spanish Chestnut *Castanea sativa.*
Spanish Dagger *Yucca carnerosana; Y. gloriosa; Y. treculeana.*
Spanish Elm *Cordia gerascanthus; Hamelia ventricosa.*
Spanish Fir *Abies pinsapo.*
Spanish Flag *Ipomoea lobata.*
Spanish Garlic *Allium scorodoprasum.*
Spanish Gorse *Genista hispanica.*
Spanish Guava *Catesbaea spinosa.*
Spanish Heath *Erica australis.*
Spanish Iris *Iris xiphium.*
Spanish Jasmine *Jasminum officinale* f. *grandiflorum.*
Spanish Juniper *Juniperus thurifera.*
Spanish Lime *Melicoccus bijugatus.*
Spanish Moss *Tillandsia usneoides.*
Spanish Needles *Bidens.*
Spanish Oak *Catalpa longissima; Inga laurina; Quercus pyrenaica; Quercus texana.*
Spanish Oyster Thistle *Scolymus hispanicus.*
Spanish Plum *Spondias purpurea.*
Spanish Psyllium *Plantago psyllium.*
Spanish Shawl *Heterocentron elegans.*
Spanish-stopper *Eugenia foetida.*
Spanish Tamarind *Vangueria madagascariensis.*
Spanish Tea *Chenopodium ambrosioides.*
Spanish Thyme *Plectranthus amboinicus.*
Spanish Tree Heath *Erica australis.*
Spanish Woodbine *Merremia tuberosa.*

Sparattosperma Mart. ex Meissn. Bignoniaceae. 2 trees. Lvs digitate. Cymes loose term., cal. tubular, membranous, split; cor. tube widening to limb, limb bilabiate, lobes 5, undulate-crispate; sta. 4, included. Trop. S Amer. Z10.
S. rosea (Bertol.) Miers = *Tabebuia rosea.*
S. vernicosum (Cham.) Bur. and Schum. Erect buttressed tree. Petioles 10–15cm; lfts 15cm, ovate, apex acute, membranous, slightly vernicose, stalked. Pan. borne on bare tree, puberulent; cor. yellow, lightly puberulent, c3cm. Braz.
→*Spathodea.*

Sparaxis Ker-Gawl. Iridaceae. 6 cormous perenn. herbs. St. unbranched or branched, with axill. cormlets. Lvs ribbed. Spike laxy 1- to several-fld; bracts scarious, lacerate; fls regular or slightly irregular; perianth tube short, narrow then funnel-shaped, seg. 6, ± equal; style with 3 br. S Afr. Z9.
S. bulbifera (L.) Ker-Gawl. 15–50cm, usually with 1–3 br., with numerous cormlets in lf axils after flowering. Lvs distichous, 4–10mm wide, sword-shaped. Spike laxly 1–6-fld; fls irregular, tube yellow, green at base, seg. white or cream, exterior with purple median streak, rarely wholly, plum-coloured 25–28mm, lanceolate; anth. white. Late winter–spring.
S. elegans (Sweet) Goldbl. St. 10–30cm, unbranched, 2–5 per corm, with some cormlets at lowest nodes. Lvs forming a fan, 8–25×0.5–1.5cm, sword-shaped. Fls regular, tube yellow, seg. vermilion fading to pink, with violet band sometimes marked yellow at edge inside at base, 18–22mm, ovate, obtuse; sta. maroon or brown. Spring. 'Coccinea': fls orange-red with near-black centre.
S. fragrans (Jacq.) Ker-Gawl. St. 1–3, 8–45cm, unbranched, with a few cormlets in lowest axils. Lvs distichous, 4–13mm wide,

lanceolate or falcate. Spike 1–6-fld; fls irregular, tube yellow, purple or black, seg. cream, yellow, red-purple or violet-purple with or without dark blotches and streaks, seg. 24–40mm, lanceolate, ovate or spathulate, subacute or obtuse. Late winter–spring. ssp. *acutiloba* Goldbl. Fls purple, or yellow sometimes with the outside of lobes marked with black, seg. 25–29mm, lanceolate, acute. ssp. *grandiflora* (Delaroche) Goldbl. Fls usually red-purple, sometimes white with purple marks, the tube yellow inside, purple outside; seg. 25–30mm, spathulate, obtuse. ssp. *fimbriata* (Lam.) Goldbl. Tube yellow, purple outside, seg. cream or pale yellow, usually with large black blotches at base and streaked on outside with purple, 28–40mm, narrowly ovate, obtuse. ssp. *violacea* (Ecklon) Goldbl. Tube yellow or cream, seg. white with or without violet marks, or violet with white at base and apex 22–26mm, spathulate, obtuse.
S. pillansii L. Bol. St. 2–4, 25–65cm, unbranched, with cormlets in lower axils. Lvs distichous, narrowly sword-shaped. Spike laxly 4–9-fld; fls regular, tube yellow, seg. rose-pink with yellow mark edged purple at base, 22–29mm; anth. purple-red. Spring.
S. tricolor (Schneev.) Ker-Gawl. St. 1–5, 10–40cm, with few cormlets below. Lvs arranged in fan, 1–2cm wide, sword-shaped. Spike laxly 2–5-fld; fls regular, tube yellow, seg. vermilion or salmon, almost always with black arrow-shaped mark at base, 25–33mm, lanceolate, acute; anth. yellow or white. 'Alba': fls white to 5cm across, seg. yellow at throat with dark centre stripe. 'Honneur de Haarlem': fls large, deep crimson, pet. blotched black in middle with yellow markings. Magic Border Hybrids: colours in one bloom; seed race.
S. violacea Ecklon = *Sparaxis fragrans* ssp. *violacea.*
→*Ixia, Sparaxis* and *Streptanthera.*

SPARGANIACEAE Rudolphi. See *Sparganium.*

Sparganium L. Sparganiaceae. 21 aquatic or marginal perenn. herbs. Roots often inflated. St. emergent. Lvs distichous, linear, floating or emergent, flattened to V-shaped, or triangular in section, sometimes carinate or keeled. Fls unisexual, arranged tightly in 2 or 3 compact rac. in globose heads; in simple or branched rac. Fruits crowded in a burr-like head. N & S temp.
S. californicum Greene = *S. eurycarpum.*
S. emersum Rehmann. Robust to slender, submerged, floating or erect, lvs usually erect and emergent, 20–50cm×0.4–1cm, carinate. Flowering st. simple, erect, 20–80cm. ♀ heads, 1.6–2.5(–3.5)cm diam., appearing white to yellow-green at anthesis. ♂ heads (3–)4–7(–10), pale yellow-green, remote and distinct at anthesis. Eur., Asia, N Amer. Z5.
S. erectum L. Robust, erect, emergent, rarely floating or submerged. Basal lvs fan-like, usually emergent, often pink at base, to 150(–350)×1–2(–2.8)cm, carinate. Flowering st. erect, 20–100cm, branched; ♀ heads 12–20mm diam. at anthesis; dark brown to black; ♂ heads green before anthesis with black flecks, at anthesis 10–12mm diam. Old World. Z6.
S. eurycarpum Engelm. Robust, erect, emergent. Basal lvs obliquely erect and fan-like, 50–100(–260)×0.6–2cm, carinate below, flattened towards apex. Flowering st. erect, 50–150(–260)cm, branched; ♀ heads dark brown to black at the apex, 2–3.5cm diam., in fr.; ♂ heads green before anthesis with black flecks, at anthesis 1.2cm diam. N Amer. Similar to *S. erectum* but fruits sessile, cuneate-obpyramidal. N Am. Z5.
S. minimum Fries = *S. natans.*
S. natans L. Slender with vegetative parts usually submerged or floating. Basal lvs thin, translucent, deep green, 6–40(–60)×0.2–10cm, flat to somewhat concave, apex rounded. Flowering st. (6–)8–40(–100)cm, decumbent or ascending, usually floating, flexuous, rarely erect and emergent. Infl. simple, 1.5–8cm, ♀ heads (5–)7–10(–15)mm diam. ♂ heads term., solitary. Arc. and boreal N Amer. and Eurasia. Z2.
S. ramosum f. *simplicior* Rothert = *S. erectum.*
S. simplex Huds. = *S. emersum.*

Sparmannia L. f. Tiliaceae. 4 shrubs or trees. Lvs toothed, unlobed or with 3–7 lobes. Fls in long-stalked axill. or subterminal umbels with short, involucral bracts; sep. 4, decid.; pet. 4, oblanceolate; sta. many in a showy boss, dilating if touched. Fr. a prickly capsule. Trop., S Afr. Z10.
S. africana L. f. AFRICAN HEMP. To 6m. Lvs 15–30cm, cordate-ovate, acuminate, irregularly toothed, bright green, white-pubesc., unlobed or with v. shallow lobes or angles; petioles 10–15cm. Pet. to 2cm, white; sta. v. numerous, yellow, with red to purple tips. Fr. a 5-celled, globose capsule. S Afr. 'Flore Pleno' ('Plena'): fls double. 'Variegata': lvs marked with white.
S. palmata E. Mey. ex Harv. = *S. ricinicarpa.*
S. ricinicarpa (Ecklon & Zeyh.) Kuntze. To 2.7m. Lvs with 3–7, slender, acuminate, unequally toothed lobes. Pet. to 1.5cm,

white or tinged purple. Fr. a 4-celled, ellipsoid, capsule. NE to S Afr.

Spartina Schreb. MARSH GRASS; CORD GRASS. Gramineae. 15 rhizomatous, perenn. grasses. Sts rigid, erect. Lvs flat to convolute, tough; ligules ciliate. Infl. racemos;e rac. digitate, secund; spikelets sessile, adpressed to spreading, pectinate, distichous. W & S Eur., NW & S Afr., Amer., S Atlantic Is.

S. michauxiana A. Hitchc. = *S. pectinata*.

S. pectinata Link. PRAIRIE CORD GRASS; FRESHWATER CORD GRASS; SLOUGH GRASS. To 2m. St. tufted, robust. Lvs elongate, flat, to 120×1.5cm, scabrous, tapering, turning yellow in autumn. Infl. narrow, compact, erect; spikes to 30, to 10cm. Autumn–winter. N Amer. 'Aureomarginata' ('Variegata'): lvs arching, olive green edged golden yellow; fl. spikes narrow, sta. purple and hanging. Z5.

Spartium L. Leguminosae (Papilionoideae). 1 decid. shrub to 3m; st. crowded, erect, terete, rush-like, glab., dark green. Lvs 1(–3)×0.25–0.5cm, sparse, linear, caducous. Fls to 2.5cm, pealike, highly fragrant, golden-yellow; in term. rac. to 45cm. Fr. 4–8×0.6cm, flat; seeds 10–18. Summer–autumn. Medit. regions and SW Eur.; nat. Calif. Z8.

S. aetnense Raf. ex Biv. = *Genista aetnensis*.

S. aspalathoides Desf. = *Genista aspalathoides*.

S. cinereum Vill. = *Genista cinerea*.

S. corsicum Lois. = *Genista corsica*.

S. erinacoides Lois. = *Genista lobelii*.

S. ferox Poir. = *Genista ferox*.

S. gasparrinii Guss. nom. nud. = *Genista ephedroides*.

S. gymnopterum Viv. = *Genista aspalathoides*.

S. horridum Vahl = *Genista horrida*.

S. horridum Sibth. & Sm. non Vahl = *Genista acanthoclada*.

S. junceum L. SPANISH BROOM; WEAVER'S BROOM. 'Ochroleucum': fls palest yellow. 'Plenum': fls double.

S. radiatum L. = *Genista radiata*.

S. scorpius L. = *Genista scorpius*.

→*Genista*.

Spathicarpa Hook. Araceae. 6 everg. thickly rhizomatous herbs. Lvs lanceolate or ovate to hastate- or sagittate-cordate, or 3-lobed, membranous; petioles slender. Peduncle slender; spathe convolute below, limb spreading, blade-like, facing upwards, pale green, semi-translucent; spadix adnate to spathe with longitudinal rows of foul-smelling fls attached to its upper surface. Trop. S Amer. Z10.

S. sagittifolia Schott. Lvs to 12.5cm, sagittate to hastate, bright green with conspicuous reticulation; petioles to 30cm. Peduncle to 40cm, spathe lanceolate, 6cm. Braz., Parag., Arg.

Spathipappus (C.B. Clarke) Tzvelev.

S. griffithii Tzvelev = *Tanacetum griffithii*.

Spathiphyllum Schott. PEACE LILY. Araceae. 36 everg. rhizomatous perennials. Lvs usually radical, lanceolate to oblong-ovate, acuminate, dark green; midrib prominent, main lat. veins numerous, impressed; petiole subequal to or exceeding lamina, geniculate. Peduncle exceeding foliage; spathe cuspidate, convolute becoming spreading, flat to concave, oblong to oblong-lanceolate, white or green; spadix greenwhite, shorter than spathe, stipe largely adnate to spadix. Trop. Amer., Philipp., Indon. Z10.

S. blandum Schott. Lvs 25×10cm, elliptic to elliptic-oblong, acute; petiole 12cm. Spathe decurrent on peduncle, ellipticoblong, cuspidate, pale green, to 25cm. Belize to Hond.

S. candidum (Bull) N.E. Br. = *S. patinii*.

S. candidum misapplied = *S. wallisii* 'Clevelandii'.

S. cannifolium (Dryand.) Schott. Lvs 25–45×8–16cm, oblanceolate to narrow-elliptic, shortly-acuminate, membranous, glossy dark green above, pale green beneath; petiole to 40cm. Spathe to 22cm, oblong to elliptic, spreading and recurved, coriaceous, white above, green below, not deucrrent along peduncle. N S Amer., Trin.

S. clevelandii see *S. wallisii*.

S. cochlearispathum (Liebm.) Engl. Lvs to 65×23cm, oblong, oblong-lanceolate or narrow-elliptic, undulate, ± membranous; petiole to 75cm, sheath mottled white. Peduncle 120cm; spathe erect, oblanceoalte to elliptic, concave, to 33cm, yellow-green; spatix to 11.5cm. Mex.

S. commutatum Schott. Close to *S. cannifolium* but lvs elliptic, 35–50×11–24cm. Spathe broader, to 24cm, creamy-white with green margin, sometimes decurrent along peduncle. Indon. (Sulawesi), Philipp.

S. floribundum (Lind. & André) N.E. Br. SNOWFLOWER. Lvs to 12–20×5.5–(cm, elliptic to oblong or lanceolate, acuminate, velvety dark green above; petioles to 15cm, sheaths wing-like.

Peduncle to 25cm; spathe recurved, spreading, lanceolate to oblong-elliptic, to 8cm, white or green, base clasping peduncle; spadix to 5cm. Colomb. 'Mauna Loa': compact; lvs deep green; infl. white, fragrant. 'Mauna Loa Supreme': upright, tall; lvs rich green.

S. friedrichsthalii misapplied. = *S. phryniifolium*.

S. kochii misapplied. = *S. wallisii* 'Clevelandii'.

S. 'Marion Wagner'. (*S. cochlearispathum* ×*S.* 'Clevelandii'.) Large. Lvs glossy, quilted, spathe to 20cm, white tinted lime green; spadix adnate.

S. 'McCoy'. (Probably *S. cochlearispathum* ×*S.* 'Clevelandii'.) Vigorous, to 1.5m. Lvs large, glossy; spathes to 30cm, thick, white to pale cream, later pale green; spadix thin, club-like.

S. patinii (Hogg) N.E. Br. Close to *S.floribundum* but lvs to 12–21cm, narrower, oblong-lanceolate, acuminate, glossy green, not velvety above. Peduncle 35–50cm; spathe spreading or recurved, oblong-lanceolate, to 7.5cm, cream below with midrib green; spadix white. Colomb.

S. phryniifolium Schott. Lvs 25–50×8–16cm, lanceolate or oblong-elliptic, base rounded. Peduncle short; spathe lanceolate to oblong-elliptic, to 25×9cm, slightly deucrrent on peduncle, membranous, green-yellow; spadix to 8cm, white. Panama, Costa Rica.

S. wallisii Reg. Lvs 24–36×5–10cm, lanceolate- to oblong-elliptic, undulate, bright green; petiole to 20cm. Peduncle to 30cm; spathe ovate to oblong, elliptic, concave, to 17×7.5cm, white, becoming green; spadix to 8cm, white, scented, stipe to 5cm, largely adnate. Panama, Costa Rica. The plant usually grown is cv. Clevelandii: lvs 36–42×9–12cm, drooping, membranous, glossy green, petiole exceeding lamina; spathe erect to slightly spreading, ovate, acuminate, 18×8.5cm, white, somewhat decurrent on peduncle; spadix to 8.5cm.

S. cvs. 'Petite': small, upright, to 15cm; lvs thin, glossy green. 'Tasson': lvs deep green, glossy, margins undulate; fls white.

Spathodea Beauv. Bignoniaceae. 1 buttressed tree to 20m. Lvs imparipinnate; pinnae 4–9 pairs, 15×5.5cm, oblong or oblong-ovate, semi-rigid. Rac. term., brown-tomentose; cal. 7.5cm, yellow to brown-tomentose; cor. 12cm, scarlet to blood-red, campanulate abruptly narrowed towards cylindrical base, tube 5–7cm, lobes 3cm, ovate, crispate. Capsule 15–21×3.5–6cm, woody. Trop. Afr. Z10.

S. alba Sim = *Dolichandrone alba*.

S. andenantha G. Don = *Newbouldia laevis*.

S. campanulata Beauv. AFRICAN TULIP.

S. corymbosa Vent. = *Phryganocydia corymbosa*.

S. gigantea Bl. = *Radermachera gigantea*.

S. glandulosa Bl. = *Radermachera glandulosa*.

S. indica Pers. = *Oroxylum indicum*.

S. jenischii Sonder = *Newbouldia laevis*.

S. laevis P. Browne = *Newbouldia laevis*.

S. longiflora Vent. = *Dolichandrone spathacea*.

S. loureiriana DC. = *Dolichandrone spathacea*.

S. lutea Benth. = *Markhamia lutea*.

S. nilotica Seem. = *S. campanulata*.

S. pentandra Hook. = *Newbouldia laevis*.

S. rheedii Spreng. = *Dolichandrone spathacea*.

S. speciosa Brongn. = *Newbouldia laevis*.

S. stipulata Wallich = *Markhamia stipulata*.

S. vernicosa Cham. = *Sparattosperma vernicosum*.

Spathodeopsis Dop = *Fernandoa*.

Spathoglottis Bl. Orchidaceae. 40 terrestrial orchids. Pbs conical to ovoid. Lvs linear-lanceolate, plicate, stalked and sheathing. Rac. lat.; fls many; tep. spreading, erect, sepalls narrower than pet.; lip midlobe lanceolate to spathulate, bilobed below, with pubesc. callus. Asia to Aus. Z10.

S. aurea Lindl. Lvs 100cm. Infl. to 60cm+, 4–10 fld; fls to 7cm diam., golden, lip spotted crimson; tep. elliptic to ovate; lip midlobe lanceolate. Summer. Malaysia.

S. ixioides (D. Don) Lindl. Lvs to 20cm. Infl. erect, slender, lax; fls yellow, minutely pubesc.; tep. elliptic to oblong; lip base saccate, midlobe obcordate. India.

S. lilacina Griff. = *S. plicata*.

S. petri Rchb. f. Lvs to 45cm. Infl. to 60cm, dense; fls 9–12, to 4cm diam., lilac, sep. ligulate, sep. elliptic; lip cuneate, dilated, midlobe short, callus 2 lines of yellow to ochre hairs, lat. lobes ligulate, purple, disc white. Pacific.

S. plicata Bl. Lvs to 120cm. Infl. to 1m, fls purple, rose or lilac; dors. sep. elliptic to 0.6cm, lat. sep. falcate; pet. elliptic-ovate; lip midlobe clawed, cuneate, callus cordate, yellow, villous. India, SE Asia to Philipp.

S. pubescens Lindl. Lvs to 30cm. Infl. axis downy to 45cm; fls to 2.5cm diam., dull yellow, lip basally violet, saccate, midlobe cuneate or obcordate with 2 tubercles at base. Autumn–winter. India, Burm., China.

S. tomentosa Lindl. Lvs to 60cm. Infl. to 35cm, axis velutinous; fls to 4.5 diam., deep pink to mauve, white or yellow, centre dappled red; lat. sep. elliptic-oblong, to 2.5cm; pet. ovate; lip midlobe slender, apex reniform. Philipp.

S. grexes.
   S. Kewensis: fls rich deep purple.
   S. Penang Beauty: fls clear pale yellow.
S. trivalvis Wallich = *Acriopsis javanica.*

Spatterdock *Nuphar.*
Speargrass *Aciphylla squarrosa.*
Spear Grass *Poa; Stipa.*
Spearhead *Senecio kleiniiformis.*
Spear Lily *Doryanthes.*
Spearmint *Mentha spicata.*
Spearwood *Acacia doratoxylon.*
Speckled Alder *Alnus rugosa.*
Speckled Wood Lily *Clintonia umbellulata.*

Specularia A. DC.
S. hybrida (L.) A. DC. = *Legousia hybrida.*
S. pentagonia (L.) A. DC. = *Legousia pentagonia.*
S. speculum-veneris (L.) A. DC. = *Legousia speculum-veneris.*

Speedwell *Veronica.*

Speirantha Bak. Liliaceae (Convallariaceae). 1 perenn. rhizomatous herb. Lvs to 15×3cm in a basal rosette, oblanceolate, tapered toward base, apex acute. Scape 7–10cm, slender with scale-like lvs; rac. loose, 20–30-fld; pet. 4–5mm, 6, spreading, white; sta. 6. Fr. a berry. Spring–summer. China. Z8.
S. convallarioides Bak.
S. gardenii Baill. = *S. convallarioides.*

Spenceria Trimen. Rosaceae. 2 erect, perenn., woody-rhizomatous herbs. Lvs pinnate, mostly basal in rosettes. Fls racemose, subtended by a cup-shaped involucre of 2 connate, dentate bracts; cal. 5-lobed; pet. 5; sta. 15–40. W China, Bhutan. Z6.
S. passiflora Stapf. V. close to *S. ramalana*, fls slightly smaller. Bhutan.
S. ramalana Trimen. Pilose to villous herb. Basal lvs to 10cm; lfts 0.3–1.5cm, 11–17, obovate-elliptic; st. lvs simple, reduced. Rac. erect, 10–20-fld; pet. to 5mm, obovate, yellow. W China.
S. ramalana var. **passiflora** (Stapf) Kit. = *S. passiflora.*

Spergula L. SPURREY. Caryophyllaceae. 6 small herbs, much-branched, with pairs of linear lvs and conspicuous clusters of axill. lvs. Fls small, in lax dichasial cymes; sep. 5, free; pet. 5, small, white, entire; sta. 5–10. Mediterranean area and S Asia. One sp. (*S. arvensis*) an almost cosmopolitan weed, probably originally European.
S. arvensis L. CORN SPURREY. Ann. St. weak, geniculate, glandular-hairy to 50cm. Lvs linear, fleshy, apparently in whorls. Infl. a forked pan., often umbel-like; pet. to 5mm, obovate, white. Summer.

Spergularia (Pers.) Presl. & C. Presl SAND SPURREY; SEA SPURREY. Caryophyllaceae. c40 ann. or perenn. herbs. Lvs linear, paired, with connate stipules. Fls cymose; sep. 5, free; pet. 5 (sometimes 0); sta. 5–10. Cosmop.
S. rubra (L.) Presl & C. Presl. Ann. or bienn. St. decumbent, branched, ± hairy, often gland., to 20cm. Sep. 3–4mm; pet. ovate, shorter than sep., pink with a paler base. Summer. Widespread throughout much of Eur. and Asia; also in N Afr. and N Amer.; introd. in Aus.
S. rupicola Lebel ex Le Jolis. Like *S. rubra*, but perenn. with larger fls with deep pink pet. exceeding sep. Summer. Eur. (Atlantic coast).

Spermadictyon Roxb. Rubiaceae. 1 everg. shrub to 3m. Lvs to 25cm, elliptic to lanceolate or ovate, acute, rigid, leathery, petioles to 2.5cm. Fls white or blue to lilac or pink, sweetly scented, clustered, in loose pan.; cal. lobes linear or awl-shaped, often gland.; cor. tube to 1.5cm, hairy, lobes spreading, pubesc.; sta. 5, included or exserted. Autumn–spring. Himal. Z10.
S. suaveolens (Roxb.) Roxb.
→*Hamiltonia.*

Sphacele Benth.
S. blochmanae Eastw. = *Lepechinia calycina.*
S. calycina var. *glabella* A. Gray = *Lepechinia calycina.*

S. calycina Benth. = *Lepechinia calycina.*
S. campanulata Benth. = *Lepechinia chamaedryoides.*
S. chilensis (Molina) Briq. = *Lepechinia chamaedryoides.*
S. gracilis Eastw. = *Lepechinia calycina.*
S. lindleyi Benth. = *Lepechinia salviae.*

Sphaeralcea St.-Hil. GLOBE MALLOW; FALSE MALLOW. Malvaceae. 60 stellate-pubesc., coarse ann. or perenn. herbs and subshrubs. Lvs linear-lanceolate to orbicular to deeply palmately lobed. Fls in small axill. clusters or usually 3; racs or pan.; cal. 5-lobed; pet. 5, cupped; sta. united in a tubular column. Arid N & S Amer.
S. ambigua A. Gray. DESERT MALLOW. Suffrutescent perenn. to 1m, white- or yellow-canescent. Lvs thick, ovate to suborbicular, slightly 3-lobed, apex blunt. Fls in open paniculate infl.; pet. 1.2–3cm, orange. SW US. Z4.
S. angustifolia (Cav.) G. Don. Suffrutescent perenn. to 2m, grey-canescent. Lvs 5–10cm, thick, often revolute, lanceolate to oblong-lanceolate, rarely lobed. Fls in long, narrow leafy thyrses; pet. to 1.5cm, pink or lavender. W US, Mex. Z4.
S. bonariensis (Cav.) Griseb. Suffrutescent perenn. to 1m. Lvs ovate, slightly 3-lobed. Fls in dense axillary clusters; pet. 1.2–1.8cm, apricot, salmon-pink to brick-red, usually darker spotted at the base. S Amer. Z9.
S. cisplatina St.-Hil. = **S. bonariensis.**
S. coccinea (Pursh) Rydb. PRAIRIE MALLOW; RED FALSE MALLOW. Woody-based, decumbent. Perenn. to 60cm, grey or white stellate-pubesc. Lvs pinnately parted or divided. Fls in short racemose infl.; pet. 1–1.8cm, orange to red. C & W N America. Z5.
S. elegans (Cav.) D. Don = *Anisodontea elegans.*
S. emoryi Torr. Suffrutescent perenn. to 1.2m, grey-canescent. Lvs thick, ovate-oblong, crenate-dentate. Fls in leafy, narrow thyrses; pet. 1–2cm, grenadine, pink or lavender. SW US. Z5.
S. fasciculata (Nutt. ex Torr. & A. Gray) Arth. = *Malacothamnus fasciculatus.*
S. fendleri A. Gray. FENDLER GLOBE MALLOW. Suffrutescent perenn. to 1.2m, grey- or white-canescent, erect or ascending. Lvs shallowly to deeply 3-lobed below middle, crenate-dentate or cleft. Fls in narrow thyrses; pet. orange-red to violet, 0.8–1.2cm. SW US, N Mex. Z4.
S. grossulariifolia (Hook. & Arn.) Rydb. Woody-based perenn. to 1m, densely white-canescent, erect or ascending. Lvs deltoid to broadly ovate, divided nearly to the midvein, lobes coarsely dentate. Fls in interrupted, many-fld thyrses; pet. 1–2cm, orange-red. W US. Z4.
S. hastulata A. Gray. Woody-based perenn. to 2m, pubesc. Lvs thin, ovate-oblong to ovate-lanceolate, hastate-dentate or shallowly lobed near base, entire to crenate, the midlobe sometimes pinnately cleft. Fls mostly solitary, forming a racemose infl.; pet. 1.5–2cm, pink. SW US, Mex. Z6.
S. miniata (Cav.) Spach = **S. fendleri.**
S. munroana (Douglas) Spach ex Gray. Perenn. to 1m, with grey-stellate pubescence, erect. Lvs ovate to subrhombic, shallowly 3- or 5-lobed, crenate. Fls in many-fld, narrow thyrses; pet. 1.5–2cm, apricot-pink to pale red or orange. W US. var. **subrhomboides** (Rydb.) Kearney Lvs cleft beyond the middle or 3-parted, divisions cleft or parted, cuneate. Wyom., Utah and Nevada. Z4.
S. nutans Scheid. ex Planch. Shrub to 60cm. Lvs cordate, lobes 5, acute, irregularly toothed, stellate-hairy. Fls on axill. 3-fld peduncles, exceeding lvs; pet. red-purple. Guat. ?. Z8.
S. obtusiloba (Hook.) G. Don. BLUNT-LEAVED CHILEAN MALLOW. Shrub to 1.2m, stellate-pubesc. Lvs cordate, obscurely 5-lobed, crenate. Fls in axill. and term. 4–6-fld corymbose infl.; pet. 2.2cm, rose-purple, apex notched, base dark-spotted. Chile. Z9.
S. philippiana Krapov. TRAILING MALLOW. Trailing woody-based perenn. herb, grey-pubesc.; st. to 45cm. Lvs small, 3- or 5-lobed, serrate-crisped. Fls in axill., 1–3-fld cymes; pet. orange. Arg. Z9.
S. remota (Greene) Fern. = *Iliamna remota.*
S. rosea (DC.) Standl. = *Phymosia rosea.*
S. subhastata J. Coult. Perenn. herb to 50cm, canescent, decumbent to erect. Lvs lanceolate-ovate, base hastate, entire or irregularly dentate. Fls 1–3 in upper lf axils; pet. 1–1.8cm, orange-red. W Tex., S Ariz., N Mex. Z8.
S. subrhomboides Rydb. = **S. munroana** var. **subrhomboides.**
S. umbellata (Cav.) G. Don = *Phymosia umbellata.*
S. vitifolia (Zucc.) Hemsl. = *Phymosia rosea.*
→*Malvastrum.*

Sphaeropteris Wallich non Bernh.
S. celebica (Bl.) Tryon = *Cyathea celebica.*
S. cooperi (F. Muell.) Tryon = *Cyathea cooperi.*
S. insignis (D.C. Eaton) Tryon = *Cyathea insignis.*
S. medullaris (Forst. f.) Bernh. = *Cyathea medullaris.*

Sphaerostephanos J. Sm. Thelypteridaceae. *c*150 terrestrial ferns. Rhiz. erect and arborescent to long-creeping. Frond-blades 1–2-pinnate, pinnae crenate to deeply lobed, rarely sub-entire, sinus-membrane distinct; basal pinnae usually abruptly reduced. E Afr., Masc. Is., Trop. Asia, Aus., E to Tahiti. Z10.

S. penniger (Hook.) Holtt. Rhiz. short-creeping. Stipe 8–10cm, densely scaly. Frond-blade to 100cm, with 25 pairs pinnae, largest to 20×2–8cm, lobes oblique, broadly pointed. Thail., to Celebes, Lambok & Sumatra.

→*Dryopteris, Nephrodium* and *Thelypteris.*

Sphaerostigma (Ser.) Fisch. & C.A. Mey. = *Camissonia.*

Sphalmanthus N.E. Br. Aizoaceae. 100 succulent subshrubs. St. prostrate, often rooting, some sp. forming tubers at nodes. Lvs linear, ± terete, papillose, v. soft and fleshy, often withering to form spines. Fls solitary or 3 together. S Afr. Z9.

S. canaliculatus (Haw.) N.E. Br. Freely branching prostrate shrub. Lvs linear, obtuse, convex beneath, channelled above, green, papillose. Fls pale red or flesh-coloured. S Cape.

S. micans L. Bol. To 20cm diam. Caudex large, crowned with crowded, simple, prostrate, papillose shoots. Lvs 4.5–7cm, tapered, green. Fls green-yellow. W Cape.

S. resurgens (Kensit) L. Bol. Caudex giving rise to many shoots. Lvs 4–5cm, prostrate, rosulate, upper surface flat, rounded beneath, papillae translucent. Fls pale yellow. W Cape.

S. salmoneus (Haw.) N.E. Br. Shrubby, prostrate. Lvs 1.2–2cm, linear-lanceolate, tapered toward both ends, upper surface channelled, lower surface v. convex, fresh green, papillose. Fls yellow to red. Cape Prov.

S. splendens (L.) L. Bol. Freely branching, cushion-forming. Lvs 1.5–2cm, cylindric, recurved at tip, light green, smooth with several dark green tubercles, slightly pruinose. Fls yellow-white. S Cape.

→*Aridaria, Mesembryanthemum, Nycteranthus* and *Phyllobolus.*

Sphedamnocarpus Planch. ex Benth. Malpighiaceae. 18 shrubs or climbers. Fls in term. umbel. or axill. pan.; bracts and bracteoles present; sep. 5, eglandular; pet. 5, clawed, yellow, entire or fimbriate; sta. 10. Fr. a samara. Trop. & S Afr., Madag. Z10.

S. pruriens (A. Juss.) Szyszyl. Climber to 4m. Br. white-tomentose. Lvs 3.5–7.5cm, ovate, mucronate, glabrate above, silver-sericeous beneath; petioles biglandular. Umbels term., 2–6-fld, pet. 8–12mm yellow. Samaras 3, sericeous, wings to 1cm. Autumn. S Afr.

Sphenomeris Maxon. Dennstaedtiaceae. 18 terrestrial or epilithic ferns. Rhiz. short-creeping to ascending, scaly. Fronds stipitate, uniform, erect, 3–4-pinnate or -pinnatifid, glab., pinnules deltoid, base decurrent, seg. cuneate or linear to spathulate. Trop. Z10.

S. chinensis (L.) Maxon. Fronds to 40×20cm, 3–4-pinnate or -pinnatifid, ovate to lanceolate, thin-textured, ultimate, seg. cuneate, toothed to lobed, lobes to 3mm, cuneate, toothed; stipes to 25cm, grey or green to brown. Madag., Trop. Asia (Malaysia to Jap.), Polyn.

S. chusana (L.) Ching = *S. chinensis.*

S. clavata (L.) Maxon. Fronds to 30×15cm, 3–4-pinnate, ovate or deltoid to linear, thin and firm-textured, glab., ultimate, seg. oblique, cuneate to linear, apex truncate, entire to toothed and fimbriate at apex; stipes to 20cm, lustrous, straw-coloured. Trop. Amer.

→*Adiantum, Davallia, Lindsaea, Odontosoria, Stenoloma* and *Trichomanes.*

Spiceberry *Ardisia crenata.*
Spicebush *Calycanthus; Lindera benzoin.*
Spice Guava *Psidium montanum.*

Spiculaea Lindl.
S. irritabilis (F. Muell.) Schltr. = *Arthrochilus irritabilis.*

Spicy Jatropha *Jatropha integerrima.*
Spicy Wintergreen Checkerberry *Gaultheria procumbens.*
Spider Aloe *Aloe humilis.*
Spider Brake *Pteris multifida.*
Spider Fern *Pteris multifida.*
Spider Flower *Cleome hassleriana; Grevillea.*
Spider Ivy *Chlorophytum comosum.*
Spider Lily *Hymenocallis; Lycoris radiata; Tradescantia.*
Spider Orchid *Brassia lawrenceana; B. verrucosa; Caladenia dilatata.*
Spider Plant *Chlorophytum comosum; Cleome hassleriana.*
Spiderwort *Tradescantia.*

Spigelia L. PINK ROOT; WORM GRASS. Loganiaceae. *c*50, ann. or perenn. herbs or subshrubs. Lvs opposite, connected by stipules or transverse membrane, entire. Infl. of few- to many-fld, cincinni; fls 5-parted; cal. seg. narrow; cor. tubular or salver-form, lobes spreading. Trop. & N Amer.

S. anthelmia L. PINK ROOT OF DEMERARA. Ann. to 45cm. Lvs ovate-oblong, tapering to both ends, sppikes 1–4 in upper lf axils; cor. 6.5–15mm, purple-white. Summer. Mex. to Peru and Braz., nat. Afr., Indon. Z10.

S. marilandica (L.) L. INDIAN PINK; MARYLAND PINKROOT; WORM GRASS. Perenn. to 60cm. Lvs ovate-lanceolate, acute, spikes solitary; cor. 3–5cm, exterior red, interior yellow. Spring-summer. US. Z8.

S. splendens hort. Wendl. ex Hook. Perenn. 30–60cm. Lvs ovate to obovate, acute to acuminate. Spikes solitary to several; cor. 1.5–3.5cm, bright scarlet. Summer. Mex., Guat. Z10.

Spignel *Meum athamanticum.*
Spiked Loosestrife *Lythrum salicaria.*
Spiked Rampion *Phyteuma spicatum.*
Spiked Speedwell *Veronica spicata.*
Spike Grass *Uniola.*
Spike Heath *Bruckenthalia spiculifolia.*
Spike Moss *Selaginella.*
Spikenard *Aralia californica; Nardostachys grandiflora.*
Spike Rush *Eleocharis.*
Spike Wattle *Acacia oxycedrus.*
Spike Witch-hazel *Corylopsis spicata.*

Spilanthes Jacq.
S. oleracea L. = *Acmella oleracea.*
S. americana L. = *Acmella oppositifolia.*
S. oppositifolia (Lam.) D'Arcy = *Acmella oppositifolia.*

Spiloxene Salisb.
S. canaliculata (Garside) Geer. = *Hypoxis neocanaliculata.*
S. capensis (L.) Garside = *Hypoxis capensis.*

Spinach *Spinacia* (*S. oleracea*).
Spinach Beet *Beta vulgaris.*
Spinach Dock *Rumex patentia.*
Spinach Rhubarb *Rumex abyssinicus.*

Spinacia L. SPINACH. Chenopodiaceae. 3 ann. or bienn. glab. herbs. Lvs large, flat. Fls small 4–5 lobed, in dense spicate infl., ♀ axill., perianth 0; bracteoles 2–4, enlarging, hardening and becoming connate in fr. SW Asia. Z5.

S. oleracea L. SPINACH. St. to 1m+, erect. Lvs bright green, glossy, ovate to triangular-hastate, entire or dentate, undulate, bullate. Origin obscure, possibly SW Asia.

Spindle Palm *Hyophorbe verschaffeltii.*
Spindle Tree *Euonymus europaeus.*
Spine Bush *Acacia colletioides.*
Spine Palm *Aiphanes caryotifolia.*
Spinning Gum *Eucalyptus perriniana.*
Spiny Bitter Cucumber *Momordica cochinchinensis.*
Spiny-club Palm *Bactris.*
Spiny-leaf Podocarp *Podocarpus spinulosus.*
Spiny Thrift *Armeria pungens.*
Spiny Wattle *Acacia spinescens.*
Spiraea *Astilbe* (*A. japonica*); *Spiraea.*

Spiraea L. SPIREA; SPIRAEA; BRIDAL-WREATH. Rosaceae. *c*80 decid. shrubs. Lvs simple, serrate, dentate, or lobed, rarely entire. Fls in rac., pan. or corymbs; cal. cupulate, campulate or turbinate, lobes 5, short; pet. 4–5, small; sta. 15–60. Asia, Eur., N Amer., Mex.

S. aemiliana C. Schneid. = *S. betulifolia* var. *aemiliana.*
S. aitchisonii Hemsl. = *Sorbaria tomentosa* var. *angustifolia.*
S. alba Duroi. MEADOWSWEET. To 1.5m. Br. erect to spreading, angled, finely rusty-tomentose. Lvs 2.5–6.25cm, oblong-oblanceolate, acute, serrate. Fls 8mm diam., white, rarely pink, in leafy pyramidal to conical pan. to 20cm+. Summer. E N Amer. Z5.
S. albiflora (Miq.) Zab. = *S. japonica* 'Albiflora'.
S. altaiensis Laxm. = *Sibiraea altaiensis.*
S. amoena Spae. Erect, to 2m. Branchlets slender, terete, downy. Lvs 3.5–10cm, ovate-oblong to ovate-lanceolate, acute to acuminate, coarsely serrate in apical half, soft-pubesc. beneath. Fls white or pink, in corymbs 3–8–12cm diam. at ends of long shoots. Summer. Himal. Z8.
S. amurensis Maxim. = *Physocarpus amurensis.*
S. aquilegiifolia hort. = *S. trilobata.*
S. aquilegiifolia var. *vanhouttei* Briot = *S.* × *vanhouttei.*

S. arborea (C. Schneid.) Bean = *Sorbaria kirilowii.*

S. arbuscula Greene = *S. densiflora* ssp. *splendens.*

S. arcuata Hook. f. Short vigorous. Br. arching, purple, striate, finely woolly at first. Lvs 0.8–2.5cm, oblong-elliptic, entire or sparsely shallow-toothed, veins pubesc. beneath, ciliate. Fls 6mm diam., pink, sometimes white, in umbels to 2cm diam. on short, leafy shoots. Early summer. Himal. (Sikkim). Z9.

S. × *arguta* Zab. (*S.* × *multiflora* × *S. thunbergii?*) GARLAND SPIRAEA. Erect, to 2m, rounded, bushy. Br. slender, arching. Lvs to 4cm, oblanceolate, acute, light green, usually biserrate, initially downy beneath. Fls 8mm diam., snow-white, in crowded corymbs. Spring. 'Compacta': compact, to 1m tall; br. arching; fls small, early spring. 'Graciosa': fls white, v. early-flowering. Z4.

S. aruncus L. = *Aruncus dioicus.*

S. aruncus var. *astilboides* Maxim. = *Aruncus dioicus* var. *astilboides.*

S. baldschuanica B. Fedtsch. Low-growing, rounded and intricately branching shrub. Branchlets slender, glab. Lvs obovate, small, serrate in apical half, blue-green. Fls white in small corymbs at br. tips. Summer. SE Russia. Z6.

S. beauverdiana C. Schneid. = *S. betulifolia* var. *aemiliana.*

S. bella Sims. 1–2.5m. Br. slender, spreading, angular, initially downy. Lvs 2.5–6cm, elliptic to ovate, apex acuminate, biserrate, grey-green, glab. above, veins pubesc. beneath. Fls 6.5mm diam., pink to white, in pubesc., term. corymbs 2–7cm diam. Summer. Himal. Z7.

S. bethlehemensis hort. = *S. latifolia.*

S. betulifolia Pall. non auct. To 1m, rounded, closely branching. Branchlets ± flexuous, terete or angled, red-brown, striate, glab. Lvs 2–5cm, broad-ovate to elliptic, apex rounded to obtuse, crenate or bicrenate, grey-green and reticulately veined beneath, usually glab. Fls to 8mm diam., white or rose, in dense, term., many-fld corymbs to 6cm diam. Summer. NE Asia to C Jap. 'Rosabella': to 4m; fls pink, in flat cymes. 'Summer Snow' (*S. betulifolia* × *S. media*): low; to 60cm; fls white, in flat cymes. var. *aemiliana* (C. Schneid.) Koidz. Dwarf to 30cm. Young br. usually short-pubesc. Lvs to 1.5cm, broad-rounded, crenate. Fls to 5mm diam., in short-pubesc. infl. to 2.5cm diam. Summer. Jap., Kurile Is., Kamchatka. var. *corymbosa* (Raf.) Maxim. 0.3–1m. St. terete, sparsely branched, red-brown. Lvs to 3–7.5cm, broadly elliptic, biserrate in apical half, glab., glaucous beneath. Fls white, 4mm diam., in rounded corymbs to 10cm diam. E US. var. *lucida* (Douglas ex Greene) C. Hitchc. To 1m. sparsely branched. Rootstock creeping. Branchlets terete, glab., buff or brown. Lvs 2–6cm, broad-ovate to ovate-oblong, apex usually acute, coarsely serrate or sharply biserrate, pale beneath. Fls white, in crowded, glab. flat cymes to 10cm diam. W N Amer. Z5.

S. betulifolia sensu auct., non Pall. = *S. betulifolia* var. *corymbosa.*

S. × *billardii* Hérincq. (*S. douglasii* × *S. salicifolia.*) Closer to *S. douglasii* but with lvs acute at apex and base, downy grey beneath. To 2m. Branchlets brown, pubesc. Lvs 5–8cm, oblong-lanceolate, apex sharply serrate, grey-green tomentose beneath. Fls bright pink, in narrow, dense, tomentulose pan. to 20cm. Summer. Gdn origin. 'Alba': fls white. 'Lenneana': shoots glab.; lvs to 8cm, oblong-elliptic to obovate, serrate to biserrate, light green tinted grey; fls pink, in pan. 'Triumphans': lvs to 6cm, serrate, lightly pubesc. beneath; fls rose tinted purple, in dense conical pan. to 20cm. Z4.

S. × *blanda* Zab. (*S. nervosa* × *S. cantoniensis.*) 1.5–2m. Br. angular, striate, brown, thinly pubesc. Lvs 2.5–6cm, ovate-oblong, apex acute, base cuneate, rough-edged to serrate, grey tomentose beneath. Fls 1cm diam., pure white, in pubesc., 4cm diam., corymbs. Spring–summer. Gdn origin, before 1876. Z6.

S. blumei G. Don. Variable sp. sometimes confused with *S. trilobata*. To 1.5m. Br. spreading, glab. Lvs 2–4cm, ovate to rhombic-ovate, apex obtuse to subrounded or subacute, base broad-cuneate to obtuse, incised crenate-serrate, pale blue-green conspicuously veined beneath. Fls 8mm diam., white, in many-fld, small corymbs. Summer. Jap., Korea. Z6.

S. bodinieri Lév. = *S. japonica* var. *acuminata.*

S. boursieri Carr. = *Holodiscus boursieri.*

S. × *brachybotrys* Lange. (*S. canescens* × *S. douglasii.*) Vigorous, to 2.5m. Br. arching; branchlets brown, angular striate, downy. Lvs 3–4.5cm, narrowly elliptic-oblong to ovate, apex sparsely serrate dull dark green, ± lanuginose above, paler, grey lanuginose-tomentose beneath. Fls pale rose-pink, small, crowded, in stout 3–8cm pan. on short side shoots. Summer. Gdn origin. Z4.

S. bracteata Zab. non Raf. = *S. nipponica.*

S. bullata Maxim. = *S. japonica* 'Bullata'.

S. bumalda Burvénich. = *S. japonica* 'Bumalda'.

S. caespitosa Nutt. = *Petrophytum caespitosum.*

S. caespitosa var. *elatior* S. Wats. = *Petrophytum caespitosum*

var. *elatius.*

S. calcicola W.W. Sm. To 1.5m. Br. arching, ribbed, red-brown, initially downy. Lvs 4–7mm, obovate to elliptic, obtuse, entire. Fls white tinted pink, small, in few-fld, reduced corymbs to 12cm. Summer. SW China. Z5.

S. callosa Thunb. = *S. japonica.*

S. callosa Lindl., non Thunb. = *S. japonica* var. *fortunei.*

S. camtschatica Pall. = *Filipendula kamtschatica.*

S. cana Waldst. & Kit. Densely branching, to 1m. Br. slender, initially downy. Lvs 1–2.5cm, narrow-oval or ovate, tapering at both ends, apex entire or sparsely toothed, grey sericeous-lanuginose. Fls 6.5mm diam., dull white, in dense, umbellate rac. to 2.5cm diam. Spring. NW Balk. Z5.

S. canescens D. Don. To 4.5m, habit domed; br. thin, arching or pendulous, ribbed to angled, downy when young. Lvs 1–2.5cm, oval or obovate, apex usually blunt and dentate, dull green and sparsely lanuginose above, grey and dense-lanuginose beneath. Fls white or dull cream-white, to 5mm diam., in 15–20-fld hemispherical corymbs to 5cm diam. Summer. Himal. 'Myrtifolia': lvs oblong, to 1.5cm, dark green, glaucescent beneath; fls small.

S. cantoniensis Lour. REEVES SPIRAEA. To 2m, wide-spreading, graceful. St. arching, glab.; branchlets slender. Lvs 2.5–6.5cm, rhombic-lanceolate, coarsely serrate or irregularly trifid, blue-green with distinct reticulate veins beneath. Fls 8.5mm diam., white, crowded in hemispheric corymbs to 5cm diam., terminating young branchlets. Spring–summer. China, Jap. 'Lanceolata' ('Flore Pleno'): lvs lanceolate, to 6cm; fls double, snow-white. Z6.

S. capitata Pursh = *Physocarpus capitatus.*

S. carpinifolia Willd. = *S. latifolia.*

S. chamaedryfolia L. Erect, to 2m, suckering. Br. often bowed outwards; branchlets winged, ± flexuous, yellow, glab. Lvs 4–7.5cm, ovate or ovate-lanceolate, acute, irregularly biserrate, slightly glaucous beneath. Fls 8.5mm diam., white, crowded in 4cm diam. domed corymbs or corymbose rac. on short side br. Spring–summer. E Alps, Carpath., Balk. to Sib. and C Asia. var. *flexuosa* (Fisch.) Maxim. Smaller. St. conspicuously flexuous and winged. Lvs smaller, narrower, subentire or with apex toothed. Fls fewer, clustered. Sib. var. *ulmifolia* (Scop.) Maxim. Taller; br. more rigid and upright. Lvs coarsely biserrate above, oval. Fls 13mm diam., white, in a more elongated racemose infl. to 5cm. Eur. Z5.

S. chinensis Maxim. = *S. nervosa* var. *angustifolia.*

S. cinerascens Piper = *Petrophytum cinerascens.*

S. × *cinerea* Zab. (*S. hypericifolia* × *S. cana.*) To 1.5m+. Br. angular, lined brown, tomentose. Lvs 2.5–3.5cm, oblong, acuminate, entire or 1–2-toothed at apex, with short, recurved tip. Fls 6.5mm diam., white, in small, sessile, terminal umbels and pedunculate umbels on lower br. axils. Spring. Gdn origin. 'Grefsheim': br. nodding; lvs lanceolate, acute, to 2.5cm, soft sea-green, pubesc. beneath; fls white, profuse, on short stalks, grouped to 6, early-flowering. Z5.

S. confusa Reg. & Körn. = *S. media.*

S. × *conspicua* Zab. (*S. japonica* × *S. latifolia.*) Erect, to 1m. Young shoots dark brown, pubesc. Lvs 3–6cm, elliptic-oblong, acute, serrate or biserrate, subglabrous. Fls shell-pink in broad pan. Summer–autumn. Gdn origin. Z6.

S. corymbosa Raf., non Muhlenb. = *S. betulifolia* var. *corymbosa.*

S. corymbosa var. *lucida* (Douglas ex Greene) Zab. = *S. betulifolia* var. *lucida.*

S. crenata L. To 1m, densely bushy. Br. erect, ± angular, red-brown. Lvs 2–4cm, lanceolate to obovate, acute, entire or bluntly toothed, distinctly 3-veined, grey-green, downy at first. Fls 5–8mm diam., white, in 2cm diam., 10–20-fld, leafy, domed umbels. Spring. SE Eur. to Cauc. and Altai Mts. Z6.

S. crenifolia C.A. Mey. = *S. crenata.*

S. dasyantha sensu auct. Japon., non Bunge = *S. nervosa.*

S. dasyantha var. *angustifolia* Yatabe = *S. nervosa* var. *angustifolia.*

S. decumbens Koch. Low-growing shrublet to 25cm. Br. wiry, prostrate then ascending, glab. Lvs 1–4cm, obovate or oval, shortly tapering, sharply, 1–2-toothed toward apex. Fls 6.5mm diam., white, in 5cm diam., many-fld corymbs on leafy young branchlets. Summer. SE Alps. ssp. *tomentosa* (Poech) Dostál. To 30cm. Shoots procumbent, grey-pubesc. Lvs to 2.5cm, elliptic, denticulate, grey-tomentose beneath. Fls in umbels to 3.5cm diam. Spring. It. (Venetian Alps). Z5.

S. decumbens var. *tomentosa* Poech = *S. decumbens* ssp. *tomentosa.*

S. densiflora Nutt. ex Rydb. To 60cm. Branchlets terete, red-brown. Lvs 2–4cm, elliptic, rounded, tip crenate or serrate, pale beneath. Fls pink, crowded in glab. corymbs to 4cm diam. Summr. NW US. ssp. *splendens* (Baumann ex K. Koch) Abrams. To 120cm. Branchlets puberulous. Lvs oval to elliptic-oblong, serrate or biserrate, entire toward base. Fls in fine-puberulous or subglabrous corymbs. US (Oreg. to Calif.).

Z6.

S. digitata Willd. = *Filipendula palmata*.

S. discolor Pursh = *Holodiscus discolor*.

S. douglasii Hook. Erect, to 2.5m, habit compact, freely suckering. Br. slender, brown, initially pubesc. Lvs 4–10cm, oblong, apex usually obtuse and serrate, dark green above, felty white beneath. Fls deep pink, crowded in erect, tomentose narrow and irregularly conical, term. pan. to 20cm. Summer. W N Amer. cf. *S. tomentosa*. ssp. *menziesii* (Hook.). Seldom exceeding 1m, suckering v. freely. Young growths and undersides of lvs glab. or lanuginose, not tomentose. Lvs 3–7cm. Infl. finer and less densely pubesc. N Oreg. to Alask. Z5.

S. dumosa Nutt. = *Holodiscus dumosus*.

S. esquirolii Lév. = *S. japonica* var. *acuminata*.

S. expansa K. Koch = *S. amoena*.

S. fastigiata Schneid. = *S. amoena*.

S. filipendula L. = *Filipendula vulgaris*.

S. flagelliformis hort. = *S. canescens*.

S. flexuosa Fisch. = *S. chamaedryfolia* var. *flexuosa*.

S. fontenaysiensis Dipp. = *S.* ×*fontenaysii*.

S. ×*fontenaysii* Lebas. (*S. canescens* ×*S. salicifolia*.) Upright, to 2m. Brnaches slender; branchlets angled, pubesc. when young. Lvs 2–5cm, elliptic-oblong, apex rounded, crenate, pale bluegreen and subglabrous beneath. Fls white, in pubesc., conic pan. to 8×8cm on short side br. Summer. Gdn origin. 'Rosea': fls pale pink. Z6.

S. fortunei Planch. = *S. japonica* var. *fortunei*.

S. ×*foxii* (Vos) Zab. (*S. japonica* ×*S. betulifolia*.) Branchlets flexuous, subglabrous, brown. Lvs 5–8cm, elliptic, upper biserrate, dull green above, sometimes mottled bronze-brown, pale green beneath, glab. Fls above, sometimes mottled bronze-brown, pale green beneath, glab. Fls 6mm diam., offwhite, sometimes suffuses pink, in broadly branching, finepubesc. corymbs. Summer. Z5.

S. gemmata Zab. Differs from *S. mollifolia* in st. and lvs glab., not sericeous. To 2.5m. St. angular, arching, slender. Lvs to 2.5cm, narrow-oblong, abrupt-acuminate, apex usually blunt, entire or 3-tootehd. Fls to 8mm diam., white, in 2.5cm diam., 2–6-fld umbels. Spring. NW China. Z5.

S. ×*gieseleriana* Zab. (*S. cana* ×*S. chamaedryfolia*.) Branchlets cinereous, bluntly angular, somewhat flexuous. Lvs 3–4cm, ovate, acute, upper two thirds serrate, sometimes entire, softly downy. Fls to 0.8cm diam., pure white, in corymbs on leafy stalks 3–6cm long. Gdn origin c1880. Z6.

S. grandiflora Hook. non Sweet = *Exochorda racemosa*.

S. grandiflora Sweet = *Sorbaria grandiflora*.

S. grossulariifolia vera hort. = *S. trilobata*.

S. hacquetii Fenzl & Koch = *S. decumbens* ssp. *tomentosa*.

S. hendersonii Canby = *Petrophytum hendersonii*.

S. henryi Hemsl. To 3m, lax, spreading. Br. red-brown, initially pubesc. Lvs 3–9cm, narrow-oblong or oblanceolate, apex coarse-toothed (entire in smaller, earlier lvs), glab. or puberulous above, loose woolly grey beneath. Fls 6.5mm diam., white, in rounded, 5cm diam., compound corymbs terminating short leafy side br. Summer. C & W China. *S. wilsonii* differs in infl. glab., not downy. Z6.

S. hookeri hort. ex Zab. = *S.* ×*nudiflora*.

S. hypericifolia L. To 1.6m. St. subterete to angular, ascending to arching, pubesc. or glab. Lvs to 3.5cm, narrow-elliptic or obovatem, acute or obtuse and entire or crenulate at apex, blue-green, sometimes slightly downy beneath with 3–5 conspicuous veins. Fls to 8mm diam., white, 5 or more per sessile cluster. Spring. Eur. to Sib. and C Asia. 'Nana': dwarf and compact. ssp. *obovata* (Waldst. & Kit. ex Willd.) H. Huber. To 1.8m. Br. graceful, arching, twiggy, brown and fine-lanuginose when young, later grey. Lvs to 3cm, obovate, entire or 3–5-wavy-toothed at apex. Fls 6.5mm diam., pure white. N Spain, S Fr. Z5.

S. incisa Thunb. = *Stephanandra incisa*.

S. japonica L. f. JAPANESE SPIRAEA. To 1.5m. Br. rigid, erect, usually terete, glab. or initially pubesc. Lvs 2–8cm, lanceolate to ovate, acute to acuminate, biserrate, glaucescent with downy veins beneath. Fls 6–9.5mm diam., rose-pink to carmine, rarely white, crowded in flat, sometimes short-pubesc., term. corymbs to 30.5cm diam. in uppermost lf axils. Summer. Jap., China. 'Albiflora': to 60cm; lvs pale green; fls white. 'Allgold': lvs clear gold. 'Alpina': mound-forming; fls rose, in tiny heads. 'Anthony Waterer': upright, dwarf; lvs deep green, occas. cream and pink variegated. 'Bullata': dwarf; lvs dark olive-green, coarsely serrate, crinkled; fls crimson. 'Bumalda': habit dwarf; lvs toothed, often cream and pink variegated; fls dark pink, in pan. 'Bumalda Ruberrima': to 50cm; lvs ovate, slightly wrinkled; fls large, pink to dusky red. 'Crispa': lvs strongly serrated and twisted. 'Fastigiata': tall, upright and open; fls small, white, in loose clusters. 'Froebelii': tall and broad, habit open; fls deepest burgundy. 'Goldflame': lvs tinted rich bronze-red when young,

yellow, strong copper and orange in autumn; fls v. red. 'Limemound': lvs lime-green, tinted russet when young, vibrant orange on red st. in autumn. 'Little Princess': dwarf; lvs light green, delicate, tinted red in autumn. 'Shirobana': fls white, pink and crimson flat-topped heads on the same plant. 'Snowmound': dwarf; lvs dark green; fls white, profuse. var. *acuminata* Franch. Lvs oval-oblong to lanceolate, acuminate. Fls pink, in corymbs to 14cm diam. C & W China. var. *fortunei* (Planch.) Rehd. Usually exceeding 1.5m. Branchlets terete, initially pubesc. Lvs 5–10cm, oblong-lanceolate, acuminate, coarsley biserrate, teeth callouys-tipped, rugose above, glaucescent. Fls pink, in many-branched, puberulous corymbs. E & C China. Z5.

S. kamtschatica auct. = *Filipendula kamtschatica*.

S. kirilowii Reg. = *Sorbaria kirilowii*.

S. kiusiana Nak. = *S. nervosa*.

S. laevigata L. = *Sibiraea altaiensis*.

S. lanceolata Borkh. = *S. alba*.

S. lancifolia Hoffsgg. = *S. decumbens* ssp. *tomentosa*.

S. latifolia (Ait.) Borkh. MEADOWSWEET. To 1.5m. Branchlets glab., ridged, red-brown. Lvs 3–7cm, broadly elliptic or obovate to oblong, usually acute, biserrate, somewhat blue and glab. beneath. Fls white to shell pink, in pyramidal, glab. pan. Summer. N Amer. Z2.

S. ×*lemoinei* Zab.) = *S. japonica* 'Bumalda Ruberrima'.

S. lindleyana Wallich ex Loud. = *Sorbaria tomentosa*.

S. lobata Gronov. ex Jacq. = *Filipendula rubra*.

S. longigemmis Maxim. To 1.5m. Br. ascending to spreading, angular, glab. with long-flattened buds. Lvs to 3–7.5cm, ovate-lanceolate, to oblong, acute, light green above, glaucous and pubesc. beneath when young, teeth gland-tipped. Fls to 6.5mm diam., white, in broad, rounded, lax, pubesc. corymbose pan. Summer. W China. Z5.

S. lucida Douglas ex Greene = *S. betulifolia* var. *lucida*.

S. ×*macrothyrsa* Dipp. (*S. douglasii* ×*S. latifolia*.) Lvs to 5cm, elliptic to obovate-elliptic, subglabrous above, light green and tomentulose beneath. Fls bright pink, in dense horizontally branching pan. to 20cm. Gdn origin. Z4.

S. media Schmidt. Similar to *S. chamaedryfolia* but with terete br. in a more erect and compact arrangement. To 1.5m. St. buff to brown, initaiy pubesc. Lvs to 5cm, broad-elliptic to ovate-oblong, obtuse, sparse-pubesc. or grey-tomentose beneath, entire or 6–8-toothed toward apex. Fls to 8mm diam., white or pale yellow, in subspherical, many-fld rac. to 4cm at tips of leafy shoots, sometimes grouiped together. Spring. E Eur. to NE Asia. ssp. *polonica* (Blocki) Pawl. Fls in soft-pubesc. infl., ivory to buttermilk-yellow, pet. fimbriate. Poland, Czech. Z5.

S. menziesii Hook. = *S. douglasii* ssp. *menziesii*.

S. menziesii var. *macrothyrsa* Zab. = *S.* ×*macrothyrsa*.

S. micrantha Hook. f. 1.5–2m. Lvs 8–15cm, ovate-lanceolate, long acuminate, scabrous or biserrate, pubesc. beneath. Fls 4–5mm diam., white or pale pink, in brown-tomentose, lax, leafy corymbs to 15cm diam. Summer. E Himal. Z6.

S. millefolium Torr. = *Chamaebatiaria millefolium*.

S. miyabei Koidz. Upright, to 1m. Branchlets ± angled, puberulous. Lvs 3–7cm, ovate to ovate-oblong, acute or acuminate, base rounded, biserrate, initially minutely pubesc. beneath. Fls 8mm diam., white, in short-pubesc., many-fld, compound, term. corymbs to 6cm diam. Summer. Jap. Z6.

S. mollifolia Rehd. Differs from *S. gemmata* in overall silky pubescence. To 2m. Br. nodding, v. angular, red-purple. Lvs 1–2cm, elliptic-obovate to oblong, apex sometimes toothed, densely sericeous. Fls white, 8mm diam., in pubesc., 2.5cm diam. umbels on short, leafy stalks. Summer. W China. Z6.

S. mongolica sensu Koehne, non Maxim. = *S. gemmata*.

S. monogyna Torr. = *Physocarpus monogynus*.

S. ×*multiflora* Zab. (*S. crenata* ×*S. hypericifolia*.) SNOW GARLAND SPIRAEA. To 1.5m. Branchlets slender, brown, downy at first. Lvs 2–3cm, obovate, obtuse, base long-cuneate, almost entire, grey-green, fine-pubesc. when young beneath. Fls white, in leafy, many-fld umbels. Spring. Gdn origin. Z4.

S. nervosa Franch. & Savat. Br. terete, initially hirsute. Lvs to 4cm, ovate to rhombic-oblong, apex subacute to obtuse, incised-dentate to obscurely trilobed, yellow-pubesc. beneath. Fls to 8mm diam., white, in many-fld, short-pubesc. clusters. Spring–summer. var. *angustifolia* (Yatabe) Ohwi. Yellow-pubesc. throughout. Lvs narrow. Jap., China. Z6.

S. nicondiertii hort. = *S.* ×*pikoviensis*.

S. nipponica Maxim. To 2.5m, rounded, bushy. Br. angled, glab. Lvs 1.5–2.75cm, thin-textured, broadly obovate, oval or elliptic, obtuse, with a few broad, rounded teeth, entire, dark green above, blue-green beneath. Fls to 8.5mm diam., pure white, subtended by leafy bracts, crowded in term., rounded or conical, clusters to 4cm diam. Jap. 'Halward's Silver': erect and compact, to 1.2m; fls to 9mm wide, white, profuse, grouped in corymbs of 8–12. 'June Bride': dwarf; br. short, arching; lvs oval; fls white, in small corymbs. 'Snowmound': upright; lvs green tinted blue; fls white, abundant, in small corymbs along br. var. **tosaensis** (Yatabe) Mak. Lvs 1–3cm, oblanceolate to oblong-obovate, entire or slightly crenate at apex. Fls small,er in dense umbels. Jap. Z4.

S. nobleana Hook. = *S. ×sanssouciana.*

S. nobleana Zab. non Hook. = *S. ×watsoniana.*

S. **×notha** Zab. (*S. betulifolia* ×*S. latifolia.*) Lvs 3–6cm, ovate to elliptic, obtuse or acute, coarsely or doubly serrate, base broadly cuneate or rounded, ± glab.; fls white or pink in pyramidal pan.

S. **×nudiflora** Zab. (*S. chamaedryfolia* var. *ulmifolia* ×*S. bella.*) Lvs to 6.5cm, ovate, biserrate or deeply incised, subglabrous. Fls rose in racemose umbels to 7.5cm diam. Z6.

S. obovata Waldst. & Kit. ex Willd. = *S. hypericifolia* ssp. *obovata.*

S. obtusa Nak. = *S. blumei.*

S. opulifolia L. = Physocarpus opulifolius.

S. palmata Thunb. pro parte non Pall. = *Filipendula purpurea.*

S. palmata Murray non Pall. nec Thunb. = *Filipendula rubra.*

S. palmata Thunb. pro parte non L. f., nec Pall. = *Filipendula multijuga.*

S. palmata Pall. = *Filipendula palmata.*

S. pectinata Torr. & A. Gray = *Luetkea pectinata.*

S. **×pikoviensis** Besser. (*S. crenata* ×*S. media.*) Differs from *S. crenata* in shoots terete, buff, subglabrous, lvs 2.5–5cm, oblong, apex denticulate or entire, subglabrous, infl. subglabrous, crowded, pet. shorter than sta. W Ukraine. Z6.

S. polonica Blocki = *S. media* ssp. *polonica.*

S. procumbens hort. = *S. decumbens.*

S. pruinosa Zab. = *S. ×brachybotrys.*

S. **prunifolia** Sieb. & Zucc. BRIDALWREATH SPIRAEA. Upright, to 2m, dense, bushy. Br. slender, arching; branchlets initially lanuginose. Lvs 2.5–4.5cm, ovate, obtuse or acute, denticulate, bright green above, downy grey beneath. Fls to 1cm diam., pure white, double in 3–6-fld, sessile clusters along br. Spring. China; nat. Jap. f. *simpliciflora* Nak. Fls single. China, Taiwan. Z4.

S. prunifolia var. *plena* Schneid. = *S. prunifolia.*

S. **pubescens** Turcz. 1–2m. Br. terete, slender, arching, tomentose at first. Lvs 3–4cm, oval to rhombic-elliptic, deeply serrate to obscurely 3-lobed, pubesc. above, grey-tomentose. Fls to 8mm diam., white, in domed and rounded, glab. corymbs. Spring. N China. Z6.

S. pumila hort. ex Zab. = *S. japonica.*

S. **×pyramidata** Greene. (*S. betulifolia* var. *lucida* ×*S. douglasii* ssp. *menziesii.*) Upright, to 1m. Branchlets terete, red-brown, glab. Lvs 3–8cm, elliptic to oblong, apex obtuse or subacute, coarsely serrate subglabrous. Fls white to pale dusty pink, crowded in conical downy or glab. pan. Summer. N Amer. Z6.

S. reevesiana Lindl. = *S. cantoniensis.*

S. **×revirescens** Zab. (*S. amoena* ×*S. japonica.*) To 1m. Branchlets brown, striate to to strongly angled, initially downy. Lvs to 9cm, oval-oblong, incised to biserrate, light green above, bluegreen beneath with veins yellow-pubesc. Fls 4–7mm diam., pink, in flat, pubesc. term. corymbs. Summer–autumn. Gdn origin. Z5.

S. rosea Raf. = *S. densiflora* ssp. *splendens.*

S. **rosthornii** Pritz. To 2m. Br. widely spreading, initially pubesc.; buds long, as in *S. longigemmis.* Lvs 3–7.5cm, ovate to lanceolate, apex acuminate, deeply and sharply lacerate-biserrate to obscurely lobed, downy. Fls to 6.5mm diam., white, in long stalked flat corymbs to 9cm diam. Summer. W China. Z6.

S. rotundifolia hort. = *S. canescens.*

S. **salicifolia** L. BRIDEWORT. To 2m. Br. erect, lanky, suckering, puberulent when young, buff to dark brown. Lvs 4–8cm, elliptic to oblong-lanceolate, acuminate to acute, closely serrate, thin-textured, pale green above, paler still beneath, glab. Fls pink, to 8mm diam., crowded in narrowly pyramidal, erect, term., somewhat downy pan. to 12cm. Summer. C & EC Eur. to NE Asia and Jap.; rarely nat. GB. Z5.

S. salicifolia var. *latifolia* Ait. = *S. latifolia.*

S. **×sanssouciana** K. Koch. (*S. japonica* ×*S. douglasii.*) To 1.5m. Branchlets striate to angular-ridged, tomentulose when young. Lvs 6–9cm, oblong to oblong-lanceolate, apex usually obtuse, strongly biserrate, light green above, woolly grey beneath. Fls rose, in term., tomentulose corymbs in dense, pyramidal, obtuse pan. Summer. Gdn origin. Z6.

S. **sargentiana** Rehd. To 2m. Shoots long thin, arching, terete, (not ribbed or angled as in similar *S. canescens*) initially lanuginose. Lvs 1–2.5cm, narrow-oval to narrow-obovate, serrulate, dull green puberulent above, paler and more densely pubesc. beneath. Fls to 6.5mm diam., ivory in dense rounded clusteres to 4.5cm at ends of short, leafy twigs. Summer. W China. Z6.

S. **×schinabeckii** Zab. (*S. chamaedryfolia* ×*S. trilobata.*) Twiggy

bush to 2m. Shoots flexuous, buff, striate above. Lvs to 5cm, round to ovate-rhombic, biserrate, dark green above, bluegreen beneath, glab. Fls white, large, in stalked umbels. Summer. Z6.

S. **×semperflorens** Zab. (*S. japonica* ×*S. salicifolia.*) To 1.5m. Branchlets terete, fine-striate. Lvs 5.5–10cm, oblong-lanceolate, acuminate, scabrous, biserrate, blue-green, subglabrous beneath. Fls pink, large, in freely branching, conical-pyramidal pan. Summer–autumn. Gdn origin. 'Syringiflora': spreading shrub to 1.2m; lvs lanceolate to lanceolate-oblong, to 7.5cm, acuminate, toothed; fls light pink in a broad, conical infl. Z4.

S. silvestris Nak. = *S. miyabei.*

S. sinobrahuica W.W. Sm. = *S. yunnanensis.*

S. sorbifolia L. = Sorbaria sorbifolia.

S. sorbifolia var. *angustifolia* Wenz. = Sorbaria tomentosa var. *angustifolia.*

S. spicata Dipp. = *S. ×semperflorens.*

S. splendens Baumann ex K. Koch = *S. densiflora* ssp. *splendens.*

S. stipulata Muhlenb. ex Willd. = Gillenia stipulata.

S. subvillosa Rydb. = *S. douglasii* ssp. *menziesii.*

S. ×**superba** Froebel ex Zab. = *S. ×foxii.*

S. **thunbergii** Sieb. ex Bl. Densely branching shrub to 1m. Branchlets wiry, angled, bright green, initially downy. Lvs 2.5–4cm, linear-lanceolate, acuminate to acute, sparsely and sharply serrulate, pale green, glab. Fls 6.5–8mm diam., pure white, 2–5-clustered in sessile infl. closely set on slender, nodding br. Spring. China, Jap. Z4.

S. **tomentosa** L. HARD HACK; STEEPLEBUSH. To 1.5m, suckering. St. erect; branchlets angled, brown-tomentose when young. Lvs to 7.5cm, ovate, coarse- and irregular-serrate, dark green, subglabrous above, yellow-grey tomentose beneath. Fls rose to purple-rose, in term., pyramidal pan. to 18×6.5cm; ovaries lanuginose, not glab. as in similar *S. douglasii.* Summer–autumn. N & C Eur., E US. 'Alba': fls white. Z3.

S. tosaensis Yatabe = *S. nipponica* var. *tosaensis.*

S. **trichocarpa** Nak. 1–2m. Br. rigid, spreading, young branchlets angled, glab. Lvs 3–6.5cm, oblong to lanceolate, abrupt-acuminate, few-toothed or entire, vivid green above, somewhat glaucous beneath. Fls to 8.5mm diam., white, in rounded corymbs to 5cm diam. ends of short, leafy twigs, forming a graceful spray. Fr. pubesc. Summer. Korea. 'Snow White' (*S. trichocarpa* ×*S. trilobata*): bushy, to 1.5m; twigs drooping; lvs large, light green; fls large, creamy white, in umbrella-shaped heads. Z5.

S. trifoliata L. = Gillenia trifoliata.

S. **trilobata** L. Intricately branching to 1.2m, broad, compact. St. often flexuous; young branchlets slender, glab. Lvs 1.5–2.75cm, ± circular, sometimes cordate, coarse-serrate, occas. 3–5-lobed, blue-green. Fls white, small, crowded in umbels to 4cm diam. at the ends of short, leafy twigs. Summer. N Sib., Turkestan to N China. 'Fairy Queen': compact to 1m; lvs lobed, dark green; fls flat-topped, white, abundant. 'Swan Lake': compact, to 1m; br. arching; lvs lobed, deep green; fls white, profuse, wreathing br. Z5.

S. ulmaria L. = Filipendula ulmaria.

S. ulmifolia Scop. = *S. chamaedryfolia* var. *ulmifolia.*

S. ×**vanhouttei** (Briot) Zab. (*S. trilobata* ×*S. cantoniensis.*) To 2m. St. slender, virgate, arching, brown, glab. Lvs 3–4cm, rhomboid or obovate, occas. 3–5-lobed, apical half, coarse-serrate, dark green above, somewhat glaucous beneath, glab. Fls to 8.5mm diam., white, in umbellate clusters to 5cm diam. borne profusely along br. Spring–summer. Z4.

S. **veitchii** Hemsl. Strong-growing, to 3.5m. Shoots arching, young br. tinted red, ± lanuginose, striate. Lvs to 5cm, oblong or obovate, entire, sometimes slightly lanuginose beneath. Fls to 5mm diam., white, in crowded, finely lanuginose dense corymbs to 6.5cm diam. Summer. W & C China. Z5.

S. venusta hort. ex Otto & A. Dietr. = Filipendula rubra.

S. vestita Wallich ex G. Don = Filipendula vestita.

S. **virginiana** Britt. Densely branched shrubto 1m; shoots glab. Lvs 2–5cm, oblong-lanceolate, apex acute, entire or few-toothed, base rounded or cuneate, bright green above, glaucescent beneath. Fls white, crowded in glab. corymbs to 5cm diam. Summer. E US. Z5.

S. ×**watsoniana** Zab. (*S. douglasii* ×*S. densiflora.*) Resembles *S. ×sanssouciana*, but lvs elliptic-oblong, apex serrate, obtuse, base rounded, grey-tomentose beneath. Fls pink, in dense, conic, tomentulose pan. NW US. Z6.

S. **wilsonii** Duthie. Differs from *S. henryi* in glab., not pubesc. infl. To 2.5m. Br. arching; branchlets dull purple, initially downy. Lvs 2–5.5cm, oval to obovate or oblong, obtuse or acute, toothed or entire, dull green, pubesc. above, grey-green, villous beneath. Fls to 6mm diam., pure white, in dense, glab., domed, term. corymbs to 5cm diam. on short, leafy shoots. Summer. C & W China. Z5.

S. **yunnanensis** Franch. To 2m. Branching gracefully; young shoots tawny-lanuginose. Lvs 1.25–2.75cm, broadly ovate or obovate, lobed and serrate in apical half, dull green and lanuginose above, ashy to tawny-velutinous beneath. Fls 8.5mm diam., creamy white, 10–20 per rounded, 2.5cm diam. cluster at tips of short leafy twigs. Summer. SW China. Z7.

S. cvs. 'Dart's Profusion': to 1.5m; lvs vivid grey-green; fls white, spring. 'Dart's White Pearl': to 1.5m; growth and lf shape as S. ×vanhouttei; fls creamy white, late spring. 'Dolchina': habit rounded, to 60cm tall, to 1m wide; lvs sharply serrated, dark green, tinted red when young; fls purple flushed pink. 'Margaritae': small; fls bright rose, in large flattened heads. 'Pink Ice': dense and compact, to 1m high, to 1m wide; lf shoots pale pink when young, cream, later cream variegated; fls white, in heads. 'Summersnow' (probably S. trilobata ×S. ×vanhouttei): habit broad; lvs light green; fls white, in umbrella-shaped heads, profuse, long-lasting. 'Wynbrook Gold': dwarf, to 60cm; lvs yellow, tinted orange when young.

Spiral Flag Costus; C. spiralis.
Spiral Ginger Costus afer; C. malortieanus.

Spiranthes Rich. Orchidaceae. c150 tuberous largely terrestrial or epiphytic orchids. Lvs in a basal rosette or reduced and sheathing erect flowering st. Rac. term.; fls usually arranged spirally; dors. sep. narrow, usually erect, lat. sep. erect or spreading; pet. narrow; lip sessile or clawed, simple to 3-lobed, concave or gibbous. Cosmop.

S. cernua (L.) Rich. Lvs to 25cm, linear to linear-lanceolate. Infl. to 60cm, downy, densely fld, apically fld; fls fragrant, white, dors. sep. to 11×3mm, oblong-lanceolate, lat. sep. to 11×2mm, lanceolate, pet. to 11×3mm, linear-lanceolate; lip to 10×6mm, ovate-oblong, recurved, apex dilated, erose-crispate. E Canada to S Flor. and Tex. Z3.

S. cinnabarina (La Ll. & Lex.) Hemsl. Lvs to 23cm, linear-lanceolate to oblanceolate. Infl. to 90cm, erect, downy, many-fld; fls tubular, yellow-orange to golden-scarlet; sep. to 25×3mm, lanceolate, pet. to 22×2mm, linear-lanceolate; lip to 25×6mm, elliptic-lanceolate, long-acuminate. Tex., Mex., Guat. Z9.

S. gracilis (Bigelow) Beck. Lvs to 6.5cm, ovate to ovate-lanceolate. Infl. to 65cm, sometimes downy above, loosely or densely-fld; fls white, faintly scented; tep. to 5.5mm, dors. sep. oblong-elliptic to oblong-lanceolate, lat. sep. lanceolate, pet. linear; lip to 6×2.5cm, with a central green stripe, oblong-elliptic to oblong-quadrate, crenulate to erose. SE Canada to US. Z3.

S. lanceolata (Aubl.) Léon = Stenorrhynchos lanceolatus.
S. speciosa (Gmel.) A. Rich. = Stenorrhynchos speciosus.
S. spiralis (L.) Chevall. LADY'S TRESSES. Lvs to 2.5cm, ovate. Infl. to 10cm, slender, downy; fls to 5mm diam., sparkling snow-white except for lime-green veins on lip, numerous, strongly spirally arranged tep. projected forward, hooding channelled and crenate lip. Eur. Z6.

S. tortilis (Sw.) Rich. Lvs to 30cm, narrowly linear. Infl. to 75cm, erect, densely fld; fls often scented, white; sep to 6×2mm, dors. sep. oblong-elliptic to oblong-lanceolate, lat. sep. lanceolate; lip to 6×3mm, ovate to subquadrate, recurved, undulate-crenulate. S US to W Indies, Guat. Z10.

S. vernalis Engelm. & Gray. Lvs to 30cm, narrowly lanceolate to linear. Infl. to 85cm, v. downy above, densely fld; fls usually scented, yellow or white, sometimes green; sep. to 10×3mm, lanceolate to oblong-lanceolate, pet. to 9×2mm, linear to linear-elliptic; lip to 8×6mm, fleshy, recurved, broadly ovate to ovate-rhombic, slightly undulate. Flor. to Tex., Mex., Guat. Z9.

Spirodela Schleid. DUCKWEED. Lemnaceae. 3 minute aquatic herbs, floating on the water surface, consisting of a shiny leaflike frond with roots from undersurface. Cosmop. Z5.

S. polyrrhiza (L.) Schleid. GREAT DUCKWEED; WATER FLAXSEED. Fronds 1.5–10×1.5–8mm, rounded or pointed at tip, usually thin. Roots 7–21. Cosmop. except most of S Amer., NZ and some oceanic islands.

Spironema Lindl.
S. fragrans Lindl. = Callisia fragrans.

Spleenwort Asplenium.
Splendid Everlasting Helipterum splendidum.
Splitbeard Bluestem Andropogon ternarius.
Split Jack Capparis lasiantha.
Split-leaf Philodendron Monstera deliciosa.
Split Pea Lens culinaris.
Split Rock Pleiospilos.
Splitrock Pleiospilos nelii.

Spodiopogon R. Br. Gramineae. 9 perenn. or ann. grasses. Lvs linear to lanceolate, flat, occas. appearing petiolate; ligules membranous. Infl. paniculate, open to compact; br. flexible, racemose; spikelets paired. Temp., subtrop. Asia. Z7.

S. sibiricus Trin. Perenn., erect to 1.5m. Lvs linear-lanceolate, to 38×1.8cm, green, tinged purple, usually glab. Infl. narrow-lanceolate, to 20cm. Summer. Sib., Manch., Korea, China, Jap. →Andropogon.

Spondias L. Anacardiaceae. 10 ± decid. trees. Lvs spiral, imparipinnate, rarely bipinnate or simple. Infl. a pan. or rac.; cal. usually 5-lobed; pet. usually 5; sta. 10, rarely 8. Fr. a drupe, endocarp slightly woody. Indo-Malesia and trop. Amer., widely nat. Z10.

S. borbonica hort. = Poupartia borbonica.
S. cytherea Sonn. = S. dulcis.
S. dulcis Parkinson. OTAHEITE APPLE; AMBARELLA; GOLDEN APPLE. To 25m. Lfts 11–23, elliptic to oblong, entire or slightly serrate. Pan. term., large; fls small, cream to yellow-green. Fr. 4–10×3–8cm, ellipsoid or oblong, bright orange. Indomalesia, widely nat. in tropics.
S. dulcis Blanco non Forst. f. = S. purpurea.
S. dulcis var. acida (Bl.) Engl. = S. pinnata.
S. lutea L. = S. mombin.
S. mangifera Willd. = S. pinnata.
S. mombin L. MOMBIN; HOG PLUM; JOBO. To 25m. Lfts 7–20, chartaceous, ovate-elliptic to elliptic-oblong, entire, acuminate. Pan. loose, fls white. Fr. orange. Trop. Amer.
S. mombin Burck non L. = S. purpurea.
S. pinnata (L. f.) Kurz. To 25m. Lfts 11–17, elliptic-oblong, oblique, abruptly cuneate, entire or serrate. Pan. usually term. to 40cm. Fr. orange-yellow. Java. Java, Philipp., nat. through-out Indomalesia.
S. purpurea L. SPANISH PLUM; RED MOMBIN; JOCOTE. To 25m. Lfts 7–23, elliptic to oblong, entire or slightly serrate, obliquely cuneate, acute to acuminate. Pan. or rac. axillary; fls red-purple. Fr. oblong to ovoid, yellow. Trop. Amer., widely cult.
S. solandri Benth. = Pleiogynium timoriense.
→Mangifera and Pourpartia.

Spoon-leaf Sundew Drosera spathulata.
Spoon-leaf Yucca Yucca filamentosa.

Sporobolus R. Br. DROPSEED; RUSHGRASS. Gramineae. c100 ann. and perenn. grasses. Infl. an open or contracted pan.; spikelets 1-fld, small, stalked. Cosmop.

S. cryptandrus (Torr.) A. Gray. SAND DROPSEED. St. to 1m clumped. Lvs flat or rolling when dry, sheaths with an apical tuft of long pale hairs. Infl. to 25cm, lax, term., br. spreading; spikelets to 0.3cm, pale to leaden grey. N Amer. Z5.

S. pulchellus R. Br. St. to 32cm, clumped. Lvs somewhat rigid, flat or keeled, ciliate. Infl. to 8cm, pyramidal, br. slender, whorled; spikelets to 0.3cm, lustrous. Aus. Z9.
→Agrostis.

Spotted Cat's Ear Hypochoeris radicata.
Spotted Dracaena Dracaena surculosa.
Spotted Fig Ficus virens.
Spotted Gentian Gentiana punctata.
Spotted Gum Eucalyptus maculata.
Spotted Hemlock Conium maculatum.
Spotted Laurel Aucuba japonica.

Spraguea Torr. Portulacaceae. 9 taprooted herbs. Lvs mostly basal and rosulate, spathulate. Flowering st. v. short; infl. compact, head-like, made up of umbels of cymes; fls small; sep. 2, scarious; pet. 4. Z7.

S. multiceps J.T. Howell = S. umbellata.
S. umbellata Torr. PUSSY-PAWS. Ann. to perenn. to 15cm, spreading to suberect. Basal lvs to 4cm, st. lvs reduced. Infl. 1–3.5cm diam., fls white or pink. W N Amer.

Spreading Clubmoss Selaginella kraussiana.
Spreading Coneflower Isopogon divergens.
Spreading Dogbane Apocynum androsaemifolium.
Spreading Fan Fern Sticherus lobatus.
Spreading Pogonia Cleistes divaricata.
Spreading Wattle Acacia genistifolia.

Sprekelia Heist. Amaryllidaceae. 1 bulbous herb. Lvs to 45cm, narrow. Scape to 30cm, erect; fls solitary, term., bright scarlet to deep crimson or white; perianth seg. 6, the lower 3 lanceolate, declinate, subequal, partly inrolled at their bases into a waisted cylinder, the upper 3 seg., the central one to 2.5cm across; sta. declinate, exserted, with large drooping versatile anth. Mex. Z9.

S. cybister Herb. = *Hippeastrum cybister.*

S. formosissima (L.) Herb. JACOBEAN LILY; ST JAMES LILY; AZTEC LILY; ORCHID LILY. 'Glauca': fls small, pale red. 'Karwinskii': fls vivid scarlet, edged white. 'Ringens': lvs somewhat glaucous; fls pendent, the central seg. with a vertical golden stripe.
→*Amaryllis.*

Spring Beauty *Claytonia* (*C. virginica*).
Spring Bell *Olsynium douglasii.*
Spring Bloodwood *Eucalyptus ptychocarpa.*
Spring Cherry *Prunus subhirtella.*
Spring Cleavers *Galium aparine.*
Spring Gentian *Gentiana verna.*
Spring Sedge *Carex caryophyllea.*
Spring Snowflake *Leucojum vernum.*
Spring Starflower *Ipheion uniflorum.*
Spring Vetch *Lathyrus vernus.*
Spring Vetch *Vicia sativa.*
Spruce *Picea.*
Spruce Pine *Pinus glabra.*
Spurge *Euphorbia.*
Spurge Laurel *Daphne laureola.*
Spurge Nettle *Cnidoscolus* (*C. urens*).
Spurge Olive *Cneorum tricoccon.*
Spur Pepper *Capsicum frutescens.*
Spurred Gentian *Halenia.*
Spurred Snapdragon *Linaria.*
Spurrey *Spergula.*
Spurwort *Sherardia arvensis.*
Square Bamboo *Chimonobambusa quadrangularis.*
Square-stack Cranesbill *Pelargonium tetragonum.*
Squawbush *Rhus trilobata* var. *malacophylla.*
Squaw Carpet *Ceanothus prostratus.*
Squaw Currant *Ribes cereum.*
Squaw Grass *Xerophyllum tenax.*
Squaw Huckleberry *Vaccinium caesium*; *V. stramineum.*
Squaw Root *Caulophyllum thalictrioides.*
Squill *Urginea maritima.*
Squinancy Wort *Asperula cynanchica.*
Squirrel Corn *Dicentra canadensis.*
Squirrel's Foot Fern *Davallia mariesii*; *D. trichomanoides.*
Squirrel-tail Barley *Hordeum jubatum.*
Squirrel-tail Grass *Hordeum jubatum.*
Squirting Cucumber *Ecballium elaterium.*

Sredinskya (Stein) Fed. Primulaceae. 1 rhizomatous perenn., v. closely related to *Primula.* Lvs 12–30cm, broadly ovate, crenate, membranous, veins impressed; petiole narrowly winged, long. Peduncles 30–60cm; umbel 15–40-fld.; pedicels 4–5cm; cal. to 1.5cm, tubular, farinose, lobes ovate; cor. to 1.25cm, pale yellow, much reduced, lobes narrowly linear. Cauc.
S. grandis (Trautv.) Fed.
→*Primula.*

Stachyphrynium Schum. Marantaceae. 8 herbaceous perennials. St. erect, branching, sheathed by bases of long petioles. Infl. terminal, spicate, sparingly branched; bracts distichous, subtending paired fls.; sep. short and narrow; cor. exceeding sep.; outer staminodes 2, obovate, callose and cucullate; anth. with petaloid appendage. India, Malaysia. Z10.
S. jagorianum (K. Koch) Schum. Lvs to 20×8cm, suboblong, acute, mid-green with bands of darker green above, pubesc. beneath; petiole 10–20cm. Bracts to 2cm; fls white; sep. to 3cm; cor. tube to 1.7cm; outer staminodes tipped yellow. India.
→*Phrynium.*

Stachys L. BETONY; HEDGE NETTLE; WOUNDWORT. Labiatae. c300 woolly to hairy herbs or subshrubs. Lvs often of 3 types: stalked in basal rosettes, narrower and short-stalked on ascending flowering sts., reduced and sessile among fls. Fls in false whorls or verticillasters in term. spikes; bracteoles present or 0; cal. often campanulate, rarely 2-lipped; cor. often 2-lipped, upper lip hooded and sometimes 2-lobed, often erect or spreading, lower lip longer than upper, sometimes 3-lobed with central lobe longest. Summer. Widespread, esp. in temp. zones and E hemis.; also Australasia and trop./subtrop. mts.
S. adenocalyx K. Koch = *S. annua.*
S. affinis Bunge. CHINESE ARTICHOKE; CROSNES DU JAPON; CHOROGI; JAPANESE ARTICHOKE; KNOTROOT. Erect, hairy perenn. herb to 50cm with many slender, knotty white tubers produced just below soil level. Lvs ovate to ovate-lanceolate, rough; fls white, light red. China. Z5.
S. alopecuros (L.) Benth. Erect perenn. herb, 20–60cm. Lvs 3–7×3–10cm, ovate and cordate at base, coarsely crenate to

crenate-dentate. Verticillasters in dense spikes; cor. 15–20mm, pale yellow, upper lip 2-lobed. S & C Eur. Z5.
S. alpina L. Erect perenn. herb, 30–100cm. Differs from *S. germanica*, *S. cretica* and *S. byzantina* in st. glandular-hairy. Lvs 5–18×3–9cm, oblong-opvate and cordate at base, crenate-serrate, often hairy or woolly only above. Verticillasters many-fld, widely spaced; cor. 15–22mm, dull purple, occas. tinged yellow, woolly. W, C & S Eur., N to Wales. Z5.
S. annua L. Erect to sprawling, hairy ann. or short-lived perenn., 10–40cm. Basal lvs 1–4.5×0.5–2.5cm, petioled, ovate-oblong to ovate-lanceolate, acute at tips, rounded at base, crenate or crenate-dentate, sometimes smooth. Verticillasters 4–8-fld, close above, widely spaced below, cor. 13–19mm, white or pale yellow, occas. with red spots, hairy. Medit. 'Alba': fls white. 'Robusta': lvs broad, pubesc.; fls large, purple, in dense heads. Z5.
S. balbissii Link = *S. annua.*
S. betonica Crantz = *S. annua.*
S. betonica Benth. non Crantz = *S. officinalis.*
S. bullata Benth. Sprawling perenn. spreading to 90cm. Lvs 0.4–2cm, petioled, ovate to ovate-oblong, mostly obtuse, crenate to serrate. Verticillasters 6-fld, widely spaced; cor. c15mm, purple. Calif. Z5.
S. byzantina K. Koch. LAMB'S TONGUE; LAMB'S TAILS; LAMB'S EARS; WOOLLY BETONY. Erect perenn. to 90cm; st. and lvs v. densely white-woolly. Differs from *S. cretica* in lvs white-woolly throughout. Lvs thick, 3–10×1.5–4cm, narrowed at base and tips, scarcely crenate, rugose oblong-spathulate to elliptical. Verticillasters 15–20-fld, distant below; cor. 15–25mm, white-woolly, purple or pink. Cauc. to Iran. 'Big Ears': large; lvs to 25cm long, tinted grey; fls purple, in tall spikes. 'Cotton Ball': fls none, spikes of woolly clusters. 'Margery Fish': lvs silver; fls mauve. 'Primrose Heron': lvs bright gold in spring; fls light magenta. 'Sheila Macqueen': low; lvs large; fls sterile. 'Silver Carpet': low; lvs grey, woolly; fls none. 'Striped Phantom' ('Variegata'): lvs broadly striped cream; fls small, purple-pink, bracts striped. Z5.
S. candida Bory & Chaub. Differs from *S. chrysantha* in cor. 15–18mm, white with purple marking. S Greece. Z5.
S. chrysantha Boiss. & Heldr. Sprawling or erect, woody-based, white-woolly perenn., 10–20cm. Lvs 1–2.5×0.8–1.5cm, suborbicular to ovate-orbicular, obscurely crenate, white-woolly. Verticillasters 4–6-fld, closely spaced; cor. 12–14mm, yellow, woolly. S Greece. Z5.
S. ciliaris Boiss. = *S. libanotica.*
S. ciliata Douglas ex Benth. Erect perenn., 100–120cm, glab. to pubesc. Lvs ovate, dentate. Verticillasters few-fld, distant; cor. dull red-purple. BC to Oreg. Z5.
S. citrina Boiss. & Heldr. Grey-hairy woody-based perenn.; flowering st. to 35cm. Lvs hairy 0.7–5×0.5–2cm, petioled, elliptic to ovate-oblong, tip obtuse, base attenuate to cuneate, obscurely crenulate. Verticillasters 6–8-fld, in short, dense heads, lower sometimes widely spaced; cor. 20–25mm, sulphur yellow, hairy. Greece, Turk. Z5.
S. coccinea Jacq. Softly hairy perenn. to 50cm. Lvs petioled crenate, ovate-lanceolate with acute base or oblong-deltoid with obtuse base. Verticillasters distant; cor. scarlet, cylindrical and narrow. Tex. to Mex. Z7.
S. cordata Riddell non Gilib. = *S. riddelli.*
S. corsica Pers. Sparsely hairy, slender, creeping, short-lived perenn. Lvs bright green, 0.5–1.7cm, petioled, suborbicular to orbicular-ovate with rounded-cordate base, broadly crenate. Verticillasters 2–4-fld, widely spaced; densely hairy; cor. white to purple or pale pink, 12–18mm. Mts of Corsica and Sardinia, Medit. region. Z5.
S. cretica L. Erect perenn., 20–80cm; differs from *S. byzantina* in lvs only moderately woolly above. Basal lvs 3–10×1–3cm, petioled, oblong-ovate to ovate, tip obtuse to acute, base attenuate to rounded, ± crenate, densely woolly and grey beneath. Verticillasters 10–16-fld, widely spaced; cor. 15–20mm, rose pink. S Eur. Z5.
S. decumbens Willd. non Pers. = *S. annua.*
S. discolor Benth. Perenn. to 30cm, woody at base and coarsehairy. Basal lvs 2.5–3.5cm, petioled, oblong-lanceolate, obtuse, deeply crenate, rugose above, white-woolly beneath. Verticillasters many-fld; cor. rose or yellow, white-tomentose. Cauc. Z5.
S. ehrenbergii Boiss. Woolly perenn., to 90cm. Basal lvs 9–14×3.5–4.5cm, petioled, ovate-oblong, grey woolly and rugose throughout. Verticillasters 12–16-fld, distant below, closer above; cor. 12–14mm, rose pink with white marking, densely hairy. Leb. Z5.
S. germanica L. DOWNY WOUNDWORT. Densely white-woolly perenn. to 1.2m, woody at base; differs from *S. cretica* and *S. byzantina* in lvs with truncate or cordate base, not cuneate. Lvs 3–12×1–5cm, long-petioled, oblong to oblong-ovate,

crenate to serrate; grey-woolly beneath, green above. Verticillasters 10–20-fld, widely spaced; cor. 14–16mm, rose pink to purple, densely hairy. Eur., N Afr., C Asia. Z5.

S. germanica ssp. *italica* var. *boissieri* Briq. = *S. cretica*.

S. grandiflora Willd. = *S. macrantha*.

S. hyssopifolia Michx. Stoloniferous, glab. perenn. to 75cm. Lvs to 3.5cm, linear to linear-lanceolate, ± sessile. Verticillasters distant; cor. 2–3×length of cal., pink. Mass. to Georgia. Z5.

S. italica Benth. non Mill. = *S. cretica*.

S. iva Griseb. White-lanate perenn., 15–40cm, somewhat woody at base. Lvs 1.5–6×0.4–1.5cm, linear-lanceolate to obovate-elliptic, base cuneate, apex obtuse, crenate, densely white-lanate. Verticillasters crowded, 4–6-fld; cor. 15–20mm, yellow, somewhat tomentose. N Greece, Balk.

S. jacquinii (Godron) Fritsch = *S. alopecuros*.

S. lanata Jacq., non Crantz = *S. byzantina*.

S. lavandulifolia Vahl. Sprawling perenn. to 45cm, woody at base. Basal lvs 2–6×0.4–1.5cm, ± sessile, oblong-lanceolate and narrowed at both ends, entire to slightly serrate, grey-woolly. Verticillasters 2–6-fld, widely spaced; cor. 13–15mm, purple to mauve, hairy outside. Armenia. Z5.

S. libanotica Benth. Erect hairy perenn. to 1m, often with stiff red hairs. Lvs 3–10cm, petioled, oblong, rounded at base, rugose and softly hairy. Verticillasters 6–15-fld, widely spaced, cor. rose. Leb. Z5.

S. macrantha (K. Koch) Stearn. Erect perenn. to 60cm, hairy. Basal lvs to 1.5×1cm, petioled, broadly ovate, obtuse tipped and cordate, crenate, rugose and roughly hairy. Verticillasters 10–15-fld, closely spaced above, distant below cor. purple-pink, 30–35mm. Cauc., NW Iran. 'Rosea': fls rose. 'Superba': fls darker. 'Violacea': fls violet. Z5.

S. macrostachya (Wendl.) Briq. Perenn. to 60cm, erect, usually unbranched, stellate-hirsute. Basal lvs 3–10×1–3cm, oblong-lanceolate, crenate, apex acute to obtuse, base cordate, petiole 4–9cm. Verticillasters 12–16-fld, ± approximate; cor. 17–22m, purple-pink. Transcauc.

S. maritima Urv. non Gouan = *S. annua*.

S. micrantha K. Koch = *S. annua*.

S. neglecta Klokov = *S. annua*.

S. nivea Labill. = *S. discolor*.

S. officinalis (L.) Trev. BISHOP'S WORT; WOOD BETONY. Erect perenn. to 1m subglabrous to densely hairy. Basal lvs 3–12×1.5–5cm, petioled, oblong to ovate-oblong with cordate base, crenate or crenate-dentate. Verticillasters 15–20-fld, in dense spikes; cor. 12–18mm, red-purple, pink or white. Eur., Asia. 'Alba': fls white. 'Grandiflora': fls larger, soft pink. 'Rosea Superba': lvs corrugated; fls rose pink. Z5.

S. olympica Briq., vix Poir. = *S. byzantina*.

S. pubescens Ten. = *S. annua*.

S. pumila Banks & Sol. Suffrutescent perenn. Flowering st. usually simple, to 35cm, tomentose. Basal lvs to 5.5×3.5cm, oblong-elliptic, crenulate, apex obtuse, base cordate, sericeous to grey-tomentose, petiole to 2.5cm. Verticillasters 6–10-fld, in a dense spike; cor. 12–14mm, white or pale lemon yellow, streaked and spotted brown. S Anatolia.

S. riddellii House. Tuberous perenn. to 1.4. Lvs to 9cm, petioled, ovate, apex attenuate base cordate, crenate to dentate. Verticillasters widely spaced; cor. *c*12mm, purple with darker marking. Ill. to N Carol. and Tenn. Z5.

S. salviifolia Ten. = *S. cretica*.

S. sieboldii Miq. = *S. affinis*.

S. sylvestris Forssk. 'Iles Flottantes': lvs cream with central green island.

S. taurica Zefirov = *S. byzantina*.

S. tenuifolia Willd. Sprawling, variable perenn. to 1m, ultimately glab. Lvs short-petioled, lanceolate to ovate. Verticillasters few-fld; cor. to 9mm, dull purple. NY to Minn. and S to Alab. and Tex. Z5.

S. tuberifera Naudin = *S. affinis*.

S. velata Klokov = *S. cretica*.

→*Betonica*.

Stachytarpheta Vahl. FALSE VERVAIN; SNAKEWEED. BASTARD VERVAIN. Verbenaceae. 65 sp. of ann. herbs or low shrubs. Lvs usually toothed, often rugose. Infl. spicate, slender, term.; fls sessile or immersed in depressions in the rachis, solitary in axils of bracts; cal. narrowly tubular, 5-lobed or 5-toothed; cor. gamopetalous, tube cylindrical, limb spreading, lobes broad. C & S Amer., SE Asia, Pacific, nat. trop. Z10.

S. cajanensis Rich. = *S. cayennensis*.

S. cayennensis (Rich.) Vahl. BRAZILIAN TEA. Shrubby ann. or perenn. to 2m. St. slender, 4-ridged. Lvs to 10×5cm, thin or papery, pale green, elliptic to ovate-oblong, apex acute or acuminate, base narrowly acuminate, densely puberulent to scabrellous above, strigillose or glabrate beneath, scarcely rugose or bullate. Infl. to 45cm, often almost black, slender rachis hardly incrassate, white-pilose, fls sunk in furrows as broad as rachis; bracts to 5×2mm, lanceolate, striate, scarious; cor. blue, violet, rose, lilac, purple or mauve. C & S Amer., nat. in the Trop. elsewhere.

S. dichotoma (Ruiz & Pav.) Vahl = *S. cayennensis*.

S. indica hort. non Vahl. = *S. jamaicensis*.

S. indica hort. non Vahl. = *S. urticifolia*.

S. × intercedens Danser. (*S. jamaicensis* × *S. urticifolia*.) Natural hybrid. Weak erect herbs, more closely resembling *S. jamaicensis* but lvs darker green, cor. larger and darker, habit more erect. SE Asia, Pacific.

S. jamaicensis (L.) Vahl. BLUE SNAKEWEED; COMMON SNAKE-WEED; JAMAICA VERVAIN. Low, spreading shrub to 1.2m, often flushed purple. Lvs to 8×5cm, fleshy, blue or grey-green, ovate to oblong, coarsely serrate, apex acute or obtuse, base narrowly cuneate. Infl. to 50cm, stout, stiff, rachis conspicuously incrassate, furrows narrower than rachis; bracts to 8×2mm, lanceolate to oblong-lanceolate, striate; cor. to 11mm, light blue. Pantrop. weed originating in subtrop. and trop. Amer.

S. mutabilis (Jacq.) Vahl. PINK SNAKEWEED. Slender straggling shrub subshrub or shrub to 3m; br. 4-angled, crisply pubesc. Lvs to 1cm, thick-chartaceous to leathery, ovate, ovate-oblong or elliptic, or silky beneath. Infl. to 60cm, rachis stout, shallowly incrassate, pubesc.; bracts 8–12mm, pubesc.; cor. large, showy, scarlet, crimson or red, fading to pink. C & S Amer. var. *violacea* Mold. Cor. blue or violet.

S. urticifolia Sims. BLUE RAT'S TAIL; SNAKEWEED. Coarse herb or subshrub to 2m, weakly erect, intricately branched. Lvs to 8×4.5cm, membranous, bullate and dark glossy green (sometimes silvered) above, lighter beneath, ovate to broadly elliptic, apex abruptly acute, base cuneate, glab., midrib often purple beneath. Infl. to 40cm, slender; rachis weakly incrassate, above as wide as furrow; bracts to 7mm; cor. indigo go dark purple with a white throat. SE Asia, Pacific. Often confused in the literature with *S. jamaicensis*.

STACHYURACEAE J. Agardh. See *Stachyurus*.

Stachyurus L. Stachyuraceae. 10 decid. shrubs or small trees. Shoots slender, glossy, red-brown. Lvs alt., simple, serrate. Fls 4-merous, small, in drooping, term. and axill. catkin-like rac., usually before lvs. E Asia, Himal.

S. chinensis Franch. Shrub to 2.5m. Lvs 3–15cm, ovate to oval-oblong, slender-acuminate, crenate, base rounded to sub-cordate. Rac. 5–10cm; cor. pale yellow, more spreading than in *S. praecox* and opening later; style equalling or exceeding pet. China. 'Magpie': lvs grey-green above, spotted pale green or pink, with an irregular ivory edge. Z7.

S. himalaicus Hook. f. & Thoms. ex Benth. Robust, semi-evergreen shrub, to 3m. Lvs to 23cm, oblong to oblong-lanceolate, long-acuminate, finely serrate, petiole tinged red. Rac. 4–5cm; cor. cupshaped, claret to pink-red. W China, Taiwan. Z9.

S. japonicus Steud. = *S. praecox*.

S. lancifolius Koidz. = *S. praecox* var. *matsuzakii*.

S. matsuzakii Nak. = *S. praecox* var. *matsuzakii*.

S. ovalifolius Nak. = *S. praecox* var. *matsuzakii*.

S. praecox Sieb. & Zucc. Shrub to 2m. Lvs to 14cm, ovate or ovate-lanceolate, long-acuminate, base rounded, serrate, glossy beneath. Rac. 5–8cm; cor. 8mm, campanulate, yellow; style included. Jap. var. *matsuzakii* (Nak.) Mak. Shoots thicker, light green-blue. Lvs 13–25cm, pale green above, blue-green beneath. Honshu. Z7.

Stackhousia Sm. Stackhousiaceae. 20 perenn. herbs. Pet. fused only in middle, claws and tips free; sta. 5, unequal enclosed in cor. tube. Aus., NZ, Philipp. Z9.

S. linarifolium A. Cunn. = *S. monogyna*.

S. monogyna Labill. Perenn. to 50cm; st. slender, simple or slightly branched. Lvs 1–5cm, linear or lanceolate. Rac. lengthening to 10–12.5cm; cor. white, tube 0.5mm. Spring. Aus.

STACKHOUSIACEAE R. Br. 3/28. *Stackhousia*.

Staehelina L. Compositae. 8 small tufted, gland. shrubs or sub-shrubs. Lvs often rosulate and crowded near br. apices, leathery. Cap. discoid, solitary or term. corymbs; flts cor. deeply 5-fid. Medit.

S. elegans Walter = *Liatris elegans*.

S. gnaphaloides L. = *Helipterum gnaphaloides*.

S. uniflosculosa Sibth. & Sm. St. to 50cm; br. white-tomentose. Lvs 1.5–4cm, ovate, acute, minutely toothed, dark green and glabrescent above, white-tomentose beneath. Cap. in corymbose cymes; flts 1–2, pink. S & W Balk.

Staff Tree *Celastrus scandens*.

Staff Vine *Celastrus orbiculatus*; *C. scandens.*
Stagger Bush *Lyonia fruticosa*; *L. mariana.*
Staggerweed *Dicentra eximia.*
Staghorn Fern *Platycerium* (*P. grande*; *P. superbum*).
Staghorn Sumac *Rhus typhina.*
Stag's Garlic *Allium vineale.*
Standing Cypress *Ipomopsis rubra.*
Stanford Manzanita *Arctostaphylos stanfordiana.*

Stangeria T. Moore. Stangeriaceae. 1 fern-like cycad. St. to 35×30cm, swollen, turnip- or trunk-like, largely subterranean. Lvs 50–70cm, in a loose apical rosette, pinnate, scurfy at first; pinnae 8–45×2–7cm in 6–17 pairs, lanceolate to oblong, apex acuminate to rounded, base narrowed to a v. short petiolule, entire to sinuate or laciniate, midrib prominent above, olive to dark green, papery to leather, glab. to downy; petiole thick, scurfy at base. ♂ cones 10–30×2–3.5cm, elongate-cylindrical, with ash to tan felt. ♀ cones 9–18×4–7.5cm, elliptic-ovoid, with obovate-rhombic scales. Seed to 2.5cm, subglobose, coating orange or scarlet. S Afr. Z9.
S. eriopus (Kunze) Nash. var. *katzeri* (Reg.) Marloth. Compact, tough-leaved, erect-growing. f. *schizocodon* (Bull) Schust. Foliage v. luxuriant; pinnae deeply and irregularly incised.
S. paradoxa T. Moore = *S. eriopus.*

STANGERIAGEAE (Pilg.) L.A.S. Johnson. See *Stangeria.*

Stanhopea Frost ex Hook. Orchidaceae. *c*30 epiphytic orchids. Pbs to 7cm, apically 1–2-lvd, ovoid to pyriform, sulcate. Lvs to 45cm, elliptic to oblong-lanceolate, plicately veined, subcoriaceous, contracted at base to petiole. Rac. basal, strongly pendent, few-fld; bracts large, chartaceous, imbricate, fls short-lived, large, fragrant, fleshy; sep. oblong to ovate-oblong, often revolute, spreading-reflexed or recurved, undulate, lat. sep. wider; pet. narrower and thinner; lip thickly fleshy, hypochile subglobose or calceiform, concave; mesochile short, entire or divided, usually with 2 fleshy horns; epichile, entire or 3-lobed, variously shaped; column long, arching usually winged clavate. Mex. to Braz. Z10.
S. aurea Lodd. ex Lindl. = *S. wardii.*
S. candida Barb. Rodr. Fls pure white to ivory, vanilla-scented; sep. to 5×2cm; lip pure white, variously tinted and spotted rose-purple, to 3.5cm, mesochile lacking horns. Venez., Colomb., Peru, Braz.
S. convoluta Rolfe = *S. tricornis.*
S. eburnea Lindl. Fls ivory-white variously dotted purple; sep. to 7×4cm; lip to 7cm, hypochile interior tinged orange-brown, exterior tinged pale pink; mesochile hornless. Summer. Braz., Guyana, Venez., Trin., Colomb.
S. grandiflora Lindl. non HBK = *S. eburnea.*
S. graveolens Lindl. = *S. warszewicziana.*
S. hernandezii (Kunth) Schltr. = *S. tigrina.*
S. jenischiana Kramer ex Rchb. f. Tep. orange-yellow dotted and marked dark maroon, tinged maroon at base; sep. to 7×4cm; lip hypochile orange-yellow, tinged dark purple-brown, exterior orange-brown, almost white apically with deep purple blotch on each side; mesochile and epichile spotted white, epichile tinged deep purple-brown at base. Panama, Venez., Colomb., Ecuad.
S. marshii Rchb. f. = *S. saccata.*
S. oculata (Lodd.) Lindl. Fls white or yellow, spotted red-purple; sep. to 7×5cm; lip to 6.5cm, with 2 large basal spots; mesochile with 2 porrect horns. Mex., Guat., Hond., Belize.
S. pulla Rchb. f. Fls small, to 7cm diam., sep. apricot yellow; pet. bright yellow; lip simple, light brown with red-brown markings, base widely inflated, broadly concave ventrally, red-brown elongate keel on inner disc, apex terminating in a fleshy, short, subcordate protuberance; column wingless. Summer. Costa Rica, Panama.
S. radiosa Lem. = *S. saccata.*
S. randii Rolfe = *S. candida.*
S. saccata Batem. Fls scented of orange or cinnamon, green-yellow to cream, flecked brown and purple; sep. to 6.5×4.3cm.; lip hypochile deeply saccate, orange marked red; mesochile horns to 3cm, slightly incurved, epichile yellow-white flecked red. Mex., Guat., El Salvador.
S. tigrina Batem. ex Lindl. Fls strongly fragrant; tep. to 8×5cm, deep yellow massively barred or blotched purple-brown; lip to 7.5cm; hypochile golden-yellow, each side dotted brown-purple, rounded; mesochile ivory-white, spotted purple on horns; epichile, ivory spotted purple. Summer–autumn. Mex. to Braz.
S. tricornis Lindl. Sep. to 6.5×3.6cm, pet. orange-tipped or tinged pink; lip to 4cm, yellow-interior ornage; hypochile with white lines, interior dotted puprle; mesochile orange with 2 lat. horns and one porrect horn at base. Peru, Colomb., Ecuad.
S. venusta Lindl. = *S. wardii.*

S. wardii Lodd. ex Lindl. Fls overpoweringly scented of spice or chocolate, green-white to pale yellow or peach, dotted red-purple, orange-yellow at base; sep. to 5.5×3.5cm; lip hypochile orange, each side with large purple-brown spot, saccate; mesochile cream to pale yellow-green, with 2 erect horns. Venez. to Peru, Mex. to Panama.
S. warszewicziana Klotzsch. Fls strongly and muskily scented, green-white to cream-yellow spotted maroon or purple; sep. to 6.5×4.5cm; lip to 5.5cm, deep apricot-yellow at base with maroon blotch on each side, cream-white above; mesochile with 2 curved horns. Mex., Guat., Braz., Hond.

Stanleya Nutt. PRINCE'S PLUME. Cruciferae. 6 ann. or perenn. herbs and subshrubs. Lvs mostly radical, usually rosulate, pinnatifid to entire. Fls 4-merous, racemose; pet. 4, white-yellow. Silique compressed. W N Amer. Z7.
S. elata M.E. Jones. Perenn., 60–150cm. Lvs 10–20cm, obovate-lanceolate, petiolate, pet. 8–10mm, yellow-white. Fr. 5–10cm. Early summer. Nevada, Ariz., Calif.
S. pinnata (Pursh) Britt. Subshrub to 180cm. Lvs 5–20cm, pinnatifid, seg. lanceolate, rarely bipinnate, cauline lvs 3–6cm, oblanceolate, entire to pinnatifid. Pet. 12–16mm, yellow, blade oval. Fr. 3–8cm. Autumn. Calif. to N Dak., Kans., Tex.
→*Cleome.*

Stapelia L. CARRION FLOWER; STARFISH FLOWER. Asclepiadaceae. 99 succulent, perenn. herbs. St. branching from base, clump-forming, ascending, 4–6-angled, fleshy, ridges flattened, toothed. Lvs rudimentary short lived. Fls solitary or in a short cyme, usually basal, carrion-scented; pedicels long; cor. 5-lobed, flat ± circular, rarely campanulate or cup-shaped; lobes triangular, acute, fleshy, rugose or swollen; corona 2-whorled. S, C & E Afr. to E India. Z9.
S. acuminata Masson. St. to 15×2cm, angles puberulous, teeth small. Fls 2–5, 3.5–4.5cm diam., dark purple-brown, flat, lobes ovate-lanceolate, narrowly attenuate, rugae yelow, fine, apex dark brown, filiform, white-ciliate; corona purple-brown, mottled yellow. Namaqualand.
S. adscendens Roxb. = *Caralluma adscendens.*
S. albocastanea Marloth = *Orbeopsis albocastanea.*
S. ambigua Masson. St. 20–25×2–2.5cm, minutely hairy, teeth distant. Fls 11–13cm diam., flat, lobes recurved, lanceolate, glab. above, margins with projecting cilia, purple-brown. SW Cape.
S. aperta Masson = *Tridentea aperta.*
S. arenosa Lückh. St. 15×1cm, puberulous. Fls few together 3cm diam., thickened and rugulose toward the centre, lobes margins recurved above, deep red-brown to purple-black, rugae white. W Cape.
S. asterias Masson. St. 10–20cm, angles softly pubesc., teeth small. Fls 1–5; to 4.5×11cm, flat, star-like, lobes narrowly lanceolate, attenuate, often twisted, interior dark red-brown, glossy, slightly rugose, often lined white or yellow, revolute, densely red-ciliate, red-brown, sometimes with yellow stripes, bases sparsely red-hairy; corona black-purple. Cape Prov.
S. beukmanii Lückh. = *S. stultitioides.*
S. campanulata Masson = *Huernia campanulata.*
S. caroli-schmidtii Dinter & A. Berger = *Orbeopsis albocastanea.*
S. caudata Thunb. = *Brachystelma caudatum.*
S. choanantha Lavranos & Hall = *Tridentea choanantha.*
S. ciliata Thunb. = *Orbea ciliata.*
S. cincta Marloth = *Tridentea jucunda* var. *cincta.*
S. clavicorona Verdoorn. St. to 30×2.5cm, puberulous, teeth stout. Fls 6cm diam., exterior puberulous, interior glab., rugulose, with a few white hairs at centre, lobes ovate-attenuate, light yellow with purple lines, ciliate in lower half. Transvaal.
S. concinna Masson. St. to 10×0.8cm, often reddened, with 4 rounded angles with small teeth, minutely hairy. Fls flat, 3.5cm diam., lobes ovate-tapered, dull yellow with minute red stripes, reticulately marked at tip, densely white-hairy. Karroo. var. *paniculata* (Willd.) N.E. Br. Fls dull purple-brown, lobes with transverse lines.
S. conformis N.E. Br. St. 12–25×2–3cm, with 4 v. compressed dentate angles. Fls 9–10cm diam., exterior puberulous, lobes, 2.5–3.5cm, lanceolate, acute, minutely wrinkled, hairy around tube and along margins, green-yellow below, with red-brown transverse stripes, margins and upper half red-brown with a yellow or green blotch at tips. E Cape. var. *abrasa* N.E. Br. Fls not ciliate, colour more intense, lobes with yellow transverse stripes for two-thirds of length, margins with a 2mm red-brown line.
S. cooperi N.E. Br. = *Orbea ciliata.*
S. cruciformis hort. = *S. olivacea.*
S. desmetiana N.E. Br. St. 25×3–3.5cm, with 4 sinuate, dentate, puberulous wings. Fls 12–16cm diam., lobes oblong-lanceolate,

tapered, exterior green or red, pubesc., interior pale to brown-red, rugulose with yellow transverse lines and hairs, long-ciliate. SE Cape Prov. var. *apicalis* N.E. Br. Lobes glab. above with yellow lines extending to tips. var. *fergusoniae* R.A. Dyer. Cor. 12cm diam., lobes 4.5cm, ovate, brown-yellow, white-ciliate, not rugulose throughout. var. *pallida* N.E. Br. Lobes edged purple-red, green-yellow, cilia pale grey or off-white.

S. digitalliflora Pfersd. = *Tavaresia angolense.*

S. dinteri A. Berger = *Tridentea* var. *dinteri.*

S. divaricata Masson. St. 10–18×1.2cm, minutely hairy, angles blunt, often tinged, red, teeth small. Fls 3–5cm diam., flat, deeply lobed, dull purple to pale flesh-pink, glossy, tube short, paler, lobes lanceolate-attenuate, smooth, reflexed, minutely white ciliate, tips green. S Afr.

S. dummeri N.E. Br. = *Pachycymbium dummeri.*

S. dwequensis Lückh. = *Tridentea dwequensis.*

S. engleriana Schltr. = *Tromotriche engleriana.*

S. erectiflora N.E. Br. St. 10–15×1cm, angles pubesc. rounded, teeth small, blunt. Fls to 1.3cm diam., red-purple, lobes, densely white-hairy. Cape Prov.

S. europaea Webb = *Caralluma europaea* var. *confusa.*

S. flavirostris N.E. Br. St. 17×2–3cm, with 4 compressed angles with small teeth, velvety-pubesc. Fls 13–16cm diam., deeply cleft, tube short, flat, lobes lanceolate, exterior pubesc., interior dull purple-red, lower part hairy with pale yellow or dull purple lines, tips dull purple, margins with red or white hairs. Cape Prov., Les.

S. flavopurpurea Marloth. St. 5–6×1.5cm, minutely hairy, teeth small, scale-like. Fls sometimes honey-scented, 3–4cm diam., deeply lobed, tube short, flat, white-yellow with red, clavate hairs, lobes linear-lanceolate, ochre-yellow, rugose, sometimes flushed pink or red, revolute; corona white-yellow. W Cape. var. *fleckii* (A. Berger & Schltr.) A. White & B.L. Sloane Fls more densely hairy in tube mouth, lobes ochre to green-yellow, often pink or red, honey scented. Nam.: Great Namaqualand.

S. fleckii A. Berger & Schltr. = *S. flavopurpurea* var. *fleckii.*

S. fucosa N.E. Br. = *Orbea verrucosa.*

S. fuscopurpurea N.E. Br. St. 15–20×2–2.5cm, puberulous, 4-angled with small teeth. Cor. 10cm diam., exterior puberulous, lobes ovate-lanceolate, dark red-brown, minutely wrinkled, tube with a cushion of long purple hairs, ciliate. S Afr.

S. gariepensis Pill. St. prostrate to erect with 4 compressed angles and small teeth, puberulous. Fls 8–9cm diam., lobes ovate-lanceolate, purple-ciliate, exterior glab., interior rugose, glossy red-purple with yellow lines below, tube mouth densely purple-hairy. W Cape.

S. gemmiflora Masson = *Tridentea gemmiflora.*

S. gettliffei Pott. St. 20–25×1.5cm, downy, teeth incurved. Fls 1–3, 14–16cm diam., flat, deeply lobed, exterior green-yellow, short-pubesc., interior cream-yellow, tube blotched purple, lobes lanceolate, mauve pubesc., banded purple, rugose, margins pale purple or white-ciliate; corona dark purple. Transvaal, Bots., Zimb., Moz.

S. gigantea N.E. Br. GIANT STAPELIA. St. 15–20×3cm, angles winged, teeth small. Fls malodorous, 25–35cm diam., flat to subcampanulate, tube short, dark red, rugose, lobes deep, ovate-acuminate, attenuate, pale ochre-yellow with tiny crimson rugae, sparsely red-pubesc., white-ciliate; corona dark purple-brown. S Afr. to Tanz. 'Schwankart': fls unscented.

S. glabricaulis N.E. Br. St. 15–20cm, glab., often tinged-red, angles crenate, teeth small. Fls 6–8.5cm diam., centre ochre-yellow, lilac-pubesc., tube flat, lobes ovate-lanceolate, attenuate, exterior green, glab., with 5 longitudinal red veins, interior red-purple, rugose, with long red cilia; corona black-purple. E Cape.

S. glanduliflora Masson. St. 9–15×2cm, 4–6-angled, downy, teeth small. Fls 3–3.5cm diam., flat, pale sulphur-yellow finely spotted and lined maroon, flat, tube short, lobes ovate-attenuate or oblong, exterior green-purple, with long white, clavate hairs on lower half and margins, slightly rugose; corona yellow or orange, tipped. Namaqualand.

S. grandiflora Masson. St. 20–30×4cm, downy, angles winged, teeth few, erect. Fls 15–16cm diam., exterior blue-green, interior dark purple-brown, flat deeply lobed, tube wide, short, lobes triangular-lanceolate, attenuate, banded purple or yellow and covered in purple hairs below, rugose, white-pubesc. towards apex and on margins; outer corona dark purple-brown, inner corona pale yellow. Cape Prov., Transvaal.

S. grandiflora var. *lineata* N.E. Br. = *S. flavirostris.*

S. herrei Nel = *Tridentea herrei.*

S. hirsuta L. Variable. St. to 20×1.5cm, depressed between angles, teeth small. Fls 10–12cm diam., covered in soft, purple hairs, lobes deep, ovate-lanceolate, attenuate, exterior blue-green, interior red-yellow, dark red or maroon, papillose, white- or purple-ciliate; corona black-purple. Cape Prov.

S. irrorata Lodd. = *Orbea irrorata.*

S. juttae Dinter. St. 5–12×1–2cm, with 4 rounded angles with small teeth, puberulous, mottled. Fls 1.5–2cm diam., lobes triangular, brown to black, coarsely wrinkled above, exterior puberulous, margins recurved. Nam.: Great Namaqualand.

S. juvencula Jacq. = *S. vetula.*

S. kwebensis N.E. Br. St. to 13×1.3cm, minutely papillose, angles rounded, teeth short. Fls carion-scented, 2.5 to 3.2cm diam., flat, exterior minutely hairy, interior glab., chestnut or chocolate-brown to maroon or ochre in centre, tube small, cylindrical, annular in appearance, lobes broadly ovate, rugose, apices sparsely pubesc. Transvaal, Bots., Nam., Zimb., Moz. var. *longipedicellata* A. Berger. Fls long-stalked, lobes black-brown with numerous dark wrinkles.

S. leendertziae N.E. Br. St. 8–10×1.2cm, hairy, slightly furrowed, teeth small. Fls 7.5–10cm diam., purple-black or dark brown, tube 7–8cm, cup-shaped to campanulate, sparsely purple-pubesc., lobes narrowly deltoid, slightly spreading, exterior pubesc., interior rugose, rough, apex slender, purple-ciliate; corona dark purple. Transvaal.

S. lepida Jacq. = *Orbea lepida.*

S. longidens N.E. Br. = *Orbea longidens.*

S. longii Lückh. = *Tridentea longii.*

S. longipedicellata N.E. Br. = *S. kwebensis* var. *longipedicellata.*

S. longipes Lückh. = *Tridentea longipes.*

S. macloughlinii Verdoorn. = *Orbea macloughlinii.*

S. macrocarpa A. Berger = *Huernia macrocarpa* var. *penzigii.*

S. maculata Masson = *Orbea maculata.*

S. margarita B.L. Sloane = *S. pulvinata* f. *margarita.*

S. marientalensis Nel = *Tridentea marientalensis.*

S. miscella N.E. Br. = *Stultitia miscella.*

S. molonyae A. White & B.L. Sloane = *Orbea semota.*

S. namaquensis N.E. Br. = *Orbea namaquensis.*

S. nobilis N.E. Br. = *S. gigantea.*

S. nouhuysii Philippi. St. 8×1cm, with 4 rounded angles and small white teeth. Fls 2cm diam., tube cup-shaped, lobes ovate, acute, tube and lobes densely red-hairy at base, smooth above, ciliate. W Cape.

S. nudiflora Pill. St. 10–15×1–1.5cm, with 4 rounded, slightly compressed angles. Fls 5cm diam., glab., tube plate-shaped, light purple-brown banded yellow, lobes ovate-lanceolate, tapered, with purple rugae above, yellow in lower half. W Cape.

S. ocellata Schult. = *Huernia ocellata.*

S. olivacea N.E. Br. St. 7–13×1cm, felty, angles rounded, teeth small. Fls 3.5–4cm diam., flattened, exterior dark green, downy, lobe ovate, long-attenuate, recurved, olive green or dark red, with red-brown rugae, white-ciliate; corona dark purple. S Afr., Nam.

S. olivacea N.E. Br. St. 7–13×1cm, with 4 v. rounded angles, puberulous, teeth small. Fls 3.5–4cm diam., exterior dirty green, puberulous, lobes long-ovate, tapered, interior glab., light or dark olive-green or dull red, densely brown wrinkled. Cape Prov.

S. pachyrrhiza Dinter = *Tridentea pachyrrhiza.*

S. paniculata Willd. = *S. concinna* var. *paniculata.*

S. parviflora Masson = *Quaqua parviflora.*

S. parvipuncta var. *truncata* Luckh. = *Tridentea parvipuncta* var. *truncata.*

S. pearsonii N.E. Br. St. 4–8×0.6–1.2cm, with 4 obtuse, slightly dentate angles, puberulous. Fls 3.5cm diam., lobes stellate-spreading, lanceolate, interior slightly rough, glab., brown-purple, exterior puberulous, margins recurved. Nam.

S. peculiaris Lückh. = *Tridentea peculiaris.*

S. pedunculata Masson = *Tridentea pedunculata.*

S. peglerae N.E. Br. St. 12–15×1.2cm, glab., teeth small. Fls 6cm diam., flat, glossy dark brown-purple, lobes lanceolate, rugae faintly white or yellow or concolorous, margins purple-ciliate glab. or with floccose sinuses; corona dark purple-brown. Transkei.

S. penzigii N.E. Br. = *Huernia macrocarpa* var. *penzigii.*

S. pillansii N.E. Br. St. 8–13×1.2cm, bluntly angled, concave between angles, velvety, teeth small. Fls 10–20cm diam., flat, v. deeply lobed, interior glab., dark purple, exterior sparsely hairy, lobes lanceolate-ovate, attenuate, star-like, smooth, revolute, purple-ciliate; corona glossy black. Cape Prov.

S. portae-taurinae Dinter & A. Berger. St. 5–20×1cm, with 4 rounded, small-toothed angles, puberulous. Fls 2.5cm diam., tube broad-campanulate with an annular depression in mouth, lobes ovate-triangular, tapered, pale yellow with brown transverse ridges, margins recurved. Namaqualand.

S. prognatha Bally = *Orbea prognatha.*

S. pruinosa Masson = *Quaqua pruinosa.*

S. pulchella Masson = *Orbea pulchella.*

S. pulvinata Masson. St. 10–20cm, soft-pubesc., teeth erect. Fls 9cm diam., dark maroon, flat, covered in purple-red hairs in centre and at lobs bases, lobes triangular-ovate, slender, abruptly attenuate, reflexed, rugae cream-yellow, margins densely puurple-ciliate; corona purple-brown, with paler tips. Cape Prov. f. *margarita* (B.L. Sloane) G. Rowley. Fls more densely pink-hairy at the centre, lobe tips glab.

S. revoluta Masson = *Tromotriche revoluta.*

S. rubiginosa Nel. St. 3–12×1cm, 4–6angled, canescent angles rounded, teeth sharp, subulate. Fls 2–2.5cm diam., flat, tube cream to green, thickened, lobes ovate, acute, exterior green striped purple, interior yellow-purple spotted dark purple, rugose below, pubesc., red-ciliate; corona brown. Namaqualand.

S. rufa Masson. St. 10–15×2cm, 4–6-angled, minutely downy, angles blunt, teeth small. Fls 3–4cm diam., red-brown, campanulate, tube short, with a broad, black-violet annulus at mouth, covered in tiny rugae, lobes triangular, long-attenuate, finely banded olive-green revolute, ciliate; outer corona orange to brown, inner whorl red-brown to black. Cape Prov.

S. ruschiana Dinter = *Tridentea ruschiana.*

S. schinzii A. Berger & Schltr. St. to 8×1.8cm, often mottled purple, minutely downy, tetragonal, winged, toothed. Fls 10–22cm diam., flat, black-brown to dull green, rugae dense, red-purple, tube short, lobes ovate-lanceolate, tapering, with purple, clavate cilia; outer corona garnet, inner red with white-tipped filiform horns. Bots., Nam., S Angola.

S. semota N.E. Br. = *Orbea semota.*

S. simsii Haw. Schult. = *S. vetula.*

S. stultitioides Lückh. St. 9×1cm, acutely 4-angled, green-pruinose, teeth sharp. Fls 4cm diam., exterior puberulous, green with purple blotches, interior rough, deep purple-black with an indistinct annualus, lobes spreading ovate, tapered above, with white hairs below. W Cape.

S. subulata Forssk. = *Caralluma subulata.*

S. surrecta N.E. Br. St. 7×1cm, with 4 obtuse angles, green-puberulous. Fls to 3cm diam., interior glab., wrinkled, tube short, bowl-shaped, lobes v. long-tapered, exterior with 3 distinct veins. W Cape. Laingsburg and Ceres Districts. var. *primosii* Lückh. Fls smooth, pale yellow or wholey brown-purple. SE Cape.

S. tapscottii Verdc. = *Orbea tapscottii.*

S. thudichumii Pill. = *Tromotriche thudichumii.*

S. tsomoensis N.E. Br. St. 10–15. Angles sinuate and minutely hairy, teeth small. Fls 6–7.5cm diam., smoky-purple, base flat, softly purple-red-hairy, lobes ovate-lanceolate, recurved, with concolorous or green-ochre rugae, red-ciliate; corona black-purple. Transkei.

S. umbellata Roxb. = *Caralluma umbellata.*

S. umbonata Pill. = *Tridentea pachyrrhiza.*

S. vaga N.E. Br. = *Orbeopsis lutea* ssp. *vaga.*

S. variegata L. = *Orbea variegata.*

S. verrucosa Masson = *Orbea verrucosa.*

S. vetula Masson. St. 10–15×1.3cm, with 4 small dentate angles, puberulous. Fls 6–8cm diam., tube campanulate, glab., lobes ovate-lanceolate, long-tapered, interior black-red, rugulose, with distinct longitudinal nerves. SW Cape.

S. virescens N.E. Br. = *Tridentea virescens.*

S. wilmaniae Lückh. = *S. leendertziae.*

S. youngii N.E. Br. = *S. gigantea.*

→*Tridentea.*

Stapelianthus Choux ex A. White & B.L. Sloane. Asclepiadaceae. 9 small succulents, to 20cm, closely related to *Huernia.* Cor. campanulate to almost flat with a significant tube, lobes, triangular or deltoid with teeth in sinuses. S & SW Madag. Z10.

S. arenarius Bosser & Morat. St. to 15×1cm, creeping, glab., tetragonal, tubercles with a 1–2mm, retorse point. Fls 2–2.5cm diam., white, blotched red-brown; lobes triangular, hairy-papillose, tips slightly reflexed; corona red-brown.

S. baylissii Leach = *Tridentea baylissii.*

S. choanantha (Lavranos & Hall) Dyer = *Tridentea choanantha.*

S. decaryi Choux. St. to 10×1cm, forming dense clumps, to 8-angled, tubercles square or hexagonal, apex spiny. Fls to 2.5cm, tube 1–1.3cm, base dark purple, mouth papillose, lobes broadly triangular, recurved, yellow-grey blotched purple, red-papillate-hairy; corona purple.

S. hardyi Lavranos. St. dense, procumbent to ascending, to 0.8cm diam., elongate, tubercles in 4–6 rows with small rudimentary lvs at apices. Fls 1.3cm diam., campanulate, fleshy, outer surface covered in tiny calli, glab., yellow-pink spotted purple-brown, inner surface glab. and yellow-pink with circular, dark purple-brown spots at base, elsewhere dark purple-brown, covered in club-shaped hairs; lobes deltoid; corona dark purple-brown.

S. insignis Descoings. St. to 20×1cm, prostrate, mat-forming, 4-angled, red-grey, dark-blotched, tubercles oblong. Lvs apical, 1.5–2mm. Fls to 2cm diam., cylindric-campanulate, expanding toward apex then narrowing again, fleshy, exterior dappled red-purple, interior pink stained garnet, mouth green with dark-

er markings outside, black to purple, yellow-reticulate within, lobes triangular, black-purple with paler central stripe corona deep violet.

S. keraudrenae Bosser & Morat. St. to 40×1cm, erect, bright green, spotted dark green or red, 6–7-angled, tubercles acute. Fls 3–3.5cm diam., flat, yellow-orange blotched wine-red to yellow-green blotched dark purple, annulus, fleshy, purple-blotched or wholly dark purple; lobes triangular-acute, papillose, apices recurved, ciliate; corona dark purple.

S. madagascarensis (Choux) Choux. St. creeping to ascending, elongate, grey-green blotched dark red, to 0.8cm diam., tubercles in 6 rows with tiny apical lvs. Fls 2cm diam., broad-campanulate, pale yellow blotched wine-red, lobes broadly deltoid, spreading, recurved, sparsely blotched, apex long, intense red, papillose; outer corona black-purple.

S. montagnacii (Boit.) Boit. & Bertrand. St. prostrate, to 1cm diam. Fls *c*2cm diam., dish-shaped, white, exterior blotched wine-red, interior streaked pale maroon, lobes erect, with large, overlapping wine-red blotches, apices short, white, papillae with bright red tips.

S. pilosus Lavranos & Hardy. St. 9–12×1.2cm, creeping to ascending, often rerooting, tubercles in dense, spiral rows, small, conical, apex with a soft, white hair, 2–5cm. Fls 1.4cm diam., fleshy, campanulate, pale yellow blotched wine-red, lobes broadly triangular, attenuate, spreading, red-tipped; papillae cylindrical, yellow or red-purple, 0.75mm; outer corona dark maroon.

Stapeliopsis Pill. Asclepiadaceae. 6 dwarf, succulent, leafless herbs. St. minutely papillose-pubescent, thick, tetragonal in section, blotched purple, ridges toothed. Fls at bases of young shoots; cor. 5-lobed, urn-shaped, hairy-papillose within. S Afr., Nam. Z10.

S. ballyi Marn.-Lip. = *Echidnopsis ballyi.*

S. breviloba (R.A. Dyer) P.V. Bruyns. St. to 5×1cm, produced from underground stolons, erect, bluntly 4-angled with pointed tubercles bearing a sharp acute tooth, grey-brown. Cor. tubular to ellipsoid, 1–1.3×0.5–0.6cm, exterior grey-brown with fine translucent veins, interior dark purple-red, yellow on lobes, lobes joined at tips. SW Cape.

S. exasperata (P.V. Bruyns) P.V. Bruyns. St. 1cm diam. produced from underground stolons, erect, pyramidal, quad-rangular, teeth small, deltoid. Cor. 1×1–1.2cm narrow-campanulate, inner surface with columnar papillae, lobes erect to spreading, exterior flesh-coloured. W Cape.

S. neronis Pill. St. to 7×3.5cm in dense clusters, angles blunt, compressed, teeth broadly deltoid, abruptly acute. Cor. 1.7–2×1.75–2cm, fleshy, tube dark purple, exterior covered in dagger-shaped, hair-tipped papillae, underside subspherical with 5 longitudinal furrows, throat mauve to white, lobes triangular-ovate, white or mauve inside. Namaqualand.

S. pillansii (N.E. Br.) P.V. Bruyns. St. prostrate, 15×1cm, forming dense clumps, acutely 4-angled, teeth conical, recurved, 3–4mm, surface shiny dark green. Cor. 7mm diam., depressed-pyriform, exterior glab. and smooth, interior light red with watery papillae, lobes thick, fleshy, deltoid, erect to spreading. SE Cape.

S. saxatilis (N.E. Br.) P.V. Bruyns. St. 2–6×2.5cm, prostrate, sometimes burrowing, acutely tetragonal, sometimes spotted red, teeth to 8mm, acute. Cor. to 0.7×1cm, broadly ovate to subcampanulate, dark maroon, cup-shaped to ovoid or conical with tiny subconical papillae, lobes black-purple, ovate-lanceolate, minutely downy, usually joined at apices. Cape Prov. ssp. *stayneri* (Bayer) P.V. Bruyns. St. 1cm thick. Cor. subcampanulate, 6mm diam. at widest, pale pink becoming off-white near base, small straight hairs toward base of tube interior; lobes joined at ip. W Cape.

S. tulipiflora Lückh. = *S. saxatilis.*

S. urniflora Lavranos. St. semi-subterranean, 7×2cm, grey-green with brown blotches, minutely papillose, 4 rounded, bluntly dentate, angles, teeth laterally compressed. Cor. urn-shaped, 15×8mm below, constricted to 5mm wide below midway, wine-coloured, exterior glab., interior with dense papillae, lobes triangular, erect. Nam.

→*Pectinaria.*

Staphylea L. BLADDERNUT. Staphyleaceae. 11 ± decid. shrubs or small trees; branchlets with smooth striped bark. Lvs trifoliolate to pinnate. Pan. term. sep. green to yellow-white, ± equalling 5 linear-spathulate to oblong, free, erect pet.; sta. 5, about as long as pet. Fr. a membranous, obovoid to subglobose inflated capsule, usually 2–3-lobed. N temp. regions.

S. bolanderi A. Gray. Glab. shrub to 3m or slender tree to 6m. Lfts to 7cm, 3, broad-elliptic or suborbicular, finely serrate, acute, glab. Fls 9–15 in pan. white. Fr. to 6cm, 3-lobed. Spring. W US. Z7.

S. bumalda DC. Shrub to 2m. Lfts 6cm, 3, ovate to ovate-lanceolate, sharply serrulate, downy on veins beneath. Fls in loose term. clusters 4–7.5cm wide, dull white. Fr. to 2.5cm, usually 2-lobed. Spring. Jap. Z4.

S. colchica Steven. Shrub to 4m. Lfts 3 or 5, 5–8cm, ovate-oblong acuminate, finely toothed, shining green, glab. and lustrous beneath. Fls fragrant, to 1.5cm in pan. 5–10cm long and wide, white; fil. glab. Fr. to 8cm, 2–3-lobed. Spring. Cauc. 'Coulomberi' ('Elegans'): lfts 3 or 5, term. leaflet to 15cm, dark green, long-acuminate; fls white, in pan. more compact than those of *S. colchica*; fr. to 10cm, with spreading lobes; possibly *S. colchica* ×*S. pinnata*. 'Grandiflora': pan., lvs and fls longer. var. **kochiana** Medv. Fil. pubesc. var. **laxiflora** Baas-Beck. Lfts usually 3. Infl. long, slender, pendulous. Z6.

S. coulombieri (André) Zab. = *S. colchica* 'Coulomberi'.

S. ×elegans Zab. = *S. colchica* 'Coulomberi'.

S. emodi Wallich. Shrub to 4m or small tree to 6.5m. Lfts 3, 5–14cm, elliptic to oblong, finely serrulate, pubesc. or subglabrous. beneath. Fls 1.2cm in term. drooping pan. to 10cm, white. Fr. 5–8cm. Early summer. Himal. Z9.

S. holocarpa Hemsl. Shrub to 5m or tree to 10m. Lfts 3–10cm, 3 elliptic to oblong, glab. and dark green above, pubesc. beneath. Fls 0.8cm, rose in bud becoming pure white, in drooping axill. pan. to 10cm. Fr. to 5cm. Spring. China. var. **rosea** Rehd. & Wils.. Lvs more downy beneath. Fls rose. Z6.

S. pinnata L. BLADDERNUT. Shrub to 5m. Lfts 5–10cm, 3, 5 or 7, ovate-oblong, acuminate, serrulate, glab. and glaucescent beneath. Fls c1cm, in pan. to 12cm, white, sep tipped red. Fr. to 3cm. Late spring–early summer. Eur., Asia Minor. Z6.

S. trifolia L. Shrub to 5m. Lfts 3.5–8cm, 3, elliptic to ovate, sharply and finely toothed, slender-pointed, pubesc. beneath, middle leaflet long-stalked. Fls 0.8cm, dull white, in drooping pan. to 5cm. Fr. 3–4cm, usually 3-lobed. Spring. E US. Z5.

STAPHYLEACEAE Lind. 5/27. *Euscaphis, Staphylea.*

Star Anise *Illicium anisatum.*
Star Apple *Chrysophyllum cainito.*
Star Begonia *Begonia heracleifolia; B. ×ricinifolia.*
Star Bush *Turraea.*
Star Cluster *Pentas lanceolata.*
Star Cucumber *Sicyos angulatus.*
Star Daisy *Lindheimera taxana.*
Star Duckweed *Lemna trisulca.*
Starfish Cactus *Orbea variegata.*
Starfish Flower *Stapelia.*
Starfish Plant *Cryptanthus acaulis.*
Star-flowered Lily of the Valley *Smilacina stellata.*
Starflower *Calytrix; Smilacina stellata; Trientalis borealis.*
Starfruit *Averrhoa carambola.*
Star-glory *Ipomoea quamoclit.*
Star Grass *Aletris; Chloris truncata; Cynodon dactylon; Hypoxis.*
Star Ipomoea *Ipomoea coccinea.*
Star Jasmine *Trachelospermum jasminoides.*
Star-leaf Begonia *Begonia heracleifolia.*
Star Lily *Leucocrinum; Zigadenus fremontii.*
Star Magnolia *Magnolia stellata.*
Star of Bethlehem *Campanula isophylla; Eucharis ×grandiflora; Ornithogalum pyrenaicum (O. umbellatum).*
Star of Bethlehem Orchid *Angraecum sesquipedale.*
Star of Persia *Allium christophii.*
Starry Saxifrage *Saxifraga stellaris.*
Star-spine *Euphorbia stellaespina.*
Star Thistle *Centaurea.*
Star Tulip *Calochortus (C. uniflorus).*
Star Zygadene *Zigadenus fremontii.*
Statice *Goniolimon tataricum; Limonium.*

Statice L.
S. acerosa Willd. = *Acantholimon acerosum.*
S. arborea Brouss. = *Limonium fruticans.*
S. arborescens Brouss. = *Limonium arborescens.*
S. arenaria Pers. = *Armeria arenaria.*
S. aristata Sm. = *Limonium echioides.*
S. armeria var. *sibirica* (Turcz. ex Boiss.) Ostenf. & Lund = *Armeria sibirica.*
S. armeria f. *arctica* (Cham.) Ledeb. = *Armeria arctica.*
S. armeria L. (in part). = *Armeria maritima.*
S. aurea L. = *Limonium aureum.*
S. australis Spreng. = *Limonium australe.*
S. bellidifolium (Gouan) DC. = *Limonium bellidifolium.*
S. bourgaei Webb = *Limonium bourgaei.*
S. bracteata Girard = *Acantholimon bracteatum.*
S. brasiliensis A. Gray non Boiss. nec. Chapm. = *Limonium carolinianum.*
S. brasiliensis Chapm. non Boiss. nec A. Gray = *Limonium angu-*

statum.
S. brassicifolia Webb & Berth. = *Limonium brassicifolium.*
S. caesia Girard = *Limonium caesium.*
S. caespitosa Cav. = *Armeria caespitosa.*
S. callicoma C.A. Mey. = *Goniolimon callicomum.*
S. caroliniana Walter = *Limonium carolinianum.*
S. caroliniana Boiss. in part non Walter = *Limonium angustatum.*
S. caspia Willd. = *Limonium bellidifolium.*
S. collina Griseb. = *Goniolimon incanum.*
S. confusa Gren. & Godron = *Limonium confusum.*
S. confusa Rchb. f. non Gren. & Godron = *Limonium ramosissimum* ssp. *tommasinii.*
S. confusa Gren. & Godron = *Limonium ramosissimum* ssp. *confusum.*
S. cordata L. = *Limonium cordatum.*
S. cosyrensis Guss. = *Limonium cosyrense.*
S. delicatula Girard = *Limonium delicatulum.*
S. dodartii Girard = *Limonium binervosum.*
S. doerfleri Hal. = *Limonium ramosissimum* ssp. *doerfleri.*
S. dregeana Presl = *Limonium dregeanum.*
S. echioides L. = *Limonium echioides.*
S. eximia Schrenk = *Goniolimon eximium.*
S. fasciculata Vent. = *Armeria pungens.*
S. ferulacea L. = *Limonium ferulaceum.*
S. filicaulis Boiss. = *Armeria filicaulis.*
S. frutescens Lem. = *Limonium fruticans.*
S. fruticans Webb = *Limonium fruticans.*
S. globulariifolia (Desf.) Kuntze = *Limonium ramosissimum.*
S. glumacea Jaub. & Spach = *Acantholimon glumaceum.*
S. gmelinii Willd. = *Limonium gmelinii.*
S. gougetiana Girard = *Limonium gougetianum.*
S. halfordii hort. = *Limonium macrophyllum.*
S. hohenackeri Jaub. & Spach = *Acantholimon hohenackeri.*
S. imbricata Webb ex Girard = *Limonium imbricatum.*
S. incana L. = *Goniolimon incanum.*
S. incana Ledeb. non L. = *Goniolimon callicomum.*
S. japonica Sieb. & Zucc. = *Limonium tetragonum.*
S. kotschyi Jaub. & Spach = *Acantholimon kotschyi.*
S. labradorica (Wallr.) Hubb. & Blake = *Armeria labradorica.*
S. latifolia Sm. = *Limonium latifolium.*
S. leptostachya Boiss. = *Psylliostachys leptostachya.*
S. limonium var. *bellidifolium* Gouan = *Limonium bellidifolium.*
S. limonium L. = *Limonium vulgare.*
S. lychnidifolia Girard = *Limonium auriculaeursifolium.*
S. lyrata M.B. Talb. = *Psylliostachys spicata.*
S. macrophylla Brouss. = *Limonium macrophyllum.*
S. macroptera Webb & Berth. = *Limonium macropterum.*
S. majellensis (Boiss.) Hubb. = *Armeria majellensis.*
S. maritima ssp. *arctica* (Cham.) Hullen = *Armeria arctica.*
S. maritima var. *labradorica* (Wallr.) Hult. = *Armeria arctica.*
S. maritima Mill. = *Armeria maritima.*
S. minuta L. = *Limonium minutum.*
S. mouretii Pitard = *Limonium mouretii.*
S. monopetala L. = *Limoniastrum monopetalum.*
S. myosuroides Reg. = *Psylliostachys ×myosuroides.*
S. nebrodensis Guss. = *Armeria canescens* ssp. *nebrodensis.*
S. occidentalis J. Lloyd = *Limonium binervosum.*
S. ornata Ball = *Limonium ornatum.*
S. otolepis Schrenk = *Limonium otolepis.*
S. pectinata Ait. = *Limonium pectinatum.*
S. peregrina Bergius = *Limonium peregrinum.*
S. perezii Stapf = *Limonium perezii.*
S. perfoliata Karel. = *Limonium reniforme.*
S. preauxii Webb = *Limonium preauxii.*
S. profusa hort. = *Limonium ×profusum.*
S. pseudarmeria Murray = *Armeria pseudarmeria.*
S. psiloclada Boiss. = *Limonium ramosissimum* ssp. *provinciale.*
S. puberula Webb = *Limonium puberulum.*
S. reniformis Girard = *Limonium reniforme.*
S. reticulata Fisch. ex Boiss. = *Limonium caspium.*
S. reticulata Bieb. = *Limonium bellidifolium.*
S. rosea Sm. = *Limonium peregrinum.*
S. sibirica auct. = *Armeria sibirica.*
S. sieberi Boiss. = *Limonium sieberi.*
S. sinuata L. = *Limonium sinuatum.*
S. smithii Gand. = *Limonium sieberi.*
S. spathulata var. *emarginata* (Willd.) Boiss. = *Limonium emarginatum.*
S. spathulata Desf. = *Limonium spathulatum.*
S. speciosa L. = *Goniolimon incanum.*
S. spicata Willd. = *Psylliostachys spicata.*
S. suworowii Reg. = *Psylliostachys suworowii.*
S. tenuifolia Jaub. & Spach = *Acantholimon hohenackeri.*
S. tetragona Thunb. = *Limonium tetragonum.*
S. tetragona Drège non Thunb. = *Limonium dregeanum.*

S. thouinii Viv. = *Limonium thouinii*.
S. tomentella Boiss. = *Limonium tomentellum*.
S. tournefortii Jaub. & Spach. = *Acantholimon ulicinum*.
S. ulicina Willd. ex Schult. = *Acantholimon ulicinum*.
S. undulata Bory & Chaub. = *Armeria undulata*.
S. virgata Willd. = *Limonium virgatum*.

St. Augustine Grass *Stenotaphrum secundatum*.

Stauntonia DC. Lardizabalaceae. 16 everg., twining shrubs. Lvs palmately compound. Rac. few-fld axill.; sep. 6, fleshy, acuminate; pet. and nectaries 0, ♂ fls with sta. connate ♀ fls with 3 carpels and staminodes. Berry edible, ellipsoid. Burm. to Taiwan and Jap.
S. hexaphylla Decne. To 10m. Lfts 3–7, to 14cm, ovate to elliptic, apex acute to acuminate, dark green, glossy, coriaceous. Fls to 2cm, white tinted violet, fragrant. Fruits 2.5–5cm, purple. Summer. S Korea, Jap., Ryukyu Is. var. *obovata* Wu. Lfts 6–10cm, obovate to oblong-lanceolate, apex caudate. Mts of Jap. and Taiwan. Z9.
S. latifolia (Wall.) Wall. = *Holboellia latifolia*.
→*Holboellia*.

Stauranthera Benth. Gesneriaceae. 10 erect, fleshy perenn. herbs. Lvs in unequal, opposite pairs, smaller lf caducous. Infl. axill. corymbose; cal. broadly campanulate, 5-fld, plicate between lobes; cor. tube short, gibbous or spurred at base, limb ± 2-lipped. Malaysia, SE Asia. Z10.
S. grandifolia Benth. St. to 30cm, succulent, branching, glab. Lvs to 25×10cm, lustrous above, one side distended into a rounded sinuate-lobate lobe at base, ciliate; petiole to 10cm. Fls to 2.5cm; cor. tube white, tinged with purple and cream-yellow, throat with broad, yellow spot. Malaysia.

Stave Wood *Heritiera trifoliolata*.
St. Barbara's Herb *Barbarea*.
St. Bernard's Lily *Anthericum liliago*.
St. Bruno's Lily *Paradisea liliastrum*.
St. Catherine's Lace *Eriogonum* (*E. giganteum*).
St. Dabeoc's Heath *Daboecia cantabrica*.
St. Domingo Oak *Catalpa longissima*.
Steedman's Gum *Eucalyptus steedmanii*.
Steel Acacia *Acacia macracantha*.
Steelhead *Callitris monticola*.
Steeplebush *Spiraea tomentosa*.
Steer's Head *Dicentra uniflora*.

Stegnogramma Bl. Thelypteridaceae. 15 terrestrial ferns. Rhiz. short-creeping or erect. Stipes densely hairy. Frond blades pinnate. Trop. Amer., Afr., Asia. Z9.
S. pozoi (Lagasca) Iwatsuki. Rhiz. erect, to 3mm wide; scales pale brown. Stipes to 25cm. Lamina ovate-lanceolate to narrowly elliptic, to 45×25cm, herbaceous, pubesc. beneath, pinnae to 4–12×1–3cm, oblong or linear-lanceolate, lobed. Spain, Azores, Madeira, Trop. & S Afr., Comoros Is.
→*Dryopteris*, *Hemionitis* and *Thelypteris*.

Steirodiscus Less. Compositae. 5 ann. herbs. Lvs alt. and spirally arranged, sometimes imbricate, appearing rosulate, coriaceous. Cap. radiate; disc flts yellow. S Afr.
S. tagetes (L.) Schltr. St. to 30cm, arching, branched above. Lvs to 5cm, pinnatipartite, seg. linear. occas. pinnatisect. Cap. to 2cm diam., on peduncles to 7.5cm; ray flts bright yellow or orange. S Afr.

Steiroglossa DC.
S. rigidula DC. = *Brachycome rigidula*.

Stelis Sw. Orchidaceae. 250+ small epiphytic or lithophytic orchids. St. short, slender, tufted, erect, unifoliate. Lvs fleshy or coriaceous, oval to linear. Rac. long, slender, usually axill.; fls small or minute, numerous; sep. subequal, variously connate, usually spreading; pet. much smaller; lip simple to trilobed, fleshy. Braz. and Peru to W Indies and Mex. Z10.
S. allenii L.O. Williams. St. to 15cm. Lvs to 19×7cm, elliptic to ovate-elliptic. Rac. to 30cm, bearing 1 to several fls to base; fls to 3cm diam., largest of genus, near-black. Panama.
S. aprica Lindl. St. to 10cm. Lvs to 8×1cm, linear-oblanceolate or linear-elliptic, obtuse, apex obliquely tridentate. Rac. solitary, to 15cm, few to many-fld; bracts to 11cm, tubular-cucullate, acute to obtuse; fls to 0.3cm diam., spreading, secund, lightly pendent, green-white to green-yellow. Summer. Mex. to Panama.
S. argentata Lindl. Secondary st. short, to 5.5cm, slender. Lvs to 10×2.5cm, oblanceolate or elliptic-ligulate, apex obtuse to rounded, subsessile, coriaceous, clear green above, dull pale

green beneath. Rac. to 20cm, loosely many-fld, suberect; fls to 0.8cm diam., pale pink to red-purple or red-green. Mex. to Panama, Braz. and Mex.
S. barbata Rolfe. To 15cm, glab.; secondary st. to 1.5cm. Lvs to 50×8mm, linear-oblanceolate to narrowly spathulate, acute or obtuse, 3-cusped at apex. Rac. densely-fld, filiform; fls to 0.4cm diam, yellow green or red-brown. Guat., Costa Rica, Panama.
S. bidentata Schltr. To 15cm, glab.; secondary st. to 4cm, erect. Lvs to 80×7mm, narrowly oblanceolate to linear, erect, apically bi- or tridentate. Rac. loosely few-fld, to 11cm, erect, filiform; fls to 0.7cm diam., purple or white tinged green, purple or red-brown. Summer. Mex., Guat., Hond.
S. ciliaris Lindl. To 30cm, glab.; secondary st. to 3cm, stout. Lvs to 15×3cm, broadly oblong to linear, obtuse, apex tridentate or retuse. Rac. exceeding lvs, many-fld; bracts red, to 2mm; fls to 0.8cm diam., deep purple. Winter. Mex., Guat., Hond., Costa Rica.
S. compacta Ames = *Platystele compacta*.
S. cresenticola Schltr. To 20cm; secondary st. to 2cm, slender, clustered. Lvs to 9×1cm, coriaceous, oblanceolate, acute or obtuse. Rac. densely many-fld, suberect to arcuate; bracts minute, in fls to 0.4cm diam. green to yellow-green. Costa Rica, Panama.
S. dusenii Garay. To 15cm; secondary st. to 4cm, densely fasciculate. Lvs to 90×8mm, variably fleshy, linear-lanceolate to linear-elliptic, obtuse, mid-nerve slightly sulcate. Rac. to 10cm, many-fld, erect to arcuate; fls to 0.3cm diam., pale yellow often tinged green. Venez., Guyana, Braz., Peru, Boliv.
S. fragrans Schltr. To 12cm. Rhiz. short; secondary st. to 3cm, slender. Lvs to 6×1cm, oblanceolate-ligulate, subacute. Rac. erect, exceeding lvs, 8–15-flds; fls to 1cm diam., fragrant, grey tinged rose. Braz.
S. inaequisepala Hoehne & Schltr. Secondary st. to 8cm. Lvs to 14×2.5cm, light green, subcoriaceous, oblong to elliptic-oblong, lightly recurved, apex rounded; petiole terete, to 9cm. Rac. to 20cm, slender, many-fld; fls to 0.6cm diam., brown tinged dark maroon to purple. Venez., Guyana, Braz.
S. ophioglossoides (Jacq.) Sw. Secondary st. to 7cm, erect or ascending. Lvs to 14×1.5cm, elliptic-oblong to linear-oblong, subcoriaceous, tridentate at apex. Rac. to 20cm, slender, densely many-fld; fls to 0.6cm diam., yellow-green tinged purple. Early autumn. W Indies, Braz.
S. ovalifolia Focke = *Platystele ovalifolia*.
S. purpurascens A. Rich. & Gal. To 43cm, stout, glab.; secondary st. to 19cm, erect or ascending, clustered. Lvs to 20×4cm, linear-oblanceolate to oblong-lanceolate, apex obtuse and refuse, usually sessile. Rac. to 33cm, 1 or 2, loosely many-fld; fls red-brown or purple to purple-green, to 1cm diam. Winter. Mex., Guat., Hond., El Salvador, Costa Rica.

Stellaria L. CHICKWEED; STITCHWORT. Caryophyllaceae. *c*120 branching ann. to perenn. herbs. Fls in dichasial cymes or solitary; sep. usually 5, free; pet. usually 5, white, deeply bifid (sometimes rudimentary or 0); sta. 1–10. Cosmop., esp. the familiar ann. chickweed, *S. media*. Z5.
S. holostea L. STITCHWORT. Perenn. with slender creeping stock and weak, ascending st. to 60cm, glab. or ± hairy above. Lvs 4–8cm, lanceolate, acuminate, slightly glaucous, margins rough. Infl. a loose dichasium with leaf-like bracts; pet. 8–12mm, deeply bifid, white. Spring, early summer. Most of Eur., rare in Medit., also in W Asia and N Afr.; nat. N Amer.
S. media L. CHICKWEED. Ann. to short-lived perenn. to 40cm, with weak st. showing one line of hairs down each internode lvs ± ovate, acute subglabrous. Fls numerous; pet. 3–5mm, white, often v. small or 0. Throughout the year. Cosmop., probably native to Eurasia.
S. pubera Michx. Differs from *S. holostea* in lvs elliptic, not lanceolate, to 10×4cm, and capsule much shorter than, not equalling cal. Spring. E N Amer.

Stellera L. Thymelaeaceae. 8 perenn. herbs, subshrubs or shrubs. Lvs alt., flat, simple. Fls in term. heads or dense spikes; perianth tube cylindrical, lobes spreading, 4–6; sta. 8–12, in 2 rows. Fr. a small nut. Temp. Asia from Persia to China. Z5.
S. chamejasme L. Subshrub or perenn. herb. St. to 30cm, many, arising from a thick rhiz. Lvs 1–2cm, lanceolate or oblong, acute. Fls fragrant, rose to white to 7mm diam., in dense globose heads to 4cm diam. Summer. Himal., C Asia.

Stem Ginger *Zingiber officinale*.
Stemless Carline Thistle *Carlina acaulis*.
Stemless Gentian *Gentiana acaulis*.

Stemmadenia Benth. Apocynaceae. 7 everg. or decid. trees and shrubs with milky sap, dichotomously branched. Lvs oval to elliptic-ovate opposite, thin-textured. Infl. forked, cymose; sep.

leafy; cor. showy, salver- or funnelform, tube with 5 narrow wings, lobes overlapping to the left. Trop. Amer. Z10.

S. galeottiana (Rich.) Miers = *S. litoralis*.

S. glabra Benth. = *S. obovata*.

S. grandiflora (Jacq.) Miq. Cor. yellow, orange or sometimes white, almost cylindrical, lobes 0.6–1× length of tube. Guyana, Venez.

S. litoralis (HBK) Allorge. Cor. white, tube 45–66mm, tubular-funnelform, lobes 0.15–0.8× length of tube. Mex. to Colomb.

S. mollis Benth. = *S. obovata*.

S. obovata (Hook. & Arn.) Schum. Plant usually pubesc.; cor. bright yellow, tube 35–55mm, funnelform, lobs 0.7–1×length of tube. Mex. to Ecuad.

S. palmeri Rose ex Greenman = *S. tomentosa*.

S. sinoloana Woods. = *S. tomentosa*.

S. tomentosa Greenman. Plant usually glab. Cor. pale yellow, tube 33–45mm, lobes 0.65–1× length of tube. Mex., probably also Guat.

→*Tabernaemontana*.

Stenandrium Nees. Acanthaceae. *c*25 ± stemless herbs. Infl. a spike; fls small; cal. 5-lobed; cor. tubular, slender, lobes 5. Trop. & subtrop. Amer. Z10.

S. lindenii Nees. Dwarf herb. Lvs obovate to broadly elliptic, low-lying, metallic bronze-green with yellow-green veins above, purple-green beneath. Spike sto 8cm, erect; fls yellow. Peru.

Stenanthera R. Br.

S. pinifolia R. Br. = *Astroloma pinifolium*.

Stenanthium (A. Gray) Kunth. Liliaceae (Melanthiaceae). 5 bulbous perenn. herbs. St. slender, erect. Lvs grass-like, mostly basal, arching; st. lvs few, bract-like, toward summit. Flowrs in term. rac. or pan.; perianth narrowly campanulate, tube short, free lobes 6, linear. W N Amer., Mex., Sakhalin. Z6.

S. angustifolium Kunth = *S. gramineum*.

S. gramineum (Ker-Gawl.) Morong. Basal lvs to 30–40×1.8cm, channelled. Flowering st. to 1.5m, channelled; infl. a dense pan., 30–60cm, apex dense, spicate, lower regions furnished with spreading or nodding br.; fls 1.2–1.8cm diam., white to white-green to purple, fragrant, starry, tep. briefly connate at base. Late summer. SE US. var. *robustum* (S. Wats.) Fern. Lvs to 2.5cm wide. Flowering st. to 1.8m, pan. denser, with ascending to spreading br.

S. occidentale A. Gray. Basal lvs 15–30×1.8cm, slightly keeled. Flowering st. to 60cm; infl. a loose rac. to 20cm, sometimes with a few short br. at base; fls 1.2–1.8cm, campanulate, brown-purple, nodding, tep., fused for half their length. Summer. W N Amer.

S. robustum S. Wats. = *S. gramineum* var. *robustum*.

Stenia Lindl. Orchidaceae. 3 epiphytic orchids. Pbs small or concealed, clustered. Lvs term. and sheathing subcoriaceous, elliptic to oblong-obovate, midvein prominent. Infl. basal, short, recurved, 1-fld; fls large; tep. free, spreading; lip fleshy, concave to saccate, simple to 3-lobed, disc with a transverse crest or lamellae, cristate. C & N S Amer. Z10.

S. guttata Rchb. f. Lvs to 13×3.5cm. Fls thin-textured, bright yellow-green to straw-yellow, spotted dark purple or brown; tep., ovate-oblong, to 26mm; lip, midlobe ovate-triangular. Peru.

S. pallida Lindl. Lvs to 15×4cm; sep. and pet. pale yellow-green, thin-textured, translucent, elliptic-ovate, to 35mm; lip white to pale yellow-green, lateral lobes erect, rounded, spotted maroon, midlobe subtriangular. Guyana, Venez., Trin., Braz., Peru.

Stenocactus (Schum.) A.W. Hill. Cactaceae. *c*10 low-growing cacti, usually unbranched; st. subglobose to short cylindric; ribs acute, usually v. numerous, thin and often sinuate areoles usually widely spaced; spines central and radial, the former often strongly flattened. Fls small, shortly funnelform or campanulate; pericarpel with scales; floral areoles naked; tube usually short. Mex.

S. coptonogonus (Lem.) A. Berger ex A.W. Hill. Simple; st. depressed-globose to globose, 5–10×7–15cm, grey to blue-green; ribs 10–15, acute, notched at areoles; spines 3–5(–7). Fl. 3×4cm, tube v. short; tep. striped white, pink-purple or violet. Spring. NC Mex., Z9.

S. crispatus (DC.) A. Berger ex A.W. Hill. Resembling *S. multicostatus* but st. dark or blue-green; ribs 25–60; spines 6–10. Fl. to 4cm; tube well developed. Summer. C to S Mex. Z9.

S. multicostatus (Hildm. ex Schum.) A. Berger ex A.W. Hill. Simple or clustering; st. depressed-globose to globose, 6–10×6–12cm, pale green; ribs to 120, v. thin; spines 6–18. Fl.

to 2.5cm; tube short; tep. white with faint pink to purple mid-stripe, or purple-pink. Spring. NE Mex. Z9.

S. obvallatus (DC.) A. Berger ex A.W. Hill. Differs from *S. multicostatus* in st. blue-green; ribs 20–50; spines 5–12. Spring. N & EC Mex. Z9.

S. ochoterenanus Tiegel. Differs from *S. multicostatus* in ribs 30–50; spines 11–26+. Fl. to 4cm; tube well developed. Spring. NC Mex. Z9.

S. phyllacanthus (A. Dietr.) A. Berger ex A.W. Hill. Usually simple; st. depressed-globose to short-cylindric, 4–10cm diam., dark green; ribs 26–60; spines 2–7. Fl. 1–2.3cm, yellow; tube short. Summer. NC Mex. Z9.

S. sulphureus (A. Dietr.) H. Bravo. Differs from *S. phyllacanthus* in spines 8–16. Fl. to 3.5cm; tube well developed. EC Mex. Z9.

S. vaupelianus (Werderm.) Backeb. & F. Knuth. Simple; st. depressed-globose to globose, pale green, apex v. woolly; ribs 27–40+, v. thin; spines 14–27. Fl. to 2.5cm, pale yellow; tube short. Spring. EC Mex. Z9.

→*Echinocactus* and *Echinofossulocactus*.

Stenocarpus R. Br. Proteaceae. 22 trees and shrubs. Lvs simple or pinnatifid. Fls in axillary umbels; perianth 1–3.5cm, tube slit on lower side, limb subglobose, recurved. Fr. a narrow, coriaceous follicle. Aus., Malaysia, New Caledonia. Z10 unless specified.

S. angustifolius C.T. White. Large shrub to small tree to 5m. Lvs 10cm, divided into fine narrow-linear seg. in juvenile stage, narrow-lanceolate, 5–10(18)cm in adult stage. Fls cream white, in axill. 12–20-fld umbels; perianth hairy. Summer. E Aus.

S. cryptocarpus D. Foreman & Hylander. Large, buttressed tree to 25m. Lvs simple to bipinnate, juvenile lvs to 1cm, adult lvs thick, elliptic to obovate, to 14cm on an 8cm petiole. Fls cream, strongly scented, in axill. umbels of to 16; perianth rusty-hairy. E Aus.

S. cunninghamii R. Br. Tall rounded shrub to 4m. Lvs to 10cm, oblong-lanceolate, shiny. Fls cream in upper lf axils. Autumn. N Aus.

S. davallioides D. Foreman & Hylander. Tall tree to 40m. Lvs 3–4× pinnately divided with 1cm lanceolate lfts to simple and lanceolate to pinnately divided into 8–20cm lfts. Fls creamy-green in 12-fld umbels; perianth sparsely hairy. Late spring. E Aus. Z9.

S. salignus R. Br. SCRUB BEEFWOOD. Tall shrub to 30m tree. Lvs to 10cm, ovate to narrow-elliptic, shiny. Fls creamy-white, fragrant, in simple or branched umbels in upper lf axils. Spring–summer. E Aus.

S. sinuatus Endl. FIREWHEEL TREE. Medium to tall tree to 30m. Lvs 20–45cm, glossy, pinnately lobed to entire, obovate or oblanceolate. Fls red in term. 12–20-fld, wheel-like umbels in upper lf axils. Summer–autumn. E Aus.

Stenocereus Riccob. Cactaceae. *c*25 tree-like or shrubby cacti; st. stout, ribbed, often heavily spined; flowering areoles usually discrete. Fls funnelform or campanulate; pericarpel with numerous areoles and usually small spines; tube flared or not, with decurrent scales. Mex., N. Amer., W Indies, Venez. and Colomb.

S. beneckei (Ehrenb.) F. Buxb. Sparsely branched; st. erect or decumbent, 1–2m×5–7cm, pruinose above; ribs 7–9, tuberculate; spines usually 1–3, black at first, uppermost longer, to 4cm, the lower 3–15mm. Fl. nocturnal, narrowly funnelform, 6.5–8cm×4–5cm; inner tep. white, tinged green or pink. W Mex. Z9.

S. dumortieri (Scheidw.) F. Buxb. Tree 5–6(–10)m, with short trunk; br. numerous erect, 5–10cm diam., glaucous; ribs 5–7; spines relatively slender; central spines 1–4, to 4cm; radial spines 9–11+, to 1cm. Fl. nocturnal, 5×3cm; outer tep. red-brown, inner white. C & S Mex. Z9.

S. eruca (Brandg.) Gibson & Horak. St. prostrate, creeping, occas. branching, to 1.5m×4–10cm, the apical 20–30cm ascending, the older st. rooting adventitiously and dying back from the base; ribs 10–12; spines *c*20, pale yellow to white, one to 35mm, flattened and directed backwards, dagger-like, the remainder ascending and radiating, 10–25mm. Fl. tubular-funnelform, 10–14×7–8cm, tube elongate, inner tep. white, creamy yellow or tinged pink. NW Mex. Z9.

S. griseus (Haw.) F. Buxb. Large shrub or small tree to 6–9m, sometimes branching at base, sometimes with a trunk; br. erect, 8.5–15cm diam., dark green or glaucous, at least above; ribs 7–8(–10), 2.5–3cm high; central spine 1, 1.5–2.5(–6)cm; radial spines 7 or more, *c*1cm. Fl. 7–8cm; outer tep. tinged pink; inner tep. white. Fr. subglobose, *c*5cm diam., spiny, red, edible; pulp red. N Venez. and adjacent islands. Z9.

S. gummosus (Engelm. ex Brandg.) Gibson & Horak. Large shrub forming thickets to 1–3×10m; br. arching to prostrate,

5–8cm diam., dark green, often tinged purple; ribs 7–8, low-obtuse; spines stout, black-brown or red-tinged, fading to grey; central spines 3–9, flattened, to 4cm; radial spines 8–12, 8–15mm. Fl. tubular-funnelform, 10–14cm; tep. white (also purple). Fr. ovoid or globose, 6–8cm diam., bright red, spiny, edible; pulp purple. NW Mexico. Z9.

S. *martinezii* (Gonz. Ortega) Bravo. Small tree, 3–5m; trunk 1–2m×30cm; br. cylindric; ribs 9; spines black; central spines 2–3, 2–5cm, the upper much shorter; radial spines 7–11, 2–10mm. Fl. not described. NW Mex. Z9.

S. *pruinosus* (Pfeiff.) F. Buxb. Large shrub or small tree, to 4–5m, much branched; st. 8–10cm diam., white-pruinose above; ribs 5–6(–8); central spines 1–4, 2–3cm, grey; radial spines 5–8, 1–2cm. Fl funnelform, c9×7cm; inner tep. white or tinged pink. S Mex. Z9.

S. *queretaroensis* (F.A.C. Weber) F. Buxb. Tree 5–6m or more with short trunk; br. numerous, ascending, to 15cm diam., green or tinged red; ribs 6–8; areoles with gland. hairs; central spines 2–4, to 4cm, stout; radial spines 6–9, unequal, to 3cm. Fl. funnelform, 10–12cm; inner tep. white, tinged pink. C Mex. Z9.

S. *stellatus* (Pfeiff.) Riccob. Usually shrubby, branching from base; st. to 4m×6–9cm, dull green; ribs 8–12, obtuse, notched; central spines u to 2.5cm, slender, dark brown-black at first, fading to grey; radial spines c8–13, to 12mm, spreading star-like. Fl. tubular-campanulate, 5–6×3–4cm; tep. clear pink. S Mex. Z9.

S. *thurberi* (Engelm.) F. Buxb. Massive shrub, branching near base; st. numerous, erect, cylindric, to 3–7m×10–15(–20)cm; ribs 12–19; areoles with gland. hairs; spines 11–19, 1.2–2.5(–5)cm, almost black or brown. Fl nocturnal, funnelform, 6–7.5×c5cm; inner tep. clear purple-pink or pink. SW US & NW Mex. Z9.

S. *treleasei* (Britt. & Rose) Backeb. Resembling S. *stellatus*, but few-branched, mainly from the base; ribs more numerous, c20. S Mex. Z9.

→*Cereus*, *Lemaireocereus* and *Machaerocereus*.

Stenochlaena J. Sm. Blechnaceae. Some 5 large, usually epiphytic, climbing ferns. Rhiz. woody, scandent, chaffy. Fronds dimorphic: sterile fronds pinnate, lat. pinnae usually articulate to the rachis, with basal glands, firm, glab., usually cartilaginous-serrate; fertile fronds pinnate or bipinnate, pinnae linear, entire. Trop. Afr., Asia and Australasia. Z10.

S. *heteromorpha* J. Sm. = *Blechnum filiforme*.

S. *palustris* (Burm.) Bedd. CLIMBING FERN. Fronds 90×30cm, always 1× pinnate, glossy, sterile pinnae 10–20×2–6cm, ± sessile fertile pinnae to 15×30×0.3–0.4cm, lower pinnae distant. India, S China, Australasia.

S. *scandens* J. Sm. = S. *palustris*.

S. *sorbifolia* (L.) J. Sm. Rhiz. occas. spiny. Fronds 30–45×15–30cm, always 1× pinnate, sterile pinnae 3–20 pairs, 12–15×1.5cm, entire or dentate, fertile pinnae 5–10×1.5cm, 2.5–5cm apart. Trop. Amer.

S. *tenuifolia* (Desv.) Moore. Sterile fronds 90×150×30–45cm, pinnae 15–23×2–4cm, short-stalked; fertile fronds bipinnate, glossy, with numerous distant pinnules. Trop. Afr.

→*Acrostichum*.

Stenocoryne Lindl.
S. *wageneri* (Rchb. f.) Kränzl. = *Teuscheria wageneri*.

Stenodraba O. Schulz. Cruciferae. 6 dwarf, perenn. herbs. Lvs obovate to narrow-spathulate, leathery or fleshy. Infl. a rac.; fls v. small; pet. 4, white, narrow-obovate; sta. 6, free, fil. thin. Fr. a silique, slightly compressed. S Andes. Z8.

S. *colchaguensis* (Barnéoud) O. Schulz. St. to 9cm, tufted, cushion-forming. Lvs rosulate, to 2cm, grey-green obovate to oblong-elliptic, apex toothed (st. lvs narrower, entire). Rac. compact; pet. often spotted blue, 3mm. Chile.

→*Draba*.

Stenoglottis Lindl. Orchidaceae. 4 fleshy-rooted, usually terrestrial orchids. Lvs in a basal rosette. Rac. erect, term., dense, slender, scape with scattered bract-like lvs. Sep. free or shortly joined to base of column; pet. lying forwards over column; lip longer than, 3- or 5-lobed, sometimes spurred. Trop. & S Afr. Z9.

S. *fimbriata* Lindl. 10–40cm. Lvs 2.5–5×0.5–1.5cm, lanceolate or oblong, undulate, spotted dark purple-brown. Fls rose-lilac with purple spots on lip and sometimes also on sep. and pet; pet. 3–6×2–4mm, oblong-obovate, sometimes fimbriate; lip 6–15mm, trilobed at about half-way, midlobe longer and narrower than lat. lobes, all lobes acute; spur 0. S Afr., Swaz.

S. *longifolia* Hook. f. 30–100cm. Lvs 9–24×1–4cm, lanceolate or oblong, slightly undulate. Fls pale rose-lilac heavily spotted purple, pet. 4–6mm, ovate, acute; lip 12–16mm, 5-lobed in

apical third, all lobes acute, midlobe longer than lat. lobes; spur 0. S Afr. (Natal and Transvaal).

S. *woodii* Schltr. 10–20cm. Lvs 5–15×1–3cm, lanceolate-elliptic or ovate-lanceolate, often glaucous green. Fls white, pale pink or rose-crimson, lip usually with some purple spots; sep. 4–6mm, ovate, obtuse; pet. 3–5mm, ovate; lip 10–14mm, triblobed in apical half, mid-lobe narrow, acute, lat. lobes much wider and truncate; spur 1.5–3mm. S Afr., Zimb.

S. *zambesiaca* Rolfe. 10–35cm. Lvs 4–12×1–2cm, ligulate-lanceolate or oblanceolate, undulate, sometimes spotted dark brown. Fls pink or lilac, lip with purple spots or streaks; pet. 5–6×3–4mm; lip 5–12mm, triblobed in apical third, lat. lobes with truncate apex, midlobe acute, narrower and longer than lat. lobes; spur 0. Tanz., Malawi, Zimb., Moz., S Afr.

Stenolema Fée = *Odontosoria*.

Stenolobium D. Don.
S. *alatum* (DC.) Sprague = *Tecoma* × *smithii*.
S. *ariquipense* Sprague = *Tecoma arequipensis*.
S. *castaneifolium* D. Don = *Tecoma castaneifolia*.
S. *incisum* Rose & Standl. = *Tecoma stans*.
S. *molle* (HBK) Seem. = *Tecoma stans* var. *velutina*.
S. *quinquejugum* Loes. = *Tecoma stans*.
S. *stans* var. *apiifolium* (DC.) Seem. = *Tecoma stans*.
S. *stans* var. *pinnatum* Seem. = *Tecoma stans*.
S. *stans* (L.) Seem. = *Tecoma stans*.
S. *tronadora* Loes. = *Tecoma stans*.

Stenoloma Farw.
S. *chinense* (L.) Bedd. = *Sphenomeris chinensis*.
S. *clavata* (L.) Fée = *Sphenomeris clavata*.

Stenomesson Herb. Amaryllidaceae. 20 bulbous herbs. Lvs radical, linear to lanceolate, occas. channelled or keeled. Umbels scapose; perianth tubular, often contracted or suddenly dilating from middle; tep. 6, ovate, hooded; cup-like corona formed from united fil. bases present and toothed in some sp.; sta. 6, included or exserted. High Andes. Z9.

S. *aurantiacum* (HBK) Herb. Lvs after fls, lanceolate, to 33cm. Scape to 30cm; fls 2–5, pendulous, funnel-shaped, scarlet or cinnabar; floral tube to 9mm; tep. narrowly elliptic, to 1.25cm, joined for 1cm, apex acute or obtuse; fil. joined forming staminal cup, coronal teeth 0. N Peru to N Ecuad.

S. *coccineum* (Ruiz & Pav.) Herb. Lvs after fls, to 30cm, thick. Scape to 30cm; fls 4–8, crimson; floral tube to 4cm; tep. to 4cm, joined to 2.3cm, abruptly dilated, free portion 1.5×0.7cm, lanceolate, acute. Spring–summer. Peru.

S. *croceum* Herb. Lvs solitary, linear-lanceolate or ovate-lanceolate. Scape 30cm; fls 4, suberect, 3.5cm long, golden-yellow, tube curved, seg. connivent. Spring–summer. Peru.

S. *curvidentatum* (Lindl.) Herb. Lvs oblanceolate, to 30cm; sub-sessile. Scape to 30cm; fls 4–6, 3.5–5cm, tube abruptly dilated from midpoint, bright yellow; sta. united to form staminal cup. Spring–summer.

S. *flavum* (Ruiz & Pav.) Herb. Like S. *curvidentatum* but lacking corona. Spring–summer. Peru, Arg.

S. *fulvum* (Herb.) Ravenna. = S. *variegatum*.
S. *hartwegii* Lindl. = S. *aurantiacum*.

S. *humile* (Herb.) Bak. Lvs lanceolate, 30cm. Fl. 1, to 8cm, scarlet; floral tube abruptly dilated from midpoint; tep. slightly spreading. Spring. Peru, Boliv., Arg.

S. *incarnatum* (HBK) Bak. = S. *variegatum*.
S. *incarnatum* var. *acutum* (Herb.) Bak. = S. *variegatum*.
S. *latifolium* Herb. = S. *flavum*.
S. *luteoviride* Bak. = S. *variegatum*.

S. *luteum* (Herb.) Bak. Lvs linear, to 21cm. Scape equals lvs; fls 2, to 5cm, ascending, yellow; fil. winged at base, without coronal teeth. Peru.

S. *miniatum* (Herb.) Ravenna. Lvs ligulate, to 40cm, after fls. Scape to 30cm; fls cinnabar-red; floral tube to 1.3cm, cylindrical, then urceolate above for 2cm; tep. to 1cm, recurved. Spring–summer. Peru, Boliv.

S. *pauciflorum* var. *curvidentatum* (Herb.) Macbr. = S. *curvidentatum*.

S. *pearcei* Bak. Lvs lorate-lanceolate, 45cm; petiole to 7.5cm. Scape to 90cm; fls 6–8, pendent, funnel-shaped, tube green-yellow, seg. primrose-yellow, tinged green externally, oblong, erecto-patent. Spring–summer. Boliv.

S. *recurvatum* Bak. Lvs linear, 30cm. Scape 30–45cm; fls 6–12 to 6.5cm, red-yellow, seg. short. S Amer.

S. *suspensum* Bak. = S. *aurantiacum*.

S. *variegatum* (Ruiz & Pav.) Macbr. Lvs ligulate, to 75cm. Scape to 66cm, spathes yellow-green edged white; fls 6–8, tawny banded red, pink, scarlet or crimson banded darker pink, or green on tep., or green and yellow; floral tube to 7cm; tep.

ovate, unequal, 2.4×1.1 or 3×1.4cm; sta. white, united into cup, alternating with green teeth. Spring.

S. viridiflorum (Ruiz & Pav.) Benth. Lvs sword-shaped, to 2cm across. Scape to 180cm; fls 1, pale green; floral tube cylindrical, slightly widened at apex. Spring–summer.
→*Coburgia, Pancratium* and *Urceolina.*

Stenorrhynchos Rich. ex Spreng. Orchidaceae. 50 terrestrial orchids. Rhiz. short. Pbs 0. Lvs basal, membranaceous, often in a low rosette, conduplicate. Rac. term., erect, with large bracts; sep. free, dors. sep. erect forming hood with pet., lat. sep. erect or spreading, concave at base; pet. narrower; lip basally saccate, entire to trilobed, disc often pubesc. C & S Amer. Z10.
S. lanceolatus (Aubl.) Rich. Lvs to 40×5cm, oblong-lanceolate to elliptic-oblong, petiolate. Infl. to 23cm; peduncle light green, finely white-pubesc.; fls showy, suberect, white or green-white to orange-red or crimson; sep. to 3×0.7cm, narrowly to broadly lanceolate, exterior glandular-pilose; lip to 2.5×1cm, simple to obscurely 3-lobed, obovate-lanceolate to rhombic-lanceolate, acuminate or acute. Trop. Amer.
S. speciosus (Gmel.) Rich. Lvs to 25×6cm, ovate-orbicular to elliptic-oblong or oblanceolate, sessile or petiolate, dark green often spotted or lined silver. Infl. held clear or lvs; peduncle coral pink to bright red; fls bright orange-red to fleshy pink; sep. to 2×0.6cm, lanceolate or elliptic-lanceolate; lip to 2×1cm, obscurely 3-lobed, triangular-lanceolate or rhombic-lanceolate, acute to apiculate. Mex. to N S Amer., W Indies.
→*Spiranthes.*

Stenospermation Schott. Araceae. 20 everg. somewhat shrubby epiphytic perennials. St. erect, 2m, densely leafy, with adventitious roots. Lvs simple, in two ranks, oblong-elliptic or lanceolate, to 30cm, coriaceous; petiole geniculate. Spathe cymbiform, soon decid., facing outwards from peduncle; spadix stipitate, shorter than spathe. Trop. S Amer. Z10.
S. multiovulatum N.E. Br. St. to 2m. Lvs to 30cm, oblong to narrow-elliptic-oblong; petiole to 25cm. Peduncle to 45cm; spathe broad-elliptic, 12.5–15cm, white. Guat. to Colomb.
S. popayanense Schott. St. to 1m. Lvs to 30cm, oblong-elliptic to oblong-lanceolate; petiole to 18cm. Peduncle to 30cm; spathe 8–12cm, white. Colomb., Ecuad.
S. spruceanum var. *multiovulatum* Engl. = *S. multiovulatum.*
S. wallisii Mast. = *S. popayanense.*

Stenotaphrum Trin. Gramineae. 7 ann. or perenn. grasses. St. creeping or ascending, rooting at nodes. Lvs linear or lanceolate, flat or folded, basally sheathing, blades perpendicular to st. Rac. short term. and axillary, embedded in swollen infl. axis; spikelets subsessile, 2-fld. New & OW Trop. Z9.
S. americanum Schrank = *S. secundatum.*
S. secundatum (Walter) Kuntze. ST AUGUSTINE GRASS; BUFFALO GRASS. Perenn., to 30cm. St. slender, creeping. Lvs in term. fans linear-oblong, flat to folded, to 15×1.5cm, glab.; sheaths overlapping, flattened. Summer–autumn. Trop. Amer., W Afr., Pacific Is. 'Variegatum' lvs longitudinally striped pale green and ivory.

Stenotus Nutt. Compositae. 18 low, caespitose everg. subshrubs. St. numerous, crowded, scapose or leafy. Lvs entire, ± leathery, mostly basal. Cap. radiate, solitary, term.; involucre campanulate or hemispheric; flts yellow; disc flts deeply 5-toothed. W N Amer.
S. acaulis Nutt. Perenn., to 15cm, forming mats to 30cm diam. Lvs to 5cm, oblanceolate, base attenuate, acute to acuminate, mucronate, mostly glab. Cap. to 3.5cm diam.; involucre hemispheric or somewhat campanulate; ray flts to 12mm, c6–15. Mts of W US. Z3.
S. andersonii Rydb. Like *S. lanuginosus* but lvs usually green, ± glab., lower lvs linear-spathulate. Summer. Mont. and Idaho. Z3.
S. armerioides Nutt. Perenn., to 20cm, glab. Lvs to 7cm, linear or narrowly spathulate, acute. Cap. 2–3cm diam.; involucre campanulate; ray flts to 12mm, 8–10. Summer. Rocky Mts of S Mont. to New Mex. and Ariz. Z5.
S. lanuginosus (A. Gray) Greene. WOOLLY STENOTUS. Perenn., to 20cm. Lvs floccose to tomentose, in dense tufts, to 10cm, narrowly oblanceolate to linear. Cap. to 3.5cm diam.; involucre hemispheric; ray flts to 10mm, 10–20. Late spring–summer. NW US. Z5.
S. pygmaeus Torr. & A. Gray = *Tonestus pygmaeus.*
→*Haplopappus.*

Stephanacoma Less.
S. barbata Less. = *Berkheya barbata.*
S. carduoides Less. = *Berkheya carduoides.*

Stephanandra Sieb. & Zucc. Rosaceae. 4 graceful decid. shrubs. Lvs alt., serrate to incised, often shallow-lobed, veins impressed above; stipules leafy, persistent. Fls small in term. rac. or corymbose pan.; cal. persistent, cup-shaped, lobes 5, triangular-ovate; pet. 5, spathulate; sta. 10–20. E Asia, Taiwan.
S. chinensis Hance. Branchlets flexuous, glab., pale brown. Lvs ovate-lanceolate, narrowly acuminate, biserrate, bright green, sparsely pilose. Fls to 4mm diam., white in crowded rac. China. Z7.
S. flexuosa Sieb. & Zucc. = *S. incisa.*
S. incisa (Thunb.) Zab. Much-branched shrub to 2.5m. Branchlets slender, flexuous, terete, pubesc. then glossy brown. Lvs to 5×3cm, ovate or triangular-ovate, caudate-acute, cordate at base, lobes incised or serrate, pilose to glabrescent, pale green below; petioles to 0.8cm. Fls 4mm diam., cream-white or yellow, in short, term. rac. Spring–summer. Jap., Korea, Taiwan. 'Crispa' ('Prostrata'): dwarf, mound-forming; br. arching; lvs small, crinkled, fern-like, tinted maroon in autumn. Z5.
S. tanakae (Franch. & Savat.) Franch. & Savat. Shrub to 2m. Shoots slender, arching, smooth; branchlets terete or angled. Lvs to 9×6cm, ovate, shallowly 3- to several-lobed, caudate-acuminate, subcordate at base, orange and scarlet or bright yellow in autumn, scabrous, biserrate, glab. above, somewhat pubesc. on veins beneath or subglabrous; petioles to 1.5cm. Fls off-white, 5mm diam., in glab., term. pan. to 10cm. Spring–summer. Jap. Z6.
→*Neillia* and *Spiraea.*

Stephanocereus A. Berger. Cactaceae. 2 cacti; st. cylindric or ovoid, ribbed, low. Flowering areoles with dense bristles; fls 1 to several, tubular; pericarpel and tube red-brown to green; scales few, minute; floral areoles naked; tep. short, spreading, white. E Braz.
S. leucostele (Gürke) A. Berger. Simple, or tree-like with 1–6 br., 2–6m; st. cylindric, to 7.5cm diam., ultimately jointed, seg. interrupted by rings of wool and long bristles from whch fls emerg; ribs 12–18; areoles with long white hairs; spines 25–30, to c2cm, white. Fl. to 10×5.3cm. Summer. E Braz. Z9.
S. luetzelburgii (Vaup.) N.P. Taylor & Eggli. Differs from *S. leucostele* in st. unbranched; fls emerging from slender, neck-like apical portion of st.
→*Cephalocereus* and *Cereus.*

Stephanotis Thouars. Asclepiadaceae. 5 twining, glab., everg. shrubs. Lvs opposite, coriaceous. Fls in short-stalked umbel-like axill. cymes; cal. 5-parted; cor. salver- to funnelform, tube cylindrical, often slightly inflated at base, throat dilated, lobes 5, spreading. OW Trop. Z10.
S. floribunda (R. Br.) Brongn. MADAGASCAR JASMINE; BRIDAL WREATH; CHAPLET FLOWER; WAXFLOWER; FLORADORA. To 4m. Lvs to 15cm, oval to oblong-elliptic, thickly coriaceous, dull sage to dark green. Fls highly fragrant; cor. to 6cm, waxy, pure white to ivory, lobes ovate-oblong. Madag.
S. jasminoides hort. = *S. floribunda.*

Stepladder Plant *Costus malortieanus.*
Stepmother's Flower *Viola* × *wittrockiana.*
Steppe Cherry *Prunus fruticosa.*

Sterculia L. Sterculiaceae. c200 decid. or everg. trees, sometimes unbranched pachycauls. Lvs unlobed or palmately lobed. Fls in axill. rac. or pan.; cal. 5-lobed,often campanulate; cor. 0; ♂ fls with 5–20 anth., on a slender androgynophore terminated by vestigial carpels; ♀ and ♂ fls with 3–6 free or slightly coherent carpels. Fr. 5 or fewer follicles, free, woody or leathery. Old and New World tropics and subtrop., esp. Asia. Z10.
S. acerifolia Cunn. ex G. Don = *Brachychiton acerifolius.*
S. alata Roxb. = *Pterygota alata.*
S. apetala (Jacq.) Karst. PANAMA TREE; BELLOTA. Decid. tree, to 40m; crown umbrella-like. Lvs to 20–30cm, cordate in outline, deeply 5-lobed, woolly then ± glab. above; petioles long. Fls in clusters near br. ends; cal. 2.5cm, yellow inside, spotted pink or purple. Follicles 5, to 10cm, tomentose, dark brown. Trop. Amer.
S. austro-caledonica Hook. f. = *Acropogon austro-caledonicus.*
S. balanghas L. Lvs 8–18cm, ovate to elliptic, caudate, base rounded to subcordate, subcoriaceous, bright green, glab.; petiole 1–2cm. Fls in pan. to 12cm; cal. pale blue inside, densely stellate-pubesc., tube 1–2×2–3mm, obconical; lobes 5–7mm, lanceolate. Burm., Malay Penins. and adjacent islands.
S. barteri Mast. = *Hildegardia barteri.*
S. bidwillii (Hook.) Hook. = *Brachychiton bidwillii.*
S. carthaginensis Cav. = *S. apetala.*
S. colorata Roxb. = *Firmiana colorata.*

S. discolor (F. Muell.) Benth. = *Brachychiton discolor*.

S. diversifolia G. Don = *Brachychiton populneus*.

S. foetida L. INDIAN ALMOND; JAVA OLIVES. Tree to 30m, bark grey or brown. Lvs 10–30cm, compound-digitate, lfts 5–15, lanceolate to ovate-lanceolate, glabrescent; petiole 10–30cm. Fls malodorous, 1.2×2.5cm, in pan. to 30cm, orange-red to scarlet, lobes linear, woolly inside. Follicles 2–5, to 10cm, in star-like clusters, ovoid, dark-red. OW Trop.

S. lanceolata Cav. Small tree to 6m. Lvs 8–15cm, ovate or obovate, entire, shortly actue, veins prominent, glab. Fls in axill. pan. 2.5–5cm long; cal. 1.2cm diam., red, deeply lobed, spreading. China.

S. macrophylla Vent. Decid. tree to 45m; bark smooth, grey-white to grey-brown. Lvs 10–30cm, leathery, broadly ovate-orbicular to obovate-orbicular, entire, obtuse to acute, base deeply cordate, glab. above, softly pubesc. beneath; petiole 3–10cm; lvs on young trees to 75×100cm, with petioles to 80cm. Flowrs in pan. to 30cm; cal. 5–6mm, cup-shaped, yellow, stellate-pubesc., with sugar-secreting hairs inside, lobes short. Follicles 3–5, 3–5.5cm, woody, ripening bright red. Trop. Asia.

S. monosperma Vent. Tree to 30m; twigs thick, glab. Lvs 8–30cm, broadly oblong to ovate, shortly acuminate, base rounded, coriaceous; petiole 2–6cm. Fls in drooping pan. 15–40cm; cal. green-white or pale yellow-red, thinly pubesc. outside, tube campanulate. Follicles 1–5, 4–10cm. China.

S. nobilis Sm. = *S. monosperma*.

S. platanifolia L. f. = *Firmiana simplex*.

S. rubiginosa Vent. Tall shrub or small tree to 6m; twigs brown stellate-pubesc. Lvs 8–30cm, narrowly rounded or cordate to obovate-lanceolate, acute to acuminate, base narrowed, rounded to cordate, brown-stellate-pubesc. beneath; petiole 1–4cm. Fls in term. or subterminal pan. to 10cm; cal. 2cm, tube minutely pubesc. inside, lobes pilose. Follicles 3–5 to 10cm. India to Java.

S. rupestris (Mitch. ex Lindl.) Benth. = *Brachychiton rupestris*.

S. tragacantha Lindl. Tree to 25m, sometimes buttressed bark grey, corky. Lvs 10–20 elliptic, oblong-elliptic or obovate, short acuminate, rounded or slightly cordate at the base, stellate-tomentose beneath; petiole 2–7cm. Fls in axill. congested pan.; cal. 7mm, green with red momentum, lobes cohering at tips. Follicles 6cm, bright red turning brown, bristly tomentose inside. Trop. W Afr., Congo Basin.

S. trichosiphon Benth. = *Brachychiton australis*.

S. urens Roxb. Tree; outer bark white. Lvs 12–30cm, orbicular, base cordate, palmately and shallowly 5-lobed, lobes entire, acuminate, velvety beneath; petiole 12–22cm. Fls in dense term. glandular-pubesc. pan. to 20cm; cal. 6mm, yellow, campanulate, lobes acute, spreading. Follicles 4–5, to 8cm, oblong, red, with stinging hairs. India.

S. villosa Roxb. Decid. tree, to 18m; bark white. Lvs 20–45cm, deeply palmately 5–7-lobed, base cordate, lobes sometimes 3-fld, acuminate, glabrescent or thinly stellate-pilose above; petiole to 40cm. Fls in rusty-pubesc. pan. to 35cm; cal. 1.2cm, yellow, broadly campanulate, stellate-pubesc. outside, lobes spreading. Follicles 4–5, oblong, spreading, rusty-villous. India, Burm.

STERCULIACEAE Bartal. 72/1500. *Acropogon, Brachychiton, Cola, Corchoropsis, Dombeya, Firmiana, Fremontodendron, Guichenotia, Helicteres, Heritiera, Hermannia, Hildegardia, Kleinhovia, Pterospermum, Pterygota, Reevesia, Sterculia, Theobroma, Triplochiton, Trochetia, Waltheria.*

Stereospermum Cham. Bignoniaceae. 15 decid. trees. Bark grey, flaking. Lvs simple or pinnate. Fls in term. thyrses, sometimes fragrant; cal. campanulate, lobes short, cor. funnelform, bilabiate, upper lip 2-lobed, lower lip 3-lobed, lobes rounded, crisped or dentate; sta. 4, included. Trop. Afr., Madag., S & SE Asia, Malaya, to E Java. Z10.

S. banaibanai Rolfe = *Radermachera pinnata*.

S. caudatum Miq. = *S. personatum*.

S. chelonoides (L. f.) A. DC. To 30m. Lvs to 50cm, pinnae to 23cm, 3–4 pairs, sticky-haired then glab., scabrid above, ovate to oblong, entire to denticulate. Thyrses to 25cm across, glandular-hairy, fls fragrant; cor. deep red to purple, lined yellow inside, to 3cm, sticky-hairy, funnelform, mouth long-pubesc., lobes equalling tube, abundant. Summer–autumn. SE Asia.

S. chelonoides sensu (Roxb.) DC. = *S. personatum*.

S. fimbriatum (Wallich ex G. Don) A. DC. To 30m. Lvs to 75cm, sticky pubesc., purple when young; pinnae to 16cm, 2–4 pairs, ovate-oblong, long-acuminate. Fls in sticky-pilose clusters to 30cm across; cor. white to pink or pale purple, narrow-funnelform, tube to 5cm, lobes 2cm, long-fimbriate. Spring–summer. Mainland SE Asia, Malay Penins. and Sumatra.

S. glandulosum Miq. = *Radermachera glandulosa*.

S. hypostictum Miq. = *Radermachera gigantea*.

S. kunthianum Cham. PINK JACARANDA. To 13m. Pinnae 8cm, 5, oblong, softish-pubesc., entire, rarely toothed; petiole to 7cm. Fls precocious, fragrant; cor. pale pink streaked red, campanulate tube to 4cm diam. Summer–autumn. Trop. Afr.

S. personatum (Hassk.) Chatterj. To 30m. Lvs to 50cm, glab., pinnae 5–15cm, 3–6 pairs, elliptic-oblong. Thyrses to 40cm; cor. 3×1.75cm, dirty yellow outside, striped cream and red inside; tube 0.5cm, campanulate above but mouth closed, lobes crisped, mustard yellow with purple lines inside, pink to purple outside. Spring–summer. Sri Lanka through SE Asia, to Yunnan and Indochina, Malaya and Sumatra.

S. pinnatum Fernandez-Villar = *Radermachera pinnata*.

S. seemannii Rolfe = *Radermachera pinnata*.

S. suaveolens A. DC. = *S. chelonoides*.

S. tetragonum A. DC. = *S. personatum*.

S. xylocarpum Benth. & Hook. f. = *Radermachera xylocarpa*.

→*Dipterosperma, Hieranthes* and *Tecoma*.

Sternbergia Waldst. & Kit. AUTUMN DAFFODIL. Amaryllidaceae. 8 bulbous perenn. herbs. Lvs basal, linear or lorate to narrowly lanceolate. Scapes 1-to several, elongating in fr.; spathe membranous; fls solitary; perianth lobes 6, in 2 whorls, oblanceolate to obovate, basally united into a narrow cylindrical tube, equal; sta. 6 in 2 unequal whorls. Turk., W to Spain and E to Kashmir.

S. candida B. Mathew & Baytop. Like *S. fischeriana*, but scape 12–20cm; perianth lobes 4.3–5×0.9–1.8cm, obovate, apex rounded, white. Winter–spring. SW Turk. Z7.

S. clusiana (Ker-Gawl.) Spreng. Lvs 5–12, appearing long after fls, 8–16mm, wide, lorate, obtuse, flat, often twisted, glaucescent. Scape below ground at flowering; perianth lobes 3.7–7.5×1.1–3.3cm, obovate to oblanceolate, bright yellow-green. Autumn. Turk., Jord., Isr., Iran. Z6.

S. colchiflora Waldst. & Kit. Lvs 4–6, narrow-linear, erect, twisted, keeled, obtusely callous, 10cm, borne after fls. Scape below ground at flowering; perianth lobes 2–3.4×0.4–1.2cm, linear, pale yellow. Autumn. SE Spain, It., W to Iran. Z5.

S. fischeriana (Herb.) Rupr. Lvs 4–7, appearing before fls, 15×1.2cm wide, lorate, flat, scarcely keeled, dark grey-green. Scape 3–15cm; perianth lobes 2–3.5×0.5–0.8cm, oblanceolate, bright yellow. Spring. Cauc. to Kashmir. Z6.

S. lutea (L.) Spreng. Lvs to 30×1.2mm, 4–6, borne with or just after fls, narrowly lanceolate, slightly channelled above, keeled beneath, bright lustrous green. Scape 2.5–20cm, spathe 3–6cm; perianth lobes 3–5.5×1–2cm, oblanceolate to obovate, deep yellow. Autumn. Spain to Iran and C Asia. 'Angustifolia': lvs narrow; fls bright yellow. Z7.

S. lutea ssp. *sicula* (Tineo) Webb = *S. sicula*.

S. lutea var. *angustifolia* hort. = *S. sicula*.

S. lutea var. *graeca* Rchb. = *S. sicula*.

S. macrantha M. = *S. clusiana*.

S. sicula Guss. Similar to *S. lutea*. Lvs 6–12mm wide, appearing before fls, lorate, flat or scarcely keeled, dark grey-green. Scape to 7cm; perianth lobes 2–3.4×0.4–1.2cm, yellow. Autumn. It., Greece, Aegean Is., W Turk. 'Dodona': lvs prostrate, narrow; fls funnel-shaped, upright, vivid yellow. Z7.

Stetsonia Britt. & Rose. Cactaceae. 1 tree-like cactus, 5–10m; trunk short, thick; br. numerous, erect or ascending, cylindric, 10–15cm diam., blue-green; ribs 8–9; spines 7–9, unequal, to 5cm, subulate. Fls funnelform, 12–15×8–10cm, nocturnal; tube elongate; perianth limb broad, spreading to rotate; inner tep. white; sta. numerous. NW Arg., S Boliv. Z9.

S. coryne (Salm-Dyck) Britt. & Rose.

Stevensonia J. Duncan ex Balf. f. = *Phoenicophorium*.

Stevia Cav. Compositae. c150 ann. to perenn. herbs and shrubs. Cap. small, discoid, in pan. or corymbs; involucre cylindric; disc flts few, tubular. Trop. and warm Amer. Z9.

S. eupatoria Willd. Perenn. herb to 50cm, velvety-hairy. Lvs alt., to 4cm, lanceolate to obovate, channelled, base attenuate, apex dentate. Cap. in fastigiate corymbs; flts white to purple. Summer. Mex.

S. ivifolia Willd. = *S. serrata*.

S. ovata Willd. Perenn. herb to 60cm. Lvs oblong to ovate, base cuneate, dentate to subentire. Cap. in compact fastigiate corymbs; flts white. Summer. Mex.

S. plummerae A. Gray. Perenn. herb, to 50cm. Lvs generally few, mostly opposite, to 9cm, elliptic to narrowly oblong, dentate. Cap. in corymbs; flts fragrant, white to pink.

S. purpurea Pers. = *S. eupatoria*.

S. rebaudiana Bertoni. Ann. herb, to 50cm, puberulous. Lvs opposite, oblanceolate, dentate to crenulate. Cap. v. small, in corymbs; flts white. Parag.

S. salicifolia Cav. Shrub to 70cm, glab. Lvs opposite, linear-lanceolate, almost connate, at base. Cap. in spreading corymbs; flts white. Summer–autumn. Mex.

S. serrata Cav. Perenn. herb, to 1m. Lvs alt., to 5cm, lancolate, deeply and sharply toothed, base entire. Cap. in fastigiate corymbs; flts white or pink. Summer. S US to C Amer. The name *S. serrata* is often to misapplied *Piqueria trinervia*.

S. serrata hort. non Cav. = *Piqueria trinervia*.

✕ Stewartara. (*Ada* ✕ *Cochlioda* ✕ *Odontoglossum*.) Orchidaceae.

Gdn. hybrids with long elegant sprays of small slender fls in shades of ginger-brown and orange; tep. slender, tip large.

Stewartia L. Theaceae. 9 decid. trees and shrubs. Bark often red, exfoliating. Lvs simple, toothed; petioles short. Fls usually solitary, rarely 2–3, in lf axils on current season's growth; sep. 5(–6); pet. 5(–8), spreading, white or cream, sometimes flushed, exterior silky; sta. numerous. E N Amer., E Asia.

S. koreana Rehd. = *S. pteropetiolata* var. *koreana*.

S. malacodendron L. SILKY CAMELLIA. Shrub or small tree to 5m. Shoots downy. Lvs 5–10cm, ovate to elliptic, finely toothed, downy beneath. Fls to 10cm diam.; pet. white, obovate, fringed, silky beneath; fil. purple, anth. blue-grey. Summer. SE US. Z7.

S. monadelpha Sieb. & Zucc. Tree to 25m. Young shoots downy. Lvs 4–8cm, ovate-lanceolate, finely toothed, densely silky-pubesc. along veins beneath, carmine in autumn. Fls 2.5–4cm diam.; pet. white, spreading; sta. united at base, fil. white, anth. violet. Jap., Korea. Z6.

S. ovata (Cav.) Weatherby. MOUNTAIN CAMELLIA. Shrub to 5m. Shoots glab. Lvs 7–13cm, oval to ovate, acute, rounded at base, sparsely toothed to almost entire, downy beneath. Fls 6–8cm across, cup-shaped; pet. 5–6, creamy white, wavy-edged, one often deformed; fil. yellow-white; anth. white, orange or tinted purple. SE US. var. **grandiflora** (Bean) Kobusi. Fls to 12cm diam.; fil. purple, anth. orange. Z5.

S. pentagyna L'Hérit. = *S. ovata*.

S. pseudocamellia Maxim. JAPANESE STEWARTIA. Tree to 20m, usually a shrub to 4m in cult. Shoots glab. Lvs 5–9cm, elliptic-lanceolate to obovate, cuneate at base, sparsely toothed, sometimes silky beneath, bright red in autumn. Fls 5–6cm diam., broadly cup-shaped; bracts small; pet. white, suborbicular, concave with jagged edges, silky beneath; fil. white, anth. orange-yellow. Jap. Z5.

S. pteropetiolata Cheng. Everg. shrub or tree to 6m or taller. Shoots sericeous. Lvs 7–12cm, elliptic to ovate, acute, base rounded, darkly glandular-toothed; petiole winged. Fls 2–3cm diam.; pet. white, rounded, margins jagged; fil. united at base, anth. yellow. S China. var. **koreana** (Rehd.) Sealy. Scaly. To 15m. Shoots somewhat flexuous. Lvs broader. Fls to 7cm diam., more spreading; pet. broadly ovate to rounded, somewhat undulate. Korea. Z5.

S. rostrata Spongb. Differs from *S. sinensis* in its shallowly furrowed bark and subglobose capsule, downy at base and abruptly beaked, with 4, not 2, seeds in each chamber. E China. Z7.

S. serrata Maxim. Large shrub or small tree to 10m. Shoots tinted red, slightly hairy when young. Lvs 5–8cm, elliptic to obovate, apex acute, base cuneate, serrate, downy on veins beneath. Fls 5–6cm diam., cup-shaped; pet. cream stained red beneath, margin jagged; fil. white, anth. yellow. S Jap. Z7.

S. sinensis Rehd. & Wils. Tree to 10m. Shoots initially downy. Lvs 5–10cm, ovate or ovate-oblong, apex acuminate, base cuneate to rounded, toothed, initially downy, ultimately glossy. Fls 4–5cm diam., cup-shaped, fragrant; pet. broadly ovate, white; fil. joined at base, downy, anth. yellow. China. Z6.

S. virginica Cav. = *S. malacodendron*.
→*Malachodendron* and *Stuartia*.

Sticherus Presl. Gleicheniaceae. 100 terrestrial ferns. Rhiz. stout, scaly or almost smooth. Fronds pinnate to bipinnate, with growth of term. node suppressed, giving fan-like pseudodichotomous branching. Trop. & S Temp. regions. Z10.

S. cunninghamii (Heward ex Hook.) Ching. UMBRELLA FERN. Stipes to 20cm, densely clad in large pale brown scales when young. Fronds repeatedly forked, spreading horizontally, superimposed, dark green and glab. above, glaucous and pubesc. beneath; pinnae 15–30cm, narrowly lanceolate; pinnules 1–2cm, linear. NZ.

S. flabellatus (R. Br.) St. John. FAN FERN. Stipes to 40cm, almost smooth. Fronds several, ascending, pinnate, repeatedly forked, sometimes 2–3 layers of fronds superimposed, dark shining green above, paler green beneath; pinnae 10–30cm, lanceolate, ascending; pinnules 3–5cm, linear, serrulate above. Australasia.

S. lobatus Wakef. SPREADING FAN FERN. Fronds 15–180cm, repeatedly dichotomous or trichotomous with each br. terminating in a pair of pinnae; pinnae 8–30cm, divided almost to midrib; pinnules 6–18mm, linear, entire. Summer. Aus.
→*Gleichenia*.

Stickseed *Hackelia*.
Stick-tight *Bidens*.
Sticky Boronia *Boronia anemonifolia*.
Sticky Nightshade *Solanum sisymbrifolium*.
Sticky Tail Flower *Anthocercis viscosa*.
Sticky Wattle *Acacia dodonifolia*.

Stictocardia Hallier f. Convolvulaceae. 12 perenn., woody or herbaceous climbers. Lvs petiolate, usually ovate, base cordate, with tiny, black, gland. hairs beneath. Infl. axill.; sep. 5, orbicular to ovate, subequal, sometimes with black gland. hairs; cor. 4.5–10cm, funnel-shaped; stigma 2-lobed. Pantrop. Z9.

S. beraviensis (Vatke) Hallier f. Woody climber to 10m, young growth densely hairy. Lvs to 16–23cm; petioles to 17cm. Infl. many-fld; cor. 4.5–5cm, bright crimson, tube orange-yellow at base, midpetaline areas with tufts of hairs at apices. W Afr. to Ethiop. and Zimb., Madag.

S. campanulata (L.) Merrill. Woody climber to 12m. Lvs 8–25cm; petioles 3–14cm. Infl. 1–4-fld; cor. 5–8cm, funnel-shaped, crimson with orange or yellow stripes inside. Pantrop.

S. maculosoi (Mattei) Verdc. Woody climber to 8m, with ridged, yellow, hairy st. Lvs 6.5–11cm; petioles 2–8cm. Infl. 2- to several-fld; cor. 5.5–7cm, scarlet, tube paler, midpetaline areas hairy at apex. S Somalia.

S. tiliifolia (Desr.) Hallier f. = *S. campanulata*.
→*Argyreia*.

Stiff Beard-tongue *Penstemon strictus*.
Stiff Bottlebrush *Callistemon rigidus*.
Stiff Dogwood *Cornus stricta*.
Stiff-haired Saxifrage *Saxifraga aspera*.

Stifftia Mikan. Compositae. 7 trees, shrubs and vines. Lvs simple, entire, leathery. Cap. discoid, large and solitary or few together, or small in pan.; flts narrow, tubular. NE Braz. Z10.

S. chrysantha Mikan. Everg. shrub, to 3m. Lvs lanceolate, acuminate, rigid, petiole short. Cap. to 10×6cm, solitary on short br.; flts orange-yellow; styles conspicuous. Winter–spring. Braz.

Stigmaphyllon A. Juss. Malpighiaceae. 60–100 lianes. Lvs simple or lobed, entire or dentate; glands 2 usually on petioles. Racs short, dense, corymbiform axill. or terminal short; sep. 5, lat. 4 with 2 glands; pet. 5, clawed, unequal, yellow, lat. 4 concave, dentate or fimbriate; sta. 10. Trop. Americas, Carib. Z10.

S. aristatum Lindl. Lvs sagittate-hastate to oblong, acute, glab. Fls few in pedunculate umbels, pet. fimbriate. Summer. Braz.

S. ciliatum (Lam.) A. Juss. GOLDEN VINE. Lvs 4–9.5cm, broad-ovate, base deeply auriculate with rounded overlapping lobes, ciliate. Fls 3–8 pet. fimbriate. Belize to Urug.

S. diversifolium (Kunth) A. Juss. Lvs 2–8cm, suborbicular to ovate or elliptic to linear, base cuneate to rounded or cordate, apex acute to rounded, apiculate, coriaceous, tomentose beneath. Fls 6–20 per cluster; pet. dentate. Cuba, Lesser Antilles.

S. fulgens (Lam.) A. Juss. Lvs to 17cm, orbicular to ovate, base reniform or cordate, apex rounded, short acuminate or apiculate, coarsely crenate or subentire, glab. above, sericeous beneath. Fls 15–17mm diam.; pet. terracotta, spotted yellow at middle. N Braz. to Carib.

S. heterophyllum Hook. Lvs ovate, apex obtuse, mucronate, undulate, sometimes cordate or 3-lobed, lobes oblong. Fls in axill. umbels; pet. orbicular. Arg.

S. humboldtianum A. Juss. Lvs 5–11cm, ovate to suborbicular or cordate, apex acute or rounded, mucronate, base truncate, rounded or cordate, glabrate above, pubesc. beneath. C & S Amer.

S. jatrophifolium A. Juss. Lvs palmately 5–7-cleft, acute, serrate-ciliate, light green. Fls many in umbels; pet. fimbriate. Urug.

S. littorale A. Juss. Lvs 4–12.5cm, opposite or alt., variable in shape, long-petiolate. Fls many, to 2.5cm across, in axill. corymbs. S Braz.

Stingaree-bush *Pickeringia*.
Stinging Nettle *Urtica* (*U. dioica*).
Stink Bells *Fritillaria agrestis*.
Stink Currant *Ribes bracteosum*.
Stinking Ash *Ptelea trifoliata*.
Stinking Bean Trefoil *Anagyris foetida*.
Stinking Benjamin *Trillium*.

Stinking Cedar *Torreya taxifolia.*
Stinking Chamomile *Anthemis cotula.*
Stinking Elder *Sambucus pubens.*
Stinking Gladwyn *Iris foetidissima.*
Stinking Hellebore *Helleborus foetidus.*
Stinking Iris *Iris foetidissima.*
Stinking Madder *Putoria calabrica.*
Stinking Nightshade *Hyoscyamus niger.*
Stinking Weed *Senna occidentalis.*
Stink-net *Oncosiphon piluliferum.*
Stink Pod *Scoliopus bigelowii.*
Stinkweed *Thlaspi arvense.*
Stinkwood *Eucryphia moorei.*
Stinkwort *Helleborus foetidus.*

Stipa L. NEEDLE GRASS; SPEAR GRASS; FEATHER GRASS. Gramineae. *c*300 perenn., rarely ann. grasses. St. clumped. Lvs narrow, rough, convolute or plicate, occas. flat, veins prominent above. Infl. narrow-paniculate; spikelets stipitate, flattened, fls solitary, narrow-ellipsoid; callus bearded; glumes membranous; palea 2-ribbed; lemma membranous to leathery, shorter than glumes, awn usually bent. Temp., warm temp. regions.
S. arundinacea Hook. f. NEW ZEALAND WIND GRASS; PHEASANT'S TAIL GRASS. Perenn., to 1.5m. St. clumped, upright or arching. Lvs to 30×0.6cm, coriaceous, involute, dark green, becoming orange- or pale brown-striped, margin ciliate.Infl. pendent spikelets sparse, tinged purple; awn to 0.8cm. E Aus., NZ. 'Autumn Tints': lvs flushed red in late summer. 'Golf Hues': lvs flushed golden yellow in late summer. Z8.
S. barbata Desf. Perenn., to 70cm. Lvs convolute, sickle-shaped, glab. above, sparsely pubesc. beneath. Infl. narrow; glumes linear-lanceolate; awn to 1.9cm. S Eur. Z8.
S. calamagrostis (L.) Wahl. Perenn., to 120cm. St. clumped, robust. Lvs to 30×0.5cm, attenuate. Infl. to 80cm, lax, appearing secund; spikelets to 0.9cm, tinged purple. Summer. C & S Eur. Z7.
S. capillata L. To 80cm. St. upright, clumped. Lvs thread-like, convolute, blue-green, glaucous, scabrous. Infl. loose; awn to 2cm. Summer–autumn. S & C Eur., Asia. Z7.
S. elegantissima Labill. Perenn. to 1m, tussock-forming. Lvs to 3mm diam., acuminate, yellow-green, inrolled above base. Pan. initially ovoid, spreading with age, to 20cm; spikelets to 1.3cm, tinged purple; awn to 4.5cm, terminal, pilose. Temp. Aus.
S. gigantea Link. Perenn., to 250cm. St. clumped. Lvs to 70×0.3cm, involute when dry, smooth to slightly rough. Pan. open, to 50cm; spikelets yellow; awn to 12cm, rough. C & S Spain, Port., NW Afr. Z8.
S. lasiagrostis Nichols. = *S. calamagrostis.*
S. pennata L. EUROPEAN FEATHER GRASS. Perenn., to 60cm. Lvs to 60×0.6cm, smooth, glab. above. Infl. compact, to 10cm; spikelets yellow; awn to 2.8cm, plumose. Summer. S & C Eur. to Himal. Z7.
S. pulcherrima K. Koch. Perenn., tufted. St. to 1m, smooth, glab. Lf sheaths glab., smooth, to 4mm diam., flat, involute, smooth or scabrous. Awn to 5cm. C & S Eur.
S. pulchra Hitchc. PURPLE NEEDLEGRASS. St. to 1m. Lvs long, narrow, flat or involute. Pan. to 20cm, nodding, loose, with slender, spreading br.; glumes, tinged purple; awn to 9cm. W US.
S. spartea Trin. St. about 1m. Lvs to 30×5cm, flat, involute. Pan. to 20cm, narrow, nodding; br. slender, bearing 1 or 2 spikelets; awn to 2cm, stout. US.
S. splendens Trin. CHEE GRASS. Perenn., to 2.5m. St. stout, robust, clumped. Lvs scabrous. Infl. to 2m, pan. to 50cm, tinged purple to white; awn bent. Summer. C Asia, Sib. Z7.
S. tenacissima L. ESPARTO GRASS. Perenn., to 2m. St. v. stout. Lvs convolute, to 1mm diam., glab., smooth above, minutely pubesc. beneath. Infl. narrow, compact, to 35cm; awn to 4cm, plumose below bend. W Medit. Z8.
S. tenuissima Trin. St. to 70cm, slender, in large tufts. Lvs to 30cm or more, filiform, wiry, closely involute. Pan. to 30cm, narrow, soft, nodding; awn about 5cm. US (Tex. & New Mex.), Mex., Arg.
S. tirsa Steven. Perenn. St. v. stout. Lvs to 1m, convolute. Infl. compact; awn to 4cm. Summer. C, S, E Eur. Z7.
→*Lasiagrostis.*

Stipagrostis Nees Gramineae. *c*50 perenn. grasses. St. erect, sometimes clumped. Lvs narrow, elongated, flat or convolute, sometimes pungent; ligule ciliate. Infl. narrow-paniculate; spikelets solitary, laterally flattened; lemmas with 3 plumose, abscising awns. Middle East, C Asia, Pak.
S. pennata (Trin.) De Winter. Perenn. to 50cm. St. branched basally, glab., smooth. Lvs linear, convolute, to 0.2cm wide, scabrous, short-pubesc.; above, acuminate. Pan. v. loose, to 20cm; spikelets plumose, to 1.5cm; awn to 1.5cm. C, S & W

Asia, SE Russia. Z8.
→*Aristida.*

Stirlingia Endl. Proteaceae. 3 shrubs or undershrubs. Lvs coriaceous. Infl. a pan. or a globular head, long-pedunculate, axis pubesc.; fls subtended by a small bract; perianth recurved above middle, separating into seg. W Aus. Z10.
S. latifolia (R. Br.) Steud. BLUEBOY. Leafy, almost unbranched shrub to 1m. Lvs 15–30cm, 1–2× bifid or trifid, seg. flat, linear to oblong-lanceolate. Fls brown-yellow, in globose spikes or heads, many on leafless flowering st. to 150cmm high. Late winter–spring.
S. simplex Lindl. Soft-leaved, small shrub to 30cm. Lvs to 12cm, intensively and dichotomously dissected. Fls light yellow in dense fl. heads, solitary on peduncles to 30cm. Late winter–spring.
S. tenuifolia (R. Br.) Steud. Leafy, erect shrublet 20–70cm. Lvs and fls as for *S. simplex* except fl. heads in pan. Late winter–spring.

Stirling Range *Isopogon baxteri.*
Stitchwort *Stellaria* (*S. holostea*).

Stizolobium P. Browne.
S. alterrimum Piper & Tracy = *Mucuna pruriens* var. *utilis.*

Stizophyllum Miers. Bignoniaceae. 3 lianes. Lvs trifoliolate, pellucid punctate, glandular-scaly beneath, term. leaflet often replaced by a tendril. Fls in axillary rac.; cal. campanulate, inflated, bilabiate to regularly 5-lobed, pubesc.; cor. tubular-campanulate. Mex. to Braz. Z10.
S. perforatum Miers. Lfts to *c*20cm, ovate, apex subacuminate, tomentose beneath. Cal. margin lacerate; cor. white to cream marked pink 5cm, pubesc. Braz.

St. James Lily *Sprekelia formosissima.*
St John's Bread *Ceratonia.*
St. John's Lily *Crinum asiaticum* var. *sinicum.*
St. Lucie Cherry *Prunus mahaleb.*
St. Martin's Flower *Alstroemeria ligtu.*

Stobaea Thunb.
S. purpurea DC. = *Berkheya purpurea.*
S. radula Harv. = *Berkheya radula.*

Stock *Matthiola.*
Stokes' Aster *Stokesia.*

Stokesia L'Hérit. STOKES' ASTER. Compositae. 1 erect, perenn. herb to 1m. Lvs to 20cm, alt., elliptic to oblong-lanceolate, entire or spinose toward base. Cap. radiate, to 10cm diam., solitary and term. or few to many in a corymb; phyllaries with leafy appendages; flts white, yellow to pale lavender to deep indigo. SE US.
S. cyanea L'Hérit. = *S. laevis.*
S. laevis (Hill) Greene. Cvs include varieties with cap. of varying size and in colours ranging from white ('Alba', 'Silver Moon') and yellow to blue ('Blue Danube', deep blue fls; 'Wyoming', deep dark blue), lilac ('Blue Star', cap. large) and purple; some early-flowering.

Stomatium Schwantes. Aizoaceae. *c*30 highly succulent stemless plants, forming dense clumps. Lf pairs often of unequal length, decussate, thick, fleshy, shortly 3-angled or broadly spathulate or elongate-lanceolate, semi-cylindric at base, the lower surface keeled toward apex, margins with short and broad teeth. Fls sessile or short-stalked, nocturnal, fragrant. Summer. S Afr., Bots. Z10.
S. agninum (Haw.) Schwantes. Lvs 40–50×10–15mm, soft, oblong, somewhat obtuse, v. convex beneath and keeled-triquetrous, margins often with 3–5 short teeth, dull grey-green, rough with green papillae. Fls 2.5cm diam., light yellow. Cape Prov.
S. ermininum (Haw.) Schwantes. Lvs 16–20×8–12mm, obtuse, lower surface convex at base, keeled toward apex, light grey-green, with numerous prominent dots, margins with 3–4 short teeth above. Fls 2–2.5cm diam., yellow, scented. W Cape.
S. loganii L. Bol. Lvs 12–20×7–11×6mm, oblong, tip rounded, widest at middle, entire or with 2–3 bristle-tipped marginal teeth. Fls 1.6cm diam., yellow. W Cape.
S. meyeri L. Bol. Lvs 18–20×6mm, slightly expanded at tip, lower surface semi-cylindric, carinate toward tip, keel pulled forward, light grey-green with coarse rough dots, angles tuberculate at tip. Fls 2.4cm diam., interior white, pink exterior. W Cape.
S. murinum (Haw.) Schwantes. Lvs projecting and incurved, thickened toward tip, keel pulled forward, margins and keel

with 3 teeth, grey-green with white, transparent, prominent dots. Fls 2–2.5cm diam., yellow. W Cape.

S. musculinum (Haw.) Schwantes = *Chasmatophyllum musculinum*.

S. mustellinum (Salm-Dyck) Schwantes. Lvs rosulate, to 2×1cm, rhombic to broadly spathulate, obtuse, keeled towards tip with 5–7 small acute teeth on angles, light grey-green, rough with minute dots. Fls 2cm diam., yellow. OFS, Bots.

S. niveum L. Bol. Lvs 20×10×6mm, dissimilar, spathulate, with prominent white dots and 3 obscure marginal teeth. Fls 1.8cm diam., white, nocturnal. W Cape.

S. suaveolens Schwantes. Lvs 10–20×9–15mm, v. soft and fleshy, thickened and expanded above, v. rounded below and pulled forward over tip, margins entire or with 1–5 teeth, light grey-green to copper-coloured with light rough dots. Fls 2.5cm diam., yellow. SE Cape.

→*Agnirictus*.

Stone Cress *Aethionema*.
Stone Crop *Sedum acre*.
Stoneface *Lithops*.
Stone Mimicry Plant *Pleiospilos*.
Stone Mountain Oak *Quercus georgiana*.
Stone Pine *Pinus pinea*.
Stoneplant *Lithops; Pleiospilos*.
Stone Root *Collinsonia*.
Stone Wood *Backhousia hughesii*.
Stonewort *Nitella*.
Stopper *Eugenia*.
Storax *Styrax*.
Storksbill *Erodium*.
Strainer Vine *Luffa*.
Strangler Fig *Ficus aurea*.

Stransvaesia Lindl.
S. davidiana Decne. = *Photinia davidiana*.
S. davidiana var. *undulata* (Decne.) Rehd. & Wils. = *Photinia davidiana* Undulata group.
S. davidiana var. *salicifolia* (Hutch.) Rehd. = *Photinia davidiana* Salicifolia group.
S. glaucescens Lindl. = *Photinia nussia*.
S. nussia (D. Don) Decne. = *Photinia nussia*.
S. undulata Decne. = *Photinia davidiana* Undulata group.

Strap Cactus *Epiphyllum*.
Strap Waterfern *Blechnum patersonii*.

Stratiotes L. Hydrocharitaceae. 1 perenn. aquatic herb, submerged, rising to the surface at anthesis; stolons radiating from v. short-stemmed main growth. Lvs to 50×2cm, basal, rosulate, erect to spreading soft, deep green, sword-shaped, long-acuminate, pungent, serrate. Fls short-stalked, axill.; pet. 15–25mm, 3, obovate, white; sta. 12 or 0 in ♀. Eur. to Sib. Z5.
S. aloides L. WATER SOLDIER.
S. nymphoides Willd. = *Hydrocleys nymphoides*.

×**Stravinia** hort.
×*S.* 'Redstart' = *Photinia* 'Redstart'.

Strawbell *Uvularia sessilifolia*.
Strawberry *Fragaria*.
Strawberry Blite *Chenopodium capitatum*.
Strawberry Bush *Euonymus americanus*.
Strawberry Cactus *Mammillaria prolifera*.
Strawberry Geranium *Saxifraga stolonifera*.
Strawberry Shrub *Calycanthus floridus*.
Strawberry Tomato *Physalis pruinosa; P. pubescens*.
Strawberry Tree *Arbutus* (*A. unedo*).
Strawflower *Acroclinium; Helichrysum bracteatum; Helipterum*.
Straw Foxglove *Digitalis lutea*.
Streaked Wattle *Acacia lineata*.
Stream Violet *Viola glabella*.

Strelitzia Banks ex Dryand. BIRD OF PARADISE. Strelitziaceae. 4 large, perenn., everg. herbs, ± stemless and clump-forming or bearing multiple, stout pseudostems. Lvs resembling *Musa* but more rigid, oblong to lanceolate; petioles long, bases partially sheathing or strongly overlapping. Infl. axill., long or short-stalked, usually horizontal; fls emerging sequentially from waxy, rigid beak- or boat-like spathes, producing copious nectar; cal. seg. 3, erect, petaloid; cor. arrow-shaped forming a projecting 'tongue' enclosing sta. and style. S Afr. Z9.
S. alba (L.) Skeels. St. usually solitary, to 6m. Lvs to 2×0.6m, oblong-lanceolate; petiole 1m. Spathe purple-red, glaucous 25–30cm; fls white, 20cm. Spring. Cape Prov.
S. augusta Wright = *S. alba*.

S. caudata Dyer. St. clumped, to 6m. Lvs to 1.75×0.8m, ovate to oblong, petiole equalling blade. Spathe dark purple-red, glaucous, 30cm; fls 20cm; cal. white; cor. white or blue-purple at base. Spring. Transvaal, Swaz.
S. ×*kewensis* Skan. (*S. alba* ×*S. reginae*.) Trunk to 1.5m or 0. Spathe long-stalked; cal. pale yellow; cor. blue, lilac-pink at base. Gdn origin.
S. nicolai Reg. & Körn. St. to 10m, clumped. Lvs to 2×0.8m, oblong or ovate-oblong; petiole to 2m. Infl. short-stalked, spathes chestnut-red, pruinose, 40–45cm; cal. 20cm, white; cor. light purple-blue, v. gummy. Spring. Natal, NE Cape.
S. parvifolia Ait. f. = *S. reginae*.
S. reginae Banks ex Dryand. BIRD OF PARADISE; CRANE FLOWER. ± stemless. Lvs 25–70×10–30cm, glaucescent, oblong-lanceolate; petiole, about 1m. Infl. long-stalked, equalling lvs; spathe about 12cm, green tinted purple and orange, glaucous; cal. to 10cm, orange; cor. dark blue. Winter–spring. S Afr. 'Farinosa': lvs v. glaucous, oblong, base truncate; petioles long. 'Glauca': lvs large, glaucous, oblong-lanceolate. 'Humilis' ('Pygmaea'): dwarf (to 80cm), closely clump-forming; lvs ovate-oblong, short-petioled; fls disproportionately large, short-stalked. 'Kirstenbosch Gold': fls pale orange-gold. 'Rutilans': lvs with red or purple midrib; fls brilliantly coloured. var. *juncea* (Ker-Gawl.) H.E. Moore. Lf blades 0 or much reduced, narrowly lanceolate or spathulate; plant appears spiky, rush-like.

STRELITZIACEAE (Schumann) Hutch. 3/7. *Phenakospermum, Ravenala, Strelitzia*.

Streptanthera Sweet.
S. elegans Sweet = *Sparaxis elegans*.

Streptanthus Nutt. TWIST FLOWER. Cruciferae. 35 ann. herbs. St. simple or branched. Lvs simple, ± succulent, ovate to linear, sometimes sessile. Fls sometimes irregular; sep. 4, suffused purple; pet. 4, narrow and red-brown or large and purple. W and S N Amer. Z6.
S. hyacinthoides Hook. To 1m, glab. Lvs to 15cm, cauline, linear-lanceolate, ± sessile. Pet. magenta. Early summer. Tex. and Okl.
S. maculatus Nutt. Similar to *S. hyacinthoides* except to 80cm, lvs oblong to ovate, clasping, pet. purple, spotted magenta. Spring. NE Tex., E Okl., W Ark.
→*Euklisia*.

Streptocalyx Beer Bromeliaceae. 14 terrestrial or epiphytic perenn. herbs. Lvs linear, toothed, leathery, in a dense rosette. Scape term., long or v. short; infl. 2–4-pinnate, densely subglobose to laxly paniculate; sep. broad, free to fused; pet. free, narrow. E Braz., Fr. Guiana, Peru, Ecuad. Z10.
S. longifolius (Rudge) Bak. Lvs 40–120cm, turning maroon in full sun, sheaths small, broad, dark brown, scaly, blades with flat 2.5mm spines, pale-scaly below. Scape short or 0; infl. 7–15cm, ovoid or ellipsoid, bipinnate, with pale red-brown scales; bracts 2–2.5cm, ovate or ellipsoid, pink to rusty-red; sep. 14–20mm, toothed; pet. white with dark margins. Colomb. to Amazonian Boliv. and Braz.
S. poeppigii Beer. Lvs to 1.6m, sheaths large, dark brown, covered in buff scales, blades with dark, curved, 4mm spines. Scape curved red to 3m; bracts bright pink, linear; infl. densely bipinnate, slenderly cylindric or pyramidal, white-scurfy; sep. 16–19mm wing, apex purple, mucronate; pet. bright purple to violet. Colomb. to Amazonian Boliv. and Braz.

Streptocarpus Lindl. CAPE PRIMROSE. Gesneriaceae. *c*130 ann., perenn. or monocarpic herbs, rarely subshrubs, often hairy. St. usually 0; fleshy and branching in subgenus *Streptocarpella*. Lvs pubesc., puckered, tough, ± sessile, tufted in stemless spp., usually paired ± fleshy, short-stalked in *Streptocarpella*. Infl. axill. or from base of lf, branching, cymose; cal. divided ×5; pet. united into a 5-lobed tube, limb 2-lipped; sta. 2. Fr. a narrow, twisted, cylindrical capsule. Trop., C & E Afr., Madag., Thail., SW China to E Indies. Z10.
S. baudertii L.L. Britten. Differs from *S. johannis* in lvs prostrate, rosulate, fls with white patch at base of lower lip. S Afr.
S. candidus Hilliard. Perenn. Rhiz. vertical. Lvs in rosettes, to 6×20cm, round-toothed. Fls to 25, fragrant, several opening simultaneously; cor. tube subcylindrical, to 4cm, white, sometimes tinged pale violet, base of tube streaked yellow and spotted violet, lower lip with 2 violet, V-shaped bars. Summer. S Afr. (Natal).
S. caulescens Vatke. Perenn. St. upright, branched, fleshy, to 60cm. Lvs elliptic or ovate, softly hairy, to 6.5×3cm. Fls 6–12; cor. to 2cm diam., tube to 8mm, violet or pale lilac.

Autumn–winter. Tanz., Kenya. var. *pallescens* Cor. violet, or striped violet on white.

S. confusus Hilliard. Differs from *S. haygarthii* in cor., lobes strongly spreading. Spring–summer. Transvaal, Natal, Swaz.

S. cooksonii B.L. Burtt. Monocarpic. Scapes stout. Lf solitary, to 40×30cm, hairy, round-toothed, base cordate, fls abundant on peduncles to 10cm; cor. to 4cm, dark mauve with white patch in throat. Summer–autumn. S Afr.

S. cooperi C.B. Clarke. Monocarpic. Lf solitary, to 70×70cm, cordate at base, hairy, round-toothed. Fls many on peduncle to 50cm; cor. to 7cm, violet with white patches on base of tube and lip. Late summer. Natal.

S. cyaneus S. Moore. Rosulate perenn. Lvs to 40×10cm, obtuse, round-toothed. Infl. to 15cm, 1–2-fld; cor. funnel-shaped, to 7.5cm, bright mauve, pink or white, tube striped yellow and streaked deep lilac within. Spring–summer. S Africa.

S. cynandrus B.L. Burtt. Tufted hairy, perenn. Lvs several, linear-oblong to lanceolate, crimson beneath, toothed, ± sessile. Infl. 1–2, to 4.5cm, fls few; cor. to 3.5cm, brilliant pink above, paler below, lobes with 3 magenta stripes, tube spotted and grooved within. Zimb.

S. daviesii N.E. Br. ex C.B. Clarke. Perenn. Lf solitary, dying back after flowering, to 20×20cm, cordate, softly hairy, pale green or purple beneath, round-toothed. Infl. to 20cm; cal. a leafy, bell-shaped tube; cor. 4.5cm, pale violet, sometimes white or pink, tube tinged green and violet. Summer. S Africa.

S. denticulatus Turrill. Monocarpic, covered in fine, red granules. Lf solitary, thin, subglabrous, rugose, serrate. Infl. hairy, to 25cm; fls numerous; cor. 3cm, mauve to pink-red, lower lobes white at base and streaked crimson, entire or denticulate, tube decurved, green, spotted and streaked crimson. Summer. S Africa.

S. dunnii Hook. f. Monocarpic or perenn., red-granullar except upper lf surface. Lvs solitary or several, oblong, to 20×30cm, silver-grey with adpresed hairs above, thickly hairy beneath. Infl. to 30cm, fls many; cor. 5cm, pink to brick-red, lobes rounded, tube interior pink, floor striped red. Early summer. S Africa.

S. erubescens Hilliard & B.L. Burtt. Monocarpic, covered in spreading hairs. Lf solitary, to 15×12cm, crenate, base cordate to cuneate, deep green above, sometimes purple beneath. Fls few; cor. to 4cm, white, suffused pink, lobes striped and spotted bright crimson within. Mid summer. Malawi, Moz.

S. eylesii S. Moore. Monocarpic. Lvs solitary, rarely several, to 30×20cm, hairy, irregularly toothed. Infl. to 30cm, fls fragrant; cor. to 6.5cm, violet, sometimes white outside, throat white, occas. with yellow patch, tube curved. Late spring–summer. Tanz. to Zimb.

S. fanniniae Harv. Perenn., creeping, rooting; upright st. to 15cm. Lvs numerous, oblong, to 90×20cm. Infl. to 1m, fls fragrant, many; cor. to 4cm, pale blue to white, tube striped yellow and spotted mauve on floor. Winter. Natal.

S. galpinnii Hook. f. Monocarpic or perenn. Lvs solitary or several, upright or prostrate, 2–15×1–12cm, cordate to cuneate at base, hairy, sometimes crimson beneath. Infl. to 16cm, 1 to many, slender; cor. to 3cm, mauve, white in throat. Summer. S Afr.

S. gardenii Hook. Rosulate perenn. Lvs petiolate, narrow-oblong, cordate at base, to 30×7cm, sometimes red-purple beneath, crenate. Infl. 1–6-fld, to 15cm; cor. to 5cm, tube decurved, interior pale green, lobes pale lilac, streaked purple. Winter. E Cape, Natal.

S. glandulosissimus Engl. Perenn. St. weak and straggling, hairy when young. Lvs in unequal pairs, elliptic or ovate, to 13×5cm, sparsely hairy, entire. Infl. to 15cm, glandular-hairy; cor. to 3cm, violet to violet-blue, glandular-hairy. Rift Valley.

S. goetzei Engl. Monocarpic. Lf solitary, usually 15×12cm, covered in upright hairs. Infl. hairy, to 10cm; cor. to 3.5cm, mauve, 2 darker blotches at mouth, tube curved, mouth compressed between upper lobes. Winter. CE Afr.

S. gracilis B.L. Burtt = *S. prolixus*.

S. grandis N.E. Br. Monocarpic. Lf solitary, sometimes stalked, cordate at base, hairy, round-toothed, to 40×35cm. Infl. to 40cm, fls numerous; cor. to 4.5cm, white, mauve or pink, throat and base of lower lip often darker with white patches. Summer. Natal, E Zimb.

S. haygarthii N.E. Br. ex C.B. Clarke. Monocarpic. Lf solitary, to 40×55cm, softly hairy, deep green above, often red-purple beneath, round-toothed, base cordate. Infl. slender, to 45cm, fls many; cor. to 4.5cm, white to blue-white, tube slightly curved, upper and lower lobes divergent. Early summer. S Africa.

S. hilsenbergü R. Br. Perenn. St. thickly hairy, straggling and woody at base, to 60cm. Lvs opposite, ovate to elliptic-lanceolate, serrate, to 6.5×3.5cm, hairy; petiole glandular-pubesc. Infl. axill., fls 1 to many; cor. pale mauve to bright red, usually darker with white blotches in throat, to 4.5cm, tube

curved. Winter. Madag.

S. holstii Engl. Erect, branching herb to 60cm. St. fleshy. Lvs opposite, to 4.5×3cm, ovate or ovate-elliptic, somewhat hairy, glab. above, paler beneath. Infl. axill., to 10cm; cor. bright blue, throat white. Winter. Tanz.

S. ×hybridus Voss. A group of hybrids derived from *S. rexii* with *S. dunnii*, *S. cyaneus*, *S. polyanthus*, *S. saundersii*, *S. wendlandii* and *S. woodii*, often backcrossed to *S. rexii*. Habit generally like *S. rexii*; fls large, mauve-purple to rosy crimson. 'Constant Nymph': fls pale blue-mauve with darker lines in throat. 'Merton Blue': fls blue-mauve, throat white with yellow patch. 'Eira': fls small, semidouble to double, white, tinged mauve on lower pet.; 'Lisa': fls shell-pink with a white centre; 'Nicola': fls small, semidouble, free, deep pink; 'Falling Stars': fls small, numerous, sky-blue; 'Wiesmoor': fls trumpet-shaped, bright ruby.

S. insignis B.L. Burtt = *S. primulifolius*.

S. johannis L.L. Britten. Rosulate perenn. Lvs many, semi-erect, tufted, hairy, oblong, obtuse, to 35×10cm. Infl. to 30cm, fls 1–2; cor. to 4.5cm, tube curved, white to pale mauve, white or yellow in throat. Spring. E Cape to S Natal.

S. kentaniensis L.L. Britten & Story. Rosulate perenn. Lvs numerous, to 20×2cm, dark green and hairy above, paller beneath, crenate. Infl. to 12cm, 2–5-fld; cor. to 3cm, tube nearly straight, pale mauve, floor striped pale yellow and dotted purple. Winter. Cape Prov.

S. kirkii Hook. f. Perenn. St. erect, young tips hairy and fleshy, older parts woody, to 40cm. Lvs opposite, obovate-oblong to suborbicular, to 6.5×3.5cm, hairy, crenate to entire; petiole 1–1.5cm. Fls to 10 in loose, axillary cymes; cor. lilac, to 18mm, throat occas. spotted purple. Winter. Kenya, Tanz.

S. luteus C.B. Clarke = *S. parviflorus*.

S. mahonii Hook. f. = *S. goetzei*.

S. meyeri B.L. Burtt. Rosulate perenn. Lvs several, softly hairy, prostrate, elliptic, to 20×7.5cm. Infl. 2–12-fld; cor. tube to 3cm, narrow-cylindrical, straight, exterior mauve, interior deeper striped and spotted purple, limb almost white, throat yellow. Late summer. E Cape.

S. michelmorei B.L. Burtt. Monocarpic. Lf solitary with thick, cordate at base, to 30×30cm. Infl. to 30cm, fls many; cor. mid-violet with deeper patch on mouth of tube and yellow band in throat, tube slightly curved. Summer. S Zimb.

S. molweniensis Hilliard. Differs from *S. wendlandii* in lf usually sessile, only 1–2 fls opening at a time, cor. tube 1–3.5cm, mauve, striped white. Summer. S Africa.

S. montigena L.L. Britten. Perenn. Lvs in a flat rosette, ovate, 15×10.5cm, pale green, hairy, crenate. Infl. to 40cm, 2–12-fld; cor. to 5cm, pale lilac and cream with 2 coalescing yellow patches at base of lower lip, tube slightly curved. Summer. Cape Prov.

S. muddii C.B. Clarke = *S. wilmsii*.

S. orientalis Craib. Herb to 40cm. St. unbranched, glandular-hairy. Lvs opposite, ovate to suborbicular, densely hairy, to 9×7cm, crenate. Infl. axill. to 13cm, fls pendulous; cor. to 4cm, exterior purple, inteerior paler, dark-lined, tube slightly curved. Spring. N & C Thail.

S. parviflorus Hook. f. Rosulate perenn. Rhiz. thick. Lvs many, strap-shaped, semi-upright, to 45×7cm, thickly hairy, paler beneath, crenate. Infl. to 20-fld; to 25cm; cor. to 3cm, narrowly funnel-shaped, white, sometimes tinged pale mauve, purple lines on lower lobes and palate, yellow stripe in tube. Summer. S Africa.

S. polackii B. L. Burtt. = *S. cyaneus*.

S. polyanthus Hook. Monocarpic or perenn. Lvs thick, hairy, to 25×20cm, pale green above, often red-purple beneath. Infl. many-fld; cor. to 4.5cm, chalky violet, throat streaked white, yellow or green, tube narrow, bent. Late winter–summer. S Afr. ssp. *dracomontanus* Hilliard. Lvs 2–3. Fls few, cor. limb, less than 2cm wide.

S. primulifolius Gand. Rosulate perenn. Lvs many, to 45×11cm, hairy. Infl. to 25cm, 1–4-fld; cor. to 10cm, tube narrowly funnel-shaped, pale blue-mauve. Summer. S Africa. ssp. *primulifolius* Cor. tube and base of lower lip deep mauve with 5 red-purple lines entering tube, lobes pale blue-mauve within. ssp. *formosus* Hilliard & B.L. Burtt. Cor. lobes white, tube minutely spotted purple, with a patch of bright yellow and purple streaks.

S. prolixus C.B. Clarke. Perenn. Lvs 2–3, to 23×15cm, dark green above, often red-purple beneath, softly hairy, crenate cordate at base, usually prostrate. Infl. to 36-fld, slender; cor. to 2.5cm, white to pale violet often with yellow patch in throat, tube subcylindrical, bent. Spring. S Africa.

S. pusillus Harv. ex C.B. Clarke. Monocarpic, hairy. Lf solitary, to 20×15cm, crenate, cordate at base. Infl. to 12cm, fls to 30; cor. to 1.8cm, white, tube 1cm, cylindrical, almost straight. Early summer. S Africa.

S. rexii Hook.   Rosulate perenn. Lvs obovate-strap-shaped, obtuse, to 30×6.5cm, short-pubesc., bullate, wavy-crenate. Infl. 1–2-fld, rarely 6-fld, to 20cm; cor. to 7.5cm, tube to 5.5cm, almost straight, white or pale mauve, palate and lower lip striped purple. S Africa.

S. ruwenzoriensis Bak. = S. glandulosissimus.

S. saundersii Hook.   Monocarpic. Lf solitary, cordate at base, dark green above, red-purple and densely hairy beneath, crenate, to 30×22cm. Infl. to 30cm; fls many; cor. to 4cm, blue-mauve, throat pale lilac with yellow midline flanked by 2 purple patches, tube slightly curved, limb glandular-pubesc. Summer. Natal.

S. saxorum Engl.   Perenn. St. prostrate, hairy, few-branched, fleshy to ± woody. Lvs opposite, elliptic to ovate, 1.5–3cm, fleshy, hairy; petioles to 1cm. Fls 1–2 in axill. cymes; cor. 3.5cm, tube white, lobes pale lilac. Kenya, Tanz.

S. silvaticus Hilliard.   Similar to S. daviesii but without large leafy cal. Early summer.

S. solenanthus Mansf.   Monocarpic. Lf solitary, to 15×35cm, usually smaller. Infl. to 15cm, fls in 1 plane; cor. white, tube interior pale to mid-violet, often with darker violet in throat. Summer. Tanz. to Zimb.

S. stomandrus B.L. Burtt.   To 25cm. St. downy. Lvs opposite, softly hairy, elliptic-ovate, 3×2cm. Infl. axill., tall, loosely branched; cor. pale mauve, 3cm, tube 1.5cm, curved, palate spotted along midline, ciliate. Winter. Tanz.

S. vanderleurii Bak. f. & S. Moore.   Monocarpic. Lf to 30×30cm, base cordate, crenate, hairy. Infl. to 30cm, fls many, fragrant; cor. 5.5cm, white, yellow-green patch at base of lower lip, tube downward-curving at narrowest point. Summer. S Africa.

S. wendlandii Spreng.   Monocarpic. Lf solitary, to 75×60cm, dark purple-green above, red-purple beneath, hairy, crenate. Infl. to 30cm; fls many; cor. tube 18×3.5cm, exterior rough, flushed blue-purple, interior smooth, white, limb blue-purple with 2 deep purple patches flanking a white stripe on palate. Summer. S. Afr.

S. wilmsii Engl.   Monocarpic. Lf solitary, cordate, to 25×18cm. Fls similar to S. candidus, fragrant, but without markings on lower lip. Early summer. S Africa.

Streptopus Rich. TWISTED STALK. Liliaceae.   7 rhizomatous perenn. herbs, allied to Polygonatum. St. erect, leafy. Lvs alt. Fls solitary or in pairs, nodding; pedicels partly fused to st., deflexed at midpoint or twisted; perianth bell-shaped, to spreading, 6-lobed; sta. 6. Fr. berry. Summer. Temp. N hemis.

S. amplexifolius (L.) DC. LIVER BERRY; SCOOT BERRY; WHITE MANDARIN.   St. 40–100cm, branched above, glab. Lvs to 12cm, lanceolate-ovate to oblong-vate, broad- to narrow-cordate, amplexicaul, glab., glaucous beneath. Fls paired; pedicels 5–7.5cm, abruptly bent above middle; perianth lobes c1cm, green-white, widely spreading or recurved. Fr. red-orange to crimson-black. C & S Eur., N Asia, Jap., N Amer. (var. *americanus* Schult.). Z5.

S. roseus Michx. ROSE MANDARIN.   St. 25–60cm, br. thinly downy to hispidulous. Lvs to 8.25cm, lanceoalte to narrow-ovate, sessile, not amplexicaul, finely ciliate. Fls solitary; pedicels 1–2.5cm, slightly deflexed (hairy in var. *perspectus* Fassett); perianth lobes 6–12mm, rose-purple, bell-shaped or tips strongly recurved in var. *curvipes* (Vail) Fassett. Fr. red. NE N Amer. Z3.

S. simplex D. Don.   Differs from S. amplexifolius in lvs to 9cm, oblong-acuminate, base deeply cordate, glaucescent beneath; fls white, broadly funnelform, usually solitary. N India, Nepal, Burm., China. Z9.

S. streptopoides (Ledeb.) Frye & Rigg.   Differs from S. roseus in perianth lobes 3–4mm, pink or rose at base, tips yellow-green recurved. Fr. red to maroon or black. N N Amer., E Sib., N Jap., Korea, China. Z3.

Streptosolen Miers. Solanaceae.   1 everg., scabrous, pubesc. shrub, to 2.5m. Br. slender. Lvs to 5cm, ovate to elliptic, acute, entire; petiole to 1cm. Infl. term., corymbose; cal. to 1cm, tubular, teeth 5, cor. orange-red, funnel-shaped, tube long, spirally twisted, yellow to orange yellow, limb spreading, lobes 5, broad-oblong, appearing 2-lipped, deeper orange than tube. Colomb., Peru. Z9.

S. jamesonii (Benth.) Miers. ORANGE BROWALLIA; MARMALADE BUSH; FIREBUSH.

→Browallia.

Streptostigma Reg.

S. viridiflorum Thwaites = Harpullia arborea.

Strickland's Gum Eucalyptus stricklandii.

String Bean Phaseolus vulgaris.

String Bean Plant Hoya longifolia.

String-of-beads Senecio rowleyanus.

String-of-buttons Crassula perforata.

String-of-hearts Ceropegia linearis ssp. woodii.

Stringy-bark Callitris macleayana.

Striped Garlic Allium cuthbertii.

Striped Inch Plant Callisia elegans.

Striped Maple Acer pensylvanicum.

Striped Mexican Marigold Tagetes tenuifolia.

Striped Squill Pushkinia scilloides.

Striped Toadflax Linaria repens.

Striped Torch Guzmania monostachia.

Striped Violet Viola striata.

Strobilanthes Bl. Acanthaceae.   250 perenn. herbs and sub-shrubs. Lvs frequently in unequal pairs. Fls in heads or cone-like or interrupted spikes or pan.; cal. lobes 5; cor. tubular, in-flated, lobes 5, ovate to round, subequal. Asia.

S. atropurpureus Nees. MEXICAN PETUNIA.   Erect, branching perenn. herb to 1.25m. St. slender. Lvs ovate, serrate, long-stalked. Fls to 4cm, indigo to deep purple, packed in spikes. Sib. Z5.

S. dyerianus Mast. PERSIAN SHIELD.   Everg. soft-stemmed shrub to 1.2m. Lvs to 15cm, ovate-lanceolate, toothed, dark green flushed purple above with iridescent silvering, dark purple beneath. Spikes short, axill.; cor. to 3.2cm, pale blue, funnelform. Burm. Z10.

S. isophyllus (Nees) Anderson. BEDDING CONEHEAD.   Subshrub to 1m. Lvs to 10cm, linear-lanceolate, toothed, glab. Fls clustered in groups of 4 in packed term. heads; cor. to 2.5cm, lavender, tube curved, swollen from a short narrow base, lobes round. NE India. Z10.

→Goldfussia.

Stromanthe Sonder. Marantaceae.   15 caulescent or tufted, branched herbs, 1–3m. Lvs basal and cauline or cauline only, ovate-oblong to elliptic; petioles long, sheathing. Rac. or pan., 1 to several per shoot; bracts leathery, cupped or folded, sub-tending 1–5 stalked, bracteolate cymules; sep. 3, fibrous, usually elliptic; cor. lobes, 3, obtuse; outer staminodes, 2, sometimes 0, callose staminode fleshy, sometimes with a petaloid margin, cucullate staminode with a flat basal appendage. C Amer. to S Braz. Z10.

S. amabilis E. Morr. = Ctenanthe amabilis.

S. jacquinii (Roem. & Schult.) H. Kenn. & Nicols. Lvs to 35cm, elliptic to oblong; petiole to 6.5cm, sheath auriculate.Infl. branching, subtended by a lf; bracts decid.; sep. yellow; cor. pale yellow. C Panama to Colomb. and Venez.

S. lubbersiana E. Morr. = Ctenanthe lubbersiana.

S. lutea Jacq. = S. jacquinii.

S. porteana Gris.   Lvs ovate-oblong to lanceolate, green with white veins above, red beneath. Infl. a rac., sometimes wjth a single basal br.; bracts red; cor. violet. E Braz.

S. sanguinea (Hook.) Sonder.   Lvs to 50cm, elliptic-oblong, dark green above, purple beneath; petioles to 25cm, sheaths pink or red. Infl. a pan.; bracts red; cal. orange-red; cor. white. Braz. var. *spectabilis* (Lem.) Eichl.   More robust; lvs usually green beneath.

S. spectabilis Lem. = S. sanguinea var. spectabilis.

S. tonckat (Aubl.) Eichl.   Lvs to 13cm, ovate-lanceolate to oblong, pubesc.; petiole and sheath villous, pan. to 11cm; bracts linear-lanceolate; cor. white. Braz., Guyana, Colomb., Venez.

→Maranta and Phrynium.

Strombocactus Britt. & Rose. Cactaceae.   1 low-growing cactus; st. simple, depressed to globose or turbinate, 2–8×3–17cm; tubercles spiralled, irregularly rhomboid, pale grey-green; areoles woolly at first; spines weak, 1–5, to 15mm, erect, off-white, dark-tipped, often caducous. Fls apical, short-funnelform, to 3.2×3.2cm, pale yellow to almost white with red throat. Summer. EC Mex. Z9.

S. disciformis (DC.) Britt. & Rose. E Mex. Z9.

S. klinkerianus (Backeb. & Jacobsen) Buining = Neolloydia schmiedickeana var. klinkeriana.

S. macrochele (Werderm.) Backeb. = Neolloydia schmiedickeana var. macrochele.

S. pseudomacrochele Backeb. = Neolloydia pseudomacrochele.

S. schmiedickianus Boed. = Neolloydia schmiedickeana.

→Echinocactus and Mammillaria.

Strombocarpa Engl. & A. Gray.

S. pubescens (Benth.) A. Gray = Prosopis pubescens.

Strong Back Bourreria ovata.

Strongylocaryum Burret.

S. latius Burret. = Ptychosperma salomonense.

Strongylodon Vogel. Leguminosae (Papilionoideae). *c*20 robust everg. or decid. shrubs or lianes. Fls papilionaceous, usually in long rac. Fr. a large legume. SE Asia to Polyn. Z10.

S. macrobotrys A. Gray JADE VINE; EMERALD CREEPER. Vigorous liane to 13m. St. glossy, purple-green, hardening to black-brown. Lvs dark green, emerging pink-bronze, trifoliolate, lfts to 12.5cm, oblong-obovate. Rac. pendulous, cylindrical to 90cm; fls to 7.5cm, paired or whorled, long-stalked, aquamarine to luminous jade green, claw-like, keel tapering finely, apex strongly curved. Philipp.

Strophanthus DC. Apocynaceae. 38 shrubs and small trees, often climbing. Fls corymbose clusters; cal. 5-lobed; cor. funnel-form or salverform, with 10 claw-like scales in the mouth, lobes 5, often produced into v. long, twisted, thread-like tails; sta. in tube mouth, forming cone around stigma. Fr. of 2, divergent, fusiform follicles. Trop. to S Afr., Trop. Asia. Z10.

S. capensis A. DC. = *S. speciosus.*

S. caudatus (Burm. f.) Kurz. Trailing or climbing shrub to 6m. Lvs 7.5–20cm, slightly leathery, oblong or oblong-obovate, apex abruptly acuminate. Fls yellow-white, sometimes stained purple; cor. tube 2.5cm, lobe tails 7.5–20cm. Trop. Asia.

S. divaricatus (Lour.) Hook. & Arn. Lax climbing shrub 1–3m. Lvs 3.5–9cm, glab., elliptic-oblong, mucronate. Fls malodorous; cor. green-yellow, striped red in throat, lobes to 10cm, thread-like. S China and Vietnam.

S. divergens Graham = *S. divaricatus.*

S. grandiflorus (N.E. Br.) Gilg = *S. petersianus.*

S. gratus (Wallich & Hook.) Baill. CLIMBING OLEANDER. Robust climber to 8m+. Lvs 5–18cm, apex shortly acuminate, leathery, olive-green; petiole short, stained red. Fls white tinted red or purple, ultimately yellow; cor. tube 1.5–4.5cm, lobes 1.4–3.5cm, obovate, obtuse, slightly crisped, not prolonged into tails, scales in mouth rose-pink, exserted. Trop. W Afr.

S. petersianus Klotzsch. Glab. woody climber. Lvs 2.8–11cm, acuminate, wavy, pale beneath. Fls dull yellow streaked with red, tube 3cm wide at mouth, lobe tails 15cm or more, reflexed, loosely twisted, yellow stained red. S Trop. Afr.

S. preussii Engl. & Pax. Climber to 4m or more. Lvs 5–12.5cm, elliptic or oblong, acuminate or abruptly pointed, glab. Fls fragrant, cream to orange with purple spots and streaks in throat; cor. tube 1.5cm, tinged purple below, lobes ovate, tails purple to 30cm; scales in mouth, short, deep yellow. Trop. W Afr.

S. sarmentosus DC. Scrambling shrub. Lvs 2–15cm, ovate to oval, apex acuminate. Fls 10cm, white striped purple in mouth, cor. tube 1.7–4cm, tails 3–11cm, scales in mouth purple. Trop. Afr.

S. speciosus (Ward & Harv.) Reber. CORKSCREW-FLOWER. Erect or rambling glab. shrub. Lvs 2–11cm, oblong-lanceolate to lanceolate, acute or obtuse, leathery. Fls cream-yellow spotted red; cor. tube 1–1.5cm, lobes 2–5cm, spirally twisted, scales in mouth short. S Afr.

Strophocactus Britt. & Rose.

S. wittii (Schum.) Britt. & Rose = *Selenicereus wittii.*

Stropholirion Torr. = *Dichelostemma.*

Strumaria Jacq. ex Willd. Amaryllidaceae. 8 bulbous perenn. herbs. Lvs with fls. Umbel to 15-fld scape, slender; perianth infundibuliform, cut to ovary; tep. 6, oblanceolate; sta. exserted. S Afr. Z9.

S. truncata Jacq. Lvs erect, ovate, obtuse, to 15×1.5cm. Scape to 30cm; fls 6–15, unscented; spathe green; tep. to 1.5cm, white-pink; sta. united. Spring. S Afr.

Struthiola L. Thymelaeaceae. 30 everg. shrubs and undershrubs. Lvs small, often heath-like. Fls small, sessile, solitary or in pairs in upper lf axils, forming leafy spikes; cal. tube cylindrical, lobes 4; pet. 4, 8 or 12, usually minute; sta. 4, included. S & Trop. Afr. Z9.

S. erecta L. 50cm; shoots glab. Lvs 6×1mm, erect, linear-lanceolate, acute. Fls fragrant, pink or white; cal. tube 8mm, lobes ovate-oblong, pointed, 3mm; pet. 8, minute, surrounded by hairs. Spring, autumn. S Afr.

S. imbricata hort. 60cm; st. downy when young. Lvs 6×3mm, ovate, blunt, hairy beneath when young. Fls white; cal. tube 8mm, downy, lobes in 2 pairs, outer ovate, acute, 4mm, inner pair oblong, blunt, narrower. S Afr.

S. juniperina Retz. = *S. lineariloba.*

S. lineariloba Meissn. 2m; shoots glab. Lvs 6×1mm, linear, pointed. Fls fragrant, white; cal. tube 8mm, lobes linear, 4mm; pet. 8, minute, oblong, tinged red. Summer. S Afr.

S. longiflora Lam. To 1m; shoots quadrangular, downy. Lvs densely set, 8×1.5–3mm, ovate- to linear-lanceolate. Cal. red,

tube v. slender, 16mm, lobes ovate-oblong, blunt 4mm; pet. 8, 2mm, yellow. Early summer. S Afr.

S. lucens Poir. To 60cm; shoots downy at first. Lvs 10–20×2mm, lanceolate to narrow-oblong, pointed, ciliate. Fls yellow; cal. tube 12mm, downy, lobes broadly ovate, acute, 2mm; pet. 8, 1.5mm, surrounded by hairs. Summer. S Afr.

S. ovata Thunb. To 60cm; shoots glab. Lvs overlapping, to 12×5mm, ovate. Fls fragrant, white or pink; cal. tube glab., slender, 2mm, lobes ovate, pointed, 4mm; pet. 8, oblong, 1.5mm. Spring. S Afr.

S. pubescens Retz. = *S. virgata.*

S. striata Lam. To 60cm; young shoots downy. Lvs 6–12×2–3mm, closely overlapping, ovate-oblong, ciliate. Fls fragrant; cal. white, tube downy, 8mm lobes 3×1mm; pet. 4, yellow, 1.5mm. Spring, with a second flush in summer. S Afr.

S. tomentosa Andrews. To 60cm; shoots hairy at first. Lvs to 12×6mm, closely overlapping, oval-oblong, tomentose at first. Fls yellow, hairy; cal. white tube cylindrical, 6mm, lobes oblong, 1mm; pet. 12, longer than cal. lobes. Late summer. S Afr.

S. virgata L. To 60cm; shoots white-downy at first. Lvs 8–15×1.5mm, oblong, blunt, white-ciliate at first. Fls white; cal. tube 12mm, downy, lobes ovate, obtuse, 3mm; pet. 8, oblong, 1mm. Late spring. S Afr.

Struthiopteris Willd.

S. niponica (Kunze) Nak. = *Blechnum nipponicum.*

S. orientalis Hook. = *Matteuccia orientalis.*

S. spicant Weiss. = *Blechnum spicant.*

Strychnine *Strychnos nux-vomica.*

Strychnos L. STRYCHNINE; CLEARING NUT; CURARE. Loganiaceae. *c*190 trees, shrubs and lianes climbing by woody hook-tendrils. Thyrses axil. and/or term., crowded or loose, with 1 to many fls; fls 4–5-parted, usually symmetrical; cor., salverform to rotate, lobes thickened, erect or recurved, triangular to oblong. Fr. a berry with a hard shell and juicy pulp. Circumtrop. Z10.

S. nux-vomica L. STRYCHNINE; NUX-VOMICA TREE. Tree to 20m. Lvs ovate, 7.5–15×6.5–11cm. Cymes term. 2.5–5cm diam., fls tinged green, numerous, 10–12mm. Fr. 3–6cm diam. India, Burm.

S. potatorum L. f. CLEARING NUT; WATER FILTER TREE. Tree to 18m. Lvs elliptic to narrow-elliptic or ovate to narrow-ovate, 6–15×3–9cm. Cymes axill. 2cm diam; fls fragrant, cream, white or yellow 4.5–7.5mm. Fr. 15–25mm diam., ripening black. India, Sri Lanka, Burm., E & S Afr., Madag.

S. spinosa Lam. KAFFIR ORANGE; NATAL ORANGE. Small thorny tree or shrub 1–6m. Lvs obovate or rotund, leathery, tip pointed, 4–9.5×1.2–7.5cm. Cymes term., compound, fls tinged green 4–5mm. Fr. 7–11cm diam., green ripening yellow, pulp fragrant. Madag., Trop. & S Afr.

St. Thomas Tree *Bauhinia tomentosa.*

Stuartia L'Hérit. = *Stewartia.*

Stultitia Phillips. Asclepiadaceae. 2 succulents differing from *Stapelia* in distinct annulus around cor. tube mouth, and deeply divided outer corona lobes. S Afr.

S. conjuncta A. White & B.L. Sloane = *Orbeanthus conjunctus.*

S. hardyi R.A. Dyer = *Orbeanthus hardyi.*

S. miscella (N.E. Br.) Lückh. St. creeping underground, aerial shoots erect, 2–3×0.3–0.5cm, obtusely tetragonal, suffused purple, with sharp teeth. Fl. solitary, 1.5cm diam.; annulus, 0.8cm diam., glab., dark purple-brown, paler in centre. Cape Prov. Z9.

S. paradoxa Verdc. = *Orbea paradoxa.*

S. tapscottii (Verdc.) Phillips = *Orbea tapscottii.*

→*Caralluma* and *Stapelia.*

Sturt's Desert Pea *Clianthus formosus.*
Sturt's Desert Rose *Gossypium sturtianum.*
St. Vincent Cistus *Cistus ladanifer* f. *latifolius.*
St. Vincent Lilac *Solanum seaforthianum.*

STYLIDIACEAE R. Br. 5/170. *Candollea, Forstera.*

Stylidium Sw. ex Willd. Stylidaceae. *c*100 mostly herbaceous perennials. Fls in scapose rac., pan. or corymbs; cal. lobes 5, ± united into 2 lips; cor. lobes 5, irregular, the labellum much smaller and turned or nearly as long and curved upwards, the other 4 ascending in pairs, staminal column elongate, bent down or folded. Aus., Trop. Asia, E Indies; all spp. described below are Australian. Z9.

S. adnatum R. Br. Scape 5–30cm. Lvs 0.5–3.5cm, scattered, linear, narrow or wide. Fls pink, in dense pan. or rac. 15–25cm long.

S. brunonianum Benth. Scape 30–50cm. Lvs 2–5cm, in 2–5 whorls, linear to oblanceolate, acute, ± flaccid. Fls pink, in a loose rac. 5–10cm long.

S. bulbiferum Benth. Scape to 15cm. Lvs 0.5–1cm, v. narrow-linear, in dense tufts at apex and base of br. Fls green-purple, in loose, 3–7-fld corymbs.

S. ciliatum Lindl. Scape 15–30cm. Lvs 2–3.5cm, linear, with a hair-like point. Fls yellow, occas. white or pink, in short, pyramidal pan. or rac. 2.5–10cm long.

S. crassifolium R. Br. Tall, rigid, erect, nearly glab.; scape 60cm, with many small br. Lvs 10–20cm, linear, fleshy. Fls 1.5cm diam., pink, 4-lobed.

S. dichotomum DC. Scape to 10cm, glandular-pubesc. Lvs to 2cm, crowded at base and tip of br., scattered between the tufts, narrow-linear, acute. Fls yellow, in a thyrse or pan.

S. graminifolium Sw. TRIGGER PLANT. Scape 15–60cm. Lvs 5–24cm, linear, rigid, nearly flat, sometimes with cartilaginous teeth.Fls pink, in a narrow rac. or interrupted spike.

S. hirsutum R. Br. Scape 15–30cm, with spreading hairs. Lvs 5–20cm, narrow-linear, acute, glab. or glandular-pubesc. Fls pink or red, to 2cm, in a dense, spike-like rac., heavily pubesc.; cor. lip crisped.

S. hookeri Planch. = *S. dichotomum.*

S. laricifolium Rich. Shrub to 30cm. Lvs 1–2cm, crowded along br., narrow-linear, mucronate. Fls pink, in a loose rac. or pan. to 30cm.

S. mucronifolium Hook. = *S. dichotomum.*

S. replicatum R. Br. Scape 15–50cm, with spreading hairs. Lvs 7.5–30cm, basal, linear, acuminate, narrowed to a long petiole, flat, revolute, glab. or minutely glandular-pubesc. Fls yellow-white or pale pink, in short, loose rac.

S. saxifragoides Lindl. = *S. ciliatum.*

S. scandens R. Br. Climber to 60cm. Lvs 2–5cm+ in dense, whorled, distant tufts, linear. Fls pink; rac. term., solitary or 2–3 together; peduncles short.

S. spathulatum R. Br. Scape 15–50cm. Lvs 1–3.5cm including petiole, in a basal rosette, obovate to oblong-spathulate, obtuse or acute, ± hairy or gland. Fls pale yellow, in loose, unbranched rac.

Stylomecon G. Tayl. WIND POPPY; FLAMING POPPY. Papaveraceae. 1 ann. herb, to 60cm. Sap yellow. St. erect, simple or branched. Lvs to 12cm, alt., pinnatisect or pinnatifid; segments entire or dissected. Fls on axill. stalks to 20cm, fragrant; sep. 2, to 1cm; pet. 4, to 2cm, orange-red with purple basal spot and green claw; sta. many, style slender. Capsule clavate-obovoid to 1.5cm, yellow-ribbed. Summer. Calif. Z8.

S. heterophyllum (Benth.) G. Tayl.
→*Papaver.*

Stylophorum Nutt. Papaveraceae. 3 perenn. herbs to 45cm, sap yellow or red. St. erect, ridged, downy. Lvs basal, rosulate and few on st., glaucous beneath, pinnatifid; seg. incised; basal lvs with long petioles; st. lvs sessile. Fls saucer-shaped, in a term. umbel or corymb; sep. 2; pet. to 2cm, 4, valvate to overlapping, suborbicular; sta. 20+; style columnar. Capsule ovate or linear, bristly. Spring–summer. E Asia, E N Amer. Z7.

S. diphyllum (Michx.) Nutt. CELANDINE POPPY; WOOD POPPY. To 50cm, downy. St. without lvs below. Lvs 20–55cm, deeply incised, lobes 5–7, ovate-oblong, sinuate, scalloped and toothed; basal lvs often with a distinct basal pair of lobes. Fls ochre in terminal clusters. E US.

S. lasiocarpum (Olivier) Fedde. To 45cm. Latex red. Basal lvs lyrate-pinnatifid, to 45cm, thin, lobes 4–7, oblong-ovate, acute, irregularly toothed. Fls yellow in terminal clusters. C & E China.

S. sutchuenense (Franch.) Fedde. To 37.5cm, densely hairy. Basal lvs to 30cm; lobes 4–5, ovate-lanceolate, acute, irregularly toothed, term. lobe trifid. Fls yellow in a term. cluster. W China.

Stylophyllum Britt. & Rose.
S. densiflorum Rose = *Dudleya densiflora.*
S. edule Britt. & Rose = *Dudleya edulis.*
S. hassei Rose = *Dudleya virens.*
S. orcuttii Rose = *Dudleya attenuata* ssp. *orcuttii.*
S. virens Rose = *Dudleya virens.*
S. viscidum Britt. & Rose = *Dudleya viscida.*

Stypandra R. Br. Liliaceae (Phormiaceae). 6 perenn. herbs, differing from *Dianella* in woolly sta. and fr. an oblong capsule, not a berry. Aus.

S. caespitosa R. Br. To 60cm. Lvs 10–35×0.5–0.8cm, mostly basal, erect, rigid. Fls blue sometimes shaded yellow within, occas. white, 3–4 per cluster. Summer. SE Aus.

Styphelia Sm. Epacridaceae. 12 erect or spreading shrubs. Lvs ± sessile, rigid, pungent. Fls axill., solitary or 2–3-grouped, forming a pseudoraceme; bracts several, imbricate; cal. 5-parted; cor. tube cylindric, usually 5-angled with 5 tufts of hair inside below middle, lobes linear, recurved to rolled back exposing sta. Fr. a drupe with a hard bony endocarp. Aus., New Guinea. Z9.

S. australis (R. Br.) F. Muell. = *Leucopogon australis.*
S. ciliata (R. Br.) F. Muell. = *Brachyloma ciliatum.*
S. collina Labill. = *Leucopogon collinus.*
S. cordata Labill. = *Acrotriche cordata.*
S. daphnoides Sm. = *Brachyloma daphnoides.*
S. ericoides Sm. = *Leucopogon ericoides.*
S. humifusa Cav. = *Astroloma humifusum.*
S. longifolia R. Br. Small shrub, 1–1.25m; br. softly downy to hirsute. Lvs 2–5cm, lanceolate, tapering to a long fine point. Cor. tube to 2.5cm, green tinged yellow, lobes rolled back, tomentose. Spring–summer. SW Aus.
S. ovalifolia (R. Br.) Spreng. = *Acrotriche cordata.*
S. parviflora Lindl. = *Cyathodes parviflora.*
S. richei Labill. = *Cyathodes parviflora.*
S. triflora Andrews. PINK FIVECORNER. Erect shrub to 1–1.2m, glabrescent. Lvs to 3cm, narrow to broad-lanceolate to oblong lanceolate, sharply pointed, rigid; cor. to 2cm, pink suffused yellow, lobes strongly recurved, pubesc. Summer. SW Aus.
S. tubiflora Sm. Shrub to 1.5m; br. glab. or puberulous. Lvs to 1.5cm, oblong-linear, apex mucronate, base cuneate. Cor. tube to 2.5cm, conspicuously 5-angled, red or rose to white, interior pubesc., lobes short, strongly rolled back, bearded; sta. far exserted. Summer. SW Aus.
S. virgata Labill. = *Leucopogon virgatus.*
S. viridis Andrews. GREEN FIVECORNER. Shrub to 1.5m; br. glab. or minutely pubesc. Lvs to 3cm, broad-lanceolate to obovate-oblong, apex obtuse, abruptly pungent, base cuneate to truncate, paler beneath. Cor. yellow-green, tube to 2cm, lobes strongly recurved, bearded; sta. and pistil far exserted. Summer. SW Aus.

Styptic Weed *Senna occidentalis.*

STYRACACEAE Dumort. 12/165. *Alniphyllum, Halesia, Pterostyrax, Rehderodendron, Sinojackia, Styrax.*

Styrax L. SNOWBELL; SILVERBALLS; STORAX. Styracaceae. *c*100 ± stellate-pubesc. decid. or ever-green shrubs and small trees. Lvs short-stalked. Fls fragrant, white, often hanging below lvs., in rac., pan. or clusters or solitary and axillary; cal. bell- or cup-shaped, shallowly 5–10-lobed or truncate; cor. deeply 5-lobed, rarely to 10-lobed; sta. 10, rarely to 16. Drupe subglobose; seeds 1–2, large. Americas, Asia, Eur.

S. americanum Lam. Shrub to 3m; br. grey to golden-downy when young. Lvs elliptic to oblong, 7cm, acute or acuminate, base cuneate, serrulate, dark green above, paler beneath, sparsely stellate-pubesc. Fls pendulous, 1–4 at end of short branchlets; pedicels 6–12mm, puberulent; cal. lobes triangular; cor. 1–5cm, lobes oblong-lanceolate. SE US. Z6.

S. benzoin Dryand. Tree to 7.5m, 0.6–1m diam., bark grey and resinous; br. grey stellate-tomentose when young. Lvs ovate-oblong, 10–14cm, base rounded, minutely toothed, glab. above. Rac. or pan. 5.5–9cm; pedicel 2–4mm, grey-tomentose; fls 10–20, 1–3cm; cal. cupuliform, 3×3mm; cor. tube 2mm. Sumatra. Z10.

S. californicum Torr. = *S. officinale* var. *californicum.*

S. dasyanthum Perkins. Shrub or small tree to 8m; br. dark brown, grey-tomentose when young. Lvs obovate to elliptic-oblong, 6–10cm, acuminate, base cuneate, minutely toothed often hanging below lvs. 5–10cm, sometimes branched; pedicels 6–8mm; cal. cupuliform, felted, 0.5cm; cor. 1–1.5cm, lobes lanceolate. Summer. C China. var. *cinerascens* Rehd. Branchlets and lower surface of lvs more densely and persistently ashy-downy. Z9.

S. grandifolium Ait. Shrub to 4m; shoots and rac., yellow-pubesc. Lvs elliptic to obovate, 6–18cm, short-acuminate, slightly toothed or entire, grey-tomentose or pubesc. beneath. Infl. slender, stellate-tomentose, racemose, 5–12cm; fls fragrant; pedicel 5mm, grey-tomentose; cor. lobes oblong 2–2.5cm across. Spring. SE US. Z8.

S. hemsleyanum Diels. Tree to 10m; br. stellate-pubesc. when young. Lvs obovate or obliquely ovate, 7–13cm, oacuminate, cuneate or rounded at base, finely, remotely serrate, glab. and pale green above, sparsely stellate-pubesc. beneath. Fls in pubesc. rac. or pan. 8–15cm; pedicels 3–4mm; cal. campanulate,

0.5cm, slender-toothed; cor. 1.5–2cm, lobes elliptic-oblong. Summer. China. Z7.

S. japonicum Sieb. & Zucc. Shrub or small tree to 10m; br. slender, stellate-pubesc. when young. Lvs elliptic-oblong, 2–8cm, acute to acuminate, shallowly toothed, dark glossy green above, ± glab. beneath. Fls 3–6 on short lat. shoots, pendulous on glab. stalks to 3.5cm; cal. glab.; cor. lobes elliptic-oblong, 1.5×2cm, pubesc. Summer. China, Jap. 'Benibana': a name applied in Japan to all pink-fld , seed-raised forms. 'Fargesii': habit robust, tree-like; lvs large. 'Pink Chimes': br. sometimes weeping; fls pale pink, v. freely produced. Z5.

S. laevigatum Ait. = S. americanum.

S. langkongense W.W. Sm. = S. limpritchii.

S. limpritchii Lingl. To 1.8m. Lvs alt., ovate or obovate, 1–2.5cm, acuminate, remotely denticulate, dark dull green and downy above, white and downy beneath. Fls 1–2 axill. or in short, term. rac.; cal. cupuliform, 4mm; cor. tubular at base, lobes spreading, white tinted cream or gold at base, downy. W China. Z8.

S. obassia Sieb. and Zucc. To 10m; br. ascending, stellate-pubesc. when young. Lvs broad-obovate to orbicular, 7–20cm, acuminate, usually rounded at base, remotely denticulate above middle, deep green and glab. above, densely pubesc. beneath. Fls in term. rac., 10–20cm; pedicels 8–10mm, pubesc.; cal. pubesc., with 5–10 shallow lobes; cor. lobes 2×0.5cm. Summer. Jap. Z6.

S. officinale L. Low-growing shrub or small tree to 7m; br. slender, tomentose at first. Lvs ovate, cordate at base, 4–6cm, entire, white-pubesc. when young. Fls pendulous, 3–8 in short drooping clusters; cal. cupuliform, 5–7mm; cor. 3.2cm wide, lobes 5–6–7, narrow oblong, pubesc., tube 6–7mm. Summer. SE Eur., Asia Minor. var. **californicum** (Torr.) Rehd. Lvs glab. or slightly woolly beneath. N Calif. Z9.

S. philadelphoides Perkins. To 2m; br. slender, weakly grey-pubesc. when young. Lvs oblong to sublanceolate, 3–8.5cm, apex acuminate, teeth minute, irregular. Fls 4–6, in 6–10cm rac.; pedicels 1–2cm; cal. cupuliform, exterior yellow-stellate-tomentose; cor. tube 4mm. China. Z8.

S. pulverulentum Michx. = S. americanum.

S. serrulatum hort. = S. dasyantha var. cinerascens.

S. schweliense Sm. Shrub to 7.5m. Lvs elliptic, 5–10cm, cuneate, acute, shallowly toothed, velvety, dark green above, tinged grey beneath. Fls 2.5–5×2.5cm, single or paired forward tips of branchlets; cal. campanulate, 6mm, densely pubesc., minutely toothed or subentire; cor. downy. Summer. W China. Z9.

S. shiraianum Mak. Small tree; br. slender, tomentose at first, bark purple-grey. Lvs thombic-orbicular or suborbicular, 4–8cm, cuneate or rounded at base, unevenly dentate, sparsely pubesc. at first. Rac., short stalked, 8–10-fld. cal. campanulate, pubesc.; cor. lobes ovate, 6mm, half length of tube, downy. Jap. Z6.

S. veitchiorum Hemsl. & Wils. Small tree to 9m; branchlets slender, initially yellow-stellate-pubesc. Lvs lanceolate-ovate to oblong, 7–11cm, apex acuminate, base rounded or cuneate, unevely toothed. Infl. racemose, 9–20cm; fls 1.5cm; pedicel 0.6–1cm, yellow-pilose; cal. cupuliform, golden-tomentose, minutely toothed; cor. tube 2.5–3mm. China. Z6.

S. wilsonii Rehd. Shrub or small tree to 3m; branchlets initially stellate-tomentose. Lvs rhombic-ovate to elliptic, 1–2.5cm, obtuse or acute, subentire to 3- or 5-toothed, sparingly pubesc. above, tomentose beneath. Fls 3–5, 1.5–1.8cm across, short-stalked; cal. stellate-pubesc., lobes 3mm; cor. lobes ovate-oblong, 8mm, acute. W China. Z7.

Subalpine Fir Abies lasiocarpa.
Subalpine Larch Larix lyallii.

Subularia L. AWLWORT. Cruciferae. 2 aquatic superficially rush-like snnual or perenn. herbs. Lvs in a basal rosette, simple, awl-shaped. Rac. leafless, few-fld; fls minute, opening at water's surface, sep. 4, erect; pet. 4, white, sometimes 0. N temp. regions, mts of trop. Afr.

S. aquatica L. Glab., ann. or perenn. Lvs 2–7cm, terete. Fls 2–12. Circumboreal. Z5.

S. purpurea Forssk. = Schouwia purpurea.

Succisa Haller. Dipsacaceae. 1 erect or decumbent perenn. herb, 15–100cm. Basal lvs to 30cm, rosulate, oblong-oval to elliptic, thinly pubesc., tapering to a short petiole, st. lvs narrower, occas. toothed. Flowerheads 1.5–2.5cm diam., indigo to purple or pink or white, semi-spherical, subtended by lanceolate, leaf-like bracts with purple tips. Eur., W Asia, Afr.; nat. NE N Amer. Z5.

S. praemorsa (Gilib.) Asch. = S. pratensis.

S. pratensis Moench. BLUE BUTTONS DEVIL'S BIT SCABIOUS.

'Alba': fls white. 'Nana': to 25cm, dwarf; fls mauve.
→Scabiosa.

Succory Cichorium intybus.
Suckling Clover Trifolium dubium.
Sudan Gum Arabic Acacia senegal.
Sugar Apple Annona squamosa.
Sugar Berry Celtis laevigata.
Sugar Bush Rhus ovata.
Sugar Candy Orchid Caladenia hirta.
Sugar Cane Saccharum officinarum.
Sugard-almond Plant Pachyphytum oviferum.
Sugar Gum Eucalyptus cladocalyx.
Sugar Huckleberry Vaccinium vaccillans.
Sugar Maple Acer saccharum.
Sugar Palm Arenga pinnata.
Sugar Pea Pisum sativum var. macrocarpon.
Sugar Pine Pinus lambertiana.
Sugarplum Amelanchier.
Sugar Scoop Tiarella.
Sugar Sumac Rhus ovata.
Sugar Trough Gourd Lagenaria siceraria.
Sugi Cryptomeria.
Suji-giboshi Hosta undulata.

Suksdorfia Gray. Saxifragaceae. 3 perenn. herbs with bulbiliferous rhiz. Lvs orbicular to reniform, long-petiolate, shallowly lobed or deeply divided, somewhat succulent, becoming reduced and sessile on st. Fls 5-merous in terminal pan.; cal., campanulate free portions triangular; pet. obovate, borne on the rim of floral cup. NW Amer., Andes of S Boliv. and N Arg. Z6.

S. ranunculifolia (Hook.) Engl. 10–40cm. Basal lvs reniform to cordate, deeply divided into 3 large lobes, entire to serrate. Infl. many-fld; sep. 2–3mm; pet. twice as long as sep., cream or purple at base, fading to white, clawed. Summer. NW Amer.

S. violacea Wheelock. 5–30cm. Basal lvs cleft, broadly crenate with obtuse teeth. Infl. few-fld; sep. 2–4mm; pet. violet to pink or white, long-clawed, 2–4×length of sep. Early summer. NW Amer.

→Saxifraga.

Sulcorebutia Backeb. = Rebutia.
S. rauschii G. Frank = Rebutia pulchra.

Sullivantia Torr. & A. Gray. Saxifragaceae. 6 stoloniferous perenn. herbs. Basal lvs reniform, cordate at base, lobed, toothed, long-stalked, st. lvs. smaller, sessile. Flowering st. leafy; pan. cymose; fls small; cal. fused at base, lobes five triangular; pet. 5. C US. Z6.

S. oregona S. Wats. Lvs to 10cm broad, yellow-green, lobes 7–9, sharply toothed. Flowering st. bearing 1–3 lvs, glandular-pubesc. above with purple-tipped hairs; fls white. Late spring-early summer. WC US.

Sulphur Flower Eriogonum kennedyi; E. umbellatum.
Sulphur Rose Rosa hemispherica.
Sultana Impatiens (I. walleriana).
Sumac, Sumach Rhus.
Sumatran Pine Pinus merkusii.
Summer Cohosh Cimicifuga americana.
Summer Copper Cups Pileanthus filifolius.
Summer Cypress Bassia scoparia.
Summer Damask Rose Rosa ×damascena.
Summer Forget-me-not Anchusa capensis.
Summer Grape Vitis aestivalis.
Summer Haw Crataegus flava.

Summerhayesia Cribb. Orchidaceae. 2 epiphytic monopodial orchids. St. short. Lvs fleshy, distichous, folded. Rac. axill.; fls fleshy; sep. and pet. similar; lip entire, concave, spurred. Trop. Afr. Z10.

S. laurentii (De Wildeman) Cribb. Lvs 10–22×0.6–1cm, linear or narrowly ligulate, fleshy. Rac. 13–40cm; fls yellow-white or cream; sep. and pet. 7–8mm, elliptic; lip 8mm, ovate; spur 6–7.5cm. Liberia, Ghana, Ivory Coast, Zaire.

S. zambesiaca Cribb. Lvs to 15×1–1.5cm, linear-ligulate, fleshy, folded. Rac. to 15cm; fls creamy yellow, exterior rusty-hairy; sep. and pet. 11–14mm, ovate; lip 11–12mm, ovate, v. concave; spur 16–20cm. Zam., Malawi, Zimb., Moz.

Summer-holly Arctostaphylos diversifolia.
Summer Hyacinth Galtonia candicans.
Summer Lilac Buddleja davidii.
Summer Marsh Afrikaner Gladiolus tristis var. aestivalis.
Summer Phlox Phlox paniculata.

Summer Pumpkin *Cucurbita pepo.*
Summer Savory *Satureja hortensis.*
Summer Snowflake *Leucojum aestivum.*
Summer Squash *Cucurbita pepo.*
Summer Sundrops *Oenothera fruticosa* ssp. *glauca.*
Summer-sweet *Clethra* (*C. alnifolia*).
Summit Cedar *Athrotaxis × laxifolia.*
Sunberry *Solanum × burbankii.*
Sun Bush *Bossiaea.*
Suncups *Oenothera* (*O. fruticosa; O. perennis; O. pilosella*).

Sundacarpus (Buchholz & Gray) Page. Podocarpaceae. 1 everg. coniferous tree to 40m or more. Crown conic to columnar; br. whorled. Lvs flattened, spreading, oblong, 5–15cm, to 25cm on vigorous young trees, midrib grooved above, 2 stomatal bands visible beneath. Seed cones to 1.5×1cm, drupe-like, fleshy, glaucous blue-black; seed receptacle not fleshy. Sumatra, Philipp. to N Queensld. Z10.
S. amarus (Bl.) Page.
→*Podocarpus* and *Prumnopitys.*

Sunflower *Helianthus.*

Sunipia Lindl. Orchidaceae. 16 epiphytic orchids. Pbs bearing a single coriaceous lf at apex. Rac. lat.; sep. equal, lat. sep. fused; pet. spreading; lip entire, ± tongue-shaped, concave, margins recurved. India, SE Asia to Taiwan. Z10.
S. palacea (Lindl.) P. Hunt. Pbs ovoid. Lvs linear-oblong. Fls 4–6, pendent; sep. pale green, striped red, dors. sep. lanceolate, arched, lat. sep. fused, projecting under the lip; pet rounded, pale yellow-green; lip red-brown, cuneate. Autumn. India.
→*Bulbophyllum.*

Sun Marigold *Dimorphotheca.*
Sun Pitcher *Heliamphora.*
Sun Plant *Portulaca grandiflora.*
Sunray *Enceliopsis.*
Sunrise Horsechestnut *Aesculus × neglecta.*
Sun Rose *Helianthemum.*
Sunshine Rose *Rosa setigera.*
Sunshine Wattle *Acacia terminalis.*
Sun Spurge *Euphorbia helioscopia.*
Suntwood *Acacia nilotica.*
Supple Jack *Berchemia scandens.*
Surinam Cherry *Eugenia uniflora.*

Sutera Roth. Scrophulariaceae. 130 herbs, subshrubs and small shrubs. Fls. in racs, spikes or cymes; cal. 5-toothed; cor. tube straight or curved, lobes 5, subequal or forming 2 lips. Macaronesia, S Afr. Z9.
S. grandiflora (Galpin) Hiern. PURPLE GLORY PLANT. Woody-based glandular-pubesc. perenn. herb to 1m. Lvs to 2.5cm, toothed, hispid. Rac. to 30cm, term.; cor. lavender to deep purple, tube to 2.5cm, slender, widening and curved upwards toward white throat, limb to 2.5cm diam., seg. obovate, spreading. Summer–autumn. S Afr.

Sutherlandia R. Br. Leguminosae (Papilionoideae). 5 shrubs. Lvs imparipinnate. Rac. slender, axill.; fls pea-like, rose to scarlet or purple. Fr. bladder-like. Summer. S Afr. Z9.
S. frutescens (L.) R. Br. BALLOON PEA; DUCK PLANT. To 1.25m; br. virgate. Lvs 6.4–8.9cm; lfts 7–19mm, 13–21, lanceolate to oblong, thinly pubesc. Rac., 2.5–8cm, 6–10-fld. cor. to 3.2cm, scarlet to deep purple. Fr. inflated, to 5×3.2cm. Summer. Plants offered as *S. montana* may belong here.

Suttonia A. Rich.
S. chathamica (F. Muell.) Mez = *Myrsine chathamica.*
S. nummularia Hook. f. = *Myrsine nummularia.*

Suurberg Cycad *Encephalartos longifolius.*

Swainsona Salisb. Leguminosae. *c*50 herbs and subshrubs. Lvs imparipinnate. Fls pea-like in erect, axill. rac. Aus., NZ. Z9.
S. galegifolia (Andrews) R. Br. SMOOTH DARLING PEA; SWAN FLOWER; WINTER SWEETPEA. Erect or trailing perenn. to 2m. Lfts 0.6–2cm, 21–25, narrowly obovate to linear, rounded, truncate or retuse, mucronulate. Cal. 4–6mm, glab. or thinly woolly; cor. blue through vivid purple to darker purple or crimson, standard 15–20mm diam. Spring–summer. E Aus. 'Albiflora': lvs light green; fls pure white. 'Violacea': lvs small; fls violet row.
S. grandiflora R. Br. = *S. greyana.*
S. greyana Lindl. DARLING PEA; HAIRY DARLING PEA. Shrubby perenn., 1–2m. Lfts 0.5–3.5cm, 11–23, narrow-oblong or elliptic, retuse, woolly beneath. Cal. 5–9mm, white-tomentose;

standard 15–22mm diam., lavender or vivid mauve with a median grey spot, keel and wings red or pink. S Aus.

Swallow Wort *Asclepias curassavica; Chelidonium majus.*

Swammerdamia DC.
S. antennaria DC. = *Ozothamnus antennaria.*
S. glomerata Raoul = *Ozothamnus glomeratus.*

Swamp Ash *Fraxinus caroliniana.*
Swamp Banksia *Banksia littoralis; B. paludosa; B. robur; B. seminuda.*
Swamp Bay *Magnolia virginiana.*
Swamp Blackberry *Rubus hispidus.*
Swamp Blueberry *Vaccinium corymbosum.*
Swamp Bottlebrush *Beaufortia sparsa.*
Swamp Candleberry *Myrica pensylvanica.*
Swamp Chestnut Oak *Quercus michauxii.*
Swamp Cypress *Taxodium* (*T. distichum*).
Swamp Daisy *Actinodium cunninghamii.*
Swamp Dewberry *Rubus hispidus.*
Swamp Fly Honeysuckle *Lonicera oblongifolia.*
Swamp Foxtail Grass *Pennisetum alopecuroides.*
Swamp Gooseberry *Ribes lacustre.*
Swamp Gum *Eucalyptus ovata.*
Swamp Heath *Epacris paludosa.*
Swamp Hibiscus *Hibiscus diversifolius.*
Swamp Hickory *Carya cordiformis.*
Swamp Holly *Ilex amelanchier.*
Swamp Horsetail *Equisetum fluviatile.*
Swamp Immortelle *Erythrina fusca.*
Swamp Laurel *Kalmia polifolia; Magnolia virginiana.*
Swamp Lily *Saururus cernuus.*
Swamp Locust *Gleditsia aquatica.*
Swamp Mahogany *Eucalyptus robusta.*
Swamp Mallee *Eucalyptus spathulata.*
Swamp Mallet *Eucalyptus spathulata.*
Swamp Maple *Acer rubrum.*
Swamp Meadowgrass *Poa palustris.*
Swamp Milkweed *Asclepias incarnata.*
Swamp Onion *Allium validum.*
Swamp Paperbark *Melaleuca ericifolia.*
Swamp Pink *Arethusa bulbosa; Helonias bullata.*
Swamp Red Currant *Ribes triste.*
Swamp Red Oak *Quercus falcata.*
Swamp Rose *Rosa palustris.*
Swamp Rose Mallow *Hibiscus moscheutos.*
Swamp Sedge *Carex acutiformis.*
Swamp Selaginela *Selaginella uliginosa.*
Swamp Sunflower *Helianthus angustifolius.*
Swamp Tupelo *Nyssa sylvatica* var. *biflora.*
Swamp Wattle *Acacia elongata.*
Swamp White Oak *Quercus bicolor.*
Swamp Willow *Salix myrtilloides.*
Swamp Yate *Eucalyptus occidentalis.*
Swan Flower *Swainsona galegifolia.*
Swan Orchid *Cycnoches.*
Swan Plant *Asclepias physocarpa.*
Swan River Daisy *Brachycome* (*B. iberidifolia*).
Swan River Everlasting *Rhodanthe manglesii.*
Swan River Myrtle *Hypocalymma robustum.*
Swan River Pea *Brachysema.*

Swartzia Gmel. non Schreb. = *Solandra.*

Swatow Mustard *Brassica juncea.*
Sweat Plant *Selaginella pallescens.*
Swede *Brassica napus* Napobrassica group.
Swedish Birch *Betula pendula* 'Dalecarlica'.
Swedish Ivy *Pectranthus.*
Swedish Whitebeam *Sorbus intermedia.*
Sweet Acacia *Acacia farnesiana.*
Sweet Alison *Lobularia maritima.*
Sweet Alyssum *Lobularia maritima.*
Sweet Balm *Melissa officinalis.*
Sweet Basil *Ocimum basilicum.*
Sweet Bay *Laurus nobilis; Magnolia virginiana.*
Sweet Bells *Leucothoë racemosa.*
Sweet Birch *Betula lenta.*
Sweet Box *Sarcococca.*
Sweet Brier *Rosa rubiginosa.*
Sweet Brush *Cercocarpus montanus* var. *glaber.*
Sweet Buckeye *Aesculus flava.*
Sweet Calabash *Passiflora maliformis.*
Sweet Calamus *Acorus calamus.*
Sweet Cassava *Manihot dulcis.*

Sweet Cherry *Prunus avium.*
Sweet Chestnut *Castanea sativa.*
Sweet Cicely *Myrrhis odorata; Osmorhiza.*
Sweet Coltsfoot *Petasites.*
Sweet Coneflower *Rudbeckia subtomentosa.*
Sweet Corn *Zea mays.*
Sweetcup *Passiflora maliformis.*
Sweet Elder *Sambucus canadensis.*
Sweet False Chamomile *Matricaria recutita.*
Sweet Fern *Comptonia peregrina; Pteris macilenta.*
Sweet Flag *Acorus calamus.*
Sweet Gale *Myrica gale.*
Sweet Garlic *Tulbaghia fragrans.*
Sweet Granadilla *Passiflora ligularis.*
Sweet Grass *Glyceria.*
Sweet Gum *Liquidambar (L. styraciflua).*
Sweetheart Geranium *Pelargonium echinatum.*
Sweetheart Ivory *Hedera hibernica.*
Sweetheart Ivy *Hedera helix* 'Deltoidea'
Sweetheart Vine *Ceropegia linearis* ssp. *woodii.*
Sweet-hurts *Vaccinium angustifolium.*
Sweet Jarvil *Osmorhiza (O. claytonii).*
Sweet Lemon *Citrus limetta.*
Sweet Lime *Citrus limetta.*
Sweet Mace *Tagetes lucida.*
Sweet Marjoram *Origanum majorana.*
Sweet Melon *Cucumis melo.*
Sweet Nancy *Achillea ageratum.*
Sweet Olive *Osmanthus.*
Sweet Orange *Citrus sinensis.*
Sweet Pea *Inga laurina.*
Sweetpea *Lathyrus odoratus.*
Sweet Pea Shrub *Polygala* × *dalmaisiana.*
Sweet Pepper *Capsicum annuum* var. *annuum.*
Sweet Pepper Bush *Clethra alnifolia.*
Sweet Pignut *Carya ovalis.*
Sweet Pitcher Plant *Sarracenia rubra.*
Sweet Potato *Ipomoea batatas.*
Sweet Reseda *Reseda odorata.*
Sweet Rocket *Hesperis matronalis.*
Sweet Scabious *Scabiosa atropurpurea.*
Sweet-scented Geranium *Pelargonium graveolens.*
Sweet-scented Marigold *Tagetes lucida.*
Sweet-scented Mexican Marigold *Tagetes lucida.*
Sweet-scented Wattle *Acacia suaveolens.*
Sweetshade *Hymenosporum flavum.*
Sweetsop *Annona squamosa.*
Sweetspire *Itea virginica.*
Sweet Sultan *Amberboa moschata.*
Sweet Tea *Osmanthus fragrans.*
Sweet Tea Vine *Gynostemma pentaphyllum.*
Sweet Trumpet Plant *Sarracenia rubra.*
Sweet Unicorn Plant *Proboscidea fragrans.*
Sweet Vernal Grass *Anthoxanthum odoratum.*
Sweet Vetch *Hedysarum boreale.*
Sweet Viburnum *Viburnum odoratissimum.*
Sweet Violet *Viola odorata.*
Sweet Wattle *Acacia farnesiana; A. suaveolens.*
Sweet White Violet *Viola blanda.*
Sweet William *Dianthus barbatus.*
Sweet Winter Grape *Vitis cinerea.*
Sweetwood *Glycyrrhiza glabra.*
Sweet Woodruff *Galium odoratum.*
Sweet Wormwood *Artemisia annua.*

Swertia L. Gentianaceae. *c*50 ann., monocarpic or perenn. herbs. Lvs basal, usually stalked to opposite then alt., smaller, ± sessile on erect st. Fls in cymes or pan., 4- or 5-merous, cor. and cal. tubes v. short, cor., usually rotate, nectaries 1–2 at base of each, sometimes fringed lobe. Mts of N Amer., Eurasia (esp. Sino-Himal.), Afr. Z7 unless specified.

S. **alata** Hayata. Ann. to 60cm st. angled. Lvs to 5cm, ovate-lanceolate. Fls in terminal pan., lurid green-yellow spotted purple; cor. lobes to 0.7cm, 4; nectaries 1 per lobe. Autumn. Himal.

S. **albicaulis** (Douglas ex Griseb.) Kuntze = *Frasera albicaulis.*

S. **atroviolacea** H. Sm. Perenn. to 30cm. Lvs to 10cm, broad-ovate to spathulate long petiolate. Fls in pan., deep purple-maroon, green within, 5-merous; cor. to 2cm, lobes narrow-ovate; nectaries 2 per lobe. Autumn. China.

S. **aucheri** Boiss. = *S. longifolia.*

S. **bella** Hemsl. Ann. to 30cm. Lvs to 2.5cm, ovate, thick. Fls in pan., purple-blue, 5-merous; cor. lobes to 2.5cm, oblong to obovate; nectary 1 per lobe, fringed. Summer. China.

S. **bimaculata** Hook. f. & Thoms. Ann. to 2m; st. 4-angled. Lvs to 15cm, elliptic to ovate. Fls long-pedicelled, in crowded corymbs, 4- to 5-merous, dull white or yellow, spotted black; cor. lobes to 12.5mm, elliptic; nectaries bright green. Autumn. E Himal.

S. **calicina** Franch. Erect perenn. to 45cm. Lvs narrow-oblong to spathulate. Fls in pan., 5-merous, white to pale yellow, veined purple; cor. lobes to 2.5cm; nectaries 2 per lobe, fringed. Autumn. China.

S. **chinensis** Franch. Erect ann. Lvs to 10cm, lanceolate. Fls in large, dense pan., 5-merous, yellow with purple at centre; cor. lobes ovate; nectaries 2 per lobe, fringed. Autumn. China.

S. **chirata** Hamilt. Ann. to 1.5m. Lvs to 15cm, ovate to elliptic. Fls many in large, leafy pan., 4-merous, lurid green-yellow veined purple; cor. lobes 18mm, ovate, acuminate; nectaries 2 per lobe, fringed. Autumn. Himal.

S. **coerulea** Royle. Perenn. to 30cm. Lvs to 7.5cm, spathulate to oblong. Fls in dense pan., 5-merous, pale blue veined green; cor. lobes to 2cm, ovate nectaries fringed. Autumn. W Himal.

S. **cordata** Wallich. Ann. to 75cm; st. 4-angled. Lvs to 3.5cm, ovate, base cordate. Fls many in large pan., 4- to 5-merous, cream, veined purple; cor. lobes 8mm, elliptic to oblong; nectaries viscous, yellow. Autumn. Himal.

S. **corymbosa** Wight. Perenn. to 45cm; st. 4-winged. Lvs to 3cm, obovate to spathulate. Fls in term. flat corymb, 4-merous, white or pale blue, blue-veined; cor. lobes 8mm, broad-oblong; nectary solitary, margin pubesc. Autumn. S India (mts).

S. **decora** Franch. Ann. to 40cm. Lvs to 5cm, oblong to obovate, obtuse. Fls in pan., 5-merous, violet-blue; cor. lobes to 2.5cm, lanceolate to ovate-lanceolate, to 2.5cm; nectaries 2 per lobe. Autumn. China.

S. **delavayi** Franch. Erect ann.; st. to 35cm. Lvs to 5cm, narrow-ovate to lanceolate. Fls many, in spreading pan., 5-merous, pale purple-blue; cor. lobes 7mm, narrow ovate, nectaries 2 per lobe, shortly fringed. Autumn. China.

S. **dilatata** Wallich. Ann. to 75cm. Lvs to 3.5cm, lanceolate. Fls in pan., 4- or 5-merous, green-yellow, banded purple at base; cor. lobes 15mm, ovate, acute; nectary 1 per lobe, horseshoe-shape. Autumn. Himal.

S. **elata** H. Sm. Erect perenn. to 75cm. Lvs to 23cm, narrow-ovate to spathulate, long-petiolate. Fls in dense pan., 5-merous, pale blue, spotted green; cor. lobes 15mm, broadly ovate; nectaries 2 per lobe, much fringed. Autumn. China.

S. **handeliana** H. Sm. Tufted perenn. to 5cm. Lvs to 2.5cm, round to reniform, petiolate. Fls term., solitary, pale purple-blue; cor. lobes 18mm, ovate to rounded. Autumn. SE Tibet, W China.

S. **hookeri** C.B. Clarke. Robust perenn. to 1.3m. Lvs 15–20cm, spathulate-elliptic to ovate. Fls in dense whorls and term. cluster, 4-merous, maroon, veined dark blue; cor. campanulate, lobes 1.8cm, erect, ovate; nectary solitary, large. E Nepal to SE Tibet.

S. **kingii** Hook. f. Stout perenn. to 60cm. Lvs to 30cm, petiolate, elliptic to oblong-ovate. Fls in dense spike, 5-merous, green-white; cor. lobes 2.5cm, oblong, obtuse; nectaries 2 per lobe, long-fringed. Himal.

S. **longifolia** Boiss. Robust perenn. to 90cm. Lvs to 30cm, narrow-spathulate to spathulate-elliptic, tapering gently to petiole. Infl. spicate, interrupted; fls 4–merous, pale yellow to yellow-white; nectaries fringed, 1 per lobe. Summer. W Asia.

S. **marginata** Schrenk. Perenn. to 45cm. Lvs to 15cm, ovate to oblong, long-petiolate. Fls in pan., 5-merous, green, edged yellow; cor. lobes to 2cm, elliptic. Summer. N Asia.

S. **multicaulis** D. Don. Low perenn. to 15cm. Lvs 5cm, narrowly spathulate, tapering to broad petiole. Fls in compound cymes, long-pedicelled, 5-merous, slate-blue; cor. lobes to 13mm, oblong; nectary solitary, fringed. Summer–autumn. C Nepal to SE Tibet.

S. **palustris** Nels. Erect perenn. to 45cm. Lvs to 15cm, oblong to oblanceolate, long-periolate. Fls in pan., 5-merous, deep blue to purple blue; cor. lobes to 2cm, oblong; nectaries 2 per lobe, fringed. Summer. N Amer.

S. **paniculata** Wallich. Erect ann. 1m. Lvs to 5cm, oblong to lanceolate. Fls in pan., 5-merous, white, spotted purple at base; cor. lobes 7mm, ovate, acute; nectary 1 per lobe. Autumn. W Himal.

S. **parryi** (Torr.) Kuntze = *Frasera parryi.*

S. **perennis** L. MARSH FELWORT. Perenn. to 60cm, st. 4–angled. Lvs to 15cm, ovate to elliptic. Fls in pan., 5-merous, wet slate blue or dirty violet, occas. yellow-green or white; cor. lobes to 2cm, ovate; nectaries 2 per lobe, fringed. Summer–autumn. Mts of Eurasia, N Amer. Z5.

S. **perfoliata** Royle ex G. Don = *S. speciosa.*

S. **petiolata** Royle ex D. Don. Perenn. to 60cm. Lvs to 8cm, lanceolate along petiolate. Fls in clusters of 3–5 within spike-like term. pan., 4- or 5-merous, grey; cor. lobes 1cm, narrow-elliptic; nectaries 1 or 2 per lobe, fringed, yellow. Summer. Afghan. to W Nepal, SE Tibet.

S. pubescens Franch. Erect ann. to 60cm. Lvs to 5cm, lanceolate to linear. Fls in pan., 5-merous, white, purple at base; cor. lobes ovate; nectaries 1 per lobe. Autumn. China.

S. purpurascens Wallich. Ann. to 1m. Lvs to 6.5cm, oblong to lanceolate. Fls many, in pan., 5-merous deep red-purple; cor. lobes 7mm, ovate, acute, reflexed; nectaries horseshoe-shaped. Autumn. W Himal.

S. radiata (Kellogg) Kuntze = *Frasera speciosa.*

S. speciosa Wallich ex D. Don non G. Don. Robust perenn. to 1.3m. Lvs to 20cm, elliptic-lanceolate, bases of st. lvs united around st. Fls in cymose pan., 5-merous, grey; cor. lobes 1.5–2cm, spathulate-oblong; nectaries 2 per lobe, long-fringed. Summer. Pak. to Bhutan.

S. speciosa G. Don non Wallich ex D. Don = *S. petiolata.*

S. tetragona C.B. Clarke. Ann. to 60cm; st. 4-angled. Lvs to 2.5cm, lanceolate to linear. fls in pan., 5-merous, white; cor. lobes 2cm, ovate acute; nectaries 2 per lobe, fringed. Autumn. W Himal.

S. thomsonii C.B. Clarke. Robust perenn. to 75cm, lvs 7.5cm, oblong to elliptic. Fls in pan., long-pedicelled, 5-merous, blue-grey; cor. lobes 8mm, oblong to ovate; nectaries 2 per lobe, minute. Summer. W Himal.

S. tibetica Batal. Stout perenn. to 1m. Basal lvs to 20cm, long-petiolate, cauline lvs broader. Fls solitary, long-pedicelled, 5-merous, yellow-white, pale blue at base; cor. lobes broadly ovate; nectaries 2 per lobe. Autumn. E Tibet, W China.

S. umpquaensis (Peck & Appleg.) St. John = *Frasera umpquaensis.*

S. wardii Marq. Stout perenn. to 40cm. Basal lvs to 12.5cm oblong. Fls solitary or paired, long-pedicelled, 5-merous, slate grey; cor. lobes to 2.5cm, oblong; nectary 1 per lobe, fringed. Summer. SE Tibet, W China.

Swida Opiz.

S. alba (L.) Opiz = *Cornus alba.*
S. amomum (Mill.) Small = *Cornus amomum.*
S. australis (C.A. Mey.) Pojark. ex Grossh. = *Cornus australis.*
S. baileyi Rydb. = *Cornus stolonifera* 'Bailey'.
S. baileyi Rydb. = *Cornus baileyi.*
S. controversa (Hemsl.) Soják = *Cornus controversa.*
S. foemina Rydb. = *Cornus stricta.*
S. glabrata Heller = *Cornus glabrata.*
S. hemsleyi Soják = *Cornus hemsleyi.*
S. hessei Soják = *Cornus hessei.*
S. macrophylla Soják = *Cornus macrophylla.*
S. microcarpa (Nash) Small = *Cornus asperifolia.*
S. monbeigii Soják = *Cornus monbeigii.*
S. oblonga Soják = *Cornus oblonga.*
S. paucinervis Soják = *Cornus paucinervis.*
S. racemosa Mold. = *Cornus racemosa.*
S. rugosa Rydb. = *Cornus rugosa.*
S. sanguinea Opiz = *Cornus sanguinea.*
S. stolonifera Rydb. = *Cornus stolonifera.*
S. stricta (Lam.) Small = *Cornus stricta.*
S. walteri Soják = *Cornus walteri.*

Swiss Chard *Beta vulgaris* var. *flavescens.*
Swiss-cheese Plant *Monstera.*
Swiss-cheese Plant *Monstera deliciosa.*
Swiss Mountain Pine *Pinus mugo.*
Swiss Pine *Pinus cembra.*
Swiss Willow *Salix helvetica.*
Switch Cane *Arundinaria gigantea.*
Switch Grass *Panicum virgatum.*
Switch Ivy *Leucothoë fontanesiana.*
Sword Brake *Pteris ensiformis.*
Sword Fern *Nephrolepis.*
Swordfish Banksia *Banksia elderiana.*
Sword-leaf Phlox *Phlox buckleyi.*
Sword-leaf Wattle *Acacia gladiiformis.*
Sword-leaved Helleborine *Cephalanthera longifolia.*
Sword Lily *Iris.*

Syagrus Mart. Palmae. 32 palms. St. solitary or clustered, subterranean to erect, sometimes swollen at base, clothed with persistent lf bases, becoming bare. Lvs pinnate, reduplicate; sheath becoming a woven fibrous mass; pinnae single-fold, regularly or irregularly spaced and held in differing planes on rachis, linear. S Amer. Z10.

S. allenii Glassm. = *S. orinocensis.*

S. botryophora (Mart.) Mart. PATI; PATIOBA. 15–18m. Trunk 15–25cm diam. Lvs to 5m, arching to pendent; pinnae 76–80 per side, slender-pointed, median pinnae 58–62cm. Braz.

S. brachyrhyncha Burret = *S. cocoides.*

S. campestris (Mart.) H. Wendl. = *S. flexuosa.*

S. cocoides Mart. JATA-UBA; CUNHAM-HEN; PIRIRIMA; UAPERIMA; PATI. 5–6m. Trunk to 7cm diam. Lvs 2m, lax, arching; pinnae 56 to 63 per side, usually in clusters of 2–4, median pinnae 60–92cm, linear, narrow, slightly curled, glab. Braz.

S. comosa (Mart.) Mart. GUARIROBA DO CAMPO; PALMITO AMARGOSO; BABAO; CATOLE; JERIVA; PATI. To 7m. Trunk to 10cm diam., sometimes clustered. Lvs 1–1.25m, spreading; pinnae crowded, 78–82 per side, usually in clusters of 2–4, erect, lanceolate, median pinnae 38–44cm. Braz.

S. coronata (Mart.) Becc. LICURI; NICURY; OURICURY; LICURYSEIRO; COQUIERI DICORI; CABECUDO. 3–12m. Pinnae 80–119 per side, in clusters of 3–4, narrow, slender-pointed, median pinnae 60–72cm. Braz.

S. drudei (Becc.) Becc. = *S. cocoides.*

S. flexuosa (Mart.) Becc. ACUMA; COQUIERO DO CAMPO; PALMITO DO CAMPO; COCO DO VAQUIERO. 2–4.5m; trunks often tufted. Pinnae 70–79 per side, in clusters of 2–4, median pinnae 30–36×0.5–1.6cm. Braz.

S. glazoviana (Dammer) Becc. = *S. petraea.*

S. macrocarpa Barb. Rodr. MARIA ROSA; BARBA DE BOI GRANDE; HARYOB; JURUA. Trunk to 20cm diam. Pinnae to 60cm, in clusters of 3–4, spreading, crisped. Braz.

S. orinocensis (Spruce) Burret. COCOCITO; COQUITO. 8–12m. Trunk to 15cm diam. Pinnae *c*100 per side, in clusters of 2–3, median pinnae 50–56cm. Colomb., Venez.

S. petraea (Mart.) Becc. ACUMO RASTEIRO; INDAYA RASTEIRO; COQUIERO DO CAMPO; INDAYA DO CAMPO; ARIRY; GURIRY. Usually stemless. Lvs 45–90cm, few, slender; pinnae not clustered, median pinnae 15–40cm, linear, slender-pointed. Boliv., Braz.

S. quinquefaria Becc. = *S. coronata.*

S. romanzoffiana (Cham.) Glassm. QUEEN PALM. 10–20m. Trunk to 40cm diam., sometimes swollen at middle. Lvs 3–5m; petiole 40–45cm; median pinnae 70–85cm, acute or acuminate, in clusters of 1–5. Braz.

S. stenopetala Burret = *S. orinocensis.*

S. urbaniana (Dammer) Becc. = *S. flexuosa.*

→*Arecastrum* and *Cocos.*

Sycamore *Acer pseudoplatanus; Ficus sycomorus; Platanus.*
Sycamore Fig *Ficus sycomorus.*

×**Sycoparrotia** Endress & Aulinker. (*Parrotia persica* ×*Sycopsis sinensis.*) Hamamelidaceae. Semi-evergreen shrub to 4m. Lvs to 12cm, obovate, leathery, with 5 small teeth per side toward apex. Fls have intermediate between parents; pet. brown-woolly, anth. bright red. Spring. Gdn origin. Z7.

×*S. semidecidua* Endress & Aulinker.

Sycopsis Oliv. Hamamelidaceae. 7 everg. shrubs or small trees. Fls small, apetalous, ♂ or hermaphrodite, in rac. or heads; floral tube urceolate, 5-lobed, enclosing superior ovary; ♂ fls. with sep. minute, sta. 6–10. Himal., China, Malaysia. Z8.

S. sinensis Oliv. To 6m. Lvs to 12cm, leathery, ovate to elliptic-lanceolate, tips occas. serrulate, dark green above, pale beneath; petioles warty. Fls in thick clusters to 2.5cm; bracts red-brown, woolly; fil. fine, yellow, anth. red. Early spring. C China.

Sydney Blue Gum *Eucalyptus saligna.*
Sydney Golden Wattle *Acacia longifolia.*
Sydney Peppermint *Eucalyptus piperita.*
Sydney Rock Rose *Boronia serrulata.*

Symphoricarpos Duh. SNOWBERRY; CORALBERRY. Caprifoliaceae. 17 decid. shrubs differing from *Lonicera* in regular cor. and 2-seeded fr. St. usually branching and suckering freely. Lvs opposite, simple. Fls small, solitary, or in dense rac.; cal. cupulate, 4–5-lobed; cor. campanulate or funnelform, 4–5-lobed; cor. campanulate or funnelform, 4–5-lobed. Fr. a globose, ovoid or ellipsoid, berry-like drupe. N & C Amer., China.

S. acutus Dipp. = *S. hesperius.*

S. albus (L.) Blake. SNOWBERRY; COMMON SNOWBERRY; WAX-BERRY. To 120cm. Shoots slender, erect, slightly lanuginose. Lvs to 5cm, oval to oval-oblong, blunt, rounded at base, sometimes lacerate, dark green above, lighter and finely downy beneath. Fls pink, in spikes or clusters. Fr. 12.5mm diam., globose or ovoid, snow-white. Summer. N Amer. 'Constance Spry': fr. large, white. 'Turesson': br. distinctly nodding; cor. to 5mm, pink, pubesc. inside; fr. ellipsoid. f. *ovatus* (Späth) Rehd. To 2m+. Vigorous. Lvs broad-ovate, cuneate to rounded at base, dark blue-green. Fls light pink. Fr. slightly larger. var. *laevigatus* (Fern.) Blake. To 180cm, forming dense thickets. St. erect, many-branched, glab. Lvs to 7.5cm, glab. Fls in short rac. Fr. larger profuse. W N Amer. (Alask. to Calif.). 'Taff's Variegated': lvs variegated yellow; fls pink; fr. white. Z3.

S. ×*chenaultii* Rehd. (*S. microphyllus* ×*S. orbiculatus.*) Erect, to 2m+. Shoots densely downy. Lvs to 2cm, ovate, dark green above, blue-green beneath, densely soft-pubesc. Fls pink, in short, term. spikes. Fr. globose, red and white-spotted, or often white stippled with red on exposed side. Summer. 'Elegance': habit erect, dense; shoot tips red-brown; lvs oblong, to 27mm long, dark green above, blue tinted beneath, young growth flushed red; fls pink; fr. red, infrequent. 'Hancock': dwarf to 50cm, of procumbent habit. Z4.

S. ×*doorenbosii* Krüssm. (*S. albus* var. *laevigatus* ×*S.* ×*chenaultii.*) also known as the Doorenbos Hybrids. V. vigorous, to 2m. Shoots downy. Lvs to 4cm, elliptic to broadly ovate, obtuse, dark green and glab. above, paler and pubesc. beneath. Fls white flushing pink, in short rac. Fr. to 13mm diam., globose, white flushed pink on exposed side. 'Erect': habit upright, compact, vigorous; fr. lilac-pink. 'Magic Berry': habit spreading, compact, to 2m; fr. small, lilac-carmine, abundant. 'Mother of Pearl': habit semi-pendulous, to 1.5m high; fr. large, white marbled pink. 'White Hedge': erect, compact; fr. small, white, abundant, in upright clusters. Z4.

S. giraldii Hesse = *S. orbiculatus.*

S. glomeratus Pursh = *S. orbiculatus.*

S. hesperius Jones. Low-growing or decumbent to 3m. Young shoots downy. Lvs to 3cm, oval, sinuate to coarsely shallow-lobed, apex acute or obtuse, base broadly cuneate to rounded, dark green and glab. above, paler with veins short-pilose beneath. Fls pink, in small, term. rac. Fr. to 6mm diam., white, subglobose. Summer. W N Amer. Z6.

S. heyeri Dipp. = *S. occidentalis* var. *heyeri.*

S. microphyllus HBK. Erect, much-branched, to 2m. Shoots somewhat woolly. Lvs to 2.5cm, oval, acute or apiculate, dark green and glab. or fine-pubesc. above, grey-green and short-pilose beneath. Fls pink, solitary or paired, or in short spikes. Fr. to 8.5mm diam., translucent white flushed pink, globose. Late summer. Mex. Z9.

S. mollis Nutt. Low shrub to 90cm. Young shoots velutinous. Lvs to 2.5cm, rounded to oval, sometimes shallow-lobed, velutinous and dense grey-lanuginose, eesp. beneath. Fls pink-white, small, few, solitary or clustered. Fr. globose, 6.5mm diam., white. Spring. W US. Z7.

S. montanus HBK = *S. microphyllus.*

S. nanus Greene = *S. mollis.*

S. occidentalis Hook. WOLFBERRY. To 2m. Shoots pubesc. Lvs to 5cm+, subcoriaceous, oval or oblong, conspicuously veined, obtuse, entire to undulate, grey blue-green above, lighter and glab. or lanuginose beneath. Fls pale pink, in dense spikes or rac. to 3cm. Fr. globose, 8.5mm diam., dull green-white soon discolouring bruised-brown. Summer. W N Amer. var. *heyeri* Dieck. Lvs thinner-textured, slightly more obtuse, more obscurely veined. Colorado. Z3.

S. orbiculatus Moench. CORALBERRY; INDIAN CURRANT. St. to 2m, erect. Br. thin, pubesc. at first. Lvs to 3cm, oval or ovate, rounded at base, full dark green above, pubesc., grey-green beneath, tinted red in autumn. Fls ivory flushing dull pink, in short clusters. Fr. to 0.6cm diam., ovoid-globose, grey-white becoming opaque wine-red. Summer–autumn. E US, Mex. 'Albovariegatus' ('Argenteovariegatus'): lvs rounded, irregular margin of white. 'Aureovariegatus' ('Variegatus', 'Follis Variegatis'): lvs small, irregularly emarginated yellow. 'Bowles' Gold Variegated': lvs with wide gold margin. 'Leucocarpus': fls yellow tinted green; fr. white. Z2.

S. oreophilus Gray. Erect to 1.5m. Br. slender, spreading. Lvs to 2.5cm, ovate-orbicular, acute or subacute, entire or dentate, thin-textured, glab., paler beneath. Fls rose, mostly paired, or in few-fld, terminal spikes. Fr. to 1cm, ovoid or ellipsoid, white. Summer. SW US. Z6.

S. ovatus Späth = *S. albus* f. *ovatus.*

S. pauciflorus Britt. = *S. albus.*

S. racemosus Michx. non hort. = *S. albus.*

S. racemosus hort. non Michx. = *S. albus* var. *laevigatus.*

S. racemosus var. *laevigatus* Fern. = *S. albus* var. *laevigatus.*

S. rivularis Suksd. = *S. albus* var. *laevigatus.*

S. rotundifolius A. Gray. Erect, to 90cm. Shoots minutely downy. Lvs to 2.5cm, rounded to oval or ovate, obtuse, sometimes sinuae, pubesc. above, downy grey beneath. Fls pink-white, in 2–5-fld spikes. Fr. oval or subglobose, 6.5mm diam., white. Summer. SW US. Z7.

S. sinensis Rehd. Erect to 1.5m. Br. slender, glab. Lvs to 5cm, oval to rhombic-ovate, acute or subobtuse, cuneate at base, glab., green above, glaucescent beneath. Fls white, solitary. Fr. ovoid, 7mm, blue-black, pruinose, beaked. Summer. C & SW China. Z6.

S. vulgaris Michx. = *S. orbiculatus.*

Symphyandra A. DC. RING BELLFLOWER. Campanulaceae. 12 perenn. herbs. Lower lvs often cordate, denticulate, long-petiolate, upper lvs few. Fls in pan. or rac.; cal. deeply 5-lobed; cor. campanulate, 5-lobed. E Medit.

S. armena (Steven) A. DC. Erect or sprawling herb to 60cm, tomentose; st. erect or drooping thin, flexuous. Lower lvs to 25cm, cordate-acuminate, incised, long-petiolate. Fls erect or pendulous, solitary or term., corymbose, white sometimes flushed blue. Summer. Cauc. Z7.

S. asiatica Nak. Erect, to 80cm. Lvs elliptic to ovate-lanceolate, irregularly dentate, pilose above, glab. beneath. Infl. lax, 5-fld; fls violet. Summer. Korea. Z8.

S. cretica A. DC. Erect, glab. perenn., to 40cm. Lover lvs to 10cm, cordate to reniform to elliptic, undulate, petiolate, upper lvs smaller, sessile. Fls pendulous, in few-fld rac., blue to white. Crete, Greece. Z8.

S. hoffmannii Pantocsek. Perenn., to 60cm, pubesc. Lvs ovate to lanceolate, narrowing at base, incised, to 15cm including winged petiole. Fls pendulous in terminal rac., white to cream or pale yellow. Summer. Balk. Z4.

S. pendula (Bieb.) A. DC. Similar to *S. hoffmannii*, to 60cm, pendulous, pubesc. Lvs cordate-lanceolate to linear, crenate, velutinous. Infl. racemose; fls. cream. Cauc. Z6.

S. wanneri (Rochel) Heuff. Erect perenn., to 35cm, pubesc. Lvs narrowly elliptic to linear-oblong, irregularly dentate, with a winged petiole or sessile. Fls in term. or axill. pan. Violet. Alps. Z7.

→*Campanula.*

Symphyglossum Schltr. Orchidaceae. 6 epiphytic orchids. Pbs ovoid. Lvs sheathing and 1–2 per apex linear, erect or suberect. Rac. or a pan. term., arching to pendent, many-fld; sep. oblong or oblanceolate; pet. wider than sep.; lip simple, unguiculate, reflexed above, callusw carinate. Venez., Colomb., Ecuad., Peru. Z10.

S. sanguineum (Rchb. f.) Schltr. Pbs to 5cm. Lvs to 22×1.5cm, linear. Infl. to 50cm; tep. rose-red; sep. to 1.2cm, narrowly elliptic or ovate-lanceolate; lip rose pink, white at base, to 1cm, ovate to subtriangular, callus bicarinate. Autumn–spring. Ecuad.

→*Cochlioda* and *Mesospinidium.*

Symphytum L. COMFREY. Boraginaceae. 35 rhizorcatous perenn. herbs, often hispid. Lvs mostly radical and long-stalked, shorter, ± sessile on st. Infl. of short scorpioid, racemose term. cymes, bracteate; cal. tubular or campanulate, 5-lobed, accrescent; cor. tube cylindrical to narrowly clavate; lobes 5, short, triangular to semicircular, throat with 5 scales; sta. 5, usually included; style exserted. Eur. to Cauc. and Iran. Z5.

S. asperrimum Sims = *S. asperum.*

S. asperum Lepech. PRICKLY COMFREY. St. to 150cm, branched, sparingly pubesc. Lvs ovate or elliptic-lanceolate to oblong, base cordate or rounded to cuneate, petiolate to sessile, setose. Infl. many-fld; cor. to 17mm, pink at first, becoming blue or lilac. Eur., Cauc., Iran.

S. bulbosum C. Schimper. Rhiz. slender, tuberous. St. to 50cm, slightly branched, sparingly setose. Lvs ovate to elliptic-lanceolate or spathulate, petiolate. Infl. several- to many-fld; cor. to 12mm, yellow or white, lobes erect. S Eur.

S. caucasicum Bieb. St. to 60cm, branched, pilose. Basal lvs to 20×8cm, ovate-lanceolate to oblong-lanceolate. Cymes paired, scorpioid; cor. to 14mm, red-purple becoming blue. Cauc., Iran. 'Eminence': habit low, spreading, to 45cm high; lvs velvety, tinted grey; fls rich blue, in short branched spikes, early summer.

S. cordatum Waldst. & Kit. ex Willd. St. to 50cm, simple, sparsely pubesc. Lvs cordate, long-petiolate. Infl. many-fld; cor. to 18mm, pale yellow. Eur.

S. ×*ferrariense* C. Massalongo. (*S. officinale* ×*S. orientale.*) Intermediate between parents; fls dirty white or pinkish.

S. ×*floribundum* Bucknall. = *S.* ×*ferrariense.*

S. grandiflorum A. DC.. St. to 40cm, ascending-decumbent, shortly pubesc. Lvs elliptic or ovate to ovate-lanceolate, base rounded or subcordate, petiolate. Infl. many-fld; cor. to 16mm, pale yellow or cream. Eur., Cauc. 'Lilacinum': fls white, tinted pink and blue.

S. ibericum Steven = *S. grandiflorum.*

S. leonhardtianum Pugsley = *S. tuberosum* ssp. *nodosum.*

S. nodosum Schur = *S. tuberosum* ssp. *nodosum.*

S. officinale L. Herb usually densely pubesc., setose. St. to 120cm, winged, erect, stout, often branched. Lvs large, ovate-lanceolate or lanceolate. Infl. many-fld; cor. to 18mm, white, pink or purple-violet, lobes deflexed. Eur. 'Bohemicum': to 30cm; fls off-white, occas. tinted purple, pendent. 'Variegatum': lvs edged white and cream; fls cream, red in bud. ssp. *uliginosum* (A. Kerner) Nyman. St. and lvs sparingly setose, densely verrucose-hispid. EC Eur.

S. orientale L. St. to 70cm, much-branched, shortly villous. Lvs ovate to ovate-oblong, base rounded to truncate, densely pubesc. throughout, often subtomentose beneath. Cymes forked, scorpoid, many-fld; cor. 14–18mm, white. Eur.

S. ottomanum Friv. St. 30–80cm, much branched, hairy. Lvs ovate to ovate-lanceolate, base cuneate-rounded. Infl. many-fld; cor. to 7mm, pale yellow to white. Eur.

S. peregrinum Ledeb. = *S. × uplandicum.*

S. tauricum Willd. St. 20–60cm, much branched, not winged. Basal lvs to 8×5cm, ovate or ovate-oblong, cordate or rounded at base. cor. 9–14mm, pale yellow. SE Eur.

S. tuberosum L. Rhiz. tuberous. St. to 60cm, slightly branched, densely pubesc. Infl. usually 8- to 6-fld; cor. to 19mm, pale yellow, lobes deflexed. Eur. ssp. *nodosum* (Schur) Soó. Rhiz. slender, with remote, not closely spaced tuberous portions. St. sparingly pilose. Infl. usually 1 to 9-fld. Cor. scales shorter (to 6mm), triangular-subulate. W Eur.

S. × uplandicum Nyman. (*S. asperum × S. officinale.*) St. to 2m. Lvs oblong to elliptic-lanceolate, shortly decurrent or amplexicaul, pubesc. Fls to 2cm, rose becoming blue or purple; throughout cor. to 18mm. Cauc.

S. cvs. 'Goldsmith' ('Jubilee'): to 30cm; lvs dark green, edged and splashed gold and cream; fls blue, white and pink. 'Hidcote Blue': spreading, vigorous, to 45cm high; lvs rough; fls soft blue and white, fading later, red in bud. 'Hidcote Pink': to 45cm; fls pink and white. 'Langthorn's Pink' ('Roseum'): to 1.2m, vigorous; fls pink, in clusters on high st., (possibly a hybrid of *S.* 'Rubrum' and *S. × uplandicum*). 'Pink Robins': to 45cm; lvs dark green; fls narrowly tubular, strong pink, in clusters. 'Rubrum': to 30cm; fls deep red, early summer.

SYMPLOCACEAE Jacq. See *Symplocos*.

Symplocarpus Salisb. SKUNK CABBAGE; POLECAT WEED; FOETID POTHOS. Araceae. 1 herbaceous perenn. Rhiz. short, stout, vertical. Lvs to 55×40cm, ovate-cordate, produced after fls in large, rosette-like clumps, dark green, soft-textured, musky; petioles to 25cm, thick, grooved above. Spathe to 15cm, borne at ground level among thick bracts, fleshy, strongly inflated, apex sharply pointed, incurved, dull yellow-green heavily mottled and flecked liver-red; spadix barrel-shaped to semi-globose, short-stalked, usually dark. Late winter–early spring. NE N Amer., NE Asia. Z4.

S. foetidus (L.) Salisb.

Symplocos Jacq. Symplocaceae. *c*250 everg. and decid. trees and shrubs. Fls in rac., pan. or clusters; cal. usually 5-lobed; cor. with 3–5 or more lobes; sta. 4 to many. Fr. a drupe or berry. N & S Amer., Australasia, E Asia.

S. paniculata (Thunb.) Miq. SAPPHIRE BERRY; ASIATIC SWEETLEAF. Decid. shrub or tree to 5m. Young shoots downy. Lvs ovate to obovate, to 8cm, finely bristle-toothed, hispidulous with veins impressed above, sparsely pubesc. beneath. Fls fragrant, in pan. to 8cm; cor. 7mm across, white, with 5+ lobes; sta. numerous, exserted, fil. white, anth. yellow. Fr. rounded, bright blue to black, 8mm. Late spring. Himal., E Asia. Z5.

Synadenium Boiss. Euphorbiaceae. 19 shrubs or small trees. Br. fleshy, containing milky latex. Lvs alt., fleshy. Cyathia stipitate, axill.; involucre shallow-cupulate, entire or lobed, lobes ciliate to dentate, fringed with a rim of glands. Trop. Amer. to Masc. Z9.

S. arborescens E. Mey. = *S. cupulare.*

S. compactum N.E. Br. Shrub or tree, to 7m+. Lvs to 18cm obovate, acute, glab., keeled beneath, glossy green, occas. flecked purple. Infl. a pseudoumbel of 2–6 cymes, yellow-green tinged pink; cyathia 7×2mm. Kenya. var. *rubrum* S. Carter. Lvs purple-red beneath. Infl. dark red.

S. cupulare (Boiss.) Wheeler. Shrub, to 1.5m+. Lvs to 10cm, obovate, apex acute to cuspidate. Umbels to 3cm diam.; involucre to 6mm diam., green-yellow. S Afr.

S. glaucescens Pax. Shrub or tree, to 9m. Lvs 18cm, obovate to oblanceolate, obtuse, entire or dentate near apex, glaucescent. Cymes 3–5, to 3× forked; cyathia 6×2.5mm, gland rim yellow. Tanz.

S. grantii Hook. f. Succulent shrub, to 3m. Lvs to 18cm, oblanceolate to obovate, blunt to apiculate. Cyathia borne in cymes to 15×10cm, thinly pubesc.; involucre to 6mm diam., rim deep red, base pubesc. Uganda to Zimb., Moz. 'Rubrum': lvs red above, purple-red beneath, finely toothed; fls red.

S. grantii Jex-Blake non Hook. f. = *S. compactum* var. *rubrum.*

S. synadenia Baill. = *S. cupulare.*

Synammia Presl = *Polypodium.*

Synaphea R. Br. Proteaceae. 10 shrubs or lignotuberous undershrubs. Lvs coriaceous, often deeply lobed, lower lvs long-petiolate. Spike terminal, simple or branched; fls small, subtended by small, bract; perianth tube *c*5mm. W Aus. Z9.

S. petiolaris R. Br. Low, almost branchless shrub to 30cm. Lvs 30cm, 3-lobed, each seg. entire or 2–3-fld. Fls yellow. Midwinter–early summer.

S. polymorpha R. Br. Multi-stemmed, leafy shrub to 30–60cm. Lvs to 20cm, 3-lobed, further 3-segmented, seg. pungent. Fls deep yellow. Late winter–spring.

Syngonium Schott. Araceae. 33 everg. epiphytic or terrestrial perennials. St. climbing, rooting. Lvs simple, sagittate to ovate when juvenile, becoming larger and more sagittate as premature lf, adult lvs 3–5-lobed, or pedate, with 3–13 unequal seg., median seg. largest; petioles long. Infl. clustered in axils; spathe margins overlapping below forming inflated tube, limb expanded, cymbiform, green to yellow and white, often marked red or purple; spadix shorter than spathe. Frit a group of berries. Trop. Amer. Z10. Juvenile plants are usually offered.

S. albolineatum Bull = *S. angustatum.*

S. angustatum Schott. Juvenile lvs to 6cm, cordate, median lobe ovate, lat. lobes suborbicular, dark green, marked grey-green along veins above; intermediate lvs sagittate to hastate; adult lvs pedatisect, seg. 3–11, free, median seg. to 31cm, elliptic to oblong-elliptic to oblanceolate; petiole 15–40cm. Mex. to Costa Rica.

S. auritum (L.) Schott. Juvenile lvs ovate or sagittate to hastate, acute; adult lvs trisect to 5-pedatisect, seg. confluente, median 10–30cm, broad-elliptic, acuminate, auriculate at base, somewhat glossy above, petioles to 48cm. Jam., Cuba, Hispan. 'Fantasy': lvs deep green, shiny, mottled white; petiole streaked cream.

S. erythrophyllum Birdsey ex Bunting. Juvenile lvs 3–9cm, ovate, cordate, lobes rounded, black-green above, violet-purple beneath; adult lvs trisect, seg. free, spreading or slightly overlapping, median seg. 10–22cm, lanceolate-elliptic to ovate, subcoriaceous, glossy dark green above, violet-purple beneath; petioles to 20cm. Panama.

S. gracile (Miq.) Schott = *S. podophyllum.*

S. hoffmannii Schott. Juvenile lvs sagittate, 4–18cm, green with grey veins; adult lvs trisect, seg. free or confluent at base, 9–28cm; median seg. oblong-elliptic to ovate-oblong or lanceolate, lat. seg. v. inequilateral, auriculate at base, glossy above; petiole to 33cm. Costa Rica to Panama.

S. macrophyllum Engl. Juvenile lvs broad-ovate, to 16cm; adult lvs pedatisect, seg. 7–9, free or outermost confluent, median seg. 17–47cm, oblanceolate, elliptic to ovate-elliptic, acuminate to acute, downturned at apex, outer seg. auriculate, light green above; petioles to 60cm. Mex. to Ecuad.

S. mauroanum Birdsey ex Bunting. Juvenile lvs to 16cm, sagittate, marked grey- or yellow-green along main veins; adult lvs 3(-5)-sect, seg. free or confluent, median seg. 12–21cm, elliptic to ovate-elliptic, acuminate, lat. seg. inequilateral, sometimes auriculate. Costa Rica, Panama.

S. oerstedianum Schott = *S. angustatum.*

S. peliocladum Schott = *S. podophyllum* var. *peliocladum.*

S. podophyllum Schott. Juvenile lvs 7–14cm, cordate, acuminate at apex, becoming sagittate or hastate, median seg. somewhat constricted at base, basal seg. triangular; intermediate lvs to 27cm; adult lvs pedatisect, seg. 3–11, confluent to free, median seg. 16–38cm, obovate to broad-elliptic, acuminate, lowermost seg. auriculate, dark green above, pale or glaucescent beneath; petioles to 60cm. Mex. to Braz. and Boliv. 'Albolineatum' ('Angustatum'): lvs heart-shaped with white centre and veins when young, later palmate and green. 'Albovirens': lvs slender, hastate when young, ivory flushed green, edge green. 'Atrovirens': lvs hastate when young, dark green with sage green shading around veins. 'Dot Mae': cultigen of 'Albolineatum', with lvs broader and more boldly marked. 'Emerald Gem': lvs fleshy, sagittate when young, shiny dark green; petioles short. 'Emerald Gem Variegated': compact; lvs thin, white to pale gray with irregular variegation. 'Imperial White': lvs tinted blue, veins white. 'Roxanne': rosette form, later creeping; petioles pinky brown; lvs hastate, when young, glossy dull green with muddy green centre and shading along the white ribs. 'Ruth Fraser': selection from 'Albolineatum', variegation bolder and longer-lasting. 'Silver Knight': lvs silver-green. 'Tricolor': lvs hastate and trilobed when young, dark green with light green and white variegation; fls purple, light pink and cream. 'Trileaf Wonder': lvs marked ash green along lat. veins and midrib. 'Variegatum': lvs splashed pale green. var. *peliocladum* (Schott) Croat. St. covered in tuberculate excrescences. Lvs trisect to 5-lobed. Costa Rica to Panama.

S. riedelianum Schott = *S. podophyllum.*

S. salvadorense Schott. Juvenile lvs to 19cm, hastate or sagittate, lobes inequilateral; intermediate lvs to 30cm, ovate; adult lvs 3(-5)-sect, confluent to almost free, median seg. 14–28cm, broad-ovate to ovate-elliptic, acuminate, lat. seg. ovate, unequal; petioles to 42cm. Mex. to El Salvador.

S. standleyanum Bunting. Juvenile lvs to 10cm, elliptic, acuminate, intermediate lvs elliptic to oblong or lanceolate, subhastate or cordate at base; adult lvs trisect, seg. free, median 18–28cm, inequilateral, elliptic to oblong, acuminate, lat. seg. to 24cm, elliptic-oblong, sometimes slightly auriculate on outer margin; petioles to 35cm. Hond. to Costa Rica. 'Lancetilla': lvs matt green, ovate and unequal when young, erect, later 3-lobed.

S. vellozianum Schott = **S. podophyllum.**

S. wendlandii Schott. Juvenile lvs to 10cm, cordate-hastate, median seg. ovate, acuminate, lat. seg. triangular, velvety green above, veins streaked silver-grey; adult lvs trisect, median seg. 8–20cm, elliptic to oblong-elliptic, acuminate, lat. seg. to 15cm, oblong-elliptic to narrow-ovate, dark velvety green; petiole to 32cm. Costa Rica.

S. cvs. 'Jenny': lvs pale silver flushed green. 'Maya Red': lvs entirely tinted pink. 'White Butterfly': lvs silver flushed green, edged green.

S. xanthophilum Schott = **S. podophyllum.**

Synnema Benth.
S. triflorum (Roxb. ex Nees) Kuntze = *Hygrophila difformis.*

Synnotia Sweet. Iridaceae. 5 perenn. cormous herbs. St. branched or unbranched; lvs 2-ranked sheathing. Fls irregular, spicate, perianth tube curved, lobes 6, the topmost erect or arched, the other shorter, spreading or recurved; style br. 3 short. Spring. S Afr. Z9.

S. bicolor Sweet = **S. villosa.**
S. galeata Sweet = **S. villosa.**
S. metelerkampiae L. Bol. St. branched, 15–25cm. Lvs 5–10cm, broadly linear, arranged in a fan. Fls violet, 3 lowest tep. blotched white.
S. parviflora G. Lewis. St. 15–30cm, sometimes branched. Lvs shorter than st. Spike 2–4-fld; fls cream and yellow.
S. variegata Sweet. St. 15–40cm, usually unbranched. Lvs to 15cm, ovate-lanceolate. Spike 2–7-fld; fls yellow and violet, or purple with yellow marks.
S. villosa (Burm.) N.E. Br. St. 15–30cm, glab. Lvs 2–13cm, linear. Fls slightly scented, yellow-cream, the topmost tep. mauve.

Synotis (C.B. Clarke) C. Jeffrey & Y.L. Chen. Compositae. c50 perenn. herbs and subshrubs. Cap. radiate, disciform or discoid, few to many in corymbs; ray flts or outer filiform flts to c20, yellow; disc flts 1 to many, yellow, pale yellow or cream. Sino-Himal. Z10.

S. alata (Wallich ex DC.) C. Jeffrey & Y.L. Chen. Tomentose or villous, erect perenn. herb, to 60cm. Basal lvs to 20cm, broadly ovate-cordate to lanceolate, acuminate, sinuate, dentate, base truncate to broadly cuneate, pubesc. beneath, petioles to 10cm. Cap. disciform, in pyramidal corymbs; involucre to 7×2mm; ray flts 2, to 4mm; disc flts 2–4, yellow. Late summer–autumn. Himal.

Synphyostemon Miers.
S. biflorus (Thunb.) Dusén = *Olsynium biflorum.*
S. narcissoides (Cav.) Miers ex Klatt = *Olsynium biflorum.*

Synsepalum (A. DC.) Baill. Sapotaceae. 8 everg. shrubs and trees. Lvs clustered at ends of br., lanceolate, coriaceous. Fls small, clustered in axils, sep. 5, fused below; cor. 5-lobed, sta. and staminodes 5. Berry ovoid, 1-seeded. W Afr. Z10.

S. dulcificum (Schum. & Thonn.) Daniell. MIRACULOUS BERRY. Shrub to 4m. Lvs 5–15cm, broadly lanceolate to obovate-lanceolate, glab., vein pairs about 8. Fls white, subsessile; cor. to 0.5cm, narrowly tubular. Fr. c2×1cm, red. W Afr.

Synthyris Benth. Scrophulariaceae. 14 perenn. low-growing herbs. Lvs radical, petiolate or reduced and bract-like on st.; sep. 4, distinct; cor. blue to violet, tube short, campanulate-rotate, 4-lobed; sta. 2, exserted. Spring. US.

S. flavescens A. Nels. = *Besseya ritteriana.*
S. gymnocarpa (A. Nels.) Heller = *Besseya wyomingensis.*
S. missurica (Raf.) Pennell. To 40cm, glab. except for rusty pubesc. petioles. Lvs to 7cm, dark green, coriaceous, orbicular-cordate to reniform, shallowly lobed, bluntly dentate. Spring–summer. Canada (Arc.) to NE Calif. Z2.
S. plantaginea (James) Benth. = *Besseya plantaginea.*
S. reflexa Eastw. = *Besseya ritteriana.*
S. reniformis (Douglas ex Benth.) Benth. SNOW-QUEEN; ROUND-LEAVED SYNTHYRIS. To 10cm, pilose to hirsute. Lvs cordate-orbicular, shallowly round-lobed, paler and glabrescent be-

neath. Rac., to 3cm, cor. to 9mm, campanulate, tube exceeding limb. Spring. US (Washington, Oreg.). 'Alba': fls white. 'Olallic Violet': fls violet. Z7.

S. rotundifolia A. Gray = **S. reniformis.**
S. rubra (Douglas) Benth. = *Besseya rubra.*
S. schizantha Piper. FRINGED SYNTHYRIS. To 25cm. Lvs to 10cm diam., cordate-orbicular, shallowly lobed, bidentate, pilose on petiole. Rac. to 9cm, cor. 1cm wide, subrotate, lobes deeply cleft exceeding tube. Summer. NW US. Z7.
S. stellata Pennell. COLUMBIA SYNTHYRIS. To 22cm. Lvs cordate-orbicular, deeply double-toothed; stem-lvs pectinate. Rac. 8–15cm; cor. 1cm wide, subrotate, lobes rounded. Spring–summer. NW US. Z7.

→*Veronica* and *Wulfenia.*

Synurus Iljin. Compositae. 1–8 perenn. herbs. Cap. discoid, nodding in fr.; receptacle bristly; involucre globose-campanulate; outer phyllaries recurved; flts white to pale purple. Temp. E Asia. Z7.
S. deltoides (Ait.) Nak. To c1m. Lvs deltoid to ovate or oblong, dentate, base cordate apex acuminate, white-tomentose beneath. Cap. few. E Asia.

→*Onopordum* and *Serratula.*

Syrian Bean Caper *Zygophyllum fabago.*
Syrian Juniper *Juniperus drupacea.*

Syringa L. LILAC. Oleaceae. 20+ decid. trees and shrubs, rarely everg. Lvs simple or lobed, to pinnate. Fls in paniculate thyrses, fragrant, small, waxy; cor. 4-lobed, tubular with 2 sta. inserted on tube. E Asia, SE Eur.

S. adamiana Balf. & W.W. Sm. = **S. tomentella.**
S. affinis L. Henry = **S. oblata** var. *alba.*
S. afghanica hort. non Schneid. = **S. laciniata.**
S. amurensis Rupr. = **S. reticulata** var. *mandschurica.*
S. amurensis var. *japonica* (Maxim.) Franch. & Savat. = **S. reticulata.**
S. bretschneideri Lemoine = **S. villosa.**
S. ×chinensis Willd. (S. ×persica ×S. vulgaris.) CHINESE LILAC. To 3m. Br. dense, slender, arching. Lvs to 8cm, ovate, apex acuminate, base rounded or broad-cuneate. Fls in long, nodding axillary pan., fragrant, lilac; cor. tube to 8mm, lobes obtuse or acute. Late spring. Gdn origin. 'Alba': fls white. 'Bicolor': fls slate-grey, throat with violet tint. 'Duplex': fls double, lilac-purple. 'Metensis': fls opalescent. 'Nana': dwarf. 'Saugeana': fls lilac flushed wine-red; paler reversions may appear. Z4.
S. +correlata Braun (S. chinensis + S. vulgaris.) Graft hybrid between white form of S. vulgaris and pale mauve S. ×chinensis. Pan. erect; fls palest lilac to white. Sporadic reversions to typical S. chinensis. Gdn origin.
S. dielsiana Schneid = **S. microphylla.**
S. ×diversifolia Rehd. (S. oblata var. giraldii ×S. pinnatifolia.) Medium to tall shrub. Lvs both entire and pinnatifid. Gdn origin. Z5. 'William H. Judd': fls white, fragrant.
S. emodi Wallich ex Royle. HIMALAYAN LILAC. Robust shrub, upright to 5m. Br. v. erect, thick, warty. Lvs to 15cm, oblong-elliptic, dark above, pale grey beneath, glab. Fls in columnar pan. to 15cm, term., pale lilac, malodorous; cor. 5mm. Early summer. Afghan., Himal. 'Aurea': lvs soft yellow. 'Variegata': lvs large, bordered gold-green. Z6.
S. emodi var. *rosea* Cornu = **S. villosa.**
S. formosissima Nak. = **S. wolfii.**
S. ×henryi Schneid. (S. josikaea ×S. villosa.) Shrub resembling S. villosa in most respects. Fls pale mauve to red; cor. tube funnel-shaped; pan. larger and more lax than parents. Gdn origin. 'Alba': fls white. 'Lutece': fls mauve to white. 'Prairial' (S. ×henyri ×S. tomentella): fls pale lavender in large pan. Z4.
S. ×hyacinthiflora (Lemoine) Rehd. (S. oblata ×S. vulgaris.) Lvs broad-ovate, emerging bronze as in S. oblata, turning purple in Autumn. Fls scented as in S. vulgaris, single or double with lobes somewhat incurved. S. ×hyacinthiflora embraces the Early-Flowering Hybrids or Praecox Hybrids, where one parent is S. oblata var. giraldii. These produce looser pan. of bloom a fortnight before S. vulgaris. Gdn origin. 'Alice Eastwood': double; garnet in bud, blooming magenta. 'Assessippi': early flowering, fls single, profuse, fragrant, pale lavender. 'Blue Hyacinth': single; lilac to powder blue. 'Clarke's Giant': single; pan. to 30cm, fls large, purple in bud opening lilac. 'Esther Staley': single, free-flowering; buds red-mauve, blooming pink. 'Mount Baker': vary hardy, early-flowering, autumn lvs tinted purple, fls in single white cluster. 'Plena': the original cross. 'Pocahontas': v. hardy and vigorous, upright, fls profuse, red tinted purple, buds slightly darker. Z4.
S. japonica Decne. = **S. reticulata.**
S. ×josiflexa Preston ex Pringle. (S. josikaea ×S. reflexa.) Close to S. reflexa, but offering a range of colours on pendent rac. and

improved cold-hardiness. Gdn origin. 'Bellicent': pan. large; fls strong pink. Z5.

S. josikaea Jacq. f. ex Rchb. HUNGARIAN LILAC. Erect shrub to 4m. Br. rigid, warty. Lvs to 12cm, elliptic, ciliate, glossy above, glaucous beneath. Fls in slender pan. to 15cm, pubesc., carried erect, deep violet; cor. to 15mm, lobes held forward. Summer. Hung., Galicia. 'Eximia': fls and pan. large, light red, later tinted pink. 'H. Zabel': compact; fls red fading to white. 'Pallida': fls pale violet. 'Rosea': fls pink. 'Rubra': fls violet, tinted red. Z5.

S. julianae Schneid. Sprawling shrub to 1.5m. Br. wiry, bark appearing woolly. Lvs to 6cm, oval, finely acuminate, deep green, hairy above with dense grey tomentum beneath. Fls in pubesc. pan. to 10cm, highly fragrant, mauve; cor. tube to 8mm. Early summer. W China. Cvs include: 'Alba': white; 'George Eastman': fls darker; 'Hers Variety': pale-fld. Z6.

S. koehneana Schneid. = S. patula.

S. komarowii Shneid. Tall vigorous shrub close to S. reflexa. Lvs to 18cm, oval to ovate-lanceolate, deep green. Pan. nodding, cylindrical; fls strong rose-pink. Late spring to early summer. China. Z5.

S. laciniata hort. non Mill. = S. protolaciniata.

S. ×laciniata Mill. (S. protolaciniata ×S. vulgaris.) CUT LEAF LILAC. Shrub to 2m. First lvs pinnately cleft or lobed ×3–9, later lvs entire. Fls deep lilac in bud, opening faded mauve with a violet centre, in loose axill. pan. to 7cm, fragrant. Summer. SW Asia. Z5.

S. meyeri Schneid. Compact shrub to 1.5m. Shoots 4-sided, downy when young. Lvs to 4cm, elliptic, veins pubesc. beneath. Fls in broad pubesc. axill. pan. to 8cm; cor. tube to 15mm, v. narrow, purple, faintly scented, sometimes flowering twice in a season. Early summer. N China. 'Palibin': compact with fls fading from violet to rose pink on profuse short pan. Z5.

S. microphylla Diels. Bushy, upright shrub, 1–1.5m; br. thinly pubesc. Lvs 1–4cm, rounded to elliptic-ovate, slightly hairy and ciliate. Pan. 4–7cm, finely pubesc.; fls v. fragrant; cor. to 1cm, lilac-pink, exterior darker, tube narrow. Early summer and early autumn. China. 'Superba': fine, free-flowering form, rose-pink fls produced from spring to autumn. Z5.

S. microphylla 'Minor' = S. meyeri 'Palibin'.

S. 'Minuet'. Small, dense and slow-growing, to 2m after 10 years. Lvs profuse, large, dark green. Fls profuse, light purple.

S. 'Miss Canada'. Vigorous and late-flowering. Lvs large. fls profuse, bright pink.

S. ×nanceiana McKelv. (S. ×henryi ×S. sweginzowii.) 'Floréal': open, arching, habit; fls fragrant, lavender. 'Rutilant': fls in pan., to 25×22cm, cyclamen-purple.

S. oblata Lindl. Shrub or small tree 2.5–4m, related to S. vulgaris. Lvs 4–10cm, rounded-cordate, apex narrowly acuminate, emerging bronze-green, later glossy mid green, red-tinted in fall. Pan. 6–12cm, lax, broad; fls fragrant; cor. 1–1.5cm, lilac blue to pale mauve. Late spring. China. var. alba hort. ex Rehd. Lvs smaller; fls white. var. dilatata (Nak.) Rehd. Habit open. Lvs ovate-acuminate, bronze at first, colouring well in fall. Fls purple-violet. var. giraldii (Lem.) Rehd. Taller. Pan. larger, looser; fls purple-violet. 'Nana': dwarf; fls lilac-blue. Z7.

S. palibiniana hort. non Nak. = S. meyeri 'Palibin'.

S. palibiniana Nak. = S. patula.

S. patula (Palib.) Nak. Decid. shrub to 3m. Young br. flushed purple, sparsely pubesc. or glab., gland. Lvs to 8cm, ovate to rhombic or lanceolate, acuminate, glab. or minutely downy above, paler, pubesc. beneath. Fls fragrant in cylindric, term. paired pan. to 15cm; cor. to 10mm, slender, lilac, white within, lobes narrow, reflexed. Early summer. Korea, N China. Z5.

S. pekinensis Rupr. Decid. tree to 5m, arching gracefully. Lvs to 10cm, ovate-lanceolate, narrow-acuminate, base cuneate, deep green, glab. above ± glaucous beneath. Fls cream, privet-scented, in paired, loose pan. to 15cm. Summer. N China. 'Pendula': br. pendulous. Z6.

S. ×persica L. PERSIAN LILAC. To 2m, branching densely. Br. ridged, glab. Lvs to 6cm, lanceolate, rarely pinnate or 3-lobed. Fls in pan. to 5×5cm, lilac, fragrant, Late spring. Long history of cult. in W Asia, nat. Asia Minor, thought to be a backcross between S. ×laciniata and S. vulgaris. 'Alba': white to rose pink. 'Laciniata': see S. ×laciniata. 'Rosea', 'Rubra': fls light to dark pink. Z5.

S. persica var. laciniata (Mill.) West. = S. ×laciniata.

S. pinetorum W.W. Sm. Differs from S. julianae, in lvs to 3.5cm, veins pilose beneath. Summer. SW China. Z7.

S. pinnatifolia Hemsl. Slender-branched shrub 1.5–3m; bark exfoliating. Lvs to 8cm, pinnate; lfts 1–3cm, 9–11, ovate to lanceolate. Pan. 3–7cm, axill., nodding; cor. to 1cm, white or pink-tinted, narrow. Late spring. W China. Z6.

S. potaninii Schneid. Close to S. julianae. To 3m. Lvs 3–6cm, ovate to elliptic, shortly acuminate, sparsely hairy above, more shaggily so beneath. Pan. 7–15cm, erect, lax, conical; fls fra-

grant, rose-purple to white; cal. sometimes pubesc.; anth. yellow. Early summer. W China. Z6.

S. protolaciniata P. Green & M.-C. Chang. Small shrub; st. slender, dark. Lvs delicately pinnately cut. Pan. narrow; fls lilac. Late spring. W China. The clone in cult originated in Afghanistan and is called 'Kabul'. Z7.

S. ×prestoniae McKelv. (S. reflexa ×S. villosa.) Lvs close to S. villosa. Fls rose-white to deep lilac in dense, nodding pan. Hardy. Summer. Gdn origin. 'Audrey': fls pink, single. 'Desdemona': fls magenta to blue, single. 'Donald Wyman': sturdy, dense and upright; fls in large pyramidal pan., lavender tinted purple. 'Elinor': fls in erect pan., pale lavender, tinted purple in bud. 'James MacFarlane': v. hardy and adaptable, free-flowering, fls clear pink. 'Hecla': fls magenta, single. 'Hiawatha': fls mauve-red, opening rose pink. 'Isabella': fls purple-pink in erect pan. 'Regan': fls rose-mauve, single. 'Red-wine': fls in erect pan., tinted claret. Z4.

S. pubescens Turcz. Shrub to 2m, erect, spreading. Br. ridged, slender, glab.; new growth red-green. Lvs to 7cm, ovate, abruptly acuminate, dark green, glossy above, canescent beneath, ciliate. Fls in pan. to 12cm, lilac, throat white, lobes incurved, highly fragrant; cor. tube narrow, to 15mm. Spring. N China. Z6.

S. reflexa Schneid. Upright shrub to 3m. Lvs to 15cm, oval-oblong, acuminate, veins prominent, pubesc. beneath. Fls in slender, pendent, semi-pyramidal pan. to 16cm, damask, tube interior white or pale rose-pink. Early summer. C China. 'Alba': fls white. 'Pallens': fls pale lilac. Z5.

S. reticulata (Bl.) Hara. JAPANESE TREE LILAC. Small tree with low, domed crown, to 10m. Br. shaggy with exfoliating bark. Lvs to 15cm, ovate, narrow-acuminate, shiny light green above, initially downy beneath. Fls cream, strongly scented of musk in pan. to 30cm. Summer. N Jap. 'Ivory Silk': sturdy and compact, bark with cherry-pink tint; fls cream. 'Miss Kim' ('Kim'): hardy and compact dwarf; lvs glossy dark green, burgundy in autumn; fls late, pale lilac. var. mandschurica (Maxim.) Hara. AMUR LILAC. Large shrub to 4m. Bark exfoliating. Lvs ovate-acuminate, glab. Fls white, in shorter pan., unscented. Early summer. Manch. Z5.

S. rothomagenesis hort. = S. ×chinensis.

S. sargentiana Schneid. = S. komarowii.

S. schneideri Lingl. = S. microphylla.

S. ×swegiflexa Hesse. (S. reflexa ×S. sweginzowii.) Resembles S. reflexa but infl. larger and more crowded; fls red to damask pink, fading once open. Gdn origin. 'Fountain': pan. nodding; fls light pink, fragrant. Z6.

S. sweginzowii Koehne & Lingl. Shrub to 3m. Br. slender, upright, dark, glossy with scattered lenticels. Lvs to 10cm, ovate-oblong, short-acuminate, deep green, glab. above, paler beneath ciliate. Fls in erect pan. to 20cm; cor. exterior rose-pink, lobes paler, tube to 8mm, interior flushed crimson. Early summer. NW China. 'Albida' ('Pink Pearl'): pale pink. 'Superba': pan. longer. Z6.

S. tigerstedtii H. Sm. Resembles a lower, narrow and divaricately branched S. yunnanensis. Fls scented, white tinted lilac to pale lilac in erect pan. Summer. W China. Z6.

S. tomentella Bur. & Franch. Shrub to 3m. Branchlets olive, slender, pilose with darker lenticels. Lvs oblong, ciliate, tomentose beneath. Fls in term. leafy pan. to 15×12cm; cor. pale lilac exterior, white interior, to 10mm, lobes narrow. Early summer. W China. 'Aurea': lvs golden; 'Rosea': fls darker; 'Superba': selection for improved colour and vigour. Z6.

S. velutina Komar. = S. patula.

S. verrucosa Schneid. = S. julianae.

S. villosa Vahl. Shrub to 4m. Br. dense, smooth. Lvs to 15cm, ovate, dark green, glab. above, ± glaucous, slightly pubesc. beneath. Fls lilac-magenta, profuse, in pubesc., pyramidal pan. to 20cm; cor. tube to 12mm. Early summer. N China. 'Alba': white; 'Lutea': yellow; 'Rosea': darker-fld; 'Semiplena': semi-double. Z4.

S. villosa Hook. f., non Vahl = S. pubescens.

S. villosa Komar. non Vahl = S. wolfii.

S. vulgaris L. COMMON LILAC. Small tree to 7m. Lvs ovate, acuminate, to 12cm, glab. Fls in pyramidal, term. pan., to 12cm, lilac, highly fragrant; cor. tube to 10mm, lobes concave; cal. minutely gland. SE Eur. 'Alba': fls white. 'Aurea': lvs opening yellow-green. Other cvs include early- and late-flowering, single- and double-fld whites, pinks, magentas, lilac-mauves and blues, some with white throats or a different colour tone in bud, and fls and pan. of varying sizes and shapes. Z5.

S. wilsonii Schneid. = S. tomentella.

S. wolfii Schneid. Shrub to 5m. Br. smooth or with few lenticels. Lvs to 10cm, oval to lanceolate, narrow-acuminate, downy beneath. Fls in term. pan., leafy, pubesc. to 30cm, tapering, pale mauve, fragrant; cor. to 15mm. Summer. Korea, Manch. Z5.

S. yunnanensis Franch. Decid. shrub to 3m, erect, narrow; br. slender. New growth pubesc., red-green, warty. Lvs to 8cm, oval or narrow obovate, acuminate, tapering to base, olive green above, glaucous beneath, ciliate. Fls in term. pubesc. pan., to 15cm, fragrant, shell-pink, fading. Early summer. SW China. 'Alba': fls white. 'Rosea': fls pink in long, slender pan. Z6.

Syringodea Hook. Iridaceae. 7 *Crocus*-like cormous perenn. herbs. Scape short or buried; spathe valves 2, thin; fls 1–2; perianth salver- or funnelform, tube long, slender, straight or declinate, lobes spreading; style slender, br. 3, simple or divided. S Afr. Z9.
S. filifolia Bak. = *S. longituba*.
S. longituba (Klatt) Kunze. Lvs 15–60cm, 8, curled. Fls. blue-purple, orange-yellow in throat; perianth tube 2–3.3cm, above, seg. 1–1.5cm. S Afr. (Cape Prov.).
S. pulchella Hook. Lvs 6.5–10cm, 4–6, arched to strongly curved. Fls pale purple, slightly fragrant, perianth tube 3–5cm, seg. 1–1.25cm, triangular to obovate, cleft. Autumn. S Afr.

Syrup Palm *Jubaea*.

Syzygium Gaertn. Myrtaceae. *c*500 aromatic trees or shrubs. Lvs oil-dotted. Infl. term., axill., usually panicular, occas. umbullatge or racemose, sometimes cymose; fls (4–5)-merous, rarely 3- or 6-merous; buds clavate to obovoid; pet. free, usually orbicular, oil-dotted; staminal fil. short to v. long. Fruits ± baccate, thick fleshy, occas. spongy, leathery or brittle. Americas. Z10.
S. aqueum (Burm. f.) Alston. WATER ROSE-APPLE. Tree to 20m. St. buttressed. Lvs 8.5–16cm, lanceolate, elliptical to ovate, acute to acuminate. Fr. red, campanulate 2.5×2.5cm. Aus., Penins. Malaysia, Borneo and New Guinea.
S. aromaticum (L.) Merrill & Perry. CLOVE; ZANZIBAR RED HEAD. Tree of conical habit, reaching *c*20cm. Lvs 8–13cm, oval-lanceolate, slenderly tapered upper surface dark green, lower duller and paler. Fl. buds tinted rose (these when dried are cloves of commerce). Fr. ellipsoid, purple, 2.5–3×1.3–1.5cm. Bruised parts smelling stronglyof cloves. Moluccas, now cult. in many trop. countries.
S. buxifolium Hook. & Arn. Small tree or shrub. Lvs 1–4cm, oval-lanceolate to elliptic, slenderly tapered. Fr. globose, shining, orange-coloured to black, 1.5cm wide. Chile.
S. coolminianum (C. Moore) L. Johnson = *S. oleosum*.
S. cumini (L.) Skeels. JAMBOLAN. Tree, to 20m. Lvs 7–18cm, oblong-ovate or elliptic-oblong or ovate-rotund. Fr. *c*2×1.8cm, oblong-ellipsoid, deep purple to black, edible. India and Java; introd. elsewhere.
S. eucalyptoides (F. Muell.) B. Hyland. Tree to 18m or shrub 2–5m. Lvs 7–15cm, linear to lanceolate, often slightly falcate. Fr. red, pink, green flushed pink, cream flushed pink, globose. N Aus.
S. grandis (Wight) Walp. SEA APPLE. Tall tree to 35m with a obconical crown. St. fluted not buttressed at base; bark flaking,

pink and yellow. Lvs to 25cm, broadly elliptic with a distinct recurved apex. Fr. to 4×3cm, oblong, green, dry but edible. Malaya, Siam, Borneo.
S. jambos (L.) Alston. ROSE APPLE; JAMBU MAWAR. Bush or small tree to 8m. Lvs 10–18cm, lanceolate, narrow, tapered at each end. Fr. 3–4×6cm, depressed globose, dull yellow tinged pink, ovoid, fragrant with a strong taste of rose water. S China, SE Asia to Aus.; widely cult. in tropics.
S. malaccense (L.) Merrill & Perry. MALAY APPLE; POMERAC. Tree to 25m. St. generally buttressed; bark flaking, pink to brown. Lvs 11.2–14.6cm, elliptical, apex recurved and shortly acuminate. Fr. 1.8–2×1.8–2.6cm, globose, pink to red but turning maroon to black when ripe. Aus., Penins. Malaysia.
S. nervosum DC. Tree to 25m. St. buttressed; bark cream to pink-brown. Lvs 9.6–17.5cm, elliptical, acuminate. Fr. 1×1.5cm, globose, black, drak purple or dark blue. India to China S to Indochina, Sumatra, Borneo, Java, Philipp. and Aus.
S. oblatum (Roxb.) Wallich. Bush or tree to 15m. Bark becoming flaky, light grey-green or brown or pale grey-buff. Lvs 7.5–16.5cm, broadly lanceolate to oblong elliptic, acuminate. Fr. 1.75×2cm, depressed globose or oblong globose, suffused dull purple. Himal., SE Asia, Borneo.
S. oleosum (F. Muell.) B. Hyland. BLUE LILLY PILLY. Tree to 12m, usually a shrub. Bark flaky, somewhat rusty brown. Lvs 3.1–11cm, lanceolate, elliptic or ovate, acuminate. Fr. 1–2×1–1.6cm, globose to ovoid, blue, blue-purple or purple. Aus.
S. operculatum (Roxb.) Merrill & Perry = *S. nervosum*.
S. paniculatum Gaertn. BRUSH CHERRY. Tree to 15m, generally smaller and shrubby. Bark flaky to ± tessellated, cream and pale brown or pink. Lvs 4.7–8.9cm, lanceolate to slightly obovate, acuminate. Fr. globular to ovoid, usually magenta but may be white, pink, red or dark purple. Aus.
S. polycephaloides (C. Robinson) Merrill Small burly tree to 15m. Lvs *c*15cm, oblong or subelliptic. Fr. irrgularly globose, gleshy, red-purple, edible. Philipp.
S. polycephalum (Miq.) Merrill & Perry. Tree. Lvs 11–25cm, oblong, oblong-lanceolate or subobovate, acuminate, sub-amplexicaul, young lvs purple. Fr. 2.5–3.5cm diam., dark purple. Java.
S. pycnanthum Merrill & Perry. WILD ROSE. Tree to 16m or shrubby. Bark rather variable, scaly or smooth. Lvs to 28cm, usually elliptic-oblong. Fr. 2–3cm diam., globose, pink to purple, fringed with persistent enlarged erect sep. Siam, Sumatra, Borneo, Java.
S. samarangense (Bl.) Merrill & Perry. JAVA APPLE; WAX APPLE; JAMBOSA; JUMROOL. Small to medium-sized tree to 12m; bark smooth, brown. Lvs to 25cm, broad-oblong, elliptic-oblong, elliptic-lanceolate to elliptic. Fr. 4–6cm long and broad often larger., green or white or red when ripe, shining, slightly ribbed. Malay Penins. and Archipel.
→*Eugenia*, *Jambos* and *Myrtus*.

Szechuan Birch *Betula szechuanica*.

T

Taaibos *Rhus.*
Tabasco Pepper *Capsicum frutescens.*

Tabebuia Gomes ex DC. Bignoniaceae. 100 trees or shrubs. Lvs simple or digitate. Fls in pan.; cal. campanulate, 3–5-lobed or truncate; cor. tubular-campanulate, 5-lobed. C & S Amer., W Indies. Z10.
T. aesculifolia (HBK) Hemsl. = *Godmania aesculifolia.*
T. argentea Britt. TREE OF GOLD; SILVER TRUMPET TREE; PARA-GUAYAN SILVER TRUMPET TREE. To 8m. Lfts 5–7, 6–18cm, silver scaly. Fls to 6.25cm, golden yellow. Parag., Arg., Braz.
T. avellanedae Lorentz ex Griseb. = *T. impetiginosa.*
T. calderonii Standl. = *Adenocalymma inundatum.*
T. chrysantha (Jacq.) Nichols. To 30m. Lfts 5, oblong-elliptic to obovate, gland.-scaly, pubesc. beneath. Fls to 8cm, yellow lined red in mouth. Venez. and Colomb. to Mex.
T. chrysea S.F. Blake = *Cybistax chrysea.*
T. chrysotricha (Mart. ex DC.) Standl. Small tree. Lfts 5, elliptic to obovate-elliptic, densely pubesc. beneath. Fls to 6cm, yellow, densely red-tomentose. Colomb., Braz.
T. crassifolia Britt. = *T. dubia.*
T. dominicensis Urban = *T. pallida.*
T. donnell-smithii Rose = *Cybistax donnell-smithii.*
T. dubia (C. Wright) Britt. ex Seib. ROBLE NEGRO; CUCHARILLO. 5–6cm. Lvs 6–18cm, simple, oblong-elliptic, leathery, densely scaly beneath. Fls 5cm, pink. Cuba.
T. dugandii Standl. = *T. impetiginosa.*
T. eximia (Miq.) Sandw. = *T. impetiginosa.*
T. fuscata (Moc. ex DC.) Hemsl. = *Godmania aesculifolia.*
T. gaudichaudii hort. = *Tecoma castaneifolia.*
T. guayacan (Seem.) Hemsl. To 50m. Lfts 5–7, oblong-ovate to lanceolate, veins scaly and pubesc. beneath. Fls 6–11cm, yellow. Mex. to Colomb.
T. haemantha DC. ROBLE CIMARRON. 3–7m. Lfts 3–5, elliptic, leathery, glab. or minutely scaly. Fls 5cm at mouth, deep red. Puerto Rico.
T. heptaphylla (Vell.) Tol. = *T. impetiginosa.*
T. heterophylla Britt. PINK TRUMPET TREE; WHITE CEDAR; PINK MANJACK; PINK CEDAR; ROBLE BLANCO. To 10m. Lfts oblong-lanceolate 1–5, scaly, shining above, paler beneath. Fls 5–8cm, white to mauve, usually dark pink. Puerto Rico, Cuba, Antilles.
T. heterophylla ssp. *dominicensis* (Urban) Stehlé = *T. pallida.*
T. heterophylla ssp. *pallida* (Lindl.) Stehlé = *T. pallida.*
T. hypodictyon (DC.) Standl. = *T. ochracea.*
T. impetiginosa (Mart. ex DC.) Standl. To 20m. Lfts 5–7, ovate to oblong-ovate, acuminate, entire or finely dentate, papery, scaly, ± pubesc. beneath. Fls 4–7.5×1.2–5cm, rose to deep purple, throat yellow becoming purple. N Mex. to Arg.
T. ipe Mart. = *T. impetiginosa.*
T. leucoxyla DC. Lvs simple, glab., oblong-elliptic. Fls to 8cm, lobes crispate-dentate. Braz.
T. longiflora (hort. non Griseb.) Greenman ex Combs = *T. vellosoi.*
T. mexicana (Mart. ex DC.) Hemsl. = *T. rosea.*
T. nicaraguensis Blake = *T. impetiginosa.*
T. nodosa (Griseb.) Griseb. MARTIN GIL; PALO CRUZ; UINAJ; TOROGUATAY. 2–10m. Lvs simple, leathery, densely scaly, spathulate to oblanceolate. Fls 2.5–4.5cm, yellow, lobes pubesc. Braz., Parag., Boliv., Arg.
T. nodosa var. *parviflora* Griseb. = *T. nodosa.*
T. obtusifolia (Cham.) Bur. = *T. leucoxyla.*
T. ochracea (Cham.) Standl. Young branchlets tawny-tomentose. Lfts 5, to 6.25cm, yellow-tomentose beneath. Fls 2.5cm, yellow, ventricose, with lines of indumentum outside. Braz.
T. odontodiscus (Bur. & K. Schum.) Toledo. = *T. roseoalba.*
T. pallida (Lindl.) Miers. Shrub or tree to 35m. Lvs simple or lfts 3, 5.5–16×4–5.9cm, oblong to elliptic, scaly. Fls 5–8cm, white-lavender, throat yellow. W Indies.
T. palmeri Rose = *T. impetiginosa.*
T. papyrophloios (Schum.) Melch. = *T. roseoalba.*
T. pentaphylla auct. non L. = *T. rosea.*
T. punctatissima (Kränzl.) Standl. = *T. rosea.*
T. rosea (Bertol.) DC. Tree to 27m. Lfts 5, 3.5–33×1.5–18cm, oblong to ovate-elliptic, leathery, scaly. Fls 5–10cm, white, pink or lilac, eye yellow becoming white. Mex. to Colomb. and N Venez.

T. roseoalba (Ridl.) Sandw. Tree. Lfts 3, lanate-barbate beneath. Fls white to pink or mauve splashed yellow on lower lip. Parag., Boliv., Braz.
T. serratifolia (Vahl) Nichols. YELLOW POUI; GUAYACAN; GUAYACAN POLVILLO; CURARIRE. Shrub to large tree. Lfts 3–5, 4–17cm, oblong-lanceolate to ovate, crenate-serrate. Fls 6–8cm, yellow, hairy inside. S Amer., Trin. and Tob.
T. shunkerigoi Simps. = *T. impetiginosa.*
T. spectabilis (Planch. & Lind. ex Planch.) Nichols. Lfts 5, 5–10cm, oblong-ovate to ovate, densely golden lanate beneath. Fls 5–6cm, yellow to orange, with hairy lines outside. Colomb., Venez.
T. triphylla DC. = *T. heterophylla.*
T. umbellata (Sonder) Sandw. Lfts 5–7, 4–10×1.5–3.5cm, elliptic, ovate-elliptic or oblanceolate, pubesc. Fls 5–7×3–6cm, yellow, glab. outside except for lobes, pilose inside. Braz.
T. vellosoi Tol. Lfts 5–7, to 8.75cm, serrate. Fls to 10cm, yellow, fragrant. Braz.
→*Bignonia, Couralia, Sparattosperma* and *Tecoma.*

Tabernaemontana L. Apocynaceae. 100 everg. trees and shrubs with milky sap. Lvs opposite, thin-textured or coriaceous. Infl. usually term. in br.-forks; cal. small, 5-parted; cor. salverform, fleshy, lobes contorted. Trop. Z10.
T. coronaria (Jacq.) Willd. = *T. divaricata.*
T. cumingiana A. DC. = *T. pandacaqui.*
T. divaricata (L.) R. Br. ex Roem. & Schult. CREPE JASMINE; CREPE GARDENIA; PINWHEEL FLOWER; EAST INDIAN ROSEBAY; ADAM'S APPLE; NERO'S CROWN; COFFEE ROSE. Shrub to 1.75m. Lvs 7–10cm, elliptic-oblong, thin-textured. Fls fragrant, 4–6 in short, paired cymes; cor. white, tube 1.5–2.7cm, not twisted, lobes oblong, 0.7–1.3× as long as tube. N India to Yunnan and N Thail. 'Flore Pleno': fls double. 'Grandifolia': lvs large; fls double.
T. divaricata hort. non (L.) R. Br. = *T. pandacaqui.*
T. grandiflora Jacq. = *Stemmadenia grandiflora.*
T. holstii Schum. = *T. pachysiphon.*
T. pachysiphon Stapf. Shrub or tree to 15m. Lvs to 25cm, oblong to elliptic-oblong, acute or apiculate, coriaceous. Fls in loose corymbs, fragrant; cor. white with yellow throat, fleshy, tube 1.8–3.5cm, hairy within. Trop. E Afr.
T. pandacaqui Lam. Shrub or tree 1–14m. Lvs 3–25cm, elliptic, acuminate, thin-textured. Fls in cymes, sometimes slightly scented; cor. white with yellow throat, tube 0.8–2.2cm, slightly twisted, lobes 0.25–1× length of tube. SE Asia to Aus.
T. populifolia Lam. = *Logania populifolia.*
→*Conopharyngia* and *Ervatamia.*

Table Fern *Pteris.*
Table Mountain Pine *Pinus pungens.*
Tacamahac *Populus balsamifera.*

Tacca Forst. & Forst. f. Taccaceae. 10 perenn., terrestrial, largely rhizomatous herbs. Lvs entire or palmately or pinnately lobed, ± glossy, veins impressed; petioles erect. Infl. scapose, umbellate; involucral bracts 4–22, leaflike; bracteoles filiform, tail-like; fls nodding, fleshy, campanulate; perianth lobes 6 in 2 whorls, star-like; ovary obpyramidal, ribbed. SE Asia, W Afr. Z10.
T. artocarpifolia Seem. = *T. leontopetaloides.*
T. aspera Roxb. = *T. integrifolia.*
T. borneensis Ridl. = *T. integrifolia.*
T. chantrieri André. DEVIL FLOWER; BAT FLOWER; CAT'S WHISKERS. Lvs to 55×22cm, oblong-lanceolate, entire. Infl. to 25-fld; scape to 63cm; bracts 4, purple-green to black, bracteoles to 25cm, green to violet-black. Thail.
T. choudhuriana Deb = *T. integrifolia.*
T. cristata Jack = *T. integrifolia.*
T. dubia Schult. = *T. leontopetaloides.*
T. gaogao Blanco = *T. leontopetaloides.*
T. integrifolia Ker-Gawl. BAT PLANT; BAT FLOWER. Lvs to 65×24cm, oblong or lanceolate, entire. Infl. to 30-fld; scape to 100cm; bracts 4, to 14cm, green to dark purple-black, inner 2 thinner, white or green to purple, veined or suffused black, bracteoles to 20cm, green to dark purple. E India to S China, S to Sumatra, Borneo, W Java.
T. involucrata Schum. & Thonn. = *T. leontopetaloides.*

T. laevis Roxb. = *T. integrifolia.*

T. lancifolia Zoll. & Moritzi = *T. chantrieri.*

T. leontopetaloides (L.) Kuntze INDIAN ARROWROOT. Tuberous. Lvs to 1m, palmately divided, divisions 1–2-pinnatifid, seg. oblong-lanceolate. Afr. to E Pacific (Easter Is.)

T. macrantha Limpr. = *T. chantrieri.*

T. maculata Seem. = *T. leontopetaloides.*

T. oceanica Nutt. = *T. leontopetaloides.*

T. paxiana Limpr. = *T. chantrieri.*

T. pinnatifida Forst. & Forst. f. = *T. leontopetaloides.*

T. pinnatifida Gaertn. = *T. leontopetaloides.*

T. plantaginea (Hance) Drenth. Differs from *T. integrifolia* in lf bases decurrent on petiole; inner involucral bracts decussate, not inserted in axil of 1 outer bract.

T. quanzensis Welw. = *T. leontopetaloides.*

T. roxburghii Limpr. = *T. chantrieri.*

T. samoensis Reinecke = *T. leontopetaloides.*

T. sumatrana Limpr. = *T. integrifolia.*

TACCACEAE Dumort. See *Tacca.*

Taccarum Brongn. ex Schott. Araceae. 4 tuberous perennials. Lvs long-stalked solitary, radical, hastate-ovate in outline, 3-lobed and 2–3-pinnatifid. Infl. short-stalked; spathe tubular at base, limb expanded, recurved, exceeded by ♂ portion of spadix. Trop. Amer. Z10.

T. weddellianum Brongn. ex Schott. Tuber large. Lvs to 60cm across, seg. small; petiole to 120cm, purple to green streaked white. Spathe to 15cm, yellow-grey-green, prominently veined; spadix to 50cm, ♂ fls yellow, spicily fragrant. Braz., Boliv., Parag.

Tachi-giboshi *Hosta rectifolia.*

Tacinga Britt. & Rose. Cactaceae. 2 weakly scandent shrubs; st. cane-like, not segmented, succulent, then woody, hollow; lvs small, decid.; spines few or 0. Fls term. or lat.; tube 0; tep. few, spreading to recurved, separated from exserted sta. by ring of hairs. E Braz.

T. funalis Britt. & Rose. St. terete, to 3(–12)m×1–2cm, green or blue-green, pink-brown in full sun. Fls 7–8×c3cm, pale yellow or yellow-green. E Braz. Z9.

Tacsonia Juss.

T. insignis Mast. = *Passiflora insignis.*

T. jamesonii Mast. = *Passiflora jamesonii.*

T. manicata Juss. = *Passiflora manicata.*

T. mixta (L. f.) Juss. = *Passiflora mixta.*

T. mollissima HBK = *Passiflora mollissima.*

T. psilantha Sodiro = *Passiflora psilantha.*

T. umbilicata Griseb. = *Passiflora umbilicata.*

Tadohae-bibich'u *Hosta jonesii.*

Taeniophyllum Bl. Orchidaceae. 100 epiphytic orchids seeming to lack any vegetative parts and appearing as a mass of flattened, pale grey, adhesive roots. Fls minute in lateral rac. Mostly New Guinea. Z10.

T. filiforme J.J. Sm. Roots elongate, to 1.5m, subcylindrical. Infl. to 6.5cm, slender; fls short-lived, pale yellow. Malay Penins., Sumatra, Java, Celebes.

Taenitis Willd. ex Schkuhr.

T. microphyllum (Presl) Mett. = *Lemmaphyllum microphyllum.*

T. miyoshiana Mak. = *Drymotaenium miyoshianum.*

T. niphoboloides Luerssen = *Drymoglossum niphoboloides.*

Taffeta Plant *Hoffmannia bullata.*

Tagasaste *Chamaecytisus palmensis.*

Tagetes L. MARIGOLD. Compositae. *c*50 ann. or perenn. herbs. Conspicuously gland-dotted. Cap. usually radiate, solitary and term. or in leafy cymose infl., pedunculate. Trop. and warm Amer., inc. one sp. from Afr. Z9.

T. corymbosa Sweet = *T. patula.*

T. erecta L. AFRICAN MARIGOLD; AZTEC MARIGOLD; BIG MARIGOLD. Stout ann. to 1.5m. St. angular, glab. Lvs pinnate, sparsely gland., seg. 1–5cm, 11–17, narrowly lanceolate to lanceolate, acute, sharply toothed. Cap. 5–12cm diam., terminal; peduncles 5–10cm; ray flts 5–8+, orange to lemon-yellow disc flts numerous. Summer. Mex., C Amer. AFRICAN MARIGOLDS: 'Crackerjack': lvs deep green, deeply cut; fls in shades of orange and yellow. Inca Hybrids: fls fully double, to 10cm across, in orange, gold and yellow; early flowering. Jubilee Hybrids: habit tall, to 55cm; fls double in white, yellow, orange or cream. Lady Hybrids: habit bushy, compact, spread to 50cm; st. strong; fls large, fully double in shades of orange and yellow. 'Moonbeam': habit compact; fls double, large, bright yellow; early flowering. 'Toreador': to 90cm; fls large, rich orange, long-lasting. Nugget Hybrids (*T. erecta* × *T. patula*): to 30cm; fls fully double in gold and orange. Fireworks Hybrids: to 36cm, bushy; fls double in range of bright colours. Super Star Orange Hybrids: to 40cm; fls double, bright orange, early flowering.

T. ficifolia hort. = *T. filifolia.*

T. filifolia Lagasca. IRISH LACE. Ann., 20–40cm, slender. St. shortly branched above, glabrus or minutely downy. Lvs 1–2-pinnatifid, seg. linear-filiform, glab. or slightly rough. Cap. to 1cm diam., many; peduncles 1–2cm; (0–)1–3, inconspicuous, to 1.5mm, yellow or white, disc flts few. Mex., Costa Rica.

T. florida Sweet = *T. lucida.*

T. glandulifera Schrank = *T. minuta.*

T. lacera Brandg. Glab. ann. or subshrubby perenn., to 1m+. St. terete, several from the base. Lvs 10–15cm, pinnate, seg. 7–11, lanceolate, acute, sharply toothed. Cap. many, in loose term. pan.; peduncles 5–15cm; ray flts 8–10mm, few, orange-yellow to yellow, disc flts 7–8mmk. Late winter–late spring. W Mex.

T. lucida Cav. SWEET MACE; SWEET-SCENTED MARIGOLD; SWEET-SCENTED MEXICAN MARIGOLD. Glab. perenn., 30–80cm, with a thick woody base. St. branched above, striate. Lvs 4–10cm, ± sessile, narrowly lanceolate, usually blunt, sharply toothed. Cap. 1cm diam., many, in flat cymose infl.; peduncles v. short; ray flts usually 3, yellow, disc flts 5–7. Late summer. Mex., Guat.

T. minuta L. MUSTER-JOHN-HENRY. Glab. ann., 30–100cm. STems shortly branched, v. leafy, striate. Lvs 5–15cm, pinnate, seg. 2–6cm, 11–17, narrowly lanceolate, sharply toothed, gland. Cap. 5mm diam., many, subsessile, in dense, cymose infl.; ray flts mostly 3, pale yellow, ± circular, disc flts 4–5. Autumn. C & S Amer.

T. patula L. FRENCH MARIGOLD. Glab. ann.; 20–50cm. St. terete, stained purple. Lvs 5–10cm, pinnate, seg. 1–3cm, lanceolate to narrowly lanceolate, toothed. Cap. to 5cm diam., solitary, in cymose infl.; peduncles 5–10cm; ray flts 8–10mm, few to many, red-brown, orange, yellow or particoloured, disc flts usually several. Mex., Guat. FRENCH MARIGOLDS. Disco Hybrids: habit compact; fls large, single, golden-yellow and red, early flowering. 'Harmony': habit compact; fls double, orange and maroon. 'Naughty Marietta': habit semi-dwarf to 40cm, bushy; fls golden-yellow, deep red eye. Pretty Joy Hybrids: habit dwarf to 17cm; fls fully double, mahogany red and pale yellow, early flowering. 'Rusty Red': habit somewhat dwarf; lvs finely dissected; fls double, rich brown, fragrant. 'Spry': habit dwarf to 25cm; fls double, anemone crest golden-yellow over red-brown guard pet. 'Yellow Pigmy': dwarf to 22cm, compact, bushy; lvs fringed; fls fully double, rounded, pale yellow.

T. rotundifolia Mill. = *Tithonia rotundifolia.*

T. signata Bartling = *T. tenuifolia.*

T. tenuifolia Cav. SIGNET MARIGOLD; STRIPED MEXICAN MARIGOLD. Ann., 30–80cm. St. terete, barely to extremely branched above, glab. Lvs pinnate, seg. 1–2cm, 13–23, v. narrowly lanceolate, toothed. Cap. many, about 2.5cm diam., in cymose infl.; peduncles 5–10cm, slender; ray flts 7–8mm, few, yellow, 7–*mm, disc flts few to several. Summer. C Mex. to Colomb. Pumila Hybrids: habit dwarf, bushy, spreading to 20cm; lvs finely fringed with lemon scent; fls single in a range of colours. Gem Hybrids: habit dwarf to 20cm; fls single in shades of orange and yellow.

Tailflower *Anthurium.*

Tail Grape *Artabotrys.*

Tailwort *Borago officinalis.*

Tainia Bl. Orchidaceae. 25 terrestrial or epiphytic orchids. Pbs sheathed. Lf solitary, apical, long-stalked, fleshy, plicate. Rac. erect, basal; tep. ± lanceolate, spreading; lip trilobed or entire, base saccate or spurred. Indomal., China. Z10.

T. hookeriana King & Pantl. Pbs to 8cm, ovoid. Lf to 50cm, lanceolate to elliptic-lanceolate. Infl. to 90cm; fls yellow, striped brown, lip white tinted yellow, spotted red, spur brown; tep. to 2.5cm; lip trilobed. India, N Thail.

T. speciosa Bl. Pbs to 6cm, rectangular. Lf to 20cm, ovate-lanceolate. Infl. to 45cm; fls pale green to green-white, narrowly striped purple; tep. to 3cm; lip entire. Malaysia, Java, Borneo.

Taiwan Cedar *Chamaecyparis formosensis.*

Taiwan Cherry *Prunus campanulata.*

Taiwan Cypress *Chamaecyparis formosensis.*

Taiwan Douglas Fir *Pseudotsuga wilsoniana.*

Taiwan Fir *Abies kawakamii.*

Taiwania *Taiwania cryptomerioides.*

Taiwania Hayata. Cupressaceae. 1 everg. conifer to 55m. Crown conic to columnar; bark brown suffused grey, exfoliating in strips. Juvenile lvs subulate to falcate, to 18mm, keeled, blue-green; adult lvs scale-like, to 5mm, triangular, blue-green. ♀ cones term. to 17mm, narrow-ovoid, scales 12–20. Taiwan, China, Burm.

T. cryptomerioides Hayata. TAIWANIA. var. *flousiana* (Gauss.) Silba. COFFIN TREE. ♀ cones oblong-ovoid, at first grey-green stained maroon-mauve, to 22mm; scales to 40. SW China, Upper Burm. Z9.

T. flousiana Gauss. = *T. cryptomerioides* Hayata.

Taiwan Juniper *Juniperus formosana*.
Taiwan Pine *Pinus taiwanensis*.
Taiwan Spruce *Picea morrisonicola*.
Taiwan White Pine *Pinus morrisonicola*.
Taka-no-tsume *Gamblea innovans*.
Tala Palm *Borassus flabellifer*.

Talauma Juss.
T. coco Lour. = *Magnolia coco*.

Talbotia Balf. Velloziaceae. 1 xerophytic herb. St. decumbent, short. Lvs c14cm, lanceolate, distichous, sheathing at base, serrate, glab. Fls solitary, pedicel 10–14cm, slender; perianth seg. 6, in 2 whorls, ovate-oblong, lilac then white veined green; sta. 6, short. S Afr. (Natal, E Transvaal). Z9.

T. elegans Balf.
→*Vellozia* and *Xerophyta*.

Talinum Adans. FAMEFLOWER. Portulacaceae. 50 ann. or perenn. herbs. Lvs ± fleshy. Fls ephemeral, solitary or in cymes or pan.; sep. 2; pet. 5–8/10; sta. 5 to many. Tropics & Subtropics. Z10.

T. arnottii Hook. f. Subshrub to 13–20cm. Lvs c4cm, orbicular-oblong, apiculate, fleshy. Fls to 2.5cm diam., solitary, pale golden yellow. S Afr.

T. caffrum (Thunb.) Ecklon & Zeyh. Bienn. or perenn. to 50cm; br. spreading from stout rootstock. Lvs 2.5–13cm, lanceolate to oval or linear, fleshy. Fls 1–2cm diam., usually solitary, yellow or sulphur. S & Trop. Afr.

T. calycinum Engelm. Perenn. to 10cm, with thick, spherical roots. Lvs 1–8cm, subterete, rather sparse. Fls 2–3cm diam., pink, in rac. N Amer.

T. cuneifolium Willd. = *T. portulacifolium*.

T. guadalupense Dudley. Compact, shrublet to 60cm, root globose or cylindrical, st. knotted. Lvs to 5cm, ovate-spathulate, fleshy, blue-green, edged red. Fls pink, in pan. Guadalupe Is., Baja Calif.

T. mengesii W. Wolf. Similar to *T. teretifolium*, differing in taller habit and fls to 2.5cm diam. N Amer.

T. okanoganense English. Cushion-forming perenn. Lvs to 1cm, ± cylindrical, fleshy, grey-green, midrib bases persisting. Fls solitary, white, to 2cm diam. W N Amer.

T. paniculatum (Jacq.) Gaertn. JEWELS-OF-OPAR; FAMEFLOWER. Perenn. to 1m; roots tuberous; st. erect. Lvs to 10cm, elliptic or obovate. Fls red to yellow, 1.2–2.5cm diam., in term. pan. S US to C Amer.; widely introd. elsewhere.

T. parviflorum Nutt. Perenn. to 20cm, roots fleshy. Lvs to 5cm, ± terete linear. Fls pink, c1cm diam. N Amer.

T. patens (L.) Willd. = *T. paniculatum*.

T. portulacifolium Asch. ex Schweinf. Subshrub, st. 45cm, erect. Lvs flat, wedge-shaped, mucronate. Fls red-violet in a term. pan. C Amer.

T. reflexum Cav. Erect bienn., 30cm. Lvs flat, lanceolate or oval. Fls yellow, in dichotomous branched term. pan. S Amer.

T. rugospermum Holzing. Perenn. to 25cm, with deep root. Lvs to 5cm, basal, cylindrical, linear. Fls 1.5cm diam., pink. N Amer.

T. spinescens Torr. Cushion-forming perenn. Lvs 1–3cm, cylindrical, midribs persisting as spines; fls 1.2–1.6cm diam., rose to deep crimson-magenta in cymes. W N Amer.

T. teretifolium Pursh. Perenn., with fleshy roots. St. to 50cm, tufted, much-branched. Lvs 1–6cm, cylindrical, linear. Fls purple or bluish, 1–1.3cm diam., in loose pan. on slender. E N Amer.

T. triangulare (Jacq.) Willd. Perenn. to 60cm, stout and fleshy. Lvs c7.5cm, obovate or narrower. Fls red to white or yellow, in rac. Trop. Amer.

Talipot Palm *Corypha umbraculifera*.
Tall Baeckea *Baeckea virgata*.
Tall Bilberry *Vaccinium ovalifolium*.
Tall Boronia *Boronia molloyae*.
Tall Cinquefoil *Potentilla arguta*.
Tall Cupflower *Nierembergia scoparia*.

Tallerack *Eucalyptus tetragona*.
Tall Groundberry *Acrotriche divaricata*.
Tallhedge Buckthorn *Rhamnus frangula* 'Columnaris'
Tall Kangaroo Paw *Anigozanthos flavidus*.
Tall Mallow *Malva sylvestris*.
Tall Melic *Melica altissima*.
Tallow Gourd *Benincasa hispida*.
Tallow Tree *Sapium*.
Tallow-wood *Eucalyptus microcorys*.
Tall Sand Mallee *Eucalyptus eremophila*.
Tall Spurge *Euphorbia altissima*.
Tall Thoroughwort *Eupatorium altissimum*.
Tall Verbena *Verbena bonariensis*.
Tall White Everlasting Flower *Helichrysum elatum*.
Tall White Violet *Viola canadensis*.
Tall Yellow-eye *Xyris operculata*.
Tamano-giboshi-kanzashi *Hosta plantaginea*.
Tamarack *Larix laricina*.

TAMARICACEAE Link. 5/78. *Myricaria, Tamarix*

Tamarillo *Cyphomandra crassicaulis*.
Tamarind, Tamarindo *Tamarindus indica*.
Tamarind of the Indies *Vangueria madagascariensis*.

Tamarindus L. Leguminosae. 1 everg. tree to 24m; bark rough, grey or black. Lvs 5–10cm, paripinnate; lfts 8–32×3–11mm, narrow-oblong, glab. or downy. Rac. to 15cm, drooping; bracts and bracteoles coloured; sep. 8–12mm, 4, flushed red outside, yellow inside; pet. 5, upper 3 9–13mm, crenate, yellow cream veined red or rose, lower 2 bristle-like. Fr. 3–15cm, oblong, compressed becoming swollen, pink-fleshy becoming leathery. Probably originating in trop. Afr. now widely naturalized throughout trop and subtrop. Z10.

T. indica L. TAMARIND; TAMARINDO; INDIAN DATE. As for the genus.

Tamarisk *Tamarix*.

Tamarix L. TAMARISK; SALT CEDAR. Tamaricaceae. 54 decid. shrubs or small trees; br. slender, feathery and cypress-like. Lvs small, often scale-like or needle-shaped. Rac. simple or compound; fls small, 4- or 5-merous; sta. 4–5, rarely 8–12. W Eur. and the Medit. to E Asia and India.

T. aestivalis hort. = *T. ramosissima*.

T. africana Poir. Shrub or bushy tree. Rac. thick and dense, 5–8×0.9cm; fls pink, nearly sessile. Medit. region, Canary Is, N Afr. Z8.

T. algeriensis hort. = *T. gallica*.

T. amurensis hort. ex H.F. Chow = *T. chinensis*.

T. anglica Webb. ENGLISH TREE. Upright shrub, 1–5m. Fls white, sometimes tinged red, in 3–5cm, slender rac. Engl., W Fr. Z7.

T. aphylla (L.) Karst. ATHL; TARFA. Tall shrub or tree, to 10m. Infl. on current year's growth; in term. rac. to 6cm; fls sessile, pale pink to white. NE Afr. and W Asia. Z8.

T. aralensis Bunge. Shrub or tree. Rac. densely flowered, to 6cm; fls pink. S to C Russia and Iran. Z5.

T. articulata Vahl = *T. aphylla*.

T. canariensis Willd. Bushy tree. Rac. densely-fld, to 5cm, fls pale pink. Medit., Canary Is. Z8.

T. caspica hort. ex Dipp. = *T. chinensis*.

T. chinensis Lour. CHINESE TREE. Shrub or small tree to 5m. Infl. on current year's growth; fls pink, in slender rac. 3–5cm long, forming large and loose usually pendulous pan. Temp. E Asia. 'Plumosa': habit dense, gaunt; br. plumose, branchlets v. thin; lvs pale; fls bright pink in bud turning paler. Z7.

T. chinensis sensu Sieb. & Zucc. non Lour. = *T. juniperina*.

T. davurica Willd. = *Myricaria davurica*.

T. dioica Roxb. ex Roth. Small tree, to 3m. Bark red-brown. Lvs sheathing. Infl. simple or loosely compound; fls rose or white, 5-merous. India, Pak., Afghan., Iran. Z8.

T. elegans Spach = *T. chinensis*.

T. gallica L. FRENCH TREE; MANNA PLANT. Shrub or small tree to 10m, with slender erect or spreading br. Fls pink, in dense cylindric rac. 3–5cm long, mostly on current season's growth. Medit. region. Z5.

T. gallica var. *canariensis* (Willd.) Ehrenb. = *T. canariensis*.

T. germanica L. = *Myricaria germanica*.

T. hispida Willd. KASHGAR TREE. Shrub or small tree usually c1m but rarely to 5m, usually hairy throughout. Fls pink, nearly sessile, in dense rac. 5–7cm long, forming term. pan. on current year's growth. Caspian Sea to Manch. Z6.

T. indica hort. non Willd. = *T. chinensis* or *T. ramosissima*.

T. japonica hort. ex Dipp. = *T. chinensis*.

T. juniperina Bunge. Tree-like in habit or a tall dense shrub. Foliage v. leathery. Fls light pink, in 3cm long, slender rac. on the previous year's shoots. China. Z6.

T. kashgarica Lemoine = *T. hispida*.

T. libanotica hort. ex K. Koch = *T. chinensis*.

T. odessana Steven ex Bunge = *T. ramosissima*.

T. orientalis Forssk. = *T. aphylla*.

T. parviflora DC. Shrub or small tree to 5m. Fls light pink in 2–4cm rac. on br. of previous year. SE Eur. Z5.

T. pentandra Pall. Shrub or small tree, 3–5m. Fls pink-red, in small spikes, grouped into large, term. pan. SE Eur. to C Asia. 'Rubra': fls darker. Z5.

T. plumosa hort. = *T. juniperina*.

T. ramosissima Ledeb. Shrub or small tree to 6m. Fls pink, in slender 3cm rac. on current year's growth. E Eur. to C & E Asia. 'Pink Cascade': vigorous; fls rich pink. 'Rosea' ('Aestivalis'): to 4.5m; br. slender, plumose; fls rose pink, densely arranged. 'Rubra': fls dark pink. 'Summer Glow': hardy, to 3m; lvs dense, feathery, blue tinged silver; fls bright pink. Z2.

T. tetrandra Pall. Shrub to 4m. Fls light pink. SE Eur., W Asia. Z6.

Tampala *Amaranthus tricolor*.

Tamy's Palm *Pinanga maculata*.

Tanacetum L. Compositae. *c*70 mostly scented, ann. or perenn. herbs, occas. slightly woody. Cap. radiate or discoid, solitary or in corymbose infl.; receptacle flat; ray flts white or yellow, small, apex 3-lobed; disc flts tubular, yellow. N temp. regions.

T. abrotanifolium (L.) Druce. St. to 1m, erect, pubesc. Lvs to 18cm, ovate, 2- or 3-pinnatisect, primary seg. in 5–9 pairs, to 3cm, secondary seg. in 4–5 pairs, linear, sessile, Cap. radiate, numerous, in corymbs; ray flts inconspicuous, yellow. Summer. Turk. to N Iran. Z7.

T. achilleifolium (Bieb.) Schultz-Bip. Perenn., to 60cm. St. creeping, ascending, erect. Lvs oblong, 2-pinnatisect, seg. to 2×0.5cm, linear, acute, white silky-hairy, petiolate, entire or slightly lobed. Cap. in loose corymbs; ray flts 1–2mm, 7–8, yellow. Summer. S Russia. Z7.

T. adenanthum Diels = *Ajania adenantha*.

T. argenteum (Lam.) Willd. St. to 30cm, white-tomentose. Lvs 2–7cm, ovate or orbicular, 2-pinnate to entire, seg. 5–9 pairs, divided to linear-lanceolate. Cap. discoid, solitary or in term. corymbs; ray flts white. Summer. E Medit. Z5.

T. atkinsonii (C.B. Clarke) Kitam. Aromatic loosely woolly, perenn., to 30cm. Lvs 10–15cm, oblong to linear-oblong, 2–3-pinantisect, seg. linear, acute. Cap. solitary, 3–4cm diam.; ray flts *c*1mm, oblong, white. Summer. Nepal to Bhutan. Z7.

T. balsamita L. ALECOST; COSTMARY; MINT GERANIUM. Aromatic, rhizomatous perenn. St. 30–80cm, pubesc. Lvs 12–30cm, oblong to elliptic, base often cordate, silver-pubesc., crenate-serrate. Cap. numerous in term. corymbs; ray flts 4–7mm, white. Late summer–autumn. Eur. to C Asia. Z6.

T. bipinnatum (L.) Schultz-Bip. Perenn. with creeping rootstock. St. *c*30cm, hirsute. Lvs oval or elliptic, 2–3-pinnatisect, seg. 2–4cm, acute, with lanceolate lobes, villous. Cap. 1–2; ray flts 3–7mm, yellow. Arc. and Subarc. Z2.

T. camphoratum Less. Camphor-scented perenn., to 80cm, tomentose. Lvs 10–20cm, 2-pinnatifid, revolute, seg. oblong. Cap. in dense corymbs; ray flts inconspicuous. Summer. Calif Z8.

T. cinerariifolium (Trev.) Schultz-Bip. PYRETHRUM; DALMATIA PYRETHRUM. Glaucous perenn., to 45cm. St. slender. Lvs 10–20cm, lanceolate to oblong, seg. narrow-lanceolate to oblong-lanceolate, deeply pinnatisect, glandular-punctate, white silky-hairy beneath. Cap. solitary; ray flts to 16mm, white. Summer. Balk., Albania. Z6.

T. coccineum (Willd.) Grierson. PYRETHRUM; PAINTED DAISY. Glab. perenn., to 60cm. St. usually simple. Lvs elliptic-oblong, 1–2-pinnatisect, seg. to 10cm, linear-lanceolate, dark green. Cap. solitary, to 7cm diam.; ray flts white to pink-purple or red, occas. yellow at apex. SW Asia, Cauc. Over 30 cvs, some dwarf (from 30cm), most around 80cm, from pale pink to dark red, single, semi-double and double; dwarfs include the double, dark rose 'Pfingstgruss', and 'Gartenschatz' with yellow-centred pink fls; notable single-fld cvs of normal form include the 60cm cerise 'Red King' and deep scarlet 'James Kelway', the large, 80cm, pink 'Eileen May Robinson' and bright rose 'Brenda'; notable doubles include the 70cm pink 'Queen Mary' and dark red 'Alfred'; seed formulas include the 90cm Double Mixed Improved and T&M Superb Mixture with semi-double and single fls in white, pink, rose and red. Z5.

T. compactum H.M. Hall. Tufted perenn., silvery-silky. Lvs to 1.5cm, pinnate, lobes 2–5mm, 4–9, elliptic-oblong, upper lvs few-lobed or entire. Cap. solitary; flts pale yellow. Summer. NW US. Z7.

T. corymbosum (L.) Schultz-Bip. Perenn., to 1m. Lvs 10–30cm, elliptic-oblanceolate, pinnatisect, seg. 1.5–3cm, in 6–10 pairs, ovate-lanceolate, pubesc., dentate. Cap. 3–15, in corymbs; ray flts white, around 10mm. Summer. S & C Eur., C Russia. ssp. *clusii* (Fisch. ex Rchb.) Heyw. Lvs green, shiny, serrate. Phyllary margins black-brown; ray flts 15–20mm. Carpath., E Alps, Balk.

T. densum (Labill.) Schultz-Bip. Erect subshrub, 15–30cm, leafy. Lvs 2–5cm, ovate to broadly elliptic, 2-pinnatisect, seg. to 9mm, 10–25, lobes in 3–12 pairs, white-tomentose. Cap. 3–7, in corymbs, occas. solitary; ray flts to 5mm, 12–15 yellow. Turk. Z7.

T. douglasii DC. Stout, rhizomatous perenn., to 60cm, tomentose. Lvs to 5–20cm, 2–3-pinnatifid. Cap. 5–20, in corymbs; ray flts conspicuous, yellow. Summer. Calif. to BC. Z7.

T. ferulaceum (Webb & Berth.) Schultz-Bip. Resembles *T. ptarmiciflorum*, but lvs 1–2-pinnatisect, pubesc. to nearly glab.; cap. in more dense corymbs, ray flts white. Canary Is. Z9.

T. grandiflorum Thunb. = *Oncosiphon grandiflorum*.

T. haradjanii (Rech. f.) Grierson. Subshrub to 30cm. St. silvery white-tomentose, leafy. Lvs to 5cm, oblong-elliptic to ovate, 2–3-pinnatisect, seg. in 4–5 pairs, secondary seg. entire or divided into linear-lanceolate lobes. Cap. in loose corymbs; ray flts 0. Late summer. Syr., Turk. Z8.

T. herderi Reg. & Schmalh. = *Hippolytia herderi*.

T. huronense Nutt. Perenn., to 60cm, hairy at first. Lvs 10–30cm, elliptic or oval, 2-pinnatisect, seg. 2–6cm, oblong, lobed. Cap. few, corymbose; ray flts to 3mm. Summer. N Amer. Z3.

T. macrophyllum (Waldst. & Kit.) Schultz-Bip. Perenn., to 1m. Lvs 15–20cm, ovate or elliptic, pinnatisect, seg. in 5–6 pairs, lanceolate, acute, gland., pubesc. beneath. Cap. numerous, in dense corymbs; ray flts, 2–3mm, white. Summer. C Eur., S Russia. Z6.

T. nuttallii Torr. & A. Gray. Grey-white-tomentose perenn., 10–20cm. St. slender. Lvs to 1.5cm, cuneate, 3-lobed at apex or entire, st. lvs few, narrower, entire. Cap. few, in term. clusters; ray flts small, bright yellow. Summer. NW US. Z4.

T. parthenifolium (Willd.) Schultz-Bip. Resembles *T. parthenium*, but lvs ovate to oblong-elliptic, 2-pinnatisect, seg. narrow, more regular; cap. smaller, 4–10, in loose corymbs; ray flts shorter. Summer. Armenia, N Iran, Turk. Z8.

T. parthenium (L.) Schultz-Bip. FEVERFEW. Aromatic perenn., to 60cm. Lvs 2.5–8cm, ovate, 1–2-pinnatisect, seg. 1–3.5cm, in 3–5 pairs, pubesc., glandular-punctate, crenate or entire. Cap. 5–20, in dense corymbs; ray flts to 7mm, 12–20, white. Summer. SE Eur., Cauc. 'Aureum': fls single, tinted yellow. 'Ball's Double White': to 60cm; fls double-centred; white; from seed. 'Golden Ball': dwarf and compact, to 30cm; fls rounded, in clusters, rich lemon. 'Gold Star': dwarf, to 20cm; pet. white, centre yellow. 'Golden Moss': carpet-forming, to 10cm; lvs moss-like, light gold. 'Silver Ball': dwarf and compact, to 30cm; fls pure white. 'Sissinghurst': to 60cm; fls double, pom-pom, pure white. 'Snowball': to 30cm; fls pom-pom, ivory. 'White Bonnet': to 60cm; fls with tight central cone and a ruff of surrounding flts, white. 'White Stars': dwarf, to 23cm; fls double, ray flts flat, white. Z6.

T. potentilloides A. Gray. CINQUEFOIL TANSY. Silky-hairy perenn. St. to 30cm, decumbent at base. Basal lvs 4–8cm, in tufts, 2–3-pinnate, seg. linear, 3–8mm. Cap. solitary or few; ray flts 0. Summer. W US. Z6.

T. poteriifolium (Ledeb.) Grierson. Perenn. to 60cm, pubesc. Lower lvs to 15cm, oblong pinnatisect, seg. to 3cm, oblong-lanceolate, pinnatifid or pinnatisect, sparsely tomentose. Cap. few in loose corymbs; ray flts 15–25, white. Summer. Turk., Cauc. Z6.

T. praeteritum (Horw.) Heyw. Slightly woody. St. erect, to 30cm, leafy. Lvs 3–4cm, elliptic or oblanceolate, 2-pinnatisect, seg. in 10–25 pairs, linear-lanceolate, obtuse, grey-white-tomentose, crenate-dentate. Cap. solitary, to 2cm diam.; ray flts 12–20, white. Summer. E Medit. Z7.

T. ptarmiciflorum (Webb & Berth.) Schultz-Bip. DUSTY MILLER; SILVER-LACE. Shrubby perenn. St. to 50cm. Lvs to 10cm, elliptic to oblong-ovate, 2–3-pinnatisect, silvery grey-tomentose. Cap. to 2.5cm diam., in dense corymbs; ray flts white. Canary Is. Z9.

T. suffruticosum L. = *Oncosiphon suffruticosum*.

T. vulgare L. TANSY; GOLDEN BUTTONS. Aromatic perenn. St. to 120cm, sparsely pubesc. Lvs 5–15cm, pinnatipartite to pinnatisect, seg. in 7–10 pairs, lanceolate, pinnately lobed or toothed, glab. to sparsely pubesc., glandular-punctate. Cap. 10–70, in dense corymbs; ray flts 0. Summer. Eur., temp. Asia. var. *crispum* DC. Lvs larger, more finely cut; plants often non-flowering. Z4.

→*Achillea*, *Balsamita*, *Chrysanthemum*, *Matricaria* and *Pyrethrum*.

Tanakaea Franch. & Savi. Saxifragaceae. 1 everg., perenn. herb to 30cm. Lvs basal, 2–8×1–5cm, long-petioled, ovate to lanceolate, rounded or cordate at base, ± leathery, toothed. Scape to 30cm; infl. 5–15cm, paniculate, dense; fls minute, white; sep. 4–7; pet. 0; sta. 10. Late spring–early summer. Jap. Z8.

T. radicans Franch. & Savi.

Tanaribe *Pourouma cecropiifolia.*
Tanbark Oak *Lithocarpus* (*L. densiflorus*).
Tanekaha *Phyllocladus trichomanoides.*
Tangelo *Citrus × tangelo.*
Tangerine *Citrus reticulata.*
Tangier Pea *Lathyrus tingitanus.*
Tangled Honeypot *Dryandra pteridifolia.*
Tanglefoot Beech *Nothofagus gunnii.*
Tangle Orchid *Plectorrhiza tridentata.*
Tangor *Citrus nobilis.*
Tanjong Tree *Mimusops elengi.*
Tanner's Cassia *Senna auriculata.*
Tanner's Dock *Rumex hymenosepalus.*
Tanner's Sumac *Rhus coriaria.*
Tannia *Xanthosoma* (*X. sagittifolium*).

Tanquana Hartmann & Liede. Aizoaceae. 3 succulent perenn. herbs. Lvs solitary or in 2–3 pairs, upper surface flat to convex, lower surface rounded, sometimes keeled. Fls solitary, golden yellow. S Afr. Z9.

T. archeri (L. Bol.) Hartmann & Liede. Plants branching, each shoot with 1 pair lvs. Lvs 15–25×8–12×6–10mm, narrowing toward rounded apex, keeled beneath, grass-green to yellow-green or dark purple-brown, scarcely spotted. Fls 2.5–3.5cm diam., sometimes with a white centre. W Cape.

T. hilmarii (L. Bol.) Hartmann & Liede. Slowly clump-forming; shoots with 1–2 pairs lvs. Lvs 25×16×12mm, slightly narrowing toward apex, upper surface flat, semicylindric beneath, angles rounded, red-green or purple-green with small green spots merging as indistinct window at tip. Fls 2.5cm diam. W Cape.

T. prismatica (Schwantes) Hartmann & Liede. Cushion-forming, each shoot with 1–2 pairs of unequal lvs. Lvs 35–40×20–30×12mm, shortly triangular, apex obtuse, flat-convex beneath, rounded-carinate toward apex, apex indistinctly windowed, green. Fls 4cm diam. W Cape.

→*Punctillaria, Pleispilos* and *Punctillaria.*

Tansy *Tanacetum vulgare.*
Tansy-leaved Rocket *Hugueninia tanacetifolia.*
Tansy-leaved Thorn *Crataegus tanacetifolia.*
Tansy Leaf Aster *Machaeranthera tanacetifolia.*
Tan Wattle *Acacia hemiteles.*
Tapao Shan Spruce *Picea asperata* var. *retroflexa.*
Tape Grass *Vallisneria spiralis.*

Tapeinanthus Herb.
T. humilis (Cav.) Herb. = *Narcissus humilis.*

Tapeinochilus Miq. Zingiberaceae. 15 rhizomatous perenn. herbs. St. reed-like. Lvs arranged spirally. Infl. term. on leafy shoot or on scape; bracts overlapping; fls largely enclosed, lip and lat. staminodes small. Malaysia, Indon., New Guinea, NE Aus. Z10.

T. ananassae Hassk. PINEAPPLE GINGER. To 2m. Lvs 15cm, narrowly obovate. Scape to 1m; infl. to 20cm; bracts waxy, scarlet to crimson, recurved in a pineapple-like arrangement; fls yellow. Moluccas.

T. pungens Teijsm. & Binnend. = *T. ananassae.*

Tapeinostelma Schltr.
T. caffrum Schltr. = *Brachystelma caffrum.*

Tapioca *Manihot* (*M. esculenta*).

Tara Molina.
T. spinosa (Molina) Britt. & Rose = *Caesalpinia spinosa.*

Tarajo *Ilex latifolia.*

Taraktagenos Hassk.
T. kurzii King = *Hydnocarpus kurzii.*

Tarata *Pittosporum eugenioides.*
Tara Vine *Actinidia arguta.*

Taraxacum Weber. DANDELION; BLOWBALLS. Compositae. *c*60 perenn. or bienn. herbs, with a taproot and milky sap. St. usually v. short. Lvs in a basal rosette, entire to laciniate-dentate or variously lobed, often coarsely serrate with basally pointing teeth. Cap. ligulate, usually solitary, sometimes 2–3, term., on a scape; receptacle ± flat; flts, yellow, or rarely tinged white, often dark-striped beneath, truncate. N temp. and Arc. regions, temp. S Amer. Z5.

T. albidum Dahlst. Lvs 20–30cm, oblanceolate to lanceolate, deeply pinnatifid, obtuse or ± acute, pale green. Cap. 3.5–4.5cm diam.; scape *c*30cm, glab., with soft white hairs beneath head; flts white, rarely pale yellow. Jap., Korea.

T. alpicola Kitam. Lvs 15–30cm, ligulate, usually incised, obtuse or rounded, base ± decurrent. Cap. *c*4cm diamm.; scape over 30cm, short-hairy, shaggy beneath head; flts orange-yellow. Summer. Jap.

T. alpinum Hegetschw. = *T. apenninum.*

T. apenninum (Ten.) Ten. Lvs variable, 3–10cm, entire or lobed, spreaidng, base attenuate, petiolate, lobes *c*10, narrow, recurved, acute, mid-green, subglabrous to cobwebby. Cap. 1.5–2cm diam.; flts short, yellow, striped grey or brown beneath. C & S Eur. mts.

T. bicorne Dahlst. = *T. glaucanthum.*

T. dens-leonis Desf. = *T.* sect. *Ruderalia* sp.

T. glaucanthum (Ledeb.) DC. RUSSIAN DANDELION. Lvs few, 10–15cm, oblanceolate, sharply lobed or remotely sinuous-toothed, green-grey or -brown, erect, fleshy, lobes recurved or spreading, slightly toothed or entire, term. lobe hastate, long. Cap. 2.5–3cm diam.; scapes 15–25cm; flts pale to bright yellow, striped grey beneath. S Russia to C Asia.

T. megalorhizon (Forssk.) Hand.-Mazz. Lvs 5–15cm, obovate to oblanceolate, spreading, entire to pinnatifid, lobes *c*13, blunt, toothed, purple towards base, hairy beneath or glab. Cap. 1–2.5cm diam.; scapes 5–10cm, sparsely hairy; flts short, pale yellow, striped brown, purple or red beneath. Autumn. S Eur.

T. officinale sensu auct., non Weber = *T.* sect. *Ruderalia.*

T. **sect. *Ruderalia* sp.** Kirschner, H. Øllg. & Stepánek. COMMON DANDELION. (The correct specific name for the common dandelion has yet to be established. *T. officinale* Weber, long used for this taxon, does not apply to it.) Lvs 5–40cm, oblong to spathulate, entire to variously toothed or cut, often large and coarse, lobes usually ± triangular, the term. largest, petiole often winged. Cap. 2.5–7.5cm diam.; scapes 5–40cm, stout, usually hairy; flts long, medium to deep yellow, usually striped brown. Spring–autumn. N hemis. Cvs include 'Amélioré à Coeur Plein' (multiple-leaved, almost self-blanching); 'Amélioré Géant' (lvs large); 'Catalogna Special'; 'Mayses's Trieb' (bred to be forced like chicory); 'Thick Leaved Improved' ('Broad Leaved', 'Cabbage Leaved'); 'Vert de Montagny'.

→*Leontodon.*

Taraxia (Nutt. ex Torr. & A. Gray) Raim. = *Camissonia.*

Tare *Vicia* (*V. sativa*).

Tarenna Gaertn. Rubiaceae. 300 or more shrubs or small trees. Lvs opposite, often leathery or papery. Fls in pan. or corymbose cymes, usually bracteate and bracteolate; cal. tubular, lobes 4–6; cor. cylindric, funnel- or salver-shaped, lobes 4–6, spreading; sta. 4–6. Fr. a berry, globose. OW Trop. Z10.

T. zeylanica Gaertn. Everg. shrub or small tree. Lvs to 20cm, elliptic or oblong-lanceolate, lustrous above; cor. white, tube to 12mm, lobes reflexed, oblong, sta. exserted. Fr. to 1cm, black. India, Sri Lanka, Malaysia, to Taiwan, Jap.

→*Rondeletia.*

Tarfa *Tamarix aphylla.*
Taro *Colocasia* (*C. esculenta*).
Tarragon *Artemisia dracunculus.*

Tarrietia Bl.
T. argyrodendron Benth. = *Heritiera trifoliolata.*
T. trifoliolata (F. Muell.) F. Muell. = *Heritiera trifoliolata.*

Tartarian Dogwood *Cornus alba.*
Tartarian Statice *Goniolimon tataricum.*
Tartogo *Jatropha; J. podagrica.*
Tarweed *Cuphea viscosissima; Grindelia.*
Tarwood *Halocarpus bidwilli.*
Tasman Celery Pine *Phyllocladus asplenifolius.*
Tasman Dwarf Pine *Microstrobus niphophilus.*
Tasmanian Alpine Yellow Gum *Eucalyptus subcrenulata.*
Tasmanian Blue Gum *Eucalyptus globulus.*
Tasmanian Christmas Bells *Blandfordia punicea.*
Tasmanian Cypress-pine *Callitris oblonga.*
Tasmanian Laurel *Anopterus glandulosus.*
Tasmanian Podocarp *Podocarpus alpinus.*
Tasmanian Sassafras *Atherosperma moschatum.*

Tasmanian Snow Gum *Eucalyptus coccifera.*
Tasmanian Tree Fern *Dicksonia antarctica.*
Tasmanian Waratah *Telopea truncata.*
Tasmanian Yellow Gum *Eucalyptus johnstonii.*
Tassel Cherry *Prunus litigiosa.*
Tassel Fern *Polystichum polyblepharum.*
Tassel Flower *Amaranthus caudatus*; *Emilia coccinea.*
Tassel Grape Hyacinth *Muscari comosum.*
Tassel Hyacinth *Muscari comosum.*
Tassel Maidenhair *Adiantum raddianum* 'Grandiceps'
Tassel Smokebush *Conospermum crassinervium.*
Tassel Tree *Garrya.*
Tassel-white *Itea virginica.*
Tatarian Dogwood *Cornus alba.*
Tatarian Maple *Acer tataricum.*
Tatting Fern *Athyrium filix-femina.*
Tauhero *Weinmannia sylvicola.*

Tavaresia Welw. ex N.E. Br. Asclepiadaceae. 3 succulent perennials; st. cylindric, grey-green, ribbed with toothed, bristly angles. Fls at base of young shoots, campanulate to funnel-shaped. Angola, Nam., Bots., Zimb., S Afr. Z10.

T. **angolensis** Welw. St. mat-forming, angles 6–8. Cor. campanulate to funnel-shaped, to 8×3cm, lobes triangular, exterior dull yellow-green minutely spotted and striped red-brown, interior paler with circular or oblong red-brown markings.

T. **barklyi** (Dyer) N.E. Br. St. mat-forming, angles 10–14. Cor. campanulate to funnel-shaped, 5–14×4.5cm, lobes triangular, exterior yellow to yellow-green, interior yellow, spotted and striped red or red-brown. S Afr., Nam., Bots., Angola.

T. **grandiflora** (Schum.) A. Berger = *T. barklyi.*

T. **meintjesii** Dyer. St. 8–10cm tall, angles 6–8. Cor. tubular at base, to 7×8cm, interior cream with blotches and chestnut-brown bands, margins brown, long-hairy, lobes triangular-lanceolate, white to red-ciliate. S Afr.

→*Decabelone, Hoodia, Huernia* and *Stapelia.*

Tawhiwhi *Pittosporum tenuifolium.*
Tawny Daylily *Hemerocallis fulva.*

TAXACEAE Gray. 6/20. *Austrotaxus, Pseudotaxus, Taxus*

TAXODIACEAE Warm. See Cupressaceae.

Taxodium Rich. SWAMP CYPRESS; BALD CYPRESS. Cupressaceae. 3 decid. or semi-evergreen conifers to 45m. Trunk often buttressed and producing 'knees' (pneumatophores); bark fissured, peeling in strips; crown broadly conic, or columnar. Lateral shoots decid.; term. shoots persistent. Lvs alt., radial or 2-ranked, narrow-lanceolate to linear. ♂ cones in slender pendulous groups, to 20cm. ♀ cones scattered, globose, short-pedunculate. US, Mex.

T. **ascendens** Brongn. POND CYPRESS. To 25m. 'Knees' rarely produced. Crown columnar; br. short; bark pale brown. Branchlets erect, feathered. Lvs radial, closely adpressed, subulate, to 1cm, bright green, fox red in autumn. SE US. 'Nutans': shoots pendulous. Z7.

T. **distichum** (L.) Rich. SWAMP CYPRESS; BALD CYPRESS. To 40m. Crown conic, becoming broad; bark pale rust brown; 'knees' often present. Lvs distichous, spreading, near-opposite, linear-lanceolate, pale green, rust brown in autumn, to 2cm. SE US. 'Hursley Park': dwarf, dense, bushy (originally a witches broom). 'Pendens': shoots pendulous. Z6.

T. distichum var. *imbricarium* Croom = *T. ascendens.*

T. distichum var. *nutans* (Ait.) Sweet = *T. ascendens* 'Nutans'.

T. distichum var. *nutans* Carr. non Sweet = *T. distichum* 'Pendens'.

T. **heterophyllum** Brongn. = *Glyptostrobus lineatus.*

T. **mucronatum** Ten. MEXICAN SWAMP CYPRESS. To 45m. Differs from *T. distichum* in semi-everg. habit, bowed, branched, slender twigs and longer, pendent shoots which drop in second year. Mexican Highlands. Z9.

T. **sempervirens** D. Don = *Sequoia sempervirens.*

Taxus L. YEW. Taxaceae. 3–10 everg. conifers. Bark red-brown, exfoliating in plates. Lvs narrow, dark green above, glossy, spirally arranged, appearing distichous. ♂ strobili solitary, borne below shoot, axill. ♀ fls solitary, borne below shoots, scales in 3 pairs. Seeds ovoid, with fleshy red aril open at apex. N temp. zone to Mex., C Malesia.

T. **baccata** L. YEW. Tree to 15m, rarely 28m. Crown ovoid-conic, becoming domed; trunk heavily branched. Lvs linear, 1.5–3(–4)cm×2–2.5mm, glossy dark green, spreading in 2 ranks in shade, denser and more erect in full light. Fr. aril red, 7–10×6–9mm, usually extending beyond the seed by 1–2mm.

Eur., Atlas Mts, Asia Minor, Cauc. Over 100 cvs, dwarf to robust, pendulous to fastigiate, lvs v. short, yellow, variegated; these traits singly or in combination; only most common and distinct cvs listed here. 'Adpressa': lvs v. short and broad, 6–12×2–3mm, dark green. 'Adpressa Aurea': similar, golden, slow growing. 'Adpressa Erecta': same, dark green, fastigiate. 'Aurea': lvs golden at margins, green-gold midrib. 'Aureovariegata': midrib green. 'Compacta': globose dwarf to 1.3m. 'Dovastoniana': br. gently downswept, branchlets pendulous, to 17m. 'Fastigiata' IRISH YEW: fastigiate, densely branched, to 20m. 'Fastigiata Aurea': same, lvs golden. 'Fructu Luteo': fr. orange-yellow. 'Glauca': lvs glaucous. 'Nana': dwarf, to 60cm. Z6.

T. baccata ssp. *cuspidata* (Sieb. & Zucc.) Pilger = *T. cuspidata.*

T. baccata ssp. *cuspidata* var. *chinensis* Pilger = *T. chinensis.*

T. baccata ssp. *globosa* (Schldl.) Pilger = *T. globosa.*

T. baccata ssp. *wallichiana* (Zucc.) Pilger = *T. wallichiana.*

T. baccata var. *brevifolia* (Nutt.) Koehne = *T. brevifolia.*

T. baccata var. *canadensis* (Marshall) Gray = *T. canadensis.*

T. baccata var. *cuspidata* (Sieb. & Zucc.) Carr. = *T. cuspidata.*

T. baccata var. *floridana* (Chapm.) Elwes & Henry = *T. floridana.*

T. **brevifolia** Nutt. PACIFIC YEW; WESTERN YEW. To 15m; v. similar to *T. baccata*. Differs in slightly shorter and narrower lvs; 1.2–2.5cm×2mm; fr. with aril shorter than wide, 4–7×6–9mm, seed extending 0–1mm beyond aril. Z6.

T. **canadensis** Marshall. CANADIAN YEW. ± Procumbent shrub. Lvs densely arranged, 1–2cm×1–2mm. Seed depressed; aril bright red. E N Amer. 'Pyramidalis': dwarf, narrow upright; lvs green in summer, bronzed in winter. Z4.

T. **celebica** (Warb.) Li (in part). = *T. chinensis.*

T. **celebica** (Warb.) Li (in part). = *T. mairei.*

T. **chienii** Cheng = *Pseudotaxus chienii.*

T. **chinensis** (Pilger) Rehd. CHINESE YEW. Resembles *T. wallichiana*, but lvs short-acuminate, to 22×3mm. Shrub to 6m. Bark red-brown. Lvs convex above, pungent, flat to involute. China. Z6.

T. **chinensis** Rehd. (in part). = *T. mairei.*

T. **cuspidata** Sieb. & Zucc. JAPANESE YEW. To 20m, often a shrub in cult. Lvs distichous, upswept, linear, 15–25×2–3mm, banded yellow-green beneath. Fr. aril 7–8mm, scarlet. Jap. Numerous cvs, esp. in E US where hardier than *T. baccata*; v. rarely seen in GB. 'Aurescens': compact, to 30×90cm; young lvs yellow, later green. 'Capitata': strongly erect. 'Densa': ♀ form, slow-growing, broad and v. flat. 'Green Mountain': broad, open when young, fast-growing, bright green; v. frost tolerant. 'Luteobaccata': arils yellow. 'Minima': v. dwarf, upright, slow-growing, to 30cm, br. irregular, lvs 4–12mm, lanceolate, glossy dark green. 'Nana': irregularly branched spreading dwarf shrub to 2m×3m; shoots short; lvs dense. 'Prostrata': ♂, to 1×3m, br. spreading to ascending, lvs in V-arrangement, somewhat falcate. 'Robusta': habit slender-columnar, side shoots stout; lvs deep green. 'Stricta': short, narrow-columnar form, branching irregular. f. *latifolia* (Pilger) Fitschen. Dense shrub; lvs slightly broader, seeds shorter. N Jap., Sakhalin & SE Sib. to E Manch. Z6.

T. cuspidata var. *chinensis* (Pilger) Rehd. & Wils., in part. = *T. chinensis.*

T. **floridana** Chapm. FLORIDA YEW. To 8m. Trunk branched from base. Lvs dark green, short acuminate, linear to slightly falcate, 2–2.5cm×1.5mm. Fr. resembles *T. baccata*. N Flor. Z9.

T. **globosa** Schldl. MEXICAN YEW. To 15m. Lvs linear, straight or falcate, 1.5–3cm, narrow, light green. Fr. aril red, globose, large, to 1cm+ diam. Mex.; Guat.; Hond., El Salvador (mts). Z8.

T. **harringtonia** Knight ex Forbes = *Cephalotaxus harringtonia.*

T. **×hunnewelliana** Rehd. (*T. canadensis* ×*T. cuspidata.*) As for *T. cuspidata*, but habit more slender. Lvs narrower, pointing towards br. tips; stomatal bands pale green. Gdn origin. Z4.

T. **mairei** (Lemée & Lév.) Hu ex Liu. To 15m, bushy in cult. Lvs sparse, falcate, linear-lanceolate, 1.5–4cm×2–3mm, yellow-green above. Seeds ovoid, or triangular, aril red, but not ripening in cult. in GB, to 8×4mm. S China to Philipp. & Indon. Z8.

T. **mairei** auct. non Lemée & Lév. = *T. chinensis.*

T. **×media** Rehd. (*T. baccata* ×*T. cuspidata.*) Bush, pyrammidal, spreading. Lvs as for *T. cuspidata*. Seeds to 1×1cm; aril scarlet. Gdn origin. Numerous cvs include forms ranging in height from dense to narrow-columnar, in lf colour from dark glossy green to grass green; widely cultivated US, v. rare in GB where frost tolerance less important. 'Hicksii': commonest cv; similar to *T. baccata* 'Fastigiata', but lvs longer to 3cm. 'Hatfieldii': similar but broader; lvs bright green. Z5.

T. **mexicana** Senilis = *T. globosa.*

T. **procumbens** Lodd. = *T. canadensis.*

T. **speciosa** Florin = *T. mairei.*

T. **sumatrana** (Miq.) Laub. = *T. mairei.*

T. verticillata Thunb. = *Sciadopitys verticillata*.

T. wallichiana Zucc. HIMALAYAN YEW. Tree or shrub. Lvs linear, to 1.5–3.5×0.25cm, apex sharp, margins revolute, midrib papillose beneath. Fr. as *T. baccata*, seed often slightly larger, to 7mm. India, Himal. to Afghan. Z8.

T. wallichiana var. *chinensis* (Pilger) Florin = *T. chinensis*.

Tchihatchewia Boiss.

T. isatidea Boiss. = *Neotchihatchewia isatidea*.

Tea *Camellia sinensis*.

Teaberry *Gaultheria procumbens*.

Teak *Tectona*; *T. grandis*.

Tea Rose *Rosa* ×*odorata*.

Teasel *Dipsacus*.

Teasel Banksia *Banksia pulchella*.

Teasel Gourd *Cucumis dipsaceus*.

Tea Tree *Camellia sinensis*; *Leptospermum* (*L. scoparium*).

Tecate Cypress *Cupressus guadalupensis*.

Tecoma Juss. TRUMPET BUSH; YELLOW BELLS. Bignoniaceae. 12 trees or shrubs. Lvs imparipinnate, or trifoliolate. Fls in terminal rac. or pan.; cal. cupular, 5-lobed; cor. tubular-funnelform. Ariz. and Flor. to Arg. Z10.

T. africana G. Don = *Kigelia africana*.

T. alata DC. = *T.* ×*smithii*.

T. arequipensis (Sprague) Sandw. Pinnae 1–2.5cm, 6–9 pairs, oblong-obovate, serrate. Fls 5–7cm, golden-yellow. Peru.

T. argentea Bur. & Schum. = *Tabebuia argentea*.

T. australis R. Br. = *Pandorea pandorana*.

T. brycei N.E. Br. = *Podranea brycei*.

T. capensis (Thunb.) Lindl. = *Tecomaria capensis* ssp. *capensis*.

T. castaneifolia (D. Don) Melch. Lvs 12.5–17.5cm, entire, elliptic, leathery, apex acute, tomentose beneath. Fls to 5cm, yellow. Ecuad.

T. chinensis (Lam.) Koch. = *Campsis grandiflora*.

T. chrysantha (Jacq.) DC. = *Tabebuia chrysantha*.

T. chrysotricha Mart. ex DC. = *Tabebuia chrysotricha*.

T. cuspidata Bl. = *Nyctocalos cuspidata*.

T. digitata HBK = *Godmania aesculifolia*.

T. diversifolia G. Don = *Pandorea pandorana*.

T. dubia C. Wright = *Tabebuia dubia*.

T. evenia F.D. Sm. = *Tabebuia rosea* or *T. chrysantha*.

T. filicifolia Nichols. = *Pandorea pandorana*.

T. floribunda Cunn. ex DC. = *Pandorea pandorana*.

T. fulva G. Don. Pinnae 9–13, linear-oblong, serrate. Fls 5cm, red above, tawny below, curved. Peru, Boliv.

T. fuscata Moc. ex DC. = *Godmania aesculifolia*.

T. garrocha Hieron. GARROCHA; GUARAN COLORADO. Pinnae 3–11, to 5cm, lanceolate to oblong, serrate. Fls 4–5cm, cor. tube scarlet or vermilion, yellow inside, curved, limb yellow, lobes undulate. Arg.

T. gaudichaudii DC. = *T. castaneifolia*.

T. grandiflora (Thunb.) Loisel. = *Campsis grandiflora*.

T. guarumae DC. Pinnae 5 pairs, 2.5cm, oblong, serrate. Fls scarlet. Peru.

T. guayacan Seem. = *Tabebuia guayacan*.

T. hassleri Spreng. = *Tabebuia ochracea*.

T. hybrida hort. ex Dipp. = *Campsis* ×*tagliabuana*.

T. hypodictyon DC. = *Tabebuia ochracea*.

T. incisa Sweet = *T. stans*.

T. intermedia hort. ex Beissn. = *Campsis* ×*tagliabuana*.

T. jasminoides Lindl. = *Pandorea jasminoides*.

T. longiflora (Vell.) Bur. & Schum. = *Tabebuia vellosoi*.

T. mackersii Will. Wats. = *Podranea ricasoliana*.

T. mairei Lév. = *Incarvillea mairei*.

T. mexicana Mart. ex DC. = *Tabebuia rosea*.

T. mollis HBK = *T. stans* var. *velutina*.

T. nyassae Oliv. = *Tecomaria capensis* ssp. *nyassae*.

T. nyikensis Bak. = *Tecomaria capensis* ssp. *nyassae*.

T. ochracea Cham. = *Tabebuia ochracea*.

T. palmeri Kränzl. = *Tabebuia chrysantha*.

T. punctatissima Kränzl. = *Tabebuia rosea*.

T. radicans (L.) Juss. = *Campsis radicans*.

T. reginae-sabae Francheschi = *Podranea brycei*.

T. ricasoliana Tanf. = *Podranea ricasoliana*.

T. rosea Bertol. = *Tabebuia rosea*.

T. sambucifolia HBK. Pinnae 2–3 pairs, to 5cm. Fls 3.75cm, yellow. Peru, N Boliv.

T. serratifolia G. Don = *Tabebuia serratifolia*.

T. shirensis Bak. = *Tecomaria capensis* ssp. *nyassae*.

T. ×**smithii** Will. Wats. (*T. arequipensis* ×*T. stans*.) Pinnae 11–17, to 5cm, oblong, serrate. Fls to 5cm, yellow tinged orange, cor. lobes reflexed at tips. Aus., NZ, Singapore.

T. sorbifolia HBK = *T. stans* var. *velutina*.

T. spectabilis Planch. & Lindl. ex Planch. = *Tabebuia spectabilis*.

T. stans (L.) Juss. ex HBK. Pinnae 2.4–15cm, lanceolate, serrate, scaly. Fls 3.5–5.8cm, yellow, mouth and upper lobes lines red. US, Mex. to N Venez. and Arg. var. **angustata** Rehd. Pinnae narrower, incised. N Mex. var. *velutina* DC. Whole plant pubesc. Lvs velvety beneath. Mex., Guat.

T. stans var. *angustatum* Rehd. = *T. stans*.

T. stans var. *apiifolia* hort. ex DC. = *T. stans*.

T. suaveolens G. Don = *Stereospermum chelonoides*.

T. tagliabuana Vis. = *Campsis* ×*tagliabuana*.

T. tenuiflora (A. DC.) Fabris. Pinnae 2.5–4.5cm, ovate or elliptic, serrate, white-tomentose, or glabrescent. Fls 5–6cm, straight, red or scarlet, yellow inside, cor. lobes undulate. Boliv. to NE Arg.

T. umbellata Sonder = *Tabebuia umbellata*.

T. undulata (Sm.) G. Don = *Tecomella undulata*.

T. valdiviana Philippi = *Campsidium valdivianum*.

T. whytei C.H. Wright = *Tecomaria capensis* ssp. *nyassae*.

→*Bignonia, Gelseminum, Stenolobium, Tabebuia* and *Tecomaria*.

Tecomanthe Baill. Bignoniaceae. 5 lianes. Lvs pinnate. Fls in pendent rac.; cal. 5-lobed; cor. funnelform; 5-lobed. Moluccas, Papuasia, Aus., NZ.

T. acutifolia Steenis = *T. dendrophila*.

T. amboinensis Steenis = *T. dendrophila*.

T. dendrophila (Bl.) Schum. Pinnae 1–2 pairs, 3–13cm, ovate or oblong-lanceolate, entire or notched. Cor. 7–11cm, tube pale to deep pink, lobes 0.75–1.5cm, cream lined purple, or pink throughout. Moluccas, New Guinea, Solomon Is. Z10.

T. gloriosa S. Moore = *T. dendrophila*.

T. speciosa W. Oliv. Pinnae 2 pairs, 8–18cm, obovate, apex rounded, often divided. Cor. 6–8cm, cream to green, lobes 2–2.5cm, exterior woolly. Three Kings Is. (NZ). Z9.

T. venusta S. Moore = *T. dendrophila*.

→*Campana, Campsis* and *Pandorea*.

Tecomaria Spach. Bignoniaceae. 1 erect or scrambling shrub. Lvs imparipinnate; lfts 2–3cm, elliptic-ovate to rhombic, serrate. Fls in term. thyrses or rac.; cal. tubular-campanulate; cor. yellow, orange or scarlet, slender, tube 3–4cm, limb to 3cm diam., deeply bilabiate. S Afr. Z9.

T. capensis (Thunb.) Spach. CAPE HONEYSUCKLE. 'Apricot': compact, to 1.5m tall; fls vivid orange. 'Aurea': fls to 5cm, bright gold. 'Coccinea': fls scarlet. 'Lutea': fls strong yellow. 'Salmonea': fls pale pink to orange. ssp. *nyassae* (Oliv.) Brummitt. Usually trees to 7m. Lfts 3–6 pairs. Tanz., Zaire, NE Angola, Zam., Malawi, N Moz.

T. fulva Baill. = *Tecoma fulva*.

T. krebsii Klotzsch = *T. capensis*.

T. nyassae (Oliv.) Schum. = *T. capensis* ssp. *nyassae*.

T. petersii Klotzsch = *T. capensis*.

T. rupium Bullock = *T. capensis* ssp. *nyassae*.

T. shirensis (Bak.) Schum. = *T. capensis* ssp. *nyassae*.

→*Bignonia* and *Tecoma*.

Tecomate *Crescentia alata*.

Tecomella Seem. SHAJRAT AL'ASAL; HONEY TREE. Bignoniaceae. 1 tree or shrub, 2–6m. Lvs 2–8cm, oblong to elliptic, entire. Fls in lat. rac. to 3cm; cal. 1cm, campanulate, 5-lobed; cor. 5–8cm, tubular-campanulate, yellow to rich orange, limb expanded, bilabiate; sta. 4, exserted. Spring–summer. SW Arabia, Iran, Pak., Afghan., NW India. Z10.

T. arabica Velen. = *T. undulata*.

T. undulata (Sm.) Seem.

→*Bignonia* and *Tecoma*.

Tecophilaea Berter ex Colla. Liliaceae (Tecophilaeaceae). 2 perenn. cormous herbs. Lvs basal linear-lanceolate. Fls scapose, usually solitary; tep. overlapping to form short tube. Andes of Chile. Z9.

T. cyanocrocus Leyb. Lvs to 12.5cm. Scapes 2.5–5cm; fls 3–3.5cm, royal blue, veined, often tinted white in neck, sometimes with a white margin. Chile. 'Leichtlinii': fls paler blue, with broad white central zone. 'Violacea': fls deep purple.

Tectaria Cav. Dryopteridaceae. 200 ferns. Rhiz. short-creeping to erect, covered with scales and roots. Fronds stipitate, uniform or dimorphous, simple to 1–3-pinnate or -pinnatifid, thin-textured. Trop. and subtrop. Z10.

T. brachiata (Zoll. & Moritzi) Morton. Rhiz. short-creeping. Fronds to 30cm, 1–2-pinnate or -pinnatifid, deltoid, glab. Trop. Asia (Indochina to Indon.), Aus., New Guinea.

T. caudata Cav. = *Diplazium caudatum*.

T. cicutaria (L.) Copel. BUTTON FERN. Rhiz. short-creeping to erect. Fronds to 55cm, 1–2-pinnate or -pinnatifid, term. lobe lanceolate, undulate, lat. pinnae to 16cm, 1–5 pairs, deltoid or oblong; secondary lobes toothed to notched. Jam.

T. crenata Cav. Rhiz. erect. Fronds to 70cm, pinnate to pinnatifid at apex, papery, terminal lobes 1–4, linear to oblong, somewhat undulate, lat. pinnae to 30cm, 4–8 pairs, narrowly acute, entire to undulate. Trop. Asia (Malaysia to Philipp.), Polyn.

T. decurrens (Presl) Copel. Rhiz. short-creeping or erect. Fronds to 60cm, simple to pinnatifid, terminal pinnule 1, lat. pinnules to 25cm, 2–5 pairs, linear to oblong, caudate, undulate to lobed. Trop. Asia, Polyn.

T. gemmifera (Fée) Alston. Rhiz. erect. Fronds proliferous to 90cm, arched, 3-pinnate or -pinnatifid, ovate to deltoid, pinnae deltoid, seg. subfalcate, oblong, notched. Trop. Afr. (Ethiop., Sudan, to S Afr.), Madag.

T. heracleifolia (Willd.) Underw. HALBERD FERN. Rhiz. sub-erect. Fronds to 45cm, simple and 3-lobed, then pinnate or pinnatifid, deltoid to pentagonal, papery, term. pinna deltoid, lateral pinnae to 25cm, 1–2 pairs, ± falcate, ovate to pentagonal, toothed to lobed, entire to undulate. Trop. Amer.

T. incisa Cav. Rhiz. erect. Fronds to 75cm, pinnate or pinnatifid, ovate or deltoid to oblong, thin-textured, pinnae to 25cm, 2–10 pairs, linear to oblong, entire to undulate, occas. proliferous. Trop. Amer.

T. macrodonta (Fée) C. Chr. BUTTON FERN. Rhiz. short-creeping. Fronds to 80cm, pinnate to pinnatifid at apex, thin-textured, lat. pinnae to 30cm, lanceolate, toothed. Trop. Asia (India).

T. mexicana (Fée) Morton. Rhiz. short-creeping or erect. Fronds to 50cm, 2-pinnate or pinnatifid, deltoid, pinnae to 38cm, 3–6 pairs, deltoid, pinnules to 20cm. Mex. to N Amer.

T. muelleri (C. Chr.) C. Chr. Rhiz. short-creeping. Fronds to 50cm, 1–3-pinnate or -pinnatifid, deltoid, lustrous, pinnae deltoid, pinnules lanceolate, uppermost linear to lanceolate, notched to undulate. Aus.

T. plumieri (Presl) Copel. = *T. trifoliata*.

T. subtriphylla (Hook. & Arn.) Copel. Rhiz. short-creeping. Fronds to 45cm, pinnate to pinnatifid at apex, ovate to deltoid, term. lobes falcate, linear, lat. pinnae 1–2 pairs, lobed at base. Trop. Asia.

T. trifoliata (L.) Cav. Rhiz. short-creeping. Fronds to 70cm, simple and 3-lobed to pinnate or pinnatifid, papery, lobes or pinnules ovate or deltoid to oblong, entire to undulate or lobed, term. lobe broad, ovate, subentire to toothed or lobed; lat. pinnae 1–4 pairs. Trop. Amer.

T. trifoliata (Hook. & Bauer) Millsp. non (L.) Cav. = *T. heracleifolia*.

T. trifoliata var. *heracleifolia* (Willd.) Farw. = *T. heracleifolia*.

T. variolosa (Wallich) C. Chr. = *T. brachiata*.

→*Nephrodium* and *Sagenia*.

Tectona L. f. TEAK. Verbenaceae. 4 decid. trees. Br. tetragonal, stellate-pubescent. Lvs v. large. Fls small in large term.; cal. campanulate, shortly 5–7-lobed, accrescent; cor. white or blue, 5–6-lobed; sta. 5–6, exserted. SE Asia, nat. elsewhere in Trop. Z10.

T. grandis L. f. TEAK; INDIAN OAK; SAGA; SAIGUN; TEKA. Tree to 50m, strongly aromatic. Lvs to 75cm, elliptic to broadly elliptic, subentire, pubesc.; pan. term. to 30cm; cor. to 0.6cm. SE Asia.

Teddy-bear Cactus *Opuntia bigelovii.*
Teddy-bear Cholla *Opuntia bigelovii.*
Teddy-bear Vine *Cyanotis kewensis.*

Teedia Rudolphi. Scrophulariaceae. 2 bienn. or perenn. shrubs, semi-woody, foetid. St. tetragonal. Lvs opposite, finely dentate; petioles winged. Infl. bracteate, cymose; cal. 5-lobed, seg. linear-lanceolate; cor. tube cylindrical, bearded, limb 5-lobed; sta. 4, included. S Afr. Z9.

T. lucida Rud. 50–100cm, glab. Lvs to 12cm, papery, shiny, ovate or elliptic, terminal or axill.; cor. 1cm, lilac to rose, tube almost cylindrical, slightly exceeding cal., lobes suborbicular, with a dark purple, stellate spot at base. Spring. S Afr.

T. pubescens Burchell. To 50cm, pubesc. Lvs to 8.5cm, ovate, apiculate or acute, papery, minutely dentate; cor. tube white flushed pink, exterior pubesc., limb 1cm diam., with black-purple stellate spot at base of lobes. Summer. S Afr.

→*Capraria* and *Solanum*.

Teesdale Violet *Viola rupestris.*
Teff *Eragrostis tef.*
Teka *Tectona grandis.*

Telanthera R. Br. = *Alternanthera*.

Telanthophora H. Robinson & Brettell. Compositae. 14 small trees and shrubs. St. few branched. Cap. discoid or radiate, in

term., frequently corymbose or subumbellate infl.; flts yellow, ray flts conspicuous or 0. C Amer. Z10.

T. grandifolia (Less.) H. Robinson & Brettell. Shrubs to 2m. St. pubesc. Lvs sinuately lobed to entire, sometimes dentate; petioles 5–15cm. Disc flts 8–12. Mex.

→*Senecio*.

Telegraph Plant *Codariocalyx motorius.*

Telekia Baumg. Compositae. 2 tall, coarse perenn. herbs. Lvs alt., ovate, cordate below, petiolate, upper lvs ± amplexicaul. Cap. radiate, usually in loose receme; peduncles long, leafy; receptacle convex; ray flts yellow; disc flts tubular, yellow. C Eur. to Cauc. Z6.

T. speciosa (Schreb.) Baumg. To 2m. Strongly scented, branched above. Basal lvs to 32cm, coarsely crenate-serrate, subglabrous above, shortly pubesc. beneath, petioles to 20cm. Cap. 5–6cm diam., 2–8 in a corymbose infl.; ray flts to 35–c1mm. Summer-autumn. C Eur., C & S Russia, Cauc. Balk.

T. speciosissima (L.) Less. Like *T. speciosa* but to 50cm, st. simple, upper st. lvs cordate, sessile, semiamplexicaul; cap. solitary, pubesc. Summer. N It.

→*Buphthalmum*.

Telephium L. Caryophyllaceae. 6 procumbent woody-based, glaucous, perennials. Lvs fleshy, lanceolate to obovate. Fls small, in term. heads; sep. 5, green edged white; pet. 5, white. Medit., SW Asia, N Afr., Madag.

T. imperati L. Rhiz. stout, woody; st. procumbent to ascending, to 40cm. Lvs obovate. Sep. 4–7mm, oblong-lanceolate; pet. slightly exceeding sep. Spring. S Eur. Z8.

Telesonix Raf.

T. heucheriformis (Rydb.) Rydb. = *Boykinia heucheriformis*.

T. jamesii (Torr.) Raf. = *Boykinia jamesii*.

Telfairia Hook. Cucurbitaceae. 3 perenn. climbers. St. usually herbaceous. Tendrils bifid. Lvs pedate. Fls 5-merous; cal. tubular; pet. free; ♂ in dense rac., ♀ solitary, larger. Fr. large, fleshy, ribbed; seeds oily. Afr. Z9.

T. occidentalis Hook. f. Climber to 15m. Lfts 3–5, elliptic, entire to sinuate. ♂ infl. to 30cm; pet. white, purple at base, about 2.5cm. Fr. white, ellipsoid. Sierra Leone to Zaire and Angola.

T. pedata (Sims) Hook. Climber, to 30m. Lfts 3–7, lanceolate to elliptic, occas. lobed. ♂ infl. to 25cm; pet. purple to about 2cm. Fr. green, ellipsoid. Moz., Tanz., widely cult. in Afr.

→*Fevillea*.

Teline Medik.

T. linifolius (L.) Webb & Berth. = *Genista linifolia*.

T. maderensis Webb. = *Genista maderensis*.

T. monspessulana (L.) K. Koch. = *Genista monspessulana*.

Telingo Potato *Amorphophallus paeoniifolius.*

Telipogon HBK. Orchidaceae. 60 epiphytic or terrestrial orchids. St. slender, erect or rambling. Lvs subcoriaceous or fleshy, 2-ranked, basally sheathing. Rac. terminal, suberect, 1- to several flowered; sep. subequal, small, concave; pet. larger, spreading triangular-ovate, prominently veined; lip similar to pet., usually simple; column usually bristly-hairy. Costa Rica, Northern S America. Z10.

T. andicola Rchb. f. Lvs to 10×1.5cm. Infl. to 10cm; sep. to 14×5mm, pale green; pet. to 15×14mm, pale green, veined dark green; lip to 15×17mm, veined dark green; callus maroon; column bristly, purple to yellow. Venezuela, Columbia, Ecuador.

T. biolleyi Schltr. = *T. bruchmuelleri*.

T. bruchmuelleri Rchb. f. Lvs to 6×1.5cm. Infl. to 10cm; sep. to 20×6mm, bright yellow-green; pet. to 22×11mm, light yellow-green, flushed pink-maroon at base; lip to 19×20mm, light yellow-green, callus maroon; column hairy, maroon. Nicaragua to Colombia and Venezuela.

T. croesus Rchb. f. Lvs to 7.5×1cm. Infl. to 11cm; sep. to 25×9mm, pale yellow or green-white, veined pale pink; pet. to 22×25mm, tip white to bright yellow, base pink; lip to 30×40mm, similar to pet., callus densely pubesc.; column glab., maroon. Venezuela, Colombia.

T. dendriticus Rchb. f. Lvs to 2×0.3cm. Infl. to 6cm; sep. to 10×3mm; pet. to 12×12mm, pale yellow-green veined brown; lip to 15×19mm, callus pilose; column densely bristly. Panama, Colombia.

T. gnomus Schltr. Lvs to 10×2cm. Infl. to 17cm; fls thin-textured, spreading, pale yellow veined red-brown or purple; sep. to 23×7mm; pet. to 27×24mm; lip to 26×32mm; column densely bristly. Peru.

T. klotzschyanus Rchb. f. Lvs to 3.5×1.5cm. Infl. to 23cm; fls pale green, veined purple or dark green; sep. to 20×6mm; pet. to 28×18mm; lip to 27×28mm, callus purple; column hairy, maroon-pink. Colombia, Venezuela.

T. nervosus (L.) Druce. Lvs to 2×1cm. Infl. to 25cm; sep. to 10×5mm, pale green; pet. to 14×12mm, yellow-green or cream-brown, veined brown or purple; lip to 14×17mm, similar colour to pet., callus pubesc.; column purple-maroon hairy or bristly. Venezuela, Colombia, Ecuador.

T. papilio Rchb. f. & Warsc. Lvs to 6×1.7cm. Infl. to 17cm; fls thin-textured, yellow or orange-yellow, veined red; sep. to 18×7mm; pet. to 19×18mm; lip to 19×25mm; column v. hairy. Peru.

T. radiatus Rchb. f. Lvs to 6×1cm. Infl. to 9cm; golden-yellow, striped rich brown; sep. to 15×5mm; pet. to 25×21mm; lip to 20×27mm, callus densely pilose; column densely bristly. Peru, Colombia, Panama.

Tellima R. Br. FRINGE CUPS. Saxifragaceae. 1 glandular-hairy, perenn. herb. Lvs mostly basal, cordate, triangular to reniform, 3–10cm broad, 5–7 lobed, crenate-dentate; petioles 5–20cm. Flowering st. to 80cm with 1–3 lvs; fls small, in 10–35-fld rac.; -calyx 5-lobed, campanulate, 6–8mm, green; pet. fringed, white tinged green to red; sta. 10. Summer. Western N America. Z6.

T. grandiflora Pursh Douglas ex Lindl. 'Alba': fls white. 'Odorata': fls scented. 'Perky': lvs small; fls red. 'Pinky': cal. pink; pet. red. 'Purpurteppich': lvs washed and veined burgundy in summer; fls large, green fringed pink. 'Rubra' ('Purpurea'): st. and lvs tinted bronze, fls green fringed pink.

T. affinis A. Gray. = *Lithophragma affine*.

T. bracteata Torr. = *Heuchera bracteata*.

T. breviflora Rydb. = *T. grandiflora*.

T. glabra (Nutt.) Walp. = *Lithophragma glabrum*.

T. heterophylla Hook. & Arn. = *Lithophragma heterophyllum*.

T. heterophylla var. *bolanderi* (A. Gray) Jeps. = *Lithophragma bolanderi*.

T. odorata Howell. = *T. grandiflora*.

T. parviflora Hook. = *Lithophragma parviflorum*.

T. racemosa (S. Wats.) Greene. = *Elmera racemosa*.

T. scabrella (Greene.) = *Lithophragma bolanderi*.

→*Mitella* and *Tiarella*.

Telopea R. Br. Proteaceae. 4 everg. shrubs. Lvs coriaceous. Rac. dense, term., head-like; fls nectariferous, in pairs, often subtended by coloured bracts; perianth tube incurved, slender, slit on lower side, lobes revolute; stigma large, capitate. Australia. Z9.

T. 'Braidwood Brilliant'. (*T. speciossima* ×*T. mongaensis*.) Compact shrub to 3m. Lvs to 20cm, oblanceolate, ± toothed at apex. Fls red in term. 6–8cm diam. heads. Spring. Gdn origin.

T. mongaensis Cheel. Shrub, 2–3m, or tree-like to 4–5m. Lvs 10–15cm, entire or toothed, lobed, oblanceolate. Fls red, in short compact rac. forming 9cm diam. flattened head; perianth 2.5cm. Spring. E Australia.

T. oreades F. Muell. Shub to 3m, or tree to 10m. Lvs to 20cm, oblanceolate to obovate. Fls red, in compact rac. forming a 9cm diam. flattened head; bracts green to pink. Spring. E Australia.

T. speciosissima (Sm.) R. Br. WARATAH. Straggling shrub to 3m. Lvs to 2.5cm, narrow-obovate, entire or toothed. Fls red in dense, globular rac. to 15cm wide; floral bracts red; perianth to 2.5cm; style long, incurved. Spring. E Australia.

T. truncata (Labill.) R. Br. TASMANIAN WARATAH. Low spreading shrub, or tree to 8m. Lvs 5–12cm, oblanceolate, tough, dull green above, blue-green beneath, apex rounded or acute, sometimes sparsely toothed or lobed, base acuminate. Fls rich crimson in 5–8cm heads; perianth to 2.5cm. Summer. Tasmania. f. *lutea* A.M. Gray. Fls pale yellow; 'Essie Huxley' is a selected clone.

Templetonia (Vent.) R. Br. Leguminosae (Papilionoideae). 11 shrubs or subshrubs, sometimes spiny. Lvs 0, scale-like, or simple, digitate or pinnate. Fls 1 to several, in axils; cal. lobes 4–5, short, ciliolate; standard reflexed, ovate or orbicular, wings narrow, shorter than standard, keel blunt, narrow, shorter than or equal to standard; sta. 10. Australia. Z10.

T. retusa (Vent.) R. Br. COCKIES TONGUE; FLAME BUSH; CORAL BUSH. Shrub, 1–3. Lvs 1.5–4cm, obovate to oblong-cuneate, coriaceous, glaucous, notched or blunt. Fls red or yellow to white, standard 15–20mm diam. S & W Australia.

Tephrocactus Lem.
T. pentlandii (Salm-Dyck) Backeb. = *Opuntia pentlandii*.

Tephroseris (Rchb. Rchb. TEAK. Compositae. *c*50 erect perenn., rarely ann. to bienn. herbs. St. usually subscapiform, leafy, often arachnoid-tomentose, at least at first. Lvs simple,

radical and cauline. Cap. usually few to numerous, in term., subumbelliform corymbose cymes, usually radiate, pedunculate; phyllaries often purple; ray flts usually oblong, apex usually 3-dentate.

T. flammea Rhizomatous perenn., to 60cm, white-arachnoid-tomentose at first. Basal lvs elliptic-oblong, base cuneate-attenuate, petiole long, lower st. lvs to 15×3cm, oblong-oblanceolate, irregularly mucronate-toothed above, petioles winged, slightly decurrent. Cap. *c*3cm diam., 2–9 in corymbs; peduncles fluvous-pubesc. and usu-ally white arachnoid-tomentose; ray flts dark-orange; disc flts yellow or purple-yellow.

T. integrifolia Perenn., to 1m, floccose. Basal lvs to 15×5cm, oblong-elliptic to suborbicular, entire, petiolate, ± adpressed to the ground, st. lvs small, lanceolate with a short, winged petiole to linear, sessile. Cap. to 2.5cm diam., solitary or to 15 in a corymb; peduncles to 1.5cm. ssp. *aurantiaca* Usually glab. or sparsely pubesc. or some-times floccose. Cap. sometimes discoid, to 10; ray flts orange to brown-red. EC Eur. (mts). ssp. *capitata* (Wahlenb.) B. Nord. to 40cm, usually densely grey-white-woolly or tomentose, esp. above. Basal lvs elliptic to ovate-oblong, st. lvs numerous. Cap. often discoid; ray flts yellow to red. Albania, Alps, Carpath. Z6.

T. palustris (L.) Fourr. Ann. or bienn., to 60cm, glandular-pubesc. or glabrescent below. Middle st. lvs to 15×2cm, sessile, linear-lanceolate to oblong, obtuse, coarsely sinuate-serrate to repand-dentate or entire, base semi-amplexicaul, glandular-pubesc. Cap. radiate, few to many, in dense to lax corymbs, peduncles densely glandular-pubesc.; ray flts pale yellow; disc flts yellow. Circumboreal, except NW Eur. and Greenland. Z4.

T. takedanus (Kitam.) Holub. Rhizomatous perenn., to 40cm, arachnoid and sometimes shortly pubesc. Lower and middle st. lvs to 10×3cm, oblong-spathulate, obtuse, amplexicaul irregularly mucronate-dentate, upper smaller, linear-spathulate, base broadly amplexicaul. Cap. to 2.5cm diam., radiate, usually 4–5, in umbels, peduncles purple-pubesc.; ray flts dark orange-red; disc flts yellow. Jap. Z7.

→*Othonna* and *Senecio*.

Temple Bells *Smithiantha cinnabarina*.

Tephrosia Pers. Leguminosae (Papilionoideae). HOARY PEA. 400 prostrate or erect perenn. herbs or shrubs. Lvs imparipinnate. Fls paired or in clusters, in term. or axill. rac.; cal. lobes 5; pet. clawed, standard suborbicular, keel blunt, sometimes downy, incurved, wings somewhat adnate to keel; sta. 10. Cosmop.

T. glomeruliflora Meissn. PINK TEPHROSIA. Erect shrub to *c*2m, white-adpressed-downy. Lfts 15–40mm, generally 11–12, obovate. Cor. 16–25mm, pink. S Afr. Z9.

T. grandiflora (L'Hérit. ex Ait.) Pers. Shrub or woody-based perenn., 0.5–2m, stiffly white or rusty-pubesc. Lfts 10–24mm, 9–15, oblanceolate to oblong, cor. rose, standard 16–18mm diam., orange on dors. surface, finely downy. S Afr.; nat. Jam. Z9.

T. pubescens Ewart & A. Morrison. Subshrub, rusty pubesc. Lfts 25mm, 3, ovate to obovate. Standard to 16mm, yellow-white veined purple. N Aus. Z9.

T. supina Domin. Perenn. herb or subshrub to 30cm, downy. Lfts 10–20mm, 5–15, obovate to cuneate. Cor. pink-purple, standard *c*7mm, ovate-orbicular. Late summer–early autumn. Aus. Z9.

T. virginiana (L.) Pers. GOAT'S RUE; CATGUT; RABBIT'S PEA. Erect, perenn. herb 70cm. Lfts 11–31mm, 9–31, elliptic to linear-oblong, glab. or downy. Standard 14–19mm, lemon to white, wings rose, keel rose. Spring–summer. E US; S Canada. Z4.

Terebinte *Pistacia terebinthus*.
Terebintho *Pistacia terebinthus*.

Terminalia L. Combretaceae. 200 trees, mostly decid., frequently buttressed. Lvs entire, transparent-punctate, often minutely verrucose, frequently with glands near base. Spike or pan. with ♂ fls at tip, ♀ below; cal. tubular-campanulate; pet. 0; sta. usually 10, exserted. Fr. a drupe, 1-seeded. Trop.

T. alata Heyne ex Roth = *T. tomentosa*.

T. arjuna (Roxb. ex DC.) Wight & Arn. Tree to 60m. Lvs to 12×5cm, oblong or oblanceolate-obovate, crenate-serrate, glab., with 2 basal glands. Spike or pan. axill:, to 15cm; cal. cream, tube to 2mm, pubesc., lobes to 2mm, triangular, glab. Fr. to 6cm, 5-winged. Sri Lanka, India.

T. bellirica (Gaertn.) Roxb. Tree to 50m. Lvs to 18×11cm, oblanceolate to elliptic-obovate, glabrate. Spike axill. to 15cm; cal. yellow, tube to 6mm, sericeous, lobes to 2mm, deltoid. Fr.

to 28mm, ellipsoid to subglobose, sericeous or velvety, 5-angled. Ceylon, India, Burm., Indochina, Siam, Malaysia.

T. calamansanai (Blanco) Rolfe. Tree to 30m. Lvs to 20×9cm, obovate to elliptic, minutely verrucose, glabrescent, with 2 basal glands. Spike axill. to 20cm; cal. cream or yellow-green, tube to 5mm, sericeous; lobes to 1mm, deltoid, tomentose. Fr. to 10cm, pubesc. 2-winged. Burm., Thail., Indochina, Malaysia.

T. catappa L. INDIAN ALMOND. Tree to 35m. Lvs to 25×14cm, obovate or elliptic-obovate, glossy glabrescent, with 2 basal glands. Spike axill. to 16cm; cal. white, tube to 10mm, sericeous or glab., lobes to 2mm, triangular-ovate. Fr. to 7cm, ellipsoid to ovoid, red, green or yellow, compressed, glabrescent. Trop. Asia, N Aus., Polyn., Malaysia.

T. chebula Retz. Tree to 25m. Lvs to 12×6.5cm, ovate or obovate-elliptic, glab. above, woolly beneath, with 2 basal glands. Spike axill. to 8.5cm; cal. cream, tube to 2mm, villous, lobes to 2mm, triangular. Fr. to 4cm, ellipsoid to obovoid, glab., slightly angled. Sri Lanka, India, Burm., Nepal.

T. erythrophylla Burchell = *Combretum erythrophyllum*.

T. latifolia Blanco non Sw. = *T. catappa*.

T. mauritania Blanco non Lam. = *T. catappa*.

T. muelleri Benth. Tree. Lvs to 18cm, obovate, slightly pubesc. beneath. Spike loose, axill.; cal. interior lanate, exterior glab. Fr. to 2.5cm, tinged blue, ovoid, wings 0. Aus. (Queensld).

T. myriocarpa Heurck & J. Muell. Everg. tree. Lvs to 20×8cm, lanceolate-oblong or elliptic-oblong, glabrescent, often with 1 or 2 basal glands. Pan. term.; cal. tube to 2mm, glab. to sericeous; lobes minute, deltoid. Fr. to 4×2mm, ellipsoid, sericeous, 2-winged. India, Burm., Indochina, China (Yunnan), Malaysia.

T. sericea Burchell. Everg. tree to 13m. Lvs to 10cm, narrowly oblong to obovate or oblanceolate, mucronulate, adpressed-pubesc. Spike axill., silky-pubesc. Fr. to 3cm, red, compressed, glab., broadly winged. S Afr.

T. tomentosa Wright & Arn. Tree. Lvs to 20cm, oblong to elliptic-oblong, grey-pubesc. beneath, with 2 basal glands. Pan. term. or axill., tomentose; cal. white, yellow or green, pubesc. Fr. to 3.5cm, glab. or downy, 5-winged. India, Burm., Sri Lanka.

→*Myrobalanus* and *Pentaptera*.

Ternstroemia Mutis ex L. f. Theaceae. 85 everg. trees or shrubs. Lvs coriaceous, entire or crenate-serrate. Fls solitary or clustered; sep. 5, imbricate; pet. 5; sta. numerous. Asia, Americas, Afr. Z9.

T. gymnanthera (Wight & Arn.) Sprague. Glab. shrub or small tree to 3.5m; br. rusty-grey. Lvs 4–7cm, narrowly cuneate-obovate, rounded, dark green, leathery. Pet. white, obovate-cuneate. Fr. c1cm diam. red, globose. Summer. Jap. 'Variegata': lvs margined cream, later tinted rose, centre marbled grey.

T. japonica Thunb. = *Cleyera japonica* or *T. gymnanthera*.

Testudinaria Salisb.

T. elephantipes (L'Hérit.) Burchell = *Dioscorea elephantipes*.

T. macrostachya (Benth.) Rowley = *Dioscorea macrostachya*.

TETRACENTRACEAE Tieghem. See *Tetracentron*.

Tetracentron Oliv. Tetracentraceae. 1 decid. tree to 30m. Shoots dark, with pale lenticels. Lvs 4.5–13cm, ovate or cordate-acuminate, crenate, deep red in fall; petioles with stipule-like flanges. Fls ♂, small, yellow, apetalous in term. pendulous spikes 10–15cm. Summer. SW & C China, N Burm., Nepal.

T. sinense Oliv.

Tetraclinis Mast. Cupressaceae. 1 everg. conifer to 15m. Crown conic; branchlets in flat, open sprays. Lvs decussate, lat. pair overlapping and larger than the facial pair, adnate, scale-like. Cones term., erect on pendulous shoots, solitary, globose, 10–16mm diam., woody, glaucous; scales 4, stout. NW Afr., Malta, SE Spain. Z10.

T. articulata (Vahl) Mast. ARAR; ALERCE; THUYA.

→*Callitris* and *Thuja*.

Tetradenia Benth. Labiatae. 5 aromatic, perenn. shrubs. St. semi-succulent, tetragonal, gland.-pubescent. Lvs cordate to round, crenate or rhombic. Fls in whorled pan., subtended by lvs; cal. campanulate, divided into 3; cor. tubular, bilabiate–upper lip 4-lobed, lower entire. Madag., S Afr. Z10.

T. riparia (Hochst.) Codd. To 3m. Lvs to 8×7cm, ovate to round, thinly pubesc. Fls to 3.5mm white to mauve, pubesc. S Afr.

→*Basilicum* and *Iboza*.

Tetradium Lour. Rutaceae. 9 trees or shrubs. Lvs usually imparipinnate, lfts stalked. Corymb or a pan., term. or axill.;

sep. 4 or 5, connate at base; pet. 4 or 5, erect, usually cucullate. S & E Asia, W Malesia. Z10.

T. daniellii (Benn) Hartley. Shrub or tree to 20m. Lvs to 44cm, lfts 2–5 pairs, to 18.5×10.5cm, elliptic, ovate or lanceolate, subentire to crenulate, subglabr. Infl. to 19cm; pet. white, to 5mm, glab. to densely pubesc. SW China to Korea.

T. fargesii Dode = *T. glabrifolium*.

T. fraxinifolium (Hook.) Hartley. Tree to 12m. Lvs to 67cm, lfts 2–7 pairs, to 25×8.5cm, subcoriaceous to chartaceous, lanceolate or ovate, glab. to puberulent, crenulate. Infl. to 24cm; pet. green to pale yellow, to 6.5mm, glab. to slightly villous. Nepal to SW China, N Thail. and N Vietnam.

T. glabrifolium (Champ. ex Benth.) Hartley. Shrub or tree to 20m. Lvs to 38cm, lfts 1–9 pairs, to 15×6cm, lanceolate or ovate to elliptic-oblong, entire to crenulate, subglab. Infl. to 19cm; pet. white to yellow or green, to 4mm, glab. to pubesc. SE Asia, Malesia.

T. glauca Miq. = *T. glabrifolium*.

T. officinalis Dode = *T. ruticarpum*.

T. ruticarpum (A. Juss.) Hartley. Shrub or small tree to 9m. Lvs to 40cm, lfts 1–7 pairs, to 17×8cm, ovate or elliptic to oblanceolate, entire or crenulate, subglabr. to densely pubesc. Infl. to 18cm; pet. white to yellow or green, to 5mm, subglabr. or sparsely pubesc. China, Taiwan.

→*Boymia*, *Evodia* and *Xanthoxylum*.

Tetragonolobus L.

T. maritimus (L.) Roth = *Lotus maritimus*.

T. purpureus Moench. = *Lotus purpureus*.

Tetramicra Lindl. Orchidaceae. 10 epiphytic or terrestrial orchids. Rhiz. elongate; secondary st. short, slightly thickened, leafy. Lvs fleshy, subterete, equitant. Rac. term., slender; fls small, showy; sep. similar, spreading; pet. somewhat narrower; lip larger than tep., trilobed. W Indies, Flor. Z10.

T. canaliculata (Aubl.) Urban St. to 2cm, 1–4-lvd. Lvs to 18×1cm, cylindrical, recurved, canaliculate above. Infl. to 60cm; fls to 2.5cm, long-lived, fragrant, green tinged red, the lip bright rose, often striped violet. Late spring–early summer. Flor., Greater Antilles.

T. elegans (Hamilt.) Cogn. = *T. canaliculata*.

→*Cyrtopodium*.

Tetranema Benth. ex Lindl. Scrophulariaceae. 2 low, shrubby, perenn. herbs. Lvs basal or opposite, glab. Infl. subumbellate, long-stalked; cal. 5-lobed; cor. bilabiate, lower lip 3-lobed, upper lip 2-lobed. 4. Summer. Mex., Guat. Z9.

T. mexicanum Benth. ex Lindl. = *T. roseum*.

T. roseum (M. Martens & Gal.) Standl. & Steyerm. MEXICAN FOXGLOVE; MEXICAN VIOLET. Lvs to 12cm, obovate, obscurely serrulate, dark green, subcoriaceous. Flowering st. to 20cm; cor. to 1.5cm, lilac to mauve with darker marking. Mex.

Tetraneuris Greene. Compositae. c35 aromatic ann. or perenn. herbs. Lvs alt., crowded near base or scattered along st., narrow, entire or lobed. Cap. usually radiate; peduncles slender; receptacle convex or conical; ray flts broadly oblong, yellow; disc flts yellow. W US.

T. acaulis (Pursh) Greene. Perenn. to 15cm. Lvs 2–8cm, crowded, narrowly linear-oblanceolate, acute. Cap. to 2cm diam.; ray flts 6–8mm, 10–12, oblong, cuneate, yellow with orange veins. C US. Z3.

T. grandiflora (Torr. & A. Gray) K.F. Parker. Perenn., 15–22cm, white-lanate. St. arising fromm woody base, erect, stout, leafy. Lvs 5–6cm, 1–2-pinnate, petiolate, seg. linear, broad and scarious at base. Cap. 5–7.5cm diam.; ray flts oblong, truncate, bright yellow. US (Rocky Mts). Z5.

T. linearifolia (Hook.) Greene. Ann. or bienn., 15–30cm, hirsute-villous or glabrate, cap. smelling of chamomile when bruised. St. erect and simmple or diffusely branched. Lvs 1–4cm, linear or linear-spathulate, entire. Cap. 12–18mm diam., on slender or filiform peduncles to 12cm; flts 5–8mm, 8–9, obovate-oblong, pale yellow. Spring–summer. S US. Z5.

T. scaposa (DC.) K.F. Parker. Perenn. with woody base, 15–22cm. St. solitary. Lvs 5–7.5cm, basal, linear-lanceolate, entire or pinnatifid, punctate, glabrate. Cap. solitary, to 2.5cm diamm.; ray flts 6–8mm, 12, cuneate-obovate, bright yellow. S & W US (Colorado to Tex.). Z4.

→*Actinella*, *Cephalophora*, *Gaillardia* and *Hymenoxys*.

Tetrapanax K. Koch. RICE-PAPER PLANT; CHINESE RICE-PAPER PLANT; TUNG-TSAU. Araliaceae. Suckering everg. shrubs or small trees. Young growth floccose. Lvs large, palmately lobed, floccose-hairy. Infl. term., paniculate, woolly, with conspicuous bracts; fls in small, stalked umbels; pet. 4–5. Taiwan.

T. papyrifer (Hook.) K. Koch. St. to 7m, slender. Lvs top of st., to 50cm or more across; seg. 5–11, scurfy green above, pale, felty beneath. Infl. 3× compound, white; primary br. 3–4, secondary br. numerous, each with 10–15 umbels about 12mm diam. Autumn. Taiwan; possibly China. 'Variegata': lvs variegated with cream to white and shades of bright to dark green. Z8.
→*Aralia* and *Fatsia*.

Tetraplasandra A. Gray. Araliaceae. 6 unarmed, everg. trees with thick ascending br. Lvs pinnately compound; lfts entire. Infl. sometimes umbelliform, usually compound; primary br. spreading or radiating, ultimate br. racemose; fls in umbels or rac. Hawaiian Is. Z10.
T. kaalae (Hillebrand Harms = *T. oahuensis*.
T. kavaiensis (H. Mann) Sherff. Tree to 25m. Lvs 40–90cm; lfts 11–21, to 20cm, narrowly oblong to ovate, scurfy-hairy. Infl. 2× compound, scurfy-hairy; axis to 15cm; primary rays 3–5, to 30cm, radiating, secondary rays clusterered at ends or racemosely arranged; fls not forming distinct umbels. Hawaiian Is.
T. meiandra hort., non (Hillebrand) Harms = *T. kavaiensis*.
T. meiandra (Hillebrand) Harms = *T. oahuensis*.
T. micrantha Sherff = *T. kavaiensis*.
T. oahuensis (A. Gray) Harms. Glab. shrub or tree to 10m. Lvs to 45cm; lfts 7–15, to 13cm, elliptic to ovate to oblong-elliptic. Infl. umbelliform, 1–2× compound; axis to 4cm or 0; primary rays 3–5, to 15cm, secondary rays springing from ends or in pseudowhorl below; fls in umbels. Hawaiian Is.
→*Dipanax*.

Tetrastigma (Miq.) Planch. JAVAN GRAPE. Vitaceae. 90 vigorous decid. or everg. vines. Tendrils simple or forked. Lvs 1–3-foliolate or pedately 4–6-foliolate. Cymes axillary; cal. lobed, dentate or truncate; pet. to 4mm, free, with broad base and saccate apex, green; ♂ fls with sta. inserted under receptacle; ♀ fls with minute staminodes. Fr. a berry, globose or ellipsoid. Indomal. to trop. Aus. Z10.
T. harmandii Planch. AYO. Tendrils simple. Lfts 5, 5–12cm, elliptic-oblong, remotely dentate, glab. and glossy. Infl. 4–10cm; fls pale green, faintly fragrant. Indochina, Philipp.
T. obovatum (Lawson) Gagnep. Tomentose throughout. Tendrils simple, long. Lfts 5, 8–25cm, obovate, obtuse to rounded at base, mucronate-dentate, firm to chartaceous. Infl. corymbose, 11cm diam.; fls numerous, white. SE Asia.
T. obtectum (Wallich ex Lawson) Planch. White to pink-hirsute, tendrils small, forked, with adhesive pads. Lfts 5, 5–8cm, obovate to elliptic, glab. mucronate-crenate. Infl. umbellate, slender; fls tinged green. Himal., W & C China.
T. planicaule (Hook. f.) Gagnep. Tendrils simple, stout. Lfts 5, 12–20cm, oblong-lanceolate, obtusely serrate. Infl. sub-corymbose. Fr. cherry-sized, red. Himal. (Sikkim).
T. serrulatum (Roxb.) Planch. Tendrils simple or forked. Lfts 5, 4–7.5cm, glab. lanceolate to ovate, bristly-serrate. Infl. with conspicuous scarious bracts. Fr. currant-sized, black. Temp. Himal., W China.
T. voinieranum (Pierre ex Nichols. & Mottet) Gagnep. CHESTNUT VINE; LIZARD PLANT. Densely tomentose. Tendrils simple. Lfts 3–5, 10–20cm, obovate to cordate rhombic, weakly serrate to crenate-serrate. Infl. 5cm, corymbose. Laos.
→*Cissus* and *Vitis*.

Tetratheca Sm. Tremandraceae. 20 low everg. shrubs. Lvs alt. to opposite or whorled. Fls nodding, solitary in axils forming pseudoracemes; pet. 4–5, c1cm. Aus., Tasm. Z9.
T. ciliare Lindl. Shrub to 50cm; st. tufted, hairy below. Lvs 0.4cm, in whorls of 3, broad-ovate. Pet. rose-pink, oblong. S Aus.
T. ericifolia Sm. Heath-like shrub, 30–75cm, downy and bristly. Lvs to 1cm, 4–6 in a whorl, narrow-linear. Pet. rose-pink, obovate, rounded. Summer. Aus. (NSW).
T. ericoides Planch. = *T. pilosa*.
T. glandulosa Labill. Shrub to 90cm, glab. and glandular-pubesc. Lvs 0.5–1cm, alt. or opposite, glandular-ciliate or -toothed. Pet. dark rose, obovate, rounded. Aus., Tasm.
T. hirsuta Lindl. Shrub to 60cm, downy. Lvs 1–2cm, alt. or in whorls, elliptic-oblong. Pet. bright rose, ovate. Spring. W Aus.
T. juncea Sm. Glab. shrub to 90cm; shoots long, slender, angled or winged. Lvs sparse, 0.5–1cm, linear. Pet. rose, obovate, rounded. Summer. NSW.
T. pilosa Labill. Heath-like shrub to 75cm, glab. to bristly. Lvs linear to broad-lanceolate, strongly revolute. Pet. rose, obovate-oblong. Aus., Tasm.
T. thymiflora Sm. Shrub to 90cm, downy or bristly. Lvs 0.5–1cm, in whorls of 3–4, oval-lanceolate, revolute, bristly. Pet. deep rose, obovate to oval. Summer. Aus.

Teucrium L. GERMANDER; WOOD SAGE. Labiatae. 300 perenn. herbs, shrubs or subshrubs, often aromatic. St. terete or 4-angled. Lvs simple or pinnatisect, entire, toothed, or incised. Fls whorled in pan., rac., spikes or heads; cal. 2-lipped or simple, tubular to bell-shaped, teeth 5; cor. ± 2-lipped, upper lip reduced, lower lip 5-lobed. Cosmop.; esp. Medit. to W Asia.
T. aroanum Orph. ex Boiss. Shrub or subshrub, to 10cm. St. ascending, stoloniferous, tomentose. Lvs to 2×1cm, ovate or elliptic to oblong, base subentire, tomentose, whorls 2–6-fld; cor. to 2cm. Greece. Z8.
T. betonicum L'Hérit. Shrub, to 90cm. St. tomentose. Lvs to 9cm, ovate to oblong, notched, tomentose, whorls 2-fld in loose rac. to 15cm; cor. purple, tube curved, pubesc. Spring–summer. Madeira. Z9.
T. bicolor Sm. Perenn. herb or subshrub, to 2m. St. 4-angled, minutely pubesc. Lvs to 4×1.5cm, ovate-lanceolate, simple or to 3-pinnatifid, seg. narrow, leathery, minutely pubesc. Fls axill. and solitary, or in loose rac.; cor. to 1cm, white to pink or violet flecked purple. Summer. Peru, Chile, Arg. Z9.
T. canadense L. AMERICAN GERMANDER; WOOD SAGE. Perenn. herb, to 1m. St. erect and stiff, pubesc. Lvs to 10×4cm, ovate, elliptic or lanceolate to oblong, notched, papillose above, 4–6-fld, in dense simple, spicate or thyroid rac. to 20cm; cor. to 2cm, cream to pink or purple. Summer. N Amer. Z4.
T. chamaedrys L. WALL GERMANDER. Perenn. herb or subshrub, to 50cm. St. ascending, pubesc. Lvs to 4×2cm, ovate to oblong, notched or toothed or lobed, herbaceous, pubesc. Whorls 8-fld, distant, in loose or dense, term. spikes or rac.; cor. to 18mm, pink or red to purple or, rarely, white, pubesc. Summer–autumn. Eur. to Cauc. 'Nanum': habit dwarf. 'Variegatum': lvs variegated cream; fls plume-like. Z5.
T. chamaedrys var. *pubescens* N. Popov = *T. krymense*.
T. chilense Desf. ex Steud. = *T. bicolor*.
T. creticum L. Shrubby, erect perenn. to 1m, young br. densely tomentose. Lvs linear-oblanceolate, strongly revolute, tomentose beneath. Fls 1–3 per axil; cor. 12–15mm, mauve. S Anatolia, Cyprus, W Syr. Z8.
T. flavum L. Shrub, to 50cm. St. much-branched, pubesc. Lvs to 4×2.5cm, ovate or obovate, notched, leathery. Whorls 3-fld, in spikes or rac. to 20cm; cor. to 2cm, yellow. Summer. Medit. Z8.
T. fruticans L. TREE GERMANDER. Perenn. shrub, to 2.5m. St. 4-angled, white-tomentose. Lvs to 2.2×0.6cm, ovate to lanceolate, entire, lustrous above, tomentose beneath. Whorls 2-fld, in loose term. rac.; cor. to 2.5cm, blue to lilac. Summer. Iberia. 'Album': fls white. 'Azureum': fls darker blue. Z8.
T. heterophyllum L'Hérit. Shrub, to 2m. St. tomentose. Lvs ovate or lanceolate to oblong, subentire to notched, pubesc. to tomentose. Whorls 1–4-fld, distant; cor. pink or red to purple. Canary Is. Z9.
T. heterophyllum Cav., non L'Hérit. = *T. bicolor*.
T. hyrcanicum L. Perenn. herb, to 75cm. St. sparsely branched, woody at base, pubesc. Lvs to 8×5cm, ovate or lanceolate to oblong, toothed to notched, minutely pubesc. to tomentose. Whorls in dense, term., spicate rac. to 20cm; cor. to 3cm, red to purple, pubesc. Autumn. W Asia, Cauc. Z6.
T. krymense Juz. Perenn. subshrub, to 40cm. St. pubesc. Lvs to 2×1cm, ovate to oblong, notched, pubesc. to tomentose. Whorls 3–6-fld, distant, in loose simple rac.; cor. to 12mm, purple. Summer. Crimea. Z6.
T. littorale E. Bickn. = *T. canadense*.
T. lucidum L. Perenn. to 60cm. St. 4-angled, woody at base, ± glab. Lvs to 4×3cm, ovate or lanceolate to oblong, toothed to lobed. Whorls distant, in loose rac.; cor. to 17mm, pink to purple. Eur. (Alps). Z6.
T. marum L. CAT THYME. Shrub, to 50cm. St. erect, tomentose. Lvs to 1cm, ovate, rhomboid to linear, entire or toothed, pubesc. Whorls 2–4-fld, in dense, subsecund, cylindric rac. to 5cm; cor. to 12mm, purple, pubesc. Summer. W Medit. Is. Z9.
T. massiliense L. Subshrub, to 1m. St. erect, tomentose. Lvs 5cm, ovate to oblong, notched. Whorls in rac.; cor. to 1cm, pink to purple. W Medit. Z6.
T. montanum L. Subshrub, to 25cm. St. suberect to creeping, white-pubesc. Lvs to 3cm, linear or oblong to elliptic, entire, glab. above, pubesc. beneath. Whorls few, in dense, term. heads; cor. to 12mm, white to cream or yellow. Summer. C to S Eur. and N Afr. to W Asia. Z6.
T. occidentale A. Gray. HAIRY GERMANDER. Perenn. herb, to 90cm. St. gland.-pubesc. Lvs to 9cm, ovate or lanceolate to oblong, pubesc. Whorls in dense or interrupted spikes to 15cm; cor. to 12mm, purple. N Amer. Z7.
T. officinale Lam. = *T. chamaedrys*.
T. orientale L. Perenn. herb, to 50cm. St. erect, 4-angled. Lvs to 5cm, 2–3-pinnatifid, ovate to suborbicular, lobes linear, entire to notched. Whorls in loose, thyrsoid pan.; cor. to 2cm, blue. Summer. E Medit. Z7.
T. polium L. Perenn. subshrub, to 45cm. St. procumbent, terete,

woody at base, tomentose. Lvs to 3.5×1.8cm, linear to oblanceolate, entire to notched, rugose and tomentose. Whorls in dense, term., heads to 2cm wide; cor. to 8mm, white or yellow to pink or purple. Summer. Medit. to W Asia. Z7.

T. prostratum Hal., non Schur = *T. montanum*.

T. pyrenaicum L. Perenn. herb, to 30cm. St. ascending, pubesc. Lower lvs to 2.5cm, suborbicular to linear-oblong, notched, pubesc. Whorls few, in dense, term. heads to 3cm wide; cor. to 15mm, white or yellow, tipped purple. Summer. Pyren. Z6.

T. sandrasicum O. Schwarz. Perenn. erect, subshrub, to 30cm. Lvs to 3cm, linear to lanceolate, entire, white-pubesc. beneath. Whorls in simple rac.; cor. blue. E Medit. Z8.

T. scorodonia L. Perenn. subshrub, to 1m. St. ascending, stoloniferous, pubesc. Lvs to 5cm, ovate to deltoid or lanceolate, notched, rugose. Whorls in loose, simple or branched, paniculate rac. to 15cm; cor. to 16mm, yellow to green, occas. white or red. Eur. 'Crispum': lvs crimped, edges frilly. 'Crispum Marginatum': lvs small, crimped, margins spotted white, tinted purple in winter; fls cream. 'Rosea': fls pink. 'Winterdown': lvs mottled yellow-white. Z6.

T. subspinosum Pourr. ex Willd. Perenn. shrub, to 50cm. St. twisted, white-tomentose, branchlets short-spiny. Lvs to 7×1mm, deltoid to lanceolate or linear, white-tomentose beneath. Whorls 2–4-fld, in loose rac.; cor. to 8mm, pale. Balearics (Majorca). Z9.

Teuscheria Garay. Orchidaceae. 3 epiphytic orchids. Pbs to 3cm, distant or clustered, ovoid or pyriform enveloped by several lf sheaths, 1-leaved at apex. Lvs to 35cm oblong to linear-lanceolate. Fls large, solitary, borne basally; sep. fleshy; pet. subsimilar to sep.; lip trilobed. Mex., C Amer., Venez., Ecuad., Colomb. Z10.

T. venezuelana Garay = *T. wageneri*.

T. wageneri (Rchb. f.) Garay. Infl. to 10cm, pendent; fls bronze tinged maroon, lip white flushed pink; sep. elliptic, dors. to 19×7mm, laterals to 25×8mm; pet. to 18×5mm, oblanceolate; lip to 23×18mm, cuneate-flabellate, dentate-crenulate, callus, golden-farinose. Venez.

→*Bifrenaria* and *Stenocoryne*.

Texan Umbrella Tree *Melia azedarach*; *Sophora secundifolia*.
Texan Walnut *Juglans microcarpa*.
Texas Almond *Prunus texana*.
Texas Bluebonnet *Lupinus subcarnosus*; *L. texensis*.
Texas Ebony *Pithecellobium flexicaule*.
Texas Groundsel *Senecio ampullaceus*.
Texas Mountain Laurel *Sophora secundiflora*.
Texas Mud Baby *Echinodorus cordifolius*.
Texas Mulberry *Morus microphylla*.
Texas Palmetto *Sabal mexicana*.
Texas Porlieria *Porlieria angustifolia*.
Texas Ranger *Leucophyllum*.
Texas Redbud *Cercis canadensis* var. *texensis*.
Texas Sotol *Dasylirion texanum*.
Texas Star *Lindheimera texana*.
Texas Umbrella Tree *Sophora secundiflora*; *Melia azedarach*.

Textoria Miq. = *Dendropanax*.

Thalia L. Marantaceae. 12 tall aquatic perenn. herbs. Lf blades ovate-lanceolate; petioles long, bases sheathing, overlapping. Fls 2-ranked on flexuous, tassel-like br. of a long-stalked pan. exceeding lvs; cor. and petaloid staminodes showy. Trop. and subtrop. Americas, Trop. Afr. Z9.

T. canniformis Forst. = *Donax canniformis*.

T. dealbata J. Fraser. Lvs c50×25cm, white-farinose, grey-green throughout; petiole to 2m. Infl. br. to 20cm on a stalk to 3m; fls violet, to 8cm. S US, Mex.

T. divaricata Chapm. = *T. geniculata*.

T. geniculata L. Differs from *T. dealbata* in longer, narrower lvs with less farina, on petioles to 3m, and larger, remote, violet fls in more strongly pendulous pan. br. Trop. Amer., Trop. Afr.

T. steudneri Koch = *Ctenanthe pilosa*.

Thalictrum L. MEADOW RUE. Ranunculaceae. 130 perenn. herbs, rhizomatous or tuberous. Lvs basal and cauline, 2–4 pinnate or ternate; lfts lobed or toothed. Infl. an axill. or term. pan., rac. or corymb; fls small; sep. 4–5, petaloid; pet. 0; sta. many, often conspicuous. N temp. zones, trop. S Amer., trop. and S Afr., Indon.

T. alpinum L. To 15cm. Lvs biternate, glab.; lfts 3–8mm, orbicular, toothed or lobed ×3–5. Infl. racemose, 8–20cm; fls 5mm; sep. 4, green-purple; sta. to 6, pendulous, exceeding sep., fil. threadlike, violet. Early summer. Eur., Asia, N Amer. Z5.

T. anemonoides Michx. = *Anemonella thalictroides*.

T. angustifolium hort. non L. = *T. lucidum*.

T. angustifolium L. non hort. = *T. simplex*.

T. aquilegiifolium L. To 1.5m. Lvs glab., 2–3-ternate; lfts to 30mm, obovate, sinuate. Infl. paniculate; sep. 4–5, green-white, 4mm; sta. erect, exceeding sep., fil. clavate, mauve to white, pink or deep purple. Early summer. Eur. to temp. Asia. 'Atropurpureum': fls dark purple. 'Aurantiacum': fls tinged orange. 'Purpureum': fls purple. 'Roseum': fls lilac-rose. 'Thundercloud' ('Purple Cloud'): fls rose-purple. Z6.

T. calabricum Spreng. Differs from *T. aquilegiifolium* in fls few, fil. purple; fr. short (not long-) stalked, not winged. Early summer. It., Sicily. Z7.

T. chelidonii DC. 30–250cm. Lvs 2–3-pinnate or ternate; lfts 1–4cm, ovate to suborbicular, 7–13-lobed or toothed. Infl. paniculate; sep. 4, pink to lilac, to 12mm; sta. pendulous, not exceeding sep., fil. threadlike. Summer. Himal. Z7.

T. coreanum non Lév. = *T. ichangense*.

T. delavayi Franch. To 120cm. St. almost black. Lvs 2–3-pinnate or ternate; lfts to 15mm, entire or 3-lobed. Infl. loose, paniculate; sep. 4, lilac to white, 15mm; sta. pendulous, not exceeding sep., fil. threadlike. Summer. W China to E Tibet. 'Album': fls white. 'Hewitt's Double': fls purple, double. 'Magnificum': fls large, pan. more open. 'Minus': habit semi-dwarf. Z7.

T. diffusiflorum Marq. & Airy Shaw. To 1m. Lvs 2–3-pinnate or ternate; lfts suborbicular, to 5mm diam., 3–5-toothed, grey-green. Infl. large, paniculate; sep. to 2cm, mauve, greatly exceeding sta.; sta. pendulous, fil. threadlike. Summer. SE Tibet. Z7.

T. dipterocarpum hort. non Franch. = *T. delavayi*.

T. fendleri Engelm. ex A. Gray. To 2m. Lvs 2–4-ternate; lfts rounded to subcordate at base. Fls green-white; fil. threadlike. NW US. Z5.

T. flavum L. YELLOW MEADOW RUE. To 1m. Lvs 2–3-pinnate, usually glab. Infl. narrow-ovoid, paniculate; sep. 4, yellow, 3mm; sta. erect, exceeding sep.; fil. threadlike. Summer. Eur. to E Medit. 'Illuminator': lvs bright green; fls pale yellow. ssp. *glaucum* (Desf.) Battand. St. and lvs glaucous. SW Eur. to N Afr. Z6.

T. foeniculaceum Bunge. To 45cm. Lvs 3–5-ternate; lfts narrow to cylindric, to 1mm wide. Infl. corymbose, loose, sep. to 14mm, white to shell pink, exceeding sta.; sta. erect, fil. threadlike. Late spring. E China. Z6.

T. foetidum L. To 60cm, densely glandular-pubesc., malodorous. Lvs 3–4-pinnate; lfts ovate to orbicular, emarginate to lobed. Infl. paniculate, lax; sep. 3mm yellow-green; sta. pendulous, exceeding sep., fil. threadlike. Summer. Eur. to temp. Asia. Z6.

T. glaucum Desf. = *T. flavum* ssp. *glaucum*.

T. ichangense Oliv. To 20cm. Lvs biternate; lfts ovate to orbicular, to 4cm diam., sinuate, usually peltate. Infl. corymbose, loose, sep. white or mauve, 3mm; sta. erect, exceeding sep., fil. clavate. Summer. E to N China. Z7.

T. japonicum Thunb. = *Coptis japonica*.

T. javanicum Bl. To 2m. Lvs 3–4-pinnate; lfts ovate to sub-orbicular, 5–25mm, 3–7-toothed glaucous. Infl. paniculate; sep. 4, white or mauve within, 4mm; sta. erect, exceeding sep., fil. clavate. Summer. Himal., India, W China, Indon. Z9.

T. kiusianum Nak. To 15cm. Lvs biternate; lfts ovate to 15mm, 3–5-lobed. Infl. few-fld; sep. to 3mm, white to purple; sta. lilac, exceeding sep., fil. clavate. Summer. Jap. Z8.

T. lucidum L. To 1m. Lvs 2–3-pinnate; lfts narrow-oblong to narrow-linear, entire or lobed. Infl. paniculate many-fld, erect; sep. 4, yellow-green, 3mm; sta. erect, exceeding sep., fil. threadlike. Summer. Eur. to temp. Asia. Z7.

T. minus L. To 1.5m. Lvs glab. or gland., sometimes glaucous, 3–4-pinnate; lfts suborbicular to ovate, lobed. Infl. many-fld paniculate; sep. 4–5, yellow or green-purple; sta. pendulous, exceeding sep., fil. threadlike. Summer. Eur. to temp. Asia. 'Adiantifolium': lvs slightly glaucous, finely cut, fern-like. Z6.

T. orientale Boiss. To 30cm. Lvs biternate, glab.; lfts sub-orbicular, to 2cm, trilobed, sinuate. Infl. few-fld, corymbose; sep. to 12mm, white to lilac; sta. erect, not exceeding sep., fil. threadlike. Early summer. Greece to Asia Minor. Z7.

T. psilotifolium anon. = *T. foeniculaceum*.

T. reniforme Wallich. Similar to *T. chelidonii* but infl. gland. or pubesc., lfts over 1cm diam.; fls usually larger. Summer. Himal. Z7.

T. rochebrunianum Franch. & Savat. To 1m. Lvs 3–4-ternate; lfts 2–3cm, obovate to elliptic, entire or lobed. Infl. loose, paniculate; sep. 7mm, lavender or white; sta. much shorter than sep., pendulous; fil. threadlike. Jap. Z8. 'Lavender Mist': hardy, vigorous; fls small, bell-shaped, violet, in large heads, sta. gold.

T. rugosum Ait. = *T. flavum* ssp. *glaucum*.

T. simplex L. Variable; resembles *T. lucidum*, lfts broad-ovate, pan. loose, sta. pendulous. Summer. Eur. to temp. Asia. Z7.

T. speciosissimum L. = *T. flavum* ssp. *glaucum*.

T. tuberosum L. To 50cm. Lvs mostly basal, 2–3-pinnate, glab.; lfts orbicular, 3-lobed. Infl. few-fld, corymbose; sep. 4–5, white or cream, to 15mm; sta. erect, not exceeding sep., fil. thread-like. Spain to SW Fr. Z8.

Thamnocalamus Munro. Gramineae. 6 clumping bamboos. Culms terete, thick-walled; sheaths decid. with auricles and dark scabrous bristles; br. many. Lvs tessellate, glab., sheaths glab. with auricles and bristles. Himal., S Afr. Z6.

T. aristatus (Gamble) Camus. Culms 3–10m×1–6cm, yellow-green, speckled brown with age; sheaths sometimes with dark markings, sparsely hairy; ligule short, nodes with white bloom below; br. and branchlets usually red-lined. Lvs 6.5–13.5×0.6–1.8cm, scaberulous. NE Himal.

T. falcatus (Nees) Camus = *Drepanostachyum falcatum*.

T. falconeri Hook. ex Munro = *Drepanostachyum falconeri*.

T. spathaceus (Franch.) Söderstr. UMBRELLA BAMBOO. Differs from *Sinarundinaria nitida* in its white powdery, soon yellow-green, later yellow culms, pale brown sheaths. Lvs 6–15×0.5–1.8cm, apple-green, with long drawn-out apex, slightly scaberulous on one margin. C China.

T. spathiflorus (Trin.) Munro. Differs from *T. aristatus* in its somewhat flexuous grey culms, white-bloomed at first, flushed pink in strong sunlight; sheaths with fewer or no hairs, ciliate, blades often longer; lvs greyer with no callus. NW Himal.

T. spathiflorus ssp. *aristatus* (Gamble) D. McClintock = *T. aristatus*.

T. tessellatus (Nees) Söderstr. & R.P. Ellis. BERGBAMBOES. Culms 2.5–7m×1–6cm, unbranched below; sheaths usually exceeding internodes, pale, papery, ligule large, fringed; nodes with a pink-purple ring below; br. tinted purple. Lvs 5–21×0.5–1.9cm, scaberulous on one margin. S Afr. Z8.

→*Arundinaria*, *Fargesia* and *Sinarundinaria*.

Thamnopteris Presl.

T. antiqua (Mak.) Mak. = *Asplenium antiquum*.

T. nidus (L.) Presl = *Asplenium nidus*.

Thamnosma Torr. & Frém. Verbenaceae. 6 aromatic herbs or shrubs, usually gland. Lvs caducous, entire, narrow. Fls racemose, 4-merous, perfect; disc entire or crenate; sta. 8, inserted on disc. N Amer., S Afr. Z9.

T. montana Torr. & Frém. TURPENTINE BROOM. Gland., to 60cm. Lvs to 1.5cm, oblanceolate to oblong-linear. Sep. to 4mm, yellow-green or purple; pet. to 12mm, purple, or white, ovate to oblong. W N Amer. to Mex.

Thanneb *Cordia africana*.

Thatch *Thrinax parviflora*.

Thatch Leaf Palm *Howea forsteriana*.

Thatch Pole *Coccothrinax* (*C. crinita*); *Thrinax*; (*T. parviflora*).

Thaumatococcus Benth. Marantaceae. 1 herbaceous perenn., to 1m. Lvs to 30×23cm, ovate to suborbicular, acuminate, leathery; petiole to 10cm. Fls to 2.5cm, paired in basal spikes. Sierra Leone, Guinea. Z10.

T. daniellii (Benn) Benth.

→*Monostiche* and *Phrynium*.

Thea L.

T. assimilis (Champ.) Seem. = *Camellia assimilis*.

T. bohea L. = *Camellia sinensis*.

T. brevistyla Hayata = *Camellia brevistyla*.

T. camellia var. *lucidissima* Lév. = *Camellia saluensis*.

T. camellia Hoffm. = *Camellia japonica*.

T. caudata (Wallich) Seem. = *Camellia caudata*.

T. connata Craib = *Camellia connata*.

T. cuspidata Kochs = *Camellia cuspidata*.

T. euryoides (Lindl.) Booth = *Camellia euryoides*.

T. forrestii Diels = *Camellia forrestii*.

T. furfuracea Merrill = *Camellia furfuracea*.

T. grijsii (Hance) Kuntze = *Camellia grijsii*.

T. honkongensis (Seem.) Pierre = *Camellia honkongensis*.

T. hozanensis Hayata = *Camellia japonica*.

T. japonica (L.) Baill. = *Camellia japonica*.

T. miyagii Koidz. = *Camellia miyagii*.

T. nokoensis (Hayata) Mak. & Nem. = *Camellia nokoensis*.

T. rosiflora var. *pilosa* Kochs = *Camellia fraterna*.

T. rosiflora (Hook.) Kuntze = *Camellia rosiflora*.

T. salicifolia (Champ.) Seem. = *Camellia salicifolia*.

T. sasanqua (Thunb.) Cels = *Camellia sasanqua*.

T. sinensis L. = *Camellia sinensis*.

T. taliensis W.W. Sm. = *Camellia taliensis*.

T. transarisanensis Hayata = *Camellia transarisanensis*.

T. transnokoensis (Hayata) Mak. & Nem. = *Camellia trans-*

nokoensis.

T. tsaii (Hu) Gagnep. = *Camellia tsaii*.

T. viridis L. = *Camellia sinensis*.

T. yunnanensis Pitard ex Diels = *Camellia yunnanensis*.

THEACEAE D. Don. 28/520. *Camellia, Cleyera, Eurya, Franklinia, Gordonia, Schima, Stewartia, Ternstroemia, Tutcheria*.

Thelesperma Less. GREENTHREADS. Compositae. 12 ann. to perenn. herbs, occas. woody. Lvs pinnate, seg. linear or filiform. Cap. small, usually radiate, solitary on long peduncles; receptacle flat. W N Amer., S S Amer.

T. burridgeanum (Reg., Körn. & Rach) S.F. Blake. Branched ann. to c80cm. Lvs to 10cm, 1-pinnate, seg. filiform. Cap. to 3cm diam.; ray flts red-brown, yellow-orange at apex; disc flts purple-brown. Summer. Tex.

T. filifolium (Hook.) A. Gray. Ann., bienn. or weak perenn. to 60cm. Lvs to 13cm, 2-pinnate, ultimate seg. oblanceolate to linear, upper lvs occas. simple. Cap. several, 5cm diam.; ray flts yellow, tinged red-brown; disc flts red-brown. Summer. C & S US.

T. hybridum Voss = *T. burridgeanum*.

T. trifidum (Poir.) Britt. Slender branched ann. or bienn. to 1m. Lvs to 12cm, bipinnate, ultimate seg. filiform. Cap. c4cm diam.; ray flts deep orange-yellow; disc flts brown-purple. C & S US. →*Cosmidium*.

Thelocactus Britt. & Rose. Cactaceae. 11 low-growing cacti. St. depressed-globose to short-cylindric, ribbed or tuberculate, areoles sometimes nectariferous, ± spiny. Fls apical, funnelform; scales of pericarpel and tube conspicuous. Fr. globose, dark green or brown and dry or bright red, and fleshy and indehiscent. C & N Mex., SW US.

T. bicolor (Gal. ex Pfeiff.) Britt. & Rose. St. simple, rarely clustering, depressed-globose, ovoid or cylindric, 5–38×5–14cm; ribs 8–13, tuberculate; areoles nectariferous, spines tinged red, yellow or white, to 3.5cm. Fl. 3.5–7×4–8cm, pink to magenta, throat red; tube well-developed. Summer. N & NE Mex., S Tex. Z9.

T. buekii (Klein) Britt. & Rose = *T. tulensis*.

T. conothelos (Reg. & Klein) F. Knuth. St. simple, globose or elongate, 6–25×7–17cm; ribs replaced by spiralled tubercles, central spines 1–5cm, black-brown to grey. Fl. c5×4cm, magenta or orange-yellow; tube narrow. Spring. NE Mex. Z9.

T. ehrenbergii (Pfeiff.) F. Knuth = *T. leucacanthus*.

T. flavidispinus (Backeb.) Backeb. = *T. bicolor*.

T. fossulatus (Scheidw.) Britt. & Rose = *T. hexaedrophorus*.

T. gielsdorfianus (Werderm.) Borg = *Neolloydia gielsdorfiana*.

T. hastifer (Werderm. & Boed.) F. Knuth. St. simple, cylindric, 10–30×2.5–5cm, crown woolly; ribs 12–18, tubercles vertical or spiralled; areoles sometimes nectariferous, spines 10–14(–26)mm, white to yellow-brown, longest becoming dark brown. Fl. 3.5–5×2.5–3cm, magenta. EC Mex. Z9.

T. heterochromus (F.A.C. Weber) Oosten. St. depressed-globose, 4–7×6–15cm; ribs 7–11, with large rounded tubercles; spines 1–4, to 3cm, stout and flattened, pale yellow and red. Fl. like those of *T. bicolor* but to 10cm diam., with orange-red throat. Summer. N Mex. Z9.

T. hexaedrophorus (Lem.) Britt. & Rose. St. simple, globose 3–8×8–15cm; ribs 8–13, obscure, tubercles large blunt; spines 4–10, to 2.5cm, stout, red, pink, yellow or grey. Fl. 2.7–3.5×3.3–5.5cm, white; tube v. short. Summer. N Mex. Z9.

T. horripilus (Lem.) Klad. = *Neolloydia horripila*.

T. knuthianus (Boed.) Borg = *Neolloydia knuthiana*.

T. leucacanthus (Zucc. ex Pfeiff.) Britt. & Rose. St. simple then clustered, globose to cylindric, 4.5–15×2.5–5cm; ribs 7–14, tuberculate, vertical or slightly spiralled; areoles nectariferous; spines variable; central 0–3, to 5cm, yellow, red or black, radial 6–20 to 1cm, yellow or red-tinged. Fl. to 5×5cm or more, yellow or magenta; tube short. Summer. CE Mex. Z9.

T. lophothele (Salm-Dyck) Britt. & Rose = *T. rinconensis*.

T. macdowellii (Quehl) Glass. Resembling *T. conothelos*, but sometimes clustering, tubercles smaller; st. globose to clavate, 4–15×5–12cm; spines pale yellow or white. Fl. to 5cm+diam., magenta; tube short. Summer. NE Mex. Z9.

T. mandragora (Fric ex A. Berger) A. Berger = *Neolloydia mandragora*.

T. nidulans (Quehl) Britt. & Rose = *T. rinconensis*.

T. phymatothelos (Ruempl.) Britt. & Rose = *T. rinconensis*.

T. porrectus (Lem.) F. Knuth = *T. leucacanthus*.

T. pottsii Britt. & Rose, not *Echinocactus pottsii* Salm-Dyck = *T. heterochromus*.

T. pseudopectinatus (Backeb.) E.F. Anderson & Boke = *Neolloydia pseudopectinata*.

T. rinconensis (Poselger) Britt. & Rose. Resembling *T. hexaedrophorus*, but with more numerous ribs and tubercles, the latter pointed (not blunt), and fls 3–4×2.7–3cm, white or pale pink, sometimes pale yellow in the throat. Summer. NE Mex. Z9.

T. roseanus (Boed.) Borg = *Escobaria roseana*.

T. saussieri (F.A.C. Weber) A. Berger = *T. conothelos*.

T. schottii (Engelm.) Kaldiwa & Fittkau = *T. bicolor*.

T. setispinus (Engelm.) E.F. Anderson. St. simple or clustering, globose to cylindric, c7–12×5–9cm; ribs 12–15, well-defined, acute, not tuberculate but sometimes sinuous; areoles nectariferous; central spine 1, to 27mm, pale yellow to red-tinged, hooked; radial spines 9–17, 9–24mm, white or tinged red. Fl. c5×5cm, yellow with red throat; tube well-developed. Summer–autumn. NE Mex., SW US. Z9.

T. subterraneus (Backeb.) Backeb. & F. Knuth = *Neolloydia mandragora*.

T. tulensis (Poselger) Britt. & Rose. St. simple, rarely clustering, globose, 5–25×6–18cm; ribs c10, indistinct, strongly tuberculate; central spines 1–7, 5–55mm, brown then grey; radial spines 5–8, 7–15mm, pale brown to almost white. Fl. 2.5–5×3.5–8cm, almost white or magenta; tube v. short. Spring–summer. NE Mex. Z9.

T. valdezianus (H. Möller) Bravo = *Neolloydia valdeziana*.

T. viereckii (Werderm.) Bravo = *Neolloydia viereckii*.

T. wagnerianus A. Berger = *T. bicolor*.

→*Echinocactus, Echinomastus, Ferocactus, Hamatocactus* and *Neolloydia*.

Thelycrania (Endl.) Fourr.

T. alba (L.) Pojark. = *Cornus alba*.

T. australis (C.A. Mey.) Sanadze = *Cornus australis*.

T. sanguinea Fourr. = *Cornus sanguinea*.

T. stolonifera Pojark. = *Cornus stolonifera*.

Thelymitra Forst. & Forst. f. Orchidaceae. 45 tuberous, terrestrial orchids. Lf solitary, channelled. Rac. term., erect; tep. similar; column prominent, erect, wings united, forming a hood with appendage. Aus., Malaysia, New Caledonia, NZ. Z10.

T. carnea R. Br. To 35cm. Lf linear. Fls bright salmon pink or cream (sep. darker); column pale green or pink, apex yellow, wings slender, smooth. E & SW W Aus.

T. ixioides Sw. To 60cm. Lf linear to lanceolate. Fls white, blue, pink, mauve or violet, sep. often spotted dark blue; column wings, trilobed, edged yellow with a crest of clavate glands. NZ, New Caledonia, temp. Aus.

T. pauciflora R. Br. To 50cm. Lf linear to lanceolate. Fls pale to bright blue, rarely pink or white; column white or blue, wings erect, tip white, mauve or pink-pubesc. E & SW W Aus., NZ.

T. venosa R. Br. To 75cm. Lf linear. Fls blue, rarely pink or white, veins distinct; column wings white, inrolled. SE Aus.

Thelypodium Endl. Cruciferae. 19 taprooted ann., bienn. or perenn. herbs. St. erect, simple or branched. Lvs in a basal rosette, simple, sometimes pinnatisect. Fls 4-merous, racemose, white-purple, sta. equal or 4 long, 2 short. Fr. a narrow-linear silique. W N Amer.

T. laciniatum (Hook.) Endl. Bienn., to 150cm. Basal lvs glaucous, 6–30cm, lanceolate, pinnately to irregularly deeply lobed. Rac. dense, elongating in fr. to 90cm; pet. 6–20mm, white-purple, linear. Fr. somewhat compressed, 2.5–13cm. Spring–summer. S BC. Z4.

→*Macropodium*.

THELYPTERIDACEAE Pichi-Serm. 30 genera. *Amauropelta, Ampelopteris, Amphineuron, Christella, Cyclosorus, Goniopteris, Macrothelypteris, Meniscium, Oreopteris, Parathelypteris, Phegopteris, Pneumatopteris, Pseudocyclosorus, Sphaerostephanos, Stegnogramma, Thelypteris*.

Thelypteris Schmidel. Thelypteridaceae. 2 terrestrial ferns. Rhiz. creeping or erect, with soft hairlike scales. Fronds lanceolate, or deltoid, bipinnatifid, ± grey pubesc., often gland. beneath. Temp. regions.

T. acuminata (Houtt.) C. Morton = *Christella acuminata*.

T. angustifolia (Willd.) Proctor = *Meniscium angustifolium*.

T. aspera (Presl) Reed = *Pronephrium asperum*.

T. decursive-pinnata (Van Hall) Ching = *Phegopteris decursive-pinnata*.

T. dentata (Forssk.) St. John = *Christella dentata*.

T. dryopteris (L.) Slosson = *Gymnocarpium dryopteris*.

T. glanduligera (Kunze) Ching = *Parathelypteris glanduligera*.

T. hexagonoptera (Michx.) Weatherby = *Phegopteris hexagonoptera*.

T. interrupta (Willd.) Iwatsuki = *Cyclosorus interruptus*.

T. limbosperma (All.) H.P. Fuchs = *Oreopteris limbosperma*.

T. megaphylla (Mett.) Iwatsuki = *Sphaerostephanos penniger*.

T. nevadensis (Bak.) Clute ex Morton = *Parathelypteris nevadensis*.

T. noveboracensis (L.) Nieuwl. = *Parathelypteris noveaboracensis*.

T. opulenta (Kaulf.) Fosb. = *Amphineuron opulentum*.

T. oreopteris (Ehrh.) Slosson = *Oreopteris limbosperma*.

T. palustris Schott. MARSH FERN. Rhiz. long, creeping. Sterile frond blades, 8–38×5–15cm, lanceolate, pinnate, membranous, pinnae to 25 pairs, linear-lanceolate, pinnatifid to subpinnate, seg. oblong-ovate, stipes equalling lamina; fertile fronds 30–100cm, stouter and stiffer then sterile, pinna seg. narrower, stipes generally longer than rachis. Cosmop. var. *pubescens* (Lawson) Fern. MEADOW FERN; SNUFFBOX FERN. Plant more hairy; indusia pilose, not gland. SE Canada, E & C US. Z4.

T. parasitica (L.) C. Morton = *Christella parasitica*.

T. patens (Sw.) Small = *Christella patens*.

T. pennigera (Forst. f.) Allan = *Pneumatopteris pennigera*.

T. phegopteris (L.) Slosson = *Phegopteris connectilis*.

T. pozoi (Lagasca) Morton = *Stegnogramma pozoi*.

T. reptans (Gmel.) Morton = *Goniopteris reptans*.

T. resinifera (Desv.) Proctor = *Amauropelta resinifera*.

T. reticulata (L.) Proctor = *Meniscium reticulatum*.

T. robertiana (Hoffm.) Slosson = *Gymnocarpium robertianum*.

T. tetragona (Sw.) Small = *Amauropelta tetragona*.

T. torresiana (Gaudich.) Alston = *Macrothelypteris torresiana*.

T. totta (Thunb.) Schelpe = *Cyclosorus interruptus*.

T. triphylla (Sw.) Iwatsuki = *Pronephrium triphyllum*.

→*Aspidium, Dryopteris* and Lastrea.

Themeda Forssk. Gramineae. c19 ann. or perenn. grasses. Lvs linear; ligule much reduced. Infl. racemose, with sheathing spatheoles. OW Trop. & Subtrop. Z10.

T. australis (R. Br.) Stapf = *T. triandra*.

T. triandra Forssk. Tufted perenn. to 2m. Lvs compressed, to 30×0.8cm. Infl. to 30cm; spatheoles to 3.5cm, russet. OW Trop. & Subtrop.

Theobroma L. Sterculiaceae. 20 trees. Lvs alt., simple, palmately nerved. Fls in axils of fallen lvs or in caulifloral fascicles, 5-merous; cal. deeply lobed; pet. clawed, spathulate to strap-shaped, hooded; staminal tube urceolate, anth. in 5 bundles alternating with 5 filiform staminodes. Fr. large, hard-fleshy, 10-ribbed; endocarp pulpy; seeds numerous. Lowland trop. Amer. Z10.

T. cacao L. CACAO; CHOCOLATE NUT TREE. Everg. tree to 8m. Lvs 10–40cm, oblong-obovate, red-brown then mid-green, thinly coriaceous. Pedicels 1–2.5cm; cal. 0.6–1cm, pink, lobes lanceolate; pet. pale yellow, shorter. Fr. 12–30cm, oblong-ellipsoid, yellow, brown or purple. C & S Amer.

Theodorea Barb. Rodr. Orchidaceae. 1 epiphytic orchid. Pbs small, clustered, compressed. Lvs to 15×1.5cm, linear-lanceolate. Infl. secund, arching; fls to 3cm; nodding, fragrant, tep. narrow, green-yellow to green-brown; lip ovate-oblong to pandurate, white to yellow-white tipped brown, calli downy, yellow. Braz. Z10.

T. gomesioides Barb. Rodr.

Theophrasta L.

T. longifolia Jacq. = *Clavija longifolia*.

THEOPHRASTACEAE Link. 5/90. *Clavija, Deherainia, Jacquinia*.

Thermopsis R. Br. Leguminosae (Papilionoideae). 23 rhizomatous erect perenn. herbs. Lvs 3-foliolate; stipules persistent, often leaf-like. Fls pea-like in bracteate rac. S & W US, Sib., N India, E Asia.

T. barbata Benth. To 40cm, hairy. Lfts oblanceolate. Fls dark purple 6–12, usually opposite, in erect term. rac. Summer. Himal. Z7.

T. caroliniana Curtis = *T. villosa*.

T. fabacea (Pall.) DC. To 1m; st. with axill. spines. Lfts broadly elliptic to obovate. Fls yellow in erect, axill. rac. Summer. Kamchatka, Kurile Is. Z5.

T. gracilis Howell = *T. macrophylla*.

T. lanceolata R. Br. ex Ait. f. 30–80cm, yellow, softly downy at first. Lfts ovate, obovate or elliptic. Fls yellow, crowded in elongate rac. Spring–summer. Sib., Alask., Jap., Korea, US. Z3.

T. lupinoides (L.) Link = *T. lanceolata*.

T. macrophylla Hook. & Arn. GOLDEN PEA; FALSE LUPINE. 30cm–2m, solitary or grouped. Lfts elliptic, broadly ovate to oblanceolate, downy beneath. Fls yellow, 6 to many in term. rac. W US. Z7.

T. *mollis* (Michx.) Curtis ex Gray. 30–150cm. Lfts rhombic-obovate to oblanceolate, downy beneath. Fls vivid yellow, 3 to many in term. rac. SE US. Z6.

T. *montana* Nutt. = *T. rhombifolia*.

T. *rhombifolia* (Pursh) Richardson. 20–100cm, downy or glab. Lfts broadly ovate, ovate to oblong-oblanceolate, pilose or villous beneath. Fls yellow, loosely to densely packed in term. rac. Rocky Mts to New Mex. Z4.

T. *villosa* (Walter) Fern. & Schubert. CAROLINA LUPIN. Generally stout, 50–150cm. Lfts elliptic, obovate or oblanceolate, somewhat glaucous and downy on veins beneath. Fls yellow, loosely-to densely-packed in term., downy, spike-like rac. Spring-–summer. SE US. Z6.

Therofon Raf.

T. *major* (A. Gray) Kuntze = *Boykinia major*.

T. *rotundifolium* (Parry) Wheelock = *Boykinia rotundifolia*.

Theropogon Maxim. Liliaceae (Convallariaceae). 1 tufted, herbaceous perenn. Lvs strap-shaped, to 15cm, persistent, glab., ribbed, glaucous beneath. Flowering st. shorter than lvs; rac. 10–20-fld, term., 5–7.5cm; fls 6–8mm, white, sometimes tinged red, perianth seg. 6, broad. Early summer. Himal.

T. *pallidus* (Kunth) Maxim.

Thespesia Sol. ex Corr. PORTIA TREE. Malvaceae. 17 trees and shrubs, mostly everg. Lvs cordate, ovate or trilobulate, unlobed or palmately 5–9-lobed. Fls long-stalked, solitary or clustered in axils; epical. seg. 3–15; cal. truncate to 5-lobed; pet. 5; staminal column conspicuous. Trop. Z10.

T. *garckeana* F. Hoffm. Tree or shrub to 10m. Lvs to 20×20cm, suborbicular in outline, palmately 3–5-lobed, stellate-pubesc. to glabrescent above, stellate-tomentose beneath, entire. Epical cupuliform, 9–10-toothed, teeth to 1.2cm; pet. 6×4cm, obliquely obovate, stellate-pubesc. outside. Trop. E & S Afr.

T. *grandiflora* DC. Tree to 15m. Lvs to 25×19cm, orbicular-ovate, palmately 5–7-nerved, base cordate, entire to undulate. Epical. seg. 3, 1.8cm, linear; pet. 7–11×5–7.5cm, obliquely triangular-obovate, deep rose to crimson inside, orange outside, with black spots or lines along the central veins, densely stellate to tomentose outside. Puerto Rico.

T. *grandiflora* DC. = *Montezuma speciosissima*.

T. *lampas* (Cav.) Dalz. ex Dalz. & A. Gibson. Shrub to 3m. Lower lvs to 20×20cm, deeply 3- or 5-lobed, upper lvs smaller, often unlobed. Epical. seg. 4–6, to 1cm, subulate; pet. to 8cm, yellow with a dark purple centre. E Afr., S & SE Asia to the Philipp.

T. *populnea* (L.) Sol. ex Corr. PORTIA TREE. Tree to 12m. Lvs 6–12cm, cordate-ovate, unlobed, glabrate, minutely gland-dotted eesp. on veins, nectariferous near base of midrib. Epical. seg. 3, to 1.2cm, oblong-lanceolate; pet. 4–6cm, yellow, with a maroon basal spot, gland-dotted. Pantrop.

→*Hibiscus*.

Thevenotia L. = *Genipa*.

Thevetia L. Apocynaceae. 8 everg. shrubs and trees. Fls showy, in cymes; cal. 5-parted, lobes spreading; cor. tube cylindric, dilating to campanulate throat, lobes broad, twisted. Trop. Amer., W Indies. Z10.

T. *neriifolia* A. Juss. ex Steud. = *T. peruviana*.

T. *peruviana* (Pers.) Schum. YELLOW OLEANDER. Shrub or small tree to 8m. Lvs to 15cm, linear-lanceolate, glossy dark green. Cymes shorter than lvs; fls fragrant; cor. to 7×5cm, yellow to orange or peach. Trop. Amer. 'Alba': fls white.

Thick-leaf Phlox *Phlox carolina*.
Thick-leaved Whortleberry *Vaccinium crassifolium*.
Thimbleberry *Rubus occidentalis*; *R. odoratus*; *R. parviflorus*.
Thimbleweed *Anemone riparia*.
Thin-leaf Alder *Alnus tenuifolia*.
Thin-leaf Pine *Pinus maximinoi*.
Thin-leaf Sunflower *Helianthus decapetalus*.
Thin-leaf Wattle *Acacia aculeatissima*.
Thin-leaved Bilberry *Vaccinium membranaceum*.
Thin-leaved Stringybark *Eucalyptus eugenioides*.
Thinwin *Pongamia pinnata*.
Thirty Thorn *Acacia seyal*.
Thistle *Carduus*.
Thistle Sage *Salvia carduacea*.
Thitmin *Podocarpus neriifolius*.

Thladiantha Bunge. Cucurbitaceae. 23 tuberous-rooted ann. and perenn. sprawlers or climbers. Tendrils simple or 2-fid. Lvs simple, ovate, or pedately 3–7-foliolate. Fls yellow, ♂ in rac., cymes, or solitary; cal. short-campanulate, lobes 5, narrow; cor. campanulate, pet. 5; sta. 5; ♀ fls solitary or clustered,

staminodes 5; ovary oblong. Fr. to 4cm, oblong-ovoid, fleshy, red, smooth or ribbed. E Asia to Malesia, Afr.

T. *dubia* Bunge. Perenn. St. villous. Tendrils simple. Lvs 5–10cm, ovate-cordate, pubesc. mucronate-dentate. ♂ fls solitary; pet. 2.5cm. Summer. Korea, NE China. Z7.

T. *nudiflora* Hemsl. ex Forbes & Hemsl. Perenn. St. sulcate. Tendrils 2-fid. Lvs 8–15cm, ovate-cordate, denticulate, scabrous above, with brown hairs beneath. ♂ fls in rac.; cal. lobes ovate-lanceolate, c5mm; pet. 1.2cm. China. Z9.

T. *oliveri* Cogn. ex Mottet. Ann. St. glab. Tendrils 2-fid. Lvs c20cm, rounded-cordate, denticulate, scabrous, paler green beneath. ♂ fls 30–40 in cymes; pet. to 2.5cm. Summer. China. Z9.

Thlaspi L. Cruciferae. 60 ann. or perenn., low-growing herbs. Lvs usually rosette-forming, simple, entire or toothed. Fls 4-merous, in rac.; sta. 6; anth. usually yellow. N temp. regions. Z6.

T. *alpestre* L. Bienn. or perenn., 10–50cm. Basal lvs obovate-spathulate to elliptic, entire. Pet. white-purple; sta. equal pet., anth. often violet. Summer. SW & C Eur. Z6.

T. *alpinum* Krantz = *T. alpestre*.

T. *arvense* L. PENNYCRESS; FRENCH WEED; STINKWEED; MITHRIDATE MUSTARD. Foetid ann., 10–60cm. Basal lvs obovate to oblanceolate, entire or toothed, not rosette-forming. Pet. 3–4mm, white, exceeding sta. N hemis.

T. *bellidifolium* Griseb. Tufted perenn. Basal lvs in a rosette, to 6mm wide, narrow-obovate, shallow-toothed; pet. 8mm, lilac. Albania, Balk. Z6.

T. *bulbosum* Sprun. Bienn. or perenn., 6–20cm. Root turbinate. Basal lvs ovate-orbicular, entire to toothed, in a loose rosette. Pet. 6–9×2–3mm, deep violet. Greece, Aegean Is. Z8.

T. *bursa-pastoris* L. = *Capsella bursa-pastoris*.

T. *cepifolium* (Wulf.) Koch. Perenn., 2.5–5cm. Stock with long stolons. Basal lvs obovate-spathulate or elliptic, entire. Pet. purple, 6mm, twice length of sep. E Alps. Z6.

T. *densiflorum* Boiss. & Kotschy. Similar to *T. violascens* except infl. not elongating in fr., wings of fr. pointed not round. Turk. Z7.

T. *goesingense* Hal. Tufted perenn., 15–40cm, much branched. Basal lvs obovate-spathulate or elliptic, entire. Pet. 6–8mm, white, 3× sep. length. E & C Eur., Balk. Penins. Z6.

T. *kerneri* Huter. Loose, mat-forming perenn., 5–15cm. Basal lvs round, glaucous. Pet. 5mm, white. SE Alps, C & N Balk. Z6.

T. *macrophyllum* Hoffm. = *Pachyphragma macrophyllum*.

T. *montanum* L. MOUNTAIN PENNYCRESS. Loose, mat-forming perenn. Basal lvs obovate to orbicular, entire or crenate; pet. 5–7mm, white, sta. much shorter. C Eur. Z5.

T. *perfoliatum* L. PENNYCRESS. Ann. or bienn., 5–30cm. Basal lvs narrow-obovate, sparsely toothed. Pet. 2–3mm, white, exceeding sta. Spring. Eur.

T. *praecox* Wulf. Densely tufted perenn., 10–20cm. Basal lvs in crowded rosettes, oblong-ovate, often violet beneath. Pet. 5–8mm, narrow, white, much exceeding sta. S Austria, It., Balk. Z6.

T. *stylosum* (Ten.) Mutel. Dwarf tufted perenn. to 3cm. Basal lvs 5–10mm, elliptic, entire. Pet. 5mm, lilac; anth. violet. C It. Z6.

T. *violascens* Boiss. Bienn., to 35cm in fr. Basal lvs narrow-obovate, long-stalked, somewhat glaucous, often tinged violet or red. Pet. 3×1mm, white-violet, just exceeding sep. Turk. Z7.

Thompsonella Britt. & Rose. Crassulaceae. 2 rosulate perenn. herbs to 3cm. Lvs sessile. Sep. 5, upright; pet. 5, joined toward base, thin, dark red, edged yellow. Summer. Mex. Z9.

T. *minutiflora* (Rose) Britt. & Rose. Lvs 2–10×1–2.5cm, 10–20, elliptic-obovate, grooved, entire to sinuous. Scape 5–35cm; fls 1–3–7, 6–10mm diam. Mex.

→*Echeveria* and *Graptopetalum*.

Thorn *Crataegus* (*C. calpodendron*); *Prunus spinosa*.
Thorn Apple *Datura*.
Thornless Rose *Rosa* 'Zéphirine Drouhin'.
Thorn Pear *Scolopia ecklonii*.
Thoroughwort *Eupatorium perfoliatum*.
Thorow-wax *Bupleurum* (*B. rotundifolium*).
Thread Agave *Agave filifera*.
Thread Fern *Blechnum filiforme*.
Threadleaf False Aralia *Schefflera elegantissima*.
Thread-leaved Sundew *Drosera filiformis*.
Thread Palm *Washingtonia robusta*.
Three-birds-flying *Linaria triornithophora*.
Three Birds Toadflax *Linaria triornithophora*.
Three-cornered Leek *Allium triquetrum*.
Three-flowered Maple *Acer triflorum*.
Three-in-one Fern *Asplenium dimorphum*.
Three-lobed Leaf Violet *Viola triloba*.
Three-parted Triloba *Viola triloba*.

Three-toothed Maple *Acer buergerianum.*
Three-veined Wattle *Acacia trineura.*
Thrift *Armeria.*

Thrinax Sw. THATCH PALM; KEY PALM. Palmae. 7 palms. St. erect, solitary, smooth or clothed with fibres, ringed; roots form fibrous mass. Crownshaft 0. Lvs palmate, sheath tomentose; petiole long; seg. cut to halfway, lanceolate, shallowly divided, glab. above, scaly beneath, semi-rigid. Infl. interfoliar, erect or arched, branched ×2, br. pendent; fls sometimes fragrant. Fr. to 1cm diam., white. Jam., Belize, Mex., N Carib. to Virgin Is. Z10.

T. argentea Chapm. non Lodd. ex Schult. = *Coccothrinax argentata.*

T. argentea Lodd. ex Schult. = *Coccothrinax argentea.*

T. bahamensis Cook = *T. morrisii.*

T. barbadensis Lodd. ex Mart. = *Coccothrinax dussiana.*

T. crinita Griseb. & H. Wendl. ex Kerch. = *Coccothrinax crinita.*

T. drudei Becc. = *T. morrisii.*

T. ekmanii Burret = *T. morrisii.*

T. excelsa Lodd. ex Griseb. St. 3–11m×12.5–16cm. Petiole 1.6–2.2m, white to tan soft-scaly beneath; blades with densely overlapping fringed scales beneath, seg. 52–65, 114–172cm. Jam.

T. excelsa L.H. Bail. = *T. radiata.*

T. floridana Sarg. = *T. radiata.*

T. keyensis Sarg. = *T. morrisii.*

T. martii Griseb. & Wendl. ex Griseb. = *T. radiata.*

T. microcarpa Sarg. = *T. morrisii.*

T. morrisii Wendl. KEY PALM; BRITTLE THATCH; BUFFALO TOP; BUFFALO-THATCH. St. 1–10.5m×5–35cm. Petiole 27–84cm, densely white scaly beneath, becoming glab.; blades scaly as in *T. excelsa* at first, becoming glab., blue-green, seg. 33–58, 55–75cm. S Flor., W Indies, Cuba.

T. multiflora sensu Read = *T. radiata.*

T. parviflora Sw. THATCH; THATCH POLE; BROOM PALM. St. 1–13m×5–15cm. Petiole 35–160cm, densely tan scaly beneath becoming glab.; blades sparsely scaly beneath, seg. 35–60, 38×96cm. Jam.

T. ponceana Cook = *T. morrisii.*

T. praeceps Cook = *T. morrisii.*

T. pumilio Mart. = *T. radiata.*

T. punctulata Becc. = *T. morrisii.*

T. radiata Lodd. ex Schult. & Schult. f. FLORIDA THATCH; JAMAICAN THATCH. St. 1.5–12m×12cm, base enlarged. Petiole to 94cm, scaly at first beneath; blades dull and grey-scurfy beneath, seg. 51–63, 73–115cm. Flor., W Indies, Mex., Hond.

T. rex Britt. & W. Harris. = *T. excelsa.*

T. wendlandiana Becc. = *T. radiata.*

→*Coccothrinax.*

Thrixanthocereus Backeb.
T. blossfeldiorum   (Werderm.)   Backeb. = *Espostoa blossfeldiorum.*

T. senilis Ritter = *Espostoa senilis.*

Thrixspermum Lour. Orchidaceae. 100 epiphytic monopodial orchids. Lvs fleshy, coriaceous, strap-shaped, alt. along st. Rac. bracteate, axill.; fls in 2 rows or scattered, short-lived; tep. narrow; lip 3-lobed, fleshy, ± saccate. Indomal. to Taiwan and W Pacific. Z10.

T. amplexicaule (Bl.) Rchb. f. St. climbing to 2m. Lvs ovate, to 6.5cm. Infl. 10–25cm; fls white or pale lilac; tep. ovate, to 1.6cm; lip midlobe white, fleshy, callus yellow, basal patch orange-red-pubesc. Sumatra to Philipp.

T. arachnites (Bl.) Rchb. f. St. to over 15cm. Lvs linear to ligulate, to 12cm. Infl. to 10cm; fls to 7.5cm across, lime green to pale yellow, lip white, basally spotted rusty orange; tep. narrow-lanceolate, with pendulous tips; lip sac spotted mauve within. Malaysia, Burm.

T. calceolus (Lindl.) Rchb. f. St. creeping or hanging. Lvs oblong. Infl. to 3cm; fls few, white, fragrant, fleshy; sep. to 2.5cm; pet. smaller, lip tipped orange-yellow, lat. lobes white, callus white with an orange, yellow-spotted patch. Sumatra, Borneo, Malaysia.

T. lilacinum Rchb. f. = *T. amplexicaule.*

Throatwort *Campanula trachelium.*

Thuja L. THUJA; RED CEDAR. Cupressaceae. 5 everg. coniferous trees to 70m. Bark red-brown, exfoliating in strips. Crown conic; br. horizontal to ascending; branchlets flattened. Lvs small, imbricate, addressed, scale-like, lateral lvs overlapping facial pair. ♂ cones solitary, term., spherical; ♀ cones solitary, ovoid to oblong; scales 6–12, 2–6 fertile, overlapping, with a minute

apical bract. N Amer., E Asia.

T. articulata Vahl = *Tetraclinis articulata.*

T. koraiensis Nak. KOREAN THUJA. Tree to 15m. Crown conic, often dense; branchlets often trailing, tips ascending; shoots flattened. Lvs deltoid on main shoots, rhombic on younger shoots, green gland. above, covered with silvery stomatal bands beneath, facial lvs sometimes with a green midrib beneath; lateral lvs with green margins below, scented when crushed. ♀ cones ellipsoid, 8–14mm, brown; scales in 4 pairs, linear-obovate, spreading widely on opening (as for genus). N & C Korea. Z5.

T. occidentalis L. To 20m. Crown slender conic; br. horizontal; branchlets crowded, flattened, spreading. Lvs scale-like, dense on lat. branchlets, more distant on main shoots, obtuse, ovate, yellow-green above, grey-green beneath, becoming yellow-brown; facial lvs with dors. gland. ♀ cones erect, ovoid, 6–14mm, scales in 3–5 pairs. E N Amer. Cvs variable: dwarf, globose to large, columnar or weeping, narrow or conical; foliage scale-like or needles, some having both types; colour ranges from yellow-white to green, occas. brown, often only in winter. Z2.

T. orientalis L. f. = *Platycladus orientalis.*

T. plicata D. Don. WESTERN RED CEDAR. To 70cm. Aromatic. Bole often buttressed at base. Crown conic to columnar, br. horizontal to drooping, tips erect. Lvs in planar sprays, scale-like decussate on term. growths, ovate, acuminate, gland., more obtuse on lat. shoots, dark green above, grey-white below. ♀ cones oblong-ellipsoid, 10–20mm, green, scales in 4–5 pairs. W N Amer. Cvs variable: habit· dwarf, conical, columnar or globose, dense or lax; branchlets variously filamentous, dark green to bronze-yellow to golden yellow or white-variegated. Z6.

T. standishii (Gordon) Carr. JAPANESE THUJA. To 30m. Crown broad conic, open; br. irregularly arranged, spreading, horizontal, ascending at tips; branchlets flattened. Lvs gland., dark green to yellow-green, matt; lat. lvs somewhat incurved at apex; facial lvs obtuse. ♀ cones ovoid, to 1cm, scales 8–10. C Jap. Z6.

T. sutchuenensis Franch. Shrub to tree. Branchlets ascending, flattened, Lvs bright green, glands inconspicuous or possibly 0; facial lvs sulcate; lat. lvs obtuse. ♀ cones brown, coriaceous, scales 4 pairs. China (v. rare and endangered in wild, doubtfully in cult). Z6.

Thujopsis Sieb. & Zucc. Cupressaceae. 1 everg. conifer to 30m. Bark red-brown, exfoliating in long strips. Crown conic. St. often layering; br. spreading, upswept at tips; branchlets erect with drooping side-shoots; shoots horizontal. Lvs 4-ranked, scale-like, thick, waxy, glossy green above, white beneath, to 5×4–6mm. ♂ cones cylindric, solitary, 5mm, term. ♀ cones solitary; scales 8–10, somewhat succulent, erect, ovoid, grey-brown or red-brown, glaucous, 9–16mm, then woody. C & S Jap. Z6.

T. dolobrata (L. f.) Sieb. & Zucc. HIBA. var. **hondai** Mak. To 30m. Branchlets more densely arranged. Lvs smaller, lat. lvs not apically incurved. Cones larger, globose. N Jap. Z5.

Thunbergia Retz. Acanthaceae. 100 erect or twining ann. or perenn. herbs and shrubs. Lvs opposite, simple. Fls solitary in lf axils or in term., pendent rac.; cal. minute, enclosed in paired bracts, annular or 10–15 toothed; cor. tube curved, ventricose, lobes 5; sta. 4. S & Trop. Afr., Madag., warm Asia. Z10.

T. alata Bojer. BLACK-EYED SUSAN. Twining perenn. herb (ann. in cult.). Lvs to 7.5cm, ovate-elliptic to ovate, dentate. Fls 3.75cm, solitary, creamy-white or yellow-orange with or without dark purple-brown throat. Summer–early autumn. Trop. Afr. 'Alba': fls white, centre dark. 'Aurantiaca': fls orange to yellow, centre dark. 'Bakeri': fls snow white. Suzie Hybrids: fls orange, yellow or white, eye dark.

T. coccinea Wallich. Perenn. woody climber to 8m. Lvs 15cm, narrowly ovate-elliptic, toothed, thick-textured. Fls 3cm, in loose pendent rac. 15–45cm, orange-red, lobes reflexed. Winter–spring. India, Burm.

T. erecta (Benth.) Anderson. KING'S MANTLE; BUSH CLOCK VINE. Erect or twining shrub to 2m. Lvs 3–6cm, ovate to oblong, sub-entire to toothed. Fls solitary, 7cm, tube yellow-cream, lobes dark blue-violet. Summer. Trop. W to S Afr. 'Alba': fls white.

T. fragrans Roxb. Perenn. woody climber. Lvs 5–7.5cm, triangular-ovate to oblong, base cordate to hastate, margin sub-entire to toothed. Fls to 3×5cm, solitary, fragrant, white. India, Ceylon. 'Angel Wings': fls snow white, to ×5cm, lightly scented.

T. gibsonii S. Moore = *T. gregorii.*

T. grandiflora (Roxb. ex Rottl.) Roxb. BLUE TRUMPET VINE; CLOCK VINE; BENGAL CLOCK VINE; SKY VINE; SKYFLOWER; BLUE SKYFLOWER. Large perenn. twining shrub. Lvs 10–20cm, ovate-elliptic, pubesc., toothed or lobed. Fls 7.5×7.5cm, solitary or in rac., blue-violet. Summer. N India. 'Alba': fls white.

T. gregorii S. Moore. Perenn. twining climber, ann. in cult. Lvs to 7.5cm, triangular-ovate, hairy, toothed. Fls solitary, 4.5×4.5cm, orange. Summer. Trop. Afr.

T. mysorensis Anderson ex Bedd. Twining shrubby climber to 6m. Lvs 10–15cm, narrowly elliptic, toothed, glabrate. Fls in pendent rac., to 3.75×5cm, tube yellow, lobes red-brown. Spring. India.

Thunia Rchb. f. Orchidaceae. 6 terrestrial or epiphytic orchids. Pbs to 80cm, clustered, cane-like. Lvs to 12cm, 2-ranked, sheathing cones. Rac. short, term.; fls fragrant, generally resembling the more showy *Cattleya* spp.; tep. lanceolate; lip rolled, bell-shaped or tubular, frilled and expanded. Himal. to Burm. Z10.

T. alba (Lindl.) Rchb. f. Lvs elliptic-lanceolate, thinly fleshy, glaucous. Fls often not opening fully; tep. white, 6–7cm, narrow-oblong; lip entire, orange or yellow, striped purple, tubular to funnelform, margins undulate or crispate. India, Burm., China.

T. bensoniae Hook. f. Lvs linear-lanceolate. Fls v. fragrant, tep. to 7cm, white tipped rose-purple, linear-lanceolate, spreading; lip trilobed, white tinted rose-purple, ruffled, disc yellow. NE India.

T. marshalliana Rchb. f. = *T. alba*.

T. pulchra Rchb. f. Lvs fleshy, lanceolate. Fls pure white, throat pale cinnabar red; lip entire, margins irregular, crests yellow and brown. Burm., Vietnam.

Thurberia A. Gray.
T. thespesioides A. Gray = *Gossypium thurberi*.

Thuya *Tetraclinis articulata*.

Thymbra L. Labiatae. 3 low-growing shrubs, glandular-punctate. Lvs sessile, opposite, overlapping, entire. Spikes term., with leafy bracts and fls in whorls; cal. 2-lipped; cor. 2-lipped, tube plane, upper lip erect, emarginate, lower lip spreading, 3-lobed; sta. 4. E Medit. Z8.

T. spicata L. To 50cm. St. pubesc. Lvs to 23×3mm, stiff, linear to lanceolate, glandular-punctate and glab. to sparsely ciliate. Spikes to 10cm, ovoid or obovoid; whorls 6–10-fld; cor. to 16mm, pink to mauve, glandular-punctate. Spring–summer. Greece, Turk., Isr.

Thyme *Thymus*.
Thyme Broomrape *Orobanche alba*.
Thyme Heath *Epacris serpyllifolia*.

Thymelaea Mill. Thymelaeaceae. 30 everg. shrubs, subshrubs, and herbs. Lvs small and narrow. Fls small, solitary or clustered in axils; perianth urceolate or, (in ♂ fls), with a slender, cylindrical tube; lobes 4, spreading; sta. 8, fil. v. short. Fr. dry. E Medit., Canary Is., C Asia, Eur. Z8.

T. hirsuta (L.) Endl. Small, divaricately branching shrub, to 1m. Lvs 3–8mm, overlapping, obtuse, dark green. Fls yellow, v. small. Autumn–winter. Greece, Crete.

T. tartonraira (L.) All. Small, much-branched shrub, to 60cm. Lvs 1–2cm, overlapping, apiculate, leathery, thickly silver-sericeous. Fls yellow-white; cor. tube 6mm, sericeous. Summer. S Eur.
→*Passerina*.

THYMELAEACEAE Juss. 50/720. *Dais, Daphne, Dirca, Drapetes, Edgeworthia, Ovidia, Passerina, Pimelea, Stellera, Struthiola*.

Thyme-leaved Eriogonum *Eriogonum thymoides*.
Thyme-leaved Speedwell *Veronica serpyllifolia*.
Thyme-leaved Willow *Salix serpyllifolia*.

Thymophylla Lagasca. Compositae. 10–12 ann. to perenn. herbs and shrubs. Lvs alt. or opposite, entire to pinnatisect, cap. radiate in corymbs; phyllaries in 1–many series; ray flts yellow-orange; disc flts yellow. Fr. terete; pappus of scales or occas. awns. US to C Amer. Z9.

T. tenuiloba (DC.) Small. GOLDEN FLEECE. Ann. to bienn. or short lived perenn. to 50cm. Lvs deeply pinnatisect. Tex., Mex.
→*Dyssodia*.

Thymus L. THYME. Labiatae. 350 aromatic perenn. herbs and subshrubs. Lvs opposite, entire. Fls crowded in term. bracteate heads or in lf axils; cal. cylindrical or campanulate, upper lip 3-lobed, lower lip cleft; cor. tubular. Eurasia.

T. acicularis Waldst. & Kit. = *T. striatus*.

T. adamovicii Velen. Resembles *T. longicaulis* but st. pubesc. throughout. Lvs larger, elliptic, 9×2.5mm, densely hairy. C Balk. Z7.

T. aestivus Reut. ex Willk. = *T. vulgaris*.

T. algarbiensis Lange = *T. camphoratus*.

T. alpestris auct., non Tausch ex A. Kerner = *T. pulegioides*.

T. alsarensis Ronn. = *T. thracicus*.

T. austriacus Bernh. ex Rchb. = *T. glabrescens* ssp. *glabrescens*.

T. azoricus Lodd. = *T. caespititius*.

T. billardieri Boiss. = *T. integer*.

T. boissieri Hal. = *T. cherlerioides*.

T. bracteosus Vis. ex Benth. Dwarf shrub, partly decid. St. to 10cm, mat-forming, pubesc. Lvs spathulate, ciliate below. Fls sessile in dense heads, bracts ovate, to 13mm, purple-green; cor. to 8mm, purple. Summer. W Balk. Z7.

T. broussonetii Boiss. Perenn. subshrub; shoots erect, tetragonal, pubesc. throughout or on two sides. Lvs to 2cm, ovate or elliptic. Infl. to 4cm, semiglobose; bracts large, purple-green, ciliate; cor. to 2cm, red-green. Moroc. Z9.

T. buschianus Klokov & Desj.-Shost. = *T. nummularius*.

T. caespititius Brot. Dwarf mat-forming shrub. Flowering st. upright to 5cm. Lvs to 6mm, narrow, spathulate, glab., ciliate. Infl. lax, small heads flattened against mat; bracts similar to lvs; cor. to 6mm, rose, lilac or white. Late spring–summer. Port., NW Spain, Azores. 'Aureus': lvs narrow, lightly golden. Z7.

T. camphoratus Hoffm. & Link. To 40cm, camphor-scented. Lvs narrow-ovate, woolly above. Infl. globose, 10–18mm diam.; bracts ovate, purple-green and woolly; cor. green-white. Port. Z7.

T. capitatus (L.) Hoffm. & Link. Compact, ascending, woody. Lvs to 12mm, linear, fleshy, gland. Fls in term., conical clusters; bracts to 6mm, overlapping, tinged red, ciliate; cor. to 10mm, pink. Mid and late summer. Medit. Eur. and Turk. Z7.

T. capitellatus Hoffm. & Link. Resembles *T. camphoratus* but fl. heads smaller, bracts green. Summer. Coastal Port. Z7.

T. carnosus Boiss. Woody, erect, to 40cm. Lvs in cluster, ovate, light to grey-green, fleshy, pubesc. beneath. Infl. to 40cm; bracts ovate, green; cor. white, lilac or pink. S Port. Z7.

T. cephalotus L. Woody, erect, to 30cm. Lvs to 1cm, linear, pubesc., ciliate, revolute. Infl. to 4cm, oblong to conical; bracts to 2cm, ovate, coriaceous; cor. 15mm, purple. Spring. S Port. Z8.

T. chamaedrys Fries = *T. pulegioides*.

T. cherlerioides Vis. Shoots caespitose, creeping. Flowering st. to 8cm, erect. Lvs linear, sessile, puberulent to velutinous, revolute and ciliate. Bracts to 2.5mm wide, occas. purple; cor. 6mm, pink. C Balk. Penins. Z6.

T. ciliatus Desf. & Benth. non Lam. Lvs oval, on flowering st., basal lvs linear, ciliate. Fls in whorls to 2cm; cor. to 1cm, red or violet. NW Afr. ssp. *euciliatus* Maire. Bracts green; fls larger. ssp. *coloratus* (Boiss. & Reut.) Battand. Bracts tinged purple. Z9.

T. cilicicus Boiss. & Bail. To 15cm. Lvs linear, ciliate, deep green. Infl. term., dense, hemispherical; bracts purple; cor. to 8mm, mauve or lilac. Mid-summer. Asia Minor. Z7.

T. cimicinus Blum ex Ledeb. St. procumbent, woody. Lvs to 7mm, oblong, glab., ciliate. Fls axillary; bracts leaf-like; cor. and cal. equal, green to red. S Russia. Z5.

T. ×citriodorus (Pers.) Schreb. ex Schweig. & Körte. (*T. pulegioides* ×*T. vulgaris*.) Lemon-scented. St. erect, to 30cm, pubesc. Lvs to 1cm, rhombic-oval to lanceolate. Infl. oblong, interrupted; bracts leaf-like; cor. pale lilac. Gdn origin. 'Anderson's Gold': dwarf, carpeting, foliage bright golden all winter. 'Archer's Gold': compact; lvs bright yellow. 'Argenteus': lvs silver. 'Argenteus Variegatus': compact; lvs narrow, edged silver. 'Aureus': erect small bush to 15cm; lvs green dappled gold, most apparent in winter and early spring; liable to revert to a green form. 'Doone Valley': prostrate, lvs dark green splashed gold, tinted red in winter. 'Fragrantissimus': upright, slender; lvs grey-green; orange-scented; fls pale pink on white. 'Golden King': upright, bushy; lvs edged gold. 'Golden Queen': loose; lvs pale green lightly variegated gold; fls mauve. 'Minus': miniature. 'Nyewoods': minute lvs intricately veined, pale green-yellow and bearing a green central stripe. 'Silver Queen': variably variegated from finely marbled cream to dull silver; term. lf buds turn rose-pink in winter. Z7.

T. comosus Heuff. ex Griseb. St. mat-forming; flowering st. to 14cm, pubesc. Lvs to 17mm, ovate, ciliate below, glab. or slighty hairy. Infl. to 7cm; bracts similar to lvs; cor. to 9mm, pink or purple. Mid-summer. C Eur. Z5.

T. comptus Friv. Procumbent hairy subshrub, flowering st. to 15cm. Lvs to 1.5cm, linear-lanceolate, ciliate near apex. Infl. to 10cm, bracts like lvs; cor. to 6mm, rose. Bulg., Greece, Turk. Z5.

T. comptus auct. non Friv. = *T. striatus*.

T. doerfleri Ronn. Dwarf carpeting shrub. Flowering st. to 10cm. Lvs to 14mm, linear, densely hairy, subcoriaceous. Infl. term.; bracts like lvs; cor. soft pink or purple. Early summer. NE Albania. 'Bressingham Pink': grey green, prostrate, fls clear pink. Z5.

T. drucei Ronniger = *T. praecox* ssp. *arcticus*.

T. dzevanoskyi Klokov & Desj.-Shost. = *T. pannonicus*.

T. ericaefolius Roth. = *Micromeria varia*.

T. funkii Coss. = *T. longiflorus*.

T. glaber Mill. = *T. pulegioides*.

T. glabrescens Willd. Subshrub to 15cm, usually herbaceous. Lvs elliptic or lanceolate to obovate, ciliate. Infl. term., rounded and interrupted; bracts like lvs. SE & EC Eur. ssp. *glabrescens*. Upper lvs on flowering st. larger, usually over 3mm. ssp. *decipiens* (A. Braun) Domin. Lvs on flowering st. less than 3mm, elliptic. ssp. *urumovii* (Velen.) Jalas. Lvs on flowering st. less than 3mm, linear-lanceolate. Z6.

T. herba-barona Lois. CARAWAY THYME. Dwarf subshrub to 25cm, wiry, forming loose carpet. Lvs minute, dark green, pubesc. Fls in lax low-lying heads; cor. pink or mauve. Midsummer. Corsica & Sardinia. 'Caraway-scented': v. heavily scented. 'Lemon-scented': strongly scented of lemons.

T. hirsutus Bieb. Shoots prostrate, woody; flowering st. to 70mm, pubesc. Lvs to 1cm, linear, grey-pubesc., revolute. Infl. hemispherical; bracts lanceolate to ovate; cor. to 6mm, lilac. Crimea. Z5.

T. hirsutus auct. non Bieb. = *T. cherlerioides*.

T. hirsutus var. *doerfleri* (Ronn.) Ronn. = *T. doerfleri*.

T. hyemalis Lange. Resembles *T. vulgaris* except in grey-green lvs to 1mm wide, densely clustered at nodes, and mauve fls with hispid cal. Spring and winter. SE Spain. Z5.

T. ilerdensis Gonzalez ex Costa = *T. vulgaris*.

T. illyricus Ronn. = *T. longicaulis*.

T. integer Sartori ex Nyman. Low-growing shrub; br. spreading, gnarled; flowering st. to 8cm, pubesc. Lvs to 7mm, linear, acute, tomentose, margins thickened, ciliate. Infl. subglobose, sparse; cor. pink, to 12mm. Late winter, early spring. Cyprus. Z5.

T. kosanii Ronn. = *T. longicaulis*.

T. lanuginosus Mill. Herbaceous perenn. to 8cm. Plants sold under this name are usually *T. pseudolanuginosus*.

T. latifolius (Besser) Andrz. = *T. pannonicus*.

T. leucotrichus Hal. Creeping dwarf shrub to 10mm. Lvs linearlanceolate, pubesc., subsessile. Infl. subglobose; bracts greenpurple; cor. pink to purple, barely exceeding cal. Greece, Turk. Z5.

T. loevyanus Opiz = *T. glabrescens* ssp. *glabrescens*.

T. longicaulis C. Presl. Dwarf long-creeping shrub; flowering st. pubesc., to 10cm. Lvs linear-lanceolate, to 1mm wide, soft and short-lived, sometimes fleshy, ciliate. Bracts like lvs; cor. purple. S Eur.

T. longidens Velen. = *T. thracicus*.

T. longiflorus Boiss. St. closely branching, ascending to 30cm. Lvs to 12mm, linear, pubesc., revolute. Infl. subglobose, bracts large, ovate coriaceous and green-purple. Summer. SE Spain. Z5.

T. lykae Deg. & Jáv. = *T. longicaulis*.

T. malyi Ronn. = *T. longicaulis*.

T. marschallianus Willd. = *T. pannonicus*.

T. mastichina L. St. erect to 50cm. Lvs ovate to ellipticlanceolate, often crenulate, pubesc. Infl. subglobose, to 2cm diam.; bracts like lvs; cor. off-white. Spain and Port. Z7.

T. membranaceus Boiss. Resembles *T. longiflorus* except bracts and cor. white. SE Spain. Z7.

T. micans Sol. ex Lowe = *T. caespititius*.

T. moesiscus Velen. = *T. longicaulis*.

T. montanus Waldst. & Kit. St. woody at base, to 25mm, pubesc. Lvs to 1.8cm, ovate or oblong-lanceolate, ciliate below. Infl. divided; bracts like lvs; cor. pink or purple, to 6mm. Eur. Z5.

T. moroderi Martinez = *T. longiflorus*.

T. nikolovii (Deg. & Urum.) Stoj. & Stef. = *T. thracicus*.

T. nummularius Bieb. Subshrub to 13cm, procumbent then ascending. Lvs to 15×9mm, ovate, ciliate. Infl. term.; bracts 12×7.5mm, leaflike, purple; cor. to 7mm, lilac-purple. Summer. Iran. Z7.

T. odoratissimus Bieb. St. erect to procumbent, to 15cm. Lvs to 2cm, linear part-ciliate. Infl. capitate; bracts as lvs; cor. pale pink. S Russia. Z6.

T. pallasianus H. Braun. Closely resembles *T. odoratissimus* but with lvs slightly wider, wholly glab. and cal. lacking purple flush. S Russia. Z7.

T. pannonicus All. Usually herbaceous perenn. to 20cm. Lvs to 15×3.5mm, lanceolate; cor. pale pink or red. SW & C Eur. Z5.

T. praecox Opiz. St. woody, to 5cm, mat-forming. Lvs lanceolate-obovate, ciliate. Infl. capitate; bracts like lvs but purple; cor. mauve to purple, rarely off-white, to 7mm. Summer. S, W & C Eur. ssp. *arcticus* (Dur.) Jalas. St. pubesc.,

cor. to 6mm. W Eur. 'Albus': creeper with white fls and small faintly-scented bright green lvs. 'Minus': prostrate, lvs minute, green; fls pink. 'Porlock': lvs rounded, dark green, fragrant; fls pink. Z5.

T. pseudoatticus Ronn. = *T. striatus*.

T. pseudolanuginosus Ronn. St. prostrate, tetragonal, with 2 opposite sides pubesc. Lvs elliptic, grey, pubesc. Fls few, axill.; cor. pale pink. Mid-summer. Origin unknown. 'Hall's Variety': to 10cm; lvs grey; fls lavender-pink. Z6.

T. pseudonummularius Klokov & Desj.-Shost. = *T. nummularius*.

T. pulegioides L. Dwarf shrub, highly aromatic; shoots to 20cm, ascending; st. tetragonal, ridges pubesc. Lvs to 1.8×1cm, ovalelliptic, ciliate below. Infl. interrupted; bracts like lvs; cor. pink to purple, to 6mm. Eur. Z5.

T. quinquecostatus Čelak. St. to 10cm, creeping, wiry, terete, pubesc. Lvs to 7mm, ovate, obtuse, entire, glab., ciliate, dotted with glands. Infl. a spike; cor. rose pink. Mong. and Jap. (deserts). Z5.

T. richardii Pers. Creeping dwarf shrub to 12cm. Lvs to 12×6mm, ovate. Infl. capitate, cymose; cor. to 9mm, purple. Balearics, Sicily, Balk. 'Peter Davis': shrubby dwarf, lvs grey, profuse pink fls. Z7.

T. rohlenae Velen. = *T. longicaulis*.

T. sabulicola Coss. = *T. zygis*.

T. serpyllum L. WILD THYME. Intensely aromatic dwarf shrub. St. to 10cm, creeping, pubesc. Lvs oval, pubesc., ciliate below. Fls crowded or whorled in a rounded head; cor. pink or purple. N Eur. Over 40 cvs with many variations: habit ranges from creeping to bushy, 3 to 10cm high; lvs from deep olive or tinted bronze to yellow variegation; fls white to pink, red or purple. 'Annie Hall' (low; fls palest pink), 'Aureus' (creeping; lvs gold), 'Carol Ann' (mat-forming; lvs variegated gold; fls lilac), 'Coccineus' (creeping; lvs dark green; fls dark red), 'Coccineus' (creeping; lvs dark green; fls dark red), 'Elfin' (trailing; lvs tiny, rounded), 'Goldstream' (vigorous; lvs variegated light green and yellow; fls lilac), 'Mountain' (creeping; lvs glossy; fls deep plum), 'Pink Chintz' (low; lvs woolly, deep olive; fls salmon pink), 'Russetings' (lvs tinted bronze), 'Rainbow Falls' (lvs variegated gold, flushed red; fls lilac), 'Snowdrift' (creeping; fls white, profuse). ssp. *serpyllum*. Lvs uniform. Fls larger than *T. serpyllum*. ssp. *tanaensis* (N. Hylander) Jalas. Lvs larger toward fls. Z5.

T. serpyllum (Willd.) Lyka non L. = *T. glabrescens* ssp. *glabrescens*.

T. serpyllum ssp. *angustifolius* (Pers.) Arcang. = *T. serpyllum* ssp. *serpyllum*.

T. serpyllum ssp. *auctus* Lyka = *T. pannonicus*.

T. serpyllum ssp. *brachyphyllus* Lyka = *T. pannonicus*.

T. serpyllum ssp. *carniolicus* (Borb.) Lyka = *T. pulegioides*.

T. serpyllum ssp. *dalmaticus* (Rchb.) Nyman = *T. longicaulis*.

T. serpyllum *effusus* (Host) Lyka = *T. pulegioides*.

T. serpyllum ssp. *marschallianus* (Willd.) Nyman = *T. pannonicus*.

T. serpyllum ssp. *parviflorus* (Opiz ex H. Braun) Lyka = *T. pulegioides*.

T. stepposus Klokov & Desj.-Shost. = *T. pannonicus*.

T. striatus Vahl. St. pubesc., prostrate, to 6cm. Lvs to 12×1mm, spathulate, pubesc. Infl. of interrupted whorls beneath a rounded head; bracts narrow-ovate, purple-green; cor. to 6mm, pink, purple or white. Balk., It., Sicily, Turk. Z7.

T. sylvestris Hoffsgg. & Link = *T. zygis*.

T. thracicus Velen. Resembles *T. praecox* but to 12cm, with basal clusters of small lvs. Infl. capitate; bracts to 2.5cm; cor. to 7.5mm, mauve to purple. Spring, early summer. Balk., Turk. Z8.

T. tschernjajevii Klokov & Desj.-Shost. = *T. glabrescens* ssp. *glabrescens*.

T. turkeviczii Knorr. = *Marrubium kotschyi*.

T. ucrainicus Klokov & Desj.-Shost. = *T. pulegioides*.

T. valentinus Rouy = *T. vulgaris*.

T. villosus L. St. erect, woody, to 30cm. Lvs to 1cm, linear to lanceolate, woolly, revolute. Infl. conical; bracts to 20×10mm, green; cor. to 10mm, purple. Summer–early autumn. Spain, Port. Z7.

T. vulgaris L. St. to 30cm, vertical, woody below. Lvs to 8×2.5mm, linear to lanceolate, pubesc. beneath, revolute. Fls crowded in whorls; bracts similar to lvs; grey green; cor. white or purple. W. Medit. 'Argenteus': lvs edged silver. 'Aureus': foliage yellow-gold; fls rose-purple. 'Compactus': dense, to 10cm high; lvs pale green tinted grey. 'Erectus': distinctive growth, like a slow-growing miniature yew, camphor-scented; foliage narrow and green-grey, term. heads of fls white. 'French': lvs narrow, tinted grey, sweeter fragrance. 'Silver Posie': lvs silver-variegated; fls delicate mauve. Z7.

T. webbianus Rouy = *T. vulgaris*.

T. zygis L. Shoots 30cm, ascending or erect; st. woody, slightly pubesc. Lvs to 1cm, linear, revolute, pubesc. Infl. to 10cm, interrupted; bracts leaflike, longer than fl. whorls; cor. off-white. Spain, Port. Z7.
→*Coridothymus* and *Satureja*.

Thyrsacanthus Nees.
T. rutilans Planch. = *Odontonema schomburgkianum*.
T. schomburgkianus Nees = *Odontonema schomburgkianum*.

Thyrse-fld Reevesia *Reevesia thyrsoidea*.

Thyrsopteris Kunze. Dicksoniaceae. 1 tree-fern to 4m. Fronds to 2m, ovate in outline, glab., somewhat dimorphous (those with modified, contracted fertile pinnae bear them in lower parts), 2–3-pinnate, pinnae lanceolate, dentate; stipes approximate and clustered, with russet trichomes at base. Chile. Z9.
T. elegans Kunze.

Thysanocarpus Hook. LACEPOD; FRINGEPOD. Cruciferae. 5 ann. herbs, to 50cm. St. erect, simple or branched. Lvs mostly basal. Fls 4-merous, v. small, white-purple, in slender rac.; sep. ovate; pet. spathulate-triangular. Fr. a flattened silicle, margin winged, entire to crenate, often perforate. NW Amer. Z6.
T. curvipes Hook. Lvs 2–10cm, oblong, st. lvs lanceolate, clasping. Fr. to 0.5cm, obovate-orbicular. Spring.
T. pulchellus Fisch. & Mey. = *T. curvipes*.

Thysanolaena Nees. Gramineae. 1 perenn. grass, to 3.6m. St. clumped, erect. Lvs narrow-lanceolate to oblong-lanceolate, to 60×6cm, flat, glab. Infl. an ovoid pan. to 60×30cm, green, tinged yellow or brown; spikelets lanceolate, laterally compressed, to 0.3cm, 2-fld. Summer–autumn. Trop. Asia. Z9.
T. acarifera Arn. & Nees = *T. maxima*.
T. agrostis Nees = *T. maxima*.
T. latifolia (Roxb.) Honda = *T. maxima*.
T. maxima (Roxb.) Kuntze. TIGER GRASS.

Thysanotus R. Br. Liliaceae (Asphodelaceae). FRINGE FLOWER; FRINGE LILY; FRINGE VIOLET. 47 rhizomatous or tuberous perennials. Lvs radical, grasslike, with papery, sheathing wings at base. Fls in scapose pan. or umbels; perianth seg. 6, free, inner whorl wider than outer, margins coloured and densely fringed. Aus., 2 sp. SE Asia. Z10.
T. dichotomus (Labill.) R. Br. Lvs 5–10, 8–14cm, narrow-lanceolate, ciliate. Scape to 60cm, branched; umbel 1–3-fld; perianth seg. purple, to 1.8cm. W Aus.
T. divaricatus R. Br. = *T. dichotomus*.
T. elatior R. Br. = *T. tuberosus*.
T. elongatus R. Br. = *T. dichotomus*.
T. flexuosus R. Br. = *T. dichotomus*.
T. intricatus Lindl. = *T. dichotomus*.
T. multiflorus R. Br. Lvs 3–30, linear to narrowly lanceolate, 20–30cm, occas. ciliate. Scape 15–30cm; umbel 4–20-fld (with 2 large umbels, one above the other in var. *prolifer*); perianth seg. blue-violet, 0.7–1.7cm. W Aus.
T. proliferus Lindl. = *T. multiflorus* var. *prolifer*.
T. tuberosus R. Br. Lvs 5–15, radical, 20–30cm, glab., linear. Scape 20–60cm; umbel 1–5-fld; perianth seg. to 2cm, purple. Queensld, NSW, Vict., S Aus.
→*Chlamysporum* and *Ornithogalum*.

Ti, Ti Tree *Cordyline terminalis*; *Leptospermum*.

Tiarella L. FALSE MITREWORT; SUGAR SCOOP. Saxifragaceae. 5 rhizomatous peren. herbs. Lvs basal, orbicular, cordate, trifoliolate or palmate, dentate; petiole long. Rac. scapose, usually term.; fls small, white or red; cal. campanulate, lobes 5; pet. 5, clawed; sta. usually 10. Summer. E & NW N Amer., 1 sp. Asia.
T. alternifolia Fisch. ex Ser. = *Tellima grandiflora*.
T. bracteata Torr. = *Heuchera bracteata*.
T. colorans Graham = *Heuchera glabra*.
T. cordifolia L. FOAM FLOWER. Stoloniferous to 30cm. Lvs 10×3–8cm, ovate-cordate, 3–5-lobed, pubesc., dentate. Scape sometimes leafy; cal. lobes 2–4mm; pet. lanceolate, twice sep. length. Nova Scotia, Appalachian Mts to Alab., W to Minn. 'Albiflora': fls white. 'Major': fls salmon pink to wine red. 'Marmorata': lvs bronze turning dark green with purple flecks, fls maroon. 'Purpurea': lvs bronze-purple, fls rose. Z3.
T. cordifolia var. *collina* Wherry = *T. wherryi*.
T. polyphylla D. Don. To 40cm. Lvs 2–7cm diam., 5-lobed, crenate. Scape with 2–3 subsessile lvs; rac. branching once at base, fls numerous, nodding; cal. lobes 1–2mm, slightly shorter than pet. China, Jap., Himal. Z7.

T. rhombifolia Nutt. = *T. trifoliata*.
T. stenopetala C. Presl = *T. trifoliata*.
T. trifoliata L. Lvs 3–8×2.5cm, trifoliolate, central leaflet 3-lobed, laterals 2-lobed, dentate. Scape with 2–3 short-petioled lvs; infl. a narrow pan.; cal. lobes 1–2mm; pet. twice sep. length. NW N Amer. 'Incarnadine': fls pink. Z5.
T. unifoliata Hook. To 45cm. Lf lobes 3–5, acute, crenate. Scape gland.-pubesc. bearing 1–3 lvs often with secondary infl. in axils; cal. lobes 1–2mm; pet. to 2× length cal., with twisted tips. W Mont. to Alberta and S Alask. Z3.
T. wherryi Lakela. Differs from *T. cordifolia* in stolons 0, more slender rac. and narrower pet. Appalachians. Z6.
→*Blondia*.

Tibetan Cherry *Prunus mugus*.
Tibetan Peony *Paeonia lutea* var. *ludlowii*.
Tibig *Ficus nota*.

Tibouchina Aubl. GLORY BUSH. Melastomataceae. 350 hispid shrubs or subshrubs or perenn. herbs. Lvs large, leathery, ovate or oblong, conspicuously 3–9-veined. Fls showy, usually a term. 3-forked pan., sometimes with involucral bracts; cal. tubular, 5-lobed; pet. 5, obovate, spreading to slightly cupped; sta. 10. Summer. Trop. S Amer., mostly Braz. Z10.
T. alba hort., non Cogn. = *Melastoma candidum*.
T. benthamiana Cogn. About 120cm; st. 4-winged. Lvs oblong-lanceolate, 9-veined, subglabrous above. Fls c5cm diam., 7 or more in term. pan., dark purple with white centre. S Braz.
T. bicolor (Naudin) Cogn. To 2m; br. densely velutinous. Lvs 3.5–7.5cm, oblong-lanceolate, 5-veined, densely strigose above, pilose beneath. Fls 2cm diam., orange and red. Boliv.
T. elegans (Naudin) Cogn. To 180cm; st. terete, hairy. Lvs c5×3cm, 3–(5)-veined, glossy green and glab. above. Fls 4–6cm diam., purple, solitary or few; sta. purple. S Braz.
T. gaudichaudiana Baill. 60–180cm; st. obtusely 4-angled or grooved. Lvs ovate-lanceolate, 5-veined, sericeous above. Fls 2.5cm diam., rose-purple. Braz.
T. gayana Cogn. To 60cm; st. terete. Lvs c4cm, ovate-oblong, 7-veined, sericeous above. Fls 2cm diam., white. Peru.
T. grandiflora hort. = *T. urvilleana*.
T. grandifolia Cogn. To 2.5m; st. obtusely 4-angled, scabrous to pilose. Lvs 12–22×7.5–15cm, 5–7-veined, sericeous; densely pubesc. beneath. Fls 2.5cm diam. in 3-branched pan., violet. Braz.
T. heteromalla Cogn. 90–150cm; st. terete to obtusely angled. Lvs broad-ovate-cordate, 7-veined, sericeous above. Fls 2.5–4cm diam., blue to purple or rose. Braz.
T. holosericea Baill. 60–180cm; st. 4-angled. Lvs ovate, acute, 5-nerved, sericeous, sessile. Fls 3–3.5cm diam., purple. Braz.
T. langsdorffiana (Bonpl.) Baill. St. 4-angled, bristly. Lvs 10–15×5cm, ovate-oblong, 5–7-veined, membranous, finely setose above, sericeous beneath. Fls 5–8cm diam., purple-violet. Braz.
T. laxa (Desr.) Cogn. To 2.2m; st. terete, hirtellous. Lvs to 5cm, ovate-cordate, 7-veined. Fls 5cm diam., few, in clusters or rac., deep violet to violet-purple. Peru.
T. multiflora (Gardn.) Cogn. To 180cm; st. 4-angled to 4-winged. Lvs to 15×7.5cm, 5–7-veined, sericeous above, ashy-tomentose beneath. Fls to 3cm diam., violet, in pan. to 50cm. Braz.
T. semidecandra hort. non (DC.) Cogn. = *T. urvilleana*.
T. urvilleana (DC.) Cogn. GLORYBUSH; LASIANDRA; PLEROMA; PRINCESS FLOWER; PURPLE GLORY TREE. Shrub to 5m; br. 4-angled, red-hairy. Lvs 5–10cm, ovate to oblong-ovate, acute, 5-veined, finely bristly above, more softly hairy and paler beneath. Fls 7–10cm diam., silky, mauve, indigo or violet; sta. purple. Braz.
T. viminea Cogn. To 180cm; st. obtusely 4-angled. Lvs 5–10cm, ovate-lanceolate, acute, 5-veined, hairy. Fls 4cm diam., violet-purple. S Braz.

Tickseed *Bidens*; *Coreopsis*.
Tick-trefoil *Desmodium*.
Tickweed *Cleome viscosa*.

Ticoglossum Rodriguez ex Halbinger. Orchidaceae. 2 epiphytic orchids. Pbs ovoid to discoid, compresed with leafy basal sheaths, apex 1-lvd. Lvs elliptic-lanceolate. Rac. lateral, few-fld; fls showy; sep. ovate to elliptic, apiculate, similar to pet.; lip short-clawed, variously shaped, callus fleshy, pubesc. Costa Rica. Z10.
T. krameri (Rchb. f.) Rodriguez & Halbinger. Pbs to 5cm, sub-rotund or ovoid. Lvs to 25×4cm. Infl. to 25cm, porrect or pendent, 2–3-fld; fls to 4.5cm diam., glossy, tep. violet, lilac or ivory-white, elliptic-ligulate to oblanceolate; lip to 2×1.5cm, violet or rose-violet, marked and spotted purple, with white and red-brown bands, callus yellow spotted red or purple. Costa

Rica. var. *album* (Rodriguez) Halbinger. Fls ivory-white; callus yellow.

T. oerstedii (Rchb. f.) Rodriguez ex Halbinger. Pbs to 5cm, ovoid, compressed. Lvs to 12.5×3cm. Infl. to 17cm, erect, 2–5-fld; fls to 4cm diam., fragrant, waxy; tep. white, spreading, elliptic-oblong to obovate-oblong; lip to 2.5×2.5cm white with golden-yellow base, obscurely 3-lobed, callus white spotted orange. Spring. Costa Rica.
→*Odontoglossum*.

Tidy Tips *Layia platyglossa*.

Tieghemopanax R. Vig.
T. sambucifolius (Sieb.) R. Vig. = *Polyscias sambucifolia*.

Tiger Aloe *Aloe variegata*.
Tiger Flower *Tigridia*.
Tiger Grass *Thysanolaena maxima*.
Tiger Jaws *Faucaria*.
Tiger Lily *Lilium catesbaei*; *L. lancifolium*.
Tiger Orchid *Rossioglossum grande*.
Tiger Palm *Pinanga maculata*.
Tiger-tail Spruce *Picea torano*.

Tigridia Juss. PEACOCK FLOWER; TIGER FLOWER; FLOWER OF TIGRIS. Iridaceae. 23 perenn. bulbous herbs. Basal lvs linear-lanceolate to ensiform, plicate, equitant. Flowering st. erect, spathaceous; perianth shallowly cupped, outer seg. 3, broadly obovate, spreading, clawed, inner seg. alternating with outer smaller, ± erect, ovate, undulate, appearing pandurate; fil. united in a cylindrical tube, sta. 3, stigmas 3. Mex., Guat.

T. chiapensis Molseed. Basal lvs 40–50cm. Flowering st. to 30cm; fls to 5cm diam., white, spotted purple at base, perianth cup yellow with purple spots. Mex.

T. dugesii S. Wats. Basal lvs to 13cm. Flowering st. 9–13cm; fls 2–4cm diam., yellow, spotted red-brown. Mex.

T. durangense Molseed ex Cruden. Basal lvs linear, to 12cm. Flowering st. 3–15cm; fls 3–4.5cm diam., lavender to deep lilac, spotted and straked white; inner seg. golden yellow. Mex.

T. meleagris (Lindl.) Nichols. Basal lvs usually 0; cauline lvs 2, 20–30cm. Flowering st. 25–60cm, branched; fls 3cm diam., pendent, silver-pink to dark maroon, usually spotted darker; inner seg. tipped yellow. Mex.

T. mexicana Molseed. Basal lvs 30cm. Flowering st. 10–30cm, branched; fls 2.5–5cm diam., yellow, spotted red-brown at centre with shallow cup. Mex. ssp. *passiflora* Molseed. Fls 4–6cm diam., white, spotted purple in cup. Mex.

T. multiflora (Herb.) Rav. Basal lvs 40cm, linear. Flowering st. to 40cm, branched; fls 3–4cm diam., brown-orange or purple, with deep perianth cup. Mex.

T. pavonia (L. f.) DC. Basal lvs, 20–50cm. Flowering st. 80–125cm, outer perianth seg. 6–10cm, orange, bright pink, red, yellow or white, variously spotted red, brown or maroon at base, inner seg. to one-third length of outer seg., more distinctly marked. Mex. 'Alba' ('Alba Grandiflora'): fls white with flesh-pink spots. 'Alba Immaculata': fls pure white. 'Aurea': fls yellow and red. 'Canariensis': to 75cm; lvs lanceolate, plaited; fls to 15cm across; pale yellow spotted red, lasting one day only. 'Carminea': fls pink-red with darker spots. 'Grandiflora': fls large in a var. of colours. 'Liliacea': fls red-purple variegated with white. 'Liliacea Immaculata': fls pure yellow. 'Lutea': fls yellow. 'Red Giant': fls bright red with red and yellow centre. 'Rosea': fls pale pink, centre variegated with yellow. 'Rubra': fls orange-red. 'Speciosa': bright red, centred spotted, in both red and yellow. 'Watkinsonii': fls deep orange shaded yellow, often marked with red. 'Wheeleri': fls bright red, centre yellow, brightly spotted.

T. pringlei Wats. = *T. pavonia*.

T. seleriana (Loesener) Ravenna. Basal lvs few. Flowering st. 2–10cm; fls 3.5–5cm diam., lavender, spotted darker blue in cup. Guat., Mex.

T. vanhouttei Roezl. ex Van Houtte. Lvs to 50cm. Flowering st. to 65cm, branched; fls many per spathe, 2–3cm diam., dull yellow-green, strongly streaked purple. Mex. ssp. *roldanii* Molseed. Fls pendent, campanulate, pale yellow, veined purple. Mex. Z8.

T. violacea Schldl. Basal lvs to 50cm. Flowering st. 12–35cm; outer perianth seg. 2.5–3cm, violet to rose-purple, claw white, dotted purple, inner seg. somewhat saccate, white spotted purple or rose. Mex. Z9.

Tigrina *Calathea ecuadoriana*.

Tilia L. LIME; LINDEN; BASSWOOD. Tiliaceae. 45 decid. trees. Bark smooth silver-grey, fissured on old trees. Young br. glossy. Lvs alt., in 2 ranks, simple, apex acute to acuminate, base

cordate, serrate; petiole slender. Fls ♂♀, often fragrant, 5-merous, in short pendulous cymes with stalks fused to large thin-textured oblong bracts; staminodes 5, petaloid or 0; sta. numerous. E & C N Amer., Eur., W, C & E Asia.

T. alba K. Koch non Michx. nec Ait. = *T.* 'Petiolaris'.

T. alba Ait. non K. Koch = *T. tomentosa*.

T. americana L. AMERICAN BASSWOOD; AMERICAN LIME. To 40m, crown broad, ovate to rounded. Lvs 6–16×5–13cm, broadly ovate to orbicular, ± truncate at base, abruptly acuminate, serrate, dark green and glab. above, paler with prominent venation and pubesc. tufts in vein axils beneath. Fls pale yellow, 5–15 per cyme. Summer. C & E N Amer. 'Ampelophylla': lvs large, lobed; coarsely, irregularly serrate; teeth acuminate. 'Convexifolia': lvs to 12cm, spathulate-convex. 'Dentata': st. straight; lvs large, irregular, often biserrate. 'Fastigiata': crown narrow, conical; br. ascending. 'Legend': habit pyramidal; lvs dark green, glossy. 'Macrophylla': lvs to 25cm. 'Pyramidalis': narrow, conical. 'Redmond': habit dense, conical. 'Sentry': habit uniform, symmetrical; br. silver when young. 'Wandell': broadly pyramidal; lvs dark green; winter buds and bracts bright vermilion. var. *vestita* (Döll) V. Engl. Lvs glab. or rarely with scattered pubescence on the veins beneath, but not with tufts in vein axils. Z3.

T. americana var. *heterophylla* Vent. = *T. heterophylla*.

T. amurensis Rupr. Distinguished from *T. cordata* by its thin bark. To 30m. Lvs broad-ovate, coarsely serrate, teeth acuminate. Cymes 5–20-fld, erect; fls pale yellow, v. fragrant. Summer. Manch., Korea, SE Sib. Z4.

T. argentea DC. = *T. tomentosa*.

T. argentea var. *mandshurica* (Rupr. & Maxim.) Reg. = *T. mandshurica*.

T. baroniana Diels = *T. chinensis*.

T. begoniifolia Steven = *T. dasystyla*.

T. ×*blechiana* Dieck. ex Dipp. = *T.* 'Spectabilis'.

T. canadensis Michx. = *T. americana*.

T. ×*carlsruhensis* Simonkai. (*T. americana* ×*T. platyphyllos*.) Close to *T. platyphyllos*. Lvs 6–12cm, round-ovate, abruptly acuminate, obliquely cordate, serrate, slightly pilose with hairs in tufts in vein axils beneath. Cymes 3-fld, pendulous. 'Diversifolia': to 6m, narrowly upright; lvs large, dark green.

T. caroliniana Mill. CAROLINA BASSWOOD. To 20m, close in habit to *T. americana*. Lvs 5–15cm, ovate, truncate to cordate, acuminate coarsely serrate, dark green and slightly lustrous above, tomentose when young and yellow or blue-green beneath, slender. Cyme shorter than bract; fls pale yellow; pedicel pubesc. SE US. Z7.

T. caucasica Rupr. To 30m+. Crown conical to rounded. Lvs 8–14cm, ovate, rounded to slightly cordate, apex abruptly acuminate, serrate, glab. and lustrous above, paler beneath with pubesc. in axill. tufts. Cymes pendulous, 3- or 6-fld; fls pale yellow. Cauc., Crimea, N Anatolia. Often confused with *T. dasystyla*. Z5.

T. chinensis Maxim. non Schneid. To 15m. Lvs 6–10cm, broadly ovate, acuminate serrate, glab. above, with thin ashy indumentum beneath and russet tufts in vein axils. China. Z5.

T. chinensis Schneid. non Maxim. = *T. tuan* var. *chinensis*.

T. chingiana Hu & Cheng. To 15m. Lvs 5–10×5–9cm, broadly ovate, short-acuminate, sometimes truncate at base, dark green above, paler and sometimes with stellate pubesc. beneath. Cyme 4–10-fld. China. Z7.

T. cordata Mill. SMALL-LEAVED LIME; LITTLELEAF LINDEN. To 40m, usually smaller, crown outspread, often suckering. Lvs 3–7×3–7cm, suborbicular, abruptly acuminate, serrate, glossy dark green above, glaucescent with tufts in vein axils beneath. Cyme pendulous to semi-erect, slender-stalked, 5–7-fld; fls pale yellow, fragrant. Midsummer. Engl. and Wales, NE Spain, Sweden to W Russia and S Cauc. 'Chancellor': habit upright, compact, narrow. 'Corinthian': habit pyramidal; dense branching; lvs small, thick, glossy; fls ivory, fragrant. 'Degroot': slow-growing, compact, pyramidal. 'Erecta': br. parallel, clustered and erect. 'Fairview': strong growing; lvs large, tough, dark green. 'Glenleven': fast-growing, pyramidal. 'Greenspire': growth strong, crown narrowly oval, uniform. 'Handsworth': bark light yellow on new growth. 'June Bride': narrowly conical, dense; lvs glossy; fls abundant. 'Olympic': vigorous growth, broadly pyramidal. 'Pyramidalis': dense, narrowly conical. 'Rancho': to 9m high, 5m wide; crown dense, conical; well-branched. 'Shamrock' ('Baileyi'): vigorous growth, broadly conical, uniform; lvs thick. 'Swedish Upright': compact, becoming pyramidal. Z3.

T. cordata var. *japonica* Miq. = *T. japonica*.

T. cordata var. *mandschurica* Maxim. = *T. amurensis*.

T. cordifolia Besser = *T. platyphyllos* ssp. *cordifolia*.

T. dasystyla Steven non Rehd. To 30m. Lvs 8–14cm, firm, ovate, abruptly acuminate, obliquely cordate, serrate, glossy dark green above, lighter with white tufts in vein axils beneath. Cyme

3–7-fld. Cauc. to N Iran. Z5.

T. dasystyla Rehd. non Steven = *T. caucasica.*

***T.* 'Euchlora'.** (*T. cordata* ×*T. dasystyla?*) CAUCASIAN LIME; CRIMEAN LINDEN. To 20m; crown rounded, br. nodding to pendulous. Lvs 5–10×6–12cm, circular-ovate, abruptly acuminate, obliquely cordate, finely serrate, glossy dark green above, paler with tawny tufts in vein axils beneath. Cyme 5–9cm, 3–7-fld. Crimea. 'Laurelhurst': vigorous growth, compact, broadly pyramidal; lvs glossy, dark green.

T. ×*euchlora* K. Koch = *T.* 'Euchlora'.

T. ×*europaea* L. emend Sm. = *T.* ×*vulgaris.*

T. ×*europaea* var. *alba* (Ait.) Loud. = *T. tomentosa.*

T. europaea var. *dasystyla* Loud. = *T.* 'Euchlora'.

T. ×*flaccida* Host = *T.* ×*carlsruhensis.*

***T.* 'Flavescens'.** (*T.* ×*americana* ×*T. cordata.*) To 30m. Crown rounded, noticeably straight-stemmed. Lvs 6–8cm, coarsely serrate, glab. throughout, persisting long into autumn. Cyme many-fld. Gdn origin. Z3. 'Dropmore': uniform habit, trunk straight, hardy. 'Wascana': fast-growing, hardy; br. spreading.

T. floridana (V. Engl.) Small = *T. caroliniana.*

T. glabra Vent. = *T. americana.*

T. grandifolia Ehrh. = *T. platyphyllos.*

T. grata Salisb. = *T. caroliniana.*

T. henryana Szyszyl. To 25m. Lvs 5–12×3–7cm, broad-ovate, abruptly acuminate, base obliquely cordate to truncate, teeth bristle-like, veins pubesc. above, brown stellate-pubesc. with axill. tufts beneath. Cyme pendulous, about 20-fld; fls cream. Late summer. C China. var. *subglabra* V. Engl. Lvs subglabrous below. Z7.

T. heterophylla Vent. WHITE BASSWOOD. To 30m; crown conical. Lvs 8–12×6–12cm, ovate, apex tapering finely, base obliquely truncate, or subcordate, lustrous dark green above, silver-tomentose beneath with rusty tufts, teeth slightly incurved. Cymes 8–20-fld. E US. var. *michauxii* (Nutt.) Sarg. Lvs 8–15cm, rounded oblong, apex acute to acuminate, base cordate, sometimes obliquely truncate, serrate, pale-pubesc. beneath. Z5.

T. hollandica K. Koch = *T.* ×*vulgaris.*

T. houghii Rose = *T. mexicana.*

T. insularis Nak. To 25m; closely allied to *T. japonica.* Lvs 5–8×5–9cm, round-ovate to subreniform, cordate, coarsely serrate, with pale downy tufts in vein axils. Korea. Z7.

T. intermedia DC. = *T.* ×*vulgaris.*

T. intonsa Rehd. & Wils. To 20m. Twigs densely tawny pubesc. Lvs 4–10×3–8cm, cordate, often obliquely and abruptly acuminate, grey-green and stellate-pubesc. beneath, vein axils pubesc. Bract downy; fls 1–3 per infl., pale yellow. SW China. Z7.

T. japonica (Miq.) Simonkai. JAPANESE LIME. To 20m. Lvs 5–8cm, suborbicular, base cordate, serrate, slightly glaucous beneath, vein axils pubesc. when young. Summer. Jap. Z6.

T. kinasha Lév. & Vaniot = *T. miqueliana.*

T. kiusiana Mak. & Shiras. Slender-stemmed shrub to tree to 10m. Lvs 5–8×3–5cm, ovate to ovate-elliptic, apex acuminate, base occas. obliquely subcordate, finely serrate, downy, dark green above, paler with tufts in vein axils beneath. Cyme to 36-fld. S Jap. Z7.

T. latifolia Salisb. = *T. americana.*

T. laxiflora Michx. = *T. caroliniana.*

T. mandshurica Rupr. & Maxim. MANCHURIAN LINDEN. To 20m. Lvs to 15cm, orbicular-ovate, apex abruptly acuminate, base cordate, coarsely serrate, teeth triangular, sometimes subdivided, sparsely pubesc. above, grey-tomentose beneath. Cymes 15–22cm, pendulous, 7-fld, brown-tomentose. NE China, SE Sib., N Korea. Z4.

T. mandshurica Miq. non Rupr. & Maxim. = *T. miqueliana.*

T. maximowicziana Shiras. 20–30m. Lvs 3–6×2–5cm, round-ovate, apex abruptly acuminate, base cordate, coarsely serrate, dark green and slightly downy above, grey stellate-pubesc. beneath, ultimately with only brown tufts in axils of veins. Cyme 10–18-fld, tomentose. Midsummer. N Jap. Has been confused with *T. miqueliana.* var. *yesoana* (Nak.) Tatew. Generally less pubesc. Lvs green beneath. Possibly a juvenile state. Z5.

T. mexicana Schldl. MEXICAN BASSWOOD. To 20m. Lvs 8–16×5–13cm, ovate, base truncate or cordate, apex briefly acuminate, lustrous dark green above, grey- or brown-pubesc. beneath. Cyme, 6–12-fld, bract pubesc.; fls cream-yellow. Late spring. Mex. Z7.

T. microphylla Vent. = *T. cordata.*

T. miqueliana Maxim. To 15m. Lvs 5–11×3–7cm, ovate, apex acute or acuminate, base obliquely cordate, with broad, mucronate teeth, lustrous dark green above, grey-tomentose beneath. Cymes about 20-fld, tomentose. E China. cf. *T. mandshurica*, *T. maximowicziana.*

T. miyabei Jack = *T. maximowicziana.*

***T.* 'Moltkei'.** (*T. americana* ×*T.* 'Petiolaris'.) To 25m, open-

crowded; br. somewhat arching. Lvs 5–13×4–12cm, subcircular to ovate, abruptly acuminate, base cordate or truncate, coarsely serrate, dark green and glab. above, resembling *T. americana* but grey-pubesc. beneath, particularly on veins. Cyme compact, 5–8-fld.

T. mongolica Maxim. MONGOLIAN LIME. To 20m, usually less. Br. arching. Lvs 4–7cm, broadly ovate, mostly 3–5-lobed, apex abruptly acuminate, base truncate to cordate, with slender teeth, flushed red at first, hardening lustrous dark green above, glaucescent with tiny downy tufts in veins axils beneath; petiole tinged red. Cyme 6–30- or more fld. Late summer. N China, Mong., E Russia. Z3.

T. monticola Sarg. = *T. heterophylla.*

T. multiflora Ledeb. = *T. dasystyla.*

T. nigra Borkh. = *T. americana.*

T. nobilis Rehd. & Wils. To 12m or more. Lvs 14–21×11–16cm, ovate, apex abruptly acuminate, base truncate or obliquely cordate, bristly-serrate, subcoriaceous, lustrous dark green above, paler beneath, with raised reticulate veins, pubesc. in axils. Cyme 2–5-fld. China. Z7.

T. occidentalis Sarg. non Small = *T. mexicana.*

T. officinarum Crantz = *T.* ×*vulgaris.*

T. oliveri Szyszyl. To 25m. Lvs 7–11×5–10cm, broad-ovate, apex abruptly acuminate, base cordate or truncate, with sparse gland.-tipped teeth, dark green and glab. above, white-tomentose beneath. Cymes 7–10-fld. C China. Z6. 'Chelsea Sentinel': broad, columnar, br. weeping.

***T.* 'Orbicularis'.** (*T.* 'Euchlora' ×*T.* 'Petiolaris'.) Distinguished from *T.* 'Petiolaris' by its less pendulous habit. To 25m. Crown conical; br. slightly pendulous. Lvs 5–7cm, ovate-cordate, short-acuminate, scabrous, serrate, dark green above, pale grey-tomentose beneath. Gdn origin (Metz, 1868). Z6.

T. parvifolia Ehrh. = *T. cordata.*

T. paucicostata Maxim. Small tree. Lvs 4–7×3–5cm, ovate, oblique, slightly cordate to truncate, acuminate, serrate but entire at apex and base, dull green, glab. above. Cymes 7–15-fld. W China.

T. pendula V. Engl. non Rupr. & Maxim. = *T. oliveri.*

***T.* 'Petiolaris'.** PENDENT WHITE LIME; WEEPING LIME. To 30m. Crown domed; br. pendulous and graceful. Lvs 5–10×4–8cm, oval-orbicular, apex acute, base cordate, sharply serrate, dark green and slightly downy above, white-tomentose beneath. Cyme 3–10-fld; fls cream-white. Origin obscure, possibly from SE Eur. or Asia Minor, most probably a selection of *T. tomentosa.*

T. platyphyllos Scop. BROAD-LEAVED LIME; LARGE-LEAVED LIME. To 40m. Crown conical to broadly columnar. Lvs 4.5–11×4–10cm, orbicular-ovate, apex abruptly acuminate, base cordate, sharply serrate, dull dark green and puberulous or glab. above, light green with pale pubesc. beneath. Cymes 3–6-fld; fls pale yellow. Early summer. Eur. to SW Asia. 'Asplenifolia': small to medium-sized; lvs deeply and irregularly divided. 'Aurea': bracts yellow. 'Compacta': habit rounded, compact. 'Fastigiata': habit narrow, pyramidal. 'Filicifolia Nova': lvs narrowly triangular, irregularly lobed, glab. 'Laciniata': small; lvs narrow, irregularly toothed. 'Obliqua': lvs oblique at base. 'Örebro': habit narrow, conical; br. dense, upright. 'Prince's Street': strong grower; br. broadly ascending, bracts red in winter. 'Pyramidalis': habit narrow, pyramidal. 'Rubra' ('Corallina'): bracts red. 'Tortuosa': young br. twisted and curled. 'Vitifolia': lvs somewhat 3-lobed, scabrous serrate. ssp. *cordifolia* (Besser) Schneid. Twigs, petioles and underside of lvs downy to densely downy. NE part of range. ssp. *pseudorubra* Schneid. Virtually glab. throughout. SE Eur. to S Alps. Z5.

T. praecox A. Br. non Host = *T.* ×*carlsruhensis.*

T. rubra DC. = *T. caucasica.*

T. rubra Steven non DC. = *T. dasystyla.*

T. rubra var. *euchlora* Dipp. = *T.* 'Euchlora'.

T. silvestris Desf. = *T. cordata.*

T. spaethii Schneid. = *T.* 'Flavescens'.

***T.* 'Spectabilis'.** (*T. americana* ×*T. tomentosa?*) Similar to *T.* 'Moltkei' except br. and buds stellate-pubesc.

T. tomentosa Moench. SILVER LIME. To 35m. Crown dense, ovoid-conical, becoming domed with age; br. erect. Lvs 5–11×5–10cm, rounded, apex abruptly and finely-acuminate, base cordate, coarsely serrate, or biserrate, sometimes lobed, dark green above, grey-tomentose beneath. Cyme 3–5cm, 5–10-fld; fls dull white. Mid-summer. SE Eur. to Asia Minor. 'Brabant': habit broadly conical, strong-stemmed. 'Green Mountain': fast-growing, dense, hardy; lvs dark green above, white beneath. 'Princeton': uniform habit, vigorous growth. 'Rhodopetala': buds red, pet. pink-mauve tinged yellow at base, many-fld. infl.; fr. large. 'Sterling Silver': broadly pyramidal, symmetrical; lvs round, thick. 'Wandell': neat, broadly pyramidal; lvs dark green, silver undersurface. Z6.

T. tomentosa var. *petiolaris* (DC.) Kirchn. = *T.* 'Petiolaris'.

T. tonsura hort. Veitch = *T. intonsa*.

T. tuan Szyszyl. To 16m. Lvs 5–12×3–8cm, thin, broadly ovate, base oblique or ± cordate, usually entire, apex acuminate, serrulate, glab. above, grey-tomentose beneath, tufted in vein axils. Cyme 15–20-fld; fls pale yellow. Summer. C China. var. *chinensis* (Schneid.) Rehd. & Wils. Young shoots tomentose. Lvs oblong-ovate. Z6.

T. ulmifolia Scop. = *T. cordata*.

T. ×varsaviensis (Kob.) Kobendza. (*T. platyphyllos* ×*T. tomentosa*.) To 30m. Crown more compact than in *T. tomentosa*, conical. Lvs closer to *T. tomentosa*, rounded-cordate, short-acuminate, lustrous green above, grey-green beneath, toothed, with tooth enlarged on either half of the lf blade. Gdn origin (Warsaw Botanic Gdn., 1924). 'Mrs Stenson': broadly conical; shoots dark red, tomentose, becoming glab.; lvs tomentose.

T. ×vulgaris Hayne. (*T. cordata* ×*T. platyphyllos*.) LIME; COMMON LIME; EUROPEAN LINDEN. To 40m. Crown conical, usually broadly. Lvs 5–9×4–8cm, broadly ovate, apex abruptly acuminate, base obliquely cordate, dark green and glab. above, paler and tufted in vein axils beneath. Cymes 5–10-fld. 'Long-evirens': lvs persistent, new growth tinged yellow. 'Pendula': br. somewhat drooping. 'Wratislaviensis': lvs golden when young. 'Zwarte Linde': crown broadly ovoid; lower br. horizontal, twigs dark.

TILIACEAE Juss. 48/725. *Corchorus, Entelia, Grewia, Sparmannia, Tilia.*

Tillandsia L. Bromeliaceae. 400 epiphytic or terrestrial perenn. herbs. St. usually v. short, simple; roots few, wiry. Lvs in a bundle, rosette or 2 rows, usually covered with absorbent grey scales, ligulate to narrow-triangular or linear, entire. Fls rarely solitary, usually in term., scapose spikes with colourful bracts; pet. forming tube or spreading; sta. exserted. S US, C & S Amer., W Indies.

T. acaulis Lindl. = *Cyrtanthus acaulis*.

T. aeranthos (Lois.) L.B. Sm. To 30cm, with a well-developed st. Lvs to 14cm, dense, grey-scaly, rigid, narrowly triangular. Infl. simple, ovoid or short-cylindric; bracts pink-purple; pet. 2cm, dark blue. S Braz., Parag., Urug., NE Arg. Z9.

T. aloifolia Hook. = *T. flexuosa*.

T. anceps Lodd. To 30cm. Lvs 15–40cm, dark green, recurving, narrow-triangular. Infl. elliptic, flattened, bracts leathery; pet. to over 6cm, claw white, blade blue. Trin. Z10.

T. araujuei Mez. To 30cm in fl. St. sprawling, simple or branched. Lvs 3–7cm, curved upwards, linear, rigid, with brown-centred scales. Infl. 3–5cm, simple, loose, bracts pink; pet. 2–3cm, white. CE Braz. Z10.

T. argentea Griseb. To 25cm in fl., st. short, branching. Lvs 6–9cm, linear-filiform, silvery-scaly, dense. Infl. simple, slender, bent, bracts green or red; pet. 3cm, bright red. C Amer., W Indies. Z10.

T. atroviridipetala Matuda = *T. plumosa*.

T. baileyi Rose ex Small. To 40cm, clump-forming. Lvs to 35cm, grey-scaly, linear, twisted, involute, base thickened, bulb-like. Infl. compound or simple, bracts leaf-like or rose pink; pet. 3cm, purple. S Tex. to Nic. Z9.

T. balbisiana Schult. f. 13–65cm. Lvs to 60cm, recurved, edged purple, linear-triangular, base bulbous. Infl. subdigitate or pinnate, bracts bright red; pet. 3–4.5cm, violet. Throughout range, S to Colomb. Z9.

T. brachycaulos Schldl. To 20cm. Lvs 12–26cm, decurved or spreading in a loose rosette, densely scaly, red in fl., linear. Infl. few-fld, capitate or subcorymbose, compound or simple; scape short; bracts leaf-like; pet. 5–7cm, violet. S Mex., C Amer. Z9.

T. bryoides Griseb. ex Bak. Clump-forming, many-stemmed, to 6cm. Lvs 4–9mm, dense, subtriangular, grey-scaly. Fls solitary; bracts papery; pet. yellow. Peru, Boliv., Arg. Z9.

T. bulbosa Hook. To 22cm, clump-forming. Lvs to 30cm, subterete, pungent, twisted, marked red-maroon, base bulb-like. Infl. subdigitate or simple, on an erect scape; bracts red; pet. 3–4cm, violet-blue. Mex. to Braz., Ecuad., W Indies. Z10.

T. butzii Mez. To 50cm, forming thick clumps. Lvs awl-shaped, long-tapered, twisted, green spotted red; bases bulb-like. Infl. compound; bracts green-red; pet. 3–3.5cm, blue. C Amer. to S Mex.

T. cacticola L.B. Sm. To 60cm. Lvs to 25cm, linear-triangular, pliant, margins curved, grey-scaly. Infl. comprising 3–7 elliptical flattened spikes; bracts green-white becoming deep lavender; pet. cream, tips blue, becoming red-lavender with age. N Peru.

T. caput-medusae E. Morr. To 25cm, base bulbous. Lvs contorted, linear-triangular, involute, densely white-scaly. Infl. 6-digitate or simple, bracts leaf-like, red; br. to 18cm, curved; floral bracts papery, red, pink and green; pet. 3–4cm, violet. Mex., C Amer. Z10.

T. carinata (Wawra) Bak. = *Vriesea carinata*.

T. chiliensis Bak. = *T. paleacea*.

T. chlorophylla L.B. Sm. To 20cm. Lvs to 50cm, linear-triangular, glab. above, scaly beneath. Infl. to 12cm, compound, slender-pyramidal, bracts leaflike with pink sheaths; floral bracts pink, papery; pet. 2.5cm, purple. NE Guat., Belize. Z10.

T. circinalis Griseb. = *T. duratii*.

T. circinnata Schldl. 10–45cm, base bulb-like. Lvs to 20cm, thick, scaly, curved, twisted or coiled, involute. Infl. pinnate, digitate or simple, bracts pink, leaflike; floral bracts papery; pet. to 4cm, violet. Throughout range. Z9.

T. coarctata Gillies ex Bak. = *T. bryoides*.

T. coccinea Platzm. = *T. geminiflora*.

T. concolor L.B. Sm. To 25cm. Lvs 20–30cm, triangular-filiform, fleshy, scaly, ringed below, in a funnel-shaped rosette. Infl. digitate or simple, scape short; bracts leaflike, bases yellow, floral bracts fleshy, red or green; pet. 6cm, violet. Mex., El Salvador. Z10.

T. contorta Mez & Pittier ex Mez. To 35cm. Lvs 10–25cm, narrowly triangular, involute, grey-scaly, sometimes blotched purple, base bulb-like. Infl. laxly pinnate or digitate; floral bracts green; pet. 0.6cm, white-yellow. Nic. to Panama. Z10.

T. cucaensis Wittm. = *T. makoyana*.

T. cyanea Lind. ex K. Koch. To 25cm. Lvs to 35cm, linear-triangular, smooth, dark green, mauve below, recurved at apex. Infl. simple, flattened, elliptic; bracts waxy, densely overlapping, pink to magenta, keeled; pet. to 3cm, dark violet, spreading. Ecuad., Peru. Z9.

T. deppeana Steud. To 2m. Lvs 60–100×8cm, ribbon-shaped, flat, soft, green, bases brown-scaly forming a funnel-shaped rosette. Infl. much-branched; spikes laterally flattened; bracts 2.5–4.5cm, thorny, bright rose; pet. bright blue-violet. Mex., C Amer. and W Indies to Columbia and Ecuad.

T. duratii Vis. To 1m in fl., st. to 30cm, stout, curved. Lvs in many rows, dense, grey-scaly, narrowly triangular, thick, involute, often spiralling. Infl. to 60cm, 2–3-pinnate, bracts grey-scaly; fls fragrant; pet. 2.5cm, lavender or violet-blue. S extent of range. Z9.

T. duvaliana Bak. = *Vriesea guttata*.

T. erubescens H. Wendl. = *T. ionantha*.

T. erythrea Lindl. & Paxt. = *T. bulbosa*.

T. fasciculata Sw. To 1m. Lvs 30–70cm, narrow-triangular, rigid, scaly, involute, bases broad, brown-scaly. Infl. digitate or simple, compressed; lower bracts leaflike, upper red or red-green; floral bracts red or red-yellow; pet. to 6cm, white or purple. Mex. to N S Amer., W Indies. Z10.

T. favillosa Bak. = *T. paleacea*.

T. filifolia Schldl. & Cham. To 30cm. Lvs to 30cm, filiform, silvery, in a dense rosette. Infl. 15cm, bipinnate, broadly pyramidal; bracts membranous; pet. 1cm, pale lilac-blue. C Mex. to Costa Rica. Z10.

T. flabellata Bak. To 30cm. Lvs narrowly triangular, arching, in a dense rosette, densely scaly beneath, flat. Infl. digitate with large, leaflike bracts; pet. 4cm, blue-violet. Mex., Guat., El Salvador. Z10.

T. flexuosa Sw. 20–150cm. Lvs 20–50cm, banded white in a dense, bulb-like rosette, rigid, involute. Infl. bipinnate or simple, bracts elliptic, inrolled; pet. 4cm, white, rose pink or purple. Throughout range S to Braz. Z9.

T. fusca Bak. = *T. paleacea*.

T. geminiflora Brongn. 15–20cm. Lvs 10–15cm, triangular-lanceolate, long-tapered, involute, grey-scaly. Infl. compound, spikes 10–15, spiralling; floral bracts pink, scaly; pet. 1.7cm, red violet. Braz., Parag., Uraguay, Arg.

T. grandis Schldl. To 3.3m. Lvs to 1.3m, blue-green, thick, ligulate, glab. above. Infl. bipinnate with leaflike bracts; floral bracts leathery; fls nocturnal; pet. to 1.2cm, green or green-white. S Mex. to Nic. Z10.

T. guttata Bak. = *Vriesea guttata*.

T. inanis Lindl. & Paxt. = *T. bulbosa*.

T. inflata Bak. = *Vriesea heterostachys*.

T. ionantha Planch. To 10cm. St. short, clumped. Lvs to 6cm, narrowly triangular, stout, midgreen, coarsely grey scaly, inner flushed red before flowering. Infl. simple, ± sessile; bracts rose to scarlet; pet. to 4cm, violet-blue. Mex. to Nic. Z9.

T. ixioides Griseb. To 20cm; st. 3–12cm. Lvs to 15cm, dense along st., narrowly triangular, grey-scaly, grooved. Infl. simple, bracts straw-yellow, thin, ovate; pet. 3cm, bright yellow. S extent of range. Z9.

T. juncea (Ruiz & Pav.) Poir. To 40cm. Lvs 30–40cm, scaly, in a bundle-like rosette, linear, filiform, involute, base red-brown. Infl. ovoid, simple or digitate; bracts red; pet. to 4cm, blue-violet. Throughout range S to Boliv. Z9.

T. krameri Bak. = *T. stricta*.

T. lampropoda L.B. Sm. 50–60cm. Lvs 25–30cm, narrowly-triangular, base purple-black. Infl. simple, sword-shaped; bracts distichous, overlapping, yellow or red-green; pet. 5–6cm. Guat., Hond., S Mex.

T. lanata Mez. = *T. paleacea.*

T. latifolia Meyen. To 60cm, mat-forming. Lvs to 20cm, grey-scaly, triangular-filiform. Infl. simple or bipinnate, bracts grey-scaly; pet. to 2cm, pink to lavender-blue. Peru, Ecuad. Z9.

T. lindenii Reg. To 80cm. Lvs to 40cm, linear-ligulate, arching, dark green, smooth, purple below. Infl. to 20cm, simple, flattened, oblong-lanceolate; bracts waxy, densely overlapping, pink or green, keeled; pet. to 7cm, royal blue, base white, spreading. NW Peru. Z10.

T. magnusiana Wittm. To 15cm. Lvs 11cm, triangular-linear, thread-like, covered in grey scales, base bulbous. Infl. simple; bracts green, grey-scaly; pet. violet. Mex., Guat., Hond., El Salvador.

T. makoyana Bak. 50–100cm, mat-forming. Lvs 6.5cm; triangular, awl-shaped, dull green to green-brown, short-scaly, ribbed beneath. Infl. simple or branched; floral bracts blunt-oval; pet. 5cm, blue or green. Mex., Guat., Hond., Costa Rica.

T. meridionalis Bak. To 20cm. Lvs 9–12cm, curved (often to one side), grey- or red-scaly, narrow-triangular. Infl. simple, bracts overlapping, lower leaflike, upper membranous; floral bracts bright pink; pet. to 2cm, white. Braz. to Arg. Z9.

T. microxiphion Bak. = *T. aeranthos.*

T. morreniana Reg. = *T. cyanea.*

T. multiflora Benth. To 80cm. Infl. loosely tripinnate, bracts straw-yellow, scaly; pet. 0.6cm. Ecuad., N Peru. Z9.

T. paleacea Presl. 10–70cm. Lvs to 12cm, spiralling, twisted, heavily scaled. Infl. simple, dense, narrowly-lanceolate, flattened; bracts distichous, overlapping; pet. blue or violet. Columbia, Peru, Boliv., Chile.

T. plumosa Bak. To 18cm. Clump-forming. Lvs to 18cm, grey- or rusty-scaly, dense, thread-like. Infl. simple or compound, capitate or corymbose; bracts rose pink, thin, leaflike; pet. 1.8cm, violet. C Mex. Z9.

T. polytrichoides E. Morr. = *T. tricholepis.*

T. ponderosa L.B. Sm. 50–65cm. Lvs forming a cistern rosette, 40×6cm, ribbon-like, green, naked or sparsely scaly. Infl. compound, broadly ellipsoid; floral bracts red or orange; pet. purple. Guat.

T. pruinosa Sw. To 20cm. Lvs to 20cm, grey-scaly, linear, recurved, involute, bases bulb-like, dark brown. Infl. digitate or simple; infl. bracts ovate, scaly; floral bracts pink; pet. 3cm, blue-violet. Throughout range, S to Braz. Z9.

T. pulchella Hook. = *T. tenuifolia.*

T. pulchra Hook. = *T. tenuifolia.*

T. pumila Lindl. & Paxt. = *T. bulbosa.*

T. punctulata Schldl. & Cham. To 45cm. Lvs recurved, in a scaly linear-triangular, base bulb-like, brown. Infl. digitate or simple, with red-brown, leaflike bracts; floral bracts leathery; pet. dark violet tipped white. Mex. to Panama. Z10.

T. recurvata (L.) L. BALL MOSS. Dwarf, st. v. short, clump- or ball-forming. Lvs distichous, 3–17cm, linear, terete, recurved, dark green. Infl. v. short 1–5-fld, with 1 or 2 bracts; pet. 1–1.3cm, white or pale blue-violet. Throughout range. Z8.

T. reichenbachii Bak. 20cm, with a curved, stout st. Lvs to 14cm, dense, in many rows, recurved, narrow-triangular, red-brown-scaly, involute. Infl. bipinnate or simple, bracts elliptic, papery; pet. 0.7cm, blue-violet. S Boliv., NW Arg. Z9.

T. rodrigueziana Mez. 1m. Lvs 50cm, densely scaly, rigid, keeled, involute. Infl. subthyrsiform, pinnate, bracts leaflike; floral bracts leathery; pet. 4cm. S Mex. to Nic. Z10.

T. roland-gosselinii Mez. 17–40cm. Lvs 25–45cm, pale-scaly, in a cupped rosette, narrow-triangular, inner lvs red in fl. Infl. pinnate, narrowly ellipsoid, bracts large, red, linear, recurved; pet. to 5cm. S Mex. Z10.

T. rubida Lindl. = *T. geminiflora.*

T. scalarifolia Bak. = *T. paleacea.*

T. schenckiana Wittm. = *T. paleacea.*

T. schiedeana Steud. To 40cm; st. fleshy. Lvs to 25cm, densely scaly; narrow-triangular, apex filiform, involute. Infl. distichous; bracts rose pink toward apex; floral bracts pink, thin; pet. yellow or red-yellow. C Amer., W Indies S to Venez. Z10.

T. seleriana Mez. To 25cm. Lvs coarsely grey- or brown-scaly, twisted, linear-triangular, involute, base bulb-like. Infl. 6–10cm, digitate or subpinnate bracts, leaflike, green or pink; floral bracts pink or green, grey-scaly; pet. violet, 3.5cm. S Mex. to Hond. Z10.

T. sessiliflora Ruiz & Pav. = *Catopsis sessiliflora.*

T. setacea Sw. To 30cm, clump-forming. Lvs to 50cm, stiff, needle-like. Infl. simple to bipinnate, bracts lanceolate, clasping; floral bracts tough, imbricate; pet. 2cm, blue-violet. Flor. to Braz., W Indies. Z9.

T. spiculosa Griseb. To 80cm. Lvs to 40cm, green or spotted purple, in an almost tubular rosette, sparsely scaly. Infl. 2–3

pinnate; bracts scaly; br. resembling ears of wheat; pet. orange or yellow to white. C Amer. to N Braz., Boliv. var. *ustulata* (Reitz) L.B. Sm. Lvs banded dark purple. Infl. usually 2-pinnate. Trin., Guyana, Colomb. to S Braz., Peru, Boliv. Z10.

T. staticeifolia E. Morr. = *T. filifolia.*

T. streptophylla Scheidw. ex E. Morr. To 45cm. Lvs to 50cm, ribbon-like, grey-scaly, strongly twisted, bulb-like at base. Infl. to 30cm, pinnate, laxly pyramidal; bracts red; pet. 3–4cm, purple. S Mex. to Hond. Z10.

T. stricta Sol. To 22cm, clump-forming. Lvs 6–18cm, grey-scaly, forming a rosette, narrow-triangular. Infl. simple; bracts red to cream; pet. 1.5–2.4cm, violet-blue or purple, later red. Venez. and Trin. to N Arg. and Parag. Z9.

T. tectorum E. Morr. To 50cm. St. long or short. Lvs 20cm, linear-filiform, scaly in many rows along st. Infl. digitate with red bracts; floral bracts red and green or pink; pet. 2–2.5cm, white tipped pale blue. Ecuad., N Peru. Z9.

T. tenuifolia L. Mat-forming, st. to 25cm. Lvs 5–10cm in many rows, densely scaly, triangular, pungent. Infl. simple, ovoid, bracts pink to red; pet. 2cm, pink, white or blue. W Indies to Arg. Z9.

T. tricholepis Bak. To 20cm forming clumps and strands. Lvs 1cm, needle or awl-shaped, succulent, scaly. Infl. simple; bracts green, grey-scaly; pet. 0.7cm, yellow-green. Braz., Boliv., Parag., Arg.

T. tricolor Schldl. & Cham. To 40cm. Lvs to 40cm, recurved, dark red in strong sun, glaucous, linear-triangular. Infl. sub-digitate or simple; bracts red; pet. 7cm, blue-violet. C Amer. Z9.

T. usneoides (L.) L. SPANISH MOSS; OLD MAN'S BEARD. Forming dense mossy festoons to 3m. St. wiry, flexuous, internodes to 6cm. Lvs to 5 per growth, 3cm, densely grey-scurfy, terete, linear. Floral bract scale-like; fl. solitary, fragrant; pet. 0.5 to 1cm, pale blue or green. SE US to C Arg., Chile. Z8.

T. utricularia L. To 2cm. Lvs 40–100cm in a dense, inflated ros-ette, densely scaly, linear-triangular, recurved. Infl. simple, 2- and 3-pinnate; bracts inrolled, grey-green to dark red or violet; floral bracts green, edged purple; pet. creamy-white, 3–4cm. Throughout range S to Venez. Z8.

T. variegata Schldl. = *T. butzii.*

T. 'Victoria'. (*T. ionantha* × *T. brachycaulos.*) To 15cm. Lvs cerise in fl. Fls large, purple.

T. wagneriana L.B. Sm. To 40cm. Lvs 45cm, strap-like, un-dulate, bright green, naked above, green-red, scaly beneath. Infl. open, compound; floral bracts naked, pink; pet. 2cm, dark blue. Peru.

T. warmingii (E. Morr.) Bak. = *Vriesea ensiformis* var. *warmingii.*

T. xiphostachys Griseb. = *T. anceps.*

Timbe *Acacia angustissima.*

Timber Bamboo *Phyllostachys bambusoides.*

Timothy *Phleum pratense.*

Tinantia Scheidw. WIDOW'S TEARS; FALSE DAYFLOWER. Commeli-naceae. 10–12 ann. or short-lived perenn. herbs. Lvs usually subsessile, lanceolate to obovate. Fls many, in cincinni; sep. 3, free; pet. 3, free, sta. 6, upper 3 shorter, basally united, bearded, the lower 3 longer, bearded or glab. US (Tex.), W In-dies, Mex. to Arg.

T. anomala (Torr.) C.B. Clarke. Erect tufted ann. to 80cm, somewhat glaucous. Lower lvs to 35cm, linear-lanceolate, base ciliate, upper to 20cm, narrowly to broadly lanceolate, often amplexicaul. Cincinnus solitary few-fld, bracteate; upper 2 pet. 15–18mm, lavender blue, lower 3–4mm, white. Summer. Tex. Z8.

T. erecta (Jacq.) Schldl. Erect ann. to 1m; st. fleshy. Lvs 6–16cm, elliptic to broadly ovate, with scattered hairs. Cincinni 1–4, gland.-pubesc., 3–20-fld; fls 2–3cm diam., blue, purple or pink. Summer–autumn. Trop. Amer. Z9.

T. fugax Scheidw. = *T. erecta.*

T. pringlei (S. Wats.) Rohw. Short-lived perenn., ascending or decumbent, to c50cm. Lvs to 10×4cm, broadly lanceolate to broadly ovate, petiolate, thin, flushed and blotched purple be-neath, often undulate. Infl. axill. with lavender blue fls to 1.5cm diam., or geocarpic with a single cleistogamous fl. Spring–autumn. NE Mex. Z8.

→*Commelinantia.*

Tindoori *Trichosanthes dioica.*

Tineo *Weinmannia trichosperma.*

Tingiringi Gum *Eucalpytus glaucescens.*

Tinker's Weed *Triosteum perfoliatum.*

Tinnea Kotschy & Peyr. Labiatae. 25 herbs, shrubs, or sub-shrubs. Lvs opposite or whorled, entire, often gland. Fls axill.

and solitary, or paired in loose, verticillate term. rac.; cal. 2-lipped; cor. 2-lipped, tube usually gland.-pubesc., upper lip reduced, lower lip spreading, 3-lobed. Trop. or subtrop. Afr. Z10.

T. aethiopica Kotschy & Peyr. Shrub or subshrub to 3m. St. terete, ribbed, ± tomentose. Lvs to 3cm, ovate to elliptic or lanceolate, entire, gland.-punctate. Fls fragrant, solitary or in verticillasters; cor. to 12mm, maroon to purple, tube pubesc., upper lip entire or emarginate, midlobe of lower lip emarginate. Trop. W Afr.

Tinnevelly Senna *Senna alexandrina.*
Tintern Spurge *Euphorbia stricta.*
Tipa Tree *Tipuana tipu.*

Tipuana Benth. Leguminosae (Papilionoideae). 1 everg. tree to 35m. Branchlets downy. Lvs imparipinnate; lfts 2.5–6cm, in 3–11 pairs, oblong to elliptic-ovate, incised, subcoriaceous, downy beneath. Pan. pendulous, term.; standard *c*2×2cm, reflexed, yellow to apricot, lined rusty-red, wings oblong, ± exceeding standard and keel. Braz., Arg., Boliv. Z10.

T. speciosa Benth. = *T. tipu.*

T. tipu (Benth.) Kuntze. YELLOW JACARANDA; TIPU TREE; ROSE WOOD; PRIDE OF BOLIVIA.

Tipu Tree *Tipuana tipu.*
Tiru-malu *Euphorbia tirucalli.*

Tischleria Schwantes.
T. peersii Schwantes = *Carruanthus peersii.*

Tisseranthodendron Sillans = *Fernandoa.*

Titan Arum *Amorphophallus titanum.*

Titanopsis Schwantes. Aizoaceae. 6 highly succulent, rosulate and clump-forming 'stone-like' herbs. Lvs 6–8 in a rosette, opposite and decussate, spathulate-obtriangular, tip tuberculate. Fls solitary, subsessile. S Afr., Nam. Z9.

T. calcarea (Marloth) Schwantes. Lvs 2.5cm, spathulate, truncate, tinged white or green-blue with green-red to grey-white tubercles. Fls 2cm diam., golden-yellow to almost orange. W Cape.

T. crassipes (Marloth) L. Bol. = *Aloinopsis spathulata.*

T. fulleri Tisch. Lvs 2cm, spathulate, tip rounded, blue-green to green-red with dark, prominent dots and grey-brown tubercles on purple margins. Fls 16mm diam., dark yellow. W Cape.

T. hugo-schlechteri (Tisch.) Dinter & Schwantes. Lvs 1.5cm, spathulate-triangular, slightly glossy, red-tinged to grey-green or grey-brown, tip with numerous light grey or brown to red tubercles. Fls orange or yellow. Nam.: Great Namaqualand.

T. luckhoffii L. Bol. = *Aloinopsis luckhoffii.*

T. luederitzii Tisch. Similar to *T. schwantesii* but lvs narrower, tip covered with large tubercles, ochre-yellow, tinged red at base. Fls to 2cm diam., yellow. Nam.: Great Namaqualand.

T. 'Primosii'. Resembles *T. schwantesii* except fls 2.5cm diam., canary yellow with flesh-coloured tips. Gdn origin.

T. schwantesii (Dinter) Schwantes. Lvs to 3cm long, tip rounded-triangular, light grey to blue-green, sometimes tinged red, tip covered with yellow-brown tubercles. Fls 1.5–1.8cm diam., light yellow. Nam.

T. setifera L. Bol. = *Aloinopsis setifera.*

T. spathulata (Thunb.) L. Bol. = *Aloinopsis spathulata.*

→*Mesembryanthemum* and *Verrucifera.*

Titanotrichum Soler. Gesneriaceae. 1 pubesc. perenn. herb, 25–50cm. Lvs 12–21cm, paired, elliptic, dentate towards apex, white-pubesc. Fls dimorphic, perfect in term. rac., large, sterile in short pan. v. small; peduncles white-pubesc.; cal. 5-parted, lobes narrow, to 1cm; cor. cylindric-campanulate, 5-lobed, yellow; sta. 4. S China, Ryukyus, Taiwan. Z9.

T. oldhamii (Hemsl.) Soler.

→*Rehmannia.*

Tithonia Desf. ex Juss. MEXICAN SUNFLOWER. Compositae. 10 erect, robust ann. or perenn. herbs and shrubs. Cap. radiate, mostly solitary, on long peduncles. Mex., C Amer.

T. diversifolia (Hemsl.) A. Gray. Perenn. to 5m. Lvs to 35cm, ovate to triangular-ovate, 3–5-lobed, glab. to pubesc., tapering to petiole to 6cm or sessile. Cap. to 13mm diam.; ray flts, orange-yellow, to 6cm. Autumn. Mex., C Amer., nat. OW Trop. Z9.

T. excelsa DC. = *Viguiera excelsa.*

T. ovata Hook. = *Lasianthaea helianthoides.*

T. rotundifolia (Mill.) S.F. Blake. Ann. to 4m. Lvs to 30cm, ovate to triangular-ovate, entire to 3–5-lobed, base cordate, sparsely hairy beneath, crenate to serrate, petiole to 10cm. Cap.

to 7cm diam.; ray flts to 3.5cm, orange or orange-scarlet. Autumn. C Mex. to Panama. 'Goldfinger': to 75cm; fls large, to 75mm diam., vivid rich orange. 'Sundance': large and compact, to 90cm; fls large, to 75mm diam., daisy-like, bright orange. 'Torch': vigorous, to 2m; fls single, to 8cm diam., vivid fire-red. 'New Hybrids': to 45cm; lvs finely divided, light green; fls to 5cm diam. in bright orange and yellow, some with purple disc; seed formula.

T. tubiformis (Jacq.) Cass. Ann. to 3m. Lvs to 25cm, deltoid, acuminate, crenate to serrate; petiole to 11cm. Cap. to 11cm diam.; ray flts yellow, to 4.5cm. Summer–autumn. Mex.

→*Helianthus* and *Tagetes.*

Titi *Cliftonia monophylla; Oxydendrum arboreum.*
Ti Tree *Cordyline terminalis; Leptospermum.*
Titoki *Alectryon excelsus.*
Ti-tree *Leptospermum.*
Toad Cactus *Orbea variegata.*
Toadflax *Linaria.*
Toad Lily *Tricyrtis.*
Toad Rush *Juncus bufonius.*
Toadshade *Trillium sessile.*
Toatoa *Phyllocladus glaucus.*
Tobacco *Nicotiana (N. rustica; N. tabacum).*
Tobacco Brush *Ceanothus velutinus.*
Tobacco Sumac *Rhus virens.*
Tobago Cane *Bactris guineensis.*
Tobira *Pittosporum tobira.*
Tobosa Grass *Hilaria mutica.*
Toddy Palm *Borassus flabellifer; Caryota urens.*

Todea Willd. ex Bernh. Osmundaceae. 2 ferns. Rhiz. massive, erect forming a fibrous trunk. Fronds in an apical crown, bipinnate, coriaceous. Australasia, S Afr. Z10.

T. africana Willd. = *T. barbara.*

T. barbara (L.) T. Moore. CREPE FERN; KING FERN. Rhiz. to 1.5m, stout, black and fibrous. Stipes to 30cm, stout, quadrangular. Fronds erect, 90–120cm, bright glossy green, pinnules 2.5–4cm, lanceolate, serrate. Aus., NZ, S Afr.

T. hymenophylloides A. Rich. = *Leptopteris hymenophylloides.*

T. superba Colenso = *Leptopteris hymenophylloides* and *Leptopteris superba.*

Toe Toe *Cortaderia richardii.*

Tofieldia Huds. FALSE ASPHODEL. Liliaceae (Melanthiaceae). 18 rhizomatous perenn. herbs. Lvs mostly basal, tufted, 2-ranked, narrow-lanceolate. Scapes erect; fls racemose or spicate; perianth seg. 6, free or briefly united; sta. 6, free; ovary superior; styles 3. Summer. N temp. regions, S Amer. Z6.

T. alpina Sm., non Sternb. & Hoppe = *T. calyculata.*

T. alpina Sternb. & Hoppe, non Sm. = *T. pusilla.*

T. borealis (Wahlenb.) Wahlenb. = *T. pusilla.*

T. calyculata (L.) Wahlenb. To 30cm. Basal lvs to 15cm. Fls green-yellow. Summer. Eur.

T. glacialis Gaudin = *T. calyculata.*

T. glutinosa (Michx.) Pers. To 50cm. St. densely dark brown-gland. Basal lvs to 20cm. Fls white. N Amer. ssp. *montana* St. shortly viscid-hairy, seeds off-white. C. Hitchc.

T. intermedia Rydb. in part. = *T. glutinosa* ssp. *montana.*

T. intermedia Rydb. in part. = *T. glutinosa.*

T. japonica Miq. To 50cm. St. viscid-glandular toward summit. Basal lvs to 40cm, margins coarse. Fls white. Jap.

T. nuda Miq. To 35cm. St. glab. Basal lvs to 12.5cm. Fls white. Jap.

T. palustris Huds. in part. = *T. calyculata.*

T. palustris Huds. in part. = *T. pusilla.*

T. pusilla (Michx.) Pers. SCOTCH ASPHODEL. To 25cm. Basal lvs 1–8cm. Fls white or white-green. N Eur., Alps, W Carpath., C Urals.

T. rubra F. Braun. = *T. calyculata.*

→*Triantha.*

Tokudama-giboshi *Hosta tokudama.*
Tokyo Cherry *Prunus* ×*yedoensis.*
Tollon *Heteromeles.*

Tolmiea Torr. & A. Gray. PICKABACK PLANT. Saxifragaceae. 1 perenn. herb, gland.-pubesc. Lvs 10cm wide, reniform, pale to lime green, cordate, shallowly 5–7 lobed, crenate; petioles 20cm; plantlets produced at junction of petiole and lamina. Fls in erect rac.; cal. green suffused purple, 8–14mm, 5-lobed; pet. 4, chocolate, twice length of cal. lobes; sta. 3. Late spring–summer. W N Amer. Z7.

T. menziesii Torr. & A. Gray. 'Taff's Gold' ('Maculata',

'Variegata'): lvs pale lime green finely spotted, mottled or washed cream to gold.

Tolpis Adans. Compositae. 20 ann. to perenn. herbs, with milky latex. St. solitary to several, usually branched. Lvs mostly basal. Cap. ligulate, few to many in subcymose pan.; peduncles bracteate; receptacle flat, flts yellow, inner occas. purple-brown. Medit., Macaronesia, NE Afr.

T. altissima Pers. = *T. virgata*.

T. barbata (L.) Gaertn. Ann., 3–90cm, slightly pubesc. St. simple or branched, br. over-topping main st. Basal lvs 2–10cm, lanceolate to oblong-obovate, entire or dentate to lobed, st. lvs often linear. Cap. 1 to several, 1–3cm diam.; peduncles thickened, bracteate, bracts grading into phyllaries; inner flts sometimes purple-brown. Spring–early summer. Medit.

T. macrorhiza (Lowe) Lowe. Shrub to 50cm, glab. St. branched. Lvs to 20cm, oblong, sessile, slightly fleshy, lustrous dark green, strongly dentate. Cap. numerous, small, in loosely branched, leafy pan.; peduncle with small bracts. Summer. Madeira. Z9.

T. staticifolia (All.) Schultz-Bip. Rhizomatous perenn., 10–50cm, ± glab. St. simple or sparingly branched not overtopping main st. Basal lvs 4–10cm, linear to linear-oblanceolate, acute, glab., entire or remotely toothed, st. lvs few or 0, entire. Cap. few, commonly solitary, peduncles thickened. Summer. Alps or Albania. Z6.

T. umbellata Bertol. = *T. barbata*.

T. virgata (Desf.) Bertol. Pubesc. perenn. or bienn. to 1m. St. br. overtopping main st. Basal lvs 5–20cm, oblong-lanceolate to elliptic, entire to serrate, dentate or lobed, st. lvs linear, entire or toothed. Cap. 1 to several, 1–3cm diam.; peduncles thickened below cap., bracts few or 0, small; inner phyllaries yellow. Early summer–autumn. Medit. Z8.

→*Crepis* and *Hieracium*.

Tolu Balsam Tree *Myroxylon balsamum*.
Tomatillo *Physalis ixocarpa*; *P. philadelphica*.
Tomato *Lycopersicon esculentum*.
Tomato Fern *Blotiella lindeniana*.

Tonella Nutt. ex A. Gray. Scrophulariaceae. 2 slender, ann. herbs, differing from the related *Collinsia* in its opposite, occas. 3-partite st., lvs and cor. lobes spreading, rotate, 3 not 2. Summer. SW US. Z7.

T. collinsioides Nutt. ex A. Gray = *T. tenella*.

T. tenella (Benth.) A.A. Heller. St. ascending, glab., to 30cm. Lvs to 1cm, orbicular to ovate, entire or notched or narrowly tripartite. Fls small white or pale blue, often spotted purple.

Tonestus Nels. Compositae. 5 low, perenn. herbs, with short, leafy st. Lvs alt., shortly petiolate. Cap. radiate, solitary, term.; outer phyllaries often leaf-like; ray flts yellow; disc flts yellow. US.

T. eximius (H.M. Hall) Nels. & Macbr. To 20cm, forming mats. St. glandular-puberulent. Lvs to 5cm, spathulate, glandular-puberulent, apex dentate. Involucre to 1.5cm diam.; phyllaries not imbricate. Summer. SW US. Z8.

T. lyallii (A. Gray) Nels. To 15cm, forming loose mats. St. somewhat glandular-hairy. Lvs to 7cm, oblanceolate or spathulate, glandular-puberulent, entire to slightly dentate. Involucre to 1.2cm diam., phyllaries imbricate. Summer. NW N Amer. Z7.

T. pygmaeus (Torr. & A. Gray) Nels. to 10cm, forming dense tufts or cushions. St. not gland. Lvs to 4cm, linear-spathulate to spathulate-oblong, sparsely puberulent, entire. Involucre to 1.5cm diam.; phyllaries not imbricate. Summer. Rocky Mts. Z5.

→*Haplopappus* and *Stenotus*.

Tonga Plant *Epipremnum mirabile*.
Tongue Fern *Pyrrosia lingua*.
Tongue Orchid *Serapias*.
Tonkin Cane *Pseudosasa amabilis*.

Toona (Endl.) M. Roem. Meliaceae. 6 everg. or decid. trees formerly included in *Cedrela* (now confined to Neotropics). E Asia to Australasia. Z9.

T. sinensis (A. Juss.) M. Roem. Decid. tree to 20m. Shoots initially downy. Lvs 30–60cm, pinnate; lfts 10–24, 6–14cm, ovate-lanceolate to ovate, acuminate, emerging pink-bronze, then deep green, gold in autumn. Fls fragrant, white to cream, to 0.5cm, in pendulous pan. China. 'Flamingo': lvs emerging vivid pink, turning creamy yellow then bright green.

→*Cedrela*.

Toothache Tree *Zanthoxylum americanum*.
Toothbrush Tree *Salvadora persica*.
Toothed Lancewood *Pseudopanax ferox*.
Toothed Orchid *Orchis tridentata*.

Toothed Sword Fern *Nephrolepis pectinata*.
Toothwort *Cardamine diphylla*; *Lathraea squamaria*; *Plumbago scandens*.
Toowomba Canary Grass *Phalaris aquatica*.
Topal Holly *Ilex* ×*attenuata*.
Torch Cactus *Echinopsis spachiana*.
Torches *Verbascum thapsus*.
Torch Ginger *Etlingera elatior*.
Torch Lily *Kniphofia*.
Torch Plant *Aloe arborescens*; *A. aristata*.
Torch Tree *Ixora pavetta*.
Torchwood *Bursera*.

Torenia L. Scrophulariaceae. *c*40 perenn. or ann. herbs. Lvs opposite, entire, crenate. Fls in short term. or axill. rac.; cal. tubular; cor. tubular 2-lipped. Summer. Afr., Asia; some spp. nat. US. Z9.

T. asiatica L. Lvs 3–6cm, ovate-cordate or -lanceolate, serrate; cor. 3–5cm, tube dark purple-blue, lat. lobes deep violet blotched dark purple. Summer. India, Sri Lanka, Java, China.

T. baillonii Godef.-Leb. = *T. flava*.

T. bicolor Dalz. in Hook. = *T. asiatica*.

T. flava Buch.-Ham. Lvs to 5cm ovate or obovate, entire or crenate; cor. 2–3cm, tube yellow, upper lip red-purple, lower lobes yellow with single purple spot. Summer. Indochina, China.

T. fournieri Lind. ex Fourn. WISHBONE FLOWER; BLUEWINGS. Lvs 4–7cm, narrowly ovate or ovate-cordate, dentate; cor. tube violet blue, limb 2–5cm diam., upper lip pale blue, throat lilac purple marked yellow, lower lobes velvety, deep violet purple. Summer. Asia.

→*Mimulus*.

Tor Grass *Brachypodium pinnatum*.
Torn's Herb *Dorstenia contrajerva*.
Toroguatay *Tabebuia nodosa*.

Torreya Arn. NUTMEG-YEW. Cephalotaxaceae. 7 everg. coniferous shrubs or trees, bark red-brown, finely scaling or shredding. Lvs in two ranks, decussate, flattened, hard, lanceolate, spine-tipped, stomata in two bands beneath. ♂ cones singly or in a loose row under the shoot, 3–5mm, globular. ♀ fr. drupe-like, ovoid, green, red or yellow, 1-seeded. N Amer. (Calif., Flor.) and Asia (Jap. to SW China).

T. californica Torr. CALIFORNIA NUTMEG-YEW. Tree to 20m; crown broad conic, br. level, shoots pendulous. Lvs in 2 sparse pectinate ranks, 3–5cm×3mm, aromatic when crushed. Fr. 3–4cm, flesh purple-green, seed nearly smooth. Calif. 'Spreadeagle': side-shoot propagation lacking apical dominance; procumbent. 'Variegata': some shoots blotched yellow-green. Z7.

T. fargesii Franch. Tree to 20m in wild. Similar to *T. nucifera* but lvs more tapered, 13–30×2–3mm; seed deeply rugose. China. Z7.

T. grandis Fort. ex Lindl. CHINESE NUTMEG-YEW. Tree to 25m or shrub, closely related to *T. nucifera*. Lvs 15–30×3mm, almost scentless when crushed. Fr. 2–3cm, seed smooth to flat furrowed. SE China. Z8.

T. jackii Chun. Tree to 10m or shrub. Lvs 5–9cm×4–5mm, falcate with long-spined apex; v. aromatic when crushed. Fr. 25–30mm, seed deeply rugose and ribbed. China. Z8.

T. nucifera (L.) Sieb. & Zucc. JAPANESE NUTMEG-YEW. Tree to 25m. Lvs 15–30×3mm, linear, spined at apex, glossy dark green above, two narrow blue-white stomatal bands beneath; aromatic when crushed. Fr. 2–3cm, seed nearly smooth. Jap. 'Prostrata': procumbent. var. *radicans* Nak. Shrubby to prostrate. Z7.

T. taxifolia Arn. STINKING CEDAR. Tree to 12m, crown as *T. californica*. Lvs 25–40mm, glossy green, convex above, two pale stomatal bands beneath; foetid when crushed. Fr. 25–30mm, seed nearly smooth. N Flor. Z9.

T. yunnanensis Cheng & Fu. YUNNAN NUTMEG-YEW. Tree to 15m or shrub. Lvs short, 20–35×3–4mm. Fr. globose, apiculate; seed ± rugose. SW China. Z8.

Tortoiseshell Bamboo *Phyllostachys edulis* f. *heterocycla*.
Tortuguero *Polygala cowellii*.
Totara *Podocarpus totara*.
Totter *Briza media*.
Touch-me-not *Impatiens noli-tangere*; *Mimosa pudica*.

Toumeya Britt. & Rose.

T. macrochele (Werderm.) Bravo & W.T. Marshall =<*Neolloydia schmiedickeana* var. *macrochele*.

T. papyracantha (Engelm.) Britt. & Rose = *Sclerocactus papyracanthus*.

T. pseudomacrochele (Backeb.) Bravo & W.T. Marshall

= *Neolloydia pse* ... *rochele*.
T. schmiedickiana ... Bravo & W.T. Marshall = *Neolloydia schmiedickeana*.
T. schwarzii (Shurly) ... = *Neolloydia schmiedickeana* var. *schwarzii*.

Toumey's Oak *Quercus* ...

Tournefortia L. Boragina... ... 50 shrubs, often scandent. Lvs usually broad, petiolate. ... in scorpioid rac. or pan. usually dichotomous; cal. 5-lo... ... tubular, lobes 5, spreading; sta. usually 5, included. Tro... ... btrop.
T. cordifolia André. Robust ... erect, short-pubesc. Lvs to 30cm, ovate, cordate, rug... ...dulate. Corymb much-branched, many-fld; cor. white... ...or pubesc., lobes short, rounded. Americas.
T. fruticosa (L.) Ker-Gawl. = *Helio...* ...*messerschmidioides*.

Tovara Adans.
T. virginiana (L.) Raf. = *Polygonum v...* ...*m*.

Tower Cress *Turritis glabra*.
Tower-of-jewels *Echium wildpretii*.

Townsendia Hook. Compositae. *c*21 ann. ... ... herbs. Cap. radiate, solitary; receptacle convex. W N A...
T. alpina (A. Gray) Rydb. Stemless, tufted, p... ...vs rosulate, to 1cm, spathulate, strigose. Involucre to 18... ...m.; ray flts to 10mm, pink; disc flts yellow. WC US. Z5.
T. eximia A. Gray. Bienn. to 40cm, hairy strigo... ...to 13cm, linear-spathulate to -oblanceolate, strigose. Inv... ...o 40mm diam.; ray flts to 18mm, blue-purple; disc flts ... ...occas. purple-tinged. Summer. WC & SC US. Z4.
T. exscapa (Richards) Porter. EASTER DAISY. Stem... ...enn., to 7cm. Lvs rosulate, to 5cm, oblanceolate, silky-s... ...In-volucre to 30mm; ray flts to 22mm, white to pale pin... ...flts yellow, often pink- or purple-tipped. Early summer. C... ...la to Mex. Z3.
T. florifera (Hook.) A. Gray. Ann. to bienn., to 25cm. B... to 6cm, narrowly spathulate. Involucre to 35mm diam.; r... to 16mm, white or pink; disc flts yellow, often tipped or t... pink. Winter. NW US. Z4.
T. formosa Greene. Erect, rhizomatous perenn., to 40cm. Ba... lvs to 8cm, spathulate to obolanceolate, glab., midrib pubesc., margin ciliate. Involucre to 30mm diam.; ray flts to 26mm, white above, mauve beneath; disc flts yellow. SW US.
T. grandiflora Nutt. Bienn., to 10cm, densely strigose. Lvs to 5cm, spathulate to oblanceolate, strigose to glab. beneath. In-volucre to 30mm diam.; ray flts 15–20mm, white above, rose-purple beneath; disc flts yellow, apex pink. Summer. C US. Z5.
T. hookeri Beaman. EASTER DAISY. Short tufted perenn. Lvs to 4.5cm, linear to narrowly oblanceolate, densely silky-strigose. Involucre to 18mm diam.; ray flts to 12mm, white above, tinged pink beneath; disc flts yellow, apex occas. pink. Spring. C US to Canada. Z4.
T. leptotes (A. Gray) Osterh. ± Stemless, tufted perenn. Lvs to 6cm, linear to oblanceolate, fleshy, glab. to silky-strigose. In-volucre to 20mm diam.; ray flts to 14mm, white to pink or blue; disc flts yellow. Summer. W US. Z7.
T. montana M.E. Jones. Low perenn. Lvs to 3cm, spathulate, fleshy, glab. or sparingly strigose. Involucre to 12mm diam.; ray flts to 8mm, pink-purple; disc flts yellow. Early summer. NW US. Z6.
T. parryi D.C. Eaton. Bienn. or short-lived perenn. to 35cm, pubesc. Lvs to 10cm, spathulate, fleshy, glab. above, strigose beneath. Involucre to 30mm diam.; ray flts 25mm, violet or blue-purple; disc flts yellow. Early summer. NW N Amer. Z5.
T. parryi var. *alpina* A. Gray = *T. alpina*.
T. rothrockii A. Gray ex Rothr. Stemless perenn., to 8cm. Lvs rosulate, to 3.5cm, spathulate-oblanceolate, fleshy, glab. In-volucre to 20mm diam.; ray flts to 16mm, blue-purple; disc flts yellow. Summer. C US. Z4.
T. sericea Hook. = *T. exscapa*.
T. sericea var. *leptotes* A. Gray = *T. leptotes*.
T. wilcoxiana Wood = *T. exscapa*.
T. wilcoxii hort. = *T. rothrockii*.

Toxicodendron (Tourn.) Mill. Anacardiaceae. 9 toxic, irritant decid. trees, shrubs or lianes. Lvs trifoliolate or imparipinnate. Infl. a pan. or rac.; sep. 5, imbricate; pet. green-white to cream-yellow, ascending, often reflexed; ovary unilocular by abortion, stigma tripartite; sta. 5. Fr. a compressed drupe. N Amer. to N S Amer.
T. diversilobum (Torr. & A. Gray) Greene. WESTERN POISON OAK. Shrub or vine. Lfts 3, to 5 or more, 3–7cm, ovate-oblong to suborbicular, entire, undulate, crenate or dentate, glab. above,

subpilose beneath. Pan. to 10cm. NW US to Vancouver. Z5.
T. eximia Greene = *T. radicans* ssp. *eximium*.
T. laurinum Kuntze = *Malosma laurina*.
T. negundo Greene = *T. radicans* ssp. *negundo*.
T. orientale Greene = *T. radicans* ssp. *orientale*.
T. quercifolium Greene = *T. diversilobum*.
T. radicans (L.) Kuntze. POISON IVY; MARKWEED; POISON MERCURY. Shrub or vine. Lfts 3, rarely 5 or 7, 2.5–18cm, ovate-elliptic, entire or serrate. Pan. to 10cm. S Canada and E US to Guat., C China to Taiwan and Jap. Z5. ssp. *barkleyi* Gillis. Lfts entire or subentire, term. leaflet elliptic or lanceolate. Mex., Guat. Z8. ssp. *eximium* (Greene) Gillis. Lfts deeply incised, base rounded. Mex. ssp. *hispidum* (Engl.) Gillis. Term. leaflet twice as long as broad, attenuate. Fr. hispid, hairs to 1mm. ssp. *negundo* (Greene) Gillis. Lfts ovate or lanceolate. US. ssp. *orientale* (Greene) Gillis. Term. leaflet ×1.2–1.7 as long as broad, cuneate. Jap. ssp. *pubescens* (Engelm. ex Wats.) Gillis. Lfts serrate, term. lft broadly ovate. ssp. *verrucosum* (Scheele) Gillis. Lfts with lobed or deeply cut margins. Okl., Tex. Z7.
T. radicans ssp. *diversiloba* (Torr. & A. Gray) Thorne = *T. diversilobum*.
T. succedaneum (L.) Mold. Shrub or small tree to 9m, lfts 9–11, 6–12cm, elliptic-oblong to lanceolate, glab., glossy green above, tinged blue below. Pan. 9–12cm. China, Jap., Himal. Z5.
T. terebinthifolium (Schltr. & Champ.) Kuntze. = *Rhus terebinthifolia*.
T. vernicifluum (Stokes) F. Barkley. VARNISH TREE; CHINESE LACQUER TREE; JAPANESE LACQUER TREE. Tree 15–20m. Lfts 7–13, 7–15×3–6cm, ovate-oblong, entire, pubesc. along midrib beneath. Pan. loose, pendulous, 15–20cm. Jap. and China to Himal. Z9.
T. vernix (L.) Shafer. POISON SUMAC. Shrub to 3m. Lfts 7–13, 4–10cm, elliptic to oblong, entire, pubesc., later glab., tinged blue beneath. Pan. pendulous, narrow, 10–20cm. E N Amer. Z3.
T. verrucosa Scheele = *T. radicans* ssp. *verrucosum*.
→*Rhus*.

Toxicoscordion Rydb.
T. gramineum (Rydb.) Rydb. = *Zigadenus venenosus* var. *gramineus*.
T. nuttallii A. Gray = *Zigadenus nuttallii*.
T. paniculatum (Nutt.) Rydb. = *Zigadenus paniculatus*.

Toyon *Heteromeles*.
Trac *Dalbergia cochinchinensis*.

Tracheliopsis Buser.
T. postii (Boiss.) Buser = *Trachelium postii*.

Trachelium L. Campanulaceae. 7 perenn. herbs, usually woody-based. Lvs simple. Fls in corymbs, pan. or solitary, axill.; cal. tubular; cor. tubular; style exserted. Medit. Z8 unless specified.
T. asperuloides Boiss. & Orph. Tufted, to 3cm. Lvs minute, ovate-orbicular, overlapping, glossy. Fls solitary or in clusters of up to 5; cor. lobes narrowly ovate, suffused, pink. Greece.
T. caeruleum L. Erect to 1m. Lvs lanceolate, biserrate, occas. pubesc. beneath. Fls in umbellate clusters; cor. tube narrow, lobes 5, to 5mm, blue or mauve. W & C Medit. 'Album': fls white. 'Blue Veil': fls violet-blue. 'Purple Umbrella': habit upright; fls purple, borne in a loose umbel. 'White Umbrella': fls white. 'White Veil': habit large; fls pure white, borne in umbels. Z9.
T. jacquinii (Sieber) Boiss. Glab. or finely pubesc. Lvs linear to lanceolate, sinuate to serrate. Fls in dense term. pan.; cor. tube to 5mm, blue to lilac. Greece, Aegean.
T. lanceolatum Guss. To 20cm. Lvs to 10cm, mainly basal, narrowly ovate, dentate, glab. Fls in corymbs; cor. tube narrow, lobes short, violet to blue. S Sicily.
T. myrtifolium Boiss. Tufted. Lvs minute ovate, pubesc. Fls solitary or in term. clusters of up to 5; cor. tomentose, mauve to white, lobes short, deltoid. S Turk.
T. postii Boiss. Erect, to 30cm; branchlets robust, pubesc. Fls with canescent toothed sep.; cor. pale violet. Syr.
T. rumelianum Hampe. St. to 30cm, sprawling. Lvs to 3cm, lanceolate to oblong, remotely dentate. Fls in cymose rac.; cor. to 1cm, blue to mauve. Bulg., Greece.
T. tubulosum Boiss. Erect, to 15cm. Lvs ovate, dentate, glab. or finely tomentose. Infl. corymbose; cor. lobes deltoid, spreading, cream to white. Leb., S Turk.
→*Diosphaera* and *Tracheliopsis*.

Trachelospermum Lem. Apocynaceae. 20 everg. climbing shrubs with milky sap. Lvs leathery, entire. Fls cymose; cal. 5-

lobed; cor. tube cylindrical, lobes 5, spreading, twisted overlapping to the right; sta. short. India to Jap.

T. asiaticum (Sieb. & Zucc.) Nak. Shoots persistently hairy. Lvs 2–5cm, elliptic or orvate, dark glossy green, glab. Fls in term. cymes; cor. yellow-white, tube 0.7–0.8cm, 2cm across limb, lobes obovate; sta. slightly exserted. Summer. Jap., Korea. Z7.

T. jasminoides (Lindl.) Lem. Shoots becoming glab. Lvs 4–7.5cm, oval-lanceolate, dark shining green, downy beneath at first. Fls intensely fragrant, in axill. and term. cymes; cor. white, tube 0.75–1cm, 2.5cm across limb, lobes narrow, sta. included. Summer. China. Z8. 'Japonicum': lvs veined white, turning bronze in autumn. 'Minimum': habit dwarf; lvs mottled. 'Variegatum': lvs ovate to almost linear-lanceolate, with white and milk-green stripes, often tinged pink to red-bronze. 'Wilsonii': lvs ovate to linear-lanceolate, veins distinct, flushing red-bronze to maroon in winter.
→*Rhynchospermum*.

Trachomitum Woodson.
T. venetum (L.) Woodson = *Apocynum venetum*.

Trachycarpus H.A. Wendl. FAN PALM; CHINESE WINDMILL PALM; CHUSAN PALM. Palmae. 6 palms. St. solitary or clustering, erect, clothed with fibrous lf bases becoming bare. Lvs palmate; petiole often armed; blade circular to fan-shaped, deeply divided into single-fold seg. Infl. interfoliar, branched ×4, bracts 1–4, overlapping brown to white; rachillae stiff, crowded; ♂ and ♀ fls similar, cream to yellow, in clusters of 2–3. Fr. spherical to reniform, purple-black or orange, pruinose. Subtrop. Asia. Z9.

T. excelsus hort. = *T. fortunei*.
T. fortunei (Hook.) H.A. Wendl. Trunk to 20m. Petiole to 1m, margins sharply dentate; blade to 85cm long, 1.25m diam., circular, divided almost to base; seg. semi-rigid, apices drooping. Probably from N Burm., C & E China; nat. China and Jap. 'Nanus': fronds rigid, 30cm diam. var. *surculosus* Henry. St. clustered.

T. khasyanus (Griff.) H.A. Wendl. = *T. martianus*.
T. martianus (Wallich.) H.A. Wendl. Trunk to 15m; petiole to 1m; lf blades to 1.5m, blue-green beneath, divided to half way; seg. drooping at apices. Himal., from Nepal to Burm.
T. takil Becc. Resembles *T. fortunei*, but trunk fibres closely addressed to trunk, not loose; lf blades orbicular; seg. 45–50, ensiform, apex shallowly to deeply divided. W Himal.
T. wagnerianus Becc. To 7m. Resembles *T. fortunei* but lvs smaller, to 45cm diam., rigid, leathery; fibres more closely attached to trunk. Only known in cult., from China and Jap.
→*Chamaerops*.

Trachymene Rudge. Umbelliferae. 12 ann., bienn. or perenn. herbs. Lvs ternately divided; st. lvs less divided to entire, petioles sheathing. Umbels simple, terminal; involucre of linear bracts; pet. ovate, outer pet. longer. Aus., W Pacific.

T. coerulea Graham. BLUE LACE FLOWER. Ann. or bienn. to 60cm. Lvs to 10cm, ternate to 2-ternate, seg. linear-cuneate, incisid. Umbels long-stalked; involucral bracts numerous, linear; fls blue. Summer. W Aus.
T. pilosa Sm. Ann., 3–15cm hirsute to glabrate. Lvs palmatisect, seg. linear, entire to lobed. Umbels short-stalked; involucral bracts 6–10, linear-lanceolate; fls white, tinged purple. Summer. Aus.
→*Didiscus*.

Trachyphrynium Benth. ex Milne-Redh. Marantaceae. 1 rhizomatous scandent herb. Lvs to 20cm, blades elliptic, acuminate, cordate. Spike branching to 20cm; bracts oblong-lanceolate; fls white, sometimes pink, in pairs with 2 fleshy bracteoles; cor. tubular, lobes oblong, longer than tube; outer staminodes 2, petaloid. Trop. W Afr. Z10.
T. braunianum (Schum.) Bak.
→*Bamburanta* and *Hybophrynium*.

Trachystemon D. Don. Boraginaceae. 2 stout, hispidulous perenn. herbs. Fls pendent in lax bracteate pan.; cal. 5-lobed, cup-shaped; cor. funnel-shaped, lobes 5, linear; sta. 5, exserted. E Eur. Z6.
T. orientalis (L.) G. Don. To 60cm. Rhiz. black, creeping. Lvs to 20cm, ovate-cordate, hispidulous. Cor. blue-purple, tube 6mm, lobes 8mm; fil. pink.
→*Borago*.

Tracy's Maidenhair *Adiantum ×tracyi*.

Tradescantia L. SPIDER-LILY; SPIDERWORT. Commelinaceae. 70 perenn., ann. or short-lived herbs; roots fibrous or tuberous. Infl. paired cincinni subtended by boat-shaped bracts; fls usually

actinomorphic; sep. 3; pet. 3, equal, usually free; sta. 6, similar. Amer.

T. ×andersoniana W. Ludw. & Rohw. An invalid name for hybrids of the parentage *T. virginiana* × *T. canaliculata* (= *T. ohiensis*) × *T. subaspera*. See. *T. virginiana*.
T. blossfeldiana Mildbr. = *T. cerinthoides*.
T. brachyphylla Greenman = *Callisia navicularis*.
T. canaliculata Raf. = *T. ohiensis*.
T. caricifolia Raf. = *T. ohiensis*.
T. cerinthoides Kunth. FLOWERING INCH PLANT. St. decumbent, rooting at nodes. Lvs to 15×3.5cm, elliptic-oblong to ovate, sessile, ± fleshy, glossy dark green and hairy to glab. above, green or purple, hairy beneath. Infl. term. and lat.; peduncles to 5cm; bracts 2–2.5cm; fls 1.5–2cm diam.; pet. purple-pink, white towards base or wholly white. Spring–autumn. SE Braz. 'Variegata': lvs variegated. Z7.
T. crassifolia Cav. St. to 60cm or more from tuberous roots, villous. Lvs 3–16×1.5–3.5cm, elliptic or oblong-lanceolate, ± channelled, glabrescent to lanate above, lanate beneath and on margins, somewhat succulent. Cincinni paired sessile in axils of reduced upper lvs; fls 2–3cm diam., purple-pink or violet blue; sta. bearded. NW Mex. to Guat. Z9.
T. crassifolia var. *acaulis* (Martens & Gal.) C.B. Clarke = *T. iridescens*.
T. crassifolia var. *glabrata* hort. non C.B. Clarke = *T. tepoxtlana*.
T. crassula Link & Otto. St. decumbent, rooting at nodes. Lvs to 15×3cm, oblong-elliptic, channelled, somewhat fleshy, shiny green, glab., margins ciliolate, sometimes minutely pubesc. beneath. Infl. term. and lat.; bracts unequal, to c4cm; fls 1–2cm diam., white. Winter–spring. SE Braz. Z9.
T. cumanensis sensu C.B. Clarke non Kunth = *Tripogandra serrulata*.
T. discolor L'Hérit. = *T. spathacea*.
T. diuretica Mart. = *Tripogandra diuretica*.
T. fluminensis Vell. Conc. St. ascending and decumbent or pendent, rooting at nodes. Lvs 1.5–12×1–3.5cm, broadly ovate to oblong-lanceolate, glab., green or flushed purple beneath, often variegated. Infl. term. and lateral on peduncles c1–5cm; bracts folded, 1–2cm; fls 12–18mm diam., white. Spring–summer. SE Braz. Z9. The popular cv. with sessile, white-striped lvs, known as *T. albiflora* 'Albovittata', is intermediate in habit between *T. fluminensis* and *T. crassula*. The decorative, non-rhizomatous, ann. or short-lived plant with small, yellow-variegated lvs and slender, often purple-tinged st., known as *T. fluminensis* 'Argenteo-variegata', is not this sp.; it may be *T. mundula* Kunth or *T. anagallidea* Seub. from S Brazil–N Argentina; individual plants are self-fertile, but most of their seedlings have normal green lvs. 'Aurea': lvs yellow. 'Laekenensis Rainbow': st. creeping; lvs small, ovate, pale green striped and banded white tinged purple; fls white. 'Tricolor Minima': lvs small, variegated pink, white and green, red beneath. 'Variegata': lvs with yellow and white stripes.
T. geniculata Jacq. = *Gibasis geniculata*.
T. iridescens Lindl. Lvs usually basal, rosulate. Lvs to 8–13×2.5–4cm, ovate-elliptic to suborbicular, succulent, bright or blue-green above, glab. or pilose beneath, margins ciliate. Infl. capitate; fls 2.5–3cm diam., purple-pink. Summer. Mex. Z8.
T. karwinskyana Schult. f. = *Gibasis karwinskyana*.
T. laekenensis hort. A variegated cv. of *T. fluminensis*.
T. linearis Benth. = *Gibasis linearis*.
T. martensiana Kunth = *Callisia multiflora*.
T. micrantha Torr. = *Callisia micrantha*.
T. montana Shuttlew. ex Small & Vail = *T. subaspera*.
T. navicularis Ortgies = *Callisia navicularis*.
T. ohiensis Raf. Related to *T. virginiana*, differing in narrower, nearly glab. sep., and generally glaucous appearance. Lvs 8–45×0.5–4.5cm, linear-lanceolate. Fls pink, purple, blue or white. Summer. US. 'Alba': fls white, sta. blue. Z7.
T. pallida (Rose) D. Hunt. St. to 40cm, ascending or decumbent. Lvs 7–15×2–3.5cm, oblong-elliptic to elliptic-lanceolate, trough-shaped, slightly succulent, glaucous green, tinged red, glab., rarely pilose. Infl. term., solitary; peduncles to 6–11cm; bracts to 7cm, ovate-acuminate; fls 2–3cm diam., pink or pink with white midline, rarely white. Summer. E Mex. 'Purple Heart' ('Purpurea'): lvs deep mauve to purple. Z8.
T. paludosa E. Anderson & Woodson = *T. ohiensis*.
T. pellucida Martens & Gal. = *Gibasis pellucida*.
T. pexata H.E. Moore = *T. sillamontana*.
T. pilosa Lehm. = *T. subaspera*.
T. quadricolor hort. = *T. zebrina* var. *flocculosa* 'Quadricolor'.
T. reflexa Raf. = *T. ohiensis*.
T. rosea Vent. = *Callisia rosea*.
T. schiedeana Kunth = *Gibasis pellucida*.
T. sellowiana Kunth = *Tripogandra diuretica*.
T. sillamontana Matuda. St. ascending or decumbent, to 30cm.

Lvs 3–7×2–2.5cm, distichous, elliptic-ovate to broadly ovate-lanceolate, ampelxicaul at base, somewhat succulent, green flushing purple-red, densely villous-lanate. Fls 1.5–2.5cm diam., purple-pink, short-stalked, solitary. Summer. NE Mex. Z9.

T. spathacea Sw. OYSTER PLANT; BOAT LILY; CRADLE LILY; MOSES IN HIS CRADLE; MOSES ON A RAFT; MOSES IN THE BULRUSHES; MEN IN A BOAT. St. usually short, stout, simple. Lvs 20–35×3–5.5cm, linear-lanceolate, in an apical rosette, semi-succulent, glab., green or dark blue-green above, purple beneath. Infl. axill.; peduncle 2–4.5cm; bracts 2–4.5cm, paired, waxy, boat-shaped; fls 1–1.5cm diam., white, scarcely exserted. Throughout the year. S Mex., Belize, Guat. 'Vittata' (Variegata'): lvs striped cream above, deep purple beneath. 'Concolor': lvs green throughout. Z9.

T. striata hort. A name used for a variegated cv. of *T. fluminensis* and for *Callisia elegans*.

T. subaspera Ker-Gawl. Close to *T. virginiana*. To 1m, with stout, flexuous st., broad, dark green lvs, 6–25×1–5cm. Infl. with mixed gland. and egland. hairs; fls 2–3cm diam., light to deep blue. Summer. US. Z7.

T. tampicana hort. = *T. pallida* 'Purple Heart' ('Purpurea').

T. tepoxtlana Matuda. Resembling *T. crassifolia* but lvs lanceolate, amplexicaul, 8–12×1.5–2cm, ± succulent, glaucous, glab. or thinly hairy, hairs beneath. Fls c1.5cm diam.; pet. white or blue-violet. Summer. S Mex. Z9.

T. tumida Lindl. = *T. iridescens*.

T. velutina hort. non Kunth & Bouché = *T. sillamontana*.

T. virginiana L. St. tufted, to 60cm. Lvs 15–35×0.5–2.5cm, linear-lanceolate, slightly fleshy, green, glab. Bracts similar to the lvs; fls numerous, 2.5–3.5cm diam.; pet. blue or purple, pink or white. Summer. E US. A complex of closely related N American spp. includes *T. bracteata*, *T. gigantea*, *T. hirsuticaulis*, *T. hirsutiflora*, *T. humilis*, *T. longipes*, *T. occidentalis*, *T. ohiensis*, *T. ozarkana*, *T. subaspera*, *T. tharpii*. The hardy gdn tradescantias are mostly hybrids of *T. virginiana*. The group name *T. ×andersoniana* is invalid. 'Alba': fls white. 'Caerulea Plena': to 45cm; fls double, royal blue. 'Carnea': fls tinged pink. 'Iris Pritchard': fls white tinged pale blue. 'Isis': fls deep blue. 'Lilacina Plena': fls double, lilac-blue. 'Major': fls double. 'Osprey': to 60cm; fls pure white centred purple-blue. 'Pauline': fls pale pink. 'Purple Dome': to 60cm; fls rich purple. 'Red Cloud': to 45cm; fls cerise-red. 'Valour': to 45cm; fls red tinged purple. 'Zwanenberg Blue': to 50cm; fls v. large, pure blue. Z7.

T. warszewicziana Kunth & Bouché = *Callisia warszewicziana*.

T. zanonia (L.) Sw. Stout, erect or decumbent herb to 1m, st. simple. Lvs to 35×8cm, towards top of st., lanceolate to oblanceolate, membranous, dark green above, pale or silvery beneath, subglabr. Infl. to 20cm, axill.; bracts 2.5–6cm; pet. 6–10×5–8mm, usually white. Summer–winter. Mex. to Braz. and Boliv., W Indies. 'Mexican Flag' (syn. *Dichorisandra albomarginata*): lvs longitudinally striped creamy yellow.

T. zebrina hort. ex Bosse. St. decumbent or creeping, rooting at the nodes. Lvs 2.5–10×1.5–3.5cm, ovate-oblong, somewhat succulent, green and/or purple above, often striped silver, usually purple beneath. Infl. solitary; bracts 2, 1.5–6cm; pet. tube to 10×1.3mm, white, lobes 5–10×3–7mm, purple-pink or violet-blue. Mex. 'Purpusii': trailing or mat-forming to 10cm; lvs tinged purple; fls small, pink. 'Quadricolor': lvs striped green, pink, red and white. var. *flocculosa* (Brückn.) D. Hunt. St. and lvs softly villous. Lvs seldom or scarcely striped. Pet. lobes violet-blue, pink or purple. S Mex., Belize, Guat., Hond. Z9.

→*Campelia*, *Rhoeo*, *Setcreasea* and *Zebrina*.

Tragopogon L. GOAT'S BEARD. Compositae. c50 taprooted, ann. to bienn. or perenn. herbs, with milky sap. Lvs linear-lanceolate to linear, entire. Cap. ligulate, solitary or few, term.; involucre narrow, campanulate or cylindrical; flts yellow or purple. Temp. Eurasia, Medit. Z5.

T. crocifolius L. Ann. to bienn. to 80cm. Lvs to 5×0.5cm, narrowly-linear. Peduncle not inflated below head; phyllaries 5–12, equalling flts, outer flts violet with yellow base, inner yellow, occas. violet. Summer. S Eur.

T. dubius Simps. Glab. perenn., to over 1m. Lvs linear-lanceolate, slightly glaucous, hairy at first. Peduncles strongly inflated below head; flts lemon yellow. Late spring. Eur.

T. glaber Hill = *T. crocifolius*.

T. major Jacq. = *T. dubius*.

T. ×mirus Ownb. (*T. dubius* × *T. porrifolius*.) Lvs to 5×1cm, linear-lanceolate, slightly clasping at base. Peduncles inflated below head, to 15mm diam.; flts yellow, apex lilac. Gdn origin (US).

T. ×miscellus Ownb. (*T. dubius* × *T. pratensis*.) Lvs to 3×0.8cm, linear-lanceolate, apex recurved, margin crisped. Peduncle inflated below head, to 10mm diam.; phyllary margins purple, far exceeding flts; flts yellow. Gdn origin (US).

T. porrifolius L. SALSIFY; VEGETABLE OYSTER; OYSTER PLANT. Glab. bienn., to 1–5m. Lvs to 30×2cm, linear-lanceolate, attenuate, glaucous, clasping at base. Peduncles strongly inflated below head; flts rose-purple. Fr. 3–4mm; pappus pale brown. Late spring–summer. Medit.

T. pratensis L. GOAT'S BEARD; JOHNNY-GO-TO-BED-AT-NOON; SHEPHERD'S CLOCK. Ann. to perenn., to 70cm. Lvs to 10×1cm, linear-lanceolate, attenuate to slightly clasping base, margins crisped. Peduncles scarcely inflated below head; phyllaries edged purple; flts yellow. Summer. Eur. Z3.

T. roseus Trev. = *T. ruber*.

T. ruber S.G. Gmel. Woolly perenn., to 40cm. Lvs linear-lanceolate, glaucous, slightly undulate. Peduncles not distinctly inflated; flts rose-purple. Sib. to E Russia. Z3.

Trailing Abutilon *Abutilon megapotamicum*.
Trailing African Daisy *Osteospermum fruticosum*.
Trailing Arbutus *Epigaea repens*.
Trailing Azalea *Loiseleuria procumbens*.
Trailing Bellflower *Cyananthus*.
Trailing Chinquapin *Castanea alnifolia*.
Trailing Maidenhair *Adiantum caudatum*.
Trailing Mallow *Sphaeralcea philippiana*.
Trailing Phlox *Phlox nivalis*.
Trailing Spike Moss *Selaginella kraussiana*.
Trailing Velvet Plant *Ruellia makoyana*.
Trailing Violet *Viola hederacea*.
Trailing Watermelon Begonia *Pellionia repens*.
Trailing Wolf's-bane *Aconitum reclinatum*.
Tramp's Spurge *Euphorbia corollata*.
Transcaucasian Birch *Betula medwediewii*.
Transvaal Daisy *Gerbera* (*G. aurantiaca*).
Transvaal Kafferboom *Erythrina lysistemon*.

Trapa L. WATER CHESTNUT. Trapaceae. 15 aquatic, perenn. herbs. St. submerged, with plume-like roots. Floating lvs to 3cm, rosulate, broadly ovate to rhombic, toothed above; petiole inflated, spongy. Fls small, white, 4-merous, axill., solitary, short-stalked. Fr. a hardened, sculpted 2–4-horned nut. C Eur. to E Asia, Afr. Z5.

T. bicornis Osbeck. LING. Fr. with 2 large, decurved horns. China.

T. bicornuta hort. = *T. bicornis*.

T. natans L. WATER CHESTNUT; WATER CALTROP; JESUITS' NUT. Fr. 2.25cm diam., with 4 spiny angles of unequal length. W sector of the genus range, inc. the Nile Region. *Trapa* may constitute a single sp. varying in lf pubescence and serration and the spiny teeth on the fr., in which case *T. bicornis*, *T. bispinosa*, the Singhara nut plant from the Indian subcontinent, and *T. verbanensis* from Lake Maggiore would be united within *T. natans*.

TRAPACEAE Dumort. See *Trapa*.

Trapper's Tea *Ledum glandulosum*.

Trautvetteria Fisch. & Mey. Ranunculaceae. 2 perenn. herbs. Lvs palmatifid, basal lvs long-petiolate; st. lvs smaller, ± sessile. Corymbs rounded; sep. 4 or 5, green-white, elliptic; pet. 0; sta. numerous. E Asia, N US. Z5.

T. carolinensis (Walter) Vail. FALSE BUGBANE. 50–100cm. Lvs to 30cm, mostly basal, reniform, palmately 5–11-lobed, base cuneate, lobed or toothed. Fls c1cm diam. Summer. NE US.

T. grandis Nutt. ex Torr. & A. Gray. To 1m, resembles *T. carolinensis*, but lower lvs 10–20cm, more deeply cleft, lobes deeply toothed. Summer. NW US.

T. palmata (Michx.) Fisch. & C.A. Mey. = *T. carolinensis*.

Traveller's Joy *Clematis vitalba*.
Traveller's Tree *Ravenala*.
Trazel *Corylus* ×*colurnoides*.
Treacleberry *Smilacina racemosa*.
Tread-softly *Cnidoscolus* (*C. urens*).
Treasure Flower *Gazania* (*G. rigens*).
Tree Anemone *Carpenteria californica*.
Tree Aralia *Kalopanax septemlobus*.
Treebine *Cissus*.
Tree Calabash *Crescentia cujete*.
Tree Caper *Capparis mitchellii*.
Tree Celandine *Bocconia frutescens*; *Macleaya cordata*.
Tree Cotoneaster *Cotoneaster frigidus*.
Tree Cotton *Gossypium arboreum*.
Tree Dracaena *Dracaena arborea*.
Tree Fern *Cibotium*; *Cyathea*; *Blechnum*; *Dicksonia*.
Tree Fuchsia *Schotia brachypetala*.
Tree Germander *Teucrium fruticans*.

Tree **Hakea** *Hakea eriantha*.
Tree **Heath** *Erica arborea; Richea pandanifolia*.
Tree **Indigofera** *Indigofera cylindrica*.
Tree **Lavatera** *Lavatera olbia; L. thuringiaca*.
Treelet **Spike Moss** *Selaginella braunii*.
Tree **Lupin** *Lupinus arboreus*.
Tree **Maidenhair Fern** *Didymochlaena trunculata*.
Tree **Mallow** *Lavatera arborea*.
Tree **Medick** *Medicago arborea*.
Tree of **Damocles** *Oroxylum indicum*.
Tree of **Gold** *Tabebuia argentea*.
Tree of **Heaven** *Ailanthus altissima*.
Tree **Onion** *Allium cepa*.
Tree **Oxalis** *Oxalis ortgiesii*.
Tree **Peony** *Paeonia potaninii*.
Tree **Petrea** *Petrea arborea*.
Tree **Poppy** *Dendromecon*.
Tree **Purslane** *Atriplex halimus*.
Tree **Smokebush** *Conospermum triplinervium*.
Tree **Tobacco** *Nicotiana glauca*.
Tree **Tomato** *Cyphomandra crassicaulis*.

Trema Lour. Ulmaceae. 14 everg. trees. Lvs alt., often distichous, serrate. Fls in small axill. clusters or cymes; cal. 5- or 4-parted; cor. 0; sta. 5, rarely 4. Trop. and warm Amer., Afr. and Asia. Z9.
T. amboinensis (Willd.) Bl. = *T. cannabina*.
T. bracteola Bl. = *T. orientalis*.
T. cannabina Lour. Similar to *T. orientalis* except lvs green and glab. to hirsute beneath. S Jap., Taiwan, S China, India, Aus.
T. guineensis (Schum. & Thonn.) Ficalho. Small tree or shrub. Lvs 6–12×2.5–5cm, ovate, attenuate, rounded or subtruncate at base, pubesc. or softly tomentose. Trop. Afr.
T. orientalis (L.) Bl. Small tree. Lvs 7–15×1.5–5cm, narrowly ovate-oblong to broadly lanceolate, serrulate, slenderly acuminate, basally obliquely cordate, scabrous and adpressed short-pubesc. above, white and densely sericeous beneath. Jap., Taiwan, S China to India, Malesia and Aus.
T. virgata Bl. = *T. cannabina*.

TREMANDRACEAE R. Br. ex DC. 3/43. *Tetratheca*.

Trentpohlia Boeck.
T. integrifolia Roth = *Heliophila amplexicaulis*.

Trevesia Vis. Araliaceae. 12 prickly or unarmed pachycaul shrubs or trees, often clump-forming. Lvs large, clustered towards tops of br., palmately lobed or pseudo-digitately compound. Infl. term., 1–2× compound; fls in stalked umbels; pet. 7–13, valvate; sta. the same number as the pet. Himal. to S China, S to W Malesia. Z10.
T. burckii Boerl. Shrub or small, sparsely branched tree to 10m; br. prickly. Juvenile lvs simple or palmately lobed with central portion (web) and lobes differentiated, but sessile; adult lvs dull olive green, pseudo-digitately compound, with foliaceous central web and pseudo-petiolate, oblong-lanceolate or elliptic toothed lobes; petiole shortly bristly or prickly. Infl. red- or brown-hairy, umbelliform-paniculate, 1× compound; umbels terminating primary br. Penins. Malaysia, Sumatra and W Borneo. Cultivated plants are often *T. sanderi* (*T. burckii* auct.; *T. palmata* auct.; *T. palmata* var. *sanderi* hort.) which differs in young parts pale-hairy, juvenile lvs pseudo-digitate with discrete false petiolules and pinnately lobed, oblong-ovate seg., adult lvs with wavy pinnately lobed seg. SE Asia. Z11.
T. cheirantha (C.B. Clarke) Kuntze = *T. burckii*.
T. eminens Bull = *Osmoxylon eminens*.
T. micholitzii hort. = under *T. palmata*.
T. palmata (Roxb. ex Lindl.) Vis. Large shrubs or small trees to 9m, st. usually branching thorny, hairy. Juvenile lvs pseudo-digitately compound as in *T. sanderi*, the outer seg. incompletely separated from the central web; adult lvs lustrous, palmately lobed, lobes to 60cm, glab. above, red pubesc. beneath; petioles sometimes prickly. Infl. 2× compound, erect, to 45cm, red-brown-pubesc. when young. Spring. India to S China, S to Vietnam and N Thail. 'Micholitzii' (SNOWFLAKE PLANT, SNOWFLAKE TREE): lvs pseudo-digitate in adult plants, seg. ± irregularly pinnatifid; young foliage white-hairy, later glossy green with silvery-white patches or dots; petioles unarmed. Z10.
T. palmata var. *cheirantha* C.B. Clarke = *T. burckii*.
T. sanderi hort. = *T. burckii*.
T. sundaica Miq. Shrub or tree to 8m, branched or not, sometimes offsetting, br. spreading, shortly prickly. Young parts hairy. Lvs 7–11-lobed, in adults to 60×60cm, glab., the upper surface glossy; lobes to 40cm, upper margins serrate; petioles to 60cm, unarmed or with a few prickles at base.Infl. 1×

compound, main axis to 60cm; umbels at ends of axis and primary br. Malesia. Z10.
T. sundaica auct., non Miq. = *T. burckii*.
→*Gastonia*.

Triangular-leaved Violet *Viola ×emarginata*.
Triangular Staghorn Fern *Platycerium stemaria*.

Triantha (Nutt.) Bak.
T. glutinosa (Michx.) Bak. = *Tofieldia glutinosa*.

Trias Lindl. Orchidaceae. 10 epiphytic orchids. Rhiz. creeping; pbs almost spherical. Lvs fleshy, solitary. Fls fleshy, solitary; sep. spreading; pet. small; lip mobile, narrow, apex dilated. SE Asia. Z10.
T. picta Parish. Pbs 1.5cm diam. Lvs 5.5–7.5cm, coriaceous, lanceolate. Fls borne basally, to 2cm across; sep. ovate to triangular, yellow-green, spotted red; pet. broadly ovate, emarginate; lip small, oblong, maroon or olive, spotted red, rough to papillose. Burm., Thail.

Tribulus L. Zygophyllaceae. 25 herbs or subshrubs. Lvs pinnate; lfts entire. Fls solitary, axill.; sep. 5, occas. persistent; pet. 5, fugacious; disc annular, 10-lobed; sta. 10. Fr. flattened, 5-angled, splitting into 5 spiny nutlets. Throughout trop. and warm regions.
T. terrestris L. CALTROP; DEVIL'S WEED. Ann., procumbent; st. 15–60cm, pubesc. Lvs 2.5–4×1–1.5cm; lfts 5–8 pairs, elliptic to oblong-lanceolate, pale glossy green. Fls yellow, 4–10mm diam. Fr. about 1cm, yellow-brown. Trop. and warm regions.

Trichantha Hook. Gesneriaceae. 26 subshrubs, epiphytes and climbers, often pubesc. St. branching. Lvs paired, equal or unequal. Fls solitary, paired or in clusters, cal. 5-lobed, often marked red; cor. ventricose to tubular, spurred, upper lip 3-lobed, lower 2-lobed, sinuses sometimes appendaged. C & S Amer. Z10.
T. ambigua (Urban) Wiehler. St. descending, brown-green. Lvs subequal to 5cm, elliptic, serrate, lustrous. Cal. lobes tipped red; cor. bright yellow. Puerto Rico.
T. angustifolia Wiehler. St. ascending, pink-pilose. Lvs unequal, 15–18cm, narrowly lanceolate, hirsute, blue-green above, marked maroon beneath. Cal. fringed; cor. yellow with maroon stripes. Ecuad.
T. anisophylla (DC.) Wiehler. Lvs markedly unequal, larger lf to 15cm, oblanceolate, hairy. Cal. dentate, green-brown-hairy; cor. bright red outside, bright yellow inside, sparsely red-pilose. Peru, Ecuad., Colomb., Costa Rica.
T. brenneri Wiehler. Erect or spreading, hirsute. Lvs 7.5–15cm, glossy blue-green above, maroon beneath. Cal. flushed or completely maroon; cor. bright yellow, faintly blotched or striped maroon. Ecuad.
T. calotricha (J.D. Sm.) Wiehler. St. arching or descending, pilose. Lvs to 11cm, elliptic, slightly serrate, maroon beneath. Cal. light green, pilose, lobes tipped red. Guat., Colomb., Guyana, N Braz.
T. cerropirrana Wiehler. St. spreading or descending, to 2m. Lvs unequal, 4–8cm, red-purple beneath. Cal. red; cor. red, pilose, limb yellow. Panama.
T. ciliata Wiehler. St. to 1m, spreading or descending, brown-hairy. Lvs strongly unequal pairs, larger lf 12–14cm, obovate or elliptic, marked red. Cor. red, yellow or white, hairy between lobes. Ecuad., E Peru.
T. citrina Wiehler. St. ascending, spreading or descending, to 50cm. Lvs in markedly unequal pairs, larger lf 7–10cm, elliptic, green, pubesc. above, red beneath. Fls pendent; cal. pubesc.; cor. pale yellow, glabrate. Panama.
T. dissimilis (Morton) Wiehler. St. to 1m, erect and spreading, red to orange hispid. Lvs in unequal pairs; larger lf to 11cm, elliptic-oblong, red pilose beneath. Cor. orange or red, red-sericeous outside, lobes yellow. Panama, Costa Rica.
T. domingensis (Urban) Wiehler. Climber. Lvs to 5×2.1cm, dentate, red-pilose, often flushed red beneath. Cal. toothed, red. Hispan.
T. erythrophylla (Hanst.) Wiehler. St. pendent or descending. Lvs markedly unequal, larger lf to 10cm, copper-green above, bright orange, lustrous beneath. Cal. green marked with orange; cor. orange. Venez.
T. filifera Wiehler. St. to 70cm, erect or spreading, red-pilose. Lvs 7–11cm, subequal, elliptic or ovate, hirsute. Cal. pilose; cor. cream, densely orange-red pilose, with red-hairy appendages. Colomb.
T. illepida (H.E. Moore) Morton. St. erect, pubesc. Lvs strongly unequal, larger lf oblanceolate to obovate, hairy, red beneath. Cor. tube yellow, maroon-striate, lobes marked with maroon spots or stripes, with yellow appendages. Panama.

T. lehmannii (Mansf.) Wiehler. St. slender, erect, brown. Lvs markedly unequal, larger lf to 7.5cm. Cal. bright orange; cor. bright yellow. Colomb.

T. minor Hook. St. wiry. Lvs strongly unequal, to 8cm, hairy. Cal. fimbriate, orange or maroon; cor. red, maroon often with dark stripes, appendaged. Ecuad., Colomb.

T. mira (Morley) Wiehler. St. red-purple hirsute. Lvs unequal, larger lf to 9cm, oblanceolate, serrate, red-purple beneath. Cal. green, red-hirsute; cor. yellow, striped red or brown, red-pilose outside. Panama.

T. moorei (Morton) Morton. St. pendent. Lvs to 1.5cm, broadly elliptic, lustrous above. Cor. tube red, red-hairy, lobes yellow, with minute yellow appendages. Panama.

T. parviflora (Morton) Wiehler. St. descending, spreading, finely white-pubesc. Lvs to 4cm, ovate, serrate, lustrous green. Cal. bright orange; cor. bright yellow. Ecuad., Panama, Colomb.

T. pulchra Wiehler. St. to 80cm, erect or ascending, spreading, red-hairy. Lvs markedly unequal, larger lf 7–13cm, oblanceolate or elliptic, flushed pink beneath. Cal. orange-red, gland. red-pilose; cor. pale yellow. Panama.

T. purpureovittata Wiehler. St. to 30cm, branching at base. Lvs strongly unequal, to 20cm, lanceolate-elliptic, overlapping, bullate, glossy blue-green above, red beneath. Cal. green or red-flushed, red-tipped; cor. bright yellow, lobes striped purple. Ecuad., Peru.

T. sanguinolenta (Klotzsch ex Ørst.) Wiehler. St. erect. Lvs strongly unequal, larger lf to 12cm, oblanceolate, marked red beneath. Cal. fimbriate, densely red- or maroon-pubesc.; cor. orange-red to maroon. Panama, Costa Rica.

T. segregata (Morley) Wiehler. St. purple-brown villous. Lvs unequal, larger lf to 13.6cm, oblanceolate, glab. above, spotted or completely red beneath. Cal. red-flushed, red-pilose; cor. yellow, outside red-pilose, lobes flushed red. Panama, Costa Rica.

T. tenensis Wiehler. St. to 40cm, ascending, branching at base. Lvs strongly unequal, larger lf to 20cm, elliptic, blue-green above, spotted or completely red-maroon beneath. Cal. green, marked purple; cor. bright yellow with 5 purple stripes. Ecuad.
→*Alloplectus* and *Columnea*.

Trichinium R. Br.
T. exaltatum (Nees) Benth. = *Ptilotus exaltatus*.
T. manglesii (Lindl.) F. Muell. = *Ptilotus manglesii*.
T. spathulatum Nees = *Ptilotus spathulatus*.
T. stirlingii Lindl. = *Ptilotus stirlingii*.

Trichloris Fourn. Gramineae. 2 perenn. grasses. St. tufted. Lvs linear, ligules ciliate. Infl. feathery. Rac. digitate; spikelets short-stipitate, to 5-fld, dorsally flattened. Summer–autumn. S Amer. Z8.
T. crinita (Lagasca) L. Parodi. To 90cm. Lvs to 45cm, scabrous, glaucous. Infl. erect, compact, setaceous; br. to 13cm; spikelets to 2-fld; awns to 1.3cm.
T. mendocina (Philippi) Kurtz = *T. crinita*.
→*Chloris*.

Trichocaulon N.E. Br. Asclepiadaceae. 20 v. succulent perennials. St. spherical or cylindric, with tubercles arranged on ribs or spirals. Lvs 0 or rudimentary. Fls small, clustered between tubercles; cor. cupped or rotate, lobes 5, ovate, sometimes annular at centre; corona lobed, conspicuous. S Afr. (Cape Prov.), Nam. Z9.
T. alstonii N.E. Br. St. 15×3-4.5cm, tinged blue, angles many, spiny-tuberculate. Cor. 3×3mm lobes sharply tapered, erect to slightly spreading. W Cape.
T. annulatum N.E. Br. St. cylindric, 14–45×3-4.5cm, bristle-tipped in many rows. Cor. 20mm diam., with a prominent annulus, exterior glab., interior papillose except base, dark red-brown, lobes short-tapered. E Cape.
T. cactiforme (Hook.) N.E. Br. St. globose to cylindric, conical to clavate, 4–15×4-6cm, tubercles in spirals, spineless. Cor. 6–13mm diam., campanulate-rotate, interior minutely papillate-rugulose, white-yellow to cream tinged with red-brown or dark brown lines, lobes ovate-triangular, abruptly tapered. NW Cape, Nam.
T. cinereueum Pill. = *T. perlatum*.
T. clavatum (Willd.) H. Huber = *T. cactiforme*.
T. columnaris Nel = *Notechidnopsis columnaris*.
T. delaetianum Dinter. St. 10–20×4-5cm, tubercles purple-spined in many rows. Cor. 12mm diam., broadly campanulate, exterior brown-red, interior brown-yellow, lobes tapered. Nam.: Great Namaqualand.
T. dinteri A. Berger. St. globose to columnar, 4–15×4-6cm, grey-green to yellow-brown. Cor. 5–10mm diam., campanulate-rotate, interior smooth, creamy white with red to

red-brown spots and stripes. Cape Prov. to Nam.
T. engleri Dinter = *T. simile*.
T. flavum N.E. Br. St. 15×4-5cm, blue-green with brown-spined tubercles in numerous rows. Cor. 10–12mm diam., flat-rotate, exterior smooth, interior minutely papillose, yellow, lobes triangular-tapered. Karroo.
T. grande N.E. Br. St. 45–60×5cm, grey-green, tubercles spiny in rows. Cor. 14–16mm diam., campanulate, exterior glab., interior densely papillose, green-yellow, lobes broad-ovate, short-tapered. W Cape.
T. halenbergense Dinter. St. 100×5-6cm, angles 16, spiny-tuberculate. Cor. yellow. Namaqualand.
T. keetmanshoppense Dinter = *T. marlothii*.
T. kubusense Nel = *T. perlatum*.
T. marlothii N.E. Br. St. globose to columnar, 4–15×4-6cm, grey-green. Cor. to 14mm diam., rotate, lobes ovate-triangular, interior white spotted and blotched red or red-brown. NW Cape to Nam.
T. meloforme Marloth = *T. simile*.
T. officinale N.E. Br. St. 20–30×6-7cm, blue-green with 20–25 hook-spined ribs. Cor. 8–9mm diam., rotate, interior red-brown with a yellow centre, minutely hairy, lobes triangular-ovate, tapered. SE Cape, Nam.
T. pedicellatum Schinz. St. cylindric, 2cm thick, angles spiny-tuberculate. Cor. rotate, 8–10mm diam., interior dark brown-red, lobes lanceolate, tapered, minutely papillose. Nam.
T. perlatum Dinter. St. 5–16cm, globose to columnar, tinged blue, tubercles grey, irregular, tesselate. Cor. 3–10mm diam., interior densely papillose with a distinct annulus, cream or grey-green with small to large red-purple spots, lobes reflexed or adpressed. NW Cape to SW Nam.
T. pictum N.E. Br. St. columnar to globose, 4–7×4-5cm, subterete, tessellate-tuberculate, grey-green. Cor. 10mm diam., smooth outside, papillose inside, white or white-yellow, blotched and lined red-brown, lobes triangular. NW Cape.
T. piliferum (L. f.) N.E. Br. St. 20×4.5cm, clump-forming, blue-green to grey-green, tubercles, spine-tipped. Cor. 18mm diam., campanulate to funnel-shaped, light yellow-red inside, dark red-brown or purple-brown outside, minutely tuberculate. SE Cape.
T. pillansii N.E. Br. St. 12–18×3-5cm, grey-green, angled, tubercles bristled. Cor. 9mm diam., exterior light white-yellow, glab., interior minutely papillose except glab. tube, lobes triangular-ovate, sharply acute. W Cape.
T. pubiflorum Dinter. St. 15×4cm, dark blue-green, angles regular, tubercles bristled. Cor. 11mm diam., hairy in centre, lobes yellow with red blotches, grading to green, margins violet to brown, red-brown below. Nam.: Great Namaqualand.
T. rusticum N.E. Br. St. 12–13×4cm, conical, tubercles in vertical rows, each with a spiny tip. Cor. 18mm diam., glab., lobes triangular-ovate, dark red-brown, minutely pubesc. Cape.
T. simile N.E. Br. St. ovoid-spherical to columnar, 4.5×4cm, grey-green, tubercles rounded, spine-tipped. Cor. campanulate, 9mm diam., glab., papillose inside, white with red to red-brown spots or lines; lobes recurved. NW Cape, S Nam.
T. somaliense Guill. = *Echidnopsis scutellata* ssp. *planiflora*.
T. triebneri Nel. St. slender, columnar, 60×4cm, blue-green to grey-green, furrowed, tubercles spiny. Cor. 15mm diam., campanulate, black-purple or red-purple; cor. lobes triangular, tapered, papillose. Nam., NW of Windhoek.
T. truncatum Pill. = *T. perlatum*.

Trichocentrum Poepp. & Endl. Orchidaceae. 12 epiphytic orchids. Rhiz. short. Pbs clustered, small or obsolete. Lvs fleshy to coriaceous. Infl. lat., short-stalked, 1- to few-fld; fls large, spreading; sep. similar, subequal to pet.; lip fleshy, suberect, simple to obscurely 3-lobed or pandurate, spurred, callus crested. Trop. Amer. Z10.
T. albococcineum Lind. Lvs to 9×4cm, elliptic or oblong-lanceolate. Infl. to 7.5cm; tep. yellow-brown above, yellow-green below, dors. sep. to 2×1cm, obovate-oblong, pet. smaller, narrower; lip to 2.5cm, pale or deep purple, base blotched dark purple, subquadrate-pandurate. Mostly summer–autumn. Ecuad., Peru, Braz.
T. candidum Lindl. Lvs to 7×2cm, elliptic to ovate-elliptic. Infl. to 2cm; tep. white marked yellow, sep. to 1.3×0.5cm, narrowly elliptic to elliptic-oblanceolate, pet. shorter; lip to 1.8cm, white marked yellow, pink-purple near base, elliptic-obovate, undulate. Mex., Guat.
T. capistratum Rchb. f. Lvs to 10×2.5cm, elliptic-lanceolate to oblong-lanceolate. Fls solitary; tep. to 1.2×0.4cm, yellow-green or pink-maroon, waxy, oblanceolate to oblong-lanceolate; lip to 1.7cm, white blotched pink-purple at base, elliptic to ovate-elliptic, emarginate. Summer–autumn. Panama, Costa Rica, Venez., Colomb.
T. panamense Rolfe = *T. capistratum*.

T. pulchrum Poepp. & Endl. Lvs to 10×2.5cm, linear-oblong or oblong-elliptic. Infl. to 4.5cm; fls white spotted red-purple; tep. concave, to 2×1.4cm, ovate-elliptic; lip to 3cm, obovate to elliptic, emarginate, crenulate. Colomb., Venez., Ecuad., Peru.

T. tigrinum Lind. & Rchb. f. Lvs to 12×3cm, elliptic-oblong. Infl. to 15cm; tep. yellow-green spotted and irregularly banded maroon-brown, sep. 3.6×1.2cm, narrowly elliptic-oblong; pet. longer, narrower; lip to 4.5cm, white, blotched rose-red towards base, broadly ovate, apex bilobulate. Spring–early summer. Ecuad.

Trichocereus Riccob.

T. andalgalensis (F.A. Weber ex Schum.) Hosseus = *Echinopsis huascha*.

T. auricolor Backeb. = *Echinopsis huascha*.

T. bertramianus Backeb. = *Echinopsis bertramiana*.

T. bridgesii (Salm-Dyck) Britt. & Rose = *Echinopsis lageniformis*.

T. camarguensis Cárdenas = *Echinopsis camarguensis*.

T. candicans (Salm-Dyck) Britt. & Rose = *Echinopsis candicans*.

T. chalaensis Rauh & Backeb. = *Echinopsis chalaensis*.

T. chiloensis (Colla) Britt. & Rose = *Echinopsis chilensis*.

T. coquimbanus (Molina) Britt. & Rose = *Echinopsis coquimbana*.

T. courantii (Schum.) Backeb. = *Echinopsis candicans*.

T. cuzcoensis Britt. & Rose = *Echinopsis cuzcoensis*.

T. fascicularis Britt. & Rose, misapplied = *Haageocereus weberbaueri*.

T. fulvilanus Ritter = *Echinopsis deserticola*.

T. gladiatus Lem. = *Echinopsis candicans*.

T. grandiflorus (Britt. & Rose) Backeb., invalid. = *Echinopsis huascha*.

T. herzogianus Cárdenas = *Echinopsis herzogiana*.

T. huascha (F.A. Weber) Britt. & Rose = *Echinopsis huascha*.

T. knuthianus Backeb. = *Echinopsis knuthiana*.

T. lamprochlorus (Lem.) Britt. & Rose = *Echinopsis lamprochlorus*.

T. litoralis (Johow) Looser = *Echinopsis litoralis*.

T. macrogonus (Salm-Dyck) Riccob. = *Echinopsis macrogona*.

T. neolamprochlorus Backeb. = *Echinopsis candicans*.

T. orurensis Cárdenas = *Echinopsis bertramiana*.

T. pachanoi Britt. & Rose = *Echinopsis pachanoi*.

T. pasacana (F.A. Weber ex Ruempl.) Britt. & Rose = *Echinopsis pasacana*.

T. peruvianus Britt. & Rose = *Echinopsis peruvianus*.

T. poco Backeb. = *Echinopsis tarijensis*.

T. purpureopilosus (Weingart) Backeb. = *Echinopsis purpureopilosa*.

T. santiaguensis (Speg.) Backeb. = *Echinopsis spachiana*.

T. schickendantzii (F.A. Weber) Britt. & Rose = *Echinopsis schickendantzii*.

T. shaferi Britt. & Rose = *Echinopsis schickendantzii*.

T. spachianus (Lem.) Riccob. = *Echinopsis spachiana*.

T. strigosus (Salm-Dyck) Britt. & Rose = *Echinopsis strigosa*.

T. taquimbalensis Cárdenas = *Echinopsis taquimbalensis*.

T. tarijensis (Vaupel) Werderm. = *Echinopsis tarijensis*.

T. terscheckii (Parmentier ex Pfeiff.) Britt. & Rose = *Echinopsis terscheckii*.

T. tetracanthus (Labouret) Borg = *Harrisia tetracantha*.

T. thelegonoides (Speg.) Britt. & Rose = *Echinopsis thelegonoides*.

T. thelegonus (F.A. Weber ex Schum.) Britt. & Rose = *Echinopsis thelegona*.

T. trichosus Cárdenas = *Echinopsis trichosa*.

T. uyupampensis Backeb. = *Echinopsis uyupampensis*.

T. vollianus Backeb. = *Echinopsis volliana*.

T. werdermannianus Backeb. = *Echinopsis terscheckii* or *E. pasacana*.

Trichoceros HBK. Orchidaceae. 6 small epiphytic orchids. Pbs small, ellipsoid. Lvs elliptic-oblong, fleshy or thinly coriaceous, sheathing. Rac. lat.; fls insect-like; spreading tep.; lip usually trilobed; column with long dark cilia, resembling antennae. Colomb., Ecuad., Peru, Boliv., Venez. Z10.

T. parviflorus HBK. FLY ORCHID. Infl. 12–30cm, slender; tep. white-green to yellow-brown, spotted purple-black, sep. to 1.3×0.7cm, ovate-lanceolate, pet. shorter, elliptic; lip to 1.3cm, intensely marked, lat. lobes, dark ciliate, midlobe ovate-elliptic, darkly hairy at base; column with long dark bristles. Peru, Colomb., Boliv., Ecuad.

Trichodiadema Schwantes. Aizoaceae. 36 succulent shrubs with woody or tuberous roots. St. long, slender, or short, tufted habit. Lvs slightly connate at base, semi-terete to subterete, papillose, with a tuft of bristles at tip. Fls solitary, short-pedicellate. Spring–late autumn. S Afr., Nam. Z9.

T. barbatum (L.) Schwantes. St. prostrate; roots napiform. Lvs 8–12×3–4mm, grey-green with 8–10 black bristles. Fls 3cm diam., deep red. Karroo, S Nam.

T. bulbosum (Haw.) Schwantes. St. to 20cm; caudex tuberous. Lvs 5–8×2.5–3mm, grey-papillose, with 8–11 white bristles. Fls 2cm diam., deep red. E Cape.

T. densum (Haw.) Schwantes. St. short, mat-forming; caudex fleshy, thickened. Lvs 10×4–5mm, green covered with pointed papillae, with 20–25 long white bristles. Fls 4–5cm diam., crimson. Karroo.

T. intonsum (Haw.) Schwantes. St. prostrate. Lvs 12–13×4mm, covered with acute papillae, with 8–10 brown bristles, margins ciliate. Fls 2cm diam., tinged red to white; cal. tube with white hairs. E Cape.

T. mirabile (N.E. Br.) Schwantes. St. white-bristly, forming a shrublet to 8cm. Lvs 12–26×4–6mm, green, covered with rhombic, acute papillae, with 8–14, stiff, dark brown bristles. Fls 4cm diam., white. W Cape, Karroo.

T. stellatum (Mill.) Schwantes. St. forming dense small mats; roots fleshy. Lvs 10×3–4mm, grey-green, rough-papillose, with 12–15 3–4mm bristles. Fls 3cm diam., light violet to red. W Cape.

Trichoglottis Bl. Orchidaceae. 60 epiphytic orchids. St. climbing or pendent. Lvs tough. Infl. axill.; fls large; pet. narrower than lat. sep.; lip fleshy, partly pubesc., base saccate or spurred, midlobe simple or trilobed. Indo-Malaya to Taiwan, Polyn. Z10.

T. brachiata Ames. Lvs 3–8cm, oblong to oblong-elliptic. Fls solitary, to 4.5cm diam.; tep. oblong-lanceolate, dark purple; lip 5-lobed, spurred, white lined purple. Philipp.

T. luzonensis Ames. Lvs to 20cm, ligulate. Fls paniculate, ivory-yellow spotted red, to 3.2cm diam.; tep. spathulate; lip 3-lobed, saccate, pubesc. Philipp.

T. philippinensis Lindl. Lvs to 6cm, oblong to oblong-ovate. Fls to 3cm diam., fragrant; tep. oblong-lanceolate, yellow marked brown; lip white, cruciform. Philipp.

Tricholaena Schräd. Gramineae. 4 perenn. or ann. grasses. Lvs glaucous, frequently inrolled; ligule ciliate. Infl. a pan.; spikelets oblong, compressed, awnless. Afr. and Medit. to India. Z9.

T. repens (Willd.) A. Hitchc. = *Rhynchelytrum repens*.

T. rosea Nees = *Rhynchelytrum repens*.

T. teneriffae (L. f.) Link. Tussock-forming perenn. to 60cm. Lvs flat or inrolled, 2–15×0.5cm. Pan. narrowly oblong, to 15cm; spikelets to 4mm. S Eur., Afr., India.

Trichomanes L. Hymenophyllaceae. BRISTLE FERN; KIDNEY FERN. 25 filmy ferns. Rhiz. creeping; stipes long. Fronds erect, tripinnate to tripinnatifid, finely divided, v. thinly textured, often translucent. Cosmopolitan. Z10 unless specified.

T. aethiopicum Burm. f. = *Asplenium aethiopicum*.

T. bipunctatum Poir. Rhiz. widely creeping. Frond blade 5–7×2–3cm, oblong-lanceolate to deltoid-oblong, tripinnatifid, pinnae lanceolate, seg. ligulate, 3–4mm, rachis winged; stipes to 5cm, ± winged. Maur.

T. chinense L. = *Sphenomeris chinensis*.

T. elegans Rich. Rhiz. tufted. Sterile fronds 15–45×5–30cm, pendulous, broadly lanceolate, pinnatifid, pinnae crowded, dentate, occas. caudate; fertile fronds 15–30×1–1.5cm, erect, simple, entire; stipes 5–20cm. Trop. Amer.

T. humile Forst. Rhiz. forming dense mat, ferruginous-tomentose when young. Frond blades 2.5–5×1–1.5cm, lanceolate-oblong, irregularly bipinnatifid, dark dull green; seg. pinnatifid, lobes linear, simple or forked; rachis winged; stipes slender, to 1.2cm, winged above. Malaysia, Australasia, Polyn.

T. meifolium Bory. Fronds to 60cm, tufted, lanceolate, v. finely divided; seg. narrowly linear, variously angled, giving fronds a luxuriously soft texture. Malaysia, Polyn.

T. radicans Sw. Rhiz. creeping, clad in black hair-like rhizoids. Frond blades 15–40×5–20cm, lanceolate-oblong to ovate, 3–4-pinnatisect; pinnae numerous, close; pinnules many, linear-oblong, truncate or forked; stipes short, winged above, pubesc. at first. Pantrop.

T. reniforme Forst. Rhiz. creeping. Frond blades orbicular-reniform, entire, with deep basal sinus, 5–10cm wide; stipes to 20cm, naked. NZ.

T. scandens L. Rhiz. sinuous, creeping, setose when young. Frond blades 15–40×10–25cm, oblong-lanceolate to ovate-oblong, 3-pinnate to 3-pinnatifid, light green, membranous, ferruginous-pilose; pinnae oblong-trapezoid; pinnules sometimes lobed or pinnatifid; rachis terete; stipe to ½ blade length, tomentose at first. W Indies.

T. speciosum Willd. KILLARNEY FERN. Rhiz. rather stout, black pubesc. Frond blades 10–20cm, ovate-triangular, deeply 3–4-pinnatisect, seg. oblong, entire; stipes equalling blades, winged. Extreme W of Eur. Z9.

T. squarrosum Forst. f. = *Dicksonia squarrosa.*

T. strigosum Thunb. = *Microlepia strigosa.*

T. venosum R. Br. Rhiz. filiform, minutely pubesc. Frond blades 2–10cm, lanceolate to elliptic, translucent; pinnae 1–3cm; rachis occas. winged above; stipes 1–5cm, unwinged. Australasia.

Trichopetalum Lindl. Liliaceae (Asphodelaceae). 1 perenn. herb to 1m. Rhiz. stout; roots fleshy. Lvs to 30cm, usually basal, grass-like, glab. Rac. loose to 15cm; fls to 15mm diam., white to green-white; perianth seg. 6, inner seg. fringed with white hairs. Chile. Z10.

T. plumosum (Ruiz & Pav.) Macbr.

→*Anthericum* and *Bottionea.*

Trichopilia Lindl. Orchidaceae. 30 epiphytic orchids. Pbs ovoid-oblong, laterally compressed, clustered. Lvs oblong to ovate-lanceolate, fleshy or coriaceous, sheathing and apical. Infl. lat., often several on one pb.; fls fragrant; tep. narrow, sometimes spiralling or undulate, the pet. and dors. sep. broader than lat. sep.; lip simple to trilobed, inrolled and funnel-shaped, wavy-margined. Trop. C & S Amer. Z10.

T. candida Lem. ex Lindl. = *T. fragrans.*

T. coccinea Warsc. ex Lindl. = *T. marginata.*

T. fragrans (Lindl.) Rchb. f. Lvs to 30×7cm, oblong-ligulate to oblong-lanceolate. Infl. to 30cm, pendent, few-fld; tep. to 4×0.8cm, white or light green, narrowly linear-lanceolate, undulate; lip to 3cm, white with a central golden-yellow blotch, erose-undulate. Winter. W Indies, Venez., Colomb., Ecuad., Peru, Boliv.

T. galeottiana A. Rich. Resembles *T. tortilis* except tep. yellow to olive-brown, edged pale green, lanceolate; lip striped and barred purple-crimson, throat pale yellow, margins white, disc deep yellow, sometimes spotted red-brown. Late summer–autumn. Mex.

T. kienastiana Rchb. f. = *T. suavis.*

T. laxa (Lindl.) Rchb. f. Lvs to 40×5cm, linear-oblong to oblong-elliptic. Infl. to 30cm, erect to pendent, few to several-fld; tep. to 3.6×0.5cm, dull rose tinted or striped green or buff, linear-lanceolate; lip to 2.6cm, white to white-green. Autumn–early winter. Venez., Colomb. Peru.

T. leucoxantha L.O. Williams. Lvs to 20×6cm, elliptic-lanceolate. Infl. to 7cm, arching to pendent, 1 to few-fld; tep. to 3.5×1cm, white, oblanceolate; lip to 3.5cm, white blotched yellow, undulate. Summer. Panama.

T. maculata Rchb. f. Lvs to 14×3cm, elliptic-lanceolate to oblong-lanceolate. Infl. to 6cm, arching to pendent, 1-, rarely 2-fld; tep. to 4×0.6cm, linear-lanceolate, pale yellow to olive, strong twisted; lip to 4cm, white, throat yellow striped red, undulate. Mostly winter. Guat., Panama.

T. marginata Henfr. Lvs to 30×5cm, lanceolate to elliptic-lanceolate. Infl. arching to pendent, few-fld; tep. to 6×1cm oblanceolate; fleshy pink to red, margins strongly undulate; lip to 8cm, white, deep red-rose within, undulate. Guat. to Colomb.

T. oicophylax Rchb. f. Lvs to 12×3cm, oblong-lanceolate. Infl. to 16cm, arching to pendent, 1- to few-fld; tep. 5×0.7cm, translucent pale green, linear-lanceolate; lip to 5cm, white, pale yellow at base, undulate. Venez., Colomb.

T. powellii Schltr. = *T. maculata.*

T. suavis Lindl. & Paxt. Lvs to 40×8cm, elliptic-lanceolate to elliptic-oblong. Infl. short, pendent, few-fld; tep. to 5.5×1cm, white or cream-white, spotted pale violet-rose or red, lanceolate, undulate; lip to 6.5cm, white or cream-white, spotted violet-rose or spotted and lined yellow on disc (*T. kienastiana*), throat yellow or yellow-orange, undulate-crisped. Mostly spring. Costa Rica, Panama, Colomb.

T. subulata (Sw.) Rchb. f. = *Leucohyle subulata.*

T. tortilis Lindl. Lvs to 22×5cm, elliptic-lanceolate to elliptic-oblanceolate. Infl. 4–10cm, arching to pendent, 1–2-fld; tep. to 8×1cm, off-white tinted pale lavender to fleshy purple-brown or yellow-grey with livid blotches, linear, strongly spirally twisted; lip to 6.5cm, white to pale yellow, throat yellow spotted brown or crimson, crisped, undulate. Winter. Mex., Guat., Hond., El Salvador.

T. turialvae Rchb. f. Lvs to 20×5cm, elliptic-lanceolate. Infl. short, pendent, 1- to few-fld; tep. to 3×0.8cm, white or clear yellow, lanceolate to ovate-lanceolate; lip to 4cm, white to yellow, throat lined or spotted orange-brown, undulate. Summer. Costa Rica, Panama.

T. wagneri (Rchb. f.) Rchb. f. = *T. fragrans.*

Trichosalpinx Luer. Orchidaceae. Tufted or sprawling epiphytic orchids. Pbs 0. St. erect, slender terminating in 1 lf. Rac. term.; fls small, resupinate; dors. sep. free, lat. sep. free or connate; pet. smaller; lip simple to trilobed. C & S Amer. Z10.

T. ciliaris (Lindl.) Luer. Lvs to 6.5×1.5cm, linear-lanceolate to elliptic. Infl. to 2.5cm, few-fld; fls purple-red, sometimes yellow-green; dors. sep. to 4×2mm, ovate-oblong, concave, ciliate; pet. minute; lip to 2×1mm, simple, oblong-spathulate, ciliate. Mex. to Costa Rica.

T. dura (Lindl.) Luer. Lvs to 2×0.6cm, ovate to elliptic-oblong. Infl. to 8cm, many-fld; dors. sep. to 4mm, ovate-lanceolate, deeply concave; pet. to 2mm; lip subequal to pet., oblong to ovate-oblong. Peru, Ecuad.

→*Pleurothallis.*

Trichosanthes L. Cucurbitaceae. 15 climbing ann. or perenn. herbs. Tendrils simple or 2–5-fid. Lvs 2–5-lobed or simple. ♂ fls white, usually racemose; cal. cylindric, 5-lobed; cor. rotate, lobes 5, fimbriate or deeply laciniate; sta. 3. ♀ fls solitary or clustered; ovary inferior, stigmas 3, entire or 2-fid. Fr. ovoid or globose, fleshy, smooth. Indomal. to Pacific. Z10 unless specified.

T. anguina L. = *T. cucumerina* var. *anguina.*

T. bracteata (Lam.) Voigt = *T. tricuspidata.*

T. colubrina Jacq. f. = *T. cucumerina* var. *anguina.*

T. cordata Roxb. Perenn. climber; roots tuberous. Tendrils usually simple. Lvs 12–20cm, broadly ovate-cordate, entire to angular-lobed. Fr. globose, bright red streaked orange. Summer. Indomal.

T. cucumerina L. Ann. Tendrils 2–3-fid. Lvs 6–13cm diam., orbicular-reniform to broadly ovate, 5–7-lobed, slightly toothed. Fr. ovoid, conical, 5–6cm. Summer. India to Malaysia, Aus. var. *anguina* (L.) Haines. SERPENT CUCUMBER; CLUB GOURD; SNAKE GOURD; VIPER GOURD. Lvs 10–15cm, shallowly to deeply 3–5-lobed. Fr. 30–200cm, elongate, cylindrical, twisted, striped white when young, orange when ripe. Summer. India to Pak.

T. cucumeroides Maxim. ex Franch. & Savat. = *T. ovigera.*

T. dioica Roxb. Perenn. Tendrils 2-fid, short. Lvs 7–10cm, ovate-oblong, lobed, sinuate-dentate, cordate. Fr. oblong, 5–12cm, orange-red, smooth. Summer. Indomal.

T. foetidissima Jacq. = *Kedrostis foetidissima.*

T. japonica Reg. = *T. kirilowii* var. *japonica.*

T. kirilowii Maxim. Perenn. Tendrils 3–5-fid. Lvs 10–12cm, orbicular, often deeply 5-lobed, lobulate. Fr. to 10cm, ovoid to oblong, orange-red. China, Mong., Vietnam. var. *japonica* (Miq.) Kitam. Lvs ovate to orbicular, 3–5-lobed. Fr. to 10cm, ovoid-globose, yellow. Jap. Z9.

T. ovigera Bl. SNAKE GOURD. Perenn. Tendrils 2-fid, short. Lvs 10–15cm, broadly ovate, cordate, entire or 3-lobed, denticulate. Fr. ovoid, 4–7cm, red. Summer. India, Burm., Malaysia, Java.

T. palmata Roxb. non L. = *T. tricuspidata.*

T. palmata L. non Roxb. = *Ceratosanthes palmata.*

T. tricuspidata Lour. Perenn. Tendrils often 2-fid. Lvs 9–18cm, ovate, pentagonal or deeply 3–5-lobed, denticulate. Fr. 6–9×2.5–6cm, subglobose, red streaked orange. Asia, Indomal., Aus.

T. tuberosa Roxb. non Willd. = *Ceratosanthes palmata.*

→*Gymnopetalum.*

Trichosma Lindl.

T. coronaria Lindl. = *Eria coronaria.*

T. suavis Lindl. = *Eria coronaria.*

Trichostema Gronov. ex L. BLUE CURLS. Labiatae. 16 aromatic, ann. herbs or small shrubs. Lvs entire. Fls in axillary cymes becoming racemose; cal. equally 5-lobed, campanulate; cor. bilabiate, tube usually slender, geniculate and curved below the limb; sta. 4, long-exserted. N Amer.

T. arizonicum A. Gray. Subshrub to 1m. Lvs ovate. Infl. cymose, in upper lf axils; cor. 2× length of cal. N Mex., Ariz. and New Mex. Z6.

T. lanatum Benth. WOOLLY BLUE CURLS; CALIFORNIA ROMERO. Shrub, 50–150cm. Lvs 2.5–7cm, linear-lanceolate, glab. above, lanate beneath. Infl. a whorled spike to 40cm, covered in blue, pink or white wool; cor. blue, tube 9–14mm, tomentose. Calif.

T. lanceolatum Benth. TURPENTINE CAMPHOR WEED. Ann. to 45cm. Lvs 2–5cm, lanceolate, villous-pubesc., gland. Infl. often unstalked, cymose; cor. light blue, tube abruptly recurved towards the apex. Late summer. W US.

T. ovatum Curran. ALKALI BLUE CURLS. Erect ann. to 50cm. Lvs 1.5cm, ovate, apiculate, villous. Cor. 6–8mm, tube somewhat exserted. Calif.

T. parishii Vasey = *T. lanatum.*

Trichostigma A. Rich. Phytolaccaceae. 3 erect or climbing shrubs. Lvs oval or elliptic, entire. Fls racemose; sep. free, reflexed in fr.; pet. 0; sta. 8–25. Fr. globose, berry-like. Trop. S Amer. Z10.

T. peruvianum H. Walter. Erect to scrambling shrub to 2m. St. slender, angular, purple-red. Lvs 25cm, elliptic, velvety grey-green above, purple-maroon beneath, veins deeply sunken. Fls small, white, in long pendulous rac. Andes.

Trichotosia Bl. Orchidaceae. 50 epiphytic orchids. Rhiz. creeping. Pbs to 80cm, stem-like. Lvs to 15cm, paired or several clothing pb., rac. nodal, arching or pendulous; sep. red-hirsute beneath, green, cream or pale pink above; lip entire or weakly trilobed, often papillose. India, Malaysia, Thail. Z10.

T.dasyphylla (Parish & Rchb. f.) Kränzl. Lvs elliptic to obovate. Infl. to 5cm; fls green-yellow, disc on lip with 2 maroon patches. India, Nepal, Vietnam, Thail.

T.ferox Bl. Lvs lanceolate hirsute. Infl. to 10cm; sep. redpubesc., lip white or pale yellow edged red. Malaysia, Thail., Borneo.

T.velutina (Lodd. ex Lindl.) Kränzl. Lvs to 75cm, oblonglanceolate downy. Infl. to 2cm; fls green-white or cream to pale pink, lip white-yellow, base often marked purple. Burm., Malaysia, Vietnam, Borneo.

T.vestita (Lindl.) Kränzl. Lvs lanceolate, hirsute. Infl. to 15.5cm, flexuous; sep. orange-red, hisute curved, pet. and lip white. Malaysia.

→*Eria.*

Tricuspidaria Ruiz & Pav.
T.dependens Ruiz & Pav. = *Crinodendron patagua.*
T.hookeriana auct. = *Crinodendron hookeranum.*
T.lanceolata Miq. = *Crinodendron hookeranum.*

Tricyrtis Wallich. TOAD LILY. Liliaceae (Tricyrtidaceae). 16 perenn. herbs. Rhiz. creeping. St. erect or arched. Lvs usually cauline, ovate to lanceolate, alt., sometimes amplexicaul or subsesile, ± plicate. Infl. terminal or in upper lf axils; fls solitary or cymes, tep. 6, free, outer 3 basally saccate, inner 3 flat. E Himal. to Jap. and Taiwan.

T.affinis Mak. Differs from *T.macropoda* in fls borne on separate stalks. Z6.

T.bakeri Koidz. = *T.latifolia.*
T.dilatata Nak. = *T.macropoda.*

T.flava Maxim. St. 20–30cm, erect, hairy. Lvs to 12.5cm, elliptic to oblanceolate, amplexicaul, blotched. Fls erect, 1 to few, in upper lf axils; tep. to 2.5cm, yellow, with brown-red spots inside. Jap. Z6.

T.flava var. *nana* Mak. = *T.nana.*

T.formosana Bak. St. erect, somewhat hairy. Lvs 1–1.5cm, oblanceolate, veins pubesc. beneath, cordate-amplexicaul. Infl. branched, term., cymose; tep. to 3cm, white to pink with dense crimson spots inside, tinged yellow towards base. Taiwan. 'Amethystina': to 1.2m; fls clustered, amethyst, throat white, speckled maroon, stained yellow. Z7.

T.hirta (Thunb.) Hook. St. thickly hairy, to 80cm. Lvs 15cm, lanceolate, pale green, cordate-amplexicaul, pubesc. Fls erect, solitary or 2–3 per axil; tep. 2.5–3cm, white with large purple spots. Jap. Plants in cult. under this name are sometimes *T.macropoda.* 'Alba': fls white flushed green. 'Lilac Towers': as 'White Towers', but fls lilac. 'Miyazaki': to 90cm; st. arching; lvs pointed; fls white spotted lilac, all along st. 'Miyazaki Gold': as 'Miyazaki', but lvs edged gold. 'White Towers': to 60cm; st. arching; fls in most leaf-axils, white. Z5.

T.japonica Miq. = *T.hirta.*
T.kyusyuensis Masum. = *T.flava.*
T.kyusyuensis var. *pseudoflava* Masum. = *T.nana.*

T.latifolia Maxim. St. 40–90cm, erect, hairy. Lvs 8–15cm, broadly ovate, heart-shaped at base, amplexicaul. Infl. erect, cymose, branched, in upper lf axils; tep. 2.5–3cm, yellow to yellowgreen, spotted purple. Jap., China. Z5.

T.macrantha Maxim. To 90cm, arched, brown-pubesc. Lvs to 10cm, ovate-oblong to lanceolate, amplexicaul. Fls axill., pendulous; tep. 3cm, yellow with chocolate spots inside. Jap. Z6.

T.macranthopsis Masum. St. 40–80cm, arching in fl. Lvs 7–17cm, narrowly oblong-ovate, cordate or amplexicaul at base, glossy green, subglabr., or hairy on veins. Fls pendulous, 1–4 per axil; tep. 3–4cm, oblanceolate, clear yellow with fine brown spots. Jap.

T.macropoda Miq. St. to 70cm, erect, occas. pubesc. Lvs 10–12.5cm, oblong to ovate, rounded at base, minutely pubesc. beneath. Fls to 2cm, in erect branching cymes; tep. to 2cm, white-purple with small purple spots. China. Z5.

T.macropoda var. *glabrescens* Koidz. = *T.macropoda.*
T.macropoda var. *hirsuta* Koidz. = *T.macropoda.*

T.maculata D. Don. Close to *T.macropoda*, differs in its looser infl. and spreading tep. Z5.

T.nana Yatabe. St. 5–15cm, shortly hairy. Lvs lanceolate to ovate or elliptic, blotched dark green, in basal rosette. Fls erect, solitary in leaf-axils; tep. to 2cm, yellow with brown-red spots, banded orange-brown across base. Jap. Z6.

T.ohsumiensis Masum. St. 20–50cm, erect, subglabr. Lvs 5–20cm, elliptic to oblong, amplexicaul, glab., pale green. Fls erect, 1–2 per axil; tep. 2.5cm, narrow-ovate or obovate-oblong, primrose-yellow, faintly spotted. Jap.

T.perfoliata Masum. St. 50–70cm, arched, glab. Lvs 2.5–4cm, lanceolate, perfoliate. Fls ascending, solitary in lf axils; tep. 2.5–3cm, yellow with red-purple spots inside. Jap. Z6.

T.puberula Nak. & Kit. = *T.latifolia.*
T.stolonifera Matsum. = *T.formosana.*
T.yatabeana Masum. = *T.flava.*

Tridactyle Schltr. Orchidaceae. 36 epiphytic or lithophytic, monopodial orchids. Lvs distichous, sheathing st. usually ligulate and coriaceous. Fls spurred, 2-ranked on short rac. in lf axils or on lower, bare st. Trop. & S Afr. Z10.

T.anthomaniaca (Rchb. f.) Summerh. St. long, pendent. Lvs 4.5–7.5×1–1.5cm, oblong, slightly succulent. Infl. about 1cm, 3–4-fld; fls straw-coloured; tep. 5×1.5–2mm, lanceolate; lip 5×2mm, entire, rhomboid; spur 10mm. Trop. Afr. (widespread).

T.bicaudata (Lindl.) Schltr. St. 30–50cm, usually erect. Lvs about 15×1.5cm, ligulate, slightly folded. Infl. to 10cm, 18–20-fld; fls yellow or green-yellow; tep. 4×1.5mm, oblong; pet. narrower; lip 5–6mm, trilobed, midlobe narrowly triangular; spur 1.5–2mm. Trop. Afr. (widespread), S Afr.

T.citrina Cribb. St. to 6cm, erect. Lvs 3–4, forming a fan, 7–14×1–1.5cm folded. Infl. 9–10cm, to 10-fld; fls creamy yellow or green-yellow; dors. sep. 10×2.5mm, lanceolate, lat. sep. slightly wider; pet. similar to lat. sep.; lip 15mm, trilobed, midlobe lanceolate; spur 4–5cm. Tanz., Malawi, Zam.

T.gentilii (De Wildeman) Schltr. St. long, branched, pendent. Lvs ligulate, to 10×1.5cm. Infl. 6cm, 7–12-fld; fls pale green, scented in the evening; dors. sep. 8×2mm, lanceolate, lat. sep. longer and wider; pet. longer and narrower; lip 15–18mm, trilobed; spur 5–8cm. Trop. & subtrop. Afr.

T.tricuspis (Bol.) Schltr. St. short and erect. Lvs toward top of st., 7–13×1.5–2cm, ligulate, slightly folded. Infl. 6–15cm manyfld; fls green-white or yellow-white; dors. sep. 7×1mm, lanceolate; pet. slightly shorter; lip 8mm, trilobed, midlobe triangular; spur 15mm. Trop. Afr. (widespread).

T.tridactylites (Rolfe) Schltr. St. to 60cm, erect or pendent. Lvs 16–18×1.5–2cm, distichous, ligulate. Infl. 4–5cm, 8–10-fld; fls pale straw-orange or green-cream, scented; dors. sep. 6×2mm, lanceolate, pet. shorter; lip 5mm, trilobed, midlobe triangular; spur 9–10mm. Trop. Afr. (widespread).

T.tridentata (Harv.) Schltr. St. woody, to 40cm, erect or pendent. Lvs to 10, 7–10cm×2–4mm, terete, grooved. Infl. 15–20mm, 4–8-fld; fls dull straw-orange; dors. sep. 3–3.5×1.5mm, ovate, lat. sep. slightly shorter and broader; pet. narrower; lip 4×1mm, trilobed, midlobe triangular; spur 6–9mm. Trop. Afr. (widespread), S Afr.

T.wakefieldii Rolfe = *Solenangis wakefieldii.*
→*Angraecum.*

Tridax L. Compositae. 26 sp. of ann. to perenn. herbs. Cap. radiate, small, solitary or few in cymose pan.; receptacle flat to convex; phyllary tips often tinged purple; ray flts 2-lipped, outer lip 2–3-toothed, inner lip smaller, 1–2-lobed; disc flts yellow. N Amer., esp. Mex.

T.bicolor A. Gray. Viscous ann. to 50cm, short-hirsute. Lvs to 9cm, ovate to lanceolate, serrate-dentate to entire, short-pilose, viscid, petiole to 2.5cm. Cap. 2.5cm diam.; ray flts 10, 14mm, rose or purple; disc flts yellow. Summer. Mex.

T.coronopifolium (Kunth) Hemsl. Ann. to perenn., to 30cm, pubesc. Lvs to 7cm, 1–2-pinnately dissected or lobed, pubesc. Cap. to 1.5cm diam.; ray flts to 8m, short, yellow; disc flts yellow. Summer. Mex. Z9.

T.trilobata (Cav.) Hemsl. Ann., to 35cm, hirsute. Lvs to 9cm, ovate to oblong, 3- to pinnately lobed, sometimes toothed, sparsely hirsute, petioles to 3cm. Cap. to 2cm diam.; ray flts 6–8, to 8mm, orange-yellow; disc flts yellow. Summer. Mex.
→*Galinsoga.*

Tridentea Haw. Asclepiadaceae. 17 dwarf, succulent, perenn. herbs. St. clumped, erect to prostrate, tuberculate, with toothed angles. Lvs subulate, decid. Fls borne laterally; cor. flat to campanulate, wrinkled, lobes with motile, clavate cilia; outer corona lobes with a large central tooth and a shorter tooth on each side, inner lobes with 2 club-shaped or slender horns. S Afr., Nam., Bots. Z9.

T.aperta (Masson) Leach. Fls 2.5–3.5cm diam.; pedicel 5cm, base tubular; lobes oblong, blunt, margins replicate, interior finely papillose, dark brown at base, off-white or yellow-white above with red-brown furrows and spots. W Cape.

T.baylissii (Leach) Leach. Fls in clusters; cor. 12–15mm, 12–13mm diam.; campanulate, exterior yellow below, deep purple toward lobe tips, glab., interior red-purple, glab. with soft silky sheen, lobes grooved. Cape Prov.

T. choanantha (Lavranos & Hall) Leach. Fls 2–6 together; cor. campanulate, tube 16×11mm, cupular to 5-angled, exterior pink, interior red-purple, glab., lobes triangular-acute, 6×7mm, revolute. Cape Prov.

T. dwequensis (Lückh.) Leach. Fls 2–4 together; cor. 4cm diam., tube campanulate, 12×12mm, exterior glab., light green, lobes 13mm, spreading, triangular, lemon yellow with red spots, tube with smaller spots, minutely papillose. Cape Prov.

T. gemmiflora (Masson) Haw. Fls 1–4, near st. base; cor. 4.5–10cm diam., flat, green, glab. and nerved below, black-brown to violet-brown, finely rugose above, lobes ovate, acute, 3.5cm, blotched yellow at base and marbled with paler brown, margins ciliate. S Afr., Nam.

T. herrei (Nel) Leach. Fls solitary; cor. 3–4cm diam., campanulate, lobes 15mm, lanceolate, exterior buff, interior white, wrinkled with the sapces between light brown-purple, paler in the tube. W Cape.

T. jucunda (N.E. Br.) Leach. Fls 1–3; cor. 2–3.5cm diam., pale green marked purple below, cream blotched sienna above, flat, glab., tube obconic, lobes to 7mm, triangular-ovate, finely wrinkled, markings merging toward margins, cilia purple. S Afr. var. *cincta* (Marloth) Leach. Fls solitary; cor. 2–4–3.6cm diam., tube hemispheric, lobes 10–5–6mm, ovate, tapered, rough, ochre densely blotched chestnut-brown, margins concolorous. 1.5–2mm wide. var. *dinteri* (A. Berger) Leach. Inner lobes shorter, with a prominent wing-like dors. projection.

T. longii (Lückh.) Leach. Fl. solitary; cor. to 2.5cm diam., glab., dull green below, yellow to cinnamon above, wrinkled and lined paler yellow around mouth of short tube, lobes to 8mm, ovate-acute, cilia purple. Cape Prov.

T. longipes (Lückh.) Leach. Fl. solitary; cor. 3–7cm diam., flat, pale green and glab. below, tube 5-angled, about 2mm deep, with inflated scales around mouth, lobes 2.4cm, base purple with broad, smooth white rugae, often coalescing, apical two-thirds magenta, dark maroon or brown, margins red-ciliate towards base. Nam.

T. marientalensis (Nel) Leach. Fls solitary to few, near st. bases, musky; cor. to 7.5cm diam., yellow-green, smooth with 6 dark green ribs below, pale yellow above, annulus at tube mouth covered in white-yellow papillae, lobes 2.5cm, triangular, reflexed, mottled purple, papillose at base, black-purple toward apex, margins with long, white to purple cilia. S Afr.

T. pachyrrhiza (Dinter) Leach. Fls in clusters, 7–7.5cm diam.; cor. lobes 2cm, angular, ovate, exterior brown-red, interior striped red on yellow ground or concolorous, velvety black or green-yellow densely blotched purple, cilia red. Nam., W Cape.

T. parvipuncta (N.E. Br.) Leach. Fls several, near st. apex; cor. to 3cm diam., flat to shallow-campanulate, glab., pale green, blotched maroon below, pale sulphur-yellow, spotted red or purple above, lobes to 1cm, triangular-ovate, margins red-brown, purple clavate-ciliate. Cape Prov. var. *truncata* (Lückh.) Leach. Lobe margins not ciliate, tips truncate.

T. peculiaris (Lückh.) Leach. Fls 1–3 together from base of young shoots; cor. 2.5–4cm diam., rotate, dull yellow-green with dense, pale purple-brown blotches, or yellow, minutely papillose, lobes 7.5–15mm, acute, with motile, purple hairs along margin. W Cape.

T. pedunculata (Masson) Leach. Fls 5–6, long-stalked; cor. 4–4.5cm diam., flat, v. deeply lobed, with an ash-white centre, tube 2mm, 5-ridged, dark maroon, with globular scales at mouth, lobes to 3cm, lanceolate, brown or olive-green to yellow-green, with clusters of dark red cilia in sinuses and at lobe bases. W Cape.

T. ruschiana (Dinter) Leach. Fls solitary or paired; cor. broad, campanulate, 3.6cm diam., lobes 14mm, green-red, dark red below with dense, black-red, clavate hairs at base, then white with red spots, lobes scarred above, red-brown, margins between lobes with curly red-brown clavate hairs. Nam.

T. umdausensis (Nel) Leach. Fls 1–2; cor. to 2.5cm diam., about 5mm deep, deeply lobed, yellow-green, with darker margins and a red central vein below, tube magenta inside, with radial, white, shallow rugulae, lobes to 11mm, ovate-lanceolate, acute, bases lime-green, tips darker, sometime bronze. Namaqualand.

T. vetula (Masson) Haw. = *Stapelia vetula*.

T. virescens (N.E. Br.) Leach. Fls in clusters of 6–9; cor. 2.5–3cm diam., deeply 5-cleft, lobes 10mm, ovate-tapered, curved slightly inwards, off-white blotched red, interior yellow-green, roughly papillose. Nam., Cape Prov. (Karroo).

→*Caralluma, Orbea, Stapelia* and *Stapelianthus*.

Trident Maple *Acer buergerianum.*

Trientalis L. CHICKWEED; WINTERGREEN. Primulaceae. 4 perenn. herbs. Rhiz. slender; st. simple, erect. Lvs in term. whorls or

smaller, sparse below. Fls 5(–7)-merous, solitary, axill.; pedicels long, slender; cal. cut nearly to base; cor. rotate, cut nearly to base; fil. long, slender, united at base. Summer. N temp.

T. americana Pursh = *T. borealis.*

T. arctica Fisch. ex Hook. St. to 20cm. Apex sparsely gland.-pubesc. Lvs to 4cm, obovate, entire. Cor. white, to 0.5cm diam., lobes obovate or lanceolate; anth. orange. N Russia, N US, Jap. Z5.

T. borealis Raf. STARFLOWER. St. to 22cm, naked or scaly below. Lvs to 10cm, lanceolate, minutely crenulate. Cor. white or pale pink, to 1cm diam., lobes obovate or oblong. N Amer. Z4.

T. europaea L. St. to 30cm, glab. Lvs to 9cm, obovate to lanceolate, entire to minutely dentate at apex. Cor. to 2cm, diam., white or tinged pink, lobes ovate. N Eur. Z4.

T. europaea var. *latifolia* (Hook.) Torr. = *T. latifolia.*

T. latifolia Hook. St. to 15cm. Lvs to 7cm, ovate, entire. Cor. to 1.75cm diam., rose pink to white. W N Amer. Z3.

Trifoliate Orange *Poncirus trifoliata.*

Trifolium L. CLOVER. Leguminosae. 230 ann., bienn. or perenn. herbs, sometimes woody. Lvs with palmately arranged lfts; usually stipulate. Fls small, pea-like in axill. or term. infl., often capitate, spike-like or umbellate. Temp. and subtrop. regions excluding Australasia.

T. alpinum L. ALPINE CLOVER. Glab., tufted, taprooted perenn. St. v. short. Lfts 3, to 4cm, lanceolate or linear, petioles to 5cm. Peduncles 0.5–15cm; fls strongly fragrant; cor. pink, purple or cream. Summer. S Eur. 'Album': fls off-white. Z3.

T. aureum Pollich. Erect, robust, downy bienn., 20–60cm. Lfts 3, to 1.5cm, oblong-ovate or rhombic, brown-yellow. Peduncles to 5cm; cor. 0.6–0.7cm, golden-yellow. Cauc., N Iran, Sib. Z3.

T. badium Schreb. BROWN TREFOIL. Taprooted perenn. to 25cm. St. many, ascending, hirsute or glabrescent. Lfts 3, 1–2cm, elliptic, rhombic or deltate. Infl. to 2.5cm; cor. 0.7–0.9cm, golden-yellow. C & S Eur. Z4.

T. dubium Sibth. SUCKLING CLOVER; LESSER YELLOW TREFOIL; LOW HOP CLOVER; YELLOW CLOVER; SHAMROCK. Erect or ascending ann., 20–40cm; st. hirsute. Lfts 3, to 1cm, obcordate or obovate. Infl. to 1cm, hemispherical; cor. yellow 0.3–0.4cm. Spring–autumn. Eur., extending E to Cauc., not extreme N.

T. incarnatum L. ITALIAN CLOVER; CRIMSON CLOVER. Erect to ascending ann., 20–50cm; st. downy. Lfts 3, 1–2cm, obovate-cuneate to suborbicular, denticulate toward apex. Infl. 1–1.5cm, oblong; cor. 1–1.2cm, yellow-white to deep red. Summer. S & W Eur.

T. macrocephalum (Pursh) Poir. Shrubby, rhizomatous erect perenn. to 30cm. Lfts 5–9, to 2–5cm, oblanceolate to obcordate. Infl. to 5cm diam., capitate, usually term.; cor. 2.5cm, pink. Eur., C US. Z4.

T. nanum Torr. Tufted bushy perenn. to 8cm. Lfts to 1cm, narrowly oblanceolate, finely denticulate. Fls usually in groups of 3; peduncles to 3cm; cor. rose-pink to purple-red. US. Z4.

T. pallescens Schreb. Glab., tufted, taprooted perenn. Lfts 3, 0.6–2cm, elliptic or obovate, bright green. Infl. 1.5–2.5cm, globose at first; peduncles 2–9cm, stout; fls sweetly fragrant; cor. 0.6–1cm, yellow-white to pink. C & S Eur. (mts). Z5.

T. pannonicum L. HUNGARIAN CLOVER. Bushy erect perenn. Lvs near base with obovate lfts, those above with oblong-lanceolate lfts. Infl. 10cm, capitate; fls yellow. E Eur. Z5.

T. parryi A. Gray. Low-growing tufted perenn. Lfts to 4.5cm, elliptic to obovate, entire or dentate. Peduncles 5–15cm; conspicuous bracts; cor. purple. W US. Z4.

T. pratense L. RED CLOVER; PURPLE CLOVER. Erect to decumbent short-lived perenn., 20–60cm. Lfts 1.5–3cm, obovate, or oblong-lanceolate to suborbicular, hirsute beneath. Infl. to 2.2cm wide, globose to ovoid, usually sessile; cor. 1.3–1.8cm, red-purple to pink, sometimes cream. Summer. Eur., except extreme N & S; nat. US. 'Susan Smith' ('Dolly North', 'Goldnet': lfts laced gold; fls pink. 'Silverwhite': fls pure white. var. *sativum* Schreb. More robust, to 70cm, with larger lfts and fl. heads. Commonly grown forage crop. Z6.

T. procumbens L. = *T. dubium.*

T. repens L. WHITE CLOVER; DUTCH CLOVER; SHAMROCK. Glab. or glabrescent perenn., 10–30cm, st. creeping. Lfts 3(–4), 1–2cm, broadly obovate to orbicular, truncate or notched serrulate. Infl. 1.5–3.5cm, umbellate, subglobose, fragrant; cor. 0.8–1.3cm, white or pink. Spring–autumn. Eur., nat. in US. 'Atropurpureum': habit dwarf; lfts red tinted bronze edged green. 'Aureum': lfts large, golden-veined. 'Purpurascens': robust form with long rhiz. and large, erect, remote lvs, the lfts each with a persistent central zone of dark maroon covering almost the entire blade. 'Purpurascens Quadrifolium' ('Tetraphyllum Purpurascens'): lfts usually 4, deep purple tinted brown, edged green; fls white. 'Quadrifolium': lfts usually 4, chocolate brown; fls white. 'Quinquefolium' ('Pentaphyllum'):

lfts usually 5, chocolate brown, golden-veined; fls yellow. 'Variegatum': lfts golden-veined; fls pinky red. 'Wheatfen': lfts purple; fls red. Z4.

T. thalii Vill. Similar to *T. pallescens*, but st. shorter. Lfts obovate, dull green. Peduncles 5–12cm; standard to 3cm. Alps, Apennines, Pyren. and mts of N Spain. Z5.

T. uniflorum L. Rhizomatous, procumbent perenn., 5–10cm. Lfts 0.4–1cm, orbicular, obovate or rhombic, strongly veined with cusped teeth, often adpressed-pubesc. beneath. Infl. 1, 2 or 3-fld; cor. 1.5–3cm yellow-white to pink, standard tinted purple-blue, keel purple. Spring–autumn. E Medit. to Sicily. Z7.

T. virginicum Small. Densely tufted, st. to 10cm, arising from a stout rootstock. Lfts 2–7cm, narrowly oblong to oblanceolate, pilose. Peduncles v. pilose, short; infl. 2–3cm, globose; cor. white. Summer. E US. Z5.

Trifurcia Herb.
T. amatorum (Wright) Goldbl. = *Herbertia amatorum*.
T. caerulea Herb. = *Alophia drummondii*.
T. lahue (Molina) Goldbl. = *Herbertia lahue*.
T. pulchella (Sweet) Goldbl. = *Herbertia pulchella*.

Trigger Plant *Stylidium graminifolium*.
Triglav Gentian *Gentiana terglouensis*.

Triglochin L. ARROW GRASS. Juncaginaceae. 15 perenn. or ann. herbs of wet places and salt marshes. St. stout. Lvs sheathing, semi-terete, linear-ligulate. Fls small, in scapose rac.; perianth of 6 sepaloid seg. Cosmop.
T. bulbosa L. To 20cm+. Lvs to 30×0.4cm. Scape smooth, erect; fls to 2.5mm, tinted purple. Medit., Asia Minor, S Afr. Z7.
T. maritima L. To 60cm. Lvs to 50×0.4cm. Scape curved; fls to 4mm, green edged purple. Cosmop. Z5.
T. palustris L. To 70cm. Lvs to 30×0.2cm, channelled. Fls to 3mm. Cosmop. Z5.
T. striata Ruiz & Pav. To 60cm. Lvs to 25×0.5cm. Scape to 20cm, usually angled; fls to 2mm. Americas, Afr., Aus., nat. Port. Z8.

Trigonachras Radlk. Sapindaceae. 9 trees. Lvs pinnate. Fls in axill. and term. pan., 5-merous; pet. with ciliate basal scales; sta. 8. Fr. drupaceous, 3-angled, 3-celled. Malay Penins. Z10.
T. acuta (Hiern) Radlk. Lvs 15–30cm, lfts to 11cm, 11–15, oblong-lanceolate. Fr. to 5cm, pyriform, orange, tomentose.

Trigonanthe (Schltr.) Brieger = *Dryadella*.

Trigonella L. Leguminosae (Papilionoideae). 80 ann. or perenn. herbs, frequently annual. Lvs trifoliolate; stipules adnate to petiole. Fls solitary or in heads, umbels or short rac.; cal. tube short, campanulate, lobes ovate; pet. distinct, standard obovate or oblong, wings oblong, keel oblong. OW.
T. caerulea (L.) Ser. Ann., to 60cm. Lfts ovate, toothed; stipules toothed at base. Fls blue and white in dense, long-stalked, globose heads. Summer. S & C Eur.
T. foenum-graecum L. FENUGREEK; GREEK CLOVER; GREEK HAY. Ann. to 60cm. Lfts obovate, toothed at apex; stipules entire. Fls off-white, 1–2 per axil. Summer. S Eur., Asia.

Trigonidium Lindl. Orchidaceae. 11 epiphytic or lithophytic orchids. Pbs slightly compressed, grooved, usually 2-leaved at apex. Lvs coriaceous or subcoriaceous, conduplicate. Fls solitary, large, arising from base of pbs and rhiz.; sep. united at base forming a triquetrous tube, free portions spreading or reflexed; pet. smaller than sep.; lip smaller than pet., trilobed. Mex. to Braz. & Peru.
T. acuminatum Batem. ex Lindl. Pbs to 4cm. Lvs to 27×1.5cm, linear-oblanceolate. Infl. to 18cm; tep. straw-coloured to green-brown, interior striped and veined deep brown, sometimes wholly purple-brown; sep. to 28×10mm, oblanceolate to ovate-lanceolate; pet. to 12×3mm, oblong-obovate; lip to 8×4.5mm, concave, midlobe obovate, rounded. Venez., Colomb., Peru, Surinam, Braz., Guyana.
T. brachyglossum (A. Rich. & Gal.) Schltr. = *T. egertonianum*.
T. egertonianum Batem. ex Lindl. Pbs to 9×4cm. Lvs to 60×3cm, linear-lanceolate. Infl. to 30cm; tep. yellow-green to pink-tan flecked and veined brown, dors. sep. to 4.5×2cm, elliptic-oblanceolate to obovate-spathulate; pet. to 22×6mm, oblong-lanceolate; lip to 10×4mm, yellow-tan or pink-tan with brown venation, midlobe broadly ovate, verrucose. Mostly spring. Mex. to Panama and Colomb.
T. lankesteri Ames. Pbs to 8×4cm. Lvs to 27×4cm, oblong-lanceolate. Infl. to 16cm; sep. to 5×2cm, light green-brown to cinnamon, elliptic-oblanceolate; pet. to 2.5×1cm, green-brown, sometimes spotted purple; lip to 15×5mm, white spotted brown, midlobe ovate, verrucose below. Spring–summer. Costa

Rica, Panama.
T. monophyllum Griseb. = *Neocogniauxia monophylla*.
T. obtusum Lindl. Pbs to 6×4cm. Lvs to 35×6cm, linear-lanceolate to oblanceolate. Infl. to 15cm; sep. to 4.2×1.2cm, yellow-green shaded pale maroon or pale brown veined light maroon, lanceolate or oblong-lanceolate; pet. to 2.2×1.7cm, white veined rose or purple; lip to 1×0.5cm, white marked red-maroon, margins red, midlobe yellow. Venez., Guyanas, Colomb., Boliv., Braz.
T. ringens Lindl. = *Mormolyca ringens*.
T. tenue Lodd. ex Lindl. = *T. acuminatum*.

Trillidium Kunth.
T. govanianum D. Don = *Trillium govanianum*.
T. japonicum Franch. & Savat. = *Kinugasa japonica*.

Trillium L. WOOD LILY; BIRTHROOT; WAKE ROBIN; STINKING BENJAMIN. Liliaceae (Trilliaceae). 30 decid., perenn. herbs. Rhiz. stout, subterranean. St. single, erect, procumbent or scarcely emerging. Lvs 3 in a term. whorl, glab., elliptic to ovate, sometimes mottled, somewhat undulate. Fls solitary, term., at junction of lvs, stalked or sessile; sep. 3, leafy, lanceolate; pet. 3; sta. 6; ovary superior. N Amer., W Himal., NE Asia.
T. albidum Freeman. Related to *T. chloropetalum*. To 50cm. Lvs to 20cm, sessile, lanceolate-ovate, obtuse, mottled silver-white. Fls sessile, fragrant; sep. to 6cm, narrow-ovate, spreading to reflexed; pet. to 10×4.5cm, obovate, semi-erect or incurving, white flushed rose pink at base. Spring. W US. Z6.
T. × amabile Miyabe & Tatew. (*T. smallii* × *T. kamtschaticum*.) Lvs to 12cm, sessile, ovate to rhombic. Pedicels to 6cm, erect; sep. to 3cm, mauve, elliptic; pet. to 2.5cm, dark purple, ovate-orbicular to reduced or 0, fused with or replaced by bright mauve anth. Spring. Jap. Z5.
T. angustipetalum (Torr.) Freeman. To 60cm. Lvs to 20×8.5cm, subsessile, broadly ovate, obtuse, mottled. Fls sessile, aromatic; sep. to 6cm, linear-lanceolate; pet. 5–10cm, narrow lanceolate, erect, maroon. Spring. Calif. Z8.
T. catesbaei Elliott. To 50cm. Lvs to 7cm, subsessile, ovate. Pedicel to 5cm, deflexed below lvs; sep. reflexed; pet. to 5cm, reflexed, ovate to cordate, acuminate, rose pink or darker. Spring. SE US. Z8.
T. cernuum L. To 50cm. Lvs short-petiolate, rhombic, acute. Pedicels to 2cm, deflexed below lvs; pet. to 2cm, undulate, white sometimes flushed rose; anth. dark purple. Spring. E N Amer. Z6.
T. chloropetalum (Torr.) Howell. St. thick, to 50cm. Lvs 10–20cm, sessile, broadly ovate-rhombic, mottled maroon. Fls sessile, fragrant, erect or incurved; pet. obovate, green to yellow to purple. Spring. Calif. var. **giganteum** (Hook. & Arn.) Munz. Pet. white to maroon and red. Z6.
T. cuneatum Raf. St. thick, to 50cm. Lvs to 20cm, sessile, broadly ovate-orbicular, obtuse or acuminate, mottled pale or silver green. Fls sessile, musky; sep. olive green tipped purple; pet. to 5×2.5cm, wedge-shaped, maroon. Spring. SE US. Z6.
T. declinatum (A. Gray) Gleason non Raf. = *T. flexipes*.
T. decumbens Harb. St. minutely pubesc., to 15cm, procumbent. Lvs to 12cm, sessile, ovate-orbicular, mottled silver. Fls sessile; sep. elliptic, to 5cm, tinged maroon; pet. to 10cm, lanceolate, erect, cupped, wavy or recurved, dark maroon often tipped golden-green. Spring. Spring SE US. Z6.
T. discolor Hook. To 18cm. Lvs to 12cm, sessile, elliptic-orbicular, acuminate, mottled jade green. Fls scented, sessile; sep. to 3cm, lanceolate, reflexed; pet. to 5cm, ovate, acute, deflexed, twisted, golden yellow with green or violet basal patches. Spring. SE US. Z6.
T. erectum L. To 50cm. Lvs to 20cm, sessile, broadly ovate. Pedicel to 10cm; fls malodorous; sep. to 5cm, light green suffused red-purple; pet. to 8cm, elliptic, acute, garnet to white. Late spring. E N Amer. 'Ochroleucum' ('Viridiflorum'): fls tinged green. var. **album** Pursh. Pet. white, occas. flushed rose; anth. golden yellow. f. **albiflorum** Hoffm. Fls white, stained lime green. f. **luteum** Lal. Short-stemmed; pet. green-yellow, blood red above. Z4.
T. erythrocarpum Michx. = *T. undulatum*.
T. flexipes Raf. To 40cm. Lvs to 20cm, sessile, ovate, acute. Fls on slender pedicel to 10cm, held horizontally; sep. reflexed; pet. to 5cm, ovate, spreading, white to pale pink. Spring. N US. Z4.
T. gleasonii Fern. = *T. flexipes*.
T. govanianum D. Don. To 20cm. Lvs to 10cm, ovate, acute, dark green. Fls erect on slender pedicel; sep. to 1.5cm, green flushed maroon, linear-lanceolate; pet. to 2×0.5cm, narrow, yellow-green to pale, uneven maroon. Spring. Himal. Z5.
T. grandiflorum (Michx.) Salisb. To 45cm. Lvs subsessile, ovate to orbicular. Fls erect on pedicels to 5cm; sep. to 5cm, dark green; pet. to 8cm, broad-ovate, bases overlapping, then

spreading widely, undulate, opening white, flushing pale pink; anth. golden. Late spring. E N Amer. 'Flore pleno': fls double. 'Roseum': fls flushing pink almost immediately, ageing damask. f. *parvum* Gates. Far smaller with fls ultimately violet-pink. f. *variegatum* Sm. Pet. with bright green midrib or green with white margins. Z5.

T. hibbersonii auct. = *T. ovatum* f. *hibbersonii*.

T. hugeri Small = *T. cuneatum*.

T. japonicum (Franch. & Savat.) Matsum. = *Kinugasa japonica*.

T. kamtschaticum Pall. To 30cm. Lvs to 15cm, sessile, ovate to rhombic, acute. Pedicel erect; sep. to 5cm, ovate-acuminate, dark green; pet. to 4.5cm, ovate, acute, white ageing purple. Early summer. E Asia. Z5.

T. luteum (Muhlenb.) Harb. To 45cm. Lvs to 15cm, sessile, broadly ovate, abrupt-acuminate, silver-mottled. Fls sessile, scented; sep. to 6cm, lanceolate, green; pet. to 9cm, elliptic, cupped, golden or bronzy green. Spring. SE US. Z5.

T. nervosum Elliott = *T. catesbaei*.

T. nivale Riddell. Dwarf, st. erect. Lvs to 3.5cm, petiolate, ovate, deep green. Pedicel to 2.5cm, erect at first; sep. green, to 2cm, lanceolate, pet. to 4cm, brilliant white. Early spring. SE US. Z5.

T. ovatum Pursh. To 50cm. Lvs to 15cm, sessile, rhombic, acute, with 5 conspicuous, sunken veins. Fls erect on pedicel to 8cm, muskily fragrant; sep. to 5cm, green; pet. ovate, spreading, rather than erect to spreading as in *T. grandiflorum*, white later pink or red. Spring. W N Amer. 'Kenmore': fls double, pale pink. f. *hibbersonii* Tayl. & Szcz. Smaller with pet. rose pink fading to white stained pink. Spring. BC. Z5.

T. petiolatum Pursh. To 20cm. Lvs to 15cm, petiolate, ovate, obtuse. Fls sessile; sep. to 5cm, oblanceolate, reflexed; pet. to 5cm, linear, acute, erect, incurved at apex, green flushed purple to maroon. Spring. Midwest US. Z5.

T. recurvatum Beck. To 45cm. Lvs to 8cm, lanceolate-elliptic, petiolate, mottled. Fls sessile; sep. to 4cm, green, lanceolate, sharply reflexed; pet. to 5cm, erect, dark purple rarely, yellow-green, ovate, clawed. Spring. E US. Z5.

T. rivale Wats. To 5cm. Lvs to 3cm, ovate, acute, petioles to 2cm. Fls on erect pedicels to 5cm; sep. to 1.5cm, ovate to oblanceolate, green; pet. to 2.5cm, rhombic to ovate, white flushed pink, spotted purple toward base. Spring. W US. 'Purple Heart': basal markings of pet. form a solid, central 'eye' of colour. Z5.

T. sessile L. 30cm, erect. Lvs to 12cm, sessile, elliptic to orbicular, with dark mottling. Fls sessile, musky; sep. to 4cm, elliptic, green flushed maroon, reflexed; pet. to 4.5cm, erect, lanceolate, maroon. Late spring. NE US. 'Rubrum': fls crimson-purple. 'Snow Queen': fls white. f. *viridiflorum* Beyer. Fls green-bronze to yellow. Z4.

T. sessile hort. non L. = *T. cuneatum*.

T. sessile var. *angustipetalum* Torr. = *T. angustipetalum*.

T. sessile var. *luteum* Muhlenb. = *T. luteum*.

T. smallii Maxim. To 40cm. Lvs to 12cm, sessile, rhombic, acute. Fls on pedicel to 4cm, held obliquely at opening, later upright; sep. green; pet. equal sep. in length, to 2cm, semi-erect, maroon, fleshy, sometimes reduced or 0. Spring. Jap. Z5.

T. stylosum Nutt. = *T. catesbaei*.

T. tschonoskii Maxim. Resembles *T. kamtschaticum* except seldom exceeding 20cm; pet. to 3.5cm; pedicel horizontal. Late spring. NE Asia. Z5.

T. underwoodii Small. To 20cm. Lvs to 15cm, sessile, ovate, acuminate, mottled, lax, somewhat pendent. Fls sessile, malodorous; sep. to 5cm, narrow-ovate, green, outspread; pet. to 6cm, often smaller than sep., elliptic, mauve-maroon. Spring. SE US. Z6.

T. undulatum Willd. To 30cm. Lvs to 15cm, petiolate, narrow-acuminate. Fls on upright pedicel to 3cm; sep. to 1cm, dark green bordered maroon; pet. to 3cm, undulate, white or pale rose pink, stained maroon at base. Late spring. E N Amer. Z4.

T. vaseyi Harb. St. robust, to 60cm. Lvs to 20cm, sessile, rhombic, broad. Fls on nodding pedicel; pet. to 4.5cm, broad, overlapping, spreading to reflexed, dark red to maroon, obtuse. Early summer. SE US. Z6.

T. viride Beck. To 40cm, st. sometimes minutely pubesc. Lvs sessile, lanceolate to elliptic, acute to obtuse, rarely mottled, spotted white above. Fls sessile, foetid; sep. lanceolate, acuminate, to 6cm, reflexed; pet. to 6cm, often less, erect, oblanceolate, somewhat revolute, green-yellow with maroon basal patch or entirely maroon. Spring. N US. Z4.

T. viride Beck var. *luteum* Muhlenb. = *T. luteum*.

→*Trillidium*.

Trimezia Herb. Iridaceae. 5 perenn. herbs. Rhiz. bulbous. Lvs few, usually basal, rush-like. Fls ephemeral, produced in succession in 1–3 spathaceous clusters on a slender st.; perianth seg. 6,

in 2 unequal whorls; outer erect to incurved. C & Trop. S Amer., W Indies. Z10.

T. martinicensis (Jacq.) Herb. Lvs to 30cm, linear, in an erect fan. Flowering st. to 30cm; fls 4–6 per cluster, outer perianth seg. to 2cm, yellow spotted brown or purple at base, inner smaller. Throughout the year. S Amer., W Indies, nat. elsewhere.

Trim Shield Fern *Lastreopsis decomposita*.
Trinidad Flame Bush *Calliandra tweedii*.
Trinity Flower *Trillium*.

Triosteum L. HORSE-GENTIAN; FEVERWORT. Caprifoliaceae. 6 rhizomatous perenn. herbs. St. clumped, erect. Lvs sessile, obovate to oblanceolate, entire or pinnatifid. Fls 5-merous, sessile, bracteate, axill., or in a term. spike; cal. tubular; cor. tubular-bilabiate, lobes 5. Fr. a drupe. E Asia, E N Amer.

T. aurantiacum E. Bickn. WILD COFFEE. To 120cm. Lvs to 25cm, ovate-oblong to oblong-lanceolate, entire or sinuate. Cor. to 2cm, maroon, glandular-puberulent, saccate at base. Fr. orange-red. Spring. N Amer. Z4.

T. erythrocarpum H. Sm. To 40cm. St. gland. Lvs to 13cm, ovate to rounded, amplexicaul. Cor. to 1.8cm, exterior green, purple within. Fr. red. Summer. W China. Z6.

T. perfoliatum L. WILD COFFEE; FEVERROOT; TINKER'S WEED. To 120cm. St. soft-pubesc. Lvs to 23cm, ovate or elliptic, often perfoliate, lanuginose beneath. Cor. purple or dull red, 2cm. Fr. orange-yellow. N Amer. Z6.

T. pinnatifidum Maxim. To 40cm. St. densely pubesc. Lvs to 12cm, rhombic-ovate, pinnatifid. Cor. 1cm, curved, light green, dark purple-tinged. Fr. white. Spring–summer. Jap., N & W China. Z4.

T. rosthornii Diels & Gräbn. = *T. pinnatifidum*.

Tripetaleia Sieb. & Zucc. Ericaceae. 2 decid. shrubs. Fls in term. bracteate pan. or rac.; cal. small, cup shaped, sep. 3, 4 or 5; cor. lobes 4–5, narrow, spirally recurved. Jap. Z6.

T. bracteata Maxim. MIYAMA-HO-TSUTSUJI; HAKO-TSUTSUJI. To 180cm. Lvs 2.5–6cm, obovate. Fls 3–8 in downy rac. 6–15cm long; cor. 8–10mm, green-white. Summer. Jap.

T. paniculata Sieb. & Zucc. HO-TSUTSUJI. To 2m. Lvs 3–8cm, obovate to narrowly ovate-elliptic. Fls packed in erect, downy pan. 5–15cm long; cor. 6–8mm, white tinged pink. Summer. Jap.

→*Elliottia*.

Triphasia Lour. LIMEBERRY. Rutaceae. 3 shrubs or small trees, with paired spines. Lvs simple or 3-foliolate, small, with oil-glands. Fls solitary or clustered, axill.; cal. 3–5-merous, cupulate; pet. 3–5, to 1cm, white; sta. free, twice as many as pet. Fr. a small hesperidium. SE Asia, New Guinea. Z10.

T. aurantiola Lour. = *T. trifolia*.

T. brassii (White) Swingle. Bush to 2m. Lvs simple, ovate-rhombic, crenate, 4–3cm. Fls 5-merous, fragrant. Fr. ellipsoid to pyriform or obovoid, to 3cm, red. New Guinea.

T. glauca Lindl. = *Eremocitrus glauca*.

T. trifolia (Burm. f.) P. Wils. LIME BERRY; MYRTLE LIME. Shrub or small tree. Lvs 3-foliolate; lfts ovate, term., 2–4cm, laterals smaller. Fls 3-merous, fragrant. Fr. ovoid or subglobose, to 1.5cm, dull orange-red or crimson. SE Asia.

→*Echinocitrus*.

Triphysaria Fisch. & C.A. Mey.

T. versicolor Fisch. & C.A. Mey. = *Orthocarpus erianthus* var. *roseus*.

Triplaris Loefl. ex L. ANT TREE; LONG JOHN. Polygonaceae. 17 trees. St. hollow. Lvs entire, gland.-punctate beneath. Infl. enclosed in a spathe-like stipule, tomentose, with racemose main axis and cymose br.; staminate fls 3–5(–7) per br., sessile; perianth seg. 6, ovate or lanceolate, forming a tube; sta. 9, exserted; pistillate fls one per br., stalked; perianth seg. forming an urceolate-campanulate to globose tube, enlarged into wings in fr. In the wild the st. are often inhabited by ants. Z10.

T. americana L. ANT TREE. To 30m. Lvs 25–35cm, ovate to oblong, glab. above, glab. to brown-tomentose beneath. Infl. densely grey-yellow to light brown-yellow velutinous. Panama to SE Braz.

T. cumingiana Fisch. & Mey. ex C.A. Mey. To 30m. Lvs 15–25cm, oblong to oblong-elliptic, glab. except for strigose midrib. Infl. yellow-grey to olive strigose-tomentose. Panama and N Colomb. to N Peru.

T. guanaiensis Rusby = *T. americana*.

T. surinamensis Cham. = *T. weigeltiana*.

T. weigeltiana (Rchb. f.) Kuntze. LONG JACK. To 35m. Lvs 20–25cm, glab. except for yellow-brown tomentose-velutinous midrib. Infl. glab. or puberulous to -pilose. Amaz. basin, NE Venez., Guiana.

Triplet Lily *Triteleia laxa.*

Tripleurospermum Schultz-Bip. SCENTLESS FALSE CAMOMILE; TURFING DAISY. Compositae. *c*30 ann. to perenn. herbs. Lvs 1–3-pinnatisect. Cap. discoid or radiate, usually solitary, scapose; receptacle hemispheric to conical; ray flts white, rarely 0, occas. tinged pink; disc flts usually yellow. N temp. regions.
T. caucasicum (Willd.) Hayek. Rhizomatous perenn., to 30cm. Lvs to 7×2.5cm, 1–2-pinnatisect, lobes acute. Cap. radiate, often solitary; peduncles glab.; ray flts c1.5cm; disc flts occas. black-brown. Summer. Cauc., N Iran, Afghan.
T. inodorum (L.) Schultz-Bip. SCENTLESS HAYWEED. Ann., to 80cm. Lvs 2–3-pinnatisect, lobes linear. Cap. to 4.5cm diam., radiate, numerous; ray flts to 1cm. Summer. Eur. 'Bridal Robe': fls double.
T. oreades (Boiss.) Rech. f. Rhizomatous perenn., to 40cm. Lvs oblong, 1–2-pinnatisect, lobes linear, acute. Cap. radiate, commonly solitary; peduncles often pilose. Spring–summer. Turk., Syr., Leb. var. *tchihatchewii* (Boiss.) E. Hoss. Glab., mat-forming perenn., to 30cm. Turk.
T. tchihatchewii (Boiss.) Bornm. = *T. oreades* var. *tchihatchewii.*
→*Chamaemelum*, *Chrysanthemum*, *Matricaria* and *Pyrethrum.*

Triplochiton Schum. Sterculiaceae. 3 trees. Lvs palmately lobed. Fls in axill. cymes or cymose pan., each subtended by an epical.; cal. campanulate, 5-lobed; pet. 5, clawed; sta. many, on a conspicuous androgynophore; staminodes 5. Trop. Afr. Z10.
T. scleroxylon Schum. Tree to 35m, buttressed. Lvs to 15cm, palmately 5–7-lobed. Fls in cymose pan. to 7.5cm; cal. to 1cm; pet. to 1×1cm, white with a red centre, densely pilose. Trop. C & W Afr.
T. zambesiacus Milne-Redh. Tree to 18m, sometimes multi-stemmed. Lvs to 14cm, palmately 5–9-lobed. Fls 1–4 per axill. or term. cyme; cal. to 2cm; pet. 3.5×2.5cm. Zam., Zimb.

Triplochlamys Ulbr.
T. multiflora (Juss.) Ulbr. = *Pavonia multiflora.*

Tripogandra Raf. Commelinaceae. 22 ann. or perenn. herbs, erect or trailing. Lvs ovate, oblong-lanceolate or linear. Cincinni paired and fused, borne on a common peduncle; fls zygomorphic; sep. 3, free; pet. 3, free; sta. 6, outer whorl fertile, shorter, fil. glab. or bearded, inner fertile or staminodal, longer, fil. curved, glab. or bearded. Trop. Amer.
T. diuretica (Mart.) Handlos. Decumbent perenn., to 1m or more. Lvs to 14×2.5cm, narrowly ovate to ovate. Infl. 1–10; fls to 2cm diam. pink. Summer–autumn. Braz.; also Parag., Boliv., Urug., Arg. Z9.
T. grandiflora (J.D. Sm.) Woodson. Subscandent perenn. to 3m. Lvs to 15×4.5cm, narrowly ovate to elliptic. Infl. paniculate cincinni to 7-fld; fls fragrant, to 2cm diam., white. Autumn––spring. S Mex., Belize, Guat. Z9.
T. multiflora (Sw.) Raf. Trailing perenn.; flowering st. to 80cm, erect. Lvs 8×3cm, narrowly to broadly ovate. Infl. numerous; fls 3–8mm diam., white or pink. Trop. Amer. Z9.
T. serrulata (Vahl) Handlos. Trailing perenn.; flowering st. to 1m erect. Lvs to 13×3cm, narrowly ovate. Cincinni to 9-fld; fls 7–12mm diam., white or pale pink. Throughout the year. Mex. to Surinam and Peru, W Indies. Z9.
→*Callisia* and *Tradescantia.*

Tripteris Less.
T. hyoseroides DC. = *Osteospermum hyoseroides.*

Tripterocalyx (Torr.). Hook.
T. crux-maltae Standl. = *Abronia crux-maltae.*
T. cyclopterus (A. Gray) Standl. = *Abronia cyclopterus.*

Tripterygium Hook. f. Celastraceae. 2 decid. scandent shrubs. Lvs alt., petiolate, large. Fls 5-merous, small, in large term. pan. Fr. broadly 3-winged; seed 1. E Asia.
T. regelii Sprague & Tak. To 10m; shoots slightly angled. Lvs 5–15cm, ovate to elliptic, obtusely serrate, glab. above, sometimes papillose-pilose beneath. Fls to 6mm diam., white tinged green. Fr. to 18mm diam., pale green. Summer. Jap., Korea, Manch. Z5.
T. wilfordii Hook. f. To 13m; shoots angled. Lvs 6–15cm, oblong-elliptic to ovate, finely crenate, glab., usually glaucous beneath. Fls to 6mm diam., pale green. Fr. to 12mm diam., purple-red. Autumn. Taiwan, E China. Z9.

Triptilion Ruiz & Pav. Compositae. 12 ann. to perenn. herbs. St.

branched. Cap. discoid, small, in leafy pan. or corymbs; phyllaries spiny. Chile, Patagonia. Z9.
T. cordifolium Lagasca. HEART-LEAVED TRIPTILION. Ann., to 30cm, erect. St. tinged brown-purple, puberulent, leafy. Basal lvs spathulate, st. lvs orbicular-ovoid, bright green, scarious, glab., amplexicaul, toothed, with 3–4 spines. Flts white, inner lip yellow. Autumn. Chile.
T. spinosum Ruiz & Pav. Perenn., to 20cm. St. woolly below, glab. above. Basal lvs pinnatifid, spiny; st. lvs oblong, pilose amplexicaul, spinose-dentate. Flts purple-blue, inner lip white. Summer. Chile.

Tripterospermum Bl.
T. japonica (Sieb. & Zucc.) Maxim. = *Gentiana trinervis.*

Triquetrous Leek *Allium triquetrum.*

Trisetella Luer. Orchidaceae. 20 diminutive tufted epiphytic orchids resembling *Masdevallia* in habit. Rac. few-fld, erect; fls small; sep. long-tailed, thin-textured, lat. sep. forming a synsepalum; pet. small, v. thin-textured; lip simple to trilobed, ovate-oblong to subpandurate. Trop. C & S Amer. Z10.
T. tridactylites (Rchb. f.) Luer = *T. triglochin.*
T. triglochin (Rchb. f.) Luer. Infl. to 90mm; dors. sep. to 6×6mm, yellow to red-brown or purple, ovate, tail to 15mm, yellow, synsepalum to 21×11mm, orange-brown or purple, tails to 12mm; pet. to 4×2mm, yellow tinged purple, equalling purple lip. Ecuad., Panama, Costa Rica, Peru, Venez., Colomb., Boliv.
→*Masdevallia.*

Tristagma Poepp. Liliaceae (Alliaceae). 5 bulbous perenn. herbs. Lvs few, basal, linear. Fls few in a scapose umbel; perianth tube cylindrical, seg. tightly inrolled. Chile, S Arg. Z9.
T. nivale Poepp. Lvs to 25×0.3cm, glossy. Scape 5–18cm; perianth olive green, tube to 12.5mm, twice length of lobes; anth. yellow. Midsummer. Patagonia, Tierra del Fuego, S Chile.

Tristania R. Br. Myrtaceae. 1 shrub or small tree. Lvs to 9cm, narrow-lanceolate, opposite, almost white beneath. Fls in axill. triads or cymes; sep. 2–3mm; 5; pet. 6–10/3–6mm, 5, yellow; sta. 3–7mm, 3–4 per fascicle, in one whorl. Aus. (NSW). Z9.
T. bakerana Gand. = *Tristaniopsis laurina.*
T. lactiflua F. Muell. = *Lophostemon lactifluus.*
T. laurina (Sm.) R. Br. = *Tristaniopsis laurina.*
T. neriifolia (Sims) R. Br. WATER GUM.
T. suaveolens (Sol. ex Gaertn.) Sm. = *Lophostemon suaveolens.*

Tristaniopsis Brongn. & Gris. Myrtaceae. 30 trees or shrubs. Lvs alt., petiolate. Infl. cymose, axill.; sep. 5; pet. 5; sta. numerous, fascicled. E Aus., New Caledonia, New Guinea, Indon., Philipp., Malaysia, Burm. and Thail. Z10.
T. laurina (Sm.) P.G. Wils. & J.T. Waterhouse. Tree to 30m, with smooth, pale bark exfoliating in strips. Lvs to 14cm, narrowly oblanceolate, dark green above, grey-white beneath, with oil glands. Infl. 7–15-fld; pet. 5×3mm, yellow; sta. 12–20 per fascicle, shorter than pet. Aus. (Queensld and Vict.).
→*Melaleuca* and *Tristania.*

Tristemon Klotzsch.
T. texanum Scheele = *Cucurbita texana.*

Triteleia Lindl. Liliaceae (Tricyrtidaceae). 15 perenn., cormous herbs. Lvs 1 to 2 per corm, linear, basal, grooved above. Fls slender-stalked, funnelform, in scapose umbels, with scarious spathe valves; tep. spreading; fertile sta. 6. W US.
T. bridgesii (Wats.) Greene. Scape to 50cm. Perianth 2.5–4cm, lilac or blue; tube gradually expanded, with slender base, lobes spreading, usually longer than base. W US. Z7.
T. candida (Bak.) Greene = *T. laxa.*
T. grandiflora Lindl. Scape to 70cm. Perianth 1.5–3cm, bright blue or rarely white, tube rounded at base, as long as or exceeding lobes. US (BC, Oreg., N Utah.). Z5.
T. hendersonii Howell ex Greene. Scape to 35cm. Perianth 2–2.5cm, lobes twice as long as tube, yellow with a dark purple midrib, tube narrow-funnelform, tapered below. W US. Z7.
T. hyacintha (Lindl.) Greene. Scape to 70cm. Perianth 0.8–1.8cm, white, blue or lilac, bowl-shaped, lobes twice as long as tube or longer, tube spreading away from the base. W US. Z4.
T. ixioides (Ait.) Greene. Scape to 60cm. Perianth 1–2.5cm, golden-yellow with dark midribs, tube about half the length of lobes. W US. Z7.
T. laxa Benth. GRASSNUT; TRIPLET LILY. Scape to 75cm. Perianth 2–5cm, violet-blue or white, tube usually slightly exceeding lobes, narrowing below. W US. 'Königin Fabiola' ('Queen

Fabiola'): fls pale violet blue.

T. lutea Davidson & Moseley = *T. hyacintha*.

T. peduncularis Lindl. Scape to 40cm. Perianth to 3cm, broadly funnelform, white, blue, or tinged lavender, tube equal to or shorter than lobes. Z6.

T. uniflora Lindl. = *Ipheion uniflorum*.

→*Brodiaea*.

Trithrinax Mart. Palmae. 5 palms. St. erect, with persistent lf sheaths, sometimes spiny, becoming bare, grooved. Lvs palmate; sheath tubular, becoming fibrous; petiole convex beneath; blade fan-shaped to circular, sometimes costapalmate, seg. single-fold, rigid, glab. above, waxy and tomentose beneath. Spikes interfoliar, curved, branched ×3, amid 4 bracts; rachillae bearing solitary trimerous fls. Fr. 1-seeded, white to black, globose. Boliv., W & S Braz., Parag., Urug., Arg. Z10.

T. acanthocoma Drude BURITI PALM. St. 2–4.5m×10cm, spiny. Lvs to 90cm, palmate; seg. 40, apex divided to 2.5–5cm laciniate. S Braz., Arg.

T. brasiliensis Mart. SARO; SAHO. St. 2–5m×8–11cm. Lvs to 2m, seg. to 70cm, apex divided to 20cm. Braz., Arg.

Tritoma Ker-Gawl. = *Kniphofia*.

Tritonia Ker-Gawl. Iridaceae. 28 cormous perenn. herbs. Lvs several, distichous, usually linear or lanceolate. Spike distichous or secund; fls irregular, rarely almost regular; tube longer or shorter than seg., upper seg. sometimes broader; sta. set in tube; style long, with 3 short recurved br. Trop. & S Afr. Z9.

T. aurantiaca Ecklon = *T. deusta* ssp. *miniata*.

T. aurea (Hook.) Planch. = *Crocosmia aurea*.

T. bakeri Klatt. St. to 80cm, simple or branched. Lvs 15–60cm, ± terete. Spike distichous; fls cream, pale yellow or mauve-pink, outer lobes with dark veins. Spring–early summer. S Afr.

T. capensis (Houtt.) Ker-Gawl. = *T. flabellifolia*.

T. chrysantha Fourc. St. 10–15cm, sometimes with 1–2 br. Lvs 5–20cm, lanceolate. Spike distichous; fls bright yellow. Winter–spring. S Afr.

T. cooperi (Bak.) Klatt. St. to 60cm, sometimes with 1 br. Lvs 20–50cm, terete or 4-ridged. Spike secund; fls irregular white or cream turning pink with age, often pink outside, with red or purple marks in throat. Late spring–early summer. S Afr.

T. crispa (L. f.) Ker-Gawl. St. 15–45cm, simple with 1–3-branches. Lvs 10–40cm, linear-lanceolate, often crisped. Spike secund; fls irregular, cream, pale yellow, pale pink or salmon pink, red or purple in centre and with red or purple median stripe on 3 lower lobes. Spring–summer. S Afr.

T. crocata (L.) Ker-Gawl. St. 20–50cm tall, sometimes branched. Lvs 5–30cm, lanceolate. Spike secund or distichous; fls regular, rather cup-shaped, bright orange, orange-red or pink-orange, the 3 lower lobes with a yellow mid-line which sometimes forms a low callus. Spring. S Afr.

T. deusta (Ait.) Ker-Gawl. St. to 50cm, sometimes 1–2-branched. Lvs to 30cm, lanceolate. Spike secund or distichous; fls regular, cup-shaped, bright orange-red or orange-salmon, the tube with a yellow star-shaped mark inside, lobes often marked with dark or yellow blotches. Spring. S Afr. ssp. *miniata* (Jacq.) De Vos. Outer lobes without dark blotch or stripe; lower lobes often with yellow blotch sometimes edged with red, or dark spot or mid-line.

T. disticha (Klatt) Bak. St. 20–100cm, sometimes with 1–3 br. Lvs 25–70cm, linear or linear-lanceolate. Spikes distichous then ± secund; fls slightly irregular, funnel-shaped red, orange-red or pink, the lower lobes with a small yellow blotch sometimes edged red. Summer. S Afr., Swaz. ssp. *rubrolucens* (Fost.) De Vos. Fls red, orange-red or pink.

T. fenestrata (Jacq.) Ker-Gawl. = *T. crocata*.

T. flabellifolia (Delaroche) G. Lewis. St. 20–60cm, unbranched or with 1–3 br. Lvs 10–45cm, linear or linear-lanceolate. Spikes secund; fls irregular, white, cream or pale pink with red or yellow stripe or blotch on lower 3 lobes, often magenta in throat. Spring–summer. S Afr. var. *major* (Ker-Gawl.) De Vos. Fls larger.

T. flava (Ait.) Ker-Gawl. = *T. securigera*.

T. karooica De Vos. 10–20cm, sometimes with 1 br. Lvs 4–15cm, falcate. Spike distichous; fls scented, slightly irregular, dull yellow or yellow-brown, cream, salmon pink or orange, dark-veined, flushed with pink or orange on outside. Winter–spring. S Afr.

T. laxifolia (Klatt) Benth. ex Bak. To 60cm, sometimes with 1–2 br. Lvs 10–50cm, linear-lanceolate. Spike secund, fls salmon-pink, orange or brick red, the 3 lower lobes with peg-like yellow callus 3–5mm high set on a yellow blotch. Summer–autumn. Tanz., Malawi, Zam., S Afr. (E Cape).

T. lineata (Salisb.) Ker-Gawl. To 80cm, sometimes branched. Lvs 15–50cm, linear-lanceolate. Spike ± secund; fls slightly

irregular, cream, pale yellow or pale apricot with darker veins, sometimes flushed with apricot outside. Winter–Spring. S Afr., Les.

T. masonorum Bol. = *Crocosmia masonorum*.

T. miniata (Jacq.) Ker-Gawl. = *T. deusta* ssp. *miniata*.

T. nelsonii Bak. 25–90cm, sometimes branched. Lvs 20–90cm, linear, ± rigid. Spike ± secund; fls red or orange-red, the 3 lower lobes each with a tall yellow-green callus. Summer–autumn. S Afr.

T. pallida Ker-Gawl. 15–60cm, often branched. Lvs 10–50cm, linear-lanceolate. Spike distichous; fls irregular, white, cream or pale lilac, yellow-green in throat, the tube purple-veined. Spring. S Afr.

T. pottsii Bak. = *Crocosmia pottsii*.

T. rosea (Jacq.) Ait. non Klatt = *T. flabellifolia* var. *major*.

T. rosea Klatt non (Jacq.) Ait. = *T. disticha* ssp. *rubrolucens*.

T. rubrolucens Fost. = *T. disticha* ssp. *rubrolucens*.

T. securigera (Ait.) Ker-Gawl. 10–35cm, sometimes with 1 br. Lvs 7–25cm, lanceolate or linear-lanceolate. Spike ± secund; fls usually apricot or orange-red, yellow in throat, but sometimes all yellow. Spring–early summer. S Afr.

T. squalida (Ait.) Ker-Gawl. 20–50cm, sometimes branched. Lvs 5–30cm, lanceolate. Spike secund or distichous; fls regular, cup-shaped, pale pink to deep mauve-pink, sometimes almost white, often veined with deeper pink. Spring. S Afr.

T. watermeyeri L. Bol. 10–30cm. Lvs 5–15cm, linear-lanceolate, undulate, sometimes spirally twisted. Spike distichous; fls almost 2-lipped, slightly scented, orange or orange-pink, upper lobes often buff or salmon inside, lower lobes with a yellow mark edged with red in the throat. Late winter–spring. S Afr.

Tritoniopsis L. Bol. Iridaceae. 20 perenn. herbs. St. simple or branched. Basal lvs few, sometimes 0 at flowering, petiolate, linear or lanceolate. Spike bracteate, distichous or spirally arranged; fls mostly irregular, often almost bilabiate; perianth tubular, seg., 6 clawed; sta. arising in perianth tube; style long 3-branched. S Afr. (Cape Prov.). Z9.

T. antholyza (Poir.) Goldbl. St. 20–90cm, unbranched. Basal lvs 15–30cm, short-stalked. Spike *c*12cm, usually spirally twisted; fls many, pink, salmon-pink or red, almost bilabiate. Summer–autumn. S, W, SW & E Cape.

T. burchellii (Burm. f.) Goldbl. St. to 90cm, unbranched. Basal lf to 35cm, long-stalked. Spike to 18cm; fls many, red. Summer. S & SW Cape.

T. caffra (Ker-Gawl. ex Bak.) Goldbl. St. 20–80cm, sometimes with 1 or 2 short br. Basal lvs to 50cm, long-stalked. Spike 7–30cm; fls 7–25, distichous, deep red or scarlet, almost bilabiate. Spring–summer. S & SE Cape.

T. intermedia (Bak.) Goldbl. St. 30–45cm, unbranched. Basal lvs 10–15cm, v. short-stalked. Spike to 24cm; fls 10–25, distichous, almost bilabiate, bright red, the 3 lower lobes with a purple-black blotch at base. E Cape.

T. pulchra (Bak.) Goldbl. St. 22–50cm, sometimes with 1 short br. Basal lvs 20–40cm, short-stalked. Spike 5–15cm, the fls 7–20, spirally arranged carmine-red, purple-red or deep pink-red, the lower 3 lobes usually with red and white lines. Autumn–winter. SW Cape.

→*Anapalina*, *Antholyza* and *Chasmanthe*.

Trixis P. Browne.

T. neriifolia Bonpl. ex Humb. = *Libanothamnus neriifolius*.

Trochetia DC. Sterculiaceae. 6 everg. shrubs and small trees. Lvs alt. crowded near ends of shoots, entire, or toothed. Fls 1–3 per axil; epical. of 1–2 bracts; sep. 5, deltoid, free or slightly connate; pet. 5, free, obdeltoid; staminal tube with 5 groups of 3 sta. each, alternating with 5 staminodes. Maur., Réunion. Z10.

T. blackburniana Bojer ex Bak. Shrub. Lvs to 15×10cm, ovate to broadly ovate, elliptic, obovate or suborbicular, serrate, stellate-hairy on veins. Fls solitary, drooping, on peduncles 2–9cm; cor. 2–3cm, pale pink to white, rosy-crimson along the margins and towards the apex. staminal tube 1.2–1.4cm. Maur.

T. grandiflora Bojer = *T. triflora*.

T. triflora DC. Tree to 8m. Lvs to 15×7cm, ovate to elliptic, dentate, stellate-pubesc., throughout. Fls in pendulous, 3-fld cymes 5–10cm; cor. 3.5cm, white; staminal tube 3cm. Maur.

→*Dombeya*.

Trochocarpa R. Br. Epacridaceae. 12 everg. shrubs and trees. Lvs elliptic or ovate, usually petiolate, coriaceous. Fls in short spikes; cal. 5-parted; cor. tube cylindric or campanulate, lobes recurved; sta. 5, inserted near throat. Fr. a drupe. Aus., Tasm., Malaysia, N Borneo. Z9.

T. laurina (R. Br. ex Rudge) R. Br. Shrub or small tree to 9m. Lvs 4–10cm, oval-elliptic, glossy green, veins 5–7, prominent, longitudinal. Fls small, white in nodding term. spikes. Fr. to

0.8cm diam., almost black. Spring–summer. Aus.
→*Cyathodes*.

TROCHODENDRACEAE Prantl. See *Trochodendron*.

Trochodendron Sieb. & Zucc. Trochodendraceae. 1 everg., glab. tree or shrub to 20m. Lvs 5–14cm, spirally arranged, ovate to ovate-oblong, acuminate or cuspidate, crenulate-serrulate, dark green above, paler beneath; petiole 3–7cm. Cyme 5–13cm, racemose, term.; fls 10–20, to 18mm diam., vivid green; perianth 0; sta. 3–7mm, 40–70, on a broad disc. Early summer. Jap., Korea, Taiwan. Z8.
T. aralioides Sieb. & Zucc.

Trochomeria Hook. f. Cucurbitaceae. 7 tuberous perennials, prostrate or climbing by tendrils. Lvs palmately 3–5-lobed or dissected. ♂ fls in axill. clusters or rac., or solitary, yellowgreen; cal. cylindrical to campanulate, lobes minute; cor. rotate, lobes 5, free; sta. 3; ♀ fls solitary, with 3 staminodes. Fr. an indehiscent berry. Afr. Z10.
T. debilis (Sonder) Hook. f. St. climbing by tendrils. Lvs 1.5–6×2–11cm, 3–7-lobed, lobes elliptic to linear, entire to pinnatifid. Fr. subglobose to ellipsoid, 2.5–3.5cm, red. S Afr., Nam.
→*Zehneria*.

Trogon Ixora *Ixora concinna*.

Trogostolon Copel. Davalliaceae. 1 epiphytic fern. Rhiz. creeping, branched; scales dark brown. Stipes remote, grooved; frond blades to 15cm, to 4× finely pinnately divided, deltoid, glab., pinnules oblong, lobed, final seg. subfalcate, lanceolate, on fertile fronds, bifid at apex. Trop. Asia (Philipp.). Z10.
T. falcinellus (Presl) Copel.
→*Davallia* and *Leucostegia*.

Trollius L. GLOBE FLOWER. Ranunculaceae. 31 perenn. herbs. Roots thick, fibrous. Lvs basal and cauline, palmately lobed or divided seg. toothed. Fls bowl-shaped, terminal, usually solitary; sep. 5–15 or more, petaloid; pet. 5–15, each with a basal nectary; sta. numerous. N Temp. region.
T. acaulis Lindl. 8–30cm. Basal lvs 3–5cm, 3–5-parted, seg. cut to oblong-lanceolate lobes, toothed. Fls 3.5–5cm diam., golden yellow; sep. *c*8, broad-oval; pet. 12–16, oblong; sta. yellow. Summer. Himal. Z6.
T. albiflorus (A. Gray) Rydb. = *T. laxus* var. *albiflorus*.
T. altaicus C.A. Mey. 15–60cm. Basal lvs close to *T. europaeus*. Fls to 4cm diam., golden-yellow to orange; sep. 15–20, occas. tinged red below; pet. to 1cm, rounded; anth. purple. Summer. W Sib. Z4.
T. americanus Muhlenb. = *T. laxus*.
T. anemonifolius (Brühl) Stapf = *T. yunnanensis* ssp. *anemonifolius*.
T. asiaticus L. 20–80cm. Basal lvs 4–12cm, usually 5-parted; seg. rhombic, lobed and toothed. Fls 3–5cm diam., golden yellow to orange; sep. 10–20, elliptic to obovate, slightly longer than pet; pet. 20–40, rounded, orange. Spring–summer. Sib., Turkestan, N Mong., NW China. Forms of this sp. with esp. large fls have been named *T. giganteus*. See also *T. europaeus*. 'Fortunei': fls double, sep. many. Z4.
T. buddhae Schipcz. = *T. papavereus*.
T. caucasicus Steven = *T. ranunculinus*.
T. chinensis Bunge. To 1m. Basal lvs 6–12cm, 5-lobed, seg. broad lanceolate, lobed, toothed. Fls 5–6cm diam., golden-yellow; sep. variable in number, broadly oval; pet. *c*20, exceeding sta. and sep.; sta. yellow. Summer. Russia, NE China. Z5.
T. ×*cultorum* Bergmans. A group of gdn hybrids between *T. europaeus*, *T. asiaticus* and *T. chinensis* to 1m with orange fls. Spring–summer. Over 20 cvs: height to 90cm; fl. colour ranges from light lemon yellow to deep orange. 'Alabaster': fls light primrose. 'Earliest of All': to 50cm; fls golden yellow, earlyflowering. 'Fire Globe': to 65cm; fls deep orange. 'First Lancers': to 70cm; fls large, deep orange shaded red. 'Golden Queen': fls globe-shaped, orange. 'Goldquelle' ('Golden Fountain'): to 70cm; fls yellow; late. 'Lemon Queen': to 60cm; fls large, pale yellow. 'Orange Globe': to 60cm; fls golden orange. 'Orange Princess': to 90cm; fls orange tinted yellow. 'Pritchard's Giant': to 90cm, robust; fls golden-orange. 'Salamander': to 75cm; fls v. deep orange. Z5.
T. dschungaricus Reg. Close to *T. europaeus*, but fls open, not globe-like, exterior stained red. Basal lvs 3–7cm, 3–5-sect, seg. obovate, 3-lobed, dentate. Fls 3.5–6cm diam., golden-yellow to pale orange; sep. *c*15, somewhat mucronate; pet. *c*10, often v. narrow, apex rounded, orange. C Asia, W China. Z6.
T. europaeus L. GLOBEFLOWER. To 80cm. Basal lvs 5–12cm, 3–5-lobed, seg. cuneate, often 3-lobed, incised. Fls 1.5–5cm

diam., globose, lemon yellow; sep. 10–20, occas. tinged green below; pet. *c*10, nearly equal to sta., pale orange; sta. yellow. Spring–summer. Eur., Russia, N Amer. Large-fld variants of this sp. have been named *T. giganteus* cf *T. asiaticus*. 'Giganteus': strong habit. 'Grandiflorus': fls large, brightly coloured. 'Loddigesii': fls deep yellow. 'Superbus': to 60cm; fls pale yellow, late flowering. Z5.
T. farreri Stapf. 5–20cm. Basal lvs 1.5–2cm, 3-sect, seg. 3-lobed, sharply toothed. Fls 2–3cm diam., open yellow; sep. 5–6, rhomboidal to rounded, often tinged purple below; pet. rounded, pale yellow-orange, shorter than sta. Summer. China, N India. Z7.
T. hybridus nom illegit. = *T.* ×*cultorum*.
T. japonicus Miq. To 60cm. Basal lvs 4–10cm, 3–5-parted, seg. cuneate, toothed. Fls 3–4cm diam., yellow; sep. 5–6, broad, spreading; pet. linear, exceeding sta. Spring–summer. Jap. Z6.
T. laxus Salisb. To 50cm. Basal lvs 4–10cm, 5-parted, seg. cuneate, lobes 3, narrow, toothed. Fls 3–4.5cm diam., open, cream to yellow or tinged green; sep. 5–10; pet. *c*15, shorter than sta. Spring–summer. N Amer. var. *albiflorus* A. Gray. Fls white, pet. nearly as long as sta. N Amer. (Rocky Mts). Z4.
T. ledebourii Rchb. f. non Hort. To 1m. Basal lvs 6–10cm, 5-parted, seg. rhomboid to oval, lobed, dentate. Fls 3–5cm diam., shallowly bowl-shaped, orange-yellow; sep. 5–10, broad; pet. 10–15, linear, exceeding sta., orange. Spring–summer. E Sib., N Korea, N Mong. Z6.
T. ledebourii hort. non Rchb. f. = *T. chinensis*.
T. lilacinus Bunge. 5–25cm. Basal lvs 2–5cm, 3–5-parted, seg. broad-oval, lobed. Fls 2–4.5cm diam., open, tinged lilac; sep. 15–20; pet. 10–15, rounded, shorter than sta., pale yellowgreen. Summer. Mts of C Asia, W Sib., NW Mong. Z5.
T. papavereus Schipcz. 20–40cm. Basal lvs 3–8cm, 3-parted, seg. rhomboid, lobed. Fls 3–4.5cm, open, yellow; sep. 5–6, rounded; pet. orange. cf. *T. pumilus*. SW China, NE Burm. Z7.
T. patulus Salisb. = *T. ranunculinus*.
T. pumilis ssp. *anemonifolius* Brühl = *T. yunnanensis* ssp. *anemonifolius*.
T. pumilus D. Don. Resembles *T. acaulis*, but lvs 4–5cm, usually basal only. Fls smaller, 2–3.5cm diam., interior yellow-orange, exterior dark wine red or crimson; pet. shorter than sta. Summer. Himal. and E Tibet. Z5.
T. ranunculinus (Sm.) Stearn. 20–55cm. Basal lvs 3–10cm, 5–7-parted, seg. deeply toothed and cut. Fls 3–5.5cm diam., bowlshaped; sep. yellow, 5–16, spreading; pet. *c*10–12, linear and rounded, nearly equal to sta., dark yellow to orange. Summer. Turk., Cauc., NW Iran. Z6.
T. riederianus var. *japonicus* (Miq.) Ohwi = *T. japonicus*.
T. stenopetalus (Reg.) Egor & Sipliv. = *T. papavereus*.
T. yunnanensis (Franch.) Ulbr. To 70cm. Basal lvs 4–10cm, 3-parted, occas. 5-parted, seg. ovate to obovate, lobed and toothed. Fls 4–8cm diam.; sep. *c*5, golden-yellow, spreading; pet. *c*12, rounded, nearly equal to sta., pale orange. Summer. W China. ssp. *anemonifolius* (Brühl) Dorosz. Lvs to 12cm, rounded in outline, 3-sect, seg. round-oval, overlapping, dentate. Fls 1–7cm diam. W China. Z5.

Tromotriche Haw. Asclepiadaceae. 3 dwarf, leafless, succulent herbs to 30cm. Fls solitary or in small pseudoterminal clusters; cor. tube pentagonal, with an annulus at mouth, lobes revolute; corona lobes bifid or linear. S Afr. (Cape Prov.). Z9.
T. engleriana (Schltr.) Leach. St. to 25×2cm, grey-green, minutely hairy, angles slightly sinuate. Fls solitary; cor. 2–4cm diam., rounded, chocolate-brown, with cream-yellow furrows and rugae, lobes to 1.4cm.
T. pruinosa (Masson) Haw. = *Quaqua pruinosa*.
T. revoluta (Masson) Haw. St. to 30×1.8cm, pruinose, angles sinuate, toothed. Fls near st. apex; cor. to 4.5cm diam., smooth, pale maroon to purple-brown, with white or lime-green central markings, lobes deep, triangular-ovate, reflexed with purple cilia.
T. thudichumii (Pill.) Leach. St. 10×1.5cm with 4 obtuse, minutely dentate angles, green with purple blotches. Fls solitary; cor. 1.3cm diam., rugose, purple-brown, lobes to 1cm, triangular, recurved, margins purple-brown with motile hairs. SE Cape.
→*Stapelia*.

Tronador *Oreopanax sanderianus*.

TROPAEOLACEAE DC. 3/88. *Tropaeolum*.

Tropaeolum L. NASTURTIUM; INDIAN CRESS; CANARY BIRD VINE; CANARY BIRD FLOWER; FLAME FLOWER. Tropaeolaceae. 86 ann. or perenn. herbs, sometimes tuberous, often climbing by leafstalks. Lvs stalked, shield-shaped, 5-angled, or lobed and dissected. Fls solitary, axill., long-stalked, spurred; sep. 5; pet. 5, obovate-spathulate, clawed, upper 2 usually smaller with darker veins, lower 3 often with bearded claws. S Mex. to Braz. and Patagonia.

T. albiflorum Lem. = *T. leptophyllum*.

T. azureum Miers. Climber to 1.2m, with small tubers. Lvs 5-lobed, to 3cm across, lobes linear-lanceolate to obovate. Fls purple-blue, 1–2cm in diam. Chile. Z9.

T. brachyceras Hook. & Arn. Climber with small tubers. Lvs 5–7-lobed, to 3cm across, often less, lobes obovate to linear-lanceolate. Fls yellow, to 1.3cm upper pet. with purple lines. Chile. Z9.

T. canariense hort. ex Lindl. & Moore = *T. peregrinum*.

T. chrysanthum Planch. & Lind. = *T. pendulum*.

T. edule Paxt. = *T. leptophyllum*.

T. elegans G. Don = *T. tricolorum*.

T. hookerianum Barnéoud. Climber. Lvs 7-lobed, to 1.5cm across. Fls yellow, to 2cm across, v. long-stalked, muskily scented. Chile. Z9.

T. incisum (Spreng.) Sparre. Perenn. herb, prostrate to procumbent. Lvs 5-lobed, to 2.5cm diam., lobes trilobed. Fls yellow, to 2.5cm diam. long-spurred. Arg. Z10.

T. jarrattii Paxt. = *T. tricolorum*.

T. × leichtlinii hort Leichtl. (*T. leptophyllum × T. polyphyllum*.) Fls bright orange-yellow, spotted red. Gdn origin. Z8.

T. leptophyllum G. Don. Climber with large tubers. Lvs long-stalked, 6- or 7-lobed. Fls c3.5cm, orange, yellow, or pink-white, v. long-stalked. Chile and Boliv. Z9.

T. lobbianum hort. Veitch ex Hook. = *T. peltophorum*.

T. majus L. NASTURTIUM; INDIAN CRESS. Glab. ann. climber. Lvs orbicular, margins sinuate, rarely lobed. Fls to 6cm, v. variable in colour, shades of red, orange, or yellow; pet. rounded; spur long. Colomb. to Boliv. Many variations have resulted from hybrids with *T. peltophorum*, *T. minus* and, less frequently, with *T. moritzianum* and *T. peregrinum*. 'Hermine Grashoff': to 20cm; lvs round, pale green; fls double, orange-scarlet. 'Peach Melba': compact; fls cream-yellow blotched at throat. 'Salmon Baby': compact; fls deep salmon pink, fringed. 'Variegatum': to 1.2m, trailing; lvs variegated; fls orange or red. Florepleno Series: fls double. Climbing Hybrids Improved: trailing to 1.8m; fls in wide range of colours. Double Gleam Hybrids: to 30cm, somewhat trailing; fls semi-double in golden yellow, orange and scarlet, scented. 'Dwarf Cherry Rose': lvs dark green; fls semi-double, cerise. 'Fiery Festival': fls deep scarlet, abundant, fragrant. 'Golden Gleam': fls double or semi-double, rich yellow. 'Strawberries and Cream': compact; pet. cream splashed bright red. Gleam series: semi-trailing habit; fls double, in single or a mixture of colours that includes scarlet, yellow and orange. 'Nanum': non-climbing, dwarf, compact form with smaller fls. Alaska Hybrids: lvs light green, marbled and striped cream; fls in wide range of colours. 'Burpeei': fls fully double, without seeds. Dwarf Compact Hybrids: habit dwarf, dense; fls in range of colours. 'Empress of India': lvs deep green; fls bright scarlet. Tom Thumb Hybrids: habit dwarf, compact; fls single in wide range of colours. Whirlybird Hybrids: low-growing; fls semi-double in range of colours.

T. minus L. Non-climbing glab. ann. Lvs rounded-reniform, nerves projecting in a point. Fls smaller than in *T. majus*, deep yellow; pet. ending in a bristle-like point, lower spotted; spur curved. Peru, Ecuad.

T. mucronatum Meyen = *T. tuberosum*.

T. myriophyllum (Poepp. & Endl.) Sparre. Climber. Lvs to 9-lobed, to 3cm diam., lobes lanceolate. Fls pale yellow-orange, to 3cm diam., spur to 2cm. Chile. Z9.

T. peltophorum Benth. Pubesc. ann. spreading climber to 0.3m. Lvs rounded, long-stalked, veins projecting beyond margins. Fls long-stalked, medium to large, orange-red or yellow; lower pet. toothed, fringed below. Colomb., Ecuad. 'Spitfire': fls deep orange-red. Z9.

T. pentaphyllum Lam. Tall glab. perenn. climber to 6m with long, beaded tubers. Lvs 5-lobed, lobes elliptical, obtuse; petioles purple. Fls 2–3cm, in pendent masses; upper sep. spotted, red; pet. scarlet. S Amer. Z8.

T. peregrinum L. CANARY CREEPER. Half-hardy ann. or perenn., climber to 2.5m. Lvs usually 5-lobed, to 5cm across, pale green. Fls long-stalked, to 2cm diam.; pet. sulphur or lemon-yellow, upper erect, fimbriate-lacerate, red-spotted at base, spur hooked. Peru, Ecuad. Z9.

T. polyphyllum Cav. Grey-green herbaceous ann. or perenn.; st. to 3m, trailing. Lvs large, 5- to 7- or more lobed, glaucous. Fls to 2.5cm diam. long-stalked in long masses; pet. obovate, clawed yellow, orange or ochre, upper notched; spur long, slender. Chile, Arg. Z8.

T. quinatum Hellen. = *T. pentaphyllum*.

T. sessilifolium Poepp. & Endl. Climber with tuberous roots. Lvs 3–5-lobed, to 1.5cm diam., lobes ovate. Pet. dark red shaded with violet, bright red towards the base, to 1.5cm, spur conical,

to 1.2cm. Chile. Z9.

T. smithii DC. Climber, half-hardy ann. or perenn. Lvs 5-lobed, to 6cm across, lobes sometimes cut. Fls bright orange-red, bristle-fringed, sometimes with darker nerves. Trop. S Amer. Z10.

T. speciosum Poepp. & Endl. FLAME NASTURTIUM; SCOTTISH FLAME FLOWER. Perenn. climber to 3m, rhiz. fleshy. Lvs 5–7 lobed, to 5cm across, hairy, lobes obovate, notched. Fls to 2cm diam., bright scarlet, upper pet. wedge-shaped, cleft, lower pet. ± rounded, bluntly cleft, spur to 3cm. Fr. blue. Chile. Z8.

T. tricolorum Sw. Perenn. climber to 2m, with small tubers. Lvs 5–7-lobed, to 3cm across, lobes linear-obovate. Cal. obconical-turbinate, orange-scarlet, tipped black, or blue-yellow within; pet. short, yellow-orange; spur 1.5–2.3cm. Boliv., Chile. Z8.

T. tuberosum Ruiz & Pav. Perenn. climber, 2–3m, with large yellow tubers marbled purple. Lvs bluntly (3–)5-lobed to mid-way, grey-green. Fls long-stalked, cup-shaped; sep. red; pet. orange or scarlet, spur narrow-conical. Peru, Boliv., Colomb. and Ecuad. 'Ken Aslet': fls orange. Z8.

T. violiflorum A. Dietr. = *T. azureum*.

Tropical Almond *Terminalia catappa.*
Tropical Banksia *Banksia dentata.*
Tropical Pitcher Plant *Nepenthes.*
Tropic Laurel *Ficus benjamina.*
Trout Begonia *Begonia × argenteoguttata.*
Trout-leaf Begonia *Begonia × argenteoguttata.*
Trout Lily *Erythronium* (*E. americanum*).

Troximon Nutt.

T. aurantiacum Hook. = *Agoseris auriantiaca.*

T. glaucum var. *dasycephalum* Torr. & A. Gray = *Agoseris glauca* var. *dasycephala.*

T. glaucum Pursh = *Agoseris glauca.*

Trudelia Garay. Orchidaceae. 5 epiphytic, monopodial orchids. St. slender, clothed with overlapping bases of 2-ranked strap-shaped, conduplicate lvs to 20cm. Rac. few-fld, shorter than lvs, axill.; tep. obovate-spathulate; lip oblong-triangular, 3-lobed, saccate to spurred, crested. India, Thail. Z9.

T. alpina (Lindl.) Garay. Fls to 2.5cm diam., tep. green-yellow, lip yellow streaked maroon or purple, lat. lobes purple. India, Himal.

T. cristata (Lindl.) Sengh. Fls 4–5cm diam.; tep. green or yellow, lip white or gold, crested and striped purple. Himal., Bangladesh.

T. griffithii (Lindl.) Garay. Fls to 4cm diam.; tep. yellow-brown above, chequered, lip lilac, basally blotched deep yellow. Bhutan.

T. pumila (Hook. f.) Sengh. Fls 5–6.2cm diam., fragrant, tep. yellow or cream, lip paler, streaked purple. India, Bhutan, Thail.

→*Vanda.*

True Jasmine *Jasminum officinale.*
True Laurel *Laurus nobilis.*
True Senna *Senna alexandrina.*
Trumpet Bush *Tecoma.*
Trumpet Creeper *Campsis.*
Trumpet Flower *Bignonia capreolata.*
Trumpet Gentian *Gentiana clusii.*
Trumpet Gourd *Lagenaria siceraria.*
Trumpet Honeysuckle *Lonicera sempervirens.*
Trumpet Narcissus *Narcissus pseudonarcissus.*
Trumpets *Sarracenia flava.*
Trumpet Tree *Cecropia peltata.*
Trumpet Vine *Campsis radicans.*
Trumpet Weed *Eupatorium purpureum.*
Tsangpo Cypress *Cupressus gigantea.*
Tsani *Dolichandrone alba.*
Tsiela *Ficus amplissima.*
Tsubomi-giboshi *Hosta clausa.*

Tsuga Carr. HEMLOCK; HEMLOCK SPRUCE. Pinaceae. 10 everg. conifers. Br. horizontal, branchlets arranged in fine sprays. Lvs spirally arranged, appearing pectinate in ranks, linear to acicular, flat. ♂ cones axill., globose to cylindric. ♀ term., becoming pendulous. Himal., China, Jap., N Amer.

T. blaringhemii Flous = *T. diversifolia.*

T. brunoniana (Wallich) Carr. = *T. dumosa.*

T. calcarea Downie = *T. dumosa.*

T. canadensis (L.) Carr. EASTERN HEMLOCK. To 40m. Crown conic; bark purple-brown, fissured. Lvs 6–20×1–2mm, dull green and grooved above, two grey-white bands beneath, serrulate. Cones sessile, obtuse-ovoid, 12–24mm, scales grey buff. N Amer. Cvs, variable, mostly dwarf, some compact and globose ('Broughton', 'Bennet', 'Dwarf Pyramid', 'Minuta'), some prostrate ('Cole', 'Prostrata'), conical ('Dwarf Whitetip', 'Fremdii') or flat-topped ('Armistice', 'Gracilis'); of the larger selections, some conical ('Jenkinsii', 'Meyers'), some narrow-upright ('Mansfield') and some pendulous ('Pendula', 'Taxifolia'). Variegated forms include the yellow-stippled 'Aurea' and the white-stippled 'Albospica' and 'Dwarf White-tip'; weeping forms include 'Gable Weeping' and 'Kelsey's Weeping'. Z4.

T. caroliniana Engelm. CAROLINA HEMLOCK. To 40m in wild. Crown dense conic. Shoots shiny brown tinged red above, pink beneath. Lvs 8–15×2mm, dark green, grooved above, entire; apex occas. notched. Cones sessile or short-stalked, cylindric-oblong, 15–32×8mm; scales thinly pubesc. SE US. 'Arnold Pyramid': pyramidal, dense; apex rounded. 'Compacta': dwarf, dense; br. horizontal. 'Le Bar Weeping': foliage dense, pendulous. Z6.

T. chinensis (Franch.) Pritz. CHINESE HEMLOCK. Broad conic to domed tree to 45m, often shrubby in cult. Bark buff pink, heavily ridged. Lvs entire or serrate, slightly tapered, glossy, 5–25×2–3mm, apex dentate, stomatal bands beneath light green to white. Cones sessile or short-stalked to 1.5–2.5cm, glossy yellow-buff, scales broadly rounded. C China. var. *formosana* (Hayata) Li & Keng. Needles linear, not tapered. Taiwan. var. *oblongisquamata* Cheng & L.K. Fu. Cones slenderer with narrow, oblong scales. NE Sichuan, W Hubei. var. *robusata* Cheng & L.K. Fu. Cones larger, to 4cm; scales stouter. NE Sichuan, W Hubei; 2800m. Z6.

T. crassifolia Flous = *T. mertensiana* ssp. *grandicona*.

T. diversifolia (Maxim.) Mast. NORTH JAPANESE HEMLOCK. To 25m, often a shrub in cult. Crown ovoid-conical. Lvs perpendicular to shoot, 5–15×2–2.5mm, tips often hooded, linear-oblong, shiny above, grooved, stomatal bands white beneath. Cones subsessile, ovoid, 1.5–2.5cm, dark brown; scales flat, striated. Jap. 'Gotelli': dwarf form. Z5.

T. dumosa (D. Don) Eichl. HIMALAYAN HEMLOCK. To 45m in wild, often a shrub in cult. Lvs largely pectinate, 1–3.5cm, long-acuminate, dentate, blue-green above, two vivid white stomatal bands beneath, acute. Cones sessile, ovoid-acute, 18–28mm; fertile scales circular. Himal. (NW India & Nepal to Yunnan & SW Sichuan) Z8.

T. formosana Hayata = *T. chinensis* var. *formosana*.

T. forrestii Downie. To 35m in wild often shrubby in cult. Lvs pectinate, 10–25×2–3mm, tapering, broadest near base, grooved strongly only on basal half, green above, two broad white stomatal bands beneath. Cones larger than *T. chinensis*, 2–4cm, scales shiny brown, slightly striated. SW China. Z8.

T. heterophylla (Raf.) Sarg. WESTERN HEMLOCK. To 70m. Crown v. regular conic; bark thick, purple-brown. Lvs loosely arranged, 5–23mm, grooved, matt bright green above, two white stomatal bands beneath, dentate, apex bluntly acute. Cones sessile, 1.5–3cm, apex acute; scales obovate, slightly pubesc. S Alask. to N Calif. 'Argenteovariegata': young shoots white. 'Conica': dwarf, ovoid; br. ascending, tips pendent. 'Dumosa': bushy dwarf; foliage dark green above. 'Flaccida': branchlets pendulous. 'Laursen's Column': narrow, columnar tree. Z6.

T. hookeriana (A. Murray) Carr. = *T. mertensiana* ssp. *grandicona*.

T. ×jeffreyi (Henry) Henry = *T. mertensiana* var. *jeffreyi*.

T. longibracteata Cheng = *Nothotsuga longibracteata*.

T. mertensiana (Bong.) Carr. MOUNTAIN HEMLOCK. To 45m. Crown narrow conic. Lvs radially arranged, 15–25×1.5–2mm, thick, keeled or slightly grooved above, often terete, entire, grey-green to blue-green, stomatal bands on both surfaces, apex acute, blunt. Cones sessile, cylindric to oblong, tapering at both ends, 3.5–6×1cm, purple when young, ripening dark brown, scales densely pubesc. S Alask. to Oreg. & W Mont. 'Argentea': foliage silvery. 'Blue Star': foliage vivid blue. 'Cascade': compact, dense, slow growing. 'Elizabeth': dwarf, spreading. 'Glauca': dwarf, slow growing; foliage silver-grey. var. *jeffreyi* (Henry) Schneid. Lvs greener above with fewer stomata, and whiter beneath with more stomata. Cones identical to type. Scattered in range of type; often considered a hybrid with *T. heterophylla*. ssp. *grandicona* Farjon. Lvs similar to type but more often strongly glaucous blue, terete and often thicker; cones stouter. US (Calif.). Z4.

T. patens Downie = *T. chinensis*.

T. pattoniana (Jeffrey) Engelm. = *T. mertensiana*.

T. pattoniana var. *jeffreyi* Henry = *T. mertensiana* var. *jeffreyi*.

T. sieboldii Carr. SOUTHERN JAPANESE HEMLOCK. To 30m, or shrub in cult. Crown conical to ovoid. Lvs in loose ranks, 7–20×2mm, yellow-green above, pale green or dull white beneath, lateral lvs longer than those above shoot, emarginate. Cones short-stalked, ovoid, 14–26mm, shiny yellow-buff, scales vertically ribbed, incurved. S Jap. Z6.

T. tchekiangensis Flous = *T. chinensis*.

T. yunnanensis (Franch.) Pritz. = *T. dumosa*.

T. yunnanensis hort. non (Franch.) Pritz. = *T. forrestii*.

Tsushima-giboshi *Hosta tsushimensis*.

Tsusiophyllum Maxim. Ericaceae. 1 prostrate, semi-evergr. shrub, 30–45cm. Lvs 1–2cm, ovate to lanceolate, hirsute above. Fls in umbellate clusters; cor. white, tubular, pubesc., tube *c*10mm, limb *c*6mm diam., lobes 5, short, corrugated. Summer. Jap. Z7.

T. tanakee Maxim.

Tuart *Eucalyptus gomphocephala*.

Tuba Root *Derris elliptica*.

Tuberaria (Dunal) Spach. Cistaceae. 12 ann. or perenn. rock-rose-like herbs with erect flowering st. and basal lf rosettes. Fls in term. cymes. Early–late summer. C & S Eur. Z8.

T. annua Spach = *T. guttata*.

T. globulariifolia (Lam.) Willk. Perenn. to 40cm. Lvs 2.5–5cm, spathulate, pubesc. or glab. above; fls 3–5cm diam.; pet. yellow, basal spot purple-brown. Early–late summer. NW Spain, Port.

T. guttata (L.) Fourr. Hairy ann. to 30cm. Lvs obovate to lanceolate or oblong, pubesc. Fls 1–2cm diam.; pet. (where present), small, yellow with maroon basal spot. Early–late summer. C & S Eur.

T. lignosa (Sweet) Samp. Perenn. to 40cm. Lvs ovate-lanceolate to elliptic, with scattered hairs above. Fls to 3cm diam., yellow, unspotted. Early–late summer. W Medit.

T. melastomatifolia Grosser = *T. lignosa*.

T. praecox Grosser. Unbranched grey-pubesc. ann. Lvs 2.5–3.5cm. Fls yellow, unspotted. Early–late summer. C Medit.

T. variabilis Willk. = *T. guttata*.

T. vulgaris Willk. = *T. lignosa*.

→*Helianthemum* and *Cistus*.

Tuberose *Polianthes tuberosa*.

Tuberous Pea *Lathyrus tuberosus*.

Tuberous Vetch *Lathyrus tuberosus*.

Tuber Root *Asclepias tuberosa*.

Tuckermannia Klotzsch.

T. maritima Nutt. = *Coreopsis maritima*.

Tufted California Poppy *Eschscholzia caespitosa*.

Tufted Fescue *Festuca amethystina*.

Tufted Fishtail Palm *Caryota mitis*.

Tufted Hair Grass *Deschampsia cespitosa*.

Tufted Sedge *Carex elata*.

Tufted Vetch *Vicia cracca*.

Tuftroot *Dieffenbachia*.

Tulbagh Bell *Gladiolus inflatus*.

Tulbaghia L. WILD GARLIC; SOCIETY GARLIC. Liliaceae (Alliaceae). *c*20 perenn. bulbous or rhizomatous herbs with a garlic-like scent. Lvs basal ligulate. Fls star-like in a loose scapose umbel; perianth urceolate, lobes 6 spreading, throat with fleshy corona; anth. 6, sessile 2-ranked. Summer. S Afr.

T. acutiloba Harv. Lvs 10–15×0.2cm. Scape to 15cm; fls 8mm; perianth tube oblong, seg. lanceolate, green; corona purple, crenate. E Cape, Transvaal. Z9.

T. alliacea L. Lvs 15–22×0.3–0.6cm. Scape to 45cm; perianth green or white, tube to 6mm, lobes oblong, 2–5×1.5mm; corona orange-brown, crenate. Cape Prov. Z8.

T. capensis L. Lvs 30×1–1.5cm. Scapes to 60cm; perianth olive green; corona maroon, deeply cleft with 3 bifid lobes. Z8.

T. cominsii Vosa. Lvs to 20×0.1cm, glaucous. Scape 22cm; fls nocturnally fragrant, 0.5cm diam., white, tube pale purple. Spring–summer. S Afr. (Cape Prov.).

T. daviesii C.H. Grey = *T. fragrans*.

T. fragrans Verdoorn. SWEET GARLIC; PINK AGAPANTHUS. Lvs 30×2cm. Scape to 60cm; fls sweet-scented; perianth light purple, tube to 9mm, lobes to 8mm, sometimes with involute margins; corona purple-pink, cylindric, split into 3 bifid lobes. NE Transvaal. Z8.

T. natalensis Bak. To 30cm. Scape 30cm; fls fragrant; perianth tube to 4mm, white sometimes tinged lilac; perianth lobes to 7mm; corona yellow-orange or green-white with 3-toothed lobes. NE Transvaal, Natal. Z8.

T. violacea Harv. Lvs to 30×1cm ± grey-green. Scape to 60cm; fls sweet-scented, bright lilac; perianth tube to 1.5cm, slightly inflated at base, lobes to 2cm, with deeper median stripe; corona with 3 lobes, purple tinged red or white. E Cape, Transvaal. 'Silver Lace': fls large. 'Variegata': lvs striped cream. Z7.

Tulipa L. Liliaceae (Liliaceae). 100 bulbous, perenn. herbs, some stoloniferous; bulb tunics papery to coriaceous. St. simple. Lvs alt., linear-lanceolate to broadly ovate, sometimes undulate or crispate. Fls usually solitary, erect, campanulate to cup-shaped; tep. 6, free, in 2 whorls, often blotched near base; sta. 6, stigma 3-lobed, prominent. 'Broken' colours, i.e. irregular splashes of colour, are due to virus infections. Spring–flowering, unless otherwise stated. N temp. OW, esp. C Asia.

T. acuminata Vahl ex Hornem. St. 30–45cm. Lvs to 20×5cm, 3, lanceolate, ± undulate, glaucous. Fls yellow, sometimes streaked red; tep. 7.5–13cm, v. narrowly tapering; apex often convoluted. Known only in cult. Z5.

T. agenensis DC. St. to 20cm. Fls red, basal blotch black, edged yellow; outer tep. 6–8.5×1–3cm, oblong to elliptic, inner tep. 5–7.5cm, elliptic, acute. W & S Turk., NW Iran, nat. S Fr. and It. Z6.

T. aitchisonii Hall = *T. clusiana*.

T. aitchisonii ssp. *cashmeriana* Hall = *T. clusiana* var. *chrysantha*.

T. aitchisonii ssp. *chrysantha* Hall = *T. clusiana* var. *chrysantha*.

T. alberti Reg. St. to 20cm. Lvs to 14×6cm, 3–4, broadly lanceolate, crispate, glaucous, margins white. Fl. 1, glossy vermilion, orange or yellow; tep. rhombic, inner cup-shaped, outer reflexed, tinged purple, tapering, basal blotch black or dark purple, heart-shaped, bordered yellow. C Asia. Z6.

T. aleppensis Hall. St. 20cm. Lvs 4–5, to 30×6cm, glaucous, ciliate. Fl. 1, cup-shaped, crimson; inner tep. to 7cm, outer to 9cm, basal blotch black, edged yellow. Syr., S Turk. Z7.

T. altaica Spreng. St. 10–25cm. Lvs to 15×4cm, 3, lanceolate, erect, plicate, glaucous. Fl. 1, spreading; tep. 5cm, oblong, acuminate, lemon-yellow, exterior tinted red and green. C Asia. Z6.

T. armena Boiss. St. to 25cm. Lvs to 16×2.5cm, 3–6, lanceolate, glaucous, recurved, undulate, ciliate. Fl. 1, cup- to bowl-shaped, crimson, vermilion, yellow or multi-coloured; tep. to 6cm, rhombic to long-obovate, basal blotch black, navy or yellow-green, sometimes fan-shaped or bordered yellow. Turk. to Transcauc. Z7.

T. aucheriana Bak. Close to *T. humilis* but fls star-shaped, pink, tep. 3×1cm, basal blotch yellow. Iran. Z5.

T. australis Link. Like *T. sylvestris* but st. slender, outer tep. shorter, 2–3.5cm, outside flushed red. Distrib. as for *T. sylvestris*. Z7.

T. baeotica Boiss. & Heldr. = *T. undulatifolia*.

T. bakeri Hall. Like *T. saxatilis* but fls deeper in colour, lilac to purple. Crete. Z6.

T. batalinii Reg. Close to *T. linifolia* but tep. pale yellow, golden to bronze at centre. 'Apricot Jewel': fls apricot-orange, interior yellow. 'Bright Gem': fls sulphur yellow, flushed orange. 'Bronze Charm': fls sulphur, feathered apricot-bronze. 'Red Gem': fls bright red, long-lasting. 'Yellow Jewel': fls pale lemon tinged pink. Z5.

T. biflora Pall. St. to 10cm, glaucous. Lvs to 15×1cm, 2, linear, channelled, decurved, feathered glaucous, margins and tips claret. Fls fragrant, 1–2, broad-campanulate; tep. to 3cm, narrowly rhombic, cream to ivory, exterior grey-green or green-violet, inner tep. acute, basal blotch yellow, fringed with yellow cilia. Late winter–spring. S Balk., SE Russia. Z5.

T. billietiana Jordan = *T. gesneriana*.

T. bonarotiana Reboul = *T. gesneriana*.

T. borszczowii Reg. St. to 20cm, sometimes tinged red. Lvs to 18×4cm, 3, lanceolate, reflexed, undulate, margins white ciliate. Fl. 1; tep. yellow, orange or vermilion, outer tep. to 6cm, rhombic inner tep. to 7cm, obtriangular, basal blotch black. C Asia, Iran.

T. butkovii Z. Botsch. Like *T. armena* but st. downy and fls ox-blood to jasper red with deep red basal blotches. C Asia. Z6.

T. carinata Vved. St. to 48cm. Lvs to 21×6.5cm, 3–4, broadly lanceolate, blue-green, pubesc., upper part often twisted around keel, margins ciliate, yellow or pink. Fl. 1, tep. to 9cm, obovate to subrhombic, tapering, crimson flushed pink, basal blotch small, yellow or black bordered yellow. C Asia. Z6.

T. celsiana DC. Resembles *T. sylvestris* but st. shorter, to 15cm, lvs often prostrate, lying twisted along the ground, fls appearing later, outer tep. shorter, outside flushed red. Z5.

T. chrysantha Boiss. ex Bak. = *T. clusiana* var. *chrysantha*.

T. clusiana DC. LADY TULIP. St. to 30cm. Lvs to 30×1cm, 2–5, linear, glaucous. Fls 1(–2), opening to form a star; tep. tapering, white to cream, outer tep. to 6cm, exterior carmine, edged white, elliptic, acuminate, basal blotch purple or red. Iran to Afghan., nat. S Eur. 'Cynthia': fls cream, exterior red with green edge, base purple. 'Tubergen's Gem': fls yellow, exterior red. var. *chrysantha* (Hall) Sealy. Fls golden-yellow, exterior of tep. stained red or purple-brown, basal blotch 0. NW India. var. *stellata* (Hook.) Reg. Fls v. starry, basal blotch yellow.

T. cornuta Delile = *T. acuminata*.

T. cretica Boiss. & Heldr. St. to 20cm. Lvs 2–3, lanceolate. Fls 1–3; tep. to 3cm, white flushed pink, basal blotch yellow, outer tep. spreading, inner erect. Crete. Z7.

T. cuspidata Reg. = *T. stapfii*.

T. cypria Turrill. Related to *T. agenensis*. St. to 35cm. Fls deep crimson, exterior flushed green at base, basal blotch navy, usually edged yellow. Cyprus. Z7.

T. dasystemon (Reg.) Reg. St. to 5cm. Lvs to 10×1cm, 2, semi-subterranean at flowering, narrowly lanceolate, blue-green. Fl. 1; tep. to 2cm, narrowly lanceolate, bright yellow, exterior of outer tep. with a broad, brown-claret or green band along mid-rib, interior pure yellow, inner tep. streaked brown-green along midrib. C Asia. Z5.

T. dasystemon auct. non (Reg.) Reg. = *T. tarda*.

T. didieri Jordan. St. to 40(–50)cm. Lvs 15–20×3cm, 3–4, lanceolate, undulate, glaucous. Fl. 1; tep. usually bright crimson, occas. white, rounded, basal blotch black, bordered pale yellow. S Eur. Z7.

T. dubia Vved. St. short; peduncle to 25cm. Lvs to 14×6cm, 2–4, in a rosette, falcate, glaucous, undulate, ciliate. Fl. 1; tep. to 4cm, lanceolate to rhombic, yellow, outside streaked blue-pink, widely stellate, fragrant, outer tep. acute, basal blotch orange, inner tep. obtuse, lemon-yellow to orange at base. C Asia. Z5.

T. edulis (Miq.) Bak. St. to 15cm. Lvs to 25×1cm, to 6. Fls 1–2; tep. to 3cm, ivory, veined claret or mauve, basal blotch purple-black edged yellow. Late winter–spring. S Jap., NE China, Korea. var. *latifolia* Mak. Lvs shorter and wider, to 15×1.5cm. Z7.

T. eichleri Reg. = *T. undulatifolia*.

T. elegans hort. ex Bak. Close to *T. gesneriana*. St. to 45cm, pubesc. Lvs to 25cm, lanceolate. Tep. scarlet, tapering, basal blotch yellow. Known only in cult. 'Alba': tep. white edged pink. Z6.

T. etrusca Levier = *T. gesneriana*.

T. ferganica Vved. St. to 25cm, pubesc., glaucous, sometimes tinged red. Lvs to 16×7cm, 3–5, broadly to narrowly lanceolate, reflexed, glaucous, undulate to crispate, margins ciliate, pale yellow. Fls 1–2, star-shaped, yellow, exterior blue-pink or pale chocolate-pink; tep. 5cm, lanceolate, acuminate. C Asia. Z5.

T. florentina hort. ex Bak. = *T. sylvestris*.

T. fosteriana Hoog ex W. Irv. St. 15–50cm, tinted pink. Lvs to 30×16cm, 3–5, oblong to broadly ovate, glossy green. Fl. 1, faintly scented; tep. to 18cm, lustrous vivid red, long-ovate to narrowly rhombic to broadly lanceolate, basal blotch black, fan-shaped or 2–3-pointed, edged yellow. Fosteriana Hybrids (*T. fosteriana* × *T. greigii* or *T. kaufmanniana*): fls large, white or yellow. 'Princeps': resembles 'Red Emperor' but st. shorter, fls later. 'Red Emperor' ('Mme Lefeber'): fls large, tep. to 15cm, brilliant red, glossy, basal blotch black with irregular yellow border. Crossed with Darwin tulips to produce Darwin Hybrids, which include Mendel tulips (fls large, st. stout). Z5.

T. fulgens Bak. As for *T. elegans* but st. glab.; anth. yellow, not purple. Probably of gdn origin. Z5.

T. galatica Freyn. St. 15cm. Lvs to 12cm, 4, linear-lanceolate, undulate. Fls campanulate; tep. to 7cm, obovate, reflexed, pale yellow, exterior tinged green-brown, basal blotch yellow-grey or olive. Turk. (not known in the wild). Z5.

T. gesneriana L. St. to 60cm, glab. or finely pubesc. Lvs to 15cm, 2–7, lanceolate to ovate-lanceolate, glaucous. Fl. 1, cup-shaped, opening to form a star; tep. 4–8cm (inner tep. wider), purple to dull crimson to yellow, sometimes variegated ('broken'), sometimes with yellow or dark olive, yellow-edged basal blotch. E Eur., Asia Minor. Z5.

T. goulimyi Sealy and Turrill. Resembles *T. ferganica* but tep. orange to brick-red. S Greece. Z7.

T. greigii Reg. St. to 45cm, often tinged pink or brown, densely pubesc. Lvs to 32×16cm, 3–5, usually reflexed, lanceolate-oblong to lanceolate, glaucous, stained and streaked maroon above. Fl. 1; tep. to 16cm, vermilion to yellow or multi-coloured, rhombic to oblong-obovate, basal blotch rhombic, black or red. C Asia. Z5.

T. grengiolensis Thommsen. As for *T. gesneriana* except st. shorter, 25–40cm; tep. pale yellow, edged crimson. Switz. Z7.

T. grisebachiana Pant. = *T. sylvestris*.

T. hageri Heldr. As for *T. orphanidea*, but fls dull red, exterior tinted or marked green. 'Splendens': fls bronze tinted red, exterior dark red. Z5.

T. heterophylla (Reg.) Bak. As for *T. kolpakowskiana* but st. 5–15cm; tep. 1.5–3cm, yellow, exterior stained purple or green. C Asia. Z6.

T. hoogiana B. Fedtsch. St. to 40cm, glaucous, dark red-brown. Lvs to 25×10cm, 3–5, lanceolate, clasping, falcate, grey-green, margins long-hairy. Fl. 1, glossy dark crimson or orange-pink, cup-shaped; outer tep. 9.5cm, broadly elliptic, ± toothed and undulate, inner upright, spoon-shaped, basal blotch ± triangular, black to dark crimson or grey-green edged yellow. C Asia. Z6.

T. humilis Herb. Highly variable. St. to 20cm. Lvs 10–15×1cm, 2–5, channelled, ± glaucous. Fls 1 to 3, cup-shaped opening to a star, pale pink, yellow at centre; tep. 2–5cm, inner longer than outer. SE Turk., N & W Iran, N Iraq, Azerbaidjan. 'Eastern Star': fls rose, flamed bronze green on outer tep., base yellow. 'Magenta Queen': fls lilac with yellow centre, exterior lush green flame. 'Odalisque': fls light purple, base yellow. 'Persian Pearl': fls cyclamen-purple, base yellow, exterior light magenta. 'Violacea': fls deep violet, centre yellow. Z7.

T. iliensis Reg. As for *T. kolpakowskiana* but st. pubesc.; fls 1–5; tep. to 3.5cm, yellow, exterior stained crimson or dull yellow-green. C Asia. Z6.

T. ingens Hoog. St. to 40cm. Lvs 3–6, narrowly lanceolate, glaucous, usually downy and undulate. Fl. 1, opening to a star; tep. to 12cm, red-purple, outer broadly-elliptic, tip densely pubesc. reflexed, basal blotch black, rhombic, inner tep. narrowly obovate, basal blotch black, sometimes edged yellow. C Asia. Z6.

T. julia K. Koch. St. to 15cm. Lvs to 13.5×5cm, 4, lanceolate, slightly glaucous, channelled, crispate. Fl. 1, opening to a wide cup; tep. to 5cm, dull crimson to orange-red, exterior tinted salmon or orange, subrhombic, basal blotch elliptic or obtriangular, green-black, edged yellow. Transcauc., NW Iran, E Turk. Z6.

T. kaufmanniana Reg. St. to 50cm, often tinged red. Lvs to 20cm wide, 2–5, often rosulate, lanceolate to oblanceolate, slightly undulate, pale grey-green. Fls 1–5, star-shaped to campanulate to cup-shaped, often fragrant; tep. to 11cm, white or cream, occas. yellow to brick-red, outer tep. lanceolate to broad-lanceolate, basal blotch yellow, outside red or pink along midrib, inner tep. often erect, long-elliptic, sometimes multi-coloured, midrib often green or red, basal blotch bright yellow. C Asia. 'Lady Killer': fls white, exterior central crimson flame, centre and anth. purple. Z5.

T. kolpakowskiana Reg. St. 15–35cm, glaucous. Lvs to 20×3cm, 2–4, erect, deeply channelled, glaucous, undulate, ciliate. Fls 1(–2–4) cup-shaped; tep. 5–8cm, long-rhombic, yellow, exterior marked green, basal blotch 0. C Asia, Afghan. Z6.

T. kurdica Wendelbo. Close to *T. orphanidea* but with shorter st. (6–15cm) and solitary, vivid, jasper-coloured fls with tep. blotched green-black at base. NE Iraq. Z7.

T. kuschkensis B. Fedtsch. St. 14–45cm, glaucous. Lvs to 25×9cm, 3–5, lanceolate, apical half falcate and recurved, margins crispate, ciliate. Fls resembling those of *T. hoogiana*, but with revolute outer tep. C Asia, Afghan. Z6.

T. lanata Reg. St. 13–60cm, pubesc. pale green. Lvs to 16×5.5cm, 4, lanceolate, reflexed, purple, margins red, undulate, ciliate. Fl. 1; tep. to 12×6cm, exterior silver-pink, interior bright red, outer tep. rhombic, tapering, inner tep. obovate, basal blotch black, elliptic to rhombic, edged pale yellow. C Asia. Z7.

T. latifolia (Mak.) Mak. = *T. edulis* var. *latifolia*.

T. lehmanniana Bunge. St. to 25cm. Lvs undulate. Fls yellow, vermilion or crimson, flushed scarlet or red-brown, basal blotch black, olive-green or purple. C Asia, Afghan., NE Iran. Z7.

T. linifolia Reg. St. to 30cm. Lvs to 8×1cm, 3–8, linear, falcate, margin often wavy, ciliate and pink. Fl. 1, star-shaped; tep. to 6cm, rhombic to subovate, scarlet, basal blotch blue-black, often edged cream to lemon-yellow. C Asia, N Iran, Afghan. Z5.

T. lortetii Jordan = *T. agenensis*.

T. marjolettii Perrier & Song. Close to *T. gesneriana*. To 50cm. Tep. pale yellow to cream edged pink, exterior flushed rose-mauve. SE Fr. Z6.

T. maurania Jordan & Fourn. = *T. mauritania*.

T. mauritania Jordan. St. to 40cm. Lvs 20×4–8cm, 3–4, lanceolate, undulate. Fl. 1, campanulate; tep. 3.5–5cm, oblong, red, basal blotch yellow or black edged yellow. SE Fr. Z6.

T. maximowiczii Reg. Close to *T. linifolia* but basal blotch black edged white. Z5.

T. micheliana Hoog. St. to 35cm. Lvs to 30×2cm, 3–5, lanceolate, grey-green with garnet or maroon stripes, usually ciliate, undulate. Fl. 1; tep. to 16cm, rhombic to obovate, vermilion to dark crimson, wavy, basal blotch rectangular to elliptic, purple-black often thinly edged pale yellow. NE Iran, C Asia. Z6.

T. montana Lindl. St. 5–15cm. Lvs to 15×1.5cm, 3–6, narrowly lanceolate, channelled, glaucous, undulate-crispate, purple. Fls cup-shaped; tep. to 5cm, subrhombic to narrowly obovate, brilliant red, basal blotch green or purple-black. N Iran, C Asia. Z6.

T. oculis-solis St.-Amans = *T. agenensis*.

T. orphanidea Heldr. St. 10–35cm. Lvs to 30×1.5cm, 2–7, lanceolate, margin oft. claret. Fls 1–4, globose; tep. 3–5cm, elliptic, vermilion to brick-red, outside of outer tep. buff stained green or purple, basal blotch olive to black, sometimes edged

yellow. E Medit. The plant usually offered as *T. orphanidea* has dull orange-brown fls, the exterior suffused green and mauve. 'Flava': fls yellow, flushed red; similar to *T. sylvestris*. Z5.

T. ostrowskiana Reg. St. to 35cm. Lvs to 15×3cm, 2–4, strongly decurved, lanceolate, channelled, glaucous, undulate-crispate, white, ciliate. Fl. 1, cup- to star-shaped; tep. 5–8cm, long-rhombic, vermilion, orange, yellow or multi-coloured, outer tep. with an opaline lustre, often with 3-peaked yellow basal blotch, inner tep. with 2 brighter stripes parallel with midrib, basal blotch yellow, sometimes with a central brown spot. C Asia. Z6.

T. passeriniana Levier = *T. gesneriana*.

T. platystigma Jordan. Lvs 20–30×5cm, 3–4, lanceolate, slightly wavy. St. slender, 40–55cm. Fl. 1, campanulate, fragrant; tep. 8×3cm, elliptic, pink-violet, basal blotch or zone blue, edged orange. SE Fr. Z7.

T. polychroma Stapf. Close to *T. biflora*. St. 10–15cm. Lvs to 15cm, 1–2, channelled. Fls 1–2, nodding, white with yellow base inside, exterior green with red veins. Iran, Afghan. Z7.

T. polychroma Stapf = *T. biflora*.

T. praecox Ten. St. to 65cm. Lvs to 35×7cm, 3–5, lanceolate, glaucous. Fl. 1; tep. orange-red, outside streaked green, basal blotch green-brown, edged yellow, outer 4–10cm, ovate to elliptic, inner 4–7cm, ovate, midrib bordered yellow. Probably Middle E, nat. S Eur. and W Turk. Z5.

T. praestans Hoog. St. 10–60cm. Lvs 3–6, oblong or lanceolate, pale grey-green, keeled, ciliate. Fls 1–5, cupped; tep. orange-red, outer 7cm, broadly elliptic or subovate, tinged yellow toward base, inner shorter. C Asia. 'Fusilier': fls glowing orange-red, to 4 per st. 'Unicum': lvs broadly edged white; fls to 5 per st., red, base small, yellow, anth. black. 'Van Tubergen's Variety': fls red, several per st. 'Zwanenburg': fls large, striking red. Z5.

T. primulina Bak. Lvs grey-green. Fls 1–2, occas. nodding; tep. off-white to ivory or pale yellow, outer suffused rose or pale green. Alg. Z8.

T. pubescens Willd. = *T. gesneriana*.

T. pulchella (Reg.) Bak. As for *T. humilis* but tep. to 3cm, strongly cupped, mauve, central (basal) blotch navy edged white. Turk. var. *albocaerulea-occulata* Tuberg. Fls white-mauve, basal blotch navy, fls earlier. Z5.

T. retroflexa Bak. Close to *T. gesneriana*. Tep. 7.5–10cm, golden yellow, long-acuminate, upper half reflexed. SE Fr. Z7.

T. rhodopea (Velen.) Velen. = *T. urumoffii*.

T. saxatilis Spreng. CANDIA TULIP. St. 15–45cm. Lvs 10–30×2–5, 2–4, glab., lustrous, rarely glaucous. Fls 1–4, fragrant; tep. 4–5cm, elliptic, pink to mauve, basal blotch yellow edged white. Crete, W Turk. Material offered as *T. saxatilis* will usually have lilac fls, those named '*T. bakeri*' have deeper mauve tones. 'Lilac Wonder': fls rosy lilac, base large, lemon-yellow, anth. yellow. Z6.

T. scabriscopa Strangw. = *T. gesneriana*.

T. schrenkii Reg. = *T. armena*.

T. sharonensis Dinsm. As for *T. praecox* and *T. agenensis* but basal blotch larger, deep olive, edged yellow. Isr. Z8.

T. sommieri Levier = *T. gesneriana*.

T. spathulata Bertol. = *T. gesneriana*.

T. sprengeri Bak. St. to 30cm. Lvs to 25×3cm, 3–6, linear. Fl. 1; tep. brilliant red, acute, outer 6cm, buff beneath, inner to 2.5cm wide, basal blotch 0. Late spring–early summer. N Turk. Z5.

T. stapfii Turrill. St. to 30cm. Lvs glaucous. Fls red, basal blotch dark violet, edged yellow. W Iran, N Iraq. Z8.

T. stellata Hook. = *T. clusiana* var. *stellata*.

T. stellata var. *chrysantha* (Hall) Sealy = *T. clusiana* var. *chrysantha*.

T. strangulata Reboul = *T. gesneriana*.

T. suaveolens Roth = *T. armena*.

T. subpraestans Vved. St. to 40cm, glaucous, pubesc. Lvs 3–4, lanceolate to oblong-lanceolate, falcate, reflexed, undulate, ciliate. Fls 2–3(–6), tep. narrow, opening to form a star, glossy orange-red, tinged yellow at base. C Asia. Z6.

T. sylvestris L. St. to 45cm. Lvs to 24×2.5cm, 2–4, declinate, linear, channelled, dark green, glaucous. Fls 1–2, starry; tep. to 7×2.5cm, lanceolate to subrhombic, golden, midrib bordered green, inner convex, sometimes tinged pink. Origin unknown; nat. from Eur. and N Afr. to C Asia and Sib. 'Major': fls to 3 per st., gold, abundant, larger, with 8 pet. 'Tabriz': tall; fls large, lemon-yellow, sweetly scented. Z5.

T. sylvestris ssp. *australis* (Link) Pamp. = *T. australis*.

T. systola Stapf. As for *T. agenensis* but lvs v. waxy, nestling close to ground, tep. deep tomato-red, outside streaked grey. Iran. Z8.

T. tarda Stapf. St. to 5×11cm. Lvs to 12×1.5cm, 3–7, lanceolate, recurved, bright green, margins claret, often ciliate. Fls 4–15, broadly star-shaped, fragrant; outer tep. to 3.5cm, broadly lanceolate, white, midrib edged with a broad green stripe shading to purple and yellow, inner 3.5cm, spoon-shaped, often yellow toward base. C Asia. Z5.

T. tetraphylla Reg. St. to 25cm. Lvs to 14×9cm, 3–7, lanceolate, reflexed, falcate, ligulate, glaucous, margins crispate, often white-ciliate. Fls 1–4, double cup-shaped; tep. to 8cm, yellow, outer broadly lanceolate, reflexed, exterior tinted lime-green along midrib surrounded by a broad crimson band, inner narrowly obovate, attenuate, basal blotch green. C Asia. Z6.

T. tschimganica Z. Botsch. St. to 26cm. Lvs to 24×7cm, 3–4, lanceolate, declinate, falcate, channelled, ciliate, glaucous. Fl. 1, conical or star-shaped; tep. yellow with crimson V-shaped markings: outer to 7cm, broadly lanceolate to narrowly ovate, inner rounded, often notched. C Asia. Z6.

T. tubergeniana Hoog. St. 5–60cm, short-hairy, sometimes tinted red-pink. Lvs to 18×2.5cm, 3–4, lanceolate to linear, glaucous, falcate, reflexed, undulate. Fl. 1; tep. to 10cm, rhombic to obovate, long-acuminate, red, basal blotch elliptic, black or black-claret, edged yellow. C Asia. Z5.

T. turkestanica Reg. V. close to *T. biflora*. St. to 30cm, white-pubesc. Lvs 2–4 exceeding infl. Fls to 12, smaller than *T. biflora*, white, centre yellow or orange, sometimes malodorous. C Asia. Z5.

T. undulatifolia Boiss. St. to 50cm. Lvs to 19×5.5cm, 3–4, linear to lanceolate, reflexed, glaucous, pubesc., margins crispate, ciliate. Fl. 1, cup-shaped to campanulate; tep. to 7cm, broadly lanceolate to obovate, crimson to dark red, basal blotch elliptic to rhombic, black to purple, often edged yellow. Balk., Greece, Turk., Iran, C Asia. 'Clare Benedict': fls bright red, base black, edge yellow, early-flowering. 'Excelsa': fls large, scarlet, base black, edge yellow. Z5.

T. urumiensis Stapf. St. 1–2, to 20cm, mostly subterranean. Lvs 10–12×1cm, 2–4 in a flat rosette, plicate, glaucous. Fls 1–2, cup-shaped, opening to a star; tep. to 4cm, yellow, outside streaked green or red. NW Iran. Z5.

T. urumoffii Hayek. St. to 30cm. Lvs 3–5, glaucous. Fls 1(–3); tep. to 6cm, yellow to red-brown, basal blotch black edged yellow, often 0. S Bulg. Z6.

T. variopicta Reboul = *T. gesneriana*.

T. violacea Boiss. & Buhse. As for *T. humilis* but fls more rounded, tep. 3–5cm, violet-pink, basal blotch black, edged yellow. N Iran, SE Turk. var. *pallida* Bornm. Fls paler mauve, basal blotch navy, fls earlier; may be identical with *T. pulchella* var. *albocaerulea-occulata*. Z5.

T. viridiflora anon. As for *T. gesneriana* but tep. green-white or yellow-green fading to cream or white at edges. Z6.

T. vvedenskyi Z. Botsch. St. 15–20cm, sometimes tinged maroon, densely short-hairy. Lvs to 25×6cm, 4–5, lanceolate, reflexed, glaucous, crispate. Fl. 1, cup-shaped; outer tep. to 10cm, crimson, basal blotch yellow, often with brown spot, inner tep. obovate, base yellow, basal blotch black-brown to claret. C Asia. 'Tangerine Beauty': fls bright red with grey-brown and lemon-yellow basal blotches, exterior light orange to flame. Z6.

T. whittallii Hall. To 35cm, fls vivid orange-bronze, otherwise v. similar to *T. orphanidea*. Z5.

T. wilsoniana Hoog = *T. montana*.

HYBRIDS AND CULTIVARS.

CLASSIFICATION. There are currently 15 subdivisions in the classification of garden tulips. The groups can be arranged into early, mid-season and late-flowering, plus the 'botanical' and other species tulips.

EARLY TULIPS. (1) Single Early. Height 15–40cm; fls 8–14cm long, white to deep purple with coloured edges, flecks or exterior central flame; late March–early April. 'Apricot Beauty': salmon pink flushed orange. 'Bellona': globular, butter yellow, fragrant. 'Brilliant Star': low; fls scarlet vermilion. 'Couleur Cardinal': deep red washed purple with white bloom. 'Diana': white, central flame tinted cream. 'Generaal de Wet': tall; fls gold washed and flecked dark orange, fragrant. 'Joffre': yellow with red flushes. 'Keizerkroon' ('Grand Duc'): scarlet broadly edged yellow and cream. 'Pink Beauty': deep pink edged white. 'Prince of Austria': orange flecked scarlet with tawny bloom. 'Prins Carnaval' ('Prince Carnival'): yellow with exterior red flame and feathering. 'Prinses Irene': orange with exterior purple flame. 'Van der Neer': deep purple.

(2) Double Early. Height 30–40cm; fls fully double bowl-shaped, 8–10cm across, white through yellow to red with coloured edges or flecks; early to mid-April. 'Electra': deep pink-mauve edged lighter. 'Madame Testout': rose. 'Maréchal Niel': yellow tinted tawny orange. 'Monte Carlo': clear yellow. 'Mr Van der Hoef': golden yellow. 'Murillo': white flushed pale pink. 'Orange Nassau': dark red flushed brilliant red. 'Peach Blossom': deep pink with creamy exterior flame and flecks. 'Schoonoord' ('Purity'): white. 'Triumphator': rosy red. 'Wilhelm Kordes': orange-red edged white.

MID-SEASON. (3) Triumph. Height 45–50cm; fls single, white through yellow, orange, pink, red to deep purple, with coloured edges or flecks; late April. 'Abu Hassan': cardinal red edged yellow. 'African Queen': deep burgundy with fine white edge. 'Athlete': white. 'Douglas Bader': exterior rose, paler within on white ground. 'Dreaming Maid': raspberry pink with white edge. 'Fidelio': magenta shading to orange. 'Garden Party': carmine pink with white base and central flame. 'Lustige Witwe' ('Merry Widow'): deep red edged silvery white. 'Negrito': deep purple with grey bloom. 'New Design': cream with white edging tinted pink and apricot. 'Orange Wonder': orange-bronze with scarlet shading. 'Paul Richter': geranium red. 'Pax': white. 'Peerless Pink': satin pink. 'Reforma': sulphur yellow edged golden yellow. The Mendel tulips, now no longer included in the classification, were the less sturdy forerunners of the Triumphs, raised in the 1920s by crossing Duc Van Tol with Darwins and about 37cm tall.

(4) Darwin Hybrid Tulips. Chiefly the result of hybridization between Darwin tulips (see Single Late) with *Tulipa fosteriana* and also other tulips of the same habit. Height 60–70cm; fls single, vividly coloured yellow through orange to bright red, often with coloured edges and base; May. 'Apeldoorn': scarlet, base black, bordered yellow. 'Beauty of Apeldoorn': orange, exterior flushed red, base and anth. black. 'Daydream': golden apricot. 'Elizabeth Arden': deep pink tinted salmon. 'Golden Oxford': pure yellow edged red. 'Gudoshnik': cream flushed pink-apricot and flecked red, base and anth. black. 'Holland's Glorie': large, tep. pointed, outside deep carmine, edged red, inside mandarin red, base greenish black. 'Ivory Floradale': pale ivory yellow. 'Jewel of Spring': creamy yellow edged red outside, inside creamy yellow, anth. purple, base green-black. 'Oranjezon' ('Orange Sun'): pure orange, fragrant. 'Oxford': red rounded, bright orange-red, base yellow. 'Spring Song': bright red tinted salmon, base white.

LATE TULIPS. (5) Single Late. This class includes those originally known as Darwin and Cottage tulips. Darwin tulips were over 60cm tall, bearing large squarish fls on sturdy st. Cottage tulips, a shorter and much older race, had long tep., often waisted, some cvs being multi-headed. Height 60–75cm; fls of rectangular outline, ivory through yellow, salmon, pink, red to black, often with coloured edges or feathering. 'Aristocrat': soft violet edged white. 'Bleu Aimable': vivid mauve. 'Clara Butt': rosy salmon pink. 'Halcro': fls oval, carmine red. 'Maureen': fls oval, marble white. 'Mrs John T. Scheepers': vivid yellow. 'Picture': bright cerise flushed lilac, edges laciniate. 'Queen of Bartigons': clear salmon-pink, base white edged blue. 'Queen of Night': deepest maroon to black. 'Renown': bright rouge red, yellow based edged blue. 'Rosy Wings': pink, v. long, waisted tep. 'San Marino': yellow with central red flame. 'Scarlett O'Hara': scarlet, base black with yellow ring. 'Shirley': ivory, spotted and finely edged purple. 'Sorbet': creamy white feathered red. 'Sweet Harmony': pale yellow edged cream. 'Wallflower': dark red, up to 5 fls per st. 'Zomerschoon': fls goblet-shaped, raspberry pink feathered white.

(6) Lily-fld. Height 45–60cm; fls long, waisted, tep. pointed, white to deep violet with coloured edges. 'Astor': bronze-pink. 'Ballade': violet edged white. 'Burgundy': deep violet-purple. 'China Pink': clear pink, white base. 'Elegant Lady': cream flushed yellow, edged rose. 'Golden Duchess': deep primrose yellow. 'Marilyn': low; cream feathered strawberry red. 'Mariette': large, deep pink. 'Queen of Sheba': red edged golden orange. 'Red Shine': deep ruby. 'West Point': clear primrose. 'White Triumphator': pure white.

(7) Fringed. Fls with fringed tep., fringes often crystal-like and of contrasting colour. 'Aleppo': pink and apricot, bright yellow base. 'Bellflower': pink, base white tinged blue. 'Blue Heron': violet-purple, marked white, base white. 'Burgundy Lace': claret edged white. 'Fancy Frills': pink shading to white edges, ivory white base. 'Fringed Beauty': vermilion edged gold, base black. 'Maja': golden yellow, base bronze-yellow. 'Noranda': blood red, edges tinted orange, base green-yellow. 'Redwing': cardinal red, edges lighter.

(8) Viridiflora. Around 45cm tall, the tep. with varying amounts of green. 'Angel': off-white, flare apple green, reaches tep. tip. 'Artist': deep rose, edges wavy. 'Esperanto': china rose, flamed green fading into red brown, base green-yellow, lvs edged white. 'Golden Artist': gold with red flushes. 'Green Eyes': yellow-green with darker markings. 'Groenland': pale pink with vivid green flare surrounded by cream. 'Humming Bird': clear yellow, flare apple green. 'Pimpernel': vivid claret. 'Praecox': pale yellow, edges wavy, early. 'Spring Green': ivory, flare pale green.

(9) Rembrandt. 'Broken' tulips having striped or feathered markings in brown, bronze, black, red, pink or purple on a white, yellow or red ground. The term Rembrandts included 'Bizarres' or 'Bizards', mostly marked with brown, bronze or black on yellow ground; and 'Bybloemens', striped pink, violet or purple on white ground. 'Absalon': coffee brown on yellow. 'Beauty of Volendam': deep crimson on white. 'Cordell Hull': rose on white. 'May Blossom': deep maroon on cream. 'Pierette': purple on pale violet. 'Striped Bellona': vivid red on yellow.

(10) Parrot. Sports (mutations) from other tulips in which the large fls are deeply laciniate or slashed, with even bands of colour. Height 50–60cm; fls to 20cm diam., often bicoloured, edges fringed, shredded or wavy. 'Apricot Parrot': apricot flushed pink and sometimes green. 'Bird of Paradise': deep cardinal red shading to orange tips, base bright yellow, edges shredded. 'Blue Parrot': mauve, bronzed outside, tep. ruffled. 'Black Parrot': deepest maroon, heavily fringed. 'Estella Rijnveld' ('Gay Presto'): white flushed yellow with heavy red markings, edges shredded. 'Fantasy': pale salmon edged and flecked rose, occasional green flushes, edges wavy. 'Karel Doorman': cherry red, edged yellow. 'Orange Parrot': gold and mahogany, fragrant. 'Texas Gold': deep gold, red on tips, flushes of green. 'White Parrot': white, tep. edges wavy.

(11) Double Late or Peony-fld. Huge peony-like fls of many tep. Height 45–60cm; fls to 10cm diam. 'Allegretto': red tipped yellow. 'Angélique': pale pink flushed darker, edges pale and ruffled. 'Bonanza': deep red edged gold. 'Brilliant Fire': cherry flushed orange. 'Carnaval de Nice': white feathered deep red, lvs edged white. 'Eros': deep pink with faint blue hints. 'Golden Medal': compact, deep yellow. 'Golden Nizza': gold lightly feathered rich violet. 'Maywonder': rose pink. 'Mount Tacoma': compact, pure white. 'Miranda': vermilion with darker flames, base yellow. 'Wirosa': bright claret edged cream.

SPECIES ('BOTANICAL TULIPS'). The first three of these groups arose from the wild spp. which give each group its name; however, recent interbreeding of the many original selections has almost rendered the groupings meaningless. All fl. in March–April.

(12) Kaufmanniana. V. early flowering with strap-shaped tep. opening flat in sunlight, hence the name waterlily tulips. Height 15–25cm; lvs plain or marked dark green-brown; fls white to currant-red with coloured edges, throat, base or central flame on exterior. tep. 'Alfred Cortot': lvs streaked purple-brown; fls bright scarlet, base black. 'Ancilla': white with red ring and yellow throat, exterior red edged rose. 'Berlioz': red-brown edged yellow, yellow exterior. 'Chopin': lvs mottled; fls lemon-yellow, base black. 'Fair Lady': lvs mottled; fls cream, base yellow, occasional red streaks, exterior carmine edged cream. 'Franz Léhar': lvs mottled; fls lemon white, base yellow, occasional red flecks. 'Fritz Kreisler' ('Yolanda'): cream to deep pink throat, exterior salmon pink edged sulphur. 'Glück': yellow, throat gold, exterior red edged yellow-cream. 'Heart's Delight': lvs mottled; fls pink, throat gold, exterior carmine broadly edged milky pink. 'Shakespeare': salmon streaked yellow and red. 'Showwinner': lvs mottled; fls cardinal red, base yellow. 'Stresa': lvs mottled; fls yellow, red mark at throat, exterior with currant red flame. 'The First': ivory, throat yellow, exterior with carmine flame. 'Vivaldi': lvs mottled bronze; fls sulphur, base gold, exterior carmine rose edged yellow.

(13) Fosteriana. Height 20–65cm; lvs apple to dark green or variegated; fls oval to oblong, white through yellow to pink or dark red, sometimes with coloured edges central flame or base. 'Candela': fls large, oblong, rich lemon yellow, anth. black. 'Cantata': to 20cm; lvs apple green; fls deep scarlet. 'Golden Eagle': fls oval, rich yellow with exterior burnt orange flame, base black and soft orange tints. 'Juan': to 45cm; lvs mottled; fls orange-scarlet marked with red-brown bands, base yellow. 'Madame Lefeber' ('Red Emperor'): fls large, bright red. 'Orange Emperor': fls large, rich vivid orange, base yellow. 'Purissima' ('White Emperor'): to 50cm; fls large, clear creamy white with yellow centre, long-lasting. 'Robassa': lvs striped cream near edge; fls vibrant red, base bluish black edged yellow. 'Spring Pearl' ('Pink Emperor'): fls pink-red with pearl sheen, centre yellow. 'Sweetheart': yellow central flame and wide white edge, slightly frilled. 'Tender Beauty': soft yellow, tep. sides with pinky red margin. 'Zombie': carmine-rose, edges yellow, exterior yellow tinted rose, red ring and black throat.

(14) Greigii. Height 20–30cm; lvs lightly to heavily mottled brown-purple; fls yellow through apricot to red, base and edges coloured. 'Cape Cod': exterior apricot edged yellow with thin red central stripe, interior flushed bronze, base black. 'Corsage': bright rose edged yellow, interior feathered gold. 'Donna Bella': cream, base black with scarlet ring, exterior carmine flame. 'Large Copper': tall; fls orange-red. 'Margaret Herbst' ('Royal Splendour'): fls large, vivid scarlet. 'Oratorio': rose, interior tinted apricot, base black. 'Oriental Splendour': fls large, deep yellow with broad scarlet flame. 'Pandour': pale yellow with red flames. 'Perlina': rose tinted orange, shading to yellow. 'Plaisir': cream with broad vermilion flame and yellow flushes. 'Red Riding Hood': fls scarlet, base black edged yellow, exterior darker. 'Toronto': multistemmed; fls deep salmon pink, interior tangerine-red, base bronze-green on yellow. 'Zampa': primrose, base bronze and green.

(15) Other spp., including selections and hybrids, including *T. batalinii*, *T. clusiana*, the Lady Tulip, *T. praestans* and *T. sprengeri*, the last to fl., around midsummer.

→*Amana*.

Tulip Orchid *Anguloa*.
Tulip Poplar *Liriodendron tulipifera*.
Tulip Tree *Liriodendron tulipifera*; *Magnolia* × *soulangiana*.
Tulip-wood Tree *Harpullia pendula*.
Tumbledown Gum *Eucalyptus dealbata*.
Tumbling Ted *Saponaria ocymoides*.
Tumbling Waters *Saxifraga* 'Calabrica'
Tuna *Opuntia*.
Tunbridge Wells Filmy Fern *Hymenophyllum tunbrigense*.
Tung-tsau *Tetrapanax*.

Tunica Hall.
T. saxifraga (L.) Scop. = *Petrorhagia saxifraga*.

Tunic Flower *Petrorhagia saxifraga*.
Tunka *Benincasa hispida*.
Tupelo *Nyssa*.

Tupidanthus Hook. f. & Thoms.
T. calyptratus Hook. f. & Thoms. = *Schefflera puckleri*.
T. puckleri K. Koch = *Schefflera puckleri*.

Turawera *Pteris tremula*.

Turbinicarpus (Backeb.) F. Buxb. & Backeb. = *Neolloydia*.

Turfing Daisy *Tripleurospermum*.
Turkestan Rose *Rosa rugosa*.
Turkey Beard *Xerophyllum asphodeloides*.
Turkey Corn *Dicentra eximia*.
Turkey Oak *Quercus cerris*.
Turkish Black Pine *Pinus nigra* var. *caramanica*.
Turkish Hazel *Corylus colurna*.
Turkish Pine *Pinus brutia*.
Turk's-cap *Aconitum napellus*; *Lilium martagon*; *Malvaviscus arboreus* var. *mexicanus*.
Turk's-cap Gourd *Cucurbita maxima*.
Turk's-cap Lily *Lilium superbum*.
Turmeric *Curcuma longa*.
Turmeric Root *Hydrastis canadensis*.

Turnera L. Turneraceae. 60 short-lived perenn. herbs or weedy small shrubs. Lvs entire, toothed or pinnatifid, with 1–2 pairs of glands at base. Fls 5-merous, solitary in lf axils, clustered or in short rac.; pet. spreading, largely free; sta. inserted at base of pet. C & S Amer., Nam. Z10.
T. ulmifolia L. WEST INDIAN HOLLY; SAGE ROSE. Subshrub to 70cm. Lvs to 10cm, lanceolate-oblong, crenate to serrate, downy above, canescent beneath, with 1 pair of glands. Peduncles connate to petioles; fls ephemeral, to 5cm diam., pet. bright yellow, sometimes flushed red or mauve; obovate to rounded. Subtrop. & trop. Americas.

TURNERACEAE DC. 10/110. *Turnera*

Turnip *Brassica rapa* Rapifera group.
Turnip Fern *Angiopteris*.
Turnip-rooted Celery *Apium graveolens* var. *rapaceum*.
Turnip-rooted Chervil *Chaerophyllum bulbosum*.
Turnip-rooted Parsley *Petroselinum crispum* var. *tuberosum*.
Turnsole *Heliotropium*.
Turpentine *Trichostema lanceolatum*.
Turpentine Broom *Thamnosma montana*.

Turraea L. Meliaceae. 70 trees and shrubs. Lvs entire or lobed. Fls in axils or on spurs; cal. cup-shaped, 5-toothed; pet. 5, long, ivory to white, strap-shaped; sta. 10, connate in a long tube, toothed at summit. Fr. a capsule splitting to reveal brightly coloured arils; seeds glossy, black. Trop. & S Afr., Trop. Asia, Aus. Z10.
T. floribunda Hochst. Lvs 3–5cm, ovate, glossy. Fls fragrant, in twos or threes on spurs; pet. *c*2cm linear, rolled in upper half. S Afr.
T. heterophylla Sm. Lvs 5–9cm, ovate, often angularly lobed. Fls clustered at end of br.; pet. *c*1cm. Upper Guinea.
T. obtusifolia Hochst. Lvs 2–4.5cm, obovate, entire or bluntly 3-lobed. Fls solitary, axilliary; pet. 2–5cm. S Afr.

Turritis L. Cruciferae. 3 ann. or bienn. herbs resembling *Arabis*. Fls small, sep. 4, not saccate at base; pet. 4; sta. 6, free, fil. without appendages. Eur. to SW Asia. Z7.
T. glabra L. TOWER CRESS. Ann. or bienn., 60–120cm. St. erect, simple, hairy below. Lvs lyrate to sinuate, entire on st. Pet.

4–6mm, pale yellow. Range as for the genus.
→*Arabis*.

Turtle Bone *Lonchocarpus*.
Turtlehead *Chelone glabra*.

Tussaca Rchb. = *Chrysothemis*.

Tussilago L. COLTSFOOT. Compositae. 15 rhizomatous perenn. herbs. Lvs mostly basal, rounded, cordate, produced after fls. Cap. scapose, radiate; involucre campanulate; ray flts numerous, ligulate, yellow; disc flts few, tubular. N temp. regions. Z5.
T. alba L. = *Petasites albus*.
T. alpina L. = *Homogyne alpina*.
T. farfara L. Rhiz. long, white, scaly. Lvs 10–30cm, in basal rosettes, suborbicular, petiolate, green, thinly floccose above when young, white-woolly beneath, shallowly lobed, irregularly toothed. Scapes 4–15cm, floccose, with purple scales; involucre 1cm diam.; phyllaries tinged purple, white-hairy. Early spring. Eur., W & N Asia, N Afr.
T. hybrida L. = *Petasites hybridus*.
T. japonicum L. = *Farfugium japonicum*.

Tussock Bellflower *Campanula carpatica*.
Tussock Grass *Deschampsia cespitosa*.

Tutcheria Dunn. Theaceae. 2 everg. trees. Fls showy, axill.; sep. imbricate, silky, inner series petaloid; pet. 5, large; sta. many, connate at base. SE China. Z9.
T. spectabilis Dunn. Small tree. Lvs 12.5–15cm, ovate-lanceolate, glossy. Fls white, c7.5cm diam., slightly scented; pet. broadly obovate, emarginate. SE China.

Tutsan *Hypericum androsaemum*.
Twayblade *Listera ovata*.

Tweedia Hook. & Arn. Asclepiadaceae. 1 twining subshrub to 90cm. Shoots sparsely branched, minutely white-pubesc. Lvs to 10cm, oblong or cordate. Fls to 2.5cm diam., solitary to few, axill., powder-blue when young, lilac with age. S Braz., Urug. Z10.
T. caerulea D. Don.
→*Oxypetalum*.

Twiggy Baeckea *Baeckea virgata*.
Twiggy Mullein *Verbascum virgatum*.
Twinberry *Lonicera involucrata*.
Twin-flower *Linnaea*.
Twin-flowered Violet *Viola biflora*.
Twining Brodiaea *Dichelostemma volubile*.
Twining Fire Cracker *Manettia luteorubra*.
Twining Snapdragon *Asarina*.
Twin Leaf *Jeffersonia*.
Twinspur *Diascia barberae*.
Twisted-leaf Pine *Pinus teocote*.
Twisted-leaf Yucca *Yucca rupicola*.
Twisted Stalk *Streptopus*.
Twist Flower *Streptanthus*.
Twistwood *Viburnum lantana*.
Two-eyed Berry *Mitchella repens*.
Two-eyed Violet *Viola ocellata*.
Two-flowered Pea *Lathyrus grandiflorus*.
Two-veined Hickory Wattle *Acacia binervata*.
Two-winged Gimlet *Eucalyptus diptera*.

Tylecodon Toelken. Crassulaceae. 28 succulent perenn. subshrubs. Lvs fleshy, spirally arranged, decid. Cymes manybranched; sep. 5, fused toward base; pet. 5, fused for more than half their length; sta. 10 in 2 whorls of 5. S Afr., Nam. Z9.
T. cacalioides (L. f.) Toelken. Foliage similar to *T. walichii*. Sep. 10–12mm, yellow, gland.-hairy; cor. 31–43mm, sulphur-yellow, lobes recurved. Cape Prov.
T. mollis Dinter = *T. paniculatus*.
T. paniculatus (L. f.) Toelken. To 1.5m. Lvs 6–20cm, obovate, glab. to gland.-hairy. Sep. 4–6mm, sparsely hairy, red; cor. 20–30mm, tube orange-red, lobes orange, spotted red and yellow at base, nectaries orange-yellow. W S Afr.
T. papillaris (L.) G. Rowley = *T. cacalioides*.
T. reticulatus (L. f.) Toelken. Lvs 1.5–5cm, linear-oblanceolate, terete or compressed, gland.-hairy to glab. Sep. 3–4mm, yellow-green; cor. 9–13mm, yellow-green, gland.-hairy outside, urn-shaped, lobes pale yellow, deflexed. W S Afr.
T. schaeferianus (Dinter) Toelken. To 25cm. Lvs 0.5–2cm, obovate-elliptic, tinged red. Sep. 2–3.5mm, green; cor. 10–16mm, glab. outside, yellow-green, lobes pink, occas. white;

nectaries yellow-green. Nam.
T. spuria L. = *T. paniculatus*.
T. wallichii (Harv.) Toelken. To 140cm. Lvs 4–12cm, grey-green or brown, linear, terete, glab. or hairy. Sep. 3–5mm, greenyellow; cor. 13–17mm, gland.-hairy or glab. outside; nectaries yellow. S Afr.
→*Cotyledon*.

Typha L. BULLRUSH; REEDMACE; CAT TAIL. Typhaceae. 10 aquatic and marginal perenn. herbs; st. erect, simple. Lvs distichous, usually basal, thick or spongy at base, linear to ligulate, sheathing. Spike scapose, dense, narrow-oblong to cylindric, apppearing velvety, terminating in a point. Fls small, packed, lacking perianth, ♂ above ♀, with floss-like hairs, or scales. Cosmop.
T. angustata Bory & Chaub. = *T. domingensis*.
T. angustifolia L. LESSER BULLRUSH; NARROW-LEAVED REEDMACE; SOFT FLAG. To 2m. Lf sheaths closed at base, auriculate. Scape shorter than lvs; ♂ and ♀ fls separated on flowering stalk by 3–8cm; scales of ♀ fls dark brown opaque. Amer., Eur., N Afr., N & C Asia. Z3.
T. domingensis (Pers.) Steud. To 3m, robust. Lf sheath open at base. Scape equal to or slightly shorter than lvs; ♂ and ♀ fls separated on stalk by 1–6cm; scales of ♀ fls obovate, apiculate, pale brown, translucent. Amer., Eur., Asia. Z5.
T. latifolia L. CAT'S TAIL; BULLRUSH; NAILROD. To 2m. Lf sheaths usually open at throat. Scape shorter than lvs; ♂ and ♀ parts ± contiguous; ♀ part dark brown mottled white later, with fls lacking scales, pubesc. N Amer., Eur., Asia, N Afr. Z3.
T. laxmannii Lepech. To 1.5m, slender. Lf sheath usually open at thriat, auriculate. Scape shorter than or equal to lvs; ♂ and ♀ parts separated by 1–6cm; ♀ portion 5–10cm, pale brown; fls pubesc., lacking scales. Eurasia. Z4.
T. minima Hoppe. To 8cm, slender. Lvs to 2mm wide. Scape shorter than lvs; ♂ part contiguous with ♀ or separated; ♀ part 2–5cm, cylindric to oblong, dark brown, sometimes bracteate; fls scaly, pubesc. Eurasia. Z6.
T. shuttleworthii Koch & Sonder. To 1.5m. Lf sheath open at throat. Scape shorter than lvs; ♂ part of infl. contiguous with ♀; ♀ part 5–15cm, brown becoming silver-grey; fls pubesc. S Eur. Z5.
T. stenophylla Fisch. & C.A. Mey. = *T. laxmannii*.

TYPHACEAE Juss. See *Typha*.

Typhoides Munch.
T. arundinacea (L.) Moench = *Phalaris arundinacea*.

Typhonium Schott. Araceae. 30 tuberous perenn. herbs. Lvs long-stalked, basal, sagittate-hastate, 3-lobed to pedatisect. Peduncle shorter than petioles; spathe forming short tube below, limb expanded above constricted tube-neck, ovatelanceolate to lanceolate; spadix exserted from but shorter than spathe, ♂ and ♀ fls separted by zone of sterile fls, appendix long. S & SE Asia to Aus., nat. elsewhere. Z10.
T. blumei Nicols. & Sivadasan. Lvs 5–15cm, sagittate or cordate to 3-lobed; petiole to 20cm. Spathe 15–20cm, tube green externally, purple within, limb spreading, apex twisted, dark purple; spadix appendix to 13cm, dark purple. E & SE Asia, nat. Pacific Is., Afr., Neotrop.
T. brownii Schott. Lvs 7.5–15cm, hastate in outline, 3-lobed, seg. elongate-lanceolate. Spathe tube subglobose, limb to 10cm, ovate, acuminate, dark purple. Spring. Aus.
T. divaricatum Bl. = *T. blumei* or *T. roxburghii*.
T. diversifolium Wallich ex Schott. Lvs 8–15cm, v. variable, entire, cordate to sagittate or hastate, or 3–5-lobed or pedatisect with 5–7 narrow seg.; petiole to 30cm. Spathe 5–20cm, tube green, limb lanceolate, acuminate, green externally, purple within, sometimes yellow-green striped, spotted or netted purple; spadix appendix to 8cm, dark purple. Summer. Himal.
T. flagelliforme (Lodd.) Bl. Lvs narrow-hastate with spreading basal lobes, or elliptic, median lobe 6–25cm; petiole to 30cm. Spathe narrow, to 30cm, limb white; spadix appendix greenyellow. NE India to SE China; Malaysia, Indon. to Queensld.
T. giganteum Engl. Lvs to 30cm+, hastate; petiole to 60cm. Spathe to 25cm, limb deep maroon. Summer. China. var. *giraldii* (Engl.) Baroni. Spathe to 12.5cm.
T. giraldii Engl. = *T. giganteum* var. *giraldii*.
T. roxburghii Schott. Lvs 5–15cm, 3-lobed, broader than long; petiole to 30cm. Spathe to 30cm, limb tapering, apex twisted, dark red to purple within; spadix appendix to 15cm, dark red. India to Malaysia, Indon. to Moluccas; nat. Braz., Zanzibar.
T. trilobatum (L.) Schott. Lvs deeply 3-lobed, median lobe to 20×10cm, lat. lobes smaller; petiole to 40cm. Spathe 10–20cm, tube green, purple within; limb dark red; spadix appendix to 10cm, dark red. Summer. India, Nepal to SE China, Sri Lanka, N Malaysia.

U

Uaperima *Syagrus cocoides.*
Ubatake-giboshi *Hosta pulchella.*
Udo *Aralia cordata.*

Uebelmannia Buining. Cactaceae. 5 cacti; st. simple, small, globose to cylindric, ribbed, spiny. Fl. apical, shortly funnelform, small, yellow; areoles woolly and bristly. Fr. globose to cylindric yellow-green or red, naked below, apex woolly and bristly. Mts of E Braz.
U. buiningii Donald. Resembling *U. gummifera*, but st. redbrown to deep chocolate brown; ribs *c*18; spines 4–8, some incurved, yellow-brown, black-tipped. Fl. 27mm. Summer. E Braz. Z9.
U. gummifera (Backeb. & Voll) Buining. St. globose to slightly elongate, to 12×9cm, grey-green; ribs *c*32, strongly tuberculate; spines *c*4–6, 3–15mm, ± erect, grey, tipped brown. Fl. *c*20mm. Summer. E Braz. Z9.
U. meninensis Buining. Resembling *U. gummifera*, but st. light to dark green or red-tinged; ribs to 40; spines 2–4, to 20mm. Fl. 22–35mm. Summer. E Braz. Z9.
U. pectinifera Buining. St. globose to cylindric, to 85×10–17cm, light grey-green to red-brown, with minute off-white scales (sometimes 0); ribs 11–20, not tuberculate; spines 3–6, 5–15mm, acicular, ± erect, light grey, to near black. Fl. 14–18mm. Summer. E Braz. Z9.
→*Parodia.*

Ugli Fruit *Citrus* ×*tangelo.*

Ugni Turcz. Myrtaceae. 5–15 shrubs. Lvs opposite, persistent, coriaceous. Fl. solitary, nodding, axill., usually 5-merous; cor. campanulate exceeding sta., fil. short. Fr. a berry. Americas. Z9.
U. molinae Turcz. Shrub to *c*2m, young growth white-pubesc. Lvs 1.4–3.6cm, ovate, lanceolate or elliptic, glab., midvein impressed above. Pet. suborbicular, fleshy, 5–8mm, pink; sta. 40–60. Fr. *c*1cm diam., dark red. Chile, W Arg.
→*Eugenia, Myrtus.*

Uinaj *Tabebuia nodosa.*
Uke-yuri *Lilium alexandrae.*

Ulex L. Leguminosae (Papilionoideae). 20 spiny, dense shrubs. Lvs 3-foliolate on seedlings, in adults reduced to a rigid spine. Spines and young shoots green, giving shrub everg. appearance. Fls pea-like, fragrant, solitary or in small clusters. W Eur., N Afr., nat. mid US.
U. europaeus L. IRISH GORSE; COMMON GORSE; FURZE; GORSE; WHIN. 60cm–2m, erect or ascending, densely branched, dead foliage persisting, young twigs and spines somewhat glaucous, hirsute to tomentose. Spines to 1.3cm, rigidly linear, sharply pointed. Fls 2.2cm, golden-yellow, marked red at base, scented of coconut. Throughout the year. W Eur. 'Aureus': vegetation gold. 'Flore Pleno' ('Plenus'): fls double. 'Strictus': habit erect and slender, dense. Z6.
U. gallii Planch. To 60cm. As for *U. europaeus*, br. hairy and branchlets stoutly spiny; spines to 2.5cm. Fls to 1.6cm, goldenyellow. Summer–autumn. W Eur. Z8.
U. hibernicus hort. = *U. europaeus.*
U. hispanicus hort. non Pourr. ex Willk. & Lange = *Genista hispanica.*
U. jussiaei (D. A. Webb) D.A. Webb = *U. parviflorus.*
U. micranthus Lange. To 50cm, erect to spreading or arching, sparingly branched, dark green, young twigs pubesc.; petioles and spines glab.; spines to 1.2cm, recurved, rather stout. Fls 1.5cm yellow. NW Port. to NW Spain. Z8.
U. minor Roth. DWARF GORSE. To 1m, often procumbent; young twigs and spines not glaucous, hirsute, spines 0.8–1.5cm, slender, straight or curved, villous at base. Fls to 1.3cm, golden-yellow. Autumn. W Eur. Z7.
U. nanus T.F. Forst. ex Symons = *U. minor.*
U. parviflorus Pourr. To 1.5m. Long shoots villous, crispatepubesc. or glabrescent; spines to 3cm, woolly or glab., straight or recurved. Fls to 1.4cm, yellow. Autumn. Port. to S Fr. Z7.
U. strictus (Mackay) D.A. Webb = *U. europaeus.*

Ullucus Caldas. Basellaceae. 1 twining perenn. herb. Tubers to 3cm, rose-purple, white, yellow or red. Lvs to 20cm across, cordate or reniform, fleshy with small aerial tubers at axils. Fls small, yellow in axill. rac. with red bracteoles. Fr. a berry. N Andes, cult. throughout S Amer. Z9.
U. tuberosus Loz.
→*Basella.*

ULMACEAE Mirb. 16/140. *Aphananthe, Celtis, Hemiptelea, Holoptelea, Planera, Pteroceltis, Trema, Ulmus, Zelkova*

Ulmo *Eucryphia cordifolia.*

Ulmus L. ELM. Ulmaceae. 45 trees or shrubs, decid. or semievergreen. Lvs entire, serrate, veins pinnate. Fls inconspicuous; cal. campanulate, 4–5-lobed; cor. 0, sta. 4–5. Fr. a samara, ovoid or oblong, wing membranaceous. N Temp. to N Mex. and C Asia.
U. abelicea (Lam.) Sm. = *Zelkova abelicea.*
U. alata Michx. SMALL LEAVED ELM; WINGED ELM. Small, to 15m, young twigs bearing corky wings. Lvs 3–6cm, small, oblong to oblong-lanceolate, somewhat coriaceous, glab. above, pubesc. on veins beneath; petiole to 3mm. Fr. about 1cm, ovoidellipsoid, narrowly winged, white-pubesc. with 2 incurved beaks at the apex. E & Central N Amer. Z4.
U. alba Raf. = *U. americana.*
U. americana L. AMERICAN ELM; WHITE ELM; WATER ELM. To 35m; br. pendulous towards tips; bark ash-grey, furrowed, twigs downy at first. Lvs 7–15cm, oblong-ovate to elliptic, acuminate, base unequal, glab. or scabrous above, downy beneath; petiole to 8mm. Fr. to 1cm, ovoid or obovoid, notched, fringed. E N Amer. 'Ascendens': narrowly upright. 'Augustine': columnar, br. obliquely spreading, vigorous. 'Aurea': lvs yellow. 'Columnaris': columnar. 'Delaware II': broadly ovate, fast-growing; resistant to Dutch elm disease. 'Incisa': lvs deeply serrate. 'Littleford': narrow, vase-shaped. 'Moline': narrow; older br. horizontal. 'Nigricans': lvs dark. 'Pyramidata': habit pyramidal. 'Vase': habit vase-shaped. Z3.
U. androssowii Litv. NARWAN. Crown spherical; older br. corky. Lvs 5–6cm, ovate-elliptic to subovate, acuminate, unequally rounded at base, biserrate, glab. to downy above, hairs in vein axils beneath; petiole pubesc. Fr. 2–5cm diam., angularorbicular, glab. Turkestan. Z6.
U. androssowii 'Koopmannii'. = *U.* 'Koopmannii'.
U. angustifolia (Weston) Weston. GOODYER'S ELM. To 30m, crown rounded at top with age. Lvs 4–7cm, broadly ovate, glossy above, with hair tufts in vein axils beneath; petiole 9–11mm. Fr. 12–15mm, mostly sterile. Engl., Fr. (Brittany). Z7.
U. angustifolia var. *cornubiensis* (Weston) Melville = *U. carpinifolia* var. *cornubiensis.*
U. antarctica Kirchn. = *U.* 'Viminalis'.
U. belgica Weston = *U.* ×*hollandica* 'Belgica'.
U. bergmanniana Schneid. 10–20m; bark grey, furrowed and flaking. Lvs 8–14cm, oblong-ovate, acuminate, unequal at base, serrate to denticulate, ± coriaceous, bright green, glabrescent above; petiole *c*1cm. Fr. obovoid, notched, wings ovate, pubesc. long-stalked. C China. Z6.
U. ×*brandisiana* Schneid. (*U. chumlia* × *U. wallichiana.*) Natural hybrid intermediate between parents. Himal. (W Nepal to SE Kashmir). Z6.
U. 'Camperdownii' = *U. glabra* 'Camperdownii'.
U. campestris L. = *U. carpinifolia, U. glabra* or *U. procera.*
U. campestris 'Major' = *U.* ×*hollandica* 'Major'.
U. campestris 'Sarniensis' = *U.* 'Sarniensis'.
U. campestris 'Wheatleyi' = *U.* 'Sarniensis'.
U. campestris 'Stricta' = *U.* 'Viminalis'.
U. campestris var. *angustifolia* Weston = *U. angustifolia.*
U. campestris var. *japonica* Sarg. ex Rehd. = *U. japonica.*
U. campestris var. *nuda* 'Dampieri' = *U.* 'Dampieri'.
U. campestris var. *parvifolia* Loud. non Jacq. = *U. pumila.*
U. campestris var. *stricta* Ait. = *U. carpinifolia* var. *cornubiensis.*
U. campestris var. *cornuta* David = *U. glabra* f. *cornuta.*
U. campestris var. *viminalis* Loud. = *U.* 'Viminalis'.
U. canescens Melville. Similar to *U. carpinifolia* except twigs and lvs densely downy when young; lvs elliptic-ovate, bluntly serrate. NE Medit. Z7.

U. carpinifolia Rupp ex Suckow. EUROPEAN FIELD ELM; SMOOTH-LEAVED ELM. To 30m, pyramidal or upright. Lvs 4–10cm, obliquely oval to ovate, biserrate, glab. above, downy on veins beneath; petiole *c*1cm. Fr. about 1cm, ovoid to obovoid, glab., notched. S & C Eur. 'Dicksonii': narrowly upright; lvs gold. 'Høersholmiensis': tall, narrowly ovate; trunk short; lvs to 14cm wide, tips pointed. 'Myrtifolia': lvs to 5cm, ovate to rhomboid, rough, usually serrate, slightly pubesc. 'Pendula': shoots thin, pendulous; lvs glab. 'Propendens': br. spreading, nodding, corky. 'Purpurascens': lvs similar to 'Myrtifolia', tinted red. 'Purpurea': lvs 5–6cm, dark red then green. 'Ruepellii': dense, rounded; br. corky; lvs small, rough above. 'Silvery Gem': lvs margin cream. 'Umbraculifera': small; rounded, dense; br. thin, somewhat pubesc. when young; lvs elliptic to ovate, to 7cm, fairly rough above. 'Umbraculifera Gracilis': habit rounded, br. thin; lvs small. 'Variegata': lvs speckled white. 'Webbiana': narrowly conical; lvs folded longitudinally. var. *cornubiensis* (Weston) Rehd. CORNISH ELM. To 30m, slender, conical. Lvs narrowly to broadly ovate, subcoriaceous, glossy dark green and smooth above, conspicuously tufted beneath. Fr. narrower. S & SW Engl. Z5.

U. carpinifolia 'Dampieri' = *U.* 'Dampieri'.
U. carpinifolia 'Italica' = *U.* ×*hollandica* 'Australis.
U. carpinifolia var. *cornubiensis* (Weston) Rehd. = *U. angustifolia* var. *cornubiensis*.
U. carpinifolia var. *koopmannii* (Späth.) Rehd. = *U.* 'Koopmannii'.
U. carpinifolia var. *plottii* (Druce) Tutin = *U. plottii*.
U. carpinifolia f. *sarniensis* (Lodd.) Rehd. = *U.* 'Sarniensis'.
U. chinensis Pers. = *U. parvifolia*.
U. chumlia Melville & Heybr. Tree to 25m, spreading; br. sinuous. Shoots slender, grey tomentose then glab., ± corky. Lvs 5.5–10cm, narrow obovate-acuminate to elliptic-acuminate, finely biserrate, base rounded, smooth above, grey-white tomentose beneath. Fr. 10–12mm, notched. Himal. Z9.
U. crassifolia Nutt. CEDAR ELM. To 30m, rounded; young twigs downy, often winged. Lvs to 5cm, ovate to oblong, dentate, firm to coriaceous, blunt or rounded at apex, obliquely rounded or cordate at base, rough above, downy beneath; petiole *c*3mm. Fr. about 8mm, ellipsoid, notched, downy. S US. Z7.
U. 'Dampieri'. Medium-sized; narrowly pyramidal; branchlets short, slender, glab. Lvs 5–6cm, elliptic to broadly ovate, crispate, basally oblique, firm, dentate, glab. except in axill. tufts beneath. 'Dampieri Aurea' ('Wredei') has broad, gold-suffused lvs. Gdn origin. Z5.
U. davidiana Schneid. To 15m; bark grey, fissured; br. ridged or winged, yellow-pubesc. when young. Lvs 5–10cm, biserrate, acuminate, cuneate at base, coriaceous, pubesc. becoming rough; petiole 1cm. Fr. oblong-ovoid, notched, silky. China. Z6.
U. davidiana var. *japonica* (Rehd.) Nak. = *U. japonica*.
U. ×*dippeliana* Schneid. = *U.* ×*hollandica*.
U. ×*dippeliana* f. *dampieri* Schneid. = *U.* 'Dampieri'.
U. diversifolia Melville = *U. carpinifolia*.
U. effusa Willd. = *U. laevis*.
U. elegantissima Horw. = *U.* ×*hollandica* 'Elegantissima'.
U. elliptica K. Koch = *U. glabra*.
U. erosa Wallich non Roth = *U. wallichiana*.
U. exoniensis hort. = *U. glabra* 'Exoniensis'.
U. foliacea Gilib. = *U. carpinifolia*.
U. fulva Michx. = *U. rubra*.
U. glabra Huds. WYCH ELM; SCOTCH ELM. To 40m; spreading and open; young shoots pubesc.; bark fissured in old age. Lvs 5–16cm, oval to obovate, acuminate, occas. 3-lobed at apex, base unequally auriculate, biserrate, rough above, downy beneath, petiole to 5mm. Fr. to 2.5cm, obovate to broadly elliptic, downy, apex notched. N & C Eur. to Asia Minor. f. *nitida* (Fries) Rehd. Young shoots glab. Lvs smooth above. Norway. f. *cornuta* (David) Rehd. Lvs bearing 1 or 2 cusp-like lobes either side of apex. 'Atropurpurea': lvs dark russet, then green in summer. 'Camperdownii': compact, dome-shaped, br. drooping. 'Crispa': loose, slow growing; lvs narrow, folding upwards, serrate. 'Exoniensis': erect, to 7m, conical; lvs irregularly serrate. 'Horizontalis': br. horizontal or low arching. 'Insularis': rounded; br. dense; lvs large. 'Lutescens': lvs yellow-green, later bronze. 'Monstrosa': compact; lvs to 8cm, frequently connate at base. 'Nana': dwarf globose bush, to only 2m; lvs 5–9cm, obovate, often with 1–2 rounded apical teeth. 'Pendula': umbrella-shaped; br. horizontally spreading. 'Purpurea': lvs large; shoots with red and blue tints, later dark green. 'Rubra': inner bark, red tinted. 'Serpentina': weeping; br. twisted, corkscrew-like. 'Variegata': lvs variegated. Z5.
U. glabra Mill. non Huds. = *U. carpinifolia*.
U. glabra 'Vegeta' = *U.* 'Vegeta'.
U. glabra var. *pubescens* Schneid. = *U. procera*.
U. glabra var. *pendula* Loud. = *U.* 'Pendula'.

U. heyderi Späth = *U. rubra*.
U. ×*hollandica* Mill. (*U. glabra* ×*U. carpinifolia*.) DUTCH ELM. 'Australis': lvs tough, conspicuously and heavily veined, occurs wild in S Fr., Switz., Ital. 'Bea Schwarz': resistant to Dutch elm disease. 'Belgica' (BELGIAN ELM): large, upright tree, trunk straight, crown wide, bark rough; lvs obovate-elliptic long, serrate. 'Christine Buisman': disease-resistant. 'Elegantissima': slender. 'Groenveldt': tall, strong-growing, crown rectangular; resistant to Dutch elm disease. 'Hillieri': weeping miniature to 1.2m. 'Hollandica': large tree to 35m, with long, erect, sinuous br. from low in crown. 'Jacqueline Hillier': densely branched shrub, slow growing, to 2m; lvs to 3.5cm, distichous, elliptic to lanceolate. 'Major' (DUTCH ELM): large, wide-spreading; young shoots somewhat glab.; lvs elliptic, wide, serrate. Z5.
U. ×*hollandica* 'Dampieri' = *U.* 'Dampieri'.
U. ×*hollandica* 'Klemmer' = *U.* 'Klemmer'.
U. ×*hollandica* 'Pendula' = *U.* 'Pendula'.
U. ×*hollandica* 'Smithii' = *U.* 'Pendula'.
U. ×*hollandica* 'Vegeta' = *U.* 'Vegeta'.
U. ×*hollandica* 'Wredei' = *U.* 'Dampieri Aurea'.
U. hookeriana Planch. = *U. lanceifolia*.
U. humilis Gmel. = *U. pumila*.
U. integrifolia Roxb. = *Holoptelea integrifolia*.
U. japonica (Rehd.) Sarg. To 35m; apex broad, br. pendent; young twigs v. downy, corky-winged; bark yellow-brown. Lvs 7–12cm, oval to obovate, coarsely biserrate, abruptly acuminate, pubesc. then rough above, downy beneath; petiole *c*4mm. Fr. 1.5×1cm, elliptic-obovate, notched and partially ciliate. NE Asia, Jap. Z5.
U. keakii Sieb. = *Zelkova serrata*.
U. 'Klemmer'. To 35m; narrow, conical; bark smooth; young twigs short-pubesc. Lvs 5–10cm, ovate, short acuminate, crispate, rough glab. above, finely pubesc. beneath; petiole to 1cm. Belgium. Z5.
U. klemmeri Späth = *U.* 'Klemmer'.
U. 'Koopmannii'. Small tree; crown ovate, dense; young twigs partially pubesc., often becoming corky. Lvs *c*3cm, elliptic to ovate, green and rough above, grey-green beneath; petiole about 4mm. Z5.
U. koopmannii Späth = *U.* 'Koopmannii'.
U. laciniata (Trautv.) Mayr. Small tree to 10m; young twigs glab. then yellow-brown. Lvs 8–18cm, obovate to oblong, biserrate, 3–5-lobed at apex, basally oblique, dark green and rough above, downy beneath; petiole 2–5mm. Fr. 2cm, elliptic, glab. E temp. Asia to Jap. var. *nikkoensis* Rehd. Lvs smaller, obovate, tinged red when young. Z5.
U. laevigata Royle = *U. villosa* or *U. wallichiana*.
U. laevis Pall. To 30m; crown open, spreading; bark brown to grey; young twigs downy. Lvs 6–12cm, suborbicular to ovate, biserrate, acuminate, glab. above, grey pubesc. beneath, base v. unequal; petiole to 5mm. Fr. *c*1cm, oval, ciliate, with incurved horns at apex, in long-stalked drooping crowded clusters. France to E Eur. and Cauc. Z5.
U. lanceifolia Roxb. ex Wallich Tree to 45m; bark brown, flaky. Shoots white to rusty pubesc. at first. Lvs 3–8cm, ovate-lanceolate, sometimes persistent, crenate-serrate, acuminate; glossy above, glab. beneath or with white tufts. Fr. 12–30mm, oval, deeply notched. SE Asia. Z9.
U. macrocarpa Hance. Shrub or tree to 10m; young twigs pubesc.; later corky-winged. Lvs 3–8cm, elliptic to ovate, biserrate, abruptly acuminate, tapering abruptly at base, rough above, pubesc. beneath. Fr. orbicular, slightly notched, bristly. NE Asia. Z5.
U. manschurica Nak. = *U. pumila*.
U. microphylla Pers. = *U. pumila*.
U. minor Mill. = *U. carpinifolia*.
U. minor var. *cornubiensis* (Weston) Richens = *U. carpinifolia* var.*cornubiensis*.
U. minor var. *lockii* (Druce) Richens = *I. plotii*.
U. minor var. *sarniensis* (Loud.) Druce = *U.* 'Sarniensis'.
U. minor var. *vulgaris* (Ait.) Richens = *U. procera*.
U. minor 'Viminalis' = *U.* 'Viminalis'.
U. montana Stokes = *U. glabra*.
U. montana 'Dampieri' = *U.* 'Dampieri'.
U. montana 'Vegeta' = *U.* 'Vegeta'.
U. montana var. *klemmeri* Gillek. = *U.* 'Klemmer'.
U. montana var. *nitida* Fries = *U. glabra* f. *nitida*.
U. montana var. *pendula* hort. = *U.* 'Pendula'.
U. nitens Moench = *U. carpinifolia*.
U. parvifolia Jacq. CHINESE ELM; LACEBARK. To 25m, semi-evergr.; crown rounded or globose; branchlets slender; bark smooth, flaking in rounded pieces. Lvs 2–5cm, elliptic to obovate, serrate, coriaceous, acute, with tufts in vein axils beneath; petiole 2–4mm. Fr. elliptic-ovate, glab., notched. China, Korea, Jap. 'Catlin': medium-sized, graceful tree; bark attractive; lvs small. 'Chessins': shrubby, to 1m; lvs to 1cm,

white variegated. 'Cork Bark': medium-sized, fast-growing; bark corky. 'Drake': habit spreading; lvs rich dark green. 'Frosty': slow-growing, shrubby; lvs v. small, neatly arranged, bearing white teeth. 'Geisha': habit low, spreading; lvs creamy when young. 'Hansen': vigorous growth; shoots ascending, ring-shaped bulge beneath br. base; lvs to 8cm, ovate, serrate, base rounded. 'Hokkaido': slow-growing; bark corky when older; lvs v. small. 'Pendens': shoots drooping; lvs semi-evergr. in mild climates. 'Seiju': bark v. corky lvs large. 'Sempervirens': habit weeping, medium-sized; crown rounded; br. broadly arching; lvs small, finely toothed. 'True Green': everg.; lvs small, v. glossy. Z5.

U. pedunculata Foug. = *U. laevis*.

U. **'Pendula'**. DOWNTON ELM. Small tree; branchlets pendulous, pubesc., later corky. Lvs 8cm, elliptic, subcoriaceous, smooth, long acuminate, biserrate, glossy above, downy beneath; petiole c1cm. Fr. 2cm, obovate, notched. Z5.

U. pendula W. Mast. = *U.* 'Pendula'.

U. pinnato-ramosa Dieck ex Koehne = *U. pumila* 'Pinnato-Ramosa'.

U. **plotii** Druce. LOCK ELM. Tree to 30m, related to *U. carpinifolia*; crown more open, apex notching. Lvs similar to *U. carpinifolia* var. *cornubiensis* but rougher above, 8×4cm, obovate, acuminate, pubesc. in vein axils. England. Z7.

U. **procera** Salisb. ENGLISH ELM. Tree to 35m, trunk long and straight, crown tall, with rounded heads of foliage on few large br.; bark rectangular fissured. Lvs 3–7cm, rounded ovate, scabrous above, bristly beneath; petiole 2–3mm, densely hairy. Fr. mostly sterile. England. 'Argenteovariegata': lvs veined and speckled with white. 'Louis van Houtte': lvs yellow tinged green. Origin unknown. Z6.

U. procera 'Australis' = *U.* ×*hollandica* 'Australis'.

U. procera var. *viminalis* (Loud.) Rehd. = *U.* 'Viminalis'.

U. propinqua Koidz. = *U. japonica*.

U. pubescens Walter = *U. rubra*.

U. **pumila** L. SIBERIAN ELM. Tree or shrub to 10m; bark rough. Lvs 2–7cm, ovate or ovate-lanceolate, serrate, acute to acuminate, glabrescent beneath, base near-equal, deep green and glab. above; petiole to 4mm, downy. Fr. c1cm, circular to obovate, notched. E Sib., N China, Turkestan. var. *arborea* Litv. Tall tree, branchlets downy. Lvs distichous, elliptic-ovate, biserrate; petiole to 8mm. 'Berardii': small bushy tree, br. slender, upright; lvs to 5cm, elliptic-oblong. 'Coolshade': slow-growing. 'Den Haag': to 20m high; crown loose, open; resistant to Dutch elm disease. 'Mopheads': st. to 120cm; crown rounded. 'Pendula': br. slender, drooping. 'Pinnato-Ramosa': elegant, fast growing; lvs small, acuminate, bright green, pinnately arranged. 'Regal': upright, pyramidal; lvs small, rich deep green; resistant to Dutch elm disease, drought-tolerant. Z3.

U. racemosa Borkh. non Thomas = *U. laevis*.

U. racemosa Thomas non Borkh. = *U. thomasii*.

U. rotundifolia Carr. = *U. macrocarpa*.

U. **rubra** Muhlenb. SLIPPERY ELM; RED ELM. To 20m; broad, rounded; young twigs downy. Lvs 7–18cm, ovate-oblong to oblong-lanceolate, sometimes falcate, acute or acuminate, biserrate, base uneven, tinged red at first, firm, dark green and rough above, paler pubesc. beneath. Fr. to 2cm, broad elliptic to rounded, slightly notched, red-brown pubesc. C & S US. Z3.

U. **'Sarniensis'**. (*U. carpinifolia* ×*U.* ×*hollandica*.) JERSEY ELM; WHEATLEY ELM. Similar to *U. carpinifolia* var. *cornubiensis* except crown tapering, br. more stiffly erect. Lvs broader, less pubesc. beneath, teeth bearing 1–3 secondary teeth. Fr. mostly sterile. Z7.

U. sarniensis (Loud.) Bancroft = *U.* 'Sarniensis'.

U. scabra Mill. = *U. glabra*.

U. scabra 'Dampieri' = *U.* 'Dampieri'.

U. **serotina** Sarg. RED ELM; SEPTEMBER ELM. To 20m; spreading, broad; young twigs glab. then corky. Lvs 6–9cm, oblong to somewhat obovate, biserrate, acuminate, base v. unequal, dark green and rough above, yellow-tinged, white-pubesc. beneath; petiole to 6mm. Fr. about 1cm, oblong-elliptic, deeply incised, silver pubesc. along margin. SE US. Z6.

U. sieboldii = *U. parvifolia*.

U. smithii Henry = *U.* 'Pendula'.

U. stricta Lindl. = *U. carpinifolia* var. *cornubiensis*.

U. stricta var. *sarniensis* (Lodd.) Moss = *U.* 'Sarniensis'.

U. suberosa Moench = *U. carpinifolia*.

U. **thomasii** Sarg. ROCK ELM. To 30m; narrow, rounded; young twigs downy; branchlets often corky. Lvs 5–11cm, elliptic to oblong-ovate, biserrate, short acuminate, base unequal, sometimes partially covering petiole. Fr. c2cm, elliptic, slightly notched. SE Canada, NE & C US. Z2.

U. tonkinensis Gagnep. = *U. lanceifolia*.

U. tricuspis hort. = *U. glabra* f. *cornuta*.

U. tridens Hort. = *U. glabra* f. *cornuta*.

U. turkestanica Reg. = *U. pumila* var. *arborea*.

U. **'Vegeta'**. HUNTINGDON ELM; CHICHESTER ELM. To 40m; trunk thick short, branching low down; crown open, bark rough. Lvs 8–12cm, elliptic, acuminate, biserrate, basally uneven, glab. above, axils downy beneath. Fr. oval about 1cm, notched. Gdn origin. Z5.

U. vegeta (Loud.) Ley = *U.* 'Vegeta'.

U. **villosa** Brandis ex Gamble. CHERRY BARK ELM; MARN ELM. To 25m; spreading; bark smooth, dark grey to brown with bands of lenticels; young twigs yellow-red. Lvs 5–11cm, obovate, acute, rounded at base, biserrate, partially red pubesc., at first with tufts remaining in vein axils beneath. Himal. 5.

U. **'Viminalis'**. Small, 7–10m; crown narrow; br. graceful, drooping; young twigs slightly downy. Lvs 3–6cm, oblanceolate to narrow-ovate, long acuminate, deeply serrate, v. rough above. Of uncertain origin, possibly one parent being *U. carpinifolia*. *U.* 'Viminalis Aurea': lvs tinged yellow. *U.* 'Viminalis Marginata': lf margins variegated white. Z5.

U. viminalis Lodd. = *U.* 'Viminalis'.

U. **wallichiana** Planch. To 35m; branchlets slender, glabrescent; bark grey, rough, scaly. Lvs 6–20cm, elliptic to obovate, acuminate, biserrate, rough above, downy beneath. Fr. 18mm, elliptic, occas. pubesc. NW Himal. ssp. *xantheroderma* Melville & Heybr. Branchlets orange- or yellow-brown, gland. then glab. var. *tomentosa* Melville & Heybr. Buds, young twigs and lf undersides densely downy. Z6.

U. wheatleyi (Bean) Druce = *U.* 'Sarniensis'.

U. **wilsoniana** Schneid. To 25m; young twigs downy, often corky. Lvs 4–10cm, elliptic to obovate, acute, base obliquely uneven, biserrate, dark green, rough above, paler, ± pubesc. beneath. Fr. obovate, glab., notched. W China. Z6.

U. 'Wredei Aura' = *U.* 'Dampieri Aurea'.

U. **cvs**. 'Clusius': large, upright; lvs bright green. 'Commelin': habit narrow, growth regular; lvs oval, short tip. 'Dodoens': strong, upright tree; br. stiff. 'Homestead': pyramidal, later arching, rapid growing; lvs dark green; resistant to Dutch elm disease. 'Lobel': habit small. 'Pioneer' (*U. glabra* ×*U. carpinifolia*): moderately globe-shaped, rapid growing; lvs large, dark green; resistant to Dutch elm disease. 'Plantijn': habit narrow, upright; br. more flexible. 'Sapporo Autumn Gold': moderately pyramidal, low, upright branching, fast-growing; lvs dense, gold in autumn; resistant to Dutch elm disease and tolerant of urban conditions.

UMBELLIFERAE Juss. 418/3100. *Aciphylla, Actinotus, Aegopodium, Ammi, Anethum, Angelica, Anisotome, Anthriscus, Apium, Artedia, Astrantia, Athamanta, Azorella, Bolax, Bupleurum, Carum, Chaerophyllum, Conium, Coriandrum, Crithmum, Cryptostegia, Cryptotaenia, Cuminum, Daucus, Erigenia, Eryngium, Ferula, Ferulago, Foeniculum, Hacquetia, Heracleum, Hydrocotyle, Levisticum, Ligusticum, Melanoselinum, Meum, Monizia, Myrrhis, Oenanthe, Osmorhiza, Pastinaca, Petroselinum, Peucedanum, Pimpinella, Pleurospermum, Sanicula, Selinum, Seseli, Sium, Smyrnium, Trachymene, Zizia*.

Umbel Lily *Lilium* ×*hollandicum*.

Umbellularia Nutt. Lauraceae. 1 aromatic, everg. tree. Lvs entire, coriaceous. Fls ♂, in stalked umbels toward br. tips; cal. shortly tubular, lobes 6, cor. 0; sta. 9, with orange basal glands. Berry purple. W N Amer.

U. **californica** (Hook. and Arn.) Nutt. MYRTLE; OREGON MYRTLE; CALIFORNIA BAY; CALIFORNIA LAUREL; CALIFORNIA OLIVE; PEPPERWOOD; HEADACHE TREE. To 25m. Lvs 5–12cm, ovate-oblong to lanceolate, glossy dark green, intensely aromatic. Umbels to 2cm diam. Fr. 2.5cm. Calif., Oreg. Z8.

Umbilicus DC. Crassulaceae. 18 perenn., succulent herbs. Lvs mostly basal, long-stalked, round-peltate, with a central dimple, glab. Fls small, 5-merous in dense term. rac. S Eur. to SW Asia. Z7.

U. **erectus** DC. 30–80cm. Lvs 3–7cm across, broad-toothed. Rac. 8–25cm, occas. branched; pet. 9–14mm, yellow-green, fused for half length, pointed. S Eur., N Afr., SW Asia.

U. erubescens Maxim. = *Orostachys erubescens*.

U. **horizontalis** (Guss.) DC. Similar to *U. rupestris* except rac. covering less than half the st., fls horizontal. Medit. var. *intermedius* (Boiss.) Chamberl. Pet. long-pointed.

U. intermedius Boiss. = *U. horizontalis* var. *intermedius*.

U. libanoticus Náb. = *Rosularia rechingeri*.

U. pallidus Schott & Kotschy = *Rosularia aizoon*.

U. pendulinus DC. = *U. rupestris*.

U. **rupestris** (Salisb.) Dandy. NAVELWORT; PENNY WORT. Lvs 15–70cm across, crenate. Rac. simple, covering more than half the st.; fls pendent; pet. 7–9mm, fused for three-quarters length, white-green, sometimes tinged pink. Widespread Eur. to SW

Asia.
→*Cotyledon.*

Umbrella Arum *Amorphophallus rivieri.*
Umbrella Bamboo *Thamnocalamus spathaceus.*
Umbrella Dracaena *Dianella ensifolia.*
Umbrella Fern *Sticherus cunninghamii.*
Umbrella Leaf *Diphylleia cymosa.*
Umbrella Magnolia *Magnolia tripetala.*
Umbrella Palm *Hedyscepe.*
Umbrella Pine *Sciadopitys.*
Umbrella Plant *Cyperus alternifolius, Darmera peltata; Eriogonum (E. allenii).*
Umbrella Tree *Magnolia macrophylla*; *M. tripetala*; *Musanga (M. cecropioides)*; *Polyscias murrayi*; *Schefflera.*
Umbrellawort *Mirabilis.*
Umkokola *Dovyalis caffra.*
Umsenge *Cussonia.*

Uncinia Pers. Cyperaceae. 35 tufted grass-like herbs. Infl. simple, the term. portion staminate; ♀ fls enclosed in a utricle; styles 3. Malesia, Pacific, C & S Amer., S Indian & Atlantic Is.
U. egmontiana Hamlin. Culms to 40cm, smooth, angled to terete. Lvs to 30cm×1.5mm, flat, dull red or green, ± scabrous on margins. Spikes to 12cm; pistillate fls 10–17; glumes membranous, red, persistent; utricles to 6mm subtrigonous. NZ.
U. rubra Boott. Whole plant dark red. Culms to 35cm, scabrous on angles. Lvs to 35cm×2mm, flat or involute, margins somewhat scabrous. Spikes to 6cm; pistillate fls 6–13; glumes coriaceous; utricles to 6mm, fusiform or convex, striate. NZ.
U. uncinata (L. f.) Kukenthal. Culms to 4.5cm, smooth, angled. Lvs to 45cm×0.4cm, flat, strongly scabrous. Spikes to 20cm; pistillate fls 60–120+; glumes coriaceous, yellow to dark brown; utricles to 5mm, convex, smooth. NZ.
→*Carex.*

Ungernia Schott. & Endl. Amaryllidaceae. 8 bulbous bulbs similar to *Lycoris*. Lvs lorate. Fls in a scapose umbel; perianth regular, tube funnel-shaped; lobes 6, oblong, keeled, with many close ribs near throat of perianth tube. C Asia to Jap.
U. trisphaera Bunge. Bulb to 7.5cm diam., long-necked. Scape 15–30cm; fls 6–15, 2.5–4cm, red; perianth lobes acute. Turkestan.

Ungnadia Endl. Sapindaceae. 1 decid. shrub or tree to 9m. Lvs imparipinnate, pinnae 8–12cm, ovate to lanceolate, crenulate, dark green above, pubesc. beneath. Fls scented, many, in pubesc. lat. clusters; cal. pink, campanulate, 5-lobed; cor. to 2.5cm wide; pet. 4, obovate, crenulate, pink, comb-like disc at the base; sta. 7–10, exserted, red. Fr. 5cm diam., red-brown. Tex. Z9.
U. speciosa Endl. MEXICAN BUCK-EYE.

Unicorn Plant *Ibicella*; *Martynia*; *Proboscidea.*
Unicorn Root *Aletris farinosa.*

Uniola L. SPANGLE GRASS; SPIKE GRASS. Gramineae. 4 rhizomatous, perenn. grasses. St. stoloniferous, clumped. Lvs linear to narrow-lanceolate, flat, scabrous. Rac. crowded; spikelets sessile, flattened, few- to many-fld; glumes rigid, keeled, persistent. S & E US to Ecuad. Z7.
U. latifolia Michx. = *Chasmanthium latifolium.*
U. paniculata L. NORTH AMERICAN SEA OATS; SEASIDE OATS. To 240cm. Lvs to 75×8cm, rigid. Pan. to 60cm, br. arching to drooping; spikelets to 3cm, ovate to oblong, laterally flattened, golden brown, glumes overlapping. Summer. E US to W Indies.

Upas Tree *Antiaris toxicaria.*
Upland Boneset *Eupatorium sessilifolium.*
Upland Cotton *Gossypium hirsutum.*
Upright Bugle *Ajuga genevensis.*
Upright Spurge *Euphorbia stricta.*
Urajiro-giboshi *Hosta hypoleuca.*

Urbinia Rose.
U. agavoides (Lem.) Rose = *Echeveria agavoides.*
U. corderoyi (Bak.) Rose = *Echeveria agavoides* var. *corderoyi.*
U. obscura Rose = *Echeveria agavoides.*
U. purpusii Rose = *Echeveria purpusorum.*

×**Urbiphytum** Gossot = ×*Pachyveria.*

Urceolina Rchb. Amaryllidaceae. 6 bulbous perenn. herbs. Lvs ovate to oblong, petiole long, grooved. Scape solid, terete; to

45cm; spathe valves 2; infl. umbellate; perianth tubular, 6-lobed, with corona of short teeth. Andes. Z9.
U. bakeriana (N.E. Br.) Traub = *Eucharis bakeriana.*
U. bouchei (Woodson & Allen) Traub = *Eucharis bouchei.*
U. candida (Planch. & Lind.) Traub = *Eucharis candida.*
U. grandiflora (Planch. & Lind.) Traub = *Eucharis* ×*grandiflora.*
U. latifolia Benth. and Hook. Lvs to 25cm ovate or elliptic, acute, channelled. Fls 6–8; perianth funnel-shaped, yellow shaded orange and tipped green; tep. erect. Winter. Peruvian Andes.
U. mastersii Bak. = *Eucharis* ×*grandiflora.*
U. miniata (Herb.) Benth. = *Stenomesson miniatum.*
U. pendula Herb. = *Stenomesson miniatum.*
U. peruviana (Presl) Macbr. = *Stenomesson miniatum.*
U. sanderi (Bak.) Traub = *Eucharis sanderi.*
U. subedentata (Bak.) Traub = *Eucharis subedentata.*
U. urceolata (Ruiz & Pav.) Green. Lvs to 50cm, ovate to oblong. Scape to 30cm; perianth tube to 10cm, urceolate above; tep. recurved, apex green, sometimes with white margins. Spring–summer. Peru.
→*Pancratium.*

Urera Gaudich. Urticaceae. 35 shrubs or small trees with vicious stinging hairs. Lvs toothed or lobed. Fls insignificant, 4–5-merous, in axill. pan. Trop. and subtrop.
U. baccifera (L.) Wedd. To 6m; st. and br. with recurved spines. Lvs to 30cm, ovate, with stinging hairs and prickly veins shallow-dentate. Fls white or pink. Spring. C & S Amer., W Indies.

Urginea Steinh. Liliaceae (Hyacinthaceae). 100 bulbous perenn. herbs. Lvs basal, narrow-linear to lorate or oblong. Rac. scapose, term., many-fld; tep. 6, free, spreading. Mostly Afr., 3 spp. Medit. Z9.
U. maritima (L.) Bak. SEA ONION; SQUILL. Bulb 5–15cm diam., ovoid-globose, part-exposed. Lvs 30–100cm, narrow-lanceolate, fleshy, glaucous. Scape 50–150cm, tinted red; rac. 30cm+; tep. 6–8mm, oblong, white, keel green or purple. Summer. Medit., Port.
→*Drimia.*

Urn Gum *Eucalyptus urnigera.*
Urn Plant *Aechmea fasciata.*

Urospermum Scop. Compositae. 2 ann. to perenn. herbs with milky latex. St. solitary, sparsely branched. Lvs basal or alt. on st. Cap. few, ligulate, large, solitary on long peduncles; receptacle domed; flts yellow, occas. striped red, apex 5-toothed. Medit.
U. dalechampii (L.) Scop. ex F.W. Schmidt. Perenn. or bienn., forming a spreading clump to 40cm. Lvs 5–19cm, hairy, lower lvs oblanceolate to obovate, usually runcinate-pinnatifid, petiole winged, upper lvs ovate to lanceolate, amplexicaul. Cap. to 5cm diam.; flts often striped red below. Summer. Medit., E to Balk. Z6.

Ursinia Gaertn. Compositae. *c*40 ann. and perenn. herbs, subshrubs and shrubs. Lvs alt., pinnatisect to pinnatifid, rarely entire, glandular-punctate. Cap. radiate, term., solitary or rarely few to many in loose pan.; receptacle flat or convex, scaly; ray flts yellow, orange or white, rarely red, often coppery beneath; disc flts yellow or purple or coppery at apex. S Afr. (Cape Prov.), Nam., Ethiop. Z9.
U. abrotanifolia (R. Br.) Spreng. Shrub to 40cm, pubesc. Lvs 2–5cm, ovate, 3–4-pinnate, pinnatisect toward base, seg. linear. Cap. solitary, to 3.5cm diam.; scape to 30cm; flts yellow. S Afr.
U. anethoides (DC.) N.E. Br. Bushy shrub, to 50cm, glab. to thinly arachnid. Lvs 0.5–2cm, lanceolate or obovate, 1–2-pinnatisect, seg. filiform. Cap. solitary, 2.5cm diam.; scape to 16cm; ray flts golden-yellow, disc flts yellow. S Afr.
U. anthemoides (L.) Poir. Ann. to 40cm. Lvs 2–6cm, ovate, 1–2-pinnatisect, seg. linear, lobes small, slightly pubesc. Cap. solitary, 1.5–6cm diam.; scape to 20cm; ray flts yellow or dark purple toward base or purple-coppery beneath; disc flts yellow or purple at apex. Summer. S Afr. ssp. *versicolor* (DC.) Prassler. To 25cm. Ray flts orange-yellow, brown-purple toward base. Nam.
U. cakilefolia DC. Ann., to 45cm. Lvs to 5cm, 2-pinnatisect, seg. obovate, lobes linear. Cap. solitary, to 5cm diam.; scape to 20cm; ray flts yellow to orange; disc flts yellow, dark purple towards apex. S Afr.
U. calenduliflora (DC.) N.E. Br. Ann., to 35cm. Lvs to 6cm, ovate, pinnatisect, seg. linear to ovate, occas. pinnate, glab. Cap. solitary, 6cm diam.; scape to 20cm; ray flts yellow, often dark purple toward base; disc flts yellow, apex purple. S Afr.
U. chrysanthemoides (Less.) Harv. Ann. to shrubby perenn. to 1m, pubesc. Lvs to 5cm, often clustered, lanceolate to ovate,

1–2-pinnatisect, seg. lanceolate to ovate, pubesc. Cap. solitary, 2.5–6cm diam.; scape 20cm; ray flts yellow or red throughout, or yellow or white above and coppery beneath; disc flts yellow, or dark purple at apex. S Afr. 'Geyeri': ray flts bright red throughout.

U. crithmifolia (R. Br.) Spreng. = *U. crithmoides.*

U. crithmoides (P. Bergius) Poir. Shrubby perenn., to 60cm, glab. Lvs to 6cm, lanceolate or obovate, pinnatisect, seg. linear-filiform. Cap. solitary, to 5cm diam.; scape to 30cm; ray flts yellow throughout or yellow above, coppery beneath; disc flts yellow. Summer. S Afr.

U. dentata (L.) Poir. Shrubby perenn. to 60cm, glab. to slightly hirsute. Lvs to 25cm, oblong, 2-pinnatisect, seg. oblong, glab., punctate. Cap. solitary, to 4cm diam.; scape to 20cm; ray flts yellow throughout or yellow above, coppery beneath; disc flts yellow. Summer. S Afr.

U. geyeri Bol. & Hall = *U. chrysanthemoides* 'Geyeri'.

U. pilifera (A. Berger) Poir. Perenn. to 35cm, glab. to slightly arachnoid. Lvs to 2.5cm, 1–2-pinnate, seg. linear, bristle-tipped, lobes 2–4, linear, slightly pubesc. Cap. solitary, to 6cm diam.; scape to 20cm; ray flts white or yellow above, purple or coppery beneath, coppery at apex. Winter. S Afr.

U. pulchra N.E. Br. = *U. anthemoides.*

U. pygmaea DC. Ann., to 6cm, glab. Lvs to 3cm, ovate, 1–2-pinnatisect, seg. linear or ovate. Cap. 2–3.5cm diam.; scape to 5cm. S Afr.

U. sericea (Thunb.) N.E. Br. Often procumbent shrub to 70cm, pubesc. Lvs to 8cm, lanceolate or obovate, pinnatisect, seg. linear, silvery-pubesc. Cap. solitary, 1–3cm diam.; scape to 60cm; flts yellow. S Afr.

U. speciosa DC. Ann., to 40cm, glab. Lvs to 5cm, ovate, 2-pinnatisect, seg. linear to oblong. Cap. solitary, 2–5cm diam.; scape to 2–12cm; ray flts yellow or orange, rarely white; disc flts yellow, apex purple. Nam.

U. versicolor (DC.) N.E. Br. = *U. anthemoides* ssp. *versicolor.* →*Arctotis.*

Urtica L. STINGING NETTLE. Urticaceae. 100 ann. or perenn. herbs, with copious stinging hairs. Lvs coarsely serrate or toothed. Fls 4-merous unisexual, green, inconspicuous, in axill. pan., cymes or rac. N hemis.

U. dioica L. STINGING NETTLE. Dioecious perenn. to 1.5m. Lvs to 15cm, ovate, acuminate, base cordate to truncate. Fls clustered in nodding, lax rac. or pan. Summer. N hemis., widely nat.

U. pilulifera L. ROMAN NETTLE. Monoecious, ann. herb to 60cm. Lvs 2.5–7.5cm, ovate, deeply serrate or entire. ♂ fls in branched cymes; ♀ fls in dense spherical heads. Summer–autumn. S Eur.

U. urens L. Like *U. pilulifera* but lvs blue-green not midgreen, ♂ and ♀ fls mixed in clustered axill. cymes. Summer–autumn. N hemis.

URTICACEAE Juss. NETTLE FAMILY. 52/1050. *Boehmeria, Debregeasia, Myriocarpa, Pellionia, Pilea, Soleirolia, Urera, Urtica*

Uruguay Grass *Chloris berroi.*
Uruguay Pennisetum *Pennisetum latifolium.*
Usambara Violet *Saintpaulia ionantha.*
Utah Ash *Fraxinus anomala.*
Utah Bugler *Penstemon utahensis.*
Utah Juniper *Juniperus osteosperma.*

Utricularia L. BLADDERWORT. Lentibulariaceae. 214 terrestrial, epiphytic or aquatic, carnivorous herbs. Rhizoids often present. Tubers sometimes present. St., (stolons), spreading, capillary to fleshy. Lvs erect, entire, linear to reniform, sometimes peltate; in aquatic spp. v. finely dissected or 0. Traps inserted on vegetative parts, hollow, globose or ovoid, mouth small with sensitive hinged door. Infl. a rac.; cal. lobes 2–4; cor. bilabiate, upper lip smaller than lower, with basal sac, lower lip spurred, with distinct palate. Cosmop.

U. alpina Jacq. Terrestrial or epiphytic perenn.; rhizoids 0. Stolons to 20cm, slender, tubers forming at base of scape. Lvs 5–10cm, elliptic or obovate, coriaceous. Traps numerous on stolon br. Scape to 40cm, erect or spreading; fls 1–4 in lax rac.; 4–6cm, white or pale pink, blotched yellow at base of lower lip. Antilles, N S Amer. Z10.

U. australis R. Br. Aquatic; rhizoids present. Stolons to 50cm+, filiform. Lvs v. numerous, to 4cm, bifurcate then dichotomously and finely 2–3× divided. Traps on secondary to penultimate seg. of lvs, or base of primary seg. Scape 10–30cm, emergent; fls 4–10 to 2cm, yellow, with swollen part of lower lip darker with red brown lines and spots. Eur., Asia to China and Jap., trop. and S Afr., trop. Asia, Aus. and NZ. Z7.

U. caerulea L. Terrestrial ann. or perenn., rhizoids present. Stolons slender. Lvs to 1×0.2cm, petiolate, obovate. Traps on stolons and lvs. Scape 5–30cm; fls 1–20, 2–8mm, white or yellow to pink or violet, with yellow at base of lower lip. Madag., Asia (India to Jap.) to NSW. Z9.

U. coerulea auct. = *U. caerulea.*

U. dichotoma Labill. Terrestrial perenn. rhizoids numerous. Stolons slender, sometimes fleshy and tuberous. Lvs to 14×0.5cm, linear to broadly elliptic. Traps on stolons. Scape to 50cm, fls to 2.2cm, dark violet with yellow at base and on ridges of lower lip. Aus. Z10.

U. exoleta R. Br. = *U. gibba.*

U. forgetiana hort. Sander = *U. longifolia.*

U. gibba L. Ann. or perenn. aquatic; rhizoids 0, or present, short and branched. Stolons to 20cm, mat-forming. Lvs to 1.5cm dichotomously branched into capillary ultimate seg. Traps on lf seg. Scape to 20cm, emergent; fls 2–6, to 2.5cm, yellow with red-brown veins. Pantrop., N to Canada and US, Iberia, N Afr., Isr., China and Jap., S to Arg., S Afr., Aus. and NZ. Z4.

U. graminifolia Vahl. Terrestrial or subaquatic perenn.; rhizoids present. Stolons slender, mat-forming. Lvs to 4×0.6cm, linear to narrow-obovate. Traps on rhizoids and lvs. Scape to 30cm, sometimes twining; fls to 1.8cm, mauve or violet. India, Sri Lanka to China (Yunnan). Z10.

U. ianthina Hook. f. = *U. reniformis.*

U. intermedia Hayne. Aquatic perenn.; rhizoids present. Stolons to 30cm, filiform. Lvs polymorphic; on floating stolons to 2cm, imbricate, circular in outline, trap-bearing, palmately divided into up to 15 seg.; on buried stolons, fewer with single elongate primary seg. with few short ultimate seg. at base and apex. Scape to 20cm, emergent; fls 2–3 to 1.6cm, yellow. Summer. Circumboreal. Z2.

U. janthiana hort. = *U. reniformis.*

U. lateriflora R. Br. Terrestrial perenn.; rhizoids few. Stolons filiform, rather fleshy. Lvs to 5×0.5cm, narrow-obovate. Traps on rhizoids, stolons and petioles. Scape erect; fls 1cm, pale lilac to mauve or violet, with white or yellow blotch at base of lower lip. E & S Aus. Z10.

U. livida E. Mey. Terrestrial ann. or perenn.; rhizoids present. Stolons capillary. Lvs to 7×0.6cm, cuneate or obovate to reniform. Traps on rhizoids, stolons and lvs. Scape to 80cm, erect; fls to 15mm, pale to dark violet, with or without yellow blotch at base of lower lip, or yellow or white. Trop. & S Afr., Madag., Mex. Z10.

U. longifolia Gardn. Terrestrial or lithophytic perenn.; rhizoids rather fleshy. Stolons filiform. Lvs 2–115×0.25–6cm, lorate or obovate to elliptic. Traps on rhizoids and stolons. Scape 30–60cm; fls to 3cm, violet with orange-yellow blotch at base of lower lip. Braz. Z10.

U. macroceras A. DC. in DC. = *U. menziesii.*

U. major Schmidel non Cariot & St.-Lager = *U. australis.*

U. major Cariot & St.-Lager non Schmidel = *U. vulgaris.*

U. menziesii R. Br. REDCOATS. Terrestrial perenn. Rhizoids numerous. Stolons 0; tubers to 1.5cm. Lvs to 4cm, obovate, rounded, somewhat succulent. Traps numerous on st. Scape to 7cm; fls to 2.5cm, bright red, marked yellow at base of lower lip, spur v. long. W Aus. Z10.

U. minor L. LESSER BLADDERWORT. Aquatic perenn. Rhizoids 0. Stolons filiform, green and floating or buried. Lvs to 1.5cm, on floating stolons semicircular in outline, palmately divided into 7–22 filiform seg., 1–2 primary seg. with few v. short seg. at base and apex. Traps on lf seg., especially on buried-stolon lvs, ovoid, mouth lat. Scape to 28cm; fls to 8mm, lemon-yellow. Summer. Circumboreal, inc. GB, S to Himal., Burm. and New Guinea. Z2.

U. monanthos Hook. f. Terrestrial perenn.; rhizoids simple, v. short. Stolons capillary. Lvs to 3cm, linear or narrow-elliptic. Traps on stolons. Scape 1–4(–15)cm; fls to 1cm, deep violet with yellow blotch at base of lower lip. Aus. (Vict., NSW, Tasm.), NZ. Z9.

U. montana Poir. = *U. alpina.*

U. nelumbifolia Gardn. Perenn. aquatic in crowns of bromeliads; rhizoids 0. Submerged stolons few, fleshy, aerial stolons to 1m+, rigid. Lvs 3–10cm diam., circular, peltate, coriaceous, long-stalked. Traps on submerged stolons. Scape to 1.2m; fls 3–4cm, blue-violet. Braz. Z10.

U. peltata Spruce ex Oliv. = *U. pubescens.*

U. prehensilis E. Mey. Terrestrial perenn., rhizoids filiform, short. Stolons filiform. Lvs to 10cm, linear. Traps on rhizoids, stolons and lvs. Scape to 35cm, erect or twining; fls to 2cm, yellow. Trop. & S Afr. (Ethiop. to Cape Prov.), Madag. Z10.

U. pubescens Sm. Terrestrial or lithophytic ann., rhizoids v. short. Lvs circular, peltate, 1–8mm diam.; petiole to 1cm. Traps on rhizoids, stolons and petioles. Scape 2–35cm; fls 5–10mm, white or pale lilac with yellow blotch and dark violet mark on ridged lower lip. India, Trop. Afr., C & S Amer. Z10.

U. purpurea Walter. Aquatic perenn. Rhizoids 0. Stolons slender. Lvs to 4cm, repeatedly divided into whorled capillary seg. bearing traps. Scape to 20cm, fls to 1.8cm, rose-pink with yellow blotch at base of lower lip. Spring–autumn. N & C Amer. (Canada to Costa Rica), Antilles, Jam. Z3.

U.reniformis A. St.-Hil. Terrestrial or epiphytic perenn.; rhizoids 0. Stolons branched, massive and fleshy. Lvs to 14cm diam., long-petiolate, reniform, coriaceous. Traps on stolon br. Scape to 1m; fls 2–4cm, blue violet with 2 yellow, purple-edged lines on swollen base of lower lip. Braz. Z10.

U. sandersonii Oliv. Perenn. lithophyte; rhizoids few, simple. Stolons capillary. Lvs to 1.5cm, petiolate, cuneate, obovate or flabellate. Traps on stolons and lvs. Scape to 6cm; fls to 1.5cm, white or v. pale mauve with darker mauve markings on upper lip and base of lower lip, spur long. S Afr. Z9.

U. subulata L. Terrestrial ann.; rhizoids short, filiform. Stolons capillary, branched. Lvs to 2cm, narrow-linear. Traps on stolons and lvs. Scape 10–50cm; fls 2mm, white to red if cleistogamous, or to 1cm, yellow. Pantrop. and subtrop., to temp. zones. Z6.

U. volubilis R. Br. Aquatic perenn.; rhizoids to 10cm, rather fleshy. Stolons 0. Lvs 1–10cm, linear. Traps on st. and rhizoid nodes. Scape to 1m; fls violet with 7–9 bright yellow ridges, upper lip paler, to 2.5cm, lower lip semicircular, to 4cm wide. W Aus. Z10.

U. vulgaris L. GREATER BLADDERWORT. Suspended aquatic perenn.; rhizoids present. Stolons filiform. Lvs 1.5–6cm, bifurcate then repeatedly divided into filiform seg., bearing traps. Scape to 25cm, fls to 2cm, yellow with red-brown streaks on swollen base of lower lip. Summer. Eur., N Afr., temp. Asia, W Sib., Tibet. Z5.

Uva Del Monte *Pourouma cecropiifolia.*
Uva Grass *Gynerium sagittatum.*

Uvularia L. BELLWORT; WILD OATS; MERRY-BELLS. Liliaceae (Uvulariaceae). 5 perenn., rhizomatous herbs. St. simple or branched, arching. Lvs 2-ranked along st., oblong-lanceolate to elliptic, entire to minutely serrulate. Fls solitary and term. or in axill. clusters, narrowly campanulate, pendulous; tep. 6, lanceolate-ovate, slightly twisted, free; sta. 6. S & SE US.

U. caroliniana (Gmel.) Wilbur. St. to 45cm, minutely hairy. Lvs to 7.5cm, glaucous, elliptic, sessile, minutely serrulate. Fls pale yellow, to 3cm. Spring–summer. Z5.

U. grandiflora Sm. St. to 75cm, glab. Lvs to 13cm, perfoliate, pubesc. beneath, glab. above. Fls yellow sometimes tinted green, to 5cm. Spring–summer. Z3. 'Citrina': fls clear yellow.

U. perfoliata L. St. to 60cm. Lvs to 11cm, perfoliate, oblong-lanceolate, glaucous, glab. Fls to 3.5cm, tep. v. papillose above. Late spring–summer. Z4.

U. puberula Michx. = *U. caroliniana.*
U. pudica (Walter) Fern. = *U. caroliniana.*

U. sessilifolia L. SESSILE BELLWORT; STRAWBELL. Resembles *U. caroliniana* but st. glab. Lvs to 9cm, sessile, oblong-lanceolate, sap green above, pale to grey-green beneath. Fls lemon to golden yellow; tep. v. papillose above. Late spring –summer. Z4.

U. sessilis Thunb. = *Disporum sessile.*

V

Vaccaria Medik. COW-COCKLE. Caryophyllaceae. 3 glab. ann. Branching dichotomous. Lvs oblong-lanceolate. Fls axillary; cal. inflated, 5-angled; cor. 5; sta. 10. Medit., SW Asia.
V. hispanica (Mill.) Rausch. To 60cm, glaucous. Pet. 3–8mm, wedge-shaped, toothed, pink-purple. Summer. S & C Eur.; introd. N Amer.
V. pyramidata Medik. = *V. hispanica*.
V. segetalis Asch. = *V. hispanica*.
→*Saponaria*.

Vaccinium L. Ericaceae. 450 shrubs, small trees or vines. Lvs simple, entire or serrate, often coloured in autumn. Fls solitary or in rac. or clusters; cal. 4–5-parted; cor. urceolate, campanulate or cylindric, 4–5-lobed; sta. 8–10. Fr. a berry, usually globose, often edible. N Hemis., from Arc. Circle to trop. mts, with a few spp. in S Afr.
V. alto-montanum Ashe. Shrub, 50–100cm. Lvs 3–5cm, narrowly elliptic to elliptic-lanceolate, entire, glab. Cor. 5–7mm, white tinged green or pink. Fr. 7–10mm diam., blue, pruinose. SE US. Z5.
V. amoenum Ait. LARGE-CLUSTER BLUEBERRY. Similar to *V. virgatum*, except larger in all parts. SE US. Z5.
V. angustifolium Ait. LOW-BUSH BLUEBERRY; LATE SWEET BLUEBERRY; LOW SWEET BLUEBERRY; SWEET-HURTS. Shrublet, 8–20cm, decid. Lvs 1–3cm, lanceolate, minutely bristly-serrate, glab. Cor. 6–7mm, white tinged green, often streaked red. Fr. globose, 6–12mm, blue-black, pruinose, edible. Spring. NE N Amer. var. **laevifolium** House. 50–60cm. Lvs 1.5–3.5cm, oblong-lanceolate to elliptic. Cor. 6mm, white. Fr. 10–12mm, light blue. E US. Z2.
V. arboreum Marshall. FARKLEBERRY. Shrub or tree to 5m, everg. or decid. Lvs 2–5cm, oval-elliptic to obovate, entire or obscurely minutely dentate, glossy above, somewhat pubesc. beneath. Cor. 6mm, white. Fr. 6mm diam., black, inedible. Summer. S & SE US. Z7. var. **glaucescens** (Greene) Sarg. Lvs glaucescent. US. Z7.
V. arctostaphylos L. CAUCASIAN WHORTLEBERRY Shrub, 1–3m, decid. Lvs 3–10cm, elliptic to oval-oblong, undulate and finely serrate, carmine in autumn, somewhat pubesc. on veins. Cor. 6–7mm, white tinged green, faintly flushed red. Fr. 8–10mm, purple. Late spring–summer. N Asia Minor, W Cauc. Z6.
V. ashei Reade. RABBIT-EYE BLUEBERRY. Shrub, 1–5m, generally decid. Lvs 4–8cm, broadly elliptic to broadly obovate, entire to serrate, gland. and pubesc. to glab. above. Cor. 1cm, white or light pink to red. Fr. 8–16mm, black, edible. SE US. Z8.
V. ×atlanticum E. Bickn. (*V. angustifolium × V. corymbosum*.) To 1m. Lvs 3–5cm, elliptic-oblong to lanceolate, finely serrate and ciliate. Cor. strongly urceolate. Fr. blue, pruinose. E US. Z3.
V. atrococcum (Gray) Heller. DOWNY SWAMP HUCKLEBERRY; BLACK HUCKLEBERRY; BLACK HIGHBUSH BLUEBERRY. Shrub, 1.5–3m, decid. Lvs 3.5–7cm, elliptic to oblong, entire, glab. above, pubesc. beneath. Cor. pink or green flushed red. Fr. 6–8mm, dull black, sweet. Late spring. Canada to Alab. Z4. 'Leucoccum': fr. translucent, white.
V. australe Small. Shrub, 2–4m, decid. Lvs 5–8cm, elliptic to ovate-lanceolate, entire, glaucous, glab. Cor. 8–11mm, white or flushed pink. Fr. 7–12mm diam., blue, edible. E US. Z6.
V. bracteatum Thunb. Shrub, to 1m, everg. Lvs 2.5–6cm, elliptic to oblong, remotely dentate, coriaceous. Cor. 6mm, white. Fr. 6mm, red, pubesc. Summer. China, Jap. Z7.
V. buxifolium Hook. f. = *V. stapfianum*.
V. caesium Greene. DEERBERRY; SQUAW HUCKLEBERRY. Shrub to 1m, decid. Lvs to 5cm, ovate to elliptic, glaucous beneath. Cor. white; sta. long-exserted. Fr. dark blue, glaucous. E US. Z5.
V. caespitosum Michx. DWARF BILBERRY. Spreading shrub, 10–25cm high, decid. Lvs 1.5–3.5cm, elliptic to obovate, entire to finely serrate, glab. Cor. 5mm, pink to off-white. Fr. 6mm, blue-black, pruinose, edible. Late spring–summer. N and W N Amer. Z2.
V. canadense Rich. = *V. myrtilloides*.
V. candicans Michx. Shrub to 2m, decid. Lvs elliptic to ovate or obovate, glaucous beneath, pubesc. Cor. 6mm, white; sta. long-exserted. Fr. to 1cm, tinged green or blue. Late spring–early summer. SE US. Z5.
V. ciliatum G. Don non Thunb. = *V. oldhamii*.

V. corymbosum L. BLUEBERRY; AMERICAN BLUEBERRY; SWAMP BLUEBERRY; HIGH-BUSH BLUEBERRY. Shrub, 1–2m, decid. Lvs 3–8cm, ovate to lanceolate, entire, orange to scarlet in autumn. Cor. 6–10mm, white to slightly red-tinted. Fr. 8–15mm, blue-black, pruinose, edible. Late spring. E US. Z2. var. **albiflorum** (Hook.) Fern. Lvs finely serrate to ciliate-serrate; fls pure white. var. **glabrum** A. Gray. Lvs minutely serrate-ciliate, glaucous, glab. beneath. 'Blue Ray': lvs dark green in summer, burgundy in winter. 'Blue Crop': hardy; lvs bright green in summer, fiery red in winter. 'Tomahawk': lvs brilliant orange in autumn.
V. crassifolium Andrews. CREEPING BLUEBERRY; THICK-LEAVED WHORTLEBERRY. Procumbent, everg. shrub to 60cm. Lvs 8–15mm, oval-elliptic, remotely finely serrate, thick and coriaceous. Cor. 4mm, pink or white with pink stripes. Fr. 3–4mm, purple-black. Late spring–summer. SE US. Z7. 'Bloodstone': good groundcover. 'Well's Delight': habit trailing, broad.
V. cylindraceum Sm. Shrub, medium-sized to large, usually decid. Lvs narrowly elliptic to oblong, finely dentate, veins reticulate. Cor. 12mm, yellow-green with red tinge. Fr. oblong, blue-black, pruinose. Summer–autumn. Azores. Z10.
V. delavayi Franch. Shrub, 30–50cm, everg. Lvs 6–12mm, obovate-cuneate to broadly obovate, incised at apex. Cor. 4mm, creamy white or flushed pink. Fr. 5mm, carmine or tinged purple. Early summer. SW China. Z7.
V. deliciosum Piper. Shrub, spreading, dense, to 30cm, decid. Lvs 1.5–3.5cm, elliptic to obovate, finely serrate, glaucous beneath, glab., tough. Cor. 5mm, pink. Fr. 6mm, black, sweet. Late spring–summer. Washington and Oreg. Z6.
V. donnianum Wight = *V. sprengelii*.
V. dunalianum Merrill. Shrub to 6m. Lvs 8–12cm, oval to oblong-lanceolate, caudate-acuminate, entire, glab., coriaceous. Cor. 5mm, white. Fr. 4mm, black. Himal. (NE India and W China). Z8.
V. elliottii Chapm. Shrub, 2–4m, forming clumps. Lvs 1.5–3cm, elliptic, minutely serrate, thin, glabrate. Cor. 6–7mm, pink. Fr. 5–8mm, dark blue to black, dull or glossy, rarely glaucous. Spring. SE US. Z6.
V. erythrinum Hook. Erect shrub, to 45cm, everg. Lvs 4–5cm, ovate, entire, glossy, red when young. Cor. deep coral red. Autumn. Java. Z10.
V. erythrocarpum Michx. SOUTHERN MOUNTAIN CRANBERRY. Shrub, 70–150cm, decid. Lvs 2.5–7cm, oval-oblong to lanceolate, bristly-serrate, pubesc. on veins. Cor. 1cm, pink to light red. Fr. red to maroon, sour. Early summer. SE US. Z6.
V. floribundum HBK = *V. mortinia*.
V. fragile Franch. Shrub, 30–50cm, everg. Lvs 1.5–3cm, oval-elliptic, finely serrate, glandular-pubesc. Cor. 6mm, white to deep pink. Fr. 6mm, black. Summer. W China. Z9.
V. fuscatum Ait. Shrub to 3m, everg. or semi-decid. Lvs to 5cm, elliptic to lanceolate, entire, coriaceous. Cor. to 9mm, pink to red. Fr. to 9mm diam., almost black. SE US. Z8.
V. gaultheriifolium Hook. f. Shrub, small to medium-sized, everg. Lvs 8–13cm, elliptic, entire or minutely dentate, glossy above, pruinose beneath. Cor. 5–6mm, white. Fr. 6mm, black. Late summer–autumn. Sikkim. Z10.
V. glaucoalbum Hook. f. ex C.B. Clarke. Shrub, 0.5–1m, everg. Lvs 3–8cm, ovate-oblong to ovate, bristly-serrate, glaucous and hispid on veins beneath. Cor. 5–6mm, white tinged pink. Fr. 6mm, black, pruinose. Late spring–summer. Sikkim. Z9.
V. hirsutum Buckl. WOOLLY BERRY; WOOLLY BERRY; HAIRY-FRUITED BLUEBERRY; HAIRY HUCKLEBERRY. Shrub to 60cm, decid. Lvs 2–6cm, ovate to elliptic-oblong, entire, pubesc. Cor. 10–12mm, white flushed pink. Fr. 6mm, red tinged black, glandular-hispid, scarcely edible. Late spring–early summer. SE US. Z6.
V. hirtum Thunb. Similar to *V. smallii*, to 50cm; lvs 1.5–3.5cm, elliptic-lanceolate, softly pubesc. Jap. Z6.
V. ×intermedium Ruthe (*V. myrtillus × V. vitis-idaea*.) Shrub to 25cm, everg. or semi-everg. Lvs 1.5–2.5cm, obovate-elliptic, finely dentate, sparsely spotted beneath. Cor. pink. Fr. 6mm, dark violet. Early summer. Eur. inc. Britain. Occurs among parents and resembles one or the other. Z6.
V. japonicum Miq. Shrub, 50–70cm. Lvs 2–6cm, oval-oblong-cordate, finely bristly-serrate, somewhat glaucous beneath, glab., rugose. Cor. 8mm, pink. Fr. 6mm, red. Summer. Jap., Korea. Z6.

V. lamarckii Camp. = *V. angustifolium*.

V. lanceolatum Dunal = *V. ovatum*.

V. leucobotrys ????. Shrub, 1–2m, everg. Lvs oblong-lanceolate, dentate. Cor. waxy white, almost diaphanous. Fr. 6mm, white with 5 dark spots. Bengal. Z10.

V. macrocarpon Ait. CRANBERRY; AMERICAN CRANBERRY; LARGE CRANBERRY. Procumbent shrub, everg. to 1m. Lvs 1–2cm, elliptic-oblong, dark green above, tinged white beneath. Cor. 1cm, light purple; sta. strongly exserted. Fr. 1–2cm, red. Summer. E N Amer., N Asia. 'Hamilton': dwarf; fls small, pink. Z2.

V. maderense Link = *V. padifolium*.

V. marianum Wats. Shrub 2–3m. Lvs 5–7cm, elliptic, entire. Cor. 6–8mm, dull white. Fr. 6–10mm diam., black, dull or glaucous. E US. Z6.

V. melanocarpum (Mohr) Mohr. SOUTHERN GOOSEBERRY; GEORGIA BLUEBERRY. Shrub to 1m, decid. Lvs ovate to elliptic or oblanceolate, acute, 3–10cm, canescent at least beneath. Cor. 6mm, white or slightly tinged green. Fr. 8–10mm, red-violet, glossy, edible. Late spring–summer. SE US. Z6.

V. membranaceum Douglas THIN-LEAVED BILBERRY; BLUE HUCKLEBERRY; MOUNTAIN BLUEBERRY; BILBERRY. Shrub, 0.5–1m, decid. Lvs 2.5–6cm, elliptic to oval-oblong, finely serrate, membranous. Cor. 6mm, white tinged green or pale pink. Fr. dark purple, not pruinose, edible. Summer. Mich., Alask. to Calif. Z6.

V. merrillianum Hayata. Shrub, often prostrate or epiphytic, 20–30cm, everg. Lvs 8–10mm, obovate, emarginate, entire, thinly coriaceous, glab. Cor. white to pink. Fr. 5–6mm, purple. Taiwan. Z9.

V. modestum W.W. Sm. Dwarf shrub, to 15cm, creeping. Lvs 2–3cm, ovate to obovate or elliptic, sometimes notched, entire, slightly glaucous beneath. Cor. 4–5mm, rosy pink. Fr. violet, glaucous, edible. W Yunnan, Burm.–Tibet. Z8.

V. mortinia Benth. MORTITIA. Shrub, procumbent, 30–100cm, everg. Lvs 8–15mm, v. crowded, ovate, finely glandular-serrate, coriaceous, sparsely glandular-pubesc. beneath. Cor. 5–8mm, v. pale pink. Fr. 5mm, red, pruinose, edible. Early summer. Ecuad. Z9.

V. moupinense Franch. Shrub, dense, 30–60cm, everg. Lvs 6–12mm, elliptic-oblong to obovate, entire, coriaceous, glab. Cor. 5mm, red to brown. Fr. 6mm, black-red. Late spring–early summer. China. Z9.

V. myrsinites Lam. EVERGREEN BLUEBERRY. Shrub, ± procumbent, to 50cm, everg. Lvs 1–2cm, elliptic-oblong to obovate, finely glandular-serrate, glab. above, sparsely pubesc. beneath. Cor. 6mm, white to pink. Fr. 6mm, blue-black. Spring. SE US. Z7. var. *glaucum* Lam. Plant glab. throughout; lvs and fr. glaucous.

V. myrtilloides Michx. CANADIAN BLUEBERRY; VELVET-LEAF BLUEBERRY; SOURTOP. Shrub, 30–50cm, decid. Lvs 2–4cm, lanceolate to narrowly oblong, entire, finely pubesc. Cor. 4–6mm, white tinged green or rose. Fr. 6–8mm, blue-black, pruinose. Late spring–early summer. N Amer. Z2.

V. myrtilloides Hook. non Michx. = *V. membranaceum*.

V. myrtillus L. BILBERRY; WHORTLEBERRY; WHINBERRY; BLAEBERRY. Shrub, erect, 30–50cm, semi-decid. Lvs 1–3cm, oval-elliptic, finely serrate, glandular-pubesc. on veins beneath. Cor. 6mm, tinged green, becoming red. Fr. 6–10mm, blue-black, pruinose, edible. Eur. to N Asia. Z3. 'Leucocarpum': fr. dirty white.

V. neglectum (Small) Fern. DEERBERRY. Shrub to 1.5m, decid. Lvs 2.5–8cm, oval-lanceolate to obovate, entire, tinged blue beneath, glab. Cor. 6mm, pink to white. Fr. 6mm, green to yellow. Late spring. SE US. Z9.

V. nitidum Andrews = *V. myrsinites*.

V. nummularium Hook. f. & Thoms. Shrub, 30–40cm, everg. Lvs 12–25mm, suborbicular to elliptic, finely serrate, rugose above, smooth beneath, bristly. Cor. pink. Fr. 6mm, black, edible. Spring. Sikkim, Bhutan. Z7.

V. occidentale A. Gray WESTERN BLUEBERRY. Shrub, compact, to 75cm, decid. Lvs to 2cm, obovate to oblanceolate, entire, glaucous. Cor. 4–5mm, white or flushed pale pink. Fr. 6mm diam., blue-black, glaucous. BC to Calif., E to Rocky Mts. Z6.

V. oldhamii Miq. Shrub, bushy, 1–2m in cult., decid. Lvs 3–8cm, oval-elliptic to obovate, finely ciliate and pubesc, carmine-red in autumn, veins hispid. Cor. 4mm, green-yellow tinged red. Fr. 6mm, black, edible. Summer. Jap., Korea. Z6.

V. ovalifolium Sm. MATHERS; TALL BILBERRY; OVAL-LEAVED BILBERRY. Shrub, 1–3m, decid. Lvs 2.5–6cm, elliptic to ovate, entire, tinged blue beneath. Cor. 9mm, pink. Fr. 1cm, dark blue, pruinose, edible. Early summer. Canada, N US. Z3.

V. ovatum Pursh. CALIFORNIAN HUCKLEBERRY; EVERGREEN HUCKLEBERRY; SHOT HUCKLEBERRY. Shrub, erect, spreading, 1–4m, decid. Lvs 1.2–3cm, oval-oblong, serrate, coriaceous, sparsely pubesc. above, setose on main vein beneath. Cor.

6mm, white tinged red. Fr. 6mm, black, sour. Spring. BC to Calif. Z7.

V. oxycoccos L. EUROPEAN CRANBERRY; SMALL CRANBERRY. Dwarf shrub, prostrate, everg. Lvs 5–10mm, ovate-oblong, tinged blue beneath. Cor. light purple. Fr. 6mm, dark red, rather sour. N Amer., N Eurasia. Z2.

V. padifolium Sm. MADEIRAN WHORTLEBERRY. Shrub, erect, to 2m or more, everg. or semi-everg. Lvs 2.5–5cm, ovate to elliptic-oblong, pubesc. beneath. Cor. 1cm, yellow with red stripes. Fr. 12mm, black. Early summer. Madeira. Z9.

V. pallidum Ait. DRYLAND BERRY. Shrub to 1m, decid. Lvs 3–5cm, elliptic-ovate, finely serrate and ciliate, tinged blue beneath. Cor. 5–8mm, white or rufescent. Fr. 6–8mm, dark blue, pruinose. Late spring. E US. Z4.

V. parvifolium Sm. RED BILBERRY; RED HUCKLEBERRY. Shrub, erect, to 2m or more, decid. Fls generally solitary, pendulous, shortly pedicellate; cor. flattened-globose, 6mm, tinged green with hint of red, minutely 5-lobed, lobes reflexed. Fr. 12mm, coral-red, slightly translucent, edible. Late spring–early summer. W N Amer. (Alask. to Calif.). Z6.

V. pennsylvanicum var. *angustifolium* (Ait.) Gray = *V. angustifolium*.

V. pensylvanicum Lam. non Mill. = *V. angustifolium* var. *laevifolium*.

V. praestans Lamb. KAMCHATKA BILBERRY. Dwarf shrub, to 15cm, decid., creeping. Lvs 2.5–5cm, broadly elliptic to obovate, obscurely serrate, somewhat pubesc. on veins beneath. Cor. campanulate, 6mm, white flushed pink. Fr. 12mm, bright red. Early summer. NE Asia. Z4.

V. reflexum (Klotzsch) Hook. f. Shrub, everg. to 60cm, pendulous. Lvs 1–2cm, oblong-lanceolate, acutely dentate, pale red when young. Cor. somewhat pentagonal, red. Winter. Boliv. Z9.

V. retusum Hook. f. Shrub to 30cm, everg. Lvs oblong, obovate or elliptic, apex sometimes incised. Cor. 5mm, white with red stripes. Fr. 5mm, black. Late spring. Himal. Z9.

V. rollisonii Hook. Shrub, erect, 60cm+, everg. Lvs 2cm, obovate, entire, occas. retuse, subglaucous beneath, coriaceous. Cor. rich scarlet. Java. Z10.

V. scoparium Leiberg ex Coville. GROUSEBERRY; DWARF RED WHORTLEBERRY; RED ALPINE BLUEBERRY; SMALL-LEAVED HUCKLEBERRY. Shrub, 10–20cm, br. compact forming broom-like tufts. Lvs 7–11mm, elliptic to ovate-lanceolate, minutely serrate. Cor. 3–4mm, pink. Fr. 4–6mm diam., red. NW Amer. Z3.

V. setosum Wright = *V. fragile*.

V. smallii Gray. Shrub, to 1.5m, decid. Lvs 3–6cm, elliptic to lanceolate, pubesc. on main vein beneath. Cor. 5–6mm, white to red-tinted. Fr. 5–7mm, blue-black. Late spring–early summer. Jap. Z6.

V. sprengelii (G. Don) Sleumer. Shrub to 3m, erect, decid. or everg. Lvs 3–7cm, oblong-lanceolate, finely serrate. Cor. 6mm, white to pink, pubesc. within. Fr. 5mm, black-red to purple-black. Late spring. NE India to W & C China. Z7.

V. stamineum var. *neglectum* Small = *V. neglectum*.

V. stapfianum Sleumer. Shrub, erect, 0.5–1m, robust. Lvs oblong, entire, to 1cm, v. thick, black-punctate beneath. Cor. 3mm, white or pink. Borneo. Z10.

V. stramineum L. DEERBERRY; SQUAW HUCKLEBERRY. Shrub, 80–150cm, decid. Lvs 3–6cm, elliptic to oval-oblong, entire, pubesc. Cor. 6–8mm, green tinged yellow to off-white or rose. Fr. 8–10mm, green or yellow, unpalatable. Spring–early summer. E & SE US. Z5.

V. tenellum Ait. SMALL CLUSTER BLUEBERRY; SOUTHERN BLUEBERRY. Shrub, 20–45cm. Lvs 2–3cm, spathulate to elliptic, serrate, gland. beneath, pubesc. Cor. 6–8mm, white flushed pink or red. Fr. 6–8mm diam., black, glossy, ± edible. SE US. Z8.

V. torreyanum Camp. = *V. vaccillans*.

V. uliginosum L. BOG WHORTLEBERRY; BOG BILBERRY; MOORBERRY. Shrub, stiffly erect, to 50cm, decid. Lvs 1–3cm, elliptic to obovate, entire, pubesc. beneath. Cor. 4mm, v. pale pink. Fr. 6mm, blue-black, pruinose, edible. Late spring–early summer. N Amer., N Eur. Z2.

V. urceolatum Hemsl. Shrub, to 180cm, everg. Lvs 5–10cm, oval-oblong, dark green, veins deeply impressed. Cor. 6mm, pink. Fr. 6mm, black. Early summer. W China. Z9.

V. vaccillans Torr. DRYLAND BLUEBERRY; SUGAR HUCKLEBERRY; LOW BLUEBERRY; EARLY SWEET BILBERRY; LOW BLUEBERRY; LOW SWEET BLUEBERRY. Shrub 20–50cm. Lvs 1.5–3cm, elliptic-spathulate to broadly elliptic, entire to finely serrate, glab. or minutely pubesc. Cor. 5–7mm, yellow-green, somewhat red-tinted. Fr. 4–5mm, dark blue, ± pruinose, edible. Late spring. E US. Z6. var. *crinitum* Fern. Twigs and underside of lvs pubesc.

V. varingiifolium (Bl.) Miq. Lvs 4–5cm, elliptic to elliptic-lanceolate, acute, coriaceous, glab., gland. at base. Infl. racemose, leafy, glab. Java. Z10.

V. virgatum Ait. SOUTHERN BLACK BLUEBERRY; RABBIT-EYE BLUE-BERRY. Shrub, erect, to 4m, decid. Lvs 3–6cm, oblanceolate to narrowly elliptic, scabrous-serrate, gland. above, glab. or pub-esc. on veins beneath. Cor. 5mm. Fr. 5mm, black. Late spring–early summer. E & SE US. Z6.

V. vitis-idaea L. COWBERRY; FOXBERRY; MOUNTAIN CRANBERRY; CRANBERRY. Shrub, creeping, 10–30cm high, everg. Lvs 1–1.5cm, obovate to ovate, often emarginate, black-punctate beneath, coriaceous. Cor. white to pink. Fr. 6mm, bright red, edible. Late spring–early summer. N Eurasia, Jap., N Amer, 'Koralle': free-fruiting; fr. large, bright red. Z5. var. *majus* Lodd. Fls larger. Lvs to 4cm. var. *minus* Lodd. MOUNTAIN CRANBERRY; ROCK CRANBERRY; LINGBERRY; LINGEN; LINGEN-BERRY; LINGONBERRY. Forming dense mats 10–20cm thick. Lvs 8–15mm. Fls pink to red. Arc. N Amer. 'Variegata': lvs edged creamy-white. Z2.

V. ornamental cvs. 'Beckyblue': st. deep red; lvs blue tinged green turning blue-yellow in autumn. 'Elliott': habit upright to 2.1m; lvs blue-green turning orange-red in autumn, long-lasting; late-flowering. 'Friendship': growth vigorous; lvs brilliant orange-red in autumn, long-lasting. 'Ornablue': lvs dense, slender, red in autumn, long-lasting; fr. dark blue. 'Premier': lvs bright green in summer. 'Top Hat': dwarf, hardy; fls abundant.

→*Cyanococcus* and *Oxycoccus*.

Vagaria Herb. Amaryllidaceae. 4 bulbous perenn. herbs. Lvs ligulate, linear, to 60cm, green banded white. Scape obscurely tetragonal; infl. umbellate; fls funnel-shaped, tep. 6, lanceolate; corona teeth 12, paired between fil.; fil. included. Autumn. N Afr., Syr. and Isr.

V. parviflora Herb. 6–9-fld. Scape to 25cm, 6–9-fld; perianth seg. to 3.5cm, white with green keel. Syr., Isr. Z9.

Valerian *Valeriana*.

Valeriana L. VALERIAN. Valerianaceae. 150–200 perenn. herbs or subshrubs. Lvs simple, pinnatifid or pinnatisect. Fls small, in clusters or paniculate cymes; cal. initially inrolled, forming a feathery crown in fr.; cor. rotate, funnelform or campanulate; sta. usually 3. Widely distrib., except Aus.

V. alliariifolia Adams. To 90cm, glab. Lower lvs to 20cm diam., ovate, cordate, entire, crenate or shallowly dentate. Fls pink in a corymbose compound infl. E Greece.

V. alpestris Steven. To 15cm, glab. Lower lvs ovate-oblong, toothed. Fls tinged pink, in numerous small heads. Cauc.

V. arizonica A. Gray. To 10cm, glab. Lvs about 2.5cm, rather fleshy, ovate to suborbicular, simple or pinnatifid. Fls pink to white, in a 1.25cm corymb. Ariz.

V. bertiscea Pančić. Close to *V. montana* but to 25cm, lower lvs occas. pinnately lobed, upper pinnatifid. Balk. Penins.

V. capitata Pall. ex Lind. To 60cm. Lvs to 7cm, mostly cauline, ovate to obovate. Fls white to pink. Arc. Alask. and Sib.

V. celtica L. To 25cm, glab. Lower lvs obovate, oblanceolate, or linear, entire, cauline lvs oblanceolate or linear. Fls tinged yellow or brown in a narrow pan. Alps.

V. coccinea hort. = *Centranthus ruber*.

V. dioica L. To 40cm. Lower lvs simple, ovate, oblong or elliptic, entire. Fls pink or white. W & C Eur. ssp. *simplicifolia* (Rchb.) Nyman. Cauline lvs simple, entire or irregularly toothed.

V. elongata Jacq. To 25cm, glab. Lvs simple, lower lvs ovate or oblong, ± entire; cauline lvs ovate-elliptic, crenate or with a few large obtuse teeth. Fls tinged brown or green in a narrow pan. E Alps.

V. excelsa Poir. = *V. officinalis* ssp. *sambucifolia*.

V. globulariifolia Ramond & DC. To 25cm, glab. Lower lvs simple or 3-fid, entire, oblanceolate to spathulate, upper lvs pinnatifid to finely pinnatisect. Fls pink in dense compounds or simple cymes. Pyren., Cordillera Cantabrica.

V. longiflora Willk. To 5cm. Lvs simple, entire, orbicular, ovate or broadly elliptic. Fls few, pink. NE Spain.

V. montana L. To 50cm, pubesc. or subglabrous. Lower lvs en-tire, ovate, orbicular, elliptic or cordate, upper lvs simple, 3-fid, ovate, entire or toothed. Fls lilac, pink or white. Alps, Cauc.

V. officinalis L. COMMON VALERIAN; GARDEN HELIOTROPE. To 1.5m, pubesc. or glab. Lvs pinnate or pinnatisect; lfts linear, lanceolate or elliptic, entire or toothed. Fls pink or white. Eur., W Asia. ssp. *sambucifolia* (Mikan f.) Čelak. Glab., cauline lvs with 5–9 lanceolate, dentate lfts. N, NC & EC Eur. ssp. *collina* (Wallr.) Nyman. Densely patent-hairy below, cauline lvs with 15–27 linear, entire lfts. E & C Eur. to Ukraine and SE Russia.

V. pancicii Hal. & Bald. = *V. saxatilis* ssp. *pancicii*.

V. phu L. Close to *V. officinalis* but differing in its mostly un-divided lower lvs. Fls white in a paniculate corymb. Cauc., Eur. 'Aurea': lvs golden-yellow turning lime to midgreen by summer.

V. pyrenaica L. To 1.1m, pubesc. at nodes. Lower lvs to 20cm, simple, ovate or suborbicular, cordate, deeply and irregularly dentate, upper lvs with 1 or 2 pairs of small lat. lfts. Fls pink. Pyren.

V. rosea hort. = *Centranthus ruber* 'Roseus'.

V. rubra L. = *Centranthus ruber*.

V. saliunca All. To 15cm. Lower lvs simple, spathulate, entire, linear-lanceolate, st. lvs lanceolate or linear, 3-fid. Fls pink in simple corymbs. S Eur., Alps.

V. sambucifolia Mikan f. = *V. officinalis* ssp. *sambucifolia*.

V. saxatilis L. Glab. Lvs simple, elliptic-oblanceolate or lanceolate to linear, entire or crenate. Infl. compound; fls white. E & EC Alps. ssp. *pancicii* (Hal. & Bald.) Ockend. To 15cm. Basal lvs narrow, glab. Albania.

V. simplicifolia (Rchb.) Kabath = *V. dioica* ssp. *simplicifolia*.

V. supina Ard. To 12cm, pubesc. Lvs simple, lower lvs spathulate to orbicular, entire or crenate, cauline lvs spathulate or oblanceolate. Infl. dense, simple; cor. pink. E & EC Alps.

V. tuberosa L. Tuberous, to 60cm, glab. Lower lvs elliptic or ovate, simple, entire, st. lvs usually pinnatifid, 3-fid or entire, upper lvs finely pinnatisect. Infl. simple or branched; fls pink. Eur., SE Russia.

VALERIANACEAE Batsch. *Centranthus, Fedia, Nardostachys, Patrinia, Plectritis, Valeriana, Valerianella*.

Valerianella Mill. CORN SALAD. Valerianaceae. 50 ann. and bienn. herbs. Lvs simple, rather succulent. Fls in term., capitate cymes; cal. minute or 0; cor. small, 5-lobed, salverform to tubular; sta. 2 or 3. US, Eur., N Afr., Asia.

V. eriocarpa Desv. ITALIAN CORN SALAD. Lvs to 12.5cm, linear to spathulate, ± entire. Cal. obliquely coroniform, with 6 deep subequal teeth. N Afr., S Eur.

V. locusta (L.) Betcke. COMMON CORN SALAD; LAMB'S LETTUCE. Lvs to 7.5cm, linear-oblong to oblong-spathulate, entire to remotely sinuate-dentate. Cal. reduced to a minute tooth. Eur. 'Blonde Shell': lvs golden.

V. olitoria (L.) Pollich = *V. locusta*.

Vallaris Burm. f. Apocynaceae. 3 twining shrubs with milky sap. Lvs entire, punctate. Fls white in cymes or clusters; cal. 5-lobed; cor. salverform, lobes broad; sta. at top of tube. Trop. Asia. Z10.

V. dichotoma (Roxb.) Wallich ex A. DC. = *V. solanacea*.

V. heynei Spreng. = *V. solanacea*.

V. solanacea (Roth) Kuntze. Tall climbing shrub. Lvs 2–15cm, elliptic or linear-oblong, slender-pointed. Fls in forked cymes, fragrant, 1.5cm across. India, Sri Lanka.

Vallea Mutis ex L. f. Elaeocarpaceae. 1 everg. shrub to 5m. Br. slender, glab. Lvs 2.5–12cm, lanceolate to broadly ovate, base rounded to cordate, thin or subcoriaceous, dark green; stipules reniform. Cymes short; sep. 5, ovate-lanceolate, pale rose with darker veins; pet. to 1.25cm, 5, obovate, cupped, 3-lobed, crimson to dark rose; sta. many, to half length of pet. Summer–early autumn. Andes. Z9.

V. stipularis L.

Vallesia Ruiz & Pav. Apocynaceae. 8 shrubs and small trees. Lvs entire. Fls small, in cymes; cal. 5-parted; cor. salverform, throat hairy, lobes 5, spreading, ovate or lanceolate; sta. included. Fr. drupaceous. Trop. Amer. Z10.

V. flexuosa Woodson. Tree to 10m. Lvs to 15cm, narrowly ovate. Fls white tinged green. Costa Rica.

Valley Oak *Quercus lobata*.
Vallis *Vallisneria*.

Vallisneria L. EEL GRASS; VALLIS. Hydrocharitaceae. 2 aquatic, perenn., bottom-rooting grass-like herbs. St. short. Lvs basal, submerged, tips floating just below surface, ribbon-like, translucent, tessellated. ♂ infl. a spadix, spathe reflexed; fl. minute, free-floating; sep. 3; pet. 1. ♀ on longer scapes, some-times coiled. Widespread in cool temp. and warm zones.

V. americana Michx. FLUMINE MISSISSIPPI. Lvs to 2m×2cm, entire to denticulate. ♂ fls with sta. partially or completely united; ♀ fls with stigmas not fringed. E US, E Asia to Aus. Z9.

V. asiatica Miki = *V. americana*.

V. gigantia Gräbn. = *V. americana*.

V. spiralis L. EEL GRASS; TAPE GRASS. Lvs to 2m×1cm, entire to denticulate. ♂ fls with free sta. Stigmas of ♀ fls fringed. Eur., Asia, Afr., Aus. 'Torta': lvs wider, tightly spiralled. Z8.

V. verticillata (L. f.) Roxb. = *Hydrilla verticillata*.

Vallonea Oak *Quercus ithaburensis*.

Vallota Salisb. & Herb.

V. purpurea (Ait.) Herb. = *Cyrtanthus elatus*.

V. speciosa (L. f.) T. Dur. & Schinz = *Cyrtanthus elatus*.

Valoradia Hochst.

V. abyssinica Hochst. = *Ceratostigma abyssinicum*.

V. patula Prain = *Ceratostigma abyssinicum*.

Vancouveria Morr. and Decne. Berberidaceae. 3 perenn. herbs. Rhiz. slender, creeping. Lvs slender-stalked, radical, 2-ternate. Flowering st. usually naked; fls nodding; sep. 12–15, in two sets, outer set small, soon falling, inner set larger, petaloid, reflexed; pet. 6, reflexed; sta. 6. W US. Z7.

V. chrysantha Greene. Differs from *V. hexandra* in fls yellow. SW Oreg. Z7.

V. hexandra (Hook.) Morr. and Decne. 10–40cm. Lvs decid., lfts ovate, ± 7cm across, glaucous beneath. Infl. exceeding foliage, 6–45-fld; fls 10–3mm diam., white; sep. spotted red. Washington to Calif. Z5.

V. planipetala Calloni. Differs from *V. hexandra* in lvs everg., lfts 6×5cm, somewhat leathery, sparsely hairy. Fls white, suffused lavender. Oreg. to mid Calif. Z7.

→*Epimedium*.

Vanda Jones ex R. Br. Orchidaceae. Some 35 epiphytic, monopodial orchids. St. leafy. Lvs rigid, strap-shaped, in 2 opposite ranks, often keeled beneath. Infl. an axillary rac.; sep. and pet. obovate to spathulate, often clawed, spreading; lip fused to the column base, 3-lobed, spur short. Himal. to Malaysia. Z9.

V. alpina (Lindl.) Lindl. = *Trudelia alpina*.

V. amesiana Rchb. f. = *Holcoglossum amesianum*.

V. bensonii Batem. Lvs 18–25cm. Rac., to 45cm; fls to 5cm diam., yellow-green dotted and veined red-brown, lip pink or rose-purple. Burm., Thail.

V. brunnea Rchb. f. Lvs narrow. Fls olive above, lip pale yellow-white. India, Burm.

V. cathcartii Lindl. = *Esmeralda cathcartii*.

V. clarkei (Rchb. f.) N.E. Br. = *Esmeralda clarkei*.

V. coerulea Griff. ex Lindl. Lvs 8–25cm. Infl. 20–60cm; fls 7–10cm diam., pale to deep lilac-blue, obscurely chequered, lip darker. India, Burm., Thail.

V. coerulescens Griff. Lvs 12.5–20cm. Infl. to 50cm+; fls 2.5–3.5cm diam., pale lilac, pale blue or white, lip darker. Burm., Thail.

V. cristata Lindl. = *Trudelia cristata*.

V. dearei Rchb. f. Lvs 40–45×4.5cm. Rac. pendent; fls 3–5, lemon yellow or cream, veined brown, fragrant. Sunda Is.

V. denisoniana Bens. & Rchb. f. (including var. *hebraica* Rchb. f.). Lvs to 30×2cm. Rac. to 15cm, fls to 5cm diam., lime green, to ivory, often mottled or spotted ginger, strongly vanilla-scented; lip base marked cinnamon to orange. Burm., Thail.

V. gigantea Lindl. = *Vandopsis gigantea*.

V. griffithii Lindl. = *Trudelia griffithii*.

V. helvola Bl. Rac. short, shorter than lvs, 3–5-fld; fls 4–5cm diam., yellow to burgundy, shading to purple. Java.

V. hookeriana Rchb. f. = *Papilionanthe hookeriana*.

V. insignis Bl. Lvs 22.5–30×2.5cm. Infl. pendent, shorter than lvs; fls 5–5.5cm diam., tawny-yellow, spotted chocolate-brown, lip midlobe white, limb rose-purple. Moluccas.

V. kimballiana Rchb. f. = *Holcoglossum kimballianum*.

V. lamellata Lindl. Lvs 30–42cm. Infl. erect or suberect; fls 2.5–5cm diam., pale yellow, blotched chestnut, lip lat. lobes white. Philipp., N Borneo.

V. lilacina Teijsm. & Binnend. Lvs 4–8, oblong, arched. Infl. erect; fls lilac, rarely mottled purple, lip base white. Thail., Burm., Laos to China.

V. limbata Bl. St. to 90cm+. Lvs linear 15–20cm. Infl. 15–20cm; fls cinnamon, blotched and chequered dark red-brown, edged yellow, tinged lilac above, lip rose-lilac, edged white. Java.

V. lowii Lindl. = *Dimorphorchis lowii*.

V. luzonica Loher. Lvs 15–35cm. Infl. erect, to 20cm+; fls to 5cm diam., white, base banded, purple, spotted violet to crimson-purple, lip violet-purple or amethyst. Philipp.

V. merrillii Ames & Quis. Lvs 25–32cm. Infl. lax; fls 3–3.5cm, waxy, fragrant, yellow suffused carmine or red, lip midlobe yellow blotched red, lat. lobes white, dotted purple. Philipp.

V. pumila Hook. f. = *Trudelia pumila*.

V. roeblingiana Rolfe. Lvs linear-oblong, 20–30cm. Fls to 5cm diam., yellow striped red-brown, lip midlobe yellow. Philipp.

V. Rothschildiana. Fls large, deep lavender blue with darker chequered markings. Gdn origin. Midwinter.

V. roxburghii R. Br. = *V. tessellata*.

V. sanderiana Rchb. f. = *Euanthe sanderiana*.

V. spathulata Spreng. Lvs 5–10cm. Infl. 30–45cm; fls few, to 3cm diam., golden yellow. India, Sri Lanka.

V. suavis Rchb. f. = *V. tricolor* var. *suavis*.

V. teres (Roxb.) Lindl. = *Papilionanthe teres*.

V. tessellata (Roxb.) D. Don Lvs conduplicate, strongly arching, 15–20cm. Infl. 15–25cm; fls 4–5cm diam., tep, yellow-green or v. pale blue, chequered brown, lip violet to blue, edged white. India, Burm. to Malaysia.

V. tricolor Lindl. Lvs 37–45cm. Infl. 7–+10-fld; fls fragrant, 5–7.5cm diam., variable in colour, usually pale yellow, densely dotted bright red-brown, lip bright magenta above, white streaked red-brown beneath, spur white. Java, Laos. var. *suavis* (Rchb. f.) Lindl. Rac. longer; fls white, dots few, red-purple; lip purple.

V. undulata Lindl. Lvs flat 7–10×2cm. Infl. 15–20cm; fls 3–4cm diam., white suffused pink, tips green, lip yellow-green, striped pink. Himal.

V. grexes and cvs. There are many hybrids and cvs recorded. These fall roughly into 2 groups, plants with strap-shaped lvs (true Vandas) and those with a narrow, scrambling habit, terete lvs and butterfly-like fls (derived from *V.* (now *Papilionanthe*) *teres*). Fl. colour ranges through white, yellow-green, gold, apricot, brick red, tan, red, purple-red, pink, rose, lilac, lavender and 'blue', often veined, marked or bicoloured.

Vandopsis Pfitz. Orchidaceae. 10 epiphytic monopodial orchids. Lvs tough, strap-shaped. Rac. erect or pendent; fls fleshy; sep. and pet. oblong-ovate to spathulate, clawed; lip base concave, sometimes spurred; lat, lobes erect. SE Asia to Malaysia. Z10.

V. gigantea (Lindl.) Pfitz. Lvs to 60×7cm. Infl. pendent, to 40cm; fls to 7cm diam., yellow, blotched red, violet beneath; lip ribbed white. Burm.

V. lissochiloides (Gaudich.) Pfitz. Lvs to 60×5cm. Infl, erect, to 120cm; fls to 20cm diam., yellow above, speckled violet, violet-red beneath. E Malaysia.

→*Vanda*.

Vanguiera Juss. Rubiaceae. 30 shrubs or small trees. Lvs simple; stipules united at base, persistent or caducous. Fls in axill. clusters or pan.; tube globose or turbinate, 4–5-parted; cor. bell-shaped or cylindric or globose, lobes 5 or, rarely, 4 or 6; sta. 5. Fr. a drupe, ovoid or subglobose. Trop. Afr., Madag. Z10.

V. edulis Vahl = *V. madagascariensis*.

V. infaustia Burchell WILD MEDLAR. Shrub or tree, to 4m. Lvs to 25×15cm, elliptic to ovate, oval or orbicular with soft, golden to russet hairs. Fls clustered, to 6mm, white-green to yellow. Fr. to 4cm diam., leathery, pale yellow to brown. S Afr.

V. madagascariensis J.F. Gmel. TAMARIND OF THE INDIES; SPANISH TAMARIND. Shrub or tree, to 6m. Lvs to 22×11cm, ovate or elliptic, glab. Fls in pan., 6mm, white-green. Fr. to 4cm diam., fleshy. Madag.

V. tomentosa Hochst. = *V. infaustia*.

Vanheerdia L. Bol. Aizoaceae. 4 highly succulent, clump-forming herbs. Lvs united to form nearly globose to elongated bodies, keels and edges mostly denticulate. Fls to 3 together, long-pedicellate, yellow. S Afr. (Cape Prov.). Z9.

V. divergens (L, Bol.) L. Bol. Lf pairs united for 20–25mm, 40–60×25–30×16–25cm, keel and angles denticulate, grey-green, tinted red in resting period. Fls 2–4cm diam.

Vanilla *Vanilla planifolia*.

Vanilla Mill. Orchidaceae. 100 scandent orchids; roots adventitious, aerial or clinging. St. often succulent, cylindrical, jointed, climbing or trailing. Lvs fleshy, borne at nodes or vestigial and scale-like or 0. Rac. or pan. usually axillary; fls large; tep. oblong-lanceolate, free, similar; lip funnel-shaped. Capsules long-cylindrical. Trop. and subtrop. of Old and New World. Z10.

V. anaromatica Griseb. = *V. inodora*.

V. articulata Northr. = *V. barbellata*.

V. barbellata Rchb. f. St. 1cm diam., green, succulent. Lvs to 4cm, lanceolate, short-lived. Fls yellow-green or buff, lip white, purple towards apex; with disc of white hairs, becoming yellow papillae near apex. Summer. S Flor., Cuba, W Indies.

V. fragrans (Salisb.) Ames = *V. planifolia*.

V. grandiflora Lindl. = *V. pompona*.

V. humboldtii Rchb. f. St. 1–1.5cm diam., green-brown. Lvs vestigial, scale-like. Fls bright yellow, lip with chestnut-brown patch in throat, with short brown papillae and red hairs over 1cm long in throat. Comoros Is.

V. imperialis Kränzl. St. green, succulent, thick. Lvs to 28×12cm, succulent, elliptic. Fls yellow or cream, lip blotched with rose-pink or purple. W, C & Trop. E Africa.

V. inodora Schiede. St. to 8mm diam., green, succulent. Lvs to 25×12cm, broadly ovate. Fls yellow-green, lip white with yellow crest. Spring-autumn. Flor., C Amer., W Indies, NE S Amer.

V. phaeantha Rchb. f. St. to 8mm diam., green. Lvs 10–12×3.5cm, oblong. Fls pale green, the lip white striped with yellow. Late spring–summer. Flor., W Indies.

V. phalaenopsis Rchb. f. St. 10–20mm diam., succulent. Lvs vestigial, brown, to 3cm. Fls white flushed pink, salmon, coral-pink or yellow in the throat, sweet-scented. Seych., Kenya, Tanz., Moz., S Afr. (Natal).

V. planifolia Andrews. VANILLA. St. 1cm diam., green. Lvs 15×5cm, oblong. Fls pale yellow-green, the lip with yellow hairs. Spring. Flor., W Indies, C & S Amer. 'Variegata': lvs striped yellow and cream.

V. polylepis Summerh. St. 1–1.5cm diam., succulent, bright green. Lvs to 24×6.5cm, lanceolate to ovate. Fls white or green-white, lip yellow in throat, usually maroon-purple towards apex. C Afr.

V. pompona Schiede. St. thick. Lvs to 25×10cm, ovate to oblong. Fls green-yellow with orange-yellow marks on lip. C Amer.

V. roscheri Rchb. f. = *V. phalaenopsis*.

Vanilla Trumpet Vine *Distictis laxiflora*.
Van Volxem's Maple *Acer velutinum* var. *vanvolxemii*.
Vaquero Blanco *Cydista aequinoctialis*.
Variable Sallow Wattle *Acacia mucronata*.
Variable Smoke Bush *Conospermum taxifolium*.
Variegated Creeping Soft Grass *Holcus mollis* 'Albovariegatus'.
Variegated Ginger *Alpinia vittata*.
Variegated Ginger Lily *Kaempferia gilbertii*.
Variegated Gout Weed *Aegopodium podagraria* 'Variegatum'.
Variegated Ground Ivy *Glechoma hederacrea* 'Variegata'.
Variegated Iris *Iris variegata*.
Variegated Leyland Cypress ×*Cupressocyparis leylandii* 'Harlequin'.
Variegated Oncidium *Oncidium variegatum*.
Various-leaved Pondweed *Potamogeton gramineus*.
Varnished Gum *Eucalyptus vernicosa*.
Varnish Tree *Koelreuteria paniculata*; *Toxicodendron vernicifluum*.
Varnish Wattle *Acacia verniciflua*.

×**Vascostylis**. (*Ascocentrum* ×*Rhynchostylis* ×*Vanda*.) Orchidaceae. Gdn hybrids with strap-shaped lvs in 2 ranks along erect st. Fls rounded, purple-blue to red-purple in erect spikes.

Vase Vine *Clematis* (*C. viorna*).
Vass's Laburnum *Laburnum* ×*watereri* 'Vossii'.
Vegetable Fern *Diplazium esculentum*.
Vegetable Humming-bird *Sesbania grandiflora*.
Vegetable Marrow *Cucurbita pepo*.
Vegetable Mercury *Brunfelsia uniflora*.
Vegetable Oyster *Tragopogon porrifolius*.
Vegetable Pear *Sechium edule*.
Vegetable Sheep *Haastia* (*H. pulvinaris*).
Vegetable Spaghetti *Curcurbita pepo*.
Vegetable Sponge *Luffa cylindrica*.
Veined Verbena *Verbena rigida*.
Veitch Fir *Abies veitchii*.

Veitchia H.A. Wendl. CHRISTMAS PALM; MANILA PALM. Palmae. 18 large monoecious palms. St. straight or basally swollen, ringed. Crownshaft conspicuous. Lvs 2.5–4m, pinnate, erect to spreading; petiole channelled above, tomentose, often with black-brown scales; pinnae single-fold, lanceolate. Fr. ovoid, to c6cm, red to orange-red. Philipp., New Hebrides, New Caledonia, Fiji. Z10.

V. arecina Becc. To 12m. Pinnae to 60×2.5cm, c60 each side of rachis, green beneath. Fr. to 4.5cm, crimson. New Hebrides.

V. joannis H.A. Wendl. To 32m. Pinnae to 80 each side of rachis, pendent, glab. Fr. to 6cm, orange-red. Fiji.

V. merrillii (Becc.) H.E. Moore. MANILA PALM; CHRISTMAS PALM. To c5m. Pinnae 48–63 per side, ascending, with pale green scales beneath. Fr. to 3.3cm, crimson. Palawan Is.

V. montgomeryana H.E. Moore. St. to 12m. Pinnae 50–60 per side, spreading, minutely scaly beneath. Fr. to 4cm, red. Origin unknown, possibly New Hebrides.

V. winin H.E. Moore. Resembles *V. montgomeryana*, but fr. to 1.9cm. New Hebrides.

→*Actinorhytis, Adonidia, Kentia* and *Normanbya*.

Veitch's Screw Pine *Pandanus veitchii*.

Vella L. Cruciferae. 4 shrublets. St. much-branched. Lvs simple, sessile. Fls 4-merous, in loose rac. Medit. Z8.

V. pseudocytisus L. Everg. Lvs obovate-lanceolate, slightly leathery, hispidulous. Pet. 8mm, obovate-orbicular, pure yellow. Early summer. C & S Spain.

V. spinosa Boiss. Decid. Br. pilose, spine-tipped. Lvs linear-lanceolate, grey-green, fleshy. Pet. 4–6mm, obovate, yellow, veined violet. Summer. S & SE Spain.

Vellozia Vand. Velloziaceae. 124 shrub- or tree-like perennials; st. fibrous, erect. Lvs in a terminal tuft, linear-ensiform, sheaths persistent, fibrous. Fls in term. clusters of 1–2; perianth campanulate or funnel-shaped, seg. 6, ovate or oblong. Trop. Amer. Z10.

V. candida Mikan. Tufted; br. short. Lvs linear, tip filiform, keeled, spiny-toothed. Fls bright white. Summer. Braz.

V. elegans (Balf.) Oliv. = *Talbotia elegans*.

V. elegans var. *minor* Bak. = *Talbotia elegans*.

V. flaviscans Mart. = *V. squamata*.

V. squamata Pohle. St. short, forked, scaly. Lvs glaucous, keeled. Fls orange-red. Summer. Braz.

V. talbotii Balf. = *Talbotia elegans*.

V. tertia Spreng. = *V. candida*.

→*Barbacenia*.

VELLOZIACEAE Endl. 6/252. *Talbotia, Vellozia, Xerophyta*.

Veltheimia Gled. Liliaceae (Hyacinthaceae). 2 bulbous perenn. herbs. Bulbs large, ovoid, with concentric scales. Lvs in a rosette, thick, undulate. Rac. cylindrical, scapose, resembling *Kniphofia*; perianth tubular, declinate, lobes 6, tooth-like. Spring. S Afr. Z9.

V. bracteata Bak. Lvs to 35cm, strap-shaped, glossy-green. Scape to 45cm, purple spotted yellow; perianth 3–4cm, pink-purple, sometimes tinged yellow. E Cape.

V. capensis (L.) DC. Lvs to 30cm, lanceolate, glaucous. Scape to 30cm+, flecked purple, glaucous; perianth 2–3cm, from white with red spots to dull pink tipped cream or pink with green or claret apex. SW Cape. 'Rosalba': fls white spotted pink. 'Rubescens': fls deeper in colour. Plants cultivated as *V. deasii* are variants of *V. capensis*, of more compact habit (to 25cm) and with shorter, grey-green, crispate lvs.

V. capensis misapplied = *V. bracteata*.

V. glauca (Ait.) Jacq. = *V. capensis*.

V. roodeae Phillips = *V. capensis*.

V. viridifolia Jacq. = *V. bracteata*.

Velvet Bean *Mucuna pruriens*.
Velvet Bells *Bartsia alpina*.
Velvet Bent Grass *Agrostis canina*.
Velvet-berry *Guettarda scabra*.
Velvet Flower *Amaranthus caudatus*.
Velvet Leaf *Abutilon theophrasti*.
Velvet-leaf Blueberry *Vaccinium myrtilloides*.
Velvet Plant *Gynura* (*G. aurantiaca*).
Velvet Rose *Aeonium canariense*.
Velvet Sumac *Rhus typhina*.
Venetian Sumac *Cotinus coggygria*.
Venezuela Treebine *Cissus rhombifolia*.

×**Venidioarctotis** hort.
×*V. hybrida* hort. = *Arctotis* ×*hybrida*.

Venidium Less.
V. calendulaceum Less. = *Arctotheca calendula*.
V. decurrens Less. = *Arctotheca calendula*.
V. fastuosum (Jacq.) Stapf. = *Arctotis fastuosa*.
V. macrocephalum DC. = *Arctotis fastuosa*.
V. wyleyi Harv. = *Arctotis fastuosa*.

Ventenatia Beauv.
V. humifusa Cav. = *Astroloma humifusum*.

Venus' Fly Trap *Dionaea*.
Venus' Looking Glass *Legousia hybrida*; *L. speculum-veneris*.
Venus Maidenhair *Adiantum capillus-veneris*.
Venus' Mouse Trap *Dionaea*.
Venus' Navelwort *Omphalodes linifolia*.
Venus' Slipper *Paphiopedilum*.

Veratrum L. Liliaceae (Melanthiaceae). 20 perenn. herbs. Rhiz. thick. St. stout, erect, leafy. Lvs often plicate. Fls usually small, 6-merous, packed in term. racemose pan. N temp. regions.

V. album L. To 20cm, downy. Lvs to 30×15cm, oblong to elliptic, plicate. Infl. to 60cm; fls tinted white outside, green inside. Eur., N Afr., N Asia. Z5.

V. californicum Dur. To 2m. Lvs to 35×20cm, elliptic-ovate to lanceolate. Infl. tomentose; fls to 2cm, green to off-white. W US. Z5.

V. eschscholtzii A. Gray = *V. viride*.

V. nigrum L. 60–120cm. Lvs to 30×20cm, plicate, broadly elliptic to linear-lanceolate. Infl. to 90cm; fls black-purple. S Eur., Asia, Sib. Z6.

V. viride Ait. To 2m. Lvs to 30cm, elliptic to ovate. Pan. hirsute with drooping lower bracts; fls yellow-green, to 2.5cm diam. N US. Z3.

V. wilsonii O. Loes. ex C.H. Wright. To 90cm. Lvs to 60×2.5cm, ligulate. Pan. pyramidal, to 60cm; fls white banded green, *c*2.5cm diam. S China. Z6.

Verbascum L. Scrophulariaceae. 300 ann., bienn. or perenn. herbs and subshrubs, often hairy or gland. St. short or erect, branching. Lvs basal and rosulate or cauline. Infl. an erect term. spike, pan. or rac.; cal. 5-parted; cor. rotate, short-tubular, pet.5; sta. 5, fil. woolly. Eur., N Afr., W and C Asia; nat. N Amer.

V. abietinum Borb. = *V. nigrum.*
V. acutifolium Hal. = *V. pulverulentum.*
V. atroviolaceum Somm. & Lév. = *V. phoeniceum.*
V. australe Schräd. = *V. phlomoides.*
V. austriacum Schott ex Roem. & Schult. = *V. chaixii.*
V. baldacci Degen. Bienn., to 210cm, green, sticky-glandular. Basal lvs obovate to oblong-elliptic. Cor. 31–50mm diam., yellow, exterior tomentose; fil. woolly. Greece, Balk. Z7.
V. banaticum Schräd. Bienn., to 180cm, grey-green. St. much-branched, glabrescent. Basal lvs 10–30×3–12cm, obovate-oblong, usually pinnately lobed towards base, tomentose beneath. Cor. 15–22mm diam., yellow, exterior tomentose; fil. with white-yellow wool. Summer. SE Eur., Balk. Z7.
V. blattaria L. MOTH MULLEIN. Bienn. to 180cm, glab. below, glandular-pubesc. above. St. simple or branched. Basal lvs 8–25×2.5–4cm, oblong to lanceolate, crenate-sinuate to pinnatifid, glab. Infl. simple, lax; cor. to 20mm diam., white, silky; fil. with mauve wool. Eur., Asia; nat. N Amer. 'Albiflorum': fls wholly white.
V. boerhavii L. Bienn. to 120cm, white-floccose at first. Basal lvs 10–30×4–12cm, obovate-elliptic, obtuse or subacute, crenate-dentate, sometimes lobed at base. Infl. simple; cor. 22–32mm diam., yellow; fil. violet-pubesc. SE Eur., W Medit. Z7.
V. bombyciferum Boiss. Bienn., to 180cm, white-felted. Basal lvs 40–50×20cm, forming large rosettes, ovate-oblong to obovate. Infl. spicate, much-branched, v. woolly; cor. 30–40mm diam., sulphur yellow, fil. with white-yellow wool. Asia Minor. 'Arctic Summer': lvs silver; fls yellow. 'Silver Lining': to 2m; lvs silver; fls cool yellow. Z6.
V. bornmuelleri Velen. = *V. nigrum.*
V. bulgaricum Velen. = *V. phlomoides.*
V. calvescens Schur. = *V. phlomoides.*
V. cardifolium Murb. ex Hayek = *V. blattaria.*
V. chaixii Vill. NETTLE-LEAVED MULLEIN. Perenn. to 100cm, grey-tomentose to pubesc. Basal lvs 10–30×4–12cm, ovate-oblong, crenate and sometimes lobed towards base. Infl. usually branched; cor. 5–25mm diam., yellow; fil. violet-pubesc. SC Eur., W to NE Spain, N to S Poland, C Russia. 'Album': fls white with mauve eyes. 'Vernale': to 120cm; cor. 15–22mm diam., yellow ssp. *orientale* Hayek. Cor. 20–25mm diam. ssp. *austriacum* (Schott ex Roem. & Schult.) Hayek. Basal lvs not lobed. Cor. 15–22mm diam. Z5.
V. condensatum Schräd. = *V. phlomoides.*
V. crenatifolium Boiss. = *V. ovalifolium* ssp. *ovalifolium.*
V. densiflorum Bertol. Resembles *V. phlomoides* except cauline lvs long-decurrent. Eur., Sib. Z5.
V. dumulosum P.H. Davis. Resembles *V. pestalozzae* except basal lvs 1.5–5×0.7–3cm, entire, crenate or crenulate. Infl. 10–35-fld; cor. 10–15mm diam., lemon-yellow with a partial central ring of coral red. SW Turk. Hybrids have been made between *V. dumulosum*, *V. pestalozzae* and *V. phoeniceum*. Z8.
V. epirotum Hal. = *V. longifolium.*
V. flaccosum Waldst. & Kit. = *V. pulverulentum.*
V. hinkei Friv. = *V. lanatum.*
V. ×hybridum Brot. A hybrid between *V. pulverulentum* and *V. sinuatum*. Plants offered as *V. ×hybridum* may not be of this parentage. Z7.
V. insigne Boiss. & Bal. = *V. widemannianum.*
V. lanatum Schräd. Perenn. or bienn. to 120cm, white-woolly. Basal lvs 8–22×5–13cm, broadly ovate to oblong, crenate to incised-dentate, green above, grey-tomentose beneath. Infl. simple; cor. 16–2mm diam., dull yellow; fil. violet-pubesc. EC Eur., N It., N Bulg. Z6.
V. leianthum Benth. Bienn. 150cm, loosely woolly-tomentose below, glabrescent above. Basal lvs 30–50×15–25cm, broadly ovate to elliptic, coarsely crenate. Infl. with numerous erect-spreading br.; cor. 10–16mm, yellow; fil. with white-yellow wool. S Anatolia. Z8.
V. longifolium Ten. Bienn. or perenn. to 150cm, densely white to yellow-tomentose, floccose above. Basal lvs 20–50×5–15cm,

elliptic-oblong to ovate-lanceolate, entire to slightly crenate. Infl. usually simple; cor. 25–35mm diam., golden yellow; upper fil. densely villous, hairs white, yellow or pale violet. Balk. Penins., C & S It. var. *pannosum* (Vis.) Murb. More woolly, fls larger. Often grown for the large rosette of grey-felted lvs. Z7.
V. lychnitis L. WHITE MULLEIN. Bienn. to 150cm, sparsely grey-tomentose. Basal lvs 15–30×6–15cm, ovate-oblanceolate to oblong, subentire to crenate, green above, white beneath. Infl. a narrow pan.; cor. 12–20mm diam., bright yellow or white; fil. with yellow or white hairs. Eur., W Asia. A sp. with several varieties and a parent of hybrids. Z6.
V. macrantherum Hal. = *V. densiflorum.*
V. nemorosum Schräd. = *V. phlomoides.*
V. nigrum L. DARK MULLEIN. Perenn. to 100cm, sparingly pub-esc., rarely tomentose. Basal lvs 15–40×5–25cm, ovate-oblong, cordate, crenate. Infl. simple or branched; cor. 18–25mm diam., yellow; fil. violet-pubesc. Eur., Asia. 'Album': fls white. ssp. *nigrum.* Infl. simple, or with a few erect br. ssp. *abietinum* (Borb.) I.K. Ferg. Infl. with suberect to ascending br. Z5.
V. olympicum Boiss. Bienn. or perenn. to 180cm, densely white-woolly throughout. Basal lvs 15–70×5–13cm, lanceolate, entire. Infl. branching near base, candelabriform; cor. 20–30mm diam., bright golden yellow; fil. with white-yellow wool. Turk. Z6.
V. orientale (L.) All. Allied to *V. chaixii*. Ann. to 70cm, pub-erulent to glabrescent below, glandular-puberulent above. Basal lvs obovate-oblong, coarsely crenate to pinnatifid, often withered at time of flowering; cauline lvs pinnatisect. Infl. lax, simple; cor. 14–20mm diam., slightly spotted brown; fil. yellow-pubesc. Balk. Penins. Z6.
V. orientale Bieb., non (L.) All. = *V. chaixii.*
V. ovalifolium Donn ex Sims. Bienn. to 100cm, yellow to grey-tomentose, glabrescent below, eglandular. Basal lvs 5–20×2–9cm, ovate to oblong-lanceolate, glabrate above, densely tomentose beneath, incised-crenate or bicrenate. Infl. dense, simple or branched; cor. 20–40mm diam., yellow; fil. with yellow wool. SE Eur. ssp. *ovalifolium.* Indumentum yellow. Infl. usually unbranched. ssp. *thracicum* (Velen.) Murb. Indumentum grey. Infl. branched. Z7.
V. pachyurum Bornm. = *V. longifolium.*
V. paniculatum Wulf. Bienn. to 105cm, grey stellate-pubesc. Basal lvs to 20cm, oblong, crenate-sinuate. Infl. paniculate; cor. to 13mm diam., yellow; fil. violet-purple pubesc. S Cauc. 'Album': fls white. Z7.
V. pannosum Vis. = *V. longifolium* var. *pannosum.*
V. pestalozzae Boiss. Dwarf perenn. to 30cm, much-branched subshrub, white or yellow to brown pannose. Basal lvs 2.5–4×1–2.5cm, elliptic to lanceolate, entire or crenate. Infl. racemose, 5–15 fld; cor. 15–22mm diam., yellow; fil. white-yellow pubesc. Asia Minor. Z7.
V. phlomoides L. Bienn. 30–200cm, grey- or yellow-tomentose. Basal lvs 5–45×3–15cm, oblong to broadly elliptic, crenate, sometimes lobed near base. Infl. dense, usually simple; cor. 30–55mm diam., yellow, sometimes pellucid-glandular; fil. white-yellow woolly. C, S & E Eur., nat. E US.
V. phoeniceum L. PURPLE MULLEIN. Bienn. or perenn., to 100cm, crispate-villous, glandular-pubesc. above. St. simple or slightly branched. Basal lvs 4–17×2.5–9cm, ovate or oblong, entire, sinuate to slightly crenate, sparsely pubesc. or glab. Infl. racemose, elongate, gland., sometimes branched; cor. 20–30mm diam., usually red or violet, sometimes white, pink, lilac, rose or yellow; fil. violet-pubesc. S Eur., N Asia. Z6.
V. pinnatifidium Vahl. Bienn. subshrub to 50cm. St. several, branched from base, tomentose then glabrescent. Basal lvs 6–17×2.5–6cm, oblong, incised-dentate to deeply pinnatisect, seg. entire, dentate or pinnatifid. Infl. a slender rac., lax, usually simple; cor. 25–30mm diam., yellow; fil. white or yellow pubesc. Summer. Cauc. Z6. Z6.
V. pulchrum Velen. = *V. ovalifolium* ssp. *ovalifolium.*
V. pulverulentum Vill. To 120cm, habit of *V. lychnitis* except lvs wider, sessile, crenulate, matted with white, woolly hairs then glabrescent. Infl. a pyramidal pan.; cor. 18–25mm diam., bright yellow; fil. white-pubesc. Eur. Z6.
V. pyramidatum Bieb. Perenn., 60–150cm, adpressed-pubesc. Basal lvs 12–30×5–10cm, obovate-oblong, crenate-dentate to slightly pinnatifid, glandular-pubesc. above. Infl. a narrowly pyramidal pan.; cor. 20–30mm diam., yellow; fil. violet-pubesc. S Russia, Cauc. Z6.
V. repandum Willd. = *V. blattaria.*
V. rhinanthifolium Davidov = *V. blattaria.*
V. rotundifolium ssp. *conocarpum* (Morris) I.K. Ferg. = *V. boerhavii.*
V. ×rubiginosum Waldst. & Kit. (*V. chaixii ×V. phoeniceum.*) Basal lvs crenate, pubesc. beneath. Infl. a loose rac.; fls yellow and red. Hung. Z6.
V. rugulosum Willd. = *V. phlomoides.*
V. samaritanii Heldr. ex Boiss. = *V. longifolium.*

V. sartorii Hausskn. = *V. phlomoides*.
V. schraderi Mey. = *V. thapsus*.
V. simplex Hoffsgg. & Link = *V. thapsus*.
V. sinuatum L. Bienn. 50–100cm, shortly and densely grey- to yellow-tomentose, sometimes floccose. Basal lvs 15–35×6–15cm, oblong-spathulate, sinuate-pinnatifid, usually undulate, subsessile. Infl. a pyramidal pan. with long twiggy br.; fls in rounded clusters; cor. 15–30mm diam., yellow or sometimes white; fil. violet-pubesc. S Eur., Medit., Canary Is. Z8.
V. speciosum Bienn. to 2m, persistently tomentose. Basal lvs 12–40×3–14cm, oblong-oblanceolate to obovate, entire. Infl. freely branched; cor. 18–30mm diam., yellow; fil. white-pubesc. SE Eur., Asia Minor, Cauc., nat. Oreg. ssp. *speciosum*. Lvs grey-tomentose. ssp. *megaphlomos* (Boiss. & Heldr.) Nyman. Lvs white- or yellow-tomentose, soft, thick. Z6.
V. spectabile Bieb. Bienn. 50–120cm, lanate below, glandular-hirsute above. Basal lvs 8–20×5–8cm, oblong-ovate, crenate-dentate, glab. to sparsely pubesc., pubesc. on veins beneath. Infl. simple; cor. 35–40mm diam., yellow, base of upper lobes spotted purple; upper fil. violet-pubesc. Crimea, Cauc.
V. spinosum L. Freely branching shrub to 50cm, shoots woody, grey with term. spines. Lvs to 1.5×1cm, oblong-lanceolate, dentate or lobed, white-grey-tomentose. Cor. 10–18mm diam., yellow; fil. with short lilac hairs. Crete. Z8.
V. ×tauricum Hook. A hybrid of *V. phoeniceum*. Resembles *V. ×rubiginosum*. Z6.
V. thapsus L. AARON'S ROD; HAG TAPER; TORCHES. Bienn. to 2m, grey- to white-tomentose. St. usually unbranched. Basal lvs 8–50×2.5–14cm, obovate-oblong, obtuse, entire or crenate. Cor. 12–35mm diam., yellow; fil. white-pubesc. Eur., Asia, nat. N Amer. Z3.
V. thaspiforme Schräd. = *V. densiflorum*.
V. thracicum Velen. = *V. ovalifolium* ssp. *thracicum*.
V. velenovskyi Horák = *V. densiflorum*.
V. vernale hort. = *V.* 'Densiflorum'.
V. virgatum Stokes in With. TWIGGY MULLEIN. Similar to *V. blattaria* except more gland. Upper lvs shortly decurrent. Rac. more densely-fld; fls clustered. W Eur. Z7.
V. widemannianum Fisch. & Mey. Bienn. 35–125cm, with dense cobweb-like indumentum below, short-pubesc. and gland. above. St. simple or branched. Basal lvs 4–20×1.5–8cm, oblong to elliptic, crenate. Infl. lax, simple or branched; cor. 25–40mm diam., purple-violet; fil. violet-purple pubesc. Asia Minor. Z7.
V. cvs. 'Boadicea' (*V. phoeniceum* × *V. longiflorum*): to 1.8m; fls copper with violet anth., in thick spikes. 'C.L. Adams': to 2m; fls yellow with magenta sta., in tall, thick spikes. 'Cotswold Beauty': to 1.2m; fls pale buff to amber, anth. purple. 'Cotswold Gem': to 1.4m; fls pale oatmeal tinted bronze, anth. lilac. 'Cotswold Queen': to 1.4m; fls salmon-amber to bronze, with pale lilac anth. (*V. densiflorum* × *V. nigrum*): to 1.8m, vigorous; lvs dark green; fls yellow, anth. lilac, infl. erect and many-branched. 'Gainsborough': to 1.4m; lvs silvery-grey; fls sulphur to primrose yellow. 'Golden Dawn' (*V. pestalozzae* × *V. spinosum*): habit compact, to 60cm; fls yellow. 'Jackie': fls buff pink, with purple eye. 'Letitia' (*V. dumulosum* × *V. spinosum*): low subshrub, to 30cm, fls clear yellow, v. abundant. 'Mont Blanc': to 1.1m; lvs silky white; fls pure white. 'Pink Domino': to 1.2m; fls rosy pink with dark eye. 'Royal Highland': to 1.2m; fls apricot-yellow. 'Silverkandelaber': to 1.5m, widely branched; fls white. 'Sunrise' (*V. pestalozzae* × *V. dumulosum* × *V. spinosum*): fls yellow.
→*Celsia*.

Verbena L. VERVAIN. Verbenaceae. 250 ann. or perenn. herbs and subshrubs, glab. or variously pubesc. Lvs mostly lobed, toothed, or dissected, rarely entire. Fls in spikes, erect, term., 1-several, or in apicate corymbs, pan. or cap.; cal. tubular, 5-ribbed, usually 5-toothed; cor. salverform or funnelform, limb 5-lobed; sta. 4, rarely 2. Trop. & subtrop. Amer.
V. alata Cham. Perenn. to 2m, broom-like. St. tetragonal, winged. Lvs ovate or triangular-oblong, amplexicaul, entire or serrate. Pan. term., spicate; cor. blue, lobes elliptic, obtuse, unequal. Braz. Z10.
V. alpina hort. = *V. tenera* var. *maonettii*.
V. aubletia Jacq. = *V. canadensis*.
V. bipinnatifida Nutt. Perenn. herb. St. diffuse, bristly. Lvs to 6cm, bipinnate or tripartite, lobes linear or oblong, hairy. Infl. capitate or in pseudofascicles; cor. pink, purple, lavender or violet, lobes emarginate. N Amer. Z3.
V. bonariensis L. PURPLE TOP; SOUTH AMERICAN VERVAIN; TALL VERBENA. Ann. or perenn. herb to 2m. St. erect, slender, tetragonal, scabrous. Lvs to 13×2cm, lanceolate or oblong-lanceolate, amplexicaul, serrate toward apex, rugose, pubesc. beneath. Fls in short spikes terminating the slender br. of a dichotomously branched pan.; cor. blue, violet, purple, and lavender, tube exceeding cal., limb inconspicuous. S Amer. Z8.

V. bracteata Lagasca & Rodriguez. CREEPING VERVAIN. Ann. or short-lived perenn. St. diffuse to 60cm, forming mats, strigose. Lvs to 5×3cm, lanceolate or ovate-lanceolate, toothed and cleft. Infl. spicate; cor. lavender, pink or white, tube slightly exerted from cal. N & C Amer. Z4.
V. bracteosa Michx. = *V. bracteata*.
V. brasiliensis Vell. Perenn. herb close to *V. bonariensis*. St. to 2m, to hispid. Lower lvs to 8×3cm, rhombic-lanceolate, amplexicaul, entire or serrate, upper lvs narrower, toothed. Infl. paniculate, spicate; cor. exceeding cal. by one third. S Amer. Z10.
V. canadensis (L.) Britt. ROSE VERVAIN. Ann. or perenn. herb. St. decumbent to ascending, glabrate to thirsute. Lvs to 9×4cm, incised, pinnatifid or 3-cleft, ovate to elongate-ovate, hairy or glabrate. Infl. fasciculate, cor. twice length of cal., broad, rose-purple to dark purple (var. *atroviolacea* Dermen), lobes emarginate. N Amer. 'Candidissima': fls white. 'Compacta': habit dense, shorter. 'Grandiflora': fls large. 'Rosea': fls red. Z4.
V. carolina L. Perenn. herb. St. to 1m, usually solitary, tetragonal, hispid. Lvs 2.5–9cm, oblong-lanceolate or lanceolate, strigose, somewhat pustulate above, serrate. Infl. paniculate; cor. about 2mm broad, pale blue, mauve, lavender or purple. N & C Amer. Z5.
V. caroo Speg. = *V. teucroides*.
V. chamaedrifolia Juss. = *V. peruviana*.
V. chamaedrioides Juss. = *V. peruviana*.
V. citriodora (Ortiz & Palau) ex L'Hérit. = *Aloysia triphylla*.
V. coccinea hort. = *V. peruviana*.
V. corymbosa Ruiz & Pav. Perenn. herb to 1m. St. much-branched, tetragonal. Lvs to 3.5×2cm, oblong or ovate, to triangular, serrate, base lobulate, rigid, hispidulous, veins impressed above. Pan. corymbose, spicate; cor. red-purple, tube twice as long as the cal. S Amer. Z9.
V. drummondii Lindl. = *V. canadensis*.
V. elegans HBK. Procumbent ann. Br. hispidulous, often purple. Lvs to 6×1cm, ovate, pinnatifid-laciniate. Infl. spicate, to 3.5cm, heads compact; cor. magenta-purple to rose, tube 2 ×length cal., limb to 12mm wide, lobes emarginate. US, Mex.
V. ×engelmannii Mold. ENGELMANN'S VERVAIN. (*V. hastata* × *V. urticifolia*.) Lvs coarsely serrate; spikes dense; fls blue to purple. NE US. Z5.
V. erinoides Lam. = *V. laciniata*.
V. gooddingii Briq. Perenn. herb to 60cm, gland. and hairy. St. erect or decumbent. Lvs to 5×4.5cm, with a few deeply cleft or toothed lobes. Infl. dense, capitate; cor. pink, lavender or blue-violet, rarely white, tube longer than cal., limb to 12mm wide. US, N Mex. Z9.
V. gracilis Desf. Ann. or perenn. herb. St. mostly erect, to 50cm. Lvs to 1.5×0.5cm, obovate or oblanceolate, incised-pinnatifid to bipinnatifid, hairy. Infl. slender, sparsely fld; cor. lilac, rose or blue, tube equalling cal., limb to 3mm wide. US (Tex., Ariz.), Mex. Z9.
V. hastata L. AMERICAN BLUE VERVAIN; WILD HYSSOP. Perenn. herb to 1.5m. St. erect, branched or unbranched. Lvs to 15×4cm, lanceolate or oblong-lanceolate, serrate, rarely lobed, rough above. Pan. dense, term., spicate; cor. blue or lavender to purple, or white, tube to 4mm, longer than cal. N Amer. 'Alba': fls pure white. 'Rosea': fls pale pink. Z3.
V. hispida Ruiz & Pav. HAIRY VERVAIN; HAIRY VERBENA. Perenn. herb to 50cm, sometimes suffrutescent. St. rigid, tetragonal. Lvs to 10×2.5cm, lanceolate or oblong-lanceolate, amplexicaul, cordate, serrate or incised. Infl. spicate, often ternate, dense, hairy; cor. blue, purple or pink-mauve, tube exserted from cal., limb deeply 5-lobed. S Amer. Z10.
V. hortensis Vilm. = *V. hybrida*.
V. ×hybrida Groenl. & Ruempl. COMMON GARDEN VERBENA; FLORIST'S VERBENA. Perenn. herb grown as ann. St. to 1m, compact to mat-like, or lax and trailing, to erect, tetragonal, densely hairy. Lvs to 8×6cm, rough, dark green, ovate to lanceolate, incised and toothed. Infl. large, a flat corymb or elongated spike; fls fragrant; white to shades of purple, blue, vermilion, scarlet, crimson, red, pink and yellow, usually with a white or yellow mouth, limb to 2.5cm wide. Known from cult.; nat. US. Thought to be a multiple hybrid involving *V. incisa*, *V. peruviana*, *V. phlogiflora* and *V. teucroides*. Many cvs. 'Amethyst': fls small, blue with white eyes. 'Aveyron': habit bushy, vigorous; fls bright pink fading with age. 'Blue Knight': fls lilac-blue. 'Cardinal': fls red. 'Carousel': pet. striped with purple and white. 'Compacta': compact. 'Defiance': fls deep red with white eye. Derby series: habit compact; fls in wide range of colours including red, pink, blue, mauve and white. 'Dwarf Jewels': habit dwarf; fls in range of vivid colours. 'Foxhunter': fls bright red. 'Gravetye': habit spreading; fls in clusters, pale purple, cal. tinged red, abundant. 'La France': habit tall; fls pale lavender-blue. 'Lavender Blue': fls rich lavender. 'Lawrence

Johnston': fls brilliant red. 'Loveliness': fls pale lavender. 'Mme du Barry': fls crimson-pink. Romance Hybrids: habit low, dense, spreading; fls with white eyes in blend of scarlet, white, burgundy, violet and rose. 'Rosea Stellata': fls pink. 'Royal Purple': fls purple. 'Showtime': habit somewhat spreading; fls in range of colours. 'Silver Ann': habit vigorous, spreading to 90cm; fls both pale and deep pink. 'Sissinghurst': mat-forming; fls magenta-pink. 'Springtime': habit spreading; fls in range of bright colours. 'Violacea Stellata': fls bright pink. 'White Knight': fls white. Z9.

V. incisa Hook. Perenn. herb to 70cm. St. ascending, br. weak. Lvs oblong-ovate or triangular to lanceolate, incised-serrate, hoary-hispid. Infl. spicate, often ternate or in a corymbose pan.; cor. scarlet to pink, eye yellow, limb to 1cm wide, lobes bifid. S Amer. Z10.

V. laciniata (L.) Briq. Ann. herb. St. creeping, much-branched. Lvs to 2.5cm, ovate, 3-parted or pinnatifid-laciniate, entire or dentate. Infl. capitate, elongating; cor. red-violet to lavender, tube slightly longer than cal. S Amer.

V. lambertii Sims = V. canadensis.

V. lasiostachys Link. VERVAIN. Perenn. herb. St. to 80cm, procumbent, villous. Lvs to 6cm, oblong to broadly ovate, coarsely serrate or incised, often trifid at base. Infl. a term. spicate pan.; cor. purple, tube barely exserted from cal., limb to 4mm wide. N Amer. Z9.

V. litoralis HBK. Similar to V. bonariensis but lvs shorter, sharply and coarsely serrate, spikes more laxly fld, fls slightly smaller. Z9.

V. macdougalii A.A. Heller. MACDOUGAL'S VERVAIN. Perenn. herb to 1m. St. erect, simple or sparsely branched. Lvs to 1×0.4cm, oblong-elliptic to ovate-lanceolate, coarsely serrate, softly hirsute. Infl. spicate, 1 to several; cor. deep purple, showy, tube scarcely exserted from cal., limb to 7mm wide. SW US. Z8.

V. menthifolia Benth. Perenn. herb. St. decumbent or ascending, sparsely hispidulous. Lvs to 6cm, ovate to lanceolate, incised or cleft, serrate-dentate, strigillose. Infl. paniculate, spikes elongate; cor. blue, light purple or lilac, tube slightly longer than cal., limb to 6mm wide, lobes ± truncate. N & C Amer. Z10.

V. monacensis Mold. MUNICH VERBENA. Perenn. herb, usually prostrate. St. tetragonal, sparsely pilose. Lvs to 3.5×2cm, elliptic to oblanceolate, deeply trifid, divisions incised. Infl. condensed, elongating to 5cm; cor. salverform, pink, limb 1cm wide, lobes. Known only in cult., esp. in Indian gardens. Z10.

V. montana hort. pro parte. = V. bipinnatifida.

V. nodiflora L. = Phyla nodiflora.

V. officinalis L. COMMON VERBENA; COMMON VERVAIN. Perenn. herb. St. to 80cm, tetragonal. Upper lvs to 7×3cm, deeply incised or 2–2-pinnatifid, lower lvs subentire. Infl. paniculate, spikes dense; cor. lilac or pale pink, tube to 3.5mm, limb to 3.5mm wide. S Eur., widely nat. around the world. Z4.

V. patagonica auct. = V. bonariensis.

V. peruviana (L.) Britt. Small, procumbent perenn. St. slender, creeping. Lvs to 5cm, ovate to oblong-lanceolate, serrate to crenate, scabrous. Spikes solitary, asecnding; cor. bright scarlet or crimson, limb to 10mm diam. Arg. to S Braz. 'Alba': fls white. 'Chiquita': habit trailing; lvs small; fls in clusters, striped lavender with white. 'Saint Paul': low-branching; lvs heavily matted; fls bright pink. Z9.

V. phlogiflora Cham. Sprawling perenn., st. ascending. Lvs oblong or lanceolate, serrate. Spike solitary or ternate; cor. purple, lilac, red or blue, tube to 2.5cm, limb to 1.8cm diam. S S Amer. Z10.

V. platensis Spreng. = V. teucroides.

V. rigida Spreng. VEINED VERBENA. Stiff perenn. herb to 60cm, erect or spreading. Lvs to 7.5cm, oblong, dentate, amplexicaul. Spikes often ternate, term.; cor. purple or magenta, limb to 5mm diam. S Braz., Arg. 'Alba': fls white. 'Flame': habit low, carpet-forming; lvs rough, crenate; fls in clusters, bright scarlet. 'Lilacina': fls blue. 'Polaris': dense, tough; fls silver-blue, abundant. Z8.

V. robusta E. Greene. Similar to V. lasiostachys but lvs scabrous, spikes denser, to 10cm, cal. and cor. limbs shorter. W US. Z7.

V. runyonii Mold. RIO GRANDE VERVAIN. Perenn. herb to 1.5m. St. erect, stout, tetragonal, hirtellous. Lvs to 6×3cm, amplexicaul, ± 3-parted, pinnatifid-incised. Infl. paniculate, spicate; cor. blue, limb to 4mm wide. US. Z6.

V. simplex Lehm. NARROW-LEAVED VERVAIN. Perenn. herb to 50cm. St. erect, simple or sparingly branched, sparsely strigose. Lvs to 10cm, linear, narrowly oblong, or narrowly lanceolate, sparsely serrate. Infl. spicate, 1–3; cor. lavender to purple. N Amer. Z4.

V. stricta Vent. HOARY VERVAIN. Perenn. herb to 1m. St. erect, densely pubesc. Lvs to 9.5×5cm, elliptic to broadly ovate to suborbicular, rough, serrate or incised-serrate, canescent be-

neath. Infl. spicate, thick, erect, 1–5; cor. deep lavender or purple, rarely white. N Amer. Hybridizes with V. hastata. Z4.

V. tenera Spreng. Shrubby perenn. St. caespitose, decumbent. Lvs to 2.5cm, pubesc., pinnatifid. Spikes elongating; cor. rose-violet. Braz. to Arg. var. maonetii Reg. Lvs finely cut; fls red-violet edged white. var. pulchella Sims. St. to 30cm, slender, sparsely hairy. Lvs to 3cm, tripartite, pinnatisect, lobes linear. Infl. spicate; cor. rose-violet, tube to 12mm, limb 6–7mm wide. S Amer. Z9.

V. tenuifolia K. Bauhin. = V. supina.

V. tenuisecta Briq. MOSS VERBENA. Ann. or perenn. herb. St. to 50cm, prostrate to decumbent, or erect, tetragonal, aromatic. Lvs to 3.5×3cm, tripartite-pinnatifid, seg. narrow, entire or toothed, revolute. Infl. term., spicate; cor. lilac, mauve, purple, white, blue, and white, limb to 1cm wide, lobes broadly obcordate, emarginate. S Amer. var. alba Mold. White-fld. var. rubella Mold. Pink-fld. Z9.

V. teucroides Gillies & Hook. Lvs small, to 2.5mm, clustered, tripartite, seg. rigid, spiny, lanceolate, with small, rounded succulent stipules. Cor. white to lilac, tube to 10mm, limb to 7mm diam. Arg. 'Matre Negra': to 2cm; lvs to 5mm, black tinged green, dense; fls white tinged lilac; fragrant. Z9.

V. tridens Speg. = V. teucroides.

V. triphylla L'Hérit. = Aloysia triphylla.

V. tweediana Niven = V. phlogiflora.

V. urticifolia L. WHITE VERVAIN; NETTLE-LEAVED VERVAIN. Perenn. herb to 25cm, erect. Lvs to 14×7cm, ovate, elliptic or lanceolate, thin, serrate, gland. above, hairy beneath. Infl. paniculate, spikes many, slender; cor. white, scarcely exserted from cal. var. leiocarpa Perry & Fern. Densely puberulent throughout or lvs velvety beneath; infl. br. v. slender, ascending, divergent, puberulent. E N Amer. Z5.

V. venosa Gillies & Hook. = V. rigida.

V. xutha Lehm. GULF VERVAIN. Perenn. herb. St. erect, to 2m, stout, obtusely tetragonal, hirsute. Lvs to 10cm, oblong-elliptic to broadly ovate, incised-pinnatifid or 3-lobed, serrate, hairy beneath. Infl. spicate, 1 to few, dense; cor. blue, lilac or purple, tube scarcely exceeding cal., limb to 6mm wide. S US. Z8.

→Buchnera, Glandularia and Junellia.

VERBENACEAE St.-Hil. 91/1900. Aloysia, Amasonia, Callicarpa, Caryopteris, Citharexylum, Clerodendrum, Coleonema, Congea, Cornutia, Crowea, Diostea, Duranta, Gmelina, Holmskioldia, Hymenopyramis, Lantana, Lippia, Oxera, Petrea, Phyla, Raphithamnus, Rhaphithamnus, Stachytarpheta, Tectona, Thamnosma, Verbena, Vitex.

Verbesina L. CROWN BEARD. Compositae. c150 ann. to perenn. herbs, shrubs and trees. Cap. radiate or discoid, solitary or several in clusters; receptacle often conical; ray flts white or yellow; disc flts tubular, 5-lobed, yellow or white. Warm Amer.

V. alternifolia (L.) Britt. ex C. Mohr. WINGSTEM; YELLOW IRONWEED. Perenn., to 2m. St. branched, commonly winged. Lvs 10–25cm, lanceolate to lanceolate-elliptical or ovate, serrate. Cap. 2–5cm, diam., radiate, in loose corymbs; ray flts to 1cm, 2–10, yellow; disc flts yellow. Summer. E US. Z5.

V. crocata (Cav.) Less. ex DC. Shrub to 1m. St. 4-winged, wings brown and brittle at flowering. Lvs 8–16cm, pinnatisect or coarsely toothed, lobes triangular to ovate, petiole winged. Cap. discoid, solitary or in small clusters, globose; disc flts orange-yellow. Summer. Mex. Z9.

V. encelioides (Cav.) A. Gray. BUTTER DAISY; GOLDEN CROWN BEARD. Ann. to 1m. Lvs 5–12cm, ovate to lanceolate, white-hairy below, petiole 2–3cm, winged, auriculate. Cap. 2.5–5cm diam., radiate, numerous, in pan.; ray flts 1–2cm, deep yellow; disc flts yellow. Summer. SW US, Mex. Z10.

V. greenmanii Urban. Shrub or small tree, to 6m. St. and br. broadly winged. Lvs 20–50×10–30cm, ovate, base cuneate, decurrent, pinnately lobed, white-hairy beneath, scabrous above, petiole winged or sessile, upper lvs entire or lobed. Cap. in a corymb; ray flts 3–4mm, 8–12, yellow; disc flts yellow. Summer. Mex.

V. helianthoides Michx. Perenn. to over 1m. St. winged. Lvs to 20cm, alt., ovate-lanceolate, sessile, margin serrate or toothed. Cap. to 4cm diam., few, clustered in a compact cymose infl.; phyllaries narrowly lanceolate; ray flts 18–30mm, sterile, yellow. Summer. S & SC US. Z5.

V. pinnatifida Cav. = V. greenmanii.

V. purpusii Brandg. Ann. or perenn., to 30cm. Lvs to 5×3cm, basal, ovate or obovate, sessile, often hairy, crenate-toothed. Cap. solitary, to 3cm diam.; ray flts to 15mm, golden yellow. Mex. Z9.

V. sativa Roxb. ex Sims = Guizotia abyssinica.

V. virginica L. FROSTWEED. Perenn. herb, to 20cm, pubesc. St. winged. Lvs to 30cm, lanceolate to ovate or oval, acute or acuminate, downy beneath, entire to serrate, petioles winged.

Cap. clustered in corymbose infl.; ray flts 4–7mm, 3–4, oval, white. Late summer. S US. Z6.
→*Actinomeris*.

Vernal Grass *Anthoxanthum*.

Vernonia Schreb. IRONWEED. Compositae. *c*1000 ann. to perenn. herbs, shrubs and trees. Cap. discoid, in term., corymbose or paniculate clusters; receptacle flat; flts tubular, purple to rose, rarely white. Trop. and warm regions, to N Amer.

V. acaulis (Walter) Gleason. Perenn. herb, to 1m, leafy below. Lvs to 3cm, oblong to ovate, pubesc. or slightly rough above, coarsely toothed, petiole short. Cap. in loose clusters, to 30cm diam. Summer. SE US. Z7.

V. acutifolia Hook. = *V. sericea*.

V. altissima Less. = *V. gigantea*.

V. angustifolia Michx. Perenn. herb, to 1m, glab. to hirsute. Lvs to 10cm, crowded, linear, revolute, scabrous above, pubesc. beneath. Cap. in compact corymbs, to 30cm diam.; flts purple. Summer. SE US. Z7.

V. arkansana DC. Perenn. herb, 1–3m, ± glab., glaucous. Lvs to 18cm, linear to linear-lanceolate, entire to toothed, glandular-punctate beneath. Cap. in corymbs, to 20cm diam.; flts violet-purple. Pappus purple. Summer. SC US. Z5.

V. axilliflora Mart. ex Less. = *V. cotoneaster*.

V. baldwinii Torr. WESTERN IRONWEED. Perenn. to 1.5m, pubesc. to tomentose. Lvs to 15cm, elliptic to ovate-lanceolate, acuminate, toothed, resinous beneath. Cap. in loose corymbs; flts purple. Summer. C & CS US. Z5.

V. brasiliana (L.) Druce. Shrub to 2m, br. puberulent. Lvs obovate-oblong, obtuse, crenulate to entire, scabrous above, grey-puberulent beneath. Cap. in large, branched pan.; flts pale purple. Autumn. Braz., Venez. Z10.

V. calvoana (Hook. f.) Hook. f. Shrub to 3.5m often tomentose. Lvs to 35cm, oblanceolate to elliptic, acuminate, toothed, base unequally auricled. Cap. in large, branched corymbs; flts purple. Winter. Cameroun. Z10.

V. capensis (Houtt.) Druce. Ann. to perenn. herb to 60cm, simple, leafy, woody below. Lvs to 7cm, crowded, filiform, acute, revolute, glab. or sparsely hairy above, silky beneath, sessile. Cap. in corymbose pan.; flts purple. Summer. SC Afr. Z9.

V. conferata Benth. Tree to 8m; br. tomentose, leafy. Lvs to 50cm, crowded toward br. tips, obovate or elliptic-oblong, membranous, lobate-dentate, petiole to 7cm. Cap. small, in pan.; longer flts white. Trop. Afr. Z10.

V. cotoneaster (Willd.) Less. Shrub to 1m, branched, white-pubesc. Lvs to 50cm, oblong-lanceolate, acute, entire,, glab. and scabrous above, white-hairy beneath, petiole short. Cap. in pan.; flts violet-purple. Autumn. Braz. Z10.

V. crinita Raf. = *V. arkansana*.

V. fasciculata Michx. Ann. to perenn. herb, to 2m, glab., green-purple. Lvs to 15cm, linear to lanceolate, long-acuminate to acute, toothed, punctate beneath, sessile. Cap. in dense, flattened clusters. Summer–early autumn. SC Canada to C and E US. Z3.

V. flexuosa Sims. ZIG-ZAG VERNONIA. Perenn. to 60cm, sparsely pubesc. Lvs to 14cm, mostly basal, lanceolate, acute, entire, glab. to pubesc., scabrous, sessile. Cap. in br. axils; flts purple or white. Autumn. S Braz., Parag., NE Arg. and Urug. Z10.

V. gerberiformis Oliv. & Hiern. Perenn., to 60cm, glab. to pubesc. Lvs to 20cm, often radical, spathulate, entire to denticulate, glab., sessile. Cap. often solitary, to 2cm; flts purple-violet to blue. Sudan. Z10.

V. gigantea (Walter) Trel. ex Branner & Colville. Perenn. to 2m, glab. Lvs to 20cm, lanceolate to elliptic, acute to acuminate, serrate, glab. above, puberulent and resinous beneath, petiole to 2cm. Cap. small, in loose clusters, to 40cm diam.; flts purple. Summer–autumn. SE US. Z4.

V. glabra (Steetz) Vatke. Ann. to 60cm, glab., leafy. Lvs to 10cm, oblanceolate to oblong, membranous, serrate, sessile. Cap. in large corymbose pan.; flts bright pink-purple. Spring–summer. Trop. Afr.

V. glauca (L.) Willd. Perenn. to 1.5m, glab. or pubesc. Lvs to 25cm, ovate-lanceolate to elliptic-lanceolate, glab. or scabrous above, sparsely hairy beneath. Summer. CE to SE US. Z3.

V. karaguensis Oliv. & Hiern. Ann. to perenn. herb, to 1m. Lvs to 3.5cm, narrowly elliptic to lanceolate, acute, scabrous above, pubesc. beneath. Cap. in corymbose clusters; flts purple. Winter. E Trop. Afr. Z10.

V. lettermannii Engelm. ex A. Gray. Ann. to 50cm, glab. Lvs to 8cm, linear, acute, entire, glandular-punctate beneath. Cap. crowded in clusters. Summer. WC US. Z5.

V. lindheimeri A. Gray & Engelm. WOOLLY IRONWEED. Perenn. to 80cm, white to grey tomentose. Lvs to 8cm, linear, entire,

revolute, white-woolly beneath. Cap. in clusters, densely woolly; flts purple. Summer. Tex. Z8.

V. marginata (Torr.) Raf. PLAINS IRONWEED. Perenn. to 80cm. Lvs to 10cm, linear to linear-lanceolate, acute to acuminate, glab., glandular-punctate beneath. Cap. in a flat corymb; flts purple. Summer. SC US. Z4.

V. melleri Oliv. & Hiern. Small shrub, to 1m, br. puberulent below, scabrous above. Lvs to 15cm, oblong to linear, acute, denticulate, scabrous, clasping and sessile. Cap. few to many in corymbs, to 15cm diam. S E Trop. Afr. Z10.

V. missurica Raf. Perenn. to 1.5m, finely grey-tomentose. Lvs to 15cm, lanceolate to ovate, entire to dentate, grey-tomentose beneath. Cap. in clusters, to 50cm diam., arachnoid-ciliate. Summer. SC Canada to CS US. Z3.

V. myriantha Hook. f. Tree to 6m, ± glab. Lvs to 30cm, elliptic to oblong-lanceolate, acute to acuminate, serrulate, petiole to 5cm. Cap. in corymbose pan., to 30cmm diam.; flts pink. Autumn. SW Afr. Z10.

V. noveboracensis (L.) Michx. Perenn., to 2m, glab. to sparsely pubesc. Lvs to 18cm, lanceolate, acuminate, entire to serrate, glab. or scaberulous above, slightly hairy beneath, petiole short or sessile. Cap. in a loose cluster, to 30cm diam.; often resinous; flts purple. Summer. E & SE US. Z5.

V. odoratissima Kunth = *V. brasiliana*.

V. pinifolia (Lam.) Less. = *V. capensis*.

V. podocoma Schultz-Bip. = *V. myriantha*.

V. praealta Michx. = *V. noveboracensis*.

V. scabra Pers. = *V. brasiliana*.

V. sericea Rich. Perenn. herb or subshrub, to 1m. Lvs to 8cm, oblong-lanceolate to ovate, acute, entire, nearly glab. above, silky-pubesc. and resinous beneath, petiole to 5mm. Cap. 1–2 in loose pan.; flts rose-purple. Winter. Braz. Z10.

V. stenostegia (Stapf) Hutch. Perenn. herb, to 50cm, grey-tomentose. Lvs to 13cm, variable acute, toothed, base cuneate, glandular-punctate above, tomentose beneath, petiole to 4cm. Cap. 2–4 in clusters; flts purple-rose, becoming white, tinged rose. Winter. Nigeria. Z10.

→*Baccharis, Candidea, Erigeron* and *Serratula*.

Veronica L. SPEEDWELL; BIRD'S-EYE. Scrophulariaceae. 250 herbs, ann. or perenn., some woody-based. St. 0 or prostrate or erect. Lvs basal or cauline, oval to lanceolate, entire to pinnatisect. Fls solitary, axill. or in narrow or broad branched rac.; cal. lobes 4–5; cor. campanulate to rotate, 4-lobed; sta. 2. N Temp. regions, particularly Eur. and Turk.

V. allionii Vill. Perenn., mat-forming; st. 5–15cm, procumbent, woody at base. Lvs 0.8–2cm, ovate to elliptic, entire to minutely crenate. Infl. 2–5cm, erect, dense, minutely crispate-pubesc.; cor. 8mm diam., deep blue to violet. SW Alps (Fr., It.). Z4.

V. alpina L. Perenn. with creeping rootstock; st. 5–15cm, ascending. Lvs 1–2.5cm, ovate to elliptic, entire to weakly crenate-dentate, ± glab. Infl. subcapitate; cor. 7mm diam., deep blue or violet. Late spring–early summer. Arc. Eur., Eurasia, N Amer. Z2.

V. americana (Raf.) Schwein. ex Benth. BROOKLIME; AMERICAN BROOKLIME. Perenn., rather fleshy, glab.; st. 20–60cm, prostrate. Lvs 3–7cm, ovate- to triangular-ovate, shallowly serrate. Rac. 5–12cm, axill., dense, soon elongating; cor. 4–6mm diam., v. pale violet to lilac. Summer. N Amer., NE Asia. Z2.

V. amethystina Willd. = *V. spuria*.

V. anagallis-aquatica ssp. *michauxii* (Lam.) Elenevsky = *V. michauxii*.

V. aphylla L. Perenn., pubesc. throughout; st. 1–4cm, procumbent. Lvs 1–1.5cm, near st. apex in loose rosette, elliptic-oblong to broadly obovate-spathulate, obscurely crenate; rac. 1–2, axillary or pseudoterminal, corymbose, 2–6-fld; cor. 6–8mm diam., deep blue, occas. pink. C & S Eur. Z5.

V. armena Boiss. & Huet. Perenn. to 15cm; st. suberect to decumbent, woody at base, pubesc. Lvs 0.5–1.2cm, sub-palmatisect, lobes 5–7, linear to subulate, revolute, minutely pubesc. or glab. Rac. 2–5cm, 5–15-fld; cor. 7–12mm diam., blue. SW Asia. Z4.

V. arvensis L. Ann. or perenn. St. 5–40cm, procumbent, pubesc. and often gland. above. Lvs 0.2–1.5cm, triangular-ovate, truncate or cordate at base, crenate-serrate, pubesc. or sub-glabrous. Fls in rac.; cor. 2–3mm diam., blue. Eur. Z5.

V. australis Schräd. = *V. spicata*.

V. austriaca L. Perenn.; st. 25–50cm, generally erect or procumbent, ± hairy. Lvs linear-lanceolate to suborbicular, 1–2-pinnatisect. Infl. axill.; cor. 10–13mm diam., bright blue. Summer. Mainland Eur., except Fennoscandia and extreme S. ssp. *teucrium* (L.) D.A. Webb. Lvs ovate to oblong, truncate to subcordate at base, crenate to incised-serrate, sessile. Throughout range, except parts of W Eur. 'Blue Fountain': to 60cm; flts bright blue. 'Crater Lake Blue': to 25cm high, neatly mound-forming; fls blue. 'Kapitan': fls gentian blue. 'Knall Blue': to 25cm; fls gentian blue. 'Royal Blue': to 45cm, habit dense bushlet; fls blue. 'Shirley Blue': to 25cm high; fls bright blue. Z6.

V. bachofenii Heuff. = *V. grandis*.

V. bandaiana (Mak.) Tak. = *V. senanensis*.

V. beccabunga L. BROOKLIME; EUROPEAN BROOKLIME. Perenn., glab.; st. decumbent. Lvs 1–4cm, orbicular or ovate to oblong, subentire to crenate-serrate, rather thick and fleshy. Rac. axill.; cor. 5–7mm diam., pale to deep blue, occas. flushed pink. Summer. Eurasia; sparsely nat. in N Amer. Z5.

V. bellidioides L. Perenn., pubesc.; st. 5–20cm, base procumbent, upper part erect. Lvs to 4×1.5cm, oblong-obovate, subentire to crenate-serrate, tinged grey. Infl. term. rac., capitate to corymbose; cor. to 1cm diam., pale blue or lilac to violet-blue. Late spring–early summer. Pyren., mts of C Eur. and Balk., S to Bulg. Z6.

V. biebersteinii Richt. ex Stapf = *V. multifida*.

V. bombycina Boiss. & Kotschy. Tufted perenn., forming cushions 2–12cm diam., densely white-tomentose; st. woody at base. Lvs 0.4–0.9cm, linear to oblanceolate. Rac. pseudoterminal, 6–10-fld; cor. 10–14mm diam. pale lilac-blue to deep blue or occas. tinged redp Summer. Turk. to Leb. Z6.

V. bonarota L. = *Paederota bonarota*.

V. caespitosa Boiss. Perenn., stoloniferous, forming cushions to 7cm diam.; st., woody at base, glab. or strigose. Lvs 0.6–1.3cm, linear to oblanceolate, entire, revolute, gland., hairy above, glab. beneath. Rac. 1–2, 2–5-fld, hairy; cor. 8–14mm diam., blue-mauve or sky blue. Late spring–early summer. Anatolia. Z4.

V. candida hort. = *V. incana*.

V. caucasica Bieb. V. similar to *V. multifida*, except pedicels longer than 5mm; cor. white, sometimes with blue streaks. Early summer. Cauc. Z6.

V. chamaedrys L. ANGELS' EYES; BIRD'S EYE; GOD'S EYE; GERMANDER SPEEDWELL. Perenn.; st. to 25cm, hairy. Lvs 1–4cm, oblong-lanceolate to ovate-dletate, crenate-serrate to pinnatifid, subglabrous to sparsely hairy. Rac. 4–12cm, 15–30-fld; cor. 1cm diam., blue with darker striations and white throat. Late spring–summer. Eur., Cauc., Sib.; nat. S Canada and N US. 'Miffy Brute' ('Variegata'): to 20cm high, trailing; lvs yellow-variegated; fls clear blue, abundant. Z3.

V. chaubardii Boiss. & Reut. = *V. glauca*.

V. cinerea Boiss. & Bal. Perenn., subshrubby, ± caespitose, white-tomentose. Lvs 0.6–1.6cm, linear, entire or minutely crenate, revolute, silvery hoary-tomentose. Rac. 2–6, 2–3cm, 10–25-fld; cor. 8–10mm diam., dark blue or tinged purple, white in centre. Summer. E Medit., Asia Minor. Z5.

V. cinerea Raf. = *Besseya wyomingensis*.

V. crassifolia Wierzb. ex Heuff. Perenn.; st. to 60cm, erect or ascending, ± glandular-hirsute. Lvs 2–8cm, ovate-lanceolate, crenate to subentire, thick, glab. Infl. term., to 30cm, dense; cor. 4–8mm diam., bright blue. Summer. S Carpath., mts of N Balk. Penins. Z6.

V. crinita Kit. ex Schult. Perenn.; st. 25–60cm, erect, simple, villous. Lvs 2–3cm, broadly ovate, rounded at apex, cordate to truncate at base, crenate, pubesc. Rac. 2–4, 30–60-fld; cor. 10–14mm, diam., blue to violet-blue. S Russia, N Balk. Penins. Z6.

V. cuneifolia D. Don. Perenn. to 7cm; st. 5–20cm, decumbent, woody at base. Lvs, 0.4–1cm suborbicular to elliptic or oblanceolate, crenate to serrate, pubesc., gland. or subglabrous. Rac. 2–4cm, axill., 1–3, 5–20-fld, ± secund; cor. 7–11mm diam., blue or purple. Spring–summer. Turk. 'Villosa': lvs pubesc. beneath; fls blue. Z5.

V. daubneyi Hochst. in Seub. Perenn., mostly glab.; st. 10–50cm, procumbent to ascending. Lvs 1.5–5cm, oblong, serrate, dark green, coriaceous. Infl. axillary, rac. to 12cm, pubesc.; cor. 10–12mm diam., pale pink with darker veining. Azores. Z9.

V. exalata Maund = *V. longifolia*.

V. filiformis Sm. Perenn. or ann., often mat-forming, pubesc.; st. procumbent, slender. Lvs 0.5–1cm, reniform, crenate. Fls solitary in lf axils; cor. 1–1.5cm diam., pale lilac-blue. Late spring–summer. Cauc. & N Anatolia, nat. NW & C Eur. Z3.

V. flexuosa hort. = *V. longifolia*.

V. fruticans Jacq. ROCK SPEEDWELL. Perenn.; st. 5–15cm, ascending, base woody. Lvs 0.8–2cm, obovate to narrowly oblong, entire to crenate-serrate, glab. or minutely pubesc. Infl. short, ± capitate, 4–10-fld; cor. 11–15mm diam., deep blue tinged red in centre. Summer–early autumn. NW Eur., mts of S & C Eur. to Spain, Corsica and Balk. Z5.

V. fruticulosa L. Similar to *V. fruticans*, except cor. 9–12mm diam., pink or v. rarely deep blue. Summer. W & SC Eur. Z3.

V. gentianoides Vahl. Perenn., 30–80cm; st. erect, pubesc. above. Lvs to 7×1.5cm, linear-oblanceolate to broadly ovate, entire to obscurely crenate, glab. or minutely pubesc. Infl. 6–30cm, term.; cor. 1cm diam., white or pale blue with dark

blue veining to wholly dark blue. Early summer. SW Asia, Cauc. 'Alba': fls white with hint of blue. 'Nana': habit spreading; fls pale blue. 'Variegata': lvs marked with broad cream stripes. Z4.

V. glauca Sibth. & Sm. Ann.; st. erect, crispate-pubesc. Lvs to 1cm, triangular-ovate, crenate-serrate to lobed, ± pubesc. Rac. term.; cor. 1–1.5cm diam., deep blue with white eye. S Balk.

V. grandis Fisch. ex Spreng. Similar to *V. longifolia* except lvs smaller, broader and more cordate at base, more deeply obtuse serrate. Summer. C & NE Asia. Z5.

V. hybrida L. = *V. spicata*.

V. incana L. SILVER SPEEDWELL. Similar to *V. spicata* except plant eglandular, grey- to white-tomentose. Summer. E Eur. 'Baccarole': to 45cm, fls rose-pink. 'Candidissima': lvs silvergrey, pubesc.; fls deep violet-blue. 'Nana': habit spreading; lvs white, velvety; fls deep purple-blue. 'Red Fox': fls deep pink. 'Romilley Purple': to 60cm, habit bushy; fls dark blue. 'Saraband': lvs silver-grey, pubesc.; fls deep violet-blue. 'Silver Carpet': to 15cm; lvs large, silver-grey; fls dark blue. 'Wendy': habit loose; lvs grey. Z3.

V. kelleri Deg. & Urum. Perenn. with semi-woody rhiz.; st. densely leafy above. Lower lvs ovate, upper suborbicular, entire, thick, pilose beneath. Rac. terminal; cor. sky blue. Macedonia. Z7.

V. kotschyana Benth. in DC. Perenn., woody at base; st. 4–10cm, decumbent to erect. Lvs 0.5–1.2cm, linear-oblong to oblanceolate, entire to minutely serrate, subcoriaceous, hirsute above, ± glab. beneath. Infl. terminal, 15–30-fld, hairy; cor. 10–14mm diam., bright blue to violet. Summer. E Medit. Z7.

V. latifolia L. = *V. austriaca*.

V. liwanensis K. Koch. Perenn.; st. 3–10cm, creeping, woody at base. Lvs 0.4–1cm, ovate, crenate, coriaceous, slightly glaucous, sparsely ciliate. Rac. 1–4, axill., globose, 10–30-fld; cor. 10–14mm diam. Spring–summer. NE Anatolia, Cauc. Z6.

V. longifolia L. Perenn.; st. 40–120cm, erect, glab. or minutely pubesc. Lvs 3–12cm, lanceolate to linear-lanceolate, biserrate, glab. or sparsely hairy. Infl. term., with few lat. br.; to 25cm, pubesc.; cor. 6–8mm diam., pale blue to lilac. Summer–early autumn. N, E & C Eur.; nat. NE Amer. 'Alba': to 90cm; lvs bright green; fls white. 'Blaueriesin' ('Blue Giantess'): to 80cm, vigorous; fls bright blue. 'Forster's Blue': to 75cm, habit bushy; fls deep blue. 'Romiley Purple': fls rich purple in long slender spikes. 'Schneeriesin' ('Snow Giantess'): vigorous to 80cm; fls white. Z4.

V. longifolia var. *subsessilis* Miq. = *V. subsessilis*.

V. maritima L. = *V. longifolia*.

V. maxima Mill. = *V. austriaca*.

V. michauxii Lam. Perenn. or ann.; st. to 60cm, erect. Lvs 2–10cm, lanceolate, subentire to crenate-serrate, glab. or pubesc. above. Rac. axillary, glandular-pubesc.; cor. to 1cm diam., white with pink eye or veining, or pale blue. Summer. Turk., Iran, C Asia. Z7.

V. missurica Raf. = *Synthyris missurica*.

V. multifida L. Similar to *V. austriaca* except smaller and more delicate; st. to 30cm, decumbent to ascending; lvs 1cm, bipinnatisect. Early summer. SE Eur., SW Asia. Z6.

V. nummularia Gouan. Perenn.; st. 5–15cm, procumbent, matted, woody below, ascending, crispate-pubesc. Lvs 0.4–0.5cm, broadly elliptic to ovate-orbicular, entire, base ciliate. Infl. capitate, 5–10-fld; cor. 6mm diam., blue or pink. Early summer. S Fr., Spain. Z7.

V. officinalis L. COMMON SPEEDWELL; GYPSYWEED. Perenn.; st. 10–50cm, procumbent to ascending, hirsute to villous. Lvs 1.5–5cm, broadly ovate to elliptic, serrate, pubesc. Rac. 3–6cm, glandular-pubesc.; cor. 8mm, diam., dull lilac-blue. Late spring–early summer. Eur. Z3.

V. orientalis Mill. Perenn.; st. to 25cm, ascending, woody below, pubesc. above. Lvs 1–2cm, linear-oblong to oblanceolate, entire to pinnatisect. Infl. axillary, rac. to 8cm, 10–50-fld, pubesc.; cor. 10–12mm diam., blue or occas. pink or white. Summer. E Medit., SW Asia. Z7.

V. parviflora var. *arborea* (Buch.) T. Kirk = *V. arborea*.

V. pectinata L. Perenn., everg. subshrub, forming mat 7–15cm tall, pubesc. Lvs 1–2.5cm, elliptic to oblong, incised-serrate. Infl. axill., rac. to 20cm, gland.; cor. 10–12mm diam., deep blue with white eye. Late spring–early summer. E Balk., Asia Minor, Syr. 'Rosea': to 10cm, spreading; lvs pubesc.; fls pink. Z3.

V. peduncularis Bieb. Perenn., sparsely pubesc.; st., prostrate, then ascending. Lvs 0.7–2.5cm, lanceolate to broadly ovate, serrate to pinnatifid. Rac. 5–10cm, lax.; cor. 10–12mm diam., blue or pink to white with rose-pink veining. Late spring–early summer. SE Russia, S Ukraine, Cauc., Asia Minor. Z4.

V. pedunculata Vahl = *V. peduncularis*.

V. peloponnesiaca Boiss. & Orph. = *V. glauca*.

V. perfoliata R. Br. = *Parahebe perfoliata*.

V. petraea Steven. Plant caespitose, pubesc.; 10–12cm, ascending. Lvs to 2cm, elliptic to oblong, crenate-serrate or entire. Rac. axill., corymbose, 10–20-fld; cor. 4mm, blue or pink. Cauc. Z6.

V. pinnata L. Perenn. with woody rootstock, glab. to canescent; st. to 30cm, ascending. Lvs to 6cm, verticillate, pinnatisect to pinnatifid, glossy. Rac. term., many-fld; cor. blue. Sib. Z3.

V. pinnatifida Salisb. = *V. pinnata*.

V. prostrata L. Perenn., mat-forming; st. procumbent, short. Lvs 0.8–2.5cm, linear-oblong to ovate, subentire to crenate-serrate, ± pubesc. Spikes axill., dense; cor. 6–11mm diam., pale to deep blue. Late spring–summer. Eur. 'Alba': fls white. 'Kapitan': dense, mat-forming, fls bright deep blue in erect spikes. 'Loddon Blue': fls bright blue. 'Mrs Holt': fls pale pink. 'Rosea': fls pale pink. 'Royal Blue': fls dark blue. 'Spode Blue': fls rich royal blue. 'Silver Queen': fls silver-blue. 'Trehane' to 20cm; lvs golden; fls violet-blue. Z5.

V. purshii G. Don = *Synthyris missurica*.

V. reniformis Pursh non Douglas ex Benth. = *Synthyris missurica*.

V. repens Clarion ex DC. in Lam. & DC. Perenn., glab. below infl.; st. 5–10cm, procumbent 0.4–0.8cm, ovate to elliptic or suborbicular, entire to crenate-serrate, bright green. Infl. short, often corymbose, 3–6-fld, pubesc., or fls solitary; cor. 1cm diam., pink, or pale blue to white. Spain and Corsica. Z5.

V. rupestris hort. = *V. prostrata*.

V. satureioides Vis. Perenn., mat-forming; st. 10–30cm, woody below, pubesc. above. Lvs 6–9mm, suborbicular to oblanceolate, entire or slightly dentate, somewhat succulent, ± ciliate. Infl. capitate, 6–12-fld, villous; cor. 7mm diam., bright blue. Mid-late spring. Balk. Z3.

V. saxatilis Scop. = *V. fruticans*.

V. schmidtiana Reg. Perenn.; st. 10–25cm, simple, pubesc. Lvs 2–4cm, rosulate, ovate, pinnately incised, somewhat fleshy, ± glab.; lobes 2–4-dentate. Rac. 5–10cm, lax, 10–30-fld, pubesc.; cor. 10–12mm diam., pale blue-mauve with darker streaks. Summer. Jap. Z5.

V. schmidtiana var. *bandaiana* Mak. = *V. senanensis*.

V. schmidtiana var. *senanensis* (Maxim.) Ohwi = *V. senanensis*.

V. schmidtii Pohl ex Schult. = *V. chamaedrys*.

V. scutellata L. MARSH SPEEDWELL. Perenn., glab. or st. to 60cm, weak. Lvs 1.5–5cm, linear to oblong, entire to serrate, often tinged red-brown. Rac. to 7cm, lax; cor. 5–6mm diam., white or blue-lilac to pale pink. Eur., but rare near Medit.; N Amer. Z6.

V. senanensis Maxim. Similar to *V. schmidtiana* except lvs with shallow subacute lobes. Jap. Z6.

V. senanensis var. *yezoalpina* Koidz. = *V. schmidtiana*.

V. serpyllifolia L. THYME-LEAVED SPEEDWELL. Perenn., creeping, delicate. Lvs to 2.5cm, ovate, entire to crenate, glab. or minutely pubesc. Infl. 2–5cm, term., 8–40-fld, pubesc.; cor. 6–10mm diam., white or pale blue to bright blue, sometimes with darker blue veining. Spring–summer. Eur.; nat. Jap. Z3.

V. spicata L. Perenn.; st. to 60cm, erect or ascending, gland., pubesc. Lvs 2–8cm, linear-lanceolate to ovate, crenate to subentire, hairy. Infl. to 30cm, term., dense; cor. 4–8mm diam., clear blue; sta. purple. Eur., but rare in W. 'Alba': fls white. 'Alpina': habit low, dense. 'Blue Fox': to 60cm; fls deep blue. 'Caerulea': fls sky blue. 'Corymbosa': with axill. spikelets. 'Erica': to 30cm; fls pink. 'Heidekind': fls wine-red, in short spikes. 'Rosea': to 45cm; fls soft rose-pink. 'Rubra': fls rose-red. Z3.

V. spicata ssp. *crassifolia* (Nyman) Hayek = *V. crassifolia*.

V. spicata ssp. *incana* (L.) Walters = *V. incana*.

V. spuria L. Perenn., densely pubesc.; st. 30–90cm, erect. Lvs 2.5cm, oblong-lanceolate to linear-oblong, crenate-dentate towards apex, smooth. Infl. large, paniculate; cor. to 12mm diam., blue. Early summer. SE Eur. Z3.

V. subsessilis (Miq.) Carr. Perenn.; st. 40–80cm, densely branched, ± pubesc. Lvs 5–10cm, narrowly ovate to ovate-deltoid, finely dentate, pubesc. Rac. 10–20cm, axill., pubesc.; cor. 8–10mm diam., purple-blue. Summer. Jap. Z6.

V. surculosa Boiss. & Bal. Perenn., dwarf, 1–4cm; st. decumbent. Lvs 0.5–1cm near st. apex, oblong-oblanceolate to subspathulate, subentire to crenate, revolute, glandular-pubesc. Infl. 1cm, 3–10-fld; ± corymbose; cor. 7–11mm diam., blue or purple. Summer. E Medit. Z6.

V. telephiifolia Vahl. Perenn., mat-forming, glab., glaucous. Lvs 0.3–0.6cm, crowded, imbricate, orbicular to obovate, glab., sometimes ciliate. Infl. term., erect, 4–10-fld; cor. 7–9mm diam., pale blue. Summer. Cauc. Z6.

V. teucrium L. = *V. austriaca* ssp. *teucrium*.

V. turrilliana Stoj. & Stef. Perenn.; st. to 40cm, decumbent, woody at base, with 2 lines of hairs. Lvs 1.2–2cm, elliptic, crenate, glab., coriaceous. Infl. axillary, lax, ovoid-globose in fl.; cor. 8–10mm diam., deep blue. E Balk. Z6.

V. virginica L. = *Veronicastrum virginicum*.

V. wormskjoldii Roem. & Schult. AMERICAN ALPINE SPEEDWELL.

Perenn. with slender rhiz.; st. 10–30cm, erect, pilose. Lvs oval-rounded, crenate to entire, pilose. Rac. term.; cor. 6–7mm diam., blue-violet. N Amer., Greenland. Z4.

V. yezoalpina (Koidz.) Tak. = *V. schmidtiana*.

→*Pseudolysimachium*.

Veronicastrum Moench. Scrophulariaceae. 2 erect, perenn. herbs. Lvs simple, whorled. Rac. term., spicate; cal. 4–5-lobed; cor. salverform; sta. 2. NE Asia, NE Amer.

V. virginicum (L.) Farw. CULVER'S ROOT; BLACKROOT; BOWMAN'S ROOT. St. 60–180cm. Lvs 4–7, lanceolate to oblanceolate, serrate, glab. Fls in dense, slender spikes to 30cm, blue or white; fil. exserted. Summer. NE Amer. 'Album': fls white. 'Roseum': fls soft pink. Z3.

→*Leptandra* and *Veronica*.

Verrucifera N.E. Br.

V. hugo-schlechteri (Tisch.) N.E. Br. = *Titanopsis hugo-schlechteri*.

V. luederitzii (Tisch.) N.E. Br. = *Titanopsis luederitzii*.

V. schwantesii (Dinter) N.E. Br. = *Titanopsis schwantesii*.

Verschaffeltia H.A. Wendl. LATANIER LATTE. Palmae. 1 palm. St. to 22×0.3m, erect, armed with rings of long reflexed spines, supported on stilt roots. Lvs to 2.7m, petiole black-spined in juveniles; blade pinnately ribbed and entire or irregularly divided, apex cleft, becoming split to half depth into irregular several-fold seg., glab. above, sparsely scaly beneath. Seych. Z10.

V. splendida H.A. Wendl.

Verticordia DC. FEATHER FLOWER. Myrtaceae. 50 everg. heath-like shrubs. Lvs small, entire. Fls in upper lf axils, forming leafy corymbs, spikes or rac.; cal. lobes 5, plumose; pet. 5, entire, fringed or digitate; sta. 10. Aus. Z10.

V. brownii (Desf.) DC. WILD CAULIFLOWER. Shrub to 0.6m. Lvs 3mm, round. Fls creamy white, c0.5cm diam., in dense cauliflower-like clusters.

V. chrysantha Endl. Shrub to 0.6m. Lvs narrow and linear to oblong. Fls yellow, fringed, in crowded clusters.

V. conferta Benth. = *V. fastigiata*.

V. densiflora Lindl. Shrub to 0.6m. Lvs 0.4cm, slender. Fls rosy pink to purple, fringed and fragrant, in dense heads.

V. fastigiata Turcz. Shrub to 0.6m. Lvs blue-green. Fls brilliant red, cup-shaped, profuse.

V. fontanesii DC. = *V. plumosa*.

V. grandis J.L. Drumm. ex Meissn. SCARLET FEATHER FLOWER. Shrub to 2m. Lvs 1cm, grey-green, rounded. Fls scarlet, 2.5cm in diam., fringed, in vertical spikes in upper lf axils.

V. habrantha Schauer. Shrub to 0.6m. Lvs thick, rounded. Fls white, fringed, with pink centres, in dense masses.

V. humilis Benth. Mat-forming shrub to 0.2m. Lvs grey-green. Fls deep red, pendent, tubular, fringed.

V. insignis Endl. Shrub to 0.5m. Lvs 0.4cm, grey-green, succulent. Fls pink, fringed, in loose term. heads.

V. nitens (Lindl.) Endl. MORRISON FEATHER FLOWER. Shrub to 1.2m. Lvs 2.5cm, v. narrow, blue-green. Fls orange-yellow, fringed, in flat-topped clusters.

V. pennigera Endl. Shrub to 1m. Lvs minute, narrow. Fls rose-pink, fringed, c1cm diam., in small dense clusters.

V. plumosa (Desf.) Druce. FEATHER FLOWER. Shrub to 0.5m. Lvs 0.6cm, grey-green, terete. Fls pink or purple, fringed, in dense, axill. spikes.

Vervain *Salvia verbenaca*; *Verbena* (*V. lasiostachys*).

Vesicaria Adans.

V. brevistyla Torr. & A. Gray = *Lesquerella grandiflora*.

V. globosa Desv. = *Lesquerella globosa*.

V. grandiflora Hook. = *Lesquerella globosa*.

V. montana A. Gray = *Lesquerella montana*.

V. sinuata (L.) Poir. = *Aurinia sinuata*.

V. shortii Torr. & Gray = *Lesquerella globosa*.

Vestia Willd. Solanaceae. 1, everg., glab. shrub to 3.6m. Lvs to 5cm, persistent, elliptic to elliptic-oblong, glossy, foetid. Fls clustered or solitary in upper lf axils, pendent; cal. campanulate, 5-lobed, green; cor. tubular to funnel-shaped, tube to 3cm, yellow green, interior pubesc., lobes 5, triangular; sta. 5, protruding. Spring–summer. Chile. Z9.

V. foetida (Ruiz & Pav.) Hoffsgg.

V. lycioides Willd. = *V. foetida*.

Vetch *Vicia*.

Vetchling *Lathyrus*.

Vetiver *Vetiveria zizanoides*.

Vetiveria Bory. Gramineae. 10 perenn. grasses. St. clumped. Infl. narrowly paniculate; br. whorled, each bearing a rac.; spikelets to 20 per rac., laterally flattened, 2-fld. Trop. Asia. Z9.

V. zizanoides (L.) Nash. VETIVER; KHUS KHUS GRASS; KHAS KHAS. St. and rhiz. fragrant. St. to 180cm, erect, clumped. Lvs linear, to 90cm, rigid. Infl. lanceolate-oblong, to 45cm, condensed; rac. to 80cm, slender.
→*Andropogon*.

Viborgia Thunb. = *Wiborgia*.

Viburnum L. ARROW-WOOD; WAYFARING TREE. Caprifoliaceae. 150+ decid. or everg. shrubs or small trees. Lvs simple, entire or toothed, sometimes lobed. Fls in corymbs, sometimes with sterile and showy ray fls, or in umbels or pan.; cal. minute, 5-toothed; cor. rotate, campanulate, rarely cylindric, 5-lobed; sta. 5. Fr. a drupe, 1-seeded. Temp. N hemis., extending into Malaysia and S Amer.

V. acerifolium L. DOCKMACKIE. Decid. shrub to 180cm. Lvs to 10cm, rounded or cordate at base, lanuginose and black-punctate beneath, carmine in fall, trilobed, serrate. Fls white, 5mm diam., in long-stalked term. cymes to 7.5cm diam. Fr. ovoid, red, later purple-black. Summer. E N Amer. Z3.

V. affine Bush = V. rafinesquianum var. *affine*.
V. alnifolium Marsh. = V. lantanoides.
V. americanum sensu Dipp. = V. trilobum.

V. atrocyaneum C.B. Clarke. Everg. shrub to 3m. Lvs to 5cm, ovate, glab., glandular-dentate, green-bronze in winter. Fls in sparse term. cymes. Fr. ellipsoid, blue-black. Spring–summer. Himal. Z9.

V. betulifolium Batal. Decid. shrub to 3.5m. Lvs to 10cm, ovate to rhomboid or elliptic-oblong, long-acuminate, coarsely serrate, glab. and rich green above, paler beneath, veins downy. Fls white, in cymes to 10cm diam. Fr. rounded, bright red. Summer. W & C China. 'Trewithen': fr. abundant, long-lasting. Z5.

V. bitchiuense Mak. Decid. shrub to 3m. Lvs to 7cm, ovate or oblong, usually obtuse, subcordate at base, dentate, densely pubesc. beneath. Fls large, pink, later white, in lax infl. to 7cm diam. Fr. black. Spring. S Jap., Korea. Z6.

V. ×bodnantense Stearn. (*V. farreri* × *V. grandiflorum*.) Decid. shrub to 3m. Lvs to 10cm, lanceolate to ovate or obovate, acute, serrate, soon glab. Fls sweetly fragrant, rich rose-red to white-pink, in dense 7cm diam. clusters. Autumn–spring. Gdn origin. 'Charles Lamont': fls bright pink; infl. slightly larger. 'Deben': fls delicate shell-pink, later white and flushed pink; cor. tube longer; winter. 'Dawn': the type of the cross. 'Pink Dawn': fls pink, rose in bud; fr. dark blue. Z7.

V. bracteatum Rehd. Decid. shrub to 3m. Lvs to 12cm, orbicular to ovate, cordate at base, coarse- and sinuate-dentate, pubesc. on veins beneath. Fls white in distinctly bracteate cymes to 8cm diam. Fr. blue-black. Spring. SE US. Z6.

V. buddleifolium C.H. Wright. Decid. or semi-evergreen shrub, 180cm. Lvs to 12.5cm, oblong-lanceolate, acute, rounded or cordate at base, shallow-serrate, pubesc. above, light grey, densely lanuginose beneath. Fls 8.5mm diam., funnelform, white, in closely branched, 7.5cm diam., cymes. Fr. ovoid, red, later black. Spring–summer. C China. Z6.

V. burejaeticum Reg. & Herd. Decid. shrub to 5m. Lvs to 10cm, ovate, oval or obovate, apex acute to obtuse, tapered, rounded or cordate at base, serrate, scattered stellate-pubesc. beneath. Fls 6.5mm diam., white, in usually 5-rayed, 5cm diam., pubesc., white cymes. Fr. ellipsoid, black. Spring. N China, Korea, Russia (Ussuri region). Z5.

V. ×burkwoodii Burkwood & Skipwith. (*V. carlesii* × *V. utile*.) Semi-everg. shrub to 2.5m. Lvs to 10cm, ovate to elliptic, acute, rounded or cordate at base, obscurely toothed, glossy, scabrous above, pale brown, lanuginose beneath. Fls pink-white, later pure white, fragrant, 12.5mm diam., in rounded, 5-rayed, term., clusters to 9cm. Spring. Gdn origin. 'Anne Russell' (backcross with *V. carlesii*): to 1.5m tall; fls in globose corymbs, pink in bud, opening white, fragrant. 'Chenault': habit more compact; lvs more everg., more grey-pubesc., often bronze-brown in autumn; fls pale pink, later white. 'Fulbrook': as 'Anne Russell' but lvs pale green, infl. larger, conical, later-flowering. 'Mohawk' (a backcross with *V. carlesii*): compact; lvs glossy dark green, deep orange in autumn; fls white with red blotch, dark red in bud, in cymes to 8cm wide, spicy fragrance; fr. red to black. 'Park Farm': habit broader; fls more pink initially, later pure white, in cymes to 12cm diam. Z5.

V. calvum Rehd. Large everg. shrub similar to *V. tinus*. Lvs ovate or elliptic, undulate, sage-green. Infl. a corymb of small, white fls. Fr. lustrous blue-black. W China. Z8.

V. canbyi Sarg. = V. dentatum.

V. ×carlcephalum Burkwood & Skipwith ex A.V. Pike. (*V. carlesii* × *V. macrocephalum* f. *keteleeri*.) Decid. shrub to

2.5m. Lvs resemble *V. carlesii*, but to 12cm, somewhat glossy, paler beneath, tinged red in autumn. Fls pink, later white and pink-flushed, in dense trusses to 15cm diam. Spring. Gdn origin. Z5.

V. carlesii Hemsl. Decid. shrub to 2.5m. Lvs to 9cm, broad-ovate, acute, cordate at base, serrate, dull to grey-green, stellate-lanuginose. Fls to 12.5mm diam., pink, later white, in term., rounded clusters to 7.5cm diam. Fr. ovoid, compressed, black. Spring. Korea, Jap. (Tsushima Is.). 'Aurora': lvs sometimes copper-flushed; fls red, then pure light pink, later white. 'Cayuga' (*V. carlesii* × *V. ×carlcephalum*): lvs to 12cm, ovate-elliptic, sandy orange in autumn; fls pink opening white, outermost darker, profuse, scented; fr. burgundy to black. 'Cayuga' ×*V. utile* has produced *V.* 'Eskimo', a dwarf, dense, mound-forming shrub with semi-persistent dark, glossy lvs and tight globose heads of white fls (cream-pink in bud). *V.* 'Chesapeake', from the same cross is a dense, mounded, small shrub with ± persistent dark glossy lvs, fls pink in bud opening white and red to black fr. 'Charis': vigorous; fls red, then pink, later white. 'Compactum': habit dense; lvs dark green; fls profuse, white. 'Diana': vigorous, of compact habit; lvs tinged chocolate when young; fls red, then pink, somewhat purple-flushed, later white. Z9.

V. cassinoides L. WITHE-ROD. Decid. shrub to 2.5m, sometimes a small tree. Lvs to 11.5cm, stout, ovate to oval, short and slender-acute, often blunt, crenate or sinuate, dull dark green, bronze-tinted when young, red in autumn, subglabrous above, scurfy beneath. Fls 5mm diam., yellow-white, in dense, flat-arched cymes to 12cm diam. Fr. blue-black. Summer. E N Amer. 'Nanum': habit compact; br. and shoots twisted; lvs crispate and curved, rich autumn colours. Z2.

V. ceanothoides C.H. Wright = V. foetidum.

V. cinnamonifolium Rehd. Everg. shrub, or tree, to 6m. Lvs to 15cm, elliptic-oblong, acuminate, subentire, coriaceous, dark green above, conspicuously 3-veined, paler beneath. Fls cream-white, in lax, 7-rayed cymes to 15cm diam. Fr. ovoid, blue, shiny. Summer. China. Z7.

V. cordifolium Wallich. Differs from *V. sympodiale* in lvs distinctly cordate at base, fls pure white, sterile fls 0. W China, E Himal. Z9.

V. coriaceum Bl. = V. cylindricum.

V. corylifolium Hook. f. & Thom. Decid. shrub to 3m. Lvs to 8cm, suborbicular to obovate, abruptly short-acuminate, base cordate, dentate, pubesc. above, densely so beneath. Fls white, v. small, in cymes to 7cm. Fr. ovoid, scarlet-red. Summer. W China, E Himal. Z6.

V. cotinifolium D. Don. Decid. shrub to 3.5m. Lvs to 12.5cm, ovate, oval or suborbicular, apex acuminate or rounded, crenate to subentire, rugulose and thinly hairy above, more so beneath. Fls white, tinged pink, funnelform, 6.5mm, in rounded, 5-rayed cymes to 7.5cm diam. Fr. ovoid, red, later black. Spring–summer. Himal. (Bhutan to Baluchistan). Z6.

V. cylindricum Buch.-Ham. ex D. Don. Everg. shrub, sometimes a tree to 15m. Lvs to 20.5cm, oval, oblong or obovate, acuminate, apex dentate, base cuneate or rounded, dark green waxy, glab. Fls white, 5mm, in 7-rayed cymes to 12.5cm diam. Fr. 4mm, ovoid, black. Summer–autumn. Himal., China. Z6.

V. dasyanthum Rehd. Decid. shrub to 2.5m. Lvs to 12cm, oval-elliptic to oblong, acuminate, base rounded, shallow-dentate, shiny above, axillary-pubesc. in veins beneath. Fls white, in lax, 7-rayed cymes to 10cm diam. Fr. ovoid, bright red. Summer. C China. Z6.

V. davidii Franch. Everg. shrub to 1.5m. Lvs to 15cm, coriaceous, narrow-oval or somewhat obovate, acuminate, shallow-dentate toward apex, dark green, glab. except for pubesc. veins beneath, clearly 3-veined. Fls dull white, 3mm diam., in dense, stiff, usually 7-rayed cymes to 7.5cm diam. Fr. narrow-ovoid, blue. Summer. W China. Z7.

V. davuricum Pall. = V. mongolicum.

V. dentatum L. ARROW WOOD; SOUTHERN ARROW WOOD. Decid. shrub to 4.5m. Lvs to 11.5cm, thin, oval to rounded, subglabrous above, sparsely lanuginose beneath, teeth large, triangular. Fls white, 4mm diam., in corymbs to 11.5cm diam. Fr. rounded-ovoid, blue-black. Summer. E N Amer. var. *pubescens* Ait. Lvs thicker, more hairy beneath. Z2.

V. dentatum auct., non L. = V. recognitum.
V. dentatum var. *lucidum* Ait. = V. recognitum.
V. dentatum var. *venosum* (Britt.) Gleason = V. venosum.

V. dilatatum Thunb. Decid. shrub to 3m+. Lvs to 12.5cm, broad-ovate, rounded or obovate, short-acuminate, base cordate, coarse-dentate, pubesc. Fls pure white, 6.5mm diam., v. abundant, in pubesc. usually 5-rayed cymes to 12cm diam. Fr. rounded-ovoid, bright red. Summer. Jap., China. 'Catskill': to 180cm, broad; lvs to 14cm, oval to obovate, finely dentate, slightly pubesc., orange-yellow to red in autumn; cymes to 10cm diam.; fr. dark red. 'Erie': to 180cm, broad; lvs turning yellow, orange and red in autumn; fr. pale pink, later coral-pink. 'Iroquois': to 2.5m, bushy; lvs to 16cm, rounded to broad-ovate or -obovate, short-acuminate, coarse-dentate, orange-red in autumn; infl. to 12cm diam.; fls cream-white; fr. coral-red; spring. 'Oneida' (*V. dilatatum* × *V. lobophyllum*): habit rounded, to 3m; lvs dark green, yellow and red in autumn; fls off-white, abundant; fr. dark red, glossy, long-lasting. 'Xanthocarpum': fr. yellow. Z5.

V. edule (Michx.) Raf. Decid. shrub to 1.5m. Lvs to 8cm, suborbicular to broad-elliptic, 3-lobed at apex, irregularly serrate, shiny, ± glab. Fls in cymes to 2.5cm diam. Fr. ovoid-globose, red. Spring. NE Asia, N Amer. Z5.

V. ellipticum Hook. Decid. shrub to 2.5m. Lvs to 7cm, subcoriaceous, elliptic-oblong, obtuse apex coarse-serrate, 3-veined at base, pubesc. beneath, at least on veins. Fls in pubesc. cymes to 5cm diam.; cor. to 1cm diam. Fr. ellipsoid, black. W N Amer. Z6.

V. erosum Thunb. Erect decid. shrub to 180cm. Lvs to 9cm, ovate or obovate, acuminate, dentate, stellate-lanuginose, esp. beneath. Fls white, 4mm diam., in slender, somewhat pubesc., usually 5-rayed cymes to 9mm diam. Fr. rounded-ovoid, red. Spring–summer. Jap., China. Z6.

V. erosum var. *ichangense* Hemsl. = *V. ichangense*.

V. erubescens Wallich. Decid. or semi-evergreen shrub or small tree. Lvs to 10cm, elliptic, elliptic-ovate or oblong, serrate, sometimes lanuginose beneath; petioles tinged red. Fls 10mm diam., white, pink-flushed, in pendulous, 5cm pan. Fls red, later black. Summer. Himal., W China, N Burm., Ceylon, India. var. *gracilipes* Rehd. Lvs elliptic, usually glab. Pan. longer, fls fragrant. Free-fruiting. Z6.

V. 'Eskimo' see *V. carlesii* 'Cayuga'.

V. farreri Stearn. Decid. shrub to 3m+. Lvs to 10cm, obovate or ovate, acute, scabrous-serrate, tough, glab. except for veins beneath. Fls white or pink-tinged, fragrant, to 16mm diam., in dense pan. to 5cm diam. Fr. red, later black. Winter. N China. 'Candidissimum': shoots green; lvs light green; fls pure white, slightly larger; fr. light yellow. 'Farrer's Pink': fls pink in bud, held in open clusters. 'Nanum': dwarf, to 50cm; lvs small; fls pink, scented, sparse. Z6.

V. foetens Decne. Closely related to *V. grandiflorum*, but to 1.5m, of wider and more open habit. Lvs large, glab. or subglabrous beneath. Fls white, in lax, 5cm pan. Fr. red, later black. Winter. Himal., Kashmir, Korea. Z6.

V. foetidum Wallich. Everg. shrub to 4m. Lvs to 7.5cm, ovate to oblong, entire or dentate, often 3-lobed at apex, dark green, glab. above, hair tufts beneath. Fls white, crowded in rounded clusters to 5cm diam. Fr. scarlet-crimson, ovoid-globose. Himal., W China. Z9.

V. fragrans Bunge, non Lois. = *V. farreri*.

V. furcatum Bl. Closely resembles *V. lantanoides*, decid. shrub to 3.5m+. Lvs to 15cm, orbicular to ovate, abruptly acuminate, cordate at base, brilliant scarlet to maroon in autumn. Fls white, to 2.5cm diam., in flat infl. to 25cm diam., sterile fls strictly peripheral, to 2.5cm diam., white; sta. to ½ length cor. Jap., Taiwan. Z6.

V. × *globosum* Coombes. (*V. davidii* × *V. lobophyllum*.) 'Jermyn's Globe': habit rounded, dense; lvs leathery; fls small, white. Z7.

V. grandiflorum Wallich. Decid. shrub or small tree. Lvs to 10cm, firm, narrow-oval, acute, toothed, lanuginose beneath; petiole tinged purple. Fls to 2cm diam., bright rose-pink at first, later nearly pure white, in many-fld corymbs to 7.5cm diam. Fr. large (to 2cm), ovoid, black-purple. Winter–spring. Himal., W China. 'Snow White': cor. tube white, sometimes becoming pink, in rac. to 7cm wide, scented. Z7.

V. harryanum Rehd. Everg. shrub to 2.5m. Lvs to 2.5cm, orbicular to obovate or broad-ovate, mucronulate, entire or dentate, glab., dark green; petiole tinged red. Fls pure white, 3mm diam., in term., usually 7-rayed, 4cm diam. umbels. Fr. ovoid, acute, shiny black. W China. Z9.

V. henryi Hemsl. Everg. or semi-everg. shrub to 3m, of tree-like habit. Lvs to 12.5cm, narrow-oval, oblong or obovate, acute, dentate, shiny above, paler beneath, glab. or lanuginose on midrib. Fls white, 6.5mm diam., in a pyramidal pan. to 10×10cm. Fr. ovoid, red, later black. Summer. C China. Z7.

V. hessei Koehne = *V. wrightii* var. *hessei*.

V. × *hillieri* Stearn. (*V. erubescens* × *V. henryi*.) Everg. shrub to 2m. Lvs to 15cm, narrow-elliptic, broader, sparsely shallow-serrate. Fls white, in conical, ascending pan. to 6×6cm. Fr. red to black. Summer. 'Winton': the type of the cross. Z6.

V. hupehense Rehd. Decid. shrub. Lvs to 7.5cm, broad-elliptic or rounded-ovate, long-acuminate, dentate, dark green, above, paler and more lanuginose beneath. Fls white, downy in 5-rayed, long-pubesc. corymbs to 5cm diam. Fr. ovoid, red. Spring–summer. China. Z6.

V. ichangense (Hemsl.) Rehd. Decid. shrub to 3m. Lvs to 6cm,

ovate to ovate-lanceolate, acuminate, broadly dentate, scabrous above, pubesc. beneath. Fls yellow-white, fragrant, in pubesc., 4–5-rayed, term. cymes to 4cm diam. Fr. red, pubesc. Summer. C & W China. Z6.

V. involucratum Wallich = *V. mullaha*.

V. × *jackii* Rehd. (*V. lentago* × *V. prunifolium*.) Resembles *V. lentago*, but more densely branched, lvs broader, obtuse, finely serrate, and petiole less broad-winged. Gdn origin. Z5.

V. japonicum (Thunb.) Spreng. Everg. shrub to 180cm. Lvs to 15cm, coriaceous, ovate, oval or subobovate, abruptly acuminate, shallow-dentate or sinuate toward apex, glab., shiny above, dark-spotted beneath. Fls 9.5mm diam., white, in rounded, usually 7-rayed cymes to 11.5cm diam. Fr. ovoid, bright red. Summer. Jap. Z7.

V. × *juddii* Rehd. (*V. bitchiuense* × *V. carlesii*.) Broad, decid. shrub to 1.5m. Lvs more oblong than in *V. carlesii*, fls more numerous, in somewhat laxer and broader corymbs. Spring. Gdn origin. Z5.

V. kansuense Batal. Decid. shrub to 2.5m. Lvs to 5cm, ovate to rounded, deeply 3- or 5-lobed, lobes coarsely toothed, dark green, adpressed-pubesc. above, paler with woolly tufts in axils beneath, dull red in autumn. Fls pink-white, 6.5mm diam., in usually 7-rayed corymbs to 4cm. Fr. ovoid-globose, red. China. Z6.

V. keteleeri Carr. = *V. macrocephalum* f. *keteleeri*.

V. lanatophyllum hort. = *V.* × *rhytidophylloides*.

V. lantana L. WAYFARING TREE; TWISTWOOD. Decid. shrub to 4.5m, occas. tree-like. Lvs to 12.5cm, broad-ovate to oblong, acute or blunt, denticulate, velvety above at first, densely stellate-hairy beneath. Fls white, 6.5mm diam., in usually 7-rayed cymes to 10cm diam. Fr. oblong, red, later black, glossy. Spring–summer. Eur., N Afr., Asia Minor, Cauc., NW Iran. 'Alleghany' see *V.* × *rhytidophylloides*. 'Aureum': young shoots and lvs golden-yellow, later green and yellow-traced. 'Mohican': to 1.5×2.5m, of esp. dense and compact habit; fr. orange-red, ultimately black. 'Variegatum': lvs variegated yellow. 'Versicolor': lvs gold, pale yellow when young. 'Willow Wood' see *V.* × *rhytidophylloides*. var. *discolor* Huter. Lvs smaller, white or grey-tomentose beneath. Z3.

V. lantanoides Michx. HOBBLE BUSH. Shrub to 4m, usually straggling. Lvs to 20cm, broadly ovate or orbicular, acuminate, finely serrate, glabrescent above, downy beneath. Cymes sessile, to 15cm; fls white, marginal fls sterile, to 2.5cm diam.; sta. equalling cor. Fr. red or scarlet, becoming black-purple. E N Amer. Z3.

V. lentago L. SHEEPBERRY. Decid. shrub or small tree to 9m. Lvs to 10cm, ovate to obovate, long-acuminate, sharply toothed, glossy dark green, glab. except for scurfy veins, red in autumn; petiole winged. Fls creamy white, 6.5mm diam., in sessile, term. cymes to 11.5cm diam. Fr. ovoid, blue-black, pruinose. Spring–summer. Canada to Georgia, W to Missouri. 'Pink Beauty': fr. pink, later almost violet. Z2.

V. lobophyllum Gräbn. Closely related to *V. betulifolium*. Decid. shrub to 5m. Lvs to 11cm, broadly ovate to -obovate, acuminate, shallow-toothed, glab. except for pubesc. veins beneath. Fls in 7-rayed, gland. cymes to 10cm diam. Fr. subglobose, red. Summer. C & W China. Z5.

V. macrocephalum Fort. Decid. or semi-everg. shrub to 6m. Lvs to 10cm, thin, ovate, sometimes oval or oblong, acute or obtuse, scattered-pubesc. above, lanuginose beneath. Fls pure white, to 3cm diam., all sterile, in globose, dense trusses to 15cm diam. Spring. The typical form is a selection, sometimes named *V.* 'Sterile'. Its dense, globose heads of sterile fls distinguish it from the wild state named f. *keteleeri* (Carr.) Rehd. which has fls small and fertile, except for marginal, showy sterile fls, in rather flat cymes to 12.5cm diam. China. Z6.

V. macrophyllum Bl. = *V. japonicum*.

V. molle Michx. Decid. shrub to 3.5m. Lvs to 12.5cm, ovate to rounded, slender-acuminate, deeply cordate, dentate, glab. above, paler and lanuginose beneath; petiole glandular-stipulate. Fls white, 6.5mm diam., in cymes to 10cm diam. Fr. ovoid, flattened, blue-black. Summer. E to Central N Amer. Z6.

V. mongolicum (Pall.) Rehd. Decid. shrub to 2m. Lvs to 6cm, broadly ovate, usually obtuse, shallow-dentate, stellate-pubesc. beneath. Fls in flat, sparse, umbellate cymes to 4cm diam. Fr. ellipsoid, black. Spring. E Sib. Z5.

V. mullaha Hamilt. Tall shrub. Lvs to 15cm, ovate to oval-lanceolate, long-acuminate, sparsely dentate, glab. above, chaffy- pubesc. beneath. Fls white, small, in somewhat sessile cymes. Fr. yellow-red. Spring–summer. Himal. (Kashmir to Sikkim). Z9.

V. nervosum Hook. f. & Thoms., non D. Don = *V. grandiflorum*.

V. nudum L. Upright decid. shrub to 3m. Lvs to 11.5cm, oval, ovate or lanceolate, thin, denticulate to entire, shiny dark green, glab. above, lighter sometimes scurfy beneath, turning scarlet in autumn. Fls yellow-white, 5mm diam., in cymes to 10cm diam. Fr. ovoid, blue-black. Summer. E N Amer. Z6.

V. odoratissimum Ker.-Gawl. Shrub to 10m, everg. Lvs to 14cm, coriaceous, glab., ovate to obovate, lustrous. Fls to 8mm diam., white, fragrant, in term. cymes to 10cm diam. Fr. oblong-ovoid, compressed. India, Burm., China to Jap. & Philipp. 'Nanum': habit dwarf. Z9.

V. opulus L. GUELDER ROSE; EUROPEAN CRANBERRYBUSH; CRAMPBARK. Decid. shrub to 4.5m, thicket-forming. Lvs to 10cm, 3-, sometimes 4- or 5-lobed, coarsely toothed, glab. above, lanuginose beneath, wine-red in autumn; petiole 2.5cm, gland., stipules linear. Fls to 2cm diam., cream-white, small and fertile, and sterile and showy, in flat cymes to 7.5cm diam., anth. yellow. Fr. 8.5mm diam., globose, bright red. Summer. Eur., NW Afr., Asia Minor, Cauc., C Asia. 'Aureum': lvs bronze when young, then dark yellow, finally green. 'Compactum': compact, to 1.5m; lvs small, glossy, maroon in autumn; fls and fr. abundant. 'Flore Pleno': to 3m tall; fls sterile, white, in globose clusters. 'Fructuluteo': fr. yellow, tinted pink. 'Harvest Gold': like 'Aureum' but lvs are richer yellow. 'Nanum': habit rounded, compact, to 80cm high; rich autumn colour; fls and fr. seldom produced. 'Notcutt's Variety': fls and fr. larger. 'Park Harvest': like 'Aureum' but lvs stronger yellow. 'Roseum' ('Sterile', 'Snowball'): habit rounded, to 4m; lvs tinted purple in autumn; fls large, double, sterile, in globose clusters, white or green tinted, sometimes turning pink. 'Tatteri': lvs variegated white; fls all sterile. 'Variegatum': lvs variegated white. 'Xanthocarpa': lvs pale; fr. pale ochre. Z3.

V. opulus var. *americanum* Ait. = *V. trilobum*.

V. opulus var. *sargentii* Tak. = *V. sargentii*.

V. orientale Pall. Closely resembles *V. acerifolium* but somewhat more vigorous, to 2.5m; lvs pubesc. only on vein axils beneath, and not black-puncticulate beneath. Summer. W Cauc., Asia Minor. Z6.

V. pauciflorum Raf. = *V. edule*.

V. phlebotrichum Sieb. & Zucc. Decid. shrub to 2.5m. Lvs to 9cm, slender, ovate or elliptic, base tapered, with coarse and sharp mucronulate teeth, glab. or somewhat lanuginose above, adpressed-pubesc. on veins beneath, crimson in autumn, vein pairs 6–9; petiole to 16mm. Fls white, small, in few-fld, 5cm diam., pendulous infl.; sta. v. short, fil. shorter than anth. Fr. ovoid, red. Spring–summer. Jap. Z6.

V. plicatum Thunb. Decid. tiered shrub to 3m. Lvs to 10cm, broad-ovate to elliptic-obovate, short-acuminate, crenate, stellate-pubesc. beneath, dark red to maroon in autumn, veins deeply impressed. Fls white, small and fertile or sterile and showy (to 4cm diam.), in flat lace cap umbels to 10cm diam. Fr. rounded-ovoid, coral red, later blue-black. Summer. Jap., China. f. *tomentosum* (Thunb.) Rehd. Br. horizontal and overlapping. Lvs ovate or oval, wine-red in autumn. Fr. blue-black. Spring–summer. Jap., China. 'Cascade': broad; infl. large, umbrella-shaped, sterile fls outermost, v. large, fr. red, profuse; a seedling of 'Rowallane'. 'Dart's Red Robin': broadly spreading, to 1.5m; lvs dark green; fls clear white, profuse; fr. deep red, in umbrella-shaped clusters, profuse, long-lasting. 'Grandiflorum': lvs wide, veins tinted red beneath; fls large, white occas. tinted pink at margins. 'Lanarth': spreading, to 4m; br. often ascending; lvs large, more acute; otherwise as 'Mariesii'. 'Mariesii': horizontally spreading; branching strongly tiered; infl. large, outer fls larger, sterile; fr. rarely produced. 'Newport' ('Newzam'): rounded, to 1m; lvs dense, burgundy in autumn; fls white, in upright clusters. 'Nanum Semperflorens' ('Nanum', 'Watanabe'): to 0.5m; lvs richly coloured in autumn; fls white, a fine 'lacecap' form. 'Pink Beauty': lvs small; fls white, later flushed pink, infl. small. 'Rosacea': lvs bronze when young; fls white and pale pink together, sterile. 'Roseum': fls white, later deep pink, infl. umbrella-shaped, outer fls sterile. 'Rotundifolium': to 2.3m high; lvs colouring well in fall; fls sterile, heads rounded. 'Rowallane': br. slightly pendulous, similar to 'Lanarth' lvs small; infl. umbrella-shaped, sterile fls tinted pink; fr. red later black, regularly produced. 'Shasta': spreading, to 2m high, lvs plum in autumn; fls large, white; fr. scarlet. 'St. Keverne': broad to 4m; infl. umbrella-shaped. 'Sterile' (JAPANESE SNOWBALL): medium-sized, spreading. Fls large, sterile, white, in globose heads in 2 rows along spreading to arching br. Often listed as *V. plicatum*. 'Summer Snowflake': habit tiered, compact, to 2m; lvs burgundy to purple in autumn; infl. lacecap; fls pure white, long-lasting. Z4.

V. ×pragense Vik. (*V. rhytidophyllum ×V. utile*.) Everg. shrub, 2.5m. Lvs to 10cm, elliptic or elliptic-lanceolate, shiny green and somewhat rugose above, densely stellate-tomentose beneath. Gdn origin. Z6.

V. propinquum Hemsl. Everg. shrub, 1m. Lvs to 9cm, thin, ovate-lanceolate to oval, acute, denticulate, distinctly 3-veined, shiny dark green, lighter beneath, glab. Fls green-white, 4mm diam., in usually 7-rayed cymes to 7.5cm diam. Fr. ovoid, glossy

blue-black. Summer. C & W China, Taiwan, Philipp. 'Lanceolatum': lvs narrower. Z7.

V. prunifolium L. BLACK HAW. Decid. shrub, sometimes small tree, to 9m. Lvs to 9cm, ovate, oval or obovate, occas. rounded, acute, serrate, glab., paler beneath, red and yellow in autumn. Fls pure white, 6.5mm diam., in cymes to 10cm diam. Fr. ovoid, dark blue, pruinose. Spring–summer. E & East-Central N Amer. Z3.

V. pubescens (Ait.) Pursh. = *V. dentatum* var. *pubescens*.

V. rafinesquianum Schult. Decid. shrub to 2.5m. Lvs to 5cm, ovate to subelliptic, acuminate or acute, coarsely toothed, lanuginose beneath, scarlet in autumn. Fls in 5–7-rayed, dense, glab. cymes to 7.5cm diam. Fr. ellipsoid, blue-black. Spring–summer. E N Amer. var. *affine* (Blake) House. Lvs to 8cm, glab. or slightly pubesc. on veins beneath. Z2.

V. recognitum Fern. ARROW-WOOD. Closely related to *V. dentatum* but glab., lvs thin, oval-lanceolate to rounded, scabrous, short-acuminate, sharply toothed. E US. Z5.

V. reticulatum hort. = *V. sieboldii*.

V. ×rhytidocarpum Lemoine. (*V. rhytidophyllum ×V. buddleifolium*.) Semi-everg. or decid. shrub. Foliage intermediate between parents. Infl. like that of *V. buddleifolium*. Fr. ultimately black and rugose. Gdn origin. Z6.

V. ×rhytidophylloides J. Sur. (*V. rhytidophyllum ×V. lantana*.) Resembles *V. rhytidophyllum*, but ± decid., lvs to 20cm, more ovate-elliptic, larger, less rugose, finely toothed. Gdn origin. 'Alleghany': lvs dark green. Fr. bright red ripening black. 'Holland': the type of the cross. 'Willow Wood': lvs leathery; fr. abundant in large clusters colouring from green to white to pink to black. Z5.

V. rhytidophyllum Hemsl. Everg. shrub to 6m. Lvs to 20cm, ovate-oblong, acute or blunt, shiny and distinctly rugose above, grey to tawny-felted beneath. Fls dull yellow-white, 6.5mm diam., in 7–11-rayed, umbellate trusses to 20.5cm diam. Fr. ovoid, red, later, black. Spring–summer. C & W China. 'Aldenhamense': lvs tinted ochre. 'Pragense' (*V. rhytidophyllum ×V. utile*:): spreading, to 2.5m tall; lvs to 10cm, elliptic, dark glossy green and rugose above, white-felted beneath; fls cream, buds pink. 'Roseum': vigorous; fls intense pink-red, later white flushed pink. 'Variegatum': lvs speckled yellow. Z6.

V. rigidum Vent. Differs from the closely related *V. tinus* in open habit, larger lvs hairy throughout. Lax everg. shrub to 3m. Lvs to 15cm, ovate or oval, acute to obtuse, entire, ciliate, dark green, ± scabrous, pubesc. above, paler grey-pubesc. beneath. Fls white, 5mm diam., in a somewhat flat corymb to 11.5cm diam. Fr. ovoid, blue, later black. Winter–spring. Canary Is. Z9.

V. rufidulum Raf. SOUTHERN BLACK HAW. Decid. shrub or tree to 12m. Lvs to 10cm, rigid, coriaceous, oval, ovate or obovate, obtuse or short-acuminate, serrulate serrate above, rusty lanuginose beneath. Fls white, 8.5mm diam., in cymes to 12.5cm diam. Fr. ellipsoid, dark blue, pruinose. Spring–summer. S US. Z5.

V. rugosum Pers. = *V. rigidum*.

V. sandankwa Hassk. = *V. suspensum*.

V. sargentii Koehne. Decid. shrub to 3m. Lvs to 12cm, trilobed, emerging dark brown, later rich yellow-green, paler and pubesc. beneath; petiole gland. Fls white to cream fertile and sterile, to 3cm diam., in cymes to 6×10cm, anth. purple, not yellow (cf. *V. opulus*). Fr. subglobose, light red. Spring–summer. NE Asia. 'Flavum' (Fructuluteo'): fr. yellow. 'Onondaga': rounded, to 3m; br. grey, corky; lvs to 14cm, maroon when young, purple-red in autumn; fl. buds red opening blush pink, marginal fls sterile, white. 'Susquehanna': habit rounded, to 2m; bark v. corky; lvs dark green; fls cream, with a crown of outer sterile fls; fr. yellow becoming red. Z4.

V. scabrellum (Torr. & A. Gray) Chapm. = *V. dentatum*.

V. schensianum Maxim. Decid. shrub. Lvs to 7cm, oval or ovate, obtuse, finely toothed, lanuginose beneath. Fls 6.5mm diam., dull white, in 5-rayed cymes to 9cm diam. Fr. ovoid, red, ultimately black. Spring–summer. NW & C China. Z6.

V. schneiderianum Hand.-Mazz. = *V. calvum*.

V. sempervirens K. Koch. Tall everg. shrub. Lvs to 9cm, elliptic-lanceolate, coriaceous, shiny above, paler and finely black-punctate beneath. Fls in cymes to 5cm diam. Fr. red. Hong Kong, SW China. Z9.

V. setigerum Hance. Decid. shrub to 3.5m. Lvs to 15cm, orange yellow in fall, ovate-lanceolate, long-acuminate, sparsely dentate, dark green above, paler beneath, veins long-pubesc. Fls white, 6.5mm diam., in term., 5-rayed cymes to 5cm diam. Fr. ovoid, orange turning bright red. C & W China. 'Aurantiacum': fr. bright orange. Z5.

V. sieboldii Miq. Decid. shrub to 3m, or small tree. Lvs to 12.5cm, obovate, or obovate-oblong, acute or obtuse, serrate, lustrous, glab. above, glab. or lanuginose beneath. Fls cream-white, 8.5mm diam., in long-stalked cymes to 10cm diam. Fr.

ovoid, pink, later blue-black. Spring–summer. Jap. 'Seneca': to 10m, broadly spreading; lvs to 20cm, elliptic to lanceolate-obovate, crenate; fls white, waxy, in many-fld pan. to 12cm; fr. in large drooping clusters, orange-red, later blood-red, ultimately blue-black. Spring–summer. Z4.

V. stellulatum Wallich ex DC. = *V. mullaha.*

V. 'Sterile' see *V. macrocephalum.*

V. suspensum Lindl. Everg. shrub to 3.5m. Lvs to 12.5cm, ovate to oval, coriaceous, acute, entire or dentate, shiny, glab. Fls 9mm diam. white, faintly rose-tinted, in corymbose pan. to 10×10cm. Fr. globose, red to black. Spring. Ryukyu Is. Z9.

V. sympodiale Gräbn. Closely resembles *V. furcatum,* but lvs smaller, more ovate, round to subcordate at base, more finely serrate, petioles with small stipules, infl. to 9cm diam. China. Z6.

V. ternatum Rehd. Everg. shrub to 4m. Lvs to 22cm, usually 3-clustered, thin, elliptic to obovate-oblong, glab. except for veins beneath. Fls yellow-white, small, in lax infl. to 17cm diam. Fr. red. W China. Z9.

V. theiferum Rehd. = *V. setigerum.*

V. tinus L. LAURUSTINUS. Everg. shrub to 3.5m. Lvs to 10cm, ovate to ovate-oblong, entire, shiny dark green, paler with axill. hair tufts in veins beneath. Fls pink-brown in bud, opening white to pink-white, 6.5mm diam., in convex, term. cymes to 10cm diam. Fr. ovoid, indigo to black. Winter–spring. S Eur., N Afr. 'Bewley's Variegated': lvs pale green deeply edged bright cream; fls blush pink. 'Clyne Castle': lvs glossy, large; hardy. 'Compactum': erect, compact; lvs small, v. dark green. 'Eve Price': dense, compact; lvs small; fls tinged pink, carmine in bud. 'French White': vigorous; fls white, in large heads. 'Froebellii': v. compact; lvs light green; fls snow white. 'Gwenllian': to 3m; lvs dull green, short; fls rich pink in bud, opening blush. 'Israel': lvs large; fls waxy, clear white. 'Lucidum': open, vigorous; lvs large, shiny; fl. heads large. 'Pink Prelude': fls white, becoming deep pink. 'Purpureum': lvs dark green tinted red, purple when young. 'Robustum': upright, dense; lvs deep green; fls blush white. 'Strictum' ('Pyramidale'): habit erect, narrowly and tightly conical. 'Variegatum': lvs variegated creamy yellow; fls pink. f. *hirtum* hort. Lvs larger, thicker, v. ciliate; shoots bristly-hairy. ssp. *rigidum* (Vent.) P. Silva see *V. rigidum.* Z7.

V. tomentosum Thunb., non Lam. = *V. plicatum* f. *tomentosum.*

V. trilobum Marsh. AMERICAN CRANBERRY BUSH; HIGHBUSH CRANBERRY; CRANBERRY. Decid. shrub to 3m. Lvs to 12cm, broad-ovate, trilobed, toothed or entire, light green above, paler and slightly pubesc. beneath, red in fall; petiole gland. Fls white, in cymes to 10cm diam. Fr. subglobose, scarlet-red. Spring–summer. N Amer. 'Alfredo': habit broader and denser than in 'Compactum'; fls and fr. sparse. 'Bailey Compact': habit dense; lvs deep red in fall. 'Compactum': habit compact, low; st. upright, spreading, slender; lvs lustrous; fls white; fr. edible. 'Spring Green': habit somewhat upright, to 1.5m tall; lvs orange-red in fall. 'Spring Red': habit somewhat upright; lvs red when young to green, orange-red in fall; fr. rare. Z2.

V. urceolatum Sieb. & Zucc. Procumbent decid. shrub to 1m. Lvs to 12cm, ovate to lanceolate, acuminate, crenate, slightly lepidote on veins beneath. Fls pink-white, to 4mm, in glab., 5-rayed long-stalked cymes to 6cm diam. Fr. ovoid black. Spring. Jap. Z6.

V. utile Hemsl. Everg. shrub to 180cm. Lvs to 7.5cm, firm, narrow-ovate or suboblong, obtuse, entire, dark green, glab. above, white and densely lanuginose beneath. Fls white, 8.5mm diam., in dense, terminal, 7.5cm diam., rounded trusses. Fr. ovoid, blue-black. Spring. China. Z7.

V. veitchii C.H. Wright. Decid. shrub, 1.5m. Lvs to 12.5cm, ovate, acuminate, sharply and sparsely toothed, sparsely lanuginose, rugose above, densely so beneath. Fls white, 6.5mm diam., in flat, v. scurfy, usually 7-rayed cymes to 12.5cm diam. Fr. ellipsoid, red, later black. Spring–summer. C China. Z5.

V. venosum Britt. Closely resembles *V. dentatum,* but lvs tough, circular, often broader than long, densely stellate-pubesc., veins raised beneath. E US. Z5.

V. venulosum Benth. = *V. sempervirens.*

V. wilsonii Rehd. Decid. shrub to 3m. Lvs to 9cm, ovate to rounded-oval, long- or caudate-acuminate, dentate, dark green somewhat pubesc. Fls white, 6.5mm diam., in term., yellow-pubesc., 5–6-rayed corymbs to 7.5cm diam. Fr. ovoid, bright red, ± pubesc. Summer. W China. Z7.

V. wrightii Miq. Decid. shrub to 3m. Lvs to 12.5cm, ovate or obovate, abrupt-acuminate, coarsely toothed, bright green, subglabrous above, paler beneath with hairs in vein axils, red in autumn. Fls white, in 5-rayed cymes to 10cm diam. Fr. round-ovoid, shiny bright red. Spring–summer. Jap. var. *hessei* (Koehne) Rehd. Smaller. Lvs to 11cm, more ovate and sparsely toothed, brilliant red in autumn. Fls in smaller, flat-arched infl., to 6cm diam. Z5.

Vicia L. VETCH; TARE. Leguminosae (Papilionoideae). 140 ann. or perenn. herbs, often climbing by tendrils. Lvs pinnate. Fls pea-like solitary and axill. or in axill. fascicles and rac. Fr. a legume, ± oblong, dehiscent. Eur., S Amer., Hawaii, trop. E Afr.

V. canescens Labill. Perenn. 38–46cm; st. erect, woolly. Lfts in 8–12 pairs, linear-elliptic, upper lvs sometimes with short tendril. Fls blue in a dense rac. Summer. Leb. Z8.

V. cracca L. TUFTED VETCH; BIRD VETCH; CANADA PEA. Scrambling or climbing perenn. to 180cm, glab. or pubesc. with branched tendrils; lfts in 6–15 pairs, linear to ovate-oblong. Fls indigo in dense rac. Summer. Eurasia, US. Z5.

V. faba L. BROAD BEAN; ENGLISH BEAN; EUROPEAN BEAN; FIELD BEAN. Robust erect ann. to 2m; lacking tendrils. Lfts alt. or in 1–3 pairs, oval to oblong, glaucous. Fls to 2.5cm, solitary or in clusters, white with purple stain. Fr large; unripe seeds reniform-oblong, edible. Late spring–summer. N Afr., SW Asia.

V. gerardii (All.) Gaudin = *V. cracca.*

V. hirsuta (L.) S.F. Gray. Pubesc. ann., 20–70cm. Lfts in 4–10 pairs, linear- or obovate-oblong. Fls buff tinged pale purple, to 8 per rac. Eur.

V. incana Gouan = *V. cracca.*

V. onobrychioides L. Glab. or pubesc. perenn., 30–120cm. Lfts 4–11 pairs, linear- or oblong-lanceolate; fls violet with pale keel, 4–12 per rac. S Eur. Z7.

V. oroboides Wulf. in Jacq. Subglabrous or sparsely pubesc. perenn., 25–50cm. Lvs lacking tendrils. Lfts in 1–4 pairs, ovate. Fls pale yellow or blue 2–12 per rac. Summer. E Alps to W Hung. and C Balk. Z5.

V. orobus DC. in Lam. & DC. BITTER VETCH. Pubesc. perenn. to 60cm. Lvs lacking tendrils; lfts in 6–15 pairs, oblong to elliptic, mucronate. Fls white veined purple, 6–20 per rac. Summer–early autumn. Eur. Z6.

V. pyrenaica Pourr. Glab., creeping perenn., 5–30cm. Lfts 3–6 pairs, oblong to suborbicular, truncate or emarginate; tendrils usually simple. Fls solitary, bright violet-purple. Mts of Spain and Fr. Z8.

V. sativa L. SPRING VETCH; TARE. Pubesc. ann. or bienn. to 80cm. Lfts in 3–8 pairs, linear to obcordate, acute, mucronate or cleft. Fls purple, usually paired. Eur., nat. N Amer. Z5.

V. sepium L. BUSH VETCH. Usually pubesc. perenn., 30cm–1m. Lfts 3–9 pairs, ovate to ovate-oblong, obtuse, mucronate or emarginate. Fls 2–6 together, dull blue, indigo or violet. Eur. to Himal. Z6.

V. tenuifolia Roth. FINE-LEAVED VETCH. St. glab. or addressed-pubesc. Lfts 5–13 pairs, linear or linear-oblong. Fls purple, pale lilac or lilac-blue, 15–30 per rac. Eur. Z6.

V. unijuga A. Braun. Erect perenn. 30–38cm, tangled, lacking tendrils. Lfts 2, lanceolate to ovate. Fls deep violet-purple or blue, in many-fld rac. Summer. NE Asia. Z7.

Victoria Lindl. GIANT WATER LILY; WATER-PLATTER. Nymphaeaceae. 2 giant aquatic herbs with stout rhiz. Lvs floating, orbicular, peltate, undersurface puckered and netted with prominent veins, margins upturned in a distinct, continuous rim. Fls floating, v. large, white, becoming pink or red; sep. 4; pet. numerous; sta. c200. Trop. S Amer. Z10.

V. amazonica (Poepp.) Sowerby. AMAZON WATER LILY; ROYAL WATER LILY; WATER MAIZE. Lvs to 2m diam., spiny and tinged red-purple beneath; lf rim to 15cm. Sep. prickly, exterior tinged red-purple. Amaz. region.

V. cruziana Orb. SANTA CRUZ WATER LILY. Differs from *V. amazonica* in lvs green, densely soft-pubesc. beneath, rim to 20cm. Sep. with basal prickles only, exterior green. N Arg., Parag., Braz., Boliv.

V. 'Longwood Hybrid' (*V. amazonica* × *V. cruziana.*) Intermediate between parents.

V. regia Lindl. = *V. amazonica.*

V. trickeri Tricker = *V. cruziana.*

Victoria Box *Pittosporum undulatum.*
Victoria Christmas Bush *Prostanthera lasianthos.*
Victoria Dogwood *Prostanthera lasianthos.*
Victoria Eurabbie *Eucalyptus globulus.*

Vigna Savi. Leguminosae (Papilionoideae). 150 erect, twining or creeping herbs. Lvs trifoliate; lfts ovate to elliptic. Fls pea-like, clustered or racemose. Fr. linear, straight or curved. Trop. Afr., S & C Amer., S US, Asia.

V. aconitifolia (Jacq.) Maréchal. MOTH BEAN. Shoots erect to diffuse. Lfts to 5cm, mostly deeply 3-lobed. Fls to 0.6cm. Fr. cylindrical, 2.5–5cm. S Asia.

V. angularis (Willd.) Ohwi and Ohashi. ADZUKI BEAN; ADUKI BEAN. Erect or scandent. Lfts to 10cm, ovate, term. leaflet 3-

lobed. Fls c2cm. Fr. 10cm; seeds pink-red, with small black hilum. Asia. Z10.

V. caracalla (L.) Verdc. SNAIL FLOWER; CORKSCREW FLOWER; SNAIL BEAN. Twining perenn. to 6m. Lfts to 13cm, ovate, pub-esc. Fls to 5cm, fragrant white or yellow, wings pink-purple, keel coiled like a small snail's shell. Fr. to 18cm, linear. Trop. S Amer.

V. catjang (Burm. f.) Walp. = *V. unguiculata* ssp. *cylindrica*.

V. radiata (L.) R. Wilcz. MUNG BEAN; GREEN GRAM; GOLDEN GRAM. Hirsute ann., freely branching. Lfts to 10cm, ovate to rhomboidal. Fls yellow. Fr. to 10cm, slender, short-hairy; seeds green, subglobose. India, Indon., US.

V. sinensis (L.) Savi ex Hassk. = *V. unguiculata* ssp. *unguiculata*.

V. unguiculata (L.) Walp. COWPEA; HORSE GRAM; CHERRY BEAN. Ann. erect or scandent. Lfts to 15cm, central leaflet to 12cm, hastate, smooth. Fr. 10–23cm, pendulous, smooth with thick, decurved beak; seeds 10–15, variable in size and colour. S Asia. ssp. *unguiculata*. BLACK-EYED PEA. Fr. pendent, to 25cm; seeds usually with a dark hilum. ssp. *cylindrica* (L.) Eselt. ex Verdc. CATJANG; JERUSALEM PEA; MARBLE PEA. Fr. to 12cm. Afr., India. ssp. *sesquipedalis* (L.) Verdc. ASPARAGUS BEAN; YARDLONG BEAN. Lfts rhombic. Fr. pendent, to 90cm, soft and swollen. S Asia.
→*Phaseolus*.

Viguiera Kunth. Compositae. c150 herbs and shrubs. Cap. radiate c5cm diam., solitary and long-stalked, cymose or paniculate; receptacle flat to slightly conic, scaly; flts usually yellow. N & S Amer. Z10.

V. excelsa Hemsl. Erect herb to 2.5m, scabrid. Lvs elliptic, apex dentate, scabrid, acute. Summer. Mex.

V. laciniata A. Gray. Shrub to 120cm, resinous. Lvs to 3.5cm, triangular-lanceolate, dentate, hastate at base and shortly petiolate. Summer. N Mex., W Calif.

V. linearis (Cav.) Hemsl. Erect perenn. herb to 60cm, scabrid. Lvs usually alt., linear, entire, revolute, veins strigose. Early autumn. Mex.

V. multiflora (Nutt.) S.F. Blake Perenn. herb to 1m; st. slender, branching. Lvs lanceolate to ovate-lanceolate, entire or remotely dentate. Summer. SC to SW US.
→*Helianthus* and *Tithonia*.

Villadia Rose. Crassulaceae. 25–30 perenn., or ann., succulent herbs. Roots frequently tuberous. St. often prostrate. Lvs small, ovate-spathulate or linear, subterete. Fls small, 5-merous, in bracteate pan., spikes or cymes; sta. 10. Summer. New Mex. to Peru. Z8.

V. batesii (Hemsl.) Baehni & Macbr. Perenn., 10–25cm. Lvs 10mm, in dense rosettes, linear-lanceolate to cylindrical, minutely tuberculate. Infl. a flat cyme; fls few, red-white. Late summer. C Mex.

V. cucullata Rose. Perenn., 10–30cm. Roots tuberous. Lvs to 25mm, cylindrical, glab. Infl. 10–15cm, a spike; fls white tinged red-orange, subtended by small ovate bracts. Autumn. New Mex.

V. elongata (Rose) Clausen. Perenn. to 25cm. St. creeping, rooting, thin, pubesc. Lvs 6mm, pubesc., ovate-linear. Infl. a pan.; fls white-red. Summer. Mex.

V. grandyi (Hamet) Baehni & Macbr. Perenn. to 10cm. St. creeping to erect, glab., occas. rooting. Lvs 5mm, packed, broad-ovate, blunt. Infl. a pan. or a cyme; fls few, white, tinged red-yellow. Peru.

V. guatemalensis Rose. Glab. perenn. to 50cm. St. prostrate. Lvs 15–25mm, dense, linear, cylindrical at right angles to st. Fls in a narrow thryse, yellow-green. Late autumn. S Mex., Guat.

V. imbricata Rose. Tuft- or mat-forming perenn. Lvs 5–6mm, overlapping, adpressed, oval, keeled, minutely tuberculate. Infl. a compact spike, fls white. Mex.

V. jurgensenii (Hemsl.) Jacobsen. Pubesc. perenn. St. branched at base. Lvs 3–4mm, oblong-ovate or lanceolate. Infl. a rac.; fls red-white or purple. Summer–autumn. Mex.

V. levis Rose = *V. guatemalensis*.

V. texana Rose = *Lenophyllum texanum*.
→*Altamiranoa, Cotyledon* and *Sedum*.

Village Oak Geranium *Pelargonium quercifolium*.

Villanova Lagasca.
V. chrysanthemoides A. Gray = *Bahia dissecta*.

Villaresia Ruiz. & Pav.
V. mucronata Ruiz. & Pav. = *Citronella mucronata*.

Villarsia Vent. Menyanthaceae. 16 perenn. herbs of marshy places. St. simple or stoloniferous. Lvs ovate to orbicular, entire to toothed, long-stalked. Fls in loose erect cymes; cal. 5-parted;

cor. 5-parted, broadly campanulate to rotate; fil. slender. SE Asia to Aus., S Afr. Z10.

V. aquatica J.F. Gmel. = *Nymphoides aquatica*.

V. capitata Nees. St. to 15cm. Lvs to 2.5cm, usually smaller, cau-line, broadly ovate, orbicular or reniform, entire or sinuately toothed. Fls to 1.2cm diam., yellow. Aus.

V. crista-galli Hook. = *Nephrophyllidium crista-galli*.

V. exaltata F. Muell. St. 15–100cm. Lvs 2.5–5cm, radical, ovate or orbicular or reniform, cordate at base, entire or repand. Fls 1.85–2.5cm diam., yellow, bearded or fringed at base within. Aus.

V. ovata Vent. St. to 15cm. Lvs mostly radical, oval, entire, tough. Fls lemon-yellow, crenate-fimbriate at base within. S Afr.

V. parnassifolia R. Br. St. 30–60cm. Lvs mostly radical, to 2.5cm, ovate to suborbicular, base rounded to cordate, entire to sinuate-crenate. Fls yellow. Aus.

V. reniformis R. Br. = *V. exaltata*.

Villous Fig *Ficus villosa*.

Viminaria Sm. GOLDEN SPRAY; RUSH BROOM. Leguminosae (Papilionoideae). 1 glab. shrub, to 6m; st. slender; br. drooping. Lvs 8–23cm, reduced to filiform petioles or with 1–3 lfts. Rac. term., 8–15cm; fls to 1.3cm; standard 0.8–1cm, orbicular, yellow with a red stain at base, wings smaller, yellow, keel smaller, red. Summer. SE Aus. Z8.

V. denudata Sm. = *V. juncea*.

V. juncea (Schräd.) Hoffm.

Vinca L. PERIWINKLE. Apocynaceae. 6 low everg. subshrubs or herbaceous perennials with long trailing shoots and shorter, erect fertile shoots. Lvs entire. Fls solitary, long-stalked, in leaf-axils; sep., 5 narrow; cor. funnelform, tube almost cylindrical, lobes spreading; sta. 5.

V. acutiflora Bertol. = *V. difformis* ssp. *difformis*.

V. difformis Pourr. Everg.; barren shoots, long prostrate; flower-ing shoots to 30cm high. Lvs 2.5–7cm, narrowly lanceolate. Sep. 5–14mm; cor. tube 12–18mm; limb 30–70mm across, pale violet-blue or almost white; lobes sharply pointed. ssp. *difformis*. Lf margin smooth and glab. SW Eur., Moroc., Alg. This is sometimes sold as *V. major* var. *alba* but lacks the hairs on lvs and sep. characteristic of *V. major*. ssp. *sardoa* Stearn. Lf margin and sep. scabrid, with microscopic hairs. Z9.

V. herbacea Waldst. & Kit. Herbaceous perenn. Shoots trailing or ascending. Lvs 6–50mm, elliptic to lanceolate and ovate. Sep. 3–10mm; cor. tube 10–20mm; limb 25–35mm across, blue-violet or white. E Eur., W Asia (to Iran). Z5.

V. libanotica Zucc. = *V. herbacea*.

V. major L. Everg.; shoots long, prostrate or to 30cm, arching. Lvs 2.5–9cm, ovate to lanceolate, ciliate; sep. 7–18mm, ciliate. Cor. tube 12–15cm; limb 30–50mm, blue-purple or violet; lobes acute. ssp. *major*. Petioles sparsely pubesc. Lvs mostly broadly ovate. Sep. hairs to about 0.5mm. Fr., It., Balk. 'Jason Hill': lvs plain dark green; cor. lobes to 1cm broad, pointed, dark violet. 'Maculata' ('Oxford' 'Aureo-maculata'): lvs with large, median, yellow-green blotch; fls large, pale blue. 'Major': lvs plain dark green; cor. lobes a little longer than broad, 10–20mm broad, blue-violet. 'Oxyloba': lvs plain dark green, predominantly lanceolate; cor. lobes much longer than broad, pointed, dark violet, 3–10mm broad. 'Reticulata': lvs with yellow veining con-spicuous when young, later becoming green. 'Variegata' ('Elegantissima'): lvs dark green with pale irregular yellow-white margin. ssp. *hirsuta* (Boiss.) Stearn. Lvs mostly lanceolate. Sep. with hairs to about 1cm. NE Asia Minor and adjacent W Cauc. Z7.

V. major var. *pubescens* (D'Urv.) Boiss. = *V. major* ssp. *hirsuta*.

V. media Hoffsg. & Link = *V. difformis* ssp. *difformis*.

V. minor L. Everg. shoots long, prostrate or fertile and erect to 20cm. Lvs lanceolate, elliptic or ovate 1.5–4.5cm, glab. Sep. 3–4mm, glab.; cor. tube 9–11mm; limb 25–30mm across. Eur., from Spain and Fr. over central and E Eur. to S Russia and N Cauc. Single-fld variants with unvariegated lvs include 'Atropurpurea' ('Burgundy') (fls red-purple), 'Alba' (fls white), 'Gertrude Jekyll' (fls creamy white), 'Bowles's Variety' ('La Grave') (fls large, violet-blue, to 2.5cm across) and 'Oland Blue' (fls light violet-blue). Double-fld variants include 'Alboplena' (fls white), 'Multiplex' (fls purple) and 'Plena' (fls blue). Variegated variants include 'Argenteovariegata' (margin white) and 'Aureovariegata' (yellow variegation). 'Grüner Teppich' ('Green Carpet') forms dense masses of foliage; fls rarely produced, light violet-blue, 3.5cm across. Z4.

V. pubescens D'Urv. = *V. major* ssp. *hirsuta*.

V. pumila Clarke = *V. herbacea*.

V. sardoa (Stearn) Pign. = *V. difformis* ssp. *sardoa*.

Vincetoxicum Wolf. Asclepiadaceae. 15 erect or twining perenn. herbs or subshrubs formerly listed under *Cynanchum* L. Infl. umbelliform, cymose; cal. 5-parted; cor. round-campanulate, deeply 5-cleft, corona attached to staminal tube, subentire to 5–10-lobed. Temp. & warm regions.

V. nigrum Moench. BLACK SWALLOWWORT. To 90cm, ultimately twining. Lvs ovate-lanceolate, ciliate. Pedicels scarcely exceeding peduncle; cor. brown, bearded. S Eur. Z8.

V. officinale Moench. Erect to 90cm. Lvs ovate, ciliate. Pedicels 3× longer than peduncle; cor. white, unbearded. Eur.

Vine *Vitis.*
Vine Cactus *Fouquieria splendens.*
Vinegar Pear *Passiflora laurifolia.*
Vinegar Tree *Rhus glabra.*
Vine Lilac *Hardenbergia violacea.*
Vine Maple *Acer circinatum.*
Vine Of Sodom *Citrullus colocynthis.*
Vine Rattany *Berchemia scandens.*
Vining Pepper *Peperomia dahlstedtii.*

Viola L. VIOLET. Violaceae. 500 ann. or perenn. herbs and shrublets. St. extended, leafy, or short with basal lvs. Lvs stipulate, lanceolate to cordate to reniform, entire to palmatifid. Fls 1 to few, nodding to facing outwards on slender axill. stalks, sometimes cleistogamous; sep. 5; pet. 5, free, unequal, uppermost pair ± erect, lat. pair spreading, lowermost pet. spurred or pouched and rather lip-like; sta. 5. Fr. a 3-chambered capsule, lobes carinate. Temp., esp. N Temp. & Andes, Sandwich Is.

V. adunca Sm. WESTERN DOG VIOLET; HOOKED-SPUR VIOLET. Perenn., to 10cm, procumbent. Lvs ovate to 4cm, glab. to pubesc. stipules dentate, or entire. Fls violet to lavender, veined purple with a white patch, then red-purple; pet. to 13mm+; spur to 18mm. Spring. NW to E US. Z4. 'Alba': lvs small; fls white.

V. aetolica Boiss. & Heldr. Perenn., to 40cm. Lvs ovate to lanceolate, crenate, to 2cm; stipules ciliate, pinnatifid. Fls to 2cm; pet. yellow, upper pet. occas. violet; spur to 6mm. SW Balk. Z8.

V. affinis Le Conte. Stemless perenn. Lvs narrow-ovate or cordate. Fls borne above lvs; pet. lavender to red tinged violet, throat pubesc., base white, veins dark violet. Spring. NE US. Z3.

V. alata hort. = *V. elatior.*

V. alba Besser. Perenn., to 15cm, or stoloniferous, prostrate to ascending. Lvs oblong to triangular-ovate, cordate, to 10cm+, pubesc., or glab., entire; stipules linear-lanceolate, fimbriate. Fls to 2cm, fragrant; pet. white or violet, lat. pet. pubesc. Spring. C & S Eur. ssp. *dehnhardtii* (Ten.) W. Becker. Stolons 0; lvs glab. to sparsely pubesc. ssp. *scotophylla* (Jordan) Nyman. Fl. spur violet. Z6.

V. allchariensis G. Beck. Perenn., to 25cm. St. clustered, thickened at base. Lower lvs elliptic-oblong, to 5cm, dentate, cuneate, upper lvs linear; stipules divided. Fls blue-violet; pet. to 15mm across; spur to 5mm. Macedonia, E Albania. ssp. *allchariensis*. Fls violet or yellow. ssp. *gostivarensis* W. Becker & Bornm. Fls to 25mm, yellow. Z6.

V. alpina Jacq. Stemless perenn., to 10cm. Lvs to 3.5cm, oblong-ovate to ovate-orbicular, truncate to cordate, glab., crenate; stipules oblong to lanceolate. Fls to 3cm, violet, occas. with a white eye, spur to 4mm. Spring–summer. NE Alps, Carpath. Z7.

V. altaica Ker-Gawl. Perenn., to 13cm, creeping. Lvs elliptic to broadly ovate, cuneate, crenate; stipules deeply dentate. Fls to 4cm, yellow, occas. violet; spur to 5mm. Summer. Asia Minor, Crimea, Altai mts.

V. appalachiensis L. Henry. Perenn. St. prostrate, to 6.5cm. Lvs ovate to orbicular to 2.5cm, coriaceous, cordate, crenate, occas. pubesc. Fls to 13mm, dark to pale violet, lower pet. white, veined violet. US.

V. arborescens L. Low shrubby perenn., to 30cm, grey-pubesc. Lvs ovate to linear-lanceolate. Fls to 15mm, white to pale violet; spur to 4mm. W Medit., S Port. Plants sold under this name are frequently *V. elatior*. Z9.

V. arenaria DC. = *V. rupestris.*

V. arkansana Greene = *V. sagittata.*

V. arsenica G. Beck. Perenn. to 25cm, ascending, glab. Lvs ovate to orbicular, to 4cm, truncate to cordate, crenate; stipules lanceolate. Fls 2cm, deep yellow, with darker lines, spur bowed upwards. Balk. (S Macedonia) Z7.

V. arvensis Murray. FIELD PANSY. Ann., to 40cm. St. erect, short pubesc. Lvs oblong-spathulate, to 5cm, crenate. Fls to 15mm; lower pet. cream to yellow to blue-violet, spur short, blunt. Eur.

V. bakeri Greene = *V. nuttalii* var. *bakeri.*

V. beckwithii Torr. & A. Gray. GREAT BASIN VIOLET. As for *V. trinervata* but lvs more divided, veins inconspicuous. W US.

Z5.

V. bellidifolia Greene = *V. adunca.*

V. bertolonii Pio. Glab. perenn., to 30cm. St. clumped, lower lvs orbicular to ovate, upper lvs narrow-linear; stipules narrow, divided ×3–5. Fls to 3cm diam., violet or yellow, square; spur equals pet., straight. S It., NE Sicily. Z10.

V. bertolonii Salisb. non Pio = *V. corsica.*

V. biacuta W. Becker = *V. yesoensis.*

V. biflora L. Perenn. to 20cm. St. erect, flimsy. Lvs reniform to cordate, dentate; stipules narrow-ovate. Fls to 15mm, yellow, not fragrant, lower pet. streaked, purple black; spur to 3mm. Spring. Eur. to N Asia, Alask., Rocky Mts.

V. biflora var. *crassifolia* Mak. = *V. crassa.*

V. blanda Willd. WILLDENOW VIOLET; WOODLAND WHITE VIOLET; SWEET WHITE VIOLET. Stemless perenn., to 10cm; stolons bearing cleistogamous fls. Lvs ovate, cordate to 6cm, pubesc. above, subentire; stipules lanceolate, ± dentate. Fls white, veins purple; pet. narrow, to 1cm; spur to 3mm, blunt. Spring. N Amer. Z2.

V. bosniaca Forman = *V. elegantula.*

V. brittoniana Pollard. COAST VIOLET. Stemless perenn., to 20cm. Lvs reniform, palmatisect, lobes with 2–4 narrow seg. Fls large; pet. dark violet tinged red, lower pet. white. E US. Z3.

V. calcarata L. Perenn., to 5cm+. Rhiz. ± filiform, subterranean. Lvs elliptic or lanceolate, to 4cm, base cuneate, to 4cm across, shallow-crenate, glab. or ciliate; stipules narrow-dentate. Fls blue or yellow, spur slender, to 15mm. Spring–summer. C Eur. (Alps), W Balk. ssp. *zoysii* (Wulf.) Merxm. To 7.5cm. Lvs ovate. Fls to 3cm across, yellow, rarely lilac; spur to 8mm. Z5.

V. calcarea (Bab.) E.S. Gregory = *V. hirta.*

V. calceolaria L. = Hybanthus calceolaria.

V. canadensis L. CANADA VIOLET; TALL WHITE VIOLET. Perenn., to 30cm; st. erect. Lvs ovate, sparse-pubesc., subglabrous beneath, dentate; stipules lanceolate, entire. Fls white above, yellow in centre, violet beneath, lower pet. frequently tinged violet above, to 18mm, lat. pet. bearded; spur inconspicuous. Spring–summer. N Amer. 'Alba': fls white. 'Alba Minor': dwarf habit; fls pure white. var. *rugulosa* (Greene) C. Hitchc. Rhiz. slender. Lvs wider than long, ciliate, pubesc. beneath.

V. canina L. DOG VIOLET; HEATH VIOLET. Perenn., to 40cm, decumbent to erect, glab. Lvs ovate-lanceolate to ovate, to 2cm wide, base cordate to reniform; stipules lanceolate, subentire. Fls blue or white; pet. to 1cm; spur yellow, straight. Summer. N Temp. Eur. and Asia. ssp. *montana* (L.) Hartm. Erect, to 40cm. Stipules longer, to ½ petiole length. Fls blue or white. ssp. *schultzii* (Billot) Kirschl. Erect, to 20cm. Pet. obovate; spur straight. Z6.

V. capensis Thunb. = Hybanthus capensis.

V. cazorlensis Gand. Shrubby perenn., to 15cm, woody-based. Lvs narrow-elliptic to oblanceolate, to 15mm; stipules entire or seg. 2. Fls rosy-lilac to violet-red; pet. narrow, to 10mm, lower pet. deeply emarginate; spur bowed, to 3cm. Summer. SE Spain.

V. cenisia L. Perenn. to 9cm, procumbent, glab. to pubesc. Lvs oblong, entire, to 10mm, lower lvs ovate; stipules leafy. Fls bright violet; pet. to 13mm; spur graceful. Summer. SW Alps. Z6.

V. chaerophylloides Mak. Stemless perenn., to 13cm. Lvs tripartite, seg. 2–3-lobed, dentate, lanceolate-ovate in older plants, ± pale. Fls violet or white; pet. to 13mm; spur stout, to 5mm. SE Asia. Z8.

V. chrysantha Hook. = *V. douglasii.*

V. colliculina anon. = *V. hirta.*

V. comollia Massara. As for *V. cenisia* but fls pale purple, with an orange to yellow spot. N It. Alps.

V. conspersa Rchb. AMERICAN DOG VIOLET. As for *V. canina* but taller, more rounded. Lvs to 4cm wide. Fls pale violet to white; veins dark violet; spur tinged purple, to 5mm. E N Amer. Z4.

V. cornuta L. VIOLA; HORNED VIOLET; BEDDING PANSY. Perenn., to 30cm, prostrate then ascending. Lvs ovate, to 25mm wide, pubesc. beneath, glab. above, base cordate to truncate, shallow-crenate; stipules triangular, leafy, segmented. Fls violet; pet. obovate to obtuse, to 18mm, spur slender, to 13mm, slightly bowed. Summer. Pyren., Spain. 'Alba': fls white. 'Atropurpurea': pet. dark violet with yellow eye. 'Bessie Cawthorne': fls rounded, deep purple with white eye. 'Evelyn Cawthorne': habit compact; fls cream later mottled mauve, thin rays. 'Leora Hamilton': fls white somewhat suffused pale blue. 'Lilacina': fls soft silver lilac. 'Minor': habit miniature, compact; fls pale violet. 'Papilio': fls large, pet. violet with lavender eye. 'Purpurea': pet. purple. 'Tony Venison': lvs variegated with golden-yellow; fls pale blue lightly striped white. 'Variegata': lvs yellow ageing to green; fls pale blue. 'Victoria Cawthorne': hardy; fls star-shaped, purple-pink, on long st. Z7.

V. corsica Nyman. Perenn., to 20cm, glab., flimsy. Lvs rhombic to orbicular; upper lvs oblong to linear, to 3cm, subcrenate to entire; stipules linear. Fls rectangular, to 35mm, violet, occas. yellow; spur to 15mm, somewhat bowed. Corsica, Sardinia. Z9.

V. crassa Mak. Perenn., to 12cm, subglabrous, creeping. Lvs reniform to cordate to 4.5cm across, rounded, waxy-toothed; stipules ovate. Fls deep yellow; pet. to 12mm, lower pet. striped dark brown. Jap.

V. cucullata Ait. = *V. obliqua.*

V. cuneata S. Wats. As for *V. ocellata,* but lower lf bases cuneate. W US. Z5.

V. cunninghamii Hook. f. Stemless, glab. perenn., to 15cm. Lvs ovate to triangular, to 25mm wide, entire to crenate; stipules adnate, lanceolate. Fls white to pale violet; pet. to 1cm; spur to 2mm. Spring. NZ. Z8.

V. curtisii E. Forst. = *V. tricolor.*

V. cyanea Čelak. = *V. suavis.*

V. declinata Waldst. & Kit. Perenn., to 30cm+; stoloniferous, ascending. Lvs ovate, to 3cm, crenate, glab. to ciliate, base truncate to subcordate; stipules pinnately segmented. Fls violet, throat yellow; pet. to 15mm; spur to 4mm, bowed. E Eur. (E to S Carpath.). Z5.

V. delphinantha Boiss. Clumped perenn., to 10cm. St. erect. Lvs lanceolate or linear, to 15mm, entire. Fls purple tinged pink to red; pet. narrow; spur to 18mm+. N Greece, Bulg. Z6.

V. delphinifolia Nutt. = *V. pedatifida.*

V. dissecta Ledeb. Stemless perenn., to 10cm. Lvs tripartite, seg. divided, lanceolate, slightly pubesc.; stipules adnate, lanceolate. Fls pale rose, fragrant; pet. to 18mm; spur to 5mm. Spring. Jap.

V. dissecta var. *chaerophylloides* (Reg.) Mak. = *V. dissecta.*

V. dissecta var. *eizanensis* Mak. = *V. dissecta.*

V. douglasii Steud. St. leafy, to 15cm. Lvs bipinnate, pubesc., seg. linear; stipules lanceolate. Pet. to 15mm+, bright orange yellow, veins violet, upper 2 pet. exterior yellow-brown, lat. pet. bearded; spur to 2mm. Spring. W US. Z5.

V. dubyana Burnat ex Gremli. St. to 30cm. Lvs orbicular, to 4cm; upper lvs narrow; stipules pinnately divided to ×6. Fls to 25mm, violet; lower pet. with a yellow spot; spur to 6mm, slender, bowed. N It. (Alps).

V. eizanensis Mak. = *V. dissecta.*

V. elatior Fries. As for *V. pumila* but erect, larger, to 50cm. Lvs to 9×2cm; stipules to 5cm; fls to 2.5cm. Spring–summer. C & E Eur., W Asia. Z5.

V. elegantula Schott. Perenn., frequently grown as bienn., to 30cm. St. ascending. Lvs ovate to subcordate, to 2cm, upper lvs ovate to lanceolate, base cuneate; stipules ovate, pinnately divded to ×10. Fls to 25mm; pet. rose-violet, yellow or part-striped, occas. white to pink; spur slender, to 8mm, ± bowed. Summer. W Balk., Albania. Z6.

V. ×emarginata (Nutt.) Le Conte. TRIANGULAR LEAVED VIOLET. (*V. affinis* ×*V. sagittata.*) Variable hybrids, usually as for *V. sagittata,* but lvs narrow triangular, base not conspicuously toothed. US.

V. epipsila Ledeb. As for *V. palustris,* but larger. Lvs paired, orbicular-cordate to reniform. Infl. stalk bracteate in top third; fls to 2cm. EC & C Eur. Z5.

V. eriocarpa Schwein. = *V. pubescens* var. *eriocarpa.*

V. fimbriatula Sm. FRINGED VIOLET; RATTLESNAKE VIOLET; NORTHERN DOWNY VIOLET. Stemless perenn., to 10cm. Lvs ovate to oblong-ovate, pubesc. beneath, base cordate, serrulate. Fls to 18mm; pet. purple to blue-violet, lower pet. veins darker violet. Spring. US.

V. flavicornis E. Forst. ex Nyman = *V. canina.*

V. flettii Piper. ROCK VIOLET; OLYMPIC VIOLET. Perenn., to 15cm, creeping. Lvs ovate to reniform, to 4cm wide, glab. to pubesc., base cordate, dentate; stipules lanceolate. Fls violet; pet. to 13mm, base yellow, veined dark violet; spur yellow, inconspicuous. Washington.

V. ×florariensis Correv. (*V. cornuta* ×*V. tricolor.*) As for *V. cornuta,* but fls purple, lower pet. base yellow, striped purple; spur inconspicuous. Spring–autumn. Gdn origin.

V. glabella Nutt. STREAM VIOLET. Perenn., to 30cm. St. occas. pubesc. Lvs reniform to ovate, base cordate; stipules narrow-ovate. Fls yellow, veins purple; pet. to 13mm; spur to 2mm. Spring. NE Asia, W N Amer. Z5.

V. gracilis Sibth. & Sm. As for *V. bertolonii* but lvs oblong to broad-ovate, ± dentate; stipules 4–8 parted, short pubesc. Fls large, deep violet, lower pet. to 13mm; spur slender, to 7mm. Greece, Balk. Penins. to Asia Minor. 'Alba': fls white. 'Lutea': fls yellow. 'Major': large; fls velvet-mauve. 'Roem van Aalsmeer': fls violet-blue.

V. grandiflora hort. An invalid name used for many cvs.

V. grisebachiana Vis. Perenn., to 8cm, stemless. Lvs orbicular to ovate, to 3cm, base cuneate; stipules oblanceolate, leafy. Fls to yellow or blue; pet. to 15mm, lat. pet. pointing upwards; spur to 4mm, blunt. C Balk. Penins.

V. hallii A. Gray. As for *V. beckwithii,* but 2 upper pet. violet, 3

lower pet. yellow or white. W US. Z5.

V. hastata Michx. HALBERD-LEAVED VIOLET. Perenn. to 25cm. Lvs narrow-lanceolate to ovate, or hastate, to 35mm wide, base cordate, often lobed. Fls yellow; pet. to 8mm, lower pet. to 13mm, veins purple; spur to 1mm. Spring–summer. E N Amer. Z3.

V. hederacea Labill. AUSTRALIAN VIOLET; TRAILING VIOLET. Stemless perenn., to 7.5cm. Lvs ovate to reniform, to 35mm wide, entire to dentate, base cordate to cuneate. Fls blue-violet to white; pet. to 13mm, lat. pet. bearded; spur inconspicuous. Summer. Aus.

V. heterophylla Bertol. non Poir. = *V. bertolonii.*

V. hiemalis hort. A name of no botanical standing.

V. hirta L. As for *V. odorata,* but stolons 0; lvs narrower, more conspicuously pubesc.; fls less noticeably perfumed. Spring–summer. C & N Eur.

V. hispida Lam. ROUEN PANSY. As for *V. tricolor,* but st. pubesc. Spring–summer. Fr. Z8.

V. hortensis Wettst. & auct. = *V. ×wittrockiana.*

V. hybrida Wulf. ex Roem. & Schult. = *V. uliginosa.*

V. incognita Brainerd. LARGE-LEAVED WHITE VIOLET. As for *V. blanda* but lat. pet. pubesc.; petioles and peduncles, pubesc.; lvs pubesc. beneath, basal lobes longer. US.

V. incognita var. *forbesii* Brainerd = *V. incognita.*

V. japonica Langsd. Subglabrous perenn. Lvs ovate to triangular-ovate, 5(–8)cm, dentate, glab. above. Fls purple; pet. to 15mm, lat. pet. interior pubesc.; spur to 8mm. Spring. Jap., S Korea, Ryukyus.

V. jooi Janka. Stemless perenn., to 7.5cm. Lvs ovate, to 3cm wide, base cordate, glab., crenate; stipules adnate, linear-lanceolate. Fls mauve with purple streaks; pet. to 13mm; spur to 5mm. Spring–summer. SE Eur., Transylvania. Z5.

V. juressi (Link ex Wein) Cout. = *V. palustris.*

V. kitaibelina var. *rafinesquii* (Greene) Fern. = *V. rafinesquii.*

V. kosaninii (Deg.) Hayek. As for *V. cazorlensis* but fls pale pink-purple; lower pet. emarginate; spur to 12mm. N Albania, N Macedonia. Z6.

V. labradorica Schrank. LABRADOR VIOLET. As for *V. adunca* but smaller, to 7.5cm, glab. N US, Greenland, Canada. 'Purpurea': lvs purple; fls spurred, violet-purple. Z2.

V. lactea Sm. PALE DOG VIOLET. As for *V. canina* but st. more erect. Lvs narrow, ovate lanceolate to lanceolate, to 3cm. Fls pale blue-white; spur green. Spring–summer. W Eur. Z7.

V. lanceolata L. EASTERN WATER VIOLET. Creeping, glab. perenn. Lvs narrow-lanceolate to linear or elliptic, to 7.5cm, glab., subentire; stipules lanceolate; petiole red. Fls white; lower pet. to 1.5cm, veined purple, lat. pet. pubesc. or glab.; spur to 1mm. Spring–summer. E N Amer.

V. langsdorfii (Reg.) Fisch. ALASKA VIOLET. Glab. perenn., to 20cm. Lvs ovate-cordate to reniform, undulate to dentate; stipules streaked red. Fls blue or violet to white; pet. to 2.5cm, lower pet. white at base, lat. pet. white-pubesc.; spur broad. Spring. NE Asia, Sib., N Amer., Alask. to Oreg.

V. lobata Benth. YELLOW WOOD VIOLET. Perenn., to 38cm. Lvs pinnately divided, seg. 3–7, oblong; stipules ovate, dentate. Fls yellow, exterior violet; pet. to 13mm, lower 3 to 18mm, veined brown; spur to 2mm. Spring–summer. W US. Z5.

V. lutea Huds. MOUNTAIN PANSY. As for *V. tricolor* but creeping perenn., to 20cm; fls to 3cm, bright yellow, upper 2 pet. sometimes purple, or whole fl. purple. Spring–summer. W & C Eur. ssp. *lutea.* To 10cm+. Lvs conspicuously pubesc. Lower pet. to 1.5cm wide. ssp. *sudetica* (Willd.) W. Becker. To 15cm+. Lvs glab. or subglabrous; lower pet. to 2cm wide. Z5.

V. macedonica Boiss. & Heldr. = *V. tricolor* ssp. *macedonica.*

V. macloskeyi F. Lloyd. WESTERN SWEET WHITE VIOLET. Stemless perenn., to 15cm; stolons leafy. Lvs cordate to orbicular, base reniform, subentire to crenate. Fls white; lower pet. veined purple, lat. pet. glab. to pubesc. E & W US (mts). var. *pallens* (Banks) C. Hitchc. Lvs crenate, to 25mm+.

V. mandshurica W. Becker. Stemless perenn., to 20cm. Lvs triangular to oblong-lanceolate, to 7.5cm. Fls dark purple or white with purple stripes; spur to 6mm. SE Eur., E Asia. Z8.

V. metajaponica Nak. = *V. japonica.*

V. mirabilis L. As for *V. riviana* but to 20cm. St. with a line of hairs. Fls to 2cm, pale violet; spur to 8mm, tinged white. Eur., N Asia. Z5.

V. missouriensis Greene. BANDED VIOLET; MISSOURI VIOLET. Stemless, glab. perenn., to 15cm. Lvs deltoid to ovate-cordate, base cordate, dentate. Fls pale violet, with a white eye, veined dark violet, lat. pet. pubesc. US. Z5.

V. montanensis Rydb. = *V. adunca.*

V. munbyana Boiss. & Reut. Perenn., to 20cm, ascending. Lvs subcordate to ovate, to 15×25mm, base subcordate, crenate; stipules pinnatifid, seg. 3–5. Fls dark violet to yellow; pet. to 18mm; spur straight, to 13mm. N Afr., NW Sicily.

V. nana. hort. Name of no botanical standing.

V. nephrophylla Greene. NORTHERN BOG VIOLET. Glab. perenn. Lvs cordate-ovate or reniform, undulate-dentate or crenate. Fls deep blue-violet, to 25mm+; pet. base white, densely pubesc., lower pet. veined dark violet; spur to 3mm. N Amer.

V. nicolai Pantl. = *V. orphanidis* ssp. *nicolai*.

V. nuttalii Pursh. YELLOW PRAIRIE VIOLET. To 13cm; rhiz. erect. Lvs oblong-elliptic to lanceolate ovate, to 4cm, subentire to entire; stipules narrow-lanceolate. Fls yellow, to 15mm; lower pet. to 6mm, veins brown; spur inconspicuous. W N Amer. var. **bakeri** (Greene) C. Hitchc. Lvs to 5cm. Fls to 12mm; upper pet. yellow beneath.

V. obliqua Hill. MARSH BLUE VIOLET. Stemless perenn., to 15cm. Lvs ovate to reniform, to 9cm wide, glab., base cordate, shallowly crenate; stipules lanceolate. Fls blue-violet, base white; lat. pet. to 18mm, short-pubesc.; spur to 2mm. Spring–summer. N Amer. 'Alba': fls white. 'Alice Witter': fls large, white with red eye. 'Bicolor': fls white, eye violet. 'Gloriole': fls white with sky-blue eye. 'Red Giant': fls large, deep red. 'Rosea': fls rose-pink. 'Snow Princess': fls pure white.

V. ocellata Torr. & A. Gray. TWO-EYED VIOLET. Short-stemmed perenn., to 30cm. Lvs lanceolate to cordate, to 13mm wide, pubesc., crenate; stipules lanceolate. Fls white; upper 2 pet. exterior violet, lower 3 pet. to 18mm, veined purple, lowermost with a yellow basal patch; spur short. US (Calif., S Oreg.). Z5.

V. odorata L. SWEET VIOLET; GARDEN VIOLET; ENGLISH VIOLET. Stoloniferous perenn., to 15cm. Lvs broad-ovate to suborbicular, or reniform, to 6cm wide, pubesc., crenate; stipules narrow ovate, glandular-toothed. Fls fragrant, dark violet, lilac or white, or yellow; peduncle bracteate at or above middle; pet. to 13mm+; spur to 5mm. Winter–spring. S, SC & W Eur., widely nat. Many cvs available, varying in size and fl. colour; double-fld forms available. Z8.

V. oedemansii W. Becker = *V. japonica*.

V. olympica Boiss. = *V. gracilis*.

V. orbiculata Geyer ex Hook. WESTERN ROUND LEAVED VIOLET. As for *V. sempervirens* but stolons 0; lvs ± round, decid. W N Amer.

V. orphanidis Boiss. Perenn., to 70cm, soft-pubesc., erect to prostrate. Lvs ovate or orbicular to subcordate, to 4cm, serrate to crenate; stipules ovate, laciniate. Fls blue to violet; lower pet. to 15mm with yellow patch; spur to 5mm, curved. Balk. ssp. **nicolai** (Pantl.) Valent. Fls to 3cm, violet. Z9.

V. pallens (Banks) Brainerd = *V. macloskeyi* var. *pallens*.

V. palmata L. EARLY BLUE VIOLET; WILD OKRA. Stemless perenn., to 14cm. Lvs palmately lobed, pubesc. beneath, seg. 5–11, toothed. Fls violet; pet. to 18mm, lower pet. base white, veins darker violet. Spring. US. Z4.

V. palustris L. MARSH VIOLET; ALPINE MARSH VIOLET. Stemless perenn., to 13cm. Lvs orbicular, reniform, to 6.5cm wide, glab., undulate to dentate; stipules ovate or lanceolate sometimes dentate. Fls pale to dark lavender, white, veins dark violet; stalks long, bracteate in upper half; pet. to 1cm; spur to 2mm, pale lavender, glab. Eur., Asia, N Amer.

V. papilio hort. = *V. cornuta* 'Papilio'.

V. papilionacea Pursh = *V. sororaria*.

V. papilionacea var. *priceana* (Pollard) Alexander = *V. sororaria*.

V. parviflora Mutis = *Hybanthus parviflorus*.

V. patrinii DC. Stemless perenn., to 15cm. Lvs triangular-ovate to linear-oblong, to 25mm wide, glab., subentire to crenate or serrate, base truncate or subcordate. Fls lilac, or white tinged; pet. to 1cm; spur to 2mm. Sib. to Jap.

V. pedata L. BIRD'S FOOT VIOLET; PANSY VIOLET; CROWFOOT VIOLET. Stemless perenn., to 15cm. Lvs palmately divided, glab., seg. 3–5, narrow, split near apex, ± ciliate; stipules linear-lanceolate, adnate, fimbriate. Pet. pubesc., to 15mm, upper pet. dark violet, lower 3 pet. pale violet, veins dark violet; spur to 2mm. Spring–summer. E N Amer. 'Bicolor': fls bicolored, pale lilac and dark violet. Z4.

V. pedata var. *concolor* Holm = *V. pedata*.

V. pedata var. *lineariloba* DC. = *V. pedata*.

V. pedatifida G. Don. LARKSPUR VIOLET; PURPLE PRAIRIE VIOLET. As for *V. pedata*, but fls smaller, resembling a peaflower or butterfly; lower pet. white-pubesc. Spring–summer. N Amer. Z2.

V. pedunculata Torr. & A. Gray. CALIFORNIA GOLDEN VIOLET; GRASS PANSY; JOHNNY-JUMP-UP; GALLITO. Perenn., to 30cm. Lvs broad-ovate to triangular, to 5cm wide, ± glab., base truncate to subcordate, crenate; stipules narrow elliptic-oblong, ± entire. Fls yellow, interior veins purple; pet. 12–18mm, lower pet. veins brown; spur 1–2mm. Spring. W US. Z8.

V. pennsylvanica Michx. = *V. pubescens* var. *eriocarpa*.

V. ×permixta Jordan. (*V. hirta* x *V. odorata*.) Resembles *V. hirta* but shorter, lvs shorter, blunter, less conspicuously pubesc. Fls more precocious, frequently flowering in autumn; stolons present. C & S Eur.

V. persicifolia Schreb. As for *V. pumila*, but lvs triangular-lanceolate to cordate; fls smaller, white, occas. tinged blue, veined violet. Spring–summer. Eur. (except Medit.), N Asia. Z5.

V. pinnata L. Perenn., to 10cm. Lvs to 6cm, deeply pinnatifid, subglabrous to minutely pubesc., seg. narrow; stipules adnate, lanceolate. Fls fragrant; pet. to 13mm, blue-violet to pale violet; spur to 5mm. C Eur. Alps, N Asia. Z5.

V. pontica W. Becker = *V. suavis*.

V. praemorsa Douglas ex Lindl. Lvs cuneate, width to over one-third of length, densely pubesc. var. **vallicola** (Nels.) St. John. Lf width greater than one-third of length, base truncate or subcordate, glab. to scantily pubesc.

V. pratensis Mert. & Koch = *V. pumila*.

V. priceana Pollard = *V. sororaria*.

V. primulifolia L. PRIMROSE-LEAVED VIOLET. Perenn., to 25cm; rhiz. erect; stolons leafy. Lvs ovate to oblong-ovate, to 4cm wide, subglabrous, base cuneate to subcordate, crenate; stipules narrow-lanceolate. Fls white; pet. to 8mm, lower pet. veined purple, bearded, petioles winged; spur to 2mm. E N Amer. Z4.

V. pringlei Rose & House = *V. blanda*.

V. pubescens Ait. DOWNY YELLOW VIOLET. Perenn., to 25cm. St. pubesc. Lvs broad-ovate to reniform or cordate, pubesc., shallow-crenate; stipules ovate to narrow-lanceolate. Fls yellow; pet. to 12mm, lower pet. veined brown, lateral pet. bearded; spur to 2mm. Spring. E N Amer. var. **eriocarpa** (Schwein.) N. Russell. SMOOTH YELLOW VIOLET. To 15cm. Lvs glab. to fine-pubesc. Z4.

V. pumila Chaix. As for *V. elatior*, but smaller, to 15cm (occas. more), subglabrous. Lvs to 3×1cm; lf bases cuneate, occas. rounded. Fls to 15mm, light to dark blue-violet. Eur., W Asia. Z5.

V. purpurea Kellogg. PINE VIOLET. Short-pubesc. perenn., to 20cm. Lvs rounded, ovate, base cuneate, undulate; stipules entire to dentate. Pet. yellow to 12mm, 2 upper pet. exterior red to purple-brown, lat. pet. pubesc., lower pet. veined brown-purple; spur pouch-like. Spring. SW US. Z5.

V. rafinesquii Greene. FIELD PANSY. Ann., to 38cm. St. glab. Lvs spathulate to obovate above, dentate base rounded; stipules pectinate, lat. pet. pubesc. Fls to 13mm across, cream to blue-white; lower pet. veined dark purple, lat. pet. pubesc. E US. Z4.

V. reichenbachiana Jordan ex Boreau. As for *V. riviana* but smaller; fls to 18mm, pale violet; pet. narrower, spur slender, to 6mm, dark purple. Spring. S, W & C Eur., N Afr., Asia. 'Rosea': fls pink. Z8.

V. renifolia A. Gray. NORTHERN WHITE VIOLET; KIDNEY-LEAVED WHITE VIOLET. Glab. to softly pubesc. perenn., to 10cm. Lvs orbicular to reniform, to 7.5cm wide, crenate to serrate. Fls white; lower 3 pet. veined brown. Spring–summer. C US. Z5.

V. riviana Rchb. WOOD VIOLET; DOG VIOLET. Perenn., to 20cm+. Lvs broad-ovate to orbicular, to 4cm, base cordate, crenate; stipules lanceolate. Fls blue-violet; pet. to 12mm; spur pale blue-violet, to 5mm. Spring–summer. Eur., N Afr. Z5.

V. rosacea Brainerd = *V. affinis*.

V. rostrata Pursh. LONG-SPURRED VIOLET. Perenn., to 20cm. Lvs broad-ovate, to 3cm wide, glab., base cordate, crenate; stipules lanceolate, dentate, ciliate. Fls to 15mm, pale lavender, lower pet. marked violet; spur 13mm. Spring–summer. E N American. Z4.

V. rothomagensis auct. = *V. hispida*.

V. rotundifolia Michx. EASTERN ROUND-LEAVED VIOLET; EARLY YELLOW VIOLET. Perenn., to 7.5cm, sparsely pubesc. Lvs stiffly pubesc. above, orbicular to ovoid, to 5cm wide, base cordate, crenate; stipules ovate. Fls yellow; lower pet. veined purple-brown, lat. pet. pubesc. Spring. E N Amer. Z4.

V. rugulosa Greene = *V. canadensis* var. *rugulosa*.

V. rupestris F.W. Schmidt. TEESDALE VIOLET. As for *V. riviana* but smaller, to 5cm; lvs cordate to reniform. Fls violet, occas. tinged red or blue, lower pet. notched. Eur., Asia, N Amer. ssp. **relicta** Jalas. Lower pet. scarcely notched.

V. sagittata Ait. ARROW-LEAF VIOLET. Perenn., to 10cm. Lvs oblong to sagittate, to 4cm wide, purple beneath, base toothed. Fls blue to violet, veins dark blue to violet; lower 3 pet. bases white; spur pubesc. at base. Spring–summer. US. Z5.

V. sarmentosa Douglas ex Hook. = *V. sempervirens*.

V. saxatalis var. *aetolica* (Boiss. & Heldr.) Hayek = *V. aetolica*.

V. saxatilis F.W. Schmidt = *V. tricolor* ssp. *subalpina*.

V. scabriuscula Schwein. ex Torr. & A. Gray = *V. pubescens* var. *eriocarpa*.

V. scotophylla Jordan = *V. alba* ssp. *scotophylla*.

V. sempervirens Greene. REDWOOD VIOLET; EVERGREEN VIOLET. Perenn., to 8cm, stoloniferous. Lvs persistent, broad-ovate, to 3cm across, base cuneate, ± pubesc. above, speckled dark brown, dentate; stipules lanceolate. Pet. to 13mm, yellow, lower pet. veined brown; spur inconspicuous. W N Amer.

V. sepincola Jordan = *V. suavis*.

V. septemloba Le Conte. SOUTHERN COAST VIOLET. As for *V. brittoniana* but lvs pedately incised, later lvs frequently uncut; pet. red-violet. E US. Z7.

V. septentrionalis Greene. NORTHERN BLUE VIOLET. Perenn., to 14cm+; rhiz. creeping. Lvs ovate to cordate or reniform, crenate, ciliate. Fls lavender to violet or white, veins dark violet; lower pet. densely pubesc., base white. Spring–summer. N Amer. Z4.

V. sheltonii Torr. Glab. to sparsely pubesc. perenn., to 15cm. Lvs orbicular, glab., 3-lobed, lobes segmented, veins purple beneath. Fls yellow, marked purple; 2 upper pet. exterior brown, lower pet. veined purple. Spring. W N Amer. Z5.

V. sororaria Willd. WOOLLY BLUE VIOLET. Villous or glab. perenn. to 8cm. Lvs ovate to rounded, crenate, to 10cm across, densely pubesc. beneath, crenate; stipules linear-lanceolate. Fls deep blue violet to white; pet. to 13mm, lower pet. white at base, veins dark violet, lat. pet. white-pubesc.; spur to 3mm. Spring–summer. E N Amer. 'Albiflora' ('Immaculata'): fls pure white. 'Freckles': fls white flecked blue. Z4.

V. stagnina Kit. = *V. persicifolia*.

V. stojanowii W. Becker. Stiffly pubesc. perenn., to 10cm. Lvs linear-spathulate, to 2cm, entire; stipules linear-spathulate. Fls yellow; pet. to 8mm, upper pet. occas. tinged violet; spur to 5mm. Balk. Penins. Z9.

V. striata Ait. PALE VIOLET; STRIPED VIOLET; CREAM VIOLET. Perenn., to 25cm+. Lvs orbicular to ovate, to 5cm across, base cordate, sparsely pubesc. above, crenate; stipules linear-lanceolate, dentate. Fls white or creamy white; pet. to 13mm, lower pet. striped purple; spur to 6mm. Spring. E N Amer. Z4.

V. suavis Bieb. RUSSIAN VIOLET. Stemless stoloniferous perenn. Lvs cordate-ovate glab., pale green, shiny, crenate, long-stalked, stipules lanceolate, fimbriate. Fls blue to violet; pet. 13mm, lower pet. notched; spur to 10mm. Spring. E Eur. Z5.

V. sudetica Willd. = *V. lutea* ssp. *sudetica*.

V. sylvatica (Hartm.) Fries ex Hartm. = *V. reichenbachiana*.

V. sylvestris Lam., in part. = *V. reichenbachiana*.

V. tricolor L. WILD PANSY; HEART'S-EASE; LOVE-IN-IDLENESS; JOHNNY JUMP UP; PINK OF MY JOHN. Ann., bienn. or perenn. to 30cm+. Lvs ovate to lanceolate, base cordate to cuneate, crenate; stipules pinnately lobed. Fls violet, yellow, pale violet or bicoloured; pet. to 13mm, 2 upper pet. violet or mauve, lat. pet. white striped black, lowest pet. white, base yellow, striped black; spur to 7mm. Eur., Asia. 'Blue Elf': deep violet and pale blue with golden eye. 'E.A. Bowles' ('Bowles Black'): fls velvety black. 'Helen Mount': fls violet, lavender and pale yellow. 'Maxima': st. long; lvs glaucous; fls v. large, normally tricoloured, deep indigo, yellow or white with dark eye, or combination of other colours. 'Prince Henry': fls purple with golden-yellow eye. 'Prince John': fls golden-yellow. The above may be hybrids assignable to *V.* × *wittrockiana*. ssp. *tricolor*. Usually ann., to 40cm+. Fls blue-violet, occas. yellow, spur to 5mm. ssp. *curtisii* (E. Forst.) Syme. Usually perenn., to 15cm. Lvs and stipules narrow. Fls variable. ssp. *macedonica* (Boiss. & Heldr.) A. Schmidt. Usually perenn., to 20cm. St. erect. Pet. yellow, upper pet. vivid violet, lat. pet. veins 0. ssp. *subalpina* Gaudin. Usually perenn., to 30cm+. Fls to 35mm, yellow, upper pet. occasionaly violet. Z4.

V. tricolor var. *hortensis* DC. = *V. tricolor*.

V. triloba Schwein. THREE-LOBED LEAF VIOLET; THREE-PARTED TRILOBA. As for *V. sororaria* but lvs entire, cordate to reniform or 3-lobed at flowering, lat. lobe seg. 2, lower seg. coarse-dentate on lower margin. Spring. E US. var. *dilatata* (Elliott) Brainerd. CUT-LEAVED TRILOBA. Lf middle seg. narrower, lat. lobe seg. 3. Z4.

V. trinervata T.J. Howell. SAGEBRUSH VIOLET. Perenn., to 7.5cm. Lvs palmately divided, seg. 3–7, narrow, glab., stipitate; stipule adnate. Fls small; upper pet. violet, lower pet. pale blue to white; spur yellow, to 2mm. NW US. Z5.

V. uliginosa Besser. As for *V. palustris* but lvs cordate; fls larger, to 3cm, violet. C, W Russia. Z4.

V. valderia All. As for *V. cenisia* but to 7.5cm, more conspicuously pubesc.; lf stipule seg. 2–7. Fls vivid lilac-purple. It., Fr. (maritime Alps). Z7.

V. vallicola Nels. = *V. praemorsa* var. *vallicola*.

V. variegata Vukot. = *V. tricolor*.

V. verecunda A. Gray. Glab. perenn. Lvs reniform to cordate, to 2cm, obtuse; stipules lanceolate. Fls white; pet. to 1cm, lat. pet. base pubesc.; spur to 3mm. Spring. Korea, China, Manch. var. *yakusimana* (Nak.) Ohwi. Dwarf; lvs to 7mm across. Pet. to 5mm.

V. viarum Pollard. PLAINS VIOLET. Glab. perenn., to 20cm. Lvs triangular, 3–7-lobed, sinuate-dentate, long-stalked. Fls to 18mm, buff red-violet to deep violet; 2 upper pet. emarginate, spreading, lat. pet. pubesc. W US. Z5.

V. walteri House. PROSTRATE BLUE VIOLET; PROSTRATE SOUTHERN VIOLET. Fine-pubesc. perenn., to 20cm, procumbent. Lvs

ovate to orbicular, to 4cm wide, apex rounded, mottled dark green, occas. tinged red or purple. Fls blue-violet, lower pet. base white, veins dark violet, lateral pet. pubesc., spur to 8mm. Spring. S US. Z8.

V. × *williamsii* auct. = *V.* × *wittrockiana*.

V. × *wittrockiana*** Gams. PANSY; LADIES'-DELIGHT; HEART'S EASE; STEPMOTHER'S FLOWER. Ann. or short-lived perenn., to 30cm. Lvs ovate to subcordate, crenate, upper lvs elliptic-lanceolate, base cuneate, entire; stipules pinnately cut. Fls to 5cm+ across; pet. orbicular, lat. pet. overlapped by lower pet.; spur to 5mm. Gdn origin. 'Azure Blue': fls sky-blue. 'Beaconsfield': upper pet. pale blue, lower pet. deep blue; winter flowering. 'Black Prince': habit dwarf; fls large, creped, black with yellow eye. 'Bruno': fls mahogany red, pet. margins yellow. Crystal Bowl Hybrids: habit compact; lvs small; fls large in range of colours, without marking, abundant. 'Gemini': fls purple, pet. margins ivory. 'Glacier Ice': fls deep blue, darkly blotched, yellow and white centre. 'Love Duet': fls large, cream-yellow blotched raspberry-red. 'Jolly Joker': habit compact, tolerant of heat; upper pet. purple, lower orange. Lyric Hybrids: fls v. large in range of colours including shades of white, yellow, red and blue, often with dark mask; early spring flowering. 'Rippling Waters': fls dark purple edged white. 'Silver Bride': fls white with violet blotch. Universal Hybrids (including 'Beaconsfield'): habit compact, hardy; fls in range of colours including white, yellow, red, blue and purple, some blotched; winter flowering.

V. yakusimana Nak. = *V. verecunda* var. *yakusimana*.

V. yatabei Mak. = *V. yesoensis*.

V. yesoensis Maxim. Stemless perenn. Lvs ovate, to 6cm, or larger after flowering, base cordate, bluntly-dentate. Fls white, striped purple; pet. to 2cm, lateral pet. bearded; spur to 8mm. Spring. Jap.

VIOLET CULTIVARS. Derived from the cross-breeding of *V. odorata* with *V. suavis* and the French 'La Violette de Quatre Saisons', it is now unclear to what extent present-day cvs are derived from *V. odorata*. Numerous cvs display a wide range of characteristics with fl. colour and form as the main distinguishing features; fls single, semi-double and double in shades of white, pink, mauve, blue and purple, occas. striped or variously marked; sweetly scented.

Scented Single Violets: 'Amiral Avellan' ('Admiral Avellan'): hardy; fls red tinged purple, tending to fade, abundant, strongly scented. 'Baronne Alice de Rothschild' ('Baron/Baroness Rothschild'): st. long; fls v. large, blue; early flowering. 'Coeur de Alsace': fls rosy salmon. 'The Czar': st. long; fls deep purple. 'Governor Herrick': disease-resistant; fls deep blue shaded purple, unscented, long-lasting. 'Mrs R. Barton': st. long; fls white marked in varying shades of violet, abundant. 'Perle Rose': habit compact; fls deep coral-pink; late flowering. 'Princess of Wales': fls v. large, lilac-blue. 'Rawson's White': fls white, early blooms tinged pink, abundant. 'Sulphurea': fls cream centred deep apricot, unscented.

Scented Semi-double Violets: 'Countess of Shaftesbury': st. long; outer pet. blue, inner pet. rose-pink. 'Cyclope': st. long; pet. blue with white and orange rosette. 'Mrs David Lloyd George': outer pet. blue with large rosette in various colours. 'Reine des Blanches': fls white. *Scented Double Violets*: 'Alba Plena de Chevreuse': buds rose opening to white fls. 'Brandyana': st. somewhat short; fls deep blue striped rose. 'Champlatreux': fls white; long-flowering. 'Double Red': fls copper-red; long-flowering. 'Patrie': fls blue tinged purple streaked red. 'Purple King': fls black tinged purple.

SCENTED PARMA VIOLETS. A large number of cvs possibly derived from *V. suavis*; habit compact, tender; lvs small, glossy, pointed; fls generally double in range of colours including shades of white, pink, mauve and blue, occas. marked or striped. 'Comte Brazza' ('White Parma', 'Swanley White'): fls white with faint pale blue shading. 'Evelyn Kelly': fls dark blue. 'Lady Hume Campbell': disease resistant; fls lavender; late-flowering. 'Madame Millet': fls lilac-rose. 'Marie Louise': fls potentially v. large, deep lavender-mauve, heavily scented. 'Mrs J.J. Kettle': fls mauve tinged silver blotched red. 'Perfection': fls pale blue; early flowering. 'Queen Mary': fls deep violet blue.

HYBRID VIOLAS. A large number of cvs for which the seed-bearing parents *V. lutea*, *V. amoena* and *V. cornuta* were crossed with most of the Show and Fancy pansies. Habit compact, perenn., free-flowering; st. neat, short-jointed; fls in range of colours including white and black and shades of cream, yellow, blue, mauve and purple, often with contrasting centres, striped or marked, frilled. 'Achilles': fls white with hint of mauve. 'Admiration': fls dark purple centred yellow. 'Ardross Gem': fls dusky gold and light blue. 'Buxton Blue': habit compact; fls blue with blue-black centre. 'Huntercombe Purple': fls elongated, purple-violet centred white. 'Iden Gem': growth vigorous; st. long; fls deep violet; long-flowering. 'Irish Molly': fls rayed, khaki tinged yellow centred bronze-khaki. 'Jackanapes': fls rayed, top 2 pet. rich brown, bottom 3 pet. yellow. 'Julian': fls pale lilac-blue centred yellow, fragrant. 'Lord Plunkett': fls large, maroon-purple centred yellow; long-flowering. 'Maggie Mott': habit somewhat tall; fls mauve shaded silver with pale cream centre. 'Martin': fls elongated, deep violet-blue centred yellow. 'Mollie Sanderson': habit low, compact; fls jet black centred yellow. 'Moonlight': st. long; fls elongated, cream-yellow self. 'Nellie Britten' ('Haslemere'): fls lavender-pink, rayed. 'Pickering Blue': fls large, sky-blue centred orange and deeply rayed. 'Vita': fls small, pale pink self centred yellow.

HYBRID VIOLETTAS. Derived from *V. cornuta* and *V. c.* var. *alba* crossed with named violas, these violettas are of more compact habit than the violas with small, oval fls carried on erect st. above bright green lvs; fls in clear colours with golden-yellow eyes; vanilla-like fragrance. 'Boy Blue': v. hardy; fls mid blue, self. 'Buttercup': fls deep yellow, self; heavily scented. 'Carina': ground colour white, upper pet. mauve, yellow eye. 'Delicia': habit compact, v. hardy; ground colour pale yellow, upper pet. mauve. mauve. 'Isata': habit compact; fls circular, violet-blue, lightly rayed. 'Little David': hardy; fls cream, self, frilled; heavily scented. 'Luna': v. hardy; fls v. pale yellow, self; heavily scented. 'Myntha': fls yellow tinged violet. 'Rebecca': fls cream, outer edged flecked violet, slightly frilled; heavily scented. scented. 'Thalia': ground colour cream, upper pet. tinged violet.

V. zoysii Wulf. = *V. calcarata* ssp. *zoysii*.

Viola *Viola cornuta.*

VIOLACEAE Batsch. 23/830. *Hybanthus, Hymenanthera, Melicytus, Viola.*

Violet *Viola.*
Violeta *Polygala cowellii.*
Violet Banksia *Banksia violacea.*
Violet Cabbage *Moricandia.*
Violet Cress *Ionopsidium acaule.*
Violet-flowered Horned Poppy *Roemeria hybrida.*
Violet-flowered Petunia *Petunia integrifolia.*
Violet Helleborine *Epipactis purpurata.*
Violet Pea *Baphia racemosa.*
Violet Tree *Polygala cowellii; Securidaca longipedunculata.*
Violet Trumpet Vine *Clytostoma binatum.*
Violet Twining Snapdragon *Asarina antirrhinifolia.*
Violet Willow *Salix daphnoides.*
Violetwood *Acacia omalophylla; Oxalis violace.*

Viorna Rchb.
V. baldwinii (Torr. & A. Gray) Small = *Clematis baldwinii.*
V. fremontii (Wats.) Heller = *Clematis fremontii.*
V. ochroleuca (Ait.) Small = *Clematis ochroleuca.*

Viper Gourd *Trichosanthes cucumerina* var. *anguina.*

Virchowia Schenk.
V. africa Valke ex Schum. nom nud. = *Echidnopsis virchowii.*

Virgilia Poir. Leguminosae (Papilionoideae). 2 trees. Lvs imparipinnate; lfts narrow, with thorn-like points. Rac. axill., profuse; fls pea-like. S Afr. Z9.
V. capensis (L.) Poir. = *V. oroboides.*
V. divaricata Adamson. KEURBOOM. Spreading everg. shrub or tree to 9m. Lvs 8–20cm; lfts 3–13 pairs, narrowly oblong, term. lft, blunt with a small, thorn-like tip, dark green, glab. above, pale hirsute beneath. Fls to 1.3cm diam., white to deep rose, highly fragrant. Spring.
V. oroboides (Bergius) Salter. Tree to 9m, often multistemmed; young parts red-downy. Lvs to 20cm; lfts in 6–10 pairs, linear-oblong, pale and tomentose beneath. Fls to 1.6cm diam., white, pink, purple or crimson, fragrant. Early summer–autumn.

Virginia Avens *Geum virginianum.*
Virginia Bluebells *Mertensia virginica.*
Virginia Creeper *Parthenocissus quinquefolia.*
Virginia Mallow *Sida hermaphrodita.*
Virginian Bird Cherry *Prunus virginiana.*
Virginian Chain Fern *Woodwardia virginica.*
Virginian Pokeweed *Phytolacca americana.*
Virginian Sumac *Rhus typhina.*
Virginian Witch-hazel *Hamamelis virginiana.*
Virginia Pine *Pinus virginiana.*
Virginia Snakeroot *Aristolochia serpentaria.*
Virginia Stock *Malcolmia maritima.*
Virginia Waterleaf *Hydrophyllum virginianum.*
Virginia Wild-rye *Elymus virginicus.*
Virginia Willow *Itea virginica.*
Virgin's Bower *Clematis virginiana.*

Virgin's Palm *Dioon edule.*

VISCACEAE Miers. 8/450. *Phoradendron, Viscum.*

Viscaria Roehl.
V. alpina (L.) G. Don = *Lychnis alpina.*
V. sartorii Boiss. = *Lychnis viscaria* ssp. *atropurpurea.*
V. vulgaris Bernh. = *Lychnis viscaria.*

Viscid Nightshade *Solanum sisymbrifolium.*

Viscum L. Viscaceae. 70 parasitic, everg. shrubs. Lvs occas. flattened or reduced to teeth or scales. Fls inconspicuous in sessile clusters. Fr. a 1-seeded berry. Temp. zones.
V. album L. MISTLETOE. Everg., unisexual shrub to 1m, parasitic on trees. Br. pendulous, dichotomous. Lvs yellow-green, 3–5cm, oblong-spathulate, opposite, leathery. Fls tinged yellow. Fr. white, translucent, glutinous. Eur., temp. Asia. Z7.

VITACEAE Juss. *13/800. Ampelopsis, Cayratia, Cissus, Cyphostemma, Parthenocissus, Pterisanthes, Rhoicissus, Tetrastigma, Vitis.*

Vitaliana Bertol. Primulaceae. 1 tufted perenn. herb, forming mats or cushions. Lvs basal, to 10mm, linear to oblong-lanceolate, entire. Fls 5-merous, solitary; cal. to 10mm, obconical, glab. or pubesc., lobes linear-lanceolate; cor. to 2cm diam., yellow, tube cylindric. Summer. Mts of S & WC Eur. to SE Alps, C Apennines. Z5.
V. primuliflora (L.) Bertol. As above. ssp. *cinerea* (Sünderm.) I.K. Ferg. Lvs silver. ssp. *praetutiana* (Buser ex Sünderm.) J.K. Fergus. Loosely carpet-forming; lvs grey-tomentose, blunt or rounded at tip; fls more freely produced than in type, slightly smaller, cal. always pubesc.
→*Androsace* and *Douglasia.*

Vitex L. Verbenaceae. 250 trees or shrubs. Lvs digitately 1 to 7-foliolate; lfts entire or toothed. Fls in pan., rac. or cymes, perfect; cal. campanulate or tubular, truncate or 5-dentate; cor. hypocrateriform, bilabiate, upper lip bifid, lower lip trifid; sta. 4, usually exserted. Fr. a drupe. Trop., sometimes temp. regions. Z10 unless specified.
V. altissima L. f. Tree to 33m. Lfts 3, to 20×6.6cm, elliptic to obovate-elliptic, dark green and glabrescent above, paler and densely short-pubesc. beneath. Pan. to 23cm; cor. to 6mm, white or pink to blue-purple, exterior puberulent, lower lip usually blue or dark violet. India, Bangladesh, Sri Lanka through Indochina to Java, Sumatra and New Guinea.
V. agnus-castus L. CHASTE TREE. Aromatic shrub or small tree to 5m. Lfts 5–9, to 11.5×2cm, narrowly elliptic, glabrescent and grey-brown above, grey-white and densely adpressed-pubesc. beneath. Pan. to 31cm; fls fragrant; cor. tube to 2.5mm, lilac to lavender, white-puberulent. f. *alba* (Weston) Rehd. Fls white. f. *latifolia* (Mill.) Rehd. More vigorous and hardy; lvs broader, larger. S Eur., nat. in trop. regions. Z7.
V. capitata Vahl. Small tree to 15m. Lfts 3, to 12×3.5cm, narrowly elliptic, glab. above, subglabrous beneath. Infl. of capituliform cymes; cor. to 10mm, blue or purple, exterior densely adpressed-pubesc. Trin., Venez., Surinam, Braz.
V. cofassus Reinw. ex Bl. Tree to 40m, trunk often buttressed. Lfts 1–3, to 20×9cm, elliptic, glab., lustrous dark green above, paler beneath. Pan. to 17cm; cor. blue, lilac, lavender or purple, tube to 6mm, lobes to 1.5mm, glandular-pubesc. E Malay Archipel., W Polyn.
V. divaricata Sw. Shrub or tree to 18m, bark much fissured, lfts 1–3, to 20×7.5cm, oblong to elliptic, glab. or with few hairs on midrib. Infl. of axill. cymes to 15cm; cor. pale blue or blue-purple to violet, finely pubesc., tube to 6mm, lobes spreading. W Indies, Venez.
V. doniana Sw. Tree to 20m. Lfts 5, to 15×7.5cm, coriaceous, obovate, rounded, base cuneate, dark to light green. Infl. of axill. cymes, brown-puberulent; fls fragrant; cor. white or yellow to blue-purple, pubesc. Sierra Leone.
V. incisa Lam. Differs from *V. negundo* in lfts smaller, to 7cm, deeply and irregularly incised or pinnatisect, mealy-white above. India to Jap. and Java.
V. laciniata hort. ex Schauer = *V. incisa.*
V. latifolia Mill. = *V. angus-castus* f. *latifolia.*
V. leichthardtii F. Muell. = *Gmelina leichthardtii.*
V. leucoxylon L. f. Tree to 20m; bark light grey to light brown. Lfts 3–5, to 14.5×4.5cm, elliptic to oblong, acute or obtuse, densely pubesc. beneath when young, bright green. Infl. of axill. cymes, to 17cm; cor. white or yellow-white, lower lip and throat with purple-blue hairs, tube to 4.5mm, lobes to 3.5mm, densely villous. India.

V. lignum-vitae Cunn. ex Schauer. Tree to 40m. Lvs unifoliate, to 15×4.5cm, narrowly ovate or obovate to elliptic, lustrous above, dull beneath. Infl. of axill. cymes shorter than lvs; cor. to 10mm, exterior tomentose. Aus.

V. lindenii Hook. f. Shrub or small tree; lfts to 6.5×3cm, obovate-elliptic to elliptic, glab., dark green. Infl. of axill. cymes, few-fld, grey-pubesc.; cor. pale violet, interior streaked purple, limb to 16mm diam., lobes suborbicular. Colomb.

V. lucens T. Kirk. PURURI. Tree to 20m. Lfts 3–5, to 12.5×5cm, coriaceous, obovate to oblong-elliptic, acute or acuminate, lustrous dark green. Pan. axillary; cor. red or pink, to 35mm, pubesc. NZ. Z9.

V. macrophylla hort. = *V. angus-castus* f. *latifolia*.

V. negundo L. Aromatic shrub or small tree to 8.5m. Lfts 3–5, to 12×3cm, lanceolate, green-white and glab. above, white and densely short-pubesc. beneath, entire or slightly dentate. Pan. term. to 25cm, densely grey-pubesc.; cor. lilac to lavender, tube to 4mm, pubesc. E Afr., Madag., E Asia, Philippine Is. Z8.

V. negundo var. *heterophylla* (Franch.) Rehd. = *V. incisa*.

V. negundo var. *incisa* (Lam.) Clarke = *V. incisa*.

V. ovata Thunb. = *V. rotundifolia*.

V. parviflora Juss. Tree to 16m. Lfts 3, to 15×5.5cm, oblong or oblong-lanceolate, glab. or subglabrous, undulate. Pan. term. to 20cm; cor. blue to purple, tube to 6mm. Malesia, Philippine Is., Hawaii.

V. peduncularis Wallich. Shrub or tree to 3.2m, bark white to dark brown; lfts 3–5, to 16×5cm, oblong, lanceolate or elliptic, entire, bright green. Pan. axill.; cor. white to yellow or pale pink, white-strigose. India to Bangladesh, Burm., Thail., Indochina and Malaysia.

V. quinata (Lour.) F.N. Williams. Tree or shrub to 14m; lfts 3–5, to 19×7cm, elliptic-obovate or ovate to oblong, subglabrous. Pan. term. to 25cm, pubesc.; cor. violet, tube to 7mm, subglabrous or pubesc. SE Asia, Philippine Is. Z9.

V. rotundifolia L. f. Closely resembles *V. trifolia* except prostrate, creeping or sprawling. Lvs usually unifoliate, to 4.5×3.5cm, broadly oblong, suborbicular or obovate-spathulate, puberulent above, tomentose to glab. beneath. Asia to Aus.

V. trifolia L. Shrub or tree to 7m. Lfts 1–3, to 9×2.5cm, oblong to obovate or lanceolate, white-tomentose beneath, entire. Pan. term.; fls fragrant; cor. blue to purple, tube to 8mm, glab. to pubesc. Asia to Aus.

V. trifolia var. *simplicifolia* Cham. = *V. rotundifolia*.

V. zeyheri Sonder ex Schauer. Tree to 3.2m, bark black. Lfts 3–5, to 7.5cm, oblong or oblong-lanceolate, densely gland. Infl. of axill. cymes, densely tomentose; cor. exterior densely glandular-pubesc., interior villous. S Afr.

→*Cornutia*.

Vitis L. VINE. Vitaceae. 65 decid. vines or shrubs climbing by tendrils. Bark peeling in strips. Lvs mostly dentate, simple or lobed. Pan. axill.; fls small; pet. 5, united at ends into cap shed at anthesis; sta. 5. Fr. a berry; seeds 2–4, pear-shaped, pointed at base. N Hemis., particularly N Amer.

V. acerifolia Raf. BUSH GRAPE. Vine, vigorously climbing; shoots densely lanate when young. Lvs 5–11cm, cordate to reniform, 3-lobed, dentate, green tinged blue, lanate above at first, persistently so beneath. Fr. 16mm diam., globose, purple. Late spring to summer. SC US. Z6.

V. aconitifolia (Bunge) Hance = *Ampelopsis aconitifolia*.

V. acuminata (A. Gray) Seem. = *Cayratia acuminata*.

V. aegirophylla (Bunge) Boiss. = *Ampelopsis vitifolia*.

V. aestivalis Michx. SUMMER GRAPE. Vine, high-climbing; st. round, sparsely pilose to glab. when mature. Lvs 10–30cm, broadly ovate to subrotund, cordate at base, deeply 3–5-lobed or entire, dull green, red to tawny, tomentose when young, persistently floccose beneath, glaucous above. Fr. 5–10mm diam., globose, dark purple or black, sweet. Summer. NE Amer. var. *argentifolia* (Munson) Fern. Surface blue-green or silvery, young twigs blue-white. N and inland parts of range. Z3.

V. amurensis Rupr. Vine or strong-growing shrub, to 15m; young shoots tinged red, tomentose. Lvs 10–25cm, 5-lobed, midlobe broadly ovate, acuminate, rich crimson and purple in autumn, somewhat pubesc. beneath. Fr. 16×10mm, subglobose ovoid, black, glaucous, usually bitter. Late spring to midsummer; fruits late summer. NE Asia. Z7.

V. antarctica (Vent.) Benth. = *Cissus antarctica*.

V. arborea L. = *Ampelopsis arborea*.

V. argentifolia Munson = *V. aestivalis* var. *argentifolia*.

V. arizonica Engelm. CANYON GRAPE. Vine, not vigorously climbing, somewhat shrubby; st. v. slender, angled, grey tomentose when young becoming charcoal grey. Lvs 5–10cm, ovate-cordate, irregularly dentate, 3-lobed, tomentose to floccose. Fr. 8–10mm diam., ovoid to globose, black, slightly glaucous. Summer. SW US, N Mex. Z8.

V. armata Diels & Gilg = *V. davidii*.

V. austrina Small = *V. cinerea* var. *floridana*.

V. baileyana Munson. Vine, high-climbing; st. angled, arachnoid-tomentose when young. Lvs 6–10cm, unlobed or shortly 3-lobed, sparsely arachnoid-pubesc. particularly along veins. Fr. 4–7mm diam., black. SE US. Z6.

V. bainesii Hook. f. = *Cyphostemma bainesii*.

V. berlandieri Planch. Robust vine; young shoots angular, hairy, later minutely floccose. Lvs 8–10cm, broadly cordate, notched to 3-lobed, with broad teeth, dark green above, initially grey-pubesc. beneath. Fr. small, succulent, black, slightly bitter. Summer; fruits late summer. N Amer. Z7.

V. betulifolia Diels & Gilg. Vigorous vine; young shoots lanate. Lvs to 10cm, ovate, simple or slightly 3-lobed, dentate, red when young, dark green when mature, red or bronze in autumn, downy on veins above, ± tomentose beneath when young. Fr. 8mm diam., globose, blue-black, somewhat glaucous. C & W China. Z7.

V. bicolor Le Conte. BLUE GRAPE. Vine, climbing vigorously; shoots white tinged blue, glab. Lvs 10–30cm, broadly ovate, 3-5-lobed, green above, v. glaucous beneath, glab. or subglab. Fr. 12mm diam., v. dark purple tinged black. C & E US. Z5.

V. bicolor Gray non Le Conte = *V. aestivalis* var. *argentifolia*.

V. bodinieri Lév. & Vaniot = *Cyphostemma bainesii*.

V. bourquiniana Munson = *V. aestivalis*.

V. 'Brant'. (*V.* 'Clinton' (*V. labrusca* ×*V. riparia*) ×*V. vinifera* 'Black St. Peters'). V. popular fruiting vine growing vigorously to 12m+, the fr. are sweet, purple-black and bloomy but the ornamental value lies in lvs deeply 3–5 lobed, large, turning dark purple-red in fall with veins edged yellow-green. Gdn origin. Z6.

V. californica Benth. Vine, climbing 6–9m; shoots grey-tomentose, later glabrate. Lvs 5–10cm, rounded-cordate or reniform, occas. 3-lobed, rounded at apex, dentate, deep crimson in autumn, glab. above, tomentose beneath. Fr. 8mm diam., black, purple-glaucous. Early summer. W US. Z7.

V. candicans Engelm. ex A. Gray = *V. mustangensis*.

V. capensis Thunb. = *Rhoicissus capensis*.

V. capriolata D. Don = *Tetrastigma serrulatum*.

V. chaffanjonii Lév. & Vaniot = *Ampelopsis chaffanjonii*.

V. cinerea (Engelm. ex A. Gray) Millardet in Bushberg. SWEET WINTER GRAPE. High-climbing vine, br. angular, tomentose when young, twigs densely pubesc. when mature. Lvs 10–20cm, broadly ovate to subrotund, shallowly 3-lobed or unlobed, serrate, tomentose then cinereous-floccose beneath. Fr. 4–6mm diam., almost black, scarcely glaucous. Early summer. C & E US. var. *floridana* Munson. Lvs rusty, floccose beneath. SE US. Z5.

V. cirrhosa Thunb. = *Cyphostemma cirrhosa*.

V. citrulloides Dipp. = *Ampelopsis brevipedunculata* var. *maximowiczii* 'Citrulloides'.

V. coignetiae Pull. ex Planch. CRIMSON GLORY VINE. Vine, climbing vigorously and rapidly; young shoots round, ribbed, loosely grey lanate at first. Lvs to 30×25cm, rounded, obscurely 3- or 5-lobed, dentate, thick-textured, rather puckered, glab. above, thickly tomentose beneath, turning pale bronze then fiery red to deep scarlet in fall. Fr. 12mm diam., purple-black, glaucous, scarcely edible. Jap., Korea. Z5.

V. cordifolia Michx. CHICKEN GRAPE; FROST GRAPE. Vine, growing v. vigorously; young shoots ± smooth. Lvs broadly ovate-cordate, irregularly dentate, unlobed or obscurely 3-lobed, glossy above, sometimes pubesc. on veins beneath. Fr. 8–12mm diam., globose, black, sweet after frost. SE US. Z5.

V. davidiana (Carr.) Nichols. = *Ampelopsis brevipedunculata* or *Ampelopsis humulifolia*.

V. davidii (Carr.) Foex. Vine, of luxuriant growth; young shoots with spiny gland. bristles. Lvs 10–25cm, cordate, dentate, tapered, shining dark green above, tinged blue or grey beneath, brilliant red in autumn, glandular-setose beneath, downy in vein axils. Fr. 16mm diam., black, pleasantly flavoured. China. 'Veitchii': lvs shiny, tinged bronze in summer. var. *cyanocarpa* (Gagnep.) Sarg. St. less prickly; lvs larger colouring well; fr. blue-pruinose. Z7.

V. delavayana (Planch.) Franch. ex Bean = *Ampelopsis delavayana*.

V. discolor (Bl.) Dalz. = *Cissus discolor*.

V. dissecta Carr. = *Ampelopsis aconitifolia*.

V. doaniana Munson = *V. acerifolia*.

V. elegans Koch = *Ampelopsis brevipedunculata* var. *maximowiczii* 'Elegans'.

V. elegantissima Jaeger = *Ampelopsis brevipedunculata* var. *maximowiczii* 'Elegans'.

V. endresii (Veitch) Nichols. = *Cissus endresii*.

V. erosa Bak. = *Cissus erosa*.

V. ficifolia Bunge = *V. thunbergii*.

V. ficifolia var. *pentagona* (Diels) Pamp. = *V. pentagona*.

V. flexuosa Thunb. Elegant vine; st. slender, slightly striate; young shoots red-brown-downy. Lvs 4–10cm, rounded-ovate, cordate or triangular-truncate at base, thin, glossy above, veins downy beneath. Fr. 7mm diam., globose, black tinged blue. Early summer. China, India, Jap., Java, Korea. Z6.

V. flexuosa var. *major* Veitch = *V. pulchra*.

V. flexuosa var. *parvifolia* (Roxb.) Gagnep. = *V. parvifolia*.

V. flexuosa var. *wilsonii* hort. = *Ampelopsis bodinieri*.

V. girdiana Munson. Vine, vigorously climbing, 2–12m, initially white-tomentose. Lvs 5–10cm, broadly ovate, deeply lobed, irregularly dentate, apex triangular, ± cordate, green and glab. above, cinereous beneath. Fr. globose, 4–7mm diam., black, slightly glaucous. Early summer. Calif., Baja Calif. Z8.

V. gongylodes Burchell ex Bak. = *Cissus gongylodes*.

V. hederacea Ehrh. = *Parthenocissus quinquefolia*.

V. henryana Hemsl. = *Parthenocissus henryana*.

V. henryi hort. = *Parthenocissus henryana*.

V. heterophylla Thunb. = *Ampelopsis brevipedunculata* var. *maximowiczii*.

V. heterophylla var. *maximowiczii* Reg. = *Ampelopsis brevipedunculata* var. *maximowiczii*.

V. himalayana (Royle) Brandis = *Parthenocissus himalayana*.

V. himalayana var. *semicordata* (Wallich) M. Lawson = *Parthenocissus semicordata*.

V. hypoglauca (A. Gray) F. Muell. = *Cissus hypoglauca*.

V. inconstans Miq. = *Parthenocissus tricuspidata*.

V. inserta Kerner = *Parthenocissus inserta*.

V. japonica Thunb. = *Cayratia japonica*.

V. labrusca L. FOX GRAPE; SKUNK GRAPE. Vigorous vine; shoots lanate when young. Lvs 10–20cm, rounded-cordate, usually shallowly 3-lobed, serrate, deep green, glab. above, rusty tomentose beneath. Fr. 1–2cm diam., globose, dark red to almost black, with musky aroma. Early summer; late summer. NE US. Z5.

V. labrusca Thunb. non L. = *V. thunbergii*.

V. labrusca var. *sinuata* Reg. = *V. thunbergii* var. *sinuata*.

V. labruscana Bail. Cultigen derived from *V. labrusca*, often crossed with *V. vinifera*. Differs from *V. labrusca* in tendrils intermittent; fr. larger, with less foxy flavour. Z5.

V. laciniosa L. = *V. vinifera* 'Apiifolia'.

V. lanata Roxb. Young shoots lanate. Lvs 8–15cm, broadly ovate, cordate at base, acute to obtuse, dentate, occas. broadly shortly lobed, green, scarlet in autumn, glab. above, tomentose beneath, rather thick. Fr. 5mm diam., globose, purple. Himal., China, India, Taiwan. Z9.

V. lecontiana House = *V. bicolor*.

V. leeoides Maxim. = *Ampelopsis leeoides*.

V. linecumii Buckl. POST-OAK GRAPE. Vine, climbing or forming bushy clumps; st. sparsely pilose to glab. Lvs to 30cm, broadly ovate to subrotund, cordate at base, ± deeply 3–5-lobed or entire, thick cinereous, sometimes glaucous beneath. Fr. 1–2.5cm diam., dark purple or black. Summer. E N Amer. Z4.

V. longii Prince = *V. acerifolia*.

V. megalophylla Veitch = *Ampelopsis megalophylla*.

V. micans (Rehd.) Bean = *Ampelopsis bodinieri*.

V. monosperma Michx. ex Sarg. = *V. palmata*.

V. monticola Buckl. Vine, climbing to 9m; branchlets slender, angled, slightly downy. Lvs 5–10cm, rounded, cordate at base, ± acute, coarsely dentate, slightly 3-lobed, lustrous, thin, tinged grey and lanate on veins beneath. Fr. 12mm diam., globose, black, sweetly flavoured. SW Tex. Z6.

V. mustangensis Buckl. MUSTANG GRAPE. Vigorous vine; shoots lanate. Lvs 5–11cm, broadly cordate to reniform, entire to sinuate or obscurely 3-lobed, or (lobes distinct in juveniles) ± dentate, dull dark green, lanate above at first, persistently tomentose beneath. Fr. 16mm diam., globose, purple, inedible. US (Okl. and Ark. to Tex.). Z5.

V. oblonga Benth. = *Cissus oblonga*.

V. obovata Lawson = *Tetrastigma obovatum*.

V. obtecta Lawson = *Tetrastigma obtectum*.

V. odoratissima Donn = *V. vulpina*.

V. oligocarpa Lév. & Vant. = *Cayratia oligocarpa*.

V. oratissima Raf. = *V. riparia*.

V. orientalis (Lam.) Boiss. = *Ampelopsis orientalis*.

V. pagnuccii Romanet = *V. piasezkii* var. *pagnuccii*.

V. palmata Vahl RED GRAPE; CAT GRAPE. Vine, high climbing; br. maroon to red, glab. Lvs 8–14cm, triangular-ovate to subrotund, 3–5-lobed, sparsely pubesc. Fr. black, glaucescent. Early summer. S & C US. Z5.

V. parvifolia Roxb. Slender vine; st. slightly striate; shoots laxly tomentose when young. Lvs to 8×5cm, rounded-ovate, cordate at base, apex sometimes broadly 3-lobed, dentate, shining bronze-green above, tinged purple and sometimes downy beneath. Fr. 7mm diam., globose, black tinged blue. Himal. to C China and Taiwan. Z7.

V. pentagona Diels & Gilg. Vigorous vine; shoots white-tomentose. Lvs 8–15cm, ovate base cordate or truncate, apex acute, shallowly dentate, shallowly 3–5-lobed, dark green above, bright white adpressed-tomentose beneath. Fr. 8mm diam., globose, blue-black. W & C China. var. *bellula* Rehd. Lvs 4–6.5cm. Z6.

V. persica Boiss. = *Ampelopsis vitifolia*.

V. piasezkii Maxim. Vigorous vine; young shoots lanate. Lvs 8–15cm, simple at base of shoot, 3-lobed or 3–5-parted toward summit, red-tinged when young, brown-tomentose beneath, red in autumn. Fr. 8mm diam., globose, v. dark purple tinged black. W & C China. var. *pagnuccii* (Romanet) Rehd. Shoots and lvs more glab. Z6.

V. planicaulis Hook. f. = *Tetrastigma planicaule*.

V. polita Miq. = *Pterisanthes polita*.

V. pterophora Bak. = *Cissus gongylodes*.

V. pulchra Rehd. (Possibly *V. amurensis* × *V. coignetiae*.) Vigorous vine; shoots tinged red, glabrescent. Lvs 7–15cm, rounded-ovate, sometimes somewhat 3-lobed, coarsely dentate, cordate at base, apex acute, tinged red at first, purple and blood-red in autumn, glab. above, grey pubesc. beneath. Summer. Origin unknown, but probably NE Asia. Z7.

V. quadrangularis Rehd. = *V. pentagona*.

V. quadrangularis (L.) Wallich ex Wight & Arn. non Rehd. = *Cissus quadrangularis*.

V. quinquefolia (L.) Lam. = *Parthenocissus quinquefolia*.

V. repens Veitch = *Ampelopsis bodinieri*.

V. reticulata Pamp. non M.A. Laws = *V. wilsoniae*.

V. rhombifolia Bak. = *Cissus rhombifolia*.

V. riparia Michx. FROST GRAPE; RIVERBANK GRAPE. Vine, climbing or scrambling; young shoots glab. Lvs 10–20cm, broadly cordate, generally 3-lobed, serrate, lustrous, pubesc. beneath when young. Fls fragrant. Fr. 6–12mm, globose, black tinged purple, blue-glaucous. Early summer. E & SE N Amer. Z2.

V. romanetii Romanet ex Foex. Vine, climbing vigorously; young shoots pubesc. with scattered gland. setae. Lvs 15–25cm, 3-lobed, with bristle-tipped teeth, dark green, subglabrous above, grey-tomentose beneath, with scattered gland. setae. Fr. 8–12mm diam., black. China. Z6.

V. rotundifolia Michx. MUSCADINE GRAPE; BULLACE; FOX GRAPE. Vine, vigorously climbing; bark tight, non-shredding; young shoots warted. Lvs 6–12cm, rounded to broadly ovate, coarsely serrate, occas. lobed, apex acute, base cordate, dark green above, green tinged yellow beneath, glossy, subglab. except in vein axils. Fr. 1–2.5cm diam., rounded, dull purple, not glaucous, musky flavoured. Early summer. SE US. Z5.

V. rubra Michx. = *V. palmata*.

V. rubrifolia Lév. & Vant. = *Parthenocissus himalayana* var. *rubrifolia*.

V. rupestris Scheele. BUSH GRAPE; SAND GRAPE. Vine or shrub, usually prostrate; young shoots glab.; tendrils few or 0. Lvs 5–10cm, reniform, usually unlobed, coarsely dentate, often ± folded, green tinged blue, paler beneath, ± glab. Fr. 6–12mm diam., subglobose, purple-black, slightly glaucous. Early summer. SC US. Z5.

V. rutilans Carr. = *V. romanetii*.

V. semicordata Wallich in Roxb. = *Parthenocissus semicordata*.

V. serjaniifolia (Reg.) Maxim. = *Ampelopsis japonica*.

V. sieboldii hort. ex K. Koch = *V. thunbergii*.

V. simpsonii Small = *V. cinerea* var. *floridana*.

V. sinensis Veitch = *V. piasezkii*.

V. striata (Ruiz & Pav.) Miq. = *Cissus striata*.

V. succulenta Galpin = *Cissus cactiformis*.

V. sylvestris C. Gmel. = *V. vinifera* ssp. *sylvestris*.

V. texana Munson = *V. monticola*.

V. thomsonii Lawson = *Parthenocissus thomsonii*.

V. thomsonii Veitch non Lawson = *Parthenocissus henryana*.

V. thunbergii Sieb. & Zucc. Vine, moderately climbing; young shoots angled, ± lanate. Lvs 7–15cm diam., 3–5-lobed, cordate at base, lobes ovate, dentate, dull dark green, rich crimson in autumn, glab. above, tomentose beneath. Fr. to 9mm diam., black, purple-glaucous. Summer. China, Jap., Korea, Taiwan. var. *sinuata* (Reg.) Rehd. Lvs deeply lobed, lobes coarsely sinuate. China, Jap. Z6.

V. thunbergii hort. non Sieb. & Zucc. = *V. coignetiae*.

V. tinctoria Poit. & Turpin = *V. vinifera* 'Purpurea'.

V. treleasii Munson ex L.H. Bail. Vine, much-branched, somewhat shrubby; young st. pale green, glabrescent. Lvs 6–10cm, broadly ovate to cordate, lobes 3, sometimes v. small, dentate, bright green and glab. above, paler and hairy along veins beneath. Fr. 6–8mm diam., globose, slightly glaucous. Late spring–summer. SW US. Z7.

V. veitchii Lynch = *Parthenocissus tricuspidata* 'Veitchii'.

V. vinifera L. COMMON GRAPE VINE. Vine, high climbing; young shoots glab. or lanate. Lvs 5–15cm, orbicular, palmately 3–7-lobed, dentate, base cordate, glabrescent above, often persistently hairy beneath. Late spring to early summer; fruits late summer. S & C Eur. ORNAMENTAL CVS. 'Apiifolia' ('Laciniosa'): lvs finely and deeply lobed. 'Brant' see *V.* 'Brant'. 'Ciotat': lvs v. deeply incised. 'Incana': lvs densely veined white. 'Madame Mathias Muscat': lvs and shoots glossy purple. 'Purpurea' (TENTURIER GRAPE): lvs white-downy when young, becoming plum-purple, deepening to rich dark purple in autumn. ssp. *vinifera*. Monoecious cultigen. Fr. 6–22mm, ellipsoid to globose, green, yellow, red or purple-black, sweet. ssp. *sylvestris* (C. Gmel.) Hegi. Dioecious; foliage dimorphic, more deeply lobed in ♂ plants. Fr. 6mm, ellipsoid, black tinged blue, acid. SE & SC Eur. to Asia Minor, Cauc., N Iran, Turkestan. Z6.

V. vinifera ssp. *sativa* Hegi = *V. vinifera* ssp. *vinifera*.

V. vinifera var. *purpurea* Bean = *V. vinifera* 'Purpurea'.

V. vinifera var. *purpurea* Veitch = *V. vinifera* 'Purpurea'.

V. vinifera var. *sylvestris* (C. Gmel.) Willd. = *V. vinifera* ssp. *sylvestris*.

V. virginana Poir. = *V. riparia*.

V. virginiana Munson non Poir. = *V. baileyana*.

V. vitacea (Knerr) Bean = *Parthenocissus inserta*.

V. voinieriana Pierre ex Nichols. & Mottet = *Tetrastigma voinierianum*.

V. vomerensis hort. = *Tetrastigma obovatum*.

V. vulpina L. FROST GRAPE; CHICKEN GRAPE. Vine, high-climbing. Lvs 10–15cm, rounded, unlobed or slightly 3-lobed, coarsely serrate, pale green, glab. above, pubesc. beneath when young. Fls fragrant. Fr. 5–10mm, black or dark blue, epruinose, sweet and edible after exposure to frost. Early summer. C & E US. Z5.

V. vulpina Lecomte non L. = *V. riparia*.

V. vulpina Torr. ex A. Gray non L. = *V. rotundifolia*.

V. wilsoniae Veitch. Vine, climbing vigorously; shoots lanate when young. Lvs ± rounded-ovate, cordate at base, apex acute, sinuate-dentate, 7.5–15cm diam., deep red in autumn, lanate when young, becoming glab. above. Fr. 10–12mm, black, purple-glaucous. C China. Z6.

→*Muscadinia* and *Parthenocissus*.

Vittadinia A. Rich. Compositae. *c*15 perenn. herbs or shrubs. Lvs alt., usually simple. Cap. radiate, small, 1 or few; phyllaries in many series, imbricate; ray flts white or blue. Fr. ± compressed; pappus of copious bristles. Aus., NZ. Z9.

V. australis hort. = *V. cuneata*.

V. cuneata DC. Subshrub to 30cm. Lvs to 1.5cm. Cap. to 1.5cm diam., 1; ray flts white. Summer. Aus., Tasm., NZ.

V. tricolor hort. = *V. cuneata*.

V. triloba hort. = *Erigeron karvinskianus*.

Vittaria Sm. Vittariaceae. 50 epiphytic ferns. Rhiz. creeping, with black scales. Fronds pendent, simple, linear or lanceolate. Trop. Z10.

V. elongata Sw. Fronds 30–60×0.7–2m, gradually tapered to both ends, main vein distinct throughout above, less so beneath; stipe distinct. E Asia to Aus.

V. ensiformis Sw. Fronds to 35×0.6cm, slightly ascending when young, pendulous with age, gradually narrowed to base, revolute, tinged red when young, main vein distinct only near base; stipe 0. Masc. Is., Malaya.

V. isoetifolia Bory. Fronds to 50×0.5cm, linear, obtuse at apex, v. gradually narrowed to base, dark green, coriaceous, main vein prominent; stipe short. Afr.

V. lineata (L.) J. Sm. Fronds to 90×0.5cm, linear, v. gradually narrowed towards base, firm, often revolute, main vein prominent; stipe indistinct. Trop. Amer.

V. scolopendrina (Bory) Thwaites. Fronds 40–90×1.5–3.5cm, linear-lanceolate, tapering v. gradually to both ends, slightly fleshy, veins visible on upper surface; stipe 0. Madag. to Samoa.

VITTARIACEAE (C. Presl) Ching. 8 genera. *Vittaria*.

Vogel's Fig *Ficus lutea*.

Voglera P. Gaertn., Mey. & Scherb.

V. spinosa Gaertn. = *Genista germanica*.

Volkameria L.

V. aculeata L. = *Clerodendrum aculeatum*.

V. fragrans Vent. = *Clerodendrum philippinum*.

V. heterophylla Poir. = *Clerodendrum heterophyllum*.

V. inermis L. = *Clerodendrum inerme*.

V. kaempferi Jacq. = *Clerodendrum kaempferi*.

V. odorata Hamilt. = *Caryopteris odorata*.

V. spinosa Juss. = *Rhaphithamnus spinosus*.

Voodoo Lily *Sauromatum venosum*.

Vriesea Lindl. Bromeliaceae. 249 perenn., stemless, mostly epiphytic herbs. Lvs strap-shaped in a funnel-like rosette, usually sparsely scaly or smooth. Infl. term., mostly erect, usually with fls in 2 rows; floral bracts brightly coloured, long-lasting; sep. free or almost free; pet. with 2 basal scales, free or fused into a tube, shorter than sep. Mex. and W Indies to S Braz., N Arg. and Boliv. Z10.

V. barilletii E. Morr. To 60cm in fl. Lvs to 40×5cm, linear, unspotted. Infl. erect, simple; bracts 2-ranked, keeled, closely overlapping, yellow-olive densely spotted deep purple-red; fls to 5cm; sta. exserted. Braz.

V. botafogensis Mez = *V. saundersii*.

V. brachystachys Reg. = *V. carinata*.

V. carinata Wawra. LOBSTER CLAWS. To 36cm, in fl. Lvs 15–27cm, virtually smooth, 12–24 in a small, funnel-shaped rosette, flat, thin, pale green. Infl. to 6cm, laterally compressed; floral bracts to 4cm, base bright red, margins and apex bright yellow or green, keeled; pet. bright yellow, tipped green. Late autumn. E Braz.

V. ensiformis (Vell.) Beer. To 1m in fl. Lvs 30–90cm, in a broad rosette, scaly, green. Infl. 20–70cm, sword-shaped; floral bracts to 6cm, bright red, broadly subelliptic, leathery; pet. yellow. E Braz. var. *warmingii* (E. Morr.) L.B. Sm. Floral bracts yellow, apices green. E Braz.

V. fenestralis Lind. & André. To 1m in fl. Lvs to 50cm, in a broad rosette, pale green netted with dark green lines, sometimes spotted red-brown and scaly beneath. Infl. distichous, to 50cm; floral bracts to 3cm, green, spotted, broadly ovate; pet. white-green. SE Braz.

V. fosteriana L.B. Sm. 1–2m in fl. Lvs 70cm, in a vase-like, spreading rosette, banded maroon beneath, green and smooth above. Infl. to over 40cm, linear; floral bracts to 4cm, yellow, leathery, inflated; pet. pale green tipped purple. Braz.

V. gigantea Gaudich. To 2m in fl. Lvs to 100cm, flat, glaucous, with faint yellow-green reticulation. Infl. to over 1m, laxly bipinnate; scape bracts leafy; floral bracts to 3cm, leathery, broadly elliptic; pet. yellow-green. E Braz.

V. glutinosa Lindl. To 2m in fl. Lvs to 70cm, pale green, densely purple-crossbanded, sparsely scaly. Infl. to over 1m, laxly bipinnate; scape bracts imbricate, crimson-spotted; br. to 50cm, glossy red; floral bracts to 6cm, pink, imbricate, elliptic; pet. bright red to orange. N Trin.

V. guttata Lind. & André. To 30cm in fl. Lvs 10–15cm in dense, upright rosette, green irregularly spotted red or lavender. Infl. simple, pendulous, loose, 20×4cm; scape bracts closely overlapping, green to lavender, chalky-scaled; floral bracts 3.5×2.5cm, green, scaly; pet. yellow. Braz.

V. heterostachys (Bak.) L.B. Sm. To 35cm in fl. Lvs to 40cm, suberect, green, scaly at margins. Infl. to 20cm, elliptic or oblong; floral bracts to 5cm, shiny orange, broad; pet. yellow, tipped green. E Braz.

V. hieroglyphica (Carr.) E. Morr. To 2.5m in fl. Lvs to 80cm, broadly banded dark green or purple. Infl. to 80cm, 2–3 pinnate; scape bracts leaflike; floral bracts yellow-green, broadly ovate, in flated; pet. yellow.

V. longibracteata (Bak.) Mez = *V. splendens* var. *formosa*.

V. × mariae André. (*V. carinata* ×*V. barilletii*.) PAINTED FEATHER. Resembles *V. carinata*, but lvs often flushed pink, margins inrolled; infl. larger; floral bracts often green toward apex. Gdn origin.

V. oligantha (Bak.) Mez. To 90cm in fl. Lvs to 30cm, blades narrowly subtriangular, ash-grey scaly, tinted violet. Infl. to 19cm, few-fld; floral bracts 24mm, ovate, fleshy and leathery. Braz. Z10.

V. petropolitana L.B. Sm. = *V. heterostachys*.

V. psittacina (Hook.) Lindl. To 50cm in fl. Lvs to 50cm, pale-sclay. Infl. to 23cm with overlapping bracts, lower green, upper yellow tipped green; floral bracts red tipped bright yellow, wholly red or green, ovate-elliptic; pet. yellow sometimes tipped green. Summer. E Braz.

V. saundersii (Carr.) E. Morr. ex Mez. To 60cm in fl. Lvs to 30cm, ash-grey scaly, densely blotched maroon beneath. Infl. to 14cm, densely bipinnate; scape bracts red-brown-spotted; floral bracts to 2cm, in 2 rows, pale green or yellow, rounded; pet. sulphur-yellow. E Braz.

V. schwackeana Mez. To 100cm in fl. or taller. Lvs to 60cm, sparsely scaly beneath, glab. above, green, sometimes flecked maroon. Infl. to 40cm, laxly bipinnate, dark red, broadly ovate; floral bracts to 3.2cm, broadly elliptic, overlapping; pet. to 4cm yellow. E Braz.

V. speciosa Hook. = *V. splendens*.

V. splendens (Brongn.) Lem. FLAMING SWORD. To 1m in fl. Lvs to 80cm, v. sparsely scaly with broad, dark purple-brown crossbands. Infl. to 55cm, strongly compressed, lanceolate or oblong; scape bracts imbricate, clasping, red-brown, banded, broadly ovate; floral bracts to 8cm, bright scarlet to orange, narrowly triangular; pet. to 8cm, yellow. E Venez. to Fr. Guiana. var. *formosa* Sur. ex Witte. Lf blades green. N Venez., Guyana, Trin. & Tob.

V. **cvs.** 'Favorite' (*V. ensiformis* ✕*?*): plum. 'Perfecta' (*V. carinata* ✕*V.* 'Poelmannii'): yellow, bracts bright red. 'Poelmannii' (*V. gloriosa* ✕*V. vangeertii*): green apex.

→*Tillandsia.*

✕**Vuylstekeara.** (*Cochlioda* ✕*Miltonia* ✕*Odontoglossum.*) Orchidaceae.

Gdn hybrids with strap-shaped lvs and erect to arching sprays of large, frilly fls in shades of white, yellow, rose and red usually spotted or mottled darker red. The most typical coloration is white heavily overlaid with a deep velvety red; e.g. the popular ✕*V.* Cambria 'Plush'.

W

Wadalee-gum Tree *Acacia catechu.*
Wafer Ash *Ptelea.*

Wagatea Dalz. Leguminosae (Caesalpinioideae). 1 robust, climbing shrub to 30m; br. hooked and prickly. Lvs bipinnate; pinnae 4–6 pairs; lfts oblong, pubesc. beneath. Rac. or pan. densely flowered, spike-like; cal. scarlet, campanulate, lobes 5; pet. 5, orange, oblong-spathulate; sta. 10. SW India, introd. Java. Z10.
W. spicata Dalz. As for the genus.

Wahlenbergia Schräd. ex Roth. ROCK BELL. Campanulaceae. 150 ann. or perenn. herbs. Fls solitary or in leafy cymes; cal. tubular, lobes 5; cor. campanulate to rotate, lobes valvate; sta. free. Eur., trop. and S Afr., Madag., India, China, Jap., NZ, Aus.
W. albomarginata Hook. f. Tufted perenn., to 30cm. Lvs to 2cm, rosulate, elliptic to lanceolate or ovate-spathulate, denticulate, hirsute, glaucous. Fls white to pale blue. Summer. NZ. 'Blue Mist': fls grey-blue. Z7.
W. capillacea A. DC. Ann. or perenn. to 40cm. Lvs in alt. clusters up st., filiform. Fls deep blue in a term. rac. Summer. S Afr. Z9.
W. cartilaginea Hook. f. Perenn. Lvs to 2cm, rosulate, spathulate to elliptic, margins thickly cartilaginous, usually glaucous. Fls white suffused with pale blue or mauve, fragrant. NZ. Z8.
W. congesta (Cheesem.) N.E. Br. Perenn. forming dense mats. Lvs to 2.5cm, rosulate, orbicular to elliptic-spathulate, glab. Fls solitary, pale blue to white. NZ. Z9.
W. consimilis Loth. Perenn., to 70cm. Lvs opposite or alt., to 5cm, lanceolate to spathulate, entire to dentate, pubesc. Fls large, deep blue. Aus. Z9.
W. dalmatica A. DC. = *Edraianthus dalmaticus.*
W. gracilis (Forst. f.) A. DC. Slender perenn. to 30cm; st. loosely pilose at base. Lvs crowded, broadly spathulate or oblanceolate, undulate, pubesc. Fls few, small, blue. New Caledonia, Polyn., SE Asia. Z10.
W. grandiflora (Jacq.) Schräd. = *Platycodon grandiflorus.*
W. hederacea (L.) Rchb. IVY-LEAVED BELLFLOWER. Slender ann. or perenn., glab., creeping. Lvs orbicular, angled or lobed. Fls small, solitary, pale blue. Summer. W Eur. Z7.
W. lobeliodes (L. f.) Link. Ann., to 30cm, glab. Lvs to 7cm, narrow-ovate to ovate, serrulate. Fls small, blue. Madeira, Canary Is. Z9.
W. marginata (Thunb.) A. DC. = *W. gracilis.*
W. matthewsii Ckn. Perenn., tufted, glab. Lvs to 4cm, rosulate, narrow-oblong, entire to dentate. Fls white to pale mauve. Summer–autumn. NZ. Z9.
W. multicaulis Benth. Ann. or perenn., to 50cm. Lvs oblanceolate, margins thickened and cartilaginous, entire to denticulate, glab. Fls small, blue. Autumn and winter. W Aus. Z9.
W. pendula Schräd. = *W. lobeliodes.*
W. pumilio (Portenschlag) A. DC. = *Edraianthus pumilio.*
W. saxicola (R. Br.) A. DC. = *W. albomarginata.*
W. stricta Sweet = *W. consimilis.*
W. tasmanica (R. Br.) A. DC. = *W. albomarginata.*
W. trichogyna Stearn = *W. gracilis.*
W. tuberosa Hook. f. Tuberous, glab. perenn. Lvs to 2.5cm, linear, denticulate. Fls white with 5 parallel pink stripes. NZ. Z9.
W. vinciflora Decne. = *W. consimilis.*

Wahoo *Euonymus atropurpureus.*
Waiawi *Psidium littorale* var. *littorale.*
Wait-a-while *Acacia colletioides; Calamus (C. muelleri.)*

Waitzia Wendl. Compositae. 6 erect, ann. herbs. Lvs alt., entire, usually amplexicaul. Cap. discoid, solitary or in corymbose clusters; involucre subglobose to cylindrical, phyllaries in many series, coloured, petaloid; receptacle flat; flts white, yellow or orange. S & W Australia.
W. acuminata Steetz. ORANGE IMMORTELLE. To 60cm, branched, pubesc. Lvs 7cm, linear, undulate. Cap. few, in a loose cluster; phyllaries yellow to orange.
W. aurea Steetz. To 50cm, simple or branched, woolly. Lvs to 8cm, linear to obovate, mucronate. Cap. few, in a loose corymb; phyllaries golden with green claw; flts yellow. Early summer.

W. citrina (Benth.) Steetz. To 40cm, simple or branched. Lvs to 7cm, linear to obovate, acute. Cap. few, in a loose corymb; phyllaries golden with a green floccose claw; flts yellow or white. Early summer.
W. corymbosa sensu Auct. = *W. acuminata.*
W. nivea Benth. = *W. suaveolens.*
W. odontolepis Turcz. = *W. suaveolens.*
W. steetziana Lehm. ex Steetz = *W. citrina.*
W. suaveolens (Benth.) Druce. To 30cm, glab. to woolly. Lvs to 8cm, obovate to linear, mucronate. Cap. solitary or few, in a loose corymb; phyllaries white or pink with green claw; flts cream. Early summer.
W. tenella Hook. = *W. citrina.*

Wake Robin *Trillium.*

Waldheimia Karel. & Kir.
W. tomentosa Reg. = *Allardia tomentosa.*

Waldsteinia Willd. Rosaceae. 6 tufted perenn. herbs; rhiz. creeping. Lvs lobed or trifoliolate, toothed. Fls solitary or several together; cal. funnel-shaped, lobes 5; pet. 5, yellow; sta. numerous. N temp. regions.
W. fragarioides (Michx.) Tratt. BARREN STRAWBERRY. Mat-forming. Lvs bronze, lfts 3, to 8×6cm, obovate, lobed and crenate. Fls 3–8, to 2cm diam., in paired, helicoid cymes. Spring–summer. E US. Z3.
W. geoides Willd. Creeping then ascending. Lvs to 25.5cm, sub-rhombic, shallow-lobed or broadly cordate-reniform, coarsely bicrenate, pubesc. Fls long-stalked 2cm diam., in lax infl. Spring. C Eur., Balk., Asia Minor. Z5.
W. lobata Torr. & A. Gray. Rhiz. slender. Lvs to 20.5cm, sub-orbicular, cordate, usually 3–5-lobed, crenate, hirsute. Fls on 4–8-fld, slender, ascending, cymose scapes to 20.5cm. Spring–summer. SE US. Z8.
W. parviflora Small. Rhiz. horizontal. Lfts 3, to 8cm, cuneate-obovate or broad-rhomboid, crenate or lobed. Fls to 0.7cm diam., starry, scapose. Spring. SE US. Z6.
W. sibirica Tratt. = *W. ternata.*
W. ternata (Stephan) Fritsch. Stoloniferous. Radical lvs ternate, pubesc.; lat. lfts to 3cm, subrhombic, crenate, term. lft broad-obovate or suborbicular, crenate-dentate. Fls 1.5cm diam., 3–7 per infl. Spring–summer. Jap., China. Z3.
W. trifolia Rochel ex Koch = *W. ternata.*
→*Dalibarda.*

Walking Fern *Asplenium rhizophyllum.*
Walking Maidenhair Fern *Adiantum caudatum.*
Walking Stick Palm *Linospadix monostachya.*
Wallaby Grass *Danthonia setacea.*
Wallangarra Wattle *Acacia adunca.*
Wall Fern *Polypodium vulgare.*
Wall Flag *Iris tectorum.*
Wallflower *Erysimum cheiri.*
Wall Germander *Teucrium chamaedrys.*

Wallichia Roxb. Palmae. 3 palms. St. tall, solitary or short and clustered. Lvs pinnately cut, scurfy. Fr. oblong-ovoid, red to purple. India, SE Asia, S China. Z9.
W. caryotoides Roxb. St. short, clustered, or 0. Lvs to 2.7m; pinnae oblong, lobed and sharply toothed. Burm., India.
W. densiflora (Mast.) Mast. St. v. short, clustered. Lvs to 3.6m; pinnae to 60cm, linear-oblong or oblong, sinuately lobed.
W. disticha Anderson. St. to 6m. Lvs to 3m; pinnae to 60cm, linear-lanceolate, toothed near apex, clustered. India, Burm., Himal.
→*Didyosperma.*

Wallowa *Acacia calamifolia.*
Wall Pepper *Sedum acre.*
Wall Rocket *Diplotaxis.*
Wall Rue *Asplenium ruta-muraria.*
Wall Spray *Cotoneaster horizontalis.*
Wallum Banksia *Banksia aemula.*
Wallum Bottlebrush *Callistemon pachyphyllus.*
Wallwort *Sambucus ebulus.*
Walnut *Juglans.*

Waltheria L. Sterculiaceae. 67 downy perenn. herbs and sub-shrubs. Lvs simple, serrate or dentate. Fls small, in clusters or cymes forming paniculate or racemose infl.; cal., 5-lobed; pet. narrowly obovate to spathulate; sta. 5, opposite pet.; staminodes 0. Trop. Z10.
W. americana L. = *W. indica.*
W. indica L. Subshrub to 2m, velvety throughout. Lvs 2–15×1–6cm, ovate to oblong-ovate. Fls fragrant, in clusters; pet. 4–6mm, yellow. Pantrop.

Waluewa Reg.
W. pulchella Reg. = *Oncidium waluewa.*

Wampee *Pontederia* (*P. cordata*).
Wampi *Clausena lansium.*
Wandering Jew *Tradescantia fluminensis.*
Wand Flower *Dierama.*
Wandflower, Wandplant *Galax.*
Wangrangkura *Eleutherococcus sessiliflorus.*
Wanza *Cordia africana.*
Wapato *Sagittaria cuneata; S. latifolia.*
Waratah *Telopea speciosissima.*
Waringin *Ficus benjamina.*

Warmingia Rchb. f. Orchidaceae. 2 epiphytic orchids. Pbs 1-lvd. Lvs coriaceous, oblong. Rac. lat., pendent; fls small; pet. denticulate; lip 3-lobed. Braz. Z10.
W. eugenii Rchb. f. Pbs to 2cm. Lvs to 10cm, oblong to sub-spathulate. Infl. to 12cm; fls translucent white; pet. to 1.4cm, fimbriate, long-acuminate; lip to 1.1cm, lat. lobes rounded, irregularly lacerate; callus yellow. E Braz.

Warminster Broom *Cytisus* ×*praecox.*

Warrea Lindl. Orchidaceae. 4 terrestrial orchids. Pbs cylindrical to ovoid or ellipsoid. Lvs few, distichous, plicate. Rac. lat.; fls fleshy, showy; sep. concave; pet. smaller than sep.; lip concave, simple to trilobed; disc fleshy, carinate or crested. C & S Amer. Z10.
W. costaricensis Schltr. Pbs ± obscured, cylindrical. Lvs to 60cm, lanceolate. Fls red-bronze, the lip pale copper with darker markings; sep. to 3.5×1.5cm; lip to 3×3cm, suborbicular, entire. Summer. Costa Rica, Panama.
W. cyanea Lindl. = *Warreella cyanea.*
W. tricolor Lindl. = *W. warreana.*
W. warreana (Lodd. ex Lindl.) Schweinf. Pbs to 12cm, ovoid to ellipsoid. Lvs to 60cm, oblong- to elliptic-lanceolate. Fls nodding, yellow-brown to white, the lip ivory, edged white with a purple blotch; sep. to 3.5×2.5cm; lip to 3.5×3.5cm, suborbicular to obovate-rhombic, ± cleft and crenate. Colomb., Venez., Braz., Peru.
→*Aganisia.*

Warreella Schltr. Orchidaceae. 1 epiphytic or terrestrial orchid. Pbs to 5cm, ovoid. Lvs to 40cm, lanceolate-acuminate, equitant. Rac. to 60cm, basal; fls to 3.5cm diam., many, white flushed pink, lip flushed rose or purple. Colomb., Venez. Z10.
W. cyanea (Lindl.) Schltr. As for the genus.
→*Maxillaria* and *Warrea.*

Warscewiczella Benth. & Hook.
W. flabelliformis (Sw.) Cogn. = *Cochleanthes flabelliformis.*
W. marginata Rchb. f. = *Cochleanthes marginata.*
W. wendlandii (Rchb. f.) Schltr. = *Zygopetalum wendlandii.*

Warszewiczia Klotzsch. Rubiaceae. 4 shrubs or trees, usually downy. Lvs with connate intrapetiolar stipules, gland. within. Fls in cymose pan.; cal. 5-lobed, one lobe occas. enlarged, leaflike; cor. funnel-shaped, lobes 5; sta. 5. Trop. Amer. Z10.
W. coccinea (Vahl) Klotzsch. To 6m. Lvs 60×30cm, obovate to obovate-oblong, somewhat lustrous above, densely pubesc. beneath. Pan. dense cymose to 50cm; cal. with enlarged lobe to 7cm, scarlet; cor. 6mm, yellow-orange. C to S Amer., W Indies. 'David Auyong': fls yellow, encircled by enlarged red cal.
→*Calycophyllum* and *Mussaenda.*

Wart Fern *Microsorium scolopendrium.*
Wart Leaf Ceanothus *Ceanothus papillosus.*
Warty Birch *Betula pendula.*
Warty-stem Ceanothus *Ceanothus verrucosus.*
Warty Yate *Eucalyptus megacornuta.*
Wasabi *Wasabia.*

Wasabia Matsum. WASABI; JAPANESE HORSERADISH. Cruciferae. 2 rhizomatous perenn. herbs. Lvs round-cordate, crenate to toothed. Fls 4-merous white, in a rac. Jap. Z8.

Washington Grass *Cabomba caroliniana.*

Washingtonia H.A. Wendl. Palmae. 2 palms. St. solitary, swollen at base, clothed with old lvs and rusty fibre above, grey, ringed below. Lvs costapalmate, blade divided to one-third depth, seg. single-fold, linear. SW US and N Mex.
W. filamentosa (Fenzi) Kuntze = *W. filifera.*
W. filifera (Lind. ex André) H.A. Wendl. COTTON PALM; DESERT FAN PALM; NORTHERN WASHINGTONIA; CALIFORNIAN WASHINGTONIA. To 15m. Petioles to 2m, margins toothed below; lf blades to 2m, seg. narrow-acuminate, apex with white fil. S Calif., SW Ariz., NW Mex.
W. gracilis Parish = *W. robusta.*
W. robusta H.A. Wendl. SOUTHERN WASHINGTONIA; MEXICAN WASHINGTONIA. To 25m. Petioles to 1m, margins toothed throughout; lf blades to 1m, seg. acuminate, pendent, with white fil. in young plants. NW Mex.
W. sonorae Wats. = *W. robusta.*

Washington Thorn *Crataegus phaenopyrum.*
Wassuk Penstemon *Penstemon rubicundus.*
Watch Chain Cypress *Crassula muscosa.*
Water Arum *Calla.*
Water Ash *Ptelea trifoliata.*
Water Avens *Geum rivale.*
Waterberg Cycad *Encephalartos eugene-maraisii.*
Water Betony *Scrophularia auriculata.*
Water Birch *Betula fontinalis.*
Water Bush *Bossiaea* (*B. aquifolium*).
Water Caltrop *Trapa natans.*
Water Carpet *Chrysosplenium americanum.*
Water Chestnut *Trapa* (*T. natans*): *Pachira aquatica.*
Water Chinquapin *Nelumbo lutea.*
Water Clover *Marsilea.*
Water Collard *Nuphar.*
Watercress *Nasturtium.*
Water Crowsfoot *Ranunculus aquatilis.*
Water Dragon *Calla.*
Water Elm *Planera.*
Water Elm *Ulmus americana.*
Waterer's Gold *Ilex aquifolium* 'Wateriana'.
Waterfall Gladiolus *Gladiolus cardinalis.*
Water Fern *Azolla; Ceratopteris; Salvinia; Scrophularia auriculata.*
Water Filter Tree *Strychnos potatorum.*
Water Flaxseed *Spirodela polrrhiza.*
Water Forget-me-not *Myosotis scorpioides.*
Water Fringe *Nymphoides peltata.*
Water Gladiolus *Butomus.*
Water Gum *Tristania neriifolia.*
Water Hawthorn *Aponogeton distachyos.*
Water Hickory *Carya aquatica.*
Water Horehound *Lycopus americanus.*
Water Hyacinth *Eichhornia* (*E. crassipes*).
Water Hyssop *Bacopa.*
Water Island Sand Crinum *Crinum arenarium.*
Waterleaf *Hydrophyllum.*
Water Lemon *Passiflora laurifolia.*
Water Lettuce *Pistia.*
Water Lily *Nymphaea.*
Water Lily Tulip *Tulipa kaufmanniana.*
Water Lobelia *Lobelia dortmanna.*
Water Locust *Gleditsia aquatica.*
Water Maize *Victoria amazonica.*
Water Mat *Chrysosplenium americanum.*
Water Meal *Wolffia.*
Water Melon *Citrullus lanatus.*
Watermelon Begonia *Peperomia argyreia.*
Watermelon Pepper *Peperomia argyreia.*
Watermint *Mentha aquatica.*
Water Moss *Fontinalis.*
Water Nymph *Najas.*
Water Oak *Quercus nigra.*
Water Oats *Zizania.*
Water Orchid *Eichhornia* (*E. crassipes*).
Water Parsnip *Sium suave.*
Water Pennywort *Hydrocotyle umbellata.*
Water Plantain *Alisma plantago-aquatica.*
Water-platter *Victoria.*
Water Poppy *Hydrocleys nymphoides.*
Water Purslane *Ludwigia palustris.*
Water Rice *Zizania aquatica; Z. latifolia.*
Water Rose-apple *Syzygium aqueum.*
Water Smartweed *Polygonum coccineum.*
Water Snowflake *Nymphoides indica.*
Water Soldier *Stratiotes aloides.*

Water Star Grass *Heteranthera dubia.*
Water Starwort *Callitriche.*
Water Trumpet *Cryptocoryne.*
Water Violet *Hottonia palustris.*
Waterweed *Elodea.*
Waterwheel Plant *Aldrovanda.*
Water Willow *Justicia.*
Water Wisteria *Hygrophila difformis.*
Waterwood *Lonchocarpus.*
Water Yam *Dioscorea alata.*
Watkins Fig *Ficus watkinsiana.*

Watsonia Mill. Iridaceae. 52 cormous perenn. herbs. Lvs distichous, sword-shaped, sheathing an erect st. terminating in a simple or branched spike; fls 2-ranked, regular or zygomorphic; perianth tube curved, tep. 6. S Afr., Swaz. Z9.

W. aletroides (Burm. f.) Ker-Gawl. 25–60cm. Lvs 5–10mm wide, linear or lanceolate. Spike to 20-fld; fls slightly irregular, usually orange-red, occas. pink or purple, tep. 10mm. Late winter–spring. SW & W Cape.

W. alpina G. Lewis = *W. strubeniae.*

W. amabilis Goldbl. 8–30cm. Lvs lanceolate, about half the height of the plant and 5–20mm wide. Spike 4–16-fld; fls slightly irregular, rose-pink, darker in centre; tep. spreading, 19–25mm. Spring–early summer. SW Cape.

W. ardernei Sander = *W. borbonica.*

W. beatricis Mathews & L. Bol. = *W. pillansii.*

W. borbonica (Pourr.) Goldbl. 1–2m. Lvs to two-thirds as long as spike, 2–4cm wide, lanceolate. Spike to 20-fld; fls slightly scented, somewhat irregular, rarely white, usually pale to deep pink or purple with white lines at base of each tep.; tep. 30–36mm. Spring–summer. SW Cape. ssp. *ardernei* (Sander) Goldbl. Fls pink or white.

W. brevifolia Ker-Gawl. = *W. laccata.*

W. bulbilifera Mathews & L. Bol. = *W. meriana.*

W. coccinea Herb. ex Bak. 15–40cm. Lvs 2–8mm wide, linear or lanceolate. Spike 3–6-fld; fls red, purple or pink, tep. sometimes with dark central line; tep. 16–23mm. Winter–spring. SW Cape.

W. comptonii L. Bol. = *W. zeyheri.*

W. densiflora Bak. 60–150cm. Lvs about half as long as spike, 10–18mm wide, linear or lanceolate. Spike many-fld; fls irregular, ± 2-lipped, pink, usually with darker mid-line on tep., rarely white; tep. 18–24mm. Summer. SE Cape coastal area and into Natal midlands. 'Alba': fls white.

W. fourcadei Mathews & L. Bol. 90–180cm. Lvs to about one-third height of plant, 1.5–4cm wide, sword-shaped. Spike 25–40-fld; fls rather irregular, pink, orange or vermilion, rarely purple, sometimes with tube paler; tep. 24–33mm. Spring–summer. SW Cape.

W. galpinii L. Bol. 1–2m. Lvs to 30×1–2cm, lanceolate or sword-shaped. Spike branched, densely-fld; fls somewhat irregular, orange-red or mauve-pink; tep. 15–20mm. Summer–autumn. S Cape.

W. humilis Mill. 10–30cm. Lvs usually about half length of st., 8–15mm wide, lanceolate. Spike 6–12-fld; fls slightly irregular, white or pale pink tinged with darker pink, the tube and outside of tep. darker; tep. 15–22mm. Spring–early summer. SW Cape.

W. laccata (Jacq.) Ker-Gawl. 20–65cm. Lvs one third to two thirds as long as plant, linear or lanceolate. Spike to 20-fld; fls irregular, pale pink, pale orange or purple; tep. 14–16mm. Late winter–spring. S Cape.

W. latifolia N.E. Br. 70–150cm. Lvs broadly lanceolate, 5–9cm wide. Spike 15–25-fld; fls slightly irregular, maroon-red; tep. 20–30mm. N Natal & SE Transvaal, Swaz.

W. marginata (L. f.) Ker-Gawl. To 2m. Lvs shorter than st., 2–5cm wide, lanceolate, margins thickened. Spike several to many-fld; fls almost regular, mauve-pink or magenta, each tep. with a white line edged with purple towards base (sometimes entirely white); tep. 14–22mm. Spring–early summer. W Cape.

W. meriana (L.) Mill. 50cm–2m. Lvs to about half the height of plant; 1–3.5cm wide, lanceolate. Spike to 25-fld; fls irregular, orange, red, pink or purple, rarely yellow; tep. 21–26mm. Spring. Cape winter rainfall area. 'Bulbilifera': a large-fld form with axill. cormlets; nat. Australia, Mauritius and Réunion.

W. pillansii L. Bol. 50–120cm. Lvs about half length of plant, 7–18mm wide. Spike 20–35-fld; fls ± irregular, orange or orange-red; tep. 20–26mm. Summer. S & E Cape, Natal, Transkei. Z7.

W. pyramidata (Andrews) Klatt = *W. borbonica.*

W. roseoalba (Jacq.) Ker-Gawl. = *W. humilis.*

W. socium Mathews & L. Bol. = *W. pillansii.*

W. spectabilis Schinz. 20–50cm. Lvs almost as long as st., 2–8mm wide, linear. Spike 2–5(-10)-fld; fls irregular, red or orange; tep. 30–35mm. Winter–spring. SW Cape.

W. stanfordiae L. Bol. = *W. fourcadei.*

W. stenosiphon L. Bol. 20–45cm. Lvs to half height of plant, 5–12mm wide, linear or lanceolate. Spike several-fld; fls irregular, salmon-orange or mauve, lower 3 tep. sometimes with dark, median line; tep. 17–20mm. Spring. S Cape coast.

W. strictiflora Ker-Gawl. 24–40cm. Lvs about half length of spike, about 1.5cm wide, lanceolate. Spike few to several-fld; fls somewhat irregular, pink with a dark red-purple streak near base of each tep.; tep. 22–25mm. Late spring–early summer. SW Cape.

W. strubeniae L. Bol. 60–100cm. Lvs 1.5–2cm wide, lanceolate, margins thickened. Main spike 25–35-fld; fls irregular, pale pink; tep. 17–19mm. Late summer–autumn. E Transvaal.

W. tabularis Mathews & L. Bol. To 1.5m. Lvs sword-shaped, about half as long as st., 2–3.5cm wide. Spike 20–30-fld; fls irregular, orange-red, or pink (inner tep. paler), tep. 20–26mm. Winter. Cape Penins. and Cape Flats.

W. transvaalensis Bak. To 50cm. Lvs equalling st., 8–25mm wide, lanceolate, margins somewhat thickened. Spike 10–16-fld; fls irregular, deep pink; tep. 20–25mm. Late summer–autumn. NE Transvaal.

W. versfeldii Mathews & L. Bol. 1–2m. Lvs shorter than st., 2.5–4cm wide, lanceolate. Main spike to 24-fld; fls irregular, purple-pink; tep. 33–46mm. Spring. SW Cape.

W. wilmanii Mathews & L. Bol. 80–150cm. Lvs about half length of st., 1.5–3cm wide, lanceolate. Spike dense; fls cream, pink, red, purple or orange; tep. 18–22mm. Late spring–summer. S Cape.

W. wilmsii L. Bol. 45–75cm. Lvs about half length of st., 1–2.5cm wide, lanceolate. Spike to about 25-fld; fls deep pink, the lower tep. with a darker median line; tep. 22–24mm. Summer–autumn. E Transvaal.

W. zeyheri L. Bol. To 80cm. Lvs about half as long as st., 12–18mm wide, linear or lanceolate. Spike few to several-fld; fls irregular, salmon-orange, tep. base with darker mid-line; tep. 20–22mm. Spring–early summer. SW Cape.

W. cvs. 'Dazzler': fls bright red. 'Malvern': fls large, clear orchid-pink. 'Mrs. Bullard's White': fls pure white. 'Rubra': fls deep crimson.

Wattakaka (Decne.) Hassk.
W. sinensis (Hemsl.) Stapf. = *Dregea sinensis.*

Wattle *Acacia.*
Wavy Cloak Fern *Cheilanthes sinuata.*
Wavy Hair Grass *Deschampsia flexuosa.*
Wavy leaf Ceanothus *Ceanothus foliosus.*
Wavy-leaf Fig *Ficus septica.*
Wavy-leaf Oak *Quercus undulata.*
Wavy-leaved Spurge *Euphorbia undulatifolia.*
Wax Apple *Syzygium samarangense.*
Wax Bean *Phaseolus vulgaris.*
Wax Begonia *Begonia schulziana.*
Waxberry *Gaultheria hispida; Symphoricarpos albus.*
Waxflower *Hoya; Jamesia; Stephanotis floribunda.*
Wax Gourd *Benincasa hispida.*
Wax Mallow *Malvaviscus arboreus.*
Wax Myrtle *Myrica cerifera.*
Wax Palm *Copernicia; Ceroxylon.*
Wax Plant *Hoya carnosa.*
Wax Privet *Peperomia glabella.*
Wax Rosette *Echeveria ×gilva.*
Wax Tree *Toxicodendron succedaneum.*
Wax Vine *Senecio macroglossus.*
Waxwork *Celastrus scandens.*
Wayfaring Tree *Viburnum lantana.*
Weasel's Snout *Misopates.*
Weather Prophet *Dimorphotheca pluvialis.*
Weaver's Broom *Spartium junceum.*

Weberbauerocereus Backeb.
W. weberbaueri (Schum. ex Vaupel) Backeb. = *Haageocereus weberbaueri.*

Weberocereus Britt. & Rose. Cactaceae. 9 epiphytic or epilithic shrubs; st. terete, angled or flattened, ribs 2–5; spines short, or 0, no. per areole given below. Fls nocturnal, funnelform. Fr. globose to oblong, red or yellow, fleshy, bristly or naked. Mex., C Amer. (mainly Costa Rica), Panama and Ecuad.

W. biolleyi (F.A.C. Weber) Britt. & Rose. Climbing or pendent; mature st. terete or angled, 4–6mm diam.; juvenile growth flattened or 3-angled; spines usually 0, rarely 1–3. Fl. 3–5cm; inner tep. pale pink. Costa Rica. Z9.

W. bradei (Britt. & Rose) Rowley. Epiphytic; st. segmented; seg. terete at base, flattened above, to 1m×5–12cm, margins crenate; spines usually 2–4, 3–6mm. Fl. 5.5–7cm; outer tep. pale pink, inner white. Spring–autumn. Costa Rica. Z9.

W. glaber (Eichlam) G. Rowley. Climbing; st. slender, 3-angled, 2.5–4.5cm broad; spines 2–4, 1–3mm. Fl. 9–11cm; tep. white. Guat., S Mex. Z9.

W. imitans (Kimnach & Hutchison) F. Buxb. Epiphyte; st. terete at base, flat and deeply pinnately lobed above, to 90×10–15cm overall; spines usually 0(–3), 2–4mm. Fl. 6–7cm; outer tep. maroon, inner pale yellow. Costa Rica. Z9.

W. panamensis Britt. & Rose. St. 1–2cm broad, 3-angled or flat, margins indented; spines 0–3, short. Fl. 4–7cm; outer tep. yellow-green, inner white. Panama. Z9.

W. rosei (Kimnach) Britt. & Rose. Epilithic; st. ascending or pendulous, flat above, to 65×4–10cm, crenate; spines 0–5, 1–4mm. Fl. 5.5–7cm; outer tep. pink-green, fleshy; inner pale yellow-green or white. Ecuad. Z9.

W. tonduzii (F.A.C. Weber) G. Rowley. St. climbing, or pendent; seg. 3- or 4-angled or winged, 10–40×2–3(–5)cm; spines 0(–1–2) to 2mm. Fl. 6–8cm; outer tep. pale yellow, tinged green or brown, inner creamy white. Winter. Costa Rica. Z9.

W. trichophorus H. Johnson & Kimnach. St. scandent and pendent, to 1m or more, terete or 5–7-angled, 8–12mm diam.; spines 2–4 (juv.), up to 20 (adults), 3–12mm, pale yellow. Fl. solitary, 5.5–6cm; outer tep. amber-pink or purple-pink, inner light pink. Costa Rica. Z9.

W. tunilla (Weber) Britt. & Rose. Climber; st. 5–12mm diam.; ribs (2–)4(–5), pronounced, juvenile ± terete; spines 6–12, 6–8mm. Fl. 5–6cm; outer tep. tinged brown, inner pink. Costa Rica. Z9.

→*Cryptocereus*, *Eccremocactus*, *Selenicereus* and *Werckleocereus*.

Wedding-cake Tree *Cornus controversa 'Variegata'*

Wedelia Jacq. Compositae. *c*70 hirsute ann. to perenn. herbs, subshrubs or shrubs; st. erect to prostrate or sometimes scandent, often rooting at nodes. Cap. radiate, axill. or term., solitary or in small clusters, on long peduncles; receptacle flat to convex; ray flts usually yellow; disc flts usually yellow. Trop. and subtrop. Z10.

W. aurea D. Don ex Hook. = *Lasianthaea aurea*.

W. hispida Kunth. Perenn. herb to 45cm. Lvs lanceolate to obovate-lanceolate, dentate, base cuneate, apex acute to acuminate. Cap. solitary. Summer. Mex.

W. radiosa Ker-Gawl. Subshrub to 60cm. Lvs ovate to oblong-lanceolate, dentate, apex acute, softly downy. Cap. 1–3; peduncles longer than lvs. Summer. Braz.

W. trilobata (L.) Hitchc. Creeping perenn. to 2m+, rooting at nodes. Lvs to 12cm, elliptic or oblong-obovate to obovate, apex 3-lobed, sometimes entire to weakly lobed or toothed. Cap. to 2cm diam., solitary. Trop. Amer. to S Flor.

Wedgeleaf Fig *Ficus semicordata*.
Wedge-leaved Dryandra *Dryandra cuneata*.
Weeping Aspen *Populus tremula* 'Pendula'.
Weeping Baeckea *Baeckea linifolia*.
Weeping Boerboon *Schotia brachypetala*.
Weeping Boree *Acacia vestita*.
Weeping Bottlebrush *Callistemon viminalis*.
Weeping Fig *Ficus benjamina*.
Weeping Gum *Eucalyptus sepulcralis*.
Weeping Larch *Larix ×pendula*.
Weeping Lime *Tilia* 'Petiolaris'.
Weeping Love Grass *Eragrostis curvula*.
Weeping Myall *Acacia pendula*.
Weeping Pinyon *Pinus pinceana*.
Weeping Pittosporum *Pittosporum phillyreoides*.
Weeping Spleenwort *Asplenium flaccidum*.
Weeping Teatree *Melaleuca leucadendra*.
Weeping Ti-tree *Leptospermum trinervium*.
Weeping Tree Broom *Chordospartium*.
Weeping Willow *Salix babylonica*; *S. ×sepulcralis* (*S. ×sepulcralis* 'Chrysocoma').

Weigela Thunb. Caprifoliaceae. 10 decid. shrubs. Lvs simple, serrate. Fls in axill. and terminal corymbs; cal.-tube narrow, sep. 5; cor. campanulate-funnelform, 5-lobed; sta. 5. E Asia.

W. amabilis Van Houtte = *W. coraeensis*.
W. arborea hort. = *W. coraeensis*.
W. arborea var. *grandiflora* hort. = *W. coraeensis* 'Alba'.

W. coraeensis Thunb. To 5m. Lvs to 15×10cm, broad-elliptic or obovate-elliptic, abruptly-acuminate, crenate, subglabrous, veins pubesc. Fls 2–8 per cyme; cor. to 4cm, white or light pink, to carmine red; style not exserted. Spring–summer. Jap. 'Alba': fls yellowish white, later pale rose. 'Gustave Mallet' (*W. coraeensis* ×*W. florida*): fls large, long-tubed, limb wide, buds bright pink opening pink tinted red. Z6.

W. decora (Nak.) Nak. To 5m. Lvs to 10×6cm, obovate-elliptic, abruptly acuminate, subglabr. above, veins short-pilose be-

neath. Fls paired or 3-together; cor. to 3.5cm, white then red; style exserted. Spring–summer. Jap. Z6.

W. floribunda (Sieb. & Zucc.) K. Koch. To 3m. Lvs to 12×6cm, elliptic, ovate-oblong or ovate, acuminate, serrate, pilose above, white pilose on veins beneath. Fls 1–3-clustered; cor. to 3.5cm, dark carmine-red, style exserted. Spring–summer. Jap. 'Grandiflora': fls large, brown tinted carmine. 'Abel Carrière': fls large, rosy carmine, throat spotted yellow, buds darker, early-flowering. 'Deboisii': fls small, v. open, deep red, limb lobe base spotted yellow, buds blood red. Z6.

W. florida (Bunge) A. DC. To 3m+. Lvs to 10×4cm, ovate-oblong or obovate, acuminate, serrate, glab. above, pubesc. on veins beneath. Fls solitary; cor. to 4cm, dark rose red, paler inside; style exserted. Spring–summer. Korea, N China, Jap. 'Alba': fls white. 'Bicolor': fls white, cream, fading to pink. 'Biformis': fls of 2 types, large fls dark pink, small pink, sometimes striped. 'Bristol Ruby' (*W. florida* ×*W.* 'Eva Rathke'): habit erect, to 2m; lvs rich green, fls ruby red, buds v. dark, profuse, long-lasting. 'Bristol Snowflake': to 1.2m; fls white, profuse; hardy. 'Dropmore Pink': fls pink. 'Eva Rathke': fls crimson to red tinted brown, abundant; weak-growing. 'Eva Supreme' ('Newport Red' ×'Eva Rathke'): habit dwarf, compact and bushy, to 1.5m high, to 1.5m wide; fls tube long and wide, deep crimson, interior lighter; strong-growing. 'Fiesta' ('Eva Rathke' ×'Newport Red'): habit open, vigorous; fls red, tube narrow, cor. to 3cm wide. 'Foliis Purpureus' ('Purpurea'): habit dwarf, compact; lvs red-purple-maroon; fls dark pink. 'Java Red': mound-forming, compact, to 1.2m high; lvs deep green, tinted maroon; fls dark pink, carmine in bud. 'Madame Teiller': habit upright; lvs pubesc. beneath; fls large, chalky pink later dark carmine. 'Minuet': habit dwarf, to 75cm; lvs dark green tinted purple; fls fragrant, cor. tube and outer cor. dark rose, lobes lilac, throat yellow; hardy. 'Mont-Blanc': fls large, snow white later lightly tinted pink, buds tinged green. 'Nana Variegata' ('Variegata Nana'): neatly rounded form; lvs soft green edged cream; fls pale pink. 'Pink Delight': habit small, to 1.3m; fls deep pink, colour lasts well; hardy. 'Pink Princess': habit rounded, to 2m high; fls brilliant pink, abundant; hardy. 'Purpurea Nana': habit small; lvs flushed purple; fls dark pink. 'Red Prince': habit low and wide; st. slender; lvs rich green; fls deep coral red, colour lasts well. 'Rosabella' ('Eva Rathke' ×'Newport Red'): habit open, rather stiff; fls large, v. open, tube short, pink, limb tinted white, profuse. 'Rosea': fls pink. 'Rumba': habit compact, to 1.2m high, to 1.2m wide; lvs yellow-green tinted purple, abundant; fls red, throats yellow, free-flowering. 'Van Houttei': fls carmine tinted pink, throat deep lilac, limb white. 'Variegata' ('Aureovariegata', 'Variegata Aurea'): habit compact; lvs edged cream; fls deep rose. 'Versicolor': fls cream and red. 'Victoria': habit bushy, compact, to 90cm high; lvs flushed purple; fls narrowly tubular, dusky pink to red. var. *venusta* (Rehd.) Nak. Lvs to 5cm, oblong-elliptic, subglabr. Fls purple-pink, dense-clustered; cor. campanulate at apex, narrowing to a long-cylindric tube, lobes small, obtuse, equal. Korea. Z5.

W. grandiflora (Sieb. & Zucc.) K. Koch = *W. coraeensis*.

W. hortensis (Sieb. & Zucc.) K. Koch. To 3m. Lvs to 10×5cm, ovate-elliptic, oblong or obovate, acuminate, serrate, subglabr. above, dense pubesc. beneath. Fls 2–3-clustered; cor. to 3.5cm, rose; style subexserted. Spring–summer. Jap. 'Nivea': fls large, white. Z7.

W. japonica Thunb. To 5m. Lvs to 10×5cm, oblong, ovate-oblong or elliptic, acuminate, serrulate, loose-pubesc. above when young, veins pubesc. beneath. Fls solitary or paired; cor. to 3.5cm; white then red; style exserted. Spring. Jap. 'Alba': fls white. 'Dart's Colour Dream': habit sturdy; fls of 2 types, cream and pink to rose with white stigma and sta. Z6.

W. maximowiczii (S. Moore) Rehd. To 3m, densely branched. Lvs to 10×3cm, ovate-oblong, narrow-obovate or ovate, abrupt-acuminate, serrate, loosely pubesc. Fls solitary or paired in cymes; cor. to 4cm, yellow; style long-exserted. Spring–summer. Jap. Z6.

W. middendorffiana (Carr.) K. Koch. To 1.5m, densely branched. Lvs to 11.5×5cm, oblong or narrow-ovate, acute or abrupt-acuminate, serrate, short-pilose above, coarse-pubesc. beneath. Fls solitary or paired; cor. to 4cm, yellow; style short-exserted. Summer. Jap., N China, Manch. Z4.

W. praecox (Lemoine) L.H. Bail. To 2m, habit tightly upright, densely branched. Lvs to 7×3cm, ovate or ovate-oblong, prominently pubesc., esp. on veins. Fls solitary or paired; cor. to 4cm, purple-pink to carmine. Spring–summer. Jap., Korea, Manch. 'Avalanche': fls snow white, outside tinted pale pink, profuse. 'Avante-garde': fls large, interior pink marbled and yellow flecked, later striking pink. 'Bouquet Rose': fls large, carmine, darker in bud, limb chalky pink, throat striped yellow. 'Conquérant': fls large, interior burgundy, exterior and throat carmine. 'Esperance': fls large, white flushed salmon, buds darker, early-flowering. 'Fleur de Mai': fls with exterior purple and pink, interior white marbled pink, fading buds purple, profuse, early-flowering. 'Floreal': fls large, rosy pink, throat tinted red, limb interior flushed white, buds purple. 'Fraicheur': fls slightly larger, exterior pink with limb white, interior cream. 'Glorieux': fls deep red in bud opening carmine, limb light coloured. 'Gracieux': habit erect; fls large, pale pink, throat sulphur, cor. limb tinted white, buds salmon. 'Le Printemps': fls pink, limb flushed white, pale carmine in bud. 'Seduction': fls strong red tinted carmine, limb lighter, buds deep red. 'Variegata': lvs variegated cream and white. Z5.

W. rosea Lindl. = *W. florida.*
W. splendens Carr. = *Diervilla* × *splendens.*
W. cvs. 'Ballet': fls wide, deep pink, profuse. 'Boskoop Glory': fls large, pink tinted salmon. 'Candida': lvs light green, fls pure white. 'Carnival': fls pink and white. 'Evita': habit broad and compact, fls red, abundant. 'Jean Mace': fls large, darkest purple. 'Lavellei': fls small, strong crimson. 'Looymansii Aurea': lvs light gold, fls carmine, profuse. 'Lucifer': fls large, red, late-flowering. 'Majestueux': tall, fls madder pink, carmine-throated, abundant. 'Olympiad' ('Rubidor'): tall, lvs soft yellow, fls red. 'Rumba': fls dark red, free-flowering. 'Stelzneri': fls red tinted purple, clustered to 20, profuse. 'Styriaca': low, lvs light green, fls bright carmine, abundant. →*Diervilla.*

Weingartia Werderm. = *Rebutia.*

Weinmannia L. Cunoniaceae. 150 everg. trees or shrubs. Lvs coriaceous, simple or odd-pinnate; lfts toothed. Fls small in a wand-like rac. or pan.; cal. 4- or 5-lobed; pet. 4 or 5, ovate or obovate to spathulate; sta. 8 to 10. Fr. a capsule with glossy seeds. Cosmop.

W. australis A. Cunn. = *Calycomis australis.*
W. benthamii (F. Muell.) Bail. = *Geissois benthamii.*
W. paniculata Cav. = *Caldcluvia paniculata.*
W. paniculosa F. Muell. = *Caldcluvia paniculosa.*
W. pinnata L. Shrub or tree to 10m. Lvs to 7cm, lfts to 2×1cm, elliptic to elliptic-oblong, serrate. Pet. to 2mm, white. Mex. to Braz. and W Indies. Z10.
W. racemosa L. f. KAMAHI. Tree to 25m. Lvs to 10cm, simple, broadly ovate or ovate-elliptic to elliptic, serrate. Pet. to 3mm, white or cream to pale rose. NZ. Z9.
W. sylvicola Sol. ex A. Cunn. TAUHERO. Tree to 15m. Lvs simple or with 3–5 lfts to 7×3cm, elliptic, serrate to crenate. Pet. to 2.5mm, white to pale rose. NZ. Z9.
W. trichosperma Cav. TINEO; MADEN. Tree or shrub to 20m. Lvs to 10cm; lfts 11–13, to 3cm, broadly elliptic or obovate, dentate. Pet. to 2mm, white. Chile, Arg. Z9.
W. trifoliatus Thunb. = *Platylophus trifoliatus.*

Weldenia Schult. f. Commelinaceae. 1 tuberous-rooted stemless perenn. Lvs 5–20cm, linear-lanceolate or lorate, rosulate. Infl. a term. thyrse of several cincinni; cor. tube 4–6.5cm, lobes ovate, 1–2×c1cm, white. Spring–autumn. Mts of Mex. and Guat. Z9.
W. candida Schult. f. As above. f. **caerulea** Matuda. Fls blue.

Wellingtonia Lindl. non Meissn. = *Sequoiadendron.*

Welsh Onion *Allium fistulosum.*
Welsh Polypody *Polypodium cambricum.*
Welsh Poppy *Meconopsis cambrica.*

Welwitschia Hook. f. Welwitschiaceae. 1. Long-lived xerophytic gymnosperm. Taproot deep, massively swollen, crown an exposed, turnip-like bole to 1m across. Lvs to 2m, 2, opposite, arising from crown margins, leathery, strap-like, growing continuously, twisting and tattered at tips. Cones in axill. cymes; ♂ to 2cm, ♀ to 6cm, red. Nam., S Angola. Z9.
W. bainesii (Hook. f.) Carr. = *W. mirabilis.*
W. mirabilis Hook. f.

WELWITSCHIACEAE Markgr. See *Welwitschia*

Wendlandia Bartling. Rubiaceae. 50 shrubs or small trees. Lvs opposite or in whorls of 3, stipulate. Fls, in bracteate term., paniculate cymes; cal. lobes 4–5; cor. funnel- or salver-shaped, or tubular, lobes 4–5; sta. 4–5. Trop. & subtrop. Asia. Z10.
W. exserta DC. Tree, everg. or decid., woolly throughout. Lvs to 23cm, lanceolate to ovate-lanceolate, leathery. Fls 6mm wide, white, fragrant in pyramidal pan. to 25cm. India.
W. speciosa Cowan. Shrub or tree, to 10m, initially pubesc. Lvs to 13cm, ovate, leathery. Fls to 2cm, cream fragrant, in paniculate cymes. Winter. SE Asia.
W. tinctoria DC. Tree to 2m. Lvs to 20cm, elliptic to lanceolate

or ovate or obovate, lustrous above, minutely pubesc. beneath. Fls 6mm diam., white, in pan. Summer. India.

Wercklea Pittier & Standl. Malvaceae. 2 shrubs or small trees. Lvs simple. Fls solitary or paired; epical. seg. 3–10; cal. seg. 5; pet. 5; sta. united in tubular column. Costa Rica, Panama. Z10.
W. insignis Pittier & Standl. Everg. tree, 5–18m, crown rounded. Lvs 20–35cm, rounded, cordate or reniform, entire to sinulate or undulate-dentate. Fls long-stalked; pet. to 12cm, rose-lilac or purple, paler or yellow at base. Costa Rica.

Werckleocereus Britt. & Rose.
W. glaber (Eichlam) Britt. & Rose = *Weberocereus glaber.*
W. imitans Kimnach & Hutchison = *Weberocereus imitans.*
W. tonduzii (F.A.C. Weber) Britt. & Rose = *Weberocereus tonduzii.*

Werckle's Rubber Tree *Ficus americana.*
Western Australia Coral Pea *Hardenbergia comptoniana.*
Western Balsam Poplar *Populus trichocarpa.*
Western Black Wattle *Acacia hakeoides.*
Western Blueberry *Vaccinium occidentalis.*
Western Bracken *Pteridium aquilinum* var. *pubescens.*
Western Burning Bush *Euonymus occidentalis.*
Western Buttercup *Ranunculus occidentalis.*
Western Catalpa *Catalpa speciosa.*
Western Chokeberry *Prunus virginiana* var. *demissa.*
Western Coastal Wattle *Acacia cyclops.*
Western Cornel *Cornus glabrata.*
Western Desert Willow *Chilopsis linearis* var. *arcuata.*
Western Dog Violet *Viola adunca.*
Western Hemlock *Tsuga heterophylla.*
Western Holly Fern *Polystichum scopulinum.*
Western Ironweed *Vernonia baldwinii.*
Western Juniper *Juniperus occidentalis.*
Western Larch *Larix occidentalis.*
Western Milfoil *Myriophyllum hippuroides.*
Western Mountain Banksia *Banksia oreophila.*
Western Mugwort *Artemisia ludoviciana.*
Western Poison Oak *Toxicodendron diversilobum.*
Western Polypody *Polypodium hesperium.*
Western Poppy *Papaver californicum.*
Western Prickly Moses *Acacia pulchella.*
Western Prince's Pine *Chimaphila umbellata.*
Western Redbud *Cercis occidentalis.*
Western Red Cedar *Thuja plicata.*
Western Round Leaved Violet *Viola orbiculata.*
Western Sand Cherry *Prunus besseyi.*
Western Silver Wattle *Acacia decora.*
Western Sweet White Violet *Viola macloskeyi.*
Western Tea Myrtle *Melaleuca nesophila.*
Western Wall Flower *Erysimum asperum.*
Western White Pine *Pinus monticola.*
Western Wild Plum *Prunus subcordata.*
Western Wild Rose *Rosa woodsii.*
Western Woody Pear *Xylomelum occidentale.*
Western Yellow Pine *Pinus ponderosa.*
Western Yew *Taxus brevifolia.*
West Himalayan Birch *Betula utilis* var. *jacquemontii.*
West Himalayan Fir *Abies pindrow.*
West Himalayan Spruce *Picea smithiana.*
West Indian Dogwood *Piscidia piscipula.*
West Indian Gherkin *Cucumis anguria.*
West Indian Gourd *Cucumis anguria.*
West Indian Holly *Leea coccinea; Turnera ulmifolia.*
West Indian Jasmine *Plumeria* (*P. alba*).
West Indian Laurel Fig *Ficus americana.*
West Indian Snowberry *Chiococca alba.*
West Indian Tree Fern *Cyathea arborea.*
West Indian Walnut *Juglans jamaicensis.*
Westland Pine *Lagarostrobus colensoi.*

Westringia Sm. Labiatae. 27 shrubs. Lvs whorled, entire. Fls axill. and solitary or in terminal heads; cal. campanulate, teeth 5; cor. 2-lipped, upper lip erect, plane, 2-lobed, lower lip spreading, 3-lobed. Aus. Z10.
W. amabilis Boiv. To 3m. Lvs to 2cm, 3-whorled, ovate to lanceolate or elliptic. Fls white or pink to lavender. Queensld, NSW.
W. angustifolia R. Br. To 2m. Lvs 3–4-whorled, linear. Fls axill. and solitary, white to lilac and yellow- to red-flecked. Tasm.
W. angustifolia J.M. Black, non R. Br. = *W. eremicola.*
W. breviflora Benth. = *W. raleighii.*
W. dampieri R. Br. To 1m. Lvs to 5cm, 3–4-whorled, linear, pubesc. to tomentose beneath. Fls white and yellow- to purple-flecked. Autumn. S & W Aus.

W. eremicola Cunn. ex Benth. To 2m. Lvs to 2.5cm, 3-whorled, linear, toothed, rough. Fls white or blue to mauve or violet. Queensld, NSW, Vict., S Aus.

W. glabra R. Br. Lvs to 2cm, 3-whorled, oblong to elliptic or lanceolate, lustrous above. Fls mauve to violet. Queensld, NSW.

W. grevillina Muell. = *W. dampieri.*

W. longifolia R. Br. To 2m. Lvs to 2.5cm, 3-whorled, linear, lustrous, glab. Fls white or, rarely, mauve to lilac. NSW.

W. raleighii Boiv. To 1m. Lvs to 1.2cm, 4-whorled, oblong to elliptic or lanceolate, white-pubesc. beneath. Fls mauve. Tasm.

W. rigida R. Br. To 1m. St. stiff. Lvs to 1cm, 3–4-whorled, linear to ovate, rough and lustrous or, initially pubesc. above, pubesc. beneath. Fls white or violet and purple-flecked. Aus., Tasm. 'Variegata': lvs variegated white.

Weymouth Pine *Pinus strobus.*
Whauwhaupaku *Pseudopanax arboreus.*
Wheately Elm *Ulmus* 'Sarniensis'.
Wheatgrass *Agropyron.*
Wheel Lily *Lilium medeoloides.*
Whin *Ulex europaeus.*
Whinberry *Vaccinium myrtillus.*

Whipplea Torr. Hydrangeaceae (Philadelphaceae). 1 decid. trailing subshrub. St. to 60cm, pubesc., rooting. Lvs to 3cm, ovate, sparsely toothed, sessile. Fls white, to 0.5cm diam. in dense term. clusters on erect stalks; cal. turbinate, lobes 5–6; pet. 5–6, spreading; sta. 10–12. Summer. Calif. to Ore. Z8.
W. modesta Torr. YERBA DE SELVA.

Whisk Fern *Psilotum.*
Whispering Bells *Emmenanthe penduliflora.*
Whistling Pine *Casuarina.*
Whistling Tree *Acacia seyal.*
White Alder *Alnus rhombifolia; Clethra; Platylophus trifoliatus.*
White Arrow Arum *Peltandra sagittifolia.*
White Ash *Fraxinus americana.*
White Asphodel *Asphodelus albus.*
White Avens *Geum canadense.*
White Bachelor's Buttons *Ranunculus aconitifolius.*
White-backed Hosta *Hosta hypoleuca.*
White Baneberry *Actaea alba.*
Whitebark Pine *Pinus albicaulis.*
White Basswood *Tilia heterophylla.*
White Beach *Gmelina leichthardtii.*
Whitebeam *Sorbus aria.*
White Bedstraw *Galium mollugo.*
White Berry Yew *Pseudotaxus chienii.*
White Birch *Betula papyrifera, B. pubescens.*
White Bottlebrush *Callistemon salignus.*
White Box *Eucalyptus albens.*
White Broom *Retama raetam.*
White Bryony *Bryonia alba.*
White Caladenia *Caladenia alba.*
White Camas *Zigadenus elegans; Z. glaucus.*
White Cedar *Chamaecyparis thyoides; Tabebuia heterophylla.*
White Chervil *Cryptotaenia canadensis.*
White Chinese Birch *Betula albosinensis.*
White Cinnamon *Canella.*
White Clover *Trifolium repens.*
White Corallita *Porana paniculata.*
White Correa *Correa alba.*
Whitecup *Nierembergia repens.*
White Cypress *Chamaecyparis thyoides.*
White Cypress-pine *Callitris glaucophylla.*
White Dead Nettle *Lamium album.*
White Dipladenia *Mandevilla boliviensis.*
White Dog's-tooth Violet *Erythronium albidum.*
White Dutch Runner *Phaseolus coccineus.*
White Elm *Ulmus americana.*
White Evening Primrose *Oenothera speciosa.*
White Everlasting *Helichrysum baxteri.*
White False Hellebore *Veratrum album.*
White False Indigo *Baptisia lactea.*
White Field Currant *Ribes cereum.*
White Fir *Abies concolor.*
White-flowered Gourd *Lagenaria siceraria.*
White-flowered Penstemon *Penstemon pratensis.*
White-flowered Currant *Ribes indecorum.*
White Forget-me-not *Cryptantha.*
White Forsythia *Abeliophyllum.*
White Fritillary *Fritillaria liliacea.*
White Gardenia *Gardenia thunbergia.*
White Ginger *Hedychium coronarium.*
White Ginger Lily *Hedychium coronarium.*

White Gourd *Benincasa hispida.*
White Gum *Eucalyptus alba.*
White-haired Cycad *Encephalartos friderici-guilielmi.*

Whiteheadia Harv. Liliaceae (Hyacinthaceae). 1 perenn. bulbous herb. Lvs to 30×20cm, 2, opposite, spreading, rounded-oblong, succulent, smooth. Spike to 15cm, condensed, short-scapose; spathe bracts 2, 2.5–4cm; perianth green, seg. 6; sta. 6. S Afr., S Nam. Z10.
W. bifolia (Jacq.) Bak.
→*Melanthium.*

White Heart Hickory *Carya tomentosa.*
White Heather *Cassiope mertensiana.*
White Helleborine *Cephalanthera damasonium.*
White Honeysuckle *Lonicera albiflora.*
White Hoop Petticoat Daffodil *Narcissus cantabricus.*
White Horehound *Marrubium vulgare.*
White Horse Nettle *Solanum elaeagnifolium.*
White Ironbark *Eucalyptus leucoxylon.*
White Ixora *Ixora thwaitesii.*
White Lady *Cephalanthera longifolia.*
White-leaf Oak *Quercus hypoleucoides.*
White-leaved Rock Rose *Cistus albidus.*
White Lettuce *Nabalus albus.*
White Lily *Lilium candidum; Nymphaea lotus.*
White Lupine *Lupinus albus.*
White Madder *Galium mollugo.*
White Mahogany *Eucalyptus acmenoides.*
White Mallee *Eucalyptus dumosa.*
White Mallow *Althaea officinalis.*
White Mandarin *Streptopus amplexifolius.*
White-man's Foot *Plantago major.*
White-margined Nightshade *Solanum marginatum.*
White Mexican Rose *Echeveria elegans.*
White Monterey Ceanothus *Ceanothus rigidus.*
White Mountain Ash *Eucalyptus fraxinoides.*
White Mugwort *Artemisia lactiflora.*
White Mulberry *Morus alba.*
White Mullein *Verbascum lychnitis.*
White Mustard *Brassica hirta; Sinapis alba.*
White Myrtle *Hypocalymma angustifolium.*
White Needles *Ixora nigricans.*
White Oak *Quercus alba.*
White Paper-daisy *Helichrysum elatum.*
White Pepper *Piper nigrum.*
White Peppermint *Eucalyptus pulchella.*
White Popinac *Leucaena leucocephala.*
White Poplar *Populus alba.*
White Potato *Solanum tuberosum.*
White Prairie Aster *Aster falcatus.*
White Prairie Clover *Dalea candida.*
White Prairie Mallow *Sidalcea candida.*
White Prairie Rose *Rosa foliolosa.*
White Purslane *Claytonia australasica.*
White Rocket *Diplotaxis erucoides.*
White Rose *Rosa ×alba.*
White Rosebay *Epilobium angustifolium* 'Album'.
White Rose of York *Rosa ×alba.*
White Sage *Artemisia ludoviciana.*
White Sails *Spathiphyllum wallisii.*
White Sallow *Acacia floribunda.*
White Sally *Eucalyptus pauciflora.*
White Sandalwood *Santalum album.*
White Sapote *Casimiroa edulis.*
White Silk-cotton Tree *Ceiba pentandra.*

Whitesloanea Chiov. Asclepiadaceae. 1 dwarf, succulent perenn. Plant bodies mitre-shaped, 10–15cm, usually solitary, 6–7cm across, pale green with toothed angles. Fls 4cm diam., tubular, campanulate, lobes spreading, exterior white-green with purple blotches, interior pale yellow with dark red blotches, tube with some hairs. Somalia. Z10.
W. crassa (N.E. Br.) Chiov.
→*Caralluma.*

White Snakeroot *Ageratina altissima.*
White Spanish Broom *Cytisus multiflorus.*
White Spruce *Picea glauca.*
White Star Grass *Hypoxis capensis.*
White Stemmed Filaree *Erodium moschatum.*
White Stringybark *Eucalyptus eugenioides; E. globoidea.*
White Thistle *Atriplex lentiformis.*
White Thorn *Crataegus laevigata.*
White Trumpet *Sarracenia leucophylla.*
White Trumpet Lily *Lilium longiflorum.*

White Upright *Reseda alba.*
White-veined Wintergreen *Pyrola picta.*
White Vervain *Verbena urticifolia* var. *leiocarpa.*
White Walnut *Juglans cinerea.*
White Waratah *Agastachys odorata.*
White Water Lily *Nymphaea alba.*
White Wax Tree *Ligustrum lucidum.*
White Wicky *Kalmia cuneata.*
White Willow *Salix alba.*
White Winter Heather *Erica* × *hiemalis.*
White Yam *Dioscorea alata.*
Whitey Wood *Acradenia frankliniae; Melicytus ramiflorus.*

Whitfieldia Hook. Acanthaceae. 10 shrubs. Lvs opposite, entire. Rac. bracteate, term.; cal. lobes 5; cor. bilabiate, lobes 5, twisted. Trop. Afr.
W. lateritia Hook. Spreading everg. shrub to 1m. Lvs oblong-ovate, coriaceous. Rac. short; fls paired or in threes; cal. conspicuous, brick red; cor. to 3cm, brick red to dull scarlet. Sierra Leone. Z10.

Whitlavia Harv.
W. grandiflora Harv. = *Phacelia minor.*
W. minor Harv. = *Phacelia minor.*

Whitlow-wort *Paronychia.*
Whorled Penstemon *Penstemon triphyllus.*
Whorled Solomon's Seal *Polygonatum verticillatum.*
Whorled Water Milfoil *Myriophyllum verticillatum.*
Whorlflower *Morina longifolia.*
Whortleberry *Vaccinium myrtillus.*
Whortle Willow *Salix myrsinifolia.*

Wiborgia Thunb. Leguminosae (Papilionoideae). 10 shrubs, often spiny. Lvs trifoliolate. Rac. term., often secund; pet. long, narrow-clawed, standard ovate. S Afr. Z9.
W. obcordata Thunb. Shrub to 1.8m. Shoots slender, grooved, sericeous. Lfts to 1cm, silky. Rac. many-fld; fls 1cm, creamy yellow. Summer.

Wickaawee *Castilleja coccinea.*
Wickson Plum *Prunus* × *sultana.*
Wickup *Epilobium angustifolium.*
Wicopy *Dirca palustris.*

Widdringtonia Endl. AFRICAN CYPRESS. Cupressaceae. 3 everg. coniferous trees. Bark grey, tinged red, thin, fibrous. Lvs dimorphic: juvenile foliage needles; mature foliage scale-like. ♂ cones term., sessile on short shoots. ♀ cones solitary or clustered, term. on leading growths; scales 4, in two opposite pairs, warty with resin blisters, bract often forming a prominent horn near apex. S & SE Afr.
W. cedarbergensis J. Marsh. CLANWILLIAM CEDAR. Tree to 20m. Crown conic, later spreading. Adult lvs ovate, to 4mm, adnate, slightly pubesc. Cones globose, to 2.5cm diam. S Afr. (Cape Prov.). Z9.
W. cupressoides L. Endl. = *W. nodiflora.*
W. dracomontana Stapf = *W. nodiflora.*
W. juniperoides Endl. = *W. cedarbergensis.*
W. nodiflora (L.) Powrie. SAPREE WOOD; MLANJI CEDAR. Tree or shrub to 45m. Crown conic, later spreading. Adult lvs 1–2mm, glaucous green, adnate to shoot for about half length. Cones subglobose to ovoid, to 2cm diam. S Afr., Moz., Zimb. to Malawi. Z9.
W. schwarzii (Marloth) Mast. WILLOWMORE CEDAR. Tree to 35m. Crown conic. Adult lvs 2mm, spreading, adnate for greater part of length. Cones to 1.8cm diam. S Afr. Z10.
W. whytei Rendle = *W. nodiflora.*

Widdy *Potentilla fruticosa.*
Wide-throated Yellow Monkey Flower *Mimulus brevipes.*
Widow Iris *Hermodactylus tuberosus.*
Widow's Tears *Commelina; Tinantia.*
Wier Maple *Acer saccharinum* f. *laciniatum.*

Wigandia Kunth. Hydrophyllaceae. 5 perenn. herbs, subshrubs or small trees. Lvs large, simple, toothed, covered in stinging hairs. Cyme term., scorpioid; cal. lobes 5, slender; cor. showy, funnel- to salverform, 5-lobed; sta. 5. Trop. Amer. Z10.
W. caracasana HBK. Robust shrubby herb to 4m, tawny or silky-pubesc. throughout. Lvs 45–60×40–45cm, ovate-cordate, crenate. Fls to 2cm, lilac-violet with cor. tube white. Mex. to Colomb. A form of *W. caracasana* is sometimes grown as *W. vigieri* with larger, broader pan. and fls turning from lilac to garnet or bronze. *W. macrophylla*, another form, has white, not tawny indumentum.

W. kunthii hort. = *W. urens.*
W. macrophylla Cham. & Schldl. see *W. caracasana.*
W. urens (Ruiz & Pav.) HBK. To 5m, coarsely hispid. Lvs to 30cm, sharply biserrate. Fls violet to indigo. Peru.

Wigginsia D.M. Porter.
W. corynodes (Otto ex Pfeiff.) D.M. Porter = *Parodia erinacea.*
W. erinacea (Haw.) D.M. Porter = *Parodia erinacea.*
W. horstii Ritter = *Parodia neohorstii.*
W. sellowii (Link & Otto) Ritter = *Parodia erinacea.*
W. sessiliflora (Pfeiff.) D.M. Porter = *Parodia erinacea.*
W. tephracantha (Link & Otto) D.M. Porter = *Parodia erinacea.*
W. vorwerkiana (Werderm.) D.M. Porter = *Parodia erinacea.*

Wig Tree *Cotinus coggygria.*
Wig Tree Fern *Cyathea baileyana.*

Wikstroemia Endl. Thymelaeaceae. 70 decid. or everg. shrubs or trees. Lvs simple. Fls in terminal heads; perianth tube long, lobes 4, spreading; sta. 8, in 2 rows. Fr. a drupe. Trop. & E Asia, Aus., Pacific Is.
W. canescens Meissn. Shrublet. Lvs to 7.5cm, oblong-lanceolate, downy. Fls yellow, to 8mm. Himal., China, Sri Lanka. Z10.
W. shikokiana Franch. & Savat. Shrub. Lvs to 5cm, oblong-lanceolate, silky. Fls yellow, silky, 8mm. Summer. Jap. Z9.

Wilcoxia Britt. & Rose.
W. albiflora Backeb. = *Echinocereus leucanthus.*
W. australis hort. = *Echinocereus poselgeri.*
W. diguetii (F.A.C. Weber) Peebles = *Peniocereus striatus.*
W. poselgeri (Lem.) Britt. & Rose = *Echinocereus poselgeri.*
W. schmollii (Weingart) Backeb. = *Echinocereus schmollii.*
W. striata (Brandg.) Britt. & Rose = *Peniocereus striatus.*
W. tamaulipensis Werderm. = *Echinocereus poselgeri.*
W. viperina (F.A.C. Weber) Britt. & Rose = *Peniocereus viperinus.*

Wild Angelica *Angelica sylvestris.*
Wild Balsam *Ibervillea lindheimeri.*
Wild Balsam Apple *Echinocystis lobata.*
Wild Basil *Clinopodium vulgare.*
Wild Bean *Apios americana.*
Wild Begonia *Rumex venosus.*
Wild Bergamot *Monarda.*
Wild Bird's Nest Fern *Asplenium serratum.*
Wild Bleeding Heart *Dicentra formosa.*
Wild Broom *Lotus scoparius.*
Wild Buckwheat *Eriogonum.*
Wild Cabbage *Brassica oleracea.*
Wild Calabash *Amphitecna latifolia; Crescentia cujete.*
Wild Calla *Calla.*
Wild Carrot *Daucus carota.*
Wild Cassia *Senna singueana.*
Wild Cauliflower *Verticordia brownii.*
Wild Celery *Apium graveolens.*
Wild Chamomile *Matricaria recutita.*
Wild Cherry *Prunus avium.*
Wild Chestnut *Pachira insignis.*
Wild China Tree *Sapindus drummondii.*
Wild Cinnamon *Canella.*
Wild Clary *Salvia verbenaca.*
Wild Climbing Hemp-weed *Mikania scandens.*
Wild Coco *Anthurium grandifolium.*
Wild Coffee *Coffea racemosa; Polyscias guilfoylei; Psychotria; Triosteum aurantiacum, T. perfoliatum.*
Wild Cucumber *Echinocystis lobata.*
Wild Daffodil *Narcissus pseudonarcissus.*
Wild Date *Phoenix sylvestris.*
Wild Date Palm *Phoenix rupicola.*
Wild Fennel *Nigella (N. arvensis).*
Wild Garlic *Allium ursinum; Tulbaghia.*
Wild Ginger *Asarum (A. canadense); Costus speciosus.*
Wild Guava *Alibertia edulis.*
Wild Hollyhock *Iliamna.*
Wild Hop *Bryonia dioica.*
Wild Hyacinth *Camassia scilloides; Dichelostemma multiflorum, D. pulchellum; Lachenalia contaminata.*
Wild Hydrangea *Rumex venosus.*
Wild Hyssop *Verbena hastata.*
Wild Indigo *Baptisia (B. tinctoria).*
Wild Iris *Dietes grandiflora.*
Wild Irishman *Discaria toumatou.*
Wild Leek *Allium ampeloprasum; A. tricoccum.*
Wild Lilac *Ceanothus sanguineus.*
Wild Lily-of-the-valley *Pyrola rotundifolia.*
Wild Lime *Zanthoxylum fagara.*

Wild Liquorice *Astragalus glycyphyllos.*
Wild Lupine *Lupinus perennis.*
Wild Madder *Rubia peregrina.*
Wild Mandrake *Podophyllum peltatum.*
Wild Marjoram *Origanum vulgare.*
Wild Meadow Lily *Lilium canadense.*
Wild Medlar *Vangueria infaustia.*
Wild Mignonette *Reseda alba.*
Wild Morning-glory *Calystegia sepium.*
Wild Oats *Uvularia.*
Wild Okra *Viola palmata.*
Wild Olive *Elaeagnus angustifolia; E. latifolia.*
Wild Olive *Olea europaea* var. *oleaster.*
Wild Onion *Allium cernuum.*
Wild Orange *Capparis mitchellii; Prunus caroliniana.*
Wild Pansy *Viola tricolor.*
Wild Papaya *Polyscias nodosa.*
Wild Parsnip *Angelica archangelica.*
Wild Passion Flower *Passiflora incarnata.*
Wild Pea *Lathyrus.*
Wild Peach *Kiggelaria africana.*
Wild Pineapple *Ananas bracteatus.*
Wild Plantain *Heliconia (H. bihai; H. caribaea).*
Wild Plum *Harpephyllum caffrum; Prunus americana.*
Wild Pomegranate *Burchellia bubalina.*
Wild Potato *Chlorogalum pomeridianum; Solanum jamesii.*
Wild Potato Vine *Ipomoea pandurata.*
Wild Quinine *Parthenium integrifolium.*
Wild Raspberry *Rubus idaeus.*
Wild Rhubarb *Rumex hymenosepalus.*
Wild Rice *Zizania.*
Wild Rose *Syzygium pycnanthum.*
Wild Rum Cherry *Prunus serotina.*
Wild Rye *Dampiera rosmarinifolia; Elymus; Ledum palustre.*
Wild Saffron *Crocus cartwrightianus.*
Wild Sage *Gmelina philippensis.*
Wild Sarsparilla *Aralia nudicaulis; Schisandra coccinea.*
Wild Senna *Senna hebecarpa; S. marilandica.*
Wild Service Tree *Sorbus torminalis.*
Wild Snapdragon *Linaria vulgaris.*
Wild Snowball *Ceanothus americanus.*
Wild Spaniard *Aciphylla colensoi.*
Wild Spinach *Chenopodium bonus-henricus.*
Wild Spurge *Euphorbia corollata.*
Wild Strawberry *Fragaria vesca.*
Wild Sweet Potato Vine *Ipomoea pandurata.*
Wild Sweet William *Phlox divaricata; P. maculata.*
Wild Tamarind *Lysiloma latisiliqua.*
Wild Tea *Camellia sinensis* var. *assamica.*
Wild Tea Leaves *Adiantum philippense.*
Wild Thyme *Thymus serpyllum.*
Wild Tobacco *Nicotiana rustica.*
Wild Water Lemon *Passiflora foetida.*
Wild Wisteria *Bolusanthus speciosus.*
Wild Yellow Lily *Lilium canadense.*
Wilga *Geijera.*

Willardia Rose. Leguminosae (Papilionoideae). 6 decid. shrubs and small trees. Lvs imparipinnate or bipinnate. Rac. axill.; . fls pea-like. Mex., C Amer. Z10.
W. mexicana (S. Wats.) Rose. Tree to 12m. Lvs pinnate; lfts to 3cm, oblong-elliptic, downy. Fls to 1.3cm, lilac. Mex.
W. schiediana (Schldl.) F.J. Herm. Shrub with pendulous br. Lvs bipinnate; lfts to 3cm, elliptic, glaucous beneath. Fls to 1.5cm, red-purple. Panama.

Willdenovia Gmel. = *Rondeletia.*

Willdenow Violet *Viola blanda.*
Willow *Salix.*
Willow Bell *Campanula persicifolia.*
Willow Bottlebrush *Callistemon salignus.*
Willow Gentian *Gentiana asclepiadea.*
Willow Grass *Polygonum amphibium.*
Willow Herb *Epilobium.*
Willow-leaf Magnolia *Magnolia salicifolia.*
Willow-leaf Podocarp *Podocarpus salignus.*
Willow-leaved Fig *Ficus cordata.*
Willow-leaved Foxglove *Digitalis obscura.*
Willow-leaved Jessamine *Cestrum parqui.*
Willow-leaved Poplar *Populus angustifolia.*
Willow-leaved Sunflower *Helianthus salicifolius.*
Willowmore Cedar *Widdringtonia schwarzii.*
Willow Moss *Fontinalis antipyretica.*
Willow Myrtle *Agonis flexuosa.*
Willow Oak *Quercus phellos.*

Willow Peppermint *Agonis flexuosa.*
Willow Podocarp *Podocarpus salignus.*
Willow Rhus *Rhus lancea.*
Willow Wattle *Acacia salicina.*

Wilmattea Britt. & Rose.
W. minutiflora (Britt. & Rose) Britt. & Rose = *Hylocereus minutiflorus.*

✕**Wilsonara**.   (*Cochlioda* ✕*Odontoglossum* ✕*Oncidium*.) Orchidaceae. Gdn hybrids with long branching sprays of small to medium-sized fls usually with crisped tep. in shades of yellow, cream and white marked brown to deep mauve, lip usually stained yellow.

Wilson's Spruce *Picea wilsonii.*
Windflower *Anemone; Zephyranthes.*
Wind Grass *Apera interrupta.*
Windmill Grass *Chloris.*
Windmill Palm *Trachycarpus fortunei.*
Windowleaf *Monstera.*
Window Palm *Reinhardtia gracilis.*
Wind Poppy *Stylomecon.*
Wind Rose *Roemeria hybrida.*
Wineberry *Rubus phoenicolasius.*
Winecups *Babiana rubrocyanea.*
Wine Palm *Borassus flabellifer; Caryota urens.*
Winged Bean *Psophocarpus tetragonolobus.*
Winged Elm *Ulmus alata.*
Winged Everlasting *Ammobium.*
Winged Pea *Lotus tetragonolobus; Psophocarpus tetragonolobus.*
Winged Spindle Tree *Euonymus alatus.*
Winged Wattle *Acacia alata.*
Wingnut *Pterocarya.*
Wingstem *Verbesina alternifolia.*

Wintera Murray.
W. colorata (Raoul) Tieghem = *Pseudowintera colorata.*

WINTERACEAE Lindl. 5/60. *Drimys, Pseudowintera.*

Winter Aconite *Eranthis.*
Winterberry *Ilex decidua; I. verticillata.*
Winter Cherry *Physalis alkekengi; Solanum pseudocapsicum.*
Winter Creeper *Euonymus fortunei.*
Winter Cress *Barbarea vulgaris.*
Winter Currant *Ribes sanguineum.*
Winter Daphne *Daphne odora.*
Winter Fern *Conium maculatum.*
Winter-flowering Begonia *Begonia* ✕*hiemalis.*
Winter-flowering Cherry *Prunus subhirtella.*
Wintergreen *Gaultheria procumbens; Pyrola; Trientalis.*
Winter Hazel *Corylopsis.*
Winter Heath *Erica carnea.*
Winter Heliotrope *Petasites fragans.*
Winter Iris *Iris unguicularis.*
Winter Jasmine *Jasminum nudiflorum.*
Winter Pea *Lathyrus hirsutus.*
Winter Purslane *Montia (M. perfoliata).*
Winter Savory *Satureja montana.*
Winter's Bark *Drimys winteri.*
Winter Squash *Cucurbita maxima; C. moschata.*
Wintersweet *Acokanthera oblongifolia; Chimonanthus.*
Winter Sweetpea *Swainsona galegifolia.*
Winter Wattle *Acacia iteaphylla.*
Wire Grass *Eleusine indica; Schizachyrium scoparium.*
Wire Netting Bush *Corokia cotoneaster.*
Wire Vine *Muehlenbeckia complexa.*
Wirilda *Acacia retinodes.*
Wiry Wattle *Acacia extensa.*
Wisconsin Weeping Willow *Salix* ✕*pendulina.*
Wishbone Flower *Torenia fournieri.*

Wisteria Nutt. Leguminosae (Papilionoideae). 10 decid., twining, strongly woody vines. Lvs imparipinnate; lfts entire. Fls pea-like in pendulous rac. China, Jap., E US.
W. brachybotrys Sieb. & Zucc. = *W. venusta* var. *violacea.*
W. chinensis DC. = *W. sinensis.*
W. floribunda (Willd.) DC. JAPANESE WISTERIA. St. twining clockwise to 8m. Lvs to 35cm, downy then glab.; lfts to 8cm, 11–19, ovate-elliptic to oblong. Rac. 40–120cm, flowering gradually from the base; fls 1.7–1.9cm diam., fragrant, violet, blue, lilac, pink, red or white. Early summer. Jap. A wide range of cvs has been developed, particularly in Japan, exhibiting variation as follows: rac. length 17cm ('Sekine's Blue') to 90cm ('Macrobotrys'); fls may be double ('Violacea-Plena'), standard

from cobalt-violet ('Macrobotrys') to white ('Geisha'), wings and keel blue-violet ('Sekine's Blue') to pale violet ('Naga Noda') to pale rose with a yellow-stained standard ('Rosea') to white ('Alba'), slightly fragrant ('Beni Fugi') to v. fragrant ('Naga Noda'). Z5.

W. ×formosa Rehd. (*W. floribunda × W. sinensis.*) St. twining clockwise. Lvs silky then glab.; lfts 9–15, commonly 13. Rac. to 25cm; deeply fragrant, blooming all at once; fls 2cm diam., standard pale violet, wings and keel darker. Early summer. Gdn origin. Z5.

W. frutescens L. (Poir.) AMERICAN WISTERIA. To 12m. Lvs to 30cm; lfts 3–6cm, 9–15, oval-lanceolate, downy when young. Rac. 4–10cm, sometimes held horizontally to semi-erect, villous; fls to 2cm, gently fragrant, pale purple-lilac sometimes with a yellow spot on the standard. Summer–early autumn. E US. 'Magnifica': fls lilac with a large sulphur-yellow blotch on the standard. 'Nivea': fls pure white; stalks short, v. pubesc.; early-flowering. Z5.

W. japonica Sieb. & Zucc. Br. slender. Lvs 15–20cm, glab., glossy; lfts 3–6cm, 9–13, ovate. Rac. 15–30cm, often branching; fls to 1.3cm diam., white or cream. Summer. Jap., Korea. Z8.

W. macrostachys (Torr. & A. Gray) Nutt. KENTUCKY WISTERIA. To 8m; young shoots somewhat villous. Lfts 3–7cm, usually 9, ovate-elliptic to lanceolate, ultimately pubesc., beneath. Rac. 20–30cm, gland.; fls densely packed, opal-rose. Summer. C US. Z6.

W. magnifica Henriq. = *W. frutescens*.
W. multijuga Van Houtte = *W. floribunda*.
W. sinensis (Sims) Sweet. CHINESE WISTERIA. St. twining anti-clockwise to 10m. Shoots glab. Lvs 25–30cm; lfts 5–8cm, 7–13, usually 11, elliptic or ovate, glab. above, hirsute beneath, mid-rib esp. Rac. 15–30cm; fls to 2.5cm, diam., faintly scented, blue-violet. Late spring. China. Notable for rapidity of growth and abundance of blossom. 'Alba': fls white. 'Black Dragon': fls semi-double, v. dark purple. 'Caroline': fls deep blue-purple, v. fragrant. 'Jako': rac. to 30cm, v. dense, fragrant; lfts 11. 'Plena': fls double, rosette-shaped, lilac. 'Sierra Madre': fls v. fragrant, standard white-tinged, wing and keel, lavender-violet. Z5.

W. venusta Rehd. & Wils. SILKY WISTERIA. St. twining anticlock-wise to 9cm. Shoots pubesc. when young. Lvs 20–35cm; lfts to 10cm, 9–13, elliptic to ovate, pubesc. Rac. 10–15cm, pendulous; pedicels v. pubesc.; fls 2–2.5cm diam. white, highly fragrant. Early summer. var. *violacea* Rehd. The wild form. Infl. to 15cm; fls purple. Jap. Z5.

W. violaceo-pleno (C. Schneid.) L.H. Bail. = *W. floribunda*.

Witch Alder *Fothergilla gardenii*.
Witch Grass *Panicum capillare*.
Witch-hazel *Hamamelis*.
Withe-rod *Viburnum cassinoides*.
Witloof *Cichorium intybus*.

Witsenia Thunb. Iridaceae. 1 shrubby perenn. St. leafy, to 2m, ± branched. Lvs to 22×1cm, distichous, lanceolate. Fl. clusters term., spathaceous; fls to 7cm, lobes 6, yellow-green at base, blue-green above, outer lobes with yellow hairs. S Afr. (Cape Prov.). Z9.

W. corymbosa Ker-Gawl. = *Nivenia corymbosa*.
W. maura Thunb.

Wittia Schum. non Pant. = *Disocactus*.

Wittiocactus Rausch. = *Disocactus*.

Wittmackia Mez. = *Aechmea*.

Wittrockia Lindm. Bromeliaceae. 7 terrestrial, epiphytic or lithophytic perenn. herbs. Lvs in a rosette, toothed, strap-shaped. Infl. scapose, bracteate, compound. Fr. berry-like, small. Coastal SE Braz. Z10.

W. superba Lindm. Lvs 80–100cm, shiny, apex blood-red, with red spiny teeth. Scape stout; bracts red, massed below dense, hemispheric infl.; sep. 23mm, ovate, pungent, pet. shorter, white tipped blue. Braz.

Woad *Isatis*.
Woadwaxen *Genista*.
Wolf Bean *Lupinus albus*.
Wolfberry *Symphoricarpos occidentalis*.

Wolffia Horkel. WATER MEAL. Lemnaceae. 8 minute, floating herbs. Fronds thick, globular, 1–2 cohering. Fls 1 per frond, arising in a central cavity. Throughout the warmer regions of the world.

W. arrhiza (L.) Horkel. Fronds 0.5–1.5×0.4–1.2mm, spherical to ellipsoid, bright green above. Eur., Afr., W Asia, E Braz. Z7.

W. brasiliensis Wedd. Fronds 0.5–1.6×0.7–1.5mm, broadly ovate to suborbicular, with a prominent papule. Americas. Z8.

W. columbiana Karst. COMMON WOLFFIA. Fronds 0.5–1.4×0.4–1.2mm, almost spherical, pale green beneath. Americas. Z8.

W. microscopica (Griff.) Kurz. Fronds 0.4–1.0×0.3–0.8mm, with a cylindrical projection from the lower surface, pale green. India. Z10.

W. punctata Griseb. = *W. brasiliensis*.

Wolffiella Hegelm. Lemnaceae. 8 minute, floating herbs. Fronds flat, thin, orbicular to ovate or linear, ribbon-shaped or sickle-shaped. Fls 1–2 per frond, arising in a central cavity. Amer., Afr. Z8.

W. gladiata (Hegelm.) Hegelm. MUD MIDGET; BOGMAT. Fronds 3–9×0.25–0.80mm, narrow, sickle-shaped, tapering, submerged. N Amer.

Wolfsbane *Aconitum lycoctonum*.
Wolf's Milk *Euphorbia esula*.
Wonder Bean *Canavalia ensiformis*.
Wonderberry *Solanum ×burbankii*.
Wonder Flower *Ornithogalum thyrsoides*.
Wonder Lemon *Citrus ponderosa*.
Wonga-wonga Vine *Pandorea pandorana*.
Wood Anemone *Anemone nemorosa*.
Wood Apple *Limonia acidissima*.
Wood Avens *Geum urbanum*.
Wood Betony *Pedicularis* (*P. canadensis*); *Stachys officinalis*.
Woodbine *Clematis virginiana*; *Lonicera periclymenum*.
Woodbine *Parthenocissus quinquefolia*.
Wood Club Rush *Scirpus sylvaticus*.
Woodcock Orchid *Ophrys scolopax*.
Wood False Brome *Brachypodium sylvaticum*.
Wood-fern *Dryopteris*.

Woodfordia Salisb. Lythraceae. 2 spreading shrubs. Lvs decussate, leathery, lanceolate, gland.-punctate. Rac. axill.; fls 5–6-merous; cal. tube red with short lobes and callus like appendages; pet. small; sta. 12, exserted. Ethiop., Madag., S Asia. Z9.

W. floribunda Salisb. = *W. fruticosa*.
W. fruticosa (L.) Kurz. To 5m. Lvs to 14cm. Infl. to 5cm, cal. tube to 1.5cm, smooth or puberulent; pet. dark rose-pink. Early summer. Madag., S Asia.
→*Lythrum*.

Wood Garlic *Allium ursinum*.
Wood Grass *Sorghastrum nutans*.
Wood Hyacinth *Hyacinthoides*.
Woodland Star *Lithophragma*.
Woodland White Violet *Viola blanda*.
Wood Lily *Lilium philadelphicum*; *Trillium*.
Wood Meadowgrass *Poa nemoralis*.
Wood Melic *Melica uniflora*.
Wood Millet *Milium effusum*.
Wood Nymph *Moneses*.
Wood Poppy *Stylophorum diphyllum*.
Wood Rose *Merremia tuberosa*; *Rosa gymnocarpa*.
Woodruff *Asperula*; *Galium odoratum*.
Wood-rush *Luzula*.
Wood Sage *Teucrium* (*T. canadense*).
Wood's Cycad *Encephalartos woodii*.
Wood Sedge *Carex sylvatica*.

Woodsia R. Br. Woodsiaceae. 25 lithophytic or terrestrial ferns. Rhiz. short to creeping. Fronds 1–2-pinnate to -pinnatifid, ovate to linear or oblanceolate; stipes tufted. Temp. and trop. regions.

W. alpina (Bolton) S.F. Gray. NORTHERN WOODSIA. Fronds to 20×2cm, linear or oblong to lanceolate, papery to leathery, pubesc., pinnae to 15×8mm, 7–18 pairs, obtuse marginal lobes 1–4 pairs; stipes to 8cm, sparsely pubesc. and scaly, red or brown to purple. N Amer., N Eur. to C Asia. Z5.

W. appalachiana Tayl. = *W. scopulina*.
W. belli (Lawson) Porsild = *W. alpina*.
W. brandtii Franch. & Savat. = *W. intermedia* and *W. polystichoides*.
W. brownii (Hook.) Mett. = *Hypoderris brownii*.
W. caucasica J. Sm. = *W. fragilis*.
W. fragilis (Trev.) Moore. Fronds to 43×5cm, lanceolate to oblong, leathery to papery, pinnae to 31×12mm, 15–34 pairs, lanceolate to oblong, apex acute, pinnules oblong, apex acute, margin notched; stipes to 10cm, lustrous, straw-coloured to red-brown. Cauc. Z6.

W. fragilis Liebm., non (Trev.) Moore = *W. mollis*.

W. frigida Gand. = *W. ilvensis*.

W. glabella R. Br. SMOOTH WOODSIA. Fronds to 15×1cm, linear to lanceolate, acute, glab., pinnae to 11×8mm, 5–16 pairs, orbicular to ovate to rhomboid, acute or obtuse, margin toothed to lobed, pinnules 1–5 pairs, elliptic to obovate, entire to toothed; stipes to 6cm, base scaly, straw-coloured. N Amer., Arc. and subarc. Eur. to Asia and E Asia. Z1.

W. guatamalensis Hook. = *W. mollis*.

W. hyperborea (Litjeblad) R. Br. = *W. alpina*.

W. hyperborea var. *rifidula* Koch = *W. ilvensis*.

W. ilvensis (L.) R. Br. RUSTY WOODSIA; FRAGRANT WOODSIA. Fronds to 25×4cm, lanceolate to oblong, leathery to papery, pubesc. pinnae to 15×9mm, 7–23 pairs, ovate to deltoid to lanceolate, pinnules 4–8 pairs, elliptic to oblong, obtuse, sub-entire to toothed; stipes to 10cm, pubesc. and scaly, occas. lustrous, red-brown to purple. N Amer., Eur. to Asia. Z1.

W. insularis Hance = *W. manchuriensis*.

W. intermedia Tag. Fronds to 13×4cm, lanceolate, pubesc., pinnae to 25×10mm, 4–12 pairs, spreading, ovate to oblong, un-dulate to lobed; stipes to 12cm, pubesc. and scaly, straw-coloured to brown. Korea, Jap. Z6.

W. lapponica Angstrom = *W. glabella*.

W. manchuriensis Hook. Fronds to 40×10cm, lanceolate to oblong, glab., occas. white to glaucous, pinnae to 46×18mm, 11–29 pairs, deltoid to lanceolate or oblanceolate, undulate and notched to lobed or incised, pinnules spreading, oblong, obtuse, toothed; stipes to 5cm, glab. to pubesc., base scaly, lustrous, straw-coloured to brown. E Asia. Z6.

W. mexicana Fée. Fronds to 35×5cm, lanceolate to oblong, acute, occas. gland., pinnae to 31×17mm, 6–25 pairs, deltoid or lanceolate to oblong, pinnules elliptic, obtuse, decurrent, toothed and ciliate; stipes to 12cm, glab. to scaly at base, straw-coloured to brown. SW US, Mex. Z9.

W. mexicana R. Br., non Fée = *W. mollis*.

W. mollis (Kaulf.) J. Sm. Fronds to 60×12cm, elliptic or lanceolate to oblong, acute, gland.-pubesc., pinnae to 6×2cm, 20–55 pairs, deltoid or lanceolate to oblong, obtuse, pinnules oblong, obtuse, lobes ovate to suborbicular, obtuse, subentire to notched; stipes to 10cm, pubesc. and scaly, lustrous, straw-coloured to brown. C Amer. Z9.

W. obtusa (Spreng.) Torr. BLUNT-LOBED WOODSIA; LARGE WOODSIA; COMMON WOODSIA. Fronds to 60×12cm, ovate or lanceolate to oblong, attenuate, gland.-pubesc., pinnae to 9×3cm, 8–17 pairs, deltoid to lanceolate, pinnules oblong, obtuse, notched to lobed; stipes to 18cm, occas. lustrous, straw-coloured to brown. N Amer. Z4.

W. obtusa var. *glandulosa* D.C. Eaton = *W. plummerae*.

W. oregana D.C. Eaton. Fronds to 27×3cm, linear or oblong to lanceolate, apex attenuate, glab. to minutely gland., pinnae to 23×13mm, 10–17 pairs, ovate or lanceolate to oblong, obtuse, pinnules distant, oblong, obtuse, notched; stipes to 11cm, glab., occas. lustrous, straw-coloured to purple. N Amer. Z4.

W. perriniana (Spreng.) Hook. & Grev. = *W. obtusa*.

W. plummerae Lemmon. Fronds to 32×6cm, ovate, lanceolate or elliptic to oblong, narrowly acute, gland.-pubesc, pinnae to 44×15mm, 6–16 pairs, lanceolate or deltoid to oblong, attenuate to acute or obtuse, pinnules oblong to elliptic, obtuse, toothed ciliate; stipes to 13cm, base scaly, straw-coloured to purple. SW US, Mex. Z9.

W. polystichoides D.C. Eaton. Fronds to 35×5cm, lanceolate or elliptic to linear, pubesc., scaly beneath, pinnae to 22×10mm, 11–38 pairs, falcate, lanceolate or oblong, entire to toothed, notched, or undulate; stipes to 10cm, scaly, red-brown. E Asia. Z4.

W. pulchella Bertol. Fronds to 12×3cm, lanceolate, acute, glab., pinnae to 1cm, 5–16 pairs, ovate or lanceolate to orbicular, pinnules 2–7 pairs, subacute or obtuse, entire to toothed; stipes sparsely pubesc., base scaly. Eur. (Alps). Z5.

W. pusilla Fourn. = *W. mexicana*.

W. scopulina D.C. Eaton. ROCKY MOUNTAIN WOODSIA. Fronds to 36×8cm, linear or oblong to lanceolate, attenuate, gland.-pubesc., pinnae to 35×23mm, 10–25 pairs, lanceolate to oblong, pinnules strap-shaped to oblong, notched; stipes to 13cm, minutely pubesc., red-brown. Alask. to Calif. Z3.

W. yazawae Mak. = *W. glabella*.

→*Acrostichum, Aspidium, Dicksonia* and *Protowoodsia*.

WOODSIACEAE (Diels) Herter. 21 genera. *Athyrium, Cystopteris, Deparia, Diplazium, Gymnocarpium, Hypodematium, Matteuccia, Onoclea, Woodsia*.

Wood Small-reed *Calamagrostis epigejos*.

Wood-sorrel *Oxalis acetosella; O. caprina*.

Wood Spurge *Euphorbia amygdaloides*.

Wood Vamp *Decumaria barbara*.

Wood Violet *Viola riviana*.

Woodwardia Sm. CHAIN FERN. Blechnaceae. 10 ferns. Rhiz. short-creeping to erect, stout, woody. Fronds in a crown sometimes dimorphic; blades uniform, pinnate; pinnae lobed or pinnatifid, linear. Eurasia, N Amer. Z10 unless specified.

W. angustifolia Sm. = *W. areolata*.

W. areolata (L.) Moore. Rhiz. 3mm thick. Fronds to 80cm, dimorphic: sterile deltoid-ovate, pinnatifid to pinnate, to 17cm wide, seg. 7–10 pairs, serrulate, to 2cm wided, stipe mostly stramineous; fertile fronds taller, seg. narrowly linear, stipe shining, purple-black. N Amer. Z5.

W. chamissoi Brack. = *W. fimbriata*.

W. fimbriata Sm. GIANT CHAIN FERN. Rhiz. oblique. Fronds to 3m, linear-oblong to oblanceolate, pinnate, to 50cm wide; pinnae deeply pinnatifid, linear-oblong to ovate, long-acuminate, seg. narrowly triangular to linear, undulate-crenate or shallowy lobed, spinulose; stipe short, stramineous. BC to S Calif. and Ariz. Z8.

W. harlandii Hook. Rhiz. slender, creeping. Fronds dimorphic: fertile blades 10–17×8–15cm, deltoid, pinnate, pinnae 5–7 pairs, lanceolate, acuminate to acute, minutely dentate, 7–15mm wide, lobe rounded to obtuse, pinnules 5×0.4–0.8cm, lanceolate, rachis winged, stipe to 35cm, slender, pale brown to stramineous, ± glab. toward base; sterile fronds, with pinnae wider, stipes shorter. Hong Kong, Jap., Taiwan, S China.

W. japonica (L. f.) Sm. Rhiz. short, stout. Fronds 40–80×20–35cm, oblong-ovate, pinnae 10–15 pairs, 15–22×2–4.5cm, lanceolate to linear-lanceolate, minutely dentate, pinnately lobed to cleft; pinnules 0.7–2.5×0.6–1.2cm, oblong-ovate, lobed at base, stipes stout, to 50cm, stramineous or somewhat rubescent, prominently scaly. E Asia.

W. orientalis Sw. Rhiz. short-creeping, stout. Fronds 30–100×20–35cm, ovate to broadly ovate-lanceolate, bipinnatipartite, with adventitious plantlets above; pinnae 12–30×4–10cm, ovate-lanceolate to deltoid-lanceolate; pinnules 7–10cm, lanceolate, minutely dentate; stipes 30–80cm, stramineous, base scaly. Jap., China.

W. radicans (L.) Sm. Fronds to 2m, triangular to ovate-lanceolate, bearing 1–few large plantlets at tip, to 40cm wide; pinnae ovate-lanceolate, pinnatifid, to 30cm; pinnules to 4cm, lanceolate, curved, finely serrate. E Eur. Z8.

W. radicans var. *japonica* (L. f.) Luerssen = *W. japonica*.

W. radicans var. *orientalis* (Sw.) Luerssen = *W. orientalis*.

W. spinulosa Mart. & Gal. Rhiz. oblique. Fronds to 3m, linear oblong to oblong-ovate or oblanceolate, pinnate, to 50cm wide, with glands beneath; pinnae deeply pinnatifid, linear-oblong to ovate, middle ones to 30cm; seg. triangular to linear-attenuate, subfalcate, undulate-crenate or shallowly lobed, serrate-spinulose; stipes stout, stramineous from a brown base. Mex., Guat.

W. unigemmata (Mak.) Nak. Rhiz. stout. Fronds 30–100×20–30cm, broadly ovate-lanceolate, bipinnatifid; pinnae 20–30×5–9cm, ovate-lanceolate to deltoid-lanceolate, caudate; plantlets borne on upper pinnae; pinnules 1.5–3×0.6–1cm, ovate-deltoid to deltoid-lanceolate, minutely spine-toothed; stipe stout, to 50cm, glabrate except at base, stramineous to pale brown. SE Asia.

W. virginica (L.) Sm. Rhiz. 60–10mm. Fronds 50×25cm, oblong-lanceolate, pinnate to pinnatifid; pinnae 15–20 pairs, sessile, pinnatifid; seg. 15–20 pairs, ovate to broadly oblong, margins cartilaginous. N Amer. Z4.

Woody Orchid *Magnolia liliiflora*.
Woody Pear *Xylomelum pyriforme*.
Woolflower *Celosia*.
Wool Grass *Scirpus cyperinus*.
Woolly Banksia *Banksia baueri*.
Woolly Bear Begonia *Begonia subvillosa* var. *leptotricha*.
Woolly Berry *Vaccinium hirsutum*.
Woolly Betony *Stachys byzantina*.
Woolly Blue Curls *Trichostema lanatum*.
Woolly Blue Violet *Viola sororaria*.
Woollybush *Adenanthos sericeus*.
Woolly Butia Palm *Butia eriospatha*.
Woollybutt *Eucalyptus longifolia*.
Woolly Butterweed *Packera flettii*.
Woolly Cycad *Encephalartos heenanii*.
Woolly Heath *Epacris lanuginosa*.
Woolly Ironweed *Vernonia lindheimeri*.
Woolly-leaf Ceanothus *Ceanothus tomentosus*.
Woolly Manzanita *Arctostaphylos tomentosa*.
Woolly Milkvetch *Oxytropis pilosa*.
Woolly Morning Glory *Argyreia nervosa*.
Woolly Netbush *Calothamnus villosus*.
Woolly Orange Banksia *Banksia victoriae*.

Woolly-podded Broom *Cytisus grandiflorus.*
Woolly Senna *Senna multiglandulosa.*
Woolly Stenotus *Stenotus lanuginosus.*
Woolly Sunflower *Eriophyllum.*
Woolly Sweet Cicely *Osmorhiza claytonii.*
Woolly Willow *Salix lanata.*
Worcesterberry *Ribes uva-crispa*; *R.* ×*succirubrum.*
Worm Grass *Spigelia*; *S. marilandica.*

Wormia Rottb.
W. burbidgei Hook. 'f. = *Dillenia suffruticosa.*
W. suffruticosa Griff. = *Dillenia suffruticosa.*

Wormseed *Chenopodium ambrosioides.*
Wormseed Mustard *Erysimum cheiranthoides.*
Wormwood *Artemisia.*
Wormwood Cassia *Senna artemisioides.*
Wormwood Senna *Senna artemisioides.*

Worsleya (Traub) Traub. Amaryllidaceae. 1 everg., bulbous, perenn. Bulbs usually clumped with thick aerial necks to 1m. Lvs to 100×10cm, strap-shaped, 2-ranked, decurved. Umbel term. scapose; perianth funnelform lilac to heliotrope or opalescent blue, mauve within, white at base, tube to 2cm, lobes 6, to 15cm, curving. S Braz. Z10.
W. rayneri (Hook.) Traub & Mold. BLUE AMARYLLIS.
→*Amaryllis* and *Hippeastrum.*

Woundwort *Stachys.*

Wrightia R. Br. Apocynaceae. 23 shrubs or small trees. Lvs simple. Fls in term. or subaxillary cymes; cal. short, 5-parted; cor. salverform or rotate, tube short, throat with overlapping scales; sta. carried at top of tube. Trop. Afr., Asia, Aus. Z10.
W. coccinea (Lodd.) Sims. Small tree. Lvs 9–15cm, elliptic or elliptic-lanceolate, caudate, thin. Fls to 2.5cm across, dark red, scales crimson. India, Pak., Yunnan.
W. tinctoria R. Br. PALA INDIGO PLANT. Small tree. Lvs 6–24cm, elliptic-ovate to obovate-oblong, abruptly caudate. Fls to 2cm across, white, scales ciliate. India.

Wulfenia Jacq. Scrophulariaceae. 5 perenn. herbs. Lvs mostly basal, simple, crenate to lobed. Rac. term., spicate, bracteate, scapose; fls small; cal. equally 5-lobed; cor. obscurely bilabiate, tube short. SE Eur., W Asia, Himal.
W. alpina (Gray) Greene = *Besseya alpina.*
W. amherstiana Benth. Lvs 5–15cm, obovate-oblong to oblanceolate, crenate, glab. above, sparsely villous beneath. Flowering st. 12–30cm; cor. purple-blue, lobes narrow, acuminate. Summer. W Himal., Afghan. Z5.
W. baldacii Deg. Lvs to 10cm, elliptic to broadly ovate, crenate or dentate or lobed, sparsely villous, almost glab. beneath. Flowering st. 15–30cm; cor. bright lilac-blue, lobes broad, obtuse. Summer. N Albania. Z7.
W. carinthiaca Jacq. To 20cm, oblong, bicrenate, glab. except midrib. Flowering st. to 50cm; cor. dark violet-blue, lobes obtuse. Summer. SE Alps, Albania. 'Alba': fls white. Z5.
W. plantaginea (James) Greene = *Besseya plantaginea.*
W. reniformis Douglas ex Benth. = *Synthyris reniformis.*

W. rubra (Douglas) Greene = *Besseya rubra.*

Wulffia Necker ex Cass. Compositae. 4 scabrous perenn. herbs. Lvs opposite, simple, dentate, petiolate. Cap. radiate or discoid, solitary or in a corymb; receptacle somewhat convex. Fr. a fleshy cypsela, resembling a blackberry. Trop. Amer. Z10.
W. baccata (L. f.) Kuntze. Erect, to 1.3m. Lvs to 16cm, ovate to oblong-lanceolate, dentate, cuneate at base, acute to acuminate at apex, scabrous above. Cap. radiate, to 2.5cm diam., in term. clusters of 3, peduncles to 1.5cm; flts orange-yellow. Fr. to 5mm. Summer. Braz.
W. stenoglossa DC. = *W. baccata.*
→*Coreopsis.*

Wunschmannia Urban = *Distictis.*

Wurmbea Thunb. Liliaceae (Colchicaceae). 37 cormous perenn. herbs. Lvs cauline, 2-ranked, lanceolate, conduplicate. Fls in a short-stalked spike; perianth 6-lobed, tube short, lobes long and spreading, each with a sunken basal nectary; sta. 6; styles 3. S Afr., Aus. Z10.
W. capensis Thunb. To 30cm. Fls *c*1.5cm, lobes pale with purple margin to entirely dark purple with black glands near base; anth. yellow. S Afr. A variable sp. that may include *W. spicata* (Burm.) Dur. & Shinz and *W. campanulata* Willd.
W. dioica R. Br. EARLY NANCY. To 30cm. Fls to 1.1cm, lobes usually white with lilac gland; anth. red or purple. Aus.

Wyalong Wattle *Acacia cardiophylla.*
Wych Elm *Ulmus glabra.*

Wyethia Nutt. Compositae. 14 erect or ascending, coarse, leafy perenn. herbs. Cap. radiate or discoid, solitary to few, term. or axill.; receptacle flat or convex, scaly; flts yellow. W N Amer.
W. amplexicaulis Nutt. To 80cm, glab., balsamic-resinous. St. ascending, simple. Lvs to 50cm, oblong to obovate, base cuneate to rounded, entire or serrate, firm, shortly petiolate. Cap. to 10cm diam., 1–8; ray flts 8–18. Summer. SW Canada to C & W US. Z5.
W. angustifolia (DC.) Nutt. To 1m, pilose and hirsute or ± resinous. St. ascending, usually simple. Lvs to 50cm, linear-lanceolate to oblong, base long-cuneate, entire to serrate, papery, hirsute, petioles to 11cm. Cap. to 9cm diam., solitary or to 4k; ray flts 10–18. Summer–autumn. W US. Z9.
W. helenioides (DC.) Nutt. To 60cm, grey floccose-tomentose at least when young. St. simple. Lvs to 35cm, oblong or ovate, cuneate to rounded base, entire, petioles to 10cm. Cap. to 9cm diam., 1–3; ray flts 13–20. Spring–summer. Calif. Z5.
W. mollis A. Gray. To 1m, densely floccose-tomentose, becoming green and glabrescent. St. simple. Lvs to 50cm, elliptic to oblong-ovate, base cuneate to subcordate, entire, petioles 4–20cm. Cap. to 9cm diam., solitary or to 4; ray flts 5–9. Summer. Oreg. to Calif. Z8.
W. ovata Torr. & A. Gray. To 30cm, tomentose to glabrate. St. simple or sparingly branched. Lvs to 20cm, suborbicular to broadly ovate, entire, base subcordate, coriaceous. Cap. to 6cm diam., usually solitary; ray flts 5–9. Summer. Calif., Baja Calif. Z9.

X

Xantheranthemum Lindau Acanthaceae. 1. Prostrate perenn. herb. Lvs dark green veined yellow, ± purple beneath. Fls 5-merous, yellow, tubular in term. spikes with toothed, overlapping bracts. Peru. Z9.
X. igneum (Lind.) Lindau. As for the genus.
→*Chamaeranthemum* and *Eranthemum*.

Xanthisma DC. Compositae. 1 ann. herb to 90cm. Lvs alt., linear to lanceolate, usually sessile, lower lvs to 6cm, pinnatisect to deeply dentate, upper lvs smaller, usually entire. Cap. radiate, to 6cm diam., solitary, term., closing at dusk; involucre hemispheric; flts lemon yellow. Spring–summer. Tex. Z7.
X. texana DC. SLEEPY DAISY.

Xanthoceras Bunge. Sapindaceae. 2 small, erect decid. trees or shrubs; wood yellow. Lvs pinnate. Fls 5-merous in rac. or pan.; disc with 5 horn-like projections. Fr. a 3-valved, thick-walled capsule. N China. Z6.
X. sorbifolium Bunge. Erect shrub to 7.5m. Lvs to 30cm, lfts 9–17, 5cm, narrow-elliptic to lanceolate, serrate. Fls 2cm wide, white with centre stained green to yellow then red, in dense, erect pan. to 25cm. Spring–summer.

Xanthorhiza Marshall. Ranunculaceae. 1. Decid., running, suckering 'shrub' to 80cm, wood yellow. Lvs to 18cm, 1–2 pinnate, purple then green, bronze in fall, lfts ovate, lobed and toothed. Fls small, brown-purple in slender drooping pan. E N Amer. Z4.
X. apiifolia   (L'Hérit.)   Guimpel,   Otto   & Hague = *X. simplicissima*.
X. simplicissima Marshall. As for the genus.
→*Zanthorhiza*.

Xanthorrhoea Sm. Liliaceae (Xanthorrhoeaceae). 10–15 everg. perennials. St. ultimately thick, dark, fibrous, woody. Lvs narrow-linear, in a dense crown. Fls small, white, in dense, long-stalked cylindrical spikes. Aus. 10.
X. arborea R. Br. BOTANY BAY GUM. St. to 1.5m× 22cm. Lvs to 100×0.5cm, flat or triangular. Spikes to 150×3cm. Queensld.
X. preisii Endl. BLACKBOY. St. to 4m× 60cm. Lvs to 100×0.4cm, rigid, v. brittle when young. Spikes to 1.5m×2.5–3cm. W Aus.
X. quadrangulata F. Muell. St. to 3m. Lvs to 90cm, quadrangular. Spikes 90cm–1.2m×3cm. S Aus.

Xanthosoma Schott. YAUTIA; TANNIA; MALANGA. Araceae. 45–50 tuberous or caulescent perenn. herbs. Tubers starchy, white to orange to purple within; st. stout, sap milky. Lvs sagittate to hastate, or pedate, somewhat fleshy; petiole long. Peduncle short; spathe tubular below, limb expanded, cymbiform; spadix shorter than spathe. Trop. Amer. Z10.
X. atrovirens K. Koch = *X. sagittifolium*.
X. barilletii Carr. = *X. hoffmannii*.
X. belophyllum Kunth = *X. sagittifolium*.
X. brasiliense (Desf.) Engl. Tubers small. Lvs 40×15cm, ovate-sagittate to hastate; petiole to 40cm. Spathe tube to 5cm, oblong-ovoid, limb to 12cm, oblong-lanceolate, yellow-green. Neotrop., original range unknown, widely cult. for lvs.
X. hastifolium K. Koch = *X. brasiliense*.
X. helleborifolium (Jacq.) Schott. Tuberous. Lvs reniform, deeply pedatisect, seg. 5–18, median seg. to 36×9cm; petiole to 85cm, mottled purple. Spathe tube to 6cm, elliptic-ovoid, limb oblong-ovate, to 10cm, yellow-green to white. C Amer. to Peru and Guianas, Carib. Is.
X. hoffmannii Schott. Tuberous or short-stemmed. Lvs reniform deeply pedatisect, seg. 5–9, median seg. to 50×53cm; petiole to 1m, stained purple at base. Spathe tube to 7cm, oblong, green, limb to 12cm, lanceolate, white. C Amer., Surinam.
X. holtonianum Schott = *X. pilosum*.
X. jacquinii Schott = *X. undipes*.
X. lindenii (André) Engl. = *Caladium lindenii*.
X. mafaffa Schott = *X. sagittifolium*.
X. pilosum K. Koch & Augustin. Tuberous, pubesc. Lvs 35×20cm, sagittate-ovate to cordate-ovate, green, often spotted white; petiole to 40cm. Spathe tube to 7cm, oblong, green, limb to 10cm, oblong-lanceolate, white. Costa Rica to Colomb.
X. sagittifolium (L.) Schott. TANNIA. St. to 1m+, fleshy, edible. Lvs to 90cm, sagitate-ovate, glaucous above; petiole to 1m,

glaucous. Spathe tube to 7cm, oblong-ovoid, green, limb to 15cm, acuminate, green-white. Neotrop.; natural range unknown, widely cult. in Americas and Afr. 'Albomarginatum': lvs tinted blue, veins off-white, edged white. 'Albomarginatum Monstrosum': lvs small, divided into lobes, variegated green, white, gold and yellow. 'Maculatum': lvs broadly sagittate, to 30cm, pale green splashed white.
X. undipes (K. Koch) K. Koch. St. to 2m. Lvs 50–200cm, broadly cordate-sagittate; petiole to 1m. Spathe tube to 7cm, ovoid, yellow-green within, limb to 25cm, yellow-green, cream within. Mex. to Peru, cult. in Carib.
X. violaceum Schott. BLUE TANNIA; BLUE TARO. Tubers large, edible. Lvs to 70×45cm, oblong-ovate, sagitate, glaucous, margin and veins flushed dark purple; petiole to 30–200cm, glaucous, dark brown-purple. Spathe tube to 10cm, oblong, green-violet, cream within, limb to 20cm, sulphur-white. Neotrop., natural range unknown, widely cult. and nat.

Xanthoxylum Mill.
X. daniellii Benn = *Tetradium daniellii*.

Xeranthemum L. Compositae. 6 erect ann. herbs. Lvs alt., entire. Cap. discoid, solitary, term., pedunculate; innermost phyllaries coloured, simulating ray flts, outermost short, brown; flts white, rose, lilac or mauve, unequally 5-lobed. Medit. to SW Asia.
X. annuum L. St. 25–75cm, erect, branched below, suberect. Lvs 2–6cm, linear to oblong, sparsely white-tomentose above, densely so beneath. Cap. 3–5cm diam.; inner phyllaries oblong, spreading 17–25mm, bright pink or white; flts numerous. Summer–autumn. SE Eur. to Cauc. and Iran, nat. elsewhere. Mixed Hybrids: lvs velvety, white; fls to 4cm diam., ranging from white, pink, rose to red and purple. 'Purple Violet': to 60cm; fls semi-double, rich purple. 'Snowlady': to 60cm; fls single, snow-white.
X. annuum var. *inapertum* L. = *X. inapertum*.
X. canescens L. = *Helipterum canescens*.
X. cylindraceum Sm. St. 15–65cm; br. spreading, erect. Lvs 1.5–4cm, linear to elliptic-oblong, sparsely white-tomentose above, densely so beneath. Cap. ovoid, 8–15mm diam.; inner phyllaries 10–13mm, pink, outer with a central patch of white hairs; flts few. Summer. S Eur. to Syr. and Cauc.
X. inapertum (L.) Mill. Differs from *X. annuum* in st. 10–40cm, cap. 1–2cm, diam., inner phyllaries, erect, 13–17mm, pale pink and flts fewer. Summer. S Eur., NW Afr. to Cauc.
X. pinifolium Lam. = *Edmondia pinifolia*.
X. sesamoides L. = *Edmondia sesamoides*.
X. speciosissimum L. = *Helipterum speciosissimum*.

Xeromphis Raf.
X. nilotica (Stapf) Keay = *Catunaregam nilotica*.
X. obovata (Hochst.) Keay = *Catunaregam spinosa*.
X. retzii Raf. = *Catunaregam spinosa*.

Xeronema Brongn. & Gris. Liliaceae (Phormiaceae). 2 perenn. herbs. Rhiz. short; roots fibrous. Basal lvs narrow-linear, conduplicate. Fls sessile crowded in tall-stemmed unbranched rac.; tep. narrow, erect. New Caledonia, Poor Knights Is. Z10.
X. callistemon Oliv. POOR KNIGHTS LILY. Lvs to 100cm. Scape erect to 90cm; rac. to 30cm, almost horizontal; fls red. Hen and Poor Knights Is., on E coast of Auckland.
X. moorei Brongn. & Gris. Lvs 30–40cm. Rac. secund; fls bright crimson. Fr. deep purple. New Caledonia.

Xerophyllum Michx. Liliaceae (Melanthiaceae). 3 perenn. herbs. Rhiz. stout, woody. St. simple, erect. Lvs basal, tufted, long-linear, margins rough. Fls long-stalked in dense terminal pyramidal rac.; tep. 6 in 2 whorls, ovate. Summer. N Amer.
X. asphodeloides (L.) Nutt. TURKEY BEARD; MOUNTAIN ASPHODEL. To 150cm. Lvs to 45×0.25cm. Rac. 7.5–15cm; fls 0.9cm across, yellow-white, fragrant, sta. shorter than tep. E & SE US. Z6.
X. tenax (Pursh) Nutt. ELK GRASS; BEAR GRASS; INDIAN BASKET GRASS; SQUAW GRASS. To 180cm. Basal lvs to 90×0.6cm. Rac. to 60cm; fls 1.5cm across, white to cream; sta. equalling or exceeding tep., violet. BC to C Calif. Z5

Xerophyta Juss. Velloziaceae. 28 shrubs. St. fibrous, with adventitious roots. Lvs clustered at tips of br., linear-subulate; firm; sheaths fibrous and persisting. Fls showy, lat., solitary; tep. 6. Afr., Madag. Z10.

X. elegans (Balf.) Bak. = *Talbotia elegans.*

X. equisetoides Bak. ELEPHANT'S GRASS. To 1m. St. sheaths ribbed dark grey, toothed. Lvs 14×0.6cm. Pedicel 5–10cm, wiry, bristly below ovary; perianth seg. to 3.5cm. S Trop. Afr.

X. retinervis Bak. To 3m. St. sheaths fan-like fibrous. Lvs to 14×0.5cm. Pedicel 7–1cm, wiry; perianth seg. to 3.5. S Afr. (Natal).

X. viscosa Bak. Lvs about 15×0.5cm. Pedicel 14–18cm, matted with black glutinous down; perianth seg. to about 1cm, rose pink spotted with black glands. S Afr.

Xerosicyos Humbert. Cucurbitaceae. 4 climbing perennials. Tendrils oft. bifid. Lvs suborbicular to oval, entire, thick, fleshy. ♂ fls small, green-yellow, in axillary, umbelliform clusters; sta. 4; ♀ fls in umbelliform clusters or loose pan., staminodes 4. Fr. compressed-obconic, apex truncate or broadly emarginnate. Madag. Z10.

X. danguyi Humbert. Lvs 3.5–5.5×2.5–5cm suborbicular, glaucous. ♂ fls numerous, yellow-green, cal. lobes 1–2mm, pet. 3×1mm, recurved, glab.; ♀ fls slightly larger than males. Fr. 2cm yellow-brown.

X. decaryi Guill. & Keraudren. Resembles *X. danguyi*, but lvs 2.5×1cm, oblong-elliptic, light green.

X. perrieri Humbert. Lvs suborbicular, 1.8–2×1.6–2cm, light green. Fr. 2.5cm, yellow-brown.

Xiat *Chamaedorea graminifolia.*

Xylobium Lindl. Orchidaceae. 30 epiphytic or terrestrial orchids. Rhiz. short. Pbs short to elongate. Lvs large, plicate. Rac. basal, erect or arching; sep. subequal, spreading; pet. smaller; lip loosely hinged, entire to 3-lobed. Trop. Amer. Z10.

X. bractescens (Lindl.) Kränzl. Pbs to 3cm, oblong to ovoid-conical. Lvs to 30cm, oblong-elliptic. Infl. to 45cm; tep. to 2cm, dull yellow or green-yellow; lip to 1.8cm, red-brown. Ecuad., Peru.

X. elongatum (Lindl. & Paxt.) Hemsl. Pbs to 27cm, cylindrical. Lvs to 40cm, elliptic to oblong-lanceolate. Infl. to 30cm; tep. to 2.5cm, fleshy, white to pale yellow, often marked brown or purple; lip to 2cm with numerous red-purple papillae. Mex., Guat., Costa Rica, Panama.

X. foveatum (Lindl.) Nichols. Pbs to 10cm, ovoid to oblong-conical. Lvs to 45cm, elliptic to oblanceolate. Infl. to 30cm, tep. to 1.5cm, white to yellow; lip white, sometimes striped red. Mex., Guat. to Panama, N S Amer.

X. gracile Schltr. = *X. leontoglossum.*

X. leontoglossum (Rchb. f.) Rolfe. Pbs to 9cm, ovoid-fusiform. Lvs to 90cm, elliptic-lanceolate; tep. to 2.5cm, cream to golden-yellow spotted pale red, sometimes tinged maroon; lip to 2cm, white to pale yellow, dotted pink. Colomb., Peru, Ecuad., Venez.

X. pallidiflorum (Hook.) Nichols. Pbs to 18cm, cylindrical or stem-like. Lvs to 41cm, elliptic to oblong-elliptic. Infl. to 18.5cm; tep. to 1.8cm, white to yellow-green, lip to 1.4cm, white to yellow-orange. W Indies, Venez. to Peru.

X. palmifolium (Sw.) Fawcett. Pbs to 7.5cm, ovoid-cylindrical. Lvs to 42cm, lanceolate to oblong-lanceolate. Infl. to 10cm; fls fragrant; tep. to 2cm, white to yellow-white, lip 1.6cm, white. W Indies.

X. squalens (Lindl.) Lindl. = *X. variegatum.*

X. variegatum (Ruiz & Pav.) Garay & Dunsterv. Pbs to 8cm,

ovoid to pyriform. Lvs to 70cm, oblong-lanceolate to oblong-elliptic. Infl. to 20cm; tep. to 2.6cm, yellow-white to flesh; lip to 1.9cm, flesh, flushed maroon, apex maroon-violet. Costa Rica, Venez., Colomb., Ecuad., Peru, Boliv., Braz.

→*Maxillaria.*

Xylomelum Sm. Proteaceae. 4 trees or shrubs. Lvs entire or dentate. Pan. or rac. to 10cm, spicate, axill., bracteate; fls paired; per. limb dilated. Fr. a woody, felty follicle to 12cm. Aus. Z10.

X. angustifolium Kipp. Small tree to 7m, bark smooth, grey. Lvs to 15cm, linear-lanceolate, grey-green, entire. Fls creamy-white, hairy. Summer. W Aus.

X. occidentale R. Br. WESTERN WOODY PEAR. Tree to 8m with dark, flaky bark. Lvs to 8cm, oak-like, broadly-oblong, prickly toothed. Fls creamy-white, villous. Summer. W Aus.

X. pyriforme (Gaertn.) J. Knight. WOODY PEAR. Shrub to small tree, 4–5m. Juvenile lvs rusty brown, toothed, adult lvs to 20cm, lanceolate, entire. Fls creamy-white, covered in rusty hairs. Spring. E Aus.

Xylopia L. Annonaceae. 100 everg. trees or shrubs. Lvs coriaceous. Fls solitary or in clusters; sep. to 0.3cm, 3, swollen, conuate; pet. slender, ivory to green, 6, in 2 whorls; sta. crowded. Fr. to 6cm, a cylindric or obovoid schizocarp. Trop., mostly Afr. Z10.

X. aethiopica (Dunal) A. Rich. NEGRO PEPPER; GUINEA PEPPER. To 10m. Lvs 8–18×4–7cm, oblong-elliptic, puberulent beneath, base cuneate. Fls 2–6 per axil; pet. to 5cm; carpels to 32, ovules 6–8. Trop. W Afr.

X. quintasii Engl. & Diels. To 8m in cult. Lvs 6–10×3–5cm, oblong to obovate. Fls fragrant; solitary, or 3–11 per axil; pet. to 2cm; carpels to 4, ovules 4. Trop. W Afr.

Xylorhiza Nutt.

X. tortifolia Greene = *Machaeranthera tortifolia.*

Xylosma Forst. f. Flacourtiaceae. 100 spiny, everg. trees and shrubs. Lvs simple, sometimes toothed. Fls small in rac. or clusters; sep. 4–5, usually connate; pet. 0; sta. numerous. Berry small. Trop. and Subtrop., except Afr.

X. bahamensis (Britt.) Standl. Shrub to 3.6m, rarely to 5m; spines sharp, often branched. Lvs to 2.5cm, elliptic to ovate, entire or with 1–4 small teeth. Fr. red. W Indies. Z10.

X. congestum (Lour.) Merrill. Shrub or small tree to 4.5m; spines slender. Lvs c9cm, ovate-acuminate, serrate, glossy. Fls fragrant. Fr. black. China. Z8.

X. flexuosum (HBK) Hemsl. Shrub or small tree to 5m. Lvs to 6.5cm, elliptic-oblong, serrate, coriaceous. Fr. red. Mex., C Amer. Z10.

X. heterophyllum (Karst.) Gilg. Shrub; spines 0. Lvs to 6.5cm, ovate-acute, serrate, coriaceous. Fr. red. Colomb. Z10.

X. racemosum (Miq.) Sieb. & Zucc. = *X. congestum.*

X. senticosum Hance = *X. congestum.*

→*Myroxylon.*

Xylotheca Hochst.

X. kraussiana Hochst. = *Oncoba kraussiana.*

XYRIDACEAE Agardh. 5/260. *Xyris*

Xyris L. YELLOW-EYED GRASS. Xyridaceae. 240 perenn. or ann. rush-like herbs. Fls 3-merous in globose or cylindrical bracteate spikes. Trop. and warm regions (except Eur.). Z10.

X. operculata Labill. TALL YELLOW-EYE. Lvs to 15cm, narrow, flat, sheathing. Fls yellow. Aus.

Y

Yacca Podocarp *Podocarpus coriaceus.*

Yadakea Mak.
Y. *japonica* (Sieb. & Zucc. ex Steud.) Mak. = *Pseudosasa japonica.*

Yam *Dioscorea.*
Yama-yuri *Lilium auratum.*
Yamazakura *Prunus serrulata* var. *spontanea.*
Yam Bean *Pachyrhizus erosus*; *P. tuberosus.*
Yampee *Dioscorea trifida.*
Yang-tao *Actinidia arguta*; *A. deliciosa.*

Yangua Spruce.
Y. *tinctoria* Spruce = *Cybistax antisyphilitica.*

Yanquapin *Nelumbo lutea.*
Yard Grass *Eleusine indica.*
Yardlong Bean *Vigna unguiculata.*
Yarey *Copernicia baileyana*; *C. berteroana.*
Yarey Hediondo *Copernicia yarey.*
Yarey Hembra *Copernicia baileyana.*
Yareyon *Copernicia baileyana.*
Yarran *Acacia omalophylla.*
Yarrow *Achillea.*

Yatabea Maxim. ex Yatabe.
Y. *japonica* (Itô) Maxim. = *Ranzania japonica.*

Yatay Palm *Butia* (*B. yatay*).
Yate *Eucalyptus cornuta.*
Yaupon *Ilex vomitoria.*
Yautia *Xanthosoma.*
Yellow Adder's Tongue *Erythronium americanum.*
Yellow Ageratum *Lonas.*
Yellow Anacyclus *Anacyclus radiatus.*
Yellow Archangel *Lamium galeobdolon.*
Yellow Asphodel *Asphodeline lutea.*
Yellow Asphodel *Narthecium americanum.*
Yellow Avens *Geum aleppicum*; *G. macrophyllum.*
Yellow Bachelor's-button *Polygala lutea.*
Yellow Bachelor's Buttons *Ranunculus acris.*
Yellow Bauhinia *Bauhinia tomentosa.*
Yellow Bedstraw *Galium verum.*
Yellow Bee Orchid *Ophrys lutea.*
Yellow Bells *Emmenanthe penduliflora*; *Tecoma.*
Yellow-berried Holly *Ilex aquifolium.*
Yellow-berry *Rubus chamaemorus.*
Yellow Birch *Betula alleghaniensis.*
Yellow Bloodwood *Eucalyptus eximia.*
Yellow Blue Stem *Bothriochloa ischaemum.*
Yellow Box *Eucalyptus melliodora*; *E. melliodora.*
Yellow Bristle Grass *Setaria glauca.*
Yellow Broomrape *Orobanche flava.*
Yellow Buckeye *Aesculus flava.*
Yellow Bugle *Ajuga chamaepitys.*
Yellow Butterfly Palm *Chrysalidocarpus lutescens.*
Yellow Buttons *Helichrysum apiculatum.*
Yellow Cattley Guava *Psidium littorale* var. *littorale.*
Yellow Chamomile *Anthemis tinctoria.*
Yellow Chestnut Oak *Quercus muehlenbergii.*
Yellow Clover *Trifolium dubium.*
Yellow Cucumber Tree *Magnolia acuminata* var. *subcordata.*
Yellow Cypress *Chamaecyparis nootkatensis.*
Yellow Devil's Claw *Ibicella lutea.*
Yellow Drumsticks *Craspedia chrysantha.*
Yellow Elder *Tecoma stans.*
Yellow Everlasting Flower *Helichrysum arenarium.*
Yellow-eyed Flame Pea *Chorizema dicksonii.*
Yellow-eyed Grass *Xyris.*
Yellow Flag *Iris pseudacorus.*
Yellow Flamboyant *Peltophorum pterocarpum.*
Yellow Flax *Reinwardtia indica.*
Yellow Floating Heart *Nymphoides peltata.*
Yellow Foxglove *Digitalis grandiflora.*
Yellow Fritillary *Fritillaria pudica.*
Yellow Fruited Thorn *Crataegus flava.*

Yellow Giant Hyssop *Agastache nepetoides.*
Yellow Ginger *Hedychium flavescens.*
Yellow Gorse *Aspalathus carnosa.*
Yellow Granadilla *Passiflora laurifolia.*
Yellow-groove Bamboo *Phyllostachys aureosulcata.*
Yellow Guava *Psidium guajava.*
Yellow Gum *Eucalyptus leucoxylon.*
Yellow Haw *Crataegus flava.*
Yellow Honeysuckle *Lonicera flava.*
Yellow Horned Poppy *Glaucium flavum.*
Yellow Ironweed *Verbesina alternifolia.*
Yellow Jacaranda *Tipuana tipu.*
Yellow Jasmine *Jasminum humile.*
Yellow Jessamine *Gelsemium.*
Yellow Kangaroo Paw *Anigozanthos pulcherrimus.*
Yellow Lady's Slipper Orchid *Cypripedium calceolus.*
Yellow Latan *Latania verschaffeltii.*
Yellow-leaf Dieffenbachia *Dieffenbachia maculata.*
Yellow Locust *Robinia pseudoacacia.*
Yellow Loosestrife *Lysimachia vulgaris.*
Yellow Lupine *Lupinus luteus.*
Yellow Mariposa *Calochortus luteus.*
Yellow Meadow Rue *Thalictrum flavum.*
Yellow Milk Bush *Euphorbia mauritanica.*
Yellow Milkwort *Polygala lutea.*
Yellow Monkey Flower *Mimulus luteus.*
Yellow Morning Glory *Merremia tuberosa.*
Yellow Mountain Heather *Phyllodoce glanduliflora.*
Yellow Mountain Saxifrage *Saxifraga aizoides.*
Yellow Musk *Mimulus luteus.*
Yellow Oleander *Thevetia peruviana.*
Yellow Onion *Allium moly.*
Yellow Ox-eye *Buphthalmum salicifolium.*
Yellow Oxytropis *Oxytropis campestris.*
Yellow Pagoda *Aphelandra chamissoniana.*
Yellow Palm *Chrysalidocarpus lutescens.*
Yellow Paper Daisy *Helichrysum bracteatum.*
Yellow Parilla *Menispermum canadense.*
Yellow Pea *Crotalaria capensis.*
Yellow Penstemon *Penstemon confertus.*
Yellow Pimpernel *Lysimachia nemorum.*
Yellow Pitcher Plant *Sarracenia flava.*
Yellow Pond Lily *Nuphar.*
Yellow Poplar *Liriodendron tulipifera.*
Yellow Popola *Solanum linnaeanum.*
Yellow Poui *Tabebuia serratifolia.*
Yellow Prairie Violet *Viola nuttalii.*
Yellow Rattle *Rhinanthus minor.*
Yellow Rocket *Barbarea vulgaris.*
Yellow-root *Xanthorhiza simplicissima.*
Yellow Root *Hydrastis canadensis.*
Yellow Sand Verbena *Abronia latifolia.*
Yellow Saxifrage *Saxifraga aizoides.*
Yellow Scabious *Cephalaria gigantea.*
Yellow Shrunk Cabbage *Lysichiton americanus.*
Yellow Silver Pine *Lepidothamnus intermedius.*
Yellow Strawberry Guava *Psidium littorale* var. *littorale.*
Yellow Stringybark *Eucalyptus muelleriana.*
Yellow-top Mallee Ash *Eucalyptus luehmanniana.*
Yellow Trefoil *Medicago lupulina.*
Yellow Trumpet *Sarracenia flava.*
Yellow Trumpet Flower *Tecoma stans.*
Yellow Trumpet Vine *Anemopaegma.*
Yellow Trumpet Vine *Macfadyena.*
Yellow Tuft *Alyssum murale.*
Yellow Turkscap Lily *Lilium pyrenaicum.*
Yellow Twining Snapdragon *Asarina filipes.*
Yellow Veronica *Paederota lutea.*
Yellow Vetchling *Lathyrus aphaca*; *L. pratensis.*
Yellow Water Crowfoot *Ranunculus flabellaris.*
Yellow Water Lily *Nuphar lutea.*
Yellow Water Lily *Nymphaea mexicana.*
Yellow Whitlow Grass *Draba aizoides.*
Yellowwood *Afrocarpus*; *Podocarpus* (*P. latifolius*); *Rhodosphaera rhodanthema.*
Yellow Wood Violet *Viola lobata.*
Yerba Buena *Micromeria chamissonis.*

Yerba De Selva *Whipplea modesta.*
Yerba Mansa *Anemopsis californica.*
Yerba Matá *Ilex paraguariensis.*
Yerba Santa *Eriodictyon californicum.*
Yertchuk *Eucalyptus consideniana.*
Yesterday-today-and-tomorrow *Brunfelsia australis.*
Yew *Taxus (T. baccata).*
Yew-leaf Sickle Pine *Falcatifolium taxoides.*
Yew Pine *Podocarus macrophyllus.*
Yezo Spruce *Picea jezoensis.*
Ying Tao Cherry *Prunus pseudocerasus.*
Yoke Wood *Catalpa longissima.*
York And Lancaster Rose *Rosa* ×*damascena* var. *semperflorens.*
Yorkshire Fog *Holcus lanatus.*
Yoshino Cherry *Prunus* ×*yedoensis.*
Young's Weeping Birch *Betula pendula* 'Youngii'
Youth-and-old-age *Aichryson* ×*domesticum.*
Youth-on-age *Tolmiea menziesii.*

Ypsilopus Summerh. Orchidaceae. 4 epiphytic orchids; st. short. Lvs 15–25cm linear, fls white or green in axill. rac.; tep. free, spreading, lip rhomboid-lanceolate, spurred. E Afr. to Zimb. Z10.
Y. **erectus** (Cribb) Cribb & Joyce Stewart. St. 2–3cm, erect. Lvs 4–5 forming fan, linear, folded. Rac. 1–2, arched, to 12cm; fls white, scented; tep. to 8mm, lanceolate; lip entire, 7mm, rhombic; spur 5–6cm. Tanz., Malawi, Zam., Zimb.
Y. **longifolius** (Kränzl.) Summerh. St. to 4cm pendent. Lvs several, narrowly linear. Rac. pendent, fls white, turning green toward tips of tep.; tep. 7–9mm, ovate-lanceolate; lip 6.5–7.5mm, ovate or rhombic, obscurely trilobed, spur 3.5–4cm. Kenya, Tanz.
Y. **viridiflorus** Cribb & Joyce Stewart. St. to 3cm, pendent. Lvs iris-like, linear, folded. Rac. 2–6cm, 1–2-fld; fls green-white or pale yellow-green, exterior scabrid; tep. 6–8mm, lanceolate; lip entire, 7–8mm, lanceolate; spur 15–18mm. Tanz.

Yuca *Manihot.*

Yucca L. Agavaceae. 40 everg. perenn. herbs or trees, st. woody, simple or branched. Lvs in apical rosettes, sword shaped, flexible to rigid, pungent. Infl. paniculate, axill. or apical; fls nocturnally fragrant, campanulate to globose, often pendent; tep. incurved, white or tinged purple, fleshy. N & C Amer., W Indies. Z10.
Y. **achrotriche** Schiede = *Dasylirion acrotrichum.*
Y. **aloifolia** L. SPANISH BAYONET; DAGGER PLANT. St. to 8m, simple or branched, slender. Lvs to 40×6cm, rigid, flat, pungent, denticulate. Infl. rounded, nodding, to 6m; fls to 5×10cm; tep. oval, cream, tinged purple or lined green at base. Winter. SE US, W Indies. 'Marginata': lf margins yellow. 'Quadricolor': lvs green striped yellow and white. 'Tricolor': lvs striped yellow or with central white stripe. var. *draconis* (L.) Engelm. Trunk branching. Lvs to 5cm across, more flexible; recurved. Z8.
Y. **angustifolia** Pursh = *Y. glauca.*
Y. **angustissima** Engelm. ex Trel. St. 0 or short. Lvs to 45×4.5cm, margins scarious, entire. Infl. to 1.4m, slender; fls to 6cm, campanulate, pale green tinged purple. NW Ariz. to NW New Mex., and SW Utah. Z8.
Y. **arborescens** (Torr.) Trel. = *Y. brevifolia.*
Y. **argyrophylla** hort. = *Furcrea bedinghausii.*
Y. **arizonica** McKelv. St. to 2.5m, many, simple, with dead lvs. Lvs to 80×9cm, rigid, concave, smooth, margins with needle-like spines, becoming blunt. Infl. to 1.5m, elongate; fls to 13cm, white to cream, globose to campanulate. Ariz. Z9.
Y. **baccata** Torr. SPANISH BAYONET; BLUE YUCCA; BANANA YUCCA. St. 0 or procumbent, to 1.5m, covered with dead lvs. Lvs to 75×7cm, ensiform, twisted, scabrous, dark green, margins filiferous. Infl. to 75cm+; fls campanulate, pendent, to 13cm, white to cream, often tinged purple. SW US, N Mex. Z9.
Y. **boerhaavii** Bak. = *Y. flexilis* var. *boerhaavii.*
Y. **brevifolia** Engelm. JOSHUA TREE. St. to 9m or more, often branching. Bark fissured, forming plates. Lvs to 40×4cm, stiletto-shaped; finely striate, denticulate. Infl. to 50cm; fls to 7cm, green tinged yellow to cream, malodorous. Calif. to SW Utah. var. *jaegerana* McKelv. To 3.6m. Lvs to 20cm, reflexed. Infl. to 20cm. Z7.
Y. **canaliculata** Hook. = *Y. treculeana.*
Y. **carnerosana** (Trel.) McKelv. SPANISH DAGGER. St. to 3.5m, solitary or clumped. Lvs to 120×9cm, ensiform, rigid, entire, base red. Infl. to 2m, bracts white; fls to 10cm, white or tinged violet. Tex., N Mex. Z9.
Y. **circinata** Bak. = *Y. baccata.*
Y. **concava** Haw. = *Y. filamentosa.*

Y. **constricta** Buckley. St. 0, or to 1.5m, procumbent. Lvs to 50×4cm, linear, flexible, pale to dark green tinged blue, ending in spine to 13mm, margin white, scarious or filamentous. Infl. to 2m+; fls to 5cm, base cup-shaped to tubular. Tex. to Gulf of Mex. Z9.
Y. **desmetiana** Bak. Differs from *Y. gloriosa* in lvs rigid, apical spine 0. St. to 1.8m. Lvs to 4cm wide, crowded, recurved, green tinged purple, margin scabrous at base. Mex. Z9.
Y. **elata** Engelm. SOAP TREE; SOAP WEED; PALMELLA. St. to 3m, suckering, with dead lvs. Lvs to 70×2cm, linear, pliable, surface striate, white-filiferous. Infl. to 2m; fls to 5cm, cream, white, or tinged green to rose. W Tex., Ariz., N Mex. Z9.
Y. **elephantipes** Reg. Differs from *Y. aloifolia* in st. to 10m, densely branched. Lvs to 100×7cm, rigid, base swollen, denticulate. Fls to 4cm, globose, pendent, white or cream. Summer–autumn. Mex., C Amer., Guat. Z10.
Y. **ellacombei** hort. ex Bak. = *Y. gloriosa* 'Nobilis'.
Y. **filamentosa** L. SPOONLEAF YUCCA; ADAM'S NEEDLE; NEEDLE PALM. St. ± 0, clumped, suckering. Lvs to 75×10cm, sword-shaped, stiff, margins filiferous. Infl. to 4.5m; fls pendent, to 5cm, white tinged yellow. US. 'Bright Edge': to 60cm; lvs broadly edged rich yellow. 'Bright Eye': lf margins bright yellow. 'Elegantissima': erect, to 1.2m; fls white. 'Glock-enriese': fls large, cream. 'Rosenglocken': fls tinted pink. 'Schellenbaum': fls milk white. 'Schneefichte': fls white. 'Schneetanne': fls white flushed yellow. 'Starburst': low, rosette-forming; lvs broad, edged cream. 'Variegata': lf margins white, becoming pink-tinged, centre glaucous green. Z7.
Y. **filamentosa** Small non L. = *Y. smalliana.*
Y. **filamentosa** var. *flaccida* (Haw.) Engelm. = *Y. filifera.*
Y. **filifera** Chabaud. Many-branched. Shrub to 10m. Lvs to 55×4cm, linear-oblanceolate, glaucous, somewhat flexible, reflexed above middle, margins with straight (not curling) threads. Infl. cylindric, to 1.5m, fls to 5×2.5cm cream-white. 'Golden Sword': lf margins yellow. 'Ivory': free-flowering. 'Orchioides': infl. simple; lvs stiff, erect. Z7.
Y. **flaccida** Haw. = *Y. filifera.*
Y. **flexilis** Carr. Resembles *Y. recurvifolia* but lvs narrower, pan. long-stalked. St. short. Lvs to 75×4cm, denticulate or entire. Pan. to 120cm; fls to 9cm, white. SW US. var. *boerhaavii* (Bak.) Trel. Lvs flat, recurved, scarcely pungent. var. *peacockii* (Bak.) Trel. Lvs more rigid. Z9. 'Garland's Gold': to 60cm. Lvs long, fleshy, reflexed, with a broad central gold stripe.
Y. **funifera** K. Koch = *Hesperaloe funifera.*
Y. **gigantea** Bak. = *Y. elephantipes.*
Y. **gilbertiana** (Trel.) Rydb. Acaulescent, clump-forming. Lvs to 45×4cm, margins brown to white, becoming filiferous. (threads curled). Infl. to 75cm; fls to 6cm, yellow to green tinged yellow or violet. Utah. Z8.
Y. **glauca** Nutt. ex J. Fraser. St. to 30cm or 0. Lvs to 60×5cm, linear, rigid, smooth, glaucous, margins white to grey, slightly filiferous (threads straight). Infl. to 1m; fls campanulate to globose; cream-white tinged green or brown. WC US. 'Rosea': fls tinged rose. Z7.
Y. **gloriosa** L. SPANISH DAGGER; ROMAN CANDLE; PALM LILY. St. to 2.5m, fleshy, simple or, rarely, branching. Lvs to 60×7.5cm, narrowly lanceolate, smooth, stiff, glaucous, entire. Inf. to 2.4m; fls campanulate, pendent, to 7cm, creamy white, sometimes tinged green or red. Autumn. SE US. 'Garland's Gold': to 60cm; lvs long, fleshy, reflexed, broad central gold stripe. 'Mediostriata': lvs with central yellow stripe. 'Nobilis': lvs v. glaucous, outer lvs recurved, sometimes twisted; fls tinted red. 'Superba': lvs ridged, pan. shorter, fls white. 'Variegata': lvs striped cream-yellow. 'Vittorio Emmanuel II': low and compact; fls strongly tinted red in bud. Z7.
Y. **gloriosa** var. *recurvifolia* (Salisb.) Engelm. = *Y. recurvifolia.*
Y. **gracilis** Otto = *Dasylirion acrotrichum.*
Y. **graminifolia** Zucc. = *Dasylirion graminifolium.*
Y. **guatemalensis** Bak. = *Y. elephantipes.*
Y. **harrimaniae** Trel. St. 0 or short. Lvs to 45×2.5cm, linear-lanceolate to -spathulate, pale to blue-green, flexible, margins scarious, filiferous, then entire. Infl. to 1m; fls globose, to 6cm. C US. Z7.
Y. **jaegerana** McKelv. = *Y. breviflora* var. *jaegerana.*
Y. ×**karlsruhensis** Gräbn. (*Y. filamentosa* × *Y. glauca.*) Lvs blue-grey, margins filiferous. Fls white, tinged red.
Y. **lenneana** Bak. = *Y. elephantipes.*
Y. **longifolia** Schult. = *Nolina longifolia.*
Y. **louisianensis** Trel. Resembles *Y. tenuistyla* but stemless. Lvs to 45×2cm, margins white. Infl. to 2.7m, glab. or pubesc.; fls white tinged green. S US. Z7.
Y. **meldensis** Engelm. = *Y. filifera.*
Y. **mohavensis** Sarg. = *Y. schidigera.*
Y. **neomexicana** Wooton & Standl. Shrub to small tree, to 5m. Lvs to 1cm wide, elongate, linear, v. filiferous. Infl. to 1.5m; fls cream, to 4cm. N Mex. Z8.

Y. pallida McKelv. Stemless. Lvs to 35×3.5cm, flat, acuminate at both ends, glaucous, margin and apical spike yellow. Infl. to 2.5m; fls campanulate, to 6.5cm. S Tex. Z8.

Y. parmentieri Roezl = *Furcrea bedinghausii*.

Y. parvifolia Torr. = *Hesperaloe parviflora*.

Y. pendula Groenl. = *Y. recurvifolia*.

Y. puberula Haw. non Torr. = *Y. filifera*.

Y. puberula Torr. non Haw. = *Y. arizonica*.

Y. radiosa Trel. = *Y. angustissima*.

Y. recurvifolia Salisb. St. to 2.5m, sometimes branched. Lvs to 90×6cm, glaucous. Infl. more open than in *Y. gloriosa*: fls to 7.5cm. SE US. 'Marginata': lvs bordered yellow. 'Variegata': lvs with a central yellow line. Z8.

Y. reverchonii Trel. SAN ANGELO YUCCA. Stemless, solitary or forming clumps. Lvs to 55×1.8cm, rigid, pale glaucous green, denticulate. Infl. to 1m; fls campanulate to globose, pendent, white or tinged green. Summer. Infl. dense; fls to 6cm. Z8.

Y. rigida (Engelm.) Trel. St. to 5m, simple or branched, with persistent dead lvs. Lvs to 60×3cm, rigid, concave, glaucous, margins denticulate. Infl. to 1.5m, fls to 6cm. Mex. Z8.

Y. rostrata Engelm. ex Trel. St. to 3m, solitary to several. Lvs to 60×1.3cm, linear, ensiform, smooth, thickened, ± rigid, margin yellow, denticulate to entire. Infl. to 1.5m, fls to 6.5cm, thin, white. Autumn. Autumn. N Mex., S US. Z8.

Y. rupicola Scheele. TWISTED LEAF YUCCA. Stemless. Lvs to 60×5cm, undulate, glaucous, margins yellow, becoming red, apical spine to 5mm, brown tinged yellow. Infl. to 3.5m or more; fls to 8cm, campanulate, pendent, white to cream, tinged yellow-green. Autumn. Tex. Z9.

Y. schidigera Roezl ex Ortgies. St. to 4.5m, usually branched, often clumped. Lvs to 150×4cm, smooth, margins thick, filiferous, threads curved then straight. Infl. to 1.2m; fls to 7cm, globose, cream, narrowed near base, waxy. Calif., NW Ariz., SE Nevada. Z8.

Y. schottii Engelm. St. to 5m, 1–3. Lvs to 100×6cm, lanceolate, concave, entire, thin, glossy, glaucous with a narrow red line. Infl. to 75cm; fls to 5cm, globose; white. Autumn. SW New Mex., to SE Ariz. Z9.

Y. serratifolia Karw. ex Schult. f. = *Dasylirion serratifolium*.

Y. smalliana Fern. ADAM'S NEEDLE; BEAR GRASS. Resembles *Y. filamentosa* L. but lvs thinner, flatter, narrower, stiff, marginal threads, curled. Infl. finely pubesc.; fls to 5cm, white. Autumn. S Calif. to Flor. 'Maxima': scape with large, leafy bracts. 'Rosea': fl. tinged pink. 'Variegata': lvs marked yellow. Z9.

Y. stricta Sims = *Y. glauca*.

Y. tenuistyla Trel. = *Y. constricta*.

Y. thompsoniana Trel. St. to 2.5m, sparsely branched, with dead reflexed lvs. Lvs to 45×0.7cm, flexible, margin scarious, dentate, yellow or brown. Infl. 1.5m; fls to 6cm, white to cream, tinged green near base, glossy. S Tex. Z9.

Y. tonelliana hort. = *Furcrea bedinghausii*.

Y. torreyi Shafer. St. to 6m, usually simple, with dead lvs. Lvs to 150×10cm, narrow-lanceolate, rigid, scabrous, dark green tinged yellow, filiferous. Infl. to 1.3m; fls campanulate, to 10cm, creamy, waxy, sometimes tinged purple. Autumn. SW US, Mex. Z9.

Y. treculeana Carr. SPANISH DAGGER; PALMA PITA. St. to 5m, simple or branched. Lvs to 120×7.5cm, narrow-lanceolate, rigid, ± filiferous, blue-green. Infl. dense; fls globose, to 5cm, white or tinged purple. Summer. Tex., W Mex. Z9.

Y. treleasei Macbr. = *Y. arizonica*.

Y. ×vomerensis Spreng. (*Y. aloifolia* × *Y. gloriosa*.) Differs from *Y. gloriosa* in thicker lvs. Infl. to 2.5m; fls white tinged green, often rose pink outside. Summer. Raised by Sprenger at Vomero, It. Z8.

Y. whipplei Torr. OUR LORD'S CANDLE. St. usually 0. Lf rosettes dense, lvs to 90×7cm, rigid, somewhat scaberulous, straight or curved, glaucous, long-acuminate, finely denticulate. Infl. to 4.5m; fls pendent, to 6.5cm, white to cream, often tipped green. Summer. W Calif., Ariz., Mex., Baja. Z8.

→*Hesperaloe*.

Yukon White Birch *Betula neoalaskana*.

Yulan *Magnolia denudata*.

Yunnan Cypress *Cupressus duclouxiana*.

Yunnan Nutmeg-yew *Torreya yunnanensis*.

Yunnan Plum Yew *Cephalotaxus lanceolata*.

Yusan *Hosta plantaginea*.

Yushania Keng f. Gramineae. 2 bamboos differing from *Sinarundinaria* in clumping rhiz. and larger lvs. E Asia. Z9.

Y. anceps (Mitford) Yi. Culms 2–5m×0.5–1.2cm, branchlets pendulous, developed in 2nd year; sheaths not long persistent, hairless, sometimes with auricles and bristles. Lvs 6–14×0.5–1.8cm, not or hardly scaberulous. C & NW Himal. 'Pitt White': graceful; to twice height of type.

Y. aztecorum McClure & E.W. Sm. = *Otatea acuminata*.

Y. humilis (Mitford) W.C. Lin = *Pleioblastus humilis*.

Y. maling (Gamble) Stapleton. Culms 3–10m×2–5cm; sheaths persistent, bristly hairy, without auricles or bristles. Lvs 8.5–18×0.8–1.6cm, scaberulous. NE Himal.

→*Arundinaria, Chimonobambusa, Fargesia* and *Sinarundinaria*.

Z

Zabelia (Rehd.) Mak.
Z. integrifolia (Koidz.) Mak. = *Abelia integrifolia*.
Z. triflora (Wallich) Mak. = *Abelia triflora*.

Zabel Laurel *Prunus laurocerasus* 'Zabeliana'

Zaluzianskya F.W. Schmidt. Scrophulariaceae. 35. Viscid ann. or perenn. herbs or subshrubs. Lvs entire or toothed. Fls to 4cm tubular, 5-lobed, in term. spikes. S & E Afr. Z9.
Z. capensis Walp. NIGHT PHLOX. Ann. or perenn. to 45cm. Lvs linear. Fls purple-black, white within. S Afr.
Z. lychnidea Walp. Subshrub to 30cm. Lvs broad. Fls pale yellow. S Afr.
Z. maritima Walp. Sprawling perenn. herb. Lvs oblong-lanceolate. Fls red-maroon, white within. S Afr.
Z. selaginoides Walp. = *Z. villosa*.
Z. villosa F.W. Schmidt. Sprawling ann. or perenn. Lvs obovate. Fls purple, white-lilac within. S Afr.
→*Nycterinia*.

Zamang *Albizia saman*.

Zamia L. Zamiaceae. 30. Cycads. St. caudiciform or tuberous. Lvs pinnate, in apical whorls. Cones pseudoterminal. Americas.
Z. amplifolia Mast. = *Z. wallisii*.
Z. angustifolia Jacq. = *Z. pumila*.
Z. debilis Ait. = *Z. pumila*.
Z. fischeri Miq. To 50cm. St. short, narrow. Pinnae to 6cm, thin, ovate-lanceolate, finely toothed. Mex. Z10.
Z. floridana A. DC. = *Z. pumila*.
Z. forestii hort. = *Z. fischeri*.
Z. furfuracea L. f. in Ait. CARDBOARD PALM. To 1m. St. stout, short. Pinnae to 12cm, obovate-oblong, rigid, bluntly toothed, scurfy. Mex. Z9.
Z. integrifolia Ait. = *Z. pumila*.
Z. kickxii Miq. = *Z. pumila* ssp. *pygmaea*.
Z. latifolia Lodd. = *Z. loddigesii* var. *latifolia*.
Z. lindenii Reg. ex André. To 3m. St. tall, thick. Pinnae to 30cm, narrow-lanceolate, serrate, veins distinct. Ecuad. Z10.
Z. loddigesii Miq. To 1.5m. St. short. Pinnae falcate-lanceolate, serrate. Mex. var. *latifolia* (Lodd.) Schust. Pinnae to 23cm, obovate-lanceolate. var. *spartea* (A. DC.) Schust. Pinnae to 30cm, linear-lanceolate. Mex., Guat. Z10.
Z. media Jacq. = *Z. pumila*.
Z. mexicana Miq. = *Z. loddigesii*.
Z. ottonis Miq. = *Z. pumila* ssp. *pygmaea*.
Z. pseudoparasitica Yates in Seem. To 3m. St. often procumbent. Pinnae to 50cm, linear-lanceolate, veins distinct. Panama. Z10.
Z. pumila L. COONTIE; COMPTIE; FLORIDA ARROWROOT; GUAYIGA; SEMINOLE BREAD. To 1.25m. St. short, swollen. Pinnae to 12cm, linear to oblanceolate, apex obscurely toothed. W Indies, Flor., Cuba. ssp. *pygmaea* (Sims) Eckenw. Dwarf. Pinnae to 5cm, narrow-oblong. Cuba. Z9.
Z. pygmaea Sims = *Z. pumila* ssp. *pygmaea*.
Z. silicea Britt. = *Z. pumila* ssp. *pygmaea*.
Z. silvatica Chamberl. = *Z. loddigesii* var. *latifolia*.
Z. silvicola Small = *Z. pumila*.
Z. skinneri Warsc. To 2m. St. tall, narrow. Pinnae to 20cm, broadly obovate, cuspidate, serrate, veins distinct, sunken above. Panama, Costa Rica. Z10.
Z. spartea A. DC. = *Z. loddigesii* var. *spartea*.
Z. tenuifolia Fisch. = *Z. fischeri*.
Z. wallisii A. Braun. To 1.5m. St. short, swollen. Pinnae to 35cm, broadly oblanceolate, veins distinct, sunken above. Colomb. Z10.

ZAMIACEAE Rchb. 9/100. *Bowenia, Ceratozamia, Dioön, Encephalartos, Lepidozamia, Macrozamia, Microcycas, Zamia*

Zamioculcas Schott. Araceae. 1. Rhizomatous perenn. herb. Lvs to 28cm, pinnate, glossy, succulent, pinnae rounded to narrow, dark green. E Afr., Kenya to NE S Afr. Z10.
Z. zamiifolia (Lodd.) Engl.

Zan *Cordia africana*.

Zannichellia L. Zannichelliaceae. 1, perenn. aquatic herb. St. long, slender. Lvs to 10cm, linear-filiform. Cosmop. Z2.
Z. aschersoniana Gräbn. = *Z. palustris*.
Z. palustris L. HORNED PONDWEED.

ZANNICHELLIACEAE Dumort. 4/7. *Zannichellia*

Zantedeschia Spreng. ARUM LILY; CALLA LILY. Araceae. 6. Rhizomatous perenn. herbs. Lvs long-stalked, lanceolate to ovate, base usually cordate to sagittate, sometimes spotted. Infl. long-stalked, spathe funnel-shaped, enclosing spadix. S Afr. to Angola, Malawi, some widely nat. elsewhere. Z9 unless specified.
Z. aethiopica (L.) Spreng. Lvs to 40cm, unspotted. Spathe to 25cm, white, spadix yellow. S Afr. Les., widely nat. in trop. and temp. regions. This is the Calla Lily or White Arum. 'Crowborough': to 90cm; spathe large, white; fully hardy when established. 'Green Goddess': to 90cm; lvs dull green; spathe large, green marked white. 'Little Gem': habit dwarf, to 45cm; free-flowering. 'White Sail': to 90cm; spathe v. open. Z8.
Z. albomaculata (Hook.) Baill. Lvs to 45cm, with pale spots or blotches or plain. Spathe to 12cm, white to ivory, pale yellow or pink. S Afr., Trop. E Afr. ssp. *albomaculata*. Lvs spotted. ssp. *macrocarpa* Engl. Lvs sometimes unspotted. ssp. *valida* Letty. Lvs unspotted. Spathe to 15cm.
Z. elliotiana (Wats.) Engl. Lvs densely spotted. Spathe golden yellow. Not known in wild, possibly of hybrid origin.
Z. jucunda Letty. Lvs flecked white. Spathe golden yellow, stained purple at base within. S Afr.
Z. melanoleuca Engl. = *Z. albomaculata*.
Z. oculata (Lindl.) Engl. = *Z. albomaculata*.
Z. pentlandii (Wats.) Wittm. Lvs usually plain. Spathe chrome yellow stained purple at base within. S Afr.
Z. rehmannii Engl. Lvs to 40cm, lanceolate, base acuminate, unspotted. Spathe to 12cm, white, pink or plum. S Afr., Swaz.
Z. sprengeri (Davy) Davy = *Z. pentlandii*.
Z. cvs. 'Apple Court': habit dwarf; spathe white. 'Aztec Gold': spathe bright orange to red. 'Best Gold': spathe large, gold. 'Black Magic': spathe yellow, throat black. 'Black-eyed Beauty': spathe cream, throat black. 'Bridal Blush': spathe cream washed pink. 'Cameo': spathe peach, throat black. 'Carmine Red': spathe deep carmine. 'Dusky Pink': spathe light pink. 'Giant White': spathe white, v. large. 'Golden Affair': spathe bright gold. 'Harvest Moon': spathe pale lemon. 'Lady Luck': spathe rich yellow faintly washed orange. 'Lavender Petite': spathe plum edged fading to blush pink centre. 'Majestic Red': spathe strong crimson red. 'Maroon Dainty': spathe plum, throat paler.
→*Calla* and *Richardia*.

Zanthorhiza L'Hérit.
Z. apifolia L'Hérit. = *Xanthorhiza simplicissima*.

Zanthoxylum L. PRICKLY ASH. Rutaceae. 250 everg. or decid. trees and shrubs, many with stipular spines. Lvs imparipinnate or simple, lfts sometimes toothed, gland., aromatic. Fls small in cymose pan. Cosmop. in warmer areas.
Z. ailanthoides Sieb. & Zucc. Tree to 18m. Lfts 11–12, to 15cm ovate to oblong-lanceolate, serrulate. Fls white to yellow-green. China, Jap. Z9.
Z. alatum Roxb. Lfts 3–15. cf. Himal. Z6.
Z. alatum var. *planispinum* (Sieb. & Zucc.) Rehd. & Wils. = *Z. planispinum*.
Z. americanum Mill. TOOTHACHE TREE. Shrub or tree to 8m. Lfts 5–11, to 8cm, ovate to oblong, entire or toothed. Fls yellow-green. E N Amer. Z3.
Z. bungei Planch. = *Z. simulans*.
Z. capense (Thunb.) Harv. SMALL KNOBWOOD. Tree to 7m. Lfts 9–17, to 4cm, ovate to elliptic, bluntly toothed. Fls green-white. S Afr. Z9.
Z. clava-herculis L. HERCULES-CLUB; SEA ASH; PEPPERWOOD. Shrub or tree to 17m, v. spiny. Lfts 5–19, to 5cm ovate to lanceolate, petiolules winged. Fls white. SE N Amer. var. *fruticosum* (A. Gray) S. Wats. Smaller. Tex. Z6.
Z. fagara (L.) Sarg. WILD LIME. Shrub or tree to 10m, everg. Lfts 5–13, to 3cm, ovate to rounded, crenulate. Fls white. SE US to S Amer. and W Indies. Z8.

Z. *fraxineum* Willd. = Z. *americanum*.

Z. *hirsutum* Buckl. = Z. *clava-herculis* var. *fruticosum*.

Z. *piperitum* DC. JAPAN PEPPER. Shrub or tree to 6m. Lfts 11–23, to 3.5cm, ovate, emarginate, dentate. Fls yellow-green. N China, Korea, Jap. Z6.

Z. *planispinum* Sieb. & Zucc. Shrub to 4m. Lfts 3–7, to 10cm, narrow-oblong to lanceolate, entire or toothed. Fls pale yellow. Jap., China, Korea. Z6.

Z. *schinifolium* Sieb. & Zucc. Shrub or small tree. Lfts 13–23, to 5cm, narrowly ovate to broadly lanceolate, emarginate, toothed. Fls green. China, Korea, Jap. Z6.

Z. *simulans* Hance. Spreading shrub or small tree to 3m; br. hirsute, spines flattened. Lfts 7–11, to 5cm, ovate-oblong, glab. serrate, midrib prickly. Cymes slender. China, Taiwan. Z6.

→*Fagara*.

Zanzibar Red Head *Syzygium aromaticum*.

Zauschneria Presl.

Z. *californica* ssp. *latifolia* (Hook.) Keck = *Epilobium canum* ssp. *latifolium*.

Z. *californica* var. *angustifolia* Keck = *Epilobium canum* ssp. *canum*.

Z. *californica* var. *microphylla* A. Gray = *Epilobium canum* ssp. *canum*.

Z. *californica* C. Presl = *Epilobium canum* ssp. *canum*.

Z. *cana* Greene = *Epilobium canum* ssp. *canum*.

Z. *garrettii* A. Nels. = *Epilobium canum* ssp. *garrettii*.

Z. *latifolia* Hook. = *Epilobium canum* ssp. *latifolium*.

Z. *mexicana* Presl = *Epilobium canum* ssp. *canum*.

Z. *microphylla* (A. Gray) Moxl. = *Epilobium canum* ssp. *canum*.

Z. *septentrionalis* Keck = *Epilobium septentrionale*.

Zea L. Gramineae. 4 ann. grasses. ♀ infl. axill., a dense cylindrical spathaceous rac. C Amer.

Z. *curagua* Molina = Z. *mays*.

Z. *gracillima* hort. = Z. *mays* var. *gracillima*.

Z. *mays* L. MAIZE; CORN; MEALIE; SWEET CORN. To 4m. St. robust. Lvs to 90cm, 2-ranked, bases sheathing, strap-like, apex acuminate. ♀ infl. to 20cm. Grains to 1cm, yellow. Cultigen, first cult. in Mex. 'Cutie Blues': grains small, dark blue. 'Fiesta': grains long, coloured white, yellow, red, blue and purple in patches. 'Harlequin': lvs striped green, red, grains deep red. 'Indian Corn': grains contain multicoloured. 'Quadricolor': lvs striped green, white, yellow, pink. 'Strawberry Corn': grains small, burgundy; husks yellow. 'Variegata': lvs longitudinally striped pale yellow, pink. 'Variegata': lvs striped white. var. *gracillima* Körn. Dwarf form; lvs narrow. var. *japonica* Alph. Wood. To 120cm. Lvs striped white. Z7.

Zebra Grass *Miscanthus sinensis*.

Zebra Haworthia *Haworthia fasciata*.

Zebra Leaf Aloe *Aloe zebrina*.

Zebra Orchid *Caladenia cairnsiana*.

Zebra Plant *Aphelandra squarrosa*; *Calathea zebrina*; *Cryptanthus zonatus*.

Zebrina Schnizl.

Z. *flocculosa* Brückn. = *Tradescantia zebrina* var. *flocculosa*.

Z. *pendula* Schnizl. = *Tradescantia zebrina*.

Z. *purpusii* Brückn. = *Tradescantia zebrina*.

Zedoary *Curcuma zedoaria*.

Zehneria Endl. Cucurbitaceae. 30 perenn. herbs. St. climbing. Tendrils simple. Lvs simple or palmately lobed. ♂ fls small, white tinged yellow, solitary or in clusters, sta. 2–3; ♀ fls solitary or in clusters, staminodes 3. Fr. small, baccate, red. OW Trop. Z10.

Z. *debilis* Sonder = *Trochomeria debilis*.

Z. *indica* (L.) Keraudren. St. striate, sparsely hairy to glab. Lvs simple, cordate, pentagonal or lobes 3, acuminate, sinuate, scabrid above, veins pubesc. beneath, petiole to 2cm. Fr. to 5mm. E Asia.

Z. *scabra* (L. f.) Sonder. St. subglabrous to crisped-pubesc. Lvs ovate-cordate or shallowly 3–5-lobed, scabrid above, sparsely hairy to densely grey-tomentose beneath; petiole to 8cm. Fr. 6–12mm. Distrib. as for the genus.

→*Melothria*.

Zelkova Spach. Ulmaceae. 5 decid. trees or shrubs. Lvs simple, coarsely serrate, prominently penninerved, stipulate. Fls 4–5 merous, in axils, inconspicuous, green, ♂ clustered, ♀ solitary or few; ovary superior. Fr. a dry, nut-like drupe, ridged, short stalked; ± persistent cal. and stigmas. Spring. Cauc., E Asia, Taiwan, Jap.

Z. *abelicea* (Lam.) Boiss. Small tree or shrub to 15m; branchlets white-pubesc. Lvs 1–2.5×1–2cm, ovate-oblong, obtuse, sub-sessile, cordate to rounded at base, triangular-toothed, somewhat pubesc. esp. beneath, becoming glab. Crete. Z8.

Z. *acuminata* (Lindl.) Planch. = Z. *serrata*.

Z. *carpinifolia* (Pall.) K. Koch. CAUCASIAN ELM. Tree to 35m, often multistemmed; crown ellipsoid; bark grey; branchlets densely downy. Lvs 2–7×1.5–5cm, elliptic-oblong, acute, rounded or subcordate at base, teeth obtuse, ciliate, with scattered pubescence above, paler and downy along veins beneath. Cauc. Z5. 'Verschaffeltii': slow-growing, to 10m; lvs deeply serrate; fr. smaller.

Z. *crenata* Spach = Z. *carpinifolia*.

Z. *cretica* Spach = Z. *abelicea*.

Z. *davidii* Bean = *Hemiptelea davidii*.

Z. *formosana* Hayata = Z. *serrata*.

Z. *keaki* (Sieb.) Maxim. = Z. *serrata*.

Z. *schneiderana* Hand.-Mazz. CHINESE ZELKOVA. Tree to 30m, similar to Z. *sinica*. Lvs 2–5×2cm, broad-ovate, acuminate, teeth apiculate, downy-pubesc., veins beneath. SW China. Z7.

Z. *serrata* (Thunb.) Mak. JAPANESE ZELKOVA; SAW LEAF ZELKOVA. To 35m; bark grey-white; branchlets tinged purple-grey, lenticellate, slightly pubesc. Lvs c3–7.5×2–3cm, oblong-elliptic, acuminate, rounded or subcordate at base, teeth acute, ciliate, subcoriaceous, sometimes sparsely pubesc. above, pale green and lustrous beneath, pubesc. on veins; petiole 2–6mm. Jap., Taiwan, E China. 'Goblin': neat rounded bush, to 1m. 'Green Vase': tall, vase-shaped, fast growing; lvs large, bronze in autumn. 'Pulverulenta': lvs small, yellow variegated. 'Spring Grove': similar to *Ulmus americana* but far smaller. 'Village Green': habit vase-shaped, trunk straight, fast growing; lvs red in autumn. var. *tarokoensis* (Hayata) Li. Lvs ovate-oblong, 2–3×1–1.3cm, obtuse, suborbicular at base, glab.; petiole 2–3mm. Z5.

Z. *sinica* Schneid. Tree to 20m; bark grey-brown, somewhat scaly; branchlets dark grey, slender, glabrate. Lvs 2–5×1.5cm, elliptic-ovate, acuminate, base rounded, coriaceous, glab. above, paler, ± downy beneath; petiole 3–5mm. E China. Z6.

Z. *ulmoides* Schneid. = Z. *carpinifolia*.

Z. *verschaffeltii* (Dipp.) Nichols. = Z. *carpinifolia* 'Verschaffeltii'.

→*Ulmus*.

Zenobia D. Don. Ericaceae. 1. Decid. or semi-evergreen shrub, 50–180cm. Branchlets ± glaucous. Lvs 2–7cm, ovate-oblong to elliptic, apex acute or rounded, entire, scalloped or blunt-toothed, blue-green, ± glaucous. Fls to 1.25cm, white, waxy, deeply campanulate, shallowly 5-lobed, sweetly scented, long-stalked, nodding in clusters. Late spring–summer. SE US. Z5.

Z. *pulverulenta* (Bartr. ex Willd.) Pollard. 'Quercifolia': lvs shallowly lobed.

Z. *speciosa* (Michx.) D. Don = Z. *pulverulenta*.

Zephyranthes Herb. ZEPHYR FLOWER; FAIRY LILY; RAIN LILY. Amaryllidaceae. 71 perenn. bulbous herbs. Lvs strap-shaped to grass-like, appearing with fls. Scape hollow, spathe membranous; fls solitary, funnel-shaped, usually tubular with 6 subequal lobes. Americas.

Z. *andersonii* (Herb.) Bak. = *Habranthus tubispathus*.

Z. *atamasca* (L.) Herb. ATAMASCO LILY. Lvs to 40×5cm, 4–6, channelled, glossy. Scape to 30cm; fl. to 8cm, pure white or tinged purple. SE US. Z8.

Z. *aurea* Benth. & Hook. f. = *Pyrolirion aureum*.

Z. *beustii* Schinz = Z. *flava*.

Z. *bifolia* (Aubl.) M. Roem. Lvs 11–35×0.5cm, curved. Scape to 8cm; fl. 6.5cm, cardinal red, green in throat. Hispan. Z10.

Z. *brasiliensis* (Traub) Traub = Z. *drummondii*.

Z. *brazosensis* Traub. Lvs to 33×0.2cm, channelled, twisted. Scape 11cm; fls to 12cm, white striped red, long-tubular. S US. Z9.

Z. *candida* (Lindl.) Herb. Lvs to 30×0.3cm, everg. Scape to 25cm; fls to 5cm, pure white or slightly rose-tinged outside, green at the base, closing in shade; perianth tube 0. Arg., Urug. 'Major': fls large. Z9.

Z. *cardinalis* C.H. Wright = Z. *bifolia*.

Z. *carinata* Herb. = Z. *grandiflora*.

Z. *citrina* Bak. Lvs to 30×0.4cm, channelled above. Scape 13cm; fls to 5cm, bright yellow. Trop. Amer. 'Ajax' (Z. *citrina* ×Z. *candida*): lvs erect, narrow, dark green, to 25cm; fls dark cream to yellow, solitary. Z10.

Z. *concolor* (Lindl.) Benth. & Hook. f. = *Habranthus concolor*.

Z. *cubensis* Urban = Z. *wrightii*.

Z. *drummondii* D. Don. Lvs linear, to 6mm wide, twisted, prostrate, glaucous. Scape 12.5–20cm, fl. to 7.5cm, white, tinged red, fragrant, opening at night. Tex., Mex. Z7.

Z. *eggersiana* Urban = Z. *citrina*.

Z. flava (Herb.) Bak. Lvs 1 or 2, dark green, channelled. Scape to 30cm+, fls to 10cm, yellow. Peru. Z10.

Z. gracilifolius (Herb.) Bak. = *Habranthus gracilifolius*.

Z. grandiflora Lindl. Lvs to 30cm. Scape 30cm; fl. 8cm, bright pink with a white throat. Mex. Z9.

Z. insularum Hume. Lvs to 21×0.7cm, striate beneath, slightly keeled. Scape to 15cm; fls to 3cm, white, flushed pink. Cult. in Flor. and Cuba; origin not known. Z9.

Z. jonesii (Cory) Traub. Lvs to 35×3cm, slightly glaucous. Scape to 30cm; per. tube to 5.5cm, green-white tinged rose, lobes 4cm, yellow. S US. Z9.

Z. lindleyana Herb. Lvs to 50×0.3cm, linear, spreading. Scape to 15cm; fls to 5cm, rose. Mex. Z9.

Z. longifolia Hemsl. Lvs to 30cm, linear. Scape to 15cm; fls to 2.5cm, yellow, coppery outside. Tex. to New Mex. Z8.

Z. longipes Bak. = *Habranthus longipes*.

Z. macrosiphon Bak. Lvs to 30×3cm, fleshy. Scape equalling lvs; fls to 6cm, bright rose-red. Mex. Z10.

Z. mesochloa Herb. Lvs 0.6cm wide, channelled. Scape 18cm; fls to 4.2cm, the lower half of tube green, the upper half white, stained red. Arg. Z9.

Z. plumieri Hume = *Habranthus plumieri*.

Z. pseudocolchicum Kränzl. = *Z. pusilla*.

Z. pulchella J.G. Sm. Lvs to 25×0.2cm. Scape to 20cm; fls 2cm, bright yellow stalked. S US. Z9.

Z. pusilla (Herb.) Dietr. Lvs v. narrow, channelled. Scape usually buried; fls to 3cm, yellow. S Braz., Urug., Arg. Z10.

Z. robusta (Herb.) Bak. = *Habranthus robustus*.

Z. rosea Lindl. Lvs to 15×6cm, glab., striate. Scape to 15cm; fls rose, funnel-shaped, to 3cm diam. Cuba. Z10.

Z. smallii (Alexander) Traub. Lvs to 15×0.3cm, bright green, channelled above. Scape to 20cm, fls to 2cm diam. lemon-yellow, ± tinted red, green at base. S US. Z9.

Z. striata Herb. = *Z. verecunda*.

Z. texana Herb. = *Habranthus tubispathus*.

Z. timida Holmb. = *Z. traubii*.

Z. traubii (Hayward) Mold. Lvs to 13×0.2cm, channelled above, keeled beneath. Scape to 14cm; fls to 4cm, white, exterior with rose band, green veins. Arg. Z7.

Z. treatiae S. Wats. Lvs to 30×0.2cm, thick, semi-terete. Scape to 25cm; fls to 10cm, white pink with age. SE US. Z8.

Z. tsouii Hu = *Z. grandiflora*.

Z. tubiflora Schinz. = *Pyrolirion aureum*.

Z. tubispatha Herb. = *Habranthus tubispathus*.

Z. verecunda Herb. Lvs to 30×0.6cm, purple-tinged below. Scape to 12cm; fls to 5cm, sessile, white, becoming pale pink, green at the base. Mex. Z10.

Z. versicolor Bak. = *Habranthus versicolor*.

Z. wrightii Bak. Lvs to 25×0.4cm, linear, erect. Scape to 30cm; fls to 6cm, pink. Cuba. Z10.

→*Amaryllis, Argyropsis, Cooperia, Habranthus, Haylockia* and *Pyrolirion*.

Zephyr Flower *Zephyranthes*.

Zerumbet Wendl. = *Alpinia*.

Zeuxine Lindl. Orchidaceae. 40 terrestrial orchids lacking pbs. St. creeping, ascending. Lvs thin-textured, alt. or loosely rosulate. Infl. terminal; fls small; tep. forming hood; lip base often saccate, apex dilated. Trop. Afr. to Trop. Asia and Fiji Is. Z10.

Z. goodyeroides Lindl. Lvs to 5×2cm, ovate, acute, deep velvety green, often flushed purple beneath, midvein white-green. Fls to 6mm diam., interior white, exterior red. Himal.

Z. regia (Lindl.) Trimen. Lvs to 6.5×1.5cm, deep velvety green, midvein white-green. Fls to 6mm diam.; tep. green; lip white. S India, Sri Lanka.

Z. strateumatica (L.) Schltr. Lvs to 7cm, linear, often flushed purple. Fls to 10mm diam.; stained white, green-white or pink; lip bright yellow to yellow-green. Afghan. to S China, SE Asia to Malay Penins., nat. Flor.

Z. violascens Ridl. Lvs to 2.5×1cm, dark purple-green, midvein paler. Fls to 12mm diam., white or rose; lip stained yellow. Sumatra, Borneo, Malay Penins.

Zigadenus Michx. DEATH CAMAS; ZYGADENE. Liliaceae (Melanthiaceae). 18 bulbous or rhizomatous perenn. herbs. Lvs mostly basal, linear. Fls in term. pan. or rac., green-white to yellow-white; tep. 6, free, spreading with green basal glands. Summer. N Amer., N Asia.

Z. elegans Pursh. WHITE CAMAS; ALKALI GRASS. Bulbous, to 90cm. Lvs to 30×1cm, keeled beneath, grey-green. Rac. loose, sometimes branched; tep. 8–12mm, green-white above, green beneath. Minn. W to Alask. and Ariz. Z3.

Z. fremontii (Torr.) S. Wats. STAR ZYGADENE; STAR LILY. Bulbous, to 90cm. Lvs to 60×7.5cm, scabrid; apex pungent. Pan. or rac. often corymbose; tep. 10–16mm, off-white to ivory. S Oreg. to N Baja Calif. Z8.

Z. glaucus Nutt. WHITE CAMAS. Like *Z. elegans* but lvs glaucous, not pungent; tep. white to white-green, suffused brown or purple. N Amer. Z3.

Z. gramineus Rydb. = *Z. venenosus* var. *gramineus*.

Z. muscitoxicum (Walter) Reg. = *Amianthum muscitoxicum*.

Z. nuttallii A. Gray. DEATH CAMAS; POISON CAMAS; MERRYHEARTS. Bulbous, to 75cm. Lvs to 45×2.5cm, linear-falcate, keeled. Infl. rac., or pan.; tep. 6–8mm, yellow-white. N Amer. Z6.

Z. paniculatus (Nutt.) S. Wats. SAND CORN. Bulbous, to 60cm. Lvs to 50×2cm, conduplicate, margins scarious. Infl. a pan.; tep. 3mm, yellow-white. W US. Z4.

Z. toxicoscordion var. *venenosus* (S. Wats.) Rydb. = *Z. venenosus*.

Z. venenosus S. Wats. DEATH CAMAS. Bulbous, to 70cm. Lvs to 30×1cm, rac. sometimes branched near base; tep. 3–6mm, off-white. W Canada to Utah and New Mex. var. *gramineus* (Rydb.) Walsh ex Peck. GRASSY DEATH CAMAS. Habit grassy. Tep. slightly longer than in type. Z4.

→*Anticlea* and *Toxicoscordion*.

Zig-zag Vernonia *Vernonia flexuosa*.
Zig-zag Wattle *Acacia macradenia*.
Zimbabwe Climber *Podranea brycei*.

Zingiber Boehm. GINGER. Zingiberaceae. 100 perenn. herbs. Rhiz. aromatic. Sts. leafy, reed-like. Lvs lanceolate, 2-ranked. Infl. scapose, cone-like, with overlapping waxy bracts; pet. 3, lip 3-lobed, staminodes usually 0. Summer. Trop. Asia. Z10.

Z. cassumunar Roxb. = *Z. purpureum*.

Z. cliffordiae Andrews = *Z. purpureum*.

Z. dubium Afzel. = *Costus dubius*.

Z. fairchildii hort. = *Z. zerumbet*.

Z. mioga (Thunb.) Roscoe JAPANESE GINGER; MIOGA GINGER. To 1m. Lvs to 30cm, linear-lanceolate. Infl. 10cm, ellipsoid, scape v. short; bracts white or green with red spots; pet. white; lip yellow. Jap.

Z. officinale Roscoe. COMMON GINGER; CANTON GINGER; STEM GINGER. To 1.5m. Lvs 15cm, lanceolate. Infl. 5cm, ellipsoid; scape 15–20cm; bracts pale green to ochre; pet. yellow-green, lip deep purple with yellow spots and stripes. Trop. Asia, widely cult. Exact origin unknown.

Z. purpureum Roscoe. BENGAL GINGER; CASSUMAR GINGER. To 1.5m. Lvs to 40cm, downy beneath. Infl. 12cm, ellipsoid; scape 15–25cm; bracts purple-brown; pet. pale yellow; lip pale yellow. India, Malaysia.

Z. spectabile Griff. To 2m. Lvs to 50cm, downy beneath. Infl. to 30cm, loose-cylindric; scape 30–100cm; bracts yellow turning scarlet; pet. yellow-white; lip dark purple spotted yellow. Malaysia.

Z. uncinatum Stokes = *Renealmia jamaicensis*.

Z. zerumbet (L.) Sm. To 2m. Lvs to 35cm, hairy beneath. Infl. 13cm, conical; scape 20–45cm; bracts pale green turning red; pet. white; lip pale yellow or darker towards base. India. 'Darceyi': lvs striped cream.

ZINGIBERACEAE Lindl. 53/1200. *Aframomum, Alpinia, Amomum, Boesenbergia, Brachychilum, Burbidgea, Camptandra, Cautleya, Costus, Curcuma, Dimerocostus, Elettaria, Etlingera, Globba, Hedychium, Kaempferia, Renealmia, Roscoea, Scaphochlamys, Siphonochilus, Tapeinochilus, Zingiber*

Zinnia L. Compositae. *c*20 ann. or perenn. herbs or low shrubs. Cap. usually radiate; involucre cylindric to hemispheric; ray flts 1–3-lobed, white, lemon, yellow, orange, red, purple or lilac; disc flts tubular, usually yellow. SC US to Arg., particularly Mex.

Z. acerosa (DC.) A. Gray. Perenn. subshrub to 16cm; st. slender, tomentose. Lvs to 2cm, needle-shaped to linear, strigose to glab. Cap. radiate, 6mm high, on peduncles to 2.5cm; ray flts 4–6, oblong to suborbicular, to 10mm, white, green-nerved below; disc flts yellow. Summer. S US, Mex. Z9.

Z. angustifolia Kunth. Erect ann. herb, to 40cm. STems strigose-hispid. Lvs to 7cm, linear to linear-lanceolate, ± sessile, strigose-scabrous. Cap. radiate, 1cm diam., on peduncles to 7cm; ray flts 7–9, oblong, to 15mm, bright orange, pubesc. in distal third; disc flts orange with yellow and black or deep purple hairs. SE US, Mex. 'Orange Star': to 25cm; fls tangerine, long-flowering.

Z. angustifolia hort. non Kunth = *Z. haageana*.

Z. dahliiflora hort. ex Kilgus = *Z. elegans*.

Z. elegans Jacq. Erect ann. to 1m. St. green, becoming yellow to purple, pilose-strigose. Lvs to 8cm, lanceolate, ovate or oblong, ± sessile, hirsute to strigose. Cap. radiate, to 22mm diam., on peduncles to 9cm; ray flts 8–60, spathulate to obovate, to 22mm, red, white, yellow, orange, pink, scarlet, lilac or purple; disc flts numerous, yellow and black. Summer. Mex. Over 80 cvs and seed races, mostly American; fls mostly double, in a wide colour range; height from dwarf (20cm) to large (75cm). Notable dwarfs include the 25cm light pink 'Fantastic Light Pink', the 30cm fully double Parasol Mixed, the early-flowering Dasher Hybrid Mixed with bright cherry, scarlet, orange, pink and white fls, the 32cm rich salmon, fully double 'Rose Starlight', and the 35cm Pulcino Mixed and Starlight Mixed with double and semi-double fls and a wide colour range; the 30cm 'Rose Pinwheel' seed formula is a cross of *Z. elegans* and *Z. angustifolia*, offering mildew-resistant, single, daisy-like pink to dark rose fls. Notable taller cvs include the 55cm Burpee's Bouquet Series with semi-ruffled, fully double fls to 9cm diam., the 60cm dahlia-fld 'Envy Double', with chartreuse-green fls, with Peppermint Stick Mixed and stippled and striped fls in a var. of colours; the large (75cm) long-flowering, cactus-fld Burpee's Zenith Series has fls to 15cm diam., dark green lvs and wide colour range, and the 70cm tetraploid Tetra Ruffled Jumbo Zinnias, with fls to 18cm diam., are available in a wide colour range.

Z. gracillima hort. = *Z. elegans*.

Z. grandiflora Nutt. Subshrub to 22cm. St. green, strigose-hispid. Lvs 2.5cm, linear, strigose-scabrous. Cap. radiate, on peduncles to 1cm; ray flts 3–6, to 18mm, ovate to orbicular, yellow; disc flts red or green. Summer. S US, N Mex. Z4.

Z. haageana Reg. Erect ann. to 60cm. St. slender, becoming purple, strigose-pilose. Lvs to 3.5cm, lanceolate, sessile, hispid. Cap. radiate, to 1cm diam., on peduncles to 6cm; ray flts 8–9k, oblong, to 17mm, bright orange and velvety above, dull orange to yellow and hirsute below; disc flts numerous, orange, darker below. Summer. Mex. 'Old Mexico': habit mound-forming, to 45cm; fls large, to 7cm diam., bright yellow, red and mahogany. Persian Carpet Mixed: to 45cm; fls double, to 5cm diam., bicoloured in gold, maroon, purple, chocolate, pink and cream.

Z. linearis Benth. = *Z. angustifolia*.

Z. mexicana hort. = *Z. haageana*.

Z. multiflora L. = *Z. peruviana*.

Z. pauciflora L. = *Z. peruviana*.

Z. peruviana (L.) L. Erect ann. to 90cm. St. green becoming yellow or purple, strigose to hirsute. Lvs to 7cm, linear-lanceolate to ovate or elliptic, glandular-punctate. Cap. radiate, to 18mm high, on peduncles to 7cm; ray flts 6–15, linear to spathulate or suborbicular, to 25mm, scarlet or yellow; disc flts 12–50, yellow and purple to black. Summer. S US to Arg.

Z. pumila A. Gray = *Z. acerosa*.

Z. tenuiflora Jacq. = *Z. peruviana*.

Z. verticillata Andrews = *Z. peruviana*.

→*Chrysogonum*.

Zitherwood *Citharexylum*.

Zit-kwa *Benincasa hispida*.

Zizania L. WILD RICE; WATER OATS. Gramineae. 3 ann. or perenn. aquatic grasses. Lvs linear, flat. Infl. term., paniculate; spikelets oblong, 1-fld. N Amer., E Asia. Z6.

Z. aquatica L. ANNUAL WILD RICE; WATER RICE; CANADIAN WILD RICE. Ann., erect, to 3.6m. Lvs to 1.2m×3cm, scabrous, deep green. Infl. pyramidal, to 75cm; ♀ spikelets to 0.5cm, with awn to 8cm, ♂ spikelets to 1cm, awns 0. N Amer.

Z. caducifolia Hand.-Mazz. = *Z. latifolia*.

Z. latifolia (Griseb.) Turcz. MANCHURIAN WILD RICE; WATER RICE. Stoloniferous perenn., to 3.6m. Lvs to 1.5m×3.5cm, scabrous. Infl. narrow-pyramidal, to 60cm; ♀ spikelets to 2cm, with awn to 3cm, ♂ spikelets to 1.3cm, tinged purple, with awn to 1cm. Summer–autumn. E Asia. Z9.

Z. palustris L. = *Z. aquatica*.

Zizia Koch. Umbelliferae. 4 perenn. herbs. Lvs ternate, seg. serrate to dentate. Umbels compound; involucre 0; bracteoles few, small; fls yellow. N Amer. Z3.

Z. aurea (L.) Koch. GOLDEN ALEXANDERS. To 75cm. Lvs 6–10cm, ovate to orbicular in outline, 2-ternate, seg. ovate-lanceolate, toothed, to pinnatifid; petiole c10cm. Umbel rays to 3.5cm, 10–15. Spring–early summer. E Canada to S US.

Ziziphus Mill. Rhamnaceae. 86 decid. and everg. shrubs and trees with stipular spines. Lvs alternate-distichous, entire to serrate. Fls small, 5-merous, yellow, in axill. cymes. Fr. sub-globose to oblong. Widely distrib. in trop. and subtrop. areas, with 1 Medit. sp. and 1 from temp. Asia.

Z. jujuba Mill. COMMON JUJUBE; CHINESE DATE; CHINESE JUJUBE. Shrub or tree to 9m, twigs flexuous. Lvs 2.5–6cm, oval-lanceolate to elliptic, apex rounded, leathery, glab., crenate. Fr. 1.5–2.5cm, edible, ovoid, dark red, later black. Temp. Asia, frequently nat. elsewhere. Z6. 'Lang': fr. small, sweet, melting flesh, tree large, early-bearing. 'Li': fr. v. large, tree large. 'Sherwood'; fr. v. large. 'Silverhill': fr. large, elongated, sweet, good for drying. 'Silverhill Round': fr. large, plum-shaped, v. sweet.

Z. jujuba Lam. non Mill. = *Z. mauritanica*.

Z. mauritanica Lam. INDIAN JUJUBE; COTTONY JUJUBE. Shrub or tree to 6m, with white or rusty-brown tomentose. Lvs to 8cm, broadly elliptic, apex rounded. Fr. to 2.5cm diam., globose to suboblong, acidic. India, nat. elsewhere. Z10.

Z. sativa Gaertn. = *Z. jujuba*.

Z. vulgaris Lam. = *Z. jujuba*.

Zoapatle *Montanoa tomentosa*.

Zonal Pelargonium *Pelargonium ×hortorum*.

Zootrophion Luer. Orchidaceae. 5 epiphytic orchids. Pbs 0. St. tufted. Lf. term., single, elliptic to obovate. Fls solitary, oft. small; synsepalum exceeding pet.; lip 3-lobed. Trop. S Amer. Z10.

Z. atropurpureum (Lindl.) Luer. St. to 50cm. Lvs to 9×3cm. Fl. deep crimson; sep. to 1.5cm. Jam., Panama, Colomb., Ecuad., Peru.

Z. dayanum (Rchb. f.) Luer. St. to 11cm. Lvs to 10×5.5cm. Fl. pendent, yellow or golden-yellow, marked dark purple; sep. to 4cm. Peru, Colomb.

→*Cryptophoranthus, Masdevallia* and *Pleurothallis*.

Zosterella Small.

Z. dubia (Jacq.) Small = *Heteranthera dubia*.

Zosterostylis Bl.

Z. arachnites Bl. = *Cryptostylis arachnites*.

Zoysia Willd. Gramineae. 5 creeping perenn. grasses. Rac. short, term., spike-like, slender; spikelets 1-fld. SE Asia, NZ.

Z. japonica Steud. KOREAN GRASS; KOREAN LAWN GRASS; JAPANESE LAWN GRASS. Lvs to 22.5cm. Spikelets to 5mm, ovate, pale purple-brown. Jap., China, Korea. Z7.

Z. matrella (L.) Merrill. JAPANESE CARPET GRASS; MANILA GRASS; FLAWN. Lvs to 10cm, filiform. Spikelets to 3.5cm, lanceolate to oblong, tinged green. Trop. Asia. Z9.

Z. pungens Willd. = *Z. matrella*.

Z. tenuifolia Willd. ex Trin. MASCARENE GRASS; KOREAN VELVET GRASS. Lvs to 5cm, filiform involute. Spikelets to 5cm, narrowly oblong-lanceolate. Asia, introd. S Flor., S Calif. Z10.

Zucchini *Cucurbita pepo*.

Zulu Fig *Ficus lutea*.

Zygadene *Zigadenus*.

Zygocactus Schum.

Z. delicatus N.E. Br. = *Schlumbergera truncata*.

Z. truncatus (Haw.) Schum. = *Schlumbergera truncata*.

Zygopetalum Hook. Orchidaceae. 20 epiphytic or terrestrial orchids. Lvs lanceolate, ± ribbed, sheathing and terminating stout pbs. or (in some spp.) elongate st. Rac. lat.; fls showy, waxy, sometimes fragrant; tep. lanceolate to obovate; pet. usually somewhat shorter and narrower than sep; lip deeply or obscurely triloboed, obovate to flabellate. Mex. to Peru & Braz. Z10.

Z. aromaticum Rchb. f. = *Z. wendlandii*.

Z. brachypetalum Lindl. Pbs to 5cm, ovoid-oblong. Lvs to 60cm. Infl. surpassing lvs; fls waxy, fragrant; tep. to 3cm, green mottled brown or purple-brown; lip to 3×2.5cm, white, streaked red-violet or blue-violet. Braz.

Z. brachystalix Rchb. f. = *Otostylis brachystalix*.

Z. burkei Rchb. f. = *Mendoncella burkei*.

Z. cerinum (Lindl.) Rchb. f. = *Pescatorea cerina*.

Z. cochleare Lindl. = *Cochleanthes flabelliformis*.

Z. crinitum Lodd. Pbs to 7cm, elongate-ovoid. Lvs to 40cm. Infl. to 50cm; fls strongly fragrant, waxy; tep. to 2.7cm grey-green or yellow-green, streaked and spotted chestnut-brown; lip to 5cm, white veined red or purple, veins pubesc. E Braz.

Z. gramineum Lindl. = *Kefersteinia graminea*.

Z. graminifolium Rolfe. Pbs to 5cm. Lvs to 40cm, grass-like. Infl. equalling lvs; tep. to 3cm green, densely marked and blotched grey-maroon or black-brown; lip to 2.3cm, violet streaked white. Braz.

Z. grandiflorum (A. Rich.) Benth. & Hook. ex Hemsl. = *Mendoncella grandiflora*.

Z. intermedium Lindl. Pbs to 8cm, ovoid-conical. Lvs to 50cm. Infl. to 50cm; fls waxy, scented strongly of hyacinths; tep. to 3.75cm, green or yellow-green, blotched red-brown or crimson; lip to 3.5cm, white with radiating purple-violet lines. Peru, Boliv., Braz.

Z. jorisianum Rolfe = *Mendoncella jorisiana*.

Z. lacteum Rchb. f. = *Kefersteinia lactea*.

Z. lindeniae Rolfe = *Zygosepalum lindeniae*.

Z. mackaii Hook. Differs from *Z. intermedium* in taller infl. and lip ± subquadrate. Braz.

Z. mackaii var. **crinitum** (Lodd.) Lindl. = *Z. crinitum*.

Z. maxillare Lodd. Pbs to 7.5cm, ovoid-oblong. Lvs to 35cm. Infl. to 35cm; fls waxy, fragrant; tep. to 2.5cm light green blotched and barred bronze-brown; lip violet-blue or purple-blue. Braz., Parag.

Z. mosenianum Barb. Rodr. Pbs 0. St. to 150cm, scandent, leafy. Lvs to 25cm. Infl. to 40cm; fls waxy, fragrant; tep. to 2.5cm, pale green blotched purple-brown; lip white, with radiating violet lines. Braz.

Z. murrayanum Gardn. = *Neogardneria murrayana*.

Z. prainianum Rolfe = *Mendoncella burkei*.

Z. pubescens Hoffsgg. = *Z. crinitum*.

Z. rostratum Hook. = *Zygosepalum labiosum*.

Z. sanguinolentum (Rchb. f.) Rchb. f. = *Kefersteinia sanguinolenta*.

Z. tatei Ames & Schweinf. = *Zygosepalum tatei*.

Z. tricolor Lindl. = *Koellensteinia tricolor*.

Z. wendlandii Rchb. f. Pbs 0. Lvs to 30cm. Infl. to 9cm; fls solitary, tep. to 3.2cm; white, pale green or yellow-green; lip to 2.5cm, undulate, lavender or violet, margins white. Costa Rica, Panama.

→*Chondrorhyncha* and *Warscewiczella*.

ZYGOPHYLLACEAE R. Br. 27/250. *Guaiacum, Larrea, Peganum, Porlieria, Tribulus, Zygophyllum*

Zygophyllum L. CAPER BEAN. Zygophyllaceae. 80 herbs or shrubs; br. fleshy, sometimes jointed. Lvs sometimes pinnate; lfts usually 2; stipules 2, often spiny. Fls axill., solitary or paired, 4–5-merous; sep. fleshy; pet. blunt, overlapping, disc fleshy, 8–10-angled. Fr. a capsule, angular or winged. Medit. to C Asia, S Afr., Aus. Z10.

Z. album L. f. St. to 40cm, procumbent. Lfts 1 pair, fleshy, cylindrical to ellipsoid, cobwebby. Fls solitary, white. Fr. to 1cm, 5-angled obcordate to subspherical. Arabia, N & C Afr.

Z. fabago L. SYRIAN BEAN CAPER. Fleshy-rooted perenn., to about 1m. Lfts 1 pair, obovate to elliptic, flat smooth, surpassed by rachis. Fls solitary, yellow-copper. Fr. 2–3cm, oblong-

cylindric. Summer. Syr. to Afghan.

Z. prismatothecum F. Muell. Ann. Lfts 1 pair. Fls yellow. Fr. to 1.5cm, narrow-oblong, angles 4, horned. Winter–spring. C Aus.

Z. proliferum Forssk. = *Z. album*.

Zygosepalum Rchb. f. Orchidaceae. 4 epiphytic orchids. Pbs often remote on rhiz., sheathed, to 6cm. Lvs plicate. Infl. lat., 1- to few-fld; fls showy; tep. similar, free, lip, simple to trilobed, ovate to suborbicular-obovate. Venez., Colomb., Peru, Braz., Guianas. Z10.

Z. labiosum (Rich.) Garay. Pbs, ovoid-oblong. Lvs to 25cm, oblong to lanceolate. Infl. to 20cm, usually 1-fld, recurved or ascending; fls to 5cm diam., green to yellow, suffused maroon at centre, lip 5.5cm, white striped violet at base. Colomb., Venez., Guianas, Braz.

Z. lindeniae (Rolfe) Garay & Dunsterv. Pbs ovoid to ellipsoid. Lvs to 25cm, lanceolate. Infl. to 20cm, arching to pendent, fls white to rose, lip to 4.5cm, white veined and edged rose-purple; tep. ovate-lanceolate, white, cream or green, lip. fimbriate. Venez., Peru, Braz.

Z. rostratum (Hook.) Rchb. f. = *Z. labiosum*.

Z. tatei (Ames & Schweinf.) Garay & Dunsterv. Pbs cylindrical. Lvs to 16cm, oblong to oblanceolate. Infl. to 50cm, erect, few-fld, fls green or yellow-green to dull lavender-brown, marked dark brown, lip 2.5cm, white flushed pink-violet at base. Venez., Guyana, Braz.

→*Zygopetalum*.

Zygosicyos Humbert. Cucurbitaceae. 2 tuberous climbers. St. slender. Tendrils often bifid. Lvs 3-partite or 3-foliolate. Fls 4-merous. ♂ solitary or in rac.; ♀ solitary. Fr. obconical, leathery. E Asia, Madag. Z10.

Z. tripartitus Humbert. St. slightly woody, ribbed. Lvs to 3cm, 3-lobed, stiffly pubesc. above, glabrescent beneath, entire to sinuate-dentate. Fls yellow-green. Fr. c2cm×1.5cm, pendulous. Madag.

→*Melothria*.

Zygostates Lindl. Orchidaceae. 4 dwarf epiphytic orchids. Lvs thick, imbricate, pbs scarcely distinguishable. Fls v. small, racemose; tep. free, spreading or reflexed; lip concave, spreading, with fleshy, basal appendage. Braz. Z10.

Z. alleniana Kränzl. Lvs to 3cm, linear. Infl. to 4cm, erect, few-fld; tep. obovate-spathulate, pellucid, lip entire. Braz.

Z. lunata Lindl. Lvs to 7cm, oblong-spathulate. Infl to 15cm, ± arching, many-fld; tep. ovate-lanceolate, white, cream or green, lip. fimbriate. Braz.

→*Ornithocephalus*.